Abbreviations Used in this Dictionary
Abréviations utilisées dans ce dictionnaire

marketing	*Mktg*	marketing
masculine plural noun	*mpl*	nom masculin pluriel
music	*Mus*	musique
mythology	*Myth*	mythologie
noun	*n*	nom
shipping	*Naut*	nautisme
term used in Northern England	*NEng*	terme utilisé dans le nord de l'Angleterre
feminine noun	*nf*	nom féminin
feminine plural noun	*nfpl*	nom féminin pluriel
masculine noun	*nm*	nom masculin
masculine and feminine noun	*nmf*	nom masculin et féminin
masculine plural noun	*nmpl*	nom masculin pluriel
plural noun	*npl*	nom pluriel
proper noun	*npr*	nom propre
nuclear	*Nucl*	nucléaire
New Zealand English	*NZ*	anglais de Nouvelle-Zélande
obstetrics	*Obst*	obstétrique
officially recommended term	*Offic*	recommandation officielle
onomatopoeia	*onomat*	onomatopée
optics	*Opt*	optique
computing	*Ordinat*	informatique
birds	*Orn*	oiseaux
parliament	*Parl*	parlement
pejorative	*Pej, Péj*	péjoratif
petroleum industry	*Petr, Pétr*	industrie pétrolière
pharmacy	*Pharm*	pharmacie
philosophy	*Phil*	philosophie
photography	*Phot*	photographie
physics	*Phys*	physique
physiology	*Physiol*	physiologie
plural	*pl*	pluriel
politics	*Pol*	politique
past participle	*pp*	participe passé
predeterminer	*predet*	prédéterminant
prefix	*pref, préf*	préfixe
preposition	*prep, prép*	préposition
proper noun	*pr n*	nom propre
pronoun	*pron*	pronom
proverb	*Prov*	proverbe
psychology, psychiatry	*Psy*	psychologie, psychiatrie
past tense	*pt*	prétérit
something	*qch*	quelque chose
somebody	*qn*	quelqu'un
registered trademark	®	marque déposée
radio	*Rad*	radio
rail	*Rail*	chemins de fer

religion	*Rel*	religion
South African English	*SAfr*	anglais d'Afrique du Sud
somebody	*sb*	quelqu'un
school	*Sch, Scol*	scolaire
Scottish English	*Scot*	anglais d'Écosse
term used in Southern England	*SEng*	terme utilisé dans le sud de l'Angleterre
singular	*sing*	singulier
specialist term	*Spec, Spéc*	vocabulaire de spécialité
Stock Exchange	*St Exch*	Bourse
something	*sth*	quelque chose
suffixe	*suff*	suffixe
superlative	*superl*	superlatif
technology	*Tech*	technologie
telecommunications	*Tel, Tél*	télécommunications
textiles	*Tex*	textile
theatre	*Theat, Théât*	théâtre
transport	*Transp*	transports
television	*TV*	télévision
typography, printing	*Typ*	typographie, imprimerie
European Union	*UE*	Union européenne
university	*Univ*	université
verb	*v*	verbe
intransitive verb	*vi*	verbe intransitif
reflexive verb	*vpr*	verbe pronominal
transitive verb	*vt*	verbe transitif
transitive verb used with a preposition [eg **parvenir à** (to reach); ils sont **parvenus à** un accord (they reached an agreement)]	*vt ind*	verbe transitif indirect [par exemple: **parvenir à**; ils sont **parvenus à** un accord]
inseparable transitive verb [phrasal verb where the verb and the adverb or preposition cannot be separated, eg **look after**; he **looked after** the children]	*vt insep*	verbe transitif à particule inséparable [par exemple: **look after** (s'occuper de); he **looked after** the children (il s'occupait des enfants)]
separable transitive verb [phrasal verb where the adverb and preposition can be separated, eg **send back**; she **sent** the present **back** *or* she **sent back** the present]	*vt sep*	verbe transitif à particule séparable [par exemple: **send** back (rendre); she **sent** the present **back** *ou* she **sent** back the present (elle a rendu le cadeau)]
veterinary medicine	*Vet, Vét*	médecine vétérinaire
vulgar	*Vulg*	vulgaire
zoology	*Zool*	zoologie

HARRAP'S

UNABRIDGED DICTIONARY DICTIONNAIRE

Volume 1

English–French
Anglais–Français

HARRAP

First published in Great Britain 2001
by Chambers Harrap Publishers Ltd
7 Hopetoun Crescent, Edinburgh EH7 4AY

Dépôt légal: juillet 2001

This volume
ISBN 0245 50434 6 (France)
ISBN 0245 60661 0 (UK)

Volume 2 (French - English)
ISBN 0245 50455 9 (France)
ISBN 0245 60702 1 (UK)

Designed and typeset by Chambers Harrap Publishers Ltd, Edinburgh
Printed and bound in France by Jouve

Contributors/Collaborateurs

Editor-in-Chief/Rédacteur en chef

Patrick White

Managing Editor/Coordination éditoriale

Anna Stevenson

Senior Editors/Rédacteurs seniors

Gearóid Cronin
Laurence Larroche
Georges Pilard

Editors/Rédaction

Lola Busuttil
Isabelle Elkaim
Stuart Fortey
Frances Illingworth
Lesley Johnston
Stéphanie Marchand
Françoise de Peretti
Susan Steinberg

with/avec

Dougal Campbell
Lynda Carey
Daniela Delas
Pat Dunn
Gilla Evans
Kay L. Hawkins
Lynn Hubble
Anne Kansau
David Kennedy
Sophie Marin
Claude Moureau-Bondy
Ruth Noble
Elaine O'Donoghue
Martine Pierquin
Rose Rociola
Deborah Sanders
Alan Seaton
Megan Thomson
Sheilagh Wilson

Canadian French Consultant/Spécialiste pour les canadianismes

Louis B. Mignault,
Associate Professor (retired),
University of Toronto

Swiss French Consultant/Spécialiste pour les helvétismes

André Thibault,
Université de Strasbourg

Reading Panel/Comité de lecture

Louis B. Mignault,
Associate Professor (retired),
University of Toronto

Philip O'Prey,
Université Catholique de l'Ouest,
Angers

Kathleen Shields,
University College of Maynooth

Computing Support/Informatique éditoriale

Siri Hansen

Prepress/Prépresse

Clair Good
David Reid

ACKNOWLEDGEMENTS/REMERCIEMENTS

Acknowledgements

Acknowledgements are due to the Chambers editorial team for material used in the English chronology, to Martyn Back for the original idea for the inclusion of allusions, to Joe de Miribel for his advice on military ranks, to Mónica Tamariz for lists of biochemistry terminology, to Peter Walton for his help with financial terms, to Scott Forbes and SULA for Australian and American material respectively, and to Emmanuelle Jowa for her advice on Belgian French.

Remerciements

L'éditeur tient à remercier l'équipe éditoriale des éditions Chambers pour les documents fournis lors de la rédaction de la chronologie du monde anglophone, Martyn Back, qui eut l'idée de créer des notes explicatives sur les allusions, Joe de Miribel pour l'aide apportée lors de la rédaction du tableau comparatif des grades militaires, Mónica Tamariz pour les termes de biochimie, Peter Walton pour les termes financiers, Scott Forbes pour les termes australiens, SULA pour les termes américains et Emmanuelle Jowa pour les termes de français de Belgique.

Trademarks

Words considered to be trademarks have been designated in this dictionary by the symbol ®. However, no judgement is implied concerning the legal status of any trademark by virtue of the presence or absence of such a symbol.

Marques déposées

Les termes considérés comme des marques déposées sont signalés dans ce dictionnaire par le symbole ®. Cependant, la présence ou l'absence de ce symbole ne constitue nullement une indication quant à la valeur juridique de ces termes.

Contents/Table des matières

Supplement/Appendice

Preface

Gone are the days when a dictionary was just a long series of words arranged in alphabetical order, to be consulted hurriedly and closed afterwards with a smile of gratitude as soon as you had found the answer to your query. There were no such smiles, however, when the word being looked up did not feature in the dictionary because it was too old-fashioned, too specialized or too rare.

Fortunately, this problem was unlikely to occur with the four-volume Harrap ***Standard*** French dictionary. Its comprehensiveness guaranteed that users who had searched in vain through other bilingual dictionaries could be assured of finding the word in its pages. However, the ***Standard*** was a dictionary in the traditional mould. Although there was much to admire in the detailed way in which translations were presented, and the variety of illustrative examples and expressions shown, the entries were listed in a tried-and-tested sequence and according to a deliberately uniform model.

Harrap, the "grande dame" of British lexicography, has been publishing dictionaries which have been valued by students, translators and the general public for a century. Now, twenty years after the last revision of the ***Standard***, Harrap is marking its centenary with the publication of the Harrap ***Unabridged*** French-English dictionary. This worthy successor to the ***Standard*** is published in two large volumes, whose contents are not only better presented and more accessible but also richer and enhanced by new distinctive features.

It is immediately apparent on opening the book that it represents a new concept of what a bilingual dictionary should be. This is made evident by the new layout which draws the attention to certain features, as if to underline the greater importance of certain words and to highlight interesting aspects of usage associated with them.

The impressive new look of the text could be seen as simply a presentation gimmick, designed to break up the monotony of the traditional dictionary page layout, but in fact the new design reflects a genuine desire to go beyond the scope of a traditional bilingual dictionary. In order to provide real help to a translator, a good bilingual dictionary should be more than just a collection of words with their matching equivalents in the other language. It should also constitute a means of discovering the associations of words and the ways in which they are used in the other culture.

So, for example, at the entry for **Carnaby Street**, a boxed note gives the user an added insight into the cultural connotations of this street, once a symbol of London in the swinging sixties and today a centre for second-hand clothes shops. On the French-English side of the dictionary, you can find, for example, information about **Canal+**, informing the user not only that this is a pay TV channel which can be viewed at certain hours by non-subscribers, but also that it plays a prominent role in funding international film-making. Such information, which the user will not necessarily expect to come across in a bilingual dictionary but is bound to find both welcome and useful, gives the dictionary an added encyclopedic dimension and at the same time makes it more interesting to browse through.

In this way the dictionary entertainingly reveals the associations of many proper names that the user may have often read or heard without knowing exactly to what they refer. The connotations of these words remain opaque as they are usually not translated. In a sense, the dictionary performs the role of a guide, charting a path through the cultural landscape of another country and arousing the curiosity of the reader who may previously have been unaware of these connotations.

The dictionary breaks further new ground in the notes in grey-tinted boxes that highlight phrases that are used allusively – often ones that have originated in literature, the cinema or popular culture. These are the kinds of phrases that we hear in everyday conversations and usually have little idea that they are in fact famous quotations. For example, we are reminded that the phrase "Qu'importe le flacon pourvu qu'on ait l'ivresse" is an allusion to a play by Alfred de Musset in which the protagonist argues that the fact of being in love is more important than the person you love. Similarly, on the English-French side of the dictionary, the note on the phrase "I have a dream" describes how this phrase was used by Martin Luther King in Washington in 1963, and his dream of an America where all citizens would be equal and would live together in harmony. Another example is the phrase "Smile, you're on Candid Camera", translated as "Souriez, c'est pour le caméra invisible", a reference to our own era where people's lives are so dominated by television.

The same concern with presenting language as it is used in real life is reflected in the prominent position given in this dictionary to the international dimension and the diversity of linguistic use. Comprehensive coverage of the standard varieties of both languages is rightly complemented by extensive coverage of French as it is used in Belgium, Canada and Switzerland, and English as it is used not only in the United States but also in Scotland, Ireland and Australia.

Last but not least: what dictionary user has not been confronted with the difficulty of trying to guess what a shortened form is short for (for example **specs** for **spectacles** in English or **réa** for **réanimation** in French), or, even more cryptically, to decipher abbreviations? Shortened forms and abbreviations are equally impenetrable, in either language, for anyone who has not lived in the country concerned. The dictionary offers help in the form of supplements which contain list of these items. Browsing through these lists, it is striking to note at an entry like **ENT** (ear, nose and throat) how pragmatic and down-to-earth English is, while the French equivalent **ORL** (oto-rhino-laryngologiste) illustrates the tendency of French towards erudite abstraction. Fortunately, hundreds of shortened forms and abbreviations – so frequently criticized nowadays as a curse – are explained and translated here. The explanations may sometimes be surprising, but they are always enlightening.

An overview of this dictionary would not be complete without mentioning the fact that it also faithfully records terms from new technologies and the latest scientific discoveries, and includes the titles of numerous works of art from the fields of literature, painting, music and cinema. Taking all of this into account, it is fair to say that this centenary edition really does represent the dawn of a new era in lexicography. Dictionaries are no longer simply useful but rather off-putting weighty tomes to be consulted only in moments of dire necessity; as the *Unabridged* proves, they are now user-friendly books which have the additional merit of being enjoyable to read.

Henriette WALTER
Emeritus Professor of Linguistics,
Université de Haute-Bretagne,
Member of the Conseil Supérieur
de la langue française

Préface

Le temps n'est plus où un dictionnaire n'était qu'une longue suite de mots classés dans l'ordre alphabétique, que l'on consultait fébrilement à la recherche d'une précision et que l'on refermait avec un sourire de reconnaissance dès que l'on avait trouvé l'information recherchée. Il faut toutefois ajouter que la déception était grande quand le mot, trop désuet, trop spécialisé ou trop rare, n'y figurait pas.

Cette dernière expérience avait peu de chances de se produire avec le dictionnaire bilingue Harrap['s ***Standard***], où la générosité de la nomenclature a toujours été un gage pour trouver ce que l'on avait cherché en vain dans les autres dictionnaires bilingues. Mais il demeurait un dictionnaire classique, où l'on appréciait, certes, l'abondance des précisions dans la traduction des formes et où l'on admirait la diversité des expressions retenues, mais où toutes les entrées se suivaient sagement, dans un ordre immuable et rassurant, et selon un modèle volontairement uniforme.

Après un siècle de publications de dictionnaires fort appréciés des étudiants, des traducteurs et du grand public, et vingt ans après les derniers remaniements, voici que nous est présenté, en cadeau d'anniversaire, le tout dernier enfant de cette grande dame de la lexicographie anglaise, aujourd'hui centenaire: le Harrap's ***Unabridged***, en deux forts volumes où l'information est encore plus riche, plus diversifiée, mieux mise en valeur et plus accessible.

Cette fois, c'est dès le premier coup d'œil que l'on perçoit l'avènement d'une nouvelle conception lexicographique. Elle se signale d'abord visuellement par des espaces imprimés d'une façon un peu différente et qui se détachent clairement du reste, comme pour souligner l'importance plus grande de certains mots et pour attirer l'attention sur certains développements qui ne sont que leur prolongement naturel.

Cette nouvelle disposition spectaculaire du texte pourrait n'être qu'un artifice de présentation, uniquement destiné à rompre la monotonie de la page de dictionnaire traditionnelle. En fait, cette maquette originale répond à un véritable désir d'aller plus loin qu'un dictionnaire bilingue habituel. Pour apporter une aide plus efficace à la traduction, un dictionnaire bilingue, en effet, se doit de ne pas être seulement un répertoire de mots avec leurs équivalents dans l'autre langue mais de constituer aussi un meilleur moyen d'imaginer ce qui peut être évoqué derrière les mots.

C'est ainsi, par exemple, qu'à l'entrée **Carnaby Street**, un encadré permet à l'utilisateur d'entrer en quelque sorte dans cette rue de Londres, naguère haut-lieu des milieux branchés et aujourd'hui spécialisée dans la vente des vêtements d'occasion. Côté français-anglais, on trouve, entre autres, des informations sur **Canal+**, chaîne de télévision privée à péage, mais qui peut être captée en clair à certaines heures, et qui finance aussi la production cinématographique. Ces renseignements, inattendus mais bienvenus dans un dictionnaire bilingue, lui apportent de ce fait une dimension encyclopédique supplémentaire tout en lui donnant un surcroît de vie.

Derrière de nombreux noms propres, souvent lus ou entendus sans savoir exactement ce qu'ils recouvrent et qui risquent de n'évoquer aucune image puisqu'on ne les traduit généralement pas, se profilent ainsi des réalités que l'on prend plaisir à connaître : le dictionnaire joue alors d'une certaine manière le rôle d'un guide inattendu, qui ouvre une brèche enrichissante dans le paysage culturel du voisin et parvient à piquer la curiosité du lecteur resté jusque-là indifférent.

Un pas de plus est franchi avec d'autres encadrés, cette fois sur fond grisé, qui s'attardent sur certaines allusions littéraires, picturales ou cinématographiques. On les a souvent entendues dans des conversations familières et sans soupçonner la plupart du temps que ce sont des citations de phrases célèbres. Ainsi, par exemple, nous rappelle-t-on que la phrase «Qu'importe le flacon pourvu qu'on ait l'ivresse», est une allusion à une pièce de Musset où le personnage soutient que ce qui compte, c'est le sentiment amoureux et non pas la personne aimée. Dans la partie anglais-français, l'encadré «I have a dream» évoque Martin Luther King à Washington en 1963 et son rêve d'une Amérique où tous les citoyens seraient égaux et vivraient ensemble en bonne intelligence. Voici aussi, avec «Smile, you're on Candid Camera», traduit par «Souriez, c'est pour la caméra invisible», un clin d'œil à notre époque où la vie de chacun est plus ou moins rythmée par des émissions de télévision.

Dans le même désir de mieux coller à la réalité, la dimension géographique et la diversité des usages sont dans cet ouvrage maintes fois soulignées : à côté de la norme d'usage de plus large diffusion, une place légitime y a été consacrée, pour le français, aux variétés lexicales de Belgique, de Suisse et du Canada, et pour l'anglais, aux usages d'Écosse, d'Irlande, d'Australie et des États-Unis.

Enfin, qui ne s'est jamais trouvé confronté avec le redoutable problème d'avoir à deviner le mot suggéré par une abréviation (par exemple **specs** pour **spectacles** en anglais ou **réa** pour **réanimation** en français), ou, question plus insoluble encore, d'essayer de comprendre ce qui se cache derrière les sigles ? Abréviations et sigles sont tout aussi impénétrables, dans l'une et l'autre langue, pour qui n'a pas vécu dans le pays. À parcourir les annexes très utiles qui leur sont consacrées dans cet ouvrage, il est piquant de retrouver, par exemple, sous **ENT** (ear, nose and throat) le côté pragmatique et toujours proche des gens de l'anglais, tandis qu'avec l'équivalent français **ORL** (oto-rhino-laryngologiste), c'est plutôt la tendance savamment abstraite de la langue française qui apparaît au grand jour. Fort heureusement, des centaines d'abréviations et de sigles – cette plaie si souvent dénoncée des temps modernes – sont ici développés et traduits : ils étonnent parfois et ils rassurent toujours.

Si l'on ajoute que ce dictionnaire se fait aussi très largement l'écho attentif des nouvelles techniques et des dernières découvertes scientifiques, et qu'il rappelle en outre les titres de nombreuses œuvres de littérature, de peinture, de musique ou de cinéma, on peut dire que cette édition du centenaire marque vraiment l'entrée de la lexicographie dans une ère nouvelle : celle des dictionnaires qui ne sont plus uniquement de gros volumes très savants, très utiles mais parfois un peu rébarbatifs, et que l'on consulte seulement par nécessité, mais des ouvrages accueillants, qu'on lit aussi vraiment pour le plaisir.

Henriette WALTER
Professeur émérite de linguistique à l'université de Haute-Bretagne,
Membre du Conseil Supérieur de la langue française

Introduction (English)

When the editors set out to produce a new large French-English English-French dictionary for publication in Harrap's centenary year, they were very aware of the illustrious footsteps in which they were following. Professor Jean Mansion's ***Standard Dictionary***, conceived by George Harrap in the early years of the company and published in two parts in 1935 and 1939, is a monumental work that for many years has enjoyed an enviable reputation. The editors of the ***Unabridged*** have endeavoured to preserve many of the characteristics which earned the ***Standard*** its high reputation, including its coverage of literary language and technical terms. At the same time, they have sought to draw on all the advances in modern bilingual lexicography.

The writing of the dictionary

The computerization of the editorial process, and the existence of texts in searchable databases, have allowed this dictionary to be produced in a fraction of the time required to write the ***Standard***. If Professor Mansion were alive today, he would surely have relished the opportunities for rapid searching offered by the Internet, and for better communication with contributors and consultants through e-mail. At the same time, the Internet has spawned a host of new vocabulary, generously represented in this book, and has consolidated the international nature of both English and French. For example, in searching for a French term on the Internet one is just as likely to find oneself consulting a Canadian or Swiss website as one produced in France. This dictionary has responded to this trend by giving fuller international coverage of both languages than will be found in any other general bilingual available.

Much of this international coverage was supplied by consultants with specialist knowledge of the different varieties of each language. Consultants' input was also invaluable in the creation of the specialist language databases in such areas as IT, finance and slang which were exploited in the writing of this book. An experienced reading panel of university lecturers brought fresh insights to the text and made many valuable suggestions.

Whilst all those who contributed to the dictionary played a valuable role, particular credit must go to the in-house editorial team which laboured long and hard to ensure the successful completion of a project initiated four years ago, and to the prepress team for their design input and skilful handling of over 10,000 pages of proofs.

Comprehensive?

In producing a dictionary of the size of the ***Unabridged***, the editors have sought to include as many terms and phrases as possible. It would, however, be wrong to assert that the ***Unabridged*** gives comprehensive coverage of the English and French languages, as such an achievement would be beyond a dictionary even twice as large. What can be reasonably claimed, however, is that the ***Unabridged*** gives a full and wide-ranging view of the two languages as they are spoken and written at the beginning of the 21st century.

Organization of entries

Headwords are presented in blue type in this dictionary and appear in alphabetical order. Note that it is the style in this dictionary to place a word beginning with an upper-case letter before one beginning with a lower-case one; thus **March** will precede **march**.

■ Grammatical divisions

The grammatical classification of an entry is marked with an italic label, eg ***n***, ***vi***, or ***prép***. All the abbreviated labels are included in the list of abbreviations at the front and back of the dictionary. When an entry has more than one part of speech, each part of speech is introduced by a bold Arabic numeral.

> **malvoyant, -e** [malvwajɑ̃, -ɑ̃t] **1** *adj* partially-sighted **2** *nm,f* partially sighted person; **les malvoyants** the partially sighted

▪ Semantic divisions

The different senses of a word are each introduced by a lower-case letter in bold type:

> **snood** [snuːd] *n* (**a**) *(for hair)* résille *f* (**b**) *(hood)* cagoule *f* (**c**) *Fishing* empile *f* (**d**) *Scot Hist (headband)* = bandeau porté autrefois dans les cheveux par les jeunes femmes célibataires

Nuances of senses, or semantic splits required to show different translations for the same sense, are shown within the same sense category by using indicating material in brackets. This material may consist of a synonym or typical collocating words, eg the objects of a transitive verb, or the nouns with which an adjective is commonly used. In some cases, both are given, with an arrow preceding the collocating words:

> **debase** [dɪˈbeɪs] *vt* (**a**) *(degrade → person, sport)* avilir, abaisser; *(→ reputation)* ternir; *(→ tradition, profession, politics)* dévaloriser (**b**) *(make less valuable → object)* dégrader, altérer; *(→ metal, currency, coinage)* déprécier

In some more complex entries with many senses, the senses are subdivided first into larger sense groups, each of which is then further divided. In these cases, a bold upper-case letter indicates the major sense division and indicating material in capitals describes it:

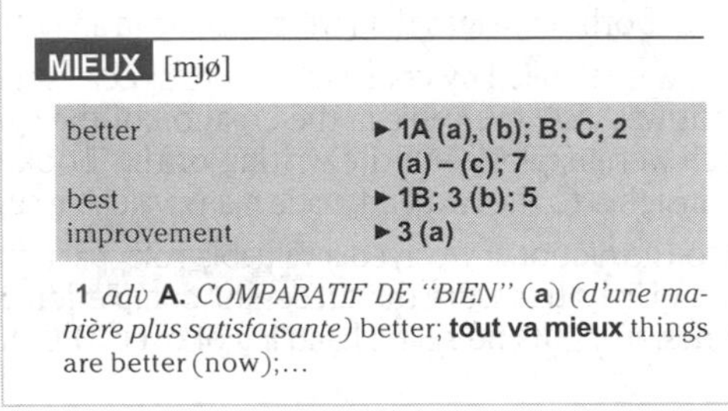

MIEUX [mjø]

better	► **1A (a), (b); B; C; 2 (a) – (c); 7**
best	► **1B; 3 (b); 5**
improvement	► **3 (a)**

1 *adv* **A.** *COMPARATIF DE "BIEN"* (**a**) *(d'une manière plus satisfaisante)* better; **tout va mieux** things are better (now);...

▪ English compounds

In this dictionary English compounds of two or more words have been presented under the entry for the first word of the compound. They appear in bold italic type in alphabetical order in a block at the end of the entry. The block is introduced by the symbol ►►.

> **editorial** [edɪˈtɔːrɪəl] **1** *adj (decision, comment)* de la rédaction; *(job, problems, skills)* de rédaction, rédactionnel
> **2** *n* (**a**) *(article)* éditorial *m* (**b**) *(department)* service *m* de la rédaction, rédaction *f*
> ►► ***editorial changes*** corrections *fpl*; ***editorial content*** contenu *m* rédactionnel; ***editorial department*** *(in press)* service *m* de la rédaction, rédaction *f*, direction *f* de la rédaction;...

The rule of entering a compound under its first element means, for example, that **sedge warbler, melodious warbler** and **garden warbler** will be found under **sedge, melodious** and **garden** respectively, and not at the entry **warbler.**

Hyphenated words in both English and French, however, appear as entries in their own right, in the relevant alphabetical order.

Grammatical information

■ **Plurals**

When a French noun has an irregular plural, this is shown immediately after the headword, sometimes in brackets:

> **linteau, -x** [lɛ̃to] *nm* lintel

> **trullo** [trulo] (*pl* **trullos** *ou* **trulli**) *nm Archit* trullo

Note that the plural of hyphenated French nouns is always given, unless the noun does not change its form in the plural, in which case it is marked **inv**:

> **protège-tibia** [prɔtɛʒtibja] (*pl* **protège-tibias**) *nm* shin pad

Similarly, English irregular plurals are also given after the headword, placed in brackets:

> **salmon** ['sæmən] (*pl* **inv** *or* **salmons**) *n Ich* saumon *m*; **young salmon** tacon *m*
> ►► ***salmon farm*** élevage *m* de saumons, ***salmon fillet*** filet *m* de saumon; ***salmon ladder, salmon leap*** échelle *f* à saumon(s); ***salmon pink*** (rose *m*) saumon *m*; ***salmon steak*** darne *f* de saumon; *Ich* ***salmon trout*** truite *f* saumonée

> **emissary** ['emɪsərɪ] (*pl* **emissaries**) *n* émissaire *m*

> **madwoman** ['mædwʊmən] (*pl* **madwomen** [-wɪmɪn]) *n* folle *f*, aliénée *f*

■ **English verb forms**

Irregular forms of English verbs are given after the headword for that verb:

> **edify** ['edɪfaɪ] (*pt & pp* **edified**) *vt Formal* édifier

> **seek** [siːk] (*pt & pp* **sought** [sɔːt]) **1** *vt* (**a**) (*search for → job, woman, solution*) chercher, rechercher; **he constantly sought her approval** il cherchait constamment à obtenir son approbation; ...

■ **French verb conjugations**

A number in square brackets is given after each French verb in volume 2. Users should refer to the conjugation model indicated by this number in the list of French conjugations on page xxix in volume 2 in order to read the full conjugation of the verb.

INTRODUCTION (ENGLISH)

Pronunciation

Pronunciation information has been given for all words using the International Phonetic Alphabet (IPA). An explanation of the symbols used can be found on page xxvii. In contrast to most bilingual dictionaries, a phonetic transcription has been given for all abbreviations, unless they are only used in written language. Thus it will be clear whether the abbreviation is an acronym or its letters are pronounced individually.

Register

The register of all words and phrases in the source language is clearly indicated in this dictionary. Register labels are used to indicate the level of language - whether formal (***Formal/Formel***), informal (***Fam***), very informal (***very/très Fam***), or vulgar (***Vulg***) - and also to indicate usage, showing whether a word is, for example, pejorative, ironic or euphemistic. All abbreviated labels are included in the list of labels on the inside cover of the book. As far as possible, the translations given match the register of the word in the source language and no register markers are therefore applied to translations, as the user can assume that the translation is a close register match of the source language item. For example:

> **macchabée** [makabe] *nm Fam (cadavre)* stiff

In cases where it has proved impossible to find an exact equivalent in terms of register for a word that is informal, or where it is considered desirable to include a neutral alternative translation, the neutral register of the translation is indicated by a superscript symbol (❑) that comes immediately after the translation. For example:

> **adman** ['ædmæn] (*pl* **admen** [-men]) *n Fam* publicitaire❑ *m*

> **quat'zyeux** [katzjø] **entre quat'zyeux** *adv Fam* in private❑

> **savater** [3] [savate] *vt Fam* to kick❑, to boot

Those French terms which are examples of verlan (the process of inverting syllables to create a slang word) have been labelled as such, with the original form indicated in brackets:

> **keuf** [kœf] *nm très Fam* (*verlan de* **flic**) cop; **les keufs** the fuzz, the cops

Similarly, those British slang words which are examples of rhyming slang have been labelled, with both the full form of the original phrase and the word with which it rhymes indicated. Note that where, as in the example below, the term is not widely used in Britain but restricted to southern England, and particularly the London area, it is labelled ***SEng***.

> **dustbin** ['dʌstbɪn] *n* (**a**) *Br (for rubbish)* poubelle *f* (**b**) *SEng Fam* **dustbins** (*rhyming slang* **dustbin lids = kids)** gosses *mpl*, mômes *mpl*
> ►► ***dustbin lid*** couvercle *m* de poubelle; ***dustbin liner*** sac-poubelle *m*; *Br* ***dustbin man*** éboueur *m*

Many terms from the Canadian French dialect joual have been included in this dictionary. They have all been labelled ***CanJoual*** but do not have any additional labelling as to the level of language. This labelling should be understood, however, to imply that the term is non-standard and of a colloquial level of language.

Register labels can occur in various combinations. A word can be either archaic or literary, old-fashioned or humorous, for example. In such cases the presentation is as follows:

abysm [ə'bɪzəm] *n Arch or Literary* abîme *m*

enamouré, -e [ɑ̃namure], **énamouré, -e** [enamure] *adj Vieilli ou Hum (regard, sourire)* amorous; **être enamouré de qn** to be enamoured of sb

mater ['meɪtə(r)] *n Br Old-fashioned or Hum* **(the) mater** ma mère, maman *f*

A word which is simultaneously informal and old-fashioned, or informal and euphemistic, will be presented as follows with the labels in sequence:

Mae West [meɪ'west] *n Am Fam Old-fashioned* gilet *m* de sauvetage (gonflable) ❑

untruth [ʌn'tru:θ] *n Euph Formal (lie)* mensonge *m*, invention *f*; **to tell an untruth** mentir, dire un mensonge

In the cases of certain words belonging to a particular variety of slang such as drugs or crime slang, the register label ***Fam*** or ***very Fam*** etc is accompanied by labels indicating the variety to which the term in question belongs. For example:

coked up [kəʊkt-] *adj Fam Drugs slang* défoncé à la coke

Poulaga [pulaga] *nf Fam Arg crime* **la maison Poulaga** the cops, *Br* the pigs, the fuzz

In instances where a term is given two translations, one technical and the other non-technical, the technical translation is placed second and preceded by the label ***Spec*** or ***Spéc*** in the English-French and French-English volumes respectively. The technical translation has been given in addition to the neutral one where the word being translated can be used in both technical and non-technical contexts.

drug ...
... ***drug dependency*** dépendance *f* à l'égard des drogues, toxicomanie *f*, *Spec* pharmacodépendance *f*; ...

mastiquer[1] [3] [mastike] *vt (pain, viande)* to chew, *Spéc* to masticate

Some French words in this dictionary are marked with the label ***Offic***. This indicates that the word in question is an officially recommended form, used less commonly than an alternative term which is often derived from English:

caravanette [kærəvə'net] *n* camping-car *m*, *Offic* autocaravane *f*

Specialist language

The *Unabridged* features a vast number of specialized items of vocabulary relating to areas as diverse as computing, finance, law, science and medicine. Many technical terms have been retained from the Harrap ***Standard***, which was used as a source for this dictionary, while a great many new terms have been added, particularly terminology created by the growth of the Internet or connected with fast-evolving areas like the stock market or genetic engineering.

A full list of the abbreviated field labels used to mark these specialist terms is to be found on the inside cover of the book. Field labels are used primarily to indicate specialist vocabulary, or to differentiate the various meanings of the headword. In cases where a word has several meanings in different domains, all with the same translation, field labels are combined in sequence to show that the translation works for all the senses indicated. For example:

palette ['pælət] *n Art & Comput* palette *f*
►► ***palette knife*** *Art* couteau *m* (à palette); *Culin* spatule *f*

hybride [ibrid] **1** *adj* (**a**) *Bot, Zool & Ling* hybrid (**b**) *(mêlé)* hybrid, mixed; **une solution un peu hybride** a rather hybrid solution; **une architecture hybride** a patchwork of architectural styles
2 *nm* hybrid

Navigating long entries

Long entries, consisting as they do of large blocks of dense text, tend not to be very user-friendly. One innovation in this dictionary that should help the user is the inclusion of "menus" at the beginning of many such entries. The aim of these menus is twofold: (i) to summarize the main translations of the entry; and (ii) to make use of the knowledge that the user already has to help them find the sense they want more quickly. Experienced dictionary users will want to consult the entries for common words to look for phrases and examples, rather than to learn that, for example, "pour" is a translation of "for". Thus in consulting, for example, the entry **care** the user can refer to the menu to locate quickly the "souci" sense of the word, and hence the phrases given at that category.

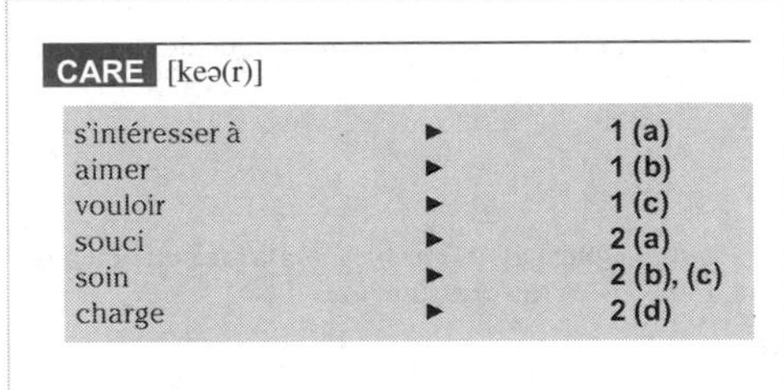
CARE [keə(r)]

s'intéresser à	►	**1 (a)**
aimer	►	**1 (b)**
vouloir	►	**1 (c)**
souci	►	**2 (a)**
soin	►	**2 (b), (c)**
charge	►	**2 (d)**

International coverage

This dictionary differs from its competitors in giving very full coverage of the international varieties of both English and French. In the English-French volume of the dictionary, thorough treatment of English as it is used in Britain and in America is complemented by extensive coverage of Australian, Irish and Scottish English. Thus, terms which the user might search for in vain in other bilingual dictionaries – such as **beyond the Black Stump**, **gurrier** and **muckle** (Australian, Irish and Scottish, respectively) to cite but three – will be found within the pages of the Harrap *Unabridged*.

Similarly, in the French-English volume, Canadian French is well represented, as are Belgian French and Swiss French. This reflects the dictionary's policy of ensuring coverage of the French language as it is used outside France. While this coverage cannot claim to be exhaustive, the editors of the dictionary hope that they have succeeded in their aim of including a substantial quantity of words and expressions from each of these French-speaking countries. As mentioned above, Canadian French joual terms have been included, as have terms particular to Acadian, the dialect spoken in the Maritime Provinces (Nova Scotia, New Brunswick, Prince Edward Island). These latter terms have been labelled (*en acadien*). Likewise, when a term is specific to a certain French-speaking canton of Switzerland, it is labelled accordingly:

lambouri [lãburi] *nm Can (en acadien)* navel

In all these cases, work done by a team of consultants from the countries concerned, combined with material drawn from monolingual sources, has formed the basis for a final selection of words and expressions associated with each country. Regional varieties of both languages are also covered, with terms from, for example, Southern France or Northern England featuring among the entries and expressions treated.

As far as target language is concerned, in the French-English volume of the dictionary, British and American variant translations are shown systematically, marked as ***Br*** and ***Am*** respectively:

> **sapeur-pompier** [sapœrpɔ̃pje] (*pl* **sapeurs-pompiers**) *nm Br* fireman, *Am* firefighter; **les sapeurs-pompiers** *Br* the fire brigade, *Am* the fire department

In the English-French volume, Belgian, Canadian and Swiss variant translations are also shown where appropriate:

> **mobile ...**
> ... ***mobile phone*** (téléphone *m*) portable *m*, *Belg* GSM *m*, *Suisse* Natel *m inv*, *Can* cellulaire *m*; ...

> **logjam** [ˈlɒgdʒæm] *n* (**a**) *(in river)* bouchon *m* de bois flottés, *Can* digue *f* (**b**) *Fig (deadlock)* impasse *f*

Cultural notes

The Harrap ***Unabridged*** contains over five hundred notes on cultural topics, where extra information that could not be conveyed in a conventional translation or gloss format is highlighted in a boxed entry integrated into the main text. Many of these notes concern "culture-specific" items, that is to say topics whose relevance or implications may not be immediately obvious to non-native speakers; other more encyclopedic-style notes provide the user with information on terms relating to the politics or history of the country. Examples in the English-French volume are the notes at **devolution, countryside debate** and **gun control**. In the French-English volume **bizutage, charentaises** and **cohabitation** are similarly explained for the non-native user. In line with the dictionary policy of comprehensive international coverage, the boxes include information on items of Canadian, Irish and Scottish relevance as well as French Canadian, Belgian and Swiss items.

DEVOLUTION

Le projet de décentralisation pour l'Écosse et le pays de Galles ("devolution"), soumis à référendum dans les années soixante-dix, fut abandonné par le parti conservateur, à la tête de la Grande-Bretagne de 1979 à 1998. Cependant, à la suite de la victoire des travaillistes en 1997, Tony Blair honora sa promesse électorale et organisa un nouveau référendum dans les deux régions. Les Écossais se déclarèrent en faveur de la décentralisation à une écrasante majorité. Le "oui" l'emporta également au Pays de Galles mais de façon moins convaincante. Moins de deux ans plus tard, le 6 mai 1999, l'Écosse retrouvait un parlement après 300 ans d'interruption et les Gallois disposaient d'une assemblée pour la première fois en 500 ans. *voir aussi encadrés sous* **Scottish Parliament** *et* **Welsh Assembly**

LA COHABITATION 

Originally, this term refers to the period (1986-1988) during which the socialist President (François Mitterrand) had a right-wing Prime Minister (Jacques Chirac), following the victory of the RPR in the legislative elections and Mitterrand's decision not to resign as President. It has since been used to refer to the similar situation which arose following the 1993 elections (with Édouard Balladur as Prime Minister) and more recently the 1997 elections (with the left-wing government of Lionel Jospin co-ruling with the President Jacques Chirac).

Allusions

A major innovative feature of this dictionary is the inclusion of notes on allusions, explaining to non-native speakers how certain phrases are used allusively in the other language. The allusions are often literary but many also derive from areas such as advertisements and popular culture. These notes are designed to enable the user to decode areas of language which might otherwise remain opaque. In each case, the origin of the phrase is explained in addition to its contemporary usage. Examples in the English-French volume are **come up and see me some time, dark Satanic mills** and **magical mystery tour,** and in the French-English volume **le mot de Cambronne, le degré zéro** and **faire avancer le schmilblick**.

A total of 250 allusions have been selected for the dictionary. Our selection has been guided by the degree to which the phrase is used in the language and its origin is recognized by native speakers.

Works of art

The dictionary contains almost a thousand titles of works of art with their equivalents in the target language. Famous paintings as well as films, works of literature and music are covered. These are to be found at the end of the entry for the first important word in the title (for example Dickens' ***Hard Times*** is at the end of the entry **hard,** and Proust's ***À l'ombre des jeunes filles en fleur*** at **ombre**) and are preceded by an icon designating the genre to which the work of art belongs. While many of these items have perfectly straightforward translations, it will be found that others are translated in quite unexpected ways.

'Le Blé en herbe' Colette 'The Ripening Seed'
'À bout de souffle' Godard 'Breathless'
'The End of the Affair' Greene, Jordan 'La Fin d'une liaison'

The titles included are a selection of those judged to be either culturally significant or which generate interesting translations.

Introduction (français)

La parution du présent ouvrage coïncide avec le centenaire de la maison Harrap. Au moment de se mettre à la tâche, les lexicographes qui travaillèrent à la rédaction de ce nouveau grand dictionnaire anglais-français français-anglais eurent une pensée émue pour leurs illustres prédécesseurs. En effet, le Harrap's ***Standard***, conçu par George Harrap, dirigé par le professeur Jean Mansion et publié en deux parties en 1935 et 1939, est un ouvrage monumental qui jouit depuis de nombreuses années d'une réputation inégalée. Les rédacteurs du Harrap's ***Unabridged*** se sont efforcés de préserver les caractéristiques qui ont fait le succès du ***Standard***, et notamment son traitement en profondeur des termes techniques et littéraires. Ils ont également su tirer le maximum des innovations qui ont révolutionné le domaine de la lexicographie bilingue depuis l'époque du professeur Mansion.

L'élaboration du dictionnaire

Grâce à l'outil informatique et à l'existence de textes sur bases de données interrogeables, la rédaction de ce dictionnaire n'a nécessité qu'une fraction du temps qui fut consacré à l'élaboration du ***Standard***. Nul doute que toutes les possibilités de recherche qu'offre l'Internet au lexicographe d'aujourd'hui auraient ravi le professeur Mansion, et que celui-ci aurait su faire bon usage du courrier électronique pour communiquer avec ses nombreux collaborateurs.

L'Internet a donné naissance à toute une nouvelle terminologie, très bien représentée dans le présent ouvrage, et a contribué à rendre accessible au plus grand nombre les différentes variétés de français et d'anglais. À titre d'exemple, lorsque l'on recherche un terme anglais sur l'Internet on peut être amené à consulter un site américain, canadien ou australien aussi bien que britannique. De même, lors d'une recherche de termes français, l'on peut consulter des sites canadiens, belges ou suisse au même titre que des sites franco-français. C'est pourquoi nous avons décidé de rendre compte de la richesse des deux langues au-delà de leur pays d'origine et l'***Unabridged*** propose ainsi un panorama linguistique des mondes francophone et anglophone d'une richesse inégalée.

Des spécialistes ont assuré le traitement des diverses variétés de français et d'anglais qui figurent dans ce dictionnaire. Par ailleurs, nos consultants ont joué un rôle déterminant lors de l'élaboration de bases de données spécialisées dans des domaines tels que l'informatique, la finance et l'argot, bases de données largement exploitées lors de la conception de l'***Unabridged***. Enfin, un comité de lecture composé d'universitaires francophones et anglophones nous a fait part de ses remarques et suggestions tout au long de la rédaction de ce livre.

Pour finir, il convient de rendre hommage aux lexicographes de la société Harrap qui n'ont pas ménagé leurs efforts pour que soit mené à bien ce projet entamé il y a quatre ans, sans oublier l'équipe prépresse qui a assuré la composition de l'ouvrage et le traitement de plus de 10 000 pages d'épreuves.

Un dictionnaire complet?

Les rédacteurs se sont efforcés d'inclure autant de termes et d'expressions que possible dans les deux volumes de l'***Unabridged***. Cependant cet ouvrage ne peut prétendre à l'exhaustivité tant il est vrai que même un dictionnaire deux fois plus volumineux ne pourrait rendre compte des deux langues dans leur intégralité. Ce qui est indéniable, c'est que l'***Unabridged*** présente un panorama complet et très large des deux langues telles qu'on les parle et qu'on les écrit en ce début de XXIème siècle.

La structure des entrées

Les entrées du dictionnaire apparaissent en bleu et sont classées par ordre alphabétique. Il faut noter que les homographes comportant une majuscule à l'initiale sont placés avant ceux dont la première lettre est une minuscule. Ainsi **Pépin (le Bref)** apparaît avant **pépin**.

■ Le classement en fonction des catégories grammaticales

Les différentes catégories grammaticales sont indiquées en italique et en abrégé; par exemple: ***nm, nf, vi, prép.*** La liste des abréviations des indicateurs de catégories grammaticales utilisées figure en début et en fin de dictionnaire. Lorsqu'un mot comporte plusieurs catégories grammaticales, ces dernières sont précédées d'un chiffre arabe en gras.

> **hand-knit 1** *n* pull *m/etc* tricoté à la main
> **2** *vt* tricoter à la main

■ Les divisions sémantiques

Les différents sens du mot sont précédés d'une lettre minuscule en gras:

> **snood** [snu:d] *n* (**a**) *(for hair)* résille *f* (**b**) *(hood)* cagoule *f* (**c**) *Fishing* empile *f* (**d**) *Scot Hist (headband)* = bandeau porté autrefois dans les cheveux par les jeunes femmes célibataires

Les nuances et les distinctions sémantiques qui nécessitent des traductions différentes au sein d'une même catégorie sont signalées par des indicateurs de sens qui apparaissent entre parenthèses. Ces indicateurs peuvent être des synonymes ou des collocations. Pour les verbes transitifs ces collocations sont des compléments d'objet typiques, pour les adjectifs il s'agit des noms qui leur sont associés le plus fréquemment. Dans certains cas figurent un indicateur synonymique ainsi que des collocations, ces dernières étant précédées d'une flèche.

> **debase** [dɪ'beɪs] *vt* (**a**) *(degrade → person, sport)* avilir, abaisser; *(→ reputation)* ternir; *(→ tradition, profession, politics)* dévaloriser (**b**) *(make less valuable → object)* dégrader, altérer; *(→ metal, currency, coinage)* déprécier

Lorsqu'un mot est particulièrement complexe, ses sens principaux sont divisés en grandes sous-catégories dont chacune est elle-même subdivisée. Une lettre majuscule en gras signale chaque grande sous-catégorie et est suivi d'explications en capitales d'imprimerie:

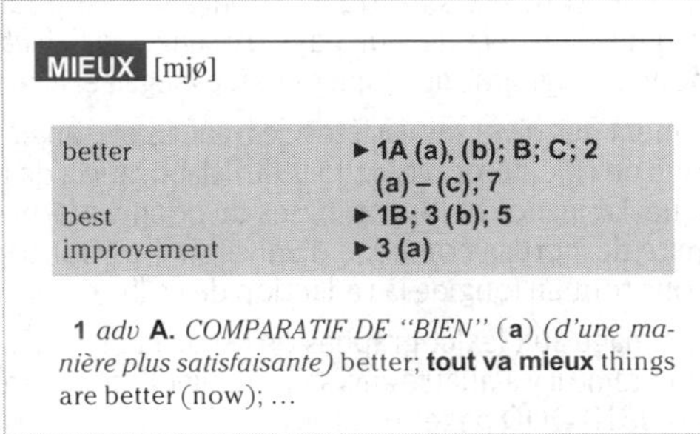

MIEUX [mjø]

better	► **1A (a), (b); B; C; 2 (a) – (c); 7**
best	► **1B; 3 (b); 5**
improvement	► **3 (a)**

1 *adv* **A.** *COMPARATIF DE "BIEN"* (**a**) *(d'une manière plus satisfaisante)* better; **tout va mieux** things are better (now); ...

■ Les mots composés anglais

Dans ce dictionnaire, les noms composés anglais de deux éléments ou plus apparaissent dans l'article consacré au premier élément du mot composé. Ils sont présentés en italique à la fin de l'article et sont classés par ordre alphabétique. Pour les entrées concernées, la section des mots composés est signalée par le symbole ►►.

> **editorial** [edɪ'tɔ:rɪəl] **1** *adj (decision, comment)* de la rédaction; *(job, problems, skills)* de rédaction, rédactionnel
> **2** *n* (**a**) *(article)* éditorial *m* (**b**) *(department)* service *m* de la rédaction, rédaction *f*
> ►► ***editorial changes*** corrections *fpl*; ***editorial content*** contenu *m* rédactionnel; ***editorial department*** *(in press)* service *m* de la rédaction, rédaction *f*, direction *f* de la rédaction; ...

Puisque que les mots composés apparaissent sous le premier élément, il faut, à titre d'exemple, chercher les mots **sedge warbler, melodious warbler** et **garden warbler** respectivement aux articles **sedge, melodious** et **garden,** et non à l'article **warbler**.

Cependant, les mots composés avec trait d'union sont présentés en tant qu'entrées à part entière, selon l'ordre alphabétique.

Les informations d'ordre grammatical

■ Le pluriel

Dans le volume français-anglais, le pluriel irrégulier des noms est indiqué juste après l'intitulé de l'entrée.

> **linteau, -x** [lɛ̃to] *nm* lintel

> **trullo** [trulo] (*pl* **trullos** *ou* **trulli**) *nm Archit* trullo

Le pluriel des noms composés avec trait d'union est donné systématiquement, sauf pour les noms invariables; dans ce cas la mention **inv** figure juste après l'abréviation qui indique la catégorie grammaticale.

> **protège-tibia** [prɔtɛʒtibja] (*pl* **protège-tibias**) *nm* shin pad

De même, dans le volume anglais-français, les pluriels irréguliers apparaissent entre parenthèses, à la suite de l'entrée:

> **salmon** ['sæmən] (*pl* **inv** *or* **salmons**) *n Ich* saumon *m*; **young salmon** tacon *m*
> ►► ***salmon farm*** élevage *m* de saumons; ***salmon fillet*** filet *m* de saumon; ***salmon ladder, salmon leap*** échelle *f* à saumon(s); ***salmon pink*** (rose *m*) saumon *m*; ***salmon steak*** darne *f* de saumon; *Ich* ***salmon trout*** truite *f* saumonée

> **emissary** ['emɪsərɪ] (*pl* **emissaries**) *n* émissaire *m*

> **madwoman** ['mædwʊmən] (*pl* **madwomen** [-wɪmɪn]) *n* folle *f*, aliénée *f*

■ La conjugaison des verbes anglais

La forme irrégulière de chaque verbe anglais est donnée juste après l'entrée correspondante:

> **edify** ['edɪfaɪ] (*pt & pp* **edified**) *vt Formal* édifier

> **seek** [si:k] (*pt & pp* **sought** [sɔ:t]) **1** *vt* (**a**) (*search for* → *job, person, solution*) chercher, rechercher; **he constantly sought her approval** il cherchait constamment à obtenir son approbation; ...

■ La conjugaison des verbes français

Dans le volume français-anglais un numéro entre crochets apparaît à la suite de chaque verbe. Pour consulter la conjugaison complète d'un verbe, il faut se reporter au numéro correspondant du tableau des conjugaisons du volume 2 [pages xxix à xl].

La prononciation

La prononciation de toutes les entrées est donnée en alphabet phonétique international (API). La liste des symboles de l'API utilisés dans ce dictionnaire figure en page xxvii. Contrairement à la plupart des autres dictionnaires bilingues, notre ouvrage indique la phonétique de toutes les abréviations, sauf lorsqu'il s'agit d'abréviations utilisées uniquement à l'écrit. Ainsi, l'utilisateur sait s'il a à faire à un acronyme ou à une abréviation dont les lettres se prononcent séparément.

Les niveaux de langue

Le registre de toutes les expressions et tous les mots donnés en langue source est clairement indiqué dans le dictionnaire. Des indicateurs de registre sont donnés pour préciser le niveau de langue, qu'il soit soutenu (***Formal*/*Formel***), familier (***Fam***), très familier (***very Fam*/*très Fam***), ou vulgaire (***Vulg***). Les nuances d'emploi sont également indiquées lorsqu'un terme est employé en tant qu'euphémisme ou de façon péjorative ou ironique. La liste de toutes les abréviations utilisées comme indicateurs figure à l'intérieur de la couverture. D'une manière générale les traductions reflètent le niveau de langue des mots et expressions de la langue source et elles ne sont donc pas accompagnées d'indicateurs de registre, comme dans l'exemple suivant:

> **macchabée** [makabe] *nm Fam (cadavre)* stiff

Lorsqu'il s'est avéré impossible de trouver une traduction qui corresponde au registre familier d'un terme de la langue source, ou lorsqu'il est souhaitable de faire figurer également en traduction un terme de registre non familier, la traduction est accompagnée d'un symbole en exposant (❑) qui indique qu'il ne s'agit pas d'un terme familier, comme dans les exemples suivants:

> **adman** ['ædmæn] (*pl* **admen** [-men]) *n Fam* publicitaire❑ *m*

> **quat'zyeux** [katzjø] **entre quat'zyeux** *adv Fam* in private❑

> **savater** [3] [savate] *vt Fam* to kick❑, to boot

Dans le volume français-anglais, les termes de verlan sont indiqués comme tels, et la forme originelle du mot est indiquée entre parenthèses:

> **keuf** [kœf] *nm très Fam* (*verlan de* **flic**) cop; **les keufs** the fuzz, the cops

De même, dans le volume anglais-français, les termes de "rhyming slang" sont clairement indiqués et sont accompagnés de leur forme complète ainsi que du terme avec lequel ils riment. Il faut noter que lorsqu'un terme n'est pas employé dans l'ensemble de la Grande-Bretagne mais uniquement dans le sud de l'Angleterre et particulièrement dans la région de Londres, il est accompagné de l'abréviation ***SEng***, comme dans l'exemple suivant:

> **dustbin** ['dʌstbɪn] *n* (**a**) *Br (for rubbish)* poubelle *f* (**b**) *SEng Fam* **dustbins** (*rhyming slang* **dustbin lids = kids**) gosses *mpl*, mômes *mpl*
> ►► ***dustbin lid*** couvercle *m* de poubelle; ***dustbin liner*** sac-poubelle *m*; *Br* ***dustbin man*** éboueur *m*

De nombreux termes de joual figurent dans ce dictionnaire. Ils sont tous accompagnés de la mention ***Can Joual***, sans indication supplémentaire de niveau de langue, car le joual est par définition une langue de registre familier.

Un terme peut comporter plusieurs indicateurs de registre. À titre d'exemple, un mot archaïque peut également être utilisé pour ses accents littéraires, et l'on peut choisir d'employer un terme vieilli de façon à produire un effet humoristique. La présentation est alors la suivante:

abysm [ə'bɪzəm] *n Arch or Literary* abîme *m*

enamouré, -e [ɑ̃namure], **énamouré, -e** [enamure] *adj Vieilli ou Hum (regard, sourire)* amorous; **être enamouré de qn** to be enamoured of sb

mater ['meɪtə(r)] *n Br Old-fashioned or Hum* **(the) mater** ma mère, maman *f*

Les termes qui sont à la fois familiers et vieillis, ou bien familiers et euphémistiques sont présentés comme suit, avec les indicateurs les uns à la suite des autres:

Mae West [meɪ'west] *n Am Fam Old-fashioned* gilet *m* de sauvetage (gonflable) ☐

untruth [ʌn'tru:θ] *n Euph Formal (lie)* mensonge *m*, invention *f*; **to tell an untruth** mentir, dire un mensonge

Lorsqu'un terme appartient à une variété d'argot particulier (comme l'argot de la drogue ou du milieu), les indicateurs de niveau de langue ***Fam*** ou ***très Fam*** sont suivis d'une mention où figure le type d'argot dont il s'agit, comme dans les exemples suivants:

coked up [kəʊkt-] *adj Fam Drugs slang* défoncé à la coke

Poulaga [pulaga] *nf Fam Arg crime* **la maison Poulaga** the cops, *Br* the pigs, the fuzz

Dans le cas où un mot de la langue source comporte deux traductions, l'une de registre technique et l'autre qui s'utilise dans la langue de tous les jours, la traduction technique est placée en seconde position et précédée de l'abréviation ***Spéc*** dans le volume français-anglais et ***Spec*** dans le volume anglais-français. Une traduction technique est fournie en plus de la traduction habituelle lorsque le mot traduit s'utilise dans des contextes techniques et non techniques.

drug ...
... ***drug dependency*** dépendance *f* à l'égard des drogues, toxicomanie *f*, *Spec* pharmacodépendance *f*;...

mastiquer[1] [3] [mastike] *vt (pain, viande)* to chew, *Spéc* to masticate

Certains mots français sont accompagnés de la mention ***Offic***. Cette abréviation indique que l'emploi du mot en question est recommandé à la place de l'anglicisme correspondant, pourtant souvent d'un usage plus courant:

> **caravanette** [kærəvə'net] *n* camping-car *m*, *Offic* autocaravane *f*

Le vocabulaire de spécialité

Le Harrap's ***Unabridged*** comporte un très grand nombre de termes techniques liés à toutes sortes de domaines tels que l'informatique, la finance, le droit, les sciences et la médecine. Un nombre non négligeable de termes provient du Harrap's ***Standard***, qui est l'une des sources utilisées lors de la rédaction de l'***Unabridged***. De très nombreux termes nouveaux ont été ajoutés notamment dans des domaines dont la terminologie évolue rapidement, tels que l'Internet, la finance et le génie génétique.

La liste complète des abréviations des domaines de spécialité utilisés dans le dictionnaire figure à l'intérieur de la couverture. Les indicateurs de domaines de spécialité servent à signaler les termes techniques ou à distinguer les différentes acceptions d'un terme. Lorsqu'un mot s'utilise dans différents domaines et que sa traduction est la même dans tous les cas, les indicateurs sont présentés les uns à la suite des autres et précèdent la traduction, comme dans les exemples suivants:

> **palette** ['pælət] *n Art & Comput* palette *f*
> ►► ***palette knife*** *Art* couteau *m* (à palette); *Culin* spatule *f*

> **hybride** [ibrid] **1** *adj* (**a**) *Bot, Zool & Ling* hybrid (**b**) *(mêlé)* hybrid, mixed; **une solution un peu hybride** a rather hybrid solution; **une architecture hybride** a patchwork of architectural styles
> **2** *nm* hybrid

La consultation des articles longs

Les longs articles de dictionnaire se présentent souvent sous forme de blocs de texte particulièrement denses et rébarbatifs. Une des innovations de cet ouvrage consiste à faire figurer des "menus" en tête des articles longs pour faciliter la recherche de l'utilisateur. L'utilité de ces menus est double: 1/ ils présentent en résumé les traductions d'un terme suivant ses différentes acceptions 2/ ils permettent au lecteur de repérer facilement le sens qu'il recherche en faisant appel à ses connaissances. Les utilisateurs de dictionnaires chevronnés consultent les articles longs davantage pour trouver des expressions et des exemples qui illustrent les différents usages d'un terme, que pour apprendre que le mot "pour" se traduit par "for". Ainsi un lecteur qui consulte l'article **care**, par exemple, pourra trouver immédiatement le sens qui correspond au français "souci" et toutes les expressions qui s'y rapportent grâce au menu.

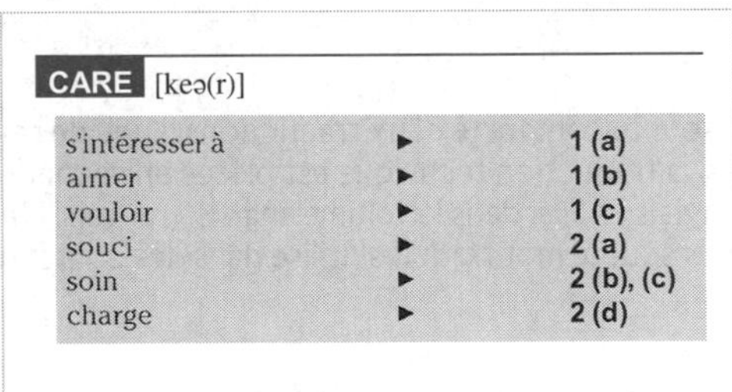

CARE [keə(r)]

s'intéresser à	►	**1 (a)**
aimer	►	**1 (b)**
vouloir	►	**1 (c)**
souci	►	**2 (a)**
soin	►	**2 (b), (c)**
charge	►	**2 (d)**

Le français et l'anglais d'ailleurs

Ce dictionnaire se distingue de ses concurrents par son traitement en profondeur des différentes variétés d'anglais et de français dans le monde. Dans le volume anglais-français, l'anglais de Grande-Bretagne et des États-Unis est traité de manière exhaustive, et les mots et expressions propres à l'anglais d'Australie, d'Irlande et d'Écosse sont également très bien représentés. À titre d'exemple, des termes tels que **gurrier**, **muckle** et **beyond the Black Stump**, qui proviennent respectivement de l'anglais d'Irlande, d'Écosse et d'Australie et que l'on chercherait en vain dans d'autres dictionnaires bilingues, se trouvent dans le Harrap's ***Unabridged***.

De même, dans le volume français-anglais, le français du Canada est très bien représenté, tout comme le français de Suisse et de Belgique. Un des buts de ce dictionnaire bilingue est de donner droit de cité au français que l'on parle hors de France. Sans prétendre à l'exhaustivité, les rédacteurs du présent ouvrage ont inclus un nombre non négligeable de termes et expressions originaires des pays cités plus haut. Des termes de joual ont été inclus ainsi que des termes d'acadien (le parler franco-canadien utilisé dans les Provinces Maritimes) qui sont précédés de la mention (*en acadien*). De même, le fait que tel ou tel terme suisse est propre à un canton particulier est clairement indiqué.

> **lambouri** [lɑ̃buri] *nm Can (en acadien)* navel

La liste des mots et expressions de chacun des pays mentionnés a été établie par des consultants originaires des pays en question et s'est enrichie de termes issus de sources monolingues. Les variantes régionales des deux langues telles qu'on les parle en France et en Grande-Bretagne sont également représentées avec entre autres des termes et expressions originaires du sud de la France et du nord de l'Angleterre.

Dans le volume français-anglais, les variantes britanniques et américaines des traductions sont systématiquement données et clairement indiquées par les abréviations *Br* et *Am*:

> **sapeur-pompier** [sapœrpɔ̃pje] *(pl* **sapeurs-pompiers***) nm Br* fireman, *Am* firefighter; **les sapeurs-pompiers** *Br* the fire brigade, *Am* the fire department

Dans le volume anglais-français, des traductions en français de Belgique, du Canada et de Suisse sont fournies lorsque nécessaire:

> **mobile** ...
> ... ***mobile phone*** (téléphone *m*) portable *m*, *Belg* GSM *m*, *Suisse* Natel *m inv*, *Can* cellulaire *m*; ...

> **logjam** ['lɒgdʒæm] *n* (**a**) *(in river)* bouchon *m* de bois flottés, *Can* digue *f* (**b**) *Fig (deadlock)* impasse *f*

Les encadrés culturels

Le Harrap's *Unabridged* contient plus de cinq cents encadrés intégrés au texte qui portent sur des points de culture; des explications y sont données lorsqu'une traduction ou une glose ne suffisent pas à fournir les informations nécessaires. Ces encadrés culturels concernent le plus souvent des thèmes propres à une culture ou à un pays particuliers, qui ne sont pas nécessairement connus en dehors du pays en question. D'autres encadrés fournissent des informations de nature encyclopédique sur des termes liés à l'histoire et à la politique des différents pays concernés. À titre d'exemple, dans le volume français-anglais, des notes en anglais éclaireront les lecteurs anglophones sur des sujets tels que le **bizutage**, la **cohabitation** ou le **Pacs**, et dans le volume anglais-français, les utilisateurs francophones pourront lire des notes en français sur la **devolution**, le **countryside debate** et le problème des armes à feu aux États-Unis (**gun control**). Les encadrés culturels comprennent également des informations sur l'Irlande, l'Écosse, le Canada, la Belgique et la Suisse.

DEVOLUTION

Le projet de décentralisation pour l'Écosse et le pays de Galles ("devolution"), soumis à référendum dans les années soixante-dix, fut abandonné par le parti conservateur, à la tête de la Grande-Bretagne de 1979 à 1998. Cependant, à la suite de la victoire des travaillistes en 1997, Tony Blair honora sa promesse électorale et organisa un nouveau référendum dans les deux régions. Les Écossais se déclarèrent en faveur de la décentralisation à une écrasante majorité. Le "oui" l'emporta également au Pays de Galles mais de façon moins convaincante. Moins de deux ans plus tard, le 6 mai 1999, l'Écosse retrouvait un parlement après 300 ans d'interruption et les Gallois disposaient d'une assemblée pour la première fois en 500 ans. *voir aussi encadrés sous* **Scottish Parliament** *et* **Welsh Assembly**

LA COHABITATION 

Originally, this term refers to the period (1986-1988) during which the socialist President (François Mitterrand) had a right-wing Prime Minister (Jacques Chirac), following the victory of the RPR in the legislative elections and Mitterrand's decision not to resign as President. It has since been used to refer to the similar situation which arose following the 1993 elections (with Édouard Balladur as Prime Minister) and more recently the 1997 elections (with the left-wing government of Lionel Jospin co-ruling with the President Jacques Chirac).

Les allusions

L'une des grandes innovations de ce dictionnaire est la présence de notes explicatives qui portent sur de nombreuses expressions anglaises et françaises qui sont en fait des allusions culturelles. Les allusions sont souvent issues de la littérature mais nombreuses sont celles qui proviennent également de la culture populaire. Ces notes explicatives sont destinées à permettre à l'utilisateur de comprendre des expressions a priori impénétrables utilisées dans l'autre langue. Dans chaque cas, la note explicative éclaire le lecteur sur l'origine de l'expression et la façon dont on l'emploie. Parmi les allusions présentes dans le volume anglais-français notons **come up and see me some time, dark Satanic mills** et **magical mystery tour,** et dans le volume français-anglais **le mot de Cambronne, le degré zéro** et **faire avancer le schmilblick**.

Le dictionnaire compte au total 250 allusions. Elles ont été retenues car elles sont d'un emploi relativement fréquent et sont reconnues comme allusions par la plupart de ceux qui les utilisent.

Les œuvres littéraires et les œuvres d'art

Ce dictionnaire compte près de mille titres d'œuvres littéraires et d'œuvres d'art avec leur équivalent dans l'autre langue. Les beaux-arts, la musique, le cinéma et la littérature sont représentés. Le titre d'une œuvre se trouve à la fin de l'article de dictionnaire correspondant au premier mot important du titre en question. Ainsi, ***Hard Times,*** de Dickens, est traité à la fin de l'article **hard,** et ***À l'ombre des jeunes filles en fleurs*** apparaît à la fin de l'article **ombre**. Les titres sont signalés par des symboles représentant le genre d'œuvre dont il s'agit. Souvent les traductions sont prévisibles, parfois elles le sont beaucoup moins...

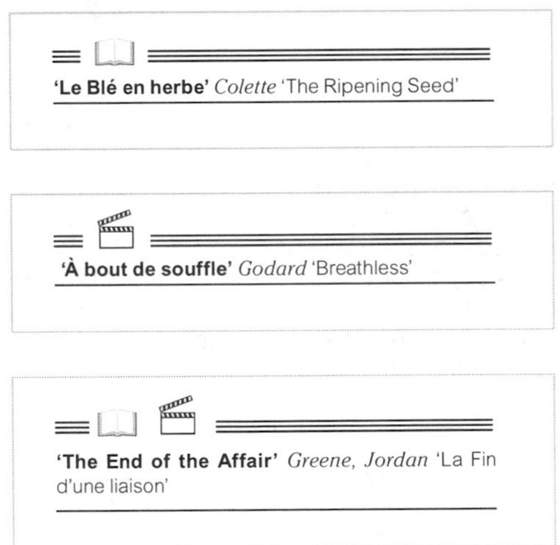

'Le Blé en herbe' Colette 'The Ripening Seed'
'À bout de souffle' Godard 'Breathless'
'The End of the Affair' Greene, Jordan 'La Fin d'une liaison'

Ont été inclus les titres d'œuvres jugées importantes d'un point de vue culturel, ou dont la traduction est particulièrement intéressante.

Prononciation de l'anglais

Pour indiquer la prononciation anglaise, nous avons utilisé dans ce dictionnaire les symboles de l'API (Alphabet phonétique international). Pour chaque son anglais, vous trouverez dans le tableau ci-dessous des exemples de mots anglais, suivis de mots français présentant un son similaire. Une explication est donnée lorsqu'il n'y a pas d'équivalent en français.

Caractère API	Exemple en anglais	Exemple en français
Consonnes		
[b]	babble	bébé
[d]	dig	dent
[dʒ]	giant, jig	jean
[f]	fit, physics	face
[g]	grey, big	gag
[h]	happy	h aspiré : à quelques rares exceptions près, il est toujours prononcé en anglais
[j]	yellow	yaourt
[k]	clay, kick	car
[l]	lip, pill	lilas
[m]	mummy	maman
[n]	nip, pin	né
[ŋ]	sing	parking
[p]	pip	papa
[r]	rig, write	Pas d'équivalent français : se prononce en plaçant le bout de la langue au milieu du palais
[(r)]		Seulement prononcé en cas de liaison avec la voyelle qui suit comme dans : faraway; the car is blue
[s]	sick, science	silence
[ʃ]	ship, nation	chèvre
[t]	tip, butt	tartine
[tʃ]	chip, batch	atchoum
[θ]	thick	Son proche du /s/ français, il se prononce en plaçant le bout de la langue entre les dents du haut et celles du bas
[ð]	this, with	Son proche du /z/ français, il se prononce en plaçant le bout de la langue entre les dents du haut et celles du bas
[v]	vague, give	vie
[w]	wit, why	whisky
[z]	zip, physics	rose
[ʒ]	pleasure	je
[χ]	loch	Existe seulement dans certains mots écossais. Pas d'équivalent français : se prononce du fond de la gorge, comme Bach en allemand ou la 'jota' espagnole.
Voyelles		
[æ]	rag	natte
[ɑː]	large, half	pâte
[e]	set	/e/ moins ouvert que le [ɛ] français
[ɜː]	curtain, were	heure
[ə]	utter, about	cheval

Caractère API	Exemple en anglais	Exemple en français
[ɪ]	b*i*g, wom*e*n	/i/ bref, à mi-chemin entre les sons [ɛ] et [i] français (plus proche de 'n*e*t' que de 'v*i*te')
[iː]	l*ea*k, w*ee*	/i/ plus long que le [i] français
[ɒ]	l*o*ck	b*o*nne – mais plus ouvert et prononcé au fond du palais
[ɔː]	w*a*ll, c*o*rk	b*au*me – mais plus ouvert et prononcé au fond du palais
[ʊ]	p*u*t, l*oo*k	Son à mi-chemin entre un /ou/ bref et un /o/ ouvert
[uː]	m*oo*n	Son /ou/ prolongé
[ʌ]	c*u*p	À mi-chemin entre un /a/ et un /e/ ouverts
Diphtongues : Elles sont rares en français et sont la combinaison de deux sons.		
[aɪ]	wh*y*, h*igh*, l*ie*	*aï*e
[aʊ]	h*ow*	mi*aou*, *aoû*tat – mais se prononce comme un seul son
[eə]	b*ear*, sh*are*, wh*ere*	fl*ai*r
[eɪ]	d*ay*, m*a*ke, m*ai*n	merv*eille*
[əʊ]	sh*ow*, g*o*	Combinaison d'un /o/ fermé et d'un /ou/
[ɪə]	h*ere*, g*ear*	Combinaison d'un /i/ long suivi d'un /e/ ouvert bref
[ɔɪ]	b*oy*, s*oi*l	langue d'*oï*l
[ʊə]	*sure*	Combinaison d'un son /ou/ suivi d'un /e/ ouvert bref

Verbes anglais irréguliers

Infinitif	Prétérit	Participe passé
arise	arose	arisen
awake	awoke	awoken
awaken	awoke, awakened	awakened, awoken
be	were/was	been
bear	bore	borne
beat	beat	beaten
become	became	become
begin	began	begun
bend	bent	bent
beseech	besought, beseeched	besought, beseeched
bet	bet, betted	bet, betted
bid	bade, bid	bidden, bid
bind	bound	bound
bite	bit	bitten
bleed	bled	bled
blow	blew	blown
break	broke	broken
breed	bred	bred
bring	brought	brought
build	built	built
burn	burnt, burned	burnt, burned
burst	burst	burst
bust	bust, busted	bust, busted
buy	bought	bought
cast	cast	cast
catch	caught	caught
chide	chided, chid	chided, chidden
choose	chose	chosen
cleave	cleaved, cleft, clove	cleaved, cleft, cloven
cling	clung	clung
clothe	clad, clothed	clad, clothed
come	came	come
cost	cost	cost
creep	crept	crept
crow	crowed, crew	crowed
cut	cut	cut
deal	dealt	dealt
dig	dug	dug
dive	dived, *Am* dove	dived
do	did	done
draw	drew	drawn
dream	dreamt, dreamed	dreamt, dreamed
drink	drank	drunk
drive	drove	driven
dwell	dwelt	dwelt
eat	ate	eaten
fall	fell	fallen
feed	fed	fed
feel	felt	felt
fight	fought	fought
find	found	found
flee	fled	fled
fling	flung	flung
fly	flew	flown
forget	forgot	forgotten
forgive	forgave	forgiven
forsake	forsook	forsaken
freeze	froze	frozen
get	got	got, *Am* gotten
gild	gilded, gilt	gilded, gilt
gird	girded, girt	girded, girt
give	gave	given
go	went	gone
grind	ground	ground
grow	grew	grown
hang	hung/hanged	hung/hanged

Infinitif	Prétérit	Participe passé
have	had	had
hear	heard	heard
hew	hewed	hewn, hewed
hide	hid	hidden
hit	hit	hit
hold	held	held
hurt	hurt	hurt
keep	kept	kept
kneel	knelt	knelt
knit	knitted, knit	knitted, knit
know	knew	known
lay	laid	laid
lead	led	led
lean	leant, leaned	leant, leaned
leap	leapt, leaped	leapt, leaped
learn	learnt, learned	learnt, learned
leave	left	left
lend	lent	lent
let	let	let
lie	lay	lain
light	lit	lit
lose	lost	lost
make	made	made
mean	meant	meant
meet	met	met
mow	mowed	mown
pay	paid	paid
plead	pleaded, *Am* pled	pleaded, *Am* plead
prove	proved	proved, proven
put	put	put
quit	quit	quit
read	read	read
rend	rent	rent
rid	rid	rid
ride	rode	ridden
ring	rang	rung
rise	rose	risen
run	ran	run
saw	sawed	sawn, sawed
say	said	said
see	saw	seen
seek	sought	sought
sell	sold	sold
send	sent	sent
set	set	set
sew	sewed	sewn
shake	shook	shaken
shear	sheared	shorn, sheared
shed	shed	shed
shine	shone	shone
shit	shitted, shat	shitted, shat
shoe	shod	shod
shoot	shot	shot
show	showed	shown
shrink	shrank	shrunk
shut	shut	shut
sing	sang	sung
sink	sank	sunk
sit	sat	sat
slay	slew	slain
sleep	slept	slept
slide	slid	slid
sling	slung	slung
slink	slunk	slunk
slit	slit	slit
smell	smelled, smelt	smelled, smelt
smite	smote	smitten
sow	sowed	sown, sowed
speak	spoke	spoken
speed	sped, speeded	sped, speeded

Infinitif	Prétérit	Participe passé
spell	spelt, spelled	spelt, spelled
spend	spent	spent
spill	spilt, spilled	spilt, spilled
spin	span	spun
spit	spat, *Am* spit	spat, *Am* spit
split	split	split
spoil	spoilt, spoiled	spoilt, spoiled
spread	spread	spread
spring	sprang	sprung
stand	stood	stood
stave in	staved in, stove in	staved in, stove in
steal	stole	stolen
stick	stuck	stuck
sting	stung	stung
stink	stank, stunk	stunk
strew	strewed	strewed, strewn
stride	strode	stridden
strike	struck	struck
string	strung	strung
strive	strove	striven
swear	swore	sworn
sweep	swept	swept
swell	swelled	swollen, swelled
swim	swam	swum
swing	swung	swung
take	took	taken
teach	taught	taught
tear	tore	torn
tell	told	told
think	thought	thought
thrive	thrived, throve	thrived
throw	threw	thrown
thrust	thrust	thrust
tread	trod	trodden
wake	woke	woken
wear	wore	worn
weave	wove, weaved	woven, weaved
weep	wept	wept
wet	wet, wetted	wet, wetted
win	won	won
wind	wound	wound
wring	wrung	wrung
write	wrote	written

DICTIONARY
DICTIONNAIRE

English-French
Anglais-Français

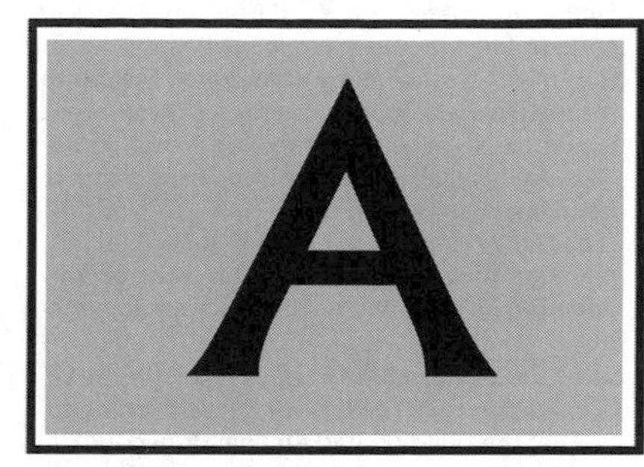

A[1], **a**[1] [eɪ] **1** *n* (**a**) *(letter)* A, a *m inv*; **two a's** deux a; **A for Andrew** ≃ A comme Anatole; **6A Bothwell Street** 6 bis Bothwell Street; **I'm not going because a) I've no money and b) I've no time** je n'y vais pas parce que primo je n'ai pas d'argent et secundo je n'ai pas le temps; *Br* **the A5** *(road)* ≃ la RN 5; **from A to Z** de A à Z; **from A to B** de A à B; **the car's old, but it gets me from A to B** c'est une vieille voiture mais elle me permet de me déplacer; **the train is the best way of getting from A to B** le train c'est le meilleur moyen de se déplacer d'un endroit à un autre; **the roads are so crowded that it takes forever to get from A to B** les routes sont si encombrées que le moindre trajet prend une éternité; **from point A to point B** d'un point A à un point B

(**b**) *Sch* **to get an A** avoir une très bonne note, ≃ avoir entre 16 et 20; *Am Sch & Univ* **he got straight A's** *(top marks)* il a eu de très bonnes notes partout

(**c**) *Br Formerly Cin* = film interdit aux moins de 14 ans (maintenant remplacé par "PG")

(**d**) *Mus* la *m inv*; **in A flat** en la bémol

2 *adj Mus (string)* de la

►► *Br* ***A road*** route *f* nationale

A[2] *Elec* (*written abbr* **ampere**) A

a[2] [ə, *stressed* eɪ]

> **a** devient **an** [ən, *stressed* æn] devant voyelle ou h muet

indef art (**a**) *(before countable nouns)* un (une); **a book** un livre; **a car** une voiture; **a hotel** [ə͵həʊ'tel], *Old-fashioned* **an hotel** [ən͵əʊ'tel] un hôtel; **an hour** [ən'aʊə(r)] une heure; **a unit** [ə'juːnɪt] une unité; **an uncle** [ən'ʌŋkəl] un oncle; **an MP** [ən'em'piː] un député; **a man and (a) woman** un homme et une femme; **a cup and saucer** une tasse et sa soucoupe; **a wife and mother** *(same person)* une épouse et mère; **I can't see a thing** je ne vois rien; **he has a broken leg** il a une jambe cassée; **would you like a coffee?** voulez-vous un café?; **an expensive German wine** un vin allemand cher

(**b**) *(before professions, nationalities)* **she's a doctor** elle est médecin; **he is an Englishman/a father** il est anglais/père; **have you seen a doctor?** as-tu vu un médecin?

(**c**) *(before numbers)* **a thousand dollars** mille dollars; **a dozen eggs** une douzaine d'œufs; **a third/fifth** un tiers/cinquième; **a twentieth of a second** un vingtième de seconde; **an hour and a half** une heure et demie

(**d**) *(per)* **£2 a dozen/a hundred grammes** deux livres la douzaine/les cent grammes; **five francs a head** cinq francs par tête; **three times a year** trois fois par an; **fifty kilometres an hour** cinquante kilomètres à l'heure

(**e**) *(before terms of quantity, amount)* **a few weeks/months** quelques semaines/mois; **a lot of money** beaucoup d'argent; **a great many visitors** de très nombreux visiteurs; **have a little more wine** reprenez donc un peu de vin; **he raised a number of interesting points** il a soulevé un certain nombre de questions intéressantes

(**f**) *(before periods of time)* un (une); **I'm going for a week/month/year** je pars (pour) une semaine/un mois/un an; **we talked for a while** nous avons parlé un moment

(**g**) *(before days, months, festivals)* un (une); **the meeting was on a Tuesday** la réunion a eu lieu un mardi; **it was an exceptionally cold March** ce fut un mois de mars particulièrement froid; **we had an unforgettable Christmas** nous avons passé un Noël inoubliable

(**h**) *(before nouns in apposition)* **Caen, a large town in Normandy** Caen, ville importante de Normandie; **forty years a sailor and he still gets seasick!** il a beau être marin depuis quarante ans, il lui arrive toujours d'avoir le mal de mer

(**i**) *(in generalizations)* **a triangle has three sides** le triangle a trois côtés; **a cheetah can outrun a lion** le guépard court plus vite que le lion; **a computer is a useful machine** les ordinateurs sont des machines bien utiles

(**j**) *(before uncountable nouns)* **a wide knowledge of the subject** une connaissance approfondie du sujet; **he felt a joy he could not conceal** il éprouvait une joie qu'il ne pouvait dissimuler

(**k**) *(before verbal nouns)* **there's been a general falling off in sales** il y a eu une chute des ventes

(**l**) *(taking definite article in French)* **to have a red nose** avoir le nez rouge; **I have a sore throat/back/knee** j'ai mal à la gorge/au dos/au genou; **to have a taste for sth** avoir le goût de qch

(**m**) *(before personal names)* **a Miss Jones was asking for you** une certaine Miss Jones vous a demandé; **he's been described as a new James Dean** on le donne pour le nouveau James Dean; **her mother was a Sinclair** sa mère était une Sinclair

(**n**) *(before names of artists)* **it's a genuine Matisse** c'est un Matisse authentique; **there's a new Stephen King/Spielberg out next month** il y a un nouveau Stephen King/Spielberg qui sort le mois prochain

(**o**) *(after half, rather, such, what)* **half a glass of wine** un demi-verre de vin; **she's rather an interesting person** c'est quelqu'un d'assez intéressant; **you're such an idiot!** tu es tellement bête!; **what a lovely dress!** quelle jolie robe!

(**p**) *(after as, how, so, too + adj)* **that's too big a slice for me** cette tranche est trop grosse pour moi; **how big a bit do you want?** combien en veux-tu?; **she's as nice a girl as you could wish to meet** c'est la fille la plus gentille du monde

---

a. *Agr* (*written abbr* **acre**) = 4047m², ≃ demi-hectare *m*

A-1 [͵eɪ'wʌn] *adj* (**a**) *(first-class, perfect)* **everything's A-1** tout est parfait (**b**) *(in health)* **to be A-1** être en pleine santé *ou* forme (**c**) *Naut* en excellent état

A3 ['eɪ'θriː] *Typ* **1** *n (paper size)* format *m* A3
2 *adj* **A3 paper** papier *m* (format) A3

A4 ['eɪ'fɔː(r)] *Typ* **1** *n (paper size)* format *m* A4
2 *adj* **A4 paper** papier *m* (format) A4

AA[1] [͵eɪ'eɪ] **1** *adj Mil* (*abbr* **anti-aircraft**) DCA *f*; **AA fire/guns** tir *m*/canons *mpl* de DCA

2 *n* (**a**) (*abbr* **Automobile Association**) = automobile club britannique et compagnie d'assurances, qui garantit le dépannage de ses adhérents et propose des services touristiques et juridiques, ≃ ACF *m*, ≃ TCF *m*

(**b**) (*abbr* **Alcoholics Anonymous**) AA *mpl*; **an AA meeting** une réunion des alcooliques anonymes

(**c**) (*abbr* **Advertising Association**) = organisme britannique dont le rôle est de veiller à la qualité des publicités et de défendre les intérêts des annonceurs et des agences de publicité

(**d**) *Am Univ* (*abbr* **Associate in Arts**) *(person)* = titulaire d'un diplôme universitaire américain de lettres; *(qualification)* diplôme *m* universitaire américain de lettres

AA[2] *n Banking & St Exch* (notation *f*) AA *f*

AAA[1] *n* (**a**) [͵θriː'eɪz] *Formerly Sport* (*abbr* **Amateur Athletics Association**) = ancien nom de la fédération britannique d'athlétisme (remplacé en octobre 1991 par la "British Athletics Federation") (**b**) [͵eɪeɪ'eɪ] (*abbr* **American Automobile Association**) = automobile club américain, ≃ ACF *m*, ≃ TCF *m*

AAA[2] [͵trɪpəl'eɪ] *n Banking & St Exch* (notation *f*) AAA *f*

Aachen ['ɑːkən] *n* Aix-la-Chapelle

A & E [͵eɪənd'iː] *n Med* (*abbr* **accident and emergency**) service *m* des urgences, urgences *fpl*

aardvark ['ɑːdvɑːk] *n Zool* oryctérope *m*

aardwolf ['ɑːdwʊlf] *n Zool* protèle *m*

Aargau ['ɑːgaʊ] *n* Argovie *f*; **in Aargau** en Argovie

Aaron ['eərən] *pr n Bible* Aaron

AARP [͵eɪeɪɑː'piː] *n* (*abbr* **American Association of Retired Persons**) = association américaine de retraités *(constituant un groupe de pression)*

AAU [͵eɪeɪ'juː] *n Am Sport* (*abbr* **Amateur Athletic Union**) = organisme chargé de superviser les manifestations sportives, en particulier dans les universités

AAUP [͵eɪeɪjuː'piː] *n* (*abbr* **American Association of University Professors**) = syndicat américain des professeurs d'université

AB[1] [͵eɪ'biː] *n* (**a**) *Am Univ* (*abbr* **Artium Baccalaureus**) *(person)* = titulaire d'une licence de lettres; *(qualification)* licence *f* de lettres (**b**) *Br Naut* (*abbr* **able-bodied seaman**) matelot *m* de deuxième classe

AB[2] (*written abbr* **Alberta**) Alberta *f*

ABA [͵eɪbiː'eɪ] *n* (**a**) (*abbr* **Amateur Boxing Association**) Association *f* de boxe amateur (**b**) *Law* (*abbr* **American Bar Association**) = association d'avocats américains qui sert de centre d'information et de formation continue à ses membres

abaca [ə'bækə] *n Bot* abaca *m*

aback [ə'bæk] *adv* **to be taken aback** être pris au dépourvu, être interloqué; *Naut* être pris bout au vent; **I was quite taken aback by what he said** j'étais très surpris par ce qu'il m'a dit

abacus ['æbəkəs] (*pl* **abacuses** *or* **abaci** [-saɪ]) *n* (**a**) *(counting device)* boulier *m* (**b**) *Archit* abaque *m*, tailloir *m*

abaft [ə'bɑːft] *Naut* **1** *adv* à l'arrière
2 *prep* en arrière de

abalone [͵æbə'ləʊnɪ] *n Ich* oreille-de-mer *f*, ormeau *m*

abandon [ə'bændən] **1** *vt* (**a**) *(leave → person, object)* abandonner; *(→ post, place)* déserter, quitter; *Naut* **to abandon ship** abandonner *ou* quitter le navire; **we had to abandon the car in the snow** nous avons dû abandonner la voiture dans la neige; **they were abandoned to their fate** on les abandonna à leur sort; *Fig* **to abandon oneself to despair** se laisser aller *ou* s'abandonner au désespoir

(**b**) *(give up → search)* abandonner, renoncer à; *(→ studies, struggle)* renoncer à; *(→ idea, cause)* laisser tomber; *Comput (file, routine)* abandonner; **we abandoned the struggle** nous avons renoncé à lutter; *Sport* **to abandon play** *(temporarily)* interrompre la partie; *(permanently)* annuler la partie; **several runners abandoned the race** plusieurs coureurs ont abandonné; **the match was abandoned because of bad weather** on a interrompu le match en raison du mauvais temps; **to abandon all hope (of doing something)** abandonner tout espoir (de faire qch); **Abandon Hope, All Ye Who Enter Here** laissez tout espoir vous qui entrez *(phrase tirée de* *l'Enfer de Dante, parfois utilisée ironiquement pour signaler un lieu prétendu dangereux)*

(**c**) *(for insurance)* **they abandoned the car to the insurance company** ils ont cédé la voiture à la compagnie d'assurances

2 *n* (**a**) *(neglect)* abandon *m*; **in a state of abandon** laissé à l'abandon

(**b**) *(lack of inhibition)* désinvolture *f*, laisser-aller *m*; **they leapt about with wild** *or* **gay abandon** ils sautaient de joie sans aucune retenue

abandoned [ə'bændənd] *adj* (**a**) *(person)* abandonné, délaissé; *(house, car, settlement)* abandonné; **the building had an abandoned look** le bâtiment avait l'air abandonné (**b**) *Old-fashioned (dissolute → behaviour, person)* débauché; *(→ life)* de débauche (**c**) *(unrestrained → laughter, gaiety)* sans retenue

abandonment [ə'bændənmənt] *n* (**a**) *(of place, person, project)* abandon *m* (**b**) *(of right)* cession *f*

abase [ə'beɪs] *vt Literary* **to abase oneself** s'humilier, s'abaisser

abasement [ə'beɪsmənt] *n Literary* humiliation *f*

abashed [ə'bæʃt] *adj* penaud; **to be** *or* **to feel abashed (at sth)** avoir honte (de qch)

abate [ə'beɪt] **1** *vi (storm, fear, anger)* s'apaiser; *(pain)* se calmer; *(flood)* baisser; *(noise)* s'atténuer

2 *vt (tax)* baisser, réduire

abatement [ə'beɪtmənt] *n* (**a**) *(of tax, rent)* réduction *f*, abattement *m* (**b**) *(of storm, fear, anger)* apaisement *m*; *(of pain, of noise)* atténuation *f*; *(of flood)* abaissement *m*

abattoir ['æbətwɑː(r)] *n* abattoirs *mpl*

abaxial [ˌæb'æksɪəl] *adj Bot* désaxé

abbess ['æbes] *n* abbesse *f*

Abbevillian [ˌæb'vɪlɪən] *Archeol* **1** *adj* abbevillien

2 *n* abbevillien *m*

abbey ['æbɪ] **1** *n* abbaye *f*; **the Abbey, Westminster Abbey** l'abbaye de Westminster

2 *comp (grounds)* de l'abbaye

abbot ['æbət] *n* abbé *m (dans un monastère)*

abbr, abbrev (**a**) *(written abbr* **abbreviation**) abréviation *f* (**b**) *(written abbr* **abbreviated**) abrégé

abbreviate [ə'briːvɪeɪt] *vt (text, title)* abréger; **"for example" is abbreviated to "eg"** "par exemple" est abrégé en "p. ex."; **the term most often appears in abbreviated form** le terme se rencontre le plus souvent dans sa forme abrégée

abbreviation [əˌbriːvɪ'eɪʃən] *n (of expression, title, word)* abréviation *f*; **"Dr" is an abbreviation for "doctor"** "Dr" est l'abréviation de "docteur"

ABC[1] [ˌeɪbiː'siː], *Am* **ABCs** [eɪbiː'siːz] **1** *n* (**a**) *(rudiments)* rudiments *mpl*, B.A. Ba *m*; **the ABC of woodwork** le B.A. Ba de la menuiserie (**b**) *(alphabet)* alphabet *m*; **it's as easy as ABC** c'est simple comme bonjour

ABC[2] *n* (**a**) *Banking (abbr* **activity-based costing**) coûts *mpl* par activité (**b**) *(abbr* **American Broadcasting Company**) = chaîne de télévision américaine (**c**) *(abbr* **Australian Broadcasting Corporation**) = chaîne de télévision australienne

ABC1 [ˌeɪbiːsiː'wʌn] *Mktg* **1** *n* = catégorie sociale allant du cadre supérieur au cadre moyen, au pouvoir d'achat élevé *(dans le cadre du système de classification sociale britannique ABC1)*

2 *adj* au pouvoir d'achat élevé; **the magazine has been targeted at ABC1 men aged 25 – 44** le magazine s'adresse aux hommes de 25 à 44 ans au pouvoir d'achat élevé

ABD [ˌeɪbiː'diː] *n Am Univ (abbr* **all but dissertation**) = personne qui n'a plus qu'à rédiger sa thèse pour obtenir son doctorat

abdicate ['æbdɪkeɪt] **1** *vt* (**a**) *(of monarch)* **to abdicate the throne** abdiquer (**b**) *(right)* renoncer à; *(responsibility)* abandonner

2 *vi* abdiquer

abdication [ˌæbdɪ'keɪʃən] *n* (**a**) *(of throne)* abdication *f* (**b**) *(of right)* renonciation *f*; *(of responsibility)* abandon *m*

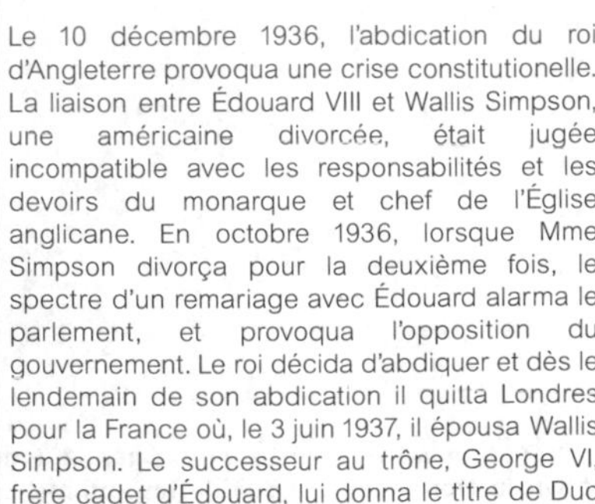

THE ABDICATION CRISIS OF 1936

Le 10 décembre 1936, l'abdication du roi d'Angleterre provoqua une crise constitutionelle. La liaison entre Édouard VIII et Wallis Simpson, une américaine divorcée, était jugée incompatible avec les responsabilités et les devoirs du monarque et chef de l'Église anglicane. En octobre 1936, lorsque Mme Simpson divorça pour la deuxième fois, le spectre d'un remariage avec Édouard alarma le parlement, et provoqua l'opposition du gouvernement. Le roi décida d'abdiquer et dès le lendemain de son abdication il quitta Londres pour la France où, le 3 juin 1937, il épousa Wallis Simpson. Le successeur au trône, George VI, frère cadet d'Édouard, lui donna le titre de Duc de Windsor.

abdicator ['æbdɪkeɪtə(r)] *n* (**a**) *(of throne)* abdicataire *mf* (**b**) *(of right)* renonciateur(trice) *m,f*

abdomen ['æbdəmən] *n Anat* abdomen *m*

abdominal [æb'dɒmɪnəl] *adj Anat* abdominal

►► ***abdominal muscles*** abdominaux *mpl*

abduct [æb'dʌkt] *vt* enlever, kidnapper

abductee [æb'dʌk'tiː] *n* = personne qui prétend avoir été enlevée par des extraterrestres

abduction [æb'dʌkʃən] *n* rapt *m*, enlèvement *m*

'The Abduction from the Seraglio' *Mozart*
'L'Enlèvement au sérail'

abductor [əb'dʌktə(r)] *n* (**a**) *(of person)* ravisseur(euse) *m,f* (**b**) *Anat* (muscle *m*) abducteur *m*

abeam [ə'biːm] *adv Naut & Aviat* par le travers

abed [ə'bed] *adv Literary* dans son lit, au lit

Abel ['eɪbəl] *pr n Bible* Abel

Aberdeen Angus ['æbəˌdiːn'æŋgəs] *n Agr (breed)* aberdeen-angus *m*

Aberdonian [ˌæbə'dəʊnɪən] **1** *n* habitant(e) *m,f* d'Aberdeen

2 *adj* d'Aberdeen

aberrant [æ'berənt] *adj (gen) & Biol* aberrant

aberration [ˌæbə'reɪʃən] *n* (**a**) *(action, idea)* aberration *f*; **a mental aberration** une aberration mentale; **it's an aberration** c'est aberrant; **in a moment of aberration** dans un moment de folie (**b**) *Astron & Opt* aberration *f*

abet [ə'bet] *(pt & pp* **abetted**, *cont* **abetting**) *vt (aid)* aider; *(encourage)* encourager; *Law* **to abet sb in a crime** encourager *ou* pousser qn à un crime

abetting [ə'betɪŋ] *n Law* **aiding and abetting** complicité *f*

abeyance [ə'beɪəns] *n Formal* (**a**) *(disuse)* désuétude *f*; **to fall into abeyance** tomber en désuétude; **the law is in temporary abeyance** la loi a momentanément cessé d'être appliquée; *Law* **estate in abeyance** succession *f* vacante (**b**) *(suspense)* suspens *m*; **the question was left in abeyance** la question a été laissée en suspens; **the final decision on the project is still in abeyance** la décision finale concernant le projet reste en suspens

abhor [əb'hɔː(r)] *(pt & pp* **abhorred**, *cont* **abhorring**) *vt Formal* détester, avoir en horreur; **nature abhors a vacuum** la nature a horreur du vide

abhorrence [əb'hɒrəns] *n Formal* aversion *f*, horreur *f*; **to have an abhorrence of sth, to hold sth in abhorrence** avoir horreur de qch *ou* une aversion pour qch, avoir qch en horreur

abhorrent [əb'hɒrənt] *adj Formal* (**a**) *(detestable → practice, attitude)* odieux, exécrable; **I find their attitude abhorrent, their attitude is abhorrent to me** je trouve leur attitude détestable (**b**) *(contrary)* contraire; *(incompatible)* incompatible; **such economic considerations are abhorrent to socialism** des considérations économiques de ce genre sont contraires au *ou* incompatibles avec le socialisme

abide [ə'baɪd] *(pt & pp* **abode** [ə'bəʊd] *or* **abided**) **1** *vt* (**a**) *(tolerate)* supporter; **she can't abide him** elle ne peut pas le souffrir *ou* supporter; **I can't abide people smoking in restaurants** je ne peux pas supporter les gens qui fument au restaurant; **if there's one thing I can't abide, it's hypocrisy** s'il y a quelque chose que je ne supporte pas, c'est l'hypocrisie; **I can't abide it when you talk to me like that** je ne supporte pas que tu me parles comme ça

(**b**) *Literary (wait for)* attendre; **I abide my time** j'attends l'occasion

2 *vi Literary* (**a**) *(live)* demeurer, habiter; *Rel* **abide with me** restez avec moi

(**b**) *(endure)* continuer, durer

►**abide by** *vt insep (decision, law)* se conformer à, respecter; *(promise)* tenir; *(result)* supporter, assumer; **will he abide by the new regulations?** respectera-t-il le nouveau règlement?; **I abide by my decision/what I said** je maintiens ma décision/ce que j'ai dit

abiding [ə'baɪdɪŋ] *adj* constant, permanent; *(impression)* durable; **an abiding sense of gratitude** un sentiment de gratitude éternelle

Abidjan [ˌæbɪ'dʒɑːn] *n Geog* Abidjan

abigail ['æbɪgeɪl] *n Arch (lady's maid)* camériste *f*, femme *f* de chambre; *(handmaiden)* suivante *f*

ability [ə'bɪlətɪ] *(pl* **abilities**) *n* (**a**) *(mental or physical)* capacité *f*, capacités *fpl*, aptitude *f*; **he has great ability** il a beaucoup de capacités, il est très capable; **to lack ability** manquer de capacités; **do you feel you have the necessary ability to run the project?** croyez-vous avoir les capacités nécessaires pour gérer le projet?; **children at different levels of ability/of different abilities** des enfants de niveaux intellectuels différents/aux compétences diverses; **I'll do it to the best of my ability** je le ferai du mieux que je peux, je ferai de mon mieux

(**b**) *(special talent)* capacités *fpl*, aptitude *f*; *(artistic or musical)* dons *mpl*, capacités *fpl*; **her acting ability** *or* **abilities remained unrecognized** ses talents d'actrice sont restés méconnus

abiogenesis [ˌeɪbaɪəʊ'dʒenɪsɪs] *n Bot & Zool* abigénèse *f*

abiotic [ˌeɪbaɪ'ɒtɪk] *adj Biol* abiotique

abject ['æbdʒekt] *adj* (**a**) *(despicable → person, deed)* abject, vil (**b**) *(servile → apology, flattery)* servile (**c**) *(miserable)* misérable; **they live in abject poverty** ils vivent dans une misère noire

abjection [æb'dʒekʃən] *n* (**a**) *(despicable nature)* abjection *f* (**b**) *(servility)* servilité *f* (**c**) *(misery)* misère *f* (**d**) *Bot (of spores)* projection *f*

abjectly ['æbdʒektlɪ] *adv* (**a**) *(despicably → act, refuse)* de manière abjecte (**b**) *(in a servile manner)* avec servilité, servilement (**c**) *(miserably)* misérablement

abjectness ['æbdʒektnɪs] *n* (**a**) *(despicable nature)* abjection *f* (**b**) *(misery)* misère *f*

abjuration [ˌæbdʒʊə'reɪʃən] *n Formal (of belief, faith)* reniement *m*; *(of religion)* abjuration *f*; *(of right)* renonciation *f*; *(of alliance)* refus *m*

abjure [əb'dʒʊə(r)] *vt Formal (belief, faith)* renier; *(religion)* abjurer; *(right)* renoncer à; *(alliance)* refuser, renier

Abkhazia [æb'keɪzɪə] *n Geog* Abkhazie *f*

Abkhazian [æb'keɪzɪən] **1** *n* (**a**) *(person)* Abkhaze *mf* (**b**) *(language)* Abkhaze *m*

2 *adj* abkhaze

ablation [æb'leɪʃən] *n* (**a**) *Med* ablation *f* (**b**) *Geol & Tech* ablation *f* (**c**) *Astron* ablation *f*

ablative ['æblətɪv] *n Gram* ablatif *m*

►► ***ablative absolute*** ablatif absolu; ***the ablative case*** l'ablatif *m*

ablaut ['æblaʊt] *n Ling* alternance *f* vocalique, ablaut *m*

ablaze [ə'bleɪz] **1** *adj* (**a**) *(on fire)* en flammes; **the factory was already ablaze when the firemen arrived** l'usine était déjà en flammes lorsque les pompiers sont arrivés (**b**) *(luminous)* **ablaze with light** brillant de lumière; **the offices were ablaze with light** toutes les lumières brillaient dans les bureaux (**c**) *(face)* brillant; *(eyes)* enflammé, pétillant; **her eyes were ablaze with anger** ses yeux étaient enflammés de colère

2 *adv* **to set sth ablaze** embraser qch

able ['eɪbəl] *(compar* **abler**, *superl* **ablest**) *adj* (**a**) *(capable of)* **to be able to do sth** *(know how)* savoir faire qch, être capable de faire qch; *(be physically capable)* pouvoir faire qch; *(succeed)* réussir à faire qch; **I won't be able to come** je ne pourrai pas venir; **I wasn't able to see** je ne voyais pas; **she wasn't able to explain** elle était incapable d'expliquer; **I'll be able to visit you**

more often now je pourrai te rendre visite plus souvent désormais; **I haven't been able to find out very much** je n'ai pas pu savoir grand-chose; **I'm not able to tell you** je ne suis pas en mesure de vous le dire; **she's better** *or* **more able to explain than I am** elle est mieux à même de vous expliquer que moi

(**b**) *(competent)* capable; **an able piece of work** un travail compétent *ou* bien fait

(**c**) *(talented)* talentueux, de talent

►► *Naut* ***able seaman*** matelot *m* breveté

able-bodied *adj* robuste, solide; **every able-bodied person helped in the search** toute personne en état de le faire a participé aux recherches

►► *Naut* ***able-bodied seaman*** matelot *m* breveté

abloom [ə'blu:m] *adj Literary* en fleur(s); **all nature is abloom once more** toute la nature est refleurie

ablush [ə'blʌʃ] *adj Literary* rougissant

ablutions [ə'blu:ʃənz] *npl* (**a**) *Rel* ablution *f* (**b**) *Hum (washing)* **to do** *or* **to perform one's ablutions** faire ses ablutions (**c**) *Fam Mil slang (building)* lavabos □ *mpl*

ably ['eɪblɪ] *adv* d'une façon compétente; **she performed ably in the 100 metres** elle s'est bien comportée dans le 100 mètres; **ably assisted by** efficacement assisté par

ABM [ˌeɪbi:'em] *n Mil (abbr* **anti-ballistic missile***)* ABM *m*

abnegate ['æbnɪgeɪt] *vt Formal* renoncer à

abnegation [ˌæbnɪ'geɪʃən] *n Formal* abnégation *f*

abnormal [æb'nɔ:məl] *adj* anormal

►► *Psy* ***abnormal psychology*** psychopathologie *f*

abnormality [ˌæbnɔ:'mælətɪ] *(pl* **abnormalities***) n* (**a**) *(abnormal state, condition etc)* anormalité *f*, caractère *m* anormal (**b**) *(abnormal feature) & Med & Biol* anomalie *f*; *(physical deformity)* malformation *f*; **behavioural abnormalities** troubles *mpl* du comportement

abnormally [æb'nɔ:məlɪ] *adv* anormalement; **he was abnormally shy** il était d'une timidité maladive

abo ['æbəʊ] *(pl* **abos***) n Austr Fam* = terme injurieux désignant un aborigène

aboard [ə'bɔ:d] **1** *adv* à bord; **to go aboard** monter à bord; **to take sth aboard** embarquer qch; **life aboard** la vie à bord; **all aboard!** *Naut* tout le monde à bord!; *Rail* en voiture!; **welcome aboard!** *(onto ship, aeroplane)* bienvenue à bord!; *Fig (onto team)* bienvenue dans l'équipe!

2 *prep (ship, aeroplane)* à bord de; *(train, bus)* dans; **aboard ship** à bord du bateau

abode [ə'bəʊd] **1** *pt & pp of* **abide**

2 *n Formal or Literary* demeure *f*; **he took up his abode in Tunisia** il s'est installé en Tunisie; *Law* **place of abode** domicile *m*; *Law* **to have the right of abode in a country** avoir le droit de séjour dans un pays

aboil [ə'bɔɪl] *adj Literary* (**a**) *(liquid → very hot)* bouillant; *(→ at boiling point)* en ébullition (**b**) *Fig (person)* furieux

abolish [ə'bɒlɪʃ] *vt (privilege, slavery, custom)* abolir; *(right)* supprimer; *(law)* supprimer, abroger

abolishing [ə'bɒlɪʃɪŋ], **abolishment** [ə'bɒlɪʃmənt] *n (of privilege, slavery, custom)* abolition *f*; *(of right)* suppression *f*; *(of law)* suppression *f*, abrogation *f*

abolition [ˌæbə'lɪʃən] *n (of* [illegible]*)* abolition *f*; *(of right)* suppression *f*; *(of law)* suppression *f*, abrogation *f*

abolitionism [ˌæbə'lɪʃənɪzəm] *n* abolitionnisme *m*; *Hist (in USA)* antiesclavagisme *m*

abolitionist [ˌæbə'lɪʃənɪst] **1** *n* abolitionniste *mf*; *Hist (in USA)* antiesclavagiste *mf*

2 *adj* abolitionniste; *Hist (in USA)* antiesclavagiste

abomasum [ˌæbəʊ'meɪsəm] *n Zool* caillette *f*, abomasum *m*

A-bomb *n Mil (abbr* **atom bomb***)* bombe *f* A

abominable [ə'bɒmɪnəbəl] *adj* (**a**) *(very bad)* abominable, lamentable, affreux; **her handwriting is abominable** son écriture est abominable (**b**) *(odious)* abominable, odieux

►► ***the abominable snowman*** l'abominable homme *m* des neiges

abominably [ə'bɒmɪnəblɪ] *adv* (**a**) *(very badly)* abominablement, lamentablement, affreusement (**b**) *(as intensifier)* extrêmement, abominablement; **it's abominably difficult** c'est abominablement difficile (**c**) *(odiously)* abominablement, odieusement

abominate [ə'bɒmɪneɪt] *vt Formal* détester, exécrer

abomination [əˌbɒmɪ'neɪʃən] *n* (**a**) *Formal (loathing)* abomination *f*; **we hold such behaviour in abomination** ce genre de comportement nous fait horreur *ou* nous horrifie (**b**) *Formal (detestable act)* abomination *f*, acte *m* abominable (**c**) *(awful thing)* abomination *f*, chose *f* abominable; **the building is an abomination** l'immeuble est une abomination

aboriginal [ˌæbə'rɪdʒənəl] **1** *adj* (**a**) *(culture, legend)* aborigène, des aborigènes (**b**) *Bot & Zool* aborigène

2 Aboriginal 1 *adj* aborigène, des aborigènes

2 *n (person)* aborigène *mf* (d'Australie)

aborigine [ˌæbə'rɪdʒənɪ] **1** *n (original inhabitant)* aborigène *mf*

2 *adj* aborigène, des aborigènes

3 Aborigine *n* (**a**) *(person)* aborigène *mf* (d'Australie) (**b**) *(language)* langue *f* aborigène

4 aborigines *npl Bot & Zool* flore *f* et faune *f* aborigènes

abort [ə'bɔ:t] **1** *n* (**a**) *(of mission, spacecraft)* interruption *f*

(**b**) *Comput (of program)* suspension *f* d'exécution, abandon *m*

2 *vt* (**a**) *(mission, flight)* interrompre, mettre un terme à; *(plan)* faire échouer

(**b**) *Med (woman)* avorter; **the foetus was aborted** la grossesse a été interrompue

(**c**) *Comput (program)* suspendre l'exécution de, abandonner

3 *vi* (**a**) *(mission, plans)* avorter, échouer; *Aviat (flight)* avorter; **the controller gave the order to abort** l'aiguilleur du ciel a donné l'ordre d'abandonner *ou* de suspendre le vol

(**b**) *Med (woman)* avorter; *(foetus)* ne pas tenir

abortifacient [əˌbɔ:tɪ'feɪʃənt] *Med* **1** *n* abortif *m*

2 *adj* abortif

abortion [ə'bɔ:ʃən] *n* (**a**) *Med* avortement *m*, interruption *f* (volontaire) de grossesse; **to have an abortion** se faire avorter; **to perform an abortion** faire un avortement; **abortion on demand** avortement *m* libre (**b**) *(of plans, mission)* avortement *m* (**c**) *very Fam (person, animal)* avorton *m*, monstre *m*

►► ***abortion clinic*** clinique *f* d'avortement; ***abortion law*** loi *f* sur l'avortement; ***abortion pill*** pilule *f* abortive

abortionist [ə'bɔ:ʃənɪst] *n* (**a**) *Med (practitioner)* avorteur(euse) *m,f* (**b**) *(advocate)* partisan *m* de l'avortement (légal)

abortive [ə'bɔ:tɪv] *adj* (**a**) *(plan, mission)* avorté, manqué; *(attempt)* manqué (**b**) *Biol (agent, organism, process)* abortif

abortively [ə'bɔ:tɪvlɪ] *adv* (**a**) *(unsuccessfully)* sans succès; **after trying abortively to help them** après avoir essayé sans (aucun) succès de les aider (**b**) *Biol (be born)* avant terme, prématurément

aboulia [ə'bu:lɪə] *n Psy* aboulie *f*

abound [ə'baʊnd] *vi (fish, resources)* abonder; *(explanations, ideas)* abonder, foisonner; **to abound in** *or* **with sth** abonder en qch, regorger de qch; **the area abounds in** *or* **with natural** [illegible] abonde en *ou* regorge de ressources naturelles

ABOUT [ə'baʊt]

à propos de	►1 (a)
au sujet de	►1 (a)
concernant	►1 (a)
partout	►1 (d)
autour de	►1 (e)
environ	►2 (a)
à peu près	►2 (a)
dans les parages	►2 (b)
par ici	►2 (b)
sur le point de	►2 (e)

1 *prep* (**a**) *(concerning, on the subject of)* à propos de, au sujet de, concernant; **she's had a letter about the loan** elle a reçu une lettre concernant le prêt; **I'm worried about her** je suis inquiet à son sujet; **what are they talking about?** de quoi parlent-ils?; **what are you talking about? of course I remembered!** qu'est-ce que tu racontes? bien sûr que j'y ai pensé!; **I don't know about you, but I fancy a drink** toi, je ne sais pas, mais moi je boirais bien un verre; **I'm not happy about her going** ça ne me plaît pas qu'elle y aille; **there's no doubt about it** cela ne fait aucun doute, il n'y a aucun doute là-dessus; **now, about your request for a salary increase...** bon, en ce qui concerne votre demande d'augmentation...; **OK, what's this all about?** bon, qu'est-ce qui se passe?; **what's the book about?** c'est un livre sur quoi?; **it's a book about the life of Mozart** c'est un livre sur la vie de Mozart; **I don't know what all the fuss is about** je ne vois pas pourquoi tout le monde se met dans cet état; **what do you want to see me about?** vous voulez me voir à quel sujet?; **that's what life's all about** c'est ça la vie; **he asked us about the war** il nous a posé des questions sur la guerre; **she asked me about my mother** elle m'a demandé des nouvelles de ma mère; **you should do something about your headaches** vous devriez faire quelque chose pour vos maux de tête; **I can't do anything about it** je n'y peux rien; **what do YOU know about it?** qu'est-ce que vous en savez, vous?; **I don't know much about Egyptian art** je ne m'y connais pas beaucoup en art égyptien; **I didn't know about your accident** je ne savais pas que vous aviez eu un accident; **she talked to them about her holidays** elle leur a parlé de ses vacances; **tell me about your holidays** parle-moi de tes vacances; **what do you think about modern art?** que pensez-vous de l'art moderne?; **I was thinking about my mother** je pensais à ma mère; **I'd like you to think about my offer** j'aimerais que vous réfléchissiez à ma proposition; **I warned them about the political situation** je les ai mis en garde en ce qui concerne la situation politique; **how** *or* **what about a game of bridge/going to Paris?** si on faisait un bridge/allait à Paris?

(**b**) *(in the character of)* **what I like about her is her generosity** ce que j'aime en *ou* chez elle, c'est sa générosité; **what I don't like about the house is all the stairs** ce qui me déplaît dans cette maison, ce sont tous les escaliers; **she found something amusing about the situation** elle a trouvé que la situation avait quelque chose d'amusant; **there's something about the house that I don't like** il y a quelque chose que je n'aime pas dans cette maison; **there's something about the place that reminds me of Rome** il y a quelque chose ici qui me fait penser à Rome; **there's something strange about her** il y a quelque chose de bizarre chez elle

(**c**) *(busy with)* **while I'm about it** pendant que j'y suis; **be quick about it!** faites vite!, dépêchez-vous!

(**d**) *(in phrasal verbs)* partout; **there were clothes lying all about the room** il y avait des vêtements qui traînaient partout; **you mustn't leave money lying about the house** il ne faut pas laisser de l'argent traîner dans la maison; **the children were running about the garden** les enfants couraient dans le jardin

(**e**) *(surrounding)* autour de; **the people about us** les gens auprès de nous, les gens qui nous entourent; **it's good to have a few** [illegible] **about the place** c'est bien de voir de nouvelles têtes par ici; **there is a high wall about the castle** un rempart entoure le château

(**f**) *Formal (on)* **to have sth about one's person** avoir qch sur soi; **he had a dangerous weapon about his person** il portait une arme dangereuse

2 *adv* (**a**) *(more or less)* environ, à peu près; **about a year** environ *ou* à peu près un an; **about £50** 50 livres environ; **about five o'clock** vers cinq heures; **she's about my age** elle a à peu près mon âge; **that looks about right** ça a l'air d'être à peu près ça; **he's about as tall as you** il est à peu près de ta taille; **you've got about as much intelligence as a two-year-old!** tu es à peu près aussi futé qu'un gamin de deux ans!; **I've just about finished** j'ai presque fini; **I've had just about enough!** j'en ai vraiment assez!; **it's about time** il serait *ou* est temps; **it's about time you started** il serait grand temps que vous vous y mettiez; **that's about it for now** c'est à peu près tout pour l'instant

(**b**) *(somewhere near)* dans les parages, par ici; **is there anyone about?** il y a quelqu'un?; **is Jack about?** est-ce que Jack est là?; **there was no one about when I left the building** il n'y avait personne dans les parages quand j'ai quitté l'immeuble; **my keys must be about somewhere** mes clés doivent être quelque part par ici; **there's never a policeman about when you need one** il n'y a jamais un seul agent de police dans les parages quand on en a besoin; **there weren't many people about** il n'y avait pas grand monde

(**c**) *(in all directions, places)* **there's a lot of flu about** il y a beaucoup de grippe en ce moment; **watch out, there are pickpockets about** méfie-toi, il y a beaucoup de pickpockets qui traînent; **have you seen many of the new coins about?** tu en as vu beaucoup de ces nouvelles pièces?; **there are some terrible rumours going about** il court des rumeurs terribles; **to run about** courir dans tous les sens; **to follow sb about** suivre qn partout; **don't leave your money lying about** ne laissez pas traîner votre argent; **they've been sitting about all day** ils ont passé toute la journée assis à ne rien faire; **she was waving her arms about** elle agitait les bras dans tous les sens

(**d**) *(in opposite direction)* **to turn about** se retourner; **the other way about** en sens inverse, dans le sens contraire

(**e**) *(expressing imminent action)* **to be about to do sth** être sur le point de faire qch; **what were you about to say?** qu'est-ce que vous alliez dire?; **I was just about to leave** j'allais partir, j'étais sur le point de partir

(**f**) *(expressing reluctance)* **I'm not about to answer that kind of question** je ne suis pas prêt à répondre à ce genre de question; **he's not about to change his ways just because of that** il n'y a pas de risque qu'il change ses manières de faire rien que pour ça

---

about-turn, *Am* **about-face 1** *exclam Mil (to right)* demi-tour...droite!; *(to left)* demi-tour... gauche!

2 *vi* (**a**) *Mil* faire un demi-tour (**b**) *(change opinion)* faire volte-face

3 *n* (**a**) *Mil* demi-tour *m*; **to do an about-turn** faire un demi-tour (**b**) *(change of opinion)* volte-face *f inv*; **to do an about-turn** faire volte-face

---

ABOVE [ə'bʌv]

au-dessus de	▸**1 (a), (b), (f), (h)**
plus que	▸**1 (c)**
au-delà de	▸**1 (d)**
par-dessus	▸**1 (g)**
ci-dessus	▸**2**
au-dessus	▸**3 (a)**
en haut	▸**3 (c)**
plus haut	▸**3 (d)**

1 *prep* (**a**) *(in a higher place or position than)* au-dessus de; **above our heads** au-dessus de nos têtes; **in the sky above us** dans le ciel au-dessus de nous; **smoke rose above the town** de la fumée s'élevait au-dessus de la ville; **above the equator** au-dessus de l'équateur; **above ground** en surface; **above sea level** au-dessus du niveau de la mer; **the water reached above their knees** l'eau leur montait jusqu'au-dessus des genoux; **skirts are above the knee this year** les jupes se portent au-dessus du genou cette année; **they live above the shop** ils habitent au-dessus du magasin; **a village on the river above Oxford** un village (situé) en amont d'Oxford; **his name appeared three lines above mine** son nom figurait trois lignes au-dessus du mien

(**b**) *(greater in degree or quantity than)* au-dessus de; **above 40 kilos** au-dessus de 40 kilos; **above $100** plus de 100 dollars; **it's above my price limit** c'est au-dessus du prix *ou* ça dépasse le prix que je me suis fixé; **his temperature is above normal** sa température est supérieure à *ou* au-dessus de la normale; **the temperature didn't rise above 10°C** la température n'a pas dépassé 10°C; **above average** au-dessus de la moyenne

(**c**) *(in preference to)* plus que; **he values friendship above success** il accorde plus d'importance à l'amitié qu'à la réussite; **he respected her above all others** il la respectait entre toutes

(**d**) *(beyond)* au-delà de; **the discussion was all rather above me** la discussion me dépassait complètement

(**e**) *(morally or intellectually superior to)* **she's above that sort of thing** elle est au-dessus de ça; **above suspicion/reproach** au-dessus de tout soupçon/reproche; **he's not above cheating** il irait jusqu'à tricher; **I'm not above asking for favours** je ne répugne pas à demander des faveurs; **she's not above telling the occasional lie** il lui arrive de mentir de temps en temps

(**f**) *(superior in rank, quality to)* au-dessus de; **to marry above one's station** se marier au-dessus de son rang; **she's ranked above the other athletes** elle se classe devant les autres athlètes; **to get above oneself** ne pas se prendre pour n'importe qui

(**g**) *(in volume, sound)* par-dessus; **it's difficult to make oneself heard above all this noise** il est difficile de se faire entendre avec tout ce bruit; **his voice was heard above the shouting** on entendait sa voix par-dessus le tumulte; **a scream rose above the noise of the engines** un cri se fit entendre par-dessus le bruit des moteurs

(**h**) *Mus (in pitch)* au-dessus de

2 *adj Formal* ci-dessus; *Admin* précité; **the above facts** les faits cités plus haut; **the names on the above list** les noms qui figurent sur la liste ci-dessus

3 *adv* (**a**) *(in a higher place or position)* au-dessus; **the stars above** le ciel constellé; **the people in the flat above** les voisins du dessus; **to fall from above** tomber d'en haut; **two lines above** deux lignes plus haut

(**b**) *(greater in degree or quantity)* **aged 20 and above** âgé de 20 ans et plus; **£5 and above** 5 livres ou plus

(**c**) *(a higher rank or authority)* en haut; **we've had orders from above** nous avons reçu des ordres d'en haut

(**d**) *(in book, document)* plus haut; **mentioned above** cité plus haut *ou* ci-dessus; **the paragraph above** le paragraphe ci-dessus; **as above** comme ci-dessus

(**e**) *Rel (in heaven)* là-haut, au ciel; **the angels above** les anges du ciel

(**f**) *Mus (in pitch)* **the note above** un ton plus haut *ou* au-dessus

4 *n Formal* **the above** *(fact, item)* ce qui se trouve ci-dessus; *(person)* le (la) susnommé(e); *(persons)* les susnommé(e)s; **can you explain the above?** pouvez-vous expliquer ce qui précède?; **the above is a quotation from Hamlet** le passage ci-dessus est une citation de Hamlet

5 above all *adv* avant tout, surtout

---

above-average *adj* au-dessus de la moyenne

above-board 1 *adj* (**a**) *(person)* honnête, régulier (**b**) *(action, behaviour)* franc (franche), honnête

2 *adv* (**a**) *(openly)* ouvertement, au grand jour (**b**) *(honestly)* honnêtement, de façon régulière (**c**) *(frankly)* franchement, cartes sur table

aboveground [ə,bʌv'graʊnd] *adj* en surface; *Am Fig Fin (income, earnings)* déclaré

above-mentioned [-'menʃənd] *(pl* **inv**) *Formal*

1 *adj* cité plus haut, susmentionné; *Admin* précité

2 *n* **the above-mentioned** *(person)* le susmentionné, la susmentionnée

above-named *(pl* **inv**) *Formal* **1** *adj* susnommé

2 *n* **the above-named** *(person)* le susnommé, la susnommée

abovestairs [ə'bʌv,steəz] **1** *adj Am (room)* (situé) à l'étage supérieur

2 *adv* (**a**) *Am (upstairs)* en haut (**b**) *(as opposed to the servants' quarters)* chez les maîtres

above-the-line 1 *n Mktg* publicité *f* média

2 *adj Acct (expenses)* au-dessus de la ligne

▸▸ *Acct* ***above-the-line accounts*** comptes *mpl* de resultats courants; *Mktg* ***above-the-line advertising*** publicité *f* média; *Acct* ***above-the-line costs*** dépenses *fpl* au-dessus de la ligne; *Mktg* coûts *mpl* média; *Acct* ***above-the-line expenditure*** dépenses *fpl* de création; *Mktg* dépenses *fpl* média

abracadabra [,æbrəkə'dæbrə] **1** *exclam* abracadabra!

2 *n* (**a**) *(magical word)* formule *f* magique (**b**) *(gibberish)* charabia *m*

abrade [ə'breɪd] *vt* (**a**) *Tech* user par abrasion *ou* par frottement (**b**) *(skin)* érafler (**c**) *Geol* éroder

Abraham ['eɪbrəhæm] *pr n Bible* Abraham; **to sham Abraham** faire le malade

abranchiate [ə'bræŋkɪeɪt] *adj Zool* abranche, dépourvu de branchies

abrasion [ə'breɪʒən] *n* (**a**) *Tech (on surface)* abrasion *f* (**b**) *(on skin)* éraflure *f*, écorchure *f* (**c**) *Geol* abrasion *f*

abrasive [ə'breɪsɪv] **1** *adj* (**a**) *Tech (surface, substance)* abrasif (**b**) *(character)* rêche; *(criticism, wit)* corrosif; *(person, voice)* caustique

2 *n Tech* abrasif *m*

abreact [,æbrɪ'ækt] *Psy* **1** *vt* libérer par abréaction

2 *vi* abréagir

abreaction [,æbrɪ'ækʃən] *n Psy* abréaction *f*

abreast [ə'brest] **1** *adv (march, ride)* côte à côte, de front; **the children were riding three abreast** les enfants faisaient du vélo à trois de front; *Naut* **(in) line abreast** en ligne de front

2 abreast of *prep* (**a**) *(alongside)* à la hauteur de, au même niveau que; *Naut* **their ship came** *or* **drew abreast of ours** leur navire est arrivé à la hauteur du nôtre

(**b**) *(in touch with)* **to be abreast of sth** être au courant de qch; **to keep abreast of recent research** rester informé *ou* au courant des recherches récentes; **she likes to keep abreast of current affairs/the latest fashions** elle aime se tenir au courant de l'actualité/de la dernière mode

abridge [ə'brɪdʒ] *vt (book)* abréger; *(article, play, speech)* écourter, abréger

abridged [ə'brɪdʒd] *adj* abrégé

abridgment, abridgement [ə'brɪdʒmənt] *n* (**a**) *(result)* résumé *m*, abrégé *m* (**b**) *(action)* abrègement *m*

abroad [ə'brɔːd] *adv* (**a**) *(overseas)* à l'étranger; **to go abroad** aller à l'étranger; **to live/to study abroad** vivre/faire ses études à l'étranger

(**b**) *(over wide area)* au loin; *(in all directions)* de tous côtés, partout; **there are rumours abroad about possible redundancies** le bruit court qu'il va y avoir des licenciements; **the news got abroad** la nouvelle s'est répandue; **when it got abroad that...** quand la nouvelle s'est répandue que...

(**c**) *Literary (out of doors)* (au) dehors; **to venture abroad** sortir (de la maison)

abrogate ['æbrəgeɪt] *vt Law* abroger, abolir

abrogation [,æbrə'geɪʃən] *n Law* abrogation *f*

abrupt [ə'brʌpt] *adj* (**a**) *(sudden → change, drop, movement)* brusque, soudain; *(→ laugh, question)* brusque; *(→ departure)* brusque, précipité, brutal; **the evening came to an abrupt end** la soirée s'acheva brusquement; **there was an abrupt change in the weather** le temps a changé brutalement (**b**) *(behaviour, person → on one occasion)* brusque; *(→ character trait)* bourru, abrupt (**c**) *(style)* haché, décousu (**d**) *(slope)* abrupt, raide

abruptly [ə'brʌptlɪ] *adv* (**a**) *(change, drop, move)* brusquement, tout à coup; *(ask, laugh, interrupt)* abruptement; *(depart)* brusquement, précipitamment (**b**) *(behave, speak)* avec brusquerie, brusquement (**c**) *(fall, rise)* en pente raide, à pic

abruptness [ə'brʌptnɪs] *n* (**a**) *(of change, drop, movement)* soudaineté *f*; *(of departure)* précipitation *f* (**b**) *(of behaviour, person)* brusquerie *f*, rudesse *f* (**c**) *(of style)* décousu *m* (**d**) *(of slope)* raideur *f*

Abruzzi [ə'brʊtsiː] *npl Geog* **the Abruzzi** les Abruzzes *fpl*

ABS [,eɪbiː'es] *n Aut (abbr* **Anti-lock Braking System**) ABS *m*

abs [æbz] *npl Fam (abdominal muscles)* abdos *mpl*

Absalom ['æbsələm] *pr n Bible* Absalon

abscess ['æbsɪs, 'æbses] *n Med* abcès *m*

abscissa [æb'sɪsə] *(pl* **abscissas** *or* **abscissae** [-siː]) *n Math* abscisse *f*

abscond [əb'skɒnd] *vi Formal* s'enfuir, prendre la fuite; **to abscond from prison** s'échapper de prison, s'évader; *Hum* **he absconded with our money** il s'est enfui avec notre argent

absconder [əb'skɒndə(r)] *n Formal (gen)* fugitif(ive) *m,f*; *(from prison)* évadé(e) *m,f*

absconding [əb'skɒndɪŋ] *n Formal (gen)* fuite *f*; *(from prison)* évasion *f*

abseil ['æbseɪl] *Sport* **1** *n* (descente *f* en) rappel *m*
2 *vi* descendre en rappel

►**abseil down** *vi Sport* descendre en rappel

abseiling ['æbseɪlɪŋ] *n Sport* (descente *f* en) rappel *m*

absence ['æbsəns] *n* (**a**) *(state of being away)* absence *f*; **in** *or* **during my absence** pendant mon absence; **in the absence of the manager** en l'absence du directeur; *Prov* **absence makes the heart grow fonder** l'éloignement renforce l'affection
(**b**) *(instance of being away)* absence *f*; **unexcused absences from school** absences *fpl* injustifiées
(**c**) *(lack)* absence *f*; **in the absence of adequate information** en l'absence d'informations satisfaisantes, faute de renseignements
(**d**) *Law* non-comparution *f*, défaut *m*; **he was tried in his absence** il fut jugé par contumace

absent 1 *adj* ['æbsənt] (**a**) *(not present)* absent; **he was absent from the meeting** il n'a pas participé à la réunion; *Mil* **to be** *or* **to go absent without leave** être absent sans permission, être porté manquant; **to absent friends!** *(toast)* à tous nos amis absents!
(**b**) *(lacking)* absent; **all signs of warmth were absent from her voice** il n'y avait aucune chaleur dans sa voix
(**c**) *(inattentive → person)* distrait; *(→ manner)* absent, distrait
2 *vt* [æb'sent] **to absent oneself (from sth)** *(leave)* s'absenter (de qch); *(not attend)* être absent (à qch)

absentee [,æbsən'ti:] **1** *n (someone not present)* absent(e) *m,f*; *(habitually)* absentéiste *mf*
2 *adj* absentéiste
►► *Pol* ***absentee ballot*** vote *m* par correspondance; **to vote by absentee ballot** voter par correspondance; *Law* ***absentee landlord*** propriétaire *m* absentéiste; *Admin & Ind* ***absentee rate*** taux *m* d'absentéisme; *Pol* ***absentee voter*** électeur(trice) *m,f* votant par correspondance

absenteeism [,æbsən'ti:ɪzəm] *n* absentéisme *m*

absently ['æbsəntlɪ] *adv* distraitement

absent-minded [-'maɪndɪd] *adj (person)* distrait; *(manner)* absent, distrait; *Fam* **he's the perfect example of an absent-minded professor** c'est un vrai professeur Tournesol

absent-mindedly [-'maɪndɪdlɪ] *adv* distraitement, d'un air distrait; **she absent-mindedly left it on the train** elle l'a laissé dans le train par distraction

absent-mindedness [-'maɪndɪdnɪs] *n* distraction *f*, absence *f*

absinth, absinthe ['æbsɪnθ] *n* absinthe *f*

absolute ['æbsəlu:t] **1** *adj* (**a**) *(as intensifier)* absolu, total; **what absolute nonsense!** quelles bêtises, vraiment!; **he's an absolute idiot** c'est un parfait crétin *ou* imbécile; **the whole thing is an absolute mess** c'est un véritable gâchis *ou* un vrai fatras
(**b**) *(entire → secrecy, truth)* absolu
(**c**) *(unlimited → power)* absolu, souverain; *(→ ruler)* absolu
(**d**) *(definite, unconditional → decision, refusal)* absolu, formel; *(→ fact)* indiscutable; *(→ proof)* formel, irréfutable
(**e**) *(independent, not relative)* absolu; **in absolute terms** en valeurs absolues
(**f**) *Chem (alcohol)* absolu, anhydre
(**g**) *Gram (adjective)* substantivé; *(verb)* absolu
(**h**) *Law (court order, decree)* définitif; **the decree was made absolute** le décret a été prononcé
2 *n Phil* **the absolute** l'absolu *m*
►► *Mktg* ***absolute frequency*** fréquence *f* absolue; *Pol* ***absolute majority*** majorité *f* absolue; *Am Mus* ***absolute pitch*** oreille *f* absolue; *Phys* ***absolute temperature*** température *f* absolue; *Law & Pol* ***absolute veto*** véto *m* formel; *Phys* ***absolute zero*** zéro *m* absolu

'Absolute Beginners' *Macinnes, Temple* 'Les Blancs-Becs'

absolutely ['æbsəlu:tlɪ] *adv* (**a**) *(as intensifier)* vraiment; **she's absolutely adorable!** elle est vraiment adorable!
(**b**) *(in expressing opinions)* absolument; **I absolutely agree** je suis tout à fait d'accord; **it's absolutely nothing to do with you** cela ne vous regarde absolument pas; **but he's an excellent teacher – oh, absolutely!** mais c'est un excellent professeur – oh, absolument *ou* mais certainement!; **do you agree? – absolutely not!** êtes-vous d'accord? – absolument pas!
(**c**) *(deny, refuse)* absolument, formellement; **I absolutely insist that you attend the meeing** je tiens absolument à ce que vous soyez présent à la réunion; **it is absolutely forbidden** c'est absolument *ou* formellement interdit

absolution [,æbsə'lu:ʃən] *n (forgiveness)* absolution *f*; *Rel* absolution *f*, remise *f* des péchés; **to grant sb absolution** promettre à qn l'absolution; *Rel (in liturgy)* **the Absolution** l'absoute *f*

absolutism ['æbsəlu:tɪzəm] *n Pol* absolutisme *m*; *Rel* = forme intransigeante de prédestination

absolutist [,æbsə'lu:tɪst] *Pol* **1** *n* absolutiste *mf*
2 *adj* absolutiste

absolve [əb'zɒlv] *vt* (**a**) *(from blame, sin etc)* absoudre (**from** *or* **of** de); *(from obligation)* décharger, délier; (**from** *or* **of** de); **to absolve sb from** *or* **of all blame** décharger qn de toute responsabilité (**b**) *Law* acquitter; **to absolve sb of sth** acquitter qn de qch

absorb [əb'sɔ:b] *vt* (**a**) *also Fig (changes, cost, light, liquid, heat)* absorber; *(surplus)* absorber, résorber; *(idea, information)* absorber, assimiler; *(loss)* essuyer; **black absorbs heat** le noir absorbe la chaleur; **the project absorbed all my time** ce projet a pris tout mon temps; **it's too much to absorb all in one day** cela en fait trop à absorber pour une seule journée
(**b**) *(shock, sound)* amortir
(**c**) *Com (incorporate → company)* absorber, incorporer; *(→ group, people)* absorber, assimiler; *Fin (→ debts)* absorber; **the newcomers were quickly absorbed into the community** les nouveaux venus ont été rapidement intégrés *ou* assimilés à la communauté
(**d**) *(usu passive) (engross)* absorber; **to be absorbed in sth** être absorbé par qch; **she was absorbed in what she was doing** elle était absorbée par ce qu'elle faisait; **he was utterly absorbed in the project/in his reading** il était entièrement absorbé par son projet/sa lecture; **the task completely absorbed our attention** ce travail a complètement accaparé notre attention

absorbance [əb'sɔ:bəns] *n Chem* absorbance *f*

absorbency [əb'sɔ:bənsɪ] *n (gen)* pouvoir *m* absorbant; *Chem & Phys* absorptivité *f*

absorbent [əb'sɔ:bənt] **1** *n* absorbant *m*
2 *adj* absorbant
►► *Am* ***absorbent cotton*** coton *m* hydrophile

absorbing [əb'sɔ:bɪŋ] *adj (activity, book)* fascinant, passionnant; *(work)* absorbant, passionnant

absorption [əb'sɔ:pʃən] *n* (**a**) *(of light, liquid, heat)* absorption *f*; *(of energy)* absorption *f* (**b**) *(of shock, sound)* amortissement *m* (**c**) *Com (of company)* absorption *f*, incorporation *f*; *(of group, people)* absorption *f*, assimilation *f* (**d**) *(fascination)* passion *f*, fascination *f*; *(concentration)* concentration *f* (d'esprit); **her absorption in the book was so great that...** elle était tellement absorbée dans son livre que...
►► *Acct* ***absorption costing*** méthode *f* du coût de revient complet

abstain [əb'steɪn] *vi* (**a**) *(refrain)* s'abstenir; **to abstain from sth/doing sth** s'abstenir de qch/faire qch; **to abstain from alcohol** s'abstenir de boire de l'alcool (**b**) *Pol (not vote)* s'abstenir; **ten members voted for the proposal and three abstained** dix députés ont voté pour le projet et trois se sont abstenus

abstainer [əb'steɪnə(r)] *n* (**a**) *(teetotaller)* abstinent(e) *m,f*; **to be a total abstainer** ne pas boire d'alcool; **he's become a total abstainer** il a complètement arrêté de boire (**b**) *Pol (person not voting)* abstentionniste *mf*

abstaining [əb'steɪnɪŋ] *n (from action)* abstention *f*; *(from drink, food)* abstinence *f*

abstemious [æb'sti:mɪəs] *adj (person)* sobre, abstinent; *(diet, meal)* frugal

abstemiously [əb'sti:mɪəslɪ] *adv* sobrement; *(eat)* frugalement

abstemiousness [æb'sti:mɪəsnɪs] *n (of person)* sobriété *f*, frugalité *f*; *(of diet, meal)* frugalité *f*

abstention [əb'stenʃən] *n* (**a**) *(from action)* abstention *f*; *(from drink, food)* abstinence *f*; **their abstention from making any comment** le fait qu'ils se soient abstenus de tout commentaire (**b**) *Pol (in vote)* abstention *f*

abstinence ['æbstɪnəns] *n* abstinence *f* (**from** de); *Rel* **day of abstinence** jour *m* d'abstinence

abstinent ['æbstɪnənt] *adj* sobre, frugal; *Rel* abstinent

abstinently ['æbstɪnəntlɪ] *adv* sobrement, frugalement; *Rel* d'une manière abstinente

abstract 1 *adj* ['æbstrækt] (**a**) *(number, noun, art)* abstrait
(**b**) *(obscure)* abstrait, abstrus
2 *n* ['æbstrækt] (**a**) *(idea, term)* abstrait *m*; **in the abstract** dans l'abstrait
(**b**) *(summary)* résumé *m*, abrégé *m*; *Fin* **an abstract of accounts** un extrait de comptes
(**c**) *Art (work of art)* œuvre *f* abstraite
3 *vt* [æb'strækt] (**a**) *Formal (remove)* extraire (**from** de)
(**b**) *Euph or Hum (steal)* soustraire, dérober
(**c**) *Phil (regard theoretically)* abstraire
(**d**) *(summarize)* résumer, abréger
4 *vi* [æb'strækt] (**a**) *(theorize)* se livrer à des abstractions
(**b**) *(summarize)* résumer
►► *Art* ***abstract artist*** artiste *m* abstrait, abstrait *m*; *Art* ***abstract expressionism*** expressionnisme *m* abstrait

abstracted [æb'stræktɪd] *adj* (**a**) *(preoccupied)* préoccupé, absorbé; *(absent-minded)* distrait (**b**) *(extracted)* extrait

abstractedly [æb'stræktɪdlɪ] *adv* distraitement, d'un air distrait

abstractedness [æb'stræktɪdnɪs] *n (preoccupation)* préoccupation *f*; *(absent-mindedness)* distraction *f*

abstraction [æb'strækʃən] *n* (**a**) *(concept)* idée *f* abstraite, abstraction *f* (**b**) *Phil* abstraction *f* (**c**) *Formal (act of removing)* extraction *f* (**d**) *(preoccupation)* préoccupation *f*; *(absent-mindedness)* distraction *f*; **she wore her customary look of abstraction** elle avait son air distrait habituel (**e**) *Art (work of art)* œuvre *f* abstraite

abstractionism [æb'strækʃənɪzəm] *n* (**a**) *Phil* abstractionnisme *m* (**b**) *Art* l'art *m* abstrait

abstractionist [æb'strækʃənɪst] **1** *n* (**a**) *Phil* abstractionniste *mf* (**b**) *Art* abstrait *m*
2 *adj* (**a**) *Phil* abstractionniste (**b**) *Art* abstrait

abstruse [æb'stru:s] *adj* abstrus

abstrusely [æb'stru:slɪ] *adv* d'une manière abstruse

abstruseness [æb'stru:snɪs] *n* caractère *m* abstrus

absurd [əb'sɜ:d] **1** *adj (unreasonable)* absurde, insensé; *(ludicrous)* absurde, ridicule; **don't be absurd!** ne sois pas ridicule!; **the idea is utterly absurd** c'est une idée complètement ridicule ou idiote; **I feel/I look absurd in this get-up** je me sens/j'ai l'air ridicule dans cet accoutrement
2 *n* absurde *m*; **he has a nice sense of the absurd** il a un bon sens de l'absurde; *Theat* **the theatre of the absurd** le théâtre de l'absurde

absurdity [əb'sɜ:dɪtɪ] (*pl* **absurdities**) *n* absurdité *f*; **the absurdity of paying people not to work** l'absurdité consistant à payer des gens à ne pas travailler

absurdly [əb'sɜ:dlɪ] *adv (behave, dress)* d'une manière insensée, d'une façon absurde; *(as intensifier)* ridiculement; **rather absurdly I seem to have forgotten your name** c'est absurde mais je crois bien que j'ai oublié votre nom; **it was absurdly complicated** c'était d'une complexité absurde

ABTA ['æbtə] *n* (*abbr* **Association of British Travel Agents**) = association des agences de voyage britanniques

Abu Dhabi [ˌæbuːˈdɑːbɪ] *n Geog* Abou Dhabi

abulia [əˈbuːlɪə] *n Psy* aboulie *f*

abundance [əˈbʌndəns] *n* (**a**) *(plenty)* abondance *f*, profusion *f*; **there was food in abundance** il y avait à manger à profusion; **she has an abundance of talent** elle est bourrée de talent (**b**) *Biol (of species etc)* abondance *f* (**c**) *Cards (in solo whist)* abondance *f*

abundant [əˈbʌndənt] *adj (plentiful)* abondant (**in** en); **he gave abundant proof of his devotion** il a largement fait la preuve de son dévouement; **there's an abundant supply of food** il y a des provisions (de nourriture) en quantité; **there is abundant evidence that he's guilty** il y a de nombreuses preuves qui démontrent qu'il est coupable

abundantly [əˈbʌndəntlɪ] *adv* (**a**) *(profusely)* abondamment; *(eat, serve)* abondamment, copieusement; *(grow)* à foison (**b**) *(as intensifier)* extrêmement; **it became abundantly clear that we had been mistaken** il devint tout à fait clair que nous nous étions trompés; **she made it abundantly clear that I was not welcome** elle me fit comprendre très clairement que j'étais indésirable; **is that clear? – abundantly** c'est clair? – limpide

abuse 1 *n* [əˈbjuːs] (**a**) *(misuse)* abus *m* (**of** de); **such positions are open to abuse** de telles situations incitent aux abus; *Law* **abuse of authority** abus *m* d'autorité *ou* de pouvoir; *Parl* **abuse of privilege** abus *m* de droit
(**b**) *(UNCOUNT) (insults)* injures *fpl*, insultes *fpl*; **to heap** *or* **shower abuse on sb** accabler qn d'injures
(**c**) *(UNCOUNT) (cruel treatment)* mauvais traitements *mpl*
(**d**) *(unjust practice)* abus *m*
2 *vt* [əˈbjuːz] (**a**) *(authority, position, someone's trust, patience)* abuser de; **a much abused word** un mot employé abusivement
(**b**) *(insult)* injurier, insulter
(**c**) *(treat cruelly)* maltraiter, malmener; *(sexually)* faire subir des sévices à
(**d**) *Formal (masturbate)* **to abuse oneself** se masturber

abuser [əˈbjuːzə(r)] *n* (**a**) *(gen)* **abusers of the system** ceux qui profitent du système (**b**) *(of child)* personne *f* coupable de mauvais traitements à enfant; *(sexual)* = personne coupable de sévices sexuels infligés à un enfant (**c**) *(of drugs)* **(drug) abuser** drogué(e) *m,f*

Abu Simbel [ˌæbuːˈsɪmbəl] *n Geog* Abou-Simbel

abusive [əˈbjuːsɪv] *adj* (**a**) *(language)* offensant, grossier; *(person)* grossier; *(phone call)* obscène; **to be abusive to sb** être grossier envers qn (**b**) *(behaviour, treatment)* brutal (**c**) *(incorrectly used)* abusif, mauvais

abusively [əˈbjuːsɪvlɪ] *adv* (**a**) *(speak)* grossièrement (**b**) *(behave, treat)* brutalement (**c**) *(use)* abusivement

abusiveness [əˈbjuːsɪvnɪs] *n* (**a**) *(of language)* grossièreté *f* (**b**) *(of behaviour, treatment)* brutalité *f*

▸**abut on, abut against** [əˈbʌt] *(pt & pp* **abutted**, *cont* **abutting**) *vt insep* (**a**) *Formal (adjoin)* être adjacent *ou* contigu à (**b**) *Archit & Constr* s'appuyer contre, buter contre

abutment [əˈbʌtmənt], **abuttal** [əˈbʌtəl] *n* (**a**) *(point of junction)* jointure *f*, point *m* de jonction (**b**) *Archit & Constr (support)* contrefort *m*; *(on bridge)* butée *f*, culée *f*; *(of arch)* piédroit *m*

abuzz [əˈbʌz] *adj* bourdonnant; **abuzz with activity** en effervescence; **abuzz with conversation** résonnant du bruit des conversations

abysm [əˈbɪzəm] *n Arch or Literary* abîme *m*

abysmal [əˈbɪzməl] *adj* (**a**) *(immeasurable)* infini, abyssal; **abysmal ignorance** une ignorance crasse (**b**) *(very bad)* épouvantable, exécrable

abysmally [əˈbɪzməlɪ] *adv* atrocement; *(fail)* lamentablement; **abysmally ignorant** d'une ignorance profonde; **the area is abysmally lacking in good restaurants** le quartier est absolument dépourvu de bons restaurants

abyss [əˈbɪs] *n* (**a**) *Geol (chasm)* abîme *m*, gouffre *m*; *(in sea)* abysse *m* (**b**) *Fig* abîme *m*; **a great abyss seemed to open up between us** il y avait comme un abîme entre nous

abyssal [əˈbɪsəl] *adj Geol* abyssal

Abyssinia [ˌæbɪˈsɪnɪə] *n Geog* Abyssinie *f*; **in Abyssinia** en Abyssinie

Abyssinian [ˌæbɪˈsɪnɪən] 1 *n* (**a**) *(person)* Abyssinien(enne) *m,f* (**b**) *(language)* abyssinien *m*
2 *adj* abyssinien, abyssin
▸▸ ***Abyssinian cat*** chat *m* abyssin; *Hist* ***the Abyssinian Empire*** l'empire *m* d'Éthiopie

AC [ˌeɪˈsiː] *n* (**a**) *Br Sport (abbr* **athletics club**) club *m* d'athlétisme (**b**) *Elec (abbr* **alternating current**) courant *m* alternatif (**c**) *Tech (abbr* **air conditioning**) climatisation *f*

.ac [ˌeɪˈsiː, æk] *Comput (abbr* **academic**) = abréviation désignant les universités et les sites éducatifs dans les adresses électroniques britanniques

a/c *Br Banking & Fin (written abbr* **account**) c

acacia [əˈkeɪʃə] *n Bot* acacia *m*; **false acacia** faux acacia *m*
▸▸ *Br* ***Acacia Avenue*** = terme évoquant la banlieue tranquille et résidentielle

academe [ˈækədiːm] *n Formal or Literary* (**a**) *(academic life)* le milieu universitaire (**b**) *Pej (person)* pédant(e) *m,f*

academia [ˌækəˈdiːmɪə] *n* le milieu universitaire

academic [ˌækəˈdemɪk] 1 *adj* (**a**) *Sch & Univ (related to formal study → of school)* scolaire; *(→ of university)* universitaire; **we aim for academic excellence** notre objectif est l'excellence de notre enseignement; **her academic achievements are impressive** elle a fait de brillantes études; **the first academic study of...** la première étude faite par un universitaire de...
(**b**) *(intellectual → standard, style, work)* intellectuel; *(→ person)* studieux, intellectuel; *(→ subjects)* d'enseignement général
(**c**) *Phil (theoretical)* théorique, spéculatif; *(not practical)* sans intérêt pratique, théorique; **their speculations were purely academic** leurs spéculations étaient purement théoriques; **out of academic interest** par simple curiosité; **whether he comes or not is all academic** qu'il vienne ou pas, cela n'a pas d'importance
(**d**) *(conventional)* académique; *Art* **an academic painter** un peintre académique
2 *n Univ (university teacher)* universitaire *mf*; *(intellectual)* intellectuel(elle) *m,f*
▸▸ *Am* ***academic advisor*** directeur(trice) *m,f* d'études; ***academic dress*** toge *f* d'étudiant; ***academic freedom*** liberté *f* d'enseignement; *Am* ***academic rank*** grade *m*; ***academic year*** année *f* universitaire

academically [ˌækəˈdemɪkəlɪ] *adv (advanced, competent, talented)* sur le plan intellectuel; *(sound)* intellectuellement; **to be academically qualified** posséder les diplômes requis; **to be academically gifted** être doué intellectuellement; **she's not very academically inclined** elle n'est pas très douée pour les études; **the school doesn't have a tremendous reputation academically** l'école n'est pas fabuleusement cotée pour la qualité de son enseignement

academicals [ˌækəˈdemɪkəlz] *npl Univ* toge *f* et accessoires *mpl* d'universitaire

academician [əˌkædəˈmɪʃən] *n* académicien(enne) *m,f*

academicism [ˌækəˈdemɪsɪzəm], **academism** [əˈkædəmɪzəm] *n esp Pej Art* académisme *m*

academy [əˈkædəmɪ] *(pl* **academies**) *n* (**a**) *(society)* académie *f*, société *f* (**b**) *(school) Scot* ≃ lycée *m*; *Eng & Am (private)* ≃ collège *m* privé; **an academy of music** un conservatoire de musique; **riding academy** académie *f* d'équitation
▸▸ *Cin* ***Academy Award*** oscar *m*

Acadia [əˈkeɪdɪə] *n* Acadie *f*; **in Acadia** en Acadie

Acadian [əˈkeɪdɪən] 1 *n* Acadien(enne) *m,f*
2 *adj* acadien

acanthus [əˈkænθəs] *(pl* **acanthuses** *or* **acanthi** [-θaɪ]) *n* (**a**) *Bot* acanthe *f* (**b**) *Archit* (feuille *f* d')acanthe *f*

a cappella [ˌɑːkəˈpelə] *Mus* 1 *adj* a cappella; **a cappella singing** chant *m* a cappella
2 *adv* a cappella

acariasis [ˌækəˈraɪəsɪs] *n Med* acariose *f*

acarid [ˈækərɪd] *n Entom* acarien *m*

acarus [ˈækərəs] *n Entom* acarus *m*

ACAS [ˈeɪkæs] *n Ind (abbr* **Advisory, Conciliation and Arbitration Service**) = organisme britannique de conciliation et d'arbitrage des conflits du travail, ≃ conseil *m* de prud'hommes

acaulescent [ˌækɔːˈlesənt] *adj Bot* acaule

accede [ækˈsiːd] *vi Formal* (**a**) *(agree)* agréer, accepter; **to accede to sth** *(demand, request)* donner suite *ou* accéder à qch; *(plan, suggestion)* accepter *ou* agréer qch (**b**) **to accede to sth** *(attain)* accéder à qch; **to accede to the throne** monter sur le trône; **to accede to office** entrer en fonction; **to accede to the directorship** accéder à la direction (**c**) *Law* **to accede to a treaty** adhérer à un traité

accelerate [əkˈseləreɪt] 1 *vt (pace, process, rhythm)* accélérer; *(decline, event)* précipiter, accélérer; *(work)* activer
2 *vi* (**a**) *(move faster)* s'accélérer (**b**) *Aut (of driver)* accélérer

accelerated [əkˈseləreɪtɪd] *adj (pace, process, rhythm)* accéléré
▸▸ *Sch & Univ* ***accelerated classes*** cours *mpl ou* niveaux *mpl* accélérés; *Acct* ***accelerated depreciation*** amortissement *m* dégressif, amortissement *m* accéléré; *Phys* ***accelerated motion*** accéléré *m*

acceleration [əkˌseləˈreɪʃən] *n* accélération *f*; **the car has good acceleration** cette voiture a une bonne accélération
▸▸ *Fin* ***acceleration clause*** clause *f* accélératrice; *Fin* ***acceleration premium*** prime *f* de rendement

accelerator [əkˈseləreɪtə(r)] *n* (**a**) *Aut (in vehicle)* accélérateur *m*; **step on the accelerator!** appuie sur l'accélérateur! (**b**) *Phys & Comput* accélérateur *m*
▸▸ *Comput* ***accelerator board, accelerator card*** carte *f* accélératrice; *Aut* ***accelerator pedal*** pédale *f* d'accélérateur

accelerometer [ækˌseləˈrɒmɪtə(r)] *n Phys* accéléromètre *m*

accent 1 *n* [ˈæksent] (**a**) *Ling (way of speaking)* accent *m*; **she has** *or* **she speaks with a Spanish/Liverpool accent** elle a l'accent espagnol/de Liverpool; **she speaks French with/without an accent** elle parle français avec un/sans accent; **he has a strange accent** il a un drôle d'accent
(**b**) *Gram & Mus (stress)* accent *m*; **the accent is on the final syllable** l'accent est sur la dernière syllabe
(**c**) *Fig (emphasis)* accent *m*; **the accent here is on team work** ici on met l'accent sur le travail d'équipe; **fashion with the accent on youth** mode qui met l'accent sur la jeunesse
(**d**) *Gram (written mark)* accent *m*
(**e**) *(contrasting detail)* accent *m*; **the room is painted white with green accents** la pièce est peinte en blanc avec des touches de vert
2 *vt* [ækˈsent] *Gram* (**a**) *(stress → syllable)* accentuer, appuyer sur; *(→ word)* accentuer, mettre l'accent sur
(**b**) *(mark with accent)* mettre un accent sur, accentuer

accented [ˈæksentɪd] *adj Gram* accentué
▸▸ ***accented character*** caractère *m* accentué

accentor [ækˈsentə(r)] *n Zool* accenteur *m*

accentuate [ækˈsentjʊeɪt] *vt* (**a**) *(word)* accentuer, mettre l'accent sur (**b**) *(feature, importance)* souligner, accentuer; *(contrast)* accuser; **to accentuate the need for sth** accentuer la nécessité de qch; **the thin dress only accentuated her frailness** la robe légère ne faisait qu'accentuer *ou* que souligner son air fragile

accentuated [ækˈsentjʊeɪtɪd] *adj* accentué; *(limp, stutter)* fortement marqué; *Mus* **the offbeat is accentuated** le temps faible est accentué

accentuation [ækˌsentjʊˈeɪʃən] *n* accentuation *f*

accept [əkˈsept] *vt* (**a**) *(take when offered → apology, gift, invitation)* accepter; *(→ advice, suggestion)* accepter, écouter; **he proposed and she accepted (him)** il la demanda en mariage et elle accepta; **please accept my apologies** je vous prie de bien vouloir accepter mes excuses; **the machine only accepts coins** la machine n'accepte que les pièces
(**b**) *(believe as right, true)* accepter, admettre; **I can't accept what he says** je ne peux accepter *ou* admettre ce qu'il dit; **I refuse to accept that**

he's guilty je me refuse à le croire coupable, je refuse de croire qu'il soit coupable; **it is generally accepted that...** il est généralement reconnu que...; **while we accept that this may be more expensive...** tout en admettant que ceci puisse être plus cher...

(**c**) *(face up to → danger)* faire face à, affronter; *(→ challenge)* accepter, relever; *(→ one's fate)* se résigner à; **she hasn't really accepted his death** elle n'a pas vraiment accepté sa mort; **you have to accept the inevitable** il vous faut accepter l'inévitable; **we have to accept the fact that war is imminent** nous devons accepter le fait que la guerre est imminente; **they refused to accept the appalling working conditions** ils ont refusé de travailler dans des conditions aussi épouvantables

(**d**) *(take on → blame, responsibility)* accepter, prendre; *(→ job, task)* se charger de, accepter; **to accept responsibility for sth** prendre *ou* accepter la responsabilité de qch; **to accept no responsibility** décliner toute responsabilité

(**e**) *(admit → to job, school)* accepter, prendre; *(→ to club, university)* accepter, admettre; **they accepted her into the club** ils l'ont admise au club; **she's been accepted** *Br* **at** *or Am* **to Harvard** elle a été admise à Harvard

(**f**) *Com (goods)* prendre livraison de; *Fin (bill of exchange)* accepter

acceptability [əkˌseptə'bɪlɪtɪ] *n* acceptabilité *f*, admissibilité *f*

acceptable [ək'septəbəl] *adj* (**a**) *(satisfactory)* acceptable, convenable; *(tolerable)* acceptable, admissible; **her behaviour just isn't socially acceptable** son attitude est tout simplement intolérable en société; **they found her work acceptable** ils ont trouvé son travail convenable; **are these conditions acceptable to you?** ces conditions vous conviennent-elles?

(**b**) *(welcome)* bienvenu, opportun; **flowers always make an acceptable gift** les fleurs sont toujours une bonne idée de cadeau *ou* font toujours plaisir; **your cheque was most acceptable** votre chèque était fort apprécié

►► *Comput* ***Acceptable Use Policy*** = code de conduite défini par un fournisseur d'accès à l'internet

acceptably [ək'septəblɪ] *adv (suitably)* convenablement; *(tolerably)* passablement; **he works acceptably well** il ne travaille pas mal (du tout); **inflation has remained acceptably low** l'inflation est restée assez faible

acceptance [ək'septəns] **1** *n* (**a**) *(of gift, invitation, apology)* acceptation *f*

(**b**) *(assent → to proposal, suggestion)* consentement *m*; **his acceptance of his fate** sa résignation devant son sort

(**c**) *(to club, school, university, group)* admission *f*; *Univ* **she's got two provisional acceptances** *(for university)* elle a été provisoirement admise dans deux universités

(**d**) *(approval, favour)* approbation *f*, réception *f* favorable; **his suggestion met with everyone's acceptance** tout le monde approuva sa suggestion; **the idea is gaining acceptance** l'idée fait son chemin

(**e**) *(belief)* **there is general acceptance now that smoking causes cancer** il est généralement reconnu maintenant que le tabac provoque le cancer

(**f**) *Com (of goods)* réception *f*; *Fin (of bill of exchange)* acceptation *f*; *(document)* effet *m* accepté, effet *m* à payer; *Fin* **to present a bill for acceptance** présenter un effet *ou* une traite à l'acceptation

►► *Am Banking* ***acceptance bank*** banque *f* d'acceptation; *Fin* ***acceptance bill*** effet *m ou* traite *f* contre acceptation; *Fin* ***acceptance fee*** commission *f* d'acceptation; *Am Banking* ***acceptance house*** maison *f* d'acceptation; ***acceptance speech*** discours *m* de réception; *Comput & Tech* ***acceptance test, acceptance trial*** test *m* d'acceptabilité

acceptation [ˌæksep'teɪʃən] *n Ling (of term, word)* acception *f*, signification *f*; **in the full acceptation of the word** dans toute l'acception du mot

accepted [ək'septɪd] *adj* (**a**) *(generally held)* **accepted ideas** les idées généralement répandues *ou* admises; **contrary to accepted belief** contrairement à la croyance établie; **it's an accepted fact that too much sun ages the skin** il est généralement reconnu que le soleil à haute dose accélère le vieillissement de la peau (**b**) *Fin (written on accepted bill of exchange)* accepté, bon pour acceptation

►► *Fin* ***accepted bill*** effet *m* accepté, acceptation *f*

accepting house [ək'septɪŋ-] *n Br Banking* maison *f* d'acceptation, banque *f* d'acceptation

acceptor [ək'septə(r)] *n* (**a**) *Chem, Elec & Phys* accepteur *m* (**b**) *Fin (of bill of exchange)* accepteur *m*, tiré *m*

Access® ['ækses] *n Fin* = carte de crédit britannique; **to put sth on Access**® payer qch avec la carte Access®

►► ***Access***® ***card*** carte *f* Access®

access ['ækses] **1** *n* (**a**) *(means of entry)* entrée *f*, ouverture *f*; *(means of approach)* accès *m*, abord *m*; *Law* droit *m* de passage; **there is easy access to the beach** on accède facilement à la plage; **the kitchen gives access to the garage** la cuisine donne accès au garage; **how did the thieves gain access?** comment les voleurs se sont-ils introduits?; **access only** *(sign)* sauf riverains (et livreurs)

(**b**) *(right to contact, use)* accès *m*; **to have access to sb/sth** avoir accès auprès de qn/à qch; **I have access to confidential files** j'ai accès à des dossiers confidentiels; **he has direct access to the minister** il a ses entrées auprès du ministre; *Law* **the father has access to the children at weekends** le père a droit de visite le week-end pour voir ses enfants

(**c**) *Br Literary (bout → of illness)* accès *m*, attaque *f*; *(→ of fever, anger)* accès *m*; **in an access of despair** dans un accès de désespoir

(**d**) *Comput* accès *m*; **to have access to a file** avoir accès à un fichier; **up to 56K access** accès *m* jusqu'à 56K; **access denied** *(DOS message)* accès refusé

2 *comp Transp (port, route)* d'accès

3 *vt* accéder à

►► *Comput* ***access authorization code*** code *m* d'autorisation d'accès; *TV* ***access broadcasting*** télévision *f* ouverte; *TV* ***access channel*** canal *m* d'accès; *Comput* ***access code*** code *m* d'accès; *Comput* ***access level*** *(in network)* niveau *m* d'accès; *Comput* ***access number*** *(to ISP)* numéro *m* d'accès; *Comput* ***access privileges*** droits *mpl* d'accès; *Comput* ***access provider*** fournisseur *m* d'accès; ***access ramp*** bretelle *f* d'accès; *Law* ***access rights*** *(to child)* droits *mpl* de visite; ***access road*** *(gen)* route *f* d'accès; *(to motorway)* bretelle *f* d'accès *ou* de raccordement; *Comput* ***access speed*** vitesse *f* d'accès; *TV* ***access television*** télévision *f* ouverte; *Comput* ***access time*** temps *m* d'accès

accessary [ək'sesərɪ] *(pl* **accessaries***) Law* **1** *n* complice *mf* (**to** de); **an accessary after/before the fact** un complice par assistance/par instigation

2 *adj* complice

accessibility [əkˌsesə'bɪlətɪ] *n* accessibilité *f*

accessible [ək'sesəbəl] *adj* (**a**) *(place)* accessible, d'accès facile; *(person)* d'un abord facile; **the teacher's very accessible** ce professeur est facile à aborder *ou* est d'un abord facile (**b**) *(available)* accessible; **computers are now accessible to everyone** maintenant les ordinateurs sont accessibles à tous (**c**) *(easily understandable → novel, style)* à la portée de tous, accessible (**d**) *(open, susceptible)* ouvert, accessible

accession [æk'seʃən] **1** *n* (**a**) *(to office, position, power)* accession *f* (**to** à); *(to fortune)* accession *f*, entrée *f* en possession; **Queen Victoria's accession (to the throne)** l'accession *f* au trône *ou* l'avènement *m* de la reine Victoria

(**b**) *(addition to collection)* nouvelle acquisition *f*

(**c**) *(increase)* augmentation *f*, accroissement *m*

(**d**) *Law (to property)* accession *f*

(**e**) *Law (consent)* assentiment *m*, accord *m*; *(of treaty)* adhésion *f*

2 *vt* enregistrer

►► ***accession number*** *(of book)* numéro *m* de catalogue

accessioning [æk'seʃənɪŋ] *n (of library book)* inscription *f* au registre des additions

accessorize, -ise [ək'sesəraɪz] *vt* accessoiriser

accessory [ək'sesərɪ] *(pl* **accessories***)* **1** *n* (**a**) *(usu pl) (supplementary article)* accessoire *m*; **car accessories** accessoires *mpl* automobiles; **a suit with matching accessories** un ensemble avec (ses) accessoires coordonnés

(**b**) *Law* complice *mf* (**to** de); **an accessory after/before the fact** un complice par assistance/par instigation

2 *adj* (**a**) *(supplementary)* accessoire (**to** à)

(**b**) *Law* complice

►► *Phot* ***accessory shoe*** fiche *f* pour accessoires

acciaccatura [əˌtʃækə'tʊərə] *n Mus* acciaccatura *f*

accidence ['æksɪdəns] *n Ling & Gram* morphologie *f* flexionnelle

accident ['æksɪdənt] **1** *n* (**a**) *(mishap)* accident *m*, malheur *m*; *(unforeseen event)* événement *m* fortuit, accident *m*; **to have an accident** avoir un accident; **her son had a car accident** son fils a eu un accident de voiture; **she was killed in an accident** elle s'est tuée dans un accident; **their last child was an accident** leur dernier enfant est un accident; **accidents in the home** accidents *mpl* domestiques; **it was an accident waiting to happen** c'est un accident qui devait arriver; *Prov* **accidents will happen** on ne peut pas parer à tout

(**b**) *(chance)* hasard *m*, chance *f*; **it was purely by accident that we met** nous nous sommes rencontrés tout à fait par accident; **any success we had was more by accident than by design** notre réussite a été plus accidentelle qu'autre chose; **it's no accident that she made the film here** ce n'est pas par hasard si elle a tourné le film ici

(**c**) *Phil* accident *m*

(**d**) *Law* cas *m* fortuit

2 *comp (figures, rate)* des accidents

►► *Med* ***accident and emergency (unit)*** *(in hospital)* service *m* des urgences, urgences *fpl*; ***accident insurance*** assurance *f* (contre les) accidents; ***accident prevention*** la prévention des accidents; ***accident victim*** victime *f* d'un/de l'accident

accidental [ˌæksɪ'dentəl] **1** *adj* (**a**) *(occurring by chance → death, poisoning)* accidentel; *(→ meeting)* fortuit (**b**) *Formal (nonessential)* accessoire, extrinsèque (**c**) *Phil* accidentel (**d**) *Mus* accidentel

2 *n Mus* accident *m*

'Accidental Hero' *Frears* 'Héros malgré lui'

'The Accidental Tourist' *Tyler, Kasdan* 'Le Voyageur malgré lui'

---

accidentally [ˌæksɪ'dentəlɪ] *adv (break, drop)* accidentellement; *(meet)* par hasard; **she accidentally tore the page** elle a déchiré la page sans le vouloir; *Hum* **he did it accidentally on purpose** il l'a fait "exprès sans le vouloir"

accident-prone *adj* **to be accident-prone** être prédisposé aux accidents

acclaim [ə'kleɪm] **1** *vt* (**a**) *(praise)* acclamer, faire l'éloge de; *(applaud)* acclamer, applaudir; **her acclaimed portrayal of Cleopatra** sa représentation acclamée de Cléopâtre (**b**) *(proclaim)* proclamer; **Charlemagne was acclaimed emperor** Charlemagne fut acclamé *ou* proclamé empereur

2 *n (UNCOUNT)* acclamation *f*, acclamations *fpl*; **his play met with great critical acclaim** sa pièce a été très applaudie par la critique; **the acclaim of his peers** la reconnaissance de ses pairs

acclamation [ˌæklə'meɪʃən] *n (UNCOUNT)* acclamation *f*, acclamations *fpl*; **to be elected by acclamation** être plébiscité; **to win by acclamation** gagner par acclamation

acclamatory [ə'klæmətərɪ] *adj* acclamatif

acclimate ['æklɪmeɪt] *Am* = **acclimatize**

aclimation [ˌæklɪ'meɪʃən] *Am* = **acclimatization**

acclimatization [əˌklaɪmətaɪ'zeɪʃən] *n (to climate)*

acclimatation *f*; *(to conditions, customs)* accoutumance *f*, acclimatement *m*

acclimatize, -ise [əˈklaɪmətaɪz] **1** *vt (animal, plant)* acclimater; **to acclimatize oneself to sth, to become acclimatized to sth** *(climate)* s'habituer à qch, s'accoutumer à qch; *(conditions, customs)* s'acclimater à qch, s'habituer à qch, s'accoutumer à qch

2 *vi* **to acclimatize to sth** *(climate)* s'habituer à qch, s'accoutumer à qch; *(conditions, customs)* s'acclimater à qch, s'habituer à qch, s'accoutumer à qch

acclivity [əˈklɪvɪtɪ] *n Geol* montée *f*

accolade [ˈækəleɪd] *n* (**a**) *(praise)* acclamation *f*, acclamations *fpl*; *(approval)* marque *f* d'approbation; *(honour)* honneur *m*; **the prize is the highest accolade a writer can receive** ce prix est le plus grand honneur qu'un écrivain puisse recevoir (**b**) *(in conferring knighthood)* accolade *f* (**c**) *Archit* accolade *f*

accommodate [əˈkɒmədeɪt] **1** *vt* (**a**) *(provide lodging for)* loger; *(provide with something needed)* équiper, pourvoir; *(provide with loan)* prêter de l'argent à; **can you accommodate me until my cheque comes through?** pouvez-vous me prêter de l'argent en attendant que je reçoive mon chèque?

(**b**) *(have room for → of car)* contenir; *(→ of house, room)* contenir, recevoir; **the restaurant can accommodate 150 people** le restaurant peut recevoir 150 personnes; **the cottage accommodates up to six people** dans la villa, on peut loger jusqu'à six (personnes)

(**c**) *(oblige)* répondre aux besoins de; **we will try to accommodate you** nous essaierons de vous satisfaire; **to do sth to accommodate sb** faire qch pour arranger qn; **the management refused to accommodate the union** la direction a refusé de prendre en compte les exigences du syndicat; **the bill is designed to accommodate special interest groups** cette loi vise à prendre en compte les besoins de groupes d'intérêts particuliers

(**d**) *(adapt)* accommoder, adapter; **she soon accommodated herself to the new working conditions** elle s'est vite adaptée aux nouvelles conditions de travail

2 *vi* **to accommodate to sth** s'accommoder *ou* s'habituer à qch

accommodating [əˈkɒmədeɪtɪŋ] *adj (willing to help)* obligeant; *(easy to please)* accommodant, complaisant

accommodatingly [əˈkɒmədeɪtɪŋlɪ] *adv* complaisamment

accommodation [əˌkɒməˈdeɪʃən] **1** *n* (**a**) *(UNCOUNT) (lodging)* logement *m*; *(lodging and services)* prestations *fpl*; **to look for accommodation** *(flat to rent)* chercher un logement; *(hotel room)* chercher une chambre (d'hôtel); **the hotel has no accommodation available** l'hôtel est complet; **furnished accommodation** chambre *f* meublée, (logement *m*) meublé *m*; **the high cost of rented accommodation** le prix élevé des locations; *Admin* **office accommodation** bureaux *mpl* à louer; **sleeping accommodation** chambres *fpl*

(**b**) *(settlement of disagreement)* accord *m*, accommodement *m*; *(compromise)* compromis *m*; **to come to an accommodation** arriver à un compromis; *Fin (with one's creditors)* parvenir à un arrangement

(**c**) *Formal (willingness to help)* obligeance *f*; *(willingness to please)* complaisance *f*

(**d**) *Anat & Psy* accommodation *f*

(**e**) *Com & Fin (loan)* prêt *m* de complaisance

2 accommodations *npl Am* (**a**) *(lodging, food and services)* hébergement *m*

(**b**) *Naut & Rail (on boat, train)* place *f*

►► *Br* ***accommodation address*** adresse *f (utilisée uniquement pour la correspondance)*; ***accommodation agency*** agence *f* de logement; ***accommodation allowance*** indemnité *f* de logement; *Fin* ***accommodation bill*** traite *f ou* effet *m* de complaisance; ***accommodation bureau*** agence *f* de logement; *Naut* ***accommodation ladder*** échelle *f* de coupée; *Transp* ***accommodation road*** route *f* de desserte

accommodative [əˈkɒmədeɪtɪv] *adj (willing to help)* obligeant; *(easy to please)* accommodant, complaisant

accompaniment [əˈkʌmpənɪmənt] *n* (**a**) *(gen)* accompagnement *m*; **he entered to the accompaniment of wild applause** il entra sous un tonnerre d'applaudissements (**b**) *Culin* accompagnement *m*, garniture *f* (**c**) *Mus* accompagnement *m* (**on** à); **guitar/piano accompaniment** accompagnement *m* à la guitare/au piano

accompanist [əˈkʌmpənɪst] *n Mus* accompagnateur(trice) *m,f*

accompany [əˈkʌmpənɪ] *(pt & pp* **accompanied***)* *vt* (**a**) *(escort)* accompagner, escorter; **she was accompanied by her brother** elle était accompagnée de son frère; **she accompanied me to the door** elle m'a raccompagné jusqu'à la porte

(**b**) *(supplement)* accompagner; **she accompanied her advice with a warning** ses conseils s'accompagnaient d'une mise en garde; **her photos accompany the text** ses photos accompagnent le texte; **the hot weather is often accompanied by afternoon thunderstorms** la chaleur s'accompagne souvent d'orages dans l'après-midi

(**c**) *Culin* accompagner, garnir

(**d**) *Mus* accompagner (**on** à); **he accompanies her on the piano** il l'accompagne au piano

accompanying [əˈkʌmpənɪɪŋ] *adj* **the accompanying documents** les documents ci-joints; **children will not be allowed in without an accompanying adult** l'entrée est interdite aux enfants non accompagnés

accompanyist [əˈkʌmpənɪɪst] *n Am Mus* accompagnateur(trice) *m,f*

accomplice [əˈkʌmplɪs] *n (gen) & Law* complice *mf*; **to be an accomplice to** *or* **in sth** être complice de qch

accomplish [əˈkʌmplɪʃ] *vt* (**a**) *(manage to do → task, work)* accomplir, exécuter; *(→ desire, dream)* réaliser; *(→ distance, trip)* effectuer; **the talks accomplished nothing** les pourparlers n'ont pas abouti; **we hope to accomplish a great deal during our discussions** nous espérons obtenir des résultats durant ces débats (**b**) *(finish successfully)* venir à bout de, mener à bonne fin

accomplished [əˈkʌmplɪʃt] *adj* (**a**) *(cook, singer)* accompli, doué; *(performance)* accompli (**b**) *(successfully completed)* accompli; **an accomplished fact** un fait accompli

accomplishment [əˈkʌmplɪʃmənt] *n* (**a**) *(skill)* talent *m*; **speaking fluent French is just one of her many accomplishments** elle parle français couramment, entre autres talents (**b**) *(feat)* exploit *m*, œuvre *f* (accomplie); **that's quite an accomplishment** c'est un véritable exploit, c'est une véritable prouesse (**c**) *(completion → of task, trip)* accomplissement *m*; *(→ of ambition)* réalisation *f*

accord [əˈkɔːd] **1** *n* (**a**) *(consent)* accord *m*, consentement *m*; **to be in accord with sb** être d'accord avec qn; **I'm in complete accord with you** je suis totalement d'accord avec vous

(**b**) *(conformity)* accord *m*, conformité *f*; **to be in accord with sth** être en accord *ou* en conformité avec qch

(**c**) *(harmony)* accord *m*, harmonie *f*

(**d**) *Law & Pol (agreement)* accord *m*; *(treaty)* traité *m*; **to reach an accord** parvenir à un accord

2 *vt (permission, significance, status)* accorder; *(welcome)* réserver; **to accord sb permission** accorder une autorisation *ou* une permission à qn; **he accorded her a warm welcome** il lui a réservé un accueil chaleureux

3 *vi* s'accorder, concorder; **what he said did not accord with our instructions** ce qu'il a dit n'était pas conforme à nos instructions

4 of one's own accord *adv* **to do sth of one's own accord** faire qch de son plein gré; **the table seemed to be moving of its own accord** la table avait l'air de bouger toute seule

5 with one accord *adv* d'un commun accord

accordance [əˈkɔːdəns] **1** *n* (**a**) *(conformity)* accord *m*, conformité *f* (**b**) *Formal (granting)* octroi *m*

2 in accordance with *prep* conformément à; *Law* **in accordance with the law** aux termes de *ou* conformément à la loi; **her statement is not in accordance with company policy** sa déclaration n'est pas dans la ligne de l'entreprise

accordant [əˈkɔːdənt] *adj Formal* **accordant with** conformément à

according [əˈkɔːdɪŋ] **1 according as** *conj Formal* selon que, suivant que; **according as they pass or fail the exam** suivant *ou* selon qu'ils ont réussi ou échoué à l'examen

2 according to *prep* (**a**) *(on the evidence of)* selon, d'après; **according to John, it's too late** selon *ou* pour John, il est trop tard; **according to what you say** d'après ce que vous dites; *Bible* **the Gospel according to St Luke** l'Évangile selon saint Luc; **according to the figures** d'après les chiffres

(**b**) *(in relation to)* **arranged according to height** disposés par ordre de taille; **prices vary according to how long the job will take** le prix varie selon le temps qu'il faut pour effectuer le travail

(**c**) *(in accordance with)* suivant, conformément à; **according to instructions** conformément aux *ou* suivant les instructions; **everything went according to plan** tout s'est passé comme prévu

accordingly [əˈkɔːdɪŋlɪ] *adv* (**a**) *(appropriately)* en conséquence (**b**) *(consequently)* par conséquent; **accordingly, I wrote to him** je lui ai donc écrit, par conséquent je lui ai écrit

accordion [əˈkɔːdɪən] *n Mus* accordéon *m*

►► ***accordion player*** accordéoniste *mf*; *Sewing* ***accordion pleat*** pli *m* (en) accordéon

accordionist [əˈkɔːdɪənɪst] *n Mus* accordéoniste *mf*

accost [əˈkɒst] *vt (gen)* accoster, aborder; *(of prostitute)* racoler

account [əˈkaʊnt] **1** *n* (**a**) *(report)* récit *m*, compte rendu *m*; **to give an account of sth** faire le récit de qch; **her account differs from her husband's** sa version diffère de celle de son mari, son récit diffère de celui de son mari; **an interesting account of his travels** un récit intéressant de ses voyages; **his latest book contains an amusing account of how he learned to drive** son dernier livre relate de façon amusante la manière dont il a appris à conduire; **he gave his account of the accident** il a donné sa version de l'accident; **by his own account he had had too much to drink** à l'en croire, il avait trop bu

(**b**) *(explanation)* compte rendu *m*, explication *f*; **to bring** *or* **to call sb to account (for sth)** demander des comptes à qn (de qch); **to be brought to account** devoir rendre des comptes; **you will be held to account for all damages** il vous faudra rendre des comptes pour tous les dommages causés

(**c**) *(consideration)* importance *f*, valeur *f*; **a town of little account** une ville de peu d'importance *ou* insignifiante; **what you think is of no account to me** ce que vous pensez ne m'intéresse pas; **to take sth into account, to take account of sth** tenir compte de qch, prendre qch en compte; **he took little account of her feelings** il ne tenait pas compte *ou* faisait peu de cas de ses sentiments; **taking everything into account** tout bien calculé; **does this estimate take all the costs into account?** est-ce que cette estimation prend en compte toutes ces dépenses?; **the rising cost of living must also be taken into account** il faut aussi prendre en compte l'augmentation du coût de la vie

(**d**) *(advantage, profit)* profit *m*; **to put** *or* **to turn one's skills to good account** tirer parti de ses compétences; **to turn sth to account** tirer parti *ou* avantage de qch, mettre qch à profit

(**e**) *(responsibility)* **to set up in business on one's own account** s'établir à son compte; **I started working on my own account** j'ai commencé à travailler à mon compte

(**f**) *(rendition)* interprétation *f*, version *f*; **the pianist gave a sensitive account of the concerto** le pianiste a donné du concerto une interprétation d'une grande sensibilité; **to give a good account of oneself** bien se débrouiller; **she gave a good account of herself in the interview** elle a réussi à bien se définir au cours de cette entrevue

(**g**) *Com (with shop)* compte *m*; **to close/to open an account** fermer/ouvrir un compte; **we have an account at the garage** nous avons un compte chez le garagiste; **put it on** *or* **charge it to my account** mettez cela sur mon compte; **I'd like to settle my account** je voudrais régler ma note; **cash or account?** vous payez *ou* réglez comptant ou est-ce que vous avez un compte chez nous?; *Fig* **to settle** *or* **to square accounts with sb** régler ses comptes avec qn; **to account rendered** suivant compte remis

(**h**) *Banking* compte *m*; **to open/close an account** ouvrir/fermer un compte; **to pay money into one's account** verser de l'argent sur son compte; **to pay sb's salary directly into his/her account** verser le salaire de qn par virement direct sur son compte; **to overdraw an account** mettre un compte à découvert

(**i**) *Fin, Com & Acct (of expenses)* état *m*, note *f*; *(of transactions)* exposé *m*; **as per** *or* **to account rendered** *(on statement)* suivant compte *ou* relevé remis

(**j**) *Com & Mktg (in advertising, marketing, PR)* budget *m*; **one of our major accounts** un de nos plus gros clients; **the agency secured the Brook account** l'agence s'est assuré le budget Brook

(**k**) *Comput (with Internet service provider)* abonnement *m* (**with** auprès de); **to set up an account with sb** s'abonner auprès de qn

(**l**) *St Exch* **the Account** la liquidation

2 *vt Formal (consider)* estimer, considérer; **she accounts herself my friend** elle se considère mon amie; **to account sb guilty** tenir qn pour coupable

3 accounts *npl Acct (of company)* comptabilité *f*; **to keep the accounts** tenir les livres *ou* les écritures *ou* la comptabilité; **to enter sth in the accounts** comptabiliser qch; **who does your accounts?** qui est-ce qui fait votre comptabilité?

4 by all accounts *adv* au dire de tout le monde, d'après ce que tout le monde dit

5 on account *adv Com & Fin* à crédit; **we bought the car on account** nous avons acheté la voiture à crédit; **payment on account** paiement *m* à compte *ou* à crédit; **I paid £100 on account** j'ai versé un acompte de 100 livres

6 on account of *prep* en raison de; *(in negative contexts)* à cause de; **on account of the weather** à cause du temps; **don't leave on account of me** *or* **on my account** ne partez pas à cause de moi; **I did it on your account** *(to help you)* je l'ai fait pour vous; **I did it on account of you** *(reproaching)* je l'ai fait à cause de vous; **we didn't go on account of there being a storm** nous n'y sommes pas allés à cause de la tempête

7 on no account *adv* en aucun cas, sous aucun prétexte; **on no account do I want to talk to her** je ne veux lui parler en aucun cas *ou* sous aucun prétexte

►► ***account balance*** *(status)* situation *f* de compte; *Acct (after audit)* reliquat *m* de compte; *Acct* ***account book*** livre *m* de comptes, registre *m* de comptabilité; ***account card*** *Fin (record of charges)* fiche *f* de compte *ou* de facture; *Com (for use in department store)* carte-clients *f*; ***account charges*** frais *mpl* de tenue de compte; ***accounts clerk*** employé(e) *m,f* aux écritures; ***account credit*** avoir *m* de compte; *St Exch* ***account day*** (jour *m* de) liquidation, (jour de) règlement *m*; ***accounts department*** (service *m* de la) comptabilité *f*; *Com & Mktg* ***account director*** *(in advertising, marketing, PR)* directeur(trice) *m,f* des comptes-clients; *Am* ***account executive*** agent *m* de change; ***account fee*** commission *f* de compte; *Com & Mktg* ***account handler*** *(in advertising, marketing, PR)* responsable *mf* des comptes-clients; ***account handling fee*** commission *f* de tenue de compte; ***account holder*** titulaire *mf*; ***account manager*** *Banking & Fin* chargé(e) *m, f* de compte; *Com & Mktg (in advertising, marketing, PR)* responsable *mf* de budget; ***account number*** numéro *m* de compte; *Acct* ***account payable*** compte *m* créditeur, dette *f* fournisseur; *Acct* ***accounts payable*** dettes *fpl* passives, dettes *fpl* fournisseurs; *Acct* ***accounts payable ledger*** livre *m* des créanciers; *Acct* ***account receivable*** compte *m* client, compte *m* débiteur; *Acct* ***accounts receivable*** dettes *fpl* actives, créances *fpl* (clients); *Acct* ***accounts receivable ledger*** livre *m* des débiteurs; *Acct* ***accounts receivable turnover*** taux *m* de rotation des comptes clients; *Comput* ***accounts software*** logiciel *m* de comptabilité; ***account statement*** relevé *m ou* état *m ou* bordereau *m* de compte

►**account for** *vt insep* (**a**) *(explain)* expliquer, rendre compte de; **that accounts for his interest in baseball** voilà qui explique son intérêt pour le baseball; **there's no accounting for his recent odd behaviour** il n'y a aucune explication à son comportement bizarre des derniers temps; **there's no accounting for taste** les goûts et les couleurs, ça ne se discute pas

(**b**) *(answer for)* rendre compte de; **he has to account for every penny he spends** il doit rendre compte de chaque franc qu'il dépense; **all the children are accounted for** aucun des enfants n'a été oublié; **two hostages have not yet been accounted for** deux otages n'ont toujours pas été retrouvés

(**c**) *(represent)* représenter; **wine accounts for 5 percent of all exports** le vin représente 5 pour cent des exportations totales; **the North Sea accounts for a large proportion of our petroleum** la mer du Nord produit une grande partie de notre pétrole

(**d**) *Formal (shoot, kill)* abattre, tuer; *(catch)* attraper

accountability [ə,kaʊntə'bɪlɪtɪ] *n* responsabilité *f* (**to** envers); **the public wants more police accountability** le public souhaite que la police réponde davantage de ses actes; **public accountability** transparence *f*

accountable [ə'kaʊntəbəl] *adj* (**a**) *(responsible)* responsable; **to be accountable to sb for sth** être responsable de qch envers qn; **to be accountable for a sum of money** être redevable d'une somme d'argent; **to hold sb accountable (for sth)** tenir qn (pour) responsable (de qch); **she is not accountable for her actions** elle n'est pas responsable de ses actes; **I'm accountable to your mother for you** je suis responsable de toi devant ta mère; **I am accountable to no one** je n'ai de comptes à rendre à personne; **they cannot be held accountable for the accident** on ne peut les tenir responsables de l'accident

(**b**) *(explainable)* explicable

►► *Fin* ***accountable receipt*** quittance *f* comptable, reçu *m* certifié

accountably [ə'kaʊntəblɪ] *adv (explicable)* d'une manière explicable

accountancy [ə'kaʊntənsɪ] *n Br (subject, work)* comptabilité *f*, expertise *f* comptable; *(profession)* profession *f* de comptable; **a degree in accountancy** un diplôme de comptabilité

accountant [ə'kaʊntənt] *n* comptable *mf*, agent *m* comptable; **he works as an accountant** il est comptable

accounting [ə'kaʊntɪŋ] *n* comptabilité *f*, expertise *f* comptable; **she does the accounting** *(for business)* elle fait *ou* tient la comptabilité; *(for the family)* elle tient les comptes

►► ***accounting clerk*** commis *m* aux écritures; ***accounting control*** contrôle *m* de la comptabilité; ***accounting day*** journée *f* comptable; ***accounting entry*** écriture *f* comptable; ***accounting entry form, accounting entry sheet*** bordereau *m* de saisie; ***accounting firm*** cabinet *m* d'expertise comptable *ou* d'expert comptable; ***accounting method*** méthode *f* de comptabilité, procédé *m ou* mode *m* comptable; ***accounting period*** exercice *m* (financier), période *f* comptable; ***accounting policy*** politique *f* comptable; ***accounting procedure*** pratique *f* comptable; *Comput* ***accounting program*** logiciel *m* de comptabilité; ***accounting rate of return*** taux *m* de rendement comptable; ***acccounting records*** états *mpl* comptables; *Comput* ***accounting software*** logiciel *m* de comptabilité; ***accounting system*** système *m ou* plan *m* comptable; ***accounting year*** exercice *m* (financier), année *f* comptable

accoutre, *Am* **accouter** [ə'ku:tə(r)] *vt Formal* équiper; **to be accoutred with sth** être équipé de qch

accoutrements, *Am* **accouterments** [ə'ku:trəmənts] *npl (equipment)* attirail *m*; *Mil* équipement *m*

Accra [ə'krɑ:] *n Geog* Accra

accredit [ə'kredɪt] *vt* (**a**) *(credit)* attribuer; **they accredited the discovery to him** on lui a attribué cette découverte; **she is accredited with having discovered radium** on lui attribue la découverte du radium (**b**) *(provide with credentials)* accréditer; **he's the ambassador accredited to Morocco** c'est l'ambassadeur accrédité au Maroc (**c**) *(recognize as bona fide)* agréer

accreditation [ə,kredɪ'teɪʃən] *n* accréditation *f*; **to seek accreditation** chercher à se faire accréditer *ou* reconnaître

accredited [ə'kredɪtɪd] *adj* (**a**) *(idea, rumour)* admis, accepté (**b**) *(official, person)* accrédité, autorisé; **the accredited representative to the United Nations** le représentant accrédité aux Nations unies (**c**) *(recognized as bona fide)* agréé; *Agr* **accredited dairy herds** troupeaux *mpl* tuberculinés; **accredited schools** = établissements délivrant des diplômes reconnus par l'État

accresecent [æ'kresənt] *adj Bot* accrescent

accrete [ə'kri:t] *Literary* **1** *vt* **to accrete followers to one's party** s'attirer des partisans

2 *vi* (**a**) *(increase)* s'accroître

accretion [æ'kri:ʃən] *n* (**a**) *(growth → in size)* accroissement *m*; *(→ of dirt, wealth)* accroissement *m*, accumulation *f* (**b**) *(addition)* addition *f*; *Law* **accretion of property** accumulation de biens (**c**) *Astron & Geol* accrétion *f* (**d**) *Zool (adhesion)* accrétion *f*; *(deposit)* concrétion *f*

accretionary [ə'kri:ʃənərɪ], **accretive** [ə'kri:tɪv] *adj Geol* qui s'accroît par addition

►► ***accretionary process*** procédé *m* d'addition

accrual [ə'kru:əl] *n* (**a**) *Fin (of interest, debt, cost)* accumulation *f* (**b**) *Acct* **accruals** *(expenses)* charges *fpl* à payer; *(income)* produits *mpl* à recevoir

►► *Acct* ***accrual accounting*** comptabilité *f* d'engagements; ***accruals concept*** principe *m* d'indépendance des exercices *ou* de rattachement à l'exercice; ***accrual of dividend*** échéance *f* de dividende; ***accrual rate*** taux *m* d'accumulation *ou* d'accroissement

accrue [ə'kru:] *Formal* **1** *vi* (**a**) *Fin (increase)* s'accroître, s'accumuler; *(interest)* s'accumuler, courir; **interest accrues (as) from the 5th of the month** les intérêts courent à partir du 5 du mois (**b**) *(benefit, gain)* **to accrue to sb** revenir à qn; **advantages accruing to property owners** les avantages revenant aux propriétaires fonciers

2 *vt* accumuler; *Fin (interest)* produire

►► ***accrued benefits*** *(under pension scheme)* points *mpl* de retraite; ***accrued charges*** effets *mpl* à payer; ***accrued dividends*** dividendes *mpl* accrus; ***accrued expenses*** frais *mpl* cumulés *ou* accumulés; ***accrued income*** recettes *fpl* échues, effets *mpl ou* produit *m* à recevoir; ***accrued interest*** intérêts *mpl* courus

acculturate [ə'kʌltʃəreɪt] *vt* acculturer

acculturation [ə,kʌltʃə'reɪʃən] *n* acculturation *f*

accumulate [ə'kju:mjʊleɪt] **1** *vt* accumuler; *(objects)* amonceler, entasser; *Phys & Elec (heat, electricity)* emmagasiner

2 *vi* s'accumuler

accumulated [ə'kju:mjʊleɪtɪd] *adj* accumulé

►► *Fin* ***accumulated depreciation*** amortissement *m* cumulé

accumulation [ə,kju:mjʊ'leɪʃən] *n* (**a**) *(process)* accumulation *f* (**b**) *(things collected → objects)* amas *m*, tas *m*; *(→ facts, evidence)* accumulation *f* (**c**) *Fin (of capital)* accroissement *m*; *(of interest)* accumulation *f*

accumulative [ə'kju:mjʊlətɪv] *adj* cumulatif, qui s'accumule; *Fin* cumulatif

accumulator [ə'kju:mjʊleɪtə(r)] *n* (**a**) *Elec (battery)* accumulateur *m* (**b**) *Br Horseracing (bet)* = pari par report (**c**) *(person)* **he's an accumulator of useless gadgets** il accumule les gadgets inutiles

accuracy ['ækjʊrəsɪ] *n (of description, report)* précision *f*, justesse *f*; *(of aim, instrument, weapon)* précision *f*; *(of figures, watch)* exactitude *f*; *(of estimate, prediction)* justesse *f*; *(of memory, translation)* fidélité *f*, exactitude *f*

accurate ['ækjʊrət] *adj (description, report)* précis, juste; *(aim, instrument, weapon)* précis; *(figures, watch)* exact; *(estimate, prediction)* juste; *(memory, translation)* fidèle; **the report was accurate in every detail** le compte rendu était fidèle jusque dans les moindres détails; **to be more accurate, there were 15 of them** pour être plus précis, ils étaient 15; **she's very accurate in her calculations** elle est très précise dans ses calculs

accurately ['ækjʊrətlɪ] *adv (count, draw, aim)* avec précision; *(tell)* exactement; *(judge, estimate, predict)* avec justesse; *(remember, translate)* fidèlement

accurateness ['ækjʊrətnɪs] *n (of description, report)* précision *f*, justesse *f*; *(of aim, instrument, weapon)* précision *f*; *(of figures, watch)* exactitude *f*; *(of estimate, prediction)* justesse *f*; *(of memory, translation)* fidélité *f*, exactitude *f*

accursed [ə'kɜːsɪd] *adj Literary (cursed)* maudit; *(hateful)* maudit, exécrable

accusal [ə'kjuːzəl] *n Law* accusation *f*

accusation [,ækjuː'zeɪʃən] *n* **(a)** *(gen)* accusation *f*; **to make an accusation (against sb)** porter une accusation (contre qn); **there was a note of accusation in her voice** sa voix prenait des accents un tant soit peu accusateurs; **she had no answer to the accusation that her fiscal policies had failed** elle n'avait rien à répondre aux accusations selon lesquelles sa politique fiscale avait échoué

(b) *Law* accusation *f*, plainte *f*; **they brought an accusation of theft against him** ils ont porté plainte contre lui pour vol

accusative [ə'kjuːzətɪv] **1** *n Gram* accusatif *m*; **in the accusative** à l'accusatif

2 *adj* **(a)** *Gram* accusatif **(b)** *(look, tone)* accusateur

accusatorial [ə,kjuːzə'tɔːrɪəl], **accusatory** [ə'kjuːzətərɪ] *adj* **(a)** *(look, tone)* accusateur **(b)** *Law (system)* accusatoire

accuse [ə'kjuːz] *vt* accuser; **to accuse sb of sth/doing sth** accuser qn de qch/de faire qch; **he is** *or* **he stands accused of tax fraud** il est accusé de fraude fiscale; *Ironic* **no one could accuse her of being punctual** on ne peut pas l'accuser d'être ponctuelle

'I accuse!' *Ferrer* 'L'Affaire Dreyfus'

accused [ə'kjuːzd] *(pl* **inv***) n Law* **the accused** l'accusé(e) *m,f*, l'inculpé(e) *m,f*

accuser [ə'kjuːzə(r)] *n* accusateur(trice) *m,f*

accusing [ə'kjuːzɪŋ] *adj* accusateur

accusingly [ə'kjuːzɪŋlɪ] *adv* de façon accusatrice; *(look, stare)* d'un air *ou* d'un œil accusateur

accustom [ə'kʌstəm] *vt* habituer, accoutumer (**to sth/to doing sth** à qch/à faire qch); **to accustom sb to sth** habituer qn à qch; **to accustom oneself to sth** s'habituer *ou* se faire *ou* s'accoutumer à qch; **she's gradually accustoming herself to her new way of life** elle s'habitue peu à peu à son nouveau style de vie

accustomed [ə'kʌstəmd] *adj* **(a)** *(familiar)* habitué, accoutumé; **to get** *or* **to grow accustomed to sth** s'habituer *ou* s'accoutumer à qch; **they weren't accustomed to strangers/politeness** ils n'étaient pas habitués aux étrangers/à la politesse; **her eyes had got accustomed to the dark** ses yeux s'étaient accoutumés à l'obscurité; **I'm not accustomed to getting up so early** je n'ai pas l'habitude de me lever si tôt; **she's not accustomed to being interrupted** elle n'a pas l'habitude qu'on l'interrompe

(b) *(regular)* habituel, coutumier

AC/DC [,eɪsiː'diːsiː] **1** *n Elec (abbr* **alternating current/direct current***)* CA/CC *m*

2 *adj Fam (bisexual)* **to be AC/DC** marcher à voile et à vapeur

ACE [,eɪsiː'iː] *n Am Mil (abbr* **Army Corps of Engineers***)* **the ACE** le Génie

ace [eɪs] **1** *n* **(a)** *(on card, dice, dominoes)* as *m*; *Cards* **the ace of spades** l'as *m* de pique; *Fig* **to have an ace up one's sleeve, to have an ace in the hole** avoir un atout en réserve; **to hold all the aces** avoir tous les atouts dans son jeu; **to come within an ace of doing sth** être à deux doigts de faire qch

(b) *(expert)* as *m*; **she's an ace at chess** c'est un as aux échecs

(c) *(in tennis)* ace *m*; **to serve an ace** servir un ace

(d) *Aviat & Mil (pilot)* as *m*

2 *adj Fam* super, génial; **she's an ace skier, she's ace at skiing** c'est une skieuse formidable; **the film was really ace!** le film était vraiment super!

3 *vt* **(a)** *(in tennis)* **he aced his opponent** il a servi un ace contre son adversaire; *Fig* il n'a pas laissé une chance à son adversaire

(b) *Am Golf* **to ace a hole** faire un trou en un

(c) *Am Fam* **to ace an exam** réussir un examen les doigts dans le nez

4 aces *adj Am Fam (excellent)* super, génial

Ace bandage® *n Am* bande *f* Velpeau®

acellular [,eɪ'seljʊlə(r)] *adj Biol* acellulaire

acephalous [,eɪ'sefələs] *adj* acéphale

acer ['eɪsə(r)] *n Bot* acéracée *f*

acerbic [ə'sɜːbɪk] *adj (taste)* âpre; *(person, tone)* acerbe

acerbity [ə'sɜːbətɪ] *n (of taste)* âpreté *f*; *(of person, tone)* aigreur *f*

acetabulum [,æsə'tæbjʊləm] *n Zool* acétabule *f*, acétabulum *m*

acetaldehyde [,æsɪ'tældɪhaɪd] *n Chem* alcool *m* éthylique, éthanol *m*

acetate ['æsɪteɪt] *n Chem* acétate *m*

acetic [ə'siːtɪk] *adj Chem* acétique

►► ***acetic acid*** acide *m* acétique

acetification [æ,siːtɪfɪ'keɪʃən] *n Chem* acétification *f*

acetify [æ'siːtɪfaɪ] *Chem* **1** *vt* acétifier

2 *vi* s'acétifier

acetone ['æsɪtəʊn] *n Chem* acétone *f*

acetyl ['æsətaɪl] *n Chem* acétyle *m*

acetylation [æ,sɪtɪ'leɪʃən] *n Chem* acétylation *f*

acetylene [ə'setɪliːn] *Chem* **1** *n* acétylène *m*

2 *comp (burner, lamp, torch)* à acétylène; *(welding)* à l'acétylène

acetylsalicylic acid ['æsɪtaɪl,sælɪ'sɪlɪk-] *n Chem* acide *m* acétylsalicylique

acey-deucy [,eɪsɪ'djuːsɪ] **1** *n (game)* jacquet *m*

2 *adj Am Fam* super, génial

ACGB [,eɪsiː,dʒiː'biː] *n (abbr* **Arts Council of Great Britain***)* = organisme public britannique de promotion des arts

ACH [,eɪsiː'eɪtʃ] *n Banking (abbr* **automated clearing house***)* chambre *f* de compensation automatisée

Achates [æ'keɪtiːz] *pr n Literature* Achate; *Literary* **his fidus Achates** son fidèle Achate

ache [eɪk] **1** *vi* **(a)** *(feel pain)* faire mal, être douloureux; **I ache all over** j'ai mal partout; **my head/tooth aches** j'ai mal à la tête/aux dents; *Fig* **her heart ached to see them so unhappy** elle souffrait de les voir si malheureux **(b)** *(feel desire)* avoir très envie; **she was aching for them to leave** elle mourait d'envie de les voir partir

2 *n (physical)* douleur *f*; *(emotional)* peine *f*; **a dull ache** une douleur sourde; **aches and pains** douleurs *fpl*, maux *mpl*

achievable [ə'tʃiːvəbəl] *adj* faisable, réalisable

achieve [ə'tʃiːv] *vt (gen)* accomplir, faire; *(desire, dream, increase)* réaliser; *(level, objective)* arriver à, atteindre; *(independence, success)* obtenir; *(honour, notoriety)* acquérir; *(reputation)* se faire; **she achieved the impossible** elle a accompli l'impossible; **he'll never achieve anything in life** il n'arrivera jamais à rien dans sa vie; **we really achieved something today** on a vraiment bien avancé aujourd'hui; **we achieved what we set out to do** nous avons rempli nos objectifs; **the demonstration achieved nothing** la manifestation n'a servi à rien; **the plan achieved its objectives** le plan a atteint ses objectifs; **this policy achieved very little** cette politique n'a pas donné de grands résultats; **what will that achieve?** *(suggestion etc)* qu'est-ce que ça fera de plus?, pour en venir à quoi?

achievement [ə'tʃiːvmənt] *n* **(a)** *(deed)* exploit *m*, réussite *f*; **convincing her to come was quite an achievement** c'est un véritable exploit d'avoir réussi à la convaincre de venir; **a lasting achievement** une réalisation durable **(b)** *(successful completion)* accomplissement *m*, réalisation *f*; **I felt a real sense of achievement** j'ai vraiment eu le sentiment d'avoir accompli quelque chose

►► *Sch* ***achievement tests*** tests *mpl* de niveau

achievement-orientated, *Am* **achievement-oriented** *adj* **to be achievement-orientated** mettre l'accent sur la réussite

achiever [ə'tʃiːvə(r)] *n* fonceur(euse) *m,f*

Achilles [ə'kɪliːz] *pr n Myth* Achille

►► *Myth* ***Achilles' heel*** talon *m* d'Achille; *Fig* **gambling is his Achilles' heel** le jeu est son point faible; *Anat* ***Achilles' tendon*** tendon *m* d'Achille

aching ['eɪkɪŋ] *adj* douloureux, endolori; **oh, my aching head!** oh, ma pauvre tête!; **to have an aching heart** avoir une peine de cœur; **her death left an aching void in his life** sa mort a laissé un vide douloureux dans sa vie

achingly ['eɪkɪŋlɪ] *adv Fam* **achingly funny** tordant; *Fam* **achingly hip** *(person, bar, clothes)* hyper branché

achondroplasia [eɪ,kɒndrəʊ'pleɪʒə] *n Med* achondroplasie *f*

achromat ['ækrəʊmæt] *n Opt* achromat *m*

achromatic [,ækrəʊ'mætɪk] *adj Opt* achromatique

achy ['eɪkɪ] *adj* douloureux, endolori; **I feel achy all over** je suis tout courbaturé, j'ai mal partout; **I have an achy feeling in my joints** j'ai mal aux articulations

acicular [eɪ'sɪkjʊlə(r)] *adj Bot & Miner* aciculaire

acid ['æsɪd] **1** *n* **(a)** *Chem* acide *m* **(b)** *Fam (LSD)* acide *m*

2 *adj* **(a)** *(drink, taste)* acide **(b)** *(remark, tone, wit)* mordant, acide; *(person)* revêche, caustique **(c)** *Chem* acide

►► ***acid drop*** bonbon *m* acidulé; *Mus* ***acid house*** house *f*; ***acid indigestion*** aigreurs *fpl* d'estomac; *Mus* ***acid jazz*** acid jazz *m*; *Ecol* ***acid rain*** pluies *fpl* acides; ***acid test*** épreuve *f* à la pierre de touche; *Fig* épreuve *f* décisive; *Acct* ***acid test ratio*** ratio *m* de liquidité immédiate

acidhead ['æsɪd,hed] *n Fam Drugs slang* drogué(e) *m,f* au LSD ❏

acidic [ə'sɪdɪk] *adj Chem* acide

acidification [ə,sɪdɪfɪ'keɪʃən] *n Chem* acidification *f*

acidify [ə'sɪdɪfaɪ] *(pt & pp* **acidified***) Chem* **1** *vt* acidifier

2 *vi* s'acidifier

acidity [ə'sɪdətɪ] *n Chem* acidité *f*; *Fig* aigreur *f*, acidité *f*

acidly ['æsɪdlɪ] *adv Chem* aigrement; *Fig* d'un ton acide

acidness ['æsɪdnɪs] *n Chem* acidité *f*; *Fig* aigreur *f*, acidité *f*

acidosis [,æsɪ'dəʊsɪs] *n Med* acidose *f*

acid-proof *adj Chem* résistant aux acides

acidulous [ə'sɪdjʊləs] *adj* acidulé

acinus ['æsɪnəs] *n Bot* acine *m*, acinus *m*

ack-ack [,æk'æk] *Br Fam Mil slang Old-fashioned* **1** *n* défense *f* contre avions ❏, DCA ❏ *f*

2 *comp* de DCA ❏, antiaérien ❏

►► ***ack-ack fire*** tir *m* de DCA ❏; ***ack-ack weapons*** armes *fpl* de DCA ❏

ackee ['ækɪ] *n Bot (tree, fruit)* ackee *m*

ackemma [,æk'emə] *adv Fam Mil slang Old-fashioned* au matin ❏

acknowledge [ək'nɒlɪdʒ] *vt* **(a)** *(admit truth of)* reconnaître, admettre; *(defeat, mistake)* reconnaître, avouer; **we acknowledge (the fact) that we were wrong** nous admettons notre erreur; **she acknowledged her guilt** elle a avoué *ou* reconnu sa culpabilité; **the candidate acknowledged himself defeated** le candidat a reconnu *ou* admis sa défaite; **acknowledged as the** *or* **to be the best Chinese restaurant in the city** reconnu comme le meilleur restaurant chinois de la ville

(b) *(show recognition of → person)* **he didn't even acknowledge my presence** il a fait comme si je n'étais pas là; **she acknowledged him with a nod** elle lui a adressé un signe de la tête; **they acknowledged him as their leader** ils l'ont reconnu comme leur chef; **he acknowledged her child (as his)** il a reconnu l'enfant (comme étant le sien)

(c) *(confirm receipt of → greeting, message)* répondre à; *Admin (→ letter, package)* accuser réception de; **sign here to acknowledge receipt** *(on form)* signez ici pour accuser réception (**d**) *(express gratitude for)* **he acknowledged the cheers of the crowd** il a salué en réponse aux applaudissements de la foule; **I'd like to acknowledge the help given me by my family** j'aimerais remercier ma famille pour l'aide qu'elle m'a apportée

►► *Comput* ***acknowledge character*** *(in datacommunications)* caractère *m* d'accusé de réception

acknowledged [ək'nɒlɪdʒd] *adj (expert, authority)* reconnu

acknowledgment, acknowledgement [ək'nɒlɪdʒmənt] **1** *n* (**a**) *(admission)* reconnaissance *f*; *(of mistake)* reconnaissance *f*, aveu *m*; **I waved/smiled at him, but received no acknowledgement** je lui ai fait signe/ai souri mais il ne m'a pas répondu; **in acknowledgement of your letter** en réponse à votre lettre; **he received a watch in acknowledgement of his work** il a reçu une montre en reconnaissance *ou* remerciement de son travail

(**b**) *Admin & Fin (letter, receipt)* accusé *m* de réception; *(for payment)* quittance *f*, reçu *m*

2 acknowledgements *npl (in article, book)* remerciements *mpl*

►► *Admin* ***acknowledgement of receipt*** accusé *m* de réception

ACL [ˌeɪsiː'el] *n Anat* (*abbr* **anterior cruciate ligament**) ligament *m* croisé antérieur

ACLU [ˌeɪsiːˌel'juː] *n Pol* (*abbr* **American Civil Liberties Union**) = ligue américaine des droits du citoyen

acme ['ækmɪ] *n* apogée *m*, point *m* culminant; **to reach the acme of one's desires** parvenir au comble de ses désirs; **to attain the acme of perfection** arriver à la perfection même; **to be at the acme of one's glory** être à l'apogée de la gloire

acne ['æknɪ] *n* acné *f*

acolyte ['ækəlaɪt] *n (gen) & Rel* acolyte *m*

aconite ['ækənaɪt] *n* (**a**) *Bot* aconit *m* (**b**) *Chem* aconitine *f*

ACORN ['eɪkɔːn] *n Mktg* (*abbr* **A Classification Of Residential Neighbourhoods**) = classement des différents types de quartiers résidentiels existant en Grande Bretagne en 39 catégories, utilisé par les entreprises pour mieux cibler leurs clients potentiels lors de campagnes commerciales

acorn ['eɪkɔːn] *n* gland *m*

►► ***acorn cup*** cupule *f*

acotyledon [ˌeɪkɒtɪ'liːdən] *n Bot* acotylédone *f*, acotylédonée *f*

acotyledonous [ˌeɪkɒtɪ'liːdənəs] *adj Bot* acotylédone, acotylédoné

acoustic [ə'kuːstɪk] *adj (feature, phonetics, nerve)* acoustique

►► *Comput & Tel* ***acoustic coupler*** coupleur *m* acoustique; *Tech* ***acoustic engineer*** acousticien(enne) *m,f*; ***acoustic feedback*** effet *m* Larsen, rétroaction *f* acoustique, bouclage *m* acoustique; ***acoustic guitar*** guitare *f* sèche; ***acoustic hood*** capot *m* antibruit; ***acoustic tile*** carreau *m* acoustique

acoustically [ə'kuːstɪkəlɪ] *adv* du point de vue de l'acoustique

acoustics [ə'kuːstɪks] **1** *n (UNCOUNT) (subject)* acoustique *f*

2 *npl (of room, theatre)* acoustique *f*; **to have bad/good acoustics** avoir une mauvaise/bonne acoustique

ACP [ˌeɪsiː'piː] *n* (**a**) *Geog* (*abbr* **African, Caribbean and Pacific**) **the ACP countries** les pays africains, des Caraïbes et du Pacifique (**b**) (*abbr* **American College of Physicians**) = académie de médecine aux États-Unis

ACPO ['ækpəʊ] *n* (*abbr* **Association of Chief Police Officers**) = syndicat d'officiers supérieurs de la police britannique

acquaint [ə'kweɪnt] *vt* (**a**) *(inform)* aviser, renseigner; **I'll acquaint you with the facts** je vais vous mettre au courant des faits; **let me acquaint you with the situation** laissez-moi vous mettre au fait de la situation; **a stay in the jungle had acquainted him with these dangers** un séjour dans la jungle l'avait familiarisé avec ces dangers; **she acquainted herself with their customs** elle s'est familiarisée avec leurs habitudes

(**b**) *(familiarize)* **to be acquainted with** *(person, place, subject)* connaître; *(fact, situation)* être au courant de; **she is well acquainted with the mayor** elle connaît très bien le maire; **I got acquainted with him later** j'ai fait sa connaissance plus tard; **we were just getting acquainted** on venait juste de faire connaissance; **to become acquainted with the facts** prendre connaissance des faits; **I'm fully acquainted with the facts** je suis tout à fait au courant des faits

acquaintance [ə'kweɪntəns] *n* (**a**) *(person)* connaissance *f*, relation *f*; **he is an acquaintance (of mine)** c'est quelqu'un que je connais; **he has a wide circle of acquaintances** il a des relations très étendues

(**b**) *(knowledge)* connaissance *f*; **to make sb's acquaintance** faire la connaissance de qn; **pleased to make your acquaintance** enchanté de faire votre connaissance; **during our brief acquaintance** pendant la courte période où nous avons été en contact; **on closer** *or* **further acquaintance he seems quite intelligent** quand on le connaît un peu mieux, il semble assez intelligent; **to have a nodding** *or* **passing acquaintance with sb/sth** connaître vaguement qn/qch

►► ***acquaintance rape*** = viol commis par une personne connue de la victime

acquaintanceship [ə'kweɪntənʃɪp] *n* (**a**) *(relationship)* relations *fpl* (**b**) *(people)* relations *fpl*, cercle *m* de connaissances; **he has a wide acquaintanceship** il a de nombreuses relations

acquest [æ'kwest] *n Law* acquêt *m*

acquiesce [ˌækwɪ'es] *vi* acquiescer, consentir (**in** *or* **to** à); **she finally acquiesced** elle a finalement acquiescé; **they acquiesced to our demands** ils ont consenti à nos exigences; **he acquiesced in the terms we had drawn up** il a consenti aux conditions que nous avions établies

acquiescence [ˌækwɪ'esəns] *n* acquiescement *m*, consentement *m* (**in** *or* **to** à)

acquiescent [ˌækwɪ'esənt] *adj* consentant

acquire [ə'kwaɪə(r)] *vt* (**a**) *(advantage, experience, possession, success)* acquérir; *(reputation, friend)* se faire; **they have recently acquired the house next door** ils ont récemment acquis *ou* se sont récemment rendus acquéreurs de la maison d'à côté; **we seem to have acquired a cat** il semble qu'on ait hérité d'un chat

(**b**) *(information, language)* apprendre; *(knowledge)* acquérir; **it took her years to acquire fluency in German** ça lui a pris des années pour apprendre couramment l'allemand

(**c**) *(habit)* prendre, contracter; **I've acquired a taste for champagne** j'ai pris goût au champagne

(**d**) *Com & Fin (other company)* prendre le contrôle de, racheter; *(shares)* acheter; **to acquire an interest in a company** prendre une participation dans une société

acquired [ə'kwaɪəd] *adj* acquis; **it's an acquired taste** on finit par y prendre goût

►► *Biol* ***acquired characteristic*** caractère *m* acquis; *Med* ***acquired immune deficiency syndrome*** syndrome *m* immunodéficitaire acquis; *Fin* ***acquired surplus*** surplus *m* acquis

acquirement [ə'kwaɪəmənt] *n* acquisition *f*

acquirer [ə'kwaɪərə(r)] *n* acquéreur(euse) *m,f*

acquisition [ˌækwɪ'zɪʃən] *n* acquisition *f*; *Fin (of company)* acquisition *f*, prise *f* de contrôle; **the acquisition of knowledge** l'acquisition *f* de connaissances; **she's the team's latest acquisition** elle est la dernière acquisition de l'équipe

►► *Acct* ***acquisition accounting*** = base de préparation des comptes consolidés où une société a pris le contrôle d'une autre; *Acct* ***acquisition cost*** coût *m* d'acquisition

acquisitive [ə'kwɪzɪtɪv] *adj (greedy)* avide; *(for money)* avide, âpre au gain, cupide

acquisitively [ə'kwɪzɪtɪvlɪ] *adv (greedily)* avidement; *(for money)* avidement, cupidement

acquisitiveness [ə'kwɪzɪtɪvnɪs] *n (greed)* avidité *f*; *(for money)* avidité *f*, âpreté *f* au gain, cupidité *f*

acquit [ə'kwɪt] (*pt & pp* **acquitted**, *cont* **acquitting**) *vt* (**a**) *(release → from duty, responsibility)* acquitter, décharger (**b**) *Law* acquitter, relaxer; **to acquit sb of sth** acquitter qn de qch (**c**) *(perform)* **to acquit oneself well/badly** bien/mal s'en sortir; **he acquitted himself well during the trial** il s'est bien conduit pendant le procès; **how did he acquit himself?** comment s'en est-il sorti? (**d**) *Fin (debt)* acquitter, s'acquitter de, régler

acquittal [ə'kwɪtəl] *n* (**a**) *(of duty, responsibility)* accomplissement *m* (**b**) *Law* acquittement *m* (**c**) *Fin (of debt)* acquittement *m*, décharge *f*, quittance *f*

acquittance [ə'kwɪtəns] *n Fin (of debt)* acquittement *m*, décharge *f*, quittance *f*

acre ['eɪkə(r)] *n* = 4047m², ≃ demi-hectare *m*; **acres of forest** des hectares *mpl* de forêts; *Fig* **they have acres of room** ils ont des kilomètres de place; *Fig* **forty acres and a mule** quarante acres de terre et une mule, = minimum garanti par l'État américain aux esclaves affranchis au lendemain de la guerre de Sécession

acreage ['eɪkərɪdʒ] *n* aire *f*, superficie *f (en mesures agraires)*; **how much acreage do you have here?** combien avez-vous d'hectares ici?

acrid ['ækrɪd] *adj* (**a**) *(smell, taste, smoke)* âcre (**b**) *(language, remark)* acerbe, mordant

acridity [æ'krɪdɪtɪ] *n* (**a**) *(of smell, taste, smoke)* âcreté *f* (**b**) *(of language, remark)* acerbité *f*

acridly ['ækrɪdlɪ] *adv (say, remark)* avec acerbité

acridness ['ækrɪdnɪs] *n* (**a**) *(of smell, taste, smoke)* âcreté *f* (**b**) *(of language, remark)* acerbité *f*

Acrilan® ['ækrɪlæn] *n Tex* Acrilan® *m*

acrimonious [ˌækrɪ'məʊnɪəs] *adj (person, remark)* acrimonieux, hargneux; *(attack, dispute)* virulent; **the discussion was becoming acrimonious** la discussion s'envenimait

acrimoniously [ˌækrɪ'məʊnɪəslɪ] *adv (say)* avec acrimonie; **the meeting ended acrimoniously** la réunion s'est terminée dans l'amertume

acrimony ['ækrɪmənɪ] *n* acrimonie *f*, hargne *f*

acrobat ['ækrəbæt] *n* acrobate *mf*

acrobatic [ˌækrə'bætɪk] *adj* acrobatique

acrobatics [ˌækrə'bætɪks] *npl* acrobatie *f*; **to do** *or* **to perform acrobatics** faire des acrobaties *ou* de l'acrobatie

acromegalic [ˌækrəʊmə'gælɪk] *adj Med* acromégalique

acromegaly [ˌækrəʊ'megəlɪ] *n Med* acromégalie *f*

acronym ['ækrənɪm] *n Gram* acronyme *m*

acrophobia [ˌækrə'fəʊbɪə] *n Psy* acrophobie *f*

Acropolis [ə'krɒpəlɪs] *n Archit* Acropole *f*

acrosome ['ækrəsəʊm] *n Biol* acrosome *m*

across [ə'krɒs] **1** *prep* (**a**) *(from one side to the other of)* d'un côté à l'autre de; **she drew a line across the page** elle a tiré un trait en travers de la page; **to walk across sth** traverser qch; **she swam across the lake** elle a traversé le lac à la nage; **I ran across the street** j'ai traversé la rue en courant; **can you help me across the road?** pouvez-vous m'aider à traverser la rue?; **they built a bridge across the lake** ils ont construit un pont sur le lac; **she threw it across the room** elle l'a jeté en travers de *ou* de l'autre côté de la pièce; **he lay across the bed** il était couché *ou* allongé en travers du lit; **she felt a pain across her chest** une douleur lui a traversé la poitrine; **he's very broad across the shoulders** il est très large d'épaules

(**b**) *(on the other side of)* en face de, de l'autre côté de; **the house across the street** la maison d'en face; **we live across the street from them** nous habitons en face de chez eux; **the woman from across the street** la femme d'en face; **there's a supermarket just across the road from us/our house** il y a un supermarché juste en face/en face de notre maison; **just across the border** de l'autre côté *ou* au-delà de la frontière; **he sat across the table from me** il s'assit en face de moi; **she glanced across the room at us** elle nous lança un regard de l'autre bout de la pièce

(**c**) *(so as to cover)* **he leaned across my desk** il s'est penché par-dessus mon bureau; **a smile spread across her face** un sourire a éclairé son visage

(**d**) *(so as to cross)* en travers de, à travers; **the study of literature across cultures** l'étude de la littérature à travers différentes cultures; **the lines cut across each other** les lignes se coupent

(**e**) *(throughout)* **he gave speeches all across Europe** il a fait des discours dans toute l'Europe; **across the political spectrum** dans l'ensemble de la classe politique
(**f**) *(on)* **he hit me across the face** il m'a frappé au visage
2 *adv* (**a**) *(from one side to the other)* d'un côté à l'autre; **the room is 3 metres across** la pièce fait 3 mètres de large; **I helped him across** je l'ai aidé à traverser
(**b**) *(on or to the other side)* de l'autre côté; **he reached across and picked the pen up** il a tendu le bras et a pris le stylo; **she walked across to Mary** elle s'est dirigée vers Mary; **I looked across at my mother** j'ai regardé ma mère
(**c**) *(in crosswords)* horizontalement; **what's 23 across?** *(clue)* quelle est la définition du 23 horizontal *ou* horizontalement?; *(solution)* quelle est la réponse du 23 horizontal *ou* horizontalement?
3 across from *prep* en face de; **the man sitting across from me** l'homme qui était assis en face de moi; **the house across from ours** la maison située en face de la nôtre
4 across the board *adv* systématiquement; **stock prices have fallen across the board** le prix des actions a baissé de façon systématique; **the policy applies to everybody in the company across the board** cette politique concerne tous les employés de l'entreprise quelle que soit leur position

across-the-board *adj* général, systématique; **an across-the-board salary rise** une augmentation de salaire générale

acrostic [ə'krɒstɪk] *n* acrostiche *m*

acrylic [ə'krɪlɪk] *Chem & Tex* **1** *adj* acrylique; *(garment)* en acrylique
2 *n (fabric)* acrylique *m*; *(paint)* acrylique *m*

ACS [ˌeɪsiː'es] *n (abbr* **American Cancer Society**) = association américaine de lutte contre le cancer

ACT [ˌeɪsiː'tiː] *n Sch (abbr* **American College Test**) = examen de fin d'études secondaires aux États-Unis

ACT [ækt]

agir	▸1 (a), (c), (e)
jouer	▸1 (d); 2
servir de	▸1 (b)
acte	▸3 (a), (d), (f)
numéro	▸3 (b), (c)
comédie	▸3 (b)
loi	▸3 (e)

1 *vi* (**a**) *(take action)* agir; **we must act quickly to stop her** nous devons agir rapidement pour l'arrêter; **they acted for the best** ils ont agi pour le mieux; **to act out of fear/greed/selfishness** agir sous l'emprise de la peur/par cupidité/par égoïsme; **she has a good lawyer acting for her** elle est représentée par un bon avocat; **to act on behalf of sb, to act on sb's behalf** agir au nom de qn
(**b**) *(serve)* **to act as** servir de, faire office de; **she acted as my interpreter** elle m'a servi d'interprète; **the trees act as a windbreak** les arbres servent de barrière contre le vent; **the smell acts as a warning to other animals** les autres animaux sont avertis par l'odeur; **the engine acts as a brake** le moteur fait fonction de frein; **to act as a warning** servir d'avertissement
(**c**) *(behave)* agir, se comporter; **they acted very sensibly/responsibly** ils ont agi de façon très raisonnable/responsable; **they act as if nothing had happened** ils se comportent *ou* ils font comme si rien ne s'était passé; **she just acts dumb** elle fait l'innocente; **to act stupid/all innocent** faire l'idiot/l'innocent; **you acted like a fool** vous vous êtes conduit comme un imbécile; **he acts as though he were bored** il agit comme s'il s'ennuyait; **she's just acting like she's angry** elle joue à *ou* fait celle qui est en colère
(**d**) *Cin, Theat & TV (perform a part)* jouer; **he's been acting since he was a child** il joue depuis son enfance; **he can't act** c'est un mauvais acteur; **I always wanted to act** j'ai toujours voulu être acteur; **to act in a film** tourner dans un film
(**e**) *(produce an effect, work)* agir
2 *vt Cin, Theat & TV (part)* jouer, tenir; *(play)* jouer; **he's acting (the part of) King Lear** il joue le rôle du Roi Lear; *Fig* **he tries to act the dutiful husband** il essaie de jouer les maris parfaits; **stop acting the fool!** arrête de faire l'imbécile!; **act your age!** arrête de faire l'enfant!
3 *n* (**a**) *(action, deed)* acte *m*; **the act of a criminal/madman** l'action d'un criminel/fou; **to be caught in the act** être pris sur le fait; **she was caught in the act of taking the money** on l'a surprise en train de voler l'argent; **to get in on the act** être dans le coup; **to be/to let sb in on the act** être/mettre qn dans le coup
(**b**) *(pretence)* comédie *f*, numéro *m*; **to put on an act** jouer la comédie; **it's all an act** tout ça c'est de la comédie; **I'm not fooled by your worried mother act!** ton numéro de mère anxieuse ne prendra pas avec moi!
(**c**) *(in circus, show)* numéro *m*; **a comedy act** un numéro de comédie; *Fam Fig* **to get one's act together** se reprendre ☐; *Am Fam* **to queer the act** tout faire foirer
(**d**) *Mus & Theat (part of play, opera)* acte *m*; **Act I, scene 1** Acte I, scène 1
(**e**) *Law & Pol* loi *f*; **an act of Congress/Parliament** une loi du Congrès/Parlement
(**f**) *Mil* **an act of war** un acte de guerre
▸▸ *Bible* ***the Acts of the Apostles*** les Actes *mpl* des Apôtres; *Rel* ***an act of faith*** un acte de foi; ***act of God*** *Rel* acte *m* divin; *Ins & Law* cas *m* de force majeure; *Br Hist* ***the Act of Settlement*** = loi promulguée en 1701 interdisant à l'héritier de la couronne britannique d'épouser une personne de confession catholique; *Br Hist* ***the Act of Supremacy*** l'Acte *m* de suprématie; *Br Hist* ***the Act of Union*** l'Acte *m* d'union *(traité de 1707 unissant l'Angleterre et l'Écosse, et constituant ainsi le Royaume-Uni de la Grande-Bretagne)*

▸**act on** *vt insep* (**a**) *(advice, suggestion)* suivre; *(order)* exécuter; *(letter)* donner suite à; **she acted on the information we gave her** elle a suivi les *ou* s'est conformée aux indications que nous lui avons données; **acting on your instructions, we have cancelled your account** selon vos instructions, nous avons fermé votre compte
(**b**) *Chem & Phys (chemical, drug)* agir sur; **acid acts on metal** l'acide agit sur le métal; **to act on the brain/the bowels** exercer une action sur *ou* agir sur le cerveau/l'intestin

▸**act out 1** *vt sep (fantasy)* réaliser; *(emotions)* extérioriser; *(event, story)* reconstituer; **local people act out scenes from the town's history** les gens du coin jouent des scènes de l'histoire de leur ville
2 *vi Psy* passer à l'acte

▸**act up** *vi Fam (person)* faire l'idiot, déconner; *(child)* faire des siennes; *(engine, machine)* déconner; **my knee/back is acting up again** mon genou/dos recommence à me faire souffrir

▸**act upon** = **act on**

Actaeon ['æktɪən] *pr n Myth* Actéon

actin ['æktɪn] *n Biol & Chem* actine *f*

acting ['æktɪŋ] **1** *n* (**a**) *(profession)* profession *f* d'acteur, profession *f* d'actrice; **I've done a bit of acting** *(theatre)* j'ai fait un peu de théâtre; *(cinema)* j'ai fait un peu de cinéma (**b**) *(performance)* interprétation *f*, jeu *m*; **the acting was superb** l'interprétation était superbe
2 *comp (lessons, school)* de comédien
3 *adj (temporary)* intérimaire, par intérim; *Com* **acting director** directeur(trice) *m,f* intérimaire *ou* par intérim; *Com* **acting president** président(e) *m,f* intérimaire *ou* par intérim

actinic [æk'tɪnɪk] *adj Phys* actinique
▸▸ ***actinic balance*** bolomètre *m*; ***actinic rays*** rayons *mpl* actiniques *ou* chimiques; ***actinic spectrum*** spectre *m* chimique

actinide ['æktɪnaɪd] *n Chem* actinide *m*

actinium [æk'tɪnɪəm] *n Chem* actinium *m*

actinometer [ˌæktɪ'nɒmɪtə(r)] *n Phys* actinomètre *m*

actinometry [ˌæktɪ'nɒmɪtrɪ] *n Phys* actinométrie *f*

actinomycete [ˌæktɪnəʊ'maɪsiːt] *n Biol* actinomycète *f*

actinomycin [ˌæktɪnəʊ'maɪsɪn] *n Med* actinomycine *f*

ACTION ['ækʃən]

action	▸1 (a) – (i); 2
acte, geste	▸1 (b)
effet	▸1 (c)
activité	▸1 (d)
intrigue	▸1 (e)
mécanique, mécanisme	▸1 (g)
procès	▸1 (h)
combat	▸1 (i)

1 *n* (**a**) *(process)* action *f*; **it's time for action** il est temps d'agir, passons aux actes; **to go into action** entrer en action; **to take action** prendre des mesures; **a man of action** un homme d'action; **we must take action to stop them** nous devons agir pour les arrêter; **we want action not words** nous voulons des actes non des paroles; **to put sth into action** *(idea, policy)* mettre qch en pratique; *(plan)* mettre qch à exécution; *(machine)* mettre qch en marche; **she's an excellent dancer, you should see her in action** c'est une excellente danseuse, vous devriez la voir en action; **out of action** *(machine)* hors de service, hors d'usage; *(person)* hors de combat; *Br* **the car is out of action** la voiture est en panne; **the storm put the telephone out of action** le téléphone est en dérangement à cause de l'orage; **her accident will put her out of action for four months** son accident va la mettre hors de combat pour quatre mois; **freedom of action** liberté d'action
(**b**) *(deed)* acte *m*, geste *m*, action *f*; **she defended her action in dismissing him** elle a défendu son geste en le congédiant; **he's not responsible for his actions** il n'est pas responsable de ses actes; **don't judge her by her actions alone** ne la jugez pas seulement sur ses actes; *Prov* **actions speak louder than words** les actes en disent plus long que les mots
(**c**) *(of chemical, drug, force)* effet *m*, action *f*
(**d**) *(activity, events)* activité *f*; *Fam (excitement)* action ☐ *f*; *Fam* **he wants to be where the action is** il veut être au cœur de l'action; *Fam* **they were looking for some action** ils cherchaient un peu d'animation; *Fam* **where's the action around here?** où est-ce que ça bouge par ici?; *Fam* **we want a piece of the action** nous voulons notre part du gâteau
(**e**) *(of book, film, play)* intrigue *f*, action *f*; **the action takes place in a barber's shop** l'action se situe *ou* se passe chez un coiffeur
(**f**) *(movement* → *of person)* gestes *mpl*; *(*→ *of animal)* allure *f*; *(*→ *of heart)* fonctionnement *m*
(**g**) *Tech (operating mechanism* → *of clock)* mécanique *f*, mécanisme *m*; *(*→ *of gun)* mécanisme *m*; *(*→ *of piano)* action *f*, mécanique *f*; *(*→ *of pump, lock)* jeu *m*
(**h**) *Law* procès *m*, action *f* en justice; **to bring an action against sb** intenter une action contre qn; **action at law** action *f* en justice; *(trial)* procès *m*; **action for libel** procès *m ou* plainte *f* en diffamation; **action for damages** action *f* en dommages et intérêts
(**i**) *Mil (fighting)* combat *m*, action *f*; **to go into action** engager le combat; **he saw a lot of action** il a vu de nombreux combats; **killed in action** tué au combat; **ready for action** prêt à combattre; **to send troops into action** faire intervenir *ou* faire donner des troupes
2 *exclam Cin* action!
3 *comp Cin & Phot (photography)* d'action
4 *vt (idea, suggestion)* mettre en action *ou* en pratique; *(plan)* mettre à exécution
▸▸ *Pol* ***action group*** groupe *m* de pression; ***action movie*** film *m* d'action; *Art* ***action painting*** peinture *f* gestuelle; ***action plan*** plan *m* d'action; *Br TV* ***action replay*** = répétition immédiate d'une séquence; ***action stations*** *Mil* **1** *npl* postes *mpl* de combat
2 *exclam* à vos postes!

actionable ['ækʃənəbəl] *adj (allegations, deed, person)* passible de poursuites; *(claim)* recevable

action-packed *adj (film, novel, match)* bourré

d'action; *(day, holiday)* rempli d'activités, bien rempli

activate ['æktɪveɪt] *vt* (**a**) *(gen) & Chem & Tech* activer; *(mechanism, alarm)* déclencher (**b**) *Phys* rendre radioactif

activated ['æktɪveɪtɪd] *adj Chem* actif
►► ***activated carbon*** charbon actif *ou* activé

activation [,æktɪ'veɪʃən] *n* activation *f*

activator ['æktɪveɪtə(r)] *n Chem* activeur *m*

active ['æktɪv] **1** *adj* (**a**) *(lively → person)* actif, dynamique; *(→ imagination)* vif, actif; **to be still active** *(of elderly person)* être encore alerte *ou* actif
(**b**) *(busy, involved → person)* actif, énergique; *(→ life, stock market)* actif; **to be active in sth, to take an active part in sth** prendre une part active à qch; **she's very active in the party** elle est très active au sein du parti; **he was very active in seeing that the measure was passed** il a contribué très activement à l'approbation de cette mesure; **to be politically active** être engagé; **to be sexually active** avoir une activité sexuelle; **how much of the population is in active employment?** quel pourcentage de la population a un emploi?
(**c**) *(keen → encouragement, interest, dislike)* vif; **to take an active dislike to sb** se prendre d'une vive aversion contre qn; **the proposal is under active discussion** la proposition fait l'objet d'une vive discussion; **they took his suggestion into active consideration** ils ont soumis sa proposition à une étude attentive; **you have our active support** vous avez notre soutien total
(**d**) *(in operation → account)* actif; *(→ case, file)* en cours; *(→ law, regulation)* en vigueur; *Geol (→ volcano)* en activité
(**e**) *Chem (chemical, ingredient)* actif
(**f**) *Gram* actif
(**g**) *Mil* actif; **to be on active** *Br* **service** *or Am* **duty** être en service actif; **he saw active** *Br* **service** *or Am* **duty in the Far East** il a servi en Extrême-Orient; **to be on the active list** faire partie de l'armée active
(**h**) *Phys & Nucl* actif, radioactif
(**i**) *St Exch (shares)* actif; *(market)* animé, actif; **there is an active demand for oils** les valeurs pétrolières sont très recherchées, il y a une forte demande de valeurs pétrolières
2 *n Gram (voice)* actif *m*; *(verb)* verbe *m* actif; **a verb in the active** un verbe à l'actif
►► *Comput* ***active desktop*** bureau *m* actif; *Comput* ***active file*** fichier *m* actif; *Comput* ***active matrix screen*** écran *m* à matrice active; *Pol* ***active minority*** minorité *f* agissante; *Banking & Fin* ***active money*** monnaie *f* circulante; *Fin & Com* ***active partner*** *(in company)* associé(e) *m,f* gérant(e), commandité(e) *m,f*; *Comput* ***active program*** programme *m* en cours d'exécution; *Gram* ***the active voice*** la voix active, l'actif *m*; **in the active voice** à l'actif; *Comput* ***active window*** fenêtre *f* active *ou* activée

actively ['æktɪvlɪ] *adv* (**a**) *(involve, participate)* activement; **they were actively seeking peace** ils cherchaient activement à faire la paix (**b**) *(disagree, discourage)* vivement, activement; **to actively dislike sb** avoir une vive aversion pour qn

activism ['æktɪvɪzəm] *n Pol* activisme *m*

activist ['æktɪvɪst] *n Pol* militant(e) *m,f*, activiste *mf*; **anti-nuclear/peace activists** activistes anti-nucléaires/en faveur de la paix

activity [æk'tɪvətɪ] (*pl* **activities**) *n* (**a**) *(of brain, person)* activité *f*; *(of place, bank account)* mouvement *m*; **this week has seen a lot of activity on the Stock Market** la Bourse a été très active cette semaine; **economic/political activity** activité économique/politique
(**b**) *(occupation)* activité *f*; **activities** *(at holiday camp)* animation *f*; **leisure activities** activités *mpl* de loisir
►► ***activity accounting*** comptabilité *f* par centres de responsabilité; ***activity book*** livre-jeu *m*; ***activity break*** (courtes) vacances *fpl* actives; ***activity centre*** centre *m* aéré; ***activity chart*** graphique *m* des activités; *Br* ***activity holiday*** vacances *fpl* actives; *Acct* ***activity ratio*** ratio *m ou* coefficent *m* d'activité, ratio *m* de gestion

activity-based costing *n Fin* coûts *mpl* par activité

actor ['æktə(r)] *n* acteur(trice) *m,f*, comédien(enne) *m,f*; **I'm a terrible actor** je suis un piètre comédien
►► ***Actors' Studio*** = école d'art dramatique fondée à New York en 1947

actress ['æktrɪs] *n* actrice *f*, comédienne *f*; **she's a good actress** c'est une bonne comédienne; *Br Fam Hum* **he's got a huge one, as the actress said to the bishop** il en a une énorme, si j'ose dire

actressy ['æktrɪsɪ] *adj Pej* théâtral

ACTT [,eɪsi:,ti:'ti:] *n Formerly* (*abbr* **Association of Cinematographic, Television and Allied Technicians**) = ancien syndicat britannique des techniciens du cinéma et de l'audiovisuel, aujourd'hui remplacé par "BECTU"

actual ['æktʃʊəl] **1** *adj* (**a**) *(genuine)* réel, véritable; *(existing as a real fact)* concret(ète); **what were her actual words?** quels étaient ses mots exacts?; **to take an actual example** prendre un exemple concret; **the actual result was quite different** le résultat véritable était plutôt différent; **the actual cost was £1,000** le coût exact était de 1000 livres; **what's the actual cash value of the car?** quelle est la valeur réelle de la voiture?
(**b**) *(emphatic use)* même; **the actual ceremony doesn't start until 10.30** la cérémonie même ne commence pas avant 10 heures 30; **this is the actual house where she was born** voici en fait la maison où elle est née
2 actuals *npl* (**a**) *Acct & Fin (real figures)* chiffres *mpl* réels; **to compare budgeted amounts with actuals** comparer les prévisions budgétaires et les résultats obtenus
(**b**) *St Exch* livraisons *fpl* physiques, marchandises *fpl* livrées au comptant
3 in actual fact *adv* en fait
►► *Law* ***actual bodily harm*** coups *mpl* et blessures *fpl*; *Acct & Fin* ***actual cost*** prix *m* de revient *ou* d'achat; ***actual figures*** chiffres *mpl* réels; *St Exch* ***actual quotations*** cours *mpl* effectifs; *Ins* ***actual total loss*** perte *f* totale effective; ***actual value*** valeur *f* réelle

actuality [,æktʃʊ'ælətɪ] (*pl* **actualities**) *n* réalité *f*; **in actuality** en réalité; **the actualities of the situation** les conditions réelles de la situation

actualization [,æktʃʊəlaɪ'zeɪʃən] *n* (**a**) *Phil* actualisation *f* (**b**) *(of idea, project)* réalisation *f* (**c**) *Psy* actuation *f*

actualize, -ise ['æktʃʊəlaɪz] *vt* (**a**) *Phil* actualiser (**b**) *(idea, project)* réaliser

actually ['æktʃʊəlɪ] *adv* (**a**) *(establishing a fact)* vraiment; **I haven't actually read the book** à vrai dire, je n'ai pas lu le livre; **what did he actually say?** qu'est-ce qu'il a dit vraiment?; **what actually happened?** que s'est-il passé au juste?; **what he actually means is…** ce qu'il veut vraiment dire, c'est…; **I didn't actually see it myself** en réalité, je ne l'ai pas vu de mes propres yeux; **the piano's just for decoration, no one actually plays it** le piano fait partie du décor, en fait personne n'en joue; **yes, but what will the government actually do?** oui, mais que va vraiment faire le gouvernement?
(**b**) *(emphatic use)* vraiment; **did you actually say that?** vous avez vraiment dit cela?; **you mean she actually speaks Latin!** tu veux dire qu'elle parle vraiment le latin!; **he actually swore** il est (même) allé jusqu'à lâcher un juron; **she actually said good morning to me** à mon grand étonnement elle m'a dit bonjour; **he was actually on time for once** pour une fois il était à l'heure
(**c**) *(contradicting or qualifying)* en fait; **she's actually older than she looks** en fait, elle est plus âgée qu'elle n'en a l'air; **I don't agree, actually** en fait, je ne suis pas d'accord; **he's not a very nice person actually** il n'est pas très gentil à vrai dire; **actually, it's a bit more complicated than that** en fait, c'est un peu plus compliqué que cela; **actually, yes, I do mind, very much!** à vrai dire, oui, ça m'ennuie beaucoup!; **I suppose you've never been there – I have, actually** je suppose que vous n'y êtes jamais allé – si, en fait
(**d**) *(in requests, advice etc)* en fait; **actually, you could set the table** en fait, tu pourrais mettre la table

actuarial [,æktjʊ'eərɪəl] *adj Fin & Ins* actuariel
►► ***actuarial tables*** tables *fpl* de mortalité

actuary ['æktjʊərɪ] (*pl* **actuaries**) *n Fin & Ins* actuaire *mf*

actuate ['æktjʊeɪt] *vt* (**a**) *(machine, system)* mettre en marche, faire marcher (**b**) *Formal (person)* faire agir, inciter

actuation [,æktjʊ'eɪʃən] *n (of machine, system)* mise *f* en marche

actuator ['æktjʊeɪtə(r)] *n Tech* actionneur *m*

Act-Up *n* Act Up *m*

acuity [ə'kju:ətɪ] *n (of hearing, sight)* acuité *f*; *(of person, thought)* perspicacité *f*

acumen ['ækjʊmən] *n* perspicacité *f*, flair *m*

acuminate [ə'kju:mɪnət] *adj Bot* acuminé

acuminous [æ'kju:mɪnəs] *adj* (**a**) *Bot* acuminé (**b**) *Literary (person)* perspicace

acupressure ['ækjʊpreʃə(r)] *n Med* acupressing *m*

acupuncture ['ækjʊpʌŋktʃə(r)] *Med* **1** *n* acupuncture *f*, acuponcture *f*
2 *comp (needle, treatment)* d'acupuncture, d'acuponcture

acupuncturist ['ækjʊpʌŋktʃərɪst] *n Med* acupuncteur(trice) *m,f*, acuponcteur(trice) *m,f*

acute [ə'kju:t] **1** *adj* (**a**) *(hearing, sense)* fin; *(sight)* pénétrant, perçant; **an acute sense of hearing** l'ouïe fine; **an acute sense of smell** l'odorat subtil *ou* développé
(**b**) *(perceptive → mind, person)* perspicace, pénétrant; *(→ intelligence)* fin, vif; *(→ analysis)* fin; **she has an acute awareness of their problems** elle a une perception pénétrante de leurs problèmes
(**c**) *(severe → pain)* aigu(uë), vif; *(→ anxiety, distress)* vif; *(→ shortage)* critique, grave; **to suffer acute embarrassment** être vivement embarrassé; **the problem was made more acute** le problème a été intensifié
(**d**) *(attack, illness)* aigu(uë); **acute appendicitis** appendicite *f* aiguë
(**e**) *Geom (angle)* aigu(uë)
(**f**) *Ling (accent)* aigu(uë); **it's spelled with an "e" acute** ça s'écrit avec un "e" accent aigu
2 *n Gram* accent *m* aigu

acute-angled *adj Geom* à angle(s) aigu(s)

acutely [ə'kju:tlɪ] *adv* (**a**) *(intensely → be aware, feel)* vivement; *(→ suffer)* intensément; **he felt the loss acutely** il ressentit cette perte intensément; **we are acutely aware** *or* **conscious of that** nous en sommes extrêmement conscients (**b**) *(extremely → embarrassing, unhappy)* très, profondément (**c**) *(shrewdly)* avec perspicacité

acuteness [ə'kju:tnɪs] *n* (**a**) *(of hearing, sense)* finesse *f* (**b**) *(of mind, person)* perspicacité *f*, pénétration *f*; *(of analysis, observation)* finesse *f* (**c**) *(of anxiety, pain, distress)* violence *f*, intensité *f*; *(of shortage)* sévérité *f*, gravité *f* (**d**) *(of illness)* violence *f* (**e**) *Geom (of angle)* caractère *m* aigu

acyl ['eɪsɪl] *n Chem* acyle *m*

AD [,eɪ'di:] **1** *adv* (*abbr* **Anno Domini**) apr. J.-C.; **in 3 AD** en l'an 3 (après Jésus-Christ *ou* de notre ère)
2 *n* (**a**) *Mil* (*abbr* **active duty**) service *m* actif (**b**) *Cin & Theat* (*abbr* **art director**) directeur(trice) *m,f* artistique

ad [æd] *n Fam (for job, event, accommodation)* (petite) annonce *f*; *(for product, service)* pub *f*; **to put an ad in the newspaper** passer une annonce dans le journal; **an ad for toothpaste, a toothpaste ad** une pub pour du dentifrice; **while the ads are on** pendant la pub
►► ***ad agency*** agence *f* publicitaire; ***ad break*** coupure *f* publicitaire

adage ['ædɪdʒ] *n* adage *m*

adagio [ə'dædʒɪəʊ] *Mus* **1** *n* adage *m*, adagio *m*
2 *adj* adagio
3 *adv* adagio

Adam ['ædəm] **1** *pr n Bible* Adam; **I don't know him from Adam** je ne le connais ni d'Ève ni d'Adam
2 *adj Archit* dans le style Adam *(style architectural créé par les Écossais Robert et James Adam au XVIIIème siècle)*
►► *Br Fam Hum* ***Adam's ale*** flotte *f*, château-la-pompe *m*; ***Adam's apple*** pomme *f* d'Adam; ***Adam Smith Institute*** = formation libéraliste au sein du parti conservateur britannique

'Adam's Rib' *Cukor* 'Madame porte la culotte'

adam ['ædəm] *Fam* **1** *n Drugs slang (ecstasy)* ecstasy❑ *f*, exta *f*
 2 *vt Br* **adam and eve** *(rhyming slang* **believe***)* croire❑; **would you adam and eve it!** tu te rends compte?

adamant ['ædəmənt] *adj* résolu, inflexible; **she is adamant that she saw him** elle affirme l'avoir vu et ne veut pas en démordre

adamantine [ˌædə'mæntaɪn] *adj* (**a**) *Miner* adamantin (**b**) *Literary (impenetrable → person, face)* impénétrable; *(invincible → courage, fortitude)* indomptable
 ►► *Miner* ***adamantine spar*** diamant *m* spathique, spath *m* adamantin

adamantly ['ædəməntlɪ] *adv (say, maintain)* de façon catégorique; *(refuse)* catégoriquement

adamsite ['ædəmzaɪt] *n Chem* adamsite *f*

adapt [ə'dæpt] **1** *vt* (**a**) *(adjust)* adapter, ajuster (**b**) *(book, play)* adapter; **the play was adapted for television** la pièce a été adaptée pour la télévision; **adapted from Shakespeare** d'après Shakespeare; **to adapt oneself to circumstances/new surroundings** s'adapter aux circonstances/à un nouvel environnement
 2 *vi* s'adapter; **she adapted well to the change** elle s'est bien adaptée au changement; **children adapt easily** les enfants s'adaptent facilement; **it was adapt or die** il fallait s'adapter à tout prix

adaptability [əˌdæptə'bɪlɪtɪ] *n (of person)* faculté *f* d'adaptation, adaptabilité *f*

adaptable [ə'dæptəbəl] *adj* (**a**) *(adjustable)* adaptable, ajustable (**to** à) (**b**) *(person)* souple, qui s'adapte facilement; *Bot & Zool (species)* qui s'adapte facilement

adaptation [ˌædæp'teɪʃən] *n (of person, work)* adaptation *f*; **to make an adaptation of a play for radio** faire l'adaptation d'une pièce pour la radio

adapter, adaptor [ə'dæptə(r)] *n* (**a**) *(plug)* transformateur *m*; *(with several sockets)* prise *f* multiple (**b**) *Tech (connecting pipes)* raccord *m* (**c**) *(person)* adaptateur(trice) *m,f*
 ►► *Comput* ***adapter card*** carte-adaptateur *f*

adaptive [ə'dæptɪv] *adj Biol (mechanism)* adaptif
 ►► *Aut* ***adaptive engine controls*** commandes *fpl* adaptatives moteur

adaptiveness [ə'dæptɪvnɪs] *n* adaptation *f*

ADC [ˌeɪdiː'siː] *n* (**a**) *Mil (abbr* **aide-de-camp***)* aide *m* de camp (**b**) *Am (abbr* **Aid to Dependent Children***)* = aide pour enfants assistés (**c**) *Tech (abbr* **analogue-digital converter***)* CAN *m*

add [æd] **1** *vt* (**a**) *(put together)* ajouter; **add her name to the list** ajoute son nom à la liste; **this book adds little to the debate** ce livre n'apporte pas grand-chose au débat; *Fig* **to add fuel to the fire** jeter de l'huile sur le feu
 (**b**) *(say)* ajouter; **I have nothing to add** je n'ai rien à ajouter
 (**c**) *(figures)* additionner; *(column of figures)* totaliser; **add 4 and** *or* **to 9** additionnez 4 et 9; **add these numbers together** additionnez ces nombres, faites l'addition de ces nombres; **it will add (on) another £100 to the cost** cela augmentera le coût de 100 livres; **they added (on) 10 percent for service** ils ont ajouté 10 pour cent pour le service
 2 *vi* faire des additions

►**add on** *vt sep* ajouter

►**add to** *vt insep (building)* faire une addition à, agrandir; *(difficulty, surprise etc)* augmenter, ajouter à; *(beauty)* rehausser; *(crisis)* accentuer; **inflation only added to our worries** l'inflation ne faisait qu'ajouter à nos soucis; **this will add to the cost** ceci va venir s'ajouter au prix; **to add to my misfortune** pour mettre le comble à mon malheur; **to add to what we were saying yesterday...** pour compléter ce que nous disions hier...

►**add up 1** *vt sep (find the sum of → figures)* additionner; *(→ bill, column of figures)* totaliser; **we added up the advantages and disadvantages** nous avons fait le total des avantages et des inconvénients; **when you add it all up it was quite cheap** si on fait le total, c'était assez bon marché; **you've added this up wrong** tu t'es trompé dans l'addition
 2 *vi* (**a**) *(give correct total)* se recouper; **these figures don't add up** ces chiffres ne font pas le compte; **the bill doesn't add up** la note n'est pas juste; *Fig* **it just doesn't add up** il y a quelque chose qui cloche *ou* qui ne marche pas
 (**b**) *(calculate)* additionner; **that boy can't add up** ce garçon ne sait pas additionner

►**add up to** *vt insep* (**a**) *(of figures)* s'élever à, se monter à; **it adds up to £22** cela s'élève à 22 livres
 (**b**) *Fig (of results, situation)* signifier, se résumer à; **it all adds up to our having to leave** autrement dit, nous devons partir; **his qualifications add up to an impressive CV** ses qualifications constituent un CV impressionnant; **what evidence we've got doesn't add up to much really** les preuves dont nous disposons ne constituent pas vraiment grand-chose; **is that all you've done? it doesn't add up to much** est-ce que c'est tout ce que tu as fait? ça ne fait pas beaucoup

addax ['ædæks] *n Zool* addax *m*

add-back *n Acct* réintégration *f*

added ['ædɪd] *adj* (**a**) *(gen)* supplémentaire; **the tax is just an added financial burden** l'impôt constitue simplement un fardeau financier supplémentaire (**b**) *(on food package)* **added ingredients** autres ingrédients; **no added sugar** sans ajout de sucre; **no added preservatives** sans conservateurs
 ►► *Com, Mktg & Acct* ***added value*** valeur *f* ajoutée

addend [ə'dend] *n Math* nombre *m ou* nombres *mpl* à ajouter

addendum [ə'dendəm] (*pl* **addenda** [-də]) *n* addendum *m*, addenda *mpl*

adder ['ædə(r)] *n* (**a**) *(snake)* vipère *f* (**b**) *(machine)* additionneur *m*
 ►► *Bot* ***adder's tongue*** langue-de-serpent *f*

addict ['ædɪkt] *n* (**a**) *(to drugs)* intoxiqué(e) *m,f* (**b**) *Fig* fanatique *mf*, fana *mf*, mordu(e) *m,f*; **she's a film addict** c'est une fana *ou* mordue de cinéma; **I'm a coffee addict** je suis accro au café; **I never miss an episode, I'm a complete addict** je ne rate jamais un épisode, je suis complètement accro

addicted [ə'dɪktɪd] *adj* (**a**) *(to drugs)* **to be addicted to heroin/cocaine** être héroïnomane/cocaïnomane; **he became addicted to morphine** il a formé une dépendance à la morphine; **you can easily get addicted to coffee** c'est facile de devenir accro au café (**b**) *Fig* **to be addicted to sth** s'adonner à qch, se passionner pour qch; **she's addicted to exercise/hard work** c'est une mordue d'exercice/de travail

addiction [ə'dɪkʃən] *n (to drugs)* dépendance *f*; *Fig* penchant *m* fort, forte inclination *f*; **coffee at 4 o'clock had become something of an addiction with her** elle ne pouvait plus se passer du café de 4 heures
 ►► *Psy* ***addiction therapy*** cure *f* de désintoxication

addictive [ə'dɪktɪv] *adj* qui crée une dépendance; **chocolate is very addictive** le chocolat, c'est une vraie drogue, on devient vite accro au chocolat; **it could become addictive** on prend vite l'habitude; **to have an addictive personality** avoir tendance à devenir dépendant

adding ['ædɪŋ] *n* addition *f*
 ►► ***adding machine*** calculatrice *f*, machine *f* à calculer; ***adding up*** addition *f*

Addis Ababa ['ædɪs'æbəbə] *n* Addis-Ababa, Addis-Abeba

Addison's disease ['ædɪsənz-] *n Med* maladie *f* bronzée d'Addison

addition [ə'dɪʃən] **1** *n* (**a**) *(gen) & Math* addition *f* (**b**) *(something or someone added)* addition *f*, ajout *m*; **they're going to have an addition to the family** leur famille va s'agrandir; **she's a welcome new addition to our staff** nous sommes heureux de la compter au sein du personnel; **a last-minute addition to the programme** un ajout de dernière minute au programme (**c**) *Am Constr (to house)* annexe *f*
 2 in addition *adv* de plus, de surcroît
 3 in addition to *prep* en plus de

additional [ə'dɪʃənəl] *adj* additionnel; *(supplementary)* supplémentaire; *Fin (investment, expenses)* supplémentaire; **additional information can be found on page 28** se référer à la page 28 pour des informations complémentaires; **this will require additional investment** cela nécessitera un investissement supplémentaire; **additional advantages** des avantages supplémentaires; **there is an additional charge on certain trains** il y a un supplément à payer pour certains trains; **for** *or* **at no additional charge** sans supplément
 ►► *Law* ***additional clause*** avenant *m*; *Fin* ***additional payment*** supplément *m*; ***additional postage*** surtaxe *f* postale; *Fin* ***additional voluntary contribution*** supplément *m* de cotisation retraite *(payé volontairement)*

additionally [ə'dɪʃənəlɪ] *adv* (**a**) *(further, more)* davantage, plus (**b**) *(moreover)* en outre, de plus

additive ['ædɪtɪv] **1** *adj* additif
 2 *n* additif *m*

addle ['ædəl] **1** *vt* embrouiller
 2 *vi* (**a**) *(person)* s'embrouiller (**b**) *(egg)* pourrir

addled ['ædld] *adj* (**a**) *(person)* aux idées confuses, brouillon; *(brain)* fumeux, brouillon; *(ideas)* confus (**b**) *(egg)* pourri

add-on 1 *n Comput* produit *m* supplémentaire, extension *f*
 2 *adj* additionel
 ►► *Comput* ***add-on board*** carte *f* d'extension; *Transp* ***add-on fare*** supplément *m*

address [ə'dres] **1** *vt* (**a**) *(envelope, letter, package)* adresser, mettre l'adresse sur; **the letter is addressed to you** cette lettre vous est adressée; **it's incorrectly addressed** l'adresse est incorrecte
 (**b**) *(direct)* adresser; **address all complaints to the manager** adressez vos doléances au directeur; **his remarks were addressed to you** ses remarques vous étaient adressées
 (**c**) *(speak to)* s'adresser à; *(write to)* écrire à; **she stood up and addressed the audience** elle s'est levée et a pris la parole devant l'assistance; **a judge should be addressed as "your honour"** on devrait s'adresser à un juge en disant "votre honneur"; **to address the chair** s'adresser au président
 (**d**) *(deal with → subject, theme)* traiter, examiner; *(→ issue, problem)* aborder; **to address oneself to a problem** aborder un problème; **to address oneself to a task** s'attaquer *ou* se mettre à une tâche
 (**e**) *(take position facing)* faire face à
 (**f**) *Comput* adresser, accéder à
 (**g**) *Golf (ball)* viser
 2 *n* (**a**) *(of building, person, letter)* adresse *f*; **a Glasgow address** une adresse à Glasgow; **what is your address?** quelle est ton adresse?; **we've changed our address** nous avons changé d'adresse; **have you notified him of any change of address?** lui avez-vous fait part d'éventuels changements d'adresse?; **they left no (forwarding) address** ils n'ont pas laissé d'adresse; **not known at this address** *(on returned letter)* inconnu à cette adresse
 (**b**) *(speech)* discours *m*, allocution *f*
 (**c**) *Comput* adresse *f*
 (**d**) *(title)* **form of address** titre *m*; **what's the correct form of address for a bishop?** comment doit-on s'adresser à un évêque?
 (**e**) *Formal or Arch (skill)* habileté *f*, doigté *m*; **she showed considerable address in her handling of the situation** elle fit preuve d'une grande habileté dans la façon dont elle traita l'affaire
 (**f**) *Br Pol (message to sovereign)* adresse *f*
 (**g**) *Arch (way of speaking)* conversation *f*; *(way of behaving)* abord *m*
 (**h**) *Arch (usu pl) (expression of affection)* **addresses** galanteries *fpl*; **to pay one's addresses to sb** faire la cour à qn
 ►► *(gen) & Comput* ***address book*** carnet *m* d'adresses; *Comput* ***address bus*** bus *m* d'adresse; *Comput* ***address file*** fichier *m* d'adresses; ***address label*** étiquette *f* d'adresse

addressable [ə'dresəbəl] *adj Comput* adressable
 ►► *Mktg* ***addressable audience*** audience *f* utile; *Mktg* ***addressable market*** marché *m* utile

addressee [ˌædre'siː] *n* destinataire *mf*

addressing [ə'dresɪŋ] *n* adressage *m*

▸▸ ***addressing machine*** machine *f* à adresser

Addressograph® [ə'dresə,grɑ:f] *n* Adressographe® *m*

adduce [ə'dju:s] *vt (explanation, proof, reason)* fournir, apporter; *(expert)* invoquer, citer

adduct [ə'dʌkt] *vt Anat (muscle)* déterminer l'adduction de

adduction [ə'dʌkʃən] *n Physiol* adduction *f*

adductor [ə'dʌktə(r)] *n Anat* adducteur *m*

Adelaide ['ædəleɪd] *n* Adélaïde

Adélie ['ædeɪlɪ] *adj*

▸▸ *Geog* ***Adélie Land*** terre Adélie *f*; **in Adélie Land** en terre Adélie; ***Adélie penguin*** manchot *m* d'Adélie

Aden ['eɪdən] *n Geog* Aden

adenine ['ædəni:n] *n Biol & Chem* adénine *f*

adenoidal [,ædɪ'nɔɪdəl] *adj Physiol* adénoïde

adenoids ['ædɪnɔɪdz] *npl Anat* végétations *fpl* (adénoïdes)

adenoma [,ædə'nəʊmə] *n Med* adénome *m*

adenopathy [,ædə'nɒpəθɪ] *n Med* adénopathie *f*

adenosine ['ædənəʊsaɪn] *n Biol & Chem* adénosine *f*

▸▸ ***adenosine diphosphate*** adénosine *f* diphosphate; ***adenosine triphosphate*** adénosine *f* triphosphate

adept 1 *adj* [ə'dept] habile, adroit; **to be adept at doing sth** être adroit à faire qch; **she's adept in mathematics** elle est douée en mathématiques

2 *n* ['ædept] expert *m*

adequacy ['ædɪkwəsɪ] *n* (**a**) *(of amount, payment, sum)* fait *m* d'être suffisant (**b**) *(of person)* compétence *f*, compétences *fpl*, capacité *f*, capacités *fpl*; *(of description, expression)* justesse *f*; **they doubted her adequacy as a mother** ils doutaient de ses capacités de mère

adequate ['ædɪkwət] *adj* (**a**) *(in amount, quantity)* suffisant, adéquat; **adequate supplies** des réserves suffisantes; **to be given adequate warning** être suffisamment averti; **to have adequate time to do sth** avoir suffisamment de temps pour faire qch; **the money we were given was more than adequate** l'argent que l'on nous avait donné était plus que suffisant

(**b**) *(appropriate)* adéquat, approprié; **he proved adequate to the task** il s'est révélé être à la hauteur de la tâche; **this flat is hardly adequate for a family of six** cet appartement ne convient guère à une famille de six personnes; **this one is quite adequate** celui-ci fera très bien l'affaire

(**c**) *(just satisfactory)* acceptable, satisfaisant

adequately ['ædɪkwətlɪ] *adv* (**a**) *(sufficiently)* suffisamment (**b**) *(satisfactorily)* convenablement

ADHD [,eɪdi:,eɪtʃ'di:] *n Med (abbr* **attention deficit hyperactivity disorder**) syndrome *m* hyperkinétique de l'enfant, syndrome *m* de l'enfant hyperactif

adhere [əd'hɪə(r)] *vi* (**a**) *(stick)* coller, adhérer; **to adhere to sth** coller à qch

(**b**) *(remain loyal)* **to adhere to** *(party, treaty)* adhérer à; *(rule)* observer; *(plan)* se conformer à; *(belief, idea)* adhérer à, souscrire à; **they undertook to adhere to the agreement** ils décidèrent de se conformer *ou* d'agir conformément à l'accord; **I don't adhere to that philosophy at all** je n'adhère pas du tout à cette philosophie

(**c**) *(join)* **to adhere to a political party** adhérer à un parti politique

adherence [əd'hɪərəns] *n (to treaty, political party)* adhésion *f* (**to** à); *(to rule)* observation *f* (**to** de)

adherent [əd'hɪərənt] **1** *adj (gen) & Bot* adhérent

2 *n (to party)* adhérent(e) *m,f*, partisan(e) *m,f*; *(to agreement)* adhérent(e) *m,f*; *(to belief, religion)* adepte *mf*

adhesion [əd'hi:ʒən] *n* (**a**) *(stickiness)* adhérence *f* (**to** à) (**b**) *(of person)* adhésion *f* (**to** à) (**c**) *Phys* adhésion *f* (**d**) *Med* adhérence *f*

adhesive [əd'hi:sɪv] **1** *n* adhésif *m*

2 *adj* adhésif, collant; *(label)* gommé

▸▸ ***adhesive tape*** *(sticky tape)* ruban *m* adhésif, Scotch® *m*; *(sticking plaster)* sparadrap *m*

adhesiveness [əd'hi:sɪvnɪs] *n* adhérence *f*

ad hoc [,æd'hɒk] **1** *adj (committee, market research)* ad hoc *(inv)*; *(decision, solution)* adapté aux circonstances, ponctuel; **the board meets on an ad hoc basis** le conseil se réunit de façon ad hoc

2 *adv* à l'improviste

ad hominem [,æd'hɒmɪnem] **1** *adj* ad hominem

2 *adv* ad hominem

adieu [ə'dju:] *(pl* **adieus** *or* **adieux** [-'dju:z]) *Arch or Literary* **1** *exclam* adieu!

2 *n* adieu *m*; **I bid you adieu** je vous fais mes adieux

ad infinitum [,ædɪnfɪ'naɪtəm] *adv* à l'infini; *Fam* **he went on talking ad infinitum** il parlait à n'en plus finir

ad interim [,æd'ɪntərɪm] **1** *adj (measures)* provisoire

2 *adv* par intérim

adipocyte ['ædɪpəʊ,saɪt] *n Physiol* adipocyte *m*

adipopexia [,ædɪpəʊ'peksɪə] *n Physiol* adipopexie *f*

adipose ['ædɪpəʊs] *adj Biol* adipeux

▸▸ *Anat* ***adipose tissue*** tissu *m* adipeux

adiposis [,ædɪ'pəʊsɪs] *n Physiol* adipose

adiposity [,ædɪ'pɒsɪtɪ] *n Physiol* adiposité *f*

adipsia [æ'dɪpsɪə] *n Med* adipsie *f*

Adirondacks [,ædɪ'rɒndæks] *npl* = région montagneuse dans le nord-est de l'État de New York

adj. *Mil (written abbr* **adjutant**) adjt

adjacency [ə'dʒeɪsənsɪ] *n* (**a**) *(common boundary* → *of houses, rooms, buildings)* contiguïté *f*; *(of countries, territories)* confinité *f* (**b**) *(proximity)* proximité *f* (**c**) *Math* adjacence *f* (**d**) *Comput* proximité

▸▸ *Comput* ***adjacency matrix*** matrice *f* d'incidence

adjacent [ə'dʒeɪsənt] *adj* (**a**) *(sharing common boundary* → *house, room)* contigu(uë), voisin; *(*→ *building)* qui jouxte, mitoyen; *(*→ *country, territory)* limitrophe; **their house is adjacent to the police station** leur maison jouxte le commissariat de police; **the two rooms are adjacent** les deux pièces sont contiguës (**b**) *(nearby* → *street)* adjacent; *(*→ *town)* proche, avoisinant (**c**) *Math* adjacent

adjectival [,ædʒɪk'taɪvəl] *adj Gram* adjectif, adjectival

adjectivally [,ædʒɪk'taɪvəlɪ] *adv Gram* adjectivement; **present participle used adjectivally** participe présent adjectivé

adjective ['ædʒɪktɪv] *n Gram* adjectif *m*

adjoin [ə'dʒɔɪn] **1** *vt (house, land, room)* être contigu(uë) à, toucher à, attenir à; **they had rooms adjoining mine** leurs chambres étaient contiguës à la mienne; **Kansas adjoins Colorado** le Kansas est un état limitrophe du Colorado

2 *vi* être contigu; **the two buildings adjoin** les deux bâtiments sont contigus

adjoining [ə'dʒɔɪnɪŋ] *adj* contigu(uë), attenant; *(state, country)* limitrophe; **the adjoining room** la pièce voisine *ou* à côté; **adjoining rooms** des pièces contiguës; **at the adjoining table** à la table voisine

adjourn [ə'dʒɜ:n] **1** *vt* (**a**) *(break off)* suspendre; **the president adjourned the meeting** le président a levé la séance

(**b**) *(defer)* ajourner, remettre, reporter; **let's adjourn this discussion until tomorrow** reportons cette discussion à demain; **the trial was adjourned until the next day** le procès fut ajourné au lendemain

2 *vi* (**a**) *(person, committee, court* → *break off)* suspendre la séance; *(*→ *end)* lever la séance

(**b**) *(meeting etc* → *be closed)* être levé; *(*→ *be interrupted)* être suspendu

(**c**) *(move elsewhere)* se retirer, passer; **shall we adjourn to the living room for coffee?** passerons-nous au salon pour prendre le café?

adjournment [ə'dʒɜ:nmənt] *n (of discussion, meeting)* suspension *f*, ajournement *m*; *Law (of trial)* ajournement *m*; **to call for an adjournment** demander un ajournement; **to move the adjournment** demander la clôture

▸▸ *Br Parl* ***adjournment debate*** = débat de clôture à la Chambre des Communes

adjt. *Mil (written abbr* **adjutant**) adjt

adjudge [ə'dʒʌdʒ] *vt Formal* (**a**) *(pronounce)* déclarer (**b**) *Law (judge)* prononcer, déclarer; *(award)* adjuger, accorder; **he was adjudged guilty of the murder** il a été déclaré coupable du meurtre; **the court adjudged damages in favour of the defendant** le tribunal a accordé des dommages et intérêts au défendeur

adjudicate [ə'dʒu:dɪkeɪt] **1** *vi* (**a**) *(give a decision)* se prononcer (**on** sur) (**b**) *Law (serve as judge)* arbitrer

2 *vt (claim, issue)* décider; *(competition)* juger; *Law* **to adjudicate sb bankrupt** déclarer *ou* mettre qn en faillite

adjudication [ə,dʒu:dɪ'keɪʃən] *n* (**a**) *Law (process)* jugement *m*, arbitration *f*; **the matter is up for adjudication** l'affaire est en jugement (**b**) *(decision)* jugement *m*, décision *f*; *Law* arrêt *m*

▸▸ *Law* ***adjudication of bankruptcy*** déclaration *f* de faillite

adjudicative [ə'dʒu:dɪkətɪv] *adj Law* déclaratif, déclaratoire

adjudicator [ə'dʒu:dɪkeɪtə(r)] *n (of competition)* juge *m*, arbitre *m*; *(of dispute)* arbitre *m*

adjunct ['ædʒʌŋkt] *n* (**a**) *(addition)* accessoire *m* (**b**) *(subordinate person)* adjoint(e) *m,f*, auxiliaire *mf* (**c**) *Gram* complément *m*

adjunctive [ə'dʒʌŋktɪv] *adj (additional)* accessoire

adjure [ə'dʒʊə(r)] *vt Formal (appeal to)* supplier; **to adjure sb to do sth** supplier qn de faire qch

adjust [ə'dʒʌst] **1** *vt* (**a**) *(regulate* → *heat, height, speed, pressure)* ajuster, régler; *(*→ *knob, loudness)* ajuster; *(*→ *brakes, machine, television)* régler, mettre au point; *(*→ *clock, watch)* régler; *(*→ *valve)* tarer; *Naut (*→ *compass)* compenser, corriger

(**b**) *(alter* → *plan, programme)* ajuster, mettre au point; *(*→ *length, size)* ajuster; *Com (*→ *prices)* ajuster; *Fin (*→ *figures, salaries)* rajuster, réajuster; *Acct (*→ *accounts)* régulariser; *Fin* **the government has adjusted prices downwards/upwards** le gouvernement a relevé/baissé les prix; *Fin* **pensions have been adjusted upwards/downwards** les pensions ont été revues à la hausse/à la baisse *ou* ont été augmentées/diminuées; *Fin* **income adjusted for inflation** revenu réel compte tenu de l'inflation; *Fin* **figures adjusted for inflation** chiffres en monnaie constante

(**c**) *(correct)* rectifier; **the figures have been seasonally adjusted** les chiffres sont les données corrigées des variations saisonnières

(**d**) *(position of clothing, hat)* rajuster; *Old-fashioned* **please adjust your dress before leaving** *(sign)* rajustez vos vêtements avant de sortir, SVP

(**e**) *(adapt)* ajuster, adapter (**to** à); **to adjust oneself to sth** s'adapter à qch

(**f**) *Ins* **to adjust a claim** régler *ou* répartir une demande d'indemnité; **to adjust an average** répartir une avarie

2 *vi* (**a**) *(adapt)* s'adapter; **to adjust to sth** s'adapter à qch

(**b**) *(chair, machine)* se régler, s'ajuster; **the cover adjusts to fit all sizes** le couvercle se règle pour s'adapter à toutes les tailles

adjustable [ə'dʒʌstəbəl] *adj (chair, height, speed)* ajustable, réglable; *(shape, size)* ajustable, adaptable; *(hours, rate)* flexible; **the seat is adjustable for height** la hauteur du siège est réglable

▸▸ *Tech Br* ***adjustable spanner,*** *Am* ***adjustable wrench*** clé *f* à molette ou anglaise

adjusted [ə'dʒʌstɪd] *adj* **well adjusted** équilibré; **badly adjusted** pas équilibré

adjuster [ə'dʒʌstə(r)] *n Tech (device)* appareil *m* de réglage; *Aut (on brake)* régleur *m*

▸▸ *Tech* ***adjuster nut*** écrou *m* de réglage; *Tech* ***adjuster screw*** vis *f* de réglage

adjusting [ə'dʒʌstɪŋ] *n* = **adjustment**

▸▸ *Acct* ***adjusting entry*** écriture *f* de régularisation; *Tech* ***adjusting screw*** vis *f* de réglage

adjustment [ə'dʒʌstmənt] *n* (**a**) *(to heat, height, speed, pressure)* ajustement *m*, réglage *m*; *(to knob, loudness)* ajustement *m*; *(to brakes, machine, television)* réglage *m*, mise *f* au point; *(to clock, watch)* réglage *m*; **to make an adjustment to sth** régler qch, ajuster qch; **a slight adjustment improved the picture** une légère mise au point a amélioré l'image

(**b**) *(to plan, programme)* ajustement *m*, mise *f* au point; *(to length, size)* ajustement *m*; *Fin (of figures, salaries)* rajustement *m*, réajustement (**c**) *(correction)* rectification *f*; **no adjustment was made for seasonal variation** il n'y a pas eu de corrigé des variations saisonnières; **some adjustments had been made to the text** des modifications avaient été apportées au texte

(**d**) *(adaptation → of person)* adaptation *f*; **a period of adjustment** une période *ou* un temps d'adaptation

►► *Acct* ***adjustment account*** compte *m* collectif

adjustor *Am* = **adjuster**

adjutant ['ædʒʊtənt] *n (assistant)* assistant(e) *m,f*, auxiliaire *mf*; *Mil* adjudant-major *m*

►► ***adjutant bird*** marabout *m*; ***adjutant general*** adjudant général

adjuvancy ['ædʒəvənsɪ] *n Literary* aide *f*, secours *m*

adjuvant ['ædʒəvənt] *n Med & Pharm* adjuvant *m*

Adlerian [æd'leərɪən] *adj Psy* adlérien

ad-lib [,æd'lɪb] *(pt & pp* **ad-libbed**, *cont* **ad-libbing***)*
1 *vt* improviser
2 *vi* improviser
3 *adj* improvisé, impromptu
4 **ad lib 1** *n (improvised performance)* improvisation *f*, improvisations *fpl*; *(witticism)* mot *m* d'esprit **2** *adv* (**a**) *(without preparation)* à l'improviste; **to speak ad lib** improviser (**b**) *(without limit)* à volonté (**c**) *Mus* ad libitum

ad-libbing [,æd'lɪbɪŋ] *n* improvisation *f*

adman ['ædmæn] *(pl* **admen** [-men]*)* *n Fam* publicitaire ❑ *m*

admass ['ædmæs] *Br Mktg* **1** *n* grand public *m*
2 *comp (culture, society)* de grande consommation

admin ['ædmɪn] *n Fam (abbr* **administration***)* *(work)* travail *m* administratif ❑; *(department)* administration ❑ *f*; **admin tasks** tâches *fpl* administratives; **are you (in) sales or admin?** vous êtes au service des ventes ou à l'administration?

administer [əd'mɪnɪstə(r)] **1** *vt* (**a**) *(manage → business, institution)* diriger, administrer, gérer; *(→ finances, fund)* gérer; *(→ country, territory, public institution)* administrer; *(→ estate)* régir

(**b**) *Formal (dispense → blow, medicine, punishment, test, last rites)* administrer; *Law (→ law)* appliquer; **to administer justice** rendre la justice; *Law* **to administer an oath (to sb)** faire prêter serment (à qn)

2 *vi Formal* **to administer to sb** subvenir aux besoins de qn

►► *Fin* ***administered price*** prix *m* imposé

administrate [əd'mɪnɪstreɪt] *vt (manage → business, institution)* diriger, administrer, gérer; *(→ finances, fund)* gérer; *(→ country, territory, public institution)* administrer; *(→ estate)* régir

administration [əd,mɪnɪ'streɪʃən] **1** *n* (**a**) *(process → of business, institution)* direction *f*, administration *f*, gestion *f*; *(→ of finances, fund)* gestion *f*; *(→ of country, territory, public institution)* administration *f*; *(→ of estate)* curatelle *f*

(**b**) *(administrative work)* travail *m* administratif; *(administrative department)* administration *f*; **you will need some experience of administration** vous devrez avoir une certaine expérience de l'administration

(**c**) *(people → of business, institution)* direction *f*, administration *f*; *(→ of country, public institution)* administration *f*

(**d**) *(of help, justice, medicine, punishment)* administration *f*; *Law* **letters of administration** lettres *fpl* d'administration

(**e**) *Law (of oath)* prestation *f*

(**f**) *Com & Law (receivership)* **to go into administration** être placé sous contrôle judiciaire

2 Administration *n Am Pol* **the Administration** le gouvernement *m*; **under the last Administration** sous le dernier gouvernement; **the Clinton Administration** le gouvernement Clinton

►► ***administration costs*** frais *mpl* d'administration, frais *mpl* de gestion; ***administration fee*** frais *mpl* de dossier

administrative [əd'mɪnɪstrətɪv] *adj (work, skills)* administratif; *(error)* d'administration

►► ***the administrative body*** le corps administratif; ***administrative costs*** frais *mpl* d'administration, frais *mpl* de gestion; *Br* ***the administrative grade*** *(in civil service)* les fonctionnaires *mpl* supérieurs; ***administrative headquarters*** siège *m* administratif; ***administrative law*** loi *f* administrative; ***administrative staff*** personnel *m* administratif; ***administrative unit*** unité *f* administrative

administratively [əd'mɪnɪstrətɪvlɪ] *adv* administrativement

administrator [əd'mɪnɪstreɪtə(r)] *n* (**a**) *(of business, institution)* directeur(trice) *m,f*, administrateur(trice) *m,f*; *(of area, public institution)* administrateur(trice) *m,f*; *(of estate)* curateur(trice) *m,f* (**b**) *Comput* administrateur *m*

admirable ['ædmərəbəl] *adj* admirable, excellent

admirably ['ædmərəblɪ] *adv* admirablement; **she coped admirably** elle s'en est tiré admirablement bien

admiral ['ædmərəl] *n* (**a**) *Mil & Naut* amiral *m*; **admiral of the fleet, fleet admiral** ≃ amiral *m* de France (**b**) *Entom (butterfly)* vanesse *f*; **red admiral** vulcain *m*

►► *Sport* ***the Admiral's Cup*** l'Admiral's Cup *f* *(course de voiliers en Angleterre)*

admiralty ['ædmərəltɪ] *(pl* **admiralties***)* *n Mil & Naut* amirauté *f*; *Br* **the Admiralty** ≃ le ministère de la Marine; **First Lord of the Admiralty** ≃ Ministre *m* de la Marine

►► *Br* ***the Admiralty Board*** ≃ le ministère de la Marine; *Law* ***admiralty court*** tribunal *m* maritime; ***Admiralty Islands*** îles *fpl* de l'Amirauté; *Law* ***admiralty law*** droit *m* maritime

THE ADMIRALTY

Ce nom désignait autrefois la Direction de la marine nationale britannique au ministère de la Défense. Aujourd'hui il désigne les bâtiments abritant le siège de la Fonction publique à Londres.

admiration [,ædmə'reɪʃən] *n* (**a**) *(feeling)* admiration *f* (**for** pour); **to be full of admiration for sb/sth** être plein d'admiration pour qn/qch, avoir une grande admiration pour qn/qch (**b**) *(person, thing)* **she was the admiration of the entire class** elle faisait l'admiration de la classe entière

admire [əd'maɪə(r)] *vt* admirer; **he admired (her for) the way she dealt with the press** il admirait la façon dont elle savait s'y prendre avec la presse; **I admire her as a leader** je l'admire en tant que dirigeante; **they admire him for sticking to his principles** ils l'admirent de s'en tenir à ses principes; **to admire oneself in the mirror** s'admirer dans le miroir; **you have to admire his persistence!** on ne peut qu'admirer sa persévérance!

admirer [əd'maɪərə(r)] *n* (**a**) *(gen)* admirateur(-trice) *m,f*; **he's one of her many admirers** il est un de ses nombreux admirateurs (**b**) *Old-fashioned (suitor)* soupirant *m*; *Fam* **is that a letter from one of your admirers?** est-ce que c'est une lettre de l'un de tes admirateurs?

admiring [əd'maɪərɪŋ] *adj* admiratif

admiringly [əd'maɪərɪŋlɪ] *adv* avec admiration

admissibility [əd,mɪsə'bɪlətɪ] *n (of behaviour, plan, argument)* admissibilité *f*; *Law (of appeal, testimony, claim, evidence)* recevabilité *f*

admissible [əd'mɪsəbəl] *adj (behaviour, plan, argument)* admissible; *(document)* valable; *Law (appeal, testimony, claim, evidence)* recevable

admission [əd'mɪʃən] *n* (**a**) *(entry)* admission *f*, entrée *f*; *(to school)* admission *f*, accès *m*; *(to career)* accès *m*; **the admission of Poland to the EU** l'entrée de la Pologne dans l'Union européenne; **admission is free** l'entrée est gratuite; **no admission to minors** *(sign)* entrée interdite aux mineurs; **to gain admission to a club** être admis dans un club; **he gained admission to the minister's office** il a été admis dans le bureau du ministre; **they granted women admission to the club** ils ont admis les femmes dans le club

(**b**) *(fee)* droit *m* d'entrée; **admission £4.50** *(sign)* entrée £4.50

(**c**) *(person admitted → to theatre)* entrée *f*; *(→ to school)* candidat(e) *m,f* accepté(e); *(→ to club)* membre *m* accepté

(**d**) *(statement)* déclaration *f*; *(confession)* aveu *m*; *(of allegation)* reconnaissance *f*; *(of crime)* confession *f*; **an admission of guilt** un aveu; **by** *or* **on one's own admission** de son propre aveu

(**e**) *Law (of evidence)* acceptation *f*, admission *f*

(**f**) *Tech (of steam, gas)* admission *f*, adduction *f*, entrée *f*; *(of water)* injection *f*

►► ***admissions form*** dossier *m* d'inscription; *Sch & Univ* ***admissions office*** service *m* des inscriptions; ***admissions officer*** responsable *mf* des inscriptions; ***admissions procedure*** procédure *f* d'inscription; ***admissions tutor*** responsable *mf* des inscriptions

admit [əd'mɪt] *(pt & pp* **admitted**, *cont* **admitting***)* *vt* (**a**) *(concede)* admettre, reconnaître, avouer; **I admit I was wrong** je reconnais que j'ai eu tort; **I must admit it's more difficult than I thought** je dois admettre que c'est plus difficile que je ne pensais; **he admitted (that) he had failed** il a reconnu qu'il avait échoué; **she refused to admit defeat** elle a refusé de reconnaître sa défaite; **no one would admit doing it** personne ne voulait admettre l'avoir fait; **we had to admit the validity of his reasoning** nous avons dû admettre la validité de son raisonnement; **it is generally admitted that women live longer than men** il est généralement admis que les femmes vivent plus longtemps que les hommes

(**b**) *(confess)* avouer; **he admitted taking bribes** il a reconnu avoir accepté des pots-de-vin; **I had to admit to myself that...** j'ai dû m'avouer à moi-même que...

(**c**) *(allow to enter → person)* laisser entrer, faire entrer; *(→ air, light)* laisser passer, laisser entrer; **admit two** *(on ticket)* valable pour deux personnes; **children are not admitted** les enfants ne sont pas admis; **he was admitted to hospital** il a été hospitalisé; **to be admitted to university** être admis à l'université

(**d**) *(accommodate)* (pouvoir) contenir *ou* recevoir

(**e**) *Formal (allow)* admettre, permettre; **the facts admit no other explanation** d'après les faits, il n'y a pas d'autre explication possible

(**f**) *Law (claim)* faire droit à; *(evidence)* admettre comme valable

►**admit of** *vt insep Br Formal* admettre, permettre; **her behaviour admits of no excuse** son attitude est inexcusable; **the text admits of only one interpretation** le texte n'admet *ou* ne permet qu'une seule interprétation

►**admit to** *vt insep (acknowledge)* admettre, reconnaître; *(confess)* avouer; **he admits to having opened the letter** il a avoué avoir ouvert la lettre; **she did admit to a feeling of loss** elle a effectivement avoué ressentir un sentiment de perte

admittance [əd'mɪtəns] *n* (**a**) *(permission to enter)* admission *f*, entrée *f*; **no admittance** *(sign)* accès interdit au public; **to refuse sb admittance** refuser de laisser entrer qn; **his supporters gained admittance to the courtroom/to the president** ses supporters ont réussi à entrer dans le tribunal/à s'approcher du président; **she was denied admittance to the club** on lui a refusé l'entrée au club (**b**) *Elec* admittance *f*

admittedly [əd'mɪtɪdlɪ] *adv* de l'aveu général; **admittedly, he's weak on economics, but he's an excellent manager** d'accord, l'économie n'est pas son point fort, mais il fait un excellent gestionnaire; **our members, although admittedly few in number, are very keen** nos membres, peu nombreux il faut le reconnaître, sont très enthousiastes; **they got there, two hours late admittedly, but...** ils sont arrivés là-bas, avec deux heures de retard, j'en conviens, mais...

admitting office [ad'mɪtɪŋ-] *n Am (in hospital)* service *m* des admissions

admixture [æd'mɪkstʃə(r)] *n* (**a**) *Chem, Metal & Tech (mixture)* mélange *m* (**b**) *(ingredient)* ingrédient *m*; *Fig* **it's mainly comedy with an admixture of satire** c'est principalement de la comédie avec un élément de satire

admonish [əd'mɒnɪʃ] *vt* (**a**) *(rebuke)* réprimander, admonester; **he was admonished for not having acted more promptly** il a été réprimandé pour ne pas avoir agi plus rapidement (**b**) *(warn)* avertir, prévenir; *Law* admonester; **to admonish sb against sth** mettre qn en garde contre qch

admonishing [ˌæd'mɒnɪʃɪŋ], **admonishment** [ˌæd'mɒnɪʃmənt], **admonition** [ˌædmə'nɪʃən] *n* (**a**) *(rebuke)* réprimande *f*, remontrance *f*, admonestation *f* (**b**) *(warning)* avertissement *m*; *Law* admonition *f*

admonitory [ˌæd'mɒnɪtərɪ] *adj* (**a**) *(rebuking)* de réprimande (**b**) *(warning)* d'avertissement; *Law* d'admonition

adnate ['ædneɪt] *adj Bot* adné, adhérent

ad nauseam [ˌæd'nɔːzɪæm] *adv* jusqu'à la nausée; *Fig* à satiété; **she went on about her holiday ad nauseam** elle nous a raconté ses vacances à n'en plus finir

adnominal [əd'nɒmɪnəl] *Gram* **1** *n* adnominal *m*
2 *adj* adnominal

ado [ə'duː] *n* **without more** *or* **further ado** sans plus de cérémonie *ou* de manières

'Much Ado about Nothing' *Shakespeare*
'Beaucoup de bruit pour rien'

adobe [ə'dəʊbɪ] *Constr* **1** *n* adobe *m*
2 *comp (house, wall)* d'adobe

adolescence [ˌædə'lesəns] *n* adolescence *f*

adolescent [ˌædə'lesənt] **1** *n* adolescent(e) *m,f*
2 *adj (boy, girl)* adolescent; *Pej (childish)* enfantin, puéril; **in his adolescent years** quand il était adolescent

Adonis [ə'dɒnɪs] *pr n Myth* Adonis; *Fig* **a young Adonis** un jeune Apollon

adonize, -ise ['ædənaɪz] *vi Literary* faire l'Adonis

adopt [ə'dɒpt] *vt* (**a**) *(child)* adopter
(**b**) *(choose → plan, technique, guideline)* adopter, suivre, choisir; *(→ country, name)* adopter, choisir; *(→ measures, method)* adopter, instaurer; *(→ career)* choisir, embrasser; *Pol (→ candidate)* choisir; *Mktg (→ product)* adopter; **he adopted the suggestion as his own** il a repris la proposition à son compte
(**c**) *(assume → position)* prendre; *(→ accent, tone)* adopter, prendre
(**d**) *Formal Admin (approve → minutes, report)* approuver; *Pol (→ bill, motion)* adopter

adopted [ə'dɒptɪd] *adj (child)* adopté; *(son, daughter)* adoptif; *(country)* d'adoption, adoptif

adopter [ə'dɒptə(r)] *n* (**a**) *(of child)* adoptant(e) *m,f* (**b**) *(of plan, measure, guideline)* **the number of adopters of the policy** le nombre de ceux qui ont adopté cette politique; **they were one of the most enthusiastic adopters of the scheme** ils sont parmi ceux qui ont adopté le système avec le plus d'enthousiasme

adoption [ə'dɒpʃən] *n* (**a**) *(of child, country, custom)* adoption *f*; **she's an American by adoption** elle est américaine d'adoption; **they have two children of their own and another by adoption** ils ont deux enfants à eux et un enfant adopté
(**b**) *(of candidate, career, plan)* choix *m*; *(of measures, method)* instauration *f*; *Mktg (of product)* adoption *f*
(**c**) *Formal Pol (of bill, motion)* adoption *f*
►► ***adoption agency*** agence *f* d'adoption; ***adoption laws*** lois *fpl* sur l'adoption; ***adoption procedure*** procédure *f* d'adoption

adoptive [ə'dɒptɪv] *adj (child, parent)* adoptif; *(country)* d'adoption, adoptif

adorable [ə'dɔːrəbəl] *adj* adorable

adorably [ə'dɔːrəblɪ] *adv* adorablement; **adorably beautiful** beau à ravir

adoration [ˌædə'reɪʃən] *n* adoration *f*; **in adoration** en adoration

adore [ə'dɔː(r)] *vt* (**a**) *Rel* adorer (**b**) *Fam (like)* adorer[❑]; **I adore walking in the rain** j'adore marcher sous la pluie

adorer [ə'dɔːrə(r)] *n Rel* adorateur(trice) *m,f*

adoring [ə'dɔːrɪŋ] *adj (look)* d'adoration; *(smile)* rempli d'adoration; *(mother)* dévoué; *(fans)* fervent; **a letter signed "your adoring daughter"** une lettre signée "ta fille qui t'adore"

adoringly [ə'dɔːrɪŋlɪ] *adv* avec adoration

adorn [ə'dɔːn] *vt Formal or Literary* (**a**) *(decorate → dress, hair)* orner, parer; *(→ room, table)* orner; **adorned with flowers** orné de fleurs; **she adorned herself with jewels** elle s'est parée de bijoux (**b**) *(story)* embellir

adornment [ə'dɔːnmənt] *n Formal or Literary* (**a**) *(act, art)* décoration *f* (**b**) *(of dress, hair)* parure *f*; *(of room, table)* ornement *m*

ADP [ˌeɪdiː'piː] *n Comput (abbr* **automatic data processing**) traitement *m* automatique des données

ADR [ˌeɪdiː'ɑː(r)] *n Fin (abbr* **American Depositary Receipt**) certificat *m* américain de dépôt

adrenal [ə'driːnəl] *Anat* **1** *n* surrénale *f*
2 *adj* surrénal
►► ***adrenal cortex*** corticosurrénale *f*; ***adrenal gland*** surrénale *f*

adrenalin(e) [ə'drenəlɪn] *n Chem & Physiol* adrénaline *f*; **it really gets the adrenalin(e) flowing** ça donne un bon coup d'adrénaline; **he runs on adrenalin(e)** il marche à l'adrénaline

adrenergic [ˌædren'ɜːdʒɪk] *adj Physiol* adrénergique

Adriatic [ˌeɪdrɪ'ætɪk] *n* l'Adriatique *f*, la mer Adriatique
►► ***the Adriatic Sea*** l'Adriatique *f*, la mer Adriatique

adrift [ə'drɪft] **1** *adv* (**a**) **to run** *or* **go adrift** *(boat)* aller à la dérive, dériver; **their boat had been cut adrift** leur bateau avait été détaché; *Fig* **his parents turned him adrift** ses parents l'ont laissé se débrouiller tout seul; *Fig* **to cut oneself adrift from sb** rompre avec qn
(**b**) *Br (undone)* **to come** *or* **to go adrift** se détacher, se défaire; **our holiday plans seem to have gone adrift** il semble que nos projets de vacances soient tombés à l'eau
2 *adj (boat)* à la dérive; *Fig* abandonné; *Fig* **she was (all) adrift** elle divaguait complètement

adroit [ə'drɔɪt] *adj* adroit, habile

adroitly [ə'drɔɪtlɪ] *adv* adroitement, habilement

adroitness [ə'drɔɪtnɪs] *n* adresse *f*

adscititious [ˌædsɪ'tɪʃəs] *adj Literary* surajouté

ADSL [ˌeɪdiːˌes'el] *n Comput (abbr* **asymmetric digital subscriber line**) LNPA *f*

ADT [ˌeɪdiː'tiː] *n (abbr* **Atlantic Daylight Time**) = heure d'été des Provinces Maritimes du Canada et d'une partie des Caraïbes

aduki bean [ə'duːkɪ-] *n* haricot *m* adzuki

adulate ['ædjʊleɪt] *vt Literary* aduler

adulation [ˌædjʊ'leɪʃən] *n* adulation *f*

adulatory ['ædjʊˌleɪtərɪ] *adj* adulateur

adult ['ædʌlt] **1** *n* adulte *mf*; **for adults only** *(sign)* interdit aux moins de 18 ans
2 *adj* (**a**) *(fully grown)* adulte
(**b**) *(mature)* adulte; **she's very adult for her age** elle est très sérieuse *ou* elle a beaucoup de maturité pour son âge; **try and be a little more adult about this** essaie de faire preuve d'un peu plus de maturité
(**c**) *(book, film, subject)* pour adultes
►► *Euph* ***adult bookstore*** sex shop *m*; ***adult education*** enseignement *m* pour adultes; ***adult fare*** tarif *m* adulte

adulterate [ə'dʌltəreɪt] **1** *vt (substance)* dénaturer; *(wine)* frelater; *(language)* corrompre; **they adulterated the wine with water** ils ont coupé le vin (avec de l'eau)
2 *adj Formal* frelaté

adulteration [əˌdʌltə'reɪʃən] *n (of substance)* dénaturation *f*; *(of wine)* frelatage *m*; *(of language)* corruption *f*

adulterer [ə'dʌltərə(r)] *n* adultère *m (personne)*

adulteress [ə'dʌltərɪs] *n* adultère *f*

adulterine [ə'dʌltəraɪn] *adj (child)* adultérin

adulterous [ə'dʌltərəs] *adj* adultère

adulterously [ə'dʌltərəslɪ] *adv* par adultère; *(live)* en état d'adultère; *(lust)* dans une passion adultère

adultery [ə'dʌltərɪ] *n* adultère *m (acte)*; **to commit adultery** commettre l'adultère
►► ***adultery laws*** lois *fpl* sur l'adultère

adulthood ['ædʌlthʊd] *n* âge *m* adulte; **to reach adulthood** devenir adulte, atteindre l'âge adulte

adumbrate ['ædʌmbreɪt] *vt Formal or Literary* (**a**) *(outline)* ébaucher, esquisser (**b**) *(foreshadow)* faire pressentir (**c**) *(obscure)* obscurcir, voiler

adumbration [ˌædʌm'breɪʃən] *n Formal or Literary* (**a**) *(outline)* ébauche *f*, esquisse *f* (**b**) *(foreshadowing)* signes *mpl* précurseurs (**c**) *(obscurity)* obscurcissement *m*

adust [ə'dʌst] *adj Arch or Literary* (**a**) *(scorched)* desséché, aduste (**b**) *(melancholy)* atrabilaire, maussade

ad valorem [ædvə'lɔːrəm] *adj Fin (tax)* proportionnel, ad valorem

advance [əd'vɑːns] **1** *vt* (**a**) *(move forward → clock, tape, film)* faire avancer; *(→ time, event, chess piece)* avancer; **the date of the meeting was advanced by one week** la réunion a été avancée d'une semaine
(**b**) *(further → project, work)* avancer; *(→ interest, cause)* promouvoir; *(→ growth, development)* accélérer; **this discovery has advanced our research by months** cette découverte nous a fait gagner plusieurs mois de recherches
(**c**) *(suggest → idea, proposition)* avancer, mettre en avant; *(→ opinion)* avancer, émettre; *(→ explanation)* avancer
(**d**) *Fin (money)* avancer, faire une avance de; **we advanced her £100 on her salary** nous lui avons avancé 100 livres sur son salaire; **we will advance him £500 before completion of the contract** nous lui verserons un acompte de 500 livres avant l'achèvement des travaux; **sum advanced** avance *f*, acompte *m*
(**e**) *Formal (increase)* augmenter, hausser
2 *vi* (**a**) *(go forward)* avancer, s'avancer; **to advance on** *or* **towards sth** avancer *ou* s'avancer vers qch; **the army advanced on Paris** l'armée avançait *ou* marchait sur Paris
(**b**) *(make progress)* avancer, progresser, faire des progrès
(**c**) *(time)* avancer, s'écouler; *(evening, winter)* avancer
(**d**) *Formal Com & Fin (price, shares, rent)* augmenter (de prix), monter; **the shares advanced to their highest point in May** les actions ont atteint leur valeur la plus haute au mois de mai
(**e**) *(be promoted)* avancer, obtenir de l'avancement; *Mil* monter en grade
3 *n* (**a**) *(forward movement)* avance *f*, marche *f* en avant; *Mil* avance *f*, progression *f*; **the enemy planned their advance on the city** l'ennemi a organisé son avance *ou* sa marche sur la ville; *Fig* **the advance of old age** le vieillissement
(**b**) *(progress)* progrès *m*; **the great advance in medicine** le progrès *ou* les progrès en médecine
(**c**) *Fin (of funds)* avance *f*, acompte *m*; **he asked for an advance of £200 on his salary** il a demandé une avance de 200 livres sur son salaire; **an advance on royalties** une avance sur droits d'auteur; **advances on securities** *or* **against collateral** prêts *mpl* sur titres
(**d**) *Formal Com & Fin (in price, rent)* hausse *f*, augmentation *f*
(**e**) *Com (increase at auction)* **any advance?** qui dit mieux?; **any advance on a hundred?** cent, qui dit mieux?
4 *comp (prior)* préalable
5 advances *npl* avances *fpl*; **to make advances to sb** faire des avances à qn
6 in advance *adv (beforehand → pay, thank)* à l'avance, d'avance; *(→ prepare, reserve, write, know)* à l'avance; **well in advance** largement à l'avance; **we had to pay two weeks in advance** il a fallu qu'on paie deux semaines d'avance; **the agency asked for £50 in advance** l'agence a demandé 50 livres d'avance; **thanking you in advance** *(in letter)* en vous remerciant à l'avance, avec mes remerciements anticipés; **he sent the messenger on in advance** *(ahead)* il a envoyé le messager devant
7 in advance of *prep* avant; **they arrived in advance of their guests** ils sont arrivés en avance sur *ou* avant leurs invités; **their computer technology is far in advance of anything we have** ils sont très en avance sur nous en matière d'informatique
►► *Fin* ***advance account*** compte *m* d'avances; ***advance booking*** réservation *f* à l'avance; **advance booking is advisable** il est recommandé de réserver à l'avance; ***advance booking office*** guichet *m* de location; ***advance copy*** *(of book)* exemplaire *m* de lancement; *(of speech)* texte *m* distribué à l'avance; *Fin* ***advance dividend*** dividende *m* anticipé; ***advance group*** *(gen)* groupe *m* de reconnaissance; *Mil* détachement *m* précurseur; *Mil* ***advance guard*** avant-garde *f*; *Am Pol* ***advance man*** organisateur *m* de la publicité *(pour une campagne politique)*; ***advance notice*** préavis *m*, avertissement *m*; ***advance party*** *(gen)* groupe *m* de reconnaissance;

Mil détachement *m* précurseur; *Fin* ***advance payment*** paiement *m* anticipé, paiement *m* par anticipation; *Mil* ***advance post*** poste *m* avancé; ***advance publicity*** publicité *f* d'amorçage; ***Advance Purchase Excursion*** = tarif préférentiel sujet à des restrictions de délai d'achat; ***advance warning*** avertissement *m*

advanced [əd'vɑːnst] *adj* (**a**) *(course, education)* supérieur; *(child, country, pupil, ideas)* avancé; *(research, work)* poussé; *(equipment, technology)* avancé, de pointe; **the system is very advanced technologically** le système est très en avance au niveau technologique; **he's advanced for his age** il est avancé *ou* très en avance pour son âge; **she's very advanced for two** elle est très avancée *ou* en avance pour une enfant de deux ans; **advanced mathematics** mathématiques *fpl* supérieures

(**b**) *(afternoon, season)* avancé; **a woman of advanced years, a woman advanced in years** une femme d'un âge avancé; **the evening was already far advanced** il était déjà tard dans la soirée

(**c**) *(model, engine, reactor)* perfectionné; *(technique)* avancé;

(**d**) *Mil (post)* avancé

►► *Nucl* ***advanced gas-cooled reactor*** réacteur *m* à gaz avancé; *Sch* ***Advanced level*** *(in England, Wales and Northern Ireland)* ≃ baccalauréat *m*; *Rail* ***advanced passenger train*** train *m* à grande vitesse, TGV *m*

advancement [əd'vɑːnsmənt] *n* (**a**) *(promotion)* avancement *m*, promotion *f*; **there is little scope for advancement** il y a peu de possibilités d'avancement (**b**) *(improvement)* progrès *m*, avancement *m*

advancing [əd'vɑːnsɪŋ] *adj* qui approche, qui avance; **the advancing army** l'armée en marche *ou* qui avance; **the advancing tide** la marée qui monte

advantage [əd'vɑːntɪdʒ] **1** *n* (**a**) *(benefit)* avantage *m*; **her experience gives her an advantage over the other candidates** son expérience lui donne un avantage sur les autres candidats; **they have an advantage over us** *or* **the advantage of us** ils ont un avantage sur nous; **the plan has the advantage of being extremely cheap** le plan présente l'avantage d'être extrêmement bon marché; **it's to your advantage to learn another language** c'est (dans) ton intérêt d'apprendre une autre langue; **that would be to their advantage** cela leur serait avantageux, ils y auraient intérêt; **the recession/weather worked to their advantage** la récession/le temps les a avantagés *ou* a travaillé pour eux; **to turn sth to advantage** tirer parti de qch, mettre qch à profit; **she turned the situation to her advantage** elle a tiré parti de la situation, elle a tourné la situation à son avantage; **to turn out to sb's advantage** *(event)* tourner à l'avantage de qn, profiter à qn; **to take advantage of sth (to do sth)** profiter de qch (pour faire qch); **we took advantage of the holiday weekend to do some gardening** nous avons profité du long week-end pour faire du jardinage; **to take advantage of sb** *(make use of)* profiter de qn; *(exploit)* exploiter qn; *(abuse sexually)* abuser de qn; **they'll only take advantage** *(of your generosity etc)* ils ne feront qu'en profiter; **that would be taking advantage!** ce serait abuser!; **she uses her charm to great advantage** elle sait user de son charme; **that colour shows her eyes off to great advantage** cette couleur met ses yeux en valeur; **this lighting shows the pictures to their best advantage** cet éclairage met les tableaux en valeur; *Br Formal* **you have the advantage of me** à qui ai-je l'honneur?

(**b**) *Sport (in tennis)* avantage *m*; **advantage Henman** avantage Henman

(**c**) *Sport* **to play advantage** *(in football, rugby)* laisser l'avantage, appliquer la règle de l'avantage

2 *vt* avantager

►► *Sport* ***advantage rule*** *(in football, rugby)* règle *f* de l'avantage; **to play the advantage rule** laisser l'avantage, appliquer la règle de l'avantage

advantaged [əd'vɑːntɪdʒd] *adj* favorisé, aisé

advantageous [,ædvən'teɪdʒəs] *adj* avantageux; **to be advantageous to sb** être avantageux pour qn, avantager qn

advantageously [,ædvən'teɪdʒəslɪ] *adv* de façon avantageuse

advent ['ædvənt] **1** *n (of spring, rainy season etc)* arrivée *f*; *(of era, computer age)* avènement *m*; *(of railways, the motor car, computerization)* introduction *f*

2 Advent *n Rel* l'Avent *m*; **the Second Advent** le second Avènement

►► ***Advent calendar*** calendrier *m* de l'Avent; ***Advent Sunday*** le premier dimanche de l'Avent

adventitious [,ædven'tɪʃəs] *adj* (**a**) *Formal (chance)* fortuit (**b**) *Phil* adventice (**c**) *Bot* adventif

adventure [əd'ventʃə(r)] **1** *n* (**a**) *(experience)* aventure *f*; **to have an adventure** avoir une aventure; **after many adventures** après bien des péripéties

(**b**) *(excitement)* aventure *f*; **he has no spirit of adventure** il n'a pas le goût du risque; **where's your sense of adventure?** où est ton sens de l'aventure?; **to look for adventure** chercher l'aventure

(**c**) *Fin (financial operation)* spéculation *f* hasardeuse

2 *comp (film, novel)* d'aventures

3 *vt Formal* (**a**) *(risk → fortune, life)* hasarder, risquer

(**b**) *(proffer → opinion, suggestion)* hasarder, avancer, risquer

(**c**) *(dare)* oser; **to adventure to do sth** s'aventurer *or* se hasarder à faire qch

4 *vi Formal* (**a**) *(embark)* se lancer; **the government has adventured on a new defence policy** le gouvernement s'est lancé dans *ou* a entrepris une nouvelle politique de défense; **to adventure into politics** se lancer dans la politique

(**b**) *(dare to go)* **to adventure in/out** prendre le risque d'entrer/de sortir, se risquer à entrer/à sortir; **the explorers adventured forth into the jungle** les explorateurs se sont lancés dans la jungle

►► ***adventure holiday*** = vacances organisées avec des activités sportives; *Br* ***adventure playground*** = sorte d'aire de jeux

adventurer [əd'ventʃərə(r)] *n* aventurier(ère) *m,f*, *Pej* aventurier(ère) *m,f*, intrigant(e) *m,f*

adventuresome [əd'ventʃəsəm] *adj Am* aventureux, téméraire

adventuress [əd'ventʃərɪs] *n* aventurière *f*, *Pej* aventurière *f*, intrigante *f*

adventurism [əd'ventʃərɪzəm] *n* aventurisme *m*

adventurous [əd'ventʃərəs] *adj (person, spirit)* aventureux, audacieux; *(life, project)* aventureux, hasardeux; **we had an adventurous trip** nous avons eu un voyage plein d'aventures; **be adventurous, try the duck** sois un peu plus aventureux et essaie le canard

adventurously [əd'ventʃərəslɪ] *adv* aventureusement, audacieusement

adventurousness [əd'ventʃərəsnɪs] *n* hardiesse *f*, audace *f*; *(liking adventure)* esprit *m* d'aventure

adverb ['ædvɜːb] *n Gram* adverbe *m*

adverbial [əd'vɜːbɪəl] *adj Gram* adverbial; **adverbial phrase** locution *f* adverbiale

adverbially [əd'vɜːbɪəlɪ] *adv Gram* adverbialement

adversarial [,ædvə'seərɪəl] *adj* antagoniste, hostile

adversary ['ædvəsərɪ] (*pl* **adversaries**) *n* adversaire *mf*

adverse ['ædvɜːs] *adj* (**a**) *(comment, criticism, opinion)* défavorable, hostile; *(circumstances, report)* défavorable; *Fin (balance, budget)* déficitaire

(**b**) *(effect)* opposé, contraire; *(wind)* contraire, debout; **the match was cancelled due to adverse weather conditions** le match a été annulé à cause du mauvais temps; **the stock markets showed an adverse reaction to the Chancellor's budget** les différentes places financières ont mal réagi au budget annoncé par le Chancelier de l'Échiquier

adversely ['ædvɜːslɪ] *adv (affect)* **the harvest was adversely affected by frost** la récolte a été très touchée par les gelées

adversity [əd'vɜːsətɪ] (*pl* **adversities**) *n* (**a**) *(distress)* adversité *f*; **in the face of adversity** dans l'adversité (**b**) *(incident)* malheur *m*; **they met with many adversities** ils ont eu bien des malheurs

advert¹ ['ædvɜːt] *n Br Fam (for job, event, accommodation)* (petite) annonce *f*; *(for product)* pub *f*, *Can* annonce *f*; **you're a walking advert for Benetton** tu as l'air tout droit sorti d'une pub pour Benetton; **the adverts** *(on TV, in cinema)* la pub

advert² [əd'vɜːt] *vi Formal (refer)* se rapporter, se référer; **he adverted to the incident in his report** il a fait allusion à l'incident dans son rapport

advertence [əd'vɜːtəns], **advertency** [əd'vɜːtənsɪ] *n Literary* attention *f*

advertently [əd'vɜːtəntlɪ] *adv Literary* attentivement, avec attention

advertise ['ædvətaɪz] **1** *vt* (**a**) *(publicize → product, service)* faire de la publicité pour; **I heard his new record advertised on the radio** j'ai entendu la publicité pour son nouveau disque à la radio; **I saw it advertised in a magazine** j'ai vu une annonce là-dessus *ou* pour ça dans une revue; **as advertised on TV** vu à la télé

(**b**) *(job)* mettre une (petite) annonce pour; *(event)* annoncer; **they advertised the job in all the nationals** ils ont mis *ou* inséré une annonce pour le poste dans toute la presse; **we advertised our house in the local paper** nous avons mis *ou* passé une annonce pour vendre notre maison dans le journal local

(**c**) *(make known)* afficher; **don't go advertising the fact that we're thinking of leaving** ne va pas crier sur les toits que nous pensons partir; **you needn't advertise the fact** vous n'avez pas besoin de le crier sur les toits; **you needn't advertise your ignorance** ce n'est pas la peine d'étaler ton ignorance; **he didn't want to advertise his presence** il ne voulait pas se faire remarquer

2 *vi* (**a**) *(to sell product, service)* faire de la publicité; **to advertise in the press/on radio/on TV** faire de la publicité dans la presse/à la radio/à la télé; **it pays to advertise** la publicité paie

(**b**) *(place advertisement)* mettre une (petite) annonce

(**c**) *(make a request)* chercher par voie d'annonce; **we advertised for a cook** nous avons mis *ou* fait paraître une annonce pour trouver une cuisinière

advertised ['ædvətaɪzd] *adj* **the advertised time of departure** *(of train, bus, plane)* l'heure *f* prévue pour le départ; *TV* **in a change to the advertised programme** contrairement à ce qu'annonçait le programme

advertisement [*Br* əd'vɜːtɪsmənt, *Am* ,ædvə'taɪzmənt] *n* (**a**) *(for product, service)* annonce *f* publicitaire, publicité *f*; *(on television)* spot *m* publicitaire; **are the advertisements effective?** la publicité est-elle efficace?; **an advertisement for toothpaste, a toothpaste advertisement** une publicité pour du dentifrice; **she made a cup of tea while the advertisements were on** elle est allée se faire une tasse de thé pendant la publicité

(**b**) *(for job, event, accommodation)* (petite) annonce *f* (**for** pour); *(on wall etc)* affiche *f*; **to put an advertisement in the paper** passer une annonce dans le journal; **I got the job through an advertisement** j'ai eu le poste grâce à une annonce

(**c**) *Fig (example)* **this company is a good/poor advertisement for public ownership** la situation de cette société plaide/ne plaide pas en faveur de la nationalisation; **you're not a good advertisement for your school** vous ne faites pas honneur à votre école

advertiser ['ædvətaɪzə(r)] *n* annonceur *m* (publicitaire)

advertising ['ædvətaɪzɪŋ] **1** *n (UNCOUNT)* (**a**) *(promotion)* publicité *f*

(**b**) *(advertisements)* publicité *f*

(**c**) *(business)* publicité *f*; **he works in advertising** il travaille dans la publicité

2 *comp (budget, material)* publicitaire

►► ***advertising agency*** agence *f* de publicité; ***advertising agent*** agent *m* de publicité; ***Advertising Association*** = organisme britannique dont le rôle est de veiller à la qualité des publicités et de défendre les intérêts des annonceurs et des agences de publicité; *Mktg* ***advertising awareness*** notoriété *f* publicitaire; *Comput* **advertising banner** *(on web page)* bandeau *f* publicitaire; ***advertising brochure*** plaquette *f* publicitaire; ***advertising campaign*** campagne *f* publicitaire *ou* de publicité; ***advertising concept*** idée *f* publicitaire; ***advertising consultant*** conseil *m* en publicité; ***advertising copy*** texte *m* publicitaire; ***advertising department*** service *m* de la publicité; ***advertising director*** directeur(trice) *m,f* de la communication *ou* de la publicité; ***advertising effectiveness*** efficacité *f* publicitaire; ***advertising executive*** chef *m* de la publicité; ***advertising expenditure*** dépenses *fpl* publicitaires; ***advertising gimmick*** gadget *m* publicitaire; ***advertising jingle*** jingle *m*, *Offic* sonal *m*; ***advertising medium*** média *m ou* support *m* publicitaire; ***advertising rates*** tarif *m* des insertions; ***advertising revenue*** recettes *fpl* publicitaires; ***advertising sales agency*** régie *f* publicitaire; ***advertising schedule*** programme *m* des annonces; ***advertising space*** espace *m* publicitaire; ***advertising standards*** normes *fpl* publicitaires; *Br* ***Advertising Standards Authority*** ≃ Bureau *m* de vérification de la publicité; ***advertising strategy*** stratégie *f* publicitaire

advertize, advertized *etc* = **advertise, advertised** *etc*

advertorial [,ædvə'tɔːrɪəl] *n Press* publireportage *m*

advice [əd'vaɪs] *n* (**a**) *(UNCOUNT) (counsel)* conseil(s) *m(pl)* (**on** sur); **a piece of advice** un conseil; **he asked his father's advice, he asked his father for advice** il a demandé conseil à *ou* a consulté son père; **let me give you some advice** permettez que je vous donne un conseil *ou* que je vous conseille; **to take** *or* **follow sb's advice** suivre le conseil de qn; **take my advice and say nothing to her** suis mon conseil, ne lui dis rien; **when I want your advice I'll ask for it!** quand j'aurai besoin de tes conseils, je saurai te les demander!; **if you take my advice you'll not have anything to do with them** suis mon conseil, ne te mêle pas de leurs affaires; **my advice to you would be to write a letter of apology** je te conseille d'envoyer une lettre d'excuses; **I took** *or* **followed your advice and called him** suivant votre conseil, je l'ai appelé; **to take legal/medical advice** consulter un avocat/un médecin

(**b**) *Admin (notification)* avis *m*; **advice of delivery/payment** avis *m* de livraison/de paiement; **as per advice** suivant avis; **letter of advice** lettre *f* d'avis

►► *Press* ***advice column*** *(agony column)* courrier *m* du cœur; *(for practical advice)* rubrique *f* pratique; *Fin* ***advice note*** lettre *f* d'avis

advisability [əd,vaɪzə'bɪlətɪ] *n* opportunité *f*, bien-fondé *m*; **they discussed the advisability of performing another operation** ils ont discuté de l'opportunité d'une nouvelle opération; **I question the advisability of contacting the police** je doute qu'il soit opportun de faire appel à la police

advisable [əd'vaɪzəbəl] *adj* conseillé, recommandé; **it would be advisable to lock the door** il serait prudent *ou* préférable que vous fermiez la porte à clé; **it is advisable to book early** il est recommandé de réserver à l'avance; **I'm going in my old car – is that advisable?** j'y vais dans ma vieille voiture – est-ce que c'est bien prudent?; **I don't think it's advisable to go out** je ne vous conseille pas de sortir; **it would perhaps be advisable to warn them** peut-être conviendrait-il de les prévenir; **she thought it advisable to call him** elle a cru bien faire en l'appelant; **if you consider** *or* **think it advisable** si bon vous semble

advise [əd'vaɪz] *vt* (**a**) *(give advice to)* conseiller, donner des conseils à; *(recommend)* recommander; **to advise sb to do sth** conseiller à qn de faire qch; **I strongly advise you to...** je vous recommande instamment de...; **customers are advised to book early** il est recommandé *ou* conseillé aux clients de réserver à l'avance; **what do you advise me to do?** que me conseillez-vous?; **we advised them to wait** nous leur avons conseillé d'attendre; **she advised caution** elle a recommandé la prudence; **I advised him against signing the contract** je lui ai conseillé de ne pas signer le contrat; **he advised them against taking legal action** il leur a déconseillé d'intenter une action en justice; **they were well advised to go by air** ils ont bien fait de prendre l'avion

(**b**) *(act as counsel to)* conseiller; **she advises the government on education** elle conseille le gouvernement en matière d'éducation

(**c**) *Formal (inform)* aviser, informer; **we are pleased to advise you that...** nous avons le plaisir de vous informer que...; **we advised them of our arrival** nous les avons prévenus de notre arrivée, nous leur avons fait part de notre arrivée; **keep me advised of your progress** tenez-moi au courant de vos progrès; **she advised him of the cost** elle l'a informé du coût

(**d**) *Banking & Fin* **to advise a draft** aviser d'une traite, donner avis d'une traite

advisedly [əd'vaɪzɪdlɪ] *adv* délibérément, en connaissance de cause

advisement [əd'vaɪzmənt] *n Am (consultation)* **the matter is still under advisement** aucune décision n'a encore été prise

adviser, *Am* **advisor** [əd'vaɪzə(r)] *n* conseiller(ère) *m,f*; *Sch & Univ* conseiller(ère) *m,f* pédagogique

advising bank [əd'vaɪzɪŋ-] *n* banque *f* notificatrice

advisor *Am* = **adviser**

advisory [əd'vaɪzərɪ] *adj (role, work)* consultatif, de conseil; **he's employed in an advisory capacity** il est employé à titre consultatif

►► ***advisory board, advisory body*** organe *m* consultatif; ***advisory bulletin*** bulletin *m* de renseignements; *Banking* ***advisory committee*** comité *m* de restructuration; *Am Law* ***advisory opinion*** avis *m* consultatif de la cour; ***advisory service*** service *m* de renseignements

advocaat ['ædvəkɑː] *n* advocaat *m*

advocacy ['ædvəkəsɪ] *n* soutien *m* appuyé, plaidoyer *m*; **she speaks in advocacy of educational reform** elle prône *ou* préconise une réforme scolaire

advocate 1 *vt* ['ædvəkeɪt] prôner, préconiser; **he advocates reducing** *or* **a reduction in defence spending** il préconise une réduction des dépenses militaires

2 *n* ['ædvəkət] (**a**) *(supporter)* défenseur *m*, avocat(e) *m,f*; **a strong advocate of free enterprise** un fervent partisan de la libre entreprise; **they are advocates of civil rights** ils défendent les droits civiques

(**b**) *Scot Law (barrister)* avocat(e) *m,f* (plaidant(e))

advt *(written abbr* **advertisement***) (for product, service)* publicité *f*; *(for job, event, accommodation)* (petite) annonce *f*

adze, *Am* **adz** [ædz] *n Tech* herminette *f*

adzuki bean [əd'zuːkɪ-] *n* haricot *m* adzuki

AEA [,eɪiː'eɪ] *n* (**a**) *Br* (*abbr* **Atomic Energy Authority**) ≃ CEA *f* (**b**) *Am* (*abbr* **Actors' Equity Association**) = syndicat de comédiens aux États-Unis

AEC [,eɪiː'siː] *n Am* (*abbr* **Atomic Energy Commission**) ≃ CEA *f*

aedes [eɪ'iːdiːz] *n Entom* stégomyie *f*

AEEU [,eɪiː,iː'juː] *n* (*abbr* **Amalgamated Engineering and Electrical Union**) = syndicat britannique de l'industrie mécanique

Aegean [iː'dʒiːən] **1** *n* **the Aegean** la mer Égée

2 *adj* égéen

►► ***the Aegean Islands*** les îles *fpl* de la mer Égée; ***the Aegean Sea*** la mer Égée

Aegeus ['iːdʒɪəs] *n Myth* Égée

Aegina [iː'dʒaɪnə] *n Geog* Égine

aegis ['iːdʒɪs] *n Fig* égide *f*; **under the aegis of** sous l'égide de; **under the aegis of the European Parliament** sous l'égide du Parlement européen

aegrotat ['iːgrəʊtæt] *n Br Univ* = équivalence d'un diplôme accordée à un bon étudiant qui était malade lors des examens

Aeneas [ɪ'niːəs] *pr n Myth* Énée

Aeneid [ɪ'niːɪd] *n*

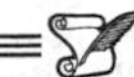

'The Aeneid' *Virgil* 'L'Énéide'

aeolian, *Am* **eolian** [iː'əʊlɪən] *adj Agr, Geol & Met* éolien

►► *Mus* ***aeolian harp*** harpe *f* éolienne; ***the Aeolian Islands*** les îles *fpl* Éoliennes

Aeolus [iː'əʊləs] *pr n Myth* Éole

aeon, *Am* **eon** ['iːən] *n* (**a**) *(age)* période *f* incommensurable; *Astron* milliard *m* d'années; *Fam* **I haven't seen him in aeons** je ne l'ai pas vu depuis une éternité *ou* des lustres; **for aeons upon aeons** pendant des siècles *ou* des éternités (**b**) *Phil* éon *m*

aerate ['eəreɪt] *vt* (**a**) *(soil, water)* aérer (**b**) *(mineral water, liquid)* gazéifier (**c**) *Physiol (blood)* oxygéner

aerated [eə'reɪtɪd] *adj* (**a**) *(soil, water)* aéré (**b**) *(mineral water, liquid)* gazeux (**c**) *Br Fam (excited, upset)* **to be aerated (about sth)** être énervé (à cause de qch)❑; **to get aerated (about sth)** s'énerver (à cause de qch)❑

aeration [eə'reɪʃən] *n* (**a**) *(of soil, water)* aération *f* (**b**) *(of mineral water, liquid)* gazéification *f* (**c**) *Physiol (of blood)* artérialisation *f*

aerial ['eərɪəl] **1** *adj* (**a**) *(in the air)* aérien

(**b**) *Bot* aérien; *(orchid)* aéricole

(**c**) *Literary (imaginary)* imaginaire

(**d**) *Literary (delicate)* aérien, éthéré

2 *n Br (for TV, radio)* antenne *f*

►► ***aerial acrobatics*** voltige *f* aérienne; ***aerial cable car*** téléphérique *m*; *Mil* ***aerial combat*** combat *m* aérien; ***aerial engineer*** antenniste *mf*; *Am Tech* ***aerial ladder*** échelle *f* pivotante; ***aerial photograph*** photographie *f* aérienne; ***aerial railway*** téléphérique *m*; *Bot* ***aerial root*** racine *f* aérienne; ***aerial socket*** prise *f* d'antenne; ***aerial walkway*** passerelle *f*; *Mil* ***aerial warfare*** combat *m* aérien

aerialist ['eərɪəlɪst] *n Am (tightrope walker)* funambule *mf*; *(trapeze artist)* trapéziste *mf*

aerially ['eərɪəlɪ] *adv* d'une manière aérienne

aerie ['eərɪ] *n Am* aire *f (d'aigle)*

aero-bars ['eərəʊ,bɑːz] *npl Cycling* guidon *m* de triathlon

aerobatics [,eərəʊ'bætɪks] *n (UNCOUNT)* acrobatie *f* aérienne, acrobaties *fpl* aériennes

►► ***aerobatics display*** démonstration *f* aérienne

aerobe ['eərəʊb] *n Biol* aérobie *m*

aerobic [eə'rəʊbɪk] *adj Biol* aérobie

aerobics [eə'rəʊbɪks] **1** *n (UNCOUNT)* aérobic *m*; **to do aerobics** faire de l'aérobic; **are you going to aerobics tonight?** est-ce que tu vas au cours d'aérobic ce soir?

2 *comp (class, teacher)* d'aérobic

aerobiologic [,eərəʊbaɪə'lɒdʒɪk], **aerobiological** [,eərəʊbaɪə'lɒdʒɪkəl] *adj Biol* aérobiologique

aerobiology [,eərəʊbaɪ'ɒlədʒɪ] *n Biol* aérobiologie *f*

aerodrome ['eərədrəʊm] *n Aviat* aérodrome *m*

aerodynamic [,eərəʊdaɪ'næmɪk] *adj Phys* aérodynamique; **the car has a very aerodynamic shape** la voiture a une forme très aérodynamique

►► ***aerodynamic drag*** résistance *f* de l'air; ***aerodynamic noise*** bruit *m* aérodynamique

aerodynamically [,eərəʊdaɪ'næmɪklɪ] *adv Phys* aérodynamiquement

aerodynamics [,eərəʊdaɪ'næmɪks] *n (UNCOUNT) Phys* aérodynamique *f*

aero-engine ['eərəʊ-] *n Aviat* moteur *m* d'avion

aerofoil ['eərəʊfɔɪl] *n Aviat* surface *f* portante, plan *m* de sustentation

aerogram ['eərəgræm] *n* (**a**) *(letter)* aérogramme *m* (**b**) *(radiotelegram)* radiotélégramme *m*

aerolite ['eərəʊlaɪt] *n Astron* aérolithe *m*

aeromodeller, *Am* **aeromodeler** ['eərəʊ,mɒdələ(r)] *n Tech* aéromodéliste *mf*

aeromodelling ['eərəʊ,mɒdəlɪŋ] *n Tech* aéromodélisme *m*

aeronaut ['eərənɔːt] *n* aéronaute *mf*

aeronautic [,eərə'nɔːtɪk], **aeronautical** [,eərə'nɔːtɪkəl] *adj* aéronautique

aeronautics [,eərə'nɔːtɪks] *n (UNCOUNT)* aéronautique *f*

aeronomy [,eə'rɒnəmɪ] *n Chem & Phys* aéronomie *f*

aerophagia [ˌeərə'feɪdʒɪə] *n Med* aérophagie *f*

aerophysics [ˌeərə'fɪsɪks] *n (UNCOUNT)* aérophysique *f*

aeroplane ['eərəpleɪn] *n Br* avion *m*

aerosol ['eərəsɒl] **1** *n* (**a**) *(suspension system)* aérosol *m* (**b**) *(container)* bombe *f*, aérosol *m*
2 *comp (container)* aérosol; *(hairspray, paint)* en aérosol, en bombe
►► ***aerosol spray*** atomiseur *m*

aerosolized ['eərəsɒˌlaɪzd] *adj (medicine)* sous forme d'aérosol

aerospace ['eərəʊˌspeɪs] **1** *n* aérospatiale *f*
2 *comp (industry, research)* aérospatial

aerostat ['eərəʊstæt] *n* aérostat *m*

aerostatic [ˌeərəʊ'stætɪk] *adj* aérostatique

aerostatics [ˌeərəʊ'stætɪks] *n (UNCOUNT)* aérostatique *f*

Aertex® ['eəteks] *n Tex* Aertex® *m (tissu synthétique)*

Aeschylus ['iːskɪləs] *pr n Myth* Eschyle

Aesculapius [ˌiːskjʊ'leɪpɪəs] *pr n Myth* Esculape

Aesop ['iːsɒp] *pr n Myth* Ésope; **Aesop's Fables** les Fables *fpl* d'Ésope

aesthete, *Am* **esthete** ['iːsθiːt] *n Art & Phil* esthète *mf*

aesthetic, *Am* **esthetic** [iːs'θetɪk] **1** *adj Art & Phil* esthétique; **in aesthetic terms** en termes d'esthétique
2 *n* esthétique *f*

aesthetically, *Am* **esthetically** [iːs'θetɪkəɪ] *adv Art & Phil* esthétiquement

aesthetician, *Am* **esthetician** [ˌiːsθə'tɪʃən] *n* (**a**) *Art & Phil* esthéticien(enne) *m,f* (**b**) *Am (beautician)* esthéticien(enne) *m,f*

aestheticism, *Am* **estheticism** [iːs'θetɪsɪzəm] *n Art & Phil* esthétisme *m*

aesthetics, *Am* **esthetics** [iːs'θetɪks] *n (UNCOUNT) Art & Phil* esthétique *f*

aestivate, *Am* **estivate** ['iːstɪveɪt] *vi Zool* estiver

aestivation, *Am* **estivation** [ˌiːstɪ'veɪʃən] *n Bot & Zool* estivation *f*

aetiological, *Am* **etiological** [ˌiːtɪə'lɒdʒɪkəl] *adj Med & Phil* étiologique

aetiology, *Am* **etiology** [ˌiːtɪ'ɒlədʒɪ] (*pl* **aetiologies**) *n Med & Phil* étiologie *f*

AF [ˌeɪ'ef] *n Am* (*abbr* **Air Force**) armée *f* de l'air

afar [ə'fɑː(r)] *Literary* **1** *adv* au loin, à (grande) distance
2 from afar *adv* de loin

AFB [ˌeɪef'biː] *n Am* (**a**) (*abbr* **air force base**) base *f* aérienne (**b**) (*abbr* **American Foundation for the Blind**) = institution américaine pour les aveugles

AFC [ˌeɪef'siː] *n* (**a**) *Aviat & Tech* (*abbr* **automatic flight control**) commande *f* automatique de vol (**b**) *Rad* (*abbr* **automatic frequency control**) correcteur *m* automatique de fréquence (**c**) (*abbr* **American Football Conference**) = division de la fédération nationale de football américain (NFL), comprenant quinze équipes

AFDC [ˌeɪefˌdiː'siː] *n Admin* (*abbr* **Aid to Families with Dependent Children**) = type d'allocations familiales destinées tout particulièrement aux familles monoparentales

afeared, afeard [ə'fɪəd] *adj Arch* effrayé, apeuré; **to be afeared (of)** avoir peur (de)

affability [ˌæfə'bɪlətɪ] *n* affabilité *f*, amabilité *f*

affable ['æfəbəl] *adj (person)* affable, aimable; *(conversation, interview)* chaleureux

affably ['æfəblɪ] *adv* affablement, avec affabilité

affair [ə'feə(r)] **1** *n* (**a**) *(event)* affaire *f*; **the meeting was a noisy affair** la réunion était bruyante; **the festival was a dull affair** le festival était dépourvu d'intérêt; **it was a sorry affair** c'était une histoire lamentable; **what kind of affair was it?** c'était comment?; **it was one of those black tie affairs** c'était une de ces soirées habillées; *Hist* **the Watergate affair** l'affaire *f* du Watergate; *Arch* **affair of honour** affaire *f* d'honneur, duel *m*
(**b**) *(business, matter)* affaire *f*; **the affair in hand** l'affaire qui nous occupe
(**c**) *(concern)* affaire *f*; **whether I go or not is my (own) affair** que j'y aille ou non ne regarde que moi; **it's no affair of his** ça ne le regarde *ou* ne le concerne pas, ça n'est pas son affaire
(**d**) *(sexual)* liaison *f*, aventure *f*; **to have an affair with sb** avoir une liaison *ou* aventure avec qn
(**e**) *Fam (thing)* truc *m*; **he was driving one of those sporty affairs** il conduisait une de ces voitures genre sport; **the cake's one of those fresh-cream affairs** c'est un de ces gâteaux à la crème fraîche; **the house is a three-storey affair** il s'agit d'une maison à trois étages
2 affairs *npl (business, matters)* affaires *fpl*; **he's looking after her financial affairs** il gère son argent; **I'm not interested in your private affairs** je ne m'intéresse pas à votre vie privée; **don't meddle in my affairs** ne vous mêlez pas de mes affaires, mêlez-vous de vos affaires; **to put one's affairs in order** mettre de l'ordre dans ses affaires; **given the current state of affairs** étant donné la situation actuelle, les choses étant ce qu'elles sont; **it's an embarrassing state of affairs** la situation est gênante; *Ironic* **this is a fine state of affairs!** c'est du propre!; *Pol* **affairs of state** affaires *fpl* d'État

affect[1] **1** *vt* [ə'fekt] (**a**) *(have effect on → person, life)* avoir un effet sur, affecter; *(influence → decision, outcome)* influer sur, avoir une incidence sur; **how will these changes affect you?** en quoi serez-vous affecté *ou* concerné par ces changements?; **I don't see how your decision affects her** je ne vois pas ce que votre décision change pour elle; **she doesn't seem to be particularly affected by the noise** elle ne semble pas être particulièrement dérangée par le bruit; **roads have been seriously affected by the flooding** les routes ont été fortement touchées par l'inondation; **these plants were badly affected by a late frost** ces plantes ont beaucoup souffert des gelées tardives; **the bad weather has affected sporting events this weekend** le mauvais temps a eu des répercussions sur les événements sportifs du week-end; **high interest rates are affecting the housing market** le niveau élevé des taux d'intérêts affecte (le marché de) l'immobilier; **one of the factors that will affect the outcome of the next election** l'un des facteurs qui influera sur le résultat des prochaines élections; **to what extent does price affect your choice?** dans quelle mesure *ou* jusqu'à quel point le prix influence-t-il votre choix?
(**b**) *(concern, involve)* toucher, concerner; **this new law affects everyone** cette nouvelle loi concerne *ou* touche tout le monde; **the strike didn't affect us** nous n'avons pas été touchés par la grève; **they are directly affected** ce sont eux les premiers intéressés, ils sont directement concernés
(**c**) *(emotionally)* affecter, émouvoir, toucher; **he was deeply affected by her death** il a été très affecté *ou* touché par sa mort; **don't let it affect you** ne vous laissez pas abattre par cela
(**d**) *(of illness, epidemic)* atteindre; *(of drug)* agir sur; **it has been proved that smoking affects your health** il est prouvé que le tabac est nocif pour la santé; **thousands of people are affected by this incurable disease** des milliers de gens sont touchés *ou* concernés par cette maladie incurable; **it's a condition that particularly affects young children** c'est une maladie qui affecte *ou* touche particulièrement les jeunes enfants; **a disease that affects the kidneys** une maladie qui affecte les reins; **she has had a stroke, but her speech is not affected** elle a eu une attaque, mais les fonctions du langage ne sont pas atteintes
2 *n* ['æfekt] *Psy* affect *m*

affect[2] *vt* (**a**) *Formal (pretend, feign → indifference, surprise, interest)* affecter, feindre; *(→ illness, pain)* feindre, simuler; **he affected a strong foreign accent** il affectait un fort accent étranger; **she affected not to see him** elle fit semblant de ne pas l'avoir vu (**b**) *Arch or Literary (be fond of)* affectionner, avoir un penchant pour (**c**) *Bot & Zool (climate, habitat)* être un habitué *ou* des habitués de, affecter

affectation [ˌæfek'teɪʃən] *n* (**a**) *(in behaviour, manners)* affectation *f*, manque *m* de naturel; *(in language, style)* manque *m* de naturel; **without affectation** simple, sans manières (**b**) *(mannerism)* pose *f* (**c**) *(pretence)* semblant *m*, simulacre *m*; **with an affectation of interest/boredom** en simulant l'intérêt/l'ennui

affected[1] [ə'fektɪd] *adj* (**a**) *Med* atteint; **the lung is affected** le poumon est atteint *ou* touché; **apply to the affected part** appliquer sur la partie malade (**b**) *(emotionally)* ému, touché

affected[2] *adj* (**a**) *Pej (person, behaviour)* affecté, maniéré; *(accent, dress, language)* affecté, recherché (**b**) *(pretended, fake)* simulé, feint

-affected [ə'fektɪd] *suff* affecté par; **famine-/drought-affected** affecté par la famine/sécheresse

affectedly [ə'fektɪdlɪ] *adv Pej* avec affectation, d'une manière affectée

affectedness [ə'fektɪdnɪs] *n (UNCOUNT) Pej* affectation *f*, manque *m* de naturel

affecting [ə'fektɪŋ] *adj* touchant, émouvant

affection [ə'fekʃən] *n* (**a**) *(liking)* affection *f*, tendresse *f*; **to show sb affection** montrer de l'affection *ou* de la tendresse pour qn; **to feel affection for sb** avoir de l'affection *ou* de la tendresse pour qn; **a rare display of affection** une rare manifestation d'affection *ou* de tendresse; **she has (a) deep affection for him** elle a une profonde affection pour lui, elle l'aime profondément; **with much affection** *(in letter)* (bien) affectueusement; **he is held in great affection** il est très aimé
(**b**) *(usu pl)* affection *f*; **to gain** *or* **to win (a place in) sb's affections** gagner l'affection *ou* le cœur de qn; **she transferred her affections to another man** elle a reporté son affection sur un autre homme; **this town has a special place in my affections** j'aime tout particulièrement cette ville
(**c**) *Med* affection *f*, maladie *f*

affectionate [ə'fekʃənət] *adj* affectueux, tendre (**towards** avec *ou* envers); *Old-fashioned* **your affectionate niece** *(in letter)* votre nièce affectionnée

affectionately [ə'fekʃənətlɪ] *adv* affectueusement; **yours affectionately** *(in letter)* (bien) affectueusement

affective [ə'fektɪv] *adj Ling & Psy* affectif

afferent ['æfərənt] *adj Physiol* afférent

affiance [ə'faɪəns] *vt Literary* **to become affianced to sb** se fiancer à *ou* avec qn; **to be affianced** être fiancé

affidavit [ˌæfɪ'deɪvɪt] *n Law* déclaration *f* écrite sous serment; **a sworn affidavit** une déclaration écrite sous serment

affiliate 1 *vt* [ə'fɪlɪeɪt] affilier; **to affiliate oneself to** *or* **with** s'affilier à; **the local group decided not to affiliate itself to the national organization** la section locale a décidé de ne pas s'affilier au mouvement national
2 *vi* [ə'fɪlɪət] **to affiliate to** *or* **with a society** s'affilier à une société
3 *n* [ə'fɪlɪət] *(person)* affilié(e) *m,f*; *(organization)* groupe *m* affilié; *Com (company)* société *f* affiliée, filiale *f*
4 *comp (member, organization)* affilié

affiliated [ə'fɪlɪeɪtɪd] *adj (member, organization)* affilié; **to be affiliated to** *or* **with** être affilié à
►► *Com* ***affiliated company*** société *f* affiliée, filiale *f*

affiliation [əˌfɪlɪ'eɪʃən] *n* (**a**) *Com (company)* affiliation *f*, société *f* affiliée, filiale *f* (**b**) *Law* attribution *f* de paternité (**c**) *(connection)* attache *f*; **his political affiliations** ses attaches *fpl* politiques
►► *Law* ***affiliation order*** = injonction au père putatif de verser une pension pour l'entretien de son enfant

affinity [ə'fɪnətɪ] (*pl* **affinities**) *n* (**a**) *(connection, link)* lien *m*, affinité *f*; **the affinities between the English and German languages** la ressemblance *ou* la parenté entre l'anglais et l'allemand; **the artist's work shows a clear affinity with that of his former teacher** on voit clairement le lien entre l'œuvre de cet artiste et celle de son maître; **there are many affinities between the two regions** les deux régions ont énormément de choses en commun
(**b**) *(attraction)* affinité *f*, attraction *f*; **to have an affinity with sb/sth** avoir des affinités avec qn/qch; **he has little affinity for** *or* **with modern art** il est peu attiré par l'art moderne; **she feels a strong sense of affinity with** *or* **for him** elle se sent beaucoup d'affinités avec lui; **there is a strong affinity between them** ils ont beaucoup de choses en commun *ou* d'affinités
(**c**) *Biol* affinité *f*, parenté *f*; *Chem* affinité *f*
(**d**) *Law (relation)* affinité *f*

►► ***affinity card*** (**a**) *Br Com & Fin* = carte de crédit émise en collaboration avec une association caritative, afin qu'une part de chaque transaction revienne à ladite association, *Can* carte *f* d'affinité (**b**) *Am Com & Fin* = carte de crédit résultant de la collaboration entre un organisme de crédit et une entreprise commerciale

affirm [ə'fɜːm] **1** *vt* (**a**) *(state)* affirmer, soutenir; **she affirms that it's the truth** elle affirme *ou* soutient que c'est la vérité; **"I will be there," he affirmed** "j'y serai," assura-t-il

(**b**) *(profess → belief)* professer, proclamer; *(→ intention)* proclamer; **she affirmed her intention to sell** elle proclamait son intention de vendre

(**c**) *(support → person)* soutenir

(**d**) *Law (verdict)* confirmer, homologuer

2 *vi Law* faire une affirmation *ou* déclaration solennelle

affirmation [ˌæfə'meɪʃən] *n* (**a**) *(statement)* affirmation *f*, assertion *f* (**b**) *Law (of verdict)* confirmation *f*, homologation *f* (**c**) *Law (declaration)* déclaration *f ou* affirmation *f* solennelle; **to make a solemn affirmation** faire une déclaration solennelle

affirmative [ə'fɜːmətɪv] **1** *n* (**a**) *Gram* affirmatif *m*; **in the affirmative** à l'affirmatif, à la forme affirmative

(**b**) *(in reply)* **the answer is in the affirmative** la réponse est affirmative; **to answer in the affirmative** répondre affirmativement *ou* par l'affirmative

2 *adj* affirmatif; **to give an affirmative answer** répondre affirmativement

3 *exclam* affirmatif!

►► *Am* ***affirmative action*** *(UNCOUNT)* mesures *fpl* d'embauche anti-discriminatoires *(en faveur des minorités)*; **to take affirmative action** prendre des mesures anti-discriminatoires

affirmatively [ə'fɜːmətɪvlɪ] *adv* affirmativement

affix 1 *vt* [ə'fɪks] *(seal, signature)* apposer; *(stamp)* coller; *(poster)* afficher, poser

2 *n* ['æfɪks] *Ling* affixe *m*

afflict [ə'flɪkt] *vt* affecter; **to be afflicted with a disease** souffrir d'une maladie; **she was afflicted by acute feelings of guilt** elle était accablée d'un fort sentiment de culpabilité; *Ironic* **the family I'm afflicted with** la famille dont je suis affligé; *Fig* **the economic problems that afflict the nation** les problèmes économiques qui accablent le pays

afflicted [ə'flɪktɪd] **1** *adj* affligé; *(part, area → by illness)* atteint

2 *npl* **the afflicted** les affligés *mpl*; **don't mock the afflicted** ne te moque pas de moi/lui/*etc*; *Fam Hum* **he can't help being stupid, don't mock the afflicted** ce n'est pas de sa faute s'il est bête, le pauvre

affliction [ə'flɪkʃən] *n* (**a**) *(suffering)* affliction *f*; *(distress)* détresse *f*; **people in affliction** les gens dans la détresse *ou* dans l'affliction (**b**) *(misfortune)* affliction *f*, souffrance *f*; **blindness is a terrible affliction** la cécité est une grande infirmité

affluence ['æflʊəns] *n* (**a**)*(wealth)* richesse *f*; **to live in affluence** vivre dans l'aisance; **in times of affluence** en période de prospérité (**b**) *Literary (abundance)* abondance *f*

affluent ['æflʊənt] **1** *adj* (**a**) *(wealthy)* aisé, riche; **to be affluent** vivre dans l'aisance; **the affluent society** la société d'abondance (**b**) *Literary (abundant)* abondant

2 *n Geog* affluent *m*

'The Affluent Society' *Galbraith* 'L'Ère de l'opulence'

affluently ['æflʊəntlɪ] *adv (live)* dans l'aisance

afflux ['æflʌks] *n* (**a**) *Formal (of visitors, traffic)* affluence *f*, afflux *m* (**b**) *Med* afflux *m*

afford [ə'fɔːd] *vt* (**a**) *(have enough money for)* **to be able to afford sth** avoir les moyens d'acheter qch; **I can't afford a holiday** je n'ai pas les moyens de prendre des vacances; **she couldn't afford to buy a car** elle n'avait pas les moyens d'acheter *ou* elle ne pouvait pas se permettre d'acheter une voiture; **can you afford it?** en avez-vous les moyens?, pouvez-vous vous le permettre?; **how much can you afford?** combien pouvez-vous mettre?, jusqu'à combien pouvez-vous aller?; **I can't afford £50!** je ne peux pas mettre 50 livres!; **I can afford to eat out twice a week** je peux me permettre d'aller au restaurant deux fois par semaine; **give what you can afford** donnez selon vos possibilités; **it's more than we can afford** c'est au-dessus de nos moyens

(**b**) *(have enough time, energy for)* **I can afford to wait** je peux attendre; **the doctor can only afford (to spend) a few minutes with each patient** le médecin ne peut pas se permettre de passer plus de quelques minutes avec chaque patient; **I'd love to come, but I can't afford the time** j'aimerais beaucoup venir mais je ne peux absolument pas me libérer

(**c**) *(allow oneself)* se permettre; **I can't afford to take any risks** je ne peux pas me permettre de prendre des risques; **we can't afford another delay** nous ne pouvons pas nous permettre encore un retard; **I can't afford not to** je n'ai pas vraiment le choix

(**d**) *Literary or Formal (provide)* fournir, offrir; **to afford sb the opportunity to do sth** donner *ou* fournir à qn l'occasion de faire qch; **this affords me great pleasure** ceci me procure un grand plaisir; **the bell tower afforded a panoramic view of the city** le clocher offrait une vue panoramique de la ville; **the trees afforded us very little shelter** les arbres ne nous fournissaient qu'un piètre abri

affordable [ə'fɔːdəbəl] *adj (price, rent)* abordable; *(house, trip etc)* (d'un prix) abordable

afforest [æ'fɒrɪst] *vt Agr* boiser, reboiser

afforestation [æˌfɒrɪ'steɪʃən] *n Agr* boisement *m*

affranchise [ə'fræntʃaɪz] *vt Formal* affranchir

affranchisement [ə'fræntʃaɪzmənt] *n Formal* affranchissement *m*

affray [ə'freɪ] *n* échauffourée *f*

affreightment [ə'freɪtmənt] *n Com* affrètement *m*

affricate ['æfrɪkət] *n Ling* affriquée *f*

affright [ə'fraɪt] *Arch* **1** *n* effroi *m*, terreur *f*

2 *vt* effrayer, terrifier

affront [ə'frʌnt] **1** *n* affront *m*, insulte *f*; **to suffer an affront** essuyer un affront; **it was an affront to her dignity** c'était un affront à sa dignité

2 *vt (offend)* faire un affront à, insulter, offenser; *(embarrass)* gêner; **to be** *or* **feel affronted** *(offended)* se sentir offensé; *(embarrassed)* se sentir gêné; *Scot Fam* **to be black affronted** *(angry)* être furax; *(embarrassed)* ne plus savoir où se mettre

Afghan ['æfgæn] **1** *n* (**a**) *(person)* Afghan(e) *m,f* (**b**) *(language)* afghan *m* (**c**) *(dog)* lévrier *m* afghan (**d**) *(coat)* afghan *m* (**e**) *Am (blanket)* couverture *f* en lainage

2 *adj* afghan

3 *comp (embassy)* d'Afghanistan; *(history)* de l'Afghanistan; *(teacher)* d'afghan

►► ***Afghan hound*** lévrier *m* afghan

Afghani [æf'gænɪ] **1** *n* (**a**) *(person)* Afghan(e) *m,f* (**b**) *(language)* afghan *m*

2 *adj* afghan

Afghanistan [æf'gænɪˌstæn] *n* Afghanistan *m*; **in Afghanistan** en Afghanistan

aficionado [əˌfɪsjə'nɑːdəʊ] *(pl* **aficionados***)* *n* aficionado *m*, amoureux(euse) *m,f*; **theatre aficionados, aficionados of the theatre** les aficionados du théâtre; **a tennis aficionado** un (une) mordu(e) de tennis

afield [ə'fild] *adv* **to go far afield** aller loin; **people came from as far afield as Australia** les gens venaient même d'Australie; **don't go too far afield** n'allez pas trop loin; **we didn't need to look very far afield** nous n'avions pas besoin de chercher très loin; **they travelled further afield for their holidays this year** ils sont allés bien plus loin cette année pour leurs vacances; *Fig* **this remark carried them even farther afield from the subject under debate** cette remarque les fit s'éloigner encore plus du sujet

afire [ə'faɪə(r)] *Literary* **1** *adj* (**a**) *(burning)* en feu, en flammes (**b**) *Fig (with emotion)* enflammé; **she was afire with passion** elle était enflammée par la passion

2 *adv* **to set sth afire** mettre le feu à qch; *Fig* embraser qch

AFL [ˌeɪef'el] *n Sport (abbr* **American Football League***)* = ligue professionnelle de football américain

aflame [ə'fleɪm] *Literary* **1** *adj* (**a**) *(burning)* en flammes, en feu

(**b**) *(emotionally)* enflammé; **to be aflame with desire/anger** être enflammé de désir/colère; **her cheeks were aflame with excitement** elle avait les joues rouges d'excitation, l'excitation lui enflammait les joues

(**c**) *(in colour)* **the sky was aflame with colour** le ciel flamboyait de couleurs vives; **the countryside was aflame with autumn reds and yellows** la campagne était embrasée de rouges et de jaunes d'automne

2 *adv* **to set aflame** mettre le feu à; *Fig* exciter, enflammer; **he set her heart aflame** il a fait battre son cœur

aflatoxin [ˌæflə'tɒksɪn] *n Med* aflatoxine *f*

AFL-CIO [ˌeɪef'elˌsiːaɪ'əʊ] *n Admin & Ind (abbr* **American Federation of Labor and Congress of Industrial Organizations***)* = la plus grande confédération syndicale américaine

afloat [ə'fləʊt] **1** *adj* (**a**) *(swimmer)* qui surnage; *(boat)* à flot; *(cork, oil)* flottant; *Fig (business)* à flot

(**b**) *(flooded)* inondé; **the bottom of the boat was afloat with water** le fond du bateau était inondé

2 *adv* (**a**) *(floating)* à flot, sur l'eau; **we managed to get** *or* **to set the raft afloat** nous avons réussi à mettre le radeau à flot; **to stay afloat** *(swimmer)* garder la tête hors de l'eau, surnager; *(boat)* rester à flot; **to keep afloat** rester à flot; **to keep sb/sth afloat** maintenir qn/qch à flot; *Fig* **to get a business afloat** *(from the start)* mettre une entreprise à flot; *(after financial difficulties)* renflouer une entreprise; **small businesses struggling to stay afloat** des petites entreprises qui luttent pour se maintenir à flot; **to get** *or* **to set a scheme afloat** lancer un projet; *Fin* **to keep bills afloat** faire circuler des effets

(**b**) *(on boat)* **a holiday spent afloat** *(on barge)* des vacances en péniche; *(at sea)* des vacances en mer

aflutter [ə'flʌtə(r)] **1** *adj* **to be (all) aflutter with excitement** tressaillir d'excitation; **my heart was all aflutter** j'avais le cœur qui battait la chamade

2 *adv* **she set my heart aflutter** elle fit battre mon cœur

AFM [ˌeɪef'em] *n TV (abbr* **assistant floor manager***)* régisseur *m* de plateau adjoint

afoot [ə'fʊt] **1** *adj* (**a**) *(in preparation)* **there's something afoot** il se prépare *ou* il se trame quelque chose; **there is a scheme afoot to build a new motorway** on a formé le projet *ou* on envisage de construire une nouvelle autoroute; **there was trouble afoot** des ennuis se préparaient (**b**) *Literary or Arch (on foot)* à pied

2 *adv Literary or Arch* à pied

afore [ə'fɔː(r)] *Arch* = **before**

aforementioned [ə'fɔːˌmenʃənd] *adj Formal* susmentionné, précité; **the aforementioned persons** lesdites personnes

aforenamed [ə'fɔːneɪmd] *adj Formal* susnommé, précité

aforesaid [ə'fɔːsed] *adj Formal* susdit, précité

aforethought [ə'fɔːθɔːt] *adj Formal* prémédité

a fortiori [ˌɑː'fɔːtɪɔːrɪ] *adv* a fortiori

afoul [ə'faʊl] *adv Literary* **to run afoul of sb** se mettre qn à dos, s'attirer le mécontentement de qn; **to run afoul of the law** avoir des ennuis avec la police

afraid [ə'freɪd] *adj* (**a**) *(frightened)* **to be afraid** avoir peur; **don't be afraid** n'ayez pas peur, ne craignez rien; **to make sb afraid** faire peur à qn; **to be afraid of sb/sth** avoir peur de qn/qch; **she is afraid of the dark** elle a peur du noir; **there's nothing to be afraid of** il n'y a rien à craindre; **she was afraid (that) the dog would** *or* **might bite her** elle avait peur *ou* elle craignait que le chien (ne) la morde; **he is afraid for his life** il craint pour sa vie; **she was afraid for her daughter** elle avait peur pour sa fille

(**b**) *(indicating reluctance, hesitation, worry)* **to be afraid that...** avoir peur *ou* craindre que + *subjunctive*...; **he isn't afraid of work** le travail ne lui fait pas peur; **don't be afraid to speak** *or*

of speaking your mind n'ayez pas peur de dire ce que vous pensez; **I'm afraid (that) I'll say the wrong thing** je crains *ou* j'ai peur de ne pas dire ce qu'il faut; **I was afraid that might happen** c'est bien ce que je craignais qu'il arrive; **that's (exactly) what I was afraid of!** c'est bien ce que je craignais!; **he was afraid to open his mouth** il n'osait pas dire un mot

(**c**) *(indicating regret)* **I'm afraid I won't be able to come** je regrette *ou* je suis désolé de ne pouvoir venir; **I'm afraid I can't help you** je regrette *ou* je suis désolé, mais je ne peux pas vous aider; **I'm afraid I cannot grant your request** je regrette de ne pas pouvoir accéder à votre requête; **I can't help you, I'm afraid** je suis désolé, je crois que je ne peux rien faire pour vous; **I'm afraid to say...** j'ai le regret de dire...; **I'm afraid so** j'ai bien peur que oui, j'en ai bien peur; **I'm afraid not** j'ai bien peur que non, j'en ai bien peur

'Who's Afraid of Virginia Woolf?' *Nichols, Albee* 'Qui a peur de Virginia Woolf?'

afresh [ə'freʃ] *adv* de nouveau; **to look at a problem afresh** jeter un nouveau regard sur un problème; **we'll have to start afresh** il va falloir recommencer *ou* reprendre à zéro

Africa ['æfrɪkə] *n* Afrique *f*; **in Africa** en Afrique

African ['æfrɪkən] **1** *n* Africain(e) *m,f*

2 *adj* africain

►► ***African American*** **1** *n* Noir(e) *m,f* américain(e) **2** *adj* noir américain; *Bot* ***African marigold*** rose *f* d'Inde; *Pol* ***African National Congress*** Congrès *m* national africain, ANC *m*; *Bot* ***African violet*** saintpaulia *m*

Africanism ['æfrɪkənɪzəm] *n* africanisme *m*

Africanist ['æfrɪkənɪst] *n* africaniste *mf*

Africanization [,æfrɪkənaɪ'zeɪʃən] *n* africanisation *f*

Africanize, -ise ['æfrɪkənaɪz] *vt* africaniser

Afrikaaner [,æfrɪ'kɑ:nə(r)] **1** *n* Afrikaner *mf*, Afrikaander *mf*

2 *adj* afrikaner, afrikaander

Afrikaans [,æfrɪ'kɑ:ns] *n (language)* afrikaans *m*

Afrikaner [,æfrɪ'kɑ:nə(r)] *n* Afrikaner *mf*, Afrikaander *mf*

Afro ['æfrəʊ] *(pl* **Afros***)* **1** *adj (hairstyle)* afro

2 *n* coiffure *f* afro

Afro-American 1 *n* Afro-Américain(e) *m,f*

2 *adj* afro-américain

Afro-Asian 1 *n* Afro-Asiatique *mf*

2 *adj* afro-asiatique

Afro-Caribbean 1 *n* Afro-antillais(e) *m,f*

2 *adj* afro-antillais

Afro-Cuban 1 *n* Afro-cubain(e) *m,f*

2 *adj* afro-cubain

AFT [,eɪef'ti:] *n (abbr* **American Federation of Teachers***)* = syndicat américain d'enseignants

aft [ɑ:ft] **1** *adv Naut & Aviat* à *ou* vers l'arrière; **to go aft** aller à *ou* vers l'arrière; **aft of the mast** sur l'arrière du mât; **to have the wind dead aft** avoir le vent en poupe

2 *adj Naut (deck)* arrière

AFTER ['ɑ:ftə(r)]

après	► 1 (a) – (g); 2; 3
derrière	► 1 (e)
d'après	► 1 (h)
ensuite	► 2
après que	► 3

1 *prep* (**a**) *(in time → gen)* après; *(→ period)* après, au bout de; **after a while** au bout d'un moment, après un moment; **after breakfast** après le petit déjeuner; **after dark** après la tombée de la nuit; **the day after the battle** le lendemain de la bataille; **after which she left** après quoi elle est partie; **it is after six o'clock already** il est déjà six heures passées *ou* plus de six heures; **shortly after midday/three** peu après midi/trois heures; *Am* **it's twenty after eight** il est huit heures vingt; **the day after tomorrow** après-demain *m*; **after this date** passé *ou* après cette date

(**b**) *(in space)* après; **the shopping centre is just after the church** le centre commercial est juste après l'église; **there ought to be a comma after "however"** il devrait y avoir une virgule après "however"

(**c**) *(in series, priority etc)* après; **Rothman comes after Richardson** Rothman vient après Richardson; **I would put Racine after Molière** pour moi Racine passe après Molière; **after you** *(politely)* après vous (je vous en prie); **after you with the paper** tu peux me passer le journal quand tu l'auras fini

(**d**) *(following consecutively)* **day after day** jour après jour; **time after time** maintes (et maintes) fois; **(for) mile after mile** sur des kilomètres et des kilomètres; **he's made mistake after mistake** il a fait erreur sur erreur; **generation after generation of farmers** des générations entières de fermiers; **there was street after street of apartment blocks** rue après rue, les immeubles se succédaient; **it's been one crisis after another ever since she arrived** on va de crise en crise depuis son arrivée

(**e**) *(behind)* après, derrière; **close the door after you** fermez la porte derrière vous; **he locked up after them** il a tout fermé après leur départ *ou* après qu'ils soient partis; **don't expect me to clean up after you** ne croyez pas que je vais nettoyer derrière vous

(**f**) *(in view of)* après; **I'll never speak to him again, after what he said to me** je ne lui parlerai plus jamais après ce qu'il m'a dit; **after the way I've been treated** après la façon dont on m'a traité; **after what you told me** après ce que vous m'avez dit; **and after all I've done for them!** et après tout ce que j'ai fait pour eux!

(**g**) *(in spite of)* **after all the trouble I took, no one came** après *ou* malgré tout le mal que je me suis donné, personne n'est venu

(**h**) *(in the manner of)* **after Rubens** d'après Rubens

(**i**) *(in search of)* **to be after sb/sth** chercher qn/qch; **she's after you** elle te cherche; *(angry with)* elle t'en veut; *(attracted to)* tu l'intéresses; **the police are after him** la police est à ses trousses, il est recherché par la police; **their mother always seems to be after them** leur mère a l'air de ne jamais les laisser tranquilles; **he's after her money** il en veut à son argent; *Fam* **what's he after?** *(want)* qu'est-ce qu'il veut?❑; *(looking for)* qu'est-ce qu'il cherche?❑; *(intend)* qu'est-ce qu'il a derrière la tête?; *Fam* **I know what she's after** je sais où elle veut en venir; **she's after a full-time job** elle cherche un travail à temps plein

(**j**) *(as verb complement)* **to ask** *or* **to inquire after sb** demander des nouvelles de qn; *Br* **to name a child after sb** donner à un enfant le nom de qn; **to run after sb** courir après qn; **they ran after him** ils lui ont couru après

2 *adv* après, ensuite; **the day after** le lendemain, le jour suivant; **the night after** la nuit d'après; **two days after** deux jours après *ou* plus tard; **the week after** la semaine d'après *ou* suivante; **for months after** pendant des mois après; **soon after** peu après; **long after** longtemps après; **to follow (on) after** suivre

3 *conj (when subject changes)* après que + *indicative ou Fam subjunctive; (when subject stays the same)* après + *infinitive*; **come and see me after you have spoken to him** venez me voir quand vous lui aurez parlé; **I came after he had left** je suis arrivé après qu'il soit parti; **after I had seen him I went out** après l'avoir vu, je suis sorti; **after saying goodnight to the children** après avoir dit bonsoir aux enfants; **was that before or after you'd signed the contract?** était-ce avant ou après que vous ayez signé le contrat?

4 *adj* (**a**) *(later)* **in after life** *or* **years** plus tard dans la vie

(**b**) *Naut (cabin, hold, mast)* arrière

5 afters *npl Br Fam* dessert❑ *m*; **what's for afters?** qu'est-ce qu'il y a pour le dessert *ou* comme dessert?; **there was ice cream for afters** il y avait de la glace en dessert *ou* pour le dessert

6 after all *adv* (**a**) *(when all's said and done)* après tout; **after all, she is very young** après tout, elle est très jeune; **that, after all, is why we came** après tout, c'est pour ça qu'on est venus; **it only costs £5 after all** ça ne coûte que cinq livres après tout

(**b**) *(against expectation)* après *ou* malgré tout; **so she was right after all** alors elle avait raison en fait; **so you went to the party after all?** alors, finalement, tu es allé à la soirée?

7 one after another, one after the other *adv* l'un après l'autre; **one after another they got up and left the room** l'un après l'autre, ils se levèrent et quittèrent la pièce; **he made several mistakes one after the other** il a fait plusieurs fautes d'affilée *ou* à la file

afterbirth ['ɑ:ftəbɜ:θ] *n Obst* placenta *m*

afterburner ['ɑ:ftəbɜ:nə(r)] *n Aviat* dispositif *m* de postcombustion; *Aut* catalyseur *m* de postcombustion

afterburning ['ɑ:ftəbɜ:nɪŋ] *n Aviat & Aut* postcombustion *f*, réchauffe *f*

aftercare ['ɑ:ftəkeə(r)] *n* (**a**) *Med (after treatment)* postcure *f*; *Obst (after giving birth)* soins *mpl* post-natals; *(after operation)* soins *mpl* postopératoires; **good aftercare facilities** un bon suivi médical (**b**) *(of prisoner)* suivi *m (après la sortie de prison)*

afterdamp ['ɑ:ftədæmp] *n Chem & Mining* gaz *mpl* délétères

afterdeck ['ɑ:ftədek] *n Naut* plage *f* arrière

after-dinner *adj (speaker, speech)* de fin de dîner *ou* banquet; **an after-dinner drink** ≃ un digestif

after-effect ['ɑ:ftərɪ,fekt] *n (usu pl) (of drug)* effet *m* secondaire; *Fig (of remark, event etc)* répercussion *f*, contrecoup *m*; **the after-effects of war** les séquelles *fpl ou* les répercussions *fpl* de la guerre; **I'm still feeling the after-effects of last night's drinking** je ne me suis toujours pas remis de ce que j'ai bu hier soir

afterglow ['ɑ:ftəgləʊ] *n* (**a**) *(of sunset)* dernières lueurs *fpl*, derniers reflets *mpl*; *Fig (of pleasure)* sensation *f* de bien-être *(après coup)*; *Fig* **he was basking in the warm afterglow of his triumph** il savourait le sentiment de volupté dans lequel son triomphe l'avait laissé (**b**) *Comput (on screen)* rémanence *f*

aftergrass ['ɑ:ftəgrɑ:s] *n Agr* regain *m*

aftergrowth ['ɑ:ftəgrəʊθ] *n Agr* regain *m*; *Fig (aftermath)* développement *m*

afterheat ['ɑ:ftəhi:t] *n Phys* chaleur *f* résiduelle

after-hours 1 *adj (after closing time)* qui suit la fermeture; *(after work)* qui suit le travail; *Br* **after-hours drinking** = verres servis après l'heure de fermeture légale des pubs; *Am* **an after-hours bar** un bar de nuit

2 after hours *adv (after closing time)* après la fermeture; *(after work)* après le travail

►► *St Exch* ***after-hours dealing*** transactions *fpl* hors Bourse; *St Exch* ***after-hours market*** marché *m* hors Bourse; *St Exch* ***after-hours trading*** transactions *fpl* hors Bourse

afterimage ['ɑ:ftər,ɪmɪdʒ] *n Opt* image *f* récurrente *ou* consécutive; *TV* rémanence *f* à l'extinction

afterlife ['ɑ:ftəlaɪf] *n Rel* au-delà *m*, vie *f* après la mort; **we shall meet in the afterlife** nous nous retrouverons dans l'au-delà

after-lunch *adj* qui suit le déjeuner; **to have an after-lunch nap** faire la sieste

aftermarket ['ɑ:ftəmɑ:kɪt] *n St Exch* marché *m* secondaire

aftermath ['ɑ:ftəmæθ] *n* (**a**) *(of event)* séquelles *fpl*, suites *fpl*; **the aftermath of war** *(after-effects)* les répercussions *fpl ou* le contrecoup de la guerre; *(period)* l'après-guerre *m*; **in the aftermath of the military coup** à la suite du coup d'État militaire; **in the immediate aftermath** tout de suite après, dans la foulée (**b**) *Agr (second mowing or crop)* regain *m*

aftermost ['ɑ:ftəməʊst] *adj Naut* le plus en arrière, le plus à l'arrière

afternoon [,ɑ:ftə'nu:n] **1** *n* après-midi *m inv or f inv*; **this afternoon** cet après-midi; **every afternoon** tous les après-midi; **all afternoon** tout l'après-midi; **tomorrow/yesterday afternoon** demain/hier après-midi; **in the afternoon** *(in general)* l'après-midi; *(of particular day)* (dans) l'après-midi; **on Friday afternoons** le vendredi après-midi; **on Friday afternoon** *(in general)* le vendredi après-midi; *(of particular day)* vendredi après-midi; **in the early afternoon** tôt dans l'après-midi; **at two o'clock in the afternoon** à deux heures de l'après-midi; **on the afternoon**

of 16 May (dans) l'après-midi du 16 mai; **on a summer afternoon** par un après-midi d'été; **good afternoon** *(hello)* bonjour; *(goodbye)* au revoir; **have a nice afternoon!** bon après-midi!

2 *comp (class, train)* de l'après-midi; *(walk)* qui a lieu dans l'après-midi

3 **afternoons** *adv esp Am* (dans) l'après-midi

►► ***afternoon nap*** sieste *f*; *Cin & Theat* ***afternoon performance*** matinée *f*; ***afternoon snack*** goûter *m*; ***afternoon tea*** = thé pris avec une légère collation dans le cours de l'après-midi; **to have afternoon tea** prendre le thé *(dans le cours de l'après-midi)*

afterpains ['ɑːftəpeɪnz] *npl Obst* tranchées *fpl* utérines

after-sales *adj Mktg* après-vente *(inv)*

►► ***after-sales department*** service *m* après-vente; ***after-sales marketing*** marketing *m* après-vente, MAV *m*; ***after-sales service*** service *m* après-vente

after-school *adj (activities)* extrascolaire

aftershave ['ɑːftəʃeɪv] *n* (lotion *f*) après-rasage *m*, (lotion *f*) after-shave *m*

►► ***aftershave lotion*** (lotion *f*) après-rasage *m*, (lotion *f*) after-shave *m*

after-shaving lotion *n Am* (lotion *f*) après-rasage *m*, (lotion *f*) after-shave *m*

aftershock ['ɑːftəʃɒk] *n Geol* réplique *f* (d'un séisme)

aftersun ['ɑːftəsʌn] *n* crème *f* après-soleil

►► ***aftersun cream*** crème *f* après-soleil

aftertaste ['ɑːftəteɪst] *n also Fig* arrière-goût *m*

after-tax *adj Fin (profits)* après impôts, net d'impôt; *(salary)* net d'impôt

afterthought ['ɑːftəθɔːt] *n* pensée *f* après coup; **I had an afterthought** j'ai pensé après coup; **I only mentioned it as an afterthought** j'en ai seulement parlé après coup, quand l'idée m'est venue; **the west wing was added as an afterthought** l'aile ouest a été ajoutée après coup

afterwards ['ɑːftəwədz], *Am* **afterward** ['æftərwərd] *adv* après, ensuite; **afterwards they went home** ensuite *ou* après ils sont rentrés chez eux; **a long time afterwards** longtemps après; **soon** *or* **shortly afterwards** peu de temps après; **I only realized afterwards** je n'ai compris qu'après coup *ou* que plus tard

afterword ['ɑːftəwɜːd] *n (postscript)* postface *f*; *(epilogue)* épilogue *m*

afterworld ['ɑːftəwɜːld] *n Rel* **the afterworld** l'au-delà *m*

AG *Am (written abbr* **Attorney General**) ≃ ministre *m* de la Justice

Aga® ['ɑːgə] *n* = cuisinière en fonte à l'ancienne

►► *Br Hum* ***Aga saga*** = roman ayant pour thème la vie sentimentale d'une femme au foyer aisée

AGAIN [ə'gen]

encore (une fois)	► (a)
ne ...plus	► (b)
re- + *verbe*	► (c)
déjà	► (d)
d'ailleurs	► (f)

adv (**a**) *(once more)* encore une fois, de nouveau; **once again** encore une fois, une fois de plus; **it's me again!** c'est encore moi, me revoici!; **here we are back home again!** nous revoilà chez nous!; **you'll soon be well again** vous serez bientôt remis; **(the) same again please!** *(in bar)* remettez-nous ça *ou* la même chose s'il vous plaît!; **yet again** encore une fois

(**b**) *(with negative)* ne... plus; **I didn't see them again** je ne les ai plus revus; **not again!** encore?; **not you again!** encore vous?; **never again!** *(after bad experience)* plus jamais!; **again and again, time and (time) again** maintes et maintes fois, à maintes reprises; **I have told you so again and again** je vous l'ai dit vingt fois *ou* cent fois; **she read the passage through over and over again** elle a lu et relu le passage

(**c**) *(with verbs)* **to begin again** recommencer; **to come again** revenir; **to do again** refaire; **if I had to do it again** si c'était à refaire; **don't do it again!** ne recommencez pas!; **can you say it again?** pouvez-vous répéter?; **don't make me have to tell you again!** et que je n'aie pas à vous le répéter!

(**d**) *(indicating forgetfulness)* déjà; **what's her name again?** comment s'appelle-t-elle déjà?; **what did he say again?** qu'est-ce qu'il a dit déjà?

(**e**) *(in quantity)* **as much/many again** encore autant; **half as much again** encore la moitié de ça; **half as many pages again** la moitié plus de pages; **it's as long/wide/far again as that** ça fait encore la même longueur/largeur/distance que ça

(**f**) *(furthermore)* d'ailleurs, qui plus est; **again, I am not sure that...** d'ailleurs je ne suis pas sûr que...

AGAINST [ə'genst]

contre	► 1 (a) – (c), (e) – (h), (l); 2
à l'encontre de	► 1 (d)
en prévision de	► 1 (i)
par rapport à	► 1 (k)
en échange de	► 1 (l)

1 *prep* (**a**) *(indicating position)* contre; **he leant his bike (up) against the wall** il appuya son vélo contre le mur; **she had her nose pressed against the window** elle avait le nez écrasé au carreau; **put the chairs (back) against the wall** remettez les chaises contre le mur; **he was standing with his back against the wall** il était adossé contre le mur *ou* au mur

(**b**) *(indicating impact)* contre; **I banged my knee against the chair** je me suis cogné le genou contre la chaise; **the shutter was banging against the window** le volet claquait contre la fenêtre

(**c**) *(in the opposite direction to → current, stream, grain)* contre

(**d**) *(contrary to → rules, principles)* à l'encontre de; **to go against a trend** s'opposer à une *ou* aller à l'encontre d'une tendance; **it's against the law** c'est illégal *ou* contraire à la loi; **it's against the law to steal** le vol est interdit par la loi; **there's no law against it** il n'y a pas de loi qui s'y oppose; **they sold the farm against my advice/wishes** ils ont vendu la ferme sans tenir compte de mes conseils/de ce que je souhaitais

(**e**) *(indicating opposition to → person, proposal, government)* contre; **the fight against inflation/crime** la lutte contre l'inflation/la criminalité; **to decide against sth** décider de ne pas faire qch; **to vote against sth** voter contre qch; **you're either for us or against us** tu dois être avec nous ou contre nous; **she's against telling him** elle trouve qu'on ne devrait pas le lui dire; **I advised her against going** je lui ai déconseillé d'y aller; **what have you got against him/the idea?** qu'est-ce que vous avez contre lui/l'idée?; **what have you got against going?** pourquoi vous n'avez pas envie d'y aller?; **to have nothing against sth** ne rien avoir contre qch; **I've nothing against it** je n'ai rien contre

(**f**) *(unfavourable to)* contre; **conditions were against them** les conditions leur étaient défavorables; **his appearance is against him** son physique ne joue pas en sa faveur

(**g**) *(in competition with)* contre; *Ftbl* **United against Everton** United contre Everton; *Sport* **to run against sb** courir contre qn; *Pol* se présenter contre qn; **a race against time** *or* **the clock** une course contre la montre

(**h**) *(indicating defence, protection, precaution etc)* contre; **protected against the cold** protégé contre le froid; **an injection against measles** une injection contre la rougeole; **to insure against accidents** *(insurer)* assurer contre les accidents; *(client)* s'assurer contre les accidents; **to be insured against theft** être assuré contre le vol; **against all risks** contre tous les risques

(**i**) *Formal (in preparation for)* en vue de, en prévision de; **to save money against one's retirement** faire des économies en prévision de *ou* pour la retraite

(**j**) *(in contrast to)* contre, sur; **to stand against the light** être à contre-jour; **the tall chimneys stood out against the sky** les hautes cheminées se détachaient sur le ciel; **yellow flowers against a green background** des fleurs jaunes sur un fond vert; **the red stood out against the grey** le rouge contrastait avec le gris; *Fig* **these events took place against a background of political violence** ces événements ont eu lieu dans un climat de violence politique

(**k**) *(in comparison to, in relation to)* en comparaison de, par rapport à; **to check sth against a list** vérifier qch d'après une liste; **they cost £10 here (as) against only £7 at the supermarket** ils coûtent 10 livres ici contre *ou* au lieu de 7 livres au supermarché; *Fin* **the dollar rose/fell against the yen** le dollar a augmenté/baissé par rapport au yen; **to plot the number of passengers against distance travelled** *(in graph)* relever le nombre de voyageurs par rapport à la distance parcourue

(**l**) *(in exchange for)* contre, en échange de; **to issue a ticket against payment of...** remettre un ticket en contrepartie du paiement de...; **cash is available against presentation of the voucher** ce bon peut être échangé contre de l'argent

2 *adv* contre; **are you for or against?** êtes-vous pour ou contre?; **the odds are 10 to 1 against** *(gen)* il y a une chance sur dix; *(in horseracing)* la cote est à 10 contre 1

Agamemnon [ˌægə'memnən] *pr n Myth* Agamemnon

agami [ə'gɑːmɪ] *n Orn* agami *m*, oiseau-trompette *m*

agamic [eɪ'gæmɪk] *adj Bot* agame

agapanthus [ˌægə'pænθəs] *n Bot* agapanthe *f*

agape [ə'geɪp] *adj* bouche bée *(inv)*; **to stand agape** rester bouche bée

agar ['eɪgə(r)], **agar-agar** [ˌeɪgə'eɪgə(r)] *n Bot & Culin* agar-agar *m*, gélose *f*

agaric ['ægərɪk] *n Bot* agaric *m*

agate ['ægɪt] 1 *n Miner* agate *f*

2 *comp (brooch)* en agate

agave [ə'geɪvɪ] *n Bot* agave *m*

AGC [ˌeɪdʒiː'siː] *n Rad & Elec (abbr* **Automatic Gain Control**) antifading *m*

AGE [eɪdʒ]

âge	► 1 (a), (c), (d)
vieillesse	► 1 (c)
époque	► 1 (d)
éternité	► 1 (e)
vieillir	► 2; 3

1 *n* (**a**) *(of person, animal, tree, building)* âge *m*; **what age is he?** quel âge a-t-il?; **he is twenty-five years of age** il est âgé de vingt-cinq ans; **at the age of twenty-five** à l'âge de vingt-cinq ans; **when I was your age** quand j'avais votre âge; **she's the same age as me** *or* **as I am** elle a le même âge que moi; **his wife is only half his age** sa femme n'a que la moitié de son âge; **she's twice my age** elle a le double de mon âge; **I have a son your age** j'ai un fils de votre âge; **she's the same age as me** *or* **as I am** elle a le même âge que moi; **they're the same age** ils sont du même âge, ils ont le même âge; **people of all ages** des gens de tout âge; **people over the age of fifty** les gens de plus de cinquante ans; **he lived to a ripe old age** il a vécu jusqu'à un bel âge *ou* très vieux; **she doesn't look her age** elle ne fait pas son âge; **I'm beginning to feel my age** je commence à me sentir vieux; **act** *or* **be your age!** *(be reasonable)* sois raisonnable!; *(don't be silly)* ne sois pas stupide!; **he is at** *or* **of an age when he should consider settling down** il est à un âge où il devrait penser à se ranger; **the two of them were of an age** ils étaient tous les deux à peu près du même âge; **at your age you should know** à ton âge, tu devrais savoir; **at that age children need a lot of attention** c'est un âge où les enfants demandent beaucoup d'attention; **fifteen is the worst age** quinze ans est l'âge le plus difficile

(**b**) *(adulthood) Law* **to be of age** être majeur; **to come of age** atteindre sa majorité, devenir majeur; *Fig* **this way of thinking has at last come of age** c'est un point de vue qui a fait son chemin; *Law* **to be under age** être mineur; *(not old enough to buy alcohol etc)* ne pas avoir l'âge

(**c**) *(old age → of person)* âge *m*, vieillesse *f*; *(→ of wood, paper, wine)* âge *m*; **bent with age** courbé par l'âge; **yellow** *or* **yellowed with age** jauni par l'âge; **wisdom comes with age** la sagesse vient avec l'âge; **age has not been kind to her** elle est marquée par l'âge; **the house is falling to pieces with age** la maison tombe de vieillesse *ou* de vétusté; **the car's beginning to show its age** la voiture commence à donner des signes de vieillesse; **you're showing your age!** *(remembering things like that)* tu es d'un autre âge!; *(you've lost touch)* tu te fais vieux!; *Hum* **age before beauty!** *(when letting someone enter first)* c'est le privilège de l'âge

(**d**) *(period → historical)* époque *f*, âge *m*; *Geol* âge *m*; **the age we live in** notre siècle, le siècle où nous vivons; **in our age** à notre époque; **in an earlier age this wouldn't have been tolerated** il fut un temps où on n'aurait pas toléré cela; **she is the product of an earlier age** elle est d'un autre temps; **in this age of consumerism** en cette ère de consumérisme; **through the ages** à travers les âges

(**e**) *(usu pl) (long time)* éternité *f*; **she was an age getting dressed, it took her an age to get dressed** elle a mis un temps fou à s'habiller; **I haven't seen you for** *or* **in ages!** cela fait une éternité que je ne vous ai (pas) vu!; **I've been waiting (for) ages** cela fait une éternité que j'attends; **it took him ages to do the work** il a mis très longtemps à faire le travail; **it's expensive, but it lasts for ages** c'est cher, mais ça dure très longtemps

2 *vi* vieillir, prendre de l'âge; **he's beginning to age** il commence à se faire vieux; **to age ten years** vieillir de dix ans; **he had aged beyond recognition** il avait tellement vieilli qu'on ne le reconnaissait plus; **to age well** *(person)* vieillir bien; *(wine, cheese)* s'améliorer en vieillissant; **he has aged a lot** il a beaucoup vieilli

3 *vt* (**a**) *(person)* vieillir; **the years had aged him** il avait beaucoup vieilli; **illness has aged her** la maladie l'a vieillie

(**b**) *(wine, cheese)* laisser vieillir *ou* mûrir; **aged in the wood** vieilli en fût

►► ***age bracket*** tranche *f* d'âge; ***Age Concern*** = association caritative britannique d'aide aux personnes âgées; *Law* ***the age of consent*** = l'âge où les rapports sexuels sont autorisés; **they are below the age of consent** ils tombent sous le coup de la loi sur la protection des mineurs; ***the age of discretion*** = âge auquel une personne est jugée apte à prendre ses responsabilités; ***age group*** tranche *f* d'âge; **the twenty to thirty age group** la tranche d'âge des vingt à trente ans; **the younger age group** les jeunes *mpl*; ***age limit*** limite *f* d'âge; ***the age of reason*** l'âge *m* de raison; *Hist* ***Age of Reason*** siècle *m* des lumières; ***age ring*** *(on tree)* cerne *m*

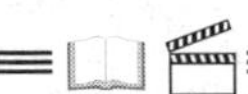

'The Age of Innocence' *Wharton, Scorsese* 'L'Âge de l'innocence' (roman), 'Le Temps de l'innocence' (film)

aged 1 *adj* (**a**) [eɪdʒd] *(of the age of)* **a man aged fifty** un homme (âgé) de cinquante ans (**b**) ['eɪdʒɪd] *(old)* âgé, vieux (vieille); **my aged aunt** ma vieille tante

2 *npl* ['eɪdʒɪd] **the aged** les personnes *fpl* âgées, les vieux *mpl*

ageing ['eɪdʒɪŋ] **1** *adj* (**a**) *(person)* vieillissant, qui se fait vieux (vieille); *(society)* de vieux; *(machinery, car)* qui se fait vieux (vieille); **the ageing process** le processus du vieillissement (**b**) *(clothes, hairstyle)* qui vieillit

2 *n* (**a**) *(of society, population)* vieillissement *m* (**b**) *(of wine, cheese)* vieillissement *m*

ageism ['eɪdʒɪzəm] *n* âgisme *m*

ageist ['eɪdʒɪst] **1** *adj (action, policy)* qui relève de l'âgisme

2 *n* = personne qui fait preuve d'âgisme

ageless ['eɪdʒlɪs] *adj (person)* sans âge, qui n'a pas d'âge; *(work of art)* intemporel; *(beauty)* toujours jeune

agency ['eɪdʒənsɪ] (*pl* **agencies**) *n* (**a**) *(for employment)* agence *f*, bureau *m*; *(for travel, accommodation)* agence *f*

(**b**) *Admin* service *m*, bureau *m*; **international aid agencies** des organisations *fpl* d'aide internationale; **a government agency** une agence gouvernementale

(**c**) *(intermediary → of person)* intermédiaire *m*, entremise *f*; *(→ of fate)* jeu *m*; *(→ of light, water)* action *f*; **through her agency** par son entremise, grâce à elle; **by the agency of direct sunlight** par l'action directe des rayons du soleil

►► *Com* ***agency agreement*** accord *m* de représentation; ***agency fee*** frais *mpl* d'agence; *Banking* commission *f* de gestion; *Am* ***Agency for International Development*** = agence américaine pour le développement international; *Com* ***agency work*** travail *m* pour une agence

agenda [ə'dʒendə] *n* (**a**) *(for meeting)* ordre *m* du jour; *(for activities)* programme *m*; **what's on today's agenda?, what's on the agenda (for) today?** *(for meeting)* quel est l'ordre du jour?; *(for activities)* qu'est-ce qu'il y a au programme pour aujourd'hui?; *Fig* **drugs are back on the agenda** la drogue revient à la une de l'actualité; **the problem of the homeless doesn't come very high on the government's agenda** le problème des sans-abri ne figure pas parmi les priorités du gouvernement; *Fig* **it was top of the agenda** c'était prioritaire; **to set the agenda** mener le jeu

(**b**) *(set of priorities)* **to have one's own agenda** avoir son propre programme

agent ['eɪdʒənt] *n* (**a**) *Com* agent *m*, représentant(e) *m,f*; *(for travel, insurance)* agent *m*; *(for firm)* concessionnaire *mf*; *(for brand)* dépositaire *mf*; **he acted as my local agent** il agissait en tant qu'agent local; **the firm are sole agents for Pitkins** la société est agent exclusif de Pitkins; **where's the nearest Jaguar agent?** où est le concessionnaire Jaguar le plus proche?

(**b**) *(for actor, sportsman, writer)* agent *m*

(**c**) *(spy)* agent *m*

(**d**) *(means)* agent *m*, moyen *m*; **by the working of some outside agent** par l'opération de quelque agent extérieur; **to be the agent of sth** être le moteur *ou* la cause de qch; **an agent of change** *(key person)* un acteur *m*; **the agent of change was the revolution** la révolution était le moteur du changement; **her forceful nature turned out to be the agent of her downfall** son naturel énergique fut aussi la cause *ou* à l'origine de sa chute

(**e**) *Chem & Ling* agent *m*

(**f**) *Comput (software)* logiciel *m* client

►► *Chem & Mil* ***Agent Orange*** agent *m* orange *(défoliant utilisé par les Américains pendant la guerre du Viêt-nam)*; ***agent provocateur*** (agent *m*) provocateur *m*

agentive ['eɪdʒəntɪv] *n Gram* agentif *m*

age-old *adj* séculaire, antique

ageratum [ædʒə'reɪtəm] *n Bot* agérate *m*

agg assault [æg-] *n Am Fam* coups *mpl* et blessures *fpl*❑

agglomerate 1 *vt* [ə'glɒməreɪt] agglomérer

2 *vi* [ə'glɒməreɪt] s'agglomérer

3 *n* [ə'glɒmərət] *Geol* agglomérat *m*

4 *adj* [ə'glɒmərət] aggloméré

agglomeration [ə,glɒmə'reɪʃən] *n* agglomération *f*

agglomerative [ə'glɒmərətɪv] *adj* agglomératif

agglutinant [ə'glu:tɪnənt] **1** *n* agglutinant *m*

2 *adj* agglutinant

agglutinate 1 *vt* [ə'glu:tɪneɪt] agglutiner

2 *vi* [ə'glu:tɪneɪt] s'agglutiner

3 *adj* [ə'glu:tɪnət] agglutiné

agglutinating [ə'glu:tɪneɪtɪŋ] *adj* agglutinant

agglutination [ə,glu:tɪ'neɪʃən] *n* agglutination *f*

agglutinative [ə'glu:tɪnətɪv] *adj* agglutinant

aggrandize, -ise [ə'grændaɪz] *vt Pej* agrandir; *(one's importance, role)* grossir, grandir

aggrandizement [ə'grændɪzmənt] *n Pej* agrandissement *m*; **personal aggrandizement** volonté *f* de se pousser en avant

aggravate ['ægrəveɪt] *vt* (**a**) *(worsen → illness, conditions)* aggraver; *(→ situation, problem)* aggraver, envenimer; *(→ quarrel)* envenimer (**b**) *Fam (irritate → person)* agacer❑, exaspérer❑

►► *Law* ***aggravated assault*** coups *mpl* et blessures *fpl*; *Law* ***aggravated burglary*** cambriolage *m* aggravé de coups et blessures

aggravating ['ægrəveɪtɪŋ] *adj* (**a**) *(worsening → situation, illness, conditions)* aggravant (**b**) *Fam (irritating → person, problem)* agaçant❑, exaspérant❑; **I've had a very aggravating day** j'ai passé une journée atroce

aggravatingly ['ægrəveɪtɪŋlɪ] *adv Fam (irritatingly)* d'une manière agaçante *ou* exaspérante❑; **he's aggravatingly smug** il est d'une suffisance insupportable

aggravation [,ægrə'veɪʃən] *n* (**a**) *(of situation, crime, illness)* aggravation *f*; *(of wound, quarrel)* envenimement *m* (**b**) *Fam (irritation)* agacement❑ *m*, exaspération❑ *f*; **he does nothing but cause aggravation** il ne fait qu'embêter le monde; **I don't want to give** *or* **cause any more aggravation** je ne veux plus embêter qui que ce soit (**c**) *Fam (cause of irritation)* circonstance *f* agaçante *ou* exaspérante❑

aggregate 1 *n* ['ægrɪgət] (**a**) *(total)* ensemble *m*, total *m*; **in the aggregate, on aggregate** dans l'ensemble, globalement; *Sport* **to win on aggregate** gagner au total des points ou des buts

(**b**) *Constr & Geol* agrégat *m*

2 *adj* ['ægrɪgət] (**a**) *(total)* global, total; **for an aggregate period of three years** pendant trois ans en tout

(**b**) *Bot & Geol* agrégé

3 *vt* ['ægrɪgeɪt] (**a**) *(bring together)* rassembler (**b**) *(add up to)* s'élever à, se monter à

►► *Fin* ***aggregate amount*** montant *m* global; *Com & Econ* ***aggregate economic activity*** ensemble *m* des activités économiques; *Fin* ***aggregate figure*** chiffre *m* global; *Fin* ***aggregate income*** revenus *mpl* globaux; *Fin* ***aggregate net increment*** accroissement *m* global net; *Com* ***aggregate output*** production *f* globale

aggression [ə'greʃən] *n* (**a**) *(attack)* agression *f* (**b**) *(aggressiveness)* agressivité *f*

aggressive [ə'gresɪv] *adj* (**a**) *(gen) & Psy* agressif (**towards** envers) (**b**) *Mil (action, weapon)* offensif (**c**) *(businessperson)* combatif, dynamique; *(campaign)* énergique

aggressively [ə'gresɪvlɪ] *adv* (**a**) *(behave)* agressivement, avec agressivité; *(say)* d'un ton agressif; *(look at)* d'un air agressif (**b**) *(sell)* énergiquement, avec dynamisme; *(campaign)* avec dynamisme

aggressiveness [ə'gresɪvnɪs] *n* (**a**) *(gen)* agressivité *f* (**b**) *(of businessperson)* combativité *f*; *(of campaign)* dynamisme *m*, fougue *f*

aggressor [ə'gresə(r)] *n* agresseur *m*

aggrieved [ə'gri:vd] *adj* (**a**) *(gen)* contrarié (**at** *or* **about** par), mécontent (**at** *or* **about** de) (**b**) *Law* lésé; **the aggrieved party** la partie lésée

aggro ['ægrəʊ] *n Br Fam (UNCOUNT)* (**a**) *(violence, fighting)* grabuge *m*, bagarre *f*; **there was a bit of aggro at the pub last night** il y a eu du grabuge *ou* ça a chauffé au pub hier soir

(**b**) *(fuss, bother)* histoires *fpl*; **people don't complain because they don't want any aggro** les gens ne se plaignent pas parce qu'ils ne veulent pas d'histoires; **there has been a lot of aggro at work recently** il y a eu pas mal d'histoires au boulot dernièrement; **my Mum's giving me so much aggro at the moment** ma mère est toujours sur mon dos en ce moment

aghast [ə'gɑ:st] *adj (astounded)* interloqué, pantois; *(horrified)* horrifié, atterré; **she was aghast at the news** elle était atterrée par la nouvelle; **I stared at him aghast** je l'ai regardé, atterré

agile [*Br* 'ædʒaɪl, *Am* 'ædʒəl] *adj* (**a**) *(person, animal)* agile, leste (**b**) *(brain, mind)* vif

agilely [*Br* 'ædʒaɪllɪ, *Am* 'ædʒəllɪ] *adv* (**a**) *(move, jump)* agilement, avec agilité (**b**) *(argue, reason)* adroitement

agility [ə'dʒɪlətɪ] *n* (**a**) *(physical)* agilité *f*, souplesse *f*; **to move with great agility** se déplacer avec une grande agilité (**b**) *(mental)* vivacité *f*

Agincourt ['ædʒɪnkɔ:t] *n* Azincourt

aging, agism *etc* = **ageing, ageism** *etc*

agio ['ædʒɪəʊ] (*pl* **agios**) *n Fin* (**a**) *(price)* agio *m*, prix *m* du change (**b**) *(business)* commerce *m* du change

►► ***agio account*** compte *m* d'agio

agiotage ['ædʒətɪdʒ] *n Fin* agiotage *m*

agitate ['ædʒɪteɪt] **1** *vi* **to agitate for/against sth** faire campagne en faveur de/contre qch; **they are agitating for better working conditions** ils réclament de meilleures conditions de travail

2 *vt* (**a**) *Chem (liquid)* agiter, remuer (**b**) *(emotionally)* agiter, troubler

agitated [ˈædʒɪteɪtɪd] *adj* agité, troublé; **she was very agitated** elle était très agitée *ou* dans tous ses états; **to become** *or* **to get agitated** se mettre dans tous ses états

agitatedly [ˈædʒɪteɪtɪdlɪ] *adv (act)* de manière agitée; *(say)* avec agitation, d'une voix agitée

agitating [ˈædʒɪteɪtɪŋ] *adj* agitateur, troublant

agitation [ˌædʒɪˈteɪʃən] *n* (**a**) *(emotional)* agitation *f*, émoi *m*, trouble *m*; **to be in a state of agitation** être dans tous ses états (**b**) *(unrest)* agitation *f*, troubles *mpl*; *Pol (campaign)* campagne *f* mouvementée; **there was a lot of agitation in favour of nuclear disarmament** il y avait un fort mouvement de contestation pour réclamer le désarmement nucléaire (**c**) *(of sea)* agitation *f*

agitato [ˌædʒɪˈtɑːtəʊ] *adv Mus* agitato

agitator [ˈædʒɪteɪtə(r)] *n* (**a**) *(person)* agitateur(-trice) *m,f* (**b**) *Tech (machine)* agitateur *m*

agitprop [ˈædʒɪtprɒp] *Pol* **1** *n* agit-prop *f inv*
2 *comp (art, theatre)* de l'agit-prop

agleam [əˈgliːm] *adj Literary* luisant; **her eyes were agleam with joy** ses yeux brillaient de joie

aglet [ˈæglət] *n (on shoelace)* ferret *m*

aglitter [əˈglɪtə(r)] *adj* brillant; **her eyes were aglitter with mischief** ses yeux pétillaient de malice

aglow [əˈgləʊ] *adj (fire)* rougeoyant; *(sky)* embrasé; **to be aglow with colour** briller de couleurs vives; *Fig* **his face was aglow with excitement/health** son visage rayonnait d'émotion/de santé

AGM [ˌeɪdʒiːˈem] *n Br Admin (abbr* **annual general meeting**) AGA *f*

agnate [ˈægneɪt] **1** *n* agnat(e) *m,f*
2 *adj* apparenté par les hommes de la famille

agnostic [ægˈnɒstɪk] *Rel* **1** *n* agnostique *mf*
2 *adj* agnostique

agnosticism [ægˈnɒstɪsɪzəm] *n Rel* agnosticisme *m*

Agnus Dei [ˌænjʊsˈdeɪiː, ˌægnʊsˈdeɪiː] *n Rel (prayer)* Agnus-Dei *m inv*; *(medallion)* agnus-Dei *m inv*

ago [əˈgəʊ] *adv* **they moved here ten years ago** ils ont emménagé ici il y a dix ans; **how long ago did this happen?** cela c'est produit il y a combien de temps?, il y a combien de temps que cela s'est produit?; **that was years ago** ça fait des années de cela; **a little while ago, a short time ago** tout à l'heure; **not so long ago** il n'y a pas si longtemps; **no longer ago than the last century** pas plus loin qu'au siècle dernier; **a long time ago, long ago** il y a longtemps; **as long ago as 1900** en 1900 déjà, dès 1900

agog [əˈgɒg] *adj* en émoi (**about sth** à cause de qch); **everyone was agog** tout le monde était en émoi; **the children were all agog (with excitement)** les enfants étaient tout excités; **I was agog to discover what had happened** je brûlais d'impatience de savoir ce qui s'était passé; **the scandal set the whole town agog** le scandale a mis la ville entière en émoi

agonize, -ise [ˈægənaɪz] *vi* (**a**) *(worry)* se tourmenter; **to agonize over** *or* **about a decision** hésiter longuement avant de prendre une décision; **don't agonize over it!** n'y passe pas trop de temps!; **to agonize over how to do sth** se ronger les sangs ou se tracasser pour savoir comment faire qch (**b**) *Literary (suffer)* être au supplice *ou* au martyre

agonized [ˈægənaɪzd] *adj (behaviour, reaction)* angoissé, d'angoisse; *(look)* angoissé, plein d'angoisse; *(cry)* déchirant; **with an agonized expression (on her face)** le visage déchiré par l'angoisse

agonizing [ˈægənaɪzɪŋ] **1** *adj (pain, worry, death)* atroce; *(sight)* navrant, angoissant; *(situation, silence, wait)* angoissant; *(decision, choice, dilemma)* pénible; **we had an agonizing half-hour** nous avons connu une demi-heure d'angoisse
2 *n* angoisse *f*; **why all this agonizing about something that can't be helped?** pourquoi se tourmenter à propos de quelque chose qu'on ne peut pas changer?

agonizingly [ˈægənaɪzɪŋlɪ] *adv* atrocement; **an agonizingly difficult decision** une décision atrocement difficile

agony [ˈægənɪ] *(pl* **agonies**) *n* (**a**) *(physical → pain)* douleur *f* atroce; *(→ suffering)* souffrance *f* atroce, souffrances *fpl* atroces; **to be in agony** souffrir le martyre; **to cry out in agony** crier de douleur; **it was agony to stand up** je souffrais le martyre pour me lever; **death agony** agonie *f* (de la mort); *Fam* **it's agony walking in these shoes** c'est un véritable supplice de marcher avec ces chaussures
(**b**) *(emotional, mental)* supplice *m*, angoisse *f*; **to be in an agony of doubt/remorse** être torturé par le doute/le remords; **it was agony just listening to him** le seul fait de l'écouter était un vrai supplice; *Fam* **to pile** *or* **put on the agony** forcer la dose
►► *Br* ***agony aunt*** = responsable du courrier du cœur; ***agony column*** courrier *m* du cœur

agora [ˈægərə] *(pl* **agorae** [-riː] *or* **agoras**) *n Antiq* agora *m*

agoraphobia [*Br* ˌægərəˈfəʊbɪə, *Am* əˌgəʊrəˈfəʊbɪə] *n Psy* agoraphobie *f*; **to have agoraphobia** souffrir d'agoraphobie

agoraphobic [ˌægərəˈfəʊbɪk] *Psy* **1** *n* agoraphobe *mf*
2 *adj* agoraphobe

agouti [əˈguːtɪ] *(pl* **inv** *or* **agoutis**) *n Zool* agouti *m*

AGR [ˌeɪdʒiːˈɑː(r)] *n Tech (abbr* **advanced gas-cooled reactor**) AGR *m*

agrarian [əˈgreərɪən] *Agr* **1** *n* agrarien(enne) *m,f*
2 *adj* agraire

agrarianism [əˈgreərɪəˌnɪzəm] *n Agr* agrarianisme *m*

agree [əˈgriː] **1** *vt* (**a**) *(share opinion)* **to agree that...** être d'accord avec le fait que...; **we all agree that he's innocent** nous sommes tous d'accord pour dire qu'il est innocent, nous sommes tous d'avis qu'il est innocent, **everyone agrees that the party was a success** tout le monde s'accorde à reconnaître que la fête était un succès; **I don't agree that the police should be armed** je ne suis pas d'accord pour que la police soit armée
(**b**) *(consent)* **to agree to do sth** accepter de *ou* consentir à faire qch
(**c**) *(admit)* admettre, reconnaître; **they agreed that they had made a mistake** ils ont reconnu *ou* convenu qu'ils avaient fait une faute
(**d**) *(reach agreement on)* convenir de; **to agree a date** convenir d'une date; **to agree a price** se mettre d'accord sur un prix; **to be agreed** *(date)* à convenir; *(price)* à débattre; **to agree to do sth** se mettre d'accord pour faire qch; **they agreed to share the cost** ils se sont mis d'accord pour partager les frais; **they agreed to take a taxi** ils ont décidé d'un commun accord de prendre un taxi; **it was agreed to continue the next day** il a été convenu que l'on poursuivrait le lendemain; **we agreed to differ** nous sommes restés chacun sur notre position; **it was agreed that the money should be invested** il a été convenu que l'argent serait investi; **the budget has been agreed** le budget a été adopté; **as agreed** comme convenu; **unless otherwise agreed** sauf accord contraire
(**e**) *(accept, approve → statement, plan)* accepter; *Acct* **to agree the accounts** *or* **the books** faire accorder les livres; **the figures were agreed between the accountants** les chiffres ont été acceptés (d'un commun accord) par les experts comptables
2 *vi* (**a**) *(share same opinion)* être d'accord (**about** sur); **I quite agree** je suis tout à fait d'accord (avec vous); **don't you agree?** n'êtes-vous pas d'accord?; **I think it's too expensive and Peter agrees** je pense que c'est trop cher et Peter est d'accord avec moi *ou* est du même avis; **to agree about sth** être d'accord sur qch; **I agree about going on a holiday** je suis d'accord pour partir en vacances; **I think we agree on** *or* **about the basic facts** je pense que nous sommes d'accord sur l'essentiel; **to agree with sb** être d'accord avec *ou* être du même avis que qn; **I agree with you entirely** je suis entièrement d'accord avec vous; **I agree with you about the decor** je suis d'accord avec vous pour ce qui est du décor; **they agree with me that it's a disgrace** ils trouvent comme moi que c'est une honte; **I couldn't agree (with you) more** je suis entièrement d'accord avec vous
(**b**) *(assent)* consentir, donner son adhésion; **to agree to a proposal** donner son adhésion à *ou* accepter une proposition; **to agree to sb's request** consentir à la requête de qn; **her parents have agreed to her going abroad** ses parents ont consenti à ce qu'elle aille *ou* sont d'accord pour qu'elle aille à l'étranger
(**c**) *(reach agreement)* se mettre d'accord (**about** sur); **the doctors couldn't agree about the best treatment** les médecins n'arrivaient pas à se mettre d'accord sur le traitement à suivre; **to agree on** *or* **upon a date** convenir d'une date; **they agreed on Italy for the honeymoon** ils se sont mis d'accord sur l'Italie pour la lune de miel; **that was the price we agreed on** c'était le prix dont nous avions convenu *ou* sur lequel nous nous étions mis d'accord
(**d**) *(correspond → account, estimate, totals)* concorder; **your statement doesn't agree with hers** ta version *ou* ta déclaration ne correspond pas à la sienne, vos deux versions ne concordent pas
(**e**) *Gram* s'accorder; **the verb agrees with the subject** le verbe s'accorde avec le sujet

►**agree with** *vt insep* (**a**) *(be in favour of)* **I don't agree with censorship** je suis contre *ou* je n'admets pas la censure; **I don't agree with people smoking in public places** je ne suis pas d'accord pour que les gens fument dans les lieux publics
(**b**) *(be suitable for)* **the climate here agrees with me** le climat d'ici me réussit *ou* me convient très bien; **rich food doesn't agree with me** la nourriture riche ne me réussit pas

agreeable [əˈgrɪəbəl] *adj* (**a**) *(pleasant → situation)* plaisant, agréable; *(→ person)* agréable
(**b**) *(willing)* consentant; **to be agreeable to sth** accepter qch, consentir à qch; **to be agreeable to doing sth** accepter de *ou* bien vouloir faire qch; **I am quite agreeable to his** *or* **him going** je veux bien *ou* je suis d'accord pour qu'il y aille; **are you agreeable to the proposal?** consentez-vous à la proposition?, êtes-vous d'accord avec la proposition?; **if you are agreeable** si cela vous convient, si vous êtes d'accord; **if she's agreeable** si elle veut bien
(**c**) *(acceptable)* acceptable, satisfaisant; **I hope the terms are agreeable to you** j'espère que les conditions vous conviennent

agreeably [əˈgrɪəblɪ] *adv* agréablement; **I was agreeably surprised** je fus agréablement surpris

agreed [əˈgriːd] **1** *adj* (**a**) *(in agreement)* d'accord; **is everyone agreed?** est-ce que tout le monde est d'accord?; **it's agreed that we leave on Friday** il est entendu *ou* convenu que nous partons vendredi; **we are agreed on** *or* **about the conditions** nous sommes d'accord sur les conditions
(**b**) *(fixed → time, place, price)* convenu; **as agreed** comme convenu; **at the agreed time** à l'heure convenue; *Journ* **agreed statement** *(in the media)* déclaration *f* commune
2 *exclam* (c'est) d'accord *ou* entendu!

agreement [əˈgriːmənt] *n* (**a**) *(gen)* accord *m*; **to be in agreement (with sb/about sth)** être d'accord (avec qn/sur *ou* au sujet de qch); **we are both in agreement on this point** nous sommes tous les deux d'accord *ou* du même avis à ce sujet; **to reach agreement** parvenir à un accord; **by agreement with the management** en accord avec la direction; **the proposal met with unanimous agreement** la proposition a été reçue à l'unanimité; **there was agreement on all sides that a change would be welcome** de toute part on convenait de l'opportunité d'un changement
(**b**) *Com & Pol* accord *m*; **under the (terms of the) agreement** selon les termes de l'accord; **to enter into** *or* **conclude an agreement with sb** passer un accord *ou* un contrat avec qn; **an agreement has been concluded between the two parties** un accord est intervenu entre les deux parties; **to have an agreement with sb** avoir conclu *ou* passé un accord avec qn; **to hold sb to an agreement** faire respecter un accord à qn; **to come to an agreement** tomber d'accord, parvenir à un accord; **to break an agreement** rompre un accord; *Law* **to sign a legal agreement (to do sth)** s'engager (par) devant notaire (à faire qch)
(**c**) *Gram* accord *m*

agrestic [əˈgrestɪk] *adj Literary* agreste, rustique

agribusiness [ˈægrɪˌbɪznɪs] *n (company)* agro-industrie *f*; *(sector)* agro-industries *fpl*

agrichemical [ˌægrɪˈkemɪkəl] **1** *n* produit *m* agrochimique

2 *adj* agrochimique

agricultural [ˌægrɪˈkʌltʃərəl] *adj (produce, machinery, land, society)* agricole; *(expert)* agronome; **East Anglia is very agricultural** l'East Anglia est une région très agricole

►► ***agricultural college*** = école supérieure d'agriculture et d'agronomie; ***agricultural economics*** agro-économie *f*; ***agricultural economy*** économie *f* du secteur agricole; ***agricultural engineer*** ingénieur *m* agronome; ***agricultural labourer*** ouvrier(ère) *m,f* agricole; ***agricultural show*** *(national)* salon *m* de l'agriculture; *(local)* foire *f* agricole; ***agricultural worker*** ouvrier(ère) *m,f* agricole

agriculturalist [ˌægrɪˈkʌltʃərəlɪst] *n (specialist)* agronome *mf*; *(farmer)* agriculteur(trice) *m,f*

agriculture [ˈægrɪˌkʌltʃə(r)] *n* agriculture *f*

agriculturist [ˌægrɪˈkʌltʃərɪst] *n* agriculteur(-trice) *m,f*

agriforestry [ˌægrɪˈfɒrəstrɪ] *n* agroforesterie *f*

Agrigento [ˌægrɪˈdʒentəʊ] *n Geog* Agrigente

agrimony [ˈægrɪmənɪ] *n Bot* aigremoine *f*

Agrippa [əˈgrɪpə] *pr n* Agrippa

Agrippina [ˌægrɪˈpiːnə] *pr n* Agrippine

agritourism [ˈægrɪˌtʊərɪzəm] *n* tourisme *m* agricole

agrobiology [ˌægrəʊbaɪˈɒlədʒɪ] *n* agrobiologie *f*

agrochemical [ˌægrəʊˈkemɪkəl] **1** *n* produit *m* agrochimique

2 *adj* agrochimique

agrochemist [ˌægrəʊˈkemɪst] *n* agrochimiste *mf*

agrochemistry [ˌægrəʊˈkemɪstrɪ] *n* agrochimie *f*

agroclimatology [ˌægrəʊklaɪməˈtɒlədʒɪ] *n* agroclimatologie *f*

agroforestry [ˌægrəʊˈfɒrəstrɪ] *n* agroforesterie *f*

agro-industrial [ˌægrəʊɪ-] *n* agro-industriel

agro-industry *n* agro-industrie *f*

agrology [æˈgrɒlədʒɪ] *n* agrologie *f*

agronomic [ˌægrəˈnɒmɪk], **agronomical** [ˌægrəˈnɒmɪkəl] *adj* agronomique

agronomist [əˈgrɒnəmɪst] *n* agronome *mf*

agronomy [əˈgrɒnəmɪ] *n* agronomie *f*

aground [əˈgraʊnd] **1** *adj (ship)* échoué; **to be aground** toucher le fond, être échoué

2 *adv* **to run** *or* **to go aground** *(ship)* s'échouer; *Fig (policy, project etc)* échouer

ague [ˈeɪgjuː] *n Arch* (**a**) *Med (malarial fever)* fièvre *f* paludéenne (**b**) *Physiol (shivering)* frissons *mpl*

ah [ɑː] *exclam* ah!; **ah, yes, now you come to mention it** euh, oui, maintenant que tu m'en parles

AHA [ˌeɪeɪtʃˈeɪ] *Chem (abbr* **alpha-hydroxy acid***)* **1** *n* AHA *m*

2 *comp (moisturizer, product)* aux acides de fruits

aha [ɑːˈhɑː] *exclam* ah, ah!, tiens!

Ahab [ˈeɪhæb] *pr n* **Captain Ahab** Achab *(personnage de 'Moby Dick' de Melville, qui mène un combat symbolique contre la baleine blanche)*

AHEAD [əˈhed]

en avant	► **1 (a)**
à venir, à l'avenir	► **1 (b)**
en avance, d'avance	► **1 (c); 2 (b)**
devant	► **2 (a)**

1 *adv* (**a**) *(in space)* en avant, devant; **to send sb ahead** envoyer qn en avant; **the road ahead** la route devant nous/eux/*etc*; **there's a crossroads about half a mile ahead** il y a un croisement à environ 800 mètres (d'ici); **go/drive on ahead and I'll catch you up** vas-y *ou* pars en avant, je te rattraperai; **to push** *or* **press ahead with a project** poursuivre un projet

(**b**) *(in time)* **the years ahead** les années à venir; **what lies ahead?** qu'est-ce qui nous attend?; **to look ahead** penser à l'avenir; **looking ahead to the future** en pensant à l'avenir; **to plan ahead** faire des projets; **you have to plan ahead for a big wedding** il faut s'organiser à l'avance pour un grand mariage; **how far ahead should one book?** combien de temps à l'avance faut-il retenir?; **we must think ahead** nous devons prévoir

(**c**) *(in competition, race)* en avance; **three lengths/five points ahead** trois longueurs/cinq points d'avance; **to be ahead on points** avoir des points d'avance; *Fig* **it's better to quit while you're ahead** mieux vaut te retirer du jeu pendant que tu as l'avantage

(**d**) *Naut* sur l'avant, en avant *(du navire)*; **the ship was right ahead** le navire était droit devant; **to go ahead** aller de l'avant

2 ahead of *prep* (**a**) *(in front of)* devant; **there were ten people ahead of us in the queue** il y avait dix personnes devant nous dans la queue

(**b**) *(in time)* **he arrived ten minutes ahead of me** il est arrivé dix minutes avant moi; **to finish ahead of schedule** terminer plus tôt que prévu *ou* en avance; **the rest of the team are two months ahead of us** les autres membres de l'équipe ont deux mois d'avance sur nous; **French time is one hour ahead of British time** la France a une heure d'avance sur la Grande-Bretagne; **to arrive ahead of time** arriver en avance *ou* avant l'heure; *Fig* **to be ahead of one's time** être en avance sur son époque; **you've got your best years ahead of you** vous avez vos meilleures années devant vous

(**c**) *(in competition, race)* **he is five points ahead of his nearest rival** il a cinq points d'avance sur son rival le plus proche, il devance son rival le plus proche de cinq points; **to be ahead of one's competitors** devancer ses concurrents; *Sch* **he is ahead of his class** il est en avance sur sa classe

ahem [əˈhem] *exclam* hum!

ahoy [əˈhɔɪ] *exclam* ohé!, holà!; **ship ahoy!** ohé du navire!

AI [ˌeɪˈaɪ] *n* (**a**) *(abbr* **Amnesty International***)* Amnesty International (**b**) *Comput (abbr* **artificial intelligence***)* IA *f* (**c**) *Biol (abbr* **artificial insemination***)* insémination *f* artificielle

AIB [ˌeɪaɪˈbiː] *n (abbr* **Accident Investigation Bureau***)* = commission d'enquête sur les accidents en Grande-Bretagne

AID [ˌeɪaɪˈdiː] *n* (**a**) *Biol (abbr* **artificial insemination by donor***)* IAD *f* (**b**) *Am Admin & Econ (abbr* **Agency for International Development***)* = agence américaine pour le développement international

aid [eɪd] **1** *n* (**a**) *(help, assistance)* aide *f*; **with the aid of sb** avec l'aide de qn; **with the aid of sth** à l'aide de qch; **with the aid of half a dozen helpers** avec l'aide d'une demi-douzaine d'assistants; **I managed to open the tin with the aid of a screwdriver** à l'aide d'un tournevis, j'ai réussi à ouvrir la boîte; **to come to sb's aid** venir à l'aide de qn; **to go to sb's aid** se porter au secours de *ou* porter secours à qn

(**b**) *Pol & Fin (to developing countries, for disaster relief)* aide *f*; **food aid** aide *f* alimentaire; **overseas aid** aide *f* au tiers-monde; **the government gives aid to depressed areas** le gouvernement octroie des aides aux régions en déclin

(**c**) *(helpful equipment)* aide *f*, support *m*; **teaching aids** supports *mpl ou* aides *fpl* pédagogiques; **visual aids** supports *mpl* visuels

(**d**) *(assistant)* aide *mf*, assistant(e) *m,f*

(**e**) *Sport (for climber)* piton *m*

2 *vt* (**a**) *(help → person)* aider, venir en aide à; *(→ financially)* aider, secourir; *(→ digestion)* faciliter; **to aid sb with sth** aider qn pour qch; **I refuse to aid you in any illegal enterprise** je refuse de vous aider dans une quelconque entreprise illicite; **they aided one another** ils se sont entraidés, ils se sont aidés les uns les autres

(**b**) *(give support to → region, industry)* aider, soutenir

(**c**) *(encourage → development, understanding, recovery)* contribuer à

(**d**) *Law* **to aid and abet sb** être (le) complice de qn; *Fig* **aided and abetted by her sister** avec la complicité de sa sœur

3 in aid of *prep* **a collection in aid of the homeless** une collecte au profit des sans-abri; *Br Fam Fig* **what are all these levers in aid of?** à quoi servent tous ces leviers?❑; *Br Fam Fig* **what are the cakes in aid of?** les gâteaux sont en l'honneur de quoi?; *Fam* **what's all this noise in aid of?** qu'est-ce que c'est que tout ce bruit?❑

►► ***aid agency*** organisation *f* humanitaire; *Sport* ***aid climbing*** escalade *f* artificielle; *Admin* ***aid organization*** organisme *m* d'aide; ***aid worker*** *(voluntary)* volontaire *mf*; *(paid)* employé(e) *m,f* d'une organisation humanitaire

AIDA [aɪˈiːdə] *n Mktg (abbr* **attention-interest-desire-action***)* AIDA *m*

aide [eɪd] *n* aide *mf*, assistant(e) *m,f*; *(to president etc)* conseiller(ère) *m,f*

aide-de-camp [eɪddəˈkɒŋ] *(pl* **aides-de-camp** [ˌeɪdz-]*) n Mil* aide *m* de camp

aided [ˈeɪdɪd] *adj*

►► *Mktg* ***aided recall*** notoriété *f* assistée; *Br* ***aided school*** = école privée qui reçoit une aide de l'Etat mais garde un certain pouvoir de décision, notamment sur le contenu des cours d'instruction religieuse et le choix des enseignants

aide-mémoire [ˌeɪdmemˈwɑː(r)] *(pl* **aides-mémoire** [ˈeɪdz-]*) n* aide-mémoire *m inv*

aiding [ˈeɪdɪŋ] *n Law* **aiding and abetting** complicité *f*

AIDS, Aids [eɪdz] *Med (abbr* **acquired immune deficiency syndrome***)* **1** *n* sida *m*, SIDA *m*, Sida *m*

2 *comp (clinic)* pour sidéens

►► ***Aids patient*** sidéen(enne) *m,f*; ***Aids research*** recherche *f* sur le sida; ***Aids specialist*** sidologue *mf*; ***Aids sufferer*** sidéen(-enne) *m,f*, malade *mf* atteint(e) du sida; ***the Aids virus*** le virus du sida

AIDS-related *adj Med* lié au sida

►► ***AIDS-related complex*** ARC *m*; ***AIDS-related virus*** ARV *m*

AIH [ˌeɪaɪˈeɪtʃ] *n Biol (abbr* **artificial insemination by husband***)* IAC *f*

aikido [aɪˈkiːdəʊ] *n Sport* aïkido *m*

ail [eɪl] **1** *vt Literary* **what ails you?** qu'avez-vous?, quelle mouche vous a piqué?

2 *vi* être souffrant

aileron [ˈeɪlərɒn] *n Aviat* aileron *m*

ailing [ˈeɪlɪŋ] *adj (person)* souffrant, en mauvaise santé; *(economy, industry)* malade; **the ailing state of the economy/country** la mauvaise passe dans laquelle se trouve l'économie/le pays

ailment [ˈeɪlmənt] *n* mal *m*, affection *f*; **she has all kinds of ailments** elle souffre de toutes sortes de maux

ailurophile [eɪˈljʊərəʊfaɪl] *n* ailurophile *mf*

ailurophilia [ˌeɪljʊərəʊˈfɪlɪə] *n* ailurophilie *f*

ailurophobe [eɪˈljʊərəʊfəʊb] *n* ailurophobe *mf*

ailurophobia [ˌeɪljʊərəʊˈfəʊbɪə] *n* ailurophobie *f*

AIM [ˌeɪaɪˈem] *n Br St Exch (abbr* **Alternative Investment Market***)* = marché hors-cote rattaché à la Bourse de Londres

aim [eɪm] **1** *n* (**a**) *(intention, purpose)* but *m*; **with the aim of** afin de, dans le but de; **she came to the meeting with the aim of causing trouble** elle est venue à la réunion dans le but de faire des histoires; **his aim is to get rich quickly** il a pour but *ou* il s'est donné comme but de s'enrichir rapidement; **her ultimate aim is to beat the world record** son but final est de battre le record du monde; **her aim in going to London was to find a job** elle était allée à Londres dans le but de trouver du travail; **you need an aim in life** il faut un but dans la vie

(**b**) *(with weapon)* **to take aim (at sb/sth)** viser (qn/qch); *Mil* **take aim!** en joue!; **to have a good aim** bien viser; **your aim isn't very good** vous ne visez pas très bien; **to miss one's aim** manquer la cible *ou* son but

2 *vt* (**a**) *(gun)* braquer; *(missile)* pointer; *(stone)* lancer; *(blow)* allonger, décocher; *(kick)* donner; **he aimed his gun at the man's head** il a braqué son pistolet sur la tête de l'homme; **he was aiming stones at the tree** il lançait des cailloux sur l'arbre; **there are missiles aimed at all the major cities** des missiles ennemis sont pointés sur toutes les grandes villes; **the man aimed a kick at the dog** l'homme donna un coup de pied au chien

(**b**) *Fig (criticism, product, programme)* destiner; **was that remark aimed at me?** est-ce que cette remarque m'était destinée?; **the programme is aimed at a teenage audience** l'émission est destinée à un public d'adolescents;

these measures are aimed at reducing unemployment ces mesures visent une réduction du chômage

3 *vi* (**a**) *(take aim)* **to aim at sb/sth** viser qn/qch; **he aimed at the target** il visait la cible; **she aimed at** *or* **for the post, but missed** elle a visé le poteau, mais elle l'a manqué

(**b**) *(have as goal)* **she's aiming to become a millionaire by the age of thirty** son but, c'est d'être millionnaire à trente ans; **we aim to arrive before midnight** nous avons l'intention *ou* nous nous sommes fixés d'arriver avant minuit; **he's aiming at quick promotion** il vise une promotion rapide; **we're aiming for Rouen before stopping** nous nous sommes fixés Rouen comme but avant de nous arrêter; **to aim high** viser haut

aimless ['eɪmlɪs] *adj (person)* sans but, désœuvré; *(life)* sans but; *(occupation, task)* sans objet, futile

aimlessly ['eɪmlɪslɪ] *adv (walk around)* sans but; *(stand around)* sans trop savoir quoi faire; **he wandered aimlessly through the streets** il errait dans les rues

aimlessness ['eɪmlɪsnɪs] *n* **the aimlessness of their existence** leur existence sans but

ain't [eɪnt] *Fam* (**a**) = **am not** (**b**) = **is not** (**c**) = **are not** (**d**) = **has not** (**e**) = **have not**

Aintree ['eɪntrɪ] *n* = champ de courses dans la banlieue de Liverpool, où se déroule le "Grand National"

AIO [ˌeɪaɪ'əʊ] *n Mktg (abbr* **activities, interests and opinions**) AIO

►► ***AIO research*** étude *f* AIO

air [eə(r)] **1** *n* (**a**) *(gen)* air *m*; **I need some (fresh) air** j'ai besoin de prendre l'air; **I went out for a breath of (fresh) air** je suis sorti prendre l'air; *Literary* **to take the air** prendre le frais; **the divers came up for air** les plongeurs sont remontés à la surface pour respirer; *Fig* **I need a change of air** j'ai besoin de changer d'air; **to disappear** *or* **vanish into thin air** se volatiliser, disparaître sans laisser de traces

(**b**) *(sky)* air *m*, ciel *m*; **the smoke rose into the air** la fumée s'éleva vers le ciel; **to throw sth up into the air** lancer qch en l'air; **to fly through the air** voler *ou* voltiger en l'air; **seen from the air, the fields looked like a chessboard** vus d'avion, les champs ressemblaient à un échiquier; **to take to the air** *(bird)* s'envoler; *(plane)* décoller

(**c**) *Aviat* **to travel by air** voyager par avion; **mail that is sent by air** le courrier (envoyé) par avion

(**d**) *Rad & TV* **to be on (the) air** *(person)* être à *ou* avoir l'antenne; *(programme)* être à l'antenne; *(station)* émettre; **to go on the air** *(person)* passer à l'antenne; *(programme)* passer à l'antenne, être diffusé; **you're on the air** vous avez l'antenne; **to go off the air** *(person)* rendre l'antenne; *(programme)* se terminer; *(station)* cesser d'émettre; **the station goes off the air at midnight** les programmes finissent à minuit

(**e**) *(manner, expression)* air *m*; **he has an air about him** il en impose; **there is an air of mystery about her** elle a un air mystérieux; **with a triumphant air** d'un air triomphant; **she smiled with a knowing air** elle sourit d'un air entendu

(**f**) *Mus* air *m*

2 *comp Aviat & Mil (piracy, traffic, attack, defence)* aérien; *(travel, traveller)* par avion

3 *vt* (**a**) *(ventilate → room, bed)* aérer; *(dry → linen)* faire sécher

(**b**) *(express → opinion, grievance)* exprimer, faire connaître; *(→ suggestion, idea)* exprimer, avancer

(**c**) *Am Rad & TV* diffuser

4 *vi Am Rad & TV* **the film airs next week** le film sera diffusé la semaine prochaine

5 airs *npl* **to put on** *or* **to give oneself airs** se donner de grands airs; *Br* **airs and graces** minauderies *fpl*

6 in the air *adv* **there's a rumour in the air that they're going to sell** le bruit court qu'ils vont vendre; **there's something in the air** il se trame quelque chose; **everything's up in the air** *(uncertain)* rien n'a été décidé pour l'instant; **our holiday plans are still (up) in the air** nos projets de vacances sont encore assez vagues; **the project is still very much (up) in the air** le projet n'est encore qu'à l'état d'ébauche *ou* est encore vague

►► ***air alert*** alerte *f* aérienne; ***air ambulance*** avion *m* sanitaire; ***air bladder*** vessie *f* natatoire; *Constr* ***air brick*** brique *f* creuse; ***air bubble*** *(in wallpaper, liquid)* bulle *f* d'air; *(in plastic, metal)* soufflure *f*; ***air cargo*** fret *m* aérien; *Tech* ***air chamber*** chambre *f* à air; *Br Mil* ***air chief marshal*** ≃ général *m* d'armée aérienne; *Br Mil* ***air commodore*** ≃ général *m* de brigade aérienne, *Can* ≃ brigadier-général *m*; ***air compressor*** compresseur *m* d'air; *Aviat* ***air corridor*** couloir *m* aérien; *Mil & Aviat* ***air cover*** couverture *f* aérienne; *Met* ***air current*** courant *m* atmosphérique; *Tech* ***air curtain*** store *m* d'air *(chaud ou froid)*; ***air cushion*** *(gen)* coussin *m* pneumatique; *Tech* coussin *m ou* matelas *m* d'air; *Tech* ***air cylinder*** cylindre *m* à air comprimé; *Tech* ***air duct*** conduite *f* d'air, amenée *f* d'air; *Aviat* ***air ferry*** avion *m* transbordeur; ***air filter*** filtre *m* à air; *Aviat* ***air freighter*** avion-cargo *m*; ***air freshener*** désodorisant *m (pour la maison)*; *Tech* ***air gauge*** micromètre *m* pneumatique; ***air hostess*** hôtesse *f* de l'air; *Aviat* ***air lane*** couloir *m* aérien *ou* de navigation aérienne; *Aviat* ***air letter*** aérogramme *m*; *Aviat* ***air link*** liaison *f* aérienne; *Br Mil* ***air marshal*** ≃ général *m* de corps aérien, *Can & Belg* ≃ lieutenant-général *m*; *Met* ***air mass*** masse *f* d'air; ***air mattress*** matelas *m* pneumatique; *Aviat* ***air mile*** mille *m* marin; ***air miles*** = points que l'on peut accumuler lors de certains achats et qui permettent de bénéficier de réductions sur des billets d'avion; **to collect air miles** accumuler des points; *Hist* ***Air Ministry*** ≃ Ministère *m* de l'Air; *Aviat* ***air miss*** quasicollision *f* (aérienne); *Tech* ***air passage*** conduit *m* aérifère; ***air pistol*** pistolet *m* à air comprimé; *Bot* ***air plant*** plante *f* aéricole, (plante *f*) épiphyte *m*; ***air pocket*** *Met & Aviat (affecting plane)* trou *m* d'air; *Tech (in pipe)* poche *f* d'air; *Ecol* ***air pollution*** pollution *f* atmosphérique; *Mil & Aviat* ***air power*** puissance *f* aérienne; *Met & Tech* ***air pressure*** pression *f* atmosphérique; *Tech* ***air pressure gauge*** manomètre *m*; *Tech* ***air pump*** compresseur *m*, pompe *f* à air; *Met* ***Air Quality Index*** indice *m* de pollution de l'air; *Aviat* ***air rage*** = comportement agressif de certains passagers d'avion; *Mil* ***air raid*** attaque *f* aérienne, raid *m* aérien; ***air rifle*** carabine *f* à air comprimé; *Aviat* ***air route*** route *f* aérienne; *Aviat* ***air service*** liaison *f* aérienne; *Golf* ***air shot*** air-shot *m*; ***air show*** *Com (exhibition)* salon *m* de l'aéronautique; *Aviat (display)* meeting *m* aérien; *Astrol* ***air sign*** signe *m* d'air; ***air speed*** vitesse *f* du vol; *Mil* ***air supremacy*** suprématie *f* aérienne; *Aviat* ***air tanker*** avitailleur *m*; *Aviat* ***air taxi*** avion-taxi *m*; ***air temperature*** température *f* ambiante; *Aviat* ***air terminal*** aérogare *f*; *Aviat* ***air ticket*** billet *m* d'avion; *Aviat* ***air traffic*** circulation *f* aérienne, trafic *m* aérien; *Aviat* ***air transport*** transport *m* aérien *ou* par avion; *Aviat* ***air travel*** voyages *mpl* en avion; ***air travel organiser*** organisateur *m* de voyages par avion; *Tech* ***air valve*** soupape *f (pour l'air)*; *Br Mil* ***air vice-marshal*** ≃ général *m* de division aérienne, *Can* ≃ major-général *m*, *Belg* ≃ général-major; *Mil* ***air war*** guerre *f* aérienne; *Com* ***air waybill*** lettre *f* de transport aérien, connaissement *m* aérien

airbag ['eəbæg] *n Aut* Air Bag® *m*

airbase ['eəbeɪs] *n* base *f* aérienne

airbed ['eəbed] *n* matelas *m* pneumatique

airborne ['eəbɔːn] *adj* (**a**) *Aviat (plane)* en vol; *(balloon)* en l'air; **to become airborne** *(plane)* décoller; **once we are airborne** une fois que nous aurons décollé (**b**) *(particles, seeds)* en suspension dans l'air; *(disease)* présent dans l'air (**c**) *Mil (troops, division, regiment)* aéroporté (**d**) *Aviat (equipment, radar)* de bord

►► *Mil* ***airborne attack*** attaque *f* exécutée par des troupes aéroportées, assaut *m* vertical

airbrake ['eəbreɪk] *n Aut* frein *m* à air comprimé; *Aviat* aérofrein *m*, frein *m* aérodynamique

airbrush ['eəbrʌʃ] *Art & Comput* **1** *n* aérographe *m*

2 *vt* retoucher à l'aérographe

►**airbrush in** *vt sep Art & Comput* ajouter à l'aérographe

►**airbrush out** *vt sep Art & Comput* effacer à l'aérographe; *Fig* **to airbrush sb out of history** faire disparaître qn de l'histoire officielle

airbrushing ['eəbrʌʃɪŋ] *n Art & Comput* peinture *f ou* retouchage *m* à l'aérographe

Airbus® ['eəbʌs] *n* Airbus® *m*

air-conditioned *adj* climatisé; **fully air-conditioned** entièrement climatisé

'The Air-Conditioned Nightmare' *Henry Miller*
'Le cauchemar climatisé'

---

air-conditioner *n* climatiseur *m*

air-conditioning *n* climatisation *f*

air-cooled [-kuːld] *adj* (**a**) *Aut & Tech (engine)* à refroidissement par air (**b**) *Am Tech (room)* climatisé

air-cooling *n Tech* refroidissement *m* par air

aircraft ['eəkrɑːft] *(pl* **inv**) *n Aviat* avion *m*

►► *Naut & Mil* ***aircraft carrier*** porte-avions *m inv*; *Aviat* ***aircraft engineering*** ingénierie *f* aéronautique; ***aircraft factory*** usine *f* d'aviation; ***aircraft hangar*** hangar *m* à avions

aircraft(s)man ['eəkrɑːft(s)mən] *(pl* **aircraft(s)men** [-mən]) *n Br Mil* ≃ aviateur *m*, *Can* ≃ soldat *m*, *Belg* ≃ premier soldat *m*

aircraft(s)woman ['eəkrɑːft(s)ˌwʊmən] *(pl* **aircraft(s)women** [-ˌwɪmɪn]) *n Br Mil* femme *f* soldat de deuxième classe *(dans l'armée de l'air)*

aircrew ['eəkruː] *n Aviat* équipage *m (d'avion)*

airdrome ['eədrəʊm] *n Am Aviat* aérodrome *m*

airdrop ['eədrɒp] *(pt & pp* **airdropped**, *cont* **airdropping**) *Aviat* **1** *n* parachutage *m*

2 *vt* parachuter

air-dry *vt* sécher à l'air

Airedale ['eədeɪl] *n* airedale *m*, airedale-terrier *m*

►► ***Airedale terrier*** airedale *m*, airedale-terrier *m*

airer ['eərə(r)] *n Br (for clothes)* séchoir *m*

airfare ['eəfeə(r)] *n* prix *m* du billet (d'avion), tarif *m* aérien

airfield ['eəfiːld] *n Aviat* terrain *m* d'aviation, (petit) aérodrome *m*

airflow ['eəfləʊ] *n* (**a**) *Tech* écoulement *m* d'air; **smooth/turbulent airflow** écoulement *m* régulier/turbulent

►► *Am Aut* ***airflow body*** carrosserie *f* aérodynamique; ***airflow meter*** débitmètre *m* d'air

airfoil ['eəfɔɪl] *n Am* surface *f* portante, plan *m* de sustentation

airforce ['eəfɔːs] *n* armée *f* de l'air

►► ***airforce blue*** **1** *n* bleu *m* pétrole **2** *adj* bleu pétrole; *Am Mil* ***airforce cadet*** ≃ aspirant *m*; ***Air Force One*** = l'avion du président des États-Unis

airframe ['eəfreɪm] *n Aviat* cellule *f* (d'avion)

airfreight ['eəfreɪt] *Aviat & Com* **1** *n (cargo)* fret *m* aérien; *(transport)* transport *m* aérien; **to send sth by airfreight** expédier qch par voie aérienne *ou* par avion

2 *vt* expédier par fret aérien

►► *Aviat & Com* ***airfreight container*** conteneur-avion *m*; ***airfreight services*** messageries *fpl* aériennes

air/fuel mixture *n Aut* mélange *m* air/carburant

airgun ['eəgʌn] *n (rifle)* carabine *f ou* fusil *m* à air comprimé; *(pistol)* pistolet *m* à air comprimé

airhead ['eəhed] *n Fam* écervelé(e) *m,f*; *(woman)* évaporée *f*

airhole ['eəhəʊl] *n Tech* trou *m* d'aération

airily ['eərəlɪ] *adv* avec désinvolture; *(to say)* d'un ton dégagé *ou* désinvolte

airiness ['eərɪnɪs] *n* (**a**) *(of building, flat)* caractère *m* spacieux (**b**) *(of tone, manner)* désinvolture *f*

airing ['eərɪŋ] *n* (**a**) *(of linen, room)* aération *f*; **the room needs an airing** la pièce a besoin d'être aérée; **give the clothes an airing outside** mets ces habits à l'air dehors

(**b**) *Fig* **to give an idea an airing** agiter une idée, mettre une idée sur le tapis; **to give one's grievances/feelings an airing** exposer ses griefs/ses sentiments

(**c**) *Am Rad & TV (of programme)* diffusion *f*, transmission *f*

►► ***airing cupboard*** = placard chauffé où l'on fait sécher le linge

air-kiss *vi* = faire semblant de faire la bise

airless ['eəlɪs] *adj* (**a**) *(room)* qui manque d'air, qui sent le renfermé (**b**) *(weather)* lourd

airlessness ['eəlɪsnɪs] *n* (**a**) *(of room)* manque *m* d'air *ou* d'aération (**b**) *(of weather)* lourdeur *f*

airlift ['eəlɪft] *Aviat* **1** *n* pont *m* aérien
2 *vt (passengers, troops → out)* évacuer par pont aérien; *(→ in)* faire entrer par pont aérien; *(supplies, cargo)* acheminer par pont aérien

airline ['eəlaɪn] *n* **(a)** *Aviat & Com (company)* compagnie *f* aérienne **(b)** *Naut & Tech (tube)* tuyau *m* d'air
►► *Aviat* ***airline club*** = programme de fidélisation de la clientèle d'une compagnie aérienne; *Aviat & Com* ***airline operator*** compagnie *f* aérienne; *Aviat* ***airline passenger*** passager(ère) *m,f* des compagnies aériennes; *Aviat* ***airline pilot*** pilote *m* de ligne

airliner ['eəlaɪnə(r)] *n Aviat* avion *m* de ligne

airlock ['eəlɒk] *n Tech* **(a)** *(in spacecraft, submarine)* sas *m* **(b)** *(in pipe)* poche *f ou* bulle *f* d'air

airmail ['eəmeɪl] *Aviat* **1** *n (service)* poste *f* aérienne; *(letters etc)* courrier *m* par avion; **by airmail** *(on envelope)* par avion
2 *comp (parcel)* par avion
3 *adv* par avion
4 *vt* expédier *ou* envoyer par avion
►► ***airmail letter*** *(letter sent by airmail)* lettre *f* par avion; *(bought at post office)* aérogramme *m*; ***airmail paper*** papier *m* avion; ***airmail sticker*** étiquette *f* par avion

airman ['eəmən] *(pl* **airmen** [-mən]) *n* **(a)** *(gen)* aviateur *m* **(b)** *Am Mil* ≃ aviateur *m* de première classe, *Can* ≃ soldat *m*, *Belg* ≃ premier soldat *m*; **airman first class** ≃ caporal *m*

airmobile ['eəməˌbiːl] *adj Am Aviat* aéroporté

airpass ['eəpɑːs] *n Aviat* carte *f* d'abonnement de transport aérien

airplane ['eəpleɪn] *Am* avion *m*

airplay ['eəpleɪ] *n Rad* **that record is getting a lot of airplay** on entend souvent ce disque à la radio

airport ['eəpɔːt] *n Aviat* aéroport *m*
►► *Mktg* ***airport advertising*** publicité *f* dans les aéroports; ***airport apron*** aire *f* de stationnement (des avions); ***airport hotel*** hôtel *m* d'aéroport; *Fin* ***airport landing tax*** taxe *f* d'atterrissage; ***airport lounge*** hall *m* d'aéroport; ***airport shop*** boutique *f* d'aéroport; *Fin* ***airport tax*** taxe *f* d'aéroport; *Transp* ***airport taxi*** taxi *m* desservant l'aéroport; ***airport terminal*** aérogare *f*

air-raid *adj*
►► *Mil* ***air-raid precautions*** défense *f* passive; *Mil* ***air-raid shelter*** abri *m* antiaérien; *Mil* ***air-raid warden*** préposé(e) *m,f* à la défense passive; *Mil* ***air-raid warning*** alerte *f* antiaérienne

airscrew ['eəskruː] *n Br Old-fashioned Aviat* hélice *f* (d'avion)

air-sea rescue *n Aviat* sauvetage *m* air-mer
►► ***air-sea rescue helicopter*** hélicoptère *m* de sauvetage en mer

airship ['eəʃɪp] *n Aviat* dirigeable *m*

airsick ['eəsɪk] *adj Aviat & Med* **to be** *or* **to get airsick** avoir le mal de l'air

airsickness ['eəˌsɪknɪs] *n Aviat & Med* mal *m* de l'air

airsock ['eəsɒk] *n Met* manche *f* à air

airspace ['eəspeɪs] *n Aviat* espace *m* aérien

airspeed ['eəspiːd] *n Aviat* vitesse *f* relative

airstream ['eəstriːm] *n Met* courant *m* atmosphérique

airstrike ['eəstraɪk] *n Mil* raid *m* aérien, attaque *f* aérienne

airstrip ['eəstrɪp] *n Aviat* terrain *m ou* piste *f* d'atterrissage

airtight ['eətaɪt] *adj* hermétique, étanche (à l'air); *Fig* **I don't think his argument is completely airtight** je ne crois pas que son argument soit totalement irréfutable

airtime ['eətaɪm] *n Rad & TV* **(a)** *(time allotted on programme)* **that record is getting a lot of airtime** on entend souvent ce disque à la radio; **the subject didn't get much airtime** on n'a pas consacré beaucoup de temps au sujet pendant l'émission **(b)** *(starting time)* heure *f* où commence l'émission; **five minutes to airtime** on est à l'antenne dans cinq minutes

air-to-air *adj Mil* air-air *(inv)*, avion-avion *(inv)*

air-to-ground *adj Mil* air-sol *(inv)*, air-terre *(inv)*

air-to-surface *adj Mil* air-sol *(inv)*

air-traffic *adj*
►► *Aviat* ***air-traffic control*** contrôle *m* du trafic aérien; *Aviat* ***air-traffic controller*** contrôleur(euse) *m,f* du trafic aérien, aiguilleur *m* du ciel

airvent ['eəvent] *n Tech* prise *f* d'air

airwaves ['eəweɪvz] *npl Phys & Rad* ondes *fpl* (hertziennes); **on the airwaves** sur les ondes, à la radio

airway ['eəweɪ] *n* **(a)** *Aviat (route)* voie *f* aérienne; *Com (company)* ligne *f* aérienne **(b)** *Med* voies *fpl* respiratoires; **make sure the airways aren't blocked** assurez-vous que les voies respiratoires ne sont pas obstruées **(c)** *Tech (shaft)* conduit *m* d'air **(d)** *Am Rad & TV* chaîne *f*

airwoman ['eəˌwʊmən] *(pl* **airwomen** [-ˌwɪmɪn]) *n* **(a)** *(gen)* aviatrice *f* **(b)** *Mil* (femme *f*) auxiliaire *f (de l'armée de l'air)*

airworthiness ['eəˌwɜːðɪnɪs] *n Aviat* tenue *f* en l'air, navigabilité *f*; **certificate of airworthiness** certificat *m* de navigabilité

airworthy ['eəˌwɜːðɪ] *adj Aviat* en état de navigation

airy ['eərɪ] *(compar* **airier**, *superl* **airiest**) *adj* **(a)** *(room)* clair et spacieux **(b)** *Fig (casual → manner)* insouciant, désinvolte; *(→ ideas, plans, promises)* en l'air

airy-fairy *adj Br Fam (person, notion)* farfelu

aisle [aɪl] *n* **(a)** *(in church)* bas-côté *m*, nef *f* latérale; **her father led her up the aisle** c'est son père qui l'a menée à l'autel; **to walk up** *or* **down the aisle** *(before ceremony)* entrer dans l'église; *(after ceremony)* sortir de l'église; *Fig* **to walk up the aisle** se marier
(b) *(in cinema, supermarket)* allée *f*; *(on train, aeroplane)* couloir *m* (central)
►► *Mktg* ***aisle end display*** tête *f* de gondole; ***aisle seat*** *(in train, aeroplane)* siège *m* côté couloir

aisled [aɪld] *adj (church)* à bas-côtés

aitch [eɪtʃ] *n* H, h *m inv*; **to drop one's aitches** ne pas prononcer (correctement) les h

aitchbone ['eɪtʃbəʊn] *n Culin* culotte *f (de bœuf)*

ajar [ə'dʒɑː(r)] **1** *adj (door, window)* entrouvert, entrebâillé
2 *adv* **the door stood ajar** la porte était entrouverte; **to swing ajar** s'entrouvrir, s'entrebâiller

Ajax ['eɪdʒæks] *pr n Myth* Ajax

AK *(written abbr* **Alaska**) Alaska *m*

aka [ˌeɪkeɪ'eɪ] *adv (abbr* **also known as**) alias

Akela [ɑː'keɪlə] *n Br (in cub scouts)* cheftaine *f*

akimbo [ə'kɪmbəʊ] *adv* **with arms akimbo** les mains *ou* poings sur les hanches

akin [ə'kɪn] *adj* **akin to** *(like)* qui ressemble à, qui tient de; *(related to)* apparenté à; **feeling akin to fear** sentiment voisin de la peur; **this is akin to treachery** cela s'apparente à de la traîtrise

AL *(written abbr* **Alabama**) Alabama *m*

Alabama [ˌælə'bæmə] *n* l'Alabama *m*; **in Alabama** en Alabama

alabaster [ˌælə'bæstə(r)] **1** *n Cer* albâtre *m*
2 *comp Cer (figurine, vase etc)* en albâtre; *Fig (complexion, hands etc)* d'albâtre

alabastrine [ˌælə'bæstraɪn] *adj Literary (figurine, vase etc)* en albâtre; *Fig (complexion, hands etc)* d'albâtre

alack [ə'læk] *exclam Arch* hélas!

alacritous [ə'lækrɪtəs] *adj Literary* empressé

alacrity [ə'lækrətɪ] *n Formal* empressement *m*; **with great alacrity** avec beaucoup d'empressement

Aladdin [ə'lædɪn] *pr n* Aladin; **the shop is an Aladdin's cave** *(full of wonderful things)* cette boutique est une véritable caverne d'Ali Baba

alalia [æ'leɪlɪə] *n Med* aphasie *f*

Alamo ['æləməʊ] *n Hist* **the Alamo** *(fort)* Fort Alamo; *(battle)* la bataille de Fort Alamo

> **THE ALAMO**
>
> Fort situé au Texas où, en 1836, pendant la guerre d'Indépendance de cet État contre le Mexique, une poignée d'Américains, parmi lesquels Davy Crockett, résistèrent jusqu'à la mort à l'assaut d'une troupe mexicaine. "Remember the Alamo" devint le cri de ralliement des Texans au moment de l'indépendance de leur État. Le Texas fut annexé par les États-Unis en 1845.

à la mode [ælæ'məʊd] *adj Am Culin (with ice cream)* (servi) avec de la crème glacée

alanine ['ælənɪːn] *n Chem* alanine *f*

Al Anon [æl-] *n* = association d'aide aux personnes ayant des proches alcooliques

alarm [ə'lɑːm] **1** *n* **(a)** *(warning)* alarme *f*, alerte *f*; **to sound** *or* **to raise the alarm** donner l'alarme *ou* l'alerte *ou* l'éveil; **false alarm** fausse alerte
(b) *(for fire, burglary)* sonnette *f ou* sonnerie *f* d'alarme
(c) *(anxiety)* inquiétude *f*, alarme *f*; **the news caused them some alarm** la nouvelle leur a causé une certaine inquiétude; **there is no cause for alarm** il n'y a aucune raison de s'alarmer; **the government viewed events with increasing alarm** le gouvernement s'est montré de plus en plus inquiet face à ces événements
(d) *(clock)* réveil *m*, réveille-matin *m inv*
2 *comp (signal)* d'alarme
3 *vt* **(a)** *(frighten, worry → person)* alarmer, faire peur à; *(→ animal)* effaroucher, faire peur à; **I don't want to alarm you unduly** je ne veux pas vous alarmer sans raison
(b) *(warn)* alerter
►► ***alarm bell*** sonnerie *f* d'alarme; *Fig* **to set (the) alarm bells ringing** donner l'alerte; ***alarm call*** *(to wake sleeper)* réveil *m* téléphonique; ***alarm clock*** réveil *m*, réveille-matin *m inv*; **he set the alarm clock for eight o'clock** il a mis le réveil à sonner à huit heures *ou* pour huit heures; **the alarm clock went off at six o'clock** le réveil a sonné à six heures; ***alarm signal*** signal *m* d'alarme

alarmed [ə'lɑːmd] *adj* **(a)** *(anxious)* inquiet(ète); **don't be alarmed** ne vous alarmez *ou* effrayez pas; **the parents looked alarmed** les parents semblaient très inquiets; **to become alarmed** *(person)* s'alarmer; *(animal)* s'effaroucher, prendre peur **(b)** *(vehicle, building)* équipé d'une alarme

alarming [ə'lɑːmɪŋ] *adj* alarmant

alarmingly [ə'lɑːmɪŋlɪ] *adv* d'une manière alarmante; **the shots were coming alarmingly close** les tirs se rapprochaient dangereusement; **to develop alarmingly fast** se développer à une vitesse alarmante

alarmism [ə'lɑːmɪzəm] *n* alarmisme *m*

alarmist [ə'lɑːmɪst] **1** *adj* alarmiste
2 *n* alarmiste *mf*; **don't be such an alarmist** ne sois pas aussi alarmiste

alarum [ə'lærəm] *n Arch* timbre *m*, sonnerie *f* (du réveil)

Alas. *(written abbr* **Alaska**) Alaska *m*

alas [ə'læs] *exclam Literary* hélas!

Alaska [ə'læskə] *n* l'Alaska *m*; **in Alaska** en Alaska
►► ***the Alaska Highway*** la route de l'Alaska; ***the Alaska Range*** la chaîne de l'Alaska

Alaskan [ə'læskən] **1** *n* habitant(e) *m,f* de l'Alaska
2 *adj* de l'Alaska; *Petr* **the Alaskan pipeline** = oléoduc traversant l'Alaska

alastrim [ə'læstrɪm] *n Med* alastrim *m*

alb [ælb] *n Rel* aube *f (d'un prêtre)*

albacore ['ælbəkɔː(r)] *n Ich* germon *m*

Albania [æl'beɪnɪə] *n* Albanie *f*; **in Albania** en Albanie

Albanian [æl'beɪnɪən] **1** *n* **(a)** *(person)* Albanais(e) *m,f* **(b)** *(language)* albanais *m*
2 *adj* albanais
3 *comp (embassy)* d'Albanie; *(history)* de l'Albanie; *(teacher)* d'albanais

albatross ['ælbətrɒs] *n* **(a)** *Orn* albatros *m* **(b)** *Fig (handicap)* boulet *m*; **their past was an albatross round their necks** ils traînaient leur passé comme un boulet; **this issue has become an albatross around the government's neck** ce problème est devenu un gros handicap pour le gouvernement **(c)** *Golf* albatros *m*

albeit [ˌɔːl'biːɪt] *conj* bien que, encore que, quoique; **an impressive, albeit flawed work of art** une œuvre impressionnante bien qu'imparfaite *ou* quoiqu'imparfaite; **we managed, albeit with great difficulty** nous y sommes arrivés, quoiqu'avec grande difficulté

Albert ['ælbət] *pr n*
►► *Mus* ***the Albert Hall*** = salle de concert à Londres; ***the Albert Memorial*** = monument à Londres érigé en l'honneur du prince Albert

> **THE ALBERT HALL**
>
> Cette grande salle londonienne accueille concerts et manifestations diverses, y compris sportives; elle a été nommée ainsi en l'honneur du prince Albert, époux de la reine Victoria.

Alberta [æl'bɜːtə] *n* l'Alberta *f*; **in Alberta** dans l'Alberta

albescent [æl'besənt] *adj Literary (whitish)* qui tend vers le blanc; *(becoming white)* pâlissant

Albigensian [ˌælbɪ'dʒensɪən] *Hist & Rel* **1** *n* Albigeois(e) *m,f*
  2 *adj* albigeois
  ►► ***the Albigensian crusade*** la croisade des Albigeois

albinism ['ælbɪnɪzəm] *n Physiol & Zool* albinisme *m*

albino [æl'biːnəʊ] *Physiol & Zool* **1** *n* albinos *mf*
  2 *adj* albinos *(inv)*

Albion ['ælbɪən] *n Literary* Albion *f*; **perfidious Albion** la perfide Albion

album ['ælbəm] *n (book, LP)* album *m*
  ►► ***album cover (of LP)*** pochette *f* de disque

albumen ['ælbjʊmɪn] *n* (**a**) *(egg white)* albumen *m*, blanc *m* de l'œuf (**b**) *Biol (in blood)* albumine *f*

albumin ['ælbjʊmɪn] *n Biol* albumine *f*; **albumin deficiency** carence *f* en albumine

albuminous [æl'bjuːmɪnəs] *adj Biol* albumineux

Alcatraz ['ælkətræz] *n Hist* Alcatraz

Alcestis [æl'sestɪs] *pr n Myth* Alceste

alchemic [æl'kemɪk], **alchemical** [æl'kemɪkəl] *adj* alchimique

alchemist ['ælkəmɪst] *n* alchimiste *m*

alchemy ['ælkəmɪ] *n* alchimie *f*

Alcibiades [ˌælsɪ'baɪədiːz] *pr n Hist* Alcibiade

alcohol ['ælkəhɒl] *n* alcool *m*; **to have an alcohol problem** être alcoolique
  ►► ***alcohol abuse*** abus *m* d'alcool; ***alcohol content*** teneur *f* en alcool

alcohol-free *adj* sans alcool
  ►► *Br* ***alcohol-free beer*** bière *f* sans alcool

alcoholic [ˌælkə'hɒlɪk] **1** *n* alcoolique *mf*
  2 *adj (drink)* alcoolisé; *(person)* alcoolique
  ►► ***Alcoholics Anonymous*** Alcooliques *mpl* anonymes, ligue *f* antialcoolique

alcoholism ['ælkəhɒlɪzəm] *n* alcoolisme *m*

alcoholization [ˌælkəhɒlaɪ'zeɪʃən] *n* alcoolisation *f*

alcoholize, -ise ['ælkəhɒlaɪz] *vt* alcooliser

alcopop ['ælkəʊpɒp] *n* prémix *m*

alcove ['ælkəʊv] *n (in room)* alcôve *f*; *(in wall)* niche *f*; *(in garden)* tonnelle *f*; **dining alcove** coin *m* des repas, coin *m* salle à manger

Aldeburgh ['ɔːldbrə] *n* = ville de l'est de l'Angleterre où se tient chaque année un festival de musique

aldehyde ['ældɪhaɪd] *n Chem* aldéhyde *m*

al dente [ˌæl'dentɪ] *Culin* **1** *adj* al dente *(inv)*
  2 *adv* al dente

alder ['ɔːldə(r)] *n Bot* aulne *m*, aune *m*

alderman ['ɔːldəmən] *(pl* **aldermen** [-mən]*)* *n* (**a**) *Br Formerly & Am Admin (town councillor)* alderman *m*, conseiller *m* municipal; *Br (magistrate)* magistrat *m* (**b**) *Hist* ≃ échevin *m*

ALDERMAN

Ce mot désigne un haut magistrat de la **City** (voir ce mot) à Londres; jusqu'en 1974, il désignait également un conseiller municipal (sens qu'il a conservé aux États-Unis et au Canada).

Aldermaston ['ɔːldə mɑːstən] *n* = village dans le Berkshire où se trouve une agence de recherche sur l'armement nucléaire et qui a été le siège de nombreuses manifestations antinucléaires (les "Aldermaston marches")

Alderney ['ɔːldənɪ] *n* Aurigny; *(cow)* vache *f* d'Aurigny
  ►► ***Alderney cow*** vache *f* d'Aurigny

Aldershot ['ɔːldəʃɒt] *n* = ville-garnison dans le sud de l'Angleterre

aldose ['ældəʊs] *n Biol & Chem* aldose *m*

ale [eɪl] *n* (**a**) *(type of beer)* bière *f* anglaise, ale *f*; **pale/brown ale** = ale de couleur claire/foncée (**b**) *Br (beer)* bière *f*

aleatoric [ˌælɪə'tɒrɪk], **aleatory** ['eɪlɪətərɪ] *adj (gen) & Mus* aléatoire

alehouse ['eɪlhaʊs, *pl* -haʊzɪz] *n Arch* taverne *f*

Alemannic [ˌælə'mænɪk] *adj Geog & Ling* alémanique

aleph ['ɑːlef] *n Ling* aleph *m*

Aleppo [ə'lepəʊ] *n* Alep
  ►► *Bot* **Aleppo pine** pin *m* d'Alep *ou* de Jérusalem

alert [ə'lɜːt] **1** *n* alerte *f*; **to give the alert** donner l'alerte; **to be on the alert** *(gen)* être sur le qui-vive; *Mil* être en état d'alerte; **the sentries were told to be on the alert for an attack** les sentinelles avaient ordre de se tenir prêtes en cas d'attaque; **the navy has been put on full alert** l'alerte générale a été déclarée dans la marine; **they're always on the alert for interesting stories** ils sont toujours à l'affût d'histoires intéressantes
  2 *adj* (**a**) *(vigilant)* vigilant, sur le qui-vive; **you should be alert to the possible dangers** soyez conscient des éventuels dangers
  (**b**) *(lively → child, mind)* vif, éveillé
  3 *vt* alerter, donner l'alerte à; **to alert sb to a danger** avertir qn d'un danger; **a noise alerted her to the presence of an intruder** un bruit l'avertit de la présence d'un intrus
  ►► *Comput* ***alert box*** message *m* d'alerte

alertly [ə'lɜːtlɪ] *adv* avec vigilance

alertness [ə'lɜːtnɪs] *n* (**a**) *(vigilance)* vigilance *f* (**b**) *(liveliness)* vivacité *f*, esprit *m* éveillé

aleuron(e) [ə'lʊərən] *n Biol & Bot* aleurone *f*

Aleut [æ'luːt] *n (language)* aléoute *mf*

Aleutian Islands [ə'luːʃən-] *npl* **the Aleutian Islands** les îles *fpl* Aléoutiennes; **in the Aleutian Islands** aux îles Aléoutiennes

A level *n (abbr* **Advanced level***)* *(in England, Wales and Northern Ireland)* **A levels, A level exams** ≃ baccalauréat *m*; **he teaches A level physics** ≃ il est professeur de physique en terminale; **he has an A level in Maths** il a un diplôme de maths niveau bac; **to take one's A levels** ≃ passer son bac

A LEVEL

Cet examen, qui ouvre l'accès aux études supérieures en Grande-Bretagne, est beaucoup plus spécialisé que le baccalauréat français; il ne comprend que deux ou trois matières (exceptionnellement quatre). D'autre part, les mentions sont très importantes pour pouvoir choisir l'université où l'on souhaite faire ses études.

alewife ['eɪlwaɪf] *n Ich* alose *f*

Alexander [ˌælɪg'zɑːndə(r)] *pr n*
  ►► ***Alexander the Great*** Alexandre le Grand; *Med* ***Alexander technique*** technique *f* Alexander *(visant à limiter les tensions exercées sur le corps en travaillant sur le maintien et les mouvements)*

Alexandra Palace [ˌælɪg'zɑːndrə-] *n* = salle d'exposition et de concert de Londres

ALEXANDRA PALACE

Cet édifice de style victorien, situé à Alexandra Park au nord de Londres, abritait autrefois les studios de télévision de la BBC. C'est maintenant un centre d'expositions et de loisirs.

Alexandria [ˌælɪg'zɑːndrɪə] *n Geog* Alexandrie

Alexandrian [ˌælɪg'zɑːndrɪən] **1** *adj* alexandrin
  2 *n* Alexandrin(e) *m,f*
  ►► *Antiq* ***the Alexandrian Library*** la bibliothèque d'Alexandrie; *Phil* ***the Alexandrian School*** l'école *f* d'Alexandrie

alexandrine [ˌælɪg'zændraɪn] *Literature* **1** *adj* alexandrin
  2 *n* alexandrin *m*

alexandrite [ˌælɪg'zændraɪt] *n Miner* alexandrite *f*

alexia [ə'leksɪə] *n Med* alexie *f*, cécité *f* verbale

ALF [ˌeɪel'ef] *n (abbr* **Animal Liberation Front***)* = mouvement britannique militant pour la défense des droits des animaux

alfalfa [æl'fælfə] *n Bot* luzerne *f*

Alf Garnett [ˌælf'gɑːnɪt] *pr n TV* = personnage comique d'une série télévisée anglaise, stéréotype de l'ouvrier réactionnaire, raciste et sexiste

Alfred ['ælfrɪd] *pr n* Alfred
  ►► ***Alfred the Great*** Alfred le Grand

alfresco [æl'freskəʊ] **1** *adj* en plein air
  2 *adv* en plein air

alga ['ælgə] *(pl* **algae** [-dʒiː]*)* *n Bot* algue *f*; **algae** algues *fpl*

algal ['ælgəl] *adj*
  ►► *Bot* ***algal bloom*** bloom *m ou* prolifération *f* d'algues

Algarve [æl'gɑːv] *n* **the Algarve** l'Algarve *f*

algebra ['ældʒɪbrə] *n* algèbre *f*

algebraic [ˌældʒɪ'breɪɪk] *adj* algébrique

Algeciras [ˌældʒɪ'sɪərəs] *n Geog* Algésiras *m*

Algeria [æl'dʒɪərɪə] *n* Algérie *f*; **in Algeria** en Algérie

Algerian [æl'dʒɪərɪən] **1** *n* Algérien(enne) *m,f*
  2 *adj* algérien
  3 *comp (embassy)* d'Algérie; *(histoire)* de l'Algérie

algid ['ældʒɪd] *adj Med* algide

algidity [æl'dʒɪdɪtɪ] *n Med* algidité *f*

Algiers [æl'dʒɪəz] *n* Alger

alginate ['ældʒɪneɪt] *n Chem* alginate *m*

alginic [æl'dʒɪnɪk] *adj Chem* alginique
  ►► ***alginic acid*** acide *m* alginique

ALGOL, Algol ['ælgɒl] *n Comput (abbr* **algorithmic oriented language***)* ALGOL *m*

algology [æl'gɒlədʒɪ] *n Bot* algologie *f*

Algonkin [æl'gɒŋkɪn] *(pl* **inv** *or* **Algonkins***)*, **Algonquin** [æl'gɒŋkwɪn] *(pl* **Algonkin** *or* **Algonquins***)* **1** *n* (**a**) *(person)* Algonkin(e) *m,f*, Algonquin(e) *m,f* (**b**) *(language)* algonkin *m*, algonquin *m*
  2 *adj* algonquin

algorithm ['ælgərɪðəm] *n Math* algorithme *m*

algorithmic [ˌælgə'rɪðmɪk] *adj Math* algorithmique

Alhambra [æl'hæmbrə] *n Hist* Alhambra *f*

alias ['eɪlɪəs] **1** *adv* alias; **Burke, alias Brown** Burke, alias Brown
  2 *n* (**a**) *(name)* nom *m* d'emprunt, faux nom *m*; *(of author)* nom *m* de plume, pseudonyme *m*; **he has several aliases** il a plusieurs pseudonymes (**b**) *Comput (in e-mail, on desktop)* alias *m*

aliasing ['eɪlɪəsɪŋ] *n Comput* aliassage *m*, crénelage *m*

alibi ['ælɪbaɪ] **1** *n* alibi *m*; *Fig* alibi *m*, excuse *f*; **to produce an alibi** fournir un alibi; **to establish an alibi** prouver *ou* établir son alibi
  2 *vt Am Fam (person, action)* trouver des excuses à ☐

Alice ['ælɪs] *pr n* Alice
  ►► ***Alice band*** bandeau *m (pour les cheveux)*

'Alice in Wonderland' *Carroll* 'Alice au pays des merveilles'

alicyclic [ˌælɪ'saɪlɪk] *adj Chem* alicyclique

alien ['eɪljən] **1** *n* (**a**) *Admin (foreigner)* étranger(ère) *m,f*; **illegal alien** clandestin(e) *m,f*, immigré(e) *m,f* clandestin(e)
  (**b**) *(in science fiction)* extraterrestre *mf*
  2 *adj* (**a**) *(foreign → customs, environment)* étranger
  (**b**) *(contrary)* **alien to sth** contraire *ou* opposé à qch; **violence is completely alien to his nature** la violence n'est absolument pas dans sa nature
  (**c**) *(from outer space)* extraterrestre; **alien abduction** enlèvement *m* par des extraterrestres; **alien life forms** d'autres formes *fpl* de vie

alienable ['eɪljənəbəl] *adj Law (property)* aliénable

alienate ['eɪljəneɪt] *vt* (**a**) *(support, friends)* aliéner; **he has alienated all his former friends** il s'est aliéné tous ses anciens amis; **this tax will alienate the people** avec cet impôt, ils vont s'aliéner la population; **no government wishes to alienate voters** aucun gouvernement ne souhaite s'aliéner les électeurs; **she has become alienated from her parents** elle s'est détachée de ses parents (**b**) *Law & Psy* aliéner

alienated ['eɪljəneɪtɪd] *adj* exclu; **most unemployed people feel alienated from society** la plupart des chômeurs se sentent exclus de la société

alienation [ˌeɪljə'neɪʃən] *n* (**a**) *(of support, friends)* fait *m* de décourager *ou* d'éloigner; **this measure resulted in the alienation of many of the party's traditional voters** avec cette mesure, le parti s'est aliéné une grande partie de son électorat traditionnel; **a sense of alienation** un sentiment d'exclusion *ou* d'isolement (**b**) *Law & Psy* aliénation *f*

►► *Theat* **alienation effect** distanciation *f*

alienist ['eɪljənɪst] *n Am* aliéniste *mf*, psychiatre *mf*

alight [ə'laɪt] **1** *vi (bird)* se poser; *(person → from bus, train)* descendre; *(→ from bike, horse)* descendre, mettre pied à terre

2 *adj (fire)* allumé; *(house)* en feu; *Fig* **his face was alight with happiness** son visage rayonnait de joie

3 *adv* **to set sth alight** mettre le feu à qch; **to catch alight** prendre feu

►**alight on** *vt insep Formal (idea)* avoir soudain; *(information)* apprendre par hasard; *(lost object)* trouver par hasard

align [ə'laɪn] **1** *vt* **(a)** *(place in line → points, objects)* aligner, mettre en ligne; *(→ paper in printer)* mettre bien droit

(b) *Pol* aligner; **to align oneself with sb** s'aligner sur qn

(c) *Tech* aligner; *Aut* régler le parallélisme de

(d) *Comput & Typ (characters, graphics)* aligner, cadrer

(e) *Fin (currencies)* aligner (**on** sur)

2 *vi* **(a)** *(points, objects)* être aligné; *(persons, countries)* s'aligner; **to align with sb** s'aligner sur qn

(b) *(shafts)* coïncider

alignment [ə'laɪnmənt] *n* **(a)** *(of points, objects)* alignement *m*; **to be in/out of alignment** être/ne pas être dans l'alignement, être aligné/désaligné; **to bring sth into alignment with the new regulations** aligner qch sur la nouvelle réglementation; **this is not in alignment with current practice** ceci n'est pas conforme à ce qui se pratique actuellement

(b) *Pol* alignement *m*

(c) *Tech* alignement *m*; *Aut* parallélisme *m*; **the wheels are in/out of alignment** le parallélisme des roues est bien/mal réglé; **steering alignment** parallélisme *m* des roues avant

(d) *(of railway)* tracé *m*

(e) *Comput & Typ (of characters, graphics)* alignement *m*, cadrage *m*

(f) *Fin (of currencies)* alignement *m*

alike [ə'laɪk] **1** *adj* semblable; **the brothers are very alike** les deux frères se ressemblent beaucoup *ou* sont très semblables; **no two are alike** il n'y en a pas deux pareils; **you are all alike!** vous êtes tous les mêmes!; **they're very alike in the way they dress** leur façon de s'habiller se ressemble beaucoup

2 *adv (act, speak, dress)* de la même façon *ou* manière; **they look alike** ils se ressemblent; **we don't think alike** nous ne sommes pas d'accord, nous ne sommes pas du même avis; **she treats them all alike** elle les traite tous de la même manière; **two different words that sound alike** deux mots différents qui se ressemblent phonétiquement; **this affects Peter and his brother alike** cela touche Peter aussi bien que son frère; **every day, summer and winter alike** tous les jours, été comme hiver

aliment ['ælɪmənt] *n Scot Law* pension *f* alimentaire

alimentary [,ælɪ'mentərɪ] *adj* alimentaire

►► *Anat* **alimentary canal** tube *m* digestif

alimentation [,ælɪmen'teɪʃən] *n Formal* alimentation *f*

alimony ['ælɪmənɪ] *n Law* pension *f* alimentaire

►► **alimony suit** demande *f* d'aliments

A-line *adj (skirt, dress)* trapèze *(inv)*

aliphatic [,ælɪ'fætɪk] *adj Chem* aliphatique

►► **aliphatic compound** composé *m* aliphatique

aliquot ['ælɪkwɒt] *adj Math* aliquote

A-list *adj (star, celebrity, guest)* très en vue

alive [ə'laɪv] *adj* **(a)** *(living)* vivant, en vie; **he is still alive** il est toujours vivant *ou* en vie; **while he was alive** de son vivant; **to be burnt alive** être brûlé vif; **to bury sb alive** enterrer qn vivant; **no one got out of the building alive** personne n'est sorti vivant de l'immeuble; **to keep alive** *(person)* maintenir en vie; *(hope)* garder; *(tradition)* préserver; **they kept her memory alive** ils sont restés fidèles à sa mémoire; **to stay alive** rester en vie, survivre; **he felt that he was the luckiest man alive** il se sentit l'homme le plus heureux du monde; **no man alive could endure such pain** personne au monde ne pourrait endurer de telles souffrances; **it's good to be alive** il fait bon vivre; **he's still alive and kicking** *(not dead)* il est toujours bien en vie; *(lively)* il est toujours d'attaque *ou* plein de vie; **to be alive and well** *(person)* être bien vivant; *(attitude, prejudice, custom)* être vivace; **Mr Evans was last seen alive on 21 June** c'est le 21 juin qu'on a vu M. Evans vivant pour la dernière fois; **the oldest man alive** l'homme le plus vieux au monde

(b) *(lively, full of life)* plein de vie, vif, actif; **he came alive when someone mentioned food** il s'est réveillé quand quelqu'un a parlé de manger; **the town centre comes alive after lunchtime** le centre-ville s'anime après l'heure du déjeuner; *Fam* **look alive!** grouille-toi!, remue-toi!

(c) *(alert, aware)* conscient, sensible; **to be alive to the dangers of sth** être conscient des *ou* sensible aux dangers de qch; **he was fully alive to the risk he was taking** il était pleinement conscient *ou* avait pleinement conscience du risque qu'il encourait; **I am alive to the fact that...** je n'ignore pas que...

(d) *(full, crowded)* **the evening air was alive with insects** il y avait des nuées d'insectes dans l'air ce soir-là; **the streets were alive with people** les rues fourmillaient *ou* grouillaient de monde

alkali ['ælkəlaɪ] *n Chem* alcali *m*

►► **alkali metal** métal *m* alcalin

alkaline ['ælkəlaɪn] *adj Chem* alcalin

alkalinity [,ælkə'lɪnətɪ] *n Chem* alcalinité *f*

alkaloid ['ælkəlɔɪd] *n Chem* alcaloïde *m*

alkalosis [,ælkəl'əʊsɪs] *n Physiol* alcalose *f*

alkane ['ælkeɪn] *n Chem* alcane *m*

alkene ['ælkiːn] *n Chem* alcène *m*

alkie, alky ['ælkɪ] *(pl* **alkies**) *n Fam* **(a)** *(abbr* **alcoholic**) alcolo *mf*, poivrot(e) *m,f* **(b)** *Am (abbr* **alcohol**) gnôle *f*

►► *Am* **alkie cooking** = fabrication clandestine d'alcool

alkylation [,ælkɪ'leɪʃən] *n Chem* alcoylation *f*, alkylation *f*

ALL [ɔːl] **1** *adj* **(a)** *(the whole of)* tout; **all expenses will be reimbursed** tous les frais seront remboursés; **all night** toute la nuit; **all day and all night** toute la journée et toute la nuit; **all six of us want to go** nous voulons y aller tous/toutes les six; **to be all things to all men** être tout à tous

(b) *(every one of)* tous (toutes); **all kinds of people** toutes sortes de gens; **for children of all ages** pour les enfants de tous les âges; *Sport* **the British all-comers 100 m record** le record britannique de l'épreuve du 100 m ouverte à tous

(c) *(the utmost)* **(with) all my love** *(at end of letter)* bien affectueusement; **with all speed** à toute vitesse; **in all fairness (to sb)** pour être juste (avec qn)

2 *predet* **(a)** *(the whole of)* tout(e) *m,f*; **all the butter** tout le beurre; **all the beer** toute la bière; **all my life** toute ma vie; **all five women** les cinq femmes; **all the way** *(of journey)* tout le long du chemin; *(of course of action)* jusqu'au bout; **is that all the luggage you're taking?** c'est tout ce que vous emportez comme bagages?; **for all his wealth** en dépit de *ou* malgré sa fortune; *Fam* **and all that** et tout cela, et tout le reste; **you're not as ill as all that** vous n'êtes pas aussi *ou* si malade que ça; **it's not all that pleasant** ce n'est pas tellement agréable; **of all the stupid things to say/do!** de toutes les idioties possibles!; **of all times to phone!** il/elle/*etc* a bien choisi son/*etc* heure pour téléphoner!; **you, of all people, should know what I mean** toi au moins tu devrais savoir ce que je veux dire; **in all honesty/sincerity** pour être honnête/sincère; **what's all that noise?** qu'est-ce que c'est que tout ce bruit?; **all that's nonsense** tout ça, c'est des bêtises; **for all that they say he's a genius, I think...** ils ont beau dire que c'est un génie, moi, je pense...

(b) *(with comparative adjectives)* **all the better!** tant mieux!; **you will feel all the better for a rest** un peu de repos vous fera le plus grand bien; **all the sooner** d'autant plus vite

3 *pron* **(a)** *(everything)* tout; **I gave all I had** j'ai donné tout ce que j'avais; **take it all** prenez tout; **all I want is to rest** tout ce que je veux c'est du repos; **that's all I have to say** c'est tout ce que j'ai à dire; **all will be well** tout ira bien; **will that be all?** ce sera tout?; **I did all I could** j'ai fait tout ce que j'ai pu; **it was all I could do not to laugh** j'ai eu du mal à m'empêcher de rire; **it's all his fault** c'est sa faute à lui; **for all I know** autant que je sache; **for all I care** pour (tout) ce que cela me fait; **you men are all the same!** vous les hommes, vous êtes tous pareils *ou* tous les mêmes!; **all or nothing** tout ou rien; **all in good time** chaque chose en son temps; **when all is said and done** en fin de compte, au bout du compte; **best/worst of all,...** le mieux/pire, c'est que...; **most of all** surtout, en particulier; *Prov* **all's well that ends well** tout est bien qui finit bien

(b) *(everyone)* tous (toutes); **all are agreed that...** tous sont d'accord que...; **all of us** nous tous; **we all love him** nous l'aimons tous; **we all came** nous sommes tous venus; **good evening, all!** bonsoir à tous!, bonsoir, tout le monde!; **don't all speak at once!** ne parlez pas tous en même temps!; **they all made the same mistake** ils ont tous fait la même erreur; **the children were all hoping to go** les enfants espéraient tous y aller; **all who knew her loved her** tous ceux qui la connaissaient l'aimaient; **all together** tous à la fois, tous ensemble

(c) *Sport* **the score is 5 all** le score est de 5 partout; **30 all** *(in tennis)* 30 partout, 30 à

(d) *(as quantifier)* **all of** tout; **all of the butter/the cakes** tout le beurre, tous les gâteaux; **all of London** Londres tout entier; **all of it was sold** (le) tout a été vendu; **how much wine did they drink? – all of it** combien de vin ont-ils bu? – tout ce qu'il y avait; **I want all of it** je le veux en entier; **all of you can come** vous pouvez tous venir; **listen, all of you** écoutez-moi tous; **she knows all of their names** elle connaît tous leurs noms; **he must be all of sixty** il doit avoir au moins soixante ans; **the book cost me all of £10** le livre ne m'a coûté que 10 livres; *Hum* **it's all of five minutes' walk away!** c'est au moins à cinq minutes à pied!

4 *adv (as intensifier)* tout; **she was all alone** elle était toute seule; **she was all excited** elle était tout excitée; **she was all dressed** *or* **she was dressed all in black** elle était habillée tout en noir; **all along the road** tout le long de la route; **all around the edge** tout le long du bord; **I forgot all about the meeting** j'ai complètement oublié qu'il y avait une réunion; **the soup went all down my dress** la soupe s'est répandue partout sur ma robe; **the jacket's split all up the sleeve** la veste a craqué tout le long de la manche; *Fam* **don't get your hands all dirty** ne va pas te salir les mains!; *Fam* **the motor's all rusty inside** le moteur est tout rouillé à l'intérieur; **all at one go** (tout) d'un seul coup; **all in one piece** *(furniture)* tout d'une pièce; *Fig (person)* sain et sauf; **I'm all for it** moi, je suis tout à fait pour; **she's all for giving children their freedom** elle est tout à fait convaincue qu'il faut donner aux enfants leur liberté; **my wife was all for calling in a doctor** ma femme voulait à toute force *ou* à tout prix appeler un médecin; **he's not all bad** il n'est pas entièrement mauvais; **that's all to the good!** tout va pour le mieux!; **all the better/worse (for me)** tant mieux/pis (pour moi); **you will be all the better for it** vous vous en trouverez (d'autant) mieux; **all the harder** encore plus dur; **the time came all too soon** l'heure n'arriva que trop tôt; *Fam* **it's all up with him** il est fichu

5 *n* tout; **I would give my all to be there** je donnerais tout ce que j'ai pour y être; **the team gave their all** l'équipe a donné son maximum; **to stake one's all on sth** tout miser sur qch

6 at all *adv* du tout; **do you know him at all?** est-ce que vous le connaissez (un peu)?; **I didn't speak at all** je n'ai pas parlé du tout; **I'm not at all astonished** je n'en suis aucunement étonné; **he's not at all patient** il n'est pas du tout patient; **not at all** pas du tout, *Fam* du tout; *(when thanked)* je vous en prie; **nothing at all** rien du tout; **if he comes at all** s'il vient; **it**

seemed to worry him very little, if at all ça n'a pas eu l'air de l'inquiéter le moins du monde; **he comes rarely if at all** il vient très rarement, voire jamais; **if you had any feelings at all** si vous aviez le moindre sentiment; **if we had any money at all** si nous avions le moindre argent *ou* ne serait-ce qu'un peu d'argent; **if you do any travelling at all, you'll know what I mean** si vous voyagez un tant soit peu, vous comprendrez ce que je veux dire; **if it is at all cold** s'il fait un (tant soit) peu froid; **if it is at all possible** si c'était possible; **why do it at all?** pourquoi se donner la peine de le faire?

7 all along *adv* depuis le début; **that's what I've been saying all along** c'est ce que je dis depuis le début

8 all at once *adv* (**a**) *(suddenly)* tout d'un coup (**b**) *(all at the same time)* à la fois, en même temps

9 all but *adv* presque; **all but finished** presque *ou* pratiquement fini; **I all but missed it** j'ai bien failli le rater, c'est tout juste si je ne l'ai pas raté

10 all in 1 *adj Fam (exhausted)* **I'm all in** je suis mort **2** *adv (everything included)* tout compris; **the rent is £250 a month all in** le loyer est de 250 livres par mois tout compris

11 all in all *adv* tout compte fait

12 all out *adv* **to go all out** y aller à fond; **to go all out to do sth** se donner à fond pour faire qch

13 all over 1 *adj (finished)* fini; **that's all over and done with now** tout ça c'est bien terminé maintenant; **it's all over between them** tout est fini entre eux **2** *prep* partout; **there were toys scattered all over the floor** il y avait des jouets éparpillés partout sur le sol; **you've got ink all over you!** tu t'es mis de l'encre partout!; **all over the world** dans le monde entier; **we have agencies all over Europe** nous avons des agences dans toute l'Europe *ou* partout en Europe; **it'll be all over town tomorrow morning!** demain matin, toute la ville sera au courant!; *Fam* **all over the place** *(everywhere)* partout❑, dans tous les coins; *(very erratic, inaccurate)* pas au point❑; *Fam* **their filing system's all over the place** leur système de classement n'est pas du tout au point; *Fam* **the team was all over the place** l'équipe a joué n'importe comment❑; *Fam* **he was all over her** il ne l'a pas laissée tranquille un instant; *Fam* **he was all over us when he heard we were from the BBC** il ne nous a plus laissés tranquilles quand il a appris que nous étions de la BBC❑; *Fam Hum* **he was all over her like a rash** *or* **a cheap suit** il l'a draguée de façon flagrante **3** *adv (everywhere)* partout; **painted green all over** peint tout en vert; **covered all over in blossoms** tout en fleur *ou* en fleurs; **it was like being a child all over again** c'était comme retomber en enfance; *Fam* **that's him all over!** ça c'est lui tout craché!

14 all round *adv* **taken all round** tout bien considéré

15 all square *adj* (**a**) *(financially)* **we're all square now** nous ne sommes plus en compte maintenant (**b**) *Sport (level)* à égalité

16 all that *adv* **it isn't all that difficult** *or* **as difficult as all that** ce n'est pas si difficile que ça

17 all the more 1 *adj* **all the more reason for doing it again** raison de plus pour recommencer **2** *adv* encore plus; **it makes her all the more interesting** ça la rend encore plus intéressante; **it's all the more unfair since** *or* **as he promised not to put up the rent** c'est d'autant plus injuste qu'il a promis de ne pas augmenter le loyer

18 all the same 1 *adv (nevertheless)* tout de même, quand même; **he paid up all the same** il a payé quand même **2** *adj* **it's all the same to me** ça m'est complètement égal, peu m'importe; **if it's all the same to you** si cela ne vous gêne pas

19 all told *adv* tout compris; **there were six of us all told** nous étions six en tout

20 all too *adv* **all too soon** bien trop vite; **the holidays went all too quickly** les vacances ne sont passées que trop vite; **it's all too easy to forget that** c'est tellement facile de l'oublier

►► ***the All Blacks*** les All Blacks *mpl (l'équipe nationale de rugby de la Nouvelle-Zélande)*; ***all clear* 1** *n* (signal *m* de) fin *f* d'alerte; **to sound the all clear** sonner la fin de l'alerte; *Fig* **he received** *or* **was given the all clear on the project** on lui a donné le feu vert pour le projet; **the tests came back negative and he's been given the all clear** les résultats des tests sont revenus et tout est normal **2** *exclam* fin d'alerte!; ***All Fools' Day*** le premier avril; ***All Hallows*** Toussaint *f*; ***All Hallows' Eve*** la veille de la Toussaint; ***All Saints' Day*** (le jour de) la Toussaint; ***All Souls' Day*** le jour *ou* la fête des Morts

'All That Fall' *Beckett* 'Tous ceux qui tombent'

'All That Jazz' *Fosse* 'Que le spectacle commence!'

'All About Eve' *Mankiewicz* 'Ève'

'All Quiet on the Western Front' *Remarque, Milestone* 'À l'Ouest, rien de nouveau'

'All's Well That Ends Well' *Shakespeare* 'Tout est bien qui finit bien'

'All the King's Men' *Warren, Rossen* 'Les Fous du Roi'

all- [ɔ:l] *pref* entièrement; **all-male/female** entièrement masculin/féminin; **the first all-French baseball team** la première équipe de baseball entièrement française

all-absorbing *adj* absorbant, passionnant; **of all-absorbing interest** fascinant

Allah ['ælə] *pr n Rel* Allah

all-American *adj* cent pour cent américain; **the all-American boy** le jeune américain type

allantois [æ'læntɔɪs] *n Anat, Orn & Zool* allantoïde *f*

all-around *adj Am* (**a**) *(versatile → athlete, player)* complet(ète); *(→ ability)* complet(ète), polyvalent; *(expert)* dans tous les domaines (**b**) *(comprehensive → improvement)* général, sur toute la ligne

allay [ə'leɪ] *vt (fear)* apaiser; *(doubt, suspicion)* dissiper; *(pain, grief)* soulager, apaiser

all-conquering *adj* qui triomphe de tout

all-consuming *adj (passion, ambition)* dévorant

all-day *adj* qui dure toute la journée

all-devouring *adj (passion)* dévorant; *(time)* qui consume tout

allegation [,ælɪ'geɪʃən] *n* allégation *f*; **to make an allegation** alléguer *ou* avancer quelque chose; **you're making allegations you can't prove** vous avancez des choses que vous ne pouvez pas prouver

allege [ə'ledʒ] *vt* alléguer, prétendre; **he alleges that he was beaten up** il prétend avoir été roué de coups; **are you alleging police brutality?** est-ce que vous prétendez avoir été victime de violences policières?; **it is alleged that...** on prétend que... + *indicative;* **the incident is alleged to have taken place the night before** l'incident aurait eu lieu *ou* on prétend que l'incident a eu lieu la veille au soir

alleged [ə'ledʒd] *adj (motive, incident, reason)* allégué, prétendu; *(thief)* présumé

allegedly [ə'ledʒɪdlɪ] *adv* **they allegedly broke in and stole £300** ils seraient entrés par effraction et auraient volé 300 livres; **she allegedly stabbed her husband** elle aurait poignardé son mari; **allegedly he's the greatest violinist since Paganini** on dit que c'est le plus grand violoniste depuis Paganini

allegiance [ə'li:dʒəns] *n* allégeance *f*; **political allegiance** allégeance *f* politique; **to swear allegiance** faire serment d'allégeance; **to switch allegiance** changer de bord; **to owe allegiance to sb** devoir fidélité et obéissance à qn

allegoric [,ælɪ'gɒrɪk], **allegorical** [,ælɪ'gɒrɪkəl] *adj* allégorique

allegorically [,ælɪ'gɒrɪkəlɪ] *adv* sous forme d'allégorie, allégoriquement

allegorist ['ælɪgərɪst] *n* allégoriste *mf*

allegorize, -ise ['ælɪgəraɪz] **1** *vi* allégoriser **2** *vt* allégoriser

allegory ['ælɪgərɪ] (*pl* **allegories**) *n* allégorie *f*

allegretto [,ælɪ'gretəʊ] *Mus* **1** *n* allegretto *m* **2** *adv* allegretto

allegro [ə'legrəʊ] *Mus* **1** *n* allegro *m* **2** *adv* allegro

allel, allele [æ'li:l], **allelomorph** [æ'li:ləʊmɔ:f] *n Biol* allèle *m*

alleluia [,ælɪ'lu:jə] *exclam Rel* alléluia!

all-embracing *adj (study, survey)* exhaustif, complet(ète); *(term)* global; **all-embracing knowledge** vaste érudition *f*

All-England Club *n Sport* = club de tennis où se déroule le tournoi de Wimbledon

Allen key, *Am* **Allen wrench** ['ælən-] *n Tech* clé *f* Allen, clé *f* à six pans creux, clé *f* hexagonale

allergen ['ælədʒən] *n Med* allergène *m*

allergenic [ælə'dʒenɪk] *adj Med* allergisant

allergic [ə'lɜ:dʒɪk] *adj (reaction, person)* allergique; **I'm allergic to cats** je suis allergique aux chats; *Hum* **he's allergic to hard work** il est allergique au travail

►► ***allergic reaction*** réaction *f* allergique; *Med* ***allergic rhinitis*** rhinite *f* allergique

allergist ['ælədʒɪst] *n Med* allergologiste *mf*, allergologue *mf*

allergy ['ælədʒɪ] (*pl* **allergies**) *n* allergie *f*

alleviate [ə'li:vɪeɪt] *vt (pain, suffering)* alléger, apaiser, soulager; *(problem, difficulties, poverty)* réduire; *(effect)* réduire, atténuer

alleviation [əli:vɪ'eɪʃən] *n (of pain, suffering)* apaisement *m*, soulagement *m*; *(of problem, difficulties)* amenuisement *m*; *(of poverty)* réduction *m*

all-expenses-paid *adj* tous frais payés

all-expense tour *n* voyage *m* à forfait

alley ['ælɪ] *n* (**a**) *(street)* ruelle *f*, passage *m*; *(in park, garden)* allée *f*; *Fig* **that's right up my alley** c'est tout à fait mon rayon; **I wouldn't like to meet him in a dark alley!** je n'aimerais pas le rencontrer au coin d'un bois! (**b**) *Am Sport (on tennis court)* couloir *m* (**c**) *Sport (for tenpin bowling, skittles)* bowling *m*, prise *f* de jeu (**d**) *(marble)* (grosse) bille *f*, calot *m*

►► ***alley cat*** chat *m* de gouttière

alleyway ['ælɪweɪ] *n* ruelle *f*, passage *m*

all-fired *Am Fam* **1** *adj* infernal **2** *adv* vachement, super

alliance [ə'laɪəns] *n* (**a**) *(agreement)* alliance *f*; **to enter into** *or* **to form an alliance with sb** s'allier *ou* faire alliance avec qn; *Pol* **electoral alliance** apparentement *m*, alliance *f* électorale (**b**) *(by marriage)* alliance *f*

allied ['ælaɪd] *adj* (**a**) *(force, nations)* allié (**b**) *(related → subjects)* connexe, du même ordre; *Econ & Fin (→ product, industry)* assimilé; *Biol* voisin (**c**) *(connected)* allié; **allied with** allié à; **his natural talent, allied with his good looks, made him a star** son talent naturel allié à un physique agréable ont fait de lui une star

►► ***the Allied forces*** *(in World War II)* les forces *fpl* alliées; ***the Allied Powers*** les Puissances *fpl* alliées

alligator ['ælɪgeɪtə(r)] **1** *n* alligator *m* **2** *comp (bag, shoes)* en (peau d')alligator; *(skin)* d'alligator

all-important *adj* de la plus haute importance, d'une importance primordiale *ou* capitale; **she found the all-important solution** elle a trouvé la solution essentielle; **it is all-important that we get this contract** il est capital que nous obtenions ce contrat

all-in *adj (price, tariff)* net, tout compris, forfaitaire; *(insurance policy)* tous risques

all-inclusive *adj (price, tariff)* net, tout compris, forfaitaire

►► ***all-inclusive holiday*** forfait *m* vacances tout compris

all-in-one 1 *n (garment)* combinaison *f* **2** *adj* tout-en-un *(inv)*

all-in wrestling *n* lutte *f* libre, catch *m*

alliteration [ə,lɪtə'reɪʃən] *n Ling* allitération *f*

alliterative [ə'lɪtərətɪv] *adj Ling* allitératif

all-merciful *adj Rel* infiniment miséricordieux

all-night *adj (party, film)* qui dure toute la nuit; *(shop, restaurant)* de nuit, ouvert la nuit; **an all-night sitting of Parliament** une session parlementaire de nuit

▸▸ *Mil* ***all-night pass*** permission *f* de (la) nuit; *Cin* ***all-night showing*** = projection ininterrompue durant toute la nuit

all-nighter [-'naɪtə(r)] *n Am* **we pulled an all-nighter for the physics exam** on a passé la nuit à réviser l'examen de physique; **the party will be an all-nighter** la fête va durer toute la nuit

allocate ['æləkeɪt] *vt* (**a**) *(assign → resources, money, capital, duties)* affecter, attribuer (**to** à); *(→ role, part)* attribuer (**to** à); *St Exch (→ shares)* attribuer, allouer (**to** à); **funds allocated to research** des crédits affectés à la recherche; **10 percent of profits are allocated to investment/advertising** 10 pour cent des bénéfices ont été affectés aux investissements/à la publicité; **allocated budget** enveloppe *f* budgétaire; **in the time allocated** dans le temps *ou* le délai imparti; **you'll need to allocate your time carefully** il va falloir que tu répartisses ton temps avec précaution

(**b**) *(share out)* répartir, distribuer

(**c**) *Law* ventiler

(**d**) *Comput (memory)* attribuer

allocation [ælə'keɪʃən] *n* (**a**) *(assignment → of resources, money, capital, duties)* affectation *f*, attribution *f*; *(→ of role, part)* attribution *f*; *St Exch (→ of shares)* attribution *f*, allocation *f* (**b**) *(sharing out)* répartition *f* (**c**) *(share → of money)* part *f*; *(→ of space)* portion *f* (**d**) *Law* ventilation *f* (**e**) *Comput (of memory)* attribution *f*

allogamy [ə'lɒgəmɪ] *n Bot* allogamie *f*

allograft ['æləʊˌgrɑːft] *n Med* allogreffe *f*

allometry [ə'lɒmətrɪ] *n Biol* allométrie *f*

allomorph ['æləmɔːf] *n Chem* allomorphe *m*

allomorphism [ˌæləʊ'mɔːfɪzəm] *n Chem* allomorphie *f*

allopath ['æləpæθ] *n Med* allopathe *mf*

allopathic [ælə'pæθɪk] *adj Med* allopathique

allopathy [ə'lɒpəθɪ] *n Med* allopathie *f*

allophone ['æləfəʊn] *n Ling* allophone *m*

all-or-none order *n St Exch* ordre *m* tout ou rien

allosaur ['æləsɔː(r)], **allosaurus** [ˌælə'sɔːrəs] *n Zool* allosaure *m*

allosteric [ˌæləʊ'stɪərɪk] *adj Biol & Chem* allostérique

allot [ə'lɒt] *(pt & pp* **allotted**, *cont* **allotting**) *vt* (**a**) *(assign → money, duties, time)* allouer, assigner, attribuer (**to** à); *St Exch (→ shares)* attribuer, allouer (**to** à); **in the allotted time** dans le délai *ou* temps imparti; **the farmers were allotted a few acres each** on a attribué aux fermiers quelques hectares chacun; **allotted budget** enveloppe *f* budgétaire (**b**) *(share out)* répartir, distribuer

allotment [ə'lɒtmənt] *n* (**a**) *(of money, duties, time)* allocation *f*, attribution *f*; *St Exch (of shares)* attribution *f*, allocation *f*; *St Exch* **letter of allotment** (lettre *f* d') avis *m* d'attribution (**b**) *Br (land)* jardin *m* ouvrier

▸▸ *St Exch* ***allotment letter*** (lettre *f* d')avis *m* d'attribution; *St Exch* ***allotment right*** droit *m* d'attribution

allotrope ['ælətrəʊp] *n Chem* variété *f* allotropique

allotropic [ˌæləʊ'trɒpɪk], **allotropical** [ˌæləʊ'trɒpɪkəl] *adj Chem* allotropique

allotropy [æ'lɒtrəpɪ] *n Chem* allotropie *f*

allottable [ə'lɒtəbəl] *adj (funds, land)* à distribuer, à répartir

all-out 1 *adj (strike, war)* total; *(effort)* maximum

2 *adv Fam* **to go all-out** y aller tous azimuts *ou* à fond; **he's going all-out to win the gold medal** il est en train de se donner à fond pour avoir la medaille d'or; **we're working all-out to finish on time** on travaille comme des fous pour terminer dans les temps

all-over *adj* qui s'étend sur toute la surface; **an all-over tan** un bronzage intégral

allow [ə'laʊ] *vt* (**a**) *(permit)* permettre, autoriser; **to allow sb to do sth** permettre à qn de faire qch, autoriser qn à faire qch; **he wasn't allowed to see her** il n'a pas été autorisé à la voir, il n'a pas eu le droit de la voir; **is he allowed sweets/help?** est-ce qu'il a le droit de manger des sucreries/de recevoir de l'aide?; **he was allowed a final cigarette** on lui a permis (de fumer) une dernière cigarette; **we weren't allowed in** on ne nous a pas permis d'entrer; **the dog is not allowed in the house** on ne laisse pas le chien entrer dans la maison, l'accès de la maison est interdit au chien; **smoking is not allowed** *(sign)* défense de fumer; **gambling is not allowed** les jeux d'argent sont interdits; **she allowed herself to be manipulated** elle s'est laissé manipuler; **he decided to allow events to take their course** il a décidé de laisser les événements suivre leur cours; **I won't allow such behaviour!** je ne tolérerai pas une telle conduite!; *Formal* **allow me to make a suggestion** permettez-moi de faire une suggestion; **if I may be allowed to make a point** si je peux me permettre (de faire) une remarque; **allow me!** vous permettez?

(**b**) *(enable)* permettre; **the ramp allows people in wheelchairs to enter the building** la rampe permet l'accès de l'immeuble aux personnes en fauteuil roulant

(**c**) *(grant → money, time)* accorder, allouer; *(→ opportunity)* donner; *(→ claim)* admettre; **to allow sb a discount** faire un escompte *ou* une remise à qn; **three hours are allowed for the exam** trois heures sont accordées pour l'examen; **he is allowed £5 pocket money** on lui accorde *ou* donne 5 livres d'argent de poche; **she allowed herself a cream cake as a special treat** comme petit plaisir, elle s'est offert un gâteau à la crème; **how much time/money are we allowed?** de combien de temps/d'argent disposons-nous?; **the bank allows 5 per cent interest on deposits** la banque alloue *ou* attribue 5 pour cent d'intérêt sur les dépôts

(**d**) *(take into account)* prévoir, compter; **allow a week for delivery** il faut prévoir *ou* compter une semaine pour la livraison; **you need to allow a few extra inches for the hem** il faut laisser *ou* prévoir quelques centimètres de plus pour l'ourlet

(**e**) *Literary (admit)* admettre, convenir; **you must allow that she is gifted** vous devez admettre *ou* reconnaître qu'elle est douée

(**f**) *Am Fam (maintain)* affirmer ❑

▸**allow for** *vt insep* (**a**) *(take into account)* tenir compte de; **allowing for the bad weather** compte tenu du mauvais temps; **we allowed for every possibility in our calculations** nous avons tenu compte de *ou* paré à toute éventualité dans nos calculs; **we must allow for the fact that she has been ill** il faut tenir compte du fait qu'elle a été malade

(**b**) *(make allowance or provision for)* **remember to allow for the time difference** n'oublie pas de compter le décalage horaire; **we hadn't allowed for these extra costs** nous n'avions pas prévu ces frais supplémentaires; **after allowing for travel expenses** déduction faite des frais de voyage

▸**allow of** *vt insep Formal* admettre, souffrir, autoriser; **the evidence allows of no other conclusion** les éléments dont nous disposons n'autorisent aucune autre conclusion

allowable [ə'laʊəbəl] *adj* admissible, permis; *(claim)* recevable; *(expense)* déductible, remboursable; *Fin* **expenses allowable against tax** dépenses *fpl* fiscalement déductibles

allowance [ə'laʊəns] *n* (**a**) *Admin (grant)* allocation *f*; *Fin (for housing, travel, food)* indemnité *f*; *Law (alimony)* pension *f* alimentaire; *(for student → from state)* bourse *f*; *(→ from parents)* pension *f* alimentaire; *(pension)* pension *f*; *(income, salary)* revenu *m*, appointements *mpl*; **his parents give him a monthly allowance of £100** ses parents lui versent une mensualité de 100 livres; **he gets a monthly allowance of £300** il touche 300 livres par mois; **she makes an allowance of £1,000 a year to her nephew** elle verse une rente *ou* une pension de 1000 livres par an à son neveu; **rent allowance** allocation *f* (de) logement

(**b**) *Fin (discount)* déduction *f*, concession *f*; *(for tax)* abattement *m*

(**c**) *(entitlement)* **(free) baggage** *or* **luggage allowance** *(on plane, coach etc)* bagages *mpl* en franchise; **there is an allowance of one item of luggage per passenger** chaque passager a droit à un bagage; **what's the duty-free allowance?** qu'est-ce qu'on a droit de ramener hors taxe?; *Sport* **time allowance** concession *m* de temps

(**d**) *Am (pocket money)* argent *m* de poche

(**e**) *(idioms)* **to make allowances for sb** être indulgent avec qn; **to make allowance** *or* **allowances for sth** tenir compte de qch, prendre qch en considération; **we must make allowance** *or* **allowances for the children's age** il faut tenir compte de *ou* il ne faut pas oublier l'âge des enfants; **you have to make allowances for inflation** il faut faire la part de l'inflation; **some allowance must be made for shrinkage** il faut tenir compte du rétrécissement

alloy 1 *n* ['ælɔɪ] *Metal* alliage *m*

2 *vt* [ə'lɔɪ] (**a**) *Metal (metal)* allier, faire un alliage de (**b**) *Fig* dévaloriser, souiller

3 alloys *npl* ['ælɔɪz] *Aut* roues *fpl* en alliage léger

▸▸ *Metal* ***alloy steel*** acier *m* allié *ou* spécial; *Aut* ***alloy wheels*** roues *fpl ou* jantes *fpl* en alliage léger

alloyed [ə'lɔɪd] *adj Metal* allié (**with** à *ou* avec)

all-party committee *n Pol* = comité où tous les partis sont représentés

all-pervading, all-pervasive *adj (stench)* envahissant, qui se répand partout; *(fear, corruption, influence)* omniprésent

all-points bulletin *n Am* = message radio diffusé par la police concernant une personne recherchée

all-powerful *adj* tout-puissant

all-purpose *adj (gen)* qui répond à tous les besoins, passe-partout *(inv)*; *(tool, vehicle, room, building)* polyvalent; **all-purpose cleaning fluid** détachant *m* tous usages

all right 1 *adj* (**a**) *(adequate)* (assez) bien, pas mal; **the film was all right** le film n'était pas mal; **the money is all right, but it could be better** le salaire est correct, mais ça pourrait être mieux

(**b**) *(in good health)* en bonne santé; *(safe)* sain et sauf; **I hope they'll be all right on their own** j'espère qu'ils sauront se débrouiller tout seuls; **are you all right?** *(are you well?)* ça va?; *(did you hurt yourself?)* ça va?, vous ne vous êtes pas blessé?; *Ironic* tu ne te sens pas bien?; **she's had an accident, but she's all right** elle a eu un accident mais ça va; **he was quite ill, but he's all right now** il a été assez malade, mais ça va *ou* il est rétabli maintenant; **do you think the car will be all right?** tu crois que ça ira avec la voiture?

(**c**) *(indicating agreement, approval)* **is it all right if they come too?** ça va s'ils viennent aussi?; **it's all right** *(no problem)* ça va; *(no matter)* ça ne fait rien, ce n'est pas grave; **I've come to see if everything is all right** je suis venu voir si tout va bien; **is everything all right, Madam?** *(in shop, restaurant etc)* tout va bien, madame?; *Br Fam* **it'll be all right on the night** tu verras, tout se passera bien ❑; **it's all right by me** moi, ça me va; **it's all right for YOU to laugh!** tu peux rire, moi, ça ne m'amuse pas!

(**d**) *(pleasant)* bien, agréable; *(nice-looking)* chouette; **the boss is all right** le patron est bien *ou* n'est pas trop mal; **she's all right** elle est pas mal

(**e**) *(financially etc)* à l'aise, tranquille; **I'll see that you're all right** je veillerai à ce que vous ne manquiez de rien; **I'm all right until Monday** ça ira jusqu'à lundi; **are you all right for cash/cigarettes?** tu as assez de liquide/de cigarettes?

2 *adv* (**a**) *(well, adequately)* bien; **the radio works all right** la radio marche bien; **they're doing all right** *(progressing well)* ça va (pour eux); *(succeeding in career, life)* ils se débrouillent bien; **everything went off all right** tout a bien marché

(**b**) *(without doubt)* **it's rabies all right** c'est bien la rage; **he was listening all right** ça, pour écouter, il écoutait

3 *exclam (indicating agreement, understanding)* entendu!, d'accord!; *(indicating approval)* c'est ça!, ça va!; *(indicating impatience)* ça va!, ça suffit!; *(indicating change or continuation of activity)* bon!; *Am (expressing great enthusiasm)* génial!; **all right, all right, I'm coming!** *(expressing irritation)* oui, oui, j'arrive!

all-right *adj* **he's an all-right guy** c'est un type réglo; **it was an all-right film** le film n'était pas mal

all-risks insurance *n* assurance *f* tous risques

all-round, *Am* **all-around** *adj* (**a**) *(versatile → athlete, player)* complet(ète); *(→ ability)* complet(ète), polyvalent; *(expert)* dans tous les domaines (**b**) *(comprehensive → improvement)* général, sur toute la ligne

all-rounder *n Br* **he's a good all-rounder** *(gen)* il est doué dans tous les domaines, il est bon en tout; *Sport* c'est un sportif complet

all-seater *adj*

►► ***all-seater stadium*** = stade ayant uniquement des places assises

All-Share Index *n Br St Exch* = indice du *Financial Times* et de l'Institut des actuaires britannique

all-singing all-dancing *adj Fam (model, system, technology)* hypersophistiqué

allspice [ˈɔːlspaɪs] *n* poivre *m* de la Jamaïque, toute-épice *m*

all-star *adj (show, performance)* avec beaucoup de vedettes, à vedettes; **with an all-star cast** avec une distribution prestigieuse; *Sport* **an all-star game** = un match dont les équipes réunissent les meilleurs joueurs professionnels

all-state *adj Am (player, team)* = sélectionné pour représenter un État

all-terrain *adj Aut* tout-terrain

all-time *adj (record)* absolu; **sales figures have reached an all-time high/low** les chiffres de vente n'ont jamais été aussi bons/mauvais; **this film is one of the all-time greats** ce film est l'un des meilleurs de tous les temps; **an all-time best-seller** un best-seller jamais égalé

allude [əˈluːd] *vi* **to allude to sb/sth** faire allusion à qn/qch; **I am not alluding to anybody in particular** je ne vise personne

allure [əˈljʊə(r)] **1** *n* attrait *m*, charme *m*; **it holds no allure for me** ça ne m'attire pas du tout

2 *vt* attirer, séduire

alluring [əˈljʊərɪŋ] *adj* séduisant, attrayant

alluringly [əˈljʊərɪŋlɪ] *adv* d'une manière séduisante *ou* attirante

allusion [əˈluːʒən] *n* allusion *f*; **to make an allusion to sth** faire allusion à qch

allusive [əˈluːsɪv] *adj* allusif, qui contient une allusion/des allusions

allusively [əˈluːsɪvlɪ] *adv* par allusion

allusiveness [əˈluːsɪvnɪs] *n* caractère *m* allusif; **allusiveness of style** style *m* plein d'allusions

alluvial [əˈluːvɪəl] *adj Geol (ground)* alluvial; **alluvial deposits** alluvions *fpl*, dépôts *mpl* alluvionnaires

►► ***alluvial plain*** plaine *f* alluviale

alluvium [əˈluːvɪəm] *(pl* **alluviums** *or* **alluvia** [-vɪə]) *n Geol* alluvions *fpl*

all-weather *adj (surface)* de toute saison, tous temps

►► *Sport* ***all-weather court*** *(for tennis)* (terrain *m* en) quick *m*; ***all-weather pitch*** terrain *m* tous temps

all-wheel drive *n Aut* quatre roues *fpl* motrices

ally *(pl* **allies**) **1** *n* [ˈælaɪ] allié(e) *m,f*; **to become allies** s'allier; **the two countries were allies** les deux pays étaient alliés

2 *vt* [əˈlaɪ] allier, unir; **to ally oneself with sb** s'allier avec qn; **Italy was allied with Germany** l'Italie était alliée avec *ou* à l'Allemagne; **we must ally ourselves with other unions** nous devons nous allier à *ou* nous associer avec d'autres syndicats

3 Allies *npl Hist* **the Allies** les Alliés

Ally Pally [ˌælɪˈpælɪ] *n* = surnom du "Alexandra Palace"

Alma Mater, alma mater [ælməˈmɑːtə(r)] *n Sch & Univ (institution)* = école ou université où l'on a fait ses études; *Am (anthem)* = hymne d'une école ou d'une université

almanac [ˈɔːlmənæk] *n* almanach *m*

almighty [ɔːlˈmaɪtɪ] **1** *adj* (**a**) *(omnipotent)* tout-puissant, omnipotent (**b**) *Fam (as intensifier → row, racket)* formidable, sacré; **an almighty din** un vacarme de tous les diables (**b**) *Rel* **Almighty God, God Almighty** Dieu Tout-Puissant

2 *adv Am Fam* extrêmement❑, énormément❑

3 *n Rel* **the Almighty** le Tout-Puissant

almond [ˈɑːmənd] **1** *n* (**a**) *(nut)* amande *f*; **sweet/bitter almond** amande *f* douce/amère; **ground almonds** amandes *fpl* pilées (**b**) *(tree)* amandier *m*

2 *comp (icing, essence)* d'amandes; *(cake)* aux amandes

►► ***almond eyes*** yeux *mpl* en amande; ***almond oil*** huile *f* d'amande; ***almond paste*** pâte *f* d'amande; ***almond tree*** amandier *m*

almond-eyed *adj* aux yeux en amande

almond-shaped *adj (eyes)* en amande

almoner [ˈɑːmənə(r)] *n* (**a**) *Hist* aumônier(ère) *m,f* (**b**) *Br Arch (social worker)* assistant(e) *m,f* social(e) *(dans un hôpital)*

almost [ˈɔːlməʊst] *adv* presque; **almost all the people** presque tous les gens, la quasi-totalité des gens; **it's almost cooked/finished** c'est presque cuit/terminé; **he is almost thirty** il a presque trente ans; **I can almost reach it** j'arrive presque à l'atteindre; **I almost cried** j'ai failli pleurer; **he was almost crying with frustration** il pleurait presque de rage; **I almost believed him** j'ai bien failli le croire, j'étais près de le croire; **we're almost there** nous sommes presque arrivés; **you're almost there** *(in answering question)* tu y es presque

alms [ɑːmz] *npl Hist* aumône *f*; **to give alms to sb** faire l'aumône *ou* la charité à qn

►► *Hist* ***alms box*** tronc *m* (pour les pauvres)

almsgiving [ˈɑːmzgɪvɪŋ] *n Hist* aumône *f*

almshouse [ˈɑːmzˌhaʊs, *pl* -haʊzɪz] *n Br Hist* hospice *m (géré par des religieux ou par une association caritative)*

aloe [ˈæləʊ] *n Bot* aloès *m*; **bitter aloes** amer *m* d'aloès

►► *Bot & Pharm* ***aloe vera*** aloe vera *m*

aloft [əˈlɒft] *adv* **(up) aloft** *(gen)* en haut, en l'air; *Aviat* en l'air; *Naut* dans la mâture

aloha [əˈləʊhɑː] *exclam (Hawaiian greeting)* salut!

►► ***the Aloha State*** = surnom donné à Hawaii

alone [əˈləʊn] **1** *adj* (**a**) *(on one's own)* seul; **to be alone** être seul; **I like being alone** j'aime la solitude *ou* être seul; **alone at last!** enfin seul(s)!; **I'm not alone in thinking that it's unfair** je ne suis pas le seul à penser que c'est injuste

(**b**) *(only)* seul; **she alone knows the truth** elle seule connaît la vérité; **time alone will tell** qui vivra verra; **every decision was, in the end, his alone** quand il y avait une décision à prendre, c'était toujours lui qui avait le dernier mot; **with that charm which is his alone** avec ce charme qui lui est propre; **the frame alone is worth £50** le cadre seul vaut 50 livres

(**c**) *(lonely)* seul; **she felt very alone** elle se sentait très seule

2 *adv* (**a**) *(on one's own)* seul; **he came alone** il est venu seul; **he lives (all) alone** il vit (tout) seul; **she managed to open the box alone** elle a réussi à ouvrir la boîte toute seule; **I'd like to speak to you alone** je voudrais vous parler seul à seul; **to stand alone** *(person)* rester seul; *(house)* être situé à l'écart; *Fig* **she stands alone as the most successful politician this century** elle est la seule depuis le début du siècle à avoir aussi bien réussi politiquement *ou* en politique; **to go it alone** faire cavalier seul

(**b**) *(undisturbed)* **to leave** *or* **to let sb alone** laisser qn tranquille; **leave me alone** *(on my own)* laissez-moi seul; *(in peace)* laissez-moi tranquille, laissez-moi en paix; **to let** *or* **leave sth alone** *(not get involved)* ne pas se mêler de qch; **leave these things alone** *(don't touch)* ne touchez pas à tout ça; **leave the bag alone!** laissez le sac tranquille!, ne touchez pas au sac!; **if I were you I would let well alone** si j'étais vous, je ne m'en mêlerais pas; **a subject better left alone** un sujet qu'il vaut mieux ne pas aborder

3 let alone *conj* sans parler de; **he's never been to London, let alone Paris** il n'a jamais été à Londres, sans parler de Paris; **she can't even walk, let alone run** elle ne peut même pas marcher, alors encore moins courir; **the soup wasn't even warm, let alone hot!** la soupe ne risquait pas d'être chaude, elle était à peine tiède!

> **I want to be alone**
> Il s'agit d'une phrase prononcée par Greta Garbo dans le film *Grand Hotel* (Grand Hôtel) (1932), qui évoque immanquablement la célèbre actrice.
> On prononce cette phrase avec l'accent scandinave, en référence à Greta Garbo et souvent par dérision, lorsque quelqu'un annonce qu'il désire qu'on le laisse seul de façon quelque peu théâtrale.

along [əˈlɒŋ] **1** *prep* (**a**) *(the length of)* le long de; **we walked along the road** nous avons marché le long de la route; **there were trees all along the road** il y avait des arbres tout le long de la route, des arbres bordaient la route; **the railway runs along the coast** la ligne de chemin de fer longe la côte; **to look along the street/corridor** regarder dans la rue/le couloir

(**b**) *(at or to a certain point in)* **could you move further along the row** pourriez-vous vous déplacer vers le bout du rang?; **her office is along here somewhere** son bureau est quelque part par ici; **the toilets are just along the corridor** les toilettes sont juste un peu plus loin dans le couloir; **somewhere along the way** en route, en chemin

2 *adv* (**a**) *(in phrasal verbs)* **I was driving/strolling along on a sunny afternoon, when...** je roulais/me baladais par un après-midi ensoleillé, quand...; **she was pulling a trolley along** elle tirait *ou* traînait un chariot derrière elle; **just then along came a policeman** c'est alors qu'un policier est arrivé; **bring a tent along (with you)** apportez une tente; **can I bring a friend along?** est-ce que je peux amener un ami?

(**b**) *(indicating progress)* **how far along is the project?** où en est le projet?; **we're further along than expected** nous en sommes plus loin que prévu; **things are going** *or* **coming along nicely, thank you** les choses ne se présentent pas trop mal, merci

(**c**) *(indicating imminent arrival)* **I'll be along in a minute** j'arrive tout de suite; **she'll be along later** elle viendra plus tard; **there'll be another bus along shortly** un autre bus va passer bientôt

3 along by *prep* en passant par; **we went strolling along by the river** on s'est baladé le long de la rivière

4 along with *prep* avec; **along with hundreds of others** avec des centaines d'autres; **I put the coat away along with the rest of my winter clothes** j'ai rangé le manteau avec mes autres vêtements d'hiver

alongshore [əˌlɒŋˈʃɔː(r)] **1** *adv* le long de la côte

2 *adj (current, tide)* côtier

alongside [əlɒŋˈsaɪd] **1** *prep* (**a**) *(along)* le long de; **to come** *or* **to draw alongside the quay** accoster le quai; **the railway runs alongside the road** la ligne de chemin de fer longe la route

(**b**) *(beside)* à côté de; **the car drew up alongside me** la voiture s'est arrêtée à côté de moi

(**c**) *(together with)* avec; **I worked alongside her for two years** j'ai travaillé avec elle pendant deux ans; **if you look at it alongside his earlier work** si vous le comparez à ses travaux plus anciens

2 *adv* (**a**) *Naut* **to come alongside** *(two ships)* naviguer à couple; *(at quayside)* accoster

(**b**) *(gen → at side)* **they're going to build a patio with a flower bed alongside** ils vont construire un patio bordé d'un parterre de fleurs; **a police car pulled up alongside** une voiture de police s'est arrêtée à côté

aloof [əˈluːf] *adj* distant; **she is very aloof** elle est très distante, elle est d'un abord difficile; **to keep** *or* **to remain aloof** garder ses distances; **he keeps** *or* **remains aloof from his colleagues** il ne se mêle guère à ses collègues; **I try to keep aloof from such matters** j'essaie de ne pas me mêler à ces histoires

aloofly [əˈluːflɪ] *adv* d'une manière distante *ou* réservée

aloofness [əˈluːfnɪs] *n* attitude *f* distante, réserve *f*

alopecia [æləˈpiːʃə] *n (UNCOUNT) Med* alopécie *f*

aloud [əˈlaʊd] *adv (read)* à haute voix, à voix haute; *(think)* tout haut

alp [ælp] *n (mountain)* montagne *f*; *(pasture)* alpage *m*, alpe *f*

alpaca [æl'pækə] **1** *n Zool* alpaga *m*

2 *comp (coat)* en alpaga, d'alpaga; *(wool)* d'alpaga

alpenhorn ['ælpənhɔ:n] *n* cor *m* des Alpes

alpenstock ['ælpənstɒk] *n* alpenstock *m*

alpha ['ælfə] *n* **(a)** *(Greek letter)* alpha *m*; *Fig* **alpha and omega** l'alpha et l'oméga, le commencement et la fin **(b)** *Br Sch* ≃ mention *f* bien; **alpha plus** ≃ mention *f* très bien

►► *Zool* ***alpha male*** mâle *m* alpha; *Fig* **he's the alpha male of the group** c'est lui qui domine le groupe; ***alpha order*** ordre *m* alphabétique; *Zool* ***alpha pair*** couple *m* alpha; *Phys* ***alpha particle*** particule *f* alpha; *Phys* ***alpha ray*** rayon *m* alpha; *St Exch* ***alpha stocks*** valeurs *fpl* de père de famille *ou* de premier ordre; *Comput* ***alpha version*** version *f* alpha; *Physiol* ***alpha wave*** rythme *m* alpha

alphabet ['ælfəbet] *n* alphabet *m*; **the Greek alphabet** l'alphabet grec

►► ***alphabet soup*** *Culin* soupe *f* aux petites pâtes en forme de lettres; *Fig (speech, writing)* = charabia bourré de sigles et d'abréviations; *Am Fam* ***alphabet soup agency*** = formule humoristique qui désigne toute agence gouvernementale dont le nom est un sigle, du type CIA et FBI

alphabetical [,ælfə'betɪkəl] *adj* alphabétique; **in alphabetical order** par ordre *ou* dans l'ordre alphabétique

alphabetically [,ælfə'betɪkəlɪ] *adv* alphabétiquement, par ordre alphabétique

alphabetization [,ælfəbetaɪ'zeɪʃən] *n* classement *m* par ordre alphabétique

alphabetize, -ise ['ælfəbə,taɪz] *vt* classer par ordre alphabétique

alphameric [,ælfə'merɪk], **alphamerical** [,ælfə'merɪkəl] = **alphanumeric**

alphametic [,ælfə'metɪk] *n* alphamétique *f*

alphanumeric [,ælfənju:'merɪk], **alphanumerical** [,ælfənju:'merɪkəl] *adj* alphanumérique

►► *Comput* ***alphanumeric characters*** caractères *mpl* alphanumériques; *Comput* ***alphanumeric code*** code *m* alphanumérique; *Comput* ***alphanumeric filing*** classement *m* alphanumérique; *Comput* ***alphanumeric key*** touche *f* alphanumérique; *Comput* ***alphamumeric keyboard, alphamumeric keypad*** clavier *m* alphanumérique

alphanumerics [,ælfənjʊ'merɪks] *npl* caractères *mpl* alphanumériques

alphasort ['ælfə,sɔ:t] *Comput* **1** *n* tri *m* alphabétique; **to do an alphasort on sth** trier qch par ordre alphabétique

2 *vt* trier par ordre alphabétique

alphatest ['ælfə,test] *Comput* **1** *n* alpha-test *m*, essai *m* préliminaire

2 *vt* conduire les alpha-tests sur, conduire les essais préliminaires sur

alpine ['ælpaɪn] **1** *n (plant → at low altitude)* plante *f* alpestre; *(→ at high altitude)* plante *f* alpine

2 *adj* **(a)** *Geog* des Alpes **(b)** *(climate, landscape)* alpestre; *(club, skiing, troops)* alpin

►► *Orn* ***alpine accentor*** accenteur *m* alpin; *Orn* ***alpine chough*** chocard *m* à bec jaune, chocard *m* des Alpes; *Bot* ***alpine clematis*** clématite *f* des Alpes; *Bot* ***alpine meadow-rue*** pigamon *m* des Alpes; ***alpine plants*** *(at low altitude)* plantes *fpl* alpestres; *(at high altitude)* plantes *fpl* alpines; ***alpine range*** chaîne *f* de montagnes alpine; *Orn* ***alpine swift*** martinet *m* alpin

alpinism ['ælpɪnɪzəm] *n Sport* alpinisme *m*

alpinist ['ælpɪnɪst] *n Sport* alpiniste *mf*

Alps [ælps] *npl* **the Alps** les Alpes *fpl*; **in the Alps** dans les Alpes; **the Southern Alps** les Alpes *fpl* du Sud

already [ɔ:l'redɪ] *adv* déjà; **ten o'clock already!** déjà dix heures!; *Am Fam* **enough, already!** ça suffit comme ça!

alright [ɔ:l'raɪt] = **all right**

Alsace [æl'sæs] *n* Alsace *f*; **in Alsace** en Alsace

Alsatian [æl'seɪʃən] **1** *n* **(a)** *(person)* Alsacien(enne) *m,f* **(b)** *(language)* alsacien *m* **(c)** *(dog)* berger *m* allemand

2 *adj (person)* d'Alsace, alsacien; *(wine)* d'Alsace

►► ***Alsatian dog*** berger *m* allemand

also ['ɔ:lsəʊ] *adv* **(a)** *(as well)* aussi, également; **she also speaks Italian** elle parle aussi *ou* également l'italien; **the other two books are also out of print** les deux autres livres sont aussi *ou* également épuisés; **he's lazy and also stupid** il est paresseux et en plus il est bête **(b)** *(furthermore)* en outre, de plus, également; **also, it must be pointed out that...** en outre *ou* de plus, il faut signaler que..., il faut également signaler que...

also-ran *n* **(a)** *Sport (gen)* concurrent(e) *m,f* non classé(e); *Horseracing* cheval *m* non classé **(b)** *Fig (person)* perdant(e) *m,f*

alstroemeria [,ælstrə'mɪərɪə] *n Bot* alstrœmère *f*

alt [ɔ:lt] *n Comput (key)* touche *f* alt; **e acute is alt 130** pour e accent aigu, il faut taper Alt 130

►► ***alt key*** touche *f* Alt

.alt [ɔ:lt] *n Comput (abbr* **alternative***) (in newsgroups)* = abréviation désignant des forums de discussion qui peuvent porter sur toutes sortes de sujets

Alta. *(written abbr* **Alberta***)* Alberta *f*

Altaic [æl'teɪɪk] *adj Ling* altaïque

altar ['ɔ:ltə(r)] *n Rel* autel *m*; *Fig* **to lead sb to the altar** conduire *ou* mener qn à l'autel; *Fig* **to be sacrificed on the altar of success** être sacrifié sur l'autel du succès

►► ***altar boy*** enfant *m* de chœur; ***altar candle*** cierge *m*; ***altar cloth*** nappe *f* d'autel; ***altar rail*** balustrade *f (devant l'autel)*; **at the altar rail** devant l'autel

altarpiece ['ɔ:ltəpi:s] *n Rel* retable *m*

alter ['ɔ:ltə(r)] **1** *vt* **(a)** *(change → appearance, plan)* changer, modifier; *(→ person)* changer; **this doesn't alter the fact that you should have known** cela ne change pas le fait que vous auriez dû être au courant; **this alters matters considerably** cela change vraiment tout; *Naut & Aviat* **to alter course** changer de cap *ou* de route **(b)** *Sewing (garment)* faire une retouche *ou* des retouches à, retoucher; **the dress needs to be altered at the neck** la robe a besoin d'être retouchée au col **(c)** *(falsify → evidence, facts, figures, document)* falsifier, fausser **(d)** *Am Euph (castrate)* châtrer

2 *vi* changer, se modifier; **the town has altered a lot in the past few years** la ville a beaucoup changé ces dernières années; **to alter for the better** *(situation)* s'améliorer; *(person)* changer en mieux; **to alter for the worse** *(situation)* s'aggraver, empirer; *(person)* changer en mal; **her whole outlook has altered** elle a complètement changé d'horizon

alterable ['ɔ:ltərəbəl] *adj* sujet à modification

alteration [ɔ:ltə'reɪʃən] *n* **(a)** *(changing)* changement *m*, modification *f*; *(touching up)* retouche *f* **(b)** *(change)* changement *m*, modification *f*; *(reorganization)* remaniement *m*; *(transformation)* transformation *f*; **to make an alteration to sth** modifier qch, apporter une modification à qch; **subject to alteration** *(programme, timetable etc)* susceptible de révisions, sauf modifications **(c)** *Sewing (of garment)* retouche *f*; **to make alterations to a dress** faire des retouches à une robe **(d)** *(falsification → of evidence, facts, figures, document)* falsification *f* **(e)** *Constr* aménagement *m*, transformation *f*; **to have alterations done** faire faire des aménagements; **they've made major alterations to their house** ils ont fait des transformations importantes dans leur maison

altercation [,ɔ:ltə'keɪʃən] *n Formal* altercation *f*; **to have an altercation with sb** se disputer *ou* avoir une altercation avec qn

altered ['ɔ:ltəd] *adj* **he is greatly altered** il est bien changé; **they were surprised by her altered appearance** ils furent surpris par son nouveau genre

alter ego *n* alter ego *m*

altering ['ɔ:ltərɪŋ] *adj* changeant, variable

alternate 1 *adj* [*Br* ɔ:l'tɜ:nət, *Am* 'ɔ:ltərnət] **(a)** *(by turns)* alterné; **alternate spells of good and bad weather** des périodes alternées de beau et de mauvais temps; **we visit her on alternate weekends** nous lui rendons visite le week-end à tour de rôle **(b)** *(every other)* tous les deux; **on alternate days** un jour sur deux, tous les deux jours **(c)** *Bot* alterne **(d)** *Geom* alterne **(e)** *Am (alternative)* alternatif

2 *vi* ['ɔ:ltəneɪt] **(a)** *(happen by turns)* alterner; **wet days alternated with fine days** les jours pluvieux alternaient avec les beaux jours, les jours pluvieux et les beaux jours se succédaient **(b)** *(take turns)* se relayer; **two actors alternated in the leading role** deux acteurs jouaient le rôle principal en alternance *ou* à tour de rôle **(c)** *(vary)* alterner; **an economy that alternates between periods of growth and disastrous slumps** une économie où alternent la prospérité et le marasme le plus profond; **he alternates between depression and euphoria** il passe de la dépression à l'euphorie **(d)** *Elec* changer périodiquement de sens

3 *vt* ['ɔ:ltəneɪt] (faire) alterner, employer alternativement *ou* tour à tour; *Agr (crops)* alterner

4 *n Am* ['ɔ:ltərnət] remplaçant(e) *m,f*, suppléant(e) *m,f*

alternately [ɔ:l'tɜ:nətlɪ] *adv* alternativement, en alternance, tour à tour; **the film is alternately comic and tragic** le film est tour à tour comique et tragique, le film est tantôt comique, tantôt tragique; **the meetings are held alternately in Paris and Edinburgh** les réunions se tiennent en alternance à Paris et à Édimbourg; **they alternately welcomed his help and saw it as an intrusion** tantôt ils appréciaient son aide, tantôt ils la ressentaient comme une intrusion

alternating ['ɔ:ltəneɪtɪŋ] *adj* **(a)** *(gen)* alternant, alterné **(b)** *Elec & Tech* alternatif **(c)** *Geom* alterné

►► *Elec* ***alternating current*** courant *m* alternatif

alternation [,ɔ:ltə'neɪʃən] *n* alternance *f*

alternative [ɔ:l'tɜ:nətɪv] **1** *n* **(a)** *(choice)* solution *f*, choix *m*; **you have no other alternative** vous n'avez pas d'autre solution *ou* choix; **he had no alternative but to accept** il n'avait pas d'autre solution *ou* choix que d'accepter; **you leave me with no alternative** vous ne me laissez pas le choix; **what's the alternative?** quelle est l'autre solution?; **there are several alternatives** il y a plusieurs possibilités; **the country has chosen the democratic alternative** le pays a choisi la solution démocratique; **there are alternatives to nuclear power** le nucléaire n'est pas la seule solution possible; **the alternative was starvation** c'était ça ou mourir de faim **(b)** *Phil* terme *m* d'une alternative

2 *adj* **(a)** *(different, other → solution, government)* autre, de rechange; **you'll have to find an alternative solution** il faudra trouver une autre solution; **an alternative proposal** une contre-proposition; **to make alternative arrangements** s'arranger autrement; **an alternative route** un itinéraire bis *ou* de délestage **(b)** *(not traditional → lifestyle)* peu conventionnel, alternatif; *(→ press, theatre)* parallèle, alternatif **(c)** *Phil* alternatif

►► ***alternative comedian*** nouveau(elle) comique *mf*; ***alternative comedy*** nouvelle comédie *f*; *Ecol* ***alternative energy*** énergies *fpl* de substitution; *Br St Exch* ***Alternative Investment Market*** = marché hors-cote rattaché à la Bourse de Londres; ***alternative medicine*** médecines *fpl* douces *ou* parallèles; ***the alternative society*** la société alternative; ***alternative technology*** technologies *fpl* douces; ***alternative tourism*** tourisme *m* vert

alternatively [ɔ:l'tɜ:nətɪvlɪ] *adv* **(a)** *(on the other hand)* sinon; **you could travel by train, or alternatively by bus** vous pourriez voyager en train ou bien en autobus **(b)** *(in a different way)* autrement; **I've been alternatively employed** j'étais occupé à autre chose

alternator ['ɔ:ltəneɪtə(r)] *n Elec* alternateur *m*

althaea, *Am* **althea** [æl'θi:ə] *n Bot* althée *m*, altha *m*

although [ɔ:l'ðəʊ] *conj* **(a)** *(despite the fact that)* bien que + *subjunctive*, quoique + *subjunctive*; **although (he is) old, he is still active** bien qu'il soit vieux il est toujours actif; **although I have never liked him, I do respect him** bien que *ou* quoique je ne l'aie jamais aimé je le respecte, je ne l'ai jamais aimé, néanmoins je le respecte; **although not beautiful, she was attractive** sans être belle elle plaisait

(**b**) *(but, however)* mais; **I don't think it will work, although it's worth a try** je ne crois pas que ça va marcher, mais ça vaut la peine d'essayer; **the scar will become less visible, although it will never completely disappear** la cicatrice va s'estomper, mais elle ne disparaîtra jamais complètement

altimeter ['æltɪmiːtə(r)] *n Tech* altimètre *m*

altimetry [æl'tɪmɪtrɪ] *n Tech* altimétrie *f*

altitude ['æltɪtjuːd] *n* altitude *f*; *(in mountains)* altitude *f*, hauteur *f*; **to fly at an altitude of 8,000 metres** voler à une altitude de 8000 mètres; **at high altitude** *or* **altitudes** en altitude, en hauteur; **at these altitudes** à cette altitude, à ces hauteurs

►► *Tech* ***altitude recorder*** enregistreur *m* d'altitude; ***altitude sickness*** mal *m* d'altitude

altitudinal [ˌæltɪ'tjuːdɪnəl] *adj* altitudinaire

alto ['æltəʊ] (*pl* **altos**) *Mus* **1** *n (voice → female)* contralto *m*; *(→ male)* haute-contre *f*; *(instrument)* alto *m*

2 *adj (voice → female)* de contralto; *(→ male)* de haute-contre; *(instrument)* alto *(inv)*

►► ***alto clef*** clef *f* d'ut; ***alto recorder*** flûte *f* alto; ***alto saxophone*** saxophone *m* alto

altocumulus [ˌæltəʊ'kjuːmjʊləs] *n Met* altocumulus *m*

altogether [ɔːltə'geðə(r)] **1** *adv* (**a**) *(entirely)* tout à fait, entièrement; **I don't altogether agree with you** je ne suis pas tout à fait *ou* entièrement d'accord avec vous; **he isn't altogether reliable** on ne peut pas toujours compter sur lui; **it's altogether out of the question** il n'en est absolument pas question; **that's a different matter altogether** c'est un tout autre problème; **I was not altogether pleased** ça ne me faisait pas exactement plaisir

(**b**) *(as a whole)* en tout; **I owe him £100 altogether** je lui dois 100 livres en tout; **taken altogether** à tout prendre

(**c**) *(in general)* somme toute, tout compte fait; **altogether, it was an enjoyable evening** somme toute, c'était une soirée agréable

2 *n Br Fam Hum* **in the altogether** tout nu ❑, à poil

Alton Towers ['ɔːltən-] *n* = parc d'attractions en Angleterre

altostratus [ˌæltəʊ'struːtəs] *n Met* altostratus *m*

altricial [æl'trɪʃəl] *adj Orn* nidicole

altruism ['æltrʊɪzəm] *n* altruisme *m*

altruist ['æltrʊɪst] *n* altruiste *mf*

altruistic [ˌæltrʊ'ɪstɪk] *adj* altruiste

ALU [ˌeɪel'juː] *n Comput (abbr* **arithmetic and logic unit**) unité *f* arithmétique et logique

alula ['æljʊlə] *n Orn* alule *f*

alum ['æləm] *n Chem & Miner* alun *m*

►► *Phot* ***alum bath*** bain *m* aluné

alumina [ə'luːmɪnə] *n Chem* alumine *f*

aluminium [ˌæljʊ'mɪnɪəm], *Am* **aluminum** [ə'luːmɪnəm] **1** *n* aluminium *m*

2 *comp (utensil)* en aluminium

►► ***aluminium foil*** papier *m* aluminium; *Chem* ***aluminium oxide*** alumine *f*

aluminize, -ise [ə'luːmɪnaɪz] *vt* (**a**) *Metal* combiner avec de l'aluminium (**b**) *(mirror)* aluminer [illegible]

►► ***aluminized steel*** acier *m* à l'aluminium

aluminosilicate [əˌluːmɪnəʊ'sɪlɪkət] *n Chem & Miner* aluminosilicate *m*

aluminous [ə'luːmɪnəs] *adj Chem* alumineux

aluminum [ə'luːmɪnəm] *Am* = aluminium

alumna [ə'lʌmnə] (*pl* **alumnae** [-niː]) *n Sch* ancienne élève *f*; *Univ* ancienne étudiante *f*

alumnus [ə'lʌmnəs] (*pl* **alumni** [-naɪ]) *n Sch* ancien élève *m*; *Univ* ancien étudiant *m*

alveolar [æl'vɪələ(r)] *adj Anat & Ling* alvéolaire

►► ***alveolar ridge*** alvéoles *fpl* (dentaires)

alveolus [æl'vɪələs] (*pl* **alveoli** [-laɪ]) *n Anat* alvéole *f* pulmonaire

always ['ɔːlweɪz] *adv* toujours; **she always comes on Mondays** elle vient toujours le lundi; **has she always worn glasses?** a-t-elle toujours porté des lunettes?; **you can always try phoning** vous pouvez toujours essayer de téléphoner; **she's always complaining** elle est toujours en train de se plaindre; **I'll always remember you!** je ne t'oublierai jamais!; **there's always tomorrow** demain il fera jour

alyssum ['ælɪsəm] *n (UNCOUNT) Bot* alysse *f*

Alzheimer's disease ['æltsˌhaɪməz-] *n Med* maladie *f* d'Alzheimer

AM [ˌeɪ'em] *n* (**a**) *Am Univ (abbr* **Master of Arts**) *(person)* = titulaire d'une maîtrise de lettres; *(qualification)* maîtrise *f* de lettres (**b**) *Tel (abbr* **amplitude modulation**) AM (**c**) *Pol (abbr* **(Welsh) Assembly Member**) = membre de l'assemblée galloise

am [æm] *see* **be**

a.m. [ˌeɪ'em] *adv (abbr* **ante meridiem**) du matin; **at 2 a.m.** à 2 heures du matin

AMA [ˌeɪem'eɪ] *n* (**a**) *Med (abbr* **American Medical Association**) = ordre américain des médecins (**b**) *Mktg (abbr* **American Marketing Association**) = institut américain de marketing

amalgam [ə'mælgəm] *n* (**a**) *(gen)* amalgame *m*; **it is an amalgam of several ideas** c'est un amalgame d'idées (**b**) *Chem & Med (in dentistry)* amalgame *m*

amalgamate [ə'mælgəˌmeɪt] **1** *vt* (**a**) *Com (companies, businesses)* fusionner, unir (**b**) *(ideas, metals)* amalgamer; **their findings were amalgamated with ours to produce the final report** leurs conclusions et les nôtres ont été réunies pour constituer le rapport final

2 *vi* (**a**) *Com (of companies, businesses)* fusionner (**b**) *(of races)* se mélanger; *(of ideas, metals)* s'amalgamer

amalgamation [əˌmælgə'meɪʃən] *n* (**a**) *Com (of companies, businesses)* fusion *f* (**b**) *(of races)* mélange *m*; *(of ideas, metals)* amalgamation *f*

amanita [ˌæmə'niːtə] *n Bot* amanite *f*

amanuensis [əˌmænjʊ'ensɪs] (*pl* **amanuenses** [-siːz]) *n Formal (secretary)* secrétaire *mf*, sténographe *mf*; *(transcriber, copyist)* copiste *mf*

amaranth ['æmərænθ] *n Bot* amarante *f*

amaretto [ˌæmə'retəʊ] *n* amaretto *m*

amaryllid [ˌæmə'rɪlɪd] *n Bot* amaryllidacée *f*

amaryllis [ˌæmə'rɪlɪs] *n Bot* amaryllis *f*

amass [ə'mæs] *vt (fortune, objects, information)* amasser, accumuler

amateur ['æmətə(r)] **1** *n (gen) & Sport* amateur *m*; **he's a keen amateur** c'est un amateur enthousiaste

2 *adj (sport, photographer, musician)* amateur; *(painting, psychology)* d'amateur; **amateur championship** championnat *m* amateur; **he has an amateur interest in psychology** il s'intéresse à la psychologie en amateur; *Pej* **they did a rather amateur job** ils ont fait du travail d'amateur

►► *Theat* ***amateur dramatics*** théâtre *m* amateur

amateurish ['æmətərɪʃ] *adj Pej* d'amateur

amateurishly ['æmətərɪʃlɪ] *adv Pej* en amateur; *(presented, written)* avec amateurisme

amateurishness ['æmətərɪʃnɪs] *n Pej (lack of professionalism)* amateurisme *m*, dilettantisme *m*

amateurism ['æmətərɪzəm] *n* (**a**) *Sport* amateurisme *m* (**b**) *Pej (lack of professionalism)* amateurisme *m*, dilettantisme *m*

amative ['æmətɪv] *adj Literary (person)* porté à l'amour

amatory ['æmətərɪ] *adj Literary (letter, verse, intentions, ambitions)* galant; *(feelings)* amoureux

amaurosis [ˌæmɔː'rəʊsɪs] *n Med* amaurose *f*

amaze [ə'meɪz] *vt* stupéfier, ébahir; **I was amazed at** *or* **by his intelligence** j'étais très impressionné par son intelligence, son intelligence m'a stupéfait *ou* ébahi; **you never cease to amaze me!** tu m'étonneras toujours!; *Ironic* **go on, amaze me!** vas-y, surprends-moi!

amazed [ə'meɪzd] *adj (expression, look)* de stupéfaction, ahuri, éberlué; *(person)* stupéfait, ahuri

amazedly [ə'meɪzɪdlɪ] *adv* avec stupéfaction, d'un air stupéfait

amazement [ə'meɪzmənt] *n* stupéfaction *f*, stupeur *f*; **to our amazement** à notre stupéfaction; **I watched in amazement** j'ai regardé, complètement stupéfait

amazing [ə'meɪzɪŋ] *adj* (**a**) *(astonishing)* stupéfiant, étonnant; **it's amazing that no one was hurt** c'est étonnant que personne n'ait été blessé; **it's amazing how fast they work** je ne reviens pas de la vitesse à laquelle ils travaillent; **that's amazing!** je n'en reviens pas!; *Com* **amazing offer** *(sign)* offre exceptionnelle (**b**) *(brilliant, very good)* extraordinaire, sensationnel

amazingly [ə'meɪzɪŋlɪ] *adv* incroyablement, extraordinairement; **he's amazingly patient** il est d'une patience extraordinaire *ou* étonnante; **he was amazingly good as Cyrano** il était absolument extraordinaire dans le rôle de Cyrano; **amazingly enough, she believed him** aussi étonnant que ça puisse paraître, elle l'a cru

Amazon ['æməzən] **1** *n* (**a**) *(river)* **the Amazon** l'Amazone *f* (**b**) *(region)* **the Amazon** l'Amazonie *f*; **in the Amazon** en Amazonie

2 *pr n Myth* Amazone *f*

3 amazon *n Fig* **she's a bit of an amazon** *(strong)* c'est une grande bonne femme; *(athletic)* c'est une vraie athlète; *(aggressive)* c'est une vraie virago

►► *Entom* ***Amazon ant*** fourmi *f* amazone; *Geog* ***the Amazon Basin*** le bassin amazonien; *Orn* ***Amazon parrot*** amazone *m*; ***the Amazon rainforest*** la forêt (tropicale) amazonienne

Amazonia [ˌæmə'zəʊnɪə] *n* Amazonie *f*

Amazonian [ˌæmə'zəʊnɪən] *adj* amazonien

ambassador [æm'bæsədə(r)] *n also Fig* ambassadeur(drice) *m,f*; **the Spanish ambassador to Morocco** l'ambassadeur d'Espagne au Maroc; **the ambassador's wife** l'ambassadrice *f*

ambassador-at-large *n Am* ambassadeur *m* extraordinaire, chargé *m* de mission

ambassadorial [æmˌbæsə'dɔːrɪəl] *adj* d'ambassadeur

ambassadorship [æm'bæsədəʃɪp] *n* fonction *f* d'ambassadeur

ambassadress [æm'bæsədrɪs] *n* ambassadrice *f*

amber ['æmbə(r)] **1** *n (colour, resin)* ambre *m*; *Fig* **the interior was unchanged, preserved as if in amber** *or* **like a fly in amber** l'intérieur de la maison était resté inchangé, comme figé dans le passé

2 *comp (necklace, ring)* d'ambre

3 *adj (colour)* ambré; *Br* **the (traffic) lights turned amber** le feu est passé à l'orange

►► *Br Fam Aut* ***amber gambler*** = automobiliste qui passe à l'orange; ***amber light*** feu *m* orange; *Br Fig* **to see the amber light** se raviser; *Br & Austr Fam Hum* ***amber nectar*** bière ❑ *f*, mousse *f*

amber-coloured *adj* ambré

ambergris ['æmbəgriːs] *n Chem* ambre *m* gris

ambiance = **ambience**

ambidextrous [ˌæmbɪ'dekstrəs] *adj* ambidextre

ambidextrousness [ˌæmbɪ'dekstrəsnɪs], **ambidexterity** [ˌæmbɪdek'sterɪtɪ] *n* ambidextérité *f*

ambience ['æmbɪəns] *n* ambiance *f*

ambient ['æmbɪənt] *adj (temperature, noise, light etc)* ambiant

►► ***ambient sound*** son *m* d'ambiance

ambiguity [ˌæmbɪ'gjuːɪtɪ] (*pl* **ambiguities**) *n* (**a**) *(uncertainty)* ambiguïté *f*, équivoque *f*; *(of expression, word)* ambiguïté *f*; **to avoid any ambiguity** pour éviter tout malentendu (**b**) *(phrase)* expression *f* ambiguë

ambiguous [æm'bɪgjʊəs] *adj* ambigu(uë), équivoque

ambiguously [æm'bɪgjʊəslɪ] *adv* de façon ambiguë *ou* équivoque

[illegible] ambiguïté *f*, équivoque *f*; *(of expression, word)* ambiguïté *f*

ambisexual [ˌæmbɪ'seksjʊəl] *adj* (**a**) *Biol* bisexué (**b**) *Psy* ambisexué

ambit ['æmbɪt] *n Formal (of regulation)* étendue *f*, portée *f*; *(of study)* champ *m*; *(of person)* compétences *fpl*, capacités *fpl*

ambition [æm'bɪʃən] *n* ambition *f*; **her ambition was to become a physicist** elle avait l'ambition *ou* son ambition était de devenir physicienne, elle ambitionnait de devenir physicienne; **he has political ambitions** il a des ambitions politiques; **to lack ambition** manquer d'ambition; **my parents had great ambitions for me** mes parents avaient de grandes ambitions pour moi

ambitious [æm'bɪʃəs] *adj* ambitieux; **she's very ambitious for her children** elle a de grandes ambitions pour ses enfants; **an ambitious film** un film ambitieux; **our holidays were nothing more ambitious than a fortnight in Brighton**

nos ambitions de vacances se sont bornées à aller passer quinze jours à Brighton

ambitiously [æm'bɪʃəslɪ] *adv* ambitieusement

ambitiousness [æm'bɪʃəsnɪs] *n (of project, design)* caractère *m* ambitieux; *(of person)* ambition *f*

ambivalence [æm'bɪvələns] *n* ambivalence *f*

ambivalent [æm'bɪvələnt] *adj* ambivalent; **to be** *or* **to feel ambivalent about sth** être *ou* se sentir indécis à propos de qch; **I have rather ambivalent feelings about him** j'éprouve des sentiments partagés à son égard

amble ['æmbəl] **1** *vi (person)* marcher *ou* aller d'un pas tranquille; *(horse)* aller l'amble; **he ambled through the park** il a traversé le parc d'un pas tranquille; **we ambled home** nous sommes rentrés lentement *ou* sans nous presser; **she whistled as she ambled along** elle flânait en sifflant; **he just ambles in at half-past ten** il arrive à dix heures et demie les mains dans les poches *ou* en se baladant

2 *n (of person)* pas *m* tranquille; *(of horse)* amble *m*; **to walk at an amble** marcher sans se presser

ambler ['æmblə(r)] *n (person)* flâneur(euse) *m,f*; *(horse)* cheval *m* ambleur

ambling ['æmblɪŋ] *adj (horse)* ambleur, qui va l'amble; **with an ambling gait** à l'amble

amblyopia [,æmblɪ'əʊpɪə] *n Med* amblyopie *f*

amblyopic [,æmblɪ'əʊpɪk] *n Med* amblyope

ambrosia [æm'brəʊzɪə] *n* ambroisie *f*

ambrosial [æm'brəʊzɪəl] *adj Literary* ambrosiaque

ambulance ['æmbjʊləns] *n* ambulance *f*

►► *Am Fam Pej* ***ambulance chaser*** = avocat qui ne s'occupe que d'affaires de demandes de dommages et intérêts pouvant rapporter gros; ***ambulance crew*** ambulanciers *mpl*; ***ambulance driver*** ambulancier(ère) *m,f*; ***ambulance man*** *(driver)* ambulancier; *(nurse)* infirmier *m* d'ambulance; *(stretcher carrier)* brancardier *m*; ***ambulance nurse*** infirmier(ère) *m,f* d'ambulance; ***ambulance woman*** *(driver)* ambulancière *f*; *(nurse)* infirmière *f* d'ambulance; *(stretcher carrier)* brancardière *f*; ***ambulance ship*** navire *m* hôpital; ***ambulance train*** train *m* sanitaire

ambulant ['æmbjʊlənt] *adj* ambulatoire

ambulatory ['æmbjʊlətərɪ] *(pl* **ambulatories**) **1** *n Archit & Rel* déambulatoire *m*

2 *adj* ambulatoire

►► ***ambulatory medical care*** traitement *m* ambulatoire

ambush ['æmbʊʃ] **1** *vt* **(a)** *(lie in wait for)* tendre une embuscade à **(b)** *(attack)* attirer dans une embuscade; **they were ambushed** ils sont tombés dans une embuscade

2 *n* embuscade *f*, guet-apens *m*; **to lie in ambush** se tenir en embuscade; *Fig* être à l'affût; **to lay** *or* **set an ambush for sb** tendre une embuscade à qn; **troops lying in ambush** troupes embusquées; **the battalion was caught in an ambush** le bataillon est tombé dans un guet-apens

ambusher ['æmbʊʃə(r)] *n* = personne qui tend une embuscade

ameba, amebic *Am* = **amoeba, amoebic**

ameliorate [ə'mi:ljə,reɪt] *Formal* **1** *vt* améliorer

2 *vi* s'améliorer

amelioration [ə,mi:ljə'reɪʃən] *n Formal* amélioration *f*

ameliorative [ə'mi:ljərətɪv] *adj* d'amélioration

amen [ɑ:'men] *Rel* **1** *n* amen *m inv*

2 *exclam* amen!; **to say amen to sth** exprimer son accord avec qch; *Fig* **amen to that!** bien dit!

amenability [ə,mi:nə'bɪlɪtɪ] *n (of person → gen)* soumission *f*, docilité *f*; *Law* justiciabilité *f* (**to** de), responsabilité *f* (**to** envers)

amenable [ə'mi:nəbəl] *adj* **(a)** *(cooperative)* accommodant, souple; **to be amenable to sth** être disposé à qch; **to be amenable to reason** être raisonnable *ou* disposé à entendre raison; **the disease is amenable to treatment** la maladie peut être traitée; **amenable to kindness** sensible à la bonté

(b) *Law (accountable)* responsable; **she is amenable for her actions to the committee** elle est responsable de ses actes devant le comité; **all citizens are amenable to the law** tout citoyen est responsable devant la loi

(c) *(able to be tested)* vérifiable; **this data is amenable to analysis** c'est données sont susceptibles d'être vérifiées par analyse

amenably [ə'mi:nəblɪ] *adv (react, behave)* d'une façon soumise *ou* docile

amend [ə'mend] *vt* **(a)** *(rectify → mistake, text)* rectifier, corriger; *(→ behaviour, habits)* réformer, *Formal* amender **(b)** *(change → law, rule)* amender, modifier; *(constitution)* amender

►► *Fin* ***amended invoice*** facture *f* rectificative

amendment [ə'mendmənt] *n* **(a)** *(correction)* rectification *f*, correction *f*; *(modification)* modification *f*, révision *f* **(b)** *(to bill, constitution)* amendement *m*; *(to contract)* avenant *m*; **an amendment to the law** une révision de la loi; *Pol* **to move an amendment (to sth)** proposer un amendement (à qch); **the third Amendment** *(to the American Constitution)* le troisième amendement

amends [ə'mendz] *npl* réparation *f*, compensation *f*; **to make amends** faire amende honorable; **nothing could make amends for what they had done** rien ne pouvait réparer ce qu'ils avaient fait; **we'll try and make amends** nous allons essayer de réparer nos torts; **I'd like to make amends for my rudeness to you** j'aimerais réparer mon impolitesse envers vous

amenhorrhoea, *Am* **amenhorrhea** [ə,menə'rɪə] *n Med* aménorrhée *f*

amenity [ə'mi:nətɪ] **1** *n Formal (pleasantness)* charme *m*, agrément *m*

2 amenities *npl* **(a)** *(features)* agréments *mpl*; *(facilities)* équipements *mpl*; **urban** *or* **public amenities** *(water, gas and electricity)* l'eau, le gaz et l'électricité; *(facilities)* équipements *mpl* collectifs; **close to all amenities** *(in advertisement for accommodation)* proximité tous commerces

(b) *(social courtesy)* civilités *fpl*, politesses *fpl*

►► *Br Med* ***amenity bed*** = dans un hôpital, catégorie de lits réservés aux malades qui paient pour avoir plus de confort et d'intimité

amenorrhoea, *Am* **amenorrhea** = **amenhorrhoea**

Amen-Ra [,ɑ:mən'rɑ:] *pr n* Amon-Rê

Amerasian [,æmə'reɪʒən] **1** *n* Amérasien(enne) *m,f*

2 *adj* de parents américain et asiatique, amérasien

America [ə'merɪkə] **1** *n* Amérique *f*; **North/South America** Amérique du Nord/Sud; **in America** en Amérique

2 Americas *npl* **the Americas** les Amériques *fpl*

►► *Sport* ***America's Cup*** coupe *f* de l'America

American [ə'merɪkən] **1** *n* Américain(e) *m,f*

2 *adj* américain

3 *comp (embassy, history)* des États-Unis

►► ***American Association for Retired Persons*** = association américaine de retraités *(constituant un groupe de pression)*; ***American Automobile Association*** = société de dépannage pour les automobilistes, ≃ Touring Club *m* de France; *Law* ***American Bar Association*** = association d'avocats américains qui sert de centre d'information et de formation continue à ses membres; *Orn* ***American bittern*** butor *m* d'Amérique; *Zool* ***American black bear*** baribal *m*, ours *m* noir; *Pol* ***American Civil Liberties Union*** = ligue américaine des droits du citoyen; *Hist* ***the American Civil War*** la guerre de Sécession; *Tex* ***American cloth*** toile *f* cirée; *Orn* ***American coot*** foulque *f* américaine; *Orn* ***American crow*** corneille *f* américaine; *Fin* ***American depositary receipt*** certificat *m* américain de dépôt; ***the American Dream*** le rêve américain; *Orn* ***American eagle*** aigle *m* d'Amérique; ***American English*** (anglais *m*) américain *m*; *Fin* ***American Express***® American Express®; **to pay by American Express**® payer par American Express®; ***American Express***® ***card*** carte *f* American Express®; *Br* ***American football*** football *m* américain; ***American football player*** joueur(euse) *m,f* de football américain; *Orn* ***American golden plover*** pluvier *m* doré américain; ***American Indian*** Indien(enne) *m,f* d'Amérique, Amérindien(enne) *m,f*; *Sport* ***American League*** = l'une des deux ligues professionnelles de base-ball aux États-Unis; ***American organ*** harmonium *m*; *Am* ***American plan*** *(in hotel)* pension *f* complète; *Orn* ***American redstart*** fauvette *f* flamboyante; *Orn* ***American robin*** merle *m* migrateur; ***American Samoa*** Samoa *fpl* américaines; ***the American Way*** le mode de vie américain; *Orn* ***American wigeon*** canard *m* siffleur d'Amérique; *Orn* ***American woodcock*** bécasse *f* américaine

Americana [əmerɪ'kɑ:nə] *npl* = objets ou documents faisant partie de l'héritage culturel américain

Americanism [ə'merɪkənɪzəm] *n Ling* américanisme *m*

Americanist [ə'merɪkənɪst] *n* américaniste *mf*

Americanization [ə,merɪkənaɪ'zeɪʃən] *n* américanisation *f*

Americanize, -ise [ə'merɪkə,naɪz] *vt* américaniser

American-style option *n St Exch* option *f* américaine

americium [,æmə'rɪsɪəm] *n Chem* américium *m*

Amerind ['æmərɪnd], **Amerindian** [,æmə'rɪndɪən] **1** *n* Indien(enne) *m,f* d'Amérique, Amérindien(enne) *m,f*

2 *adj* amérindien

amethyst ['æmɪθɪst] **1** *n* **(a)** *(stone)* améthyste *f* **(b)** *(colour)* violet *m* d'améthyste

2 *(necklace, ring)* d'améthyste

3 *adj (colour)* violet d'améthyste *(inv)*

Amex ['æmeks] *n* **(a)** *St Exch (abbr* **American Stock Exchange**) = deuxième place boursière des États-Unis **(b)** *Fin (abbr* **American Express**®) American Express®

Amharic [æm'hærɪk] *Ling* **1** *n (language)* amharique *m*

2 *adj* amharique

amiability [,eɪmɪə'bɪlətɪ] *n* amabilité *f*

amiable ['eɪmɪəbəl] *adj* aimable, gentil

amiably ['eɪmɪəblɪ] *adv* avec amabilité *ou* gentillesse, aimablement

amianthus [,æmɪ'ænθəs] *n Miner* amiante *m*

amicability [,æmɪkə'bɪlɪtɪ] *n* nature *f ou* disposition *f* amicale; **the amicability of his nature** sa nature amicale

amicable ['æmɪkəbəl] *adj (feeling, relationship)* amical, d'amitié; *(agreement, settlement, end)* à l'amiable; **to settle a dispute in an amicable way** régler un différend à l'amiable

amicably ['æmɪkəblɪ] *adv* amicalement; *(part)* bons amis, en bons termes; **they welcomed me very amicably** ils m'ont reçu très amicalement, leur accueil fut très amical; **let's try and settle this amicably** essayons de régler ce problème à l'amiable; **to live amicably together** vivre en harmonie

amid [ə'mɪd] *prep* au milieu de, parmi; **the news came amid revelations of corruption** la nouvelle survint en plein milieu *ou* au moment des révélations de corruption; **amid all the noise and confusion, she escaped** dans la confusion générale, elle s'est échappée; **share prices fell amid rumours of a change of government** le prix des actions a baissé face aux rumeurs selon lesquelles il allait y avoir un changement de gouvernement

amide ['æmaɪd] *n Chem* amide *m*

amidships [ə'mɪdʃɪps] *adj & adv Naut* au milieu *ou* par le milieu du navire

amidst [ə'mɪdst] = **amid**

amine ['æmi:n, 'æmaɪn] *n Chem* amine *f*

amino acid [ə'mi:nəʊ-] *n Chem* acide *m* aminé, aminoacide *m*

Amish ['ɑ:mɪʃ] **1** *adj* amish

2 *npl* **the Amish** les Amish *mpl (communauté mennonite vivant en Pennsylvanie, austère et fidèle aux traditions)*

amiss [ə'mɪs] **1** *adv* **(a)** *(incorrectly)* de travers, mal; **to take sth amiss** mal prendre qch, prendre qch en mauvaise part; **don't take this criticism amiss** ne prenez pas cette critique en mauvaise part

(b) *(out of place)* **a few words of explanation may not come amiss here** il conviendrait ici de donner une petite explication; **a little tact and diplomacy wouldn't go amiss** un peu de tact et de diplomatie seraient les bienvenus *ou* ne feraient pas de mal; **a cup of coffee wouldn't come** *or* **go amiss** une tasse de café serait la bienvenue

2 *adj* **(a)** *(wrong)* **something seems to be amiss with the engine** on dirait qu'il y a quelque chose qui ne va pas dans le moteur;

there's something amiss with our calculations il y a quelque chose qui ne va pas dans nos calculs

(**b**) *(out of place)* déplacé; **have I said something amiss?** ai-je dit quelque chose qu'il ne fallait pas?; **would it be amiss to send her some flowers?** est-ce qu'il serait malvenu *ou* déplacé de lui offrir des fleurs?

amitosis [,æmɪ'təʊsɪs] *n Biol* amitose *f*

amity ['æmətɪ] (*pl* **amities**) *n Formal (friendship)* amitié *f*; *(good relations)* bonnes relations *fpl*, bons rapports *mpl*; **to live in amity with one's fellow man** vivre en paix *ou* en bonne intelligence avec ses semblables

Amman [ə'mɑːn] *n Geog* Amman

ammeter ['æmɪtə(r)] *n Elec* ampèremètre *m*

ammo ['æməʊ] *n (UNCOUNT) Fam* munitions□ *fpl*

ammonia [ə'məʊnɪə] *n (gas)* ammoniac *m*; *(liquid)* ammoniaque *f*

ammoniac [ə'məʊnɪæk] **1** *n* ammoniac *m*, gomme-ammoniaque *f*

2 *adj (substance)* ammoniacal; *(smell)* d'ammoniaque

Ammonite ['æmənaɪt] *n Bible* Ammonite *mf*

ammonite ['æmənaɪt] *n* (**a**) *Zool (mollusc)* ammonite *f* (**b**) *(explosive)* ammonal *m*

ammonium [ə'məʊnɪəm] *n Chem* ammonium *m*

►► *Chem* ***ammonium carbonate*** carbonate *m* d'ammonium; ***ammonium sulphate*** sulfate *m* d'ammonium

ammunition [,æmjʊ'nɪʃən] *n (UNCOUNT) Mil* munitions *fpl*; **live ammunition** munitions *fpl* réelles *ou* pour tir réel; **round of ammunition** cartouche *f*; *Fig* **the letter could be used as ammunition against them** la lettre pourrait être utilisée contre eux

►► *Mil* ***ammunition belt*** ceinturon *m*; *Mil* ***ammunition box*** coffre *m* à munitions; *Mil* ***ammunition dump*** dépôt *m* de munitions

amnesia [æm'niːzɪə] *n Med* amnésie *f*; **to have** *or* **suffer (from) amnesia** être atteint d'amnésie, être amnésique

amnesiac [æm'niːzɪæk], **amnesic** [æm'niːzɪk] *Med* **1** *n* amnésique *mf*

2 *adj* amnésique

amnesty ['æmnəstɪ] (*pl* **amnesties**) **1** *n* amnistie *f*; **to declare an amnesty** déclarer une amnistie; **under an amnesty** en vertu d'une amnistie

2 *vt* amnistier

►► ***Amnesty International*** Amnesty International

amniocentesis [,æmnɪəʊsen'tiːsɪs] (*pl* **amniocenteses** [-siːz]) *n Obst* amniocentèse *f*

amniography [,æmnɪ'ɒgrəfɪ] *n Obst* amniographie *f*

amnion ['æmnɪən] *n Anat & Zool* amnios *m*

amnioscope ['æmnɪəʊskəʊp] *n Obst* amnioscopie *f*

amniotic [,æmnɪ'ɒtɪk] *adj Anat & Obst* amniotique

►► ***amniotic fluid*** liquide *m* amniotique

amoeba, *Am* **ameba** [ə'miːbə] (*Br pl* **amoebae** [-biː] *or* **amoebas**, *Am pl* **amebae** [-biː] *or* **amebas**) *n Biol* amibe *f*

amoebic, *Am* **amebic** [ə'miːbɪk] *adj Biol* amibien

►► *Med* ***amoebic dysentery*** dysenterie *f* amibienne

amok [ə'mɒk] *adv* **to run amok** être pris d'une crise de folie meurtrière *ou* furieuse; *Fig* devenir fou furieux, se déchaîner; **the football fans ran amok** les supporters de foot se sont déchaînés; **defence spending has run amok** les dépenses militaires ont dérapé

among [ə'mʌŋ], **amongst** [ə'mʌŋst] *prep* (**a**) *(in the midst of)* au milieu de, parmi; **I moved among the spectators** je circulais parmi les spectateurs; **she was lost among the crowd** elle était perdue dans la foule; **it was found among the rubble** on l'a trouvé parmi les gravats; **to be among friends** être entre amis; **murmurings of discontent arose among the students/the crowd** des murmures de mécontentement s'élevèrent parmi les étudiants/dans la foule

(**b**) *(forming part of)* parmi; **among those who left was her brother** parmi ceux qui sont partis, il y avait son frère; **several members abstained, myself among them** plusieurs membres se sont abstenus, dont moi; **it is among her most important plays** c'est une de ses pièces les plus importantes; **that is only one among many possible options** ce n'est qu'une option parmi bien d'autres; **among other things** entre autres, entre autres choses; **he said among other things that...** il a dit entre autres choses que...

(**c**) *(within a specified group)* parmi, entre; **it's a current expression among teenagers** c'est une expression courante chez les jeunes; **we discussed it among ourselves** nous en avons discuté entre nous; **I count her among my friends** je la compte parmi *ou* au nombre de mes amis; **that cake won't go far among twelve** ce gâteau ne donnera pas grand-chose, divisé entre douze personnes

(**d**) *(to each of)* parmi, entre; **share out the sweets among the children** partagez les bonbons entre les enfants; **share the books among you** partagez les livres entre vous, partagez-vous les livres

amontillado [ə,mɒntɪ'lɑːdəʊ] *n* amontillado *m*

amoral [eɪ'mɒrəl] *adj* amoral

amorality [,eɪmɒ'rælətɪ] *n* amoralisme *m*, amoralité *f*

Amorites ['æməraɪts] *npl* Amorrhéens *mpl*

amorous ['æmərəs] *adj (person, couple)* amoureux; *(glance)* amoureux, ardent; *(letter)* d'amour; **amorous advances** des avances *fpl*; **to be of an amorous disposition** être romantique; **he became quite amorous** il a commencé à me/lui/*etc* faire des avances

amorously ['æmərəslɪ] *adv* amoureusement

amorphous [ə'mɔːfəs] *adj Biol & Chem* amorphe; *(shapeless)* amorphe; *Fig (personality)* amorphe, mou (molle); *(ideas)* informe, sans forme; *(plans)* vague

amorphousness [ə'mɔːfəsnɪs] *n Biol & Chem* amorphie *f*; *(of substance)* état *m* amorphe

amortizable [əmɔː'taɪzəbəl] *adj Fin (debt)* amortissable

amortization [əmɔːtɪ'zeɪʃən] *n Fin (of debt)* amortissement *m*

amortize, -ise [ə'mɔːtaɪz] *vt Fin (debt)* amortir

amortizement [ə'mɔːtaɪzmənt] *n* (**a**) *Archit* amortissement *m* (**b**) *Fin (of debt)* amortissement *m*

Amos ['eɪmɒs] *pr n Bible* Amos

amount [ə'maʊnt] *n* (**a**) *(quantity)* quantité *f*; **great** *or* **large amounts of money** beaucoup d'argent; **a massive amount of time** énormément de temps; **in small/large amounts** en petites/grandes quantités; **no amount of talking can bring him back** on peut lui parler tant qu'on veut, ça ne le fera pas revenir; **I have a certain amount of respect for them** j'ai un certain respect pour eux; **a modest amount** une quantité modeste; **any amount of** des quantités de, énormément de; **that shop has any amount of books** il y a des masses de livres dans ce magasin; **you'll have any amount of time for reading on holiday** tu auras tout ton temps pour lire pendant les vacances

(**b**) *(sum, total)* montant *m*, total *m*; *(of money)* somme *f*; **do you have the exact amount?** avez-vous le compte (exact)?; **she billed us for the amount of £50** elle nous a présenté une facture d'un montant de *ou* qui se montait à 50 livres; **you're in credit to the amount of £100** vous avez un crédit de 100 livres; **please find enclosed a cheque to the amount of $100** veuillez trouver ci-joint un chèque (d'un montant) de 100 dollars; **amount due** *(on bill)* montant à régler; **no amount (of money) could make up for what I've lost** rien ne pourrait compenser ce que j'ai perdu; *Acct* **amount brought forward** montant *m* à reporter

►**amount to** *vt insep* (**a**) *(total)* se monter à, s'élever à; **he left debts amounting to over £1,800** il a laissé des dettes qui s'élèvent *ou* se montent à plus de 1800 livres; **profits last year amounted to several million dollars** les bénéfices pour l'année dernière se chiffrent à plusieurs millions de dollars; **after tax it doesn't amount to much** après impôts ça ne représente pas grand-chose; **he'll never amount to much** il ne fera jamais grand-chose

(**b**) *(be equivalent to)* **it amounts to something not far short of stealing** c'est pratiquement du vol; **it amounts to the same thing** cela revient au même; **what his speech amounts to is an attack on democracy** en fait, avec ce discours, il attaque la démocratie

amour [ə'mʊə(r)] *n Literary or Hum* aventure *f* amoureuse, liaison *f*

amp [æmp] *n* (**a**) *Elec (abbr* **ampere***)* ampère *m*; **13-amp plug** fiche *f* de 13 ampères (**b**) *Fam (abbr* **amplifier***)* ampli *m*

ampelopsis [,æmpə'lɒpsɪs] *n Bot* ampélopsis *m*

amperage ['æmpərɪdʒ] *n Elec* intensité *f* de courant

ampere ['æmpeə(r)] *n Elec* ampère *m*

ampersand ['æmpəsænd] *n* esperluette *f*

amphetamine [æm'fetəmiːn] *n Pharm* amphétamine *f*

►► ***amphetamine addiction*** dépendance *f* aux amphétamines

amphibia [æm'fɪbɪə] *npl Zool* batraciens *mpl*, amphibiens *mpl*

amphibian [æm'fɪbɪən] **1** *n* (**a**) *Zool* amphibie *m* (**b**) *(plane)* avion *m* amphibie; *(car)* voiture *f* amphibie; *(tank)* char *m* amphibie

2 *adj* amphibie

amphibious [æm'fɪbɪəs] *adj* amphibie

►► *Bot* ***amphibious bistort*** renouée *f* amphibée

amphibolic [,æmfɪ'bɒlɪk] *adj Biol & Chem* amphibole

amphipatic [,æmfɪ'pætɪk] *adj Biol & Chem* amphipatique

amphipod ['æmfɪpɒd] *n Zool* amphipode *m*

amphisbaena [,æmfɪz'biːnə] *n Zool* amphisbène *m*

amphitheatre, *Am* **amphitheater** ['æmfɪ,θɪətə(r)] *n* amphithéâtre *m*; **natural amphitheatre** cirque *m*

amphora ['æmfərə] (*pl* **amphorae** [-riː] *or* **amphoras**) *n Antiq* amphore *f*

amphoteric [,æmfə'terɪk] *adj Chem* amphotère

ampicillin [,æmpɪ'sɪlɪn] *n Pharm* ampicilline *f*

ample ['æmpəl] *adj* (**a**) *(large → garment)* ample; *(→ garden, lawn)* grand, vaste; *(→ helping, stomach)* grand; **a woman of ample proportions** une femme forte

(**b**) *(more than enough → supplies)* bien *ou* largement assez de; *(→ proof, reason)* solide; *(→ fortune, means)* gros (grosse); **this will be ample** ceci sera amplement suffisant, ceci suffira amplement; **he was given ample opportunity to refuse** il a eu largement l'occasion de refuser; **we have ample reason to suspect foul play** nous avons de solides *ou* de bonnes raisons de soupçonner quelque chose de louche; **you'll have ample time to finish** vous aurez largement le temps de finir; **you'll be given ample warning** vous serez averti longtemps à l'avance

ampleness ['æmpəlnɪs] *n (gen)* ampleur *f*; *(of resources)* abondance *f*

amplexicaul [,æm'pleksɪkɔːl] *adj Bot* amplectif

amplification [,æmplɪfɪ'keɪʃən] *n* (**a**) *(of power, current, sound)* amplification *f* (**b**) *(further explanation)* explication *f*, développement *m*; **the facts require no amplification** les faits ne demandent pas plus d'explications (**c**) *Opt (using lens)* grossissement *m*

amplifier ['æmplɪfaɪə(r)] *n* (**a**) *(for sound system)* amplificateur *m* (**b**) *Opt* (lentille *f*) amplificatrice *f*

amplify ['æmplɪfaɪ] *vt* (**a**) *(power, sound)* amplifier (**b**) *(facts, idea, speech)* développer

►**amplify on** *vt insep* développer

amplitude ['æmplɪtjuːd] *n* (**a**) *(breadth, scope → of dimensions, resources)* ampleur *f*; *(→ of operation)* envergure *f*; *Astron & Phys* amplitude *f* (**b**) *(expanse → of sky, ocean)* étendue *f*

►► ***amplitude modulation*** modulation *f* d'amplitude

amply ['æmplɪ] *adv* amplement, largement; **amply built** *(person)* bien bâti; **amply proportioned** aux dimensions généreuses; **amply rewarded** largement récompensé; **as has been amply shown** comme il a été amplement démontré

ampoule, *Am* **ampule** ['æmpuːl] *n* ampoule *f (de médicament)*

amputate ['æmpjʊteɪt] *vt* amputer; **they had to amputate her arm** ils ont dû l'amputer du bras; **her right arm was amputated** elle a été amputée du bras droit

amputation [ˌæmpjʊ'teɪʃən] *n* amputation *f*
amputee [ˌæmpjʊ'tiː] *n* amputé(e) *m,f*
Amsterdam [ˌæmstə'dæm] *n* Amsterdam
amt (*written abbr* **amount**) (*quantity*) quantité *f*; (*sum*) montant *m*
Amtrak® ['æmtræk] *n Rail* = société nationale de chemins de fer aux États-Unis (pour le transport des voyageurs)
amuck [ə'mʌk] = **amok**
amulet ['æmjʊlɪt] *n* amulette *f*, fétiche *m*
Amur [ə'mʊə] *n* **the (River) Amur** l'Amour *m*
amuse [ə'mjuːz] *vt* (**a**) (*occupy*) divertir, amuser, distraire; **he amused himself (by) building sandcastles** il s'est amusé à faire des châteaux de sable; **you'll have to amuse yourself this afternoon** il va falloir trouver de quoi t'occuper cet après-midi
(**b**) (*make laugh*) amuser, faire rire; **he amuses me** il me fait rire; **does the idea amuse you?** l'idée vous amuse-t-elle?
amused [ə'mjuːzd] *adj* (**a**) (*occupied*) occupé, diverti; **to keep oneself amused** s'occuper, se distraire; **the game kept them amused for hours** le jeu les a occupés pendant des heures
(**b**) (*delighted, entertained*) amusé; **they were greatly amused at** *or* **by the cat's behaviour** le comportement du chat les a bien fait rire; **I was greatly amused to hear about his adventures** cela m'a beaucoup amusé d'entendre parler de ses aventures; **she was not (at all) amused** elle n'a pas trouvé ça drôle (du tout); **an amused look/smile** un regard/sourire amusé; **she looked at him, amused** elle l'a regardé d'un air amusé; *Fam* **we are not amused** très drôle!

> **We are not amused**
> Cette expression fait allusion à une réflexion qu'aurait faite la reine Victoria pour marquer sa désapprobation, après avoir entendu une histoire osée de la bouche d'un de ses courtisans.
> De nos jours, il est courant de l'employer en réponse à quelqu'un qui a fait une remarque qu'on ne trouve pas drôle ou qu'on juge malvenue.

amusedly [ə'mjuːzɪdlɪ] *adv* d'un air amusé
amusement [ə'mjuːzmənt] *n* (**a**) (*enjoyment*) amusement *m*, divertissement *m*; **she smiled in amusement** elle a eu un sourire amusé; **I listened in amusement** amusé, j'ai écouté; **we've arranged a party for your amusement** nous avons prévu une soirée pour vous divertir *ou* vous distraire; **much to everyone's amusement** au grand amusement de tous; **there was much amusement at her untimely entrance** son entrée intempestive a fait rire tout le monde
(**b**) (*pastime*) distraction *f*, amusement *m*; **there are few amusements in small towns** les petites villes offrent peu de distractions; **what amusements do you have for the children?** qu'est-ce que vous avez pour distraire les enfants?
(**c**) (*at funfair*) attraction *f*; **to go on the amusements** monter sur les manèges
►► ***amusement arcade*** salle *f* de jeux électroniques; ***amusement park*** parc *m* d'attractions
amusing [ə'mjuːzɪŋ] *adj* amusant, drôle
amusingly [ə'mjuːzɪŋlɪ] *adv* d'une façon amusante
Amway® ['æmweɪ] *n* = marque américaine de produits d'entretien vendus par des particuliers lors de réunions à domicile
amygdalin [ə'mɪgdəlɪn] *n Chem* amygdaline *f*
amyl ['æmɪl] *n Chem* amyle *m*
►► ***amyl nitrate*** nitrite *m* d'amyle
amylase ['æmɪleɪz] *n Biol & Chem* amylase *f*
amylene ['æmɪliːn] *n Chem* amylène *m*
amyloid ['æmɪlɔɪd] *n Chem* amyloïde *f*
amyloidosis [ˌæmɪlɔɪ'dəʊsɪs] *n Med* amylose *f*
amylose ['æmɪləʊz] *n Chem* amylose *m*
amyotrophy [æmɪ'ɒtrəfɪ] *n Med* amyotrophie *f*
an [ən, *stressed* æn] **1** *indefinite art see* **a²**
2 *conj Arch* si
ANA [ˌeɪen'eɪ] *n* (**a**) *Press* (*abbr* **American Newspaper Association**) = syndicat américain de la presse écrite (**b**) *Med* (*abbr* **American Nurses Association**) = syndicat américain d'infirmiers
Anabaptism [ˌænə'bæptɪzəm] *n Rel* anabaptisme *m*
Anabaptist [ˌænə'bæptɪst] *Rel* **1** *n* anabaptiste *mf*
2 *adj* anabaptiste
anabiosis [ˌænəbaɪ'əʊsɪs] *n Bot* anabiose *f*
anableps ['ænəbleps] *n Ich* anableps *m*
anabolic [ˌænə'bɒlɪk] *adj Chem* anabolisant
►► *Pharm* ***anabolic steroid*** stéroïde *m* anabolisant; ***anabolic steroid abuse*** prise *f* excessive d'anabolisants
anabolism [ə'næbəlɪzəm] *n Physiol* anabolisme *m*
anabolite [ə'næbəlaɪt] *n Physiol* anabolite *m*
anachronism [ə'nækrənɪzəm] *n* anachronisme *m*; **to be an anachronism** faire figure d'anachronisme
anachronistic [əˌnækrə'nɪstɪk] *adj* anachronique
anachronistically [əˌnækrə'nɪstɪkəlɪ] *adv* anachroniquement
anacoluthon [ˌænəkəʊ'luːθɒn] (*pl* **anacolutha** [-θə]) *n Gram* anacoluthe *f*
anaconda [ænə'kɒndə] *n* anaconda *m*
Anacreon [ə'nækrɪən] *pr n Antiq* Anacréon
anadromous [ə'nædrəməs] *adj Ich* anadrome
anaemia, *Am* **anemia** [ə'niːmɪə] *n Med & Fig* anémie *f*; **to suffer from anaemia** être anémique
anaemic, *Am* **anemic** [ə'niːmɪk] *adj* (**a**) *Med & Fig* anémique; **to become anaemic** s'anémier (**b**) (*pale*) anémique, blême
anaerobe [æ'neərəʊb] *n Biol* anaérobie *m*
anaerobic [ˌænə'rəʊbɪk] *adj Biol* anaérobie; **anaerobic exercise** exercice *m* d'anaérobie
anaesthesia, *Am* **anesthesia** [ˌænɪs'θiːzɪə] *n* anesthésie *f*
anaesthesiologist, *Am* **anesthesiologist** [ˌænɪsˌθiːzɪ'ɒlədʒɪst] *n* anesthésiologiste *mf*
anaesthesiology, *Am* **anesthesiology** [ˌænɪsθiːzɪ'ɒlədʒɪ] *n* anesthésiologie *f*
anaesthetic, *Am* **anesthetic** [ˌænɪs'θetɪk] **1** *n* anesthésique *m*, anesthésiant *m*; **under anaesthetic** sous anesthésie; **to give sb an anaesthetic** anesthésier qn
2 *adj* anesthésique, anesthésiant
anaesthetist, *Am* **anesthetist** [ə'niːsθətɪst] *n* anesthésiste *mf*
anaesthetization, *Am* **anesthetization** [əˌniːsθətaɪ'zeɪʃən] *n* administration *f* d'un anesthésique
anaesthetize, -ise, *Am* **anesthetize** [æ'niːsθətaɪz] *vt* anesthésier; *Fig* anesthésier, insensibiliser
anagram ['ænəgræm] *n* anagramme *f*
anagrammatic [ˌænəgrə'mætɪk], **anagrammatical** [ˌænəgrə'mætɪkəl] *adj* anagrammatique
anagrammatist [ˌænə'græmətɪst] *n* anagrammatiste *mf*, faiseur(euse) *m,f* d'anagrammes
anagrammatize, -ise [ˌænə'græmətaɪz] *vt* anagrammatiser
anal ['eɪnəl] *adj* (**a**) *Anat* anal (**b**) *Psy* anal; *Fam* **he's so anal** il est très maniaque ▫
►► ***anal intercourse, anal sex*** sodomie *f*
analepsis [ˌænə'lepsɪs] *n Literature & Ling* analepse *f*
analeptic [ˌænə'leptɪk] *Pharm* **1** *n* analeptique *m*
2 *adj* analeptique
analgesia [ˌænæl'dʒiːzɪə] *n Physiol* analgésie *f*
analgesic [ˌænæl'dʒiːsɪk] *Pharm* **1** *n* analgésique *m*
2 *adj* analgésique
analog *Am* = **analogue**
analogic [ˌænə'lɒdʒɪk], **analogical** [ˌænə'lɒdʒɪkəl] *adj* analogique
analogically [ˌænə'lɒdʒɪkəlɪ] *adv* analogiquement, par analogie; **analogically speaking** analogiquement parlant
analogous [ə'næləgəs] *adj* analogue; **to be analogous to** *or* **with sth** être analogue à qch
analogously [ə'næləgəslɪ] *adv* d'une manière analogue
analogue, *Am* **analog** ['ænəlɒg] **1** *n* analogue *m*
2 *comp* (*clock, watch, computer*) analogique
analogy [ə'nælədʒɪ] (*pl* **analogies**) *n* analogie *f*; **the author draws an analogy between a fear of falling and the fear of death** l'auteur établit une analogie entre la peur de tomber et la peur de mourir; **by analogy with sth** par analogie avec qch; **reasoning from analogy** raisonnement par analogie
analphabetic [ˌænælfə'betɪk] *adj* analphabète
analysable, *Am* **analyzable** [ˌænə'laɪzəbəl] *adj* analysable
analysand, *Am* **analyzand** [ə'nælɪsænd] *n Psy* patient(e) *m,f* en analyse
analyse, *Am* **analyze** ['ænəlaɪz] *vt* (**a**) (*examine*) analyser, faire l'analyse de; *Gram* (*sentence*) analyser, faire l'analyse logique de (**b**) *Psy* psychanalyser
analysis [ə'næləsɪs] (*pl* **analyses** [-siːz]) *n* (**a**) (*examination*) analyse *f*; *Gram* (*of sentence*) analyse *f* logique; **our analysis is that...** notre analyse démontre que...; **to hold up under** *or* **to withstand analysis** résister à l'analyse; **in the final** *or* **last** *or* **ultimate analysis** (*ultimately*) en dernière analyse, en fin de compte
(**b**) *Psy* psychanalyse *f*, analyse *f*; **to be in analysis** être en analyse, suivre une analyse
►► *Acct* ***analysis ledger*** journal *m* analytique
analyst ['ænəlɪst] *n* (**a**) (*specialist*) analyste *mf* (**b**) *Psy* analyste *mf*, psychanalyste *mf*
analytic [ænə'lɪtɪk], **analytical** [ænə'lɪtɪkəl] *adj* analytique; **to have an analytical mind** avoir l'esprit d'analyse
►► ***analytical geometry*** géométrie *f* analytique; *Ling* ***analytical language*** langue *f* analytique; ***analytical psychology*** psychologie *f* analytique
analytics [ænə'lɪtɪks] *n* (*UNCOUNT*) analytique *f*
analyzable, analyzand *etc Am* = **analysable, analysand** *etc*
analyzer ['ænəlaɪzə(r)] *n Comput* analyseur *m*
anamnesis [ˌænæm'niːsɪs] *n* (**a**) *Psy* (*recollection of past events*) anamnésie *f*, retour *m* de mémoire (**b**) *Med* (*case history*) anamnèse *f* (**c**) *Rel* (*prayer*) anamnèse *f*
anamorphic [ˌænə'mɔːfɪk] *adj Bot & Opt* anamorphosique
anamorphosis [ˌænə'mɔːfəsɪs] *n Bot & Opt* anamorphose *f*
anapaest ['ænəpiːst], **anapest** ['ænəpest] *n* anapeste *m*
anaphase ['ænəfeɪz] *n Biol* anaphase *f*
anaphora [ə'næfərə] *n Ling & Rel* anaphorique *m*; (*in rhetoric*) anaphore *f*
anaphoric [ˌænə'fɒrɪk] *adj Ling* anaphorique
anaphylactic [ˌænəfə'læktɪk] *adj Med* anaphylactique
►► *Med* ***anaphylactic shock*** choc *m* anaphylactique; **to go into anaphylactic shock** faire un choc anaphylactique
anaphylaxis [ˌænəfɪ'læksɪs], **anaphylaxy** [ˌænəfɪ'læksɪ] *n Med* anaphylaxie *f*
anaplastic [ˌænə'plæstɪk] *Med* **1** *adj* (*surgery*) anaplastique
2 anaplastics *n* autoplastie *f*
anaplasty ['ænəˌplæstɪ] *n Med* autoplastie *f*
anarchic [æ'nɑːkɪk] *adj* anarchique
anarchically [æ'nɑːkɪkəlɪ] *adv* anarchiquement
anarchism ['ænəkɪzəm] *n* anarchisme *m*
anarchist ['ænəkɪst] *n* anarchiste *mf*
anarchistic [ænə'kɪstɪk] *adj* anarchiste
anarchize, -ise ['ænəːkaɪz] *vt* anarchiser
anarcho-syndicalism [ə'nɑːkəʊ-] *n Pol* anarcho-syndicalisme *m*
anarcho-syndicalist *Pol* **1** *n* anarcho-syndicaliste *mf*
2 *adj* anarcho-syndicaliste
anarchy ['ænəkɪ] *n* anarchie *f*
anastigmatic [ˌænæstɪg'mætɪk] *adj Med* anastigmat, anastigmatique
anastigmatism [ˌænæs'tɪgmətɪzəm] *n Med* anastigmatisme *m*
anastomosis [əˌnæstə'məʊsɪs] (*pl* **anastomoses** [-siːz]) *n Med* anastomose *f*
anathema [ə'næθəmə] *n* (**a**) *Formal* (*detested thing*) abomination *f*; **such ideas are anathema to the general public** le grand public a horreur de ces idées; **his books are anathema to her** ses livres lui sont insupportables, elle a ses livres en abomination (**b**) *Rel & Fig* anathème *m*
anathematize, -ise [ə'næθəmətaɪz] *vt Rel* anathématiser, frapper d'anathème; *Fig* jeter l'anathème sur
Anatolia [ænə'təʊlɪə] *n* Anatolie *f*; **in Anatolia** en Anatolie
Anatolian [ænə'təʊlɪən] **1** *n* Anatolien(enne) *m,f*
2 *adj* anatolien
anatomical [ˌænə'tɒmɪkəl] *adj* anatomique; **anatomical specimen** pièce *f* d'anatomie, préparation *f* anatomique
anatomically [ˌænə'tɒmɪkəlɪ] *adv* anatomiquement; **anatomically correct** (*doll, model*)

réaliste du point de vue anatomique

anatomist [ə'nætəmɪst] *n* anatomiste *mf*

anatomize, -ise [ə'nætəmaɪz] *vt Med & Fig* disséquer

anatomy [ə'nætəmɪ] *n* (**a**) *(of animal, person)* anatomie *f*; *Fig (of situation, society)* structure *f* (**b**) *Biol (science)* anatomie *f*; *Fig (analysis)* analyse *f* (**c**) *Hum (body)* anatomie *f*; **every part of his anatomy hurt** il était plein de courbatures, il avait mal partout

'The Anatomy of Melancholy' *Burton*
'L'Anatomie de la mélancolie'

Anaxagoras [ˌænæk'sægərəs] *pr n Antiq* Anaxagore

Anaximander [əˌnæksɪ'mændə(r)] *pr n Antiq* Anaximandre

Anaximenes [ˌænæk'sɪmənɪ:z] *pr n Antiq* Anaximène

ANC [ˌeɪen'si:] *n Pol (abbr* **African National Congress**) ANC *m*

ancestor ['ænsestə(r)] *n (forefather) & Fig (of computer, system)* ancêtre *m*; **his ancestors** ses ancêtres, *Literary* ses aïeux *mpl*

►► ***ancestor worship*** culte *m* des ancêtres

ancestral [æn'sestrəl] *adj* ancestral

►► ***ancestral home*** demeure *f* ancestrale

ancestress ['ænsestrɪs] *n* ancêtre *f*

ancestry ['ænsestrɪ] *(pl* **ancestries**) *n* (**a**) *(lineage)* ascendance *f*; **both families were of French ancestry** les deux familles étaient d'ascendance française; **this custom is of more recent ancestry** cette coutume est d'apparition plus récente (**b**) *(ancestors)* ancêtres *mpl*, *Literary* aïeux *mpl*

anchor ['æŋkə(r)] **1** *n* (**a**) *Naut (for boat)* ancre *f*; **to lie** *or* **to ride at anchor** être à l'ancre, être au mouillage; **to cast** *or* **to come to** *or* **to drop anchor** jeter l'ancre, mouiller; **up** *or* **weigh anchor!** levez l'ancre!

(**b**) *(fastener)* attache *f*

(**c**) *Fig (mainstay)* soutien *m*, point *m* d'ancrage; **religion is her anchor in life** la religion est son soutien dans la vie; **many people need the anchor of family life** beaucoup de gens ont besoin de la vie de famille comme point d'ancrage

(**d**) *TV* présentateur(trice) *m,f*

(**e**) *Sport* pilier *m*, pivot *m*

(**f**) *(in mountaineering)* point *m* d'assurage

(**g**) *Comput* ancre *f*

2 *vi* (**a**) *Naut (boat)* jeter l'ancre, mouiller

(**b**) *(fasten)* s'ancrer, se fixer

(**c**) *(settle)* se fixer, s'installer; **they remain firmly anchored in tradition** ils restent fermement ancrés dans la tradition

3 *vt* (**a**) *Naut (boat)* ancrer

(**b**) *(fasten)* ancrer, fixer; *Fig* **to be anchored to the spot** *(by indecision, terror)* être cloué sur place

(**c**) *TV (programme)* présenter

►► *Naut* ***anchor buoy*** bouée *f* de mouillage *ou* d'ancre

Anchorage ['æŋkərɪdʒ] *n* Anchorage

anchorage ['æŋkərɪdʒ] *n* (**a**) *Naut (place)* mouillage *m*, ancrage *m*; *(fee)* droits *mpl* de mouillage *ou* d'ancrage (**b**) *(fastening)* ancrage *m*, attache *f* (**c**) *Fig (mainstay)* soutien *m*, point *m* d'ancrage

anchored ['æŋkəd] *adj Naut* ancré, mouillé, à l'ancre

anchoring ['æŋkərɪŋ] *n Naut* ancrage *m*, mouillage *m*

anchorite ['æŋkəraɪt] *n* ermite *m*, solitaire *m*; *Rel* anachorète *m*

anchorless ['æŋkəlɪs] *adj* (**a**) *Naut* sans ancre (**b**) *Fig (person)* désemparé, qui n'a pas de racines

anchorman ['æŋkəmæn] *(pl* **anchormen** [-men]) *n* (**a**) *TV* présentateur *m* (**b**) *Sport* dernier partant *m*

anchorwoman ['æŋkəˌwʊmən] *(pl* **anchorwomen** [-ˌwɪmɪn]) *n TV* présentatrice *f*

anchovy [*Br* 'æntʃəvɪ, *Am* 'æntʃəʊvɪ] *(pl* **inv** *or* **anchovies**) *n* anchois *m*

►► ***anchovy butter*** beurre *m* d'anchois; ***anchovy paste*** pâte *f* d'anchois; ***anchovy sauce*** sauce *f* aux anchois

ancient ['eɪnʃənt] **1** *adj* (**a**) *(custom, ruins)* ancien; *(civilization, world)* antique; *(relic)* historique

(**b**) *Hum (very old → person)* très vieux (vieille); *(→ thing)* antique, antédiluvien; **she drives an ancient Volkswagen** elle conduit une Volkswagen qui a fait la guerre; **her husband's absolutely ancient** son mari est vraiment très vieux

2 *n* (**a**) *Hist* **the ancients** les anciens *mpl*

(**b**) *Arch or Hum (old man)* vieillard *m*; *(old woman)* vieille *f*

►► ***ancient Greece*** la Grèce antique; *also Fig* ***ancient history*** histoire *f* ancienne; *Br* **their affair is ancient history now** leur liaison est maintenant de l'histoire ancienne; ***ancient monument*** monument *m* historique *ou* classé; ***ancient Rome*** la Rome antique; ***ancient times*** les temps *mpl* anciens, l'antiquité *f*; ***the ancient world*** le monde antique

ancillary [æn'sɪlərɪ] *(pl* **ancillaries**) **1** *n* (**a**) *(helper)* auxiliaire *mf*; **hospital ancillaries** personnel *m* des services auxiliaires, agents *mpl* des hôpitaux

(**b**) *(of firm)* filiale *f*

2 *adj* (**a**) *(supplementary)* auxiliaire; **local services are ancillary to the national programme** les services locaux apportent leur aide *ou* contribution au programme national

(**b**) *(subsidiary → reason)* subsidiaire; *(→ advantage, cost)* accessoire

►► ***ancillary staff*** *(gen)* personnel *m* auxiliaire; *(in hospital)* personnel *m* des services auxiliaires; *(in school)* personnel *m* auxiliaire, auxiliaires *mfpl*

Ancona [æŋ'kəʊnə] *n* Ancône

AND [ænd] *n Comput*

►► ***AND circuit*** circuit *m* ET; ***AND element*** élément *m* ET;

and [ənd, ən, *stressed* ænd] **1** *conj* (**a**) *(in addition to)* et; **brother and sister** frère et sœur; **get your hat and coat** va chercher ton manteau et ton chapeau; **he went out without his shoes and socks on** il est sorti sans mettre ses chaussures ni ses chaussettes; **he goes fishing winter and summer (alike)** il va à la pêche en hiver comme en été; **I have to interview and assess people as part of my job** mon travail consiste en partie à m'occuper des entretiens et à évaluer les capacités des gens; **you can't work for us AND work for our competitors** vous ne pouvez pas travailler ET pour nous ET pour nos concurrents; **and/or** et/ou; **I got a letter from the bank – and?** j'ai reçu une lettre de la banque – (et) alors?; **there are books and books** il y a livres et livres; **there are champions and (there are) great champions** il y a les champions et (il y a) les grands champions; **he speaks English, and very well too** il parle anglais et même très bien

(**b**) *(then)* **he opened the door and went out** il a ouvert la porte et est sorti; **I fell and cut my knee** je me suis ouvert le genou en tombant

(**c**) *(with infinitive)* **go and look for it** va le chercher; **try and understand** essayez de comprendre

(**d**) *(but)* mais; **I want to go and he doesn't** je veux y aller, mais lui ne veut pas

(**e**) *(in numbers)* **one hundred and three** cent trois; **five pounds and ten pence** cinq livres (et) dix (pence); **two hours and ten minutes** deux heures dix (minutes); **three and a half years** trois ans et demi; **four and two thirds** quatre deux tiers

(**f**) *(indicating continuity, repetition)* **he cried and cried** il n'arrêtait pas de pleurer; **for hours and hours** pendant des heures (et des heures); **over and over again** maintes et maintes fois; **he goes on and on about politics** quand il commence à parler politique il n'y a plus moyen de l'arrêter

(**g**) *(with comparative adjectives)* **fainter and fainter** de plus en plus faible; **louder and louder** de plus en plus fort

(**h**) *(as intensifier)* **her room was nice and sunny** sa chambre était bien ensoleillée; **the soup is good and hot** la soupe est bien chaude; *Fam* **he's good and mad** il est fou furieux

(**i**) *(with implied conditional)* **one move and you're dead** un geste et vous êtes mort

(**j**) *(introducing questions)* et; **and how's your family?** et comment va la famille?; **I went to New York – and how did you like it?** je suis allé à New York – et alors, ça vous a plu?; **and what if I AM going?** et si j'y allais?

(**k**) *(introducing statement)* **and now it's time for "Kaleidoscope"** et maintenant, voici l'heure de "Kaléidoscope"; **and another thing...!** ah! autre chose *ou* j'oubliais...; **they started taking drugs, so I came home – and a good thing too!** ils ont commencé à prendre de la drogue alors je suis rentré – tu as bien fait!

(**l**) *(what's more)* **and you still owe me money!** et tu me dois encore de l'argent!; **and that's not all...** et ce n'est pas tout...

2 *n* **I want no ifs, ands or buts** je ne veux pas de discussion

3 and all *adv* (**a**) *(and everything)* et tout (ce qui s'ensuit); **the whole lot went flying, plates, cups, teapot and all** tout a volé, les assiettes, les tasses, la théière et tout (**b**) *Br Fam (as well)* aussi ▫; **you can wipe that grin off your face and all** tu peux aussi arrêter de sourire comme ça

4 and so on (and so forth) *adv* et ainsi de suite

Andalusia [ˌændəˈlu:zɪə] *n* Andalousie *f*; **in Andalusia** en Andalousie

Andalusian [ˌændəˈlu:zɪən] **1** *n* Andalou(se) *m,f*

2 *adj* andalou

andalusite [ˌændəˈlu:saɪt] *n Miner* andalousite *f*

andante [ˌæn'dæntɪ] *Mus* **1** *n* andante *m*

2 *adv* andante

andantino [ˌændæn'ti:nəʊ] *Mus* **1** *n* andantino *m*

2 *adv* andantino

Andean ['ændi:ən] *adj* des Andes, andin

Anderson shelter ['ændəsən-] *n* = abri antiaérien enterré, utilisé au Royaume-Uni pendant la seconde Guerre mondiale

Andes ['ændi:z] *npl* **the Andes** les Andes *fpl*, la cordillère des Andes; **in the Andes** dans les Andes

andesite ['ændɪzaɪt] *n Geol* andésite *f*

andiron ['ændaɪən] *n* chenet *m*

Andorra [æn'dɔ:rə] *n* Andorre *f*; **in Andorra** en Andorre; **the principality of Andorra** la principauté d'Andorre

Andorran [æn'dɔ:rən] **1** *n* Andorran(e) *m,f*

2 *adj* andorran

3 *comp (embassy)* d'Andorre; *(history)* de l'Andorre

andradite ['ændrədaɪt] *n Miner* andradite *f*

androcentric [ˌændrəʊ'sentrɪk] *adj* androcentrique

Androcles ['ændrəʊkli:z] *pr n Myth* Androclès

androgen ['ændrədʒən] *n Biol* androgène *m*

androgynous [æn'drɒdʒɪnəs] *adj Biol & Bot* androgyne

androgyny [æn'drɒdʒɪnɪ] *n Biol* androgynie *f*

android ['ændrɔɪd] **1** *n* androïde *m*

2 *adj* androïde

andrologist [æn'drɒlədʒɪst] *n Med* andrologue *mf*

andrology [æn'drɒlədʒɪ] *n Med* andrologie *f*

Andromache [æn'drɒməkɪ] *pr n Myth* Andromaque

Andromeda [æn'drɒmɪdə] **1** *pr n Myth* Andromède

2 *n Astron* Andromède

Andronicus [æn'drɒnɪkəs] *pr n Hist* Andronic

androsterone [æn'drɒstərəʊn] *n Biol* androstérone *f*

Andy Capp [ˌændɪ'kæp] *pr n* = personnage de bande dessinée incarnant, sous une forme caricaturale, un ouvrier machiste, paresseux et irrévérencieux

anecdotal [ænek'dəʊtəl] *adj* anecdotique

►► *Law* ***anecdotal evidence*** preuve *f* *ou* témoignage *m* anecdotique

anecdote ['ænɪkdəʊt] *n* anecdote *f*

anecdotist ['ænɪkdəʊtɪst] *n* anecdotier(ère) *m,f*

anechoic [ˌænə'kəʊɪk] *adj Tech* anéchoïque

anemia, anemic *Am* = **anaemia, anaemic**

anemometer [ˌænɪ'mɒmɪtə(r)] *n Met* anémomètre *m*

anemone [ə'nemənɪ] *n Bot* anémone *f*

anencephalic [ˌænense'fælɪk] *adj Med* anencéphale

anencephaly [ˌænen'sefəlɪ] *n Med* anencéphalie *f*

aneroid ['ænərɔɪd] *adj* anéroïde

►► *Met* ***aneroid barometer*** baromètre *m* anéroïde

anesthesia, anesthesiology *etc Am* = **anaesthesia, anaesthesiology** *etc*
anestrus *Am* = **anoestrus**
aneurism, aneurysm ['ænjʊrɪzəm] *n Med* anévrisme *m*, anévrysme *m*
anew [ə'nju:] *adv Literary* (**a**) *(again)* de nouveau, encore; **to begin anew** recommencer; **the fighting began anew** le combat reprit (**b**) *(in a new way)* à nouveau; **to create sth anew** créer qch à nouveau; **to start life anew** repartir à zéro
Anfield ['ænfi:ld] *n* = stade de football à Liverpool
angel ['eɪndʒəl] *n* (**a**) *Rel* ange *m*; **fallen angel** ange *m* déchu; **to be on the side of the angels** être du bon côté; **to go where angels fear to tread** s'aventurer en terrain dangereux
(**b**) *(person)* ange *m*, amour *m*; **you angel!, you're an angel!** tu es un ange *ou* un amour!; **be an angel and fetch me a glass of water** sois gentil, va me chercher un verre d'eau
(**c**) *Fam Fin (investor)* commanditaire❑ *mf*, bailleur(eresse) *m,f* de fonds❑
(**d**) *Fam Aviat* écho *m* radar non identifié❑
(**e**) *Culin* **angels on horseback** brochettes *fpl* d'huîtres à l'anglaise *(huîtres entourées d'une tranche de bacon et grillées)*
►► *Culin* ***angel cake*** ≃ gâteau *m* de Savoie; ***the Angel of Darkness*** l'ange *m* des ténèbres; *Fam Drugs slang* ***angel dust*** poudre *f* d'ange; *Am Culin* ***angel food cake*** ≃ gâteau *m* de Savoie; ***angel of mercy*** ange *m* de miséricorde; *Culin* ***angel hair noodles, angel hair pasta*** cheveux *mpl* d'ange; ***the Angel of the North*** = sculpture géante située non loin de Newcastle-upon-Tyne, symbolisant la tradition industrielle de la région
Angeleno [,ændʒə'li:nəʊ] *n* = habitant de Los Angeles
angelfish ['eɪndʒəlfɪʃ] *(pl* **inv** *or* **angelfishes**) *n (aquarium fish)* scalaire *m*; *(shark)* ange *m*
angelic [æn'dʒelɪk] *adj* angélique; **she looks absolutely angelic** elle a vraiment l'air d'un ange *ou* angélique
angelica [æn'dʒelɪkə] *n Bot & Culin* angélique *f*
angelically [æn'dʒelɪkəlɪ] *adv* comme un ange
angelus ['ændʒələs] *n Rel (bell, prayer)* angélus *m*
anger ['æŋgə(r)] **1** *n* colère *f*; **she felt intense anger** elle était très en colère; **in a fit** *or* **a moment of anger** dans un accès *ou* un mouvement de colère; **he later regretted words spoken in anger** il regretta ensuite les paroles qu'il prononça sous le coup de la colère; **his family reacted with anger and disbelief at the verdict** sa famille a réagi avec colère et incrédulité à l'annonce du verdict; **she spoke with barely suppressed anger** elle parla avec une colère à peine dissimulée *ou* en réprimant mal sa colère; **to move sb to anger** mettre qn en colère
2 *vt* mettre en colère, énerver; **he's easily angered** il se met facilement en colère, il s'emporte facilement; **he is angered by suggestions that he took bribes** cela le met en colère qu'on suggère qu'il ait pu accepter des pots-de-vin; **these remarks have angered Christians** ces commentaires ont provoqué la colère de la communauté chrétienne
Angevin ['ændʒəvɪn] *adj* Angevin, d'Anjou
angina [æn'dʒaɪnə] *n (UNCOUNT) Med* angine *f* de poitrine
►► ***angina pectoris*** angine *f* de poitrine
anginal ['ændʒaɪnəl], **anginose** ['ændʒɪnəʊs], **anginous** ['ændʒɪnəs] *adj Med* angineux
angiocardiography [,ændʒɪəʊkɑ:dɪ'ɒgrəfɪ] *n Med* angiocardiographie *f*
angiocholitis [,ændʒɪəʊkə'laɪtəs] *n Med* angiocholite *f*
angiogenesis [,ændʒɪə'dʒenɪsɪs] *n Med* angiogenèse *f*
angiogram ['ændʒɪəʊgræm] *n Med* angiogramme *m*
angiographic [,ændʒɪəʊ'græfɪk] *adj Med* angiographique, angéiographique
angiography [,ændʒɪ'ɒgrəfɪ] *n Med* angiographie *f*, angéiographie *f*
angiology [,ændʒɪ'ɒlədʒɪ] *n Med* angiologie *f*, angéiologie *f*
angioma [,ændʒɪ'əʊmə] *n Med* angiome *m*
angioneurotic [,ændʒɪəʊnjʊə'rɒtɪk] *adj Med* angioneurotique
angioplasty ['ændʒɪə,plæstɪ] *n Med* angioplastie *f*
angiosperm ['ændʒɪəʊspɜ:m] *n Bot* angiosperme *m*
angiotensin [,ændʒɪə'tensɪn] *n Med* angiotensine *f*
Angkor ['æŋkɔ:(r)] *n* Angkor
Angle ['æŋgəl] *n Hist* Angle *mf*
angle ['æŋgəl] **1** *n* (**a**) *(gen) & Geom* angle *m*; **at an angle of…** formant un angle de…; **the roads intersect at an angle of 90°** les routes se croisent à angle droit; **the car hit us at an angle** la voiture nous a heurtés de biais; **she wore her hat at an angle** elle portait son chapeau penché; **cut at an angle** coupé en biseau; **the shop stands at an angle to the street** le magasin fait l'angle
(**b**) *(corner)* angle *m*, coin *m*
(**c**) *Fig (point of view)* point *m* de vue; *(aspect)* angle *m*; **seen from this angle** vu sous cet angle; **he examined the issue from all angles** il a étudié la question sous tous les angles; **from an economic angle** d'un point de vue économique; **what's your angle on the situation?** comment voyez-vous la situation?; **we need a new angle** il nous faut un éclairage *ou* un point de vue nouveau
(**d**) *Fam (trick)* **she knows all the angles** elle en connaît un bout *ou* un rayon
(**e**) *Fam (motive)* raison❑ *f*, motif❑ *m*; **what's his angle in all this?** qu'est-ce qu'il espère y gagner?
2 *vt* (**a**) *(move)* orienter; **I angled the light towards the workbench** j'ai orienté *ou* dirigé la lumière sur l'établi
(**b**) *Fig (slant)* présenter sous un certain angle; **the article was deliberately angled to provoke a certain response** l'article était rédigé de façon à provoquer une réaction bien précise; **it's angled towards the 16-18 age group** cela vise les 16-18 ans, c'est destiné aux 16-18 ans; **studies are angled towards exams** les études sont très axées sur les examens
(**c**) *Sport* **to angle a shot** envoyer la balle en diagonale
3 *vi* (**a**) *(slant)* s'orienter; **the road angled (off) to the right** la route tournait à droite
(**b**) *Fishing* pêcher à la ligne; **to go angling** aller à la pêche (à la ligne); *Fig* **to angle for sth** chercher (à avoir) qch; **stop angling for compliments!** arrête de chercher des compliments!; **he's always angling for an invitation/a job** il est toujours en train de chercher à se faire inviter/à se faire embaucher
►► *Mil* ***angle of altitude*** angle *m* de hausse *ou* de tir positif; *Aviat* ***angle of attack*** angle *m* d'attaque; *Constr* ***angle bar*** cornière *f*, équerre *f*; *Constr* ***angle brace*** *(tool)* foret *m* à angle; *Typ* ***angle bracket*** crochet *m* en chevron; *Aviat & Mil* ***angle of climb*** angle *m* de montée; *Mil* ***angle of deflection*** angle *m* de dérive; *Mil* ***angle of depression*** angle *m* de dépression; *Phys* ***angle of dip*** inclinaison *f* magnétique; ***angle of elevation*** *Mil* angle *m* de hausse *ou* de tir positif; *Archit* angle *m* d'élévation; *Phys* ***angle of incidence*** angle *m* d'incidence; *Constr* ***angle iron*** cornière *f*, équerre *f*; *Constr* ***angle plate*** équerre *f*; *Mil* ***angle of sight*** angle *m* de mire *ou* de visée
angled ['æŋgəld] *adj (slanted → report, account)* partial, tendancieux; *Sport* **angled shot** coup *m* en diagonale
Anglepoise® ['æŋgəlpɔɪz] *n (lamp)* lampe *f* d'architecte
►► ***Anglepoise® lamp*** lampe *f* d'architecte
angler ['æŋglə(r)] *n* (**a**) *Fishing* pêcheur(euse) *m,f* (à la ligne) (**b**) *Ich* baudroie *f*, lotte *f* de mer
anglerfish ['æŋgləfɪʃ] *n Ich* baudroie *f*, lotte *f* de mer
Anglesey ['æŋgəlsɪ] *n* Anglesey
Anglican ['æŋglɪkən] **1** *n* anglican(e) *m,f*
2 *adj* anglican
►► ***the Anglican Church*** l'Église *f* anglicane; ***the Anglican Communion*** la communauté anglicane
Anglicanism ['æŋglɪkənɪzəm] *n Ling* anglicanisme *m*
anglicism ['æŋglɪsɪzəm] *n Ling* anglicisme *m*
Anglicist ['æŋglɪsɪst] *n Ling* angliciste *mf*
anglicization [,æŋglɪsaɪ'zeɪʃən] *n Ling* anglicisation *f*
anglicize, -ise ['æŋglɪsaɪz] *vt Ling* angliciser
angling ['æŋglɪŋ] *n Fishing* pêche *f* à la ligne
Anglo ['æŋgləʊ] *(pl* **Anglos**) *n* (**a**) *Am* Américain(e) *m,f* blanc (blanche) (**b**) *Can* Canadien(enne) *m,f* anglophone
Anglo- ['æŋgləʊ] *pref* anglo-
Anglo-American 1 *n* Américain(e) *m,f* d'origine anglaise
2 *adj* anglo-américain
Anglo-Arab 1 *n* (cheval *m*) anglo-arabe *m*
2 *adj (horse)* anglo-arabe
Anglo-Canadian *n* Canadien(enne) *m,f* anglophone
Anglo-Catholic *n* anglo-catholique *mf (anglican acceptant les préceptes de l'Église catholique sans pour autant se convertir)*
Anglo-French *adj* anglo-français, franco-anglais, franco-britannique
Anglo-Indian 1 *n* (**a**) *(person of mixed British and Indian descent)* métis(isse) *m,f* d'origine anglaise et indienne (**b**) *(English person living in India)* Anglais(e) *m,f* des Indes
2 *adj* anglo-indien
Anglo-Irish 1 *npl* **the Anglo-Irish** l'aristocratie *f* irlandaise d'origine anglaise
2 *n (language)* anglais *m* parlé en Irlande
3 *adj* anglo-irlandais
►► *Pol* ***the Anglo-Irish Agreement*** = accord conclu en 1985 entre le Royaume-Uni et la république d'Irlande pour garantir la paix et la stabilité en Irlande du Nord
Anglomania [,æŋgləʊ'meɪnɪə] *n* anglomanie *f*
Anglo-Norman 1 *n* (**a**) *(person)* Anglais(e) *m,f* d'origine normande (**b**) *(language)* anglo-normand *m*
2 *adj* anglo-normand
Anglophile ['æŋgləʊfaɪl] **1** *n* anglophile *mf*
2 *adj* anglophile
anglophilia [,æŋgləʊ'fɪlɪə] *n* anglophilie *f*
Anglophobe ['æŋgləʊfəʊb] **1** *n* anglophobe *mf*
2 *adj* anglophobe
anglophobia [,æŋgləʊ'fəʊbɪə] *n* anglophobie *f*
Anglophone ['æŋgləfəʊn] *Ling* **1** *n* anglophone
2 *adj* anglophone
Anglo-Saxon 1 *n* (**a**) *(person)* Anglo-Saxon(onne) *m,f* (**b**) *(language)* anglo-saxon *m*; *Euph* **he used some choice Anglo-Saxon** il a juré comme un charretier
2 *adj* anglo-saxon
Angola [æŋ'gəʊlə] *n* Angola *m*; **in Angola** en Angola
Angolan [æŋ'gəʊlən] **1** *n* Angolais(e) *m,f*
2 *adj* angolais
3 *comp (embassy)* d'Angola; *(history)* de l'Angola
angora [æŋ'gɔ:rə] **1** *n* (**a**) *(animal)* angora *m* (**b**) *(cloth, yarn)* laine *f* angora, angora *m*
2 *comp (coat, sweater)* en angora
3 *adj (animal)* angora *(inv)*
►► ***angora cat*** chat *m* angora; ***angora goat*** chèvre *f* angora; ***angora rabbit*** lapin *m* angora
Angostura bitters® [,æŋgə'stjʊərə-] *npl* bitter *m* à base d'angustura
angrily ['æŋgrəlɪ] *adv (deny, speak)* avec colère *ou* emportement; *(leave, stand up)* en colère
angry ['æŋgrɪ] *(compar* **angrier**, *superl* **angriest**) *adj* (**a**) *(person)* en colère, fâché; **to be angry at** *or* **with sb** être fâché *ou* en colère contre qn; **she's angry about** *or* **at not having been invited** elle est en colère parce qu'elle n'a pas été invitée; **they're angry at the price increase** ils sont très mécontents de l'augmentation des prix; **I'm angry with myself for having forgotten** je m'en veux d'avoir oublié; **to get angry** se mettre en colère, se fâcher; **to get angry with sb** se fâcher *ou* se mettre en colère contre qn; **her remarks made me angry** ses observations m'ont mis en colère; **his insolence made her very angry** son insolence l'a mise hors d'elle
(**b**) *(look, tone)* irrité, furieux; *(outburst, words)* violent; **in an angry voice** d'un ton irrité *ou* furieux; **he wrote her an angry letter** il lui a écrit une lettre dans laquelle il exprimait sa colère; **angry words were exchanged** il y eut un échange assez virulent
(**c**) *Fig (sky)* menaçant; *(sea)* mauvais, démonté

(**d**) *(inflamed)* enflammé, irrité; *(painful)* douloureux; **she has an angry-looking scar on her cheek** elle a une vilaine cicatrice sur la joue
►► ***angry young man*** jeune rebelle *m*

> **Angry Young Men**
> Il s'agit du nom qui fut donné à un groupe de jeunes auteurs britanniques dans les années 50 parmi lesquels figuraient John Osborne, John Arden, Alan Sillitoe et Kingsley Amis. "Les Jeunes Gens en colère" explorèrent le thème de l'aliénation sociale et s'insurgèrent contre les valeurs et le conformisme de la société anglaise de l'époque.
> Aujourd'hui on utilise cette expression à propos de toute jeune personne exprimant des opinions radicales.

angst [æŋst] *n* angoisse *f*
angstrom ['æŋstrəm] *n Phys* angström *m*, angstroem *m*
angsty ['æŋstɪ] *adj Fam* stressé
Anguilla [æn'gwɪlə] *n* Anguilla *f*
anguish ['æŋgwɪʃ] **1** *n (mental, physical)* douleur *f* immense, tourment *m*; **to be in anguish** être au supplice; **her indifference caused him great anguish** son indifférence le faisait beaucoup souffrir
2 *vt* tourmenter, faire souffrir
anguished ['æŋgwɪʃt] *adj* plein de souffrance
angular ['æŋgjʊlə(r)] *adj* (**a**) *(features, room)* anguleux; *(face, body)* anguleux, osseux (**b**) *(movement)* saccadé, haché (**c**) *(velocity, distance)* angulaire
angularity [,æŋgjʊ'lærɪtɪ] *n* angularité *f*
angwantibo [,æŋwæn'tiːbəʊ] *n Zool* potto *m* (de Calabar)
anhydride [æn'haɪdraɪd] *n Chem* anhydride *m*
anhydrite [æn'haɪdraɪt] *n Miner* anhydrite *f*
anhydrous [æn'haɪdrəs] *adj Chem* anhydre
aniline ['ænɪliːn] *n Chem* aniline *f*
►► ***aniline dye*** colorant *m* d'aniline
animadversion [,ænɪmæd'vɜːʃən] *n Formal* animadversion *f*, critique *f*; **to make animadversions on sth** critiquer qch, se répandre en critiques sur qch
animadvert [,ænɪmæd'vɜːt] *vi Formal* critiquer; **to animadvert on** *or* **upon sth** critiquer qch
animal ['ænɪməl] **1** *n* (**a**) *Zool* animal *m*; *(excluding humans)* animal *m*, bête *f*; **man is a social animal** l'homme est un animal sociable; **she's a political animal** elle a la politique dans le sang
(**b**) *Pej (brute)* brute *f*; **he's like an animal when he gets drunk** c'est une brute lorsqu'il est ivre
(**c**) *(thing)* chose *f*; **French socialism is a very different animal** le socialisme à la française est complètement différent; **there's no such animal** ça n'existe pas
2 *adj* (**a**) *Zool (products, behaviour)* animal; **they wore simple clothes made of animal hides** ils se vêtaient de peaux de bêtes; **he specializes in animal photography** c'est un spécialiste de la photographie animalière
(**b**) *(desire, needs)* animal, bestial; *(courage, instinct)* animal; **animal high spirits** vivacité *f*, entrain *m*
►► *Am* ***animal cracker*** = biscuit en forme d'animal; ***animal experimentation*** expérimentation *f* animale *ou* sur les animaux; ***animal house*** *(in zoo)* ménagerie *f*; ***animal husbandry*** élevage *m*; ***Animal Liberation Front*** = mouvement britannique militant pour la défense des droits des animaux; ***animal life*** faune *f*; ***animal lover*** ami(e) *m,f* des animaux *ou* des bêtes; ***animal magnetism*** *(charm)* magnétisme *m*, charme *m*; *(form of hypnosis)* magnétisme *m* animal; ***animal painter*** animalier(ère) *m,f*; ***animal programme*** émission *f* sur les animaux; ***animal rights*** droits *mpl* des animaux; ***animal testing*** expérimentation *f* animale *ou* sur les animaux; ***animal therapy*** zoothérapie *f*

'**Animal Farm**' *Orwell* 'La Ferme des animaux'

animalcule [,ænɪ'mælkjuːl] *n Zool* animalcule *m*
animalism ['ænɪməlɪzəm] *n* (**a**) *(animal trait)* animalité *f* (**b**) *(sensuality)* animalité *f*, sensualité *f* (**c**) *Phil (theory)* animalisme *m*
animalist ['ænɪməlɪst] *n* (**a**) *(sensualist)* sensualiste *mf* (**b**) *Phil* animaliste *mf* (**c**) *Art* animalier(ère) *m,f*
animality [ænɪ'mælɪtɪ] *n* animalité *f*
animalize, -ise ['ænɪməlaɪz] *vt* (**a**) *(excite the animal passions of)* **to animalize sb** réveiller l'animal en qn (**b**) *Art* représenter sous la forme d'un animal
animate 1 *vt* ['ænɪmeɪt] (**a**) *(give life to)* animer (**b**) *Fig (enliven* → *face, look, party)* animer, égayer; *(→ discussion)* animer, stimuler (**c**) *(move to action)* motiver, inciter (**d**) *Cin & TV* animer
2 *adj* ['ænɪmət] vivant, animé; **to become animate** s'animer
animated ['ænɪmeɪtɪd] *adj* animé; **to become animated** s'animer
►► ***animated cartoon*** dessin *m* animé; ***animated film*** film *m* d'animation; *Comput* ***animated GIF*** (fichier *m*) GIF *m* animé
animatedly ['ænɪmeɪtɪdlɪ] *adv (behave, participate)* avec vivacité *ou* entrain; *(talk)* d'un ton animé, avec animation
animatic [,ænɪ'mætɪk] *n (storyboard)* animatique *f*
animation [ænɪ'meɪʃən] *n* (**a**) *(of discussion, party)* animation *f*; *(of place, street)* activité *f*, animation *f*; *(of person)* vivacité *f*, entrain *m*; *(of face, look)* animation *f* (**b**) *Cin & TV* animation *f*
animator ['ænɪmeɪtə(r)] *n* animateur(trice) *m,f*
animatronic [,ænɪmə'trɒnɪk] **1** *adj (figure, character, puppet)* animé électroniquement
2 animatronics *n* animatronique *f*
animism ['ænɪmɪzəm] *n Phil & Rel* animisme *m*
animist ['ænɪmɪst] *Phil & Rel* **1** *n* animiste *mf*
2 *adj* animiste
animistic [ænɪ'mɪstɪk] *adj Phil & Rel* animiste
animosity [ænɪ'mɒsətɪ] (*pl* **animosities**) *n* animosité *f*, antipathie *f*; **she felt great animosity towards politicians** elle ressentait de l'animosité à l'égard des hommes politiques; **I sensed the animosity between them** je sentais une certaine animosité entre eux
animus ['ænɪməs] *n* (**a**) *(hostility)* animosité *f*, antipathie *f* (**b**) *(motive)* animus *m* (**c**) *Psy* animus *m*
anion ['ænaɪən] *n Phys* anion *m*
anionic [,ænaɪ'ɒnɪk] *adj Phys* anionique
anise ['ænɪs] *n Bot* anis *m*
aniseed ['ænɪsiːd] *Bot & Culin* **1** *n* graine *f* d'anis; **aniseed-flavoured** anisé
2 *comp (cake, sweet)* à l'anis
►► ***aniseed ball*** bonbon *m* à l'anis
anisette [ænɪ'zet] *n* anisette *f*
anisotropic [,ænɪsəʊ'trɒpɪk] *adj Biol & Phys* anisotrope
anisotropism [,ænɪsəʊ'trɒpɪzəm], **anisotropy** [,ænɪ'sɒtrəpɪ] *n Biol & Phys* anisotropie *f*
Ankara ['æŋkərə] *n* Ankara
ankle ['æŋkəl] *n* cheville *f*
►► ***ankle boot*** bottine *f*; ***ankle chain*** bracelet *m* de cheville; ***ankle joint*** articulation *f* du pied; ***ankle sock*** socquette *f*; ***ankle strap*** bride *f*; ***ankle support*** chevillière *f*
ankle-biter *n Fam (child)* gosse *mf*
anklebone ['æŋkəlbəʊn] *n* astragale *m*
ankle-deep *adj* **she was ankle-deep in mud** elle était dans la boue jusqu'aux chevilles; **the water is only ankle-deep** l'eau monte *ou* vient seulement jusqu'à la cheville; *Am Fig* **to be ankle-deep in sth** *(involved)* être impliqué dans qch
ankle-length *adj* qui descend jusqu'à la cheville; **ankle-length boot** bottine *f*
anklet ['æŋklɪt] *n* (**a**) *(chain)* bracelet *m* de cheville (**b**) *Am (ankle sock)* socquette *f*
ankylose ['æŋkɪləʊz] *Med* **1** *vt* ankyloser
2 *vi* s'ankyloser
ankylosis [,æŋkɪ'ləʊsɪs] *n Med* ankylose *f*
annalist ['ænəlɪst] *n* annaliste *mf*
annals ['ænəlz] *npl* annales *fpl*
Annam [æn'æm] *n* Annam *m*
Annamese [ænə'miːz] **1** *n* Annamite *mf*
2 *adj* annamite
Annapurna [,ænə'pɜːnə] *n* l'Annapurna *m*
Anne [æn] *pr n* **Anne of Austria** Anne d'Autriche; **Anne Boleyn** Anne Boleyn; **Anne of Cleves** Anne de Clèves
anneal [ə'niːl] *vt Tech (glass)* recuire; *(metal)* tremper, recuire
annealing [ə'niːlɪŋ] *n Tech (of glass)* recuit *m*, recuite *f*; *(of metal)* adoucissement *m*, recuit *m*, recuite *f*; **box** *or* **close annealing** recuit en vase clos
►► ***annealing furnace*** four *m* à recuire
annelid ['ænəlɪd] *n Zool* annélide *f*
►► ***annelid worm*** annélide *f*
annex 1 *n* ['æneks] *Am (building, supplement to document)* annexe *f*
2 *vt* [æ'neks] annexer (**sth to sth** qch à qch)
annexation [,ænek'seɪʃən] *n (act)* annexion *f*; *(country)* pays *m* annexé; *(document)* document *m* annexe, annexe *f*
annexe, *Am* **annex** ['æneks] *n (building, supplement to document)* annexe *f*
annihilate [ə'naɪəleɪt] *vt* (**a**) *(destroy* → *enemy, race)* anéantir; *(→ argument)* démolir; *(→ effort)* réduire à néant (**b**) *(defeat)* pulvériser, anéantir
annihilating [ə'naɪəleɪtɪŋ] *adj* annihilant, annihilateur
annihilation [ənaɪə'leɪʃən] *n* (**a**) *(destruction* → *of argument, enemy, effort)* anéantissement *m* (**b**) *(defeat)* défaite *f* (totale) (**c**) *Phys* annihilation *f*
annihilator [ə'naɪəleɪtə(r)] *n* (**a**) *(person)* annihilateur(trice) *m,f* (**b**) *Math* annulateur *m*
anniversary [ænɪ'vɜːsərɪ] (*pl* **anniversaries**) **1** *n* anniversaire *m (d'un événement)*, commémoration *f*
2 *comp (celebration, dinner)* anniversaire, commémoratif
►► ***anniversary card*** carte *f* d'anniversaire (de mariage); ***anniversary present*** cadeau *m* d'anniversaire (de mariage)
Anno Domini [,ænəʊ'dɒmɪnaɪ] *adv Formal* après Jésus-Christ
annotate ['ænəteɪt] *vt* annoter
annotation [,ænə'teɪʃən] *n (action)* annotation *f*; *(note)* annotation *f*, note *f*
annotator ['ænəteɪtə(r)] *n* annotateur(trice) *m,f*
announce [ə'naʊns] **1** *vt* annoncer; **to announce sth to sb** annoncer qch à qn; **we are pleased to announce the birth/marriage of our son** nous sommes heureux de vous faire part de la naissance/du mariage de notre fils; **a whistle announced the arrival of the train** un coup de sifflet annonça l'arrivée du train; **management have announced a cut in pay** l'administration a annoncé une réduction des salaires
2 *vi Am Pol* **to announce for the presidency** se déclarer candidat à la présidence
announcement [ə'naʊnsmənt] *n (public statement)* annonce *f*; *Admin* avis *m*; *(notice of birth, marriage)* faire-part *m*; **here is a passenger announcement** avis voyageurs; **here is a staff announcement** appel de service
announcer [ə'naʊnsə(r)] *n (gen)* annonceur(euse) *m,f*; *Rad & TV (newscaster)* journaliste *mf*; *(introducing programme)* speaker (speakerine) *m,f*, annonceur(euse) *m,f*
annoy [ə'nɔɪ] *vt* (**a**) *(irritate)* ennuyer, agacer, embêter; **is this man annoying you?** cet homme vous ennuie-t-il *ou Formal* vous importune-t-il?; **it's his constant boasting that annoys me** ce sont ses fanfaronnades perpétuelles qui m'agacent; **he only did it to annoy you** il l'a fait uniquement pour vous ennuyer *ou* contrarier
(**b**) *(disturb* → *noise, music)* déranger; **is the light/noise annoying you?** est-ce que la lumière/le bruit te dérange?
annoyance [ə'nɔɪəns] *n* (**a**) *(displeasure)* contrariété *f*, mécontentement *m*; **with a look of annoyance** d'un air contrarié *ou* mécontent; **"no, I won't", she said with some annoyance** "non, je ne le ferai pas", déclara-t-elle d'un ton agacé; **to my great annoyance** à mon grand mécontentement *ou* déplaisir; **to cause annoyance to sb** contrarier qn (**b**) *(source of irritation)* ennui *m*, désagrément *m*
annoyed [ə'nɔɪd] *adj* **to be/to get annoyed with sb** être/se mettre en colère contre qn; **to be annoyed with oneself** s'en vouloir; **I felt really annoyed with him** j'étais vraiment en colère contre lui; **she was annoyed that he hadn't called** elle n'était pas contente qu'il n'ait pas appelé
annoying [ə'nɔɪɪŋ] *adj (bothersome)* gênant, ennuyeux; *(irritating)* énervant, agaçant, fâcheux; **the annoying thing is...** ce qui est

énervant dans l'histoire, c'est…; **how annoying!** que c'est ennuyeux!

annoyingly [ə'nɔɪŋlɪ] *adv* de manière gênante *ou* agaçante; **she was annoyingly vague** elle était si vague que c'en était agaçant; **annoyingly, he was late** il était en retard, ce qui était ennuyeux

annual ['ænjʊəl] **1** *n* (**a**) *(publication)* publication *f* annuelle; *Com (of association, firm)* annuaire *m*; *(for children)* album *m* (de bandes dessinées) (**b**) *Bot* plante *f* annuelle

2 *adj* annuel; **what's your annual income?** combien gagnez-vous par an?

►► *Acct & Fin* ***annual accounts*** bilan *m* annuel, comptes *mpl* de clôture *ou* de fin d'exercice; ***annual budget*** budget *m* annuel; *Fin* ***annual contribution*** *(to pension scheme)* cotisation *f* annuelle; *Acct* ***annual depreciation*** dépréciation *f* annuelle, amortissement *m* annuel; ***annual earnings*** *(of company)* recette(s) *f(pl)* annuelle(s); *(of person)* revenu *m* annuel; *Com* ***annual general meeting*** assemblée *f* générale (annuelle); ***annual income*** revenu *m* annuel; ***annual instalment*** annuité *f*; *Admin* ***annual leave*** congé *m* annuel; *Fin* ***annual percentage rate*** taux *m* effectif global; ***annual profit*** profit *m* annuel; *Fin* ***annual report*** rapport *m* annuel de gestion; *Fin* ***annual returns*** déclarations *fpl* annuelles; *Fin* ***annual statement of results*** déclaration *f* annuelle de résultats; *Acct & Fin* ***annual turnover*** chiffre *m* d'affaires annuel; *Acct* ***annual writedown*** dépréciation *f* annuelle, amortissement *m* annuel

annualize, -ise ['ænjʊə,laɪz] *vt Acct & Fin* annualiser; **the annualized figures** le montant total pour un an

►► ***annualized percentage rate*** taux *m* effectif global

annually ['ænjʊəlɪ] *adv (in a year)* par an, annuellement; *(every year)* tous les ans; **he earns £20,000 annually** il gagne 20 000 livres par an

annuity [ə'nju:ɪtɪ] *(pl* **annuities***) n Fin (regular income)* rente *f* (annuelle); **annuity for life, life annuity** viager *m*, rente *f* viagère; **to purchase an annuity** placer de l'argent en viager; **to pay sb an annuity** servir *ou* faire une rente à qn

►► ***annuity payment*** versement *m* d'annuité; *(investment)* viager *m*, rente *f* viagère

annul [ə'nʌl] *(pt & pp* **annulled,** *cont* **annulling***) vt (law)* abroger, abolir; *(agreement)* annuler; *(contract)* résilier, annuler; *(marriage)* annuler; *(judgement)* casser, annuler

annular ['ænjʊlə(r)] *adj* annulaire

annulate ['ænjʊlət], **annulated** ['ænjʊleɪtɪd] *adj* (**a**) *Bot & Zool* annelé (**b**) *Archit* armillé

annulment [ə'nʌlmənt] *n (of law)* abrogation *f*, abolition *f*; *(of agreement)* annulation *f*; *(of contract)* résiliation *f*, annulation *f*; *(of marriage)* annulation *f*; *(of judgement)* cassation *f*, annulation *f*; **decree of annulment** décret *m* abolitif

Annunciation [ə,nʌnsɪ'eɪʃən] *n Rel* **the Annunciation** l'Annonciation *f*

anode ['ænəʊd] *n Elec* anode *f*

anodize, -ise ['ænədaɪz] *vt Metal* anodiser

anodyne ['ænədaɪn] **1** *n Med* analgésique *m*, calmant *m*; *Fig* baume *m*

2 *adj* (**a**) *Med* analgésique, antalgique; *Fig* apaisant (**b**) *(inoffensive)* anodin

anoestrus, *Am* **anestrus** [æn'i:strəs] *n Physiol* interoestrus *m*

anoint [ə'nɔɪnt] *vt (in religious ceremony)* oindre, consacrer par l'onction; **to anoint sb with oil** oindre qn d'huile; **they anointed him king** ils l'ont sacré roi; **the anointed King** le roi consacré

anointing [ə'nɔɪntɪŋ] *n* onction *f*; *(of ruler)* sacre *m*

anointment [ə'nɔɪntmənt] *n* (**a**) *(action)* onction *f*; *(of ruler)* sacre *m* (**b**) *Chem (ointment)* onguent *m*, pommade *f*

anomalous [ə'nɒmələs] *adj (effect, growth, result)* anormal, irrégulier; *Gram* anormal

anomalously [ə'nɒmələslɪ] *adv* anormalement, irrégulièrement

anomalousness [ə'nɒmələsnɪs] *n* caractère *m* anormal

anomaly [ə'nɒməlɪ] *(pl* **anomalies***) n (gen) & Astron* anomalie *f*

anomer [ə'nəʊmə(r)] *n Biol & Chem* anomère *m*

anon [ə'nɒn] *adv Arch or Literary (soon)* bientôt, sous peu; *Hum* **see you anon** à bientôt; **more of this anon** je reviendrai sur cela

anon. *(written abbr* **anonymous***)* anon.

anonymity [ænə'nɪmətɪ] *n* (**a**) *(namelessness)* anonymat *m*; **to preserve one's anonymity** garder l'anonymat, préserver son anonymat (**b**) *(unexceptional quality)* banalité *f*

anonymous [ə'nɒnɪməs] *adj* anonyme; **an anonymous caller phoned the newspaper to say that...** la rédaction du journal a reçu un appel anonyme l'informant que…; **to remain anonymous** garder l'anonymat

►► *Mktg* ***anonymous buyer*** acheteur(euse) *m,f* anonyme; *Comput* ***anonymous FTP*** protocole *m* de transfert anonyme; *Comput* ***anonymous remailer*** service *m* de courrier électronique anonyme

anonymously [ə'nɒnɪməslɪ] *adv (act, donate)* anonymement, en gardant l'anonymat; *(publish)* anonymement, sans nom d'auteur

anopheles [ə'nɒfɪli:z] *(pl* **inv***) n Entom (mosquito)* anophèle *m*

►► ***anopheles mosquito*** anophèle *m*

anorak ['ænəræk] *n* (**a**) *(garment)* anorak *m* (**b**) *Br Fam Pej (person)* ringard(e) *m,f*

anorectic [,ænə'rektɪk] *adj* anorexique

anorexia [,ænə'reksɪə] *n* anorexie *f*; **anorexia sufferer** anorexique *mf*

►► ***anorexia nervosa*** anorexie *f* mentale

anorexic [ænə'reksɪk] **1** *n* anorexique *mf*

2 *adj* anorexique

another [ə'nʌðə(r)] **1** *adj* (**a**) *(additional)* un (une)… de plus, encore un (une); **have another chocolate** prenez un autre *ou* reprenez un chocolat; **another cup of tea?** vous reprendrez bien une tasse de thé?; **another 5 miles** encore 5 miles; **can you wait another 10 minutes?** peux-tu attendre encore 10 minutes?; **another 5 minutes and we'd have missed the train** 5 minutes de plus et on ratait le train; **in another 3 weeks** dans 3 semaines; **without another word** sans un mot de plus, sans ajouter un mot; **and for another thing, he's ill** et de plus il est malade; **I don't want to see another fish as long as I live** je ne veux plus voir un seul poisson de toute ma vie

(**b**) *(second)* un (une) autre, un (une) second; **we're thinking of getting another car** *(in addition to the one we have)* nous pensons acheter une deuxième voiture; **it could be another Vietnam** ça pourrait être un second *ou* nouveau Viêt-nam; **he is another Picasso** c'est le nouveau Picasso

(**c**) *(different)* un (une) autre; **can't we do that another time?** on ne peut pas remettre ça à plus tard *ou* à une autre fois?; **let's do it another way** faisons-le autrement; **that's another matter entirely!** ça, c'est une tout autre histoire!; **we're thinking of getting another car** *(to replace the car we have)* nous pensons acheter une nouvelle voiture *ou* changer de voiture

2 *pron* (**a**) *(a similar one)* un (une) autre, encore un (une); **a glass of milk and another of water** un verre de lait et un verre d'eau; **she finished one cigarette and lit another** elle finit une cigarette et en alluma une autre; *Literary* **many another** bien d'autres, beaucoup d'autres; **one way or another** d'une façon ou d'une autre; **taking one thing with another, we just manage** l'un dans l'autre, on arrive à joindre les deux bouts; **what with one thing and another, I forgot** avec tout ça j'ai oublié

(**b**) *(a different one)* **another of the girls** une autre des filles; **bring a dessert of one sort or another** apportez un dessert, (n'importe lequel); **science is one thing, art is another** la science est une chose, l'art en est une autre

(**c**) *(reciprocal)* **one another** l'un l'autre; *(more than two people)* les uns les autres; **to help one another** s'entraider; **love one another** aimez-vous les uns les autres; **he and his wife adore one another** lui et sa femme s'adorent; **they give one another presents** ils se donnent des cadeaux

(**d**) *Arch or Literary (somebody else)* un (une) autre; **she loves another** elle en aime un autre

A. N. Other [,eɪen'ʌðə(r)] *n Br (man)* monsieur X; *(woman)* madame X

anoxia [æn'ɒksɪə] *n Biol & Med* anoxie *f*

Ansaphone® ['ɑ:nsəfəʊn] *n Tel* répondeur *m* (téléphonique)

ANSI [,eɪen,es'aɪ] *n Admin & Ind (abbr* **American National Standards Institute***)* association *f* américaine de normalisation, = AFNOR *f*

answer ['ɑ:nsə(r)] **1** *vt* (**a**) *(letter, person, telephone, advertisement)* répondre à; *(door)* aller *ou* venir ouvrir; *Literary* **he answered not a word** il n'a pas répondu, il n'a pas soufflé mot; **she answered with a shy grin** pour toute réponse elle a souri timidement; **I phoned earlier but nobody answered** j'ai téléphoné tout à l'heure mais ça ne répondait pas; **the maid answered the bell** la bonne a répondu au coup de sonnette; **to answer a prayer** exaucer une prière; **letters to be answered** courrier *m* en cours

(**b**) *(respond correctly to)* **he could only answer two of the questions** il n'a su répondre qu'à deux des questions; **few of the students answered this question well** peu d'élèves ont bien traité cette question

(**c**) *(fulfil)* répondre à, satisfaire; **the computer answers a number of requirements** l'ordinateur répond à plusieurs fonctions; **this should answer the purpose quite nicely** ceci fera très bien l'affaire; **it should answer the purposes of both students and translators** ce devrait être utile aux étudiants comme aux traducteurs; **that will answer my purpose** cela fera mon affaire

(**d**) *(description)* répondre à, correspondre à; **a man answering this description was seen in the area** un homme répondant *ou* correspondant à ce signalement a été aperçu dans la région

(**e**) *Law* **the defendant answered the charge** l'accusé a répondu à *ou* a réfuté l'accusation

(**f**) *Naut* **to answer the helm** *(ship)* obéir à la barre

2 *vi* répondre, donner une réponse; **it's not answering** *(phone)* ça ne répond pas

3 *n* (**a**) *(reply → to letter, person, request)* réponse *f*; *(→ to criticism, objection)* réponse *f*, réplique *f*; **she made no answer** elle n'a pas répondu; **he couldn't think of an answer** il n'a rien trouvé à répondre; **in answer to her question he simply grinned** pour toute réponse à sa question, il a eu un large sourire; *Formal* **in answer to your letter** en réponse à votre lettre; **did you get an answer to your letter?** as-tu obtenu une réponse à ta lettre?; **I rang the bell but there was no answer** j'ai sonné mais personne n'a répondu *ou* n'a ouvert; **I phoned but there was no answer** j'ai téléphoné mais ça ne répondait pas; **she won't take no for an answer** elle n'acceptera pas de refus; **he has an answer for everything** il a réponse à tout; **they had no answer to this** ils n'ont pas su quoi répondre; **there's no answer to that!** comment répondre à ça!; **it's the answer to the government's prayers** c'est exactement ce dont le gouvernement avait besoin; **he's the answer to our prayers** il est notre sauveur; **it's the answer to all my prayers** *or* **dreams!** c'est ce dont j'ai toujours rêvé!

(**b**) *(solution)* solution *f*; **the (right) answer** la bonne réponse; *also Fig* **there's no easy answer** il n'y a pas de solution facile; **you think you know all the answers, don't you?** tu crois que tu sais tout, c'est ça?

(**c**) *(to exam question)* réponse *f*; **write your answers on a separate sheet of paper** notez vos réponses sur une feuille séparée

(**d**) *(equivalent)* **she's England's answer to Edith Piaf** elle est *ou* c'est l'Édith Piaf anglaise; **it's the poor man's answer to lobster** c'est le homard des pauvres

(**e**) *Law* **answer to a charge** réponse *f ou* réfutation *f* à une accusation

►► *Tel* ***answer mode*** mode *m* réponse; *Tel* ***answer tone*** tonalité *f* de réponse

►**answer back 1** *vt sep* répondre (avec insolence) à, répliquer à; **don't answer (your father) back!** ne réponds pas (à ton père)!

2 *vi* répondre (avec insolence)

►**answer for** *vt insep* (**a**) *(be responsible for)* répondre de, être responsable de; **she'll answer to me for his safety** elle se portera garante envers moi de sa sécurité; **this government has a lot to answer for** ce gouvernement a bien des comptes à rendre; **he/television has a lot to answer for** il/la télévision est à l'origine de bien des problèmes; **you'll answer for that!** vous me le paierez!

(**b**) *(vouch for)* garantir; **I can't answer for the quality of her work** je ne peux pas garantir la qualité de son travail

►**answer to** *vt insep* (**a**) *(respond to)* **the cat answers to (the name of) Mitzi** le chat répond au nom de Mitzi, le chat s'appelle Mitzi

(**b**) *(correspond to)* répondre à, correspondre à; **to answer to a description** répondre à une description

(**c**) *(be accountable to)* être responsable envers, rendre compte à; **you'll have me to answer to** *(if you do that)* c'est à moi que vous devrez rendre des comptes; **to answer to sb for sth** être responsable de qch envers qn

answerable ['ɑːnsərəbəl] *adj* (**a**) *(person)* responsable, comptable; **to be answerable to sb for sth** être responsable de qch devant qn, être garant de qch envers qn; **politicians are answerable to their constituents for their actions** les hommes politiques sont responsables de leurs actions devant leurs électeurs; **you're answerable to the company for any damages** vous êtes garant envers la société de toute avarie *ou* de tout dégât; **he's answerable only to the president** il ne relève que du président; **I'm answerable to no one** je n'ai de comptes à rendre à personne

(**b**) *(question)* susceptible de réponse, qui admet une réponse; *(accusation, argument)* réfutable

answerback ['ɑːnsəbæk] *n Comput* réponse *f* en retour

answering ['ɑːnsərɪŋ] *adj*

►► *Tel* ***answering machine*** répondeur *m* (automatique *ou* téléphonique); *Tel* ***answering service*** *(manned)* permanence *f* téléphonique; *(unmanned)* répondeur *m* téléphonique

answerphone ['ænsəfəʊn] *n Br* répondeur *m* (automatique *ou* téléphonique)

ant [ænt] *n* fourmi *f*; *Fam* **to have ants in one's pants** avoir la bougeotte

►► *Entom* ***ant lion*** fourmi-lion *m*, fourmilion *m*

ANTA [ˌeɪenˌtiː'eɪ] *n* (*abbr* **American National Theater and Academy**) = organisation américaine dont le rôle est de promouvoir l'art théâtral

anta ['æntə] (*pl* **antae** [-tiː]) *n Archit* ante *f*

antacid [ænt'æsɪd] **1** *n* (médicament *m*) alcalin *m*, antiacide *m*

2 *adj* alcalin, antiacide; **antacid digestant** médicament *m* contre les maux d'estomac

antagonism [æn'tægənɪzəm] *n* antagonisme *m*, hostilité *f*; **there is considerable antagonism towards the new tax** il y a une opposition considérable au nouvel impôt

antagonist [æn'tægənɪst] *n* antagoniste *mf*, adversaire *mf*

antagonistic [ænˌtægə'nɪstɪk] *adj* *(person)* opposé, hostile; *(feelings, ideas)* antagoniste, antagonique; **he's openly antagonistic to the policy** il est ouvertement opposé *ou* hostile à la politique

antagonize, -ise [æn'tægənaɪz] *vt* contrarier, mettre à dos; **we can't afford to antagonize the voters** nous ne pouvons pas nous permettre de nous aliéner les électeurs; **don't antagonize him!** ne te le mets pas à dos!

Antalya [ɑːn'tɑːljə] *n* Antalya

Antananarivo [ˌæntəˌnænə'riːvəʊ] *n* Antananarivo

Antarctic [ænt'ɑːktɪk] **1** *n (ocean)* l'Antarctique *m*, l'océan *m* Antarctique; **in the Antarctic** dans l'Antarctique

2 *adj* antarctique

►► ***the Antarctic Circle*** le cercle polaire antarctique; ***the Antarctic Ocean*** l'Antarctique *m*, l'océan *m* Antarctique; ***the Antarctic Peninsula*** la péninsule antarctique

Antarctica [ænt'ɑːktɪkə] *n* l'Antarctique *f*, l'Antarctide *f*

Antares [æn'teəriːz] *n Astron* Antarès *m*

antbird ['æntbɜːd] *n Orn* fourmilier *m*

ante ['æntɪ] **1** *n* (**a**) *Cards* mise *f*; **a £3 ante** une mise de 3 livres; *Fam* **to up the ante** *(in gambling)* augmenter la mise❑; *Fig* placer la barre plus haut (**b**) *Fam (price)* part *f*

2 *vi Cards* faire une mise

►**ante up** *Am Fam* **1** *vt sep* casquer

2 *vi* casquer; **come on, ante up!** allez, allonge!

anteater ['ænt,iːtə(r)] *n* fourmilier *m*

antebellum [ˌæntɪ'beləm] *adj* d'avant la guerre; *Am Hist* d'avant la guerre de Sécession

antecede [ˌæntɪ'siːd] *vt* précéder

antecedence [ˌæntɪ'siːdəns] *n* (**a**) *(precedence)* antériorité *f* (**b**) *(priority)* priorité *f*

antecedent [ˌæntɪ'siːdənt] **1** *n* antécédent

2 *adj* antérieur, précédent (**to** à)

3 antecedents *npl Formal (family)* ancêtres *mpl*; *(history)* passé *m*, antécédents *mpl*

antechamber ['æntɪˌtʃeɪmbə(r)] *n* (**a**) *Archit* antichambre *f* (**b**) *Tech (in engine)* préchambre *f*; **diesel engine with antechamber** moteur *m* diesel à chambre de précombustion

antedate [ˌæntɪ'deɪt] *vt* (**a**) *(precede in time)* précéder, dater d'avant (**b**) *(give earlier date to)* antidater (**c**) *(set an earlier date for)* avancer

antediluvian [ˌæntɪdɪ'luːvɪən] *adj Literary or Hum* antédiluvien

antelope ['æntɪləʊp] (*pl* **inv** *or* **antelopes**) *n* antilope *f*

ante meridian [ˌæntɪmə'rɪdɪən], **ante meridiem** [ˌæntɪmə'rɪdɪəm] *adj Formal* du matin

antenatal [ˌæntɪ'neɪtəl] *Br Obst* **1** *adj* prénatal

2 *n Fam* consultation *f* prénatale❑

►► ***antenatal care*** soins *mpl* prénatals; ***antenatal class*** = cours de préparation à l'accouchement; ***antenatal clinic*** service *m* de consultation prénatale

antenna [æn'tenə] (*pl* **antennae** [-niː] *or* **antennas**) *n* antenne *f*

antepenult [ˌæntɪpɪ'nʌlt] *n Gram* antépénultième *f*

antepenultimate [æntɪpɪ'nʌltɪmət] **1** *n* antépénultième *f*

2 *adj* antépénultième

anterior [æn'tɪərɪə(r)] *adj Formal or Anat* antérieur (**to** à)

►► *Anat* ***anterior cruciate ligament*** ligament *m* croisé antérieur du genou

anteriority [ænˌtɪərɪ'ɒrɪtɪ] *n Formal or Anat* antériorité *f*

anteroom ['æntɪrʊm] *n Archit* antichambre *f*, vestibule *m*

anthem ['ænθəm] *n (song)* chant *m*; *Rel* motet *m*; **national anthem** hymne *m* national

anther ['ænθə(r)] *n Bot* anthère *f*

anthill ['ænthɪl] *n* fourmilière *f*

anthologist [æn'θɒlədʒɪst] *n* anthologiste *mf*

anthologize [æn'θɒlədʒaɪz] **1** *vt (poem)* mettre dans une anthologie; **a much anthologized poem** un poème qu'on trouve dans toutes les anthologies

2 *vi* faire une anthologie

anthology [æn'θɒlədʒɪ] (*pl* **anthologies**) *n* anthologie *f*

Anthony ['æntənɪ] *pr n* Antoine

►► ***Anthony Eden*** *(hat)* chapeau *m* de feutre noir; *Med* ***(St) Anthony's fire*** érysipèle *m*, feu *m* Saint-Antoine; **Anthony of Padua** Antoine de Padoue

anthracite ['ænθrəsaɪt] **1** *n* (**a**) *Miner* anthracite *m* (**b**) *(colour)* (gris *m*) anthracite *m inv*

2 *adj (colour)* (gris) anthracite *(inv)*

►► ***anthracite grey*** **1** *n* (gris *m*) anthracite *m* **2** *adj* gris anthracite *(inv)*

anthracosis [ˌænθrə'kəʊsɪs] *n Med* anthracose *f*

anthrax ['ænθræks] *n Med & Vet (disease)* charbon *m*; *(sore)* anthrax *m*

anthropocentric [ˌænθrəpəʊ'sentrɪk] *adj Phil* anthropocentrique

anthropocentrism [ˌænθrəpəʊ'sentrɪzəm] *n Phil* anthropocentrisme *m*

anthropogenesis [ˌænθrəpəʊ'dʒenɪsɪs] *n* anthropogenèse *f*, anthropogénie *f*

anthropogenic [ˌænθrəpəʊ'dʒenɪk] *adj* anthropogénique

anthropoid ['ænθrəpɔɪd] *Zool* **1** *n* anthropoïde *m*

2 *adj* anthropoïde

anthropological [ˌænθrəpə'lɒdʒɪkəl] *adj* anthropologique

anthropologist [ˌænθrə'pɒlədʒɪst] *n* anthropologue *mf*

anthropology [ˌænθrə'pɒlədʒɪ] *n* anthropologie *f*

anthropometry [ˌænθrə'pɒmɪtrɪ] *n* anthropométrie *f*

anthropomorphic [ˌænθrəpə'mɔːfɪk] *adj* anthropomorphique

anthropomorphism [ˌænθrəpə'mɔːfɪzəm] *n* anthropomorphisme *m*

anthropomorphize, -ise [ˌænθrəpə'mɔːfaɪz] *vt* anthropomorphiser

anthropomorphous [ˌænθrəpə'mɔːfəs] *adj* anthropomorphe

anthropophagi [ˌænθrə'pɒfəgaɪ] (*sing* **anthropophagus** [-gəs]) *npl* anthropophages *mpl*

anthropophagous [ˌænθrə'pɒfəgəs] *adj* anthropophage

anthropophagus [ˌænθrəpɒfəgəs] *sing of* **anthropophagi**

anthropophagy [ˌænθrə'pɒfədʒɪ] *n* anthropophagie *f*

anti ['æntɪ] *Fam* **1** *adj* **she's rather anti** elle est plutôt contre❑; **he's a bit anti all that kind of thing** il est un peu contre tout cela *ou* toutes ces choses❑

2 *n* opposant(e)❑ *m,f*

anti- ['æntɪ] *pref* anti-; **anti-American** antiaméricain; **anti-British** antibritannique

antiabortion [ˌæntɪə'bɔːʃən] *adj (movement, campaigners)* anti-avortement

antiabortionist [ˌæntɪə'bɔːʃənɪst] *n* adversaire *mf* de l'avortement

antiacarid [ˌæntɪ'ækərɪd] *adj* antiacarien

antiacid [ˌæntɪ'æsɪd] *n* antiacide *m*

antiaircraft [ˌæntɪ'eəkrɑːft] *adj (system, weapon)* antiaérien

►► ***antiaircraft defence*** défense *f* contre avions, DCA *f*

anti-aliasing *n Comput* anti-crénelage *m*, antialiassage *m*

anti-anxiety *adj (drug)* anxiolytique

antiapartheid [ˌæntɪə'pɑːthaɪt] *adj* anti-apartheid

antibacterial [ˌæntɪbæk'tɪːrɪəl] *adj Biol* antibactérien

antiballistic [ˌæntɪbə'lɪstɪk] *adj Mil* antibalistique, antimissile

►► *Mil* ***antiballistic missile*** engin *m ou* fusée *f* antimissile

antibioresistance [ˌæntɪbaɪəʊrɪ'zɪstəns] *n Biol* antibiorésistance *f*

antibiotic [ˌæntɪbaɪ'ɒtɪk] **1** *n* antibiotique *m*

2 *adj* antibiotique

antibody ['æntɪˌbɒdɪ] (*pl* **antibodies**) *n Biol* anticorps *m*

anti-burst lock *n Tech* serrure *f* renforcée

anticathode [ˌæntɪ'kæθəʊd] *n Tech* anticathode *f*

anticatholic [ˌæntɪ'kæθəlɪk] **1** *n* anticatholique *mf*

2 *adj* anticatholique

anti-cellulite *adj (cream, treatment)* anticellulite *(inv)*

antichresis [ˌæntɪ'kriːsɪs] *n Law* antichrèse *f*

Antichrist ['æntɪˌkraɪst] *n Rel* **the Antichrist** l'Antéchrist *m*

antichristian [ˌæntɪ'krɪstʃən] *adj Rel* antichrétien

anticipate [æn'tɪsɪˌpeɪt] **1** *vt* (**a**) *(think likely)* [illegible] **they anticipate meeting some opposition, they anticipate that they will meet some opposition** ils s'attendent à rencontrer une certaine opposition; **we had anticipated a price increase** nous nous attendions à *ou* nous avions prévu une hausse des prix; **I didn't anticipate leaving so early** je ne m'attendais pas à ce qu'on parte si tôt; **we don't anticipate any objections** nous n'envisageons pas d'objections; **we do not anticipate any delays** aucun retard n'est prévu; **do you anticipate visiting her?** pensez-vous lui rendre visite?; **faster than anticipated** plus vite que prévu; **as anticipated** comme prévu

(**b**) *(be prepared for → attack, decision, event)* anticiper, anticiper sur; *(→ needs, wishes)* devancer, prévenir, aller au devant de; **we anticipated our competitors by launching our product first** nous avons devancé la concurrence en lançant notre produit les premiers; **he anticipated the fall in price and sold early** il a

anticipé la baisse des prix et a vendu avant
(**c**) *(prefigure)* **her writing anticipated later developments in English fiction** son style annonçait *ou* préfigurait les développements futurs de la fiction anglaise
(**d**) *(act on prematurely → effect, success)* escompter; *Fin (→ profit, salary)* anticiper sur; *(→ happiness)* anticiper, savourer d'avance; *(→ pain)* anticiper, éprouver d'avance
(**e**) *Fin (pay in advance → bill)* anticiper
(**f**) *(mention prematurely)* anticiper, anticiper sur; **don't anticipate the end of the story** n'anticipez pas la fin de l'histoire
2 *vi* anticiper; **just wait and see, don't anticipate** attends de voir, n'anticipe pas; **do you think you'll get married? – I think you're anticipating a bit** penses-tu que tu vas te marier? – je crois que tu vas un peu vite
►► *Fin* ***anticipated profit*** profit *m* espéré

anticipation [æn,tɪsɪ'peɪʃən] *n* (**a**) *(expectation)* attente *f*; **I was all kitted out in waterproofs in anticipation of rain** pensant qu'il allait pleuvoir, je m'étais équipée d'un tas d'imperméables; **they raised their prices in anticipation of increased inflation** ils ont augmenté leurs prix en prévision d'une hausse de l'inflation
(**b**) *Formal (readiness)* anticipation *f*; **in anticipation of your wishes, I've had the fire made up** pour aller au devant de *ou* pour devancer vos désirs, j'ai demandé qu'on fasse du feu; **thanking you in anticipation** *(in letter)* en vous remerciant d'avance, avec mes remerciements anticipés
(**c**) *(eagerness)* impatience *f*, empressement *m*; **fans jostled at the gates in eager anticipation** les fans, ne tenant plus d'impatience, se bousculaient aux grilles d'entrée
(**d**) *(premature experiencing → of inheritance, profits, success)* anticipation *f*, attente *f*; *(→ of fear, pain)* appréhension *f*

anticipatory [æn,tɪsɪ'peɪtərɪ] *adj* d'anticipation
►► *Com* ***anticipatory pricing*** fixation *f* des prix par anticipation

anticlerical [,æntɪ'klerɪkəl] *Pol & Rel* **1** *n* anticlérical(e) *m,f*
2 *adj* anticlérical

anticlericalism [,æntɪ'klerɪkəlɪsəm] *n Pol & Rel* anticléricalisme *m*

anticlimactic [,æntɪklaɪ'mæktɪk] *adj* décevant; **the death of the hero is rather anticlimactic** la mort du héros était attendue

anticlimax [,æntɪ'klaɪmæks] *n* (**a**) *(disappointment)* déception *f*; **the opening ceremony was a bit of an anticlimax** la cérémonie d'ouverture a été quelque peu décevante; **after all the waiting the news almost felt like an anticlimax** après toute cette attente la nouvelle n'a pas produit tout l'effet escompté; **what an anticlimax!** quelle douche froide! (**b**) *Literature* chute *f* dans le trivial

anticlinal [,æntɪ'klaɪnəl] *adj Geol* anticlinal
►► ***anticlinal fold*** pli *m* anticlinal

anticline ['æntɪklaɪn] *n Geol* anticlinal *m*

anticlockwise [,æntɪ'klɒkwaɪz] *Br* **1** *adv* dans le sens inverse *ou* contraire des aiguilles d'une montre
2 *adj* **turn it in an anticlockwise direction** tournez-le dans le sens inverse des aiguilles d'une montre

anticoagulant [,æntɪkəʊ'ægjʊlənt] *Pharm* **1** *n* anticoagulant *m*
2 *adj* anticoagulant

anticodon [,æntɪ'kəʊdɒn] *n Biol & Chem* anticodon *m*

anticolonialism [,æntɪkə'ləʊnɪəlɪzəm] *n Pol* anticolonialisme *m*

anticolonialist [,æntɪkə'ləʊnɪəlɪst] *n* anticolonialiste *mf*

anticonstitutional [,æntɪ,kɒnstɪ'tju:ʃənəl] *adj Pol* anticonstitutionnel

anticonvulsant [,æntɪkən'vʌlsənt] *Pharm* **1** *n* antispasmodique *m*
2 *adj* antispasmodique

Anti-Corn Law League *n Br Hist* **the Anti-Corn Law League** = association fondée en 1838 hostile à la pratique des tarifs protectionnistes frappant les blés importés

anti-corrosion *adj*
►► ***anti-corrosion guarantee*** garantie *f* anticorrosion; *Tech* ***anti-corrosion primer*** apprêt *m* anti-corrosion

anti-corrosive *Chem* **1** *n* anticorrosif *m*
2 *adj* anticorrosif

antics ['æntɪks] *npl (absurd behaviour)* cabrioles *fpl*, gambades *fpl*; *(jokes)* bouffonnerie *f*, pitrerie *f*; **I'm fed up with her silly antics** j'en ai assez de son cirque ridicule; **he's up to his (old) antics again** le voilà qui fait de nouveau des siennes

anticyclone [,æntɪ'saɪkləʊn] *n Met* anticyclone *m*

anti-dazzle *adj Br Aut* **anti-dazzle headlights** phares *mpl* antiéblouissants

antidemocratic [,æntɪ,deməʊ'krætɪk] *adj* antidémocratique

antidepressant [,æntɪdə'presənt] **1** *n* antidépresseur *m*
2 *adj* antidépresseur

anti-dieselling valve [-'di:zəlɪŋ-] *n Aut* thermovalve *f*

anti-dive geometry *n Aut* géométrie *f* anti-plongée

antidote ['æntɪdəʊt] *n (gen) & Pharm* antidote *m*; **work is an antidote to** *or* **for unhappiness** le travail est un antidote à *ou* contre la tristesse

anti-dumping *adj (laws, legislation)* antidumping *inv*

anti-dust mite *adj (spray, product)* antiacarien

anti-Establishment *adj Pol* anticonformiste

antifascism [,æntɪ'fæʃɪzəm] *n Pol* antifascisme *m*

antifascist [,æntɪ'fæʃɪst] *Pol* **1** *n* antifasciste *mf*
2 *adj* antifasciste

antifebrile [,æntɪ'fi:braɪl] *Pharm* **1** *n* antipyrétique *m*, fébrifuge *m*
2 *adj* antipyrétique, fébrifuge

antifeminism [,æntɪ'femɪnɪzəm] *n* antiféminisme *m*

antifeminist [,æntɪ'femɪnɪst] *n* antiféministe *mf*

antifreeze ['æntɪfri:z] *n* antigel *m*

antifriction [,æntɪ'frɪkʃən] **1** *n* antifriction *f*
2 *adj* antifriction *(inv)*

antifungal [,æntɪ'fʌŋgəl] *adj* antifongique

anti-G *adj Phys* anti-g *(inv)*

antigen ['æntɪdʒən] *n Biol* antigène *m*

antigenic [,æntɪ'dʒenɪk] *adj* antigènique

antiglare ['æntɪgleə(r)] *adj*
►► *Comput* ***antiglare filter*** écran *m* antireflets; *Aut* ***antiglare headlights*** phares *mpl* antiéblouissants; ***antiglare mirror*** rétroviseur *m* jour/nuit; *Comput* ***antiglare screen*** écran *m* antireflets

Antigone [æn'tɪgənɪ] *pr n Myth* Antigone

Antigua [æn'ti:gə] *n* Antigua; **in Antigua** à Antigua; **Antigua and Barbuda** Antigua et Barbuda

Antiguan [æn'ti:gən] **1** *n* = habitant d'Antigua
2 *adj* d'Antigua

antihero ['æntɪ,hɪərəʊ] (*pl* **antiheroes**) *n Literature* antihéros *m*

antiheroine ['æntɪ,herəʊɪn] *n Literature* antihéroïne *f*

antihistamine [,æntɪ'hɪstəmɪn] *n Pharm* antihistaminique *m*
►► ***antihistamine tablet*** médicament *m* antihistaminique

anti-icer [-'aɪsə(r)] *n* antigivreur *m*

anti-icing **1** *n Aut* antigel *m*; *Aviat* antigivrant *m*
2 *adj* antigivre *(inv)*

anti-imperialism *n Pol* anti-impérialisme *m*

anti-imperialist *Pol* **1** *n* anti-impérialiste *mf*
2 *adj* anti-impérialiste

anti-inflammatory *Pharm* **1** *n* anti-inflammatoire *m*
2 *adj* anti-inflammatoire

anti-inflationary *adj Econ* anti-inflationniste

anti-Jewish *adj* antijuif, anti-sémitique

antiking [,æntɪ'kɪŋ] *n Hist* antiroi *m*

antiknock [,æntɪ'nɒk] *n Aut* antidétonant *m*

Antilles [æn'tɪli:z] *npl* Antilles *fpl*; **in the Antilles** aux Antilles; **the Greater/Lesser Antilles** les Grandes/Petites Antilles *fpl*

anti-lock *adj*
►► *Aut* ***anti-lock brakes*** anti-blocage *m* des freins; ***anti-lock braking system*** système *m* anti-blocage des freins

antilog ['æntɪlɒg], **antilogarithm** [,æntɪ'lɒgərɪðəm] *n Math* antilogarithme *m*

antilogy [æn'tɪlədʒɪ] *n* antilogie *f*

antimacassar [,æntɪmə'kæsə(r)] *n* têtière *f*

antimagnetic [,æntɪmæg'netɪk] *adj Phys* antimagnétique

antimalarial [,æntɪmə'leərɪəl] *Pharm* **1** *n* antipaludique *m*, antipaludéen *m*
2 *adj* antipaludique, antipaludéen

antimatter ['æntɪ,mætə(r)] *n Phys* antimatière *f*

antimilitarism [,æntɪ'mɪlɪtərɪzəm] *n Pol* antimilitarisme *m*

antimissile [,æntɪ'mɪsaɪl] *Mil* **1** *n* missile *m* antimissile
2 *adj* antimissile *(inv)*

antimitotic [,æntɪmɪ'təʊtɪk] *Biol & Med* **1** *n* antimitotique *m*
2 *adj* antimitotique

antimonarchism [,æntɪ'mɒnəkɪzəm] *n* antimonarchisme *m*

antimonarchist [,æntɪ'mɒnəkɪst] **1** *n* antimonarchiste *mf*
2 *adj* antimonarchiste

antimoniate [,æntɪ'məʊnɪeɪt] *n Chem* antimoniate *m*

antimony ['æntɪmənɪ] *n Chem* antimoine *m*

antineutrino [,æntɪnju:'tri:nəʊ] *n Phys* antineutrino *m*

antineutron [,æntɪ,nju:trɒn] *n Phys* antineutron *m*

anti-novel *n* antiroman *m*

antinuclear [,æntɪ'nju:klɪə(r)] *adj* antinucléaire

Antioch ['æntɪ,ɒk] *pr n Bible* Antioche

antioxidant [,æntɪ'ɒksɪdənt] *n Biol & Chem* antioxydant *m*

antiparallel [,æntɪ'pærələl] *adj Biol & Chem* antiparallèle

antiparliamentary [,æntɪpɑ:lə'mentərɪ] *adj* antiparlementaire

antiparticle ['æntɪ,pɑ:tɪkəl] *n Phys* antiparticule *f*

antipasto [,æntɪ'pæstəʊ] (*pl* **antipasti** [-stɪ]) *n Culin* hors-d'œuvres *mpl (dans un repas italien)*

antipathetic [,æntɪpə'θetɪk] *adj* antipathique; **he remains antipathetic to the cause** il reste hostile à la cause

antipathy [æn'tɪpəθɪ] (*pl* **antipathies**) *n* antipathie *f*; **to feel antipathy towards sb/sth** avoir *ou* éprouver de l'antipathie pour qn/qch

antipatriotic [,æntɪpætrɪ'ɒtɪk] *adj* antipatriotique

antipatriotism [,æntɪ'pætrɪətɪzəm] *n* antipatriotisme *m*

antiperistalsis [,æntɪperɪs'tælsɪs] *n Med* contraction *f* antipéristaltique

antiperistaltic [,æntɪperɪs'tæltɪk] *adj Med* antipéristaltique

antipersonnel [,æntɪ,pɜ:sə'nel] *adj Euph* antipersonnel *(inv)*

antiperspirant [,æntɪ'pɜ:spərənt] **1** *n* antiperspirant *m*
2 *adj* antiperspirant
►► ***antiperspirant deodorant*** déodorant *m* antiperspirant

antiphon ['æntɪfən] *n Mus & Rel* antienne *f*

antiphonal [æn'tɪfənəl] *Mus & Rel* **1** *n* antiphonaire *m*, antiphonal *m*
2 *adj* (en forme) d'antienne

anitiphonary [æn'tɪfənərɪ] *n* antiphonaire *m*, antiphonal *m*

antiphony [æn'tɪfənɪ] (*pl* **antiphonies**) *n Mus* chant *m* en contre-chant

antiphrasis [æn'tɪfrəsɪs] (*pl* **antiphrases** [-si:z]) *n Ling* antiphrase *f*

anti-pinch sensor *n Aut (for windows)* détecteur *m ou* capteur *m* anti-pincement

antipodal [æn'tɪpədəl] *adj Geog* des antipodes

antipodean [æn,tɪpə'dɪən] *adj* (**a**) *Geog* des antipodes (**b**) *Br (from Australia and/or New Zealand)* = d'Australie et/ou de Nouvelle-Zélande; *Hum* **our antipodean cousins** nos cousins d'Australie/de Nouvelle-Zélande; **the kangaroo and other antipodean animals** le kangourou et les autres animaux australiens

antipodes [æn'tɪpədi:z] **1** *npl* antipodes *mpl*
2 Antipodes *npl* **the Antipodes** l'Australie *f* et la Nouvelle Zélande

anti-pollution *adj* anti-pollution

antipope ['æntɪpəʊp] *n Hist & Rel* antipape *m*

antiprohibitionism [,æntɪprəʊhɪ'bɪʃənɪzəm] *n* antiprohibitionnisme *m*

antiprohibitionist [,æntɪprəʊhɪ'bɪʃənɪst] *n* antiprohibitionniste *mf*

antiprotectionist [,æntɪprə'tekʃənɪst] *n Pol* antiprotectionniste *mf*

antiproton ['æntɪˌprəʊtɒn] *n Phys* antiproton *m*
antipsychiatry [ˌæntɪsaɪ'kaɪətrɪ] *n* antipsychiatrie *f*
antipyretic [ˌæntɪpaɪ'retɪk] *Pharm* **1** *n* antipyrétique *m*, fébrifuge *m*
2 *adj* antipyrétique, fébrifuge
antiquarian [ˌæntɪ'kweərɪən] **1** *n (collector)* collectionneur(euse) *m,f* d'antiquités; *(researcher)* archéologue *mf*; *(merchant)* antiquaire *mf*
2 *adj (collection, shop)* d'antiquités; *(bookseller, bookshop)* spécialisé dans les livres anciens
antiquary ['æntɪkwərɪ] (*pl* **antiquaries**) *n (collector)* collectionneur(euse) *m,f* d'antiquités; *(researcher)* archéologue *mf*; *(merchant)* antiquaire *mf*
antiquated ['æntɪkweɪtɪd] *adj* (**a**) *(outmoded → machine, method)* vieillot, obsolète; *(→ building, installation)* vétuste; *(→ idea, manners)* vieillot, suranné; *(→ person)* vieux jeu *(inv)*; **you have such antiquated ideas** tu es tellement vieux jeu (**b**) *(ancient)* très vieux (vieille)
antique [æn'tiːk] **1** *adj* (**a**) *(very old)* ancien; *(dating from Greek or Roman times)* antique; **an antique clock** une pendule ancienne *ou* d'époque (**b**) *Fam (outmoded → machine, method)* vieillot❑, obsolète❑; *(→ building, installation)* vétuste❑
2 *n (piece of furniture)* meuble *m* ancien *ou* d'époque; *(vase)* vase *m* ancien *ou* d'époque; *(work of art)* objet *m* d'art ancien
3 *comp (lover, shop)* d'antiquités
►► ***antique dealer*** antiquaire *mf*
antiquity [æn'tɪkwətɪ] (*pl* **antiquities**) *n* (**a**) *(ancient times)* l'Antiquité *f* (**b**) *(building, ruin)* monument *m* ancien, antiquité *f*; *(coin, statue)* objet *m* ancien; *(work of art)* objet *m* d'art ancien, antiquité *f* (**c**) *(oldness)* ancienneté *f*
anti-rabies *adj* antirabique
antiracial [ˌæntɪ'reɪʃəl] *adj* antiraciste
antiracism [ˌæntɪ'reɪsɪzəm] *n* antiracisme *m*
antiracist [ˌæntɪ'reɪsɪst] *adj* antiraciste
antiraid precautions [ˌæntɪ'reɪd-] *n Fin & St Exch* barrières *fpl* antiraid
anti-religious *adj* antireligieux
anti-republican **1** *n* antirépublicain(e) *m,f*
2 *adj* antirépublicain
antiretroviral [ˌæntɪˌretrəʊ'vaɪrəl] *adj* antirétroviral
antirevolutionary [ˌæntɪrevə'luːʃənərɪ] **1** *n* antirévolutionnaire *mf*
2 *adj* antirévolutionnaire
antiriot [ˌæntɪ'raɪət] *adj* antiémeute
anti-roll bar *n Aut* barre *f* antiroulis
antirrhinum [ˌæntɪ'raɪnəm] *n Bot* muflier *m*, gueule-de-loup *f*
anti-run-on valve *n Aut* thermovalve *f*
antirust [ˌæntɪ'rʌst] *adj* antirouille *(inv)*
anti-Semite *n* antisémite *mf*
anti-Semitic *adj* antisémite
anti-Semitism *n* antisémitisme *m*
antisepsis [ˌæntɪ'sepsɪs] *n* antisepsie *f*
antiseptic [ˌæntɪ'septɪk] **1** *n* antiseptique *m*
2 *adj* antiseptique
antiserum [ˌæntɪ'sɪərəm] *n* antisérum *m*
antiskid [ˌæntɪ'skɪd] *adj Aut* antidérapant
antislavery [ˌæntɪ'sleɪvərɪ] *adj Pol* antiesclavagiste
antislip [ˌæntɪ'slɪp] *adj* antidérapant
antisocial [ˌæntɪ'səʊʃəl] *adj* (**a**) *(behaviour, measure)* antisocial (**b**) *(unsociable)* sauvage; **don't be so antisocial** ne sois pas si sauvage
antispasmodic [ˌæntɪspæz'mɒdɪk] *Pharm* **1** *n* antispasmodique *m*
2 *adj* antispasmodique
antistatic [ˌæntɪ'stætɪk] *adj* antistatique
anti-submarine *adj Mil & Naut* anti-sous-marin
anti-submarining ramp *n Aut* glissière *f* antiplongée
antitank [ˌæntɪ'tæŋk] *adj Mil* antichar
►► ***antitank grenades*** grenades *fpl* antichars
anti-terrorist *adj* antiterroriste
antitheft [ˌæntɪ'θeft] *adj* antivol; **an antitheft device** un antivol, un dispositif contre le vol *ou* antivol
antithesis [æn'tɪθɪsɪs] (*pl* **antitheses** [-siːz]) *n* (**a**) *(exact opposite)* contraire *m*, opposé *m*, antithèse *m*; **he is the antithesis of a forceful young manager** c'est tout le contraire *ou* c'est l'antithèse du jeune cadre dynamique (**b**) *(contrast, opposition)* antithèse *f*, contraste *m*, opposition *f* (**c**) *Literature* antithèse *f*
antithetic [ˌæntɪ'θetɪk], **antithetical** [ˌæntɪ'θetɪkəl] *adj* antithétique
antithetically [ˌæntɪ'θetɪkəlɪ] *adv* par antithèse
antitoxic [ˌæntɪ'tɒksɪk] *adj Med* antitoxique
antitoxin [ˌæntɪ'tɒksɪn] *n Biol & Pharm* antitoxine *f*
antitrust [ˌæntɪ'trʌst] *adj Am Law* antitrust *(inv)*; *Hist* **the Sherman Antitrust Act** la loi antitrust Sherman
►► ***antitrust law*** loi *f* anti-trust

THE SHERMAN ANTITRUST ACT

Loi fédérale de 1890 interdisant la formation de monopoles aux États-Unis et provoquant le démembrement de sociétés telles que la "Standard Oil Company" et l' "American Tobacco Company".

antitrypsin [ˌæntɪ'trɪpsɪn] *n Biol & Chem* antitrypsine *f*
antitussive [ˌæntɪ'tʌsɪv] *Pharm* **1** *n* antitussif *m*
2 *adj* antitussif
antivenin [ˌæntɪ'venɪn] *n* anavenin *m*, traitement *m* antivénéneux
antiviral [ˌæntɪ'vaɪrəl] *adj Pharm* antiviral
antivirus ['æntɪˌvaɪrəs] *n Comput* antivirus *m*
►► ***antivirus check*** vérification *f* antivirale; ***antivirus program*** programme *m* antivirus
antivivisectionist [ˌæntɪˌvɪvɪ'sekʃənɪst] *n* adversaire *mf* de la vivisection
antiworld ['æntɪwɜːld] *n Phys* monde *m* composé d'antimatière
antler ['æntlə(r)] *n* corne *f*; **the antlers** les bois *mpl*, la ramure
antlike ['æntlaɪk] *adj (movement)* de fourmi; *(activity)* fourmillant
antonomasia [ˌæntənəʊ'meɪzɪə] *n Ling* antonomase *f*
Antony ['æntənɪ] *pr n Antiq* **(Mark) Antony** (Marc) Antoine

'Antony and Cleopatra' *Shakespeare* 'Antoine et Cléopâtre'

antonym ['æntənɪm] *n Ling* antonyme *m*
antonymous [æn'tɒnɪməs] *adj Ling* antonymique
antonymy [æn'tɒnɪmɪ] *n Ling* antonymie *f*
antsy ['æntsɪ] *adj Am Fam* agité❑, nerveux❑; **I'm feeling antsy** j'ai la bougeotte
Antwerp ['æntwɜːp] *n* Anvers
anus ['eɪnəs] *n* anus *m*
anvil ['ænvɪl] *n* enclume *f*
anxiety [æŋ'zaɪətɪ] (*pl* **anxieties**) *n* (**a**) *(feeling of worry)* anxiété *f*, appréhension *f*; **rising interest rates have caused anxiety** la hausse des taux d'intérêt a suscité une vive anxiété; **to cause sb great anxiety** donner de grandes inquiétudes *ou* bien des soucis à qn; **there is no cause for anxiety** il n'y a pas de quoi s'inquiéter; **I talked openly about my anxieties** j'ai évoqué franchement mes appréhensions; **a source of deep anxiety** une source d'angoisse profonde; **to be in a state of high anxiety** être rempli d'angoisse
(**b**) *(source of worry)* souci *m*; **her son is a great anxiety to her** son fils lui donne énormément de soucis *ou* l'inquiète énormément
(**c**) *(intense eagerness)* désir *m* ardent; **in his anxiety to please her, he forgot everything else** il tenait tellement à lui faire plaisir qu'il en oubliait tout le reste
(**d**) *Psy* anxiété *f*
►► *Psy* ***anxiety attack*** crise *f* d'angoisse; *Psy* ***anxiety neurosis*** anxiété *f* névrotique
anxious ['æŋkʃəs] *adj* (**a**) *(worried)* inquiet(ète), anxieux; *(stronger)* angoissé; **she's anxious about losing her job** elle a peur de perdre son travail; **an anxious smile** un sourire anxieux *ou* inquiet; **she's anxious for their safety** elle est inquiète *ou* elle craint pour leur sécurité; **I am anxious about his health** sa santé me préoccupe, je m'inquiète de sa santé; **she's a very anxious person** c'est une anxieuse, elle est anxieuse; **anxious friends and relatives waited for news** amis et parents attendaient des nouvelles dans l'angoisse
(**b**) *(worrying)* inquiétant, angoissant; **these are anxious times** nous vivons une sombre époque; **we had one or two anxious moments** nous avons connu quelques moments d'anxiété *ou* d'inquiétude
(**c**) *(eager)* anxieux, impatient; **they're anxious to start** ils sont impatients *ou* pressés de commencer; **he was anxious for them to go** il attendait impatiemment qu'ils partent *ou* leur départ; **he was very anxious that we shouldn't be seen together** il tenait beaucoup à ce que l'on ne nous voie pas ensemble; **he's not exactly anxious to tell her** il n'a pas réellement envie de lui dire; **she's very anxious to please** elle est très désireuse *ou* anxieuse de plaire
(**d**) *Psy* anxieux
anxiously ['æŋkʃəslɪ] *adv* (**a**) *(nervously)* avec inquiétude, anxieusement (**b**) *(eagerly)* impatiemment, avec impatience
anxiousness ['æŋkʃəsnɪs] = **anxiety**

ANY ['enɪ]

du, de la, de l', des	► **1 (a), (b)**
aucun	► **1 (c)**
n'importe quel	► **1 (d)**
tout	► **1 (e)**
ne...plus	► **2 (b)**
n'importe lequel	► **3 (c)**

1 *adj* (**a**) *(some → in questions)* **have you any money?** avez-vous de l'argent?; **did you see any lions?** avez-vous vu des lions?; **do they have any others?** en ont-ils d'autres?; **have any guests arrived?** des invités sont-ils arrivés?; **were you in any danger?** étiez-vous en danger?; *Fam* **any letters for me?** il y a du courrier pour moi?; *Fam* **any news about the application?** il y a du neuf pour la candidature?
(**b**) *(some → in conditional clauses)* **if there's any cake left, can I have some?** s'il reste du gâteau, est-ce que je peux en avoir?; **if you find any children's books, let me know** si jamais vous trouvez des livres pour enfants, dites-le moi; **if you have any free time, call me** si vous avez un moment, appelez-moi; *Fam* **any nonsense from you and you'll be out!** tu n'as qu'à bien te tenir, sinon, c'est la porte!
(**c**) *(in negative phrases)* **he hasn't any change/money/cigarettes** il n'a pas de monnaie/d'argent/de cigarettes; **you haven't any reason to complain** vous n'avez aucune raison de vous plaindre; **he can't stand any noise** il ne supporte pas le moindre bruit, il ne supporte aucun bruit; **it's impossible to say with any degree of certainty** on ne peut l'affirmer avec aucune certitude; **without any warning/fuss** sans le moindre avertissement/problème; **she's forbidden to do any work** tout travail lui est interdit; **hardly** *or* **barely** *or* **scarcely any** très peu de
(**d**) *(no matter which)* n'importe quel (quelle); **ask any woman** demandez à n'importe quelle femme; **any man, woman or child** qui que ce soit, homme, femme, ou enfant; **choose any colour you like** choisissez la couleur que vous voulez, choisissez n'importe quelle couleur; **at any time of day** à n'importe quel moment ou à tout moment de la journée; **I expect him any moment now** je l'attends d'un instant à l'autre; **any one of these paintings is worth a fortune** chacun de ces tableaux vaut une fortune; **answer any two of the questions in section C** répondez à deux des questions de la section C; **any (old) cup will do** n'importe quelle tasse fera l'affaire; **she's not just any (old) pianist!** ce n'est pas n'importe quelle pianiste!
(**e**) *(all, every)* tout; **give me any money you've got** donne-moi tout l'argent que tu as; **I'll accept any help I can get** j'accepterai toute l'aide qui me sera offerte; **any latecomers should report to the office** tous les retardataires doivent se présenter au bureau; **any public-spirited citizen would have done the same** tout citoyen ayant le souci du bien public aurait fait la même chose
(**f**) *(unlimited)* **there are any number of ways of winning** il y a mille façons de gagner; **she has**

any amount *or* **number of friends to help her** elle a (une) quantité d'amis qui peuvent l'aider

2 *adv* (**a**) *(with comparative → in questions, conditional statements)* **can you walk any faster?** peux-tu marcher un peu plus vite?; **can't you walk any faster than that?** tu ne peux pas marcher plus vite que ça?; **is she any better today?** va-t-elle un peu mieux aujourd'hui?; **if she isn't any better by tomorrow, call the doctor** si elle ne va pas mieux demain, appelez le médecin; **if the wind gets any stronger, we shan't be able to set sail** si le vent se renforce, nous ne pourrons pas partir

(**b**) *(with comparative → in negative statements)* **he won't be any (the) happier** il n'en sera pas plus heureux; **we can't go any further** nous ne pouvons aller plus loin; **I don't see him any longer** *or* **more** je ne le vois plus; **I didn't do it any more than you did** je ne l'ai pas fait plus que vous; **I don't like her any more than you do** je ne l'aime pas plus que tu ne l'aimes; **it's not getting any easier to find good staff** c'est toujours aussi difficile de trouver de bons employés; **I can't get this floor any cleaner** je n'arrive pas à nettoyer le sol mieux que ça; **I can't put it any more plainly than that, can I?** je ne pourrais pas le dire plus simplement que ça, si?

(**c**) *Fam (at all)* **you're not helping me any** tu ne m'aides pas du tout□; **has the situation improved any?** la situation s'est-elle arrangée un tant soit peu?□; **she wasn't any too pleased with the press coverage she got** elle n'était pas ravie de la publicité que lui ont faite les médias□; **any old how** n'importe comment□

3 *pron* (**a**) *(some, someone → in questions, conditional statements)* **did you see any?** en avez-vous vu?; **did any of them go?** est-ce que certains d'entre eux y sont allés?; **if any of you want to help, please phone** s'il y en a parmi vous qui veulent apporter leur aide, ils n'ont qu'à téléphoner; **if any of you wants them, do take them** si quelqu'un parmi vous *ou* si l'un d'entre vous les veut, il n'a qu'à les prendre; **few, if any, of his supporters remained loyal** aucun ou presque aucun de ses supporters ne lui est resté fidèle

(**b**) *(even one → in negative statements)* **he couldn't see any of them** il ne voyait aucun d'entre eux; **he won't vote for any of the candidates** il ne votera pour aucun des candidats; **there was hardly any of it left** il n'en restait que très peu; **she's learned two foreign languages, I haven't learned any** elle a étudié deux langues étrangères, je n'en ai étudié aucune; **I have absolutely no money and don't expect to get any** je n'ai pas un sou et je ne m'attends pas à en avoir; **if you don't eat supper now, you'll go to bed without any** si tu ne manges pas immédiatement, tu iras au lit sans dîner; *Fam* **he's not having any (of it)** il ne marche pas

(**c**) *(no matter which one)* n'importe lequel (laquelle); **which chocolate shall I have? – take any, they're all the same** quel chocolat est-ce que je vais prendre? – prends n'importe lequel, ils sont tous pareils; **which dress should I wear? – any but that one** quelle robe est-ce que je mets? – n'importe laquelle sauf celle-là; **study any of her works and you will discover...** étudie n'importe laquelle de ses œuvres et tu découvriras...

(**d**) *(every one, all)* tout; **any of the suspects would fit that description** cette description s'applique à tous les suspects; **this applies to any of you who are married** ceci s'applique à tous ceux d'entre vous qui sont mariés

►► *Br Rad* ***Any Questions*** = débat radiophonique entre le public et diverses personnalités médiatiques autour de sujets d'actualité

'Any Old Iron' *Burgess* 'Ferraille à vendre'

ANYBODY ['enɪˌbɒdɪ]

quelqu'un	► (a)
personne	► (b)
n'importe qui	► (c)

pron (**a**) *(someone → in questions, conditional statements)* quelqu'un; **has anybody lost their glasses?** est-ce que quelqu'un a perdu ses lunettes?; **if anybody asks, say I've gone abroad** si quelqu'un pose la question, dis que je suis à l'étranger; **(is) anybody home?** il y a quelqu'un?; **is anybody there?** *(in seance)* esprit, es-tu là?; *Fam* **anybody for more tea?** quelqu'un reveut du thé?□; **she'll persuade them, if anybody can** si quelqu'un peut les convaincre, c'est bien elle

(**b**) *(someone → in negative statements)* personne; **she's not accusing anybody** elle n'accuse personne; **there was hardly anybody there** il n'y avait presque personne; **she left without speaking to anybody** elle est partie sans parler à personne

(**c**) *(no matter who, everyone)* **anybody who wants can join us** tous ceux qui veulent peuvent se joindre à nous; **invite anybody you want** invitez qui vous voulez; **it could happen to anybody** ça pourrait arriver à tout le monde *ou* n'importe qui; **I don't care what anybody thinks** je me fiche de ce que pensent les gens; **she's cleverer than anybody I know** c'est la personne la plus intelligente que je connaisse; **anybody who saw the accident should come forward** ceux qui ont été témoins de l'accident sont priés de se faire connaître; **anybody with any sense** *or* **in their right mind would have...** toute personne un peu sensée aurait...; **please, anybody but him!** je t'en prie, pas lui!; **anybody but him would have...** n'importe qui d'autre que lui *ou* tout autre que lui aurait...; **anybody will do** n'importe qui *ou* le premier venu fera l'affaire; **anybody would think you'd just lost your best friend** on croirait que tu viens de perdre ton meilleur ami; **he's not just anybody, he's my brother!** ce n'est pas n'importe qui, c'est mon frère!; **it's anybody's guess!** qui sait?; *Hum* **a couple of gin and tonics and you're anybody's** deux ou trois gin-tonics et on fait tout ce qu'on veut de toi

(**d**) *(important person)* quelqu'un d'important *ou* de connu; **anybody who's anybody will be there** tout le gratin sera là; **if you want to be anybody, you've got to work** si tu veux devenir quelqu'un tu dois travailler

---

anyhow ['enɪhaʊ] **1** *adv* (**a**) = **anyway**

(**b**) *(in any manner, by any means)* **you can do it anyhow, but just get it done!** tu peux le faire n'importe comment, mais fais-le!; **I had to persuade her somehow, anyhow** il fallait que je trouve un moyen de la convaincre, n'importe lequel

(**c**) *Fam (haphazardly)* n'importe comment□; **she threw her things down just anyhow** elle a jeté ses affaires en désordre par terre *ou* par terre n'importe comment

2 *adj Fam* **he left the room all anyhow** il a laissé la pièce sens dessus dessous

any more, *Am* **anymore** [ˌenɪ'mɔː(r)] *adv* **they don't live here any more** ils n'habitent plus ici; **I won't do it any more** je ne le ferai plus (jamais)

anyone ['enɪwʌn] = **anybody**

anyplace ['enɪpleɪs] *Am* = **anywhere**

anyroad ['enɪrəʊd] *adv NEng* = **anyway**

ANYTHING ['enɪθɪŋ]

quelque chose	► 1 (a), (b)
quoi que ce soit	► 1 (b)
rien	► 1 (c)
n'importe quoi	► 1 (d)
tout	► 1 (e)

1 *pron* (**a**) *(something → in questions)* quelque chose; **did you hear anything?** avez-vous entendu quelque chose?; **is there anything to eat?** est-ce qu'il y a quelque chose à manger?; **can we do anything?** est-ce qu'on peut faire quelque chose?; **can't we do anything?** est-ce qu'il n'y a rien à faire?; **are you doing anything this weekend?** avez-vous quelque chose de prévu pour ce week-end?; **have you anything to write with?** avez-vous de quoi écrire?; **is there anything in** *or* **to what she says?** est-ce qu'il y a du vrai dans ce qu'elle dit?; **can we get anything out of it?** peut-on en tirer quelque chose?; **have you heard anything from them?** avez-vous eu de leurs nouvelles?; **did you notice anything unusual?** avez-vous remarqué quelque chose de bizarre?; **will there be anything else, madam?** *(in shop)* désirez-vous autre chose, madame?, et avec cela, madame?; **is there anything more annoying than just missing a train?** y a-t-il quelque chose *ou* rien de plus agaçant que de rater un train?; *Fam* **anything good on TV tonight?** est-ce qu'il y a quelque chose de bien à la télé ce soir?; *Fam* **anything the matter?** quelque chose ne va pas?; **have you anything smaller?** *(in different size)* est-ce que vous avez la taille en-dessous?; *(money)* vous n'avez pas plus petit?

(**b**) *(in conditional statements)* **if anything should happen, take care of John for me** s'il m'arrivait quelque chose *ou* quoi que ce soit, occupez-vous de John; **if you should learn anything, let me know** si jamais vous apprenez quelque chose *ou* quoi que ce soit, dites-le moi

(**c**) *(in negative statements)* rien; **I didn't say anything** je n'ai rien dit; **you can't believe anything he says** on ne peut rien croire de ce qu'il dit; **don't do anything stupid!** ne fais pas de bêtise!; **I don't know anything about computers** je ne m'y connais pas du tout *ou* je n'y connais rien en informatique; **I didn't know anything about their divorce** je ne savais pas qu'ils avaient divorcé; **there's hardly anything left** il ne reste presque rien; **she hasn't written anything very much since last year** elle n'a pas écrit grand-chose depuis l'année dernière; **without saying anything** sans rien dire; **she's not angry or anything** elle n'est pas fâchée ni rien; **do you want a book or anything?** voulez-vous un livre ou autre chose?; **if she feels sick or anything, call the doctor** si elle se sent mal *ou* si ça ne va pas, appelez le médecin

(**d**) *(no matter what)* n'importe quoi; **just tell him anything** racontez-lui n'importe quoi; **anything you like** tout ce que vous voudrez; **anything will do** n'importe quoi fera l'affaire; **I'd give anything to know the truth** je donnerais n'importe quoi pour savoir la vérité; **he won't read just anything** il ne lit pas n'importe quoi; **anything goes!** tout est permis!

(**e**) *(all, everything)* tout; **her son eats anything** son fils mange de tout; **I like anything with chocolate in it** j'aime tout ce qui est au chocolat; **anything above 75/below 25 is a very good score** tout ce qui est au-dessus de 75/au-dessous de 25 est un très bon score; **she must earn anything between £30,000 and £40,000** elle doit gagner dans les 30 000 à 40 000 livres; **you can use it to flavour anything from jam to soup** vous pouvez l'utiliser pour parfumer n'importe quoi, de la confiture à la soupe

(**f**) *(in intensifying phrases)* **he isn't anything like his father** il ne ressemble pas du tout *ou* en rien à son père; **it doesn't taste anything like a tomato** ça n'a pas du tout le goût de tomate; **it isn't anything like as good as his last film** c'est loin d'être aussi bon que son dernier film; **they aren't producing the goods anything like fast enough** ils ne produisent pas la marchandise assez vite, loin de là; **I wouldn't miss it for anything** je ne le manquerais pour rien au monde; **it's as easy as anything** c'est facile comme tout; **to run like anything** courir comme un dératé; **he worked like anything** il a travaillé comme un fou; **they shouted like anything** ils ont crié comme des forcenés; **it rained like anything** il pleuvait des cordes

2 anything but *adv* tout sauf; **that music is anything but relaxing** cette musique est tout sauf reposante; **is he crazy? – anything but!** est-ce qu'il est fou? – bien au contraire! *ou* il est tout sauf ça!

---

anyway ['enɪweɪ], *Am* **anyways** ['enɪweɪz] *adv* (**a**) *(in any case → reinforcing)* de toute façon; **it's too late now anyway** de toute façon, il est trop tard maintenant; **what's to stop them anyway?** de toute façon, qu'est-ce qui peut les en empêcher?

(**b**) *(summarizing, concluding)* en tout cas; **anyway, that's what I think** en tout cas, c'est mon avis *ou* ce que je pense; **anyway, in the end**

she left toujours est-il qu'elle *ou* en tout cas, elle a fini par partir; **anyway, I have to go** *(I'll be late)* bon, il faut que j'y aille; *(I don't have any choice)* enfin, il faut que j'y aille

(**c**) *(nevertheless, notwithstanding)* quand même; **thanks anyway** merci quand même; **we can invite them anyway** on peut toujours *ou* quand même les inviter; **I don't care what you say, I'm going anyway** tu peux dire ce que tu veux, j'y vais quand même

(**d**) *(qualifying)* en tout cas; **that's what we all think, well, most of us anyway** c'est ce qu'on pense tous, ou presque tous en tout cas; **and that's the situation, to the best of my knowledge anyway** et voilà où on en est, autant que je sache en tout cas

(**e**) *(returning to topic)* bref; **anyway, as I was saying...** bref, comme je disais...; **anyway, let's get back to what we were saying** enfin *ou* bon, revenons à ce que nous disions

ANYWHERE ['enɪweə(r)]

quelque part	▸ **1 (a)**
n'importe où	▸ **1 (b)**
partout	▸ **1 (c)**
nulle part	▸ **1 (d)**
de... à	▸ **1 (e)**

1 *adv* (**a**) *(in questions)* quelque part; **have you seen my keys anywhere?** avez-vous vu mes clés (quelque part)?; **are you going anywhere at Easter?** vous partez à Pâques?; **are you going anywhere this evening?** est-ce que vous sortez ce soir?; **have you found anywhere to live?** avez-vous trouvé à vous loger?

(**b**) *(in positive statements → no matter where)* n'importe où; **just put it down anywhere** posez-le n'importe où; **sit anywhere you like** asseyez-vous où vous voulez; **the book could be anywhere** le livre pourrait être n'importe où; **anywhere you go it's the same story** où que vous alliez, c'est toujours pareil *ou* toujours la même chose; **I'd know her anywhere** je la reconnaîtrais entre mille

(**c**) *(everywhere)* partout; **you can find that magazine anywhere** on trouve cette revue partout

(**d**) *(in negative statements → any place)* nulle part; **I haven't been anywhere today** je ne suis allé nulle part ailleurs aujourd'hui; **I can't find my keys anywhere** je ne trouve mes clés nulle part; **we didn't go anywhere** nous ne sommes allés nulle part; **we're not getting anywhere** nous n'arrivons à rien, nous n'avançons pas; **look, this isn't getting us anywhere** écoute, tout ça ne nous mène à rien; **crying won't get you anywhere** pleurer ne te servira à rien

(**e**) *(any number within a range)* **we might receive anywhere between 60 and 600 applications** on peut recevoir entre 60 et 600 demandes; **the rate could be anywhere from 10 to 20 percent** le taux peut aller de 10 à 20 pour cent

(**f**) *(idioms)* **he isn't anywhere near as quick as you are** il est loin d'être aussi rapide que toi; **are they anywhere near completion?** ont-ils bientôt fini?

2 *pron (any place)* **do they need anywhere to stay?** ont-ils besoin d'un endroit où loger?; **she's looking for a flat, but hasn't found anywhere yet** elle cherche un appartement mais elle n'a encore rien trouvé; **they live miles from anywhere** ils habitent en pleine cambrousse

anywheres ['enɪweəz] *Am Fam* = **anywhere**

anywise ['enɪwaɪz] *adv Am (at all)* en aucune façon, aucunement

Anzac ['ænzæk] *n Mil (abbr* **Australia-New Zealand Army Corps**) = soldat néo-zélandais ou australien

▸▸ ***Anzac Day*** = date anniversaire du débarquement des alliés australiens et néo-zélandais à Gallipoli en Turquie, le 25 avril 1915

ANZUS ['ænzəs] *n Mil (abbr* **Australia, New Zealand, United States**) = alliance entre l'Australie, la Nouvelle-Zélande et les États-Unis

aob, AOB [ˌeɪəʊ'biː] *n Admin (abbr* **any other business**) ≃ divers

aocb, AOCB [ˌeɪəʊˌsiː'biː] *n Admin (abbr* **any other competent business**) ≃ affaires diverses

A-OK [ˌeɪəʊ'keɪ] *Am Fam* **1** *adj* excellent ❑; **everything's A-OK** tout baigne; **he's A-OK** c'est un type bien

2 *adv* parfaitement ❑; **to go A-OK** se passer vachement bien

AONB [ˌeɪəʊˌen'biː] *n Br (abbr* **area of outstanding natural beauty**) = zone naturelle protégée

aorist ['eərɪst] *n Ling* aoriste *m*

aorta [eɪ'ɔːtə] *(pl* **aortas** *or* **aortae** [-tiː]) *n Anat* aorte *f*

aortal [eɪ'ɔːtəl] *adj Anat* aortique

aortic [eɪ'ɔːtɪk] *adj Anat* aortique

Aosta [eɪ'ɒstə] *n* Aoste

AP [ˌeɪ'piː] *n* (**a**) *(abbr* **American Plan**) pension *f* complète (**b**) *Press (abbr* **Associated Press**) AP *f*

apace [ə'peɪs] *adv Literary* rapidement, vite; **privatization is proceeding** *or* **continuing apace** les privatisations continuent à un rythme soutenu

Apache [ə'pætʃɪ] *(pl* **inv** *or* **Apaches**) **1** *n* (**a**) *(person)* Apache *mf* (**b**) *(language)* apache *m*

2 *adj* apache

Apalachee [ˌæpə'lætʃɪ] *n* Apalache *mf*

▸▸ ***Apalachee Bay*** la baie d'Apalachie

apart [ə'pɑːt] **1** *adv* (**a**) *(separated → in space)* **a couple of metres apart** à (une distance de) deux ou trois mètres l'un de l'autre; **the houses were about 10 kilometres apart** les maisons étaient à environ 10 kilomètres l'une de l'autre; **the lines must be 10 centimetres apart** les lignes doivent être espacées de 10 centimètres; **plant the seeds fairly far apart** plantez les graines assez loin les unes des autres; **cities as far apart as Johannesburg and Hong Kong** des villes aussi éloignées l'une de l'autre que Johannesburg et Hong Kong; **he stood with his legs wide apart** il se tenait (debout) les jambes bien écartées; **they can't bear to be apart** ils ne supportent pas d'être loin l'un de l'autre *ou* séparés; **the boys and girls were kept apart** on tenait séparés les garçons et les filles; **they're living apart** *(because of circumstances)* ils n'habitent pas ensemble; *(because of divorce, break-up)* ils sont séparés, ils vivent séparément; **children born two years apart** des enfants nés à deux ans d'intervalle; *Fig* **we're miles apart when it comes to politics** nous avons des points de vue politiques très différents

(**b**) *(in pieces)* en pièces, en morceaux; **to break apart** s'émietter; **to take a machine apart** démonter *ou* désassembler une machine

(**c**) *(with verbs of motion)* **to push apart** éloigner (en poussant); **they sprang apart when I entered the room** ils se sont écartés vivement l'un de l'autre quand je suis entré dans la pièce; **to grow apart from sb** s'éloigner de qn

(**d**) *(isolated)* à l'écart; **she stood apart from the others** elle se tenait à l'écart des autres

(**e**) *(aside)* à part; **joking apart** trêve de plaisanterie; **that apart, did you enjoy yourselves?** à part ça, vous vous êtes amusés?

2 *adj (after n) (distinct and special)* à part; **they regard it as a thing apart** ils considèrent que c'est quelque chose de complètement différent

3 apart from *prep* (**a**) *(except for)* à part; **apart from my salary, we have nothing** en dehors de *ou* à part mon salaire, nous n'avons rien; **it's fine, apart from a few minor mistakes** à part *ou* sauf quelques fautes sans importance, c'est très bien; **I don't know anyone apart from you** je ne connais personne à part toi; **but apart from that, everything's fine!** mais à part ça, tout va très bien!

(**b**) *(as well as)* en plus de; **she has many interests apart from golf** elle s'intéresse à beaucoup de choses à part le *ou* en plus du golf; **quite apart from the fact that it's too big, I don't like the colour** outre (le fait) que c'est trop grand, je n'aime pas la couleur

apartheid [ə'pɑːthaɪt] *n* apartheid *m*

▸▸ ***apartheid laws*** lois *fpl* de l'apartheid

apartment [ə'pɑːtmənt] *n* (**a**) *Am (flat)* appartement *m*, logement *m*; **a one-bedroom** *or* **one-bedroomed apartment** un deux-pièces (**b**) *Br (usu pl) (room)* pièce *f*; *(bedroom)* chambre *f*; **state apartments** grands appartements *mpl*, salons *mpl* d'apparat; **the Royal apartments** la résidence royale

▸▸ *Am* ***apartment block, apartment building, apartment house*** immeuble *m (d'habitation)*, *Can* bloc-appartement *m*

apathetic [ˌæpə'θetɪk] *adj* apathique, indifférent

apathetically [ˌæpə'θetɪkəlɪ] *adv* avec apathie *ou* indifférence; **to smile apathetically** sourire mollement *ou* sans grande conviction

apathy ['æpəθɪ] *n* apathie *f*, indifférence *f*; **an air of apathy** un air apathique; **their apathy about the issue** leur indifférence à l'égard de ce problème

APB [ˌeɪpiː'biː] *n Am (abbr* **all points bulletin**) = message radio diffusé par la police concernant une personne recherchée

ape [eɪp] **1** *n* (**a**) *(monkey)* grand singe *m*, *Spec* anthropoïde *m* (**b**) *Pej (person)* brute *f* (**c**) *Fam* **to go ape (about sb/sth)** *(become angry)* piquer une crise (à propos de qn/qch); *(enthuse)* s'emballer (pour qn/qch)

2 *vt* singer

apelike ['eɪplaɪk] *adj (face, appearance, creature)* simiesque; *(noises)* de singe

ape-man *(pl* **ape-men** [-men]) *n* homme-singe *m*

Apennines ['æpɪnaɪnz] *npl* **the Apennines** l'Apennin *m*, les Apennins *mpl*

aperient [ə'pɪərɪənt] *Med & Pharm* **1** *n* laxatif *m*

2 *adj* laxatif

aperiodic [ˌeɪpɪərɪ'ɒdɪk] *adj (gen) & Phys* apériodique

aperitif [əperə'tiːf] *n* apéritif *m*

aperture ['æpəˌtjʊə(r)] *n* (**a**) *(opening)* ouverture *f*, orifice *m*; *(gap)* brèche *f*, trouée *f* (**b**) *Phot* ouverture *f* (du diaphragme)

apeshit ['eɪpʃɪt] *adv very Fam* **to go apeshit (about sb/sth)** *(become angry)* piquer une crise (à propos de qn/qch); *(enthuse)* s'emballer (pour qn/qch)

APEX ['eɪpeks] *n Br (abbr* **advance purchase excursion**) = tarif préférentiel sujet à des restrictions de délai d'achat

apex ['eɪpeks] *(pl* **apexes** *or* **apices** [-ɪsiːz]) *n Geom (of triangle)* sommet *m*, apex *m*; *Fig* point *m* culminant, sommet *m*; *Fig* **to reach the apex of one's career** atteindre le point culminant *ou* le sommet de sa carrière; *Br very Fam Hum* **to fall arse over apex** tomber cul par-dessus tête

aphaeresis, *Am* **apheresis** [ə'fɪərəsɪs] *n Ling* aphérèse *f*

aphagia [ə'feɪdʒɪə] *n Med* aphagie *f*

aphasia [ə'feɪzɪə] *n Med* aphasie *f*

aphasic [ə'feɪzɪk] *Med* **1** *n* aphasique *mf*

2 *adj* aphasique

apheresis *Am* = **aphaerisis**

aphelion [æ'fiːlɪən] *(pl* **aphelia** [-lɪə]) *n Astron* aphélie *m*

aphesis ['æfɪsɪs] *(pl* **apheses** [-siːz]) *n Ling* aphérèse *f*

aphid ['eɪfɪd] *n Entom* puceron *m*

aphidian [eɪ'fɪdɪən] *Entom* **1** *n* aphidien *m*

2 *adj* aphidien

aphis ['eɪfɪs] *(pl* **aphides** [-fɪdiːz]) *n Entom* aphididé *m*

aphonia [eɪ'fəʊnɪə] *n Med* aphonie *f*

aphonic [eɪ'fɒnɪk] *adj Med* aphone

aphorism ['æfərɪzəm] *n Ling* aphorisme *m*

aphoristic [æfə'rɪstɪk] *adj Ling* aphoristique

aphoristically [æfə'rɪstɪkəlɪ] *adv Ling* par aphorisme

aphotic [eɪ'fəʊtɪk] *adj* aphotique

aphrodisiac [ˌæfrə'dɪzɪæk] **1** *n* aphrodisiaque *m*

2 *adj* aphrodisiaque

aphrodisiacal [ˌæfrədɪzɪ'ækəl] *adj* aphrodisiaque

Aphrodite [ˌæfrə'daɪtɪ] *pr n Myth* Aphrodite

aphtha ['æfθə] *n Med* aphte *m*

API [ˌeɪpiː'aɪ] *n Press (abbr* **American Press Institute**) = association de journalistes américains

apiarist ['eɪpɪərɪst] *n Entom* apiculteur(trice) *m,f*

apiary ['eɪpɪərɪ] *(pl* **apiaries**) *n Entom* rucher *m*

apical ['æpɪkəl] *adj Bot & Geom* apical

▸▸ *Ling* ***apical consonant*** apicale *f*

apices ['eɪpɪsiːz] *pl of* **apex**

apico-alveolar [ˌeɪpɪkəʊ-] *Ling* **1** *n* apico-alvéolaire *f*

2 *adj* apico-alvéolaire

apico-dental *Ling* **1** *n* apico-dentale *f*

2 *adj* apico-dental

apiculture ['eɪpɪˌkʌltʃə(r)] *n* apiculture *f*

apiculturist [ˌeɪpɪˈkʌltʃərɪst] *n* apiculteur(trice) *m,f*

apiece [əˈpiːs] *adv* (**a**) *(for each item)* chacun(e), (la) pièce; **the plants are £3 apiece** les plantes coûtent 3 livres (la) pièce *ou* chacune (**b**) *(for each person)* chacun(e), par personne; **we had two shirts apiece** nous avions deux chemises chacun

apish [ˈeɪpɪʃ] *adj* (**a**) *(ape-like)* simiesque (**b**) *(affected, foppish)* affecté, poseur

aplasia [eɪˈpleɪzɪə] *n Med* aplasie *f*

aplastic [eɪˈplæstɪk] *adj Med* aplasique, aplastique

►► ***aplastic anaemia*** anémie *f* aplastique

aplenty [əˈplentɪ] *adv* en abondance; **she's always had money aplenty** elle a toujours eu beaucoup *ou* énormément d'argent

aplomb [əˈplɒm] *n* assurance *f*, aplomb *m*; **with great aplomb** avec un aplomb formidable

apnoea, *Am* **apnea** [æpˈnɪə] *n Med* apnée *f*

APO [ˌeɪpiːˈəʊ] *n Mil (abbr* **Army Post Office**) = service postal de l'armée

apocalypse [əˈpɒkəlɪps] *n* apocalypse *f*

2 Apocalypse *n Bible* Apocalypse *f*; **the four horsemen of the Apocalypse** les quatre cavaliers *mpl* de l'Apocalypse

apocalyptic [əˌpɒkəˈlɪptɪk] *adj* apocalyptique

►► *Bible* ***the apocalyptic number*** le nombre de la bête

apocalyptically [əˌpɒkəˈlɪptɪkəlɪ] *adv* d'une manière apocalyptique

apocopate *Ling* **1** *vt* [əˈpɒkəʊpeɪt] abréger par apocope

2 *adj* [əˈpɒkəʊpɪt] apocopé

apocope [əˈpɒkəʊpɪ] *n Ling* apocope *f*

apocrine [ˈæpəkraɪn] *adj Physiol* apocrine *f*

►► *Anat* ***apocrine glands*** glandes *fpl* apocrines

Apocrypha [əˈpɒkrɪfə] *npl Bible* **the Apocrypha** les apocryphes *mpl*

apocryphal [əˈpɒkrɪfəl] *adj* apocryphe; **the story's apocryphal** je doute que l'histoire soit vraie

apodal [ˈæpədəl] *adj Zool* apode

apodosis [əˈpɒdəsɪs] *(pl* **apodoses** [-siːz]) *n Gram* apodose *f*

apodous [ˈæpədəs] *adj Entom* apode

apogee [ˈæpədʒiː] *n Astron & Fig* apogée *m*; **to reach the apogee of one's career** atteindre le sommet *ou* le point culminant de sa carrière

apolitical [ˌeɪpəˈlɪtɪkəl] *adj* apolitique

Apollo [əˈpɒləʊ] **1** *pr n Myth* Apollon

2 *n Astron (spacecraft)* Apollo *m*

►► *Entom* ***Apollo butterfly*** apollon *m*; *Astron* ***the Apollo program*** le programme Apollo

Apollonian [ˌæpəˈləʊnɪən] *adj* apollinien

Apollonius [ˌæpəˈləʊnɪəs] *pr n Antiq* Apollonios

apologetic [əˌpɒləˈdʒetɪk] *adj* (**a**) *(person)* **she was very apologetic for being late** elle s'est excusée plusieurs fois d'être arrivée en retard; **he was most apologetic** il s'est confondu en excuses (**b**) *(letter, note)* d'excuse; *(look, smile)* contrit, désolé

apologetically [əˌpɒləˈdʒetɪkəlɪ] *adv (say)* en s'excusant, pour s'excuser; *(smile)* d'un air désolé *ou* contrit

apologetics [əˌpɒləˈdʒetɪks] *n (UNCOUNT)* apologétique *f*

apologia [ˌæpəˈləʊdʒɪə] *n* apologie *f*

apologist [əˈpɒlədʒɪst] *n* apologiste *mf*

apologize, -ise [əˈpɒlədʒaɪz] *vi* s'excuser (**for sth** de qch); **to apologize for doing sth** s'excuser d'avoir fait qch; **to apologize to sb for sth** s'excuser de qch auprès de qn, faire *ou* présenter des *ou* ses excuses à qn pour qch; **I was wrong, I apologize** j'ai eu tort, excusez-moi *ou* je m'excuse; **I apologize for having kept you waiting** excusez-moi de vous avoir fait attendre; **we apologize for any inconvenience** veuillez nous excuser pour les désagréments occasionnés; **I had to apologize for you** *or* **your behaviour** j'ai dû demander qu'on excuse ta conduite; **it's him you should be apologizing to** c'est à lui qu'il faut demander pardon, c'est auprès de lui que tu dois t'excuser; **there's no need to apologize** vous n'avez pas à vous excuser; **I can't apologize enough** je ne sais comment m'excuser

apology [əˈpɒlədʒɪ] *(pl* **apologies**) *n* (**a**) *(expression of regret)* excuses *fpl*; **to make/offer an apology** faire/présenter des excuses; **to make/send one's apologies** faire/envoyer ses excuses; **they were full of apologies** ils se sont confondus en excuses; **I owe him an apology** je lui dois des excuses; **will you accept this gift by way of an apology?** accepterez-vous ce cadeau avec mes excuses?; **we demand an apology** nous exigeons des excuses; **please accept my sincere apology** je vous présente mes plus sincères excuses; **the director sends his apologies** le directeur vous prie de l'excuser; **a letter of apology** une lettre d'excuses

(**b**) *(defence)* apologie *f*

(**c**) *Br Pej (poor example)* **he's a mere apology for a man** c'est un nul; **an apology for a dinner** un semblant de dîner

apolune [ˈæpəluːn] *n Astron* apolune *f*

apomorphia [ˌæpəʊˈmɔːfɪə], **apomorphine** [ˌæpəʊˈmɔːfiːn] *n Pharm* apomorphine *f*

apophysis [əˈpɒfɪsɪs] *n Anat* apophyse *f*

apoplectic [ˌæpəˈplektɪk] **1** *adj* apoplectique; **to be apoplectic (with rage)** s'étrangler de rage; **she was apoplectic when I told her** elle a failli avoir une attaque quand je le lui ai dit; **to have an apoplectic fit** avoir *ou* faire une attaque d'apoplexie

2 *n Med* apoplectique *mf*

apoplexy [ˈæpəpleksɪ] *n Med* apoplexie *f*

apoprotein [ˌæpəˈprəʊtiːn] *n Biol* apoprotéine *f*

apoptosis [ˌæpəpˈtəʊsɪs] *n Biol* apoptose *f*

aporetic [ˌæpəˈretɪk] *adj Phil* aporétique

aporia [əˈpɔːrɪə] *n Phil* aporie *f*

aposematic [ˌæpəsəˈmætɪk] *adj Zool* aposématique

aposiopesis [ˌæpəsaɪəʊˈpiːsɪs] *n Ling* apisiopèse *f*

apostasy [əˈpɒstəsɪ] *(pl* **apostasies**) *n Rel* apostasie *f*

apostate [əˈpɒsteɪt] *Rel* **1** *n* apostat(e) *m,f*

2 *adj* apostat

apostatize, -ise [əˈpɒstətaɪz] *vi Rel* apostasier

a posteriori [eɪpɒsˌterɪˈɔːraɪ] **1** *adj* a posteriori

2 *adv* a posteriori

apostle [əˈpɒsəl] *n Rel & Fig* apôtre *m*

►► ***the Apostles' Creed*** le Symbole des Apôtres; ***apostle spoon*** cuiller *f* avec figurine d'apôtre

apostolic [ˌæpəsˈtɒlɪk], **apostolical** [æpəsˈtɒlɪkəl] *adj Rel* apostolique

►► ***apostolic succession*** succession *f* apostolique

apostrophe [əˈpɒstrəfɪ] *n Gram* apostrophe *f*

apostrophize, -ise [əˈpɒstrəfaɪz] *vt Ling* apostropher

apothecary [əˈpɒθəkərɪ] *(pl* **apothecaries**) *n Formal or Arch* pharmacien(enne) *m,f*, *Arch* apothicaire *m*

apothem [ˈæpəθem] *n Math* apothème *m*

apotheosis [əˌpɒθɪˈəʊsɪs] *(pl* **apotheoses** [-siːz]) *n Rel* apothéose *f*

apotheosize, -ise [əˈpɒθɪəʊsaɪz] *vt Rel* apothéoser

apotropaic [æˌpɒtrəʊˈpeɪɪk] *adj Literary* apotropaïque

appal, *Am* **appall** [əˈpɔːl] *(pt & pp* **appalled,** *cont* **appalling**) *vt (scandalize)* choquer, scandaliser; *(horrify)* horrifier; **she was appalled at** *or* **by the very thought** l'idée même l'horrifiait; **I'm appalled!** c'est un scandale!

Appalachia [ˌæpəˈleɪʃə] *n* région *f* des Appalaches *(région pauvre dans le sud américain, connue pour son artisanat et sa musique traditionnelle)*

Appalachian [ˌæpəˈleɪʃən] **1** *n* **the Appalachians** *(mountains)* les (monts *mpl*) Appalaches *mpl*

2 *adj* appalachien

►► ***the Appalachian Mountains*** les monts *mpl* Appalaches

appall *Am* = **appal**

appalled [əˈpɔːld] *adj* écœuré

appalling [əˈpɔːlɪŋ] *adj (behaviour, conditions, smell)* épouvantable

appallingly [əˈpɔːlɪŋlɪ] *adv* (**a**) *(badly)* épouvantablement *ou* effroyablement mal; **he speaks French quite appallingly** son français est épouvantable *ou* effroyable; **he's appallingly badly behaved** il est effroyablement mal élevé; **to treat sb appallingly** se conduire épouvantablement mal envers qn

(**b**) *(as intensifier) (ugly, boring, rude)* effroyablement; **an appallingly bad film** un film effroyablement mauvais; **he's appallingly stupid** il est d'une stupidité effroyable *ou* extraordinaire

appaloosa [æpəˈluːsə] *n Zool* appaloosa *m*

apparatchik [ˌæpəˈrætʃɪk] *n Pol* apparatchik *m*

apparatus [ˌæpəˈreɪtəs] *(pl* **inv** *or* **apparatuses**) *n* (**a**) *(UNCOUNT) (equipment)* équipement *m*; *(set of instruments)* instruments *mpl*; **laboratory apparatus** appareils *mpl* de laboratoire; **a piece of apparatus** un appareil; *Literature* **apparatus criticus, critical apparatus** appareil *m ou* apparat *m* critique

(**b**) *(UNCOUNT) Gym (in gymnasium)* agrès *mpl*; **exercises on the apparatus, apparatus work** exercices *mpl* aux agrès

(**c**) *(machine)* appareil *m*; **heating apparatus** appareil *m* de chauffage

(**d**) *Anat* appareil *m*; **the digestive apparatus** l'appareil digestif

(**e**) *(organization)* **the apparatus of government** la machine administrative, l'administration *f*

apparel [əˈpærəl] *(Br pt & pp* **apparelled,** *cont* **apparelling,** *Am pt & pp* **appareled,** *cont* **appareling**) **1** *n* (**a**) *Literary or Arch (garb)* costume *m*, mise *f* (**b**) *Am (clothes)* habillement *m*, vêtements *mpl*; *(industry)* confection *f*

2 *vt Literary or Arch (dress)* vêtir, habiller; *(adorn)* orner; **he was apparelled in the robes of state** il avait revêtu son costume d'apparat

apparent [əˈpærənt] *adj* (**a**) *(obvious)* évident, apparent; **to make sth apparent** indiquer qch clairement; **the tension between them had become apparent to us all** nous sentions tous désormais la tension qui existait entre eux; **the truth became apparent to her** la vérité lui apparut; **it was apparent to me that...** pour moi il était évident que...; **for no apparent reason** sans raison apparente

(**b**) *(seeming)* apparent, supposé; **with apparent ease** avec une facilité apparente; **I admire the apparent ease with which she does the work** j'admire l'apparente facilité avec laquelle elle exécute le travail

apparently [əˈpærəntlɪ] *adv* (**a**) *(seemingly)* apparemment, en apparence; **she was apparently quite calm and collected** elle paraissait assez calme et sereine (**b**) *(according to rumour)* à ce qu'il paraît; **he apparently quit his job** il paraît qu'il a démissionné; **is she leaving? – apparently not** elle part? – on dirait que non; **that's apparently the reason** il paraît que c'est pour ça; **apparently, they had a huge row** il paraît qu'ils se sont violemment disputés

apparition [ˌæpəˈrɪʃən] *n* apparition *f*

appeal [əˈpiːl] **1** *n* (**a**) *(request)* appel *m*; **she made an appeal on behalf of the victims** elle a lancé un appel au profit des victimes; **we made an appeal for money to help the refugees** nous avons fait un appel de fonds pour aider les réfugiés; **an appeal for help** un appel au secours; *Com & Fin* **an appeal for funds** un appel de fonds

(**b**) *Law* appel *m*, pourvoi *m*; **to enter** *or* **to lodge an appeal** interjeter appel, se pourvoir en appel; **on appeal** en seconde instance; **notice of appeal** infirmation *f*; **right of appeal** droit *m* d'appel; **with no right of appeal** sans appel; **Court of Appeal** cour *f* d'appel

(**c**) *(attraction)* attrait *m*, charme *m*; **to have great appeal** *(thing)* être très attrayant; *(person)* avoir beaucoup de charme; **travelling has lost its appeal for me** je n'aime plus voyager, les voyages ne m'intéressent plus; **the idea does have a certain appeal** l'idée est bien séduisante; **their music has a wide appeal** leur musique plaît à toutes sortes de gens

2 *vi* (**a**) *(make request)* faire un appel; *(publicly)* lancer un appel; *(plead)* supplier, implorer; **she appealed to me to be patient** elle m'a prié d'être patient; **they're appealing for help for the victims** ils lancent un appel au profit des victimes; *Com & Fin* **to appeal for funds** faire un appel de fonds

(**b**) **to appeal to sth** *(invoke)* faire appel à qch; **she appealed to his sense of justice** elle a fait appel à son sens de la justice

(**c**) *(apply)* faire appel; **he appealed to them for help** il leur a demandé du secours; **they**

appealed to the management for better working conditions ils ont fait appel à la direction pour obtenir de meilleures conditions de travail; **he appealed against the decision** il a fait appel contre cette décision

(**d**) *Law* interjeter appel, se pourvoir en appel; **to appeal against a sentence** appeler d'un jugement, faire appel d'un jugement; **to appeal against a decision** réclamer contre une décision; faire opposition à une décision; *Law* faire appel d'une décision

(**e**) *(please)* plaire; **the programmes appeal most to children** ces émissions plaisent particulièrement aux enfants; **the book appeals to the reader's imagination** ce livre parle à l'imagination du lecteur; **the idea appealed to me** l'idée m'a séduit; **it doesn't really appeal to me** ça ne m'attire pas vraiment, ça ne me dit pas grand-chose

►► *Law* ***appeal court*** cour *f* d'appel

appealing [ə'piːlɪŋ] *adj* (**a**) *(attractive → dress)* joli; *(→ idea, plan)* séduisant, attrayant (**b**) *(likeable → person)* sympathique, attachant (**c**) *(moving)* émouvant, attendrissant; *(imploring)* suppliant, implorant; **he had sad, appealing eyes** il avait un regard triste et implorant

appealingly [ə'piːlɪŋlɪ] *adv* (**a**) *(charmingly)* de façon attrayante (**b**) *(beseechingly → look)* d'un air suppliant *ou* implorant; *(→ say)* d'un ton suppliant

appear [ə'pɪə(r)] *vi* (**a**) *(come into view → person, ghost, stars)* apparaître; **he suddenly appeared round the corner** il a soudain surgi au coin de la rue; **the sun appeared from behind a cloud** le soleil est sorti de derrière un nuage; **she appeared to him in a vision** elle lui est apparue dans une vision; **she only appears at meal times** elle n'apparaît qu'au moment des repas; **she finally appeared at about eight o'clock** elle est arrivée finalement vers vingt heures; **where did you appear from?** d'où est-ce que tu sors?; **to appear from nowhere** sortir de nulle part

(**b**) *(come into being)* apparaître; *Com (new product)* apparaître, être mis sur le marché; *(book, newspaper)* paraître, sortir, être publié

(**c**) *(feature)* paraître, figurer; **her name appears on the list** son nom figure sur la liste; **the father figure often appears in his films** le personnage du père figure souvent dans ses films

(**d**) *(be present officially)* se présenter, paraître; *Law (in court)* comparaître; **to appear before the court** *or* **the judge** comparaître devant le tribunal; **to fail to appear** faire défaut; **he appeared on a charge of murder** il a été jugé pour meurtre; **they appeared as witnesses for the defence** ils ont témoigné pour la défense; **he appeared for the accused** *(defence counsel)* il a plaidé pour l'accusé

(**e**) *(actor)* jouer; **she appeared as Antigone** elle a joué Antigone; **to appear in a play** jouer dans une pièce; **to appear on TV** passer à la télévision

(**f**) *(seem)* paraître, sembler; **he appeared to hesitate** il paraissait *ou* semblait hésiter, il avait l'air d'hésiter; **she appeared nervous** elle avait l'air nerveux *ou* nerveuse; **to appear to be lost** avoir l'air d'être perdu; **the baby appeared quite content** le bébé semblait plutôt satisfait; **how does the situation appear to you?** comment voyez-vous la situation?; **there appears to have been a mistake** il semble qu'il y ait eu erreur; **there appears to be a mistake in the bill** on dirait qu'il y a une erreur dans la facture; **it appears she never received the letter** il semble qu'elle n'ait jamais reçu la lettre; **it appears not** il semble que non; **so it appears, so it would appear** c'est ce qu'il semble, on dirait bien; **is she ill? – it appears so** est-elle malade? – il paraît (que oui); **it would appear that he was already known to the police** il semble qu'il était déjà connu des services de police; **it appeared later that he had killed his wife** il est ensuite apparu qu'il avait assassiné sa femme

appearance [ə'pɪərəns] *n* (**a**) *(act of appearing)* apparition *f*; **with the appearance of fast-food restaurants** avec l'apparition *ou* l'arrivée des fast-foods; **the antibiotics help guard against the appearance of further infections** les antibiotiques contribuent à éviter l'apparition de nouvelles infections; **she made a brief appearance at the party** elle a fait une brève apparition à la fête; **the president made a personal appearance** le président est apparu en personne; **to put in an appearance** passer; *(as token gesture)* faire acte de présence

(**b**) *(advent)* avènement *m*; *Com (of new product)* mise *f* sur le marché; *(of book, newspaper)* parution *f*

(**c**) *Law (in court)* comparution *f*; **to make an appearance before a court** *or* **a judge** comparaître devant un tribunal

(**d**) *(performance)* **this was her first appearance on the stage** c'était sa première apparition sur scène; **she's made a number of television appearances** elle est passée plusieurs fois à la télévision; **offers have flooded in since her television appearance** les propositions ont afflué depuis son passage à la télévision; **in order of appearance** par ordre d'entrée en scène

(**e**) *(outward aspect)* apparence *f*, aspect *m*; **from his appearance one would say...** à son air *ou* son extérieur on dirait...; **to have a good appearance** *(person)* présenter bien; **I tried to give the appearance that I cared** j'ai essayé de donner l'impression que ça ne m'était pas indifférent; **it has all the appearances of being a first-class show** si l'on en juge par les apparences, ce devrait être un spectacle de premier ordre; **to** *or* **by all appearances** selon toute apparence; **contrary to all appearances, against all appearances** contrairement à toute apparence; **appearances can be deceptive** les apparences sont parfois trompeuses; **don't judge by appearances** ne vous fiez pas aux apparences, il ne faut pas se fier aux apparences; **to keep up appearances** sauver les apparences; **for appearances' sake** pour la forme

appease [ə'piːz] *vt* (**a**) *(person)* apaiser, calmer (**b**) *(anger, hunger etc)* assouvir

appeasement [ə'piːzmənt], **appeasing** [ə'piːzɪŋ] *n* (**a**) *(of person)* apaisement *m*, *Pej* conciliation *f* (**b**) *(of anger, hunger etc)* assouvissement *m*

appellant [ə'pelənt] *Law* **1** *n* partie *f* appelante, appelant(e) *m,f*

2 *adj* appelant

appellate court [ə'pelɪt-] *n Law* cour *f* d'appel

appellation [ˌæpə'leɪʃən] *n Formal* appellation *f*

appellative [ə'pelətɪv] *Gram* **1** *n* appellatif *m*

2 *adj* appellatif

append [ə'pend] *vt Formal (document, note)* joindre (**to** à); *(signature)* apposer (**to** à); *Comput (to database)* ajouter (**to** à); **to append a document to a file** annexer *ou* joindre un document à un dossier

appendage [ə'pendɪdʒ] *n* appendice *m*; **I will not be treated as a mere appendage of my husband** je n'existe pas qu'en fonction de mon mari, j'existe aussi par moi-même

appendectomy [ˌæpen'dektəmɪ] (*pl* **appendectomies**), **appendicectomy** [əˌpendɪ'sektəmɪ] (*pl* **appendicectomies**) *n* appendicectomie *f*

appendices [ə'pendɪsiːz] *pl of* **appendix**

appendicitis [əˌpendɪ'saɪtɪs] *n (UNCOUNT)* appendicite *f*; **have you had appendicitis?** avez-vous eu l'appendicite?

appendix [ə'pendɪks] (*pl* **appendixes** *or* **appendices** [-siːz]) *n* (**a**) *Anat* appendice *m*; **to have one's appendix out** se faire opérer de l'appendicite; **have you had your appendix out?** est-ce que tu t'es fait opérer de l'appendicite? (**b**) *(to book)* appendice *m*; *(to report)* annexe *f*

apperceive [æpə'siːv] *vt Psy* = percevoir d'une certaine manière d'après ses expériences individuelles antérieures

apperception [æpə'sepʃən] *n Psy* aperception *f*

appertain [ˌæpə'teɪn] *vi Formal* (**a**) *(belong)* **to appertain to** appartenir à; **land appertaining to the Crown** des terres appartenant à la Couronne; **those islands appertain to the United States** ces îles font partie des États-Unis (**b**) *(relate)* **to appertain to** relever de; **the responsibilities appertaining to adulthood** les responsabilités de l'âge adulte; **duties appertaining to his position** des devoirs qui incombent à ses fonctions

appetence ['æpɪtəns], **appetency** ['æpɪtənsɪ] *n Literary* appétence *f*

appetite ['æpɪtaɪt] *n* (**a**) *(for food)* appétit *m*; **she has a good appetite** elle a bon appétit; **I've got no appetite** je n'ai pas d'appétit; **I've lost my appetite** j'ai perdu l'appétit; **don't have too many sweets, you'll spoil your appetite** ne mange pas trop de bonbons, ça va te couper l'appétit; **they've gone for a swim to work up an appetite** ils sont allés se baigner pour s'ouvrir l'appétit *ou* se mettre en appétit

(**b**) *Fig (for knowledge)* soif *f*; *(for travel)* goût *m*; *(for doing something)* envie *f*; **that whetted his appetite for travel** cela a aiguisé son goût des voyages; **appetite for revenge** soif *f* de vengeance; **she had an enormous appetite for books** elle avait une immense soif de lecture, elle était avide de lecture; **to have little appetite for a fight** être peu enclin à une querelle *ou* à se disputer; **sexual appetite** appétit *m* sexuel; *Fig* **he has an insatiable appetite for work** c'est un boulimique du travail

►► ***appetite suppressant*** coupe-faim *m*

appetizer ['æpɪtaɪzə(r)] *n Culin (food)* hors-d'œuvre *m inv*, amuse-gueule *m*; *(drink)* apéritif *m*; *Fig* **that was just an appetizer for what was to come** ce n'était qu'un avant-goût de ce qui allait suivre

appetizing ['æpɪtaɪzɪŋ] *adj (food, smell)* appétissant, alléchant; *Fig* **he doesn't look very appetizing** il n'est pas ragoûtant

appetizingly ['æpɪtaɪzɪŋlɪ] *adv* d'une façon appétissante

Appian Way ['æpɪən-] *n* **the Appian Way** la voie Appienne

applaud [ə'plɔːd] **1** *vt* applaudir, approuver; **his efforts are to be applauded** il faut applaudir ses efforts

2 *vi* applaudir

applause [ə'plɔːz] *n (UNCOUNT)* applaudissements *mpl*, acclamations *fpl*; *Fig* approbation *f*; **his performance won enthusiastic applause from the audience** son interprétation a été chaleureusement applaudie par le public; **she left the stage to thunderous applause** elle quitta la scène sous un tonnerre d'applaudissements; **to meet** *or* **be greeted with applause** *(of performance, decision etc)* être applaudi

►► ***applause meter*** applaudimètre *m*

apple ['æpəl] *n (fruit)* pomme *f*; *(tree)* pommier *m*; *Fig* **to compare apples with oranges** comparer ce qui n'est pas comparable; *Fig Literary* **the apple of discord** la pomme de discorde; **he's a rotten apple** c'est un mauvais sujet; **she's the apple of his eye** il tient à elle comme à la prunelle de ses yeux; *Prov* **an apple a day keeps the doctor away** = mangez une pomme par jour et vous resterez en bonne santé; *Br Fam* **apples and pears** *(rhyming slang* **stairs**) escaliers *mpl*; *Austr Fam* **she'll be apples!** tout ira bien!

►► ***apple blossom*** fleur *f* de pommier; *Am Culin* ***apple butter*** confiture *f* de pommes; ***apple core*** trognon *m* de pomme; ***apple corer*** vide-pommes *m inv*; ***apple juice*** jus *m* de pomme; ***apple orchard*** pommeraie *f*; *Comput* **Apple menu** menu *m* pomme; ***apple pie*** *(covered)* tourte *f* aux pommes; *(open)* tarte *f* aux pommes; **as American as apple pie** typiquement américain; *Br* ***apple sauce*** compote *f* de pommes; *Culin* ***apple strudel*** strudel *m*; ***apple tree*** pommier *m*

applecart ['æpəlkɑːt] *n Fig* **to upset the applecart** tout chambouler

apple-cheeked [-tʃiːkt] *adj* aux joues pleines et vermeilles

apple-green **1** *n* vert pomme *m inv*

2 *adj* vert pomme *(inv)*

applejack ['æpldʒæk] *n* eau-de-vie *f* de pommes

apple-pie *adj Fam* impeccable; **in apple-pie order** en ordre parfait

►► *Br* ***apple-pie bed*** lit *m* en portefeuille

apple-polisher *n Am Fam* lèche-bottes *mf*

applesauce ['æpəlsɔːs] *n Am Culin* compote *f* de pommes; *Am & Can Fam Fig* boniments *mpl*

applet ['æplət] *n Comput* appelette *f*, appliquette *f*, *Can* applet *m*

appliance [ə'plaɪəns] *n* (**a**) *(device)* appareil *m*; *(small)* dispositif *m*, instrument *m*; **domestic** *or* **household appliances** appareils *mpl* électroménagers; **electrical appliances** appareils *mpl* électriques (**b**) *(fire engine)* autopompe *f*

applicability [əˌplɪkə'bɪlɪtɪ] *n* applicabilité *f*

applicable [ə'plɪkəbəl] *adj* applicable (**to** à); **not applicable** *(on form)* sans rapport; **delete where not applicable** *(on form)* rayer les mentions inutiles

applicant ['æplɪkənt] *n* (**a**) *(for loan, funding, patent)* demandeur(euse) *m,f* (**for** de); *(for job)* candidat(e) *m,f* (**for** à), postulant(e) *m,f*; *St Exch (for shares)* souscripteur(trice) *m,f* (**for** de) (**b**) *Law* requérant(e) *m,f*

application [,æplɪ'keɪʃən] *n* (**a**) *(use)* application *f*; **the application of free market economics to communist systems** l'application de l'économie de marché aux régimes communistes; **the practical applications of the research** les applications pratiques de la recherche
(**b**) *(of lotion, paint)* application *f*; **for external application only** *(on drugs packaging)* réservé à l'usage externe
(**c**) *(request)* demande *f*; **a job application** *(spontaneous)* une demande d'emploi; *(in answer to advertisement)* une candidature à un poste; **to submit an application** faire une demande; **I submitted my application for a scholarship** j'ai fait ma demande de bourse; **further** *or* **full details on application** informations complètes sur demande; **he made an application to the committee for a hearing** il s'est adressé au comité pour obtenir une audition; **we made an application for citizenship** nous avons fait une demande de naturalisation
(**d**) *St Exch* **application for shares** demande *f* de titres en souscription, souscription *f* d'actions; **to make an application for shares** souscrire (à) des actions; **payable on application** payable à la souscription
(**e**) *(diligence)* application *f*, assiduité *f*; **this student lacks application** cet étudiant manque d'assiduité, cet étudiant n'est pas très appliqué; **to show a lot of application** faire preuve d'une grande application *ou* assiduité
(**f**) *(relevance)* pertinence *f*
(**g**) *Comput* application *f*
▸▸ ***application form*** *(for grant, benefits)* formulaire *m* de demande; *(for membership)* demande *f* d'inscription; *(detailed)* dossier *m* de candidature; *Univ* dossier *m* d'inscription; *St Exch (for shares)* bulletin *m* de souscription; *Comput* ***application program*** programme *m* d'application; *Comput* ***application software*** logiciel *m* d'application

applicator ['æplɪkeɪtə(r)] *n* applicateur *m*

applied [ə'plaɪd] *adj (maths)* appliqué; *(sciences)* expérimental
▸▸ ***applied arts*** arts *mpl* décoratifs; ***applied psychology*** psychotechnique *f*

appliqué [æ'pli:keɪ] **1** *n (decoration)* application *f*; *(decorative work)* travail *m* d'application
2 *vt* coudre en application

apply [ə'plaɪ] *(pt & pp* **applied**) **1** *vt* (**a**) *(use)* appliquer (**to** à), mettre en pratique *ou* en application; *(rule, law)* appliquer (**to** à); **we apply the same rule to all students** nous appliquons la même règle à *ou* pour tous les étudiants; **he would like to apply his experience in IT to industry** il voudrait utiliser ses compétences en informatique dans le domaine de l'industrie
(**b**) *(pressure)* **to apply pressure to sth** exercer une pression *ou* appuyer sur qch; **she applied the brakes** elle a freiné; *Fig* **the bank applied pressure on him to repay his loan** la banque a fait pression sur lui pour qu'il rembourse son emprunt
(**c**) *(paint, lotion etc)* appliquer, mettre (**to** sur); **apply antiseptic to the wound** désinfectez la plaie; **apply the paint using a roller** appliquez la peinture à l'aide d'un rouleau; **to apply heat to sth** exposer qch à la chaleur; **the doctor applied heat to her back** le médecin lui a traité le dos par la thermothérapie
(**d**) *(devote)* **to apply one's mind to sth** s'appliquer à qch; **she applied herself to her work** elle s'est lancée dans son travail; **he must learn to apply himself** il faut qu'il apprenne à s'appliquer
2 *vi* (**a**) *(make an application)* s'adresser, avoir recours; **to apply to sb for sth** s'adresser *ou* recourir à qn pour obtenir qch; **apply to the personnel office** adressez-vous au service du personnel; **apply within** *(sign)* s'adresser à l'intérieur *ou* ici; **to apply for a job** faire une demande d'emploi, poser sa candidature à un emploi, *Formal* solliciter *ou* postuler un emploi; **to apply for a loan** demander un prêt; **he applied to the Research Council for an award** il s'est adressé au conseil de la recherche pour obtenir une bourse; **we applied for a patent** nous avons déposé une demande de brevet; **to apply in writing** écrire; **to apply in person** se présenter; *Law* **the right to apply to the courts** le droit au recours juridictionnel; *St Exch* **to apply for shares** souscrire (à) des actions
(**b**) *(be relevant)* s'appliquer (**to** à); **and that applies to you too!** et ça s'applique aussi à toi!; **this law applies to all citizens** cette loi s'applique à tous les citoyens; **this doesn't apply to us** nous ne sommes pas concernés; **his criticism applies to all journalists** ses critiques s'appliquent à tous les journalistes

appoggiatura [ə,pɒdʒɪə'tʊərə] *n Mus* appoggiature *f*

appoint [ə'pɔɪnt] *vt* (**a**) *(assign)* nommer, désigner; *(committee)* constituer, nommer; *(heir)* instituer; **she was appointed to the post of director** elle a été nommée directrice; **the members appointed him president** les adhérents l'ont nommé président; **the president appointed a committee** le président a constitué un comité
(**b**) *(hire)* engager; **we have appointed a new cook** nous avons engagé un nouveau cuisinier
(**c**) *(place, date, time)* fixer, désigner; **let's appoint a time for the meeting** fixons une heure pour la réunion
(**d**) *Br Formal (furnish)* aménager
(**e**) *Arch or Law (prescribe, ordain)* ordonner, prescrire

appointed [ə'pɔɪntɪd] *adj* (**a**) *(official)* nommé; *(agent)* attitré (**b**) *Formal (agreed → place, date, time)* convenu, dit; **we met on the appointed day** nous nous sommes rencontrés au jour dit *ou* convenu

appointee [ə,pɔɪn'ti:] *n* candidat(e) *m,f* retenu(e)

appointment [ə'pɔɪntmənt] *n* (**a**) *(meeting → at doctor's etc)* rendez-vous *m*; *(for business)* rendez-vous *m*, entrevue *f*; **I made an appointment with the dentist** j'ai pris rendez-vous chez le dentiste; **I've made an appointment with the doctor for you** je t'ai pris un rendez-vous chez le docteur; **they made an appointment to have lunch together** ils se sont donné rendez-vous pour déjeuner; **he has a 4 o'clock appointment** il a un rendez-vous à 16 heures; **she didn't keep our** *or* **the appointment** elle n'est pas venue au rendez-vous; **I've got an appointment with the doctor** j'ai rendez-vous chez le médecin; *(announcing arrival to receptionist)* j'ai rendez-vous avec le médecin; **to meet sb by appointment** rencontrer qn sur rendez-vous; **by appointment only** sur rendez-vous seulement; **have you got an appointment?** avez-vous un rendez-vous?; *Admin* êtes-vous convoqué?
(**b**) *(nomination)* nomination *f*, désignation *f*; *(office filled)* poste *m*; *(posting)* affectation *f*; **his appointment to the office of Lord Chancellor** sa nomination au poste de grand chancelier; **there are still some appointments to be made** il y a encore quelques postes à pourvoir; *Com* **by appointment to Her Majesty the Queen** *(on packaging)* fournisseur de S.M. la Reine
(**c**) **appointments** *(in newspaper)* offres *fpl* d'emploi
(**d**) *Formal* **appointments** *(of house)* aménagement *m*
▸▸ ***appointments diary*** carnet *m* de rendez-vous, agenda *m*

Appomattox [,æpə'mætəks] *n Hist* = village de la Virginie, aujourd'hui parc historique, où le Général Lee se rendit aux troupes nordistes du Général Grant, marquant ainsi la fin de la guerre de Sécession

apportion [ə'pɔ:ʃən] *vt (blame, praise)* répartir; *(costs, taxes, expenses, shares)* répartir, partager; *(rations)* allouer; *(funds)* affecter; *(property)* distribuer; **to apportion sth to sb** assigner qch à qn

apportionment [ə'pɔ:ʃənmənt] *n (of blame, praise)* répartition *f*; *(of costs, taxes, expenses, shares)* répartition *f*, partage *m*; *(of rations)* allocation *f*; *(of funds)* affectation *f*; *(of property)* distribution *f*

apposite ['æpəzɪt] *adj (observation)* juste; *(action)* approprié (**to** à); **an apposite remark** une remarque très à propos

appositely ['æpəzɪtlɪ] *adv (remark)* à propos

appositeness ['æpəzɪtnɪs] *n (of observation)* justesse *f*; *(of action, remark)* à-propos *m*

apposition [,æpə'zɪʃən] *n* apposition *f*; *Gram* **a noun/phrase in apposition** un nom/une expression en apposition

appositive [ə'pɒzətɪv] *adj Gram* en apposition

appraisal [ə'preɪzəl] *n (of standards, personnel, situation)* évaluation *f*; *(of object)* estimation *f*, appréciation *f*; *(before auction)* prisée *f*; **an official appraisal** *Ins (of object)* une expertise; **performance appraisal** *(in company)* évaluation *f*

appraise [ə'preɪz] *vt (standards, personnel, situation)* évaluer; *(object)* estimer, évaluer (la valeur de); *(importance, quality)* évaluer, apprécier; **they appraised the damage after the fire** ils évaluèrent les dégâts après l'incendie

appraising [ə'preɪzɪŋ] *adj* **she shot him an appraising glance** elle lui a lancé un coup d'œil pour le jauger

appreciable [ə'pri:ʃəbəl] *adj (difference, amount, distance)* appréciable, notable; *(change, improvement)* sensible

appreciably [ə'pri:ʃəblɪ] *adv (differ)* appréciablement; *(change, improve)* sensiblement

appreciate [ə'pri:ʃɪeɪt] **1** *vt* (**a**) *(value)* apprécier; *(art)* apprécier, goûter; *(person)* apprécier (à sa juste valeur); **they appreciate good food** ils apprécient la bonne cuisine; **no one appreciates me** personne ne m'apprécie à ma juste valeur
(**b**) *(be grateful for)* être reconnaissant de, être sensible à; **I appreciate your help** je vous suis reconnaissant de votre aide; **I would appreciate a prompt reply to this letter** je vous serais obligé de bien vouloir me répondre dans les plus brefs délais; **I appreciate it** j'en suis reconnaissant; *esp Am (thanks)* je vous en remercie; **I would appreciate it if you didn't smoke in the car** je vous serais reconnaissant *ou* je vous saurais gré de ne pas fumer dans la voiture; **thanks, I'd really appreciate that** ça me rendrait vraiment service; **he greatly appreciates this honour** il est très sensible à cet honneur
(**c**) *(realize, understand)* se rendre compte de, être conscient de; **I fully appreciate (the fact) that...** je me rends bien compte que...; **I do appreciate your concern but...** votre sollicitude me touche beaucoup mais...; **do you appreciate how hard I try?** est-ce que tu te rends compte des efforts que je fais?; **we fully appreciate the situation** nous nous rendons parfaitement compte de la situation; **I hadn't appreciated how difficult it is** je ne m'étais pas rendu compte que c'était aussi difficile
2 *vi (value, price)* augmenter; *(currency)* s'apprécier; *(goods, property, investment, shares)* prendre de la valeur

appreciation [ə,pri:ʃɪ'eɪʃən] *n* (**a**) *(thanks)* reconnaissance *f*, gratitude *f*; **let me show my appreciation for your help** laissez-moi vous témoigner ma reconnaissance *ou* ma gratitude; **as a sign of our appreciation** en témoignage de notre reconnaissance *ou* gratitude; **in appreciation of what you have done** en remerciement *ou* pour vous remercier de ce que vous avez fait; **the audience showed its appreciation of the performance by cheering** le public a acclamé le spectacle
(**b**) *(understanding, awareness)* compréhension *f*; **he has a thorough appreciation of the situation** il comprend très bien la situation; **she has no appreciation of what is involved** elle ne se rend pas compte de ce que ça implique; **art appreciation course** cours *m* d'initiation à l'art; **literary appreciation** explication *f* de texte; **musical appreciation** appréciation *f* musicale; **a wine appreciation society** une société d'amateurs de vin
(**c**) *Journ & Press (review)* critique *f*; **to write an appreciation of a new play** faire la critique d'une nouvelle pièce
(**d**) *(of value, price)* augmentation *f*; *(of*

currency) appréciation *f*; *(of goods, property, investment, shares)* augmentation *f* de la valeur

appreciative [ə'pri:ʃɪətɪv] *adj* (**a**) *(grateful)* reconnaissant; **I'm very appreciative of all you've done for me** je vous suis reconnaissant de tout ce que vous avez fait pour moi; **she's a very appreciative sort of person** c'est une personne qui sait faire preuve de reconnaissance *ou* de gratitude; **in a few appreciative words** avec quelques mots de reconnaissance

(**b**) *Journ & Press (review, audience)* favorable; *(praising)* élogieux

(**c**) *(showing liking)* **I gave him the present, but he wasn't very appreciative** je lui ai donné le cadeau, mais il n'a pas beaucoup aimé; **to be appreciative of music** apprécier la musique

(**d**) *(showing understanding, awareness)* **to be appreciative of sth** comprendre l'importance de qch, être sensible à qch; **he was very appreciative of their problems** il s'est montré très sensible à leurs problèmes

appreciatively [ə'pri:ʃɪətɪvlɪ] *adv* (**a**) *(gratefully)* avec reconnaissance (**b**) *(showing understanding, praising → review)* en termes élogieux, favorablement; *(listen)* avec appréciation; **they clapped appreciatively** ils applaudirent pour montrer leur enthousiasme; **she smiled appreciatively at his joke** elle a aimé l'histoire qui l'a fait sourire; **she smiled appreciatively** elle eut un sourire approbateur; **the performance was received appreciatively** le spectacle a été bien *ou* favorablement reçu (**c**) *(showing liking)* **"excellent coffee", he said appreciatively** "excellent, ce café", dit-il avec plaisir; **"a superb brandy", she said appreciatively** "un cognac exceptionnel", dit-elle en connaisseuse

apprehend [,æprɪ'hend] *vt* (**a**) *Law (arrest)* arrêter, appréhender (**b**) *Formal (understand)* comprendre, saisir (**c**) *Arch or Literary (fear, dread)* redouter, appréhender

apprehension [,æprɪ'henʃən] *n* (**a**) *(fear)* inquiétude *f*, appréhension *f*; **there is no cause for apprehension** il n'y a pas de raison d'être inquiet (**b**) *Law (arrest)* arrestation *f* (**c**) *Formal (understanding)* compréhension *f*

apprehensive [,æprɪ'hensɪv] *adj* plein d'appréhension; **there's nothing to be apprehensive about** il n'y a aucune raison de s'inquiéter; **I'm feeling a bit apprehensive** je me sens un peu nerveux; **he is apprehensive about the interview** il appréhende l'entretien; **I am apprehensive for your safety** je crains *ou* je suis inquiet pour votre sécurité

apprehensively [,æprɪ'hensɪvlɪ] *adv* avec appréhension *ou* inquiétude

apprehensiveness [,æprɪ'hensɪvnɪs] *n* inquiétude *f*, appréhension *f*

apprentice [ə'prentɪs] **1** *n* apprenti(e) *m,f*; *(in arts and crafts)* élève *mf*; **she's an electrician's apprentice** elle est apprentie électricienne

2 *adj* **an apprentice toolmaker/butcher** un apprenti outilleur/boucher; **an apprentice draughtsman** un élève dessinateur

3 *vt* **to apprentice sb to sb** placer *ou* mettre qn en apprentissage chez qn; **he is apprenticed to a sculptor** il suit une formation chez un sculpteur; **she is apprenticed to a violin-maker** elle est en apprentissage chez un luthier

►► *Pol* ***the Apprentice Boys*** = confrérie orangiste d'Irlande du Nord qui défile chaque année dans la ville de Derry

apprenticeship [ə'prentɪʃɪp] *n* apprentissage *m*; **to serve one's apprenticeship (with sb)** faire son apprentissage (chez qn); **she did an apprenticeship as a carpenter** elle a fait un apprentissage de charpentier; *Fig* **to serve one's apprenticeship** faire ses débuts

apprise [ə'praɪz] *vt Formal* **to apprise sb of sth** apprendre qch à qn, prévenir *ou* informer qn de qch; **we were not apprised of his arrival** nous n'avons pas été informés de son arrivée

appro ['æprəʊ] *n Br Fam Com* (*abbr* **approval**) **on appro** à *ou* sous condition ☐, à l'essai ☐

approach [ə'prəʊtʃ] **1** *vt* (**a**) *(person)* s'approcher de; *(place)* approcher de; **as we approached Boston** comme nous approchions de Boston; **she is approaching fifty** elle approche de la cinquantaine; **we are approaching a time when...** le jour approche où...; **we have nothing approaching that colour** nous n'avons rien qui se rapproche de cette couleur; **speeds approaching the speed of light** des vitesses proches de celle de la lumière; **it was approaching Christmas** Noël approchait; **a feeling approaching hatred** un sentiment proche de la haine

(**b**) *(consider)* aborder; **let's approach the problem from another angle** abordons le problème d'une autre façon; **that's not the way to approach it** ce n'est pas comme cela qu'il faut s'y prendre

(**c**) *(speak to)* parler à; *(of company, group, team)* pressentir, faire des propositions *ou* des ouvertures à; **to be easy/difficult to approach** être d'un abord facile/difficile; **I was approached by a man in the street** j'ai été abordé par un homme dans la rue; **I approached him about the job** je lui ai parlé du poste; **they approached him about doing a deal** ils sont entrés en contact avec lui pour conclure un marché

2 *vi (person, vehicle)* s'approcher; *(time, event)* approcher, être proche; **Christmas/spring is approaching** Noël/le printemps approche

3 *n* (**a**) *(of person, vehicle)* approche *f*, arrivée *f*; *(of spring)* approche *f*; *(of night)* tombée *f*; *(of death)* approche(s) *f(pl)*; **she heard his approach** elle l'a entendu venir; **the pilot began his approach to Heathrow** le pilote commença sa descente sur *ou* vers Heathrow

(**b**) *(way of tackling)* méthode *f*; **another approach to the problem** une autre façon d'aborder le problème; **I don't like her approach** je n'aime pas sa façon de s'y prendre; **a new approach to dealing with unemployment** une nouvelle conception de la lutte contre le chômage, une nouvelle méthode de lutte contre le chômage; **let's try the direct approach** allons-y sans détours; **this book adopts a non-scientific approach to the subject** ce livre aborde le sujet d'une manière non scientifique

(**c**) *(proposal)* proposition *f*; **the shopkeeper made an approach to his suppliers** le commerçant a fait une proposition à ses fournisseurs

(**d**) *(access)* voie *f* d'accès; **the approaches to the town** les voies d'accès de la ville; **the approach to the house/hotel** l'allée qui mène à la maison/à l'hôtel; **the approaches to the beach** les chemins qui mènent à la plage; **the approach to the summit** le chemin qui mène au sommet

(**e**) *Formal (approximation)* **an approach to an apology/a smile** un semblant d'excuse/de sourire; **it's the nearest approach to an apology that they received** c'est ce qu'on leur a dit qui ressemblait le plus à des excuses

►► *Br Transp* ***approach road*** route *f* d'accès; *(to motorway)* voie *f* de raccordement, bretelle *f*; *Sport* ***approach shot*** *(in tennis)* coup *m* d'approche; *(in golf)* approche *f*

approachability [ə,prəʊtʃə'bɪlɪtɪ] *n* **her approachability is what makes her popular with students** c'est parce qu'elle est d'un abord facile que les étudiants l'aiment bien

approachable [ə'prəʊtʃəbəl] *adj (place)* accessible; *(person)* d'un abord facile

approaching [ə'prəʊtʃɪŋ] **1** *adj (event)* prochain, qui est proche; *(vehicle)* qui vient en sens inverse; *(storm)* qui arrive; **the approaching war would have terrible consequences** la guerre qui approchait eut des conséquences terribles

2 *prep* **there were approaching 200 people** il y avait près de 200 personnes

approbate ['æprə,beɪt] *vt Am* approuver

approbation [,æprə'beɪʃən] *n* approbation *f*, consentement *m*; **a nod/smile of approbation** un signe de tête/un sourire approbateur

appropriate 1 *adj* [ə'prəʊprɪət] *(place, decision)* approprié; *(moment)* opportun; *(remark, word)* juste; *(name)* bien choisi; *(authority)* compétent; *(behaviour)* convenable; **the level of contribution appropriate for** *or* **to each country** la contribution appropriée à chaque pays; **music/remarks appropriate to the occasion** de la musique/des propos de circonstance; **take (the) appropriate action** prenez les mesures appropriées; **it wouldn't be appropriate if she went** il ne serait pas convenable qu'elle y aille; **I am not the appropriate person to ask** ce n'est pas à moi qu'il faut poser la question

2 *vt* [ə'prəʊprɪeɪt] (**a**) *(take)* s'approprier, s'emparer de; *(keep for oneself)* s'attribuer, se réserver

(**b**) *Fin (funds)* affecter (**to** *ou* **for** à); **the funds appropriated for** *or* **to the school** l'argent affecté à l'école; **£4,000 has been appropriated to upgrading computers** 4000 livres ont été affectées à l'augmentation de mémoire des ordinateurs

appropriately [ə'prəʊprɪətlɪ] *adv (behave)* convenablement; *(speak, react)* avec à-propos, pertinemment; *(decide)* à juste titre; **appropriately dressed** habillé comme il faut *ou* pour la circonstance; **the restaurant is appropriately named** le restaurant porte bien son nom

appropriateness [ə'prəʊprɪətnɪs] *n (of moment)* opportunité *f*; *(of remark, decision, word)* justesse *f*; *(of behaviour)* correction *f*, bienséance *f*

appropriation [ə,prəʊprɪ'eɪʃən] *n* (**a**) *(taking)* appropriation *f*, prise *f* de possession (**of** de) (**b**) *Fin (of funds)* affectation *f*; *(of payment)* imputation *f*; *Am Pol* crédit *m* budgétaire; **appropriation to the reserve** dotation *f* au compte de provisions; **allotment of appropriations** répartition *f* des budgets

►► *Acct* ***appropriation account*** compte *m* d'affectation; *Pol* ***appropriations bill*** projet *m* de loi de finances; *Pol* ***Appropriations Committee*** = commission des finances de la Chambre des Représentants qui examine les dépenses

approval [ə'pru:vəl] **1** *n* (**a**) *(favourable opinion)* approbation *f*, accord *m*; **a gesture of approval** un signe approbateur; **the plan has your seal of approval, then?** alors tu donnes ton approbation pour le projet?; **to submit sth for approval (by sb)** soumettre qch à l'approbation (de qn); **to meet with sb's approval** obtenir *ou* recevoir l'approbation de qn; **does the report meet with your approval?** êtes-vous satisfait du rapport?; **subject to approval** soumis à l'approbation

(**b**) *Admin & Law (of document, treaty)* ratification *f*, homologation *f*; **for (your) approval** *(on document)* pour approbation

(**c**) *Com* **on approval** à condition, à l'essai; **a book sent on approval** un livre envoyé à l'examen

2 approvals *npl Am Com (goods)* marchandises *fpl* envoyées à l'essai

►► ***approval rating*** *(of politician)* cote *f* de popularité; *Mktg (of product)* score *m* d'agrément

approve [ə'pru:v] **1** *vt (plan, proposal etc)* approuver; *(document, treaty, decision)* ratifier, homologuer; **the plan must be approved by the committee** il faut que le projet reçoive l'approbation du comité; **approved by the government** agréé par l'État; **read and approved** *(on document)* lu et approuvé

2 *vi* être d'accord; **I told her what I had done and she seemed to approve** je lui ai dit ce que j'avais fait et elle a eu l'air de m'approuver; **I'm afraid I don't approve** je crains de ne pas être d'accord

►**approve of** *vt insep* approuver; *(person)* avoir une bonne opinion de; **I don't approve of his ideas** je n'approuve pas *ou* je désapprouve ses idées; **she doesn't approve of them smoking** ça ne lui plaît pas qu'ils fument; **do you approve of the proposal?** êtes-vous d'accord avec la proposition?; **she doesn't approve of her son's friends** les amis de son fils ne lui plaisent pas

approved [ə'pru:vd] *adj* (**a**) *(method, practice)* reconnu, admis (**b**) *(officially authorized)* agréé, autorisé

►► *Formerly* ***approved school*** = nom anciennement donné en Grande-Bretagne à un centre d'éducation surveillé (aujourd'hui appelé "community home")

approving [ə'pru:vɪŋ] *adj* approbateur, approbatif

approvingly [ə'pru:vɪŋlɪ] *adv (look)* d'un air approbateur; *(say)* d'un ton approbateur; **to react approvingly** approuver

approx. *(written abbr* **approximately***)* approx., env

approximate 1 *adj* [ə'prɒksɪmət] (**a**) *(figure, date,*

calculation) approximatif; **the approximate distance to town is 5 miles** il y a à peu près 5 miles d'ici à la ville; **he told the approximate truth** il ne disait qu'une partie de la vérité; **figures approximate to the nearest whole number** des chiffres arrondis au nombre entier le plus proche (**b**) *Biol & Phys* rapproché, proche, voisin
2 *vi* [ə'prɒksɪmeɪt] **to approximate to sth** se rapprocher de qch; **to approximate to the truth** se rapprocher de la vérité; **his answer approximated to a refusal** sa réponse était presque un refus

approximately [ə'prɒksɪmətlɪ] *adv* à peu près, environ; **a pint is approximately half a litre** une pinte correspond approximativement à un litre; **his income is approximately £20,000** son revenu est d'environ vingt mille livres

approximation [əˌprɒksɪ'meɪʃən] *n* approximation *f*; **this figure is only an approximation** ceci n'est qu'un chiffre approximatif; **his statement was no more than an approximation of the truth** sa déclaration n'avait qu'un lointain rapport avec la réalité

appurtenance [ə'pɜːtɪnəns] *n (usu pl) Formal* accessoire *m*; **the property and its appurtenances** *(buildings, gardens etc)* la propriété et ses dépendances; *Law (legal rights and privileges)* la propriété et ses circonstances et dépendances

APR [ˌeɪpiː'ɑː(r)] *n Fin* (**a**) *(abbr* **annual** *or* **annualized percentage rate**) TEG *m* (**b**) *(abbr* **annual purchase rate**) taux *m* annuel

Apr. *(written abbr* **April**) avr

apragmatic [ˌeɪpræg'mætɪk] *adj Psy* apragmatique

apragmatism [eɪ'prægmətɪzəm] *n Psy* apragmatisme *m*

apraxia [eɪ'præksɪə] *n Med* apraxie *f*

apraxic [eɪ'præksɪk] *adj Med* apraxique

après-ski [ˌæpreɪ'skiː] **1** *n* = distractions après une séance de ski
2 *comp (clothing, outfit)* = que l'on porte après une séance de ski

apricot ['eɪprɪkɒt] **1** *n* (**a**) *(fruit)* abricot *m*; *(tree)* abricotier *m* (**b**) *(colour)* abricot *m inv*
2 *comp (yoghurt, ice cream)* à l'abricot; *(jam)* d'abricots; *(tart)* aux abricots
3 *adj (colour)* abricot *(inv)*
►► ***apricot tree*** abricotier *m*

April ['eɪprəl] *n* avril *m*; *Prov* **April showers bring forth May flowers** les giboulées de mars apportent les fleurs du printemps; *see also* **February**
►► ***April fool*** *(person)* = personne à qui l'on a fait un poisson d'avril; *(trick)* poisson *m* d'avril; **April fool!** poisson d'avril!; ***April Fools' Day*** le premier avril; ***April showers*** giboulées *fpl* de mars

> **APRIL FOOLS' DAY**
>
> En Grande-Bretagne, le premier avril est l'occasion de farces en tous genres; en revanche, la tradition du poisson en papier n'existe pas.

a priori [ˌeɪpraɪ'ɔːraɪ] *adj* a priori

apriorism [eɪ'praɪərɪzəm] *n* apriorisme *m*

apron ['eɪprən] *n* (**a**) *(clothing)* tablier *m*; **he's tied to his mother's apron strings** il est pendu aux jupes de sa mère (**b**) *Aviat* aire *f* de manœuvre *ou* de stationnement; *(for plane maintenance and repair)* tablier *m*, aire *f* en dur (**c**) *Theat* avant-scène *f* (**d**) *(of reservoir)* radier *m* (**e**) *(of golf green)* tablier *m*, lisière *f*
►► *Theat* ***apron stage*** avant-scène *f*

apropos [ˌæprə'pəʊ] **1** *adj* opportun, à propos
2 *adv* à propos, opportunément
3 **apropos of** *prep* à propos de; **…he said, apropos of nothing** …dit-il, de but en blanc; **apropos of nothing, I saw Zoe yesterday** au fait, ça n'a aucun rapport mais j'ai vu Zoe hier

APS [ˌeɪpiː'es] *(abbr* **advanced photo system**) **1** *n* APS *m inv*
2 *adj (camera)* APS *(inv)*

apse [æps] *n* (**a**) *Archit (in church)* abside *f* (**b**) *Astron* apside *f*

APT [ˌeɪpiː'tiː] *n* (**a**) *Br Rail (abbr* **advanced passenger train**) = train à grande vitesse, ≃ TGV *m* (**b**) *Fin (abbr* **arbitrage pricing theory**) théorie *f* de l'évaluation arbitrage

apt [æpt] *adj* (**a**) *(person)* **to be apt to do sth** avoir tendance à faire qch; **I am apt to forget people's names** j'ai tendance à oublier le nom des gens; **people are apt to believe the worst** les gens croient facilement le pire
(**b**) *(things)* **to be apt to do sth** être susceptible de faire qch; **buttons are apt to get lost** les boutons se perdent facilement
(**c**) *(suitable)* convenable, approprié; *(remark)* juste, qui convient; **an apt expression** une expression heureuse; **it is very apt that it should end in this way** il est tout à fait approprié que cela se termine de cette manière
(**d**) *(clever)* doué, intelligent

apt. *(written abbr* **apartment**) appt

apterous ['æptərəs] *adj Zool* aptère

apteryx ['æptərɪks] *n Orn* aptéryx *m*, kiwi *m*

aptitude ['æptɪtjuːd] *n* aptitude *f*, disposition *f*; **to have an aptitude for sth** avoir une aptitude à *ou* une disposition pour qch; **he has an aptitude for languages** il a des dispositions *ou* un talent pour les langues; **a young musician who shows great aptitude** une jeune musicienne qui promet
►► ***aptitude test*** test *m* d'aptitude

aptly ['æptlɪ] *adv* à *ou* avec propos, avec justesse; **the dog, Spot, was aptly named** le chien, Spot, portait *ou* méritait bien son nom; **an aptly chosen name** un nom bien choisi; **as you so aptly pointed out…** comme tu l'as si bien fait remarquer…

aptness ['æptnɪs] *n* (**a**) *(suitability)* à-propos *m*, justesse *f* (**b**) *(tendency)* tendance *f* (**c**) *(talent)* aptitude *f*, disposition *f*

Apulia [ə'pjuːljə] *n* Pouille *f*, Pouilles *fpl*; **in Apulia** dans les Pouilles

AQ [ˌeɪ'kjuː] *n (abbr* **achievement quotient**) = quotient d'aptitude obtenu en divisant l'âge d'aptitude par l'âge réel du sujet

aquacade ['ækwəkeɪd] *n Am Archit* spectacle *m* aquatique

aquaculture ['ækwəˌkʌltʃə(r)] *n* aquaculture *f*

aqualung ['ækwəlʌŋ] *n* scaphandre *m* autonome

aquamarine [ˌækwəmə'riːn] **1** *n Miner (stone)* aigue-marine *f*; *(colour)* bleu vert *m inv*
2 *adj* bleu vert *(inv)*

aquanaut ['ækwənɔːt] *n* plongeur *m*, scaphandrier *m*

aquaplane ['ækwəpleɪn] **1** *n Sport* aquaplane *m*
2 *vi* (**a**) *Sport* faire de l'aquaplane (**b**) *Br (car)* partir en aquaplanage *ou* aquaplaning

aquaplaning ['ækwəpleɪnɪŋ] *n* (**a**) *Sport* aquaplane *m* (**b**) *Br (of car)* aquaplanage *m*, aquaplaning *m*

aquarelle [ˌækwə'rel] *n Art* aquarelle *f*

aquarellist [ˌækwə'relɪst] *n Art* aquarelliste *mf*

Aquarian [ə'kweərɪən] *Astrol* **1** *n* **to be an Aquarian** être (du signe du) Verseau
2 *adj* du Verseau; **the Aquarian male** l'homme Verseau

aquarist [ə'kweərɪst] *n* aquariophile *mf*

aquarium [ə'kweərɪəm] *(pl* **aquariums** *or* **aquaria** [-rɪə]) *n* aquarium *m*

Aquarius [ə'kweərɪəs] **1** *n* (**a**) *Astron* Verseau *m*; **it's the age of Aquarius** c'est l'ère du Verseau (**b**) *Astrol* Verseau *m*; **he's an Aquarius** il est (du signe du) Verseau
2 *adj Astrol* du Verseau; **he's Aquarius** il est (du signe du) Verseau

aquarobics [ˌækwə'rəʊbɪks] *n* aquagym *f*

aquatic [ə'kwætɪk] *adj Biol* aquatique; *(sport)* nautique
►► *Orn* ***aquatic warbler*** phragmite *m* aquatique

aquatics [ə'kwætɪks] *npl* sports *mpl* nautiques

aquatint ['ækwətɪnt] *n Art* aquatinte *f*

aquavit ['ækwəvɪt] *n* aquavit *m*, akvavit *m*

aqua vitae [ˈækwə'viːtaɪ] *n* eau-de-vie *f*

aqueduct ['ækwɪdʌkt] *n* aqueduc *m*

aqueous ['ækwɪəs, 'eɪkwɪəs] *adj Chem* aqueux
►► *Anat* ***aqueous humour*** humeur *f* aqueuse; *Chem* ***aqueous solution*** soluté *m*

aquiculture ['ækwɪˌkʌltʃə(r)] *n* aquaculture *f*

aquifer ['ækwɪfə(r)] *n Geol* nappe *f* aquifère

aquilegia [ˌækwɪ'liːdʒɪə] *n Bot* ancolie *f*

aquiline ['ækwɪlaɪn] *adj Orn* aquilin; *Anat (nose)* aquilin, en bec d'aigle

Aquitaine [ˌækwɪ'teɪn] *n* Aquitaine *f*; **in Aquitaine** en Aquitaine
►► ***the Aquitaine Basin*** le bassin d'Aquitaine

Aquitanian [ˌækwɪ'teɪnɪən] **1** *n* (**a**) *Hist (person)* Aquitain(e) *m,f* (**b**) *Geol* aquitanien *m*
2 *adj* (**a**) *Hist* aquitanique, aquitain; **the Aquitanian nobility** la noblesse aquitaine (**b**) *Geol* aquitanien

aquiver [ə'kwɪvə(r)] *adj Literary* frémissant, tremblant (**with** de)

AR *(written abbr* **Arkansas**) Arkansas *m*

ARA [ˌeɪɑː'reɪ] *n (abbr* **Associate of the Royal Academy**) = membre associé de la "Royal Academy"

Arab ['ærəb] **1** *n* (**a**) *(person)* Arabe *mf* (**b**) *(horse)* cheval *m* arabe
2 *adj* arabe
►► *Pol* ***the Arab League*** la Ligue arabe

> **ARAB**
>
> En anglais le mot "Arab" désigne l'ensemble des ressortissants des pays de culture arabe, et surtout de l'Arabie Saoudite. Il n'a pas le sens restreint de "Maghrébin" que l'on rencontre souvent en français: "the firm was bought by a wealthy Arab family".

arabesque [ˌærə'besk] **1** *n* (**a**) *(usu pl) Art* arabesque *f* (**b**) *(in ballet)* arabesque *f*
2 *adj Art (decoration)* de style arabe

Arabia [ə'reɪbɪə] *n* Arabie *f*

Arabian [ə'reɪbɪən] **1** *n* Arabe *mf*
2 *adj* arabe, d'Arabie
►► ***the Arabian Desert*** le désert d'Arabie; ***the Arabian Gulf*** le golfe Arabique; ***the Arabian Peninsula*** la péninsule d'Arabie; ***the Arabian Sea*** la mer d'Arabie

> **'The Arabian Nights'** 'Les Mille et Une Nuits'

Arabic ['ærəbɪk] **1** *n (language)* arabe *m*; **written Arabic** l'arabe *m* littéral
2 *adj* arabe
►► ***Arabic numerals*** chiffres *mpl* arabes

arabica [ə'ræbɪkə] *n Bot* arabica *m*

Arabicize, -ise [ə'ræbɪsaɪz] *vt* arabiser

Arabic-speaking *adj* arabophone

Arab-Israeli *adj* israélo-arabe; **the Arab-Israeli Wars** le conflit israélo-arabe

Arabist ['ærəbɪst] *n (scholar)* arabisant(e) *m,f*; *(politician)* pro-Arabe *mf*

Arabization [ˌærəbaɪ'zeɪʃən] *n* arabisation *f*

Arabize, -ise ['ærəbaɪz] *vt* arabiser

arable ['ærəbəl] *adj Agr* arable, cultivable; *(crops)* cultivable; *(farm)* agricole
►► ***arable farmer*** cultivateur(trice) *m,f*; ***arable farming*** culture *f*

Araby ['ærəbɪ] *n Literary* Arabie *f*

Arachne [ə'ræknɪ] *pr n Myth* Arachné

arachnid [ə'ræknɪd] *n Zool* arachnid *m*; **the arachnids** les arachnides *mpl*

arachnoid [ə'ræknɔɪd] **1** *n Anat* arachnoïde *f*
2 *adj Bot & Zool* arachnoïdien, arachnoïde

arachnoiditis [əˌræknɔɪ'daɪtɪs] *n Med* arachnoïdite *f*

arachnologist [ˌæræk'nɒlədʒɪst] *n* arachnologue *mf*

arachnology [ˌæræk'nɒlədʒɪ] *n* arachnologie *f*

arachnophobia [əˌræknə'fəʊbɪə] *n* arachnophobie *f*

Aragon ['ærəgən] *n Geog* Aragon *m*; **in Aragon** en Aragon

Aragonese [ˌærəgə'niːz] **1** *n* (**a**) *(person)* Aragonais(e) *m,f* (**b**) *(language)* aragonais *m*
2 *adj* aragonais

aragonite [ə'rægənaɪt] *n Miner* aragonite *f*

arak = **arrack**

Aral Sea ['ɑːrəl-] *n* **the Aral Sea** la mer d'Aral

ARAM [ˌeɪɑːˌreɪ'em] *n Mus (abbr* **Associate of the Royal Academy of Music**) = membre associé de la "Royal Academy of Music"

Aramaean, Aramean [ˌærə'miːən] *adj Antiq & Ling* araméen

Aramaic [ˌærə'meɪɪk] *Antiq & Ling* **1** *n* araméen *m*
2 *adj* araméen

Aramean = **Aramaean**

Aran ['ærən] *adj*
►► ***the Aran Islands*** les îles *fpl* Aran; ***Aran sweater*** pull *m* Aran *(de grosse laine naturelle)*

Ararat ['ærəræt] *see* **Mount**

Arawakan [ˌærə'wækən] *n Ling* arawak *m*

arbiter ['ɑːbɪtə(r)] *n* arbitre *m*, médiateur(trice) *m,f*; *Fig* **magazines act as arbiters of modern taste** les magazines se font les juges *ou* les arbitres des goûts de notre société

arbitrage [ˌɑːbɪ'trɑːʒ] *n Fin & St Exch* arbitrage *m*

►► ***arbitrage pricing theory*** théorie *f* de l'évaluation par arbitrage

arbitrager, arbitrageur ['ɑːbɪtrɑːʒə(r)] *n Fin & St Exch* arbitragiste *m*

arbitrarily [*Br* 'ɑːbɪtrərəlɪ, *Am* ˌɑːrbə'trerəlɪ] *adv* arbitrairement

arbitrariness ['ɑːbɪtrərɪnɪs] *n (of decision, choice)* nature *f* arbitraire

arbitrary ['ɑːbɪtrərɪ] *adj* arbitraire

arbitrate ['ɑːbɪtreɪt] **1** *vt* arbitrer, juger

2 *vi* décider en qualité d'arbitre, arbitrer

arbitration [ˌɑːbɪ'treɪʃən] *n (gen) & Ind* arbitrage *m*; **to go to arbitration** *(of union)* soumettre le différend à l'arbitrage; *(of dispute)* être soumis à l'arbitrage; **they referred the dispute to arbitration** ils ont soumis le conflit à l'arbitrage; **settlement by arbitration** règlement *m* par arbitrage

►► ***arbitration board*** commission *f* d'arbitrage; ***arbitration court*** instance *f* chargée d'arbitrer les conflits sociaux, tribunal *m* arbitral; ***arbitration clause*** clause *f* compromissoire; *Fin* ***arbitration of exchange*** arbitrage *m* de change; ***arbitration tribunal*** instance *f* chargée d'arbitrer les conflits sociaux, tribunal *m* arbitral

arbitrator ['ɑːbɪtreɪtə(r)] *n (gen) & Ind* arbitre *m*, médiateur(trice) *m,f*; **the dispute has been referred to the arbitrator** le litige a été soumis à l'arbitrage

arbor ['ɑːbə(r)] *n* (**a**) *Am Bot & Hort* tonnelle *f* (**b**) *Tech* arbre *m*, mandrin *m*

►► ***Arbor Day*** = jour férié aux États-Unis traditionnellement consacré à la plantation d'arbres

arboreal [ɑː'bɔːrɪəl] *adj Bot (relating to trees)* d'arbre(s); *(animal, technique)* arboricole

arborescence [ˌɑːbə'resəns] *n Bot* arborescence *f*

arborescent [ˌɑːbə'resənt] *adj Bot* arborescent

arboretum [ˌɑːbə'riːtəm] (*pl* **arboretums** *or* **arboreta** [-iːtə]) *n Hort* arboretum *m*

arboriculture ['ɑːbərɪkʌltʃə(r)] *n Hort* arboriculture *f*

arboriculturist [ˌɑːbərɪ'kʌltʃərɪst] *n Hort* arboriculteur(trice) *m,f*

arborio rice [ɑː'bɔːrɪəʊ-] *n* riz *m* arborio

arbour, *Am* **arbor** ['ɑːbə(r)] *n Bot & Hort* tonnelle *f*

arbutus [ɑː'bjuːtəs] *n Bot & Hort* arbousier *m*

►► ***arbutus berry*** arbouse *f*

ARC [ˌeɪɑː'siː] *n* (**a**) *Med* (*abbr* **aids-related complex**) ARC *m* (**b**) (*abbr* **American Red Cross**) **the ARC** la Croix-Rouge américaine

arc [ɑːk] **1** *n* (**a**) *Geom (of circle)* arc *m*; **to describe an arc** décrire un arc; *Mil* **arc of fire** *(of cannon etc)* champ *m* de tir (**b**) *Elec* arc *m*

2 *vi* (**a**) *(gen)* décrire un arc; **the ball arced up into the air** la balle décrivit un arc de cercle dans les airs (**b**) *Elec* faire jaillir un arc électrique

►► ***arc lamp, arc light*** *Elec* lampe *f* à arc; *Cin & TV* sunlight *m*

arcade [ɑː'keɪd] *n* (**a**) *Archit (set of arches)* arcade *f*, galerie *f* (**b**) *Com (for shopping)* galerie *f* marchande (**c**) *(amusement arcade)* salle *f* de jeux électroniques

►► ***arcade game*** jeu *m* électronique

Arcadia [ɑː'keɪdɪə] *n* Arcadie *f*; **in Arcadia** en Arcadie

Arcadian [ɑː'keɪdɪən] **1** *n* Arcadien(enne) *m,f*

2 *adj* arcadien, d'Arcadie

Arcady ['ɑːkədɪ] *n* Arcadie *f*; **in Arcady** en Arcadie

arcane [ɑː'keɪn] **1** *adj* mystérieux, ésotérique; *(knowledge, practice, ritual)* secret(ète)

2 *n* **the arcane** le mystérieux

arch [ɑːtʃ] **1** *n* (**a**) *Archit* arc *m*; *(in church)* arc *m*, voûte *f*; *Constr (of bridge, viaduct)* arche *f*

(**b**) *Anat (of eyebrows)* courbe *f*; *(of foot)* cambrure *f*, voûte *f* plantaire; **to have fallen arches** avoir les pieds plats *ou Spec* un affaissement de la voûte plantaire

2 *vt* arquer, cambrer; **he arched his back** il a cambré le dos; **the cat arched its back** le chat fit le gros dos

3 *vi* former voûte, s'arquer

4 *adj* (**a**) *(leading)* grand, par excellence; **my arch rival** mon principal adversaire; **he is an arch traitor** c'est le traître par excellence; **the arch villain in the play** le principal scélérat de la pièce

(**b**) *(mischievous)* coquin, espiègle; *(look, smile, tone)* malin(igne), espiègle

(**c**) *(supercilious → voice, manner)* condescendant

►► *Archit* ***arch stone*** claveau *m*, voussoir *m*

archaeological, *Am* **archeological** [ˌɑːkɪə'lɒdʒɪkəl] *adj* archéologique

archaeologically, *Am* **archeologically** [ˌɑːkɪə'lɒdʒɪkəlɪ] *adv* archéologiquement

archaeologist, *Am* **archeologist** [ˌɑːkɪ'ɒlədʒɪst] *n* archéologue *mf*

archaeology, *Am* **archeology** [ˌɑːkɪ'ɒlədʒɪ] *n* archéologie *f*

archaeometry, *Am* **archeometry** [ˌɑːkɪ'ɒmɪtrɪ] *n Archeol* archéométrie *f*

archaeopteryx, *Am* **archeopteryx** [ˌɑːkɪ'ɒptərɪks] *n Orn* archéoptéryx *m*

archaic [ɑː'keɪɪk] *adj* archaïque

archaism ['ɑːkeɪɪzəm] *n Ling* archaïsme *m*

archaize, -ise ['ɑːkeɪaɪz] *vt* donner une apparence archaïque à

archangel ['ɑːkˌeɪndʒəl] *n* archange *m*; **the Archangel Gabriel** l'archange Gabriel, saint Gabriel archange

archbishop [ˌɑːtʃ'bɪʃəp] *n Rel* archevêque *m*; **archbishop's palace** palais *m* archiépiscopal

►► ***the Archbishop of Canterbury*** l'archevêque *m* de Cantorbéry; ***the Archbishop of Westminster*** l'archevêque *m* de Westminster; ***the Archbishop of York*** l'archevêque *m* de York

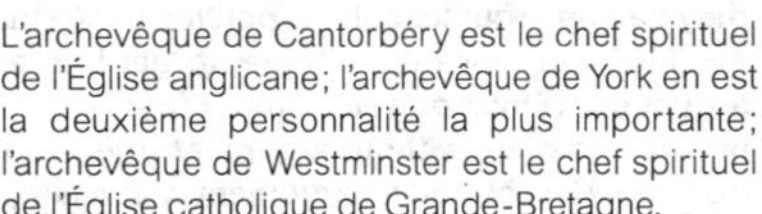

ARCHBISHOP

L'archevêque de Cantorbéry est le chef spirituel de l'Église anglicane; l'archevêque de York en est la deuxième personnalité la plus importante; l'archevêque de Westminster est le chef spirituel de l'Église catholique de Grande-Bretagne.

archbishopric [ˌɑːtʃ'bɪʃəprɪk] *n Rel* archevêché *m*

archdeacon [ˌɑːtʃ'diːkən] *n Rel* archidiacre *m*

archdiocese [ˌɑːtʃ'daɪəsɪs] *n Rel* archidiocèse *m*

archduchess [ˌɑːtʃ'dʌtʃɪs] *n* archiduchesse *f*

archduchy [ˌɑːtʃ'dʌtʃɪ] (*pl* **archduchies**) *n* archiduché *m*

archduke [ˌɑːtʃ'djuːk] *n* archiduc *m*

arched [ɑːtʃt] *adj* (**a**) *Archit (roof, window)* cintré (**b**) *Anat (back, foot)* cambré; *(eyebrows)* arqué

archenemy [ˌɑːtʃ'enɪmɪ] (*pl* **archenemies**) *n* pire ennemi *m*; *Rel* **the Archenemy** Satan

archeological, archeologically *etc Am* = **archaeological, archaeologically** *etc*

archeometry *Am* = **archaeometry**

archeopteryx *Am* = **archaeopteryx**

archer ['ɑːtʃə(r)] *n* archer *m*; *Astron* **the Archer** le Sagittaire

►► ***archer fish*** archer *m* cracheur

Archers ['ɑːtʃəz] *npl Br Rad* **The Archers** = feuilleton radiophonique fleuve qui a pour cadre un village imaginaire en Angleterre, diffusé par la BBC depuis 1951

archery ['ɑːtʃərɪ] *n* tir *m* à l'arc

archetypal [ˌɑːkɪ'taɪpəl] *adj* **the archetypal English village** l'archétype *m* du village anglais

archetype ['ɑːkɪtaɪp] *n* archétype *m*

archetypical [ˌɑːkɪ'tɪpɪkəl] = **archetypal**

archidiaconal [ˌɑːkɪdaɪ'ækənəl] *adj Rel* d'archidiacre

Archie ['ɑːtʃɪ] *n Comput* Archie *m*

Archie Bunker *pr n TV* = personnage d'un feuilleton télévisé américain des années 70, stéréotype de l'ouvrier réactionnaire et raciste

archiepiscopal [ˌɑːkɪɪ'pɪskəpəl] *adj Rel* archiépiscopal

Archimedes [ˌɑːkɪ'miːdiːz] *pr n* Archimède

►► *Phys* ***Archimedes' principle*** le principe d'Archimède; *Tech* ***Archimedes' screw*** vis *f* d'Archimède

archipelago [ˌɑːkɪ'pelɪgəʊ] (*pl* **archipelagoes** *or* **archipelagos**) *n Geog* archipel *m*

archiphoneme ['ɑːkɪˌfəʊniːm] *n Ling* archiphonème *m*

architect ['ɑːkɪtekt] *n* architecte *mf*; *Fig* artisan *m*, créateur(trice) *m,f*; **to be the architect of one's own downfall** être l'artisan de sa propre ruine

architectonic [ˌɑːkɪtek'tɒnɪk] *adj* architectonique

architectonics [ˌɑːkɪtek'tɒnɪks] *n (UNCOUNT)* architectonique *f*, architectonie *f*

architectural [ˌɑːkɪ'tektʃərəl] *adj* architectural

architecturally [ˌɑːkɪ'tektʃərəlɪ] *adv* au *ou* du point de vue architectural

architecture ['ɑːkɪtektʃə(r)] *n* architecture *f*

architrave ['ɑːkɪtreɪv] *n Archit* architrave *f*

archive ['ɑːkaɪv] **1** *n (usu pl)* **archives** archives *fpl*; **a national archive of photographs** des archives nationales de photographies

2 *comp (photo)* d'archives

3 *vt (gen) & Comput* archiver

►► *Comput* ***archive copy*** copie *f* archivée; *Comput* ***archive file*** fichier *m* d'archives; *TV* ***archive footage*** extraits *mpl* d'archives; ***archive material*** matériel *m* d'archives; *Comput* ***archive site*** site *m* FTP

archivist ['ɑːkɪvɪst] *n* archiviste *mf*

archly ['ɑːtʃlɪ] *adv* (**a**) *(mischievously)* d'un air espiègle *ou* malicieux; *(say)* d'un ton espiègle *ou* malicieux (**b**) *(condescendingly)* avec condescendance

archness ['ɑːtʃnɪs] *n* (**a**) *(mischief)* espièglerie *f*, malice *f* (**b**) *(condescension)* condescendance *f*

archpriest [ˌɑːtʃ'priːst] *n Rel* archiprêtre *m*

archway ['ɑːtʃweɪ] *n* porche *m*; *(long)* galerie *f*, arcades *fpl*

ARCM [ˌeɪɑːˌsiː'em] *n Mus* (*abbr* **Associate of the Royal College of Music**) = membre associé du "Royal College of Music"

arctic ['ɑːktɪk] **1** *adj* (**a**) *Met* arctique (**b**) *Fam (very cold)* glacial; **there was a spell of arctic weather** il a fait un froid polaire

2 *n Am (overshoe)* couvre-chaussure *m*

3 Arctic *n (ocean)* l'Arctique *m*, l'océan Arctique; **in the Arctic** dans l'Arctique; **an expedition to the Arctic** une expédition dans l'Arctique

►► ***the Arctic Circle*** le cercle polaire arctique; ***Arctic fox*** isatis *m*; ***the Arctic Ocean*** l'(océan *m*) Arctique *m*; *Orn* ***Arctic redpoll*** sizerin *m* blanchâtre; *Orn* ***Arctic skua*** labbe *m* parasite; *Orn* ***Arctic tern*** sterne *f* arctique

arctoid ['ɑːktɔɪd] *adj Zool (relating to bears)* relatif aux ours; *(bear-like)* qui ressemble à un ours

arctophile ['ɑːktəʊfaɪl] *n* arctophile *mf*

arc-weld *vt Tech* souder à l'arc

arc-welding *n Tech* soudure *f* à l'arc

ardency ['ɑːdənsɪ] *n Literary* ardeur *f*

ardent ['ɑːdənt] *adj (desire, love)* passionné, ardent; **an ardent admirer** un fervent admirateur

ardently ['ɑːdəntlɪ] *adv* ardemment, passionnément

ardour, *Am* **ardor** ['ɑːdə(r)] *n (of passion, desire)* ardeur *f*; *(religious)* ferveur *f*

arduous ['ɑːdjʊəs] *adj* ardu, difficile; *(work, task)* laborieux, pénible; *(path)* ardu, raide; *(hill)* raide, escarpé

arduously ['ɑːdjʊəslɪ] *adv* péniblement, laborieusement

arduousness ['ɑːdjʊəsnɪs] *n* difficulté *f*

are[1] [ə(r), *stressed* ɑː(r)] *see* **be**

are[2] [ɑː(r)] *n* are *m*

area ['eərɪə] **1** *n* (**a**) *(surface size)* superficie *f*, aire *f*; **the garden is 500 m² in area, the garden has** *ou* **covers an area of 500 m²** le jardin a une superficie de 500 m²

(**b**) *(region)* territoire *m*, région *f*; *(of town)* zone *f*, quartier *m*; *(of lung, brain, diskette, surface)* zone *f*; **houses were searched over a wide area** on a fouillé les maisons sur un large périmètre; **we're staying in the Boston area** nous logeons dans la région de Boston; **in the whole area** *(neighbourhood)* dans tout le quartier; *(political region)* dans toute la région; **area of operations** branche *f* d'activité; **residential area** *(in town)* quartier *m* résidentiel; **industrial/suburban area** zone *f* industrielle/suburbaine; **cotton (growing)/mining area** région *f* du coton/minière; **customs area** territoire *m* douanier; *Fin* **currency area** zone *f* monétaire; **the Manchester area** la région de Manchester; **the Greater London area** l'agglomération *f* londonienne, le grand Londres; **area of agreement** terrain *m* d'entente; *Fig* **problem area** domaine *m* problématique; **growth area** secteur *m* de croissance; *Mil etc* **forward area** zone *f* de l'avant, zone *f* avancée; **prohibited** *or* **restricted area** zone *f* prohibée; *Comput* **storage area** zone *f* de mémoire; *Transp* **service area** *(on motorway)* relais *m* d'autoroute; **a residential/shopping area** un quartier résidentiel/commercial; *Ecol* **a conservation area** un site classé; *Ecol* **a protected wildlife area** une réserve naturelle; *Ecol* **area of outstanding natural beauty** = zone naturelle protégée

(**c**) *(part, section)* partie *f*; *(of room)* coin *m*; **living/eating area** coin salon/salle à manger; **a large kitchen area** une grande cuisine; **play area** *(in park)* aire *f* de jeu; **parking area** parking *m*, aire *m ou Can* terrain *m* de stationnement; **smoking area** espace *m* fumeurs

(**d**) *(of study, investigation, experience)* domaine *m*, champ *m*; **area of expertise** domaine *m* de compétence; **in the foreign policy area** dans le domaine de la politique étrangère

2 *comp (director, office)* régional

►► *Mil* ***area bombing*** bombardement *m* sur zone; *Tel* ***area code*** indicatif *m* de zone; ***area manager*** directeur(trice) *m,f* régional(e); *Am* ***area rug*** tapis *m*, *Can* carpette *f*; *Mktg* ***area sample*** échantillon *m* par zone; *Mktg* ***area sampling*** échantillonnage *m* par zone

areaway ['eərɪəweɪ] *n* courette *f* en contre-bas

areca ['ærɪkə] *n Bot (tree)* aréquier *m*

►► ***areca nut*** noix *f* d'arec; ***areca tree*** aréquier *m*

arena [ə'ri:nə] *n* arène *f*; *Fig (economic, international etc)* scène *f*; **the challenger entered the arena** le challenger est descendu dans l'arène; *Fig* **to enter the arena** entrer dans l'arène; *Fig* **the political arena** l'arène *f* politique

aren't [ɑ:nt] (**a**) = **are not** (**b**) **aren't I?** = **am I not?**

areola [ə'ri:ələ] *(pl* **areolas** *or* **areolae** [-ˌli:]) *n Anat* aréole *f*

Arethusa [ˌærɪ'θju:zə] *pr n Myth* Aréthuse

argentiferous [ˌɑ:dʒen'tɪfərəs] *adj Miner* argentifère

Argentina [ˌɑ:dʒən'ti:nə] *n* Argentine *f*; **in Argentina** en Argentine

Argentine ['ɑ:dʒəntaɪn] **1** *n* (**a**) *Old-fashioned* **the Argentine** *(country)* l'Argentine *f* (**b**) *(person)* Argentin(e) *m,f*

2 *adj* argentin

Argentinian [ˌɑ:dʒən'tɪnɪən] **1** *n* Argentin(e) *m,f*

2 *adj* argentin

3 *comp (embassy)* d'Argentine; *(history)* de l'Argentine

argentite ['ɑ:dʒəntaɪt] *n Miner* argentite *f*, argyrose *f*

argie-bargie = **argy-bargy**

arginine ['ɑ:dʒɪnaɪn] *n Biol & Chem* arginine *f*

argon ['ɑ:gɒn] *n Chem* argon *m*

Argonaut ['ɑ:gənɔ:t] *n Myth* **the Argonauts** les Argonautes *mpl*

argosy ['ɑ:gəsɪ] *(pl* **argosies**) *n Literary or Arch Naut* (**a**) *(ship)* galion *m* de commerce (**b**) *(fleet)* flotte *f* de galions

argot ['ɑ:gəʊ] *n Ling* argot *m*

arguable ['ɑ:gjʊəbəl] *adj* (**a**) *(questionable)* discutable, contestable; **that's arguable** c'est discutable; **it is arguable whether it would have made any difference** on peut se demander si cela aurait changé quelque chose (**b**) *(plausible)* défendable; **it is arguable that...** on peut soutenir que...

arguably ['ɑ:gjʊəblɪ] *adv* possiblement; **the Beatles are arguably the most popular group of all time** on pourrait dire *ou* on peut soutenir que les Beatles sont le groupe le plus populaire de tous les temps

argue ['ɑ:gju:] **1** *vt* (**a**) *(debate)* discuter, débattre; **a well-argued case** une cause bien présentée *ou* défendue; **he argued the case for lower taxes** il a plaidé en faveur d'une baisse des impôts; *Fam* **why do you always have to argue the toss** *or* **point?** pourquoi faut-il toujours que tu ergotes *ou* chicanes?

(**b**) *(person)* **he argued me into/out of staying** il m'a persuadé/dissuadé de rester; **they argued her into continuing her studies** ils l'ont convaincue *ou* persuadée de continuer ses études

(**c**) *(maintain)* soutenir, affirmer; **she argues that war is always pointless** elle affirme *ou* soutient que la guerre ne sert jamais à rien

(**d**) *Formal (indicate)* indiquer; **their attitude argues a certain ignorance** leur attitude indique une certaine ignorance

2 *vi* (**a**) *(quarrel)* se disputer; **to argue (with sb) about sth** se disputer (avec qn) au sujet de *ou* à propos de qch; **I'm not going to argue about it** *(I refuse to discuss it)* je ne veux pas en discuter; **don't let's argue** ne nous disputons pas; **he's always arguing** c'est un argumentateur; **don't argue!** pas de discussion!; **stop arguing!** arrêtez de vous disputer!; **she argues with her sister almost constantly** elle se dispute presque constamment avec sa sœur

(**b**) *(reason)* argumenter; **she argued for/against raising taxes** elle a soutenu qu'il fallait/ne fallait pas augmenter les impôts; **we argued (about it) all day** nous (en) avons discuté toute la journée; **he argued from the historical aspect** ses arguments étaient de nature historique; **the facts argue for the evolutionary theory** les faits plaident en faveur de la théorie évolutionniste

(**c**) *Law* témoigner; **everything argues in her favour** tout témoigne en sa faveur; **the evidence argues against him** les preuves sont contre lui

►**argue away 1** *vt sep (make disappear)* nier l'importance de

2 *vi* **they've been arguing away for hours** *(quarrelling)* ils se disputent depuis des heures; *(discussing)* ils discutent depuis des heures

►**argue out** *vt sep* régler; **I left them to argue it out** je les ai laissés chercher une solution

arguing ['ɑ:gju:ɪŋ] *n* **that's enough arguing** assez discuté; *Fam* **and no arguing!** pas de discussion!

argument ['ɑ:gjʊmənt] *n* (**a**) *(quarrel)* dispute *f*; **they had an argument about politics** ils se sont disputés à propos de politique; **to get into an argument (with/about)** se disputer (avec/à propos de); **to obey without argument** obéir sans discuter; *Hum* **he had an argument with a lamppost** il a rencontré un réverbère

(**b**) *(debate)* discussion *f*, débat *m*; **for the sake of argument** à titre d'exemple; **it is open to argument whether...** on peut s'interroger pour savoir si...; **you should listen to both sides of the argument** vous devriez écouter les deux versions de l'histoire; **she got the better of the argument** elle l'a emporté dans la discussion

(**c**) *(reasoning)* argument *m*; **I didn't follow his (line of) argument** je n'ai pas suivi son raisonnement; **their argument was that the plan was too expensive** ils soutenaient que le projet était trop cher; **there is a strong argument in favour of the proposal** il y a de bonnes raisons pour soutenir *ou* appuyer cette proposition; **let us suppose for argument's sake that...** supposons à titre d'exemple que... + *subjunctive*

(**d**) *Literature & Theat (of book, play)* argument *m*, sommaire *m*

argumentation [ˌɑ:gjʊmen'teɪʃən] *n* argumentation *f*

argumentative [ˌɑ:gjʊ'mentətɪv] *adj (person)* raisonneur, disposé à argumenter *ou* à disputailler; *(tone)* polémique, agressif; **don't be so argumentative** arrête de faire le raisonneur

argumentativeness [ˌɑ:gjʊ'mentətɪvnɪs] *n* esprit *m* raisonneur, disposition *f* à argumenter

Argus ['ɑ:gəs] *pr n Myth* Argos, Argus

argus pheasant ['ɑ:gəs-] *n Orn* argus *m*

Argy ['ɑ:dʒɪ] *n Br Fam* = terme injurieux désignant un Argentin

argy-bargy [ˌɑ:dʒɪ'bɑ:dʒɪ] *n (UNCOUNT) Fam* chamailleries *fpl*; **there was a bit of argy-bargy over who should do it** il y a eu des histoires pour savoir qui devait le faire

argyle [ɑ:'gaɪl] **1** *n* chaussette *f* avec des losanges

2 *adj* à motifs de losanges

aria ['ɑ:rɪə] *n Mus* aria *f*

Ariadne [ˌærɪ'ædnɪ] *pr n Myth* Ariane

Arian[1] ['eərɪən] **1** *n (who believes in Arianism)* Arien(enne) *m,f*

2 *adj (pertaining to Arianism)* arien

Arian[2] *Astrol* **1** *n* **to be an Arian** être (du signe du) Bélier

2 *adj* du Bélier

Arianism ['eərɪənɪzəm] *n Rel* arianisme *m*

ARIBA [ə'ri:bə] *n (abbr* **Associate of the Royal Institute of British Architects**) = membre associé du "Royal Institute of British Architects"

arid ['ærɪd] *adj* (**a**) *(dry)* aride (**b**) *Fig (of no interest)* aride, ingrat; *(fruitless)* stérile

aridity [ə'rɪdɪtɪ] *n* aridité *f*

aridly ['ærɪdlɪ] *adv* aridement

aridness ['ærɪdnɪs] *n* aridité *f*

Ariel ['eərɪəl] *n St Exch* = système informatique qui rend possible les operations boursières entre souscripteurs sans passer par la Bourse de Londres

Aries ['eəri:z] **1** *n* (**a**) *Astron* Bélier *m* (**b**) *Astrol* Bélier *m*; **he's an Aries** il est (du signe du) Bélier

2 *adj Astrol* du Bélier; **he's Aries** il est (du signe du) Bélier

aright [ə'raɪt] *adv* bien, correctement; **to set things aright** arranger les choses; **his explanation set matters aright** son explication a arrangé la situation *ou* l'affaire

arise [ə'raɪz] *(pt* **arose** [-'rəʊz], *pp* **arisen** [-'rɪzən]) *vi* (**a**) *(appear, happen)* survenir, se présenter; *Literary* **there arose a great cheer** des acclamations se firent entendre; **if complications should arise** si des complications survenaient; **a doubt arose in his mind** un doute est apparu dans son esprit; **if the need arises** en cas de besoin; **if the occasion arises** si l'occasion se présente

(**b**) *(result)* résulter; **a problem that arises from this decision** un problème qui résulte *ou* découle de cette décision; **matters arising from the last meeting** des questions soulevées lors de la dernière réunion

(**c**) *Literary (person)* se lever; *(sun)* se lever, paraître; *(storm)* se lever; **arise, Sir John!** *(in knighthood ceremony)* relevez-vous, Sir John; **to arise from the dead** ressusciter (des morts)

Aristides [ˌærɪ'staɪdi:z] *pr n* Aristide

aristocracy [ˌærɪ'stɒkrəsɪ] *(pl* **aristocracies**) *n* aristocratie *f*

aristocrat [*Br* 'ærɪstəkræt, *Am* ə'rɪstəkræt] *n* aristocrate *mf*

aristocratic [*Br* ˌærɪstə'krætɪk, *Am* əˌrɪstə'krætɪk] *adj* aristocratique

aristocratically [*Br* ˌærɪstə'krætɪkəlɪ, *Am* əˌrɪstə'krætɪkəlɪ] *adv* aristocratiquement

Aristophanes [ˌærɪ'stɒfəni:z] *pr n* Aristophane

Aristotelian [ˌærɪstɒ'ti:lɪən] *Phil* **1** *n* Aristotélicien(enne) *m,f*

2 *adj* aristotélicien

Aristotelianism [ˌærɪstɒ'ti:lɪənɪzəm] *n Phil* aristotélisme *m*

Aristotle ['ærɪstɒtəl] *pr n* Aristote

arithmetic 1 *n* [ə'rɪθmətɪk] *(calculations)* calcul *m*; *(subject)* arithmétique *f*; **my arithmetic is absolutely appalling** je suis nul en calcul; **your arithmetic is spot on** tes calculs tombent pile; **it's a simple question of arithmetic** les chiffres parlent d'eux-mêmes

2 *adj* [ˌærɪθ'metɪk] arithmétique

►► ***arithmetic progression*** progression *f* arithmétique

arithmetical [ˌærɪθ'metɪkəl] *adj* arithmétique

arithmetically [ˌærɪθ'metɪkəlɪ] *adv* arithmétiquement

arithmetician [əˌrɪθmə'tɪʃən] *n* arithméticien(enne) *m,f*

arithmology [ˌærɪθ'mɒlədʒɪ] *n Math* arithmologie *f*

Ariz *(written abbr* **Arizona**) Arizona *m*

Arizona [ˌærɪ'zəʊnə] *n* l'Arizona *m*; **in Arizona** en Arizona

ark [ɑ:k] *n* arche *f*; *Br Hum* **this machine must have come out of the ark** cet appareil doit remonter au déluge *ou* est vieux comme le monde; *Bible* **the Ark of the Covenant** l'Arche *f* d'alliance

'Schindler's Ark' *Keneally* 'La Liste de Schindler'

Arkansas ['ɑ:kənsɔ:] *n* l'Arkansas *m*; **in Arkansas** en *ou* dans l'Arkansas

Ark Royal *n Naut* = porte-avions de la Marine britannique coulé en 1941 au large de Gibraltar

Arlington National Cemetery ['ɑ:lɪŋtən-] *n* =

cimetière près de Washington où est enterré John F. Kennedy

arm [ɑːm] **1** *n* (**a**) *(part of the body)* bras *m*; **he carried a book under his arm** il portait un livre sous le bras; **to hold sb/sth in one's arms** tenir qn/qch dans ses bras; **with his wife on his arm** avec sa femme à son bras; **to walk arm in arm** marcher bras dessus bras dessous; **give me your arm** donne-moi le *ou* ton bras; **he offered her his arm** il lui a offert son bras; **she flung her arms around my neck** elle s'est jetée à mon cou; **he put his arm round her** il a passé son bras autour d'elle; **she put her arm round my shoulders** elle a passé son bras autour de mes épaules; **he took her in his arms** il l'a prise dans ses bras; **with arms folded** les bras croisés; **he stood with his arms wide apart** il se tenait les bras écartés; *Fig* **to welcome sb/sth with open arms** accueillir qn/qch à bras ouverts; **within arm's reach** à portée de la main; **at arm's length** à bout de bras; *Fig* **to keep sb at arm's length** tenir qn à distance; **a list as long as your arm** une liste qui n'en finit pas *ou* interminable; **the long arm of the law** le bras de la justice; *Fam* **I'd give my right arm for that job** je donnerais cher *ou* n'importe quoi pour obtenir cet emploi

(**b**) *(of clothing)* manche *f*

(**c**) *Tech (of record player, machinery)* bras *m*; *(of chair)* bras *m*, accoudoir *m*; *(of spectacle frames)* branche *f*

(**d**) *Geog (of sea)* bras *m*

(**e**) *(section)* section *f*, branche *f*; **Sinn Fein is the political arm of the IRA** Sinn Fein est la section politique de l'IRA

2 *vt* (**a**) *(person, country)* armer; *Fig* **armed with an umbrella** muni *ou* armé d'un parapluie; *Fig* **to arm oneself with the facts/evidence** s'armer de faits/preuves

(**b**) *Mil (missile)* munir d'une (tête d')ogive; *(bomb, fuse)* armer

3 *vi* s'armer, prendre les armes

►► ***arm wrestling*** bras *m* de fer

armada [ɑːˈmɑːdə] **1** *n Naut (fleet of warships)* armada *f*

2 Armada *n Hist* **the (Spanish) Armada** l'Invincible Armada *f*

armadillo [ˌɑːməˈdɪləʊ] *(pl* **armadillos***) n* tatou *m*

Armageddon [ˌɑːməˈgedən] *n Bible* Apocalypse *f*; *Fig* apocalypse *f*

Armalite® [ˈɑːməlaɪt] *n Mil* Armalite® *m*

armament [ˈɑːməmənt] **1** *n Mil* (**a**) *(fighting force)* force *f* de frappe (**b**) *(weaponry)* armement *m*, matériel *m* de guerre (**c**) *(preparation for war)* armement *m*

2 armaments *npl* armement *m*

armature [ˈɑːməˌtjʊə(r)] *n Tech (gen)* armature *f*; *(of magnet)* armature *f*; *Elec (of motor)* induit *m*; *Biol* carapace *f*

armband [ˈɑːmbænd] *n* brassard *m*; *(for swimming)* brassard *m*, flotteur *m*; **black armband** brassard *m* de deuil

armchair [ˈɑːmtʃeə(r)] **1** *n* fauteuil *m*

2 *comp (gardener, traveller)* en chambre

Armco® [ˈɑːmkəʊ] *n Br Transp (crash barrier)* glissière *f* de sécurité

armed [ɑːmd] *adj* (**a**) *(with weapons)* armé; **they were armed with knives** ils étaient armés de couteaux; *Fig* **the minister arrived at the press conference armed with pages of statistics** le ministre est arrivé à la conférence de presse armé *ou* muni de pages entières de statistiques; **armed to the teeth** armé jusqu'aux dents

(**b**) *Mil (missile)* muni d'une (tête d')ogive; *(bomb, fuse)* armé

►► *Mil* ***armed conflict*** conflit *m* armé; ***armed forces*** forces *fpl* armées; **to be in the armed forces** être dans les forces armées; *Law* ***armed robbery*** vol *m ou* attaque *f* à main armée

-armed [ɑːmd] *suff* aux bras...; **long-armed** aux bras longs; **one-armed** à un seul bras, manchot

Armenia [ɑːˈmiːnɪə] *n* Arménie *f*; **in Armenia** en Arménie

Armenian [ɑːˈmiːnɪən] **1** *n* (**a**) *(person)* Arménien(enne) *m,f* (**b**) *(language)* arménien *m*

2 *adj* arménien

3 *comp (embassy)* d'Arménie; *(history)* de l'Arménie; *(teacher)* d'arménien

armful [ˈɑːmfʊl] *n* brassée *f*; **she had an armful of flowers** elle portait une brassée de fleurs; **in armfuls, by the armful** par pleines brassées, par brassées entières

armhole [ˈɑːmhəʊl] *n* emmanchure *f*

armistice [ˈɑːmɪstɪs] *n Mil* armistice *m*

►► ***Armistice Day*** l'Armistice *m*

ARMISTICE DAY

En Grande-Bretagne l'Armistice est maintenant célébré le dimanche le plus proche du 11 novembre, qu'on appelle "Remembrance Sunday".

armless [ˈɑːmlɪs] *adj* sans bras

armlet [ˈɑːmlɪt] *n (armband)* brassard *m*; *(bracelet)* bracelet *m*

armor, armor-clad *etc Am* = **armour, armour-clad** *etc*

armorial [ɑːˈmɔːrɪəl] *Her* **1** *n* armorial *m*

2 *adj* armorial

►► ***armorial bearings*** armoiries *fpl*

Armorica [ɑːˈmɒrɪkə] *n Antiq* Armorique *f*

Armorican [ɑːˈmɒrɪkən] **1** *n* Armoricain(e) *m,f*

2 *adj Ling* armoricain

armour, *Am* **armor** [ˈɑːmə(r)] *n (UNCOUNT)* (**a**) *Hist (of knight etc)* armure *f*; **suit of armour** armure *f* complète; **in full armour** armé de pied en cap (**b**) *Mil (of vehicle, tank etc)* blindage *m*; *(of ship)* cuirasse *f*, cuirassement *m*, blindage (**c**) *Mil (units, vehicles)* blindés *mpl* (**d**) *(of animal)* carapace *f*

armour-clad, *Am* **armor-clad** *adj Mil* blindé; *(ship)* blindé, cuirassé

armoured, *Am* **armored** [ˈɑːməd] *adj* (**a**) *Mil* blindé (**b**) *(animal)* cuirassé, à carapace

►► ***armoured car*** voiture *f* blindée; *Mil* engin *m* blindé de reconnaissance; *(for cash, gold etc)* fourgon *m* blindé; *Mil* ***armoured fighting vehicle*** blindé *m*; ***armoured personnel carrier*** véhicule *m* blindé de transport de troupes; *Mil* ***armour plate, armour plating*** blindage *m*; *(on ship)* cuirasse *f*; ***armoured reconnaissance vehicle*** véhicule *m* blindé de reconnaissance; ***armoured tank*** blindé *m*

armourer, *Am* **armorer** [ˈɑːmərə(r)] *n Mil & Her* armurier *m*

armour-piercing, *Am* **armor-piercing** *adj Mil (mine, gun)* antichar; *(shell, bullet)* perforant

armour-plated, *Am* **armor-plated** *adj Mil* blindé; **an armour-plated vehicle** un véhicule blindé

armoury, *Am* **armory** [ˈɑːmərɪ] *(Br pl* **armouries,** *Am pl* **armories***) n Mil* arsenal *m*, dépôt *m* d'armes; *Fig (resources)* arsenal *m*; *Am (arms factory)* armurerie *f*, fabrique *f* d'armes

armpit [ˈɑːmpɪt] *n* aisselle *f*; *Fam Fig* **the armpit of the universe** *(place)* un coin paumé, un trou

armrest [ˈɑːmrest] *n* accoudoir *m*

arms [ɑːmz] *npl* (**a**) *Mil (weapons)* armes *fpl*; **to arms!** aux armes!; **to bear arms** porter les armes; **lay down your arms!** déposez vos armes!; **100,000 men under arms** 100 000 hommes sous les drapeaux; **to take up arms against sb/sth** s'insurger contre qn/qch; **the villagers are up in arms over the planned motorway** la proposition de construction d'une autoroute a provoqué une levée de boucliers parmi les villageois; **the unions are up in arms over the new legislation** les syndicats s'élèvent *ou* partent en guerre contre la nouvelle législation

(**b**) *Her* armes *fpl*, armoiries *fpl*

►► ***arms control*** contrôle *m* des armements; *Mil* ***arms dealer*** armurier *m*; ***arms embargo*** embargo *m* sur les armes; ***arms limitation talks*** négociations *fpl* pour la limitation des armements; ***arms manufacturer*** fabricant *m* d'armes, armurier *m*; *Mil* ***arms race*** course *f* aux armements; ***the arms trade*** le commerce d'armes

'Arms and the Man' *Shaw* 'Le Héros et le soldat'

arm's-length *adj (not intimate)* distant, froid; **they have an arm's-length relationship** ils gardent leurs distances

►► *Com* ***arm's-length price*** = prix fixé dans les conditions normales de la concurrence

arm-twisting *n (UNCOUNT) Fam* pressions❑ *fpl*; **it took a lot of arm-twisting to convince him** ça a été une véritable partie de bras de fer pour arriver à le convaincre

arm-wrestle *vi* **to arm-wrestle with sb** faire une partie de bras de fer avec qn

army [ˈɑːmɪ] *(pl* **armies***)* **1** *n* (**a**) *Mil* armée *f* (de terre); **to go into** *or* **to join the army** s'engager; **he was drafted into the army** il a été appelé sous les drapeaux; **she is going into the army** elle s'engage; **is he in the army?** est-ce qu'il est militaire *ou* dans l'armée?; **an army of occupation** une armée d'occupation

(**b**) *Fig (multitude)* foule *f*, multitude *f*; *(of ants)* armée *f*; **there was enough food for an army** il y avait assez de nourriture pour un régiment; **an army of tourists descend on the town every summer** une armée de touristes envahit la ville tous les étés

2 *comp Mil (life, nurse, truck, uniform)* militaire; *(family)* de militaires

►► *Entom* ***army ant*** fourmi *f* légionnaire; ***army barracks*** caserne *f*, baraquement *m* militaire; *Am Fam* ***army brat*** gosse *mf* de militaire *ou* de militaires; ***army corps*** corps *m* d'armée; *Br Mil* ***Army List*** annuaire *m* militaire *ou* des officiers de carrière *(de l'armée de terre)*; ***army officer*** officier *m* de l'armée de terre

arnica [ˈɑːnɪkə] *n Bot & Pharm* arnica *f*

aroma [əˈrəʊmə] *n* arôme *m*; **an aroma of coffee** un arôme de café

aromatherapist [əˌrəʊməˈθerəpɪst] *n* spécialiste *mf* en aromathérapie, aromathérapeute *mf*

aromatherapy [əˌrəʊməˈθerəpɪ] *n* aromathérapie *f*

aromatic [ˌærəˈmætɪk] **1** *n* aromate *m*

2 *adj (herb, tea, smell)* aromatique

►► *Chem* ***aromatic compound*** carbure *m* aromatiques *ou* à noyau

aromatize, -ise [əˈrəʊmətaɪz] *vt Chem* aromatiser

arose [əˈrəʊz] *pt of* **arise**

AROUND [əˈraʊnd]

autour	► **1 (a)**
pas loin	► **1 (b)**
ici et là	► **1 (d)**
autour de	► **2 (a), (c)**

1 *adv* (**a**) *(in all directions)* autour; **the fields all around** les champs tout autour; **for five miles around** sur *ou* dans un rayon de cinq miles

(**b**) *(nearby)* pas loin; **stay** *or* **stick around** reste dans les parages; **he's around somewhere** il n'est pas loin, il est dans le coin; **will you be around this afternoon?** tu seras là cet après-midi?; **see you around!** à un de ces jours!

(**c**) *(in existence)* **that firm has been around for years** cette société existe depuis des années; **he's one of the most promising actors around at the moment** c'est un des acteurs les plus prometteurs que l'on puisse voir en ce moment; **there wasn't much money around in those days** les gens n'avaient pas beaucoup d'argent à l'époque; **he won't be around long!** il ne fera pas de vieux os!

(**d**) *(here and there)* ici et là; **to travel around** voyager; **to wander around** faire un tour; **I don't know my way around yet** je suis encore un peu perdu; *Fam* **he's been around** *(has travelled widely)* il a pas mal roulé sa bosse; *(is experienced)* il n'est pas né d'hier

2 *prep* (**a**) *(encircling)* autour de; **seated around a table** assis autour d'une table; **the people around us** les gens qui nous entourent *ou* autour de nous; **the area around Berlin** les alentours *mpl ou* les environs *mpl* de Berlin; **the tree measures two metres around the trunk** l'arbre mesure deux mètres de circonférence; *Fig* **find a way (to get) around the problem** trouvez un moyen de contourner le problème; **my keys are somewhere around here** mes clés sont quelque part par ici

(**b**) *(within)* **they travelled around Europe** ils ont voyagé à travers l'Europe; **we strolled around town** nous nous sommes promenés en ville

(**c**) *(approximately)* autour de; **around midnight** autour de *ou* vers minuit; **around five o'clock** vers cinq heures; **around 1920** vers *ou* aux alentours de 1920; **he's around your age** il a environ *ou* à peu près votre âge

'Around the World in 80 Days' *Verne, Anderson*
'Le Tour du monde en 80 jours'

around-the-clock *adj* **around-the-clock protection/surveillance** protection *f*/surveillance *f* 24 heures sur 24

arousal [ə'raʊzəl] *n* (**a**) *(stimulation)* excitation *f*, stimulation *f* (**b**) *(of interest, suspicion)* éveil *m*; *(of anger)* soulèvement *m*

arouse [ə'raʊz] *vt* (**a**) *(stimulate)* stimuler, provoquer; **the sound aroused their curiosity/suspicions** le bruit a éveillé leur curiosité/leurs soupçons; **his pleading aroused their contempt** ses implorations n'ont suscité que leur mépris; **sexually aroused** excité (sexuellement) (**b**) *(awaken)* réveiller, éveiller; **he aroused her from a deep sleep** il l'a tirée d'un profond sommeil

ARP [,eɪɑː'piː] *n Br Hist* (*abbr* **air-raid precautions**) *(measures)* = mesures de défense civile lors des bombardements aériens pendant la Deuxième Guerre mondiale; **the ARP** *(organization)* = organisation chargée de mettre en œuvre les mesures de défense civile lors des bombardements aériens pendant la Deuxième Guerre mondiale

►► ***ARP warden*** = agent chargé de faire appliquer les mesures de défense civile lors des bombardements aériens pendant la Deuxième Guerre mondiale

arpeggiate [ɑː'pedʒɪeɪt] *vt Mus (chord)* arpéger

arpeggiated [ɑː'pedʒɪeɪtɪd] *adj Mus (chord)* arpégé

arpeggio [ɑː'pedʒɪəʊ] *n Mus* arpège *m*

arquebus ['ɑːkwɪbəs] *n Mil* arquebuse *f*

arquebusier [,ɑːkwɪbə'sɪə(r)] *n Mil* arquebusier *m*

ARR [,eɪɑː'rɑː(r)] *n Acct* (*abbr* **accounting rate of return**) taux *m* de rendement comptable

arr. (*written abbr* **arrives**) *(on timetable)* arrive

arrack ['ærək] *n* arak *m*, arac *m*, arack *m*

arraign [ə'reɪn] *vt Law* traduire en justice; *Fig* accuser, mettre en cause

arraignment [ə'reɪnmənt] *n Law* (**a**) *(of person)* mise *f* en accusation *ou* en jugement (**b**) *(charges)* acte *m* d'accusation

arrange [ə'reɪndʒ] **1** *vt* (**a**) *(put in order)* ranger, mettre en ordre; *(clothing, room)* arranger; *(flowers)* arranger, disposer; **the chairs were arranged in a circle** les chaises étaient disposées en cercle; **arrange the books in alphabetical order** rangez les livres par ordre alphabétique; **the room was arranged as an office** la pièce a été aménagée en bureau

(**b**) *(organize, plan)* organiser, arranger; *(date, time)* fixer; **I can arrange a loan** je peux m'arranger pour obtenir un prêt; **I'll arrange a table for eight o'clock** je vais réserver une table pour vingt heures; **it has been arranged for us to travel by train** il a été décidé *ou* convenu que nous voyagerions en train; **let's arrange a time to meet** fixons (une heure pour) un rendez-vous; **that can be arranged** cela peut s'arranger; **arrange it amongst yourselves** arrangez cela entre vous, entendez-vous là-dessus; **the meeting is arranged for noon tomorrow** la réunion est prévue pour demain midi; **I've got nothing arranged** je n'ai rien de prévu; **here is the first instalment, as arranged** *(money)* voici le premier versement, comme convenu; **don't worry, I'll arrange it** ne vous en faites pas, je vais m'en occuper; **everything is arranged** tout est déjà arrangé; **to arrange one's affairs** mettre ses affaires en ordre; **to arrange a marriage** arranger un mariage

(**c**) *(dispute)* régler, arranger

(**d**) *Mus & Theat* adapter; **he arranged the concerto for guitar** il a adapté le concerto pour la guitare

2 *vi* **to arrange to do sth** *(make preparations)* s'arranger *ou* prendre ses dispositions pour faire qch; *(with somebody else)* convenir de faire qch; **I've arranged with the boss to leave early tomorrow** je me suis arrangé avec le patron pour partir de bonne heure demain; **we arranged to meet** nous avons prévu de nous rencontrer; **I think I'll arrange to be out when he comes** je crois que je m'arrangerai pour être sorti quand il viendra; **he's arranged for the car to be repaired** il a fait le nécessaire pour faire réparer la voiture

arranged [ə'reɪndʒd] *adj*

►► *Mktg* ***arranged interview*** entretien *m* organisé; ***arranged marriage*** mariage *m* arrangé

arrangement [ə'reɪndʒmənt] **1** *n* (**a**) *(usu pl) (plan)* disposition *f*, arrangement *m*; **what are the travel arrangements?** comment le voyage est-il organisé?; **what are the sleeping arrangements?** où est-ce qu'on dort?; **I haven't made any arrangements for the journey yet** je n'ai pas encore fait de *ou* mes préparatifs pour le voyage; **I've made all the arrangements** j'ai tout arrangé; **could you make arrangements to change the date of the meeting?** pouvez-vous faire le nécessaire pour changer la date de la réunion?; **he made arrangements to leave work early** il s'est arrangé pour quitter son travail de bonne heure; **an arrangement whereby you pay monthly** un arrangement selon lequel vous effectuez des paiements mensuels

(**b**) *(understanding, agreement)* arrangement *m*; *Fin (with creditors)* accommodement *m*; **we can come to an** *or* **some arrangement on the price** pour le prix, nous pouvons nous arranger; **he came to an arrangement with the bank** il est parvenu à un accord avec la banque; **the arrangement was that I would call you when I arrived** on s'était mis d'accord pour que je t'appelle à mon arrivée; **a private arrangement** un accord à l'amiable

(**c**) *(layout)* arrangement *m*, disposition *f*; *(of room)* aménagement *m*; *(of clothing, hair)* arrangement *m*

(**d**) *Mus & Theat* adaptation *f*, arrangement *m*

2 by arrangement *adv* **price by arrangement** prix à débattre; **we make special designs by arrangement** nous faisons autres modèles à la demande; **by prior arrangement** sur accord préalable; **by arrangement with the town hall** avec l'autorisation de la mairie; **he sold the stock by arrangement with the company** il s'est arrangé *ou* entendu avec la société pour vendre les actions; **viewing by arrangement with the owner** pour visiter, prenez rendez-vous avec *ou* contactez le propriétaire

arranger [ə'reɪndʒə(r)] *n Mus* arrangeur(euse) *m,f*

arrant ['ærənt] *adj* fini, parfait; **don't talk such arrant rubbish** comment est-ce que tu peux dire des bêtises pareilles?

arras ['ærəs] (*pl* **inv**) *n* tapisserie *f*

array [ə'reɪ] **1** *n* (**a**) *(collection)* ensemble *m* impressionnant, collection *f*; **a distinguished array of people** une assemblée de gens distingués; **there was a fine array of cakes in the window** il y avait une belle sélection de gâteaux en vitrine

(**b**) *Law, Comput & Math* tableau *m*, matrice *f*; **an array of data** un tableau de données

(**c**) *(of solar panels, batteries etc)* série *f*

(**d**) *Mil* rang *m*, ordre *m*; **in battle array** en ordre de bataille; **in close array** en rangs serrés

(**e**) *(fine clothes)* parure *f*, atours *mpl*; *(ceremonial dress)* habit *m* d'apparat

2 *vt* (**a**) *(arrange)* disposer, étaler; *Mil (troops)* déployer, disposer

(**b**) *Literary (adorn)* habiller, revêtir; **she was arrayed in silks** elle était vêtue de soie

arrears [ə'rɪəz] *npl Fin* arriéré *m*; **your arrears now amount to over £2,000** vos arriérés s'élèvent maintenant à plus de 2000 livres; **taxes in arrears** arriéré *m* d'impôts; **to get into arrears** s'arriérer; **I'm worried about getting into arrears** j'ai peur de m'endetter; **we're six months in arrears on the loan payments** nous devons six mois de traites; **to be paid a month in arrears** être payé un mois après; **she's in arrears with her correspondence** elle a du retard dans sa correspondance; **interest on arrears** intérêts *mpl* moratoires; **arrears of interest** intérêts *mpl* non payés; **arrears of work** du travail en retard

arrest [ə'rest] **1** *n* (**a**) *(detention)* arrestation *f*; **you're under arrest!** vous êtes en état d'arrestation!; **he was put under arrest** il a été arrêté; **several arrests were made** plusieurs personnes ont été arrêtées; **to make an arrest** *(of police officer)* procéder à une arrestation; *Mil* **to be under arrest** être aux arrêts; **they put him under arrest** ils l'ont mis aux arrêts; **open/close arrest** arrêts *mpl* simples/de rigueur

(**b**) *(sudden stopping)* arrêt *m*, suspension *f*

2 *vt* (**a**) *(person)* arrêter, appréhender; *Scot (property, ship)* saisir

(**b**) *Formal (growth, development → halt)* arrêter; *(→ slow down)* entraver, retarder; **in an effort to arrest unemployment/inflation** pour essayer d'enrayer le chômage/l'inflation; *Med* **arrested development** *(physical)* arrêt *m* de croissance; *(mental)* atrophie *f* de la personnalité; *Law* **to arrest judgement** surseoir à un jugement, suspendre l'exécution d'un jugement

(**c**) *Formal (attention)* attirer, retenir

3 *vi Med* avoir un arrêt cardiaque

►► *Law* ***arrest warrant*** mandat *m* d'arrêt

arrestable [ə'restəbəl] *adj (person)* qui risque d'être appréhendé; *(offence)* répréhensible

arrester [ə'restə(r)] *n Tech* intercepteur *m*, séparateur *m*; **spark arrester** pare-étincelles *m inv*

►► ***arrester gear*** *Aviat (on runway)* dispositif *m* d'arrêt; *Aviat & Naut (on carrier deck)* dispositif *m* d'appontage

arresting [ə'restɪŋ] *adj* saisissant, frappant; **the arresting officer** le policier qui a effectué/qui effectue l'arrestation

arrestingly [ə'restɪŋlɪ] *adv* **arrestingly beautiful** d'une beauté frappante

arrhythmia [ə'rɪðmɪə] *n Med* arythmie *f*

arrhythmic [ə'rɪðmɪk] *n Med* arythmique

arrival [ə'raɪvəl] *n* (**a**) *(of person, train, aeroplane etc)* arrivée *f*; **on** *or* **upon arrival** à l'arrivée; **arrivals and departures** les arrivées et les départs *mpl*

(**b**) *(newcomer)* **a new arrival** un nouveau venu (une nouvelle venue); *(baby)* un nouveau-né (une nouveau-née); *(book)* une dernière parution; **late arrivals** retardataires *mpl*

(**c**) *Com (of goods)* arrivage *m*

(**d**) *(advent)* avènement *m*; **the arrival of the motor car** l'apparition *f ou* l'avènement de l'automobile

►► ***arrivals board*** tableau *m* des arrivées; ***arrivals lounge*** salon *m* des arrivées; ***arrival time*** heure *f* d'arrivée

arrive [ə'raɪv] *vi* (**a**) *(person, train, aeroplane etc)* arriver; **I've just arrived** j'arrive à l'instant; **as soon as you arrive** dès votre arrivée, dès que vous arriverez; **as soon as he arrived** dès son arrivée; **he arrived in the nick of time** il est arrivé juste à temps; **the first post arrives at eight o'clock** le premier courrier est à huit heures; **the baby arrived three weeks early** le bébé est arrivé *ou* est né avec trois semaines d'avance; **to arrive on the scene** survenir; **to arrive unexpectedly** survenir, arriver à l'improviste; **the time has arrived for us to take action, the time for action has arrived** le moment est venu pour nous d'agir

(**b**) *Fam (achieve success)* réussir[❑], arriver; **you know you've really arrived when...** on sait qu'on a vraiment réussi le jour où...; **she finally arrived after years of singing in backstreet bars** elle connut enfin le succès après avoir chanté pendant des années dans des bars miteux

►**arrive at** *vt insep* (**a**) *(decision)* arriver *ou* parvenir à; *(perfection)* atteindre; **we finally arrived at the conclusion that...** nous en sommes finalement arrivés à la conclusion que... (**b**) *(price)* fixer; **they finally arrived at a price** ils se sont finalement mis d'accord sur un prix

arrogance ['ærəgəns] *n* arrogance *f*, morgue *f*

arrogant ['ærəgənt] *adj* arrogant, insolent

arrogantly ['ærəgəntlɪ] *adv* de manière arrogante, avec arrogance

arrogate ['ærəgeɪt] *vt Formal* (**a**) *(claim unjustly)* revendiquer à tort, s'arroger; *(victory)* s'attribuer (**b**) *(assign unjustly)* attribuer injustement (**to sb** à qn)

arrogation [,ærə'geɪʃən] *n Formal (claim)* prétention *f* mal fondée; *(act)* usurpation *f*; **the arrogation of the fortune** l'usurpation de la fortune

arrow ['ærəʊ] **1** *n* (**a**) *(missile)* flèche *f*; **to loose** *or* **to shoot** *or* **to let fly an arrow** décocher une flèche; **the ball flew as straight as an arrow into the net** la balle alla voler tout droit dans le filet; **as swift as an arrow** vif comme l'éclair

(**b**) *(indicating direction → on sign etc)* flèche *f*; *(→ of surveyor)* fiche *f*

(**c**) *Br Fam* **arrows** *(darts)* fléchettes ❑ *fpl*

2 *vt* (**a**) *(indicate → on list)* cocher; *(→ on road sign)* flécher (**b**) *(in editing)* indiquer au moyen d'une flèche; **to arrow a correction in** indiquer l'emplacement d'une correction (au moyen d'une flèche)

►► *Bot* ***arrow grass*** triglochin *m*, troscart *m*; *Comput* ***arrow key*** touche *f* fléchée, touche *f* de direction; ***arrow slit*** *(in building)* arbalétrière

arrowhead ['ærəʊhed] *n* (**a**) *(of arrow)* fer *m*, pointe *f* de flèche (**b**) *Bot (plant)* sagittaire *f*, flèche *f* d'eau

arrowroot ['ærəʊruːt] *n (plant)* marante *f*; *Culin* arrow-root *m*

arrow-shaped *adj* en forme de flèche

arroyo [ə'rɔɪəʊ] *n Am Geol* arroyo *m*

arse [ɑːs] *Br Vulg* **1** *n* (**a**) *(buttocks)* cul *m*; **move** *or* **shift your arse** pousse ton cul; **to make an arse of sth** complètement foirer qch; **to get one's arse in(to) gear** se remuer le cul; **to work one's arse off** bosser comme un nègre; **to talk out of one's arse** dire des conneries; **to be out on one's arse** *(get fired)* se faire virer; **my arse!** mon cul!; **to kiss** *or* **lick sb's arse** faire du lèche-cul à qn, *Can* lécher le cul de qn; **kiss my arse!** va te faire foutre!; **get your arse over here!** ramène ta fraise!, amène-toi!; **get your arse over to the town hall!** file à la mairie!; **it's my arse that's on the line** ça risque de me retomber sur la gueule; **he's been sitting on his arse all day** il a rien foutu de la journée; **he doesn't know his arse from his elbow** il est complètement nul; **she thinks the sun shines out of her arse** elle se prend pas pour de la merde; **you'd better get off your arse** *(move)* tu ferais bien de te bouger le cul; *(speed up)* tu ferais bien de te magner le cul; **he's a pain in the arse** c'est un emmerdeur; **it's a pain in the arse** c'est emmerdant; **he fell** *or* **went arse over tit** *or* **tip** *or* **apex** il est tombé cul par-dessus tête; **to do sth arse-backwards** faire qch à l'envers *ou* n'importe comment

(**b**) *(person)* crétin(e) *m,f*; **to make an arse of oneself** se ridiculiser ❑

2 *vt* **why don't you come with us? – I can't be arsed** tu viens avec nous? – non, j'ai trop la flemme; **he can't be arsed doing it himself** il a pas envie de se faire chier à le faire lui-même

►**arse about, arse around** *vi Br Vulg (act foolishly)* faire le con, déconner; *(waste time)* glander, glandouiller

►**arse up** *vt sep Br Vulg* **to arse sth up** foirer qch

arsehole ['ɑːshəʊl] *n Br Vulg* (**a**) *(anus)* trou *m* du cul; **the arsehole of nowhere** *or* **of the universe** *(place)* un coin paumé, un trou (**b**) *Fig (stupid person)* connard (connasse) *m,f*; *(nasty person)* salaud (salope) *m,f*; **don't be such an arsehole** ne sois pas si con; **to make an arsehole of oneself** se ridiculiser ❑

arseholed ['ɑːshəʊld] *adj Br Vulg (drunk)* bourré comme un coing, complètement pété

arse-licker [-ˌlɪkə(r)] *n Br Vulg* lèche-cul *m inv*

arse-licking *Br Vulg* **1** *n* **too much arse-licking goes on in this office** il y a un peu trop de lèche-culs dans ce bureau!

2 *adj* **he's an arse-licking little bastard!** c'est un salaud de lèche-cul!

arsenal ['ɑːsənəl] *n Mil* arsenal *m*

arsenic ['ɑːsnɪk] *n Chem* arsenic *m*

►► ***arsenic poisoning*** empoisonnement *m* à l'arsenic

'Arsenic and Old Lace' *Kesselring, Capra* 'Arsenic et vieilles dentelles'

arsenite ['ɑːsənaɪt] *n Chem* arsénite *m*

arson ['ɑːsən] *n Law* incendie *m* criminel *ou* volontaire; **to commit arson** provoquer (volontairement) un incendie; **to be charged with arson** être accusé d'avoir provoqué un incendie; **police suspect arson** la police suspecte un incendie criminel

arsonist ['ɑːsənɪst] *n Law* incendiaire *mf*; *(maniac)* pyromane *mf*

art[1] [ɑːt] **1** *n* (**a**) *(gen)* art *m*; *(school subject)* dessin *m*; **she studies art** elle est étudiante en art, elle fait des études d'art; **art for art's sake** l'art pour l'art; **African art** l'art *m* africain; **the art of ballet** l'art du ballet; **he was never any good at art at school** à l'école il n'a jamais été très doué en dessin; **a work of art** une œuvre d'art; **arts and crafts** artisanat *m* (d'art)

(**b**) *(skill)* art *m*, habileté *f*; **the art of survival** l'art *m* de survivre; **the art of war** l'art *m* militaire, l'art *m* de la guerre; **it's an art in itself** c'est tout un art; **there's an art to doing that** c'est tout un art que de faire cela; **she has got cooking down to a real** *or* **fine art** la cuisine chez elle, c'est du grand art

(**c**) *(cunning)* ruse *f*, artifice *m*; *(trick)* artifice *m*, stratagème *m*; **they used every art to persuade him** ils ont usé de tous les stratagèmes pour le convaincre

2 *comp (collection, critic)* d'art

3 arts *npl Univ* lettres *fpl*; **Faculty of Arts (and Letters)** faculté *f* des lettres (et sciences humaines)

►► ***art book*** livre *m* d'art; ***arts centre*** ≃ centre *m* culturel; ***art cinema*** cinéma *m* d'art et d'essai; ***art class(es)*** cours *m* de dessin; ***the Arts Council (of Great Britain)*** = organisme public britannique de promotion des arts; ***art deco*** art *m* déco; ***arts degree*** licence *f* de lettres; ***art desk*** bureau *m* de dessin; ***art director*** directeur(-trice) *m,f* artistique; ***art editor*** rédacteur(trice) *m,f* artistique; ***art exhibition*** exposition *f* d'art; ***arts festival*** festival *m* culturel; ***art form*** moyen *m* d'expression artistique; **painting is an art form** la peinture est un art; ***art gallery*** *(museum)* musée *m* d'art; *(shop)* galerie *f* d'art; ***art nouveau*** art *m* nouveau, modern style *m*; ***art nouveau furniture*** meuble *m* de style art nouveau; *Comput* ***art package*** logiciel *m* de dessin; ***arts programme*** programme *m* culturel; ***art school*** ≃ école *f* des Beaux-Arts; ***art student*** étudiant(e) *m,f* en art; *Univ* ***arts student*** étudiant(e) *m,f* de *ou* en lettres (et sciences humaines); ***art teacher*** professeur *m* de dessin; *Psy* ***art therapy*** art-thérapie *m*

'The Art of (the) Fugue' *Bach* 'L'Art de la fugue'

art[2] *Arch or Bible* = **are**

artefact = **artifact**

Artemis ['ɑːtəmɪs] *pr n Myth* Artémis

arterial [ɑː'tɪərɪəl] *adj Anat* artériel

►► *Br Rail* ***arterial line*** grande ligne *f*; *Br Transp* ***arterial road*** route *f ou* voie *f* à grande circulation;

arteriole [ɑː'tɪərɪəʊl] *n Anat* artériole *f*

arteriosclerosis [ɑːˌtɪərɪəʊsklɪə'rəʊsɪs] *n Med* artériosclérose *f*

arteriovenous [ɑːˌtɪərɪəʊ'viːnəs] *adj Anat* artérioveineux

►► *Med* ***arteriovenous malformation*** malformation *f* artérioveineuse

artery ['ɑːtərɪ] (*pl* **arteries**) *n* (**a**) *Anat* artère *f* (**b**) *Transp (road)* artère *f*, route *f ou* voie *f* à grande circulation

artesian well [ɑː'tiːzɪən-] *n* puits *m* artésien

Artex® ['ɑːteks] *n Constr* = sorte de plâtre utilisé comme revêtement pour les murs et les plafonds

artful ['ɑːtfʊl] *adj* astucieux, habile; *(crafty)* rusé, malin(igne)

►► ***artful dodger*** rusé(e) *m,f (du nom d'un jeune voleur habile dans le roman de Dickens 'Oliver Twist')*

artfully ['ɑːtfʊlɪ] *adv (skilfully)* habilement, avec finesse; *(craftily)* astucieusement, avec astuce

artfulness ['ɑːtfʊlnɪs] *n (skill)* habileté *f*, finesse *f*; *(cunning)* astuce *f*, ruse *f*

arthouse ['ɑːthaʊs, *pl* -haʊzɪz] **1** *n* (**a**) *(gallery)* galerie *f* (**b**) *(cinema)* cinéma *m* d'art et d'essai

2 *comp Cin (director, producer)* de films d'art et d'essai

►► ***arthouse cinema*** cinéma *m* d'art et d'essai; ***arthouse film*** film *m* d'art et d'essai

arthralgia [ɑː'θrældʒə] *n Med* arthralgie *f*

arthritic [ɑː'θrɪtɪk] *Med* **1** *n* arthritique *mf*

2 *adj* arthritique; **to have an arthritic hip** avoir de l'arthrite à la hanche

arthritis [ɑː'θraɪtɪs] *n Med* arthrite *f*; **arthritis sufferer** arthritique *mf*

arthropod ['ɑːθrəpɒd] *n Entom & Zool* arthropode *m*

arthrosis [ɑː'θrəʊsɪs] *n Med* arthrose *f*

Arthur ['ɑːθə(r)] *pr n Myth (king)* Arthur

Arthurian [ɑː'θjʊərɪən] *adj Myth* du roi Arthur

►► ***the Arthurian legend*** la légende du roi Arthur

artic [ɑː'tɪk] *n Br Fam (abbr* **articulated lorry***)* semi-remorque *m*

artichoke ['ɑːtɪtʃəʊk] *n* artichaut *m*

►► ***artichoke hearts*** cœurs *mpl* d'artichauts

article ['ɑːtɪkəl] **1** *n* (**a**) *(object)* objet *m*; **an article of clothing** un vêtement; **articles of value** des objets *mpl* de valeur; *Fam* **it's the genuine article!** c'est du vrai de vrai!

(**b**) *(in press)* article *m*

(**c**) *Law (clause, provision)* article *m*; **the articles of a contract** les stipulations *fpl* d'un contrat; **to do** *or* **to serve one's articles** faire son apprentissage; *Rel* **the Thirty-Nine Articles** = les trente-neuf articles de foi de l'Église anglicane

(**d**) *Gram* article *m*

(**e**) *Com* article *m*, marchandise *f*

(**f**) *Comput (in newsgroups)* article *m*

2 *vt Br Com & Ind (to trade)* mettre en apprentissage; *(to profession)* mettre en stage; **to article sb to a tradesman** mettre qn en apprentissage chez un commerçant

►► *Law* ***articles of apprenticeship*** contrat *m* d'apprentissage; *Com* ***articles of association*** statuts *mpl (d'une société à responsabilité limitée)*; ***articles and conditions*** *(of sale, contract)* cahier *m* des charges; *Am Hist* ***the Articles of Confederation*** = accords signés en 1781 par les 13 colonies des États-Unis, et qui servirent de loi fondamentale jusqu'à l'élaboration de la Constitution de 1788; *Rel* ***article of faith*** article *m* de foi; *Am Mil* ***articles of war*** code *m* de justice militaire

articled clerk ['ɑːtɪkəld-] *n Br Law* clerc *m* d'avoué *(lié par un contrat d'apprentissage)*

articular [ɑː'tɪkjʊlə(r)] *adj Anat* articulaire

articulate 1 *adj* [ɑː'tɪkjʊlət] (**a**) *(person)* qui s'exprime bien, *(writing, speech)* clair, net; **the child gave a very articulate account** l'enfant a fait un compte rendu très clair

(**b**) *(manner of speech)* bien articulé, distinct

(**c**) *Anat & Bot* articulé

2 *vt* [ɑː'tɪkjʊleɪt] (**a**) *(words, syllables)* articuler (**b**) *Fig (wishes, thoughts)* exprimer clairement

(**c**) *Anat & Bot* articuler

3 *vi* [ɑː'tɪkjʊleɪt] articuler

articulated lorry [ɑː'tɪkjʊleɪtɪd-] *n Br Transp* semi-remorque *f*

articulately [ɑː'tɪkjʊlətlɪ] *adv (speak)* distinctement; *(explain)* clairement; **as you so articulately put it** comme vous l'avez si bien exprimé

articulateness [ɑː'tɪkjʊlətnɪs] *n* (**a**) *(of person)* facilité *f* d'expression; *(of writing, speech)* clarté *f* (**b**) *(manner of speech)* articulation *f* nette, netteté *f* d'énonciation

articulation [ɑːˌtɪkjʊ'leɪʃən] *n* (**a**) *Anat, Bot & Ling* articulation *f* (**b**) *(of thought)* expression *f*; **you've heard his articulation of the new theory** vous avez entendu sa présentation de la nouvelle théorie

articulator [ɑː'tɪkjʊleɪtə(r)] *n Anat* organe *m* articulatoire

articulatory [ɑː'tɪkjʊlətrɪ] *adj Ling* articulatoire

►► *Ling* ***articulatory phonetics*** phonétique *f* articulatoire

artifact ['ɑːtɪfækt] *n* objet *m (fabriqué)*

artifice ['ɑːtɪfɪs] *n* (**a**) *(trick)* artifice *m*, ruse *f*; *(scheme)* stratagème *m* (**b**) *(cleverness)* art *m*, adresse *f*

artificer [ɑː'tɪfɪsə(r)] *n Mil & Tech* artilleur *m*

artificial [ˌɑːtɪ'fɪʃəl] *adj* (**a**) *(man-made)* artificiel; *Com* synthétique, artificiel; **artificial flowers** fleurs *fpl* artificielles; **a wig made from artificial hair** une perruque en cheveux artificiels; **an artificial heart** un cœur artificiel; **an artificial leg** une jambe artificielle; *Fig* **the current situation is an artificial one** la situation actuelle n'est pas naturelle *ou* est artificielle (**b**) *(affected → person)* factice, étudié; **she is very artificial** elle manque de naturel; **an artificial smile** un sourire forcé; **artificial tears** larmes *fpl* de crocodile

►► *Sport* ***artificial climbing*** escalade *f* artificielle; *Sport* ***artificial climbing wall*** mur *m* d'escalade artificielle; *Agr & Chem* ***artificial fertilizer*** engrais *m* chimique; ***artificial flavouring*** parfum *m* artificiel *ou* synthétique; *Astron* ***artificial horizon*** horizon *m* artificiel; ***artificial insemination*** insémination *f* artificielle; *Comput* ***artificial intelligence*** intelligence *f* artificielle; ***artificial kidney*** rein *m* artificiel; ***artificial language*** langage *m* artificiel; *Elec* ***artificial light*** la lumière artificielle; ***artificial limb*** prothèse *f*, membre *m* artificiel; *Law* ***artificial person*** personne *f* morale *ou* civique *ou* juridique; *Med* ***artificial respiration*** respiration *f* artificielle; **to give sb artificial respiration** faire la respiration artificielle à qn; ***artificial satellite*** satellite *m* artificiel; ***artificial sweetener*** édulcorant *m* (de synthèse)

artificiality [ˌɑːtɪfɪʃɪ'ælətɪ] *n* manque *m* de naturel

artificially [ˌɑːtɪ'fɪʃəlɪ] *adv* artificiellement; **the exchange rate is artificially high at the moment** le taux de change est maintenu artificiellement à un niveau élevé

artillery [ɑː'tɪlərɪ] (*pl* **artilleries**) *n Mil* artillerie *f*

►► ***artillery fire*** tir *m* d'artillerie; ***artillery regiment*** régiment *m* d'artillerie; ***artillery shell*** obus *m*

artilleryman [ɑː'tɪlərɪmən] (*pl* **artillerymen** [-mən]) *n Mil* artilleur *m*

artiness ['ɑːtɪnɪs] *n Fam* côté *m* artiste ❑

artisan [ˌɑːtɪ'zæn] *n* artisan *m*; **the artisans of Spain** les artisans espagnols

artist ['ɑːtɪst] *n (actor, painter, singer)* artiste *mf*; **he is an artist** *(painter)* il est artiste, il est peintre; *(footballer, athlete)* c'est un véritable artiste

artiste [ɑː'tiːst] *n* artiste *mf*

artistic [ɑː'tɪstɪk] *adj* artistique; *(design, product)* de bon goût, décoratif; *(style, temperament)* artiste; **she is an artistic child** cette enfant a des dons artistiques; **she came from an artistic family** elle venait d'une famille d'artistes; **I'm not at all artistic** je n'ai aucune inclination artistique, je n'ai pas la fibre artistique; *Sport* **mark for artistic impression** note *f* artistique

►► ***artistic director*** directeur(trice) *m,f* artistique

artistically [ɑː'tɪstɪkəlɪ] *adv* (**a**) *(tastefully)* avec art, artistiquement (**b**) *(from an artistic point of view)* d'un point de vue artistique

artistry ['ɑːtɪstrɪ] *n* art *m*, talent *m* artistique

artless ['ɑːtlɪs] *adj* (**a**) *(natural)* naturel, ingénu; **artless beauty** beauté *f* naturelle; **with an artless smile** avec un sourire candide (**b**) *(without skill)* grossier

artlessly ['ɑːtlɪslɪ] *adv* (**a**) *(naturally)* naturellement, sans artifice (**b**) *(naively)* naïvement, ingénument

artlessness ['ɑːtlɪsnɪs] *n* (**a**) *(naturalness)* naturel *m*, simplicité *f* (**b**) *(naivety)* naïveté *f*, ingénuité *f*

artsy ['ɑːtsɪ] (*compar* **artsier**, *superl* **artsiest**) = **arty**

artsy-craftsy [ˌɑːtzɪ'krɑːftsɪ] = **arty-crafty**

artsy-fartsy [ˌɑːtzɪ'fɑːtsɪ] *Am* = **arty-farty**

artwork ['ɑːtwɜːk] *n* (**a**) *(illustrations)* iconographie *f*, illustrations *fpl* (**b**) *Typ* documents *mpl*

arty ['ɑːtɪ] (*compar* **artier**, *superl* **artiest**) *adj Fam* (**a**) *(person, style, job, furniture)* artistique ❑; *(existence)* bohème ❑ (**b**) *Pej (person)* qui se veut artiste ❑; *(object, film, style)* prétentieux ❑; **he's an arty type** c'est le genre artiste; **the arty set** le milieu artiste

arty-crafty [ˌɑːtɪ'krɑːftɪ] *adj Fam Pej (person)* qui se veut artiste *ou* bohème ❑; *(object, style)* bohème ❑, qui se veut artisanal ❑

arty-farty [ˌɑːtɪ'fɑːtɪ], *Am* **artsy-fartsy** [ˌɑːtsɪˌfɑːtsɪ] *adj Fam Pej (person)* prétentieux ❑, poseur ❑; *(play, film)* prétentieux ❑

arum ['eərəm] *n Bot* arum *m*

►► ***arum lily*** calla *f*

ARV [ˌeɪɑː'viː] *n* (**a**) *Bible* (*abbr* **American Revised Version**) = traduction américaine de la Bible (**b**) *Med* (*abbr* **aids-related virus**) ARV *m*

arvo ['ɑːvəʊ] *n Austr Fam (afternoon)* après-midi ❑ *m or f*, aprème *m or f*

Aryan ['eərɪən] *Ling* **1** *n* Aryen(enne) *m,f*
2 *adj* aryen

Aryanize, -ise ['eərɪənaɪz] *vt* germaniser

AS¹ [ˌeɪ'es] *n Am Univ* (*abbr* **Associate in Science**) *(person)* = titulaire d'un diplôme universitaire américain de sciences; *(qualification)* = diplôme universitaire américain de sciences

AS² *(written abbr* **American Samoa**) Samoa *fpl* américaines

AS [əz, *stressed* æz]

alors que	► 1 (a)
comme	► 1 (b); 2
puisque	► 1 (c)
que	► 1 (e)
en tant que	► 2
contre	► 4
quant à	► 6
à partir de	► 7; 11
comme si	► 8; 13
déjà	► 9
pour ainsi dire	► 10
en plus, aussi	► 15 (a)
en plus de	► 16
encore	► 17

1 *conj* (**a**) *(while)* alors que; **the phone rang as I was coming in** le téléphone s'est mis à sonner alors que *ou* au moment où j'entrais; **I listened as she explained the plan to them** je l'ai écoutée leur expliquer le projet; **as a student, he worked part-time** lorsqu'il était étudiant, il travaillait à mi-temps; **as he advanced, I retreated** (au fur et) à mesure qu'il avançait, je reculais; **take two aspirins as needed** prenez deux aspirines en cas de douleur

(**b**) *(like)* comme, ainsi que; **A as in Abel** A comme Anatole; **as usual** comme d'habitude; **as shown by the unemployment rate** comme *ou* ainsi que le montre le taux de chômage; **as is often the case** comme c'est souvent le cas; **she is a doctor, as is her sister** elle est médecin comme sa sœur; **as I told you** comme je vous l'ai dit; **as you know, the inflation rate has gone up** comme vous le savez, le taux d'inflation a augmenté; **do as you see fit** faites comme bon vous semble; **leave it as it is** laissez-le tel qu'il est *ou* tel quel; **to buy sth as is** acheter qch en l'état; *Mil* **as you were!** repos!; *Hum* **my mistake! as you were!** c'est moi qui me trompe! faites comme si je n'avais rien dit!

(**c**) *(since)* puisque; **let her drive, as it's her car** laissez-la conduire, puisque c'est sa voiture; **as you're the one in charge, you'd better be there** étant donné que c'est vous le responsable, il faut que vous soyez là

(**d**) *Formal (concessive use)* **old as I am, I can still keep up with them** malgré mon âge, j'arrive à les suivre; **try as they might, they couldn't persuade her** malgré tous leurs efforts, ils n'ont pu la convaincre; **powerful as the president is, he cannot stop his country's disintegration** quelque pouvoir qu'ait le président, il ne peut empêcher la ruine de son pays

(**e**) *(with 'the same', 'such')* **I had the same problems as you did** j'ai eu les mêmes problèmes que toi; **at the same time as last week** à la même heure que la semaine dernière; **such a problem as only an expert can solve** un problème que seul un expert peut résoudre

2 *prep* en tant que, comme; **as her husband, he cannot testify** étant son mari, il ne peut pas témoigner; **he was dressed as a clown** il était habillé en clown; **I advised him as his friend, not as his teacher** je l'ai conseillé en tant qu'ami, pas en tant que professeur; **with Vivien Leigh as Scarlett O'Hara** avec Vivien Leigh dans le rôle de Scarlett O'Hara

3 *adv (in comparisons)* **it's twice as big** c'est deux fois plus grand; **it costs half as much again** ça coûte la moitié plus; **as... as** aussi... que; **he's as intelligent as his brother** il est aussi intelligent que son frère; **he isn't as talented as you (are)** il n'est pas aussi doué que vous; **as often as possible** aussi souvent que possible; **not as often as I would like** pas aussi souvent que je voudrais; **they aren't as innocent as they look** ils ne sont pas aussi innocents qu'ils en ont l'air; **I worked as much for you as for me** j'ai travaillé autant pour toi que pour moi

4 as against *prep* contre; **he received 39 votes as against the 17 for his rival** il a obtenu 39 votes contre 17 pour son adversaire

5 as and when 1 *conj* **we'll buy new equipment as and when it's required** nous achèterons du nouveau matériel en temps voulu *ou* quand ce sera nécessaire **2** *adv Fam* en temps voulu ❑; **you'll be sent the money as and when** on vous enverra l'argent en temps voulu

6 as for *prep* quant à; **as for me, I don't intend to go** pour ma part *ou* quant à moi, je n'ai pas l'intention d'y aller; **as for your threats, they don't scare me in the least** pour ce qui est de *ou* quant à vos menaces, elles ne me font pas peur du tout

7 as from *prep* à partir de; **as from yesterday** depuis hier; **as from tomorrow** à partir de demain; **as from next week I'll be unemployed** je serai au chômage à partir de la semaine prochaine

8 as if *conj* comme si; **he looks as if he's drunk** on dirait qu'il est soûl; **he carried on as if nothing had happened** il a continué comme si de rien n'était *ou* comme s'il ne s'était rien passé; **as if aware of my look, she turned** comme si elle avait senti mon regard, elle s'est retournée; **as if by chance** comme par hasard; **he moved as if to strike him** il a fait un mouvement comme pour le frapper; **it's not as if she were my sister** ce n'est quand même pas comme si c'était ma sœur; **as if it mattered!** comme si ça avait aucune importance!; **as if I would allow it!** comme si j'allais le permettre!; *Hum* **as if!** tu parles!; **he said he would do it – as if!** il a dit qu'il le ferait – mon œil!

9 as it is *adv* (**a**) *(in present circumstances)* les choses étant ce qu'elles sont; **she's hoping for promotion, but as it is there's little chance of that** elle espère obtenir une promotion, mais dans la situation actuelle *ou* les choses étant ce qu'elles sont, il est peu probable que cela arrive

(**b**) *(already)* déjà; **you've got enough work as it is** vous avez déjà assez de travail, vous avez assez de travail comme ça; **as it is I'm an hour late** j'ai déjà une heure de retard

10 as it were *adv* pour ainsi dire

11 as of *prep* à partir de; **as of yesterday** depuis hier; **as of tomorrow** à partir de demain; **as of next week I'll be unemployed** je serai au chômage à partir de la semaine prochaine

12 as such *adv* (**a**) *(properly speaking)* véritablement, à proprement parler; **it's not a contract as such, more a gentleman's agreement** ce n'est pas un véritable contrat *ou* pas un contrat à proprement parler *ou* pas véritablement un contrat, mais plutôt un accord entre hommes de parole

(**b**) *(in itself)* même, en soi; **the place as such isn't great** l'endroit même *ou* en soi n'est pas terrible

(**c**) *(in that capacity)* à ce titre, en tant que tel; **I'm his father and as such, I insist on knowing** je suis son père et à ce titre j'insiste pour qu'on me mette au courant

13 as though *conj* comme si; **he looks as though he's drunk** on dirait qu'il est soûl; **he carried on as though nothing had happened** il a continué comme si de rien n'était *ou* comme s'il ne s'était rien passé; **as though aware of my look, she turned** comme si elle avait senti mon regard, elle s'est retournée; **it's not as though she were my sister** ce n'est quand même pas comme si c'était ma sœur

14 as to *prep (regarding)* **to question sb as to his/her motives** interroger qn sur ses motifs; **I'm still uncertain as to the nature of the problem** j'hésite encore sur la nature du problème; **as to that** quant à cela, pour cela

15 as well *adv* (**a**) *(in addition)* en plus; *(also)* aussi; **I'd like one as well** j'en voudrais un aussi; **he bought the house and the land as well** il a acheté la maison et la propriété aussi; **and then the car broke down as well!** et par-dessus le marché la voiture est tombée en panne!

(**b**) *(with modal verbs)* **you may as well tell me the truth** autant me dire *ou* tu ferais aussi bien de me dire la vérité; **now that we're here, we**

might as well stay puisque nous sommes là, autant rester; **shall we go to the cinema? – we might as well** et si on allait au cinéma? – pourquoi pas?; **she was angry, as well she might be** elle était furieuse, et ça n'est pas surprenant; **he has a few doubts about the job, as well he might** il a quelques doutes sur cet emploi, ce qui n'est guère surprenant; **he apologized profusely – as well he should!** il s'est confondu en excuses – j'espère bien!; **perhaps I'd better leave – that might be as well** peut-être vaudrait-il mieux que je m'en aille – je crois que ça vaut mieux; **it would be as well not to break it** ce serait mieux si on pouvait éviter de le casser; **I decided not to write back – just as well really** j'ai décidé de ne pas répondre – c'est mieux comme ça; **it would be just as well if you were present** il vaudrait mieux que vous soyez là; **it's just as well he missed his flight** c'est une bonne chose qu'il ait manqué l'avion

16 as well as *conj (in addition to)* en plus de; **so she's a liar as well as a thief** alors comme ça, c'est une menteuse en plus d'être une voleuse; **Jim looks after the children as well as helping around the house** Jim s'occupe des enfants en plus de participer au ménage

17 as yet *adv* encore; **I don't have the answer as yet** je n'ai pas encore la réponse; **an as yet undisclosed sum** une somme qui n'a pas encore été révélée

'As you like it' *Shakespeare* 'Comme il vous plaira'

ASA [,eɪes'eɪ] *n* (**a**) *Br* (*abbr* **Advertising Standards Authority**) ≃ BVP *m* (**b**) (*abbr* **American Standards Association**) association *f* américaine de normalisation, ≃ AFNOR *f* (**c**) *Phot* (*abbr* **American Standards Association**) ASA *f*; **ASA/DIN exposure index** graduations *fpl* ASA/DIN; **an ASA 100 film, a 100 ASA film** une pellicule 100 ASA (**d**) *Br* (*abbr* **Amateur Swimming Association**) fédération *f* de natation

asap [,eɪeseɪ'piː] *adv* (*abbr* **as soon as possible**) aussitôt *ou* dès que possible; **we need to reply asap** il faut qu'on réponde dès que possible

asbestos [æs'bestɒs] **1** *n* amiante *f*, asbeste *f*

2 *comp (board, cord)* d'amiante

▸▸ ***asbestos cement*** amiante-ciment *m*; ***asbestos dust*** poudre *f* d'amiante; ***asbestos matting*** plaque *f* d'amiante

asbestosis [,æsbes'təʊsɪs] *n Med* asbestose *f*

ASC [,eɪes'siː] *n* (*abbr* **American Society of Cinematographers**) = société américaine des chefs-opérateurs

ascend [ə'send] **1** *vi* (**a**) *(rise)* monter; **she reached the bottom of the steps and started to ascend slowly** elle arriva en bas des escaliers et commença à monter lentement (**b**) *(in time)* remonter; **to ascend (back) to sth** remonter à qch

2 *vt (stairs)* monter; *(ladder)* monter à; *(mountain)* gravir, faire l'ascension de; *(river)* remonter; *(throne)* monter sur

ascendancy [ə'sendənsɪ] *n* (**a**) *(dominance)* ascendant *m*, empire *m*; **Japan has gained ascendancy over its competitors in the electronics market** le Japon domine ses concurrents sur le marché de l'électronique (**b**) *Hist* **the Ascendancy** – l'aristocratie d'origine anglaise en Irlande

ascendant [ə'sendənt] **1** *adj* dominant, puissant; *Astrol & Astron* ascendant

2 *n Astrol* ascendant *m*; **his star is in the ascendant** son étoile est à l'ascendant; *Fig* **his business is in the ascendant** ses affaires prospèrent

ascendency, **ascendent** = ascendancy, ascendant

ascender [ə'sendə(r)] *n* (**a**) *(in mountaineering)* ascendeur *m*, autobloqueur *m* (**b**) *Typ* hampe *f* montante

ascending [ə'sendɪŋ] *adj* (**a**) *(rising)* ascendant (**b**) *(increasing)* **in ascending order** en ordre croissant (**c**) *Bot* montant

▸▸ *Mus* ***ascending scale*** gamme *f* ascendante *ou* montante; ***ascending series*** progression *f* croissante; *Comput* ***ascending sort*** tri *m* en ordre croissant

ascension [ə'senʃən] **1** *n* ascension *f*

2 Ascension *n* (**a**) *Geog* île *f* de l'Ascension; **on Ascension** à l'île de l'Ascension (**b**) *Rel* **the Ascension** l'Ascension *f*

▸▸ *Rel* ***Ascension Day*** jour *m ou* fête *f* de l'Ascension; ***Ascension Island*** île *f* de l'Ascension; **on Ascension Island** à l'île de l'Ascension

Ascensiontide [ə'senʃəntaɪd] *n Rel* = période entre l'Ascension et le dimanche de Pentecôte

ascent [ə'sent] *n* (**a**) *(of mountain)* ascension *f* (**b**) *(incline)* montée *f* (**c**) *(in time)* retour *m*; **the line of ascent** l'ascendance *f* (**d**) *(in rank)* montée *f*, avancement *m* (**e**) **his ascent to power** son ascension jusqu'au pouvoir

ascertain [,æsə'teɪn] *vt Formal (facts)* établir, déterminer; **the police ascertained their names and addresses** la police a vérifié leurs nom et adresse; **to ascertain that sth is the case** vérifier *ou* s'assurer que qch est vrai; **I ascertained from his report that...** j'ai déduit de son rapport que...; **are we to ascertain from this that...?** devons-nous en déduire que...?; **he ascertained that it was safe to continue** il s'est assuré qu'on pouvait continuer sans danger

ascertainable [,æsə'teɪnəbəl] *adj Formal (information, fact)* qui peut être déterminé; *(truth)* vérifiable

ascertainment [,æsə'teɪnmənt] *n Formal (of information, fact)* détermination *f*; *(of truth)* vérification *f*

ascetic [ə'setɪk] *Rel & Fig* **1** *n* ascète *mf*

2 *adj* ascétique

ascetically [ə'setɪkəlɪ] *adv Rel (live)* comme un une ascète

asceticism [ə'setɪsɪzəm] *n Rel* ascétisme *m*

ASCII ['æskɪ] *Comput* (*abbr* **American Standard Code for Information Interchange**) *n* ASCII *m*; **in ASCII** en ASCII

▸▸ ***ASCII art*** art *m* ASCII; ***ASCII code*** code *m* ASCII; ***ASCII file*** fichier *m* ASCII; ***ASCII text*** texte *m* ASCII; ***ASCII value*** valeur *f* ASCII

ascorbic acid [ə'skɔːbɪk-] *n Chem* acide *m* ascorbique

Ascot ['æskət] **1** *n* = champ de courses près de Windsor

2 ascot *n Am* foulard *m (pour hommes)*

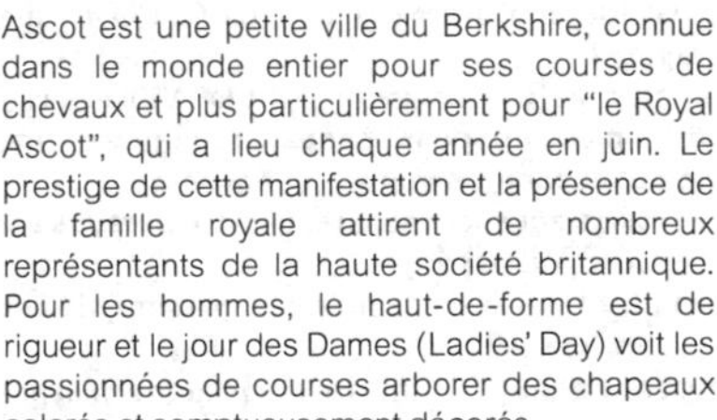

ASCOT

Ascot est une petite ville du Berkshire, connue dans le monde entier pour ses courses de chevaux et plus particulièrement pour "le Royal Ascot", qui a lieu chaque année en juin. Le prestige de cette manifestation et la présence de la famille royale attirent de nombreux représentants de la haute société britannique. Pour les hommes, le haut-de-forme est de rigueur et le jour des Dames (Ladies' Day) voit les passionnées de courses arborer des chapeaux colorés et somptueusement décorés.

ascribable [ə'skraɪbəbəl] *adj* attribuable; *(fault, blame)* imputable; **his downfall is ascribable to greed** sa chute est imputable à sa cupidité

ascribe [ə'skraɪb] *vt* attribuer (**to** à); *(fault, blame)* imputer (**to** à); **heart attacks are often ascribed to stress** les crises cardiaques sont souvent attribuées *ou* imputées au stress; **this painting is sometimes ascribed to Millet** on attribue parfois ce tableau à Millet

ascription [ə'skrɪpʃən] *n Rel* attribution *f*; *(of fault, blame)* imputation *f*

ASCU [,eɪes,siː'juː] *n Am Univ* (*abbr* **Association of State Colleges and Universities**) = association des établissements universitaires d'État aux États-Unis

asdic ['æzdɪk] *n Naut* asdic *m*

ASE [,eɪes'iː] *n* (*abbr* **American Stock Exchange**) = deuxième place boursière des États-Unis

ASEAN [,eɪes,iːeɪ'en] *n* (*abbr* **Association of South East Asian Nations**) ANASE *f*

aseismic [,eɪ'saɪzmɪk] *adj Geol & Constr* aséismique

asepsis [,eɪ'sepsɪs] *n Med* asepsie *f*

aseptic [,eɪ'septɪk] *adj Med* aseptique

asexual [,eɪ'sekʃʊəl] *adj* asexué; *Bot (flower)* neutre

▸▸ *Biol* ***asexual reproduction*** reproduction *f* asexuée

asexuality [,eɪsekʃʊ'ælɪtɪ] *n* caractère *m* asexuel, asexualité *f*

ASH [æʃ] *n* (*abbr* **Action on Smoking and Health**) = ligue antitabac britannique

ash [æʃ] **1** *n* (**a**) *(from fire, cigarette)* cendre *f*; **he dropped ash on the carpet** il a laissé tomber sa cendre sur la moquette; **the fire reduced the house to ashes** l'incendie a réduit la maison en cendres; *Rel* **ashes to ashes, dust to dust** tu es poussière, et tu retourneras en poussière; *Literary* **to rake over the ashes of the past** tisonner les cendres du passé; **to rise from the ashes** renaître de ses cendres

(**b**) *(colour)* cendré *m*, gris cendré *m (inv)*

(**c**) *(tree, wood)* frêne *m*

2 Ashes *npl Sport (in cricket)* = trophée que les équipes anglaises et australiennes se disputent

▸▸ ***ash bin*** *(for ashes)* cendrier *m*; *(for rubbish)* poubelle *f*, boîte *f* à ordures; *Rel* ***Ash Wednesday*** mercredi *m* des Cendres

'Ash Wednesday' *Eliot* 'Mercredi des cendres'

ashamed [ə'ʃeɪmd] *adj* confus, honteux; **to be ashamed (of oneself)** avoir honte; **to be ashamed of sb/sth** avoir honte de qn/qch; **to feel ashamed** être honteux *ou* confus; **he's ashamed of his behaviour/of having cried** il a honte de sa conduite/d'avoir pleuré; **I'm ashamed of you** j'ai honte de toi, tu me fais honte; **I'm ashamed to say that...** j'avoue à ma grande honte que...; **I'm not ashamed to admit it** je l'admets sans honte; **you ought to be ashamed of yourself** tu devrais avoir honte; **there is nothing to be ashamed of** il n'y a pas de quoi avoir honte

ashamedly [ə'ʃeɪmɪdlɪ] *adv* d'une façon honteuse

Ashanti [ə'ʃæntɪ] *n* (**a**) *(person)* Achanti(e) *m,f* (**b**) *(language)* achanti *m*

A-share *n St Exch* action *f* ordinaire sans droit de vote

ash-blond, ash-blonde **1** *n (colour)* blond *m* cendré; **she's an ash-blond** elle a les cheveux blond cendré

2 *adj* blond cendré *(inv)*

ashcan ['æʃkæn] *n Am* boîte *f* à ordures, poubelle *f*

ashen ['æʃən] *adj* (**a**) *(ash-coloured)* cendré, couleur de cendres; *(face)* blême, livide (**b**) *Bot (of ashwood)* en (bois de) frêne

ashen-faced *adj* blême

ashet ['æʃət] *n Scot* grand plat *m*

Ashkenazi [,æʃkə'nɑːzɪ] (*pl* **Ashkenazim** [-zɪm]) *n Rel* Ashkénase *mf*

ashlar ['æʃlə(r)] *n* (**a**) *Miner (stone)* pierre *f* de taille (**b**) *Constr (facing)* parements *mpl*, revêtement *m*

ashore [ə'ʃɔː(r)] **1** *adv* à terre; **he swam ashore** il a nagé jusqu'à la rive; **debris from the wreck was washed ashore** des morceaux de l'épave ont été rejetés sur la côte; *Naut* **to go ashore** débarquer; *Naut* **the ship put the passengers ashore at Plymouth** le navire a débarqué les passagers à Plymouth

2 *adj* à terre

ashpan ['æʃpæn] *n (for stove)* cendrier *m*

ashplant ['æʃplɑːnt] *n Bot* canne *f* en bois de frêne

ashram ['æʃrəm] *n Rel* ashram *m*

ashtray ['æʃtreɪ] *n* cendrier *m*

ashy ['æʃɪ] (*compar* **ashier**, *superl* **ashiest**) *adj* (**a**) *(ash-coloured)* cendré, couleur de cendre; *(pale)* blême, livide (**b**) *(covered with ashes)* couvert de cendres

Asia ['eɪʒə, 'eɪʃə] *n* Asie *f*; **in Asia** en Asie

▸▸ ***Asia Minor*** Asie *f* Mineure

Asian ['eɪʒən, 'eɪʃən] **1** *n* Asiatique *mf*; *(Indian)* Indien(enne) *m,f*; *(Pakistani)* Pakistanais(e) *m,f*

2 *adj* asiatique; *(Indian)* indien; *(Pakistani)* pakistanais

▸▸ ***Asian American*** **1** *n* Américain(e) *m,f* d'origine asiatique **2** *adj* américain d'origine asiatique; *Fam* ***Asian babe*** Indienne *f*/Pakistanaise *f* /Orientale *f* super belle; *Med* ***Asian flu*** grippe *f* asiatique; *Entom* ***Asian longhorn beetle*** capricorne *m* d'Asie

ASIAN

Pour les Britanniques, "Asian" désigne le plus souvent les habitants de l'Inde et des pays limitrophes: ainsi, l'expression "the Asian community in Birmingham" fait référence aux personnes d'origine indienne, pakistanaise et bangladaise qui habitent Birmingham.

Asiatic [ˌeɪʒɪ'ætɪk, ˌeɪʃɪ'ætɪk] **1** *n* Asiatique *mf*
2 *adj* asiatique

A-side *n* face *f* A *(d'un disque)*

aside [ə'saɪd] **1** *adv* de côté, à part; **she held aside the curtains** elle écarta les rideaux; **stand aside!** écartez-vous!; **I stepped aside to let her pass** je me suis écarté pour la laisser passer; **he took her aside** il l'a prise à part; **we've been putting money aside for the trip** nous avons mis de l'argent de côté pour le voyage; **would you put this dress aside for me?** pourriez-vous me mettre cette robe de côté *ou* me réserver cette robe?; **these problems aside, we have been very successful** à part ces problèmes, ce fut un véritable succès; **(leaving) politics aside, I think...** si on laisse de côté la politique, je pense...
2 *n* aparté *m*; **he said something to her in an aside** il lui a dit quelque chose en aparté; **(purely) as an aside** soit dit entre nous
3 aside from *prep* **(a)** *(except for)* sauf **(b)** *Am (as well as)* en plus de

asinine ['æsɪnaɪn] *adj* **(a)** *(person, behaviour)* stupide, sot (sotte); **that was an asinine thing to do!** là, tu as vraiment fait une bêtise! **(b)** *(like an ass)* asinien

ask [ɑːsk] **1** *vt* **(a)** *(for opinion, information)* **to ask sb sth** demander qch à qn; **I asked her the time** je lui ai demandé l'heure; **she asked him about his job** elle lui a posé des questions sur son travail; **may I ask you a question?** puis-je vous poser une question?; **ask your mother!** demande à ta mère!; **if you ask me** si vous voulez mon avis; *Fam* **but how? I ask you!** mais comment? je vous le demande!; *Fam* **don't ask me!** est-ce que je sais, moi?; *Fam* **no one asked you!** on ne t'a rien demandé!
(b) *(request)* demander, solliciter; **he asked them a favour** il leur a demandé un service; **he asked her hand in marriage** il l'a demandée en mariage; **to ask sb to do sth** demander à qn de faire qch; **I asked them to be quiet** je leur ai demandé de se taire; **she asked to have the bags brought up** elle a demandé que les bagages soient montés; **he asked to be admitted** il a demandé à être admis; **she was asked to wait outside** on lui a demandé d'attendre dehors; **that's asking a lot** c'est beaucoup demander; **that's asking too much of me** c'est trop m'en demander; *Com* **to ask a price** demander un prix; **what are you asking for it?** combien en voulez-vous *ou* demandez-vous?
(c) *(invite)* inviter; **they asked her to join them** ils l'ont invitée à se joindre à eux; **he asked her to the pictures** il l'a invitée au cinéma; **she asked us up** elle nous a invités à monter
2 *vi* demander; **he was asking about the job** il s'informait *ou* se renseignait sur le poste; **I was only asking!** je ne faisais que demander!
►► *St Exch* ***ask price*** cours *m* offert, cours *m* vendeur Shorter

►**ask after** *vt insep* **she asked after you** elle a demandé de vos nouvelles; **I asked after her health** je me suis informé de sa santé

►**ask along** *vt sep* inviter; **we asked them along (with us)** nous leur avons proposé de venir avec nous

►**ask around** *vi* se renseigner; **I asked around about cheap flights** je me suis renseigné sur les vols pas chers

►**ask back** *vt sep (invite again)* réinviter; *(for reciprocal visit)* inviter; **she asked us back for dinner** elle nous a rendu l'invitation à dîner

►**ask for** *vt insep* demander; **they asked for some water** ils ont demandé de l'eau; **you're asking for the moon** vous demandez la lune; **she asked for her book back** elle a demandé qu'on lui rende son livre; **you're just asking for trouble!** tu cherches des ennuis!; **he was asking for it!** il l'a cherché!; **she left him – he was asking for it** elle l'a quitté – il l'a voulu, il l'a eu!

►**ask in** *vt sep* inviter à entrer; **he asked us in for a drink** il nous a invités à (entrer) prendre un verre

►**ask out** *vt sep* inviter à sortir; **they asked us out for dinner/to the theatre** ils nous ont invités au restaurant/au théâtre

►**ask round** *vt sep* inviter (à venir); **we must ask him round soon** nous devrions l'inviter un de ces jours

askance [ə'skæns] *adv* **(a)** *(with distrust)* **to look askance at sb/sth** regarder qn/qch avec méfiance; **he looked askance at her** il l'a regardée d'un air méfiant **(b)** *(disapprovingly)* **to look askance at sb** regarder qn de travers

asked price *n Am St Exch* cours *m* offert, cours *m* vendeur

askew [ə'skjuː] **1** *adv* obliquement, de travers
2 *adj Am* **something's askew here** il y a quelque chose qui cloche

asking ['ɑːskɪŋ] *n* **it's yours for the asking** il n'y a qu'à (le) demander; **it was theirs for the asking** ils n'ont eu qu'à demander
►► ***asking price*** *Fin* prix *m* de départ, prix *m* demandé; *Am St Exch* cours *m* offert, cours *m* vendeur

ASL [ˌeɪes'el] *n* (*abbr* **American Sign Language**) = langage des signes utilisé aux États-Unis

aslant [ə'slɑːnt] **1** *prep* en travers de
2 *adv* de travers, de *ou* en biais

asleep [ə'sliːp] *adj* endormi; **to be asleep** dormir; **to be fast** *or* **sound asleep** dormir profondément *ou* à poings fermés; **to fall asleep** s'endormir; **you're half asleep** tu dors à moitié, tu es à moitié endormi; **he's asleep on his feet** il dort debout

ASLEF ['æzlef] *n Rail* (*abbr* **Associated Society of Locomotive Engineers and Firemen**) = syndicat des cheminots en Grande-Bretagne

A/S-level *n Sch* = examen facultatif complétant les "A-levels"

ASM [ˌeɪes'em] *n* **(a)** *Mil* (*abbr* **air-to-surface missile**) ASM *m* **(b)** *Theat* (*abbr* **assistant stage manager**) régisseur *m* général

as-new *adj* comme neuf

asocial [ˌeɪ'səʊʃəl] *adj* asocial

asp [æsp] *n* **(a)** *Zool* aspic *m* **(b)** *Arch Bot* tremble *m*

asparagina [ə'spærəˌdʒiːnə] *n Biol & Chem* asparagine *f*

asparagus [ə'spærəgəs] *n (UNCOUNT)* asperges *fpl*; **a piece** *or* **spear of asparagus** une asperge; **to eat asparagus** manger des asperges
►► ***asparagus fern*** asparagus *m*; ***asparagus tips*** pointes *fpl* d'asperges

aspartame [*Br* ə'spɑːteɪm, *Am* 'æspərteɪm] *n Chem* aspartame *m*

aspartic acid [ə'spɑːtɪk-] *n Chem* acide *m* aspartique

ASPCA [ˌeɪes,piːsiː'eɪ] *n* (*abbr* **American Society for the Prevention of Cruelty to Animals**) = société protectrice des animaux aux États-Unis, ≃ SPA *f*

aspect ['æspekt] *n* **(a)** *(of problem, subject)* aspect *m*, côté *m*; **we should examine all aspects of the problem** nous devrions étudier le problème sous tous ses aspects **(b)** *Literary (appearance)* air *m*, aspect *m*; **a young man of (a) serious aspect** un jeune homme à la mine sérieuse **(c)** *(outlook)* orientation *f*, exposition *f*; **a house with a northern/southern aspect** une maison exposée au nord/sud **(d)** *Astrol (of planets)* aspect *m* **(e)** *Gram* aspect *m*

aspectual [æ'spektjʊəl] *adj Astrol & Gram* aspectuel

aspen ['æspən] *n Bot* tremble *m*

asperity [æ'sperɪtɪ] (*pl* **asperities**) *n Formal* **(a)** *(of manner, voice)* aspérité *f*; **"certainly not", she said with some asperity** "certainement pas", dit-elle d'un ton sec **(b)** *(of person)* rudesse *f* **(c)** *(of climate)* rigueur *f*

asperse [ə'spɜːs] *vt Literary (slander)* calomnier, diffamer; **to asperse sb's honour** porter atteinte à l'honneur de qn

aspersions [ə'spɜːʃənz] *npl* **to cast aspersions on sb** dénigrer qn; **he cast aspersions on her honour** il a porté atteinte à son honneur

aspersorium [ˌæspə'sɔːrɪəm] (*pl* **aspersoria** [-rɪə]) *n Rel (basin)* bénitier *m*; *(sprinkler)* aspersoir *m*

asphalt ['æsfælt] *Constr* **1** *n* asphalte *m*
2 *comp (road, roof)* asphalté
3 *vt* asphalter
►► ***asphalt jungle*** jungle *f* urbaine

'The Asphalt Jungle' *Huston* 'Quand la ville dort'

asphalting ['æsfæltɪŋ] *n Constr* asphaltage *m*

aspheric [eɪ'sferɪk], **aspherical** [eɪ'sferɪkəl] *adj* asphérique

asphodel ['æsfədel] *n Bot* asphodèle *m*

asphyxia [əs'fɪksɪə] *n Med* asphyxie *f*

asphyxiant [əs'fɪksɪənt] *Med* **1** *n* agent *m* asphyxiant
2 *adj* asphyxiant

asphyxiate [əs'fɪksɪeɪt] *Med* **1** *vt* asphyxier
2 *vi* s'asphyxier

asphyxiating [əs'fɪksɪˌeɪtɪŋ] *adj Med* asphyxiant
►► ***asphyxiating gases*** gaz *mpl* asphyxiants

asphyxiation [əsˌfɪksɪ'eɪʃən] *n Med* asphyxie *f*; **to die by** *or* **of asphyxiation** mourir d'asphyxie

aspic ['æspɪk] *n Culin* gelée *f*; **eggs in aspic** œufs *mpl* en aspic; **salmon in aspic** aspic *m* de saumon; *Fig* **preserved in aspic** mis sous verre

aspidistra [ˌæspɪ'dɪstrə] *n Bot* aspidistra *m*

aspirant ['æspɪrənt] **1** *n* candidat(e) *m,f*; **aspirant to the throne** prétendant *m* au trône
2 *adj* **aspirant journalists/diplomats** les gens qui aspirent à devenir journalistes/diplomates

aspirate *Ling* **1** *vt* ['æspəreɪt] aspirer
2 *adj* ['æspərət] aspiré; **an aspirate h** un h aspiré
3 *n* ['æspərət] aspirée *f*

aspiration [ˌæspə'reɪʃən] *n* **(a)** *(ambition)* aspiration *f*; **young people with political aspirations** des jeunes qui ont des aspirations politiques; **to have aspirations to greater things/to become a doctor** aspirer à de grandes choses/à devenir médecin **(b)** *Ling* aspiration *f*

aspirational [ˌæspɪ'reɪʃənəl] *adj Mktg (product)* qui fait chic; *(consumer)* qui achète des produits de prestige; *(advertising)* qui joue sur le prestige d'un produit
►► ***aspirational group*** groupe *m* de référence

aspirator ['æspəreɪtə(r)] *n Med & Tech* aspirateur *m*

aspiratory [ˌæspɪ'reɪtərɪ] *adj* aspiratoire

aspire [ə'spaɪə(r)] *vi* **(a) to aspire to do sth** aspirer à *ou* ambitionner de faire qch; **to aspire to fame** briguer la célébrité; **he aspires to political power** il aspire au pouvoir politique; **she aspires to** *or* **after higher things** elle vise plus haut, ses ambitions vont plus loin **(b)** *Arch or Literary (rise)* monter, s'élever

aspirin ['æspərɪn] *n* aspirine *f*; *(tablet)* (comprimé *m* d')aspirine *f*

aspiring [ə'spaɪərɪŋ] *adj (artist etc)* en herbe; **to be an aspiring doctor/dancer** aspirer à devenir médecin/danseur

ASR [ˌeɪes'ɑː(r)] *n Am* (*abbr* **air-sea rescue**) sauvetage *m* air-mer

ass[1] [æs] *n* **(a)** *(donkey)* âne *m*; **she-ass** ânesse *f*; **an ass's foal** un ânon; **ass's milk** lait *m* d'ânesse
(b) *Fam (idiot)* imbécile *mf*; **she's such an ass** elle est bête comme ses pieds; **to make an ass of oneself** se ridiculiser; *(make an exhibition of oneself)* se donner en spectacle; **don't be such an ass** ne fais pas l'imbécile
(c) *Am Vulg (bottom)* cul *m*; **my ass!** mon cul!; **a kick in the ass** un coup de pied au cul; **to get one's ass in gear** se remuer le cul; **to work one's ass off** bosser comme un nègre; **to get one's ass in a sling** avoir des emmerdes; **to go ass over teakettle** ramasser une gamelle; **I don't want to put my ass on the line** je veux pas que ça me retombe sur la gueule; **to haul** *or* **tear ass** se grouiller; **to kiss sb's ass** faire du lèche-cul à qn, *Can* lécher le cul de qn; **kiss my ass!** va te faire foutre!; **move your ass!** pousse ton cul!; **he's been sitting on his ass all day** il n'a rien foutu de la journée; **he doesn't know his ass from his elbow** *or* **from a hole in the ground** il est complètement nul; **to be up to**

one's ass in work crouler sous le travail; **your ass is grass!** tu vas voir ce que tu vas prendre!; **you can bet your ass I'll do it!** tu peux être sûr que je le ferai!; **to be on sb's ass** être sur le dos de qn; **get your ass out of here!** casse-toi!; **get your ass over here!** amène-toi!; **to break one's ass** se crever le cul; **there's no need to bust your ass to get it finished** pas la peine de te casser le cul pour le finir; **this weather is a pain in the ass** ce temps me fait vraiment chier; **they want your ass** ils veulent ta peau; **to be out on one's ass** ne pas avoir de pot; **a piece of ass** *(sex)* une baise; *(woman)* une fille baisable; **to do sth ass-backwards** faire qch à l'envers *ou* n'importe comment

▸**ass about, ass around** *vi Am Vulg* déconner

ass² *(written abbr* **assistant***)* assistant(e) *m,f*

assagai = **assegai**

assail [ə'seɪl] *vt* attaquer, assaillir; *Fig* **he assailed her with questions** il l'a harcelée de questions; **assailed by doubt** assailli par le doute

assailable [ə'seɪləbəl] *adj* attaquable

assailant [ə'seɪlənt] *n* agresseur *m*, assaillant(e) *m,f*

Assam [æ'sæm] *n* Assam *m*; **in Assam** en Assam

Assamese [ˌæsə'miːz] *(pl* **inv***)* **1** *n* (**a**) *(person)* Assamais(e) *m,f* (**b**) *(language)* assamais *m*

2 *adj* assamais

assassin [ə'sæsɪn] *n* assassin *m*

►► *Entom* **assassin bug** triatome *m*

assassinate [ə'sæsɪneɪt] *vt* assassiner

assassination [əˌsæsɪ'neɪʃən] *n* assassinat *m*; **character assassination** diffamation *f*

►► ***assassination attempt*** attentat *m (contre quel qu'un)*

assault [ə'sɔːlt] **1** *n* (**a**) *(physical attack)* agression *f*; *Law* tentative *f* de voie de fait; **he is accused of assault** il est accusé de voie de fait; *Law* **common assault** voie *f* de fait simple; *Law* **sexual assault** agression *f* sexuelle; *Law* **assault and battery** coups *mpl* et blessures *fpl*

(**b**) *Mil* assaut *m*; **to lead an assault** se lancer à l'assaut; **they opened the assault on enemy positions** ils ont donné l'assaut aux positions ennemies; **they made** *or* **carried out an assault on the camp** ils sont montés à l'assaut du camp; *Fig* **the party launched an all-out assault on the opposition** le parti a lancé une offensive tous azimuts contre l'opposition; **they finally scored the winning try after a prolonged assault on their opponents' line** après une offensive prolongée dans le camp adverse, ils ont fini par marquer l'essai de la victoire

(**c**) *(criticism, vocal attack)* attaque *f*; **it's an assault on my reputation** c'est une atteinte à ma réputation; **a brave assault on widely held beliefs** une attaque courageuse contre des croyances très répandues; **the music is an assault on listeners' ears** cette musique est une agression pour les oreilles des auditeurs

(**d**) *(in climbing)* assaut *m*; **their assault on K2** leur tentative d'ascension du K2

2 *vt* (**a**) *(attack → person)* agresser, attaquer; *Law* se livrer à des voies de fait sur; *(sexually)* violenter; **to be assaulted** être victime d'une agression; *(sexually)* être victime d'un attentat à la pudeur

(**b**) *Mil (town, position etc)* attaquer, assaillir, [illegible]

►► *Mil* ***assault course*** parcours *m* du combattant; *Mil* ***assault craft*** engin *m* d'assaut

assay [ə'seɪ] **1** *vt* (**a**) *Metal (analyse → metal)* essayer; *(→ gold, silver)* coupeller (**b**) *Arch (attempt)* essayer, tenter

2 *n* essai *m* (scientifique)

►► ***assay office*** laboratoire *m* d'essais

assayer [ə'seɪə(r)] *n Metal* essayeur *m*

assaying [ə'seɪɪŋ] *n Metal* analyse *f*, essai *m*

assegai ['æsəgaɪ] *n Bot* sagaie *f*

assemblage [ə'semblɪdʒ] *n* (**a**) *(collection)* collection *f*, groupe *m*; *(of people)* assemblée *f* (**b**) *(process)* montage *m*, assemblage *m*

assemble [ə'sembəl] **1** *vt* (**a**) *(people)* rassembler, réunir; *(documents, evidence)* réunir; *(troops)* rassembler (**b**) *(put together)* monter, assembler; **factory assembled** monté en usine

2 *vi* se rassembler, se réunir

assembler [ə'semblə(r)] *n Comput* assembleur *m*

assembly [ə'semblɪ] *(pl* **assemblies***)* *n* (**a**) *(meeting → gen)* réunion *f*, assemblée *f*; **a place of assembly** un lieu de réunion; **unlawful assembly** attroupement *m*; **the right of assembly** la liberté de réunion

(**b**) *Pol* assemblée *f*; **National Assembly** l'Assemblée *f* nationale

(**c**) *Sch* = réunion de tous les élèves de l'établissement;

(**d**) *Mil* rassemblement *m*

(**e**) *(building → process)* montage *m*, assemblage *m*; *(→ end product)* assemblage *m*; *Aut* **the engine assembly** le bloc moteur

(**f**) *Comput* assemblage *m*

►► *Mil* ***assembly area*** zone *f* d'attente; ***assembly hall*** = hall où les enfants se réunissent le matin avant d'entrer en classe; ***assembly instructions*** instructions *fpl* de montage *ou* d'assemblage; *Comput* ***assembly language*** langage *m* d'assemblage; ***assembly language program*** programme *m* en assembleur; *Ind* ***assembly line*** chaîne *f* de montage; **to work on an assembly line** travailler à la chaîne; *Ind* ***assembly plant*** usine *f* de montage; ***assembly point*** point *m* de rassemblement; ***assembly room*** *(gen)* salle *f* de réunion; *(at town hall)* salle *f* des fêtes; *(industrial)* atelier *m* de montage; *Ind* ***assembly shop*** salle *f* de montage

assemblyman [ə'semblɪmən] *(pl* **assemblymen** [-mən]*)* *n Am Pol* = homme qui siège à une assemblée législative

assemblywoman [ə'semblɪˌwʊmən] *(pl* **assemblywomen** [-ˌwɪmɪn]*)* *n Am Pol* = femme qui siège à une assemblée législative

assent [ə'sent] **1** *vi* consentir, acquiescer; **they finally assented to the proposition** ils ont fini par donner leur assentiment à la proposition

2 *n* consentement *m*, assentiment *m*; **to give one's assent to sth** donner son assentiment à qch; **the royal assent** le consentement du souverain; **by common assent** du consentement de tous

assentation [ˌæsen'teɪʃən] *n Literary* assentiment *m* obséquieux

assenting [ə'sentɪŋ] *adj* consentant

assentor [ə'sentə(r)] *n Br Pol* = signataire à l'appui d'un candidat aux élections gouvernementales

assert [ə'sɜːt] *vt* (**a**) *(proclaim)* affirmer, maintenir; *(innocence)* affirmer, protester de; **she continues to assert her innocence/good faith** elle ne cesse de protester de son innocence/de sa bonne foi (**b**) *(defend)* défendre; *(lay claim to)* revendiquer; **we must assert our right to speak** nous devons faire valoir notre droit à la parole (**c**) *(impose)* **to assert oneself** se faire respecter, s'imposer; **I had to assert my authority** il a fallu que j'affirme mon autorité *ou* que je m'impose

assertion [ə'sɜːʃən] *n* (**a**) *(claim)* affirmation *f*, assertion *f* (**b**) *(of rights)* revendication *f*

assertive [ə'sɜːtɪv] *adj (tone, person, manner etc)* assuré; **don't be too assertive** ne te montre pas trop autoritaire; **he's not assertive enough** il n'a pas assez d'autorité, il ne s'affirme pas assez

assertively [ə'sɜːtɪvlɪ] *adv* fermement

assertiveness [ə'sɜːtɪvnɪs] *n* assurance *f*

►► ***assertiveness training*** stage *m* d'affirmation de soi

assess [ə'ses] *vt* (**a**) *(judge → effectiveness, performance)* évaluer; *(value)* estimer; **to assess the damage** évaluer les dégâts; **I had to assess the quality of their work** j'ai dû juger de la qualité de leur travail; **it is important to assess public opinion on the subject** il est important de savoir ce qu'en pense l'opinion publique; **how do you assess the team's chances?** à votre avis, quelles sont les chances de l'équipe?, quelles chances accordez-vous à l'équipe?

(**b**) *Fin (value)* fixer *ou* déterminer la valeur de; **to assess a property for taxation** évaluer *ou* calculer la valeur imposable d'une propriété; **the court assessed the damages at £2000** la cour a fixé les dommages et intérêts à 2000 livres

(**c**) *Fin (taxes)* évaluer

(**d**) *Sch & Univ (of teacher, tutor → knowledge, abilities)* évaluer; **students are continuously assessed** le niveau des étudiants est évalué par un contrôle continu

(**e**) *Med & Psy (of doctor, social worker, psychologist)* évaluer

►► *Fin* ***assessed income*** revenu *m* imposable

assessable [ə'sesəbəl] *adj* imposable

►► *Fin* ***assessable income, assessable profits*** assiette *f* de l'impôt

assessment [ə'sesmənt] *n* (**a**) *(judgement)* estimation *f*, évaluation *f*; **I don't accept his assessment of our work** je ne suis pas d'accord avec son évaluation de notre travail; **what's your assessment of the situation?** comment voyez-vous *ou* jugez-vous la situation?; **what is your assessment of their chances?** à votre avis, quelles sont leurs chances?, quelles chances leur accordez-vous?

(**b**) *Fin (valuation → of amount due)* détermination *f*, évaluation *f*; *(→ of tax)* calcul *m* (de la valeur imposable); *Law (of damages)* évaluation *f*, estimation *f*

(**c**) *Sch & Univ (by teacher, tutor)* contrôle *m* des connaissances; *(on report card)* appréciation *f* des professeurs; **methods of assessment** méthodes *fpl* d'évaluation

(**d**) *Med & Psy (by doctor, social worker, psychologist)* évaluation *f*

►► ***assessment centre*** *Ind (for job candidates)* centre *f* d'évaluation des candidats; *Med (to assess needs of disabled children)* = service hospitalier dont le rôle est d'évaluer les besoins des enfants handicapés et de conseiller les parents

assessor [ə'sesə(r)] *n* (**a**) *(for insurance)* expert *m* (**b**) *Law* (juge *m*) assesseur *m*

►► *Am Fin* ***assessor of taxes*** inspecteur(trice) *m,f* des contributions directes

asset ['æset] **1** *n* avantage *m*, atout *m*; **she's a great asset to our team** elle est un excellent atout pour notre équipe

2 assets *npl (possessions)* avoir *m*, capital *m*; *Acct, Fin & Law* actif *m*; *(personal)* patrimoine *m*; *(on liquidation after bankruptcy)* masse *f* active; **the assets amount to £5 million** l'actif s'élève à cinq millions de livres; **our total assets** tous nos biens; **total assets** total *m* de l'actif; **assets and liabilities** l'actif *m* et le passif; **excess of assets over liabilities** excédent *m* de l'actif sur le passif

►► *Fin* ***asset allocation*** répartition *f* des actifs; *Fin* ***asset management*** gestion *f* de biens, gestion *f* de capital; *(of individual's wealth)* gestion *f* de patrimoine; *Fin* ***asset swap*** swap *m* d'actifs; *Fin* ***asset turnover*** rotation *f* des capitaux; *Acct & Fin* ***asset utilization ratio*** taux *m* d'utilisation des actifs; *Acct* ***asset valuation*** réserve *f*, provision *f* pour évaluation d'actif; *Acct* ***asset value*** valeur *f* de l'actif

asset-stripper *n Fin* dépeceur *m* d'entreprise

asset-stripping [-ˌstrɪpɪŋ] *n Fin* démembrement *m* d'entreprise

asseverate [ə'sevəˌreɪt] *vt Formal* déclarer; **he asseverated his innocence** il a juré de son innocence

asseveration [əˌsevə'reɪʃən] *n Formal* déclaration *f*; *(of good faith, innocence)* protestation *f*

asshole ['æshəʊl] *n Am Vulg* (**a**) *(anus)* trou *m* du cul (**b**) *Fig (stupid person)* connard (connasse) *m,f*; *(nasty person)* salaud (salope) *m,f*; **don't be such an asshole** ne sois pas si con; **to make an asshole of oneself** se ridiculiser ❑

assibilate [ə'sɪbɪleɪt] *Ling* **1** *vt* assibiler

2 *vi* s'assibiler

assibilation [əˌsɪbɪ'leɪʃən] *n Ling* assibilation *f*

assiduity [ˌæsɪ'djuːətɪ] *n* assiduité *f*, zèle *m*

assiduous [ə'sɪdjʊəs] *adj* assidu; **she was assiduous in her attention to detail** elle portait une attention assidue aux détails

assiduously [ə'sɪdjʊəslɪ] *adv* assidûment

assiduousness [ə'sɪdjʊəsnɪs] *n* assiduité *f*, zèle *m*

assign [ə'saɪn] **1** *vt* (**a**) *(allot)* assigner, attribuer; (**to** à); *(funds)* affecter (**to** à); *(debts)* céder, transférer (**to** à); *St Exch (shares)* attribuer (**to** à); **the room was assigned to study groups** la salle fut affectée *ou* réservée aux groupes d'étude; **a date and place were assigned for the exam** la date et le lieu de l'examen ont été fixés; **to assign a duty/task to sb** assigner une responsabilité/tâche à qn; **I assigned her the task of writing the report** je l'ai chargée de la rédaction du rapport; *Am* **assigned seating** *(in theatre)* places *fpl* numérotées

(**b**) *(appoint)* nommer, désigner; **he's been assigned to Moscow** il a été affecté à Moscou

(**c**) *(ascribe)* **to assign a reason for sth** donner la raison de qch; *Math* **we assign a value to X** nous attribuons *ou* assignons une valeur à X; **the aqueduct has been assigned to the Roman period** l'aqueduc a été attribué à l'époque romaine

(**d**) *Law* céder, transférer; **the property was assigned to his daughter** la propriété fut transférée au nom de sa fille; **she assigned the copyright to the school** elle a fait cession du droit d'auteur à l'école

2 *n* cessionnaire *mf*

assignable [ə'saɪnəbəl] *adj Law* cessible

assignation [,æsɪg'neɪʃən] *n* (**a**) *(meeting)* rendez-vous *m* clandestin; *Old-fashioned or Hum* **to have an assignation with sb** avoir un rendez-vous secret avec qn (**b**) *(assignment)* attribution *f*; *(of money)* allocation *f*; *(of person)* affectation *f* (**c**) *Law* cession *f*, transfert *m*

assignee [,æsaɪ'niː] *n Law* cessionnaire *mf*

assignment [ə'saɪnmənt] *n* (**a**) *(task)* tâche *f*; *(official)* mission *f*; *Sch & Univ* devoir *m*; *Journ (of individual reporter)* reportage *m* assigné; **a dangerous assignment** une tâche dangereuse; *Journ* **to be on assignment** être en reportage

(**b**) *(of duties, responsibilities)* allocation *f*; *(of person)* affectation *f*

(**c**) *(of funds)* affectation *f*; *(of debts)* transfert *m*; *St Exch (of shares)* attribution *f*

(**d**) *Law* cession *f*, transfert *m*; *(of patent)* cession *f*

►► ***assignment of accounts receivable*** transfert *m* de créances; *Law* ***assignment of contract*** = cession des droits et obligations découlant d'un contrat; *Comput* ***assignment table*** table *f* d'affectation

assignor [ə'saɪnə(r)] *n Law* cédant(e) *m,f*

assimilate [ə'sɪmɪleɪt] **1** *vt* (**a**) *(food, information)* assimiler (**b**) *(immigrants)* intégrer; **they try very hard to assimilate newcomers** ils font tout leur possible pour intégrer les nouveaux arrivants

2 *vi* (**a**) *(become absorbed)* s'assimiler, s'intégrer (**b**) *(immigrants)* s'intégrer; **foreigners find it difficult to assimilate into a new culture** les étrangers ont du mal à s'intégrer à une autre culture (**c**) *(become similar)* **to assimilate to** *or* **with sth** s'assimiler à qch

assimilation [ə,sɪmɪ'leɪʃən] *n (gen) & Ling* assimilation *f*

Assisi [ə'siːzɪ, ə'siːsɪ] *n Geog* Assise *f*

assist [ə'sɪst] **1** *vt* (**a**) *(help)* aider, assister; *(process)* faciliter; **he assisted her up/down the stairs** il l'a aidée à monter/descendre l'escalier; **how may I assist you?** comment puis-je vous être utile?; **the two groups assisted each other with their research** les deux groupes se sont entraidés dans leur recherche; *Law* **a man is assisting police with their enquiries** la police est en train d'interroger un suspect

(**b**) *(with money)* **assisted by the town hall** avec le concours de la mairie; **assisted passage** billet *m* subventionné

2 *vi* (**a**) *(help)* aider, prêter secours; **she assisted at the operation** elle a apporté son assistance pendant l'opération

(**b**) *Arch (attend)* assister; **we assisted at his funeral** nous avons assisté à ses obsèques

3 *n Sport* = action qui permet à un coéquipier de marquer un point

assistance [ə'sɪstəns] *n* aide *f*, secours *m*; **may I be of assistance to you?** puis-je vous être utile?; **to come to sb's assistance** venir au secours de qn; **could you give me some assistance with these calculations?** pourriez-vous me venir en aide dans ces calculs?; **with the assistance of sb** avec l'aide de qn; **with the assistance of sth** à l'aide de qch; **with the financial assistance of the university** avec le concours financier de l'université

assistant [ə'sɪstənt] **1** *n* assistant(e) *m,f*, aide *mf*; *Comput (program)* assistant *m*; **(shop) assistant** vendeur(euse) *m,f*; **(foreign language) assistant** *Sch* assistant(e) *m,f* (en langue étrangère); *Univ* lecteur(trice) *m,f* (en langue étrangère); **French assistant** assistant(e) *m,f* de français; *Sch* **non-teaching assistant** auxiliaire *mf*

2 *comp (director, judge, librarian, secretary)* adjoint

►► *Com* ***assistant manager*** sous-directeur(trice) *m,f*, directeur(trice) *m,f* adjoint(e); *Br Com* ***assistant manageress*** sous-directrice *f*, directrice *f* adjointe; *Sch* ***assistant master, assistant mistress*** professeur *m (qui n'est pas responsable d'une section)*; *Am Univ* ***assistant professor*** ≃ maître-assistant *m*, *Can* ≃ professeur *m* adjoint; ***assistant referee*** *(in football)* juge *m* de touche; *Sch* ***assistant teacher*** *(primary)* instituteur(trice) *m,f*; *(secondary)* professeur *m (qui n'est pas responsable d'une section)*

assistantship [ə'sɪstənt,ʃɪp] *n Univ* assistanat *m*

assize [ə'saɪz] *n* réunion *f*; *Law* assises *fpl*; **court of assizes** cour *f* d'assises; **to be brought before the assizes** être traduit en cour d'assises

►► ***assize court*** cour *f* d'assises

ass-kisser, ass-licker *n Am Vulg* lèche-cul *m*

assoc (**a**) *(written abbr* **association**) association *f* (**b**) *(written abbr* **associated**) associé

associate 1 *vt* [ə'səʊʃɪeɪt] (**a**) *(mentally)* associer (**with sb** avec qn; **with sth** à qch); **I don't associate you with that kind of activity** je ne t'imagine pas dans ce genre d'activité; **I don't associate the two things** pour moi, les deux choses sont indépendantes

(**b**) *(in partnership etc)* **to associate oneself (with sb)** s'associer (avec qn); **to be associated with sb in an undertaking** s'associer avec qn pour une entreprise; **to be associated with sth** *(with project, research etc)* participer à qch; *(with company etc)* avoir des liens avec qch, travailler avec qch; **we are not associated in any way with that company** nous n'avons absolument rien à faire *ou* voir avec cette société; **the problems associated with nuclear power** les problèmes relatifs à l'énergie nucléaire; **that kind of behaviour is often associated with an unhappy childhood** ce type de comportement est souvent lié à une enfance malheureuse

2 *vi* [ə'səʊʃɪeɪt] **to associate with sb** fréquenter qn

3 *n* [ə'səʊʃɪət] (**a**) *(partner)* associé(e) *m,f*; *Law* complice *mf*

(**b**) *(of club)* membre *m*, associé(e) *m,f*; *(of institution)* membre *m*; *Am Univ* **Associate in Arts** *(person)* = titulaire d'un diplôme universitaire américain de lettres; *(qualification)* diplôme *m* universitaire américain de lettres; *Am Univ* **Associate in Science** *(person)* = titulaire d'un diplôme universitaire américain de sciences; *(qualification)* diplôme *m* universitaire américain de sciences

4 *adj* [ə'səʊʃɪət] associé, allié; **I'm only an associate member of the organisation** je suis seulement membre associé de l'organisation

►► *Com* ***associate company*** société *f* affiliée; *Am Univ* ***associate degree*** = diplôme universitaire obtenu au bout de deux années d'études, ≃ DEUG *m*; *Cin* ***associate director*** assistant-réalisateur (assistante-réalisatrice) *m,f*; *Journ* ***associate editor*** rédacteur(trice) *m,f* associé(e); *Law* ***associate judge*** juge *m* assesseur; *Am Law* ***Associate Justice*** juge *m* de la Cour Suprême; *Am Univ* ***associate professor*** ≃ maître *m* de conférences, *Can* professeur *m* agrégé

associated [ə'səʊʃɪeɪtɪd] *adj* associé

►► *Com* ***associated company*** société *f* affiliée; *Press* ***Associated Press*** Associated Press *f (agence de presse dont le siège est à New York)*

association [ə,səʊsɪ'eɪʃən] *n* (**a**) *(grouping)* association *f*, société *f*; **the teachers have formed an association** les enseignants ont constitué une association; *Com* **trade association** association *f* professionnelle

(**b**) *(involvement)* association *f*, fréquentation *f*; **through long association with the medical profession** à force de fréquenter la profession médicale; **to do sth in association with sb** faire qch en association avec qn; **this programme was made in association with Belgian television** ce programme a été fait en collaboration avec la télévision belge; **I have no association with that company** je n'ai pas de liens avec cette société; **the police knew about his association with the underworld** la police savait qu'il fréquentait le milieu

(**c**) *(of ideas)* association *f*; **by association of ideas** par association d'idées; **the name has unfortunate associations for her** ce nom lui évoque des pensées désagréables; **the associations of the name** ce qu'on associe à ce nom

►► *Br* ***association football*** football *m* association; *Psy* ***association test*** test *m* d'association

associationism [ə,səʊsɪ'eɪʃənɪzəm] *n Phil* associationisme *m*, associationnisme *m*

associative [ə'səʊʃɪətɪv] *adj (gen) & Comput* associatif

►► *Comput* ***associative storage*** mémoire *f* associative

assonance ['æsənəns] *n Ling* assonance *f*

assort [ə'sɔːt] **1** *vt* classer, ranger

2 *vi* s'assortir (**with** à)

assorted [ə'sɔːtɪd] *adj* (**a**) *(various)* varié, divers; **in assorted sizes** en différentes tailles; **an audience of assorted academics and businessmen** un public très varié, composé d'universitaires et d'hommes d'affaires (**b**) *(matched)* assorti; **well-/ill-assorted** bien/mal assorti

assortment [ə'sɔːtmənt] *n* assortiment *m*, collection *f*; *(of people)* mélange *m*; **there was a good assortment of cakes** il y avait un grand choix *ou* une bonne sélection de gâteaux; **she certainly has an odd assortment of friends!** ses amis forment un curieux mélange!

asst *(written abbr* **assistant**) assistant(e) *m,f*

assuage [ə'sweɪdʒ] *vt (grief, pain)* soulager, apaiser; *(hunger, thirst)* assouvir; *(person)* apaiser, calmer

assuagement [ə'sweɪdʒmənt] *n (of grief, pain)* soulagement *m*, apaisement *m*; *(of hunger, thirst)* assouvissement *m*; *(of person)* apaisement *m*

assume [ə'sjuːm] *vt* (**a**) *(presume)* supposer, présumer; **we can't assume anything** nous ne pouvons présumer de rien; **if we assume there will be no problems,...** en supposant qu'il n'y aura aucun problème,...; **I assume that he will come** je présume qu'il viendra; **he was assumed to be rich** on le supposait riche; **in the absence of proof he must be assumed to be innocent** en l'absence de preuves, il doit être présumé innocent; **don't assume that people will like you because you are rich** ne crois pas que les gens t'aimeront parce que tu es riche; **let us assume that...** mettons *ou* supposons que...; **to assume the worst** mettre les choses au pis

(**b**) *(take over → responsibility)* prendre sur soi, assumer; *(→ duty)* se charger de; *(→ power, command)* prendre; *(→ running of hotel, company etc)* prendre en main

(**c**) *(adopt → right, title etc)* s'attribuer, s'arroger, s'approprier; *(→ name)* adopter, emprunter; *Law* **to assume ownership** faire acte de propriétaire

(**d**) *(take on → air, appearance, tone)* prendre, se donner; *(→ shape, character)* affecter, revêtir; *(of problem → importance)* prendre; **his voice assumed a tone of authority** sa voix prit un ton autoritaire

(**e**) *(feign → indifference)* feindre, simuler

assumed [ə'sjuːmd] *adj* feint, faux (fausse); **with assumed indifference** avec une indifférence feinte

►► ***assumed name*** nom *m* d'emprunt; *(of author)* pseudonyme *m*; **he travels under an assumed name** il se sert d'un nom d'emprunt pour voyager

assuming [ə'sjuːmɪŋ] *conj* en admettant *ou* supposant que + *subjunctive*; **assuming he is alive** en admettant *ou* supposant qu'il soit toujours en vie

assumption [ə'sʌmpʃən] **1** *n* (**a**) *(supposition)* supposition *f*, hypothèse *f*; **the assumptions on which society is based** les idées de base qui servent de fondement à la société; **on the assumption that he agrees, we can go ahead** en supposant *ou* admettant qu'il soit d'accord, nous pouvons aller de l'avant; **we're working on the assumption that what she says is true** nous partons du principe qu'elle dit la vérité

(**b**) *(of power, responsibility etc)* prise *f*; **assumption of office** entrée *f* en fonctions; **his assumption of the role of chairman** *(after nomination)* son entrée en fonctions en tant que président; *(without consent)* le fait qu'il s'arroge la fonction de président
(**c**) *(of attitude)* affectation *f*
2 Assumption *n Rel* **the Assumption** l'Assomption *f*
►► *Rel* ***Assumption Day*** jour *m ou* fête *f* de l'Assomption

assurance [ə'ʃʊərəns] *n* (**a**) *(assertion)* affirmation *f*, assurance *f*; *(pledge)* promesse *f*, assurance *f*; **I can give you an assurance that...** je peux vous assurer *ou* vous affirmer que...; **she gave repeated assurances that she would not try to escape** elle a promis à plusieurs reprises qu'elle n'essaierait pas de s'enfuir; **he gave her a ring as an assurance of his love** il lui a donné une bague comme gage de son amour
(**b**) *(confidence)* assurance *f*, confiance *f* en soi; *(overconfidence)* arrogance *f*; **to lack assurance** manquer de confiance en soi; **she said it with such assurance, I believed her** elle l'a dit avec une telle assurance que je l'ai crue; **they set out with absolute assurance of their success** ils partirent, sûrs de leur réussite
(**c**) *Br (insurance)* assurance *f*; **life assurance** assurance sur la vie *f*, assurance-vie *f*
►► *Br* ***assurance company*** compagnie *f* d'assurances; *Br* ***assurance policy*** police *f* d'assurance

assure [ə'ʃʊə(r)] *vt* (**a**) *(affirm)* affirmer, assurer; **to assure sb of the truth of sth** assurer qn de la vérité de qch; **to assure sb of a fact** assurer *ou* affirmer un fait à qn; **he assures me that it is true** il me certifie que c'est vrai; **he assured me he was coming** il m'a assuré qu'il viendrait; **he will do it, I (can) assure you!** il le fera, je vous assure!; **she assured herself (of) a good pension** elle s'est assuré une bonne retraite
(**b**) *(ensure → peace, someone's happiness)* assurer
(**c**) *Br (insure)* assurer

assured [ə'ʃʊəd] **1** *adj* (**a**) *(certain)* assuré, certain; **they are assured of victory** ils sont certains de gagner; **she is assured a place in the finals** elle est certaine d'aller en finale; **you're assured of a warm welcome** on vous garantit un accueil chaleureux (**b**) *(self-confident)* assuré, sûr de soi; *(overconfident)* arrogant, effronté (**c**) *Br (insured)* assuré
2 *n* assuré(e) *m,f*

assuredly [ə'ʃʊərɪdlɪ] *adv* assurément, sûrement, sans aucun doute; **when she returns, as she assuredly will, ...** quand elle reviendra, ce qui ne laisse aucun doute, ...

assurer, assuror [ə'ʃʊərə(r)] *n Br Ins* assureur *m*

Assyria [ə'sɪrɪə] *n* Assyrie *f*; **in Assyria** en Assyrie

Assyrian [ə'sɪrɪən] **1** *n* Assyrien(enne) *m,f*
2 *adj* assyrien

Assyriology [ə,sɪrɪ'ɒlədʒɪ] *n* Assyriologie *f*

AST [,eɪes'tiː] *n* (*abbr* **Atlantic Standard Time**) = heure d'hiver des Provinces Maritimes du Canada et d'une partie des Caraïbes

astable [,eɪ'steɪbəl] *adj* instable

astatic [,eɪ'stætɪk] *adj (unstable)* instable; *Phys* astatique

astatine ['æstətiːn] *n Chem* astate *m*

[illegible]

asterisk ['æstərɪsk] **1** *n* astérisque *m*
2 *vt* marquer d'un astérisque

asterism ['æstərɪzəm] *n* (**a**) *Typ* = trois astérisques en triangle (**b**) *Astron & Miner* astérisme *m*

astern [ə'stɜːn] **1** *adv Naut* à *ou* sur l'arrière, en poupe; **to go astern** *(person)* aller à l'arrière *ou* en poupe; *(boat)* faire machine arrière, battre en arrière, culer; **full speed astern!** en arrière toutes!
2 *adj* à *ou* sur l'arrière

asteroid ['æstərɔɪd] *n* astéroïde *m*
►► ***asteroid belt*** ceinture *f* d'astéroïdes

asthenia [æs'θiːnɪə] *n Med* asthénie *f*

asthenosphere [əs'θiːnə,sfɪə(r)] *n Geol* asthénosphère *f*

asthma ['æsmə] *n* asthme *m*; **she has asthma** elle est asthmatique
►► ***asthma attack*** crise *f* d'asthme; ***asthma sufferer*** asthmatique *mf*

asthmatic [æs'mætɪk] **1** *n* asthmatique *mf*
2 *adj* asthmatique
►► ***asthmatic attack*** crise *f* d'asthme

astigmatic [,æstɪg'mætɪk] **1** *n* astigmate *mf*
2 *adj* astigmate

astigmatism [æ'stɪgmətɪzəm] *n* astigmatisme *m*

astir [ə'stɜː(r)] *adj Literary* (**a**) *(out of bed)* debout *(inv)*, levé (**b**) *(in motion)* animé

ASTMS ['æstiːmz, ,eɪes,tiːem'es] *n* (*abbr* **Association of Scientific, Technical and Managerial Staffs**) = ancien syndicat britannique des personnels scientifiques, techniques et administratifs

astonish [ə'stɒnɪʃ] *vt (surprise)* étonner; *(amaze)* stupéfier, ahurir; **you astonish me** vous m'étonnez; **it never fails to astonish me that...** ça m'étonnera toujours de voir que...; **to be astonished at seeing sth** être étonné *ou* s'étonner de voir qch; **I was astonished at** *or* **by the price** j'ai été étonné du prix; **I am continually astonished by her audacity** son audace ne cesse de m'étonner; **I am astonished that...** cela m'étonne que... + *subjunctive*

astonished [ə'stɒnɪʃt] *adj (surprised)* étonné; *(amazed)* stupéfait; **she had an astonished look on her face** elle avait l'air étonné *ou* stupéfait

astonishing [ə'stɒnɪʃɪŋ] *adj (surprising)* étonnant; *(amazing)* stupéfiant, ahurissant; **it's astonishing how he's changed** c'est stupéfiant comme il a changé; **with astonishing speed** à une vitesse incroyable *ou* étonnante

astonishingly [ə'stɒnɪʃɪŋlɪ] *adv* incroyablement; **she was astonishingly good at the piano** elle jouait incroyablement bien du piano; **astonishingly, they both decided to leave** aussi étonnant que cela paraisse, ils ont tous les deux décidé de partir

astonishment [ə'stɒnɪʃmənt] *n (surprise)* étonnement *m*; *(amazement)* stupéfaction *f*, ahurissement *m*; **they stared in astonishment** ils avaient l'air stupéfait; **a look of astonishment** un regard stupéfait *ou* ahuri; **to our astonishment** à notre grand étonnement, à notre stupéfaction

astound [ə'staʊnd] *vt* stupéfier, abasourdir; **we were astounded to hear the news** la nouvelle nous a stupéfaits; **I was astounded when she left like that** j'étais stupéfait qu'elle parte comme ça; *Ironic* **you astound me!** comme c'est étonnant!

astounded [ə'staʊndɪd] *adj* stupéfait

astounding [ə'staʊndɪŋ] *adj* stupéfiant, ahurissant

astoundingly [ə'staʊndɪŋlɪ] *adv* incroyablement; **astoundingly beautiful** d'une beauté incroyable; **astoundingly enough, they'd already met** chose extraordinaire, ils s'étaient déjà rencontrés

Astrakhan [,æstrə'kæn] **1** *n Geog* Astrakan, Astrakhan
2 astrakhan 1 *n Tex* astrakan *m* **2** *comp (hat, jacket)* d'astrakan

astral ['æstrəl] *adj Astron* astral
►► ***astral projection*** projection *f* astrale

astray [ə'streɪ] *adv* (**a**) *(lost)* **to go astray** s'égarer, se perdre; **the letter went astray** la lettre s'est perdue; **my pen seems to have gone astray** j'ai égaré mon stylo
(**b**) *(idioms)* **to go astray** *(morally)* se dévoyer, se détourner du droit chemin; **to lead sb astray** *(misinform)* mettre *ou* diriger qn sur une fausse piste; *(morally)* détourner qn du droit chemin; **don't be led astray by their so-called expertise** ne vous laissez pas tromper *ou* abuser par leur soi-disant compétence; **he's easily led astray** il se laisse facilement entraîner hors du droit chemin

astrict [ə'strɪkt] *vt Arch or Literary* astreindre

astride [ə'straɪd] *prep* à califourchon *ou* à cheval sur; **he sat astride the fence** il était assis à califourchon sur la barrière

astringence [ə'strɪndʒəns], **astringency** [ə'strɪndʒənsɪ] *n* astringence *f*

astringent [ə'strɪndʒənt] **1** *adj* (**a**) *(remark)* acerbe, caustique; *(criticism)* dur, sévère (**b**) *(lotion)* astringent
2 *n* astringent *m*

astringently [ə'strɪndʒəntlɪ] *adv (say, remark)* d'un ton acerbe; **astringently worded** virulent

astrodome ['æstrəʊdəʊm] *n* (**a**) *(for aircraft)* astrodôme *m* (**b**) *Am Sport* = centre sportif dont la toiture est un dôme transparent

astrodynamics [,æstrəʊdaɪ'næmɪks] *n (UNCOUNT)* astrodynamique *f*

astroid ['æstrɔɪd] *n Math* astroïde *f*

astrolabe ['æstrəleɪb] *n Astron* astrolabe *m*

astrologer [ə'strɒlədʒə(r)] *n* astrologue *mf*

astrological [,æstrə'lɒdʒɪkəl] *adj* astrologique

astrologically [,æstrə'lɒdʒɪkəlɪ] *adv* astrologiquement

astrologist [ə'strɒlədʒɪst] *n* astrologue *mf*

astrology [ə'strɒlədʒɪ] *n* astrologie *f*

astrometry [ə'strɒmətrɪ] *n Astron* astrométrie *f*

astronaut ['æstrənɔːt] *n* astronaute *mf*

astronautic [,æstrə'nɔːtɪk], **astronautical** [,æstrə'nɔːtɪkəl] *adj* astronautique

astronautics [,æstrə'nɔːtɪks] *n (UNCOUNT)* astronautique *f*

astronomer [ə'strɒnəmə(r)] *n* astronome *mf*

astronomic [,æstrə'nɒmɪk], **astronomical** [,æstrə'nɒmɪkəl] *adj (year, unit etc)* astronomique; *Fig* **an astronomic price** un prix astronomique; **an astronomic failure/disaster** un échec/désastre de proportions astronomiques

astronomically [,æstrə'nɒmɪkəlɪ] *adv* astronomiquement; *Fig (increase)* de façon astronomique; **it's astronomically expensive** ça coûte les yeux de la tête

astronomy [ə'strɒnəmɪ] *n* astronomie *f*

astrophotography [,æstrəʊfə'tɒgrəfɪ] *n* astrophotographie *f*

astrophysicist [,æstrəʊ'fɪzɪsɪst] *n* astrophysicien(enne) *m,f*

astrophysics [,æstrəʊ'fɪzɪks] *n (UNCOUNT)* astrophysique *f*

Astroturf® ['æstrəʊ,tɜːf] *n Sport* gazon *m* artificiel

Asturian [æs'tjʊərɪən] *adj* asturien

Asturias [æ'stʊərɪæs] *n Geog* Asturies *fpl*; *Hist* **the prince of Asturias** le prince des Asturies

astute [ə'stjuːt] *adj (person → shrewd)* astucieux, fin, perspicace; *(→ crafty)* malin(igne), rusé; *(investment, management)* astucieux; **how astute of you!** vous êtes malin!

astutely [ə'stjuːtlɪ] *adv* astucieusement, avec finesse *ou* perspicacité

astuteness [ə'stjuːtnɪs] *n* finesse *f*, perspicacité *f*

Asuncion [ə,sʊnsɪ'ɒn] *n Geog* Asuncion

asunder [ə'sʌndə(r)] *adv Literary (to pieces)* **to tear sth asunder** mettre qch en pièces; **the family had been torn asunder by war** la famille avait été déchirée par la guerre; **to break asunder** se casser en deux

ASV [,eɪes'viː] *n* (*abbr* **American Standard Version**) = traduction américaine de la Bible

Aswan ['æswɑːn] *n* Assouan
►► ***the Aswan (High) Dam*** le barrage d'Assouan

aswirl [ə'swɜːl] *adj Literary* tourbillonnant

asylum [ə'saɪləm] *n* (**a**) *(shelter)* (lieu *m* de) refuge *m*; *(in church etc)* asile *m* (inviolable); **to seek asylum** chercher asile; **he was granted/refused asylum** on lui a accordé/refusé l'asile; **the right to** *or* **of asylum** le droit d'asile; **political asylum** asile politique (**b**) *(mental hospital)* asile *m* (d'aliénés)

asylum-seeker *n* demandeur(euse) *m,f* d'asile

asymmetric [,eɪsɪ'metrɪk], **asymmetrical** [,eɪsɪ'metrɪkəl] *adj* asymétrique
►► *Sport* ***asymmetrical bars*** barres *fpl* asymétriques

asymmetry [,eɪ'sɪmətrɪ] *n* asymétrie *f*

asymptomatic ['eɪ,sɪmptə'mætɪk] *adj Med* asymptomatique

asymptote ['æsɪmptəʊt] *n Geom* asymptote

asymptotic ['æsɪmptəʊtɪk] *adj Geom* asymptotique

asynchronous [,eɪ'sɪŋkrənəs] *adj* asynchrone
►► *Comput* ***asynchronous transfer mode*** commutation *f* temporelle asynchrone

asyndetic [,æsɪn'detɪk] *adj Gram* asyndétique

asyndeton [,æ'sɪndətən] *adj Gram* asyndète *f*

asystole [eɪ'sɪstəlɪ] *n Med* arrêt *m* cardiocirculatoire, *Spec* asystolie *f*

asystolic [eɪsɪs'tɒlɪk] *adj Med* asystolique

AT [ət, *stressed* æt]

à	▸ **1 (a) – (c), (f) – (h)**
dans la direction de	▸ **1 (d)**
en	▸ **1 (i)**

1 *prep* (**a**) *(indicating point in space)* à; **at the door/the bus stop** à la porte/l'arrêt de bus; **at my house/the dentist's** chez moi/le dentiste; **I'm at the airport** je suis à l'aéroport; **we're at the Savoy (Hotel)** *(staying at)* nous sommes au Savoy; **she's at a wedding/a committee meeting** *(attending)* elle est à un mariage/en réunion avec le comité; **she was standing at the window** elle se tenait debout à la fenêtre; **turn left at the traffic lights/at the Town Hall** tournez à gauche au feu/à la mairie; *Rail* **change at Reading** prenez la correspondance à Reading; *Am* **where are you at with that report?** où en êtes-vous avec ce rapport?; *Fam* **this club is where it's at** ce club est très chic *ou* dans le vent; *Fam* **that's not where it's at** *(not fashionable)* ça n'est pas dans le vent; *Am (not the important thing)* là n'est pas la question; *Fam* **that's not where I'm at** c'est pas mon truc

(**b**) *(indicating point in time)* à; **at noon/six o'clock** à midi/six heures; **I work at night** je travaille de nuit; **I like to work at night** j'aime travailler la nuit; **I'm busy at the moment** je suis occupé en ce moment; **at a time when...** à un moment où...

(**c**) *(indicating age)* à; **he started working at fifteen** il a commencé à travailler à (l'âge de) quinze ans

(**d**) *(indicating direction)* vers, dans la direction de; **look at this!** regarde ça!; **he shot at the rabbit** il a tiré sur le lapin; **she grabbed at the purse** elle a essayé de s'emparer du porte-monnaie; **don't shout at me!** ne me crie pas dessus!

(**e**) *(indicating activity)* **my parents are at work** mes parents sont au travail; **he was at lunch** il était allé déjeuner; *Fam* **get me some coffee while you're at it** prenez-moi du café pendant que vous y êtes; *Fam* **she's at it again!** la voilà qui recommence!; *Fam* **don't let me catch you at it again!** que je ne t'y reprenne pas!

(**f**) *(indicating level, rate)* **the temperature stands at 30°** la température est de 30°; **at 50 mph** ≃ à 80 km/h; **he drove at 50 mph** ≃ il faisait du 80 (à l'heure); **the rise worked out at £1 an hour** l'augmentation correspondait à 1 livre de l'heure

(**g**) *(indicating price)* à; **it's a bargain at £5** à 5 livres, c'est une bonne affaire; **we sell it at (a price of) £1 a kilo** nous le vendons 1 livre le kilo

(**h**) *(with superlative)* à; **the water level was at its highest/lowest** le niveau d'eau était au plus haut/au plus bas; **she's at her most/least effective in such situations** c'est là qu'elle est le plus/le moins efficace

(**i**) *(as adjective complement)* en; **he's brilliant/hopeless at maths** il est excellent/nul en maths

(**j**) *Fam (idiom)* **to be (on) at sb** harceler qn□; **he's always (on) at his secretary to arrive earlier** il n'arrête pas de harceler sa secrétaire pour qu'elle vienne plus tôt le matin; **his mother's always (on) at him to tidy his room** sa mère est toujours après lui *ou* le harcèle toujours pour qu'il range sa chambre

(**k**) *Comput (in e-mail address)* arrobas, a commercial; **gwilson at transex, dot, co, dot, uk** gwilson, arrobas, transex, point, co, point, uk

2 at once *adv* (**a**) *(immediately)* tout de suite, immédiatement

(**b**) *(simultaneously)* en même temps; **they all came at once** ils sont tous arrivés en même temps; **don't all talk at once** ne parlez pas tous en même temps

Atacama [ætəˈkɑːmə]

►► ***the Atacama Desert*** le désert d'Atacama

ataractic [ˌætəˈræktɪk] *adj Phil* ataraxique

ataraxia [ˌætəˈræksɪə] *n Phil* ataraxie *f*

atavism [ˈætəvɪzəm] *n Biol* atavisme *m*

atavistic [ˌætəˈvɪstɪk] *adj Biol* atavique

ataxia [əˈtæksɪə] *n Med* ataxie *f*; **locomotor ataxia** ataxie *f* locomotrice progressive, tabes *m* dorsalis

ataxic [əˈtæksɪk] *adj Med* ataxique

ataxy [əˈtæksɪ] *n Med* ataxie *f*

ATB [ˌeɪtiːˈbiː] *n (abbr* **all-terrain bike***)* VTT *m*

at-bat *n Sport (in baseball)* présence *f* au bâton

ATC [ˌeɪtiːˈsiː] *n* (**a**) *(abbr* **air traffic control***)* contrôle *m* du trafic aérien (**b**) *(abbr* **Air Training Corps***)* = unité de formation de l'armée de l'air britannique

ate [eɪt] *pt of* **eat**

A-team *n Sport* **the A-team** l'équipe *f* première

atelier [æˈtelɪeɪ] *n* atelier *m*

a tempo [ɑːˈtempəʊ] *Mus* **1** *adj* a tempo

2 *adv* a tempo

Athanasian Creed [ˌæθəˈneɪʃən-] *n Rel* **the Athanasian Creed** le symbole de saint Athanase

atheism [ˈeɪθɪɪzəm] *n Rel* athéisme *m*

atheist [ˈeɪθɪɪst] *Rel* **1** *adj* athée

2 *n* athée *mf*

atheistic [ˌeɪθɪˈɪstɪk], **atheistical** [ˌeɪθɪˈɪstɪkəl] *adj* athée

athematic [ˌeɪθɪˈmætɪk] *adj* athématique

Athena [əˈθiːnə], **Athene** [əˈθiːniː] *pr n Myth* Athéna *f*

Athenaeum [ˌæθɪˈniːəm] *n Antiq* athénée *m*

Athenian [əˈθiːnɪən] **1** *n* Athénien(enne) *m,f*

2 *adj* athénien

Athens [ˈæθɪnz] *n* Athènes

►► *Naut* ***Athens Convention*** Convention *f* d'Athènes; ***the Athens of the North*** l'Athènes du Nord *(surnom donné à Édimbourg)*

athirst [əˈθɜːst] *adj Literary* assoiffé; **athirst for revenge** assoiffé de vengeance

athlete [ˈæθliːt] *n (gen)* sportif(ive) *m,f*; *(track & field competitor)* athlète *mf*

►► ***athlete's foot*** *(UNCOUNT)* mycose *f*; **to have athlete's foot** avoir une mycose

athletic [æθˈletɪk] *adj (sporty)* sportif; *(muscular)* athlétique; **she's very athletic** elle est très sportive; **an athletic-looking young man** un jeune homme athlétique; **I don't do anything very athletic** je ne fais pas beaucoup de sport

►► ***athletic support, athletic supporter*** *(underwear)* suspensoir *m*

athletically [æθˈletɪkəlɪ] *adv (swim, ride, jump)* de façon sportive; **to be athletically built** être athlétique, avoir un corps d'athlète; **she's athletically gifted** elle est douée pour le sport

athleticism [æθˈletɪsɪzəm] *n* athlétisme *m*

athletics [æθˈletɪks] **1** *n (UNCOUNT)* athlétisme *m*

2 *comp (club, meeting)* d'athlétisme; *(activity → track & field)* athlétique; *(→ other sport)* sportif

►► *Am* ***athletics coach*** entraîneur *m* (sportif)

at-home *n* = réception chez soi

athwart [əˈθwɔːt] *Literary* **1** *prep* (**a**) *(across the path of)* en travers de; *Naut* par le travers de (**b**) *(in opposition to)* contre, en opposition à

2 *adv* en travers; *Naut* par le travers

atishoo [əˈtɪʃuː] *exclam Br* atchoum!

Atlanta [ətˈlæntə] *n* Atlanta

Atlantic [ətˈlæntɪk] **1** *n* **the Atlantic** l'Atlantique *m*, l'océan *m* Atlantique

2 *adj (coast, community)* atlantique; *Met (wind)* de l'Atlantique; *(ocean)* l'Atlantique *m*, l'océan *m* Atlantique

►► *Hist* ***the Atlantic Charter*** le Pacte atlantique; *Naut* ***Atlantic liner*** transatlantique *m*; ***the Atlantic Ocean*** l'Atlantique *m*, l'océan *m* Atlantique; ***the Atlantic Provinces*** *(in Canada)* les Provinces *fpl* atlantiques; ***Atlantic Standard Time*** = heure d'hiver des Provinces Maritimes du Canada et d'une partie des Caraïbes

Atlantis [ətˈlæntɪs] *pr n Myth* Atlantide *f*

Atlas [ˈætləs] **1** *n* **the High Atlas** le Haut *ou* Grand Atlas; **the Middle Atlas** le Moyen Atlas

2 *pr n Myth* Atlas; **the Daughters of Atlas** les Atlantides *fpl*

►► *Entom* ***Atlas moth*** atlas *m*; ***the Atlas Mountains*** l'Atlas *m*

atlas [ˈætləs] *(pl sense* (**c**) **atlantes** [ətˈlæntiːz]) *n* (**a**) *(book)* atlas *m* (**b**) *Anat* atlas *m* (**c**) *Archit* atlante *m*, télamon *m*

ATM [ˌeɪtiːˈem] *n* (**a**) *Banking (abbr* **automated teller machine***)* DAB *m*, *Can* guichet *m* (bancaire) automatique, *Suisse* bancomat *m* (**b**) *Comput (abbr* **asynchronous transfer mode***)* ATM *m*, commutation *f* temporelle asynchrone

atm. *(written abbr* **atmosphere***)* atm

atmosphere [ˈætməˌsfɪə(r)] *n* (**a**) *(air)* atmosphère *f*; **the smoky atmosphere bothered her** l'atmosphère enfumée la gênait

(**b**) *(feeling, mood)* ambiance *f*, atmosphère *f*; **there was an atmosphere of elation in the room** il régnait une joyeuse ambiance dans la pièce; **the place has no atmosphere** l'endroit est impersonnel; **there's a really bad atmosphere in the office just now** il y a une très mauvaise ambiance au bureau en ce moment

(**c**) *Phys* atmosphère *f*

atmospheric [ˌætməsˈferɪk] *adj* (**a**) *(pollution, pressure)* atmosphérique (**b**) *(lighting, music)* qui met dans l'ambiance; **the film was very atmospheric** il y avait beaucoup d'atmosphère dans ce film

atmospherics [ˌætməsˈferɪks] *npl Elec & Tel* parasites *mpl*

ATOL [ˌæˈtɒl] *n (abbr* **air travel organizer's licence***)* licence *m* d'organisateur de voyages par avion

atoll [ˈætɒl] *n Geog* atoll *m*

atom [ˈætəm] *n* (**a**) *Phys* atome *m* (**b**) *Fig* **there's not an atom of truth in what you say** il n'y a pas une once *ou* un brin de vérité dans ce que tu dis; **they haven't one atom of common sense** ils n'ont pas le moindre bon sens

►► *Mil & Nucl* ***atom bomb*** bombe *f* atomique; *Fam Nucl* ***atom smasher*** accélérateur *m* de particules□

atomic [əˈtɒmɪk] *adj Phys & Nucl* atomique

►► ***atomic bomb*** bombe *f* atomique; *Tech* ***atomic clock*** horloge *f* atomique; *Med* ***atomic cocktail*** = mélange radioactif utilisé dans le traitement du cancer; ***atomic energy*** énergie *f* nucléaire *ou* atomique; ***Atomic Energy Authority*** = commissariat à l'énergie nucléaire en Grande-Bretagne; *Am* ***Atomic Energy Commission*** = commissariat à l'énergie nucléaire aux États-Unis at au Canada; ***atomic heat*** chaleur *f* atomique; ***atomic mass*** masse *f ou* poids *m* atomique; ***atomic number*** nombre *m ou* numéro *m* atomique; ***atomic pile*** pile *f* atomique, réacteur *m* nucléaire; ***atomic power*** énergie *f* atomique, réacteur *m* nucléaire; ***atomic power station*** centrale *f* nucléaire; ***atomic reactor*** réacteur *m* nucléaire; ***atomic structure*** structure *f* atomique; ***atomic theory*** théorie *f* atomique; ***atomic volume*** volume *m* atomique; ***atomic warfare*** guerre *f* nucléaire *ou* atomique; ***atomic weight*** masse *f ou* poids *m* atomique

atomicity [ætəˈmɪsɪtɪ] *n Phys* atomicité *f*

atomic-powered *adj* (fonctionnant à l'énergie) nucléaire *ou* atomique

atomism [ˈætəmɪzəm] *n Phil, Phys & Psy* atomisme *m*

atomization [ˌætəmaɪˈzeɪʃən] *n Phys (of matter)* atomisation *f*, *Chem (of fuel)* atomisation *f*, pulvérisation *f*

atomize, -ise [ˈætəmaɪz] *vt Phys (matter)* atomiser; *Chem (fuel)* atomiser, pulvériser; *Chem (in spray, liquid)* vaporiser

atomized [ˈætəmaɪzd] *adj (life, society)* fragmenté

atomizer [ˈætəmaɪzə(r)] *n* atomiseur *m*

atonal [eɪˈtəʊnəl] *adj Mus* atonal

atonality [ˌeɪtəʊˈnælətɪ] *n Mus* atonalité *f*

▸**atone for** [əˈtəʊn] *vt insep (sin, crime)* expier; *(mistake, behaviour)* racheter, réparer

atonement [əˈtəʊnmənt] *n (of crime, sin)* expiation *f*; *(of mistake, behaviour)* réparation *f*; *Rel* **to make atonement for one's sins** expier ses péchés; **they made atonement for their past mistakes** ils ont racheté leurs erreurs passées; *Rel* **Day of Atonement** (fête *f* du) Grand Pardon *m*

atonic [eɪˈtɒnɪk] *adj* (**a**) *Ling* atone (**b**) *Physiol (muscle)* atonique

atony [ˈætənɪ] *n Ling & Physiol* atonie *f*

atop [əˈtɒp] *Literary* **1** *adv* en haut

2 *prep* en haut de, sur; **sitting atop a suitcase** assis sur une valise

A to Z *n* (**a**) *(street guide)* plan *m* de ville; **an A to Z of London** un plan de Londres (**b**) *(guide)* manuel *m*; **an A to Z of gardening** le jardinage de A à Z

ATP [ˌeɪtiːˈpiː] *n Sport (abbr* **Association of Tennis Professionals***)* ATP *f*

atrabilious [ˌætrəˈbɪlɪəs] *adj Literary* atrabilaire

Atreus [ˈeɪtrɪəs] *pr n Myth* Atrée

at-risk *adj* **an at-risk group** un groupe *ou* une population à risque

atrium ['eɪtrɪəm] (*pl* **atria** [-trɪə] *or* **atriums**) *n* (**a**) *(court)* cour *f*; *Antiq* atrium *m* (**b**) *Anat* orifice *m* de l'oreillette

atrocious [ə'trəʊʃəs] *adj* (**a**) *Fam (very bad → pun, weather, journey)* atroce❑, exécrable❑; *(→ clothes, design)* affreux❑; *(→ behaviour, manners)* ignoble❑; *(→ injuries)* atroce; **his French is atrocious** son français est très mauvais; **his singing is atrocious** il chante atrocement *ou* affreusement mal (**b**) *(crime)* atroce; **an atrocious act** une atrocité

atrociously [ə'trəʊʃəslɪ] *adv* (**a**) *Fam (very badly)* exécrablement❑; **atrociously bad** atroce❑, exécrable❑ (**b**) *(cruelly)* atrocement

atrociousness [ə'trəʊʃəsnɪs] *n* (**a**) *Fam (of pun, weather)* caractère *m* exécrable❑ *ou* atroce❑; **we could scarcely believe the atrociousness of the weather** nous avions peine à croire qu'il faisait un temps aussi exécrable *ou* atroce (**b**) *(of crime)* atrocité *f*

atrocity [ə'trɒsətɪ] (*pl* **atrocities**) *n* (**a**) *(act)* atrocité *f* (**b**) *(of crime)* atrocité *f*

atrophied ['ætrəfɪd] *adj Med* atrophié

atrophy ['ætrəfɪ] (*pt & pp* **atrophied**) *Med* **1** *n* atrophie *f*

2 *vi* s'atrophier

3 *vt* atrophier

atrophying ['ætrəfɪɪŋ] *adj Med* atrophiant

atropine ['ætrəpiːn] *n Med* atropine *f*

at-sign *n Typ & Comput* arrobas *m*

attaboy ['ætəbɔɪ] *exclam Am Fam* bravo! vas-y mon petit!

attach [ə'tætʃ] **1** *vt* (**a**) *(connect → handle, label)* attacher, fixer; *(→ appendix, document)* joindre; **the attached letter** la lettre ci-jointe; **please find attached...** veuillez trouver ci-joint...

(**b**) *(associate with)* **he attached himself to a group of walkers** il s'est joint à un groupe de randonneurs; **the kitten attached himself to her** *(followed her)* le chaton l'a adoptée

(**c**) *(be part of)* **the research centre is attached to the science department** le centre de recherche dépend du *ou* est rattaché au département des sciences

(**d**) *(attribute)* attacher, attribuer (**to** à); *(blame)* imputer (**to** à); **don't attach too much importance to this survey** n'accordez pas trop d'importance à cette enquête

(**e**) *(place on temporary duty)* affecter; **an official attached to another department** un fonctionnaire détaché à un autre service; **to be attached to a unit** être affecté à une unité; **she's attached to NATO** elle est attachée à l'OTAN

(**f**) *Law (person)* arrêter, appréhender; *(property, salary)* saisir

(**g**) *Comput (file)* joindre (**to** à); **to attach a file to an e-mail message** joindre un fichier à un message électronique

2 *vi* (**a**) **to attach to** *(fix on to)* s'accrocher à; *(appliance, shelves → to wall)* se fixer à; *(rope, hook)* être relié à

(**b**) *Formal (be attributed)* être attribué, être imputé; **the benefits that attach to this position are considerable** les avantages attachés à ce poste sont énormes; **no blame attaches to you for what happened** la responsabilité de ce qui s'est produit ne repose nullement sur vous

attaché [ə'tæʃeɪ] *n Pol* attaché(e) *m,f*

▸▸ ***attaché case*** mallette *f*, attaché-case *m*

attached [ə'tætʃt] *adj* attaché; **he's very attached to his family** il est très attaché *ou* il tient beaucoup à sa famille; **she's (already) attached** elle a déjà quelqu'un dans sa vie; **I was very attached to that car** j'étais très attaché à cette voiture

attachment [ə'tætʃmənt] *n* (**a**) *(fastening)* fixation *f*

(**b**) *(accessory, part)* accessoire *m*

(**c**) *(document)* pièce *f* jointe; *Comput (to e-mail)* fichier *m* joint

(**d**) *(affection)* attachement *m*, affection *f*; *(loyalty)* attachement *m*; **to form an attachment to sb** s'attacher à qn, se prendre d'affection pour qn; **she has a strong attachment to her grandfather** elle est très attachée à son grand-père

(**e**) *(temporary duty)* détachement *m*; **he's on attachment to the hospital** il est en détachement à l'hôpital

(**f**) *Law (of person)* arrestation *f*; *(of property)* saisie *f*

(**g**) *Comput (of e-mail)* fichier *m* joint

▸▸ *Law* ***attachment of earnings*** = saisie-arrêt du salaire, des biens ou des bienfaits d'un débiteur par un créancier

attack [ə'tæk] **1** *vt* (**a**) *(assault → physically)* attaquer; *(→ verbally)* attaquer, s'attaquer à; *Mil* attaquer, assaillir

(**b**) *(tackle)* s'attaquer à; **a campaign to attack racism** une campagne pour combattre le racisme; **she attacked the problem with enthusiasm** elle s'est attaquée au problème avec enthousiasme

(**c**) *(of disease → person, organ)* s'attaquer à, atteindre; *(of rust → metal)* attaquer, s'attaquer à, ronger; *(of fear, doubts)* assaillir; **the disease mainly attacks the very young** la maladie atteint essentiellement les très jeunes enfants; **this apathy attacks the very roots of democracy** cette apathie menace les racines mêmes de la démocratie

2 *vi* attaquer

3 *n* (**a**) *(gen) & Sport* attaque *f*; *Mil* attaque *f*, assaut *m*; **attacks on old people are on the increase** les agressions contre les personnes âgées sont de plus en plus nombreuses; **to launch an attack on** donner l'assaut à; *(crime)* lancer une opération contre; *(problem, policy)* s'attaquer à; **to launch an attack on the enemy** donner l'assaut à l'ennemi; **yesterday the police launched an attack on petty theft in the area** hier la police a lancé une opération contre les larcins dans le secteur; **the newspaper launched an attack on government policy** le journal s'est attaqué à la politique gouvernementale; **the attack on her life failed** l'attentat contre elle a échoué; **the attack on drugs** le combat contre la drogue; **to return to the attack** revenir à la charge; **to go on the attack** passer à l'attaque; **the infantry was under attack** l'infanterie subissait un assaut *ou* était attaquée; **to come under attack** être en butte aux attaques; **she felt as though she were under attack** elle s'est sentie agressée; **to leave oneself wide open to attack** prêter le flanc à la critique; **attack is the best form of defence** l'attaque est la meilleure forme de défense

(**b**) *(of illness)* crise *f*; **an attack of malaria/nerves** une crise de paludisme/de nerfs; **an attack of fever** un accès de fièvre; **to have an attack of the shakes** être pris de tremblements; **to have an attack of giddiness** être pris de vertiges; **an attack of self-doubt** une crise de doute

(**c**) *Mus* attaque *f*

attacker [ə'tækə(r)] *n (gen)* agresseur *m*, attaquant(e) *m,f*; *Sport* attaquant *m*

attacking [ə'tækɪŋ] *adj* attaquant; *(game, play)* d'attaque

attagirl ['ætəgɜːl] *exclam Am Fam* bravo!, vas-y ma petite!

attain [ə'teɪn] *vt* (**a**) *(achieve → ambition, hopes)* réaliser; *(→ objectives)* réaliser, atteindre; *(→ happiness)* parvenir à; *(→ independence)* accéder à; *(→ success)* obtenir; *(→ knowledge)* acquérir (**b**) *(arrive at, reach)* atteindre, arriver à

▸**attain to** *vt insep Formal* **to attain to power** accéder au pouvoir

attainability [əˌteɪnə'bɪlɪtɪ] *n (of level, objective, profits)* caractère *m* réalisable; *(of position)* accessibilité *f*

attainable [ə'teɪnəbəl] *adj (ambition, level, objective, profits)* réalisable; *(position)* accessible; **a growth rate attainable by industrialized countries** un taux de croissance à la portée des *ou* accessible aux pays industrialisés; **they believe that independence is now attainable** ils pensent qu'il est désormais possible d'accéder à l'indépendance

attainder [ə'teɪndə(r)] *n Hist & Law* mort *f* civile

attainment [ə'teɪnmənt] *n* (**a**) *(of ambition, hopes, objectives)* réalisation *f*; *(of independence, success)* obtention *f*; *(of happiness)* conquête *f*; *(of knowledge)* acquisition *f* (**b**) *(accomplishment)* résultat *m* (obtenu); *(knowledge, skill)* connaissance *f*; **a man of considerable attainments** un homme qui a beaucoup d'instruction *ou* d'acquis; **her linguistic attainments** sa connaissance des langues

attar ['ætə(r)] *n* **attar (of roses)** huile *f* essentielle de rose

attempt [ə'tempt] **1** *n* (**a**) *(effort, try)* tentative *f*, essai *m*, effort *m*; **what do you think of my latest attempt?** que pensez-vous de mon dernier essai?; **was that an attempt at an apology?** est-ce que c'était censé être une excuse?; **her feeble attempt to justify herself** la piètre tentative qu'elle a faite pour se justifier; **without (making) any attempt at concealment** sans chercher à se cacher; **they made no attempt to help** ils n'ont pas essayé d'aider; **attempt to escape** tentative *f* d'évasion; **to make an attempt at doing sth** *or* **to do sth** essayer *ou* tâcher de faire qch; **he made an attempt at 'War and Peace'** il a essayé de lire 'Guerre et paix'; **to make an attempt on a record** *or* **to beat a record** essayer de battre un record; **to make an attempt on Everest** tenter l'ascension de l'Everest; **first attempt** coup *m* d'essai, première tentative *f*; **it wasn't bad for a first attempt** ce n'était pas mal pour une première tentative *ou* un premier essai; **at the first attempt** du premier coup; **I passed the test at my third attempt** j'ai réussi l'examen la troisième fois; **to make another attempt** renouveler ses tentatives, revenir à la charge; **to give up the attempt** y renoncer; **he died in the attempt** il est mort en essayant

(**b**) *(attack)* attentat *m*; **attempt on sb's life** tentative *f* d'assassinat; **to make an attempt on sb's life** attenter à la vie de qn

2 *vt* (**a**) *(try)* tenter, essayer; *(undertake → job, task)* entreprendre, s'attaquer à; **to attempt to do sth** essayer *ou* tenter de faire qch, chercher à faire qch; **he attempted to cross the street, he attempted crossing the street** il a essayé de traverser la rue; **she plans to attempt the record again in June** elle a l'intention de s'attaquer de nouveau au record en juin; **to attempt the impossible** tenter l'impossible; **he has already attempted suicide once** il a déjà fait une tentative de suicide

(**b**) *(in mountaineering → ascent, climb)* entreprendre; *(→ mountain)* entreprendre l'escalade de

attempted [ə'temptɪd] *adj* tenté; **attempted murder/suicide** tentative *f* de meurtre/de suicide

attend [ə'tend] **1** *vt* (**a**) *(go to → conference, meeting)* assister à; *(→ church, school)* aller à; *(→ course)* suivre; **will you be attending the meeting?** assisterez-vous à la réunion?; **she attends the same course as me** elle suit les mêmes cours que moi; **I attended a private school** j'ai fait mes études dans une école privée; **the concert was well attended** il y avait beaucoup de monde au concert

(**b**) *(look after, care for)* servir, être au service de; **he was always attended by a manservant** un valet de chambre l'accompagnait partout; **a doctor attended the children** un médecin a soigné les enfants

(**c**) *Formal (accompany)* accompagner; **serious consequences attend such an action** de telles actions entraînent de graves conséquences; **the mission was attended by great difficulties** la mission comportait de grandes difficultés

2 *vi* (**a**) *(be present)* être présent; **let us know if you are unable to attend** prévenez-nous si vous ne pouvez pas venir

(**b**) *(pay attention)* faire *ou* prêter attention

▸**attend on** *vt insep* (**a**) *(of maid)* servir, être au service de; *(of bodyguard)* accompagner; *(of doctor)* soigner; **she attended on her guests** elle s'est occupée de ses invités

(**b**) *Formal (be consequence of)* résulter de

▸**attend to** *vt insep* (**a**) *(deal with → matter)* s'occuper de; *(→ one's business)* vaquer à; *(→ one's interests)* veiller à; *(→ one's health, appearance)* soigner; *(→ order)* exécuter; **I shall attend to it** je m'en occuperai, je m'en chargerai

(**b**) *(customer)* s'occuper de; **are you being attended to?** est-ce qu'on s'occupe de vous?

(**c**) *Formal (pay attention to)* faire *ou* prêter attention à; **attend to what I'm saying** écoutez attentivement ce que je dis

▸**attend upon** = **attend on**

attendance [ə'tendəns] *n* (**a**) *(presence → at meeting)* présence *f*; **regular attendance** assiduité *f*;

school attendance fréquentation *f* scolaire; **church attendances have fallen** le nombre de personnes qui vont à l'église a baissé; **his attendance has been good/bad, he has a good/bad attendance record** il a été/il n'a pas été assidu; **poor attendance** manque *m* d'assiduité

(**b**) *(people present)* assistance *f*; **there was a good attendance at the meeting** il y avait une assistance nombreuse à la réunion; **there was a record attendance at the final** la finale a attiré un nombre record de spectateurs; **the evening class had to be cancelled because of poor attendance** le cours du soir a dû être annulé pour manque d'élèves

(**c**) **to be in attendance on** *(of doctor → sick person)* donner des soins à; *(of courtier → king etc)* être de service auprès de; **with six bodyguards in attendance** accompagné de six gardes du corps; **in close attendance** à proximité

▸▸ *Br Fin & Med* ***attendance allowance*** = allocation pour les handicapés; *Br Law* ***attendance centre*** = maison de redressement où des délinquants assistent régulièrement à des réunions; ***attendance list*** *(for meetings)* liste *f* de présence; ***attendance register*** registre *m* de présence; ***attendance sheet*** *(for meetings)* feuille *f* de présence

attendant [ə'tendənt] **1** *n* (**a**) *(official)* surveillant(e) *m,f*; *(in public lavatory, cloakroom)* préposé(e) *m,f*; *(in museum, car park)* gardien(enne) *m,f*; *(in theatre)* ouvreuse *f*; **(petrol-)pump attendant** pompiste *mf*; **swimming pool attendant** maître *m* nageur

(**b**) *(usu pl)* **attendants** *(of king etc)* gens *mpl*, suite *f*

2 *adj Formal* (**a**) *(person → accompanying)* qui accompagne; *(→ on duty)* en service; **the salesman attendant on us was a Mr Jones** le vendeur qui nous servait *ou* s'occupait de nous était un certain M. Jones

(**b**) *(related)* **there are some disadvantages attendant on working at home** le travail à domicile comporte certains inconvénients; **he talked about marriage and its attendant problems** il parla du mariage et des problèmes qui l'accompagnent

attending physician [ə'tendɪŋ-] *n Med* médecin *m* traitant

attention [ə'tenʃən] **1** *n* (**a**) *(concentration, thought)* attention *f*; **he wouldn't start until he had their full attention** il refusait de commencer tant qu'il n'avait pas toute leur attention; **may I have your attention for a moment?** pourriez-vous m'accorder votre attention un instant?; **your attention please, ladies and gentlemen** mesdames et messieurs, votre attention s'il vous plaît; **you have my undivided attention** je suis tout à vous; **she knows how to hold an audience's attention** elle sait retenir l'attention d'un auditoire; **they were all attention** ils étaient (tout yeux et) tout oreilles *ou* tout ouïe; **to pay attention (to)** prêter attention (à); **he paid careful attention to everything she said** il a prêté une extrême attention à tout ce qu'elle disait; **I paid little attention to what she said** j'ai accordé peu d'attention à *ou* j'ai fait peu de cas de ce qu'elle a dit; **we paid no attention to the survey** nous n'avons tenu aucun compte de l'enquête; **attention to detail** précision *f*, minutie *f*; **she switched her attention back to her book** elle est retournée à son livre

(**b**) *(notice)* attention *f*; **he waved to attract** *or* **catch our attention** il a fait un geste de la main pour attirer notre attention; **to draw attention to oneself** se faire remarquer; **the news came to his attention** il a appris la nouvelle; **let me bring** *or* **direct** *or* **draw your attention to the matter of punctuality** permettez que j'attire votre attention sur le problème de la ponctualité; *Formal* **it has been brought to our attention that...** il a été porté à notre connaissance que... ; **he drew attention to the rise in unemployment** il a attiré l'attention sur la montée du chômage; **let us now turn our attention to the population problem** considérons maintenant le problème démographique; **for the attention of Mr Smith** *(in letter)* à l'attention de M. Smith

(**c**) *(care)* soins *mpl*, entretien *m*; **they need medical attention** ils ont besoin de soins médicaux; **the furnace requires constant attention** la chaudière demande un entretien régulier; **the bathroom looks as if it needs some attention** la salle de bains a besoin d'être un peu retapée

(**d**) *Mil* garde-à-vous *m inv*; **to stand at/to come to attention** se tenir/se mettre au garde-à-vous

2 *exclam* garde-à-vous!

3 attentions *npl* attentions *fpl*, égards *mpl*; **she felt irritated by his unwanted attentions** elle était agacée par les attentions dont il l'entourait

▸▸ *Med* ***attention deficit disorder*** troubles *mpl* de l'attention; *Med* ***attention deficit hyperactivity disorder*** syndrome *m* hyperkinétique de l'enfant, syndrome *m* de l'enfant hyperactif; ***attention span*** capacité *f* de concentration; **a short/long attention span** une faible/bonne capacité de concentration; **his attention span is no longer than half an hour** il ne peut pas se concentrer pendant plus d'une demi-heure

attention-seeking 1 *n* **it's just attention-seeking** il/elle/*etc* ne cherche qu'à attirer l'attention sur lui/elle/*etc*, il/elle/*etc* essaie juste de se faire remarquer

2 *adj* **her attention-seeking behaviour** son besoin constant de se faire remarquer

attentive [ə'tentɪv] *adj* (**a**) *(paying attention)* attentif; **attentive to detail** méticuleux (**b**) *(considerate)* attentionné, prévenant; **to be attentive to sb** être prévenant envers qn; **she was attentive to our every need** elle était attentive à tous nos besoins

attentively [ə'tentɪvlɪ] *adv* (**a**) *(paying attention)* attentivement, avec attention (**b**) *(with consideration)* avec beaucoup d'égards

attentiveness [ə'tentɪvnɪs] *n* (**a**) *(concentration)* attention *f* (**b**) *(consideration)* égards *mpl*, prévenance *f*

attenuate 1 *vt* [ə'tenjʊeɪt] (**a**) *(attack, remark)* atténuer, modérer; *(pain)* apaiser (**b**) *(form, line)* amincir, affiner (**c**) *(gas)* raréfier

2 *vi* [ə'tenjʊeɪt] s'atténuer, diminuer

3 *adj* [ə'tenjʊɪt] *Bot* atténué

attenuated [ə'tenjʊeɪtɪd] *adj Med (virus)* atténué

attenuation [əˌtenjʊ'eɪʃən] *n* (**a**) *(of attack, remark)* atténuation *f*, modération *f*; *(of pain)* atténuation *f*, apaisement *m* (**b**) *(of form)* amincissement *m*

attenuator [ə'tenjʊeɪtə(r)] *n Tech* atténuateur *m*

attest [ə'test] *Formal* **1** *vt* (**a**) *(affirm)* attester, certifier; *(under oath)* affirmer sous serment; **the document attests the fact that...** le document atteste que...

(**b**) *(be proof of)* démontrer, témoigner de

(**c**) *(bear witness to)* témoigner; **to attest a signature** légaliser une signature

(**d**) *(put oath to)* faire prêter serment à

2 *vi* témoigner, prêter serment; **she attested to the truth of the report** elle a témoigné de la véracité du rapport; **to attest to the honesty of sb** se porter garant (de l'honnêteté) de qn

▸▸ *Com* ***attested copy*** copie *f* certifiée conforme; *Agr* ***attested herd*** troupeau *m* ayant subi une tuberculination; *Br* ***attested milk*** = lait venant d'un cheptel ayant subi une tuberculination

attestation [ˌæte'steɪʃən] *n Law* (**a**) *(statement)* attestation *f*; *(in court)* attestation *f*, témoignage *m* (**b**) *(proof)* attestation *f*, preuve *f* (**c**) *(of signature)* légalisation *f* (**d**) *(taking of oath)* assermentation *f*, prestation *f* de serment

at-the-money option *n St Exch* option *f* au cours, option *f* à la monnaie

Attic ['ætɪk] **1** *adj Antiq & Geog* attique

2 *n Ling* attique *m*, dialecte *m* attique

▸▸ ***Attic salt, Attic wit*** sel *m* attique

attic ['ætɪk] *n (space)* grenier *m*; *(room)* mansarde *f*

▸▸ ***attic room*** mansarde *f*; ***attic window*** fenêtre *f* en mansarde; *(skylight)* lucarne *f*

Attica ['ætɪkə] *n Antiq & Geog* Attique *f*; **in Attica** en Attique

Attila [ə'tɪlə] *pr n* **Attila the Hun** Attila roi des Huns

attire [ə'taɪə(r)] *Formal* **1** *n (UNCOUNT)* habits *mpl*, vêtements *mpl*; *(formal)* tenue *f*

2 *vt* vêtir, habiller, parer; **she attired herself in silk** elle se vêtit de soie

attitude ['ætɪtjuːd] *n* (**a**) *(way of thinking)* attitude *f*, disposition *f*; **what's your attitude to** *or* **towards him?** que pensez-vous de lui?; **she took the attitude that...** elle est partie du principe que...; **an attitude of mind** un état d'esprit; **he has a very positive attitude of mind** il a une attitude extrêmement positive; **what's your attitude to abortion?** que pensez-vous de l'avortement?, quelle est votre attitude face à l'avortement?; **old-fashioned attitudes** des idées *fpl* démodées

(**b**) *(behaviour, manner)* attitude *f*, manière *f*; **I don't like your attitude, young man** je n'aime pas vos manières, jeune homme; **well, if that's your attitude you can go** eh bien, si c'est comme ça que tu le prends, tu peux t'en aller; **he's got an attitude problem** il a des problèmes relationnels

(**c**) *Formal (posture)* attitude *f*, position *f*; **to strike an attitude** poser, prendre une pose affectée

(**d**) *Fam (self-assurance, assertiveness)* assurance ❑ *f*; **he's got attitude** il n'a pas froid aux yeux; **a car with attitude** une voiture qui a du caractère

(**e**) *Mktg (of consumer to product)* attitude *f*

▸▸ *Mktg* ***attitude research*** enquête *f* d'attitudes; ***attitude scale*** échelle *f* d'attitudes; ***attitude survey*** enquête *f* d'attitudes

attitudinal [ˌætɪ'tjuːdɪnəl] *adj* relatif aux attitudes

▸▸ ***attitudinal research*** enquête *f* d'attitudes

attitudinize, -ise [ˌætɪ'tjuːdɪnaɪz] *vi Pej* prendre des attitudes, poser

attn *(written abbr* **for the attention of***)* attn, à l'attention de

attorney [ə'tɜːnɪ] *(pl* **attorneys***)* *n* (**a**) *(representative)* mandataire *mf*, représentant(e) *m,f* (**b**) *Am (solicitor → for documents, sales etc)* notaire *m*; *(→ for court cases)* avocat(e) *m,f*; *(barrister)* avocat(e) *m,f*

▸▸ ***Attorney General*** *(in England, Wales and Northern Ireland)* = principal avocat de la couronne; *(in US)* ≃ ministre *m* de la Justice; *(in Canada)* procureur *m* général

attorney-at-law *n Am* avocat(e) *m,f*

attract [ə'trækt] **1** *vt* (**a**) *(draw, cause to come near)* attirer; **the proposal attracted a lot of attention/interest** la proposition a attiré l'attention/a éveillé l'intérêt de beaucoup de gens; **to attract criticism** s'attirer des critiques; **we hope to attract more young people to the church** nous espérons attirer davantage de jeunes à l'église

(**b**) *(be attractive to)* attirer, séduire, plaire; **she's attracted to men with beards** elle est attirée par les barbus; **what really attracts me to him is his sense of humour** ce qui me plaît chez lui c'est son sens de l'humour; **what is it that attracts you about skiing?** qu'est-ce qui vous plaît *ou* séduit dans le ski?

2 *vi* s'attirer; **opposites attract** les contraires s'attirent

attracter [ə'træktə] *n Phys* attracteur *m*

attraction [ə'trækʃən] *n* (**a**) *Phys (pull)* attraction *f*; *Fig* attraction *f*, attirance *f*; **I don't understand your attraction for** *or* **to her** je ne comprends pas ce qui te plaît chez *ou* en elle; **the idea holds no attraction for me** cette idée ne me dit rien; **I can't** *or* **don't see the attraction of it** je n'en vois pas l'intérêt

(**b**) *(appeal → of place, plan)* attrait *m*, fascination *f*; *(→ of person)* charme *m*, charmes *mpl*; **it's the city's chief attraction** c'est l'attrait principal de la ville; **the attractions of living in the country** les charmes de la vie à la campagne; **the main attraction of our show** le clou *ou* la grande attraction de notre spectacle; **a tourist attraction** un site touristique

attractive [ə'træktɪv] *adj* (**a**) *(pretty → person, smile)* séduisant; *(→ dress, picture)* attrayant, beau (belle); **do you find him attractive?** il te plaît?, tu le trouves séduisant? (**b**) *(interesting → idea, price)* intéressant; *(→ offer, opportunity)* intéressant, attrayant (**c**) *Phys (force)* attractif

attractively [ə'træktɪvlɪ] *adv* de manière attrayante; **to dress attractively** s'habiller de façon séduisante; **the meal was very attractively**

presented le repas était très agréablement présenté

attractiveness [ə'træktɪvnɪs] *n* (**a**) *(of person, smile)* beauté *f*, charme *m*; *(of dress, picture)* beauté *f* (**b**) *(of idea, opportunity, price)* intérêt *m*, attrait *m* (**c**) *Phys* attraction *f*

attractor = **attracter**

attributable [ə'trɪbjʊtəbəl] *adj* attribuable, imputable, dû; **to be attributable to sth** être attribuable *ou* imputable *ou* dû à qch
►► *Acct* ***attributable profit*** bénéfices *mpl* nets

attribute 1 *vt* [ə'trɪbjuːt] *(ascribe → accident, failure)* attribuer, imputer; *(→ invention, painting, quotation)* prêter, attribuer; *(→ success)* attribuer; **to what do you attribute your success?** à quoi attribuez-vous votre réussite?
2 *n* ['ætrɪbjuːt] (**a**) *(feature, quality)* attribut *m*; *(object)* attribut *m*, emblème *m* (**b**) *(in logic)* attribut *m* (**c**) *Ling* épithète *m*

attribution [,ætrɪ'bjuːʃən] *n* attribution *f*

attributive [ə'trɪbjʊtɪv] **1** *n Ling* attribut *m*
2 *adj* (**a**) *(gen)* attributif (**b**) *Gram* épithète

attributively [ə'trɪbjʊtɪvlɪ] *adv Ling* comme épithète

attrit [ə'trɪt] *vt* (**a**) *(wear down → enemy, army, defences)* affaiblir (**b**) *Euph (kill)* éliminer; *(destroy)* détruire

attrition [ə'trɪʃən] *n* (**a**) *(wearing down)* usure *f* (par friction); *Mil* **war of attrition** guerre *f* d'usure (**b**) *Econ & Ind* attrition *f*, départs *mpl* volontaires

attune [ə'tjuːn] *vt* accorder; **her ideas are closely attuned to his** ses idées sont en parfait accord avec les siennes; **to attune oneself** *or* **become attuned to sth** se faire à qch, s'accoutumer à qch

Atty. Gen. *(written abbr* **Attorney General***)* *(in US)* ≃ ministre *m* de la Justice

ATV [,eɪtiː'viː] *n (abbr* **all-terrain vehicle***)* véhicule *m* tout terrain

ATW [,eɪtiː'dʌbəljuː] *adv (abbr* **around the world***)* autour du monde

atypical [,eɪ'tɪpɪkəl] *adj* atypique; **this behaviour is atypical of him** cela ne lui ressemble pas

aubergine ['əʊbəʒiːn] *Br* **1** *n* (**a**) *(vegetable)* aubergine *f* (**b**) *(colour)* violet *m* aubergine
2 *adj* aubergine *(inv)*

aubretia [ɔː'briːʃə] *n Bot* aubrietia *m*

auburn ['ɔːbən] **1** *adj* auburn *(inv)*
2 *n* (couleur *f*) auburn *m*

auction ['ɔːkʃən] **1** *n* (vente *f* aux) enchères *fpl*; **sold at** *or* **by auction** vendu aux enchères; **to put sth up for auction** mettre qch en vente aux enchères; **they put the house up for auction** ils ont mis la maison en vente aux enchères
2 *vt (put up for auction)* mettre aux enchères; *(sell)* vendre aux enchères
►► *Cards* ***auction bridge*** bridge *m* aux enchères; ***auction room*** salle *f* des ventes
►**auction off** *vt sep* vendre aux enchères

auctioneer [,ɔːkʃə'nɪə(r)] *n* commissaire-priseur *m*

audacious [ɔː'deɪʃəs] *adj* (**a**) *(daring)* audacieux, intrépide (**b**) *(impudent)* effronté, impudent

audaciously [ɔː'deɪʃəslɪ] *adv* (**a**) *(daringly)* audacieusement, avec audace (**b**) *(impudently)* effrontément, impudemment

audaciousness [ɔː'deɪʃəsnɪs] = **audacity**

audacity [ɔː'dæsətɪ] *n* (**a**) *(daring)* audace *f*, intrépidité *f* (**b**) *(impudence)* effronterie *f*, impudence *f*; **he had the audacity to ask for a pay rise** il a eu l'audace de demander une augmentation (de salaire)

audibility [,ɔːdɪ'bɪlətɪ] *n* audibilité *f*

audible ['ɔːdəbəl] *adj (sound)* audible, perceptible; *(words)* intelligible, distinct; **the music was barely audible** on entendait à peine la musique
►► *Phys* ***audible frequency*** fréquence *f* audible

audibly ['ɔːdəblɪ] *adv* distinctement

audience ['ɔːdɪəns] **1** *n* (**a**) *(at film, match, play)* spectateurs *mpl*, public *m*; *(at concert, lecture)* auditoire *m*, public *m*; *(of author)* lecteurs *mpl*; *(of artist)* public *m*; **someone in the audience laughed** il y eut un rire dans la salle; **do we have any Americans in the audience?** y a-t-il des Américains dans la salle?; **the audience gave him a standing ovation** le public s'est levé pour l'ovationner; **was there a large audience at the play?** y avait-il beaucoup de monde au théâtre?; **his books reach a wide audience** ses livres sont lus par beaucoup de gens
(**b**) *Rad* auditeurs *mpl*, audience *f*; *TV* téléspectateurs *mpl*, audience *f*
(**c**) *Mktg (for product, advertisement)* audience *f*
(**d**) *Formal (meeting)* audience *f*; **to grant sb an audience** accorder audience à qn
2 *comp Rad & TV (figures)* de l'assistance, du public
►► *Mktg* ***audience exposure*** exposition *f* au public; *Rad & TV* ***audience participation*** participation *f* de l'assistance (à ce qui se passe sur la scène); *Rad & TV* ***audience rating*** indice *m* d'écoute, taux *m* d'écoute; *Mktg* ***audience research*** études *fpl* d'audience; *Mktg* ***audience study*** étude *f* d'audience

audio ['ɔːdɪəʊ] *n* son *m*, acoustique *f*; **the audio has gone** il n'y a plus de son
►► ***audio cassette*** cassette *f* audio; *Tel* ***audio conference*** audioconférence *f*; ***audio equipment*** équipement *m* acoustique; *Phys* ***audio frequency*** audiofréquence *f*; ***audio library*** sonothèque *f*, phonothèque *f*; ***audio recording*** enregistrement *m* sonore; ***audio response*** réponse *f* acoustique; ***audio signal*** signal *m* audio, signal *m* son; ***audio system*** système *m* audio; ***audio tape*** bande *f* magnétique audio

audiobook ['ɔːdɪəʊ,bʊk] *n* livre *f* enregistré

audiology [,ɔːdɪ'ɒlədʒɪ] *n* audiologie *f*

audiometer [,ɔːdɪ'ɒmɪtə(r)] *n* audiomètre *m*

audiometry [,ɔːdɪ'ɒmɪtrɪ] *n* audiométrie *f*

audiophile ['ɔːdɪəʊfaɪl] *n* audiophile *mf*

audio-typing *n* audiotypie *f*

audio-typist *n* audiotypiste *mf*

audiovisual [,ɔːdɪəʊ'vɪʒʊəl] *adj* audiovisuel
►► ***audiovisual aids*** supports *mpl* audiovisuels; ***audiovisual equipment*** équipement *m* audiovisuel, matériel *m* audiovisuel

audiphone ['ɔːdɪfəʊn] *n* audiophone *m*

audit ['ɔːdɪt] **1** *n Acct & Admin* vérification *f* des comptes, audit *m*
2 *vt* (**a**) *Acct (accounts)* vérifier, apurer, examiner (**b**) *Am Univ* **he audits several courses** il assiste à plusieurs cours en tant qu'auditeur libre
►► *Acct* ***audit manager*** directeur(trice) *m,f* du service d'audit; *Admin* **Audit office** ≃ Cour *f* des Comptes; ***audit trail*** *Comput* protocole *m* de vérification *ou* de contrôle; *Fin* vérification *f* à rebours

auditing ['ɔːdɪtɪŋ] *n Acct* vérification *f* des comptes, audit *m*

audition [ɔː'dɪʃən] **1** *n* (**a**) *Theat* audition *f*; *Cin & TV* (séance *f* d') essai *m*; **the director gave her an audition** *Theat* le metteur en scène l'a auditionnée; *Cin & TV* le metteur en scène lui a fait faire un essai; **to hold auditions** *Theat* organiser des auditions; *Cin & TV* organiser des essais; **to do an audition** *Theat* passer une audition; *Cin & TV* faire un essai
(**b**) *(hearing)* ouïe *f*, audition *f*
2 *vt Theat* auditionner; *Cin & TV* faire faire un essai à
3 *vi Theat (director)* auditionner; *(actor)* passer une audition; *Cin & TV* faire un essai; **I auditioned for 'Woyzeck'** *Theat* j'ai passé une audition pour un rôle dans 'Woyzeck'; *Cin & TV* j'ai fait un essai pour un rôle dans 'Woyzeck'

auditor ['ɔːdɪtə(r)] *n* (**a**) *Acct (of company)* audit *m*, auditeur(trice) *m,f*; *(officially appointed)* commissaire *m* aux comptes; *Admin (of public body)* vérificateur(trice) *m,f* des comptes, audit *m*, auditeur(trice) *m,f*; **firm of auditors** cabinet *m* d'audit, cabinet *m* comptable
(**b**) *Formal (listener)* auditeur(trice) *m,f*
(**c**) *Am Univ (student)* auditeur(trice) *m,f* libre
►► *Acct* ***auditors' report*** rapport *m* des vérificateurs

auditorium [,ɔːdɪ'tɔːrɪəm] (*pl* **auditoriums** *or* **auditoria** [-rɪə]) *n* (**a**) *(of concert hall, theatre)* salle *f* (**b**) *(large meeting room)* amphithéâtre *m*

auditorship ['ɔːdɪtəʃɪp] *n Acct* commissariat *m* aux comptes

auditory ['ɔːdɪtərɪ] *adj Physiol* auditif
►► ***auditory phonetics*** phonétique *f* auditive

Audubon Society ['ɔːdəbɒn-] *n* = ligue américaine pour la protection des oiseaux

AUEW [,eɪjuː,iː'dʌbəljuː] *n Formerly Ind (abbr* **Amalgamated Union of Engineering Workers***)* = ancien syndicat britannique de l'industrie mécanique, aujourd'hui remplacée par l'AEEU

au fait [,əʊ'feɪ] *adj* **to be au fait with sth** être au courant de qch

Aug. *(written abbr* **August***)* août *m*

Augean [ɔː'dʒiːən] *adj (filthy)* crasseux, dégoûtant; *(corrupt)* corrompu
►► *Myth* ***the Augean stables*** les écuries *fpl* d'Augias

auger ['ɔːgə(r)] *n Carp (hand tool)* vrille *f*; *Tech* foreuse *f*

aught [ɔːt] *Arch or Literary* **1** *pron* ce que; **for aught I know** (pour) autant que je sache; **for aught I care** pour ce que cela me fait
2 *n* zéro *m*

augment [ɔːg'ment] **1** *vt* (**a**) *(increase)* augmenter, accroître; **her salary is augmented by** *or* **with gratuities** à son salaire s'ajoutent les pourboires (**b**) *Mus* augmenter
2 *vi* augmenter, s'accroître

augmentation [,ɔːgmen'teɪʃən] *n* (**a**) *(increase)* augmentation *f*, accroissement *m* (**b**) *Mus* augmentation *f* (**c**) *Mktg* augmentation *f*

augmentative [ɔːg'mentətɪv] *adj Ling* augmentatif

augmented [ɔːg'mentɪd] *adj* augmenté
►► *Mktg* ***augmented product*** produit *m* augmenté

Augsburg ['aʊgzbɜːg] *n* Augsbourg

augur ['ɔːgə(r)] **1** *vi* **this weather augurs ill/well for our holiday** ce temps est de mauvais/bon augure pour nos vacances; **it doesn't augur well for the future** cela ne présage *ou* n'annonce rien de bon
2 *vt (predict)* prédire, prévoir; *(be omen of)* présager; **it augurs no good** cela ne présage *ou* n'annonce rien de bon
3 *n (prophet)* augure *m*

augury ['ɔːgjʊrɪ] (*pl* **auguries**) *n* (**a**) *(art)* art *m* augural; *(rite)* rite *m* augural (**b**) *(omen)* augure *m*, présage *m*; *(prediction)* prédiction *f*

August ['ɔːgəst] *n* août *m*, *see also* **February**
►► ***August Bank Holiday*** = jour férié tombant le dernier lundi d'août en Angleterre et au pays de Galles, le premier lundi d'août en Écosse

august [ɔː'gʌst] *adj Literary (dignified)* auguste, vénérable; *(noble)* noble

Augustan [ɔː'gʌstən] *adj Antiq* d'Auguste
►► ***the Augustan Period*** *(in Latin literature)* le siècle d'Auguste; *(in English literature)* l'époque *f* d'Auguste

Augustinian [,ɔːgə'stɪnɪən] *Rel* **1** *n (follower)* augustinien *m*; *(monk)* augustin *m*
2 *adj* augustinien, de saint Augustin

augustly [ɔː'gʌstlɪ] *adv Literary (with dignity)* augustement, vénérablement; *(nobly)* noblement

Augustus [ɔː'gʌstəs] *pr n* Auguste

auk [ɔːk] *n Orn* alcidé *m*, alque *m*

auld [ɔːld] *adj Scot* vieux (vieille)
►► *Hist* ***the Auld Alliance*** = l'ancienne alliance (XIIIème–XIVème siècle) unissant l'Écosse et la France contre l'Angleterre, dont le souvenir est encore souvent évoqué aujourd'hui; ***the Auld Enemy*** = surnom donné à l'Angleterre par les Écossais; *Mus* ***Auld Lang Syne*** = chanson sur l'air de "ce n'est qu'un au revoir" que l'on chante à minuit le soir du 31 décembre en Grande-Bretagne; *Fam* ***Auld Reekie*** = surnom donné à Édimbourg, qui signifie littéralement "la vieille enfumée"

aunt [ɑːnt] *n* tante *f*
►► *Br* ***Aunt Sally*** *(at fairground)* ≃ jeu *m* de massacre; *Fig (person)* tête *f* de Turc

auntie, aunty ['ɑːntɪ] (*pl* **aunties**) *Br Fam* **1** *n* tantine *f*, tata *f*, tatie *f*; **Auntie Susan** tante Susan
2 Auntie *n* = surnom affectueux de la BBC, perçue comme une vieille tante détentrice des valeurs morales

AUP [,eɪjuː'piː] *n Comput (abbr* **Acceptable Use Policy***)* = code de conduite défini par un fournisseur d'accès à l'Internet

au pair [,əʊ'peə(r)] (*pl* **au pairs**) **1** *n* (jeune fille *f*) au pair *f*; **she's working as an au pair** elle travaille au pair, elle est (jeune fille) au pair
2 *adj* au pair
3 *adv* **to work au pair** travailler au pair
4 *vi* travailler au pair

AUR [ˌeɪjuːˈɑː(r)] *n Acct & Fin* (*abbr* **asset utilization ratio**) taux *m* d'utilisation des actifs

aura [ˈɔːrə] (*pl* **auras** *or* **aurae** [-riː]) *n* (**a**) (*quality → of person*) aura *f*, émanation *f*; (*→ of place*) atmosphère *f*, ambiance *f*; **there's an aura of mystery about her** il y a quelque chose de mystérieux chez elle (**b**) (*surrounding body*) aura *f* (**c**) *Med* aura *f*

►► ***aura reading*** = interprétation de la personnalité d'après une photographie censée représenter l'aura

aural [ˈɔːrəl] *adj* (**a**) (*relating to hearing*) auditif, sonore (**b**) *Anat* (*relating to the ear*) auriculaire

►► ***aural comprehension*** compréhension *f* orale; ***aural skills*** aptitudes *fpl* à la compréhension orale

aurally [ˈɔːrəlɪ] *adv* du point de vue auditif; *Med* **aurally handicapped** malentendant

aureate [ˈɔːrɪət] *adj Literary* d'or, doré

aureola [ɔːˈriːələ], **aureole** [ˈɔːrɪəʊl] *n* (**a**) *Art* (*of saint*) auréole *f* (**b**) *Astron* (*of sun*) auréole *f*

auricle [ˈɔːrɪkəl] *n Anat* (**a**) (*of ear*) auricule *f* (**b**) (*of heart*) oreillette *f*

auricular [ɔːˈrɪkjʊlə(r)] *adj* auriculaire

auriferous [ɔːˈrɪfərəs] *adj Metal* aurifère

aurochs [ˈɔːrɒks] (*pl* **inv**) *n Zool* aurochs *m*

aurora [ɔːˈrɔːrə] (*pl* **auroras** *or* **aurorae** [-riː]) **1** *n Astron* aurore *f*

2 Aurora *pr n Myth* Aurore

►► *Astron* ***aurora australis*** aurore *f* australe; *Astron* ***aurora borealis*** aurore *f* boréale

auroral [ɔːˈrɔːrəl] *adj Literary* auroral, de l'aurore

aurous [ˈɔːrəs] *adj Chem* aurique

auscultate [ˈɔːskəlˌteɪt] *vt Med* ausculter

auscultation [ˌɔːskəlˈteɪʃən] *n Med* auscultation *f*

auspices [ˈɔːspɪsɪz] *npl* auspices *mpl*; **under the auspices of the UN** sous les auspices de l'ONU, sous l'égide de l'ONU

auspicious [ɔːˈspɪʃəs] *adj* (*event, start, occasion*) propice, favorable; (*sign*) de bon augure; **we made an auspicious beginning** nous avons pris un bon départ; **on this auspicious occasion** en ce jour mémorable

auspiciously [ɔːˈspɪʃəslɪ] *adv* favorablement, sous d'heureux auspices; **the meeting began auspiciously** la réunion a bien commencé

auspiciousness [ɔːˈspɪʃəsnɪs] *n* aspect *m* propice *ou* favorable; **the auspiciousness of this omen** cet heureux auspice

Aussie [ˈɒzɪ] *Fam* **1** *n* Australien(enne)[□] *m,f*

2 *adj* australien[□]

austere [ɒˈstɪə(r)] *adj* (**a**) (*person*) austère, sévère; (*life*) austère, sobre, ascétique (**b**) (*design, interior*) austère, sobre

austerely [ɒˈstɪəlɪ] *adv* (**a**) (*live*) austèrement, avec austérité, comme un ascète (**b**) (*dress, furnish*) austèrement, avec austérité, sobrement

austereness [ɒˈstɪənɪs], **austerity** [ɒˈsterətɪ] (*pl* **austerities**) *n* (**a**) (*simplicity*) austérité *f*, sobriété *f* (**b**) (*hardship*) austérité *f*; **a period of austerity** une période d'austérité, des temps difficiles; (**c**) (*usu pl*) (*practice*) austérité *f*, pratique *f* austère

►► *Econ* ***austerity measures*** mesures *fpl* d'austérité

austral [ˈɔːstrəl] *adj Astron* austral

Australasia [ˌɒstrəˈleɪʒjə] *n* Australasie *f*; **in Australasia** en Australasie

Australasian [ˌɒstrəˈleɪʒən] **1** *n* natif(ive) *m,f* de l'Australasie

2 *adj* d'Australasie

Australia [ɒˈstreɪljə] *n* Australie *f*; **in Australia** en Australie; **the Commonwealth of Australia** l'Australie

►► ***Australia Day*** = premier lundi suivant le 26 janvier (commémorant l'arrivée des Britanniques en Australie en 1788)

Australian [ɒˈstreɪljən] **1** *n* (**a**) (*person*) Australien(enne) *m,f*

(**b**) *Ling* australien *m*

2 *adj* australien

3 *comp* (*embassy*) d'Australie; (*history*) de l'Australie

►► ***the Australian Alps*** les Alpes *fpl* australiennes; ***Australian Antarctic Territory*** Antarctique *f* australienne; ***the Australian Capital Territory*** le Territoire de la Capitale australienne; **in the Australian Capital Territory** dans le Territoire de la Capitale australienne; *Sport* ***Australian Rules (football)*** football *m* australien

Australianism [ɒˈstreɪljənɪzəm] *n Ling* = terme ou expression typique de l'anglais d'Australie

Australianize, -ise [ɒˈstreɪljənaɪz] *vt* donner un caractère australien à

Austral Islands [ˈɔːstrəl-] *npl* **the Austral Islands** les îles *fpl* Australes; **in the Austral Islands** aux îles Australes

Australoid [ˈɒstrəlɔɪd] **1** *adj* australoïde

2 *n* australoïde *mf*

australopithecine [ˌɒstrələˈpɪθɪsiːn] *n Archeol* australopithèque *m*

Austria [ˈɒstrɪə] *n* Autriche *f*; **in Austria** en Autriche

Austria-Hungary *n Hist* Autriche-Hongrie *f*

Austrian [ˈɒstrɪən] **1** *n* Autrichien(enne) *m,f*

2 *adj* autrichien

3 *comp* (*embassy*) d'Autriche; (*history*) de l'Autriche

►► ***Austrian blind*** store *m* autrichien

Austro-Hungarian [ˌɒstrəʊ-] *adj Hist* austro-hongrois

►► *Hist* ***the Austro-Hungarian Empire*** l'empire d'Autriche-Hongrie

Austronesian [ˌɒstrəˈniːʒən] *adj* malayo-polynésien

AUT [ˌeɪjuːˈtiː] *n Univ* (*abbr* **Association of University Teachers**) = syndicat britannique d'enseignants d'université

autarchy [ˈɔːtɑːkɪ] (*pl* **autarchies**) *n Pol* autocratie *f*

autarky [ˈɔːtɑːkɪ] (*pl* **autarkies**) *n Econ* (**a**) (*system*) autarcie *f* (**b**) (*country*) pays *m* en autarcie

authentic [ɔːˈθentɪk] *adj* (*genuine*) authentique; (*accurate, reliable*) authentique, véridique; *Law* **each document being authentic** chaque texte faisant foi

authentically [ɔːˈθentɪkəlɪ] *adv* de façon authentique

authenticate [ɔːˈθentɪkeɪt] *vt* (*painting*) établir l'authenticité de; (*signature*) légaliser

authentication [ɔːˌθentɪˈkeɪʃən] *n* authentification *f*, certification *f*

authenticity [ˌɔːθenˈtɪsətɪ] *n* authenticité *f*

author [ˈɔːθə(r)] **1** *n* (**a**) (*writer*) auteur *m*, écrivain *m*; **have you ever read this author?** avez-vous déjà lu des livres de cet auteur? (**b**) (*of idea, plan*) auteur *m*; (*of painting, sculpture*) auteur *m*, créateur *m*; *Literary* **to be the author of one's own misfortunes** être l'artisan de ses malheurs

2 *vt* être l'auteur de

authoress [ˈɔːθərɪs] *n* (**a**) (*writer*) = femme auteur d'ouvrages s'adressant au grand public (**b**) (*of idea, plan*) auteur *m*; (*of painting, sculpture*) auteur *m*, créatrice *f*

authoring [ˈɔːθərɪŋ] *n*

►► *Comput* ***authoring language*** langage *m* auteur; ***authoring software*** logiciel *m* auteur; ***authoring tool*** outil *m* auteur

authoritarian [ɔːˌθɒrɪˈteərɪən] **1** *adj Pol* autoritaire

2 *n* personne *f* autoritaire; **the boss is a strict authoritarian** le patron est très autoritaire *ou* croit ferme à l'autorité

authoritarianism [ɔːˌθɒrɪˈteərɪənɪzəm] *n Pol* autoritarisme *m*

authoritative [ɔːˈθɒrɪtətɪv] *adj* (**a**) (*article, report, person*) qui fait autorité; **I had it from an authoritative source that...** je tiens de source sûre que... (**b**) (*official*) autorisé, officiel

authoritatively [ɔːˈθɒrɪtətɪvlɪ] *adv* avec autorité

authoritativeness [ɔːˈθɒrɪtətɪvnɪs] *n* (**a**) (*of person*) autorité *f*; **the authoritativeness of his manner** son assurance (**b**) (*of article, report*) autorité *f*

authority [ɔːˈθɒrətɪ] (*pl* **authorities**) *n* (**a**) (*power*) autorité *f*, pouvoir *m*; **who's in authority here?** qui est le responsable ici?; **in a position of authority** en position d'autorité; **she has authority** *or* **she is in authority over all the staff** elle a autorité sur tout le personnel; **he made his authority felt** il faisait sentir son autorité; *Pol* **those in authority in Haiti** ceux qui gouvernent en Haïti

(**b**) (*forcefulness*) autorité *f*, assurance *f*; **"no!" he said with authority** "non!" dit-il avec autorité; **her conviction gave authority to her argument** sa conviction a donné du poids à son raisonnement; **his opinions carry a lot of authority** ses opinions font autorité

(**c**) (*permission*) autorisation *f*, droit *m*; **to give sb authority to do sth** autoriser qn à faire qch; **who gave him (the) authority to enter?** qui lui a donné l'autorisation d'entrer?, qui l'a autorisé à entrer?; **they had no authority to answer** ils n'étaient pas habilités à répondre; **I decided on my own authority** j'ai décidé de ma propre autorité *ou* de mon propre chef; **on his authority** avec son autorisation; **on whose authority did they search the house?** avec l'autorisation de qui ont-ils perquisitionné la maison?; **without authority** sans autorisation

(**d**) (*usu pl*) (*people in command*) autorité *f*; *Pol* **the authorities** les autorités *fpl*, l'administration *f*; **the proper authorities** qui de droit, les autorités compétentes; **the education/housing authority** = services chargés de l'éducation/du logement; **we'll go to the highest authority in the land** nous nous adresserons aux plus hautes instances du pays

(**e**) (*expert*) autorité *f*, expert *m*; (*article, book*) autorité *f*; **he's an authority on China** c'est un grand spécialiste de la Chine

(**f**) (*testimony*) **I have it on his authority that she was there** il m'a certifié qu'elle était présente; **we have it on good authority that...** nous tenons de source sûre *ou* de bonne source que...

(**g**) (*permit*) autorisation *f*

authorization [ˌɔːθəraɪˈzeɪʃən] *n* (*act, permission*) autorisation *f*; (*official sanction*) pouvoir *m*, mandat *m*; **he has authorization to leave the country** il est autorisé à quitter le pays; **you can't do anything without authorization from the management** vous ne pouvez rien faire sans l'autorisation de la direction

authorize, -ise [ˈɔːθəraɪz] *vt* (**a**) (*empower*) autoriser; **she is authorized to act for her father** elle a pouvoir de représenter son père, elle est autorisée à représenter son père (**b**) (*sanction*) autoriser, sanctionner; *Fin* **to authorize a loan** consentir un prêt; *Law* **to authorize a drug for the market** homologuer un médicament

authorized [ˈɔːθəraɪzd] *adj* autorisé; *Fin & Law* **duly authorized officer** représentant(e) *m,f* dûment habilité(e)

►► *Com* ***authorized agent*** mandataire *mf*, agent *m* mandataire; *Fin* ***authorized capital*** capital *m* autorisé *ou* social *ou* nominal; *Com* ***authorized dealer*** distributeur *m* agréé; *Banking* ***authorized overdraft facility*** autorisation *f* de découvert; *Com* ***authorized representative*** mandataire *mf*, agent *m* mandataire; *St Exch* ***authorized share capital*** capital *m* autorisé; ***authorized signatory*** signataire *mf* autorisé(e) *ou* accrédité(e); *St Exch* ***authorized unit trust*** = SICAV autorisée par la commission britannique des opérations de Bourse; *Bible* ***the Authorized Version*** = la version anglaise de la Bible de 1611, autorisée par le roi Jacques I d'Angleterre

authorship [ˈɔːθəʃɪp] *n* (**a**) (*of book*) auteur *m*, paternité *f*; (*of invention*) paternité *f*; **a work of unknown authorship** un ouvrage *ou* une œuvre anonyme; **they have established the authorship of the book** ils ont identifié l'auteur du livre; **he claimed authorship of the invention** il a revendiqué la paternité de l'invention (**b**) (*profession*) profession *f* d'auteur *ou* d'écrivain

autism [ˈɔːtɪzəm] *n Med* autisme *m*

autistic [ɔːˈtɪstɪk] *adj Med* autiste

auto [ˈɔːtəʊ] *Am* **1** *n* voiture *f*, auto *f*

2 *comp* d'auto, automobile

►► ***auto accident*** accident *m* de voiture; ***auto industry*** industrie *f* automobile; ***auto parts*** pièces *fpl* détachées (pour voiture)

auto- [ˈɔːtəʊ] *pref* auto-

auto-addresser *n Comput* (*on laser printer*) adressage *m* automatique

auto-answer *n Comput* (*in datacomms*) réponse *f* automatique

autoantibody [ˌɔːtəʊˈæntɪbɒdɪ] *n Biol* autoanticorps *m*

auto-antigen *n Med* auto-antigène *m*

autobank [ˈɔːtəʊˌbæŋk] *n* distributeur *m* automatique de billets (de banque)

autobiographer [ˌɔːtəbaɪ'ɒgrəfə(r)] *n* autobiographe *mf*

autobiographical ['ɔːtəˌbaɪə'græfɪkəl] *adj* autobiographique

autobiography [ˌɔːtəbaɪ'ɒgrəfɪ] (*pl* **autobiographies**) *n* autobiographie *f*

autocade ['ɔːtəʊkeɪd] *n Am Aut* cortège *m* d'automobiles

autochton [ɔː'tɒkθɒn] *n* (**a**) *(person)* autochtone *mf* (**b**) *Bot* plante *f* indigène (**c**) *Zool* animal *m* indigène

autoclave ['ɔːtəʊkleɪv] *n* autoclave *m*

autocorrect [ˌɔːtəʊkə'rekt] *vt Comput* corriger automatiquement

autocracy [ɔː'tɒkrəsɪ] (*pl* **autocracies**) *n Pol* autocratie *f*

autocrat ['ɔːtəkræt] *n Pol (absolute ruler)* autocrate *m*; *Fig* despote *mf*

autocratic [ˌɔːtə'krætɪk] *adj Pol (government, policies)* autocratique; *(ruler)* absolu; *Fig (person)* despotique

autocratically [ˌɔːtə'krætɪkəlɪ] *adv Pol* autocratiquement; *Fig* despotiquement

autocross ['ɔːtəʊkrɒs] *n Sport* autocross *m*

Autocue® ['ɔːtəʊkjuː] *n Br TV* téléprompteur *m*

auto-da-fé [ˌɔːtəʊdɑː'feɪ] (*pl* **autos-da-fé** [ˌɔːtəʊz-]) *n Hist & Rel* autodafé *m*

autodestruct [ˌɔːtəʊdɪ'strʌkt] **1** *vi* s'autodétruire
  2 *adj* qui s'autodétruit

autodial ['ɔːtəʊdaɪəl] *n Tel* numérotation *f* automatique; **a phone with auto-dial** un poste à numérotation *f* automatique

autodialler ['ɔːtəʊˌdaɪələ(r)] *n Tel* numéroteur *m* automatique

autodidact [ˌɔːtəʊ'daɪdækt] *n* autodidacte *mf*

autodidactic [ˌɔːtəʊdaɪ'dæktɪk] *adj* autodidacte

auto-dissolve *n TV & Cin* fondu *m* enchaîné automatique

autoerotic [ˌɔːtəʊɪ'rɒtɪk] *adj* autoérotique

autoeroticism [ˌɔːtəʊɪ'rɒtɪsɪzəm], **autoerotism** [ˌɔːtəʊ'erɒtɪzəm] *n* autoérotisme *m*

autoexec.bat [ˌɔːtəʊeksek'bæt] *n Comput* **autoexec.bat (file)** fichier *m* autoexec. bat

autoflow ['ɔːtəʊfləʊ] *n Comput* passage *m* automatique à la ligne

autofocus ['ɔːtəʊˌfəʊkəs] *n Phot* autofocus *m inv*; **camera with autofocus** appareil *m* autofocus

autoformat ['ɔːtəʊˌfɔːmæt] *n Comput* composition *f* automatique

autogamous [ɔː'tɒgəməs] *adj Biol* autogame

autogenous [ɔː'tɒdʒənəs] *adj Med & Tech* autogène
  ►► *Com* ***autogenous training*** training *m* autogène, autorelaxation *f*

autogiro [ˌɔːtəʊ'dʒaɪərəʊ] *n Aviat* autogire *m*

autograft ['ɔːtəgrɑːft] *n Med* autogreffe *f*

autograph ['ɔːtəgrɑːf] **1** *n* autographe *m*
  2 *comp (letter)* autographe; *(album, collector)* d'autographes
  3 *vt (book, picture, record)* dédicacer; *(letter, object)* signer
  ►► ***autograph hunter*** collectionneur(euse) *m,f* d'autographes

autogyro = **autogiro**

autohypnosis [ˌɔːtəʊhɪp'nəʊsɪs] *n Psy* auto-hypnose *f*

auto-ignition *n* auto-allumage *m*

autoimmune [ˌɔːtəʊɪ'mjuːn] *adj Med* auto-immun
  ►► ***autoimmune disease*** maladie *f* auto-immune

autoimmunity [ˌɔːtəʊɪ'mjuːnətɪ] *n Med* auto-immunisation *f*

autoinfection [ˌɔːtəʊɪn'fekʃən] *n Med* auto-infection *f*

autokinetic [ˌɔːtəʊkɪ'netɪk] *adj Phys* automobile

autoload ['ɔːtəʊləʊd] *vi Comput* se charger automatiquement

automaker ['ɔːtəʊˌmeɪkə(r)] *n Am* constructeur *m* automobile

automat ['ɔːtəmæt] *n (machine)* distributeur *m* automatique; *Am (room)* cafétéria *f* équipée de distributeurs automatiques

automata [ɔː'tɒmətə] *pl of* **automaton**

automatable [ˌɔːtə'meɪtəbəl] *adj* automatisable

automate ['ɔːtəmeɪt] *vt* automatiser

automated ['ɔːtəmeɪtɪd] *adj* automatisé
  ►► *Banking* ***automated clearing house*** chambre *f* de compensation automatisée; ***automated reservation*** réservation *f* télématique; *Banking* ***automated teller machine*** distributeur *m* automatique (de billets); ***automated ticket*** billet *m* informatisé; *Banking* ***automated withdrawal*** retrait *m* automatique

automatic [ˌɔːtə'mætɪk] **1** *adj (machine)* automatique; *(answer, smile)* automatique, machinal
  2 *n* (**a**) *(weapon)* automatique *m*
  (**b**) *Aut* voiture *f* à boîte *ou* à transmission automatique, automatique *f*; **a Volkswagen automatic** une Volkswagen (à boîte *ou* à transmission) automatique
  ►► *Acct* ***automatic accounting*** comptabilité *f* mécanographique; *Comput* ***automatic data processing*** traitement *m* automatique des données; *Tel* ***automatic dialling*** composition *f* automatique de numéros; *Comput* ***automatic feed*** avance *f* automatique; *Rad & Elec* ***automatic gain control*** antifading *m*; *Physiol* ***automatic nervous system*** système *m* nerveux autonome; *Comput* ***automatic pagination*** séparation *f* automatique des pages; *Aviat* ***automatic pilot*** pilote *m* automatique; **on automatic pilot** en pilotage automatique; *Fig* **to do sth on automatic pilot** faire qch mécaniquement *ou* machinalement; *Fig* **I just went onto automatic pilot** j'ai poursuivi machinalement; ***automatic pistol*** pistolet *m* automatique, automatique *m*; ***automatic search*** *(on cassette player)* recherche *f* automatique (de séquences musicales); ***automatic ticket distributor*** distributeur *m* automatique de titres de transport; ***automatic ticket machine*** billetterie *f* automatique; *Banking* ***automatic transfer*** virement *m* automatique; *Aut* ***automatic transmission*** transmission *f* automatique; *Rad & Elec* ***automatic volume control*** antifading *m*

automatically [ˌɔːtə'mætɪkəlɪ] *adv* automatiquement; *Fig* automatiquement, machinalement; **teachers are automatically retired at the age of sixty-five** les enseignants sont mis à la retraite d'office à l'âge de soixante-cinq ans; *Law* **automatically void** nul de plein droit; **I just automatically assumed he was right** j'ai automatiquement supposé qu'il avait raison

automation [ˌɔːtə'meɪʃən] *n (process of making automatic)* automatisation *f*; *(state of being automatic)* automation *f*; **factory** *or* **industrial automation** productique *f*

automatism [ɔː'tɒmətɪzəm] *n Psy & Tech* automatisme *m*

automatist [ɔː'tɒmətɪst] *n Tech* automatiste *mf*

automatization [ˌɔːtəmətaɪ'zeɪʃən] *n Tech* automatisation *f*

automatize, -ise [ɔː'tɒmətaɪz] *vt Tech* automatiser

automaton [ɔː'tɒmətən] (*pl* **automatons** *or* **automata** [-tə]) *n Tech* automate *m*

automobile ['ɔːtəməbiːl] *n Am* automobile *f*, voiture *f*
  ►► ***Automobile Association*** = société *f* de dépannage pour les automobilistes, ≃ Touring Club *m* de France; ***automobile club*** club *m* automobile; ***the automobile industry*** l'industrie *f* automobile; ***automobile manufacture*** fabrication *f* d'automobiles; ***automobile workers*** ouvriers *mpl* de l'industrie automobile

automotive [ˌɔːtə'məʊtɪv] *adj Tech (self-propelled)* automoteur
  ►► *Am* ***automotive industry*** industrie *f* automobile; *Am* ***automotive engineering*** technique *f* automobile

autonomic [ˌɔːtə'nɒmɪk] *adj Biol & Physiol* autonome

autonomous [ɔː'tɒnəməs] *adj Biol & Pol* autonome

autonomy [ɔː'tɒnəmɪ] (*pl* **autonomies**) *n Pol* (**a**) *(self-government)* autonomie *f* (**b**) *(country)* pays *m* autonome

autopilot [ˌɔːtəʊ'paɪlət] *n Aviat* pilote *m* automatique; **on autopilot** en pilotage automatique; *Fig* **to do sth on autopilot** faire qch mécaniquement *ou* machinalement; *Fig* **I just went onto autopilot** j'ai poursuivi machinalement

autopsy ['ɔːtɒpsɪ] (*pl* **autopsies**) *Med* **1** *n* autopsie *f*; **to carry out an autopsy** faire une autopsie; *Fig* faire une analyse
  2 *vt* autopsier

auto-redial *n Tel* re-numérotation *f* automatique

auto-refresh *n Comput* autorafraîchissement *m*

autoreverse [ˌɔːtəʊrɪ'vɜːs] *n Tech* autoreverse *m*, inversion *f* automatique du sens de défilement

autosave ['ɔːtəʊˌseɪv] *Br Comput* **1** *n* sauvegarde *f* automatique
  2 *vt* sauvegarder automatiquement

autosome ['ɔːtəsəʊm] *n Biol (in genetics)* chromosome *m* somatique

autostart ['ɔːtəʊˌstɑːt] *n Comput* démarrage *m* automatique

autosuggestion [ˌɔːtəʊsə'dʒestʃən] *n Psy* autosuggestion *f*

autoswitch ['ɔːtəʊˌswɪtʃ] *n Comput* commutateur *m* automatique

autoteller ['ɔːtəʊtelə(r)] *n Austr* distributeur *m* automatique (de billets), DAB *m*, *Suisse* bancomat *m*

autotimer ['ɔːtəʊˌtaɪmə(r)] *n Tech* programmateur *m*

autotrophic [ˌɔːtəʊ'trəʊfɪk] *adj Biol* autotrophe

autowinder ['ɔːtəʊˌwaɪndə(r)] *n Phot* avance *f* automatique du film

autumn ['ɔːtəm] **1** *n* automne *m*; **in (the) autumn** en automne; *Literary* **he was in the autumn of his years** il était à l'automne de sa vie; **autumn leaves** *(on tree)* feuilles *fpl* d'automne; *(dead)* feuilles *fpl* mortes; **an autumn evening** une soirée d'automne
  2 *comp (colours, weather)* d'automne, automnal
  ►► *Bot* ***autumn gentian*** gentiane *f* amère; *Bot* ***autumn hawkbit*** liondent *m* hispide; *Bot* ***autumn lady's tresses*** spiranthe *f* spiralée, spiranthe *f* d'automne; *Br Pol* ***autumn statement*** = document remis au Parlement par le gouvernement britannique, généralement en novembre, traitant des prévisions économiques et des dépenses publiques pour les trois années à venir

autumnal [ɔː'tʌmnəl] *adj* automnal, d'automne; **autumnal shades** teintes *fpl* automnales; **there was an autumnal feeling in the air, it was autumnal** il y avait de l'automne dans l'air
  ►► *Astron* ***autumnal equinox*** équinoxe *m* d'automne

Auvergne [əʊ'veən] *n* Auvergne *f*; **in Auvergne** en Auvergne

auxiliary [ɔːg'zɪljərɪ] (*pl* **auxiliaries**) **1** *adj (forces, workers, engine)* auxiliaire; *(heating, lighting)* d'appoint
  2 *n* (**a**) *(assistant, subordinate)* auxiliaire *mf*; *Med* **nursing auxiliary** infirmier(ère) *m,f* auxiliaire, aide-soignant(e) *m,f*
  (**b**) *Mil* **auxiliaries** auxiliaires *mpl*
  (**c**) *Gram* (verbe *m*) auxiliaire *m*
  ►► ***auxiliary power unit*** unité *f* auxiliaire d'alimentation; ***auxiliary staff*** *(gen)* le personnel auxiliaire, les auxiliaires *mpl*; *Br Sch* personnel *m* auxiliaire non enseignant; *Gram* ***auxiliary verb*** (verbe *m*) auxiliaire *m*

auxin ['ɔːksɪn] *n Bot* auxine *f*

AV [ˌeɪ'viː] **1** *n Br Bible* (*abbr* **Authorized Version**) = la version anglaise de la Bible de 1611, autorisée par le roi Jacques Ier d'Angleterre
  2 *adj* (*abbr* **audiovisual**) audio-visuel

Av. (*written abbr* **avenue**) av

avadavat [æ'vædəvæt] *n Orn* bengali *m* rouge

avail [ə'veɪl] **1** *n* **it is of no avail to complain** il est inutile de se plaindre; **his efforts were of no avail** ses efforts n'ont eu aucun effet; **to no avail** sans effet; **they argued with her to no avail** ils ont essayé en vain de la convaincre; **to little avail** sans grand effet; **we tried but it was to little avail** nous avons essayé mais cela n'a pas servi à grand-chose; **to be of little avail** être peu utile *ou* peu avantageux
  2 *vt* **I availed myself of the opportunity to thank her** j'ai profité de l'occasion pour *ou* j'ai saisi cette occasion de la remercier
  3 *vi Literary* servir; **nothing could avail against the storm** rien ne s'avéra efficace contre l'orage

availability [əˌveɪlə'bɪlətɪ] (*pl* **availabilities**) *n* (**a**) *(accessibility)* disponibilité *f*; *Com* **offer subject to availability** dans la limite des stocks disponibles; *(of tickets)* dans la limite des places disponibles; **the widespread availability of drugs** la facilité avec laquelle on peut se procurer de la drogue; **the availability of easy credit means that many people have got into serious debt** du

fait qu'il est facile de se faire prêter de l'argent, beaucoup de gens se retrouvent couverts de dettes
(**b**) *Am Pej Pol (of candidate)* = caractère inoffensif

available [ə'veɪləbəl] *adj* (**a**) *(accessible, to hand)* disponible; *(person → for interview etc)* libre, disponible; **they made the data available to us** ils ont mis les données à notre disposition; **they used the time available to evacuate the area** ils ont utilisé le temps dont ils disposaient pour évacuer le secteur; **available for work** disponible; **when are you available to start work?** à partir de quand pouvez-vous commencer à travailler?; **we tried every available means** nous avons essayé (par) tous les moyens possibles; *Com* **they're available in three sizes** ils sont disponibles en trois tailles; *Com* **available in all bookshops** en vente *ou* disponible chez tous les libraires; *Com* **also available in white** existe également en blanc; *Com* **we regret that this offer is no longer available** nous avons le regret de vous annoncer que cette offre n'est plus valable; **available to download from our Web site** peut être téléchargé à partir de notre site web; **illegal drugs are readily available in the town** on se procure facilement de la drogue dans cette ville; **legal aid should be available to everyone** l'assistance juridique devrait être accessible à tous; **available on CD-ROM/DVD** existe en CD-ROM/DVD; **available for the Mac/PC** disponible pour Mac/PC; *Fin* **sum available for dividend** affectation *f* aux actions
(**b**) *(free)* libre, disponible; **the minister in charge was not available for comment** le ministre responsable s'est refusé à toute déclaration; **were there any available men at the party?** est-ce qu'il y avait des hommes disponibles *ou* libres à la soirée?
(**c**) *Am Pej Pol (candidate)* sûr *(en raison de son caractère inoffensif)*
►► *Fin* ***available assets*** actif *m* disponible *ou* liquide; *Fin* ***available balance*** solde *m* disponible; *Fin* ***available capital*** capitaux *mpl* disponibles; *Fin* ***available cash flow*** cash-flow *m* disponible; *Fin* ***available funds*** fonds *mpl* liquides *ou* disponibles, disponibilités *fpl*; *Phot* ***available light*** lumière *f* naturelle; *Mktg* ***available market*** marché *m* effectif; *Comput* ***available memory*** mémoire *f* disponible

aval [æ'væl] *n Banking* aval *m* bancaire

avalanche ['ævəlɑːnʃ] **1** *n also Fig* avalanche *f*
2 *vi* tomber en avalanche

avalize, -ise ['ævəlaɪz] *vt Banking* avaliser

avant-garde [ˌævɒŋ'gɑːd] **1** *n* avant-garde *f*
2 *adj* d'avant-garde, avant-gardiste; **avant-garde films** films *mpl* d'avant-garde

avant-gardism [ˌævɒŋ'gɑːdɪzəm] *n* avant-gardisme *m*

avant-gardist, avant-gardiste [ˌævɒŋ'gɑːdɪst] *n* avant-gardiste *mf*

avarice ['ævərɪs] *n* cupidité *f*

avaricious [ˌævə'rɪʃəs] *adj* cupide

avariciously [ˌævə'rɪʃəslɪ] *adv* cupidement

avariciousness [ˌævə'rɪʃəsnɪs] *n* cupidité *f*

avast [ə'vɑːst] *exclam Old-fashioned Naut* tenez bon!, baste!

avatar [ˌævə'tɑː(r)] *n* (**a**) *Rel* avatar *m*; *Fig* manifestation *f* (**b**) *Comput* avatar *m*

AVC [ˌeɪviː'siː] *n Fin (abbr* **additional voluntary contribution**) supplément *m* de cotisation retraite *(payé volontairement)*

AVCO ['ævˌkəʊ] *n Fin (abbr* **average cost**) coût *m* moyen

avdp. *(written abbr* **avoirdupois**) avoirdupoids *m*

Ave. *(written abbr* **avenue**) av

Ave (Maria) ['ɑːvɪ(mə'rɪə)] *n Rel* Ave *m* (Maria) *inv*

Avebury ['eɪvbərɪ] *n* = village du sud de l'Angleterre connu pour ses mégalithes

avenge [ə'vendʒ] *vt* venger; **he avenged his brother's death** il a vengé la mort de son frère; **he intends to avenge himself on his enemy** il a l'intention de se venger de *ou* de prendre sa revanche sur son ennemi

avenger [ə'vendʒə(r)] *n* vengeur(eresse) *m,f*

'The Avengers' 'Chapeau melon et bottes de cuir'

avenging [ə'vendʒɪŋ] *adj* vengeur; **an avenging angel** un ange exterminateur

Aventine Hill ['ævənˌtaɪn-] *n Antiq* **the Aventine Hill** le mont Aventin

avenue ['ævənjuː] *n* (**a**) *(public)* avenue *f*, boulevard *m*; *(private)* avenue *f*, allée *f (bordée d'arbres)*; *esp Am (wide street)* boulevard *m* (**b**) *Fig* possibilité *f*; **we must explore every avenue** il faut explorer toutes les possibilités; **this opens up another avenue of investigation** ceci ouvre une nouvelle voie de recherche; **an avenue to fame/wealth** un moyen de parvenir à la gloire/fortune

aver [ə'vɜː(r)] *(pt & pp* **averred**, *cont* **averring**) *vi Literary* affirmer, déclarer; **everyone avers that he was present** au dire de chacun il était présent; **this is averred to be true** on affirme que c'est vrai

average ['ævərɪdʒ] **1** *n* (**a**) *(standard amount, quality)* moyenne *f*; **an average of four to six years** une moyenne de quatre à six ans; **above/below average** au-dessus/au-dessous de la moyenne; **on (an) average** en moyenne; **we travelled an average of 100 miles a day** nous avons fait une moyenne de 100 miles par jour *ou* 100 miles par jour en moyenne; **to spend an average of £85 per week** dépenser en moyenne 85 livres par semaine; **the law of averages** la loi de la probabilité
(**b**) *Math* moyenne *f*; **to work out the average** établir la moyenne; **that gives an average of six** ça fait une moyenne de six
(**c**) *Ins & Naut (in marine insurance)* avarie(s) *f(pl)*
(**d**) *St Exch* indice *m*
2 *adj* moyen; **of average intelligence/size** d'intelligence/de taille moyenne; **ask the average man in the street** demandez à l'homme de la rue; **of average height** de taille moyenne; **the food is better than average** la nourriture est au-dessus de la moyenne; **the film was just average** le film était moyen; **in an average week** dans une semaine ordinaire; **how was your day? – average** comment s'est passée ta journée? – moyen; *Fam* **a very average singer** un chanteur de qualité très moyenne
3 *vt* (**a**) *Math* établir *ou* faire la moyenne de
(**b**) *(perform typical number of)* atteindre la moyenne de; **household spending averages £80 per week** les dépenses des ménages sont de *ou* atteignent les 80 livres par semaine en moyenne; **the factory averages ten machines a day** l'usine produit en moyenne dix machines par jour; **we average two letters a day** nous recevons en moyenne deux lettres par jour; **he averaged 100 km/h** il a fait du 100 km/h de moyenne
(**c**) *(divide up)* partager; **the company averages the profits among the staff** la firme distribue *ou* répartit les bénéfices entre le personnel
►► *Ins* ***average adjuster*** dispacheur *m*, expert-répartiteur *m*; *Ins* ***average adjustment*** dispache *f*; *Fin* ***average cost*** coût *m* moyen; *Fin* ***average due date*** échéance *f* moyenne; *Fin* ***average revenue*** produit *m* moyen; *Am Fin* ***average tax rate*** taux *m* d'imposition effectif *ou* moyen; *Fin* ***average yield*** rendement *m* moyen

►**average out 1** *vi Fin* **profits average out at 10 percent** les bénéfices s'élèvent en moyenne à 10 pour cent; **factory production averages out at a hundred and twenty cars a day** l'usine produit en moyenne cent vingt voitures par jour; **what does it average out at?** ça fait combien en moyenne?
2 *vt sep* faire la moyenne de

averment [ə'vɜːmənt] *n Literary* affirmation *f*, déclaration *f*

averse [ə'vɜːs] *adj* **to be averse to sth** *(to task, job)* répugner à qch; *(to criticism, change)* détester qch; **to be averse to doing sth** répugner à faire qch; **she's not averse to the occasional glass of wine** elle boit volontiers un verre de vin de temps à autre; **he's not averse to making money out of the crisis** ça ne le gêne pas de profiter de la crise pour se faire de l'argent

averseness [ə'vɜːsnɪs] *n* aversion *f* (**to** *or* **from** pour)

aversion [ə'vɜːʃən] *n* (**a**) *(dislike)* aversion *f*; **to have an aversion to sth** avoir une aversion pour *ou* contre qch; **she has an aversion to smoking** elle a horreur du tabac; **I have an aversion to his brother** je ne supporte pas son frère, son frère m'est insupportable; **he has a strong aversion to travelling** il déteste voyager
(**b**) *(object of dislike)* objet *m* d'aversion; *Br* **my pet aversion is housework** ma bête noire *ou* ce que je déteste le plus, c'est le ménage
►► *Psy* ***aversion therapy*** thérapie *f* d'aversion

avert [ə'vɜːt] *vt* (**a**) *(prevent)* prévenir, éviter (**b**) *(turn aside → eyes, thoughts)* détourner; *(→ blow)* détourner, parer; *(→ suspicion)* écarter; **I averted my gaze** j'ai détourné les yeux

avertable, avertible [ə'vɜːtəbəl] *adj* évitable

avian ['eɪvɪən] *adj Orn* avien

aviary ['eɪvjərɪ] *(pl* **aviaries**) *n Orn* volière *f*

aviation [ˌeɪvɪ'eɪʃən] **1** *n* aviation *f*
2 *comp (design)* d'aviation
►► ***aviation fuel*** kérosène *m*; ***aviation history*** histoire *f* de l'aviation; ***the aviation industry*** l'aéronautique *f*

aviator ['eɪvɪeɪtə(r)] *n Old-fashioned* aviateur(-trice) *m,f*, pilote *m*
►► ***aviator sunglasses*** lunettes *fpl* de soleil sport

aviatrix ['eɪvɪeɪtrɪks] *n Old-fashioned* aviatrice *f*

aviculture ['eɪvɪˌkʌltʃə] *n Orn* aviculture *f*

avid ['ævɪd] *adj* avide; **avid for revenge** avide de revanche; **avid to learn** avide d'apprendre; **avid reader** lecteur(trice) *m,f* passionné(e)

avidity [ə'vɪdətɪ] *n* avidité *f*

avidly ['ævɪdlɪ] *adv* avidement, avec avidité

avionics [ˌeɪvɪ'ɒnɪks] *Aviat & Tech* **1** *n (UNCOUNT) (science)* avionique *f*
2 *npl (instruments)* avionique *f*

avocado [ˌævə'kɑːdəʊ] *(pl* **avocados** *or* **avocadoes**) *n (fruit)* avocat *m*; *(tree)* avocatier *m*
►► ***avocado pear*** avocat *m*

avocation [ˌævə'keɪʃən] *n Am* activité *f* de loisir

avocet ['ævəˌset] *n Orn* avocette *f*

avoid [ə'vɔɪd] *vt* (**a**) *(object, person)* éviter; *(danger, task, punishment)* éviter, échapper à; *(blow)* esquiver; **she avoided my eyes** elle évita mon regard; **we can't avoid inviting them** nous ne pouvons pas faire autrement que de les inviter; **you've been avoiding me** tu m'évites; **they couldn't avoid hitting the car** ils n'ont pas pu éviter la voiture; **avoid giving them too much information** évitez de leur donner trop d'informations; **to avoid the truth** refuser de voir la réalité en face; **don't avoid the issue** n'essaie pas d'éviter *ou* d'éluder la question; *Fin* **to avoid (paying) taxes** *(legally)* se soustraire à l'impôt; *(illegally)* frauder le fisc
(**b**) *Law (void)* annuler, rendre nul

avoidable [ə'vɔɪdəbəl] *adj* évitable
►► *Fin* ***avoidable costs*** coûts *mpl* évitables

avoidance [ə'vɔɪdəns] *n* **avoidance of work** le soin que l'on met à éviter le travail; **avoidance of duty** manquements *mpl* au devoir; *Fin* **avoidance of payment** non-paiement *m*; *Fin* **tax avoidance** évasion *f* fiscale

avoirdupois [ˌævədə'pɔɪz] **1** *n* (**a**) *(system)* avoirdupoids *m* (**b**) *Am (of person)* embonpoint *m*
2 *comp (ounce, pound)* = conforme aux poids et mesures officiellement établis
►► ***avoirdupois ounce*** = 28,35g, once *f*; ***avoirdupois weight*** avoirdupoids *m*

Avon ['eɪvən] *n Formerly* l'Avon *m*, = comté dans le sud-ouest de l'Angleterre; **in Avon** dans l'Avon
►► ***Avon***® ***Lady*** démarcheuse *f* de produits Avon®

avouch [ə'vaʊtʃ] *vt Literary* affirmer, déclarer

avouchment [ə'vaʊtʃmənt] *n Literary* affirmation *f*, déclaration *f*

avow [ə'vaʊ] *vt Formal (state)* affirmer, déclarer; *(admit)* admettre, reconnaître, confesser; **to avow oneself beaten** s'avouer vaincu; **he openly avowed himself a communist** il a ouvertement reconnu qu'il était communiste

avowal [ə'vaʊəl] *n Formal* aveu *m*

avowed [ə'vaʊd] *adj (enemy)* déclaré; *(aim, purpose)* avoué; **she's an avowed Marxist** c'est une marxiste convaincue; **an avowed homosexual** un homosexuel qui se revendique comme tel

avowedly [ə'vaʊɪdlɪ] *adv* de son propre aveu

AVP [,eɪviː'piː] *n* (*abbr* **assistant vice-president**) = vice-président adjoint

avuncular [ə'vʌŋkjʊlə(r)] *adj* avunculaire

aw [ɔː] *exclam Am* oh!

AWACS ['eɪwæks] *n Aviat & Mil* (*abbr* **airborne warning and control system**) AWACS *m*

await [ə'weɪt] *vt* (**a**) (*wait for*) attendre; **a long-awaited holiday** des vacances *fpl* qui se sont fait attendre; **awaiting your instructions** (*in letter, memo*) dans l'attente de vos instructions; **soldiers awaiting discharge** soldats *mpl* en instance de libération; **mail awaiting delivery** courrier *m* en souffrance; **awaiting collection** (*parcel, mail*) en souffrance; *Law* **she's awaiting trial** elle est en instance de procès

(**b**) (*be in store for*) attendre, être réservé à; **a warm welcome awaited them** un accueil chaleureux leur fut réservé; **who knows what may await us** qui sait ce qui nous attend *ou* est réservé

awake [ə'weɪk] (*pt* **awoke** [ə'wəʊk], *pp* **awoken** [ə'wəʊkən]) **1** *adj* (**a**) (*not sleeping*) éveillé, réveillé; **to be awake** être réveillé, ne pas dormir; **are you still awake?** tu ne dors pas encore?, tu n'es pas encore endormi?; **the noise kept me awake** le bruit m'a empêché de dormir; **I lay awake all night** je n'ai pas fermé l'œil de la nuit; **to stay awake** rester éveillé; **he was wide awake** il était bien éveillé

(**b**) (*aware*) attentif, vigilant; **we're all awake to the dangers of our situation** nous sommes tous conscients des dangers de notre situation; **is the minister awake to the dangers inherent to the system?** le ministre a-t-il conscience *ou* se rend-il compte des dangers inhérents au système?

2 *vi* (**a**) (*emerge from sleep*) se réveiller, s'éveiller; **I awoke from a deep sleep** je suis sorti d'un sommeil profond; **to awake from** (*trance, unconsciousness*) sortir de; **I awoke to the sound of birds singing** à mon réveil j'ai entendu chanter les oiseaux

(**b**) (*become aware*) **to awake to** (*danger, fact etc*) se rendre compte de, prendre conscience de; (*possibility*) prendre conscience de; **he finally awoke from his illusions** il est enfin revenu de ses illusions

3 *vt* (**a**) (*person*) réveiller, éveiller

(**b**) *Fig* (*curiosity, suspicions*) éveiller; (*memories*) réveiller, faire renaître; (*hope*) éveiller, faire naître; *Fig* **to awake sb to sth** faire prendre conscience de qch à qn

awaken [ə'weɪkən] **1** *vt* éveiller

2 *vi* s'éveiller

awakening [ə'weɪknɪŋ] **1** *n* (**a**) *also Fig* (*arousal*) réveil *m*; **it was a rude awakening** c'était un réveil brutal *ou* pénible (**b**) (*beginning*) début *m*, commencement *m*

2 *adj* naissant

award [ə'wɔːd] **1** *n* (**a**) (*prize*) prix *m*; (*medal*) médaille *f*; *Mil* distinction *f* honorifique; *Sch* récompense *f*; **to make an award** décerner un prix; *Sch* décerner une récompense; **to be given an award** recevoir un prix; *Sch* recevoir une récompense; **the annual awards ceremony** la cérémonie annuelle de remise des prix; **he received an award for bravery** il a reçu une médaille en reconnaissance de son courage

(**b**) (*scholarship*) bourse *f*

(**c**) *Law* (*damages*) dommages-intérêts *mpl* accordés par le juge; (*decision*) décision *f*, sentence *f* (arbitrale); (*of contract*) adjudication *f*

(**d**) *Austr & NZ Fin* (*minimum wage*) ≃ salaire *m* minimum interprofessionnel de croissance, SMIC *m*

2 *vt* (**a**) (*mark*) accorder; (*prize*) décerner; (*scholarship*) attribuer, allouer; *Law* (*damages*) accorder; (*contract*) adjuger; (*pay increase, grant*) accorder; **she was awarded first prize** on lui a décerné le premier prix

(**b**) *Sport* (*penalty, free kick*) accorder

►► *Austr & NZ Fin* ***award rate, award wage*** ≃ salaire *m* minimum interprofessionnel de croissance, SMIC *m*

awarding [ə'wɔːdɪŋ] **1** *adj* adjudicatif; **the university is the sole awarding body for these qualifications** seule cette université est habilitée à délivrer ces diplômes

2 *n* (*of prize*) décernement *m*; (*of scholarship*) attribution *f*; *Com* (*of contract*) adjudication *f*

award-winner *n* (*person*) lauréat(e) *m,f*; (*film*) film *m* primé; (*book*) livre *m* primé

award-winning *adj* (*person*) qui a reçu un prix; (*film, book*) primé; **he gave an award-winning performance in...** il a reçu un prix pour son rôle dans...

aware [ə'weə(r)] *adj* (**a**) (*cognizant, conscious*) conscient; (*informed*) au courant, informé; **to be aware of sth** être conscient de qch; **are you aware of the problems?** êtes-vous conscient des problèmes?; **I am quite aware of his feelings** je connais *ou* je n'ignore pas ses sentiments; **he's well aware of the risks** il est tout à fait conscient des risques; **I wasn't aware of his presence** je ne m'étais pas aperçu qu'il était là; **to become aware of sth** se rendre compte *ou* prendre conscience de qch; **she made us aware of the problem** elle nous a fait prendre conscience du problème; **as far as I am aware** autant que je sache; **not that I am aware of** pas que je sache; **without being aware of it** sans s'en rendre compte; **politically aware** politisé; **socially aware** au courant des problèmes sociaux

(**b**) (*sensitive*) sensible

awareness [ə'weənɪs] *n* (*gen*) conscience *f*; **he has little awareness of the situation** il n'a guère conscience de la situation; **a heightened awareness of colour** une conscience plus aiguë des couleurs; **political awareness** politisation *f*

►► *Mktg* ***awareness rating*** taux *m* de notoriété; *Mktg* ***awareness study*** étude *f* de notoriété

awash [ə'wɒʃ] *adj* (**a**) *also Fig* (*flooded*) inondé; **awash with oil** inondé de pétrole; *Fig* **to be awash with money** (*sector, organization*) crouler sous l'argent (**b**) *Naut* (*submarine etc*) à fleur d'eau, qui affleure; **rocks awash at high tide** roches couvertes d'eau à marée haute

AWAY [ə'weɪ] **1** *adv* (**a**) (*indicating movement*) **he got into his car and drove away** il est monté dans sa voiture et il est parti; **to go away** partir, s'en aller; **to look away** détourner son regard; **to run/fly away** s'enfuir/s'envoler; **they moved away from the door** ils se sont éloignés de la porte; **they're away!** (*at start of race*) ils sont partis; *Fam* **a couple of drinks and he's away** (*talking, doing something*) deux verres et il est parti; *Fam* **well away** (*progressing*) bien en train; (*drunk*) soûl; *Arch or Literary* **we must away** il nous faut partir

(**b**) (*indicating distance, position*) **the village is 10 miles away** le village est à 10 miles; **it's less than five minutes' walk away** c'est à moins de cinq minutes à pied; **the church was set away from the road** l'église était située en retrait par rapport à la route; **away in the distance** au loin, dans le lointain; **away over there beyond the mountains** là-bas, bien loin au-delà des montagnes

(**c**) (*in time*) **the holidays are only three weeks away** les vacances sont dans trois semaines seulement; **away back in the 20s** il y a bien longtemps, dans les années 20; **away back in 1970** il y a longtemps déjà, en 1970

(**d**) (*absent*) absent; **he feeds the cat whenever we're away** il donne à manger au chat quand nous ne sommes pas là *ou* quand nous sommes absents; **the boss is away on business this week** le patron est en déplacement cette semaine; **they're away on holiday/in Madrid** ils sont (partis) en vacances/à Madrid

(**e**) (*indicating disappearance, decline*) **the water had boiled away** l'eau s'était évaporée (à force de bouillir); **we danced the night away** nous avons passé toute la nuit à danser; **to fade** *or* **die away** (*sound*) s'éteindre; (*protests*) se taire; **government support gradually fell away** le soutien de l'État a disparu petit à petit

(**f**) (*continuously*) **to work away** travailler beaucoup; **she's working away on her novel** elle travaille d'arrache-pied à son roman; **he was singing away to himself** il fredonnait

(**g**) *Sport* **the team is (playing) away this Saturday** l'équipe joue à l'extérieur *ou* en déplacement samedi

(**h**) *Formal* (*idioms*) **away with** assez de; **away with petty restrictions!** assez de restrictions mesquines; *Fam* **away with you!** (*don't be silly*) arrête tes bêtises!

2 away from *prep* (*indicating precise distance*) à...de; (*not at, not in*) loin de; **two metres away from us** à deux mètres de nous; **somewhere well away from the city** quelque part très loin de la ville; **when we're away from home** quand nous partons, quand nous ne sommes pas chez nous

►► *Sport* ***away game*** match *m* à l'extérieur; ***away goal*** = but marqué lors d'un match à l'extérieur; **they won on away goals** ils ont gagné grâce aux buts qu'ils ont marqués lors de matchs joués à l'extérieur; ***away match*** match *m* à l'extérieur; ***away strip*** = tenue portée par l'équipe qui joue à l'extérieur lorsque l'équipe qui joue à domicile a une tenue similaire; ***the away team*** l'équipe *f* qui joue à l'extérieur, les visiteurs *mpl*

Awayday [ə'weɪdeɪ] *n Br Formerly Rail* = billet de train à tarif réduit valable dans la journée

AWB [,eɪdʌbəljuː'biː] *n Com* (*abbr* **air waybill**) LTA *f*

awe [ɔː] **1** *n* admiration *f* mêlée de respect; **to be** *or* **to stand in awe of sb/sth** être impressionné par qn/qch; **he stared at her in awe** il la regardait, plein d'admiration

2 *vt* impressionner; **the children were awed by the cathedral/the tone of her voice** les enfants ont été terriblement impressionnés par la cathédrale/le ton de sa voix; **the music awed them into silence** impressionnés par la musique, ils se sont tus

awed [ɔːd] *adj* **she spoke in an awed whisper** elle chuchotait d'une voix respectueuse et intimidée

aweigh [ə'weɪ] *adv Naut* **with anchor aweigh** l'ancre dérapée; **anchors aweigh!** levez l'ancre!

awe-inspiring *adj* (*impressive*) impressionnant, imposant; (*amazing*) stupéfiant; (*frightening*) terrifiant

awesome ['ɔːsəm] *adj* (**a**) (*impressive*) impressionnant, imposant; (*amazing*) stupéfiant; (*frightening*) terrifiant

(**b**) *esp Am Fam* (*great*) génial

awe-struck *adj* (*intimidated*) intimidé, impressionné; (*amazed*) stupéfait; (*frightened*) frappé de terreur

awful ['ɔːfʊl] **1** *adj* (**a**) (*bad*) affreux, atroce; **he was simply awful to her** il a été absolument infecte *ou* horrible avec elle; **I feel awful** je me sens très mal; **she looks awful** (*ill*) elle a l'air malade; (*badly dressed*) elle est affreusement mal habillée; **how awful for you!** ça a dû être vraiment terrible (pour vous)!; **what an awful bore!** (*person*) ce qu'il/elle peut être assommant(e)!; (*task*) quelle corvée!; **you're awful!** tu es impossible!; **what awful weather!** quel temps affreux *ou* de chien!; **she's an awful woman** c'est quelqu'un d'épouvantable

(**b**) (*horrific* → *crime, news*) épouvantable, effroyable

(**c**) (*as intensifier*) **I have an awful lot of work** j'ai énormément de travail; **they took an awful chance** ils ont pris un risque énorme *ou* considérable; **he's an awful fool** il est bien bête

2 *adv Fam* (*very*) très ❑, terriblement

awfully ['ɔːflɪ] *adv* (*very*) très, terriblement; **awfully funny/nice** extrêmement drôle/gentil; **he's an awfully good writer** il écrit merveilleusement bien; **I'm awfully sorry** je suis vraiment *ou* sincèrement désolé; **thanks awfully** merci infiniment *ou* mille fois; *Fam Hum* **awfully awfully** = maniérisme utilisé pour décrire les manières et l'accent de la haute bourgeoisie britannique

awfulness ['ɔːfʊlnɪs] *n* (**a**) (*of behaviour, treatment*) atrocité *f* (**b**) (*of accident, crime*) horreur *f*

awhile [ə'waɪl] *adv Literary* (pendant) un instant *ou* un moment; **let's think about it awhile** réfléchissons-y un peu; **not yet awhile** pas encore, pas de sitôt; **wait awhile** attendez un peu

awkward ['ɔːkwəd] *adj* (**a**) *(clumsy → person)* maladroit, gauche; *(→ gesture)* maladroit, peu élégant; *(→ style)* lourd, gauche; **he's awkward with his hands** il n'est pas très habile de ses mains; **the awkward age** l'âge ingrat

(**b**) *(embarrassed → person)* gêné, ennuyé; *(→ silence)* gêné, embarrassé; **she felt awkward about going** cela la gênait d'y aller; **it would be awkward if he met her** cela serait fâcheux *ou* gênant s'il la rencontrait

(**c**) *(difficult → problem, situation)* délicat, fâcheux; *(→ task)* délicat; *(→ question)* gênant, embarrassant; *(→ person)* peu commode, difficile; **it's an awkward time for me to leave** cela me serait difficile de partir en ce moment; **you've come at an awkward time** vous êtes arrivé au mauvais moment; **an awkward moment** un moment inopportun; **they could make things awkward for her** ils pourraient lui mettre des bâtons dans les roues; *Fam* **he's an awkward customer** il n'est pas commode; **it's awkward to use** ça n'est pas facile à utiliser; **the table is at an awkward angle** la table est mal placée; **the switch is in an awkward place** l'interrupteur est situé à un endroit peu accessible; **their house is awkward to get to** leur maison est d'un accès difficile

(**d**) *(uncooperative)* peu coopératif; **he's just being awkward** il essaie seulement de compliquer les choses

awkwardly ['ɔːkwədlɪ] *adv* (**a**) *(clumsily → dance, move)* maladroitement, peu élégamment; *(→ handle, speak)* maladroitement, gauchement; **an awkwardly phrased sentence** une phrase lourde *ou* mal formulée; **to put sth awkwardly** dire qch d'une façon maladroite; **it's very awkwardly designed** c'est très mal conçu

(**b**) *(with embarrassment → behave)* d'une façon gênée *ou* embarrassée; *(→ reply, speak)* d'un ton embarrassé *ou* gêné, avec gêne; **she grinned awkwardly** elle a souri d'un air gêné

(**c**) *(inconveniently)* **the lever is awkwardly placed** le levier est mal placé; **their house is awkwardly situated** leur maison est mal située

awkwardness ['ɔːkwədnɪs] *n* (**a**) *(clumsiness → of movement, person)* maladresse *f*, gaucherie *f*; *(→ of style)* lourdeur *f*, inélégance *f* (**b**) *(unease)* embarras *m*, gêne *f*; **the awkwardness of the situation** le côté gênant *ou* embarrassant de la situation

awl [ɔːl] *n* alène *f*, poinçon *m*

awn [ɔːn] *n Bot* barbe *f*

awning ['ɔːnɪŋ] *n* (**a**) *(over window)* store *m*; *(on shop display)* banne *f*, store *m*; *(at door of hotel, theatre etc)* marquise *f*, auvent *m*; *Naut* taud *m*, taude *f* (**b**) *(tent)* auvent *m*

awoke [ə'wəʊk] *pt of* **awake**

awoken [ə'wəʊkən] *pp of* **awake**

AWOL ['eɪwɒl] *(abbr* **absent without leave***) adj Mil* **to be/to go AWOL** être absent/s'absenter sans permission; *Fig Hum* **to go AWOL** *(person)* disparaître de la circulation; *(object)* disparaître; **my keys have gone AWOL** mes clés ont disparu, impossible de retrouver mes clés

awry [ə'raɪ] **1** *adj* de travers, de guingois

2 *adv* de travers; **to go awry** mal tourner, aller de travers

axe, *Am* **ax** [æks] *(pl* **axes***)* **1** *n* (**a**) *(tool)* hache *f*; **to have an axe to grind** *(ulterior motive)* prêcher pour sa paroisse, être intéressé; *(complaint)* avoir un compte à régler; *Fam* **to get the axe** *(person)* être viré; *(programme, plan etc)* être annulé *ou* supprimé ❑; *Fig* **when the axe falls** quand le couperet tombe (**b**) *Fam (guitar)* gratte *f*, râpe *f*

2 *vt* (**a**) *(wood)* couper, hacher (**b**) *Fig (person)* virer; *(project)* annuler, abandonner; *(job, position)* supprimer; **many educational grants have been axed** un grand nombre de bourses d'études ont été supprimées; **to axe public expenditure** faire des coupes claires dans les dépenses publiques

►► ***axe murderer*** = assassin qui tue ses victimes à coups de hache

axel ['æksəl] *n Sport* axel *m*

axeman ['æksmæn] *(pl* **axemen** [-men]*) n (killer)* = assassin qui tue ses victimes à coups de hache; *Fig (in company)* cadre *m* chargé des licenciements

axes ['æksiːz] *pl of* **axis**

axial ['æksɪəl] *adj* axial

axil ['æksɪl] *n Bot* aisselle *f*

axiological [ˌæksɪəʊ'lɒdʒɪkəl] *adj Phil* axiologique

axiology [ˌæksɪ'ɒlədʒɪ] *n Phil* axiologie *f*

axiom ['æksɪəm] *n Math* axiome *m*

axiomatic [ˌæksɪə'mætɪk] *adj* (**a**) *Math* axiomatique (**b**) *(self-evident)* évident

axis ['æksɪs] **1** *n (pl* **axes** [-iːz]*)* axe *m*

2 Axis *n Hist* **the Axis** l'Axe *m*

►► *Zool* ***axis deer*** *(Axis axis)* chital *m*; *(Axis porcinus)* cerf-cochon *m*

axle ['æksəl] *n (gen)* axe *m*; *Aut* essieu *m*; **front/rear axle** essieu avant/arrière

axle-box *n Aut* boîte *f* d'essieu

axle-pin *n* esse *f*; *Aut* clavette *f* d'essieu

axletree ['æksəltriː] *n Aut* essieu *m*

Axminster ['æksmɪnstə(r)] *n Br (carpet)* = tapis fabriqué à Axminster en Angleterre

ay [aɪ] **1** *n* oui *m inv*

2 *exclam Arch or Scot & NEng* oui

ayah ['aɪə] *n* bonne *f* d'enfant

ayatollah [ˌaɪə'tɒlə] *n Rel* ayatollah *m*

aye 1 *adv* [eɪ] *Arch or Scot & NEng* toujours

2 *exclam* [aɪ] *Arch or Scot & NEng* oui; *Naut* **aye, aye sir!** oui, mon commandant!

3 *n* [aɪ] oui *m inv*; **twenty-five ayes and three noes** vingt-cinq oui et trois non, vingt-cinq pour et trois contre; **the ayes have it** les oui l'emportent

aye-aye *exclam Br* tiens donc!

Ayers Rock [eəz-] *n* = montagne sacrée des aborigènes, dans le centre de l'Australie

AYH [ˌeɪwaɪ'eɪtʃ] *n (abbr* **American Youth Hostels***)* = association américaine des auberges de jeunesse

Ayrshire ['eəʃɪə] *n Zool* Ayrshire *m (race bovine)*

AZ *(written abbr* **Arizona***)* Arizona *m*

azalea [ə'zeɪljə] *n Bot* azalée *f*

Azerbaijan [ˌæzəbaɪ'dʒɑːn] *n* Azerbaïdjan *m*; **in Azerbaijan** en Azerbaïdjan

Azerbaijani [ˌæzəbaɪ'dʒɑːnɪ] **1** *n* (**a**) *(person)* Azerbaïdjanais(e) *m,f*, Azéri(e) *m,f* (**b**) *(language)* azéri

2 *adj* azerbaïdjanais, azéri

3 *comp (embassy)* d'Azerbaïdjan; *(history)* de l'Azerbaïdjan; *(teacher)* d'azéri

Azeri [ə'zerɪ] **1** *n* Azeri *mf*

2 *adj* azeri

AZERTY keyboard [eɪ'zɜːtɪ-] *n Comput* clavier *m* AZERTY

azimuth ['æzɪməθ] *n Astron & Geog* azimut *m*

azonal [eɪ'zəʊnəl] *adj* azonal; **azonal soil** sol *m* azonal

azonic [eɪ'zəʊnɪk] *adj* azonal

Azores [ə'zɔːz] *npl* **the Azores** les Açores *fpl*; **in the Azores** aux Açores

AZT [ˌeɪzed'tiː] *n Med (abbr* **azidothymidine***)* AZT *f*

Aztec ['æztek] **1** *n* Aztèque *mf*

2 *adj* aztèque

azure ['æʒʊər] *Literary* **1** *n* azur *m*

2 *adj* azuré, d'azur

azure-winged magpie *n Orn* pie *f* bleue à calotte noire

azurine ['æʒʊəraɪn] **1** *n* (**a**) *Tex (dye)* azurine *f* (**b**) *Ich* gardon *m* bleu

2 *adj Literary* azuré, d'azur

azurite ['æʒʊraɪt] *n Miner* azurite *f*

B, b[1] [biː] **1** *n* (**a**) *(letter)* B, b *m inv*; **two b's** deux b; **B for Bob** ≃ B comme Berthe; **6B Napoleon Avenue** 6ter, Napoleon Avenue; *Br* **the B792** *(road)* ≃ la départementale 792; **grade B meat** viande de deuxième catégorie
(**b**) *Sch* **to get a B** avoir une bonne note, ≃ avoir 14 ou 15 sur 20
(**c**) *Mus* si *m inv*; **in B flat** en si bémol
2 *adj Mus (string)* de si
▸▸ *Physiol* ***B cell*** lymphocyte *m* B; *Biol* ***B chromosome*** chromosome *m* B; *Br* ***B road*** route *f* secondaire

b[2] (**a**) *(written abbr* **billion***)* milliard *m* (**b**) *(written abbr* **born***)* né

BA [ˌbiːˈeɪ] *n* (**a**) *Univ (abbr* **Bachelor of Arts***) (person)* = titulaire d'une licence de lettres; *(qualification)* licence *f* de lettres; **to have a BA in history** ≃ avoir une licence en histoire; **John Smith, BA** ≃ John Smith, licencié ès lettres/droit/*etc* (**b**) *(abbr* **British Academy***)* = organisme public d'aide à la recherche dans le domaine des lettres (**c**) *(abbr* **British Airways***)* British Airways

BAA [ˌbiːeɪˈeɪ] *n Com & Aviat (abbr* **British Airports Authority***)* = organisme autonome responsable des aéroports en Grande-Bretagne

baa [bɑː] **1** *n* bêlement *m*; **baa!** bêê!; **Baa, Baa, Black Sheep** = comptine enfantine anglaise
2 *vi* bêler

Baal [ˈbeɪəl, bɑːl] *(pl* **Baalim** [-lɪm]*) n Rel* Baal *m*; *Fig* faux dieu *m*

baa-lamb *n (in children's language)* petit agneau *m*

baba [ˈbɑːbɑː] *n Culin* **(rum) baba** baba *m* (au rhum)

Babbitt [ˈbæbɪt] *n Am Pej* bourgeois(e) *m,f* borné(e)

babble [ˈbæbəl] **1** *vi* (**a**) *(baby)* gazouiller, babiller; *(person → nervously)* bredouiller, bafouiller; *(→ foolishly)* jacasser
(**b**) *(stream)* murmurer
2 *vt* bredouiller, bafouiller
3 *n* (**a**) *(of voices)* rumeur *f*, brouhaha *m*; *(of baby)* babillage *m*, babil *m*; **she could hear the babble of conversation** elle entendait le bruit des conversations
(**b**) *(of stream)* murmure *m*, babil *m*

▸**babble away, babble on** *vi* (**a**) *(baby)* gazouiller, babiller; *(person)* jacasser; **to babble on about sth** parler de qch de façon incessante
(**b**) *(stream)* murmurer

babbler [ˈbæblə(r)] *n (gen) & Orn* bavard(e) *m,f*

babbling [ˈbæblɪŋ] **1** *n* (**a**) *(of voices)* rumeur *f*; *(of baby)* babillage *m*, babil *m*; *(of stream)* gazouillement *m*, babil *m* (**b**) *(chatter)* bavardage *m*
2 *adj* babillard; **babbling idiot** personne qui parle à tort et à travers; **I felt like a babbling idiot** j'avais l'impression que je racontais n'importe quoi

babe [beɪb] *n* (**a**) *(baby)* bébé *m*; *Fig (naive person)* innocent(e) *m,f*, naïf(ïve) *m,f*; **babe in arms** enfant *m* au berceau; *Fig* **she's a babe in arms** elle est comme l'enfant qui vient de naître; **babes in the wood** de jeunes innocents *ou* naïfs (**b**) *Fam (attractive woman)* canon *m* (**c**) *Fam (term of endearment)* chéri(e) *m,f*; **hey babe!** salut ma belle!

babel [ˈbeɪbəl] **1** *n (of voices)* brouhaha *m*
2 Babel *n Bible* **the tower of Babel** la tour de Babel

baboon [bəˈbuːn] *n* babouin *m*

babu [ˈbɑːbuː] *n Br* (**a**) *(Indian term of address)* monsieur *m* (**b**) *Pej (clerk)* employé *m* de bureau *(en Inde)*

babushka [bəˈbuːʃkə] *n* foulard *m (porté par les paysannes russes)*

baby [ˈbeɪbɪ] *(pl* **babies**, *pt & pp* **babied***)* **1** *n* (**a**) *(infant)* bébé *m*; **we've known her since she was a baby** nous l'avons connue toute petite *ou* bébé; **he's the baby of the family** il est le plus jeune *ou* le benjamin de la famille; **don't be such a baby!** ne fais pas l'enfant!; **they left him holding the baby** il l'ont laissé tomber et il a fallu qu'il se débrouille tout seul; **to throw the baby out with the bathwater** jeter le bébé avec l'eau du bain, pécher par excès de zèle
(**b**) *Am Fam (young woman)* belle gosse *f*, minette *f*
(**c**) *Am Fam (term of endearment)* chéri(e) *m,f*; **hey baby!** salut ma belle!
(**d**) *Fam (pet project)* **the new library is the mayor's baby** la nouvelle bibliothèque est un projet qui tient particulièrement à cœur au maire
(**e**) *Am Fam (person)* personne❑ *f*; **he's one tough baby** c'est un coriace *ou* un dur à cuire
(**f**) *Am Fam (machine)* merveille *f*; **this baby drives like a dream** cette voiture est une pure merveille à conduire
2 *vt* dorloter, cajoler
3 *adj (animal)* bébé, petit; **baby cat** chaton *m*, petit chat *m*; **baby elephant** éléphanteau *m*, bébé *m* éléphant; **baby brother/sister** petit frère/petite sœur; **baby girl** petite fille *f*; **baby carrots/aubergines** carottes *fpl*/aubergines *fpl* naines
▸▸ ***baby batterer*** bourreau *m* d'enfants; ***baby battering*** = violences commises sur un bébé; *Fam* ***the baby blues*** *(post-natal depression)* le baby blues; ***baby boom*** baby boom *m*; ***baby boomer*** enfant *m* du baby boom; *Br* ***baby's bottle***, *Am* ***baby bottle*** biberon *m*; *Bot* ***baby's breath*** gypsophile *f*, brouillard *m*; *Br* ***Baby buggy***® *(pushchair)* poussette *f*; *Am* ***baby buggy*** voiture *f* d'enfant, landau *m*; *Am* ***baby carriage*** voiture *f* d'enfant, landau *m*; ***baby carrier*** porte-bébé *m inv*; ***baby care*** soins *mpl* pour bébés; ***baby clothes*** layette *f*; ***baby doll*** poupée *f*; ***baby face*** visage *m* de bébé; ***baby fat*** rondeurs *fpl (chez l'enfant)*; ***baby food*** aliments *mpl* pour bébés; *Mus* ***baby grand*** (piano *m*) demi-queue *m*; ***baby linen*** layette *f*; ***baby milk*** lait *m* maternisé *ou* pour nourrissons; ***baby scales*** pèse-bébé *m*; *Aut* ***baby seat*** siège *m* auto pour bébé, siège *m* enfant; ***baby shampoo*** shampooing *m* pour bébés; ***baby sling*** porte-bébé *m*, Kangourou® *m*; ***baby talk*** langage *m* enfantin *ou* de bébé; ***baby tooth*** dent *f* de lait

baby-blue 1 *n* bleu clair *m inv*
2 *adj* bleu clair *(inv)*; **baby-blue eyes** des yeux bleus *ou* bleu clair

Baby-bouncer® *n* trotteur *m*, youpala *m*

Babycham® [ˈbeɪbɪʃæm] *n* = boisson pétillante légèrement alcoolisée

baby-changing area *n (in shop, shopping centre, airport)* coin-bébé *m*; *(on motorway)* relais-bébé *m*

baby-doll *adj* **baby-doll pyjamas, baby-doll nightdress** baby-doll *m*

baby-face, baby-faced *adj* au visage poupin

Baby-gro® [ˈbeɪbɪgrəʊ] *n Br* grenouillère *f*

babyhood [ˈbeɪbɪhʊd] *n* petite *ou* première enfance *f*

babyish [ˈbeɪbɪɪʃ] *adj Pej (features, voice)* puéril, enfantin; *(behaviour)* puéril, enfantin, infantile

babyishly [ˈbeɪbɪɪʃlɪ] *adv Pej* puérilement, comme un petit enfant

babyishness [ˈbeɪbɪɪʃnɪs] *n Pej* puérilité *f*

baby-listening *adj*
▸▸ ***baby-listening microphone*** babyphone *m*; ***baby-listening service*** service *m* de surveillance à distance des bébés, service *m* baby-phone

Babylon [ˈbæbɪlɒn] *n* Babylone

Babylonia [ˌbæbɪˈləʊnjə] *n* Babylonie *f*; **in Babylonia** en Babylonie

Babylonian [ˌbæbɪˈləʊnjən] **1** *n* (**a**) *(person)* Babylonien(enne) *m,f* (**b**) *(language)* babylonien *m*
2 *adj* babylonien

baby-minder *n* nourrice *f*

baby-sit *vi* garder des enfants, faire du baby-sitting; **she baby-sits for them** elle garde leurs enfants

baby-sitter *n* baby-sitter *mf*, *Can* gardien(enne) *m,f* d'enfants

baby-sitting *n* garde *f* d'enfants, baby-sitting *m*

baby-snatcher *n* ravisseur(euse) *m,f* de bébés; *Fig* **he's/she's a baby snatcher** il/elle les prend au berceau

baby-snatching [-ˌsnætʃɪŋ] *n* rapt *m ou* enlèvement *m* de bébés; *Fig* **I don't go in for baby snatching** moi, je ne les prends pas au berceau

baby-walker *n Br* trotteur *m*

babywipe [ˈbeɪbɪwaɪp] *n* lingette *f*

baccalaureate [ˌbækəˈlɔːrɪət] *n* (**a**) *Univ* ≃ licence *f* (**b**) *Sch* baccalauréat *m* international

baccarat [ˈbækərɑː] *n Cards* baccara *m*

Bacchae [ˈbækiː] *npl Myth* **the Bacchae** les Bacchantes *fpl*

bacchanal [ˈbækənəl] **1** *adj* bachique
2 *n* (**a**) *Myth (worshipper)* adorateur(trice) *m,f* de Bacchus; *Antiq (priestess)* bacchante *f* (**b**) *(reveller)* noceur(euse) *m,f*; *(party)* bacchanale *f*

bacchanalia [ˌbækəˈneɪlɪə] *npl Myth (rite)* bacchanales *fpl*; *(party)* bacchanale *f*

bacchanalian [ˌbækəˈneɪlɪən] *adj (gen) & Myth* bachique

bacchante [bəˈkæntɪ] *n* bacchante *f*

Bacchic [ˈbækɪk] *adj (gen) & Myth* bachique

Bacchus [ˈbækəs] *pr n Myth* Bacchus

baccy [ˈbækɪ] *n Br Fam* tabac❑ *m*

Bach [bɑːx] *pr n* Bach

bachelor [ˈbætʃələ(r)] **1** *n* (**a**) *(man)* célibataire *m*; **a confirmed bachelor** un célibataire endurci (**b**) *Univ* ≃ licencié(e) *m,f* (**c**) *Hist* bachelier *m (aspirant à la chevalerie)*; **knight bachelor** chevalier *m*
2 *adj (brother, uncle)* célibataire; *(life)* de célibataire
▸▸ ***Bachelor of Arts*** *(person)* = titulaire d'une licence de lettres; *(qualification)* licence *f* de lettres; ***bachelor's degree*** licence *f*; ***Bachelor of Education*** *(person)* = titulaire d'une licence d'enseignement; *(qualification)* = licence *f* d'enseignement; ***bachelor flat*** garçonnière *f*; ***bachelor girl*** célibataire *f*; ***bachelor pad*** garçonnière *f*; *Am* ***bachelor party*** enterrement *m* de vie de garçon; *Am* **to have a bachelor party** enterrer sa vie de garçon; ***Bachelor of Science*** *(person)* = titulaire d'une licence de sciences; *(qualification)* licence *f* de sciences; *Am* ***Bachelor of Surgery*** *(person)* = titulaire d'un diplôme sanctionnant trois années d'études de médecine; *(qualification)* = diplôme sanctionnant trois années d'études de médecine

bachelordom [ˈbætʃələdəm], **bachelorhood** [ˈbætʃələhʊd] *n (gen)* célibat *m*; *(of men)* vie *f* de garçon

bachelorette [ˌbætʃələ'ret] *n Am* célibataire *f*
►► ***bachelorette party*** enterrement *m* de vie de jeune fille

bacillary [bə'sɪlərɪ] *adj Med (disease)* bacillaire; *(shape)* bacilliforme

bacilloscopy [ˌbæsɪ'lɒskəpɪ] *n Med* bacilloscopie *f*

bacillus [bə'sɪləs] (*pl* **bacilli** [-laɪ]) *n Biol* bacille *m*

BACK [bæk]

vers l'arrière	► 1 (a)
re + *verbe*	► 1 (b), (c)
de derrière	► 2 (a)
arrière	► 2 (a), 3 (g)
dos	► 3 (a) – (c), (e), (f)
fond	► 3 (d)
reculer	► 4 (a); 5 (a)
financer	► 4 (b)
parier sur	► 4 (c)

1 *adv* (**a**) *(towards the rear)* vers l'arrière, en arrière; **he stepped back** il a reculé d'un pas, il a fait un pas en arrière; **I pushed back my chair** j'ai reculé ma chaise; **she tied her hair back** elle a attaché ses cheveux; **he glanced back** il a regardé derrière lui; **house set** *or* **standing back from the road** maison écartée du chemin *ou* en retrait

(**b**) *(into or in previous place)* **to come back** revenir; **to go back** *(return)* retourner; **to go** *or* **turn back** *(retrace footsteps)* rebrousser chemin; *Am Fam* **to go back on sb** *(betray)* doubler qn; **we went back home** nous sommes rentrés (à la maison); **my headache's back** j'ai de nouveau mal à la tête, mon mal de tête a recommencé; **they'll be back on Monday** ils rentrent *ou* ils seront de retour lundi; **I'll be right back** je reviens tout de suite; **I'll be back** *(threat)* vous me reverrez; **we expect him back tomorrow** il doit rentrer demain; **as soon as you get back** dès votre retour; **is he back at work?** a-t-il repris le travail?; **he's just back from Moscow** il arrive *ou* rentre de Moscou; **we went to town and back** nous avons fait un saut en ville; **he went to his aunt's and back** il a fait l'aller et retour chez sa tante; **the trip to Madrid and back takes three hours** il faut trois heures pour aller à Madrid et revenir; **meanwhile, back in Washington** entre-temps, à Washington; **back home, there's no school on Saturdays** chez moi *ou* nous, il n'y a pas d'école le samedi; *Com* **the back-to-school sales** les soldes *fpl* de la rentrée

(**c**) *(indicating return to previous state)* **she wants her children back** elle veut qu'on lui rende ses enfants; **he went back to sleep** il s'est rendormi; **business soon got back to normal** les affaires ont vite repris leur cours normal; **miniskirts are coming back (in fashion)** les minijupes reviennent à la mode

(**d**) *(earlier)* **six pages back** six pages plus haut; **back in the 17th century** au 17ème siècle; **as far back as I can remember** d'aussi loin que je m'en souvienne; **back in November** déjà au mois de novembre; *Fam* **ten years back** il y a dix ans ☐

(**e**) *(in reply, in return)* **you should ask for your money back** vous devriez demander un remboursement *ou* qu'on vous rembourse; **I hit him back** je lui ai rendu son coup; **if you kick me I'll kick you back** si tu me donnes un coup de pied, je te le rendrai; **she smiled back at him** elle lui a répondu par un sourire; **to write back** répondre (par écrit); **to get one's own back (on sb)** prendre sa revanche (sur qn); **that's her way of getting back at you** c'est sa façon de prendre sa revanche sur toi

2 *adj* (**a**) *(rear → door, garden)* de derrière; *(→ wheel)* arrière *(inv)*; *(→ seat)* arrière *(inv)*, de derrière; **the back legs of a horse** les pattes *fpl* arrière d'un cheval; **back entrance** entrée *f* située à l'arrière; **the back room is the quietest** la pièce qui donne sur l'arrière est la plus calme; **the back page of the newspaper** la dernière page du journal; **to put sth on the back burner** remettre qch à plus tard

(**b**) *(quiet → lane, road)* écarté, isolé

(**c**) *(overdue)* arriéré

(**d**) *Ling (vowel)* postérieur

3 *n* (**a**) *(part of body)* dos *m*; **back pain** mal *m* de dos; **to have a back problem** avoir des problèmes de dos; **she carried her baby on her back** elle portait son bébé sur son dos; **I fell flat on my back** je suis tombé à la renverse *ou* sur le dos; **we lay on our backs** nous étions allongés sur le dos; **my back aches** j'ai mal au dos; **the cat arched its back** le chat a fait le gros dos; **I only saw them from the back** je ne les ai vus que de dos; **she sat with her back to the window** elle était assise le dos tourné à la fenêtre; **sitting with one's back to the light** assis à contre-jour; **he was sitting with his back to the wall** il était assis, dos au mur; *Fig* **to have one's back to the wall** être au pied du mur; **to turn one's back on sb** tourner le dos à qn; *Fig* abandonner qn; **when my back was turned** quand j'avais le dos tourné; **you had your back to me** tu me tournais le dos; **they have the police at their backs** *(in support)* ils ont la police avec eux; *(in pursuit)* ils ont la police à leurs trousses; **with an army at his back** *(supporting him)* soutenu par une armée; **to do sth behind sb's back** faire qch dans le dos de qn; **he laughs at you behind your back** il se moque de vous quand vous avez le dos tourné *ou* dans votre dos; **to talk about sb behind their back** dire du mal de qn dans son dos; **the decision was taken behind my back** la décision a été prise derrière mon dos; **he went behind my back to the boss** il est allé voir le patron derrière mon dos *ou* à mon insu; **to be flat on one's back** *(bedridden)* être alité *ou* cloué au lit; *Fam* **get off my back!** fiche-moi la paix!; **mind your backs!** attention, s'il vous plaît!; **the rich live off the backs of the poor** les riches vivent sur le dos des pauvres; **to put sb's back up** énerver qn; **to put one's back into sth** mettre toute son énergie dans qch; *Fam* **that's it, put your back into it!** allez, un peu de nerf!; **to put one's back out** se faire mal au dos; **I'll be glad to see the back of her** je serai content de la voir partir *ou* d'être débarrassé d'elle

(**b**) *(part opposite the front → gen)* dos *m*, derrière *m*; *(→ of coat, shirt, door)* dos *m*; *(→ of vehicle, building, head)* arrière *m*; *(→ of train)* queue *f*; *(→ of book)* fin *f*; **to sit in the back** *(of car)* monter à l'arrière; **to sit at the back** *(of bus)* s'asseoir à l'arrière; **the carriage at the back of the train** la voiture en queue de *ou* du train; **at the back of the book** à la fin du livre; **the garden is out** *or* **round the back** le jardin se trouve derrière la maison; **the dress fastens at the back** *or Am* **in back** la robe s'agrafe dans le dos; **there was an advert on the back of the bus** il y avait une publicité à l'arrière du bus; *Fam* **she's got a face like the back of a bus** elle est moche comme un pou

(**c**) *(other side → of hand, spoon, envelope)* dos *m*; *(→ of carpet, coin, medal)* revers *m*; *(→ of fabric)* envers *m*; *(→ of page)* verso *m*; *Fin (→ of cheque)* dos *m*, verso *m*; **I know this town like the back of my hand** je connais cette ville comme ma poche; *Fam* **you'll feel the back of my hand in a minute!** tu vas en prendre une!

(**d**) *(farthest from the front → of cupboard, room, stage)* fond *m*; **back of the mouth** arrière-bouche *f*; **back of the throat** arrière-gorge *f*; **we'd like a table at the** *or* **in the very back** nous voudrions une table tout au fond; *Fam* **in the back of beyond** en pleine brousse, au diable vauvert; **it was always there at the back of his mind that...** l'idée ne le quittait pas que...; **it's something to keep at the back of your mind** c'est quelque chose à ne pas oublier; **I've had it** *or* **it's been at the back of my mind for ages** j'y pense depuis longtemps, ça fait longtemps que ça me travaille

(**e**) *(binding)* dos *m*

(**f**) *(of chair)* dos *m*, dossier *m*

(**g**) *Sport* arrière *m*; **(full) back** arrière *m*; **right/left back** arrière *m* droit/gauche

4 *vt* (**a**) *(move backwards → bicycle, car)* reculer; *(→ horse)* faire reculer; *(→ train)* refouler; **I backed the car into the garage** j'ai mis la voiture dans le garage en marche arrière; **she backed him into the next room** elle l'a fait reculer dans la pièce d'à côté

(**b**) *Com (support financially → company, venture)* financer, commanditer; *Fin (→ loan)* garantir; *Fin* **to back a bill** avaliser *ou* endosser un effet

(**c**) *(encourage → efforts, person, venture)* encourager, appuyer, soutenir; *Pol (→ candidate, bill)* soutenir; **we backed her in her fight against racism** nous l'avons soutenue dans sa lutte contre le racisme;

(**d**) *(bet on)* parier sur, miser sur; *Sport* **to back a winner** *(horse, team)* parier *ou* miser sur un gagnant; *Fin & Com (company, stock)* bien placer son argent; *Fig* jouer la bonne carte; *Fig* **to back the wrong horse** parier *ou* miser sur le mauvais cheval

(**e**) *(strengthen, provide backing for → curtain, material)* doubler; *(→ picture, paper)* renforcer

(**f**) *Mus (accompany)* accompagner

(**g**) *Naut (sail)* masquer

5 *vi* (**a**) *(go in reverse → car, train)* faire marche arrière; *(→ horse, person)* reculer; **the car backed into the driveway** la voiture est entrée en marche arrière dans l'allée; **I backed into my neighbour's car** je suis rentré dans la voiture de mon voisin en reculant; **I backed into a corner** je me suis retiré dans un coin

(**b**) *(wind)* tourner en sens inverse des aiguilles d'une montre

6 back and forth *adv* **to go back and forth** *(person)* faire des allées et venues; *(machine, piston)* faire un mouvement de va-et-vient; **his eyes darted back and forth** il regardait de droite à gauche

7 back to front *adv* devant derrière, à l'envers; **you've got your pullover on back to front** tu as mis ton pull devant derrière

8 in back of *prep Am* derrière

►► *Tech* ***back boiler*** = ballon d'eau chaude situé derrière un foyer; *Press* ***back copy*** vieux numéro *m*; *Austr & NZ* ***back country*** campagne *f*, arrière-pays *m inv*; ***back door*** *(of building)* porte *f* de derrière; *Fin* financement *m* déguisé; *Fig* **to get in through** *or* **by the back door** être pistonné; ***back end*** (**a**) *(of car, bus)* arrière *m*; *(of train)* queue *f* (**b**) *NEng (autumn)* arrière-saison *f*, automne *m*; **the back end of the year** l'arrière-saison; *Ling* ***back formation*** dérivation *f* régressive; *Am* ***back haul*** = trajet de retour d'un camion; *Fin* ***back interest*** arrérages *mpl*, intérêts *mpl* arriérés; *Press* ***back issue*** vieux numéro *m*; *Golf* ***the back nine*** les neuf derniers trous *mpl*; *Press* ***back number*** vieux numéro *m*; *Banking* ***back office*** back-office *m*; ***back office staff*** personnels *mpl* de back-office; *Com* ***back orders*** commandes *fpl* en souffrance; ***back page*** dernière page *f*; *Ftbl* ***back pass*** passe *f* en retrait; ***back passage*** *Anat* rectum *m*; *(alley)* ruelle *f*; ***back pay*** rappel *m* de salaire; *Cin & Theat* ***back projection*** rétroprojection *f*; ***back rent*** arriéré *m* de loyer; ***back road*** petite route *f*; ***back room*** *(in house)* pièce *f* de derrière; *(in shop)* arrière-boutique *f*; *(for research)* laboratoire *m* de recherche secret; ***back seat*** siège *m* arrière; *Fig* **to take a back seat** *(job, project)* passer au second plan; *(person)* s'effacer; ***back shift*** *(people)* = équipe du soir; **I hate the back shift** je déteste être du soir; **to work** *or* **be on the back shift** être (de l'équipe) du soir; *Ling* ***back slang*** ≃ verlan *m*; ***back straight*** ligne *f* (droite) d'en face; ***back street*** petite rue *f*; **I grew up in the back streets of Chicago** j'ai été élevé dans les mauvais quartiers de Chicago; *Horseracing* ***back stretch*** *(on race course)* ligne *f* d'en face; *Am Fam* ***back talk*** impertinence ☐ *f*, insolence ☐ *f*; *Fin* ***back taxes*** arriéré *m* d'impôts

► **back away** *vi* (**a**) *(car)* faire marche arrière

(**b**) *(person)* (se) reculer; **she backed away from him** elle a reculé devant lui; *Fig* **they have backed away from making a decision** ils se sont abstenus de prendre une décision

► **back down** *vi (accept defeat → in argument)* admettre qu'on est dans son tort; *(→ in conflict)* faire marche arrière; **he finally backed down on the issue of membership** il a fini par céder sur la question de l'adhésion

► **back off** *vi* (**a**) *(withdraw)* reculer; *Fam Fig* **back off, will you!** fiche-moi la paix!, lâche-moi les baskets!

(**b**) *Am (accept defeat → in argument)* admettre qu'on est dans son tort; *(→ in conflict)* faire marche arrière

►**back onto** *vt insep (have back facing towards)* donner sur (à l'arrière); **the house backs onto the river** l'arrière de la maison donne sur la rivière

►**back out** *vi* (**a**) *(car)* sortir en marche arrière; *(person)* sortir à reculons
(**b**) *Fig (withdraw)* se dérober, tirer son épingle du jeu; **don't back out now!** ne faites pas marche arrière maintenant!; **they backed out of the deal** ils se sont retirés de l'affaire; **to back out of a contract** se rétracter *ou* se retirer d'un contrat; **he's trying to back out (of it)** il voudrait se dédire

►**back up 1** *vi* (**a**) *(car)* faire marche arrière
(**b**) *(drain)* se boucher; *(water)* refouler
2 *vt sep* (**a**) *(car, horse)* faire reculer; *(train)* refouler
(**b**) *(support → claim, story)* appuyer, soutenir; *(→ person)* soutenir, épauler, seconder; **to back sb up in an argument** donner raison à qn; **her story is backed up by eye witnesses** sa version des faits est confirmée par des témoins oculaires; **he backed this up with a few facts** il a étayé ça avec quelques faits
(**c**) *Comput (data, file)* sauvegarder
(**d**) *(accumulate)* **traffic is backed up for 5 miles** ≃ il y a un embouteillage sur 8 km
3 *vi Comput* sauvegarder

'Back to the Future' *Zemeckis* 'Retour vers le futur'

backache ['bækeɪk] *n* mal *m* de dos; **to have backache** avoir mal au dos

backbench ['bækbentʃ] *Parl n* = banc des membres du Parlement britannique sans fonction ministérielle; **discontent on the backbenches** mécontentement parmi les députés sans fonction ministérielle

backbencher [,bæk'bentʃə(r)] *n Parl* = parlementaire sans fonction ministérielle, *Can* simple député(e) *m,f*, député(e) *m,f* d'arrière-banc

BACKBENCHER

Les "backbenchers" sont assis aux derniers rangs de la Chambre des communes, tandis que les rangs de devant sont réservés aux ministres et aux membres du "shadow cabinet" (voir aussi l'encadré sur **shadow cabinet**).

backbend ['bækbend] *n Gym* pont *m (en gymnastique)*

backbite ['bækbaɪt] **1** *vt (person)* médire de
2 *vi* médire

backbiting ['bæk,baɪtɪŋ] *n* médisance *f*

backblocks ['bækblɒks] *npl Can, Austr & NZ* **the backblocks** les régions *fpl* de l'intérieur

backboard ['bækbɔːd] *n Med & Tech (board)* planche *f*, panneau *m*; *Sport (in basketball)* panneau *m*

backbone ['bækbəʊn] *n* (**a**) *Anat* colonne *f* vertébrale; *Zool* épine *f* dorsale; *Fig* **English to the backbone** anglais jusqu'au bout des ongles
(**b**) *(of country, organization)* pivot *m*; **tourism is the backbone of the economy** le tourisme est le pivot de l'économie; **she is the backbone of the movement** elle est le moteur du mouvement
(**c**) *Fig (strength of character)* fermeté *f*, caractère *m*; **you haven't the backbone to do it** tu n'as pas assez de cran pour le faire; **he has no backbone** il n'a rien dans le ventre
(**d**) *Comput (of network)* épine *f* dorsale, réseau *m* d'interconnexion

backbreaking ['bæk,breɪkɪŋ] *adj* éreintant; **backbreaking work** un travail à vous casser les reins

backburn ['bækbɜːn] *Austr* **1** *n (to control forest fire)* contre-feu *m*
2 *vi* allumer un contre-feu

backchat ['bæktʃæt] *n Br Fam* culot *m*; **and I want none of your backchat** et je ne veux pas de discussions

backcloth ['bækklɒθ] *n Theat* toile *f* de fond; *Fig* toile *f* de fond, fond *m*

backcomb ['bækkəʊm] *vt (hair)* crêper

backcourt ['bækkɔːt] *n Sport (in basketball)* zone *f* de défense; *(in tennis)* fond *m* du court

backdate [,bæk'deɪt] *vt (cheque, document)* antidater; **the pay rise is backdated to March** l'augmentation de salaire a un effet rétroactif à compter de mars; **will it be backdated?** est-ce qu'il aura effet rétroactif?

backdoor ['bækdɔː(r)] *adj* louche, suspect; **backdoor methods** méthodes *fpl* peu respectables; **she got the job through backdoor methods** elle a été pistonnée

backdrop ['bækdrɒp] *n* (**a**) *Theat* toile *f* de fond; *(with perspective)* découverte *f* (**b**) *Fig (background)* toile *f* de fond, arrière-plan *m*; **against a backdrop of continuing violence** avec, comme arrière-plan *ou* toile de fond, un climat de violence permanente

-backed [bækt] *suff* (**a**) *(chair)* à dos, à dossier; **a high-backed chair** une chaise à dos *ou* dossier haut; **silk-backed** à dos *ou* dossier en soie; **a broad-backed man** un homme qui a le dos large
(**b**) *(supported by)* **US-backed rebels** des rebelles soutenus par les États-Unis

back-end load *n Am St Exch* frais *mpl* de sortie

backer ['bækə(r)] *n* (**a**) *(supporter)* partisan(e) *m,f*; *(financial supporter)* commanditaire *mf*, bailleur(eresse) *m,f* de fonds; *Fin (of bill)* donneur *m* d'aval, avaliseur *m*; **we need a backer** il nous faut un mécène (**b**) *Sport (punter)* parieur(euse) *m,f*

backfield ['bækfiːld] *n Sport (in American football)* = joueurs positionnés derrière la ligne de mêlée

backfill ['bækfɪl] *Constr* **1** *n (of trench)* remplissage *m*
2 *vt (trench)* remplir

backfire [,bæk'faɪə(r)] **1** *vi* (**a**) *(car)* pétarader (**b**) *(plan)* avoir l'effet inverse; **to backfire on sb** se retourner contre qn
2 *n* (**a**) *(noise)* pétarade *f*; *(explosion)* retour *m* de flamme (**b**) *(controlled fire)* contre-feu *m*

backflip ['bækflɪp] *n (in gymnastics)* culbute *f* à l'envers

backgammon ['bæk,gæmən] *n* backgammon *m*; **to play backgammon** jouer au backgammon; **let's play (a game of) backgammon** si on faisait une partie de backgammon?
►► ***backgammon board*** damier *m* de backgammon

background ['bækgraʊnd] **1** *n* (**a**) *(scene, view)* fond *m*, arrière-plan *m*; *(sound)* fond *m* sonore; *Theat* fond *m*; **yellow flowers on a green background** des fleurs jaunes sur fond vert; **in the background** dans le fond, à l'arrière-plan; **music was playing in the background** il y avait de la musique en bruit de fond; **there was a lot of noise in the background** il y avait beaucoup de bruit de fond; *Fig* **his wife remains very much in the background** sa femme est très effacée *ou* reste à l'écart; **he's rather faded into the background since then** on n'entend plus tellement parler de lui depuis
(**b**) *(of person → history)* antécédents *mpl*; *(→ family)* milieu *m* socioculturel; *(→ experience)* formation *f*, acquis *m*; *(→ education)* formation *f*, bagage *m*; **people from a working-class background** gens *mpl* de milieu ouvrier; **she has a good background in history** elle a une bonne formation en histoire; **what is the candidate's background?** *(social)* à quel milieu social appartient le candidat?; *(professional)* quelle est la formation du candidat?
(**c**) *(of event, situation)* contexte *m*, climat *m*; **the economic background to the crisis** les raisons économiques de la crise; **the talks are taking place against a background of political tensions** les débats ont lieu dans un climat de tension politique; **the report looks at the background to the unrest** le rapport examine l'historique de l'agitation
(**d**) *Comput* arrière-plan *m*; **the program works in the background** le programme est exécuté en arrière-plan
2 *adj* (**a**) *(unobtrusive → noise)* de fond; **background colour** couleur *f* de fond
(**b**) *(facts, material)* de base, de fond; **background information** éléments *mpl* de référence *ou* de base; **I need a bit more background information** j'ai besoin de plus de données
►► *Comput* ***background job*** tâche *f* de fond; ***background light*** éclairage *m* d'ambiance; *Comput* ***background (mode) printing*** impression *f* en arrière-plan; ***background music*** musique *f* d'ambiance *ou* de fond; *Cin & Theat* fond *m* sonore; *Comput* ***background processing*** traitement *m* de données en tâches de fond; *Phys* ***background radiation*** rayonnement *m* naturel; ***background reading*** lectures *fpl* complémentaires; *Comput* ***background task*** tâche *f* d'arrière-plan

backhand ['bækhænd] **1** *n* (**a**) *Sport* revers *m*; **her backhand is weak** son revers manque de puissance; **he has a wicked backhand** il a un sacré revers; **keep serving to his backhand** continue de servir sur son revers (**b**) *(writing)* écriture *f* renversée *ou* penchée à gauche
2 *adj Sport (stroke)* en revers; *(volley)* de revers
3 *adv* en revers

backhanded ['bækhændɪd] *adj* (**a**) *(blow, slap)* donné avec le revers de la main (**b**) *(compliment, remark)* équivoque
►► *Sport* ***backhanded stroke*** revers *m*

backhander ['bæk,hændə(r)] *n* (**a**) *(blow, stroke)* coup *m* du revers de la main; *Sport* revers *m* (**b**) *(comment)* remarque *f* équivoque (**c**) *Br Fam (bribe)* pot-de-vin *m*, dessous-de-table *m inv*

backheel ['bækhiːl] *Ftbl* **1** *n* talonnade *f*
2 *vt* **to backheel the ball** faire une talonnade

backhoe loader ['bækhəʊ-] *n* chargeuse-pelleteuse *f*

backing ['bækɪŋ] *n* (**a**) *(support)* soutien *m*, appui *m*; *(financial support)* financement *m*; **to give financial backing to sth** financer qch (**b**) *(material)* renfort *m* (**c**) *Mus (accompaniment)* accompagnement *m* (**d**) *Horseracing (bets)* paris *mpl*
►► *Br Mus* ***backing group*** = musiciens qui accompagnent un chanteur; ***backing track*** piste *f* de fond; ***backing vocalist*** choriste *mf*; ***backing vocals*** chœurs *mpl*

backlash ['bæklæʃ] *n* retour *m* de manivelle; **a backlash of violence** une réaction de violence

backless ['bæklɪs] *adj (dress, top)* dos nu *(inv)*

backlight ['bæklaɪt] *n Comput (of screen)* rétroéclairage *m*

backlist ['bæklɪst] *n* liste *f* des ouvrages disponibles
►► ***backlist titles*** ouvrages *mpl* de fonds

backlit ['bæklɪt] *adj Comput (screen)* rétro-éclairé

backlog ['bæklɒg] *n* accumulation *f*, arriéré *m*; **to have a backlog of correspondence/work** avoir du retard dans son courrier/travail, avoir du courrier/travail en retard; *Com* **a backlog of orders** des commandes inexécutées *ou* en souffrance

backlot ['bæklɒt] *n Am* cour *f (derrière un immeuble)*

backpack ['bækpæk] **1** *n* sac *m* à dos
2 *vt* transporter dans un sac à dos
3 *vi* voyager sac au dos

backpacker ['bækpækə(r)] *n* routard(e) *m,f*

backpacking ['bækpækɪŋ] *n* **to go backpacking** voyager sac au dos; **backpacking is very popular with students** les étudiants aiment beaucoup voyager sac au dos

backpedal [,bæk'pedəl] *(Br pt & pp* **backpedalled,** *cont* **backpedalling,** *Am pt & pp* **backpedaled,** *cont* **backpedaling)** *vi* (**a**) *(on bicycle)* rétropédaler (**b**) *Fig* [illegible] faire marche arrière; **to backpedal on a promise** revenir sur une promesse

back-pedalling, *Am* **back-pedaling** ['bæk,pedəlɪŋ] *n (on bicycle)* rétropédalage *m*; *Fig* marche *f* arrière

back-pressure *n Tech* contre-pression *f*

backrest ['bækrest] *n (support)* dossier *m*

backroom ['bækruːm] *adj (research, work)* secret(ète)
►► ***backroom boys*** *(gen)* ceux qui restent dans l'ombre *ou* dans les coulisses; *(researchers)* chercheurs *mpl* qui travaillent dans l'anonymat

back-scratcher *n (implement)* gratte-dos *m inv*

back-scratching *n Fig* échange *m* de faveurs

back-scrubber *n* lave-dos *m*

back-seat *adj*
►► *Pej* ***back-seat driver*** *(in car)* = personne qui donne toujours des conseils au conducteur; *(interfering person)* donneur(euse) *m,f* de leçons; ***back-seat passenger*** passager *m* arrière

backsheesh, backshish [ˌbæk'ʃiːʃ] *n Fam* bakchich *m*

backside ['bæksaɪd] *n Fam* derrière *m*, fesses *fpl*; **he just sits around on his backside all day** il reste assis toute la journée à ne rien faire

backsight ['bæksaɪt] *n (on rifle)* cran *m* de mire *ou* de hausse; *(in surveying)* rétrovisée *f*

backslapping ['bækˌslæpɪŋ] **1** *n (heartiness)* cordialité *f* excessive; *(congratulations)* encensement *m*

2 *adj* jovial

backslash ['bækslæʃ] *n* barre *f* oblique inversée

backslide [ˌbæk'slaɪd] (*pt* **backslid** [-'slɪd], *pp* **backslid** [-'slɪd] *or* **backslidden** [-'slɪdən]) *vi* retomber, récidiver; **no backsliding!** pas question de récidiver!

backslider ['bækˌslaɪdə(r)] *n* récidiviste *mf*

backsliding ['bækˌslaɪdɪŋ] *n* récidive *f*

backspace ['bækspeɪs] *Comput & Typ* **1** *n* espacement *m ou* retour *m* arrière

2 *vt* rappeler

3 *vi* faire un retour arrière

▸▸ ***backspace key*** touche *f* retour arrière

backspin ['bækspɪn] *n Sport* effet *m* contraire; **to put backspin on a ball** couper une balle

backstage [ˌbæk'steɪdʒ] **1** *n Theat & Fig* coulisse *f*, coulisses *fpl*

2 *adv Theat* dans la coulisse *ou* les coulisses, derrière la scène; *Fig* en coulisse, en secret; **to go backstage** aller dans les coulisses

3 *adj Fig* secret(ète), furtif

backstairs [ˌbæk'steəz] **1** *npl (for servants)* escalier *m* de service; *(secret)* escalier *m* secret *ou* dérobé

2 *adj (secret)* secret(ète); *(unfair)* déloyal

▸▸ ***backstairs gossip*** commérages *mpl (des domestiques)*

backstitch ['bækstɪtʃ] *Sewing* **1** *n* point *m* arrière

2 *vt* coudre en point arrière

3 *vi* coudre en point arrière

backstop ['bækstɒp] *n Sport* (**a**) *(screen)* panneau *m* (**b**) *(in baseball)* attrapeur *m*

backstory ['bækstɔːrɪ] *n Am* exposition *f (dans un récit)*

backstreet ['bækstriːt] *adj (secret)* secret(ète), furtif; *(underhand)* louche

▸▸ ***backstreet abortion*** avortement *m* clandestin; ***backstreet abortionist*** faiseuse *f* d'anges, *Pej* avorteur(euse) *mf*

backstroke ['bækstrəʊk] *n Swimming* dos *m* crawlé, *Can* nage *f* sur le dos; **to do (the) backstroke** nager le dos crawlé, *Can* nager sur le dos

backstroker ['bækˌstrəʊkə(r)] *n Swimming* nageur(euse) *m,f* de dos crawlé; **she's an excellent backstroker** c'est une très bonne nageuse de dos crawlé

backswept ['bækswept] *adj* rejeté en arrière

backswing ['bækswɪŋ] *n* swing *m* (en arrière)

back-to-back 1 *adj also Fig* dos à dos

2 *adv also Fig* dos à dos; **they're showing the two films back-to-back** ils passent les deux films l'un après l'autre; **to play two games back-to-back** jouer deux parties l'une à la suite de l'autre

3 *n (houses)* **back-to-backs** = rangée de maisons construites dos à dos et séparées par un passage étroit, typique des régions industrielles du nord de l'Angleterre

▸▸ *Fin* ***back-to-back credit*** crédit *m* dos-à-dos; *Fin* ***back-to-back loan, back-to-back operation*** opération *f* de face à face

backtrack ['bæktræk] *vi* revenir sur ses pas, rebrousser chemin; *Fig* faire marche arrière; **he's already backtracking from** *or* **on his agreement** il est déjà en train de revenir sur son accord

backup ['bækʌp] **1** *n* (**a**) *(support)* soutien *m*, appui *m*; **to ask for backup** *(police)* demander des renforts

(**b**) *(reserve)* réserve *f*; *(substitute)* remplaçant(e) *m,f*

(**c**) *Comput* sauvegarde *f*; **to do the backup** faire la sauvegarde; **the backup has failed** la sauvegarde a échoué

(**d**) *Am Mus* = musiciens qui accompagnent un chanteur

(**e**) *Am (traffic jam)* embouteillage *m*

2 *adj (furnace)* de secours, de réserve; *(plan)* de secours; *(supplies)* supplémentaire, de réserve

▸▸ *Comput* ***backup copy*** copie *f* de sauvegarde; *Comput* ***backup device*** unité *f* de sauvegarde; *Comput* ***backup disk*** sauvegarde *f*; *Comput* ***backup file*** fichier *m* de sauvegarde; *Am Aut* ***backup light*** phare *m* de recul; *Comput* ***backup storage*** mémoire *f* auxiliaire; *Comput* ***backup system*** *(for doing the backup)* système *m* de sauvegarde; *(auxiliary system)* système *m* de secours; ***backup team*** *(which provides support)* équipe *f* de soutien; *(which acts as replacement)* équipe *f* de remplacement; *Mil* ***backup troops*** renforts *mpl*

backward ['bækwəd] **1** *adj* (**a**) *(directed towards the rear)* en arrière, rétrograde; **without a backward look** sans jeter un regard en arrière; **backward and forward motion** mouvement *m* de va-et-vient

(**b**) *(late in development → country, society, child)* arriéré; **the backward state of the country** le retard dont souffre le pays

(**c**) *(reluctant)* hésitant, peu disposé; **he's not backward about giving his opinion** il n'hésite pas à donner son avis; *Hum* **she's not backward at coming forward** elle n'hésite pas à se mettre en avant

2 *adv* = **backwards**

▸▸ *Econ* ***backward integration*** intégration *f* en amont; *Comput* ***backward search*** recherche *f* arrière

backwardation [ˌbækwə'deɪʃən] *n Br Fin & St Exch* déport *m*

▸▸ ***backwardation rate*** taux *m* de déport

backward-compatible *adj Comput* compatible avec les versions antérieures

backward-looking *adj (ideas)* rétrograde

backwardness ['bækwədnɪs] *n* (**a**) *(in development → of country)* sous-développement *m*; *(→ of person)* retard *m* mental; *(→ of economy)* retard *m* (**b**) *(reluctance)* hésitation *f*, lenteur *f*

backwards ['bækwədz] **1** *adv* (**a**) *(towards the rear)* en arrière; *also Fig* **a step backwards** un pas en arrière; **I fell backwards** je suis tombé en arrière *ou* à la renverse

(**b**) *(towards the past)* en arrière, vers le passé; **looking backwards in time** en remontant dans le temps

(**c**) *(with the back foremost)* **to walk backwards** marcher à reculons; **you've got your sweater on backwards** tu as mis ton pull à l'envers *ou* devant derrière

(**d**) *(in reverse)* à l'envers; **now say it backwards** dis-le à l'envers maintenant

(**e**) *(thoroughly)* à fond, sur le bout des doigts; **she knows her subject backwards** elle connaît son sujet sur le bout des doigts

2 backwards and forwards *adv* **to go backwards and forwards** *(person)* aller et venir; *(machine, piston)* faire un mouvement de va-et-vient; *(pendulum)* osciller; **we walked backwards and forwards along the beach** nous avons marché de long en large sur la plage; **she goes backwards and forwards between London and Paris** elle fait la navette entre Londres et Paris

backwash ['bækwɒʃ] *n* remous *mpl*; *Naut (of ship)* sillage *m*, remous *mpl*; *(of waves)* ressac *m*; *Fig* **he was caught up in the backwash of the scandal** il s'est retrouvé pris dans les contrecoups du scandale

backwater ['bækˌwɔːtə(r)] *n (of river)* bras *m* mort; *Fig (remote spot)* coin *m* tranquille; *Pej* coin *m* perdu; **a cultural backwater** un désert culturel

backwoods ['bækwʊdz] **1** *npl (forest)* région *f* forestière *(peu peuplée)*; *Fig (remote spot)* coin *m* tranquille; *Pej* coin *m* perdu; **to live in the backwoods** habiter un trou perdu *ou* un bled

2 *adj (remote)* isolé; *(backward)* peu avancé

backwoodsman ['bækwʊdzmən] (*pl* **backwoodsmen** [-mən]) *n* (**a**) *(who lives in forest)* habitant *m* de la forêt; *Pej (uncouth person)* rustre *m*, rustaud *m* (**b**) *Br Fam Pol* = membre de la Chambre des Lords qui ne fait acte de présence que lorsqu'il s'intéresse à un vote

backyard [bæk'jɑːd] *n Br (courtyard)* cour *f* de derrière, arrière-cour *f*; *Am (garden)* jardin *m* de derrière; *Fig* **in one's own backyard** *(near where one lives)* près de chez soi; **the party leaders don't know what's going on in their own backyard** les dirigeants ne savent pas ce qui se passe au sein de leur propre parti; **the United States sees Latin America as its backyard** les États-Unis considèrent l'Amérique latine comme leur chasse gardée; **the "not-in-my-backyard" syndrome** = attitude de rejet vis à vis de la construction d'une centrale nucléaire, d'un projet de construction etc dans sa commune

baclava = **baklava**

bacon ['beɪkən] *n* lard *m* (maigre), bacon *m*; **a slice** *or* **rasher of bacon** une tranche de lard; **bacon and eggs** œufs *mpl* au bacon *ou* au lard; **bacon sandwich** sandwich *m* au bacon; *Fig* **to save sb's bacon** sauver la peau de qn; *Fam* **to bring home the bacon** *(be the breadwinner)* faire bouillir la marmite; *(succeed)* décrocher la timbale *ou* le gros lot

▸▸ ***bacon slicer*** coupe-jambon *m inv*

Baconian [beɪ'kəʊnɪən] *Phil* **1** *adj* baconien

2 *n* baconiste *mf (disciple de Lord Francis Bacon ou partisan du baconisme)*

Baconianism [beɪ'kəʊnɪənɪzəm] *n Phil* baconisme *m*

BACS [bæks] *n Banking (abbr* **Bankers' Automated Clearing Services***)* système *m* électronique de compensation de chèques; **to pay by BACS** payer par virement électronique

bacteria [bæk'tɪərɪə] *npl Biol* bactéries *fpl*

bacterial [bæk'tɪərɪəl] *adj Biol* bactérien

bactericidal [bækˌtɪərɪ'saɪdəl] *adj Biol* bactéricide

bactericide [bæk'tɪərɪsaɪd] *n Chem* (produit *m*) bactéricide *m*

bacteriological [bækˌtɪərɪə'lɒdʒɪkəl] *adj Biol* bactériologique

▸▸ *Biol & Mil* ***bacteriological warfare*** guerre *f* bactériologique

bacteriologist [bækˌtɪərɪ'ɒlədʒɪst] *n Biol* bactériologiste *mf*

bacteriology [bækˌtɪərɪ'ɒlədʒɪ] *n Biol* bactériologie *f*

bacteriolysis [bækˌtɪərɪ'ɒlɪsɪs] *n Biol* bactériolyse *f*

bacteriophage [bæk'tɪərɪəʊˌfeɪdʒ] *n Biol* bactériophage *m*

bacteriostatic [bækˌtɪərɪə'stætɪk] *adj Biol* bactériostatique

bacterium [bæk'tɪərɪəm] (*pl* **bacteria** [-rɪə]) *n Biol* bactérie *f*

Bactrian camel ['bæktrɪən-] *n* chameau *m* (bactrien)

BAD [bæd]

mauvais	▸ **1 (a), (b), (d), (e), (g), (h); 2; 3**
grave	▸ **1 (c)**
malade	▸ **1 (f)**
pourri	▸ **1 (h)**

(*compar* **worse** [wɜːs], *superl* **worst** [wɜːst]) **1** *adj* (**a**) *(unpleasant → breath, news, terms, weather)* mauvais; *(→ smell, taste)* mauvais, désagréable; **that's too bad!** *(regrettable)* c'est *ou* quel dommage!; *(hard luck)* tant pis pour toi!; **it's too bad he had to leave** quel dommage qu'il ait été obligé de partir; **there was a bad smell in the house** il y avait une odeur désagréable *ou* une mauvaise odeur dans la maison; **bad weather** mauvais temps *m*; *Naut* gros temps *m*; **I have a bad feeling about this** j'ai le pressentiment que ça va mal tourner; **he's/she's not bad-looking** il/elle n'est pas mal; **he's in a bad mood** *or* **bad temper** il est de mauvaise humeur; **she has a bad temper** elle a un sale caractère, elle a un caractère de chien *ou* de cochon; **I'm on bad terms with her** nous sommes en mauvais termes; **to come to a bad end** mal finir; **it's a bad business** *(unpleasant)* c'est une sale affaire; *(unhappy)* c'est une triste affaire; **things went from bad to worse** les choses se sont gâtées *ou* sont allées de mal en pis

(**b**) *(unfavourable → effect, result)* mauvais, malheureux; *(→ omen, report)* mauvais, défavorable; *(→ opinion)* mauvais *(before n)*; **that looks bad** *(augurs ill)* c'est mauvais signe; **things look bad** la situation n'est pas brillante;

is this a bad time to ask for leave? peut-être n'est-ce pas le moment de demander des congés?; **am I phoning at a bad time?** je vous dérange?; **it happened at the worst possible time** ça ne pouvait pas tomber plus mal; **please don't say anything bad about him** ne dis pas de mal de lui, s'il te plaît; **he's in a bad way** *(ill, unhappy)* il va mal, il est en piteux état; *(in trouble)* il est dans de sales draps

(**c**) *(severe → accident, mistake)* grave; *(→ pain)* violent, aigu(üe); *(→ headache)* violent; *(→ climate, winter)* rude, dur; **I have a bad cold** j'ai un gros rhume; **she has a bad case of flu** elle a une mauvaise grippe; **is the pain bad?** est-ce que cela fait très mal?; **that looks bad** *(injury, accident)* ça a l'air grave

(**d**) *(evil, wicked → person)* méchant, mauvais; *(→ behaviour, habit)* mauvais, odieux; **they're a bad lot** ils ne sont pas recommandables; **to call sb bad names** traiter qn de tous les noms, injurier qn; **you've been a bad girl!** tu as fait la vilaine *ou* la méchante!; **bad boy!** vilain!; **bad language** gros mots *mpl*, grossièretés *fpl*

(**e**) *(harmful)* mauvais, néfaste; **smoking is bad for your health** le tabac est mauvais pour la santé; **eating all these sweets is bad for him** c'est mauvais pour lui *ou* ça ne lui vaut rien de manger autant de sucreries; **to be** *or* **have a bad influence on sb** avoir une mauvaise influence sur qn

(**f**) *(unhealthy → leg, arm, person)* malade; *(→ tooth)* carié; **to have bad teeth** avoir de mauvaises dents; **to have a bad back** avoir des problèmes de dos; **your grandmother is bad today** ta grand-mère ne va pas *ou* ne se sent pas bien aujourd'hui; **how are you? – not so bad** comment allez-vous? – on fait aller *ou* pas trop mal; *Fam* **he was taken bad at the office** il a eu un malaise au bureau; **to have a bad heart** être cardiaque, avoir le cœur malade; **because of my bad leg** à cause de mes problèmes de jambe

(**g**) *(poor → light, work)* mauvais, de mauvaise qualité; *(→ actor, pay, performance, road)* mauvais; **to have bad hair** ne pas avoir de beaux cheveux; **he's got bad eyesight** il n'a pas de bons yeux; **that's not bad for a beginner** ce n'est pas mal pour un débutant; *Br Fam* **your painting isn't half bad** ton tableau n'est pas mal du tout ❑; **the salary isn't bad** le salaire est convenable; **it was a bad buy** ce n'était pas un bon investissement; **he speaks rather bad Spanish** il parle plutôt mal espagnol *ou* un espagnol plutôt mauvais; **it would be bad form** *or* **manners to refuse** ce serait impoli de refuser; **that looks bad** *(in eyes of other people)* c'est mal vu; **I've always been bad at maths** je n'ai jamais été doué pour les maths, j'ai toujours été mauvais en maths; **he's bad at keeping a secret** il ne sait pas garder un secret; **he's bad at helping about the house** il n'aide pas souvent aux tâches ménagères; **she's bad about paying bills on time** elle ne paie jamais ses factures à temps; *Fam* **he's always turning up like a bad penny** on n'arrive jamais à se débarrasser de lui; **don't worry, he'll turn up like a bad penny** ne t'en fais pas, tu sais bien qu'il revient toujours; *Fam* **I'm having a bad hair day** *(my hair's a mess)* je n'arrive pas à me coiffer aujourd'hui ❑; *(I'm having a bad day)* aujourd'hui c'est un jour sans, c'est pas mon jour; **bad light stopped play** *(at cricket match)* la partie a été remise à cause d'un manque de lumière

(**h**) *(food)* mauvais, pourri; **to go bad** *(milk)* tourner; *(meat)* pourrir, se gâter; **a bad apple** une pomme pourrie; *Fig* une brebis galeuse; *Fig* **one bad apple spoils the barrel** il ne faut qu'une brebis galeuse pour gâter un troupeau

(**i**) *(unhappy, uncomfortable)* **I feel bad about leaving you alone** cela m'ennuie de te laisser tout seul; **he felt bad about the way he'd treated her** il s'en voulait de l'avoir traitée comme ça; **I feel bad about firing him but I'll have to** cela m'embête d'avoir à le renvoyer, mais il faudra bien que je le fasse

(**j**) *Fam (very good)* terrible; **man, you're looking bad!** mon vieux, tu as l'air en super forme!

2 *n* mauvais *m*; **you have to take the bad with the good** il faut prendre les choses comme elles viennent, bonnes ou mauvaises; **he's gone to the bad** il a mal tourné; *Fin* **he is £5,000 to the bad** *(overdrawn)* il a un découvert de 5000 livres; *(after a deal)* il a perdu 5000 livres; *Fam* **she got in bad with her boss** elle n'a pas la cote avec son patron

3 *npl (people)* **the bad** les mauvais *mpl*

4 *adv Fam* **he wants it bad** il en meurt d'envie; **she's got it bad for him** elle l'a dans la peau; *Am* **he was beaten bad** il s'est fait méchamment tabasser

►► *Banking* ***bad cheque*** chèque *m* sans provision; *Comput* ***bad command*** commande *f* erronée; *Fin* ***bad debt*** créance *f* irrécouvrable *ou* douteuse; ***bad debt provision*** provision *f* pour créances douteuses; ***bad debts reserve*** réserve *f* pour créances douteuses; ***bad debtor*** créance *f* irrécouvrable *ou* douteuse; *Comput* ***bad file name*** nom *m* de fichier erroné; *Comput* ***bad sector*** secteur *m* endommagé

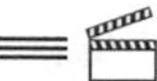

'Bad Day at Black Rock' *Sturges* 'Un homme est passé'

badass ['bædæs] *Am very Fam* **1** *n (person)* dur *m* (à cuire)

2 *adj* (**a**) *(intimidating, tough)* **to be badass** être un dur à cuire (**b**) *(excellent)* super, génial; **her new sneakers are so badass** ils sont super, ses nouveaux tennis

baddie, baddy ['bædɪ] *n Br Fam* méchant ❑ *m*; **he's the baddie** c'est lui le méchant

bade [bæd, beɪd] *pt of* **bid**

badge [bædʒ] **1** *n* (**a**) *(gen)* insigne *m*; *(metal, plastic)* badge *m*; *(fabric)* écusson *m*; *(on lapel)* pin's *m inv*; *(of scout)* badge *m*; *Mil* insigne *m* (**b**) *Fig* signe *m*, marque *f*

2 *vt Mktg (product)* donner une marque à

►► ***badge of office*** insigne *m* de fonction

badged [bædʒd] *adj (wearing a badge)* portant un badge, badgé

badger ['bædʒə(r)] **1** *n* blaireau *m*

2 *vt* harceler, persécuter; **stop badgering your mother with questions** arrête de harceler ta mère de questions; **she badgered us into going** elle nous a harcelés jusqu'à ce que nous y allions

►► ***badger sett*** terrier *m* de blaireau; ***the Badger State*** = surnom donné au Wisconsin

badger-baiting *n Hunt* chasse *f* au blaireau; *(avec des chiens)* déterrage *m* du blaireau

badinage ['bædɪˌnɑːʒ] *n Literary* badinage *m*

badlands ['bædlændz] *npl* bad-lands *fpl*; *Fig* mauvais quartiers *mpl*

badly ['bædlɪ] *(compar* **worse** [wɜːs], *superl* **worst** [wɜːst]) *adv* (**a**) *(poorly)* mal; **badly made/organized** mal fait/organisé; **badly lit** mal éclairé; **things aren't going too badly** ça ne va pas trop mal; **the candidate did** *or* **came off badly in the exams** le candidat ne s'en est pas bien sorti aux examens; **we came off worst in the deal** c'est nous qui nous en sommes le plus mal sortis dans l'affaire; **his business is doing badly** ses affaires marchent *ou* vont mal, il fait de mauvaises affaires; **I feel badly about it** *(sorry)* je le regrette beaucoup; *(embarrassed)* cela me gêne beaucoup; **don't think badly of him for what he did** ne lui en voulez pas de ce qu'il a fait; **she took the news badly** elle a mal pris la nouvelle; **to be badly off** *(financially)* être dans la gêne; **we're badly off for supplies** nous manquons de provisions

(**b**) *(behave → improperly)* mal; *(→ cruelly)* méchamment, avec cruauté

(**c**) *(severely → burn, damage)* gravement, sérieusement; *(→ hurt)* gravement, grièvement; **the town was badly affected by the storm** la ville a été sérieusement touchée par l'orage; **she had been badly beaten** elle avait reçu des coups violents; *Mil* **the army was badly defeated** l'armée a subi une sévère défaite; **badly wounded** gravement *ou* grièvement blessé

(**d**) *(very much)* énormément; **he badly needs** *or* **he's badly in need of a holiday** il a grand *ou* sérieusement besoin de (prendre des) vacances; **we badly want to see her** nous avons très envie de la voir

badman ['bædmæn] *(pl* **badmen** [-men]) *n Am (crook)* bandit *m*; *(in movie)* méchant *m*

bad-mannered *adj* mal élevé

badminton ['bædmɪntən] *n Sport* badminton *m*

►► *Horseriding* ***Badminton Horse Trials*** = prestigieux concours hippique en Angleterre; ***badminton racket*** raquette *f* de badminton

badmouth ['bædmaʊθ] *vt esp Am Fam* débiner

badness ['bædnɪs] *n* (**a**) *(wickedness)* méchanceté *f*; *(cruelty)* cruauté *f* (**b**) *(inferior quality)* mauvaise qualité *f*, mauvais état *m*

bad-tempered *adj (person)* grincheux; *(reply)* désagréable; **to be bad-tempered** *(temporarily)* être de mauvaise humeur; *(permanently)* avoir mauvais caractère

BAE [ˌbiːeɪ'iː] *n Am (abbr* **Bachelor of Arts in Education**) *(person)* = titulaire d'une licence de sciences de l'éducation; *(qualification)* licence *f* de sciences de l'éducation

Baedeker ['beɪdekə(r)] *n* guide *m (livre)*

Baffin Island ['bæfɪn-] *n* terre *f* de Baffin; **in Baffin Island** en terre de Baffin

baffle ['bæfəl] **1** *vt* (**a**) *(puzzle)* déconcerter, dérouter; **the police admit they are baffled** la police reconnaît qu'elle est perplexe; **I'm baffled as to why she said that** je ne comprends vraiment pas pourquoi elle a dit ça

(**b**) *(frustrate → effort, plans)* faire échouer, déjouer; *(→ expectations, hopes)* décevoir, tromper

2 *n Tech (deflector)* déflecteur *m*; *(acoustic)* baffle *m*, écran *m*

►► *Tech* ***baffle board, baffle plate*** *(deflector)* déflecteur *m*; *(acoustic)* baffle *m*, écran *m*

bafflement ['bæfəlmənt] *n* confusion *f*

baffling ['bæflɪŋ] *adj (behaviour)* déconcertant, déroutant; *(mystery, puzzle)* inexplicable; **a baffling problem** un casse-tête

BAFTA ['bæftə] *n Cin & TV (abbr* **British Academy of Film and Television Awards**) **BAFTA (award)** = prix récompensant les meilleurs films et émissions de télévision en Grande-Bretagne

bag [bæg] *(pt & pp* **bagged**, *cont* **bagging**) **1** *n* (**a**) *(container)* sac *m*; **paper/plastic bag** sac *m* en papier/en plastique; **a bag of sweets/groceries** un sac de bonbons/d'épicerie; *Am Fam* **he was left holding the bag** tout lui est retombé dessus; *Fam* **her promotion is in the bag** son avancement, c'est dans la poche *ou* dans le sac *ou* du tout cuit; *Fam* **to pull sth out of the bag** sortir qch du chapeau; *Fam* **the whole bag of tricks** tout le tralala; *esp Am Fam Old-fashioned* **that's not my bag** *(I'm not good at it)* ce n'est pas mon fort; *(I'm not interested in it)* ce n'est pas mon truc

(**b**) *(handbag)* sac *m* (à main); *(suitcase)* valise *f*; **bags** valises *fpl*, bagages *mpl*; **to pack one's bags** faire ses bagages; *Fig* **it's time to pack our bags** c'est le moment de plier bagage; *Fam* **they threw her out bag and baggage** ils l'ont mise à la porte avec toutes ses affaires

(**c**) *(of cloth, skin)* poche *f*; **to have bags under one's eyes** avoir des poches sous les yeux; *Fam* **bag of bones** sac *m ou* tas *m* d'os

(**d**) *Hunt* prise *f*; **did you get a good bag?** avez-vous fait bonne chasse?

(**e**) *Fam Pej (woman)* **old bag** vieille peau *f*, vieille bique *f*; **you stupid bag!** espèce d'idiote!

(**f**) *Fam Drugs slang (quantity of drugs)* dose ❑ *f (en sachet ou dans un papier plié)*

2 *vt* (**a**) *(books, groceries)* mettre dans un sac; *(apples, sweets)* ensacher; *Am (supermarket purchases)* emballer

(**b**) *Fam (seize)* mettre le grappin sur, s'emparer de ❑; *(steal)* piquer, faucher; *Br* **I bags the cakes!** les gâteaux sont à moi!; **he bagged the best seat for himself** il s'est réservé la meilleure place

(**c**) *Hunt* tuer

3 *vi* goder, faire des poches; **his trousers bag at the knees** ses pantalons font des poches aux genoux

4 bags *Fam* **1** *npl Br* (**a**) *(trousers)* pantalon ❑ *m*, fute *m* (**b**) *(lots)* **there are bags of things to do** il y a plein de choses à faire; **we have bags of time** nous avons tout notre temps; **they've bags of money** ils sont pleins aux as **2** *exclam Br* **bags I go!** c'est à moi! ❑; **bags I get the biggest one!** le plus gros est pour moi! ❑

►► *Fam* ***bag lady*** clocharde *f*

bagasse [bə'gæs] *n* bagasse *f*

bagatelle [ˌbægə'tel] *n* (**a**) *(trinket)* bagatelle *f*,

bad–bag

babiole *f*; **a mere bagatelle** une simple bagatelle (**b**) *(board game)* (sorte *f* de) flipper *m*; *(billiards)* billard *m* anglais (**c**) *Mus* bagatelle *f*

bagboy ['bægbɔɪ] *n Am* commis *m (qui aide à l'emballage des achats)*

bagel ['beɪgəl] *n Culin* petit pain *m* en couronne, *Can* bagel *m*

bagful ['bægfʊl] *n* sac *m* plein, plein sac *m*; **a bagful of sweets** un sac plein de bonbons; **he ate a whole bagful of apples** il a mangé un plein sac de pommes

baggage ['bægɪdʒ] *n* (**a**) *(luggage)* valises *fpl*, bagages *mpl*; **one piece of baggage** un bagage
(**b**) *Fig* **to have a lot of (emotional) baggage** avoir accumulé les échecs sentimentaux; **the party has jettisoned a lot of its traditional ideological baggage** le parti s'est débarrassé de son idéologie traditionnelle
(**c**) *Mil* équipement *m* (portatif)
(**d**) *Fam Old-fashioned (cheeky girl)* coquine *f*; *(prostitute)* prostituée ▫ *f*, traînée *f*
►► *Am* ***baggage car*** fourgon *m (d'un train)*; ***baggage check*** *(inspection)* contrôle *m* des bagages; *Am (ticket)* ticket *m* d'enregistrement; *Am* ***baggage checkroom*** consigne *f*; ***baggage handler*** bagagiste *m*; ***baggage reclaim*** livraison *f* des bagages; ***baggage reclaim area*** zone *f* de livraison des bagages; *Am* ***baggage room*** consigne *f*; *Am* ***baggage tag*** bulletin *m* de consigne

Baggie® ['bægɪ] *n Am* = petit sachet hermétique en plastique

bagginess ['bægɪnɪs] *n (of clothes)* ampleur *f*

bagging ['bægɪŋ] *n Tex* toile *f* à sac

baggy ['bægɪ] (*compar* **baggier**, *superl* **baggiest**) *adj (clothing → too big)* trop ample *ou* grand; *(→ loose-fitting)* ample; **baggy trousers** un pantalon bouffant

Baghdad [bæg'dæd] *n* Bagdad

bagman ['bægmən] (*pl* **bagmen** [-mən]) *n Fam* (**a**) *Br Mktg (salesman)* VRP ▫ *m*, voyageur *m ou* représentant *m* de commerce ▫ (**b**) *Am Law (racketeer)* racketteur ▫ *m*

bagpiper ['bægpaɪpə(r)] *n* joueur(euse) *m,f* de cornemuse

bagpipes ['bægpaɪps] *npl* cornemuse *f*

bag-snatcher [-snætʃə(r)] *n* voleur(euse) *m,f* à la tire

bag-snatching [-ˌsnætʃɪŋ] *n* vol *m* à l'arraché

bah [bɑː] *exclam* bah!

Baha'i [bə'hɑːɪ] *Rel* **1** *n* adepte *mf* de la religion Bahaï
2 *adj* bahaï

Bahaism [bə'hɑːɪzəm] *n Rel* bahaïsme *m*

Bahamas [bə'hɑːməz] *npl* Bahamas *fpl*; **in the Bahamas** aux Bahamas

Bahamian [bə'heɪmɪən] **1** *n* Bahamien(enne) *m,f*
2 *adj* des Bahamas, bahamien

Bahrain [bɑː'reɪn] *n* Bahreïn *m*, Bahrayn *m*; **in Bahrain** à Bahreïn; **the Bahrain Islands** les îles *fpl* Bahreïn

Bahraini [bɑː'reɪnɪ] **1** *n* Bahreïni(e) *m,f*
2 *adj* bahreïni

Bahrein = **Bahrain**

Bahreini = **Bahraini**

bail [beɪl] **1** *n* (**a**) *Law (money)* caution *f*; *(guarantor)* caution *f*, répondant(e) *m,f*; *(release)* mise *f* en liberté provisoire sous caution; **on bail** sous caution; **the judge granted/refused bail** le juge a accordé/refusé la mise en liberté provisoire sous caution; **she was released on £2,000 bail** elle a été mise en liberté provisoire après avoir payé une caution de 2 000 livres; **to stand** *or* **to go bail for sb** se porter garant de qn; **who put up bail?** qui a payé la caution?; **the prisoner jumped** *or* **forfeited bail** le prisonnier s'est soustrait à la justice *(à la faveur d'une mise en liberté provisoire)*
(**b**) *Sport (in cricket)* barre *f* horizontale *(du guichet)*
2 *vt* (**a**) *Law (of guarantor)* payer la caution pour, se porter garant de; *(of judge)* mettre en liberté provisoire sous caution
(**b**) *(water)* vider
►► *Law* ***bail bond*** cautionnement *m*; *Am* ***bail bondsman*** garant *m*
► **bail out 1** *vt sep* (**a**) *Law (of guarantor)* payer la caution pour, se porter garant de; *(of judge)* mettre en liberté provisoire sous caution
(**b**) *(help)* tirer *ou* sortir d'affaire; **his parents usually bail him out** la plupart du temps, ses parents le tirent d'affaire *ou* le renflouent
(**c**) *Naut (boat)* écoper; *(cellar, water)* vider
2 *vi Aviat (parachute)* sauter en parachute *(d'un avion en perdition)*

bailer ['beɪlə(r)] *n Naut (bucket)* écope *f*

bailey ['beɪlɪ] *n Constr (wall)* mur *m* d'enceinte; *(courtyard)* cour *f (à l'intérieur de l'enceinte)*

Bailey bridge ['beɪlɪ-] *n Mil* pont *m* Bailey

bailiff ['beɪlɪf] *n* (**a**) *Law* huissier *m* (**b**) *Br (on estate, farm)* régisseur *m*, intendant *m*; **water bailiff** garde-pêche *m* (**c**) *Br Hist (sovereign's representative)* bailli *m*

bailiwick ['beɪlɪwɪk] *n* (**a**) *Law* juridiction *f*, circonscription *f* (**b**) *Fig (interest)* domaine *m*; *Fig* **it's not my bailiwick** *(field, area of expertise)* ce n'est pas mon domaine

bailout ['beɪlaʊt] *n Fin (of company)* renflouement *m*, sauvetage *m*

bairn [beən] *n Scot* enfant *mf*

bait [beɪt] **1** *n* appât *m*, amorce *f*; *Fig* appât *m*, leurre *m*; *also Fig* **to rise to** *or* **swallow** *or* **take the bait** mordre (à l'hameçon)
2 *vt* (**a**) *(hook, trap)* amorcer; *(line)* mettre l'appât à (**b**) *(tease)* harceler, tourmenter (**c**) *Hunt (badger, bear)* lâcher les chiens sur (**d**) *(entice)* tenter

baiting ['beɪtɪŋ] *n* (**a**) *(of hook, trap, line)* amorçage *m* (**b**) *(teasing)* harcèlement *m* (**c**) *Hunt (of badger, bear)* = fait de lâcher les chiens sur la proie

baize [beɪz] **1** *n Tex (fabric)* feutre *m*; *Sport (on billiard table)* tapis *m* de billard; **green baize door** = porte recouverte de feutre vert qui sépare l'office du reste de la maison dans une demeure bourgeoise
2 *adj Tex (cloth, lining)* de feutre

baize-covered *adj* feutré

Bajan ['beɪdʒən] **1** *n* habitant(e) *m,f* de la Barbade
2 *adj* de la Barbade

bake [beɪk] **1** *vt* (**a**) *(cook in oven)* faire cuire au four; **she's baking a cake for me** elle me fait un gâteau
(**b**) *(dry, harden)* cuire; **the land was baked dry** la terre était desséchée
2 *vi* (**a**) *(person → make bread)* elle s'est mise à faire du pain; *(→ make cakes)* faire de la pâtisserie
(**b**) *(cake, pottery)* cuire (au four); **the ground was baking in the sun** le sol se desséchait au soleil
(**c**) *Fam (be hot)* **it's baking in here!** il fait une de ces chaleurs ici!; **I'm baking!** j'étouffe!, je crève de chaleur!
3 *n* (**a**) *(batch of food)* fournée *f*
(**b**) *Br (biscuit)* = sorte de biscuit
(**c**) *Am (party)* = fête où l'on sert un repas cuit au four

baked [beɪkt] *adj*
►► *Culin* ***baked Alaska*** omelette *f* norvégienne; ***baked beans*** *Br (in tomato sauce)* haricots *mpl* blancs à la sauce tomate; *Am (dish)* haricots au lard, *Can* fèves *fpl* au lard; ***baked potato*** pomme *f* de terre en robe de chambre *ou* en robe des champs

bakehouse ['beɪkhaʊs, *pl* -haʊzɪz] *n* boulangerie *f*

Bakelite® ['beɪkəlaɪt] **1** *n* Bakélite® *f*
2 *adj* en Bakélite®

baker ['beɪkə(r)] *n* boulanger(ère) *m,f*; **I'm going to the baker's (shop)** je vais à la boulangerie
►► ***a baker's dozen*** treize à la douzaine

Baker Day *n Br Sch* = journée de formation professionnelle des enseignants durant laquelle les enfants ne vont pas en classe

bakery ['beɪkərɪ] (*pl* **bakeries**) *n* boulangerie *f*

Bakewell tart ['beɪkwel-] *n Br* = fond de tarte fourré au biscuit de Savoie, à la confiture et à la pâte d'amandes

baking ['beɪkɪŋ] **1** *n* (**a**) *(process)* cuisson *f* (au four); **I'll do some baking tomorrow** *(make cakes)* demain, je ferai de la pâtisserie; *(make bread)* demain, je ferai du pain
(**b**) *(batch → of food)* fournée *f*; *(→ of bricks etc)* cuite *f*
2 *adj (hot → pavement, sun)* brûlant; *(→ day, weather)* torride
3 *adv* **a baking hot afternoon** un après-midi torride
►► ***baking dish*** plat *m* allant au four; ***baking potatoes*** pommes *fpl* de terre à cuire au four; ***baking powder*** levure *f* (chimique); ***baking sheet*** plaque *f* (de four), tôle *f*; ***baking soda*** bicarbonate *m* de soude; ***baking tin*** moule *m* à gâteau; ***baking tray*** plaque *f* de four

baklava ['bɑːkləvɑː] *n Culin* baklava *m*

baksheesh [ˌbæk'ʃiːʃ] *n Fam Old-fashioned* bakchich *m*

Baku [bæ'kuː] *n* Bakou

Balaam ['beɪlæm] *pr n Rel* Balaam

Balaclava [ˌbælə'klɑːvə] *n Geog* Balaklava

balaclava (helmet) [bælə'klɑːvə-] *n* passe-montagne *m*

Balaklava = **Balaclava**

balalaika [ˌbælə'laɪkə] *n Mus* balalaïka *f*

BALANCE ['bæləns]

équilibre	► 1 (a), (b)
balance	► 1 (c), (f)
contrepoids	► 1 (d)
solde, reste	► 1 (e)
mettre en équilibre	► 2 (a)
faire contrepoids à	► 2 (b)
peser	► 2 (c)
équilibrer, balancer	► 2 (d)
solder	► 2 (e)
être en équilibre	► 3 (a)
s'équilibrer	► 3 (b), (c)

1 *n* (**a**) *(of person → physical)* équilibre *m*, aplomb *m*; *(→ mental)* calme *m*, équilibre *m*; **she tried to keep her balance** elle a essayé de garder l'équilibre *ou* son équilibre; **I lost my balance** j'ai perdu l'équilibre *ou* mon équilibre; **off balance** *(physically, mentally)* déséquilibré; **he threw me off balance** il m'a fait perdre l'équilibre; *Fig* il m'a décontenancé; *Fig* **to catch sb off balance** prendre qn au dépourvu
(**b**) *(of situation)* équilibre *m*; *Art (of painting, sculpture)* harmonie *f*; **she tried to strike a balance between the practical and the idealistic** elle a essayé de trouver un juste milieu entre la réalité et l'idéal; **balance of nature** l'équilibre *m* de la nature; **budgetary/economic balance** équilibre *m* budgétaire/économique
(**c**) *(scales)* balance *f*; **to hang in the balance** être en jeu; **our future hangs** *or* **lies in the balance** notre avenir est en jeu; **everything is still (hanging) in the balance** rien n'est encore certain; **his remark tipped the balance in his favour** sa remarque a fait pencher la balance en sa faveur
(**d**) *(weight, force)* poids *m*, contrepoids *m*; **the balance of evidence is against him** la plupart des preuves lui sont défavorables; **she acts as a balance to his impulsiveness** elle sert de contrepoids à *ou* elle contrebalance son impulsivité
(**e**) *(remainder)* solde *m*, reste *m*; *Com & Fin* solde *m*; *Acct* balance *f*, bilan *m*; **balance in hand** solde *m* en caisse; **balance carried forward** solde *m* à reporter; *(on balance sheet)* report *m* à nouveau; **balance brought forward** solde *m* reporté; *(on balance sheet)* report *m*; **balance due** solde *m* débiteur *ou* dû; **I'd like to pay the balance of my account** j'aimerais solder mon compte
(**f**) *(on hi-fi, amplifier)* balance *f*
2 *vt* (**a**) *(put in stable position)* mettre en équilibre; *(hold in stable position)* tenir en équilibre; **she balanced the book on her head** elle a mis *ou* posé le livre en équilibre sur sa tête; **women balancing pots on their heads** des femmes portant des pots sur la tête; *Aut* **to balance the wheels** équilibrer les roues
(**b**) *(act as counterbalance, offset)* faire contrepoids à, contrebalancer; **we have to balance the right to privacy against the public's right to know** nous devons trouver le juste milieu entre le respect de la vie privée et le droit du public à être informé
(**c**) *(weigh)* peser; *Fig* mettre en balance, comparer; **you have to balance its usefulness against the actual cost** vous devez mettre en balance *ou* comparer son utilité et le coût réel; **to balance the advantages against the disadvantages** peser le pour et le contre
(**d**) *Math & Fin (equation, finances)* équilibrer,

balancer; **to balance the budget** équilibrer le budget; **to balance an adverse budget** rétablir un budget déficitaire; **to balance the books** dresser *ou* établir le bilan, arrêter les comptes; **to balance one's chequebook** faire ses comptes

(**e**) *Fin (settle, pay)* régler, solder; *(debt)* compenser; **to balance an account** solder un compte

3 *vi* (**a**) *(remain in stable position)* se maintenir en équilibre; *(be in stable position)* être en équilibre; **to balance on one foot** se tenir en équilibre sur un pied; **she was balanced precariously on the top of a ladder** elle était en équilibre instable en haut de l'échelle

(**b**) *(act as counterbalance)* **the weights balance** les poids s'équilibrent

(**c**) *Acct & Fin (budget, finances)* s'équilibrer, balancer; **I can't get the accounts to balance** je n'arrive pas à équilibrer les comptes

4 on balance *adv* à tout prendre, tout bien considéré

►► ***balance beam*** *(in gymnastics)* poutre *f*; *Fin* ***balance book*** livre *m* d'inventaire; *Constr* ***balance bridge*** pont *m* basculant; *Econ* ***balance of payments*** balance *f* des paiements; *Econ* ***balance of payments deficit*** déficit *m* de la balance des paiements, déficit *m* extérieur; *Pol* ***balance of power*** *(in government)* balance *f* *ou* équilibre *m* des pouvoirs; *(between states)* balance *f* *ou* équilibre *m* des forces; *Pol* **he holds the balance of power** il peut faire pencher la balance, tout dépend de lui; *Acct* ***balance sheet*** bilan *m*; **off the balance sheet** hors de bilan; *Acct* ***balance sheet auditing*** contrôle *m* du bilan; *Acct* ***balance sheet consolidation*** consolidation *f* de bilan; *Acct* ***balance sheet item*** poste *m* de bilan; ***balance sheet value*** valeur *f* bilantielle *ou* d'inventaire; *Econ* ***balance of trade*** balance *f* commerciale; *Tech* ***balance weight*** contrepoids *m*; *Tech* ***balance wheel*** balancier *m*

►**balance out** *vi* **the advantages and disadvantages balance out** les avantages contrebalancent *ou* compensent les inconvénients; **they balance each other out** *(because of their respective skills)* ils se complètent bien; *Fin* **the debits and credits should balance out** les débits et les crédits devraient s'équilibrer

---

balanced ['bælənst] *adj* (**a**) *(diet, scales, person)* équilibré; **to be well balanced** *(person)* être équilibré; **a (well-)balanced diet** un régime (alimentaire) équilibré (**b**) *(in strength, value)* égal; *Fin (budget)* équilibré; **the two teams were pretty well balanced** les deux équipes étaient de force à peu près égale (**c**) *(programme, report)* impartial, objectif; **a balanced view** une vue impartiale *ou* objective

balancer shaft ['bælənsə-] *n Aut* arbre *m* d'équilibrage

balancing ['bælənsɪŋ] *n* (**a**) *(physical effort)* stabilisation *f* (**b**) *Acct* **balancing of accounts** solde *m* *ou* alignement *m* *ou* arrêté *m* des comptes (**c**) *(of two things)* ajustement *m*; *(of something by something)* compensation *f*

►► ***balancing act*** numéro *m* d'équilibriste; *Fig* **it was a real balancing act keeping everyone happy** ce n'a pas été une mince affaire de contenter tout le monde

balconied ['bælkənɪd] *adj (house)* à balcon(s)

balcony ['bælkənɪ] (*pl* **balconies**) *n* (**a**) *(of apartment, house)* balcon *m* (**b**) *Theat* deuxième balcon *m*

bald [bɔːld] *adj* (**a**) *(having no hair)* chauve; **he's going bald** il devient chauve, il se dégarnit; **his bald head** son crâne chauve; **a bald patch** *(on person)* une tonsure; *(on animal)* un endroit sans poils; **he's got a bald patch** *or* **spot** il a le sommet du crâne chauve, il a une tonsure; *Fam* **as bald as a coot** chauve comme un œuf *ou* comme une boule de billard

(**b**) *(carpet)* usé, pelé; *(mountain top)* pelé; *(tyre)* lisse

(**c**) *(unadorned → facts)* brutal; **the bald truth** la pure vérité, la vérité toute nue; **a bald statement of the facts** une simple exposition des faits

►► *Orn* ***bald eagle*** pygargue *m* à tête blanche

> **BALD EAGLE**
>
> Cet oiseau est le symbole des États-Unis et figure sur le sceau officiel.

baldachin, baldaquin ['bɔːldəkɪn] *n Archit & Tex* baldaquin *m*

balderdash ['bɔːldədæʃ] *Old-fashioned* **1** *exclam* balivernes!, fadaises!

2 *n (UNCOUNT)* fadaises *fpl*; **the book is utter balderdash** le livre est un ramassis de fadaises

bald-faced *adj Am (liar, thief)* effronté; *(lie)* flagrant

bald-headed *adj* chauve; **a bald-headed man** un chauve

balding ['bɔːldɪŋ] *adj* à la calvitie naissante; **his balding head** son début de calvitie

baldly ['bɔːldlɪ] *adv* brutalement; **to put it baldly** pour parler franchement

baldness ['bɔːldnɪs] *n* (**a**) *(of person)* calvitie *f*; *(of animal)* absence *f* de poils; **premature baldness** calvitie *f* précoce (**b**) *(of mountain top)* nudité *f*; *(of carpet, tyre)* usure *f* (**c**) *(of facts)* brutalité *f*

baldric ['bɔːldrɪk] *n Arch* baudrier *m*

bale [beɪl] **1** *n* (**a**) *(of cloth, hay)* balle *f* (**b**) *Arch (evil)* mal *m*

2 *vt* (**a**) *(hay)* mettre en balles; *(cotton, merchandise)* emballer, empaqueter (**b**) *Br (water)* vider

►**bale out 1** *vt sep Naut (boat)* écoper; *(cellar, water)* vider

2 *vi Aviat (parachute)* sauter en parachute *(d'un avion en perdition)*

Balearic [ˌbælɪ'ærɪk] **1** *adj* **the Balearic Islands** les Baléares *fpl*; **in the Balearic Islands** aux Baléares

2 Balearics *npl* **the Balearics** les Baléares *fpl*; **in the Balearics** aux Baléares

baleen ['beɪliːn] *n Zool (of whale)* fanon *m* de baleine

baleful ['beɪlfʊl] *adj* (**a**) *(glance, presence)* menaçant; *(influence)* néfaste; **he looked at us with a baleful eye** il nous a regardés d'un sale œil, il nous a jeté un regard mauvais (**b**) *(gloomy)* lugubre

balefully ['beɪlfʊlɪ] *adv* (**a**) *(menacingly → look)* d'un sale œil; *(→ say)* d'un ton menaçant (**b**) *(gloomily)* d'une façon lugubre

balefulness ['beɪlfʊlnɪs] *n* caractère *m* menaçant

baler ['beɪlə(r)] *n Agr* ramasseuse-presse *f*

►► ***baler twine*** ficelle *f* agricole

Bali ['bɑːlɪ] *n* Bali; **in Bali** à Bali

Balinese [ˌbɑːlɪ'niːz] (*pl* **inv**) **1** *n* (**a**) *(person)* Balinais(e) *m,f* (**b**) *(language)* balinais *m*

2 *adj* balinais, de Bali

baling ['beɪlɪŋ] *n (of hay)* mise *f* en balles; *(of cotton, merchandise)* mise *f* en balles, empaquetage *m*

►► *Agr* ***baling machine*** botteleuse *f*

balk [bɔːk] **1** *n* (**a**) *Constr (beam)* bille *f*; *(of roof)* solive *f*

(**b**) *Agr* billon *m*

(**c**) *(hindrance)* obstacle *m*

(**d**) *Sport (in baseball)* feinte *f* irrégulière d'un lanceur

(**e**) *(in snooker)* = espace entre la bande et la ligne

2 *vt* (**a**) *(thwart)* contrecarrer, contrarier (**b**) *(avoid)* éviter

3 *vi* **the horse balked at the fence** le cheval a refusé la barrière; **she balked at the idea of executing him** elle a reculé à l'idée de le faire exécuter; **he balked at the expense** il a rechigné à la dépense

►► ***balk line*** *(in snooker)* ligne *f* de départ; *(in croquet)* position *f* de départ

Balkan ['bɔːlkən] *adj* balkanique

►► ***the Balkan Peninsula*** la péninsule balkanique, les Balkans *mpl*; ***Balkan States*** États *mpl* balkaniques, Balkans *mpl*

balkanization [ˌbɔːlkənaɪ'zeɪʃən] *n* balkanisation *f*

balkanize, -ise ['bɔːlkənaɪz] *vt* balkaniser

Balkans ['bɔːlkənz] *npl* Balkans *mpl*; **in the Balkans** dans les Balkans

ball [bɔːl] **1** *n* (**a**) *(sphere)* boule *f*; *(of wool)* pelote *f*; **he rolled up the jersey into a ball** il a roulé le pullover en boule; **the hedgehog was curled up in a ball** le hérisson était roulé en boule; **roll the wool into a ball** mets la laine en pelote; **ball of fire** boule *f* de feu; *Fig* **to be a ball of fire** déborder d'énergie

(**b**) *Sport (small)* balle *f*; *(large → for playing football, rugby, basketball)* ballon *m*; *(in snooker)* bille *f*, boule *f*; *(in croquet)* boule *f*; *(in golf, tennis)* balle *f*; **to kick the ball about** *(play football)* s'amuser avec le ballon; **to knock the ball about** *(in tennis)* faire des balles; **the children were playing ball** les enfants jouaient au ballon

(**c**) *Sport (shot → in golf, tennis)* coup *m*; *Ftbl* passe *f*; *(→ in hockey)* tir *m*; *(→ in cricket)* lancer *m*; **that was a difficult ball** c'était un tir difficile; *Ftbl* **a long ball** une passe longue, une balle en profondeur; **it was a good ball** c'était bien joué

(**d**) *(of foot)* avant-pied *m*; *(of thumb)* partie *f* charnue; **to be standing on the balls of one's feet** se tenir sur la pointe des pieds; **the ball of the thumb** la partie charnue du pouce

(**e**) *(dance)* bal *m*; **to have** *or* **to hold** *or* **to organize a ball** donner un bal; *Fam Fig* **to have a ball** se marrer comme un fou/des fous; *Fam Fig* **I'm having a ball** je me marre comme un fou, je m'éclate

(**f**) *(idioms)* **the ball is in his court now** c'est à lui de jouer maintenant, la balle est dans son camp; **to be on the ball** *(knowledgeable)* connaître son affaire; *(alert)* être sur le qui-vive; **he's well over eighty but he's still on the ball** il a plus de quatre-vingts ans mais il a toute sa tête; *Br* **to have the ball at one's feet** avoir la partie belle; **to keep the ball rolling** *(maintain interest)* maintenir l'intérêt; *(maintain activity)* assurer la continuité; *(maintain conversation)* soutenir la conversation; **to start** *or* **to set the ball rolling** *(in conversation)* lancer la conversation; *Com (in deal)* faire démarrer l'affaire; *Sport* **to play ball** jouer au ballon; *Am (baseball)* jouer au base-ball; *Fig* coopérer, jouer le jeu; *Am Fig* **that's the way the ball bounces!** c'est la vie!

2 *vi* (**a**) *(wool)* boulocher

(**b**) *Am Vulg (have sex)* baiser

3 *vt* (**a**) *(wool)* mettre en pelote; *(fists)* serrer; *Am* **to ball sth up** rouler qch en boule

(**b**) *Am Vulg (have sex with)* baiser

4 balls *Vulg* **1** *npl* (**a**) *(testicles)* couilles *fpl*; *Fig* **they've got you by the balls** t'es bien baisé; **balls to him!** qu'il aille se faire foutre! (**b**) *(courage)* **to have balls** avoir des couilles, en avoir; **that type of thing takes balls** il faut avoir des couilles pour faire ce genre de truc; **he lost his balls** il s'est dégonflé (**c**) *(rubbish)* conneries *fpl*; **what a load of balls!** c'est des conneries, tout ça! **2** *exclam* quelles conneries!

►► *Tech* ***ball bearing*** bille *f* de roulement; ***ball bearings*** roulement *m* à billes; *Sport* ***ball boy*** ramasseur *m* de balles; ***ball game*** *(with small ball)* jeu *m* de balle; *(with large ball)* jeu *m* de ballon; *(baseball)* match *m* de base-ball; *Fam Fig* **it's a whole new ball game, it's a different ball game altogether** c'est une toute autre histoire; **we're talking about a different ball game** ça n'a rien à voir avec notre sujet[❑]; *Sport* ***ball girl*** ramasseuse *f* de balles; ***ball gown*** robe *f* de bal; *Anat* ***ball joint*** joint *m* à rotule; *Met* ***ball lightning*** éclair *m* en boule; ***ball park*** *(stadium)* [illegible] **the right ball park** il avait plutôt bien deviné[❑]; *Fam Fig* **are we in the same ball park?** est-ce qu'on est sur la même longueur d'ondes?; *Tech* ***ball peen hammer*** marteau *m* à panne ronde *ou* sphérique; *Tech* ***ball valve*** robinet *m* à tournant sphérique

►**balls up,** *Am* **ball up** *vt sep very Fam* foutre la merde dans; **he completely ballsed up the job** il a complètement salopé le boulot; **we're really ballsed up now** on est dans la merde jusqu'au cou

ballad ['bæləd] *n Mus (song → narrative)* ballade *f*; *(→ popular, sentimental)* romance *f*; *(musical piece)* ballade *f*

'The Ballad of the Sad Café' *McCullers* 'La Ballade du café triste'

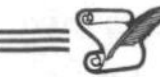

'The Ballad of Reading Gaol' *Wilde* 'La Ballade de la geôle de Reading'

ballade [bæ'lɑːd] *n Literature* ballade *f*

ball-and-socket joint *n* (**a**) *Anat* énarthrose *f* (**b**) *Tech* joint *m* à rotule, joint *m* de Cardan

Ballan wrasse ['bælən-] *n Ich* vieille *f* commune

ballast ['bæləst] **1** *n (UNCOUNT)* (**a**) *Aviat & Naut (in balloon, ship)* lest *m*; **to drop ballast** jeter du lest (**b**) *Constr (in road)* pierraille *f*; *Rail* ballast *m*

2 *vt* (**a**) *Aviat & Naut (balloon, ship)* lester (**b**) *Constr (road)* empierrer, caillouter; *Rail (railway)* ballaster

►► *Naut* ***ballast tank*** *(of submarine)* ballast *m*

ball-breaker, *Am* **ball-buster** *n very Fam* (**a**) *(problem, situation, task)* casse-tête *m* (**b**) *Pej (woman)* chieuse *f*

ballcock ['bɔːlkɒk] *n Tech* robinet *m* à flotteur

ballerina [ˌbælə'riːnə] *n* ballerine *f (danseuse)*

ballet ['bæleɪ] *n* ballet *m*; **I'm going to the ballet this evening** je vais voir un ballet *ou* un spectacle de danse classique ce soir

►► ***ballet dancer*** danseur(euse) *m,f* de ballet; ***ballet dancing*** danse *f* classique; ***ballet dress*** robe *f* de ballet; *(skirt)* tutu *m*; ***ballet lesson*** cours *m* de danse classique; ***the ballet season*** la saison *f* chorégraphique; ***ballet shoe*** chausson *m* de danse

ballistic [bə'lɪstɪk] *adj Phys* balistique; *Fam Fig* **to go ballistic** *(get angry)* piquer une crise

►► *Mil* ***ballistic missile*** missile *m* balistique

ballistics [bə'lɪstɪks] *n (UNCOUNT) Phys* balistique *f*

ballocks = **bollocks**

balloon [bə'luːn] **1** *n* (**a**) *(toy)* ballon *m*

(**b**) *(for carrying people or weather instruments)* ballon *m*, aérostat *m*; **(hot air) balloon** montgolfière *f*; **to go up in a balloon** monter en ballon; *Fam Fig* **when the balloon goes up** quand ça démarre; *Fam Fig* **the balloon went up** l'affaire a éclaté

(**c**) *(in comic strip)* bulle *f*

(**d**) *Chem (flask)* ballon *m*

(**e**) *(brandy glass)* (verre *m*) ballon *m*

(**f**) *Br Sport (shot → in tennis)* lob *m*; *(→ in football)* chandelle *f*

2 *vi* (**a**) *(billow → sail, trousers)* **to balloon (out)** gonfler

(**b**) *Fig (grow dramatically)* augmenter démesurément; **unemployment has ballooned in recent months** le chômage a considérablement augmenté ces derniers mois

3 *vt Br Sport (ball)* projeter très haut en l'air

►► ***balloon glass*** verre *m* ballon; ***balloon payment*** dernier remboursement *m (dont le montant est supérieur aux versements précédents)*; *Naut* ***balloon sail*** foc *m* d'avant; ***balloon sleeve*** manche *f* ballon; *Aut* ***balloon tyre*** pneu *m* ballon

ballooning [bə'luːnɪŋ] *n* **to go ballooning** *(regularly)* pratiquer la montgolfière; *(on one occasion)* faire un tour en montgolfière *ou* en ballon

balloonist [bə'luːnɪst] *n* aéronaute *mf*

ballot ['bælət] *(pt & pp* **ballotted,** *cont* **ballotting)** **1** *n* (**a**) *(secret vote)* scrutin *m*; **to vote by ballot** voter à bulletin secret; **in the second ballot** au deuxième tour de scrutin; **to take a ballot** procéder à un scrutin *ou* à un vote

(**b**) *(voting paper)* bulletin *m* de vote; **to cast one's ballot for sb** voter pour qn

(**c**) *St Exch (when shares are oversubscribed)* allocation *f* d'actions par tirage au sort

2 *vt* sonder au moyen d'un vote; **union members will be ballotted on Tuesday** les membres du syndicat décideront par voie de scrutin mardi

3 *vi* (**a**) *(vote)* voter par (voie de) scrutin; **to ballot for/against sb** voter pour/contre qn

(**b**) *Arch (draw lots)* tirer au sort; **to ballot for a place** tirer une place au sort

►► ***ballot box*** *(for ballot papers)* urne *f*; *Fig* système *m* électoral *ou* démocratique; **change cannot be achieved by the ballot box alone** le système électoral à lui seul ne suffit pas à faire bouger les choses; *Am* ***ballot box stuffing*** fraude *f* électorale; ***ballot paper*** bulletin *m* de vote; ***ballot rigging*** fraude *f* électorale

balloting ['bælətɪŋ] *n* (**a**) *(voting)* scrutin *m* (**b**) *Arch (drawing of lots)* tirage *m* au sort

ball-park figure *n Fam* **a ball-park figure** un chiffre approximatif[❑]

ballplayer ['bɔːlˌpleɪə(r)] *n Am Sport (basketball)* joueur(euse) *m,f* de basket; *(football)* joueur(euse) *m,f* de football américain; *(baseball)* joueur(euse) *m,f* de baseball

ballpoint ['bɔːlpɔɪnt] **1** *adj* à bille

2 *n* stylo *m* (à) bille, Bic® *m*

►► ***ballpoint pen*** stylo *m* (à) bille, Bic® *m*

ballroom ['bɔːlrʊm] *n* salle *f* de bal

►► ***ballroom dancing*** danse *f* de salon

ballsiness ['bɔːlzɪnɪs] *n Am very Fam* culot *m*

balls-up, *Am* **ball-up** *n very Fam* bordel *m*; **to make a balls-up of sth** merder qch, *Can* faire de la merde de qch; **the trip was a complete balls-up** l'excursion a complètement foiré

ballsy ['bɔːlzɪ] *adj Am very Fam* culotté, couillu

ball-up ['bɔːlʌp] *Am* = **balls-up**

bally ['bælɪ] *adj Br Fam Old-fashioned* sacré; **you bally fool!** espèce de crétin!

ballyhoo [ˌbælɪ'huː] *Fam* **1** *n (commotion)* tapage *m*; *(publicity)* battage *m*, **what's all the ballyhoo about?** pourquoi tout ce remue-ménage?

2 *vt esp Am Mktg (book, show)* faire du battage (publicitaire) pour promouvoir[❑]

balm [bɑːm] *n* (**a**) *Pharm & Fig* baume *m* (**b**) *Bot* mélisse *f* officinale

balminess ['bɑːmɪnɪs] *n (mildness)* **the balminess of the evening air** l'air embaumé du soir

Balmoral [bæl'mɒrəl] *n* = château situé dans le nord-est de l'Écosse et appartenant à la famille royale britannique

balmy ['bɑːmɪ] *adj* (**a**) *(weather)* doux (douce) (**b**) *(scented)* embaumé, parfumé; *Bot* balsamique; **the air was balmy with the scent of roses** l'air était embaumé du parfum des roses

balneology [ˌbælnɪ'ɒlədʒɪ] *n Med* science *f* de la balnéothérapie

balneotherapy [ˌbælnɪəʊ'θerəpɪ] *n Med* balnéothérapie *f*

baloney [bə'ləʊnɪ] *n* (**a**) *(UNCOUNT) Fam (nonsense)* idioties *fpl*, balivernes *fpl*; **baloney, you don't know what you're talking about!** n'importe quoi, tu ne sais pas de quoi tu parles! (**b**) *Culin* = saucisse à base de bœuf, veau et porc, mangée froide

BALPA ['bælpə] *n Aviat (abbr* **British Airline Pilots' Association**) = syndicat britannique des pilotes de ligne

balsa ['bɔːlsə] *n* balsa *m*

balsam ['bɔːlsəm] *n* (**a**) *Pharm (balm)* baume *m* (**b**) *Bot (plant)* balsamine *f* (**c**) *Chem (turpentine)* oléorésine *f*

►► *Bot* ***balsam fir*** sapin *m* baumier; *Bot* ***balsam poplar*** peuplier *m* baumier; *Bot* ***balsam spruce*** épicéa *m* du Colorado, sapin *m* bleu

balsamic vinegar [ˌbɔːl'sæmɪk-] *n Culin* vinaigre *m* balsamique

balsawood ['bɔːlsəwʊd] *n* balsa *m*

Balt [bɔːlt] *n (person)* Balte *mf*

Balthazar [bæl'θæzə(r), 'bælθəˌzɑː(r)] **1** *pr n Bible* Balthazar

2 *n (bottle)* balthazar *m*

balti ['bɔːltɪ] *n Culin* (**a**) *(container)* = récipient métallique utilisé dans la cuisine indienne (**b**) *(food)* = plat épicé prépare dans un "balti"

Baltic ['bɔːltɪk] **1** *n* **the Baltic** la Baltique

2 *adj (port, coast)* de la Baltique

►► ***the Baltic Exchange*** = bourse du commerce à Londres; ***the Baltic Republics*** les républiques *fpl* baltes; ***the Baltic Sea*** la mer Baltique; ***the Baltic States*** les pays *mpl* baltes

baltic ['bɔːltɪk] *adj Br Fam (weather)* **it's baltic** il fait un froid de canard

Baluchi [bə'luːtʃɪ] *(pl* **inv** *or* **Baluchis**) *n* (**a**) *(person)* Baloutchi *mf* (**b**) *(language)* baloutchi *m*

Baluchistan [ˌbəluːtʃɪ'stɑːn] *n* Baloutchistan *m*, Béloutchistan *m*; **in Baluchistan** au Baloutchistan

baluster ['bæləstə(r)] **1** *n* balustre *m*; **the balusters** la rampe *(d'un escalier)*

2 *adj (post, stem of glass)* en forme de balustre

balustrade [ˌbæləs'treɪd] *n* balustrade *f*

balustraded [ˌbæləs'treɪdɪd] *adj* à balustrade

Bamako [ˌbæmə'kəʊ] *n* Bamako

bamboo [bæm'buː] **1** *n* bambou *m*

2 *comp (screen, table)* de *ou* en bambou; *(forest)* de bambou

►► ***Bamboo Curtain*** rideau *m* de bambou; ***bamboo shoots*** pousses *fpl* de bambou

bamboozle [bæm'buːzəl] *vt Fam* (**a**) *(cheat)* avoir, embobiner; **they were bamboozled into signing the contract** on les a embobinés pour qu'ils signent le contrat (**b**) *(confuse)* déboussoler; **the game had him completely bamboozled** le jeu l'avait complètement déboussolé

ban [bæn] *(pt & pp* **banned,** *cont* **banning**) **1** *n* (**a**) *(prohibition)* interdiction *f*, interdit *m*; **to put** *or* **impose a ban on sth** interdire qch; **to lift the ban on sth** lever l'interdiction qui porte sur qch; **they've put a ban on smoking in the office** ils ont interdit de fumer dans le bureau; **the nuclear test ban** l'interdiction des essais nucléaires

(**b**) *Com (embargo)* embargo *m*; *(sanction)* sanctions *fpl* économiques

2 *vt* interdire; **he was banned from going into town** on lui a interdit d'aller en ville; **they are banned from the club** on leur a interdit l'accès à la boîte de nuit; **he was banned from driving for a year** il a eu une suspension de permis de conduire d'un an; **the Ban the Bomb movement** le mouvement contre la bombe atomique; **ban the bomb!** non à la bombe atomique!

banal [bə'nɑːl] *adj* banal

banality [bə'nælətɪ] *n* banalité *f*

banana [bə'nɑːnə] **1** *n (fruit)* banane *f*; *(tree)* bananier *m*; **a bunch of bananas** un régime de bananes

2 *comp (milk shake, ice-cream)* à la banane

3 bananas *adj Fam* maboul, dingue; **she's completely bananas!** elle est complètement maboule!; **to go bananas** *(crazy)* devenir dingue; *(angry)* piquer une crise

►► *Can Fam* ***banana belt*** région *f* chaude[❑]; ***banana boat*** bananier *m (bateau)*; *Chem* ***banana oil*** nitrate *m* de cellulose; ***banana plantation*** bananeraie *f*; *Fam* ***banana republic*** république *f* bananière; ***banana skin*** peau *f* de banane; *Fig* **he slipped on a banana skin** il a fait une gaffe; *Culin* ***banana split*** banana split *m*; ***banana tree*** bananier *m*

Banbury cake ['bænbərɪ-] *n Br Culin* = pâtisserie aux raisins secs

bancassurance ['bæŋkəʃʊərəns] *n Banking* bancassurance *f*

banco ['bæŋkəʊ] *exclam* banco!

band [bænd] **1** *n* (**a**) *Mus (musicians → folk, rock, jazz)* groupe *m*; *(→ brass, military)* fanfare *f*; **to be** *or* **play in a band** faire partie d'un groupe; **drinks were free to members of the band** les boissons étaient gratuites pour les musiciens

(**b**) *(group)* bande *f*, troupe *f*; **a band of dedicated reformers** une bande de réformateurs convaincus

(**c**) *(strip → of cloth, metal)* bande *f*; *(→ on hat)* ruban *m*; *(→ of leather)* lanière *f*

(**d**) *(stripe → of colour)* bande *f*; *(→ of sunlight)* rai *m*; *(→ small)* bandelette *f*

(**e**) *(as binding → around wheel)* bandage *m*; *(→ around books)* sangle *f*; *(→ on cigar)* bague *f*; *(→ on barrel)* cercle *m*

(**f**) *Tech (drive belt)* courroie *f* de transmission

(**g**) *Rad (range of frequency)* bande *f*; *Opt (in spectrum)* bande *f*; *Comput* bande *f* magnétique

(**h**) *Br (range → in age, price)* tranche *f*; **people in this age band** les gens dans *ou* de cette tranche d'âge

(**i**) *(ring)* anneau *m*; **wedding band** alliance *f*

2 *vt (usu passive) (stripe)* **a red wall banded with yellow** un mur rouge rayé de jaune

►► ***Band Aid*** *(charity)* = association caritative fondée en 1984 pour lutter contre la faim en Éthiopie qui réunit notamment des vedettes du monde de la musique pop; *Tech* ***band saw*** scie *f* à ruban; *Phys* ***band spectrum*** spectre *m* de bandes

►**band together** *vi (unite)* se grouper, se liguer; *(gang together)* former une bande

bandage ['bændɪdʒ] **1** *n* (**a**) *(strip of cloth)* bande *f*, bandage *m*; **he wrapped the bandage around her hand** il a enroulé le bandage autour de sa main

(**b**) *Med (prepared dressing)* pansement *m*

2 *vt Med (head, limb)* bander; *(wound)* mettre

un bandage sur; *(with prepared dressing)* panser

▸**bandage up** *vt sep Med (head, limb)* bander; *(wound)* mettre un bandage sur; *(with prepared dressing)* panser

bandaging ['bændɪdʒɪŋ] *n* (**a**) *(strips of cloth)* bandes *fpl*, bandages *mpl* (**b**) *Med (prepared dressings)* pansements *mpl* (**c**) *Med (action)* bandage *m*

Band-Aid® ['bændeɪd] *n Am Med* sparadrap *m*; *Fig* **a Band-Aid**® **solution/measure** une solution/une mesure provisoire *ou* en attendant

bandana, bandanna [bæn'dænə] *n* bandana *m*

b and b, B & B [ˌbiːən'biː] *n (abbr* **bed and breakfast**) chambre *f* et petit déjeuner, chambre *f* d'hôte

bandbox ['bændbɒks] *n (gen)* boîte *f* cylindrique; *(for hats)* carton *m* à chapeaux

bandeau ['bændəʊ] *(pl* **bandeaux** [-dəʊz]) *n* bandeau *m (pour retenir les cheveux)*

banded ['bændɪd] *adj (striped)* rayé

▸▸ *Com* ***banded pack*** lot *m*; ***banded pack selling*** vente *f* par lot

banderol, banderole ['bændərəʊl] *n Naut (on ship)* banderole *f*; *Archit & Her* banderole *f*; *(at funeral)* drapeau *m*

bandicoot ['bændɪˌkuːt] *n Zool* péramèle *m*

▸▸ ***bandicoot rat*** bandicoot *m*

banding ['bændɪŋ] *n Br Sch* = répartition en groupes de niveau dans le primaire

bandit ['bændɪt] *n also Fig* bandit *m*

banditry ['bændɪtrɪ] *n* banditisme *m*

bandleader ['bændˌliːdə(r)] *n Mus* chef *m* d'orchestre; *Mil* chef *m* de fanfare; *(of pop group)* leader *m*

bandmaster ['bændˌmɑːstə(r)] *n Mus* chef *m* d'orchestre

bandoleer, bandolier [ˌbændə'lɪə(r)] *n Mil* cartouchière *f*

bandsman ['bændzmən] *(pl* **bandsmen** [-mən]) *n Mus* membre *m* d'un orchestre; *Mil* membre *m* d'une fanfare

bandstand ['bændstænd] *n Mus* kiosque *m* à musique

bandwagon ['bændwægən] *n* **to jump** *or* **to climb on the bandwagon** prendre le train en marche, *Pej* suivre le mouvement

bandwidth ['bændwɪdθ] *n* (**a**) *Comput & Rad* largeur *f* de bande (**b**) *(in acoustics)* bande *f* passante

bandy ['bændɪ] *(pt & pp* **bandied,** *comp* **bandier,** *superl* **bandiest**) **1** *vt* (**a**) *(blows)* échanger (**b**) *(ideas, witticisms, insults)* échanger; **don't bandy words with me** ne discute pas

2 *adj (person)* aux jambes arquées; *(leg → of animal, person)* arqué

▸**bandy about, bandy around** *vt insep (expression, story)* faire circuler; **his name is often bandied about** on parle souvent de lui; **this is just one of the explanations being bandied around** c'est une des nombreuses explications qui circulent

bandy-legged *adj* **to be bandy-legged** avoir les jambes arquées

bane [beɪn] *n* (**a**) *(scourge, trial)* fléau *m*; **it's/he's the bane of my life** ça/il m'empoisonne la vie; **the tax has become the bane of local government** l'impôt est devenu la bête noire des collectivités locales (**b**) *Literary (poison)* poison *m*

baneberry ['beɪnˌbərɪ] *n Bot* actée *f*

baneful ['beɪnfʊl] *adj Literary* funeste; *(influence)* néfaste

banefully ['beɪnfʊlɪ] *adv Literary* funestement

bang [bæŋ] **1** *n* (**a**) *(loud noise → explosion)* détonation *f*; *(→ clatter)* fracas *m*; *(→ slam)* claquement *m*; *(→ supersonic)* bang *m*; **the door shut with a bang** la porte s'est refermée en claquant; **to shut the door with a bang** claquer la porte; **there was a big bang** il y a eu une forte détonation *ou* une explosion *Fam* **to go** *Br* **over** *or Am* **out with a bang, to go with a bang** avoir un succès fou; *Fam* **the show went (off) with a bang** le spectacle a eu un succès fou; *Am Fam* **I got a bang out of it** ça m'a fait marrer

(**b**) *(bump)* coup *m* violent; **he got a nasty bang on the head** il s'est cogné la tête assez violemment

2 *adv* (**a**) **to go bang** *(explode)* éclater; *Fam* **bang go my chances of winning!** envolées, mes chances de gagner!; *Fam* **bang goes another £10!** et pan, encore 10 livres de parties!

(**b**) *Br (exactly)* **bang in the middle** au beau milieu, en plein milieu; **the missile was bang on target** le missile a atteint sa cible en plein dans le mille; **bang on time** pile à l'heure; **I walked bang into him** je suis tombé en plein sur lui; **my desk is bang against the wall** mon bureau est contre le mur; **his flat is bang in the middle of town** son appartement est en plein centre-ville

3 *exclam (of gun)* pan!; *(of blow, slam)* vlan!; *(of explosion)* boum!

4 *vt* (**a**) *(hit → table, window)* frapper violemment; **he banged his fist on the table** il a frappé la table du poing; **I banged my head on the ceiling** je me suis cogné la tête contre le *ou* au plafond; *Fig* **we're banging our heads against a brick wall** nous perdons notre temps, nous nous dépensons en pure perte

(**b**) *(slam → door, window)* claquer; **she banged the door shut** elle a claqué la porte

(**c**) *Vulg (have sex with)* baiser

(**d**) *St Exch* **to bang the market** faire baisser les prix, écraser le marché

5 *vi* (**a**) *(slam)* claquer; **the door banged shut** la porte s'est refermée en claquant; **to bang at** *or* **on the door** frapper à la porte à grands coups; **to bang on the table with one's fist** taper du poing sur la table

(**b**) *(detonate → gun)* détoner

(**c**) *Vulg (have sex)* baiser

6 bangs *npl Am* frange *f*; **to have bangs** porter une frange

▸**bang about, bang around** *Fam* **1** *vt sep (books, crockery)* cogner les uns contre les autres ⌐; *(person)* tabasser, cogner ⌐

2 *vi* faire du bruit ⌐, faire du pétard

▸**bang away** *vi* (**a**) *(detonate → guns)* tonner (**b**) *(keep firing → soldier)* tirer sans arrêt; *(keep hammering → workmen)* faire du vacarme; *Fig (keep working)* continuer à travailler; **he was banging away on his typewriter** il tapait sans arrêt sur sa machine à écrire

▸**bang down** *vt sep (books)* jeter violemment; *(dish)* poser brutalement; **he banged the receiver down** il a raccroché brutalement; **she banged down the lid** elle a violemment rabattu le couvercle

▸**bang into** *vt insep (collide with)* se cogner contre, heurter

▸**bang on** *vi Br Fam (talk at length)* rabâcher; **he's always banging on about it** il n'arrête pas de bassiner tout le monde avec ça; **he's always banging on about his personal problems** il n'arrête pas de bassiner tout le monde avec ses problèmes personnels

▸**bang out** *vt sep Fam (tune)* jouer fort et mal ⌐

▸**bang together** *vt sep* cogner l'un contre l'autre; **I could have banged their heads together!** j'aurais pu prendre l'un pour taper sur l'autre!

▸**bang up** *vt sep Br Fam (prisoner)* boucler; **to get banged up** être mis en taule *ou* à l'ombre

banger ['bæŋə(r)] *n Br Fam* (**a**) *(sausage)* saucisse ⌐ *f*; **bangers and mash** saucisses-purée *(considéré comme un plat typiquement britannique)* (**b**) *(car)* tacot *m*, vieille guimbarde *f* (**c**) *(firework)* pétard ⌐ *m*

banging ['bæŋɪŋ] *adj Br Fam (club, party)* hyper animé

Bangkok [ˌbæŋ'kɒk] *n* Bangkok *f*

Bangladesh [ˌbæŋglə'deʃ] *n* Bangladesh *m*; **in Bangladesh** au Bangladesh

Bangladeshi [ˌbæŋglə'deʃɪ] **1** *n* Bangladais(e) *m,f*, Bangladeshi *mf*

2 *adj* bangladais, bangladeshi

bangle ['bæŋgəl] *n* bracelet *m*

bang-on *Br Fam* **1** *adv* (**a**) *(exactly)* pile; **to hit sth bang-on** frapper qch en plein dans le mille (**b**) *(punctually)* pile à l'heure; à l'heure pile

2 *adj (guess, answer, calculation)* qui tombe pile

bang-up *adj Am Fam* super, génial

banish ['bænɪʃ] *vt (person)* bannir, exiler; *(thought)* bannir, chasser; **he was banished from Rome** il a été banni de Rome; **banish all worries from your mind** chassez tout souci de votre esprit

banishment ['bænɪʃmənt] *n (of thoughts)* bannissement *m*; *(of person)* exil *m*, bannissement *m*; **after his banishment from the party** après son exclusion du parti

banister ['bænɪstə(r)] *n* rampe *f (d'escalier)*; **to slide down the banisters** glisser le long de la rampe d'escalier

banjax ['bændʒæks] *vt Ir & Scot Fam (break)* bousiller

banjaxed ['bændʒækst] *adj Ir & Scot Fam (broken)* bousillé

banjo ['bændʒəʊ] *(Br pl* **banjoes,** *Am pl* **banjos**) *n* banjo *m*

banjoist ['bændʒəʊɪst] *n* joueur(euse) *m,f* de banjo, banjoiste *mf*

bank [bæŋk] **1** *n* (**a**) *(building, institution)* banque *f*; **I asked the bank for a loan** j'ai demandé un crédit à ma banque; **she has £10,000 in the bank** elle a 10 000 livres à la banque; **what's the address of your bank?** quelle est l'adresse de votre banque?; **the Bank of England/France** la Banque d'Angleterre/de France; **the bank of issue** la banque d'émission

(**b**) *Cards* banque *f (de celui qui tient le jeu)*; *(in casino)* = argent qui appartient à la maison de jeu; **to break the bank** faire sauter la banque; *Fig* **it won't break the bank** ça ne va pas me/nous/*etc* ruiner

(**c**) *(reserve → of blood, data)* banque *f*

(**d**) *(of lake, river)* bord *m*, rive *f*; *(above water)* berge *f*; *(of canal)* bord *m*, berge *f*; **we ran along the bank** nous avons couru le long de la berge; **the river has overflowed its banks** le fleuve est sorti de son lit; **the banks of Lake Como** les rives du lac de Côme; **the Left Bank** *(in Paris)* la rive gauche

(**e**) *(embankment, mound → of earth, snow)* talus *m*; *(→ on railway)* remblai *m*; *(hill)* pente *f*; **he ran up the bank on to the road** il a grimpé la pente en courant jusqu'à la route

(**f**) *(ridge → on racetrack, road)* bord *m* relevé; *(→ by road)* talus *m*; *(→ of sand)* banc *m*; *(→ by sea)* digue *f*

(**g**) *Horseriding* banquette *f* irlandaise

(**h**) *(mass → of flowers, shrubs)* massif *m*; *(→ of cloud)* couche *f*, amoncellement *m*; *(→ of coal)* amoncellement *m*; *(→ of fog)* banc *m*, couche *f*; *(→ of sand)* banc *m*; **banks of flowers** des multitudes de fleurs

(**i**) *Mining (pithead)* carreau *m*; *(face of coal, ore)* front *m* de taille

(**j**) *Aviat* virage *m* incliné *ou* sur l'aile

(**k**) *(row → of levers, switches)* rangée *f*; *Cin (of projectors)* rampe *f*; *(of speakers, transformers etc)* groupe *m*, batterie *f*

2 *vt* (**a**) *(enclose → railway, road)* relever *(dans un virage)*; *(→ river)* endiguer

(**b**) *(heap up → earth, stone)* amonceler; *(→ fire)* couvrir; **to be banked** *(of clouds, snow)* être amoncelé

(**c**) *Aviat* **to bank an aeroplane** faire faire à un avion un virage sur l'aile

(**d**) *Fin (cheque, money)* mettre *ou* déposer à la banque

3 *vi* (**a**) *(have bank account)* **he banks with the National Bank** il a un compte à la National Bank; **where do you bank?, who do you bank with?** à quelle banque êtes-vous *ou* avez-vous votre compte?, quelle est votre banque?

(**b**) [illegible] *Aviat (tip)* s'incliner sur l'aile; *(turn)* virer (sur l'aile)

▸▸ ***bank acceptance*** acceptation *f* de banque; ***bank account*** compte *m* bancaire; **to open/close a bank account** ouvrir/fermer un compte bancaire; ***bank advance*** avance *f* bancaire; ***bank advice*** avis *m* de la banque; ***bank balance*** solde *m* bancaire; ***bank base rate*** taux *m* de base bancaire; ***bank bill*** effet *m (tiré par une banque sur une autre)*; ***bank book*** livret *m* de caisse d'épargne, carnet *m* de banque; ***bank borrowings*** emprunts *mpl* bancaires, concours *m* bancaire; ***bank branch code*** code *m* guichet; ***bank buying rate*** taux *m* de change à l'achat; ***bank card*** carte *f* (d'identité) bancaire; ***bank charges*** frais *mpl* bancaires *ou* de banque; ***bank cheque*** chèque *m* bancaire; ***bank clerk*** employé(e) *m,f* de banque; ***bank commitment*** engagement *m* bancaire; ***bank credit*** avoir *m* en banque, crédit *m* bancaire; ***bank debts*** dettes *fpl* bancaires; ***bank details*** relevé *m* d'identité bancaire, RIB *m*; ***bank discount*** escompte *m* de banque, escompte *m* en dehors; ***bank discount rate*** escompte *m* officiel; ***bank draft*** traite *f* bancaire; *Am* ***bank examiner*** inspecteur(trice) *m,f* de banque; ***bank guarantee*** garantie *f* bancaire, caution *f* de banque; ***bank holiday*** *(in UK)* jour *m* férié; *(in US)* jour *m* de fermeture des banques; ***bank holiday Monday*** lundi férié *(jour de clôture des banques)*; ***bank interest*** intérêt *m* bancaire; ***bank lending*** concours *m* bancaire; ***bank loan*** *(money lent)* prêt *m* bancaire; *(money borrowed)* emprunt *m* bancaire; **to take out a bank loan** obtenir un prêt bancaire; **to pay off a bank loan** rembourser un emprunt bancaire; ***bank manager*** *(head of bank)* directeur(trice) *m,f* de banque; **my** *or* **the bank manager** *(head of bank)* le directeur de l'agence où j'ai mon compte; *(in charge of account)* le responsable de mon compte; *Hum* **I'll have to speak to my bank manager** il faudra que j'en parle à mon banquier; ***bank money*** monnaie *f* de banque, monnaie *f* scripturale; ***bank notification*** avis *m* de la banque; ***bank overdraft*** découvert *m* bancaire; ***bank rate*** taux *m* d'escompte *ou* de l'escompte, taux *m* bancaire; ***bank reconciliation*** rapprochement *m* bancaire; ***bank reserves*** réserves *fpl* bancaires; ***bank robber*** cambrioleur(euse) *m,f* de banque; ***bank selling rate*** taux *m* de change à la vente; *St Exch* ***bank shares*** valeurs *fpl* bancaires; *Banking* ***bank sort code*** code *m* guichet; ***bank statement*** relevé *m* de compte; *Banking* ***bank teller*** guichetier(ère) *m,f*; ***bank transactions*** transactions *fpl* bancaires; ***bank transfer*** virement *m* bancaire; ***bank transfer advice*** avis *m* de virement; *Banking* ***bank treasurer*** trésorier(ère) *m,f* de banque

▸**bank on** *vt insep (count on)* compter sur; **I'm banking on it** je compte là-dessus; **he's banking on us** il compte sur nous

▸**bank up 1** *vt sep* (**a**) *(road)* relever *(dans un virage)*; *(river)* endiguer (**b**) *(fire)* couvrir; *(earth)* amonceler

2 *vi (cloud)* s'amonceler

▸**bank upon** = **bank on**

bankable ['bæŋkəbəl] *adj Fin* bancable, escomptable; *Fig* **to be bankable** être une valeur sûre

▸▸ ***bankable paper*** papier *m* bancable

banker ['bæŋkə(r)] *n* (**a**) *Fin* banquier *m* (**b**) *(in betting)* banquier *m*; **to be banker** *(in game)* tenir la banque

▸▸ ***banker's acceptance*** acceptation *f* bancaire; ***Bankers' Automated Clearing System*** = système électronique de compensation de chèques; ***banker's card*** carte *f* d'identité bancaire; ***banker's cheque*** traite *f* bancaire; ***banker's draft*** traite *f* bancaire; *Br* ***banker's order*** ordre *m* de virement bancaire

banking ['bæŋkɪŋ] *n (UNCOUNT)* (**a**) *Fin (profession)* profession *f* de banquier, la banque; *(activity)* opérations *fpl* bancaires, activité *f* bancaire; **she's in banking** elle travaille dans la banque; **international banking** opérations *fpl* bancaires internationales

(**b**) *(embankment → on river)* berge *f*; *(→ on racetrack)* bords *mpl* relevés

(**c**) *Aviat* virage *m* sur l'aile

▸▸ *Am* ***banking account*** compte *m* en banque, compte *m* bancaire; ***banking business*** trafic *m* bancaire; ***banking controls*** contrôle *m* bancaire; ***banking hours*** heures *fpl* d'ouverture des banques; ***banking house*** maison *f* de banque, établissement *m* bancaire; ***banking mechanism*** mécanisme *m* bancaire; ***banking product*** produit *m* bancaire; ***banking services*** services *mpl* bancaires; ***banking system*** système *m* bancaire

banknote ['bæŋknəʊt] *n* billet *m* de banque

bankroll ['bæŋkrəʊl] *Am Fam* **1** *n* fonds❑ *mpl*, finances❑ *fpl*

2 *vt (deal, project)* financer❑

bankrupt ['bæŋkrʌpt] **1** *n Law* failli(e) *m,f*

2 *adj Law (insolvent)* failli; *Fig (person)* ruiné; **to go bankrupt** faire faillite; **to be bankrupt** être en faillite; **to adjudicate** *or* **declare sb bankrupt** déclarer qn en faillite; **the firm was declared bankrupt** la firme a été déclarée *ou* mise en faillite; *Fig* **he is completely bankrupt of ideas** il est complètement à court d'idées; **morally bankrupt** sans moralité

3 *vt (company, person)* mettre en faillite; *Fig (person)* ruiner; **the deal bankrupted the business** la transaction a mis l'entreprise en faillite

▸▸ ***bankrupt's certificate*** concordat *m*; ***bankrupt's estate*** actif *m* de la faillite

bankruptcy ['bæŋkrʌptsɪ] *n Law* faillite *f*; *Fig (destitution)* ruine *f*; **to present** *or* **file one's petition for bankruptcy** déposer son bilan; **to bring sb to the verge of bankruptcy** amener qn au bord de la ruine; *Fig* **moral bankruptcy** ruine *f* morale

▸▸ *Br Law* ***bankruptcy court*** ≃ tribunal *m* de commerce; ***bankruptcy proceedings*** procédure *f* de faillite

banner ['bænə(r)] **1** *n* (**a**) *(flag)* étendard *m*; *(placard)* bannière *f*; *Fig* **to march/to campaign under sb's banner** se ranger/faire campagne sous la bannière de qn; **she carried the banner of women's rights** elle brandissait l'étendard des droits des femmes

(**b**) *Comput & Mktg (for advertising on Internet)* bandeau *m*, bannière *f* publicitaire

2 *adj Am (year, season)* excellent

▸▸ *Press* ***banner headline*** gros titre *m*, manchette *f*; **in banner headlines** en gros titres

bannister = **banister**

bannock ['bænək] *n Scot* = gâteau sec d'avoine ou d'orge

Bannockburn ['bænək,bɜːn] *n Hist* = village d'Écosse où Robert Bruce remporta une victoire sur les Anglais en 1314, assurant ainsi l'indépendance de l'Écosse

banns [bænz] *npl* bans *mpl*; **to publish the banns (of marriage)** publier les bans (de mariage)

banoffee pie, banoffi pie [bən'ɒfɪ-] *n Culin* = gâteau à la banane et au caramel

banquet ['bæŋkwɪt] **1** *n (formal dinner)* banquet *m*; *(big meal)* festin *m*

2 *vt (dignitary)* offrir un banquet à; *(treat lavishly)* offrir un festin à

3 *vi (dine formally)* faire un banquet; *(dine lavishly)* faire un festin

banqueting ['bæŋkwɪtɪŋ] *n*

▸▸ ***banqueting hall*** salle *f* de banquet; ***banqueting manager*** responsable *mf* des banquets; ***banqueting room*** salle *f* de banquet

banquette [bæŋ'ket] *n* (**a**) *(seat)* banquette *f* (**b**) *Constr (footbridge)* berme *f*

bans = **banns**

banshee ['bænʃiː] *n Myth* = fée de la mythologie irlandaise dont les cris présagent la mort; **the child was wailing like a banshee** l'enfant hurlait comme un putois

bantam ['bæntəm] *n (hen)* poule *f* naine; *(cock)* coq *m* nain

bantamweight ['bæntəmweɪt] **1** *n (boxer)* poids coq *m inv*

2 *adj (boxer)* poids coq *(inv)*

banter ['bæntə(r)] **1** *n (UNCOUNT)* badinage *m*, plaisanterie *f*

2 *vi* badiner; **to banter with sb** badiner avec qn

bantering ['bæntərɪŋ] *adj Br (tone)* de plaisanterie, badin

bantling ['bæntlɪŋ] *n Literary (young child)* poupon *m*, bambin *m*; *Pej* marmot *m*

Bantu [,bæn'tuː] *(pl* **inv** *or* **Bantus) 1** *n* (**a**) *(person)* Bantou(e) *m,f* (**b**) *(language)* bantou *m*

2 *adj* bantou

▸▸ ***Bantu languages*** langues *fpl* bantoues

Bantustan [,bæntuː'stɑːn] *n Formerly* bantoustan *m*

banyan ['bænɪən] *n Bot* banian *m*

baobab ['beɪəʊ,bæb] *n Bot* baobab *m*

BAOR [,biːeɪəʊ'ɑː(r)] *n Mil (abbr* **British Army of the Rhine**) = forces britanniques en Allemagne

bap [bæp] *n Br* = pain rond que l'on utilise pour faire un sandwich

baptism ['bæptɪzəm] *n Rel* baptême *m*; *Fig* **baptism of fire** baptême *m* du feu

baptismal [bæp'tɪzməl] *adj Rel* baptismal, de baptême

▸▸ ***baptismal font*** fonts *mpl* baptismaux; ***baptismal name*** nom *m* de baptême

Baptist ['bæptɪst] *n Rel* baptiste *mf*

▸▸ ***the Baptist Church*** l'église *f* baptiste

baptistery, baptistry ['bæptɪstrɪ] *(pl* **baptistries** *or* **baptisteries**) *n Rel* baptistère *m*; *(font in Baptist church)* fonts *mpl* baptismaux

baptize, -ise ['bæptaɪz, *Br* bæp'taɪz] *vt Rel & Fig* baptiser

BAR [bɑː(r)]

bar	▸ 1 (a), (p)
barre	▸ 1 (c), (i), (n), (o), (q)
interdiction	▸ 1 (d)
obstacle	▸ 1 (e)
munir de barreaux	▸ 2 (a)
barrer	▸ 2 (b)
exclure	▸ 2 (c)
sauf	▸ 3
le barreau	▸ 4

(pt & pp **barred,** *cont* **barring) 1** *n* (**a**) *(pub)* bar *m*, café *m*; *(in hotel, club)* bar *m*; *(in station)* café *m*, bar *m*; *(counter)* bar *m*; **we sat at the bar all night drinking** on est restés à boire au bar toute la nuit

(**b**) *(small shop → for coffee, tea)* buvette *f*; *(→ for sandwiches)* snack *m*

(**c**) *(long piece of metal)* barre *f*; *(on grating, cage, window)* barreau *m*; *(on door)* bâcle *f*; *Elec (element)* barre *f*; **an iron bar** une barre de fer; **behind the bars of the cage** derrière les barreaux de la cage; **push bar to open** *(on exit doors)* appuyer sur la barre pour sortir; **to be behind (prison) bars** être sous les verrous *ou* derrière les barreaux; **they put him behind bars** ils l'ont mis sous les verrous

(**d**) *(ban)* interdiction *f*; **there is a bar on bringing drink into the club** il est interdit d'introduire de l'alcool au sein du club; **there is no bar on foreign athletes** les athlètes étrangers sont autorisés à participer aux compétitions

(**e**) *(obstacle)* empêchement *m*, obstacle *m*; *(in river, harbour)* barre *f* (de sable), traverse *f*; **to be a bar to sth** faire obstacle à qch

(**f**) *(bank → in lake, river)* banc *m*; *Am Geol (alluvial deposit)* barre *f*

(**g**) *(slab → of chocolate)* tablette *f*; *(→ of gold)* lingot *m*; **a bar of soap** une savonnette, un pain de savon

(**h**) *(stripe)* raie *f*; *(of sunlight)* rayon *m*

(**i**) *Law (in court)* barre *f*; **the accused stood at the bar** l'accusé était à la barre; **the prisoner at the bar** l'accusé(e) *m,f*

(**j**) *(authority, tribunal)* tribunal *m*

(**k**) *Br Parl* = endroit au Parlement où le public peut venir s'adresser aux députés ou aux Lords

(**l**) *Mus* mesure *f*; **the opening/closing bars** les premières/dernières mesures

(**m**) *Br Mil* barrette *f (portée sur le ruban d'une médaille)*; *Am* galon *m*

(**n**) *Her* burelle *f*; *(dividing shield)* barre *f*

(**o**) *Zool (in jaw of horse)* barre *f*

(**p**) *Tech (unit of pressure)* bar *m*

(**q**) *Comput (menu bar)* barre *f*

2 *vt* (**a**) *(put bars on → window)* munir de barreaux; **bar the door** mettez la barre *ou* la bâcle à la porte; *Fig* **they barred the door against intruders** ils ont barré la porte aux intrus

(**b**) *(obstruct)* barrer; **he barred her way** *or* **her path** il lui barra le passage; *Fig* **high interest rates are barring our way out of the recession** le niveau élevé des taux d'intérêt empêche la reprise (économique)

(**c**) *(ban → person)* exclure; *(→ activity)* interdire; **members of the sect were barred from entering the country** l'entrée du pays était interdite aux membres de la secte; **he was barred from the club** il a été exclu du club

(**d**) *(stripe)* rayer

3 *prep* excepté, sauf; **bar accidents** sauf accident, sauf imprévu; **bar none** sans exception; **bar one** sauf un (une); **it's all over bar the shouting** les jeux sont faits

4 **Bar** *n Law* **the Bar** *(in UK)* le barreau; *(in US)* les avocats *mpl*; *Br* **to call sb to the Bar,** *Am* **to admit sb to the Bar** inscrire qn au barreau; **she was** *Br* **called** *or Am* **admitted to the Bar** elle s'est inscrite au barreau

▸▸ *Br* ***bar billiards*** = version du jeu de billard, couramment pratiquée dans les pubs, ≃ billard *m* russe; ***bar chart*** histogramme *m*; ***bar code*** code-barres *m*; ***bar code reader*** lecteur *m* de code-barres; ***bar diagram*** histogramme *m*; ***bar ends*** *(of bicycle)* embouts *mpl* de guidon, cornes *fpl*; *Am Law* ***Bar exam*** = examen obligatoire avant de pouvoir exercer en tant qu'avocat; ***bar food*** = repas simples servis dans les pubs; ***bar game*** = jeu pratiqué dans un pub; ***bar girl*** *Am (hostess)* entraîneuse *f* de bar; *Br (barmaid)* serveuse *f* (de bar); ***bar graph*** histogramme *m*; ***bar prices*** prix *mpl* des consommations; ***Her bar sinister*** barre *f* de bâtardise; ***bar snack*** = repas simple pris dans un pub; ***bar stool*** tabouret *m* de bar; ***bar tariff*** liste *f* des prix des consommations

-bar [bɑː(r)] *suff* **a three-bar gate** une barrière à trois barreaux; **a two-bar electric fire** un radiateur électrique à deux résistances

Barabbas [bəˈræbəs] *pr n Bible* Barabbas

barb [bɑːb] *n* (**a**) *(on fishhook)* barbillon *m*; *(on barbed wire)* barbe *f*, pointe *f*; *(on arrow)* barbelure *f*; *Orn (feather)* barbe *f* (**b**) *(dig, gibe)* trait *m*, pointe *f*; **that was a cruel barb** c'était un trait cruel (**c**) *Zool (horse)* cheval *m* barbe, barbe *m*

Barbadian [bɑːˈbeɪdɪən] **1** *n* = habitant de la Barbade

2 *adj* de la Barbade

Barbados [bɑːˈbeɪdɒs] *n* Barbade *f*; **in Barbados** à la Barbade

barbarian [bɑːˈbeərɪən] **1** *n (boor, savage)* barbare *mf*

2 Barbarians *npl Sport (rugby team)* = équipe de rugby basée en Grande-Bretagne mais composée de joueurs de différents pays

barbaric [bɑːˈbærɪk] *adj also Fig* barbare

barbarism [ˈbɑːbərɪzəm] *n* (**a**) *(state)* barbarie *f* (**b**) *(in language)* barbarisme *m*

barbarity [bɑːˈbærətɪ] *n* (**a**) *(brutality)* barbarie *f*, inhumanité *f* (**b**) *(atrocity)* atrocité *f*, acte *m* de barbarie; **the barbarities committed by the enemy** les atrocités commises par l'ennemi

barbarize, -ise [ˈbɑːbəraɪz] *vt* **to barbarize sb** faire de qn un monstre; *Ling* **to barbarize the language** estropier la langue

Barbarossa [ˌbɑːbəˈrɒsə] *pr n* Barberousse

barbarous [ˈbɑːbərəs] *adj (language, manners, tribe)* barbare

barbarously [ˈbɑːbərəslɪ] *adv (brutally)* cruellement, inhumainement; *(primitively)* d'une façon barbare

barbarousness [ˈbɑːbərəsnɪs] *n* barbarie *f*

Barbary [ˈbɑːbərɪ] *n Geog* Barbarie *f*, États *mpl* barbaresques; **in Barbary** en Barbarie

▸▸ ***Barbary ape*** singe *m* de Barbarie, magot *m*; ***the Barbary coast*** les côtes *fpl* de Barbarie; ***Barbary sheep*** mouton *m* de Barbarie, mouflon *m* à manchettes; ***Barbary States*** États *mpl* barbaresques

barbecue [ˈbɑːbɪkjuː] *(pt & pp* **barbecued,** *cont* **barbecuing)** **1** *n (grill, meal, party)* barbecue *m*; **to have a barbecue** faire un barbecue

2 *vt (steak)* griller au charbon de bois; *(pig, sheep)* rôtir tout entier

▸▸ ***barbecue sauce*** sauce *f* barbecue

barbed [bɑːbd] *adj (arrow, hook)* barbelé; *(comment)* acéré, caustique

▸▸ ***barbed wire*** (fil *m* de fer) barbelé *m*; ***barbed wire fence*** barbelés *mpl*

barbel [ˈbɑːbəl] *n Ich (fish)* barbeau *m*; *(smaller)* barbillon *m*; *(spine on fish)* barbillon *m*

barbell [ˈbɑːbel] *n* barre *f* à disques

barber [ˈbɑːbə(r)] *n* coiffeur *m* (pour hommes), *Can* barbier *m*; **to go to the barber's** aller chez le coiffeur (pour hommes)

▸▸ ***barber's pole*** enseigne *f* de coiffeur

'The Barber of Seville' *Beaumarchais, Rossini* 'Le Barbier de Séville'

barberry [ˈbɑːbərɪ] *n Bot* épine-vinette *f*, berbéris *m*

barbershop [ˈbɑːbəʃɒp] **1** *n Am* salon *m* de coiffure (pour hommes)

2 *adj (songs)* = chanté en harmonie étroite

▸▸ ***barbershop quartet*** = quatuor d'hommes chantant en harmonie étroite

barbet [ˈbɑːbɪt] *n Orn* barbu *m*

barbican [ˈbɑːbɪkən] **1** *n Archit* barbacane *f*

2 Barbican *n* **the Barbican (Centre)** = centre culturel londonien

BARBICAN

Le Barbican Centre réunit une salle de concert, un théâtre, un cinéma, un musée, une bibliothèque et des salles d'exposition.

barbie [ˈbɑːbɪ] *n Br & Austr Fam (barbecue)* barbecue ❑ *m*; **to have a barbie** faire un barbecue

Barbie doll® [ˈbɑːbiː-] *n* (poupée *f*) Barbie® *f*; *Fam Fig* **all his girlfriends have been real Barbie dolls** toutes ses petites amies ressemblent à des poupées Barbie

barbitone [ˈbɑːbɪtəʊn] *n Pharm* véronal *m*

barbiturate [bɑːˈbɪtjʊrət] *n Pharm* barbiturique *m*

▸▸ *Med* ***barbiturate addiction*** dépendance *f* aux barbituriques; *Med* ***barbiturate poisoning*** barbiturisme *m*

barbituric [ˌbɑːbɪˈtjʊrɪk] *adj Chem* barbiturique

Barbour® **jacket** [ˈbɑːbə(r)-] *n Br* = veste en toile cirée à col de velours souvent associée à un style de vie BCBG en Grande-Bretagne

barbwire [ˈbɑːbˌwaɪə(r)] *n Am* (fil *m* de fer) barbelé *m*

▸▸ ***barbwire fence*** barbelés *mpl*

barcarole, barcarolle [ˌbɑːkəˈrəʊl] *n Mus* barcarolle *f*

Barcelona [ˌbɑːsɪˈləʊnə] *n* Barcelone

Barclaycard® [ˈbɑːklɪkɑːd] *n* = carte de crédit britannique; **to put sth on Barclaycard**® acheter qch avec la Barclaycard®

bar-code *vt (item, product)* mettre un code-barres sur

bar-coded *adj (item, product)* avec code-barres

bard [bɑːd] **1** *n* (**a**) *(Celtic)* barde *m*; *(Greek)* aède *m*; *Literary (poet)* poète *m*; **the Bard of Avon** = surnom donné à William Shakespeare, originaire de Stratford-upon-Avon; **the language of the Bard** l'anglais *m* (**b**) *Culin* barde *f* (de lard)

2 *vt Culin* barder

bardic [ˈbɑːdɪk] *adj (poetry, privileges)* du barde, des bardes

bardolatry [bɑːˈdɒlətrɪ] *n Hum Pej* = admiration sans bornes pour Shakespeare et ses œuvres

bare [beə(r)] *(compar* **barer,** *superl* **barest)** **1** *adj* (**a**) *(naked → body, feet)* nu; **they were bare to the waist** ils étaient nus jusqu'à la taille; **in one's bare feet** pieds nus; **he killed a tiger with his bare hands** il a tué un tigre à mains nues; *Boxing* **to fight with bare hands** boxer à main nue

(**b**) *(unadorned, uncovered)* nu; *Elec (wire)* dénudé; **we had to sleep on bare floorboards** nous avons dû coucher à même le plancher; **his head was bare** il était nu-tête; **bare wood** bois *m* naturel; **the tree was bare of leaves** l'arbre était dépouillé *ou* dénudé; **the lawn was just a bare patch of grass** la pelouse consistait en un maigre carré d'herbe; **a wall of bare rock** une paroi de roche nue; **to lay bare one's heart** mettre son cœur à nu; **to lay bare a plot** révéler *ou* dévoiler un complot

(**c**) *(empty)* vide; **the cupboard was bare** le garde-manger était vide; **the room was bare of furniture/pictures** la pièce ne comportait aucun meuble/tableau

(**d**) *(basic, plain)* simple, dépouillé; **I just told him the barest details** je lui ai donné le minimum de détails; **the bare facts** les faits *mpl* bruts; *Fig* **the bare bones of the story** le squelette de l'histoire

(**e**) *(absolute)* absolu, strict; **the house was stripped to the bare essentials** la maison ne contenait que le strict nécessaire; **the bare necessities of life** le minimum vital; **the bare minimum** le strict minimum; **I took the barest minimum of cash** j'ai pris le minimum d'argent

(**f**) *(meagre)* **a bare 20 percent of the population is literate** à peine 20 pour cent de la population est alphabétisée; **he earned a bare £200** il a gagné tout juste 200 livres; **they won by a bare majority** ils ont gagné de justesse; **he got a bare pass** il a eu son examen en ayant juste la moyenne; **a bare pass isn't good enough in my father's eyes** pour mon père réussir un examen de justesse n'est pas suffisant; **they manage to scrape a bare living from the land** ils arrivent tout juste à vivoter en travaillant la terre

2 *vt* (**a**) *(part of body)* découvrir; *(teeth)* montrer; **to bare one's head** se découvrir la tête; **to bare one's soul** mettre son âme à nu

(**b**) *(unsheath → dagger, sword)* dégainer, tirer du fourreau; *Elec (→ wire)* dénuder

bareass [ˈbeəræs], **bareassed** [ˈbeəræst] *adj Am very Fam* à poil

bareback [ˈbeəbæk] **1** *adj Horseriding (rider)* qui monte à cru

2 *adv Horseriding* **to ride bareback** monter à cru; *very Fam Hum (have unprotected sex)* faire l'amour sans préservatif ❑

bareboat charter [ˈbeəbəʊt-] *n Naut* affrètement *m* coque nue

barefaced [ˈbeəfeɪst] *adj (liar)* effronté, éhonté; *(lie)* impudent, éhonté

barefoot [ˈbeəfʊt] *adj* aux pieds nus

▸▸ *Med* ***barefoot doctor*** médecin *m* aux pieds nus; *Sport* ***barefoot waterskiing*** ski *m* nautique pieds nus, bare-foot *m inv*; **to go barefoot waterskiing** faire du ski nautique pieds nus, faire du bare-foot

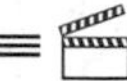

'The Barefoot Contessa' *Mankiewicz* 'La Comtesse aux pieds nus'

barefooted [ˌbeəˈfʊtɪd] **1** *adj* aux pieds nus

2 *adv* nu-pieds, (les) pieds nus; **to go barefooted** marcher pieds nus

barefooting [ˌbeəˈfʊtɪŋ] *n Sport* ski *m* nautique pieds nus, bare-foot *m inv*; **to go barefoot waterskiing** faire du ski nautique pieds nus, faire du bare-foot

bare-handed **1** *adv (fight)* à mains nues

2 *adj* aux mains nues

bareheaded [ˌbeəˈhedɪd] **1** *adv* nu-tête, (la) tête nue

2 *adj* nu-tête *(inv)*

barelegged [ˌbeəˈlegd] **1** *adv* nu-jambes, (les) jambes nues; **she goes out barelegged even in winter** même en hiver elle ne porte pas de collant

2 *adj* aux jambes nues; **it was a warm day so he was barelegged** il était en short parce qu'il faisait chaud

barely [ˈbeəlɪ] *adv* (**a**) *(only just)* à peine, tout juste; **there was barely enough to go around** il y en avait à peine assez pour tout le monde; **I had barely arrived when I heard the news** j'étais à peine arrivé que j'ai entendu la nouvelle; **he can barely read and write** c'est tout juste s'il sait lire et écrire (**b**) *(sparsely)* très peu; *(poorly)* pauvrement

bareness [ˈbeənɪs] *n* (**a**) *(nakedness → of person)* nudité *f* (**b**) *(sparseness → of style)* dépouillement *m*, *Pej* sécheresse *f*; *(→ of furnishings)* pauvreté *f*; *(→ of room)* dénuement *m* (**c**) *(simplicity)* dépouillement *m*

Barents Sea [ˈbærənts-] *n* **the Barents Sea** la mer de Barents

barf [bɑːf] *vi Fam* dégueuler

▸▸ ***barf bag*** sac *m* pour vomir ❑

barfly [ˈbɑːflaɪ] *n Am Fam* pilier *m* de bistrot

bargain [ˈbɑːgɪn] **1** *n* (**a**) *(deal)* marché *m*, affaire *f*; **a good/bad bargain** une bonne/mauvaise affaire; **to strike** *or* **to make a bargain with sb** conclure un marché avec qn; **to drive a hard bargain** marchander d'une façon acharnée; **you keep your end of the bargain and I'll keep mine** vous respectez vos engagements et je respecterai les miens; **we had a drink to seal the bargain** nous avons pris un verre pour conclure le marché

(**b**) *(good buy)* occasion *f*; **it's a real bargain!** c'est une bonne affaire!, c'est une occasion!; **to go bargain hunting** faire les soldes; *(in second-hand shops)* chiner

2 *vi* (**a**) *(haggle)* marchander; **she bargained with me over the price of the shoes** elle a marchandé avec moi au sujet du prix des chaussures

(**b**) *(negotiate)* négocier; **the unions are bargaining with management for an 8% pay rise** les syndicats négocient une hausse de salaire de 8% avec la direction; **I won't bargain with you** je ne parlementerai pas avec vous

3 into the bargain *adv* par-dessus le marché; **I was tired, hungry and had a headache into the bargain** j'étais fatigué, j'avais faim et en plus j'avais mal à la tête

▸▸ ***bargain basement*** *(in shop)* = dans certains grands magasins, sous-sol où sont regroupés les articles en solde et autres bonnes affaires; ***bargain break*** séjour *m* discompté; ***bargain counter*** rayon *m* des soldes; ***bargain offer*** promotion *f*, offre *f* exceptionnelle; ***bargain price*** prix *m* avantageux; ***bargain sale*** soldes *mpl* exceptionnels; ***bargain store*** magasin *m* bon marché

►**bargain away** *vt sep (rights, reputation)* brader; *(freedom)* sacrifier

►**bargain for** *vt insep (anticipate)* s'attendre à; **I hadn't bargained for this** je ne m'étais pas attendu à ça; **they got more than they bargained for** ils ne s'attendaient pas à un coup pareil; **things happened more quickly than he had bargained for** les choses sont allées plus vite qu'il n'avait pensé

►**bargain on** *vt insep (depend on)* compter sur; **I'm bargaining on it** je compte là-dessus; **I hadn't bargained on this happening!** je ne m'attendais pas à cela!

bargain-hunter *n* dénicheur(euse) *m,f* de bonnes affaires

bargaining ['bɑːɡɪnɪŋ] *n (haggling)* marchandage *m*; *(negotiating)* négociations *fpl*; **we are in a strong bargaining position** nous sommes en position de force pour négocier; **they have considerable bargaining power** ils ont beaucoup de poids dans les négociations; **this has reduced their bargaining power** cela a affaibli leur position dans les négociations

►► ***bargaining chip,*** *Br* ***bargaining counter*** monnaie *f* d'échange; **to use sb/sth as a bargaining chip** utiliser qn/qch comme monnaie d'échange; *Ind* ***bargaining table*** table *f* des négociations

barge [bɑːdʒ] **1** *n Naut* (**a**) *(on canal)* chaland *m*; *(larger → on river)* péniche *f*; **to live on a barge** vivre sur une péniche (**b**) *(ceremonial boat)* barque *f*; **the queen's barge** la barque de cérémonie de la reine; **the admiral's barge** la vedette de l'amiral

2 *vi* **they barge about as if they owned the place** ils vont et viennent comme si l'endroit leur appartenait; **he barged into the room** il fit irruption dans la pièce; **she barged past me** elle m'a bousculé en passant; **she barged across the room** elle a traversé la pièce en trombe

3 *vt Sport (goalkeeper, player)* écarter d'un coup d'épaule; **to barge sb out of the way** écarter qn d'un geste brusque; **to barge one's way into a room** faire irruption dans une pièce

►**barge in** *vi (enter)* faire irruption; *(interrupt)* intervenir mal à propos; **I'm sorry for barging in like this** excusez-moi de faire ainsi irruption; **he keeps barging in on our conversation** il n'arrête pas de nous interrompre dans notre conversation

►**barge into** *vt insep* (**a**) *(bump into → person)* rentrer dans; *(→ piece of furniture)* rentrer dans, se cogner contre (**b**) *(enter abruptly → room)* faire irruption dans

►**barge through** **1** *vt insep* **to barge through a door** passer une porte en trombe; **to barge through a crowd** foncer à travers la foule

2 *vt sep* **to barge one's way through the crowd** foncer à travers la foule; **just barge your way through** force le passage

bargee [bɑː'dʒiː], *Am* **bargeman** ['bɑːdʒmən] (*pl* **bargemen** [-mən]) *n Naut* batelier *m*, marinier *m*

bargepole ['bɑːdʒpəʊl] *n Naut* gaffe *f*; *Br* **I wouldn't touch it with a bargepole** *(disgusting object)* je n'y toucherais pas avec des pincettes; *(risky affair, deal)* je ne m'en mêlerais pour rien au monde

barhop ['bɑːhɒp] *vt Am Fam* faire les bars

baric ['beərɪk] *adj* (**a**) *Chem (salt)* barytique; *Miner (mineral, ore)* barytifère (**b**) *Met* de bars

►► ***baric hydroxide, baric oxide*** baryte *f*

barite ['beəraɪt] *n Am Miner* barytine *f*

baritone ['bærɪtəʊn] *Mus* **1** *n (singer, voice)* baryton *m*

2 *adj (part, voice)* de baryton

barium ['beərɪəm] *n Chem* baryum *m*

►► *Med* ***barium meal*** bouillie *f* barytée; *Med* ***barium sulphate*** barytine *f*, barytite *f*

bark [bɑːk] **1** *n* (**a**) *(of dog)* aboiement *m*; *(of fox)* glapissement *m*; *Fig (cough)* toux *f* sèche; **to give** *or* **to let out a bark** *(dog)* aboyer, pousser un aboiement; *(fox)* pousser un glapissement; **his bark is worse than his bite** il crie beaucoup mais il n'est pas méchant

(**b**) *(of tree)* écorce *f*; **to strip** *or* **take the bark off a tree** écorcer un arbre

(**c**) *Am* = **barque**

2 *vi (dog)* aboyer; *(fox)* glapir; *Fig (cough)* tousser; *(speak harshly)* crier, aboyer; *(sell)* vendre à la criée; **the dog barked at the postman** le chien a aboyé après le facteur; *Fig* **to be barking up the wrong tree** faire fausse route; *Fam Hum* **there's no point having a dog and barking yourself** ça ne sert à rien d'avoir des gens pour nous servir si c'est pour tout faire soi-même ❑

3 *vt* (**a**) *(order)* aboyer

(**b**) *(tree)* écorcer; *(skin)* écorcher; **to bark one's shins** s'écorcher les jambes

►► *Entom* ***bark beetle*** scolyte *m*, bostryche *m*

►**bark out** *vt sep (order)* aboyer

barkeep ['bɑːkiːp], **barkeeper** ['bɑːˌkiːpə(r)] *n Am Fam* barman ❑ *m*

barker ['bɑːkə(r)] *n* (**a**) *(in fairground)* bonimenteur *m* (**b**) *(animal)* **the dog is a terrible barker** ce chien n'arrête pas d'aboyer

barking ['bɑːkɪŋ] **1** *n (UNCOUNT) (of dog)* aboiements *mpl*; *(of fox)* glapissements *mpl*

2 *adj* (**a**) *(dog)* aboyeur; *(fox)* glapissant (**b**) *Br Fam* **barking (mad)** complètement cinglé

barley ['bɑːlɪ] *n* (**a**) *(crop, grain)* orge *f* (**b**) *(in cooking, distilling)* orge *m*; *(in soup)* orge *m* perlé; *(for whisky)* orge *m* mondé

►► ***barley sugar*** sucre *m* d'orge; *Br* ***barley water*** = sirop à base d'orge généralement parfumé au citron ou à l'orange; *Br* ***barley wine*** = bière très forte en alcool

barleycorn ['bɑːlɪkɔːn] *n* (**a**) *(grain)* grain *m* d'orge (**b**) *(barley)* orge *f*

barm [bɑːm] *n* levure *f* (de bière)

barmaid ['bɑːmeɪd] *n* barmaid *f*, serveuse *f (au bar)*

barman ['bɑːmən] (*pl* **barmen** [-mən]) *n* barman *m*, serveur *m (au bar)*

Barmecide ['bɑːməsaɪd] *pr n* Barmécide

►► ***Barmecide feast*** festin *m* de Barmécide

barminess ['bɑːmɪnɪs] *n Br Fam* folie ❑ *f*

bar mitzvah [ˌbɑː'mɪtsvə] *n Rel (ceremony)* bar-mitsva *f inv*; *(boy)* garçon *m* qui fait sa bar-mitsva

barmy ['bɑːmɪ] (*compar* **barmier**, *superl* **barmiest**) *adj Br Fam* maboul, dingue

barn [bɑːn] *n* (**a**) *(for hay)* grange *f*; *(for horses)* écurie *f*; *(for cows)* étable *f*; *Fig* **their house is a great barn of a place** leur maison est une énorme bâtisse; *Hum* **were you born in a barn?** on ne t'a jamais appris à fermer tes portes?; *Fig* **it's as big as a barn door** c'est gros comme une maison; *Am* **it was barn-door obvious** c'était gros comme une maison; **he couldn't hit a barn door** *(he's a poor shot)* c'est un mauvais tireur

(**b**) *(for railroad trucks)* dépôt *m*

►► ***barn dance*** = bal de campagne où l'on danse des quadrilles; *Orn* ***barn owl*** (chouette *f*) effraie *f*, chouette *f* des clochers

Barnabas ['bɑːnəbəs] *pr n Bible* Barnabé

barnacle ['bɑːnəkəl] *n* bernache *f*, bernacle *f (crustacé)*

►► *Orn* ***barnacle goose*** bernache *f* (nonnette)

Barnardo's [bə'nɑːdəʊz] *n* = association caritative britannique

BARNARDO'S

L'association, fondée en 1870 par le docteur Barnardo, aide les orphelins ainsi que les enfants défavorisés (notamment handicapés) et leurs familles. Aujourd'hui, l'association ne gère plus d'orphelinats ni d'institutions pour enfants.

barney ['bɑːnɪ] *n Br Fam* engueulade *f*; **to have a barney** avoir une engueulade *ou* une prise de bec

barnstorm ['bɑːnˌstɔːm] *vi* (**a**) *Sport* faire une tournée à la campagne; *Theat* jouer sur les tréteaux (**b**) *Am Pol* = faire une tournée électorale (dans les circonscriptions rurales)

barnstormer ['bɑːnˌstɔːmə(r)] *n* (**a**) *Theat (actor)* comédien(enne) *m,f* ambulant(e); *(acrobat)* acrobate *mf* ambulant(e) (**b**) *Am Pol* orateur(trice) *m,f* électoral(e)

barnstorming ['bɑːnˌstɔːmɪŋ] *n* (**a**) *Theat* théâtre *m* ambulant (**b**) *Am Pol* tournée *f ou* campagne *f* électorale

barnyard ['bɑːnjɑːd] **1** *n* cour *f* de ferme

2 *adj (animals)* de basse-cour; *Fig (humour)* rustre

►► ***barnyard fowls*** volaille *f*

barogram ['bærəɡræm] *n Met* barogramme *m*

barograph ['bærəʊɡrɑːf] *n Met* barographe *m*

barometer [bə'rɒmɪtə(r)] *n Met* baromètre *m*; **the barometer is showing fair** le baromètre est au beau; *Fig* **the poll is a clear barometer of public reaction** le sondage est un parfait baromètre des réactions du public

barometric [ˌbærə'metrɪk] *adj Met* barométrique

►► ***barometric pressure*** pression *f* atmosphérique

baron ['bærən] *n* (**a**) *(noble)* baron *m* (**b**) *(magnate)* magnat *m*; **a press baron** un magnat de la presse (**c**) *Culin* **a baron of beef** un double aloyau de bœuf

baroness ['bærənɪs] *n* baronne *f*

baronet ['bærənɪt] *n* baronnet *m*

baronetcy ['bærənɪtsɪ] *n (patent)* titre *m* de baronnet; *(position)* rang *m* de baronnet

baronial [bə'rəʊnɪəl] *adj* de baron

►► ***baronial hall*** demeure *f* seigneuriale

barony ['bærənɪ] *n* baronnie *f (terre)*

baroque [bə'rɒk] *Art, Archit & Mus* **1** *n* baroque *m*

2 *adj* baroque

barostat ['bærəstæt] *n Tech* barostat *m*

barouche [bə'ruːʃ] *n* calèche *f*

barperson ['bɑːˌpɜːsən] *n* serveur(euse) *m,f (au bar)*

barque, *Am* **bark** [bɑːk] *n* (**a**) *Literary* barque *f* (**b**) *Naut (with three masts)* trois-mâts *m inv*; *(with four masts)* quatre-mâts *m inv*

barrack ['bærək] **1** *vt* (**a**) *Mil (soldiers)* caserner (**b**) *Br (heckle)* chahuter (**c**) *Austr Fam (support → team)* supporter ❑; *(shout encouragement at → player, team)* encourager ❑

2 **barracks** *n Mil* caserne *f*; **infantry barracks** quartier *m* d'infanterie; **in barracks** à la caserne; **to be confined to barracks** être consigné; *Fig* **the school is a great barracks of a place** l'école est une espèce d'énorme bâtisse du genre caserne

►► *Mil* ***barrack square*** cour *f* de caserne

barracking ['bærəkɪŋ] *n Br* chahut *m*; **he got** *or* **they gave him a terrible barracking** on l'a chahuté violemment

barrack-room *adj Br (humour, joke)* de caserne; **barrack-room language** langage *m* de corps de garde *ou* de caserne

►► ***barrack-room lawyer*** chicanier(ère) *m,f*

barracuda [ˌbærə'kuːdə] *n Ich* barracuda *m*

barrage ['bærɑːʒ] **1** *n* (**a**) *Mil* tir *m* de barrage (**b**) *Fig (of punches, questions)* pluie *f*, déluge *m*; *(of insults, words)* déluge *m*, flot *m* (**c**) *Constr (dam)* barrage *m*

2 *vt* **to barrage sb with sth** *(questions, insults etc)* assaillir qn de qch

►► *Mil* ***barrage balloon*** ballon *m* de barrage

barramundi [ˌbærə'mʌndɪ] *n Ich* barramundi *m*

barratry ['bærətrɪ] *n* (**a**) *Scot Law* = délit commis par un juge qui se laisse suborner (**b**) *Law & Naut* baraterie *f*

barred [bɑːd] *adj (locked → door)* barré; *(with bars on → window)* à barreaux

barrel ['bærəl] (*Br pt & pp* **barrelled**, *cont* **barrelling**, *Am pt & pp* **barreled**, *cont* **barreling**) **1** *n* (**a**) *(cask, unit of capacity → of wine)* tonneau *m*, fût *m*; *(→ of cider)* fût *m*; *(→ of beer)* tonneau *m*; *Petr (→ of oil, tar)* baril *m*; *(→ of fish)* caque *f*; **they have a production capacity of 2 million barrels a day** leur capacité de production est de 2 millions de barils par jour; *Fam* **to have sb over a barrel** tenir qn à sa merci ❑

(**b**) *Tech (hollow cylinder → of gun, key)* canon *m*; *(→ of clock, lock)* barillet *m*; *(→ of pen)* corps *m*; *(of capstan, winch)* fusée *f*, mèche *f*, tambour *m*; *Mil (of artillery piece)* tube *m*; *Fam* **to give sb both barrels** passer un savon à qn

(**c**) *Fam (lot)* **we had a barrel of fun** *or* **a barrel of laughs** on s'est vachement amusés; **it wasn't a barrel of laughs** *(interview, project)* ça n'a pas été une partie de plaisir; *(film, show)* ce n'était pas très rigolo; **he's a barrel of fun** il est vraiment marrant; *Am* **it was more fun than a barrel of monkeys** c'était marrant comme tout

2 *vt (beer)* mettre en tonneau; *Petr (oil)* mettre en baril

3 *vi Am Fam* **to barrel (along)** foncer, aller à toute pompe

►► *Mus* **barrel organ** orgue *m* de Barbarie; *Aviat* **barrel roll** tonneau *m* en spirale; *Archit* **barrel vault** voûte *f* en berceau

barrel-chested [-'tʃestɪd] *adj* **to be barrel-chested** avoir le torse bombé

barrelful ['bærəl,fʊl] *n* tonneau *m*, fût *m*

barrelhouse ['bærəl,haʊs, *pl* -haʊzɪz] *n Am* bistrot *m*

►► *Mus* **barrelhouse jazz** jazz *m* de bastringue

barrel-roll *vi Aviat* faire un tonneau en spirale

barrel-shaped *adj* en forme de baril *ou* de tonneau

barren ['bærən] **1** *adj* (**a**) *(land → infertile)* stérile, improductif; *(→ bare)* désertique; *(→ dry)* aride (**b**) *Literary (sterile → woman)* stérile (**c**) *(dull → film, play)* aride; *(→ discussion)* stérile; *(→ writing)* aride, sec (sèche)

2 *n* lande *f*; **the pine barrens of Frankonia** les landes de la Franconie

►► *Geog* **the Barren Grounds, the Barren Lands** la toundra canadienne

barrenness ['bærənnɪs] *n* (**a**) *(of land → infertility)* stérilité *f*; *(→ bareness)* désolation *f*; *(→ dryness)* aridité *f* (**b**) *Literary (sterility → of woman)* stérilité *f* (**c**) *(dullness → of film, play, writing)* aridité *f*; *(→ of discussion)* stérilité *f*

barrette [bə'ret] *n Am* barrette *f (pour cheveux)*

barricade ['bærɪ,keɪd] **1** *n Naut & Constr* barricade *f*

2 *vt (door, street)* barricader; **they barricaded themselves in** ils se sont barricadés

►**barricade off** *vt sep (street)* barrer

barrier ['bærɪə(r)] *n* (**a**) *(fence, gate)* barrière *f*; *(at railway station)* portillon *m*

(**b**) *(obstacle)* obstacle *m*; **lack of investment is a barrier to economic growth** le manque d'investissement est un obstacle à la croissance économique; **the language barrier** le barrage *ou* la barrière de la langue

►► **barrier cream** crème *f* protectrice; **barrier ice** banquise *f*; **barrier method** méthode *f* de contraception locale; *Min* **barrier pillar** stot *m*; **barrier reef** barrière *f* de corail

barring ['bɑːrɪŋ] *prep* excepté, sauf; **barring rain the concert will take place tomorrow** à moins qu'il ne pleuve, le concert aura lieu demain; **barring accidents** sauf accident, sauf imprévu

barrio ['bærɪəʊ] *n Am* quartier *m* latino-américain

barrister ['bærɪstə(r)], **barrister-at-law** *n Br Law* ≃ avocat(e) *m,f*

bar-room *n Am* bar *m*

►► **bar-room brawl** bagarre *f* de bar

barrow ['bærəʊ] *n* (**a**) *(wheelbarrow)* brouette *f*; *(fruitseller's)* voiture *f* des quatre saisons; *(for luggage)* diable *m*; *Mining* wagonnet *m*; **I wheeled** *or* **carried the bricks in a barrow** j'ai brouetté les briques (**b**) *(burial mound)* tumulus *m*

►► *Br* **barrow boy** marchand *m* ambulant; *Br Fam* **he's a bit of a barrow boy** il est assez frimeur

barrowful ['bærəʊfʊl] *n* brouettée *f*

barrowload ['bærəʊləʊd] *n* brouettée *f*

Bart. *(written abbr baronet)* baronnet *m*

bar-tailed godwit *n Orn* barge *f* rousse

bartend ['bɑːtend] *vi Am (man)* être barman *ou* serveur *(au bar)*, *(woman)* être barmaid *ou* serveuse *(au bar)*

bartender ['bɑːtendə(r)] *n Am (man)* barman *m*, serveur *m (au bar)*; *(woman)* barmaid *f*, serveuse *f (au bar)*

barter ['bɑːtə(r)] *Com* **1** *n (UNCOUNT)* échange *m*, troc *m*; **a system of barter** une économie de troc

2 *vt* échanger, troquer; **they bartered animals for cloth** ils ont échangé des animaux contre du tissu; *Fig* **he bartered his freedom for money** il a vendu sa liberté pour de l'argent

3 *vi (exchange)* faire un échange *ou* un troc; *(haggle)* marchander

►► *Com* **a barter society** une société vivant du troc; **a barter system** une économie de troc

►**barter away** *vt sep (rights)* vendre; **he's bartered away his honour** il s'est vendu

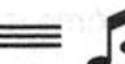

'The Bartered Bride' *Smetana* 'La Fiancée vendue'

barterer ['bɑːtərə(r)] *n Com* troqueur(euse) *m,f*; *Pej* trafiqueur *m*

Bart's [bɑːts] *n* = surnom du "Saint Bartholomew's Hospital" à Londres

barycentre, *Am* **barycenter** ['bærɪ,sentə(r)] *n Astron & Phys* barycentre *m*

barycentric [,bærɪ'sentrɪk] *adj Astron & Phys* barycentrique

baryon ['bærɪɒn] *n Phys* baryon *m*

barysphere ['bærɪ,sfɪə(r)] *n Geol* barysphère *f*

barytes [bə'raɪtiːz] *n Miner* barytine *f*

barytone = **baritone**

basal ['beɪsəl] *adj* (**a**) *Physiol* basal (**b**) *(fundamental)* fondamental

basalt ['bæsɔːlt] *n Geol* basalte *m*

►► **basalt column** colonne *f* basaltique

basaltic [bə'sɔːltɪk] *adj Geol* basaltique

bascule ['bæskjuːl] *n Tech* bascule *f*

►► *Constr* **bascule bridge** pont *m* à bascule

base [beɪs] *(compar* **baser**, *superl* **basest**) **1** *n* (**a**) *(bottom → gen)* partie *f* inférieure, base *f*; *(→ of tree, column)* pied *m*; *(→ of bowl, glass)* fond *m*; *(→ of triangle)* base *f*; **the bud grows at the base of the branch** le bourgeon pousse à la base de la branche; **the base came away from the rest** la base *ou* la partie inférieure s'est détachée du reste

(**b**) *(support, stand → of statue, pillar)* socle *m*; **she used the box as a base for her sculpture** elle s'est servie de la boîte comme socle pour sa sculpture

(**c**) *(of food, paint)* base *f*; **the stock forms the base of your sauce** le fond constitue la base de votre sauce

(**d**) *(basis → of knowledge)* base *f*; *(→ of experience)* réserve *f*

(**e**) *Econ & Pol* base *f*; **an industrial base** une zone industrielle

(**f**) *(centre of activities)* point *m* de départ; *Mil* base *f*; **the explorers returned to base** les explorateurs sont retournés au camp de base; **the visitors made central London their base** les visiteurs ont pris le centre de Londres comme point de départ; **Glasgow is a good base from which to explore the Highlands** Glasgow est un bon point d'attache pour rayonner dans les Highlands; *Com* **the company's base** le siège de la société

(**g**) *Chem, Comput, Geom & Math* base *f*

(**h**) *Sport (in baseball and rounders)* base *f*; *Am Fam Fig* **he's way off base** il est complètement à côté de la plaque; **first base** *(in baseball)* première base *f*; *Fig* **to get to first base** réussir la première étape; **we didn't even get to first base** on n'a pas fait le moindre progrès; **I just thought I'd touch base** je voulais juste garder le contact

2 *vt* (**a**) *(found → opinion, project)* baser, fonder; **the project is based on cooperation from all regions** le projet est fondé sur la coopération de toutes les régions; **the film is based on a true story/on a short story by Herman Melville** le film est tiré d'une histoire vraie/d'une nouvelle de Herman Melville

(**b**) *(locate)* baser; **where are you based?** où êtes-vous installé?; **the job is based in Tokyo** le poste est basé à Tokyo

3 *adj (motive, thoughts, conduct)* bas, indigne; *(origins)* bas; *(ingratitude)* flagrant; *(coinage)* faux (fausse)

►► *Am Tech* **base burner** = poêle où le charbon alimente le feu automatiquement; *Mil* **base camp** camp *m* de base; **base coat** *(of paint)* première couche *f*; *Ling* **base component** composant *m* de base; *Fin* **base date** date *f* de base; **base hit** *(in baseball)* = coup permettant au batteur d'atteindre la première base; *Sport* **base jumping** = saut en chute libre à partir d'un pont, d'une falaise ou d'une montagne, avec parachute plié que l'on ouvre le plus tard possible; *Fin* **base lending rate** = taux de base du crédit bancaire; *Com & Elec* **base load** charge *f* minimum; *Metal* **base metal** métal *m* vil; *Biol* **base pair** paire *f* de bases; *Am* **base pay** salaire *m* de base; *Banking* **base rate** taux *m* de base (bancaire) *(utilisé par les banques pour déterminer leur taux de prêt)*; *Am* **base salary** salaire *m* de base; *Banking* **base year** année *f* de référence

baseball ['beɪsbɔːl] *n Sport* base-ball *m*

►► **baseball cap** casquette *f* de base-ball; **baseball card** = image de joueur de base-ball à collectionner; **baseball game** match *m* de base-ball; **baseball glove, baseball mitt** gant *m* de base-ball

baseboard ['beɪsbɔːd] *n Am Constr* plinthe *f*

-based [beɪst] *suff* (**a**) *(located)* **the company is Tokyo-based** le centre d'opérations de la firme est à Tokyo (**b**) *(centred)* **a science-based curriculum** un programme basé sur les sciences; **an oil-based economy** une économie fondée sur le pétrole; **an interview-based study** une étude basée sur des entretiens (**c**) *(composed)* **a water -based paint** une peinture à l'eau

Basel ['bɑːzəl] *n* Bâle *f*

baseless ['beɪslɪs] *adj (gossip)* sans fondement; *(suspicion)* injustifié; *(fear, superstition)* déraisonnable

baselessness ['beɪslɪsnɪs] *n (of gossip)* manque *m* de fondement; *(of suspicion)* caractère *m* non justifié; *(of fear, superstition)* déraison *f*

baseline ['beɪslaɪn] *n* (**a**) *Sport (in baseball)* ligne *f* des bases; *(in tennis)* ligne *f* de fond (**b**) *(in surveying)* base *f*; *(in diagram)* ligne *f* zéro; *Art* ligne *f* de fuite (**c**) *(standard)* point *m* de comparaison (**d**) *Comput (in desktop publishing)* ligne *f* de base

►► *Fin* **baseline costs** coûts *mpl* de base; **baseline player** joueur(euse) *m,f* de fond de court; *Com* **baseline sales** ventes *fpl* de base

baseliner ['beɪslaɪnə(r)] *n Sport (in tennis)* joueur(euse) *m,f* de fond de court

basely ['beɪslɪ] *adv* bassement, vilement

baseman ['beɪsmæn] *(pl* **basemen** [-men]) *n Sport (in baseball)* **first/second/third baseman** gardien *m* base un/deux/trois

basement ['beɪsmənt] **1** *n* sous-sol *m*; **in the basement** au sous-sol

2 *adj (kitchen, bedroom)* en sous-sol

►► **basement flat** (appartement *m* en) sous-sol *m*

baseness ['beɪsnɪs] *n (of motives, thoughts, conduct, origins)* bassesse *f*

bases ['beɪsiːz] *pl of* **basis**

bash [bæʃ] *Fam* **1** *n* (**a**) *(blow)* coup ❑ *m*; *(with fist)* coup *m* de poing ❑; **he gave me a bash on the nose** il m'a donné un coup de poing sur le nez

(**b**) *(dent → in wood)* entaille ❑ *f*; *(→ in metal)* bosse ❑ *f*, bosselure ❑ *f*; **my car door got a bash** la porte de ma voiture a été cabossée

(**c**) *(party)* fête ❑ *f*; **we're having a bit of a bash** nous organisons une petite fête

(**d**) *Br (attempt)* **to have a bash at doing sth** essayer de faire qch ❑; **go on, have a bash!** vas-y, essaie!; **I'm willing to give it a bash** je vais essayer un coup

2 *vt* (**a**) *(person, one's head)* frapper ❑, cogner ❑; **she bashed him on the head** elle l'a assommé

(**b**) *(dent → wooden box, table)* entailler ❑; *(→ car)* cabosser ❑, bosseler ❑

(**c**) *Fig (criticize)* critiquer ❑; *Fig* **it's part of their campaign to bash the unions** leur campagne a en partie pour but d'enfoncer les syndicats

►**bash about, bash around** *vt sep Fam* (**a**) *(hit → person)* flanquer des coups à; *(punch)* flanquer des coups de poing à (**b**) *(ill-treat → person)* maltraiter ❑, rudoyer ❑; *(→ car)* mettre à rude épreuve ❑; **the package has been bashed about** *or* **around** le paquet a souffert

►**bash in** *vt sep Fam (door)* enfoncer ❑; *(car, hat)* cabosser ❑

►**bash on** *vi Br Fam (with journey, task)* continuer (tant bien que mal) ❑

►**bash up** *vt sep Fam (car)* bousiller; *(person)* tabasser

-basher ['bæʃə(r)] *suff Fam* **a union-basher** un(e) anti-syndicaliste ❑

bashful ['bæʃfʊl] *adj (shy)* timide; *(modest)* pudique

bashfully ['bæʃfʊlɪ] *adv (shyly)* timidement; *(modestly)* avec pudeur

bashfulness ['bæʃfʊlnɪs] *n (shyness)* timidité *f*; *(modesty)* pudeur *f*

bashing ['bæʃɪŋ] *n Fam* raclée *f*, peignée *f*; **to take** *or* **get a bashing** prendre une raclée *ou* une peignée

BASIC ['beɪsɪk] *n Comput* (*abbr* **beginner's all-purpose symbolic instruction code**) basic *m*

basic ['beɪsɪk] **1** *adj* (**a**) *(fundamental → problem, theme)* fondamental; *(→ aim, belief)* principal; **these things are basic to a good marriage** ces choses sont fondamentales *ou* vitales pour un mariage heureux
(**b**) *(elementary → rule, skill)* élémentaire; *(→ knowledge, vocabulary)* de base; **basic English** anglais *m* de base; **a basic knowledge of Greek** une connaissance de base du grec; **my French is a bit basic** mon français est plutôt rudimentaire; **basic vocabulary** vocabulaire *m* de base; **I've got the basic idea** je vois de quoi il s'agit en gros; *Math* **the four basic operations** les quatre opérations *fpl* fondamentales
(**c**) *(essential)* essentiel; **basic foodstuffs** denrées *fpl* de base; **the basic necessities of life** les besoins *mpl* vitaux; **basic precautions** précautions *fpl* élémentaires *ou* essentielles
(**d**) *(primitive → furniture, accommodation, skills)* rudimentaire; **their flat is really basic** leur appartement est très rudimentaire
(**e**) *(as a starting point → hours)* de base; **this is the basic model of the car** voici la voiture dans son modèle de base
(**f**) *Chem* basique
2 basics *npl* **the basics** l'essentiel *m*; **let's get down to basics** venons-en à l'essentiel; **I learned the basics of computing** j'ai acquis les notions de base en informatique; **they learned to cook with just the basics** ils ont appris à faire la cuisine avec un minimum; **to get back to basics** *(important things in life)* retourner aux choses essentielles; *Pol* **back to basics** = expression qui suggère un retour aux valeurs traditionnelles en matière d'éducation ou de moralité, lancée par les Conservateurs comme argument de renouveau politique au début des années 90
►► *Econ* ***basic commodity*** denrée *f* de base; *Mktg* ***basic consumer goods*** denrées *fpl* de consommation courante; *Ins* ***basic cover*** assurance *f* de garantie de base; *Fin* ***basic pay*** salaire *m* de base; *Br Fin* ***basic rate*** taux *m* de base; **most people are basic rate taxpayers** la plupart des gens sont imposés au taux de base; *Br Fin* ***basic salary*** salaire *m* de base, traitement *m* de base; *Chem* ***basic salt*** sel *m* basique; ***basic slag*** scorie *f* de déphosphoration; *Fin* ***basic wage*** salaire *m* de base

basically ['beɪsɪkəlɪ] *adv* au fond; **they are both basically the same** au fond, ils sont tous les deux identiques; **basically I agree with you** dans l'ensemble *ou* en gros je suis d'accord avec vous; **she's basically a shy person, she's basically shy** c'est une personne foncièrement timide; **basically, I think this war is wrong** globalement, cette guerre me paraît injuste; **basically, she doesn't know what to think** dans le fond, elle ne sait pas quoi penser; **basically, he only has to do two things** en gros, il n'a que deux choses à faire

basicity [beɪ'sɪsətɪ] *n Chem* basicité *f*

basil [*Br* 'bæzəl, *Am* 'beɪzəl] *n Bot & Culin* basilic *m*

basilica [bə'zɪlɪkə] *n Archit & Rel* basilique *f*

basilisk ['bæzɪlɪsk] *n Her, Myth & Zool* basilic *m*

basin ['beɪsən] *n* (**a**) *Culin* bol *m*; *(for cream)* jatte *f* (**b**) *(for washing)* cuvette *f*, bassine *f*; *(plumbed in)* lavabo *m* (**c**) *Geog (of river)* bassin *m*; *(of valley)* cuvette *f*; **the Paris Basin** le Bassin parisien (**d**) *(for fountain)* vasque *f*, coupe *f*; *(in harbour)* bassin *m*
►► ***basin cut*** *(haircut)* coupe *f* au bol

basinful ['beɪsənfʊl] *n (of milk)* bol *m*; *(of cream)* jatte *f*; *(of water)* pleine cuvette *f*; *Fam* **to have had a basinful (of sb/sth)** en avoir ras le bol (de qn/qch)

basis ['beɪsɪs] (*pl* **bases** [-si:z]) *n* (**a**) *(foundation)* base *f*; **he can't survive on that basis** il ne peut pas survivre dans ces conditions-là; **on the basis of what I was told** d'après ce qu'on m'a dit; *Fin* **the basis for assessing income tax** l'assiette *f* de l'impôt sur le revenu
(**b**) *(reason)* raison *f*; *(grounds)* motif *m*; **he did it on the basis that he'd nothing to lose** il l'a fait en partant du principe qu'il n'avait rien à perdre; **there was no rational basis for his decision** sa décision n'avait aucun fondement rationnel
(**c**) *(system, scheme)* **on a worldwide basis** à l'échelle mondiale; **employed on a part-time basis** employé à mi-temps; **paid on a weekly basis** payé à la semaine; **the centre is organized on a voluntary basis** le centre fonctionne sur la base du bénévolat; **I will be taking part on an unofficial basis** je participerai à titre non officiel

bask [bɑ:sk] *vi* (**a**) *(lie)* **to bask in the sun** lézarder; **a cat basking in the sunshine** un chat se chauffant au soleil (**b**) *(revel)* se réjouir, se délecter; **he basked in all the unexpected publicity** il se réjouissait de toute cette publicité imprévue

basket ['bɑ:skɪt] *n* (**a**) *(container → gen)* corbeille *f*; *(→ for shopping, carrying)* panier *m*; *(→ for wastepaper)* corbeille *f* à papier; *(→ for linen)* panier *m* à linge; *(→ for baby)* couffin *m*; *(→ on donkey)* panier *m*; *(→ on someone's back)* hotte *f*
(**b**) *(quantity)* panier *m*; **a basket of apples** un panier de pommes
(**c**) *(group)* assortiment *m*; *Fin* **a basket of European currencies** un panier de devises européennes
(**d**) *Sport (in basketball → net, point)* panier *m*; **to score a basket** marquer un panier
(**e**) *Ski (on pole)* rondelle *f* de ski
►► *Fam* ***basket case*** *(nervous wreck)* paquet *m* de nerfs; *(mad person)* cinglé(e) *m,f*, barjo *mf*; *Am (invalid)* grand(e) invalide *m,f*; ***basket chair*** chaise *f* en osier; *Fin* ***basket clause*** clause *f* fourre-tout; ***basket maker*** vannier *m*; ***basket making*** vannerie *f*; *Tex* ***basket weave*** armure *f* nattée

basketball ['bɑ:skɪtbɔ:l] *n Sport* basket-ball *m*, basket *m*
►► ***basketball game*** match *m* de basket; ***basketball player*** basketteur(euse) *m,f*

basketful ['bɑ:skɪtfʊl] *n* plein panier *m*

basketry ['bɑ:skɪtrɪ] *n* vannerie *f*

basketwork ['bɑ:skɪtwɜ:k] *n (UNCOUNT) (objects)* objets *mpl* en osier; *(skill)* vannerie *f*

basking shark ['bɑ:skɪŋ-] *n Ich* requin *m* pèlerin, pèlerin *m*

Basle [bɑ:l] *n* Bâle *f*

basmati rice [bæs'mætɪ-] *n* riz *m* basmati

basophile ['bæsəʊfɪl], **basophilic** [bæ'sɒfɪlɪk] *adj Physiol* basophile

Basque [bɑ:sk] **1** *n* (**a**) *(person)* Basque *mf* (**b**) *(language)* basque *m*
2 *adj* basque
►► ***the Basque Country*** le Pays basque; **in the Basque Country** au Pays basque

basque [bɑ:sk] *n* corsage *m* très ajusté; *(bodice)* guêpière *f*; *(of jacket)* basque *f*

Basra, Basrah ['bæzrə] *n Geog* Bassora *f*

bas-relief [ˌbæsrɪ'li:f] *n Art & Archit* bas-relief *m*

bass[1] [beɪs] *Mus* **1** *n* (**a**) *(part, singer)* basse *f*; **to sing bass** chanter dans les basses
(**b**) *(bass guitar)* basse *f*; *(double bass)* contrebasse *f*
(**c**) *(on stereo)* basses *fpl*, graves *mpl*; *(knob)* bouton *m* de réglage des graves
2 *adj (note, pitch)* grave, bas; **a part for a bass voice** une partie pour voix de basse; **a singer with a bass voice** un chanteur à la voix de basse, une basse
►► ***bass clarinet*** clarinette *f* basse; *Mus* ***bass clef*** clef *f* de fa; ***bass drum*** grosse caisse *f*; ***bass guitar*** guitare *f* basse; *Mus* ***bass viol*** viole *f* de gambe

bass[2] [bæs] *n Ich (freshwater fish)* perche *f*; *(sea fish)* bar *m*, loup *m*

bass[3] [bæs] *n Tex (material)* tille *f*, filasse *f*

bass-baritone *n Mus* basse *f* chantante

basset ['bæsɪt] *n* basset *m (chien)*
►► *Mus* ***basset horn*** cor *m* de basset; ***basset hound*** basset *m (chien)*

bassinet [ˌbæsɪ'net] *n* (**a**) *(cradle → wickerwork)* moïse *m*; *(→ wooden)* berceau *m* (**b**) *(pram)* voiture *f* d'enfant

bassist ['beɪsɪst] *n Mus* bassiste *mf* de basse

basso-profondo, basso-profundo ['bæsəʊprə'fʌndəʊ] *n Mus* basse *f* profonde

bassoon [bə'su:n] *n* basson *m*; **double bassoon** contrebasson *m*

bassoonist [bə'su:nɪst] *n* basson *m*, bassoniste *mf*

bast [bæst] *n Tex (material)* tille *f*, filasse *f*

bastard ['bɑ:stəd] **1** *n* (**a**) *Literary or Pej (child)* bâtard(e) *m,f*
(**b**) *very Fam Pej (nasty person)* salaud (salope) *m,f*; **some bastard traffic warden gave me a parking ticket** une salope de contractuelle m'a collé un papillon
(**c**) *very Fam (derisively)* **poor bastard!** le pauvre!; **he's a stupid bastard!** c'est un pauvre con!
(**d**) *very Fam (affectionately)* **you lucky bastard!** sacré veinard!; **how are you, you old bastard?** comment ça va, enfoiré?
(**e**) *very Fam (difficult case, job)* truc *m* chiant; **it's a bastard of a book to translate** ce livre est vachement dur à traduire; **this job's a real bastard** ce boulot est une vraie vacherie; **I can't get the bastard thing to work** j'arrive pas à faire marcher cette saloperie
2 *adj* (**a**) *Literary or Pej (child)* bâtard
(**b**) *Ling (language)* corrompu
(**c**) *Typ (character)* d'un autre œil

bastardization [ˌbɑ:stədaɪ'zeɪʃən] *n* (**a**) *Ling (of language, style)* abâtardissement *m* (**b**) *(of child)* fait *m* de déclarer illégitime *ou* naturel

bastardize, -ise ['bɑ:stədaɪz] *vt* (**a**) *Ling (language, style)* abâtardir (**b**) *(child)* déclarer illégitime *ou* naturel

bastardy ['bɑ:stədɪ] *n Literary or Pej* bâtardise *f*

baste [beɪst] *vt* (**a**) *Culin* arroser (**b**) *Sewing* bâtir, faufiler (**c**) *(beat)* rouer de coups, rosser

basting ['beɪstɪŋ] *n* (**a**) *Culin* arrosage *m* (**b**) *Sewing* bâtissage *m* (**c**) *(beating)* raclée *f*, correction *f*

bastion ['bæstɪən] *n also Fig* bastion *m*; **the last bastion of Stalinism** le dernier bastion du stalinisme

Basutoland [bə'su:təʊlænd] *n Formerly* Basutoland *m*

BASW [ˌbi:eɪˌes'dʌbəlju:] *n* (*abbr* **British Association of Social Workers**) = syndicat britannique des travailleurs sociaux

bat [bæt] (*pt & pp* **batted**, *cont* **batting**) **1** *n* (**a**) *Sport (in baseball & cricket)* batte *f*; *(in table tennis)* raquette *f*; **he's a good bat** il manie bien la batte; *Am Fam* **right off the bat** sur-le-champ ❑; *Br Fam* **to do sth off one's own bat** faire qch de sa propre initiative ❑
(**b**) *(shot, blow)* coup *m*
(**c**) *(animal)* chauve-souris *f*; *Fam Pej* **she's an old bat** c'est une vieille bique *ou* chouette; *Fam* **to have bats in the** *or* **one's belfry** avoir une araignée au plafond; *Fam* **to run/to drive like a bat out of hell** courir/conduire comme si l'on avait le diable à ses trousses
(**d**) *Am very Fam (spree)* fête ❑ *f*, bringue *f*; **to go off on a bat** aller faire la bringue
2 *vi Sport (baseball player, cricketer → play)* manier la batte; *(→ take one's turn at playing)* être à la batte; **he batted for Pakistan** il était à la batte pour l'équipe pakistanaise; **to go in to bat** aller à la batte; *Am Fam Fig* **to go to bat for sb** intervenir en faveur de qn ❑
3 *vt* (**a**) *(hit)* donner un coup à
(**b**) *(blink)* **she batted her eyelids at him** elle battit des paupières en le regardant; *Fig* **he didn't bat an eyelid** il n'a pas sourcillé *ou* bronché; *Fig* **she did it without batting an eyelid** elle l'a fait sans broncher
►► *Am Sport* ***bat boy*** *(in baseball)* = garçon qui s'occupe des battes et de l'entretien du matériel
►**bat around** *vt sep Am Fam* **to bat sth around** parler de qch à bâtons rompus

batavia lettuce [bə'teɪvɪə-] *n* batavia *f*

batch [bætʃ] **1** *n (of letters)* paquet *m*, liasse *f*; *(of people)* groupe *m*; *(of refugees)* convoi *m*; *(of bread)* fournée *f*; *(of recruits)* contingent *m*; *Com* lot *m*; **in batches of 20** *(people)* par groupes de 20; *(files etc)* par lots de 20
2 *vt* grouper
►► *Comput* ***batch command*** commande *f* séquentielle; *Comput* ***batch file*** fichier *m* de

commandes; *Comput* ***batch processing*** traitement *m* par lots; *Ind* ***batch production*** production *f* par lots

bate [beɪt] **1** *n Br Old-fashioned (temper)* accès *m* de colère, crise *f*

2 *vi Literary (abate)* diminuer

bated ['beɪtɪd] *adj* **we waited with bated breath** nous avons attendu en retenant notre souffle

BATF [ˌbiːeɪˌtiː'ef] *n Am (abbr* **Bureau of Alcohol, Tobacco and Firearms**) = organisme gouvernemental américain dont le rôle est de veiller à ce que les lois concernant les boissons alcoolisées, le tabac et les armes à feu soient respectées

bath [bɑːθ] *(pl* **baths** [bɑːðz], *pt & pp* **bathed**) **1** *n* (**a**) *(wash)* bain *m*; *(tub)* baignoire *f*, *Can* bain *m*; **to give sb a bath** donner un bain à qn; **to** *Br* **have** *or Am* **take a bath** prendre un bain; **she's in the bath** elle prend son bain, elle est dans son bain; **to run** *or Formal* **to draw a bath** se faire couler un bain; **a room with bath** *(in hotel)* une chambre avec salle de bains

(**b**) *Chem (for chemicals, dye)* bain *m*; *Phot* cuvette *f*

2 *vt (baby, person)* baigner, donner un bain à

3 *vi Br* prendre un bain

4 baths *npl Br Old-fashioned (swimming pool)* piscine *f*; *(public baths)* bains-douches *mpl*; *(at spa)* thermes *mpl*

►► *Culin* ***bath bun*** = petit pain rond aux raisins secs souvent servi chaud et beurré; *Am* ***bath cap*** bonnet *m* de bain; ***bath chair*** fauteuil *m* roulant; *Br* ***bath cube*** cube *m* de sels de bain; ***bath mat*** tapis *m* de bain; ***bath oil*** huile *f* de bain; ***bath pearls*** perles *fpl* de bain; ***bath rail*** barre *f* de soutien; ***bath salts*** sels *mpl* de bain; ***bath sheet*** drap *m* de bain; ***bath towel*** serviette *f* de bain

bathe [beɪð] *(pt & pp* **bathed**) **1** *vi* (**a**) *Br Old-fashioned (swim)* se baigner; **we bathed in the sea/the river** nous avons pris un bain de mer/dans la rivière

(**b**) *Am (bath)* prendre un bain

2 *vt* (**a**) *(wound)* laver; *(eyes, feet)* baigner; **he bathed his eyes** il s'est baigné les yeux

(**b**) *(covered)* **I was bathed in sweat** j'étais en nage, je ruisselais de sueur; **the hills were bathed in light** les collines étaient éclairées d'une lumière douce; **her face was bathed in tears** son visage était baigné de larmes

(**c**) *Am (bath)* baigner, donner un bain à

3 *n Br Old-fashioned* bain *m (dans la mer, dans une rivière)*; **to have a bathe** se baigner; **we went for a bathe** nous sommes allés nous baigner

bather ['beɪðə(r)] **1** *n (swimmer)* baigneur(euse) *m,f*

2 bathers *npl Austr Fam (costume)* maillot *m* de bain ❑

bathetic [bæ'θetɪk] *adj Literature* = qui offre un contraste ridicule avec la pensée qui précède

bathhouse ['bɑːθhaʊs, *pl* -haʊzɪz] *n* bains-douches *mpl (bâtiment)*

bathing ['beɪðɪŋ] *n (UNCOUNT)* (**a**) *Br (swimming)* baignade *f*; **not safe for bathing** *(sign)* baignade interdite; **the water isn't warm enough for bathing** l'eau n'est pas assez chaude pour se baigner

(**b**) *(washing → of wound)* lavage *m*

►► ***bathing beauty*** belle *f* baigneuse; ***bathing cap*** bonnet *m* de bain; ***bathing costume*** maillot *m* de bain; ***bathing hut*** cabine *f* de bains; ***bathing machine*** cabine *f* de bains roulante; ***bathing suit*** maillot *m* de bain; *Br* ***bathing trunks*** maillot *m* de bain

bathometer [bə'θɒmɪtə(r)] *n* bathomètre *m*, bathymètre *m*

bathos ['beɪθɒs] *n (UNCOUNT) Literature* chute *f* du sublime au ridicule

bathrobe ['bɑːθrəʊb] *n* (**a**) *(for bathroom, swimming pool)* peignoir *m* de bain (**b**) *Am (dressing gown)* robe *f* de chambre

bathroom ['bɑːθrʊm] **1** *n* salle *f* de bains; *Euph* **to use** *or* **to go to the bathroom** aller aux toilettes

2 *comp (cabinet, mirror)* de salle de bains

►► ***bathroom scales*** pèse-personne *m*; ***bathroom suite*** salle *f* de bains *(mobilier)*

Bathsheba [ˌbæθ'ʃiːbə] *pr n Bible* Bethsabée

bathtime ['bɑːθtaɪm] *n* l'heure *f* du bain

bathtub ['bɑːθtʌb] *n* baignoire *f*, *Can* bain *m*

bathwater ['bɑːθˌwɔːtə(r)] *n* eau *f* du bain

bathymetry [bə'θɪmɪtrɪ] *n* bathymétrie *f*

bathyscaphe ['bæθɪskæf] *n Naut* bathyscaphe *m*

bathysphere ['bæθɪˌsfɪə(r)] *n Naut* bathysphère *f*

batik [bə'tiːk] *Tex* **1** *n (cloth, technique)* batik *m*

2 *comp (scarf, skirt)* en batik

batiste [bæ'tiːst] *n Tex* batiste *f*

batman ['bætmən] *(pl* **batmen** [-mən]) *n Br Mil* ordonnance *m ou f*

baton ['bætən] *n* (**a**) *Mus (conductor's)* baguette *f*; **under the baton of** sous la baguette *ou* la direction de (**b**) *(policeman's → in traffic)* bâton *m*; *(→ in riots)* matraque *f* (**c**) *Sport* témoin *m*; *Fig* **to pass the baton to sb** donner le relais à qn

►► ***baton charge*** charge *f* à la matraque; ***baton gun*** fusil *m* à balles en plastique; ***baton round*** balle *f* en plastique

batrachian [bə'treɪkɪən] *Zool* **1** *n* batracien *m*

2 *adj* batrachian

bats [bæts] *adj Fam* timbré, cinglé

batsman ['bætsmən] *(pl* **batsmen** [-mən]) *n Sport* batteur *m*

battalion [bə'tæljən] *n Mil & Fig* bataillon *m*

battels ['bætəlz] *npl Univ* = compte d'un étudiant à Oxford

batten ['bætən] **1** *n Carp & Constr (board)* latte *f*, lambourde *f*; *(in roof)* volige *f*; *(in floor)* latte *f*, lame *f* de parquet; *Naut* latte *f* de voile; *Theat* herse *f*

2 *vt Carp & Constr* latter; *(floor)* planchéier; *(roof)* voliger

►► *Constr* ***batten plate*** traverse *f* de liaison

►**batten down** *vt sep* **to batten down the hatches** fermer les écoutilles, condamner les panneaux; *Fig* dresser ses batteries

►**batten on, batten upon** *vt insep Br* **she immediately battened on me for help** elle s'est immédiatement accrochée à moi comme une sangsue pour que je l'aide

Battenburg cake ['bætənˌbɜːg-] *n Br Culin* = génoise recouverte de pâte d'amandes

batter ['bætə(r)] **1** *vt* (**a**) *(beat → person)* battre, maltraiter

(**b**) *(hammer → door, wall)* frapper sur

(**c**) *(buffet)* **the ship was battered by the waves** le vaisseau était battu par les vagues; *Fig* **he felt battered by the experience** il se sentait ravagé par l'expérience

2 *vi (hammer)* **to batter at** *or* **on the door** frapper à la porte à coups redoublés; **the waves battered against the coast** les vagues s'abattaient le long de la côte

3 *n* (**a**) *Typ (plate)* cliché *m* endommagé; *(print)* tirage *m* défectueux

(**b**) *Culin* pâte *f* à crêpes

(**c**) *Sport (in baseball)* batteur *m*

►**batter about** *vt sep* (**a**) *(person)* maltraiter, rouer de coups

(**b**) *Naut (ship)* battre

►**batter down** *vt sep Agr (vegetation)* fouler; *(wall)* démolir; *(tree)* abattre

►**batter in** *vt sep (skull)* défoncer; *(door)* enfoncer; *Carp (nail)* enfoncer à grands coups

battered ['bætəd] *adj (building)* délabré; *(car, hat)* cabossé, bosselé; *(briefcase, suitcase)* cabossé; *(face → beaten)* meurtri; *(→ ravaged)* buriné; **a battered child** un(e) enfant martyr(e) *ou* battu(e); **a refuge for battered wives** un refuge pour femmes battues

battering ['bætərɪŋ] *n* (**a**) *(beating)* **he got a bad battering** on l'a rossé sévèrement (**b**) *(hammering)* **the building took a battering in the war** le bâtiment a été durement éprouvé pendant la guerre; **his confidence took a battering** sa confiance en soi en a pris un coup; **the team took a bad battering** l'équipe a été battue à plate(s) couture(s)

►► ***battering ram*** bélier *m*

Battersea ['bætəsɪ] *n* = quartier de Londres

►► ***Battersea Dogs' Home*** = centre d'accueil des chats et chiens abandonnés situé à Battersea; ***Battersea Power Station*** = centrale électrique désaffectée qui marque le paysage londonien de ses quatre grandes cheminées

battery ['bætərɪ] *(pl* **batteries**) *n* (**a**) *(in clock, radio)* pile *f*; *(in car)* batterie *f*, accumulateurs *mpl*; **batteries not included** *(on packaging, in catalogue)* livré sans piles

(**b**) *Mil (of guns, missiles)* batterie *f*

(**c**) *(barrage)* tir *m* de barrage; **a battery of insults** une pluie d'insultes; **a battery of criticism** un feu roulant de critiques

(**d**) *Law see* **assault**

(**e**) *Agr* batterie *f*

►► *Elec* ***battery charger*** chargeur *m*; *Agr* ***battery farming*** élevage *m* intensif *ou* en batterie; *Agr* ***battery hen*** poule *f* de batterie; *Elec* ***battery pack*** boîtier *m* d'alimentation par pile; ***Battery Park*** = parc de Manhattan d'où l'on embarque pour aller visiter la Statue de la Liberté

battery-operated [-ˌɒpəreɪtɪd], **battery-powered** *adj (radio, toy)* **to be battery-operated** *or* **battery-powered** fonctionner sur piles

battery-reared [-'rɪəd] *adj Agr* de batterie

batting ['bætɪŋ] *n* (**a**) *Constr (wadding)* bourre *f (pour matelas, couettes)* (**b**) *Sport* maniement *m* de la batte; **he has a high batting average** il a un score élevé à la batte

battle ['bætəl] **1** *n* (**a**) *(fight)* bataille *f*; *Fig* lutte *f*; **he was killed in battle** il a été tué au combat; **to do** *or* **to give** *or* **to join battle** livrer bataille; **to do battle with sb** livrer bataille à qn; **in battle order** en bataille; **a battle between the two companies** une lutte entre les deux entreprises; **a battle for control of the government** un combat pour obtenir le contrôle du gouvernement; **the battle between** *or* **of the sexes** la lutte des sexes; **a battle of wits** une joute d'esprit

(**b**) *(struggle)* lutte *f*; **the battle for freedom** la lutte pour la liberté; **the battle against poverty** la lutte contre la pauvreté; **life is one long battle at the moment** de nos jours la vie est un long combat; **to do battle for** lutter pour; **to do battle against** *or* **with** lutter contre; **we're fighting the same battle** nous nous battons pour la même cause; **don't fight his battles for him** ne te bats pas à sa place; **it's half the battle** la partie est presque gagnée

2 *comp Mil (dress, zone)* de combat

3 *vi* se battre, lutter; **she battled to save his life** elle s'est battue pour lui sauver la vie; **he's battling against the system** il se bat contre le système; **they battled between themselves** ils se battirent entre eux

4 *vt Am Mil* combattre

►► *Hist* ***the Battle of the Boyne*** la bataille de la Boyne *(bataille qui mit fin au rôle politique des Stuart en Irlande)*; *Hist* ***the Battle of Britain*** la bataille d'Angleterre; ***Battle of Britain Day*** = jour commémoratif de la bataille d'Angleterre; *Hist* ***the Battle of the Bulge*** la bataille des Ardennes; *Hum* ***the battle of the bulge*** la lutte contre les kilos; *Naut & Mil* ***battle cruiser*** croiseur *m* cuirassé; *Mil* ***battle cry*** cri *m* de guerre; ***battle fatigue*** psychose *f* traumatique; *Hist* ***the Battle of Hastings*** la bataille de Hastings; *Hist* ***the Battle of the Nile*** la bataille d'Aboukir; ***battle royal*** *(fight)* bagarre *f*; *(argument)* querelle *f*; *Mil* ***battle zone*** zone *f* de bataille *ou* d'engagement

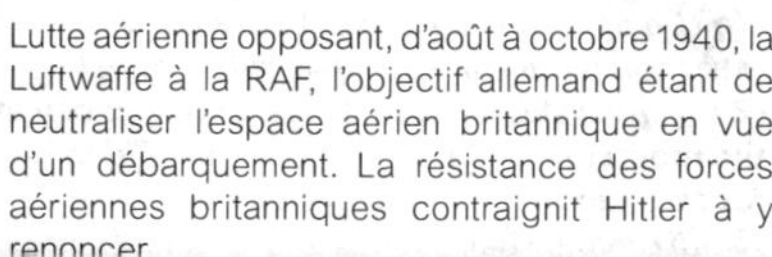

THE BATTLE OF BRITAIN

Lutte aérienne opposant, d'août à octobre 1940, la Luftwaffe à la RAF, l'objectif allemand étant de neutraliser l'espace aérien britannique en vue d'un débarquement. La résistance des forces aériennes britanniques contraignit Hitler à y renoncer.

battleaxe, *Am* **battleax** ['bætəlæks] *n* (**a**) *Hist & Mil (weapon)* hache *f* d'armes (**b**) *Fam Pej (woman)* virago *f*, mégère *f*

battledore ['bætəldɔː(r)] *n Sport (racket)* raquette *f*; **battledore (and shuttlecock)** *(game)* jeu *m* de volant

battledress ['bætəldres] *n Mil* tenue *f* de combat

battlefield ['bætəlfiːld], **battleground** ['bætəlgraʊnd] *n Mil & Fig* champ *m* de bataille

battle-hardened *adj Mil* aguerri

battlement ['bætəlmənt] **1** *n (crenellation)* créneau *m*

2 battlements *npl (wall)* remparts *mpl*

battlemented ['bætəlməntɪd] *adj* crénelé

battler ['bætlə(r)] *n Austr Fam* battant(e) *m,f*

battle-scarred *adj Mil (army, landscape)* marqué par les combats; *(person)* marqué par la vie; *Hum (car, table)* abîmé

battleship ['bætəlˌʃɪp] *n Naut & Mil* cuirassé *m*

'The Battleship Potemkin' *Eisenstein* 'Le Cuirassé Potemkine'

batty ['bætɪ] *(compar* **battier,** *superl* **battiest)** *adj Fam (crazy)* cinglé, dingue; *(eccentric)* farfelu

batwing sleeve ['bætwɪŋ-] *n* manche *f* chauve-souris

bauble ['bɔ:bəl] *n (trinket)* babiole *f*, colifichet *m*; *(jester's)* marotte *f*

baud [bɔ:d] *n Comput & Elec* baud *m*
►► ***baud rate*** débit *m* en bauds

bauhinia [bɔ:'hɪnɪə] *n Bot* bauhinie *f*

baulk = **balk**

bauxite ['bɔ:ksaɪt] *n Miner* bauxite *f*

Bavaria [bə'veərɪə] *n* Bavière *f*; **in Bavaria** en Bavière

Bavarian [bə'veərɪən] **1** *n* Bavarois(e) *m,f*
2 *adj Ling* bavarois
►► *Culin* ***Bavarian cream*** bavaroise *f*

bawbee [bɔ:'bi:] *n Scot Hist* sou *m*

bawd [bɔ:d] *n Arch (prostitute)* catin *f*

bawdily ['bɔ:dɪlɪ] *adv* de manière paillarde

bawdiness ['bɔ:dɪnɪs] *n* paillardise *f*

bawdy ['bɔ:dɪ] *adj* paillard
►► *Arch* ***bawdy house*** maison *f* close

bawl [bɔ:l] **1** *vi* **(a)** *(yell)* brailler; **to bawl at sb** crier après qn **(b)** *Fam (weep)* brailler; **the baby was bawling his head off** le bébé braillait à pleins poumons
2 *vt (slogan, word)* brailler, hurler

►**bawl out** *vt sep* **(a)** *(yell)* brailler, hurler **(b)** *Fam (reprimand)* passer un savon à; **she really bawled him out** elle lui a passé un bon savon **(c)** *Fam (weep)* **the child was bawling his eyes out** l'enfant braillait à pleins poumons

bawling ['bɔ:lɪŋ] *n* **(a)** *(yelling)* hurlements *mpl*, braillements *mpl* **(b)** *Fam (weeping)* braillement(s) *m(pl)*; **stop that bawling** arrête de brailler
►► *Fam* ***bawling out*** *(reprimand)* engueulade *f*; **to give sb a bawling out** engueuler qn; **to get a bawling out** se faire engueuler

bay [beɪ] **1** *n* **(a)** *Geog* baie *f*; *(smaller)* anse *f*
(b) *Archit* travée *f*; *(recess)* renfoncement *m*, niche *f*; *(window)* fenêtre *f* en saillie
(c) *Br (in bus station, car park)* aire *f* de stationnement; *Rail* voie *f* d'arrêt
(d) *Bot & Culin* laurier *m*; **sweet bay** laurier *m* commun, laurier *m* des poètes
(e) *Hunt & Fig* **to be at bay** être aux abois; *Hunt* **to bring an animal to bay** acculer un animal; **to keep** *or* **hold at bay** *Mil (the enemy)* tenir en échec; *(assailant)* tenir en respect; *(creditors, persistent caller etc)* tenir à distance; **to keep boredom at bay** tromper l'ennui; **I'm managing to keep my cold at bay** jusqu'ici j'ai réussi à combattre le rhume; **to keep** *or* **to hold hunger at bay** tromper la faim; **use this product to keep ants at bay** utilisez ce produit pour éloigner les fourmis
(f) *Zool (horse)* cheval *m* bai
(g) *Comput (for disk drive)* baie *f*
(h) *(compartment → in plane, ship)* soute *f*
2 *vi (bark)* aboyer, donner de la voix; **to bay at the moon** hurler *ou* aboyer à la lune; *Fig* **to bay for sb's blood** réclamer la tête de qn
3 *adj (colour)* bai
►► ***the Bay Area*** = région de la baie de San Francisco comprenant également les villes de Berkeley, Oakland et San José; ***the Bay of Bengal*** le golfe du Bengale; ***the Bay of Biscay*** le golfe de Gascogne; *Bot & Culin* ***bay laurel*** laurier *m* commun, laurier *m* des poètes; *Bot & Culin* ***bay leaf*** feuille *f* de laurier; *Hist* ***the Bay of Pigs*** la baie des Cochons; *Pharm* ***bay rum*** = lotion capillaire; ***the Bay State*** = surnom donné au Massachusetts; *Bot* ***bay tree*** laurier *m*; ***bay window*** *Archit* fenêtre *f* en saillie; *Am Fam (stomach)* gros bide *m*

THE BAY OF PIGS

On désigne ainsi la tentative de coup d'État contre Fidel Castro par des Cubains exilés aux États-Unis, en 1961. Équipés et entraînés par la CIA, ils débarquèrent dans cette baie, mais l'opération tourna au désastre.

bayberry ['beɪbərɪ] *n Bot* **(a)** *(berry)* baie *f* de laurier **(b)** *(allspice tree)* piment *m* de la Jamaïque **(c)** *Am (wax myrtle)* cirier *m*, arbre *m* à cire

baying ['beɪɪŋ] *n (UNCOUNT) (barking)* aboiement *m*

bayonet ['beɪənɪt] *(pt & pp* **bayoneted** *or* **bayonetted,** *cont* **bayoneting** *or* **bayonetting)** *Mil* **1** *n* baïonnette *f*; **with fixed bayonets** baïonnette au canon; *Mil* **at bayonet point** à la pointe de la baïonnette
2 *vt* passer à la baïonnette
►► *Mil* ***bayonet charge*** charge *f* à la baïonnette; *Tech* ***bayonet joint*** joint *m* à baïonnette; *Tech* ***bayonet socket*** douille *f* à baïonnette

bayou ['baɪu:] *n Am Geog* bayou *m*, marécages *mpl*

bazaar [bə'zɑ:(r)] *n (in East)* bazar *m*; *(sale for charity)* vente *f* de charité; *(shop)* bazar *m*

bazooka [bə'zu:kə] *n Mil* bazooka *m*

BB [ˌbi:'bi:] *n* **(a)** *(abbr* **Boys' Brigade)** = organisation protestante de scoutisme pour garçons **(b)** *(abbr* **double black)** = sur un crayon à papier, indique une mine grasse **(c)** *Am (abbr* **bail bond)** cautionnement *m*
►► *Am* ***BB gun*** fusil *m* à air comprimé

BBB [ˌbi:bi:'bi:] *n Am (abbr* **Better Business Bureau)** = organisme dont la vocation est de faire respecter la déontologie professionnelle dans le secteur tertiaire

BBC [ˌbi:bi:'si:] *n (abbr* **British Broadcasting Corporation) the BBC** la BBC *(office national britannique de radiodiffusion)*; **BBC1** = chaîne généraliste de la BBC; **BBC2** = chaîne à vocation culturelle de la BBC
►► ***BBC English*** = l'anglais tel qu'il était parlé sur la BBC et qui servait de référence pour la "bonne" prononciation; ***BBC World Service*** = émissions radiophoniques de la BBC diffusées dans le monde entier

bbl. *(written abbr* **barrel)** baril *m*

BBQ [ˌbi:bi:'kju:] *n (abbr* **barbecue)** barbecue *m*

BBS [ˌbi:bi:'es] *n Comput (abbr* **bulletin board system)** serveur *m* télématique, *Can* babillard *m*

BC[1] [ˌbi:'si:] *(abbr* **before Christ)** av. J.C.; **in the year 25 BC** en l'an 25 avant Jésus-Christ

BC[2] *(written abbr* **British Columbia)** Colombie-Britannique *f*

Bcc [ˌbi:si:'si:] *n Comput (abbr* **blind carbon copy)** copie *f* cachée

BCCI [ˌbi:si:ˌsi:'aɪ] *n Banking (abbr* **Bank of Credit and Commerce International)** BCCI *f*

BCD [ˌbi:si:'di:] *n Comput (abbr* **binary-coded decimal)** DCB *m*

BCE [ˌbi:si:'i:] *n (abbr* **Board of Customs and Excise)** = douane britannique

BCG [ˌbi:si:'dʒi:] *n Med (abbr* **bacille Calmette-Guérin)** BCG *m*
►► ***BCG vaccination*** vaccin *m* BCG

BD [ˌbi:'di:] *n* **(a)** *(abbr* **Bachelor of Divinity)** *(person)* = titulaire d'une licence de théologie; *(qualification)* licence *f* de théologie **(b)** *Am Fin (abbr* **bank draft)** traite *f* bancaire

BDS [ˌbi:di:'es] *n (abbr* **Bachelor of Dental Science)** *(person)* = titulaire d'une licence de chirurgie dentaire; *(qualification)* licence *f* de chirurgie dentaire

BE [ˌbi:'i:] *n (abbr* **Bank of England)** Banque *f* d'Angleterre

b/e *Fin (written abbr* **bill of exchange)** lettre *f* de change

BE [bi:]

être	► **1 (a) – (c), (f), (h), (i), (m), (o), (p); 2**
aller	► **1 (d)**
avoir	► **1 (e)**
mesurer	► **1 (g)**
coûter	► **1 (j)**
il y a	► **1 (k)**
voici, voilà	► **1 (l)**
faire	► **1 (n), (q)**
aller, venir	► **1 (o)**
Dans les question tags	► **2 (j)**

(pres 1st sing **am** [əm, *stressed* æm], *pres 2nd sing* **are** [ə, *stressed* ɑ:(r)], *pres 3rd sing* **is** [ɪz], *pres pl* **are** [ə, *stressed* ɑ:(r)], *pt 1st sing* **was** [wəz, *stressed* wɒz], *pt 2nd sing* **were** [wə, *stressed* wɜ:(r)], *pt 3rd sing* **was** [wəz, *stressed* wɒz], *pt pl* **were** [wə, *stressed* wɜ:(r)], *pp* **been** [bi:n], *cont* **being** ['bi:ɪŋ])

À l'oral et dans un style familier à l'écrit, le verbe **be** peut être contracté: **I am** devient **I'm, he/she/it is** deviennent **he's/she's/it's** et **you/we/they are** deviennent **you're/we're/they're**. Les formes négatives **is not/are not/was not** et **were not** se contractent respectivement en **isn't/aren't/wasn't** et **weren't**.

1 *vi* **(a)** *(exist, live)* être, exister; **I think, therefore I am** je pense, donc je suis; **to be or not to be** être ou ne pas être; **God is** Dieu existe; **the greatest scientist that ever was** le plus grand savant qui ait jamais existé *ou* de tous les temps; **there are no such things as ghosts** les fantômes n'existent pas; **she's a genius if ever there was one** c'est *ou* voilà un génie si jamais il en fut; **as happy as can be** heureux comme un roi; **that may be, but…** cela se peut, mais…, peut-être, mais…
(b) *(used to identify, describe)* être; **she is my sister** c'est ma sœur; **I'm Elaine** je suis *ou* je m'appelle Elaine; **she's a doctor/engineer** elle est médecin/ingénieur; **the glasses were crystal** les verres étaient en cristal; **he is American** il est américain, c'est un Américain; **be careful!** soyez prudent!; **to be frank…** pour être franc…, franchement…; **being the boy's mother, I have a right to know** étant la mère de l'enfant, j'ai le droit de savoir; **the situation being what** *or* **as it is…** la situation étant ce qu'elle est…; **the problem is knowing** *or* **is to know when to stop** le problème, c'est de savoir quand s'arrêter; **the rule is: when in doubt, don't do it** la règle c'est: dans le doute abstiens-toi; **seeing is believing** voir, c'est croire; **just be yourself** soyez vous-même, soyez naturel; **you be Batman and I'll be Robin** *(children playing)* on dirait que tu es Batman et moi je suis Robin
(c) *(indicating temporary state or condition)* **he was angry/tired** il était fâché/fatigué; **I am hungry/thirsty/afraid** j'ai faim/soif/peur; **my feet/hands are frozen** j'ai les pieds gelés/mains gelées
(d) *(indicating health)* aller, se porter; **how are you?** comment allez-vous?, comment ça va?; **I am fine** ça va; **he is not well** il est malade, il ne va pas bien
(e) *(indicating age)* avoir; **how old are you?** quel âge avez-vous?; **I'm twelve (years old)** j'ai douze ans; **it's different when you're fifty** ce n'est pas pareil quand on a cinquante ans; **you'll see when you're fifty** tu verras quand tu auras cinquante ans
(f) *(indicating location)* être; **the cake was on the table** le gâteau était sur la table; **the hotel is next to the river** l'hôtel se trouve *ou* est près de la rivière; **be there at nine o'clock** soyez-y à neuf heures; **where was I?** où étais-je?; *Fig (in book, speech)* où en étais-je?
(g) *(indicating measurement)* **the table is one metre long** la table fait un mètre de long; **how tall is he?** combien mesure-t-il?; **he is two metres tall** il mesure *ou* fait deux mètres; **the school is two kilometres from here** l'école est à deux kilomètres d'ici
(h) *(indicating time, date)* être; **it's five o'clock** il est cinq heures; **yesterday was Monday** hier on était *ou* c'était lundi; **today is Tuesday** nous sommes *ou* c'est mardi aujourd'hui; **what date is it today?** le combien sommes-nous aujourd'hui?; **it's the 16th of December** nous sommes *ou* c'est le 16 décembre
(i) *(happen, occur)* être, avoir lieu; **the concert is on Saturday night** le concert est *ou* a lieu samedi soir; **when is your birthday?** quand est *ou* c'est quand ton anniversaire?; **the spring holidays are in March this year** les vacances de printemps tombent en mars cette année; **how is it that you arrived so quickly?** comment se fait-il que vous soyez arrivé si vite?
(j) *(indicating cost)* coûter; **how much is this table?** combien coûte *ou* vaut cette table?; **it is expensive** ça coûte *ou* c'est cher; **the phone bill is £75** la facture de téléphone est de 75 livres
(k) *(with "there")* **there is, there are** il y a,

Literary il est; **there is** *or* **has been no snow** il n'y a pas de neige; **there are six of them** ils sont *ou* il y en a six; **what is there to do?** qu'est-ce qu'il y a à faire?; **there will be swimming** on nagera; **there is nothing funny about it** il n'y a rien d'amusant là-dedans, ce n'est pas drôle; **there's no telling what she'll do** il est impossible de prévoir ce qu'elle va faire

(**l**) *(calling attention to)* **this is my friend John** voici mon ami John; **here are the reports you wanted** voici les rapports que vous vouliez; **there is our car** voilà notre voiture; **there are the others** voilà les autres; **here I am** me voici; **there you are!** *(I've found you)* ah, te voilà!; *(take this)* tiens, voilà!; **now there's an idea!** voilà une bonne idée!

(**m**) *(with 'it')* **who is it? – it's us!** qui est-ce? – c'est nous!; **it was your mother who decided** c'est ta mère qui a décidé; *Formal* **it is I who am to blame** c'est moi le responsable

(**n**) *(indicating weather)* faire; **it is cold/hot/grey** il fait froid/chaud/gris; **it is windy** il y a du vent

(**o**) *(go)* aller, être; *(come)* être, venir; **she's been to visit her mother** elle a été *ou* est allée rendre visite à sa mère; **I have never been to China** je ne suis jamais allé *ou* je n'ai jamais été en Chine; **have you been home since Christmas?** est-ce que tu es rentré (chez toi) depuis Noël?; **has the plumber been?** le plombier est-il (déjà) passé?; **wait for us, we'll be there in ten minutes** attends-nous, nous serons là dans dix minutes; **there's no need to rush, we'll be there in ten minutes** inutile de se presser, nous y serons dans dix minutes; **he was into/out of the house in a flash** il est entré dans/sorti de la maison en coup de vent; **I know, I've been there** je sais, j'y suis allé; *Fig* je sais, j'ai connu ça; **she is from Egypt** elle vient d'Égypte; **your brother has been and gone** votre frère est venu et reparti; **someone had been there in her absence** quelqu'un est venu pendant son absence; *Br Fam* **he's only been and wrecked the car!** il est allé casser la voiture!; *Br Fam* **now you've been (and gone) and done it!** *(caused trouble, broken something)* et voilà, c'est réussi!

(**p**) *(indicating hypothesis, supposition)* **if I were you** si j'étais vous *ou* à votre place; **if we were younger** si nous étions plus jeunes; *Formal* **were it not for my sister** sans ma sœur; *Formal* **were it not for their contribution, the school would close** sans leur assistance, l'école serait obligée de fermer

(**q**) *(in calculations)* faire; **1 and 1 are 2** 1 et 1 font 2; **what is 5 less 3?** combien fait 5 moins 3?

2 *v aux* (**a**) *(forming continuous tenses)* **he is having breakfast** il prend *ou* il est en train de prendre son petit déjeuner; **they are always giggling** ils sont toujours en train de glousser; **where are you going?** où allez-vous?; **a problem which is getting worse and worse** un problème qui s'aggrave; **I have just been thinking about you** je pensais justement à toi; **we've been waiting hours for you** ça fait des heures que nous t'attendons; **when will she be leaving?** quand est-ce qu'elle part *ou* va-t-elle partir?; **what are you going to do about it?** qu'est-ce que vous allez *ou* comptez faire?; **why aren't you working? – but I AM working!** pourquoi ne travaillez-vous pas? – mais je travaille!

(**b**) *(forming passive voice)* **she is known as a good negotiator** elle est connue pour ses talents de négociatrice; **the car was found** la voiture a été retrouvée; **plans are being made** on fait des projets; **what is left to do?** qu'est-ce qui reste à faire?; **smoking is not permitted** il est interdit *ou* défendu de fumer; **socks are sold by the pair** les chaussettes se vendent par deux; **it is said/thought/assumed that...** on dit/pense/suppose que...; **to be continued** *(TV programme, serialized story)* à suivre; **not to be confused with** à ne pas confondre avec

(**c**) *(with infinitive → indicating future event)* **the next meeting is to take place on Wednesday** la prochaine réunion aura lieu mercredi; **he's to be the new headmaster** c'est lui qui sera le nouveau directeur; **she was to become a famous pianist** elle allait devenir une pianiste renommée; **we were never to see him again** nous ne devions jamais le revoir

(**d**) *(with infinitive → indicating expected event)* **they were to have been married in June** ils devaient se marier en juin

(**e**) *(with infinitive → indicating obligation)* **I'm to be home by ten o'clock** il faut que je rentre avant dix heures; **you are not to speak to strangers** il ne faut pas parler aux inconnus

(**f**) *(with infinitive → expressing opinion)* **you are to be congratulated** on doit vous féliciter; **they are to be pitied** ils sont à plaindre

(**g**) *(with infinitive → requesting information)* **are we then to assume that taxes will decrease?** faut-il *ou* doit-on en conclure que les impôts vont diminuer?; **what am I to say to them?** qu'est-ce que je vais leur dire?

(**h**) *(with passive infinitive → indicating possibility)* **bargains are to be found even in the West End** on peut faire de bonnes affaires même dans le West End; **she was not to be dissuaded** rien ne devait *ou* il fut impossible de lui faire changer d'avis

(**i**) *Formal (with infinitive → indicating hypothesis)* **if he were** *or* **were he to die** s'il venait à mourir, à supposer qu'il meure

(**j**) *(in question tags)* **he's always causing trouble, isn't he? – yes, he is** il est toujours en train de créer des problèmes, n'est-ce pas? – oui, toujours; **you're back, are you?** vous êtes revenu alors?; **you're not leaving already, are you?** vous ne partez pas déjà, j'espère?

(**k**) *(in ellipsis)* **is she satisfied? – she is** est-elle satisfaite? – oui(, elle l'est); **you're angry – no I'm not – oh yes you are!** tu es fâché – non – mais si!; **it's a touching scene – not for me, it isn't** c'est une scène émouvante – je ne trouve pas *ou* pas pour moi; **I was pleased to see him but the children weren't** (moi,) j'étais content de le voir mais pas les enfants

(**l**) *(forming perfect tenses)* **we're finished** nous avons terminé; *Rel* **Christ is risen** (le) Christ est ressucité; **when I looked again, they were gone** quand j'ai regardé de nouveau, ils étaient partis

(**m**) *(as suffix)* **the husband-to-be** le futur mari; **the father-to-be** le futur père

3 be that as it may *adv* quoi qu'il en soit

---

beach [biːtʃ] **1** *n (seaside)* plage *f*; *(shore → sand, shingle)* grève *f*; *(at lake)* rivage *m*; *Am Fam Fig* **it was no day at the beach** c'était pas du gâteau

2 *comp (ball, towel, hut)* de plage

3 *vt Naut (boat)* échouer; **beached whale** baleine *f* échouée; *Fig* **she was lying on the sofa like a beached whale** elle était là, énorme, vautrée sur le canapé

►► ***beach ball*** ballon *m* de plage; ***beach buggy*** buggy *m*; *Fam* ***beach bum*** = jeune qui passe son temps à la plage; *Am Fam* ***beach bunny*** petite pépée *f (qui passe son temps à la plage)*; ***beach hut*** cabine *f* (de bains *ou* de plage); ***beach soccer*** football *m* de plage, beach soccer *m*; ***beach umbrella*** parasol *m*; ***beach volleyball*** beach-volley *m*

> **We shall fight them on the beaches**
> Ces mots ("nous les combattrons sur les plages") furent prononcés par Churchill dans un de ses discours les plus fameux pendant la Deuxième Guerre mondiale, dans lequel il encourageait les Britanniques à se préparer à lutter en cas de débarquement nazi.
> Aujourd'hui encore on utilise cette formule métaphoriquement pour exprimer sa volonté farouche de continuer le combat et de ne jamais s'avouer vaincu.

beachchair ['biːtʃ,tʃeə(r)] *n Am* chaise *f* longue, transat *m*

beachcomber ['biːtʃ,kəʊmə(r)] *n (collector)* = personne qui ramasse des objets sur les plages; *(wave)* vague *f* déferlante

beachcombing ['biːtʃ,kəʊmɪŋ] *n* = ramassage d'objets sur les plages; **to go beachcombing** aller ramasser des choses sur la plage

beachfront ['biːtʃfrʌnt] *n* plage *f*; **on the beachfront** au bord de la plage

►► ***beachfront property*** propriété *f* qui donne sur la plage

beachhead ['biːtʃhed] *n Mil* tête *f* de pont; **to establish** *or* **to secure a beachhead** mettre en place une tête de pont sur la plage

beachwear ['biːtʃweə(r)] *n (UNCOUNT) (one outfit)* tenue *f* de plage; *(several outfits)* articles *mpl* de plage

beacon ['biːkən] **1** *n* (**a**) *(warning signal)* phare *m*, signal *m* lumineux; *(lantern)* fanal *m*; *(marking channel, runway)* balise *f*; *Fig* phare *m*; **a beacon of hope** une source d'espoir (**b**) *(bonfire on hill)* feu *m* d'alarme (**c**) *(in place names)* colline *f*

2 *vt Literary (area, coastline)* éclairer

►► ***beacon light*** balise *f*

bead [biːd] **1** *n* (**a**) *(of glass, wood)* perle *f*; *Rel (for rosary)* grain *m*; **bead necklace** collier *m* de perles (artificielles); **where are my beads?** où est mon collier?; *Rel* **to tell one's beads** égrener *ou* dire son chapelet

(**b**) *(drop → of sweat)* goutte *f*; *(→ of water, dew)* perle *f*; *(bubble)* bulle *f*; **beads of sweat stood out on her forehead** la sueur perlait sur son front

(**c**) *Tech (on gun)* guidon *m*; *Br* **to draw a bead on sb** viser qn

2 *vt* (**a**) *(decorate)* décorer de perles

(**b**) *Archit & Carp (in carpentry)* appliquer une baguette sur

3 *vi (form drops)* perler

►► ***bead curtain*** rideau *m* de perles

beaded ['biːdɪd] *adj* (**a**) *(decorated)* couvert *ou* orné de perles; **a beaded evening bag** un sac (à main) de soirée brodé de perles (**b**) *(with moisture)* couvert de gouttelettes d'eau; **beaded with sweat** couvert de gouttes de sueur

beading ['biːdɪŋ] *n* (**a**) *Archit* astragale *m*; *(in carpentry)* baguette *f* (**b**) *Sewing (trim)* garniture *f* de perles; *(over cloth)* broderie *f* perlée

beadle ['biːdəl] *n* (**a**) *Rel* bedeau *m* (**b**) *Br Univ* appariteur *m*

beady ['biːdɪ] *(compar* **beadier**, *superl* **beadiest**) *adj (eyes, gaze)* perçant; *Br Fam* **I've got my beady eye on you** je t'ai à l'œil; **I had to keep a beady eye on the sweets** il fallait que je surveille les bonbons de près; **his beady eyes never left the money** il ne détacha pas ses yeux de fouine de l'argent

beady-eyed *adj* aux yeux de fouine; *Fig (piercing)* au regard perçant; *Pej (curious)* au regard inquisiteur

beagle ['biːgəl] **1** *n* beagle *m*

2 *vi Hunt* chasser avec des beagles

3 Beagle *n Br Hist* **HMS Beagle** = nom du navire sur lequel Charles Darwin effectua un voyage scientifique autour du monde

beagling ['biːglɪŋ] *n Hunt* **to go beagling** aller à la chasse avec des beagles

beak [biːk] *n* (**a**) *(of bird, tortoise, jug, vase etc)* bec *m* (**b**) *Fam (nose)* blair *m*, tarin *m*; *(hooked)* nez *m* crochu ▫ (**c**) *Br Fam (judge)* juge ▫ *m*; *(headmaster)* dirlo *m*

beaked [biːkt] *adj (nose)* crochu

beaker ['biːkə(r)] *n* gobelet *m*; *Chem* vase *m* à bec

be-all and end-all *n Fam (aim)* but *m* suprême ▫, fin *f* des fins ▫; **it's not the be-all and end-all if it doesn't work** ce n'est pas la fin du monde si ça ne marche pas

beam [biːm] **1** *n* (**a**) *Carp & Constr (bar of wood → in house)* poutre *f*; *(→ big)* madrier *m*; *(→ small)* poutrelle *f*; *(→ in gymnastics)* poutre *f*

(**b**) *Naut (cross member)* barrot *m*; *(breadth)* largeur *f*; **on the beam** par le travers; **on the port beam** à bâbord; **on the starboard beam** à tribord

(**c**) *Tech (of scales)* fléau *m*; *(of engine)* balancier *m*; *(of loom)* ensouple *f*, rouleau *m*; *Agr (of plough)* age *m*

(**d**) *(ray → of sunlight)* rayon *m*; *(→ of searchlight, headlamp)* faisceau *m* lumineux; *Phys* faisceau *m*; *Aviat & Naut* chenal *m* de radioguidage; **to be off (the) beam** *Aviat* ne pas être dans le chenal de radioguidage; *Br Fam Fig* dérailler; *Br Fam* **he's way off beam** il déraille complètement; **to be on the beam** *Aviat* être dans le chenal radioguidage; *Br Fam Fig* être sur la bonne voie

(**e**) *(smile)* sourire *m* radieux; **he greeted her with a beam** il l'accueillit avec un sourire radieux

(**f**) *Am Aut* **high beams** phares *mpl*; **he flicked on his high beams** il a mis ses phares; **the headlights were on full beam** la voiture était en pleins phares

2 *vi* (**a**) *(smile)* faire un grand sourire; **their faces were beaming with pleasure** leurs visages étaient rayonnants de plaisir; **he beamed when he saw us** il eut un sourire radieux en nous apercevant

(**b**) *(shine → sun)* briller, darder ses rayons

3 *vt* (**a**) *Rad & TV (message)* transmettre par émission dirigée; **the pictures were beamed all over the world** les images ont été diffusées dans le monde entier

(**b**) *(smile)* **she beamed her thanks** elle a fait un grand sourire en guise de remerciement

►► *Rad & TV Br* ***beam aerial,*** *Am* ***beam antenna*** antenne *f* directive; *Tech* ***beam balance*** balance *f* à fléau; *Geom* ***beam compass*** compas *m* à verge

beam-ends *npl Naut* **on her beam-ends** couché sur le flanc; *Br Fam* **to be on one's beam-ends** tirer le diable par la queue

beaming ['bi:mɪŋ] *adj* radieux, resplendissant

bean [bi:n] **1** *n* (**a**) *Bot & Culin* haricot *m*

(**b**) *(of coffee)* grain *m*; *(of cocoa)* graine *f*, fève *f*

(**c**) *Am Fam (head)* caboche *f*, pomme *f*; *(brains)* cervelle ❑ *f*

(**d**) *Fam (idioms)* **to be full of beans** péter le feu; **I haven't got a bean** je n'ai pas un rond; *Br Old-fashioned or Hum* **hello, old bean!** salut, mon vieux!; **that car isn't worth a bean** cette voiture-là ne vaut rien; *Am* **he doesn't know beans about it** il n'y connaît rien

2 *vt Am Fam* **to bean sb** frapper qn (sur la tête) ❑

►► *Culin* ***bean curd*** pâte *f* de soja; *Orn* ***bean goose*** oie *f* des moissons

beanbag ['bi:nbæg] *n (in game)* balle *f* lestée; *(seat)* sacco *m*

bean-counter *n Am Fam* petit(e) comptable *mf*

beanery ['bi:nərɪ] (*pl* **beaneries**) *n Am Fam* gargote *f*

beanfeast ['bi:nfi:st] *n Br Fam* gueuleton *m*

beanie ['bi:nɪ] *n (skullcap)* calotte *f*

beano ['bi:nəʊ] *n Br Fam (meal)* gueuleton *m*; *(spree)* bombe *f*; **to have** *or* **to go on a beano** faire la bombe

beanpole ['bi:npəʊl] *n Agr* rame *f*; *Fig (person)* (grande) perche *f*

beanshoot ['bi:nʃu:t], **beansprout** ['bi:nspraʊt] *n Bot & Culin* germe *m* de soja

beanstalk ['bi:nstɔ:k] *n Bot* tige *f* de haricot

BEAR [beə(r)]

porter	► **1 (a), (f), (h), (i)**
supporter	► **2 (b), (c) – (e)**
donner naissance à	► **1 (g)**
diriger	► **2 (a)**
peser	► **2 (c)**
ours	► **3 (a), (b), (d)**

(*pt* **bore** [bɔ:(r)], *pp* **borne** [bɔ:n]) **1** *vt* (**a**) *(carry → goods, burden)* porter; *(→ gift, message)* apporter; *(→ sound)* porter, transporter; **a convoy of lorries bore the refugees away** *or* **off** un convoi de camions emmena les réfugiés; **they bore him aloft on their shoulders** ils le portèrent en triomphe; **they arrived bearing fruit** ils sont arrivés, chargés de fruits; **she bore her head high** elle avait un port de tête altier; *Naut* **the wind bore the ship west** le vent poussait le navire vers l'ouest; **to be borne along by the crowd/current** être emporté par la foule/le courant

(**b**) *(sustain → weight)* supporter; **the ice couldn't bear his weight** la glace ne pouvait pas supporter son poids; *Fig* **the system can only bear a certain amount of pressure** le système ne peut supporter qu'une certaine pression

(**c**) *(endure)* tolérer, supporter; **the news was more than she could bear** elle n'a pas pu supporter la nouvelle; **she can't bear the sight of blood** elle ne supporte pas la vue du sang; **I can't bear to see you go** je ne supporte pas que tu t'en ailles; **I can't bear that man** je ne supporte pas cet homme; **I can't bear the suspense** ce suspense est insupportable; **she bore the pain with great fortitude** elle a supporté la douleur avec beaucoup de courage

(**d**) *(accept → responsibility, blame)* assumer; *(→ costs)* supporter

(**e**) *(allow → examination)* soutenir, supporter; **his theory doesn't really bear close analysis** sa théorie ne supporte pas une analyse approfondie; **his language does not bear repeating** il a été si grossier que je n'ose même pas répéter ce qu'il a dit; **his work bears comparison with Hemingway and Steinbeck** son œuvre soutient la comparaison avec Hemingway et Steinbeck; **it doesn't bear thinking about** je n'ose pas *ou* je préfère ne pas y penser

(**f**) *(show → mark, name, sign etc)* porter; **the glass bore the letters "TR"** le verre portait les lettres "TR"; **the letter bore the signatures of several eminent writers** la lettre portait la signature de plusieurs écrivains célèbres; **I still bear the scars** j'en porte encore les cicatrices; **the murder bore all the marks of a mafia killing** le meurtre avait tout d'un crime mafieux; **he bears no resemblance to his father** il ne ressemble pas du tout à son père; **his account bears no relation to the truth** sa version n'a rien à voir avec ce qui s'est vraiment passé; **to bear witness to sth** *(person)* attester qch; *(thing, quality)* témoigner de qch

(**g**) *(give birth to)* donner naissance à; **she bore a child** elle a donné naissance à un enfant; **she bore him two sons** elle lui donna deux fils

(**h**) *(produce)* porter, produire; **the cherry tree bears beautiful blossom in spring** le cerisier donne de belles fleurs au printemps; *Fig* **all my efforts have borne fruit** mes efforts ont porté leurs fruits; *Fin* **his investment bore 8 percent interest** ses investissements lui ont rapporté 8 pour cent d'intérêt

(**i**) *(feel)* porter, avoir en soi; **to bear love/hatred for sb** éprouver de l'amour/de la haine pour qn; **I bear you no ill will** je ne t'en veux pas; **to bear a grudge against sb** en vouloir *ou* garder rancune à qn

(**j**) *(behave)* **he bore himself like a man** il s'est comporté en homme; **she bore herself with dignity** elle est restée très digne

(**k**) *St Exch (market, prices, shares)* chercher à faire baisser

2 *vi* (**a**) *(move)* diriger; **bear to your left** prenez sur la gauche *ou* à gauche; **we bore due west** nous fîmes route vers l'ouest; **they bore straight across the field** ils traversèrent le champ en ligne droite; *Am* **bear left ahead** *(sign)* tournez à gauche, filez à gauche

(**b**) *(tree → fruit)* produire, donner; *(→ flower)* fleurir

(**c**) *(be oppressive)* peser; **grief bore heavily on her** le chagrin l'accablait

(**d**) *St Exch* spéculer à la baisse

(**e**) *(idioms)* **to bring a gun to bear on a target** pointer un canon sur un objectif; **to bring pressure to bear on sb** faire pression sur qn; **to bring one's mind to bear on sth** s'appliquer à qch

3 *n* (**a**) *Zool (animal)* ours(e) *m,f*; *Br Fam* **he's like a bear with a sore head** il est d'une humeur massacrante; *very Fam Hum* **does a bear shit in the woods?** qu'est-ce que tu crois? ❑, à ton avis? ❑

(**b**) *Pej (person)* ours *m*; **he's a big bear of a man** *(physically)* c'est un grand costaud

(**c**) *St Exch (person)* baissier(ère) *m,f*, spéculateur(trice) *m,f* à la baisse; **to go a bear** spéculer *ou* jouer à la baisse

(**d**) *(toy)* ours *m* (en peluche)

►► *Am Culin* ***bear claw*** = chausson aux fruits portant sur le dessus des incisions semblables à des griffes d'ours; *St Exch* ***bear closing*** arbitrage *m* à la baisse; ***bear cub*** ourson *m*; ***bear garden*** *Hist* fosse *f* aux ours; *Fig* pétaudière *f*; *Br* **the place was like a bear garden** l'endroit était une véritable pétaudière, on se serait cru à la cour du roi Pétaud; *Fam St Exch* ***bear hug*** = communiqué d'information annonçant une OPA immédiate; **to give sb a bear hug** *(embrace)* serrer qn très fort dans ses bras; *St Exch* ***bear market*** marché *m* à la baisse *ou* baissier; *Zool* ***bear pit*** fosse *f* aux ours; *St Exch* ***bear position*** position *f* vendeur *ou* baissière; *St Exch* ***bear sale*** vente *f* à découvert; *St Exch* ***bear speculation*** spéculation *f* à la baisse; ***bear tracks*** empreintes *fpl* d'ours; *St Exch* ***bear trading*** spéculation *f* à la baisse; *St Exch* ***bear transaction*** transaction *f* à la baisse

►**bear down** *vi* (**a**) *(approach)* **to bear down on** *or* **upon** *(ship)* venir sur; *(person)* foncer sur; **a lorry was bearing down on me** un camion fonçait sur moi (**b**) *(press)* appuyer; *(in childbirth)* pousser

►**bear in** *vi* **to bear in on sb** s'approcher d'un air menaçant de qn

►**bear on** *vt insep (be relevant to)* se rapporter à, être relatif à; *(concern)* intéresser, concerner

►**bear out** *vt sep Br* confirmer, corroborer; **to bear sb out, to bear out what sb says** corroborer ce que qn dit; **the results don't bear out the hypothesis** les résultats ne confirment pas l'hypothèse; **he will bear me out on this matter** il sera d'accord avec moi sur ce sujet

►**bear up** *vi Br* tenir le coup, garder le moral; **she's bearing up under the pressure** elle ne se laisse pas décourager par le stress; **he's bearing up remarkably well** il tient drôlement bien le coup; **bear up!** courage!

►**bear upon** = **bear on**

►**bear with** *vt insep (be patient with)* supporter patiemment; **if you'll just bear with me a minute** je vous demande un peu de patience; **if you'll bear with me I'll explain** si vous patientez un instant, je vais vous expliquer

bearable ['beərəbəl] *adj* supportable, tolérable

bearably ['beərəblɪ] *adv* d'une façon supportable; **it was hot but bearably so** il faisait chaud mais c'était supportable

bearbaiting ['beə,beɪtɪŋ] *n* combat *m* d'ours et de chiens

beard [bɪəd] **1** *n* (**a**) *(on person)* barbe *f*; *(goatee)* barbiche *f*; **to have a beard** avoir la barbe; **a man with a beard** un (homme) barbu; **to grow a beard** se laisser pousser la barbe; **he wears a full beard** il porte la barbe; **a two-day beard** une barbe de deux jours

(**b**) *(on goat)* barbiche *f*; *Ich (on fish, oyster, mussel)* barbe *f*; *Bot (on plant)* arête *f*, barbe *f*

(**c**) *Typ* talus *m*

2 *vt Literary (confront)* affronter, braver; **to beard the lion in his den** aller braver le lion dans sa tanière

►► ***beard trimmer*** tondeuse *f* à barbe

bearded ['bɪədɪd] *adj* barbu

►► ***bearded lady*** femme *f* à barbe; *Orn* ***bearded tit*** mésange *f* à moustaches; *Orn* ***bearded vulture*** gypaète *m* barbu

beardless ['bɪədlɪs] *adj* imberbe, sans barbe; *Literary* **a beardless youth** un jeunet

bearer ['beərə(r)] *n* (**a**) *(of news, letter)* porteur(euse) *m,f*; *(of load, coffin)* porteur(euse) *m,f*; *(servant)* serviteur *m*; **I hate to be the bearer of bad tidings** j'ai horreur d'annoncer les mauvaises nouvelles

(**b**) *(of cheque, title)* porteur(euse) *m,f*; *(of passport)* titulaire *mf*; *Banking* **cheque made payable to bearer** chèque *m* (payable) au porteur

(**c**) *Constr* support *m*

►► *Fin* ***bearer bill*** effet *m* *ou* billet *m* au porteur; *St Exch* ***bearer bond*** titre *m* *ou* obligation *f* au porteur; *Banking* ***bearer cheque*** chèque *m* au porteur; *Fin* ***bearer paper*** papier *m* au porteur; *St Exch* ***bearer share*** action *f* au porteur

bearing ['beərɪŋ] **1** *n* (**a**) *(relevance)* rapport *m*, relation *f*; **his comments have some** *or* **a bearing on the present situation** ses remarques ont un certain rapport avec la situation actuelle; **the event had no bearing on the outcome of the war** l'événement n'eut aucune incidence sur l'issue de la guerre

(**b**) *(deportment)* maintien *m*, port *m*; **a man of distinguished bearing** un homme à l'allure distinguée; **her queenly bearing** son port de reine

(**c**) *(endurance)* **it's beyond** *or* **past all bearing** c'est absolument insupportable

(**d**) *(direction)* position *f*; *Constr (in surveying)* gisement *m*, azimut *m*; *Naut & Aviat* relèvement *m*, position *f*; **to take a (compass) bearing (on sth)** relever la position (de qch) au compas; *Naut* **to take a ship's bearing** faire le point; *Naut* **to get** *or* **to find one's bearings** retrouver sa direction *ou* sa route; *Fig* se repérer, s'orienter; *Naut* **to lose one's bearings** perdre sa direction *ou* sa route; *Fig* perdre le nord

(**e**) *Tech* palier *m*

2 bearings *npl Her* armoiries *fpl*

-bearing ['beərɪŋ] *suff* **rain-bearing clouds** des nuages *mpl* chargés de pluie; **fruit-bearing trees** des arbres *mpl* fructifères; **interest-bearing capital** capital *m* qui rapporte; **oxygen-bearing water** de l'eau *f* riche en oxygène

bearish ['beərɪʃ] *adj* (**a**) *Pej (person)* bourru (**b**) *St Exch (market, trend)* à la baisse, baissier; **to be bearish** *(person)* spéculer *ou* jouer à la baisse

►► *St Exch* ***bearish tendency*** tendance *f* à la baisse

bearishly ['beərɪʃlɪ] *adv Pej* de façon bourrue

bearishness ['beərɪʃnɪs] *n Pej* caractère *m* bourru

bearskin ['beəskɪn] *n* (**a**) *Tex (piece of fur)* peau *f* d'ours (**b**) *Mil (hat)* bonnet *m* à poils

beast [bi:st] *n* (**a**) *(animal)* bête *f*, animal *m*; **the king of the beasts** le roi des animaux; *Bible* **the Beast** l'Antéchrist *m* , la bête de l'Apocalypse; **beast of burden** bête *f* de somme; **beast of prey** bête *f* de proie

(**b**) *(savage nature)* **the beast in man** la bête en l'homme

(**c**) *(person → unpleasant)* chameau *m*; *(→ cruel)* brute *f*; **you beast!** vous êtes dégoûtant!

(**d**) *Fam (unpleasant thing)* **a beast of a job** un sale boulot; **I've had a beast of a day** j'ai eu une journée affreuse

(**e**) *Am Fam (ugly woman)* boudin *m*, cageot *m*

beastie ['bi:stɪ] *n Fam* (**a**) *Scot (small animal)* petit animal ❑ *m* (**b**) *(insect)* bestiole *f*

beastliness ['bi:stlɪnɪs] *n (of person)* méchanceté *f*; *(of act)* bestialité *f*; *(of language)* obscénité *f*

beastly ['bi:stlɪ] *Br Fam* **1** *adj (person, behaviour)* vache; *(food)* infect; **he's a beastly child** c'est un enfant intenable; **he was beastly to her** il a été vache avec elle; **a beastly job** *(task)* un sale boulot; **what beastly weather!** quel sale temps!

2 *adv* vachement; **it's beastly cold!** il fait vachement froid!

BEAT [bi:t] (*pt* **beat**, *pp* **beaten** ['bi:tən]) **1** *vt* (**a**) *(hit → dog, person)* frapper, battre; *(→ carpet, metal)* battre; *Culin (eggs)* battre, fouetter; **to beat sb with a stick** donner des coups de bâton à qn; **to beat sth flat** aplatir qch *(en tapant dessus)*; **to beat sb black and blue** battre qn comme plâtre; **he beat the water with his hands** il battit l'eau de ses mains; *Literary* **she beat her breast** elle se frappa la poitrine; *Am Vulg* **to beat one's meat** *(masturbate)* se branler

(**b**) *Mus* **to beat time** battre la mesure; **she beat time to the music with her foot** elle marquait le rythme de la musique avec son pied; **to beat a drum** battre du tambour

(**c**) *(move → wing)* battre; **the bird was beating its wings** l'oiseau battait des ailes; **the pigeon was beating the air with its wings** le pigeon battait l'air de ses ailes

(**d**) *(defeat → at game, sport)* battre, vaincre; **she beat him at poker** elle l'a battu au poker; **Liverpool were beaten** Liverpool a perdu; **to beat the world record** battre le record mondial; *Fig* **beat the rush hour, travel early** évitez l'heure de pointe, voyagez plus tôt; **to beat the system** tirer son épingle du jeu en magouillant; *Am Fam* **to beat the charge** échapper à l'accusation ❑; *Am Fam* **to beat the rap** échapper à la tôle; **we've got to beat racism** il faut en finir avec le racisme; **if you can't beat them, join them** mieux vaut s'allier aux gens que l'on ne peut pas vaincre; *Fam* **to beat sb hollow** *or Br* **hands down, to beat the pants off sb** battre qn à plate couture; *Fam* **the problem has me beaten** le problème me dépasse complètement; *Fam* **(it) beats me** cela me dépasse; *Fam* **it beats me** *or* **what beats me is how he gets away with it** je ne comprends pas *ou* ça me dépasse qu'il s'en tire à chaque fois; *Fam* **he beat me to it** *(arrived, telephoned before me etc)* il m'a devancé

(**e**) *(outdo)* **you can't beat the Chinese for inventiveness** on ne peut pas trouver plus inventifs que les Chinois; **nothing beats a cup of tea** rien ne vaut une tasse de thé; **beat that!** voyons si tu peux faire mieux!; *Fig* pas mal, hein?; *Fam* **that beats the lot!, that takes some beating!** ça, c'est le bouquet!; *Fam* **his answer takes some beating!** *(critically)* c'est le comble!; *(admiringly)* on n'aurait pas pu mieux dire!; *Fam* **can you beat it!** tu as déjà vu ça, toi!

(**f**) *(path)* se frayer; **to beat a way through the undergrowth** se frayer un chemin à travers la végétation; *Fig* **the new doctor soon had people beating a path to his door** très vite, les gens se pressèrent chez le nouveau docteur

(**g**) *Mil (retreat)* **to beat the retreat** battre la retraite; *Fig* **they beat a hasty retreat when they saw the police arrive** ils ont décampé en vitesse quand ils ont vu arriver la police

(**h**) *Hunt* **to beat the woods/the moors** battre les bois/les landes

(**i**) *Fam (idioms)* **to beat it**, *Am* **to beat feet** *(go away)* se tirer, se barrer; **beat it!** dégage!

2 *vi* (**a**) *(rain)* battre; *(sun)* taper; *(wind)* souffler en rafales; **to beat on** *or* **at the door** cogner à la porte; **the waves beat against the sea wall** les vagues venaient battre la digue; **the rain was beating against the roof** la pluie battait contre le toit; **he doesn't beat** *Br* **about** *or Am* **around the bush** il n'y va pas par quatre chemins; **so, not to beat** *Br* **about** *or Am* **around the bush, I've lost my job** enfin bref, j'ai perdu mon emploi

(**b**) *(heart, pulse, wing)* battre; **with beating heart** le cœur battant; **his heart was beating with terror** son cœur palpitait de terreur; **I heard the drums beating** j'entendis le roulement des tambours

(**c**) *Naut* **to beat to windward** louvoyer au plus près

3 *n* (**a**) *(of heart, pulse, wing)* battement *m*, pulsation *f*; *Mus (of drums)* battement *m*; battement *m*; *Mil* **to march to the beat of the drum** marcher au son du tambour

(**b**) *Mus (time)* temps *m*; *(in jazz and pop)* rythme *m*; **a strong/weak beat** un temps fort/faible; **a funky beat** un rythme funky

(**c**) *(of policeman)* ronde *f*, secteur *m*; *Mil (of sentry)* ronde *f*; **we need more policemen on the beat** il faudrait qu'il y ait plus de policiers à faire des rondes; **he saw the robbery when he was on his beat** il a été témoin du vol pendant qu'il effectuait sa ronde; *Fam Fig* **it's off my beat altogether** cela ne relève pas de ma compétence ❑, ce n'est pas de mon ressort ❑

(**d**) *Hunt* battue *f*

(**e**) *Fam (beatnik)* beatnik ❑ *mf*

4 *adj* (**a**) *Fam (exhausted)* crevé, vidé

(**b**) *Fam (defeated)* **you've got me beat** *(defeated)* je m'avoue vaincu; *(unable to answer)* je sèche; **this crossword's got me beat** je sèche sur ces mots croisés

(**c**) *Fam* beatnik ❑; **a beat poet** un poète beatnik

►► ***the Beat generation*** = mouvement littéraire et culturel américain des années 50–60 dont les adeptes (les "beatniks") refusaient les conventions de la société moderne

►**beat back** *vt sep Mil (enemy, flames)* repousser

►**beat down 1** *vt sep* (**a**) *(grass)* **the wind had beaten the grass down** le vent avait couché les herbes; **the horses had beaten down the crops** les chevaux avaient foulé les récoltes

(**b**) *Br Com (seller)* faire baisser; **I beat him down to £20** je lui ai fait baisser son prix à 20 livres

2 *vi (sun)* taper; *(rain)* tomber à verse *ou* à torrents; **the rain was beating down** il pleuvait à torrents; **the rain was beating down on the tin roof** la pluie s'abattait sur le toit en tôle

►**beat in** *vt sep (door)* défoncer; **I'll beat his head in!** je lui défoncerai le crâne!

►**beat off 1** *vt sep Mil (enemy, attack)* repousser

2 *vi Vulg (masturbate)* se branler

►**beat out** *vt sep* (**a**) *(flames)* étouffer

(**b**) *(metal)* étaler au marteau; *Fam Fig* **to beat one's brains out** se creuser la cervelle; *Fam* **to beat sb's brains out** défoncer le crâne à qn

(**c**) *Mus (rhythm)* marquer; **she beat the rhythm out on a drum** elle marquait le rythme *ou* elle battait la mesure sur un tambour

(**d**) *Am Sport (opponent)* battre

►**beat up 1** *vt sep* (**a**) *Fam (person)* tabasser, passer à tabac

(**b**) *Culin (egg white)* faire monter; *(cream, egg)* fouetter, battre

(**c**) *(drum up → help, volunteers)* racoler, recruter

2 *vi Naut* louvoyer *ou* gagner vers la terre

beat-'em-up *n Fam (video game)* jeu *m* vidéo violent

beaten ['bi:tən] **1** *pp of* **beat**

2 *adj* (**a**) *(gold)* battu, martelé; *(earth, path)* battu; *Culin (eggs, cream)* battu, fouetté; **a beaten track** un chemin *ou* sentier battu; *Fig* **off the beaten track** dans un endroit reculé, à l'écart (**b**) *(defeated)* vaincu, battu (**c**) *(exhausted)* éreinté, épuisé

beaten-up *adj* cabossé; **a beaten-up old bus** un vieux bus tout cabossé

beater ['bi:tə(r)] *n* (**a**) *Culin (manual)* fouet *m*; *(electric)* batteur *m* (**b**) *Tex* peigne *m*; *(for carpet)* tapette *f* (**c**) *Hunt* rabatteur *m*

beatific [,bi:ə'tɪfɪk] *adj Rel* béat; **a beatific smile** un sourire béat

beatifically [,bi:ə'tɪfɪkəlɪ] *adv Rel* avec béatitude

beatification [bi:,ætɪfɪ'keɪʃən] *n Rel* béatification *f*

beatify [bi:'ætɪfaɪ] *vt Rel* béatifier

beating ['bi:tɪŋ] **1** *adj (heart)* battant, palpitant; *(rain)* battant

2 *n* (**a**) *(thrashing)* correction *f*; **to give sb a beating** donner une correction à qn; **to get a beating** recevoir une correction

(**b**) *(defeat)* défaite *f*; **to take** *or* **get a beating** se faire battre à plate couture

(**c**) *(of wings, heart)* battement *m*

(**d**) *Fam (outdoing)* **it takes some** *or* **a lot of beating** c'est difficile de faire mieux

(**e**) *(UNCOUNT) Tech (of metal)* batte *f*; *Mus (of drums)* battement *m*, roulement *m*; *Tex (of carpet)* battage *m*

(**f**) *Hunt* battue *f*

►► *Fam* ***beating up*** passage *m* à tabac, raclée *f*

beatitude [bi:'ætɪ,tju:d] *Rel* **1** *n* béatitude *f*

2 Beatitudes *npl* **the Beatitudes** les béatitudes *fpl*

beatnik ['bi:tnɪk] **1** *n* beatnik *mf*

2 *adj* beatnik

beat-up *adj Fam (car)* bousillé, déglingué; *Am (person)* amoché

beau [bəʊ] (*pl* **beaux** [bəʊz]) *n (dandy)* dandy *m*; *(suitor)* galant *m*

Beaufort scale ['bəʊfət-] *n Met* échelle *f* de Beaufort

beaut [bju:t] *Fam* **1** *n* **that's a beaut** c'est super, c'est génial; **(what a) beaut!** super!

2 *adj Austr* super, génial

beauteous ['bju:tɪəs] *adj Literary* beau (belle)

beautician [,bju:'tɪʃən] *n* esthéticien(enne) *m,f*; *Cin, TV & Theat (make-up artist)* visagiste *mf*

beautification [,bju:tɪfɪ'keɪʃən] *n* embellissement *m*, enjolivement *m*

beautiful ['bju:tɪfʊl] **1** *adj* (**a**) *(attractive → person, dress)* beau (belle); **a beautiful woman** une belle femme; **a beautiful baby** un beau bébé; **what a beautiful photo/song!** quelle belle photo/chanson!; **the beautiful game** *(soccer)* le beau jeu; **the beautiful people** *(famous)* les gens *mpl* riches et célèbres; *Am (hippies)* les hippies *mpl*; *Fam Hum* **I'm just going to make myself look beautiful** je vais me faire belle

(**b**) *(splendid → weather, meal)* magnifique, superbe; **what a beautiful shot!** bien joué!, joli!

2 *exclam Fam* magnifique!

'The Beautiful and the Damned' *Fitzgerald* 'Les Heureux et les Damnés'

---

beautifully ['bju:təfəlɪ] *adv* (**a**) *(sing, dress)* admirablement, à la perfection (**b**) *(splendidly)* **it was a beautifully played shot** c'était bien joué, c'était une belle balle; **that will do beautifully** cela convient parfaitement (**c**) *(as intensifier → peaceful, warm)* merveilleusement

beautify ['bju:tɪfaɪ] (*pt & pp* **beautified**) *vt* embellir, orner; **to beautify oneself** se faire une beauté

beautifying ['bju:tɪfaɪɪŋ] *adj* embellissant

beauty ['bju:tɪ] (*pl* **beauties**) **1** *n* (**a**) *(loveliness)* beauté *f*; **a thing of beauty** un objet d'une rare beauté; **to spoil the beauty of sth** déparer qch; *Prov* **beauty is in the eye of the beholder** il n'y a pas de laides amours; *Prov* **beauty is only skin-deep** la beauté n'est pas tout; *Hum* **I need my beauty sleep** j'ai besoin de mon compte de sommeil pour être frais le matin

(**b**) *(beautiful person)* beauté *f*; **she's a/she's no beauty** c'est une/ce n'est pas une beauté; **the beauties of nature** les merveilles *fpl* de la nature

(**c**) *Fam (excellent thing)* merveille ❑ *f*; **this new bike's a real beauty** cette nouvelle bicyclette est une vraie merveille; *Fam* **that black eye is a real beauty** quel beau coquard!

(**d**) *(attraction)* **the beauty of the system is its simplicity** ce qui est bien dans ce système, c'est sa simplicité; **that's the beauty of it** c'est ça qui est formidable

2 *comp (cream, product, treatment)* de beauté

3 *exclam Br Fam* **(you) beauty!** super!

►► ***beauty competition, beauty contest*** concours *m* de beauté; *Br* ***beauty parlour,*** *Am* ***beauty parlor*** institut *m* de beauté; ***beauty queen*** reine *f* de beauté; ***beauty salon*** institut *m* de beauté; *Am* ***beauty shop*** institut *m* de beauté; ***beauty specialist*** esthéticien(enne) *m,f*; ***beauty spot*** *(on skin)* grain *m* de beauté; *(artificial)* mouche *f*; *(scenic place)* site *m* touristique; ***beauty therapist*** esthéticien(enne) *m,f*

'Beauty and the Beast' *Madame Leprince de Beaumont, Cocteau* 'La Belle et la bête'

beaver ['bi:və(r)] **1** *n* (**a**) *(animal, fur)* castor *m*; *Fam* **to work like a beaver** travailler d'arrache-pied (**b**) *Vulg (female genitals)* chatte *f*

2 *comp (coat, hat)* de castor

►► ***the Beaver State*** = surnom donné à l'Oregon

►**beaver away** *vi Br Fam* **to beaver away (at sth)** travailler d'arrache-pied (à qch)

Beaverboard® ['bi:və,bɔ:d] *n Constr* panneau *m* d'aggloméré

bebop ['bi:bɒp] *n Mus (music, dance)* be-bop *m*

becalm [bɪ'kɑ:m] *vt (usu passive)* **to be becalmed** être encalminé

became [bɪ'keɪm] *pt of* **become**

because [bɪ'kɒz] **1** *conj* parce que; **he came because it was his duty** il est venu parce que c'était son devoir; **if she won it was because she deserved to** si elle a gagné, c'est qu'elle le méritait; **it was all the more difficult because he was sick** c'était d'autant plus difficile qu'il était malade; **not because he was sad but because he was angry** pas parce qu'il était triste mais parce qu'il était fâché; **they only won because they cheated** ils n'ont gagné que parce qu'ils ont triché; **just because you're my sister, it doesn't mean you can boss me about** ce n'est pas parce que tu es ma sœur que tu peux me donner des ordres; **why? – just because** pourquoi? – parce que; **why can't I go? – because you can't!** pourquoi est-ce que je ne peux pas y aller? – parce que (c'est comme ça)!

2 because of *prep* à cause de; **we couldn't move because of the snow** nous étions bloqués par la neige; **I couldn't go to work because of the tube strike** je n'ai pas pu aller au travail à cause de la grève de métro; **it was all because of a silly misunderstanding** tout ça à cause d'un *ou* tout provenait d'un petit malentendu; **he's ineligible because of his age** il ne peut être élu à cause de son âge

> **Because it's there**
> Cette phrase ("parce qu'il est là") est censée être la réponse donnée par l'alpiniste britannique George Mallory lorsqu'on lui demanda pourquoi il désirait être le premier à faire l'ascension de l'Everest.
> Aujourd'hui on utilise cette formule de façon allusive pour expliquer pourquoi on décide de s'atteler à une tâche particulièrement ardue.

bechamel ['beʃəmel] *n Culin (sauce)* béchamel

►► ***bechamel sauce*** sauce *f* béchamel

Becher's Brook ['bi:tʃəz-] *n Horseracing* = obstacle réputé très difficile du "Grand National" (course hippique en Grande-Bretagne)

beck [bek] *n* (**a**) *(in Northern England) (stream)* ruisseau *m*, ru *m* (**b**) *(idioms)* **to be at sb's beck and call** être constamment à la disposition de qn; **she has him at her beck and call** elle le fait marcher à la baguette, il lui obéit au doigt et à l'œil

beckon ['bekən] **1** *vi* faire signe; **to beckon to sb** faire signe à qn; *Fig* **a glittering career beckoned for the young singer** la jeune chanteuse avait devant elle une brillante carrière; *Fig* **the bright lights of the city beckoned** les lumières de la ville étaient une tentation; **I can't stay, work beckons** il faut que je m'en aille, j'ai du travail

2 *vt* (**a**) *(motion)* faire signe à; **I beckoned them over (to me)** je leur ai fait signe d'approcher; **he beckoned me to follow him** il m'a fait signe de le suivre

(**b**) *(attract, call)* attirer; **the bright lights beckoned me to the city** j'ai été attiré par les lumières de la ville

becloud [bɪ'klaʊd] *vt Literary* couvrir de nuages, ennuager; *Fig (obscure)* voiler, obscurcir

become [bɪ'kʌm] (*pt* **became** [-'keɪm], *pp* **become**) **1** *vi* (**a**) *(grow)* devenir, se faire; **the noise became louder and louder** le bruit est devenu de plus en plus fort *ou* a continué à augmenter; **to become old** vieillir; **to become fat** grossir; **to become weak** s'affaiblir; **it became clear that we were wrong** il s'est avéré que nous nous trompions; **we became friends** nous sommes devenus amis; **she's becoming a dreadful nuisance** elle est en train de devenir vraiment gênante; **to become known** commencer à être connu

(**b**) *(acquire post of)* devenir; **to become president** devenir président; **she's become an accountant** elle est devenue comptable

2 *vt Formal* (**a**) *(suit → of hat, dress)* aller à; **that hat really becomes you** ce chapeau vous va vraiment bien

(**b**) *(befit)* convenir à, être digne de; **such behaviour doesn't become him** une telle conduite n'est pas digne de lui

►**become of** *vt insep (only following "what", "whatever")* **whatever will become of us?** qu'allons-nous devenir?; **what became of your hat?** où est passé ton chapeau?; **I wonder what became of that young man** je me demande ce qu'est devenu ce jeune homme

becoming [bɪ'kʌmɪŋ] *adj Formal* (**a**) *(fetching)* qui va bien, seyant; **that's a very becoming hat** ce chapeau vous va très bien; **you look very becoming in that dress** cette robe te va très bien (**b**) *(suitable)* convenable, bienséant; **such language is hardly becoming for a young lady!** un tel langage n'est guère convenable chez une jeune fille!

becomingly [bɪ'kʌmɪŋlɪ] *adv Formal* (**a**) *(fetchingly)* élégamment; **she was most becomingly dressed** elle était habillée à son avantage; **becomingly furnished** meublé avec goût (**b**) *(suitably)* convenablement

becquerel [,bekə'rel] *n Phys* becquerel *m*

BECTU ['bektu:] *n Cin, TV & Theat* (*abbr* **Broadcasting, Entertainment, Cinematograph and Theatre Union**) = syndicat britannique des techniciens du cinéma, du théâtre et de l'audiovisuel

BEd [,bi:'ed] *n Br* (*abbr* **Bachelor of Education**) *(person)* = titulaire d'une licence de sciences de l'éducation; *(qualification)* licence *f* de sciences de l'éducation

BED [bed]

lit	► **1 (a), (c), (d)**
parterre	► **1 (b)**
couche	► **1 (d)**

(*pt & pp* **bedded,** *cont* **bedding**) **1** *n* (**a**) *(furniture)* lit *m*; **to be in bed** *(to rest)* être couché, être au lit; *(through illness)* être alité, garder le lit; **he's in bed with the flu** il est au lit avec la grippe; **to read in bed** lire au lit; **we asked for a room with two beds** nous avons demandé une chambre à deux lits; **they sleep in separate beds** ils font lit à part; **it's time to go to** *or* **time for bed** il est l'heure d'aller au lit *ou* de se coucher; **to get out of bed** se lever; **to get into bed** se mettre au lit; *Fam Fig* **to get into bed with sb** *(form partnership with)* travailler en collaboration avec qn ❑; **did I get you out of bed?** est-ce que je vous ai tiré du lit?; **she got** *or* **put the children to bed** elle a couché les enfants *ou* mis les enfants au lit; **he took a walk before bed** il a fait une promenade avant de se coucher; **to make the bed** faire le lit; **they made me up a bed** ils m'ont préparé un lit; **she took to her bed with pneumonia** elle a dû s'aliter à cause d'une pneumonie; **the doctor recommended complete bed rest** le médecin a conseillé l'immobilité totale; *Fam* **to go to bed with sb** coucher avec qn; *Fam* **he's/she's really great in bed** c'est vraiment un bon coup; *Hum* **I wouldn't kick him out of bed** s'il voulait de moi, je ne dirais pas non; **to get out of bed on the wrong side** se lever du pied gauche *ou* du mauvais pied; *Prov* **you've made your bed, now you must lie in it** comme on fait son lit, on se couche; *Literary* **his bed of pain** son lit de douleur; *Arch* **she was brought to bed of twins** elle accoucha de jumeaux; **life's not a bed of roses** la vie n'est pas toujours une partie de plaisir; **her life isn't exactly a bed of roses** sa vie n'est pas vraiment rose; **teaching in a secondary school isn't exactly a bed of roses** enseigner dans un lycée n'a rien d'une sinécure; **bed and breakfast** *(accommodation)* chambre *f* d'hôte *ou* chez l'habitant; *esp Br* **we stayed in a bed and breakfast** nous avons pris une chambre d'hôte; **bed and breakfast** *(sign)* chambres d'hôte; *St Exch* **bed and breakfasting** aller et retour *m*

(**b**) *(plot → of flowers)* parterre *m*, plate-bande *f*; *(→ of vegetables)* planche *f*; *(→ of coral, oysters)* banc *m*

(**c**) *(bottom → of river)* lit *m*; *(→ of lake, sea)* fond *m*

(**d**) *(layer → of clay, rock)* couche *f*, lit *m*; *Miner (→ of ore)* gisement *m*; *(→ of ashes)* lit *m*; *Constr (→ of mortar)* bain *m*; **bed of nails** lit *m* à clous; *Culin* **place the roast on a bed of vegetables** placez le rôti sur un lit de légumes

(**e**) *(of machine)* base *f*, bâti *m*; *(of lorry)* plateau *m*; *(of printing press)* marbre *m*, plateau *m*; *Br Typ & Press* **to put a newspaper to bed** boucler un journal; *Br Typ* **the magazine has gone to bed** la revue est bouclée *ou* sur le marbre

2 *vt* (**a**) *(embed)* fixer, enfoncer; *Constr* asseoir

(**b**) *Hort* repiquer

(**c**) *Fam (have sex with)* coucher avec

►► ***bed bath*** toilette *f (d'un malade)*; ***bed board*** planche *f* à mettre sous le matelas; ***bed frame*** châlit *m*; *Br* ***bed jacket*** liseuse *f*; ***bed linen*** draps *mpl* de lit (et taies *fpl* d'oreiller)

►**bed down 1** *vi (go to bed)* se coucher; *(spend the night)* coucher

2 *vt sep* (**a**) *(children)* mettre au lit, coucher; *(animal)* installer pour la nuit

(**b**) *(embed)* fixer, enfoncer; *Constr* asseoir

►**bed out** *vt sep* repiquer

bedaub [bɪ'dɔ:b] *vt Formal (smear)* enduire; *(dirty)* barbouiller; **bedaubed with mud** barbouillé de boue

bedazzle [bɪ'dæzəl] *vt (dazzle)* éblouir, aveugler; *(fascinate)* éblouir

bedbug ['bedbʌg] *n* punaise *f* des lits

bedchamber ['bed,tʃeɪmbə(r)] *n Arch* chambre *f*

bedclothes ['bedkləʊðz] *npl* draps *mpl* et couvertures *fpl*; **to turn down the bedclothes** ouvrir le lit

bedcover ['bed,kʌvə(r)] *n* dessus-de-lit *m*, couvre-lit *m*

beddable ['bedəbəl] *adj Fam Hum* baisable

-bedded ['bedɪd] *suff* **single-bedded room** chambre *f* à un lit

bedder ['bedə(r)] *n* (**a**) *Br Univ* femme *f* de ménage *(qui fait les chambres à l'université de Cambridge)* (**b**) *Hort* plante *f* à repiquer

bedding ['bedɪŋ] *n* (**a**) *(bedclothes)* draps *mpl* et couvertures *fpl*; *(including mattress)* literie *f*; *Mil* matériel *m* de couchage (**b**) *(for animals)* litière *f*

►► *Hort* ***bedding out*** *(of plants)* dépotage *m*, dépotement *m*; *Hort* ***bedding plant*** plante *f* à repiquer

beddy-byes ['bedɪ,baɪz] *n Fam (in children's*

language) **to go beddy-byes** (aller) se coucher❑

Bede [biːd] *pr n Hist* **the Venerable Bede** Bède le Vénérable

bedeck [bɪ'dek] *vt Literary* orner, parer; **a balcony bedecked with flowers** un balcon orné de fleurs *ou* fleuri

bedevil [bɪ'devəl] *(Br pt & pp* **bedevilled,** *cont* **bedevilling,** *Am pt & pp* **bedeviled,** *cont* **bedeviling)** *vt* (**a**) *(plague → plans, project)* déranger, gêner; *(→ person)* harceler, tourmenter; **bedevilled by** *or* **with problems** assailli par les problèmes (**b**) *(confuse)* embrouiller (**c**) *(bewitch)* ensorceler

bedew [bɪ'djuː] *vt Literary* humecter de rosée; *Fig* **her cheeks were bedewed with tears** ses joues étaient baignées de larmes; *Fig* **her pillow was bedewed with tears** son oreiller était arrosé de larmes

bedfellow ['bedˌfeləʊ] *n* (**a**) *(bedmate)* **he was my bedfellow when we were children** nous avons partagé le même lit dans notre enfance (**b**) *(associate)* associé(e) *m,f*, collègue *mf*; **they make strange bedfellows** ils forment une drôle d'association *ou* de paire

Bedfordshire ['bedfədˌʃə(r)] *n* le Bedfordshire, = comté dans le sud de l'Angleterre; **in Bedfordshire** dans le Bedfordshire

bedhead ['bedhed] *n Br* tête *f* de lit

bed-hopper *n Fam Pej* **to be a bed-hopper** coucher à droite et à gauche

bedim [bɪ'dɪm] *vt (pt & pp* **bedimmed,** *cont* **bedimming)** *Literary* obscurcir

bedlam ['bedləm] *n* (**a**) *(chaos)* tohu-bohu *m*; *(in classroom)* chahut *m*; **utter bedlam broke out after her speech** un véritable tumulte éclata après son discours; **it's absolute bedlam in town today!** quel cirque en ville, aujourd'hui!; **the meeting was absolute bedlam** la réunion était un véritable bazar (**b**) *Arch (asylum)* maison *f* de fous *ou* d'aliénés

bedmate ['bedmeɪt] *n* partenaire *mf*

bed-night *n Com (in hotel)* nuitée *f*

Bedouin ['bedʊɪn] *(pl* **inv** *or* **Bedouins)** **1** *n* Bédouin(e) *m,f*

2 *adj* bédouin

bedpan ['bedpæn] *n* bassin *m* (hygiénique)

bedplate ['bedpleɪt] *n Tech* semelle *f*

bedpost ['bedpəʊst] *n* colonne *f* de lit; *Hum* **(just) between you, me and the bedpost** entre nous

bedraggled [bɪ'drægəld] *adj (clothing, person)* débraillé; *(hair)* ébouriffé, échevelé

bedridden ['bedˌrɪdən] *adj* alité, cloué au lit; *(permanently)* grabataire

bedrock ['bedrɒk] *n Geol* soubassement *m*, substratum *m*; *Fig* base *f*, fondation *f*; *Br* **to get down to bedrock** considérer l'essentiel

bedroll ['bedrəʊl] *n* matériel *m* de couchage *(enroulé)*

bedroom ['bedrʊm] **1** *n* chambre *f* (à coucher); **spare bedroom** chambre *f* d'ami

2 *comp (carpet, window)* de la chambre

▸▸ *Theat* ***bedroom comedy*** comédie *f* de boulevard; *Am* ***bedroom community*** cité-dortoir *f*; *Fam* ***bedroom eyes*** regard *m* sexy; *Cin & Theat* ***bedroom scene*** scène *f* d'amour

-bedroomed [ˌbedrʊmd] *suff* **two-bedroomed flat** trois pièces *m*

Beds *(written abbr* **Bedfordshire)** le Bedfordshire, = comté dans le sud de l'Angleterre

bedsettee [ˌbedse'tiː] *n Br* canapé-lit *m*

bedside ['bedsaɪd] **1** *adj (lamp, table)* de chevet

2 *n* chevet *m*; **at** *or* **by your bedside** à votre chevet; **to rush to sb's bedside** courir au chevet de qn

▸▸ ***bedside manner*** comportement *m* envers les malades; **the doctor has a good bedside manner** le médecin sait rassurer les malades

bedsit ['bedˌsɪt], **bedsitter** ['bedˌsɪtə(r)], **bedsitting room** [ˌbed'sɪtɪŋ-] *n Br* chambre *f* meublée, studette *f*

bedsocks ['bedsɒks] *npl* chaussettes *fpl (que l'on porte au lit)*

bedsore ['bedsɔː(r)] *n* escarre *f*

bedspace ['bedspeɪs] *n Com (in hotel)* capacité *f* d'accueil

bedspread ['bedspred] *n* dessus-de-lit *m inv*, couvre-lit *m*

bedsprings ['bedsprɪŋz] *npl (springs)* ressorts *mpl* de sommier; *(frame)* sommier *m* à ressorts

bedstead ['bedsted] *n* châlit *m*

bedtick ['bedtɪk] *n Am (bug)* punaise *f*

bedtime ['bedtaɪm] *n* heure *f* du coucher; **bedtime!** c'est l'heure d'aller au lit *ou* de se coucher!; **what's his bedtime?** à quelle heure se couche-t-il?; **it's your bedtime** il est l'heure d'aller te coucher; **it's long past your bedtime** il y a longtemps que tu devrais être au lit; **her mother reads to her at bedtime** sa mère lui lit une histoire avant qu'elle s'endorme; **they were allowed to stay up past their bedtime** on leur a permis de se coucher plus tard que d'habitude

▸▸ ***bedtime story*** histoire *f (qu'on lit à l'heure du coucher)*; **I'll read you a bedtime story** je vais te lire une histoire avant que tu t'endormes

Beduin *(pl* **inv** *or* **Beduins)** = **Bedouin**

bedwarmer ['bedˌwɔːmə(r)] *n* bassinoire *f*

bed-wetter [-ˌwetə(r)] *n (child)* enfant *mf* qui fait pipi au lit; **he's a bed-wetter** il fait pipi au lit

bed-wetting [-ˌwetɪŋ] *n* incontinence *f* nocturne, énurésie *f*

bee [biː] *n* (**a**) *(insect)* abeille *f*; *Fam* **he is a busy (little) bee** *(is energetic)* il déborde d'énergie; *(has a lot of work)* il a énormément de choses à faire; **to have a bee in one's bonnet (about sth)** être obsédé (par qch); *Fam* **it's the bee's knees!** c'est formidable *ou* super!; *Fam* **she thinks he's the bee's knees** elle le trouve formidable; *Fam* **he thinks he's the bee's knees** il ne se prend pas pour n'importe qui

(**b**) *Am (social event)* réunion *f (de voisins ou d'amis pour des travaux en commun)*; **quilting bee** atelier *m* de patchwork

▸▸ *Bot* ***bee balm*** monarde *f* d'Amérique; *Bot* ***bee orchid*** ophrys *f* abeille; ***bee sting*** piqûre *f* d'abeille; *Fam Hum* ***bee stings*** *(small breasts)* œufs *mpl* sur le plat

Beeb [biːb] *n Br Fam* **the Beeb** = surnom courant de la BBC

beech [biːtʃ] *(pl* **inv** *or* **beeches)** *Bot* **1** *n (tree)* hêtre *m*; *(wood)* (bois *m* de) hêtre *m*

2 *comp (chair, table)* de hêtre

▸▸ ***beech grove*** hêtraie *f*; *Bot* ***beech mast*** *(UNCOUNT)* faines *fpl (tombées par terre)*; ***beech nut*** faine *f*; ***beech tree*** hêtre *m*

beechen ['biːtʃən] *adj Literary* de hêtre

beechwood ['biːtʃwʊd] *n Bot (substance)* (bois *m* de) hêtre *m*; *(forest)* bois *m* de hêtres

bee-eater *n Orn* guêpier *m*

beef [biːf] *(Br pl sense* (**b**) **beeves** [biːvz], *Am pl sense* (**b**) **beefs**, *pl sense* (**c**) **beefs)** **1** *n* (**a**) *(UNCOUNT) (meat)* bœuf *m*; **joint of beef** rôti *m* (de bœuf), rosbif *m*

(**b**) *(animal)* bœuf *m*

(**c**) *Fam (complaint)* grief❑ *m*; **what's your beef?** c'est quoi, ton problème?; **their main beef is high taxation** ils râlent surtout parce qu'ils trouvent les impôts élevés; *Am* **to have a beef with sb/sth** avoir des ennuis avec qn/qch

(**d**) *Fam (muscle)* **put some beef into it!** allez, un peu de nerf!

2 *comp Culin (sausage, stew)* de bœuf

3 *vi Fam* râler; **to beef about sth** râler contre qch

▸▸ *Agr* ***beef cattle*** bœufs *mpl* de boucherie; ***beef farm*** élevage *m* de bœufs; ***beef farmer*** éleveur *m* de bœufs; *Culin* ***beef olives*** = chair à saucisse enrobée de fines tranches de bœuf, cuite à la cocotte; *Culin* ***beef stroganoff*** bœuf *m* stroganoff; ***beef tea*** bouillon *m* de bœuf; ***beef tomato*** ≃ marmande *f*; *Culin* ***beef Wellington*** = bœuf en croûte

▸**beef up** *vt sep Fam (army, campaign)* renforcer; *(report, story)* étoffer

beefburger ['biːfˌbɜːgə(r)] *n* hamburger *m*

beefcake ['biːfkeɪk] *n (UNCOUNT) Fam Hum (attractive men)* beaux mecs *mpl* musclés; *Br* **he's a real beefcake** il est vraiment bien foutu

Beefeater ['biːfˌiːtə(r)] *n* = surnom des gardiens de la Tour de Londres

beefing ['biːfɪŋ] *n Fam (complaining)* ronchonnements *mpl*, rouspétances *fpl*

beefsteak ['biːfˌsteɪk] *n Culin* bifteck *m*, steak *m*

▸▸ ***beefsteak tomato*** ≃ marmande *f*

beefy ['biːfɪ] *(compar* **beefier,** *superl* **beefiest)** *adj* (**a**) *(consistency, taste)* de viande, de bœuf (**b**) *Fam (brawny)* costaud; *(fat)* grassouillet

beehive ['biːhaɪv] *n* (**a**) *(for bees)* ruche *f* (**b**) *(hairstyle)* = coiffure très haute maintenue avec de la laque

▸▸ ***the Beehive State*** = surnom donné à l'Utah

beekeeper ['biːˌkiːpə(r)] *n* apiculteur(trice) *m,f*

beekeeping ['biːˌkiːpɪŋ] *n* apiculture *f*

beeline ['biːlaɪn] *n Fam* **to make a beeline for sb/sth** aller droit *ou* directement vers qn/qch❑; **he made a beeline for the kitchen** *(headed straight to)* il s'est dirigé tout droit vers la cuisine❑; *(rushed to)* il s'est précipité *ou* a filé tout droit à la cuisine❑

Beelzebub [biː'elzɪˌbʌb] *pr n Bible* Belzébuth

beemer [ˌbiːmə(r)] *n Fam (BMW car)* BM *f*

been [biːn] *pp of* **be**

beep [biːp] **1** *n (of car horn)* coup *m* de klaxon; *(of alarm, timer)* signal *m* sonore, bip *m*

2 *vt* (**a**) **to beep the** *or* **one's horn** klaxonner (**b**) *(person → on pager)* appeler au récepteur d'appel

3 *vi (car horn)* klaxonner; *(alarm, timer)* sonner, faire bip

beeper ['biːpə(r)] *n* récepteur *m* d'appels

beeping ['biːpɪŋ] *n (of alarm, timer)* bip-bip *m*; **a sudden beeping of car horns woke me up** des coups de klaxon brutaux m'ont réveillé

beer [bɪə(r)] *n* bière *f*; **to go for a beer** aller boire une bière; *Br Fig* **his life is not all beer and skittles** sa vie n'est pas toujours rose

▸▸ ***beer barrel*** tonneau *m* à bière; *Am Fam* ***beer bash*** beuverie *f* à la bière entre étudiants; *Fam* ***beer belly*** brioche *f*; ***beer bottle*** canette *f ou* bouteille *f* de bière; *Am Fam* ***beer bust*** = soirée entre étudiants où l'on consomme beaucoup de bière; ***beer can*** canette *f* de bière *(en métal)*; ***beer cellar*** *(bar)* brasserie *f*; ***beer garden*** = jardin d'un pub, où l'on peut prendre des consommations; ***beer glass*** verre *m* à bière; *Fam* ***beer gut*** brioche *f*, bide *m*; ***beer mat*** sous-bock *m inv*; *Fam* ***beer money*** argent *m* de poche❑; ***beer pump*** pompe *f* à bière; *Br* ***beer tent*** = grande tente abritant la buvette lors des manifestations sportives de plein air

beery ['bɪərɪ] *(compar* **beerier,** *superl* **beeriest)** *adj (atmosphere, smell, taste)* qui sent la bière; *(party)* où l'on boit beaucoup de bière; *(person)* qui a bu beaucoup de bière

beeswax ['biːzwæks] **1** *n* cire *f* d'abeille; *Am Fam* **mind your own beeswax!** occupe-toi de tes oignons!

2 *vt* cirer *(avec de la cire d'abeille)*

beet [biːt] *n Bot & Culin* betterave *f* (potagère); *Am* **(red) beet** betterave *f* (rouge)

▸▸ ***beet sugar*** sucre *m* de betterave

Beethoven ['beɪtˌhəʊvən] *pr n* Beethoven

beetle ['biːtəl] **1** *n* (**a**) *(insect)* scarabée *m*, coléoptère *m*

(**b**) *(game)* = jeu de dés où l'on essaye de dessiner un scarabée

(**c**) *Constr (hammer)* mailloche *f*; *Tech (machine)* mouton *m*; *Constr (for paving)* hie *f*, demoiselle *f*

2 *vi* (**a**) *(cliff, crag)* surplomber

(**b**) *Br Fam* courir précipitamment❑; **he beetled in/out of the house** il est entré dans/sorti de la maison à toute vitesse

3 **Beetle**® *n Aut* **(Volkswagen) Beetle** Coccinelle *f*

▸▸ *Br* ***beetle drive*** = tournoi au jeu du "beetle"

▸**beetle off** *vi Fam* filer

beetle-browed [-braʊd] *adj Br (with overhanging eyebrows)* aux sourcils proéminents; *(with bushy eyebrows)* aux sourcils broussailleux; *(scowling)* renfrogné

beetle-crusher *n Fam* écrase-merde *m*

beetling ['biːtlɪŋ] *adj (cliff, crag)* qui surplombe, surplombant; *(brow)* proéminent; *(eyebrows)* broussailleux

beetroot ['biːtruːt] *n Bot & Culin* betterave *f* (potagère *ou* rouge); **to go (as red as a) beetroot** devenir rouge comme une tomate

beezer ['biːzə(r)] *n Fam* (**a**) *Br Old-fashioned (person)* type *m* (**b**) *Br Old-fashioned (nose)* pif *m* (**c**) *Scot (extreme example)* comble❑ *m*; **that was a beezer of a storm last night** il y a eu une sacrée tempête hier soir

befall [bɪ'fɔːl] *(pt* **befell** [-'fel], *pp* **befallen** [-'fɔːlən]) *Literary* **1** *vt* arriver à, survenir à; **no**

harm will befall her il ne lui sera fait aucun mal

2 *vi* (**a**) *(happen)* arriver, se passer (**b**) *(be due)* échoir

befit [bɪ'fɪt] *(pt & pp* **befitted,** *cont* **befitting***) vt Formal* convenir à, seoir à; **as befits a woman of her eminence** comme il sied à une femme de son rang; **it does not befit a man to...** ce n'est pas le fait d'un homme de...

befitting [bɪ'fɪtɪŋ] *adj Formal* convenable, seyant; **in a manner befitting a statesman** d'une façon qui sied à un homme d'État; **with befitting modesty** avec la modestie qui sied

befog [bɪ'fɒg] *(pt & pp* **befogged,** *cont* **befogging***) vt* envelopper de brouillard; *Fig (confuse → person)* brouiller l'esprit *ou* les idées de, embrouiller; *(→ issue)* obscurcir; **his mind was befogged by whisky** le whisky lui avait brouillé l'esprit

BEFORE [bɪ'fɔː(r)]

avant	▸ **1 (a); 2 (a), (b)**
en avant	▸ **1 (b)**
devant	▸ **2 (c) – (e)**
avant de, avant que	▸ **3 (a)**
plutôt que de	▸ **3 (b)**
précédent	▸ **4**

1 *adv* (**a**) *(at a previous time)* avant; **you should have thought of that before** tu aurais dû y penser avant; **haven't we met before?** est-ce que nous ne nous sommes pas déjà rencontrés?; **I have never seen this film before** c'est la première fois que je vois ce film; **I have/had seen it before** je l'ai/l'avais déjà vu; **he's made mistakes before** ce n'est pas la première fois qu'il se trompe; **such things have happened before** c'est déjà arrivé; **she carries on driving as before** elle continue de conduire comme auparavant *ou* avant

(**b**) *Literary (ahead)* en avant, devant

2 *prep* (**a**) *(in time)* avant; **before the holidays** avant les vacances; **the day before the meeting** la veille de la réunion; **two days before your birthday** deux jours avant *ou* l'avant-veille de votre anniversaire; **the day before yesterday** avant-hier; **they arrived before us** ils sont arrivés avant nous; **the couch won't be delivered before next Tuesday** le divan ne sera pas livré avant mardi prochain; **it should have been done before now** ça devrait déjà être fait; **before that, she was a teacher** auparavant *ou* avant ça, elle était professeur; **that was before your time** *(you were not born)* vous n'étiez pas encore né; *(you had not arrived, joined etc)* vous n'étiez pas encore là; *Fam* **it's not before time, and not before time** ce n'est pas trop tôt

(**b**) *(in order, preference)* avant; **her name was** *or* **came before mine in the list** son nom était avant le mien sur la liste; **ladies before gentlemen** les dames avant les messieurs; **she puts family before friends** pour elle, la famille est plus importante que les amis; **they put quality before quantity** ils font passer la qualité avant la quantité; **the welfare of the people comes before private concerns** le bien-être du peuple passe avant tout intérêt privé; **before anything else, I would like to thank you** avant tout, je voudrais vous remercier

(**c**) *(in space)* devant; *Formal* **on the table before them** sur la table devant eux; *Literary* **fields stretched away before us** des champs s'étendaient devant nous; *Fig* **we have a difficult task before us** nous avons une tâche difficile devant nous; **before my very eyes** sous mes propres yeux; *Naut* **to sail before the wind** avoir le vent arrière *ou* en poupe; *Mil* **the troops fled before the enemy** les troupes se sont enfuies devant l'ennemi

(**d**) *(in the presence of)* devant, en présence de; **he said it before witnesses** il l'a dit devant *ou* en présence de témoins; *Law* **to appear before the court/judge** comparaître devant le tribunal/juge; **she appeared before the committee** elle s'est présentée devant le comité

(**e**) *(for the consideration of)* devant; **the problem before us** la question qui nous occupe; *Law* **the case before the court** l'affaire portée devant le tribunal; *Law* **to bring a case before the court** saisir le tribunal d'une affaire; **the matter went before the council** l'affaire est passée devant le conseil

3 *conj* (**a**) *(in time)* avant de, avant que; **she hesitated before answering** elle a hésité avant de répondre; **may I see you before you leave?** puis-je vous voir avant que vous ne partiez *ou* avant votre départ?; **I saw him the day before he died** je l'ai vu la veille de sa mort; **get out before I call the police!** fichez le camp avant que je n'appelle la police *ou* sinon j'appelle la police!; **it'll be a long time before he tries that again** il ne recommencera pas de sitôt, il n'est pas près de recommencer; **we should be able to finish before the boss gets back** nous devrions pouvoir terminer avant le retour du patron; **it'll be summer before she plants the garden** elle ne plantera pas le jardin avant l'été; **it'll be two years before the school is built** l'école ne sera pas construite avant deux ans; **it was almost an hour before the ambulance arrived** il a fallu presque une heure avant que l'ambulance n'arrive; **before I forget, they expect you this evening** avant que je n'oublie, il faut que je te dise qu'ils comptent sur toi ce soir; **before you know it** avant qu'on ait le temps de dire "ouf"; **I'll be back before you know it** je serai bientôt de retour; **it'll be Christmas before we know it** le temps va passer vite jusqu'à Noël

(**b**) *(rather than)* plutôt que de; **I'll die before I let him marry my daughter** je mourrai plutôt que de le laisser épouser ma fille

4 *adj* d'avant, précédent; **the day before** la veille; **the night before** la veille au soir; **the week before** la semaine d'avant *ou* précédente; **this summer and the one before** cet été et celui d'avant *ou* le précédent

beforehand [bɪ'fɔːhænd] **1** *adv* auparavant, à l'avance; **she had prepared her speech beforehand** elle avait préparé son discours au préalable *ou* à l'avance; **if you're coming let me know beforehand** prévenez-moi si vous décidez de venir

2 *adj Fam Hum (early)* **you were a bit beforehand with the congratulations!** tu t'y es pris un peu tôt pour les félicitations!

before-tax *adj Fin* brut, avant impôts; **before-tax income** revenus *mpl* bruts

beforetime [bɪ'fɔːtaɪm] *adv Literary* autrefois, jadis

befoul [bɪ'faʊl] *vt Literary* souiller, salir

befriend [bɪ'frend] *vt (make friends with)* prendre en amitié, se prendre d'amitié pour; *(assist)* venir en aide à, aider; **he was befriended by a colleague** un de ses collègues s'est pris d'amitié pour lui; **I was befriended by a stray dog** un chien perdu s'est attaché à moi

befuddle [bɪ'fʌdəl] *vt* (**a**) *(confuse → person)* brouiller l'esprit *ou* les idées de, embrouiller; *(→ mind)* embrouiller (**b**) *(muddle with alcohol)* griser, enivrer; **his mind was befuddled with drink** il était étourdi par l'alcool

beg [beg] *(pt & pp* **begged,** *cont* **begging***)* **1** *vt* (**a**) *(solicit as charity)* mendier; **to beg food** mendier de la nourriture; **she begged money from the passers-by** elle mendiait auprès des passants; **to beg, borrow or steal** se procurer par tous les moyens

(**b**) *(ask for)* demander, solliciter; *(plead with)* supplier; **I begged the doctor not to say anything** j'ai supplié le médecin de ne rien dire; **she begged to be sent back to school** elle supplia qu'on la renvoie à l'école; **she begged a favour of her sister** elle a demandé à sa sœur de lui rendre un service; **to beg sb's forgiveness** *or* **pardon** demander pardon à qn; **I beg your pardon** *(I apologize)* je vous demande pardon; *(I didn't hear you)* pardon?; *(indignantly)* pardon!

(**c**) *Formal (request politely)* **I beg to differ** permettez-moi de ne pas être de votre avis; **I beg to inform you that...** je tiens à *ou* j'ai l'honneur de vous informer que...; **to beg leave to do sth** demander la permission de faire qch

(**d**) *(idiom)* **to beg the question** *(evade the issue)* éluder la question; *(assume something proved)* considérer que la question est résolue; **that begs the question of whether...** cela pose la question de savoir si..., c'est toute la question de savoir si...; **wanting to climb Mount Everest rather begs the question 'why?'** on serait enclin à se demander pourquoi quelqu'un aurait envie d'escalader le Mont Everest

2 *vi* (**a**) *(solicit charity)* mendier; **to beg for food** mendier de la nourriture; **children begging (for money) in the street** des enfants qui mendient dans la rue; **they live by begging** ils vivent de charité *ou* d'aumône

(**b**) *(ask, plead)* supplier; **to beg for forgiveness/mercy** demander pardon/grâce

(**c**) *(dog)* faire le beau

(**d**) *Br (idioms)* **I'll have that last sandwich if it's going begging** je prendrai bien ce dernier sandwich si personne d'autre ne le veut; **there's a piece of cake going begging** il reste un morceau de gâteau; **these jobs are going begging** ce sont des emplois qui trouvent peu d'amateurs

▸**beg off** *vi Br* se soustraire; **our best player begged off pleading illness** notre meilleur joueur s'est fait excuser pour cause de maladie

began [bɪ'gæn] *pt of* **begin**

beget [bɪ'get] *(pt* **begot** [-'gɒt] *or* **begat** [-'gæt], *pp* **begotten** [-'gɒtən], *cont* **begetting***) vt Bible & Literary (father)* engendrer; *Fig (cause)* engendrer, causer; **Abraham begat Isaac** Abraham engendra Isaac; **the only begotten Son of the Father** le Fils unique du Père

begetter [bɪ'getə(r)] *n* (**a**) *Bible & Literary (father)* père *m*; *Fig (originator)* auteur *m*; *Fig (cause)* cause *f*

beggar ['begə(r)] **1** *n* (**a**) *(mendicant)* mendiant(e) *m,f*; *(pauper)* indigent(e) *m,f*; *Prov* **beggars can't be choosers** nécessité fait loi (**b**) *Br Fam (person)* type *m*; **you lucky beggar!** sacré veinard!; **poor beggar!** pauvre diable!; **you naughty little beggar!** petit coquin!; **jammy beggar!** veinard!

2 *vt* (**a**) *Formal (impoverish)* réduire à la mendicité, appauvrir (**b**) *(defy)* **to beggar (all) description** défier toute description; **it beggars belief** c'est incroyable

'The Beggar's Opera' *Gay* 'L'Opéra du gueux'

beggarly ['begəlɪ] *adj (conditions, life)* misérable, malheureux; *(meal)* maigre, piètre; *(salary, sum)* misérable, dérisoire

beggar-my-neighbour *Br* **1** *n (card game)* bataille *f*

2 *adj Com* protectionniste; **beggar-my-neighbour policies** politique *f* protectionniste *ou* du chacun pour soi

beggary ['begərɪ] *n* misère *f*, mendicité *f*; **they were reduced to beggary** ils étaient réduits à la mendicité

begging ['begɪŋ] *n* mendicité *f*; **to live by begging** vivre d'aumône

▸▸ ***begging bowl*** sébile *f (de mendiant)*; *Fig* **many sports organizations have to approach the government with a begging bowl** de nombreuses associations sportives sont obligées de demander l'aumône au gouvernement; ***begging letter*** lettre *f* de requête *(demandant de l'argent)*

BEGIN [bɪ'gɪn]

commencer	▸ **1 (a), (b); 2**
fonder, inaugurer	▸ **1 (c)**
d'abord, pour commencer	▸ **3**

(pt **began** [bɪ'gæn], *pp* **begun** [bɪ'gʌn], *cont* **beginning***)* **1** *vt* (**a**) *(start)* commencer; *(career, term)* commencer, débuter; *(task)* entreprendre, s'attaquer à; *(work)* commencer, se mettre à; **to begin to do** *or* **doing sth** commencer à faire qch, se mettre à faire qch; **I had begun to believe he was lying** j'avais commencé à croire qu'il mentait; **she began the first chapter** *(reading)* elle commença à lire le premier chapitre; *(writing)* elle commença à écrire le premier chapitre; **the quotation beginning this chapter** la citation qui ouvre ce chapitre; **she began life as a waitress** elle a débuté comme serveuse; **he soon began to complain** il n'a pas tardé à se plaindre; **I began the day all wrong** j'ai mal

commencé la journée; **the film doesn't begin to compare with the book** le film est loin de valoir le livre; **he can't begin to compete with her** il ne lui arrive pas à la cheville; **I can't begin to explain** c'est trop difficile à expliquer

(**b**) *(start to say)* commencer; **"this is unforgivable", she began** "c'est impardonnable", commença-t-elle

(**c**) *(found → institution, club)* fonder, inaugurer; *(initiate → business, fashion)* lancer; *(→ argument, fight, war)* déclencher, faire naître; *(→ conversation)* engager, amorcer; *(→ discussion, speech)* commencer, ouvrir

2 *vi* (**a**) *(start → person, career, concert, project, speech)* commencer; **work should begin in the spring** les travaux devraient commencer au printemps; **the day began badly/well** la journée s'annonçait mal/bien; **to begin again** *or* **afresh** recommencer (à zéro); **begin at the beginning** commencez par le commencement; **the night shift begins at midnight** l'équipe de nuit commence (le travail) à minuit; **when does school begin?** quand est la rentrée?; **after the film begins** après le début du film; **her career began in Hollywood** sa carrière a débuté à Hollywood; **he began in politics** il a commencé par faire de la politique; **let me begin by thanking our host** permettez-moi tout d'abord de remercier notre hôte; **let's begin with a song** commençons par une chanson; **her name begins with (a) B** son nom commence par un B; **the play begins with a murder** la pièce débute par un meurtre; **I began with the idea of buying a flat** au départ *ou* au début je voulais acheter un appartement; *Br Prov* **well begun is half done** = ce qui commence bien est à moitié fait

(**b**) *(originate → club, country, institution)* être fondé; *(→ fire, epidemic)* commencer; *(→ war)* éclater, commencer; *(→ trouble)* commencer; *(→ river)* prendre sa source; *(→ road)* commencer; *(→ fashion)* commencer, débuter; **the magazine began as a freesheet** la revue a débuté comme publication gratuite

3 to begin with *adv* (**a**) *(in the first place)* d'abord, pour commencer; **to begin with, it's too cold** d'abord, il fait trop froid; **to begin with, the statistics are wrong** pour commencer *ou* d'abord, les chiffres sont faux

(**b**) *(initially)* au départ; **everything went well to begin with** tout s'est bien passé au début *ou* au départ; **the plate was cracked to begin with** l'assiette était déjà fêlée au départ

---

beginner [bɪ'gɪnə(r)] *n* débutant(e) *m,f*; **I'm just a beginner at golf** je ne suis qu'un débutant au golf; **not bad for a beginner** pas si mal pour un débutant; **it's beginner's luck!** on a toujours de la chance au début!; **French for beginners** français pour débutants; **complete** *or* **absolute beginner** grand débutant; **beginner's class** cours *m* de débutants

beginning [bɪ'gɪnɪŋ] **1** *n* (**a**) *(start → of book, career, project)* commencement *m*, début *m*; **in** *or* **at the beginning** au début, au commencement; **from the beginning** dès le commencement *ou* le début; **this is just the beginning of our troubles** nos ennuis ne font que commencer; **let's start again from the beginning** reprenons depuis le début; **at the beginning of the academic year** au début de l'année universitaire; **from beginning to end** du début à la fin, d'un bout à l'autre; **it's the beginning of the end** c'est le début de la fin

(**b**) *(early part, stage → of book, career, war)* commencement *m*, début *m*; *(→ of negotiations)* début *m*, ouverture *f*; **the day had a good beginning** la journée avait bien commencé; **the beginning of the world** l'origine *ou* le commencement du monde; **since the beginning of time** depuis la nuit des temps; **I have the beginnings of a cold** je couve un rhume, j'ai un début de rhume

(**c**) *(origin → of event)* origine *f*, commencement *m*; **Protestantism had its beginnings in Germany** le protestantisme a pris naissance en Allemagne; **his assassination signalled the beginning of the war** son assassinat a marqué le déclenchement de la guerre

2 *adj* **beginning student** débutant(e) *m,f*

begone [bɪ'gɒn] *exclam Literary* hors d'ici!

begonia [bɪ'gəʊnɪə] *n Bot* bégonia *m*

begorrah [bɪ'gɒrə] *exclam Fam* = expression stéréotypée, souvent employée pour caricaturer la manière de parler des Irlandais

begot [bɪ'gɒt] *pt of* **beget**

begotten [bɪ'gɒtən] *pp of* **beget**

begrime [bɪ'graɪm] *vt Literary* noircir, salir; **begrimed with smoke** noirci de fumée

begrudge [bɪ'grʌdʒ] *vt* (**a**) *(envy)* envier; **to begrudge sb sth** envier qch à qn; **she begrudges him his success** elle lui en veut de sa réussite

(**b**) *(give grudgingly)* donner *ou* accorder à regret; **he begrudges every minute spent away from his family** il rechigne à passer une seule minute loin de sa famille; **you don't begrudge me the money, do you?** tu ne me donnes pas cet argent à contrecœur, n'est-ce pas?; **they begrudge him his food** ils le nourrissent à contrecœur; **to begrudge doing sth** faire qch à contrecœur; **I begrudge spending so much on rent** ça me fait mal au cœur de payer un loyer aussi cher

begrudging [bɪ'grʌdʒɪŋ] *adj* (**a**) *(envious)* envieux (**b**) *(grudging → compliment, praise)* fait *ou* donné à contrecœur; *(→ agreement)* réticent

begrudgingly [bɪ'grʌdʒɪŋlɪ] *adv* (**a**) *(enviously)* envieusement (**b**) *(grudgingly)* à contrecœur, avec réticence

beguile [bɪ'gaɪl] *vt* (**a**) *(charm)* envoûter, séduire (**b**) *(delude)* enjôler, tromper; **to beguile sb into doing sth** amener qn à faire qch; **to beguile sb out of sth** obtenir qch de qn par la séduction (**c**) *(pass pleasantly)* **to beguile (away) the hours** faire passer le temps *(agréablement)*

beguiling [bɪ'gaɪlɪŋ] *adj* charmant, séduisant

beguilingly [bɪ'gaɪlɪŋlɪ] *adv* de façon charmante *ou* séduisante

beguine [bɪ'giːn] *n Mus* = musique ou danse ressemblant au boléro

begum ['beɪgəm] *n* bégum *f*

begun [bɪ'gʌn] *pp of* **begin**

behalf [bɪ'hɑːf] *n Br* **on behalf of sb**, *Am* **in behalf of sb** *(as their representative)* de la part de *ou* au nom de qn; *(in their interest)* dans l'intérêt de *ou* pour qn; **on behalf of everyone here, I thank you** au nom de tous ceux qui sont ici présents, je vous remercie; **I'm here on behalf of the president** je viens de la part du président; **speaking on my own behalf** *or* **on behalf of myself** en mon (propre) nom; **she accepted the award on his behalf** elle a reçu le prix en son nom *ou* pour lui; **she acted on his behalf when he was ill** c'est elle qui l'a représenté quand il était malade; **your lawyer acts on your behalf** votre avocat agit en votre nom; **the commission decided on their behalf** la commission a décidé en leur nom; **don't worry on my behalf** ne vous inquiétez pas à mon sujet

behave [bɪ'heɪv] **1** *vi* (**a**) *(act)* se comporter, se conduire; **why are you behaving this way?** pourquoi agis-tu de cette façon?; **to behave badly/well** mal/bien se comporter; **what a way to behave!** quelles manières!; **to know how to behave** savoir vivre; **he behaved badly towards her** il s'est mal conduit envers elle; **she's behaving very strangely** elle se comporte de façon bizarre; **she was sorry for the way she'd behaved towards him** elle regrettait la façon dont elle l'avait traité

(**b**) *(act properly)* se tenir bien; **will you behave!** sois sage!, tiens-toi bien!

(**c**) *(function)* fonctionner, marcher; **she studies how matter behaves in extremes of cold and heat** elle étudie le comportement de la matière dans des conditions de froid ou de chaleur extrêmes; **the car behaves well on curves** la voiture tient bien la route dans les virages; **the television hasn't behaved properly since** la télévision ne marche pas bien depuis

2 *vt* **to behave oneself** se tenir bien; **behave yourself!** sois sage!, tiens-toi bien!; **to behave itself** *(machine, clock etc)* marcher, fonctionner

-behaved [bɪ'heɪvd] *suff* **well-behaved** sage, qui se conduit *ou* se tient bien; **badly-behaved** qui se conduit *ou* se tient mal

behaviour, *Am* **behavior** [bɪ'heɪvjə(r)] **1** *n* (**a**) *(of person)* comportement *m*, conduite *f*; *(of animal)* comportement *m*; **her behaviour towards her mother was unforgivable** la façon dont elle s'est comportée avec sa mère était impardonnable; **to be on one's best behaviour** se tenir *ou* se conduire de son mieux; **the child was on his best behaviour** l'enfant était d'une sagesse exemplaire

(**b**) *Phys (of atom, chemical, light)* comportement *m*; *(of machine)* fonctionnement *m*

2 *comp (modification, problem)* du comportement

►► *Psy* ***behaviour pattern*** type *m* de comportement; *Mktg* ***behaviour segmentation*** segmentation *f* comportementale; *Psy* ***behaviour therapy*** thérapie *f* comportementale

behavioural, *Am* **behavioral** [bɪ'heɪvjərəl] *adj Psy* de comportement, comportemental; *(analysis, study)* de comportement

►► ***behavioural pattern*** type *m* de comportement; ***behavioural science*** science *f* du comportement, comportementalisme *m*

behaviourism, *Am* **behaviorism** [bɪ'heɪvjərɪzəm] *n Psy* behaviorisme *m*

behaviourist, *Am* **behaviorist** [bɪ'heɪvjərɪst] *Psy* **1** *n* behavioriste *mf*

2 *adj* behavioriste

behaviouristic, *Am* **behavioristic** [bɪˌheɪvjə'rɪstɪk] *adj Psy* behavioriste

behead [bɪ'hed] *vt* décapiter

beheading [bɪ'hedɪŋ] *n* décapitation *f*

beheld [bɪ'held] *pt & pp of* **behold**

behemoth [bɪ'hiːmɒθ] *n (monster)* monstre *m*

behest [bɪ'hest] *n Formal* commandement *m*, ordre *m*; **at the behest of the Queen** sur ordre de la reine

---

BEHIND [bɪ'haɪnd]

derrière	► **1 (a), (b), (d); 2 (a); 3**
en retard sur	► **1 (c)**
en retard	► **2 (b)**

1 *prep* (**a**) *(at the back of)* derrière; **behind the house** derrière la maison; **she came out from behind the bushes** elle est sortie de derrière les buissons; **I sat down right behind him** je me suis assis juste derrière lui; **lock the door behind you** fermez la porte à clé (derrière vous); **his wife was behind the bar that night** sa femme était derrière le bar *ou* au bar ce soir-là

(**b**) *(indicating past time)* derrière; **he has ten years' experience behind him** il a dix ans d'expérience derrière lui; **your troubles are behind you now** vos ennuis sont terminés maintenant; **let's put it all behind us** oublions tout cela, n'y pensons plus; **you have to put the incident behind you** il faut que tu oublies cet incident

(**c**) *(indicating deficiency, delay)* en retard sur, derrière; **she is behind the other pupils** elle est en retard sur les autres élèves; **we're three points behind the other team** nous sommes à trois points derrière l'autre équipe; **the trains are running behind schedule** *or* **behind time** les trains ont du retard (sur l'horaire); **behind the times** *(country)* arriéré, attardé; **you're behind the times** *(old-fashioned)* tu n'es pas à la page; *(not aware of latest developments)* tu as un métro de retard

(**d**) *(responsible for)* derrière; **who was behind the plot?** qui était derrière le complot *ou* à l'origine du complot?; **what's behind all this?** qu'est-ce que ça cache?

(**e**) *(supporting)* **we're right behind you on this** vous avez tout notre soutien dans cette affaire; **the country is right behind the new policies** la population soutient tout à fait les nouvelles mesures

2 *adv* (**a**) *(at, in the back)* derrière, en arrière; **look behind** regardez derrière; **he attacked them from behind** il les a attaqués par derrière; **they followed behind** ils arrivaient derrière, ils suivaient; **to stay** *or* **remain behind** *(be at the back)* rester *ou* demeurer en arrière; *(not leave)* ne pas partir; **I'll stay behind and wait for them** je resterai derrière pour les attendre; **the teacher kept him behind** *or* **made him stay behind** le professeur l'a retenu *ou* l'a mis en retenue; **I left my umbrella behind** *(at home)* j'ai oublié mon parapluie à la maison; *(at someone else's home)* j'ai oublié mon parapluie (chez lui/eux/

etc); **disaster was not far behind** la catastrophe était imminente

(**b**) *(late)* en retard; **I'm behind in** *or* **with my rent** je suis en retard sur mon loyer; **I'm behind in** *or* **with my work** j'ai du retard dans mon travail; **she's too far behind to catch up with the others** elle a pris trop de retard pour pouvoir rattraper les autres; **our team is three points behind** notre équipe a trois points de moins; *Fam* **I'm all behind today** je suis en retard (dans mon travail) aujourd'hui ❑

3 *n Euph (buttocks)* derrière *m*, postérieur *m*; **to kick sb in the behind** botter le derrière à qn; **get up off your behind and find yourself a job!** remue-toi un peu et trouve du boulot!

---

behindhand [bɪ'haɪndhænd] *adv* en retard; **we're behindhand with the rent** nous sommes en retard sur le loyer; **I'm getting behindhand with my work** je suis en train de prendre du retard dans mon travail

behind-the-scenes *adj* secret(ète); **a behind-the-scenes look at politics** un regard en coulisse sur la politique

behold [bɪ'həʊld] (*pt & pp* **beheld** [-'held]) *vt Arch or Literary (see)* regarder, voir; *(notice)* apercevoir; **behold!** voyez!; **a sight to behold** un spectacle à voir; **behold your king** voici votre roi

beholden [bɪ'həʊldən] *adj Formal* redevable; **I am deeply beholden to him** je lui suis infiniment redevable

behove [bɪ'həʊv], *Am* **behoove** [bɪ'hu:v] *vt Arch or Literary* **it behoves them to be prudent** il leur appartient d'être prudents; **it ill behoves her to criticize** ça lui va mal de critiquer

beige [beɪʒ] **1** *n* beige *m*

2 *adj* beige

Beijing [,beɪ'dʒɪŋ] *n* Beijing

being ['bi:ɪŋ] *n* (**a**) *(creature)* être *m*, créature *f*; **a human being** un être humain; **a being from another planet** une créature (venue) d'une autre planète

(**b**) *(essential nature)* être *m*; **her whole being rebelled** tout son être se révoltait

(**c**) *(existence)* existence *f*; **already in being** déjà existant, qui existe déjà; **to bring** *or* **to call sth into being** faire naître qch, susciter qch; **they brought a new social policy into being** ils ont établi une nouvelle politique sociale; **the movement came into being in the 1920s** le mouvement est apparu *ou* fut créé dans les années 20

'Being and Nothingness' *Sartre* 'L'Être et le Néant'

Beirut [,beɪ'ru:t] *n* Beyrouth; **East Beirut** Beyrouth-Est; **West Beirut** Beyrouth-Ouest

bejewelled, *Am* **bejeweled** [bɪ'dʒu:əld] *adj (person)* paré *ou* couvert de bijoux; *(box, purse)* incrusté de bijoux

Bekaa Valley [bɪ'kɑ:-] *n* vallée *f* de la Bekaa

bel [bel] *n Elec* bel *m*

belabour, *Am* **belabor** [bɪ'leɪbə(r)] *vt* (**a**) *(beat)* rouer de coups (**b**) *(criticize)* injurier, invectiver

Belarus [,belə'ru:s] *n* la Biélorussie; **in Belarus** en Biélorussie; **the Republic of Belarus** la République de Biélorussie

Belarussian [,belə'rʌʃən] **1** *n* (**a**) *(person)* Biélorusse *mf* (**b**) *(language)* biélorusse *m*

2 *adj* biélorusse

3 *comp (embassy)* de Biélorussie; *(history)* de la Biélorussie; *(teacher)* de biélorusse

belated [bɪ'leɪtɪd] *adj* tardif; **to wish you a belated happy birthday** pour te souhaiter un bon anniversaire avec un peu de retard

belatedly [bɪ'leɪtɪdlɪ] *adv* tardivement

belaud [bɪ'lɔ:d] *vt Literary (person)* combler de louanges; *(thing)* chanter les louanges de

belay [bɪ'leɪ] **1** *n (in mountaineering → system)* relais *m*; *(→ rope)* assurance *f*

2 *vt* (**a**) *Naut* amarrer (**b**) *(in mountaineering)* assurer

►► ***belay plate*** plaquette *f* d'assurage; ***belay station*** relais *m*

belayer [bɪ'leɪə(r)] *n (in mountaineering)* assureur *m*

belaying [bɪ'leɪɪŋ] *n* (**a**) *Naut* amarrage *m* (**b**) *(in mountaineering)* assurance *f*, assurage *m*

►► ***belaying cleat, belaying pin*** cabillot *m*, taquet *m*

belch [beltʃ] **1** *n* renvoi *m*, rot *m*; **to give a belch** roter

2 *vt (expel)* cracher, vomir; **the house was belching smoke and flames** la maison crachait de la fumée et des flammes

3 *vi* roter

►**belch forth, belch out** **1** *vt sep (flames, smoke etc)* cracher, vomir

2 *vi* **smoke and flames were belching out of the house** la maison crachait de la fumée et des flammes

beldam, beldame ['beldəm] *n Literary* mégère *f*

beleaguer [bɪ'li:gə(r)] *vt* (**a**) *(harass)* harceler, assaillir; **reporters beleaguered him with questions** les journalistes le harcelèrent de questions; **she was beleaguered by problems** elle croulait sous les problèmes (**b**) *Mil (besiege → city)* assiéger; *(→ army, group)* encercler, cerner

beleaguered [bɪ'li:gəd] *adj Mil (city)* assiégé; *Fig (project, ideology)* très critiqué; *(government, politician)* assailli de toutes parts; *(parents, look, manner)* accablé

Belfast ['belfɑ:st] *n* Belfast

belfry ['belfrɪ] (*pl* **belfries**) *n (of church)* beffroi *m*, clocher *m*; *(of tower)* beffroi *m*

Belgian ['beldʒən] **1** *n* Belge *mf*

2 *adj* belge

3 *comp (embassy)* de Belgique; *(history)* de la Belgique

►► ***Belgian franc*** franc *m* belge

Belgium ['beldʒəm] *n* Belgique *f*; **in Belgium** en Belgique

Belgrade [,bel'greɪd] *n* Belgrade

Belgrano [bel'grɑ:nəʊ] *n* **the Belgrano affair** = conflit politique pendant la guerre des Malouines consécutif à la décision prise par le gouvernement britannique de couler un navire argentin

Belgravia [bel'greɪvɪə] *n* = quartier chic de Londres

belie [bɪ'laɪ] (*pt & pp* **belied**, *cont* **belying**) *vt Formal (misrepresent)* donner une fausse idée *ou* impression de; *(contradict → hope, impression)* démentir, tromper; *(→ promise)* démentir, donner le démenti à; **her youthful figure belied her age** la jeunesse de sa silhouette démentait son âge

belief [bɪ'li:f] *n* (**a**) *(feeling of certainty)* croyance *f*; **belief in God** croyance en Dieu; **I've lost any belief I had in human kindness** je ne crois plus du tout en la bonté humaine; **contrary to popular belief** contrairement à ce qu'on croit; **it's beyond belief** c'est incroyable; **he's lazy beyond belief** il est incroyablement paresseux

(**b**) *(conviction, opinion)* conviction *f*, certitude *f*; **it's my belief he's lying** je suis certain *ou* convaincu qu'il ment; **in the belief that he would help them** certain *ou* persuadé qu'il allait les aider; **in the mistaken belief that...** persuadé à tort que...; **to the best of my belief** autant que je sache

(**c**) *(religious faith)* foi *f*, croyance *f*; *(political faith)* dogme *m*, doctrine *f*

(**d**) *(confidence, trust)* confiance *f*, foi *f*

believable [bɪ'li:vəbəl] *adj (story, account)* croyable, crédible; *(character in novel, person)* crédible

BELIEVE [bɪ'li:v] **1** *vt* (**a**) *(consider as real or true)* croire; **don't believe a word she says** ne croyez pas un mot de ce qu'elle dit; **I don't believe a word of it** je n'en crois rien *ou* pas un mot; **don't you believe it!** détrompe-toi!; **he's getting married! – I don't believe it!** il va se marier! – c'est pas vrai!; **she's fifty, would you believe it!** elle a cinquante ans, figure-toi!; **he couldn't believe his ears/his eyes** il n'en croyait pas ses oreilles/ses yeux; **and, believe it or not, she left** et, crois-le si tu veux, elle est partie; **I can well believe it** je suis prêt à le croire, je veux bien le croire; **it has to be seen to be believed** il faut le voir pour le croire

(**b**) *(accept statement or opinion of)* croire; **if she is to be believed, she was born a duchess** à l'en croire, elle est duchesse; **and believe (you) me, I know what I'm talking about!** et croyez-moi, je sais de quoi je parle!; *Fam* **you'd better believe it!** bien sûr que oui!

(**c**) *(hold as opinion, suppose)* croire; **I believe he left** je crois qu'il est parti; **I don't believe we've met** je ne crois pas que nous nous connaissions; **I believe I've taken a wrong turning** je crois que je me suis trompé de route *ou* que j'ai pris la mauvaise route; *Law* **the jury believes him (to be) guilty** le jury le croit coupable; **I don't know what to believe** je ne sais que croire, je ne sais pas à quoi m'en tenir; **it is widely believed that the prisoners have been killed** on pense généralement que les prisonniers ont été tués; **she is, I believe, our greatest novelist** elle est, je crois *ou* à mon avis, notre meilleure romancière; **we have every reason to believe he's telling the truth** nous avons tout lieu de croire qu'il dit la vérité; **he'd have her believe it's an antique** il voudrait lui faire croire que c'est un objet d'époque; **I believe not** je crois que non, je ne crois pas; **I believe so** je crois que oui, je crois; **I wouldn't have believed it of him** je n'aurais pas cru cela de lui

2 *vi (have religious faith)* être croyant, avoir la foi

►**believe in** *vt insep* (**a**) *(be convinced of existence or truth of)* **to believe in miracles/in God** croire aux miracles/en Dieu

(**b**) *(be convinced of value of)* **I believe in free enterprise** je crois à la libre entreprise; **they believe in their president** ils ont confiance en *ou* font confiance à *ou* croient en leur président; **he believes in giving the public greater access to information** il est d'avis qu'il faut donner au public un plus grand accès à l'information; **I don't believe in making promises** je ne fais jamais de promesses

---

believer [bɪ'li:və(r)] *n* (**a**) *(supporter)* partisan *m*, adepte *mf*; **a believer in socialism** un partisan du socialisme; **he's a great believer in taking exercise** il est convaincu qu'il faut faire de l'exercice (**b**) *Rel* croyant(e) *m,f*; **are you a believer?** êtes-vous croyant?

belike [bɪ'laɪk] *adv Arch or Literary* probablement; **belike he will consent** il y a lieu de croire qu'il donnera son consentement

Belisha beacon [bɪ'li:ʃə-] *n Br* = globe orange clignotant marquant un passage clouté

belittle [bɪ'lɪtəl] *vt* rabaisser, dénigrer; **he's always belittling her work** il dénigre toujours son travail; **to belittle oneself** *(disparage)* se déprécier; *(demean)* se déconsidérer *(aux yeux de quelqu'un, auprès de quelqu'un)*; **a belittling remark** une remarque désobligeante

Belize [be'li:z] *n* Belize *m*; **in Belize** au Belize

Belizean [be'li:zɪən] **1** *n* Bélizien(enne) *m,f*

2 *adj* bélizien

bell [bel] **1** *n* (**a**) *(in church)* cloche *f*; *(handheld)* clochette *f*; *(on bicycle)* sonnette *f*; *(for cows)* cloche *f*, clarine *f*; *(on boots, toys)* grelot *m*; *(sound)* coup *m* (de cloche); **there goes the dinner bell** c'est la cloche qui annonce le dîner; *Rel* **has the first bell for vespers gone?** a-t-on sonné le premier coup des vêpres?; *Naut* **to sound bells** piquer la cloche *ou* l'heure; *Naut* **it sounded four/eight bells** cela a piqué quatre/huit coups (de cloche); **saved by the bell!** sauvé par le gong!; *Rel* **bell, book and candle** instruments *mpl* du culte; **bells and whistles** accessoires *mpl*

(**b**) *(electrical device → on door)* sonnette *f*; **there's the bell** il y a quelqu'un à la porte, on sonne (à la porte); **to ring the bell** sonner

(**c**) *Br Fam (telephone call)* **to give sb a bell** passer un coup de fil à qn

(**d**) *Bot (of flower)* calice *m*, clochette *f*; *Mus (of oboe, trumpet)* pavillon *m*

(**e**) *(of stag)* bramement *m*; *(of hound)* aboiement *m*

2 *vi* (**a**) *(stag)* bramer; *(hound)* aboyer

(**b**) *(bloat, distend)* ballonner

3 *vt Fig* **to bell the cat** attacher le grelot

►► *Naut* ***bell buoy*** bouée *f* à cloche; *Am* ***bell captain*** chef *m* chasseur; *Hort* ***bell glass*** cloche *f* de verre; *Bot* ***bell heather*** bruyère *f* cendrée; *Chem* ***bell jar*** cloche *f* de verre; ***Bell Laboratories, Bell Labs*** = centre américain de recherches scientifiques et techniques de haute renommée; *Am Sport* **bell lap** dernier tour *m (de piste, de circuit)*; *Am Bot & Culin* **bell pepper** poivron *m*; ***bell push*** bouton *m* de sonnette; ***bell rope*** *(to call servant)* cordon *m* de sonnette; *(in belfry)* corde *f* de cloche; ***bell tent*** tente *f* conique; ***bell tower*** clocher *m*

'The Bell Jar' *Plath* 'La Cloche de verre'

'For Whom the Bell Tolls' *Hemingway* 'Pour qui sonne le glas'

The bells, the bells
Dans *The Hunchback of Notre-Dame*, la traduction anglaise de *Notre-Dame de Paris* de Victor Hugo, Quasimodo s'exclame "the bells, the bells!" lorsqu'il entend sonner les cloches de la cathédrale.
Pour plaisanter, il arrive que l'on prononce ces paroles en prenant une grosse voix lorsque l'on entend sonner des cloches, pour évoquer le personnage de Quasimodo.

belladonna [ˌbeləˈdɒnə] *n Bot & Pharm* belladone *f*

bellbird [ˈbelbɜːd] *n Orn* oiseau-cloche *m*; *(South American)* procnia *m*

bell-bottomed [-ˌbɒtəmd] *adj* à pattes d'éléphant

bell-bottoms *npl* pantalon *m* à pattes d'éléphant

bellboy [ˈbelbɔɪ] *n (page)* chasseur *m*; *(porter)* porteur *m*

belle [bel] *n* belle *f*, beauté *f*; **the belle of the ball** la reine du bal

belletrist [belˈletrɪst] *n Literature* écrivain *m* des belles-lettres

bellflower [ˈbelˌflaʊə(r)] *n Bot* campanule *f*

bellhop [ˈbelhɒp] *n Am (page)* chasseur *m*; *(porter)* porteur *m*

bellicose [ˈbelɪkəʊs] *adj* belliqueux

bellicosely [ˈbelɪkəʊslɪ] *adv* agressivement

bellicosity [ˌbelɪˈkɒsətɪ] *n* bellicisme *m*

-bellied [ˈbelɪd] *suff* **round-/swollen-bellied** au ventre rond/enflé

belligerence [bɪˈlɪdʒərəns], **belligerency** [bɪˈlɪdʒərənsɪ] *n Mil* belligérance *f*

belligerent [bɪˈlɪdʒərənt] **1** *n* (**a**) *(in dispute)* partie *f* (**b**) *Mil* belligérant(e) *m,f*

2 *adj* (**a**) *(aggressive → person, tone of voice, attitude)* agressif, belliqueux (**b**) *Mil (at war → country)* belligérant

bellow [ˈbeləʊ] **1** *vi (bull)* beugler, meugler; *(elephant)* barrir; *(person)* brailler; **to bellow at sb** *(with rage)* brailler dans les oreilles de qn; **he bellowed with pain** il a hurlé de douleur; **the crowd bellowed with laughter** la foule hurlait de rire

2 *vt* **to bellow sth (out)** brailler qch; *Fam (song)* beugler qch

3 *n (of bull)* beuglement *m*, meuglement *m*; *(of elephant)* barrissement *m*; *(of person)* braillement *m*

bellowing [ˈbeləʊɪŋ] *n (of bull)* beuglement *m*, meuglement *m*; *(of elephant)* barrissement *m*; *(of person)* braillement *m*

bellows [ˈbeləʊz] *npl* (**a**) *Tech (for fire)* soufflet *m*; **a pair of bellows** un soufflet (**b**) *Mus (for accordion, organ)* soufflerie *f*

bellpull [ˈbelpʊl] *n (for servant)* cordon *m* de sonnette; *(on door)* poignée *f* de sonnette

bell-ringer *n Mus* sonneur *m*, carillonneur *m*

bell-ringing *n Mus* carillonnement *m*

bell-shaped *adj* en forme de cloche

Bell's palsy [belz-] *n Med* paralysie *f* de Bell

bellwether [ˈbelˌweðə(r)] *n Agr (sheep)* sonnailler *m*; *Fig (person)* meneur(euse) *m,f*, chef *m*

belly [ˈbelɪ] *(pl* **bellies**, *pt & pp* **bellied**) **1** *n* (**a**) *(stomach)* ventre *m*; **a big belly** un gros ventre; **he only thinks of his belly** il ne pense qu'à son estomac; *Fam Fig* **to go belly up** *(of company)* faire faillite ❑

(**b**) *(of plane, ship)* ventre *m*; *(of sail)* creux *m*

(**c**) *Mus (of cello, guitar)* table *f* d'harmonie

(**d**) *Culin* **belly of pork, pork belly** poitrine *f* de porc

(**e**) *Arch (womb)* ventre *m*

2 *vi* **to belly (out)** s'enfler, se gonfler

3 *vt* enfler, gonfler

►► *Fam* ***belly button*** nombril ❑ *m*; ***belly dance*** danse *f* du ventre; ***belly dancer*** danseuse *f* du ventre *ou* orientale; *Swimming* ***belly flop*** plat *m*; **to do a belly flop** faire un plat; *Fam* ***belly laugh*** gros rire ❑ *m*

bellyache [ˈbelɪeɪk] *Fam* **1** *n* (**a**) *(pain)* mal *m* au *ou* de ventre ❑; **I've got (a) bellyache** j'ai mal au ventre (**b**) *(complaint)* rogne *f*, rouspétance *f*

2 *vi* râler; **stop bellyaching!** arrête de râler!

bellyaching [ˈbelɪˌeɪkɪŋ] *n (UNCOUNT) Fam* ronchonnements *mpl*, rouspétances *fpl*; **I don't want any bellyaching** je n'accepterai aucune rouspétance; **your constant bellyaching is driving me up the wall** tes jérémiades incessantes me fatiguent

belly-dance *vi* danser *ou* faire la danse du ventre

bellyful [ˈbelɪfʊl] *n Fam (of food)* ventre *m* plein ❑; *Fig* **I've had a bellyful** j'en ai jusque-là; **I've had a bellyful of your complaints** j'en ai ras le bol de tes rouspétances

belly-land *Fam Aviat* **1** *vt* atterrir sur le ventre ❑

2 *vi* atterrir sur le ventre ❑

belly-landing *n Fam Aviat* atterrissage *m* sur le ventre ❑; **the plane made a belly-landing** l'avion a atterri *ou* s'est posé sur le ventre

Belmont Stakes [ˈbelmɒnt-] *n Horseracing* **the Belmont Stakes** = course pour chevaux de trois ans, dans l'État de New York

belong [bɪˈlɒŋ] *vi* (**a**) *(as property)* **to belong to sb** appartenir à *ou* être à qn; **the dictionary belongs to her** le dictionnaire lui appartient *ou* est à elle; *Com* **the company belongs to a large conglomerate** l'entreprise appartient à un important conglomérat; *Law* **to belong to the Crown** *(land etc)* dépendre de la Couronne

(**b**) *(as member)* **to belong to a society** faire partie d'une société; **do you belong to this club?** êtes-vous membre de ce cercle?; **he belongs to a trade union** il fait partie *ou* il est membre d'un syndicat, il est syndiqué

(**c**) *(as part, component)* appartenir; **the field belongs to that house** le champ dépend de cette maison; **this key belongs to the car** cette clé est pour la voiture; **this jacket belongs with those trousers** cette veste va avec ce pantalon; **which species do they belong to?** à quelle espèce appartiennent-ils?; **she belongs in another era** elle est d'une autre époque

(**d**) *(be in proper place)* être à sa place; **the dishes belong in that cupboard** les assiettes vont dans ce placard; **put the books back where they belong** remettez les livres à leur place; **the two of them belong together** ces deux-là sont faits pour être ensemble; **these gloves belong together** ces gants appartiennent à la même paire; **I don't belong here** je ne suis pas à ma place ici; **go back home where you belong** rentrez chez vous; **she doesn't feel she belongs** elle ne se sent pas chez elle ici; **he belongs in teaching** sa place est dans l'enseignement; **these issues belong in a court of law** ces questions relèvent d'un tribunal

belonging [bɪˈlɒŋɪŋ] **1** *n* **a sense of belonging** un sentiment d'appartenance

2 belongings *npl* affaires *fpl*, possessions *fpl*; **she packed the few belongings she had** elle a emballé le peu (de choses *ou* d'affaires) qu'elle avait; **personal belongings** objets *mpl ou* effets *mpl* personnels

Belorussia, Belorussian = **Belarus, Belarussian**

beloved [bɪˈlʌvɪd] **1** *n* bien-aimé(e) *m,f*, amour *m*; **my beloved** mon (ma) bien-aimé(e); *Rel* **dearly beloved, we are gathered here today...** mes bien chers frères, nous sommes ici aujourd'hui...

2 *adj* chéri, bien-aimé; **he was beloved by** *or* **of all his friends** il était cher à tous ses amis; **my beloved father** mon très cher père, mon père bien-aimé

below [bɪˈləʊ] **1** *prep* (**a**) *(at, to a lower position than)* au-dessous de, en dessous de; *(under)* sous; **the flat below ours** l'appartement au-dessous *ou* en dessous du nôtre; **her skirt came to below her knees** sa jupe lui descendait au-dessous du genou; **below the surface** sous la surface; **below (the) ground** sous (la) terre; **below sea level** au-dessous du niveau de la mer; **below the surface** sous la surface

(**b**) *(inferior to)* au-dessous de, inférieur à; **temperatures below zero** des températures au-dessous de *ou* inférieures à zéro; **his grades are below average** ses notes sont au-dessous de *ou* inférieures à la moyenne; **below the poverty line** en dessous du seuil de pauvreté; **children below the age of five** des enfants de moins de cinq ans; **the rank is just below that of general** le rang est juste au-dessous de celui d'un général

(**c**) *(downstream of)* en aval de

(**d**) *(south of)* au sud de

2 *adv* (**a**) *(in lower place, on lower level)* en dessous, plus bas; **we looked down onto the town below** nous contemplions la ville à nos pieds; **down below in the valley** en bas dans la vallée; **the flat below** l'appartement d'en dessous *ou* du dessous; **he could hear two men talking below** il entendait deux hommes parler en bas; **seen from below** vu d'en bas; **the title came first with her name immediately below** le titre apparaissait en premier avec son nom juste en dessous; *Arch or Literary* **here below** *(on earth)* ici-bas

(**b**) *(with numbers, quantities)* moins; *Fam* **it was twenty below** il faisait moins vingt; **children of five and below** les enfants de cinq ans et moins

(**c**) *(in text)* plus bas, ci-dessous; **see below** voir plus bas *ou* ci-dessous; **the address given below** l'adresse mentionnée ci-dessous

(**d**) *Naut* en bas; **to go below** descendre dans l'entrepont; **she went below to her cabin** elle est descendue à sa cabine

below-average *adj* en-dessous de la moyenne, *Can* sous la moyenne

below-the-line **1** *n Mktg* publicité *f* hors-média

2 *adj Acct (expenses)* au-dessous de la ligne

►► ***below-the-line accounts*** comptes *mpl* de résultats exceptionnels; *Mktg* ***below-the-line advertising*** publicité *f* hors-média; *Acct* ***below-the-line costs*** coûts *mpl* hors-média; *Mktg* ***below-the-line promotion*** promotion *f* hors-média

belt [belt] **1** *n* (**a**) *(band of leather etc) & Sport* ceinture *f*; *Mil* ceinturon *m*, ceinture *f*; *(for punishing)* lanière *f* de cuir; **a leather belt** une ceinture en cuir; **he had a gun at his belt** il portait un revolver à la ceinture; **to give sb the belt** *(at school)* donner une correction à qn *(avec une lanière de cuir)*; **to be a brown/black belt** *(in martial arts)* être ceinture marron/noire; *Fig* **to have sth under one's belt** *(move, project)* en avoir fini avec qch; *(driving licence, degree)* avoir qch en poche; **once you've got a few years' experience under your belt** une fois que tu as quelques années d'expérience à ton actif; *Boxing* **to hold the belt** être le champion; *Boxing* **no hitting below the belt** il est interdit de porter des coups bas; *Fig* **to hit sb beneath** *or* **below the belt** donner à qn un coup en traître *ou* un coup bas; **that was a bit below the belt** c'était un peu déloyal comme procédé; **to pull in** *or* **to tighten one's belt** se serrer la ceinture

(**b**) *(of machine)* courroie *f*

(**c**) *(area, zone)* région *f*; **belts of high unemployment** des régions à fort taux de chômage

(**d**) *Fam (sharp blow → with hand)* gifle ❑ *f*; *(→ with bat, stick)* coup ❑ *m*; **he gave the ball a terrific belt** il a tapé un grand coup dans la balle; **to give sb a belt in the face** flanquer un gnon *ou* un pain dans la tronche à qn

(**e**) *Fam (of whisky)* gorgée ❑ *f*

2 *vt* (**a**) *(dress, trousers)* ceinturer, mettre une ceinture à; **he had a gun belted to his waist** il avait un revolver à la ceinture; **a belted raincoat** un imperméable à ceinture

(**b**) *(hit with belt)* donner des coups de ceinture à; *(as punishment)* donner une correction à *(avec une lanière de cuir)*

(**c**) *Fam (hit with hand)* gifler ❑; *(hit with bat, stick → ball)* frapper dans ❑, taper dans ❑; *(→ person)* frapper ❑; **I belted him (one) in the eye** je lui en ai collé un dans l'œil; **she belted the ball** elle a donné un grand coup dans la balle

3 *vi Br Fam* filer; **they went belting along** ils fonçaient; **he belted into/out of the room** il est entré dans/sorti de la pièce à toute berzingue;

to belt down the stairs descendre l'escalier quatre à quatre; **they were belting down the motorway** ils fonçaient sur l'autoroute
►► ***belt buckle*** boucle *f* de ceinture; *Tech* ***belt conveyor*** transporteur *m* à courroie *ou* à ruban *ou* à bande; *Tech* ***belt drive*** transmission *f* par courroie; ***belt loop*** passant *m (de ceinture)*; *Tech* ***belt sander*** ponceuse *f* à courroie

►**belt out** *vt sep Fam (order, instructions)* gueuler; *(song)* gueuler, brailler; **she belted out the last song** elle s'est donnée à fond dans la dernière chanson

►**belt up** *vi* (**a**) *(in car, plane)* attacher sa ceinture; **belt up!** attachez votre ceinture!
(**b**) *Br Fam (be quiet)* la fermer, la boucler; **belt up!** boucle-la!

belt-and-braces *adj (policy, measures)* extrêmement prudent

Beltane ['beltem] *n* = fête d'origine celte célébrée le premier mai, notamment par des feux de joie

belt-driven *adj Tech* actionné par courroie

belted ['beltɪd] *adj* ceinturé
►► *Aut* ***belted tyre*** pneu *m* à ceinture

belter ['beltə(r)] *n Br Fam* (**a**) *(excellent thing)* **it was a real belter** c'était vraiment génial (**b**) *(singer)* = chanteur ou chanteuse qui chante à pleins poumons; *(song)* = chanson chantée à pleins poumons

belting ['beltɪŋ] *n* (**a**) *Tech (belts)* courroie(s) *f(pl)*; *Tex (material)* matériau *m* à courroies (**b**) *Fam* **to give sb a belting** *(as punishment)* donner des coups de ceinture *ou* administrer une correction à qn; *(in fight)* rouer qn de coups; *(in match, competition etc)* mettre la pâtée à qn

beltway ['beltweɪ] *n Am Transp* (boulevard *m*) périphérique *m*; *Fig Pol* **inside the beltway** à Washington

beluga [bɪ'luːgə] *n Ich & Zool (fish, whale)* bélouga *m*, béluga *m*; *Culin (caviar)* caviar *m* de bélouga *ou* béluga

belvedere ['belvɪˌdɪə(r)] *n Archit* belvédère *m*

bemired [bɪ'maɪəd] *adj Literary* embourbé

bemoan [bɪ'məʊn] *vt* pleurer, se lamenter sur; **he bemoaned the loss of this freedom** il pleura la perte de sa liberté; **to bemoan one's fate** pleurer sur son sort; **she was bemoaning the fact that they had no money** elle se lamentait de ce qu'ils n'avaient pas d'argent

bemuse [bɪ'mjuːz] *vt Literary (confuse)* déconcerter, dérouter, rendre perplexe

bemused [bɪ'mjuːzd] *adj* déconcerté, dérouté, perplexe; **she seemed bemused** elle semblait déconcertée; **he gave a bemused smile** il sourit d'un air *ou* il eut un sourire déconcerté

ben [ben] *n Ir & Scot Geog* sommet *m*, mont *m*
►► ***Ben Nevis*** = point culminant de la Grande-Bretagne, en Écosse (1343m)

Benares [bɪ'nɑːrɪz] *n Geog & Rel* Bénarès

bench [bentʃ] **1** *n* (**a**) *(seat)* banc *m*; *(caned, padded)* banquette *f*; *(in auditorium)* gradin *m*; **park bench** banc *m* public
(**b**) *Sport* banc *m (pour les joueurs qui ne sont pas sur le terrain)*; **on the bench** en réserve
(**c**) *Br Parl (in Parliament)* banc *m*; **the government benches** les bancs du gouvernement
(**d**) *(work table)* établi *m*
(**e**) *Law (seat)* banc *m*; **the bench** *(judge)* la cour, le juge; *(judges as group)* les juges, les magistrats; **address your remarks to the bench** adressez-vous à la cour; **she has been raised to the bench** elle a été nommée juge; **he serves** *or* **sits on the bench** *(permanent office)* il est juge; *(for particular case)* il siège au tribunal; **what does the bench feel about this?** qu'en pense la cour?
2 *comp (lathe, vice)* d'établi
3 *vt Am Sport* retirer du jeu
4 *vi Rel (in Judaism)* prier après le repas *(dans la religion juive)*
►► *Sport* ***bench press*** développé-couché *m*; ***bench seat*** *(in vehicle)* banquette; *Law* ***bench warrant*** mandat *m* d'arrêt

bencher ['bentʃə(r)] *n Br Law* ≃ membre *m* de l'ordre des avocats

benching ['bentʃɪŋ] *n Rel (in Judaism)* = prière après le repas *(dans la religion juive)*

benchmark ['bentʃˌmɑːk] **1** *n* repère *m*; *Constr (in surveying)* repère *m* de nivellement; *Fig* repère *m*, point *m* de référence
2 *comp (decision)* de base, de référence
►► *Mktg* ***benchmark market*** marché *m* de référence; *Can Admin* ***benchmark position*** poste-repère *m*; *Comput* ***benchmark programme*** programme *m* d'évaluation des performances; *Comput* ***benchmark test*** test *m* d'évaluation (de programme)

benchmarking ['bentʃmɑːkɪŋ] *n Ind & Tech* benchmarking *m*

bench-press *vt* **to bench-press 50 kg** soulever 50 kg *(allongé)*

benchtest ['bentʃˌtest] *Tech* **1** *n* banc *m* d'essai
2 *vt* faire passer au banc d'essai

BEND [bend]

plier	► 1 (a)
tordre, courber	► 1 (b)
se courber	► 2 (a)
céder	► 2 (c)
virage	► 3 (a)
coude	► 3 (a)
pli	► 3 (b)

(*pt & pp* **bent** [bent]) **1** *vt* (**a**) *(arm, finger)* plier; *(knee, leg)* plier, fléchir; *(back, body)* courber; *(head)* pencher, baisser; **they bent their heads over their books** ils se penchèrent sur leurs livres; *Rel* **to bend one's head in prayer** baisser la tête pour prier; **on bended knee** à genoux; **he went down on bended knee** il se mit à genoux, il s'agenouilla; **to bend sb to one's will** plier qn à sa volonté; *Br Fam* **he likes to bend the elbow** il sait lever le coude, il aime bien picoler; *Fam* **to bend sb's ear** casser les oreilles à qn
(**b**) *(pipe, wire)* tordre, courber; *(branch, tree)* courber, faire ployer; *(bow)* bander, arquer; **to bend sth at right angles** plier qch à angle droit; **she bent the stem slightly** elle a courbé un peu la tige; **he bent the rod out of shape** il a tordu la barre; **to bend the rules** faire une entorse au règlement
(**c**) *(deflect → light)* réfracter; *(→ ray)* infléchir; *(→ stream)* dériver, détourner
(**d**) *Literary (direct, turn)* diriger; **they bent their steps towards home** ils se dirigèrent *ou* ils dirigèrent leurs pas vers la maison; **he bent his attention** *or* **his mind to solving the problem** il s'appliqua à résoudre le problème; **we bent all our efforts to fighting racism** nous avons mis tous nos efforts dans la lutte contre le racisme; **they bent themselves to the task** ils se sont attelés à la tâche; **all eyes were bent on the demonstration** tous les yeux *ou* regards étaient fixés sur la démonstration
(**e**) *Naut (fasten → cable, rope)* étalinguer; *(→ sail)* enverguer
2 *vi* (**a**) *(arm, knee, leg)* plier; *(person)* se courber, se pencher; *(head)* se pencher; *(rod, wire)* plier, se courber; *(branch, tree)* ployer, plier; **to bend under the burden/the weight** ployer sous le fardeau/le poids; **she bent over the counter** elle s'est penchée par-dessus le comptoir; **he bent backwards/forwards** il s'est penché en arrière/en avant
(**b**) *(river, road)* faire un coude, tourner; **the road bends to the left** la route tourne à gauche
(**c**) *(submit)* céder; **the people refused to bend to the colonial forces** le peuple a refusé de se soumettre aux forces coloniales; **the government bent to pressure from the unions** l'administration a cédé à la pression des syndicats
3 *n* (**a**) *(in road)* virage *m*, tournant *m*; *(in river)* méandre *m*, coude *m*; *(in pipe, rod)* coude *m*; **after I rounded the first bend in the road** après (avoir pris) le premier virage; **to take a bend at speed** prendre un virage à toute vitesse; **the road makes a bend to the right** la route fait un coude vers la droite; **bends for 7 miles** *(sign)* virages sur 10 km; *Fam* **to drive sb round the bend** rendre qn dingue; *Fam* **he's completely round the bend** il est complètement dingue
(**b**) *(in arm)* pli *m*, saignée *f*; *(in knee)* pli *m*, flexion *f*; **she did a couple of forward bends** elle s'est penchée plusieurs fois en avant
(**c**) *Naut (knot)* nœud *m* (de jonction)
4 bends *npl Med* **the bends** la maladie des caissons; **to get the bends** être atteint par la maladie des caissons
►► *Her* ***bend sinister*** barre *f* de bâtardise

►**bend back 1** *vt sep* replier, recourber
2 *vi* (**a**) *(person)* se pencher en arrière
(**b**) *(blade, tube)* se recourber

►**bend down 1** *vt sep (branch, tree)* faire ployer; *(blade, tube)* replier, recourber
2 *vi* (**a**) *(person)* se courber, se baisser
(**b**) *(branch, tree)* plier, ployer

►**bend over 1** *vt sep* replier, recourber
2 *vi* se pencher; *Fig* **to bend over backwards to please (sb)** se donner beaucoup de mal pour faire plaisir (à qn)

bended ['bendɪd] *adj Literary* **on one's bended knees, on bended knee** *(ask for something)* à genoux; **to go down on bended knee** *or* **knees** *(kneel down)* se mettre à genoux, s'agenouiller; *Fig* **to go down on one's bended knees to sb** *(beg)* supplier qn

bender ['bendə(r)] *n* (**a**) *Fam (drinking session)* beuverie *f*; **to go on a bender** faire la noce (**b**) *very Fam (homosexual)* pédale *f*, tantouze *f*, = terme injurieux désignant un homosexuel (**c**) *Am Fam Sport* balle *f* à effet

bendy ['bendɪ] (*compar* **bendier**, *superl* **bendiest**) *adj* (**a**) *(road)* sinueux (**b**) *(flexible)* souple, flexible

beneath [bɪ'niːθ] **1** *prep* (**a**) *(under)* sous; **the ground beneath my feet** le sol sous mes pieds; **buried beneath tons of rubble** enfoui sous des tonnes de gravats; **the ship sank beneath the waves** le navire a sombré sous les vagues
(**b**) *(below)* **the valley was spread out beneath us** la vallée s'étalait sous nos pieds
(**c**) *(unworthy of)* indigne de; **she thinks the work is beneath her** elle estime que le travail est indigne d'elle; **beneath contempt** parfaitement méprisable
(**d**) *(socially inferior to)* inférieur *(socialement)*; **he married beneath him** il a fait une mésalliance; **she thinks everybody's beneath her** elle s'imagine que tout le monde lui est inférieur
2 *adv (underneath)* dessous, en dessous; **from beneath** d'en dessous

Benedictine 1 *n* (**a**) [benɪ'dɪktɪn] *Rel* bénédictin(e) *m,f* (**b**) [benɪ'dɪktiːn] *(liqueur)* Bénédictine® *f*
2 *adj* [benɪ'dɪktɪn] *Rel* bénédictin

benediction [ˌbenɪ'dɪkʃən] *n Rel & Fig (blessing)* bénédiction *f*; *(service)* salut *m*

benedictory [ˌbenɪ'dɪktərɪ] *adj Rel & Fig* de bénédiction; **benedictory prayer** bénédiction *f*

benefaction [ˌbenɪ'fækʃən] *n* (**a**) *(good deed)* acte *m* de bienfaisance (**b**) *(donation)* don *m*, donation *f*

benefactor ['benɪfæktə(r)] *n* bienfaiteur *m*

benefactress ['benɪfæktrɪs] *n* bienfaitrice *f*

benefice ['benɪfɪs] *n Rel* bénéfice *m*

beneficence [bɪ'nefɪsəns] *n Literary* (**a**) *(kindness)* bienveillance *f*, bienfaisance *f* (**b**) *(good deed)* acte *m* de bienfaisance, bienfait *m*

beneficent [bɪ'nefɪsənt] *adj Literary (person, regime)* bienfaisant, généreux; *(change, effect)* bienfaisant, salutaire

beneficial [ˌbenɪ'fɪʃəl] *adj (good, useful)* avantageux, profitable; **legislation beneficial to the self-employed** des lois favorables aux travailleurs non-salariés; **the holiday proved highly beneficial** les vacances ont été extrêmement bénéfiques; **vitamins are beneficial to health** les vitamines sont bonnes pour la santé; **beneficial effects** des effets salutaires
►► *Law* ***beneficial legacy*** usufruit *m*; ***beneficial owner*** usufruitier(ère) *m,f*

beneficially [ˌbenɪ'fɪʃəlɪ] *adv* avantageusement

beneficiary [ˌbenɪ'fɪʃərɪ] (*pl* **beneficiaries**) *n* (**a**) *(of insurance policy, trust)* bénéficiaire *mf*; *Law (of will)* bénéficiaire *mf*, légataire *mf*; *(of family allowance)* allocataire *mf*; *Fig* **the main beneficiaries of the new law will be working mothers** ce sont les mères qui travaillent qui bénéficieront le plus de la nouvelle loi; **beneficiary under a trust** bénéficiaire d'une fiducie (**b**) *Rel* bénéficier *m*

benefit ['benɪfɪt] (*pt & pp* **benefited** *or* **benefitted**, *cont* **benefiting** *or* **benefitting**) **1** *n* (**a**) *(advantage)* avantage *m*; **to have the benefit of sth**

bénéficier de qch; **the benefits of a good education** les avantages *mpl ou* les bienfaits *mpl* d'une bonne éducation; **she is starting to feel the benefits of the treatment** elle commence à ressentir les bienfaits du traitement; **she did it for the benefit of the whole family** elle a agi pour le bien-être de toute la famille; **I'm saying this for your benefit** je dis cela pour toi *ou* pour ton bien; **for the benefit of those who arrived late** pour les retardataires *ou* ceux qui sont arrivés en retard; **the speech she made was all for his benefit** le discours qu'elle a prononcé ne s'adressait qu'à lui; **the holiday wasn't of much benefit to him** les vacances ne lui ont pas fait tellement de bien; **our discussion was of no benefit to me** notre discussion ne m'a rien apporté; **it's to your benefit to watch your diet** il est dans votre intérêt de surveiller ce que vous mangez; **this law is to the benefit of the wealthy** cette loi favorise les gens aisés; **to offer sb the benefit of one's experience** faire profiter qn de son expérience; **with the benefit of hindsight, I now see I was wrong** avec le recul *ou* rétrospectivement, je m'aperçois que j'avais tort; **to give sb the benefit of the doubt** laisser *ou* accorder à qn le bénéfice du doute; *Fin* **benefits** *(to employee)* avantages *mpl* sociaux

(**b**) *Fin (payment)* allocation *f*, prestation *f*; **social security benefits** prestations *fpl* sociales; *Am* **tax benefit** dégrèvement *m*, allègement *m* fiscal

(**c**)*(performance)* spectacle *m (au profit d'une association caritative)*

2 *vt (do good to)* faire du bien à; *(bring financial profit to)* profiter à; **a steady exchange rate benefits trade** un change stable est avantageux pour le commerce *ou* favorise le commerce; **whom does it benefit?** qui en bénéficie?; **it will benefit mankind** c'est l'humanité toute entière qui en profitera

3 *vi* **to benefit by** *or* **from sth** bénéficier de qch, profiter de qch, tirer avantage de qch; **he will benefit from the experience** l'expérience lui sera bénéfique; **no one is likely to benefit by** *or* **from the closures** personne n'a de chance de tirer avantage des fermetures; **the novel would benefit greatly from judicious editing** le roman gagnerait beaucoup à être révisé de façon judicieuse; **you would benefit from a stay in the country** un séjour à la campagne vous ferait du bien; **who benefits most from his death?** à qui sa mort profite-t-elle le plus?

►► *Br Admin* ***Benefits Agency*** caisse *f* des allocations sociales; *Rel & Hist* ***benefit of clergy*** bénéfice *m* de clergie; ***benefit concert*** concert *m (au profit d'une association caritative)*; *Sport* ***benefit match*** match *m (au profit d'un joueur auquel on rend hommage)*; *Fin* ***benefits package*** *(to employee)* avantages *mpl* sociaux; *Theat* ***benefit performance*** représentation *f* de bienfaisance; *Mktg* ***benefit segmentation*** segmentation *f* par avantages recherchés; *Am Fin* ***benefit society*** société *f* de prévoyance, mutuelle *f*

Benelux ['benɪlʌks] *n* Bénélux *m*; **the Benelux countries** les pays du Bénélux; **in the Benelux countries** au Bénélux

benevolence [bɪ'nevələns] *n* (**a**) *(kindness)* bienveillance *f*, bienfaisance *f* (**b**) *(good deed)* acte *m* de bienfaisance, bienfait *m*

benevolent [bɪ'nevələnt] *adj* (**a**) *(kindly)* bienveillant; **to feel benevolent towards sb** être bien disposé envers qn

(**b**) *(donor)* généreux, charitable; *(organization)* de bienfaisance

►► *Hist* ***benevolent despot*** despote *m* éclairé; *Hist* ***benevolent despotism*** despotisme *m* éclairé; *Fin* ***benevolent fund*** fonds *m* de prévoyance; ***benevolent society*** association *f* de bienfaisance; *Fig Hum* **I'm not a benevolent society** je ne suis pas l'Armée du Salut

benevolently [bɪ'nevələntlɪ] *adv* avec bienveillance

BEng [,biː'eŋ] *n Br Univ (abbr* **Bachelor of Engineering**) *(person)* = titulaire d'une licence d'ingénierie; *(qualification)* licence *f* d'ingénierie

Bengal [,beŋ'gɔːl] *n* Bengale *m*; **in Bengal** au Bengale

►► *Br* ***Bengal light*** feu *m* de Bengale; ***Bengal tiger*** tigre *m* du Bengale

Bengali [,beŋ'gɔːlɪ], **Bengalese** [,beŋgə'liːz] **1** *n* (**a**) *(person)* Bengali *mf*, Bengalais(e) *m,f* (**b**) *(language)* bengali *m*

2 *adj* bengali, bengalais

3 *comp (history)* du Bangladesh; *(teacher)* de bengali

benighted [bɪ'naɪtɪd] *adj Literary (ignorant → person)* plongé dans (les ténèbres de) l'ignorance; *(→ mind)* étroit; *(→ policy)* aveugle

benign [bɪ'naɪn] *adj* (**a**) *(kind → person)* affable, aimable; *(→ smile)* bienveillant; *(→ power, system)* bienfaisant, salutaire (**b**) *(harmless)* bénin(igne) *m,f* (**c**) *(temperate → climate)* doux (douce), clément

►► *Med* ***benign illness*** maladie *f* bénigne; *Med* ***benign tumour*** tumeur *f* bénigne

benignancy [bɪ'nɪgnənsɪ] *n Literary* bienveillance *f*, bonté *f*

benignantly [bɪ'nɪgnəntlɪ] *adv Literary* avec bienveillance

benignity [bɪ'nɪgnɪtɪ] *n Literary* (**a**) *(of person)* bienveillance *f*, bonté *f* (**b**) *(of climate)* douceur *f*

benignly [bɪ'naɪnlɪ] *adv* (**a**) *(kindly → say, speak, smile)* avec bienveillance (**b**) *(harmlessly)* bénignement

Benin [be'niːn] *n* Bénin *m*; **in Benin** au Bénin

Beninese [,benɪ'niːz] **1** *n* Béninois(e) *m,f*

2 *adj* béninois

Benjamin ['bendʒəmɪn] *pr n Bible* Benjamin

Bennism ['benɪzəm] *n Pol* = politique de nationalisation de l'industrie en Grande-Bretagne (d'après Tony Benn, ministre travailliste en 1974)

benny ['benɪ] *(pl* **bennies**) *n Fam Drugs slang* (comprimé *m* de) Benzédrine® *f*

bens *Admin (written abbr* **benefits**) allocations *fpl*

bent [bent] **1** *pt & pp of* **bend**

2 *adj* (**a**) *(curved → tree, tube, wire)* tordu, courbé; *(→ branch)* courbé; *(→ back)* voûté; *(→ person)* voûté, tassé; *(out of shape → aerial, coathanger)* tordu; *(→ axle, lever)* coudé; *Am Fam Fig* **bent out of shape** *(angry, upset)* dans tous ses états

(**b**) *(dented)* cabossé, bosselé

(**c**) *Br (determined)* **he's bent on becoming an actor** il est décidé à *ou* veut absolument devenir acteur; **she's bent on winning** elle est décidée à gagner; **to be bent on self-destruction** être porté à l'autodestruction

(**d**) *Br Fam (dishonest)* pourri

(**e**) *Br very Fam Pej (homosexual)* homo, gay; **as bent as a nine bob note** *or* **as a three pound note** pédé comme un phoque

3 *n* (**a**) *(liking)* penchant *m*, goût *m*; *(aptitude)* aptitudes *fpl*, dispositions *fpl*; **they're of an artistic bent** ils sont tournés vers les arts; **she has a natural bent for music** *(liking)* elle a un goût naturel pour la musique; *(talent)* elle a des dispositions naturelles pour la musique; **he followed his (natural) bent** il a suivi son penchant *ou* son inclination

(**b**) *Br (endurance)* endurance *f*; **to the top of one's bent** au meilleur de sa forme

►► *Bot* ***bent grass*** agrostide *f*

Benthamism ['benθəmɪzəm] *n Phil* benthamisme *m*

Benthamite ['benθəmaɪt] *n Phil* adhérent(e) *m,f* du benthamisme

benthos ['benθɒs] *n Biol* benthos *m*

bentonite ['bentənaɪt] *n Miner* bentonite *f*

bentwood ['bentwʊd] *Carp* **1** *n* bois *m* courbé

2 *comp (chair, table)* en bois courbé

benumb [bɪ'nʌm] *vt Literary* engourdir; *(with cold)* transir; *Fig (with fear)* paralyser

benumbed [bɪ'nʌmd] *adj Literary* **benumbed by the** *or* **with cold** *(person)* transi de froid; *(fingers, toes)* engourdi par le froid; **her mind was benumbed with fear** elle était transie de *ou* paralysée par la peur

benzaldehyde [ben'zældɪ,haɪd] *n Chem* benzaldéhyde *m*

Benzedrine® ['benzədriːn] *n Pharm* Benzédrine® *f*

benzene ['benziːn] *n Chem* benzène *m*

►► *Chem* ***benzene ring*** noyau *m* benzénique

benzin, benzine ['benziːn, ben'ziːn] *n Chem & Ind* benzine *f*

benzodiazepine [,benzəʊdaɪ'æzəpiːn] *n Pharm* benzodiazépine *f*

benzoic [ben'zəʊɪk] *adj Chem & Pharm* benzoïque

benzoin ['benzəʊɪn] *n* (**a**) *Chem & Pharm (resin)* benjoin *m* (**b**) *Bot (tree)* styrax *m* benjoin

benzol ['benzɒl] *n Chem & Petr* benzol *m*

benzyl ['benzɪl] *n Chem* benzyle *m*

►► ***benzyl alcohol*** alcool *m* benzylique; ***benzyl cellulose*** cellulose *f* benzylique

Beowulf ['bɪəwʊlf] *pr n* = héros légendaire d'un poème épique anglo-saxon (VIIIème siècle).

bequeath [bɪ'kwiːð] *vt (pass on)* transmettre, léguer; *Law (in will)* léguer; **her father bequeathed her his fortune** son père lui a légué sa fortune; **they've bequeathed nothing to us but a ruined economy** ils ne nous ont légué qu'une économie en ruine

bequest [bɪ'kwest] *n* legs *m*; *Fin* **she made a bequest of £2,000 to her favourite charity** elle a légué 2000 livres à l'œuvre de bienfaisance qu'elle préférait

berate [bɪ'reɪt] *vt* réprimander; **he berated them for being late** il leur a reproché d'être en retard

Berber ['bɜːbə(r)] **1** *n* (**a**) *(person)* Berbère *mf* (**b**) *(language)* berbère *m*

2 *adj* berbère

bereave [bɪ'riːv] *(pt & pp* **bereaved** *or* **bereft** [-'reft]) *vt* priver, déposséder; **the war bereaved them of their two sons** la guerre leur a pris leurs deux fils, ils ont perdu leurs deux fils à la guerre

bereaved [bɪ'riːvd] **1** *adj* affligé, endeuillé; **a bereaved mother** une mère qui vient de perdre son enfant; **he's recently bereaved** il a perdu quelqu'un récemment

2 *npl* **the bereaved** la famille du défunt

bereavement [bɪ'riːvmənt] *n* deuil *m*; **owing to a recent bereavement** en raison d'un deuil récent; **she has suffered a bereavement** elle a été affligée par un deuil; **she can't get over her recent bereavement** *(husband's death)* elle n'arrive pas à accepter la mort de son mari; **in his bereavement** dans son deuil; **a tragic bereavement** une perte cruelle

►► ***bereavement counselling*** = service d'aide psychologique aux personnes frappées par un deuil

bereft [bɪ'reft] *Formal or Literary* **1** *pt & pp of* **bereave**

2 *adj* privé; **bereft of all hope** complètement désespéré; **to be bereft of reason** avoir perdu la raison; **I feel utterly bereft** je me sens totalement seul; **to leave sb bereft of speech** rendre qn muet; **she collapsed into a chair, her face bereft of colour** elle s'effondra sur une chaise, le visage livide

Berenice's Hair [,berɪ'naɪsɪz-] *n Astron* la Chevelure de Bérénice

beret ['bereɪ] *n* béret *m*

berg [bɜːg] *n (iceberg)* iceberg *m*

Bergamo ['bɜːgəməʊ] *n* Bergame

bergamot ['bɜːgəmɒt] *n Bot & Chem* bergamote *f*

►► ***bergamot oil*** essence *f* de bergamote

Bergen ['bɜːgən] *n* Bergen

Bergschrund ['bɜːgʃrʊnt] *n (in mountaineering)* rimaye *f*

Bergsonian [bɜːg'səʊnɪən] *adj Phil* bergsonien

bergy bit ['bɜːgɪ-] *n* bergy bit *m (fragment d'iceberg)*

beribboned [bɪ'rɪbənd] *adj* enrubanné

[illegible]

Bering ['berɪŋ]

►► ***the Bering Sea*** la mer de Béring; ***the Bering Strait*** le détroit de Béring

berk [bɜːk] *n Br Fam* andouille *f*, debile *mf*; **to make a complete berk of oneself** se conduire comme une andouille; **to feel a right berk** se sentir con

Berkeley Square ['bɑːklɪ-] *n* = place londonienne où vécurent des personnages célèbres au XVIIème et XVIIIème siècles

berkelium [bɜː'kiːlɪəm] *n Chem* berkélium *m*

Berks. *(written abbr* **Berkshire**) le Berkshire, = comté dans le sud de l'Angleterre

Berkshire ['bɑːkʃɪə] *n* le Berkshire, = comté dans le sud de l'Angleterre; **in Berkshire** dans le Berkshire

Berlin [bɜː'lɪn] *n* Berlin; **East Berlin** Berlin-Est; **West Berlin** Berlin-Ouest

►► ***the Berlin airlift*** le pont aérien de Berlin; ***the Berlin Wall*** le mur de Berlin

ben–ber

berlin [bɜ:ˈlɪn] *n* (**a**) *Tex* **berlin (wool)** laine *f* à broder (**b**) *Transp (carriage)* berline *f*

Berliner [bɜ:ˈlɪnə(r)] *n* Berlinois(e) *m,f*

berm, berme [bɜ:m] *n Archit* berme *f*

Bermuda [bəˈmju:də] **1** *n* les Bermudes *fpl*; **in Bermuda** aux Bermudes

2 Bermudas *npl (shorts)* bermuda *m*

►► *Am* ***Bermuda Plan*** tarif *m* chambre avec petit déjeuner anglais; *Naut* ***Bermuda rig*** gréement *m* Marconi; ***Bermuda shorts*** bermuda *m*; ***the Bermuda Triangle*** le triangle des Bermudes

Bermudan [bəˈmju:dən], **Bermudian** [bəˈmu:dɪən] **1** *n* = habitant des Bermudes

2 *adj* des Bermudes

Bern [bɜ:n] *n Geog* Berne

Bernese [ˌbɜ:ˈni:z] **1** *n* Bernois(e) *m,f*

2 *adj* bernois

►► ***the Bernese Alps*** l'Oberland *m* bernois; ***Bernese mountain dog*** chien *m* de montagne bernois

Berni Inn® [ˈbɜ:nɪ-] *n Br* = chaîne de restaurants bon marché

Bernoulli® [bɜ:ˈnu:lɪ] *n Comput*

►► ***Bernoulli disk*** cartouche *f* Bernoulli®; ***Bernoulli drive*** lecteur *m* Bernoulli®

berried [ˈberɪd] *adj* (**a**) *Bot* à baies, couvert de baies (**b**) *Zool (crustacean)* œuvé

berry [ˈberɪ] (*pl* **berries**, *pt & pp* **berried**) **1** *n* (**a**) *(fruit)* baie *f*; **to go berry picking** aller cueillir des baies (**b**) *Zool (of crustacean)* œuf *m*; **lobster in berry** homard *m* œuvé

2 *vi* (**a**) *Bot (bush)* produire des baies (**b**) *(person)* cueillir des baies; **to go berrying** aller cueillir des baies

berserk [bəˈzɜ:k] *adj* fou furieux (folle furieuse); **to go berserk** *(person)* devenir fou furieux; *(crowd)* se déchaîner

berth [bɜ:θ] **1** *n* (**a**) *Naut & Rail (bunk)* couchette *f* (**b**) *Naut (in harbour)* mouillage *m*, poste *m* d'amarrage; *(distance)* distance *f*; **to give a ship a wide berth** éviter *ou* parer un navire, passer au large d'un navire

(**c**) *Br Fam (job)* boulot *m*; **to find a soft** *or* **an easy berth** trouver un emploi pépère

(**d**) *Br (idiom)* **to give sb a wide berth** éviter qn (à tout prix); **I'd give him a wide berth if I were you** je l'éviterais (à tout prix) *ou* je me tiendrais à distance si j'étais vous

2 *vi Naut (at dock)* venir à quai, accoster; *(at anchor)* mouiller; **when do we berth?** quand accostons-nous?

3 *vt Naut (dock)* amarrer, faire accoster; *(assign place to)* donner un poste d'amarrage à

Bertha [ˈbɜ:θə] *n* (**a**) *Mil & Hist (gun)* **(Big) Bertha** la grosse Bertha (**b**) *(collar)* berthe *f*

berthing [ˈbɜ:θɪŋ] *n Naut (of ship)* abordage *m* à quai

Bertie Wooster [ˈbɜ:tɪˈwʊstə(r)] *pr n* = personnage des romans de P.G. Wodehouse, jeune aristocrate écervelé toujours tiré d'affaire par son valet Jeeves

beryl [ˈberəl] *n Miner* béryl *m*

beryllium [beˈrɪlɪəm] *n Chem* béryllium *m*

beseech [bɪˈsi:tʃ] (*pt & pp* **beseeched** *or* **besought** [-ˈsɔ:t]) *vt Formal or Literary* (**a**) *(ask for)* solliciter, implorer (**b**) *(entreat)* implorer, supplier; **to beseech sb to do sth** implorer *ou* supplier qn de faire qch; **he beseeched them to save him** il les a suppliés *ou* implorés de le sauver; **please, I beseech you** s'il vous plaît, je vous en supplie

beseeching [bɪˈsi:tʃɪŋ] **1** *n (UNCOUNT)* supplications *fpl*

2 *adj* suppliant, implorant

beseechingly [bɪˈsi:tʃɪŋlɪ] *adv* d'un air *ou* ton suppliant

beset [bɪˈset] (*pt & pp* **beset**, *cont* **besetting**) *vt (usu passive)* (**a**) *(assail)* assaillir, harceler; **I was beset by** *or* **with doubt** j'étais assailli par le doute; **the whole project is beset with financial difficulties** le projet pose énormément de problèmes sur le plan financier; **they are beset with problems** ils sont assaillis de problèmes (**b**) *(surround)* encercler; **beset by the enemy** cerné par l'ennemi

besetting [bɪˈsetɪŋ] *adj Formal (idea, thought etc)* obsédant; **his besetting sin was greed** la cupidité était son plus grand défaut

beside [bɪˈsaɪd] *prep* (**a**) *(next to)* à côté de, auprès de; **walk beside me** marchez à côté de moi; **he wanted to keep his family beside him** il voulait garder sa famille auprès de lui; **a plate with a glass beside it** une assiette avec un verre à côté; **a house beside the sea** une maison au bord de la mer

(**b**) *(as compared with)* à côté de, par rapport à; **beside him everyone else appears slow** à côté de lui, tous les autres paraissent lents; **the results don't look very brilliant beside last year's** les résultats n'ont pas l'air brillants à côté de *ou* par rapport à ceux de l'année dernière

(**c**) *(in addition to)* en plus de, outre; *(apart from)* à part, excepté; **other people beside ourselves** d'autres (personnes) que nous

(**d**) *(wide of)* **that is beside the point** *or* **question** cela n'a rien à voir (avec l'affaire en question); **whether you arrived or not is beside the point** que tu sois arrivé ou non n'est pas le problème; **beside oneself (with joy/anger)** fou (folle) (de joie/colère); **beside oneself with enthusiasm** débordant d'enthousiasme

besides [bɪˈsaɪdz] **1** *prep* (**a**) *(in addition to)* en plus de, outre; **there are three (other) candidates besides yourself** il y a trois (autres) candidats à part vous; **what other skills do you have besides languages?** quelles compétences avez-vous à part *ou* outre les langues?; **have you got it in anything besides black?** est-ce que vous l'avez dans d'autres couleurs qu'en noir?; **that's besides what you already owe me** c'est en plus de ce que tu me dois déjà; **besides being old, she's also extremely deaf** non seulement elle est vieille, mais elle est également très sourde; **besides which that book is out of print** sans compter que ce livre est épuisé

(**b**) *(with negatives) (apart from)* hormis, excepté; **nobody besides me** personne à part moi; **she said nothing besides what we knew already** elle n'a rien dit que nous ne sachions déjà

2 *adv* (**a**) *(in addition)* en plus, en outre; **and more besides** et d'autres encore; **he owns two flats and a country house besides** il est propriétaire de deux appartements ainsi que d'une maison à la campagne; **he knows the rudiments but little else besides** il connaît les rudiments mais pas grand-chose d'autre *ou* de plus

(**b**) *(furthermore)* en plus; **it's an excellent play and, besides, the tickets aren't expensive** la pièce est excellente et en plus, les billets ne coûtent pas cher; **besides, I don't even like funfairs** d'ailleurs *ou* en plus, je n'aime pas les fêtes foraines

besiege [bɪˈsi:dʒ] *vt* (**a**) *Mil (surround → town)* assiéger; *Fig (→ person, office)* assaillir; **the tourists were besieged by beggars** les touristes étaient assaillis par des mendiants (**b**) *(harass)* assaillir, harceler; **besieged by doubt** rongé *ou* assailli par le doute; **we've been besieged by requests for help** nous avons été assaillis de demandes d'aide

besieger [bɪˈsi:dʒə(r)] *n Mil & Fig* assiégeant *m*

besmear [bɪˈsmɪə(r)] *vt Literary (smear)* barbouiller, salir; *Fig (tarnish)* souiller; **to besmear sb's reputation** souiller *ou* ternir la réputation de qn

besmirch [bɪˈsmɜ:tʃ] *vt Literary (make dirty)* souiller; *Fig (tarnish)* souiller; **besmirched with mud** barbouillé de boue; **to besmirch sb's name** souiller *ou* ternir le nom de qn

besom *n* (**a**) [ˈbi:zəm] *(broom)* balai *m* (**b**) [ˈbɪzəm] *Scot Fam Pej (woman)* bonne femme *f*; **she's a cheeky besom!** elle est gonflée!

besotted [bɪˈsɒtɪd] *adj* (**a**) *(infatuated)* fou (folle), épris; **to be besotted with sb** *(in love)* être fou *ou* follement épris de qn; **to be besotted with sth** *(car, computer etc)* adorer qch; **she is besotted with her grandchildren** elle est folle de ses petits enfants (**b**) *(foolish)* idiot; **besotted with drink** abruti (par l'alcool), soûl

besought [bɪˈsɔ:t] *pt & pp of* **beseech**

bespangle [bɪˈspæŋgəl] *vt Literary* pailleter; **bespangled with diamonds** pailleté *ou* parsemé de diamants

bespatter [bɪˈspætə(r)] *vt Literary (splash)* éclabousser; **bespattered with mud** tout maculé de boue; *Fig (tarnish)* souiller, éclabousser

bespeak [bɪˈspi:k] (*pt* **bespoke** [-ˈspəʊk], *pp* **bespoke** *or* **bespoken** [-ˈspəʊkən]) *vt Literary* (**a**) *(be sign of)* démontrer, témoigner de; **her action bespeaks kindness** son geste témoigne de sa bonté; **their hesitation bespeaks moral weakness** leur hésitation révèle une faiblesse morale (**b**) *(reserve → room, table)* réserver, retenir; *(→ book, product)* commander

bespectacled [bɪˈspektəkəld] *adj* qui porte des lunettes, à lunettes

bespoke [bɪˈspəʊk] **1** *pt of* **bespeak**

2 *adj (shoemaker, tailor)* à façon; *(shoes, suit)* fait sur mesure

bespoken [bɪˈspəʊkən] *pp of* **bespeak**

besprinkle [bɪˈsprɪŋkəl] *vt Literary (with sugar, talcum)* saupoudrer; *(with liquid)* asperger, arroser

Bess [bes] *pr n Fam* **Good Queen Bess** = la reine Elisabeth Ière d'Angleterre

Bessarabia [ˌbesəˈreɪbɪə] *n Geog* Bessarabie *f*

Bessemer [ˈbesɪmə(r)] *pr n*

►► *Metal* ***Bessemer converter*** convertisseur *m* Bessemer; *Metal* ***Bessemer process*** procédé *m* Bessemer

BEST [best]

meilleur	► **1 (a)**
mieux	► **2**
le meilleur	► **3 (a), (b)**
le mieux	► **3 (b)**
au mieux	► **5**
pour le mieux	► **6**

1 *adj* (**a**) *(superl of* **good**) meilleur; **some of our best scientists will be there** certains de nos meilleurs chercheurs seront présents; **it's one of the best films I've ever seen** c'est un des meilleurs films que j'aie jamais vus; **she's my best friend** c'est ma meilleure amie; **may the best man win** que le meilleur gagne; **she gave him the best years of her life** elle lui a sacrifié les plus belles années de sa vie; **I'm doing what is best for the family** je fais ce qu'il y a de mieux pour la famille; **she knows what's best for her** elle sait ce qui lui va *ou* convient le mieux; **I only want what's best for you** je ne veux que ce qu'il y a de mieux pour toi; **do as you think best** faites pour le mieux; **they think it best not to answer** ils croient qu'il vaut mieux ne pas répondre; **it's best not to smoke at all** il est préférable de ne pas fumer du tout; **what's the best thing to do?** quelle est la meilleure chose à faire?; **the best thing (to do) is to keep quiet** le mieux, c'est de ne rien dire; **it would be best to…, the best plan would be to…** le mieux serait de…; **the best thing about it is that it's free/is that she didn't even realize** le mieux, c'est que c'est gratuit/c'est qu'elle ne s'en est même pas rendu compte; **best of all** le meilleur de tout; *Com* **best before 2002** *(on packaging)* à consommer de préférence avant 2002

(**b**) *(reserved for special occasions)* plus beau (belle); **she put out her best dishes** elle a sorti sa plus belle vaisselle; **she was dressed in her best clothes** elle portait ses plus beaux vêtements

(**c**) *(idiom)* **the best part of** la plus grande partie de; **she spent the best part of the day working** elle a passé le plus clair de la journée à travailler; **I waited for the best part of an hour** j'ai attendu près d'une heure *ou* presque une heure

2 *adv (superl of* **well**) mieux; **he does it best** c'est lui qui le fait le mieux; **Tuesday would suit me best** le mieux pour moi serait mardi; **the best-kept garden in the village** le jardin le mieux entretenu du village; **the best-preserved Renaissance theatre in Italy** le théâtre Renaissance le mieux conservé d'Italie; **the best-looking women** les femmes les plus jolies; **which film did you like best?** quel est le film que vous avez préféré?; **I liked the Fellini best** c'est le Fellini que j'ai préféré; **you know best** c'est vous (qui êtes) le mieux placé pour en juger; **he's best able to decide** il est le plus à même de décider; **do as you think best** faites comme bon vous semble(ra); **I comforted her as best I could** je l'ai consolée de mon mieux *ou* du mieux que j'ai pu; **you had best apologize to**

her vous feriez mieux de lui présenter vos excuses; **these things are best left to the police** il vaut mieux laisser à la police le soin de s'occuper de ces choses-là

3 *n* (**a**) *(most outstanding person, thing, part etc)* le (la) meilleur(e) *m,f*; **it/she is the best there is** c'est le meilleur/la meilleure qui soit; **he wants her to have the best** il veut qu'elle ait ce qu'il y a de mieux, il veut ce qu'il y a de mieux pour elle; **your parents only want the best for you** tes parents ne veulent que ce qu'il y a de mieux pour toi **only the best will do** ne fera l'affaire que ce qu'il y a de meilleur; **the best of it is the paid holidays** le mieux *ou* ce qu'il y a de vraiment bien, ce sont les congés payés; **the best of it is that...** le plus beau de l'affaire, c'est que...; **the best you can say about him is that...** le mieux qu'on puisse dire à son sujet c'est que...; **she can stand comparison with the best of them** on peut la comparer avec les meilleurs d'entre eux/les meilleures d'entre elles; **even the best of us can make mistakes** tout le monde peut se tromper; **to get** *or* **to have the best of the bargain** avoir la part belle; **to get the best of sb in an argument** l'emporter sur qn dans une discussion; **she wants the best of both worlds** elle veut tout avoir

(**b**) *(greatest, highest degree)* le mieux, le meilleur; **they're the best of friends** ce sont les meilleurs amis du monde; **to the best of my knowledge/recollection** autant que je sache/je me souvienne; **the best of luck!** bonne chance!; **(even) at the best of times** même dans les meilleurs moments; **she's not the calmest of people, (even) at the best of times** ce n'est pas quelqu'un de très calme de toute façon; **it's journalism at its best** c'est du journalisme de haut niveau; **the garden is at its best in spring** c'est au printemps que le jardin est le plus beau; **he was at his best last night** il était en pleine forme hier soir; **I'm not at my best in the morning** je ne suis pas en forme le matin; **this is Shakespeare at his best** voilà du meilleur Shakespeare; **I am in the best of health** je me porte à merveille, je suis en excellente santé; **to do one's best** faire de son mieux *ou* tout son possible; **do your best!** faites de votre mieux!, faites pour le mieux!; **do your best to finish on time** faites de votre mieux pour finir à temps; **it was the best we could do** nous ne pouvions pas faire mieux; **do the best you can** *(given the circumstances)* arrangez-vous; *(in exam)* faites de votre mieux; **to get the best out of sb/sth** tirer un maximum de qn/qch; **to bring out the best in people** faire ressortir les bons côtés des gens; **to look one's best** *(gen)* être resplendissant; **she looks her best with short hair** les cheveux courts l'avantagent; **we'll have to make the best of the situation** il faudra nous accommoder de la situation (du mieux que nous pouvons); **to make the best of a bad bargain** *or* **job** faire contre mauvaise fortune bon cœur

(**c**) *(nicest clothes)* **they were (dressed) in their (Sunday) best** ils étaient endimanchés *ou* portaient leurs habits du dimanche; **I keep it for best** *(of dress, suit etc)* je le garde pour des occasions spéciales

(**d**) *(good wishes)* **(I wish you) all the best** (je [illegible]) [illegible] **give your wife my best** mes amitiés à votre femme

(**e**) *Sport (winning majority)* **we played the best of three (games)** le jeu consistait à gagner *ou* il fallait gagner deux parties sur trois; **let's make it the best of five** le premier qui remporte trois jeux *ou* parties sur cinq a gagné

4 *vt Arch (get advantage over)* l'emporter sur; *(defeat)* vaincre

5 at best *adv* au mieux; **this is, at best, a temporary solution** c'est, au mieux, une solution temporaire; **his performance has been at best mediocre** ses résultats ont été, au mieux, médiocres

6 for the best *adv* pour le mieux; **it's all for the best** c'est pour le mieux; **he meant it for the best** il avait les meilleures intentions du monde; **we must hope for the best** il faut être optimiste

►► *TV & Cin* ***best boy*** aide-électricien *m*; ***best man*** garçon *m* d'honneur

---

BEST MAN

Dans les pays anglo-saxons, le garçon d'honneur présente l'alliance au marié et prononce un discours lors de la réception de mariage.

---

best-before date *n Culin (for foodstuffs)* date *f* limite de consommation; *Aut (for batteries, car oil etc)* date *f* limite d'utilisation

best-case scenario *n* **this is the best-case scenario** c'est le scénario le plus optimiste

bestial ['bestɪəl] *adj* bestial

bestialism ['bestɪəlɪzəm] *n* absence *f* de la faculté de raisonner

bestiality [ˌbestɪ'ælətɪ] (*pl* **bestialities**) *n* (**a**) *(of behaviour, character)* bestialité *f* (**b**) *(act)* acte *m* bestial (**c**) *(sexual practice)* bestialité *f*

bestially ['bestɪəlɪ] *adv* avec bestialité, bestialement

bestiary ['bestɪərɪ] (*pl* **bestiaries**) *n* bestiaire *m* *(recueil)*

best-in-class *n* (**a**) *(at dog show)* meilleur *m* de groupe (**b**) *Mktg (product)* chef *m* de file

best-in-show *n (at dog show)* meilleur chien *m* de l'exposition toutes races

bestir [bɪ'stɜː(r)] (*pt & pp* **bestirred**, *cont* **bestirring**) *vt* **to bestir oneself** s'activer

best-of-breed *n* (**a**) *(at dog show)* meilleur *m* de race (**b**) *Mktg (product)* nec *m* plus ultra

bestow [bɪ'stəʊ] *vt Formal (favour, gift, praise)* accorder; *(award, honour)* conférer, accorder; **to bestow sth on sb** accorder *ou* conférer qch à qn

bestowal [bɪ'stəʊəl] *n Formal (of favour, honour, title)* octroi *m*

bestower [bɪ'stəʊə(r)] *n Formal* donateur(trice) *m,f*

best-perceived *adj Mktg* mieux perçu; **the best-perceived product** le produit le mieux perçu

bestrew [bɪ'struː] (*pt* **bestrewed**, *pp* **bestrewed** *or* **bestrewn** [-'struːn]) *vt Literary* joncher; **the floor was bestrewed with flowers** le plancher était jonché de fleurs

bestride [bɪ'straɪd] (*pt* **bestrode** [-'strəʊd], *pp* **bestridden** [-'strɪdən]) *vt Literary* (**a**) *(straddle → bicycle, house)* enfourcher; *(→ chair)* se mettre à califourchon *ou* à cheval sur (**b**) *(span → river)* enjamber, franchir; *(→ obstacle)* enjamber

best-seller *n* (**a**) *(book)* best-seller *m*, succès *m* de librairie; *(hi-fi, record)* article *m* qui se vend bien; **to be on the best-seller list** être un best-seller (**b**) *(author)* auteur *m* à succès

best-selling *adj Com & Mktg (book, item)* à fort tirage; *(author)* à succès

bestudded [bɪ'stʌdɪd] *adj Literary* **bestudded with flowers/stars** parsemé de fleurs/d'étoiles

bet [bet] (*pt & pp* **bet** *or* **betted**, *cont* **betting**) **1** *n* pari *m*; **do you want to make a bet?** tu veux parier?; **we accepted** *or* **took the bet** nous avons accepté le pari; **to win/to lose a bet** gagner/perdre un pari; **he lay** *or* **put** *or* **placed a bet on the race** il a parié *ou* il a fait un pari sur la course; **place your bets!** faites vos jeux!; **all bets are off** les paris sont annulés; **they're taking bets** ils prennent des paris; *Fig* **it's a good** *or* **safe bet that they'll win** ils vont gagner à coup sûr; *Fam Fig* **your best bet is to take a taxi** tu ferais mieux de prendre un taxi; *Fig* **she's a bad/good bet as a prospective leader** elle ferait un mauvais/bon leader

2 *vt also Fig* parier; **how much did you bet on the race?** combien as-tu parié *ou* misé sur la course?; **I bet her £5 he wouldn't come** j'ai parié 5 livres avec elle qu'il ne viendrait pas; **I'll bet you anything you want** je te parie tout ce que tu veux; **I'm willing to bet she's lying** je suis prête à parier qu'elle ment; *Fam* **I bet you won't do it!** (t'es pas) chiche!; *Fam* **I'll bet my bottom dollar** *or* **my boots he loses** il va perdre, j'en mettrais ma main au feu; *Fam* **bet you I will!** chiche (que je le fais)!

3 *vi* parier, miser; **to bet against/on sth** parier contre/sur qch; **he bets on the races** il parie *ou* joue aux courses; **which horse did you bet on?** quel cheval as-tu joué?, sur quel cheval as-tu misé?; **to bet 5 to 1** parier *ou* miser à 5 contre 1; **do you want to bet?** *(as challenge)* tu paries?; *Fam* **he said he'd phone me – well, I wouldn't bet on it!** il a dit qu'il me téléphonerait – à ta place, je ne me ferais pas trop d'illusions!; *Fam* **I wouldn't bet on getting your money back** à mon avis, tu n'es pas près de revoir ton argent; *Fam* **are you going to the party? – you bet!** tu vas à la soirée? – et comment! *ou* qu'est-ce que tu crois?; *Fam* **I'll tell him off – I'll bet!** *(you will)* je vais lui dire ses quatre vérités – j'en doute pas!; *(you won't)* je vais lui dire ses quatre vérités – mon œil!

beta ['biːtə] *n Ling* bêta *m inv*

►► *Comput* ***beta release*** version *f* bêta; *Comput* ***beta test*** bêta-test *m*; *Comput* ***beta testing*** bêta-tests *mpl*; *Comput* ***beta version*** version *f* bêta; *Physiol* ***beta wave*** rythme *m* bêta

beta-blocker [-ˌblɒkə(r)] *n Med* bêtabloquant *m*

betake [bɪ'teɪk] (*pt* **betook** [-'tʊk], *pp* **betaken** [-'teɪkn]) *vt Literary* **to betake oneself to** se rendre à; **they betook themselves to the fair** ils se rendirent à la foire

Betamax® ['biːtəˌmæks] *n* Betamax® *f*

beta-test *vt Comput* conduire les bêta-tests sur, conduire les essais approfondis sur

betel ['biːtəl] *n Bot* bétel *m*

►► *Bot* ***betel nut*** noix *f* d'arec; *Bot* ***betel palm*** aréquier *m*, arec *m*

Bethany ['beθənɪ] *n Bible* Béthanie *f*

Bethel ['beθəl] *n Bible* Béthel

bethel ['beθəl] *n Naut* = lieu de recueillement pour les marins

bethink [bɪ'θɪŋk] (*pt & pp* **bethought** [-'θɔːt]) *vt Arch* **to bethink oneself of sth** *(consider)* considérer qch, songer à qch; *(remember)* se rappeler qch, se souvenir de qch

Bethlehem ['beθlɪhem] *n Bible* Bethléem

bethought [bɪ'θɔːt] *pt & pp of* **bethink**

betide [bɪ'taɪd] *vi Literary* advenir

betimes [bɪ'taɪmz] *adv Arch (early)* de bonne heure, tôt; *(in good time)* à temps; *(soon)* bientôt

betoken [bɪ'təʊkən] *vt Formal (indicate)* être l'indice de, révéler; *(augur)* présager, annoncer

betony ['betənɪ] (*pl* **betonies**) *n Bot* bétoine *f*

betook [bɪ'tʊk] *pt of* **betake**

betray [bɪ'treɪ] *vt* (**a**) *(be disloyal to → friend, principle)* trahir; *(→ husband, wife)* tromper, trahir; *(→ country)* trahir, être traître à; *Fig* **my face betrayed me** mon visage m'a trahi

(**b**) *(denounce)* trahir, dénoncer; *(hand over)* trahir, livrer; **he betrayed the rebels to the police** il a livré les rebelles à la police

(**c**) *(confidence, hope, trust)* trahir, tromper

(**d**) *(disclose → secret, truth)* trahir, divulguer; *(→ grief, happiness)* trahir, laisser voir; **her voice betrayed her nervousness** sa voix laissait deviner son inquiétude

betrayal [bɪ'treɪəl] *n* (**a**) *(of person, principle)* trahison *f* (**b**) *(act)* (acte *m* de) trahison *f*; **it's a betrayal of one's country** c'est une trahison envers son pays (**c**) *(of confidence, trust)* abus *m*, trahison *f* (**d**) *(of secret, truth)* trahison *f*, divulgation *f*

betrayer [bɪ'treɪə(r)] *n* traître(esse) *m,f*

betroth [bɪ'trəʊð] *vt Arch* promettre en mariage

betrothal [bɪ'trəʊðəl] *n Arch* fiançailles *fpl*; **her betrothal to the prince** ses fiançailles avec le prince

betrothed [bɪ'trəʊðd] *Arch* **1** *adj* fiancé, promis; **she is betrothed to our son** [illegible] avec notre fils

2 *n* fiancé(e) *m,f*, promis(e) *m,f*

BETTER ['betə(r)]

meilleur	► 1 (a)
mieux	► 1 (b); 2 (a) – (c)
le meilleur	► 3
améliorer	► 4

1 *adj* (**a**) *(compar of* **good***)* *(superior)* meilleur; **you will find no better hotel** vous ne trouverez pas mieux comme hôtel; **the marks are better than I expected** les notes sont meilleures que je ne m'y attendais; **it's better than nothing** c'est mieux que rien; **nothing could be better, it couldn't be better** cela ne peut pas être mieux, c'est on ne peut mieux; **that's better!** voilà qui est mieux!; **I'm better at languages than he is** je suis meilleur *ou* plus fort en langues que lui; **he's a better cook than you are** il cuisine mieux que toi; **she's a better painter than she is a sculptor** elle peint mieux qu'elle ne sculpte; **fruit juice is better for you than coffee** le jus de fruit est meilleur pour la santé que le café; **I had hoped for better things** j'avais espéré mieux; **to get better** *(at doing something)* faire des progrès; *(of weather, situation etc)* s'améliorer; **the weather is better** il fait meilleur; **business is (getting) better** les affaires vont mieux; **things are (getting) better and better!** ça va de mieux en mieux!; **it couldn't** *or* **nothing could be better!** c'est on ne peut mieux!; **he looks better without his glasses** il est mieux sans lunettes; **you get a better view from here** on voit mieux d'ici; **it's better if I don't see them** il vaut mieux *ou* il est préférable que je ne les voie pas; **it's better that way** c'est mieux comme ça; **it would be better if you called me tomorrow** ce serait *ou* il vaudrait mieux que tu m'appelles demain; **it would have been better to have waited a little** il aurait mieux valu attendre un peu; **you're far better leaving now** il vaut beaucoup mieux que tu partes maintenant; **to be all the better for having done sth** se trouver mieux d'avoir fait qch; **you'll be all the better for a holiday** des vacances vous feront le plus grand bien; **all the better!** tant mieux!; **better off** mieux; **they're better off than we are** *(richer)* ils ont plus d'argent que nous; *(in a more advantageous position)* ils sont dans une meilleure position que nous; **she'd be better off in hospital** elle serait mieux à l'hôpital; **he'd have been better off staying where he was** il aurait mieux fait de rester où il était

(**b**) *(compar of* **well***)* *(improved in health)* mieux; **to get better** commencer à aller mieux; **now that he's better** maintenant qu'il va mieux; **I hope you will soon be better** j'espère que vous serez bientôt rétabli; **my cold is much better** mon rhume va beaucoup mieux; **I'm feeling much better** je me sens beaucoup mieux; **you are looking better** tu as meilleure mine

(**c**) *(morally)* **she's a better person for it** ça lui a fait beaucoup de bien; *Hum* **you're a better man than I am!** tu as (bien) du mérite; **he is no better than his brother** il ne vaut pas mieux que son frère; **you're no better than a liar!** tu n'es qu'un menteur!; *Euph Old-fashioned or Hum* **she's no better than she should be** elle n'est pas d'une vertu farouche

(**d**) *(idiom)* **the better part of sth** la plus grande partie de qch; **I waited for the better part of an hour** j'ai attendu presque une heure; **we haven't seen them for the better part of a month** ça fait presque un mois *ou* près d'un mois que nous ne les avons pas vus

2 *adv* (**a**) *(compar of* **well***)* *(more proficiently, aptly etc)* mieux; **he swims better than I do** il nage mieux que moi; **she paints better than she sculpts** elle peint mieux qu'elle ne sculpte; **they speak French better than they used to** ils parlent mieux le français qu'avant; **the town would be better described as a backwater** la ville est plutôt un coin perdu; **he held it up to the light, the better to see the colours** il l'a mis dans la lumière afin de mieux voir les couleurs; **all the better to hear you with** c'est pour mieux t'entendre; **to go one better (than sb)** renchérir (sur qn)

(**b**) *(indicating preference)* **I liked his last book better** j'ai préféré son dernier livre; **I'd like nothing better than to talk to him** je ne demande pas mieux que de lui parler; **so much the better** tant mieux; **or better still** ou mieux encore; **the less he knows the better** moins il en saura, mieux ça vaudra; **the more I know him the better I like him** plus je le connais plus je l'aime; *Prov* **better late than never** mieux vaut tard que jamais

(**c**) *(with adj)* mieux, plus; **better looking** plus beau (belle); **better paid/prepared** mieux payé/préparé; **she's one of Canada's better-known authors** c'est un des auteurs canadiens les plus *ou* mieux connus

(**d**) *(idioms)* **you had better begin at the beginning** tu ferais bien de commencer par le commencement; **we'd better be going** *(must go)* il faut que nous partions; *(would be preferable)* il vaut mieux que nous partions; **I'd better not wake him** il vaut mieux que je ne le réveille pas; **you'd better not** il ne vaudrait mieux pas; **hadn't you better phone first?** est-ce qu'il ne vaudrait pas mieux que tu appelles avant?; **it'll be ready tomorrow – it'd better be!** ce sera prêt demain – il vaudrait mieux!; **you'd better be on time!** tu as intérêt à être à l'heure!

3 *n* (**a**) *(superior of two)* le (la) meilleur(e) *m,f*; **which is the better of the two?** lequel des deux est le meilleur?; **what do you think of this wine? – I've tasted better** comment trouvez-vous ce vin? – j'en ai bu de meilleurs; **there's been a change for the better in his health** son état de santé s'est amélioré; **the situation has taken a turn for the better** la situation a pris une meilleure tournure; **for better or worse** pour le meilleur ou pour le pire; **I expected better of you** je m'attendais à mieux de ta part

(**b**) *(usu pl) (person)* supérieur(e) *m,f*

(**c**) *(gambler)* parieur(euse) *m,f*

(**d**) *(idioms)* **curiosity got the better of me** ma curiosité l'a emporté; **we got the better of them in the deal** nous l'avons emporté sur eux dans l'affaire

4 *vt (position, status, situation)* améliorer; *(achievement, sales figures)* dépasser; **can you better that?** pouvez-vous faire mieux que cela?; *Com* **the company has bettered the competition for the second year running** c'est la deuxième année consécutive que l'entreprise a fait mieux que la concurrence; **she's eager to better herself** elle a vraiment envie d'améliorer sa situation

▸▸ *Com* ***Better Business Bureau*** = organisme américain de conseil aux entreprises et aux consommateurs, notamment lorsque ceux-ci veulent faire une réclamation, *Can* Bureau *m* d'éthique commerciale du Canada; *Fam Hum* ***better half*** *(husband, wife)* moitié *f*

---

betterment ['betəmənt] *n* amélioration *f*; *Law (of property)* plus-value *f*

better-off **1** *adj* aisé, riche
2 *npl* **the better-off** les riches *mpl*

betting ['betɪŋ] **1** *n* (**a**) *(bets)* pari *m*, paris *mpl*; **the betting was heavy** les paris allaient bon train; *Fig* **what's the betting they refuse to go?** je suis prêt à parier qu'ils ne voudront pas y aller

(**b**) *(odds)* cote *f*; **the betting is 5 to 1 on Blackie** (la cote de) Blackie est à 5 contre 1, la cote est à 5 contre 1 sur Blackie

2 *adj* **I'm not a betting man** je n'aime pas parier

▸▸ ***betting office*** ≃ (bureau *m* de) PMU *m*; ***betting shop*** bureau *m* de paris *(appartenant à un bookmaker)*; ***betting slip*** bulletin *m* de pari

bettor ['betə(r)] *n Am (gambler)* parieur(euse) *m,f*

Betty Crocker® ['betɪ'krɒkə(r)] *n Culin* = marque américaine de produits alimentaires et de livres de recettes

Betty Ford Clinic [-'fɔːd-] *n* = centre de désintoxication pour alcooliques et toxicomanes situé en Californie et fréquenté par des personnalités riches et célèbres

---

BETWEEN [bɪ'twiːn] **1** *prep* (**a**) *(in space or time)* entre; **the crowd stood between him and the door** la foule le séparait de la porte; **the distance between the two towns** la distance entre *ou* qui sépare les deux villes; **it happened between 3 and 4 am** cela s'est passé entre 3 heures et 4 heures (du matin); **between now and this evening** d'ici ce soir; **I'm between jobs at the moment** je suis entre deux emplois en ce moment; **you'll have an hour between trains** vous aurez une heure entre les deux trains; **you shouldn't eat between meals** tu ne devrais pas manger entre les repas *ou* en dehors des repas

(**b**) *(in the range that separates)* entre; **it will cost between 5 and 10 million** ça coûtera entre 5 et 10 millions; **children between the ages of 5 and 10** les enfants de 5 à 10 ans; **somewhere between a half and a third** (quelque chose) entre une moitié et un tiers; **something between a laugh and a groan** quelque chose entre un rire et un grognement

(**c**) *(indicating connection, relation)* entre; **a bus runs between the airport and the hotel** un bus fait la navette entre l'aéroport et l'hôtel; **it's a half-hour drive between home and the office** il y a une demi-heure de route entre la maison et le bureau; **a treaty between the two nations** un traité entre les deux États; **an argument between two experts** une dispute entre deux experts; **a contest between two heavyweight boxers** un combat entre deux poids lourds; **the difference/distinction between A and B** la différence/distinction entre A et B; **he drew a comparison between the two systems** il a établi une comparaison entre les deux systèmes; **he felt things weren't right between them** il sentait que ça n'allait pas entre eux; **no one can come between us** personne ne peut nous séparer; **between you and me, between ourselves** entre nous; *Hum* **between you, me and the gatepost** *or* **bedpost** entre nous; **this is strictly between ourselves** *or* **between you and me** que cela reste entre nous

(**d**) *(indicating alternatives)* entre; **I had to choose between going with them and staying at home** il fallait que je choisisse entre les accompagner et rester à la maison

(**e**) *(added together)* **between us we saved enough money for the trip** à nous tous nous avons économisé assez d'argent pour le voyage; **they have 7 children between them** à eux deux ils ont 7 enfants; **the 5 groups collected £1,000 between them** les 5 groupes ont recueilli 1000 livres en tout; **(in) between painting, writing and looking after the children, she was kept very busy** entre la peinture, l'écriture et les enfants, elle était très occupée

(**f**) *(indicating division)* entre; **he divided it between his children** il l'a partagé entre ses enfants; **they shared the cake between them** ils se sont partagé le gâteau

2 *adv* = **in between**

3 in between 1 *adv* (**a**) *(in intermediate position)* **a row of bushes with little clumps of flowers in between** une rangée d'arbustes intercalés de petits bouquets de fleurs; **he's neither right nor left but somewhere in between** il n'est ni de droite ni de gauche mais quelque part entre les deux; **she either plays very well or very badly, never in between** elle joue très bien ou très mal, jamais entre les deux (**b**) *(in time)* entre-temps, dans l'intervalle **2** *prep* entre

▸▸ *Br Old-fashioned* ***between maid*** bonne *f (qui aide la cuisinière et la femme de chambre)*

---

between-decks *Naut* **1** *adv* dans l'entrepont
2 *n* entrepont *m*

betweentimes [bɪ'twiːntaɪmz] *adv* dans l'intervalle, entre-temps

betwixt [bɪ'twɪkst] **1** *prep Arch* = **between**
2 *adv* **something betwixt and between** quelque chose entre les deux

BeV *Phys & Elec (written abbr* **billion electron volts***)* GeV

bevel ['bevəl] *(Br pt & pp* **bevelled**, *cont* **bevelling**, *Am pt & pp* **beveled**, *cont* **beveling***)* **1** *vt* biseauter, tailler en biseau *ou* de biais

2 *n* (**a**) *(surface)* surface *f* oblique; *(angle)* angle *m* oblique (**b**) *Carp* fausse équerre *f*

▸▸ *Mining* ***bevel cut*** fausse coupe *f*; *Carp* ***bevel edge*** biseau *m*; *Tech* ***bevel gear*** engrenage *m* conique; *Carp* ***bevel square*** fausse équerre *f*

beveled, beveling *Am* = **bevelled, bevelling**

bevelled, *Am* **beveled** ['bevəld] *adj* biseauté

bevelling, *Am* **beveling** ['bevəlɪŋ] *n* biseautage *m*

beverage ['bevərɪdʒ] *n* boisson *f*

Beverly Hills [bevəlɪ'hɪlz] *n* Beverly Hills

Bevin boy ['bevɪn-] *Hist* = conscrit choisi au sort pour le travail dans une houillère

bevvy ['bevɪ] *(pl* **bevvies***)* *Br Fam* **1** *n* (**a**) *(alcohol)* alcool□ *m* (**b**) *(alcoholic drink)* **to have a bevvy** boire un coup (**c**) *(drinking session)* beuverie *f*; **to go on the bevvy** aller se cuiter
2 *vi* picoler
3 *vt* **to get bevvied** se soûler la gueule

bevy ['bevɪ] *(pl* **bevies***)* *n (of people)* bande *f*, troupeau *m*; *(of larks, quails, swans)* volée *f*; *(of roe deer)* harde *f*; **a bevy of reports** un tas de rapports

bewail [bɪ'weɪl] *vt Literary* pleurer; **to bewail one's fate** se lamenter sur son sort

beware [bɪ'weə(r)] *(infinitive and imperative only)* **1** *vi* prendre garde; **beware!** prenez garde!; **beware of getting lost** prenez garde de ne pas vous perdre; **beware of pickpockets** attention aux pickpockets; **beware of married men** méfiez-vous des hommes mariés; **beware of making hasty decisions** gardez-vous de prendre des décisions hâtives; **beware of the dog!** *(sign)* chien méchant!

2 *vt* prendre garde; **beware what you say to her** prenez garde *ou* faites attention à ce que vous lui dites

bewhiskered [bɪ'wɪskəd] *adj Literary (with side whiskers)* qui a des favoris; *(bearded)* barbu

Bewick's swan ['bju:ɪks-] *n Orn* cygne *m* nain *ou* de Bewick

bewigged [bɪ'wɪgd] *adj Literary* portant une perruque

bewilder [bɪ'wɪldə(r)] *vt* rendre perplexe, dérouter

bewildered [bɪ'wɪldəd] *adj* perplexe; **a bewildered look** un regard perplexe

bewildering [bɪ'wɪldərɪŋ] *adj* déconcertant, déroutant

bewilderingly [bɪ'wɪldərɪŋlɪ] *adv* de manière déconcertante *ou* déroutante; **the problem is bewilderingly complex** le problème est d'une complexité déroutante; **even more bewilderingly, she didn't tell anyone** chose encore plus ahurissante, elle ne l'a dit à personne

bewilderment [bɪ'wɪldəmənt] *n* confusion *f*, perplexité *f*; **"why?" she asked in bewilderment** "pourquoi?", demanda-t-elle avec perplexité; **to my complete bewilderment, he refused** à mon grand étonnement, il a refusé

bewitch [bɪ'wɪtʃ] *vt* (**a**) *(cast spell over)* ensorceler, enchanter (**b**) *(fascinate)* enchanter, charmer

bewitched [bɪ'wɪtʃt] *adj* ensorcelé, enchanté

bewitching [bɪ'wɪtʃɪŋ] *adj (smile)* enchanteur, charmeur; *(beauty, person)* charmant, séduisant

bewitchingly [bɪ'wɪtʃɪŋlɪ] *adv* d'une façon séduisante; **she smiled at him bewitchingly** elle lui a adressé un sourire charmeur; **bewitchingly beautiful** beau (belle) à ravir

bewitchment [bɪ'wɪtʃmənt] *n* ensorcellement *m*, charme *m*

bey [beɪ] *n Hist* bey *m*

beyond [bɪ'jɒnd] **1** *prep* (**a**) *(on the further side of)* au-delà de, de l'autre côté de; **the museum is a few yards beyond the church** le musée se trouve à quelques mètres après l'église; **beyond the mountains lies China** au-delà des montagnes se trouve la Chine; **the countries beyond the sea** les pays d'outre-mer *ou* au-delà des mers

(**b**) *(outside the range of)* au-delà de, au-dessus de; **do your duties extend beyond teaching?** est-ce que vos fonctions s'étendent au-delà de l'enseignement?; **beyond one's ability** au-dessus de ses capacités; **beyond belief** incroyable; **beyond question** indiscutablement, incontestablement; **beyond repair** irréparable; **due to circumstances beyond our control** dû à des circonstances indépendantes de notre volonté; **his guilt has been established beyond (all reasonable) doubt** sa culpabilité a été établie sans aucun *ou* sans le moindre doute; **it's (gone) beyond a joke** cela dépasse les bornes; **beyond one's means** au-dessus de ses moyens; **I'm beyond caring what they do next** peu m'importe ce qu'ils feront ensuite; **it's beyond me** cela me dépasse, je n'y comprends rien; **economics is completely beyond me** je ne comprends rien à l'économie; **why he wants to go there is beyond me** je ne comprends pas pourquoi il veut y aller

(**c**) *(later than)* au-delà de, plus de; **the deadline has been extended to beyond 2002** l'échéance a été repoussée au-delà de 2002; **beyond 2005 that law will no longer be valid** après *ou* à partir de 2005, cette loi ne sera plus applicable; **don't stay out beyond midnight!** rentre avant minuit!

(**d**) *(apart from, other than)* sauf, excepté; **I know nothing beyond what I've already told you** je ne sais rien de plus que ce que je vous ai déjà dit

2 *adv* (**a**) *(on the other side)* au-delà, plus loin; **the room beyond was smaller** la pièce suivante était plus petite; **they crossed the mountains and the valleys beyond** ils ont traversé les montagnes et les vallées au-delà

(**b**) *(after)* au-delà; **major changes are foreseen for 2003 and beyond** des changements importants sont prévus pour 2003 et au-delà

3 the (great) beyond l'au-delà *m*

'Beyond the Pleasure Principle' *Freud* 'Au-delà du principe de plaisir'

'Beyond Good and Evil' *Nietzsche* 'Par-delà le bien et le mal'

Beyrouth [,beɪ'ru:t] = **Beirut**

bezel ['bezəl] (*Br pt & pp* **bezelled**, *cont* **bezelling**, *Am pt & pp* **bezeled**, *cont* **bezeling**) **1** *n* (**a**) *Tech (face → of tool)* biseau *m*; *Miner (→ of gem)* facette *f* (**b**) *Metal (rim → for gem)* chaton *m*; *(→ for watch crystal)* portée *f*

2 *vt* biseauter, tailler en biseau

Bézier curve ['bezjeɪ] *n Comput* courbe *f* de Bézier

bezique [bɪ'zi:k] *n Cards* bésigue *m*

bf[1] [,bi:'ef] *n Br Fam (abbr* **bloody fool**) crétin(e) *m,f*

bf[2] *Typ (written abbr* **boldface**) caractères *mpl* gras

b/f *Acct (written abbr* **brought forward**) reporté

BFA [,bi:ef'eɪ] *n Am (abbr* **Bachelor of Fine Arts**) *(person)* = titulaire d'un diplôme universitaire d'art, de musique ou de théâtre; *(qualification)* = diplôme universitaire d'art, de musique ou de théâtre

BFI [,bi:ef'aɪ] *n (abbr* **British Film Institute**) = organisme britannique de promotion du cinéma (aide à la réalisation notamment)

BFPO [,bi:efpi:'əʊ] *n Mil (abbr* **British Forces Post Office**) = mention figurant dans l'adresse des militaires britanniques

bhagee, bhaji ['bɑ:dʒɪ] *n Br Culin* = petite galette indienne épicée à base de légumes

bhang [bæŋ] *n* cannabis *m*

bhangra ['bæŋgrə] *n Mus* = combinaison de musique traditionnelle du Pendjab et de musique pop occidentale

Bhoys [bɔɪz] *n Br Ftbl* **the Bhoys** = surnom donné à l'équipe de football Celtic

bhp [,bi:eɪtʃ'pi:] *n Aut (abbr* **brake horsepower**) puissance *f* au frein

Bhutan [,bu:'tɑ:n] *n* Bhoutan *m*

bi *Fam* [baɪ] **1** *n* bisexuel(elle)[❑] *m,f*

2 *adj* bi *(inv)*

bi- [baɪ] *pref* bi-

BIA [,bi:aɪ'eɪ] *n Am (abbr* **Bureau of Indian Affairs**) Bureau *m* des affaires indiennes

Biafra [bɪ'æfrə] *n* Biafra; **in Biafra** au Biafra

Biafran [bɪ'æfrən] **1** *n* Biafrais(e) *m,f*

2 *adj* biafrais

biannual [,baɪ'ænjʊəl] *adj* semestriel

biannually [,baɪ'ænjʊəlɪ] *adv* deux fois par an

bias ['baɪəs] *(pt & pp* **biased** *or* **biassed**) **1** *n* (**a**) *(prejudice)* préjugé *m*; **there is still considerable bias against women candidates** les femmes qui se présentent sont encore victimes d'un fort préjugé; **they are quite without bias** ils sont sans préjugés

(**b**) *(tendency)* tendance *f*, penchant *m*; **the school has a scientific bias** l'école favorise les sciences

(**c**) *Sewing* biais *m*; **cut on the bias** taillé dans le biais

(**d**) *Sport (in bowls → weight)* = poids ou renflement d'une boule qui l'empêche d'aller droit; *(→ curved course)* déviation *f*

(**e**) *Math* biais *m*

2 *vt (influence)* influencer; *(prejudice)* prévenir; **his experience biased him against/towards them** son expérience l'a prévenu contre eux/en leur faveur; **the course is biased towards the arts** l'enseignement est plutôt orienté sur les lettres

3 *adj* en biais

4 *adv* en biais, de biais

►► *Sewing* ***bias binding*** biais *m (ruban)*

biased ['baɪəst] *adj* (**a**) *(partial)* partial; **biased opinion** opinion *f* préconçue; **you're biased in her favour** tu as un parti pris pour elle (**b**) *Sport (ball)* décentré

►► ***biased error*** erreur *f* systématique; *Math* ***biased sample*** *(in statistics)* échantillon *m* biaisé *ou* avec erreur systématique

bias-ply tire *n Am Aut* pneu *m* à structure diagonale

biassed = **biased**

biathlete [baɪ'æθli:t] *n Sport* biathlonien(enne) *m,f*

biathlon [baɪ'æθlɒn] *n Sport* biathlon *m*

bib [bɪb] *n* (**a**) *(for child)* bavoir *m*, bavette *f* (**b**) *(of apron, dungarees)* bavette *f*; *Br Fam* **in one's best bib and tucker** sur son trente et un, *Can* sur son trente-six (**c**) *(of feathers, fur)* tache *f*, touche *f* (**d**) *Sport* dossard *m*

bibcock ['bɪbkɒk] *n* robinet *m* à bec courbe

Bible ['baɪbəl] **1** *n* Bible *f*

2 bible *n Fig (manual)* bible *f*, évangile *m*; **the fisherman's bible** la bible du pêcheur

►► ***the Bible Belt*** = états du sud des États-Unis où l'évangélisme est très répandu; ***Bible class*** *(in school, church)* classe *f* d'instruction religieuse; *(in Catholic church)* catéchisme *m*; ***Bible paper*** papier *m* bible; ***Bible school*** cours *m* d'instruction religieuse; ***Bible study*** étude *f* de la Bible

Bible-basher *n Br Fam Pej* évangéliste *m* extrémiste[❑]

Bible-bashing *adj Br Fam Pej* **Bible-bashing preacher** évangéliste *m* extrémiste

Bible-thumper [-,θʌmpə(r)] *n Br Fam Pej* évangéliste *m* extrémiste

Bible-thumping *adj Br Fam Pej* **Bible-thumping preacher** évangéliste *m* extrémiste

biblical, Biblical ['bɪblɪkəl] *adj* biblique; *Fam Hum* **to know sb in the biblical sense** connaître qn au sens biblique du terme

biblically ['bɪblɪkəlɪ] *adv* bibliquement

bibliographer [,bɪblɪ'ɒgrəfə(r)] *n* bibliographe *mf*

bibliographical [,bɪblɪə'græfɪkəl] *adj* bibliographique

bibliography [,bɪblɪ'ɒgrəfɪ] *(pl* **bibliographies**) *n* bibliographie *f*

bibliomania [,bɪblɪəʊ'meɪnɪə] *n* bibliomanie *f*

bibliophile ['bɪblɪə,faɪl] *n* bibliophile *mf*

bibulous ['bɪbjʊləs] *adj Literary (person)* adonné à la boisson; *(celebration)* bien arrosé

bicameral [,baɪ'kæmərəl] *adj Pol* bicaméral

bicameralism [,baɪ'kæmərəlɪzəm] *n Pol* bicaméralisme *m*, bicamérisme *m*

bicarb [baɪ'kɑ:b] *n Fam* bicarbonate *m* (de soude)[❑]

bicarbonate [baɪ'kɑ:bənət] *n Chem* bicarbonate *m*; **bicarbonate of soda** bicarbonate *m* de soude

biccy ['bɪkɪ] *n Br Fam (biscuit)* petit gâteau[❑] *m*

bicentenary [,baɪsen'ti:nərɪ] *(pl* **bicentenaries**) *Br* **1** *n* bicentenaire *m*

2 *adj* bicentenaire

bicentennial [,baɪsen'tenjəl] **1** *n Am* bicentenaire *m*

2 *adj* bicentenaire

bicephalous [,baɪ'sefələs] *adj Biol* bicéphale

biceps ['baɪseps] *(pl* **inv**) *n* biceps *m*

bichir ['bɪtʃə(r)] *n Ich* bichir *m*, polyptère *m*

bichloride [,baɪ'klɔ:raɪd] *n Chem* bichlorure *m*

bichon frisé [illegible]

bichromate [,baɪ'krəʊmeɪt] *n Chem* bichromate *m*

bicker ['bɪkə(r)] *vi* se chamailler; **to bicker about** *or* **over sth** se chamailler à propos de qch; **he's always bickering with his sister** lui et sa sœur sont toujours en train de se chamailler

bickering ['bɪkərɪŋ] **1** *n* chamailleries *fpl*; **stop your bickering!** arrêtez de vous chamailler!

2 *adj* chamailleur

bickie = **biccy**

bicoastal [,baɪ'kəʊstəl] *adj Am (company)* établi sur les deux côtes

bicoloured, *Am* **bicolored** [,baɪ'kʌləd] *adj* bicolore

biconcave [,baɪ'kɒŋkeɪv] *adj* biconcave

biconvex [,baɪ'kɒnveks] *adj* biconvexe

bicultural [,baɪ'kʌltʃərəl] *adj* biculturel

biculturalism [,baɪ'kʌltʃərəlɪzəm] *n* biculturalisme *m*

bicuspid [,baɪ'kʌspɪd] **1** *n* prémolaire *f*

2 *adj* bicuspide

bicycle ['baɪsɪkəl] **1** *n* vélo *m*, bicyclette *f*; **I go to work by bicycle** je vais travailler à bicyclette *ou* à vélo; **do you know how to ride a bicycle?** sais-tu faire du vélo *ou* de la bicyclette?; **he went for a ride on his bicycle** il est allé faire un tour à vélo; **he was riding his bicycle** il était à bicyclette *ou* à vélo

2 *comp (bell, lamp)* de vélo, de bicyclette

3 *vi* faire du vélo *ou* de la bicyclette; **she bicycles to work** elle va travailler à bicyclette *ou* à vélo

►► ***bicycle chain*** chaîne *f* de vélo; *(for securing bike)* antivol *m inv*; ***bicycle clip*** pince *f* à vélo; *Ftbl* ***bicycle kick*** retourné *m* bicyclette; ***bicycle lock*** antivol *m*; ***bicycle path*** piste *f ou* bande *f* cyclable; ***bicycle pump*** pompe *f* à bicyclette *ou* à vélo; ***bicycle race*** course *f* de bicyclette; ***bicycle rack*** *(on pavement)* ratelier *m* à bicyclettes *ou* à vélos; *(on car)* porte-vélos *m inv*; ***bicycle shop*** magasin *m* de cycles; ***bicycle track*** piste *f* cyclable

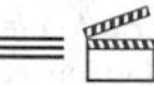

'Bicycle Thieves' (UK), **'The Bicycle Thief'** (US)
De Sica 'Le Voleur de bicyclette'

bicycler ['baɪsɪklə(r)] *n Am* cycliste *mf*

bicycling ['baɪsɪklɪŋ] *n* cyclisme *m*

bicyclist ['baɪsɪklɪst] *n* cycliste *mf*

BID [bɪd]

offrir	► **1 (a); 2 (a)**
faire une soumission	► **1 (b)**
demander, annoncer	► **1 (c)**
offre	► **3 (a)**
soumission	► **3 (b)**
demande, annonce	► **3 (c)**
tentative	► **3 (d)**

(pt & pp vi all senses and vt senses (**a**) *and* (**b**) **bid**, *pt vt senses* (**c**) *to* (**e**) **bade** [bæd], *pp vt senses* (**c**) *to* (**e**) **bidden** ['bɪdən], *cont all senses* **bidding**) **1** *vi* (**a**) *Fin (offer to pay)* faire une offre, offrir; **to bid for sth** faire une offre pour qch; **they bid against us** ils ont surenchéri sur notre offre

(**b**) *Com (tender)* faire une soumission, répondre à un appel d'offres; **several firms bid on the project** plusieurs entreprises ont soumissionné pour le projet

(**c**) *(make attempt)* **he's bidding for the presidency** il vise la présidence

(**d**) *(idiom)* **to bid fair to do sth** promettre de faire qch; **the negotiations bid fair to succeed** les négociations s'annoncent bien *ou* sont en bonne voie

2 *vt* (**a**) *Fin (offer to pay)* faire une offre de, offrir; *(at auction)* faire une enchère de; **what am I bid for this table?** combien m'offre-t-on pour cette table?; **we bid £300 for the statue** nous avons fait une enchère de 300 livres pour la statue

(**b**) *Cards* demander, annoncer

(**c**) *Literary (say)* dire; **he bade them good day** il leur souhaita le bonjour; **they bade him farewell** ils lui firent leurs adieux; **she bade them welcome** elle leur souhaita la bienvenue

(**d**) *Literary (order, tell)* ordonner, enjoindre; **he bade them enter** il les pria d'entrer; **do as you are bidden** faites ce qu'on vous dit

(**e**) *Arch (invite)* inviter, convier

3 *n* (**a**) *Fin (offer to pay)* offre *f*; *(at auction)* enchère *f*; **I made a bid of £100** *(gen)* j'ai fait une offre de 100 livres; *(at auction)* j'ai fait une enchère de 100 livres; ; **to make the first** *or* **opening bid** faire la première enchère; **a higher bid** une surenchère; **they made a higher bid** ils ont surenchéri; **to put a bid in on a flat** faire une offre pour un appartement

(**b**) *Com (tender)* soumission *f*; **the firm made** *or* **put in a bid for the contract** l'entreprise a fait une soumission *ou* a soumissionné pour le contrat; **the State invited bids for** *or* **on the project** l'État a mis le projet en adjudication

(**c**) *Cards* demande *f*, annonce *f*; **it's your bid** c'est à vous d'annoncer; **to make a bid of two hearts** demander *ou* annoncer deux cœurs; **I make no bid** je passe (parole); **"no bid"** "passe", "parole"; **he raised the bid** il a monté *ou* enchéri

(**d**) *(attempt)* tentative *f*; **to make a bid for power** *(legally)* viser le pouvoir; *(illegally)* tenter un coup d'état; **they made a bid to gain control of the movement** ils ont tenté de prendre la tête du mouvement; **the prisoners made a bid for freedom** les prisonniers ont fait une tentative d'évasion; **a rescue bid** une tentative de sauvetage; **she failed in her bid to beat the record** elle a échoué dans sa tentative de battre le record; *Press* **Birmingham fails in bid for next Olympics** *(in headlines)* Birmingham n'est pas sélectionné pour recevoir les prochains jeux Olympiques

(**e**) *Am St Exch* **the bid and asked** les cours *mpl* d'achat et de vente

►► *Fin* ***bid bond*** caution *f* d'adjudication *ou* de soumission; *St Exch* ***bid price*** cours *m* acheteur

►**bid in** *vi Fin* enchérir *ou* surenchérir sur toute offre

►**bid up** *vt sep Fin* enchérir *ou* surenchérir sur

biddable ['bɪdəbəl] *adj* (**a**) *Cards* demandable (**b**) *Br (docile)* docile, obéissant

bidden ['bɪdən] *pp of* **bid**

bidder ['bɪdə(r)] *n* (**a**) *Fin & Com (at auction)* enchérisseur(euse) *m,f*; **there were no bidders** il n'y a pas eu de preneurs, personne n'a fait d'offre; **sold to the highest bidder** vendu au plus offrant; **the lowest bidder** le moins offrant (**b**) *Com* soumissionnaire *mf*; **the highest/lowest bidder** le soumissionnaire le plus/le moins offrant (**c**) *Cards* demandeur (euse) *m,f*

bidding ['bɪdɪŋ] *n* (**a**) *Fin & Com (at auction)* enchères *fpl*; **the bidding went against me** on avait enchéri sur mon offre; **to start the bidding at £5,000** commencer les enchères à 5000 livres; **to open the bidding** ouvrir les enchères; **to raise the bidding** faire monter les enchères; **bidding was brisk** les enchères étaient vives; **the bidding is closed** l'enchère est faite, c'est adjugé

(**b**) *Com (tenders)* soumissions *fpl*

(**c**) *Cards* enchères *fpl*

(**d**) *Literary (request)* demande *f*; *(order)* ordre *m*, ordres *mpl*; **he did his mother's bidding** il respecta les volontés de sa mère; **at her brother's bidding** sur la requête de son frère

►► *Am St Exch* ***bidding price*** cours *m* acheteur

biddy ['bɪdɪ] *(pl* **biddies**) *n* (**a**) *NEng (chicken)* poulet *m*; *(hen)* poule *f* (**b**) *Fam Pej (old woman)* vieille bonne femme *f*; *(gossip)* commère[❑] *f*

bide [baɪd] *(pt* **bided** *or* **bode** [bəʊd], *pp* **bided**) *vt* **to bide one's time** attendre son heure *ou* le bon moment

bidet ['bi:deɪ] *n* bidet *m*

bidirectional [,baɪdə'rekʃənəl] *adj* bidirectionnel

►► *Typ* ***bidirectional printing*** impression *f* bidirectionnelle

Biel [bi:l] *n Geog* Bienne

biennial [,baɪ'enɪəl] **1** *adj* (**a**) *(every two years)* biennal, bisannuel (**b**) *(lasting two years)* biennal

2 *n* (**a**) *(event)* biennale *f* (**b**) *Bot (plant)* plante *f* bisannuelle

biennially [,baɪ'enɪəlɪ] *adv* tous les deux ans

bier [bɪə(r)] *n (for corpse)* bière *f*; *(for coffin)* brancards *mpl*

bifasciated lark [,baɪ'fæʃɪeɪtɪd-] *n Orn* sirli *m* du désert

biff [bɪf] *Fam* **1** *vt* flanquer un coup de poing à

2 *n* coup *m* de poing[❑], gnon *m*; **she gave him a biff on the nose** elle lui a flanqué son poing dans *ou* sur la figure

bifid ['baɪfɪd] *adj* bifide

bifocal [,baɪ'fəʊkəl] **1** *adj* bifocal

2 bifocals *npl* lunettes *fpl* bifocales *ou* à double foyer

BIFU ['bɪfu:] *n (abbr* **The Banking, Insurance and Finance Union**) = syndicat britannique des employés du secteur financier

bifunctional [,baɪ'fʌŋkʃənəl] *adj* bifonctionnel

bifurcate ['baɪfəkeɪt] **1** *vi* bifurquer

2 *adj* à deux branches

bifurcation [,baɪfə'keɪʃən] *n* bifurcation *f*

BIG [bɪg]

grand	► **1 (a), (b), (f), (g)**
gros	► **1 (a)**
aîné	► **1 (c)**
important	► **1 (e)**
à la mode	► **1 (h)**

(compar **bigger**, *superl* **biggest**) **1** *adj* (**a**) *(in size → car, hat, majority)* grand, gros (grosse); *(→ crowd, field, room)* grand; *(→ person)* grand, fort; **the crowd got bigger** la foule a grossi; **in big letters** en (lettres) majuscules; **a big A** un A majuscule; **to make sth bigger** *(garment, hole)* agrandir; **the new wallpaper makes the room look bigger** le nouveau papier peint agrandit la pièce; **we're not big eaters** nous ne sommes pas de gros mangeurs; **to earn big money** gagner gros; **advertising is where the big money is** la publicité rapporte gros; *Fig* **he has a big head** il a la grosse tête; *Fam Fig* **he has a big mouth** il faut toujours qu'il l'ouvre; *Fam* **why did you have to open your big mouth?** tu ne pouvais pas la fermer, non?; *Bible & Literary* **to be big with child** être enceinte, attendre un enfant; *Fam* **she's too big for her boots** *or* **her breeches** elle ne se prend pas pour n'importe qui

(**b**) *(in height)* grand; **to get** *or* **to grow bigger** grandir; **you're a big boy now** tu es un grand garçon maintenant; **she's big enough to look after herself** elle est assez grande pour se défendre

(**c**) *(older)* aîné, plus grand; **my big sister** ma grande sœur

(**d**) *(as intensifier)* grand, énorme; **he's just a big bully** ce n'est qu'une grosse brute; **you're the biggest fool of the lot!** c'est toi le plus bête de tous!

(**e**) *(important, significant → decision, problem)* grand, important; *(→ drop, increase)* fort, important; *(→ mistake)* grave; **the big day** le grand jour; **you've got a big day ahead of you tomorrow** tu as une journée importante devant toi demain; **this is your big scene** *(of main character)* la scène est à toi; *(of minor character)* c'est ta scène; **he's big in publishing, he's a big man in publishing** c'est quelqu'un d'important dans l'édition; **we're onto something big!** nous sommes sur une piste intéressante!; *Fam* **to be into sb/sth big time** *or* **in a big way** être dingue de qn/qch; *Fam* **he's been doing drugs big time** *or* **in a big way** depuis quelque temps il arrête pas de se droguer; *Fam* **it's going to cost them big time** ça va leur revenir vachement cher; *Fam* **he messed up his driving test big time** il s'est planté dans les grandes largeurs au permis; *Fam* **did you have fun? – big time!** vous vous êtes bien amusés? – oui, vachement bien!; *Fam* **to be in the big time, to have made the big time** être en haut de l'échelle, être le dessus du panier, être arrivé; *Fam* **to hit** *or* **to make** *or* **to reach the big time** arriver, réussir; *Fam* **once they've had a taste of the big time** une fois qu'ils ont goûté au succès; *Fam* **big deal!** tu parles!; *Fam* **it's no big deal** il n'y a pas de quoi en faire un plat!

(**f**) *(grandiose)* grand; **he has very big ideas about the future** il a de grands projets d'avenir; **don't get any big ideas about doing this yourself** ne crois pas que tu vas pouvoir faire ça tout seul; **I've got big plans for you** j'ai de grands projets pour toi; **you really do things in a big way** tu ne fais pas les choses à moitié; **he went into politics in a big way** il est entré dans la politique par la grande porte; **they entertain in a big way** ils font les choses en grand quand ils reçoivent; **big words!** ce sont de bien grands mots!

(**g**) *(generous)* grand, généreux; **he has a big heart** il a du cœur *ou* bon cœur; **he's a big spender** c'est un grand dépensier; *Ironic* **you know what he's like, the last of the big spenders!** tu le connais, toujours à faire des frais; *Ironic* **that's big of you!** quelle générosité!

(**h**) *Fam (popular)* à la mode[❑]; **Japanese food is really big just now** la cuisine japonaise est vraiment à la mode en ce moment

(**i**) *Fam (enthusiastic)* **to be big on sth** être fana de qch; **the company is big on research** l'entreprise investit beaucoup dans la recherche

2 *adv* (**a**) *(grandly)* **he talks big** il se vante, il fanfaronne; **to think big** voir grand

(**b**) *Fam (well)* **their music goes over** *or* **down big with teenagers** les adolescents adorent leur musique; **they made it big in the pop world** ce sont maintenant des stars de la musique pop

►► *Fam* ***the Big Apple*** = surnom donné à la ville de New York; *Mus* ***big band*** big band *m (grand orchestre de jazz typique des années 40-50)*; *Br Fam St Exch* ***the Big Bang*** = déréglementation de la Bourse de Londres en octobre 1986; *Fam Astron* ***the big bang*** le big-bang, le big bang; *Astron* ***the big bang theory*** la théorie du big-bang *ou* big bang; ***big bank*** grande banque *f*, enseigne *f* bancaire; ***Big Ben*** Big Ben; *Comput* ***Big Blue*** = surnom de la société IBM; *Am St Exch* ***the big board*** = la Bourse de New York; ***Big Brother*** Big Brother; **Big Brother is watching you** Big Brother vous surveille; *Com* ***big business*** *(UNCOUNT)* les grandes entreprises *fpl*; ***big cat*** fauve *m*, grand félin *m*; ***the big cats*** les fauves *mpl*, les grands félins *mpl*; *Fam Fig* ***big cheese*** gros bonnet *m*; *Am Fam* ***the Big D*** = surnom donné à la ville de Dallas; *Am Fam* ***big daddy*** = surnom donné au gouvernement américain; *Am Astron* ***the Big Dipper*** la Grande Ourse; ***big dipper*** *(in fairground)* montagnes *fpl* russes; *Am Fam* ***the Big Easy*** = surnom donné à la Nouvelle-Orléans; *Br Aut* ***big end*** tête *f* de bielle; *Br Formerly Banking* ***the Big Four*** = les quatre grandes banques anglaises *(Lloyds, National Westminster, Barclays, Midland)*; *Hunt* ***big game*** gros gibier *m*; *Br Fam Hum* ***big girl's blouse*** *(wimp)* femmelette *f*; *Am Pej Pol* ***Big Government*** = gouvernement interventionniste sur le plan social; *Fam Fig* ***big gun*** gros bonnet *m*; *Am Fam* ***big hair*** = coiffure volumineuse et apprêtée; *Am Fam* ***big house*** *(prison)* taule *f*, placard *m*; **he's gone to the big house** on l'a mis à l'ombre; *Fam Mktg* ***Big Idea, big idea*** idée-force ❑ *f*; **new product development is all about coming up with a Big Idea** le développement de nouveaux produits démarre toujours avec une idée-force; *Br Press* ***The Big Issue*** = hebdomadaire vendu au profit des sans-logis par ces derniers, ≃ le Réverbère; *Am Sport* ***Big League*** *(gen)* première division *f*; *(in baseball)* = une des deux principales divisions de baseball professionnel aux États-Unis; *Am Fam* ***big man on campus*** = étudiant jouissant d'une certaine popularité grâce à ses exploits sportifs etc; *Sport* ***big match*** grand match *m*; ***big name*** grand nom *m*; *Br Fam Fig* ***big noise*** gros bonnet *m*; *Cin* ***the big screen*** le grand écran, le cinéma; *Fam Fig* ***big shot*** gros bonnet *m*; **he thinks he's a real big shot** il croit qu'il est vraiment quelqu'un; *Br Fam* ***the Big Smoke*** *(gen)* la grande ville ❑; *(London)* = surnom donné à Londres; *Fam Fig* ***the big stick*** le bâton, la force; ***big stick diplomacy*** diplomatie *f* musclée; *Am Sport* ***the Big Ten*** = équipes sportives universitaires du Mid West, réputées de très haut niveau; *Aut* ***the Big Three*** = les trois principaux constructeurs automobiles américains (General Motors, Ford, Chrysler); ***big toe*** gros orteil *m*; ***big top*** *(tent)* grand chapiteau *m*; *(circus)* cirque *m*; *Fam Fig* ***big wheel*** gros bonnet *m*

'The Big Sleep' *Chandler, Hawks* 'Le Grand Sommeil'

'The Big Chill' *Kasdan* 'Les Copains d'abord'

Big brother is watching you

Cette formule ("Big Brother vous surveille") est tirée du roman de George Orwell *1984*, dans lequel Big Brother personnifie l'état tout-puissant et omniprésent.

Le terme Big Brother est entré dans la langue pour décrire tout état totalitaire, et l'expression **Big Brother is watching you** s'utilise souvent sur le mode humoristique à propos d'un gouvernement ou de tout autre forme d'autorité perçus comme impersonnels et envahissants.

BIG BEN

Nom de la cloche de la Tour de l'horloge à Westminster, souvent donné à tort à la tour elle-même. Elle est considérée comme un des monuments principaux de Londres.

bigamist ['bɪgəmɪst] *n* bigame *mf*

bigamous ['bɪgəməs] *adj* bigame

bigamy ['bɪgəmɪ] *n* bigamie *f*; **to commit bigamy** être coupable de bigamie

big-bellied *adj (fat)* ventru, pansu; **she's big-bellied** *(of pregnant woman)* elle a un gros ventre

big-boned *adj* fortement charpenté

big-budget *adj Fin* à gros budget

big-eared *adj* aux grandes oreilles

►► *Zool* ***big-eared bat*** mégaderme *m*

Bigfoot ['bɪgfʊt] *pr n Myth* = sorte d'abominable homme des neiges qui vivrait dans le nord des États-Unis et au Canada

big-game *adj* **big-game hunter** chasseur *m* de gros gibier; **big-game hunting** chasse *f* au gros gibier

biggie ['bɪgɪ] *n Fam (success → song)* tube *m*; *(→ film, record)* succès ❑ *m*; **his next book/film should be a biggie** son prochain livre/film devrait faire un malheur; *Am* **no biggie!** pas de problèmes!

biggish ['bɪgɪʃ] *adj (tall, large)* assez grand; *(fat)* assez gros (grosse)

Biggles ['bɪgəlz] *pr n* = pilote de guerre dans les romans de W.E. Johns (pour toute une génération de jeunes lecteurs le personnage fut un modèle de courage et de sang-froid)

bighead ['bɪghed] *n Fam* crâneur(euse) *m,f*

bigheaded [,bɪg'hedɪd] *adj Fam* crâneur; **to be bigheaded** avoir la grosse tête

bigheadedness [,bɪg'hedɪdnɪs] *n Fam* suffisance ❑ *f*

bighearted [,bɪg'hɑːtɪd] *adj* au grand cœur; **to be bighearted** avoir le cœur sur la main, avoir bon *ou* du cœur

bighorn ['bɪghɔːn] *(pl* **inv** *or* **bighorns**) *n Zool* mouflon *m* (d'Amérique)

bight [baɪt] *n* (**a**) *Geog (of shoreline)* baie *f*; **the Great Australian Bight** la Grande Baie Australienne, le Grand Golfe Australien *ou* de l'Australie (**b**) *(in rope → slack)* mou *m*; *(→ coil)* boucle *f*

bigmouth ['bɪgmaʊθ, *pl* -maʊðz] *n Fam* grande gueule *f*; **she's such a bigmouth** elle ne sait pas la fermer; **shut up, bigmouth!** la ferme!

bigness ['bɪgnɪs] *n (of person → tallness)* grande taille *f*; *(→ fatness)* grosseur *f*; *(of thing)* grandes dimensions *fpl*

bigot ['bɪgət] *n (gen)* sectaire *mf*, intolérant(e) *m,f*; *Rel* bigot(e) *m,f*, sectaire *mf*

bigoted ['bɪgətɪd] *adj (gen → person)* sectaire, intolérant; *(→ attitude, opinion)* fanatique; *Rel* bigot

bigotry ['bɪgətrɪ] *n (gen)* sectarisme *m*, intolérance *f*; *Rel* bigoterie *f*

big-shot *adj Fam* **a big-shot lawyer from London** un crack du barreau de Londres

big-ticket *adj Am (expensive)* cher

big-time *adj Fam (actor, singer)* à succès ❑; *(businessman, politician)* de haut vol; *(project)* ambitieux ❑, de grande échelle ❑

big-timer *n Fam* gros bonnet *m*

bigwig ['bɪgwɪg] *n Fam* gros bonnet *m*

bijou ['biːʒuː] *adj Br* petit mais chic

►► ***bijou flat, bijou residence*** petit appartement *m* très chic

bike [baɪk] **1** *n (bicycle)* vélo *m*, bicyclette *f*; *(motorcycle)* moto *f*; **to ride a bike** *(bicycle)* faire du vélo *ou* de la bicyclette; *(motorcycle)* faire de la moto; *Br Fam* **on your bike!** *(go away)* dégage!; *(don't be ridiculous)* mais oui, c'est ça!

2 *vi (bicycle)* faire du vélo; *(motorcycle)* faire de la moto; **we biked there** nous y sommes allés à *ou* en vélo/moto

►► ***bike lane*** piste *f* cyclable; ***bike shed*** cabane *f ou* remise *f* à vélos

biker ['baɪkə(r)] *n Fam* motard(e) *m,f*, motocycliste ❑ *mf*

►► ***biker's jacket*** blouson *m* de cuir

bikeway ['baɪkweɪ] *n Am* piste *f* cyclable

bikini [bɪ'kiːnɪ] *n* bikini *m*; **to have one's bikini line done** se faire faire une épilation maillot

►► ***Bikini Atoll*** Bikini

bilabial [,baɪ'leɪbɪəl] *Ling* **1** *n* bilabiale *f*

2 *adj* bilabial

bilateral [,baɪ'lætərəl] *adj* bilatéral

bilaterally [,baɪ'lætərəlɪ] *adv* bilatéralement

bilayer ['baɪleɪə(r)] *n Biol & Chem* bicouche *f*

bilevel [,baɪ'levəl] *adj Am* à deux niveaux; **a bilevel house** maison *f* à deux niveaux

bilberry ['bɪlbərɪ] *(pl* **bilberries**) *n Bot* myrtille *f*

bile [baɪl] *n* (**a**) *Anat* bile *f* (**b**) *Literary (irritability)* mauvaise humeur *f*, irascibilité *f*

►► ***bile duct*** canal *m* biliaire

bilestone ['baɪl,stəʊn] *n Anat* calcul *m* biliaire

bilge [bɪldʒ] *n* (**a**) *Naut (hull)* bouchain *m*, renflement *m*; *(hold)* fond *m* de cale, sentine *f*; *(water)* eau *f* de cale *ou* de sentine

(**b**) *(UNCOUNT) Fam Fig (nonsense)* âneries *fpl*, idioties *fpl*; **he talks a load of bilge** il raconte un tas de bêtises

►► *Naut* ***bilge block*** ventrière *f*; *Naut* ***bilge keel*** quille *f* de bouchain; *Naut* ***bilge pump*** pompe *f* de drain *ou* de cale; ***bilge water*** *(UNCOUNT) Naut* eau *f* de cale *ou* de sentine; *Fam Fig (nonsense)* âneries *fpl*, idioties *fpl*; *Naut* ***bilge well*** puisard *m*

bilharzia [bɪl'hɑːtsɪə] *n* (**a**) *(UNCOUNT) Med (disease)* bilharziose *f* (**b**) *Biol (parasite)* bilharzia *f*, bilharzie *f*

bilharziasis [,bɪlhɑː'tsaɪəsɪs], **bilharziosis** [bɪl,hɑːtsɪ'əʊsɪs] *n Med* bilharziose *f*

biliary ['bɪlɪərɪ] *adj Anat* biliaire

bilinear [,baɪ'lɪnɪə(r)] *adj* bilinéaire

bilingual [baɪ'lɪŋgwəl] *adj Ling* bilingue; **to be bilingual in French and English** être bilingue français-anglais

►► ***bilingual dictionary*** dictionnaire *m* bilingue; ***bilingual secretary*** secrétaire *mf* bilingue

bilingualism [baɪ'lɪŋgwəlɪzəm] *n Ling* bilinguisme *m*

bilious ['bɪlɪəs] *adj* (**a**) *Med* bilié; **bilious attack** crise *f* de foie; **bilious disorder** affection *f* hépatique (**b**) *(colour)* écœurant (**c**) *Literary (irritable)* bilieux, irascible

biliousness ['bɪlɪəsnɪs] *n* (**a**) *Med* affection *f* hépatique (**b**) *(of colour)* aspect *m* écœurant (**c**) *Literary (irritability)* mauvaise humeur *f*, irascibilité *f*

bilirubin [,bɪlɪ'ruːbɪn] *n Anat* bilirubine *f*

bilk [bɪlk] *vt Br* (**a**) *(thwart → person)* contrecarrer, contrarier les projets de; *(→ plan)* contrecarrer, contrarier (**b**) *(cheat)* escroquer; **they bilked her of her fortune** ils lui ont escroqué sa fortune

Bill [bɪl] *n Br Fam* **the (Old) Bill** les flics *mpl*

bill [bɪl] **1** *n* (**a**) *(for gas, telephone)* facture *f*, note *f*; *(for product)* facture *f*; *Br (in restaurant)* addition *f*, note *f*; *(in hotel)* note *f*; **to pay a bill** payer *ou* régler une facture; **to foot the bill** payer la note *ou* les dépenses; **to make out a bill** dresser *ou* rédiger une facture; **may I have the bill please?** l'addition, s'il vous plaît; **have you paid the telephone bill?** as-tu payé le téléphone?; **put it on my bill** mettez-le sur ma note

(**b**) *Law (draft of law)* projet *m* de loi; *Parl* **to introduce a bill in Parliament** présenter un projet de loi au Parlement; **to vote on a bill** mettre un projet de loi au vote; **to pass/reject a bill** adopter/repousser un projet de loi

(**c**) *(poster)* affiche *f*, placard *m*; **(stick) no bills!** défense d'afficher;

(**d**) *Theat* affiche *f*; **to head** *or* **to top the bill** être en tête d'affiche *ou* en vedette

(**e**) *(list, statement)* liste *f*; *Am Fam Com* **to sell sb a bill of goods** rouler *ou* avoir qn

(**f**) *Com & Fin (promissory note)* effet *m* (de commerce), traite *f*; **bill made out to bearer** effet au porteur

(**g**) *Am (banknote)* billet *m* (de banque); **a ten-dollar bill** un billet de dix dollars

(**h**) *Orn & Zool (beak)* bec *m*

(**i**) *Geog* promontoire *m*, bec *m*

(**j**) *Hist (weapon)* hallebarde *f*

(**k**) *(billhook)* serpe *f*, serpette *f*

2 *vt* (**a**) *Com & Fin (invoice)* facturer; **he bills his company for his travel expenses** il se fait rembourser ses frais de voyage par son entreprise; **bill me for the newspaper at the end**

of the month envoyez-moi la facture pour le journal à la fin du mois

(**b**) *(advertise)* annoncer; **they're billed as the best band in the world** on les présente comme le meilleur groupe du monde

(**c**) *Theat* mettre à l'affiche, annoncer; **he is billed to appear as Cyrano** il est à l'affiche dans le rôle de Cyrano

3 *vi* **to bill and coo** *(birds)* se becqueter; *(people)* roucouler

►► *Law* ***bill of attainder*** décret *m* de mort civile; *Fin* ***bill book*** livre *m* d'échéance; *Fin* ***bill broker*** agent *m ou* courtier(ère) *m,f* de change; *Fin* ***bills for collection*** effets *mpl* à l'encaissement; *Fin* ***bills for collection form*** formulaire *m* d'encaissement; *Fin* ***bill collector*** agent *m* de recouvrement; *Fin* ***bill discounter*** agent *m ou* courtier(ère) *m,f* de change; *Customs* ***bill of entry*** déclaration *f* d'entrée (en douane); *Fin* ***bill of exchange*** lettre *f* de change, effet *m* de commerce; ***bills of exchange statement*** lettre *f* de change relevé, LCR *f*; ***bill of fare*** carte *f* (du jour); ***bills in hand*** effets *mpl* en portefeuille; *Naut* ***bill of health*** patente *f* (de santé); *Fam* **the doctor gave him a clean bill of health** le médecin l'a trouvé en parfaite santé❑; *Fam* **the investigators gave the engine a clean bill of health** les enquêteurs ont conclu que le moteur était en parfait état❑; *Law* ***bill of indictment*** acte *m* d'accusation; *Com* ***bill of lading*** connaissement *m*; ***bill payable at sight*** effet *m* payable à vue *ou* à présentation; ***bills payable*** effets *mpl* à payer; ***bills payable ledger*** livre *m ou* journal *m* des effets à payer; ***bills receivable*** effets *mpl* à recevoir; ***bills receivable ledger*** livre *m ou* journal *m* des effets à recevoir; ***the Bill of Rights*** *Br Hist* = loi de 1689 déterminant les droits du citoyen anglais; *Am* = les dix premiers amendements à la Constitution américaine garantissant, entre autres droits, la liberté d'expression, de religion et de réunion; ***bill of sale*** acte *m ou* contrat *m* de vente; *Fin* ***bill 'without protest'*** traite *f* 'sans frais'

billabong ['bɪləbɒŋ] *n Austr Geog (pool)* mare *f*; *(of river)* bras *m* mort

billboard ['bɪlbɔːd] *n Mktg* panneau *m* (d'affichage)

►► ***billboard advertising*** publicité *f* sur panneaux; ***billboard site*** emplacement *m* d'affichage

billet ['bɪlɪt] **1** *n* (**a**) *Mil (accommodation)* cantonnement *m* (chez l'habitant); *(document)* billet *m* de logement (**b**) *Archit* billette *f* (**c**) *Br Old-fashioned Fam (job)* situation❑ *f*

2 *vt (gen)* loger; *Mil* cantonner, loger; **the captain billeted his men on the mayor/on the town** le capitaine a cantonné ses hommes chez le maire/dans la ville

billeting ['bɪlɪtɪŋ] *n Mil (in private house)* logement *m* chez l'habitant; *(on town)* cantonnement *m*

►► ***billeting officer*** officier *m* de cantonnement

billfold ['bɪlfəʊld] *n Am* portefeuille *m*

billhook ['bɪlhʊk] *n* serpe *f*, serpette *f*

billiard ['bɪljəd] **1** *comp* de billard

2 billiards *n (UNCOUNT)* (jeu *m* de) billard *m*; **to play billiards** jouer au billard; **to have** *or* **play a game of billiards** faire *ou* disputer une partie de billard

►► ***billiard ball*** boule *f* de billard; ***billiard cue*** queue *f* de billard; ***billiard hall*** (salle *f* de) billard *m*; ***billiard table*** (table *f* de) billard *m*

billing ['bɪlɪŋ] *n* (**a**) *Theat* affichage *m*; **to get** *or* **to have top/second billing** être en tête d'affiche/en deuxième place à l'affiche (**b**) *Am (advertising)* **to give sth advance billing** annoncer qch (**c**) *Fin* facturation *f* (**d**) *also Fig (sound)* **billing and cooing** roucoulements *mpl*

►► ***billing date*** date *f* de facturation; ***billing machine*** caisse *f* (enregistreuse); ***billing office*** bureau *m* de facturation

Billingsgate ['bɪlɪŋzgeɪt] *n* = marché au poisson à Londres

billion ['bɪljən] *(pl* **inv** *or* **billions**) *n (thousand million)* milliard *m*; *Br Old-fashioned (million million)* billion *m*

billionaire [ˌbɪljə'neə(r)] *n* milliardaire *mf*

billionth ['bɪljənθ] **1** *n* (**a**) *(ordinal)* milliardième *mf* (**b**) *(fraction)* milliardième *m*

2 *adj* milliardième

billow ['bɪləʊ] **1** *n* (**a**) *(of smoke)* tourbillon *m*, volute *f* (**b**) *(wave)* grosse vague *f*; *Literary* **the billows** les flots *mpl*

2 *vi (cloth, flag)* onduler; *(sail)* se gonfler; *(cloud, smoke)* tourbillonner, tournoyer; *(of sea)* se soulever en vagues

►**billow out** *vi (sail, cloth)* se gonfler

billowy ['bɪləʊɪ] *adj (sea)* houleux, agité; *(wave)* gros (grosse); *(sail)* gonflé; *(skirt)* tourbillonnant; **billowy clouds of smoke** de gros nuages de fumée

billposter ['bɪlˌpəʊstə(r)], **billsticker** ['bɪlˌstɪkə(r)] *n* afficheur(euse) *m,f*, colleur(euse) *m,f* d'affiches

billposting ['bɪlˌpəʊstɪŋ], **billsticking** ['bɪlˌstɪkɪŋ] *n* affichage *m*

billy ['bɪlɪ] *(pl* **billies**) *n* (**a**) *Am (weapon)* **billy (club)** matraque *f* (**b**) *Br & Austr (can)* gamelle *f*; *Austr* **to boil the billy** faire le thé *(dans une gamelle)* (**c**) *Fam (goat)* bouc❑ *m*

►► ***billy goat*** bouc *m*

Billy Bunter *pr n* = gros garçon gourmand (personnage d'une série de livres pour enfants en Grande-Bretagne)

billycan ['bɪlɪkæn] *n Br & Austr* gamelle *f*

billy-o, billy-oh ['bɪlɪəʊ] *n Br Fam Old-fashioned* **he ran like billy-o** il a couru comme un dératé

biltong ['bɪltɒŋ] *n SAfr Culin* morceaux *mpl* de viande séchée

BIM [ˌbiːaɪ'em] *n Com (abbr* **British Institute of Management**) = organisme britannique dont la fonction est de renseigner et de conseiller les entreprises en matière de gestion, ainsi que de promouvoir l'enseignement de cette discipline

bimbette [bɪm'bet], **bimbo** ['bɪmbəʊ] *(pl* **bimbos** *or* **bimboes**) *n Fam Pej* = jeune femme sexy et un peu bête

bimetallic [ˌbaɪmɪ'tælɪk] *adj* bimétallique

►► ***bimetallic strip*** bilame *m*

bimetallism [ˌbaɪ'metəlɪzəm] *n Fin* bimétallisme *m*

bimillenary [ˌbaɪmɪ'lenərɪ] *n* bimillénaire *m*

bimonthly [ˌbaɪ'mʌnθlɪ] *(pl* **bimonthlies**) **1** *adj (every two months)* bimestriel; *(twice monthly)* bimensuel

2 *adv (every two months)* tous les deux mois; *(twice monthly)* deux fois par mois

3 *n* bimestriel *m*

bimorph ['baɪmɔːf] *n Phys & Tech* cristal *m* bimorphe

bin [bɪn] *(pt & pp* **binned,** *cont* **binning**) **1** *n* (**a**) *Br (for rubbish)* poubelle *f*, boîte *f* à ordures

(**b**) *(for coal, grain)* coffre *m*; *(for bread)* huche *f*

(**c**) *Br (for wine)* casier *m* (à bouteilles)

(**d**) *Fam* **the bin** *(psychiatric hospital)* la maison de fous

2 *vt* (**a**) *(coal, grain)* mettre dans un coffre; *Br (wine)* mettre à vieillir

(**b**) *Br Fam (discard)* flanquer à la poubelle

►► ***bin bag*** sac *m* poubelle; *Br* ***bin end*** *(wine)* fin *f* de série; *Br* ***bin liner*** sac *m* poubelle

binal ['baɪnəl] *adj* double

binary ['baɪnərɪ] **1** *adj Math & Comput* binaire

2 *n Astron* binaire *f*

►► ***binary code*** code *m* binaire; ***binary file*** fichier *m* binaire; ***binary number*** nombre *m* binaire; ***binary search*** recherche *f* binaire *ou* dichotomique; *Astron* ***binary star*** binaire *f*; *Mil* ***binary weapon*** arme *f* binaire

binaural [ˌbaɪn'ɔːrəl] *adj* biaural, binaural

bind [baɪnd] *(pt & pp* **bound** [baʊnd]) **1** *vt* (**a**) *(tie)* attacher, lier; **bind him to his chair** attachez-le à sa chaise; **to bind sb hand and foot** ligoter qn; **he was bound hand and foot** il avait les pieds et les poings liés

(**b**) *(encircle)* entourer, ceindre; *Med* **to bind a wound** bander *ou* panser une blessure

(**c**) *Sewing (provide with border)* border; *(buttonhole)* brider

(**d**) *(book)* relier; **the book is bound in leather** le livre est relié en cuir

(**e**) *(stick together)* lier, agglutiner; *Culin* **add eggs to bind the sauce** ajouter des œufs pour lier la sauce

(**f**) *Fig (bond, unite)* lier, attacher; **they are bound by friendship** c'est l'amitié qui les unit; **they are very much bound up with each other** *(lovers)* ils sont très attachés l'un à l'autre; *(friends)* ils sont très liés; **the two companies are bound by commercial interests** des intérêts commerciaux lient les deux sociétés

(**g**) *(oblige)* obliger, contraindre; **we are bound to tell the truth** nous sommes obligés *ou* tenus de dire la vérité; **she bound me to my promise** elle m'a obligé à tenir ma promesse; **they bound him to secrecy** ils lui ont fait jurer le secret; *Law* **to be bound by oath** être lié par serment

(**h**) *Med (dress → wound)* bander, panser

(**i**) *(apprentice)* mettre en apprentissage

2 *vi* (**a**) *Law (agreement, promise)* engager; *(rule)* être obligatoire

(**b**) *Culin (sauce)* se lier; *Constr (cement)* durcir, prendre

(**c**) *(mechanism)* se gripper

3 *n* (**a**) *(bond)* lien *m*, liens *mpl*

(**b**) *Mus* liaison *f*

(**c**) *Fam (nuisance)* plaie *f*; **working at weekends is a real bind!** quelle corvée de devoir travailler le week-end!, c'est la plaie de devoir travailler le week-end!; **we're in a bit of a bind** nous sommes plutôt dans le pétrin

►**bind down** *vt sep (tie, truss)* lier, attacher

►**bind over** *vt sep* (**a**) *(apprentice)* mettre en apprentissage (**b**) *Br Law (order)* sommer; **they were bound over to keep the peace** ils ont été sommés de ne pas troubler l'ordre public

►**bind together** *vt sep* attacher, lier; *Fig* lier, unir

►**bind up** *vt sep (tie → gen)* attacher, lier; *Med (→ wound)* bander, panser

binder ['baɪndə(r)] *n* (**a**) *(folder)* classeur *m* (**b**) *(bookbinder)* relieur(euse) *m,f* (**c**) *(glue)* colle *f*; *Culin (for sauce)* liant *m*; *Tech* liant *m*, agglomérant *m* (**d**) *Agr (machine)* lieuse *f*

bindery ['baɪndərɪ] *(pl* **binderies**) *n* atelier *m* de reliure

binding ['baɪndɪŋ] **1** *n* (**a**) *(for book)* reliure *f*

(**b**) *Sewing* extrafort *m*

(**c**) *Constr* agglutination *f*, agrégation *f*; *(of road surface)* liant *m*, agglomérant *m*

(**d**) *(on skis)* fixation *f*; **safety (release) bindings** fixations de sécurité

2 *adj* (**a**) *(law)* obligatoire; *(contract, promise)* qui engage *ou* lie; **the agreement is binding on all parties** l'accord engage chaque partie; *Com* **it is binding on the buyer to make immediate payment** l'acheteur est tenu de payer immédiatement

(**b**) *(food)* constipant

bindweed ['baɪndwiːd] *n Bot* liseron *m*

binge [bɪndʒ] *Fam* **1** *n* (**a**) *(spree)* **to go on a binge** faire la bringue; **they went on a shopping binge** ils sont allés dépenser du fric dans les magasins; **an eating binge** une grosse bouffe (**b**) *(drinking bout)* beuverie *f*, bringue *f*

2 *vi* (**a**) *(overspend)* faire des folies❑ (**b**) *(overeat)* faire des excès❑ *(de nourriture)*; *(drink too much)* prendre une cuite; **to binge on sth** *(drink)* s'enfiler des litres de qch; *(food)* s'empiffrer de qch

bingo ['bɪŋgəʊ] **1** *n* bingo *m*, ≃ loto *m*

2 *exclam Fam* ça y est!

►► ***bingo hall*** salle *f* de bingo

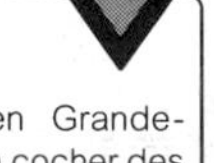

BINGO

Ce jeu d'argent très populaire en Grande-Bretagne et aux États-Unis consiste à cocher des chiffres sur une carte jusqu'à ce qu'elle soit remplie; il est souvent pratiqué dans d'anciens cinémas ou des salles municipales.

BinHex [bɪn'heks] *n Comput (abbr* **Binary Hexadecimal**) BinHex

binman ['bɪnmæn] *(pl* **binmen** [-men]) *n Br* éboueur *m*

binnacle ['bɪnəkəl] *n Naut* habitacle *m*

binocular [bɪ'nɒkjʊlə(r)] **1** *adj Opt* binoculaire

2 binoculars *npl* jumelles *fpl*

►► ***binocular vision*** vision *f* binoculaire

binomial [ˌbaɪ'nəʊmɪəl] *Math* **1** *n* binôme *m*

2 *adj* binomial

►► ***the binomial theorem*** le binôme de Newton, le théorème de Newton

bint [bɪnt] *n Br very Fam Pej* greluche *f*

binuclear [ˌbaɪ'njuːklɪə(r)] *adj Biol* binucléaire

bio ['baɪəʊ] *(pl* **bios**) *n Fam* biographie❑ *f*

bioactive [ˌbaɪəʊ'æktɪv] *adj Biol* bioactif
bioassay [ˌbaɪəʊə'seɪ] *n Chem & Pharm* essai *m ou* titrage *m* biologique
bioavailability [ˌbaɪəʊəˌveɪlə'bɪlɪtɪ] *n Pharm* biodisponibilité *f*
biochemical [ˌbaɪəʊ'kemɪkəl] **1** *n* produit *m* biochimique
2 *adj* biochimique
biochemist [ˌbaɪəʊ'kemɪst] *n* biochimiste *mf*
biochemistry [ˌbaɪəʊ'kemɪstrɪ] *n* biochimie *f*
biocide ['baɪəsaɪd] *n* biocide *m*
biocompatible [ˌbaɪəʊkəm'pætəbəl] *adj Biol* biocompatible
bioconversion [ˌbaɪəʊkən'vɜːʃən] *n Chem & Ind* bioconversion *f*
biodata ['baɪəʊdeɪtə] *n* biographie *f* succinte
biodegradability [ˌbaɪəʊdɪˌgreɪdə'bɪlɪtɪ] *n Biol* biodégradabilité *f*
biodegradable [ˌbaɪəʊdɪ'greɪdəbəl] *adj Biol* biodégradable
biodegrade [ˌbaɪəʊdɪ'greɪd] *vi Biol* biodégrader
biodiversity [ˌbaɪəʊdaɪ'vɜːsətɪ] *n Bot & Zool* biodiversité *f*
bioecology [ˌbaɪəʊɪ'kɒlədʒɪ] *n* synécologie *f*
bioengineering ['baɪəʊendʒɪ'nɪərɪŋ] *n Med* génie *f* biologique
bioethics [ˌbaɪəʊ'eθɪks] *n (UNCOUNT) Med* bioéthique *f*
biofeedback [ˌbaɪəʊ'fiːdbæk] *n Med & Psy* biofeedback *m*
biogas ['baɪəʊgæs] *n Chem* biogaz *m*
biogen ['baɪədʒən] *n Biol* protéine *f* biogène
biogenesis [ˌbaɪəʊ'dʒenɪsɪs] *n Biol* biogenèse *f*
biogeography [ˌbaɪəʊdʒɪ'ɒgrəfɪ] *n Bot & Zool* biogéographie *f*
biographer [baɪ'ɒgrəfə(r)] *n* biographe *mf*
biographical [ˌbaɪə'græfɪkəl] *adj* biographique; **biographical novel** biographie *f* romancée
biography [baɪ'ɒgrəfɪ] *n* biographie *f*
biological [ˌbaɪə'lɒdʒɪkəl] *adj* biologique
►► ***biological clock*** horloge *f* interne *ou* biologique; **my biological clock is ticking away** *(of woman)* mon temps est compté si je veux avoir des enfants; ***biological control*** *(of insects)* élimination *f* des insectes par des méthodes biologiques; *Mil* ***biological warfare*** guerre *f* bactériologique
biologically [ˌbaɪə'lɒdʒɪkəlɪ] *adv* biologiquement
biologist [baɪ'ɒlədʒɪst] *n* biologiste *mf*
biology [baɪ'ɒlədʒɪ] **1** *n* biologie *f*
2 *comp (lesson, teacher)* de biologie
bioluminescence [ˌbaɪəʊluːmɪ'nesəns] *n Bot, Entom & Ich* bioluminescence *f*
biomass ['baɪəʊmæs] *n Biol* biomasse *f*
biomaterial [ˌbaɪəʊmə'tɪərɪəl] *n Med* biomatériau *m*
biomathematics [ˌbaɪəʊmæθə'mætɪks] *n (UNCOUNT)* biomathématiques *fpl*
biome ['baɪəʊm] *n Ecol* biome *m*
biomechanics [ˌbaɪəʊmɪ'kænɪks] *n (UNCOUNT)* biomécanique *f*
biomedical [ˌbaɪəʊ'medɪkəl] *adj* biomédical
biomedicine [ˌbaɪəʊ'medɪsɪn] *n Biol & Med* biomédecine *f*
biometric [ˌbaɪəʊ'metrɪk], **biometrical** [ˌbaɪəʊ'metrɪkəl] *adj Biol* biométrique
biometrics [ˌbaɪəʊ'metrɪks] *n (UNCOUNT) Biol* biométrie *f*
biometry [baɪ'ɒmɪtrɪ] *n Biol* biométrie *f*
biomolecular [ˌbaɪəʊmə'lekjʊlə(r)] *adj Biol* biomoléculaire
biomolecule [ˌbaɪəʊ'mɒlɪkjuːl] *n Biol* biomolécule *f*
bionic [baɪ'ɒnɪk] *adj* bionique
bionics [baɪ'ɒnɪks] *n (UNCOUNT)* bionique *f*
biophysicist [ˌbaɪəʊ'fɪzɪsɪst] *n Biol & Phys* biophysicien(enne) *m,f*
biophysics [ˌbaɪəʊ'fɪzɪks] *n (UNCOUNT) Biol & Phys* biophysique *f*
biopic ['baɪəʊpɪk] *n Fam Cin* film *m* biographique ❑
biopiracy [baɪəʊ'paɪrəsɪ] *n* biopiratage *m*, biopiraterie *f*
bioprospecting [baɪəʊ'prɒspektɪŋ] *n* bioprospection *f*
biopsy ['baɪɒpsɪ] *(pl* **biopsies***)* *n Biol & Med* biopsie *f*
bioremediation [ˌbaɪəʊrəmiːdɪ'eɪʃən] *n Ecol* bioremédiation
biorhythm ['baɪəʊrɪðəm] *n Biol & Physiol* biorythme *m*
BIOS ['baɪɒs] *n Comput (abbr* **basic input/output system***)* BIOS *m*
bioscience ['baɪəʊˌsaɪəns] *n* biologie *f*
bioscope ['baɪəʊskəʊp] *n Cin* (**a**) *Old-fashioned (projector)* bioscope *m* (**b**) *SAfr (cinema)* cinéma *m*
biosphere ['baɪəʊˌsfɪə(r)] *n Biol* biosphère *f*
biosynthesis [ˌbaɪəʊ'sɪnθəsɪs] *n Chem & Biol* biosynthèse *f*
biosynthetic [ˌbaɪəʊsɪn'θetɪk] *adj Biol* biosynthétique
biotech [baɪəʊ'tek] **1** *n* biotechnologie *f*
2 *comp (industry)* de la biotechnologie; *(company)* entreprise *f* de biotechnologie
biotechnology [ˌbaɪəʊtek'nɒlədʒɪ] *n* biotechnologie *f*
bioterrorism [ˌbaɪəʊ'terərɪzəm] *n* terrorisme *m* biologique
bioterrorist [ˌbaɪəʊ'terərɪst] *n* = personne qui pratique le terrorisme biologique
biotic [baɪ'ɒtɪk] *adj Biol* biotique
biotin ['baɪətɪn] *n Chem* biotine *f*
biotope ['baɪətəʊp] *n Geog* biotope *m*
biotype ['baɪətaɪp] *n Biol* biotype *m*
biowarfare [ˌbaɪəʊ'wɔːfeə(r)] *n Mil* guerre *f* biologique
biparous ['bɪpərəs] *adj Bot & Zool* bipare
bipartisan [ˌbaɪpɑːtɪ'zæn] *adj Pol* biparti, bipartite
bipartisanship [ˌbaɪ'pɑːtɪzənʃɪp] *n* bipartisme *m*
bipartite [ˌbaɪ'pɑːtaɪt] *adj Bot & Pol* biparti, bipartite
biped ['baɪped] *Zool* **1** *n* bipède *m*
2 *adj* bipède
biphenyl [ˌbaɪ'fenɪl] *n Chem* diphényle *m*
biplane ['baɪpleɪn] *n Aviat* biplan *m*
bipod ['baɪpɒd] *n* bipied *m*
bipolar [ˌbaɪ'pəʊlə(r)] *adj* bipolaire
bipolarity [ˌbaɪpəʊ'lærɪtɪ] *n* bipolarité *f*
biquarterly [ˌbaɪ'kwɔːtəlɪ] *adj Am* deux fois par trimestre
biracial [baɪ'reɪʃəl] *adj* biracial
birch [bɜːtʃ] **1** *n* (**a**) *Bot (tree)* bouleau *m*; *(wood)* (bois *m* de) bouleau *m* (**b**) *Br (rod for whipping)* verge *f*; **to give sb the birch** fouetter qn
2 *comp (forest, furniture)* de bouleau
3 *vt Br* fouetter
►► *Agr* ***birch plantation*** boulaie *f*, plantation *f* de bouleaux; ***birch whisk*** fouet *m* en bouleau
birchen ['bɜːtʃən] *adj Literary* de bouleau
Bircher ['bɜːtʃə(r)] *n Pol* = membre de la "John Birch Society"
birching ['bɜːtʃɪŋ] *n Br* correction *f*; **to give sb a birching** fouetter qn, donner une correction à qn
Birchism ['bɜːtʃɪzəm] *n Pol* = philosophie de la "John Birch Society"
bird [bɜːd] *n* (**a**) *(gen)* oiseau *m*; *Culin* volaille *f*; **she eats like a bird** elle a un appétit d'oiseau; **a little bird told me** mon petit doigt me l'a dit; **strictly for the birds** bon pour les imbéciles; *Euph* **it's time you talked to him about the birds and the bees** *(facts of life)* il serait temps de lui expliquer que les bébés ne naissent pas dans les choux; **the bird has flown** l'oiseau s'est envolé; *Fam* **to give sb the bird** *(hiss)* huer *ou* siffler qn ❑; *(send packing)* envoyer qn paître; *Am (make fun of)* se foutre de la gueule de qn; *Am (gesture at)* faire un doigt d'honneur à qn; *Am Fam* **to flip sb the bird** faire un doigt d'honneur à qn; *Prov* **birds of a feather flock together** qui se ressemble s'assemble; **you and your father are birds of a feather** toi et ton père, vous ne valez pas mieux l'un que l'autre, toi et ton père, je vous mets dans le même sac; *Prov* **a bird in the hand is worth two in the bush** un tiens vaut mieux que deux tu l'auras
(**b**) *Br Fam (woman)* nana *f*
(**c**) *Fam (individual)* type *m*; **he's a strange bird** c'est un drôle d'oiseau; **a home bird** un(e) casanier(ère); *Fig* **night bird** noctambule *mf*
(**d**) *Br Fam Crime slang* **to do bird** faire de la taule
►► *Fam Pej* ***bird brain*** tête *f* de linotte, écervelé(e) *m,f*; *Hunt* ***bird dog*** chien *m* d'arrêt *(pour le gibier à plumes)*; ***bird droppings*** fiente *f*; *Br* ***bird fancier*** *(interested in birds)* ornithologue *mf* amateur; *(breeder)* aviculteur(trice) *m,f*; ***bird of paradise*** *(bird, flower)* oiseau *m* de paradis; *also Fig* ***bird of passage*** oiseau *m* de passage; ***bird of prey*** oiseau *m* de proie, rapace *m*; ***bird sanctuary*** réserve *f ou* refuge *m* d'oiseaux

'The Birds' *du Maurier, Hitchcock* 'Les Oiseaux'

birdbath ['bɜːdbɑːθ, *pl* -bɑːðz] *n* vasque *f (pour les oiseaux)*
bird-brained [-breɪnd] *adj Fam (person)* écervelé, qui a une cervelle d'oiseau; *(idea)* insensé ❑
birdcage ['bɜːdkeɪdʒ] *n (small)* cage *f* à oiseaux; *(large)* volière *f*
birdcall ['bɜːdkɔːl] *n* cri *m* d'oiseau
birdcatcher ['bɜːdkætʃə(r)] *n* oiseleur *m*
bird-eating spider *n* mygale *m* aviculaire
birdhouse ['bɜːdhaʊs, *pl* -haʊzɪz] *n Am* volière *f*
birdie ['bɜːdɪ] **1** *n* (**a**) *Fam (small bird)* petit oiseau ❑ *m*, oisillon ❑ *m*; *Phot* **watch the birdie!** le petit oiseau va sortir! (**b**) *Golf* birdie *m*; **a birdie 3** un birdie 3
2 *vt Golf* **to birdie a hole** faire un birdie *(jouer un trou en un coup au-dessous du par)*
birding ['bɜːdɪŋ] *n* ornithologie *f*; **to go birding** aller observer les oiseaux
birdlike ['bɜːdlaɪk] *adj (appetite)* d'oiseau; **birdlike movements/features** mouvements *mpl/* traits *mpl* semblables à ceux d'un oiseau
birdlime ['bɜːdlaɪm] *n Orn* glu *f*
birdman ['bɜːdmæn] *(pl* **birdmen** [-men]*)* *n (interested in birds)* ornithologue *m* amateur; *(breeder)* aviculteur *m*
bird-nesting *n* **to go bird-nesting** aller dénicher des oiseaux
birdseed ['bɜːdsiːd] *n* graine *f* pour les oiseaux
bird's-eye 1 *adj* **a bird's-eye view of sth** une vue panoramique de qch; *Fig* une vue d'ensemble de qch
2 *n* (**a**) *Bot (primrose)* primevère *f* farineuse (**b**) *Tex (cloth)* œil-de-perdrix *m*
►► *Bot* ***bird's-eye speedwell*** véronique *f*
bird's-foot *n Bot* pied-d'oiseau *m*
►► *Bot* ***bird's-foot trefoil*** lotier *m*, pied-de-poule *m*
bird's-nesting = **bird-nesting**
bird's-nest soup *n Culin* soupe *f* aux nids d'hirondelles
birdsong ['bɜːdsɒŋ] *n* chant *m* d'oiseau
birdstrike ['bɜːdstraɪk] *n Aviat* = collision entre un avion et un oiseau
birdtable ['bɜːdˌteɪbəl] *n* mangeoire *f (pour oiseaux)*
bird-watcher *n* ornithologue *mf* amateur
bird-watching *n* ornithologie *f*; **to go bird-watching** aller observer les oiseaux
bireme ['baɪriːm] *n Hist* birème *f*
biretta [bɪ'retə] *n Rel* barrette *f (d'un ecclésiastique)*
biriani = **biryani**
Birkenstocks® ['bɜːkənstɒks] *npl* = sandales de cuir que l'on associe volontiers à un mode de vie écologique
birling ['bɜːlɪŋ] *n (sport)* = sport pratiqué par les bûcherons, qui consiste à se maintenir debout sur un tronc d'arbre flottant que l'on fait tourner sous ses pieds, *Can* concours *m* de draveurs
Birmingham ['bɜːmɪŋəm] *n* Birmingham; **the Birmingham Six** = groupe de six Irlandais condamnés à perpétuité en Angleterre à la suite d'un attentat à la bombe qui eut lieu à Birmingham en 1974, et libérés en 1991 lorsqu'une enquête révéla qu'ils avaient été accusés à tort
Biro® ['baɪrəʊ] *(pl* **Biros***)* *n Br* stylo *m* (à) bille, ≃ Bic® *m*
birth [bɜːθ] *n* (**a**) *(of child)* naissance *f*; **deaf from birth** sourd de naissance; *Fam Hum* **he should have been drowned at birth!** on aurait dû le noyer à la naissance!
(**b**) *(act of bearing young → of person)* accouchement *m*, couches *fpl*; *(→ of animal)* mise *f* bas; **to give birth** *(woman)* accoucher; *(animal)* mettre bas; **she gave birth to a boy** elle a accouché d'un garçon; **a difficult birth** un

accouchement difficile; **will the father be present at the birth?** le père assistera-t-il à l'accouchement *ou* à la naissance?

(**c**) *Fig (origin → of movement, nation)* naissance *f*, origine *f*; *(→ of era, industry)* naissance *f*, commencement *m*; *(→ of product, radio)* apparition *f*

(**d**) *(ancestry, lineage)* naissance *f*, ascendance *f*; **he's Chinese by birth** il est chinois de naissance; **of high birth** de bonne famille, bien né; **of low birth** de basse extraction

►► ***birth certificate*** *(original)* acte *m* de naissance; *(copy)* extrait *m* de naissance; *Astrol* ***birth chart*** thème *m* astral; ***birth control*** *(contraception)* contraception *f*; *(family planning)* contrôle *m* des naissances; **to practise birth control** utiliser un contraceptif *ou* un moyen de contraception; ***birth father*** père *m* biologique; ***birth mother*** mère *f* biologique; ***birth pangs*** douleurs *fpl* de l'accouchement; *Fig* **the birth pangs of democracy** la naissance difficile de la démocratie; ***birth parent*** *(father)* père *m* biologique; *(mother)* mère *f* biologique; ***birth parents*** parents *mpl* biologiques; ***birth partner*** =proche qui assiste à l'accouchement; ***birth rate*** (taux *m* de) natalité *f*

'The Birth of Venus' *Botticelli* 'La Naissance de Vénus'

'The Birth of a Nation' *Griffith* 'La Naissance d'une nation'

birthday ['bɜːθdeɪ] **1** *n* anniversaire *m*; **her 21st birthday** ses 21 ans; **she was 42 on her last birthday** elle a 42 ans; **let me buy the birthday girl a drink** laisse-moi te payer un verre pour ton anniversaire; **they're giving him a birthday party** ils organisent une fête pour son anniversaire

2 *comp (cake, card, present)* d'anniversaire

►► ***the Birthday Honours*** = titres honorifiques et autres distinctions décernés chaque année le jour de l'anniversaire officiel du souverain britannique; *Fam Hum* ***birthday suit*** *(of man)* costume *m* d'Adam; *(of woman)* costume *m* d'Ève

'The Birthday Party' *Pinter* 'L'Anniversaire'

birthing ['bɜːθɪŋ] *n*

►► *Br Obst* ***birthing pool*** piscine *f* d'accouchement; *Obst* ***birthing room*** salle *f* d'accouchement

birthmark ['bɜːθmɑːk] *n* tache *f* de naissance

birthplace ['bɜːθpleɪs] *n (town)* lieu *m* de naissance; *(house)* maison *f* natale; *Fig* berceau *m*

birthright ['bɜːθraɪt] *n* droit *m* (acquis à la naissance); **freedom of speech is every citizen's birthright** la liberté d'expression constitue un droit pour chaque citoyen

birthstone ['bɜːθstəʊn] *n* pierre *f* porte-bonheur *(selon la date de naissance)*

biryani [ˌbɪrɪ'ɑːnɪ] *n Culin* biriani *m*; **chicken biryani** poulet *m* biriani

BIS [ˌbiːaɪ'es] *n (abbr* **Bank for International Settlements**) BRI *f*

Biscay ['bɪskeɪ] *n* Biscaye *f*

biscuit ['bɪskɪt] **1** *n* (**a**) *Br Culin* biscuit *m*, petit gâteau *m*; *Fam* **that really takes the biscuit!** ça, c'est vraiment le bouquet!; *Fam* **you really take the biscuit!** vous êtes marrant, vous!

(**b**) *Am Culin* = petit gâteau que l'on mange avec de la confiture ou avec un plat salé

(**c**) *(colour)* beige *m*

(**d**) *Cer* biscuit *m*

2 *adj* (de couleur) beige

►► ***biscuit barrel*** boîte *f* à biscuits; ***biscuit cutter*** emporte-pièce *m*; ***biscuit factory*** biscuiterie *f*; ***biscuit tin*** boîte *f* à biscuits

bisect [baɪ'sekt] **1** *vt (gen)* couper en deux; *Math* diviser en deux parties égales

2 *vi Transp (of road etc)* bifurquer

bisection [ˌbaɪ'sekʃən] *n (action)* division *f* en deux; *Math* bissection *f*

bisector [ˌbaɪ'sektə(r)] *n Math* bissectrice *f*

bisexual [ˌbaɪ'sekʃʊəl] **1** *n* (**a**) *(person)* bisexuel(elle) *m,f* (**b**) *Biol & Zool* hermaphrodite *m*

2 *adj* (**a**) *(person, tendency)* bisexuel (**b**) *Biol & Zool* bisexué, hermaphrodite

bisexuality [baɪˌseksjʊ'ælɪtɪ] *n* bisexualité *f*

bishop ['bɪʃəp] *n* (**a**) *Rel* évêque *m*; **bishop's palace** palais *m* épiscopal, évêché *m* (**b**) *Chess* fou *m* (**c**) *(drink)* bichof *m*

►► *Orn* ***bishop bird*** euplecte *m*

bishopric ['bɪʃəprɪk] *n Rel (position)* épiscopat *m*; *(diocese)* évêché *m*

Bismarck ['bɪzmɑːk] *pr n* Bismarck

bismuth ['bɪzməθ] *n Chem* bismuth *m*

►► ***bismuth glance*** bismuthine *f*

bismuthinite [bɪz'mʌθɪˌnaɪt] *n Chem* bismuthine *f*

bison ['baɪsən] *n Zool* bison *m*

bisque [bɪsk] *n* (**a**) *(colour)* beige-rosé *m* (**b**) *Cer* biscuit *m* (**c**) *Culin (soup)* bisque *f*

bissextile [bɪ'sekstaɪl] **1** *n* année *f* bissextile

2 *adj* bissextile

bister *Am* = **bistre**

bistort ['bɪstɔːt] *n Bot* **(common) bistort** renouée *f* bistorte

bistoury ['bɪstʊrɪ] *(pl* **bistouries**) *n Med* bistouri *m*

bistre, *Am* **bister** ['bɪstə(r)] *Art* **1** *n* bistre *m*

2 *adj* bistré

bistro ['biːstrəʊ] *(pl* **bistros**) *n Culin* bistro *m*

bisulphate, *Am* **bisulfate** [ˌbaɪ'sʌlfeɪt] *n Chem* bisulfate *m*

bisulphite [ˌbaɪ'sʌlfaɪt] *n Chem* bisulfite *m*; **sodium bisulphite** bisulfite *m* de sodium *ou* de soude

bisync [ˌbaɪ'sɪŋk], **bisynchronous** [ˌbaɪ'sɪŋkrənəs] *adj Comput* bisynchrone

BIT[1] [bɪt]

bout, morceau	► **1 (a)**
numéro	► **1 (c)**
mors	► **1 (f)**
mèche	► **1 (g)**
bit	► **1 (h)**
quelque temps	► **2 (a)**
un peu	► **2 (b)**
petit à petit	► **3**

1 *n* (**a**) *(piece → of paper, wood, string)* bout *m*; *(→ of land)* morceau *m*; *(→ of cake, meat, cheese)* morceau *m*; *(smaller)* bout *m*; *(→ of book)* passage *m*; *(→ of film)* séquence *f*; *(→ of jigsaw puzzle)* pièce *f*; **you missed out the best bits** *(of story, joke)* tu as oublié le meilleur; **I liked the bit where they were in the cave** *(in book)* j'aime le passage où ils sont dans la caverne; *(in film)* j'aime la séquence où ils sont dans la caverne; **this is the difficult bit** c'est là où ça se complique; **bits and pieces of sth** des morceaux de qch; **made of bits and pieces** fait de bric et de broc; **she picked up her bits and pieces** elle a ramassé ses affaires; **in bits** en morceaux; **to take sth to bits** démonter qch; **the dog tore the paper to bits** le chien a complètement déchiré le journal; **to fall to bits** *(book, clothes)* tomber en lambeaux; **the wall was falling to bits** le mur tombait en morceaux *ou* en ruine; **to come to bits** *(dismantle)* se démonter; *(break)* tomber en morceaux; *Fam* **I love him to bits!** je l'adore!❑

(**b**) *(unspecified small quantity)* **a bit of dirt** une petite saleté; **a bit of advice** un (petit) conseil; **a bit of money/time** un peu d'argent/de temps; **a little bit of tact/patience** un tout petit peu de tact/de patience; **quite a bit of rain/trouble** pas mal de pluie/d'ennuis; **there's been a bit of trouble at home** il y a eu quelques problèmes à la maison; **it's a bit of a problem** cela pose un problème; **it was a bit of a nuisance** c'était vraiment ennuyeux; **we got a bit of a shock** ça nous a fait un choc; **it's not a bit of use** cela ne sert absolument à rien; **he's a bit of a crook** il est un peu escroc sur les bords; **I've been a bit of a fool** j'ai été un peu bête; **it was a bit too much of a coincidence** c'était un peu fort comme coïncidence; **to do one's bit** y mettre du sien, faire un effort; **everyone did their bit** tout le monde y a mis du sien *ou* a fait un effort; **we did our bit to help the children** nous avons fait ce qu'il fallait pour aider les enfants; **they ate up every bit** ils ont tout mangé jusqu'au dernier morceau; **I've had quite a bit to drink** j'ai un peu trop bu; **to make quite a bit** *(earn money)* gagner pas mal d'argent *ou* de fric; **to have a bit put away** avoir un petit pécule; **that must be worth quite a bit!** ça doit valoir pas mal d'argent; **she's every bit as competent as he is** elle est tout aussi compétente que lui; *Fam* **to have a bit on the side** *(male lover)* avoir un amant; *(female lover)* avoir une maîtresse; *Br Fam* **to be a bit of all right** *(of woman)* être une jolie fille; *(of man)* être un beau mec; *Br Fam* **this is a bit of all right!** ça c'est chouette!; *Fam* **that takes a bit of doing** ça, c'est bien difficile

(**c**) *Fam (role)* numéro *m*; **he's doing his perfect father bit** il nous fait son numéro du père parfait

(**d**) *Fam (small coin)* pièce❑ *f*; **a threepenny bit** une pièce de trois pence

(**e**) *Am (coin)* = ancienne pièce de 12,5 cents; **two bits** vingt-cinq cents

(**f**) *(for horse)* mors *m*; *Fig* **to take the bit between one's teeth** prendre le mors aux dents

(**g**) *Tech (of drill)* mèche *f*

(**h**) *Comput* bit *m*; **bits per second** bits *mpl* par seconde

(**i**) *Am Fam (term of imprisonment)* peine *f* de prison❑; **he did a bit in Fort Worth** il a fait de la taule à Fort Worth

2 a bit *adv* (**a**) *(some time)* quelque temps; **let's sit down for a bit** asseyons-nous un instant *ou* un peu; **we waited a good/little bit** nous avons attendu un bon/un petit moment; **hold on** *or* **wait a bit!** attendez un peu *ou* un instant!; **he's away quite a bit** il est souvent absent; **after a bit we left** au bout de quelque temps nous sommes partis; **in a bit** dans quelques minutes

(**b**) *(slightly)* un peu; **I'm a bit late** je suis un peu en retard; **she's a good/little bit older than he is** elle est beaucoup/un peu plus âgée que lui; **it's a (little) bit more expensive** c'est un (tout petit) peu plus cher

(**c**) *(at all)* **they haven't changed a bit** ils n'ont pas du tout changé; **I don't care a bit** cela m'est bien *ou* complètement égal; **are we bothering you? – not a bit!** on vous dérange? – pas du tout!; **not a bit of it!** pas le moins du monde!; **it's asking a bit much to expect her to apologize** il ne faut pas s'attendre à des excuses, c'est trop lui demander; **that's a bit much** *or* **a bit steep!** ça c'est un peu fort!

3 bit by bit *adv* petit à petit

►► *Comput* ***bit command*** commande *f* binaire; *Cin & Theat* ***bit part*** petit rôle *m*; *Cin & Theat* ***bit player*** acteur(trice) *m,f* qui joue des petits rôles; *Comput* ***bit rate*** débit *f* binaire

bit[2] *pt of* **bite**

bitch [bɪtʃ] **1** *n* (**a**) *Zool (female canine → gen)* femelle *f*; *(dog)* chienne *f*; *(fox)* renarde *f*; *(wolf)* louve *f*; **a collie bitch** un colley femelle

(**b**) *very Fam Pej (woman)* garce *f*; **she's such a bitch** c'est une vraie garce; **you bitch!** espèce de garce!; *Br* **the poor bitch** la pauvre; **the lucky bitch** la veinarde

(**c**) *Fam (thing)* saloperie *f*; **life's a bitch!** chienne de vie!; **it's been a bitch of a day** quelle foutue journée alors!; **a bitch of a job** une saloperie de boulot; **this problem's a real bitch** c'est un vrai casse-tête!

(**d**) *Fam (complaint)* motif *m* de râler; **what's their latest bitch?** qu'est-ce qui les fait râler maintenant?

2 *vt Am Fam (spoil)* gâcher❑; **that's really bitched my day** ça m'a vraiment fichu ma journée en l'air

3 *vi Fam* (**a**) *Br (say nasty things)* déblatérer (**about** contre)

(**b**) *(complain)* râler, rouspéter; **to bitch about sb/sth** râler *ou* rouspéter contre qn/qch

►**bitch out** *vt sep very Fam* engueuler

bitchin ['bɪtʃɪn] *adj Am Fam* super, génial

bitchy ['bɪtʃɪ] *(compar* **bitchier,** *superl* **bitchiest**) *adj Fam* vache; **a bitchy remark** une vacherie; **he's in a bitchy mood** il est dans une sale humeur; **she was very bitchy to the new girl** elle a été très vache avec la nouvelle; **don't be bitchy about it!** ne sois pas vache!

BITE [baɪt]

mordre	▶ **1 (a); 2 (a), (c), (d)**
piquer	▶ **1 (a); 2 (a), (b)**
agacer	▶ **1 (b)**
morsure, piqûre	▶ **3 (a)**
bouchée	▶ **3 (b)**

(*pt* **bit** [bɪt], *pp* **bitten** ['bɪtən]) **1** *vt* (**a**) *(of animal, person)* mordre; *(subj: insect, snake)* piquer, mordre; **I bit a piece out of the pear** j'ai mordu dans la poire; **the dog bit him on the leg** le chien l'a mordu à la jambe; **the dog bit the rope in two** le chien a coupé la corde en deux avec ses dents; **to bite one's nails** se ronger les ongles; **he bit his lip** il s'est mordu la lèvre; *Fig* **they've been bitten by the photography bug** ils sont devenus des mordus de photographie; *also Fig* **to bite one's tongue** se mordre la langue; *Fig* **to bite the bullet** serrer les dents; **we're going to have to bite the bullet and fire them** il va falloir prendre le taureau par les cornes et les renvoyer; **to bite the dust** mordre la poussière; **theirs is the latest plan to bite the dust** leur projet est le dernier à être tombé à l'eau; **to bite the hand that feeds one** montrer de l'ingratitude envers qn qui vous veut du bien; *Prov* **once bitten, twice shy** chat échaudé craint l'eau froide; *Am Fam* **bite me!** va te faire voir!; *Am Vulg* **bite my ass!** va te faire foutre!

(**b**) *Fam Fig (bother)* agacer, contrarier; **what's biting him?** quelle mouche l'a piqué?

2 *vi* (**a**) *(animal, person)* mordre; *(insect, snake)* piquer, mordre; *(fish)* mordre (à l'hameçon); **I bit into the apple** j'ai mordu dans la pomme; **does the dog bite?** il mord, votre chien?; **he bit through the cord** il coupa la ficelle avec ses dents; **are they** *or* **the fish biting (today)?** alors, ça mord?; *Fig* **don't worry, I don't bite!** n'ayez pas peur, je ne mords pas!

(**b**) *(mustard, spice)* piquer

(**c**) *(air, wind)* mordre, cingler

(**d**) *Aut & Tech (clutch, screw)* mordre; *(tyre)* adhérer (à la route); **the acid bit into the metal** l'acide a attaqué le métal; **the rope bit into his wrists** la corde mordait dans la chair de ses poignets

(**e**) *(take effect)* **the law is beginning to bite** les effets de la loi commencent à se faire sentir

3 *n* (**a**) *(of animal, person)* morsure *f*; *(of insect, snake)* piqûre *f*, morsure *f*; **mosquito bites** piqûres *fpl* de moustiques; *Am Fam* **to put the bite on sb** taper du fric à qn

(**b**) *(piece)* bouchée *f*; **chew each bite 30 times** mâchez chaque bouchée 30 fois; **he swallowed the steak in three bites** il a avalé le bifteck en trois bouchées; **to take a bite of sth** *(bite into)* mordre dans qch; *(taste)* goûter (à) qch; *Fig* **the repairs took a big bite out of our savings** les réparations ont fait un trou dans nos économies; **do you want a bite?** tu veux (y) goûter?; *Br Fam* **to have** *or* **to get another** *or* **a second bite at the cherry** s'y reprendre à deux fois

(**c**) *Fam (something to eat)* **we stopped for a bite (to eat)** nous nous sommes arrêtés pour manger un morceau; **I haven't had a bite all day** je n'ai rien mangé de la journée ❑

(**d**) *Fishing* touche *f*; **did you get a bite?** ça a mordu?

(**e**) *(sharpness → of mustard, spice)* piquant *m*; *(→ of speech, wit)* mordant *m*; *(→ of air, wind)* caractère *m* cinglant *ou* mordant

(**f**) *Med* articulé *m* dentaire

▶**bite back** *vt sep* **to bite sth back** se retenir de dire qch

▶**bite off** *vt sep* arracher d'un coup de dents; **she bit off a piece of toast** elle a mordu dans la tartine; **to bite off more than one can chew** avoir les yeux plus grands *ou* gros que le ventre; *Fam* **to bite sb's head off** enguirlander qn

biter ['baɪtə(r)] *n Br Prov* **it's a case of the biter bit** c'est l'arroseur arrosé, tel est pris qui croyait prendre

bite-sized [-ˌsaɪzd] *adj* **cut the meat into bite-sized pieces** coupez la viande en petits morceaux

biting ['baɪtɪŋ] *adj* (**a**) *(insect)* piqueur, vorace (**b**) *Fig (remark, wit)* mordant, cinglant; *(wind)* cinglant, mordant; *(cold)* mordant, perçant

▶▶ ***Aut biting point*** *(of clutch)* point *m* d'attaque

bitingly ['baɪtɪŋlɪ] *adv* (**a**) *(say, speak)* d'un ton mordant *ou* cinglant (**b**) *(as intensifier)* **a bitingly cold wind** un vent glacial

bitmap ['bɪtˌmap] *Comput* **1** *n* bitmap *m*

2 *adj (image, font)* bitmap, en mode point

bitmapped ['bɪtmæpt] *adj Comput (image, font)* bitmap, en mode point

bit-slice processor *n Comput* processeur *m* en tranches

bitten ['bɪtən] *pp of* **bit**

bitter ['bɪtə(r)] **1** *adj* (**a**) *(taste)* amer, âpre; *Fig* **it's a bitter pill (to swallow)** c'est difficile à avaler

(**b**) *(resentful → person)* amer; *(→ look, tone)* amer, plein d'amertume; *(→ reproach, tears)* amer; **to be bitter about sth** être amer *ou* plein d'amertume au sujet de qch; *Fam Pej* **bitter and twisted** aigri

(**c**) *(unpleasant → disappointment, experience)* amer, cruel; *(→ argument, struggle)* violent; *(→ blow)* dur; **the bitter truth** l'amère vérité *f*; **we fought to the bitter end** nous avons lutté jusqu'au bout

(**d**) *(extreme → enemy)* acharné; *(→ opposition)* violent, acharné; *(→ remorse)* cuisant

(**e**) *(cold → wind)* cinglant, glacial; *(→ weather)* glacial; *(→ winter)* rude, dur

2 *n (beer)* = bière pression relativement amère, à forte teneur en houblon

3 bitters *npl* bitter *m*, amer *m*; *Pharm* amer *m*; **whisky and bitters** = cocktail au whisky et au bitter

▶▶ ***bitter almonds*** amandes *fpl* amères; *Pharm* ***bitter aloes*** aloès *m* (médicinal); ***bitter lemon*** Schweppes® *m* au citron; ***bitter orange*** orange *f* amère

bitterling ['bɪtəlɪŋ] *n Orn* bouvière *f*

bitterly ['bɪtəlɪ] *adv* (**a**) *(speak)* amèrement, avec amertume; *(criticize)* âprement; *(weep)* amèrement (**b**) *(intensely → ashamed, unhappy)* profondément; *(→ disappointed)* cruellement; **it was a bitterly cold day** il faisait un froid de loup; **I've regretted it bitterly ever since** je n'ai cessé de le regretter amèrement

bittern¹ ['bɪtən] *n Orn* butor *m*

bittern² *n (in salt industry)* eau *f* mère

bitterness ['bɪtənɪs] *n* (**a**) *(of disappointment, person, taste)* amertume *f*; *(of criticism, remark)* âpreté *f* (**b**) *(of opposition)* violence *f*

bittersweet ['bɪtəswiːt] **1** *adj (memory, taste)* aigre-doux (aigre-douce)

2 *n Bot* douce-amère *f*

bitty ['bɪtɪ] (*compar* **bittier**, *superl* **bittiest**) *adj* (**a**) *Br Fam (disjointed)* décousu ❑ (**b**) *Am (small)* **a little bitty town** une toute petite ville

bitumen ['bɪtjʊmɪn] *n Chem & Constr* bitume *m*

bituminize, -ise [bɪ'tjuːmɪnaɪz] *vt Chem* bitumer

bituminous [bɪ'tjuːmɪnəs] *adj Chem* bitumineux; *Miner* **bituminous coal** flambant *m*

bivalence [ˌbaɪ'veɪləns], **bivalency** [ˌbaɪ'veɪlənsɪ] *n Chem* bivalence *f*

bivalent [ˌbaɪ'veɪlənt] *adj Biol* bivalent

bivalve ['baɪvælv] *Bot & Zool* **1** *n* bivalve *m*

2 *adj* bivalve

bivouac ['bɪvʊæk] (*pt & pp* **bivouacked**, *cont* **bivouacking**) *Mil* **1** *n* bivouac *m*

2 *vi* bivouaquer

bivvy [illegible] bivouac ❑ *m*

▶▶ ***bivvy bag*** sac *m* de bivouac ❑

biweekly [ˌbaɪ'wiːklɪ] (*pl* **biweeklies**) **1** *adj (every two weeks)* bimensuel; *(twice weekly)* bihebdomadaire

2 *adv (every two weeks)* tous les quinze jours; *(twice weekly)* deux fois par semaine

3 *n* bimensuel *m*

biyearly [ˌbaɪ'jɪəlɪ] (*pl* **biyearlies**) **1** *adj (every two years)* biennal; *(twice yearly)* semestriel

2 *adv (every two years)* tous les deux ans; *(twice yearly)* deux fois par an

3 *n* biennale *f*

biz [bɪz] *n Fam* **the music biz** l'industrie *f* de la musique ❑; **he's the best in the biz** c'est le meilleur dans le business; *Br Fam* **it's the biz!** c'est impec'!

bizarre [bɪ'zɑː(r)] *adj* bizarre

bizarrely [bɪ'zɑːlɪ] *adv* bizarrement

bizarreness [bɪ'zɑːnɪs] *n* bizarrerie *f*

bk (**a**) *(written abbr* **bank**) banque *f* (**b**) *(written abbr* **book**) livre *m*

BL [ˌbiː'el] *n* (**a**) *(abbr* **Bachelor of Law(s)**) *(person)* = titulaire d'une licence de droit; *(qualification)* licence *f* de droit (**b**) *(abbr* **Bachelor of Letters**) *(person)* = titulaire d'une licence de lettres; *(qualification)* licence *f* de lettres (**c**) *Am (abbr* **Bachelor of Literature**) *(person)* = titulaire d'une licence de littérature; *(qualification)* licence *f* de littérature

bl *Com (written abbr* **bill of lading**) connaissement *m*

blab [blæb] (*pt & pp* **blabbed**, *cont* **blabbing**) *Fam*

1 *vt* laisser échapper ❑, divulguer ❑

2 *vi* (**a**) *(tell secret)* vendre la mèche (**b**) *(prattle)* jaser, babiller; **she blabbed on about her holiday** elle n'en finissait pas de nous raconter ses vacances

blabber ['blæbə(r)] *Fam* **1** *n* (**a**) *(person)* moulin *m* à paroles (**b**) *(prattle)* bavardage *m*, papotage *m*

2 *vi* jaser, babiller; **to blabber on about sth** parler de qch à n'en plus finir

blabbermouth ['blæbəˌmaʊθ, *pl* -ˌmaʊðz] *n Fam* pipelette *f*; **he's such a blabbermouth!** c'est une vraie pipelette!

black [blæk] **1** *adj* (**a**) *(colour)* noir; **as black as ink** noir comme du jais *ou* de l'encre; **black and blue** *(bruised)* couvert de bleus; **they beat him black and blue** ils l'ont roué de coups; **to be black and blue all over** être couvert de bleus, être tuméfié; *Austr Fam* **beyond the Black Stump** en pleine brousse, au diable vauvert

(**b**) *(race)* noir; **the black area of New York** le quartier noir de New York; **he won the black vote** il a gagné les voix de l'électorat noir; **black man** Noir *m*; **black woman** Noire *f*; *Br Fam* **black man's wheels** *(BMW)* BM *f*

(**c**) *(coffee)* noir; *(tea)* nature *(inv)*

(**d**) *(dark)* noir, sans lumière; **the room was as black as** *Br* **pitch** *or Am* **tar** dans la pièce il faisait noir comme dans un four

(**e**) *(gloomy → future, mood)* noir; *(→ despair)* sombre; **they painted a black picture of our prospects** ils ont peint un sombre tableau de notre avenir; **the situation is not as black as it looks** la situation n'est pas aussi désespérée qu'on pourrait le croire; **the situation looks black** les choses se présentent très mal; **in a fit of black despair** dans un moment d'extrême désespoir; **it's a black day for the UN** c'est un jour noir pour l'ONU

(**f**) *(angry)* furieux, menaçant; **he gave her a black look** il lui a jeté *ou* lancé un regard noir

(**g**) *(wicked)* noir, mauvais; **a black deed** un crime, un forfait; **he's not as black as he's painted** il n'est pas aussi mauvais qu'on le dit

(**h**) *(dirty)* noir, sale; **her hands were black with ink** elle avait les mains pleines d'encre

(**i**) *Br Ind (factory, goods)* boycotté

2 *n* (**a**) *(colour)* noir *m*; **to be dressed in black** *(gen)* être habillé de *ou* en noir; *(in mourning)* porter le deuil; **he'd swear black is white** il refuse d'admettre l'évidence

(**b**) *(darkness)* obscurité *f*, noir *m*

(**c**) **the black** *(in roulette)* le noir; *(in snooker)* la bille *ou* boule noire

(**d**) *(idioms)* **to be in the black** *(person)* être solvable; *(account)* être créditeur; **to get back into the black** sortir du rouge; **I want the agreement in black and white** *(written down)* je veux voir l'accord écrit noir sur blanc; **to put sth down in black and white** écrire qch noir sur blanc; **things aren't that black and white** les choses ne sont pas si simples

3 *vt* (**a**) *(make black)* noircir; *(shoes)* cirer *(avec du cirage noir)*; **he blacked his attacker's eye** il a poché l'œil de son agresseur; *Theat* **the actors blacked their faces** les acteurs se sont noirci le visage

(**b**) *Br Ind* boycotter

4 Black *n* (**a**) *(person)* Noir(e) *m,f*

(**b**) *Chess* noir *m*

▶▶ ***black Africa*** l'Afrique *f* noire; ***black American*** Afro-Américain(e) *m,f*; ***the black art, the black arts*** la magie noire; *Am Fam* ***black bag*** caisse *f* noire; ***black bear*** ours *m* noir; ***Black Beauty*** = pur-sang dans un célèbre roman pour enfants écrit par Anna Sewell en 1877; *Entom* ***black beetle*** cafard *m*, blatte *f*; ***black belt*** *Sport* ceinture *f* noire; *Am Fam* = zone habitée par des Noirs; **she's a black belt in judo** elle est ceinture noire de judo; *Fin* ***black book*** plan *m* de défense contre une OPA *ou* anti-OPA; *Acct & Fin* ***black bottom line*** solde *m* créditeur; ***black box*** boîte *f* noire; *Culin* ***black bread*** pain *m* de seigle; *Scot Culin* ***black bun*** = sorte de pain au raisin consommé au nouvel an; ***black cab*** taxi *m* londonien, taxi *m* anglais; ***black cherry*** *(fruit)* guigne *f* noire; *(tree)* merisier *m* américain, *Can* cerisier *m* tardif; ***black comedy*** comédie *f* noire; *Pol* ***black consciousness*** négritude *f*; ***the Black Country*** le Pays noir; *Hist* ***Black Death*** peste *f* noire; *Orn* ***black duck*** canard *m* noir; *Com* ***black economy*** économie *f* noire; ***black eye*** œil *m* poché *ou* au beurre noir; **I'll give him a black eye!** je vais lui faire un œil au beurre noir!; ***the Black Forest*** la Forêt noire; ***Black Forest gateau*** forêt-noire *f*; *Petr* ***black gold*** or *m* noir; *Orn* ***black grouse*** tétras-lyre *m*, coq *m* des bouleaux; *Orn* ***black guillemot*** guillemot *m* à miroir blanc; *Astron* ***black hole*** trou *m* noir; *Hist* ***the Black Hole of Calcutta*** = célèbre prison à Calcutta au XVIIIème siècle; *Fam* **it's like the Black Hole of Calcutta in there!** il fait horriblement sombre là-dedans!; ***black humour*** humour *m* noir; ***black ice*** verglas *m*; *Orn* ***black kite*** milan *m* noir; *St Exch* ***black knight*** chevalier *m* noir; *Orn* ***black lark*** calandre *m* nègre; *Chem & Metal* ***black lead*** graphite *m*; ***black magic*** magie *f* noire; *Zool* ***black mamba*** mamba *m* noir; *Fam* ***Black Maria*** panier *m* à salade *(fourgon)*; ***black mark*** mauvais point *m*; **it's a black mark against her** ça joue contre elle; ***black market*** **1** *n Com* marché *m* noir; **on the black market** au marché noir **2** *comp (cigarettes, whisky)* au marché noir; *Com* ***black marketeer*** vendeur(euse) *m,f* au marché noir; ***Black Mass*** messe *f* noire; *Bot* ***black medick*** luzerne *f* lupuline, minette *f*; *St Exch* ***Black Monday*** lundi *m* noir, jour *m* du krach (boursier) *(le lundi 19 octobre 1987)*; ***black money*** *(earned on black market)* argent *m* du marché noir; *(undeclared)* argent non déclaré au fisc; *Rel* ***Black Muslim*** Black Muslim *mf (membre d'un mouvement séparatiste noir se réclamant de l'Islam)*; *Pol* ***Black Nationalism*** = mouvement nationaliste noir américain; *Am Pol* ***Black Panther*** Panthère *f* noire; ***black pepper*** poivre *m* gris; *Pol* ***Black Power*** Black Power *m (mouvement séparatiste noir né dans les années 60 aux États-Unis)*; *Hist* **the Black Prince** le Prince Noir *(fils du roi Édouard III d'Angleterre et duc d'Aquitaine)*; *Culin* ***black pudding*** boudin *m* (noir); *Bot* ***black radish*** radis *m* noir; *Orn* ***black redstart*** rouge-queue *m* noir; *Parl* ***Black Rod*** = huissier chargé par la Chambre des lords britannique de convoquer les Communes; ***Black Russian*** *(cocktail)* black russian *m*; ***the Black Sea*** la mer Noire; ***black sheep*** brebis *f* galeuse; *Br Fig* ***black spot*** point *m* noir; *Orn* ***black stork*** cigogne *f* noire; *Univ* ***Black Studies*** = études afro-américaines; *Hist* ***the Black and Tans*** = forces armées britanniques envoyées en Irlande en 1920 pour lutter contre le Sinn Fein; *Orn* ***black tern*** guifette *f* épouvantail, guifette *f* noire; ***Black Thursday*** Jeudi noir *(jour du krach de Wall Street qui déclencha la crise de 1929)*; ***black tie*** = nœud papillon noir porté avec une tenue de soirée; **black tie** *(on invitation card)* tenue de soirée exigée; ***black velvet*** *(cocktail)* = cocktail de champagne et de stout; *Br Mil* ***Black Watch*** = nom populaire d'un régiment de l'armée britannique, le Royal Highland Regiment; *Orn* ***black wheatear*** traquet *m* rieur *ou* noir; ***black widow (spider)*** latrodecte *m*, veuve *f* noire; *Orn* ***black woodpecker*** pic *m* noir

►**black out** **1** *vt sep* **(a)** *(extinguish lights)* plonger dans l'obscurité; *Mil (in wartime)* faire le black-out dans
(b) *Rad & TV (programme)* interdire la diffusion de
(c) *(memory)* effacer (de son esprit), oublier
2 *vi* s'évanouir

►**black up** *vi Theat* se maquiller la peau en noir, se noircir le visage

'Black Like Me' *Griffin* 'Dans la peau d'un Noir'

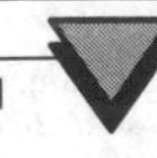

BLACK AMERICAN ENGLISH

Beaucoup d'Afro-Américains parlent un anglais particulier dont la syntaxe et le vocabulaire portent encore l'empreinte de certaines langues africaines. De nos jours certains spécialistes rejettent le terme "Black American English", se fondant sur le fait que cette langue – aujourd'hui communément appelée "ebonics" – est plus proche des structures des langues africaines parlées par les premiers esclaves que de l'anglais standard, alors que d'autres la considèrent comme un simple dialecte. Récemment, et ce particulièrement grâce à la popularité du rap, l'anglais parlé par les Afro-Américains est devenu à la mode chez les jeunes des deux côtés de l'Atlantique.

THE BLACK COUNTRY

Le Pays noir désigne, en Grande-Bretagne, la région des West Midlands, riche en aciéries et en mines de charbon.

blackamoor ['blækə,mʊə(r)] *n Arch* Noir(e) *m,f*

black-and-white **1** *adj* **(a)** *(photograph, television)* noir et blanc; *Cin* **a black-and-white film** un film en noir et blanc **(b)** *Fig (clear-cut)* précis, net; **there's no black-and-white solution** le problème n'est pas simple; **he has very black-and-white views on the war** il a des idées très arrêtées sur la guerre
2 *n Art (drawing, print)* dessin *m* en noir et blanc; *Phot (photograph)* photographie *f* en noir et blanc

blackball ['blæk,bɔːl] **1** *n* vote *m* contre
2 *vt* blackbouler

blackballing ['blæk,bɔːlɪŋ] *n* blackboulage *m*

blackberry ['blækbərɪ] *(pl* **blackberries***)* **1** *n Bot* mûre *f*
2 *comp (jam)* de mûres; *(tart)* aux mûres
3 *vi* cueillir des mûres; **to go blackberrying** aller ramasser *ou* cueillir des mûres
►► ***blackberry bush*** mûrier *m*

blackbird ['blæk,bɜːd] *n Orn* merle *m*

blackboard ['blæk,bɔːd] *n* tableau *m* (noir)
►► *Am Fam* ***blackboard jungle*** métier *m* d'enseignant ❑

'The Blackboard Jungle' *Brooks* 'Graine de violence'

black-bordered [-'bɔːdəd] *adj* à bordure noire

blackbuck ['blæk,bʌk] *n Zool* antilope *f* cervicapre

blackcap ['blæk,kæp] *n* **(a)** *Orn* fauvette *f* à tête noire **(b)** *Br Law (of judge)* bonnet *m* noir

blackcock ['blæk,kɒk] *n Orn* coq *m* de bruyère

blackcurrant [,blæk'kʌrənt] *n (bush, fruit)* cassis *m*

black-eared wheatear *n Orn* traquet *m* oreillard

blacken ['blækən] **1** *vt* **(a)** *(make black → house, wall)* noircir; *(→ shoes)* cirer *(avec du cirage noir)*; **he blackened his face** il s'est noirci le visage
(b) *(make dirty)* noircir, salir; **his fingers were blackened with ink** il avait les doigts couverts *ou* pleins d'encre; **smoke-blackened buildings** des bâtiments noircis par la fumée
(c) *Fig (name, reputation)* noircir, ternir
2 *vi (cloud, sky)* s'assombrir, (se) noircir; *(colour, fruit)* (se) noircir, devenir noir

blackening ['blækənɪŋ] *n* noircissement *m*

black-eyed pea, black-eyed bean *n* dolique *m*, dolic *m*, niébé *m*

blackface ['blæk,feɪs] *n* **(a)** *Old-fashioned (person)* = acteur blanc maquillé pour jouer un Noir **(b)** *Typ* caractère *m* gras; **in blackface** en (caractères) gras

blackfly ['blæk,flaɪ] *(pl* **inv** *or* **blackflies***)* *n Entom* puceron *m* noir

Blackfoot ['blæk,fʊt] *(pl* **inv** *or* **Blackfeet** [-fiːt]*)* *n* Blackfoot *mf*; **the Blackfoot** les Blackfoot *mpl*

blackguard ['blægɑːd] *n Old-fashioned* canaille *f*

blackguardism ['blægɑːdɪzəm] *n Old-fashioned* canaillerie *f*

blackguardly ['blægɑːdlɪ] *adj Old-fashioned* canaille, ignoble; **a blackguardly trick** un sale coup

blackhead ['blæk,hed] *n* point *m* noir

black-headed gull *n Orn* mouette *f* rieuse

black-hearted *adj* méchant, malfaisant

blacking ['blækɪŋ] *n (for shoes)* cirage *m* noir; *(for stove)* pâte *f* à noircir

blackish ['blækɪʃ] *adj* noirâtre, tirant sur le noir

blackjack ['blæk,dʒæk] **1** *n* **(a)** *(card game)* vingt-et-un *m* **(b)** *Am (truncheon)* matraque *f*
2 *vt Am (beat)* matraquer; *(compel)* contraindre (sous la menace); **they blackjacked him into paying** ils l'ont forcé à payer

blackleg ['blæk,leg] *(pt & pp* **blacklegged,** *cont* **blacklegging***)* *Br Pej* **1** *n* jaune *m*, briseur *m* de grève
2 *vi* briser la grève

blacklist ['blæklɪst] **1** *n* liste *f* noire
2 *vt* mettre sur la liste noire

blackmail ['blæk,meɪl] **1** *vt* faire chanter; **to be blackmailed** être victime d'un chantage; **I'm being blackmailed for £5,000** je suis victime d'un chantage, on me réclame 5000 livres; **he blackmailed them into meeting his demands** il les a contraints par le chantage à satisfaire ses exigences
2 *n* chantage *m*

blackmailer ['blæk,meɪlə(r)] *n* maître chanteur *m*

black-necked grebe *n Orn* grèbe *m* à cou noir

blackness ['blæknɪs] *n* **(a)** *(of colour)* noir *m*, couleur *f* noire; *Fig (of deed)* atrocité *f*, noirceur *f* **(b)** *(of night, room)* obscurité *f*, noir *m* **(c)** *(dirtiness)* saleté *f*, crasse *f*

blackout ['blækaʊt] *n* **(a)** *(power failure)* panne *f* d'électricité; *Mil (in wartime)* black-out *m inv* **(b)** *(loss of consciousness)* évanouissement *m*, étourdissement *m*; *(amnesia)* trou *m* de mémoire; **I must have had a blackout** j'ai dû m'évanouir **(c)** *Rad & TV* black-out *m inv*, censure *f*; **the army imposed a news blackout on the war** l'armée a fait le black-out sur la guerre

Blackpool ['blæk,puːl] *n* = station balnéaire du nord-ouest de l'Angleterre, célèbre pour ses attractions et pour ses illuminations nocturnes

Blackshirt ['blæk,ʃɜːt] *n Hist* Chemise *f* noire

blacksmith ['blæk,smɪθ] *n (for horses)* maréchal-ferrant *m*; *(for tools)* forgeron *m*

blackstrap molasses ['blækstræp-] *n Am* mélasse *f* noire

black-tailed godwit *n Orn* barge *f* égocéphale *ou* à queue noire

blackthorn ['blæk,θɔːn] *n Bot* prunelier *m*, épine *f* noire

black-throated [-,θrəʊtɪd] *adj*
►► *Orn* **black-throated diver** plongeon *m* arctique, lumme *m*, *Can* huard *m*; *Orn* **black-throated thrush** grive *f* à gorge noire

black-tie *adj* **it's black-tie** il faut être en smoking
►► ***black-tie dinner*** dîner *m* en smoking

blacktop ['blæk,tɒp] *n Am Transp* route *f* goudronnée

blackwater fever ['blæk,wɔːtə(r)-] *n Med* fièvre *f* bilieuse hémoglobinurique

black-winged *adj*
►► *Orn* ***black-winged pratincole*** glaréole *f* à ailes noires; *Orn* ***black-winged stilt*** échasse *f* blanche

blad [blæd] *n Typ* blad *m*

bladder ['blædə(r)] *n* **(a)** *Anat* vessie *f*; **to have a full bladder** avoir la vessie pleine **(b)** *(of leather, skin, ball)* vessie *f* **(c)** *Bot* vésicule *f*
►► *Bot* ***bladder campion*** silène *m* acaule; *Med* ***bladder infection*** cystite *f*; *Med* ***bladder stone*** calcul *m* vésical

bladderwort ['blædə,wɜːt] *n Bot* utriculaire *f*

bladderwrack ['blædə,ræk] *n Bot* fucus *m* vésiculeux

blade [bleɪd] *n* **(a)** *(cutting edge → of knife, razor, tool)* lame *f*; *(→ of guillotine)* couperet *m*
(b) *Tech (of fan)* pale *f*; *(of propeller)* pale *f*, aile *f*; *(of helicopter)* hélice *f*; *(of turbine motor, water wheel)* aube *f*; *(of plough)* soc *m* (tranchant); *(of ice skates)* lame *f*; *(of oar, paddle)* plat *m*, pale *f*; *(of windscreen wiper)* balai *m*, raclette *f*
(c) *Bot (of grass)* brin *m*; *(of wheat)* pousse *f*; *(of leaf)* limbe *m*; **wheat in the blade** blé *m* en herbe
(d) *Naut (in rowing → oar)* aviron *m*
(e) *Literary (sword)* lame *f*
(f) *Arch (young man)* gaillard *m*
(g) *Anat (of tongue)* dos *m*

(**h**) *Am Fam Crime slang (knife)* lame *f*, surin *m*

-bladed [bleɪdɪd] *suff* (**a**) *(knife, razor)* à lame…; **sharp-bladed knife** couteau *m* aiguisé (**b**) *(fan, propeller)* à pale…; **a five-bladed fan** un ventilateur à cinq pales (**c**) *(plant)* à limbe…; **broad-bladed leaf** feuille *f* à limbe large

blaeberry ['bleɪbərɪ] *(pl* **blaeberries***) n Br Bot* myrtille *f*

blag [blæg] *Br Fam* **1** *n (robbery)* braquage *m*

2 *vt* (**a**) *(steal)* piquer (**b**) *(con)* **to blag oneself sth** obtenir qch au culot; **to blag one's way in** resquiller

blah [blɑː] *Fam* **1** *n* (**a**) *(meaningless remarks, nonsense)* blabla *m*, baratin *m* (**b**) **blah, blah, blah** *(to avoid repetition)* etc etc; **he went on for half an hour about how we all had to work harder, blah, blah, blah** il nous a rabâché pendant une demi-heure qu'il fallait qu'on fasse tous plus d'efforts, etc etc (**c**) *Am (blues)* **to have the blahs** avoir le cafard

2 *adj Am* (**a**) *(uninteresting)* insipide ❑, ennuyeux ❑ (**b**) *(blue)* **to feel blah** avoir le cafard

Blairism ['bleərɪzəm] *n Pol* blairisme *m (courant politique travailliste incarné par Tony Blair)*

Blairite ['bleəraɪt] *Pol* **1** *n* partisan *m* de Tony Blair

2 *adj* partisan de Tony Blair

blamable ['bleɪməbəl] *adj* blâmable

blame [bleɪm] **1** *n* (**a**) *(responsibility)* responsabilité *f*, faute *f*; **they laid** *or* **put the blame for the incident on the secretary** ils ont rejeté la responsabilité de l'incident sur la secrétaire; **we had to bear** *or* **to take the blame** nous avons dû endosser la responsabilité; **why is it always me that gets the blame?** pourquoi est-ce que tout retombe toujours sur moi?; **I got the blame for breaking the window** c'est moi qu'on a accusé d'avoir cassé la fenêtre; **to shift the blame onto sb** rejeter la responsabilité sur qn; **where does the blame lie?** à qui la faute?; **the blame lies with her** c'est (de) sa faute

(**b**) *(reproof)* blâme *m*, réprimande *f*; **her conduct has been without blame** sa conduite a été irréprochable

2 *vt* (**a**) *(consider as responsible)* rejeter la responsabilité sur; **they blame inflation on the government** *or* **the government for inflation** ils accusent le gouvernement d'être responsable de l'inflation; **they blamed the early frost for the bad harvest** ils ont attribué leur mauvaise récolte aux gelées précoces; **he is/is not to blame** c'est/ce n'est pas de sa faute; **the bad weather was to blame** c'était à cause du mauvais temps; **I blame the parents** pour moi, ce sont les parents qui sont responsables; **don't blame me (for it)!** inutile de m'accuser!; **don't blame me if you're late** tu ne viendras pas dire que c'est de ma faute si tu es en retard; **you have only yourself to blame** tu ne peux t'en prendre qu'à toi-même, tu l'as voulu *ou* cherché

(**b**) *(reproach)* critiquer, reprocher; **to blame sb for sth** reprocher qch à qn; **I blame myself for having left her alone** je m'en veux de l'avoir laissée seule; **you have nothing to blame yourself for** tu n'as rien à te reprocher; **you can't blame her for wanting a divorce** tu ne peux pas lui reprocher de vouloir divorcer; **I wouldn't blame you if you left him** je te comprendrais si tu le quittais; **he left in disgust – I don't blame him!** il est parti dégoûté – ça se comprend!; **I don't blame you!** (comme) je te comprends!

blamed [bleɪmd] *adj Am* damné, maudit

blameless ['bleɪmlɪs] *adj* irréprochable, sans reproche; **to lead a blameless life** avoir une vie irréprochable

blamelessly ['bleɪmlɪslɪ] *adv* d'une façon irréprochable

blamelessness ['bleɪmlɪsnɪs] *n* irréprochabilité *f*

blameworthy ['bleɪm,wɜːðɪ] *adj (person)* fautif, coupable; *(action)* répréhensible

blanch [blɑːntʃ] **1** *vt (gen)* décolorer, blanchir; *Agr & Culin* blanchir; **blanched almonds** amandes *fpl* émondées *ou* épluchées

2 *vi* blêmir

blancmange [blə'mɒndʒ] *n Culin* = entremets généralement préparé à partir d'une poudre, ≃ flan *m* instantané

bland [blænd] *adj* (**a**) *(flavour, food)* fade, insipide; *(diet)* fade (**b**) *(person → dull)* insipide, ennuyeux; *(→ ingratiating)* mielleux, doucereux (**c**) *(weather)* doux (douce)

blandish ['blændɪʃ] *vt* amadouer

blandishment ['blændɪʃmənt] *n (usu pl) (coaxing)* cajoleries *fpl*; *(flattery)* flatterie *f*; **neither threats nor blandishments had any effect on him** mes menaces comme mes flatteries n'ont eu aucun effet sur lui

blandly ['blændlɪ] *adv (say → dully)* affablement, avec affabilité; *(→ ingratiatingly)* d'un ton mielleux

blandness ['blændnɪs] *n* (**a**) *(of flavour, food, diet)* fadeur *f* (**b**) *(of person → dullness)* fadeur *f*; *(→ ingratiating nature)* côté *m* mielleux (**c**) *(of weather)* douceur *f*

blank [blæŋk] **1** *adj* (**a**) *(paper → with no writing)* vierge, blanc (blanche); *(→ unruled)* blanc (blanche); *(form)* vierge, à remplir; *Admin* **fill in the blank spaces** remplissez les blancs *ou* les (espaces) vides; *Admin* **leave this line blank** n'écrivez rien sur cette ligne

(**b**) *(empty → screen, wall)* vide; *(→ cassette)* vierge; *(→ cartridge)* à blanc; *Comput (→ disk)* vide; *Comput (→ unformatted disk)* vierge; **to go blank** *(screen)* s'éteindre; *(face)* se vider de toute expression; **my mind went blank** j'ai eu un trou; *Cards* **to be blank in clubs** ne pas avoir de trèfles dans son jeu

(**c**) *(face, look → expressionless)* vide, sans expression; *(→ confused)* déconcerté, dérouté; **she looked blank** *(expressionless)* elle avait le regard vide; *(confused)* elle avait l'air déconcerté

(**d**) *(absolute → protest, refusal)* absolu, net; *(→ dismay)* absolu, profond

2 *n* (**a**) *(empty space, void)* blanc *m*, (espace *m*) vide *m*; **fill in the blanks** remplissez les blancs *ou* les (espaces) vides; **she filled in the blanks of her education** elle a comblé les lacunes de son éducation; **the rest of his life is a blank** on ne sait rien du reste de sa vie; **my mind was a total blank** j'ai eu un passage à vide complet; *Fig* **to draw a blank** *(be unsuccessful in search)* faire chou blanc; *Am (be unable to remember)* avoir un trou de mémoire; **she searched everywhere for him but drew a blank** elle l'a cherché partout mais sans succès; *Cards* **to have a blank in clubs** ne pas avoir de trèfles dans son jeu

(**b**) *(form)* formulaire *m* (vierge *ou* à remplir), imprimé *m*

(**c**) *(cartridge)* cartouche *f* à blanc; *Fam Hum* **to shoot** *or* **fire blanks** *(man)* être stérile ❑

(**d**) *(in dominoes)* blanc *m*

(**e**) *(metal disc → in minting coins)* flan *m*; *Metal & Tech* flan, masselotte *f*, galette *f*

(**f**) *Typ (to replace swear word etc)* tiret *m*

►► *Fin* ***blank cheque*** chèque *m* en blanc; *Fig* **to write sb a blank cheque** donner carte blanche à qn; *Fin* ***blank credit*** crédit *m* en blanc; *Fin* ***blank endorsement*** endossement *m* en blanc; *Literature* ***blank verse*** vers *mpl* blancs *ou* sans rime

►**blank out 1** *vt sep (parts of text, tape)* effacer; *Phot* **her face had been blanked out** *(on negative)* on avait effacé son visage; *Typ (on print)* on avait caché son visage; **she's blanked out the memory** elle a effacé cet événement de sa mémoire

2 *vi (lose consciousness)* tomber dans les pommes

blank-endorse *vt Fin* endosser en blanc

blanket ['blæŋkɪt] **1** *n* (**a**) *(for bed)* couverture *f*; *Br* **to be born on the wrong side of the blanket** être un enfant naturel, être (de naissance) illégitime

(**b**) *Fig (of clouds, snow)* couche *f*; *(of fog)* manteau *m*, nappe *f*; *(of smoke)* voile *m*, nuage *m*; *(of despair, sadness)* manteau *m*

(**c**) *Typ* blanchet *m*

2 *vt* (**a**) *(of snow)* recouvrir; *(of fog, smoke)* envelopper, voiler; **blanketed with snow** recouvert de neige

(**b**) *(noise)* étouffer, assourdir

3 *adj* général, global; **a blanket rule for all employees** un règlement qui s'applique à tout le personnel

►► *Com* ***blanket agreement*** accord-cadre *m*; ***blanket bath*** grande toilette *f (d'un malade alité)*; *Rad & TV* ***blanket coverage*** *(of event)* reportage *m* (très) complet; **our insurance policy guarantees blanket coverage** notre police d'assurance couvre tous les risques; ***blanket instruction*** consigne *f* générale; *Ins* ***blanket policy*** police *f* globale (tous risques); *Sewing* ***blanket stitch*** point *m* de feston; ***blanket term*** terme *m* général

►**blanket out** *vt sep* noyer

blanket-stitch *vt Sewing* **to blanket-stitch sth** border qch au point de feston

blankety-blank [,blæŋkətɪ-] *Fam Euph* **1** *adj* fichu

2 *n (man)* sale type *m*; *(woman)* sale bonne femme *f*; **what the blankety-blank are you doing here?** que diable fais-tu ici?

blanking ['blæŋkɪŋ] *n TV* suppression *f* de faisceau; *(erasing)* effacement *m*

blankly ['blæŋklɪ] *adv* (**a**) *(look → without expression)* avec le regard vide; *(→ with confusion)* d'un air ahuri *ou* interdit (**b**) *(answer, state)* carrément; *(refuse)* tout net, sans ambages

blankness ['blæŋknɪs] *n* (**a**) *(of person)* air *m* confus *ou* décontenancé (**b**) *(of eyes, expression)* vacuité *f*

blare [bleə(r)] **1** *n (gen)* vacarme *m*; *(of car horn, siren)* bruit *m* strident; *(of radio, television)* beuglement *m*; *(of trumpet)* sonnerie *f*

2 *vi (siren, music)* beugler; *(voice)* brailler

►**blare out 1** *vt sep (of radio, television)* beugler, brailler; *(of person)* brailler, hurler

2 *vi (radio, television)* beugler, brailler; *(person, voice)* brailler, hurler

blarney ['blɑːnɪ] *Fam* **1** *n (smooth talk)* baratin *m*; *(flattery)* flatterie ❑ *f*

2 *vt (smooth talk)* baratiner; *(wheedle)* embobiner; *(flatter)* flatter ❑

►► ***Blarney Stone*** = au château de Blarney, en Irlande, pierre censée donner des dons d'éloquence à ceux qui l'embrassent; **he's kissed the Blarney Stone** il a la langue bien pendue

blasé [*Br* 'blɑːzeɪ, *Am* blɑː'zeɪ] *adj* blasé

blaspheme [blæs'fiːm] *Rel* **1** *vi* blasphémer; **don't blaspheme against God** ne blasphémez pas contre Dieu

2 *vt* blasphémer

blasphemer [blæs'fiːmə(r)] *n Rel* blasphémateur(trice) *m,f*

blasphemous ['blæsfəməs] *adj Rel (poem, talk)* blasphématoire; *(person)* blasphémateur

blasphemously ['blæsfəməslɪ] *adv Rel* de façon impie, avec impiété

blasphemy ['blæsfəmɪ] *(pl* **blasphemies***) n Rel* blasphème *m*; **what you're saying is blasphemy** c'est blasphémer ce que vous dites là

blast [blɑːst] **1** *n* (**a**) *(explosion)* explosion *f*; *(shock wave)* souffle *m*; **the house was destroyed by the blast** la maison a été soufflée par l'explosion

(**b**) *(of air)* bouffée *f*; *(of steam)* jet *m*; **a blast (of wind)** un coup de vent, une rafale

(**c**) *(sound → of car horn, whistle)* coup *m* strident; *(→ of trumpet)* sonnerie *f*; *(→ of explosion)* détonation *f*; *(→ of rocket)* rugissement *m*; **a whistle blast** un coup de sifflet; **he blew a couple of blasts on his whistle** il a donné plusieurs coups de sifflet

(**d**) *Am Fam (fun)* **we had a blast** on s'est vraiment marrés; **he gets a blast out of teasing her** cela l'amuse de la taquiner; **it was a blast** c'était génial

(**e**) *Fam* **a blast from the past** *(song)* un vieux tube; **that's a real blast from the past** *(fashion, behaviour etc)* c'est comme autrefois; *(brings back memories)* ça me ramène des années en arrière

(**f**) *(idioms)* **she had the radio on (at) full blast** elle faisait marcher la radio à fond; **the machine was going at full blast** la machine avançait à toute allure; **we worked at full blast** nous travaillions comme des brutes

2 *vt* (**a**) *(with explosives)* faire sauter; **they blasted a tunnel through the mountain** ils ont creusé un tunnel à travers la montagne avec des explosifs

(**b**) *(with gun)* tirer sur; **the thieves blasted their way through the roadblock** les voleurs ont forcé le barrage routier en tirant des coups de feu

(**c**) *(of radio, television)* beugler

(**d**) *Bot (blight)* flétrir

bla–bla

(**e**) *(criticize)* attaquer *ou* critiquer violemment

(**f**) *(plan)* détruire; *(hope)* briser, anéantir

3 *vi (radio, television)* beugler; *(music)* retentir; **the radio was blasting away** la radio marchait à fond

4 *exclam Fam* zut!; **blast that car!** il y en a marre de cette voiture!; **blast her!** ce qu'elle peut être embêtante!

▸▸ *Tech* ***blast furnace*** haut-fourneau *m*

▸**blast off** *vi (rocket)* décoller

▸**blast out 1** *vt sep (music)* beugler

2 *vi (radio, television)* beugler; *(music)* retentir

blasted ['blɑːstɪd] **1** *adj* (**a**) *Bot (plant)* flétri; **a blasted oak** un chêne foudroyé (**b**) *Fam (as intensifier)* fichu, sacré; **you blasted fool!** espèce d'imbécile!; **it's a blasted nuisance!** c'est vraiment casse-pieds! (**c**) *Fam (drunk)* bourré, beurré; *(on drugs)* défoncé

2 *adv Fam (for emphasis)* **don't go so blasted fast!** ne va pas si vite, bon sang!

blastema [blæ'stiːmə] (*pl* **blastemas** *or* **blastemata** [-mətə]) *n Biol* blastème *m*

blasting ['blɑːstɪŋ] *n* (**a**) *(explosions)* travail *m* aux explosifs, explosions *fpl*; *Tech* minage *m*; **beware, blasting in progress** *(sign)* attention, tirs de mines (**b**) *Br Fam (verbal attack)* engueulade *f*; **he got a blasting from the boss** le patron lui a passé un sacré savon

blastoderm ['blæstəʊdɜːm] *n Biol* blastoderme *m*

blast-off *n* lancement *m*, mise *f* à feu *(d'une fusée spatiale)*; **ten seconds to blast-off** dix secondes avant la mise à feu

blastula ['blæstjʊlə] (*pl* **blastulas** *or* **blastulae** [-liː]) *n Biol* blastula *f*

blat [blæt] (*pt & pp* **blatted,** *cont* **blatting**) *Am* **1** *vt* bêler

2 *vi* bêler

blatancy ['bleɪtənsɪ] *n (obviousness)* évidence *f*, caractère *m* flagrant

blatant ['bleɪtənt] *adj (discrimination, injustice)* évident, flagrant; *(lie)* manifeste; **it was a blatant attempt to win him over** c'était une tentative évidente de s'assurer ses faveurs

blatantly ['bleɪtəntlɪ] *adv (discriminate, disregard)* de façon flagrante; *(cheat, lie)* de façon éhontée; **it's blatantly obvious that...** il est évident que...; **yes, that's blatantly obvious** oui, évidemment

blather ['blæðə(r)] *Am* **1** *n (UNCOUNT)* âneries *fpl*, bêtises *fpl*

2 *vi* raconter des bêtises *ou* des âneries

blatherskite ['blæðəskaɪt] *n Fam* moulin *m* à paroles

blaxploitation [,blæksplɔɪ'teɪʃən] *n Cin* = genre de cinéma qui exploitait les stéréotypes associés à l'identité noire américaine au cinéma, au cours des années 70

blaze [bleɪz] **1** *n* (**a**) *(flame)* flamme *f*, flammes *fpl*, feu *m*; *(large fire)* incendie *m*; **five die in blaze** *(in headline)* un incendie a fait cinq morts

(**b**) *(burst → of colour)* éclat *m*, flamboiement *m*; *(→ of light)* éclat *m*; *(→ of eloquence, enthusiasm)* élan *m*, transport *m*; *(→ of sunlight)* torrent *m*; **the street was a blaze of light** la rue était tout illuminée; **a blaze of gunfire** des coups de feu, une fusillade; **in a sudden blaze of anger** sous le coup de la colère; **she married in a blaze of publicity** elle s'est mariée sous les feux des projecteurs; **he finished in a blaze of glory** il a terminé en beauté

(**c**) *Miner (of gem)* éclat *m*, brillance *f*

(**d**) *(mark → on tree)* marque *f*, encoche *f*; *Zool (→ on animal, horse)* étoile *f*

(**e**) *Br Fam (idioms)* **what the blazes are you doing here?** qu'est-ce que tu fabriques ici?; **how the blazes would I know?** comment veux-tu que je le sache?; **we ran like blazes** nous avons couru à toutes jambes; **go** *or* **get to blazes!** va te faire voir!

2 *vi* (**a**) *(fire)* flamber; **he suddenly blazed with anger** il s'est enflammé de colère; **his eyes were blazing with anger/passion** ses yeux lançaient des éclairs de colère/passion

(**b**) *(colour, light, sun)* flamboyer; *(gem)* resplendir, briller; **the fields blazed with colour** les champs resplendissaient de mille couleurs

(**c**) *(gun)* tirer, faire feu

3 *vt* (**a**) *(proclaim)* proclamer, claironner; *(publish)* publier; **the news was blazed across the front page** la nouvelle faisait la une du journal; **it's not the kind of thing you want blazed abroad** ce n'est pas le genre de chose qu'on veut crier sur les toits

(**b**) *(lead)* **to blaze the way for sth** préparer le terrain pour qch

(**c**) *(idiom)* **to blaze a trail** frayer un chemin; **they're blazing a trail in biotechnology** ils font un travail de pionniers dans le domaine de la biotechnologie

▸**blaze away** *vi* (**a**) *(fire)* (continuer de) flamber

(**b**) *Br (gun)* faire feu; **the gangsters blazed away at the police** les gangsters maintenaient un feu nourri contre la police; **I blazed away at the target** je tirais sans cesse sur la cible

▸**blaze down** *vi (sun)* flamboyer, darder ses rayons

▸**blaze up** *vi* (**a**) *(fire)* prendre immédiatement *ou* rapidement

(**b**) *(person)* s'enflammer de colère, s'emporter; *(anger, resentment)* éclater

blazer ['bleɪzə(r)] *n* blazer *m*

blazing ['bleɪzɪŋ] *adj* (**a**) *(building, town)* en flammes, embrasé; **to sit in front of a blazing fire** s'installer devant une bonne flambée (**b**) *(sun)* brûlant, ardent; *(heat)* torride; **a blazing hot day** une journée de chaleur torride (**c**) *(light)* éclatant; *(colour)* très vif; *(gem)* brillant, étincelant; *(eyes)* qui jette des éclairs (**d**) *(argument)* violent (**e**) *(angry)* furieux

blazon ['bleɪzn] **1** *n* blason *m*

2 *vt* (**a**) *(proclaim)* proclamer, claironner; **to blazon sth abroad** proclamer qch, crier qch sur les toits; *Fig* **his name was blazoned over the front pages of all the newspapers** son nom s'étalait en grosses lettres à la une de tous les journaux (**b**) *(mark)* marquer; *Her* blasonner

▸**blazon forth, blazon out** *vt sep Formal* annoncer *ou* proclamer à son de trompe

blazonry ['bleɪzənrɪ] *n Her* blasonnement *m*

bldg *(written abbr* **building***)* bât.

bleach [bliːtʃ] **1** *n (gen)* décolorant *m*; **(household) bleach** eau *f* de Javel

2 *vt* (**a**) *(clothes, linen)* passer à l'eau de Javel

(**b**) *(of sun → bones)* blanchir; *(→ colour)* éclaircir

(**c**) *(hair → chemically)* décolorer, oxygéner; *(→ with sun)* éclaircir; **to bleach one's hair** se décolorer les cheveux; **a bleached blonde** une fausse blonde, une blonde décolorée

3 *vi* blanchir; **do not bleach** *(washing instruction)* javel interdite

▸**bleach out** *vt sep (stain)* enlever à l'aide d'un décolorant *ou* d'un blanchissant

bleachers ['bliːtʃəz] *npl Am Sport* gradins *mpl*

bleaching ['bliːtʃɪŋ] *n* blanchiment *m*; *(of hair)* décoloration *f*

▸▸ ***bleaching agent*** produit *m* blanchissant, décolorant *m*; *Chem* ***bleaching powder*** chlorure *m* de chaux

bleak [bliːk] **1** *adj* (**a**) *(place, room)* froid, austère; *(landscape)* morne, désolé (**b**) *(weather)* morne, maussade; *(winter)* rude, rigoureux (**c**) *(situation)* sombre, morne; *(life)* morne, monotone; **the bleak facts** la vérité toute nue *ou* sans fard; **the future looks bleak** l'avenir se présente plutôt mal (**d**) *(mood, person)* lugubre, morne; *(smile)* pâle; *(tone, voice)* monocorde, morne

2 *n Ich* ablette *f*

'Bleak House' *Dickens* 'La Maison d'âpre vent'

bleakly ['bliːklɪ] *adv (speak)* d'un ton morne *ou* monocorde; *(stare)* d'un air triste, lugubrement

bleakness ['bliːknɪs] *n* (**a**) *(of furnishings, room)* austérité *f*; *(of landscape)* caractère *m* morne *ou* désolé (**b**) *(of weather)* caractère *m* morne *ou* maussade; *(of winter)* rigueurs *fpl* (**c**) *(of situation)* caractère *m* sombre *ou* peu prometteur; *(of life)* monotonie *f* (**d**) *(of mood, person)* tristesse *f*; *(of voice)* ton *m* monocorde *ou* morne

blear [blɪə(r)] *vt* (**a**) *(eyes, vision)* rendre troubles

(**b**) *(make indistinct)* obscurcir, estomper

blearily ['blɪərɪlɪ] *adv* les yeux troubles

bleary ['blɪərɪ] (*compar* **blearier,** *superl* **bleariest**) *adj* (**a**) *(eyes → from fatigue)* trouble, voilé; *(→ watery)* larmoyant; *(vision)* trouble (**b**) *(indistinct)* indécis, vague

bleary-eyed *adj (from sleep)* aux yeux troubles; *(watery-eyed)* aux yeux vitreux

bleat [bliːt] **1** *vi* (**a**) *(sheep)* bêler; *(goat)* bêler, chevroter (**b**) *(person → speak)* bêler, chevroter; *(→ whine)* geindre, bêler

2 *vt (say)* dire d'un ton bêlant; *(whine)* geindre, bêler

3 *n* (**a**) *(of sheep)* bêlement *m*; *(of goat)* bêlement, chevrotement *m* (**b**) *(of person → voice)* bêlement *m*; *(→ complaint)* gémissement *m*

bleating ['bliːtɪŋ] **1** *adj (voice)* chevrotant

2 *n* (**a**) *(of sheep)* bêlement *m*; *(of goat)* bêlement, chevrotement *m* (**b**) *(of person → voice)* bêlement *m*; *(→ complaint)* gémissement *m*

bled [bled] *pt & pp of* **bleed**

bleed [bliːd] (*pt & pp* **bled** [bled]) **1** *vi* (**a**) *(lose blood)* saigner, perdre du sang; **to bleed to death** saigner à mort; **my nose is bleeding** je saigne du nez; *Fig Ironic* **my heart bleeds for you!** tu me fends le cœur!

(**b**) *Bot (plant)* pleurer, perdre sa sève

(**c**) *(cloth, colour)* déteindre

2 *vt* (**a**) *(person)* saigner

(**b**) *Fig Fin (extort money from)* saigner; **to bleed sb dry** *or* **white** saigner qn à blanc

(**c**) *Aut & Tech (brake, radiator)* purger

3 *n Comput & Typ* fond *m* perdu, plein papier *m*

▸▸ *Tech* ***bleed valve*** soupape *f* de purge

▸**bleed out** *vi Med* perdre beaucoup de sang

bleeder ['bliːdə(r)] *n Br very Fam (person → gen)* type *m*; *(→ disagreeable)* salaud *m*; **the poor bleeder** le pauvre gars; **cheeky bleeder** petit effronté *m*; **lucky bleeder** sacré veinard *m*

bleeding ['bliːdɪŋ] **1** *n* (**a**) *(loss of blood)* saignement *m*; *(haemorrhage)* hémorragie *f*; *(taking of blood)* saignée *f*; **they stopped the bleeding** ils ont arrêté l'hémorragie; **bleeding from the nose** saignement *m* de nez

(**b**) *Hort (of plant)* écoulement *m* de sève

(**c**) *Aut & Tech (of brake, radiator)* purge *f*

2 *adj* (**a**) *(wound)* saignant, qui saigne; *(person)* qui saigne

(**b**) *Br very Fam (as intensifier)* fichu, sacré; **bleeding idiot!** espèce d'imbécile!; **what a bleeding nuisance!** quelle saloperie!

3 *adv very Fam* vachement; **you're bleeding (well) coming with me!** un peu, que tu vas venir avec moi!; **that was bleeding stupid!** c'est vraiment con, ce que tu as fait/dit!

▸▸ ***bleeding heart*** *Pej (person)* sentimental *m*; *Bot* cœur-de-Jeannette *m*

bleeding-heart *adj Pej* **he's a bleeding-heart liberal** c'est un sentimental qui s'apitoie sur le sort des infortunés

bleep [bliːp] **1** *n* bip *m*, bip-bip *m*

2 *vi* émettre un bip *ou* un bip-bip

3 *vt* (**a**) *(doctor)* appeler (au moyen d'un bip *ou* d'un bip-bip); **I'm being bleeped** on m'appelle (**b**) *Rad & TV* **to bleep words (out)** masquer des paroles (par un bip)

bleeper ['bliːpə(r)] *n Br* bip *m*, bip-bip *m*

bleeping ['bliːpɪŋ] *n (of electronic device)* bip-bip *m*

blemish ['blemɪʃ] **1** *n* (**a**) *(flaw)* défaut *m*, imperfection *f*; *(on fruit)* tache *f* (**b**) *(on face → pimple)* bouton *m* (**c**) *Fig (on name, reputation)* tache *f*, *Literary* souillure *f*; **her reputation is without blemish** sa réputation est sans tache

2 *vt* (**a**) *(beauty, landscape)* gâter; *(fruit)* tacher (**b**) *Fig (reputation)* tacher, *Literary* souiller

blench [blentʃ] *vi (recoil in fear)* reculer; *(turn pale)* blêmir; **she blenched at the idea** à cette pensée, elle pâlit *ou* blêmit; **without blenching** sans broncher *ou* sourciller

blend [blend] **1** *vt* (**a**) *(mix together → gen)* mélanger, mêler; *(→ cultures, races)* fusionner; *(→ feelings, qualities)* joindre, unir; *Culin* **blend the butter and sugar (together), blend the sugar into the butter** mélangez le beurre au *ou* avec le sucre; **to blend two coffees** mélanger deux cafés, faire un mélange de deux cafés; **to blend old traditions with modern methods** faire un mélange de traditions anciennes et de méthodes modernes

(**b**) *(colours → mix together)* mêler, mélanger; *(→ put together)* marier; **to blend white and**

black mélanger du blanc avec du noir; *(in painting)* **to blend one colour into another** fondre une couleur dans une autre

2 *vi* (**a**) *(mix together → gen)* se mélanger, se mêler; *(→ cultures, races)* fusionner; *(→ feelings, sounds)* se confondre, se mêler; *(→ perfumes)* se marier; **their voices blended into one** leurs voix se confondaient;

(**b**) *(colours → form one shade)* se fondre; *(→ go well together)* aller ensemble

3 *n* (**a**) *(mixture)* mélange *m*; **house blend** *(on sign, packaging)* mélange (spécial de la) maison

(**b**) *Fig (of feelings, qualities)* alliance *f*, mélange *m*; **his speech was a blend of caution and encouragement** son discours était un mélange de prudence et d'encouragement

(**c**) *Ling* mot-valise *m*

(**d**) *Comput (in desktop publishing)* dégradé

►► *Am* ***blended family*** famille *f* recomposée; ***blended whisky*** blend *m (whisky obtenu par mélange de whiskies de grain industriels et de whiskies pur malt)*

►**blend in 1** *vi (harmonize)* s'harmoniser, se marier (**with** avec); *(of person)* s'intégrer; **the new student blended in well** le nouvel étudiant s'est bien intégré; **that new building doesn't blend in with its surroundings** ce nouveau bâtiment ne se marie pas bien *ou* ne va pas bien avec ce qui l'entoure

2 *vt sep Culin (mix)* incorporer

blender ['blendə(r)] *n Culin* mixer *m*; *Tech* malaxeur *m*

►► ***blender attachment*** accessoire *m* pour mixer

blending ['blendɪŋ] *n* (**a**) *(mixing)* mélange *m*; *(in winemaking)* coupage *m* (**b**) *Fig (of feelings, qualities)* alliance *f*

Blenheim Palace ['blenɪm-] *n* = château près d'Oxford, où naquit Winston Churchill

blennorrhoea, *Am* **blennorrhea** [ˌblenə'rɪə] *n Med* blennorrhée *f*

blenny ['blenɪ] *n Ich* blennie *f*

bless [bles] *(pt & pp* **blessed**) *vt* (**a**) *Rel (of God, priest)* bénir; **God bless (you)!, bless you!** que Dieu vous bénisse!; **bless you!** *(after sneeze)* à vos/tes souhaits!, *Suisse* santé!; *(in thanks)* merci mille fois!; **Mary, bless her, has agreed to do it** Mary, Dieu soit loué, a accepté de le faire; **he remembered her birthday, bless his heart!** et il n'a pas oublié son anniversaire, le petit chéri!; **bless your heart!** que tu es gentil!; *Fam Old-fashioned* **bless my soul!, bless me!** Seigneur!, mon Dieu!; *Fam Old-fashioned* **bless me if I didn't forget her name!** figurez-vous que j'avais oublié son nom!; *Fam* **I'm blessed if I know!** que le diable m'emporte si je sais!; **I bless the day I learnt to swim** béni soit le jour où j'ai appris à nager; **God bless America** = phrase traditionnellement prononcée par le président des États-Unis pour terminer une allocution

(**b**) *(usu passive) Formal (endow, grant)* douer, doter; **to be blessed with sth** jouir de qch, avoir le bonheur de posséder qch; **she is blessed with excellent health** elle a le bonheur d'avoir une excellente santé; **Nature has blessed him with an extraordinary memory** la nature l'a doué d'une mémoire extraordinaire; **they have been blessed with two fine children** ils ont deux enfants adorables; *Fam* **he hasn't a penny to bless himself with** il n'a pas le sou

(**c**) *Rel (glorify)* **to bless God** bénir *ou* adorer Dieu

blessed 1 [blest] *pt & pp of* **bless**

2 *adj* [blesɪd] (**a**) *Rel (holy)* béni, sacré

(**b**) *Rel (favoured by God)* bienheureux, heureux; *Bible* **blessed are the poor in spirit** heureux les pauvres d'esprit

(**c**) *(wonderful → day, freedom, rain)* béni

(**d**) *Fam (as intensifier)* sacré, fichu; **every blessed day** chaque jour que le bon Dieu fait; **the whole blessed day** toute la sainte journée; **it's a blessed nuisance having to...** quelle barbe d'avoir à...; **I can't see a blessed thing** je n'y vois rien

3 *npl* [blest] *Rel* **the blessed** les bienheureux *mpl*

►► *Rel* ***the Blessed Trinity*** la Sainte Trinité; *Rel* ***the Blessed Virgin*** la Sainte Vierge

blessedly ['blesɪdlɪ] *adv* parfaitement; **the speech was blessedly short** Dieu merci, le discours fut bref

blessedness ['blesɪdnɪs] *n* félicité *f*; *Rel* béatitude *f*

blessing ['blesɪŋ] *n* (**a**) *Rel (God's favour)* grâce *f*, faveur *f*; **the blessing of the Lord be upon you** que Dieu vous bénisse

(**b**) *Rel (prayer)* bénédiction *f*; *(before meal)* bénédicité *m*; **to give** *or* **pronounce the blessing** donner la bénédiction; **the priest said the blessing** le prêtre a donné la bénédiction

(**c**) *Fig (approval)* bénédiction *f*, approbation *f*; **with the blessing of his parents** avec la bénédiction de ses parents; **does the project have the boss's blessing?** est-ce que le patron a donné sa bénédiction au projet?

(**d**) *(advantage)* bienfait *m*, avantage *m*; *(godsend)* aubaine *f*, bénédiction *f*; **it was a blessing that no one was hurt** c'était une chance que personne ne soit blessé; **the rain was a blessing for the farmers** la pluie était un don du ciel *ou* une bénédiction pour les agriculteurs; **what a blessing!** quelle chance!; **it was a blessing in disguise** c'était une bonne chose, en fin de compte

blest [blest] *Arch or Literary* = **blessed**

blether ['bleðə(r)] **1** *n* (**a**) *(foolish talk)* âneries *fpl*, bêtises *fpl* (**b**) *Scot (chat)* causette *f*; **to have a blether (with sb)** bavarder (avec qn)

2 *vi* (**a**) *(talk foolishly)* dire des âneries *ou* des bêtises (**b**) *Scot (chat)* bavarder

bletherskate ['bleðəˌskeɪt] *n Fam* moulin *m* à paroles

blew [blu:] *pt of* **blow**

blight [blaɪt] **1** *n* (**a**) *Bot & Agr (of flowering plants)* rouille *f*; *(of fruit trees)* cloque *f*; *(of cereals)* rouille *f*, nielle *f*; *(of potato plants)* mildiou *m*

(**b**) *(curse)* malheur *m*, fléau *m*; **the accident cast a blight on our holiday** l'accident a gâché nos vacances; **her illness was a blight on their happiness** sa maladie a terni leur bonheur; **air pollution is a real blight** la pollution de l'air est un vrai fléau

(**c**) *(condition of decay)* **inner-city blight** la dégradation des quartiers pauvres

2 *vt* (**a**) *Bot & Agr (plants → gen)* rouiller; *(cereals)* nieller, rouiller

(**b**) *(spoil → happiness, holiday)* gâcher; *(→ career, life)* gâcher, briser; *(→ hopes)* anéantir, détruire; *(→ plans)* déjouer; **a marriage blighted by money problems** un mariage assombri par des problèmes d'argent

blighter ['blaɪtə(r)] *n Br Fam* type *m*; **you lucky blighter!** sacré veinard!; **silly blighters!** les imbéciles!

blighty, Blighty ['blaɪtɪ] *n Br Fam Old-fashioned (England)* l'Angleterre ❑ *f*; *Hist (wound)* = pendant la Première Guerre mondiale, une blessure suffisamment grave pour qu'elle nécessite un rapatriement en Grande-Bretagne

blimey ['blaɪmɪ] *exclam Br Fam* ça alors!, mon Dieu!

blimp [blɪmp] **1** *n Aviat (airship)* dirigeable *m*

2 Blimp *n Fam* vieux réac *m*

blimpish, Blimpish ['blɪmpɪʃ] *adj Br Fam* réactionnaire ❑

blind [blaɪnd] **1** *adj* (**a**) *(sightless)* aveugle, non voyant; **to go blind** devenir aveugle; **blind from birth** aveugle de naissance; **his sister is blind** sa sœur est aveugle; **he's blind in one eye** il est aveugle d'un œil, il est borgne; **I'm blind without my glasses** je ne vois rien sans mes lunettes; **as blind as a bat** myope comme une taupe; **to turn a blind eye to sth** fermer les yeux sur qch

(**b**) *(unthinking)* aveugle; **blind loyalty/trust** loyauté *f*/confiance *f* aveugle; **he flew into a blind rage** il s'est mis dans une colère noire; **blind with anger** aveuglé par la colère; **they were blind to the danger** le danger leur échappait; **she was blind to the consequences** elle ignorait les conséquences, elle ne voyait pas les conséquences; **love is blind** l'amour est aveugle

(**c**) *(hidden from sight → corner, turning)* sans visibilité

(**d**) *Aviat (landing, take-off)* aux appareils; **blind flying** vol *m* sans visibilité, vol *m* en P.S.V.

(**e**) *(as intensifier)* **he was blind drunk** il était ivre mort; *Fam* **he didn't take a blind bit of notice of what I said** il n'a pas fait la moindre attention à ce que j'ai dit; *Fam* **it doesn't make a blind bit of difference to me** cela m'est complètement égal

(**f**) *(without exit → window, door)* feint, aveugle

2 *vt* (**a**) *(deprive of sight)* aveugler, rendre aveugle; *(of flash of light)* aveugler, éblouir; **blinded ex-servicemen** aveugles *mpl* de guerre; **we were blinded by the smoke** on était aveuglé par la fumée

(**b**) *(deprive of judgement, reason)* aveugler; **vanity blinded him to her real motives** sa vanité l'empêchait de discerner ses véritables intentions; **love blinded her to his faults** aveuglée par l'amour, elle n'a pas vu ses défauts; *Hum* **to blind sb with science** éblouir qn par sa science

3 *n* (**a**) *(for window)* store *m*; **shop blind** *(over pavement)* banne *f*

(**b**) *Br Fam (trick)* prétexte ❑ *m*, feinte ❑ *f*; **the trip was just a blind for his smuggling activities** le voyage a servi à masquer *ou* dissimuler ses activités de contrebande

(**c**) *Am (hiding place)* cachette *f*; *Hunt* affût *m*

4 *npl* **the blind** les aveugles *mpl*, les non-voyants *mpl*; **I was told to show him how the new photocopier works but it's like the blind leading the blind** on m'a demandé de lui montrer comment se servir de la nouvelle photocopieuse mais je n'en sais pas plus long que lui

5 *adv* (**a**) *Aut & Aviat (drive, fly → without visibility)* sans visibilité; *(→ using only instruments)* aux instruments

(**b**) *(purchase)* sans avoir vu; *(decide)* à l'aveuglette

(**c**) *(as intensifier)* **I would swear blind he was there** j'aurais donné ma tête à couper *ou* j'aurais juré qu'il était là

►► *Br* ***blind alley*** impasse *f*, cul-de-sac *m*; *Fig* **the government's new idea is just another blind alley** encore une idée du gouvernement qui n'aboutira à rien *ou* ne mènera nulle part; ***blind date*** *(meeting)* rendez-vous *m ou* rencontre *f* arrangée *(avec quelqu'un qu'on ne connaît pas)*; *(person)* inconnu(e) *m,f (avec qui on a rendez-vous)*; ***blind man's buff*** *(game)* colin-maillard *m*; ***blind side*** *Sport (in rugby)* côté *m* fermé; *Aut* angle *m* mort; **on my blind side** dans mon angle mort; ***blind spot*** *Aut (in mirror)* angle *m* mort; *(in road)* endroit *m* sans visibilité; *Med* point *m* aveugle; *Fig (weak area)* côté *m* faible, faiblesse *f*; **he has a blind spot about his daughter** quand il s'agit de sa fille, il refuse de voir la vérité en face; **I have a blind spot about maths** je ne comprends rien aux mathématiques; *Mktg* ***blind test*** test *m* aveugle; *Mktg* ***blind testing*** tests *mpl* aveugles

blinder ['blaɪndə(r)] *n* (**a**) *Br Fam* **to go on a blinder** *(get drunk)* se bourrer (la gueule) (**b**) *Fam (outstanding feat)* **he played a blinder (of a game)** il a eu un jeu spectaculaire; **the first goal was a blinder** le premier but a été spectaculaire (**c**) *Am (for horse)* œillère *f*

blindfold ['blaɪndfəʊld] **1** *n* bandeau *m*

2 *vt* bander les yeux à *ou* de

3 *adv* les yeux bandés; **I could do the job blindfold** je pourrais faire ce travail les yeux bandés *ou* fermés

4 *adj* **blindfold** *or* **blindfolded prisoners** prisonniers aux yeux bandés

blindfolding ['blaɪndˌfəʊldɪŋ] *n* bandage *m* des yeux

blinding ['blaɪndɪŋ] **1** *adj* (**a**) *(light)* aveuglant, éblouissant; *Fig (speed)* éblouissant; **a blinding headache** un mal de tête effroyable; **it was a blinding revelation** ça a été une véritable révélation; **the blinding intensity of his criticism** l'intensité affolante de ses critiques (**b**) *Br Fam (excellent)* super, génial

2 *n* (**a**) *(of person, animal)* aveuglement *m* (**b**) *Constr (on road)* couche *f* de sable

blindingly ['blaɪndɪŋlɪ] *adv* de façon aveuglante; **it was blindingly obvious** ça sautait aux yeux

blindly ['blaɪndlɪ] *adv (unseeingly)* à l'aveuglette; *Fig (without thinking)* aveuglément

blindness ['blaɪndnɪs] *n* cécité *f*; *Fig* aveuglement *m*; **the government's blindness to social problems** l'aveuglement du gouvernement face aux problèmes sociaux

blindworm ['blaɪndwɜːm] *n Zool* orvet *m*

blini ['bliːnɪ] *n Culin* blinis *m*

blink [blɪŋk] **1** *vi* (**a**) *(person)* cligner *ou* clignoter des yeux; *(eyes)* cligner, clignoter; *Fig* **without blinking** *(calmly, without surprise)* sans sourciller; *Fig* **she didn't even blink at the news** elle n'a même pas sourcillé en apprenant la nouvelle; *Fig* **they blink at his heavy drinking** ils ferment les yeux sur le fait qu'il boit beaucoup; *Fig* **to blink at the facts** fermer les yeux sur la vérité

(**b**) *(light, cursor)* clignoter, vaciller

2 *vt* (**a**) **to blink one's eyes** cligner les *ou* des yeux; **to blink away** *or* **to blink back one's tears** refouler ses larmes *(en clignant des yeux)*

(**b**) *Am Aut* **to blink one's lights** faire un appel de phares

3 *n* (**a**) *(of eyelid)* clignement *m* (des yeux), battement *m* de paupières; **in the blink of an eye** *or* **eyelid** en un clin d'œil, en un rien de temps

(**b**) *(glimpse)* coup *m* d'œil

(**c**) *(of light)* lueur *f*; *(of sunlight)* rayon *m*

(**d**) *Fam (idiom)* **to be on the blink** *(machine, TV)* déconner

►► *Comput* **blink rate** *(of cursor)* vitesse *f* de clignotement

blinker ['blɪŋkə(r)] **1** *n Aut* **blinker (light)** *(turn signal)* clignotant *m*; *(warning light)* feu *m* de détresse

2 *vt* mettre des œillères à

3 blinkers *npl (for eyes)* œillères *fpl*; **when it comes to her family she wears blinkers** elle a des œillères quand il s'agit de sa famille

blinkered ['blɪŋkəd] *adj* (**a**) *(horse)* qui porte des œillères (**b**) *(opinion, view)* borné

blinking ['blɪŋkɪŋ] *Br Fam* **1** *adj* sacré, fichu; **blinking idiot!** espèce d'idiot!; **the blinking thing won't work!** pas moyen de faire marcher cette saloperie!

2 *adv* sacrément, fichtrement

blintz, blintze [blɪnts] *n Culin* crêpe *f* fourrée

blip [blɪp] **1** *n* (**a**) *(sound)* bip *m*; *(spot of light)* spot *m*; *(on graph)* sommet *m* (**b**) *(temporary problem)* mauvais moment *m* (à passer); **the company suffered a blip in February when it lost that contract** l'entreprise a subi un contretemps en février lorsqu'elle a perdu ce contrat

2 *vi* faire bip *ou* bip-bip

bliss [blɪs] *n* (**a**) *(happiness)* bonheur *m* (complet *ou* absolu), contentement *m*; **what bliss to have a lie-in!** quel bonheur de pouvoir faire la grasse matinée!; **our holiday was absolute bliss!** on a passé des vacances absolument merveilleuses *ou* divines!; **it's sheer bliss!** c'est le bonheur total!; **married bliss** le bonheur conjugal (**b**) *Rel* béatitude *f*

blissful ['blɪsfʊl] *adj* (**a**) *(person → happy)* bienheureux; *(→ peaceful)* serein; *(holiday, weekend etc)* plein de bonheur; **three blissful years** trois années de bonheur complet; **we had a blissful time in France** nous avons passé un merveilleux séjour en France; **...she said with a blissful sigh** ...dit-elle en soupirant de bonheur; **she remained in blissful ignorance** elle était heureuse dans son ignorance (**b**) *Rel* bienheureux

blissfully ['blɪsfʊlɪ] *adv (agree, smile)* d'un air heureux; *(peaceful, quiet)* merveilleusement; **he was blissfully happy** il était comblé de bonheur; **we were blissfully unaware of the danger** nous étions dans l'ignorance la plus totale du danger

blissfulness ['blɪsfʊlnɪs] = **bliss**

B-list *adj (star, celebrity, guest)* pas parmi les plus connus; **there were only B-list stars among the guests** il n'y avait aucune vedette de stature internationale parmi les invités

blister ['blɪstə(r)] **1** *n* (**a**) *(on skin)* ampoule *f*, cloque *f* (**b**) *(on painted surface)* boursouflure *f*; *(on metal surface)* soufflure *f*

2 *vi* (**a**) *(skin)* se couvrir d'ampoules (**b**) *(paint)* se boursoufler; *(metal)* former des soufflures

3 *vt* (**a**) *(skin)* donner des ampoules à (**b**) *(paint)* boursoufler; *(metal)* former des soufflures dans (**c**) *(attack verbally)* critiquer sévèrement

►► *Entom* **blister beetle** cantharide *f*; *Br* **blister pack** *(for light bulb, pens)* blister *m*; *(for pills)* plaquette *f*

blistered ['blɪstəd] *adj* couvert d'ampoules

blistering ['blɪstərɪŋ] **1** *adj* (**a**) *(sun)* brûlant, de plomb; *(heat)* torride (**b**) *(attack, criticism)* cinglant, virulent; *(remark)* caustique, cinglant; **she's setting a blistering pace** elle mène un train d'enfer

2 *n* (**a**) *(on skin)* ampoules *fpl*; **blistering is inevitable** la formation d'ampoules est inévitable (**b**) *(of paint)* cloquage *m*

blisteringly ['blɪstərɪŋlɪ] *adv* **it was a blisteringly hot day** c'était une journée d'une chaleur étouffante; **it was blisteringly hot** il faisait une chaleur étouffante

BLit [ˌbiː'lɪt] *n (abbr* **Bachelor of Literature**) *(person)* = titulaire d'une licence de littérature; *(qualification)* licence *f* de littérature

blithe [blaɪð] *adj (cheerful)* gai, joyeux; *(carefree)* insouciant; **blithe indifference** indifférence insouciante

'Blithe Spirit' *Coward* 'L'Esprit s'amuse'

blithely ['blaɪðlɪ] *adv (cheerfully)* gaiement, joyeusement; *(carelessly)* avec insouciance; **she blithely ignored him** elle l'a ignoré avec une complète désinvolture; **he was blithely unaware of the danger** il ne se doutait pas le moins du monde du danger qu'il courait

blithering ['blɪðərɪŋ] *adj Fam* sacré; **it's a blithering nuisance!** c'est la barbe!; **a blithering idiot** un crétin fini; **you blithering fool!** espèce d'imbécile!

blithesome ['blaɪðsəm] *adj Literary (cheerful)* gai, joyeux; *(carefree)* insouciant

BLitt [ˌbiː'lɪt] *n Br Univ (abbr* **Bachelor of Letters**) *(person)* = titulaire d'une licence de littérature; *(qualification)* licence *f* de littérature

blitz [blɪts] **1** *n Mil (attack)* attaque *f* éclair; *(bombing)* bombardement *m* aérien intense; *Fig* **to have a blitz on sth** s'attaquer à qch; **let's have a blitz and get this work done** attaquons-nous à ce travail pour en finir; *Fig* **the blitz of holiday advertisements starts immediately after Christmas** dès que les fêtes sont finies, on est bombardé de publicité par les agences de voyage

2 *vt Mil (attack)* pilonner; *(bomb)* bombarder; **the house was blitzed** la maison a été endommagée/détruite par un bombardement; *Fam Fig* **to blitz sb with letters/complaints** bombarder qn de lettres/plaintes

3 Blitz *n Hist* **the Blitz** le Blitz

blitzed [blɪtst] *adj Fam (drunk)* bourré; *(on drugs)* défoncé

blizzard ['blɪzəd] *n Met* tempête *f* de neige, blizzard *m*

BLM [ˌbiːel'em] *n Am Admin (abbr* **Bureau of Land Management**) = services de l'aménagement du territoire aux États-Unis

bloat [bləʊt] **1** *vt* gonfler, bouffir

2 *vi* bouffir

bloated ['bləʊtɪd] *adj (gen)* gonflé, boursouflé; *(stomach)* gonflé, ballonné; **to feel bloated** se sentir ballonné; **bloated with self-importance** imbu de soi-même, pénétré de son importance; **he suffers from a bloated ego** sa suffisance n'a pas de limites

bloater ['bləʊtə(r)] *n Ich* bouffi *m*

blob [blɒb] *n (drop)* goutte *f*; *(stain)* tache *f*; **a blob on the horizon** une forme indistincte à l'horizon

bloc [blɒk] *n Pol & Com* bloc *m*

block [blɒk] **1** *n* (**a**) *(of ice, stone, wood)* bloc *m*; *(of chocolate)* grosse tablette *f*; *(for butcher, executioner)* billot *m*; *(for athletes)* bloc *m* de départ; *Am* **the painting was on the (auctioneer's) block** le tableau était mis aux enchères; **to put** *or* **to lay one's head on the block** prendre des risques

(**b**) *(toy)* **(building) blocks** jeu *m* de construction, (jeu *m* de) cubes *mpl*

(**c**) *(of seats)* groupe *m*; *St Exch (of shares)* paquet *m*; *(of tickets)* série *f*; *Comput* bloc *m*

(**d**) *(area of land)* pâté *m* de maisons; **we walked round the block** nous avons fait le tour du pâté de maisons; *Am* **the school is five blocks away** l'école est à cinq rues d'ici; **the new kid on the block** le petit nouveau

(**e**) *Br (building)* immeuble *m*; *(of barracks, prison)* quartier *m*; *(of hospital)* pavillon *m*; **block of flats** immeuble (d'habitation)

(**f**) *(obstruction → in pipe, tube)* obstruction *f*; *Am (→ in traffic)* embouteillage *m*; *Med & Psy* blocage *m*; *Fin & Com* **to put a block on sth** *(cheque, account, prices, imports)* bloquer qch **to have a (mental) block about sth** faire un blocage sur qch; **I have a (mental) block about mathematics** je fais un blocage sur les mathématiques **he's suffering from writer's block** il n'arrive pas à écrire, c'est le vide *ou* le blocage total

(**g**) *Sport* obstruction *f*

(**h**) *Fam (head)* caboche *f*; **I'll knock your block off!** je vais te démolir le portrait!

(**i**) *(of paper)* bloc *m*

(**j**) *Tech* **block (and tackle)** palan *m*, moufles *mpl*

(**k**) *(in engraving → wood)* planche *f*, bois *m*

2 *comp (booking, vote)* groupé

3 *vt* (**a**) *(obstruct → pipe, tube)* boucher; *(→ road)* bloquer, barrer; *(→ view)* boucher, cacher; *(→ artery)* obstruer; **don't block the door!** dégagez la porte!; **to block one's ears** se boucher les oreilles; **to block sb's way** barrer le chemin à qn; **that building blocks the sun** ce bâtiment empêche le soleil d'entrer

(**b**) *(hinder → traffic)* bloquer, gêner; *(→ progress)* gêner, enrayer; *Fin (→ credit, deal, funds, account)* bloquer; *Med (→ pain)* anesthésier; *Sport (→ ball)* bloquer; *(→ opponent)* faire obstruction à; *Parl* **to block a bill** faire obstruction à un projet de loi; **the goalkeeper blocked the shot** le gardien arrêta le tir; *Tennis* **she blocked the serve magnificently** elle fit un superbe retour de service

(**c**) *(hat, knitting)* mettre en forme

(**d**) *Comput (text)* sélectionner

4 *vi Sport* faire de l'obstruction

►► *Typ* ***block capital*** (caractère *m*) majuscule *f*; **in block capitals** en majuscules; *Comput* ***block copy*** copie *f* de bloc; ***block diagram*** *Comput & Geog* bloc-diagramme *m*; *Electron* schéma *m* (de principe); *Br Admin* ***block grant*** dotation *f* *(aux collectivités locales)*; *St Exch* ***block issue*** émission *f* par série; *Typ* ***block letter*** (caractère *m*) majuscule *f*; **in block letters** en majuscules; *Am* ***block party*** fête *f* de rue; *Br Ind* ***block release*** = système de stages de formation qui alternent avec une activité professionnelle; *St Exch* ***block trading*** négociations *fpl* de bloc; *Pol & Ind* ***block vote*** = mode de scrutin utilisé par les syndicats britanniques par opposition au mode de scrutin "un homme, une voix"

►**block in** *vt sep* (**a**) *(car)* bloquer; **I've been blocked in** ma voiture est bloquée

(**b**) *(drawing, figure)* colorer; *Fig (plan, scheme)* ébaucher

►**block off** *vt sep (road)* bloquer, barrer; *(door, part of road, window)* condamner; *(view)* boucher, cacher; *(sun)* cacher

►**block out** *vt sep* (**a**) *(light, sun)* empêcher d'entrer; *(view)* cacher, boucher

(**b**) *(ideas)* empêcher; *(information)* interdire, censurer; **to block out the memory of sb/sth** refouler le souvenir de qn/qch

(**c**) *(outline)* ébaucher

►**block up** *vt sep* (**a**) *(pipe, tube)* boucher, bloquer; *(sink)* boucher

(**b**) *(hole)* boucher; *(door, window)* condamner

(**c**) *(nose)* **my nose is blocked up** j'ai le nez bouché

BLOCK VOTE

Le "block vote" donne au vote d'un délégué syndical la valeur non pas de sa seule voix, mais de toutes les voix de la section qu'il représente.

blockade [blɒ'keɪd] **1** *n* (**a**) *Mil* blocus *m*; **to lift** *or* **to raise a blockade** lever un blocus; **to be under blockade** être en état de blocus; *Hist* **to run the blockade** forcer le blocus (**b**) *Fig (obstacle)* obstacle *m*

2 *vt* (**a**) *Mil* faire le blocus de (**b**) *Fig (obstruct)* bloquer, obstruer

►► *Hist* ***blockade runner*** forceur *m* de blocus

blockage ['blɒkɪdʒ] *n (gen)* obstruction *f*; *(in*

pipe) obstruction *f*, bouchon *m*; *Med (in heart)* blocage *m*, obstruction *f*; *(in intestine)* occlusion *f*; *Psy* blocage *m*

blockboard ['blɒkbɔːd] *n Carp* panneau *m* latté, latté *m*

blockbuster ['blɒkbʌstə(r)] *n Fam* (**a**) *(success → book)* best-seller ❑ *m*, livre *m* à succès ❑; *(→ film)* superproduction ❑ *f* (**b**) *Mil (bomb)* bombe *f* de gros calibre ❑

blockbusting ['blɒkbʌstɪŋ] *adj Fam* à sensation

blocked [blɒkt] *adj Fin & Com (account, cheque, market)* bloqué

►► *Fin* ***blocked currency*** monnaie *f* bloquée *ou* non convertible

blocked-up *adj* bouché; **I have a blocked-up nose** j'ai le nez bouché

blockhead ['blɒkhed] *n Fam* imbécile *mf*, idiot(e) *m,f*

blockhouse ['blɒkhaʊs, *pl* -haʊzɪz] *n Hist & Mil* blockhaus *m*, casemate *f*

blocking ['blɒkɪŋ] *n* (**a**) *(of street)* encombrement *m*, embouteillage *m*; *(of port)* blocus *m* (**b**) *Elec (of current)* blocage *m* (**c**) *(of bookbinding)* gaufrage *m*, frappe *f* (**d**) *Theat & TV (of actor, camera)* prise *f* des marques

►► *Comput* ***blocking software*** logiciel *m* de filtrage

block-oriented *adj Comput* orienté bloc

bloke [bləʊk] *n Br Fam* type *m*; **he's a good bloke** c'est un brave type

blokeish, blokish ['bləʊkɪʃ] *adj Br Fam* = typique d'un style de vie caractérisé par de fréquentes sorties entre copains, généralement copieusement arrosées, et un goût prononcé pour le sport et les activités de groupe

blond [blɒnd] **1** *n* blond *m*

2 *adj* blond

blonde [blɒnd] **1** *n* blond(e) *m,f*

2 *adj* blond

blood [blʌd] **1** *n* (**a**) *Anat (fluid)* sang *m*; **to donate** *or* **to give blood** donner son sang; **to shed** *or* **spill blood** verser *ou* faire couler du sang; **she bit him and drew blood** elle l'a mordu (jusqu')au sang; **the blood rushed to his head** le sang lui est monté à la tête; *Fig* **his last question drew blood** sa dernière question a fait mouche; *Fig* **he has blood on his hands** il a du sang sur les mains; *Fig* **his blood is up** il est furieux; *Fam* **the mafia are after his blood** la mafia veut sa peau; *Fig* **the boss is after your blood** le patron en a après toi; **there is bad blood between the two families** le torchon brûle entre les deux familles; **the argument made for bad blood between them** la dispute les a brouillés; **his attitude makes my blood boil** son attitude me met hors de moi; **it's like getting blood out of a stone** ce n'est pas une mince affaire; **her blood froze** *or* **ran cold at the thought** rien qu'à y penser son sang s'est figé dans ses veines; **the film made my blood run cold** le film m'a donné des frissons; *Fam* **a film full of blood and guts** un film gore; **the town's blood is up over these new taxes** la ville s'élève *ou* part en guerre contre les nouveaux impôts; **to do sth in cold blood** faire qch de sang-froid; **travelling is** *or* **runs in her blood** elle a le voyage dans le sang *ou* dans la peau; **what we need is new** *or* **fresh** *or* **young blood** nous avons besoin d'un ou de sang nouveau; **they're out for blood** ils cherchent à se venger; *Prov* **blood is thicker than water** la voix du sang est la plus forte

(**b**) *(breeding, kinship)* **of noble/Italian blood** de sang noble/italien; **a prince of the blood** un prince du sang *ou* de sang royal

(**c**) *Arch (man)* **a young blood** un roué

2 *vt* (**a**) *Hunt (hound)* acharner, donner le goût du sang à; *(person)* donner le goût du sang à

(**b**) *Fig (beginner, soldier)* donner le baptême du feu à

►► *Med* ***blood bank*** banque *f* du sang; ***blood blister*** pinçon *m*; ***blood brother*** frère *m* de sang; *Anat* ***blood cell*** cellule *f* sanguine, globule *m* (du sang); *Med* ***blood count*** numération *f* globulaire; *Med* ***blood donor*** donneur(euse) *m,f* de sang; ***blood doping*** = transfusion sanguine utilisée comme méthode de dopage; ***blood feud*** vendetta *f*; *Med* ***blood group*** groupe *m* sanguin; ***blood heat*** température *f* du sang; ***blood lust*** soif *f* de sang; ***blood money*** prix *m* du sang; ***blood orange*** (orange *f*) sanguine *f*; ***blood plasma*** plasma *m* sanguin; *Med* ***blood poisoning*** septicémie *f*; *Med* ***blood pressure*** tension *f* (artérielle); **the doctor took my blood pressure** le médecin m'a pris la tension; **to have high/low blood pressure** faire de l'hypertension/de l'hypotension; **the patient's blood pressure is down/up** la tension du malade a baissé/monté; *Fig* **her blood pressure goes up every time she talks politics** elle se met en colère chaque fois qu'elle parle politique; *Hum* **watch your blood pressure!** calmez-vous!; ***blood pressure cuff*** brassard *m* de tension; *Med* ***blood product*** dérivé *m* du sang; *Culin* ***blood pudding*** boudin *m* (noir); ***blood relation*** parent(e) *m,f* par le sang; *Med* ***blood sample*** prise *f* de sang; *Culin* ***blood sausage*** boudin *m* (noir); *Med* ***blood serum*** sérum *m* sanguin; ***blood sister*** sœur *f* de sang; *Br Hunt* ***blood sport*** sport *m* sanguinaire; ***blood sugar*** glycémie *f*; **to have low blood sugar** avoir une glycémie faible; ***blood sugar level*** taux *m* de glycémie; *Med* ***blood test*** analyse *f* de sang; **to have a blood test** faire faire une analyse de sang; *Med* ***blood transfusion*** transfusion *f* sanguine *ou* de sang; *Med* ***blood type*** groupe *m* sanguin; *Anat* ***blood vessel*** vaisseau *m* sanguin

blood-and-thunder *adj Literature (adventure)* à sensation; *(melodramatic)* mélodramatique

bloodbath ['blʌdbɑːθ, *pl* -bɑːðz] *n* massacre *m*, bain *m* de sang

bloodcurdler ['blʌd,kɜːdlə(r)] *n Fam (book)* livre *m* d'horreur; *(film)* film *m* d'épouvante; *(tale)* conte *m* d'épouvante

bloodcurdling ['blʌd,kɜːdlɪŋ] *adj* terrifiant; **a bloodcurdling scream** un cri à vous glacer *ou* figer le sang

-blooded ['blʌdɪd] *suff* de sang...; **blue-blooded** de sang noble, aristocratique; **warm-blooded** à sang chaud

bloodhound ['blʌd,haʊnd] *n* (**a**) *(dog)* limier *m* (**b**) *Fam (detective)* limier *m*, détective ❑ *m*

bloodiness ['blʌdɪnɪs] *n* état *m* sanglant; **the bloodiness of war** les carnages de la guerre

bloodless ['blʌdlɪs] *adj* (**a**) *(without blood)* exsangue (**b**) *Mil & Pol (battle, victory, coup)* sans effusion de sang; *Hist* **the Bloodless Revolution** la Seconde Révolution d'Angleterre *(1688-1689)* (**c**) *(cheeks, face)* pâle

bloodlessly ['blʌdlɪslɪ] *adv Mil & Pol* sans effusion de sang

bloodletting ['blʌd,letɪŋ] *n* (**a**) *(bloodshed)* carnage *m*, massacre *m* (**b**) *Med* saignée *f*

blood-red *adj* rouge sang *(inv)*

bloodshed ['blʌdʃed] *n* carnage *m*, massacre *m*; **without bloodshed** sans effusion *f* de sang

bloodshot ['blʌdʃɒt] *adj* injecté (de sang); **her eyes became bloodshot** ses yeux se sont injectés (de sang)

blood-spattered *adj* maculé de sang

bloodstain ['blʌdsteɪn] *n* tache *f* de sang

bloodstained ['blʌdsteɪnd] *adj* taché de sang

bloodstock ['blʌdstɒk] *n Zool & Horseracing* chevaux *mpl* de race *ou* de sang

bloodstone ['blʌdstəʊn] *n Miner* héliotrope *m (pierre)*

bloodstream ['blʌdstriːm] *n Anat & Physiol* sang *m*, système *m* sanguin

bloodsucker ['blʌd,sʌkə(r)] *n Zool & Fig* sangsue *f*

bloodsucking ['blʌd,sʌkɪŋ] *adj Zool* hématophage; *Fig* vampirique

bloodthirstiness ['blʌd,θɜːstɪnɪs] *n* soif *f* de sang

bloodthirsty ['blʌd,θɜːstɪ] (*compar* **bloodthirstier,** *superl* **bloodthirstiest**) *adj (animal, person)* assoiffé *ou* avide de sang; *(film)* sanglant

bloodworm ['blʌdwɜːm] *n Entom* ver *m* de vase

bloody ['blʌdɪ] (*compar* **bloodier,** *superl* **bloodiest**) **1** *adj* (**a**) *(wound)* sanglant, saignant; *(bandage, clothing, hand)* taché *ou* couvert de sang; *(nose)* en sang; **he came home with a bloody nose** il est rentré en saignant du nez; *Fig* **to give sb a bloody nose** donner une raclée à qn

(**b**) *(battle, fight)* sanglant, meurtrier

(**c**) *(blood-coloured)* rouge, rouge sang *(inv)*

(**d**) *Br very Fam (as intensifier)* foutu; **you bloody fool!** espèce de crétin!; **bloody hell!** et merde!; **I can't get the bloody car to start** je n'arrive pas à faire démarrer cette foutue bagnole; **it's a bloody shame she didn't come** c'est vachement dommage qu'elle n'ait pas pu venir

(**e**) *Br Fam (unpleasant)* affreux ❑, désagréable ❑; **he's been perfectly bloody with me** il a été affreux avec moi

2 *adv Br very Fam* vachement; **it's bloody hot!** quelle putain de chaleur!; **you can bloody well do it yourself!** tu n'as qu'à te démerder (tout seul)!; **are you coming? – not bloody likely!** est-ce que tu viens? – pas question!; **I wish he'd bloody stop it!** quand est-ce qu'il va s'arrêter, merde!

3 *vt* ensanglanter, couvrir de sang; **they came out of it bloodied but unbowed** ils s'en sont sortis meurtris mais avec la tête haute

►► *Bot* ***bloody crane's bill*** géranium *m* sanguin; ***Bloody Mary*** *Hist (queen)* = surnom de la reine Marie Tudor, donné par les protestants qu'elle persécuta; *(cocktail)* bloody mary *m inv*; *Br Hist* ***Bloody Sunday*** = dimanche sanglant (le 30 janvier 1972) au cours duquel des soldats britanniques abattirent 13 Irlandais qui manifestaient contre la détention de présumés terroristes

bloody-minded *adj Br Fam (person)* vache; *(attitude, behaviour)* buté ❑, têtu ❑; **he's just being bloody-minded!** il le fait rien que pour emmerder le monde!

bloody-mindedness [-'maɪndɪdnɪs] *n Br Fam* caractère *m* difficile ❑; **his bloody-mindedness didn't help things** son caractère de chien n'a pas arrangé les choses; **it's sheer bloody-mindedness on your part** tu le fais uniquement pour emmerder le monde

bloom [bluːm] **1** *n* (**a**) *Bot (flower)* fleur *f*

(**b**) *Bot (state)* **the roses are just coming into bloom** les roses commencent tout juste à fleurir *ou* à s'épanouir; **to be in bloom** *(lily, rose)* être éclos; *(bush, garden, tree)* être en floraison *ou* en fleurs; **to be in full bloom** *(lily, rose)* être épanoui; *(bush, garden, tree)* être en pleine floraison

(**c**) *(of cheeks, face)* éclat *m*; **in the bloom of youth** dans la fleur de l'âge, en pleine jeunesse; *Chem* **cobalt/zinc bloom** fleur *f* de cobalt/zinc

(**d**) *Bot (on fruit)* velouté *m*

2 *vi* (**a**) *Bot (flower)* éclore; *(bush, tree)* fleurir; *(garden)* se couvrir de fleurs

(**b**) *Fig (person)* être en pleine forme; *(arts, industry)* prospérer

bloomer ['bluːmə(r)] *n* (**a**) *Bot (plant)* plante *f* fleurie; **a night bloomer** une plante qui fleurit la nuit (**b**) *Fam (blunder)* gaffe *f*, faux pas ❑ *m*; **I made a terrible bloomer** j'ai fait une gaffe terrible (**c**) *Br (loaf)* = pain cranté sur le dessus

bloomers ['bluːməz] *npl* **(a pair of) bloomers** une culotte bouffante

blooming ['bluːmɪŋ] **1** *adj* (**a**) *Bot (flower)* éclos; *(bush, garden, tree)* en fleur, fleuri (**b**) *(glowing → with health)* resplendissant, florissant; *(→ with happiness)* épanoui, rayonnant; **blooming with health** resplendissant de santé (**c**) *Br Fam (as intensifier)* sacré, fichu; **you blooming idiot!** espèce d'imbécile!; **he's a blooming nuisance** il est casse-pieds

2 *adv Br Fam* sacrément, vachement; **you can blooming well do it yourself!** tu n'as qu'à te débrouiller tout seul!

Bloomsbury Group ['bluːmzbərɪ] *n* **the Bloomsbury Group** = groupe d'écrivains, d'artistes et d'intellectuels anglais du début du XXème siècle.

BLOOMSBURY GROUP

Les membres du Bloomsbury Group habitaient le quartier du même nom à Londres; ce groupe comprenait notamment les écrivains Virginia Woolf et Lytton Strachey, les peintres Roger Fry et Vanessa Bell et l'économiste John Maynard Keynes. Ce groupe, créé en 1907, évolua en réaction contre les valeurs conservatrices et puritaines de l'époque victorienne, prônant la liberté des mœurs et des idées socialement et politiquement progressistes.

blooper ['bluːpə(r)] *n Am Fam* gaffe *f*, faux pas ❑ *m*; **what a blooper he made!** la gaffe qu'il a faite!

blossom ['blɒsəm] **1** *n* (**a**) *(flower)* fleur *f* (**b**) *(state)* **the cherry trees are just coming into**

blossom les cerisiers commencent tout juste à fleurir; **to be in blossom** être en fleurs; **the chestnut trees are in full blossom** les marronniers sont en pleine floraison

2 *vi* (**a**) *(flower)* éclorer; *(bush, tree)* fleurir (**b**) *Fig (person, friendship, relationship)* s'épanouir; *(arts, industry)* prospérer; **she blossomed into a talented writer** elle est devenue un écrivain doué

►**blossom out** = **blossom** *vi*

blossoming ['blɒsəmɪŋ] **1** *n (of flower)* éclosion *f*; *(of bush, tree)* fleuraison *f*, floraison *f* (**b**) *Fig (of person, friendship, relationship)* épanouissement *m*

2 *adj* (**a**) *(flower)* qui commence à éclore; *(bush, tree)* qui commence à fleurir (**b**) *Fig (friendship, relationship)* en herbe

blot [blɒt] *(pt & pp* **blotted**, *cont* **blotting**) **1** *n* (**a**) *(spot → gen)* tache *f*; *(→ of ink)* tache *f*, pâté *m*

(**b**) *Fig (on character, name)* tache *f*, *Literary* souillure *f*; *(on civilization, system)* tare *f*; **a blot on sb's honour/reputation** une tache faite à l'honneur/la réputation de qn; **it's a blot on the landscape** ça gâche le paysage

2 *vt* (**a**) *(dry)* sécher

(**b**) *(spot)* tacher; *(with ink)* tacher, faire des pâtés sur; **to blot one's copybook** salir sa réputation

(**c**) *(letter)* passer un buvard sur; **to blot one's lipstick** fixer son rouge à lèvres *(en pressant les lèvres sur un mouchoir à papier)*

►**blot out** *vt sep (obscure → light, sun)* cacher, masquer; *(→ memory, thought)* effacer; *(→ act, event)* éclipser

►**blot up** *vt sep (of person)* éponger, essuyer; *(of blotting paper, sponge)* boire

blotch [blɒtʃ] **1** *n (spot → of colour)* tache *f*; *(→ of ink)* tache *f*, pâté *m*;*(→ on skin)* tache *f*, marbrure *f*

2 *vi* (**a**) *(skin)* se couvrir de taches *ou* de marbrures (**b**) *(pen)* faire des pâtés

3 *vt* (**a**) *(clothing, paper)* tacher, faire des taches sur (**b**) *(skin)* marbrer; **her face was blotched with tears** son visage portait des traces de larmes

blotchy ['blɒtʃɪ] *(compar* **blotchier**, *superl* **blotchiest**) *adj (complexion, skin)* marbré, couvert de taches *ou* de marbrures; *(cloth, paper, report)* couvert de taches

blotter ['blɒtə(r)] *n* (**a**) *(paper)* buvard *m*; *(desk pad)* sous-main *m inv*; **hand blotter** tampon *m* buvard (**b**) *Am (register)* registre *m (provisoire)*

blotting ['blɒtɪŋ] *n (of ink)* séchage *m (au buvard)*

►► ***blotting pad*** (bloc *m*) buvard *m*; ***blotting paper*** (papier *m*) buvard *m*

blotto ['blɒtəʊ] *adj Fam (drunk)* parti

blouse [blaʊz] **1** *n (for woman)* chemisier *m*, corsage *m*; *(for farmer, worker)* blouse *f*; *(for sailor)* vareuse *f*

2 *vt* faire blouser; **a bloused top** un haut blousant

blouson ['blu:zɒn] *n Br* blouson *m*

BLOW [bləʊ]

coup de poing	► **1 (a)**
coup	► **1 (a), (b), (e)**
coup de vent	► **1 (c)**
souffle	► **1 (d)**
souffler	► **2 (a), (b); 3 (b)**
faire bouger	► **3 (a)**
jouer de	► **3 (d)**
faire éclater	► **3 (e)**
claquer	► **3 (g)**
gâcher	► **3 (h)**
révéler	► **3 (i)**
quitter	► **3 (j)**

(pt **blew** [blu:], *pp* **blown** [bləʊn]) **1** *n* (**a**) *(hit)* coup *m*; *(with fist)* coup *m* de poing; **to come to blows, to exchange blows** en venir aux mains; **without striking a blow** sans coup férir; *Fig* **to strike a blow for freedom** rompre une lance pour la liberté

(**b**) *(setback)* coup *m*, malheur *m*; *(shock)* coup *m*, choc *m*; **her death came as a terrible blow (to them)** sa mort a été (pour eux) un choc terrible; **to soften** *or* **to cushion the blow** amortir le choc; **to deal sb/sth a (serious) blow** porter un coup (terrible) à qn/qch; **it was a big blow to her pride** son orgueil en a pris un coup

(**c**) *(blast of wind)* coup *m* de vent; *(stronger)* bourrasque *f*; *Fig* **we went for a blow on the prom** nous sommes sortis prendre l'air sur le front de mer

(**d**) *(puff)* souffle *m*; **have a good blow** *(blow your nose)* mouche-toi bien

(**e**) *(of whistle)* coup *m*

(**f**) *Fam Drugs slang Br (cannabis)* shit *m*; *Am (cocaine)* coke *f*, neige *f*; *(heroin)* héro *f*, blanche *f*

(**g**) *Bot (bloom)* inflorescence *f*; **lilacs in full blow** des lilas en pleine floraison

2 *vi* (**a**) *(wind)* souffler; **the wind was blowing hard** le vent soufflait fort; **the wind is blowing from the north** le vent souffle du nord; **it's blowing a gale out there** le vent souffle en tempête là-bas; *Fig* **let's wait and see which way the wind blows** attendons de voir de quel côté *ou* d'où souffle le vent

(**b**) *(person)* souffler; **she blew on her hands/on her coffee** elle a soufflé dans ses mains/sur son café; **he blows hot and cold** il souffle le chaud et le froid

(**c**) *(move with wind)* **the trees were blowing in the wind** le vent soufflait dans les arbres; **papers blew all over the yard** des papiers se sont envolés à travers la cour; **the window blew open/shut** un coup de vent a ouvert/fermé la fenêtre; *Fam* **when did you blow into town?** quand est-ce que tu es arrivé? ❑

(**d**) *Mus (wind instrument)* sonner; *(whistle)* siffler

(**e**) *(explode → tyre)* éclater; *(→ fuse)* sauter; *(→ boiler)* exploser

(**f**) *Zool (whale)* souffler; **there she blows!** la voilà!

(**g**) *Fam (leave)* filer

(**h**) *Am, Scot & Austr (brag)* se vanter

(**i**) *Bot (bloom)* fleurir; *(open out)* s'épanouir

(**j**) *Am very Fam (be disgusting)* **this coffee really blows!** il est vraiment dégueulasse, ce café!

3 *vt* (**a**) *(of wind)* faire bouger; *(leaves)* chasser, faire envoler; **the wind blew the door open/shut** un coup de vent a ouvert/fermé la porte; **a gust of wind blew the papers off the table** un coup de vent a fait s'envoler les papiers de la table; **he was nearly blown off his feet** *(by wind, explosion)* il a failli être emporté; **the wind was blowing the ship southward** le vent poussait le navire vers le sud; **the hurricane blew the ship off course** l'ouragan a fait dévier *ou* a dérouté le navire

(**b**) *(of person)* souffler; **blow your nose!** mouche-toi!; **he blew the dust off the book** il a soufflé sur le livre pour enlever la poussière; **to blow sb a kiss** envoyer un baiser à qn

(**c**) *(bubbles, glass)* **to blow bubbles/smoke rings** faire des bulles/ronds de fumée; **to blow glass** souffler le verre

(**d**) *Mus (wind instrument)* jouer de; *(whistle)* faire retentir; **the policeman blew his whistle** le policier a sifflé *ou* a donné un coup de sifflet; *Fam* **to blow the gaff** vendre la mèche; *Fam* **to blow one's own trumpet** se vanter; *Fam* **to blow the whistle on sb** balancer qn; *Fam* **to blow the whistle on sth** dévoiler qch

(**e**) *Aut (tyre)* faire éclater; *(fuse, safe)* faire sauter; **the house was blown to pieces** la maison a été entièrement détruite par l'explosion; **the blast almost blew his hand off** l'explosion lui a presque emporté la main; **the gunman threatened to blow their heads off** l'homme au pistolet a menacé de leur faire sauter la cervelle; *Fig* **their plans were blown sky-high** leurs projets sont tombés à l'eau; *Fam* **he blew a gasket** *or* **a fuse when he found out** quand il l'a appris, il a piqué une crise; *Fam* **to blow sb out of the water** *(criticize)* descendre qn en flammes; *(beat)* battre qn à plates coutures

(**f**) *(egg)* vider

(**g**) *Fam (squander → money)* claquer; **he blew all his savings on a new car** il a claqué toutes ses économies pour s'acheter une nouvelle voiture

(**h**) *Fam (spoil → chance)* gâcher ❑; **I blew it!** j'ai tout gâché!; **that's blown it!** ça a tout gâché *ou* bousillé, ça a tout fait louper

(**i**) *Fam (reveal, expose)* révéler; **to blow sb's cover** griller qn; **her article blew the whole thing wide open** son article a exposé toute l'affaire au grand jour; *Fam* **to blow the lid off sth** faire des révélations sur qch ❑

(**j**) *Am Fam (leave)* quitter ❑; **they blew town yesterday** ils ont fichu le camp hier

(**k**) *Br Fam (disregard)* **let's go anyway, and blow what he thinks** allons-y quand même, je me moque de ce qu'il pense *ou* il peut penser ce qu'il veut; **blow the expense, we're going out to dinner** au diable l'avarice, on sort dîner ce soir

(**l**) *Am Fam Drugs slang (drugs)* prendre

(**m**) *Vulg (fellate)* tailler une pipe à

(**n**) *Fam (idioms)* **the idea blew his mind** l'idée l'a fait flipper; **the Grand Canyon blew my mind** quel pied le Grand Canyon!; *Br* **oh, blow (it)!** la barbe!, mince!; *Am* **blow it out your ear!** arrête tes conneries et fiche-moi le camp!; **to blow one's lid** *or* **stack** *or* **top** exploser de rage; **our team blew them out of the water** notre équipe les a complètement écrasés; **don't blow your cool** ne t'emballe pas; **blow me down!**, *Br* **well, I'll be blowed!** ça par exemple!; *Br* **I'll be** *or* **I'm blowed if I'm going to apologize!** pas question que je fasse des excuses!

►► *Am* ***blow in*** *(in newspaper)* encart *f* publicitaire volant; *Vulg* ***blow job*** *(oral sex)* pipe *f*; **to give sb a blow job** tailler une pipe à qn; ***blow wave*** brushing *m*

►**blow away** *vt sep* (**a**) *(of wind)* chasser, disperser; *Br* **let's take a walk to blow away the cobwebs** allons nous promener pour nous changer les idées

(**b**) *Fam (astound, impress)* emballer; **the film just blew me away** ce film m'a complètement retourné

(**c**) *Fam (shoot dead)* flinguer, descendre

(**d**) *Am Fam (defeat)* écraser, battre à plate couture

►**blow down 1** *vi* être abattu par le vent, tomber

2 *vt sep (of wind)* faire tomber, renverser; *(of person)* faire tomber *ou* abattre (en soufflant)

►**blow in 1** *vi Fam* débarquer à l'improviste, s'amener

2 *vt sep (door, window)* enfoncer

►**blow off 1** *vi* (**a**) *(hat, roof)* s'envoler

(**b**) *Br Fam (break wind)* péter

2 *vt sep* (**a**) *(of wind)* emporter

(**b**) *(release)* laisser échapper, lâcher; *Fam* **to blow off steam** dire ce qu'on a sur le cœur

(**c**) *Am Fam* **to blow sb off** *(not turn up)* poser un lapin à qn; *(ignore)* snober qn ❑

(**d**) *Am Vulg (perform oral sex on)* **to blow sb off** faire une pipe à qn

►**blow out 1** *vt sep* (**a**) *(extinguish → candle)* souffler; *Elec (→ fuse)* faire sauter; **to blow one's brains out** se faire sauter *ou* se brûler la cervelle; **to blow sb's brains out** faire sauter la cervelle à qn

(**b**) *(of storm)* **the hurricane eventually blew itself out** l'ouragan s'est finalement calmé

(**c**) *(cheeks)* gonfler

2 *vi Elec (fuse)* sauter; *(candle)* s'éteindre; *Aut (tyre)* éclater

►**blow over 1** *vi* (**a**) *(storm)* se calmer, passer; *Fig* **the scandal soon blew over** le scandale fut vite oublié

(**b**) *(tree)* s'abattre, se renverser

2 *vt sep (tree)* abattre, renverser

►**blow up 1** *vt sep* (**a**) *(explode → bomb)* faire exploser *ou* sauter; *(→ building)* faire sauter

(**b**) *(inflate)* gonfler

(**c**) *(enlarge)* agrandir; *(exaggerate)* exagérer; **the whole issue was blown up out of all proportion** la question a été exagérée hors de (toute) proportion

2 *vi* (**a**) *(explode)* exploser, sauter; *Fig* **the plan blew up in their faces** le projet leur a claqué dans les doigts

(**b**) *(begin → wind)* se lever; *(→ storm)* se préparer; *(→ crisis)* se déclencher; **the argument blew up out of nowhere** la dispute a commencé sans raison

(**c**) *Fam (lose one's temper)* exploser, se mettre en boule; **to blow up at sb** engueuler qn

(**d**) *Fam (athlete, cyclist)* s'essouffler ❑

blowback ['bləʊbæk] *n* retour *m* de souffle

blow-by *n Aut* fuite *f* de gaz

blow-by-blow *adj* détaillé; **she gave me a**

blow-by-blow account elle m'a tout raconté en détail

blowcock ['bləʊkɒk] *n Tech* robinet *m* d'extraction *ou* de vidange

blowdart ['bləʊdɑ:t] *n* petite flèche *f*

blow-dry 1 *vt (hair)* sécher (avec un séchoir); **to blow-dry sb's hair** faire un brushing à qn

2 *n* brushing *m*

blow-drying *n* **too much blow-drying can damage your hair** à force d'être séchés au séchoir, les cheveux s'abîment

blower ['bləʊə(r)] *n* (**a**) *Tech (device)* soufflante *f*; *(in ventilation system)* turbine *f* de ventilation; *Aut (supercharger)* soufflante *f* (**b**) *(grate)* tablier *m ou* rideau *m* de cheminée (**c**) *Mining* jet *m* de grisou (**d**) *Fam (whale)* baleine ❑ *f* (**e**) *Br Fam (telephone)* bigophone *m*; **to get on the blower to sb** passer un coup de fil à qn

blowfly ['bləʊflaɪ] (*pl* **blowflies**) *n Entom* mouche *f* à viande

blowgun ['bləʊgʌn] *n Am* sarbacane *f*

blowhard ['bləʊhɑ:d] *n Am Fam* vantard(e) *m,f*, fanfaron(onne) *m,f*

blowhole ['bləʊhəʊl] **1** *n* (**a**) *(of whale)* évent *m* (**b**) *Tech* bouche *f* d'aération, évent *m* (**c**) *(in ice)* = trou où un phoque etc vient respirer

2 blowholes *npl Metal* soufflures *fpl*

blowing ['bləʊɪŋ] *n* (**a**) *(of wind)* souffle *m*; **he could hear the blowing of the wind outside** il entendait le vent souffler dehors (**b**) *(of glass)* soufflage *m*

blowlamp ['bləʊlæmp] *n Br Metal* lampe *f* à souder, chalumeau *m*

blown [bləʊn] **1** *pp of* **blow**

2 *adj* **blown glass** verre *m* soufflé

blown-glass *adj* en verre soufflé

blow-off *n (discharge)* vidange *f*; *Tech (device)* bouchon *m* de vidange

blowout ['bləʊaʊt] *n* (**a**) *Elec (of fuse)* **there's been a blowout** les plombs ont sauté (**b**) *Aut (of tyre)* éclatement *m*; **I had a blowout** j'ai un pneu qui a éclaté (**c**) *(of gas)* éruption *f* (**d**) *Br Fam (meal)* gueuleton *m*; **let's have a blowout** faisons un gueuleton *ou* une grande bouffe

blowpipe ['bləʊpaɪp] *n* (**a**) *Br (weapon)* sarbacane *f* (**b**) *Chem & Ind (tube)* chalumeau *m*; *(in glassmaking)* canne *f* de souffleur, fêle *f*

blowsiness *Am* = **blowziness**

blowsy (*compar* **blowsier**, *superl* **blowsiest**) *Am* = **blowzy**

blowtorch ['bləʊtɔ:tʃ] *n Metal* lampe *f* à souder, chalumeau *m*

blow-up *n* (**a**) *(explosion)* explosion *f* (**b**) *Fam (argument)* engueulade *f* (**c**) *(enlargement)* agrandissement *m*

blow-valve *n Tech (on steam boiler)* reniflard *m*

blow-wave *vt* **to blow-wave sb's hair** faire un brushing à qn

blowy ['bləʊɪ] (*compar* **blowier**, *superl* **blowiest**) *adj* venté, venteux

blowziness, *Am* **blowsiness** ['blaʊzɪnɪs] *n* (**a**) *Pej (untidiness)* aspect *m* négligé; *(sluttishness)* vulgarité *f* (**b**) *(ruddiness)* aspect *m* rubicond

blowzy, *Am* **blowsy** ['blaʊzɪ] (*compar* **blowzier**, *superl* **blowziest**) *adj* (**a**) *Pej (untidy)* négligé; *(sluttish)* vulgaire (**b**) *(ruddy)* rubicond

BLS [ˌbi:el'es] *n Am* (*abbr* **Bureau of Labor Statistics**) = institut de statistiques du travail aux États-Unis

BLT [ˌbi:el'ti:] *n* (*abbr* **bacon, lettuce and tomato**) = sandwich avec du bacon, de la laitue et de la tomate

blub [blʌb] (*pt & pp* **blubbed**, *cont* **blubbing**) *vi Br Fam* pleurer comme un veau *ou* une Madeleine

blubber ['blʌbə(r)] **1** *n (of whale)* blanc *m* de baleine; *Fam Pej (of person)* graisse ❑ *f*

2 *vi Br Fam* pleurer comme un veau *ou* une Madeleine

blubbering ['blʌbərɪŋ] *n Br Fam* larmoiements *mpl*

blubbery ['blʌbərɪ] *adj Fam* plein de graisse

bludge [blʌdʒ] *vi Austr Fam* (**a**) *(shirk responsibilities)* se défiler (**b**) *(cadge)* quémander ❑ (**c**) *(live off the State)* vivre en parasite de la société ❑

bludgeon ['blʌdʒən] **1** *n* gourdin *m*, matraque *f*

2 *vt* (**a**) *(beat)* matraquer; **he was bludgeoned to death** il a été matraqué à mort (**b**) *(force)* contraindre, forcer; **they bludgeoned him into selling the house** ils lui ont forcé la main pour qu'il vende la maison

bludger ['blʌdʒə(r)] *n Austr Fam* (**a**) *(shirker)* tire-au-flanc *m* (**b**) *(cadger)* pique-assiette *mf inv*, parasite ❑ *m* (**c**) *(who lives off the State)* parasite ❑ *m* de la société

blue [blu:] (*cont* **blueing** *or* **bluing**) **1** *n* (**a**) *(colour)* bleu *m*; **dressed in blue** habillé en bleu

(**b**) **the blue** *(sky)* le ciel, *Literary* l'azur *m*; **they set off into the blue** ils sont partis à l'aventure

(**c**) *Pol* = membre du parti conservateur britannique; **a true blue** *(patriot)* un(e) patriote *m,f*, *Pol* un(e) conservateur(trice) *m,f*

(**d**) *Br Univ* **Cambridge/Oxford blue** = étudiant sélectionné dans l'équipe de l'Université de Cambridge/d'Oxford; **the Dark/Light Blues** l'équipe *f* universitaire d'Oxford/de Cambridge; **he got a blue for cricket** il a représenté son université au cricket

(**e**) *Am Fam (police officer)* flic *m*

(**f**) *(for laundry)* bleu *m*

(**g**) *Br & Austr Fam (argument)* prise *f* de bec; *(fight)* bagarre *f*

(**h**) *(idioms)* **out of the blue** sans prévenir; **he arrived out of the blue** il est arrivé à l'improviste; **the job offer came out of the blue** la proposition de travail est tombée du ciel; **her resignation was** *or* **came like a bolt from the blue** sa démission a été une véritable surprise

2 *adj* (**a**) *(colour)* bleu; **to go** *or* **turn blue** *(of sky, litmus paper)* virer au bleu; *(of person → because suffocating, near death)* devenir violacé *ou* bleu; **to be blue with cold** être bleu de froid; *Fam* **I've told you so until I'm blue in the face** je me tue à te le dire; *Fam* **you can argue until you're blue in the face but she still won't give in** vous pouvez vous tuer à discuter, elle ne s'avouera pas vaincue pour autant; *Fig* **to take a blue pencil to sth** censurer qch

(**b**) *Fam (depressed)* triste ❑, cafardeux; **to feel blue** avoir le cafard

(**c**) *Fam (obscene → language, joke)* obscène ❑, cochon; (→ *book, movie)* porno; **to tell blue jokes** en dire de vertes, en raconter des vertes et des pas mûres; *Br* **his jokes turn the air blue** ses plaisanteries sont affreusement cochonnes

(**d**) *Br Fam (idioms)* **to have a blue fit** piquer une crise; **to scream** *or* **to shout blue murder** crier comme un putois; **once in a blue moon** tous les trente-six du mois; *Am* **he talks a blue streak** il n'arrête pas de jacasser

(**e**) *Pol* conservateur(trice) *m,f*

3 *vt* (**a**) *Br Fam (squander → money)* claquer; **he blued his inheritance on the horses** il a claqué son héritage en jouant aux courses

(**b**) *(laundry)* passer au bleu

4 blues *n* (**a**) *Fam (depression)* **the blues** le cafard; **to get** *or* **to have the blues** avoir le cafard

(**b**) *Mus* le blues; **to sing the blues** chanter le blues; *Am Fig (complain)* pleurnicher

5 Blues *npl Mil* **the Blues and Royals** = section de la Cavalerie de la Maison du Souverain britannique

►► *Med* ***blue baby*** enfant *mf* bleu(e); ***blue berets*** casques *mpl* bleus; *Am* ***Blue Birds*** = section du "Camp Fire Club" réservée aux jeunes enfants; ***blue blood*** sang *m* bleu *ou* noble; ***blue book*** *Br Parl* livre *m* bleu; *Am Univ* cahier *m* d'examen; *Am (social register)* = sorte de bottin mondain, ≃ gotha *m*; ***blue cheese*** (fromage *m*) bleu *m*; ***blue chip*** *St Exch (stock)* valeur *f* de père de famille *ou* de premier ordre; *Fin (investment)* placement *m* de bon rapport; ***blue fox*** *(animal)* isatis *m*, renard *m* bleu; *(fur)* renard *m* bleu; *Br Fam* ***blue funk*** sacrée frousse *f*, peur *f* bleue; **she left in a blue funk** elle est partie complètement terrorisée; *Orn* ***blue goose*** oie *f* bleue; *Orn* ***blue jay*** geai *m* bleu; *Am* ***blue jeans*** jean *m*; *Am Fam* ***blue laws*** = lois qui, au nom de la morale, limitent certaines activités telles que l'ouverture des commerces le dimanche, la vente d'alcool etc; *Sport* ***blue line*** *(in ice hockey)* ligne *f* bleue; *Am* ***the Blue Mountain State*** = surnom donné à l'Orégon; *Mus* ***blue note*** = tierce ou septième diminuée, très utilisée dans le blues; *TV* ***Blue Peter*** = émission télévisée britannique pour enfants, à vocation pédagogique; *Naut* ***blue peter*** pavillon *m* de partance; ***the Blue Ridge Mountains*** Montagnes *fpl* bleues *(dans les Appalaches)*; ***blue rinse*** rinçage *m* à reflets bleus; *Ich* ***blue shark*** requin *m* bleu; *Zool* ***blue whale*** baleine *f* bleue

'The Blue Danube' *Johann Strauss* 'Le Beau Danube bleu'

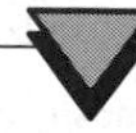

BLUE

Sur la scène politique britannique, la couleur bleue représente le parti conservateur. Dans le milieu des sports universitaires, le bleu foncé est porté par les joueurs d'Oxford, le bleu clair par ceux de Cambridge.

blue-arsed fly [-ɑ:st-] *n Br very Fam* **to run about** *or* **around like a blue-arsed fly** courir dans tous les sens

bluebag ['blu:bæg] *n* sachet *m* à *ou* de bleu

Bluebeard ['blu:ˌbɪəd] *pr n* Barbe-bleue

bluebeat ['blu:bi:t] *n Mus* = genre musical antillais des années 60, précurseur du reggae

bluebell ['blu:bel] *n Bot* jacinthe *f* des bois; *Scot (harebell)* campanule *f*; **bluebell wood** = sous-bois tapissé de jacinthes sauvages

blueberry ['blu:bərɪ] (*pl* **blueberries**) **1** *n Bot* myrtille *f*, *Can* bleuet *m*

2 *comp (jam)* de myrtilles; *(pie, tart)* aux myrtilles

bluebird ['blu:bɜ:d] *n Orn (in America)* rouge-gorge *m* bleu; *(in Australia)* langrayen *m* à face noire; **fairy bluebird** irène *f*, oiseau *m* bleu des fées; **eastern bluebird** rouge-gorge *m* bleu d'Amérique; *(in Canada)* merle *m* bleu à poitrine rouge; **mountain bluebird** merle *m* bleu des montagnes; **western bluebird** merle *m* bleu à dos marron

blue-black *adj* bleu tirant sur le noir, bleu-noir

blue-blooded *adj* aristocratique, de sang noble

bluebottle ['blu:ˌbɒtəl] *n* (**a**) *Entom (fly)* mouche *f* bleue *ou* à viande (**b**) *Bot* bleuet *m* (**c**) *Br Fam Old-fashioned (police officer)* flic *m* (**d**) *Austr Fam (Portuguese man-of-war)* physalie ❑ *f*

blue-chip *adj Com* **blue-chip company** affaire *f* de premier ordre, *St Exch* **blue-chip stocks** *or* **shares** valeurs *fpl* de père de famille *ou* de premier ordre

blue-collar *adj Ind (gen)* ouvrier; *(area, background)* populaire, ouvrier

►► ***blue-collar union*** syndicat *m* ouvrier; ***blue-collar worker*** col *m* bleu

blue-eyed *adj* aux yeux bleus; *Br Fam* **his mother's blue-eyed boy** le chouchou de sa maman, le petit chéri de sa maman; **the boss's blue-eyed boy** le chouchou du patron

bluegrass ['blu:grɑ:s] *n Bot (grass)* pâturin *m* des champs; *(music)* musique *f* bluegrass

►► ***the Bluegrass State*** = surnom donné au Kentucky

blue-gray *Am* = **blue-grey**

blue-green *adj* bleu-vert *(inv)*

►► *Bot* ***blue-green algae*** algues *fpl* bleues, *Spec* cyanophycées *fpl*

blue-grey, *Am* **blue-gray 1** *n* gris *m* bleuté

2 *adj* gris bleuté

blueness ['blu:nɪs] *n* bleu *m*

bluenose ['blu:nəʊz] *n Fam* (**a**) *(of Nova Scotia)* = personne de Nouvelle-Écosse, *Can* Néo-Écossais(e) ❑ *m,f* (**b**) *Am (prig)* prude ❑ *f* (**c**) *Scot Pej (Protestant)* protestant(e) ❑ *m,f*

blue-pencil *vt (edit)* corriger; *(censor)* censurer

blueprint ['blu:prɪnt] **1** *n* (**a**) *Archit & Tech (photographic)* bleu *m* (**b**) *Fig (programme)* plan *m*, projet *m*; *Tech (prototype)* prototype *m*; *Fig* **this project is a blueprint for success** avec ce projet, c'est le succès assuré; **the blueprint for democratic government** le modèle démocratique

2 *vt* tirer des bleus

blue rib(b)and, blue ribbon 1 *n Sport* = premier prix d'une compétition

2 *adj* de première classe

blue-ribbon *adj*

►► *Am* ***blue-ribbon committee*** comité *m* constitué par des personnalités; *Sport* ***blue-ribbon event*** épreuve *f* phare; *Law* ***blue-ribbon jury*** jury *m* d'experts

blue-rinse *adj Br Fam Hum* **the blue-rinse brigade** = vieilles bourgeoises aux idées conservatrices

blue-sky *adj*
►► *St Exch* ***blue-sky law*** = loi américaine qui protège le public contre les titres boursiers douteux; *Ind* ***blue-sky research*** recherches *fpl* sans applications immédiates; *St Exch* ***blue-sky security*** titre *m* hautement speculatif *ou* à haut risque

bluestocking ['blu:ˌstɒkɪŋ] *n Br Hist* bas-bleu *m*

bluethroat ['blu:θrəʊt] *n Orn* gorge-bleue *f*

bluetit ['blu:tɪt] *n Orn* mésange *f* bleue

bluewater ['blu:wɔ:tə(r)] *adj (fishing, sailing)* en haute mer

blue-winged teal *n Orn* sarcelle *f* soucrourou

bluff [blʌf] **1** *n* (**a**) *(deception)* bluff *m* (**b**) *(cliff)* falaise *f*, promontoire *m* (**c**) *(idioms)* **she called his bluff** elle l'a pris au mot tout en sachant qu'il bluffait; **it's time to call her bluff** il est temps de la mettre au pied du mur
2 *adj (person)* direct, franc (franche); *(landscape)* escarpé, à pic
3 *vi* bluffer
4 *vt* bluffer; **don't try to bluff me** n'essayez pas de m'en conter; **to bluff one's way through things** marcher au bluff; **to bluff one's way out of a tricky situation** se tirer d'affaire par un coup de bluff; **we'll just have to bluff it out** nous n'aurons qu'à bluffer

bluffer ['blʌfə(r)] *n* bluffeur(euse) *m,f*

bluffness ['blʌfnɪs] *n (of person)* franc-parler *m*

bluish ['blu:ɪʃ] *adj* bleuâtre, tirant sur le bleu

blunder ['blʌndə(r)] **1** *n (mistake)* bourde *f*; *(remark)* gaffe *f*, impair *m*; **I made a terrible blunder** j'ai fait une gaffe *ou* une bévue épouvantable
2 *vi* (**a**) *(make a mistake)* faire une gaffe *ou* un impair (**b**) *(move clumsily)* avancer à l'aveuglette, tâtonner; **he was blundering about in the dark** il avançait à l'aveuglette *ou* à tâtons dans le noir; **she blundered against** *or* **into the bookshelf** elle s'est heurtée *ou* cognée à la bibliothèque; **he blundered through the interview** il s'embrouillait au cours de l'entretien

blunderbuss ['blʌndəbʌs] *n Hist* tromblon *m*

blunderer ['blʌndərə(r)] *n* gaffeur(euse) *m,f*

blundering ['blʌndərɪŋ] **1** *adj (person)* maladroit, gaffeur; *(action, remark)* maladroit, malavisé
2 *n* maladresse *f*, gaucherie *f*

blunderingly ['blʌndərɪŋlɪ] *adv* avec maladresse

blunt [blʌnt] **1** *adj* (**a**) *(blade)* peu tranchant, émoussé; *(point)* émoussé, épointé; *(pencil)* mal taillé, épointé; *(instrument)* contondant (**b**) *(frank → person, reply)* direct, franc (franche); *(refusal)* catégorique; **he was quite blunt about it** il n'a pas mâché ses mots; **let me be blunt** permettez que je parle franchement
2 *vt (blade)* émousser; *(pencil, point)* épointer; *Fig (feelings, senses)* émousser

bluntly ['blʌntlɪ] *adv* carrément, franchement; **to put it bluntly,...** (pour parler) franchement,...; **he answered bluntly** il a répondu sans ménagement *ou* sans mâcher ses mots

bluntness ['blʌntnɪs] *n* (**a**) *(of blade)* manque *m* de tranchant, état *m* émoussé (**b**) *(frankness)* franchise *f*, brusquerie *f*

blur [blɜ:(r)] *(pt & pp* **blurred**, *cont* **blurring**) **1** *n* (**a**) *(vague shape)* masse *f* confuse, tache *f* floue; **without my glasses, everything is a blur** sans mes lunettes, je suis complètement dans le brouillard; **my childhood is all a blur to me now** maintenant mon enfance n'est plus qu'un vague souvenir; **when travelling at such speeds, the countryside is little more than a blur** quand on avance à une telle vitesse, le paysage n'est qu'une suite de formes confuses
(**b**) *(smudge)* tache *f*; *(of ink)* pâté *m*, bavure *f*
2 *vt* (**a**) *(writing)* estomper, effacer; *(outline)* estomper
(**b**) *(judgment, memory, sight)* troubler, brouiller; **tears blurred my eyes** mes yeux étaient voilés de larmes; **time had blurred the memory** le souvenir était devenu confus avec le temps
3 *vi* (**a**) *(inscription, outline)* s'estomper; *(judgment, memory, sight)* se troubler, se brouiller
(**b**) *(smudge → ink)* s'estomper

blurb [blɜ:b] *n Mktg* notice *f* publicitaire, argumentaire *m*; *(on book)* (texte *m* de) présentation *f*

blurred [blɜ:d] *adj* flou, indistinct

blurring ['blɜ:rɪŋ] *n* flou *m*

blurry ['blɜ:rɪ] *adj* flou, indistinct

blurt [blɜ:t] *vt* lâcher, jeter

►**blurt out** *vt sep (secret)* laisser échapper; **she blurted out his name** elle a laissé échapper son nom

blush [blʌʃ] **1** *vi* (**a**) *(person → gen)* rougir, devenir rouge; *(→ with embarrassment)* rougir; **she blushed deeply** elle est devenue toute rouge; **he blushed to the roots of his hair** il a rougi jusqu'aux oreilles; **I blush to think of it now** maintenant quand j'y pense, j'en rougis; **I blush for her** j'ai honte pour elle
(**b**) *Literary (flower, dawn)* rougir
2 *n* rougeur *f*; **the blush of a peach** la couleur rosée de la pêche; **a blush rose to her cheeks** le sang lui est monté au visage; **to hide one's blushes** baisser les yeux d'embarras; **"thank you", she said with a blush** "merci", dit-elle en rougissant; *Hum* **please, spare our blushes!** ne nous faites pas rougir, s'il vous plaît!; **the first blush of dawn** les premières rougeurs *fpl* de l'aube; **she was in the first blush of youth** elle était dans la prime fleur de l'âge; *Br* **at first blush** de prime abord, à première vue
►► ***blush wine*** vin *m* rosé très léger

blusher ['blʌʃə(r)] *n* (**a**) *(make-up)* fard *m* à joues, blush *m*
(**b**) *Bot* golmote *f*, golmotte *f*

blushing ['blʌʃɪŋ] **1** *adj* (**a**) *(person)* rougissant; **the blushing bride** la mariée (**b**) *Literary (flower, dawn)* rouge, rougissant
2 *n* rougissement *m*

blushingly ['blʌʃɪŋlɪ] *adv* en rougissant, timidement

bluster ['blʌstə(r)] **1** *vi* (**a**) *(wind)* faire rage, souffler en rafales; *(storm)* faire rage, se déchaîner
(**b**) *(speak angrily)* fulminer, tempêter
(**c**) *(boast)* se vanter, fanfaronner
2 *vt (person)* intimider; **he tried to bluster his way out of doing it** il a essayé de se défiler avec de grandes phrases
3 *n (UNCOUNT)* (**a**) *(boasting)* fanfaronnades *fpl*; **I wasn't impressed by his bluster** ses grands cris ne m'impressionnaient pas; **his threats were no more than bluster** ses menaces n'étaient en fait que du vent
(**b**) *(wind)* rafale *f*

blusterer ['blʌstərə(r)] *n* fanfaron *m*, bravache *m*

blustering ['blʌstərɪŋ] **1** *n (UNCOUNT)* fanfaronnades *fpl*
2 *adj* fanfaron

blustery ['blʌstərɪ] *adj (weather)* venteux, à bourrasques; *(wind)* qui souffle en rafales, de tempête

Blvd *(written abbr* **boulevard**) bd, boul

BM [ˌbi:'em] *n* (**a**) *(abbr* **Bachelor of Medicine**) *(person)* = titulaire d'une licence de médecine; *(qualification)* licence *f* de médecine (**b**) *(abbr* **British Museum**) **the BM** le British Museum

BMA [ˌbi:em'eɪ] *n Med (abbr* **British Medical Association**) = ordre britannique des médecins

BMJ [ˌbi:em'dʒeɪ] *n (abbr* **British Medical Journal**) = organe de la "British Medical Association"

B-movie *n Cin* film *m* de série B; **he was a B-movie actor** c'était un acteur de série B

BMus *n (written abbr* **Bachelor of Music**) *(person)* = titulaire d'une licence de musique; *(qualification)* licence *f* de musique

BMX [ˌbi:em'eks] *n (abbr* **bicycle motorcross**) *(bicycle)* VTT *m*; *(sport, activity)* cyclo-cross *m inv*

bn *(written abbr* **billion**) milliard *m*

BNP [ˌbi:en'pi:] *n Pol (abbr* **British National Party**) = parti d'extrême-droite britannique

BO [ˌbi:'əʊ] *n Fam (abbr* **body odour**) odeur *f* corporelle ☐; **he's got BO** il sent mauvais

boa ['bəʊə] *n* (**a**) **(feather) boa** boa *m* (**b**) *Zool* boa *m*
►► *Zool* ***boa constrictor*** boa constricteur *m*, constrictor *m*

Boadicea [ˌbəʊdɪ'sɪə] *pr n Antiq* Boadicée

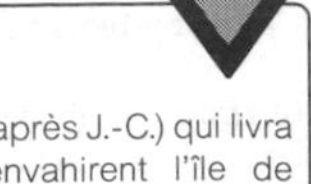

BOADICEA

Reine des Icéniens (1er siècle après J.-C.) qui livra bataille aux Romains qui envahirent l'île de Bretagne, toujours représentée dans l'imagerie populaire en train de conduire un char.

boar [bɔ:(r)] *n (male pig)* verrat *m*; *(wild pig)* sanglier *m*; **young (wild) boar** marcassin *m*
►► ***boar's head*** hure *f* de sanglier

board [bɔ:d] **1** *n* (**a**) *(plank)* planche *f*; *Theat* **the boards** la scène, les planches *fpl*
(**b**) *(cardboard)* carton *m*; **the boards** *(of book)* les plats *mpl*
(**c**) *(for games)* tableau *m*; *(for draughts)* damier *m*; *(for chess)* échiquier *m*
(**d**) *(notice board)* tableau *m*; *Sch* **to write sth on the board** écrire qch au tableau
(**e**) *Admin & Com* conseil *m*, commission *f*; **to be on the board** faire partie *ou* être membre du conseil d'administration; **the bank is represented on the board** la banque fait partie du conseil
(**f**) *(meals provided)* pension *f*; *Arch (table)* table *f*; *Br* **board and lodging,** *Am* **board and room** (chambre *f* et) pension *f*
(**g**) *Aviat & Naut* bord *m*; **to go on board** monter à bord, embarquer; **we're on board** nous sommes à bord; **they took provisions on board** ils ont embarqué des provisions; *Br* **to go by the board** être abandonné *ou* oublié; **in the excitement the normal routine went by the board** dans l'agitation la routine habituelle a été abandonnée; **his principles went by the board** il a dû abandonner ses principes; *Fig* **to take sth on board** tenir compte de qch
(**h**) *Comput (in PC)* carte *f*; *(in mainframe)* panneau *m*; **on board** installé
2 *comp Admin (decision)* du conseil d'administration
3 *vt* (**a**) *(plane, ship)* monter à bord de; *(bus, train)* monter dans; *Mil & Naut (in attack)* monter *ou* prendre à l'abordage
(**b**) *(cover with planks)* couvrir de planches
(**c**) *(provide meals, lodging)* prendre en pension
4 *vi* (**a**) *(lodge)* être en pension; **to board with sb** être pensionnaire chez qn
(**b**) *(passenger)* monter à bord, embarquer; **the flight is now boarding at gate 3** embarquement immédiat du vol porte 3
►► ***Board of Customs and Excise*** = douane britannique; ***board of directors*** conseil *m* d'administration; *Am Sch* ***Board of Education*** conseil *m* d'administration *(d'un établissement scolaire)*; ***board of examiners*** jury *m* d'examen; ***board game*** jeu *m* de société; *Br* ***board of governors*** ≃ conseil *m* d'administration *(d'un établissement scolaire)*; *Am* ***the board of health*** le service municipal d'hygiène; *Mil* le conseil de révision; ***board of inquiry*** commission *f* d'enquête; *Com* ***board meeting*** réunion *f* du conseil d'administration; *Com* ***board member*** membre *m* du conseil d'administration; *Am Univ* ***board of regents*** ≃ conseil *m* d'administration *(d'un établissement scolaire)*; *Austr Fam* ***board shorts*** slip *m* de bain ☐; *TV* ***board test*** animatique *f*; *Com* ***the Board of Trade*** *(in UK)* le ministère du Commerce; *(in US)* la chambre de commerce; ***board of trustees*** conseil *m* de gestion

►**board out** *vt sep* **she boards the children out with us** elle met les enfants en pension chez nous

►**board up** *vt sep* couvrir de planches; *(door, window)* boucher, obturer

boarder ['bɔ:də(r)] *n* pensionnaire *mf*; *Sch* interne *mf*, pensionnaire *mf*; **she takes in boarders** elle prend des pensionnaires

boarding ['bɔ:dɪŋ] *n* (**a**) *(UNCOUNT) (gen) & Fencing* planches *fpl*; *(floor)* planchéiage *m*
(**b**) *(embarking) Aviat & Naut* embarquement *m*; *Naut & Mil (in attack)* abordage *m*
►► *Aviat* ***boarding card*** carte *f* d'embarquement; ***boarding house*** pension *f*; *Sch* internat *m*; ***boarding party*** *Naut (for inspection)* détachement *m* de visite; *(of pirates)* détachement *m* d'abordage; *Aviat* ***boarding pass*** carte *f* d'embarquement; ***boarding school*** internat *m*, pensionnat *m*; **to go to boarding school** être interne; **they sent their children to boarding school** ils ont mis leurs enfants en internat

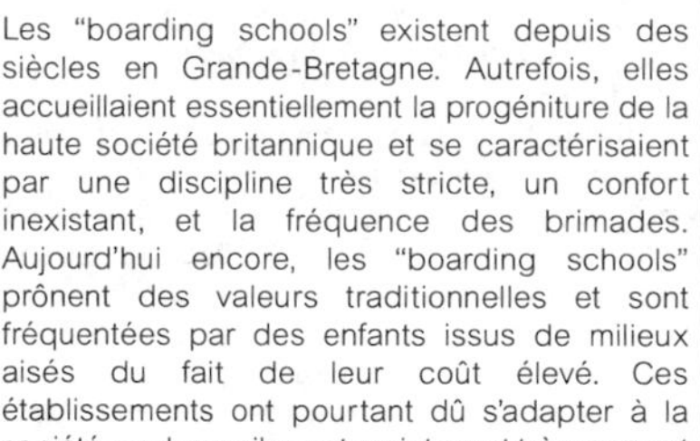

BOARDING SCHOOLS

Les "boarding schools" existent depuis des siècles en Grande-Bretagne. Autrefois, elles accueillaient essentiellement la progéniture de la haute société britannique et se caractérisaient par une discipline très stricte, un confort inexistant, et la fréquence des brimades. Aujourd'hui encore, les "boarding schools" prônent des valeurs traditionnelles et sont fréquentées par des enfants issus de milieux aisés du fait de leur coût élevé. Ces établissements ont pourtant dû s'adapter à la société moderne: ils sont maintenant très souvent mixtes et acceptent des pensionnaires d'origine sociale un peu plus variée qu'autrefois.

boarding-house reach *n Am Fam* = fait de passer le bras devant son voisin, à table

boardroom ['bɔːdrʊm] *n Com* salle *f* de conférence; *Fig (management)* administration *f*; **to be promoted to the boardroom** être promu au conseil d'administration; **the decision was taken at boardroom level** la décision a été prise au niveau de la direction

boardsail ['bɔːdseɪl] *vi Sport* faire de la planche à voile

boardsailing ['bɔːdseɪlɪŋ] *n Sport* planche *f* à voile; **to go boardsailing** faire de la planche à voile

boardwalk ['bɔːdwɔːk] *n Am* passage *m* en bois; *(on beach)* promenade *f* (en planches)

boast [bəʊst] **1** *n* (**a**) *(brag)* fanfaronnade *f*; **it's his proud boast that he has never lost a game** il se vante de n'avoir jamais perdu un jeu

(**b**) *Sport (in squash)* bosse *f*

2 *vi* se vanter, fanfaronner; **failing the exam is nothing to boast about** il n'y a pas de quoi se vanter d'avoir raté l'examen; **without boasting** *or* **wanting to boast** sans vouloir me vanter

3 *vt* (**a**) *(brag)* se vanter de; **he boasted that he could beat me** il s'est vanté de pouvoir me battre

(**b**) *(possess)* être fier d'avoir; **the town boasts an excellent symphonic orchestra** la ville se glorifie d'avoir un excellent orchestre symphonique; **the entire town boasts just one pub** il n'y a qu'un seul pub dans toute la ville

boaster ['bəʊstə(r)] *n* fanfaron(onne) *m,f*, vantard(e) *m,f*

boastful ['bəʊstfʊl] *adj* fanfaron, vantard

boastfully ['bəʊstfʊlɪ] *adv* en se vantant

boastfulness ['bəʊstfʊlnɪs] *n* fanfaronnades *fpl*, vantardise *f*

boasting ['bəʊstɪŋ] *n (UNCOUNT)* vantardise *f*, fanfaronnade *f*, fanfaronnades *fpl*

boat [bəʊt] **1** *n (gen)* bateau *m*; *(for rowing)* barque *f*, canot *m*; *(for sailing)* voilier *m*; *(ship)* navire *m*, paquebot *m*; **we're travelling by boat** nous voyageons en bateau; **I caught the boat at Singapore** j'ai embarqué *ou* pris le bateau à Singapour; **to go by boat** prendre le bateau; **they crossed the Atlantic by boat** ils ont traversé l'Atlantique en bateau; **to take to the boats** monter dans les canots de sauvetage; *Fig* **we're all in the same boat** nous sommes tous logés à la même enseigne

2 *vi* voyager en bateau; **to go boating** aller se promener en bateau; **he boated up/down the river** il a remonté/descendu le fleuve en bateau

►► *Naut* ***boat deck*** pont *m* des embarcations; ***boat drill*** manœuvres *fpl* d'évacuation; ***boat neck*** *(on dress, jumper)* encolure *f* bateau; *Hist* ***boat people*** boat people *mpl*; ***the Boat Race*** = course universitaire annuelle d'aviron sur la Tamise entre les universités d'Oxford et de Cambridge; ***boat race*** *(event)* course *f* d'avirons; *Naut* régates *fpl*; *SEng Fam (rhyming slang* **face**) tronche *f*, trombine *f*; *Am* ***boat slip*** poste *m* à quai, poste *m* d'amarrage; ***boat train*** = train qui assure la correspondance avec un bateau

boatbuilder ['bəʊt,bɪldə(r)] *n Naut* constructeur *m* naval

boater ['bəʊtə(r)] *n (hat)* canotier *m*

boathook ['bəʊthʊk] *n Naut* gaffe *f*

boathouse ['bəʊthaʊs, *pl* -haʊzɪz] *n Naut* abri *m ou* hangar *m* à bateaux

boating ['bəʊtɪŋ] *Naut* **1** *n* canotage *m*

2 *comp (accident, enthusiast, trip)* de canotage; *(lake)* de plaisance

boatkeeper ['bəʊt,kiːpə(r)] *n Naut* (**a**) *(in the navy)* homme *m* de garde *(d'une embarcation)* (**b**) *(boathouse employee)* employé *m* d'un hangar pour canots (**c**) *(person who hires out boats)* loueur *m* d'embarcations

boatload ['bəʊtləʊd] *n (merchandise)* cargaison *f*; *(people)* plein bateau *m*; **six boatloads of refugees** six bateaux pleins de réfugiés

boatman ['bəʊtmən] *(pl* **boatmen** [-mən]) *n Naut (rower)* passeur *m*; *(renter of boats)* loueur *m* de canots

boatswain ['bəʊsən] *n Naut* maître *m* d'équipage

►► ***boatswain's chair*** sellette *f*; ***boatswain's mate*** second maître *m*

boatyard ['bəʊtjɑːd] *n Naut* chantier *m* de construction navale

Bob [bɒb] *n Fam* **Bob's your uncle!** et voilà le travail!

►► ***Bob Cratchit*** = personnage du roman de Dickens 'A Christmas Carol', le type même de l'homme pauvre mais bon

bob [bɒb] *(pt & pp* **bobbed,** *cont* **bobbing,** *pl sense* (**f**) **inv**) **1** *vi* (**a**) *(move)* **to bob up and down** *(cork, buoy)* danser sur l'eau; **I could see his head bobbing up and down behind the wall** je voyais par moments sa tête surgir de derrière le mur; **to bob for apples** = essayer d'attraper avec les dents des pommes flottant dans une bassine d'eau à Halloween

(**b**) *(curtsy)* faire une petite révérence

(**c**) *(move quickly)* **to bob in/out** entrer/sortir rapidement; **to bob up and down** *(in one's seat)* s'agiter

(**d**) *Sport (bobsleigh)* faire du bobsleigh

2 *vt* (**a**) *(move up and down)* faire monter et descendre; **she bobbed a curtsy** elle a fait une petite révérence

(**b**) *(hair)* couper au carré; **to have one's hair bobbed** se faire couper les cheveux au carré

(**c**) *(horse's tail)* écourter

3 *n* (**a**) *(abrupt movement)* petit coup *m*, petite secousse *f*; *(of head)* hochement *m ou* salut *m* de tête; *(curtsy)* petite révérence *f*

(**b**) *(hairstyle)* (coupe *f* au) carré *m*; **to wear one's hair in a bob** avoir les cheveux coupés au carré; **to have a bob** avoir une coupe au carré, avoir un carré

(**c**) *(horse's tail)* queue *f* écourtée

(**d**) *(fishing float)* flotteur *m*, bouchon *m*; *(weight)* plomb *m*

(**e**) *Sport (bobsleigh)* bobsleigh *m*, bob *m*; *(runner)* patin *m*

(**f**) *Br Fam Old-fashioned (shilling)* shilling ❑ *m*; **that must cost a few bob** ça ne doit pas être donné; **he's not short of a bob or two** il n'est pas dans l'indigence, il a de quoi

(**g**) *Fam (idioms)* **all my bits and bobs** toutes mes petites affaires; **we'll deal with the bits and bobs later** nous nous occuperons des détails plus tard; **I've brought a few bits and bobs for lunch** j'ai apporté quelques bricoles pour le déjeuner

►**bob down** *vi* se baisser subitement; *(duck)* baisser la tête; **the children bobbed down out of sight** les enfants se baissèrent subitement hors de notre vue

►**bob up** *vi* remonter tout d'un coup

Bob-a-Job Week *n Br* = semaine pendant laquelle les scouts collectent des fonds en effectuant des petits travaux chez des particuliers

bobbed ['bɒbd] *adj* (**a**) *(hair)* coupé au carré (**b**) *(tail)* écourté

bobbin ['bɒbɪn] *n* (**a**) *Tex (gen)* bobine *f*; *(for lace)* fuseau *m* (**b**) *Elec* corps *m* de bobine

►► *Tech* ***bobbin frame*** bobinoir *m*; ***bobbin lace*** dentelle *f* aux fuseaux; *Tech* ***bobbin winder*** bobineuse *f*

bobble ['bɒbəl] **1** *n* (**a**) *(bobbing movement)* secousse *f*, saccade *f* (**b**) *(pompom)* pompon *m* (**c**) *Am Fam (mistake)* boulette *f*

2 *vt Am Fam* **he bobbled the ball** il n'arriva pas à bloquer la balle

3 *vi* **the ball bobbled and the player mishit his shot** il y a eu un faux rebond et le joueur a raté son tir

►► *Br* ***bobble hat*** chapeau *m* à pompon

bobby ['bɒbɪ] *(pl* **bobbies**) *n Br Fam Old-fashioned (policeman)* flic *m*

►► *Am* ***bobby pin*** pince *f* à cheveux; *Am* ***bobby socks, bobby sox*** socquettes *fpl (de fille)*

bobby-dazzler [-,dæzlə(r)] *n Br Fam Old-fashioned* **she's a right bobby-dazzler!** c'est un beau brin de fille!; **his new car's a bobby-dazzler** sa nouvelle voiture est vraiment extra

bobby-pin *vt Am* attacher *(avec une pince à cheveux)*

bobby-soxer [-,sɒksə(r)] *n Am Fam* fille ❑ *f*, minette *f*

bobcat ['bɒbkæt] *n Zool* lynx *m* roux

bobfloat ['bɒbfləʊt] *n Fishing* flotteur *m*, bouchon *m*

bobolink ['bɒbəlɪŋk] *n Orn* goglu *m*

bobskate ['bɒbskeɪt] *n Am Sport* patin *m* à double lame

bobsled ['bɒbsled], **bobsleigh** ['bɒbsleɪ] **1** *n* bobsleigh *m*, bob *m*

2 *vi* faire du bobsleigh

bobtail ['bɒbteɪl] *n (tail)* queue *f* écourtée; *(cat)* chat *m* écourté; *(dog)* chien *m* écourté

bobtailed ['bɒbteɪld] *adj* à (la) queue écourtée, écourté

bobwhite ['bɒbwaɪt] *n Orn* colin *m* de Virginie

Boccaccio [bɒ'kɑːtʃɪəʊ] *pr n* Boccace

Boche [bɒʃ] *Fam Old-fashioned Pej* **1** *n* Boche *mf*

2 *adj* boche

bock [bɒk] *n* (**a**) *Am (beer)* bière *f* brune forte (**b**) *(glass)* bock *m*

bod [bɒd] *n Fam* (**a**) *Br (person)* type *m*; **he's a bit of an odd bod** c'est plutôt un drôle d'oiseau (**b**) *(body)* physique ❑ *m*, corps ❑ *m*; **he's got a great bod!** il est vachement bien (foutu)!

bodacious [bəʊ'deɪʃəs] *adj Am Fam* génial

bode [bəʊd] **1** *pt of* **bide**

2 *vi (presage)* augurer, présager; **to bode well/ill** être de bon/de mauvais augure (**for** pour)

3 *vt Arch (predict)* présager, annoncer

bodeful ['bəʊdfʊl] *adj Arch or Literary* de mauvais augure (**for** pour)

bodge [bɒdʒ] *vt Br Fam* (**a**) *(spoil)* saboter, bousiller (**b**) *(mend clumsily)* rafistoler

bodhran [baʊ'rɑːn] *n Scot & Ir Mus* = tambourin typique de la musique folklorique irlandaise et écossaise

bodice ['bɒdɪs] *n (of dress)* corsage *m*; *(corset)* corset *m*

bodice-ripper *n Hum* = roman grivois à trame historique

-bodied [,bɒdɪd] *suff* **an able-bodied man** un homme robuste *ou* solide; *Aviat* **a short-bodied aircraft** un avion au fuselage court; **a full-bodied wine** un vin robuste

bodiless ['bɒdɪlɪs] *adj* sans corps

bodily ['bɒdɪlɪ] **1** *adj* matériel; **to cause sb bodily harm** blesser qn

2 *adv* (**a**) *(carry, seize)* à bras-le-corps; **he was carried bodily to the door** on l'a saisi (à bras-le-corps) et transporté jusqu'à la porte (**b**) *(entirely)* entièrement; **she threw herself bodily into her work** elle s'est jetée à corps perdu dans son travail

►► ***bodily functions*** fonctions *fpl* corporelles; ***bodily strength*** force *f* physique

bodkin ['bɒdkɪn] *n* (**a**) *Sewing (needle)* grosse aiguille *f*; *(for tape)* passe-lacet *m* (**b**) *Arch (dagger)* poignard *m*; *(hairpin)* épingle *f* à cheveux

Bodleian Library ['bɒdlɪən-] *n Univ* **the Bodleian Library** la bibliothèque Bodléienne *(à Oxford)*

body ['bɒdɪ] *(pl* **bodies**) *n* (**a**) *(human, animal)* corps *m*; **we belong together body and soul** nous sommes faits l'un pour l'autre; **he gave himself to her body and soul** il s'est donné à elle corps et âme; *Fig* **to have just enough to keep body and soul together** avoir tout juste de quoi vivre; **this obsession with the body beautiful** cette obsession que tout le monde a d'avoir un corps parfait

(**b**) *(corpse)* cadavre *m*, corps *m*; *Fam* **over my dead body!** il faudra me passer sur le corps!

(**c**) *(group)* ensemble *m*, corps *m*; *(organization)* organisme *m*; **the main body of voters** le gros des électeurs; **a large body of people** une foule énorme; **they came in one body** ils sont venus en masse; **taken as a body** dans leur ensemble, pris ensemble; *Law* **legislative body** corps *m* législatif

(**d**) *(mass)* masse *f*; **a body of water** un plan

d'eau; **a growing body of evidence** une accumulation de preuves; **the body of public opinion** la majorité de l'opinion publique; **there is a large body of support for the policy** un grand nombre de personnes sont en faveur de cette politique

(e) *(largest part → of document, speech, e-mail)* fond *m*, corps *m*

(f) *(of car)* carrosserie *f*; *(of plane)* fuselage *m*; *(of ship)* coque *f*; *(of camera)* boîtier *m*; *(of dress)* corsage *m*; *(of building)* corps *m*; *(of musical instrument)* coffre *m*

(g) *(fullness → of wine)* corps *m*; *(→ of hair)* volume *m*; **a wine with (a lot of) body** un vin qui a du corps; **a shampoo that gives your hair body** un shampooing qui donne du volume à vos cheveux

(h) *Fam (man)* bonhomme *m*; *(woman)* bonne femme *f*; **she's a funny little body** c'est une drôle de petite bonne femme

(i) *(garment)* body *m*

(j) *Phys* corps *m*

►► ***body armour*** vêtements *mpl* pare-balles; ***body art*** body art *m*; ***body bag*** sac *m* mortuaire; *Boxing* ***body blow*** coup *m* dur; *Fig* **to be a real body blow to sb's hopes** être un véritable coup porté aux espoirs de qn; *Sport* ***body building*** culturisme *m*; ***body clock*** horloge *f* interne *ou* biologique; *Pol* ***body corporate*** personne *f* morale; ***body count*** pertes *fpl* en vies humaines; *Cin* ***body double*** doublure *f*; ***body fascism*** culte *m* excessif de la beauté physique *(conduisant à un phénomène de discrimination)*; ***body fluids*** fluides *mpl* organiques; ***body hair*** poils *mpl*; ***body heat*** chaleur *f* animale; ***body language*** langage *m* du corps; **I could tell by his body language** je le savais d'après la façon dont il se tenait; ***body lotion*** lait *m* corporel; ***body odour*** odeur *f* corporelle; ***body paint*** peinture *f* pour le corps; ***body piercing*** piercing *m*; *Pol* ***body politic*** corps *m* politique; ***body popper*** smurfer (euse) *m,f*; ***body popping*** smurf *m*; *Sport* ***body rafting*** canyoning *m*; *Med* ***body scan*** scanographie *f*; *Med* ***body scanner*** scanner *m*, scanographe *m*; ***body scrub*** produit *m* exfoliant pour le corps; ***body search*** fouille *f* corporelle; ***body shampoo*** shampooing *m* pour le corps; ***body shop*** *Aut (for vehicles)* atelier *m* de carrosserie; *Am Fam (gym)* club *m* de gym ❑; *Hist* ***body snatcher*** déterreur(euse) *m,f* de cadavres; ***body stocking*** body *m*; ***body swerve*** feinte *f*; *Scot Fam Fig* **to give sb/sth a body swerve** éviter qn/qch ❑; ***body warmer*** gilet *m* matelassé

bodybuilder ['bɒdɪ,bɪldə(r)] *n Sport (person)* culturiste *mf*; *Tech (machine)* extenseur *m*; *Culin (food)* aliment *m* énergétique

bodycheck ['bɒdɪ,tʃek] *Sport* **1** *n (in ice hockey, football)* interception *f*

2 *vt (in ice hockey, football)* intercepter

bodyguard ['bɒdɪgɑːd] *n* garde *m* du corps

bodylock seat restraint ['bɒdɪlɒk-] *n Aut* blocage *m* de maintien du corps

bodyshell ['bɒdɪʃel] *n Aut* caisse *f*, coque *f*, carcasse *f*

body-surf *vi Sport* body-surfer

body-surfer *n Sport* body-surfer(euse) *m,f*, body-surfeur(euse) *m,f*

body-surfing *n Sport* body-surfing *m*

bodywork ['bɒdɪwɜːk] *n Aut* carrosserie *f*

Boer [bɔː] **1** *n* Boer *mf*

2 *adj* boer

►► *Hist* ***the Boer War*** la guerre des Boers

THE BOER WAR

Ce conflit opposa, à la fin du XIXème siècle, les Britanniques aux républiques sud-africaines, qui défendaient leur indépendance face aux ambitions de la "British South Africa Company" et à la suzeraineté britannique. Il s'acheva par une victoire britannique en 1902.

B of E [,biːəv'iː] *n (abbr* **Bank of England***)* Banque *f* d'Angleterre

boff [bɒf] *vt Am very Fam (have sex with)* baiser

boffin ['bɒfɪn] *n Br Fam* chercheur *m* scientifique *ou* technique ❑

bog [bɒg] *(pt & pp* **bogged,** *cont* **bogging***)* *n* (a) *(area)* marécage *m*, marais *m*; *(peat)* tourbière *f*

(b) *Br very Fam (lavatory)* chiottes *fpl*

►► *Bot* ***bog bean*** trèfle *m* d'eau; *Bot* ***bog oak*** chêne *m* des marais; *very Fam* ***bog paper, bog roll*** PQ *m*, papier-cul *m*; *Bot* ***bog rosemary*** andromède *f*; *Vet* ***bog spavin*** jarde *f*

►**bog down** *vt sep* empêcher, entraver; *(vehicle)* embourber, enliser; *Fig* **I got bogged down in paperwork** je me suis laissé déborder par la paperasserie; **let's not get bogged down in details** ne nous perdons pas dans les détails

►**bog off** *vi Br very Fam* dégager; **oh, bog off!** *(go away)* dégage!; *(expressing contempt, disagreement)* va te faire voir!

bogart ['bəʊgɑːt] *vt Fam Drugs slang* **to bogart a joint** squatter un joint

bogey ['bəʊgɪ] **1** *n* (a) *(monster)* démon *m*, fantôme *m*; *(source of fear)* spectre *m*, hantise *f*; *(pet worry)* bête *f* noire (b) *Golf* bogey *m*; **a bogey 5** un bogey 5 (c) *Br Fam (in nose)* crotte *f* de nez (d) *Rail* bogie *m*; *(trolley)* diable *m*

2 *vt Golf* **to bogey a hole** faire un bogey *(jouer un trou en un coup au-dessus du par)*

bogeyman ['bəʊgɪmæn] *(pl* **bogeymen** [-men]*)* *n Br* croque-mitaine *m*, père *m* fouettard; **the bogeyman will get you** le croque-mitaine va t'attraper

bogginess ['bɒgɪnɪs] *n (of land)* état *m* marécageux

boggle ['bɒgəl] *vi* (a) *(be amazed)* être abasourdi; **the mind boggles!** ça laisse rêveur!; **the mind** *or* **imagination boggles at the thought** ça laisse perplexe (b) *(hesitate)* hésiter; **she boggles at the idea of marriage** elle n'est pas sûre de vouloir se marier

boggy ['bɒgɪ] *(compar* **boggier,** *superl* **boggiest***)* *adj (swampy)* marécageux; *(peaty)* tourbeux

bogie ['bəʊgɪ] *n Rail* bogie *m*; *(trolley)* diable *m*

Bogota [,bɒgə'tɑː] *n* Bogota

bog-standard *adj Br Fam* tout ce qu'il y a d'ordinaire ❑

bogus ['bəʊgəs] *adj* (a) *(fake)* faux (fausse); **he's completely bogus** c'est un faux jeton (b) *Am Fam (unfashionable)* ringard

►► *Com* ***bogus company*** société *f* fantôme

bogy ['bəʊgɪ] *(pl* **bogies***)* *n Rail* bogie *m*; *(trolley)* diable *m*

Bohemia [bəʊ'hiːmɪə] *n* Bohême *f*; **in Bohemia** en Bohême

bohemian [bəʊ'hiːmɪən] **1** *n* bohème *mf*

2 *adj* bohème

3 Bohemian 1 *n (from Bohemia)* Bohémien(enne) *m,f*; *(gypsy)* bohémien(enne) *m,f* **2** *adj (of Bohemia)* bohémien; *(gypsy)* bohémien

bohemianism [bəʊ'hiːmɪənɪzəm] *n* vie *f* de bohème

bohrium ['bɔrɪəm] *n Chem* bohrium

bohunk ['bəʊhʌŋk] *n Am Fam* = terme injurieux désignant un travailleur migrant d'Europe centrale

boil [bɔɪl] **1** *n* (a) *(on face, body)* furoncle *m*

(b) *(boiling point)* **bring the sauce to the boil** amenez la sauce à ébullition; **the water was just coming to the boil** l'eau venait juste de se mettre à bouillir; *Br* **the water's on the boil** l'eau bout *ou* est bouillante; *Br* **the pan has gone off the boil** l'eau de la casserole ne bout plus; *Fig* **their romance has gone off the boil** leur histoire tourne au ralenti, leur histoire ne marche plus très fort; *Br Fig* **the project has gone off the boil** le projet a été mis en attente

2 *vt* (a) *(liquid)* faire bouillir, amener à ébullition

(b) *(laundry)* faire bouillir; *Fam* **a boiled shirt** une chemise empesée

(c) *(food)* cuire à l'eau, faire bouillir; **to boil the kettle** *(by gas)* mettre la bouilloire sur le feu; *(by electricity)* mettre la bouilloire en marche; *Br* **don't boil the kettle dry** ne laissez pas s'évaporer l'eau dans la bouilloire; **I can't even boil an egg!** je ne sais même pas faire cuire un œuf!; *Br Fam* **go (and) boil your head!** va te faire cuire un œuf!

3 *vi* (a) *(liquid)* bouillir; **the kettle's boiling** l'eau bout (dans la bouilloire); **don't let the soup boil** ne laisse pas bouillir la soupe; *Br* **the pot boiled dry** toute l'eau de la casserole s'est évaporée; *Fam* **to keep the pot boiling** *(bring in enough money)* faire bouillir la marmite; *Fam* **I'm boiling!** *(very hot)* je crève de chaleur *ou* de chaud!

(b) *(seethe → ocean)* bouillonner; *(→ person)* bouillir; **I was boiling with anger** je bouillais de rage

►**boil away** *vi (continue boiling)* bouillir très fort; *(evaporate)* s'évaporer

►**boil down 1** *vt sep Culin* faire réduire; *Fig* réduire à l'essentiel; **he boiled the speech down to the basics** il a réduit son discours à l'essentiel

2 *vi Culin (sauce)* se réduire

►**boil down to** *vt insep* revenir à; **it all boils down to money** tout cela revient à une question d'argent; **it boils down to the same thing** ça revient au même

►**boil over** *vi* (a) *(overflow)* déborder; *(milk)* se sauver, déborder

(b) *Fig (with anger)* bouillir; **he boiled over with rage** il bouillait de rage; **her resentment boiled over into outright anger** son ressentiment s'est transformé en véritable colère; **the unrest boiled over into violence** l'agitation a débouché sur la violence

►**boil up 1** *vi (milk, water)* monter; *Fig* **frustration boiled up in her** elle commençait à s'énerver sérieusement

2 *vt sep (milk, water)* monter

boiled ['bɔɪld] *adj*

►► *Culin* ***boiled beef*** *(alone)* bœuf *m* bouilli; *(dish)* pot-au-feu *m inv*; ***boiled egg*** œuf *m* à la coque; ***boiled ham*** jambon *m* blanc; ***boiled potatoes*** pommes de terre *fpl* à l'eau *ou* bouillies; *Br* ***boiled sweets*** bonbons *mpl* à sucer

boiler ['bɔɪlə(r)] *n* (a) *(furnace)* chaudière *f*; *(domestic)* chaudière *f*; *Br (washing machine)* lessiveuse *f*; *(pot)* casserole *f* (b) *Culin (chicken)* poule *f* à faire au pot (c) *very Fam Pej* **(old) boiler** *(woman)* vieille peau *f*

►► ***boiler room*** *(in building)* salle *f* des chaudières, chaufferie *f*; *Naut (in boat)* chaufferie *f*, chambre *f* de chauffe; *Am Fin* = organisation qui vend illégalement au public des produits financiers très spéculatifs ou sans valeur; *Br Ind* ***boiler suit*** *(for work)* bleu *m ou* bleus *mpl* (de travail); *(fashion garment)* salopette *f*

boilerhouse ['bɔɪləhaʊs, *pl* -haʊzɪz] *n* bâtiment *m* des chaudières

boilermaker ['bɔɪlə,meɪkə(r)] *n* (a) *Ind (workman)* chaudronnier *m* (b) *(drink) Br* bière *f* fortifiée; *Am* (verre *m* de) whisky *m* suivi d'une bière

boilermaking ['bɔɪlə,meɪkɪŋ] *n Ind* grosse chaudronnerie *f*

boilerman ['bɔɪlə,mæn] *(pl* **boilermen** [-,men]*)* *n Rail & Ind* chauffeur *m*

boilerplate ['bɔɪləpleɪt] *n* (a) *Ind & Metal* tôle *f* à chaudière (b) *(form of words)* paragraphe *m* standard *(que l'on peut insérer dans un document)*

boiling ['bɔɪlɪŋ] **1** *adj (very hot)* bouillant; **the weather here is boiling** il fait une chaleur infernale ici

2 *adv* **boiling hot** tout bouillant; **a boiling hot cup of tea** une tasse de thé bouillant; *Fam* **it's boiling hot today** il fait une chaleur à crever aujourd'hui

3 *n (action)* ébullition *f*; *(bubbling)* bouillonnement *m*

►► ***boiling point*** point *m* d'ébullition; **at boiling point** à ébullition; **to reach boiling point** arriver à ébullition; *Fig* être en ébullition

boiling-water reactor *n Nucl* réacteur *m* à eau bouillante

boil-in-the-bag *adj Culin* en sachet-cuisson

boisterous ['bɔɪstərəs] *adj* (a) *(exuberant)* tapageur, plein d'entrain; **a boisterous meeting** une réunion houleuse (b) *Naut (sea)* tumultueux, turbulent; *(wind)* violent, furieux

boisterously ['bɔɪstərəslɪ] *adv* bruyamment, tumultueusement

boisterousness ['bɔɪstərəsnɪs] *n* (a) *(exuberance)* turbulence *f* (b) *Naut (of sea)* turbulence *f*; *(of wind)* violence *f*

bok choi, bok choy [,bɒk'tʃɔɪ] *n Bot & Culin* pak-choï *m*

bold [bəʊld] **1** *adj* (a) *(courageous)* intrépide, hardi; **a bold plan** un projet audacieux *ou* osé; **a bold stroke** un coup d'audace; **he grew**

bolder in his efforts il s'est enhardi dans ses tentatives

(**b**) *(not shy)* assuré; *(brazen)* effronté; **he was** *or* **made so bold as to disagree** il a eu l'audace d'exprimer son désaccord; **may I be so bold as to ask your name?** puis-je me permettre de vous demander qui vous êtes?; **he put a bold face on it, he put on a bold front** face à cela il a fait *ou* gardé bonne contenance; *Br Fam* **to do sth as bold as brass** faire qch avec un culot pas possible; **he's as bold as brass** il a un culot pas possible

(**c**) *Ir Fam (naughty)* vilain ❑; **you bold boy!** vilain!

(**d**) *(vigorous)* puissant, hardi; **with bold strokes of the brush** avec des coups de brosse vigoureux *ou* puissants; **a bold style of writing** un style (d'écriture) hardi; **in bold relief** en puissant relief

(**e**) *(colours)* vif, éclatant; **bold stripes** des rayures éclatantes

(**f**) *Typ* gras

2 *n Typ* caractères *mpl* gras, gras *m*; **in bold** en gras

►► ***bold character*** caractère *m* gras; ***bold face*** caractères *mpl* gras, gras *m*; **in bold face** en gras; ***bold italics*** caractères *mpl* italiques gras; ***bold print*** caractères *mpl* gras; ***bold type*** caractères *mpl* gras

boldface *adj Typ* gras (grasse)

boldfaced ['bəʊldfeɪst] *adj* impudent; **a boldfaced lie** un mensonge éhonté

boldly ['bəʊldlɪ] *adv* (**a**) *(bravely)* intrépidement, audacieusement (**b**) *(impudently)* avec impudence, effrontément (**c**) *(forcefully)* avec vigueur, vigoureusement

> **To boldly go**
>
> Il s'agit certainement du "split infinitive" le plus célèbre de la langue anglaise, présent dans la formule **to boldly go where no man has gone before** ("s'aventurer là où nul n'est jamais allé") qui figure au commencement de chaque épisode de la série américaine de science-fiction *Star Trek*, qui débuta dans les années 60.
>
> On utilise fréquemment cette expression de façon humoristique en allusion à la série télévisée lorsque quelqu'un se lance dans une aventure dont l'issue est incertaine.

boldness ['bəʊldnɪs] *n* (**a**) *(courage)* intrépidité *f*, audace *f* (**b**) *(impudence)* impudence *f*, effronterie *f* (**c**) *(force)* vigueur *f*, hardiesse *f*

bole [bəʊl] *n Bot* fût *m*, tronc *m (d'arbre)*

bolero *(pl* **boleros***)* *n* (**a**) [bə'leərəʊ] *Mus (dance, music)* boléro *m* (**b**) [bə'leərəʊ, 'bɒlərəʊ] *(jacket)* boléro *m*

boletus [bə'li:təs] *(pl* **boletuses** *or* **boleti** [-taɪ]*)* *n Bot* bolet *m*

bolide ['bəʊlaɪd] *n Astron* bolide *m*

bolivar ['bɒlɪvɑ:(r)] *n* bolivar *m*

Bolivia [bə'lɪvɪə] *n* Bolivie *f*; **in Bolivia** en Bolivie

Bolivian [bə'lɪvɪən] **1** *n* Bolivien(enne) *m,f*

2 *adj* bolivien

3 *comp (embassy)* de Bolivie; *(history)* de la Bolivie

boliviano [bɒ,li:vɪ'ɑ:nəʊ] *n* boliviano *m*

boll [bəʊl] *n* [illegible] *du lin)*

►► *Entom* ***boll weevil*** anthonome *m (du cotonnier)*

bollard ['bɒlɑ:d] *n (on wharf)* bollard *m*; *Br (on road)* borne *f*

bollock ['bɒlək] *Br very Fam* **1** *adv* **bollock naked** à poil, le cul à l'air

2 bollocks 1 *n (UNCOUNT) (nonsense)* conneries *fpl*, couillonnades *fpl* **2** *npl (testicles)* couilles *fpl* **3** *exclam* quelles conneries!; **oh, bollocks, I've got no money on me!** quelle merde *ou* quelle connerie, je n'ai pas d'argent sur moi!

►**bollocks up** *vt sep Br very Fam* semer la pagaïe dans, foutre le bordel dans

bollocking ['bɒləkɪŋ] *n Br very Fam* engueulade *f*; **he got/she gave him a right bollocking** il a reçu/elle lui a passé un sacré savon

Bollywood ['bɒlɪwʊd] *n Cin* = appellation humoristique de l'industrie du film en Inde, formée à partir de "Bombay" (où sont produits la plupart des films) et "Hollywood"

Bologna [bə'ləʊnjə] *n* Bologne

bologna [bə'ləʊnɪ] *n Am Culin (sausage)* = saucisse à base de bœuf, veau et porc, mangée froide

Bolognese [,bɒlə'neɪz] *(pl* **inv***)* **1** *n* Bolonais(e) *m,f*

2 *adj* bolonais; *Culin* **spaghetti Bolognese** spaghettis *mpl* (à la) bolognaise

boloney = **baloney**

bolo tie ['bəʊləʊ-] *n Am* = cordon noué autour du cou et orné d'une boucle

Bolshevik ['bɒlʃɪvɪk] *Hist & Pol* **1** *n* bolchevik *mf*

2 *adj* bolchevique

Bolshevism ['bɒlʃɪvɪzəm] *n Hist & Pol* bolchevisme *m*

Bolshevist ['bɒlʃɪvɪst] *Hist & Pol* **1** *n* bolchevik *mf*

2 *adj* bolchevique

bolshie, bolshy ['bɒlʃɪ] *Br Fam* **1** *n Pol* rouge *mf*

2 *adj* (**a**) *(intractable)* ronchon; **she's in a bolshie mood** elle est de très mauvais poil; **she was a bit bolshie about going to school** elle a un peu rechigné pour aller à l'école (**b**) *Pol* rouge

bolson [bəʊl'səʊn] *n Geog* bolson *m*

bolster ['bəʊlstə(r)] **1** *vt* (**a**) *(strengthen)* soutenir; **he bolstered my morale** il m'a remonté le moral; **it bolstered his ego** ça a fait du bien à son amour propre (**b**) *(pad)* rembourrer

2 *n* (**a**) *(cushion)* traversin *m* (**b**) *Archit* racinal *m*, sous-poutre *f*

►**bolster up** *vt sep Fig (regime, government)* appuyer, soutenir; *(theory)* étayer; **he bolstered himself up with a few drinks** il a bu quelques verres pour se donner du courage; **bolstered up by recent successes** fort de ses récents succès; **these laws simply bolster up the system** ces lois ne font que renforcer le système; *Fin* **to bolster up the pound** soutenir la livre

bolt [bəʊlt] **1** *vi* (**a**) *(move quickly)* se précipiter; **a rabbit bolted across the lawn** un lapin a traversé la pelouse à toute allure

(**b**) *(escape)* déguerpir; *(horse)* s'emballer

(**c**) *Bot (plants)* monter en graine

2 *vt* (**a**) *(lock)* fermer à clé, verrouiller; **did you bolt the door?** avez-vous poussé *ou* mis les verrous?

(**b**) *(food)* engloutir

(**c**) *Am Pol (break away from)* abandonner, laisser tomber

(**d**) *Tech (fasten)* boulonner

(**e**) *(sift)* tamiser, passer au tamis; *Fig (examine)* passer au crible *ou* tamis

3 *n* (**a**) *(sliding bar to door, window)* verrou *m*; *(in lock)* pêne *m*

(**b**) *(for nut)* boulon *m*

(**c**) *(dash)* **we made a bolt for the door** nous nous sommes rués sur la porte; **she made a bolt for it** elle s'est sauvée à toutes jambes

(**d**) *(lightning)* éclair *m*

(**e**) *(of cloth)* rouleau *m*

(**f**) *(of crossbow)* carreau *m*; *(of firearm)* culasse *f* mobile; *Fig* **to have shot one's bolt** *(made final attempt)* avoir joué sa dernière carte

(**g**) *Sport (in mountaineering)* scellement *m*, goujon *m*

4 *adv* **bolt upright** droit comme un i; **he was standing bolt upright** il était debout, raide comme la justice [illegible]

►► ***bolt hole*** abri *m*, refuge *m*; **he used the cottage as a bolt hole** il s'est servi du cottage comme refuge

►**bolt down** *vt sep (food, meal)* avaler à toute vitesse

►**bolt in** *vt sep* enfermer au verrou

►**bolt on** *vt sep* boulonner

►**bolt out** *vi* sortir en coup de vent

bolus ['bəʊləs] *(pl* **boluses***)* *n Pharm* bol *m*

bomb [bɒm] **1** *n* (**a**) *Mil (explosive)* bombe *f*; *Nucl* **the bomb** la bombe atomique; **to release** *or* **drop a bomb** lâcher *ou* larguer une bombe; *Fam* **this room looks as if a bomb had hit it** cette pièce est un véritable champ de bataille

(**b**) *Br Fam (large sum of money)* fortune ❑ *f*; **the repairs cost a bomb** les réparations ont coûté les yeux de la tête; **to make a bomb** se faire un fric fou

(**c**) *Am Fam (failure)* fiasco ❑ *m*, bide *m*

(**d**) *(in swimming pool)* bombe *f*; **to do a bomb** faire une bombe

(**e**) *Fam (idioms)* **this car goes like a bomb** elle fonce, cette voiture; *Br* **the show went like a bomb** le spectacle a fait un malheur

2 *vt* (**a**) *Mil (drop a bomb on)* bombarder

(**b**) *Am Fam Sch & Univ (test)* se planter complètement à

3 *vi Fam* (**a**) *(go quickly)* bomber, filer à toute vitesse; **we bombed down the motorway** on bombait sur l'autoroute

(**b**) *(fail – film, show)* être un fiasco ❑, être un bide; *Am Sch & Univ (– student)* se planter complètement

►► *Mil* ***bomb bay*** soute *f* à bombes; *Mil* ***bomb disposal*** déminage *m*; ***bomb disposal expert*** démineur *m*; *Mil* ***bomb disposal squad, bomb disposal team*** équipe *f* de déminage; *Mil* ***bomb scare*** alerte *f* à la bombe; *Mil* ***bomb shelter*** abri *m*

►**bomb along** *Br Fam* **1** *vi (of car, driver)* bomber

2 *vt insep* **to bomb along the road** bomber sur la route

►**bomb out 1** *vt sep* (**a**) *Mil (destroy)* détruire par bombardement; **the whole street had been bombed out** toute la rue avait été détruite par les bombardements; **he was bombed out (of his house)** il a perdu sa maison dans le bombardement (**b**) *Br Fam (fail to keep appointment with)* **to bomb sb out** poser un lapin à qn

2 *vi Fam (fail)* foirer; **to bomb out of sth** se faire éjecter de qch ❑

bombard [bɒm'bɑ:d] *vt Mil* bombarder; *Fig* **to bombard sb with questions** bombarder *ou* assaillir qn de questions

bombardier [,bɒmbə'dɪə(r)] *n Mil (in Air Force)* bombardier *m (aviateur)*; *Br (in Royal Artillery)* caporal-chef *m* d'artillerie, brigadier-chef *m* d'artillerie

bombardment [bɒm'bɑ:dmənt] *n Mil* bombardement *m*

bombast ['bɒmbæst] *n* grandiloquence *f*, boursouflure *f*

bombastic [bɒm'bæstɪk] *adj (style)* ampoulé, grandiloquent; *(person)* grandiloquent, pompeux

bombastically [bɒm'bæstɪkəlɪ] *adv (speak)* avec grandiloquence; *(write)* dans un style ampoulé

Bombay [,bɒm'beɪ] *n* Bombay

►► *Culin* ***Bombay duck*** = petit poisson séché utilisé comme accompagnement dans la cuisine indienne; *Culin* ***Bombay mix*** = mélange apéritif épicé composé de cacahouètes et de lentilles

bombazine ['bɒmbəzi:n] *n Tex* bombasin *m*

bombe [bɒm] *n Culin (ice cream)* bombe *f* glacée

bombed [bɒmd] *adj Fam (drunk)* bourré, beurré; *(on drugs)* défoncé; **they were bombed out of their minds** ils étaient complètement bourrés

bombed-out *adj Fam* (**a**) *(exhausted)* crevé, nase (**b**) *(very crowded)* plein à craquer (**c**) *(drunk)* bourré, beurré; *(on drugs)* défoncé

bomber ['bɒmə(r)] *n* (**a**) *Mil (aircraft)* bombardier *m* (**b**) *(terrorist)* plastiqueur(euse) *m,f* (**c**) *Fam Drugs slang (large joint)* cône *m*

►► *Aviat & Mil* ***bomber command*** aviation *f* de bombardement; ***bomber jacket*** blouson *m* d'aviateur; *Aviat & Mil* ***bomber pilot*** pilote *m* de bombardier

bombing ['bɒmɪŋ] **1** *n (by aircraft)* bombardement *m*; *(by terrorist)* attentat *m* à la bombe

2 *comp (mission, raid)* de bombardement

bombproof ['bɒmpru:f] *adj* à l'épreuve des bombes

bombshell ['bɒmʃel] *n* (**a**) *Mil (explosive)* obus *m* (**b**) *Fig (shock)* **her death came as a real bombshell** sa mort nous a fait un grand choc *ou* nous a atterrés; **their wedding announcement came as a complete bombshell** l'annonce de leur mariage a fait l'effet d'une bombe; **to drop a bombshell** faire part d'une nouvelle qui fait l'effet d'une bombe (**c**) *Fam (woman)* **a blonde bombshell** une blonde incendiaire

bombsight ['bɒmsaɪt] *n Mil* viseur *m* de bombardement

bombsite ['bɒmsaɪt] *n Mil* lieu *m* bombardé; *Br* **to look like a bombsite** *(of untidy room)* ressembler à un champ de bataille

bombthrower ['bɒm,θrəʊə(r)] *n Mil* (**a**) *(device)*

bol–bom

lance-bombes *m inv* (**b**) *(person)* lanceur(-euse) *m,f* de bombes

bona fide [ˌbəʊnəˈfaɪdɪ] **1** *adj (genuine → excuse, contract, reason)* valable; *(→ agreement, offer)* sérieux; *(→ charity, refugee)* vrai, authentique

2 bona fides [-faɪdiːz] *n Law* bonne foi *f*

bonanza [bəˈnænzə] **1** *n* aubaine *f*, filon *m*; *Am Mining* riche filon *m*; **she had a real bonanza at the sales** elle a fait de véritables affaires pendant les soldes

2 *adj* exceptionnel; **1997 was a bonanza year for them** ils ont connu une année exceptionnelle en 1997

►► *Am* ***the Bonanza State*** = surnom donné au Montana

Bonaparte [ˈbəʊnəpɑːt] *pr n* Bonaparte

Bonapartism [ˈbəʊnəpɑːtɪzəm] *n* bonapartisme *m*

Bonapartist [ˈbəʊnəpɑːtɪst] **1** *n* bonapartiste *mf*

2 *adj* bonapartiste

bonce [bɒns] *n Br Fam (head)* caboche *f*

bond [bɒnd] **1** *n* (**a**) *(link)* lien *m*, liens *mpl*, attachement *m*; **marriage bonds** liens *mpl* conjugaux; **there is a very close bond between us** nous sommes très liés

(**b**) *Law (agreement)* engagement *m*, contrat *m*; **we entered into a bond to buy the land** nous nous sommes engagés à acheter la terre; **my word is my bond** je n'ai qu'une parole

(**c**) *Law (for bail)* caution *f* financière; *Austr (for rented accommodation)* caution *f*

(**d**) *Fin (certificate)* obligation *f*; **long/medium/short bond** obligation *f* longue/moyenne/courte

(**e**) *Chem (adhesion)* adhérence *f*

(**f**) *Typ (paper)* papier *m* de qualité supérieure

(**g**) *Chem* liaison *f*

(**h**) *Constr* appareil *m*

(**i**) *Com* **in bond** en entrepôt; **he put the merchandise in bond** il a entreposé les marchandises en douane; **to take goods out of bond** dédouaner des marchandises, faire sortir des marchandises de l'entrepôt

2 *vt* (**a**) *(hold together)* lier, unir

(**b**) *Com (goods)* entreposer

(**c**) *Law (place under bond)* placer sous caution; *(put up bond for)* se porter caution pour

(**d**) *Fin* lier (par garantie financière)

(**e**) *Constr* liaisonner

(**f**) *(people)* **the experience really bonded them (together)** cela a créé des liens très forts entre eux

3 *vi* (**a**) *Chem (with adhesive)* **the surfaces have bonded** les surfaces ont adhéré l'une à l'autre

(**b**) *(of people)* former des liens affectifs; **we didn't really bond** on n'a pas vraiment accroché; *Hum* **the guys have been away bonding on a fishing trip** ils sont allés pêcher entre hommes

4 bonds *npl (fetters)* chaînes *fpl*, fers *mpl*; *Fig* liens *mpl*, contraintes *fpl*

►► *Fin* ***bond equivalent yield*** = rendement équivalent à celui d'une obligation; *Fin* ***bond investment*** placement *m* obligataire; *Fin* ***bond issue*** emprunt *m* obligataire; **to make a bond issue** émettre un emprunt; *Fin* ***bond market*** marché *m* obligataire *ou* des obligations; *Fin* ***bond note*** titre *m* d'obligation; *Typ* ***bond paper*** papier *m* de qualité supérieure; ***Bond Street*** = grande rue commerçante de Londres; *Fin* ***bond yield*** rendement *m* de l'obligation

BOND STREET

Cette artère commerciale de Londres est surtout célèbre pour ses magasins de mode, ses bijouteries et ses galeries de peinture.

bondage [ˈbɒndɪdʒ] *n* (**a**) *(slavery)* esclavage *m*; *Fig* esclavage *m*, servitude *f*; *Hist* **the serfs were in bondage to the lord** les serfs étaient asservis au seigneur (**b**) *(sexual)* bondage *m (pratique sexuelle où l'un des partenaires est attaché)*

bonded [ˈbɒndɪd] *adj* (**a**) *Fin* titré (**b**) *Com* (entreposé) sous douane

►► *Com* ***bonded warehouse*** entrepôt *m* sous douane

bonder [ˈbɒndə(r)] *n Com* entrepositaire *m*

bondholder [ˈbɒndhəʊldə(r)] *n Fin* obligataire *mf*, détenteur(trice) *m,f ou* porteur(euse) *m,f* d'obligations

Bondi Beach [ˈbɒndaɪ-] *n* = plage de Sydney, célèbre pour ses surfeurs

bonding [ˈbɒndɪŋ] *n* (**a**) *(between people)* formation *f* des liens affectifs (**b**) *(of two objects)* collage *m* (**c**) *Elec* système *m ou* circuit *m* régulateur de tension (**d**) *Constr* liaison *f*

►► *Chem* ***bonding agent*** agent *m* de collage *ou* d'adhésivité

bondmaid [ˈbɒndmeɪd] *n Hist* serve *f ou* esclave *f* célibataire

bondman [ˈbɒndmən] (*pl* **bondmen** [-mən]) *n Hist (serf)* serf *m*; *(slave)* esclave *m*

bondservant [ˈbɒndˌsɜːvənt] *n Hist (serf)* serf *m*, serve *f*; *(slave)* esclave *mf*

bondsman [ˈbɒndzmən] (*pl* **bondsmen** [-mən]) *Hist* (**a**) *(serf)* serf *m*; *(slave)* esclave *m* (**b**) *Law (surety)* **to be bondsman for sb** être la caution *ou* le garant de qn, se porter caution pour qn

bondstone [ˈbɒndstəʊn] *n Constr* parpaing *m*

bondswoman [ˈbɒndzˌwʊmən], **bondwoman** [ˈbɒndˌwʊmən] (*pl* **bondswomen, bondwomen** [-wɪmɪn]) *n Hist (serf)* serve *f*; *(slave)* esclave *m*

bone [bəʊn] **1** *n* (**a**) *(of human, animal)* os *m*; *(of fish)* arête *f*; **the handle was made from bone** le manche était en os; **she's got good bone structure** elle a les pommettes saillantes; **her finger was cut to the bone** elle s'est coupé le doigt jusqu'à l'os; **to work one's fingers to the bone** se tuer au travail; **to be as dry as a bone** *(earth)* être desséché; *(well)* être à sec; *(washing)* être complètement sec (sèche); **bone of contention** pomme *f* de discorde; **chilled** *or* **frozen to the bone** glacé jusqu'à la moelle (des os); **his comments were a bit close to** *or* **near the bone** ses commentaires frôlaient l'indécence; **I have a bone to pick with you** j'ai un compte à régler avec toi; **he hasn't got a suspicious/generous bone in his body** il n'est pas méfiant/généreux pour un sou; **there's trouble ahead, I can feel it in my bones** quelque chose me dit qu'il va y avoir du grabuge; **to make no bones about doing sth** ne pas hésiter à faire qch; **he made no bones about it** il y est allé carrément, il n'y est pas allé par quatre chemins; **she made no bones about her displeasure** elle n'a pas caché son mécontentement; **he'll never make old bones** il ne fera sûrement pas de vieux os; **he's nothing but skin and bone** *or* **bones, he's nothing but a bag of bones** il est maigre comme un clou

(**b**) *(substance)* os *m*; *(in corset)* baleine *f*

(**c**) *(essential)* essentiel *m*; **the bare bones of sth** l'essentiel de qch; **to cut spending down to the bone** réduire les dépenses au strict minimum

2 *vt* (**a**) *Culin (meat)* désosser; *(fish)* ôter les arêtes de

(**b**) *Br Fam Old-fashioned (steal)* piquer, faucher

(**c**) *Am Vulg (have sex with)* baiser

3 *vi Am Vulg (have sex)* baiser, s'envoyer en l'air

4 bones 1 *npl* (**a**) *(remains)* ossements *mpl*, os *mpl*; **to lay sb's bones to rest** enterrer qn (**b**) *Am Fam (dice)* dé *m (pour jouer)* **2** *n Fam (doctor)* **the bones** le toubib

►► *Cer* ***bone china*** porcelaine *f* tendre; *Anat* ***bone marrow*** moelle *f*; *Med* ***bone marrow transplant*** greffe *f* de moelle; *Agr* ***bone meal*** engrais *m* (de cendres d'os)

►**bone up on** *vt insep Fam (study)* **to bone up on sth** potasser qch

boned [bəʊnd] *adj* (**a**) *Culin (meat, poultry)* désossé (**b**) *(corset)* baleiné

-boned [bəʊnd] *suff* **big-boned** bien charpenté; **fine-boned** aux attaches fines

bone-dry *adj (earth)* desséché; *(well)* à sec; *(washing)* complètement sec (sèche)

bonehead [ˈbəʊnˌhed] *n Fam* crétin(e) *m,f*, imbécile *mf*

boneheaded [ˈbəʊnˌhedɪd] *adj Fam (stupid)* idiot ❑; *(stubborn)* têtu ❑

bone-idle *adj Br Fam* paresseux comme une couleuvre

boneless [ˈbəʊnlɪs] *adj Culin (meat)* désossé, sans os; *(fish)* sans arêtes

boner [ˈbəʊnə(r)] *n* (**a**) *Am Fam (blunder)* gaffe *f*, bourde *f*; **to pull a boner** faire une gaffe (**b**) *very Fam (erection)* **to have a boner** bander

bonesetter [ˈbəʊnˌsetə(r)] *n Med* rebouteux(-euse) *m,f*

bonesetting [ˈbəʊnˌsetɪŋ] *n Med* reboutement *m*

boneshaker [ˈbəʊnˌʃeɪkə(r)] *n Fam (car)* tacot *m*; *Hist (bicycle)* vélocipède ❑ *m*

Boney [ˈbəʊnɪ] *pr n Hist* = surnom de Napoléon Bonaparte

bonfire [ˈbɒnˌfaɪə(r)] *n (with fireworks)* feu *m* de joie; *(for burning leaves etc)* feu de jardin; **to make** *or* **build a bonfire** *(with wood, leaves etc)* faire un feu

►► *Br* ***Bonfire Night*** le 5 novembre *(commémoration de la tentative de Guy Fawkes de faire sauter le Parlement en 1605)*

'The Bonfire of the Vanities' *Wolfe, De Palma* 'Le Bûcher des vanités'

bong[1] [bɒŋ] **1** *n (droning sound)* bourdon *m*

2 *vi (drone)* bourdonner

bong[2] *n Fam Drugs slang* pipe *f* à eau ❑, bang *m*

bongo [ˈbɒŋgəʊ] (*pl* **bongos** *or* **bongoes**) *n* bongo *m*

bonhomie [ˈbɒnəmiː] *n* bonhomie *f*

Boniface [ˈbɒnɪˌfeɪs] *pr n* Boniface

boniness [ˈbəʊnɪnɪs] *n* (**a**) *(of face, knees)* aspect *m* anguleux; *(of fingers, arms)* aspect *m* squelettique (**b**) *Culin (of fish)* abondance *f* d'arêtes; *(of meat)* forte proportion *f* d'os

bonito [bəˈniːtəʊ] (*pl* **bonitos**) *n Ich* bonite *f*

bonk [bɒŋk] *Br Fam* **1** *vi* s'envoyer en l'air

2 *vt* s'envoyer en l'air avec

3 *n* partie *f* de jambes en l'air; **to have a bonk** faire une partie de jambes en l'air

bonkbuster [ˈbɒŋkˌbʌstə(r)] *n Br Fam* = roman de gare qui se caractérise par la fréquence des scènes à caractère érotique

bonkers [ˈbɒŋkəz] *adj Br Fam* cinglé; **to go bonkers** devenir cinglé

Bonn [bɒn] *n* Bonn

bonnet [ˈbɒnɪt] *n* (**a**) *(hat → woman's)* bonnet *m*, chapeau *m* à brides; *(→ child's)* béguin *m*, bonnet *m*; *Scot (→ man's)* béret *m*, bonnet *m* (**b**) *Br Aut* capot *m*; **to have a look under the bonnet** jeter un coup d'œil sous le capot (**c**) *Archit (awning)* auvent *m*; *(of chimney)* capuchon *m* (**d**) *Naut* bonnette *f*

►► *Aut* ***bonnet release*** déverrouillage *m* du capot

bonneted [ˈbɒnɪtɪd] *adj (woman)* coiffé d'un bonnet *ou* d'un chapeau à brides

Bonnie Prince Charlie [ˌbɒnɪ-] *pr n Hist* = surnom donné à Charles Édouard Stuart, le Jeune Prétendant

bonny [ˈbɒnɪ] (*compar* **bonnier**, *superl* **bonniest**) *adj Scot & NEng (pretty)* joli, beau (belle)

bonobo [bəˈnəʊbəʊ] *n Zool* bonobo *m*

bonsai [ˈbɒnsaɪ] *n Bot & Hort* bonsaï *m*

bonus [ˈbəʊnəs] *n* (**a**) *(gen) & Com* prime *f*; **to work on a bonus system** travailler à la prime; **a Christmas bonus of £200** 200 livres de prime de fin d'année; *Fig* **the holiday was an added bonus** les vacances étaient en prime; **it's a real bonus having a theatre close by** le fait qu'il y ait un théâtre tout près constitue vraiment un plus

(**b**) *Br St Exch (dividend on shares)* dividende *m* supplémentaire, bonification *f*

(**c**) *Ins (to policy holder)* bénéfice *m* additionnel

►► *Br St Exch* ***bonus issue*** émission *f* d'actions gratuites; ***bonus number*** *(in lottery)* numéro *m* complémentaire; *Mktg* ***bonus pack*** prime *f* produit en plus; *St Exch* ***bonus scheme*** système *m* de primes; *Br St Exch* ***bonus share*** action *f* gratuite *ou* donnée en prime

bon vivant [ˌbɒnviːˈvɒŋ], **bon viveur** [ˌbɒnviːˈvɜː(r)] *n* bon vivant *m*

bony [ˈbəʊnɪ] (*compar* **bonier**, *superl* **boniest**) *adj* (**a**) *Anat* osseux; *(knees, person)* anguleux, décharné; *(fingers, arms)* squelettique (**b**) *Culin (fish)* plein d'arêtes; *(meat)* plein d'os

bonzer [ˈbɒnzə(r)] *Austr & NZ Fam* **1** *adj* vachement bien, super

2 *exclam* super!

bonzo ['bɒnzəʊ] *adj Am Fam* cinglé, fêle

boo [bu:] **1** *vt* huer, siffler; **the audience booed him off the stage** il a quitté la scène sous les huées *ou* les sifflets du public

2 *vi* pousser des huées, siffler; **to boo at sb** huer *ou* siffler qn

3 *n* huée *f*; **her arrival was greeted with boos** elle s'est fait huer à son arrivée

4 *exclam* hou!; *Br Fam* **he wouldn't say boo to a goose** c'est un grand timide ❑

boob [bu:b] *Fam* **1** *n* (**a**) *(idiot)* nigaud(e) *m,f*, ballot *m* (**b**) *Br (mistake)* gaffe *f*, boulette *f*; **to make a boob** faire une gaffe *ou* une boulette (**c**) *(breast)* nichon *m*; **to have a boob job** se faire refaire les nichons

2 *vi Br (make mistake)* gaffer

►► *Fam* ***boob tube*** *(strapless top)* bustier *m* moulant ❑; *Am (television set)* télé *f*

boo-boo (*pl* **boo-boos**) *n Fam* (**a**) *(blunder)* gaffe *f*, bourde *f*; **to make a boo-boo** faire une gaffe *ou* une bourde (**b**) *Am (injury)* bobo *m*

booby ['bu:bɪ] (*pl* **boobies**) *n* (**a**) *Fam (idiot)* nigaud(e) *m,f*, ballot *m* (**b**) *Orn* fou *m*

►► ***booby hatch*** *Naut* écoutillon *m*; *Am Fam (mental hospital)* asile *m* de dingues; *Sport* ***booby prize*** prix *m* de consolation *(attribué par plaisanterie au dernier)*; **to win** *or* **to get the booby prize** gagner *ou* recevoir le prix de consolation; ***booby trap*** *Mil* objet *m* piégé; *(practical joke)* traquenard *f*

booby-trap (*pt & pp* **booby-trapped,** *cont* **booby-trapping**) *vt Mil* piéger

boodle ['bu:dəl] *n Fam* (**a**) *Am (money)* pognon *m*, fric *m* (**b**) *(bribe)* pot-de-vin ❑ *m* (**c**) *Am* **the whole boodle** tout le bazar

booger ['bu:gə(r)] *n Am Fam* crotte *f* de nez

boogie ['bu:gɪ] *Fam* **1** *vi* (**a**) *(dance)* danser ❑, guincher; *(party)* faire la fête (**b**) *Am (leave)* mettre les bouts, s'arracher; **let's boogie on out of here** on met les bouts, on s'arrache

2 *n* (**a**) *(dance)* boogie *m*; **to have a boogie** danser ❑, guincher (**b**) *Am very Fam* nègre (négresse) *m,f*, = terme injurieux désignant un Noir

►► *Sport* ***boogie board*** boogie board *m*; *Sport* ***boogie boarding*** boogie boarding *m*; **to go boogie boarding** faire du boogie boarding; *Am* ***boogie man*** croque-mitaine *m*, père *m* fouettard, *Can* bonhomme *m* Sept Heures; **the boogie man will get you** le croque-mitaine va t'attraper

boogie-woogie [-,wu:gɪ] *n Mus* boogie-woogie *m*

boohoo [,bu:'hu:] *Fam* **1** *vi* chialer

2 *n* pleurs ❑ *mpl*

3 *exclam Hum* sniff!

booing ['bu:ɪŋ] *n (UNCOUNT)* huées *fpl*

BOOK [bʊk]

livre	► 1 (a), (b)
registre	► 1 (a); 4 (b)
carnet	► 1 (c)
pari	► 1 (e)
réserver	► 2 (a); 3 (a)
embaucher	► 2 (b)
comptabilité	► 4 (a)

1 *n* (**a**) *(gen)* livre *m*; *Com & Fin* registre *m*; *Sch* cahier *m*; **a book on** *or* **about gardening** un livre de jardinage; *Tel* **I'm in the book** *(listed in directory)* je suis dans l'annuaire; **not published in book form** inédit en librairie; *Hum* **his little black book** son carnet d'adresses; *Fig* **her face is an open book** toutes ses émotions se voient sur son visage; **his life is an open book** il n'a rien à cacher; **she's an open book** on peut lire en elle comme dans un livre; **to read sb like a book** *or* **an open book** lire à livre ouvert dans la pensée de qn; **mathematics is a closed book to me** je ne comprends rien aux mathématiques; *Br* **to bring sb to book** obliger qn à rendre des comptes; **to do things** *or* **to go by the book** faire les choses selon les règles; **to be in sb's good books** être dans les petits papiers de qn; **to be in sb's bad books** être mal vu de qn; *Fam* **in my book** à mon avis ❑; **he can read her like a book** pour lui elle est transparente; **that's one for the book** *or* **books!** il faudra marquer ça d'une pierre blanche!; **that provision is already on the books** cette disposition figure déjà dans les textes; **that law went on the books in 1979** cette loi est entrée en vigueur en 1979; *Br* **that suits my book** cela me va tout à fait; **to throw the book at sb** donner le maximum à qn

(**b**) *(section of work)* livre *m*; *(of poem)* chant *m*

(**c**) *(of stamps, tickets)* carnet *m*; *(of matches)* pochette *f*

(**d**) *(of samples)* jeu *m*, album *m*

(**e**) *(betting)* pari *m*; **to make/to start/to keep a book on sth** inscrire/engager/tenir un pari sur qch

(**f**) *(script, libretto)* livret *m*

(**g**) *Cards* contrat *m*

2 *vt* (**a**) *(reserve)* réserver, retenir; *Br (tickets)* prendre; **I've booked you on the next flight** je vous ai réservé une place sur le prochain vol; **I've booked her (a seat) through to New York** je lui ai réservé une place jusqu'à New York; **have you already booked your trip?** avez-vous déjà fait les réservations pour votre voyage?; **the tour is fully booked** l'excursion est complète; **the performance is booked up** *or* **fully booked** on joue à bureaux *ou* guichets fermés; **the restaurant is fully booked** le restaurant est complet; **I've booked myself into the best hotel in town** *(in advance)* j'ai réservé une chambre dans le meilleur hôtel de la ville; *(on the spur of the moment)* j'ai pris une chambre dans le meilleur hôtel de la ville; **I'm booked for this evening** *(have engagement)* je suis pris ce soir

(**b**) *Com (engage)* embaucher, engager; **he's booked solid until next week** il est complètement pris jusqu'à la semaine prochaine

(**c**) *Law (of police)* **he was booked for speeding** il a attrapé une contravention pour excès de vitesse

(**d**) *Sport* prendre le nom de

(**e**) *Com (order)* enregistrer

(**f**) *Am Fam* **to book it** *(leave)* mettre les bouts, s'arracher; *(move quickly)* foncer

3 *vi* (**a**) *(make a reservation)* réserver; **to book into a hotel** prendre une chambre d'hôtel; **to book through to Nice** prendre tous les billets nécessaires pour Nice

(**b**) *Am Fam (leave)* mettre les bouts, s'arracher; *(move quickly)* foncer

4 books *npl* (**a**) *Acct, Com & Fin (accounts)* livre *m* de comptes; **to keep the books** tenir les comptes *ou* la comptabilité; **to close the books** clore *ou* arrêter les comptes; **the books and records** la comptabilité; *Fam* **to cook the books** trafiquer les comptes

(**b**) *Admin (of club)* registre *m*; **he's on our books** *(member of our club etc)* c'est un de nos membres; *(player in our team)* c'est un de nos joueurs; *(employee)* il est dans nos fichiers; **I had myself taken off the books** j'ai donné ma démission

►► ***book club*** club *m* du livre; *Acct* ***book debts*** comptes *mpl* fournisseurs, dettes *fpl* compte; ***book end*** serre-livres *m inv*; *Acct* ***book entry*** écriture *f* comptable; ***book entry transfer*** transfert *m* de compte à compte; ***book fair*** salon *m* du livre; *(secondhand)* foire *f* aux livres; ***book lover*** bibliophile *mf*; ***book number*** numéro *m* ISBN numéro *m* de dépôt légal; *Acct* ***book profit*** profit *m* comptable; ***book review*** revue *f* littéraire; *Press* ***book review page*** chronique *f* littéraire; *Br* ***book token*** bon *m* d'achat de livres, chèque-livre *m*; *Fin* ***book value*** valeur *f* comptable, valeur de bilan

►**book in 1** *vi Br* se faire enregistrer; *(at hotel)* prendre une chambre

2 *vt sep* inscrire; *(at hotel)* réserver une chambre pour

►**book out 1** *vi* quitter sa chambre d'hôtel, partir

2 *vt sep* (**a**) **I booked them out at noon** *(they left)* ils ont réglé leur note à midi (**b**) *Br (library book)* emprunter

►**book up 1** *vt sep* réserver, retenir; **the restaurant is booked up** le restaurant est complet; **she's booked up (all) next week** elle est prise (toute) la semaine prochaine; **I'm booked up for this evening** *(have engagement)* je suis pris ce soir

2 *vi* réserver

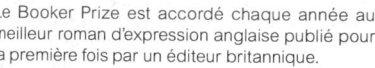

THE BOOK OF COMMON PRAYER

Édité en 1549 avec l'assentiment du Parlement, ce livre de prières introduisit une réforme du culte public, alliant la solennité des cérémonies traditionnelles à un office simplifié en anglais.

bookable ['bʊkəbəl] *adj* (**a**) *Br (seat)* qui peut être réservé d'avance (**b**) *Law (offence)* passible d'une contravention

bookbag ['bʊkbæg] *n Am* cartable *m*

bookbinder ['bʊk,baɪndə(r)] *n* relieur(euse) *m,f*

bookbinding ['bʊk,baɪndɪŋ] *n* reliure *f*

bookcase ['bʊkkeɪs] *n* bibliothèque *f (meuble)*

Booker Prize ['bʊkə-] *n* **the Booker Prize** = prix littéraire britannique

BOOKER PRIZE

Le Booker Prize est accordé chaque année au meilleur roman d'expression anglaise publié pour la première fois par un éditeur britannique.

bookie ['bʊkɪ] *n Fam* bookmaker ❑ *m*

booking ['bʊkɪŋ] *n* (**a**) *(reservation)* réservation *f*; **who made the booking?** qui a fait la réservation? (**b**) *(of actor, singer)* engagement *m*

►► ***booking agency*** agence *f* de réservation; ***booking clerk*** préposé(e) *m,f* aux réservations; ***booking fee*** frais *mpl* de réservation; ***booking office*** bureau *m* de location

bookish ['bʊkɪʃ] *adj (person)* qui aime la lecture, studieux; *(style)* livresque

bookkeeper ['bʊk,ki:pə(r)] *n Acct* comptable *mf*, teneur *m* de comptes

bookkeeping ['bʊk,ki:pɪŋ] *n Acct* tenue *f* de(s) livres, comptabilité *f*

book-learning *n (UNCOUNT)* connaissances *fpl* livresques

booklet ['bʊklɪt] *n* petit livre *m*, brochure *f*, plaquette *f*

bookmaker ['bʊk,meɪkə(r)] *n* bookmaker *m*

bookmark ['bʊkmɑ:k] **1** *n* signet *m*, marque page *m*; *Comput (for Web page)* signet *m*

2 *vt Comput (Web page)* créer un signet sur; **don't forget to bookmark this page** n'oublie pas de créer un signet sur cette page

►► *Comput* ***bookmark list*** liste *f* de signets

bookmarker ['bʊk,mɑ:kə(r)] *n* signet *m*, marque-page *m*

bookmobile ['bʊkməbi:l] *n Am* bibliobus *m*

bookplate ['bʊkpleɪt] *n* ex-libris *m*

bookrest ['bʊkrest] *n* lutrin *m*, support *m* à livres

booksack ['bʊksæk] *n Am* cartable *m*

bookseller ['bʊk,selə(r)] *n* libraire *mf*

bookselling ['bʊk,selɪŋ] *n* librairie *f*, commerce *m* du livre

bookshelf ['bʊkʃelf] (*pl* **bookshelves** [-ʃelvz]) *n* étagère *f* à livres, rayon *m* (de bibliothèque)

bookshop ['bʊkʃɒp] *n Br* librairie *f*

bookstall ['bʊkstɔ:l] *n* étalage *m* de bouquiniste; *Br (in station)* kiosque *m* à journaux

bookstand ['bʊkstænd] *n Am (furniture)* bibliothèque *f*; *(small shop)* étalage *m* de bouquiniste; *(in station)* kiosque *m* à journaux

bookstore ['bʊkstɔ:(r)] *n Am* librairie *f*

bookwork ['bʊkwɜ:k] *n* (**a**) *Acct (accounts)* comptabilité *f*; *Admin (secretarial duties)* secrétariat *m* (**b**) *Univ (academic work)* études *fpl* livresques

bookworm ['bʊkwɜ:m] *n Entom* ver *m* du papier; *Fig* rat *m* de bibliothèque

Boolean ['bu:lɪən] *adj Comput* booléen

►► ***Boolean algebra*** algèbre *f* booléenne; ***Boolean function*** fonction *f* booléenne; ***Boolean operator*** opérateur *m* booléen; ***Boolean search*** recherche *f* booléenne

boom [bu:m] **1** *vi* (**a**) *(resonate → gen)* retentir, résonner; *(→ guns, thunder)* tonner, gronder; *(→ waves)* gronder, mugir; *Mus (→ organ)* ronfler; *(→ voice)* tonner, tonitruer

(**b**) *(prosper)* prospérer, réussir; **business was booming** les affaires étaient en plein essor; **car sales are booming** les ventes de voitures connaissent une forte progression

2 *vt* (**a**) *(say loudly)* tonner; **"nonsense!" she boomed** "quelles idioties!", dit-elle d'une voix tonitruante (**b**) *Am (develop)* développer; *Mktg (publicize)* promouvoir

3 *n* (**a**) *(sound → gen)* retentissement *m*; *(→ of guns, thunder)* grondement *m*; *(→ of waves)* grondement *m*, mugissement *m*; *Mus (→ of organ)* ronflement *m*; *(→ of voice)* rugissement *m*, grondement *m*

(**b**) *(period of expansion)* (vague *f* de) prospérité *f*, boom *m*, période *f* d'essor; *(of trade)* forte hausse *f ou* progression *f*; *(of prices, sales)* brusque *ou* très forte hausse *f*, montée *f* en flèche; *(of product)* popularité *f*, vogue *f*; *Econ* **boom and bust (cycle)** cycle *m* expansion-récession

(**c**) *Naut (spar)* bôme *f*, gui *m*

(**d**) *TV & Cin (for camera, microphone)* perche *f*, girafe *f*; *Tech (for crane)* flèche *f*

(**e**) *Tech (of derrick)* bras *m*

(**f**) *Tech (barrier)* barrage *m* (de radeaux *ou* de chaînes), estacade *f*

►► *Am Fam* ***boom box*** radiocassette❑ *f*; *TV & Cin* ***boom operator*** perchiste *mf*; *Econ* ***boom town*** ville *f* en plein essor, ville-champignon *f*

►**boom out 1** *vi (guns, thunder)* gronder, tonner; *Mus (organ)* ronfler; *(voice)* tonner, tonitruer

2 *vt sep* tonner; **"of course!" he boomed out** "bien sûr!", dit-il d'une voix tonitruante

boomerang ['bu:məræŋ] **1** *n* boomerang *m*

2 *vi* faire boomerang; **his tricks will boomerang on him one day** un jour ses tours lui retomberont sur le nez

►► ***boomerang effect*** effet *m* boomerang

booming ['bu:mɪŋ] **1** *adj* (**a**) *(sound)* retentissant (**b**) *(business)* prospère, en plein essor

2 *n (gen)* retentissement *m*; *(of guns, thunder)* grondement *m*; *(of waves)* grondement *m*, mugissement *m*; *Mus (of organ)* ronflement *m*; *(of voice)* rugissement *m*, grondement *m*

boon [bu:n] *n* (**a**) *(blessing)* aubaine *f*, bénédiction *f*; **the new industrial estate is a boon to the area** la nouvelle zone industrielle est une aubaine pour la région; **her help is a real boon to me** son aide m'est tout à fait précieuse (**b**) *Arch (favour)* faveur *f*

►► ***boon companion*** bon compère *m*

boondocks ['bu:ndɒks], **boonies** ['bu:nɪz] *npl Am Fam* **the boondocks** le bled, la cambrousse; **in the boondocks** à perpète(-les-oies), en pleine cambrousse

boondoggle ['bu:n,dɒgəl] *vi Am Fam* flemmarder, peigner la girafe

boor [bʊə(r)] *n (rough)* rustre *m*; *(uncouth)* goujat *m*, malotru *m*

boorish ['bʊərɪʃ] *adj* grossier, rustre

boorishly ['bʊərɪʃlɪ] *adv* grossièrement; **he behaved boorishly** il s'est comporté en rustre

boorishness ['bʊərɪʃnɪs] *n (roughness)* rudesse *f*, manque *m* d'éducation *ou* de savoir-vivre; *(uncouthness)* goujaterie *f*

boost [bu:st] **1** *vt* (**a**) *Com (sales)* faire monter, augmenter; *Ind (productivity)* développer, accroître; *(morale, confidence)* renforcer; *(economy)* relancer; **a policy designed to boost the economy** des mesures destinées à relancer l'économie

(**b**) *Elec* survolter; *Aut* suralimenter

(**c**) *Mktg (promote)* faire de la réclame *ou* de la publicité pour

(**d**) *Am Fam (steal)* piquer, faucher

(**e**) *Am Fam (break into)* cambrioler❑

2 *n* (**a**) *(increase)* augmentation *f*, croissance *f*; *(improvement)* amélioration *f*; *Com* **a boost in sales** une brusque augmentation des ventes; *Fin* **the announcement gave the pound a boost on the foreign exchanges** la nouvelle a fait grimper la livre sur le marché des changes; **the success gave her morale a much-needed boost** le succès lui a remonté le moral, ce dont elle avait bien besoin

(**b**) *(promotion)* **the review gave his play a boost** la critique a fait de la publicité pour *ou* du battage autour de sa pièce

(**c**) *(leg-up)* **to give sb a boost** faire la courte échelle à qn; *Fig* donner un coup *m* de pouce à qn

booster ['bu:stə(r)] *n* (**a**) *Astron* **booster (rocket)** fusée *f* de lancement, moteur *m* auxiliaire (**b**) *Rad* amplificateur *m* (**c**) *Elec (device)* survolteur *m*; *(charge)* charge *f* d'appoint (**d**) *Am Fam (supporter)* supporter❑ *m* (**e**) *Med* piqûre *f* de rappel

►► ***booster cushion, booster seat*** réhausseur *m*; *Med* ***booster shot*** piqûre *f* de rappel; ***booster station*** *Tel* station *f* relais; *Tech* station *f* auxiliaire de pompage

boot [bu:t] **1** *n* (**a**) botte *f*; *(ankle-length)* bottillon *m*; *(for babies, women)* bottine *f*; *(of soldier, workman)* brodequin *m*; *Sport (for football, rugby)* chaussure *f*; *Fam* **to give sb the boot** flanquer qn à la porte; *Fam* **she got the boot** elle a été flanquée à la porte, elle a été virée; *Br Fam* **they put the boot in** ils lui ont balancé des coups de pied; *Fig* ils ont enfoncé méchamment le clou

(**b**) *Br Aut* coffre *m*, malle *f*

(**c**) *Fam (kick)* coup *m* de pied❑; **he gave the door a boot** il flanqua un coup de pied dans la porte; **he needs a boot up the backside** il a besoin d'un bon coup de pied au derrière

(**d**) *Hist (instrument of torture)* brodequin *m*

(**e**) *Br Fam Pej (ugly woman)* boudin *m*, cageot *m*

2 *vt* (**a**) *(kick)* donner des coups de pied à

(**b**) *(equip with boots)* botter

(**c**) *Comput* amorcer, faire démarrer; **to boot the system** initialiser le système

3 to boot *adv* en plus, par-dessus le marché; **she's beautiful and intelligent to boot** elle est belle, et intelligente par-dessus le marché

4 boots *npl Br* = garçon d'hôtel qui cire les chaussures

►► *Ftbl* ***boot boy*** = personne dont le rôle est de préparer les tenues des membres d'une équipe de football et de s'assurer notamment de la propreté de leurs chaussures; *Fam* ***boot camp*** *Am Mil* = camp d'entraînement pour nouvelles recrues; *Br (centre for young offenders)* = centre de redressement *(pour jeunes délinquants)*; **to go into boot camp** ≃ faire ses classes; *Comput* ***boot disk*** *(hard)* disque *m* de démarrage; *(floppy)* disquette *f* de démarrage; ***boot polish*** cirage *m*; *Br* ***boot sale*** = sorte de marché aux puces où des particuliers apportent dans leur voiture les objets de brocante qu'ils souhaitent vendre; ***boot scraper*** décrottoir *m*; *Comput* ***boot sector*** secteur *m* d'initialisation; *Comput* ***boot track*** piste *f* d'amorçage

►**boot out** *vt sep Fam* flanquer à la porte

►**boot up** *vt sep Comput* **1** *vi (computer)* s'amorcer, démarrer; *(person)* démarrer

2 *vt sep (computer)* amorcer, faire démarrer

bootable ['bu:təbəl] *adj Comput* amorçable

bootblack ['bu:tblæk] *n* cireur *m* de chaussures

bootcut ['bu:tkʌt] *adj (trousers, jeans)* trompette

booted ['bu:tɪd] *adj* botté

►► *Orn* ***booted warbler*** hypolaïs *m* russe

bootee ['bu:ti:] *n (for babies)* petit chausson *m*, bottine *f*; *(for women)* bottine *f*, bottillon *m*

booth [bu:ð] *n* (**a**) *(at fair)* baraque *f*, stand *m*; *Am (at exhibition)* stand *m* (**b**) *(cubicle → for telephone, language laboratory)* cabine *f*; *(→ for voting)* isoloir *m* (**c**) *(in restaurant)* box *m*

bootjack ['bu:tdʒæk] *n Tech* tire-botte *m*

bootlace ['bu:tleɪs] *n* lacet *m* (de chaussure)

bootleg ['bu:t,leg] *(pt & pp* **bootlegged,** *cont* **bootlegging) 1** *vi* faire de la contrebande de boissons alcoolisées

2 *vt (make)* fabriquer illicitement; *(sell)* vendre en contrebande

3 *n (gen)* marchandise *f* illicite; *(cassette, video, software etc)* pirate *m*; *Am (liquor)* alcool *m* de contrebande

4 *adj* (**a**) *(illicit)* de contrebande; **bootleg cassette/record** cassette *f*/disque *m* pirate (**b**) *(trousers, jeans)* trompette

bootlegger ['bu:t,legə(r)] *n (of cassettes, videos, software etc)* = personne qui se livre au piratage; *Am (of liquor)* bootlegger *m*

bootlegging ['bu:t,legɪŋ] *n (of cassettes, videos, software etc)* piratage *m*; *Am (of liquor)* contrebande *f*

bootless ['bu:tlɪs] *adj* (**a**) *(without boots)* sans bottes (**b**) *Literary (fruitless)* vain, infructueux

bootlick ['bu:tlɪk] *vi Fam* **he's always bootlicking** c'est un vrai lèche-bottes

bootlicker ['bu:t,lɪkə(r)] *n Fam* lèche-bottes *mf inv*

bootloader ['bu:t,ləʊdə(r)] *n Comput* chargeur-amorce *m*

bootmaker ['bu:t,meɪkə(r)] *n* bottier *m*

bootstrap ['bu:tstræp] **1** *n* (**a**) *(on boot)* tirant *m* de botte; *Fig* **she pulled herself up by her own bootstraps** elle a réussi par ses propres moyens (**b**) *Comput* programme *m* amorce, amorce *f*

2 *adj* autonome

►► *Comput* ***bootstrap program*** programme *m* amorce, amorce *f*

booty ['bu:tɪ] *n* (**a**) *(loot)* butin *m* (**b**) *Am Fam (buttocks)* cul *m*, derche *m*; *very Fam* **to get some booty** *(have sexual intercourse)* s'envoyer en l'air

booze [bu:z] *Fam* **1** *n (UNCOUNT)* alcool❑ *m*, boissons *fpl* alcoolisées❑; **bring your own booze** apportez à boire; **to go on the booze** picoler; **he's on the booze** il picole; **she's off the booze** elle a arrêté de picoler

2 *vi* picoler

►► *Austr* ***booze bus*** = patrouille de police qui arrête des automobilistes au hasard pour leur faire passer l'alcootest

boozed up [bu:zd-] *adj Fam* bourré

boozehound ['bu:zhaʊnd] *n Am Fam* poivrot(e) *m,f*

boozer ['bu:zə(r)] *n Fam* (**a**) *(drunkard)* poivrot(e) *m,f* (**b**) *Br (pub)* pub❑ *m*

booze-up *n Br Fam* beuverie *f*, soûlerie *f*; **to have a booze-up** prendre une cuite

boozily ['bu:zɪlɪ] *adv Fam* **to look at sb boozily** regarder qn à travers les vapeurs de l'alcool; **to say sth boozily** dire qch d'une voix avinée

boozy ['bu:zɪ] *(compar* **boozier,** *superl* **booziest)** *adj Fam (party, evening)* bien arrosé; **her boozy husband** son soûlard de mari

bop [bɒp] *(pt & pp* **bopped,** *cont* **bopping) 1** *n* (**a**) *(music)* bop *m* (**b**) *Fam (dance)* danse❑ *f*; **shall we have a bop?** on danse? (**c**) *Fam (punch)* coup *m* de poing❑

2 *vt Fam (hit)* cogner❑; **he bopped me on the nose!** il m'a allongé un marron sur le nez!

3 *vi Fam (dance)* danser❑; **we bopped (away) all night** on a dansé toute la nuit

bo-peep [bəʊ-] **1** *n* cache-cache *m inv*

2 Bo-Peep *pr n* **Little Bo-Peep** = dans une comptine anglaise, petite bergère qui a perdu son troupeau

Bora Bora [,bɔ:rə'bɔ:rə] *n Geog* Bora Bora; **on Bora Bora** à Bora Bora

boracic [bə'ræsɪk] *adj Chem (acid)* borique; **boracic ointment** pommade *f* boriquée

borage ['bɒrɪdʒ] *n Bot* bourrache *f*

borax ['bɔ:ræks] *n Miner & Pharm* borax *m*

Bordeaux [bɔ:'dəʊ] *n* (**a**) *(region)* le Bordelais; **an inhabitant of Bordeaux** un(e) Bordelais(e) (**b**) *(wine)* bordeaux *m*

bordello [bɔ:'deləʊ] *n* lupanar *m*

border ['bɔ:də(r)] **1** *n* (**a**) *(boundary)* frontière *f*; **on the border between Norway and Sweden** à la frontière entre la Norvège et la Suède; **they live near the Scottish border** ils habitent près de la frontière écossaise; **to cross the border** passer la frontière; **they tried to escape over the border** ils ont tenté de s'enfuir en passant la frontière; **north of the Border** *(from viewpoint of England)* en Écosse; *(from viewpoint of Ireland)* en Irlande du nord; *(from viewpoint of the US)* au Canada; **south of the Border** *(from viewpoint of Scotland)* en Angleterre; *(from viewpoint of Northern Ireland)* en République d'Irlande; *(from viewpoint of Canada)* aux États-Unis; *(from viewpoint of the US)* au Mexique

(**b**) *(outer edge → of lake)* bord *m*, rive *f*; *(→ of field)* bordure *f*, limite *f*; *(→ of forest)* lisière *f*, limite *f*

(**c**) *(edging → of dress, handkerchief, plate, notepaper)* bord *m*, bordure *f*

(**d**) *Hort (in garden)* bordure *f*, plate-bande *f*

(**e**) *Comput (of paragraph, cell)* bordure *f*

2 *comp (state)* frontière *(inv)*; *(zone)* frontière *(inv)*, frontalier; *(search)* à la frontière; *(dispute, patrol)* frontalier

3 *vt* (**a**) *(line edges of)* border; *(encircle)* entourer, encadrer

(**b**) *(be adjacent to)* toucher; **Mexico borders Texas** le Mexique touche *ou* a une frontière commune avec le Texas; **their garden is bordered on two sides by open fields** sur deux côtés, leur jardin est entouré de champs à perte de vue

4 **Borders** *npl* **the Borders** les Borders *fpl*, = région frontalière du sud-est de l'Écosse; **in the Borders** dans les Borders

►► ***Border collie*** colley *m* berger; ***border controls*** contrôles *mpl* aux frontières; ***border crossing*** passage *m* de frontière; *Mil* ***border guard*** garde-frontière *m*; ***border incident*** incident *m* de frontière; ***border police*** police *f* des frontières; *Customs* ***border post*** poste-frontière *m*; ***border region*** région *f* frontalière; ***border states*** = états américains limitrophes du Canada; ***Border terrier*** terrier *m*; ***border town*** ville *f* frontière *ou* frontalière

►**border on, border upon** *vt insep* (**a**) *(be adjacent to)* toucher, avoisiner; **my property borders on his** ma propriété touche la sienne; **Italy and Austria border on each other** l'Italie et l'Autriche ont une frontière commune *ou* sont limitrophes

(**b**) *(verge on)* friser, frôler; **to border on rudeness/a lie/the absurd** friser l'impolitesse/le mensonge/l'absurde; **his remark borders on slander** sa remarque frise la calomnie; **hysteria bordering upon madness** une crise de nerfs proche de *ou* qui frôle la folie

borderer ['bɔ:dərə(r)] *n* frontalier(ère) *m,f*; *Br (in Scotland)* Écossais(e) *m,f* frontalier(ère); *(in England)* Anglais(e) *m,f* frontalier(ère)

bordering ['bɔ:dərɪŋ] *adj (country)* contigu, limitrophe

borderland ['bɔ:dəlænd] *n (country)* pays *m* frontière; *also Fig (area)* région *f* limitrophe; **the borderland between fantasy and reality** la frontière entre l'imagination et la réalité

borderline ['bɔ:dəlaɪn] **1** *n* limite *f*, ligne *f* de démarcation; **to be on the borderline** être à la limite; **the borderline between acceptable and unacceptable behaviour** ce qui sépare un comportement acceptable d'un comportement inacceptable

2 *adj* limite; **a borderline case** un cas limite; **he is a borderline candidate** il est limite; **borderline students** *(in exam)* les étudiants qui atteignent tout juste la moyenne

bore [bɔ:(r)] **1** *pt of* **bear**

2 *n* (**a**) *(person)* raseur(euse) *m,f*; *(event, thing)* ennui *m*, corvée *f*; **what a bore she is!** ce qu'elle peut être lassante *ou* fatigante!; **visiting them is such a bore!** quelle barbe de leur rendre visite!; **homework is a real bore!** quelle corvée, les devoirs!; **the film was a bit of a bore** le film était un peu ennuyeux

(**b**) *Constr (from drilling)* trou *m* de sonde; *Tech* alésage *m*

(**c**) *Tech (diameter of gun, tube)* calibre *m*; **a twelve-bore shotgun** un fusil de calibre douze

(**d**) *(tidal flood)* mascaret *m*

(**e**) *Mining (hole)* trou *m* de sonde, sondage *m*, forage *m*

3 *vt* (**a**) *(tire)* ennuyer; *Fam* **housework bores me stiff** *or* **to tears** *or* **to death** *or* **rigid** *or* **out of my mind** faire le ménage m'ennuie à mourir; *Fam* **he bores the pants off me** il me barbe profondément; **I won't bore you with the details** je vous passe les détails

(**b**) *Tech (drill → hole)* percer; *(→ well)* forer, creuser; *(→ tunnel)* creuser; *(→ cylinder)* aléser

4 *vi* forer, sonder; **to bore through sth** percer qch; **they're boring for coal** ils forent pour extraire du charbon, ils recherchent du charbon par forage; *Fig* **I felt his eyes boring into me** je sentais son regard me transpercer

boreal ['bɔ:rɪəl] *adj Literary (forest)* boréal

bored [bɔ:d] *adj (person)* qui s'ennuie; *(expression, sigh)* d'ennui; **you look bored** tu as l'air de t'ennuyer; **to be** *or* **get bored** s'ennuyer; **to be bored with doing sth** s'ennuyer à faire qch; **I'm bored with my job** j'en ai assez de mon travail; **I'm getting bored with this conversation** j'en ai assez de cette conversation; *Fam* **to be bored stiff** *or* **to tears** *or* **to death** *or* **rigid** *or* **out of one's mind** s'ennuyer ferme *ou* à mourir

boredom ['bɔ:dəm] *n* ennui *m*; **her boredom with city life** l'ennui que lui inspirait la vie citadine

borehole ['bɔ:həʊl] *n Constr* trou *m* de sonde; *Mining (for mine)* trou *m* de mine

borer ['bɔ:rə(r)] *n* (**a**) *(person)* foreur *m*, perceur *m*; *(for wood)* vrille *f*, foret *m*; *(for metal)* alésoir *m*; *(for mine, well)* foret *m*, sonde *f* (**b**) *Entom (insect)* insecte *m* térébrant

boresome ['bɔ:səm] *adj Am* ennuyeux

boric ['bɔ:rɪk] *adj Chem* borique

boride ['bɔ:raɪd] *n Chem* borure *m*

boring ['bɔ:rɪŋ] **1** *adj (tiresome)* ennuyeux; *(uninteresting)* sans intérêt; **the meeting was so boring** cette réunion était assommante; **the street was an endless succession of boring shops** la rue n'était qu'une longue succession de magasins sans intérêt

2 *n Tech (in wood)* perforation *f*, forage *m*; *(in metal)* alésage *m*; *(in ground)* forage *m*, sondage *m*

►► *Tech* ***boring machine*** *(for wood)* perceuse *f*; *(for metal)* alésoir *m*

boringly ['bɔ:rɪŋlɪ] *adv* d'une manière ennuyeuse

bork [bɔ:k] *vt Am Fam* = s'opposer à la nomination de quelqu'un par une campagne de dénigrement dans les médias

born [bɔ:n] *adj* (**a**) *(gen)* né; **to be born** naître; **she was born blind** elle est née aveugle; **the town where I was born** la ville où je suis né, ma ville natale; **Victor Hugo was born in 1802** Victor Hugo est né en 1802; **two children were born to her** elle a mis au monde deux enfants; **born of an American father** né d'un père américain; **a child born into this world** un enfant qui vient au monde; **born and bred** né et élevé; **she was born and bred in Boston** c'est une Bostonienne de souche; **they were born to riches** ils sont nés riches; **she was born Elizabeth Hughes, but writes under the name E.R. Johnson** elle est née Elizabeth Hughes mais écrit sous le nom d'E.R. Johnson; *Fig* **the place where communism was born** le lieu où est né le communisme; **anger born of frustration** une colère née de *ou* due à la frustration; *Fam* **in all my born days** de toute ma vie ❑; *Fam* **I wasn't born yesterday!** je ne suis pas né d'hier *ou* de la dernière pluie!; **she was born with a silver spoon in her mouth** elle est née avec une cuillère en argent dans la bouche; **she was born lucky** elle est née coiffée, elle est née sous une bonne étoile; *Fam* **there's one born every minute!** il y en a toujours un qui tombe dans le panneau!

(**b**) *(as intensifier)* **he's a born musician** il est né musicien, c'est un musicien né; **you're a born fool** tu es un parfait idiot; **she's a born worrier** elle s'inquiète à tout propos; **he's a born loser** il est né sous une mauvaise étoile

'Born on the Fourth of July' *Stone* 'Né un 4 juillet'

-born [bɔ:n] *suff* originaire de; **he's New York-born** il est né à New York, il est originaire de New York; **she's English-born** elle est d'origine anglaise

born-again *adj Rel & Fig* rené; **born-again Christian** chrétien *m* rené

borne [bɔ:n] *pp of* **bear**

-borne [bɔ:n] *suff* transporté par; *Biol* **water-borne organisms** organismes *mpl* véhiculés par l'eau

Bornean ['bɔ:nɪən] **1** *n* = habitant de Bornéo

2 *adj* de Bornéo

Borneo ['bɔ:nɪəʊ] *n* Bornéo; **in Borneo** à Bornéo

Borodin ['bɒrədɪn] *pr n* Borodine

boron ['bɔ:rɒn] *n Chem* bore *m*

borosilicate [ˌbɔ:rəʊ'sɪlɪkeɪt] *n Chem* borosilicate *m*

borough ['bʌrə] *n* (**a**) *(British town)* = ville représentée à la Chambre des communes par un ou plusieurs députés (**b**) *(in London)* = une des 32 subdivisions administratives de Londres (**c**) *(in New York)* = une des 5 subdivisions administratives de New York

►► ***borough council*** = conseil municipal d'un "borough"

borrow ['bɒrəʊ] **1** *vt* (**a**) *(gen) & Fin* emprunter; **to borrow sth from sb** emprunter qch à qn; **she borrowed money from him** elle lui a emprunté de l'argent; **can I borrow the car?** est-ce que je peux prendre la voiture?; **an artist who borrows his ideas from nature** un artiste qui trouve ses idées dans la nature; **we often borrow books from the library** nous empruntons souvent des livres à la bibliothèque; **a word borrowed from Russian** un mot emprunté au russe

(**b**) *Br Math (in subtraction)* **I borrow one** je retiens un

2 *vi* emprunter (**from** à); *(money)* **to borrow from sb** faire un emprunt à qn, emprunter de l'argent à qn; **to borrow on** *or* **at interest** emprunter à intérêt

►**borrow against** *vt insep Fin (salary, property)* emprunter sur; **the company borrowed against its assets** l'entreprise a emprunté de l'argent en utilisant son actif comme garantie

borrowed ['bɒrəʊd] *adj (gen) & Fin* emprunté, d'emprunt; **borrowed capital** capitaux *mpl* empruntés *ou* d'emprunt; **the doctors say he's living on borrowed time** les médecins disent qu'il n'en a plus pour longtemps; **the company is living on borrowed time** les jours de l'entreprise sont comptés; **my grandfather is living on borrowed time** mon grand-père a de la chance d'être encore en vie; **he'd been living on borrowed time since he was caught stealing from his employer** il était en sursis depuis qu'on l'avait pris à voler son employeur

borrower ['bɒrəʊə(r)] *n (gen) & Fin* emprunteur(euse) *m,f*; *Prov* **neither a borrower nor a lender be** = il ne faut ni emprunter ni prêter d'argent

borrowing ['bɒrəʊɪŋ] *n Fin & Ling* emprunts *mpl*; **financed by borrowing** financé par des emprunts

►► ***borrowing power*** capacité *f* de crédit *ou* d'emprunt *ou* d'endettement; ***the borrowing rate*** le taux d'intérêt des emprunts; ***borrowing requirements*** besoins *mpl* de crédit

borsch [bɔ:ʃ], **borscht** [bɔ:ʃt] *n Culin* bortsch *m*, borchtch *m*

borstal ['bɔ:stəl] *n Br Formerly* = ancien nom d'une institution pour jeunes délinquants, aujourd'hui appelée "young offender institution"

borzoi ['bɔ:zɔɪ] *n* (lévrier *m*) barzoï *m*

Bosch [bɒʃ] *pr n* **Hieronymus Bosch** Jérôme Bosch

bosh [bɒʃ] *(UNCOUNT) Br Fam* **1** *n* bêtises ❑ *fpl*, âneries *fpl*

2 *exclam* n'importe quoi!, sottises!

bosk [bɒsk] *n Literary (wooded area)* bosquet *m*; *(thicket)* fourré *m*

bosky ['bɒskɪ] *adj Literary (wooded)* boisé; *(bushy)* broussailleux

bos'n ['bəʊsən] *n Naut* maître *m* d'équipage

Bosnia ['bɒznɪə] *n* Bosnie *f*; **in Bosnia** en Bosnie

Bosnia-Herzegovina [-ˌheətsəgə'vi:nə] *n* Bosnie-Herzégovine *f*

Bosnian ['bɒznɪən] **1** *n* Bosnien(enne) *m,f*, Bosniaque *mf*

2 *adj* bosnien, bosniaque

bosom ['bʊzəm] *n* (**a**) *(of woman)* seins *mpl*; *Fig Literary (of person)* poitrine *f*; **she took the child to her bosom** elle prit l'enfant sous son aile; **he harboured in his bosom feelings of deep insecurity** il nourrissait en son sein un sentiment de profonde insécurité

(**b**) *(of dress)* corsage *m*

(**c**) *Fig (centre)* sein *m*, fond *m*; **in the bosom of the community** au sein de la communauté

►► *Fam* ***bosom buddy*** meilleur pote *m*; ***bosom friend*** ami(e) *m,f* intime

-bosomed ['bʊzəmd] *suff* **big/small bosomed** qui a des gros/petits seins

bosomy ['bʊzəmɪ] *adj Fam (woman)* qui a une forte poitrine ❑

Bosporus ['bɒspərəs], **Bosphorus** ['bɒsfərəs] *n* Bosphore *m*; **in the Bosporus** dans le Bosphore

bosquet ['bɒskɪt] *n* fourré *m*

boss [bɒs] **1** *n* (**a**) *Fam (person in charge)* patron(onne) ❑ *m,f*, chef *m*; **who's the boss around here?** qui est-ce qui commande ici?; **I'll show you who's boss!** je vais te montrer qui est le chef!; **she's the boss** c'est elle qui porte la culotte; **to be one's own boss** être son propre patron; *Austr Pej* **the boss cocky** le boss

(**b**) *Fam (of gang)* caïd *m*; *Am (politician)* manitou *m* (du parti)

(**c**) *Mil (knob)* bossage *m*; *(on shield)* ombon *m*

(**d**) *Archit* bossage *m*

(**e**) *Biol* bosse *f*

(**f**) *Tech* mamelon *m*, bossage *m*; *Aviat & Naut (of propeller)* moyeu *m*

2 *vt Fam (person)* commander❑, donner des ordres à❑; *(organization)* diriger❑, faire marcher❑

3 *adj Fam Am & NEng Old-fashioned* formidable; **the party was boss!** la soirée était sensass!

▸**boss about, boss around** *vt sep Fam* mener à la baguette; **stop bossing me around!** j'en ai assez que tu me donnes des ordres!

boss-eyed *adj Br Fam* qui louche❑; **she is boss-eyed** elle louche

bossily ['bɒsɪlɪ] *adv Fam* d'une manière autoritaire❑

bossiness ['bɒsɪnɪs] *n Fam* comportement *m* autoritaire❑

bossy ['bɒsɪ] *(compar* **bossier,** *superl* **bossiest)** *adj Fam* autoritaire❑, dictatorial❑; **he's too bossy** il veut mener tout le monde à la baguette

bossy-boots *n Fam* dictateur❑ *m*

Boston ['bɒstən] **1** *n* Boston

2 boston *n* **(a)** *(card game)* boston *m* **(b)** *(dance)* **to do the boston (two-step)** danser le boston, bostonner

►► *Hist* ***the Boston Massacre*** le massacre de Boston; *Mktg* ***Boston matrix*** matrice *f* BCG; *Hist* ***the Boston Tea Party*** la "Boston Tea Party"

THE BOSTON MASSACRE

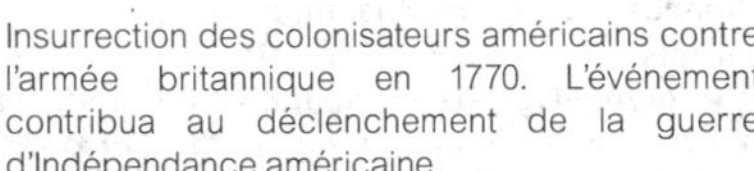

Insurrection des colonisateurs américains contre l'armée britannique en 1770. L'événement contribua au déclenchement de la guerre d'Indépendance américaine.

BOSTON TEA PARTY

Insurrection en 1773 pendant laquelle les Bostoniens jetèrent des cargaisons de thé à la mer pour protester contre les droits de douane imposés par l'Angleterre; elle marque le point de départ de la guerre d'Indépendance des États-Unis.

Bostonian [bɒ'stəʊnjən] **1** *n* Bostonien(enne) *m,f*

2 *adj* bostonien

'The Bostonians' *James* 'Les Bostoniennes'

bosun ['bəʊsən] *n Naut* maître *m* d'équipage

Bosworth Field ['bɒzwɜːθ-] *n Hist* **the Battle of Bosworth Field** = bataille finale de la guerre des Deux-Roses, en 1485, à l'issue de laquelle Henry Tudor devint Henry VII d'Angleterre

BoT [ˌbiːəʊ'tiː] *n (abbr* **Board of Trade)** *(in UK)* ministère *m* du Commerce; *(in US)* chambre *f* de commerce

botanic [bə'tænɪk], **botanical** [bə'tænɪkəl] *adj* botanique

►► ***botanic garden*** jardin *m* botanique

botanist ['bɒtənɪst] *n* botaniste *mf*

botanize, -ise ['bɒtənaɪz] *vi* herboriser

botany ['bɒtənɪ] *n* botanique *f*

►► ***Botany Bay*** Botany Bay *f*; *Tex* ***botany wool*** laine *f* mérinos

botch [bɒtʃ] *Fam* **1** *n* travail *m* salopé; **those workmen made a real botch** *or* **botch-up of the job** ces ouvriers ont fait un travail de cochon *ou* ont tout salopé

2 *vt (job)* saloper; *(interview, speech)* rater

▸**botch up** *vt sep Fam (job)* saloper; *(interview, speech)* rater

botched [bɒtʃt] *adj Fam* **a botched attempt at suicide** une tentative de suicide ratée; **his botched apology only made matters worse** ses excuses minables n'ont fait qu'empirer la situation; **a botched job** un travail de sagouin; **to make a botched job of sth** bousiller qch

botchy ['bɒtʃɪ] *(compar* **botchier,** *superl* **botchiest)** *adj Fam* bâclé

both [bəʊθ] **1** *predet* les deux, l'un (l'une) et l'autre; **both dresses are pretty** les deux robes sont jolies; **on both sides of the road** des deux côtés de la route; **hold it in both hands** tenez-le à *ou* des deux mains; **you can't have it both ways!** il faut te décider, c'est soit l'un, soit l'autre!

2 *pron* tous (toutes) (les) deux *mpl, fpl*; **both (of them) are coming** ils viennent tous les deux; **both are to blame** c'est leur faute à tous les deux; **why not do both?** pourquoi ne pas faire les deux?; **from both of us** de notre part à tous les deux; **we both said yes** nous avons dit oui tous les deux; **you're both alike** vous êtes pareils tous les deux; **both you and I like to travel** nous aimons tous les deux voyager; **Claire and I both went** Claire et moi y sommes allés tous les deux

3 both... and... *conj* **her job is both interesting and well-paid** son travail est à la fois intéressant et bien payé; **I both read and write Spanish** je sais lire et écrire l'espagnol; **both the rich and the poor voted for him** les riches et les pauvres ont voté pour lui

bother ['bɒðə(r)] **1** *n* **(a)** *(trouble)* ennui *m*; *Br* **to be in** *or* **to have a spot of bother (with sb)** avoir des ennuis (avec qn); **I hear there was a bit of bother down at the pub last night** il paraît qu'il y a eu du grabuge hier soir au pub; **he doesn't give her any bother** il ne la dérange pas; **the trip isn't worth the bother** le voyage ne vaut pas la peine; **if it's not too much bother** si cela ne vous dérange pas trop; **I hope I haven't put you to a lot of bother** j'espère que je ne vous ai pas trop dérangé; **I didn't go to the bother of cooking a meal** je n'ai pas pris la peine de cuisiner un repas; **thanks for babysitting – it's no bother!** merci pour le babysitting – de rien!

(b) *(nuisance)* ennui *m*; **homework is such a bother!** quelle corvée, les devoirs!; **sorry to be a bother** excusez-moi de vous déranger

2 *vt* **(a)** *(irritate)* ennuyer, embêter; *(pester)* harceler; *(disturb)* déranger; **I'm sorry to bother you** excusez-moi de vous déranger; **would it bother you if I opened the window?** cela vous dérange *ou* ennuie si j'ouvre la fenêtre?; **don't bother him when he's resting** laisse-le tranquille quand il se repose

(b) *(worry)* tracasser; **don't bother yourself** *or* **your head about it** ne vous tracassez pas à ce sujet; **it doesn't bother me whether they come or not** cela m'est bien égal qu'ils viennent ou pas

(c) *(hurt)* faire souffrir; **his leg is bothering him again** sa jambe le fait de nouveau souffrir

3 *vi* prendre la peine; **don't bother to answer the phone** ce n'est pas la peine de répondre au téléphone; **please don't bother getting up!** ne vous donnez pas la peine de vous lever!; **don't bother about me** ne vous en faites pas *ou* ne vous inquiétez pas pour moi; **he didn't even bother to apologize** il n'a même pas pris la peine de s'excuser; **let's not bother with the housework** laissons tomber le ménage

4 *exclam Br Fam* flûte!, mince!; **bother the lot of them!** qu'ils aillent au diable!, qu'ils aillent se faire pendre ailleurs!

botheration [ˌbɒðə'reɪʃən] *exclam Fam Old-fashioned* flûte!, mince!

bothered ['bɒðəd] *adj* **to be bothered about sb/sth** s'inquiéter de qn/qch; **I can't be bothered to write letters tonight** je n'ai pas le courage d'écrire des lettres ce soir; **he can't be bothered to do his own laundry** il a la flemme de laver son linge lui-même; **are you going out tonight? – no, I can't be bothered** tu sors ce soir? – non, j'ai pas le courage; **I'm not bothered** ça m'est égal

bothersome ['bɒðəsəm] *adj* ennuyeux, gênant

Bothnia ['bɒθnɪə] *n see* **gulf**

bothy ['bɒθɪ] *n Scot* **(a)** *(mountain shelter)* refuge *m (de montagne)* **(b)** *(farmworker's dwelling)* = petite maison très rudimentaire pour les ouvriers agricoles

botrytis [bə'traɪtɪs] *n Bot* botrytis *m*

Botswana [bɒt'swɑːnə] *n* Botswana *m*; **in Botswana** au Botswana

Botswanan [bɒt'swɑːnən] **1** *n* Botswanais(e) *m,f*

2 *adj* botswanais

bottle ['bɒtəl] **1** *n* **(a)** *(container, contents)* bouteille *f*; *(of perfume)* flacon *m*; *(of medicine)* flacon *m*, fiole *f*; *(jar)* bocal *m*; *(made of stone)* cruche *f*, cruchon *m*; **a wine bottle** une bouteille à vin; **we ordered a bottle of wine** nous avons commandé une bouteille de vin; **he drank (straight) from the bottle** il a bu au goulot; *Fam Fig* **he was too fond of the bottle** il levait bien le coude, il aimait la bouteille; *Fam* **to hit the bottle** picoler dur; *Fam* **to take to the bottle** se mettre à picoler; *Fam* **they're on the bottle** ils lèvent bien le coude; *Fam* **to be off the bottle** s'abstenir *ou* s'arrêter de boire❑

(b) *(for baby)* biberon *m*; **her baby is on the bottle** son bébé est nourri au biberon

(c) *Br Fam (nerve)* cran *m*, culot *m*; **he lost his bottle** il s'est dégonflé; **she's got a lot of bottle** elle a un sacré cran

2 *vt Ind (drinks)* mettre en bouteille; *(fruit)* mettre en bocal *ou* conserve, conserver

►► ***bottle bank*** = conteneur pour la collecte du verre usagé; *Fam Pej* ***bottle blonde*** blonde *f* décolorée; ***bottle glass*** verre *m* à bouteilles, verre *m* vert; ***bottle green*** vert *m* bouteille; ***bottle opener*** ouvre-bouteilles *m inv*, décapsuleur *m*; *Br* ***bottle party*** = soirée où chacun des invités apporte à boire; ***bottle rack*** casier *m* à bouteilles; *Austr* ***bottle shop*** magasin *m* de vins et spiritueux; *Fam* ***bottle tan*** bronzage *m* artificiel❑

▸**bottle out** *vi Br Fam* se dégonfler; **he bottled out of the fight** il s'est dégonflé au dernier moment et a refusé de se battre; **he bottled out of telling her the truth** finalement il a eu la trouille de lui dire la vérité

▸**bottle up** *vt sep* **(a)** *(emotions)* refouler, ravaler **(b)** *Mil (army)* embouteiller, contenir

bottlebrush ['bɒtəlbrʌʃ] *n* rince-bouteilles *m inv*, goupillon *m*

bottled ['bɒtəld] *adj* en bouteille *ou* bouteilles; **bottled beer** bière *f* en bouteille *ou* bouteilles; **bottled gas** gaz *m* en bouteille *ou* bouteilles

bottle-fed *adj* élevé *ou* nourri au biberon

bottle-feed *vt* nourrir au biberon

bottle-feeding *n* alimentation *f* au biberon

bottleful ['bɒtəlfʊl] *n* **a bottleful of sth** une pleine bouteille de qch; **by the bottleful** à pleine bouteille

bottle-green *adj* vert bouteille *(inv)*

bottleneck ['bɒtəlnek] **1** *n (in road)* rétrécissement *m* de la chaussée, étranglement *m*; *(of traffic)* embouteillage *m*, bouchon *m*; *(in industry)* goulet *m ou* goulot *m* d'étranglement

2 *vt Am* **strikes have bottlenecked production** les grèves ont ralenti la production

bottlenosed ['bɒtəlˌnəʊzd] *adj* à gros nez

►► ***bottlenosed dolphin*** tursiops *m*, souffleur *m*; ***bottlenosed whale*** hyperoodon *m*

bottle-warmer *n* chauffe-biberon *m*

bottle-washer *n (person)* laveur(euse) *m,f* de bouteilles; *(machine)* rince-bouteilles *m inv*

bottling ['bɒtəlɪŋ] *n (of drinks)* mise *f* en bouteille(s); *(of fruit)* mise *f* en bocaux, mise *f* en conserve

Bottom ['bɒtəm] *pr n* = personnage comique transformé en âne dans 'Le Songe d'une nuit d'été' de Shakespeare

BOTTOM ['bɒtəm] **1** *n* **(a)** *(lowest part → of garment, heap)* bas *m*; *(→ of water)* fond *m*; *(→ of hill, stairs)* bas *m*, pied *m*; *(→ of outside of container)* bas *m*; *(→ of inside of container)* fond *m*; *(→ of chair)* siège *m*, fond *m*; *Naut (→ of ship)* carène *f*; **at the bottom of my bag** au fond de mon sac; **at the bottom of the staircase** au pied *ou* bas de l'escalier; **at the bottom of page one** au bas de la page un, en bas de page un; **to send a ship to the bottom** envoyer un bâtiment par le fond; **the ship sank to the bottom** le navire a coulé; **the ship touched (the) bottom** le navire a touché le fond; *Fig* **I believe, at the bottom of my heart, that...** je crois, au fond de moi-même, que...; **he thanked them from the bottom of his heart** il les a remerciés du fond du cœur; **my reasoning knocked the bottom out of his argument** mon raisonnement a démoli son argument; **the bottom fell out of the grain market** le marché des grains s'est effondré; **the bottom dropped out of her world when he died** lorsqu'il est mort, pour elle le monde s'est effondré; **to put sth bottom up(wards)** mettre qch sens dessus dessous; *Fam* **bottoms up!** cul sec!; *Sport* **at the bottom of the fifth (inning)** *(in baseball)* à la fin de la cinquième manche

(b) *(last place)* **he's (at the) bottom of his**

class il est le dernier de sa classe; **you're at the bottom of the list** vous êtes en queue de liste; **you have to start at the bottom and work your way up** vous devez commencer au plus bas et monter dans la hiérarchie à la force du poignet

(**c**) *(far end)* fond *m*, bas *m*; **at the bottom of the street/garden** au bout de la rue/du jardin

(**d**) *Fig (origin, source)* base *f*, origine *f*; **I'm sure she's at the bottom of all this** je suis sûr que c'est elle qui est à l'origine de cette histoire; **I intend to get to the bottom of this affair** j'entends aller au fin fond de cette affaire *ou* découvrir le pot aux roses

(**e**) *(buttocks)* derrière *m*, fesses *fpl*

(**f**) *(of two-piece garment)* bas *m*; **pyjama bottoms** bas *m* de pyjama; **bikini bottom** bas *m* de maillot de bain

(**g**) *(in billiards, snooker)* **to put bottom on a ball** faire de l'effet à revenir *ou* de l'effet rétrograde

(**h**) *Br Aut (gear)* première *f*

2 *adj* **it's on the bottom shelf** il se trouve sur l'étagère du bas; **the bottom book in the pile** le livre qui est en bas de la pile; **the bottom half of the chart** la partie inférieure du tableau; **the bottom half of the class/list** la deuxième moitié de la classe/liste; **the bottom floor** le rez-de-chaussée; **the bottom stair** *(going up)* la marche du bas, la première marche; *(going down)* la dernière marche; *Sport* **the bottom end of the table** le bas de la table; *Br* **she's collecting things for her bottom drawer** elle réunit des choses pour son trousseau

3 *vi Naut (ship)* toucher le fond

4 at bottom *adv* au fond; **at bottom, their motives are purely mercenary** au fond, leurs intentions sont purement intéressées

►► ***bottom feeder*** *Ich* poisson *m* de fond; *Fig Pej (unsuccessful person)* raté(e) *m,f*; *(team, company)* ratés *mpl*; *Br Aut* ***bottom gear*** première *f* (vitesse *f*); *Am Geog* ***bottom land*** *or* ***lands*** terre *f ou* plaine *f* alluviale; *Acct & Fin* ***bottom line*** résultat *m* net, solde *m* final, résultat *m* financier; **all he's interested in is the bottom line** la seule chose qui l'intéresse c'est de faire de l'argent; *Fig* **the bottom line is we can't afford it** le fait est que nous ne pouvons pas nous le permettre; *Am Culin* ***bottom round*** gîte *m* à la noix

►**bottom out** *vi Fin (prices)* atteindre son niveau plancher; *Econ (recession, inflation, unemployment)* atteindre son plus bas niveau

bottomless ['bɒtəmlɪs] *adj* sans fond, insondable; *(unlimited → funds, supply)* inépuisable

►► *Fig* ***bottomless pit*** gouffre *m*; **it's like pouring money into a bottomless pit** c'est comme jeter de l'argent par les fenêtres; *Fam* **he's a bottomless pit** *(always hungry)* c'est un crevard

bottommost ['bɒtəm,məʊst] *adj* le plus bas

bottom-of-the-range 1 *n* modèle *m* de base

2 *adj* bas de gamme

bottom-up *adj (plan, method)* de la base au sommet, bottom-up *(inv)*; *Comput (programming)* ascendant

botulism ['bɒtjʊlɪzəm] *n Med* botulisme *m*

bouclé ['bu:kleɪ] *Tex* **1** *n* bouclé *m*

2 *comp (sweater, fabric)* en bouclette

►► ***bouclé wool*** bouclette *f*

Boudicca [bəʊ'dɪkə] = **Boadicea**

boudoir ['bu:dwɑ:(r)] *n* boudoir *m*

►► ***boudoir biscuit*** boudoir *m*

bouffant ['bu:fɒn] *adj (hairstyle)* gonflant; *(sleeve)* bouffant

Bougainville ['bu:gənvɪl] *n* Bougainville

bougainvillaea, bougainvillea [,bu:gən'vɪlɪə] *n Bot* bougainvillée *f*, bougainvillier *m*

bough [baʊ] *n* branche *f*

bought [bɔ:t] *pt & pp of* **buy**

►► *Acct & Fin* ***bought ledger*** cahier *m ou* livre *m* des achats

bouillon ['bu:jɒn] *n Culin* bouillon *m*, consommé *m*

►► *Am* ***bouillon cube*** cube *m* de bouillon; *Am* ***bouillon cup*** tasse *f* à bouillon *ou* à consommé

boulder ['bəʊldə(r)] *n* bloc *m* de roche, *Spec* boulder *m*; *(smaller)* gros galet *m*

►► *Geol* ***boulder clay*** argile *f* à blocaux

boulevard ['bu:ləvɑ:d] *n* boulevard *m*

bounce [baʊns] **1** *n* (**a**) *(rebound)* bond *m*, rebond *m*; *Sport* **he caught the ball on the bounce** il a pris la balle au bond; *Sport* **you get a better bounce on grass** cela rebondit mieux sur l'herbe

(**b**) *(spring)* **there isn't much bounce in this ball** cette balle ne rebondit pas beaucoup; **I'd like to put some bounce in my hair** je voudrais donner du volume à mes cheveux; *Fig* **he's still full of bounce at seventy** à soixante-dix ans il est encore plein d'énergie

(**c**) *Am Fam (dismissal)* **to give sb the bounce** virer qn; **he got the bounce** il s'est fait virer

(**d**) *Fam* **on the bounce** *(in succession)* à la suite

2 *vt* (**a**) *(cause to spring)* faire rebondir; **she bounced the ball against** *or* **off the wall** elle fit rebondir la balle sur le mur; **he bounced the baby on his knee** il a fait sauter l'enfant sur son genou; *Tel* **signals are bounced off a satellite** les signaux sont renvoyés *ou* retransmis par satellite; **to bounce an idea off sb** soumettre une idée à qn

(**b**) *Fam Banking (cheque)* refuser d'honorer ❑; **the bank bounced my cheque** la banque a refusé mon chèque

(**c**) *Fam (throw out)* flanquer à la porte, vider

3 *vi* (**a**) *(object)* rebondir; **the ball bounced down the steps** la balle a rebondi de marche en marche; **the knapsack bounced up and down on his back** le sac à dos tressautait sur ses épaules; **the bicycle bounced along the bumpy path** le vélo faisait des bonds sur le chemin cahoteux; **the hailstones were bouncing off the roof** les grêlons rebondissaient sur le toit

(**b**) *(person)* bondir, sauter; **we bounced up and down on the bed** nous faisions des bonds sur le lit; **she came bouncing into/out of the room** elle est entrée dans/sortie de la pièce d'un bond

(**c**) *Fam Banking (cheque)* être refusé pour non-provision ❑; **I hope this cheque won't bounce** j'espère que ce chèque ne sera pas refusé

(**d**) *Comput (e-mail)* revenir à l'expéditeur

►► *Comput* ***bounce message*** = message électronique non délivré revenu à l'expéditeur; *Sport* ***bounce pass*** *(in basketball)* passe *m* par rebond

►**bounce back** *vi (ball)* rebondir; *(person → after illness, disappointment)* se remettre rapidement; *(Stock Exchange)* reprendre, remonter; *Fin* **the pound has bounced back against the dollar** la livre a regagné du terrain par rapport au dollar; **she bounced right back after her illness** elle s'est vite rétablie après sa maladie

bouncer ['baʊnsə(r)] *n Fam (doorman)* videur ❑ *m*

bounciness ['baʊnsɪnɪs] *n* (**a**) *(of ball, mattress)* élasticité *f*; *(of hair)* souplesse *f* (**b**) *(of person)* entrain *m*, dynamisme *m*

bouncing ['baʊnsɪŋ] *adj* (**a**) *(healthy)* qui respire la santé; **a bouncing baby** un bébé en pleine santé (**b**) *(ball)* qui rebondit

►► *Hist* ***bouncing bomb*** = type de bombe utilisé par les briseurs de barrages de la RAF en 1943

bouncy ['baʊnsɪ] ([illegible] **ciest**) *adj* (**a**) *(ball, bed)* élastique; *(hair)* souple, qui a du volume (**b**) *(person)* plein d'entrain, dynamique

►► ***bouncy castle*** château *m* gonflable

BOUND [baʊnd]

sûr	► **2 (a)**
obligé	► **2 (b)**
lié	► **2 (c), (e), (g)**
relié	► **2 (f)**
à destination de	► **2 (d)**
saut, bond	► **3 (a)**
sauter, bondir	► **4**
borner, limiter	► **5**
borne, limite	► **6**

1 *pt & pp of* **bind**

2 *adj* (**a**) *(certain)* sûr, certain; **it was bound to happen** c'était à prévoir; **it's bound to rain tomorrow** il pleuvra sûrement demain; **but he's bound to say that** mais il est certain que c'est cela qu'il va dire; **he's bound to apologize** il ne va pas manquer de s'excuser; **she's up to no good, I'll be bound** je parie qu'elle ne mijote rien de bon

(**b**) *(compelled)* obligé; **they are bound by the treaty to take action** l'accord les oblige à prendre des mesures; **the teacher felt bound to report them** l'enseignant s'est cru obligé de les dénoncer; **I'm bound to say I disagree** je dois dire que je ne suis pas d'accord

(**c**) *(connected)* **bound up** lié; **his frustration is bound up with his work** sa frustration est directement liée à son travail

(**d**) *(heading towards)* **bound for** *(person)* en route pour; *(shipment, cargo etc)* à destination de; *(train)* à destination *ou* en direction de; **to be homeward bound** être sur le chemin du retour; **where are you bound for?** où allez-vous?; **I'm bound for Chicago** je suis en route pour Chicago; **all shipments bound for Madrid** toutes cargaisons à destination de Madrid; **the train is bound for Rome** le train est à destination *ou* en direction de Rome; **on a plane bound for Tokyo** dans un avion à destination de *ou* en route pour Tokyo

(**e**) *(tied)* lié; **bound hand and foot** pieds et poings liés

(**f**) *Typ (book)* relié; **bound in boards** cartonné

(**g**) *Ling* lié

3 *n* (**a**) *(leap)* saut *m*, bond *m*; **at one bound, in a single bound** d'un seul bond *ou* saut

(**b**) *Math* **lower bound** minorant *m*; **upper bound** majorant *m*

4 *vi (person)* sauter, bondir; *(animal)* faire un bond *ou* des bonds, bondir; **the children bounded into/out of the classroom** les enfants sont entrés dans/sortis de la salle de classe en faisant des bonds; **the dog bounded down the hill** le chien dévala la colline en bondissant

5 *vt* borner, limiter; **a country bounded on two sides by the sea** un pays limité par la mer de deux côtés; **an area bounded by Smith Street on the west, James Avenue on the south** une zone délimitée par Smith Street à l'ouest et James Avenue au sud

6 bounds *npl* limite *f*, borne *f*; **the situation has gone beyond the bounds of all reason** la situation est devenue complètement aberrante *ou* insensée; **her rage knew no bounds** sa colère était sans bornes; **within the bounds of possibility** dans la limite du possible; *Fig* **to keep within bounds** rester dans la juste mesure, pratiquer la modération; **out of bounds** *(gen)* dont l'accès est interdit; *(in golf)* hors du jeu; **the castle gardens are out of bounds to visitors** les jardins du château sont interdits au public; **to beat the bounds** = dans certaines régions de Grande-Bretagne, parcourir le périmètre d'une paroisse en frappant le sol de baguettes, pour en rappeler les limites

-bound [baʊnd] *suff* (**a**) *(restricted)* confiné; **snow-bound road** route *f* complètement enneigée; **fog-bound ship** navire *m* bloqué par le brouillard (**b**) *(heading towards)* **a south-bound train** un train en partance pour le Sud; **city-bound traffic** circulation *f* en direction du centre-ville

boundary ['baʊndərɪ] (*pl* **boundaries**) *n* limite *f*, frontière *f*; **boundary (line)** limite *f*; *Sport* limites *fpl* du terrain; *(in basketball)* ligne *f* de touche; **to hit** *or* **to score a boundary** *(in cricket)* envoyer la balle jusqu'aux limites du terrain

►► *Br Parl* ***boundary change*** *(of parliamentary constituency)* = modification des limites d'une circonscription; *Br Parl* ***Boundary Commission*** commission *f* de délimitation des frontières *(en Grande-Bretagne)*; *Hort* ***boundary stone*** borne *f*, pierre *f* de bornage

bounden ['baʊndən] *adj Formal* **bounden duty** devoir *m* impérieux

bounder ['baʊndə(r)] *n Fam Old-fashioned or Hum* goujat ❑ *m*, malotru ❑ *m*

boundless ['baʊndlɪs] *adj (energy, wealth)* illimité; *(ambition, gratitude)* sans bornes; *(space)* infini

boundlessly ['baʊndlɪslɪ] *adv* infiniment

boundlessness ['baundlɪsnɪs] *n* infinité *f*, immensité *f*

bot–bou

bounteous ['baʊntɪəs] *adj Literary (person)* généreux, libéral; *(harvest, supply)* abondant; *(rain)* bienfaisant

bounteously ['baʊntɪəslɪ] *adv Literary* généreusement

bounteousness ['baʊntɪəsnɪs] *n Literary (of person)* bonté *f*, générosité *f*; *(of harvest, supply)* abondance *f*

bountiful ['baʊntɪfʊl] *adj Literary (person)* généreux, libéral; *(harvest, supply)* abondant; *(rain)* bienfaisant

bountifully ['baʊntɪfʊlɪ] *adv Literary* généreusement

bountifulness ['baʊntɪfʊlnɪs] *n Literary (of person)* bonté *f*, générosité *f*; *(of harvest, supply)* abondance *f*

bounty ['baʊntɪ] *(pl* **bounties***) n* **(a)** *Literary (generosity)* munificence *f* **(b)** *(gift)* don *m* **(c)** *(reward)* prime *f*

►► ***bounty hunter*** chasseur *m* de primes

bouquet [bʊ'keɪ] *n* **(a)** *(of flowers)* bouquet *m*; *Fig* **to throw bouquets at sb** faire des compliments à qn; *TV* **bouquet of channels** bouquet *m* de chaînes **(b)** *(of wine)* bouquet *m*

►► *Culin* ***bouquet garni*** bouquet *m* garni

Bourbon ['bʊəbən] *Hist* **1** *n* Bourbon *mf*

2 *adj* bourbonien

bourbon ['bɜːbən] *n (whisky)* bourbon *m*

►► *Br* ***bourbon biscuit*** = biscuit au chocolat fourré de crème au chocolat

bourdon ['bʊədən] *n Mus (of organ, bagpipes)* bourdon *m*

bourgeois ['bɔːʒwɑː] **1** *n* bourgeois(e) *m,f*

2 *adj* bourgeois

bourgeoisie [,bɔːʒwɑː'ziː] *n* bourgeoisie *f*

Bourke [bɔːk] *n Austr Fam* **in the back of Bourke** en pleine brousse, au diable vauvert

bourn, bourne [bɔːn] *n Literary* **(a)** *(boundary, limit)* frontière *f*; **the bourn from which no traveller returns** l'au-delà *m* **(b)** *(goal)* but *m*

Bournemouth ['bɔːnməθ] *n* = station balnéaire de la côte sud de l'Angleterre

Bourse [bʊəs] *n St Exch* Bourse *f* (de valeurs)

bout [baʊt] *n* **(a)** *(of illness)* attaque *f*; *(of fever)* accès *m*; *(of rheumatism)* crise *f*; *(of coughing)* quinte *f*; *(of self-pity)* crise *f*; *(of depression, intense activity)* période *f*; **a bout of bronchitis** une bronchite; **a bout of flu** une grippe; **she's prone to frequent bouts of illness** elle est souvent malade; **a bout of drinking** une soûlerie, une beuverie **(b)** *Sport (in boxing, wrestling)* combat *m*; *Fencing* assaut *m*

boutique [buː'tiːk] *n (shop)* boutique *f*; *(in department store)* rayon *m*

bouzouki [bʊ'zuːkɪ] *n Mus* bouzouki *m*

bovid ['bəʊvɪd] *adj Zool* de la famille des bovidés

bovine ['bəʊvaɪn] **1** *n* bovin *m*

2 *adj also Fig* bovin

►► *Vet* ***bovine spongiform encephalopathy*** encéphalite *f* bovine spongiforme; *Vet* ***bovine TB*** tuberculose *f* bovine

bovinely ['bəʊvaɪnlɪ] *adv* stupidement, d'un air hébété

Bovril® ['bɒvrɪl] *n Br* = préparation à base de suc de viande utilisée comme boisson ou comme condiment

bovver ['bɒvə(r)] *n (UNCOUNT) Br Fam Old-fashioned (fighting)* bagarre *f*

►► ***bovver boots*** brodequins *mpl*, rangers *mpl*; ***bovver boy*** loubard *m*

bow¹ [bəʊ] **1** *n* **(a)** *(curve)* arc *m*

(b) *(for arrows)* arc *m*; **he drew the bow** il a tiré à l'arc

(c) *Mus (stick)* archet *m*; *(stroke)* coup *m* d'archet

(d) *(in ribbon)* nœud *m*, boucle *f*; **tie it in a bow** faites un nœud

2 *vi Mus* manier l'archet

►► ***Bow Bells*** = cloches de l'église Saint-Mary-Le-Bow à Londres; *Pol* ***the Bow Group*** = société influente de jeunes conservateurs britanniques; ***bow legs*** jambes *fpl* arquées; *Br Hist* ***Bow Street runner*** = membre de la première police londonienne, créée en 1748; ***bow tie*** nœud *m* papillon; *Br Archit* ***bow window*** fenêtre *f* en saillie, oriel *m*, bow-window *m*

> **BOW BELLS**
>
> Selon la tradition, un "vrai Londonien" (un Cockney) doit être né à portée du son des cloches de l'église de Saint-Mary-Le-Bow.

bow² [baʊ] **1** *n* **(a)** *(gen)* salut *m (fait en inclinant le buste)*; **he made her a deep** *or* **low bow** il l'a saluée profondément *ou* bien bas; **to take a bow** *(of performer)* saluer

(b) *Naut (of ship)* avant *m*, proue *f*; **on the port/starboard bow** par bâbord/tribord avant

(c) *Naut (oarsman)* nageur *m* de l'avant

2 *vt (bend)* incliner, courber; *(knee)* fléchir; *(head → in shame)* baisser; *(→ in prayer)* incliner; *(→ in contemplation)* pencher

3 *vi* **(a)** *(in greeting)* incliner la tête, saluer; **I bowed to him** je l'ai salué de la tête; **he refuses to bow and scrape to anyone** il refuse de faire des courbettes *ou* des salamalecs à qui que ce soit

(b) *(bend)* se courber; *(under load)* ployer

(c) *Fig (yield)* s'incliner; **to bow to the inevitable** s'incliner devant l'inévitable; **the government is bowing under** *or* **to pressure from the unions** l'administration s'incline sous la pression des syndicats; **I'll bow to your greater knowledge** je m'incline devant tant de savoir *ou* de science

►► ***bow oar*** aviron *m* de l'avant; ***bow rope*** amarre *f* de bout *ou* de l'avant; ***bow wave*** lame *f* d'étrave

►**bow down 1** *vt sep* faire plier; *Fig* écraser, briser

2 *vi* s'incliner; **he bowed down to her** il s'est incliné devant elle

►**bow out** *vi Fig (retire, withdraw)* tirer sa révérence

bowdlerization [,baʊdləraɪ'zeɪʃən] *n* expurgation *f*

bowdlerize, -ise ['baʊdləraɪz] *vt* expurger; *Fig* **a bowdlerized version of the party** une version tronquée de la soirée

bowed [baʊd] *adj (back)* courbé; *(head)* baissé

bowel ['baʊəl] *n (usu pl)* **(a)** *(of human)* intestin *m*, intestins *mpl*; *(of animal)* boyau *m*, boyaux *mpl* intestinaux; **a bowel disorder** troubles *mpl* intestinaux **(b)** *Fig* **the bowels of the earth** les entrailles *fpl* de la terre

►► *Med* ***bowel cancer*** cancer *m* de l'intestin; ***bowel movement*** selles *fpl*; **to have a bowel movement** aller à la selle

bower ['baʊə(r)] *n* **(a)** *(arbour)* berceau *m* de verdure, charmille *f* **(b)** *Literary (cottage)* chaumière *f*; *(boudoir)* boudoir *m*

bowerbird ['baʊəbɜːd] *n Orn* oiseau *m* à berceau

Bowery ['baʊərɪ] *n* **the Bowery** *(gen)* les bas-quartiers *mpl*; *(in New York)* = quartier pauvre de New York

bowery ['baʊərɪ] *adj Literary (shady)* ombragé

bowfin ['bəʊfɪn] *n Ich* amie *f*

bowfronted [,bəʊ'frʌntɪd] *adj (piece of furniture)* pansu; *Archit (house)* à la façade arrondie

bowhead ['bəʊhed] *n Zool (whale)* baleine *f* boréale

bowie knife ['bəʊɪ-] *n* couteau *m* de chasse

bowing¹ ['baʊɪŋ] *n (UNCOUNT) (greeting)* saluts *mpl*; **bowing and scraping** salamalecs *mpl*, courbettes *fpl*

bowing² ['bəʊɪŋ] *n Mus* technique *f* d'archet; **his bowing is perfect** il a un coup d'archet parfait

bowl [bəʊl] **1** *n* **(a)** *(receptacle, contents)* bol *m*; *(larger)* bassin *m*, cuvette *f*; *(shallow)* jatte *f*; *(made of glass)* coupe *f*; *(for washing-up)* cuvette *f*; *(of beggar)* sébile *f*; **a bowl of rice** un bol de riz; **the cat drank a bowl of milk** le chat a bu tout un bol de lait

(b) *(rounded part → of spoon)* creux *m*; *(→ of pipe)* fourneau *m*; *(→ of wine glass)* coupe *f*; *(→ of sink, toilet)* cuvette *f*

(c) *Geog* bassin *m*, cuvette *f*

(d) *Am Sport (arena)* amphithéâtre *m*; *(championship)* championnat *m*, coupe *f*; *(trophy)* coupe *f*

(e) *Sport (ball)* boule *f*

2 *vt* **(a)** *Sport (ball, bowl)* lancer, faire rouler; *(hoop)* faire rouler

(b) *Sport (score)* **I bowled 160** j'ai marqué 160 points; **to bowl the ball** *(in cricket)* servir; **he bowled (out) the batsman** il a mis le batteur hors jeu

3 *vi* **(a)** *Sport (play bowls)* jouer aux boules; *(play tenpin bowling)* jouer au bowling; *(in cricket)* lancer (la balle); **he bowls for England** *(in cricket)* il sert pour l'Angleterre; *(in bowls)* il joue pour l'Angleterre

(b) *(move quickly)* filer, aller bon train; **the kids came bowling down the street** les enfants descendaient la rue à toute allure; **the bus bowled along the country lanes** l'autocar roulait à toute vitesse sur les petites routes de campagne

4 bowls *n Br Sport* (jeu *m* de) boules *fpl*; **let's play (a game of) bowls!** et si on jouait aux boules!

►► ***bowl game*** = match de football américain, qui n'a pas lieu dans le cadre d'un championnat, qui oppose les meilleures équipes d'une région

►**bowl down** *vt sep Fam* renverser❑

►**bowl out** *vt sep Sport (in cricket)* mettre hors jeu

►**bowl over** *vt sep* **(a)** *(knock down)* renverser, faire tomber **(b)** *Fam Fig (amaze)* stupéfier❑, sidérer; **I was bowled over by the news** la nouvelle m'a abasourdi; **our success really bowled them over** notre réussite les a renversés

bow-legged [bəʊ-] *adj* à jambes arquées

bowler ['bəʊlə(r)] *n* **(a)** *Sport (in bowls)* joueur(euse) *m,f* de boules *ou* pétanque, bouliste *mf*; *(in tenpin bowling)* joueur(euse) *m,f* de bowling; *(in cricket)* lanceur(euse) *m,f* **(b)** *Br (hat)* (chapeau *m*) melon *m*

►► *Br* ***bowler hat*** (chapeau *m*) melon *m*

bowlful ['bəʊlfʊl] *n* bol *m*; **a bowlful of water** une cuvette d'eau

bowline ['bəʊlɪn] *n Naut (rope)* bouline *f*; *(knot)* nœud *m* de chaise

bowling ['bəʊlɪŋ] *n Sport (bowls)* jeu *m* de boules, pétanque *f*; *(tenpin)* bowling *m*; *(in cricket)* service *m*; **to go bowling** *(play bowls)* (aller) jouer à la pétanque; *(play tenpin bowling)* (aller) faire du bowling

►► ***bowling alley*** *(building)* bowling *m*; *(single lane)* piste *f* de bowling; ***bowling ball*** boule *f* de bowling; ***bowling green*** terrain *m* de boules *(sur gazon)*

bowl-shaped *adj (gen)* cratériforme; *(steering wheel)* en tulipe

bowman¹ ['bəʊmən] *(pl* **bowmen** [-mən]*) n Literary (archer)* archer *m*

bowman² ['baʊmən] *(pl* **bowmen** [-mən]*) n Naut* nageur *m* de l'avant

bow-saw [bəʊ-] *n Carp* archet *m (scie)*

bowser ['baʊzə(r)] *n* camion-citerne *m*

bowsprit ['bəʊsprɪt] *n Naut* beaupré *m*

bowstring ['bəʊstrɪŋ] *n Mus* corde *f*

bow-wow [,baʊ'waʊ] **1** *n (in children's language)* toutou *m*

2 *exclam* ouâ ouâ

box [bɒks] *(pl* **boxes***)* **1** *n* **(a)** *(container, contents)* boîte *f*; *(with lock)* coffret *m*; *(cardboard box)* carton *m*; *(crate)* caisse *f*; *(for money)* caisse *f*; *(collecting box)* tronc *m*; **box of chocolates** boîte *f* de chocolats; *Fig* **how can people live in these little boxes?** comment les gens font-ils pour vivre dans ces trous de souris?; *Fig* **in a pine** *or* **wooden box** *(coffin)* dans un cercueil; **if you keep on taking drugs you'll end up in a wooden box** si tu continues à te droguer, tu vas finir au cimetière; *Hum* **the only way he's leaving here is in a wooden box** il ne partira d'ici que les pieds devant; *Br Fam* **to be out of one's box** *(extremely drunk)* être complètement pété, être plein comme une barrique

(b) *(compartment)* compartiment *m*; *Theat* loge *f*; *Theat (on ground floor)* baignoire *f*; *Law (for jury, reporters)* banc *m*; *Law (for witness)* barre *f*; *(in stable)* box *m*, stalle *f*; *Hist (of coachman)* siège *m* (de cocher); **the Royal box** = loge réservée aux membres de la famille royale

(c) *(designated area → on form)* case *f*; *(→ in newspaper)* encadré *m*; *(→ frame around article)* cadre *m*; *(→ on screen)* boîte *f*, case *f*; *Comput (→ for graphic)* cadre *m*; *(→ that can be drawn)* encadré *m*; *(→ on road, sportsfield)* zone *f* quadrillée; *Ftbl (penalty box)* surface *f* de réparation

(d) *Aut & Tech (casing)* boîte *f*, carter *m*; *(of*

axle, brake) boîte *f*; *(of wheel)* moyeu *m*; *(of lock)* palâtre *m*, palastre *m*

(**e**) *Fam TV (television)* **the box** la télé; **what's on the box?** qu'y a-t-il à la télé?

(**f**) *(postal address)* boîte *f* postale

(**g**) *(blow)* **a box on the ears** une gifle, une claque

(**h**) *Gym (for vaulting)* plinth *m*

(**i**) *Sport (protector)* coquille *f*

(**j**) *Bot* buis *m*

(**k**) *Vulg (vagina)* chatte *f*

2 *comp (border, hedge)* de *ou* en buis

3 *vi (fight)* faire de la boxe, boxer

4 *vt* (**a**)*(fight)* boxer avec, boxer

(**b**) *(put in box)* mettre en boîte *ou* caisse

(**c**) *Naut* **to box the compass** réciter les aires du vent

(**d**) *(idiom)* **to box sb's ears** gifler qn; **she boxed his ears** elle l'a giflé

►► ***box calf*** box *m*, box-calf *m*; *Phot* ***box camera*** appareil *m* photographique rudimentaire; *Am Geog* ***box canyon*** cañon *m ou* canyon *m* encaissé; *Am Tech* ***box end wrench*** clef *f* polygonale; ***box file*** boîte *f* archive; *Constr* ***box girder*** poutre-caisson *f*; ***box jellyfish*** cuboméduse *f*; *Br* ***box junction*** carrefour *m (matérialisé sur la chaussée par des bandes croisées)*; ***box kite*** cerf-volant *m* cellulaire; *Am* ***box lunch*** = déjeuner à emporter, vendu dans une boîte; ***box number*** *(in newspaper)* numéro *m* d'annonce; *(at post office)* numéro *m* de boîte à lettres; **Box number 301** Référence 301, Réf. 301; *Theat & Cin* ***box office*** *(office)* bureau *m* de location; *(window)* guichet *m* (de location); **the play was a big success at the box office** *or* **was good box office** la pièce a fait beaucoup d'entrées; *Sewing* ***box pleat*** pli *m* creux; *Tech* ***box spanner*** clef *f ou* clé *f* en douille; ***box spring*** sommier *m* à ressort; *Am* ***box stall*** box *m*; ***box of tricks*** sac *m* à malices

►**box in** *vt sep (enclose)* enfermer, confiner; *(pipes, bath, wash basin)* encastrer; **the car was boxed in between two vans** la voiture était coincée entre deux camionnettes; **to feel boxed in** se sentir à l'étroit; **don't box me in!** de l'air!

►**box off** *vt sep* compartimenter, cloisonner

►**box up** *vt sep* mettre en boîte *ou* caisse; *Fig* enfermer

boxboard ['bɒksbɔːd] *n* carton *m* compact

boxcar ['bɒkskɑː(r)] *n Am Rail* wagon *m* de marchandises (couvert)

boxed [bɒkst] *adj* en boîte

►► ***boxed set*** *(of CDs, videos, books)* coffret *m*

boxer ['bɒksə(r)] **1** *n* (**a**) *(fighter)* boxeur *m* (**b**) *(dog)* boxer *m*

2 boxers *npl (boxer shorts)* caleçon *m*

►► *Aut* ***boxer engine*** moteur *m* à cylindres à plat, boxer *m*; ***boxer shorts*** caleçon *m*

boxercise ['bɒksəsaɪz] *n Sport* = type d'aérobic incluant des mouvements de boxe

boxful ['bɒksfʊl] *n* pleine boîte *f*; *(with lock)* plein coffret *m*; *(cardboard box)* plein carton *m*; *(crate)* pleine caisse *f*

boxing ['bɒksɪŋ] *n* boxe *f*

►► *Br* ***Boxing Day*** = le 26 décembre; ***boxing glove*** gant *m* de boxe; ***boxing match*** match *m* de boxe; ***boxing ring*** ring *m*

box-office *adj* **the film was a box-office success** le film a fait beaucoup d'entrées, **she's always a big box-office draw** *or* **attraction** elle est sûre de faire des entrées

►► ***box-office receipts*** recettes *fpl* en salles

box-pleated *adj Sewing* à plis creux

boxroom ['bɒksrʊm] *n Br* débarras *m*, capharnaüm *m*

boxwood ['bɒkswʊd] *n Bot* buis *m*

boxy ['bɒksɪ] *adj (jacket)* vague; *Pej (building, design)* trop carré

boy [bɔɪ] **1** *n* (**a**) *(male child)* garçon *m*, enfant *m*; **a little boy** un petit garçon, un garçonnet; **when I was a boy** quand j'étais petit *ou* jeune; **be a good boy!** sois sage!; **you bad boy!** vilain!; **an Italian boy** un petit *ou* jeune Italien; **sit down, my boy** assieds-toi, mon petit *ou* mon grand; **I've known them since they were boys** je les connais depuis leur enfance *ou* depuis qu'ils sont petits; **boys will be boys** il faut bien que jeunesse se passe; *Fig* **he's just a boy when it comes to women** ce n'est encore qu'un gamin quand il s'agit des femmes; **he's a mother's boy** c'est le petit garçon à sa maman

(**b**) *(son)* fils *m*; **the Smiths' boy** le petit Smith

(**c**) *Br Sch (student)* élève *m*

(**d**) *Fam (term of address)* **that's my boy!** je te reconnais bien là!; **my dear boy** mon cher ami; *Br* **how are you, old boy?** ça va mon vieux?

(**e**) *(male adult)* **he likes to think he's one of the boys** il aime à croire qu'il fait partie de la bande; **a local boy** un gars du coin; **come on, boys!** allons-y les gars!; **a nice old boy** un vieux monsieur sympathique; **a night out with the boys** une virée entre copains; *Fam* **the boys in blue** les flics *mpl*; **the backroom boys** ceux qui restent dans les coulisses; *Fam* **he threatened to send the boys round** il a menacé d'envoyer ses gars; *Fam* **the big boys** *(important men)* les grosses légumes *fpl*; *Fig* **to play with the big boys** jouer dans la cour des grands

(**f**) *(native servant)* boy *m*, = terme injurieux désignant un servant indigène

(**g**) *Am very Fam Pej (black man)* nègre *m*, = terme injurieux désignant un Noir

(**h**) *(used to address dog, horse etc)* mon beau; **down, boy!** couché, mon beau!

2 *exclam* **(oh) boy!** dis donc!

►► ***boy band*** boys band *m*; ***Boys' Brigade*** = organisation protestante de scoutisme pour garçons; ***Boy's Own*** = magazine d'aventures du début du siècle, dont le nom évoque toute action digne d'un héros d'aventure; *Br Fam* ***boy racer*** jeune conducteur *m* imprudent ☐; ***Boy Scout, boy scout*** scout *m*; ***boy wonder*** petit génie *m*

boycott ['bɔɪkɒt] **1** *n* boycottage *m*, boycott *m*

2 *vt* boycotter

boycotter ['bɔɪkɒtə(r)] *n* boycotteur(euse) *m,f*

boycotting ['bɔɪkɒtɪŋ] *n* boycottage *m*

boyfriend ['bɔɪˌfrend] *n* petit ami *m*, copain *m*; **to have boyfriend trouble** avoir des problèmes de cœur

boyhood ['bɔɪhʊd] *n (when very young)* enfance *f*, première jeunesse *f*; *(in teens)* adolescence *f*; **boyhood friends** amis *mpl* d'enfance

boyish ['bɔɪɪʃ] *adj* (**a**) *(youthful)* d'enfant, de garçon; *(childish)* enfantin, puéril (**b**) *(tomboyish → behaviour)* de garçon manqué; **she's very boyish** elle fait très garçon manqué

boyishly ['bɔɪɪʃlɪ] *adv* (**a**) *(youthfully, childishly)* comme un enfant (**b**) *(tomboyishly)* comme un garçon

boyishness ['bɔɪɪʃnɪs] *n* (**a**) *(of young man)* air *m* juvénil (**b**) *(of girl)* airs *mpl* de garçon manqué

boy-meets-girl *adj* **a boy-meets-girl story** une histoire d'amour conventionnelle

bozo ['bəʊzəʊ] *n Am Fam* crétin(e) *m,f*, andouille *f*

BP [ˌbiːˈpiː] *n Med (abbr* **blood pressure***)* pression *f* artérielle

Bp *Rel (written abbr* **bishop***)* Mgr

bpd [ˌbiːpiːˈdiː] *Petr (abbr* **barrels per day***)* barils *mpl* par jour

BPhil [ˌbiːˈfɪl] *n (abbr* **Bachelor of Philosophy***)* *(person)* = titulaire d'un diplôme intermédiaire entre le MA et le PhD; *(qualification)* = diplôme intermédiaire entre le MA et le PhD

bpi [ˌbiːpiːˈaɪ] *Comput (abbr* **bits per inch***)* bits *mpl* par pouce

bpm [ˌbiːpiːˈem] *Mus (abbr* **beats per minute***)* temps *mpl* par minute

bps [ˌbiːpiːˈes] *Comput (abbr* **bits per second***)* bits *mpl* par seconde

BR [ˌbiːˈɑː(r)] *n Formerly (abbr* **British Rail***)* = société des chemins de fer britanniques

Br (**a**) *(written abbr* **British***)* britannique (**b**) *Rel (written abbr* **brother***)* *(preceding name of monk)* F

bra [brɑː] *n* soutien-gorge *m*; **half-cup bra** Balconnet® *m*; **underwired bra** soutien-gorge *m* avec armature

►► ***bra strap*** bretelle *f* de soutien-gorge

braai [braɪ] *n SAfr Culin* barbecue *m*

Brabant [brəˈbænt] *n Geog* Brabant *m*; **in Brabant** dans le Brabant

brace [breɪs] *(pl senses* (**a**) *to* (**d**) *and* (**f**) **braces**, *pl sense* (**e**) **inv**) **1** *n* (**a**)*(supporting or fastening device)* attache *f*, agrafe *f*

(**b**) *(for leg)* appareil *m* orthopédique; *(for teeth)* appareil *m* dentaire *ou* orthodontique; *(for torso)* corset *m*

(**c**) *Constr* étai *m*

(**d**) *(drill)* **brace (and bit)** vilebrequin *m* à main

(**e**) *(of game birds, pistols)* paire *f*

(**f**) *Mus & Typ (bracket)* accolade *f*

2 *vt* (**a**) *(strengthen)* renforcer, consolider; *(support)* soutenir; *Constr* étayer; *(beam)* armer; *Aviat (wing)* croisillonner; **to brace a beam with sth** armer une poutre de qch

(**b**) *(steady, prepare)* **he braced his body/himself for the impact** il raidit son corps/s'arc-bouta en préparation du choc; **he braced himself to try again** il a rassemblé ses forces pour une nouvelle tentative; **the family braced itself for the funeral** la famille s'est armée de courage pour les funérailles; **brace yourself for some bad news** préparez-vous à de mauvaises nouvelles

(**c**) *(of weather)* fortifier, tonifier

3 *vi Am (prepare)* se préparer; **they braced for the attack** ils se préparèrent à soutenir l'assaut

4 braces *npl* (**a**) *Br (for trousers)* bretelles *fpl*

(**b**) *(for teeth)* appareil *m* dentaire *ou* orthodontique

►**brace up 1** *vt sep* **to brace sb up** réconforter qn

2 *vi (take heart)* reprendre courage, se ressaisir; **you have to brace up and face the situation** il faut te ressaisir et faire face

bracelet ['breɪslɪt] **1** *n* bracelet *m*

2 bracelets *npl Fam Crime slang (handcuffs)* menottes ☐ *fpl*, bracelets *mpl*

bracer ['breɪsə(r)] *n Fam* remontant *m*

brachiopod ['brækɪəpɒd] *n Zool (mollusc)* brachiopode *m*

brachiosaurus [ˌbrækɪəˈsɔːrəs] *(pl* **brachiosauruses** *or* **brachiosauri** [-raɪ]) *n Zool* brachiosaure *m*

brachycephalic [ˌbrækɪsɪˈfælɪk] *adj Anat & Zool* brachycéphale

brachylogy [bræˈkɪlədʒɪ] *(pl* **brachylogies***)* *n Ling* brachylogie *f*

bracing ['breɪsɪŋ] **1** *adj* fortifiant, tonifiant; **a bracing wind** un vent vivifiant

2 *n Constr* entretoisement *m*

►► *Constr* ***bracing strut*** jambe *f* de force

bracken ['brækən] *n Bot* fougère *f*

bracket ['brækɪt] **1** *n* (**a**) *(L-shaped support)* équerre *f*, support *m*; *(for shelf)* équerre *f*, tasseau *m*; *(lamp fixture)* fixation *f*; *Archit* console *f*, corbeau *m*

(**b**) *(category)* groupe *m*, classe *f*; *Fin (level of income, tax)* tranche *f*; **the 20-25 age bracket** le groupe des 20-25 ans; **the high/low income bracket** la tranche des gros/petits revenus; **my rise put me in the £20,000 a year bracket** mon augmentation de salaire m'a placé dans la tranche (de revenus) des 20 000 livres annuelles

(**c**) *Math & Typ (round)* parenthèse *f*; *(square)* crochet *m*; **in** *or* **between brackets** entre parenthèses; *Mus & Typ* **(brace) bracket** accolade *f*

2 *vt* (**a**) *(put in parentheses)* mettre entre parenthèses; *(put in square brackets)* mettre entre crochets

(**b**) *(in vertical list)* réunir par une accolade

(**c**) *Fig (categorize)* associer, mettre dans la même catégorie; **he is often bracketed with the Surrealists** on le range souvent parmi les surréalistes; **why bracket together two such different companies?** pourquoi mettre deux entreprises aussi différentes dans la même catégorie?

►► *Bot* ***bracket fungus*** polypore *m*

bracketing ['brækɪtɪŋ] *n* (**a**) *(in parentheses)* mise *f* entre parenthèses; *(in square brackets)* mise *f* entre crochets (**b**) *(in a vertical list)* réunion *f* par une accolade

brackish ['brækɪʃ] *adj* saumâtre

bract [brækt] *n Bot* bractée *f*

brad [bræd] *n Tech* semence *f*, clou *m* de tapissier

bradawl ['brædɔːl] *n Tech* poinçon *m*

Brady Bunch ['breɪdɪ-] *n* **The Brady Bunch** = feuilleton télévisé américain des années 60-70 racontant la famille parfaite type

bradycardia [ˌbrædɪˈkɑːdɪə] *n Med* bradycardie *f*

bradykinin [ˌbrædɪˈkaɪnɪn] *n Biol* bradykinine *f*

brae [breɪ] *n Scot (hillside)* colline *f*; *(slope)* pente *f*, côte *f*

brag [bræg] *(pt & pp* **bragged**, *cont* **bragging***)* **1** *vi* se vanter; **to brag about sth** se vanter de qch; **he's always bragging about his salary** il faut toujours qu'il se vante de son salaire; **it's nothing to brag about** il n'y a pas là de quoi se vanter

2 *n* (**a**) *(boasting)* vantardise *f*, fanfaronnades *fpl* (**b**) *(person)* vantard(e) *m,f*, fanfaron(onne) *m,f* (**c**) *(card game)* = jeu de cartes qui ressemble au poker

braggadocio [ˌbrægəˈdəʊtʃɪəʊ] *n Literary* vantardise *f*

braggart [ˈbrægət] *n* vantard(e) *m,f*, fanfaron(onne) *m,f*

bragging [ˈbrægɪŋ] **1** *adj* vantard, fanfaron

2 *n* vantardise *f*, fanfaronnades *fpl*

Brahma [ˈbrɑːmə] *pr n Rel* Brahma

Brahman [ˈbrɑːmən] *n Rel (person)* brahmane *m*

brahmanic [ˌbrɑːˈmænɪk], **brahmanical** [ˌbrɑːˈmænɪkəl] *adj* brahmanique

Brahmanism [ˈbrɑːmənɪzəm] *n Rel* brahmanisme *m*

Brahmaputra [ˌbrɑːməˈpuːtrə] *n Geog* **the Brahmaputra** le Brahmapoutre

Brahmin [ˈbrɑːmɪn] (*pl* **inv** *or* **Brahmins**) *n* (**a**) *Rel* brahmane *m* (**b**) *Am Fam* intellectuel(elle)❑ *m,f*; **she's a Boston Brahmin** elle est d'une vieille famille bostonienne❑

brahminic [ˌbrɑːˈmɪnɪk], **brahminical** [ˌbrɑːˈmɪnɪkəl] *adj Am Fam* intellectuel❑

Brahminism [ˈbrɑːmɪnɪzəm] *n Rel* brahmanisme *m*

Brahms and Liszt [ˌbrɑːmzənˈlɪst] *adj Br Fam (rhyming slang* **pissed***)* rond comme un tonneau

braid [breɪd] **1** *n* (**a**) *(trimming)* ganse *f*, soutache *f*; *(on uniform)* galon *m* (**b**) *esp Am (of hair)* tresse *f*, natte *f*; **she wears her hair in braids** elle porte *ou* se fait des nattes

2 *vt* (**a**) *esp Am (plait)* tresser, natter (**b**) *(decorate with)* soutacher, galonner

braided [ˈbreɪdɪd] *adj* (**a**) *(clothing)* passementé (**b**) *esp Am (hair)* tressé

braille, Braille [breɪl]

1 *n* braille *m*; **to read Braille** lire le braille; **in Braille** en braille

2 *comp (reader, teacher)* de braille; *(book)* en braille

►► ***Braille alphabet*** alphabet *m* braille

brailled [breɪld] *adj (switches, instructions)* en braille

brain [breɪn] **1** *n* (**a**) *(part of body)* cerveau *m*; *(mind)* cerveau *m*, tête *f*; *Culin* cervelle *f*; *Med* **she had a brain scan** on lui a fait un scanner du cerveau

(**b**) *Fam Fig* **we're going to beat his brains out** on va lui casser la figure; **to blow one's brains out** se faire sauter la cervelle; **you've got money on the brain** tu es obsédé par l'argent; **she's got it on the brain** elle ne pense qu'à ça, ça la tient

(**c**) *(intelligence)* intelligence *f*; **he's got brains** il est intelligent; **you need a good brain to solve this puzzle** il faut être intelligent pour résoudre ce problème; **I haven't got the brains to become a doctor** je ne suis pas assez intelligent pour devenir médecin; **anyone with half a brain** n'importe qui d'un tant soit peu intelligent; **can I pick your brains for a minute?** j'ai besoin de tes lumières; *Rad* **Brain of Britain** = jeu radiophonique britannique portant sur des questions de culture générale; *Br Fam Fig* **he's a real Brain of Britain** c'est une grosse tête

(**d**) *Fam (clever person)* cerveau *m*

2 *comp Med (disease)* cérébral

3 *vt Fam (hit)* assommer❑

4 brains *n Fam (clever person)* cerveau *m*; **the brains** le cerveau; **she's the brains of the family/business** c'est elle le cerveau de la famille/de l'entreprise

►► *Med* ***brain damage*** lésions *fpl* cérébrales; *Med* ***brain death*** mort *f* cérébrale; ***brain drain*** fuite *f ou* exode *m* des cerveaux; *Fam* ***brain food*** = aliments censés être bons pour la mémoire, les capacités intellectuelles etc; *Med* ***brain surgeon*** neurochirugien *m*; *Med* ***brain surgery*** neurochirurgie *f*; *Am* ***brain trust,*** *Br* ***brains trust*** *(panel of experts)* groupe *m* d'experts, brain-trust *m*; *Med* ***brain tumour*** tumeur *m* au cerveau

brainbox [ˈbreɪmbɒks] *n Br Fam (skull)* crâne❑ *m*; *(person)* cerveau *m*

brainchild [ˈbreɪnˌtʃaɪld] (*pl* **brainchildren** [-ˌtʃɪldrən]) *n Fam* bébé *m*; **the scheme is his brainchild** le projet est son bébé

brain-dead *adj Med* **to be brain-dead** *(accident victim)* être en coma dépassé; *Fam Fig (extremely stupid)* ne rien avoir dans la cervelle

braininess [ˈbreɪnɪnɪs] *n Fam* intelligence❑ *f*

brainless [ˈbreɪnlɪs] *adj (person)* écervelé, stupide; *(idea)* stupide

brainpan [ˈbreɪnpæn] *n Fam* crâne❑ *m*

brainpower [ˈbreɪnˌpaʊə(r)] *n* intelligence *f*

brainstem [ˈbreɪnstem] *n Anat* tronc *m* cérébral

brainstorm [ˈbreɪnstɔːm] **1** *n* (**a**) *Med* congestion *f* cérébrale (**b**) *Br Fam Fig (mental aberration)* idée *f* insensée *ou* loufoque (**c**) *Am Fam Fig (brilliant idea)* idée *f* géniale

2 *vi* faire du brainstorming

3 *vt* plancher sur

brainstorming [ˈbreɪnˌstɔːmɪŋ] *n* brainstorming *m*, remue-méninges *m inv*; **a brainstorming session** un brainstorming, une réunion de remue-méninges

brainteaser [ˈbreɪnˌtiːzə(r)] *n Fam* énigme❑ *f*, colle *f*

brainwash [ˈbreɪnwɒʃ] *vt* faire un lavage de cerveau à; **to brainwash sb into doing sth** faire un lavage de cerveau à qn pour qu'il fasse qch; **advertisements can brainwash people into believing anything** la publicité peut faire croire n'importe quoi aux gens; **I won't be brainwashed into buying things I don't need** je refuse de me laisser manipuler pour acheter des choses dont je n'ai pas besoin

brainwashing [ˈbreɪnˌwɒʃɪŋ] *n* lavage *m* de cerveau

brainwave [ˈbreɪnweɪv] *n* (**a**) *Med* onde *f* cérébrale (**b**) *Fam (brilliant idea)* idée *f* géniale; **I've had a brainwave!** j'ai eu un éclair de génie!

brainy [ˈbreɪnɪ] (*compar* **brainier,** *superl* **brainiest**) *adj Fam* intelligent❑, futé

braise [breɪz] *vt Culin* braiser, cuire à l'étouffée

braising [ˈbreɪzɪŋ] *n Culin* cuisson *f* à l'étouffée

►► ***braising beef*** bœuf *m* à braiser

brake [breɪk] **1** *n* (**a**) *(gen) & Aut* frein *m*; **to put on** *or* **to apply the brakes** freiner; **to slam on the brakes** écraser la pédale de frein; **release the brake** desserrez le frein; *Fig* **bad weather has put a brake on construction work** le mauvais temps a mis un frein à la construction; **high interest rates acted as a brake on borrowing** des taux d'intérêt élevés ont freiné les emprunts

(**b**) *(carriage)* break *m*

(**c**) *Bot (bracken)* fougère *f*; *(thicket)* fourré *m*

2 *comp Aut (cable)* de frein

3 *vi Aut* freiner, mettre le frein; **to brake hard** freiner brusquement, écraser la pédale de frein

►► ***brake adjuster spanner*** clé *f* de réglage des freins; *Aut* ***brake block*** sabot *m ou* patin *m* de frein; *Aut* ***brake drum*** tambour *m* de frein; *Aut* ***brake fade*** fading *m*; *Aut* ***brake fluid*** liquide *m* de freins, Lockheed® *m*; *Aut* ***brake horsepower*** puissance *f* au frein; *Aut* ***brake lamp*** feu *m* de stop; *Aut & Tech* ***brake lever*** frein *m* à main; *Aut* ***brakelight*** feu *m* de stop; *Am Rad & TV* ***brakelight function*** signal *m* de fin de temps de parole; *Aut* ***brake lining*** garniture *f* de frein; *Aut* ***brake pad*** plaquette *f* de frein; *Aviat* ***brake parachute*** parachute *m* de freinage; *Aut* ***brake pedal*** pédale *f* de frein; *Aut* ***brake shoe*** mâchoire *f* de frein; *Br Rail* ***brake van*** fourgon *m* à frein

braked trailer [ˈbreɪkt-] *n Aut* remorque *f* freinée

brakeman [ˈbreɪkmæn] (*pl* **brakemen** [-mən]) *n* (**a**) *Am Rail* garde-frein *m* (**b**) *Sport (for bobsleigh)* = équipier qui s'occupe du frein

brakesman [ˈbreɪksmən] (*pl* **brakesmen** [-mən]) *n Br Rail* garde-frein *m*

braking [ˈbreɪkɪŋ] *n Aut* freinage *m*

►► ***braking distance*** distance *f* de freinage

bramble [ˈbræmbəl] *n Bot* (**a**) *(prickly shrub)* roncier *m*, roncière *f* (**b**) *(blackberry bush)* ronce *f* des haies, mûrier *m* sauvage; **I fell among the brambles** je suis tombé dans les ronces (**c**) *(berry)* mûre *f* sauvage

►► ***bramble jelly*** gelée *f* de mûres

brambling [ˈbræmblɪŋ] *n Orn* pinson *m* du Nord

brambly [ˈbræmblɪ] *adj Bot* couvert de ronces

Bramley [ˈbræmlɪ] *n* **Bramley (apple)** pomme *f* Bramley *(variété de pomme à cuire)*

bran [bræn] *n* son *m* (de blé), bran *m*

►► ***bran flakes*** son *m* en flocons; ***bran loaf*** pain *m* au son; *Br* ***bran mash*** son *m ou* bran *m* mouillé; *Br* ***bran tub*** pêche *f* miraculeuse *(jeu)*

branch [brɑːntʃ] **1** *n* (**a**) *(of tree)* branche *f*; **the branches** le branchage, les branches

(**b**) *(secondary part → of road)* embranchement *m*; *(→ of river)* bras *m*; *(→ of railway)* bifurcation *f*, raccordement *m*; *(→ of pipe)* branchement *m*; *(→ of candlestick, artery)* branche *f*

(**c**) *(division → gen)* division *f*, section *f*; *(→ of family)* ramification *f*, branche *f*; *(→ of science)* branche *f*; *(→ of police force)* antenne *f*; *(→ of government, civil service)* service *m*; *Mil (→ of armed forces)* division *f*; *Ling* rameau *m*

(**d**) *Com (of company)* agence *f*, succursale *f*, filiale *f*; *(of shop)* succursale *f*; *(of bank)* agence *f*, succursale *f*; **where's the nearest branch of Kookaï?** où se trouve le Kookaï le plus proche?

(**e**) *Comput (of network)* branchement *m*

(**f**) *Am Geog (stream)* ruisseau *m*

2 *vi* (**a**) *(tree)* se ramifier

(**b**) *(road, river)* bifurquer

►► ***branch banking*** banque *f* à réseau; *Rail* ***branch line*** ligne *f* secondaire; ***branch manager*** *(of bank)* directeur(trice) *m,f* d'agence; *(of shop)* directeur(trice) *m,f* de succursale; ***branch office*** *(of company)* succursale *f*; *(of bank)* agence *f*, succursale *f*; *Fam* ***branch water*** eau *f* plate❑

►**branch off** *vi* (**a**) *(road)* bifurquer; **a smaller path branches off to the left** un chemin plus petit bifurque vers la gauche (**b**) *(digress)* **I'd like to branch off from my main topic for a moment** j'aimerais m'écarter un instant du sujet qui m'occupe

►**branch out** *vi* étendre ses activités; **they're branching out into the restaurant business** ils étendent leurs activités à *ou* se lancent dans la restauration; **I'm going to branch out on my own** je vais faire cavalier seul

branched [brɑːntʃt] *adj* (**a**) *Bot* branchu, rameux (**b**) *(candlestick)* à (plusieurs) branches

branchia [ˈbræŋkɪə] (*pl* **branchiae** [-kɪiː]) *n Ich & Zool* branchie *f*

branchiate [ˈbræŋkɪət] *adj Ich & Zool* branchié

branchless [ˈbrɑːntʃlɪs] *adj* sans branches, dépourvu de branches

brand [brænd] **1** *n* (**a**) *Com & Mktg (trademark)* marque *f* (de fabrique); **he always buys the same brand of cigars** il achète toujours la même marque de cigares; *Fig* **he has his own brand of humour** il a un sens de l'humour particulier; **brand X** = terme désignant "votre marque habituelle" dans la publicité comparative

(**b**) *(identifying mark → on cattle)* marque *f*; *Hist (→ on criminal)* flétrissure *f*

(**c**) *Metal (branding iron)* fer *m* à marquer

(**d**) *(burning wood)* tison *m*, brandon *m*; *Literary (torch)* flambeau *m*

2 *vt* (**a**) *(with branding iron → person, animal, goods)* marquer au fer rouge; *Hist (→ criminal)* flétrir, marquer au fer rouge; *Hist (→ slave)* marquer

(**b**) *Fig (label)* étiqueter, stigmatiser; **she was branded (as) a thief** on lui a collé une étiquette de voleuse

(**c**) *(impress indelibly)* **the experience was branded on his memory for life** l'expérience resta à jamais gravée dans sa mémoire

►► *Mktg* ***brand advertising*** publicité *f* de marque, publicité *f* sur la marque; *Mktg* ***brand awareness*** mémorisation *f* de la marque, notoriété *f* de la marque; *Mktg* ***brand image*** image *f* de marque; *Mktg* ***brand leader*** marque *f* dominante; *Mktg* ***brand loyalty*** fidélité *f* à la marque; *Com & Mktg* ***brand manager*** chef *m* de marque; *Com & Mktg* ***brand name*** marque *f* (de fabrique); *Mktg* ***brand name recall*** mémorisation *f* de la marque; *Mktg* ***brand recognition*** identification *f* de la marque

branded goods [ˈbrændɪd-] *npl Mktg* produits *mpl* de marque

Brandenburg [ˈbrændənbɜːg] *n Geog* Brandebourg

►► ***the Brandenburg Gate*** la Porte de Brandebourg

'The Brandenburg Concertos' *Bach* 'Les Concertos brandebourgeois'

branding ['brændɪŋ] *n* (**a**) *(of cattle)* marquage *m* au fer rouge (**b**) *Mktg* marquage *m*
►► ***branding campaign*** campagne *f* d'image de marque; ***branding iron*** fer *m* à marquer

brandish ['brændɪʃ] **1** *n* brandissement *m*
2 *vt* brandir

brand-led *adj Mktg* conditionné par la marque, piloté par la marque

brand-loyal *adj Mktg* fidèle à la marque

brand-new *adj* tout *ou* flambant neuf

brand-sensitive *adj Mktg* sensible aux marques

Brand's Hatch *n* = circuit de courses automobiles en Angleterre

brandy ['brændɪ] (*pl* **brandies**) *n (cognac)* cognac *m*; *(made from fruit other than grapes)* eau-de-vie *f*; **plum brandy** eau-de-vie *f* de prune; **brandy and soda** = fine à l'eau
►► *Br Culin* ***brandy butter*** = beurre mélangé avec du sucre et parfumé au cognac; ***brandy glass*** verre *m* à cognac; *Br Culin* ***brandy snap*** cigarette *f* russe au gingembre

brash [bræʃ] **1** *adj* (**a**) *(showy)* exubérant; *(impudent)* effronté, impertinent (**b**) *(colour)* criard
2 *n* (**a**) *Geol (rocks)* éboulis *m*; *(wood)* bois *m* cassant (**b**) *(ice)* glace *f* en débâcle, sarrasins *mpl*

brashly ['bræʃlɪ] *adv (showily)* avec exubérance; *(with impudence)* effrontément, avec impertinence

brashness ['bræʃnɪs] *n (showiness)* exubérance *f*; *(impudence)* effronterie *f*, impertinence *f*

Brasilia [brə'zɪljə] *n* Brasilia

brass [brɑːs] **1** *n* (**a**) *(metal)* cuivre *m* (jaune), laiton *m*
(**b**) *(objects)* **brass(es)** cuivres *mpl*; **the brass is cleaned once a week** les cuivres sont faits une fois par semaine
(**c**) *Br (memorial)* plaque *f* mortuaire (en cuivre)
(**d**) *Mus* **the brass** les cuivres *mpl*
(**e**) *Fam Mil* **the (top) brass** les huiles *fpl*
(**f**) *Br Fam (nerve)* toupet *m*, culot *m*; **he had the brass to accuse me of cheating** il a eu le toupet de m'accuser de tricher
(**g**) *Br Fam (money)* pognon *m*
(**h**) *Br very Fam (prostitute)* pute *f*
(**i**) *(idioms)* **to get down to brass tacks** en venir au fait *ou* aux choses sérieuses; *Br very Fam* **it's brass monkeys** *(very cold)* on se les gèle, on se les caille; *Br Fam* **it's not worth a brass farthing** ça ne vaut pas un clou
2 *comp (object, ornament)* de *ou* en cuivre; *(foundry)* de cuivre
►► *Mus* ***brass band*** fanfare *f*, orchestre *m* de cuivres; *Mus* ***brass ensemble*** ensemble *m* de cuivres; *Br Fam Fig* ***brass hat*** gros bonnet *m*; *Am* ***brass knuckles*** coup-de-poing *m* américain; *Br Fam* ***brass neck*** *(nerve)* toupet *m*, culot *m*; **to have a brass neck** avoir du culot, être culotté; **I don't know how you have the brass neck to say that!** je ne sais pas comment tu peux avoir le culot de dire une chose pareille!; ***brass player*** = musicien qui joue d'un instrument à vent en cuivre; *Art* ***brass rubbing*** *(picture)* décalque *m*; *(action)* décalquage *m* par frottement; *Mus* ***the brass section*** les cuivres *mpl*
►**brass off** *vt sep Br Fam* **to brass sb off** gonfler qn

brass-collar *adj Am Pol* qui soutient sans faille la ligne du parti, inconditionnel

brassed off [brɑːst-] *adj Br Fam* **to be brassed off** en avoir marre; **I'm brassed off with waiting** j'en ai marre d'attendre; **I'm brassed off with their complaints** j'en ai plein le dos de leurs récriminations

brasserie ['bræsərɪ] *n* brasserie *f*

brassica ['bræsɪkə] *n Bot* brassica *m*

brassie ['brɑːsɪ] *n Golf* brassie *m*

brassiere [*Br* 'bræzɪə(r), *Am* brə'zɪər] *n* soutien-gorge *m*

brassily ['brɑːsɪlɪ] *adv Fam (brazenly)* effrontément [❑]

brassiness ['brɑːsɪnɪs] *n* (**a**) *(of sound)* caractère *m* métallique (**b**) *Fam (brazenness)* effronterie [❑] *f*, impertinence [❑] *f*

brass-monkey *adj Br very Fam* **it's brass-monkey weather** on se les gèle, on se les caille

brassware ['brɑːsweə(r)] *n (utensils)* chaudronnerie *f* d'art

brasswork ['brɑːswɜːk] *n Metal* dinanderie *f*

brassy ['brɑːsɪ] (*compar* **brassier**, *superl* **brassiest**) **1** *adj* (**a**) *(colour)* cuivré; *(sound)* cuivré, claironnant; *Pej (yellow, blonde)* artificiel; *(cheap jewellery)* qui fait toc (**b**) *Fam (brazen)* effronté [❑], impertinent [❑]
2 *n Golf* brassie *m*

brat [bræt] *n Pej* morveux(euse) *m,f*, galopin *m*; **that kid is a real brat** un vrai morveux, ce gamin; **she brought her brats** elle a amené sa marmaille
►► ***the brat pack*** *(gen)* les jeunes loups arrogants; *Cin* = terme désignant les jeunes acteurs américains populaires des années 80

Bratislava [,brætɪ'slɑːvə] *n* Bratislava *f*

bravado [brə'vɑːdəʊ] *n* bravade *f*

brave [breɪv] **1** *adj* (**a**) *(courageous)* courageux; **be brave!** sois courageux!, du courage!; **you'll have to be brave and tell him** tu vas devoir prendre ton courage à deux mains et le lui dire; **to put on a brave face, to put a brave face on it** faire bonne contenance; **it was a brave effort nonetheless** néanmoins c'était un bel effort
(**b**) *Literary (splendid)* beau (belle), excellent; **a brave new world** une ère nouvelle
2 *vt (person)* braver, défier; *(danger, storm)* braver, affronter
3 *npl (people)* **the brave** les courageux *mpl*; **the bravest of the brave** les plus braves d'entre les braves
4 *n Hist (Indian warrior)* brave *m*, guerrier *m* indien
►**brave out** *vt sep* faire face à; **we'll just have to brave it out!** nous devrons tout simplement faire face à la situation!

> **Brave new world**
> Il s'agit du titre d'un roman de science-fiction de l'écrivain anglais Aldous Huxley (publié en 1932) et d'une allusion à un vers de Shakespeare dans *La Tempête*. Il est intéressant de noter que le titre français du roman est *Le Meilleur des mondes*, une allusion au *Candide* de Voltaire.
> L'expression **brave new world** s'utilise à propos de tout changement de société provoqué par les progrès de la science. On parlera par exemple de **the brave new world of genetic manipulation** ("l'ère de la manipulation génétique").

bravely ['breɪvlɪ] *adv* courageusement, bravement

bravery ['breɪvərɪ] *n* courage *m*, vaillance *f*; **bravery award** médaille *f* du courage

bravo [,brɑː'vəʊ] (*pl* **bravos**) **1** *exclam* bravo!
2 *n* bravo *m*

bravura [brə'vʊərə] *n (gen) & Mus* bravoure *f*

brawl [brɔːl] **1** *n* (**a**) *(fight)* bagarre *f*, rixe *f*; **a drunken brawl** une querelle d'ivrognes (**b**) *Am Fam (party)* java *f* (**c**) *Literary (of stream)* murmure *m*
2 *vi* (**a**) *(fight)* se bagarrer (**b**) *Literary (of stream)* murmurer

brawler ['brɔːlə(r)] *n* bagarreur(euse) *m,f*

brawling ['brɔːlɪŋ] *n* (**a**) *(fighting)* bagarres *fpl*, rixes *fpl* (**b**) *Literary (of stream)* murmure *m*

brawn [brɔːn] *n (UNCOUNT)* (**a**) *(muscle)* muscles *mpl*; *(strength)* muscle *m*; **to have plenty of brawn** avoir du biceps; **all brawn and no brains** tout dans les bras et rien dans la tête (**b**) *Br Culin* fromage *m* de tête

brawniness ['brɔːnɪnɪs] *n (of person)* carrure *f* musclée, forte carrure *f*

brawny ['brɔːnɪ] (*compar* **brawnier**, *superl* **brawniest**) *adj (arm)* musculeux; *(person)* musclé

bray [breɪ] **1** *n (of donkey)* braiment *m*; *Pej (of person)* braillement *m*; *Mus (of trumpet)* beuglement *m*, bruit *m* strident
2 *vi (donkey)* braire; *Pej (person)* brailler; *Mus (trumpet)* beugler, retentir

braze [breɪz] *vt Metal* braser

brazen ['breɪzən] *adj* (**a**) *(bold)* effronté, impudent; **a brazen lie** un mensonge audacieux *ou* effronté; **a brazen hussy** une effrontée (**b**) *Metal (brass)* de cuivre (jaune), de laiton; *(sound)* cuivré
►**brazen out** *vt sep* **you'll have to brazen it out** il va falloir que tu t'en tires par des fanfaronnades

brazen-faced *adj* effronté, impudent

brazenly ['breɪzənlɪ] *adv* effrontément, impudemment

brazenness ['breɪzənnɪs] *n* effronterie *f*

brazier ['breɪzɪə(r)] *n* (**a**) *(for fire)* brasero *m* (**b**) *Metal (brass worker)* chaudronnier *m*

Brazil [brə'zɪl] *n* Brésil *m*; **in Brazil** au Brésil

brazil [brə'zɪl] *n* **brazil (nut)** noix *f* du Brésil

Brazilian [brə'zɪljən] **1** *n* Brésilien(enne) *m,f*
2 *adj* brésilien
3 *comp (embassy, history)* du Brésil

breach [briːtʃ] **1** *n* (**a**) *(gap)* brèche *f*, trou *m*; *Mil* **our troops made a breach in the enemy lines** nos troupes ont percé les lignes ennemies; *Fig* **she stepped into the breach when I fell ill** elle m'a remplacé au pied levé quand je suis tombé malade; *Fam Hum* **once more into the breach (, dear friends)** encore une fois sur la brèche (, les amis)
(**b**) *(violation → of law)* violation *f* (**of** de); *(→ of discipline, order, rules)* infraction *f* (**of** de); *(→ of etiquette, friendship)* manquement *m* (**of** à); *(→ of confidence, trust)* abus *m* (**of** de); **a breach of faith** *(gen)* un manque de foi; *Law* un acte de déloyauté; **a breach of professional secrecy** une violation du secret professionnel
(**c**) *(rift)* brouille *f*, désaccord *m*
(**d**) *Zool (of whale)* saut *m*
2 *vt* (**a**) *(make gap in)* ouvrir une brèche dans, faire un trou dans; *Mil* **we breached the enemy lines** nous avons percé les lignes ennemies
(**b**) *Com & Law (agreement)* violer, rompre; *(promise)* manquer à
3 *vi (whale)* sauter hors de l'eau
►► *Law* ***breach of contract*** rupture *f* de contrat; *Law* ***breach of the peace*** atteinte *f* à l'ordre public; *Parl* ***breach of privilege*** atteinte *f* aux privilèges parlementaires; ***breach of promise*** *(gen)* manque *m* de parole; *(of marriage)* violation *f* de promesse de mariage

> **Once more into the breach, dear friends**
> Cette phrase ("encore une fois sur la brèche, les amis") est extraite d'un passage de *Henry V* de Shakespeare, lorsque le roi s'adresse à ses soldats pour les encourager avant la bataille d'Azincourt.
> Aujourd'hui on utilise cette phrase sur le mode humoristique lorsque l'on entreprend une tâche difficile, et souvent avant un deuxième essai.

bread [bred] **1** *n (UNCOUNT)* (**a**) *(foodstuff)* pain *m*; **a loaf of bread** un pain, une miche; **freshly baked bread** du pain frais; **bread and butter** du pain beurré; **a slice of bread and butter** une tartine (beurrée); **translation is her bread and butter** la traduction est son gagne-pain; **they put the prisoner on bread and water** ils ont mis le prisonnier au pain sec et à l'eau; *Rel* **the bread and wine** les espèces *fpl*; **to earn one's daily bread** gagner sa vie *ou* sa croûte; *Fig* **to put bread on the table** *(of person)* faire bouillir la marmite; *Fig* **to take the bread out of sb's mouth** ôter le pain de la bouche à qn; **I know which side my bread is buttered on** je sais où est mon intérêt; *Bible* **give us each day our daily bread** donnez-nous aujourd'hui notre pain quotidien
(**b**) *Fam (money)* pognon *m*, fric *m*
2 *vt Culin (coat in breadcrumbs)* passer à la chapelure
►► *Br* ***bread bin***, *Am* ***bread box*** *(small)* boîte *f* à pain; *(larger)* huche *f* à pain; *Culin* ***bread pudding*** gâteau *m* de pain; *Br Culin* ***bread sauce*** sauce *f* à la mie de pain

bread-and-butter *adj* (**a**) *Fam (basic)* **a bread-and-butter job** un travail qui assure le nécessaire [❑]; **the bread-and-butter issues** les questions les plus terre-à-terre [❑] (**b**) *Fam (reliable → person)* sur qui l'on peut compter [❑]
►► *Fam* ***bread-and-butter letter*** lettre *f* de remerciements; *Culin* ***bread-and-butter pudding*** pudding *m* au pain

breadbasket ['bred,bɑːskɪt] *n* (**a**) *(basket)* corbeille *f* à pain (**b**) *Geog* région *f* céréalière (**c**) *Fam Old-fashioned (stomach)* estomac [❑] *m*

breadboard ['bredbɔːd] *n* (**a**) *(for bread)* planche *f* à pain (**b**) *Electron* montage *m* expérimental

breadcrumb ['bredkrʌm] **1** *n* miette *f* de pain

2 *vt Culin (coat in breadcrumbs)* passer à la chapelure

3 breadcrumbs *npl Culin* chapelure *f*, panure *f*; **fish fried in breadcrumbs** du poisson pané

breaded ['bredɪd] *adj Culin* pané; *(before cooking)* enrobé de chapelure

breadfruit ['bredfruːt] *n Bot (tree)* arbre *m* à pain; *(fruit)* fruit *m* à pain

breadknife ['brednaɪf] (*pl* **breadknives** [-naɪvz]) *n* couteau *m* à pain

breadline ['bredlaɪn] *n* = file d'attente pour recevoir des vivres gratuits; *Fig* **to live** *or* **to be on the breadline** être sans le sou *ou* indigent

breadstick ['bredstɪk] *n Culin* gressin *m*, *Suisse* flûte *f*

breadth [bredθ] *n* (**a**) *(width)* largeur *f*; *(of cloth)* lé *m*; **the stage is 60 metres in breadth** la scène a 60 mètres de large (**b**) *(scope → of mind, thought)* largeur *f*; *(→ of style)* ampleur *f*; *Art* largeur *f* d'exécution; *Mus* jeu *m* large

breadthwise ['bredθˌwaɪz], **breadthways** ['bredθˌweɪz] *adv* dans le sens de la largeur

breadwinner ['bredˌwɪnə(r)] *n Fin* soutien *m* de famille

BREAK [breɪk]

casser	▶ 1 (a), (c)
briser	▶ 1 (a), (i), (j)
fracturer	▶ 1 (b)
enfoncer	▶ 1 (e)
violer, enfreindre	▶ 1 (f)
rompre	▶ 1 (h)
couper	▶ 1 (h)
ruiner	▶ 1 (k)
amortir	▶ 1 (l)
se casser	▶ 2 (a)
se briser	▶ 2 (a)
se fracturer	▶ 2 (b)
cassure, brisure	▶ 3 (a)
fissure, fente	▶ 3 (b)
ouverture	▶ 3 (c)
interruption	▶ 3 (d)
pause	▶ 3 (e)
évasion	▶ 3 (f)
chance	▶ 3 (g)
changement	▶ 3 (h)

(*pt* **broke** [brəʊk], *pp* **broken** ['brəʊkn]) **1** *vt* (**a**) *(split into pieces → glass, furniture)* casser, briser; *(→ branch, lace, string, egg, toy)* casser; **break the stick in two** cassez le bâton en deux; **to break sth into pieces** mettre qch en morceaux; **to get broken** se casser; **to break a safe** forcer un coffre-fort; *Rel* **to break bread** *(priest)* administrer la communion; *(congregation)* recevoir la communion; *Fig* **to break bread with sb** partager le repas de qn; *Fig* **to break sb's heart** briser le cœur à qn; **Ross broke her heart** Ross lui a brisé le cœur; **it breaks my heart to see her unhappy** ça me brise le cœur de la voir malheureuse; *Fig* **to break the ice** rompre *ou* briser la glace

(**b**) *Med (fracture)* casser, fracturer; **to break one's leg** se casser *ou* se fracturer la jambe; **to break one's neck** se casser *ou* se rompre le cou; **the fall broke his back** la chute lui a brisé les reins; *Fam Fig* **to break one's back** s'échiner; *Fam Fig* **they broke their backs trying to get the job done** ils se sont éreintés à finir le travail; *Fam* **we've broken the back of the job** nous avons fait le plus gros du travail; *Fam* **I'll break his neck if I catch him doing it again!** je lui tords le cou si je le reprends à faire ça!; *Fam Fig* **break a leg!** merde! *(pour souhaiter bonne chance)*

(**c**) *(render inoperable → appliance, machine)* casser; **you've broken the TV** tu as cassé la télé

(**d**) *(cut surface of → ground)* entamer; *(→ skin)* écorcher; *Law (seals → illegally)* briser; *(legally)* lever; **the seal on the coffee jar was broken** le pot de café avait été ouvert; **the skin isn't broken** la peau n'est pas écorchée; **to break new** *or* **fresh ground** innover, faire œuvre de pionnier; **scientists are breaking new** *or* **fresh ground in cancer research** les savants font une percée dans la recherche contre le cancer

(**e**) *(force a way through)* enfoncer; **the river broke its banks** la rivière est sortie de son lit; **to break the sound barrier** franchir le mur du son; **to break surface** *(diver, whale)* remonter à la surface; *Naut (submarine)* faire surface

(**f**) *Law (violate → law, rule)* violer, enfreindre; *(→ speed limit)* dépasser; *(→ agreement, treaty)* violer; *(→ contract)* rompre; *(→ promise)* manquer à; *Rel (→ commandment)* désobéir à; *(→ Sabbath)* ne pas respecter; **she broke her appointment with them** elle a annulé son rendez-vous avec eux; **he broke his word to her** il a manqué à la parole qu'il lui avait donnée; *Law* **to break parole** = commettre un délit qui entraîne la révocation de la mise en liberté conditionnelle; *Mil* **to break bounds** violer la consigne

(**g**) *(escape from, leave suddenly) Law* **to break jail** s'évader (de prison); **to break camp** lever le camp; **to break cover** *(animal)* être débusqué; *(person)* sortir à découvert

(**h**) *(interrupt → fast, monotony, spell)* rompre; *Elec (→ circuit, current)* couper; *Typ (→ word, page)* couper; **we broke our journey at Brussels** nous avons fait une étape à Bruxelles; **a cry broke the silence** un cri a déchiré *ou* percé le silence; **the plain was broken only by an occasional small settlement** la plaine n'était interrompue que par de rares petits hameaux; *Mil* **to break step** rompre le pas

(**i**) *(put an end to → strike)* briser; *(→ uprising)* mater; **the new offer broke the deadlock** la nouvelle proposition a permis de sortir de l'impasse; **he's tried to stop smoking but he can't break the habit** il a essayé d'arrêter de fumer mais il n'arrive pas à se débarrasser *ou* se défaire de l'habitude; **to break sb of a habit** corriger *ou* guérir qn d'une habitude; **to break oneself of a habit** se corriger *ou* se défaire d'une habitude

(**j**) *(wear down, destroy → enemy)* détruire; *(→ person, will, courage, resistance)* briser; *(→ witness)* réfuter; *(→ health)* abîmer; *(→ alibi)* écarter; **torture did not break him** *or* **his spirit** il a résisté à la torture; **this scandal could break them** ce scandale pourrait signer leur perte; **the experience will either make or break him** l'expérience lui sera ou salutaire ou fatale

(**k**) *(bankrupt)* ruiner; **her new business will either make or break her** sa nouvelle affaire la rendra riche ou la ruinera; **to break the bank** *(exhaust funds)* faire sauter la banque; *Hum* **buying a book won't break the bank!** acheter un livre ne te/nous/*etc* ruinera pas!

(**l**) *(soften → fall)* amortir, adoucir; **we planted a row of trees to break the wind** nous avons planté une rangée d'arbres pour couper le vent

(**m**) *(reveal, tell)* annoncer, révéler; **break it to her gently** annonce-le lui avec ménagement

(**n**) *(beat, improve on)* battre; **to break a record** battre un record; **the golfer broke 90** le golfeur a dépassé le score de 90

(**o**) *(solve → code)* déchiffrer

(**p**) *Sport* **to break sb's service** *(in tennis)* prendre le service de qn; **Hingis was broken in the fifth game** Hingis a perdu son service dans le cinquième jeu

(**q**) *(divide into parts → collection)* dépareiller; *(→ bank note)* entamer; **can you break a £10 note?** pouvez-vous faire de la monnaie sur un billet de 10 livres?

(**r**) *(horse)* dresser

(**s**) *Mil (demote)* casser

(**t**) *Naut (flag)* déferler

(**u**) *Euph* **to break wind** lâcher un vent

2 *vi* (**a**) *(split into pieces → glass, furniture)* se casser, se briser; *(→ branch, stick)* se casser, se rompre; *(→ lace, string, egg, toy)* se casser; **to break apart** se casser *ou* se briser (en morceaux); **the plate broke in two** l'assiette s'est cassée en deux; **to break into pieces** se casser en morceaux; *Fig* **her heart broke** elle a eu le cœur brisé

(**b**) *Med (fracture → bone, limb)* se fracturer; **is the bone broken?** y a-t-il une fracture?; *Hum* **any bones broken?** rien de cassé?

(**c**) *(become inoperable → lock, tool)* casser; *(→ machine)* tomber en panne; **the dishwasher broke last week** le lave-vaisselle est tombé en panne la semaine dernière

(**d**) *(disperse → clouds)* se disperser, se dissiper; *Mil (→ troops)* rompre les rangs; *(→ ranks)* se rompre

(**e**) *(escape)* **to break free** se libérer; **the ship broke loose from its moorings** le bateau a rompu ses amarres

(**f**) *(fail → health, person, spirit)* se détériorer; **the witness broke under questioning** le témoin a craqué au cours de l'interrogatoire; **she** *or* **her spirit did not break** elle ne s'est pas laissée abattre; **their courage finally broke** leur courage a fini par les abandonner

(**g**) *(take a break)* faire une pause; **let's break for coffee** arrêtons-nous pour prendre un café

(**h**) *(arise suddenly → day)* se lever, poindre; *(→ dawn)* poindre; *Press & TV (→ news)* être annoncé; *(→ scandal, war)* éclater

(**i**) *(move suddenly)* se précipiter, foncer

(**j**) *(weather)* changer; *(storm)* éclater

(**k**) *(voice → of boy)* muer; *(→ with emotion)* se briser; **she was so upset that her voice kept breaking** elle était tellement bouleversée que sa voix se brisait

(**l**) *(wave)* déferler; **the sea was breaking against the rocks** les vagues se brisaient sur les rochers

(**m**) *Obst* **her waters have broken** elle a perdu les eaux

(**n**) *Am Fam (happen)* se passer❑, arriver❑; **to break right/badly** bien/mal se passer

(**o**) *Ling (vowel)* se diphtonguer

(**p**) *Sport (boxers)* se dégager; **break!** break!, stop!

(**q**) *Sport (ball)* dévier

(**r**) *Sport (in billiards, snooker, pool)* donner l'acquit

(**s**) *(idiom)* **to break even** *(gen)* s'y retrouver; *Fin* rentrer dans ses frais

3 *n* (**a**) *(in china, glass)* cassure *f*, brisure *f*; *(in wood)* cassure *f*, rupture *f*; *Med (in bone, limb)* fracture *f*; *Fig (with friend, group)* rupture *f*; *(in marriage)* séparation *f*; **a clean break** *(in object)* une cassure nette; *Med (in bone)* une fracture simple; **the break with her husband was a painful experience** ça a été très pénible pour elle quand elle s'est séparée de son mari; **her break with the party in 1968** sa rupture avec le parti en 1968; **to make a clean break with the past** rompre avec le passé

(**b**) *(crack)* fissure *f*, fente *f*

(**c**) *(gap → in hedge, wall)* trouée *f*, ouverture *f*; *Geol (→ in rock)* faille *f*; *(→ in line)* interruption *f*, rupture *f*; *Typ (→ in word)* césure *f*; *(→ in pagination)* fin *f* de page; **a break in the clouds** une éclaircie

(**d**) *(interruption → in conversation)* interruption *f*, pause *f*; *(→ in payment)* interruption *f*, suspension *f*; *(→ in trip)* arrêt *m*; *(→ in production)* suspension *f*, rupture *f*; *(→ in series)* interruption *f*; *Literature & Mus* pause *f*; *(in jazz)* break *m*; **guitar break** *(in rock)* (courte) improvisation *f* de guitare; *Elec* **a break in the circuit** une coupure de courant; *Rad* **a break for commercials, a (commercial) break** un intermède de publicité; *TV* un écran publicitaire, une page de publicité; *TV* **a break in transmission** une interruption des programmes (due à un incident technique)

(**e**) *(rest)* pause *f*; *(holiday)* vacances *fpl*; *Br Sch* récréation *f*; **let's take a break** on fait une pause?; **we worked all morning without a break** nous avons travaillé toute la matinée sans nous arrêter; **he drove for three hours without a break** il a conduit trois heures de suite; **you need a break** *(short rest)* tu as besoin de faire une pause; *(holiday)* tu as besoin de vacances; **an hour's break for lunch** une heure de pause pour le déjeuner; **lunch break** pause *f* de midi; **do you get a lunch break?** tu as une pause à midi?; **a weekend in the country makes a pleasant break** un week-end à la campagne fait du bien; *Fam* **give me a break!** *(don't talk nonsense)* dis pas n'importe quoi!; *(stop nagging)* fiche-moi la paix!

(**f**) *(escape)* évasion *f*, fuite *f*; *Law* **jail break** évasion *f* (de prison); **she made a break for the woods** elle s'est élancée vers le bois; **to make a break for it** prendre la fuite

(**g**) *Fam (opportunity)* chance❑ *f*; *(luck)* (coup *m* de) veine *f*; **you get all the breaks!** tu en as du pot!; **to have a lucky break** avoir de la veine; **to have a bad break** manquer de veine; **this could be your big break** ça pourrait être la chance de ta vie; **she's never had an even break in her life** rien n'a jamais été facile dans sa vie; **give him a break** donne-lui une chance; *(he won't do it again)* donne-lui une seconde chance

(**h**) *(change)* changement *m*; **a break in the weather** un changement de temps; **the decision signalled a break with tradition** la décision marquait une rupture avec la tradition

(**i**) *(carriage)* break *m*

(**j**) *Literary* **at break of day** au point du jour, à l'aube

(**k**) *Sport* **to have a service break** *or* **a break (of serve)** *(in tennis)* avoir une rupture de service *(de l'adversaire)*; **to have two break points** *(in tennis)* avoir deux balles de break; **he made a 70 break** *(in snooker, pool etc)* il a fait une série de 70

►► *Comput* ***break character*** caractère *m* d'interruption; *Comput* ***break key*** touche *f* d'interruption

▸**break away 1** *vi* (**a**) *(move away)* se détacher; *(escape)* s'évader; **I broke away from the crowd** je me suis éloigné de la foule; **he broke away from her grasp** il s'est dégagé de son étreinte

(**b**) *(end association with)* rompre; *(province → from State)* se séparer; **a group of MPs broke away from the party** un groupe de députés a quitté le parti; **as a band they have broken away from traditional jazz** leur groupe a (complètement) rompu avec le jazz traditionnel

(**c**) *Sport (in racing, cycling)* s'échapper, se détacher du peloton

2 *vt sep* détacher; **they broke all the fittings away from the walls** ils ont décroché toutes les appliques des murs

▸**break back** *vi (in tennis)* = gagner le service de son adversaire après avoir perdu son propre service

▸**break down 1** *vi* (**a**) *(vehicle, machine)* tomber en panne; **the car has broken down** la voiture est en panne

(**b**) *(fail → health)* se détériorer; *(→ authority)* disparaître; *(→ argument, system, resistance)* s'effondrer; *(→ negotiations, relations, plan)* échouer; **radio communications broke down** le contact radio a été coupé; **their marriage is breaking down** leur mariage se désagrège

(**c**) *(lose one's composure)* s'effondrer; **to break down in tears** fondre en larmes

(**d**) *(divide)* se diviser; **the report breaks down into three parts** le rapport comprend *ou* est composé de trois parties

(**e**) *Chem* se décomposer; **to break down into sth** se décomposer en qch

2 *vt sep* (**a**) *(destroy → barrier)* démolir, abattre; *(→ door)* enfoncer; *Fig (→ resistance)* briser; **we must break down old prejudices** il faut mettre fin aux vieux préjugés

(**b**) *(analyse → idea, statistics)* analyser; *(→ reasons)* décomposer; *(→ account, figures, expenses)* décomposer, ventiler; *(→ bill, estimate)* détailler; *(→ substance)* décomposer; **the problem can be broken down into three parts** le problème peut se décomposer en trois parties

▸**break forth** *vi Literary (light)* jaillir; *(storm, buds)* éclater; *(blossom)* s'épanouir subitement

▸**break in 1** *vt sep* (**a**) *(train → person)* former; *(→ horse)* dresser; **a month should be enough to break you in to the job** un mois devrait suffire pour vous faire *ou* vous habituer au métier

(**b**) *(clothing)* porter *(pour user)*; **I want to break these shoes in** je veux que ces chaussures se fassent

(**c**) *(knock down → door)* enfoncer

2 *vi* (**a**) *Law (burglar)* entrer par effraction

(**b**) *(speaker)* interrompre; **to break in on sb/sth** interrompre qn/qch

▸**break into** *vt insep* (**a**) *(of burglar)* entrer par effraction dans; *(drawer)* forcer; **they broke into the safe** ils ont fracturé *ou* forcé le coffre-fort; **they've been broken into three times** ils se sont fait cambrioler trois fois

(**b**) *(begin suddenly)* **the audience broke into applause** le public s'est mis à applaudir; **to break into a run/sprint** se mettre à courir/à sprinter; **the horse broke into a gallop** le cheval a pris le galop

(**c**) *(conversation)* interrompre

(**d**) *(start to spend → savings)* entamer; **I don't want to break into a £20 note** je ne veux pas entamer un billet de 20 livres

(**e**) *Com (market)* percer sur; **the firm has broken into the Japanese market** l'entreprise a percé sur le marché japonais

▸**break off 1** *vi* (**a**) *(separate)* se détacher, se casser; **a branch has broken off** une branche s'est détachée (de l'arbre)

(**b**) *(stop)* s'arrêter brusquement; **he broke off in mid-sentence** il s'est arrêté au milieu d'une phrase; **they broke off from work** *(for rest)* ils ont fait une pause; *(for day)* ils ont cessé le travail; **to break off for ten minutes** prendre dix minutes de pause; **to break off for lunch** s'arrêter pour déjeuner

(**c**) *(end relationship)* rompre; **she's broken off with him** elle a rompu avec lui

2 *vt sep* (**a**) *(separate)* détacher, casser; **to break sth off sth** casser *ou* détacher qch de qch

(**b**) *(end → agreement, relationship)* rompre; **they've broken off their engagement** ils ont rompu leurs fiançailles; **to break it off (with sb)** rompre (avec qn); **Italy had broken off diplomatic relations with Libya** l'Italie avait rompu ses relations diplomatiques avec la Libye

▸**break open** *vt sep (door)* enfoncer; *(lock, safe, till)* forcer; *Fam (bottle of wine etc)* ouvrir□, déboucher□; **to break a desk open** ouvrir un bureau en forçant la serrure

▸**break out 1** *vi* (**a**) *(begin → war, storm)* éclater; *(→ disease, fire)* se déclarer; *(→ fight)* se déclencher

(**b**) *(become covered)* **to break out in spots** *or* **in a rash** avoir une éruption de boutons; **to break out in a sweat** se mettre à transpirer; **she broke out in a cold sweat** elle s'est mise à avoir des sueurs froides

(**c**) *(escape)* s'échapper; **to break out from** *or* **of prison** s'évader (de prison); **we have to break out of this vicious circle** il faut que nous sortions de ce cercle vicieux

2 *vt sep (bottle, champagne)* ouvrir

▸**break through 1** *vt insep (sun)* percer; **I broke through the crowd** je me suis frayé un chemin à travers la foule; **the troops broke through enemy lines** les troupes ont enfoncé les lignes ennemies; **she eventually broke through his reserve** elle a fini par le faire sortir de sa réserve

2 *vi* percer; *Fig & Mil* faire une percée; *Fig* **his hidden feelings tend to break through in his writing** ses sentiments cachés tendent à transparaître *ou* percer dans ses écrits

▸**break up 1** *vt sep* (**a**) *(divide up → rocks)* briser, morceler; *Law (→ property)* morceler; *(→ soil)* ameublir; *(→ bread, cake)* partager; **she broke the loaf up into four pieces** elle a rompu *ou* partagé la miche en quatre; **illustrations break up the text** le texte est aéré par des illustrations

(**b**) *(destroy → house)* démolir; *(→ road)* défoncer

(**c**) *(end → fight, party)* mettre fin à, arrêter; *Com & Law (→ conglomerate, trust)* scinder, diviser; *Com (→ company)* scinder; *Pol (→ coalition)* briser, rompre; *Admin (→ organization)* dissoudre; *(→ empire)* démembrer; *(→ family)* séparer; **his drinking broke up their marriage** le fait qu'il buvait a brisé *ou* détruit leur mariage

(**d**) *(disperse → crowd)* disperser; **break it up!** *(people fighting or arguing)* arrêtez!; *(said by policeman)* circulez!

(**e**) *Fam (distress)* bouleverser, retourner; **the news really broke her up** la nouvelle l'a complètement bouleversée

(**f**) *Am Fam (amuse)* **her stories really break me up!** ses histoires me font bien marrer!

2 *vi* (**a**) *(split into pieces → road, system)* se désagréger; *(→ ice)* craquer, se fissurer; *(→ ship)* se disloquer; **the ship broke up on the rocks** le navire s'est disloqué sur les rochers

(**b**) *(come to an end → meeting, party)* se terminer, prendre fin; *(→ partnership)* cesser, prendre fin; *(→ talks, negotiations)* cesser; **when the meeting broke up** à l'issue *ou* à la fin de la réunion; **their marriage broke up** leur mariage n'a pas marché

(**c**) *(boyfriend, girlfriend)* rompre; **she broke up with her boyfriend** elle a rompu avec son petit ami; **they've broken up** ils se sont séparés

(**d**) *(disperse → clouds)* se disperser; *(→ group)* se disperser; *(→ friends)* se quitter, se séparer

(**e**) *Br Sch* **we break up for Christmas on the 22nd** les vacances de Noël commencent le 22; **when do we break up?** quand est-ce qu'on est en vacances?

(**f**) *(lose one's composure)* s'effondrer

(**g**) *Am Fam (laugh)* se tordre de rire

▸**break with** *vt insep* (**a**) *(end association with → person, organization)* rompre avec; **the defeat caused many people to break with the party** la défaite a poussé beaucoup de gens à rompre avec le parti

(**b**) *(depart from → belief, values)* rompre avec; **she broke with tradition by getting married away from her village** elle a rompu avec la tradition en ne se mariant pas dans son village

---

breakable ['breɪkəbəl] **1** *adj* fragile, cassable

2 breakables *npl* **put away all breakables** rangez tout objet fragile

breakage ['breɪkɪdʒ] *n* (**a**) *(of metal)* rupture *f*; *(of glass)* casse *f*, bris *m* (**b**) *(damages)* casse *f*; **have there been any breakages?** est-ce qu'il y a eu de la casse?; **the insurance pays for all breakage** *or* **breakages** l'assurance paye toute la casse

breakaway ['breɪkəweɪ] **1** *n* (**a**) *(of people)* séparation *f*; *(of group)* rupture *f*; *Sport (in cycling)* échappée *f*; *(in boxing)* dégagement *m* (**b**) *Cin* accessoire *m* cassable

2 *adj* séparatiste, dissident; *Pol* **a breakaway group** un groupe dissident; *Sport (in cycling)* un groupe d'échappés; *Pol* **a breakaway republic** une république séparatiste et indépendante

breakbeat ['breɪkbiːt] *n Mus* breakbeat *m*

breakdance ['breɪkdɑːns] *Mus* **1** *n* smurf *m*

2 *vi* danser le smurf

breakdancer ['breɪk,dɑːnsə(r)] *n Mus* smurfeur(-euse) *m,f*

breakdancing ['breɪk,dɑːnsɪŋ] *n Mus* smurf *m*

breakdown ['breɪkdaʊn] *n* (**a**) *(mechanical)* panne *f*; **to have a breakdown** tomber en panne

(**b**) *(of communications, negotiations)* rupture *f*; *(of system, service)* arrêt *m* complet; *(of tradition, state of affairs)* détérioration *f*, dégradation *f*; *(of marriage, relationship)* échec *m*

(**c**) *Psy (nervous)* dépression *f* nerveuse; *Med (physical)* effondrement *m*; **to have a breakdown** faire une dépression (nerveuse)

(**d**) *(analysis → of ideas, statistics)* analyse *f*; *(→ of reasons)* décomposition *f*; *Com (→ of costs, figures)* ventilation *f*; *Fin (→ of account, expenses)* décomposition *f*, ventilation *f*; *(→ of bill, estimate)* détail *m*; *(→ of script)* pré-découpage *m*; *(→ for recording)* dépouillement *m*; **a breakdown of the population by age** une répartition de la population par âge; **give me a breakdown of the annual report** faites-moi l'analyse du rapport annuel

►► *Aut* ***breakdown gang*** équipe *f* de dépannage; *Br Aut* ***breakdown lorry*** dépanneuse *f*, camion *m* de dépannage; *Aut* ***breakdown and recovery service*** service *m* de remorquage et de dépannage; *Aut* ***breakdown service*** service *m* de dépannage; ***breakdown truck, breakdown van*** dépanneuse *f*, camion *m* de dépannage

breaker ['breɪkə(r)] *n* (**a**) *(scrap merchant)* **the ship was sent to the breaker's** le navire a été envoyé à la démolition (**b**) *(wave)* déferlante *f* (**c**) *Elec* disjoncteur *m* (**d**) *Tech (machine)* concasseur *m*, broyeur *m* (**e**) *(CB operator)* cibiste *mf*

►► ***breaker's yard*** *(for cars, boats etc)* chantier *m* de démolition

break-even *n Fin* seuil *m* de rentabilité; *Acct* point *m* mort, point *m* d'équilibre; *Fin* **to reach break-even** atteindre le seuil de rentabilité

►► *Fin* ***break-even analysis*** analyse *f* du point mort; ***break-even deal*** affaire *f* blanche; ***break-even point*** *Fin* seuil *m* de rentabilité; *Acct* point *m* mort, point *m* d'équilibre; ***break-even price*** prix *m* minimum rentable

breakfast ['brekfəst] **1** *n* petit déjeuner *m*; **to have breakfast** prendre le petit déjeuner; **what do you want for breakfast?** que veux-tu pour ton petit déjeuner?; *Fig* **she could have someone like you for breakfast** les gens comme toi, elle n'en fait qu'une bouchée

2 *comp (service, set)* à petit déjeuner; *(tea, time)* du petit déjeuner
3 *vi* prendre le petit déjeuner, déjeuner
►► ***breakfast buffet*** buffet *m* du petit déjeuner; ***breakfast cereal*** céréales *fpl*; ***breakfast chef*** chef *m* de petit déjeuner; ***breakfast cup*** déjeuner *m*; ***breakfast meeting*** réunion *f* pendant le petit déjeuner; ***breakfast room*** salle *f* du petit déjeuner; ***breakfast table*** table *f* pour le petit déjeuner; ***breakfast television*** télévision *f* du matin

'Breakfast at Tiffany's' *Capote, Edwards* 'Petit déjeuner chez Tiffany' (roman), 'Diamants sur canapé' (film)

To believe six impossible things before breakfast
Il s'agit d'une formule tirée d'un passage de l'œuvre de Lewis Carrol *Through the Looking-Glass* (De l'autre côté du miroir) (1872), dans lequel la reine confie à Alice que lorsqu'elle avait son âge il lui arrivait de croire jusqu'à six choses impossibles avant le petit déjeuner.
On utilise aujourd'hui cette phrase lorsque quelqu'un doit assimiler de nombreuses connaissances ou bien s'adapter à une situation radicalement nouvelle. Parfois on ne garde que la seconde partie de la phrase (**before breakfast**) lorsque quelqu'un a fait quelque chose très rapidement. Ainsi on pourra dire **They are only short novels, I used to read two of them before breakfast** ("ces romans sont très courts, il m'arrivait d'en lire deux avant le petit déjeuner").

break-in *n* cambriolage *m*
breaking ['breɪkɪŋ] *n* (**a**) *(shattering)* bris *m*; *(of bone)* fracture *f*; *Law (of seal → illegal)* bris *m*; *(→ legal)* levée *f*; *Aviat (of sound barrier)* franchissement *m*; *Law* **breaking and entering** effraction *f*
(**b**) *(violation → of treaty, rule, law)* violation *f* (**of** de); *(→ of promise)* manquement *m* (**of** à); *(→ of commandment)* désobéissance *f* (**of** à)
(**c**) *(interruption → of journey)* interruption *f*; *(→ of silence)* rupture *f*; *(→ of strike)* action *f* de briser
(**d**) *Ling* fracture *f*
(**e**) *(of horse)* dressage *m*
(**f**) *(of fall, force of something)* amortissement *m*
►► ***breaking in*** (**a**) *(of horse)* dressage *m*; *Fig (of new employee)* formation *f* (**b**) *(burglary)* effraction *f* (**c**) *(of door)* enfoncement *m*, défonçage *m*; ***breaking point*** point *m* de rupture; *Fig* **I've reached breaking point** je suis à bout, je n'en peux plus; **you're trying my patience to breaking point** tu pousses à bout ma patience; **the situation has reached breaking point** la situation est devenue critique; ***breaking up*** (**a**) *(of building)* démolition *f*; *(of earth, field)* défoncement *m*, premier labourage *m*; *(of rocks, substance)* broyage *m*, décomposition *f*; *(of organization, assembly)* dissolution *f*; *(of crowd)* dispersion *f*; *(of family)* désagrégation *f*; *(of estate, property, country)* morcellement *m*; *(of empire)* démembrement *m*, fragmentation *f*; *(of ship)* dépècement *m*, démembrement (**b**) *Sch* entrée *f* en vacances (**c**) *(of ice)* débâcle *f*; *Sch* ***breaking up party*** soirée *f* de fin de trimestre
breakneck ['breɪknek] *adj* **at breakneck speed** à une allure folle, à tombeau ouvert
break-out *n (from prison)* évasion *f* (de prison)
breakpoint ['breɪkpɔɪnt] *n* (**a**) *Sport (in tennis)* balle *f* de break (**b**) *Comput* point *m* de rupture
breakthrough ['breɪkθruː] *n* (**a**) *(advance, discovery)* découverte *f* capitale, percée *f* (technologique); *(in negotiations)* progrès *m*; *(in market)* percée *f*; **their latest breakthrough in computing technology** leur dernière découverte en technologie informatique; **to make a breakthrough** *(discovery)* faire une percée; *(in negotiations)* progresser; **the breakthrough came only after a week of deadlock** la situation ne s'est débloquée qu'après une semaine
(**b**) *Mil (in enemy lines)* percée *f*
break-up *n* (**a**) *(disintegration → of association)* démembrement *m*, dissolution *f*; *(→ of relationship)* rupture *f*; *Com (→ of company)* scission *f*; **before our break-up** avant que nous ne rompions (**b**) *(end → of meeting, activity)* fin *f* (**c**) *(of ship)* dislocation *f* (**d**) *(of ice)* débâcle *f*
►► *Fin* ***break-up price*** prix *m* de liquidation; *Com* ***break-up value*** valeur *f* de liquidation
breakwater ['breɪk,wɔːtə(r)] *n* digue *f*, brise-lames *m inv*
bream [briːm] (*pl* **inv** *or* **breams**) *n Ich* brème *f*
breast [brest] **1** *n* (**a**) *(chest)* poitrine *f*; *(of animal)* poitrine, poitrail *m*; *(of bird)* gorge *f*; *Culin (of chicken)* blanc *m*; *Literary* **he held her to his breast** il la tint serrée contre sa poitrine
(**b**) *(bosom → of woman)* sein *m*, poitrine *f*; *Literary (→ of man)* sein *m*; **she put the baby to her breast** elle porta le bébé à son sein; **a child at the breast** un enfant au sein
(**c**) *Mining* front *m* de taille
2 *vt* (**a**) *Literary (face → waves, storm)* affronter
(**b**) *(reach summit of)* atteindre le sommet de; **the runner breasted the tape** le coureur a franchi la ligne d'arrivée (en vainqueur)
►► ***breast cancer*** cancer *m* du sein; ***breast enlargement*** augmentation *f* mammaire; ***breast pocket*** poche *f* de poitrine; ***breast pump*** tire-lait *m*; ***breast reduction*** réduction *f* mammaire
breast-beating *n (UNCOUNT)* jérémiades *fpl*
breastbone ['brestbəʊn] *n Anat* sternum *m*; *(of bird)* bréchet *m*
-breasted ['brestɪd] *adj* **wide-/narrow-breasted** à poitrine large/étroite; **to be high-/low-breasted** avoir la poitrine haute/basse
breast-fed *adj* nourri au sein
breast-feed 1 *vt* allaiter, donner le sein à
2 *vi* allaiter, nourrir au sein
breast-feeding *n* allaitement *m* au sein
breastplate ['brestpleɪt] *n (armour)* plastron *m* (de cuirasse); *(of priest)* pectoral *m*
breaststroke ['breststrəʊk] *n Swimming* brasse *f*; **to swim (the) breaststroke** nager la brasse
breastwork ['brest,wɜːk] *n Mil* parapet *m*; *Naut* rambarde *f*
breath [breθ] *n* (**a**) *(of human, animal)* haleine *f*, souffle *m*; **to have bad breath** avoir mauvaise haleine; *Fam* **to have coffee/whisky breath** avoir l'haleine qui sent le café/le whisky ❑; **take a breath** respirez; **he took a deep breath** il a respiré à fond; **I took a deep breath and started to explain** je respirai profondément et commençai d'expliquer; **let me get my breath back** laissez-moi retrouver mon souffle *ou* reprendre haleine; **she stopped for breath** elle s'est arrêtée pour reprendre haleine; **to be out of breath** être essoufflé *ou* à bout de souffle; **to be short of breath** avoir le souffle court; **he said it all in one breath** il l'a dit d'un trait; **they are not to be mentioned in the same breath** on ne saurait les comparer; **but in the next breath he said the opposite** mais quelques secondes plus tard il a dit le contraire; **under one's breath** à voix basse, tout bas; **she laughed under her breath** elle a ri sous cape; **with her dying breath** en mourant; **he drew his last breath** il a rendu l'âme *ou* le dernier soupir; **music is the breath of life to him** la musique est toute sa vie; **to hold one's breath** retenir son souffle; **I wouldn't hold my breath!** je ne compterais pas trop là-dessus!; **don't hold your breath waiting for the money** si c'est l'argent que tu attends, ne compte pas dessus *ou* tu perds ton temps; **I'm wasting my breath** je perds mon temps, je me fatigue pour rien; **save your breath!** inutile de gaspiller ta salive!; **the sight took his breath away** la vue *ou* le spectacle lui a coupé le souffle; **it takes my breath away** je n'en reviens pas
(**b**) *(gust)* souffle *m*; **there isn't a breath of air** il n'y a pas un souffle d'air; **we went out for a breath of fresh air** nous sommes sortis prendre l'air; *Fig* **it's/she's like a breath of fresh air** c'est/elle est comme une bouffée d'air frais
(**c**) *(hint)* trace *f*; **the first breath of spring** les premiers effluves du printemps; **the faintest breath of scandal** le plus petit soupçon de scandale
►► ***breath freshener*** purificateur *m* d'haleine, spray *m* buccal; ***breath test*** Alcootest® *m*
breathable ['briːðəbəl] *adj* respirable
breathalyse, *Am* **breathalyze** ['breθəlaɪz] *vt* faire passer l'Alcootest® à
Breathalyser®, *Am* **Breathalyzer®** ['breθəlaɪzə(r)] *n* Alcootest® *m*
breathe [briːð] **1** *vi* (**a**) *(person)* respirer; **to breathe hard** haleter; **to breathe heavily** *or* **deeply** *(after exertion)* souffler *ou* respirer bruyamment; *(during illness)* il respirait péniblement; **you can't breathe in here** *(it's too hot)* on ne peut pas respirer ici; **is he still breathing?** est-il toujours en vie?, vit-il encore?; *Fig* **I breathed more easily** *or* **again after the exam** après l'examen j'ai enfin pu respirer; *Fam* **to breathe down sb's neck** *(supervise)* être sur le dos de qn; *(look over their shoulder)* regarder par-dessus l'épaule de qn; *Fig* **how can I work with you breathing down my neck?** comment veux-tu que je travaille si tu es toujours derrière moi?; *Fig* **I need room to breathe** *(in relationship)* j'ai besoin d'espace, il faut que je respire
(**b**) *(wine)* respirer
2 *vt* (**a**) *(take in oxygen)* respirer; **she breathed a sigh of relief** elle poussa un soupir de soulagement; **to breathe one's last** rendre le dernier soupir *ou* l'âme; **she breathed new life into the project** elle a insufflé de nouvelles forces au projet; **she'll be breathing fire when she finds out!** elle va se mettre dans une colère noire quand elle saura!
(**b**) *(whisper)* murmurer; **don't breathe a word!** ne soufflez pas mot!; **they didn't breathe a word about it** ils n'en ont pas soufflé mot
(**c**) *Ling* aspirer
►**breathe in 1** *vt sep* inhaler
2 *vi* inspirer
►**breathe out 1** *vt sep* expirer
2 *vi* expirer
breathed [briːðd] *adj Ling (unvoiced)* sourd, non voisé
breather ['briːðə(r)] *n (rest)* moment *m* de repos *ou* de répit; **let's take a breather** prenons le temps de souffler un peu; **I went out for a breather** je suis sorti prendre l'air
►► *Aut* ***breather pipe*** (tuyau *m* de) reniflard *m*; *Tech* ***breather port*** orifice *m* de reniflard
breathing ['briːðɪŋ] *n* (**a**) *(gen)* respiration *f*, souffle *m*; *Mus (of musician)* respiration *f*; **heavy breathing** respiration *f* bruyante
(**b**) *Ling* aspiration *f*; **rough/smooth breathing** *(in ancient Greek)* esprit *m* rude/doux
►► *Tech* ***breathing apparatus*** *(for fireman, miner etc)* masque *m* à oxygène; *(for diver)* scaphandre *m*; ***breathing space*** moment *m* de répit; *Fig* **I need some breathing space** *(in relationship)* j'ai besoin de respirer *ou* d'espace
breathless ['breθlɪs] *adj* (**a**) *(from exertion)* essoufflé, hors d'haleine; *(from illness)* oppressé, qui a du mal à respirer (**b**) *(from emotion)* **his kiss left her breathless** son baiser lui a coupé le souffle; **we waited in breathless excitement** nous attendions le souffle coupé par l'émotion *ou* en retenant notre haleine; **the film held us breathless** le film nous a tenus en haleine (**c**) *(atmosphere)* étouffant

'Breathless' *Godard* 'À bout de souffle'

breathlessly ['breθlɪslɪ] *adv (gasping)* en haletant; *Fig (hurriedly)* en toute hâte
breathlessness ['breθlɪsnɪs] *n* essoufflement *m*
breathtaking ['breθ,teɪkɪŋ] *adj* impressionnant; **with a breathtaking lack of tact** avec un manque de tact incroyable; **a breathtaking view** une vue à (vous) couper le souffle
breathtakingly ['breθ,teɪkɪŋlɪ] *adv (beautiful)* extraordinairement; *(stupid, tactless etc)* incroyablement
breathy ['breθɪ] (*compar* **breathier**, *superl* **breathiest**) *adj* qui respire bruyamment; *Mus* qui manque d'attaque; **she has a breathy voice** elle respire bruyamment en parlant
Brechtian ['brektɪən] *Literature* **1** *n* brechtien(enne) *m,f*
2 *adj* brechtien
Brecon Beacons ['brekən-] *npl* = parc national au Pays de Galles
bred [bred] **1** *pt & pp of* **breed**
2 *adj* élevé
-bred [bred] *suff* élevé; **ill/well-bred** mal/bien élevé

breech [bri:tʃ] **1** *n* (**a**) *Tech (of gun)* culasse *f* (**b**) *(of person)* derrière *m*
2 *vt Tech (gun)* munir d'une culasse
►► *Obst* ***breech birth, breech delivery*** accouchement *m* par le siège; *Obst* ***breech presentation*** présentation *f* par le siège

breechblock ['bri:tʃ,blɒk] *n Tech* bloc *m* de culasse

breechcloth ['bri:tʃklɒθ] *n Am Tex* pagne *m*

breeches, *Am* **britches** ['brɪtʃɪz] *npl* pantalon *m*; *(knee-length)* haut-de-chausses *m*; *(for riding)* culotte *f*; *Am* **to be too big for one's breeches** avoir la grosse tête
►► *Naut* ***breeches buoy*** bouée-culotte *f*

breechloader ['bri:tʃ,ləʊdə(r)] *n Tech* arme *f* chargée par la culasse

breech-loading *adj Tech* qui se charge par la culasse

breed [bri:d] (*pt & pp* **bred** [bred]) **1** *n* (**a**) *Zool (race)* race *f*, espèce *f*; *(within race)* type *m*; *Bot (of plant)* espèce *f*
(**b**) *Fig (kind)* sorte *f*, espèce *f*; **he's one of a dying breed** il fait partie d'une espèce en voie de disparition; **she is one of the new breed of executives** elle fait partie de la nouvelle race *ou* génération de cadres
2 *vt* (**a**) *(raise → animals)* élever, faire l'élevage de; *Hort (→ plants)* cultiver; *Literary or Hum (→ children)* élever; **to breed in/out a characteristic** faire acquérir/éliminer une caractéristique (par la sélection); **he was bred for the sea** on l'a élevé pour en faire un marin plus tard; **they're specially bred for racing** ils sont élevés spécialement pour la course; *Prov* **what's bred in the bone will come out in the flesh** bon chien chasse de race
(**b**) *Fig (cause)* engendrer, faire naître; **dirt breeds disease** la saleté entraîne des maladies
3 *vi* (**a**) *(animals, people)* se reproduire, se multiplier; **to breed like rabbits** se multiplier comme des lapins
(**b**) *(animal breeder)* faire de l'élevage

breeder ['bri:də(r)] *n* (**a**) *(farmer)* éleveur(euse) *m,f*; *(animal)* reproducteur(trice) *m,f* (**b**) *Pej or Hum (heterosexual)* hétéro *mf*
►► *Horseracing* ***the Breeders' Cup*** = la plus importante course hippique aux États-Unis, qui a lieu une fois par an; *Nucl* ***breeder reactor*** surgénérateur *m*, surrégénérateur *m*

breeding ['bri:dɪŋ] *n* (**a**) *(raising → of animals)* élevage *m*; *Hort (→ of plants)* culture *f*
(**b**) *Biol (reproduction)* reproduction *f*, procréation *f*
(**c**) *(upbringing)* éducation *f*; **he lacks breeding** il manque de savoir-vivre
(**d**) *Phys* surgénération *f*, surrégénération *f*
►► ***the breeding season*** *(for animals)* la saison des amours; *(for birds)* la saison des nids; ***breeding stock*** animaux *mpl* élevés en vue de la reproduction

breeding-ground *n* (**a**) *(for wild animals, birds)* lieu *m* de prédilection pour l'accouplement *ou* la ponte (**b**) *Fig* foyer *m*, terrain *m* propice; **a breeding-ground for terrorists** une pépinière de terroristes; **damp areas are a breeding-ground for germs** les zones humides sont des foyers de microbes *ou* constituent un terrain propice aux maladies

breeks [bri:ks] *npl Scot* pantalon *m*

breeze [bri:z] **1** *n* (**a**) *(wind)* brise *f*; **a gentle** *or* **light breeze** une petite *ou* légère brise; **a stiff breeze** un vent frais; **there's quite a breeze** ça souffle
(**b**) *Fam (easy task)* **it's a breeze** c'est l'enfance de l'art, c'est du gâteau
(**c**) *Miner (charcoal)* cendres *fpl* (de charbon)
2 *vi (move quickly)* **the car breezed along the country lanes** la voiture roulait à vive allure sur les routes de campagne
►► *Br Constr* ***breeze block*** parpaing *m*

►**breeze in** *vi (quickly)* entrer en coup de vent; *(casually)* entrer d'un air désinvolte

►**breeze out** *vi (quickly)* sortir en coup de vent; *(casually)* sortir d'un air désinvolte

►**breeze through** **1** *vt insep (exam)* réussir les doigts dans le nez; **to breeze through life** se laisser vivre
2 *vi (pass exam with ease)* réussir les doigts dans le nez

breezeway ['bri:zweɪ] *n Am* passage *m* couvert *(souvent entre la maison et le garage)*

breezily ['bri:zɪlɪ] *adv (casually)* avec désinvolture; *(cheerfully)* joyeusement, jovialement

breeziness ['bri:zɪnɪs] *n (of person, manner → casualness)* désinvolture *f*; *(→ cheerfulness)* jovialité *f*

breezy ['bri:zɪ] (*compar* **breezier**, *superl* **breeziest**) *adj* (**a**) *(weather, day)* venteux; *(place, spot)* éventé (**b**) *(person → casual)* désinvolte; *(→ cheerful)* jovial, enjoué

Bremen ['breɪmən] *n* Brême

Bren gun [bren-] *n Mil* fusil *m* mitrailleur

brent [brent] *n Orn* **brent (goose)** bernache *f* cravant

Brer Rabbit [breə-] *pr n* = personnage principal des histoires pour enfants de l'écrivain américain Uncle Remus

brethren ['breðrɪn] *npl Formal (fellow members)* camarades *mpl*; *Rel* frères *mpl*

Breton ['bretən] **1** *n* (**a**) *(person)* Breton(onne) *m,f* (**b**) *(language)* breton *m*
2 *adj* breton

breve [bri:v] *n Mus & Typ* brève *f*

breviary ['bri:vɪərɪ] (*pl* **breviaries**) *n Rel* bréviaire *m*

brevity ['brevɪtɪ] *n* (**a**) *(shortness)* brièveté *f* (**b**) *(succinctness)* concision *f*; *(terseness)* laconisme *m*; *Prov* **brevity is the soul of wit** = la concision est le secret d'un bon mot d'esprit

brew [bru:] **1** *n* (**a**) *(infusion)* infusion *f*; *(herbal)* tisane *f*; **a witch's brew** un brouet de sorcière
(**b**) *(beer)* brassage *m*; *(amount made)* brassin *m*
(**c**) *Br Fam (tea)* thé ❑ *m*; **do you want a brew?** tu veux du thé?
(**d**) *Am Fam (beer)* mousse *f*
2 *vt* (**a**) *(make → tea)* préparer, faire infuser; *(→ beer)* brasser
(**b**) *Fig (scheme)* tramer, mijoter
3 *vi* (**a**) *(tea)* infuser; *(beer)* fermenter
(**b**) *(make beer)* brasser, faire de la bière
(**c**) *Fig (storm)* couver, se préparer; *(scheme)* se tramer, mijoter; **there's something brewing** il se trame quelque chose, il y a quelque chose qui se prépare; **I could tell by her face there was a storm brewing** j'ai vu sur son visage qu'il y avait de l'orage dans l'air; **there's trouble brewing** il y a de l'orage dans l'air

►**brew up** *vi* (**a**) *(storm)* couver, se préparer; *(trouble)* se préparer, se tramer
(**b**) *Br Fam (make tea)* préparer *ou* faire du thé ❑

brewer ['bru:ə(r)] *n Ind* brasseur(euse) *m,f*
►► *Br Fam Hum* ***brewer's droop*** = impuissance temporaire due à l'alcool; **he had brewer's droop** il a bandé mou parce qu'il avait trop picolé; *Biol* ***brewer's yeast*** levure *f* de bière

brewery ['brʊərɪ] (*pl* **breweries**) *n* brasserie *f* *(fabrique)*

brewski ['bru:skɪ] *n Am Fam (beer)* mousse *f*

brew-up *n Br Fam* **to have a brew-up** faire du thé ❑; **we stopped work for a brew-up** nous avons fait une pause pour prendre un thé

briar ['braɪə(r)] *Bot* **1** *n* (**a**) *(thorn)* épine *f*; *(wild rose)* églantier *m* (**b**) *(heather)* bruyère *f*; *(wood)* (racine *f* de) bruyère *f* (**c**) *(pipe)* pipe *f* de bruyère
2 **briars** *npl* ronces *fpl*
►► ***briar pipe*** pipe *f* de bruyère; *Bot* ***briar root*** racine *f* de bruyère

briarwood ['braɪəwʊd] *n Bot* racine *f* de bruyère

bribable ['braɪbəbəl] *adj* corruptible

bribe [braɪb] **1** *vt* soudoyer, acheter; *(witness)* suborner; **to bribe sb into doing sth** soudoyer qn *ou* graisser la patte à qn pour qu'il fasse qch; **we bribed the guard to tell us** nous avons soudoyé le garde pour qu'il nous le dise; **I bribed him with sweets** je l'ai acheté avec des bonbons
2 *n* pot-de-vin *m*; **to take bribes** se laisser corrompre; **I offered him a bribe** j'ai tenté de le corrompre, je lui ai offert un pot-de-vin

briber ['braɪbə(r)] *n* corrupteur(trice) *m,f*; *(of witness)* suborneur *m*

bribery ['braɪbərɪ] *n* corruption *f*; *(of witness)* subornation *f*; **open to bribery** corruptible; **not open to bribery** incorruptible; *Law* **bribery and corruption** corruption *f*; *Hum* **that's bribery and corruption!** c'est une tentative de corruption!

bric-à-brac ['brɪkəbræk] **1** *n* bric-à-brac *m*
2 *comp (shop, stall)* de brocanteur

brick [brɪk] **1** *n* (**a**) *(for building)* brique *f*; **a house made of brick** une maison en brique; **to invest in bricks and mortar** investir dans l'immobilier; *Fam* **to come down on sb like a ton of bricks** passer un savon à qn; *Prov* **you can't make bricks without straw** à l'impossible nul n'est tenu; *Fam Fig* **to be one brick short of a load** ne pas être net
(**b**) *(of ice cream)* pavé *m*
(**c**) *Br (toy)* cube *m* (de construction); **a box of bricks** un jeu de construction
(**d**) *Br Fam Old-fashioned (man)* chic type *m*; *(woman)* chic fille *f*; **you're a brick!** tu es vraiment *ou* super sympa!
2 *comp (building)* en brique *ou* briques
►► ***brick red*** rouge *m* brique *inv*; ***brick wall*** mur *m* de brique; *Fig* **to come up against a brick wall** se heurter à un obstacle infranchissable; **it's like talking to a brick wall** autant (vaut) parler à un mur *ou* un sourd; **it's like banging your head against a brick wall** c'est peine perdue

►**brick in** *vt sep* murer

►**brick off** *vt sep* murer

►**brick up** *vt sep* murer

brickbat ['brɪkbæt] *n (weapon)* morceau *m* de brique; *Fig (criticism)* critique *f*; **the government has been receiving more brickbats than bouquets** le gouvernement a été plus critiqué qu'applaudi

brickfield ['brɪk,fi:ld] *n* briqueterie *f*

brickie ['brɪkɪ] *n Br & Austr Fam* maçon ❑ *m*, ouvrier-maçon ❑ *m*

brick-kiln *n* four *m* à briques

bricklayer ['brɪk,leɪə(r)] *n Constr* maçon *m*, ouvrier-maçon *m*

bricklaying ['brɪk,leɪɪŋ] *n Constr* briquetage *m*

brickmaker ['brɪk,meɪkə(r)] *n* briquetier *m*

brick-red *adj* rouge brique *(inv)*

brickwork ['brɪkwɜ:k] **1** *n Constr (structure)* briquetage *m*, brique *f*
2 **brickworks** *npl Ind* briqueterie *f*

brickyard ['brɪkjɑ:d] *n* (**a**) *Ind (where bricks are made)* briqueterie *f* (**b**) *Sport* **the Brickyard** *(racetrack)* = circuit automobile à Indianapolis

bridal ['braɪdəl] *adj (gown, veil)* de mariée; *(chamber, procession)* nuptial; *(feast)* de noce
►► ***bridal party*** la noce *(les invités)*; ***bridal suite*** suite *f* nuptiale

bride [braɪd] *n (before wedding)* (future) mariée *f*; *(after wedding)* (jeune) mariée *f*; **the bride and groom** les (jeunes) mariés *mpl*; **his bride of four months** la femme avec qui il est/était marié depuis quatre mois; *Rel* **to become a bride of Christ** prendre le voile

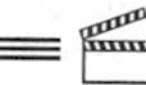

'The Bride Wore Black' *Truffaut* 'La Mariée était en noir'

bridegroom ['braɪdgrʊm] *n (before wedding)* (futur) marié *m*; *(after wedding)* (jeune) marié *m*

bridesmaid ['braɪdzmeɪd] *n* demoiselle *f* d'honneur; **always the bridesmaid, never the bride!** elle est toujours demoiselle d'honneur mais on ne l'a jamais demandée en mariage; *Fig* c'est l'éternel second!

bride-to-be *n* future mariée *f*

bridewell ['braɪd,wel] *n Old-fashioned* maison *f* de correction

bridge [brɪdʒ] **1** *n* (**a**) *(structure)* pont *m*; **the engineers built** *or* **put a bridge across the river** les ingénieurs ont construit *ou* jeté un pont sur le fleuve
(**b**) *Fig (link)* rapprochement *m*; **building bridges between East and West** efforts *mpl* de rapprochement entre l'Est et l'Ouest
(**c**) *Naut (of ship)* passerelle *f* (de commandement)
(**d**) *(of nose)* arête *f*; *(of glasses)* arcade *f*
(**e**) *Mus (of stringed instrument)* chevalet *m*
(**f**) *(dentures)* bridge *m*
(**g**) *Cards* bridge *m*; **what about a game of bridge?** et si on faisait un bridge?; **do you play bridge?** jouez-vous au bridge?; **they're playing bridge** ils bridgent
(**h**) *(in billiards, snooker, pool)* chevalet *m*

(i) *Sport (in wrestling)* pont *m*; **to make a bridge** ponter

(j) *Comput (in network)* pont *m*

2 *comp Cards (party, tournament)* de bridge

3 *vt (river)* construire *ou* jeter un pont sur; *Fig* **a composer whose work bridged two centuries** un compositeur dont l'œuvre est à cheval sur deux siècles; **to bridge the generation gap** combler le fossé entre les générations; **in order to bridge the gap in our knowledge/in our resources** pour combler la lacune dans notre savoir/le trou dans nos ressources

►► *Am Fin* ***bridge loan*** prêt-relais *m*; *Cards* ***bridge player*** bridgeur(euse) *m,f*; *Br* ***bridge roll*** petit pain *m* (au lait)

'The Bridge on the River Kwai' *Lean* 'Le Pont de la rivière Kwaï'

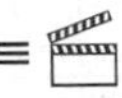

'A Bridge Too Far' *Attenborough* 'Un pont trop loin'

bridgehead ['brɪdʒhed] *n Mil* tête *f* de pont

bridgework ['brɪdʒwɜːk] *n (UNCOUNT) (in dentistry)* **to have bridgework done** se faire faire un bridge

bridging ['brɪdʒɪŋ] *n* **(a)** *(in climbing)* opposition *f* **(b)** *Constr* entretoisement *m* **(c)** *Elec* shuntage *m*

►► *Elec* ***bridging connection*** montage *m* en pont; *Br Fin* ***bridging loan*** prêt-relais *m*; *Constr* ***bridging piece*** entretoise *f*; *Fin* ***bridging value*** valeur *f* de récupération

bridle ['braɪdəl] **1** *n (harness)* bride *f*; *Fig (constraint)* frein *m*, contrainte *f*

2 *vt (horse)* brider; *Fig (emotions)* refréner; **to bridle one's tongue** tenir sa langue

3 *vi (horse)* redresser la tête; *Fig (person)* s'indigner, se scandaliser

►► ***bridle path*** piste *f* cavalière

bridleway ['braɪdəlˌweɪ] *n* piste *f* cavalière

brief [briːf] **1** *adj* **(a)** *(short in duration)* bref, court; **a brief interval** un court intervalle; **I caught a brief glimpse of her** je n'ai fait que l'entrevoir

(b) *(succinct)* concis, bref; **we exchanged a few brief words** nous avons échangé quelques mots; **please be brief** soyez bref s'il vous plaît; **to be brief, I think you're right** (en) bref, je crois que tu as raison; **a brief account** un exposé sommaire

(c) *(terse → person, reply)* laconique; *(abrupt)* brusque

(d) *(short in length)* court; **a very brief pair of shorts** un short très court

2 *vt* **(a)** *(bring up to date)* mettre au courant; *Mil (give orders to)* donner des instructions à; **the boss briefed me on the latest developments** le patron m'a mis au courant des derniers développements; **the soldiers were briefed on their mission** les soldats ont reçu leurs ordres pour la mission

(b) *Law (lawyer)* confier une cause à; *(case)* établir le dossier de

3 *n* **(a)** *Law* dossier *m*, affaire *f*; **he took our brief** il a accepté de plaider notre cause; **to hold a watching brief for sb/sth** veiller (en justice) aux intérêts de qn/qch; **to hold no brief for sb/sth** ne pas se faire l'avocat de qn/qch; *Fig* **he holds no brief for those who take drugs** il ne prend pas la défense de ceux qui se droguent

(b) *(instructions)* briefing *m*; **my brief was to develop sales** la tâche *ou* la mission qui m'a été confiée était de développer les ventes

(c) *Br Fam (lawyer)* avocat ◻ *m*

4 briefs *npl (underwear)* slip *m*

5 in brief *adv* en résumé

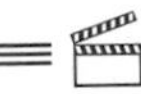

'Brief Encounter' *Lean* 'Brève rencontre'

'A Brief History of Time' *Hawking* 'Brève Histoire du Temps'

briefcase ['briːfkeɪs] *n* **(a)** serviette *f*, mallette *f* **(b)** *Comput (Windows® icon)* porte-documents *m*

briefing ['briːfɪŋ] *n* **(a)** *Mil (for mission)* instructions *fpl*, directives *fpl*; *Admin (meeting)* réunion *f* d'information, briefing *m*; *Aviat* briefing *m*; **they gave me a final briefing** ils m'ont donné les dernières directives **(b)** *Law (of lawyer)* ≃ constitution *f*

►► ***briefing room*** salle *f* de réunion

briefless ['briːflɪs] *adj (lawyer)* sans cause

briefly ['briːflɪ] *adv* **(a)** *(for a short time)* un court instant; **we spoke briefly on the telephone** nous avons échangé quelques mots au téléphone; **I visited her briefly on the way home** au retour, je lui ai rendu visite en coup de vent

(b) *(succinctly)* brièvement; *(tersely)* laconiquement; **she told them briefly what had happened** elle leur a résumé ce qui s'était passé; **put briefly, the situation is a mess** en bref, la situation est très embrouillée

briefness ['briːfnɪs] *n* **(a)** *(of time)* brièveté *f*, courte durée *f* **(b)** *(succinctness)* concision *f*; *(terseness)* laconisme *m*; *(abruptness)* brusquerie *f*

brier = **briar**

brierwood = **briarwood**

Brig. *Mil (written abbr* **brigadier***)* général *m* de brigade; **Brig. Smith** le général de brigade Smith

brig [brɪg] *n Naut* **(a)** *(ship)* brick *m* **(b)** *Am (prison on ship)* prison *f* *(à bord d'un navire)*; *Fam Fig* **they threw him in the brig** ils l'ont mis au trou **(c)** *Scot (bridge)* pont *m*

brigade [brɪ'geɪd] *n (gen) & Mil* brigade *f*; *Fig Hum Pej (group of people)* bande *f*; *Fig* **one of the old brigade** un vieux de la vieille

brigadier [ˌbrɪgə'dɪə(r)] *n Br Mil* général *m* de brigade

►► *Am Mil* ***brigadier general*** *(in army)* général *m* de brigade; *(in air force)* général *m* de brigade aérienne

brigand ['brɪgənd] *n* brigand *m*, bandit *m*

brigandage ['brɪgəndɪdʒ] *n* brigandage *m*

brigantine ['brɪgəntiːn] *n Naut* brigantin *m*

bright [braɪt] **1** *adj* **(a)** *(weather, day)* clair, radieux; *(sunshine)* éclatant; *(room)* clair; *(fire, light)* vif; *(colour)* vif, éclatant; *Met* **the weather will get brighter later** le temps s'améliorera en cours de journée; *Met* **cloudy with bright intervals** nuageux avec des éclaircies; *Met* **to become brighter** s'éclaircir; *Met* **the outlook for tomorrow is brighter** on prévoit une amélioration du temps pour demain; **bright red** rouge *m* vif; *Fig* **bright and early** tôt le matin, de bon *ou* grand matin; **'All Things Bright And Beautiful'** = chant religieux souvent chanté par les enfants

(b) *(shining → diamond, star)* brillant; *(→ metal)* poli, luisant; *(→ eyes)* brillant, vif; **she likes the bright lights** elle aime la grande ville; **the bright lights of London** les attractions de Londres

(c) *(clever)* intelligent; *(child)* éveillé, vif; **he's not very bright** ce n'est pas une lumière, il n'est pas très futé *ou* malin; **a bright idea** une idée géniale *ou* lumineuse

(d) *(cheerful)* gai, joyeux; *(lively)* animé, vif; **you're very bright this morning!** tu es bien gai ce matin!; **to be bright and breezy** avoir l'air en pleine forme; **it was the only bright spot in the day** c'était la seule chose positive de la journée

(e) *(promising)* brillant; **there are brighter days ahead** des jours meilleurs nous attendent; **to have a bright future** avoir un brillant avenir; **the future's looking bright** l'avenir est plein de promesses *ou* s'annonce bien; **to look on the bright side** prendre les choses du bon côté, être optimiste

2 *adv Literary (burn, shine)* avec éclat, brillamment

3 brights *npl Am Aut (headlights)* **to put the brights on** se mettre en pleins phares

►► *Br Fam* ***bright spark*** *(clever person)* lumière *f*; *Ironic* **you're a bright spark!** gros malin!

brighten ['braɪtən] **1** *vt* **(a)** *(decorate → place, person)* égayer; *(enliven → conversation)* animer, égayer **(b)** *(prospects)* améliorer, faire paraître sous un meilleur jour **(c)** *(polish → metal)* astiquer, faire reluire **(d)** *(colour)* aviver

2 *vi* **(a)** *(weather)* s'améliorer **(b)** *(person)* s'animer; *(face)* s'éclairer; *(eyes)* s'allumer, s'éclairer; **their mood brightened** ils se sont déridés **(c)** *(prospects)* s'améliorer

►**brighten up** = **brighten**

brightener ['braɪtənə(r)] *n* **(a)** *(of colours)* aviveur *m* **(b)** *Metal (for metals)* (agent *m*) brillanteur *m*

brightening ['braɪtənɪŋ] *n* **(a)** *(of sky, weather)* éclaircissement *m*; *Fig* **there was a momentary brightening of her mood** elle s'est égayée un moment **(b)** *(of colours)* avivage *m*

bright-eyed *adj* aux yeux brillants; *Fig (eager)* enthousiaste; *Hum* **bright-eyed and bushy-tailed** frais comme la rosée

brightly ['braɪtlɪ] *adv* **(a)** *(shine)* avec éclat; **the stars were shining brightly** les étoiles scintillaient; **the fire burned brightly** le feu flambait; **brightly polished** reluisant **(b)** *(cheerfully)* gaiement, joyeusement; **to smile brightly** sourire d'un air radieux; **to answer brightly** répondre gaiement

brightly-coloured *adj* aux couleurs vives

brightness ['braɪtnɪs] *n* **(a)** *(of sun)* éclat *m*; *(of light)* intensité *f*; *(of room)* clarté *f*, luminosité *f*; *(of colour)* éclat *m*; *TV* **brightness (control)** (dispositif *m* de réglage de la) luminosité *f* **(b)** *(cheerfulness)* gaieté *f*, joie *f*; *(liveliness)* vivacité *f*; *(of smile)* éclat *m* **(c)** *(cleverness)* intelligence *f*

Bright's disease [braɪts-] *n Med* mal *m* de Bright, *Spec* néphrite *f* chronique

brill[1] [brɪl] *(pl* **inv***)* *n Ich* barbue *f*

brill[2] *adj Br Fam (terrific)* super, sensass

brilliance ['brɪljəns], **brilliancy** ['brɪljənsɪ] *n* **(a)** *(of light, smile, performance, career)* éclat *m*, brillant *m* **(b)** *(cleverness)* intelligence *f*; **no one doubts her brilliance** il ne fait pas de doute qu'elle est d'une intelligence supérieure

brilliant ['brɪljənt] **1** *adj* **(a)** *(light, sunshine)* éclatant, intense; *(smile)* éclatant, radieux; *(colour)* vif, éclatant

(b) *(outstanding → mind, musician, writer)* brillant, exceptionnel; *(→ film, novel, piece of work)* brillant, exceptionnel; *(→ success)* éclatant; **a brilliant career** une brillante carrière

(c) *Fam (terrific)* sensationnel, super; **you were brilliant!** tu as été formidable *ou* magnifique!

(d) *(intelligent)* brillant; **that's a brilliant idea** c'est une idée lumineuse *ou* de génie

2 *n Miner (diamond, cut)* brillant *m*

brilliantine ['brɪljəntiːn] *n* brillantine *f*

brilliantly ['brɪljəntlɪ] *adv* **(a)** *(shine)* avec éclat; **brilliantly coloured** d'une couleur vive; **brilliantly lit** très bien éclairé **(b)** *(perform, talk)* brillamment; **to play brilliantly** jouer avec brio

Brillo pad® ['brɪləʊ-] *n* ≃ tampon *m* Jex®

brim [brɪm] *(pp & pt* **brimmed**, *cont* **brimming***)* **1** *n (of hat)* bord *m*; *(of bowl, cup)* bord *m*; **full to the brim** plein à ras bord

2 *vi* déborder; **eyes brimming with tears** des yeux pleins *ou* noyés de larmes; *Fig* **the newcomers were brimming with ideas** les nouveaux venus avaient des idées à revendre

►**brim over** *vi* déborder; *Fig* **to be brimming over with enthusiasm** déborder d'enthousiasme

brimful [ˌbrɪm'fʊl] *adj Br (cup)* plein à déborder *ou* jusqu'au bord; *Fig* débordant; **brimful of confidence** très *ou* excessivement confiant

brimless ['brɪmlɪs] *adj (hat)* sans bord *ou* bords

-brimmed [brɪmd] *suff* **broad-brimmed** à larges bords; **narrow-brimmed** à bords étroits

brimstone ['brɪmstəʊn] *n* **(a)** *Arch (sulphur)* soufre *m* **(b)** *Entom (butterfly)* citron *m*

brindle ['brɪndəl], **brindled** ['brɪndəld] *adj* moucheté, tavelé

brine [braɪn] *n* **(a)** *(salty water)* eau *f* salée; *Culin* saumure *f* **(b)** *Literary (sea)* mer *f*; *(sea water)* eau *f* de mer; *Culin* **mussels in brine** moules *fpl* en saumure

►► *Zool* ***brine shrimp*** artémia *f*

BRING [brɪŋ]

amener	► (a), (b), (d), (e)
apporter	► (a)
provoquer	► (c)
rapporter	► (g)

(pt & pp **brought** [brɔːt]*)* *vt* **(a)** *(take → animal, person, vehicle)* amener; *(→ object)* apporter; *(→ fashion, idea, product)* introduire, lancer; **I'll**

bring the books (across) tomorrow j'apporterai les livres demain; **her father's bringing her home today** son père la ramène à la maison aujourd'hui; **what brings you here?** qu'est-ce qui vous amène?; **can you bring me a beer, please?** vous pouvez m'apporter une bière, s'il vous plaît?; **that brings the total to £350** cela fait 350 livres en tout; **he brought his dog with him** il a emmené son chien; **did you bring anything with you?** as-tu apporté quelque chose?; **black musicians brought jazz to Europe** les musiciens noirs ont introduit le jazz en Europe; **this programme is brought to you by the BBC** ce programme est diffusé par la BBC

(**b**) *(into specified state)* entraîner, amener; **to bring sth into play** faire jouer qch; **to bring sth into question** mettre *ou* remettre qch en question; **to bring sb to his/her senses** ramener qn à la raison; **to bring sth to an end** *or* **a close** *or* **a halt** mettre fin à qch; **to bring sth to sb's attention** *or* **knowledge** *or* **notice** attirer l'attention de qn sur qch; **to bring a child into the world** mettre un enfant au monde; **to bring sth to light** mettre qch en lumière, révéler qch; **to bring sth to mind** rappeler qch; **to bring sth onto the market** introduire qch sur le marché

(**c**) *(produce)* provoquer, causer; **her performance brought wild applause** son interprétation a provoqué un tonnerre d'applaudissements; **to bring sth upon sb** attirer qch sur qn; **her foolhardiness brought misfortune upon the family** son imprudence a attiré le malheur sur la famille; **you've brought it on yourself** vous l'avez cherché; **you bring credit to the firm** vous faites honneur à la société; **it brings bad/good luck** ça porte malheur/bonheur; **he brought a sense of urgency to the project** il a fait accélérer le projet; **to bring new hope to sb** redonner de l'espoir à qn; **the story brought tears to my eyes** l'histoire m'a fait venir les larmes aux yeux; **his speech brought jeers from the audience** son discours lui a valu les huées de l'assistance; **money does not always bring happiness** l'argent ne fait pas toujours le bonheur; **the winter brought more wind and rain** l'hiver a amené encore plus de vent et de pluie; **tourism has brought prosperity to the area** le tourisme a enrichi la région; **who knows what the future will bring?** qui sait ce que l'avenir nous/lui/*etc* réserve?

(**d**) *(force)* amener; **she can't bring herself to speak about it** elle n'arrive pas à en parler; **her performance brought the audience to its feet** les spectateurs se sont levés pour l'applaudir

(**e**) *(lead)* mener, amener; **the path brings you straight (out) into the village** ce chemin vous mène (tout) droit au village; **the shock brought him to the verge of a breakdown** le choc l'a mené au bord de la dépression nerveuse; **to bring sb into a conversation/discussion** faire participer qn à une conversation/discussion; **that brings us to the next question** cela nous amène à la question suivante

(**f**) *Law* **to bring an action** *or* **a suit against sb** intenter un procès à *ou* contre qn; **to bring a charge against sb** porter une accusation contre qn; **the case was brought before the court** l'affaire a été déférée au tribunal; **he was brought before the court** il a comparu devant le tribunal; **the murderer must be brought to justice** l'assassin doit être traduit en justice; **to bring evidence** avancer *ou* présenter des preuves

(**g**) *(financially)* rapporter; **her painting only brings her a few thousand pounds a year** ses peintures ne lui rapportent que quelques milliers de livres par an

▸**bring about** *vt sep* (**a**) *(cause → changes, war)* provoquer, amener, entraîner; *(→ reconciliation)* amener; *(→ person's downfall)* entraîner; *(→ accident)* provoquer, causer; **what brought about his dismissal?** pourquoi a-t-il été renvoyé exactement?, quel est le motif de son renvoi?

(**b**) *Naut* faire virer de bord

▸**bring along** *vt sep (person)* amener; *(thing)* apporter

▸**bring around** = **bring round**

▸**bring away** *vt sep (memories, impressions)* garder

▸**bring back** *vt sep* (**a**) *(fetch → person)* ramener; *(→ thing)* rapporter; **no amount of crying will bring him back** pleurer ne le ramènera pas à la vie; *Law* **to bring a case back before the court** ressaisir le tribunal d'un dossier

(**b**) *(restore)* restaurer; **the news brought a smile back to her face** la nouvelle lui a rendu le sourire; **they're bringing back miniskirts** ils relancent la minijupe; **to bring sb back to life** ranimer qn

(**c**) *(evoke → memory)* rappeler (à la mémoire); **that brings it all back to me** ça réveille tous mes souvenirs

▸**bring by** *vt sep* **to bring sb by** amener qn

▸**bring down** *vt sep* (**a**) *(fetch → person)* amener; *(→ thing)* descendre, apporter

(**b**) *(reduce → prices, temperature)* faire baisser; *(→ currency)* déprécier, avilir; *(→ birthrate, inflation, unemployment, swelling)* réduire

(**c**) *(cause to land → kite)* ramener (au sol); *(→ plane)* faire atterrir

(**d**) *(cause to fall → prey)* descendre; *(→ plane, enemy, tree)* abattre; **her performance brought the house down** son interprétation lui a valu des applaudissements à tout rompre

(**e**) *Pol (overthrow)* faire tomber, renverser

(**f**) *Math (carry)* abaisser

(**g**) *Fam (depress)* déprimer ❑, donner le cafard à

(**h**) *Literary (provoke → anger)* attirer; **to bring down the wrath of God on sb** attirer la colère de Dieu sur qn; **stop making so much noise or you'll bring the headmaster down on us** ne fais pas tant de bruit, tu vas attirer l'attention du proviseur sur nous

▸**bring forth** *vt sep Formal* (**a**) *(produce → fruit)* produire; *(→ child)* mettre au monde; *(→ animal)* mettre bas (**b**) *(elicit)* provoquer

▸**bring forward** *vt sep* (**a**) *(present → person)* faire avancer; *(→ argument)* avancer, présenter; *Law (→ witness)* produire; *Law (→ evidence)* avancer, présenter

(**b**) *(chair etc)* avancer

(**c**) *Admin (move → date, meeting)* avancer; **the conference has been brought forward to the 28th** la conférence a été avancée au 28

(**d**) *Acct* reporter; **brought forward** reporté

▸**bring in** *vt sep* (**a**) *(fetch in → person)* faire entrer; *(→ thing)* rentrer; **to bring in the harvest** rentrer la moisson; **they want to bring a new person in** ils veulent prendre quelqu'un d'autre; **we will have to bring in the police** il faudra faire intervenir la *ou* faire appel à la police; **to bring sb in for questioning** emmener qn au poste de police pour l'interroger

(**b**) *(introduce → laws, system)* introduire, présenter; *(→ fashion)* lancer; **the government has brought in a new tax bill** le gouvernement a présenté *ou* déposé un nouveau projet de loi fiscal; **can I just bring in a new point?** est-ce que je peux faire une autre remarque?

(**c**) *(yield, produce)* rapporter; **to bring in interest** rapporter des intérêts; **tourism brings in millions of dollars each year** le tourisme rapporte des millions de dollars tous les ans; **her work doesn't bring in much money** son travail ne lui rapporte pas grand-chose

(**d**) *Law (verdict)* rendre; **they brought in a verdict of guilty** ils l'ont déclaré coupable

▸**bring off** *vt sep* (**a**) *Br Fam (trick)* réussir ❑; *(plan)* réaliser ❑; *Com (deal)* conclure ❑, mener à bien ❑; **did you manage to bring it off?** avez-vous réussi votre coup?

(**b**) *Sport (player)* faire sortir

(**c**) *(person → from ship)* débarquer; **the injured men will be brought off by helicopter** les blessés seront évacués en hélicoptère

(**d**) *Vulg (masturbate)* **to bring sb off** branler qn; **to bring oneself off** se branler

▸**bring on** *vt sep* (**a**) *(induce)* provoquer, causer; **the shock brought on a heart attack** le choc a provoqué une crise cardiaque; *Hum* **what brought this on?** *(why are you offering to help?)* qu'est-ce que tu me caches?

(**b**) *(encourage)* encourager; **the warm weather has really brought on the flowers** la chaleur a bien fait pousser les fleurs; **the idea is to bring on new tennis players** il s'agit d'encourager de nouveaux tennismen

(**c**) *Theat (person)* amener sur scène; *(thing)* apporter sur scène; **please bring on our next contestant** faites entrer le concurrent suivant

(**d**) *Sport (substitute)* faire entrer

▸**bring out** *vt sep* (**a**) *(take out → person)* faire sortir; *(→ thing)* sortir

(**b**) *Com (commercially → product, style)* lancer; *(→ record)* sortir; *(→ book)* publier

(**c**) *(accentuate)* souligner; **that colour brings out the green in her eyes** cette couleur met en valeur le vert de ses yeux; **her performance brought out the character's comic side** son interprétation a fait ressortir le côté comique du personnage; **to bring out the best/worst in sb** faire apparaître qn sous son meilleur/plus mauvais jour; *Hum* **it brings out the beast in me** cela réveille l'animal qui est en moi

(**d**) *Br Med (in rash, spots)* **strawberries bring me out in spots** les fraises me donnent des boutons

(**e**) *(encourage → person)* encourager; **he's very good at bringing people out (of themselves)** il sait très bien s'y prendre pour mettre les gens à l'aise; **the sun has brought out the roses** le soleil a fait s'épanouir les roses

(**f**) *Ind (workers)* appeler à la grève; **they're threatening to bring everyone out (on strike)** ils menacent d'appeler tout le monde à faire grève

(**g**) *St Exch (shares)* émettre; **to bring out new shares** émettre de nouvelles actions

▸**bring over** *vt sep (take → person)* amener; *(→ thing)* apporter

▸**bring round** *vt sep* (**a**) *(take → person)* amener; *(→ thing)* apporter; *Br Fig* **I brought the conversation round to marriage** j'ai amené la conversation sur le mariage

(**b**) *(revive)* ranimer

(**c**) *(persuade)* convaincre, convertir; **to bring sb round to a point of view** convertir *ou* amener qn à un point de vue

▸**bring through** *vt sep* **he brought the country through the depression** il a réussi à faire sortir le pays de la dépression; **the doctors brought me through my illness** grâce aux médecins, j'ai survécu à ma maladie

▸**bring to** *vt sep* (**a**) *(revive)* ranimer (**b**) *Naut* mettre en panne

▸**bring together** *vt sep* (**a**) *(people)* réunir; *(facts)* rassembler

(**b**) *(introduce)* mettre en contact, faire se rencontrer; **her brother brought them together** son frère les a fait se rencontrer

(**c**) *(reconcile)* réconcilier; *Ind* **an arbitrator is trying to bring the two sides together** un médiateur essaie de réconcilier les deux parties

▸**bring up** *vt sep* (**a**) *(take → person)* amener; *(→ thing)* monter

(**b**) *(child)* élever; **to be well/badly brought up** être bien/mal élevé; **I was brought up to be polite** on m'a appris la politesse

(**c**) *(mention → fact, problem)* signaler, mentionner; *(→ question)* soulever; **don't bring that up again** ne remettez pas cela sur le tapis; **we won't bring it up again** nous n'en reparlerons plus

(**d**) *(vomit)* vomir, rendre

(**e**) *Law* **to bring sb up before a judge** citer *ou* faire comparaître qn devant un juge

(**f**) *(move forward → troops)* faire avancer; *(→ reinforcements, fresh supplies etc)* faire venir

(**g**) *(raise)* **to bring sb/sth up to professional standard** élever qn/qch à un niveau professionnel

---

bring-and-buy *n Br Com* **bring-and-buy (sale)** = brocante de particuliers

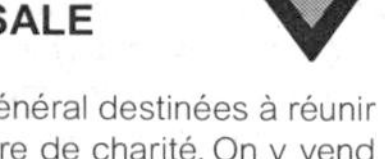

BRING-AND-BUY SALE

Ces brocantes sont en général destinées à réunir des fonds pour une œuvre de charité. On y vend des articles d'occasion et des produits faits maison.

bringing up ['brɪŋɪŋ-] *n (of child)* éducation *f*

brink [brɪŋk] *n (of precipice, river)* bord *m*; **to be on the brink of sth** *(tears, war, success, starvation etc)* être au bord de qch; *(discovery)* être à la veille de qch; *(death)* être à deux doigts de qch; *(ruin)* être au bord *ou* à deux doigts de qch; **to be on the brink of doing sth** être sur le point de faire qch; *Zool* **to be on the brink of**

extinction *(animal)* être en voie de disparition; *Fig* **to stand shivering on the brink** hésiter à faire le plongeon

brinkmanship ['brɪŋkmən,ʃɪp], **brinksmanship** ['brɪŋksmən,ʃɪp] *n Pol* politique *f* de la corde raide; **he's a master in the art of brinkmanship** c'est un maître dans l'art de savoir jusqu'où il peut aller; **the country is engaged in a tense game of diplomatic brinkmanship with the West** le pays a entamé un bras de fer diplomatique avec l'Ouest

briny ['braɪnɪ] *(compar* **brinier,** *superl* **briniest) 1** *adj* saumâtre, salé

2 *n Literary* **the briny** la mer

briquet, briquette [brɪ'ket] *n (of coal)* briquette *f*, aggloméré *m*; *(of ice cream)* pavé *m*

Brisbane ['brɪzbən] *n* Brisbane

brisk [brɪsk] *adj* **(a)** *(person)* vif, alerte; *(curt)* sec (sèche); *(manner)* brusque

(b) *(quick)* rapide, vif; **to go for a brisk walk** se promener d'un bon pas; **to go for a brisk swim** nager vigoureusement; **at a brisk pace** à vive allure

(c) *Com* florissant; **business is brisk** les affaires marchent bien; **bidding at the auction was brisk** les enchères étaient animées; **we're doing a brisk trade in this particular item** cet article se vend très bien; *St Exch* **brisk trading** marché *m* actif

(d) *(weather)* vivifiant, frais (fraîche); *(day, wind)* frais (fraîche)

brisket ['brɪskɪt] *n (of animal)* poitrine *f*; *Culin* poitrine *f* de bœuf

briskly ['brɪsklɪ] *adv* **(a)** *(move)* vivement; *(walk)* d'un bon pas; *(speak)* brusquement, sèchement; *(act)* sans délai *ou* tarder **(b)** *Com* **cold drinks were selling briskly** les boissons fraîches se vendaient très bien *ou* comme des petits pains

briskness ['brɪsknɪs] *n* **(a)** *(of person)* vivacité *f*; *(of manner)* brusquerie *f*; *(of action)* rapidité *f* **(b)** *Com* activité *f* **(c)** *(of weather)* fraîcheur *f*

brisling ['brɪzlɪŋ] *n Ich* sprat *m*

bristle ['brɪsəl] **1** *n (of beard, brush)* poil *m*; *(of boar, pig)* soie *f*; *Bot (of plant)* poil *m*, soie *f*; **a brush with nylon/natural bristles** une brosse en nylon/soie; **a pure bristle brush** une brosse pur sanglier

2 *vi* **(a)** *(hair)* se redresser, se hérisser

(b) *Fig (show anger)* s'irriter, se hérisser; **they bristled at any suggestion of incompetence** ils se hérissèrent lorsqu'on osa insinuer qu'ils étaient incompétents

▸**bristle with** *vt insep Br (swarm with)* grouiller de; **the whole subject bristles with difficulties** toute la question est hérissée de difficultés; **the town centre was bristling with police** le centre-ville grouillait de policiers; **bristling with machine guns** *(fort, trench)* hérissé de mitrailleuses

bristletail ['brɪsəlteɪl] *n Entom* lépisme *m*

bristleworm ['brɪsəlwɜːm] *n Zool* chétopode *m*

bristling ['brɪsəlɪŋ] *adj* hérissé, en bataille

bristly ['brɪslɪ] *(compar* **bristlier,** *superl* **bristliest)** *adj (beard → in appearance)* aux poils raides; *(→ to touch)* qui pique; *(chin)* piquant; **his face was all bristly** il avait une barbe de trois jours

Bristol ['brɪstəl] **1** *n (city)* Bristol; *Fam Old-fashioned* **(shipshape and) Bristol fashion** bien rangé, impeccable

2 bristols *npl Br Fam Old-fashioned* roberts *mpl*, nichons *mpl*

►► ***Bristol board*** bristol *m*; ***the Bristol Channel*** le canal de Bristol; ***Bristol Cream***® = marque de xérès

Brit [brɪt] **1** *n Fam* Britannique ❑ *mf*, British *m*

2 the Brit Awards, the Brits *npl Mus* = distinction récompensant les meilleures œuvres musicales britanniques de l'année (classique exclue)

Britain ['brɪtən] *n* **(Great) Britain** Grande-Bretagne *f*; **in Britain** en Grande-Bretagne

Britannia [brɪ'tænjə] *n* **(a)** *(figure)* = femme assise portant un casque et tenant un trident, qui personnifie la Grande-Bretagne **(b) (the Royal Yacht) Britannia** = yacht de la famille royale britannique, aujourd'hui transformé en musée

►► ***Britannia metal*** métal *m* anglais; ***Britannia silver*** argent *m* fin

Britannic [brɪ'tænɪk] *adj Formal* **His** *or* **Her Britannic Majesty** Sa Majesté Britannique

Britannicus [brɪ'tænɪkəs] *pr n* Britannicus

britches *Am* = **breeches**

briticism ['brɪtɪsɪzəm] *n Ling* anglicisme *m*

British ['brɪtɪʃ] **1** *npl* **the British** les Britanniques *mpl*, les Anglais *mpl*

2 *adj* britannique, anglais; **British goods** produits *mpl* anglais; *Br* **the best of British (luck)!** bonne chance!

►► ***the British Academy*** = organisme public d'aide à la recherche dans le domaine des lettres; *Formerly Aviat & Com* ***British Aerospace*** British Aerospace *f (principale société de construction aéronautique et spatiale britannique)*; ***British Antarctic Territory*** territoire *m* de l'Antarctique britannique; *Mil* ***British Army of the Rhine*** = forces armées britanniques établies en Allemagne de l'Ouest après la Seconde Guerre mondiale; *Cin* ***British Board of Film Classification*** = organisme britannique délivrant les visas de sortie pour les films; *Rad & TV* ***the British Broadcasting Corporation*** la BBC; ***British Columbia*** la Colombie-Britannique; **in British Columbia** en Colombie-Britannique; ***British Columbian* 1** *n* = habitant ou natif de la Colombie-Britannique **2** *adj* de la Colombie-Britannique; ***the British Commonwealth*** le Commonwealth; *Admin* ***the British Council*** = organisme public chargé de promouvoir la langue et la culture anglaises; *Hist* ***the British East India Company*** la Compagnie britannique des Indes orientales; ***the British Embassy*** l'ambassade *f* de Grande-Bretagne; *Hist* ***the British Empire*** l'Empire *m* britannique; ***British English*** anglais *m* britannique; *Cin* ***British Film Institute*** = organisme britannique de promotion du cinéma (aide à la réalisation notamment); *Formerly* ***British Gas*** = société de production et de distribution du gaz; ***(former) British Honduras*** (l'ex) Honduras *m* britannique; **in British Honduras** au Honduras britannique; ***British Institute of Management*** = organisme britannique dont la fonction est de renseigner et de conseiller les entreprises en matière de gestion, ainsi que de promouvoir l'enseignement de cette discipline; ***the British Isles*** les îles *fpl* Britanniques; **in the British Isles** aux îles Britanniques; ***British Legion*** = organisme d'aide aux anciens combattants; ***British Library*** = la bibliothèque nationale britannique; *Sport* ***the British Lions*** = équipe de rugby à quinze constituée des joueurs sélectionnés dans les quatre équipes nationales (Angleterre, pays de Galles, Écosse et Irlande); ***British Museum*** = grand musée et bibliothèque londoniens; ***British Nuclear Fuels*** = entreprise publique de production de combustibles nucléaires; ***the British Open*** = important championnat de golf qui se tient chaque année en Grande-Bretagne; *Formerly* ***British Rail*** = société des chemins de fers britanniques, ≃ SNCF *f*; ***British Standards Institution*** = association britannique de normalisation; *Formerly* ***British Steel*** = société britannique de production d'acier; ***British Summer Time*** = heure d'été britannique; ***British Technology Group*** = organisme privé britannique commercialisant des innovations technologiques élaborées par des universités ou des inventeurs; *Formerly* ***British Telecom*** = société britannique de télécommunications; *Phys* ***British thermal unit*** calorie *f* britannique, ≃ 1055,06 joules *mpl*

BRITISH COUNCIL

Le British Council est chargé de promouvoir la langue et la culture anglaises, et de renforcer les liens culturels avec les autres pays.

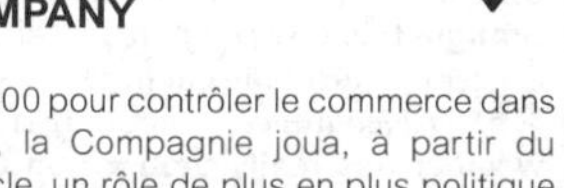

THE BRITISH EAST INDIA COMPANY

Fondée en 1600 pour contrôler le commerce dans les colonies, la Compagnie joua, à partir du XVIIIème siècle, un rôle de plus en plus politique en Inde, pour finalement devenir l'agent de l'impérialisme britannique; elle disparut dans les années 1870.

BRITISH GAS/TELECOM/RAIL

Plusieurs services britanniques autrefois publics ont été successivement privatisés. En 1984, les résaux de télécommunications sont rachetés par British Telecom. Cet opérateur privé en assure le monopole jusqu'en 1991, lorsque le marché est ouvert à la concurrence. British Telecom devient alors BT et partage le marché avec plusieurs autres compagnies. British Gas est privatisé en 1986 et a pris le nom de Centrica. British Rail est partagé dans les années 90 entre Railtrack, propriétaire des stations et lignes de chemin de fer, et plusieurs petites compagnies qui assurent le trafic ferroviaire.

Britisher ['brɪtɪʃə(r)] *n Am* Anglais(e) *m,f*, Britannique *mf*

Briton ['brɪtən] *n* Britannique *mf*, Anglais(e) *m,f*; *Hist* Breton(onne) *m,f* (d'Angleterre)

Britpop ['brɪtpɒp] *n Mus* = la musique pop britannique du milieu des années 90

Brittany ['brɪtənɪ] *n* Bretagne *f*; **in Brittany** en Bretagne

brittle ['brɪtəl] *adj* **(a)** *(breakable)* cassant, fragile **(b)** *(person)* froid, indifférent; *(humour)* mordant, caustique; *(reply)* sec (sèche); **a brittle tone of voice** un ton sec *ou* cassant **(c)** *(sound)* strident, aigu(ë)

►► *Med* ***brittle bone disease*** ostéogenèse *f* imparfaite, fragilité *f* osseuse héréditaire; *Ich* ***brittle star*** ophiure *f*

brittleness ['brɪtəlnɪs] *n* **(a)** *(fragility)* fragilité *f* **(b)** *(of person)* froideur *f*, insensibilité *f*; *(of humour)* causticité *f*, mordant *m*; **the brittleness of her voice** sa voix crispée **(c)** *(of sound)* son *m* aigu

Brittonic [brɪ'tɒnɪk] *Ling* **1** *n* brittonique *m*

2 *adj* brittonique

bro [brəʊ] *n Fam* **(a)** *(brother)* frangin *m*, frérot *m* **(b)** *Am (male friend)* pote *m*; **hey, bro!** salut mon pote!

broach [brəʊtʃ] **1** *vt* **(a)** *(subject)* aborder, entamer **(b)** *(barrel)* percer, mettre en perce; *(supplies)* entamer

2 *vi Naut* venir *ou* tomber en travers

3 *n* **(a)** *Am (jewellery)* broche *f (bijou)* **(b)** *Constr* perçoir *m*, foret *m* **(c)** *Culin* broche *f*

broad [brɔːd] **1** *adj* **(a)** *(wide)* large; **the road is 4 metres broad** la route a 4 mètres de large *ou* de largeur; **she has a broad back** elle a une forte carrure; **a broad grin** un large *ou* grand sourire; **to be broad in the shoulders, to have broad shoulders** être large d'épaules; *Fig* **he has broad shoulders, he can take it** il a les reins solides, il peut encaisser; **to be broad in the beam** *(ship)* être ventru; *Fam (person)* être large des hanches ❑; *Br Fig* **it's as broad as it's long** c'est bonnet blanc et blanc bonnet, c'est du pareil *ou* ça revient au même

(b) *(extensive)* vaste, immense; **a broad syllabus** un programme très divers; **we offer a broad range of products** nous offrons une large *ou* grande gamme de produits; **in broad daylight** au grand jour, en plein jour; *Fig* au vu et au su de tout le monde, au grand jour

(c) *(general)* général; **here is a broad outline** voilà les grandes lignes; **in the broadest sense of the word** au sens le plus large du mot; **his books still have a very broad appeal** ses livres plaisent toujours à *ou* intéressent toujours un vaste public; **to be in broad agreement** être d'accord dans les grandes lignes; *Am Law* **broad construction** interprétation *f* large

(d) *(not subtle)* évident; **a broad hint** une allusion transparente; **"surely not", she said with broad sarcasm** "pas possible", dit-elle d'un ton des plus sarcastiques; **he speaks with a broad Scottish accent** il a un accent écossais prononcé *ou* un fort accent écossais

(e) *(liberal)* libéral; **to have broad views** avoir les idées larges; **she has very broad tastes in literature** elle a des goûts littéraires très éclectiques

(f) *(coarse)* grossier, vulgaire; **broad humour** humour *m* grivois; **a broad joke** une plaisanterie osée *ou* leste

(g) *Ling* large; **broad transcription** transcription *f* large

2 *n* (**a**) *(widest part)* **the broad of the back** le milieu du dos

(**b**) *Am Fam (woman)* gonzesse *f*

▸▸ ***broad bean*** fève *f*; *Rel* ***Broad Church*** = groupe libéral à l'intérieur de l'Église anglicane; *Fig* **the party is a broad church** le parti rassemble de nombreux courants différents; *Am Sport* ***broad jump*** saut *m* en longueur

broad-backed *adj* qui a une forte carrure

broadband ['brɔːdbænd] *Rad* **1** *n* diffusion *f* en larges bandes de fréquence

2 *adj* à larges bandes

broad-bottomed [-ˌbɒtəmd] *adj* (**a**) *(boat)* à fond plat (**b**) *Fam (person)* fessu

broad-brimmed [-ˌbrɪmd] *adj* à bords larges

broad-brush *adj* **a broad-brush approach** une approche grossière

broadcast ['brɔːdkɑːst] *(pt & pp* **broadcast** *or* **broadcasted)** **1** *n Rad & TV* émission *f*; **live/recorded broadcast** émission *f* en direct/en différé; **repeat broadcast** rediffusion *f*

2 *vt* (**a**) *Rad & TV* diffuser; **the match will be broadcast live** le match sera diffusé en direct; *Fig* **you don't have to broadcast it!** ce n'est pas la peine de le crier sur les toits *ou* le carillonner partout!

(**b**) *Agr* semer à la volée

3 *vi Rad & TV (station)* émettre; *(actor)* participer à une émission, paraître à la télévision; *(show host)* faire une émission

4 *adj Rad* radiodiffusé; *TV* télévisé

5 *adv Agr* à la volée

▸▸ *Comput* ***broadcast message*** message *m* système; ***broadcast satellite*** satellite *m* de radiodiffusion; ***broadcast signal*** signal *m* de radiodiffusion; *Mktg* ***broadcast sponsorship*** parrainage *m* audiovisuel

broadcaster ['brɔːdkɑːstə(r)] *n Rad & TV (person)* personnalité *f* de la radio *ou* de la télévision; **independent broadcaster** *Rad* station *f* de radio; *TV* chaîne *f* de télévision privée

broadcasting ['brɔːdkɑːstɪŋ] *n Rad* radiodiffusion *f*; *TV* télévision *f*; **he wants to go into broadcasting** il veut faire une carrière à la radio ou à la télévision

▸▸ *Rad & TV* ***Broadcasting Complaints Commission*** = organisme britannique traitant les plaintes concernant les émissions de télévision et de radio; *Rad & TV* ***Broadcasting House*** = siège de la BBC à Londres; *Rad & TV* ***Broadcasting Standards Council*** = organisme britannique de contrôle des émissions de télévision et de radio

broadcloth ['brɔːdklɒθ] *n Tex* drap *m* fin

broaden ['brɔːdən] **1** *vt* élargir; **to broaden sb's outlook** *or* **horizons** élargir l'horizon de qn; **travel broadens the mind** les voyages ouvrent de nouveaux horizons

2 *vi* s'élargir

▸**broaden out** *vi (river, road, valley)* s'élargir

broad-leaved *adj Bot* feuillu

broadloom ['brɔːdluːm] *adj Tex (carpet)* en grande largeur

broadly ['brɔːdlɪ] *adv* (**a**) *(widely)* largement; **to smile broadly** faire un grand sourire (**b**) *(generally)* en général; **broadly speaking** d'une façon générale, en gros

broadly-based *adj* composé d'éléments variés *ou* divers

[illegible] **broad-minded** avoir les idées larges; **he has very broad-minded parents** ses parents sont très tolérants *ou* larges d'esprit

broad-mindedness [-'maɪndɪdnɪs] *n* largeur *f* d'esprit

Broadmoor ['brɔːdˌmɔː(r)] *n* = institution britannique pour les détenus souffrant de graves troubles psychiques

broadness ['brɔːdnɪs] *n* (**a**) *(width)* largeur *f* (**b**) *(coarseness)* grossièreté *f*, vulgarité *f* (**c**) *(of accent)* caractère *m* prononcé; **the broadness of his accent** son accent prononcé

Broads [brɔːdz] *npl* **the (Norfolk) Broads** = ensemble de lacs situés dans le Norfolk et le Suffolk

> **BROADS**
>
> Les Broads sont des lacs peu profonds mais navigables, reliés entre eux par des cours d'eau; ils constituent aujourd'hui un parc national et une réserve ornithologique.

broadsheet ['brɔːdʃiːt] *n* (**a**) *Press (newspaper)* journal *m* plein format; *Br* **the broadsheets** les journaux *mpl* de qualité (**b**) *Typ* placard *m*

> **BROADSHEET** 
>
> Les principaux journaux nationaux de qualité en Grande-Bretagne sont: *The Guardian* (tendance centre gauche); *The Independent*; *The Daily Telegraph* (tendance conservatrice); *The Times* (tendance centre droit); *The Financial Times*.

broad-shouldered [-'ʃəʊldəd] *adj* large d'épaules, aux larges épaules

broadside ['brɔːdsaɪd] **1** *n* (**a**) *Naut (of ship)* flanc *m* (**b**) *Mil (volley of shots)* bordée *f*; **the ship fired a broadside** le navire a lâché une bordée; *Fig (tirade)* attaque *f* cinglante; *(of insults)* bordée *f* d'injures; **to fire a broadside at sb/sth** s'en prendre violemment à qn/qch

2 *adv* **broadside (on)** par le travers; *Naut* **the ship is broadside on to the wharf** le navire présente le flanc *ou* le travers au quai; *Br Aut* **the truck hit us broadside on** le camion nous a heurtés sur le côté

broad-spectrum *adj Pharm* à large spectre

broadsword ['brɔːdsɔːd] *n Hist* sabre *m*

Broadway ['brɔːdweɪ] *n* Broadway *(rue des théâtres à Manhattan)*

broadways ['brɔːdˌweɪz], **broadwise** ['brɔːdˌwaɪz] *adv* dans le sens de la largeur

brocade [brə'keɪd] **1** *n* brocart *m*

2 *vt* brocher; **brocaded gown** robe *f* de brocart

3 *comp (curtains)* de brocart

broccoli ['brɒkəlɪ] *n (UNCOUNT)* brocolis *mpl*

brochure [*Br* 'brəʊʃə(r), *Am* brəʊ'ʃʊr] *n (gen)* brochure *f*, dépliant *m*; *Sch & Univ* prospectus *m*

brogue [brəʊg] **1** *n Ling (accent)* accent *m* du terroir; *(Irish)* accent *m* irlandais

2 brogues *npl* = chaussures basses assez lourdes ornées de petits trous

broil [brɔɪl] *Am* **1** *vt Culin* griller, faire cuire sur le gril; *Fig* griller

2 *vi Culin* griller; **broiling sun** soleil brûlant

broiler ['brɔɪlə(r)] *n Culin* (**a**) *(chicken)* poulet *m* (à rôtir) (**b**) *Am (grill)* gril *m*, rôtissoire *f*; *Fam Fig* **it's a broiler today** il fait une chaleur à crever aujourd'hui

▸▸ ***broiler house*** éleveuse *f* (de poulets)

broke [brəʊk] **1** *pt of* **break**

2 *adj Fam* (**a**) *(with no money)* fauché, à sec; **to go broke** faire faillite; **to go for broke** jouer le tout pour le tout; **to be flat** *or* **dead** *or Br* **stony broke** être fauché comme les blés, être raide comme un passe-lacet (**b**) *(broken)* bousillé; **if it ain't broke, don't fix it** s'il n'y a pas de problèmes particuliers, il ne faut rien changer ❑

broken ['brəʊkən] **1** *pp of* **break**

2 *adj* (**a**) *(damaged → chair, toy, window)* cassé, brisé; *(→ leg, rib)* fracturé, cassé; *(→ back)* brisé, cassé; *(→ biscuit)* brisé; **are there any broken bones?** y a-t-il des fractures?; *Fig* **a broken heart** un cœur brisé; **to die of a broken heart** mourir de chagrin; **she's from a broken home** elle vient d'un foyer désuni; **a broken marriage** un mariage brisé, un ménage désuni

(**b**) *(sleep → disturbed)* interrompu; *(→ restless)* agité

(**c**) *(speech)* mauvais, imparfait; **he speaks broken English** il parle un mauvais anglais; **in broken French** en mauvais français; **in a voice broken with sobs** d'une voix entrecoupée de sanglots; **in a broken voice** d'une voix brisée

(**d**) *(agreement, promise)* rompu, violé; *(appointment)* manqué

(**e**) *(health)* délabré; **her spirit is broken** elle est abattue; **he's a broken man since his wife's death** il a le cœur brisé *ou* il est très abattu depuis la mort de sa femme; **the scandal left him a broken man** le scandale l'a ruiné

(**f**) *(incomplete → set)* incomplet(ète)

(**g**) *(uneven → ground)* accidenté; *(→ coastline)* dentelé; *(→ line)* brisé, discontinu

(**h**) *(tamed → animal)* dressé, maté

(**i**) *Ling (vowel)* diphtongué

▸▸ *Mus* ***broken chord*** arpège *m*; ; ***broken cloud*** *(UNCOUNT)* éclaircie *f*; *Com* ***broken lots*** articles *mpl* dépareillés; *Math* ***broken numbers*** fractions *fpl*

broken-down *adj* (**a**) *(damaged → machine)* détraqué; *(→ car)* en panne (**b**) *(worn out)* fini, à bout

brokenhearted [ˌbrəʊkən'hɑːtɪd] *adj* au cœur brisé

brokenheartedly [ˌbrəʊkən'hɑːtɪdlɪ] *adv* le cœur brisé

brokenheartedness [ˌbrəʊkən'hɑːtɪdnɪs] *n* douleur *f* profonde

brokenly ['brəʊkənlɪ] *adv (speak)* de façon entrecoupée

broken-winded [-'wɪndɪd] *adj (horse)* poussif

broker ['brəʊkə(r)] **1** *n* (**a**) *Com (for goods)* courtier(ère) *m,f* (de commerce); *Naut* courtier(-ère) *m,f* maritime; *St Exch* ≃ courtier(ère) *m,f* (en Bourse), ≃ agent *m* de change; *Ins* **(insurance) broker** courtier(ère) *m,f ou* agent *m* d'assurances; *Com* **wine broker** négociant *m* en vins; *St Exch* **broker's commission** (frais *mpl* de) courtage *m*; **broker's contract** courtage *m* (**b**) *Com (second-hand dealer)* brocanteur *m*

2 *vt Fig* **to broker an agreement** négocier un accord en tant qu'intermédiaire

brokerage ['brəʊkərɪdʒ] *n Com* (**a**) *(fee)* (frais *mpl* de) courtage *m* (**b**) *(profession)* courtage *m*

▸▸ ***brokerage house*** *(business)* maison *f* de courtage

broking ['brəʊkɪŋ] *n (profession)* courtage *m*

brolly ['brɒlɪ] *(pl* **brollies)** *n Br Fam* pépin *m* *(parapluie)*

bromeliad [brəʊ'miːlɪæd] *n Bot* broméliacée *f*

bromide ['brəʊmaɪd] *n* (**a**) *Chem* bromure *m*; *Pharm (sedative)* bromure *m* (de potassium) (**b**) *Typ* bromure *m* (**c**) *Old-fashioned (remark)* banalité *f*, platitude *f*

bromine ['brəʊmiːn] *n Chem* brome *m*

Bromo® ['brəʊməʊ] *n Am Pharm* = médicament contre les maux d'estomac et les troubles digestifs

bronchi ['brɒŋkaɪ] *pl of* **bronchus**

bronchial ['brɒŋkɪəl] *adj Anat* des bronches, bronchique

▸▸ *Anat* ***bronchial tubes*** bronches *fpl*

bronchiole ['brɒŋkɪəʊl] *n Anat* bronchiole *f*

bronchitic [brɒŋ'kɪtɪk] *Med* **1** *n* bronchitique *mf*

2 *adj* bronchitique

bronchitis [brɒŋ'kaɪtɪs] *n (UNCOUNT) Med* bronchite *f*; **to have (an attack of) bronchitis** avoir *ou* faire une bronchite; **bronchitis sufferer** bronchitique *mf*

bronchodilator [ˌbrɒŋkəʊdaɪ'leɪtə(r)] *n Med* bronchodilatateur *m*

bronchopneumonia [ˌbrɒŋkəʊnjuː'məʊnɪə] *n Med* broncho-pneumonie *f*

bronchoscopy [ˌbrɒŋ'kɒskəpɪ] *n Med* bronchoscopie *f*

bronchus ['brɒŋkəs] *(pl* **bronchi** [-kaɪ]) *n Anat* bronche *f*

bronco ['brɒŋkəʊ] *(pl* **broncos**) *n Am* cheval *m* sauvage *(de l'Ouest)*

broncobuster ['brɒŋkəʊˌbʌstə(r)] *n Am* = cow-boy qui dompte les chevaux sauvages

broncobusting ['brɒŋkəʊˌbʌstɪŋ] *n Am* domptage *m* de chevaux sauvages

brontosaurus [ˌbrɒntə'sɔːrəs] *(pl* **brontosauruses** *or* **brontosauri** [-raɪ]) *n* brontosaure *m*

Bronx [brɒŋks] *n* **the Bronx** le Bronx *(quartier de New York)*; *Am Fam* **to give sb a Bronx cheer** ≃ [illegible] à qn

bronze [brɒnz] **1** *n* (**a**) *(alloy)* bronze *m*

(**b**) *(statue)* bronze *m*, statue *f* de *ou* en bronze

(**c**) *(medal)* médaille *f* en bronze; **he's a bronze medallist** il a remporté la médaille de bronze

(**d**) *(colour)* (couleur *f* de) bronze *m inv*

2 *comp* (**a**) *(lamp, medal, statue)* de *ou* en bronze

(**b**) *(colour, skin)* (couleur *f* de) bronze *(inv)*

3 *vt (metal)* bronzer; *(skin)* faire bronzer, brunir

4 *vi* se bronzer, brunir

▸▸ ***the Bronze Age*** l'âge *m* du bronze; ***bronze medal*** médaille *f* de bronze

bronzed [brɒnzd] *adj* bronzé, hâlé

bronzing ['brɒnzɪŋ] *n* bronzage *m*

brooch [brəʊtʃ] *(pl* **brooches**) *n* broche *f* *(bijou)*

brood [bruːd] **1** *n* (**a**) *Orn (of birds)* couvée *f*, nichée *f*; *Zool (of animals)* nichée *f*, portée *f*

(**b**) *Hum (children)* progéniture *f*; *Pej* marmaille *f* (**c**) *Fig Pej (of scoundrels etc)* race *f*, engeance *f*

2 *vi* (**a**) *Orn (bird)* couver

(**b**) *(danger, storm)* couver, menacer; *Fig* **the monument broods over the town's main square** le monument domine la grand-place de la ville

(**c**) *(person)* ruminer, broyer du noir; **to brood about things** ruminer; **all he does is sit there brooding** il passe son temps à broyer du noir; **it's no use brooding on** *or* **over the past** cela ne sert à rien de s'appesantir sur *ou* remâcher le passé

►► *Agr* ***brood mare*** (jument *f*) poulinière *f*

brooder ['bru:də(r)] *n* (**a**) *(hen)* (poule *f*) couveuse *f* (**b**) *(enclosure)* couveuse *f* (artificielle) (**c**) *Fig (person)* **he's such a brooder** il est toujours à ruminer

broodiness ['bru:dɪnɪs] *n* (**a**) *(gloominess)* mélancolie *f*; **he has always been prone to broodiness** il a toujours été enclin à la mélancolie (**b**) *(desire for child)* désir *m* d'enfant

brooding ['bru:dɪŋ] **1** *adj* menaçant, inquiétant

2 *n* **he's done a lot of brooding since he got home** depuis son retour à la maison, il a passé beaucoup de temps à ruminer

broody ['bru:dɪ] *(compar* **broodier**, *superl* **broodiest**) *adj* (**a**) *(gloomy)* mélancolique, cafardeux (**b**) *(motherly)* **a broody hen** une (poule) couveuse; *Br Fam Fig* **to feel broody** être en mal d'enfant ❑

brook [brʊk] **1** *vt (usu neg) (tolerate)* supporter, tolérer; *(answer, delay)* admettre, souffrir; **he will brook no insolence** il ne supporte pas d'impertinence

2 *n (stream)* ruisseau *m*

►► *Ich* ***brook trout*** saumon *m* de fontaine

Brookings Institution ['brʊkɪŋs-] *n* = organisme américain indépendant d'études sociales et économiques

brookite ['brʊkaɪt] *n* (**a**) *Miner* brookite *m* (**b**) *Literary (small brook)* ruisselet *m*, petit ruisseau *m*

brooklet ['brʊklɪt] *n Literary* ruisselet *m*, petit ruisseau *m*

brooklime ['brʊklaɪm] *n Bot* cresson *m* de cheval

Brooklyn ['brʊklɪn] *n* Brooklyn *(quartier populaire et industriel de New York)*

►► ***Brooklyn Bridge*** le pont de Brooklyn

broom [bru:m] *n* (**a**) *(brush)* balai *m*; *Fig* **new broom** = personne nouvellement arrivée qui veut remanier l'organisation de l'entreprise; *Prov* **a new broom sweeps clean** à nouveaux dirigeants, nouvelles méthodes (**b**) *Bot* genêt *m*

►► ***broom handle*** manche *m* à balai

broomstick ['bru:mstɪk] *n* manche *m* à balai

Bros., bros. *(written abbr* **brothers**) Frères

broth [brɒθ] *n* (**a**) *Culin* bouillon *m (de viande et de légumes)* (**b**) *Biol* bouillon *m* de culture

brothel ['brɒθəl] *n* maison *f* close *ou* de passe, *Fam* bordel *m*

►► *Br Fam* ***brothel creeper*** = chaussure de daim à semelle de crêpe pour hommes

brother ['brʌðə(r)] *(pl senses* (**b**) *and* (**c**) **brethren** ['breðrɪn] *or* **brothers**) **1** *n* (**a**) *(relative)* frère *m*; **older/younger brother** frère *m* aîné/cadet

(**b**) *Rel* frère *m*; **no, Brother** non, mon Frère; **Brother Damian** Frère Damian

(**c**) *(fellow member → of trade union)* camarade *m*; *(→ of professional group)* collègue *m*; *Mil* **brothers in arms** compagnons *mpl ou* frères *mpl* d'armes; **his brother officers** les autres officiers de sa brigade *ou Mil* de son régiment

(**d**) *Am Fam (term of address)* **hey, brother!** *(to stranger)* eh, camarade!; *(to friend)* eh, mon vieux!

(**e**) *Fam Black Am slang (fellow black man)* = nom donné par les noirs américains à un homme noir

2 *exclam Fam* **(oh) brother!** dis donc!, bigre!

►► ***the Brothers Grimm*** les frères *mpl* Grimm

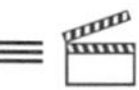

'Brother, can you spare a dime?' *Mora* 'T'as pas cent balles?'

brotherhood ['brʌðəhʊd] *n* (**a**) *(relationship)* fraternité *f*; *Fig (fellowship)* fraternité *f*, confraternité *f*; *Rel* confrérie *f*; **the brotherhood of man** la communauté humaine (**b**) *(association)* association *f*; *Rel* confrérie *f*; **the Brotherhood** *(in Freemasonry)* la franc-maçonnerie (**c**) *Am Ind (entire profession)* corporation *f*

brother-in-law *(pl* **brothers-in-law**) *n* beau-frère *m*

brotherliness ['brʌðəlɪnɪs] *n* amour *m* fraternel

brotherly ['brʌðəlɪ] *adj* fraternel; **he felt very brotherly towards her** il la considérait un peu comme une sœur

►► ***brotherly love*** amour *m* fraternel

brougham ['bru:əm] *n Hist (carriage)* voiture *f* à chevaux; *(car)* coupé *m* de ville

brought [brɔ:t] *pt & pp of* **bring**

brought-on *adj Am (imported)* importé

brouhaha ['bru:hɑ:hɑ:] *n* brouhaha *m*, vacarme *m*

brow [braʊ] *n* (**a**) *(forehead)* front *m*; **her troubled brow** son air inquiet (**b**) *(eyebrow)* sourcil *m* (**c**) *(of hill)* sommet *m* (**d**) *Mining (pithead)* tour *m* d'extraction

browband ['braʊbænd] *n Horseriding* frontail *m*

browbeat ['braʊbi:t] *(pt* **browbeat**, *pp* **browbeaten** [-bi:tən]) *vt* intimider, brusquer; **to browbeat sb into doing sth** forcer qn à faire qch en usant d'intimidation

browbeaten ['braʊˌbi:tən] *adj* persécuté

browbeating ['braʊˌbi:tɪŋ] **1** *n* intimidation *f*

2 *adj* intimidant

brown [braʊn] **1** *n* marron *m*; **dressed in brown** habillé en marron

2 *adj* (**a**) *(gen)* marron *(inv)*; *(leather)* marron *(inv)*; *(hair → light)* châtain; *(→ dark)* brun; *(eyes)* marron; **light brown hair** cheveux *mpl* châtain clair; **a light brown scarf** une écharpe marron clair; **the leaves are turning brown** les feuilles commencent à jaunir; *Am Fam* **we'll do it up brown!** nous allons fignoler ça!; **in a brown study** plongé dans ses pensées, pensif

(**b**) *(tanned)* bronzé, hâlé; **he's looking very brown after his holiday** il est rentré de vacances très bronzé; **as brown as a berry** tout bronzé

3 *vi* (**a**) *Culin* dorer

(**b**) *(skin)* bronzer, brunir

(**c**) *(plant)* roussir

4 *vt* (**a**) *Culin* faire dorer; *(sauce)* faire roussir

(**b**) *(tan)* bronzer, brunir

►► ***brown ale*** bière *f* brune; *Zool* ***brown bear*** ours *m* brun; *Sport* ***brown belt*** *(in martial arts)* ceinture *f* marron; *Orn* ***brown booby*** fou *m* brun; ***brown bread*** *(UNCOUNT)* pain *m* complet *ou* bis; *Miner* ***brown coal*** lignite *m*; *Com* ***brown goods*** = biens de consommation de taille moyenne tels que téléviseur, radio ou magnétoscope; *Orn* ***brown owl*** chat-huant *m*, chouette *f* des bois, hulotte *f*; ***brown paper*** papier *m* d'emballage; ***brown paper bag*** sac *m* en papier kraft; *Zool* ***brown rat*** surmulot *m*; ***brown rice*** riz *m* complet; ***Brown Shirt*** fasciste *mf*; *Hist (Nazi)* chemise *f* brune; ***brown sugar*** *Culin* cassonade *f*, sucre *m* roux; *Fam Drugs slang* héro *f*; *Ich* ***brown trout*** truite *f* de rivière

brownbag [ˌbraʊn'bæg] *(pp & pt* **brownbagged**, *cont* **brownbagging**) *vt Am Fam* **I brownbag it to work** j'apporte mon déjeuner tous les jours au travail; **to brownbag it** *(drink)* = boire de l'alcool au goulot, dans la rue, la bouteille étant enveloppée d'un sac en papier

►► *Am* ***brownbag seminar*** = séminaire où les participants apportent leur déjeuner

brownbagger [ˌbraʊn'bægə(r)] *n Am Fam* = personne qui apporte son déjeuner sur son lieu de travail

browned-off *adj Br Fam* **to be browned-off** *(bored)* en avoir marre; *(discouraged)* ne plus avoir le moral; **she's browned-off with her job** elle en a marre *ou* ras le bol de son travail

brown-eyed *adj* aux yeux marrons

brownfield site ['braʊnfi:ld-] *n* terrain *m* à bâtir *(après démolition de bâtiments préexistants)*

brown-haired *adj (light)* aux cheveux châtains; *(dark)* aux cheveux bruns

brownie ['braʊnɪ] **1** *n* (**a**) *(elf)* lutin *m*, farfadet *m*

(**b**) *Culin (cake)* brownie *m*; **chocolate brownies** brownies *mpl* au chocolat

(**c**) *Phot* **Brownie**® *(camera)* Brownie® *m* Kodak®

2 Brownie (Guide) *n* ≃ jeannette *f*; **to join the Brownies** s'inscrire aux jeannettes, devenir jeannette

►► *Fam Hum* ***brownie point*** bon point *m*; **to win** *or* **get brownie points** se faire bien voir; **doing the ironing should earn you a few brownie points** tu seras bien vu si tu fais le repassage

Browning ['braʊnɪŋ] *n Mil* **Browning (automatic rifle)** browning *m*

browning ['braʊnɪŋ] *n* (**a**) *(by sun)* brunissement *m*, bronzage *m* (**b**) *Culin* **the browning of the meat is important** c'est important de faire rissoler la viande (**c**) *Br Culin (substance)* colorant *m* brun (pour les sauces)

brownish ['braʊnɪʃ] *adj* qui tire sur le marron, brunâtre

brown-nose *very Fam* **1** *n* lèche-cul *mf inv*

2 *vt* faire du lèche-cul à

3 *vi* faire du lèche-cul

brown-noser [-ˌnəʊzə(r)] *n very Fam* lèche-cul *mf inv*

brownout ['braʊnaʊt] *n Am Elec (electric failure)* baisse *f* de tension; *Mil (blackout)* black-out *m* partiel, camouflage *m* partiel des lumières

brownstone ['braʊnstəʊn] *n Am (stone)* grès *m* brun; *(building)* bâtiment *m* de grès brun

browse [braʊz] **1** *vi* (**a**) *(person)* regarder, jeter un œil; **she browsed through the book** elle a feuilleté le livre; **feel free to browse** *(in shop)* vous pouvez regarder si vous voulez; *(sign)* entrée libre

(**b**) *Zool (animal)* brouter, paître

2 *n* (**a**) *(look)* **I popped into the shop to have a browse around** je suis passé au magasin pour jeter un coup d'œil *ou* regarder

(**b**) *Bot & Agr (young leaves, twigs)* broutille *f*

3 *vt Comput* **to browse the Net/Web** naviguer sur l'Internet/le Web

►► *Comput* ***browse mode*** mode *m* survol

►**browse through** *vt insep* (**a**) *Fig* **to browse through a book/magazine** feuilleter un livre/un magazine; **to browse through sb's books/records** jeter un coup d'œil aux livres/disques de qn

(**b**) *Comput* se promener dans, survoler

browser ['braʊzə(r)] *n* (**a**) *(in shop)* **browsers welcome** *(sign)* entrée libre (**b**) *Comput* navigateur *m*, logiciel *m* de navigation

browsing ['braʊzɪŋ] *n* (**a**) *(of person → through book, magazine)* feuilletage *m*; **browsing is frowned upon in that bookshop** ils n'apprécient pas trop que l'on feuillette les magazines dans cette librairie (**b**) *Zool (of animal)* broutement *m* (**c**) *Comput* navigation *f*; **fast/secure browsing** navigation *f* rapide/sécurisée

brucellosis [ˌbru:sɪ'ləʊsɪs] *n Med & Vet* brucellose *f*

Bruges [bru:ʒ] *n* Bruges

bruise [bru:z] **1** *n* (**a**) *(on person)* bleu *m*, contusion *f*; **to be covered with bruises** être couvert de bleus

(**b**) *(on fruit)* meurtrissure *f*, talure *f*

2 *vt* (**a**) *(person)* faire un bleu à, contusionner; *Fig* blesser; **to bruise one's arm** se faire un bleu au bras; **to be bruised all over** être couvert de bleus; *Fig* **he felt bruised by her harsh words** ses dures paroles l'ont blessé; *Fig* **his ego was bruised** son amour-propre en a pris un coup

(**b**) *(fruit)* taler, abîmer; *(lettuce)* flétrir

(**c**) *Culin (crush)* écraser, piler

3 *vi (fruit)* se taler, s'abîmer; **to bruise easily** *(person)* se faire facilement des bleus

bruised [bru:zd] *adj* meurtri; *Fig (pride)* blessé; **badly bruised** couvert de bleus

bruiser ['bru:zə(r)] *n Fam (big man)* malabar *m*; *Boxing (fighter)* cogneur ❑ *m*; **their baby's a real bruiser!** leur bébé est vraiment costaud!

bruising ['bru:zɪŋ] **1** *n (UNCOUNT)* contusions *fpl*, bleus *mpl*; **he suffered bruising to his arm** il a eu le bras contusionné; *Fam Hum* **to be cruising for a bruising** chercher les emmerdes

2 *adj Fig* pénible, douloureux; **it was a rather bruising experience** ce fut une expérience plutôt douloureuse

bruit [bru:t] *Literary* **1** *n (rumour)* bruit *m* (qui court), rumeur *f*

2 *vt* **to bruit sth about** ébruiter quelque chose; **it was bruited that...** le bruit courait que...

Brum [brʌm] *n Br Fam* = surnom donné à Birmingham

brumal ['bru:məl] *adj Literary* brumal, d'hiver
brumbie, brumby ['brʌmbɪ] *n Austr Fam Zool* cheval *m* sauvage ❑
Brummagem ['brʌmədʒəm] *Br Fam* **1** *n* = surnom donné à Birmingham
2 *adj (of poor quality)* à la gomme; *(showy)* clinquant
Brummie, Brummy ['brʌmɪ] *Br Fam* **1** *n* = nom familier désignant un natif de Birmingham
2 *adj* de Birmingham ❑
brunch [brʌntʃ] **1** *n* brunch *m*
2 *vi* prendre un brunch, bruncher
Brunei [bru:'naɪ] *n* Brunei *m*; **in Brunei** au Brunei
brunet [bru:'net] *Am* **1** *n* brun(e) *m,f*
2 *adj (hair)* châtain
brunette [bru:'net] **1** *n* brune *f*, brunette *f*; **she's a brunette** elle est brune
2 *adj (hair)* châtain
Brunswick ['brʌnzwɪk] *n Geog* Brunswick
brunt [brʌnt] *n* **the car took the brunt of the shock** c'est la voiture qui a tout pris; *Mil* **the village bore the full brunt of the attack** le village a essuyé le plus fort de l'attaque; **she bore the brunt of his anger** c'est elle qui a fait les frais de sa colère; **to bear the brunt of the expense** supporter la plus grande partie des frais
bruschetta [brʊs'ketə] *n Culin* bruschetta *f (pain grillé arrosé d'huile d'olive et garni de tomates grillées, de basilic etc)*
brush [brʌʃ] *(pl* **brushes***)* **1** *n* (**a**) *(gen)* brosse *f*; *(for paint)* pinceau *m*; *(bigger)* brosse *f*; *(for paste)* pinceau *m*, brosse *f*; *(shaving brush)* blaireau *m*; *(scrubbing brush)* brosse *f* dure; *(broom)* balai *m*; *(with dustpan)* balayette *f*
(**b**) *(act of brushing)* coup *m* de brosse; **to give sth a brush** *(clothes)* donner un coup de brosse à qch; *(floor)* donner un coup de balai à qch; **to give one's hair a brush** se donner un coup de brosse; **to give one's teeth a brush** se brosser les dents
(**c**) *(encounter, skirmish)* accrochage *m*, escarmouche *f*; *Fig* **to have a brush with death** frôler la mort; **to have a brush with the law** avoir des démêlés avec la justice; **she's had the odd brush with the authorities** elle a eu parfois maille à partir avec les autorités
(**d**) *(light stroke)* effleurement *m*; **she felt the brush of his lips on her neck** elle a senti ses lèvres lui effleurer le cou
(**e**) *(of fox)* queue *f*
(**f**) *Elec (in generator, dynamo)* balai *m*; *(discharge)* aigrette *f*
(**g**) *(UNCOUNT) Bot (undergrowth)* broussailles *fpl*; *Geog (scrubland)* brousse *f*
2 *vt* (**a**) *(clothes, carpet)* brosser; **to brush one's hair** se brosser les cheveux; **to brush one's teeth** se brosser les dents; **she brushed her hair back from her face** elle a brossé ses cheveux en arrière
(**b**) *(sweep → floor)* balayer
(**c**) *(touch lightly)* effleurer, frôler; *(surface)* raser
(**d**) *Tex (wool)* gratter
3 *vi* effleurer, frôler; **her hair brushed against his cheek** ses cheveux ont effleuré *ou* frôlé sa joue
►► ***brush fire*** *(fire)* feu *m* de brousse, incendie *m* de broussailles; *Mil (minor war)* conflit *m* armé; ***brush stroke*** *(gen)* coup *m* de brosse; *Art* coup *m ou* trait *m* de pinceau
►**brush aside** *vt sep* (**a**) *(move aside)* écarter, repousser (**b**) *(ignore → remark)* balayer d'un geste; *(→ report)* ignorer
►**brush away** *vt sep* (**a**) *(remove → tears)* essuyer; *(→ insect)* chasser; *(remove → from clothes)* enlever d'un coup de brosse; *(→ from floor)* enlever d'un coup de balai
(**b**) *(person, difficulty)* écarter; **to brush away criticism** mépriser les critiques
►**brush down** *vt sep (clothing)* donner un coup de brosse à; *(horse)* brosser
►**brush off** **1** *vt sep* (**a**) *(remove)* enlever *(à la brosse ou à la main)*; *(insect)* chasser
(**b**) *(dismiss → plea, challenge)* rejeter; *(→ person)* écarter, repousser
2 *vi (dirt)* s'enlever
►**brush past** *vt insep* frôler en passant
►**brush up** *vt sep* (**a**) *Fam (revise)* revoir ❑, réviser ❑; **I have to brush up my maths** il faut que je me remette à niveau en maths
(**b**) *(sweep up)* ramasser à la balayette
(**c**) *Tex (wool)* gratter
►**brush up on** *vt insep Fam* revoir ❑, réviser ❑
brushdown ['brʌʃ,daʊn] *n* **to give sb a brushdown** donner un coup de brosse à qn; **to give a horse a brushdown** brosser *ou* panser un cheval
brushed [brʌʃt] *adj Tex* gratté; **brushed cotton** pilou *m*, finette *f*; **brushed nylon** nylon *m* gratté
brushing ['brʌʃɪŋ] *n* (**a**) *(of clothes, carpet, hair)* brossage *m* (**b**) *(of floor)* balayage *m*
brush-off *n Fam* **to give sb the brush-off** envoyer promener *ou* balader qn; **I got the brush-off** on m'a envoyé sur les roses
brush-up *n* (**a**) *Br (clean-up)* coup *m* de brosse (**b**) *Fam (revision)* révision ❑ *f*; **my German could do with a brush-up** j'aurais besoin de me remettre à l'allemand
brushwood ['brʌʃwʊd] *n (UNCOUNT) Bot (undergrowth)* broussailles *fpl*; *(cuttings)* menu bois *m*, brindilles *fpl*
brushwork ['brʌʃwɜ:k] *n (UNCOUNT) (gen)* travail *m* au pinceau; *Art* touche *f*
brusque [bru:sk] *adj (abrupt)* brusque; *(curt)* brusque, bourru
brusquely ['bru:sklɪ] *adv (abruptly)* avec brusquerie; *(curtly)* avec brusquerie *ou* rudesse, brutalement
brusqueness ['bru:sknɪs] *n (abruptness)* brusquerie *f*; *(curtness)* brusquerie *f*, rudesse *f*
Brussels ['brʌsəlz] *n* Bruxelles
►► ***Brussels sprout*** chou *m* de Bruxelles
brutal ['bru:təl] *adj (cruel → action, behaviour, person)* brutal, cruel; *(uncompromising → honesty)* franc (franche), brutal; *(severe → climate, cold)* rude, rigoureux; **with brutal frankness** d'une franchise brutale
brutalism ['bru:təlɪzəm] *n Archit* brutalisme *m*
brutality [bru:'tælətɪ] *(pl* **brutalities***)* *n* (**a**) *(cruelty)* brutalité *f*, cruauté *f* (**b**) *(act of cruelty)* brutalité *f*
brutalization [,bru:təlaɪ'zeɪʃən] *n* abrutissement *m*
brutalize, -ise ['bru:təlaɪz] *vt* (**a**) *(ill-treat)* brutaliser (**b**) *(make brutal)* rendre brutal
brutalizing ['bru:təlaɪzɪŋ] *adj* qui rend brutal; **the brutalizing effects of war** l'effet déshumanisant de la guerre
brutally ['bru:təlɪ] *adv (attack, kill, treat)* brutalement, sauvagement; *(say)* brutalement, franchement; *(cold)* extrêmement; **to be brutally frank** *or* **honest with sb** être d'une franchise brutale avec qn
brute [bru:t] **1** *n* (**a**) *(animal)* brute *f*, bête *f*
(**b**) *(person → violent)* brute *f*; *(→ coarse)* brute *f* (épaisse), rustre *m*; **a great brute of a man** une grande brute
2 *adj* (**a**) *(animal-like)* animal, bestial
(**b**) *(purely physical)* brutal; **brute force** *or* **strength** force *f* brutale; **by brute force** par la force; **you'll have to use brute force** il faudra user de la manière forte
(**c**) *(mindless)* brut; **an act of brute stupidity** un acte d'une bêtise sans nom
brutish ['bru:tɪʃ] *adj* (**a**) *(animal-like)* animal, bestial (**b**) *(cruel)* brutal, violent; *(coarse)* grossier
brutishly ['bru:tɪʃlɪ] *adv* (**a**) *(like an animal)* comme une brute (**b**) *(cruelly)* brutalement, violemment; *(coarsely)* grossièrement
brutishness ['bru:tɪʃnɪs] *n* (**a**) *(animal-like quality)* bestialité *f* (**b**) *(cruelty)* brutalité *f* (**c**) *(coarseness)* grossièreté *f*
Brutus ['bru:təs] *pr n* Brutus
Bryansk [brɪ'ænsk] *n Geog* Briansk
Brylcreem® ['brɪlkri:m] *n* = marque de brillantine
bryony ['braɪənɪ] *(pl* **bryonies***)* *n Bot* bryone *f*
BS [,bi:'es] *n* (**a**) *Br (abbr* **British Standard/Standards***)* = indique que le chiffre qui suit renvoie au numéro de la norme fixée par l'Institut britannique de normalisation (**b**) *Am Univ (abbr* **Bachelor of Science***) (person)* = titulaire d'une licence de sciences; *(qualification)* licence *f* de sciences (**c**) *Am very Fam (abbr* **bullshit***)* conneries *fpl*
bs *Com (written abbr* **bill of sale***)* acte *m ou* contrat *m* de vente
BSA [,bi:es'eɪ] *n (abbr* **Boy Scouts of America***)* = association américaine de scouts
BSC [,bi:es'si:] *n (abbr* **British Steel Corporation***)* = entreprise sidérurgique, aujourd'hui privatisée
BSc [,bi:es'si:] *n Br (abbr* **Bachelor of Science***)* *(person)* = titulaire d'une licence de sciences; *(qualification)* licence *f* de sciences
BSE [,bi:es'i:] *n Vet (abbr* **bovine spongiform encephalopathy***)* EBS *f*
B-share *n St Exch* action *f* ordinaire avec droit de vote, action *f* à dividende prioritaire
BSI [,bi:es'aɪ] *n (abbr* **British Standards Institution***)* = association britannique de normalisation, ≃ AFNOR *f*
B-side *n* face *f* B *ou* 2 *(d'un disque)*; **to play the B-side of a record** passer la deuxième *ou* l'autre face d'un disque
BSkyB [,bi:skaɪ'bi:] *n TV (abbr* **British Sky Broadcasting***)* = société de diffusion de chaînes de télévision par satellite
BSM [,bi:es'em] *n Aut (abbr* **British School of Motoring***)* = école de conduite britannique
BST [,bi:es'ti:] *n (abbr* **British Summer Time***)* = heure d'été britannique
BT [,bi:'ti:] *n (abbr* **British Telecom***)* = société britannique de télécommunications
Bt. *(written abbr* **baronet***)* baronnet *m*
B-team *n Sport* **the B-team** l'équipe *f* seconde
bt/fwd *Acct (written abbr* **brought forward***)* reporté
BTU [,bi:ti:'ju:] *n Phys (abbr* **British thermal unit***)* BTU
BTW *Comput (written abbr* **by the way***) (in e-mail messages)* à propos
bubba ['bʌbə] *n Am Fam* (**a**) *(brother)* frangin *m* (**b**) *(Southern male)* plouc *m (du Sud des États-Unis)*
bubble ['bʌbəl] **1** *n* (**a**) *(of foam)* bulle *f*; **soap bubbles** bulles *fpl* de savon; *(in liquid)* bouillon *m*; *(in champagne)* bulle *f*; *(in glass)* bulle *f*, soufflure *f*; *(in paint)* boursouflure *f*, cloque *f*; *(in metal)* soufflure *f*
(**b**) *(transparent cover)* cloche *f*
(**c**) *Fig (illusion)* **to prick** *or* **to burst sb's bubble** réduire à néant les illusions de qn, enlever ses illusions à qn; **the bubble finally burst** finalement mes/ses *etc* illusions s'envolèrent
(**d**) *Com (fraudulent scheme)* affaire *f* pourrie
(**e**) *(sound)* glouglou *m*
2 *vi* (**a**) *(liquid)* bouillonner, faire des bulles; *(champagne)* pétiller; *(gas)* barboter; *Fig* **her real feelings bubbled beneath the surface** ses sentiments véritables bouillonnaient en elle
(**b**) *(gurgle)* gargouiller, glouglouter
(**c**) *(brim)* déborder; **the children were bubbling with excitement** les enfants étaient tout excités *ou* surexcités
(**d**) *Am (mumble)* marmonner
►► ***bubble bath*** bain *m* moussant; *Br Aut* ***bubble car*** = petite voiture à trois roues; ***bubble gum*** bubble-gum *m*; *Fam* ***bubble gum music*** = musique destinée aux jeunes adolescents; *Am Fam* ***bubble head*** imbécile *mf*; *Comput* ***bubble memory*** mémoire *f* à bulles; ***bubble pack*** *Com (for toy, batteries)* blister *m*, emballage *m* bulle; *(for pills)* plaquette *f*; *Com* ***bubble scheme*** affaire *f* pourri; *Br Culin* ***bubble and squeak*** = plat à base de pommes de terre et de choux, servi réchauffé; *Comput* ***bubble store*** mémoire *f* à bulles; *Com* ***bubble wrap*** bullpack® *m*
►**bubble out** *vi* sortir à gros bouillons
►**bubble over** *vi also Fig* déborder; **to bubble over with enthusiasm** déborder d'enthousiasme
►**bubble up** *vi (liquid)* monter en bouillonnant; *Fig (feeling)* monter
bubble-jet printer *n Comput* imprimante *f* à bulles
bubbling ['bʌbəlɪŋ] **1** *adj* bouillonnant
2 *n* bouillonnement *m*; *Chem & Ind* barbotage *m*; *(in paintwork)* boursouflures *fpl*
bubbly ['bʌbəlɪ] *(compar* **bubblier**, *superl* **bubbliest***)* **1** *adj* (**a**) *Chem (liquid)* pétillant, plein de bulles (**b**) *(person)* pétillant, plein d'entrain; *(personality)* plein de vitalité
2 *n Br Fam (champagne)* champ' *m*
bubo ['bju:bəʊ] *(pl* **buboes***)* *n Med* bubon *m*

bubonic [bju:'bɒnɪk] *adj Med* bubonique
►► ***bubonic plague*** peste *f* bubonique

buccal ['bʌkəl] *adj Anat* buccal

buccaneer [,bʌkə'nɪə(r)] *n* (**a**) *Hist* boucanier *m* (**b**) *(unscrupulous person)* flibustier *m*, pirate *m*

buccaneering [,bʌkə'nɪərɪŋ] **1** *n Hist* métier *m* de boucanier
2 *adj (enterprising)* entreprenant

Bucharest [,bu:kə'rest] *n* Bucarest

buck [bʌk] **1** *n* (**a**) *(male animal)* mâle *m*
(**b**) *SAfr Zool (antelope)* antilope *f*
(**c**) *Fam (young man)* jeune mec *m*; *Arch (dandy)* dandy *m*
(**d**) *Am Fam (dollar)* dollar ❑ *m*; **to be down to one's last buck** être fauché *ou* raide; **to make a buck** gagner sa croûte; **to make a fast** *or* **quick buck** faire du fric facilement
(**e**) *Fam (responsibility)* **to pass the buck onto sb** *(blame)* faire porter le chapeau à qn; *(shift responsibility)* refiler le bébé à qn; **it's far too easy to pass the buck** c'est trop facile de rejeter la responsabilité sur quelqu'un d'autre; **the buck stops here** *(with me)* en dernier ressort, c'est moi le responsable; *(with you)* en dernier ressort, c'est toi le responsable
(**f**) *(jump)* ruade *f*
(**g**) *Am Carp (sawhorse)* chevalet *m*, baudet *m*
(**h**) *Gym* cheval *m*, cheval-d'arçons *m inv*
2 *comp (goat, hare, kangaroo, rabbit)* mâle
3 *vi* (**a**) *(horse)* donner une ruade; *Am Aut (car)* cahoter, tressauter; **the truck bucked along** le camion avançait en cahotant; **we bucked to a stop** nous avons fait un arrêt brutal
(**b**) *Am (charge)* donner un coup de tête
(**c**) *Am Fam (resist)* **to buck against change** se rebiffer contre les changements
(**d**) *Am Fam (strive)* rechercher ❑; **he's bucking for promotion** il est prêt à tout pour obtenir de l'avancement
4 *vt* (**a**) *(of horse)* **the horse bucked his rider (off)** le cheval a désarçonné *ou* jeté bas son cavalier
(**b**) *Fam (resist)* **to buck the system** se rebiffer contre le système; **it takes courage to buck public opinion** il faut du courage pour aller à l'encontre de l'opinion publique
►► ***buck deer*** daim *m*, chevreuil *m*; *Br* ***buck's fizz*** = cocktail composé de champagne et de jus d'orange; *Austr* ***buck's party*** soirée *f* entre hommes

►**buck up** *Br Fam* **1** *vt sep* (**a**) *(cheer up)* remonter le moral à ❑
(**b**) *(improve)* améliorer ❑; **you'd better buck your ideas up** tu as intérêt à te remuer *ou* à en mettre un coup
2 *vi* (**a**) *(cheer up)* se secouer; **buck up! life goes on!** courage! la vie continue!
(**b**) *(hurry up)* se grouiller, se magner

buckaroo ['bʌkə,ru:] *n Am* cow-boy *m*

buckboard ['bʌkbɔ:d] *n Hist* = voiture hippomobile à quatre roues très répandue aux États-Unis à la fin du XIXème siècle

bucked [bʌkt] *adj Fam Old-fashioned* ragaillardi

bucket ['bʌkɪt] **1** *n* (**a**) *(container, contents)* seau *m*; **a bucket of water** un seau d'eau; *Fam* **it rained buckets** il a plu à seaux; *Fam* **to cry** *or* **to weep buckets** pleurer comme une Madeleine *ou* un veau; **a bucket and spade** un seau et une pelle *(symbole, pour un Britannique, de vacances familiales au bord de la mer)*
(**b**) *Tech (of dredger, grain elevator)* godet *m*; *(of pump)* piston *m*; *(of wheel)* auget *m*
2 *vt* (**a**) *(put in bucket)* mettre dans un seau; *(carry)* transporter dans un seau
(**b**) *Br (horse)* surmener; *(car)* conduire brutalement
3 *vi Br Fam* (**a**) *(rain)* pleuvoir à seaux
(**b**) *(move hurriedly)* aller à fond de train; *(car)* rouler à fond la caisse; **we were bucketing along** nous roulions à fond la caisse
►► *Tech* ***bucket elevator*** élévateur *m* à godets, noria *f*; *Aut & Aviat* ***bucket seat*** baquet *m*, siège-baquet *m*, siège *m* cuve; ***bucket shop*** *Fin* bureau *m ou* maison *f* de contrepartie, bureau *m* de courtier marron; *Br Com (travel agency)* = organisme de vente de billets d'avion à prix réduit

►**bucket down** *vi Br Fam* pleuvoir à seaux

bucketful ['bʌkɪtfʊl] *n* plein seau *m*; **a bucketful of water** un seau plein d'eau; **in bucketfuls** à seaux

buckeye ['bʌkaɪ] *n Bot (tree)* marronnier *m* d'Inde
►► ***the Buckeye State*** = surnom donné à l'Ohio

buckhorn ['bʌkhɔ:n] **1** *n* (**a**) *(horn)* corne *f* de cerf
(**b**) *Bot* plantain *m* lancéolé
2 *comp (knife)* au manche en corne de cerf

buckhound ['bʌk,haʊnd] *n* chien *m* de chasse

Buck House [bʌk-] *n Fam* = nom familier du palais de Buckingham

bucking ['bʌkɪŋ] *n (of horse)* ruades *fpl*

Buckingham Palace ['bʌkɪŋəm-] *n* le palais de Buckingham *(résidence officielle du souverain britannique)*

Buckinghamshire ['bʌkɪŋəmʃə(r)] *n* le Buckinghamshire, = comté dans le sud de l'Angleterre; **in Buckinghamshire** dans le Buckinghamshire

buckle ['bʌkəl] **1** *n* (**a**) *(clasp)* boucle *f*
(**b**) *Metal (kink → in metal)* gauchissement *m*, flambage *m*; *Aut (→ in wheel)* voilure *f*
2 *vi* (**a**) *(fasten)* se boucler, s'attacher
(**b**) *Metal (distort → metal)* gauchir, se déformer; *(→ wheel)* se voiler; **the bridge buckled under the weight of traffic** le pont s'est déformé sous le poids des véhicules
(**c**) *(give way → knees, legs)* se dérober; *Fig (person → under attack)* céder; *(→ under criticism)* se décomposer; **his knees buckled** ses jambes se dérobèrent sous lui
3 *vt* (**a**) *(fasten → suitcase, belt, shoe)* boucler; *(safety belt)* attacher
(**b**) *(distort)* déformer, fausser; *(metal)* gauchir, fausser; *(wheel)* voiler

►**buckle down** *vi Fam* s'appliquer ❑; **to buckle down to work** se mettre au travail; **come on now, buckle down!** allez, au boulot!; **she'll have to buckle down if she wants to pass** il faudra qu'elle en mette un coup si elle veut réussir

►**buckle in** *vt sep (person)* attacher

►**buckle on** *vt sep (armour)* revêtir, endosser; *(gunbelt, sword)* attacher, ceindre

►**buckle to** *vi Fam* s'y mettre, s'y atteler

►**buckle up** *vi Am Aut* **buckle up!** attachez vos ceintures!

buckler ['bʌklə(r)] *n Hist* écu *m*; *(worn on arm)* targe *f*

Buckley's ['bʌklɪz] *n Austr Fam* **you don't have a Buckley's (chance)** tu n'as aucune chance ❑

buckling ['bʌkəlɪŋ] *n Metal (of metal)* déformation *f*, gauchissement *m*; *Aut (of wheel)* voilure *f*

buckram ['bʌkrəm] *n Tex* bougran *m*

Buck Rogers [-'rɒdʒəz] *pr n* = héros de bandes dessinées de science-fiction

Bucks *(written abbr* **Buckinghamshire**) le Buckinghamshire, = comté dans le sud de l'Angleterre

bucksaw ['bʌksɔ:] *n Tech* scie *f* à bûches

buckshee [,bʌk'ʃi:] *Br Fam* **1** *adj* gratis, à l'œil
2 *adv* gratis, à l'œil

buckshot ['bʌkʃɒt] *n* chevrotine *f*, gros plomb *m*

buckskin ['bʌkskɪn] *n* peau *f* de daim

buckthorn ['bʌkθɔ:n] *n Bot* nerprun *m*, alaterne *m*

bucktooth ['bʌk,tu:θ] *(pl* **buckteeth** [-,ti:θ]) *n* dent *f* proéminente *ou* qui avance; **to have buckteeth** avoir des dents de lapin

bucktoothed ['bʌk,tu:θt] *adj* **to be bucktoothed** avoir des dents de lapin

buckwheat ['bʌkwi:t] *n Bot* sarrasin *m*, blé *m* noir
►► *Culin* ***buckwheat flour*** farine *f* de blé noir *ou* de sarrasin; *Culin* ***buckwheat pancake*** galette *f* de blé noir *ou* de sarrasin

bucolic [bju:'kɒlɪk] **1** *adj* bucolique, pastoral
2 *n Literature* bucolique *f*

bud [bʌd] *(pt & pp* **budded,** *cont* **budding**) **1** *n* (**a**) *(on shrub, tree)* bourgeon *m*; *(for grafting)* écusson *m*; **the trees are in bud** les arbres bourgeonnent
(**b**) *(of flower)* bouton *m*; **the roses are in bud** les roses sont en bouton
(**c**) *Biol & Anat* papille *f*
(**d**) *Am Fam (term of address)* **hey, bud!** *(to stranger)* eh, vous là-bas!; *(to friend)* eh, mon vieux!
2 *vi* (**a**) *(plant)* bourgeonner; *(flower)* former des boutons
(**b**) *Zool (horns)* (commencer à) poindre *ou* percer
(**c**) *Fig (talent)* (commencer à) se révéler *ou* percer
3 *vt Bot & Biol* greffer, écussonner
►► ***bud vase*** soliflore *m*

Budapest [,bju:də'pest, ,bju:də'peʃt] *n* Budapest

Buddha ['bʊdə] *pr n Rel* Bouddha

Buddhism ['bʊdɪzəm] *n Rel* bouddhisme *m*

Buddhist ['bʊdɪst] *Rel* **1** *n* Bouddhiste *mf*
2 *adj (country, priest)* bouddhiste; *(art, philosophy, temple)* bouddhique; **Buddhist monastery** monastère *m* de bonzes

budding ['bʌdɪŋ] *adj* (**a**) *(plant)* bourgeonnant, couvert de bourgeons; *(flower)* en bouton (**b**) *Fig (artist, genius)* en herbe, prometteur; *(love, talent)* naissant

buddleia ['bʌdlɪə] *n Bot* buddleia *m*

buddy ['bʌdɪ] *(pl* **buddies**) *n esp Am Fam (friend)* copain (copine) *m,f*; *(for Aids patient)* = personne qui tient compagnie à un malade du sida à son domicile et l'aide dans ses travaux ménagers; **since when are they such buddies?** depuis quand sont-ils si copains?; **they're best** *or* **big buddies** ce sont les meilleurs copains du monde; *Am* **say there, old buddy** dis donc, mon vieux *ou* mon pote
►► *Am* ***buddy movie*** film *m* qui raconte les histoires de deux copains

►**buddy up** *vi Am Fam* **to buddy up to sb** faire de la lèche à qn

buddy-buddy *adj esp Am (close, friendly)* copain (copine) (**with** avec); **since when are they so buddy-buddy?** depuis quand sont-ils si copains?; **those two are very buddy-buddy** ils sont très copain-copain

budge [bʌdʒ] **1** *vi* (**a**) *(move)* bouger; **it won't budge** c'est coincé, c'est bloqué
(**b**) *Fig (yield)* céder, changer d'avis; **she refused to budge** elle ne voulut pas en démordre; **he wouldn't budge an inch** il a tenu bon
2 *vt* (**a**) *(move)* faire bouger
(**b**) *(convince)* convaincre, faire changer d'avis; **he won't be budged** il reste inébranlable, il n'y a pas eu moyen de le faire changer d'avis

►**budge over, budge up** *vi Fam* se pousser ❑

budgerigar ['bʌdʒərɪgɑ:(r)] *n Br Orn* perruche *f*

budget ['bʌdʒɪt] **1** *n (gen) & Fin (financial plan)* budget *m*; *(allocated ceiling)* enveloppe *f* budgétaire; **to be on a tight budget** disposer d'un budget serré *ou* modeste; **it was finished well below** *or* **within budget** c'est revenu bien moins cher que prévu; **the project is already well over budget** on a déjà largement dépassé le budget qui était alloué pour le projet
2 *vt* budgétiser, inscrire au budget; **to budget one's time** bien organiser son temps
3 *vi* dresser *ou* préparer un budget
4 *adj* (**a**) *(inexpensive)* économique, pour petits budgets; **budget prices** prix *mpl* avantageux *ou* modiques
(**b**) *Econ & Fin* budgétaire
5 Budget *n Pol* **the Budget** le budget
►► ***budget account*** *(with store)* compte-crédit *m*; *(with bank)* ≃ compte *m* permanent; ***budget allocation*** enveloppe *f* budgétaire; ***budget constraint*** contrainte *f* budgétaire; ***budget cuts*** coupes *fpl* budgétaires; ***Budget Day*** = jour de la présentation du budget par le chancelier de l'Échiquier britannique; ***budget deficit*** déficit *m* budgétaire; ***budget estimates*** prévisions *fpl* budgétaires; ***budget forecast*** prévisions *fpl* budgétaires; *Am Fin* ***budget plan*** système *m* de crédit; ***budget planning*** planification *f* budgétaire; *Br & Can Pol* ***Budget speech*** = discours à l'occasion de la présentation du budget au parlement; ***budget surplus*** excédent *m* budgétaire

►**budget for** *vt insep (gen)* prévoir des frais de, budgétiser; **to budget for sth** *Acct (allow for in accounts)* inscrire qch au budget, prévoir des frais de qch; *Econ & Fin* inscrire *ou* porter au budget, budgétiser; **I'm budgeting for my holidays** je surveille mes dépenses pour pouvoir partir en vacances

budgetary ['bʌdʒɪtərɪ] *adj Fin & Econ* budgétaire
►► ***budgetary control*** gestion *f* budgétaire; ***budgetary limit*** plafond *m* des charges budgétaires; ***budgetary policy*** politique *f* budgétaire; ***budgetary variance*** écart *m* budgétaire; ***budgetary year*** exercice *m* budgétaire

budgeting ['bʌdʒɪtɪŋ] *n Fin* (**a**) *(of person, company)* budgétisation *f*, planification *f* budgétaire (**b**) *Acct* comptabilité *f* budgétaire

budgie ['bʌdʒɪ] *n Br Fam* perruche □ *f*

Buenos Aires [ˌbwenəs'aɪrɪz] *n* Buenos Aires

buff [bʌf] **1** *n* (**a**) *(colour)* (couleur *f*) chamois *m*
(**b**) *Tex (leather)* peau *f* de buffle; *(polishing cloth)* polissoir *m*
(**c**) *(enthusiast)* **a wine buff** un amateur de vin; **a history buff** un(e) mordu(e) d'histoire
(**d**) *Fam* **in the buff** *(naked)* à poil
2 *vt* polir; **to buff one's nails** se polir les ongles; **it just needs buffing up a bit** cela a juste besoin d'être un peu astiqué
3 *adj* (**a**) *(coloured)* (couleur) chamois; *(leather)* de *ou* en buffle
(**b**) *Fam (good-looking)* canon *(inv)*

buffalo ['bʌfələʊ] *(pl* **inv** *or* **buffaloes**) *Zool* **1** *n (male)* buffle *m*; *(female)* bufflesse *f*, bufflonne *f*; *(in US)* bison *m*; **a herd of buffalo** un troupeau de buffles
2 *vt Am Fam (intimidate)* intimider □; **they really had him buffaloed** ils lui en ont mis plein la vue
►► *Bot* ***buffalo grass*** = herbe courte poussant dans les régions sèches au centre des États-Unis; ***buffalo hide*** peau *f* de buffle; *Culin* ***buffalo wings*** ailes *fpl* de poulet frites

buffer ['bʌfə(r)] **1** *n* (**a**) *(protection)* tampon *m*; *Am Aut (on car)* pare-chocs *m inv*; *Rail (on train)* tampon *m*; *(at station)* butoir *m*, heurtoir *m*; *Comput* tampon *m*, mémoire *f* intermédiaire; *Fig Econ* **a buffer against inflation** une mesure de protection contre l'inflation; *Fig* **to run into** *or* **hit the buffers** tomber à l'eau; *Fam* **to act as a buffer** *(between people)* faire tampon
(**b**) *Br Fam (fool)* imbécile □ *mf*; **an old buffer** un vieux schnock; **he's a nice old buffer** c'est un gentil petit pépé
(**c**) *(for polishing)* polissoir *m*
2 *vt* tamponner, amortir (le choc); **to be buffered against reality** être protégé de la réalité *ou* des réalités (de la vie)
►► *Comput* ***buffer memory*** mémoire *f* tampon; *Pol* ***buffer state*** état *m* tampon; *Com* ***buffer stock*** stock *m* tampon; *Pol* ***buffer zone*** région *f* tampon

buffering ['bʌfərɪŋ] *n Comput (storage)* stockage *m* en mémoire tampon; *(use)* utilisation *f* de mémoire tampon

buffet[1] [*Br* 'bʊfeɪ, *Am* bə'feɪ] **1** *n* (**a**) *Culin (refreshments)* buffet *m*; **cold buffet** buffet *m* froid (**b**) *(sideboard)* buffet *m* (**c**) *Com (restaurant)* buvette *f*, cafétéria *f*; *(in station)* buffet *m ou* café *m* de gare; *(on train)* wagon-restaurant *m*
2 *comp Culin (lunch, dinner)* -buffet
►► *Rail* ***buffet car*** wagon-restaurant *m*

buffet[2] ['bʌfɪt] **1** *vt* (**a**) *(batter)* **buffeted by the waves** ballotté par les vagues; **the trees were buffeted by the wind** les arbres étaient secoués par le vent; *Fig Literary* **buffeted by misfortune** poursuivi par la malchance
(**b**) *Literary (hit → with hand)* souffleter; *(→ with fist)* donner un coup de poing à
2 *n Literary (blow → with hand)* soufflet *m*; *(→ with fist)* coup *m* de poing; *Fig* **the buffets of fate** *or* **fortune** les coups du sort

buffeting ['bʌfɪtɪŋ] **1** *n* (**a**) *(of rain, wind)* assaut *m*; **the waves gave the boat a real buffeting, the boat took quite a buffeting from the waves** le navire a été violemment ballotté par les vagues
(**b**) *Literary (beating)* bourrades *fpl*
2 *adj* violent

buffing ['bʌfɪŋ] *n* polissage *m*

bufflehead ['bʌfəlhed] *n Orn* garrot *m* albéole

buffoon [bə'fuːn] *n* bouffon *m*, pitre *m*; **to act** *or* **to play the buffoon** faire le clown *ou* le pitre

buffoonery [bə'fuːnərɪ] *n (UNCOUNT)* bouffonnerie *f*, bouffonneries *fpl*

bug [bʌg] *(pt & pp* **bugged**, *cont* **bugging**) **1** *n* (**a**) *Am (insect)* insecte *m*; *Entom (bedbug)* punaise *f*; *Fam Fig* **she's been bitten by the film bug** c'est une mordue de cinéma; *Fam* **she's been bitten by the travel bug** elle a la passion des voyages
(**b**) *Fam Biol & Med (germ)* microbe □ *m*; **to catch a bug** attraper un microbe; **the flu bug** le virus de la grippe □; **I've got a stomach bug** j'ai des problèmes intestinaux □; **there's a bug going round** il y a un virus qui se balade *ou* qui traîne
(**c**) *Fam Tech (defect)* défaut □ *m*, erreur □ *f*; **there are still a few bugs to be ironed out** il y a encore quelques petits trucs qui clochent
(**d**) *Comput* bogue *m*
(**e**) *Fam Tech (microphone)* micro *m* (caché)
(**f**) *Am Fam (car)* Coccinelle □ *f*
2 *vt* (**a**) *Fam (bother)* taper sur les nerfs de; **what's bugging him?** qu'est-ce qu'il a?; **it really bugs me to think of her having all that money** ça m'énerve vraiment de savoir qu'elle a tout cet argent
(**b**) *Tech (wiretap → room)* poser *ou* installer des appareils d'écoute (clandestins) dans; *(→ phone)* brancher sur table d'écoute

►**bug off** *vi Am Fam (leave hurriedly)* ficher le camp; **bug off!** dégage!, fiche le camp!

►**bug out** *vi Am Fam* (**a**) *(leave hurriedly)* ficher le camp (**b**) *(eyes)* être globuleux *ou* exorbité □

bugaboo ['bʌgəbuː] *n* loup-garou *m*, croque-mitaine *m*

bugbear ['bʌgbeə(r)] *n (monster)* épouvantail *m*, croque-mitaine *m*; *Fig (worry)* bête *f* noire, cauchemar *m*; **maths is my bugbear** les maths c'est mon cauchemar; *Econ* **inflation is the government's chief bugbear** l'inflation est le grand cauchemar du gouvernement

bug-eyed *adj Am Fam* aux yeux globuleux *ou* exorbités □; **she was bug-eyed in amazement** elle avait les yeux écarquillés d'étonnement

bug-free *adj* (**a**) *Comput (program)* exempt d'erreurs *ou* de bogues (**b**) *(room → without listening devices)* sans micros clandestins; *(→ having no insects)* d'où les insectes ont été chassés

bugger ['bʌgə(r)] **1** *n* (**a**) *very Fam (foolish person)* couillon *m*; *(unpleasant person)* salaud *m*; **silly bugger!** pauvre connard!; *Br* **stop playing silly buggers!** arrête de faire le con!; **poor old bugger** pauvre bougre *m*; **he can be a real bugger sometimes** c'est un vrai saligaud *ou* salopard des fois; **you little bugger!** *(to child)* petite fripouille!; **how are you, you old bugger?** comment ça va, vieille fripouille?
(**b**) *Br very Fam (thing, job)* truc *m* chiant; **this job's a real bugger** c'est une saloperie de boulot; **her house is a bugger to find** sa maison est vachement dure à trouver
(**c**) *Br very Fam (damn)* **I don't give a bugger** je m'en tape
(**d**) *Old-fashioned (sodomite)* pédéraste *m*
2 *exclam Br very Fam* merde alors!
3 *vt* (**a**) *(sodomize)* sodomiser; *Law* se livrer à la pédérastie avec
(**b**) *Br very Fam (damn)* **bugger him!** je l'emmerde!; **well, bugger me!** merde alors!; **oh, bugger it!** oh, merde!
(**c**) *Br very Fam (damage)* bousiller; **that's really buggered it!** *(broken it)* ça l'a complètement bousillé; *(spoilt things)* ça a tout gâché □
(**d**) *Br very Fam (exhaust)* mettre sur les genoux □
4 **bugger all** *adj Br very Fam* que dalle; **bugger all money/thanks** pas un sou/un merci □; **that was bugger all help** ça n'a servi à rien □

►**bugger about, bugger around** *Br very Fam* **1** *vt sep* **to bugger sb about** *or* **around** *(treat badly)* se foutre de la gueule de qn; *(waste time of)* faire tourner qn en bourrique
2 *vi* glander

►**bugger off** *vi Br very Fam* foutre le camp; **bugger off!** *(go away)* fous le camp!; *(leave me alone)* fous-moi la paix!; *(expressing contempt, disagreement)* va te faire foutre!

►**bugger up** *vt sep Br very Fam* saloper

buggered ['bʌgəd] *adj Br very Fam* (**a**) *(broken)* foutu (**b**) *(in surprise)* **well, I'll be buggered!** merde alors! (**c**) *(in annoyance)* **I'm buggered if I'll do anything to help** ils peuvent toujours courir pour que je les aide; **(I'm) buggered if I know** j'en sais foutre rien (**d**) *(exhausted)* crevé, naze (**e**) *(in trouble)* foutu; **if we don't get the money soon, we're buggered** si on a pas l'argent rapidement, on est foutus

buggery ['bʌgərɪ] **1** *n* (**a**) *(sodomy)* sodomie *f* (**b**) *very Fam* **to run like buggery** courir ventre à terre; **my plans have been shot to buggery** ça a foutu mes projets en l'air; **is he a good cook? – is he buggery!** il fait bien la cuisine? – tu veux rire!
2 *exclam Br very Fam* merde!

bugging ['bʌgɪŋ] *n (of room)* utilisation *f* d'appareils d'écoute (clandestins); *(of telephone)* mise *f* sur écoute
►► ***bugging device*** appareil *m* d'écoute (clandestin)

buggy ['bʌgɪ] *(pl* **buggies**, *compar* **buggier**, *superl* **buggiest**) **1** *n* (**a**) *(carriage)* boghei *m* (**b**) *(for baby)* poussette *f*, poussette-canne *f*; *Am (pram)* voiture *f* d'enfant (**c**) *Fam Aut (car)* bagnole *f*
2 *adj Am Fam (crazy)* cinglé

bughouse ['bʌghaʊs, *pl* -haʊzɪz] *Am Fam Pej* **1** *n* maison *f* de fous
2 *adj* dingue, cinglé

bugle ['bjuːgəl] **1** *n* clairon *m*; **to sound the bugle** faire sonner le clairon
2 *vi* jouer du clairon, sonner le clairon
►► ***bugle call*** sonnerie *f* de clairon

bugler ['bjuːglə(r)] *n* (joueur *m* de) clairon *m*

bugless ['bʌglɪs] *adj Comput* sans bogues

bug-ridden *adj Comput* bogué

build [bɪld] *(pt & pp* **built** [bɪlt]) **1** *vt* (**a**) *(dwelling)* bâtir, construire; *(temple)* bâtir, édifier; *(bridge, machine, ship)* construire; *(nest)* faire, bâtir; **houses are being built** des maisons sont en construction; **we are planning to build a new garage** nous avons l'intention de faire construire un nouveau garage; **we're building an extension on the house** nous agrandissons la maison; *Fig* **to build castles in the air** bâtir des châteaux en Espagne; *Mktg* **to build a brand** créer une marque
(**b**) *(found)* bâtir, fonder; **to build one's hopes on sth** fonder ses espoirs sur qch
2 *vi* (**a**) *(construct)* bâtir; **developers are planning to build on the land** les promoteurs envisagent de construire *ou* bâtir sur le terrain; *Fig* **to build on sand** bâtir sur le sable; *Fig* **his success is built on hard work** sa réussite repose sur un travail acharné
(**b**) *(increase)* augmenter, monter; **excitement/tension is building** l'excitation/la tension augmente *ou* monte
3 *n Anat* carrure *f*, charpente *f*; **of strong build** solidement bâti *ou* charpenté; **of heavy build** de forte corpulence *ou* taille; **of medium build** de taille *ou* corpulence moyenne; **a man of slight build** un homme fluet; **she's about the same build as I am** elle est à peu près de ma taille; **he has the build of a rugby player** il est bâti comme un joueur de rugby

►**build in** *vt sep Constr (wardrobe, beam etc)* encastrer; *Fig (include → special features)* intégrer

►**build into** *vt sep (incorporate)* intégrer à

►**build on** **1** *vt sep Constr* ajouter
2 *vt insep* **we need to build on our achievements** il faut consolider nos succès

►**build up** **1** *vt sep* (**a**) *(develop → business, theory)* établir, développer; *(→ reputation)* établir, bâtir; *(→ confidence)* donner, redonner; *(→ strength)* prendre; **you need to build up your strength, you need building up** vous avez besoin de prendre des forces; **he really helped to build up my self-confidence** il m'a vraiment aidé à me donner confiance en moi
(**b**) *Ind (increase → production)* [illegible] augmenter; *(→ excitement)* faire monter, accroître; *(→ pressure)* accumuler
(**c**) *(promote)* faire de la publicité pour; **the film wasn't as good as it had been built up to be** le film n'était pas aussi bon qu'on le prétendait
(**d**) *Constr (wall → make higher)* rehausser; *(→ rebuild)* réparer
2 *vi* (**a**) *(business)* se développer
(**b**) *(excitement)* monter, augmenter; *(pressure)* s'accumuler; **traffic is building up** il commence à y avoir beaucoup de circulation

►**build upon** = **build on** *vt insep*

builder ['bɪldə(r)] *n* (**a**) *Constr (contractor)* entrepreneur(euse) *m,f (en bâtiment)*; *(worker)* ouvrier(ère) *m,f* du bâtiment; *Com & Ind (of machines, ships)* constructeur(trice) *m,f*
(**b**) *Fig (founder)* fondateur(trice) *m,f*; **the builders of the empire** les bâtisseurs *mpl* de l'empire

▸▸ *Br Fam Hum* **builder's bum** = phénomène censé se produire communément chez les ouvriers du bâtiment, dont le pantalon a tendance à tomber, exposant le haut de leur postérieur; *Constr* **builder's merchant** fournisseur *m* de matériaux de construction; *Br Fam Hum* **builder's suntan** bronzage *m* agricole

building ['bɪldɪŋ] **1** *n* (**a**) *(structure)* bâtiment *m*; *(monumental)* édifice *m*; *(apartment, office)* immeuble *m*
(**b**) *Constr (work)* construction *f*; **building is due to start on Monday** les travaux de construction doivent commencer lundi
2 *comp Constr (land)* à bâtir; *(materials)* de construction
▸▸ **building block** *(toy)* cube *m*; *Fig* composante *f*; *Constr* **building contractor** entrepreneur *m* (en bâtiment *ou* construction); **building industry** (industrie *f* du) bâtiment *m*; **buildings insurance** assurance *f* habitation; *Am Fin* **building and loan association** ≃ société *f* de crédit immobilier; *Am* **building permit** permis *m* de construire; **building plot** terrain *m* à bâtir; **building site** chantier *m* (de construction); *Br Fin* **building society** ≃ société *f* de crédit immobilier; *Fin* **building society passbook** livret *m* d'épargne logement; **building trade** (industrie *f* du) bâtiment *m*; **building worker** ouvrier(ère) *m,f* du bâtiment

BUILDING SOCIETY

Les "building societies" fonctionnent comme des banques mais elles n'ont pas de système de compensation. Établissements consentant des prêts immobiliers aux particuliers, elles jouent un rôle important dans la vie en Grande-Bretagne. Au cours des dernières années, de nombreuses "building societies" ont abandonné leur statut de sociétés mutuelles pour devenir des banques cotées en Bourse.

build-up *n* (**a**) *(increase → in pressure)* intensification *f*; *(→ in excitement)* montée *f*; *(→ in production)* accroissement *m*; *(→ in stock)* accumulation *f*; *Mil (→ in troops)* rassemblement *m*; **nuclear arms build-up** accumulation *f* des armes nucléaires
(**b**) *(publicity)* campagne *f* publicitaire *(avant le lancement d'un produit)*; **they gave the product a big build-up** ils ont fait beaucoup de publicité pour le produit
(**c**) *(preparatory period)* **the build-up to the match** la période d'avant le match; **in the build-up to the election, there will be...** pendant la période qui précédera les élections, il y aura...

built [bɪlt] **1** *pt & pp of* **build**
2 *adj (building)* bâti, construit; *(person)* charpenté; **brick-built** en *ou* de brique; **British built** de construction britannique; **to be powerfully built** *(person)* être puissamment *ou* solidement charpenté; **to be slightly built** *(person)* être fluet

built-in *adj (beam, wardrobe)* encastré; *(device, safeguard)* intégré; *Fig (feature)* inné, ancré; *Comput* incorporé
▸▸ **built-in obsolescence** obsolescence *f* programmée

built-to-order *adj Comput* construit sur mesure

built-up *adj* (**a**) *(land)* bâti; **the area is becoming very built-up** ça se construit beaucoup *ou* on a beaucoup construit dans la région (**b**) *(in clothing)* **built-up shoulders** épaules *fpl* surhaussées; **built-up shoes** chaussures *fpl* à semelles compensées
▸▸ **built-up area** agglomération *f* (urbaine)

bulb [bʌlb] *n* (**a**) *Bot* bulbe *m*, oignon *m*; **tulip bulb** bulbe *m* de tulipe (**b**) *Elec* ampoule *f*; **a light bulb** une ampoule (**c**) *Tech (of thermometer)* réservoir *m* (**d**) *Anat* bulbe *m* (**e**) *Naut (bulbous bow)* bulb *m*, bulbe *m*

bulbar ['bʌlbə(r)] *adj* bulbaire

bulbous ['bʌlbəs] *adj Bot* bulbeux; *Anat* **a bulbous nose** un gros nez; *Naut* **a bulbous bow** un bulb, un bulbe

bulbul ['bʊlbʊl] *n Orn* bulbul *m*

Bulgaria [bʌl'geərɪə] *n* Bulgarie *f*; **in Bulgaria** en Bulgarie

Bulgarian [bʌl'geərɪən] **1** *n* (**a**) *(person)* Bulgare *mf* (**b**) *(language)* bulgare *m*
2 *adj* bulgare
3 *comp (embassy)* de Bulgarie; *(history)* de la Bulgarie; *(teacher)* de bulgare

bulge [bʌldʒ] **1** *n* (**a**) *(lump, swelling)* renflement *m*; *(on vase, jug)* panse *f*, ventre *m*; *Br Mil* saillant *m*; **he noticed a bulge in her pocket** il remarqua que sa poche faisait un renflement; **this dress shows all my bulges** on voit tous mes bourrelets avec cette robe
(**b**) *(increase)* poussée *f*; *Econ* **a population bulge** une explosion démographique
2 *vi (swell)* se gonfler, se renfler; *(stick out)* faire saillie, saillir; **his suitcase was bulging with gifts** sa valise était bourrée de cadeaux; *Fig* **the town was bulging at the seams with holidaymakers** la ville était pleine à craquer de vacanciers; **he bulged (out) at the waist** il était ventru, il avait du ventre; **his eyes bulged** il avait les yeux saillants *ou* globuleux

bulghur (wheat) ['bʌlgə(r)-] *n* boulgour *m*

bulging ['bʌldʒɪŋ] *adj (forehead, wall, ceiling)* bombé; *(stomach)* ballonné; *(muscles, waist)* saillant; *(eyes)* protubérant, globuleux; *(cheeks)* bouffi; *(bag, wallet etc)* bourré, plein à craquer; *(bag, pockets)* gonflé

bulgur = **bulghur**

bulimia [bʊ'lɪmɪə] *n Med* boulimie *f*

bulimic [bʊ'lɪmɪk] *Med* **1** *n* boulimique *mf*
2 *adj* boulimique

bulk [bʌlk] **1** *n* (**a**) *(mass)* masse *f*; *(stoutness)* corpulence *f*; **the great bulk of the cathedral loomed out of the darkness** la silhouette massive de la cathédrale se dessina dans l'obscurité; **a man of enormous bulk** un homme très corpulent; **he levered his great bulk out of the armchair** il extirpa sa grosse carcasse du fauteuil
(**b**) *(main part)* **the bulk** la plus grande partie, la majeure partie; **the bulk of the estate was woodland** la majeure partie de la propriété était boisée; **she left the bulk of her fortune to charity** elle légua le plus gros de sa fortune aux bonnes œuvres
(**c**) *(in food)* fibre *f* (végétale)
(**d**) *Naut (goods)* cargaison *f*
(**e**) *Comput (of information)* volume *m*, masse *f*
2 *comp Com (order, supplies)* en gros
3 *vt Com (packages)* grouper
4 *vi Br* **to bulk large** occuper une place importante; **the prospect of a further drop in prices bulked large in their minds** la perspective d'une autre baisse des prix les préoccupait vivement *ou* était au premier plan de leurs préoccupations
5 in bulk *adv* par grosses quantités; *Com* en gros; *Naut* en vrac
▸▸ *Com* **bulk buying** *(UNCOUNT)* achat *m* par grosses quantités; achat *m* en gros; *Naut* **bulk carrier** vraquier *m*, transporteur *m* de vrac; *Mktg* **bulk mail** *(UNCOUNT)* envois *mpl* en nombre; *Mktg* **bulk mailing** mailing *m ou* publipostage *m* à grande diffusion; *Com* **bulk rate** affranchissement *m* à forfait

bulk-buy *Com* **1** *vt* acheter en gros *ou* grande quantité
2 *vi* acheter en gros *ou* grande quantité

bulkhead ['bʌlkhed] *n Aviat & Naut* cloison *f* *(d'avion, de navire)*

bulkiness ['bʌlkɪnɪs] *n (of object)* grosseur *f*, encombrement *m*, volume *m*; *(of person)* corpulence *f*

bulky ['bʌlkɪ] *adj* (**a**) *(massive, large)* volumineux; *(cumbersome)* encombrant; **a bulky sweater** *or* **jumper** un gros pull; **a bulky package** *or* **parcel** un paquet encombrant *ou* volumineux (**b**) *(corpulent, stout)* corpulent, gros (grosse); *(solidly built)* massif

bull [bʊl] **1** *n* (**a**) *(male cow)* taureau *m*; **like a bull in a china shop** comme un éléphant dans un magasin de porcelaine; *Fig* **to take the bull by the horns** prendre le taureau par les cornes; **to go at sth like a bull at a gate** foncer tête baissée *ou* la tête la première dans qch
(**b**) *(male of a species → elephant, whale)* mâle *m*
(**c**) *Fam (large, strong man)* costaud *m*, malabar *m*; **a great bull of a man** un homme fort comme un bœuf
(**d**) *St Exch* haussier *m*, spéculateur(trice) *m,f* à la hausse
(**e**) *(centre of target)* mille *m*, centre *m* de la cible; **to hit the bull** faire mouche, mettre dans le mille
(**f**) *very Fam (nonsense)* conneries *fpl*; **that's a lot** *or* **load of bull** c'est des conneries tout ça
(**g**) *Rel* bulle *f*; **papal bull** bulle *f* papale
(**h**) *Br Fam Mil slang (polishing)* fourbissage ❑ *m*
2 *comp (elephant, whale)* mâle
3 *vt St Exch (market, prices, shares)* pousser à la hausse; **to bull the market** chercher à faire hausser les cours
4 *vi St Exch (person)* spéculer *ou* jouer à la hausse; *(stocks)* être en hausse
5 Bull *n Astrol* **the Bull** le Taureau
▸▸ *Aut* **bull bars** pare-buffles *m inv*; **bull calf** jeune taureau *m*, taurillon *m*; *St Exch* **bull market** marché *m* à la hausse *ou* haussier; **bull mastiff** = chien issu d'un métissage entre le bouledogue et le mastiff; *St Exch* **bull position** position *f* acheteur; *St Exch* **bull purchase** achat *m* à la hausse; *Hist* **Bull Run** = petite rivière de Virginie qui fut le théâtre d'une importante défaite des nordistes pendant la guerre de Sécession; *Am Fam* **bull session** causerie *f* entre hommes; *Zool* **bull shark** requin *m* bouledogue; *St Exch* **bull speculation, bull trading** spéculation *f* à la hausse; **bull terrier** bull-terrier *m*; *St Exch* **bull transaction** opération *f* à la hausse

bulldog ['bʊldɒg] *n* (**a**) *(dog)* bouledogue *m*
(**b**) *Br St Exch* **bulldog (bond)** obligation *f* bulldog *(obligation d'un emprunteur étranger à la Bourse de Londres, libellée en sterling)*
(**c**) *Br Univ (official)* appariteur *m* du censeur *(aux universités d'Oxford et de Cambridge)*
▸▸ **bulldog clip** pince *f* à dessin; **Bulldog Drummond** = dans les romans de Herman McNeile, ancien officier britannique très laid mais sympathique

bulldoze ['bʊldəʊz] *vt* (**a**) *Constr (building)* démolir au bulldozer; *(earth, stone)* passer au bulldozer; **whole villages have been bulldozed out of existence** des villages entiers ont été rasés au bulldozer (**b**) *Fig (push)* **to bulldoze sb into doing sth** forcer qn à faire qch, faire pression sur qn pour lui faire faire qch; **she bulldozed her way to the top** elle est arrivée au sommet à la force du poignet

bulldozer ['bʊldəʊzə(r)] *n Tech* bulldozer *m*

bulldyke ['bʊldaɪk] *n very Fam Pej* gouine *f* à l'allure masculine

bullet ['bʊlɪt] **1** *n* (**a**) *(from rifle, revolver)* balle *f*; *Br Fam Fig* **to get the bullet** *(get fired)* se faire virer, se faire sacquer (**b**) *Typ* puce *f* (**c**) *Am Fin (loan)* emprunt *m* remboursable in fine; *(repayment)* remboursement *m* in fine
2 *comp (hole)* de balle; *(wound)* par balle
▸▸ *Am Fin* **bullet bond** obligation *f* remboursable en une seule fois; *Rail* **bullet train** train *m* à grande vitesse *(au Japon)*

bulleted list ['bʊlɪtɪd-] *n Typ & Comput* liste *f* à puces

bullet-headed *adj* (**a**) *(with a small, round head)* à tête ronde (**b**) *Am Fig (obstinate)* entêté, têtu

bulletin ['bʊlətɪn] *n Rad & TV (announcement)* bulletin *m*, communiqué *m*; *Press (newsletter)* bulletin *m*
▸▸ **bulletin board** *Am (gen)* tableau *m* d'affichage; *Comput* serveur *m* télématique, *Can* babillard *m*; *Comput* **bulletin board service** serveur *m* télématique, *Can* babillard *m*

bulletproof ['bʊlɪt,pru:f] **1** *adj (glass, garment)* pare-balles *(inv)*; *(vehicle)* blindé
2 *vt (door, vehicle)* blinder
▸▸ **bulletproof vest** gilet *m* pare-balles

bullfight ['bʊlfaɪt] *n* corrida *f*, course *f* de taureaux

bullfighter ['bʊl,faɪtə(r)] *n* torero *m*, matador *m*

bullfighting ['bʊl,faɪtɪŋ] *n (UNCOUNT)* courses *fpl* de taureaux, corrida *f*; *(as art)* tauromachie *f*

bullfinch ['bʊlfɪntʃ] *n Orn* bouvreuil *m*

bullfrog ['bʊlfrɒg] *n Zool* grenouille *f* taureau, *Can* ouaouaron *m*

bullhead ['bʊlhed] *n Ich* meunier *m*

bull-headed *adj Fam* (**a**) *(impetuous)* d'une impétuosité de taureau; **to go at sth bull-headed** foncer la tête la première dans qch (**b**) *(obstinate)* entêté ❑, têtu ❑

bullhorn ['bʊlhɔ:n] *n Am* mégaphone *m*, porte-voix *m inv*

bullion ['bʊljən] *n (gold)* encaisse-or *f*, or *m* en lingots *ou* en barres; *(silver)* argent *m* en lingots *ou* en barres

►► *Fin* ***bullion reserve*** réserve *f* métallique

bullish ['bʊlɪʃ] *adj* (**a**) *St Exch (market, tendency)* à la hausse, haussier; **to be bullish** *(of person)* spéculer *ou* jouer à la hausse; **bullish tendency** tendance *f* à la hausse (**b**) *Br Fam (optimistic)* **to be in a bullish mood** être confiant *ou* optimiste ❑

bullishness ['bʊlɪʃnɪs] *n St Exch* tendance *f* à la hausse

bull-necked *adj* au cou de taureau

bullock ['bʊlək] *n (castrated)* bœuf *m*; *(young)* bouvillon *m*

bullpen ['bʊlpen] *n* (**a**) *Am (in police station)* = grande cellule commune (**b**) *Sport (in baseball)* = partie d'un terrain de base-ball où les lanceurs s'échauffent

bullring ['bʊlrɪŋ] *n* arène *f (pour la corrida)*

bull-roarer *n* rhombe *m*

bullrush = **bulrush**

bull's-eye *n* (**a**) *(centre of target)* mille *m*, centre *m* de la cible; **bull's-eye!** dans le mille!; **to hit the bull's-eye** faire mouche, mettre dans le mille; *Fig (person)* faire mouche, mettre dans le mille; *(remark)* faire mouche (**b**) *(sweet)* gros bonbon *m* à la menthe (**c**) *Archit (window)* œil-de-bœuf *m*, oculus *m*; *Cer (in glass)* boudine *f*

bullshit ['bʊlʃɪt] *Vulg* **1** *n (UNCOUNT)* conneries *fpl*; **don't give me that bullshit!** ne me raconte *ou* dis pas de conneries!

2 *vt* raconter des conneries à; **don't bullshit me!** ne me raconte pas de conneries!; **she bullshitted her way into the job** elle a eu le boulot au culot

3 *vi* déconner, raconter des conneries

4 *exclam* des conneries, tout ça!

bullshitter ['bʊl,ʃɪtə(r)] *n Vulg (smooth talker)* baratineur(euse) *m,f*; **he's a bullshitter** *(talks nonsense)* il raconte des conneries

bullwhip ['bʊlwɪp] **1** *n* fouet *m*

2 *vt* fouetter

bully ['bʊlɪ] **1** *n* (**a**) *(adult)* tyran *m*; *(child)* petite brute *f*; **don't be such a bully!** ne sois pas si tyrannique!; *Am* **it was an opportunity for the President to use his office as a bully pulpit** ce fut l'occasion pour le président des États-Unis de profiter de sa position pour imposer ses vues (**b**) *Sport (in hockey)* bully *m*

2 *vt (intimidate → spouse, employee)* brimer, persécuter; *(maltreat)* brutaliser; **she bullies her little sister** elle est tyrannique avec sa petite sœur; **they bullied me into going** ils m'ont forcé à y aller; **he gets bullied by the other children at school** il se fait persécuter par les autres enfants à l'école

3 *exclam Fam Ironic* **bully for you!** quel exploit!, bravo!

►► *Br Fam Old-fashioned* ***bully beef*** singe *m (corned-beef)*

►**bully off** *vi Sport (in hockey)* engager le jeu, mettre la balle en jeu

bullyboy ['bʊlɪbɔɪ] *n Br* brute *f*, voyou *m*; **bullyboy tactics** manœuvres *fpl* d'intimidation

bullying ['bʊlɪɪŋ] **1** *adj (intimidating)* agressif, brutal

2 *n (UNCOUNT)* brimades *fpl*; **the problem of bullying in** [illegible] persécutés par leurs camarades d'école

bully-off *n Sport (in hockey)* bully *m*

bulrush ['bʊlrʌʃ] *n Bot* jonc *m*

bulwark ['bʊlwək] **1** *n Archit* rempart *m*, fortification *f*; *(breakwater)* digue *f*, môle *m*; *Fig (protection)* rempart *m*, protection *f*; **a bulwark against the harsh realities of life** un rempart *ou* une protection contre les dures réalités de la vie; **a bulwark against inflation** une mesure de protection contre l'inflation

2 bulwarks *npl Naut* bastingage *m*, pavois *m*

bum [bʌm] (*pt & pp* **bummed,** *cont* **bumming**) *Fam* **1** *n* (**a**) *Br (buttocks)* fesses ❑ *fpl*; **to put bums on seats** attirer le public ❑

(**b**) *(tramp)* clochard(e) ❑ *m,f*, clodo *m*; *(lazy person)* fainéant(e) ❑ *m,f*, flemmard(e) *m,f*; *(worthless person)* minable *mf*, minus *m*; **to give sb the bum's rush** *(dismiss)* envoyer paître qn; *(from work)* virer qn; **to give sth the bum's rush** *(idea, suggestion)* rejeter qch ❑; **my idea was given the bum's rush** mon idée est passée à la trappe

(**c**) *Sport (sports fanatic)* fana *mf*, mordu(e) *m,f*; **a beach bum** un(e) fana *ou* mordu(e) des plages

(**d**) *Am (vagrancy)* **to be** *or* **live on the bum** vagabonder; **he went on the bum** il s'est mis à dormir sous les ponts

2 *adj (worthless)* minable, nul; *(injured, disabled)* patraque, mal fichu; *(untrue)* faux (fausse) ❑; **he got a bit of a bum deal** il a été très mal traité; *Am* **he was in jail on a bum rap** il était en prison pour un délit qu'il n'avait pas commis

3 *vt (beg, borrow)* **to bum sth off sb** emprunter qch à qn ❑, taper qn de qch ❑; **he's always bumming cigarettes** il est toujours à quémander *ou* mendier des cigarettes; **to bum a lift** *or* **ride** se faire accompagner en voiture ❑; **can I bum a lift** *or* **a ride to the station?** est-ce que tu peux me déposer à la gare? ❑; **they bummed a lift to the border** ils ont réussi à se faire emmener en voiture jusqu'à la frontière ❑

4 *vi Am* (**a**) *(be disappointed)* l'avoir mauvaise (**b**) *(laze about)* traîner

►► *Br* ***bum bag*** banane *f*; ***bum fluff*** *(beard)* barbe *f* très peu fournie; ***bum steer*** tuyau *m* percé; **to give sb a bum steer** donner un tuyau percé à qn

►**bum about, bum around** *Fam* **1** *vt insep (spend time in)* **to bum around Australia/the country** parcourir l'Australie/le pays sac au dos ❑; **to bum around the house** rester chez soi à glander

2 *vi* glander, glandouiller; *(travel)* vadrouiller; **they spent three months bumming around in Mexico** ils ont passé trois mois à se balader au Mexique

bumble ['bʌmbəl] *vi* (**a**) *(speak incoherently)* bafouiller; **he bumbled through his speech** il a fait un discours décousu (**b**) *(move clumsily)* **he came bumbling in** il entra, l'air gauche

bumblebee ['bʌmbəlbiː] *n Entom* bourdon *m*

bumbler ['bʌmblə(r)] *n* empoté(e) *m,f*, maladroit(e) *m,f*

bumbling ['bʌmblɪŋ] *adj Fam (person)* empoté, maladroit; *(behaviour)* maladroit; **bumbling fool** *or* **idiot** andouille *f*

bumboat ['bʌmbəʊt] *n Naut* canot *m* d'approvisionnement

bumf [bʌmf] *n Br Fam* (**a**) *(documentation)* doc *f* (**b**) *Pej (useless papers)* paperasse *f* (**c**) *(toilet paper)* papier *m* cul

bumfreezer ['bʌm,friːzə(r)] *n Br Fam (jacket)* blouson *m* court ❑; *(skirt)* jupe *f* ultra-courte ❑, jupe *f* ras la touffe

bumhole ['bʌm,həʊl] *n very Fam* trou *m* de balle

bummed [bʌmd] *adj Am Fam* **to be bummed** l'avoir mauvaise; **he's bummed (out) with his job** il en a marre de son travail

bummer ['bʌmə(r)] *n very Fam* (**a**) *(bad experience)* poisse *f*; **the film's a real bummer** ce film est vraiment nul *ou* un vrai navet; **what a bummer!** quelle poisse!; **it's a real bummer when you find out...** ça en fiche un coup quand on découvre que... (**b**) *(idiom)* **to be on a bummer** *(drug addict)* faire un bad trip; *Am (be depressed)* avoir le cafard

bump [bʌmp] **1** *n* (**a**) *(lump* [illegible] *on head, in path, road surface)* bosse *f*; **he has a big bump on his head** il a une grosse bosse au crâne; **a bump in the road** une bosse sur la route; *Aut* **to hit a bump** passer sur une bosse

(**b**) *(blow, knock)* choc *m*, coup *m*; **he felt a bump as he reversed the car into the garage** il a senti un choc en reculant la voiture dans le garage; **her head hit the shelf with a bump** il y a eu un bruit sourd quand elle s'est cogné la tête contre l'étagère; **the boat hit the jetty with a bump** le bateau a cogné contre la jetée; *Fig* **to be brought down to earth with a bump** être ramené brutalement à la réalité

(**c**) *Aviat (air current)* courant *m* ascendant

2 *vt* (**a**) *(hit)* heurter; *(elbow, head, knee)* cogner

(**b**) *Fam (get rid of)* virer; **he got bumped from the football team** il s'est fait virer de l'équipe de football; **to be bumped from a flight** perdre sa place sur un vol *(pour cause de sur-réservation)*

3 *vi* (**a**) *(move jerkily)* cahoter; **the old bus bumped along the country roads** le vieil autobus cahotait le long des petites routes

(**b**) *(collide)* se heurter; **the boat bumped against the pier** le bateau a buté contre l'embarcadère

(**c**) *Fam* **to bump and grind** *(dancer, striptease artist)* se déhancher *(en simulant l'acte sexuel)*

4 *adv* **the driver went bump into the car in front** le conducteur est rentré en plein dans la voiture de devant; **things that go bump in the night** les spectres *mpl*, les fantômes *mpl*

5 bumps *npl* (**a**) *Br* **to give sb the (birthday) bumps** = à son anniversaire, tenir à plusieurs quelqu'un par les bras et les jambes, et lui faire toucher le sol un nombre de fois correspondant à son âge, *Can* donner la bascule à qn

(**b**) *Sport (rowing race)* = à Oxford, course-poursuite dans laquelle chaque bateau doit rattraper pour le heurter le bateau qui le précède

►► *Aut* ***bump start*** = démarrage d'un véhicule en le poussant

►**bump into** *vt insep (object)* rentrer dedans, tamponner; *(person)* rencontrer par hasard, tomber sur; **he bumped into a lamppost** il est rentré dans un réverbère; **I bumped into an old school friend this morning** je suis tombé sur un ancien camarade d'école ce matin

►**bump off** *vt sep Fam (murder)* liquider, supprimer; *(with a gun)* descendre

►**bump up** *vt sep Fam (increase)* faire grimper ❑; *Com (prices)* gonfler ❑, faire grimper ❑

bumper ['bʌmpə(r)] **1** *n* (**a**) *Aut* pare-chocs *m inv*; **front/rear bumper** pare-chocs *m inv* avant/arrière

(**b**) *Am Rail (on train)* tampon *m*; *(at station)* butoir *m*

(**c**) *(full glass)* rasade *f*

2 *adj (crop, harvest)* exceptionnel, formidable; *Br* **a bumper issue** un numéro exceptionnel

►► ***bumper car*** auto *f* tamponneuse, *Belg* autoscooter *m ou f*; *Aut* ***bumper sticker*** autocollant *m (pour voiture)*

bumper-to-bumper *adj* **bumper-to-bumper traffic** circulation *f* difficile; **the cars were bumper-to-bumper on the bridge** les voitures roulaient pare-chocs contre pare-chocs sur le pont

bumpety-bump ['bʌmpɪtɪ-] *adv Fam* en cahotant; **my heart went bumpety-bump** mon cœur a battu à tout rompre

bumph = **bumf**

bumping ['bʌmpɪŋ] *n* (**a**) *(collision)* heurt(s) *m(pl)*, choc(s) *m(pl)*; *(jolting)* cahotement *m* (**b**) *(of air passenger)* bumping *m*, refus *m* d'embarquer *(suite à sur-réservation)* (**c**) *Fam* **bumping and grinding** *(of dancer, striptease artist)* déhanchements *mpl (simulant l'acte sexuel)*

bumpkin ['bʌmpkɪn] *n Fam Pej* plouc *m*, péquenaud *m*

bump-start *vt Aut* démarrer en poussant

bumptious ['bʌmpʃəs] *adj* suffisant, prétentieux

bumptiously ['bʌmpʃəslɪ] *adv* avec suffisance

bumptiousness ['bʌmpʃəsnɪs] *n* suffisance *f*

bumpy ['bʌmpɪ] (*compar* **bumpier,** *superl* **bumpiest**) *adj (road)* cahoteux; *(flight, ride)* agité (de secousses); *(surface, wall)* bosselé; **we had a bumpy flight** [illegible] l'avion; *Fig* **we've got a bumpy ride ahead of us** on va traverser une mauvaise passe

bun [bʌn] **1** *n* (**a**) *(bread)* petit pain *m* (au lait); *Br Fam Fig* **she's got a bun in the oven** elle a un polichinelle dans le tiroir

(**b**) *(in hair)* chignon *m*

2 buns *npl Am Fam (buttocks)* fesses ❑ *fpl*, miches *fpl*

►► *Br Fam Hum* ***bun fight*** *(gathering)* réception ❑ *f*

bunch [bʌntʃ] **1** *n* (**a**) *(of flowers, straw)* bouquet *m*, botte *f*; *(of grapes)* grappe *f*; *(of bananas, dates)* régime *m*; *(of feathers, hair)* touffe *f*; *(of sticks, twigs)* faisceau *m*, poignée *f*; *(of keys)* trousseau *m*; *(of papers)* liasse *f*; *Br Fam* **do you want a bunch of fives?** tu veux mon poing sur la gueule?

(**b**) *Fam (of people)* bande ❑ *f*; **they're a bunch of idiots** c'est une bande d'imbéciles; **her family are a strange bunch** elle a une drôle de famille; *Ironic* **you're a fine bunch!** quelle équipe vous faites!; **he's the best of a bad bunch** c'est le moins mauvais du lot

(**c**) *(of cyclists)* peloton *m*

(**d**) *Fam Ironic (idiom)* **thanks a bunch!** merci beaucoup!

2 *vt (straw, vegetables)* mettre en bottes, botteler; *(flowers)* botteler, mettre en bouquets

3 bunches *npl Br* couettes *fpl*; **she wears her hair in bunches** elle porte des couettes

▸**bunch together 1** *vt sep* mettre ensemble; *(flowers)* botteler, mettre en bouquets

2 *vi (people)* se serrer, se presser

▸**bunch up 1** *vt sep* mettre ensemble; *(flowers)* mettre en bouquets, botteler; *(dress, skirt)* retrousser; **your dress is bunched up at the back** le derrière de ta robe est tout retroussé

2 *vi* (**a**) *(group of people)* se serrer (**b**) *(clothing)* se retrousser

bunco ['bʊŋkəʊ] (*pl* **buncos**) *Am Fam Cards* **1** *n* arnaque *f*

2 *vt* arnaquer, rouler

bundle ['bʌndəl] **1** *n* (**a**) *(of clothes, linen)* paquet *m*; *(wrapped in a cloth)* paquet *m*; *Com (of goods)* paquet *m*, ballot *m*; *(of sticks, twigs)* faisceau *f*; *Fin & Admin (of banknotes, papers)* liasse *f*; **he's a bundle of nerves** c'est un paquet de nerfs; **a bundle of firewood** un fagot; **she's a bundle of contradictions** elle est pleine de contradictions; *Fam* **a bundle of fun** *or* **laughs** marrant, amusant; *Fam* **the trip wasn't exactly a bundle of laughs** le voyage n'était pas vraiment marrant; *Ironic* **he's a real bundle of fun** c'est fou ce qu'on s'amuse avec lui; **bundle of joy** *(baby)* bout *m* de chou

(**b**) *Fam Fin (large sum of money)* **to cost a bundle** coûter bonbon *ou* la peau des fesses; **to make a bundle** faire son beurre

(**c**) *Comput* plus produit *m*

(**d**) *Br (idioms) Fam* **to go a bundle on sth** s'emballer pour qch; *Fam Ironic* **thanks a bundle!** merci beaucoup!

2 *vt* (**a**) *(clothes)* mettre en paquet; *(for a journey)* empaqueter; *(linen)* mettre en paquet; *Com (goods)* mettre en paquet; *(banknotes, papers)* mettre en liasses; *(sticks, twigs)* mettre en faisceaux; *(firewood)* mettre en fagots; *(straw)* botteler, mettre en bottes

(**b**) *(shove)* **she bundled the papers into the drawer** elle fourra les papiers dans le tiroir; **he was bundled into the car** on l'a poussé dans la voiture brusquement *ou* sans ménagement; **he quickly bundled them out of the room** il les a poussés précipitamment hors de la pièce

(**c**) *Comput* vendre en *ou* par lot

(**d**) *Com & Mktg* **to bundle sth with sth** offrir qch en plus de qch; **to come bundled with sth** être livré avec qch; *Comput* **bundled software** logiciel *m* livré avec le matériel

▸**bundle off** *vt sep* **they bundled me off the train** ils m'ont fait descendre du train en toute hâte; **the children were bundled off to school** les enfants furent envoyés *ou* expédiés à l'école vite fait

▸**bundle up 1** *vt sep* (**a**) *(tie up)* mettre en paquet (**b**) *(dress warmly)* emmitoufler; **she bundled the baby up in a warm blanket** elle emmitoufla le bébé dans une grosse couverture

2 *vi* s'emmitoufler

bundling selling ['bʌndəlɪŋ-] *n Com* vente *f* par lots

Bundt [bʌnt] *n*

▸▸ *Am Culin* ***Bundt cake*** = gâteau en forme d'anneau, que l'on offre traditionnellement à un voisin qui vient d'emménager; *Am Culin* ***Bundt pan*** moule *m* à kouglof

bung [bʌŋ] **1** *n* (**a**) *(stopper)* bondon *m*, bonde *f*

(**b**) *(hole)* bonde *f*

(**c**) *Fam (bribe)* pot-de-vin❑ *m*

2 *vt* (**a**) *(hole)* boucher

(**b**) *Br Fam (put carelessly)* balancer; **just bung it in the rubbish bin** fiche-le à la poubelle

(**c**) *Br Fam (add)* rajouter❑; **bung it on the bill** rajoutez-le sur la note; **we'll bung in a few extras** on va rajouter quelques petits extras

▸**bung up** *vt sep Br Fam* boucher❑; **my nose is/my eyes are bunged up** j'ai le nez bouché/les yeux gonflés

bungalow ['bʌŋgələʊ] *n Archit (one-storey house)* maison *f* sans étage; *(in India)* bungalow *m*

bungee ['bʌndʒiː] *n (cord)* tendeur *m*

▸▸ ***bungee cord*** tendeur *m*; ***bungee jump*** saut *m* à l'élastique; ***bungee jumping*** saut *m* à l'élastique

bunghole ['bʌŋhəʊl] *n* bonde *f*

bungle ['bʌŋgəl] **1** *vt* gâcher; **you bungled it** *or* **the job** tu as tout gâché

2 *n Br* **to make a bungle of sth** gâcher qch

bungler ['bʌŋglə(r)] *n* incapable *mf*

bungling ['bʌŋglɪŋ] **1** *adj (person)* incompétent, incapable; *(action)* maladroit, gauche

2 *n* incompétence *f*, *Fam* bousillage *m*; **your bungling has cost us the contract** tes bourdes nous ont fait perdre le contrat

bunion ['bʌnjən] *n* oignon *m (cor)*

bunk [bʌŋk] **1** *n* (**a**) *(berth)* couchette *f*; *(bed)* lit *m* (**b**) *Br Fam* **to do a bunk** se tirer, se faire la malle (**c**) *Fam (nonsense)* foutaises *fpl*; **that's a load of bunk** ce sont des foutaises

2 *vi Fam* (**a**) *(sleep)* coucher❑; *Am (spend the night)* dormir❑, passer la nuit❑ (**b**) *(escape)* se tailler

▸▸ ***bunk bed*** lit *m* superposé

▸**bunk down** *vi* coucher *(dans un lit de fortune)*

▸**bunk off 1** *vt insep* **to bunk off school** faire l'école buissonnière

2 *vi Br Fam* (**a**) *(scram)* décamper, filer (**b**) *(from school)* sécher l'école

bunker ['bʌŋkə(r)] **1** *n* (**a**) *Mil* blockhaus *m*, bunker *m*; **nuclear bunker** abri *m* anti-atomique (**b**) *(for coal)* coffre *m*; *Naut* soute *f* (**c**) *Golf* bunker *m*

2 *vt* (**a**) *Naut (coal, oil, ship)* mettre en soute (**b**) *Golf* envoyer la balle dans un bunker

Bunker Hill *n Hist* **the Battle of Bunker Hill** la bataille de Bunker Hill

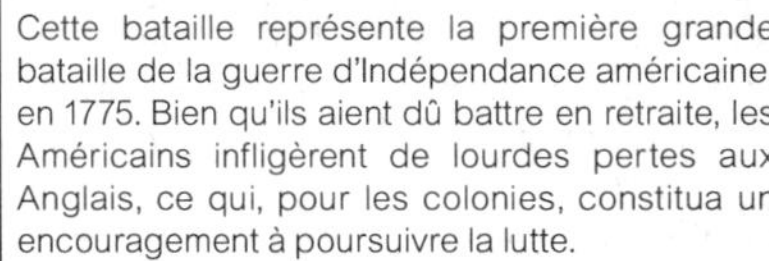

THE BATTLE OF BUNKER HILL

Cette bataille représente la première grande bataille de la guerre d'Indépendance américaine, en 1775. Bien qu'ils aient dû battre en retraite, les Américains infligèrent de lourdes pertes aux Anglais, ce qui, pour les colonies, constitua un encouragement à poursuivre la lutte.

bunkhouse ['bʌŋkhaʊs, *pl* -haʊzɪz] *n Am* baraquement *m* (pour ouvriers)

bunko ['bʌŋkəʊ] (*pl* **bunkos**) = **bunco**

bunkum ['bʌŋkəm] *n (UNCOUNT) Fam (nonsense)* foutaises *fpl*

bunk-up *n Br* **to give sb a bunk-up** faire la courte échelle à qn

bunny ['bʌnɪ] *n Fam* **bunny (rabbit)** (petit) lapin❑ *m*, Jeannot lapin *m*

▸▸ ***bunny girl*** hôtesse *f* de boîte de nuit *(habillée en lapin)*; *Am Ski* ***bunny hill*** piste *f* pour débutants

Bunsen burner ['bʌnsən-] *n* (bec *m*) Bunsen *m*

bunt [bʌnt] **1** *n* coup *m* retenu

2 *vt Sport* frapper doucement

3 *vi Sport* frapper doucement la balle

bunting ['bʌntɪŋ] *n* (**a**) *Tex (fabric)* étamine *f* (**b**) *(UNCOUNT) (flags)* fanions *mpl*, drapeaux *mpl*; **the building was decorated with blue and white bunting** le bâtiment était pavoisé de drapeaux bleus et blancs (**c**) *Orn* bruant *m*

bunyip ['bʌnjɪp] *n Austr* = créature imaginaire des marais de l'intérieur de l'Australie

buoy [*Br* bɔɪ, *Am* 'buːɪ] **1** *n Naut* bouée *f*, balise *f*; **mooring buoy** bouée *f* de corps-mort, coffre *m* d'amarrage

2 *vt (waterway)* baliser; *(vessel, obstacle)* marquer d'une bouée

▸**buoy up** *vt sep* (**a**) *Naut* faire flotter, maintenir à flot (**b**) *Fig (support, sustain)* soutenir; *(person)* remonter; *Fin (currency)* soutenir, maintenir; **her son's visit buoyed her up** *or* **buoyed up her spirits** la visite de son fils l'a remontée *ou* lui a remonté le moral

buoyancy ['bɔɪənsɪ] *n* (**a**) *(ability to float)* flottabilité *f*; *Chem (of gas, liquid)* poussée *f* (**b**) *Fig (resilience)* ressort *m*, force *f* morale; *(cheerfulness)* entrain *m*, allant *m* (**c**) *Fin (of economy, sector)* robustesse *f*, vigueur *f*; *(of prices, currency)* stabilité *f*; *St Exch (of market)* fermeté *f*

▸▸ ***buoyancy tank*** réservoir *m* de flottabilité

buoyant ['bɔɪənt] *adj* (**a**) *(floatable)* flottable, capable de flotter; *(causing to float)* qui fait flotter; **sea water is very buoyant** l'eau de mer porte très bien (**b**) *Fig (cheerful)* plein d'allant *ou* d'entrain; *(mood)* gai, allègre; **her spirits were buoyant that morning** elle était pleine d'allant *ou* d'entrain ce matin-là (**c**) *Fin (economy, sector)* sain, robuste; *(prices, currency)* stable; *St Exch (market)* ferme

buoyantly ['bɔɪəntlɪ] *adv (walk)* d'un pas allègre; *(float, rise)* légèrement; *(speak)* avec allant, avec entrain

BUPA ['buːpə] *n* (*abbr* **British United Provident Association**) = association d'assurance-maladie privée

buppie ['bʌpɪ] *n Am Fam* = yuppie de race noire

bur [bɜː(r)] **1** *n Bot* bardane *f*

2 *vt (clothing)* enlever les bardanes de

▸▸ *Bot* ***bur medick*** luzerne *f* naine

Burberry® ['bɜːbərɪ] *n Br* gabardine *f*, imperméable *m* Burberry®

burble ['bɜːbəl] **1** *vi* (**a**) *(liquid)* glouglouter, faire glouglou; *(stream)* murmurer (**b**) *Pej (person)* jacasser; **he's always burbling on about moral values** il est toujours à jacasser *ou* dégoiser sur les valeurs morales

2 *n* (**a**) *(of a liquid)* glouglou *m*; *(of a stream)* murmure *m* (**b**) *Pej (chatter)* jacasserie *f*, jacassement *m*

burbling ['bɜːblɪŋ] *adj* (**a**) *(liquid)* glougloutant; *(stream)* murmurant (**b**) *Pej (person)* qui jacasse, bavard

burbot ['bɜːbət] *n Ich* lotte *f*

burbs [bɜːbz] *npl Am Fam* **the burbs** la banlieue❑; **they live in the burbs** ils habitent en banlieue

burden ['bɜːdən] **1** *n* (**a**) *Formal (heavy weight, load)* fardeau *m*, charge *f*

(**b**) *Fig (heavy responsibility, strain)* fardeau *m*, charge *f*; **to be a burden to sb** être un fardeau pour qn; **his guilt was a heavy burden to bear** sa culpabilité était un lourd fardeau; **to increase/to relieve the tax burden** augmenter/alléger le fardeau *ou* le poids des impôts; *Law* **the burden of proof** la charge de la preuve; *Law* **the burden of proof rests with him** c'est à lui qu'il incombe d'apporter des preuves

(**c**) *Naut* tonnage *m*, jauge *f*; **a ship of 500 tons burden** un navire qui jauge 500 tonneaux

(**d**) *Br Mus (chorus, refrain)* refrain *m*; *Fig (theme, central idea)* fond *m*, substance *f*; **what is the main burden of her argument?** quel est le point essentiel de son argument?

2 *vt* (**a**) *(weigh down)* charger; **to be burdened with sth** être chargé de qch; *Fig* **to burden sb with taxes** accabler qn d'impôts

(**b**) *(trouble)* ennuyer, importuner; **I don't want to burden you with my problems** je ne veux pas vous ennuyer avec mes problèmes; **she was burdened with guilt** elle était rongée par un sentiment de culpabilité

burdensome ['bɜːdənsəm] *adj Formal (load)* pesant; *Fin (taxes)* lourd

burdock ['bɜːdɒk] *n Bot* bardane *f*

bureau ['bjʊərəʊ] (*pl* **bureaus** *or* **bureaux** [-rəʊz]) *n* (**a**) *Admin* service *m*, office *m*; *Com (in private enterprise)* bureau *m* (**b**) *Br (desk)* secrétaire *m*, bureau *m* (**c**) *Am (chest of drawers)* commode *f*

▸▸ ***bureau de change*** bureau *m* de change; ***Bureau of Indian Affairs*** = services fédéraux américains des affaires indiennes

bureaucracy [bjʊə'rɒkrəsɪ] (*pl* **bureaucracies**) *n* bureaucratie *f*

bureaucrat ['bjʊərəkræt] *n* bureaucrate *mf*

bureaucratic [ˌbjʊərə'krætɪk] *adj* bureaucratique

bureaucratically [ˌbjʊərə'krætɪkəlɪ] *adv* bureaucratiquement

bureaucratization [bjʊəˌrɒkrətaɪ'zeɪʃən] *n* bureaucratisation *f*

bureaucratize, -ise [bjʊə'rɒkrətaɪz] *vt* bureaucratiser

burette, *Am* **buret** [bjʊ'ret] *n* éprouvette *f* graduée, burette *f*

burg [bɜːg] *n Am Fam (village)* bled *m*; *(town)* ville❑ *f*; **there's nothing happening in this burg** il ne se passe rien dans ce coin *ou* bled

burgee ['bɜːdʒiː] *n Naut* cornette *m (drapeau)*

burgeon ['bɜːdʒən] *vi* bourgeonner; *(leaf, flower)* éclore

burgeoning ['bɜːdʒənɪŋ] *adj (industry, population)* en expansion, en plein essor; **a burgeoning talent** un talent en herbe; **the burgeoning movement for independence** le mouvement naissant pour l'indépendance

burger ['bɜːgə(r)] *n* hamburger *m*
▸▸ ***burger bar*** fast-food *m (où l'on sert des hamburgers)*

burgess ['bɜːdʒɪs] *n Hist (elected representative)* député *m*, représentant *m*; *(citizen)* bourgeois(e) *m,f*

burgh ['bʌrə] *n Scot Formerly* = jusqu'en 1975, ville jouissant d'un certain degré d'autonomie administrative

burgher ['bɜːgə(r)] *n Hist* bourgeois(e) *m,f*

burglar ['bɜːglə(r)] *n* cambrioleur(euse) *m,f*
▸▸ ***burglar alarm*** alarme *f* antivol

burglarize ['bɜːgləraɪz] *vt Am* cambrioler

burglarproof ['bɜːgləpruːf] *adj (safe)* inviolable; *(lock)* incrochetable; *(alarm system)* antieffraction; *(house)* à l'épreuve des cambrioleurs

burglary ['bɜːglərɪ] (*pl* **burglaries**) *n* cambriolage *m*

burgle ['bɜːgəl] *vt* cambrioler

burgomaster ['bɜːgəʊmɑːstə(r)] *n Admin* bourgmestre *m*, maire *m*

Burgundian [bɜː'gʌndɪən] **1** *n* Bourguignon(onne) *m,f*
2 *adj* bourguignon

Burgundy ['bɜːgəndɪ] **1** *n* (**a**) *(region)* Bourgogne *f*; **in Burgundy** en Bourgogne (**b**) *(wine)* bourgogne *m*
2 burgundy 1 *n (colour)* bordeaux *m* **2** *adj (colour)* bordeaux

burial ['berɪəl] **1** *n* enterrement *m*, inhumation *f*; **a Christian burial** une sépulture ecclésiastique; **he was denied a Christian burial** il n'a même pas en droit à un enterrement convenable
2 *comp (place, service)* d'inhumation
▸▸ ***burial chamber*** caveau *m*; ***burial ground*** cimetière *m*; ***burial mound*** tumulus *m*; ***burial place*** (lieu *m* de) sépulture *f*

burin ['bjʊərɪn] *n Tech* burin *m*

burk = **berk**

Burke's Peerage [bɜːks-] *n* = annuaire de l'aristocratie britannique

Burkina-Faso [bɜːˌkiːnə'fæsəʊ] *n* Burkina *m*; **in Burkina-Faso** au Burkina

burl [bɜːl] *n Austr Fam (attempt)* essai ❑ *m*; **give it a burl!** essaye!

burlap ['bɜːlæp] *n Tex* toile *f* à sac, gros canevas *m*

burlesque [bɜː'lesk] **1** *n* (**a**) *Literature & Theat* burlesque *m*, parodie *f* (**b**) *Am (bawdy comedy)* revue *f* déshabillée, striptease *m*
2 *adj* burlesque
3 *vt* parodier

burliness ['bɜːlɪnɪs] *n (of person)* forte carrure *f*

burly ['bɜːlɪ] (*compar* **burlier**, *superl* **burliest**) *adj* de forte carrure

Burma ['bɜːmə] *n Formerly* la Birmanie

Burmese [ˌbɜː'miːz] (*pl* **inv**) **1** *n* (**a**) *(person)* Birman(e) *m,f* (**b**) *(language)* birman *m*
2 *adj* birman
3 *comp (embassy)* de Birmanie; *(history)* de la Birmanie; *(teacher)* de birman
▸▸ ***Burmese cat*** burmese *m*, chat *f* birman

BURN [bɜːn]

brûlure	▸ **1 (a)**
combustion	▸ **1 (b)**
brûler	▸ **2 (a), (b); 3 (a)**
filer	▸ **2 (c)**
exploser	▸ **2 (d)**

(*Br pt & pp* **burned** *or* **burnt** [bɜːnt], *Am pt & pp* **burned**) **1** *n* (**a**) *(injury)* brûlure *f*
(**b**) *Tech (in engine)* (durée *f* de) combustion *f*
(**c**) *Fam* **to go for the burn** *(when exercising)* forcer jusqu'à ce que ça fasse mal ❑
(**d**) *Scot (brook)* ruisseau *m*
2 *vi* (**a**) *(gen)* brûler; **there was a lovely fire burning in the sitting-room** un beau feu brûlait *ou* flambait au salon; **I can't get the wood to burn** je n'arrive pas à faire brûler *ou* flamber le bois; **the toast is burning** le pain grillé est en train de brûler; **she could see a cigarette burning in the dark** elle pouvait voir une cigarette qui brûlait *ou* se consumait dans l'obscurité; **this material won't burn** ce tissu est ininflammable; **the church burned to the ground** l'église a été réduite en cendres; **a light was burning in the study** une lumière brûlait dans le bureau
(**b**) *Fig (face, person)* **my face was burning** *(with embarrassment)* j'avais le visage en feu, j'étais tout rouge; **the wind made her face burn** le vent lui brûlait le visage; **I'm burning** *(from sun)* je brûle; *(from fever)* je suis brûlant, je brûle; **she was burning with anger/impatience** elle bouillait de colère/d'impatience; **she was burning for adventure** elle brûlait du désir d'aventure
(**c**) *Fam (travel at speed)* filer, foncer; **we burned down the motorway** nous foncions *ou* nous filions sur l'autoroute
(**d**) *Tech (mixture in engine)* exploser
3 *vt* (**a**) *(paper, logs, food)* brûler; *(car, crop, forest)* brûler, incendier; **to burn coal/oil/gas** *(boiler)* marcher au charbon/au mazout/au gaz; **three people were burnt to death** trois personnes sont mortes carbonisées *ou* ont été brûlées vives; **to be burnt alive** être brûlé vif; **suspected witches were burnt at the stake** les femmes soupçonnées de sorcellerie étaient brûlées vives; **his cigarette burnt a hole in the carpet** sa cigarette a fait un trou dans la moquette; **did you burn yourself?** est-ce que tu t'es brûlé?; **I burnt my mouth drinking hot tea** je me suis brûlé (la langue) en buvant du thé chaud; **I've burnt the potatoes** j'ai laissé brûler les pommes de terre; **the house was burnt to the ground** la maison fut réduite en cendres *ou* brûla entièrement; *Fig* **to burn one's boats** *or* **bridges** brûler ses vaisseaux *ou* les ponts; *Fig* **to burn one's fingers, to get one's fingers burnt** se brûler les doigts; *Fig* **to have money to burn** avoir de l'argent à ne pas savoir qu'en faire; **money burns a hole in his pocket** l'argent lui file entre les doigts
(**b**) *Comput (CD)* graver
(**c**) *Am Fam (swindle)* arnaquer
(**d**) *Am Fam (anger)* foutre en rogne

▸**burn away 1** *vi* (**a**) *(continue burning)* **the bonfire burned away for several hours** le feu a brûlé pendant plusieurs heures (**b**) *(be destroyed by fire)* se consumer
2 *vt sep (gen)* brûler; *(paint)* brûler, décaper au chalumeau

▸**burn down 1** *vi* (**a**) *(be destroyed by fire)* brûler complètement; **the building burned down** le bâtiment fut complètement détruit par le feu *ou* brûla complètement
(**b**) *(die down)* **the fire in the stove has burned down** le feu dans le poêle est presque éteint; *(grow smaller)* diminuer, baisser; **the candle has burned down** la bougie a diminué
2 *vt sep (building)* détruire par le feu, incendier

▸**burn off** *vt sep* (**a**) *(vegetation)* brûler, détruire par le feu; *(gas)* brûler; *(paint)* décaper au chalumeau (**b**) *(calories)* brûler; **to burn off some energy** se dépenser

▸**burn out 1** *vt sep* (**a**) *(destroy by fire → building)* détruire par le feu
(**b**) *(wear out → bulb)* griller; *(→ fuse)* faire sauter; *(→ engine)* griller; *Fig* **to burn oneself out** s'épuiser
(**c**) *(die down)* diminuer, éteindre; **after twelve hours the forest fire burnt itself out** au bout de douze heures l'incendie de forêt s'est éteint
2 *vi (bulb)* griller; *(fuse)* sauter; *(brakes, engine)* griller; *(candle, fire)* s'éteindre

▸**burn up 1** *vt sep* (**a**) *(destroy by fire)* brûler
(**b**) *Fig (person → consume)* brûler, dévorer; **the desire for revenge was burning him up** il était dévoré par le désir de se venger
(**c**) *(consume)* **this car burns up a lot of petrol** cette voiture consomme beaucoup d'essence; *Physiol* **to burn up a lot of calories/energy** dépenser *ou* brûler beaucoup de calories/d'énergie; *Aut* **to burn up the miles** aller à toute vitesse, foncer
(**d**) *Am Fam (make angry)* **it really burns me up to see you like this** ça me rend dingue de te voir comme ça
2 *vi* (**a**) *(fire)* flamber
(**b**) *Aviat* se consumer, se désintégrer

burn-beat *vt Agr* écobuer

burn-beating *n Agr* écobuage *m*

burned-out ['bɜːnd-] *adj* = **burnt-out**

burner ['bɜːnə(r)] *n* (**a**) *(on a stove)* brûleur *m*; *(on a lamp)* bec *m* (**b**) *(for essential oils)* brûle-parfums *m* (**c**) *Comput* graveur *m*

burnet ['bɜːnɪt] *n Bot* sanguisorbe *f*
▸▸ *Entom* ***burnet moth*** sphinx *m* bélier

burn-in *n Comput (of machine)* rodage *m*

burning ['bɜːnɪŋ] **1** *adj* (**a**) *(on fire)* en flammes, en feu; *(arrow, torch)* enflammé; *Bible* **the burning bush** le buisson ardent
(**b**) *(hot)* ardent, brûlant; **I have a burning sensation in my stomach** j'ai des brûlures d'estomac
(**c**) *Fig (intense)* ardent, brûlant; **he had a burning desire to be a writer** il désirait ardemment être écrivain; **a burning thirst** une soif brûlante; **she has a burning interest in opera** elle s'intéresse vivement à *ou* se passionne pour l'opéra
(**d**) *(crucial, vital)* brûlant; **a burning issue** une question brûlante
2 *adv* **burning hot coals** des charbons; **her forehead is burning hot** elle a le front brûlant
3 *n* (**a**) *(sensation, smell)* **a smell of burning** une odeur de brûlé; **can anyone smell burning?** ça sent le brûlé ou quoi?; **he felt a burning in his chest** il sentit une brûlure à la poitrine
(**b**) *(destruction by fire)* **he witnessed the burning of hundreds of books** il a été témoin de l'autodafé de centaines de livres
(**c**) *Hist* **burning (at the stake)** supplice *m* du bûcher
(**d**) *Metal (overheating)* brûlure *f*

burnish ['bɜːnɪʃ] **1** *vt* (**a**) *Metal* brunir, polir (**b**) *Literary* lustrer
2 *n* (**a**) *Metal* brunissure *f* (**b**) *Literary (shine)* brillant *m*, lustre *m*

burnished ['bɜːnɪʃt] *adj* (**a**) *Metal* bruni, poli (**b**) *Literary (bright, shiny)* lustré; **her hair was like burnished gold** elle avait les cheveux d'un or cuivré

burnisher ['bɜːnɪʃə(r)] *n Metal* (**a**) *(person)* brunisseur(euse) *m,f* (**b**) *(instrument)* brunissoir *m*, polissoir *m*

burnishing ['bɜːnɪʃɪŋ] *n Metal* brunissage *m*, polissage *m*

burnous, burnouse [bɜː'nuːs] *n* burnous *m*

burnout ['bɜːnaʊt] *n* (**a**) *Astron* = arrêt par suite d'épuisement du combustible (**b**) *Elec* **what caused the burnout?** qu'est-ce qui a fait griller les circuits? (**c**) *(exhaustion)* épuisement *m* total

Burns' Night [bɜːnz-] *n* = fête célébrée en l'honneur du poète écossais Robert Burns, le 25 janvier

BURNS' NIGHT

Cette fête est célébrée par les Écossais en Écosse et à l'étranger. Les gens se réunissent en famille ou entre amis, prononcent des discours en l'honneur du poète, et mangent des plats arrosés de whisky. Le haggis, plat écossais par excellence, est servi au son de la cornemuse.

burnt [bɜːnt] **1** *pt & pp of* **burn**
2 *adj* (**a**) *(charred)* brûlé, carbonisé (**b**) *(dark)* **burnt orange/red** orange/rouge foncé
▸▸ ***burnt offering*** *Rel (sacrifice)* holocauste *m*; *Hum (food)* plat *m* calciné *ou* carbonisé

burnt-out *adj* (**a**) *(destroyed by fire)* incendié, brûlé (**b**) *Fam (person)* lessivé, vidé; **she was burnt-out by thirty** elle était usée avant (l'âge de) trente ans (**c**) *Tech (bearings)* grippé; *Elec (coil, light bulb)* grillé

burn-up *n Fam (car race)* course *f* de vitesse ❑

burp [bɜːp] *Fam* **1** *n* rot *m*; **"cheers", he said with a burp** "à ta santé", dit-il en rotant
2 *vi* roter
3 *vt* **to burp a baby** faire faire son rot à un bébé
▸▸ *Am* ***burp gun*** sulfateuse *f (mitraillette)*

burr [bɜː(r)] **1** *n* (**a**) *Metal (rough edge)* barbe *f*, bavure *f*
(**b**) *Tech (tool)* fraise *f*
(**c**) *Bot (on tree trunk)* broussin *m*; *(seed-case)* bardane *f*
(**d**) *Ling (West Country accent)* grasseyement

m; **he speaks with a soft burr** il a un léger accent du terroir

(**e**) *(noise)* ronflement *m*, vrombissement *m*

2 *vt* (**a**) *Metal (file)* ébarber, ébavurer

(**b**) *(clothing)* enlever les bardanes de

3 *vi* (**a**) *Ling (in pronunciation)* grasseyer

(**b**) *(make a noise)* ronfler, vrombir

►► ***burr walnut*** ronce *f* de noyer

Burrell Collection [ˈbʌrəl-] *n* **the Burrell Collection** = musée des beaux-arts à Glasgow où sont réunies les collections d'un grand industriel local

burrito [bəˈriːtəʊ] *n Culin* burrito *m (tortilla fourrée)*

burro [ˈbʊrəʊ] *n Am* baudet *m*

burrow [ˈbʌrəʊ] **1** *n* terrier *m*

2 *vt* (**a**) *(of person)* creuser; *(of animal, insect)* creuser, fouir; **he burrowed his way underneath the prison wall** il a creusé un tunnel sous le mur de la prison

(**b**) *Fig (nestle)* enfouir; **the cat burrowed its head into my shoulder** le chat a blotti sa tête contre mon épaule

3 *vi* (**a**) *(dig)* creuser; **they found earthworms burrowing through the soil** ils ont trouvé des vers de terre qui creusaient des galeries dans le sol

(**b**) *(search)* fouiller; **I've been burrowing through the files for clues** j'ai cherché ou fouillé dans les dossiers pour trouver des indices

(**c**) *(nestle)* s'enfouir, s'enfoncer; **she burrowed under the sheets** elle s'est enfouie sous les draps

burrowing [ˈbʌrəʊɪŋ] *adj (animal)* fouisseur; *(insect)* fossoyeur, mineur

bursar [ˈbɜːsə(r)] *n* (**a**) *Br Fin (treasurer)* intendant(e) *m,f*, économe *mf* (**b**) *Scot Univ (student)* boursier(ère) *m,f*

bursarship [ˈbɜːsəʃɪp] *n* (**a**) *Br Fin (treasury)* intendance *f*, économat *m* (**b**) *Univ (grant, scholarship)* bourse *f* (d'études)

bursary [ˈbɜːsərɪ] (*pl* **bursaries**) *n* (**a**) *Br Fin (treasury)* intendance *f*, économat *m* (**b**) *Univ (grant, scholarship)* bourse *f* (d'études)

bursitis [bɜːˈsaɪtɪs] *n Med* bursite *f*; **I have bursitis in my shoulder** j'ai une bursite à l'épaule

BURST [bɜːst]

éclatement	► **1 (a)**
éclat	► **1 (b)**
jaillissement	► **1 (b)**
éclater	► **2 (a)**
crever	► **2 (a); 3**
faire éclater	► **3**

(*pt & pp* **burst**) **1** *n* (**a**) *(explosion)* éclatement *m*, explosion *f*; *(puncture)* éclatement *m*, crevaison *f*

(**b**) *(sudden eruption → of laughter)* éclat *m*; *(→ of emotion)* accès *m*, explosion *f*; *(→ of ideas)* jaillissement *m*; *(→ of thunder)* coup *m*; *(→ of flame)* jet *m*, jaillissement *m*; *(→ of applause)* salve *f*; *Mil* **a burst of gunfire** une rafale; **he had a sudden burst of energy** il a eu un sursaut d'énergie; **to put on** *or* **to have a sudden burst of speed** faire une pointe de vitesse, accélérer soudainement; **we heard a burst of music** on entendit quelques mesures; **a burst of activity** une poussée d'activité; **to work in bursts** travailler par à-coups

2 *vi* (**a**) *(break, explode → balloon, paper bag)* éclater; *Med (→ abscess, bubble)* crever; *Aut (→ tyre)* crever, éclater; *(→ bottle)* éclater, voler en éclats; *(→ dam)* éclater, céder; **to be bursting with pride** crever d'orgueil; **to be bursting with health** déborder de santé; **to be bursting with impatience** bouillir d'impatience; **I was bursting to tell him** je mourais d'envie de le lui dire; *Fig* **his heart felt as if it would burst with joy/grief** il crut que son cœur allait éclater de joie/se briser de chagrin; *Fam* **to be bursting (for the toilet)** avoir terriblement envie d'aller aux toilettes ☐; *Hum* **I'll burst if I eat any more** je vais éclater si je mange une bouchée de plus

(**b**) *(enter, move suddenly)* **two policemen burst into the house** deux policiers ont fait irruption dans la maison; **she burst through the door** elle est entrée brusquement; **the front door burst open** la porte d'entrée s'est ouverte brusquement; **the sun suddenly burst through the clouds** le soleil perça *ou* apparut soudain à travers les nuages

3 *vt (balloon, bubble)* crever, faire éclater; *(pipe)* faire éclater; *(boiler)* faire éclater, faire sauter; *Aut (tyre)* crever, faire éclater; *Med (abscess)* crever, percer; **the river is about to burst its banks** le fleuve est sur le point de déborder; **we've got a burst pipe** *(in house)* nous avons un tuyau qui a éclaté; **to burst a blood vessel** se faire éclater une veine, se rompre un vaisseau sanguin; *Br Fam Hum* **don't burst a blood vessel to get it done** ce n'est pas la peine de te crever pour finir, ce n'est pas la peine de te tuer à la tâche

►**burst forth** *vi Literary (liquid)* jaillir; *(person)* sortir précipitamment, apparaître; **the children burst forth into the playground** les enfants se précipitèrent dans la cour de récréation; **he burst forth with a song** il se mit à chanter

►**burst in** *vi (enter violently)* faire irruption; *(interrupt conversation)* interrompre brutalement la discussion; *(intrude)* entrer précipitamment; **it was very rude of you to burst in on** *or* **upon us like that** c'était très mal élevé de ta part de faire irruption chez nous comme ça

►**burst into** *vt insep (begin suddenly)* **to burst into laughter** éclater de rire; **to burst into tears** éclater en sanglots, fondre en larmes; **to burst into song** se mettre à chanter; **to burst into flames** prendre feu, s'enflammer

►**burst open 1** *vt sep (door → open suddenly)* ouvrir brusquement; *(smash open)* enfoncer, briser; *(cover, lock)* faire sauter

2 *vi (of door)* s'ouvrir brusquement

►**burst out 1** *vi (leave suddenly)* sortir précipitamment; **two men suddenly burst out of the room** deux hommes sortirent en trombe de la pièce

2 *vt insep (exclaim)* s'exclamer, s'écrier; **to burst out laughing** éclater de rire; **to burst out crying** fondre en larmes; **they all burst out singing** ils se sont tous mis à chanter d'un coup; **"I love you", he burst out** "je t'aime", lança-t-il

bursting [ˈbɜːstɪŋ] **1** *adj* (**a**) *(full)* plein à craquer; **to be bursting at the seams** se défaire aux coutures, se découdre; *Fig* **the place was bursting at the seams (with people)** l'endroit était plein à craquer; **to be bursting with joy/pride** déborder de joie/d'orgueil; **to be bursting with health** péter la santé

(**b**) *(longing, yearning)* **to be bursting to do sth** mourir d'envie de faire qch; **they were bursting to tell us the news** ils mouraient d'envie de nous apprendre la nouvelle

2 to bursting *adv* **to be full to bursting** être plein à craquer

burton [ˈbɜːtən] *n Br Fam Old-fashioned* **to be gone for a burton** *(broken)* être fichu; *(lost)* avoir disparu ☐; *(dead)* avoir cassé sa pipe; *(fallen)* avoir ramassé une bûche

Burundi [bʊˈrʊndɪ] *n* Burundi *m*; **in Burundi** au Burundi

Burundian [bʊˈrʊndɪən] **1** *n* Burundais(e) *m,f*

2 *adj* burundais

3 *comp (embassy, history)* du Burundi

bury [ˈberɪ] (*pt & pp* **buried**) *vt* (**a**) *(in the ground)* enterrer, *Formal* inhumer; *(in water)* immerger; **to be buried alive** être enterré vivant; **he was buried at sea** son corps a été immergé en haute mer; **buried treasure** trésor *m* enterré *ou* enfoui; *Fig* **she's buried two husbands already** elle a déjà enterré deux maris; **we agreed to bury our differences** nous avons convenu d'oublier *ou* d'enterrer nos différends; *Fig* **to bury the hatchet** enterrer la hache de guerre, faire la paix

(**b**) *(of snow, landslide → town, house)* ensevelir; **she buried her feet in the sand** elle a enfoncé ses pieds dans le sable; *Fig* **to bury one's head in the sand** faire l'autruche

(**c**) *(hide)* **where have you buried my newspaper?** où as-tu fourré mon journal?; **she buried her face in the pillow** elle enfouit *ou* enfonça son visage dans l'oreiller; **to bury one's face in one's hands** enfouir son visage dans ses mains; **he always has his nose buried in a book** il a toujours le nez fourré dans un livre; *Fig* **to bury oneself in the country** s'enterrer à la campagne; **long-buried memories began to surface** des souvenirs oubliés depuis longtemps commencèrent à refaire surface; **it's buried in a drawer somewhere** c'est enfoui dans un tiroir quelque part

(**d**) *(occupy)* **to bury oneself in (one's) work** se plonger dans son travail

(**e**) *(thrust, plunge → knife)* enfoncer, plonger; **he buried his hands in his pockets** il a fourré les mains dans ses poches

(**f**) *Fam (defeat)* écraser

►**bury away** *vt sep* cacher, enfouir; **the information was buried away in the small print** l'information était perdue dans la foule des détails

burying [ˈberɪɪŋ] *adj* **a burying place** un cimetière

bus [bʌs] (*pl* **buses** *or* **busses**, *pt & pp* **bused** *or* **bussed**, *cont* **busing** *or* **bussing**) **1** *n* (**a**) *(vehicle)* bus *m*, autobus *m*; *Am (coach)* car *m*; **by bus** en bus

(**b**) *Br Fam (old car)* (vieille) bagnole *f*, guimbarde *f*

(**c**) *Comput* bus *m*

2 *comp (service, strike, ticket)* d'autobus, de bus

3 *vi* **we can walk or bus home** nous pouvons rentrer à pied ou en autobus

4 *vt* (**a**) *(transport)* emmener en autobus; **the children are bussed to school** les enfants vont à l'école en autobus

(**b**) *Am Sch (for purposes of racial integration)* **to bus children** = conduire les enfants à l'école en autobus de façon à organiser la répartition des enfants noirs et des enfants blancs afin de lutter contre la ségrégation raciale

(**c**) *(in restaurant)* **to bus tables** travailler comme aide-serveur; **he busses tables at the weekends** il travaille comme aide-serveur le week-end

►► *Mktg* ***bus advertising*** publicité *f* sur les autobus; *Comput* ***bus board*** carte *f* bus; *Br* ***bus conductor*** receveur(euse) *m,f* d'autobus; *Br* ***bus conductress*** receveuse *f* d'autobus; *Comput* ***bus controller*** contrôleur *m* de bus; ***bus depot*** dépôt *m* d'autobus; *(long-distance bus station)* gare *f* routière; ***bus driver*** conducteur(trice) *m,f* d'autobus; ***bus lane*** voie *f* ou couloir *m* d'autobus; *Mktg* ***bus mailing*** publipostage *m* groupé, multipostage *m*; ***bus route*** itinéraire *m* *ou* trajet *m* d'autobus; **are you on a bus route?** est-ce qu'il y a un bus qui passe près de chez toi?; ***bus shelter*** Abribus® *m*; ***bus station*** gare *f* routière; ***bus stop*** arrêt *m* d'autobus *ou* de bus; ***bus way*** voie *f* ou couloir *m* d'autobus

►**bus in** *vt sep* faire venir en car

►**bus out** *vt sep* évacuer en car

busbar [ˈbʌsbɑː(r)] *n Comput & Elec* bus *m*

busboy [ˈbʌsbɔɪ] *n Am* aide-serveur *m*

busby [ˈbʌzbɪ] (*pl* **busbies**) *n Br Mil* bonnet *m* de hussard

bush [bʊʃ] **1** *n* (**a**) *(shrub)* buisson *m*, arbuste *m*; **the children hid in the bushes** les enfants se cachèrent dans les fourrés; *Fig* **a bush of black hair** une tignasse de cheveux noirs

(**b**) *Geog (in Africa, Australia)* **the bush** la brousse

(**c**) *Aut & Tech* bague *f*; *(between bearing and shaft)* coussinet *m*

(**d**) *Vulg (woman's pubic hair)* barbu *m*

(**e**) *Fam Drugs slang (marijuana)* herbe *f*

2 *adv Austr* **to go bush** aller dans la brousse

►► ***Bush House*** = siège de la BBC à Londres d'où sont retransmises vers l'étranger les émissions du BBC World Service; ***bush jacket*** saharienne *f*; *Am Sport* ***bush league*** = petite équipe locale de baseball; ***bush taxi*** taxi-brousse *m*; ***bush telegraph*** téléphone *m* de brousse; *Br Fig Hum (grapevine)* téléphone *m* arabe

bushbaby [ˈbʊʃˌbeɪbɪ] *n Zool* galago *m*

bushbuck [ˈbʊʃbʌk] *n Zool* guib *m*

bushed [bʊʃt] *adj Fam* (**a**) *(exhausted)* crevé, claqué (**b**) *Austr (lost)* perdu *ou* égaré dans la brousse ☐; *Fig (bewildered)* désorienté ☐

bushel [ˈbʊʃəl] (*pt & pp* **busheled**, *cont* **busheling**) **1** *n (measure)* boisseau *m*

2 *vt Am (mend)* recoudre; *(alter)* retoucher

bushfire ['bʊʃ,faɪə(r)] *n* feu *m* de brousse

bushiness ['bʊʃɪnɪs] *n* épaisseur *f*

bushing ['bʊʃɪŋ] *n (UNCOUNT) Tech* bague *f*

bush-league *adj Pej* médiocre

Bushman ['bʊʃmən] *(pl* **inv** *or* **Bushmen** [-mən]) *n (in southern Africa)* Bochiman *m*

bushman ['bʊʃmən] *(pl* **bushmen** [-mən]) *n Austr & NZ* broussard *m*

bushpig ['bʊʃpɪg] *n Zool* potamochère *m*

bushranger ['bʊʃ,reɪndʒə(r)] *n Austr & NZ* (**a**) *Hist (rustler)* voleur *m* de bétail (**b**) *(backwoodsman)* broussard(e) *m,f*

bushwalking ['bʊʃ,wɔːkɪŋ] *n Austr* randonnée *f* dans la brousse; **to go bushwalking** aller marcher dans la brousse

bushwhack ['bʊʃ,wæk] **1** *vi* (**a**) *(clear a path)* se frayer un passage à travers la brousse (**b**) *(live in the bush)* vivre dans la brousse

2 *vt Am Mil (ambush)* tendre une embuscade à

bushwhacker ['bʊʃ,wækə(r)] *n* (**a**) *Am & Austr (backwoodsman)* broussard(e) *m,f* (**b**) *Am Mil (guerrilla)* guérillero *m*

bushwhacking ['bʊʃ,wækɪŋ] *n* (**a**) *(clearing paths)* = défrichement dans le but d'aménager des sentiers (**b**) *(life in the bush)* la vie dans la brousse (**c**) *Am Mil (ambushing)* guerre *f* d'embuscades

bushy ['bʊʃɪ] *(compar* **bushier,** *superl* **bushiest**) *adj* (**a**) *(area)* broussailleux (**b**) *(tree)* touffu; *(beard, eyebrows, hair)* touffu, fourni

busily ['bɪzɪlɪ] *adv* activement; **to be busily engaged in sth/in doing sth** être très occupé à qch/à faire qch; **she is busily collecting material for her next book** elle est très occupée à rassembler des matériaux pour son prochain livre; **he was busily scribbling in his notebook** il griffonnait sur son calepin d'un air affairé

business ['bɪznɪs] **1** *n* (**a**) *Com (company, firm)* affaire *f*, entreprise *f*; **there has been an increase in the number of small businesses throughout the country** il y a eu une augmentation du nombre des petites entreprises à travers le pays; **he's got a mail-order business** il a une affaire *ou* entreprise de vente par correspondance; **would you like to have** *or* **to run your own business?** aimeriez-vous travailler à votre compte?; **business for sale** *(on sign, in advertisement)* commerce à vendre

(**b**) *(UNCOUNT) Com & Ind (trade)* affaires *fpl*; *(commerce)* commerce *m*; **business is good/bad** les affaires vont bien/mal; **business is slow** les affaires ne vont pas; **how's business?** comment vont les affaires?; **business as usual** *(sign)* ouvert; **hours of business** *(sign)* heures d'ouverture; **to go to London on business** aller à Londres pour affaires; **a profitable piece of business** une affaire rentable *ou* qui rapporte; **we have lost business to foreign competitors** nous avons perdu une partie de notre clientèle au profit de concurrents étrangers; **we can help you to increase your business** nous pouvons vous aider à augmenter votre chiffre d'affaires; **the travel business** les métiers *ou* le secteur du tourisme; **she's in the fashion business** elle est dans la mode; **my business is pharmaceuticals** je travaille dans l'industrie pharmaceutique; **she knows her business** elle connaît son métier; **he's in business** il est dans les affaires; **this firm has been in business for 25 years** cette entreprise tourne depuis 25 ans; **she's in business for herself** elle travaille à son compte; **to set up in business** ouvrir un commerce; **he wants to go into business** il veut travailler dans les affaires; **what's his line of business?, what business is he in?** qu'est-ce qu'il fait (comme métier)?; **the best in the business** le meilleur de tous; **I'm not in the business of solving your problems** ce n'est pas à moi de résoudre tes problèmes; **this shop will be open for business from tomorrow** ce magasin ouvrira demain; **these high interest rates will put us out of business** ces taux d'intérêt élevés vont nous obliger à fermer; **to go out of business** cesser une activité, faire faillite; **he's got no business sense** il n'a pas le sens des affaires; **she has a good head for business** elle a le sens des affaires; **to do business with sb** faire affaire *ou* des affaires avec qn; *Fig* **he's a man we can do business with** c'est un homme avec lequel nous pouvons traiter; **shop that does good business** commerce qui marche bien; **I've come on business** je suis venu pour le travail *ou* pour affaires; **big business is running the country** le gros commerce gouverne le pays; **selling weapons is big business** la vente d'armes rapporte beaucoup d'argent; **from now on I'll take my business elsewhere** désormais j'irai voir *ou* je m'adresserai ailleurs; **they've put a lot of business our way** ils nous ont donné beaucoup de travail; **it's bad business to refuse credit** c'est mauvais en affaires de refuser le crédit; **we're not in the business of providing free meals** ce n'est pas notre rôle de fournir des repas gratuits; *Univ* **a degree in business, a business degree** un diplôme de gestion; **let's get down to business** passons aux choses sérieuses; **(now) we're in business!** nous voilà partis!; **to talk business** parler affaires

(**c**) *(concern)* **it's my (own) business if I decide not to go** c'est mon affaire *ou* cela ne regarde que moi si je décide de ne pas y aller; **what business is it of yours?** est-ce que cela vous regarde?; **it's none of your business** cela ne vous regarde pas; **tell him to mind his own business** dis-lui de se mêler de ses affaires; **I was just walking along, minding my own business, when...** je marchais tranquillement dans la rue quand...; **what's your business (with him)?** que (lui) voulez-vous?; **I'll make it my business to find out** je m'occuperai d'en savoir plus; **people going about their business** des gens vaquant à leurs occupations; **it's/it's not my business to...** c'est/ce n'est pas à moi de...; **you had no business reading that letter** vous n'aviez pas à lire cette lettre; **I could see she meant business** je voyais qu'elle ne plaisantait pas; **I soon sent him about his business** je l'ai vite envoyé promener; *Fam* **he drank like nobody's business** il buvait comme un trou; *Fam* **she worked like nobody's business to get it finished** elle a travaillé comme un forçat pour tout terminer; *Br Fam* **it's the business** *(excellent)* c'est impec'

(**d**) *(matter, task)* **the business of this meeting is the training budget** l'ordre du jour de cette réunion est le budget de formation; **any other business** *(on agenda)* points *mpl* divers; **any other business?** d'autres questions à l'ordre du jour?; **she had important business to discuss** elle avait à parler d'affaires importantes; **that investigation of police misconduct was a dirty business** l'enquête sur la bavure policière a été une sale affaire; **it's a bad** *or* **sad** *or* **sorry business** c'est une bien triste affaire; **this strike business has gone on long enough** cette histoire de grève a assez duré; **I'm tired of the whole business** je suis las de toute cette histoire

(**e**) *(rigmarole)* **it was a real business getting tickets for the concert** ça a été toute une affaire pour avoir des billets pour le concert

(**f**) *Theat* jeux *mpl* de scène

(**g**) *Fam Euph* **the dog did his business and ran off** le chien a fait ses besoins et a détalé

2 *comp* d'affaires

►► *Banking* ***business account*** compte *m* professionnel *ou* commercial; ***business accounting*** comptabilité *f* commerciale; ***business acumen*** sens *m* des affaires; ***business address*** adresse *f* professionnelle; ***business administration*** gestion *f* commerciale; ***business associate*** associé(e) *m,f*; ***business bank*** banque *f* d'affaires; ***business banking*** operations *fpl* des banques d'affaires; *Com* ***business card*** carte *f* de visite; ***business centre*** centre *m* des affaires; ***business class*** *(on aeroplane)* classe *f* affaires; **to travel business class** voyager en classe affaires; *Br* ***business college*** école *f* de commerce; *(for management training)* école *f* (supérieure) de gestion; ***business computing*** informatique *f* de gestion; *Journ* ***business correspondent*** correspondant(e) *m,f* financier (ère); *Fam* ***business end*** *(of knife)* partie *f* coupante ☐; *(of gun)* gueule ☐ *f*; ***Business Expansion Scheme*** ≃ plan *m* d'aide à l'investissement; ***business expenses*** *(for individual)* frais *mpl* professionnels; *(for firm)* frais *mpl* généraux; ***business failure*** défaillance *f* d'entreprise; *Comput* ***business graphics*** graphiques *mpl* de gestion; ***business hours*** *(of office)* heures *fpl* de bureau; *(of shop, public service)* heures *fpl* d'ouverture; *Comput* ***business intelligence system*** réactique *f*; *Admin* ***business letter*** lettre *f* commerciale; ***business lunch*** déjeuner *m* d'affaires; ***business manager*** *Com & Ind* directeur(trice) *m,f* commercial(e); *Sport* manager *m*; *Theat* directeur(trice) *m,f*; ***business meeting*** rendez-vous *m* d'affaires; ***business park*** zone *f* d'activités; ***business plan*** projet *m* commercial; ***business portfolio*** portefeuille *m* d'activités; ***business premises*** locaux *mpl* commerciaux; *Am* ***business reply,*** *Br* ***business reply card*** carte-réponse *f*; ***business reply envelope*** enveloppe *f* préaffranchie; ***business school*** école *f* de commerce; *Sch & Univ* ***business studies*** études *fpl* commerciales *ou* de commerce; *Am* ***business suit*** complet *m* (-veston) *m*; ***business transaction*** transaction *f* commerciale; ***business travel*** voyages *mpl* d'affaires; ***business traveller*** = personne qui voyage pour affaires; ***business trip*** voyage *m* d'affaires; **to go on a business trip** voyager pour affaires

businesslike ['bɪznɪslaɪk] *adj (professional → person, manner)* sérieux; *(systematic, methodical)* systématique, méthodique; **I was amazed at the businesslike way in which she handled the funeral arrangements** j'ai été étonné de voir avec quelle efficacité elle s'est occupée de l'enterrement; **her manner was cold and businesslike** son comportement était froid et direct; **our conversation was courteous and businesslike** notre entretien a été courtois et franc

businessman ['bɪznɪsmæn] *(pl* **businessmen** [-men]) *n* homme *m* d'affaires; **I'm not a very good businessman** je ne suis pas très doué en affaires

business-to-business *adj* intérentreprise

businesswoman ['bɪznɪs,wʊmən] *(pl* **businesswomen** [-,wɪmɪn]) *n* femme *f* d'affaires

busing = **bussing**

busk [bʌsk] *vi Br* jouer de la musique *(dans la rue ou le métro)*; **we earned money busking in the street/underground** nous avons gagné de l'argent en jouant dans la rue/le métro

busker ['bʌskə(r)] *n Br* musicien(enne) *m,f* de rue

buskin ['bʌskɪn] *n Antiq* cothurne *m*

busload ['bʌsləʊd] *n* **a busload of workers** un autobus plein d'ouvriers; **the tourists arrived by the busload** *or* **in busloads** les touristes sont arrivés par cars entiers

busman ['bʌsmən] *(pl* **busmen** [-mən]) *n Br* **to take a busman's holiday** = faire la même chose pendant ses loisirs que pendant son travail; **that's a bit of a busman's holiday** vous appelez ça des vacances!

bussing ['bʌsɪŋ] *n Am Sch* = système de ramassage scolaire aux États-Unis, qui organise la répartition des enfants noirs et des enfants blancs dans les écoles afin de lutter contre la ségrégation raciale

bust [bʌst] *(pt & pp* **busted** *or* **bust**) **1** *adj Fam* (**a**) *(broken)* fichu

(**b**) *(bankrupt)* **to go bust** faire faillite ☐

(**c**) *(broke)* **I'm bust** je suis fauché

(**d**) *(idiom)* **or bust** = expression indiquant la détermination à arriver quelque part

2 *n* (**a**) *(breasts)* poitrine *f*, buste *m*; **a large bust** une forte poitrine; **she has a small bust** elle a peu de poitrine; **what (size) bust are you?** combien est-ce que vous faites de tour de poitrine?

(**b**) *Art* buste *m*

(**c**) *Fam (by police → arrest)* arrestation ☐ *f*; *(→ raid)* descente ☐ *f*; *(→ search)* perquisition ☐ *f*; **there was a big drugs bust in Chicago** il y a eu un beau coup de filet chez les trafiquants de drogue de Chicago

(**d**) *Am Fam (failure)* fiasco *m*

3 *vt Fam* (**a**) *(break)* bousiller; *Fig* **to bust a gut** *or* **blood vessel** se casser la nénette; *Am very Fam* **to bust one's ass doing sth** se crever *ou* se casser le cul à faire qch; *Am very Fam* **I'm not going to bust my ass for him!** je ne vais pas me casser le cul pour lui!

(**b**) *Law (arrest, raid)* **he was busted on a**

drugs charge il s'est fait choper *ou* embarquer pour une affaire de drogue; **the police busted the house at 3 a.m.** la police a fait une descente dans la maison à 3 heures du matin
(**c**) *Am (tame → horse)* dresser ❑
(**d**) *Am Fam Mil slang (demote)* rétrograder ❑; **he got busted to sergeant** il est repassé sergent
(**e**) *Am (catch)* découvrir ❑; **you're busted!** je t'y prends!, je t'ai eu!
4 *vi Am* **to be busting to do sth** crever d'envie de faire qch

▸**bust out** *vi Fam (escape)* se tirer; **three prisoners have busted out (of jail)** trois prisonniers se sont fait la belle *ou* la paire

▸**bust up** *Fam* **1** *vi* (**a**) *(boyfriend, girlfriend)* rompre (après une dispute) ❑; **he's bust up with his girlfriend** il a rompu avec sa copine après une engueulade
(**b**) *Am (laugh)* éclater de rire ❑
2 *vt sep* (**a**) *(disrupt)* **demonstrators busted up the meeting** des manifestants sont venus semer la pagaïe dans la réunion
(**b**) *(damage, destroy → bar, flat)* saccager

bustard ['bʌstəd] *n Orn* outarde *f*

buster ['bʌstə(r)] *n Fam* (**a**) *Am (pal)* **thanks, buster** merci, mon pote; **now listen, buster...** écoute, mec... (**b**) *Am (tamer, breaker)* dompteur(euse) ❑ *m,f*

bustier ['bʊstɪːeɪ(r)] *n (garment)* bustier *m*

bustle ['bʌsəl] **1** *n* (**a**) *(activity)* agitation *f*; **I enjoy the hustle and bustle of working in a bank** j'aime bien travailler dans une banque à cause de tout le va-et-vient qui y règne; **the bustle of New York** l'animation des rues de New York
(**b**) *(on dress)* tournure *f*
2 *vt* **to bustle sb out of the house** faire sortir qn précipitamment
3 *vi* **he bustled about** *or* **around the kitchen** il s'affairait dans la cuisine; **the nurse came bustling in** l'infirmière entra d'un air affairé

bustling ['bʌsəlɪŋ] **1** *adj (person)* affairé; *(place)* animé; **the streets were bustling with Christmas shoppers** les rues grouillaient de gens faisant leurs achats de Noël
2 *n (activity)* agitation *f*

bust-up *n Fam* (**a**) *(quarrel)* engueulade *f*; **Craig and Claire have had another bust-up** Craig et Claire se sont encore engueulés (**b**) *(brawl)* bagarre ❑ *f*

busty ['bʌstɪ] (*compar* **bustier**, *superl* **bustiest**) *adj Fam* qui a une forte poitrine ❑; **she was a big, busty woman** c'était une femme forte, à la poitrine plantureuse ❑

busy ['bɪzɪ] (*compar* **busier**, *superl* **busiest**, *pt & pp* **busied**) **1** *adj* (**a**) *(person)* occupé; **he was too busy to notice** il était trop occupé pour s'en apercevoir; **I'm busy enough as it is!** je suis déjà assez occupé!; **she was busy painting the kitchen** elle était occupée à peindre la cuisine; **he likes to keep busy** il aime bien s'occuper; **the packing kept me busy all afternoon** j'ai été occupé à faire les valises tout l'après-midi; **I'm afraid I'm busy tomorrow** malheureusement je suis pris demain; **the bank manager is busy with a customer** le directeur de l'agence est occupé avec *ou* en rendez-vous avec un client; **you HAVE been busy!** eh bien, tu n'as pas chômé!; *Fam* **she's as busy as a bee, she's a busy bee** elle est très occupée ❑
(**b**) *(port, road, street)* très fréquenté; *(time, period, schedule)* chargé, plein; **I've had a busy day** j'ai eu une journée chargée; **he has a busy schedule** il a un emploi du temps chargé *ou* bien rempli; *Com* **this is our busiest period** c'est la période où nous sommes en pleine activité; **the office is very busy at the moment** nous avons beaucoup de travail au bureau en ce moment; **the shops are very busy today** les magasins sont pleins (de monde) aujourd'hui
(**c**) *Am (telephone line)* occupé; **I got the busy signal** ça sonnait occupé
(**d**) *Pej (excessively elaborate)* chargé
2 *vt* **he busied himself with household chores** il s'est occupé à des tâches ménagères; **she busied herself by tidying the office** elle s'est occupée en faisant le ménage dans le bureau
▸▸ *Bot* ***busy lizzie*** balsamine *f*, impatiente *f*

busybody ['bɪzɪˌbɒdɪ] (*pl* **busybodies**) *n Fam* fouineur(euse) *m,f*, fouinard(e) *m,f*; **he's an awful busybody** il se mêle des affaires de tout le monde

BUT [bʌt]

mais	▸ **1 (a) – (c), (e)**
ne... que	▸ **2 (a)**
sauf	▸ **3 (a)**
sans	▸ **5**

1 *conj* (**a**) *(to express contrast)* mais; **my husband smokes, but I don't** mon mari fume, mais moi non; **my husband doesn't smoke, but I do** mon mari ne fume pas, mais moi si; **I speak Spanish but not Italian** je parle espagnol mais pas italien; **she came home tired but happy** elle est rentrée fatiguée mais heureuse
(**b**) *(in exclamations)* mais; **but you can't do that!** mais tu ne peux pas faire ça!; **but that's absurd!** mais c'est absurde!
(**c**) *(when addressing someone politely)* **sorry, but I think that's MY umbrella** pardon, mais je crois que c'est mon parapluie; **excuse me, but there's a call for you** excusez-moi, il y a un appel pour vous
(**d**) *(used for emphasis)* **nobody, but nobody, gets in without a ticket** personne, absolument personne, n'entre sans ticket
(**e**) *(except, only)* mais; **it tastes like a grapefruit, but sweeter** ça a le goût d'un pamplemousse, mais en plus sucré; **I'll do it, but not right now** je vais le faire, mais pas tout de suite
(**f**) *Literary* **she never hears his name but she starts to weep** elle ne peut entendre son nom sans verser des larmes; **barely a day goes by but he receives another invitation** il ne se passe pas un jour sans qu'il reçoive une nouvelle invitation
2 *adv* (**a**) *(only)* ne...que; **I can but try** je ne peux qu'essayer; *Literary* **had I but known!** si j'avais su!; *Formal* **his resignation cannot but confirm such suspicions** sa démission ne fait que confirmer de tels soupçons; *Literary* **they had but recently become acquainted** ils ne se connaissaient que depuis peu (de temps); *Literary* **this life is but transitory/but a dream** cette vie n'est qu'éphémère/qu'un rêve
(**b**) *Am Fam (used for emphasis)* et ❑; **get them down here but fast!** descends-les et vite!
(**c**) *Scot Fam (in Glaswegian)* toutefois ❑; **the meal was expensive, it wasn't very nice but** le repas nous a coûté cher mais n'était pas très bon ❑
3 *prep* (**a**) *(except)* sauf, à part; **she wouldn't see anyone but her lawyer** elle ne voulait voir personne sauf *ou* à part son avocat; **who but a fool would believe his story?** il n'y a qu'un imbécile pour croire son histoire; **nobody but me knew about it** personne d'autre que moi n'était au courant; **anyone but me** tout autre que moi; **anything but that** tout plutôt que cela; **he's anything but a hero** c'est loin d'être un héros; **where but in America could you find such a gadget?** il n'y a qu'en Amérique qu'on trouve un tel gadget; **nothing but a miracle could have saved her** seul un miracle aurait pu la sauver; **he does nothing but complain** il n'arrête pas de se plaindre; **there is nothing for it but to obey** il n'y a qu'à obéir; **he is anything but happy** il n'est pas du tout heureux; **is she lazy? – anything but!** est-ce qu'elle est paresseuse? – bien au contraire!
(**b**) *Br (with numbers)* **turn right at the next corner but one** tournez à droite au deuxième carrefour; **I was the last but two to finish** j'étais l'avant-avant-dernier à finir
4 *n* **you're coming and no buts** *or* **I don't want any buts!** tu viens, et pas de mais!
5 but for *prep* sans; **but for her courage, many more people would have drowned** sans son courage, il y aurait eu beaucoup plus de noyés; **but for the rain I should have gone out** s'il n'avait pas plu je serais sorti; **he wouldn't have left but for me** *(it was my fault for being there)* il serait resté si je n'avais pas été là; *(it was for my sake)* il ne serait pas parti si ça n'avait pas été pour moi
6 but that *conj Formal* **we should have been on time, but that the train was delayed** nous aurions été à l'heure si le train n'avait pas été retardé; **I do not doubt but that we shall succeed** je ne doute pas de notre réussite
7 but then *adv* enfin; **but then, that's just the way it goes** enfin, c'est comme ça

butane ['bjuːteɪn] *n Chem* butane *m*
▸▸ ***butane gas*** gaz *m* butane, butane *m*

butch [bʊtʃ] *Fam* **1** *adj (woman)* hommasse; *(man)* macho; **a butch haircut** une coupe en brosse
2 *n (lesbian)* = lesbienne d'apparence masculine

butcher ['bʊtʃə(r)] **1** *n* (**a**) *(gen)* boucher *m*; **she's gone to the butcher's** elle est partie chez le boucher; **the butcher's wife** la bouchère; **butcher's shop** boucherie *f*; *Br* **butcher's boy** garçon *m* boucher
(**b**) *(murderer)* boucher *m*
(**c**) *Fam (surgeon, dentist)* boucher *m*, charcutier *m*
(**d**) *SEng Fam (rhyming slang* **butcher's hook = look**) **to have a butcher's (at sb/sth)** mater (qn/qch); **let's have a butcher's (at it)!** montre un peu!
2 *vt* (**a**) *(animal)* abattre, tuer
(**b**) *(person)* massacrer
(**c**) *Fam (story, joke)* massacrer
(**d**) *Fam (of surgeon, dentist → patient)* charcuter
▸▸ *Orn* ***butcher bird*** écorcheur *m*, pie-grièche *f* écorcheur; ***butcher's block*** *(for professional use)* billot *m*; *(for domestic use)* planche *f* à découper; *Bot* ***butcher's broom*** petit houx *m*, fragon *m* épineux

butcher-block *adj (kitchen, work surface)* en bois massif

butchery ['bʊtʃərɪ] *n* (**a**) *Com (profession)* boucherie *f*; *Br (slaughterhouse)* abattoir *m* (**b**) *Fig (massacre)* boucherie *f*, massacre *m*

butene ['bjuːtiːn] *n Chem* butylène *m*, butène *m*

butler ['bʌtlə(r)] *n* maître *m* d'hôtel, majordome *m*; **butler's pantry** office *f*

The butler did it
Il s'agit de la formule consacrée des romans policiers et des pièces de théâtre du début du XXème siècle dont l'action se déroule traditionnellement dans un manoir de campagne. Le majordome y est en effet le principal suspect et bien souvent l'assassin.
On utilise cette formule – que l'on peut traduire par "c'est le majordome qui a fait le coup" – pour faire allusion à ce style de récit ou bien de façon humoristique lorsqu'on essaie de deviner qui est le responsable d'une mauvaise action.

What the butler saw
A l'origine cette formule ("ce que vit le majordome") figurait sur les visionneuses à pièces installées dans les stations balnéaires anglaises et invitait le spectateur à jouer au voyeur en lui promettant des scènes osées. L'auteur dramatique Joe Orton fit de cette phrase le titre d'une de ses pièces dans les années 60.
Cette expression évoque le refoulement sexuel associé à l'époque victorienne, mais s'utilise également pour décrire une situation dans laquelle quelqu'un assiste à une scène intime à l'insu des participants ou bien a accès à des informations censées être confidentielles.

Butlin's ['bʌtlɪnz] *n* = chaîne de villages de vacances en Grande Bretagne

butt [bʌt] **1** *n* (**a**) *(end)* bout *m*; *(of rifle)* crosse *f*; *(of cigarette)* mégot *m*; **the butt end** le bout
(**b**) *esp Am Fam (buttocks)* fesses ❑ *fpl*; **why don't you get off your butt and do something?** remue-toi un peu les fesses et fais quelque chose!; **you just sit around on your butt all day!** tu ne fous rien de toute la journée!; **move your butt!** bouge-toi!
(**c**) *(in archery → target)* but *m*; *(→ mound)* butte *f*; *Mil* **the butts** le champ *ou* la butte de tir
(**d**) *(person)* **she became the butt of their teasing** elle s'est trouvée en butte à leurs taquineries; **he was the butt of all the office jokes** il était la cible de toutes les plaisanteries du bureau
(**e**) *(barrel)* tonneau *m*

2 *vt* (**a**) *(of animal)* donner un coup de corne à; *(of person)* donner un coup de tête à; **the goat butted its head against the gate** la chèvre donna un coup de corne à la barrière; *Fig* **he butted his way through the crowds** il s'est forcé un passage dans la foule
(**b**) *Tech (abut)* abouter
3 *adv Am Fam* **butt naked** à poil
►► *Tech* ***butt joint*** joint *m* abouté, soudure *f* bout à bout; ***butt welding*** soudure *f* bout à bout
►**butt in** *vi (interrupt)* **excuse me for butting in** excusez-moi de m'en mêler *ou* de vous interrompre; **she is always butting in on people's conversations** elle s'immisce toujours dans les conversations des autres
►**butt out** *vi Fam* s'occuper de ses fesses; **butt out!** occupe-toi de tes fesses!; **just butt out of my life!** laisse-moi vivre!
butte [bju:t] *n Am* butte *f*, tertre *m*
butter ['bʌtə(r)] **1** *n* beurre *m*; **she looked as if butter wouldn't melt in her mouth** on lui aurait donné le bon Dieu sans confession
2 *vt* (**a**) *(bread)* beurrer
(**b**) *Culin (potatoes, vegetables)* mettre du beurre dans
►► ***butter bean*** = sorte de haricot de Lima; *Br* ***butter biscuit,*** *Am* ***butter cookie*** galette *f* au beurre; *Culin* ***butter icing*** glaçage *m* au beurre; ***butter knife*** couteau *m* à beurre; *EU* ***butter mountain*** montagne *f* de beurre; ***butter muslin*** gaze *f* à envelopper le beurre, étamine *f*
►**butter up** *vt sep Fam* passer de la pommade à
butterball ['bʌtəbɔ:l] *n Am Fam* **he's a butterball** il est un peu grassouillet
buttercream ['bʌtə,kri:m] *n Culin* crème *f* au beurre
buttercup ['bʌtəkʌp] *n Bot* bouton *m* d'or
butterdish ['bʌtədɪʃ] *n* beurrier *m*
buttered ['bʌtəd] *adj (bread)* beurré
butterfat ['bʌtəfæt] *n* matière *f* grasse
butterfingered ['bʌtə,fɪŋgəd] *adj Fam* maladroit❑, empoté; **a butterfingered child** un enfant aux mains malhabiles❑
butterfingers ['bʌtə,fɪŋgəz] *n Fam* maladroit(e)❑ *m,f (de ses mains)*
butterfish ['bʌtəfɪʃ] *n Ich (of Pholis genus)* gon(n)elle *f*; *(of Stromateidae family)* stromatée *f*
butterfly ['bʌtəflaɪ] (*pl* **butterflies**) *n* (**a**) *Entom* papillon *m*; **she always has** *or* **gets butterflies (in her stomach) before a performance** elle a toujours le trac avant une représentation
(**b**) *Swimming* **(the) butterfly** la brasse papillon; **the 200m butterfly** le 200 mètres papillon
►► *Phys* ***butterfly effect*** effet *m* papillon; ***butterfly farm*** élevage *m* de papillons; *Ich* ***butterfly fish*** *(freshwater)* poisson *m* papillon; *Br* ***butterfly kiss*** baiser *m* de papillon *(consistant à effleurer des cils la peau de l'autre personne)*; ***butterfly museum*** = élevage de papillons en serre ouvert au public; ***butterfly net*** filet *m* à papillons; *Tech* ***butterfly nut*** papillon *m*, écrou *m* à ailettes; *Tech* ***butterfly valve*** (soupape *f* à) papillon *m*
buttermilk ['bʌtəmɪlk] *n* (**a**) *(sour liquid)* babeurre *m* (**b**) *Am (clabbered milk)* lait *m* fermenté
butterscotch ['bʌtəskɒtʃ] *n Culin* caramel *m* dur au beurre
[illegible]
butterwort ['bʌtəwɔ:t] *n Bot* grassette *f*
buttery ['bʌtərɪ] (*pl* **butteries**) **1** *adj* (**a**) *(smell, taste)* de beurre; *(fingers)* couvert de beurre; *(biscuits)* fait avec beaucoup de beurre (**b**) *Fam Fig (obsequious)* mielleux❑
2 *n Br (in college, university → storeroom)* office *m or f*; *(→ snackbar)* buffet *m*, buvette *f*; *(→ dining hall)* cantine *f*
butthead ['bʌt,hed] *n Am Fam* crétin(e) *m,f*
butting ['bʌtɪŋ] *n (by animal)* coup(s) *m(pl)* de corne; *(by person)* coup(s) *m(pl)* de tête; **he was disqualified for butting** il a été disqualifié pour avoir donné un/des coup(s) de tête
buttinski [bʌ'tɪnskɪ] *n Am Fam* fouille-merde *mf*
buttock ['bʌtək] *n* fesse *f*; **buttocks** fesses *fpl*
button ['bʌtən] **1** *n* (**a**) *(on clothing, bell, switch, sword)* bouton *m*; *Fam* **on the button** exactement❑; **$1000 on the button** très exactement 1000 dollars; **six o'clock on the button** six heures tapantes; **as bright as a button** vif, éveillé
(**b**) *Am (badge)* badge *m*
(**c**) *(sweet)* **chocolate buttons** pastilles *fpl* de chocolat
(**d**) *Comput (on mouse)* bouton *m*; *(for menu selection)* case *f*
(**e**) *Sport (in rowing)* taquet *m*
2 *vt (gen) & Fencing* boutonner; *Fam* **button it** *or* **your lip** *or* **your mouth!** ferme-la!, boucle-la!
3 *vi* se boutonner; **the blouse buttons at the back** le chemisier se boutonne par derrière *ou* dans le dos
4 buttons *n Br Old-fashioned* groom *m*, chasseur *m*
5 Buttons *pr n Theat* = ami de Cendrillon dans la pantomime 'Cinderella'
►► *Ski* ***button lift*** téléski *m*, *Fam* tire-fesses *m inv*; ***button mushroom*** champignon *m* de couche *ou* de Paris; *Orn* ***button quail*** tridactyle *m*, turnix *m*; *Bot* ***button tree*** platane *m* d'occident
►**button up 1** *vt sep* (**a**) *(piece of clothing)* boutonner (**b**) *Fam Fig (conclude)* régler❑
2 *vi* (**a**) *(piece of clothing)* se boutonner (**b**) *Fam (shut up)* **button up!** ferme-la!, boucle-la!
button-down *adj* (**a**) *(collar)* boutonné; *(shirt)* à col boutonné (**b**) *Am Fig (conventional)* **a button-down businessman** un homme d'affaires très comme il faut
buttonhole ['bʌtənhəʊl] **1** *n* (**a**) *(in clothing)* boutonnière *f*; **she gave him a carnation for his buttonhole** elle lui donna un œillet pour mettre à sa boutonnière
(**b**) *Br (flower)* **she was wearing a pink buttonhole** elle portait une fleur rose à la boutonnière
2 *vt* (**a**) *(make buttonholes in)* faire des boutonnières sur; *Sewing (sew with buttonhole stitch)* coudre au point de boutonnière
(**b**) *Fam Fig (detain → person)* retenir❑, coincer
►► *Sewing* ***buttonhole stitch*** point *m* de boutonnière
button-nosed *adj* qui a un petit nez
button-through *adj* **a button-through dress** une robe-chemisier; **a button-through skirt** une jupe boutonnée
buttonwood ['bʌtən,wʊd] *n Bot* platane *m* d'occident
buttress ['bʌtrɪs] **1** *n* (**a**) *Archit* contrefort *m* (**b**) *Geog (of mountain)* pilier *m* (**c**) *Fig (support)* pilier *m*
2 *vt* (**a**) *Archit* étayer; *(cathedral)* arc-bouter (**b**) *Fig (argument, system)* étayer, renforcer
buttressing ['bʌtrɪsɪŋ] *n Archit* étayage *m*; *(of cathedral)* arc-boutement *m*
butty ['bʌtɪ] (*pl* **butties**) *n Fam* (**a**) *Br (sandwich)* sandwich❑ *m*, casse-croûte *m* (**b**) *NEng (friend)* copain *m*
buxom ['bʌksəm] *adj (plump)* plantureux, bien en chair; *(busty)* à la poitrine plantureuse
buxomness ['bʌksəmnɪs] *n (plumpness)* ampleur *f* de formes; *(bustiness)* poitrine *f* plantureuse

BUY [baɪ] (*pt & pp* **bought** [bɔ:t]) **1** *vt* (**a**) *(purchase)* acheter; **to buy sth for sb, to buy sb sth** acheter qch à *ou* pour qn; **I'll buy it for you** je te l'achète; **can I buy you a coffee?** puis-je t'offrir un café?; **she didn't have a pen, so he bought her one** elle n'avait pas de stylo, alors il lui en a acheté un; **she bought her car from her sister** elle a racheté la voiture de sa sœur; **I'll buy it from you** je te le rachète; **they bought it for £100** ils l'ont payé 100 livres; **have you bought the plane tickets?** avez-vous pris les billets d'avion?; **you'd better buy the theatre tickets today** tu devrais prendre *ou* louer les places de théâtre aujourd'hui; **we're out of coffee – I'll go and buy some more** nous n'avons plus de café – je vais aller en racheter; **to buy sth new/second-hand/on credit** acheter qch neuf/d'occasion/à crédit; **she bought herself a pair of skis** elle s'est acheté une paire de skis; **you never buy yourself anything!** tu ne t'achètes jamais rien!; **£20 won't buy you very much these days** avec 20 livres, on ne va pas très loin de nos jours; *St Exch* **to buy earnings** investir en valeurs de croissance
(**b**) *(gain, obtain)* **to buy time** gagner du temps; **she bought their freedom with her life** elle paya leur liberté de sa vie; **a dearly bought advantage** un avantage chèrement payé; **money can't buy you love/health/happiness** l'amour/la santé/le bonheur ne s'achète pas
(**c**) *(bribe)* acheter; **I won't be bought** on ne m'achètera pas
(**d**) *Fam (believe)* **she'll never buy that story** elle ne l'avalera *ou* ne gobera jamais cette histoire; **do you think he'll buy it?** tu crois qu'il va marcher?; **OK, I'll buy that!** d'accord, je marche!
(**e**) *Fam (idioms)* **to buy it,** *Am* **to buy the farm** *(die)* passer l'arme à gauche
2 *n (purchase)* affaire *f*; **a good/bad buy** une bonne/mauvaise affaire; **this car was a great buy** cette voiture était une très bonne affaire
3 *vi* acheter; *St Exch* **to buy spot** acheter au comptant; **to buy on credit** acheter à crédit *ou* à terme; **to buy on margin** acheter à découvert
►► *St Exch* ***buy order*** ordre *m* d'achat; **to give a buy order** donner un ordre d'achat
►**buy back** *vt sep* racheter; **can I buy my bicycle back from you?** puis-je te racheter mon vélo?
►**buy in 1** *vt sep* (**a**) *Br (stockpile)* stocker, faire des provisions de; **we bought in plenty of coffee before the price increase** nous avons fait des provisions de café avant que les prix n'augmentent
(**b**) *St Exch* acheter, acquérir
(**c**) *(at auction)* racheter
2 *vi* acheter; *Fin* **to buy in against a client** exécuter un client
►**buy into** *vt insep* (**a**) *Fin* acheter une participation dans
(**b**) *(believe)* **to buy into sth** gober qch; **there's no way I'm buying into this** pas question que je marche avec ça
►**buy off** *vt sep (bribe)* acheter; **they bought off the witness for £10,000** ils ont acheté le silence du témoin pour 10000 livres
►**buy out** *vt sep* (**a**) *Fin* racheter la part de, désintéresser; **she bought out all the other shareholders** elle racheta les parts de tous les autres actionnaires; **he was bought out for £50,000** on lui a racheté sa part dans l'affaire pour 50 000 livres
(**b**) *Mil* racheter; **he bought himself out (of the army)** il a payé pour pouvoir rompre son contrat avec l'armée
►**buy over** *vt sep (bribe)* acheter
►**buy up** *vt sep* acheter en quantité; *(firm, shares, stock)* racheter; **the company bought up £50,000 worth of shares** la société racheta des actions pour une valeur de 50 000 livres

buy-back *n St Exch* rachat *m* d'actions
buyer ['baɪə(r)] *n Com* acheteur(euse) *m,f*; **I haven't found a buyer for my house** je n'ai pas trouvé d'acheteur pour ma maison; **she's a buyer at** *or* **for Harrods** elle est responsable des achats chez Harrods; **buyer beware** = principe selon lequel, lors d'une transaction, il revient à l'acquéreur de s'assurer de la qualité de l'objet acheté; **it's a case of buyer beware if you buy something from a street vendor** c'est au client de se méfier quand il achète quelque chose à un vendeur ambulant
►► *Mktg* ***buyer behaviour*** comportement *m* de l'acheteur; *Fin* ***buyer credit*** crédit acheteur *m*; *Com* ***buyers' market*** marché *m* à la baisse, marché demandeur; *(for house buyers)* marché *m* d'offre *ou* offreur; *St Exch* ***buyer's option*** prime *f* acheteur; *Mktg* ***buyer readiness*** prédisposition *f* à l'achat
buy-in *n St Exch* exécution *f*
buying ['baɪɪŋ] *n* achat *m*; *St Exch* exécution *f*; **buying and selling** l'achat et la vente
►► *Mktg* ***buying decision*** décision *f* d'achat; *Fin* ***buying power*** pouvoir *m* d'achat; *St Exch* ***buying quotation, buying rate*** *(of shares)* cours *m* d'achat
buy-out *n Com* rachat *m*
buy-sell agreement *n Com & Law* protocole *m ou* accord *m* d'achat et de vente
buzz [bʌz] **1** *n* (**a**) *(of insect)* bourdonnement *m*, vrombissement *m*; *Fig* **there was a buzz of conversation in the room** la pièce résonnait du bourdonnement des conversations; **the announcement caused a buzz of excitement**

l'annonce provoqua un murmure d'excitation
(**b**) *(of buzzer)* coup *m* de sonnette
(**c**) *Fam (telephone call)* coup *m* de fil; **to give sb a buzz** donner un coup de fil à qn
(**d**) *Fam (gossip)* **what's the buzz?** quoi de neuf?
(**e**) *(activity)* **I love the buzz of London** j'adore l'animation de Londres
(**f**) *Fam (strong sensation)* **I get quite a buzz out of being on the stage** je m'éclate vraiment quand je suis sur scène; *Am Fam* **to get a buzz on** *(take drugs)* se défoncer
2 *vi* (**a**) *(insect)* bourdonner, vrombir; *Fig* **the theatre buzzed with excitement** le théâtre était tout bourdonnant d'excitation; **the town buzzed with excitement** la ville était en effervescence; *Fam* **the party was really buzzing** la soirée était super animée
(**b**) *(ears)* bourdonner, tinter; **her head was buzzing** elle avait des bourdonnements dans la tête; **his head was buzzing with ideas** les idées bourdonnaient dans sa tête
(**c**) *(with buzzer)* **he buzzed for his secretary** il appela sa secrétaire (à l'interphone)
(**d**) *Fam (be lively → person)* tenir la forme; **he's really buzzing tonight** il tient vraiment la forme ce soir
(**e**) *Am Fam (leave)* se tirer; **I wanna buzz** je veux me tirer
3 *vt* (**a**) *(with buzzer)* **he buzzed the nurse** il appela l'infirmière d'un coup de sonnette
(**b**) *Am Fam (telephone)* passer un coup de fil à
(**c**) *Fam (building, town)* raser, frôler❑; *(aircraft)* frôler❑
▸▸ *Hist* **buzz bomb** V1 *m*; *Tech* **buzz saw** scie *f* mécanique *ou* circulaire
▸**buzz about** *vi (bees, flies)* voler en bourdonnant; *Fam (person)* s'affairer❑, s'agiter❑
▸**buzz off** *vi Fam* décamper, dégager; **buzz off, will you!** dégage *ou* fiche le camp, tu veux!

buzzard ['bʌzəd] *n Orn* (**a**) *Br (bird of prey)* buse *f* (**b**) *Am (vulture)* urubu *m*

buzzed [bʌzd] *adj Am Fam (drunk)* bourré

buzzer ['bʌzə(r)] *n* sonnette *f*; **there's the buzzer** *(on machine)* ça sonne; *(at door)* on sonne

buzzing ['bʌzɪŋ] **1** *n (of insects)* bourdonnement *m*, vrombissement *m*; *(in ears)* bourdonnement *m*, tintement *m*
2 *adj (insect)* bourdonnant, vrombissant; **a buzzing noise** *or* **sound** un bourdonnement *ou* vrombissement

buzzword ['bʌzwɜːd] *n Fam* mot *m* à la mode❑

BVDs® [,biːviː'diːz] *npl Am* sous-vêtements *mpl (pour hommes)*

BVM *(written abbr* **Blessed Virgin Mary***)* **the BVM** la Sainte Vierge

b/w *(written abbr* **black and white***)* NB

BY [baɪ]

de côté	▸ **1 (b)**
près de	▸ **2 (a)**
au bord de	▸ **2 (a)**
devant	▸ **2 (b)**
par	▸ **2 (c) – (f), (h), (o), (q)**
à	▸ **2 (d), (p), (q)**
en	▸ **2 (d), (q)**
de	▸ **2 (g), (m), (n)**

1 *adv* (**a**) *(past)* **she drove by without stopping** elle est passée (en voiture) sans s'arrêter; **he managed to squeeze by** il a réussi à passer (en se faufilant); **if you see him, just walk on by** si tu le vois, ne t'arrête pas; **two hours have gone by** deux heures ont passé; **as time went by he became less bitter** avec le temps il est devenu moins amer
(**b**) *(aside, away)* de côté; **to lay** *or* **put sth by** mettre qch de côté; **she put some money by for her old age** elle a mis de l'argent de côté pour ses vieux jours
(**c**) *(nearby)* **is there a bank close by?** y a-t-il une banque près d'ici?; **she sat** *or* **stood by while they operated** elle est restée là pendant qu'ils opéraient; *Fig* **how can you just sit** *or* **stand by while he suffers?** comment peux-tu rester là sans rien faire alors qu'il souffre?; **stand by in case of an emergency** ne vous éloignez pas au cas où il y aurait une urgence
(**d**) *(to, at someone's home)* **I'll stop** *or* **drop by this evening** je passerai ce soir; **your mother came by this morning** ta mère est passée ce matin
2 *prep* (**a**) *(near, beside)* près de, à côté de; **by a stream** au bord *ou* près d'un ruisseau; **by the sea** au bord de la mer; **she parked her car by the kerb** elle gara sa voiture au bord du trottoir; **come and sit by me** *or* **my side** viens t'asseoir près *ou* auprès de moi; **sitting by the fire** assis près du feu; **don't stand by the door** ne restez pas debout près de la porte
(**b**) *(past)* devant; **she walked right by me** elle passa juste devant moi; **I drive by the school every day** je passe (en voiture) devant l'école tous les jours
(**c**) *(through)* par; **she left by the back door** elle est partie par la porte de derrière
(**d**) *(indicating means, method)* **to pay by cheque** payer par chèque; **by letter/phone** par courrier/téléphone; **to go by bus/car/plane/train** aller en autobus/voiture/avion/train; **send it by plane/ship** envoyez-le par avion/bateau; **by land/sea** par (voie de) terre/mer; **by land and sea** par terre et par mer; **it's quicker by train** ça va plus vite en train; **I know her by name/sight** je la connais de nom/vue; *Literary* **he died by his own hand** il est mort de sa propre main; **you must wash it by hand** il faut le laver à la main; **was it made by hand/machine?** a-t-il été fait à la main/machine?; **by candlelight** à la lumière d'une bougie; **by moonlight** au clair de lune; **I can do it by myself** je peux le faire (tout) seul; **I'm all by myself tonight** je suis tout seul ce soir
(**e**) *(indicating agent or cause)* par; **it was built by the Romans** il fut construit par les Romains; **the house was surrounded by the police** la police a cerné la maison; **I was shocked by his reaction** sa réaction m'a choqué; **she had two daughters by him** elle a eu deux filles de lui; **she has a daughter by her first marriage/husband** elle a une fille de son premier mariage/mari
(**f**) *(as a result of)* par; *(with present participle)* en; **by chance/mistake** par hasard/erreur; **by working overtime he managed to pay off his debts** en faisant des heures supplémentaires il a réussi à rembourser ses dettes; **I'll lose by doing it** j'y perdrai; **he learned to cook by watching his mother** il a appris à faire la cuisine en regardant sa mère
(**g**) *(indicating authorship)* de; **a book by Toni Morrison** un livre de Toni Morrison; **a quartet by Schubert** un quatuor de Schubert
(**h**) *(indicating part of person, thing held)* par; **carry it by the handle** prends-le par la poignée; **she took her by the hand** elle l'a prise par la main; **he seized him by the collar** il l'a saisi par le col
(**i**) *(not later than, before)* **she'll be here by tonight/five o'clock** elle sera ici avant ce soir/pour cinq heures; **it must be done by tomorrow** ça doit être fait pour demain; **I'll have finished by Friday** j'aurai fini pour vendredi; **by the end of the 21st century illiteracy should be stamped out** d'ici la fin du XXIème siècle l'analphabétisme devrait avoir disparu; **by 1960 most Americans had television sets** en 1960 la plupart des Américains avaient déjà un poste de télévision; **by the time you read this letter I'll be in California** lorsque tu liras cette lettre, je serai en Californie; **by the time the police came the thieves had left** le temps que la police arrive *ou* lorsque la police arriva, les voleurs étaient déjà partis; **he should be in India by now** il devrait être en Inde maintenant; **she had already married by then** à ce moment-là elle était déjà mariée
(**j**) *(during)* **by daylight** au jour, à la lumière du jour; **he works by night and sleeps by day** il travaille la nuit et dort le jour
(**k**) *(according to)* d'après; **to call sb by his/her name** appeler qn par son nom; **they're rich, even by American standards** ils sont riches même par rapport aux normes américaines; **it's 6:15 by my watch** il est 6 heures 15 à *ou* d'après ma montre; **you can tell he's lying by the expression on his face** on voit qu'il ment à l'expression de son visage
(**l**) *(in accordance with)* selon, d'après; **by law** selon *ou* d'après la loi; *Sport & Fig* **to play by the rules** faire les choses dans les règles
(**m**) *(with regard to)* de; **to do one's duty by sb** faire son devoir envers qn; **she's Canadian by birth** elle est canadienne de naissance; **cheerful by nature** gai par nature, d'un naturel gai; **he's an actor by trade** *or* **profession** il est acteur de profession; *Fam* **it's all right by me** moi, je suis d'accord *ou* je n'ai rien contre; *Fam* **if that's okay by you** si ça te va, si tu es d'accord❑
(**n**) *(indicating degree, extent)* de; *Sport* **she won by five points** elle a gagné de cinq points; **I missed the train by less than a minute** j'ai manqué le train de moins d'une minute; **she's older than her husband by five years** elle est plus âgée que son mari de cinq ans; **increase your income by half** augmentez vos revenus de 50 pour cent; **they overcharged me by ten percent** ils m'ont compté dix pour cent en trop; **his second book is better by far** son deuxième livre est nettement meilleur
(**o**) *(in calculations, measurements)* **multiply/divide 12 by 6** multipliez/divisez 12 par 6; **the room is 6 metres by 3 (metres)** la pièce fait 6 mètres sur 3 (mètres)
(**p**) *(indicating specific amount, duration)* **to be paid by the hour/week/month** être payé à l'heure/à la semaine/au mois; *Com* **they only sell by the kilo** ils ne vendent qu'au kilo; *Com* **it sold by the thousand** ça s'est vendu par milliers; **he rents his room by the week** il loue sa chambre à la semaine
(**q**) *(indicating rate or speed)* **little by little** peu à peu; **day by day** jour par jour, de jour en jour; **year by year** d'année en année; **two by two** deux par deux
(**r**) *(used with points of the compass)* quart; **north by west** nord-quart-nord-ouest
3 by and by *adv Literary* bientôt
4 by the by 1 *adv* à propos **2** *adj* **that's by the by** ça n'a pas d'importance

bye [baɪ] **1** *n Sport* (**a**) **to get a bye** = passer au tour suivant sans avoir à jouer *(lors d'un tournoi qui oppose un nombre impair de concurrents)*; **our team have got a bye into the second round** nous sommes passés directement au tour suivant, faute d'adversaire (**b**) *(in cricket)* balle *f* passée
2 *exclam Fam* au revoir!❑, salut!; **bye for now!** à bientôt!

bye-bye *Fam* **1** *exclam* au revoir❑, salut; **say bye-bye** *(to child)* dis au revoir
2 bye-byes *n (in children's language)* dodo *m*; **go to bye-byes now** va faire dodo maintenant

byelaw = **bylaw**

by-election, bye-election *n* élection *f* (législative) partielle *(en Grande-Bretagne)*

Byelorussia [bɪ,eləʊ'rʌʃə] *n* Biélorussie *f*; **in Byelorussia** en Biélorussie

Byelorussian [bɪ,eləʊ'rʌʃən] **1** *n* (**a**) *(person)* Biélorusse *mf* (**b**) *(language)* biélorusse *m*
2 *adj* biélorusse
3 *comp (embassy)* de Biélorussie; *(history)* de la Biélorussie; *(teacher)* de biélorusse

bygone ['baɪgɒn] **1** *adj Literary* passé, révolu; **he displayed the gallantry of a bygone age** il faisait preuve d'une galanterie qui n'a plus cours aujourd'hui; **in bygone days** autrefois, jadis
2 *n* (**a**) *(object)* vieillerie *f* (**b**) *(idiom)* **let bygones be bygones** oublions le passé

bylaw ['baɪlɔː] *n* (**a**) *Br (of local authority)* arrêté *m* municipal (**b**) *Am (of club, company)* statut *m*

by-line *n Press* signature *f (en tête d'un article)*

BYO [,biːwaɪ'əʊ] *n (abbr* **bring your own***)* = restaurant non autorisé à vendre des boissons alcoolisées mais où l'on a la possibilité d'apporter sa propre bouteille

BYOB [,biːwaɪəʊ'biː] *n (abbr* **bring your own bottle***)* = "apportez une bouteille", inscription que l'on trouve sur un carton d'invitation à une soirée ou qui indique qu'un restaurant n'est pas autorisé à vendre d'alcool et que l'on peut donc en apporter pour accompagner son repas

BYOD [,biːwaɪ,əʊ'diː] *n Am (abbr* **bring your own drink***)* = **BYOB**

bypass ['baɪpɑːs] **1** *n* (**a**) *(road)* rocade *f*; **the Oxford bypass** la route qui contourne Oxford

(**b**) *Tech (pipe)* conduit *m* de dérivation, by-pass *m*
(**c**) *Elec* dérivation *f*
(**d**) *Med* pontage *m*, by-pass *m*; **he's had a heart bypass** il a subi un pontage coronarien
2 *vt (avoid → town)* contourner, éviter; *(→ problem, regulation)* contourner, éluder; *(→ superior)* court-circuiter; **I bypassed the personnel officer and spoke directly to the boss** je suis allé parler directement au directeur sans passer par le chef du personnel
►► ***bypass operation, bypass surgery*** pontage *m*

byplay ['baɪpleɪ] *n Theat* jeu *m* de scène secondaire

by-product *n Ind* sous-produit *m*, (produit *m*) dérivé *m*; *Fig* conséquence *f* indirecte, effet *m* secondaire

byre ['baɪə(r)] *n Br* étable *f* (à vaches)

byroad ['baɪrəʊd] *n (road)* chemin *m* détourné *ou* écarté

Byronic [baɪ'rɒnɪk] *adj* byronien

bystander ['baɪˌstændə(r)] *n* spectateur(trice) *m,f*

byte [baɪt] *n Comput* octet *m*, byte *m*

byway ['baɪweɪ] *n* (**a**) *(road)* chemin *m* détourné *ou* écarté (**b**) *Fig (of subject)* à-côté *m*; **the book explores the byways of Buddhist teaching** le livre explore les aspects peu connus *ou* les à-côtés de l'enseignement bouddhiste

byword ['baɪwɜːd] *n* symbole *m*, illustration *f*; **the company has become a byword for inefficiency** le nom de cette entreprise est devenu synonyme d'inefficacité

by-your-leave *n Literary or Hum* **without so much as a by-your-leave** sans même demander la permission

Byzantine [*Br* bɪ'zæntaɪn, *Am* 'bɪzəntiːn] **1** *n* Byzantin(e) *m,f*
2 *adj* byzantin, de Byzance

Byzantinism [bɪ'zæntɪnɪzəm] *n* byzantinisme *m*

Byzantium [bɪ'zæntɪəm] *n* Byzance

C[1], c[1] [siː] **1** *n* (**a**) *(letter)* C, c *m inv*; **two c's** deux c; **C for Charlie** ≃ C comme Célestin; *Fam* **the big C** *(cancer)* le cancer □ (**b**) *Sch* **to get a C** avoir une note moyenne, ≃ avoir entre 10 et 13 sur 20 (**c**) *Mus* do *m*, ut *m*; **in C sharp** en do dièse majeur (**d**) *(Roman numeral)* C *m*
2 *adj Mus (string)* de do
►► *Am Fam* **C note** billet *m* de cent dollars □

C[2] (**a**) *(written abbr* **Celsius, Centigrade**) C (**b**) *(written abbr* **century**) s; **C16** XVIème s

c[2] (**a**) *(written abbr* **cent(s)**) ct (**b**) *(written abbr* **circa**) vers

C1 [ˌsiːˈwʌn] *n Sport (abbr* **Canadian canoe 1**) C1 *m*

C2 [ˌsiːˈtuː] *n Sport (abbr* **Canadian canoe 2**) C2 *m*

C++ [ˌsiˌplʌsˈplʌs] *n Comput* C++ *m*

CA[1] [ˌsiːˈeɪ] *n* (**a**) *(abbr* **Consumers' Association**) = association britannique des consommateurs (**b**) *Br (abbr* **chartered accountant**) expert-comptable *m*

CA[2] (**a**) *(written abbr* **Central America**) Amérique *f* centrale (**b**) *(written abbr* **California**) Californie *f*

c/a (**a**) *Banking (written abbr* **capital account**) compte *m* de capitaux (**b**) *Com (written abbr* **credit account**) compte *m* créditeur (**c**) *Banking (written abbr* **current** *or* **cheque** *or Am* **checking account**) C/C *m*, CCB *m*

ca. *(written abbr* **circa**) vers

CAA [ˌsiːeɪˈeɪ] *n Aviat* (**a**) *Br (abbr* **Civil Aviation Authority**) = organisme britannique de réglementation de l'aviation civile (**b**) *Am Formerly (abbr* **Civil Aeronautics Authority**) = organisme américain de contrôle des compagnies aériennes

CAB [ˌsiːeɪˈbiː] *n* (**a**) *Br (abbr* **Citizens' Advice Bureau**) = en Grande-Bretagne, bureau où les citoyens peuvent obtenir des conseils d'ordre juridique, social etc (**b**) *Am Formerly Aviat (abbr* **Civil Aeronautics Board**) = organisme américain de réglementation de l'aviation civile

cab [kæb] *n* (**a**) *(taxi)* taxi *m*; **let's go by cab, let's take a cab** allons-y en taxi; **I didn't even have enough for my cab fare home** je n'avais même pas de quoi me payer un taxi (**b**) *(of lorry, train)* cabine *f* (**c**) *(horse-drawn)* fiacre *m*
►► ***cab driver*** chauffeur *m* de taxi; ***cab rank*** station *f* de taxis

cabal [kəˈbæl] *n* (**a**) *(plot)* cabale *f* (**b**) *(group)* coterie *f*

cabala [kəˈbɑːlə] *n Rel* cabale *f*

cabalism [ˈkæbəlɪzəm] *n Rel* cabalisme *m*

cabalistic [kæbəˈlɪstɪk] *adj Rel* cabalistique

cabana [kəˈbænə] *n Am* cabine *f (de plage)*

cabaret [ˈkæbəreɪ] *n (nightclub)* cabaret *m*; *(show)* spectacle *m*; **cabaret performer** artiste *mf* de cabaret

cabbage [ˈkæbɪdʒ] *n* (**a**) *(vegetable)* chou *m* (**b**) *Br Fam (brain-damaged person)* légume *m*; *Pej (dull person)* larve *f*; **I'd rather die than be a cabbage for the rest of my life** plutôt mourir que vivre comme un légume jusqu'à la fin de mes jours (**c**) *Am Fam (money)* fric *m*, blé *m*, oseille *f*
►► ***cabbage lettuce*** laitue *f* pommée; ***cabbage patch*** ≃ carré *m* de salade; ***cabbage rose*** rose *f* centfeuilles; ***cabbage tree*** palmiste *m*; ***cabbage white*** *(butterfly)* piéride *f* du chou

cabbala, cabbalism *etc* = **cabala, cabalism** *etc*

cabby, cabbie [ˈkæbɪ] *n Fam (taxi-driver)* chauffeur *m* de taxi □; *(coachman)* cocher *m* (de fiacre) □

caber [ˈkeɪbə(r)] *n Sport* tronc *m*; **tossing the caber** = concours de lancement d'un tronc d'arbre *(dans les jeux des Highlands)*

cabin [ˈkæbɪn] *n* (**a**) *(hut)* cabane *f*, hutte *f* (**b**) *Naut* cabine *f* (**c**) *Aviat* cabine *f*; **the first class cabin** la cabine de première classe (**d**) *Br Rail (signal box)* cabine *f* d'aiguillage (**e**) *Br (lorry, train)* cabine *f*
►► *Aviat* ***cabin attendant*** *(male)* steward *m*; *(female)* hôtesse *f* de l'air; *Naut* ***cabin boy*** mousse *m*; *Naut* ***cabin class*** deuxième classe *f*; *Aviat* ***cabin crew*** personnel *m* de cabine; *Naut* ***cabin cruiser*** cruiser *m*, yacht *m* de croisière; ***cabin fever*** = dépression ou mauvaise humeur dues à de longues périodes d'isolement; *Aviat* ***cabin staff*** personnel *m* de cabine; ***cabin trunk*** malle-cabine *f*

cabinet [ˈkæbɪnɪt] *n* (**a**) *(furniture)* meuble *m* (de rangement); *(for bottles)* bar *m*; *(for television)* meuble *m* télé; *(for stereo)* meuble *m* hi-fi; *(for precious objects)* cabinet *m*; *(with glass doors)* vitrine *f*
(**b**) *Pol* cabinet *m*; **to form a cabinet** former un cabinet *ou* un ministère; **he was in Major's cabinet** il faisait partie du cabinet *ou* gouvernement Major; **they took the decision in cabinet** ils ont pris la décision en Conseil des ministres
►► *Pol* ***cabinet meeting*** conseil *m* des ministres; *Pol* ***cabinet minister*** ministre *m* siégeant au cabinet; **he was a cabinet minister under Heath** *or* **in the Heath government** il était ministre sous (le gouvernement) Heath; *Pol* ***cabinet reshuffle*** remaniement *m* ministériel

cabinet-maker *n Carp* ébéniste *mf*

cabinet-making *n Carp* ébénisterie *f*

cabinetwork [ˈkæbɪnɪtwɜːk] *n Carp* ébénisterie *f*

cable [ˈkeɪbəl] **1** *n* (**a**) *(rope, wire)* câble *m*; **electric cable** câble *m* électrique
(**b**) *(telegram)* télégramme *m*; **we'll send you a cable** nous t'enverrons un télégramme
(**c**) *Naut (measure)* encablure *f*
(**d**) *Knitting* point *m* de torsade
(**e**) *TV* le cable; **it's only available on cable** ça n'existe que sur le câble
2 *vt* (**a**) *(lay cables in)* câbler
(**b**) *(telegraph)* télégraphier à; **I cabled them to say I needed more money** je leur ai télégraphié que j'avais encore besoin d'argent
►► ***cable car*** téléphérique *m*; *TV* ***cable company*** câblo-opérateur *m*; *TV* ***cable distribution*** câblo-distribution *f*, distribution *f* par câble; *Comput* ***cable modem*** modem-câble *m*; *Knitting* ***cable needle*** aiguille *f* à torsades; *TV* ***Cable News Network*** réseau *m* d'information américain par câble et satellite; *TV* ***cable operator*** câblo-opérateur *m*; ***cable railway*** funiculaire *m*; ***cable release*** déclencheur *m*; *Tel & Naut* ***cable ship*** câblier *m*; *Knitting* ***cable stitch*** point *m* de torsade; ***cable telephone*** téléphone *m* par câble; ***cable television*** câble *m*, télévision *f* par câble; ***cable transfer*** *(of money)* virement *m* télégraphique; ***cable TV*** câble *m*, télévision *f* par câble

cablecast [ˈkeɪbəlkɑːst] *vt Am TV* transmettre par câble

cablecasting [ˈkeɪbəlˌkɑːstɪŋ] *n Am TV* transmission *f* par câble

cabled [ˈkeɪbəld] *adj* câblé; *TV* **cabled network** réseau *m* câblé

cablegram [ˈkeɪbəlgræm] *n Old-fashioned* câblogramme *m*

cable-knit *adj Knitting (sweater)* à torsades

cableless [ˈkeɪbəllɪs] *adj* sans câble

cable-stayed bridge [-steɪd-] *n Constr* pont *m* à haubans

cable-stitch *adj Knitting (sweater)* à torsades

cableway [ˈkeɪbəlweɪ] *n* téléphérique *m*

cabling [ˈkeɪbəlɪŋ] *n* câblage *m*; *Comput* câbles *mpl*

cabman [ˈkæbmən] *(pl* **cabmen** [-mən]) *n Br* chauffeur *m* de taxi

cabochon [ˈkæbəʃɒn] *n Miner* cabochon *m*

caboodle [kəˈbuːdəl] *n Fam* **the whole (kit and) caboodle** tout le bataclan *ou* bazar

caboose [kəˈbuːs] *n* (**a**) *Am Rail* fourgon *m* de queue (**b**) *Naut* coquerie *f* (**c**) *Am very Fam (buttocks)* cul *m*, fesses □ *fpl*

cabotage [kæbəˈtɑːʒ] *n Aviat & Naut* cabotage *m*
►► ***cabotage fare*** tarif *m* de cabotage; ***cabotage route*** itinéraire *m* de cabotage

cabriole [ˈkæbrɪəʊl] *n Carp* pied *m* de biche

cabriolet [ˈkæbrɪəˌleɪ] *n Aut* cabriolet *m*

cabstand [ˈkæbstænd] *n* station *f* de taxis

CAC 40 index [kækˌfɔːtɪ-] *n St Exch* indice *m* CAC 40

ca'canny [ˌkɔːˈkænɪ] *vi Scot Fam* y aller doucement

cacao [kəˈkɑːəʊ] *(pl* **cacaos**) *n (bean)* cacao *m*; *(tree)* cacaoyer *m*, cacaotier *m*

cache [kæʃ] **1** *n* (**a**) *(hidden supply)* cache *f*; **a cache of weapons, an arms cache** une cache d'armes; **the cache had a value of one million pounds** les armes/drogues/*etc* qui ont été découvertes avaient une valeur d'un million de livres (**b**) *Comput* antémémoire *f*, mémoire-cache *f* (**c**) *(hiding place)* cachette *f*
2 *vt* (**a**) *(hide)* mettre dans une cachette (**b**) *Comput (data)* mettre en antémémoire *ou* en mémoire-cache
►► *Comput* ***cache memory*** antémémoire *f*, mémoire-cache *f*

cachectic [kəˈkektɪk] *adj Med* cachectique

cachepot [ˈkæʃpəʊ, ˈkæʃpɒt] *n* cache-pot *m*

cachet [ˈkæʃeɪ] *n also Fig* cachet *m*

cachexia [kæˈkeksɪə] *n Med* cachexie *f*

cachou [ˈkæʃuː] *n* cachou *m*

CACI [ˌsiːeɪˌsiːˈaɪ] *n Mktg (abbr* **California Analysis Centers Inc**) = institut international de sondages

cack [kæk] *Br very Fam* **1** *n* (**a**) *(excrement)* caca *m* (**b**) *(nonsense)* conneries *fpl*; **don't talk cack!** arrête de raconter n'importe quoi! (**c**) *(worthless things)* camelote *f*; **the film was a load of cack** le film était nul
2 *adj (bad)* nul; **her music is cack** sa musique est nulle
3 *vt* **he was cacking himself** *(scared)* il faisait dans son froc

cack-handed *adj Br Fam* maladroit □, gauche □

cackle [ˈkækəl] **1** *n* (**a**) *(of hen)* caquet *m*, caquètement *m* (**b**) *(of person → chatter)* caquètement *m*, jacasserie *f*; *(→ laugh)* gloussement *m*; **she gave a loud cackle** elle gloussa bruyamment; *Fam* **cut the cackle!** assez bavardé!, la ferme!
2 *vt* **"you're trapped!" cackled the old witch** "je te tiens!", glousse la vieille sorcière
3 *vi* (**a**) *(hen)* caqueter (**b**) *(person → chatter)* caqueter, jacasser; *(→ laugh)* glousser

cackling [ˈkæklɪŋ] **1** *n* (**a**) *(of hen)* caquètement *m* (**b**) *(of person → chattering)* jacassements *mpl*; *(→ laughing)* gloussements *mpl*
2 *adj* (**a**) *(hen)* qui caquette (**b**) *(person → chattering)* qui caquette, qui jacasse; *(→ laughing)* qui glousse; **I heard the sound of cackling laughter** j'ai entendu des gloussements

cacographer [kəˈkɒgrəfə(r)] *n* cacographe *mf*

cacography [kəˈkɒgrəfɪ] *n* cacographie *f*

cacophonous [kæˈkɒfənəs] *adj* cacophonique

cacophony [kæˈkɒfənɪ] *(pl* **cacophonies**) *n* cacophonie *f*

cactus [ˈkæktəs] *(pl* **cactuses** *or* **cacti** [-taɪ]) *n* cactus *m*

►► *Bot* ***cactus flower*** fleur *f* de cactus

cacuminal [kæ'kju:mɪnəl] *Ling* **1** *n* cacuminale *f*
2 *adj* cacuminal

CAD¹ [ˌsi:eɪ'di:] *n Com* (*abbr* **cash against documents**) comptant *m* contre documents

CAD² [kæd] *n Comput* (*abbr* **computer-assisted design**) CAO *f*

cad [kæd] *n Br Old-fashioned* mufle *m*; **you cad!** vous êtes ignoble *ou* indigne!

cadastral [kə'dæstrəl] *adj Admin* cadastral
►► ***cadastral register*** (registre *m* du) cadastre *m*

cadaver [kə'dævə(r)] *n Med* cadavre *m*

cadaverous [kə'dævərəs] *adj Formal or Literary* cadavéreux, cadavérique

cadaverousness [kə'dævərəsnɪs] *n Formal or Literary* pâleur *f* cadavéreuse

CADCAM ['kædkæm] *n Comput* (*abbr* **computer-assisted design and manufacture**) CFAO *f*

caddie ['kædɪ] **1** *n* (**a**) *Golf* caddie *m* (**b**) *Am (cart)* chariot *m*, Caddie® *m*
2 *vi Golf* **to caddie for sb** être le caddie de qn
►► *Golf* ***caddie car, caddie cart*** chariot *m* (*pour clubs de golf*)

caddis fly ['kædɪs-] *n Entom* trichoptère *m*
►► ***caddis fly larva*** larve *f* de trichoptère

caddish ['kædɪʃ] *adj Br Old-fashioned (behaviour)* de mufle; *(person)* mufle; **that was a caddish thing to do** c'est vraiment se comporter comme un mufle

Caddy ['kædɪ] *n Fam (Cadillac)* Cadillac ❑ *f*

caddy ['kædɪ] (*pl* **caddies**) *n* (**a**) *Br (container → for tea)* boîte *f* (**b**) *Am (cart)* chariot *m*, Caddie® *m*

cadence ['keɪdəns] *n* cadence *f*, rythme *m*; *Mus* cadence *f*

cadenced ['keɪdənst] *adj* cadencé

cadential [kə'denʃəl] *adj* (**a**) *(pertaining to a cadence)* rythmique (**b**) *Mus (pertaining to a cadenza)* d'une cadence

cadenza [kə'denzə] *n Mus* cadence *f*

cadet [kə'det] **1** *n* (**a**) *Mil* élève *mf* officier; *(police)* élève *mf* policier; *Br Sch* – élève qui reçoit une formation militaire (**b**) *(younger brother, son)* cadet *m*
2 *adj* cadet
►► *Mil* ***cadet corps*** peloton *m* d'instruction militaire; *(for police training)* corps *m* d'élèves policiers

cadge [kædʒ] *Fam* **1** *n Br* (**a**) *(person)* pique-assiette *mf inv*, parasite ❑ *m* (**b**) *(idiom)* **to be on the cadge** chercher à se faire payer quelque chose ❑
2 *vt (food, money)* se procurer ❑ *(en quémandant)*; **he cadged a meal from** *or* **off his aunt** il s'est invité à manger chez sa tante; **she cadged £10 off me** elle m'a tapé de 10 livres; **they cadged a lift home** à force de quémander ils se sont fait ramener en voiture
3 *vi* **she's always cadging off her friends** elle est toujours en train de taper ses amis

cadger ['kædʒə(r)] *n Fam* pique-assiette *mf inv*, parasite ❑ *m*

Cadiz [kə'dɪz] *n* Cadix

cadmium ['kædmɪəm] *n Chem* cadmium *m*
►► ***cadmium yellow*** jaune *m* de cadmium

cadre ['kɑ:də(r)] *n* cadre *m*

[illegible] [kə'dju:[illegible]] (*pl* **[illegible]** [illegible]) *n Myth* caducée *m*

CAE [ˌsi:eɪ'i:] *n Comput* (*abbr* **computer-aided engineering**) IAO *f*

caecal, *Am* **cecal** ['si:kəl] *adj Anat* cæcal

caecilian [si:'sɪlɪən] *n Zool* typhlonecte *m*, cécilie *f*

caecum, *Am* **cecum** ['si:kəm] (*Br pl* **caeca** [-kə], *Am pl* **ceca** [-kə]) *n Anat* cæcum *m*

Caernarfon, Caernarvon [kə'nɑ:vən] *n* = petite ville du pays de Galles dont le château sert de cadre à la cérémonie d'investiture du prince de Galles

Caesar ['si:zə(r)] *pr n* César; **Julius Caesar** Jules César
►► *Culin* ***Caesar salad*** = salade à base de romaine, de croûtons et d'une vinaigrette additionnée d'œuf

Caesarean, *Am* **Cesarean** [sɪ'zeərɪən] **1** *n Obst* césarienne *f*; **to be born** *or* **delivered by Caesarean** naître par césarienne; **she has to have a Caesarean** il va falloir lui faire une césarienne
2 *adj* césarien
►► *Obst* ***Caesarean birth*** césarienne *f*; *Obst* ***Caesarean section*** césarienne *f*; **to be born** *or* **delivered by Caesarean section** naître par césarienne

caesium, *Am* **cesium** ['si:zɪəm] *n Chem* césium *m*, cæsium *m*; **caesium 90** césium *m* 90

caesura [sɪ'zjʊərə] (*pl* **caesuras** *or* **caesurae** [-ri:]) *n Literature* césure *f*

CAF [ˌsi:eɪ'ef] *n Com* (*abbr* **cost and freight**) C et F

cafe, café ['kæfeɪ] *n (in UK)* snack *m*; *(in rest of Europe)* café *m*
►► ***cafe society*** le beau monde

CAFÉ

En Grande-Bretagne, le mot "café" désigne une sorte de snack où l'on peut prendre un repas léger et boire du thé ou du café.

cafeteria [kæfɪ'tɪərɪə] *n (self-service restaurant)* restaurant *m* self-service, self *m*; *Am (canteen)* cantine *f*

cafetiere [kæfə'tjeə(r)] *n* cafetière *f*

caff [kæf] *n Br Fam* snack ❑ *m*

caffeine ['kæfi:n] *n* caféine *f*

caffeine-free *adj* sans caféine

caftan ['kæftæn] *n* caftan *m*

cage [keɪdʒ] **1** *n* (**a**) *(with bars)* cage *f* (**b**) *(lift)* cabine *f*; *Mining* cage *f* (d'extraction) (**c**) *Sport (in basketball)* panier *m*; *(in ice hockey)* cage *f*
2 *vt* mettre en cage, encager
►► ***cage bird*** oiseau *m* d'agrément *ou* d'appartement

caged [keɪdʒd] *adj* en cage; **he was like a caged animal** il était comme un animal en cage

cagey ['keɪdʒɪ] (*comp* **cagier,** *superl* **cagiest**) *adj Fam (careful)* prudent ❑; *(reticent)* réticent ❑; **he was being cagey about his salary** il s'est montré évasif lorsqu'il s'est agi de son salaire

cagily ['keɪdʒɪlɪ] *adv Fam (carefully)* très prudemment ❑; *(reticently)* avec réticence ❑; **to answer cagily** donner une réponse vague

caginess ['keɪdʒɪnɪs] *n Fam (carefulness)* prudence ❑ *f*; *(reticence)* réticence ❑ *f*; **there was a certain caginess in her replies** elle évitait de répondre en restant dans le vague ❑

cagoule [kə'gu:l] *n Br* veste *f* imperméable (*à capuche*)

cagy = **cagey**

cahoots [kə'hu:ts] *npl Fam (idiom)* **to be in cahoots (with sb)** être de mèche (avec qn); **they discovered that the bank manager was in cahoots with the gang** on a découvert que le directeur de la banque était de mèche avec les voleurs

CAI [ˌsi:eɪ'aɪ] *n* (**a**) *Comput* (*abbr* **computer-aided instruction**) EAO *m* (**b**) *Ind* (*abbr* **Confederation of Australian Industry**) = confédération du patronat australien

Caiaphas ['kaɪəfæs] *pr n Bible* Caïphe

caiman = **cayman**

Cain [keɪn] *pr n Bible* Caïn; **the mark of Cain** la marque de Caïn; **to raise Cain** *(make noise)* faire un bruit de tous les diables; *(make scene)* faire une scène terrible

cairn [keən] *n* cairn *m*
►► [illegible]

cairngorm ['keəngɔ:m] **1** *n Miner* quartz *m* fumé
2 Cairngorm *n* **the Cairngorms** les monts *mpl* Cairngorm
►► ***the Cairngorm Mountains*** les monts *mpl* Cairngorm

Cairo ['kaɪərəʊ] *n* Le Caire

caisson ['keɪsɒn] *n* (**a**) *Constr (for working underwater)* caisson *m* (**b**) *Naut (in dry dock)* bateau-porte *m* (**c**) *Mil (for ammunition)* caisson *m*
►► *Med* ***caisson disease*** maladie *f* des caissons

cajole [kə'dʒəʊl] *vt* enjôler; **he cajoled her into accepting** il l'a amenée à accepter à force de cajoleries; **they eventually cajoled the information out of him** à force de cajoleries, ils ont réussi à lui soutirer le renseignement

cajoler [kə'dʒəʊlə(r)] *n* cajoleur(euse) *m,f*

cajolery [kə'dʒəʊlərɪ] *n (UNCOUNT)* cajoleries *fpl*

cajoling [kə'dʒəʊlɪŋ] *adj* cajoleur

cajolingly [kə'dʒəʊlɪŋlɪ] *adv* d'une manière cajoleuse; *(speak)* d'un ton cajoleur

Cajun ['keɪdʒən] **1** *n* (**a**) Cajun *mf inv* (**b**) *(language)* cajun *m*
2 *adj* cajun *(inv)*

cake [keɪk] **1** *n* (**a**) *(sweet)* gâteau *m*; *(pastry)* pâtisserie *f*; *(savoury)* croquette *f*; **a chocolate/cherry cake** un gâteau au chocolat/aux cerises; **to make** *or* **to bake a cake** faire un gâteau; *Fam* **it's a piece of cake** c'est du gâteau *ou* de la tarte; *Prov* **you can't have your cake and eat it** on ne peut pas avoir le beurre et l'argent du beurre
(**b**) *(block → of soap, wax)* pain *m*; *(→ of chocolate)* plaquette *f*
2 *comp (crumb)* de gâteau; *(dish)* à gâteau
3 *vt* **caked with mud/blood** couvert de boue/sang séché(e)
4 *vi* durcir; **the mud had caked on his boots** la boue avait séché sur ses bottes
►► ***cake decoration*** décoration *f* pour gâteau; ***cake fork*** fourchette *f* à dessert *ou* à gâteaux; ***cake mix*** préparation *f* (instantanée) pour gâteau; *Am* ***cake pan*** moule *m* à gâteau; ***cake shop*** pâtisserie *f*; ***cake stall*** *(at fair)* stand *m* à gâteaux; ***cake stand*** plat *m* à gâteaux; ***cake tin*** moule *m* à gateau

caked [keɪkt] *adj (mud, blood)* séché

cakehole ['keɪkhəʊl] *n Br Fam (mouth)* bouche ❑ *f*, clapet *m*; **shut your cakehole!** ferme-la!, ferme ton clapet!

cakewalk ['keɪkwɔ:k] *n* (**a**) *(dance)* cake-walk *m* (**b**) *Am Fam Fig (easy task)* **the exam was a cakewalk** l'examen, c'était du gâteau

CAL [ˌsi:eɪ'el, kæl] *n Comput* (*abbr* **computer-assisted learning**) EAO *m*

cal. (*written abbr* **calorie**) cal

calabash ['kæləbæʃ] *n Bot (fruit)* calebasse *f*; *(tree)* calebassier *m*

calaboose ['kæləbu:s] *n Am Fam* taule *f*, tôle *f*; **in the calaboose** en taule, en tôle

calabrese [kælə'breɪzɪ] *n Bot* brocoli *m* calabrais

Calabria [kə'læbrɪə] *n* Calabre *f*; **in Calabria** en Calabre

Calabrian [kə'læbrɪən] **1** *n* Calabrais(e) *m,f*
2 *adj* calabrais

caladium [kə'leɪdɪʌm] *n Bot* caladium *m*

calamari [ˌkælə'mɑ:rɪ] *npl Culin* calmars *mpl*, calamars *mpl*

calamine ['kæləˌmaɪn] *n Chem* calamine *f*
►► ***calamine lotion*** lotion *f* calmante à la calamine

calamitous [kə'læmɪtəs] *adj* calamiteux

calamitously [kə'læmɪˌtəslɪ] *adv* calamiteusement

calamity [kə'læmətɪ] (*pl* **calamities**) *n* calamité *f*

Calamity Jane [-dʒeɪn] *pr n* Calamity Jane; *Fig* **she's a bit of a Calamity Jane** il ne lui arrive que des catastrophes

calandra [kə'lændrə] *n Orn* **calandra (lark)** calandre *f*, alouette *f* calandrelle

calandria [kə'lændrɪə] *n Nucl* calandre *f*

calcareous [kæl'keərɪəs] *adj Chem* calcaire

calceolaria [ˌkælsɪə'leərɪə] *n Bot* calcéolaire *f*

calcic ['kælsɪk] *adj Chem* calcique

calcicole ['kælsɪkəʊl], **calcicolous** [ˌkæl'sɪkələs] *adj Bot* calcicole

calciferol [kæl'sɪfərɒl] *n Biol & Chem* calciférol *m*

calciferous [kæl'sɪfərəs] *adj Biol & Chem* calci[illegible]

calcification [ˌkælsɪfɪ'keɪʃən] *n Chem* calcification *f*

calcified ['kælsɪfaɪd] *adj Chem* calcifié

calcifuge ['kælsɪfju:dʒ] *Bot* **1** *n* plante *f* calcifuge
2 *adj* calcifuge

calcify ['kælsɪfaɪ] (*pt & pp* **calcified**) *Chem* **1** *vt* calcifier
2 *vi* se calcifier

calcination [ˌkælsɪ'neɪʃən] *n Metal* calcination *f*

calcine ['kælsaɪn] *Metal* **1** *vt* calciner
2 *vi* se calciner

calcite ['kælsaɪt] *n Miner* calcite *f*

calcium ['kælsɪəm] *n Chem* calcium *m*
►► ***calcium carbide*** carbure *m* de calcium; ***calcium carbonate*** carbonate *m* de calcium; ***calcium chloride*** chlorure *m* de calcium; ***calcium cyanamide*** cyanamide *f* calcique; ***calcium deficiency*** carence *f* en calcium; ***calcium fluoride*** fluorure *m* de calcium; ***calcium lactate*** lactate *m* de calcium; ***calcium oxide*** oxyde *m* de

calcium; ***calcium phosphate*** phosphate *m* de chaux

calculability [ˌkælkjʊlə'bɪlɪtɪ] *n* calculabilité *f*

calculable ['kælkjʊləbəl] *adj* calculable

calculably ['kælkjʊləblɪ] *adv* à ce qu'on peut estimer

calculate ['kælkjʊleɪt] **1** *vt* (**a**) *Math* calculer; *(estimate, evaluate)* calculer, évaluer; **he calculated that his chances of success were reasonably good** il calcula *ou* estima qu'il avait d'assez bonnes chances de réussir

(**b**) *(design, intend)* **her remark was calculated to offend the guests** sa réflexion était destinée à offenser les invités; **words calculated to reassure us** paroles propres à nous rassurer; **the price of the house was scarcely calculated to attract potential buyers** le prix de la maison n'a guère été calculé pour attirer d'éventuels acheteurs

2 *vi* (**a**) *Math* calculer, faire des calculs

(**b**) *Am (count, depend)* **I calculated on George lending me the money** je comptais sur George pour me prêter l'argent

calculated ['kælkjʊleɪtɪd] *adj* (**a**) *(considered)* calculé, mesuré; **a calculated risk** un risque calculé (**b**) *(deliberate, intentional)* délibéré, voulu; **a calculated insult** une insulte délibérée

calculatedly ['kælkjʊleɪtɪdlɪ] *adv* (**a**) *(in a considered manner)* d'une manière calculée (**b**) *(deliberately, intentionally)* délibérément

calculating ['kælkjʊleɪtɪŋ] *adj* (**a**) *Pej (person)* calculateur (**b**) *(cautious)* prudent, mesuré

►► *Math* ***calculating machine*** machine *f* à calculer

calculatingly ['kælkjʊleɪtɪŋlɪ] *adv Pej* de manière calculée

calculation [ˌkælkjʊ'leɪʃən] *n* (**a**) *Math & Fig* calcul *m*; **to make a calculation** effectuer un calcul; **by** *or* **according to my calculations** selon *ou* d'après mes calculs (**b**) *(UNCOUNT) Pej (scheming)* **his offer of help was free of all calculation** il a offert son aide sans la moindre arrière-pensée

calculator ['kælkjʊleɪtə(r)] **1** *n* (**a**) *(machine)* calculateur *m*; *(small)* calculatrice *f* (**b**) *(table)* table *f*

2 *comp (battery)* de calculatrice

calculus ['kælkjʊləs] *n* (**a**) *Math* calcul *m* (**b**) *Med* calcul *m*

Calcutta [kæl'kʌtə] *n* Calcutta

caldera [kæl'deərə] *n Geol* caldeira *f*, caldère *f*

caldron = **cauldron**

Caledonia [ˌkælɪ'dəʊnjə] *n Hist* Calédonie *f*; **in Caledonia** en Calédonie

Caledonian [ˌkælɪ'dəʊnjən] **1** *n* Calédonien(enne) *m,f*

2 *adj* calédonien

►► ***the Caledonian Canal*** le canal calédonien

calendar ['kælɪndə(r)] **1** *n* (**a**) *(of dates)* calendrier *m* (**b**) *(register)* annuaire *m*; **the university calendar** l'annuaire de l'université (**c**) *Am (planner)* agenda *m*

2 *comp (day, month, year)* civil, calendaire

3 *vt (event)* inscrire sur le calendrier; *Am (put in planner)* noter *(dans son agenda)*

►► ***calendar girl*** pin-up *f*

calender ['kælɪndə(r)] *Tech* **1** *n* calandre *f*, laminoir *m*

2 *vt* calandrer

calendered ['kælɪndəd] *adj Tech (paper)* calandré, satiné

calendering ['kælɪndərɪŋ] *n Tech* calendrage *m*

calends ['kælɪndz] *npl Hist* calendes *fpl*

calendula [kæ'lendjʊlə] *n Bot* celendule *f*

calf [kɑːf] *(pl* **calves** [kɑːvz]*)* *n* (**a**) *(young cow, bull)* veau *m*; **the cow is in calf** la vache est pleine (**b**) *(skin)* veau *m*, vachette *f*; **a book bound in calf** un livre relié en veau (**c**) *(buffalo)* bufflon *m*, buffletin *m*; *(elephant)* éléphanteau *m*; *(giraffe)* girafeau *m*, girafon *m*; *(whale)* baleineau *m* (**d**) *(part of leg)* mollet *m* (**e**) *Geol (of glacier)* glaçon *m*, veau *m*

►► ***calf love*** premières amours *fpl*

calf-length *adj* **calf-length boots** demi-bottes *fpl*; **calf-length skirt** jupe *f* mi-longue

calf's-foot jelly *n Culin* gelée *f* de pied de veau

calfskin ['kɑːfskɪn] **1** *n* veau *m*, vachette *f*

2 *comp* en veau, en vachette

Caliban ['kælɪbæn] *pr n* = personnage monstrueux dans 'La Tempête' de Shakespeare

caliber *Am* = **calibre**

calibrate ['kælɪbreɪt] *vt Tech (measuring instrument etc)* étalonner; *(bore)* calibrer; *(thermometer)* graduer; *Mil (piece of artillery)* vérifier le calibre de

calibration [ˌkælɪ'breɪʃən] *n Tech (of measuring instrument)* étalonnage *m*; *(of bore)* calibrage *m*; *(of thermometer)* graduation *f*

calibre, *Am* **caliber** ['kælɪbə(r)] *n* (**a**) *(of gun, tube)* calibre *m*; **a high calibre revolver** un revolver de gros calibre (**b**) *(quality)* qualité *f*; **their work is of the highest calibre** ils font un travail de grande qualité; **the two applicants are not of the same calibre** les deux candidats ne sont pas du même calibre *ou* n'ont pas la même envergure

calico ['kælɪkəʊ] *(pl* **calicoes** *or* **calicos***)* *Tex* **1** *n Br* calicot *m* blanc; *Am* calicot *m* imprimé, indienne *f*

2 *comp* de calicot

►► ***calico cat*** chat *m* tacheté

California [ˌkælɪ'fɔːnjə] *n* la Californie; **in California** en Californie; **Lower California** la Basse-Californie

►► *Orn* ***California condor*** condor *m* de Californie; *Bot* ***California lilac*** céanothe *m*, céanothus *m*; *Bot* ***California poppy*** eschscholtzie *f*; *Orn* ***California quail*** colin *m* de Californie

Californian [ˌkælɪ'fɔːnjən] **1** *n* Californien(enne) *m,f*

2 *adj* californien

californium [ˌkælɪ'fɔːnjəm] *n Chem* californium *m*

Caligula [kə'lɪgjʊlə] *pr n* Caligula

calipash ['kælɪpæʃ] *n Culin* = partie gélatineuse de la tortue, au-dessous de la carapace

calipee ['kælɪpiː] *n Culin* = partie gélatineuse du ventre de la tortue

caliper *Am* = **calliper**

caliph, Caliph ['keɪlɪf] *n Rel* calife *m*

caliphate ['keɪlɪfɪt] *n Rel* califat *m*

calisthenics = **callisthenics**

calix ['keɪlɪks] *(pl* **calices** [-lɪsiːz]*)* *n* calice *m* *(récipient)*

calk [kɔːk] **1** *n (on shoe, horseshoe)* crampon *m*

2 *vt* (**a**) *(shoe, horseshoe)* munir de crampons (**b**) *(make watertight)* calfeutrer; *Naut* calfater

CALL [kɔːl]

appeler	► **1 (a), (b), (f); 2 (a), (b), (d), (g)**
pousser un cri	► **1 (c)**
passer	► **1 (d)**
s'arrêter	► **1 (e)**
réveiller	► **2 (c)**
appel	► **3 (a) – (c)**
visite	► **3 (d)**

1 *vi* (**a**) *(with one's voice)* appeler; **if you need me, just call** si tu as besoin de moi, tu n'as qu'à (m') appeler; **she called to her son in the crowd** elle appela son fils dans la foule; **to call for help** appeler à l'aide *ou* au secours

(**b**) *(on the telephone)* appeler; **where are you calling from?** d'où appelles-tu?; **it's Alison calling** c'est Alison à l'appareil; **who's calling?** qui est à l'appareil?, c'est de la part de qui?; **may I ask who's calling?** qui est à l'appareil, je vous prie?

(**c**) *(animal, bird)* pousser un cri

(**d**) *Br (visit)* passer; **did the postman call?** est-ce que le facteur est passé?; **I'll call at the butcher's on the way home** je passerai chez le boucher en revenant à la maison; **do call again** n'hésitez pas à revenir; **I was out when they called** je n'étais pas là quand ils sont passés

(**e**) *Br (stop)* s'arrêter; **to call at** *(train)* s'arrêter à; *(ship)* faire escale à

(**f**) *Cards (in bridge)* appeler (l'atout); *(in poker)* forcer l'adversaire à déclarer son jeu

2 *vt* (**a**) *(with one's voice)* appeler; **to call sb's name** appeler qn; **can you call the children to the table?** pouvez-vous appeler les enfants pour qu'ils viennent à table?; **"be careful!", he called** "attention!", cria-t-il; *Sch* **to call the roll** faire l'appel

(**b**) *(telephone)* appeler; **who's calling?** qui est à l'appareil?; **call me tonight** appelle-moi ce soir; **don't call me at work** ne m'appelle pas au bureau; **we called his house** nous avons appelé chez lui; **to call the police/fire brigade** appeler la police/les pompiers; *Hum Euph* **don't call us, we'll call you** on vous écrira

(**c**) *(wake up)* réveiller; **can you call me at nine?** pouvez-vous me réveiller à 9 heures?

(**d**) *(name or describe as)* appeler; **he has a cat called Felix** il a un chat qui s'appelle Félix; **she was called "Ratty" as a child** on l'appelait "Ratty" quand elle était enfant; *Br* **he was called Charles after his grandfather** on l'a appelé Charles comme son grand-père; **to call oneself a colonel** s'attribuer le titre de colonel; **what's this called?** comment est-ce qu'on appelle ça?, comment est-ce que ça s'appelle?; **she called him a crook** elle l'a traité d'escroc; **are you calling me a thief?** me traitez-vous de voleur?; **to call sb names** injurier qn, invectiver qn; **they called him all sorts of names** *or* **every name in the book** ils l'ont traité de tous les noms

(**e**) *(consider)* **Denver is where I call home** c'est à Denver que je me sens chez moi; **he had no home to call his own** il n'avait pas de chez lui; **she had no time to call her own** elle n'avait pas de temps à elle; **(and you) call yourself a Christian!** et tu te dis chrétien!; **I don't call that clean** ce n'est pas ce que j'appelle propre; *Br* **let's call it £10, shall we?** disons *ou* mettons 10 livres, d'accord?; **let's call it a day** si on s'arrêtait là pour aujourd'hui?

(**f**) *(announce)* **to call an election** annoncer des élections; **to call a meeting** convoquer une assemblée; **to call a strike** appeler à la grève

(**g**) *(send for, summon)* appeler, convoquer; **he was called to the phone** on l'a demandé au téléphone; **to call the doctor** faire venir le médecin, appeler le médecin; **she was suddenly called home** elle a été rappelée soudainement chez elle; **to be called away on an emergency** être appelé en urgence; **he's been called away, his mother is ill** il a dû s'absenter parce que sa mère est malade; **he was called to his regiment** il a été rappelé à son régiment; **she was called as a witness** elle a été citée comme témoin; **he called me over** il m'a appelé; **to call sth into being** former qch

(**h**) *Fin* **to call a loan** exiger le remboursement d'un prêt

(**i**) *Sport (declare, judge)* juger; **he called it out** il a jugé qu'elle était dehors

(**j**) *Cards (in bridge)* annoncer; *(in poker)* demander

(**k**) **to call heads/tails** choisir face/pile

(**l**) *(idioms)* **to call sth to mind** rappeler qch; **the scenery calls to mind certain parts of Brittany** le paysage rappelle un peu certaines parties de la Bretagne; **to call sth into play** faire jouer qch; **market forces will soon be called into play** on fera bientôt jouer les lois du marché; **to call sth into question** remettre qch en question; **she called into question his competence as a doctor** elle a mis ses compétences de médecin en doute; *Fam* **to call the shots** *or Br* **tune** faire la loi

3 *n* (**a**) *(cry, shout)* appel *m*; *(of animal, bird)* cri *m*; *(of bugle, drum)* appel *m*; *Fig* **the call of the sea** l'appel du large; **he showed dedication (above and) beyond the call of duty** il a fait preuve d'un dévouement bien au-delà de ce qu'on était en droit d'attendre de lui; **a call for help** un appel à l'aide *ou* au secours; **to give sb a call** *(waken)* réveiller qn

(**b**) *(on telephone)* appel *m*; **can I make a call?** puis-je téléphoner?; **to put a call through** passer une communication; **to make a call** passer un coup de téléphone; **there's a call for you** on vous demande au téléphone; **to take a call** prendre un appel; **I'll give you a call tomorrow** je t'appelle demain; **how much does a call to Italy cost?** combien est-ce que ça coûte d'appeler en Italie *ou* l'Italie?; **he's on a call** il est en ligne; **to return sb's call** rappeler qn

(**c**) *(summons)* appel *m*; **to come at/answer sb's call** venir/répondre à l'appel de qn; **to be within call** être à portée de voix; **this is the last call for passengers for Bordeaux** ceci est le dernier appel pour les passagers à destination de Bordeaux; **call for tenders** appel *m* d'offres; *Euph* **to obey** *or* **answer a call of nature** satisfaire un besoin naturel

(**d**) *(visit)* visite *f*; *Br* **to make** *or* **pay a call on sb** rendre visite à qn; *Br* **she had several calls to make in the neighbourhood** elle devait rendre quelques visites dans le voisinage; **the doctor doesn't make house calls** le médecin ne fait pas de visites à domicile

(**e**) *Br (stop)* **the ship made a call at Genoa** le navire a fait escale à Gênes

(**f**) *(demand, need)* **there have been renewed calls for a return to capital punishment** il y a des gens qui demandent à nouveau le rétablissement de la peine de mort; **there is little call for unskilled labour** il n'y a qu'une faible demande de travailleurs non spécialisés; **there's no call to shout** il n'y a aucune raison de crier; **there's no call for rudeness!** pas besoin *ou* ce n'est pas la peine d'être impoli!; **you have first call on my time** je m'occuperai de vous en premier lieu

(**g**) *St Exch* option *f* d'achat, call *m*; **call of more** option *f* du double

(**h**) *Fin (for repayment)* demande *f* (d'argent); **call for capital** appel *m* de fonds; **payable at call** payable sur demande *ou* à présentation *ou* à vue

(**i**) *Sport (decision)* jugement *m*

(**j**) *Cards (in bridge)* annonce *f*; *(in solo, whist)* demande *f*

(**k**) *Rel* vocation *f*; **he felt a call (to the ministry)** il se sentait une vocation religieuse

(**l**) *(heads or tails)* **your call** pile ou face?; **it's your call!** c'est à toi de décider

4 on call *adj (doctor, nurse)* de garde; *(police, troops)* en éveil; *(car)* disponible; *Fin (loan)* remboursable sur demande

►► ***call alarm*** alarme *f (pour personne âgée ou handicapée)*; *Tel* ***call barring*** interdiction *f* d'appels; *Tel Br* ***call box*** *(telephone box)* cabine *f* téléphonique; *Am (on roadside)* borne *f* d'appel d'urgence; ***call button*** bouton *d*'appel; *Com* ***call centre*** centre *m* d'appels; *Tel* ***call connection*** établissement *m* d'appel; *Tel* ***call diversion*** transfert *m* d'appel; *St Exch* ***call feature*** = clause de remboursement anticipé au gré de l'émetteur; *Tel* ***call forwarding*** redirection *f* d'appel; *Tel* ***call forwarding device*** dispositif *m* de redirection d'appel; ***call girl*** *(prostitute)* call-girl *f*; *Tel* ***call holding*** mise *f* en attente d'appels; *Tel* ***call key*** touche *f* d'appel; ***call letter*** avis *m* d'appel de fonds; *Am Rad* ***call letters*** indicatif *m* d'appel *(d'une station de radio)*; *Fin* ***call loan*** prêt *m* à vue, prêt *m* remboursable sur demande; *Fin* ***call money*** argent *m* au jour le jour; *Am* ***call number*** *(on library book)* cote *f*; *St Exch* ***call option*** option *f* d'achat, call *m*; *St Exch* ***call price*** cours *m* du dont; *Tel* ***call screening*** filtrage *m* d'appels; *Comput* ***call sequence*** séquence *f* d'appel; *Rad* ***call sign*** indicatif *m* d'appel *(d'une station de radio)*; *Tel* ***call waiting*** signal *m* d'appel; *Tel* ***call waiting service*** signal *m* d'appel; ***call warrant*** warrant *m* à l'achat

►**call aside** *vt sep* prendre à part

►**call away** *vt sep* **she was called away from the office** on l'a appelée et elle a dû quitter le bureau; **she's often called away on business** elle doit souvent partir en déplacement ou s'absenter pour affaires

►**call back 1** *vt sep* (**a**) *(on telephone)* rappeler; **I'll call you back later** je te rappelle plus tard (**b**) *(ask to return)* rappeler; **I was already at the door when she called me back** j'étais déjà près de la porte lorsqu'elle m'a rappelé

2 *vi* (**a**) *(on telephone)* rappeler; **can you call back after five?** pourriez-vous rappeler après cinq heures? (**b**) *(visit again)* revenir, repasser; **I'll call back tomorrow** je reviendrai *ou* repasserai demain

►**call down** *vt sep* (**a**) *Literary (invoke)* **he called down the wrath of God on the killers** il appela la colère de Dieu sur la tête des tueurs (**b**) *Am Fam (reprimand)* engueuler

►**call for** *vt insep* (**a**) *Br (collect)* **he called for her at her parents' house** il est passé la chercher chez ses parents; **whose is this parcel? – someone's calling for it later** à qui est ce paquet? – quelqu'un passera le prendre plus tard

(**b**) *(put forward as demand)* appeler, demander; *(of agreement, treaty)* prévoir; **the opposition called for an official statement** l'opposition a exigé *ou* demandé une déclaration officielle; **the police are calling for tougher penalties** la police réclame des sanctions plus fermes

(**c**) *(require)* exiger; **the situation called for quick thinking** la situation demandait *ou* exigeait qu'on réfléchisse vite; **this calls for a celebration/a drink!** il faut fêter/arroser ça!; **that sort of behaviour isn't called for** on se passe bien de ce genre de comportement

►**call forth** *vt sep Formal* provoquer, susciter; **the article called forth vigorous denials** l'article suscita *ou* occasionna des démentis énergiques

►**call in 1** *vt sep* (**a**) *(send for)* faire venir; **call Miss Smith in, please** faites entrer Mlle Smith, s'il vous plaît; **an accountant was called in to look at the books** on a fait venir un comptable pour examiner les livres de comptes; **she called the children in** *(back into the house)* elle a fait rentrer les enfants; **the army was called in to assist with the evacuation** on a fait appel à l'armée pour aider à l'évacuation

(**b**) *(recall* → *defective goods)* rappeler; *(*→ *banknotes)* retirer de la circulation; *(*→ *library books)* faire rentrer

(**c**) *Fin (debt)* rappeler; **to call in one's money** faire rentrer ses fonds; **to call in a loan** *(of bank)* demander le remboursement d'un prêt

2 *vi* (**a**) *Br (pay a visit)* passer; **she called in at her sister's to say goodbye** elle est passée chez sa sœur pour dire au revoir

(**b**) *(telephone)* appeler, téléphoner; **to call in sick** téléphoner pour prévenir qu'on est malade

(**c**) *Fin (currency)* retirer de la circulation

►**call off** *vt sep* (**a**) *(appointment, meeting, match, holidays)* annuler; *(deal)* annuler, résilier; **to call off a strike** *(before it takes place)* annuler un ordre de grève; *(when it has begun)* mettre fin à une grève; **to call off one's engagement** rompre ses fiançailles; **the police called off their search** la police a arrêté ses recherches (**b**) *(dog, attacker)* rappeler

►**call on** *vt insep Br* (**a**) *(summon)* faire appel à; **to call on the experts/sb's services** faire appel aux *ou* avoir recours aux experts/services de qn

(**b**) *(urge, invite)* **to call on sb to do sth** demander à qn de faire qch; **she called on the government to take action** elle a demandé au gouvernement d'agir; **I now call on Mr Stewart** *(to speak)* je laisse la parole à M. Stewart

(**c**) *(visit)* rendre visite à; **I'll call on her this evening** je lui rendrai visite *ou* je passerai chez elle ce soir

(**d**) *(invoke)* **to call on God** invoquer le nom de Dieu

►**call out 1** *vt sep* (**a**) *(cry out)* **"over here!" he called out** "par ici!" appela-t-il; **she called out the winning number** elle a annoncé le numéro gagnant (**b**) *(summon)* appeler, faire appel à; **the army was called out to help** on a fait appel à l'armée pour aider; **the union called out its members for 24 hours** le syndicat appela ses adhérents à une grève de 24 heures

2 *vi (shout)* appeler; **she called out to a policeman** elle appela un agent de police; **to call out in anger/pain** crier de colère/douleur

►**call out for** *vt insep* exiger

►**call round** *vi Br* **can I call round this evening?** puis-je passer ce soir?; **your mother called round for the parcel** votre mère est passée prendre le paquet

►**call together** *vt sep* convoquer

►**call up 1** *vt sep* (**a**) *(telephone)* appeler (**b**) *Mil (for military service)* appeler; *(reservists)* mobiliser (**c**) *(evoke)* évoquer, faire venir à l'esprit (**d**) *(summon)* appeler, convoquer; **she was called up for jury service** elle a été appelée *ou* convoquée pour faire partie d'un jury (**e**) *Comput (help screen, menu)* rappeler

2 *vi* appeler

►**call upon** *vt insep Formal (request, summon)* faire appel à; **she may be called upon to give evidence** il est possible qu'elle soit citée comme témoin; **I called upon him for assistance** j'ai fait appel à son aide

'The Call of the Wild' *London* 'L'Appel de la forêt'

callable ['kɔːləbəl] *adj Fin (loan, debt)* remboursable sur demande

Callanetics® [kælə'netɪks] *n Sport* = sorte de gymnatisque douce

callboy ['kɒːlbɔɪ] *n* (**a**) *Theat* avertisseur *m* (**b**) *Am (bellboy)* chasseur *m*, groom *m*

called-up capital *n Fin* capital *m* appelé

caller ['kɔːlə(r)] *n* (**a**) *(visitor)* visiteur(euse) *m,f* (**b**) *Tel* personne *f* qui appelle; **the vast majority of callers just need someone to talk to** la plupart des gens qui nous appellent ont juste besoin de parler (**c**) *(in bingo)* ≃ animateur(trice) *m,f*

►► *Tel* ***caller identification*** identification *f* d'appel

calligram, calligramme ['kælɪgræm] *n* calligramme *m*

calligrapher [kə'lɪgrəfə(r)] *n* calligraphe *mf*

calligraphic [kælɪ'græfɪk] *adj* calligraphique

calligraphist [kə'lɪgrəfɪst] *n* calligraphe *mf*

calligraphy [kə'lɪgrəfɪ] *n* calligraphie *f*

call-in *n TV & Rad* émission *f* à ligne ouverte

calling ['kɔːlɪŋ] *n* (**a**) *(vocation)* appel *m* intérieur, vocation *f*; **I felt no/a calling for a religious life** je n'avais pas/j'avais la vocation (**b**) *Formal (profession)* métier *m*, profession *f*

►► *Am* ***calling card*** *(visiting card)* carte *f* de visite; *Tel* carte *f* téléphonique; *Fam Hum* **the dog left its calling card on the carpet/front doorstep** le chien a fait sa crotte sur le tapis/devant la porte d'entrée; *Fin* ***calling in*** *(of debt, loan)* demande *f* de remboursement immédiat; *(of currency)* retrait *m*; ***calling off*** *(of appointment, meeting, match, holidays)* annulation *f*; *(of deal)* rupture *f*; *(of dog, attacker)* rappel *m*; **the calling off of the strike** l'annulation de l'ordre de grève; ***calling up*** *(of memory)* évocation *f*; *(by telephone)* appel *m* au téléphone; *Mil* appel *m* (sous les drapeaux)

calliope [kə'laɪəpɪ] *n* orgue *m* à vapeur

calliper, *Am* **caliper** ['kælɪpə(r)] *n* (**a**) *Math* **a pair of calliper compasses** *or* **callipers** un compas (**b**) *Med* **calliper (splint)** attelle-étrier *f* (**c**) *Tech (for brake)* étrier *m*

callisthenics [ˌkælɪs'θenɪks] *n (UNCOUNT) Sport* gymnastique *f* rythmique

callose ['kæləʊs] *n Bot* callose *f*

callosity [kə'lɒsətɪ] *(pl* **callosities***)* *n* callosité *f*

callous ['kæləs] *adj* (**a**) *(unfeeling)* dur, sans cœur; *(behaviour, remark)* dur, impitoyable (**b**) *(skin)* calleux

calloused ['kæləst] *adj (feet, hands)* calleux, corné

callously ['kæləslɪ] *adv* durement

callousness ['kæləsnɪs] *n* dureté *f*

call-out *n (by maintenance man)* dépannage *m*;

►► ***call-out charge*** (frais *mpl* de) déplacement *m*; ***call-out maintenance insurance*** assurance *f* maintenance visite

callow ['kæləʊ] *adj* sans expérience, sans maturité; **he's a callow youth** c'est un jeune homme sans expérience *ou* maturité

callowness ['kæləʊnɪs] *n* manque *m* d'expérience

call-up *n Br Mil (conscription)* convocation *f* (au service militaire), ordre *m* d'incorporation

►► ***call-up papers*** ordre *m* d'incorporation

callus ['kæləs] *n (on feet, hands)* cal *m*, durillon *m*

calm [kɑːm] **1** *n* calme *m*; *(after upset, excitement)* accalmie *f*; **there was a strange calm after the battle** la bataille fut suivie d'une étrange accalmie; **the calm of the botanical gardens** le calme du jardin botanique; **when calm descends on the town** quand le calme revient sur la ville; **the calm before the storm** le calme qui précède la tempête

2 *adj* calme; **keep calm!** du calme!, restons calmes!; **she tried to keep calm** elle essaya de garder son calme *ou* sang-froid; **to be calm and collected** être maître de soi, garder son sang-froid

3 *vt* calmer; *(fears)* apaiser, calmer; **she tried to calm her nerves** elle essaya de se calmer

►**calm down 1** *vi* se calmer; **calm down!** calmez-vous!, ne vous énervez pas!

2 *vt sep* calmer

calmative [ˈkælmətɪv] *n* calmant *m*

calming [ˈkɑːmɪŋ] *adj* calmant; **her words had a calming effect on him** ses paroles ont réussi à le calmer

calmly [ˈkɑːmlɪ] *adv* calmement; **she received the news calmly** elle a reçu la nouvelle calmement *ou* avec calme

calmness [ˈkɑːmnɪs] *n* calme *m*; **she felt a sense of calmness** elle éprouvait une sensation de calme

Calor gas® [ˈkælə-] *n Br* butane *m*, Butagaz® *m*
▸▸ ***Calor gas*® *heater*** radiateur *m* au butane; ***Calor gas*® *stove*** réchaud *m*

caloric [kəˈlɒrɪk] *adj Phys* calorique

calorie [ˈkælərɪ] *n Phys* calorie *f*; *Fam* **to watch** *or* **count the calories** surveiller sa ligne ▫
▸▸ ***calorie count*** taux *m* de calorie

calorie-conscious *adj* **she's very calorie-conscious** elle fait très attention au nombre de calories qu'elle absorbe

calorie-controlled *adj (diet)* hypocalorique, faible en calories

calorie-free *adj* sans calories

calorific [ˌkæləˈrɪfɪk] *adj Phys* calorifique; **that cake is very calorific** ce gâteau est très riche en calories
▸▸ *Phys* ***calorific value*** valeur *f* calorifique

calorification [ˌkælərɪfɪˈkeɪʃən] *n Phys* calorification *f*

calorimeter [kæləˈrɪmɪtə(r)] *n Phys* calorimètre *m*; **electric resistance calorimeter** calorimètre *m* électrique; **bomb calorimeter** bombe *f* calorimétrique

calorimetry [kæləˈrɪmɪtrɪ] *n Phys* calorimétrie *f*

calorization [kælərarˈzeɪʃən] *n Metal* calorisation *f*

calorize, -ise [ˈkæləraɪz] *vt Metal* caloriser

calque [kælk] *n Ling* calque *m*

calumet [ˈkæljʊmet] *n* calumet *m*

calumniate [kəˈlʌmnɪeɪt] *vt Formal* calomnier

calumniation [kəˌlʌmnɪˈeɪʃən] *n Formal* calomnie *f*

calumniatory [kəˈlʌmnɪətərɪ] *adj Formal* calomnieux

calumnious [kəˈlʌmnɪəs] *adj Formal* calomnieux

calumniously [kəˈlʌmnɪəslɪ] *adv Formal* calomnieusement

calumny [ˈkæləmnɪ] (*pl* **calumnies**) *n Formal* calomnie *f*

calvados [ˈkælvəˌdɒs] *n (brandy)* calvados *m*

calvary [ˈkælvərɪ] *Rel* **1** *n* calvaire *m*
2 Calvary *n* le Calvaire

calve [kɑːv] *vi (cow, glacier)* vêler

calves [kɑːvz] *pl of* **calf**

Calvin [ˈkælvɪn] *pr n* **John Calvin** Jean Calvin

calving [ˈkɑːvɪŋ] *n (of cow)* vêlage *m*, vêlement *m*; **at calving time** pendant le vêlement

Calvinism [ˈkælvɪnɪzəm] *n Rel* calvinisme *m*

Calvinist [ˈkælvɪnɪst] *Rel* **1** *adj* calviniste
2 *n* calviniste *mf*

Calvinistic [ˌkælvɪˈnɪstɪk] *adj Rel* calviniste; *Fig* puritain

calx [kælks] *n Chem & Metal* résidu *m* de calcination

calypso [kəˈlɪpsəʊ] (*pl* **calypsos**) **1** *n Mus* calypso *m*; **calypso rhythm** rythme *m* de calypso
2 Calypso *pr n Myth* Calypso

calyx [ˈkeɪlɪks] (*pl* **calyxes** *or* **calyces** [-siːz]) *n Bot* calice *m*

calzone [kælˈtsəʊnɪ] *n Culin* calzone *m*

CAM [ˌsiːeɪˈem, kæm] *n Comput* (*abbr* **computer-aided manufacture**) FAO *f*

cam [kæm] *n Tech* came *f*

camaraderie [ˌkæməˈrɑːdərɪ] *n* camaraderie *f*

Camargue [kɑːˈmɑːg] *n* **the Camargue** la Camargue; **in the Camargue** en Camargue

camarilla [kæməˈrɪlə] *n Pol* camarilla *f*

camber [ˈkæmbə(r)] *Tech* **1** *n (in road)* bombement *m*; *(in beam, girder)* cambre *f*, cambrure *f*; *(in ship's deck)* tonture *f*
2 *vi (road)* bomber, être bombé; *(beam, girder)* être cambré; *(ship's deck)* avoir une tonture

cambered [ˈkæmbəd] *adj Tech* arqué, courbé, cambré; *(road)* bombé; *Naut (deck)* en pente; *Naut (ship)* arqué

cambium [ˈkæmbɪəm] *n Bot* cambium *m*

Cambodia [kæmˈbəʊdjə] *n* Cambodge *m*; **in Cambodia** au Cambodge

Cambodian [kæmˈbəʊdjən] **1** *n* Cambodgien(enne) *m,f*
2 *adj* cambodgien
3 *comp (embassy, history)* du Cambodge

Cambozola [ˌkæmbəˈtsəʊlə] *n* cambozola *m*

Cambrian [ˈkæmbrɪən] **1** *n* **the Cambrian** le cambrien
2 *adj* cambrien; **the Cambrian Mountains** les monts *mpl* Cambriens

cambric [ˈkeɪmbrɪk, ˈkæmbrɪk] *n Tex* batiste *f*

Cambridge [ˈkeɪmbrɪdʒ] *n* Cambridge
▸▸ ***Cambridge blue*** **1** *adj* bleu clair **2** *n* bleu *m* clair; ***Cambridge Certificate*** = diplôme d'anglais langue étrangère administré par l'Université de Cambridge

Cambridgeshire [ˈkeɪmbrɪdʒˌʃɪə] *n* le Cambridgeshire, = comté dans le sud de l'Angleterre; **in Cambridgeshire** dans le Cambridgeshire

Cambs. (*written abbr* **Cambridgeshire**) Cambridgeshire *m*

camcorder [ˈkæmˌkɔːdə(r)] *n* Caméscope® *m*

Camden [ˈkæmdən] *n* = quartier à la mode dans le nord-ouest de Londres
▸▸ ***Camden Lock*** = partie du quartier de Camden où se déroule un marché célèbre

came [keɪm] *pt of* **come**

camel [ˈkæməl] **1** *n* (**a**) *Zool* chameau *m*; *(with one hump)* dromadaire *m*; *(female)* chamelle *f* (**b**) *(colour)* fauve *m inv*
2 *comp* (**a**) *(train)* de chameaux (**b**) *(coat, jacket → of camel hair)* en poil de chameau; *(→ coloured)* fauve *(inv)*
▸▸ *Mil* ***the Camel Corps*** les compagnies *fpl* de méharistes; ***camel driver*** chamelier *m*; ***camel ride*** promenade *f* à dos de chameau

camelhair [ˈkæməlheə(r)] **1** *n* poil *m* de chameau
2 *comp (coat, jacket)* en poil de chameau
▸▸ ***camelhair brush*** *(for watercolour painting)* pinceau *m* en petit-gris

camellia [kəˈmiːlɪə] *n Bot* camélia *m*

Camembert [ˈkæməmbeə] *n* camembert *m*

cameo [ˈkæmɪəʊ] (*pl* **cameos**) **1** *n* (**a**) *(piece of jewellery)* camée *m* (**b**) *(piece of writing)* morceau *m* bref, court texte *m*; *Cin, Theat & TV (appearance)* brève apparition *f (par un acteur célèbre)*
2 *comp (brooch, ring)* monté en broche
▸▸ *Cin, Theat & TV* ***cameo performance, cameo role*** petit rôle *(joué par un acteur célèbre)*

camera [ˈkæmərə] **1** *n* (**a**) *(device → for still photos)* appareil *m* (photographique), appareil photo *m*; *(→ for film, video)* caméra *f*; **to be on camera** être à l'écran; **off camera** hors champ; **in front of the camera** devant les caméras (**b**) *Law* **in camera** à huis clos
2 *comp (battery, case)* pour appareil photo; *(shop)* de photo
▸▸ ***camera crew*** équipe *f* de tournage; ***camera lens*** objectif *m*; *Opt* ***camera obscura*** chambre *f* noire; *TV & Opt* ***camera tube*** tube *m* analyseur

cameraman [ˈkæmərəmæn] (*pl* **cameramen** [-men]) *n* cadreur *m*, cameraman *m*

camera-ready copy *n Typ & Comput* copie *f* prête pour la reproduction

camera-shy *adj* **he's camera-shy** il n'aime pas être pris en photo

camerawoman [ˈkæmərəˌwʊmən] (*pl* **camerawomen** [-ˌwɪmɪn]) *n* cadreuse *f*

camerawork [ˈkæmərəwɜːk] *n* prise *f* de vue

camerlengo [ˌkæməˈleŋgəʊ], **camerlingo** [ˌkæməˈlɪŋgəʊ] *n Rel* camerlingue *m*

Cameroon [ˌkæməˈruːn] *n* Cameroun *m*; **in Cameroon** au Cameroun

Cameroonian [ˌkæməˈruːnɪən] **1** *n* Camerounais(e) *m,f*
2 *adj* camerounais

camiknickers [ˈkæmɪˌnɪkəz] *npl Br* combinaison-culotte *f*

camisole [ˈkæmɪsəʊl] *n* caraco *m*, *Can & Suisse* camisole *f*

camogie [kəˈməʊgɪ] *n Ir Sport* = sport féminin, proche du hockey sur gazon, pratiqué en Irlande

camomile [ˈkæməmaɪl] *n Bot* camomille *f*
▸▸ ***camomile shampoo*** shampooing *m* à la camomille; ***camomile tea*** infusion *f* de camomille

camorra [kæˈmɔːrə] *n* camorra *f*

camouflage [ˈkæməflɑːʒ] **1** *n* camouflage *m*
2 *comp (material, jacket, trousers)* de camouflage
3 *vt* camoufler

camp[1] [kæmp] **1** *n* (**a**) *(place)* camp *m*; *(not permanent)* campement *m*; **to make** *or* **to pitch** *or* **to set up camp** établir un camp; **to break camp** lever le camp
(**b**) *(group)* camp *m*, parti *m*; **the conservative camp** le parti *ou* camp conservateur, les conservateurs *mpl*; **to go over to the other camp** changer de camp; **to be in the same camp** être du même bord
2 *vi* camper; **are you going to camp?** allez-vous camper *ou* faire du camping?
▸▸ ***camp bed*** lit *m* de camp; ***camp chair*** pliant *m*, chaise *f* pliante; *Am* ***camp counselor*** moniteur(trice) *m,f*; ***Camp David*** Camp David; ***the Camp David agreement*** les accords *mpl* de Camp David; ***Camp Fire Club*** = organisation américaine de scouts pour garçons et filles; ***camp follower*** *(gen)* = civil qui accompagne une armée pour rendre des services; *(prostitute)* prostituée *f*, fille *f* à soldats; *Fig (supporter)* compagnon *m* de route; *esp Am* ***camp meeting*** rassemblement *m* religieux *(qui a lieu sous des tentes)*; *Am Orn* ***camp robber*** mésangeai *m* du Canada; ***camp stool*** pliant *m*, chaise *f* pliante

camp[2] **1** *n (kitsch)* **(high) camp** kitsch *m*
2 *adj* (**a**) *(effeminate)* efféminé (**b**) *(affected)* affecté, maniéré; *(theatrical → person)* cabotin; *(→ manners)* théâtral (**c**) *(in dubious taste)* kitsch *(inv)*

▸**camp out** *vi* camper, faire du camping; *Fig* **we camped out at my parents** nous avons campé chez mes parents

▸**camp up** *vt sep Fam* **to camp it up** *(overdramatize)* cabotiner, en faire trop; *(effeminate man)* en rajouter dans le genre efféminé

Campagna [kæmˈpænjə] *n* **the Campagna** la Campagne de Rome

campaign [kæmˈpeɪn] **1** *n* campagne *f*; **to conduct** *or* **to lead a campaign against drugs** mener une campagne *ou* faire campagne contre la drogue; *Pol* **to be on the campaign trail** être en pleine campagne électorale
2 *vi* mener une campagne, faire campagne; **to campaign against/for sth** mener une campagne contre/en faveur de qch
▸▸ *Br Pol* ***Campaign Group*** = groupe de députés travaillistes de l'aile gauche du parti; *Mil* ***campaign medal*** médaille *f* commémorative; *Br* ***Campaign for Nuclear Disarmament*** = en Grande-Bretagne, mouvement pour le désarmement nucléaire; *Br* ***Campaign for Real Ale*** = association britannique d'amateurs de bières traditionnelles

campaigner [kæmˈpeɪnə(r)] *n* militant(e) *m,f*; *Mil* vétéran *m*; *Mil & Fig* **old campaigner** vétéran *m*; **campaigners in favour of/against nuclear power** des militants pronucléaires/antinucléaires

Campania [kæmˈpeɪnɪə] *n* Campanie *f*; **in Campania** en Campanie

campanile [ˌkæmpəˈniːlɪ] *n Archit* campanile *m*

campanological [ˌkæmpənəˈlɒdʒɪkəl] *adj* campanaire

campanologist [ˌkæmpəˈnɒlədʒɪst] *n* carillonneur *m*

campanology [ˌkæmpəˈnɒlədʒɪ] *n* art *m* des carillons

campanula [kəmˈpænjʊlə] *n Bot* campanule *f*

camper [ˈkæmpə(r)] *n* (**a**) *(person)* campeur(euse) *m,f* (**b**) *(vehicle)* **camper (van)** camping-car *m*

campfire [ˈkæmpˌfaɪə(r)] *n* feu *m* de camp

campground [ˈkæmpˌgraʊnd] *n Am (private)* camp *m*; *(commercial)* terrain *m* de camping, camping *m*; *(clearing)* emplacement *m* de camping, endroit *m* où camper

camphor [ˈkæmfə(r)] *n Chem* camphre *m*
▸▸ ***camphor tree*** camphrier *m*

camphorate [ˈkæmfəreɪt] *n Chem* camphorate *m*

camphorated [ˈkæmfəreɪtɪd] *adj Chem* camphré
▸▸ ***camphorated oil*** huile *f* camphrée

camping [ˈkæmpɪŋ] **1** *n* camping *m*; **to go camping** faire du camping, camper
2 *comp (equipment)* de camping

►► ***camping gas*** butane *m*; ***camping ground*** *or* ***grounds*** *or* ***site*** *(private)* camp *m*; *(commercial)* terrain *m* de camping, camping *m*; *(clearing)* emplacement *m* de camping, endroit *m* où camper; ***camping holiday*** vacances *fpl* (en) camping; ***camping stool*** pliant *m*; ***camping stove*** camping-gaz *m*

camping-caravanning *n* campage-caravanage *m*, camping-caravaning *m*

campion ['kæmpjən] *n Bot* silène *m*, lychnis *m*

campsis ['kæmpsɪs] *n Bot* campsis *m*

campsite ['kæmpsaɪt] *n (commercial)* terrain *m* de camping, camping *m*; *(clearing)* emplacement *m* de camping, endroit *m* où camper

►► ***campsite facilities*** installations *fpl* de camping

campus ['kæmpəs] (*pl* **campuses**) *n Univ (grounds)* campus *m*; *(buildings)* campus *m*, complexe *m* universitaire; **to live on campus** habiter sur le campus; **to live off campus** habiter en dehors du campus; **on-/off-campus housing** logements *mpl* sur le/en dehors du campus

►► ***campus police*** police *f* du campus; ***campus university*** université *f* regroupée sur un campus

CAMRA ['kæmrə] *n Br* (*abbr* **Campaign for Real Ale**) = association britannique d'amateurs de bières traditionnelles

camshaft ['kæmʃɑːft] *n Tech* arbre *m* à cames

camwood ['kæmwʊd] *n Bot* bois *m* de cam; camwood *m*

Can. (*written abbr* **Canada**) Canada *m*

CAN[1] [kən, *stressed* kæn]

pouvoir	► **(a), (d) – (j)**
savoir	► **(c)**

(*pt* **could** [kəd, *stressed* kʊd], *negative forms* **cannot** ['kænət, *stressed* 'kænɒt], **could not**, *frequently shortened to* **can't** [kɑːnt], **couldn't** ['kʊdənt])

Le verbe **can** n'a ni infinitif, ni gérondif ni participe. Pour exprimer l'infinitif ou le participe, on aura recours à la forme correspondante de **be able to** (**he wanted to be able to speak English**; **she has always been able to swim**).

modal aux v (**a**) *(be able to)* pouvoir; **can you come to the party?** peux-tu venir à la fête?; **I'll come if I can** je viendrai si je (le) peux; **I'll come as soon as I can** je viendrai aussitôt que possible *ou* aussitôt que je pourrai; **we'll do everything we can to help** nous ferons tout ce que nous pourrons *ou* tout notre possible pour aider; **she has everything money can buy** elle a tout ce qu'elle veut; **she can no longer walk** elle ne peut plus marcher; **five years ago I could run a mile in four minutes but I can't anymore** il y a cinq ans, je courais un mile en quatre minutes mais je ne peux plus maintenant; **can you help me?** pouvez-vous m'aider?; **can you tell me when the train leaves?** pouvez-vous me dire à quelle heure part le train?; **I can't very well accept** il m'est difficile d'accepter; **can it be true?** serait-ce vrai?; **(it) could be** c'est possible; *Fam* **no can do!** impossible!; *Am Fam* **can do!** pas de problème!

(**b**) *(with verbs of perception or understanding)* **can you feel it?** tu le sens?; **we can hear everything our neighbours say** nous entendons tout ce que disent nos voisins; **I can't understand you when you mumble** je ne te comprends pas *ou* je ne comprends pas ce que tu dis quand tu marmonnes; **I can see his point of view** je comprends son point de vue; **there can be no doubt about his guilt** sa culpabilité ne fait aucun doute

(**c**) *(indicating ability or skill)* savoir; **can you drive/sew?** savez-vous conduire/coudre?; **many people can't read or write** beaucoup de gens ne savent ni lire ni écrire; **she can speak three languages** elle parle trois langues

(**d**) *(giving or asking for permission)* pouvoir; **I've already said you can't go** je t'ai déjà dit que tu ne peux pas y aller; **can I borrow your sweater? – yes, you can** puis-je emprunter ton pull? – (mais oui,) bien sûr; **can I sit with you?** puis-je m'asseoir avec vous?

(**e**) *(used to interrupt, intervene)* pouvoir; **can I just say something here?** est-ce que je peux dire quelque chose?

(**f**) *(in offers of help)* pouvoir; **can I be of any assistance?** puis-je vous aider?; **what can I do for you?** que puis-je (faire) pour vous?

(**g**) *(indicating reluctance)* pouvoir; **we can't leave the children alone** nous ne pouvons pas laisser *ou* il nous est impossible de laisser les enfants seuls; *(indicating refusal)* pouvoir; **we cannot tolerate such behaviour** nous ne pouvons pas tolérer ce genre de comportement

(**h**) *(expressing opinions)* **you can't let him speak to you like that!** tu ne peux pas *ou* tu ne devrais pas lui permettre de te parler comme ça!; **you can't blame her for leaving him!** tu ne peux pas lui reprocher de l'avoir quitté!; **you'll have to leave, it can't be helped** il faudra que tu partes, il n'y a rien à faire

(**i**) *(used to urge or insist)* **can't we at least talk about it?** est-ce que nous pouvons au moins en discuter?

(**j**) *(indicating possibility or likelihood)* pouvoir; **they can back out of it at any time** ils peuvent se rétracter à n'importe quel moment; **the contract can still be cancelled** il est toujours possible d'annuler *ou* on peut encore annuler le contrat; **the job can't be finished in one day** il est impossible de finir le travail *ou* le travail ne peut pas se faire en un jour; **the cottage can sleep six people** on peut loger six personnes dans ce cottage; **you can always try again later** tu peux toujours réessayer plus tard; **he can be very stubborn** il lui arrive d'être *ou* il peut être très têtu; **he could have done it** il aurait pu le faire; **what can I have done with the keys?** qu'est-ce que j'ai bien pu faire des clés?; **I'm as happy as can be** je suis on ne peut plus heureux; **she was as kind as can be** elle était on ne peut plus gentille

(**k**) *(indicating disbelief or doubt)* **you can't be serious!** (ce n'est pas possible!) vous ne parlez pas sérieusement!; **he can't possibly have finished already!** ce n'est pas possible qu'il ait déjà fini!; **the house can't have been that expensive** la maison n'a pas dû coûter si cher que ça, **how can you say that?** comment pouvez-vous *ou* osez-vous dire ça?; **how COULD you!** comment avez-vous pu faire une chose pareille?; **you can't mean it!** tu ne penses pas ce que tu dis!; **what can they want now?** qu'est-ce qu'ils peuvent bien vouloir maintenant?; **who on earth can that be?** qui diable cela peut-il bien être?

(**l**) *(expressing impatience or exasperation)* **I could have wept** j'avais envie de pleurer; **I could have smacked his face!** je l'aurais giflé!; **you could have warned me!** tu aurais pu me prévenir!

(**m**) *Formal (idiom)* **his resignation cannot but confirm such suspicions** sa démission ne fait que confirmer de tels soupçons

can[2] [kæn] (*pt & pp* **canned,** *cont* **canning**) **1** *n* (**a**) *(container → for liquid)* bidon *m*; *(→ for tinned food)* boîte *f* (de conserve); *Am (→ for rubbish)* poubelle *f*, boîte *f* à ordures; **a can of tuna** une boîte de thon (en conserve); **a can of beer/soda** une boîte de bière/de soda; **a (real) can of worms** un vrai casse-tête; **to open a can of worms** mettre à jour toutes sortes d'histoires désagréables; **the film's in the can** le film est dans la boîte; *Fam* **the deal's in the can** l'affaire est conclue

(**b**) *Am Fam (prison)* taule *f*; **in the can** en taule, au placard, à l'ombre

(**c**) *Am Fam (toilet)* chiottes *fpl*

(**d**) *Am Fam (buttocks)* fesses ❑ *fpl*; **to kick sb in the can** botter les fesses à qn

(**e**) *Br (idiom)* **to carry the can** payer les pots cassés

2 *vt* (**a**) *(food)* mettre en boîte *ou* en conserve, conserver (en boîte)

(**b**) *Am Fam (dismiss from job)* virer, renvoyer ❑

(**c**) *Am Fam* **to can it** *(shut up)* la fermer, la boucler; **can it!** ferme-la!, la ferme!

►► ***can opener*** ouvre-boîtes *m inv*

Cana ['keɪnə] *n Bible* **Cana (of Galilee)** Cana (de Galilée)

Canaan ['keɪnən] *n Bible* (la Terre de) Canaan *ou* Chanaan

Canaanite ['keɪnənaɪt] *n Bible* Cananéen(enne) *m,f*, Chananéen(enne) *m,f*

Canada ['kænədə] *n* Canada *m*; **in Canada** au Canada

►► *Bot* ***Canada balsam*** baume *m* de *ou* du Canada; *Bot* ***Canada balsam fir*** sapin *m* baumier; ***Canada Day*** Fête *f* du Canada *(anniversaire de l'indépendance canadienne, le 1er juillet)*; *Orn* ***Canada goose*** bernache *f* du Canada; *Bot* ***Canada thistle*** cirsium *m*, chardon *m* des champs

Canadian [kə'neɪdjən] **1** *n* Canadien(enne) *m,f*

2 *adj (gen)* canadien

3 *comp (embassy, history)* du Canada

►► ***Canadian Broadcasting Corporation*** = office national canadien de radiodiffusion; ***Canadian canoe*** canoë *m*; ***the Canadian Confederation*** la conféderation canadienne; ***Canadian English*** anglais *m* du Canada; ***Canadian French*** français *m* canadien; *Bot* ***Canadian goldenrod*** solidage *m* du Canada

Canadianism [kə'neɪdjəˌnɪzəm] *n (expression)* canadianisme *m*

canal [kə'næl] *n* (**a**) *(waterway)* canal *m* (**b**) *Anat* canal *m*, conduit *m*

►► ***canal barge, canal boat*** péniche *f*, chaland *m*; ***canal holiday*** croisière *f* fluviale *ou* en péniche; ***canal path*** chemin *m* de halage; *Geog* ***the Canal Zone*** *(of Panama)* la zone du canal de Panama; *(of Suez)* la zone du canal de Suez

canalization [ˌkænəlaɪ'zeɪʃən] *n Fig* canalisation *f*

canalize, -ise ['kænəlaɪz] *vt Fig* canaliser

canapé ['kænəpeɪ] *n Culin* canapé *m*

canard [kæ'nɑːd] *n (false report)* fausse nouvelle *f*, canard *m*

Canaries [kə'neərɪz] *npl* **the Canaries** les Canaries *fpl*; **in the Canaries** aux Canaries

canary [kə'neərɪ] (*pl* **canaries**) **1** *n* (**a**) *(bird)* canari *m*, serin *m* (**b**) *(colour)* jaune serin *m inv*, jaune canari *m inv*

2 *adj (colour)* jaune serin *(inv)*, jaune canari *(inv)*

►► *Bot* ***canary creeper*** capucine *f* jaune canari; *Bot* ***canary grass*** alpiste *m*; ***the Canary Islands*** les (îles *fpl*) Canaries *fpl*; **in the Canary Islands** aux Canaries; *Bot* ***canary seed*** millet *m*; ***canary yellow*** **1** *n* jaune serin *m inv*, jaune canari *m inv* **2** *adj* jaune serin *(inv)*, jaune canari *(inv)*; ***Canary Wharf*** = quartier d'affaires dans l'est de Londres, dominé par la Canary Wharf Tower, l'immeuble le plus haut de Grande-Bretagne

canasta [kə'næstə] *n Cards* canasta *f*

Canberra ['kænbərə] *n* Canberra

cancan ['kænkæn] *n* cancan *m*, french cancan *m*

►► ***cancan dancer*** danseuse *f* de cancan

cancel ['kænsəl] (*Br pt & pp* **cancelled,** *cont* **cancelling,** *Am pt & pp* **canceled,** *cont* **canceling**) **1** *vt* (**a**) *(call off → event, order, reservation)* annuler; *(→ appointment)* annuler, décommander; *(→ goods)* décommander; **the flight has been cancelled** le vol a été annulé; **they cancelled the order for three warships** ils ont annulé leur commande de trois navires de guerre

(**b**) *(revoke → agreement, contract)* résilier, annuler; *(→ debt)* faire remise à; *(→ cheque)* faire opposition à

(**c**) *(mark as no longer valid → by stamping)* oblitérer; *(→ by punching)* poinçonner

(**d**) *(cross out)* barrer, rayer, biffer

(**e**) *Math* éliminer

2 *vi* (**a**) *(having made booking)* se décommander

(**b**) *Comput* s'annuler; **press "esc" to cancel** appuyez sur "Echap" pour annuler; **cancel entry** *(command)* annulation d'entrée

►► *Comput* ***cancel button*** case *f* 'annuler'

►**cancel out** *vt sep* (**a**) *(counterbalance)* neutraliser, compenser; **the factors cancel each other out** les facteurs se neutralisent *ou* se compensent (**b**) *Math* éliminer, annuler

cancellate ['kænsəleɪt], **cancellated** ['kænsəleɪtɪd] *adj Zool* réticulé, cancellé

cancellation [ˌkænsə'leɪʃən] *n* (**a**) *(calling off → of event, reservation)* annulation *f*; *(annulment → of agreement, contract)* résiliation *f*, annulation *f*; *(→ of cheque)* opposition *f*; **we only got a table**

because there had been a cancellation nous n'avons eu une table que parce que quelqu'un avait annulé sa réservation

(**b**) *(act of invalidating → by punching)* poinçonnage *m*; *(→ by stamping)* oblitération *f*

(**c**) *(crossing out)* biffage *m*

(**d**) *Math* élimination *f*

▸▸ ***cancellation charge*** frais *mpl* d'annulation; ***cancellation clause*** clause *f* d'annulation *ou* de résiliation; ***cancellation fee*** frais *mpl* d'annulation

Cancer ['kænsə(r)] **1** *n* (**a**) *Astron* Cancer *m* (**b**) *Astrol* Cancer *m*; **he's a Cancer** il est (du signe du) Cancer

2 *adj Astrol* du Cancer; **he's Cancer** il est (du signe du) Cancer

cancer ['kænsə(r)] **1** *n Med & Fig* cancer *m*; **to have cancer** avoir un *ou* le cancer; **to die of cancer** mourir (à la suite) d'un cancer; **cigarettes cause cancer** les cigarettes sont cancérigènes *ou* carcinogènes; *Fig* **we must remove the cancer of militarism** il faut enrayer le cancer du militarisme

▸▸ ***cancer cell*** cellule *f* cancéreuse; ***cancer patient*** cancéreux(euse) *m,f*; ***cancer research*** oncologie *f*, cancérologie *f*; **we're collecting money for cancer research** nous recueillons des fonds pour la recherche contre le cancer; *Fam Hum* ***cancer stick*** clope *f*; ***cancer ward*** *(wing)* service *m* oncologique; *(building)* pavillon *m* oncologique

'Cancer Ward' *Solzhenitsyn* 'Le Pavillon des cancéreux'

cancer-causing *adj* cancérigène, carcinogène

Cancerian [,kæn'seərıən] *Astrol* **1** *n* **to be a Cancerian** être (du signe du) Cancer

2 *adj* du Cancer; **the Cancerian male** l'homme Cancer

cancerologist [,kænsə'rɒlədʒıst] *n Med* cancérologue *mf*

cancerophobia [,kænsərəʊ'fəʊbıə] *n Psy* cancérophobie *f*

cancerous ['kænsərəs] *adj Med* cancéreux

cancroid ['kæŋkrɔıd] *adj Med* cancroïde

candela [kæn'di:lə] *n Phys* candela *f*

candelabra [,kændı'lɑ:brə] (*pl* **inv** *or* **candelabras**), **candelabrum** [,kændı'lɑ:brəm] *n* candélabre *m*

C&F, C and F [,si:ənd'ef] *n Com* (*abbr* **cost and freight**) C et F

C&G, C and G [,si:ən'dʒi:] *n Sch* (*abbr* **City and Guilds**) = diplôme britannique d'enseignement technique

C&I, C and I [,si:ənd'aı] *n Com* (*abbr* **cost and insurance**) C & A

candid ['kændıd] *adj (person)* franc (franche), sincère; *(smile)* franc (franche); *(account, report)* qui ne cache rien; **I'd like your candid opinion** j'aimerais que vous me disiez franchement ce que vous en pensez; **to be quite candid, I don't like it** pour parler franchement *ou* pour être franc, je ne l'aime pas

▸▸ ***candid camera*** appareil *m* photo à instantanés; ***candid camera shot*** = photo prise à l'insu de la personne photographiée

Smile, you're on Candid Camera

Il s'agit du slogan d'une émission de télévision britannique des années 70 dont l'équivalent français est la caméra invisible, dans laquelle des gens étaient filmés à leur insu dans des situations cocasses. **Smile, you're on Candid Camera** ("Souriez, c'est pour la caméra invisible") était la formule utilisée par les animateurs de l'émission pour annoncer aux participants qu'ils venaient d'être filmés. On utilise aujourd'hui cette expression de façon humoristique lorsque l'on photographie ou lorsque l'on filme quelqu'un.

candida ['kændıdə] *n Biol* candidose *f*

candidacy ['kændıdəsı] *n* candidature *f*

candidate ['kændıdət] *n* candidat(e) *m,f*; **to be a** *or* **to stand as candidate for mayor** être candidat à la mairie; **presidential candidate** candidat aux élections présidentielles; **successful candidates will have at least three years' experience** les candidats retenus auront au moins trois ans d'expérience

candidature ['kændıdətʃə(r)] *n* candidature *f*

candid-camera *adj* **a candid-camera shot** un instantané

candidiasis [,kandı'daıəsıs] *n* candidose *f*

candidly ['kændıdlı] *adv (speak)* franchement; *(smile)* candidement, avec candeur

candidness ['kændıdnıs] *n* franchise *f*

candied ['kændıd] *adj* (**a**) *Culin (piece of fruit, peel)* confit; *(whole fruit)* confit, glacé (**b**) *Fig Literary (flattering)* mielleux

candle ['kændəl] *n* (**a**) *(of wax → gen)* bougie *f*, chandelle *f*; *(→ in church)* cierge *m*, chandelle *f*; *Fig* **he can't hold a candle to you** il ne vous arrive pas à la cheville; **to burn the candle at both ends** brûler la chandelle par les deux bouts (**b**) *Phys (former unit)* bougie *f*; *(candela)* candela *f*

▸▸ ***candle grease*** suif *m*

candleberry ['kændəlbərı] *n Bot (fruit)* (noix *f* de) bancoul *m*; *(tree)* cirier *m*, bancoulier *m*

candleholder ['kændəl,həʊldə(r)] *n (single)* bougeoir *m*; *(branched)* chandelier *m*

candlelight ['kændəllaıt] **1** *n* lueur *f* d'une bougie *ou* d'une chandelle; **they had dinner by candlelight** ils ont dîné aux chandelles; **she read by candlelight** elle lisait à la lueur d'une bougie

2 *comp (dinner, supper)* aux chandelles

candlelit ['kændəllıt] *adj* éclairé aux bougies *ou* aux chandelles

Candlemas ['kændəlməs] *n Rel* la Chandeleur

candlenut ['kændəlnʌt] *n Bot* (noix *f* de) bancoul *m*

candlepower ['kændəl,paʊə(r)] *n Phys* intensité *f* lumineuse

candlestick ['kændəlstık] *n (single)* bougeoir *m*; *(branched)* chandelier *m*

candlewick ['kændəlwık] *Tex* **1** *n (yarn)* chenille *f* (de coton)

2 *comp (bedspread)* en chenille (de coton)

can-do *adj* dynamique, entreprenant; **can-do attitude** *or* **spirit** esprit *m* de battant *ou* de gagneur

candour, *Am* **candor** ['kændə(r)] *n* candeur *f*, franchise *f*

C & W [,si:ən'dʌbelju:] *n* (*abbr* **country and western (music)**) country and western *f*

candy ['kændı] (*pl* **candies,** *pt & pp* **candied**) **1** *n* (**a**) *Am (piece)* bonbon *m*; *(UNCOUNT) (sweets in general)* bonbons *mpl*, confiserie *f* (**b**) *Culin (sugar)* sucre *m* candi (**c**) *Fam Drugs slang* came *f*

2 *vt (ginger, pieces of fruit, orange peel)* confire; *(whole fruit)* glacer, confire; *(sugar)* faire candir

3 *vi* se candir, se cristalliser

▸▸ *Am* ***candy apple*** pomme *f* d'amour; *Am* ***candy bar*** barre *f* chocolatée; *Am* ***candy cane*** = sucre d'orge en forme de canne; *Am* ***candy corn*** *(UNCOUNT)* = bonbons que l'on mange à Halloween; *Br* ***candy floss*** barbe *f* à papa; *Am* ***candy store*** confiserie *f*; *Am* ***candy striper*** = bénévole qui travaille aux œuvres de bienfaisance dans un hôpital; ***candy wrapper*** papier *m* de bonbon

candy-striped *adj* à rayures multicolores

candytuft ['kændıtʌft] *n Bot* corbeille-d'argent *f*, ibéris *f*

cane [keın] **1** *n* (**a**) *(stem of plant)* canne *f*; *(in making baskets, furniture)* rotin *m*, jonc *m*

(**b**) *(rod → for walking)* canne *f*; *(→ for punishment)* verge *f*, baguette *f*; **to give sb the cane** fouetter qn; **to get the cane** être fouetté, recevoir le fouet

(**c**) *Hort (for supporting plant)* tuteur *m*

2 *comp (furniture)* en rotin; *(chair → entirely in cane)* en rotin; *(→ with cane back, seat)* canné

3 *vt* (**a**) *(beat with rod)* donner des coups de bâton à, fouetter

(**b**) *Fam (defeat)* battre à plate couture

▸▸ *Zool* ***cane rat*** aulacode *m*; ***cane sugar*** sucre *m* de canne

canescent [kæ'nesənt] *adj* (**a**) *Literary (becoming white)* blanchissant, qui tourne au blanc (**b**) *Biol* incanescent

canework ['keınwɜ:k] *n* cannage *m*

cang, cangue [kæŋ] *n* cangue *f*

canine ['keınaın] **1** *adj (gen)* canin; *Zool* de la famille des canidés

2 *n* (**a**) *Zool (animal)* canidé *m* (**b**) *Anat (tooth)* canine *f*

▸▸ *Am* ***canine corps*** équipe *f ou* brigade *f* cynophile; *Vet* ***canine distemper*** maladie *f* de Carré; *Anat* ***canine tooth*** canine *f*

caning ['keınıŋ] *n* (**a**) *(beating)* **to give sb a caning** *(gen)* donner des coups de bâton *ou* de trique à qn; *Sch* fouetter qn à la baguette (**b**) *Fam (defeat)* **to get a caning** être battu à plate couture

Canis ['keınıs] *n Astron*

▸▸ ***Canis Major*** le Grand Chien; ***Canis Minor*** le Petit Chien

canister ['kænıstə(r)] *n* (**a**) *(for flour, sugar)* boîte *f*; **flour/sugar canister** boîte *f* à farine/sucre (**b**) *(for gas, shaving cream)* bombe *f*; **tear gas canister** bombe *f* lacrymogène

▸▸ ***canister vacuum cleaner*** aspirateur-traîneau *m*

canker ['kæŋkə(r)] *n* (**a**) *(UNCOUNT) Med* ulcère *m*, chancre *m* (**b**) *Bot & Fig* chancre *m* (**c**) *Vet (of dog etc)* gale *f* de l'oreille; *(in horse's hoof)* crapaud *m*

cankered ['kæŋkəd] *adj* (**a**) *Bot (tree)* atteint par le chancre; *(wood)* pouilleux (**b**) *Fig (person)* plein d'amertume

cankerous ['kæŋkərəs] *adj Med (tissue)* chancreux; *(sore)* rongeur; *Fig* rongeur

cankerworm ['kæŋkəwɜ:m] *n* ver *m* rongeur (des plantes)

canna ['kænə] *n Bot* balisier *m*, canna *m*

cannabis ['kænəbıs] *n (plant)* chanvre *m* indien; *(drug)* cannabis *m*

▸▸ ***cannabis resin*** résine *f* de cannabis

canned [kænd] *adj* (**a**) *(food)* en boîte, en conserve (**b**) *Fam (drunk)* paf *(inv)*, rond; **to get canned** se soûler

▸▸ ***canned goods*** conserves *fpl*; ***canned laughter*** rires *mpl* préenregistrés; ***canned music*** musique *f* enregistrée *ou* en conserve

cannellini [,kænı'li:nı] *n Bot & Culin* **cannellini (bean)** cannellini *m (haricot blanc fin)*

cannelloni [,kænı'ləʊnı] *n (UNCOUNT) Culin* cannellonis *mpl*

canner ['kænə(r)] *n* conserveur *m*

cannery ['kænərı] (*pl* **canneries**) *n* conserverie *f*, fabrique *f* de conserves

'Cannery Row' *Steinbeck* 'Rue de la sardine'

cannibal ['kænıbəl] **1** *adj* cannibale, anthropophage

2 *n* cannibale *mf*, anthropophage *mf*

cannibalism ['kænıbəlızəm] *n* cannibalisme *m*, anthropophagie *f*

cannibalistic [,kænıbə'lıstık] *adj* anthropophage

cannibalization [,kænıbəlaı'zeıʃən] *n Mktg & Tech* cannibalisation *f*

cannibalize, -ise ['kænıbəlaız] *vt Tech (car, machine)* cannibaliser, récupérer des pièces détachées de; *(text)* récupérer des parties de; *Mktg (product)* cannibaliser

cannily ['kænılı] *adv (cleverly → assess)* avec perspicacité; *(→ reason)* habilement, astucieusement; *(cautiously)* prudemment, avec circonspection

canniness ['kænınıs] *n (cleverness)* perspicacité *f*, habileté *f*; *(cautiousness)* prudence *f*, circonspection *f*

canning ['kænıŋ] **1** *n* mise *f* en boîte *ou* en conserve

2 *comp (process)* de mise en boîte *ou* en conserve

▸▸ ***canning factory*** conserverie *f*, fabrique *f* de conserves; ***canning industry*** conserverie *f*, industrie *f* de la conserve

cannon ['kænən] (*pl* **inv** *or* **cannons**) **1** *n* (**a**) *(weapon)* canon *m*; *Fig* **he's a loose cannon** il n'en fait qu'à sa tête; **she's regarded as a loose cannon in the party** elle passe pour quelqu'un de peu fiable au sein du parti car elle n'en fait qu'à sa tête

(**b**) *Tech (barrel of gun, syringe)* canon *m*

(**c**) *Br (in billiards, snooker)* carambolage *m*

2 *vi* (**a**) *(bump)* **to cannon into sb/sth** se heurter contre qn/qch

(**b**) *Br (in billiards, snooker)* caramboler; **to**

cannon off the cushion *(of player)* jouer la bricole

►► ***cannon fodder*** chair *f* à canon

cannonade [ˌkænəˈneɪd] *Mil* **1** *n* canonnade *f*

2 *vt* canonner

cannonball [ˈkænənbɔːl] *n* (**a**) *Mil (ammunition)* boulet *m* de canon (**b**) *Sport* **a cannonball (service)** un service en boulet de canon

cannonshot [ˈkænənʃɒt] *n (firing)* coup *m* de canon; *(range)* **within cannonshot** à portée de canon

cannot [ˈkænɒt] = **can not**

cannula [ˈkænjʊlə] *(pl* **cannulas** *or* **cannulae** [-liː]) *n Med (for giving medication)* canule *f*, cathéter *m*; *(for draining)* sonde *f*

canny [ˈkænɪ] *(compar* **cannier,** *superl* **canniest**) *adj* (**a**) *(clever)* astucieux, habile; *(shrewd)* malin(igne), rusé (**b**) *(cautious)* prudent, circonspect (**c**) *Br (person → thrifty)* économe; *(→ nice)* sympathique; *(bargain, deal)* avantageux

canoe [kəˈnuː] *(cont* **canoeing**) **1** *n* canoë *m*; *(dugout)* pirogue *f*; *Sport* canoë *m*, canoë-kayak *m*; *Fig* **to paddle one's own canoe** mener seul sa barque

2 *vi (gen)* faire du canoë; *Sport* faire du canoë *ou* du canoë-kayak; **we canoed down the river** nous avons descendu le fleuve en canoë

canoeing [kəˈnuːɪŋ] *n Sport* canoë-kayak *m*; **to go canoeing** faire du canoë-kayak

►► ***canoeing holiday*** raid *m ou* randonnée *f* en canoë-kayak

canoeist [kəˈnuːɪst] *n Sport* canoéiste *mf*

canola [kəˈnəʊlə] *n Am* colza *m*

canon [ˈkænən] *n* (**a**) *Rel (decree, prayer)* canon *m*; *(clergyman)* chanoine *m* (**b**) *Literature* œuvre *f* (**c**) *Mus* canon *m* (**d**) *Fig (rule)* canon *m*, règle *f*

►► *Rel* ***canon law*** droit *m* canon

canonical [kəˈnɒnɪkəl] *adj* (**a**) *Rel (text)* canonique; *(practice)* conforme aux canons (de l'église); *(robe)* sacerdotal (**b**) *Mus* en canon (**c**) *Fig (accepted)* canonique, autorisé

►► ***canonical dress*** vêtements *mpl* sacerdotaux; ***canonical hours*** *(Catholic)* heures *fpl* canoniales; *(Church of England)* = heures pendant lesquelles la célébration des mariages est autorisée (entre 8 heures et 18 heures)

canonization [ˌkænənaɪˈzeɪʃən] *n Rel & Fig* canonisation *f*

canonize, -ise [ˈkænənaɪz] *vt Rel & Fig* canoniser

canoodle [kəˈnuːdəl] *vi Br Fam* se faire des mamours

canopic jar [kəˈnəʊpɪk-] *n Archeol* canope *m*

canopied [ˈkænəpɪd] *adj (bed)* à baldaquin *ou* ciel de lit; *(balcony, passageway)* à auvent *ou* marquise; *(throne)* avec dais

canopy [ˈkænəpɪ] *(pl* **canopies**) *n* (**a**) *(over bed)* baldaquin *m*, ciel *m* de lit; *(over balcony, doorway)* auvent *m*, marquise *f*; *(over throne, altar, statue)* dais *m*; *Archit (with columns)* baldaquin *m* (**b**) *(of parachute)* voilure *f* (**c**) *Aviat (of cockpit)* verrière *f* (**d**) *(in forest)* canopée *f* (**e**) *Fig (branches, sky)* voûte *f*; *Literary* **the canopy of heaven** la voûte du ciel

cant[1] [kænt] **1** *n* (**a**) *(UNCOUNT) (insincere talk)* paroles *fpl* hypocrites; *(clichés)* clichés *mpl*, phrases *fpl* toutes faites (**b**) *(jargon)* argot *m* de métier, jargon *m*

2 *vi* (**a**) *(talk → insincerely)* parler avec hypocrisie; *(→ in clichés)* débiter des clichés (**b**) *(use jargon)* parler en argot de métier, jargonner

cant[2] **1** *n* (**a**) *(slope)* pente *f*, inclinaison *f*; *(oblique surface)* surface *f* oblique, plan *m* incliné (**b**) *Archit & Carp (edge)* chanfrein *m*, biseau *m* (**c**) *(movement)* secousse *f*, cahot *m*

2 *vt* (**a**) *(tip slightly)* pencher, incliner; *(overturn)* renverser *ou* retourner (d'un seul coup) (**b**) *Archit & Carp (edge)* biseauter, écorner

3 *vi* (**a**) *(tip slightly)* se pencher, s'incliner; *(overturn)* se renverser *ou* se retourner (d'un seul coup) (**b**) *(slope)* être incliné *ou* en pente

can't [kɑːnt] = **can not**

Cantab. *Univ* (*written abbr* **Cantabrigiensis**) = de l'université de Cambridge

cantabile [kænˈtɑːbɪleɪ] *adv Mus* cantabile

Cantabrian Mountains [kænˈteɪbrɪən-] *npl* **the Cantabrian Mountains** les monts *mpl* Cantabriques

cantaloup, cantaloupe [ˈkæntəluːp] *n* cantaloup *m*

►► ***cantaloup melon*** cantaloup *m*

cantankerous [kænˈtæŋkərəs] *adj (bad-tempered)* acariâtre, revêche, grincheux

cantankerously [kænˈtæŋkərəslɪ] *adv (bad-temperedly)* d'une manière acariâtre

cantankerousness [kænˈtæŋkərəsnɪs] *n* humeur *f* acariâtre

cantata [kænˈtɑːtə] *n Mus* cantate *f*

canteen [kænˈtiːn] *n* (**a**) *(restaurant)* cantine *f* (**b**) *Am (flask)* flasque *f*, gourde *f* (**c**) *(box for cutlery)* coffret *m*; **canteen of cutlery** ménagère *f* (**d**) *Mil (mess tin)* gamelle *f*

canter [ˈkæntə(r)] **1** *n* petit galop *m*; **the horse set off at a canter** le cheval est parti au petit galop; *Fig* **to win in a canter** gagner haut la main

2 *vt* faire aller au petit galop

3 *vi* aller au petit galop

Canterbury [ˈkæntəbrɪ] *n* Cantorbéry

►► ***Canterbury bell*** campanule *f*

'The Canterbury Tales' *Chaucer* 'Les Contes de Cantorbéry'

cantharides [kænˈθærɪˌdiːz] *npl Entom* cantharides *fpl*

canticle [ˈkæntɪkəl] *n Mus & Rel* cantique *m*; **the Canticle of Canticles** le Cantique des cantiques

cantilena [ˌkæntɪˈleɪnə] *n Mus* cantilène *f*

cantilever [ˈkæntɪliːvə(r)] **1** *n* (**a**) *(beam, girder)* cantilever *m*; *(projecting beam)* corbeau *m*, encorbellement *m* (**b**) *Aviat* cantilever *m*

2 *comp (girder)* en cantilever, cantilever *(inv)*

3 *vt* mettre en cantilever

►► ***cantilever beam*** poutre *f* en porte-à-faux; ***cantilever bridge*** pont *m* cantilever; ***cantilever foundation*** montage *m* à porte-à-faux; ***cantilever wall*** mur *m* en porte-à-faux

canting [ˈkæntɪŋ] *adj* (**a**) *(hypocritical)* hypocrite (**b**) *(whining)* pleurnichard, pleurnicheur

cantle [ˈkæntəl] *n* (**a**) *(of saddle)* troussequin *m* (**b**) *(piece → of bread, cheese)* morceau *m*

canto [ˈkæntəʊ] *(pl* **cantos**) *n Literature* chant *m (d'un poème)*

Canton [kænˈtɒn] *n* Canton

canton 1 *n* (**a**) [ˈkæntɒn] *Admin* canton *m* (**b**) [ˈkæntən] *Her* canton *m*

2 *vt* (**a**) [kænˈtɒn] *Admin (land)* diviser en cantons (**b**) [kænˈtuːn] *Mil (soldiers)* cantonner

cantonal [ˈkæntənəl] *adj Admin* cantonal

Cantonese [ˌkæntəˈniːz] *(pl* **inv**) **1** *n* (**a**) *(person)* Cantonais(e) *m,f* (**b**) *(language)* cantonais *m*

2 *adj* cantonais

cantonization [ˌkæntənaɪˈzeɪʃən] *n Admin* morcellement *m (en cantons)*

cantonize, -ise [ˈkæntənaɪz] *vt Admin* diviser en plusieurs cantons

cantonment [kænˈtuːnmənt] *n Mil* cantonnement *m*

cantor [ˈkæntɔː(r)] *n Rel* chantre *m*

Canuck [kəˈnʌk] *n Am Fam (Canadian)* = terme injurieux ou humoristique désignant un Canadien (le plus souvent un Canadien français)

canula [ˈkænjələ] *n Med (for giving medication)* canule *f*, cathéter *m*; *(for draining)* sonde *f*

Canute [kəˈnjuːt] *pr n Hist* Canut, Knud

CANUTE

C'est le nom d'un roi d'Angleterre d'origine danoise (XIème siècle), dont le peuple pensait qu'il serait capable d'arrêter les vagues. On évoque Canut et les vagues pour faire allusion au caractère inéluctable d'un événement.

canvas [ˈkænvəs] *(pl* **inv** *ou* **canvasses**) **1** *n* (**a**) *(cloth)* toile *f*; *(for tapestry)* canevas *m*; **under canvas** *(in a tent)* sous une tente; *Naut* sous voiles (**b**) *(painting)* toile *f*, tableau *m* (**c**) *Boxing* **the canvas** le tapis

2 *comp (bag, cloth)* de *ou* en toile

canvasback [ˈkænvəsbæk] *n Orn* fuligule *f* aux yeux rouges

canvass [ˈkænvəs] **1** *vi* (**a**) *(seek opinions)* faire un sondage

(**b**) *Com (seek orders)* visiter la clientèle, faire la place; *(door to door)* faire du démarchage *ou* du porte-à-porte; **to canvass for customers** prospecter la clientèle

(**c**) *Pol (candidate, campaign worker)* faire campagne *(en faisant du porte-à-porte)*; **we're canvassing for the Greens** nous faisons campagne pour les Verts

2 *vt* (**a**) *(seek opinion of)* sonder; **to canvass opinions (on sth)** sonder l'opinion (à propos de)

(**b**) *Com (person)* démarcher, solliciter des commandes de; *(area)* prospecter

(**c**) *Pol (person)* solliciter la voix de; *(area)* faire du démarchage électoral dans

(**d**) *(for support in job application etc)* solliciter l'appui de

(**e**) *Am Pol (ballots)* pointer

3 *n* (**a**) *(gen) & Com* démarchage *m*

(**b**) *Pol* démarchage *m* électoral

(**c**) *Am Pol (of ballots)* pointage *m*

canvasser [ˈkænvəsə(r)] *n* (**a**) *(pollster)* sondeur(euse) *m,f*, enquêteur(euse) *m,f* (**b**) *Com (salesman)* placier *m*; *(door to door)* démarcheur *m*; **no canvassers** *(notice on door)* démarchage interdit (**c**) *Pol* agent *m* électoral *(qui sollicite des voix)* (**d**) *Am Pol (of ballots)* scrutateur(trice) *m,f*

canvassing [ˈkænvəsɪŋ] *n* (**a**) *(gen) & Com* démarchage *m* (**b**) *Pol* démarchage *m* électoral (**c**) *(for support in job application etc)* sollicitation *f* d'appui

canyon [ˈkænjən] *n* cañon *m*, canyon *m*, gorge *f*

canyoning [ˈkænjənɪŋ] *n Sport* canyoning *m*

canzone [kænˈtsəʊnɪ] *n Literature & Mus* canzone *f*

CAP [ˌsiːeɪˈpiː, kæp] *n EU* (*abbr* **Common Agricultural Policy**) PAC *f*

cap [kæp] *(pt & pp* **capped,** *cont* **capping**) **1** *n* (**a**) *(hat → with peak)* casquette *f*; *(→ without peak)* bonnet *m*; *(→ of jockey, judge)* toque *f*; *(→ of nurse, traditional costume)* coiffe *f*; *(→ of soldier)* calot *m*; *(→ of officer)* képi *m*; **cap and bells** marotte *f* (de bouffon); **cap and gown** = expression britannique évoquant le milieu universitaire; **in cap and gown** en costume d'apparat universitaire; **if the cap fits, wear it** qui se sent morveux (qu'il) se mouche; **to go to sb cap in hand** aller vers qn chapeau bas; *Old-fashioned* **to set one's cap at sb** jeter son dévolu sur qn; **to put on one's thinking cap** réfléchir, méditer la question

(**b**) *(cover, lid → of bottle, container)* capsule *f*; *(→ of lens)* cache *m*; *(→ of tyre valve)* bouchon *m*; *(→ of pen)* capuchon *m*; *(→ of mushroom)* chapeau *m*; *(→ of tooth)* couronne *f*; *(→ of column, pedestal)* chapiteau *m*

(**c**) *Br Sport* **he has been an England cap three times** il a été sélectionné trois fois dans l'équipe d'Angleterre

(**d**) *Orn (of bird)* capuchon *m*

(**e**) *(for toy gun)* amorce *f*; *Am (bullet)* bastos *f*

(**f**) *(contraceptive device)* diaphragme *m*

(**g**) *(spending limit)* plafond *m*

2 *vt* (**a**) *(cover)* couvrir, recouvrir; **the mountain was capped with snow** le sommet de la montagne était recouvert de neige

(**b**) *(tooth)* couronner, mettre une couronne à

(**c**) *(outdo)* surpasser; **he capped that story with an even funnier one** il a raconté une histoire encore plus drôle que celle-là; **to cap it all** pour couronner le tout, pour comble

(**d**) *Admin (impose limit on → spending)* limiter, restreindre; ([illegible]) limiter les dépenses de; **these measures have been effective in capping overall expenditure** ces mesures ont permis de limiter les dépenses globales

(**e**) *Br Sport* sélectionner (dans l'équipe nationale); **she was capped five times** elle a joué *ou* elle a été sélectionnée cinq fois

(**f**) *Scot & NZ Univ (graduate)* conférer un diplôme à

(**g**) *Am Fam (shoot)* descendre

►► *Tech* ***cap screw*** vis *f* à six pans creux

capability [ˌkeɪpəˈbɪlətɪ] *(pl* **capabilities**) *n* (**a**) *(gen)* aptitude *f*, capacité *f*; **the work is beyond his capabilities** ce travail est au-dessus de ses capacités (**b**) *Mil* capacité *f*, potentiel *m*; **nuclear capability** puissance *f ou* potentiel *m* nucléaire; **we have the military capability to...** notre potentiel militaire est suffisant pour...

capable [ˈkeɪpəbəl] *adj* (**a**) *(able)* capable; **they are quite capable of looking after themselves** ils sont parfaitement capables de *ou* ils peuvent très bien se débrouiller tout seuls; **he's capable**

of intense concentration il a une grande capacité de concentration; **that man's capable of anything** cet homme est capable de tout (**b**) *(competent)* capable, compétent; **the business is in capable hands** l'affaire est entre de bonnes mains

capably ['keɪpəblɪ] *adv* avec compétence, de façon compétente

capacious [kə'peɪʃəs] *adj Formal (room)* vaste, spacieux; *(clothing)* ample; *(container)* de grande capacité *ou* contenance

capaciousness [kə'peɪʃəsnɪs] *n Formal* amples proportions *fpl*

capacitance [kə'pæsɪtəns] *n Elec* capacité *f*

capacitate [kə'pæsɪteɪt] *vt Law* donner pouvoir *ou* qualité à (**to act** pour agir)

capacitor [kə'pæsɪtə(r)] *n Elec* condensateur *m*

capacity [kə'pæsɪtɪ] *(pl* **capacities***)* *n* (**a**) *(size → of container)* contenance *f*, capacité *f*; *(→ of room)* capacité *f*; **the stadium has a capacity of 50,000** le stade peut accueillir 50 000 personnes; **he has an amazing capacity for beer** il peut boire une quantité étonnante de bière; **filled to capacity** *(bottle, tank)* plein; *(ship, theatre)* plein, comble; **they played to a capacity crowd** ils ont joué à guichets fermés
(**b**) *(aptitude)* aptitude *f*, capacité *f*; **capacity to learn** aptitude à apprendre, capacité d'apprendre; **she has a great capacity for languages** elle a une grande aptitude *ou* capacité pour les langues, elle est douée pour les langues; **the work is well within our capacity** nous sommes tout à fait en mesure *ou* capables de faire ce travail
(**c**) *(position)* qualité *f*, titre *m*; *Law (legal competence)* pouvoir *m* légal; **she spoke in her capacity as government representative** elle s'est exprimée en sa qualité de *ou* en tant que représentante du gouvernement; **he's acting in an advisory capacity** il a un rôle consultatif; **they are here in an official capacity** ils sont ici à titre officiel
(**d**) *(of factory, industry)* moyens *mpl* de production; *(output)* rendement *m*; **the factory is (working) at full capacity** l'usine produit à plein rendement; **the factory has not yet reached capacity** l'usine n'a pas encore atteint son rendement maximum
(**e**) *(of engine)* capacité *f*
(**f**) *Elec* capacité *f*
►► ***a capacity audience*** une salle comble

caparison [kə'pærɪsən] *Arch or Literary* **1** *n* caparaçon *m*
2 *vt* caparaçonner

cape¹ [keɪp] *n Geog (headland)* cap *m*; *(promontory)* promontoire *m*
►► ***Cape Bon*** cap Bon; ***Cape Breton*** Cap-Breton; *Zool* ***Cape buffalo*** buffle *m* de Cafrerie, buffle *m* du Cap; ***Cape Canaveral*** cap Canaveral; ***Cape Cod*** cap Cod; ***Cape Coloured*** métis(isse) *m,f* sud-africain(e); ***the Cape of Good Hope*** le cap de Bonne-Espérance; *Bot* ***cape gooseberry*** physalis *m*; ***Cape Horn*** le cap Horn; *Zool* ***Cape hunting dog*** lycaon *m*; ***Cape Kennedy*** cap *m* Kennedy; ***the Cape Peninsula*** la péninsule du Cap, Le Cap; ***Cape Province*** province *f* du Cap; ***Cape Town*** Le Cap; ***Cape Verde*** le Cap-Vert; **in *Cape Verde*** au Cap-Vert; ***the Cape Verde Islands*** les îles *fpl* du Cap-Vert; ***Cape Verdean*** **1** *n* Capverdien(enne) *m,f* **2** *adj* capverdien

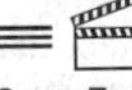

'Cape Fear' *Thompson, Scorsese* 'Les nerfs à vif'

cape² *n (cloak)* cape *f*, pèlerine *f*

caper¹ ['keɪpə(r)] **1** *vi* (**a**) *(jump, skip)* cabrioler, gambader, faire des cabrioles *ou* des gambades; **to caper down/up the road** descendre/monter la rue en gambadant (**b**) *(frolic)* faire le fou (folle)
2 *n* (**a**) *(jump, skip)* cabriole *f*, gambade *f*; *Old-fashioned* **to cut capers** faire des cabrioles (**b**) *(practical joke)* farce *f* (**c**) *Fam (nonsense)* **I haven't time for all that caper** je n'ai pas de temps à perdre avec des âneries pareilles; **what a caper!** *(fuss)* quel cirque! (**d**) *Fam (illegal activity)* coup *m*

caper² *n* câpre *f*; *(shrub)* câprier *m*
►► ***caper sauce*** sauce *f* aux câpres

capercaillie, capercailzie [ˌkæpə'keɪlɪ] *n Orn* grand tétras *m*, coq *m* de bruyère

Capernaum [kə'pɜːnjəm] *n Bible* Capharnaüm

capeskin ['keɪpskɪn] *n* peau *f* souple

Capetian [kə'piːʃən] **1** *n* Capétien(enne) *m,f*
2 *adj* capétien

capful ['kæpfʊl] *n (of liquid)* (plein) bouchon *m*

capillarity [ˌkæpɪ'lærətɪ] *n Phys* capillarité *f*

capillary [kə'pɪlərɪ] *(pl* **capillaries***)* *Biol* **1** *adj* capillaire
2 *n* capillaire *m*
►► ***capillary action*** capillarité *f*; ***capillary tube*** capillaire *m*

capital ['kæpɪtəl] **1** *n* (**a**) *(city)* capitale *f*; **the financial capital of the world** la capitale financière du monde
(**b**) *(letter)* majuscule *f*, capitale *f*; **write in capitals** écrivez en (lettres) majuscules *ou* en capitales
(**c**) *(UNCOUNT) Econ & Fin (funds)* capital *m*, capitaux *mpl*, fonds *mpl*; *(funds and assets)* capital *m* (en espèces et en nature); **to raise capital** réunir des capitaux; **capital invested, outlay of capital** mise *f* de fonds; **capital and labour** capital et main-d'œuvre; **to try and make capital out of a situation** essayer de tirer profit *ou* parti d'une situation
(**d**) *Fin (principal)* capital *m*, principal *m*
(**e**) *Archit (of column)* chapiteau *m*
2 *adj* (**a**) *(chief, primary)* capital, principal; **it's of capital importance** c'est d'une importance capitale, c'est de la plus haute importance
(**b**) *Law* capital
(**c**) *(upper case)* majuscule; **capital D** D majuscule; **in capital letters** en majuscules, en capitales; **he's an idiot with a capital "I"** c'est un imbécile avec un grand "I"
(**d**) *Br Fam Old-fashioned (wonderful)* épatant, fameux
3 *comp Fin* de capital
►► *Fin* ***capital account*** compte *m* de capitaux; *Fin* ***capital allowances*** amortissements *mpl* admis par le fisc; *Fin* ***capital asset pricing model*** modèle *m* d'évaluation des actifs; *Fin* ***capital assets*** actif *m* immobilisé, immobilisations *fpl*; *Fin* ***capital bond*** obligation *f* à coupon zéro; *Fin* ***capital budget*** budget *m* d'investissement; ***capital charge*** intérêt *m* des capitaux (investis); ***capital city*** capitale *f*; *Fin* ***capital clause*** *(in memorandum of association)* constitution *f* du capital social; *Fin* ***capital contribution*** apport *m* en capital, dotation *f* en capital, apport de capitaux; *Acct* ***capital employed*** capital *m* engagé, capitaux *mpl* pemanents; *Fin & Acct* ***capital equipment*** biens *mpl* d'équipement, capitaux fixes; *Fin* ***capital expenditure*** *(UNCOUNT)* mise *f* de fonds, investissements *mpl* (en immobilisations), dépenses *fpl* d'équipement; *Fin* ***capital gains*** plus-value *f*; *Fin* ***capital gains distribution*** distribution *f* de plus-values; *Fin* ***capital gains tax*** impôt *m* sur les plus-values; *Fin* ***capital goods*** biens *mpl* d'équipement *ou* d'investissement; *Fin* ***capital goods market*** marché *m* d'équipement; ***capital grants*** subventions *fpl* en capital; *Fin* ***capital growth*** croissance *m* du capital; *Fin* ***capital income*** revenu *m* du capital; *Fin* ***capital injection*** injection *f* de capital, injection *f* de capitaux; *Fin* ***capital investment*** mise *f* de fonds; *Fin* ***capital items*** biens capitaux; *Fin* ***capital levy*** impôt *m ou* prélèvement *m* sur le capital; *Fin* ***capital loss*** moins-value *f*; *Fin* ***capital market*** marché *m* des capitaux; *Law* ***capital offence*** crime *m* passible de la peine de mort; *Fin* ***capital outlay*** dépenses *fpl* en capital; *Fin* ***capital profits*** plus-value *f*; *Law* ***capital punishment*** peine *f* capitale, peine *f* de mort; ***Capital Radio*** = station de radio indépendante de Londres spécialisée dans les variétés; *Fin* ***capital reserves*** profits *mpl* mis en réserve, réserves *fpl* non distribuées; *Fin* ***capital share*** part *f* sociale; *Am Fin* ***capital stock*** capital *m* social, fonds *mpl* propres; *Fin* ***capital sum*** capital *m*; *Fin* ***capital tax*** impôt *m* sur le capital; *Formerly Fin* ***capital transfer tax*** droits *mpl* de mutation; *Fin* ***capital turnover*** rotation *f* des capitaux

capital-intensive *adj* à forte *or* intensité de capital, capitalistique

capitalism ['kæpɪtəlɪzəm] *n* capitalisme *m*

capitalist ['kæpɪtəlɪst] **1** *adj* capitaliste
2 *n* capitaliste *mf*

capitalistic [ˌkæpɪtə'lɪstɪk] *adj* capitaliste

capitalization [ˌkæpɪtəlaɪ'zeɪʃən] *n* (**a**) *Fin (of interest)* capitalisation *f* (**b**) *Typ* emploi *m* des majuscules; *(putting into upper case)* mise *f* en majuscules
►► ***capitalization issue*** attribution *f* d'actions gratuites; ***capitalization of reserves*** incorporation *f* de réserves au capital; ***capitalization ratio*** ratio *m* de capitalisation

capitalize, -ise ['kæpɪtəlaɪz] **1** *vt* (**a**) *Fin (convert into capital)* capitaliser; *(raise capital through issue of stock)* constituer le capital social de *(par émission d'actions)*; *(provide with capital)* pourvoir de fonds *ou* de capital; **under-/over-capitalized** sous-/sur-capitalisé; **capitalized value** valeur *f* capitalisée
(**b**) *Fin (estimate value of)* capitaliser; **they capitalized her investments at £5,000** ils ont capitalisé ses investissements à 5000 livres; **the company is capitalized at £100,000** la société dispose d'un capital de 100 000 livres
(**c**) *Typ (write in upper case → first letter)* écrire avec une majuscule; *(→ entire word)* écrire *ou* mettre en majuscules
2 *vi* **to capitalize on sth** *(take advantage of)* tirer profit *ou* parti de qch; *(make money on)* monnayer qch; **to capitalize on a situation** tirer profit *ou* parti d'une situation, exploiter une situation; **he capitalized on his opponent's mistakes** il a tiré profit des erreurs de son adversaire, il a tourné les erreurs de son adversaire à son avantage

capital-labour ratio *n* ratio *m* capital-travail

capital-output ratio *n* ratio *m* capital-travail

capitally ['kæpɪtəlɪ] *adv Br Fam Old-fashioned* fameusement, admirablement

capitation [ˌkæpɪ'teɪʃən] *n* (**a**) *Fin* capitation *f* (**b**) *Br Sch* dotation *f* forfaitaire par élève *(accordée à un établissement scolaire)*
►► *Br Sch* ***capitation allowance, capitation expenditure*** dotation *f* forfaitaire par élève *(accordée à un établissement scolaire)*; *Fin* ***capitation tax*** capitation *f*

Capitol ['kæpɪtəl] *n* (**a**) *(in Rome)* **the Capitol** le Capitole (**b**) *(in US)* **the Capitol** *(national)* le Capitole *(siège du Congrès américain)*; *(state)* le Capitole *(siège du Congrès de l'État)*
►► ***Capitol Hill*** = la colline du Capitole, à Washington, où se trouve le Congrès américain

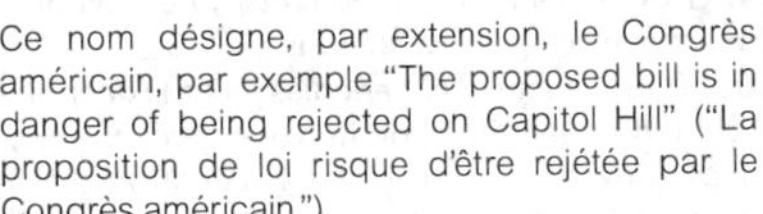

CAPITOL HILL

Ce nom désigne, par extension, le Congrès américain, par exemple "The proposed bill is in danger of being rejected on Capitol Hill" ("La proposition de loi risque d'être rejétée par le Congrès américain.").

Capitoline [kæ'pɪtəlaɪn] *adj Antiq* capitolin
►► ***the Capitoline Hill*** le mont Capitolin

capitulate [kə'pɪtjʊleɪt] *vi Mil & Fig* capituler (**to** devant)

capitulation [kəˌpɪtjʊ'leɪʃən] *n Mil & Fig* capitulation *f*

caplin 'kæplɪn] *n Ich* capelan *m* de Terre-Neuve

CAPM [ˌsiːeɪˌpiː'em, ˌkæp'em] *n* *(abbr* **capital asset pricing model***)* MÉDAF *m*

capo ['keɪpəʊ] *(pl* **capos***)* *n Mus (on guitar)* capo *m* (tasto)

capon ['keɪpən] *n* chapon *m*

Cappadocia [ˌkæpə'dəʊsjə] *n* Cappadoce *f*; **in Cappadocia** en Cappadoce

-capped [kæpt] *suff* couvert *ou* couronné de; **snow-capped mountains** montagnes *fpl* couronnées de neige

capped-rate *adj Fin (mortgage)* à taux d'intérêt plafonné

cappuccino [ˌkæpʊ'tʃiːnəʊ] *(pl* **cappuccinos***)* *n* cappuccino *m*

Capri [kə'priː] *n* Capri
►► ***capri pants*** = sorte de pantalon cigarette qui arrive au-dessus de la cheville

capriccio [kə'priːtʃɪəʊ] *n Mus* caprice *m*

caprice [kə'priːs] *n (whim)* caprice *m*; *(change of mood)* saute *f* d'humeur

capricious [kə'prɪʃəs] *adj (person)* capricieux, fantasque; *(weather)* capricieux, changeant

capriciously [kəˈprɪʃəslɪ] *adv* capricieusement
capriciousness [kəˈprɪʃəsnɪs] *n (of person, weather)* caractère *m* capricieux
Capricorn [ˈkæprɪkɔːn] **1** *n* (**a**) *Astron* Capricorne *m* (**b**) *Astrol* Capricorne *m*; **he's a Capricorn** il est (du signe du) Capricorne
  2 *adj Astrol* du Capricorne; **he's Capricorn** il est (du signe du) Capricorne
caprine [ˈkæpraɪn] *adj* caprin
caps [kæps] *npl* (**a**) *Typ & Comput (abbr* **capital letters**) majuscules *fpl*; **put in small caps** à imprimer en petites capitales (**b**) *(abbr* **capsules**) capsules *fpl*, gélules *fpl*
  ►► ***caps lock*** verrouillage *m* des majuscules; ***caps lock key*** touche *f* de verrouillage des majuscules
capsicum [ˈkæpsɪkəm] *n (fruit, plant → sweet)* poivron *m*, piment *m* doux; *(→ hot)* piment *m*
capsid [ˈkæpsɪd] *n Biol* capside *f*
capsizable [kæpˈsaɪzəbəl] *adj (gen)* renversable; *(boat)* chavirable
capsize [kæpˈsaɪz] **1** *vi (gen)* se renverser; *(boat)* chavirer; **we capsized** nous avons chaviré
  2 *vt (gen)* renverser; *(boat)* faire chavirer
capstan [ˈkæpstən] *n Naut* cabestan *m*
  ►► *Naut* ***capstan bar*** barre *f ou* bras *m* de cabestan; *Tech* ***capstan lathe*** tour *m* revolver
capstone [ˈkæpstəʊn] *n Archit* pierre *f* de faîte; *Fig* sommet *m*
capsular [ˈkæpsjʊlə(r)] *adj Biol & Bot* capsulaire
capsule [ˈkæpsjuːl] **1** *n* (**a**) *(gen) & Aviat, Anat & Bot* capsule *f* (**b**) *Pharm* capsule *f*, gélule *f*
  2 *adj* concis, bref
capsulize, -ise [ˈkæpsjʊlaɪz] *vt* résumer, récapituler
Capt. *(written abbr* **captain**) cap
captain [ˈkæptɪn] **1** *n* (**a**) *(army rank)* capitaine *m*; *Mil (of ship)* capitaine *m*; *(navy rank)* ≃ capitaine *m* de vaisseau; **captain of the fleet** capitaine *m* de pavillon; **Captain James Brown** *(in title)* le capitaine James Brown; **yes, captain!** oui, mon capitaine!
  (**b**) *(of group, team)* chef *m*, capitaine *m*; *Sport* capitaine *m* (d'équipe); **captain of industry** capitaine *m* d'industrie
  (**c**) *Am (of police)* ≃ commissaire *m* (de police) de quartier
  (**d**) *Am (head waiter)* maître *m* d'hôtel; *(of bellboys)* responsable *m* des grooms
  2 *vt* (**a**) *(gen)* diriger; *Mil* commander
  (**b**) *Sport* être le capitaine de; **he captained the side in the World Cup** c'était lui le capitaine de l'équipe pour la Coupe du Monde
captaincy [ˈkæptɪnsɪ] *(pl* **captaincies**) *n* (**a**) *Naut & Mil* grade *m* de capitaine; **to receive one's captaincy** être promu *ou* passer capitaine (**b**) *Sport* poste *m* de capitaine; **under the captaincy of Rogers** avec Rogers comme capitaine
captainship [ˈkæptɪnʃɪp] *n* (**a**) *Naut & Mil* grade *m* de capitaine; **to receive one's captainship** être promu *ou* passer capitaine (**b**) *Sport* poste *m* de capitaine (**c**) *(skill)* **he handled his troops with consummate captainship** il a dirigé ses troupes avec l'art d'un grand capitaine
caption [ˈkæpʃən] **1** *n* (**a**) *(under illustration, photograph, cartoon)* légende *f* (**b**) *(in article, chapter)* sous-titre *m* (**c**) *Cin* sous-titre *m*
  2 *vt* (**a**) *(illustration)* mettre une légende à, légender (**b**) *Cin* sous-titrer
captious [ˈkæpʃəs] *adj Formal (person)* qui trouve toujours à redire, chicanier; *(attitude)* chicanier
captivate [ˈkæptɪveɪt] *vt* captiver, fasciner
captivating [ˈkæptɪveɪtɪŋ] *adj* captivant, fascinant
captive [ˈkæptɪv] **1** *n* captif(ive) *m,f*, prisonnier(ère) *m,f*; **to take sb captive** faire qn prisonnier; **to hold sb captive** garder qn en captivité
  2 *adj (person)* captif, prisonnier; *(animal, balloon)* captif; *Mktg (audience, market)* captif; *Mktg (product)* lié; **a captive audience** *(of entertainer, show)* un public captif
  ►► *Fin* ***captive fund*** fonds *m* de capital-risque maison
captivity [kæpˈtɪvətɪ] *n* captivité *f*; **in captivity** en captivité
captor [ˈkæptə(r)] *n (gen)* personne *f* qui capture; *(unlawfully)* ravisseur(euse) *m,f*
capture [ˈkæptʃə(r)] **1** *vt* (**a**) *(take prisoner → animal, criminal, enemy)* capturer, prendre; *(→ runaway)* reprendre; *(→ city)* prendre, s'emparer de; *(in games)* prendre
  (**b**) *(gain control of → market)* conquérir, s'emparer de; *(→ attention, imagination)* captiver; *(→ admiration, interest)* gagner
  (**c**) *(succeed in representing)* rendre, reproduire; **to capture the moment** *(photographer, photograph)* saisir l'instant; **to capture sb/sth (on film)** filmer qn/qch
  (**d**) *Comput (data)* saisir
  2 *n* (**a**) *(of animal, criminal, enemy)* capture *f*, prise *f*
  (**b**) *Comput (of data)* saisie *f*
Capua [ˈkæpjʊə] *n Geog* Capoue
capuche [kæˈpuːʃ] *n* capuchon *m*, capuce *m*
Capuchin [ˈkæpjʊtʃɪn] **1** *n Rel* capucin *m*
  2 *adj Rel* capucin; **a monk of the Capuchin order** un capucin; **a nun of the Capuchin order** une capucine
  3 capuchin *n* (**a**) *(cloak)* cape *f* (avec capuchon) (**b**) *Zool* capucin *m*
  ►► *Rel* ***Capuchin monk*** capucin *m*; *Zool* ***capuchin monkey*** capucin *m*
capybara [kæpɪˈbɑːrə] *n Zool* cabiai *m*, capybara *m*
car [kɑː(r)] **1** *n* (**a**) *(automobile)* voiture *f*, automobile *f*, auto *f*; **to go by car** aller en voiture
  (**b**) *Am (of train)* wagon *m*, voiture *f*; *(in subway)* rame *f*
  (**c**) *Am (tram)* tramway *m*, tram *m*
  (**d**) *(of lift)* cabine *f (d'ascenseur)*
  (**e**) *(of airship, balloon)* nacelle *f*
  2 *comp (engine, tyre, wheel)* de voiture, d'automobile; *(journey, trip)* en voiture
  ►► ***car alarm*** alarme *f* de voiture; *Br* ***car allowance*** indemnité *f* de déplacement (en voiture); ***car body*** carrosserie *f*; ***car bomb*** voiture *f* piégée; ***car bomb attack*** attentat *m* à la voiture piégée; ***car bomber*** auteur *m* d'un attentat à la voiture piégée; *Br* ***car bonnet*** capot *m*; *Br* ***car boot*** coffre *m*, malle *f* (arrière); *Br* ***car boot sale*** = sorte de marché aux puces où des particuliers apportent dans leur voiture les objets de brocante qu'ils souhaitent vendre; ***car chase*** course-poursuite *f*; *Br* ***car coat*** manteau *m* trois-quarts; ***car dealer*** concessionnaire *m* automobile; ***car ferry*** ferry-boat *m*; *Br* ***car hire*** **1** *n* location *f* de voitures **2** *comp (company, firm)* de location de voitures; ***car hood*** *Br* capote *f*; *Am* capot *m*; ***car industry*** industrie *f* (de l')automobile; ***car insurance*** assurance *f* auto; ***car jack*** cric *m*; ***car keys*** clés *fpl* de voiture; ***car manufacturer*** constructeur *m* automobile; *Br* ***car number*** numéro *m* d'immatriculation; *Br* ***car park*** parking *m*, parc *m* de stationnement; ***car park attendant*** gardien(enne) *m,f* de parking; ***car pool*** *(of commuters)* = groupe de personnes qui s'organise pour utiliser la même voiture afin de se rendre à une destination commune; *(cars provided by company)* voitures *fpl* de fonction; *Am* ***car pool lane*** = voie d'autoroute réservée, les jours de grande circulation, aux voitures à deux passagers ou plus; ***car pooling*** covoiturage *m*; ***car radio*** autoradio *f*; *Am* ***car rental*** **1** *n* location *f* de voitures **2** *comp (company, firm)* de location de voitures; ***car rug*** plaid *m*; ***car salesman*** vendeur *m* de voitures; ***car sickness*** mal *m* des transports; **to suffer from car sickness** être malade en voiture; ***car sickness pills*** comprimés *mpl* contre le mal des transports; ***car stereo*** autoradio *m*; *Am* ***car trunk*** coffre *m*, malle *f* (arrière); ***car wash*** *(place)* portique *m* de lavage automatique (de voitures), *Can* lave-auto *m*; *(action)* lavage *m* de voitures; ***car worker*** ouvrier(ère) *m,f* de l'industrie automobile
carabid [ˈkærəbɪd] *n Entom* carabidé *m*, carabique *m*
caracal [ˈkærəkæl] *n Zool* caracal *m*
Caracas [kəˈrækəs] *n* Caracas
caracole [ˈkærəkəʊl] **1** *n* (**a**) *Horseriding* caracole *f* (**b**) *(spiral staircase)* escalier *m* en caracole
  2 *vi* (**a**) *Horseriding* caracoler (**b**) *(skip about)* caracoler
carafe [kəˈræf] *n* carafe *f*
carambola [kærəmˈbəʊlə] *n Bot & Culin* carambole *f*
caramel [ˈkærəmel] **1** *n* caramel *m*; **a (piece of) caramel** un caramel
  2 *comp (ice cream, cake)* au caramel
  ►► *Am* ***a caramel candy*** un caramel; ***caramel flavouring*** arôme *m* caramel
caramelization [ˌkærəməlaɪˈzeɪʃən] *n* caramélisation *f*
caramelize, -ise [ˈkærəməlaɪz] **1** *vt* caraméliser
  2 *vi* se caraméliser
carapace [ˈkærəpeɪs] *n Zool* carapace *f*
carat, *Am* **karat** [ˈkærət] *n* (**a**) *(for gold)* carat *m*; **an 18-carat gold ring** une bague en or 18 carats (**b**) *(for diamonds)* **metric carat** carat *m* (de 200 milligrammes)
Caravaggio [ˌkærəˈvædʒɪəʊ] *pr n* le Caravage; **a painting by Caravaggio** un tableau du Caravage
caravan [ˈkærəvæn] *(Br pt & pp* **caravanned,** *cont* **caravanning**, *Am pt & pp* **caravaned** *or* **caravaned,** *cont* **caravanning** *or* **caravaning**) **1** *n* (**a**) *Br (vehicle)* caravane *f* (**b**) *(of gipsy)* roulotte *f* (**c**) *(in desert)* caravane *f*; **to travel in caravan** voyager en convoi
  2 *vi* **to go caravanning** faire du caravaning *ou Offic* du caravanage
  ►► *Br* ***caravan site*** *(for campers)* camping *m* (pour caravanes); *(of gipsies)* campement *m*
caravanette [kærəvəˈnet] *n* camping-car *m*, *Offic* autocaravane *f*
caravanner, *Am* **caravaner** [ˈkærəvænə(r)] *n* caravanier(ère) *m,f*
caravanning [ˈkærəvænɪŋ] *n* caravaning *m*, *Offic* caravanage *m*
caravanserai [ˌkærəˈvænsəraɪ] *n (inn)* caravansérail *m*
caravel [ˈkærəvel] *n Naut* caravelle *f*
caraway [ˈkærəweɪ] *n Bot & Culin (plant)* carvi *m*, cumin *m* des prés
  ►► ***caraway seeds*** (graines *fpl* de) carvi
carb [kɑːb] *n Fam* (**a**) *Aut (carburettor)* carburateur[□] *m* (**b**) *(carbohydrate)* glucide[□] *m*
carbamate [ˈkɑːbəmeɪt] *n Chem* carbamate *m*
carbamic [ˌkɑːˈbæmɪk] *adj Chem* carbamique
carbamide [ˈkɑːbəmaɪd] *n Chem* carbamide *f*
carbide [ˈkɑːbaɪd] *n Chem* carbure *m*
carbine [ˈkɑːbaɪn] *n* carabine *f*
carbohydrate [ˌkɑːbəʊˈhaɪdreɪt] *n* (**a**) *Chem* hydrate *m* de carbone (**b**) *(usu pl) (foodstuff)* **carbohydrates** glucides *mpl*
carbolic [kɑːˈbɒlɪk] *adj Chem* phéniqué
  ►► ***carbolic acid*** phénol *m*; ***carbolic soap*** ≃ savon *m* de Marseille
carbon [ˈkɑːbən] *n* (**a**) *Chem* carbone *m* (**b**) *(copy, paper)* carbone *m*
  ►► *Tech* ***carbon arc*** arc *m* à charbon; *Chem* ***carbon black*** noir *m* de carbone; ***carbon brush*** baguette *f ou* balai *m* de charbon; ***carbon copy*** *(of document)* carbone *m*; *Fig* réplique *f*; **she's a carbon copy of her mother** c'est l'exacte réplique de sa mère; *Chem* ***carbon cycle*** cycle *m* du carbone; *Archeol* ***carbon dating*** datation *f* au carbone 14; *Chem* ***carbon dioxide*** gaz *m* carbonique, dioxyde *m* de carbone; *Chem & Tex* ***carbon fibre*** fibre *f* de carbone; *Aut* ***carbon filter*** filtre *m* au charbon; *Chem* ***carbon monoxide*** monoxyde *m* de carbone; ***carbon monoxide poisoning*** empoisonnement *m* au monoxyde de carbone; ***carbon paper*** (papier *m*) carbone *m*; *Metal* ***carbon steel*** acier *m* carburé; *Chem* ***carbon tetrachloride*** tétrachlorure *m* de carbone
carbonaceous [ˌkɑːbəˈneɪʃəs] *adj Chem* carboné
carbonade = **carbonnade**
carbonado [ˌkɑːbəˈneɪdəʊ] *n Miner* carbonado *m*
carbonara [ˌkɑːbəˈnɑːrə] *adj Culin* **spaghetti carbonara** spaghettis *mpl* (à la) carbonara
  ►► ***carbonara sauce*** sauce *f* carbonara
carbonate [ˈkɑːbənɪt] *n Chem* carbonate *m*
carbonated [ˈkɑːbəneɪtɪd] *adj Chem* carbonaté; **carbonated soft drinks** boissons *fpl* gazeuses
carbon-date *vt Archeol* dater au carbone 14
carbon(-14) dating *n Archeol* datation *f* au carbone 14
carbonic [kɑːˈbɒnɪk] *adj Chem* carbonique
  ►► ***carbonic acid*** acide *m* carbonique
carboniferous [ˌkɑːbəˈnɪfərəs] *Geol* **1** *adj* carbonifère
  2 Carboniferous 1 *n* **the Carboniferous** le Carbonifère **2** *adj* **the Carboniferous Period** le carbonifère
carbonization [ˌkɑːbənaɪˈzeɪʃən] *n Chem* carbonisation *f*

cap–car

carbonize, -ise ['kɑːbənaɪz] *vt Chem* carboniser

carbonnade [kɑːbə'nɑːd] *n Culin* **(beef) carbonnade** carbonade *f*, carbonnade *f*

carbonyl ['kɑːbənɪl] *n Chem* carbonyle *m*

▸▸ ***carbonyl chloride*** acide *m* chlorocarbonique, phosgène *m*, chlorure *m* de carbonyle

Carborundum® [ˌkɑːbə'rʌndəm] *n* carborundum® *m*

carboxyl [kɑː'bɒksɪl] *n Chem* carboxyle *m*

carboxylase [kɑː'bɒksɪleɪz] *n Biol* carboxylase *f*

carboxylic acid [kɑːbɒk'sɪlɪk-] *n Chem* acide *m* carboxylique

carboy ['kɑːˌbɔɪ] *n* bonbonne *f*, bombonne *f*

carbuncle ['kɑːˌbʌŋkəl] *n* (**a**) *Med* furoncle *m* (**b**) *Miner (gemstone)* escarboucle *f*

carburation [ˌkɑːbjʊ'reɪʃən] *n Tech* carburation *f*

carburettor, *Am* **carburetor** [ˌkɑːbə'retə(r)] *n* carburateur *m*

carbylamine [kɑː'bɪləmɪn] *n Chem* carbylamine *f*

carcass, carcase ['kɑːkəs] *n* (**a**) *(of animal)* carcasse *f*, cadavre *m*; *(for food)* carcasse *f* (**b**) *(of person → dead)* cadavre *m*; *Fam Hum* **move your carcass!** pousse un peu ta viande! (**c**) *(of building)* carcasse *f*, charpente *f*; *(of car)* carcasse *f*

carcinogen [kɑː'sɪnədʒən] *n Med* (agent *m*) cancérogène *m ou* cancérogène *m*

carcinogenesis [ˌkɑːsɪnəʊ'dʒenɪsɪs] *n Med* carcinogénèse *f*

carcinogenic [ˌkɑːsɪnə'dʒenɪk] *adj Med* carcinogène, cancérogène

carcinoma [ˌkɑːsɪ'nəʊmə] (*pl* **carcinomas** *or* **carcinomata** [-mətə]) *n Med* carcinome *m*

carcinomatous [ˌkɑːsɪ'nəʊmətəs] *adj Med* carcinomateux

card¹ [kɑːd] **1** *n* (**a**) *(for game)* carte *f*; **how about a game of cards?** et si on jouait aux cartes?; **to play cards** jouer aux cartes; *Fig* **to play one's cards right** mener bien son jeu *ou* sa barque, bien se débrouiller; **play your cards right and you could get promoted** si tu te débrouilles bien, tu peux avoir une promotion; **to play one's best** *or* **strongest** *or* **trump card** jouer sa carte maîtresse; **I still have a couple of cards up my sleeve** j'ai encore quelques atouts dans mon jeu; **to keep one's cards close to one's chest** cacher son jeu; **to hold all the (winning** *or* **best) cards** avoir tous les atouts dans son jeu *ou* en main; **to lay** *or* **to place one's cards on the table** jouer cartes sur table; **it was** *Br* **on** *or Am* **in the cards that the project would fail** il était dit *ou* prévisible que le projet échouerait

(**b**) *(with written information → gen)* carte *f*; *(→ for business)* carte *f* (de visite); *(→ for index)* fiche *f*; *(→ for membership)* carte *f* de membre *ou* d'adhérent; *(→ for library)* carte *f* (d'abonnement); *(postcard)* carte *f* (postale); *(programme)* programme *m*; **here's my card** voici ma carte; **we received a card inviting us to their wedding** nous avons reçu un carton *ou* une carte d'invitation pour leur mariage

(**c**) *(cardboard)* carton *m*

(**d**) *Fam Old-fashioned (person)* plaisantin ❑ *m*; **he's a card!** c'est un marrant *ou* un rigolo!

(**e**) *Golf* carte *f* du parcours; *Sport (list of races)* programme *m* des courses

(**f**) *Comput (circuit board)* cartet *f*

2 *vt* (**a**) *(information)* ficher, mettre sur fiche

(**b**) *Am (ask for identity card)* demander sa carte (d'identité) à

(**c**) *Golf (score)* marquer

3 *comp Fin (payment, transaction)* par carte

4 cards *npl Br (idioms)* **to ask for one's cards** quitter son travail; **to get one's cards** être mis à la porte; **the boss gave him his cards** le patron l'a renvoyé

▸▸ ***card catalogue*** fichier *m* (de bibliothèque); ***card counting*** = mémorisation des cartes qui tombent pendant une partie pour augmenter ses chances de gagner; ***card file*** fichier *m*; ***card game*** jeu *m* de cartes; ***card holder*** *(of club, political party)* membre *m*, adhérent(e) *m,f*; *(of library)* abonné(e) *m,f*; *(of credit card)* titulaire *mf*; ***card index*** fichier *m*; ***card key*** carte-clé *f*; *Am* ***card member*** titulaire *mf*; *Comput* ***card slot*** emplacement *m* pour carte; ***card table*** table *f* de jeu; ***card trick*** tour *m* de cartes; *Br* ***card vote*** vote *m* sur carte *(chaque voix représentant le nombre de voix d'adhérents représentés)*

card² *Tex* **1** *n* carde *f*

2 *vt* carder

cardamom, cardamon, cardamum ['kɑːdəməm] *n Bot & Culin* cardamome *f*

▸▸ ***cardamom seeds*** (graines *fpl* de) cardamome *f*

cardan joint ['kɑːdən-] *n Tech* joint *m* de cardan

cardboard ['kɑːdbɔːd] **1** *n* carton *m*

2 *adj* (**a**) *(container, partition)* de *ou* en carton (**b**) *Fig (unreal → character, leader)* de carton-pâte, faux (fausse)

▸▸ ***cardboard box*** (boîte *f* en) carton *m*; ***cardboard city*** quartier *m* des sans-abri; ***cardboard cutouts*** découpages *mpl* en carton

card-carrying *adj* **card-carrying member** membre *m*, adhérent(e) *m,f*; **card-carrying Communist** membre du parti communiste

cardiac ['kɑːdɪæk] **1** *n* cardiaque *mf*

2 *adj* cardiaque

▸▸ ***cardiac arrest*** arrêt *m* cardiaque; ***cardiac massage*** massage *m* cardiaque

cardialgia [ˌkɑːdɪ'ældʒɪə] *n Med* cardialgie *f*

cardie ['kɑːdɪ] *n Br Fam* cardigan ❑ *m*

Cardiff ['kɑːdɪf] *n* Cardiff

▸▸ ***Cardiff Arms Park*** = stade de rugby à Cardiff

cardigan ['kɑːdɪgən] *n Br* cardigan *m*

▸▸ *Am* ***cardigan sweater*** cardigan *m*

Cardiganshire ['kɑːdɪgənˌʃɪə(r)] *n* Cardiganshire *m*

cardinal ['kɑːdɪnəl] **1** *adj* (**a**) *(essential)* cardinal (**b**) *(colour)* rouge cardinal *(inv)*

2 *n* (**a**) *Math & Rel* cardinal *m* (**b**) *Orn* cardinal *m* (rouge) (**c**) *(colour)* rouge cardinal *m inv*

▸▸ *Ich* ***cardinal fish*** apogonidé *m*; *Math* ***cardinal number*** nombre *m* cardinal; ***the cardinal points*** les (quatre) points *mpl* cardinaux; ***cardinal red*** **1** *n* rouge cardinal *m inv* **2** *adj* rouge cardinal *(inv)*; *Rel* ***cardinal sin*** péché *m* capital; ***the cardinal virtues*** les (quatre) vertus *fpl* cardinales

card-index *vt* ficher, mettre sur fichier

card-indexing *n* mise *f* sur fiches

carding ['kɑːdɪŋ] *n Tex* cardage *m*

cardio- ['kɑːdɪəʊ] *pref* cardio-

cardiogram ['kɑːdɪəgræm] *n Med* cardiogramme *m*

cardiograph ['kɑːdɪəgrɑːf] *n Med* cardiographe *m*

cardiological [ˌkɑːdɪə'lɒdʒɪkəl] *adj Med* cardiologique

cardiologist [ˌkɑːdɪ'ɒlədʒɪst] *n Med* cardiologue *mf*

cardiology [ˌkɑːdɪ'ɒlədʒɪ] *n Med* cardiologie *f*

cardiopulmonary [ˌkɑːdɪəʊ'pʌlmənərɪ] *adj Med* cardio-pulmonaire

▸▸ ***cardiopulmonary resuscitation*** respiration *f* artificielle et massage cardiaque

cardiorenal [ˌkɑːdɪəʊ'riːnəl] *adj Med* cardio-rénal

cardiorespiratory [ˌkɑːdɪəʊrə'spɪrətərɪ] *adj Med* cardio-respiratoire

cardiovascular [ˌkɑːdɪəʊ'væskjʊlə(r)] *adj Med* cardio-vasculaire

carditis [kɑː'daɪtɪs] *n Med* cardite *f*

cardoon [kɑː'duːn] *n Bot & Culin* cardon *m*

card-operated lock *n* serrure *f* à carte perforée

cardphone ['kɑːdfəʊn] *n Br* téléphone *m* à carte

cardplayer ['kɑːdˌpleɪə(r)] *n* joueur(euse) *m,f* de cartes

cardpunch ['kɑːdpʌntʃ] *n* perforatrice *f* de cartes

Cards *(written abbr* **Cardiganshire***)* Cardiganshire *m*

cardsharp ['kɑːdˌʃɑːp], **cardsharper** ['kɑːdˌʃɑːpə(r)] *n* tricheur(euse) *m,f* professionnel(elle) *(aux cartes)*

cardy (*pl* **cardies**) = **cardie**

CARE [keə(r)] *n* (*abbr* **Cooperative for American Relief Everywhere**) = organisation humanitaire américaine

▸▸ ***CARE package*** envoi *m* humanitaire; *Fig* = colis plein de friandises envoyé par un proche

CARE [keə(r)]	
s'intéresser à	▸ **1 (a)**
aimer	▸ **1 (b)**
vouloir	▸ **1 (c)**
souci	▸ **2 (a)**
soin	▸ **2 (b), (c)**
charge	▸ **2 (d)**

1 *vi* (**a**) *(feel concern)* **to care about sth** s'intéresser à *ou* se soucier de qch; **all you care about is your work!** il n'y a que ton travail qui t'intéresse!; **they really do care about the project** le projet est vraiment important pour eux; **a book for all those who care about the environment** un livre pour tous ceux qui s'intéressent à l'environnement *ou* qui se sentent concernés par les problèmes d'environnement; **she didn't seem to care at all** elle avait l'air de s'en moquer complètement; **I don't care what people think** je me moque de ce que pensent les gens; **when do you want to tell them? – I don't care** quand veux-tu leur dire? – ça m'est égal; *Fam* **as if I cared!, I couldn't care less!** je m'en fiche éperdument, je m'en fous; *Fam* **I couldn't** *or Am* **could care less if he comes or not** ça m'est complètement égal ❑ qu'il vienne ou non; **what do I care?** qu'est-ce que ça peut me faire?; **we could be dead for all he cares** il se moque totalement de ce qui peut nous arriver; *Fam* **they don't care a damn** ils s'en fichent éperdument *ou* comme de leur première chemise; **who cares?** qu'est-ce que ça peut bien faire?

(**b**) *(feel affection)* **to care about** *or* **for sb** aimer qn; **do you still care about** *or* **for her?** est-ce que tu l'aimes toujours?; **she cares a lot about her family** elle est très attachée *ou* elle tient beaucoup à sa famille

(**c**) *Formal (like)* **would you care to join us?** voulez-vous vous joindre à nous?; **would you care to have a cup of coffee?** prendriez-vous *ou* aimeriez-vous une tasse de café?; **I was more nervous than I cared to admit** j'étais plus intimidé qu'il n'y paraissait; **the house is available whenever you care to use it** la maison est disponible quand vous voulez *ou* à n'importe quel moment; **I wouldn't care to go back there** cela ne me dit rien d'y retourner

2 *n* (**a**) *(worry)* souci *m*; **to be full of cares** avoir beaucoup de soucis; **you look as though you haven't a care in the world** on dirait que tu n'as pas le moindre souci; *Br* **weighed down by care** accablé de soucis; **cares of State** responsabilités *fpl* d'État

(**b**) *(UNCOUNT) (treatment → of person)* soin(s) *m(pl)*, traitement *m*; *(looking after → of teeth, hair etc)* soin(s) *m(pl)*; *(→ of machine, material)* entretien *m*; **nursing care** soins *mpl* à domicile; **you should take care of that cough** vous devriez (faire) soigner cette toux; **he doesn't take care of his bicycle** il ne prend pas soin de son vélo; **she needs special care** elle a besoin de soins spécialisés

(**c**) *(UNCOUNT) (attention)* attention *f*, soin *m*; **they worked with great care** ils ont travaillé avec le plus grand soin; **handle with care** *(on package)* fragile; **take care not to offend her** faites attention à *ou* prenez soin de ne pas la vexer; **take care not to spill the paint** prenez garde de *ou* faites attention à ne pas renverser la peinture; **drive with care** conduisez prudemment; **he was charged with driving without due care and attention** il a été accusé de conduite négligente; *Br Old-fashioned* **have a care!** prenez garde!, faites attention!

(**d**) *(protection, supervision)* charge *f*, garde *f*; **I'm leaving the matter in your care** je vous confie l'affaire, je confie l'affaire à vos soins; **the children are in the care of a nanny** on a laissé *ou* confié les enfants à une nurse *ou* à la garde d'une nurse; **he is under the care of a heart specialist** c'est un cardiologue qui le traite *ou* qui le soigne; **to take care of** *(invalid, child, customer, problem etc)* s'occuper de; **to take care of one's health** ménager sa santé; **who will take care of your cat?** qui va s'occuper *ou* prendre soin de ton chat?; **I'll take care of the reservations** je me charge des réservations *ou* de faire les réservations, je vais m'occuper des réservations; **I have important business to take care of** j'ai une affaire importante à expédier; **take care!** salut!; **take (good) care of yourself** fais bien attention à toi; **I can take care of myself** je peux *ou* je sais me débrouiller (tout seul); **the problem will take care of itself** le problème va s'arranger tout seul; **care of** *(in address)* chez; **address the letter to me (in) care of Mrs Barry** adressez-moi la lettre chez Mme Barry (**e**) *Br Admin* **the baby was put in care** *or* **taken into care** on a retiré aux parents la garde de leur bébé; **children in care** enfants *mpl* confiés aux services sociaux

►► *Br Admin* ***care assistant*** aide-soignant(e) *m,f*; *Br Admin* ***care attendant*** infirmier(ère) *m,f* à domicile; *Am* ***care giver*** *(professional)* aide *mf* à domicile; *(relative)* = personne s'occupant d'un parent malade ou âgé; *Br Admin* ***care in the community*** = système de soins prodigués aux malades mentaux en dehors du milieu hospitalier; ***care label*** *(on garment)* conseils *mpl* d'entretien; *Br Admin* ***care worker*** travailleur(euse) *m,f* social(e)

►**care for** *vt insep* (**a**) *(look after → child)* s'occuper de; *(→ invalid)* soigner; **I'm glad to see you're being well cared for** *(child)* je suis contente de voir qu'on s'occupe bien de toi; *(invalid)* je suis contente de voir qu'on te soigne bien; **to look well cared for** *(animal, child, hair etc)* avoir l'air soigné *ou* une apparence soignée; *(car, garden etc)* avoir l'air bien entretenu (**b**) *(like)* aimer; **he still cares for her** *(loves)* il l'aime toujours; *(has affection for)* il est toujours attaché à elle, il tient toujours à elle; **I don't care for him** il me déplaît, il ne me plaît pas; **I didn't care for his last book** son dernier livre ne m'a pas plu, je n'ai pas aimé son dernier livre; **she didn't care for the way he spoke** la façon dont il a parlé lui a déplu; *Formal* **would you care for a cup of coffee?** aimeriez-vous *ou* voudriez-vous une tasse de café?

careen [kə'riːn] **1** *vi Naut (ship)* donner de la bande (de façon dangereuse); *(car, train)* tanguer

2 *vt Naut (ship)* caréner; *(car, train)* faire tanguer

careening [kə'riːnɪŋ] *n Naut (of ship)* carénage *m*

career [kə'rɪə(r)] **1** *n* (**a**) *(profession)* carrière *f*, profession *f*; **a career in banking** une carrière dans la banque *ou* de banquier; **she made a career (for herself) in politics** elle a fait carrière dans la politique (**b**) *(life)* vie *f*, carrière *f*; **he spent most of his career working as a journalist** il a travaillé presque toute sa vie comme journaliste; **her university career** son parcours universitaire

2 *comp (diplomat, soldier)* de carrière; **it's a good/bad career move** c'est bon/mauvais pour ta/sa/*etc* carrière; **good career prospects** de bonnes possibilités d'avancement

3 *vi Br* **the car careered wildly down the hill** la voiture a descendu la colline à toute vitesse; **to career along** aller à toute vitesse *ou* à toute allure; **to career into a lorry** *(vehicle)* foncer dans un camion; **the car careered off the road** la voiture a quitté la route à vive allure

►► ***career break*** interruption *f* de carrière; **to take a career break** interrompre sa carrière *(pour élever des enfants, reprendre des études etc)*; ***career development*** évolution *f* professionnelle; *Br* ***career girl*** jeune fille *f* ambitieuse *ou* qui ne pense qu'à sa carrière; *Sch & Univ* ***careers advisor*** *or* ***adviser*** *or* ***officer*** conseiller(ère) *m,f* d'orientation professionnelle; ***careers guidance*** orientation *f* professionnelle; ***careers master*** conseiller *m* d'orientation professionnelle; ***careers mistress*** conseillère *f* d'orientation professionnelle; ***careers office, careers service*** centre *m* d'orientation professionnelle; ***career woman*** = femme *f* ambitieuse *ou* qui ne pense qu'à sa carrière

careerism [kə'rɪərɪzəm] *n Pej* carriérisme *m*

careerist [kə'rɪərɪst] *n Pej* carriériste *mf*

career-minded *adj* ambitieux

carefree ['keəfriː] *adj (person)* sans souci, insouciant; *(look, smile)* insouciant

careful ['keəfʊl] *adj* (**a**) *(cautious)* prudent; **be careful!** (faites) attention!; **be careful of the wet floor!** attention au sol mouillé!; **be careful to close the window before leaving** n'oubliez pas de fermer la fenêtre avant de partir; **be careful not to** *or* **be careful you don't hurt her feelings** faites attention à *ou* prenez soin de ne pas la froisser; **be careful (that) the boss doesn't find out** faites attention *ou* prenez garde que le patron n'en sache rien; **be careful how you hold the baby** fais attention à la façon dont tu prends le bébé; **be careful crossing the road** fais attention en traversant *ou* quand tu traverses (la route); **you can never be too careful** *(gen)* on n'est jamais assez prudent; *(in double-checking something)* deux précautions valent mieux qu'une; **he was careful not to mention her name** il a pris soin de ne pas mentionner son nom; **to be careful with one's money** *(gen)* être économe; *Pej* être près de ses sous; **we have to be careful with money this month** il faut que nous surveillions nos dépenses ce mois-ci

(**b**) *(thorough, painstaking → person, work)* soigneux, consciencieux; *(→ consideration, examination)* approfondi; **they showed careful attention to detail** ils se sont montrés très attentifs aux détails; **to be careful of one's appearance** être soucieux de son apparence

carefully ['keəfəlɪ] *adv* (**a**) *(cautiously)* avec prudence *ou* précaution, prudemment; **she chose her words carefully** elle a pesé ses mots (**b**) *(thoroughly → work)* soigneusement, avec soin; *(→ consider, examine)* de façon approfondie, à fond; *(→ listen, watch)* attentivement

carefulness ['keəfʊlnɪs] *n* (**a**) *(caution)* prudence *f* (**b**) *(thoroughness)* attention *f*, soin *m*

careless ['keəlɪs] *adj* (**a**) *(negligent → person)* négligent, peu soigneux; *(→ work)* peu soigné; **a careless mistake** une faute d'inattention; **he's very careless about his appearance** il ne se soucie pas du tout de son apparence; **careless of the consequences** insouciant des conséquences; **to be careless with money** dépenser à tort et à travers; **accused of careless driving** accusé d'imprudence au volant

(**b**) *(thoughtless → remark)* irréfléchi

(**c**) *(carefree → person)* sans souci, insouciant; *(→ look, smile)* insouciant; **she danced with careless grace** elle dansait avec une grâce naturelle

carelessly ['keəlɪslɪ] *adv* (**a**) *(negligently → work, write)* sans soin, sans faire attention; **to drive carelessly** conduire avec négligence (**b**) *(thoughtlessly → act, speak)* sans réfléchir, à la légère; *(→ dress)* sans soin, sans recherche (**c**) *(in carefree way)* avec insouciance, nonchalamment

carelessness ['keəlɪsnɪs] *n (UNCOUNT)* (**a**) *(negligence)* négligence *f*, manque *m* de soin *ou* d'attention (**b**) *(thoughtlessness → of dress)* négligence *f*; *(→ of behaviour)* désinvolture *f*; *(→ of remark)* légèreté *f*

carer ['keərə(r)] *n (professional)* aide *mf* à domicile; *(relative)* = personne s'occupant d'un parent malade ou âgé

caress [kə'res] **1** *vt* caresser

2 *n* caresse *f*

caressingly [kə'resɪŋlɪ] *adv* d'une manière caressante; **to speak caressingly** prendre un ton câlin

caret ['kærət] *n Typ* accent *m* circonflexe

caretaker ['keə,teɪkə(r)] **1** *n* (**a**) *(of building)* concierge *mf*, gardien(enne) *m,f* (**b**) *Am (carer)* **he's his grandmother's caretaker** il a sa grand-mère à charge

2 *adj (government, prime minister, manager)* intérimaire

'The Caretaker' *Pinter* 'Le Gardien'

careworn ['keəwɔːn] *adj* accablé de soucis, rongé par les soucis

carfare ['kɑːfeə(r)] *n Am* prix *m* du trajet

carfax ['kɑːfæks] *n* carrefour *m*

cargo ['kɑːgəʊ] *(pl* **cargoes** *or* **cargos**) *n* cargaison *f*, chargement *m*; **to take on** *or* **embark cargo** charger des marchandises; **cargo outward** chargement d'aller; **cargo homeward** chargement de retour

►► ***cargo boat*** cargo *m*; ***cargo plane*** avion-cargo *m*; ***cargo trousers*** pantalon *m* cargo; ***cargo vessel*** cargo *m*

carhop ['kɑːhɒp] *n Am Fam (serving food)* serveur(euse)□ *m,f (qui apporte à manger aux clients dans leur voiture)*

Carib ['kærɪb] *n* (**a**) *(person)* Caraïbe *mf* (**b**) *(language)* caraïbe *m*

Caribbean [*Br* kærɪ'biːən, *Am* kə'rɪbɪən] **1** *n* **the Caribbean** *(area)* les Antilles *fpl*; *(sea)* la mer des Caraïbes *ou* des Antilles; **in the Caribbean** dans les Caraïbes, aux Antilles

2 *adj* des Caraïbes

►► ***Caribbean cruise*** croisière aux Caraïbes; ***the Caribbean islands*** les Antilles *fpl*; ***the Caribbean Sea*** la mer des Caraïbes *ou* des Antilles

caribou ['kærɪbuː] *(pl* **inv** *or* **caribous**) *n Zool* caribou *m*

caricaturable [,kærɪkə'tjʊərəbəl] *adj* qui se prête à la caricature

caricatural [,kærɪkə'tjʊərəl] *adj* caricatural

caricature ['kærɪkə,tjʊə(r)] **1** *n also Fig* caricature *f*

2 *vt (depict)* caricaturer; *(parody)* caricaturer, parodier

caricaturist ['kærɪkə,tjʊərɪst] *n* caricaturiste *mf*

caries ['keəriːz] *(pl* **inv**) *n* carie *f*

carillon ['kærɪljən] *n* carillon *m*

carina [kə'riːnə] *n Orn & Bot* carène *f*

carinate ['kærɪneɪt] *n Orn* carinate *m*

caring ['keərɪŋ] **1** *n (loving)* affection *f*; *(kindliness)* bienveillance *f*

2 *adj* (**a**) *(loving)* aimant; *(kindly)* bienveillant; **a more caring society** une société plus chaleureuse *ou* humaine; **a caring environment** un milieu chaleureux (**b**) *(organization)* à vocation sociale; **the caring professions** les métiers *mpl* du social

Carinthia [kə'rɪnθɪə] *n Geog* Carinthie *f*; **in Carinthia** en Carinthie

cariogenic [,keərɪəʊ'dʒenɪk] *adj Med* cariant, cariogène

carious ['keərɪəs] *adj Med* carié

carjack ['kɑːdʒæk] *vt* **to carjack sb** voler la voiture de qn *(avec violences ou intimidation à l'égard du conducteur)*

carjacker [,kɑːdʒækə(r)] *n* = auteur d'un vol de voiture sous la menace d'une arme

carjacking ['kɑːdʒækɪŋ] *n* = vol de voiture sous la menace d'une arme

carless ['kɑːlɪs] *adj* sans voiture

carline ['kɑːlaɪn] *n Bot* **carline (thistle)** carline *f* vulgaire, chardon *m* doré

carload ['kɑːləʊd] *n* **a carload of boxes/people** une voiture pleine de cartons/de gens

carlot ['kɑːlɒt] *n Am* parking *m (d'un garage automobile)*

Carlovingian [,kɑːləʊ'vɪndʒɪən] *adj Hist* carolingien

Carlow ['kɑːləʊ] *n* (**a**) *(town)* Carlow (**b**) *(county)* le comté de Carlow, = comté dans le sud-est de la République d'Irlande; **in Carlow** dans le comté de Carlow

carmaker ['kɑːmeɪkə(r)] *n Am* constructeur *m* automobile

carman ['kɑːmən] *(pl* **carmen** [-mən]) *n* (**a**) *(driver → of car)* chauffeur *m*, conducteur *m*; *(→ of lorry)* camionneur *m*; *(→ of cart)* charretier *m* (**b**) *(transporter)* voiturier *m* (**c**) *Am* chauffeur *m (de tram, de métro)*

Carmel ['kɑːməl] *n* **Mount Carmel** le mont Carmel

Carmelite ['kɑːmɪlaɪt] *Rel* **1** *adj* carmélite

2 *n (nun)* carmélite *f*; *(friar)* carme *m*

carminative ['kɑːmɪnətɪv] *Med* **1** *adj* carminatif

2 *n* carminatif *m*

[illegible] **1** *adj* carmin *(inv)*, carminé

2 *n* carmin *m*

Carnaby Street ['kɑːnəbɪ-] *n* = rue de Londres

CARNABY STREET

Carnaby Street était, dans les années 60, le haut lieu des milieux branchés; c'est aujourd'hui une rue spécialisée dans la fripe.

carnage ['kɑːnɪdʒ] *n* carnage *m*

carnal ['kɑːnəl] *adj* charnel; **to have carnal knowledge of sb** *Formal or Law* avoir des rapports sexuels avec qn; *Bible* connaître qn

►► *Am* ***carnal abuse*** *(sexual assault)* attouchements *mpl* sexuels sur des enfants; *(rape)* viol *m*

carnality [kɑː'nælɪtɪ] *n* sensualité *f*

carnally ['kɑːnəlɪ] *adv* charnellement; *Formal or Law* **to know sb carnally** avoir des rapports sexuels avec qn

carnassial tooth [kɑː'næsɪəl-] *n Anat* carnassière *f*, dent *f* carnassière

carnation [kɑːˈneɪʃən] **1** *n* œillet *m*
2 *adj (pink)* rose; *(reddish-pink)* incarnat

carnauba [kɑːˈnaʊbə] *n Bot* carnauba *m*
►► ***carnauba wax*** carnauba *m*

Carnegie Hall [kɑːˈneɪgɪ-] *n* = grande salle de concert à New York

carnelian [kəˈniːljən] *n Miner* cornaline *f*

carnet [ˈkɑːneɪ] *n* **(a)** *(book of tickets)* carnet *m* **(b)** *Com & Law* passavant *m*

carnification [ˌkɑːnɪfɪˈkeɪʃən] *n Med* carnification *f*

carnify [ˈkɑːnɪfaɪ] *vi Med (of tissue)* se carnifier

carnival [ˈkɑːnɪvəl] **1** *n* **(a)** *(festival)* carnaval *m* **(b)** *(fun fair)* fête *f* foraine
2 *comp (atmosphere, parade)* de carnaval

carnivora [kɑːˈnɪvərə] *npl Zool* carnivores *mpl*

carnivore [ˈkɑːnɪvɔː(r)] *n* carnivore *m*, carnassier *m*

carnivorous [kɑːˈnɪvərəs] *adj* **(a)** *(animal)* carnivore, carnassier **(b)** *(person, plant)* carnivore

carob [ˈkærəb] *n Bot & Culin (tree)* caroubier *m*; *(pod)* caroube *f*
►► ***carob bean*** caroube *f*; ***carob cake*** gâteau *m* à la caroube; ***carob powder*** farine *f* de caroube; ***carob tree*** caroubier *m*

carol [ˈkærəl] *(Br pt & pp* **carolled**, *cont* **carolling**, *Am pt & pp* **caroled**, *cont* **caroling**) **1** *n* chant *m* (joyeux); **to go carol singing** aller chanter des chants de Noël
2 *vi (person)* chanter (joyeusement); *(baby, bird)* gazouiller; **to go carolling** chanter des chants de Noël
3 *vt* **(a)** *(sing → of person)* chanter (joyeusement); *(→ of bird)* chanter **(b)** *(praise)* célébrer (par des chants)
►► ***carol service*** = office religieux qui précède Noël; ***carol singer*** = personne qui, à l'époque de Noël, va chanter et quêter au profit des bonnes œuvres

> **CAROL SERVICE**
>
> Le "Carol Service" se tient juste avant Noël et se compose surtout de chants de Noël et de lectures de la Bible.

Carolina [ˌkærəˈlaɪnə] *n* Caroline *f*; **the Carolinas** la Caroline du Nord et la Caroline du Sud; **South/North Carolina** Caroline *f* du Sud/du Nord

Caroline Islands [ˈkærəlaɪn-] *npl* **the Caroline Islands** les îles *fpl* Carolines; **in the Caroline Islands** aux îles Carolines

Carolingian [ˌkærəˈlɪndʒɪən] *Hist* **1** *adj* carolingien
2 *n* Carolingien(enne) *m,f*

caroller [ˈkærələ(r)] *n* = personne qui chante des chants de Noël

carom [ˈkærəm] **1** *n* carambolage *m*
2 *vi* caramboler

carotene [ˈkærəˌtiːn] *n Biol & Chem* carotène *m*

carotenoid [kæˈrɒtɪnɔɪd] *Biol & Chem* **1** *n* caroténoïde *m*
2 *adj* caroténoïde

carotid [kəˈrɒtɪd] *Anat* **1** *adj (artery)* carotide; *(nerve, system)* carotidien
2 *n* carotide *f*

carotin [ˈkærətɪn] *n Biol & Chem* carotène *m*

carousal [kəˈraʊzəl] *n Literary* beuverie *f*, ribote *f*

carouse [kəˈraʊz] *vi Literary* faire ribote

carousel [ˌkærəˈsel] *n* **(a)** *Phot (for slides)* carrousel *m* **(b)** *(for luggage)* carrousel *m*, tapis *m* roulant (à bagages) **(c)** *Am (merry-go-round)* manège *m* (de chevaux de bois)

carouser [kəˈraʊzə(r)] *n Literary* noceur(euse) *m,f*

carp[1] [kɑːp] *(pl* **inv** *or* **carps**) *n Ich* carpe *f*

carp[2] *vi (complain)* se plaindre; *(find fault)* critiquer; **he's always carping on about his work** il se plaint toujours de son travail

carpaccio [kɑːˈpætʃɪəʊ] *n Culin* carpaccio *m*

carpal [ˈkɑːpəl] *Anat* **1** *n* carpe *m*
2 *adj* carpien
►► *Med* ***carpal tunnel syndrome*** syndrome *m* du canal carpien

Carpathian Mountains [kɑːˈpeɪθɪən-], **Carpathians** [kɑːˈpeɪθɪənz] *npl* **the Carpathian Mountains** les Carpates *fpl*; **in the Carpathian Mountains** dans les Carpates

carpel [ˈkɑːpel] *n Bot* carpelle *m*

carpenter [ˈkɑːpɪntə(r)] *n (for houses, large-scale works)* charpentier *m*; *(for doors, furniture)* menuisier *m*
►► *Entom* ***carpenter bee*** abeille *f* charpentière; ***carpenter pants, carpenter trousers*** pantalon *m* charpentier

carpentry [ˈkɑːpɪntrɪ] *n (large-scale work)* charpenterie *f*; *(doors, furniture)* menuiserie *f*

carpet [ˈkɑːpɪt] **1** *n* **(a)** *(not fitted)* tapis *m*; *(fitted)* moquette *f*; *Fam Fig* **to be on the carpet** *(of question)* être sur le tapis; *(of person)* être sur la sellette; *Fam* **to have** *or* **put sb on the carpet** enguirlander qn, passer un savon à qn
(b) *Br Fig (of leaves, snow)* tapis *m*
2 *vt* **(a)** *(floor)* recouvrir d'un tapis; *(with fitted carpet)* recouvrir d'une moquette, moquetter; *(house, room)* mettre de la moquette dans, moquetter; **carpeted hallway** couloir moquetté *ou* avec de la moquette; **all the rooms are carpeted** il y a de la moquette dans toutes les pièces; *Fig* **carpeted with leaves/snow** tapissé de feuilles/de neige
(b) *Br Fam (scold)* enguirlander, passer un savon à
►► ***carpet beetle*** anthrène *m* (des tapis); *Mil* ***carpet bombing*** bombardement *m* intensif; *Sport* ***carpet bowls*** = jeu de boules pratiqué en intérieur; ***carpet cleaner*** *(product)* produit *m* nettoyant pour moquette; *(machine)* shampouineuse *f*; ***carpet shampoo*** shampooing *m* pour moquette; ***carpet showroom*** magasin *m* de moquettes; ***carpet slipper*** pantoufle *f (recouverte de tapisserie)*; ***carpet sweeper*** *(mechanical)* balai *m* mécanique; *(electric)* aspirateur *m*; ***carpet tack*** fixe-tapis *m inv*; ***carpet tile*** carreau *m* de moquette

carpetbag [ˈkɑːpɪtˌbæg] *n* sac *m* de voyage *(recouvert de tapisserie)*

carpetbagger [ˈkɑːpɪtˌbægə(r)] *n Pej* **(a)** *Pol* candidat *m* étranger à la circonscription **(b)** *Am Hist* = nom donné aux nordistes qui s'installèrent dans le Sud des États-Unis après la guerre de Sécession pour y faire fortune

carpet-bomb *vt Mil* bombarder, arroser de bombes

carpeting [ˈkɑːpɪtɪŋ] *n* **(a)** *(carpets)* moquette *f* **(b)** *Fam (severe reprimand)* réprimande[□] *f*; **to give sb a carpeting** passer un savon à qn

carphone [ˈkɑːˌfəʊn] *n* téléphone *m* de voiture

carping [ˈkɑːpɪŋ] **1** *adj (person → complaining)* qui se plaint tout le temps; *(→ faultfinding)* qui trouve toujours à redire, chicanier; *(attitude)* chicanier, grincheux; *(criticism, voice)* malveillant
2 *n (UNCOUNT) (complaining)* plaintes *fpl* (continuelles); *(faultfinding)* chicanerie *f*, critiques *fpl* (malveillantes)

carpingly [ˈkɑːpɪŋlɪ] *adv (in complaining manner)* en se plaignant; *(in faultfinding manner)* de façon pointilleuse

carpology [kɑːˈpɒlədʒɪ] *n Bot* carpologie *f*

carport [ˈkɑːˌpɔːt] *n* auvent *m* (pour voiture)

carpus [ˈkɑːpəs] *n Med* carpe *m*

carrageen, carragheen [ˈkærəgiːn] *n Bot* carragheen *m*, mousse *f* d'Irlande

Carrara [kəˈrɑːrə] *n Geog* Carrare *f*
►► ***Carrara marble*** marbre *m* de Carrare, carrare *m*

carrel, carrell [ˈkærəl] *n* box *m* individuel *(dans une bibliothèque)*

carriage [ˈkærɪdʒ] *n* **(a)** *(vehicle → horse-drawn)* calèche *f*, voiture *f* à cheval; *(→ together with horses and driver)* équipage *m*; *Br* **carriage and four** voiture *ou* équipage *m* à quatre chevaux
(b) *Br Rail* voiture *f*, wagon *m* (de voyageurs); **he was leaning out of the carriage window** il se penchait par la fenêtre du compartiment
(c) *Br Com (transportation)* transport *m*; *(cost of transportation)* transport *m*, fret *m*; *Com* **carriage forward** (en) port *m* dû; *Com* **carriage free** franco de port; *Com* **carriage insurance paid** port payé, assurance comprise; *Com* **carriage paid** (en) port *m* payé
(d) *(bearing, posture)* port *m*, maintien *m*
(e) *(of typewriter)* chariot *m*; *(of gun)* affût *m*
►► *Tech* ***carriage bolt*** boulon *m* à tête ronde et collet carré; *Com* ***carriage charge, carriage charges*** frais *mpl* de port; *Br* ***carriage clock*** pendulette *f (à boîtier rectangulaire muni d'une poignée)*; *Sport* ***carriage driving*** course *f* de chevaux d'attelage; *typ* ***carriage return*** retour *m* de chariot; *Br Com* ***carriage trade*** clientèle *f* riche

carriageway [ˈkærɪdʒweɪ] *n Br* chaussée *f*

carrick bend [ˈkærɪk-] *n Naut* ajut *m*

carrier [ˈkærɪə(r)] *n* **(a)** *(container → on bicycle) (basket)* panier *m*; *(behind the saddle)* porte-bagages *m inv*; *Am (→ on car)* galerie *f*; *(→ for homing pigeon)* cartouche *f*
(b) *Com (transporter → company)* entreprise *f* de transport, transporteur *m*; *(→ aeroplane)* appareil *m*, avion *m*; *(→ ship)* navire *m*; **sent by carrier** *(by road)* expédié par camion *ou* par transporteur; *(by rail)* expédié par chemin de fer; *(by air)* expédié par avion
(c) *Med (of disease, germs)* porteur(euse) *m,f*
(d) *(for signal)* opérateur *m*
►► *Br* ***carrier bag*** sac *m* en plastique; *Comput* ***carrier detect signal*** signal *m* de détection de porteuse; ***carrier pigeon*** pigeon *m* voyageur; *Comput* ***carrier signal*** signal *m* de détection de porteuse; *Rad* ***carrier wave*** onde *f* porteuse

carrier-based *adj Aviat & Naut* embarqué

carrier-borne *adj Aviat & Naut* embarqué

carrion [ˈkærɪən] *n* charogne *f*
►► *Entom* ***carrion beetle*** bouclier *m*, silphe *m*; *Orn* ***carrion crow*** corneille *f* noire; *Orn* ***carrion hawk*** caracara *m*

carrot [ˈkærət] **1** *n* **(a)** *(plant & vegetable)* carotte *f* **(b)** *Fig (motivation)* carotte *f*; **the boss used the promise of promotion as a carrot** le patron a promis une promotion pour nous encourager; **the carrot and stick approach** la méthode de la carotte et du bâton **(c)** *Fam Hum* **carrots** *(redhead)* rouquin(e) *m,f*
2 *comp (flavour, juice)* de carotte; *(soup)* aux carottes
►► ***carrot cake*** gâteau *m* aux carottes

carrot-coloured *adj* (de couleur) carotte *(inv)*

carrot-top *n Fam Hum (redhead)* rouquin(e) *m,f*

carroty [ˈkærətɪ] *adj* carotte *(inv)*, roux (rousse); **she has carroty hair** elle est rousse *ou Hum* poil-de-carotte

carrousel = **carousel**

CARRY [ˈkærɪ]

porter	► 1 (a), (c) – (e), (h), (i); 2
transporter	► 1 (b)
transmettre	► 1 (b), (c), (f)
adopter	► 1 (k)
vendre	► 1 (l)
retenir	► 1 (m)

(pt & pp **carried**) **1** *vt* **(a)** *(bear → of person)* porter; *(→ heavy load)* porter, transporter; **she carried her baby on her back/in her arms** elle portait son enfant sur son dos/dans ses bras; **they carried the equipment across the bridge** ils ont porté le matériel de l'autre côté du pont; **could you carry the groceries into the kitchen?** pourrais-tu porter les provisions jusqu'à la cuisine?; **the porter carried the suitcases downstairs/upstairs** le porteur a descendu/monté les bagages
(b) *(convey, transport → of vehicle)* transporter; *(→ of river, wind)* porter, emporter; *(→ of pipe)* acheminer, amener; *(→ of airwaves, telephone wire)* transmettre, conduire; **she ran as fast as her legs would carry her** elle a couru à toutes jambes; **the current carried the raft out to sea** le courant a emporté le radeau au large; **she carries all the facts in her head** elle a tous les faits en mémoire; **he carried the secret to his grave** il a emporté le secret dans la tombe; **to carry a tune** chanter juste; *Fig* **to carry coals to Newcastle** porter de l'eau à la rivière
(c) *(be medium for → message, news)* porter, transmettre; *Med (→ disease, virus)* porter; **rats carry diseases** les rats sont porteurs de maladies
(d) *(have on one's person → identity card, papers)* porter, avoir (sur soi); *(→ cash)* avoir (sur soi); *(→ gun)* porter; **I don't carry much money about** *or* **on me** je n'ai jamais beaucoup d'argent sur moi
(e) *(comprise, include)* porter, comporter;

(have as consequence) entraîner; **to carry a risk** comporter un risque; **to carry responsibility** comporter des responsabilités; **our products carry a 6-month warranty** nos produits sont accompagnés d'une garantie de 6 mois; **the crime carries a long sentence** ce crime est passible d'une longue peine; **to carry weight/authority** *(of person, opinion)* avoir du poids/de l'autorité

(**f**) *(of magazine, newspaper)* rapporter; *(of radio, television)* transmettre; **all the newspapers carried the story** l'histoire était dans tous les journaux; **the banners carried anti-government slogans** les bannières portaient des slogans anti-gouvernementaux

(**g**) *(take, lead, extend)* **to carry an argument to its logical conclusion** aller au bout d'un raisonnement; **to carry sth too far** pousser qch trop loin; *Mil* **to carry the battle** *or* **fight into the enemy's camp** faire du territoire ennemi le lieu du conflit; *Fig* attaquer l'ennemi sur son propre terrain

(**h**) *(bear, hold)* porter; **to carry oneself well** *(sit, stand)* se tenir droit; *(behave)* bien se conduire *ou* se tenir; **to carry one's head high** porter la tête haute

(**i**) *(hold up, support → roof, weight)* porter, supporter, soutenir; *also Fig* **to carry a heavy load** porter un lourd fardeau

(**j**) *(win)* **she carried the audience with her** le public était avec elle; **he carried all before him** ce fut un triomphe pour lui; **to carry the day** l'emporter

(**k**) *(proposal → pass)* adopter; *(→ secure passage of)* faire adopter *ou* passer; **the motion was carried** la motion a été votée

(**l**) *Com (deal in → stock)* vendre, stocker

(**m**) *Math* retenir; **add nine and carry one** ajoute neuf et retiens un

(**n**) *(be pregnant with)* attendre; **she's carrying their fourth child** elle est enceinte de leur quatrième enfant

2 *vi (ball, sound)* porter

►**carry away** *vt sep* (**a**) *(remove)* emporter, enlever; *(of waves, wind)* emporter (**b**) *(usu passive) (excite)* **he was carried away by his enthusiasm/imagination** il s'est laissé emporter par son enthousiasme/imagination; **I got a bit carried away and spent all my money** je me suis emballé et j'ai dépensé tout mon argent; **don't get too carried away!** du calme!, ne t'emballe pas!

►**carry back** *vt sep* (**a**) *(bring → object)* rapporter; *(→ person)* ramener (**b**) *(take → object)* reporter; *(→ person)* remmener; **that carries me back to my youth** cela me ramène à l'époque de ma jeunesse

►**carry down** *vt sep* (**a**) *(from upstairs)* descendre (**b**) *(usu passive) (tradition)* transmettre

►**carry forward** *vt sep Acct* reporter; **carried forward** report, à reporter; **carried forward from the previous year** report de l'exercice précédent; **carried forward to the next year** report à l'exercice suivant

►**carry off** *vt sep* (**a**) *(remove forcibly → goods)* emporter, enlever; *(→ person)* enlever; **the thieves carried off all their jewellery** les voleurs se sont enfuis avec tous leurs bijoux

(**b**) *(award, prize)* remporter

(**c**) *(do successfully → aim, plan)* réaliser; *(→ deal, meeting)* mener à bien; **to carry it off** réussir le coup; **she carried it off beautifully** elle s'en est très bien tirée

(**d**) *Euph (kill → of disease)* emporter; **hundreds were carried off by the epidemic** des centaines de personnes ont été emportées par l'épidémie

►**carry on 1** *vi* (**a**) *Br (continue)* continuer; **I carried on working** *or* **with my work** j'ai continué à travailler, j'ai continué mon travail; **they carried on to the bitter end** ils sont allés jusqu'au bout

(**b**) *Fam (make a fuss)* faire une histoire *ou* des histoires; **the way you carry on, you'd think I never did anything around the house** à t'entendre, je n'ai jamais rien fait dans cette maison

(**c**) *Fam (have affair)* **to carry on with sb** avoir une liaison ❑ avec qn; **he's carrying on with somebody else's wife** il a une liaison avec *ou* il couche avec la femme d'un autre; **Carry On films** = série de comédies britanniques des années 60 et 70 dont le titre commence toujours par "Carry On", célèbres pour leur humour plein de sous-entendus grivois

2 *vt insep* (**a**) *Br (continue → conversation, work)* continuer, poursuivre; *(→ tradition)* entretenir, perpétuer; **we can carry on this conversation later** nous pourrons poursuivre *ou* reprendre cette conversation plus tard

(**b**) *(conduct → work)* effectuer, réaliser; *(→ negotiations)* mener; *(→ discussion)* avoir; *(→ correspondence)* entretenir

►**carry out** *vt sep* (**a**) *(take away)* emporter

(**b**) *(perform → programme, raid)* effectuer; *(→ idea, plan)* réaliser, mettre à exécution; *(→ experiment)* effectuer, conduire; *(→ investigation, research, survey)* conduire, mener; *(→ instruction, order)* exécuter; **the police carried out a search** *(of house, premises)* la police a effectué une perquisition

(**c**) *(fulfil → obligation)* s'acquitter de; *(→ wish)* satisfaire à; *(→ responsibilities)* assumer; **he failed to carry out his promise** il a manqué à sa parole, il n'a pas tenu *ou* respecté sa promesse; **to carry out one's (professional) duties** s'acquitter de ses fonctions

►**carry over** *vt sep* (**a**) *(transport)* faire traverser; *Fig (transfer)* reporter, transférer

(**b**) *(defer, postpone)* reporter; **to carry over one's holiday entitlement/tax allowance to the next year** reporter ses congés/son abattement fiscal sur l'année suivante

(**c**) *Acct* reporter; **to carry over a loss to the following year** reporter une perte sur l'année suivante

(**d**) *St Exch (shares)* reporter, prendre en report

(**e**) *Com* **to carry over goods from one season to another** stocker des marchandises d'une saison sur l'autre

►**carry through** *vt sep* (**a**) *(accomplish)* réaliser, mener à bien *ou* à bonne fin (**b**) *(support)* soutenir (dans une épreuve); **her love of life carried her through her illness** sa volonté de vivre lui a permis de vaincre sa maladie

---

carryall ['kærɪˌɔːl] *n Am* fourre-tout *m inv (sac)*

carrycot ['kærɪˌkɒt] *n Br* porte-bébé *m*

carrying ['kærɪɪŋ] *adj*

►► *Tech* **carrying axle** *(of locomotive)* essieu *m* porteur; **carrying capacity** *(of vehicle)* charge *f* utile; *(of tourist attraction)* capacité *f* d'accueil; *Am* **carrying case** boîte *f*, étui *m*; *Com* **carrying charge** *Am (extra charge)* supplément *m*; *(que l'on paye lorsqu'on achète à crédit)*; *Br (transport costs)* frais *mpl* de transport; *Acct* **carrying forward** report *m*

carrying-on *(pl* **carryings-on***)* *n Fam (of child)* cirque *m*; *(of unfaithful spouse, lover)* écart *m* de conduite ❑, incartade(s) ❑ *f(pl)*

carry-on 1 *n Br Fam* (**a**) *(fuss)* histoires *fpl*; *(commotion)* tapage ❑ *m*, agitation ❑ *f*; **what a carry-on!** que d'histoires! (**b**) *(of child)* cirque *m*; *(of unfaithful spouse, lover)* écart *m* de conduite ❑

2 *adj* **carry-on items** bagages *mpl* à main

carry-out 1 *n* (**a**) *Am & Scot (restaurant)* = restaurant qui fait des plats à emporter; *(meal)* plat *m* à emporter (**b**) *Scot (drink)* = boissons alcoolisées à emporter

2 *adj Am & Scot (dish, food)* à emporter; *Scot (drink)* à emporter

►► **carry-out menu** liste *f* des plats à emporter

carry-over *n* (**a**) *(habit, influence, trace)* vestige *m* (**b**) *Fin (amount)* report *m*

carsick ['kɑːˌsɪk] *adj* **to be** *or* **to feel carsick** être malade en voiture

cart [kɑːt] **1** *n* (**a**) *(horse-drawn → for farming)* charrette *f*; *(→ for passengers)* charrette *f* (anglaise), voiture *f*; **to put the cart before the horse** mettre la charrue avant les bœufs (**b**) *(handcart)* charrette *f* à bras

2 *vt* (**a**) *(transport by cart)* charrier, charroyer, transporter en charrette (**b**) *Fam Fig (haul)* transporter ❑, trimballer; **I've been carting this suitcase around all day** j'ai passé la journée à trimballer cette valise

►► **cart track** chemin *m* de terre

►**cart away, cart off** *vt sep (rubbish, wood)* emporter; *Fam (person)* emmener

cartage ['kɑːtɪdʒ] *n Com* (**a**) *(transport → in cart)* charroi *m*, charriage *m*; *(→ in lorry)* camionnage *m* (**b**) *(cost → by cart)* (coût *m* de) charriage *m*; *(→ by lorry)* (coût *m* de) camionnage *m*

Cartagena [ˌkɑːtə'dʒiːnə] *n* Carthagène

carte blanche [ˌkɑːt'blɑ̃ʃ] *n* carte *f* blanche; **to give sb carte blanche (to do sth)** donner carte blanche à qn (pour faire qch)

cartel [kɑː'tel] *n Com & Pol* cartel *m*; **oil/steel cartel** cartel *m* du pétrole/de l'acier

cartelization, cartellization [ˌkɑːtəlaɪ'zeɪʃən] *n Com & Pol* cartellisation *f*

carter ['kɑːtə(r)] *n* charretier(ère) *m,f*

Cartesian [kɑː'tiːzɪən] **1** *n* cartésien(enne) *m,f*

2 *adj* cartésien

►► **Cartesian coordinates** coordonnées *fpl* cartésiennes; **Cartesian diver** ludion *m*

Cartesianism [kɑː'tiːzɪənɪzəm] *n Phil* Cartésianisme *m*

Carthage ['kɑːθɪdʒ] *n Antiq* Carthage

Carthaginian [ˌkɑːθə'dʒɪnɪən] **1** *n* Carthaginois(e) *m,f*

2 *adj* carthaginois

carthorse ['kɑːthɔːs, *pl* hɔːsɪz] *n* cheval *m* de trait

Carthusian [kɑː'θjuːzjən] *Rel* **1** *n* chartreux(euse) *m,f*

2 *adj* de *ou* des chartreux; **Carthusian monastery** chartreuse *f (monastère)*; **Carthusian monk** chartreux *m*; **Carthusian nun** chartreuse *f*

cartilage ['kɑːtɪlɪdʒ] *n* cartilage *m*

cartilaginous [ˌkɑːtɪ'lædʒɪnəs] *adj* cartilagineux

►► **cartilaginous fish** poisson *m* cartilagineux

cartload ['kɑːtləʊd] *n* charretée *f*, voiturée *f* (**of** de); *(transported in tip cart)* tombereau *m*

cartogram ['kɑːtəgræm] *n* cartogramme *m*

cartographer [kɑː'tɒgrəfə(r)] *n* cartographe *mf*

cartographic [ˌkɑːtə'græfɪk], **cartographical** [ˌkɑːtə'græfɪkəl] *adj* cartographique

cartography [kɑː'tɒgrəfɪ] *n* cartographie *f*

cartomancy ['kɑːtəʊmænsɪ] *n* cartomancie *f*

carton ['kɑːtən] *n (cardboard box)* boîte *f* (en carton), carton *m*; *(of juice, milk)* carton *m*, brique *f*; *(of cream, yoghurt)* pot *m*; *(of cigarettes)* cartouche *f*

cartoon [kɑː'tuːn] *n* (**a**) *(drawing)* dessin *m* humoristique; *(series of drawings)* bande *f* dessinée; *(animated film)* dessin *m* animé (**b**) *Art (sketch)* carton *m*

►► **cartoon character** personnage *m* de bande dessinée/de dessin animé; **cartoon strip** bande *f* dessinée, BD *f*

cartoonist [kɑː'tuːnɪst] *n (of drawings)* dessinateur(trice) *m,f* humoristique; *(of series of drawings)* dessinateur(trice) *m,f* de bandes dessinées; *(for films)* dessinateur(trice) *m,f* de dessins animés, animateur(trice) *m,f*

cartouche [kɑː'tuːʃ] *n Hist* (**a**) *(for gun)* cartouche *f* (**b**) *Archit* cartouche *m* (**c**) *(in hieroglyphics)* cartouche *m*

cartridge ['kɑːtrɪdʒ] *n* (**a**) *(for explosive, gun)* cartouche *f* (**b**) *(for pen, tape deck, typewriter)* cartouche *f* (**c**) *(for stylus)* cellule *f* (**d**) *Phot* chargeur *m* (d'appareil photo) (**e**) *Comput (disk)* cartouche *f*; **ink/toner cartridge** cartouche *f* d'encre/de toner

►► **cartridge belt** *(for hunter, soldier)* cartouchière *f*; *(for machine gun)* bande *f* (de mitrailleuse); **cartridge case** *(for gun)* douille *f*, étui *m* (de cartouche); *(for cannon)* douille *f*; **cartridge clip** chargeur *m (d'une arme à feu)*; **cartridge paper** papier *m* à cartouche; **cartridge pen** stylo *m* à cartouche; **cartridge player** lecteur *m* de cartouche

cartwheel ['kɑːtwiːl] **1** *n* (**a**) *(of cart)* roue *f* de charrette (**b**) *(movement)* roue *f*; **to do** *or* **to turn cartwheels** faire la roue

2 *vi* faire la roue; **she cartwheeled across the floor** elle a traversé la pièce en faisant des roues

►► **cartwheel hat** chapeau *m* à larges bords

cartwright ['kɑːtraɪt] *n* charron *m*

caruncle ['kærəŋkəl] *n Anat, Bot & Zool* caroncule *f*

carve [kɑːv] *vt* (**a**) *(stone, wood)* tailler; **to carve a statue in** *or* **out of marble** sculpter une statue dans le marbre; **a carved lion** un lion sculpté; **she carved their names on the tree trunk** elle a gravé leurs noms sur le tronc de l'arbre; **the**

river had carved a channel through the rock la rivière s'était creusé un lit dans le rocher (**b**) *(meat)* découper

▸**carve out** *vt sep (piece)* découper, tailler; *(shape)* sculpter, tailler; **to carve a figure out of marble** tailler une silhouette dans du marbre; **the company carved out a niche in the market** la société s'est taillé une place sur le marché; *Fig* **she carved out a career for herself in the arts** elle a fait carrière dans les arts

▸**carve up** *vt sep* (**a**) *(cut up → meat)* découper; *Fig (→ country, estate)* morceler, démembrer; **they carved up the profits among them** ils se sont partagé les profits (**b**) *Fam (person)* amocher à coups de couteau; *(face)* balafrer❑, taillader❑ (**c**) *Fam (in car)* faire une queue de poisson à❑

carvel-built ['kɑːvəl-] *adj Naut (boat)* bordé à joints serrés

carver ['kɑːvə(r)] *n* (**a**) *(knife)* couteau *m* à découper; **carvers** service *m* à découper (**b**) *Br (chair)* fauteuil *m* de table *(qu'occupe le chef de famille)*

carvery ['kɑːvərɪ] *(pl* **carveries***) n* = restaurant où l'on mange de la viande découpée à table

carve-up *n Fam (of booty, inheritance)* fractionnement❑ *m*; *(of country, estate)* morcellement❑ *m*, démembrement❑ *m*

'What a Carve Up!' *Coe* 'Testament à l'anglaise'

carving ['kɑːvɪŋ] *n* (**a**) *(sculpture)* sculpture *f*; *(engraving)* gravure *f*; **wood carving** sculpture *f* sur bois (**b**) *(act)* taille *f*; *(skill)* taille *f*, art *m* de la taille (**c**) *(of meat)* découpage *m* (**d**) *Ski* carving *m*

▸▸ ***carving fork*** fourchette *f* à découper; ***carving knife*** couteau *m* à découper; *Ski* ***carving ski*** ski *m* carvé

caryatid [ˌkærɪ'ætɪd] *n Archit* cariatide *f*

caryopsis [ˌkærɪ'ɒpsɪs] *n Bot* caryopse *m*

Casablanca [ˌkæsə'blæŋkə] *n* Casablanca

Casanova [ˌkæsə'nəʊvə] **1** *pr n* Casanova

2 *n* **he's a real Casanova** c'est un vrai Don Juan

casbah ['kæzbɑː] *n* casbah *f*

Cascade [kæ'skeɪd] *n Geog* **the Cascade Range, the Cascades** la chaîne des Cascades

cascade [kæ'skeɪd] **1** *n* cascade *f*, chute *f* d'eau; *Fig (of hair)* flot *m*

2 *vi (water, hair)* tomber en cascade; **the tins came cascading down** les boîtes de conserve sont tombées les unes après les autres

▸▸ *Fin* ***cascade taxation*** imposition *f* en cascade

cascading menu [kæs'keɪdɪŋ-] *n Comput* menu *m* en cascade

cascara [kæ'skɑːrə] *n Pharm* cascara *f*

CASE [keɪs] *n Comput* (*abbr* **computer-aided software engineering**) ingénierie *f* des systèmes assistée par ordinateur

CASE¹ [keɪs]

cas	▸ **1 (a), (b), (f) – (h)**
affaire	▸ **1 (c), (d)**
arguments	▸ **1 (e)**
en tout cas	▸ **2**
au cas où	▸ **3**
en cas de	▸ **4**

1 *n* (**a**) *(instance, situation)* cas *m*, exemple *m*; **it's a clear case of mismanagement** c'est un exemple manifeste de mauvaise gestion; **it was a case of having to decide on the spur of the moment** il fallait décider sur-le-champ; **we often hear of cases where companies go bankrupt** nous entendons souvent parler de cas où des entreprises font faillite; **if it's a case of not having enough money** si c'est une question d'argent; **to put the case clearly** exposer clairement le cas *ou* la situation; **in the case of single mothers** dans le cas des mères célibataires; **in that case** dans *ou* en ce cas; **in these cases it's best to wait** dans de telles circonstances, il vaut mieux attendre; **in this particular case** en l'occurrence; **in which case** auquel cas; **in your case** en ce qui vous concerne, dans votre cas; **in Paul's case** dans le cas de Paul; **in many/most cases** dans beaucoup de/la plupart des cas; **in no case** en aucun cas; **in some cases** dans certains cas; **in the vast majority of cases** dans la plupart des cas; **in nine cases out of ten** neuf fois sur dix; **the current crisis is a case in point** la crise actuelle est un exemple typique; **it's a case of now or never** il s'agit de saisir l'occasion *ou* de faire vite; *Fam* **he's always on my case** je l'ai tout le temps sur le dos

(**b**) *(actual state of affairs)* cas *m*; **can we assume that this is in fact the case?** pouvons-nous considérer que c'est bien le cas?; **that is not the case in Great Britain** ce *ou* tel n'est pas le cas en Grande-Bretagne; **as is often/usually the case** comme c'est souvent/ordinairement le cas; **as the case** *or* **whatever the case may be** selon le cas; **if such is indeed the case** si tel est *ou* si c'est vraiment le cas

(**c**) *(investigation)* affaire *f*; **it was one of Inspector Dupont's most difficult cases** ce fut une des affaires les plus difficiles de l'inspecteur Dupont; **a murder/fraud case** une affaire de meurtre/fraude; **the case continues** affaire à suivre; **the case is closed** c'est une affaire classée; **he's on the case** *(working on it)* il s'en occupe; *(alert, informed)* il est très au courant; *Fam* **to be on sb's case** être sur le dos de qn; *Fam* **get off my case!** fiche-moi la paix!; *Am Fam* **to have a case on sb** en pincer pour qn

(**d**) *Law* affaire *f*, cause *f*, procès *m*; **a civil rights case** une affaire de droits civils; **her case comes up next week** son procès a lieu la semaine prochaine; **to try a case** juger une affaire; **he won his case for slander** *(barrister)* il a gagné le procès en diffamation; *(plaintiff)* il a gagné son procès *ou* il a eu gain de cause dans son procès en diffamation

(**e**) *(argument)* arguments *mpl*; **there is no case against him** aucune preuve n'a pu être retenue contre lui; **the case against/for the defendant** les arguments contre/en faveur de l'accusé; **there is a good case against/for establishing quotas** il y a beaucoup à dire contre/en faveur de l'établissement de quotas; **the union has a good case** le syndicat a de bons arguments *ou* de bonnes raisons; **state your case** présentez vos arguments; **there is a case to be answered here** il ne faut pas négliger cette question; **to make (out) a case for sth** présenter des arguments pour *ou* en faveur de qch

(**f**) *Med (disease)* cas *m*; *(person)* malade *mf*; **there have been several cases of meningitis recently** il y a eu plusieurs cas de méningite récemment; **the hospital could only take the most serious cases** l'hôpital ne pouvait s'occuper que des cas les plus graves; **all burns cases are treated here** tous les grands brûlés sont traités ici

(**g**) *Fam (person)* cas❑ *m*; **he's a real case!** c'est un cas *ou* un phénomène!; **he's a sad case** c'est vraiment un pauvre type

(**h**) *Gram* cas *m*

2 in any case *adv* (**a**) *(besides)* en tout cas; **in any case I shan't be coming** je ne viendrai pas en tout cas *ou* de toute façon; **in any case, that's not the point** bref *ou* en tout cas, là n'est pas la question

(**b**) *(at least)* du moins, en tout cas; **that's what I was told, or in any case was led to believe** c'est ce qu'on m'a dit ou en tout cas *ou* ou du moins, ce qu'on m'a fait croire

3 in case 1 *adv* au cas où; **I'll take my umbrella (just) in case** je vais prendre mon parapluie au cas où **2** *conj* au cas où; **in case you think I'm bluffing** au cas où tu croirais que je bluffe; **I kept a place for you, in case you were late** je t'ai gardé une place, au cas où tu serais en retard

4 in case of *prep* en cas de; **in case of emergency/fire** en cas d'urgence/d'incendie

▸▸ ***case conference*** étude *f* de cas *(par un groupe de spécialistes)*; ***case grammar*** grammaire *f* des cas; ***case history*** antécédents *mpl*; ***case law*** jurisprudence *f*, droit *m* jurisprudentiel; ***case load*** (nombre *m* de) dossiers *mpl* à traiter; ***case notes*** dossier *m*; ***case study*** étude *f* de cas

case² **1** *n* (**a**) *(container)* caisse *f*, boîte *f*; *(for bottles)* caisse *f*; *(for fruit, vegetables)* cageot *m*; *(chest)* coffre *m*; *(for jewellery)* coffret *m*; *(for necklace, watch)* écrin *m*; *(for camera, guitar, spectacles, cigarettes)* étui *m*; *(for pencils, geometry etc instruments)* trousse *f*

(**b**) *(for display)* vitrine *f*

(**c**) *Br (suitcase)* valise *f*

(**d**) *Typ* casse *f*

(**e**) *Bot & Zool (covering)* enveloppe *f*

2 *vt* (**a**) *(put in box)* mettre en boîte *ou* caisse (**b**) *(cover)* couvrir, envelopper; **cased in ice** couvert de glace

(**c**) *Fam (inspect)* examiner❑; **the robbers had thoroughly cased the joint** les voleurs avaient bien examiné les lieux (avant de faire leur coup)

▸▸ ***case knife*** couteau *m* à gaine

casebook ['keɪsbʊk] *n (gen)* = recueil de comptes rendus de cas; *Law* recueil *m* de jurisprudence

casebound ['keɪsbaʊnd] *adj* cartonné

casefile ['keɪsfaɪl] *n* dossier *m*

case-harden *vt Metal* cémenter; *Fig* endurcir

case-hardened *adj Metal* cémenté; *Fig* endurci

case-hardening *n Metal* cémentation *f*

casein ['keɪsiːn] *n Chem* caséine *f*

case-insensitive *adj Comput* qui ne distingue pas les majuscules des minuscules; **this URL is case-insensitive** le respect de majuscules et des minuscules n'est pas nécessaire pour cette URL

casemate ['keɪsmeɪt] *n Mil* casemate *f*

casemated ['keɪsmeɪtɪd] *adj Mil* casematé

▸▸ ***casemated battery*** batterie *f* blindée

casement ['keɪsmənt] *n (window)* fenêtre *f* à battant *ou* battants, croisée *f*; *(window frame)* châssis *m* de fenêtre (à deux battants); *Literary* fenêtre *f*

▸▸ ***casement window*** fenêtre *f* à battant *ou* battants, croisée *f*

case-sensitive *adj Comput* qui distingue les majuscules des minuscules; **this e-mail address is case-sensitive** il faut respecter les majuscules et les minuscules dans cette adresse électronique

casework ['keɪswɜːk] *n* = travail social personnalisé

caseworker ['keɪsˌwɜːkə(r)] *n* = travailleur social s'occupant de cas individuels et familiaux

Casey Jones ['keɪsɪdʒəʊnz] *pr n* = héros populaire américain qui perdit sa vie en sauvant les passagers d'un train fou

cash [kæʃ] **1** *n* (**a**) *(coins and banknotes)* espèces *fpl*, (argent *m*) liquide *m*; **I never carry much cash** je n'ai jamais beaucoup d'argent *ou* de liquide sur moi; **£3,000 in cash** 3000 livres en espèces *ou* en liquide; **hard** *or* **ready cash** liquide *m*; **to pay (in) cash** *(not credit)* payer comptant; *(money not cheque)* payer en liquide *ou* en espèces; **to buy/sell sth for cash** acheter/vendre qch comptant; **cash against documents** comptant contre documents; **to pay cash on the nail** payer rubis sur ongle; *Acct* **cash at bank** avoir *m* en banque; **cash in hand** fonds *mpl ou* espèces *mpl ou* argent *m* en caisse; *Acct* **cash in till** encaisse *f*, fonds *m* de caisse

(**b**) *(money in general)* argent *m*; **to be short of cash** être à court (d'argent); **I haven't got any cash** *(no money)* je n'ai pas d'argent; *(no change)* je n'ai pas de monnaie; **I ran out of cash** je n'avais plus d'argent; **they haven't any cash** ils n'ont plus un sou

(**c**) *(immediate payment)* **discount for cash** escompte *m* de caisse; **cash down** argent *m* comptant; **to pay cash down** payer comptant; *Br* **cash on delivery** paiement *m* à la livraison, (livraison *f*) contre remboursement; *Am* **cash before delivery** règlement *m* avant livraison; **cash with order** payable à la commande; **cash on shipment** comptant *m* à l'expédition

2 *comp* (**a**) *(problems, worries)* d'argent (**b**) *(price, transaction)* (au) comptant

3 *vt (cheque)* encaisser, toucher; **could you cash this cheque for me?** *(to friend)* peux-tu me donner de l'argent contre ce chèque?; *(to bank employee)* voudriez-vous m'encaisser ce chèque?

▸▸ ***cash account*** compte *m* de caisse; ***cash advance*** avance *m* en numéraire; *Br* ***cash and carry*** libre-service *m* de gros; ***cash balance*** *(status)* situation *f* de caisse; *(amount remaining)* solde *m* actif, solde de caisse; *Am* **cash bar** bar *m* payant *(à une réception)*; *Acct* ***cash basis accounting*** comptabilité *f* de caisse *ou* de gestion; ***cash benefits*** avantages *mpl* en espèces; ***cash bonus*** prime *f* en espèces; ***cash budget*** budget *m* de trésorerie; ***cash card*** carte *f* de retrait; *Acct* ***cash contribution*** apport *m* en numéraire *ou* en espèces; ***cash cow*** vache *f* à lait; ***cash crop*** culture *f* de rapport *ou* commerciale; ***cash debit*** débit *m* de caisse; ***cash deficit*** déficit *m* de trésorerie; ***cash deposit*** versement *m* en espèces; ***cash desk*** caisse *f*; ***cash discount*** escompte *m* de caisse; ***cash dispenser*** distributeur *m* (automatique) de billets, DAB *m*, *Suisse* bancomat *m*; ***cash dividend*** dividende *m* en espèces; *Fin* ***cash equivalents*** quasi-espèces *fpl*, actifs *mpl* facilement réalisables; *Acct* ***cash expenditure*** dépenses *fpl* de caisse; *Fin* ***cash flow*** cash-flow *m*, trésorerie *f*; *Acct (in cashflow statement)* marge *f* brute d'autofinancement; *Hum* **to have cash flow problems** avoir des problèmes de trésorerie; *Acct & Fin* ***cash flow forecast*** prévision *f* de trésorerie; *Fin* ***cash flow management*** gestion *f* de trésorerie; ***cash flow statement*** état *m* des mouvements de la trésorerie; ***cash incentive*** stimulation *f* financière; *Acct* ***cash inflow*** rentrées *fpl* de fonds; ***cash inflows and outflows*** encaissements *mpl* et décaissements *mpl*; *Acct* ***cash item*** article *m* de caisse; *Banking* ***cash machine*** distributeur *m* de billets; ***cash management*** gestion *f* de trésorerie; ***cash nexus*** rapports *mpl* d'argent; ***cash offer*** offre *f* d'achat avec paiement comptant; **she made us a cash offer for the flat** elle nous a proposé de payer l'appartement (au) comptant; *Acct* ***cash order*** ordre *m* au comptant; ***cash outflow*** sorties *fpl* de trésorerie; ***cash overs*** excédent *m* de caisse; ***cash payment*** *(immediate)* paiement *m* comptant; *(in cash)* paiement *m* en espèces *ou* en liquide; ***cash price*** prix *m* comptant; ***cash prize*** prix *m* en espèces; ***cash purchase*** achat *m* au comptant, achat contre espèces; *Acct* ***cash ratio*** ratio *m* de trésorerie; *Acct* ***cash receipt*** reçu *m* pour paiement en espèces, reçu *m* d'espèces; *Acct* ***cash receipts and payments*** rentrées *fpl* et sorties *fpl* de caisse; *Acct* ***cash received*** *(balance sheet item)* entrée *f* d'argent; ***cash register*** caisse *f* (enregistreuse); *Acct* ***cash report (form)*** situation *f* de caisse; ***cash reserves*** réserves *fpl* en espèces; ***cash sale*** vente *f* au comptant; *Acct* ***cash statement*** état *m* *ou* relevé *m* de caisse; *Acct* ***cash surplus*** restant *m* en caisse; ***cash terms*** conditions *fpl* au comptant; ***cash unders*** manque *m* de caisse; ***cash value*** valeur *f* vénale; *Fin* ***cash voucher*** pièce *f* de caisse, PC *f*; *Banking* ***cash withdrawal*** retrait *m* d'espèces

►**cash in 1** *vt sep (bond, certificate)* réaliser, se faire rembourser; *(coupon)* se faire rembourser; *Am Fam* **to cash in one's chips** *or* **checks** *(die)* casser sa pipe

2 *vi Fam* (**a**) *(take advantage)* **to cash in on a situation** profiter *ou* tirer profit d'une situation ❑; **to cash in on one's influence/talent** monnayer son influence/talent ❑

(**b**) *Am (die)* casser sa pipe

►**cash up** *vi Br Com* faire ses comptes

cashable ['kæʃəbəl] *adj* encaissable, payable

cash-and-carry 1 *adj* de libre-service de gros

2 *adv* dans un libre-service de gros

►► *St Exch* ***cash-and-carry arbitrage*** arbitrage *m* comptant-terme

cashback ['kæʃbæk] *n Br* (**a**) *(in mortgage lending)* = prime versée par une société de crédit immobilier au souscripteur d'un emprunt (**b**) *(in supermarket)* = espèces retirées à la caisse d'un supermarché lors d'un paiement par carte de crédit

cash-based accounting *n Acct* comptabilité *f* de caisse

cashbook ['kæʃbʊk] *n* livre *m* de caisse

cashbox ['kæʃbɒks] *n* caisse *f*

cashew ['kæʃuː] *n (tree)* anacardier *m*; *(nut)* (noix *f* de) cajou *m*

►► ***cashew nut*** (noix *f* de) cajou *m*

cashier[1] [kæ'ʃɪə(r)] *n Banking & Com* caissier(ère) *m,f*; *Am* **cashier's check** chèque *m* de banque; **cashier's desk** comptoir-caisse *m*

cashier[2] *vt Mil* casser; *Fig* renvoyer, congédier

cashless ['kæʃlɪs] *adj* **the cashless society** la société sans argent liquide *(où toutes les transactions sont effectuées en argent électronique)*; **we're moving towards a cashless society** nous nous dirigeons vers une société où l'argent liquide ne sera plus utilisé; **cashless transaction** transaction *f* sans argent

cashmere [kæʃ'mɪə(r)] **1** *n* cachemire *m*

2 *comp (coat, sweater)* de *ou* en cachemire

cashpoint ['kæʃpɔɪnt] *n Br* distributeur *m* (automatique) de billets, DAB *m*, *Suisse* bancomat *m*

casing ['keɪsɪŋ] *n* (**a**) *(gen)* revêtement *m*, enveloppe *f*; *(for tyre)* enveloppe *f* extérieure; *(of pump)* enveloppe *f*, garniture *f*; *(of machine)* cage *f*, coquille *f*; *Constr (for reinforced concrete)* coffrage *m* (**b**) *(of window)* chambranle *m*, châssis *m*; *(of door)* encadrement *m*, chambranle *m*

casino [kə'siːnəʊ] *(pl* **casinos***)* *n* casino *m*

cask [kɑːsk] *n (barrel → gen)* tonneau *m*, fût *m*; *(→ large)* barrique *f*; *(→ small)* baril *m*

casket ['kɑːskɪt] *n* (**a**) *(small box)* coffret *m*, boîte *f* (**b**) *Am (coffin)* cercueil *m*

CASM ['kæzəm] *n Br Comput (abbr* **computer-aided sales and marketing***)* vente *f* et marketing *m* assistés par ordinateur

Caspian Sea ['kæspɪən-] *n* **the Caspian Sea** la (mer) Caspienne

Cassandra [kə'sændrə] *pr n Myth & Fig* Cassandre

cassata [kə'sɑːtə] *n Culin* cassate *f*

cassava [kə'sɑːvə] *n Bot (plant)* manioc *m*; *Culin (flour)* farine *f* de manioc

casserole ['kæsərəʊl] **1** *n* (**a**) *(dish, pan)* cocotte *f* (**b**) *(stew)* ragoût *m*

2 *vt* (faire) cuire en ragoût

cassette [kæ'set] *n* (**a**) *(tape)* cassette *f* (**b**) *Phot (cartridge)* chargeur *m*

►► ***cassette case*** étui *m* de cassette; ***cassette deck*** lecteur *m* de cassettes; ***cassette head cleaner*** cassette *f* autonettoyante; ***cassette player*** lecteur *m* de cassettes; ***cassette recorder*** magnétophone *m* à cassettes; ***cassette storage rack*** rangement *m* pour cassettes

cassia ['kæsɪə] *n Bot* casse *f*

Cassini's division [kə'siːnɪz-] *n Astron* division *f* de Cassini

Cassiopeia [ˌkæsɪə'pɪə] *n Astron* Cassiopée *f*

cassis [kə'siːs] *n* cassis *m*

cassiterite [kæ'sɪtəraɪt] *n Miner* cassitérite *f*

Cassius ['kæsɪəs] *pr n Myth* Cassius

cassock ['kæsək] *n* soutane *f*

cassowary ['kæsəweərɪ] *(pl* **cassowaries***)* *n Orn* casoar *m*

CAST [kɑːst]

jeter	► **1 (a), (b)**
projeter	► **1 (b)**
perdre	► **1 (c)**
distribuer les rôles de	► **1 (d)**
mouler	► **1 (e)**
couler	► **1 (e)**
acteurs	► **2 (a)**
nuance	► **2 (b)**
moulage	► **2 (c)**
coulage	► **2 (c)**
[illegible]	[illegible]

(pt & pp **cast***)* **1** *vt* (**a**) *(throw)* jeter, lancer; *Br* **to cast lots** tirer au sort; **to cast a spell on** *or* **over sb** *(witch)* jeter un sort à qn, ensorceler qn; *Fig* ensorceler *ou* envoûter qn; **to cast one's vote for sb** voter pour qn; **the number of votes cast** le nombre de voix *ou* de suffrages; *Naut* **to cast anchor** mouiller (l'ancre), jeter l'ancre; *Literary* **the tyrant cast his enemies into prison** le tyran a jeté ses ennemis en prison; *Fig* **we'll have to cast our net wide to find the right candidate** il va falloir ratisser large pour trouver le bon candidat

(**b**) *(direct → light, shadow)* projeter; *(→ look)* jeter, diriger; **the accident cast a shadow over their lives** l'accident a jeté une ombre sur leur existence; **could you cast an eye over this report?** voulez-vous jeter un œil sur ce rapport?; **he cast an eye over the audience** il a promené son regard sur l'auditoire; **she cast a desperate glance at her mother** elle glissa à sa mère un regard désespéré, elle regarda sa mère avec désespoir; **to cast doubt on sth** jeter le doute sur qch; **this cast doubt on his ability** cela jeta un doute sur ses capacités; **to cast aspersions on sb's character** dénigrer qn; **the evidence cast suspicion on him** les preuves ont jeté la suspicion sur lui

(**c**) *(shed, throw off)* perdre; **the horse cast a shoe** le cheval a perdu un fer; **to cast its skin** *(reptile)* muer; **cast all fear/thought of revenge from your mind** oubliez toute crainte/toute idée de revanche

(**d**) *(film, play)* distribuer les rôles de; **the director cast her in the role of the mother** le metteur en scène lui a attribué le rôle de la mère; *Fig* **to cast sb in the role of the villain** donner à qn le rôle du méchant

(**e**) *Art & Tech (form, statue)* mouler; *(metal)* couler, fondre; *(plaster)* couler; *Fig* **they are all cast in the same mould** ils sont tous faits sur *ou* sont tous coulés dans le même moule

(**f**) *Astrol (horoscope)* tirer

2 *n* (**a**) *Cin & Theat (actors)* distribution *f*, acteurs *mpl*; **the cast is Italian** tous les acteurs sont italiens; **he was in the cast of 'Citizen Kane'** il a joué dans 'Citizen Kane'; **Juliette Binoche heads a strong cast** Juliette Binoche est en tête d'une très bonne distribution; *Cin & TV* **cast and credits** générique *m*

(**b**) *Art (colour, shade)* nuance *f*, teinte *f*; **white with a pinkish cast** blanc nuancé de rose

(**c**) *Art & Tech (act of moulding → metal)* coulage *m*, coulée *f*; *(→ plaster)* moulage *m*; *(→ coin, medallion)* empreinte *f*; *(mould)* moule *m*; *(object moulded)* moulage *m*; **to make a bronze cast of a statue** mouler une statue en bronze; *Fig Literary* **a man of his cast** un homme de sa trempe

(**d**) *Med (for broken limb)* plâtre *m*; **her arm was in a cast** elle avait un bras dans le plâtre

(**e**) *Med (squint)* strabisme *m*; **he had a cast in his eye** il louchait d'un œil, il avait un œil qui louchait

(**f**) *Formal (type)* **the delicate cast of her features** la finesse de ses traits; **a peculiar cast of mind** une drôle de mentalité *ou* de tournure d'esprit

(**g**) *(of earthworm)* déjections *fpl*

(**h**) *(skin of insect, snake)* dépouille *f*

(**i**) *(regurgitated food)* pelote *f* régurgitée *(par les hiboux, les faucons)*

►► ***cast iron*** fonte *f*; ***cast list*** *Cin & TV* générique *m*; *Theat* distribution *f*; ***cast steel*** acier *m* moulé

►**cast about, cast around** *vi Br* **she cast about for an idea/an excuse to leave** elle essaya de trouver une idée/un prétexte pour partir

►**cast aside** *vt sep Literary (book)* mettre de côté; *(shirt, shoes)* se débarrasser de; *Fig (person, suggestion)* rejeter, écarter; **to cast aside one's fears** oublier ses craintes; **are you going to cast all this aside for a foolish dream?** est-ce que tu vas renoncer à tout ça pour une chimère?

►**cast away** *vt sep* (**a**) *(book, letter)* jeter; *Fig (cares, principle)* se défaire de

(**b**) *Naut* **to be cast away** être naufragé

►**cast back** *vt sep* **cast your mind back to the day we met** souviens-toi du *ou* rappelle-toi le jour de notre première rencontre; **to cast one's thoughts back** se reporter en arrière

►**cast down** *vt sep* (**a**) *Formal (weapon)* déposer, mettre bas

(**b**) *Fig Literary* **to be cast down** être démoralisé *ou* découragé

►**cast off 1** *vt sep* (**a**) *(undo)* défaire; *(untie)* délier, dénouer

(**b**) *Knitting* rabattre

(**c**) *Naut (lines, rope)* larguer, lâcher; *(boat)* larguer *ou* lâcher les amarres de

(**d**) *Literary (rid oneself of → clothing)* enlever, se débarrasser de; *Fig (→ bonds)* se défaire de, se libérer de; *(→ cares, habit, tradition)* se défaire de, abandonner

2 *vi* (**a**) *Naut* larguer les amarres, appareiller

(**b**) *Knitting* rabattre les mailles

►**cast on** *Knitting* **1** *vi* monter les mailles

2 *vt sep (stitches)* monter

►**cast out** *vt sep Arch or Literary (person)* renvoyer, chasser; *Fig (fear, guilt)* bannir

►**cast up** *vt sep (of sea, tide, waves)* rejeter

castanets [ˌkæstəˈnets] *npl* castagnettes *fpl*

castaway [ˈkɑːstəweɪ] *Naut* **1** *n* naufragé(e) *m,f*; *Fig* naufragé(e) *m,f*, laissé-pour-compte (laissée-pour-compte) *m,f*

2 *adj* naufragé

caste [kɑːst] *n* (*gen*) caste *f*, classe *f* sociale; (*in Hindu society*) caste *f*; *Br Fig* **to lose caste** déchoir, déroger

casteless [ˈkɑːstlɪs] *adj* sans caste

castellated [ˈkæstəleɪtɪd] *adj Archit* à tourelles; *Tech (filament, nut)* crénelé

caster [ˈkɑːstə(r)] *n* (**a**) (*sifter*) saupoudroir *m*, saupoudreuse *f* (**b**) (*wheel*) roulette *f*

▸▸ *Aut* ***caster action*** (*of steering*) effet *m* de chasse; *Br* ***caster sugar*** sucre *m* en poudre

castigate [ˈkæstɪgeɪt] *vt Formal* (**a**) (*punish*) corriger, punir; (*scold*) réprimander, tancer (**b**) (*criticize → person*) critiquer sévèrement, fustiger; (*→ book, play*) éreinter

castigation [ˌkæstɪˈgeɪʃən] *n Formal* (*punishment*) correction *f*, punition *f*; (*scolding*) réprimande *f*; (*criticism*) critique *f* sévère

castigator [ˈkæstɪgeɪtə(r)] *n Formal* pourfendeur(euse) *m,f*; **a castigator of the abuses of his time** un critique sévère des abus de son époque

Castile [kæsˈtiːl] *n* Castille *f*

Castilian [kæsˈtɪljən] **1** *n* (**a**) (*person*) Castillan(e) *m,f* (**b**) (*language*) castillan *m*

2 *adj* castillan

casting [ˈkɑːstɪŋ] *n* (**a**) *Art (act & object)* moulage *m*; *Tech (act)* coulée *f*, coulage *m*, fonte *f*; (*object*) pièce *f* fondue

(**b**) *Cin & Theat (selection of actors)* attribution *f* des rôles, casting *m*; *Fam Fig* **he looks like a mafioso from central casting** on dirait vraiment un mafioso comme on en voit au cinéma ◻; *Fam* **she denied having got the part on the casting couch** elle a nié avoir couché avec le metteur en scène pour obtenir le rôle

(**c**) *Fishing* lancer *m*; **casting net** épervier *m*

▸▸ *Cin & Theat* ***casting director*** metteur *m* en scène (qui distribue les rôles); *Knitting* ***casting off*** arrêt *m* (de mailles); *Knitting* ***casting on*** montage *m* (de mailles); ***casting vote*** voix *f* prépondérante; **the president has a** *or* **the casting vote** le président a voix prépondérante

cast-iron *adj* (**a**) (*pot, stove*) de *ou* en fonte (**b**) *Fig (alibi)* inattaquable, en béton; (*guarantee*) en béton; (*stomach, constitution*) en béton

castle [ˈkɑːsəl] **1** *n* (**a**) (*building*) château *m* (fort); **to build castles in the air** bâtir des châteaux en Espagne (**b**) *Chess* tour *f*

2 *vi Chess* roquer

▸▸ ***castle grounds*** parc *m* (*d'un château*); ***Castle Howard*** = château de style baroque du XVIIIème siècle dans le Yorkshire

castling [ˈkɑːslɪŋ] *n Chess* roque *m*

cast-off 1 *n* (**a**) (*piece of clothing*) vieux vêtement *m*

(**b**) *Fig (person)* laissé-pour-compte (laissée-pour-compte) *m,f*; **the manager had built a team from other clubs' cast-offs** le directeur sportif avait formé une équipe avec les joueurs dont les autres équipes ne voulaient pas; **I'm not going out with one of his cast-offs** je ne veux pas sortir avec une copine dont il ne veut plus

(**c**) *Typ (in printing)* calibrage *m*

2 *adj* dont personne ne veut; **cast-off clothes** vieux vêtements *mpl*

castor[1] [ˈkɑːstə(r)] = **caster**

castor[2] **1** *n* [ˈkɑːstə(r)] (**a**) (*secretion*) castoréum *m* (**b**) *Zool (beaver)* castor *m*

2 Castor [ˈkæstə(r)] **1** *pr n Myth* Castor; **Castor and Pollux** Castor et Pollux **2** *n Astron* Castor

▸▸ ***castor oil*** huile *f* de ricin

castor-oil plant *n Bot* ricin *m*

castrate [kæˈstreɪt] *vt* châtrer, castrer; *Fig* (*weaken → person, political movement*) émasculer

castration [kæˈstreɪʃən] *n* castration *f*; *Fig* (*of political movement*) émasculation *f*

▸▸ ***castration complex*** complexe *m* de castration

castrato [kæˈstrɑːtəʊ] (*pl* **castratos** *or* **castrati** [-tiː]) *n Mus* castrat *m*

Castroism [ˈkæstrəʊɪzəm] *n Pol* castrisme *m*

Castroist [ˈkæstrəʊɪst] *n Pol* castriste *mf*

casual [ˈkæʒʊəl] **1** *adj* (**a**) (*unconcerned*) désinvolte, nonchalant; (*natural*) simple, naturel; **they're very casual about the way they dress** ils attachent très peu d'importance à leurs vêtements *ou* à la façon dont ils s'habillent; **I tried to appear casual when talking about it** j'ai essayé d'en parler avec désinvolture; **they were very casual about the danger** ils ne se sont pas souciés du danger

(**b**) (*informal → dinner*) simple, détendu; (*→ clothing*) sport (*inv*)

(**c**) (*superficial*) superficiel; **I took a casual glance at the paper** j'ai jeté un coup d'œil (rapide) au journal; **to make casual conversation** parler de choses et d'autres, parler à bâtons rompus; **it was just a casual suggestion** c'était seulement une suggestion en passant; **she's just a casual acquaintance of mine** c'est quelqu'un que je connais très peu; **a casual love affair** une aventure

(**d**) (*happening by chance → meeting*) de hasard; (*→ onlooker*) venu par hasard

(**e**) (*occasional → job*) intermittent; (*→ worker*) temporaire

2 *n* (**a**) (*farmworker → for one day*) journalier(ère) *m,f*; (*→ for harvest, season*) (travailleur(euse) *m,f*) saisonnier(ère) *m,f*; (*in construction work*) ouvrier(ère) *m,f* temporaire (**b**) *Br Fam (football supporter)* jeune supporter *m* de foot (*soucieux de sa mise et souvent responsable de violences*)

3 casuals *npl* (*clothing*) vêtements *mpl* sport; (*shoes*) chaussures *fpl* sport

▸▸ *Br* ***casual labourer*** (*for one day*) journalier(ère) *m,f*; (*for harvest, season*) (travailleur(euse) *m,f*) saisonnier(ère) *m.f*; (*in construction work*) ouvrier(ère) *m,f* temporaire; ***casual sex*** rapports *mpl* sexuels de rencontre; ***casual water*** (*in golf*) flaque d'eau

casualization [ˌkæʒʊəlaɪˈzeɪʃən] *n Br Ind* **the casualization of labour** la précarisation de l'emploi

casually [ˈkæʒʊəlɪ] *adv* (**a**) (*unconcernedly*) avec désinvolture, nonchalamment (**b**) (*informally*) simplement; **to dress casually** s'habiller sport (**c**) (*glance, remark, suggest*) en passant; **they talked casually about this and that** ils ont parlé de choses et d'autres *ou* à bâtons rompus (**d**) (*by chance*) par hasard

casualness [ˈkæʒʊəlnɪs] *n* (**a**) (*unconcern*) désinvolture *f*, nonchalance *f* (**b**) (*informality*) simplicité *f*; **the casualness of their dress** l'allure décontractée *ou* sport de leur habillement (**c**) (*haphazardness*) hasard *m*, fortuité *f*

casualty [ˈkæʒjʊəltɪ] (*pl* **casualties**) *n* (**a**) (*wounded*) blessé(e) *m,f*; (*dead*) mort(e) *m,f*; (*in accident, fire, earthquake etc*) victime *f*; **there were heavy casualties** (*gen*) il y avait beaucoup de victimes *ou* de morts et de blessés; (*dead*) il y avait beaucoup de pertes; **these children are the casualties of the divorce rate** ces enfants sont les victimes du divorce; *Fig* **truth is often a casualty in political debates** la vérité est souvent sacrifiée dans les débats politiques; *Fig* **truth is the first casualty of war** la première victime de la guerre, c'est la vérité; *Fig* **the party had many casualties in the last election** le parti a perdu beaucoup de députés aux dernières élections

(**b**) (*UNCOUNT*) *Br (hospital department)* urgences *fpl*; **she was taken to casualty** elle a été emmenée aux urgences

▸▸ *Br* ***casualty department*** (*in hospital*) service *m* des urgences; ***casualty list, casualty return*** (*gen*) liste *f* des victimes; *Mil* état *m* des pertes; *Br* ***casualty ward*** (*in hospital*) service *m* des urgences

casuist [ˈkæzjʊɪst] *n* casuiste *m*

casuistic [ˌkæzjʊˈɪstɪk], **casuistical** [ˌkæzjʊˈɪstɪkəl] *adj* de casuiste

casuistry [ˈkæzjʊɪstrɪ] *n* (*philosophy*) casuistique *f*; (*UNCOUNT*) (*reasoning*) arguments *mpl* de casuiste

casus belli [ˌkeɪzəsˈbelaɪ, ˌkɑːzəsˈbeliː] *n* casus belli *m*

CAT[1] [kæt] *n Med* (*abbr* **computerized axial tomography**) TDM *f*

▸▸ ***CAT scan*** scanographie *f*; ***CAT scanner*** scanographe *m*

CAT[2] [ˌsiːeɪˈtiː] *n Comput* (*abbr* **computer-aided teaching**) EAO *m*

cat [kæt] **1** *n* (**a**) (*animal*) chat *m*; (*female*) chatte *f*; **I'm not really a cat person** je n'aime pas beaucoup les chats; **to let the cat out of the bag** révéler un secret par mégarde; **to be like a cat on a hot tin roof** *or Br* **on hot bricks** être sur des charbons ardents; **there isn't enough room to swing a cat** il n'y a pas la place de se retourner; **he looked like something the cat brought** *or* **dragged in** il ne ressemblait à rien; **has the cat got your tongue?** tu as perdu ta langue?; **to fight like cat and dog** se battre comme des chiffonniers; *Fam* **to be the cat's pyjamas** être génial; *Br* **to put** *or* **to set the cat among the pigeons** jeter un pavé dans la mare; **to play (a game of) cat and mouse with sb** jouer au chat et à la souris avec qn; *Br* **to wait for the cat to jump** *or* **to see which way the cat will jump** attendre de voir d'où vient le vent; *Prov* **when the cat's away the mice will play** quand le chat n'est pas là les souris dansent; *Prov* **a cat may look at a king** un chien regarde bien un évêque

(**b**) *Pej (woman)* rosse *f*, chipie *f*

(**c**) *Am Fam Old-fashioned (man)* mec *m*; **what a cool cat!** vraiment cool, ce type!

(**d**) *Fam (boat)* catamaran *m*

(**e**) *Fam Tech (catalytic converter)* pot *m* catalytique

2 *comp* (*bowl, basket*) pour chats; (*breeder*) de chats; (*hair*) de chat

▸▸ ***cat burglar*** monte-en-l'air *m inv*; ***cat burglary*** vol *m* de nuit à l'escalade; ***cat door*** chatière *f*; ***the cat family*** les félidés *mpl*; ***cat flap*** chatière *f*; ***cat food*** (*UNCOUNT*) nourriture *f* pour chats; *Fam* ***cat's lick*** toilette *f* de chat, brin *m* de toilette; **to give oneself** *or* **have a cat's lick** se laver le bout du nez, faire une toilette de chat; ***cat litter*** litière *f* (pour chats); ***cat litter tray*** bac *m* à litière; *Rad* ***cat's whisker*** chercheur *m* (de détecteur à galène); *Fam* ***he thinks he's the cat's whiskers*** il se prend pour le nombril du monde

'Cat on a Hot Tin Roof' *Williams, Brooks* 'La Chatte sur un toit brûlant'

catabolic [kætəˈbɒlɪk] *adj Biol & Chem* catabolique

catabolism [kəˈtæbəlɪzəm] *n Biol & Chem* catabolisme *m*

catabolite [kəˈtæbəlaɪt] *n Biol & Chem* catabolite *m*

catachresis [ˌkætəˈkriːsɪs] *n Ling* catachrèse *f*

cataclysm [ˈkætəklɪzəm] *n* cataclysme *m*

cataclysmic [ˌkætəˈklɪzmɪk] *adj* cataclysmique

catacomb [ˈkætəkuːm] *n* (*usu pl*) catacombe *f*

catafalque [ˈkætəfælk] *n* catafalque *m*

Catalan [ˈkætəˌlæn] **1** *n* (**a**) (*person*) catalan(e) *m,f* (**b**) *Ling* catalan *m*

2 *adj* catalan

catalepsy [ˈkætəlepsɪ] *n Med* catalepsie *f*

cataleptic [ˌkætəˈleptɪk] *adj Med* cataleptique; **to have a cataleptic fit** tomber en catalepsie

catalogue, *Am* **catalog** [ˈkætəlɒg] **1** *n* catalogue *m*; (*in library*) fichier *m*; *Am Univ* guide *m* de l'étudiant; *Fig* **his life story was a catalogue of disasters** l'histoire de sa vie a été un catalogue de malheurs

2 *vt* cataloguer, faire le catalogue de

▸▸ ***catalogue number*** référence *f*; (*for library book*) référence *f* bibliographique; *Com* ***catalogue price*** prix *m* catalogue

cataloguer [ˈkætəlɒgə(r)] *n* catalogueur *m*

cataloguing, *Am* **cataloging** [ˈkætəlɒgɪŋ] *n* catalogage *m*

Catalonia [ˌkætəˈləʊnɪə] *n* Catalogne *f*; **in Catalonia** en Catalogne

Catalonian [ˌkætəˈləʊnɪən] **1** *adj* catalan

2 *n* (*person*) catalan(e) *m,f*

catalyse, *Am* **catalyze** [ˈkætəlaɪz] *vt Chem* catalyser

catalysis [kəˈtæləsɪs] (*pl* **catalyses** [-siːz]) *n Chem* catalyse *f*

catalyst [ˈkætəlɪst] *n Chem & Fig* catalyseur *m*

catalytic [ˌkætəˈlɪtɪk] *adj Chem* catalytique

▸▸ *Aut* ***catalytic converter*** pot *m* catalytique

catalyze *Am* = **catalyse**
catamaran [ˌkætəmə'ræn] *n* catamaran *m*
catamite ['kætəmaɪt] *n* mignon *m*, giton *m*
Catania [kə'teɪnjə] *n* Catane
cataphora [kə'tæfrə] *n Med* cataphore *f*
cataphoretic [kætəfə'riːtɪk], **cataphoric** [kætə'fɔːrɪk] *adj* cataphorétique
cataplasm ['kætəplæzəm] *n Med* cataplasme *m*
cataplexy ['kætəpleksɪ] *n Med* cataplexie *f*
catapult ['kætəpʌlt] **1** *n* (**a**) *Br (child's)* lance-pierres *m inv* (**b**) *Aviat & Mil* catapulte *f*
2 *vt (gen) & Aviat* catapulter; **he catapulted the stone over the wall** il a lancé la pierre par-dessus le mur; *Fig* **these reforms catapulted the country into the 20th century** ces réformes ont propulsé le pays dans le 20ème siècle; **to catapult sb to stardom** *(of film etc)* propulser qn vers la célébrité; *Fig* **she was catapulted into the leadership job** elle a été catapultée à la direction
▸▸ ***catapult launcher*** catapulte *f*; ***catapult launching*** catapultage *m*
cataract ['kætərækt] *n* (**a**) *Med* cataracte *f*; **to be operated on for a cataract** être opéré de la cataracte (**b**) *(waterfall)* cataracte *f*, cascade *f* (**c**) *(downpour)* déluge *m*
catarrh [kə'tɑː(r)] *n* catarrhe *m*; *Br* **to have bad catarrh** être très catarrheux
catarrhal [kə'tɑːrəl] *adj* catarrheux
catastasis [kə'tæstəsɪs] (*pl* **catastases** [-siːz] *n Literature* catastase *f*
catastrophe [kə'tæstrəfɪ] *n* catastrophe *f*
▸▸ *Math* ***catastrophe theory*** théorie *f* des catastrophes
catastrophic [ˌkætə'strɒfɪk] *adj* catastrophique
catastrophically [kætə'strɒfɪkəlɪ] *adv* d'une façon catastrophique
catatonia [ˌkætə'təʊnɪə] *n Med* catatonie *f*
catatonic [ˌkætə'tɒnɪk] *adj Med* catatonique
catbird ['kætbɜːd] *n* (**a**) *Orn* moqueur-chat *m* (**b**) *Am Fam* **to be in the catbird seat** être bien placé *ou* dans une situation privilégiée ❑
catboat ['kætbəʊt] *n Naut* cat-boat *m*
catcall ['kætkɔːl] *Theat* **1** *n* sifflet *m*; **the actors were greeted with catcalls** les acteurs se sont fait siffler
2 *vt (actor)* siffler
3 *vi (audience)* siffler

CATCH [kætʃ]

attraper	▸ **1 (a) – (d)**
se prendre	▸ **1 (e); 2 (c)**
saisir	▸ **1 (f), (h)**
remarquer	▸ **1 (j)**
prise	▸ **3 (a), (b)**
piège	▸ **3 (c)**
loquet	▸ **3 (d)**

(*pt & pp* **caught** [kɔːt]) **1** *vt* (**a**) *(ball, thrown object)* attraper; **to catch hold of sth** attraper qch; **the dog caught the ball in its mouth** le chien a attrapé la balle dans sa gueule; **catch!** attrape!; **to catch sb's arm** *(take hold of)* saisir *ou* prendre qn par le bras; **I caught him as he fell** je l'ai retenu *ou* attrapé au moment où il tombait
(**b**) *(trap → fish, mouse, thief)* attraper, prendre; **he got caught by the police** il s'est fait attraper par la police; **to get caught in a traffic jam** être pris dans un embouteillage; **we got caught in a shower/thunderstorm** nous avons été surpris par une averse/un orage; **to catch sb doing sth** surprendre qn à faire qch; **to catch oneself doing sth** se surprendre à faire qch; **I caught myself thinking about him** je me suis surpris à repenser à lui; **they were caught trying to escape** on les a surpris en train d'essayer de s'évader; **don't get caught!** ne te fais pas prendre!; **if I catch you talking once more I'll throw you out!** si je te prends *ou* surprends encore une fois en train de parler, je te mets à la porte!; **you won't catch me doing the washing-up!** aucun danger de me surprendre en train de faire la vaisselle!; **don't let me catch you at it again!** que je ne t'y reprenne pas!; *Br Fam* **you'll catch it when you get home!** qu'est-ce que tu vas prendre en rentrant!; **to catch sb napping** prendre qn au dépourvu; **to catch sb in the act** *or* **red-handed** prendre qn sur le fait *ou* la main dans le sac
(**c**) *(disease, infection)* attraper; *Fig (habit)* prendre; **to catch a cold** attraper un rhume; *Fig (company)* perdre de l'argent lors d'une transaction; **to catch cold** attraper *ou* prendre froid; **I caught this cold from you** c'est toi qui m'as passé ce rhume; *Fam* **he'll catch his death (of cold)!** il va attraper la crève!
(**d**) *(bus, train)* attraper, prendre; *(person)* attraper; **I have a train to catch at 6 o'clock** j'ai un train à prendre à 6 heures; *Br* **to catch the last post** arriver à temps pour la dernière levée (du courrier); **try and catch the postman before you leave** essayez d'attraper le facteur avant de partir; **you're unlikely to catch her at home** je ne pense pas que tu la trouveras chez elle; **you caught me just as I was going into a meeting** tu m'as parlé au moment où j'allais en réunion; **we caught him in a good mood** il était de bonne humeur quand nous l'avons vu; **I just caught the end of the film** j'ai juste vu la fin du film; *Fam* **catch you later!** à plus tard!
(**e**) *(on nail, obstacle)* **he caught his finger in the door** il s'est pris le doigt dans la porte; **she caught her skirt in the door** sa jupe s'est prise dans la porte; **he caught his coat on the brambles** son manteau s'est accroché aux ronces
(**f**) *(hear clearly, understand)* saisir, comprendre; **I didn't quite catch what you said** je n'ai pas bien entendu ce que vous avez dit; **I don't catch your meaning** je ne vois pas ce que vous voulez dire
(**g**) *(attract)* **to catch sb's attention** *or* **sb's eye** attirer l'attention de qn; **the idea caught her imagination** l'idée l'a inspirée; **their story caught the imagination of the public** leur histoire a passionné le public; *Br* **the house caught his fancy** la maison lui a plu; **this coat catches fluff** la poussière se voit sur ce manteau
(**h**) *(in portrait, writing → likeness, mood)* saisir; **the author has caught the mood of the time** l'auteur a su rendre l'atmosphère de l'époque
(**i**) *(hit) Br* **to catch sb a blow** donner *ou* flanquer un coup à qn; **the punch caught me in the chest** j'ai reçu le coup de poing en plein dans la poitrine; **the wave caught her sideways** la vague l'a frappée de côté; **he fell and caught his head on the radiator** il est tombé et s'est cogné la tête contre le radiateur
(**j**) *(notice)* remarquer; **did you catch the look on his face?** vous avez remarqué l'expression de son visage?; **I caught a hint of bitterness** *(in what she said)* j'ai senti un peu d'amertume dans ses paroles
(**k**) *(idioms)* **to catch one's breath** reprendre son souffle; **he had to sit down to catch his breath** il a dû s'asseoir pour reprendre son souffle; **to catch the light** refléter la lumière; **to catch the sun** *(person)* prendre des couleurs; **the garden catches the sun in the afternoon** le jardin est ensoleillé l'après-midi
2 *vi* (**a**) *(ignite → fire, wood)* prendre; *(→ engine)* démarrer
(**b**) *(bolt, lock)* fermer; *(gears)* mordre
(**c**) *(on obstacle → in door, machinery etc)* se prendre; *(→ on thorn, nail etc)* s'accrocher; **her skirt caught on a nail** sa jupe s'est accrochée à un clou; **his coat caught in the door** son manteau s'est pris dans la porte
3 *n* (**a**) *(act)* prise *f*; **good catch!** bien rattrapé!
(**b**) *(of fish)* prise *f*; **a fine catch** une belle prise; *Hum Fig* **he's a good catch** *(man)* c'est un beau parti
(**c**) *(snag)* piège *m*; **there must be a catch in it somewhere** il doit y avoir un truc *ou* un piège quelque part, ça cache quelque chose; **where's** *or* **what's the catch?** qu'est-ce que ça cache?, où est le piège?
(**d**) *(on lock, door)* loquet *m*; *(on window)* loqueteau *m*; *(on shoe-buckle)* ardillon *m*
(**e**) *(in voice)* **with a catch in his voice** d'une voix entrecoupée
(**f**) *(game)* jeu *m* de balle; **to play catch** jouer à la balle
(**g**) *Mus* canon *m*
▸▸ *Agr* ***catch crop*** culture *f* dérobée; ***catch question*** question-piège *f*, colle *f*
▸**catch at** *vt insep* (essayer d') attraper
▸**catch on** *vi* (**a**) *(fashion, trend, slogan)* devenir populaire, prendre; **this dance style caught on in the fifties** cette danse a fait un tabac *ou* était très populaire dans les années cinquante; **the game never caught on in Europe** ce jeu n'a jamais pris en Europe *ou* eu de succès en Europe
(**b**) *Fam (understand)* piger, saisir ❑; **I didn't quite catch on to what he was trying to say** je n'ai pas bien saisi ce qu'il essayait de dire; **did you catch on?** est-ce que tu as pigé?
▸**catch out** *vt sep Br (by trickery)* prendre en défaut, piéger; *(in the act)* prendre sur le fait; **he tried to catch me out with a trick question** il a essayé de me coller *ou* prendre en défaut avec une question-piège; **to catch sb out in a lie** prendre *ou* surprendre qn à mentir; **I won't be caught out like that again!** on ne m'y prendra plus!
▸**catch up 1** *vi* (**a**) *(as verb of movement)* **to catch up with sb** rattraper qn; **I had to run to catch up with him** *or* **to catch him up** j'ai dû courir pour le rattraper *ou* le rejoindre; **the police caught up with him in Zurich** la police l'a rattrapé à Zurich; *Fig* **his past will catch up with him one day** il finira par être rattrapé par son passé
(**b**) *(on lost time)* combler *ou* rattraper son retard; *(on studies)* rattraper son retard, se remettre au niveau; **to catch up on** *or* **with one's work** rattraper le retard qu'on a pris dans son travail; **he'll have to work hard to catch up with the rest of the class** il va falloir qu'il travaille beaucoup pour rattraper le reste de la classe; **I need to catch up on some sleep** j'ai du sommeil à rattraper; **we had a lot of news to catch up on** nous avions beaucoup de choses à nous dire
2 *vt sep* (**a**) *(entangle)* **the material got caught up in the machinery** le tissu s'est pris dans la machine; **they were caught up in a traffic jam for hours** ils ont été bloqués dans un embouteillage pendant des heures
(**b**) *(absorb, involve)* **to get caught up in a wave of enthusiasm** être gagné par une vague d'enthousiasme; **he was too caught up in the film to notice what was happening** il était trop absorbé par le film pour remarquer ce qui se passait; **I refuse to get caught up in their private quarrel** je refuse de me laisser entraîner dans leurs querelles personnelles
(**c**) *(seize → object)* ramasser vivement, s'emparer de; *(→ baby, child)* prendre dans ses bras
(**d**) *(person, car in front etc)* rattraper

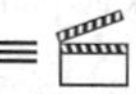

'To Catch a Thief' *Hitchcock* 'La Main au collet'

catch-22 [-twentɪ'tuː] *n* **catch-22 (situation)** situation *f* sans issue, cercle *m* vicieux

'Catch-22' *Heller, Nichols* 'Catch-22'

> **Catch-22**
> Cette formule provient du roman éponyme de Joseph Heller, publié en 1961, dans lequel **catch-22** est le nom donné à une situation sans issue. Pendant la deuxième guerre mondiale, un pilote de l'armée américaine essaie de trouver un prétexte pour ne pas partir en mission. Mais le règlement stipule que seul un pilote reconnu comme malade mental peut être dispensé de mission; tout pilote qui cherche à être exempté montre qu'il a conscience du danger encouru en mission, et fait par là même preuve de sa santé mentale, et doit donc continuer à voler. Autrement dit, seuls peuvent être dispensés ceux qui ne cherchent pas à l'être.
> On utilise cette expression pour parler de toute situation en forme de cercle vicieux. On dira par exemple **it's a catch-22 situation, I can't get a job without experience, but I can't get experience without a job** ("c'est une situation sans issue: je ne peux pas trouver de travail sans expérience préalable, mais je ne pas acquérir d'expérience sans travail").

catch-all 1 *n* fourre-tout *m inv*

2 *adj* fourre-tout *(inv)*, qui pare à toute éventualité; **catch-all phrase** expression *f* passe-partout
catch-as-catch-can 1 *n Sport* catch *m*
2 *adj Am* improvisé
catcher [ˈkætʃə(r)] *n (gen) & Sport (in baseball)* attrapeur *m*

'The Catcher in the Rye' *Salinger* 'L'Attrape-cœur'

catchfly [ˈkætʃflaɪ] *n Bot* silène *m*
catching [ˈkætʃɪŋ] 1 *n* (**a**) *(of ball)* réception *f*
2 *adj* (**a**) *Med* contagieux (**b**) *Fig (enthusiasm)* contagieux, communicatif; *(habit)* contagieux
catchline [ˈkætʃlaɪn] *n* accroche *f*; *(identification for story)* intitulé *m*
catchment [ˈkætʃmənt] *n* captage *m*
▸▸ ***catchment area*** *Geog (drainage area)* bassin *m* hydrographique; *Admin (for hospital)* = circonscription hospitalière; *(for school)* secteur *m* de recrutement scolaire; ***catchment basin*** bassin *m* hydrographique
catchpenny [ˈkætʃˌpenɪ] *(pl* **catchpennies***) Br* 1 *adj* accrocheur
2 *n* attrape-nigaud *m*
catchphrase [ˈkætʃfreɪz] *n (in advertising)* accroche *f*; *(set phrase)* formule *f* toute faite; *(of performer)* petite phrase *f*
catchup [ˈkætʃʌp] *n Am* ketchup *m*
catch-up *n Am* **to play catch-up** avoir du retard à rattraper
catchwater [ˈkætʃwɔːtə(r)] *n* fossé *m* de réception *ou* d'irrigation
▸▸ ***catchwater drain*** fossé *m* de réception *ou* d'irrigation
catchword [ˈkætʃwɜːd] *n* (**a**) *(slogan)* slogan *m*; *Pol* mot *m* d'ordre, slogan *m* (**b**) *Typ (in printing → at top of page)* mot-vedette *m*; *(→ at foot of page)* réclame *f* (**c**) *Theat* réclame *f*
catchy [ˈkætʃɪ] *(compar* **catchier**, *superl* **catchiest***) adj (tune)* qui trotte dans la tête, facile à retenir; *(title)* facile à retenir
catechetic [kætəˈketɪk], **cathechetical** [kætəˈketɪkəl] *adj Rel (gen)* catéchétique; *(instruction, method)* par demandes et réponses
catechism [ˈkætəkɪzəm] *n Rel* catéchisme *m*
catechist [ˈkætəkɪst] *n Rel* catéchiste *mf*
catechize, -ise [ˈkætəkaɪz] *vt* (**a**) *Rel* catéchiser (**b**) *Fig (examine)* interroger, questionner
catecholamine [ˌkætəˈkəʊləmaɪn] *n Biol & Chem* catécholamine *f*
categoric [ˌkætɪˈgɒrɪk], **categorical** [ˌkætɪˈgɒrɪkəl] *adj* catégorique
▸▸ *Phil* ***categorical imperative*** impératif *m* catégorique
categorically [ˌkætɪˈgɒrɪkəlɪ] *adv* catégoriquement
categorization [ˌkætəgəraɪˈzeɪʃən] *n* catégorisation *f*
categorize, -ise [ˈkætəgəraɪz] *vt* catégoriser
category [ˈkætəgərɪ] *(pl* **categories***) n* catégorie *f*
▸▸ *Mktg* ***category leader*** *(product)* chef *m* de file dans sa catégorie
cater [ˈkeɪtə(r)] 1 *vi* s'occuper de la nourriture, fournir des repas
2 *vt Am* s'occuper de la nourriture pour
▸**cater for,** *Am* **cater to** *vt insep* (**a**) *(with food)* s'occuper de la nourriture pour; **coach parties catered for** *(sign)* accueil de groupes (**b**) *(needs)* répondre à, satisfaire; *(tastes)* satisfaire; **we cater for the needs of small companies** nous répondons à la demande des petites entreprises; **the hotel doesn't cater for children** l'hôtel ne prévoit pas d'aménagements pour les enfants; **to cater for all tastes** satisfaire tous les goûts
cater-cornered *Am Fam* 1 *adj* diagonal ❑
2 *adv* diagonalement ❑
caterer [ˈkeɪtərə(r)] *n* traiteur *m*
catering [ˈkeɪtərɪŋ] 1 *n* restauration *f*; **who did the catering for the wedding?** qui a fourni le repas pour le mariage?
2 *comp (industry)* de la restauration; *(staff)* de restauration
▸▸ ***catering college*** école *f* de restauration; ***catering contract*** contrat *m* de restauration; ***catering firm*** traiteur *m*; ***catering manager*** chef *m ou* responsable *mf* de la restauration
caterpillar [ˈkætəpɪlə(r)] *n Zool & Tech* chenille *f*
▸▸ *Tech* ***caterpillar track*** chenille *f*; *Tech* ***caterpillar tractor*** tracteur *m* à chenilles
caterwaul [ˈkætəwɔːl] 1 *vi (cat)* miauler; *(person)* brailler
2 *n (of cat)* miaulement *m*; *(of person)* braillement *m*
caterwauling [ˈkætəwɔːlɪŋ] *n (UNCOUNT) (of cat)* miaulements *mpl*; *(of person)* braillements *mpl*
cat-eye glasses *npl Opt* lunettes *fpl* de star
catfight [ˈkætfaɪt] *n* (**a**) *(between cats)* bagarre *f* de chats; **there was a catfight last night** des chats se sont battus la nuit dernière (**b**) *Fam Fig (quarrel between women)* crêpage *m* de chignon; **to have a catfight** se crêper le chignon
catfish [ˈkætfɪʃ] *(pl* **inv** *or* **catfishes***) n Ich* poisson-chat *m*
catfoot [ˈkætfʊt] *vi Am* se déplacer d'une démarche féline; **he left, catfooting out of the room** il quitta la pièce de sa démarche féline
catgut [ˈkætgʌt] *n* (**a**) *(for musical instrument, racket)* boyau *m* (de chat) (**b**) *Med* catgut *m*
Cathar [ˈkæθɑː(r)] *Rel & Hist* 1 *n* cathare *mf*
2 *adj* cathare
catharsis [kəˈθɑːsɪs] *(pl* **catharses** [-siːz]*) n* catharsis *f*
cathartic [kəˈθɑːtɪk] 1 *adj* cathartique
2 *n Med* purgatif *m*, cathartique *m*
Cathay [ˈkæθeɪ] *n Geog* Cathay *m*
cathedra [kəˈθiːdrə] *n Rel* cathèdre *f*
cathedral [kəˈθiːdrəl] *n* cathédrale *f*
▸▸ ***cathedral city*** évêché *m*, ville *f* épiscopale; ***cathedral glass*** verre *m* cathédrale
Catherine [ˈkæθrɪn] *pr n* **Catherine the Great** la Grande Catherine; **Catherine de' Medici** Catherine de Médicis; **Catherine of Aragon** Catherine d'Aragon
catherine wheel [ˈkæθrɪn-] *n (firework)* soleil *m*
catheter [ˈkæθɪtə(r)] *n* cathéter *m*, sonde *f* creuse; **he has to have a catheter** il faut qu'on lui pose un cathéter
catheterize, -ise [ˈkæθɪtəˌraɪz] *vt* cathétériser
cathiodermie [ˈkæθɪəʊˌdɜːmɪ] *n* = type de soin de beauté consistant à appliquer sur le visage un courant électrique de faible intensité afin de nettoyer et d'oxygéner la peau
cathode [ˈkæθəʊd] *Elec* 1 *n* cathode *f*
2 *comp (beam, screen)* cathodique
▸▸ *Elec* ***cathode rays*** rayons *mpl* cathodiques; *Elec* ***cathode ray tube*** tube *m* cathodique; *Elec* ***cathode ray tube monitor*** moniteur *m* à tube cathodique; ***cathode sputtering*** pulvérisation *f* cathodique, ionoplastie *f*
catholic [ˈkæθlɪk] 1 *adj* (**a**) *(broad → tastes)* éclectique (**b**) *(liberal → views)* libéral (**c**) *(universal)* universel
2 **Catholic** 1 *adj* catholique; **Catholic charities** les associations caritatives catholiques; **the Catholic Church** l'Église *f* catholique 2 *n* catholique *mf*
▸▸ *Am* ***Catholic Youth Organization*** = association de jeunes catholiques aux États-Unis
Catholicism [kəˈθɒlɪsɪzəm] *n* catholicisme *m*
catholicity [kæθəˈlɪsɪtɪ] *n* (**a**) *(of tastes)* éclectisme *m* (**b**) *(liberalism → of person)* largeur *f* d'esprit (**c**) *(universality)* universalité *f* (**d**) *Rel (orthodoxy)* orthodoxie *f*; *(conformity with the Roman Catholic Church)* catholicité *f*
catholicize, -ise [kəˈθɒlɪsaɪz] *vt* catholiciser
cathouse [ˈkæthaʊs, *pl* -haʊzɪz] *n Am Fam (brothel)* bordel *m*
cation [ˈkætaɪən] *n Phys* cation *m*
catkin [ˈkætkɪn] *n Bot* chaton *m*
catlike [ˈkætlaɪk] 1 *adj* félin
2 *adv* comme un chat
catmint [ˈkætmɪnt] *n* herbe *f* aux chats
catnap [ˈkætnæp] *Fam* 1 *n* (petit) somme *m*; **to have a catnap** faire un petit somme
2 *vi* sommeiller, faire un petit somme
catnip [ˈkætnɪp] *n* herbe *f* aux chats
Cato [ˈkeɪtəʊ] *pr n* Caton
cat-o'-nine-tails *n* chat à neuf queues *m*, martinet *m*
cat's cradle [ˌkæts-] *n* jeu *m* de figures *(que l'on forme entre les doigts avec de la ficelle)*
cats-eye® *n Br Transp* catadioptre *m (marquant le milieu de la chaussée)*
cat's-eye *n (gem)* œil-de-chat *m*
cat's-foot *n Bot* pied-de-chat *m*, antennaire *f*
Catskill [ˈkætskɪl] *n* **the Catskill mountains, the Catskills** les monts *mpl* Catskill, les Catskill *mpl*
cat's-paw *n* (**a**) *(person)* dupe *f* (**b**) *(on water)* = effet de vague produit par une légère brise
catsuit [ˈkætsuːt] *n* combinaison-pantalon *f*
catsup [ˈkætsəp] *n Am* ketchup *m*
cattail [ˈkætteɪl] *n Am Bot* jonc *m*
cattery [ˈkætərɪ] *(pl* **catteries***) n* pension *f* pour chats
cattily [ˈkætɪlɪ] *adv Fam* méchamment
cattiness [ˈkætɪnɪs] *n Fam* vacherie *f*, rosserie *f*
cattle [ˈkætəl] *npl (UNCOUNT)* bétail *m*, bestiaux *mpl*, bovins *mpl*; **horned cattle** bêtes *fpl* à cornes, bovins *mpl*; **we were herded onto trucks like cattle** on nous a entassés dans des camions comme du bétail
▸▸ *Br* ***cattle breeder*** éleveur *m* (de bétail); ***cattle breeding*** élevage *m* (du bétail); *Agr* ***cattle cake*** tourteau *m*; ***cattle car*** fourgon *m* à bestiaux; *Orn* ***cattle egret*** héron *m* garde-bœufs; ***cattle grid***, *Am* ***cattle guard*** = grille destinée à empêcher le passage du bétail mais non des voitures; ***cattle market*** marché *m ou* foire *f* aux bestiaux; *Br Fam Pej* **this beauty contest is just a cattle market** ce concours de beauté n'est qu'un marché aux bestiaux; ***cattle prod*** aiguillon *m* électrique; ***cattle ranch*** ranch *m* (pour l'élevage du bétail); ***cattle rustler*** voleur *m* de bétail; ***cattle shed*** étable *f*; ***cattle show*** concours *m* agricole; ***cattle truck*** fourgon *m* à bestiaux
cattleman [ˈkætəlmən] *(pl* **cattlemen** [-mən]*) n* vacher *m*, bouvier *m*
cattleya [kætˈliːjə] *n Bot* cattleya *m*
catty [ˈkætɪ] *(compar* **cattier**, *superl* **cattiest***) adj Fam* (**a**) *(person, gossip)* méchant ❑, vache; **a catty remark** une vacherie, une réflexion désagréable ❑ (**b**) *(like a cat)* **there's a catty smell** ça sent le pipi de chat
catty-corner, catty-cornered *Am* 1 *adj* diamétralement opposé
2 *adv* diamétralement opposé
Catullus [kəˈtʌləs] *pr n* Catulle
CATV [ˌsiːeɪˌtiːˈviː] *n Am (abbr* **community antenna television***)* télévision *f* par câble
catwalk [ˈkætwɔːk] *n* (**a**) *(at fashion show)* passerelle *f* (**b**) *Naut* coursive *f*
▸▸ ***catwalk fashions*** la haute couture; ***catwalk model*** mannequin *m* qui fait des défilés de mode
Caucasia [kɔːˈkeɪzjə] *n Geog* Caucase *m*
Caucasian [kɔːˈkeɪzjən], **Caucasic** [kɔːˈkeɪzɪk] 1 *n* (**a**) *(from Caucasia)* Caucasien(enne) *m,f* (**b**) *(white person)* Blanc (Blanche) *m,f* (**c**) *Ling* caucasien *m*
2 *adj* (**a**) *(from Caucasia)* caucasien (**b**) *(white)* blanc (blanche); **the man is described as a Caucasian male in his thirties** l'individu est de type européen et aurait entre trente et quarante ans (**c**) *Ling* caucasien, caucasique
Caucasoid [ˈkɔːkəsɔɪd] 1 *n* Caucasoïde *mf*
2 *adj* caucasoïde
Caucasus [ˈkɔːkəsəs] *n Geog* **the Caucasus** le Caucase; **in the Caucasus** dans le Caucase; **the Caucasus mountains** le Caucase, la chaîne du Caucase
caucus [ˈkɔːkəs] *n Pol* (**a**) *Am (committee)* comité *m* électoral, caucus *m*; **the Democratic caucus** le groupe *ou* le lobby démocrate (**b**) *Br (party organization)* comité *m*; **the Black caucus of the Labour Party** = les personnalités noires du parti travailliste
▸▸ ***caucus meeting*** réunion *f* du comité électoral

CAUCUS

Aux États-Unis, les "Caucus" sont d'immenses rassemblements politiques, au cours desquels les deux partis nationaux choisissent leurs candidats et définissent leurs objectifs.

caudal [ˈkɔːdəl] *adj Anat* caudal
▸▸ ***caudal fin*** (nageoire *f*) caudale *f*
caught [kɔːt] *pt & pp of* **catch**
caul [kɔːl] *n* coiffe *f (de nouveau-né)*; **born with a caul** né coiffé
cauldron [ˈkɔːldrən] *n* chaudron *m*

cat–cau

cauli [ˈkɒlɪ] *n Br Fam* chou-fleur❑ *m*
cauliflower [ˈkɒlɪˌflaʊə(r)] *n* chou-fleur *m*
►► *Culin* ***cauliflower cheese*** chou-fleur *m* au gratin; ***cauliflower ear*** oreille *f* en chou-fleur
caulk [kɔːk] *vt (gen)* calfeutrer; *Naut* calfater
caulking [ˈkɔːkɪŋ] *n (gen)* calfeutrage *m*; *Naut* calfatage *m*
►► ***caulking iron*** calfait *m*, burin *m*
causal [ˈkɔːzəl] *adj (gen)* causal; *Gram* causal, causatif
causality [kɔːˈzælətɪ] *n* causalité *f*
causally [ˈkɔːzəlɪ] *adv* **the two events are causally linked** les deux événements ont la même cause
causation [kɔːˈzeɪʃən] *n (causing)* causalité *f*; *(cause-effect relationship)* relation *f* de cause à effet
causative [ˈkɔːzətɪv] **1** *adj (gen)* causal; *Gram* causal, causatif
2 *n Gram* causatif *m*
cause [kɔːz] **1** *n* (**a**) *(reason)* cause *f*; **to be the cause of sth** être (la) cause de qch; **he was the cause of all our trouble** c'est lui qui a été la cause *ou* qui a été à l'origine de tous nos ennuis; **the cause of the disease is not yet known** la cause de la maladie demeure inconnue; **she is the cause of his being in prison** c'est à cause d'elle qu'il est en prison; **the relation of cause and effect** la relation de cause à effet
(**b**) *(justification)* raison *f*, motif *m*; **there is cause for anxiety** il y a lieu d'être inquiet, il y a de quoi s'inquiéter; **we mustn't give them cause for complaint** il ne faut pas leur donner de motif de se plaindre; **they have cause to be bitter** ils ont lieu d'être amers, ils ont de quoi être amers; **to have good cause for doing sth** avoir de bonnes raisons de faire qch; **with (good) cause** à juste titre; **without good cause** sans cause *ou* raison valable
(**c**) *(principle)* cause *f*; **in the cause of justice** pour la cause de la justice; **the cause of equal rights** la cause de l'égalité des droits; **her lifelong devotion to the cause** son dévouement de toujours à la cause; *Formal* **to make common cause with sb** faire cause commune avec qn; **to work for a good cause** travailler pour une bonne cause; **it's all in a good cause!** c'est pour une bonne cause!
(**d**) *Law* cause *f*; **to plead sb's cause** plaider la cause de qn; **cause of action** fondement *m* d'une action en justice
2 *vt* causer, provoquer; **smoking can cause cancer** le tabac peut provoquer des cancers; **to cause grief** causer du chagrin; **he has caused us a lot of trouble** il nous a créé beaucoup d'ennuis; **it will only cause trouble** cela ne servira qu'à semer la zizanie; **to cause sb/sth to do sth** faire faire qch à qn/qch; **what caused him to change his mind?** qu'est-ce qui l'a fait changer d'avis?; **this caused me to lose my job** à cause de cela, j'ai perdu mon emploi
causeless [ˈkɔːzlɪs] *adj* sans cause, sans raison
causelessly [ˈkɔːzlɪslɪ] *adv* sans cause, sans raison
causeway [ˈkɔːzweɪ] *n* chaussée *f*
caustic [ˈkɔːstɪk] **1** *adj Chem & Fig* caustique
2 *n Chem* caustique *m*, substance *f* caustique
►► *Chem* ***caustic soda*** soude *f* caustique
caustically [ˈkɔːstɪkəlɪ] *adv* caustiquement, d'un ton caustique *ou* mordant
causticity [kɔːˈstɪsɪtɪ] *n Chem & Fig* causticité *f*
cauterization [ˌkɔːtəraɪˈzeɪʃən] *n* cautérisation *f*
cauterize, -ise [ˈkɔːtəraɪz] *vt* cautériser
cautery [ˈkɔːtərɪ] (*pl* **cauteries**) *n* cautère *m*
caution [ˈkɔːʃən] **1** *n* (**a**) *(care)* circonspection *f*, prudence *f*; **to proceed with caution** *(gen)* agir avec circonspection *ou* avec prudence; *(in car)* avancer lentement; **caution!** *(sign)* attention!; **to throw caution to the wind** faire fi de toute prudence
(**b**) *(warning)* avertissement *m*; *(reprimand)* réprimande *f*
(**c**) *Law* avertissement *m*; *Br* **I got off with a caution** je m'en suis tiré avec un avertissement
(**d**) *Sport* avertissement *m*; **to give sb a caution** donner un avertissement à qn
(**e**) *Br Fam Old-fashioned (person)* **he's a caution!** c'est un numéro *ou* un polisson!
2 *vt* (**a**) *(warn)* avertir, mettre en garde; **he cautioned them to be careful** il leur a conseillé d'être prudents; **to caution sb against doing sth** déconseiller à qn de faire qch; **he cautioned them against the evils of drink** il les a mis en garde contre les dangers de la boisson
(**b**) *Law* **to caution sb** *(on arrest)* informer qn de ses droits; *(instead of prosecuting)* donner un avertissement à qn
(**c**) *Sport (player)* donner un avertissement à
3 *vi* **to caution against sth** déconseiller qch
cautionary [ˈkɔːʃənərɪ] *adj* qui sert d'avertissement; **as a cautionary measure** par mesure de précaution; **a cautionary tale** un récit édifiant
cautious [ˈkɔːʃəs] *adj* circonspect; *(driver, remark, optimism)* prudent; **to be cautious about doing sth** faire qch avec circonspection
cautiously [ˈkɔːʃəslɪ] *adv* avec prudence, prudemment
cautiousness [ˈkɔːʃəsnɪs] *n (care)* circonspection *f*, prudence *f*
cavalcade [ˌkævəlˈkeɪd] *n* cortège *m*; *(on horseback)* cavalcade *f*
cavalier [ˌkævəˈlɪə(r)] **1** *n (gen) & Mil* cavalier *m*
2 *adj* cavalier, désinvolte; **he treated me in a very cavalier fashion** il s'est comporté envers moi d'une façon très cavalière
3 Cavalier *Hist* **1** *n* Cavalier *m (partisan de Charles I d'Angleterre pendant la guerre civile anglaise)*; **the Cavaliers and the Roundheads** les Cavaliers *mpl* et les Têtes *fpl* rondes **2** *adj* royaliste, Cavalier
cavalierly [ˌkævəˈlɪəlɪ] *adv* cavalièrement
cavalry [ˈkævəlrɪ] *n Mil* cavalerie *f*
►► *Mil* ***cavalry charge*** charge *f* de cavalerie; *Mil* ***cavalry officer*** officier *m* de cavalerie; ***cavalry twill*** = étoffe utilisée pour faire les culottes de cheval
cavalryman [ˈkævəlrɪmən] (*pl* **cavalrymen** [-mən]) *n Mil* cavalier *m (soldat)*
Cavan [ˈkævən] *n* (**a**) *(town)* Cavan (**b**) *(county)* le comté de Cavan, = comté dans le nord-ouest de la République d'Irlande; **in Cavan** dans le comté de Cavan
cave[1] [keɪv] *n* caverne *f*, grotte *f*
►► ***cave art*** art *m* rupestre; ***cave drawing*** peinture *f* rupestre; ***cave dweller*** *(in prehistory)* homme *m* des cavernes; *(troglodyte)* troglodyte *m*; *Ich* ***cave fish*** poisson *m* cavernicole; ***cave painting*** peinture *f* rupestre
►**cave in** *vi* (**a**) *(ceiling, floor)* s'écrouler, s'effondrer, s'affaisser; *(wall)* s'écrouler, s'effondrer, céder (**b**) *Fam (person)* flancher, céder❑; **eventually they caved in and agreed** ils ont finalement cédé et donné leur accord

♫ **'Fingal's Cave'** *Mendelssohn* 'La Grotte de Fingal'

cave[2] [ˈkeɪvɪ] *Br Fam Old-fashioned School slang*
1 *n* **to keep cave** faire le guet
2 *exclam* pet!
caveat [ˈkævɪæt] *n* avertissement *m*; *Law* notification *f* d'opposition
►► *Com & Law* ***caveat emptor*** aux risques de l'acheteur; *Com & Law* ***caveat subscriptor*** aux risques du signataire
cave-dwelling [ˈkeɪv-] *adj* cavernicole
cave-in [keɪv-] *n* (**a**) *(of ceiling, floor)* effondrement *m*, affaissement *m* (**b**) *Fam Fig* effondrement❑ *m*, dégonflage *m*
caveman [ˈkeɪvmæn] (*pl* **cavemen** [-men]) *n* homme *m* des cavernes; *Fig* brute *f*
caver [ˈkeɪvə(r)] *n* spéléologue *mf*
cavern [ˈkævən] *n* caverne *f*
cavernous [ˈkævənəs] *adj* (**a**) *Fig* **a cavernous building** un bâtiment très vaste à l'intérieur; **cavernous eyes** des yeux enfoncés; **cavernous depths** des profondeurs insondables; **a cavernous voice** une voix caverneuse (**b**) *Geol* plein de cavernes
cavetto [kəˈvetəʊ] *n Archit* cavet *m*
caviar, caviare [ˈkævɪɑː(r)] *n* caviar *m*
cavil [ˈkævəl] (*Br pt & pp* **cavilled**, *cont* **cavilling**, *Am pt & pp* **caviled**, *cont* **caviling**) **1** *vi* chicaner, ergoter; **to cavil at sth** chicaner *ou* ergoter sur qch
2 *n* chicane *f*, ergotage *m*
caving [ˈkeɪvɪŋ] *n* spéléologie *f*; **to go caving** faire de la spéléologie
cavity [ˈkævətɪ] (*pl* **cavities**) *n* (**a**) *(in rock, wood)* cavité *f*, creux *m* (**b**) *Anat* cavité *f*; *(in tooth)* cavité *f*
►► ***cavity wall*** mur *m* creux *ou* à double paroi; ***cavity wall insulation*** isolation *f* en murs creux
cavort [kəˈvɔːt] *vi* (**a**) *(frolic)* cabrioler, gambader, faire des cabrioles (**b**) *Fig* batifoler; **while his wife was off cavorting around Europe** pendant que sa femme menait une vie de bâton de chaise en Europe
cavy [ˈkeɪvɪ] *n Zool (animal)* cobaye *m*, cochon *m* d'Inde
caw [kɔː] **1** *vi* croasser
2 *n* croassement *m*
cawing [ˈkɔːɪŋ] *n* croassement *m*
cay [keɪ] *n Geog (sandbank)* banc *m* de sable; *(coral reef)* banc *m ou* récif *m* de corail
Cayenne [ˌkeɪˈen] *n Geog* Cayenne
cayenne pepper [ˌkeɪˈen-] *n* poivre *m* de cayenne
cayman [ˈkeɪmən] *n Zool* caïman *m*
Cayman Islands [ˈkeɪmən] *npl* **the Cayman Islands** les îles *fpl* Caïmans
cayuse [ˈkaɪuːs] *n Am (pony)* petit poney *m*
CB [ˌsiːˈbiː] *n* (**a**) *(abbr* **Citizens' Band**) CB *f* (**b**) *(abbr* **Companion of (the Order of) the Bath**) = distinction honorifique britannique
CBAT [ˌsiːbiːˌeɪˈtiː] *n Am Formerly (abbr* **college board achievement test**) = examen d'entrée à l'université aux États-Unis
CBC [ˌsiːbiːˈsiː] *n* (**a**) *(abbr* **Canadian Broadcasting Corporation**) = office national canadien de radiodiffusion (**b**) *Med (abbr* **complete blood count**) hémogramme *m*
CBD [ˌsiːbiːˈdiː] *n Am (abbr* **cash before delivery**) règlement *m* avant livraison
CBE [ˌsiːbiːˈiː] *n (abbr* **Companion of (the Order of) the British Empire**) = distinction honorifique britannique
CBer [ˌsiːˈbiːə(r)] *n Am* cibiste *mf*
CBI [ˌsiːbiːˈaɪ] *n (abbr* **Confederation of British Industry**) = association du patronat britannique, ≃ CNPF *m*
CBR [ˌsiːbiːˈɑː(r)] *comp Chem (abbr* **chemical, bacteriological and radiation**) chimique, bactériologique et radioactif
CBS [ˌsiːbiːˈes] *n (abbr* **Columbia Broadcasting System**) = chaîne de télévision américaine
CBT [ˌsiːbiːˈtiː] *n Am Fin (abbr* **Chicago Board of Trade**) Chambre *f* de commerce de Chicago
CC *(written abbr* **county council**) ≃ conseil *m* général
cc [ˌsiːˈsiː] **1** *n (abbr* **cubic centimetre**) cm^3
2 *vt (abbr* **carbon copy**) pcc; **to cc sb sth, to cc sth to sb** envoyer une copie de qch à qn
CCA [ˌsiːsiːˈeɪ] *n* (**a**) *Acct (abbr* **current cost accounting**) comptabilité *f* en coûts actuels (**b**) *Am Hist (abbr* **Circuit Court of Appeals**) = cour d'appel du système judiciaire des États-Unis avant 1948
CCI [ˌsiːsiːˈaɪ] *n (abbr* **Chamber of Commerce and Industry**) CCI *f*
CCTV [ˌsiːsiːˌtiːˈviː] *n (abbr* **closed-circuit television**) télévision *f* en circuit fermé
CCU [ˌsiːsiːˈjuː] *n Med (abbr* **coronary care unit**) unité *f* de soins coronariens
CD[1] [ˌsiːˈdiː] *n* (**a**) *(abbr* **compact disc**) CD *m*, **un CD** sur CD (**b**) *(abbr* **Civil Defence**) protection *f* civile (**c**) *(abbr* **certificate of deposit**) certificat *m* de dépôt
►► ***CD burner*** graveur *m* de CD; ***CD player*** lecteur *m* de CD; ***CD rack*** casier *m* de rangement pour CD; ***CD writer*** graveur *m* de CD
CD[2] *(written abbr* **Corps Diplomatique**) CD
CDC [ˌsiːdiːˈsiː] *n Am Med (abbr* **Center for Disease Control**) = aux États-Unis, institut fédéral de recherche sur les causes et la prévention des maladies
cd/fwd *Acct (written abbr* **carried forward**) reporté
CDI [ˌsiːdiːˈaɪ] *n Comput (abbr* **compact disc interactive**) CDI *m*
CD-R [ˌsiːdiːˈɑː(r)] *n* (**a**) *(abbr* **compact disc recorder)** graveur *m* de disque compact (**b**) *(abbr* **compact disc recordable)** CD-R *m*
Cdr *Mil (written abbr* **commander**) Cdt
Cdre *(written abbr* **Commodore**) (**a**) *Mil* commodore *m (officier de rang inférieur au contre-amiral*

et supérieur au capitaine de vaisseau) (**b**) *Naut (of merchant ships)* chef *m* de convoi; *(of shipping line)* doyen *m* (des capitaines); *(of yacht club)* président *m*

CD-ROM [ˌsiːdiːˈrɒm] *n Comput* (*abbr* **compact disc read-only memory**) CD-ROM *m*, CD-Rom *m*, *Offic* DOC *m*, *Offic* cédérom *m*

►► *Comput* ***CD-ROM burner*** graveur *m* de CD-ROM; *Comput* ***CD-ROM drive*** lecteur *m* de CD-ROM, *Offic* lecteur *m* de disque optique; *Comput* ***CD-ROM newspaper*** journal *m* sur CD-ROM; *Comput* ***CD-ROM reader*** lecteur de CD-ROM

CD-RW [ˌsiːdiːɑːˈdʌbəljuː] *n Comput* (*abbr* **compact disc rewritable**) CD *m* réinscriptible

CDT [ˌsiːdiːˈtiː] *n* (**a**) *Am* (*abbr* **Central Daylight Time**) = heure d'été du centre des États-Unis (**b**) *Br Sch* (*abbr* **craft, design and technology**) = matière enseignée dans le secondaire qui comprend travaux manuels et technologie

CDV [ˌsiːdiːˈviː] *n Comput* (*abbr* **compact disc video**) CDV *m*, CD vidéo *m*

CDW [ˌsiːdiːˈdʌbəljuː] *n Ins* (*abbr* **collision damage waiver**) = suppression de franchise pour les dommages causés aux véhicules

CE [ˌsiːˈiː] *n* (*abbr* **Church of England**) Église *f* anglicane

cease [siːs] **1** *vi Formal (activity, noise)* cesser, s'arrêter; **the rain eventually ceased** il a finalement cessé de pleuvoir; *Law* **to cease and desist** se désister

2 *vt (activity, efforts, work)* cesser, arrêter; **to cease doing sth** cesser de *ou* arrêter de faire qch; **it never ceases to amaze me that…** cela m'étonne toujours que…; **to cease trading** cesser ses activités; **a county that ceased to exist in 1974** un comté qui n'existe plus depuis 1974; *Mil* **to cease fire** cesser le feu; *Literary* **they have ceased to be** ils ne sont plus

3 *n Formal* **without cease** sans cesse

> **It has ceased to be**
> Il s'agit d'une formule extraite de l'un des sketchs les plus célèbres de la troupe de comiques britannique Monty Python, dans lequel le client d'un magasin d'animaux venait se plaindre qu'on lui avait vendu un perroquet mort. Le client décrivait l'état du perroquet au vendeur en utilisant de nombreuses périphrases, dont l'une était **it has ceased to be** ("il n'est plus"). Aujourd'hui on utilise cette expression de façon humoristique pour parler de quelque chose qui n'existe plus ou qui n'a plus cours.

ceasefire [ˌsiːsˈfaɪə(r)] *n Mil* cessez-le-feu *m inv*; **to declare a ceasefire** déclarer un cessez-le-feu; **to agree to a ceasefire** accepter un cessez-le-feu

►► ***ceasefire agreement*** accord *m* de cessez-le-feu; **to sign a ceasefire agreement** signer un cessez-le-feu *ou* un accord de cessez-le-feu

ceaseless [ˈsiːslɪs] *adj* incessant, continuel

ceaselessly [ˈsiːslɪslɪ] *adv* sans cesse, continuellement

ceaselessness [ˈsiːslɪsnɪs] *n* continuité *f*, persistance *f*

cecal *Am* = **caecal**

cecum *Am* = **caecum**

cedar [ˈsiːdə(r)] **1** *n* cèdre *m*

2 *comp (table, cupboard)* de *ou* en cèdre

►► *Am* ***cedar closet*** *(for protecting clothes etc against moths)* placard *m* en cèdre; ***cedar of Lebanon*** cèdre *m* du Liban

cedarwood [ˈsiːdəwʊd] *n* (bois *m* de) cèdre *m*

cede [siːd] *vt* céder (**to** à); **to cede a point** *(in argument)* concéder un point

cedilla [sɪˈdɪlə] *n Ling* cédille *f*

CEEB [ˌsiːiːˌiːˈbiː] *n Am Univ* (*abbr* **College Entry Examination Board**) = commission d'admission dans l'enseignement supérieur aux États-Unis

Ceefax® [ˈsiːfæks] *n Br* = service de télétexte de la BBC

ceilidh [ˈkeɪlɪ] *n* = soirée de danse et de musique folklorique (en Irlande et en Écosse)

ceiling [ˈsiːlɪŋ] **1** *n* (**a**) *(of room)* plafond *m*; *Fam* **to hit the ceiling** *(become angry)* sauter les plombs (**b**) *Aviat & Met* plafond *m*; **the cloud ceiling** le plafond de nuages; **to fly at the ceiling** plafonner (**c**) *Com & Econ* plafond *m*; **prices have reached their ceiling** les prix ont atteint leur plafond; **the government has set a 3 percent ceiling on wage rises** le gouvernement a limité à 3 pour cent les augmentations de salaire

2 *comp Com & Econ (charge, price)* plafond *(inv)*

►► ***ceiling fan*** ventilateur *m* de plafond; ***ceiling light*** plafonnier *m*; ***ceiling tile*** dalle *f* pour plafond

-ceilinged [ˈsiːlɪŋd] *suff* **high-/low-ceilinged room** pièce *f* haute/ basse de plafond

celadon [ˈselədən] *n Cer* céladon *m*

►► ***celadon green*** **1** *n* (vert *m*) céladon *m*

2 *adj* (vert) céladon

celandine [ˈseləndaɪn] *n Bot* chélidoine *f*

celeb [səˈleb] *n Fam* célébrité ❑ *f*

Celebes [seˈliːbɪz] *n* Célèbes

►► *Geog* ***the Celebes Sea*** la mer de Célèbes

celebrant [ˈselɪbrənt] *n Rel* célébrant *m*, officiant *m*

celebrate [ˈselɪbreɪt] **1** *vt* (**a**) *(birthday, Christmas)* fêter, célébrer; *(event, victory)* célébrer; **to celebrate the memory of sth** commémorer qch; **the city is celebrating the anniversary of its founding** la ville fête l'anniversaire de sa fondation; **let's open a bottle of wine to celebrate the occasion** ouvrons une bouteille de vin pour fêter ça (**b**) *(praise → person, sb's beauty)* célébrer, glorifier (**c**) *Rel* **to celebrate mass** célébrer la messe

2 *vi* faire la fête; **let's celebrate with a new car/ a weekend in Paris** achetons une nouvelle voiture/allons passer un week-end à Paris pour fêter ça; **will you be celebrating tonight?** tu vas arroser ça ce soir?; **let's celebrate with some champagne** on va arroser ça au champagne; **let's celebrate!** *(gen)* il faut fêter ça!; *(with drinks)* il faut arroser ça!

celebrated [ˈselɪbreɪtɪd] *adj* célèbre (**for** par)

celebration [ˌselɪˈbreɪʃən] *n* (**a**) *(of birthday, Christmas)* célébration *f*; *(of anniversary, past event)* commémoration *f*; **in celebration of Christmas** pour fêter *ou* célébrer Noël; **in celebration of forty years of peace** pour commémorer quarante ans de paix

(**b**) *Mus & Literature* éloge *m*, louange *f*; **he wrote the poem in celebration of her beauty** il a écrit le poème pour célébrer sa beauté

(**c**) *Rel (of communion, feast)* célébration *f*

(**d**) *(often pl) (occasion → of birthday, Christmas)* fête *f*, fêtes *fpl*; *(→ of historical event)* cérémonies *fpl*, fête *f*; **this calls for a celebration!** il faut fêter ça!, il faut arroser ça!; **to join in the celebrations** participer à la fête *ou* aux festivités; **birthday celebrations** fête d'anniversaire

►► ***celebration dinner*** repas *m* de fête

celebratory [ˌseləˈbreɪtərɪ] *adj (dinner)* de fête; *(marking official occasion)* commémoratif; *(atmosphere, mood)* de fête, festif

celebrity [sɪˈlebrətɪ] (*pl* **celebrities**) *n* (**a**) *(fame)* célébrité *f* (**b**) *(person)* vedette *f*, célébrité *f*

►► ***celebrity football match*** = match de football dans lequel une des équipes est composée de célébrités

celebutante [sɪˈlebjʊˌtɑːnt] *n Am Fam Hum* = jeune personne en passe de devenir célèbre

celeriac [sɪˈlerɪæk] *n* céleri-rave *m*

celerity [sɪˈlerətɪ] *n Literary* célérité *f*, rapidité *f*

celery [ˈselərɪ] **1** *n* céleri *m*; **head of celery** pied *m* de céleri; **stick of celery** branche *f* de céleri

2 *comp (plant)* de céleri; *(soup)* au céleri

►► ***celery salt*** sel *m* de céleri

celesta [sɪˈlestə] *n Mus* célesta *m*

celestial [sɪˈlestɪəl] *adj Astron & Fig* céleste

►► *Astron* ***celestial equator*** équateur *m* céleste; *Astron* ***celestial mechanics*** mécanique *f* céleste; ***celestial pole*** pôle *m* céleste; *Astron* ***celestial sphere*** sphère *f* céleste

celiac *Am* = **coeliac**

celibacy [ˈselɪbəsɪ] *n (sexual abstinence)* abstinence *f* sexuelle, chasteté *f*; *(not being married)* célibat *m*; *Rel* **to take a vow of celibacy** faire vœu de chasteté

celibate [ˈselɪbət] **1** *adj (person → chaste)* qui n'a pas de rapports sexuels, chaste; *(life → by choice)* de chasteté; *(→ forced)* sans rapports sexuels

2 *n* personne *f* qui n'a pas de rapports sexuels

cell [sel] **1** *n* (**a**) *(in prison)* cellule *f*; **he spent the night in the cells** il a passé la nuit en cellule; **she was released after two days in the cells** elle a été relâchée après deux jours de cellule (**b**) *(of monk, hermit)* cellule *f* (**c**) *Biol* cellule *f*; *(in beehive)* cellule *f*, alvéole *m* (**d**) *Elec* élément *m* (de pile) (**e**) *Pol* cellule *f* (**f**) *Comput (on spreadsheet)* cellule *f*

2 *comp Biol* cellulaire

►► *Biol* ***cell division*** division *f* cellulaire; *Biol* ***cell membrane*** membrane *f* cellulaire; *Biol* ***cell structure*** structure *f* cellulaire; *Biol* ***cell wall*** paroi *f* cellulaire

cellar [ˈselə(r)] *n (for wine)* cave *f*, cellier *m*; *(for coal, bric-a-brac)* cave *f*; *(for food)* cellier *m*; **he keeps a good cellar** il a une bonne cave

cellarage [ˈselərɪdʒ] *n* (**a**) *(storage in cellar)* emmagasinage *m* (en cave); *(for wine)* encavement *m* (**b**) *(cellars)* caves *fpl*

cellarman [ˈselәmәn] (*pl* **cellermen** [-mәn]) *n* sommelier *m*

cellist [ˈtʃelɪst] *n* violoncelliste *mf*

cell-mediated immunity *n Biol* immunité *f* à médiation cellulaire

Cellnet® [ˈselnet] *n Tel* = réseau britannique de téléphonie mobile

cello [ˈtʃeləʊ] (*pl* **cellos**) *n* violoncelle *m*

Cellophane® [ˈseləfeɪn] *n* Cellophane® *f*

cellophane noodles [ˈseləfeɪn-] *npl Culin* vermicelles *mpl* chinois

cellphone [ˈselfəʊn] *n* téléphone *m* cellulaire, *Can* cellulaire *m*

cellular [ˈseljʊlə(r)] *adj* (**a**) *Biol* cellulaire (**b**) *Constr* cellulaire (**c**) *Tex (blanket)* en cellular

►► ***cellular board*** *(cardboard)* carton *m* ondulé; *Electron & Tel* ***cellular logic*** logique *f* cellulaire; ***cellular (tele)phone*** téléphone *m* cellulaire, *Can* cellulaire *m*

cellulase [ˈseljʊleɪz] *n Biol* cellulase *f*

cellule [ˈseljuːl] *n Biol* cellule *f*

cellulite [ˈseljʊlaɪt] *n Physiol* cellulite *f*

cellulitis [ˌseljʊˈlaɪtɪs] *n Med* cellulite *f*

celluloid® [ˈseljʊlɔɪd] **1** *n* Celluloïd® *m*; *Fig* **to capture sb/sth on celluloid**® filmer qn/qch

2 *adj* en Celluloïd®

cellulose [ˈseljʊləʊs] *Chem* **1** *n* cellulose *f*

2 *adj* en *ou* de cellulose, cellulosique

►► ***cellulose acetate*** acétate *m* de cellulose; ***cellulose nitrate*** nitrocellulose *f*

Celsius [ˈselsɪəs] *adj* Celsius; **25 degrees Celsius** 25 degrés Celsius

►► ***Celsius thermometer*** thermomètre *m* de Celsius

Celt [kelt] *n* Celte *mf*

Celtic [ˈkeltɪk] **1** *n Ling* celtique *m*

2 *adj* celtique, celte

►► ***Celtic cross*** croix *f* celtique; ***the Celtic fringe*** = les pays de tradition celte en Grande-Bretagne *(pays de Galle et Écosse)*; *Mus* ***Celtic harp*** harpe *f* celtique; ***Celtic Tiger*** = surnom donné à l'Irlande depuis l'essor économique du milieu des années 90

Celticist [ˈkeltɪsɪst] *n* = spécialiste du monde celte

cement [sɪˈment] **1** *n* (**a**) *Constr & Fig* ciment *m* (**b**) *(in dentistry)* amalgame *m* (**c**) *(glue)* colle *f*

2 *vt* (**a**) *Constr & Fig* cimenter (**b**) *(in dentistry)* obturer

►► ***cement mixer*** bétonnière *f*

cementation [ˌsiːmenˈteɪʃən] *n Constr & Fig* cimentation *f*

cemetery [ˈsemɪtrɪ] (*pl* **cemeteries**) *n* cimetière *m*

cenacle [ˈsenəkəl] *n* cénacle *m*

cenotaph [ˈsenətɑːf] *n* cénotaphe *m*; **the Cenotaph** = monument aux morts des deux guerres mondiales (à Londres), où se déroulent les cérémonies de l'Armistice

Cenozoic [ˌsiːnəʊˈzəʊɪk] *Geol* **1** *n* **the Cenozoic** le cénozoïque

2 *adj* cénozoïque

censer [ˈsensə(r)] *n Rel* encensoir *m*

censor [ˈsensə(r)] **1** *n* censeur *m*; **to get past the censor** échapper à la censure

2 *vt* (**a**) *(ban → book, film, article etc)* interdire, censurer; *(→ scene)* supprimer, couper; *(→ line, word)* supprimer (**b**) *(cut parts of → film, article, newspaper)* censurer; *(→ play, book, scenario)* censurer, expurger

►► *TV & Rad* ***censor bleep*** bip *m* de censure

censoring [ˈsensərɪŋ] *n* censure *f*

censorious [senˈsɔːrɪəs] *adj Formal (comments,*

criticism) sévère; *(person)* porté à la censure

censoriousness [sen'sɔːrɪəsnɪs] *n (of comments, criticism)* sévérité *f*; *(of person)* penchant *m* à la censure, disposition *f* à critiquer

censorship ['sensəʃɪp] *n* (**a**) *(act, practice)* censure *f*; **there is no longer any censorship of his films** ses films ne sont plus censurés (**b**) *(office of censor)* censorat *m*
►► ***censorship law*** loi *f* de censure

censurable ['senʃərəbəl] *adj Formal* blâmable, qui mérite la réprobation

censure ['senʃə(r)] **1** *n* blâme *m*, critique *f*
2 *vt* blâmer, critiquer

census ['sensəs] *n Admin* recensement *m*; **to conduct** *or* **to take a census** faire un recensement; **to conduct** *or* **to take a population census** faire le recensement de la population, recenser la population
►► *Am* ***Census Bureau*** Bureau *m* des statistiques; ***census return*** formulaire *m* de recensement; ***census taker*** agent *m* recenseur

cent [sent] *n (coin)* cent *m*; *Am Fig* **it's not worth a cent** ça ne vaut rien; **I haven't got a cent** je n'ai pas un sou; *Am* **to put one's two cents in** mettre son grain de sel; *Am Fam* **I'll buy it if you give me a cent's off** *(reduction)* je l'achète si vous me faites une ristourne *ou* un prix ❑

centaur ['sentɔː(r)] *n Myth* centaure *m*

centaury ['sentɔːrɪ] *n Bot* petite centaurée *f*

centenarian [ˌsentɪ'neərɪən] **1** *n* centenaire *mf*
2 *adj* centenaire

centenary [sen'tiːnərɪ] (*pl* **centenaries**) **1** *n (anniversary)* centenaire *m*, centième anniversaire *m*; **the organization is celebrating its centenary** l'organisation fête son centenaire; **the centenary of Mozart's birth** le centenaire de la naissance de Mozart
2 *comp* centenaire; *(celebrations)* du centenaire

centennial [sen'tenjəl] **1** *n Am* centenaire *m*, centième anniversaire *m*
2 *adj* (**a**) *(in age)* centenaire, séculaire (**b**) *(every hundred years)* séculaire
►► ***the Centennial State*** = surnom donné au Colorado

center, centering *etc Am* = **centre, centring** *etc*

centerline ['sentəlaɪn] *Am* = **centreline**

centerpiece *Am* = **centrepiece**

centesimal [sen'tesɪməl] *adj* centésimal

centigrade ['sentɪgreɪd] *adj* centigrade; **25 degrees centigrade** 25 degrés centigrades
►► ***centigrade thermometer*** thermomètre *m* centigrade

centigram, centigramme ['sentɪgræm] *n* centigramme *m*

centilitre, *Am* **centiliter** ['sentɪˌliːtə(r)] *n* centilitre *m*

centime ['sɒntiːm] *n* centime *m*

centimetre, *Am* **centimeter** ['sentɪˌmiːtə(r)] *n* centimètre *m*

centipede ['sentɪpiːd] *n Entom* mille-pattes *m inv*

cento ['sentəʊ] (*pl* **centos** *or* **centones** [-'təʊniːz]) *n Mus & Literature* centon *m*

central ['sentrəl] **1** *adj* (**a**) *(in location)* central; **central Miami** le centre de Miami; **the office is very central** *(in town)* le bureau est situé en plein centre
(**b**) *(in importance)* central; **the central character** le personnage central; **central to the debate is the question of safety** la question de la sécurité se situe au cœur du débat; **of central importance** d'une importance capitale; **this concept is central to his theory** ce concept est au centre de sa théorie
2 *n Am Old-fashioned* central *m* téléphonique
►► *Banking* ***central account*** compte *m* centralisateur; ***Central African*** **1** *n* Centrafricain(e) *m,f* **2** *adj* centrafricain; ***the Central African Republic*** la République centrafricaine; **in the Central African Republic** en République centrafricaine; ***Central America*** Amérique *f* centrale; **in Central America** en Amérique centrale; ***Central American*** **1** *n* Centraméricain(e) *m,f* **2** *adj* centraméricain; *Geog* ***Central Asia*** Asie *f* centrale; **in Central Asia** en Asie centrale; ***central bank*** banque *f* centrale; *Br* ***Central Belt*** = région d'Écosse qui s'étend de Glasgow à Édimbourg; ***Central Criminal Court*** = cour d'assises du Grand Londres située dans Old Bailey; ***Central Daylight Time*** heure *f* d'été du centre des États-Unis; ***Central Europe*** Europe *f* centrale; ***Central European*** **1** *n* habitant(e) *m,f* de l'Europe centrale **2** *adj* d'Europe centrale; ***Central European Time*** heure *f* de l'Europe centrale; ***central government*** gouvernement *m* central; ***central heating*** chauffage *m* central; *Am* ***Central Intelligence Agency*** CIA *f*; *Med* ***central line*** veine *f* centrale; *Aut* ***central locking*** verrouillage *m* central; ***Central Mosque*** = principal lieu de culte musulman en Grande-Bretagne (à Londres); *Anat* ***central nervous system*** système *m* nerveux central; *Br Pol* ***Central Office*** = siège du parti conservateur britannique; *Admin* ***Central Office of Information*** = organisme public qui édite des documents d'information sur la Grande-Bretagne; ***Central Park*** Central Park *m*; *Comput* ***central processing unit*** unité *f* centrale (de traitement), processeur *m* central; ***central purchasing*** achats *mpl* centralisés; ***central purchasing department*** *(in company)* centrale *f* d'achat(s); ***central purchasing group, central purchasing office*** centrale *f* d'achat(s); ***Central Region*** le Centre, = région du centre de l'Écosse; **in Central Region** dans le Centre; *Br* ***central reservation*** *(with grass)* terre-plein *m* central, *Belg & Suisse* berme *f* centrale; *(with barrier)* bande *f* médiane; *Am Banking & St Exch* ***Central Securities Depository*** dépositaire *m* national de titres; ***Central Standard Time*** heure *f* d'hiver du centre des États-Unis

centralism ['sentrəlɪzəm] *n Pol* centralisme *m*

centrality [sen'trælətɪ] (*pl* **centralities**) *n (of argument, idea)* caractère *m* essentiel; *(of location)* situation *f* centrale

centralization [ˌsentrəlaɪ'zeɪʃən] *n* centralisation *f*

centralize, -ise ['sentrəlaɪz] **1** *vt* centraliser
2 *vi* se centraliser

centralized ['sentrəlaɪzd] *adj* centralisé
►► *Comput* ***centralized data processing*** traitement *m* centralisé de l'information; ***centralized management*** gestion *f* intégrée; ***centralized purchasing*** achats *mpl* centralisés; *Comput* ***centralized storage*** mémoire *f* centrale

centrally ['sentrəlɪ] *adv (located)* au centre; *(organized)* de façon centralisée; **centrally based** centralisé; **the flat is centrally heated** l'appartement a le chauffage central; **the house is centrally situated** la maison est située de façon centrale; *Econ* **a centrally planned economy** une économie dirigée

centre, *Am* **center** ['sentə(r)] **1** *n* (**a**) *(gen)* centre *m*; **in the centre** au centre; **centre of gravity** centre *m* de gravité; *Med* **centre of infection** foyer *m* infectueux
(**b**) *(of town)* centre *m*; **she lives in the city centre** elle habite dans le centre-ville
(**c**) *Fig (of unrest)* foyer *m*; *(of debate)* cœur *m*, centre *m*; **at the centre of the debate** au cœur du débat; **the centre of attention** le centre d'attention
(**d**) *(place, building)* centre *m*; **a sports/health centre** un centre sportif/médical
(**e**) *Pol* centre *m*; **to be left/right of centre** être du centre gauche/droit
(**f**) *Tech (of lathe)* pointe *f*; **to be off centre** *or* **out of centre** être décentré
(**g**) *Sport (pass)* centre *m*
[illegible]
2 *comp* (**a**) *(central)* central
(**b**) *Pol* du centre
3 *vt* (**a**) *(place in centre)* centrer; **to centre a line** *(when keying)* centrer une ligne
(**b**) *Cin & Phot (image)* cadrer; *Typ (text)* centrer
(**c**) *Fig (attention)* concentrer, fixer; **to centre one's hopes on sth** mettre *ou* fonder tous ses espoirs sur qch
(**d**) *Sport* **to centre the ball** centrer le ballon
►► *Ftbl* ***centre back*** arrière *m* central; *Tech* ***centre bit*** mèche *f* à bois; *Ftbl* ***centre circle*** cercle *m* central; ***the centre court*** *(in tennis)* le court central; *Am Med* ***Center for Disease Control*** = aux États-Unis, institut fédéral de recherche sur les causes et la prévention des maladies; *Am Aut* ***center divider strip*** terre-plein *m*; *Ftbl* ***centre forward*** avant-centre *m*; *Ftbl* ***centre half*** demi-centre *m*; *Tech* ***centre punch*** pointeau *m*; *Typ* ***centre spread*** double page *f* centrale; *Am Aut* ***center strip*** terre-plein *m*; *Sport* ***centre three-quarter*** *(in rugby)* trois-quarts *m* centre

►**centre around,** *Am* **center around** *vt insep* tourner autour de; **the debate centres around politics** le débat tourne autour de la politique

►**centre on,** *Am* **center on** *vt insep* se concentrer sur; **all their attention was centred on the World Cup** toute leur attention était concentrée sur la coupe du monde; **the conversation centred on politics** la conversation tournait autour de la politique

►**centre round** = **centre around**

centreboard, *Am* **centerboard** ['sentəbɔːd] *n Naut* dérive *f (d'un bateau)*

centred, *Am* **centered** ['sentəd] *adj (placed in centre)* centré; *Am Fig* **he's not very centered** il est un peu paumé

centrefold, *Am* **centerfold** ['sentəˌfəʊld] *n Press (in magazine, newspaper)* double page *f* centrale détachable; *(nude picture)* photo *f* de pin-up; **to do a centrefold** *(nude picture)* poser comme pin-up; **centrefold girl** pin-up *f*

centreline, *Am* **centerline** ['sentəlaɪn] *n* axe *m*, ligne *f* médiane; *(in tennis)* ligne *f* médiane

centrepiece, *Am* **centerpiece** ['sentəpiːs] *n (outstanding feature)* joyau *m*; *(on table)* décoration *f* de table; *(of meal)* pièce *f* de résistance

centreplate, *Am* **centerplate** ['sentəpleɪt] *n* = **centreboard**

centre-point steering, *Am* **center-point steering** *n Aut* direction *f* à point milieu

Centrica ['sentrɪkə] *n Br* = société de production et de distribution du gaz

centrifugal [ˌsentrɪ'fjʊgəl] *adj Phys* centrifuge
►► ***centrifugal force*** force *f* centrifuge

centrifugally [ˌsentrɪ'fjʊgəlɪ] *adv Tech (cast)* par centrifugation

centrifuge ['sentrɪfjuːdʒ] *Tech* **1** *n* centrifugeur *m*, centrifugeuse *f*
2 *vt* centrifuger

centring, *Am* **centering** ['sentərɪŋ] *n* (**a**) *(placing in centre)* centrage *m* (**b**) *Cin & Phot* cadrage *m*; *Typ (of text)* centrage *m*
►► ***centring tool*** centreur *m*

centriole ['sentrɪəʊl] *n Biol* centriole *m*

centripetal [ˌsentrɪ'piːtəl] *adj Phys* centripète; **centripetal force** force *f* centripète

centrism ['sentrɪzəm] *n Pol* centrisme *m*

centrist ['sentrɪst] *Pol* **1** *adj* centriste
2 *n* centriste *mf*

centromere ['sentrəʊmɪə(r)] *n Biol* centromère *m*

Centronics® [sen'trɒnɪks] *n*
►► ***Centronics® cable*** câble *m* Centronics; ***Centronics® printer*** imprimante *f* Centronics

centrosoma [sentrəʊ'səʊmə], **centrosome** ['sentrəʊsəʊm] *n Biol* centrosome *m*

centrosphere ['sentrəʊsfɪə(r)] *n Geol* centrosphère *f*

centuplicate 1 *n* [sen'tjuːplɪkət] centuple *m*
2 *adj* [sen'tjuːplɪkət] centuple
3 *vt* [sen'tjuːplɪkeɪt] centupler

centuries-old ['sentʃərɪz-] *adj* vieux (vieille) de plusieurs siècles

centurion [sen'tjʊərɪən] *n Hist* centurion *m*

century ['sentʃʊrɪ] (*pl* **centuries**) *n* (**a**) *(time)* siècle *m*; **in the 20th century** au 20ème siècle; **this house is five centuries old** cette maison a été bâtie il y a cinq siècles; **these trees are centuries old** ces arbres sont plusieurs fois centenaires (**b**) *Sport (one hundred runs)* centaine *f*, série *f* de cent (**c**) *Antiq & Mil* centurie *f*
►► *Am Fam* ***century note*** billet *m* de cent dollars ❑

CEO [ˌsiːiː'əʊ] *n Com & Ind (abbr* **chief executive officer***)* P-DG *m*

cep [sep] *n Bot & Culin* cèpe *m*

cephalic [sə'fælɪk, ke'fælɪk] *adj Anat* céphalique
►► ***cephalic index*** indice *m* céphalique

cephalopod ['sefələpɒd] *n Zool* céphalopode *m*

Cepheid variable ['siːfɪɪd-] *n Astron* céphéide *f*

Cepheus ['siːfɪəs] *n Astron* Céphée *f*

ceramic [sɪ'ræmɪk] **1** *n* (**a**) *(objects)* céramique *f* (**b**) *(object)* (objet *m* en) céramique *f*
2 *comp (art)* céramique; *(vase)* en céramique
►► *Br* ***ceramic hob*** plaque *f* vitrocéramique; ***ceramic tiles*** carrelage *m*

ceramicist [sɪ'ræmɪsɪst] *n* céramiste *mf*

ceramics [sɪ'ræmɪks] *n (UNCOUNT)* céramique *f*

cen–cer

ceramist ['serəmɪst] *n* céramiste *m*

Cerberus ['sɜːbərəs] *pr n Myth* Cerbère

cercaria [sə'keərɪə] (*pl* **cercariae** [-iiː]) *n* cercaire *f*

cereal ['sɪərɪəl] **1** *n* (**a**) *Agr (plant)* céréale *f*; *(grain)* grain *m* (de céréale) (**b**) *Culin* **(breakfast) cereal** céréales *fpl*; **baby cereal** bouillie *f*

2 *comp Agr (farming)* céréalier

►► ***cereal bowl*** assiette *f* creuse, bol *m* à céréales; ***cereal crops*** céréales *fpl*

cerebellum [ˌserɪ'beləm] (*pl* **cerebellums** *or* **cerebella** [-lə]) *n Anat* cervelet *m*

cerebral *adj* (**a**) ['serɪbrəl, *Am* sə'riːbrəl] *Anat* cérébral (**b**) ['serɪbrəl, sə'riːbrəl] *(intellectual)* cérébral

►► *Med* ***cerebral aneurism*** anévrisme *m or* anévrysme *m* cérébral; *Med* ***cerebral death*** mort *f* cérébrale; *Med* ***cerebral haemorrhage*** hémorragie *f* cérébrale; ***cerebral hemisphere*** hémisphère *m* cérébral; *Med* ***cerebral palsy*** paralysie *f* cérébrale

cerebrate [ˌserɪ'breɪt] *vi Formal* réfléchir, méditer; *Hum* cogiter

cerebration [ˌserɪ'breɪʃən] *n Formal* réflexion *f*, méditation *f*; *Hum* cogitation *f*

cerebrospinal [ˌserəbrə'spaɪnəl] *adj Anat* cérébro-spinal, céphalo-rachidien

►► *Anat* ***cerebrospinal fluid*** liquide *m* céphalo-rachidien

cerebrum ['serɪbrəm] (*pl* **cerebrums** *or* **cerebra** [-brə]) *n Anat* cerveau *m*

cerecloth ['sɪəklɒθ], **cerement** ['sɪəmənt] *n Literary* linceul *m*, suaire *m*

ceremonial [ˌserɪ'məʊnjəl] **1** *adj* (**a**) *(rite, visit)* cérémoniel; *(robes)* de cérémonie (**b**) *Am (post)* honorifique

2 *n* cérémonial *m*; *Rel* cérémonial *m*, rituel *m*

ceremonially [ˌserɪ'məʊnjəlɪ] *adv* selon le cérémonial d'usage

ceremonious [ˌserɪ'məʊnjəs] *adj* solennel; *(mock-solemn)* cérémonieux

ceremoniously [ˌserɪ'məʊnjəslɪ] *adv* solennellement, avec cérémonie; *(mock-solemnly)* cérémonieusement

ceremoniousness [serɪ'məʊnɪəsnɪs] *n* solennité *f*

ceremony [*Br* 'serɪmənɪ, *Am* 'serəməʊnɪ] (*pl* **ceremonies**) *n* (**a**) *(UNCOUNT) (formality)* cérémonie *f*, cérémonies *fpl*; **with much ceremony** avec beaucoup de cérémonie; **without ceremony** sans cérémonie *ou* cérémonies; **we don't stand on ceremony** nous ne faisons pas de cérémonies (**b**) *(event)* cérémonie *f*

Ceres ['sɪəriːz] *pr n Myth* Cérès

cerise [sə'riːz] **1** *n* cerise *m inv*

2 *adj* (de) couleur cerise, cerise *(inv)*

cerium ['sɪərɪəm] *n Chem* cérium *m*

ceroc® [ʃə'rɒk] *n (dance)* = sorte de danse, inspirée du rock

cert [sɜːt] *n Br Fam* certitude *f*; **it's a dead cert that he'll win** il va gagner, ça ne fait pas un pli *ou* c'est couru d'avance; **he's a cert for the job** il est sûr d'obtenir le poste; **if one thing's a cert it's that...** s'il y a une chose qui est sûre c'est que...

cert. *(written abbr* **certificate**) certificat *m*; **a cert. 18 film** un film interdit aux moins de 18 ans

certain ['sɜːtən] **1** *adj* (**a**) *(sure)* certain, sûr; **to be certain of sth** être sûr de qch; **I'm certain of it!** j'en suis sûr!; **she was quite certain about what she had seen** elle était tout à fait sûre de ce qu'elle avait vu; **he was certain (that) she was there** il était certain qu'elle était là; **it's certain that she will get the job** il est sûr qu'elle aura le poste; **it's still not certain that he's going to England** il n'est pas encore certain *ou* sûr qu'il aille en Angleterre; **there is certain to be some opposition to the bill** il est sûr que la loi rencontrera une opposition; **to be certain to do sth** être sûr de faire qch; **he's certain to win** il est sûr qu'il va gagner; **he's certain to come** il ne manquera pas de venir, il viendra sûrement; **I'd better make certain** je ferais mieux de m'en assurer; **to make certain of sth** *(check)* vérifier qch, s'assurer de qch; *(be sure to have)* s'assurer qch; **you ought to make certain of the time** vous devriez vérifier l'heure; **he made certain that all the doors were locked** il a vérifié que toutes les portes étaient fermées; **I made certain of a good seat** je me suis assuré une bonne place

(**b**) *(inevitable → death, failure)* certain, inévitable; **the soldiers faced certain death** les soldats allaient à une mort certaine; **they face certain dismissal** ils seront renvoyés à coup sûr

(**c**) *(definite, infallible → cure)* sûr, infaillible

2 *adj* (**a**) *(particular but unspecified)* certain; **on a certain day in June** un certain jour de juin; **in certain places** à certains endroits; **he has a certain something about him** il a un certain je ne sais quoi; **she has a certain charm** elle a un certain charme; **women of a certain age** les femmes d'un certain âge; **if I were to ask you to meet me at a certain time and in a certain place...** si je te demandais de me retrouver à telle heure, à tel endroit...

(**b**) *(not known personally)* certain; **a certain Mr Roberts** un certain M. Roberts

(**c**) *(some)* certain; **there's been a certain amount of confusion over this** il y a eu une certaine confusion à ce sujet; **to a certain extent** *or* **degree** dans une certaine mesure; **certain people** certaines personnes

3 *pron* certains (certaines) *mpl,fpl*; **certain of his colleagues** certains *ou* quelques-uns de ses collègues; **certain of the pages** certaines pages

4 for certain *adv* **I don't know for certain** je n'en suis pas certain; **I can't say for certain** je ne peux pas l'affirmer; **you'll have it tomorrow for certain** vous l'aurez demain sans faute; **that's for certain!** c'est sûr et certain!, cela ne fait pas de doute!

certainly ['sɜːtənlɪ] *adv* (**a**) *(without doubt)* certainement, assurément; *(admittedly)* certes; **he is certainly very handsome** il est très beau, ça ne fait pas de doute; **I will certainly come** je ne manquerai pas de venir, je viendrai, c'est sûr; **it will certainly be ready tomorrow** cela sera prêt demain sans faute

(**b**) *(of course)* certainement, bien sûr; **can you help me? – certainly!** pouvez-vous m'aider? – bien sûr *ou* volontiers!; **certainly, sir!** bien sûr, monsieur!; **are you angry? – I most certainly am!** êtes-vous fâché? – oui, et comment!; **certainly not!** bien sûr que non!, certainement pas!

certainty ['sɜːtəntɪ] (*pl* **certainties**) *n* (**a**) *(conviction)* certitude *f*, conviction *f*; **I cannot say with any certainty when I shall arrive** je ne peux pas dire exactement à quelle heure j'arriverai; **we can have no certainty of success** nous ne sommes pas sûrs de réussir; **moral certainty** certitude morale

(**b**) *(fact)* certitude *f*, fait *m* certain; *(event)* certitude *f*, événement *m* certain; **for a certainty** à coup sûr, sans aucun doute; **I know for a certainty that he's leaving** je sais à coup sûr qu'il part; **their victory is now a certainty** leur victoire est maintenant assurée *ou* ne fait aucun doute; **it's an absolute certainty** c'est une chose certaine, c'est une certitude absolue

CertEd [sɜːt'ed] *n Br Univ* (*abbr* **Certificate in Education**) = diplôme universitaire britannique en sciences de l'éducation

certifiable [ˌsɜːtɪ'faɪəbəl] *adj* (**a**) *(gen)* qu'on peut certifier (**b**) *Psy (insane)* dont l'état nécessite l'internement psychiatrique; *Fam* **he's certifiable** il est fou à lier

certificate [sə'tɪfɪkət] *n* (**a**) *(gen) & Admin* certificat *m* (**b**) *(academic)* diplôme *m*; *(vocational → of apprenticeship)* brevet *m*

►► *Aviat* ***certificate of airworthiness*** certificat *m* de navigabilité; *Fin* ***certificate of deposit*** certificat *m* de dépôt; *Acct* ***certificate of dishonour*** certificat *m* de non-paiement; *Br Univ* ***Certificate in Education*** = diplôme universitaire britannique en sciences de l'éducation; *Com* ***certificate of incorporation*** certificat *m* d'enregistrement de société; ***certificate of insurance*** attestation *f* d'assurance; *Com* ***certificate of origin*** certificat *m* d'origine; *Br Sch* ***Certificate of Pre-vocational Education*** = examen d'accès à une formation professionnelle pour les élèves désirant poursuivre leurs études après le "GCSE" mais ne souhaitant pas passer les "A levels"; *Com* ***certificate of quality*** certificat *m* de qualité; *Br Formerly Sch* ***Certificate of Secondary Education*** = ancien brevet de l'enseignement secondaire en Grande-Bretagne, aujourd'hui remplacé par le "GCSE", ≃ BEPC *m*; *Fin* ***certificate of transfer*** acte *m* de cession; *Com* ***certificate of value*** certificat *m* de valeur

certificated [sə'tɪfɪkeɪtɪd] *adj* diplômé

certification [ˌsɜːtɪfɪ'keɪʃən] *n* (**a**) *(act)* certification *f*, authentification *f* (**b**) *(certificate)* certificat *m*

certified ['sɜːtɪfaɪd] *adj* (**a**) *(having certificate)* diplômé

(**b**) *(guaranteed)* **certified by a notary** notarié

(**c**) *Psy (declared insane)* dont l'état nécessite l'internement psychiatrique; *(in state school)* professeur *m* diplômé; *(in private school)* professeur *m* habilité

►► ***certified accounts*** comptes *mpl* approuvés; *Am Fin* ***certified cheque*** chèque *m* certifié; ***certified copy*** copie *f* certifiée conforme, copie *f* authentique; *Com* ***certified invoice*** facture *f* certifiée; *Am* ***certified letter*** lettre *f* recommandée; *Am* ***certified mail*** envoi *m* recommandé; **to send sth by certified mail** envoyer qch en recommandé avec accusé de réception; *Am* ***certified milk*** = lait venant d'un cheptel certifié (comme ayant été tuberculinisé); *Am* ***certified public accountant*** ≃ expert-comptable *m*; *Am Sch* ***certified teacher*** *(in state school)* professeur *m* diplômé; *(in private school)* professeur *m* habilité

certify ['sɜːtɪfaɪ] (*pt & pp* **certified**) **1** *vt* (**a**) *(gen)* certifier, attester; *Med (death)* constater; *Am Fin (cheque)* certifier; *Acct* **to certify the books** viser les livres de commerce; **this is to certify that A. Gooch has...** *(on certificate, letter)* ce document certifie que A. Gooch a...; **to certify that sth is true** attester que qch est vrai (**b**) *Com (goods)* garantir (**c**) *Psy* **to certify sb (insane)** déclarer qn atteint d'aliénation mentale; *Fam* **he ought to be certified!** il est bon à enfermer!

2 *vi* **to certify to sth** attester qch

certitude ['sɜːtɪtjuːd] *n Formal* certitude *f*

cerulean [sɪ'ruːljən] *adj Literary* céruléen, azuré

cerumen [sɪ'ruːmen] *n* cérumen *m*

Cervantes [sə'væntɪz] *pr n* Cervantès

cervical [sə'vaɪkəl, 'sɜːvɪkəl] *adj Anat* (**a**) *(of the cervix)* du col de l'utérus (**b**) *(of the neck)* cervical

►► ***cervical cancer*** cancer *m* du col de l'utérus; ***cervical collar*** minerve *f*; ***cervical smear*** frottis *m* vaginal; ***cervical vertebra*** vertèbre *f* cervicale

cervicitis [ˌsɜːvɪ'saɪtɪs] *n (UNCOUNT) Med* cervicite *f*

cervine ['sɜːvaɪn] *adj* du cerf

cervix ['sɜːvɪks] (*pl* **cervixes** *or* **cervices** [-siːz]) *n* (**a**) *(of uterus)* col *m* de l'utérus (**b**) *(neck)* cou *m*

Cesarean, Cesarian *Am* = **Caesarean**

cesium *Am* = **caesium**

cessation [se'seɪʃən] *n Formal* cessation *f*, suspension *f*; *Mil* **cessation of hostilities** cessation *f ou* suspension *f* des hostilités

cession ['seʃən] *n Law* cession *f*

cesspit ['sespɪt], **cesspool** ['sespuːl] *n* fosse *f* d'aisances; *Fig* cloaque *m*; **the district is a cesspit of drug dealing and prostitution** le quartier est un cloaque où règnent le trafic de drogue et la prostitution

cesura (*pl* **cesuras** *or* **cesurae** [-riː]) = **caesura**

CET [ˌsiːiː'tiː] *n* (**a**) (*abbr* **Central European Time**) heure *f* de l'Europe centrale (**b**) *EU* (*abbr* **common external tariff**) tarif *m* externe commun

cetacean [sɪ'teɪʃən] *Zool* **1** *n* cétacé *m*

2 *adj* cétacé

cetane ['siːteɪn] *n Chem* cétane *m*

►► *Chem* ***cetane number*** indice *m* de cétane

cetology [sɪ'tɒlədʒɪ] *n Zool* cétographie *f*

Cetus ['siːtəs] *n Astron* la Baleine

Ceylon [sɪ'lɒn] *n Formerly* Ceylan; **in Ceylon** à Ceylan

Ceylonese [ˌsɪlə'niːz] *Formerly* **1** *n* (**a**) *(person)* Ceylanais(e) *m,f*, Sri Lankais(e) *m,f* (**b**) *(language)* cinghalais *m*

2 *adj* ceylanais, sri lankais

CF [ˌsiː'ef] *n Am Com* (*abbr* **cost and freight**) C et F

c/f *Acct* (*written abbr* **carried forward**) reporté

cf. (*written abbr* **confer**) cf

CFC [ˌsiːefː'siː] *n Chem* (*abbr* **chlorofluorocarbon**) CFC *m*

cfi [ˌsiːef'aɪ] *n Com* (*abbr* **cost, freight and insurance**) caf, CAF

CFL [ˌsiːef'el] *n* (*abbr* **Canadian Football League**) = ligue professionnelle canadienne de football américain

CFO [ˌsiːef'əʊ] *n Am* (*abbr* **Chief Financial Officer**) chef *m* comptable, chef *m* de la comptabilité

CFR [ˌsiːef'ɑː(r)] *n Am* (*abbr* **Code of Federal Regulations**) ≃ Journal *m* officiel

CFS [ˌsiːef'es] *n Med* (*abbr* **chronic fatigue syndrome**) encéphalomyélite *f* myalgique, syndrome *m* de fatigue chronique

CFSP [ˌsiːefes'piː] *n EU* (*abbr* **Common Foreign and Security Policy**) PESC *f*

CFTC [ˌsiːef,tiː'siː] *n Fin* (*abbr* **Commodity Futures Trading Commission**) = organisme fédéral chargé de réglementer les marchés des options et des contrats à terme de marchandises aux États-Unis

CG [ˌsiː'dʒiː] *n* (*abbr* **coastguard**) garde-côte *m*

cg (*written abbr* **centigram**) cg

CGA [ˌsiːdʒiː'eɪ] *n Phot* (*abbr* **colour graphics adapter**) adaptateur *m* graphique couleur, CGA *m*

CGI [ˌsiːdʒiː'aɪ] *n Comput* (**a**) (*abbr* **common gateway interface**) interface *f* commune de passerelle, CGI *f* (**b**) (*abbr* **computer-generated images**) images *fpl* de synthèse

CGT [ˌsiːdʒiː'tiː] *n Fin* (*abbr* **capital gains tax**) impôt *m* sur les plus-values

CH [ˌsiː'eɪtʃ] *n* (**a**) (*abbr* **Companion of Honour**) = décoration britannique remise aux citoyens qui ont rendu des services à l'État, ≃ chevalier *m* de la Légion d'honneur (**b**) *Banking & Fin* (*abbr* **clearing house**) chambre *f* de compensation

ch (*written abbr* **central heating**) ch. cent

ch. (*written abbr* **chapter**) chap

cha [tʃɑː] *n Br Fam Old-fashioned* (*tea*) thé□ *m*

Chablis ['ʃæbliː] *n* chablis *m*

cha-cha(-cha) ['tʃɑːtʃɑː('tʃɑː)] **1** *n* cha-cha-cha *m inv*

2 *vi* danser le cha-cha-cha

Chad [tʃæd] *n* Tchad *m*; **in Chad** au Tchad; **Lake Chad** le lac Tchad

Chadian ['tʃædɪən] **1** *n* Tchadien(enne) *m,f*

2 *adj* tchadien

3 *comp* (*embassy, history*) du Tchad

Chadic ['tʃædɪk] *n Ling* tchadique *m*

chador ['tʃɑːdɔː(r)] *n* tchador *m*

chaebol ['tʃeɪbɒl] *n Econ* chaebol *m*

chafe [tʃeɪf] **1** *vt* (**a**) (*rub*) frictionner, frotter

(**b**) (*irritate*) frotter contre, irriter; **his shirt collar chafed his neck** son col de chemise lui irritait le cou

(**c**) (*wear away* → *collar*) élimer, user (par le frottement); (→ *paint*) érafler; (→ *rope*) raguer

2 *vi* (**a**) (*become worn* → *gen*) s'user (par le frottement); (→ *rope*) raguer

(**b**) (*skin*) s'irriter; *Fig* (*person*) s'irriter, s'impatienter; **to chafe at** *or* **under sth** s'irriter de qch; **the media chafed under the military censorship** soumis à la censure militaire, les médias rongeaient leur frein

3 *n* friction *f*, usure *f*

chafed [tʃeɪft] *adj* (**a**) (*skin*) irrité (**b**) (*worn* → *collar*) usé; (→ *paint*) éraflé; (→ *rope*) ragué

chafer ['tʃeɪfə(r)] *n Entom* hanneton *m*

chaff [tʃæf] **1** *n* (**a**) (*of grain*) balle *f*; (*hay, straw*) menue paille *f*; *Fig* **the bulk of his collected poems is mere chaff** la plupart de ses poèmes ne valent pas grand-chose (**b**) *Old-fashioned* (*teasing*) taquinerie *f*, raillerie *f* (**c**) *Electron* ruban *m* métallique antiradar

2 *vt Old-fashioned* (*tease*) taquiner

chaffinch ['tʃæfɪntʃ] *n Orn* pinson *m*

chaffing ['tʃæfɪŋ] *n Old-fashioned* taquinerie *f*, raillerie *f*

chafing ['tʃeɪfɪŋ] *n* (**a**) (*warming* → *of limbs*) friction *f* (**b**) (*of skin*) irritation *f*

▸▸ ***chafing dish*** chauffe-plats *m*

chagrin ['ʃægrɪn] **1** *n Literary* (vif) dépit *m*, (vive) déception *f ou* contrariété *f*; **much to my chagrin** à mon grand dépit

2 *vt* contrarier, décevoir

chain [tʃeɪn] **1** *n* (**a**) (*gen*) chaîne *f*; (*small* → *for medallion etc*) chaînette *f*; **we keep the dog on a chain** notre chien est toujours attaché; **to pull the chain** (*of toilet*) tirer la chasse d'eau; **to form a human chain** former une chaîne humaine; *Aut* **(snow) chains** chaînes *fpl* (à neige); *Am Fam* **to yank sb's chain** taquiner□ qn

(**b**) *Admin* **chain of office** ≃ écharpe *f* de maire

(**c**) (*of mountains*) chaîne *f*; (*of islands*) chapelet *m*

(**d**) (*of events*) série *f*, suite *f*; (*of ideas*) suite *f*

(**e**) *Com* (*of shops, restaurants*) chaîne *f*; **fast food chain** chaîne *f* de restauration rapide; **chain of distribution** circuit *m* de distribution, réseau *m* de distribution

(**f**) *Phys & Chem* chaîne *f*

(**g**) *Tech* (*for surveying*) chaîne *f* d'arpenteur

(**h**) (*unit of measurement*) 20,1 m, chaînée *f*

2 *vt also Fig* enchaîner; (*door*) mettre la chaîne à; **the dog was chained to the post** le chien était attaché au poteau (par une chaîne); **she chained herself to the railings** elle s'est enchaînée à la grille; *Fig* **to be chained to one's desk** être rivé à son bureau; *Fig* **she is chained to the kitchen sink** elle ne sort pas de sa cuisine

3 **chains** *npl* (*for prisoner*) chaînes *fpl*, entraves *fpl*; **a prisoner in chains** un prisonnier enchaîné; *Fig* **to break** *or* **burst one's chains** rompre ses chaînes

▸▸ ***chain armour*** mailles *fpl*; (*suit*) cotte *f* de mailles; *Am* ***chain bank*** banque *f* à succursales multiples; *Tech* ***chain drive*** transmission *f* par chaîne; ***chain gang*** chaîne *f* de forçats; ***chain guard*** caiter *m* (*de bicyclette*); *Aut* ***chain guide*** guide *m* chaîne; ***chain letter*** lettre *f* faisant partie d'une chaîne; ***chain lightning*** (*UNCOUNT*) éclairs *mpl* en zigzag; ***chain link*** chaînon *m ou* maillon *m* de chaîne; ***chain mail*** (*UNCOUNT*) mailles *fpl*; (*suit*) cotte *f* de mailles; *Phys, Chem & Fig* ***chain reaction*** réaction *f* en chaîne; **to set off a chain reaction** provoquer une réaction en chaîne; ***chain saw*** tronçonneuse *f*; ***chain smoker*** fumeur(euse) *m,f* invétéré(e), gros (grosse) fumeur(euse) *m,f*; ***chain stitch*** point *m* de chaînette; ***chain store*** magasin *m* à succursales (multiples); (*individual store*) succursale *f*; *Aut* ***chain tensioner*** tendeur *m* de chaîne

▸**chain down** *vt sep* enchaîner, attacher avec une chaîne

▸**chain up** *vt sep* (*prisoner*) enchaîner; (*dog*) mettre à l'attache, attacher; (*bike, gate*) mettre une chaîne à

chaining ['tʃeɪnɪŋ] *n Comput* chaînage *m*

chainlet ['tʃeɪnlɪt] *n* chaînette *f*, petite chaîne *f*

chain-smoke **1** *vt* **he chain-smokes untipped cigarettes** il fume des cigarettes sans filtre du matin au soir; **he was chain-smoking Gitanes** il fumait Gitane sur Gitane

2 *vi* fumer cigarette sur cigarette

chain-stitch **1** *vt* coudre au point de chaînette

2 *vi* coudre au point de chaînette

chainwheel ['tʃeɪnwiːl] *n Tech* roue *f* dentée (*de vélo*), pignon *m*

chair [tʃeə(r)] **1** *n* (**a**) (*seat*) chaise *f*; (*armchair*) fauteuil *m*; **in the dentist's chair** dans le fauteuil du dentiste

(**b**) (*chairperson*) président(e) *m,f*; **to be in the chair** présider; **to take the chair** prendre la présidence; **to address the chair** s'adresser au président

(**c**) *Univ* chaire *f*; **to hold the chair in French** avoir *ou* occuper la chaire de français

(**d**) *Fam* (*for execution*) **to go** *or* **to be sent to the chair, to get the chair** passer à la chaise électrique

2 *vt* (**a**) *Admin* (*meeting*) présider

(**b**) *Br* (*hero, victor*) porter en triomphe

▸▸ ***chair back*** dossier *m* de chaise; ***chair leg*** pied *m* de chaise; ***chair rail*** antibois *m*, antebois *m*

chaircover ['tʃeəˌkʌvə(r)] *n* housse *f* de fauteuil

chairlady ['tʃeəˌleɪdɪ] (*pl* **chairladies**) *n* présidente *f* (*d'un comité*)

chairlift ['tʃeəlɪft] *n* télésiège *m*

chairman ['tʃeəmən] (*pl* **chairmen** [-mən]) *n* (**a**) (*at meeting*) président *m* (*d'un comité*); **to act as chairman** présider la séance; **Mr Chairman** Monsieur le Président; **Madam Chairman** Madame la Présidente (**b**) *Com* (*of company*) président-directeur *m* général, P-D G *m*; **chairman of the board** Président du conseil (**c**) *Pol* **Chairman Mao** le président Mao

chairmanship ['tʃeəmənʃɪp] *n* présidence *f* (*d'un comité*); **under the chairmanship of Mr Black** sous la présidence de M. Black

chairperson ['tʃeəˌpɜːsən] *n* président(e) *m,f* (*d'un comité*)

chairwoman ['tʃeəˌwʊmən] (*pl* **chairwomen** [-ˌwɪmɪn]) *n* présidente *f* (*d'un comité*); **Madam Chairwoman** Madame la Présidente

chaise [ʃeɪz] *n* cabriolet *m*

▸▸ *Br* ***chaise longue***, *Am* ***chaise lounge*** méridienne *f*

chakra ['tʃækrə] *n* chakra *m*

chalaza [kə'leɪzə] *n Biol & Bot* chalaze *f*

chalcanthite ['kælkənˌθaɪt] *n Miner* cyanose *f*, chalcanthite *f*

chalcedony [kæl'sedənɪ] *n Miner* calcédoine *f*

chalcocite ['kælkəʊˌsaɪt] *n Miner* chalcocite *f*, chalcosine *f*

chalcography [kæl'kɒgrəfɪ] *n* chalcographie *f*

Chalcolithic [ˌkælkəʊ'lɪθɪk] *n Geol* chalcolitique *m*

chalcopyrite [ˌkælkəʊ'paɪraɪt] *n Geol* chalcopyrite *f*, pyrite *f* cuivreuse

Chaldaea, Chaldea [kæl'diːə] *n Geog* Chaldée *f*

Chaldaean, Chaldean [kæl'diːən] **1** *n* Chaldéen(enne) *m,f*

2 *adj* chaldéen

chalet ['ʃæleɪ] *n* chalet *m*

▸▸ ***chalet girl*** = jeune femme qui s'occupe de l'entretien d'un chalet de sports d'hiver; ***chalet park*** parc *m* résidentiel de loisirs

chalice ['tʃælɪs] *n* (**a**) *Rel* calice *m* (**b**) (*goblet*) coupe *f*

chalk [tʃɔːk] **1** *n* (**a**) (*substance*) craie *f*; (*in rock-climbing*) magnésie *f*; **a piece of chalk** un morceau de craie; *Br* **chalk and talk** = méthode d'enseignement traditionnelle; *Br* **they're as different as chalk and cheese** c'est le jour et la nuit

(**b**) (*piece*) craie *f*; **a set of coloured chalks** un assortiment de craies de couleur

(**c**) *Br* (*idiom*) **by a long chalk** de beaucoup, de loin; **not by a long chalk** loin de là, tant s'en faut; **the best by a long chalk** le meilleur, et de loin

2 *vt* (*write*) écrire à la craie; (*mark*) marquer à la craie; (*rub with chalk* → *gen*) frotter de craie; (→ *cue*) enduire de craie; **to chalk one's name on a wall** écrire son nom sur un mur à la craie; *Carp* **to chalk a line** tringler une ligne

3 *comp* (*hills, cliffs*) crayeux; (*drawing*) à la craie

▸▸ ***chalk line*** (*drawn*) trait *m* à la craie; *Carp* (*string*) cordeau *m*; (*made by string*) ligne *f* faite au cordeau

▸**chalk out** *vt sep* (*draw* → *line, pattern*) esquisser *ou* tracer (à la craie)

▸**chalk up** *vt sep* (**a**) (*write in chalk*) écrire à la craie

(**b**) (*credit*) **chalk that one up to me** mettez cela sur mon compte; *Fig* **to chalk sth up to experience** mettre qch au compte de l'expérience; **they chalked their defeat up to lack of practice** ils ont mis leur défaite sur le compte du manque d'entraînement

(**c**) (*add up* → *points, score*) totaliser, marquer

(**d**) (*attain* → *victory*) remporter; (→ *profits*) encaisser

chalkboard ['tʃɔːkbɔːd] *n Am* tableau *m* (noir)

chalkdust ['tʃɔːkdʌst] *n* poussière *f* de craie

chalkface ['tʃɔːkfeɪs] *n Hum* expérience *f* pratique (de l'enseignement)

chalkiness ['tʃɔːkɪnɪs] *n* (**a**) (*of earth, soil*) nature *f* crayeuse (**b**) (*of complexion*) extrême pâleur *f*

chalkpit ['tʃɔːkpɪt] *n* carrière *f* de craie

chalktalk ['tʃɔːktɔːk] *n Am* conférence *f*

chalky ['tʃɔːkɪ] (*compar* **chalkier**, *superl* **chalkiest**) *adj* (*earth, water*) calcaire; (*deposit*) calcique; (*hands*) couvert de craie; (*complexion*) crayeux, blafard; (*taste*) de craie; (*colour*) pâle, terreux

challenge ['tʃælɪndʒ] **1** *vt* (**a**) (*gen* → *defy*) défier; **to challenge sb** lancer un défi à qn; **to challenge sb to do sth** défier qn de faire qch; **to challenge sb to a game of tennis** inviter qn à faire une partie de tennis; **to challenge sb to a duel** provoquer qn en duel

(**b**) (*demand effort from*) mettre à l'épreuve; **she needs a job that really challenges her** elle a besoin d'un travail qui soit pour elle une gageure *ou* un challenge

(**c**) (*contest* → *authority, findings*) contester,

mettre en cause; *(→ statement)* protester contre, disputer; **to challenge sb's right to do sth** contester à qn le droit de faire qch; **their position was challenged by younger artists** leur position a été remise en question par des artistes plus jeunes
(**d**) *Mil (of sentry)* faire une sommation à
(**e**) *Law (juror)* récuser
(**f**) *Literary (require)* requérir
2 *n* (**a**) *(in contest)* défi *m*; **to issue a challenge** lancer un défi; **to take up the challenge** relever le défi; **Jackson's challenge for the leadership of the party** la tentative de Jackson pour s'emparer de la direction du parti; *Fig* **the challenge of modern technology** le défi de la technologie moderne
(**b**) *(in job, activity)* défi *m*; **to enjoy a challenge** aimer les défis; **he needs a job that presents more of a challenge** il a besoin d'un emploi plus stimulant; **the race was a great challenge to their skill** la course a été un véritable défi pour eux; **environmental problems are the major challenge for our generation** les problèmes d'environnement constituent la principale gageure *ou* le principal défi pour notre génération
(**c**) *(to right, authority)* mise *f* en question, contestation *f*; **the new law met with a challenge from the people** la nouvelle loi s'est vue contestée par le peuple
(**d**) *Mil (by sentry)* sommation *f*; **to give the challenge** faire une sommation
(**e**) *Law (of jury member)* récusation *f*
►► *Sport* ***challenge cup*** coupe-challenge *f*; *Am* ***challenge grant*** = subvention à hauteur des fonds déjà rassemblés; *Sport* ***challenge match*** challenge *m*

challenged ['tʃælɪndʒd] *adj Euph* handicapé; **visually challenged** malvoyant; *Hum* **vertically challenged** de petite taille *(expression humoristique calquée sur "visually challenged")*

challenger ['tʃælɪndʒə(r)] *n (gen)* provocateur(trice) *m,f*; *Pol & Sport* challenger *m*; *Mktg (product, company)* challengeur *m*, prétendant(e) *m,f*

challenging ['tʃælɪndʒɪŋ] *adj* (**a**) *(defiant → look, remark)* provocateur (**b**) *(demanding → ideas, theory)* provocateur, stimulant, exaltant; *(→ job, activity)* stimulant, qui met à l'épreuve; **to find oneself in a challenging situation** se trouver face à un défi

challengingly ['tʃælɪndʒɪŋlɪ] *adv* (**a**) *(defiantly)* avec défiance; **she stared challengingly back at me** elle me lança un regard lourd de défi (**b**) *(demandingly)* **it's a challengingly difficult task** c'est une tâche difficile mais exaltante

chalybite ['kælɪbaɪt] *n Miner* chalybite *f*

chamber ['tʃeɪmbə(r)] **1** *n* (**a**) *(hall, room)* chambre *f*; *Br Pol* **the upper/lower Chamber** la Chambre haute/basse
(**b**) *Arch (lodgings)* logement *m*, appartement *m*
(**c**) *(of gun)* chambre *f*
(**d**) *Anat (of the heart)* cavité *f*; *(of the eye)* chambre *f*
(**e**) *Metal (of furnace)* laboratoire *m*; *Phys (for ionization, expansion)* chambre *f*
(**f**) *(of cave)* salle *f*
(**g**) *Fam Old-fashioned (pot)* pot *m* de chambre
2 chambers *npl Law (of barrister, judge)* cabinet *m*; *(of solicitor)* cabinet *m*, étude *f*; **in chambers** en chambre du conseil; **the case was heard in chambers** l'affaire a été jugée en référé
►► ***chamber cantata*** cantatille *f*; ***chamber concert*** concert *m* de musique de chambre; ***chamber music*** musique *f* de chambre; ***Chamber of Commerce*** Chambre *f* de commerce; ***Chamber of Commerce and Industry*** Chambre *f* de commerce et d'industrie; ***the Chamber of Horrors*** = la Chambre des horreurs du musée de cire de Madame Tussaud (à Londres), spécialement consacrée aux meurtres et aux criminels célèbres; *Mus* ***chamber orchestra*** orchestre *m* de chambre; ***chamber pot*** pot *m* de chambre; *Com* ***chamber of trade*** chambre *f* des métiers

chambered ['tʃeɪmbəd] *adj (tomb, grave)* évidé, chambré; *(shell)* à loges, chambré; **six-chambered revolver** revolver *m* à six coups

chamberlain ['tʃeɪmbəlɪn] *n* chambellan *m*

chambermaid ['tʃeɪmbə,meɪd] *n* femme *f* de chambre

chambray ['ʃæmbreɪ] *n Tex* chambray *m*

chameleon [kə'miːlɪən] *n Zool & Fig* caméléon *m*

chamfer ['tʃæmfə(r)] *Carp* **1** *n* chanfrein *m*
2 *vt* (**a**) *(bevel)* chanfreiner (**b**) *(cut grooves in)* canneler

chammy ['ʃæmɪ] *(pl* **chammies***)* *n* peau *f* de chamois

chamois *(pl* **inv***)* **1** *n* (**a**) ['ʃæmwɑː] *Zool* chamois *m* (**b**) ['ʃæmɪ] *(hide)* peau *f* de chamois
2 *vt* ['ʃæmɪ] (**a**) *(leather, skin)* chamoiser (**b**) *(polish)* polir à la peau de chamois
►► ***chamois leather*** *(cloth)* peau *f* de chamois

chamomile = **camomile**

champ [tʃæmp] **1** *vt* mâchonner
2 *vi* (**a**) *(munch)* mâchonner (**b**) *(idiom)* **to champ at the bit** ronger son frein; **we were all champing at the bit to get started** on rongeait tous notre frein en attendant de commencer
3 *n* (**a**) *Fam (champion)* crack *m* (**b**) *Culin* = plat à base de purée de pommes de terre et de petits oignons blancs ou de poireaux

Champagne [,ʃæm'peɪn] *n* Champagne *f*

champagne [,ʃæm'peɪn] **1** *n* (**a**) *(wine)* champagne *m* (**b**) *(colour)* champagne *m inv*
2 *adj (colour)* champagne *(inv)*; **a champagne-coloured sofa** un canapé couleur champagne
►► ***champagne cocktail*** cocktail *m* au champagne; ***champagne flute*** flûte *f* à champagne; ***champagne glass*** *(tall)* flûte *f* à champagne; *(broad)* coupe *f* à champagne; ***champagne reception*** réception *f* avec champagne; ***champagne socialism*** la gauche caviar; ***champagne socialist*** membre *m* de la gauche caviar

champaign ['ʃæmpeɪn] *n Literary* campagne *f* ouverte

champers ['ʃæmpəz] *n Br Fam* champ' *m*

champerty ['tʃæmpətɪ] *n Law* pacte *m* de quota litis

champion ['tʃæmpjən] **1** *n* (**a**) *(winner)* champion(onne) *m,f*; **the world chess champion** le champion du monde d'échecs; **she's a champion runner** elle est championne de course
(**b**) *(supporter)* champion(onne) *m,f*; **he's a self-proclaimed champion of the working man** il se veut le champion des travailleurs
2 *vt* défendre, soutenir; **she championed the cause of birth control** elle s'est faite la championne de la régulation des naissances
3 *adj Scot & NEng Fam (very good)* super
►► *Ftbl* ***the Champions' League*** la Ligue des Champions

championship ['tʃæmpjənʃɪp] *n* (**a**) *(contest)* championnat *m*; **he plays championship tennis** il participe aux championnats de tennis (**b**) *(support)* défense *f*
►► ***championship match*** match *m* de championnat

CHANCE [tʃɑːns]

chance(s)	►1 (a); 5 (a)
hasard	►1 (b)
occasion	►1 (c)
risque(s)	►1 (d); 5 (b)
fortuit	►2
hasarder	►4

1 *n* (**a**) *(possibility, likelihood)* chance *f*; **is there any chance of seeing you again?** serait-il possible de vous revoir?; **there was little chance of him finding work** il y avait peu de chances qu'il trouve du travail; **we have an outside chance of success** nous avons une très faible chance de réussir; **she's got a good** *or* **strong chance of being accepted** elle a de fortes chances d'être acceptée *ou* reçue; **there's a fifty-fifty chance he won't turn up** il y a une chance sur deux qu'il ne vienne pas; *Fam* **no chance!** des clous!; **he's in with a chance of getting the job** il a une chance d'obtenir le poste
(**b**) *(fortune, luck)* hasard *m*; **games of chance** les jeux *mpl* de hasard; **there was an element of chance in his success** il y a eu une part de hasard dans sa réussite; **it was pure chance that I found it** je l'ai trouvé tout à fait par hasard; **to leave things to chance** laisser faire les choses; **to leave nothing to chance** ne rien laisser au hasard; *Fam* **chance would be a fine thing!** ah, si seulement je pouvais/il pouvait/*etc*!
(**c**) *(opportunity)* occasion *f*; **I haven't had a chance to write to him** je n'ai pas trouvé l'occasion de lui écrire; **give him a chance!** donne-lui une chance!; **give her a chance to defend herself** donnez-lui l'occasion de se défendre; **give peace a chance** la paix est possible, donnez-lui *ou* laissez-lui sa chance; **it's a chance in a million** c'est une occasion unique; **I'm offering you the chance of a lifetime** je vous offre la chance de votre vie; **the poor man never had** *or* **stood a chance** le pauvre homme n'avait aucune chance de s'en tirer; **some children simply don't get a chance in life** pour certains enfants il n'y a tout simplement aucun avenir; **this is your last chance** c'est votre dernière chance; **she deserves a second chance** elle mérite une deuxième chance; **there are no second chances, there is no second chance** tu n'as pas droit à l'erreur; **he was thrown out before he had a chance to protest** il a été évincé avant même d'avoir eu l'occasion de protester; *Fam* **given half a chance she'd play tennis every day** si elle pouvait elle jouerait au tennis tous les jours
(**d**) *(risk)* risque *m*; **I don't want to take the chance of losing** je ne veux pas prendre le risque de perdre; **I'm taking no chances** je ne veux pas prendre de risques; **he took a chance on a racehorse** il a parié sur un cheval de course; *Fig* **take a chance on me** donne-moi une chance
2 *adj (encounter, meeting)* fortuit; **chance discovery** découverte *f* accidentelle *ou* fortuite; **I was a chance witness to the robbery** j'ai été un témoin accidentel du vol
3 *vi Formal or Literary (happen)* **I chanced to be at the same table as Sir Sydney** je me suis trouvé par hasard à la même table que Sir Sydney; **it chanced that no one else had heard of her** il s'est trouvé que personne d'autre n'avait entendu parler d'elle
4 *vt (risk) Literary* hasarder; **he chanced his savings on the venture** il a risqué ses économies dans l'entreprise; **I can't chance her finding out about it** je ne peux pas prendre le risque qu'elle l'apprenne; **she chanced going out despite the curfew** elle s'est hasardée à sortir malgré le couvre-feu; **let's chance it** *or* **our luck** tentons notre chance; *Fam* **to chance one's arm** *(take a risk)* risquer le coup; *(push one's luck)* exagérer, pousser
5 chances *npl* (**a**) *(possibility, likelihood)* chances *fpl*; **(the) chances are (that) he'll never find out** il y a de fortes *ou* grandes chances qu'il ne l'apprenne jamais; **what are her chances of making a full recovery?** quelles sont ses chances de se rétablir complètement?
(**b**) *(risks)* risques *mpl*; **she was taking no chances** elle ne prenait pas de risques
6 by chance *adv* par hasard; **by pure** *or* **sheer chance we were both staying at the same hotel** il se trouvait que nous logions au même hôtel; **would you by any chance know who that man is?** sauriez-vous par hasard qui est cet homme?
►**chance on, chance upon** *vt insep (person)* rencontrer par hasard; *(thing)* trouver par hasard

chancel ['tʃɑːnsəl] *n Archit* chœur *m*
►► ***chancel screen*** jubé *m*

chancellery ['tʃɑːnsələrɪ] *(pl* **chancelleries***)* *n* chancellerie *f*

chancellor ['tʃɑːnsələ(r)] *n* (**a**) *Pol* chancelier *m* (**b**) *Univ (in UK)* président(e) *m,f* honoraire; *(in US)* président(e) *m,f* (d'université)
►► ***Chancellor of the Exchequer*** Chancelier *m* de l'Échiquier, ≃ ministre *m* des Finances *(en Grande-Bretagne)*

chancellorship ['tʃɑːnsələʃɪp] *n* (**a**) *Pol* direction *f* des finances; **the economy had done extremely well under Mr Smith's chancellorship** l'économie avait montré d'excellents résultats lorsque M. Smith était au ministère des Finances (**b**) *Univ* présidence *f* (d'université)

chancer ['tʃɑːnsə(r)] *n Br Fam* filou *m*

chancery ['tʃɑːnsərɪ] *(pl* **chanceries***)* *n* (**a**) *Law (in UK)* **the suit is in chancery** l'action est en instance; **Chancery (Division)** cour *f* de la chancellerie *(une des trois divisions de la Haute cour de justice en Angleterre)*; **ward in chancery** pupille *mf* de l'État (**b**) *Law (in US)* **Court of Chancery** ≃ cour *f* d'équité (**c**) *Sport (in wrestling)* clé *f*, clef *f*

chancre ['ʃæŋkə(r)] *n Med* chancre *m*

chancroid ['ʃænkrɔɪd] *n Med* chancrelle *f*, chancre *m* mou

chancy ['tʃɑːnsɪ] *(compar* **chancier,** *superl* **chanciest)** *adj Fam* risqué[□]

chandelier [ˌʃændə'lɪə(r)] *n* lustre *m (pour éclairer)*

chandler ['tʃɑːndlə(r)] *n* (**a**) *(supplier)* fournisseur *m*; **ship's chandler** shipchandler *m* (**b**) *(candlemaker)* chandelier *m*

CHANGE [tʃeɪndʒ]

changement	▸ **1 (a), (c)**
correspondance	▸ **1 (c)**
monnaie	▸ **1 (d)**
changer	▸ **2; 3 (a), (d)**
se changer	▸ **3 (b), (c)**

1 *n* (**a**) *(alteration)* changement *m*; **we expect a change in the weather** nous nous attendons à un changement de temps; **there's been a change in the law** la loi a été modifiée; **there has been a change in thinking regarding nuclear power** il y a eu un changement d'opinion *ou* une évolution de l'opinion concernant l'énergie nucléaire; **a survey showed a radical change in public opinion** un sondage a montré un revirement de l'opinion publique; **the party needs a change of direction** le parti a besoin d'un changement de direction *ou* d'orientation; **a change for the better/worse** un changement en mieux/pire, une amélioration/dégradation; **walking to work makes a pleasant change from driving** c'est agréable d'aller travailler à pied plutôt qu'en voiture; **it'll be** *or* **make a nice change for them not to have the children in the house** cela les changera agréablement de ne pas avoir les enfants à la maison; **that makes a change!** ça change un peu!; **yes, it makes a nice change, doesn't it?** oui, ça change un peu de l'ordinaire, n'est-ce pas?; **living in the country will be a big change for us** cela nous changera beaucoup de vivre à la campagne; **there's been little change in his condition** son état n'a guère évolué; **she dislikes change of any kind** tout changement lui déplaît; **there are going to be some changes in this office!** il va y avoir du nouveau *ou* du changement dans ce bureau!; **to have a change of heart** changer d'avis; *Fig* **I need a change of scene** *or* **scenery** j'ai besoin de changer de décor *ou* d'air; **a change is as good as a rest** changer de décor fait autant de bien que de partir en vacances

(**b**) *(fresh set or supply)* **a change of clothes** des vêtements de rechange; **he had to spend a week without a change of clothes** il a dû passer une semaine sans changer de vêtements

(**c**) *(in journey)* changement *m*, correspondance *f*; **if you go by underground you'll have to make two changes** si vous y allez en métro vous serez obligé de changer deux fois; **you can get there by train with a change at Bristol** vous pouvez y aller en train avec un changement *ou* une correspondance à Bristol

(**d**) *(money)* monnaie *f*; **small** *or* **loose change** petite *ou* menue monnaie *f*; **she gave me two pounds in change** elle m'a donné deux livres en monnaie; **can you give me change for five pounds?** pouvez-vous me faire la monnaie de cinq livres?; **the machine doesn't give change** la machine ne rend pas la monnaie; *Br Fam* **you'll get no change out of him** on ne peut rien en tirer

(**e**) *Euph* **the change** *(menopause)* le retour d'âge

(**f**) *Arch (market)* marché *m*

2 *vt* (**a**) *(substitute, switch)* changer, changer de; **to change one's name** changer de nom; **she's going to change her name to Parker** elle va prendre le nom de Parker; **to change a fuse** changer un fusible; **to change one's clothes** changer de vêtements, se changer; **to change trains** changer de train; **they're going to change the guard at 11 o'clock** ils vont faire la relève de *ou* relever la garde à 11 heures; **to change sides** changer de côté; *Sport* **to change ends** changer de camp; **this old desk has changed hands many times** ce vieux bureau a changé maintes fois de mains; **to change one's mind** changer d'avis; **I've changed my mind about him** j'ai changé d'avis *ou* d'idée à son égard; **he's changed his mind about moving to Scotland** pour ce qui est de s'installer en Écosse il a changé d'avis; **you'd better change your ways** tu ferais bien de t'amender; **to change the subject** changer de sujet; **don't change the subject!** ne détourne pas la conversation!; **to change one's tune** changer de ton

(**b**) *(exchange)* changer; **when are you thinking of changing your car?** quand pensez-vous changer de voiture?; **if the shoes are too small we'll change them for you** si les chaussures sont trop petites nous vous les changerons; **to change places with sb** changer de place avec qn; *Fig* **I wouldn't want to change places with him!** je n'aimerais pas être à sa place!; **I'd like to change my pounds into dollars** j'aimerais changer mes livres contre des *ou* en dollars; **does this bank change money?** est-ce que cette banque fait le change?; **can you change a ten-pound note?** *(into coins)* pouvez-vous me donner la monnaie d'un billet de dix livres?

(**c**) *(alter, modify)* changer; **there's no point in trying to change him** c'est inutile d'essayer de le changer; **she wants to change the world** elle veut changer le monde; **he won't change anything in the text** il ne changera rien au texte; **the illness completely changed his personality** la maladie a complètement transformé son caractère; **she doesn't want to change her routine in any way** elle ne veut rien changer à sa routine; *Fig* **to change one's spots** changer *ou* modifier totalement son caractère

(**d**) *(transform)* changer, transformer; **to change sb/sth into sth** changer qn/qch en qch; **the prince was changed into a frog** le prince fut changé en grenouille; *Bible* **to change water into wine** changer l'eau en vin; **the liquid/her hair has changed colour** le liquide a/ses cheveux ont changé de couleur

(**e**) *(baby, bed)* changer; **the baby needs changing** le bébé a besoin d'être changé; **I've changed the sheets** j'ai changé les draps

(**f**) **to change gear** changer de vitesse

3 *vi* (**a**) *(alter, turn)* changer; *(luck, wind)* tourner; **to change for the better/worse** changer en mieux/pire; **nothing will make him change** rien ne le changera, il ne changera jamais; **wait for the lights to change** attendez que le feu passe au vert; **winter changed to spring** le printemps a succédé à l'hiver; **the wind has changed** le vent a changé *ou* tourné

(**b**) *(become transformed)* se changer, se transformer; **to change into sth** se transformer en qch; **the ogre changed into a mouse** l'ogre s'est transformé en souris; **the country had changed from dictatorship to democracy overnight** en une nuit, le pays était passé de la dictature à la démocratie; **the lights changed from green to amber** les feux sont passés du vert à l'orange; **to change from one system to another** passer d'un système à un autre

(**c**) *(change clothing)* se changer; **she's gone upstairs to change** elle est montée se changer; **they changed out of their uniforms** ils ont enlevé leurs uniformes; **he changed into a pair of jeans** il s'est changé et a mis un jean; **I'm going to change into something warmer** je vais mettre quelque chose de plus chaud

(**d**) *(transportation)* changer; **is it a direct flight or do I have to change?** est-ce que le vol est direct ou faut-il changer?; **we had to change twice** nous avons eu deux correspondances *ou* deux changements; **all change!** *(announcement)* tout le monde descend!

(**e**) *Br* **she changed into fourth gear** elle a passé la quatrième

(**f**) *(moon)* entrer dans une nouvelle phase

4 for a change *adv* **it's nice to see you smiling for a change** c'est bien de te voir sourire pour une fois; **he was early for a change** pour une fois il était en avance

▸▸ ***the change of life*** le retour d'âge; ***change machine*** distributeur *m* de monnaie; *Am* ***change purse*** porte-monnaie *m inv*

▸**change down** *vi Aut* rétrograder; **he changed down into third** il est passé en troisième

▸**change off** *vi Am (swap)* échanger; **to change off with sb** échanger avec qn

▸**change over** *vi* (**a**) *Br (switch)* **he changed over from smoking cigarettes to smoking cigars** il s'est mis à fumer des cigares à la place de cigarettes; **the country has changed over to nuclear power** le pays est passé au nucléaire; **one day I wash and he dries and the next day we change over** un jour je fais la vaisselle et il l'essuie et le jour d'après on change; *TV* **to change over (to another channel)** passer sur une autre chaîne; *TV* **why don't you change over to ITV?** et si on mettait ITV?

(**b**) *Sport (change positions)* changer de côté

▸**change up** *vi Aut* passer la vitesse supérieure; **he changed up into third** il a passé la troisième, il est passé en troisième

'Changing Places' *Lodge* 'Changement de décor'

changeability [ˌtʃeɪndʒə'bɪlɪtɪ] *n* (**a**) *(variability)* variabilité *f* (**b**) *(capricious, fickleness)* changements *mpl*

changeable ['tʃeɪndʒəbəl] *adj* (**a**) *(variable)* variable; **changeable weather** temps *m* variable *ou* instable (**b**) *(capricious, fickle)* changeant, inconstant

changeableness ['tʃeɪndʒəbəlnɪs] *n* (**a**) *(variability)* variabilité *f* (**b**) *(capricious, fickleness)* changements *mpl*

changed [tʃeɪndʒd] *adj* changé, différent; **he's a changed man** c'est un autre homme

changeless ['tʃeɪndʒlɪs] *adj* immuable, inaltérable

changeling ['tʃeɪndʒlɪŋ] *n* = enfant substitué par les fées au véritable enfant d'un couple

changemaker ['tʃeɪndʒˌmeɪkə(r)] *n Am (machine)* distributeur *m* de monnaie

changeover ['tʃeɪndʒˌəʊvə(r)] *n* (**a**) *(switch)* changement *m*, passage *m*; *(after election)* relève *f*; **in Australia the changeover from pounds to dollars took place in 1966** en Australie le changement monétaire qui a remplacé la livre par le dollar a eu lieu en 1966; **the changeover to computers went smoothly** le passage à l'informatisation s'est fait en douceur (**b**) *Br Sport* changement *m* de côté; *(in relay race)* passage *m* du témoin

change-ringing *n* = manière particulière de sonner les cloches, notamment dans les églises anglicanes

changing ['tʃeɪndʒɪŋ] **1** *adj* qui change; **we're living in a changing world** nous vivons dans un monde en évolution

2 *n* changement *m*

▸▸ ***the Changing of the Guard*** la relève de la garde; *Br* ***changing room*** *(in sports centre, gym)* vestiaire *m*; *(in shop)* cabine *f* d'essayage; ***changing table*** table *f* à langer

channel ['tʃænəl] *(Br pt & pp* **channelled,** *cont* **channelling**, *Am pt & pp* **channeled**, *cont* **channelling)** **1** *n* (**a**) *(broad strait)* détroit *m*, bras *m* de mer; **the Channel** la Manche; **a Channel ferry** un ferry qui traverse la Manche

(**b**) *(river bed)* lit *m*; *Naut (navigable course)* chenal *m*, passe *f*

(**c**) *(passage → for gases, liquids)* canal *m*, conduite *f*; *(→ for electrical signals)* piste *f*

(**d**) *(furrow, groove)* sillon *m*; *(on a column)* cannelure *f*; *(in a street)* caniveau *m*

(**e**) *TV* chaîne *f*; **the film is on Channel 2** le film est sur la deuxième chaîne

(**f**) *Rad* bande *f*

(**g**) *Fig (means)* canal *m*, voie *f*; **to go through (the) official channels** suivre la filière officielle; **they tried to obtain his release through diplomatic channels** ils ont essayé d'obtenir sa libération par voie diplomatique; **channels of communication** canaux *mpl* de communication; **there were still channels of communication open** la communication n'était pas totalement interrompue; **the government has**

suppressed all channels of dissent le gouvernement a supprimé tout moyen d'expression de la dissidence

(**h**) *Comput (of communication, data flow, for IRC)* canal *m*

2 *vt* (**a**) *(land)* creuser des rigoles dans; *(river)* canaliser; *(street)* construire des caniveaux dans; *(gas, water)* acheminer (par des conduites); *(column)* canneler; **the water channelled its way through the cliff** l'eau a creusé une rigole dans la falaise

(**b**) *Fig (direct)* canaliser, diriger; **the government wants to channel resources to those who need them most** le gouvernement veut affecter les ressources en priorité à ceux qui en ont le plus besoin; **she needs to channel her energies into some useful work** elle a besoin de canaliser son énergie à effectuer du travail utile

►► *Com* ***channel of distribution*** circuit *m* de distribution, canal *m* de distribution; ***Channel Four*** = chaîne de télévision privée britannique à vocation culturelle; ***Channel Five*** = chaîne de télévision privée britannique; *Br Fam* ***channel hopping*** zapping *m*; ***Channel Islander*** = habitant des îles Anglo-Normandes; ***the Channel Islands*** les îles *fpl* Anglo-Normandes; **in the Channel Islands** dans les îles Anglo-Normandes; *Fam* ***channel surfing*** zapping *m*; ***the Channel Tunnel*** le tunnel sous la Manche, l'Eurotunnel *m*

►**channel off** *vt sep* canaliser

channel-hop, channel-surf *vi Fam* zapper

chant [tʃɑːnt] **1** *n* (**a**) *Mus* mélopée *f*; *Rel* psalmodie *f* (**b**) *(slogan, cry)* chant *m* scandé

2 *vt* (**a**) *Mus* chanter; *Rel* psalmodier (**b**) *(slogans)* scander

3 *vi* (**a**) *Mus* chanter une mélopée; *Rel* psalmodier (**b**) *(crowd, demonstrators)* scander des slogans

chanterelle [ʃɒntə'rel] *n* **chanterelle (mushroom)** chanterelle *f*

chantey = **shanty**

chanticleer ['tʃæntɪklɪə(r)] *n Literary* chantecler *m*

chanting ['tʃɑːntɪŋ] **1** *adj (voice)* monotone, traînant

2 *n* (**a**) *Mus* mélopée *f*; *Rel* chants *mpl*, psalmodie *f* (**b**) *(of slogans)* slogans *mpl* (scandés)

chantry ['tʃɑːntrɪ] *n Arch Rel* chantrerie *f*, chanterie *f*

chanty (*pl* **chanties**) = **shanty**

Chanukkhah ['hɑːnəkə] *n Rel* Hanukkah *f*

chaos ['keɪɒs] *n* chaos *m*; **it'll be chaos if you try to introduce these changes** ça va être la pagaille si tu fais ces changements; **the country is in a state of chaos** le pays est dans un état de confusion totale; **our plans were thrown into chaos** nos projets ont été bouleversés

►► ***chaos theory*** théorie *f* du chaos

chaotic [keɪ'ɒtɪk] *adj* chaotique

chaotically [keɪ'ɒtɪklɪ] *adv* chaotiquement; **clothes all chaotically piled into one drawer** vêtements tous mis en pagaille dans un tiroir

chap [tʃæp] (*pt & pp* **chapped**, *cont* **chapping**) **1** *n* (**a**) *Br Fam (man)* type *m*; **he's a nice chap** c'est un brave type; **be a good chap and tell him I'm not in** sois sympa et dis-lui que je ne suis pas là; **you chaps have made a big mistake** messieurs, vous avez fait une grave erreur; **what do you think, chaps?** qu'en pensez-vous, les amis?; **he's gone broke, poor chap** il a fait faillite, le pauvre; *Old-fashioned* **how are you, old chap?** comment allez-vous, mon vieux?

(**b**) *(sore)* gerçure *f*, crevasse *f*

(**c**) *Scot & NEng (knock)* coup *m*; **there was a chap on the door** on a frappé

2 *vt* (**a**) *(skin)* gercer, crevasser

(**b**) *Scot & NEng (knock)* **to chap the door/window** frapper à la porte/au carreau

3 *vi* (**a**) *(skin)* (se) gercer, se crevasser

(**b**) *Scot & NEng (knock)* frapper; **to chap on** *or* **at the door** frapper (à la porte)

chaparral [ʃæpə'ræl] *n* chaparal *m*, chaparral *m*

chapati, chapatti [tʃə'pætɪ] *n Culin* galette *f* de pain indienne

chapel ['tʃæpəl] *n* (**a**) *(in church, school etc)* chapelle *f* (**b**) *Br (Nonconformist church)* temple *m*; *Scot (Catholic church)* église *f* catholique (**c**) *Br (of trade unionists)* = membres du syndicat dans une maison d'édition ou la rédaction d'un journal

►► *Rel* ***chapel of ease*** église *f* succursale; ***chapel of love*** = lieu où l'on célèbre des mariages rapides aux États-Unis; ***chapel of rest*** = chambre mortuaire dans une entreprise de pompes funèbres

chaperon, chaperone ['ʃæpərəʊn] **1** *n* chaperon *m*; **her aunt acted as her chaperone** sa tante lui servait de chaperon

2 *vt* chaperonner; *Fam* **don't worry, I'll chaperone you!** ne t'inquiète pas, je te servirai de chaperon

chaplain ['tʃæplɪn] *n* aumônier *m*; *(in private chapel)* chapelain *m*

chaplaincy ['tʃæplɪnsɪ] **1** *n* aumônerie *f*

2 *comp (work, duties)* de l'aumônier

chaplet ['tʃæplɪt] *n* (**a**) *(wreath)* guirlande *f* (**b**) *Rel* chapelet *m*

Chappaquiddick [tʃæpə'kwɪdɪk] *n* **the Chappaquiddick incident** l'affaire *f* de Chappaquiddick *(accident ayant coûté la vie, en 1973, à Mary-Jo Kopechne, collaboratrice du sénateur américain Edward Kennedy, dans des circonstances mal élucidées)*

chapped [tʃæpt] *adj (hands, lips)* gercé; **he has chapped lips** il a les lèvres gercées; **your hands will get chapped in this weather** vous aurez les mains gercées par ce temps

chappie ['tʃæpɪ] *Old-fashioned* = **chap** *n* (**a**)

CHAPS [tʃæps] *n Br Banking* (*abbr* **clearing house automated payment system**) ≃ SIT *m*

chaps [tʃæps] *npl (leggings)* jambières *fpl* de cuir

chapstick ['tʃæpstɪk] *n* bâton *m* de pommade pour les lèvres

chapter ['tʃæptə(r)] *n* (**a**) *(of book)* chapitre *m*; **it's in chapter three** c'est dans le troisième chapitre; **she can give** *or* **quote (you) chapter and verse on the subject** elle peut citer toutes les autorités en la matière; *Am Fin* **chapter 11** *(part of bankruptcy laws)* = ensemble de dispositions légales régissant la procédure de redressement judiciaire; *Am Fin* **to file for Chapter 11** faire une demande de redressement judiciaire

(**b**) *(era)* chapitre *m*; **this closed a particularly violent chapter in our history** ceci marqua la fin d'un chapitre particulièrement violent de notre histoire

(**c**) *(series)* succession *f*, cascade *f*; **a chapter of accidents** une série d'accidents *ou* de malheurs, une série noire

(**d**) *(of organization)* branche *f*, section *f*

(**e**) *Rel* chapitre *m*

►► *Rel* ***chapter house*** salle *f* capitulaire

char [tʃɑː(r)] (*pt & pp* **charred**, *cont* **charring**) **1** *vt* (**a**) *(reduce to charcoal)* carboniser, réduire en charbon

(**b**) *(scorch)* griller, brûler légèrement

2 *vi* (**a**) *(scorch)* brûler; *(blacken)* noircir

(**b**) *Br Fam Old-fashioned (clean)* faire des ménages ❑; **she had to go out charring to support her family** elle a dû faire des ménages pour faire vivre sa famille

3 *n* (**a**) *Fam Old-fashioned (cleaner)* femme *f* de ménage ❑

(**b**) *Br Fam Old-fashioned (tea)* thé ❑ *m*

(**c**) *Ich* omble *m* chevalier

charabanc ['ʃærəbæŋ] *n Old-fashioned* autocar *m* (de tourisme)

characin ['kærəsɪn] *n Ich* characin *m*

character ['kærəktə(r)] **1** *n* (**a**) *(nature, temperament)* caractère *m*; **the war completely changed his character** la guerre a complètement transformé son caractère; **is there such a thing as national character?** la notion de caractère national existe-t-elle?; **his remark was quite in/out of character** cette remarque lui ressemblait tout à fait/ne lui ressemblait pas du tout

(**b**) *(aspect, quality)* caractère *m*; **it was the vindictive character of the punishment she objected to** c'était le caractère vindicatif du châtiment qu'elle désapprouvait

(**c**) *(determination, integrity)* caractère *m*; **she's a woman of great character** c'est une femme qui a beaucoup de caractère; **he lacks character** il manque de caractère

(**d**) *(distinction, originality)* caractère *m*; **to have character** avoir du caractère; **the house had (great) character** la maison avait beaucoup de caractère; **her face is full of character** son visage a beaucoup de caractère

(**e**) *(unusual person)* personnage *m*; **he's a bit of a character** c'est un personnage; **she seems to attract all sorts of characters** elle semble attirer toutes sortes d'individus; **he's quite a character!** c'est un phénomène *ou* un sacré numéro!

(**f**) *Pej (person)* individu *m*; **there's a suspicious character loitering outside** il y a un individu suspect qui rôde dehors

(**g**) *Cin, Literature & Theat* personnage *m*; **the main character** le personnage principal, le protagoniste; **Chaplin plays two different characters in 'The Great Dictator'** Chaplin joue deux rôles différents dans 'Le Dictateur'

(**h**) *Typ* caractère *m*; **in Greek characters** en caractères grecs; *Typ & Comput* **characters per inch** caractères *mpl* par pouce; *Typ & Comput* **characters per second** caractères *mpl* par seconde

(**i**) *Literary (handwriting)* écriture *f*

(**j**) *Br Old-fashioned (written reference)* références *fpl*

►► *Cin & Theat* ***character actor*** acteur *m* de genre; *Cin & Theat* ***character actress*** actrice *f* de genre; ***character assassination*** diffamation *f*; *Comput* ***character code*** code *m* de caractère; *Comput* ***character generator*** générateur *m* de caractères; *Comput* ***character insert*** insertion *f* de caractère; *Mktg* ***character licensing*** cession *f* de licence sur un personnage; *Cin & Theat* ***character part*** rôle *m* de composition; *Comput* ***character recognition*** reconnaissance *f* de caractères; *Br* ***character reference*** références *fpl*; *Cin & Theat* ***character role*** rôle *m* de composition; *Comput* ***character set*** jeu *m* de caractères; ***character sketch*** portrait *m* ou description *f* rapide; *Comput* ***character smoothing*** lissage *m* de caractères; *Comput* ***character space*** espace *m*; *Comput* ***character spacing*** espacement *m* des caractères; *Law* ***character witness*** témoin *m* de moralité

character-forming, *Br* **character-building** *adj* qui forme le caractère; **it's character-forming** ça forme le caractère

characterful ['kærəktəfʊl] *adj* plein de caractère

characteristic [ˌkærəəktə'rɪstɪk] **1** *adj* caractéristique; **she refused all honours with characteristic humility** elle refusa tous les honneurs avec l'humilité qui la caractérisait; **this attitude is characteristic of him** cette attitude lui correspond bien, c'est bien de lui

2 *n* (**a**) *(feature)* caractéristique *f*; **national characteristics** les caractères *mpl* nationaux (**b**) *Math (of logarithm)* caractéristique *f*

characteristically [ˌkærəktə'rɪstɪklɪ] *adv* de façon caractéristique; **he was characteristically generous with his praise** comme on pouvait s'y attendre, il fut prodigue de ses compliments *ou* il ne ménagea pas ses éloges; **characteristically, she put her family first** elle fit passer sa famille en premier, ce qui était bien dans son caractère *ou* lui ressemblait bien

characterization [ˌkærəktəraɪ'zeɪʃən] *n* (**a**) *Formal (description)* caractérisation *f* (**b**) *Cin, Literature & Theat* représentation *f ou* peinture *f* des personnages; **he's very poor at characterization** *(writer)* ses personnages ne sont pas très convaincants; *(actor)* il n'a aucun talent pour l'interprétation

characterize, -ise ['kærəktəraɪz] *vt* caractériser; **his music is characterized by a sense of joy** sa musique se caractérise par une impression de joie; **the speaker characterized apartheid as utterly immoral** le conférencier qualifia l'apartheid de totalement immoral; **Shakespeare characterized Henry VI as a weak but pious king** Shakespeare a dépeint Henri VI comme un roi faible mais pieux; **the long pauses that characterize his speech** les longs silences qui caractérisent son discours

characterless ['kærəktəlɪs] *adj* sans caractère

charade [ʃə'rɑːd] **1** *n (pretence)* feinte *f*; **the trial was a complete charade!** c'était une véritable parodie de procès!

2 charades *npl (game)* charade *f* en action; **let's play charades** jouons aux charades

char-broil *vt Am Culin* griller au charbon de bois

char-broiled *adj Am Culin* grillé au charbon de bois

charcoal ['tʃɑːkəʊl] **1** *n* (**a**) *(fuel)* charbon *m* de bois (**b**) *Art* fusain *m*; **he drew her in charcoal** il l'a dessinée au fusain (**c**) *(colour)* gris *m* foncé *(inv)*

2 *adj* gris foncé *(inv)*

3 *comp* (**a**) *(fuel)* à charbon (**b**) *Art* au charbon, au fusain

►► ***charcoal artist*** fusainiste *mf*; ***charcoal burner*** charbonnier *m*; ***charcoal crayon*** fusain *m*; ***charcoal drawing*** croquis au fusain; ***charcoal grey*** gris *m* foncé *inv*; ***charcoal pencil*** crayon fusain; ***charcoal stove*** réchaud à charbon de bois

charcoal-broiled *adj Am Culin* grillé au charbon de bois

charcoal-grey *adj* gris foncé *(inv)*

charcoal-grilled *adj Culin* grillé au charbon de bois

chard [tʃɑːd] *n Bot & Culin* blette *f*, bette *inv*

Chardonnay ['ʃɑːdəˌneɪ] *n (wine)* chardonay *m*, chardonnay *m*

CHARGE [tʃɑːdʒ]

frais	►1 (a)
inculpation	►1 (b)
accusation	►1 (c)
responsabilité	►1 (d)
charge	►1 (e), (g), (h)
faire payer	►2 (a)
accuser	►2 (c)
inculper	►2 (d)
charger	►2 (e), (g) – (i); 3 (b), (c)

1 *n* (**a**) *Com & Fin (fee, cost)* frais *mpl*; *(to an account)* imputation *f*; **administrative charges** frais *mpl* de dossier; **postal/telephone charges** frais *mpl* postaux/téléphoniques; **there's a charge of one pound for use of the locker** il faut payer une livre pour utiliser la consigne automatique; **is there any extra charge for a single room?** est-ce qu'il faut payer un supplément pour une chambre à un lit?; **what's the charge for delivery?** la livraison coûte combien?; **there's no charge for children** c'est gratuit pour les enfants; **it's free of charge** c'est gratuit; **there's a small admission charge to the museum** il y a un petit droit d'entrée au musée; *Am* **will that be cash or charge?** vous payez comptant ou vous le portez à votre compte?

(**b**) *Law (accusation)* chef *m* d'accusation, inculpation *f*; *(judge's address to the jury)* réquisitoire *m*; **he was arrested on a charge of conspiracy** il a été arrêté sous l'inculpation d'association criminelle; **you are under arrest – on what charge?** vous êtes en état d'arrestation – pour quel motif?; **to bring** *or* **file charges against sb** porter plainte *ou* déposer une plainte contre qn; **a charge of drunk driving was brought against the driver** le conducteur a été mis en examen pour conduite en état d'ivresse; **the judge threw out the charge** le juge a retiré l'inculpation; **she was acquitted on both charges** elle a été acquittée des deux chefs d'inculpation; **some of the charges may be dropped** certains des chefs d'accusation pourraient être retirés; **he pleaded guilty to the charge of robbery** il a plaidé coupable à l'accusation de vol; **they will have to answer** *or* **face charges of fraud** ils auront à répondre à l'accusation d'escroquerie; **she's laying herself open to charges of favouritism** on risque de l'accuser de favoritisme

(**c**) *(allegation)* accusation *f*; **the government rejected charges that it was mismanaging the economy** le gouvernement a rejeté l'accusation selon laquelle il gérait mal l'économie; **charges of torture have been brought** *or* **made against the regime** des accusations de torture ont été portées contre le régime

(**d**) *(command, control)* **who's (the person) in charge here?** qui est le responsable ici?; **she's in charge of public relations** elle s'occupe des relations publiques; **can I leave you in charge of the shop?** puis-je vous laisser la responsabilité du magasin?; **she was in charge of consumer protection** elle était responsable de la protection des consommateurs; **I was put in charge of the investigation** on m'a confié la responsabilité de l'enquête; **he was put in charge of 100 men** on a mis 100 hommes sous sa responsabilité; **to take charge of sth** prendre en charge qch, prendre *ou* assumer la direction de qch; **she took charge of organizing the festival** elle a pris en charge l'organisation du festival; **he took charge of his nephew** il a pris son neveu en charge; **he had a dozen salesmen under his charge** il avait une douzaine de vendeurs sous sa responsabilité

(**e**) *Formal (burden)* **to be a charge on sb** être une charge pour qn; **she refused to be a charge on her family/the State** elle refusa d'être une charge pour sa famille/d'être à la charge de l'État

(**f**) *Formal (dependent)* = personne confiée à la garde d'une autre; *(pupil)* élève *mf*; **the governess instructed her two charges in French and Italian** la gouvernante apprit le français et l'italien à ses deux élèves; **the nanny is out for a walk with her charges** la nourrice est partie se promener avec les enfants qu'elle garde *ou* dont elle a la charge

(**g**) *(duty, mission)* charge *f*; **he was given the charge of preparing the defence** on l'a chargé de préparer la défense; *Law* **the judge's charge to the jury** les recommandations du juge au jury

(**h**) *Mil (attack)* charge *f*; **soldiers made several charges against the demonstrators** les soldats ont chargé les manifestants à plusieurs reprises

(**i**) *Elec & Phys* charge *f*; **the battery needs a charge** la batterie a besoin d'être chargée; **I left it on charge all night** je l'ai laissé charger toute la nuit; *Am Fam Fig* **to get a charge out of sth/doing sth** *(thrill)* s'éclater *ou* prendre son pied avec qch/en faisant qch

(**j**) *Mil* charge *f*; *Br Hist* **the Charge of the Light Brigade** la Charge de la brigade légère

(**k**) *Her* meuble *m*

2 *vt* (**a**) *Com & Fin (person)* faire payer; *(sum)* faire payer, prendre; *(commission)* prélever; **the doctor charged her $90 for a visit** le médecin lui a fait payer *ou* lui a pris 90 dollars pour une consultation; **how much would you charge to take us to the airport?** combien prendriez-vous pour nous emmener à l'aéroport?; **they didn't charge us for the coffee** ils ne nous ont pas fait payer les cafés; **you will be charged for postage** les frais postaux seront à votre charge

(**b**) *Com & Fin (defer payment of)* **charge the bill to my account** mettez le montant de la facture sur mon compte; **I charged all my expenses to the company** j'ai mis tous mes frais sur le compte de la société; *Am* **can I charge this jacket?** *(with a credit card)* puis-je payer cette veste avec ma carte (de crédit)?; *Am* **charge it** mettez-le sur mon compte

(**c**) *(allege)* **to charge that sb has done sth** accuser qn d'avoir fait qch; **the Opposition spokesman charged that the Employment Secretary had falsified the figures** le porte-parole de l'opposition a accusé le ministre du Travail *ou* de l'Emploi d'avoir falsifié les chiffres; **he charged his partner with having stolen thousands of pounds from the firm** il a accusé son associé d'avoir volé des milliers de livres à l'entreprise

(**d**) *Law* inculper; **I'm charging you with the murder of X** je vous inculpe du meurtre de X; **he was charged with assaulting a policeman** il a été inculpé de voies de fait sur un agent de police

(**e**) *(attack)* charger; **the police charged the crowd** les forces de l'ordre ont chargé la foule; **the troops charged the building** les troupes donnèrent l'assaut au bâtiment

(**f**) *Formal (command, entrust)* **I was charged with guarding the prisoner** je fus chargé de la surveillance du prisonnier; **I charge you to find the stolen documents** je vous confie la tâche de retrouver les documents dérobés; **she was charged with the task of interviewing applicants** on lui confia la tâche d'interroger les candidats; *Law* **the judge charged the jury** le juge a fait ses recommandations au jury

(**g**) *Elec* charger

(**h**) *Mil* charger

(**i**) *Formal (fill)* charger; **to charge sb's glass** remplir le verre de qn

3 *vi* (**a**) *(demand in payment)* demander, prendre; **how much do you charge?** combien demandez-vous *ou* prenez-vous?; **do you charge for delivery?** est-ce que vous faites payer la livraison?; **he doesn't charge** il ne demande *ou* prend rien

(**b**) *(rush → person)* se précipiter; *(→ animal)* charger; **the rhino suddenly charged** tout d'un coup le rhinocéros a chargé; **the crowd charged across the square** la foule s'est ruée à travers la place; **suddenly two policemen charged into the room** tout d'un coup deux policiers ont fait irruption dans la pièce; **she charged into/out of her office** elle entra dans son/sortit de son bureau au pas de charge

(**c**) *Mil (attack)* charger, donner l'assaut; **charge!** à l'assaut!

(**d**) *Elec* se charger *ou* recharger; **this battery won't charge** cette batterie ne veut pas se charger *ou* recharger

►► *Am Com & Fin* ***charge account*** compte *m* crédit d'achats, compte *m* accréditif; *Com & Fin* ***charge card*** carte *f* de paiement; *Br* ***charge hand*** sous-chef *m* d'équipe; *Br* ***charge nurse*** infirmier(ère) *m,f* en chef; *Br Law* ***charge sheet*** procès-verbal *m (établi par la police avant le passage d'un prévenu devant un tribunal)*

►**charge down** *vt sep Sport (ball)* contrer

►**charge off** *vt sep Am Fin (capital)* amortir, imputer à l'exercice; **we were obliged to charge off the whole operation** il a fallu imputer l'intégralité du coût de l'opération à l'exercice

►**charge up 1** *vt sep* (**a**) *Fin & Com (bill)* **to charge sth up to sb's account** mettre qch sur le compte de qn; **could you charge it up?** pourriez-vous le mettre sur mon compte?; **she charged everything up to her account** elle a mis tous les frais sur son compte

(**b**) *Elec* charger, recharger

2 *vi (battery)* se (re)charger

'The Charge of the Light Brigade' *Tennyson* 'La Charge de la brigade légère'

THE CHARGE OF THE LIGHT BRIGADE

Ce célèbre poème de lord Tennyson fut inspiré par un épisode de la guerre de Crimée, en 1854: une poignée de soldats britanniques se sacrifièrent pour sauver le port de Balaklava (tenu par les Anglais, les Français et les Turcs) d'une attaque par les Russes.

chargeable ['tʃɑːdʒəbəl] *adj* (**a**) *Com & Fin (to an account)* imputable; **to be chargeable to sb** *(payable by)* être à la charge de qn, être pris(e) en charge par qn; **the item is chargeable with duty of £10** l'article est soumis à une taxe de 10 livres; **travelling expenses are chargeable to the employer** les frais de déplacement sont à la charge de l'employeur; **could you make that chargeable to Crown Ltd?** [illegible] pourriez facturer Crown Ltd?

(**b**) *Law* **a chargeable offence** un délit; **if they refuse to give evidence they'll be chargeable with contempt of court** s'ils refusent de témoigner ils seront passibles de poursuites pour refus de comparaître

►► *Fin* ***chargeable asset*** actif *m* imposable sur les plus-values; *Fin* ***chargeable expenses*** frais *mpl* facturables; *Fin* ***chargeable gain*** bénéfice *m* imposable

charge-cooled [-kuːld] *adj Aut (engine)* suralimenté refroidi

charged [tʃɑːdʒd] *adj* (**a**) *(atmosphere)* chargé; **a voice charged with emotion** une voix pleine d'émotion; **a look charged with suspicion** un regard lourd de soupçons (**b**) *Elec* chargé

chargé d'affaires [ˌʃɑːʒeɪdæ'feə(r)] *(pl* **chargés d'affaires**) *n Pol* chargé *m* d'affaires

charger ['tʃɑːdʒə(r)] *n* (**a**) *Elec* chargeur *m* (**b**) *Arch or Literary (horse)* cheval *m* de bataille

chargrill [tʃɑː'grɪl] *vt Br Culin* griller au charbon de bois

chargrilled [tʃɑː'grɪld] *adj Br Culin* grillé au charbon de bois

charily ['tʃeərəlɪ] *adv* (**a**) *(cautiously)* précautionneusement (**b**) *(sparingly)* avec parcimonie

chariness ['tʃeərɪnɪs] *n* (**a**) *(wariness)* circonspection *f*, prudence *f* (**b**) *(in praise, speech)* parcimonie *f*

Charing Cross ['tʃærɪŋ-] *n* = une des grandes gares londoniennes

chariot ['tʃærɪət] *n* char *m*; *Hum* **your chariot awaits!** la voiture de Monsieur/Madame est avancée!

charioteer [ˌtʃærɪə'tɪə(r)] *n* aurige *m*

charisma [kə'rɪzmə] *n* charisme *m*; **to have charisma** avoir du charisme

charismatic [ˌkærɪz'mætɪk] *adj* charismatique; *Rel* **the charismatic movement** le mouvement charismatique

charitable ['tʃærətəbəl] *adj* (**a**) *(generous, kind)* charitable; *Fig* **the critics were not charitable** les critiques n'ont pas été très tendres *ou* bienveillants (**b**) *(cause, institution)* de bienfaisance, de charité; **a charitable donation** un don fait par charité; **charitable works** les bonnes œuvres

►► ***charitable organization*** œuvre *f* de bienfaisance *ou* de charité; ***charitable trust*** fondation *f* d'utilité publique

charitably ['tʃærətəblɪ] *adv* charitablement

charity ['tʃærətɪ] *(pl* **charities**) *n* (**a**) *Rel* charité *f*; *(generosity, kindness)* charité *f*; **he bought the painting out of charity** il a acheté le tableau par charité; **an act of charity** une action charitable, un acte de charité

(**b**) *(help to the needy)* charité *f*; **to live on charity** vivre d'aumônes; **I don't want your charity** je ne veux pas que tu me fasses la charité; **they're too proud to accept charity** ils sont trop fiers pour accepter la charité *ou* l'aumône; **they raised £10,000 for charity** ils ont collecté 10 000 livres pour les bonnes œuvres; *Prov* **charity begins at home** charité bien ordonnée commence par soi-même

(**c**) *(association)* **we're not a charity!** nous ne sommes pas des philanthropes *ou* une organisation de bienfaisance!

►► ***charity ball*** bal *m* de bienfaisance; ***charity card*** = carte de crédit émise par un organisme de crédit en collaboration avec une association caritative de façon à ce qu'une part de chaque transaction revienne à ladite association, *Can* carte *f* d'affinité; ***the Charity Commission*** = commission gouvernementale britannique contrôlant les associations caritatives; ***charity organization*** association *f* caritative, œuvre *f* de bienfaisance; *Br Ftbl* ***Charity Shield*** = match de football opposant l'équipe qui remporte la "FA Cup" à celle qui arrive en tête du championnat d'Angleterre; ***charity shop*** = magasin dont les employés sont des bénévoles et dont les bénéfices servent à subventionner une œuvre d'utilité publique; ***charity work*** bénévolat *m*

charlady ['tʃɑːˌleɪdɪ] *(pl* **charladies**) *n Br Old-fashioned* femme *f* de ménage

charlatan ['ʃɑːlətən] **1** *n* charlatan *m*

2 *adj* charlatanesque

charlatanism ['ʃɑːlətənɪzəm] *n* charlatanisme *m*

charlatanry ['ʃɑːlətənrɪ] *n* charlatanerie *f*

Charlemagne ['ʃɑːləmeɪn] *pr n* Charlemagne

Charles [tʃɑːlz] *pr n* **Charles the Bold** Charles le Téméraire; **Charles V** Charles Quint; *Phys* **Charles's law** loi *f* de Charles

charleston ['tʃɑːlstən] *n* charleston *m*; **to do the charleston** danser le charleston

charley horse ['tʃɑːlɪ-] *n (UNCOUNT) Am Fam* crampe ❑ *f*; **to have a charley horse** avoir des crampes

charlie ['tʃɑːlɪ] **1** *n* (**a**) *Br Fam (idiot)* cloche *f*; **I felt a proper charlie** je me suis senti vraiment cloche; **he's a right charlie** c'est une vraie cloche (**b**) *Fam Drugs slang (cocaine)* coke *f*

2 Charlie *n Am Fam Mil slang (Vietcong)* le Viêt-cong

Charlie Chaplin [tʃɑːlɪ'tʃæplɪn] *pr n (in real life)* Charlie Chaplin; *(in films)* Charlot

charlock ['tʃɑːlɒk] *n Bot* sénevé *m*

charlotte ['ʃɑːlət] *n Culin (baked)* charlotte *f*; **apple charlotte** charlotte *f* aux pommes

►► *Culin* ***charlotte russe*** charlotte *f* russe

charm [tʃɑːm] **1** *n* (**a**) *(appeal, attraction)* charme *m*; **he has great charm** il a beaucoup de charme; **to turn on the charm** faire du charme; *Ironic* **what charm school did you go to?** oh, comme tu parles bien!

(**b**) *(spell)* charme *m*, sortilège *m*; *(talisman)* amulette *f*, fétiche *m*; **a lucky charm** un porte-bonheur; **to work like a charm** marcher à merveille *ou* à la perfection

(**c**) *(piece of jewellery)* breloque *f*

2 *vt* (**a**) *(please, delight)* charmer, séduire; **I was charmed by his gentle manner** je fus charmé par ses douces manières; **she charmed him into accepting the invitation** elle l'a si bien enjôlé qu'il a accepté l'invitation

(**b**) *(of magician)* charmer, ensorceler; *(of snake charmer)* charmer

3 charms *npl* charmes *mpl*

►► ***charm bracelet*** bracelet *m* à breloques; ***charm offensive*** offensive *f* de charme

►**charm away** *vt sep* **he charmed away all their fears** il a fait disparaître toutes leurs craintes comme par enchantement

charmed [tʃɑːmd] *adj* (**a**) *(delighted)* enchanté; **she sang before a charmed audience** elle a chanté devant des spectateurs enchantés; **charmed, I'm sure!** *(in introduction)* enchanté!; *Ironic* surtout, ne vous gênez pas! (**b**) *(by magic)* charmé; *Fig* **to lead a charmed life** être béni des dieux

charmer ['tʃɑːmə(r)] *n* charmeur(euse) *m,f*

charming ['tʃɑːmɪŋ] *adj* charmant; *Ironic* **charming!** c'est charmant!

charmingly ['tʃɑːmɪŋlɪ] *adv* de façon charmante; **he seemed charmingly innocent** il paraissait d'une innocence charmante

charmless ['tʃɑːmlɪs] *adj* sans charme, dépourvu de charme

charmlessness ['tʃɑːmlɪsnɪs] *n* manque *m* de charme

charnel house ['tʃɑːnəl-] *n Literary* charnier *m*, ossuaire *m*

charr = **char** *n* (**c**)

charred [tʃɑːd] *adj* noirci (par le feu); **the charred ruins of the building** les ruines du bâtiment noircies par le feu

charring ['tʃɑːrɪŋ] *n* carbonisation *f*

chart [tʃɑːt] **1** *n* (**a**) *Naut* carte *f* marine; *Astron* carte *f* (du ciel)

(**b**) *(table)* tableau *m*; *(graph)* courbe *f*, *Med* courbe *f*

(**c**) *Astrol* horoscope *m*

(**d**) *Comput* graphique *m*

2 *vt* (**a**) *Naut (seas, waterway)* établir la carte de, faire un levé hydrographique de; *Astron (stars)* porter sur la carte

(**b**) *(record → on a table, graph)* faire la courbe de; *Fig (→ progress, development)* rendre compte de; **the patient's progress was carefully charted** l'évolution du malade fut soigneusement notée sur sa fiche; *Fig* **the book charts the rise of the labour movement** ce livre retrace la montée du mouvement travailliste; **this graph charts sales over the last ten years** ce graphique montre l'évolution des ventes au cours des dix dernières années

(**c**) *Fig (make a plan of)* tracer; **the director charted a way out of financial collapse** le directeur a établi *ou* mis au point un plan pour éviter un effondrement financier

3 charts *npl Mus* hit-parade *m*; **she's (got a record) in the charts** elle est au hit-parade; **it's number one in** *or* **it's top of the charts** c'est le numéro un au hit-parade

►► *Acct* ***chart of accounts*** plan *m* comptable général; ***chart analyst*** analyste *mf* sur graphiques; *Naut* ***chart room*** cabine *f* des cartes; ***chart topper*** numéro *m* un

charter ['tʃɑːtə(r)] **1** *n* (**a**) *(statement of rights)* charte *f*; *(of a business, organization, university)* statuts *mpl*; **the United Nations Charter** la Charte de l'Organisation des Nations unies (**b**) *(lease, licence)* affrètement *m*; *(charter flight)* charter *m*; *Br* **we've hired three coaches on charter** nous avons affrété trois autocars

2 *vt* (**a**) *(establish)* accorder une charte à (**b**) *(hire, rent)* affréter

►► ***charter company*** affréteur *m*; ***charter flight*** (vol *m*) charter *m*; ***charter member*** membre *m* fondateur; *Naut* ***charter party*** charte-partie *f*; ***charter plane*** (avion *m*) charter *m*

chartered ['tʃɑːtəd] *adj (plane, ship, coach)* affrété

►► *Br* ***chartered accountant*** expert-comptable *m*; ***chartered bank*** banque *f* privilégiée; ***chartered surveyor*** expert *m* immobilier

charterer ['tʃɑːtərə(r)] *n* affréteur *m*, nolisateur *m*

charterhouse ['tʃɑːtəˌhaʊs, *pl* -haʊzɪz] *n* chartreuse *f*

chartering ['tʃɑːtərɪŋ] *n (of plane, ship, coach)* affrètement *m*; *(at reduced rates)* charterisation *f*

►► ***chartering broker*** courtier *m* d'affrètement

Chartism ['tʃɑːtɪzəm] *n Hist* chartisme *m*

Chartist ['tʃɑːtɪst] *Hist* **1** *n* chartiste *mf*

2 *adj* chartiste

►► ***the Chartist movement*** le mouvement chartiste

THE CHARTIST MOVEMENT

Ce mouvement réformiste d'émancipation ouvrière, fondé en Angleterre en 1838, fut à l'origine d'une "Charte du peuple" réclamant, notamment, le suffrage universel. Les chartistes présentèrent successivement au Parlement trois pétitions de plus de un million de signatures, sans succès.

chartist ['tʃɑːtɪst] *n St Exch* analyste *mf* des cours des valeurs boursières, chartiste *mf*

chart-topping *adj Br* = qui est en tête du hit-parade

chartreuse [ʃɑː'trɜːz] *n (liqueur)* chartreuse *f*

charwoman ['tʃɑːˌwʊmən] *(pl* **charwomen** [-ˌwɪmɪn]) *n Fam Old-fashioned (cleaner)* femme *f* de ménage ❑

chary ['tʃeərɪ] *adj* (**a**) *(wary)* précautionneux; **he's chary of allowing strangers into his home** il hésite à accueillir des gens qu'il ne connaît pas chez lui (**b**) *(ungenerous)* parcimonieux; **he was chary of praise** il faisait rarement des éloges, il était avare de compliments

Charybdis [kə'rɪbdɪs] *n Myth* Charybde; **to be between Scylla and Charybdis** tomber de Charybde en Scylla

chase [tʃeɪs] **1** *vt* (**a**) *(pursue)* poursuivre; **two police cars chased the van** deux voitures de police ont pris la camionnette en chasse; **the dog chased the postman down the street** le chien a poursuivi le facteur jusqu'en bas de la rue; **the reporters were chased from** *or* **out of the house** les journalistes furent chassés de la maison

(**b**) *(amorously)* courir (après); **he's always chasing young women** il est toujours à courir (après) les filles

(**c**) *(try to obtain)* courir après; **there are thousands of applicants chasing only a few jobs** il y a des milliers de candidats qui courent après quelques postes seulement

(**d**) *(engrave → gold, silver)* ciseler

(**e**) *Metal (emboss)* repousser

2 *vi (rush)* **she chased all around London to find a wedding dress** elle a parcouru *ou* fait tout Londres pour trouver une robe de mariée

3 *n* (**a**) *(pursuit)* poursuite *f*; **the hounds gave chase to the fox** la meute a pris le renard en chasse; **the prisoner climbed over the wall and the guards gave chase** le prisonnier escalada le mur et les gardiens se lancèrent à sa poursuite

(**b**) *Cycling* poursuite *f*

(**c**) *Hunt (sport, land, game)* chasse *f*

(**d**) *Horseracing* steeple *m*

(**e**) *(groove)* saignée

(**f**) *Typ* châssis *m*

►**chase after** *vt insep* être à la poursuite de, poursuivre; *(amorously)* courir après; **we've been all over town chasing after that spare part** nous avons dû faire tout le tour de la ville pour trouver cette pièce détachée

►**chase away, chase off** *vt sep* chasser

►**chase down** *vt sep (runner, cyclist)* poursuivre

►**chase up** *vt sep Br* (**a**) *(information)* rechercher (**b**) *(organization, person)* relancer; **can you chase up the manager for me?** pouvez-vous relancer le directeur à propos de ce que je lui ai demandé?; **I had to chase him up for the £50 he owed me** j'ai dû lui réclamer les 50 livres qu'il me devait; **I'll chase the matter up for you** je vais tenter d'activer les choses pour vous

chaser ['tʃeɪsə(r)] *n* (**a**) *(drink)* = alcool bu après une bière ou vice versa; **a pint of beer and a whisky chaser** une pinte de bière suivie d'un whisky (**b**) *(pursuer)* chasseur *m* (**c**) *Horse-racing* cheval *m* de course

chasing ['tʃeɪsɪŋ] *n* (**a**) *(engraving → of gold, silver)* ciselage *m*, ciselure *f* (**b**) *Metal (embossing)* repoussage *m*

chasm ['kæzəm] *n also Fig* abîme *m*, gouffre *m*

chassé ['ʃæseɪ] **1** *n (dance step)* chassé *m*

2 *vi (in dancing)* chasser

chassis ['ʃæsɪ] (*pl* **inv** [-sɪz]) *n* (**a**) *Aut* châssis *m*; *Aviat* train *m* d'atterrissage (**b**) *Fam (body)* châssis *m*; *Hum* **she's got a classy chassis** elle est super bien balancée *ou* carrossée

►► ***chassis number*** numéro *m* de châssis

chassisless construction ['ʃæsɪlɪs-] *n Aut* carrosserie *f* autoporteuse

chaste [tʃeɪst] *adj* (**a**) *(sexually)* chaste (**b**) *(speech, taste, style)* sobre, simple

chastely ['tʃeɪstlɪ] *adv* (**a**) *(sexually)* chastement (**b**) *(speak, dress)* sobrement

chasten ['tʃeɪsən] *vt Formal* (**a**) *(subdue, humble)* corriger, maîtriser; *(pride)* rabaisser (**b**) *(punish, reprimand)* châtier, punir

chastened ['tʃeɪsənd] *adj* abattu; **she was chastened by her failure** elle fut abattue par son échec; **he was in a chastened mood** il était abattu

chasteness ['tʃeɪstnɪs] *n* caractère *m* chaste

chastening ['tʃeɪsənɪŋ] *adj* **prison had a chastening effect on him** la prison l'a assagi; **it's a chastening thought** c'était une pensée plutôt décourageante

chastise [tʃæ'staɪz] *vt* (**a**) *(reprimand, criticize)* réprimander (**b**) *Formal (punish)* châtier; *(beat)* corriger

chastisement ['tʃæstɪzmənt] *n Formal (punishment)* châtiment *m*; *(beating)* correction *f*

chastity ['tʃæstətɪ] *n* chasteté *f*; **to take a vow of chastity** faire vœu de chasteté

►► ***chastity belt*** ceinture *f* de chasteté

chasuble ['tʃæzjʊbəl] *n Rel* chasuble *f*

chat [tʃæt] (*pt & pp* **chatted**, *cont* **chatting**) **1** *vi* (**a**) bavarder, causer; **we were just chatting about this and that** nous causions de choses et d'autres; **he was chatting to the man next to him** il bavardait avec l'homme qui était à côté de lui (**b**) *Comput* bavarder

2 *n* (**a**) *(conversation)* petite conversation *f*, causette *f*; **to have a chat with sb** bavarder avec qn; *(about a problem, work performance etc)* dire un mot à qn; **it's time we had a little chat** il est temps que nous ayons une petite discussion; **the chat at work is all about cars** au travail, on ne discute que de voitures; **we had a nice chat over lunch** nous avons eu une conversation agréable pendant le déjeuner; [illegible] der un peu; **there's too much chat and not enough work going on here!** il y a *ou* on s'occupe trop de bavardage et pas assez de travail ici!

(**b**) *Comput (on Internet)* messagerie *f* de dialogue en direct, bavardage *m*, chat *m*

►► *Comput* ***chat room*** site *m* de bavardage, salon *m*, *Can* bavardoir *m*; *Br TV* ***chat show*** causerie *f* télévisée, talk-show *m*; ***chat show host*** présentateur(trice) *m,f* de talk-show; *Comput* ***chat software*** logiciel *m* de bavardage

►**chat up** *vt sep Br Fam* baratiner, draguer; *Fig* **to chat up a client** baratiner un client

château ['ʃætəʊ] (*pl* **châteaus** *or* **châteaux** [-əʊz]) *n* château *m*

château-bottled *adj* mis en bouteille au château

Chateaubriand [ˌʃætəʊ'briːɑ̃] *n Culin* chateaubriand *m*, châteaubriant *m*

chatline ['tʃætlaɪn] *n* réseau *m* téléphonique *(payant)*

chattel ['tʃætəl] *n Law* bien *m* meuble; **chattels** biens *mpl*; **goods and chattels** biens *mpl* et effets *mpl*

►► *Am Fin* ***chattel mortgage*** nantissement *m* de biens meubles

chatter ['tʃætə(r)] **1** *vi* (**a**) *(person)* papoter, bavarder; *(bird)* jaser, jacasser; *(monkey)* crier; **she sat quietly while Maria chattered away** elle restait tranquillement assise tandis que Maria palabrait (**b**) *(machine)* cliqueter (**c**) *(teeth)* claquer; **my teeth were chattering from** *or* **with the cold** j'avais tellement froid que je claquais des dents

2 *n* (**a**) *(of people)* bavardage *m*, papotage *m*; *(of birds)* jacassement *m*; *(of monkey)* cri *m* (**b**) *(of machines)* cliquetis *m* (**c**) *(of teeth)* claquement *m*

chatterbox ['tʃætəbɒks] *n Fam* moulin *m* à paroles

chatterer ['tʃætərə(r)] *n* (**a**) *(talkative person)* bavard(e) *m,f* (**b**) *Zool* cotinga *m*

chattering ['tʃætərɪŋ] *n (of people)* bavardage *m*; *(of birds)* caquetage *m*; *(of monkeys)* babil *m*; *(of teeth)* claquement *m*; *(of machine-gun)* martèlement *m*

►► *Pej* ***the chattering classes*** les intellectuels *mpl* qui s'écoutent parler

chattily ['tʃætɪlɪ] *adv (speak, write)* d'une façon familière

chattiness ['tʃætɪnɪs] *n* loquacité *f*

chatty ['tʃætɪ] *adj (person)* bavard; *(letter)* plein de bavardages; *(article)* écrit sur le ton de la conversation; **Mr Smith was very chatty** *or* **in a very chatty mood today** M. Smith était très bavard aujourd'hui

chat-up line *n Br Fam* = formule d'entrée en matière pour commencer à draguer quelqu'un; **that's his standard chat-up line** c'est son baratin habituel quand il drague

Chaucerian [tʃɔː'sɪərɪən] *adj* de Chaucer

chauffeur ['ʃəʊfə(r)] **1** *n* chauffeur *m*

2 *vi* travailler comme chauffeur; **he chauffeurs for a cabinet minister** il est chauffeur de ministre

3 *vt* conduire; **we were chauffeured to the airport** on nous a conduits à l'aéroport

chauffeur-driven *adj (car)* conduit par un chauffeur

chauvinism ['ʃəʊvɪnɪzəm] *n (sexism)* machisme *m*, phallocratie *f*; *(nationalism)* chauvinisme *m*

chauvinist ['ʃəʊvɪnɪst] *n (sexist)* phallocrate *m*, machiste *m*; *(nationalist)* chauvin(e) *m,f*

chauvinistic ['ʃəʊvɪ'nɪstɪk] *adj (sexist)* machiste, phallocrate; *(nationalistic)* chauvin

chaw [tʃɔː] **1** *vt* chiquer

2 *vi* chiquer

3 *n (tobacco)* chique *f*

ChB [ˌsiːeɪtʃ'biː] *n Univ* (*abbr* **Bachelor of Surgery**) *(person)* = titulaire d'un diplôme sanctionnant trois années d'études de médecine; *(qualification)* = diplôme sanctionnant trois années d'études de médecine

ChE (*written abbr* **chemical engineer**) ingénieur *m* chimiste

cheap [tʃiːp] **1** *adj* (**a**) *(inexpensive)* bon marché *(inv)*, pas cher; **labour is cheaper in the Far East** la main-d'œuvre est moins chère en Extrême-Orient; **he bought a cheap ticket to** [illegible] tarif réduit pour l'Australie; **it was the cheapest piano in the shop** c'était le piano le moins cher du magasin; **it works out cheaper to take a whole bottle** cela revient moins cher de prendre la bouteille entière; **it's cheap to run** *(car)* elle est économique à l'entretien; *Fam* **he's very cheap** *(shopkeeper)* il n'est pas cher; **cheap and cheerful** sans prétentions

(**b**) *(poor quality)* de mauvaise qualité; *Br* **the furniture was cheap and nasty** les meubles étaient de très mauvaise qualité

(**c**) *(of little value)* de peu de valeur; **human life is cheap in many countries** il y a beaucoup de pays où la vie humaine a peu de valeur; **that's how he gets his cheap thrills** c'est ça qui l'excite

(**d**) *(low, despicable)* **a cheap joke** une plaisanterie de mauvais goût; **a cheap remark** une remarque facile; **that was a cheap shot** c'était vraiment mesquin comme critique; **he made the girl feel cheap** il fit en sorte que la fille eût honte; **she had made herself cheap in her father's eyes** elle s'était rabaissée aux yeux de son père

(**e**) *esp Am (stingy)* mesquin

2 *adv (buy, get, sell)* bon marché; **I can get it for you cheaper** je peux vous le trouver pour moins cher; **clothes of that quality don't come cheap** des vêtements de cette qualité coûtent cher; **it was going cheap** c'était bon marché

3 on the cheap *adv Fam* **she furnished the house on the cheap** elle a meublé la maison pour pas cher[a]; **they've got immigrants working for them on the cheap** ils ont des immigrés qui travaillent pour eux au rabais[a]

►► *Fin* ***cheap money*** argent *m* à bon marché; ***cheap rate*** tarif *m* réduit

cheapen ['tʃiːpən] **1** *vt* (**a**) *(lower, debase)* abaisser; **I wouldn't cheapen myself by accepting a bribe** je ne m'abaisserais pas à accepter un pot-de-vin (**b**) *(reduce the price of)* baisser le prix de

2 *vi* devenir moins cher

cheapish ['tʃiːpɪʃ] *adj* d'un prix assez bas, relativement bon marché

cheap-jack *Fam* **1** *n* marchand *m* de bric-à-brac[a], camelot[a] *m*

2 *adj* (**a**) *(goods)* de pacotille (**b**) *(solution)* facile[a]; *(remark)* facile[a], mesquin[a]

cheaply ['tʃiːplɪ] *adv* à bon marché; **I can do the job more cheaply** je peux faire le travail à meilleur marché *ou* pour moins cher; **to eat out cheaply** manger dehors pour pas cher

cheapness ['tʃiːpnɪs] *n* (**a**) *(low price)* bas prix *m* (**b**) *(poor quality)* mauvaise qualité *f*

cheapo ['tʃiːpəʊ] *adj Fam* **1** *n* article *m* bas de gamme[a]

2 *adj* bas de gamme[a]

cheapskate ['tʃiːpskeɪt] *n Fam* radin(e) *m,f*, grippe-sou *m*

cheat [tʃiːt] **1** *vt* (**a**) *(defraud, swindle)* escroquer, léser; **to cheat sb out of sth** escroquer qch à qn; **to feel cheated** se sentir lésé *ou* frustré; **to cheat sb into doing sth** faire faire qch à qn en le trompant

(**b**) *Fig Literary (deceive, trick)* duper; **to cheat death** échapper à la mort

2 *vi* tricher; **he always cheats at cards** il triche toujours aux cartes; **she was expelled from university for cheating** elle fut renvoyée de l'université pour avoir triché aux examens

3 *n* (**a**) *(dishonest person)* tricheur(euse) *m,f*; *(crook, swindler)* escroc *m*, fraudeur(euse) *m,f* (**b**) *(dishonest practice)* tricherie *f*, tromperie *f* (**c**) *(in computer game)* cheat *m*

►► *Am Fam* ***cheat sheet*** antisèche *m or f*

►**cheat on** *vt insep* (**a**) *(falsify)* tricher sur; **he cheated on his income tax** il a triché sur sa déclaration d'impôts (**b**) *(be unfaithful to)* tromper; **he cheats on his wife** il trompe sa femme

cheating ['tʃiːtɪŋ] **1** *n* (**a**) *(at cards, games)* tricherie *f*; *(at exams)* copiage *m*; **that's cheating!** c'est de la triche! (**b**) *(fraud)* fraude *f* (**c**) *(UNCOUNT) (infidelity)* infidélité *f*, infidélités *fpl*

2 *adj* (**a**) *(dishonest)* malhonnête, trompeur (**b**) *(unfaithful, disloyal)* infidèle

Chechen ['tʃetʃen] **1** *n* Tchétchène *mf*

2 *adj* tchétchène

►► ***the Chechen Republic*** la République tchétchène; **in the Chechen Republic** en République [illegible]

Chechenia, Chechnya ['tʃetʃnɪə] *n* Tchétchénie *f*; **in Chechenia** *or* **Chechnya** en Tchétchénie

CHECK [tʃek]

contrôler	► 1 (a)
vérifier	► 1 (a); 2 (a)
enrayer	► 1 (b)
mettre au vestiaire/ à la consigne	► 1 (c)
cocher	► 1 (d)
correspondre	► 2 (b)
contrôle	► 3 (a)
enquête	► 3 (b)
frein	► 3 (c)
échec	► 3 (d)
addition	► 3 (e)
carreau	► 3 (f)
coche	► 3 (g)
chèque	► 3 (h)

1 *vt* (**a**) *(inspect, examine)* contrôler, vérifier; *(confirm, substantiate)* vérifier; **she didn't check her facts before writing the article** elle n'a pas vérifié les faits avant d'écrire son article; **the figures have to be checked** il faut vérifier les chiffres; **the doctor checked my blood pressure** le médecin a pris ma tension; **the inspector checked our tickets** le contrôleur a contrôlé nos billets; **check these names against the ones on the list** vérifie que ces noms sont les mêmes que ceux de la liste
(**b**) *(contain, limit → recession, inflation)* enrayer; *(→ emotions, troops)* contenir; *(→ urge)* réprimer; **to check oneself** se retenir
(**c**) *Am (coat, hat)* mettre au vestiaire; *(luggage)* mettre à la consigne
(**d**) *Am (mark, tick)* cocher
(**e**) *Chess* faire échec à
(**f**) *Scot Fam (reprimand)* réprimander□
2 *vi* (**a**) *(confirm)* vérifier; **I'll have to check with the accountant** je vais devoir vérifier auprès du comptable; **they usually have vacancies, but it's a good idea to check** d'ordinaire, ils ont de la place, mais il vaut mieux s'en assurer *ou* vérifier
(**b**) *(correspond)* correspondre, s'accorder; **his description of the killer checked with forensic evidence** sa description du tueur s'accordait avec l'expertise médico-légale
(**c**) *(pause, halt)* s'arrêter
3 *n* (**a**) *(examination, inspection)* contrôle *m*, vérification *f*; **the airline ordered checks on all their 747s** la compagnie aérienne a ordonné que des contrôles soient faits sur tous ses 747; **a routine check** une vérification de routine
(**b**) *(inquiry, investigation)* enquête *f*; **to do** *or* **to run a check on sb** se renseigner sur qn; **to keep a check on sb** observer qn
(**c**) *(restraint)* frein *m*; **the House of Lords acts as a check upon the House of Commons** la Chambre des lords met un frein au pouvoir de la Chambre des communes; *Pol* **(a system of) checks and balances** (un système d') équilibre *m* des pouvoirs; **he kept** *or* **held his anger in check** il a contenu *ou* maîtrisé sa colère; **we could no longer hold** *or* **keep the enemy in check** nous ne pouvions plus contenir l'ennemi
(**d**) *Chess* échec *m*; **in check** en échec; **check!** échec au roi!
(**e**) *Am (bill)* addition *f*; *(receipt for coats, luggage)* ticket *m*
(**f**) *(square)* carreau *m*; **a skirt in black and white check** une jupe à carreaux noirs et blancs
(**g**) *Am (mark, tick)* coche *f*; **put a check next to all the verbs** cochez tous les verbes
(**h**) *Am (cheque)* chèque *m*
4 *adj (pattern, skirt)* à carreaux
►► *Comput* ***check bit*** bit *m* de contrôle; *Comput* ***check box*** case *f* de pointage, case *f* d'option; *Comput* ***check byte*** octet *m* de contrôle; *Comput* ***check digit*** chiffre *m* de contrôle *ou* de vérification, clé *f*; *Mktg* ***check question*** question *f* de contrôle, question *f* filtre; *Mktg* ***check sample*** échantillon *m* témoin

►**check in 1** *vi* (**a**) *(at airport)* se présenter à l'enregistrement
(**b**) *(at hotel)* se présenter à la réception
(**c**) *Am (phone)* **it's a little late, I'd better check in with my parents** il se fait tard, il faudrait que je passe un coup de fil à mes parents
2 *vt sep* (**a**) *(at airport → baggage)* enregistrer
(**b**) *(at hotel)* inscrire sur le registre
(**c**) *(at cloakroom)* mettre au vestiaire; *(at left-luggage office)* mettre à la consigne
(**d**) *Am (at library)* **to check in a book at the library** rapporter un livre à la bibliothèque

►**check into** *vt insep* **to check into a hotel** descendre dans un hôtel

►**check off** *vt sep (names, numbers on list etc)* cocher

►**check on** *vt insep* (**a**) *(facts)* vérifier (**b**) *(person)* **the doctor checked on two patients before leaving** le médecin est allé voir deux patients avant de partir; **would you mind checking on the baby?** tu peux aller voir si le bébé va bien?

►**check out 1** *vi* (**a**) *(pay hotel bill)* régler sa note; *(leave hotel)* quitter l'hôtel
(**b**) *(prove to be correct)* s'avérer exact; *(correspond, match)* s'accorder, correspondre
(**c**) *Am Fam (die)* passer l'arme à gauche
2 *vt sep* (**a**) *(library book)* faire tamponner; *(hotel guest)* faire régler sa note à
(**b**) *(investigate → person)* enquêter sur, se renseigner sur; *(→ information, machine, place)* vérifier
(**c**) *Fam (try)* essayer□; **why don't we check out the restaurant that John told us about?** pourquoi ne pas essayer le restaurant dont John nous a parlé?
(**d**) *Fam (look at)* **to check sb/sth out** mater qn/qch; **check this out** *(look)* vise un peu ça; *(listen)* écoute-moi ça

►**check over** *vt sep* examiner, vérifier

►**check through** *vt sep* (**a**) *(examine → baggage etc)* contrôler, examiner (**b**) *Am (send by plane)* faire envoyer (par avion); **I'd like my luggage checked through to Los Angeles** je voudrais faire envoyer directement mes bagages à Los Angeles

►**check up on** *vt insep* **to check up on sb** enquêter *ou* se renseigner sur qn; **if you trusted me you wouldn't check up on me all the time** si tu me faisais confiance tu ne serais pas toujours en train de m'espionner; **to check up on sth** vérifier qch; **the social worker checked up on reports of child abuse** l'assistante sociale a enquêté sur les allégations de mauvais traitements à enfant

CHECKS AND BALANCES

Ce système de contrôle mutuel, garanti par la Constitution, est l'un des principes fondamentaux du gouvernement américain. Il a été élaboré afin que les pouvoirs législatif, exécutif et judiciaire n'accumulent pas trop d'influence les uns par rapport aux autres.

checkbook *Am* = **chequebook**

check-control *n Aut* appareil *m* de signalisation des défauts

checked [tʃekt] *adj* (**a**) *(pattern, tablecloth)* à carreaux, *Can* carreauté (**b**) *Ling (syllable)* fermé, entravé

checker [ˈtʃekə(r)] *n Am* (**a**) *(square)* carreau *m*; **a checker tablecloth** une nappe à carreaux (**b**) *(in draughts)* pion *m* (**c**) *(in supermarket)* caissier(ère) *m,f*; *(in left-luggage office)* préposé(e) *m,f* à la consigne; *(in cloakroom)* préposé(e) *m,f* au vestiaire
►► ***Checker cab*** = taxi américain reconnaissable au motif de damier qui en décore la carrosserie

checkerboard [ˈtʃekəbɔːd] *n Am Chess* échiquier *m*; *(in draughts)* damier *m*

checkered *Am* = **chequered**

checkers *Am* = **chequers**

check-in *n (at airport)* enregistrement *m*
►► ***check-in desk*** enregistrement *m*; ***check-in time*** *(at airport, hotel)* heure *f* d'enregistrement

checking [ˈtʃekɪŋ] *n (verification, examination)* contrôle *m*, vérification *f*; *(more detailed)* pointage *m*
►► *Am Banking* ***checking account*** compte *m* courant

checklist [ˈtʃeklɪst] *n* liste *f* de vérification; *Aviat* check-list *f*

checkmark [ˈtʃekmɑːk] *n Am* coche *f*

checkmate [ˈtʃekmeɪt] **1** *n* (**a**) *Chess* échec et mat *m* (**b**) *Fig (deadlock, standstill)* impasse *f*; *(defeat)* échec *m* total
2 *vt* (**a**) *Chess* faire échec et mat à (**b**) *Fig (frustrate, obstruct)* contrecarrer; *(defeat)* vaincre

check-out *n* (**a**) *(in supermarket)* caisse *f* (**b**) *(in hotel)* **check-out (time) is at 11 a.m.** les chambres doivent être libérées avant 11 heures
►► *Am* ***check-out assistant, checkout clerk*** caissier(ère) *m,f*; ***check-out counter*** caisse *f*, comptoir-caisse *m*; ***check-out display*** devant *m* de caisse; ***check-out girl*** caissière *f*; ***check-out operator*** caissier(ère) *m,f*

checkpoint [ˈtʃekpɔɪnt] *n* (poste *m* de) contrôle *m*
►► *Mil & Hist* ***Checkpoint Charlie*** checkpoint *m* Charlie

checkrein [ˈtʃekreɪn] *n Am Horseriding* fausses rênes *fpl*

checkroom [ˈtʃekrʊm] *n Am (for coats, hats)* vestiaire *m*; *(for luggage)* consigne *f*

checksum [ˈtʃeksʌm] *n Comput* somme *f* de contrôle

check-up *n* bilan *m* de santé, check-up *m*; **to give sb a check-up** faire un bilan de santé à qn; **to go for** *or* **to have a check-up** faire faire un bilan de santé

Cheddar [ˈtʃedə(r)] *n (cheese)* cheddar *m*
►► ***Cheddar cheese*** cheddar *m*; ***Cheddar Gorge*** = gorge située dans le sud-ouest de l'Angleterre, célèbre pour ses grottes

cheek [tʃiːk] **1** *n* (**a**) *(of face)* joue *f*; **cheek to cheek** joue contre joue; **to be/to live cheek by jowl with sb** être/vivre tout près de qn; **to turn the other cheek** tendre *ou* présenter l'autre joue
(**b**) *Fam (buttock)* fesse□ *f*
(**c**) *Br Fam (impudence)* culot *m*, toupet *m*; **he's got a cheek!** il est culotté *ou* gonflé!, quel culot!; **he had the cheek to ask her age!** il a eu le culot *ou* le toupet de lui demander son âge!; **what (a) cheek!, of all the cheek!** quel culot!, quel toupet!
2 *vt Br Fam* être insolent avec
►► *Horseriding* ***cheek piece*** montant *m*; ***cheek pouch*** abajoue *f*

cheekbone [ˈtʃiːkbəʊn] *n* pommette *f*; **high/prominent cheekbones** pommettes *fpl* hautes/saillantes

-cheeked [tʃiːkt] *suff* **rosy-cheeked** aux joues roses *ou* rouges; **round-cheeked** aux joues rebondies *ou* rondes, joufflu

cheekily [ˈtʃiːkɪlɪ] *adv Br* avec effronterie *ou* impudence, effrontément

cheekiness [ˈtʃiːkɪnɪs] *n Br* effronterie *f*, audace *f*

cheeky [ˈtʃiːkɪ] *adj Br (person)* effronté, impudent; *(attitude, behaviour)* impertinent; **don't be cheeky!** pas d'impertinence!; *Fam* **a cheeky little wine** un bon petit pinard

cheep [tʃiːp] **1** *n* pépiement *m*; *Fam* **you can't get a cheep out of her** elle ne dit jamais mot□
2 *vi* pépier

cheer [tʃɪə(r)] **1** *n* (**a**) *(cry)* hourra *m*, bravo *m*; **I heard a cheer go up** j'ai entendu des acclamations; **three cheers for the winner!** un ban *ou* hourra pour le gagnant!; **three cheers!** hourra!
(**b**) *Literary (good spirits)* bonne humeur *f*, gaieté *f*; **words of good cheer** paroles *fpl* d'encouragement; **be of good cheer!** prenez courage!
2 *vt* (**a**) *(make cheerful → person)* remonter le moral à, réconforter
(**b**) *(encourage by shouts)* acclamer
3 *vi* pousser des acclamations *ou* des hourras

►**cheer on** *vt sep* encourager (par des acclamations); **his supporters cheered him on to victory** les acclamations de ses supporters l'ont encouragé jusqu'à la victoire

►**cheer up 1** *vt sep* (**a**) *(person)* remonter le moral à, réconforter
(**b**) *(house, room)* égayer
2 *vi (become more cheerful)* s'égayer, se dérider; **cheer up!** courage!; **the weather's cheered up** le temps s'est arrangé

cheerful [ˈtʃɪəfʊl] *adj* (**a**) *(happy → person)* de bonne humeur; *(→ remark, smile)* joyeux, gai; *(→ atmosphere, mood, music)* gai, joyeux; *(→ colour, wallpaper)* gai, riant; *(→ news)* réjouissant; **she's always cheerful** elle est toujours de bonne humeur (**b**) *(enthusiastic, willing → helper, worker)* de bonne volonté; *(→ dedication)* grand

cheerfully [ˈtʃɪəfʊlɪ] *adv* (**a**) *(happily)* joyeusement, avec entrain (**b**) *(willingly)* de plein gré, avec bonne volonté; **I could cheerfully have hit him!** je l'aurais bien frappé!

cheerfulness [ˈtʃɪəfʊlnɪs] *n (of person)* bonne humeur *f*; *(of atmosphere, colour, music)* gaieté *f*; *(of remark, smile)* gaieté *f*, caractère *m* jovial

cheerily [ˈtʃɪərɪlɪ] *adv* joyeusement, avec entrain

cheeriness [ˈtʃɪərɪnɪs] *n* bonne humeur *f*

cheering [ˈtʃɪərɪŋ] **1** *n (UNCOUNT)* acclamations *fpl*, hourras *mpl*
2 *adj (remark, thought)* encourageant, qui remonte le moral; *(news, sight)* encourageant, réconfortant; *Ironic* **that's cheering!** voilà qui est réconfortant!

cheerio [ˌtʃɪərɪˈəʊ] *exclam Br Fam* (**a**) *(goodbye)* salut!, ciao!; **it's cheerio 2000** bye-bye 2000 (**b**) *Old-fashioned (toast)* à la tienne!
cheerleader [ˈtʃɪəˌliːdə(r)] *n Sport* = majorette qui stimule l'enthousiasme des supporters des équipes sportives, surtout aux États-Unis
cheerless [ˈtʃɪəlɪs] *adj (person)* triste, mélancolique; *(landscape)* morne
cheerlessly [ˈtʃɪəlɪslɪ] *adv* tristement
cheerlessness [ˈtʃɪəlɪsnɪs] *n (of person)* tristesse *f*, mélancolie *f*; *(of landscape)* aspect *m* morne
cheers [tʃɪəz] *exclam Fam (as toast)* à la tienne!; *Br (goodbye)* salut!, ciao!; *Br (thanks)* merci!❑
cheery [ˈtʃɪərɪ] *(compar* **cheerier**, *superl* **cheeriest**) *adj (person)* de bonne humeur; *(smile)* joyeux, gai
cheese [tʃiːz] **1** *n* (**a**) *(gen)* fromage *m*; **say cheese!** *(when taking photo)* souriez!❑; **a cheese and wine (evening)** = petite fête où l'on déguste du vin et du fromage
(**b**) *(individual piece)* fromage *m*; **an assortment of different cheeses** un assortiment de fromages
2 *comp (omelette, sandwich, sauce)* au fromage; *(knife)* à fromage
►► ***cheese biscuit*** *(for cheese)* biscuit *m* salé; *(cheese-flavoured)* biscuit *m* au fromage; ***cheese grater*** râpe *f* à fromage; ***the cheese industry*** l'industrie *f* fromagère; ***cheese maker*** fromager(ère) *m,f*; ***cheese mite*** mite *f* du fromage; ***cheese straw*** allumette *f* au fromage; ***cheese wire*** fil *m* à couper
► **cheese off** *vt sep Fam* **to cheese sb off** gonfler qn
cheeseboard [ˈtʃiːzbɔːd] *n (board)* plateau *m* à fromage *ou* fromages; *(on menu)* plateau *m* de fromages
cheeseburger [ˈtʃiːzˌbɜːgə(r)] *n* hamburger *m* au fromage, cheeseburger *m*
cheesecake [ˈtʃiːzkeɪk] *n* (**a**) *(dessert)* gâteau *m* au fromage (blanc), cheesecake *m* (**b**) *(UNCOUNT) Fam Hum (attractive women)* belles nanas *fpl*; *(in photo)* pin-up *f inv*; *Br* **she's a real cheesecake** elle est vraiment bien foutue
cheesecloth [ˈtʃiːzklɒθ] *n Culin & Tex* étamine *f*
cheesed off [tʃiːzd-] *adj Br Fam* **to be cheesed off (with)** en avoir marre (de); **I'm cheesed off with this job** j'en ai marre de ce boulot
cheesemonger [ˈtʃiːzˌmʌŋgə(r)] *n Br* fromager(ère) *m,f*
cheeseparing [ˈtʃiːzˌpeərɪŋ] **1** *n* parcimonie *f*
2 *adj* parcimonieux, pingre
cheesy [ˈtʃiːzɪ] *(compar* **cheesier**, *superl* **cheesiest**) *adj* (**a**) *(flavour)* qui a un goût de fromage, qui sent le fromage; *(smell)* qui sent le fromage (**b**) *Fam (tasteless)* ringard (**c**) *Fam* **a cheesy grin** un large sourire❑
cheetah [ˈtʃiːtə] *n Zool* guépard *m*
chef [ʃef] *n* chef *m* (de cuisine), cuisinier(ère) *m,f*
►► *Culin* ***chef's salad*** = salade à base de poulet, de jambon et de fromage
Chekhov [ˈtʃekɒf] *pr n* Tchekhov
chelate [ˈkiːleɪt] *n Chem* chélate *m*
Chelsea [ˈtʃelsɪ] *n* = quartier chic de Londres
►► ***Chelsea bun*** = petit pain rond aux raisins [illegible] ***Chelsea Flower Show*** = floralies ayant lieu chaque année à Londres; ***Chelsea Hospital*** l'hôpital *m* de Chelsea *(pour les vieux soldats)*; ***Chelsea Pensioner*** = ancien combattant résidant au Chelsea Royal Hospital, à Londres
Cheltenham Gold Cup [ˈtʃeltənəm-] *n Horse-racing* = course hippique annuelle à Cheltenham en Angleterre
chemical [ˈkemɪkəl] **1** *n* produit *m* chimique
2 *adj* chimique
►► ***chemical element*** élément *m* chimique; ***chemical engineer*** ingénieur *m* chimiste; ***chemical engineering*** génie *m* chimique; *Fam* ***the chemical generation*** = la génération des dix-huit à vingt-cinq ans qui fréquentent les boîtes de nuit et consomment de l'ecstasy; ***chemical reaction*** réaction *f* chimique; ***chemical symbol*** symbole *m* chimique; ***chemical toilet*** W-C *mpl* chimiques; ***chemical warfare*** guerre *f* chimique; ***chemical waste*** déchets *mpl* chimiques; ***chemical weapons*** armes *fpl* chimiques
chemically [ˈkemɪkəlɪ] *adv* chimiquement
chemiluminescence [ˌkemɪljʊmɪˈnesəns], **chemicoluminescence** [ˌkemɪkəʊljʊmɪˈnesəns] *n Chem* chimiluminescence *f*, chimioluminescence *f*
chemin de fer [ʃəˌmændəˈfeə(r)] *n Cards* chemin *m* de fer *(jeu de cartes)*
chemise [ʃəˈmiːz] *n (dress)* robe-chemisier *f*; *(undergarment)* chemise *f (de femme)*
chemist [ˈkemɪst] *n* (**a**) *(scientist)* chimiste *mf* (**b**) *Br (pharmacist)* pharmacien(enne) *m,f* (**c**) *(shop)* pharmacie *f*
►► ***chemist's shop*** pharmacie *f*
chemistry [ˈkemɪstrɪ] **1** *n* (**a**) *(science)* chimie *f* (**b**) *(affinity) Fig* **sexual chemistry** (bonne) entente *f* sexuelle; *Fig* **there was a certain chemistry between the members of the band** il y avait une certaine affinité entre les musiciens; *Fig* **there's no chemistry, the chemistry's missing** le courant ne passe pas, on n'a pas d'atomes crochus
2 *comp (lesson, teacher, degree)* de chimie
►► ***chemistry set*** panoplie *f* de chimiste
chemo [ˈkiːməʊ] *n Fam Med (abbr* **chemotherapy**) chimio *f*
chemoreceptor [ˌkiːməʊrɪˈseptə(r)] *n Biol* chémorécepteur *m*, chimiorécepteur *m*
chemosynthesis [ˌkiːməʊˈsɪnθɪsɪs] *n Biol* chimiosynthèse *f*
chemotaxis [ˌkiːməʊˈtæksɪs] *n Biol* chimiotaxie *f*
chemotherapeutic [ˌkiːməʊθerəˈpjuːtɪk] *adj Med* chimiothérapeutique
chemotherapist [ˌkiːməʊˈθerəpɪst] *n Med* chimiothérapeute *mf*
chemotherapy [ˌkiːməʊˈθerəpɪ] *n Med* chimiothérapie *f*
chemurgy [ˈkemɜːdʒɪ] *n Chem & Ind* chimiurgie *f*
chenille [ʃəˈniːl] *n Tex* chenille *f*
Cheops [ˈkiːɒps] *n* Kheops; **the great pyramid of Cheops** la grande pyramide de Kheops
cheque, *Am* **check** [tʃek] *n* chèque *m*; **a cheque for £7** *or* **to the amount of £7** un chèque de 7 livres; **will you take a cheque?** est-ce que vous acceptez les chèques?; **who should I make the cheque payable to?** à quel nom dois-je libeller le chèque?; **to pay by cheque** payer par chèque; **to cash a cheque** toucher un chèque; **to stop a cheque** faire opposition à un chèque; **to write sb a cheque** faire un chèque à qn; **a bad cheque** un chèque sans provision; *Br* **a crossed/open cheque** un chèque barré/non-barré
►► *Br* ***cheque account*** compte *m* chèques; ***cheque counterfoil*** talon *m* de chèque, souche *f*; *Br* ***cheque (guarantee) card*** = carte d'identité bancaire sans laquelle les chèques ne sont pas acceptés en Grande-Bretagne; ***cheque number*** numéro *m* de chèque; ***cheque stub*** talon *m* de chèque, souche *f*
chequebook, *Am* **checkbook** [ˈtʃekˌbʊk] *n* carnet *m* de chèques, chéquier *m*
►► ***chequebook account*** compte *m* (de) chèques; ***chequebook holder*** porte-chéquier *m*; ***chequebook journalism*** = dans les milieux de la presse, pratique qui consiste à payer des sommes importantes pour le témoignage d'une personne impliquée dans une affaire
chequerboard [ˈtʃekəˌbɔːd] *n* damier *m*
chequered, *Am* **checkered** [ˈtʃekəd] *adj* (**a**) *(pattern)* à carreaux, à damiers, *Can* carreauté (**b**) *(varied)* varié; *(life)* plein de vicissitudes; [illegible] **had a chequered career** sa carrière a connu des hauts et des bas
►► ***chequered flag*** *(in motor racing)* drapeau *m* à damiers
Chequers [ˈtʃekəz] *n* = résidence secondaire officielle du Premier ministre britannique
chequers, *Am* **checkers** [ˈtʃekəz] *n (UNCOUNT)* jeu *m* de dames; **how about (a game of) chequers?** si on jouait aux dames?
chequerwork [ˈtʃekəwɜːk] *n (pattern → of bricks, fields)* motif *m* en damier
cherish [ˈtʃerɪʃ] *vt (person)* chérir, aimer; *(ambition, hope)* caresser, nourrir; *(experience, memory, possession)* chérir; *(right, value)* tenir à; **one of my most cherished memories** un de mes souvenirs les plus chers
Chernenko [tʃɜːˈneŋkəʊ] *pr n* Tchernenko
Chernobyl [tʃɜːˈnəʊbəl] *n* Tchernobyl
chernozem [ˈtʃɜːnəzem] *n Geol* tchernoziom *m*
Cherokee [ˌtʃerəˈkiː] *(pl* **inv** *or* **Cherokees**) **1** *n* (**a**) *(person)* Cherokee *mf* (**b**) *(language)* cherokee *m*
2 *adj* cherokee
►► ***Cherokee Indian*** Indien(enne) *m,f* cherokee, Cherokee *mf*
cheroot [ʃəˈruːt] *n* petit cigare *m (à bouts coupés)*
cherry [ˈtʃerɪ] *(pl* **cherries**) *n* (**a**) *(fruit)* cerise *f*; *(tree)* cerisier *m*; *Prov* **life is just a bowl of cherries** = il faut voir la vie en rose
(**b**) *(colour)* cerise *f inv*, rouge *m* cerise *(inv)*
(**c**) *very Fam (virginity)* **to lose one's cherry** perdre sa fleur; **she's still got her cherry** elle est encore pucelle
(**d**) *very Fam (virgin)* puceau (elle) *m,f*
(**e**) *Am Fam (newcomer)* bleu *m*
2 *adj* (**a**) *(colour)* cerise *(inv)*, rouge cerise *(inv)*
(**b**) *Am Fam (in perfect condition)* en parfait état❑, impec
3 *comp (blossom, wood)* de cerisier; *(pie, tart)* aux cerises
►► *Am* ***cherry bomb*** = sorte de pétard rouge; ***cherry brandy*** cherry *m*; ***cherry orchard*** cerisaie *f*; *Tech* ***cherry picker*** plate-forme *f* élévatrice; *Bot* ***cherry plum*** myrobolan *m*; ***cherry red*** rouge *m* cerise; ***cherry stone*** noyau *m* de cerise; ***cherry tomato*** tomate *f* cerise; ***cherry tree*** cerisier *m*; *(wild)* merisier *m*

'The Cherry Orchard' *Chekhov* 'La Cerisaie'

cherry-pick *vt Fig* écrémer
cherry-picking *n* cueillette *f* des cerises; *Fig* écrémage *m*
cherry-red *adj* (rouge) cerise *(inv)*; **cherry-red lips** des lèvres *fpl* vermeilles
cherrywood [ˈtʃerɪˌwʊd] **1** *n (gen)* (bois *m* de) cerisier *m*; *(of wild or black cherry tree)* (bois *m* de) merisier *m*
2 *comp (table, cabinet etc → gen)* en (bois de) cerisier; *(→ made of wild or black cherrywood)* en (bois de) merisier
cherub [ˈtʃerəb] *(pl* **cherubs** *or* **cherubim** [-bɪm]) *n Bible* chérubin *m*; *Art* angelot *m*, ange *m* joufflu; *Fig* **a little cherub** *(child)* un petit ange
cherubic [tʃeˈruːbɪk] *adj (face)* de chérubin; *(child, look, smile)* angélique
chervil [ˈtʃɜːvɪl] *n* cerfeuil *m*
Ches. *(written abbr* **Cheshire**) Cheshire *m*
Cheshire [ˈtʃeʃə(r)] *n* le Cheshire, = comté dans le nord-ouest de l'Angleterre; **in Cheshire** dans le Cheshire; *Fam* **to grin like a Cheshire cat** avoir un sourire jusqu'aux oreilles❑
►► *Culin* ***Cheshire cheese*** fromage *m* de Chester, chester *m*
chess [tʃes] *n (UNCOUNT)* échecs *mpl*; **to play chess** jouer aux échecs; **let's play a game of chess** si on faisait une partie d'échecs?
►► ***chess player*** joueur(euse) *m,f* d'échecs; ***chess tournment*** tournoi *m* d'échecs
chessboard [ˈtʃesbɔːd] *n* échiquier *m*
chessman [ˈtʃesmæn] *(pl* **chessmen** [-men]) *n* pion *m*, pièce *f (de jeu d'échecs)*
chesspiece [ˈtʃespiːs] *n* pion *m*, pièce *f (de jeu d'échecs)*
chest [tʃest] **1** *n* (**a**) *Anat* poitrine *f*; *(of horse)* poitrail *m*; **to have a weak chest** être faible des [illegible]; *Fig* **to get something off one's chest** dire ce qu'on a sur le cœur
(**b**) *(box)* coffre *m*, caisse *f*
2 *comp (cold, measurement, voice, pain)* de poitrine
►► *Sport* ***chest bump*** = lorsque deux coéquipiers sautent en l'air et se heurtent la poitrine, en signe de félicitation; *Med* ***chest drain*** drain *m* thoracique; ***chest of drawers*** commode *f*; ***chest expander*** extenseur *m (pour développer les pectoraux)*; ***chest freezer*** congélateur *m* coffre; ***chest infection*** infection *f* des voies respiratoires; *Sport* ***chest pass*** *(in basketball)* passe *f (à la hauteur de la poitrine)*; *Sport* ***chest protector*** *(in baseball)* plastron *m* protecteur; ***chest size*** tour *m* de poitrine; ***chest X-ray*** radio *f* des poumons
-chested [ˈtʃestɪd] *suff* **broad-chested** *(person)* à large poitrine, de forte carrure; *(horse)* au poitrail large, empoitraillé; **big-chested** à forte poitrine
chesterfield [ˈtʃestəfiːld] *n* (**a**) *(coat)* pardessus

m (de ville) (**b**) *(sofa)* canapé *m* Chesterfield

chestnut ['tʃesnʌt] **1** *n* (**a**) *(tree)* châtaignier *m*; *(fruit)* châtaigne *f*; *(when cooked)* marron *m*; *Fig* **to pull sb's chestnuts out of the fire** tirer les marrons du feu à qn

(**b**) **(horse) chestnut** marron *m* (d'Inde); **(horse) chestnut tree** marronnier *m* d'Inde

(**c**) *(colour)* châtain *m*

(**d**) *(wood)* châtaignier *m*

(**e**) *(horse)* alezan(e) *m,f*

(**f**) *Fam (joke)* **old chestnut** plaisanterie *f* rebattue *ou* éculée

2 *adj (colour, hair)* châtain; *(horse)* alezan

3 *comp (blossom, wood)* de châtaignier; *(stuffing)* aux marrons

►► ***chestnut brown*** **1** *n* châtain *m inv* **2** *adj* châtain *(inv)*; ***chestnut purée*** crème *f* de marrons; ***chestnut tree*** châtaignier *m*

chesty ['tʃestɪ] *(compar* **chestier,** *superl* **chestiest)** *adj* (**a**) *(cough)* de poitrine; **to be chesty** être bronchitique (**b**) *Fam* **to be chesty** *(large-breasted)* avoir des gros seins ❑, *Hum* avoir du monde au balcon

cheval glass [ʃə'væl-] *n* psyché *f (glace)*

chevalier [ˌʃevə'lɪə(r)] *n Arch or Literary* chevalier *m*

Cheviot ['tʃiːvɪət] *n* **the Cheviot Hills, the Cheviots** les Cheviot

chevron ['ʃevrən] *n Archit, Her & Mil* chevron *m*

chevrotain ['ʃevrəʊˌteɪn] *n Zool* chevrotain *m*

Chevy ['ʃevɪ] *n Fam (Chevrolet® car)* Chevrolet ❑ *f*

chevy ['tʃevɪ] *n* (jeu *m* de) barres *fpl*

chew [tʃuː] **1** *vt* mâcher, mastiquer; *(cigar, end of pen etc)* mâchonner; **to chew tobacco** chiquer, mâcher du tabac; **to chew one's nails** se ronger les ongles; *also Fig* **to chew the cud** ruminer; *Fam* **to chew the fat** *or* **the rag (with sb)** tailler une bavette (avec qn)

2 *n* (**a**) *(act)* mâchement *m*, mastication *f*; **to have a chew at sth** mâchonner qch

(**b**) *(piece of tobacco)* chique *f*

(**c**) *(sweet)* bonbon *m*

(**d**) *(for cat, dog)* aliment *m* à mâcher

►**chew on** *vt insep* (**a**) *(food)* mâcher, mastiquer; *(bone)* ronger; *(tobacco)* chiquer; *(cigar, end of pen etc)* mâchonner; **he chewed on his pipe** il mâchouillait sa pipe

(**b**) *Fam (problem, question)* ruminer ❑, retourner dans sa tête ❑

►**chew out** *vt sep Am Fam* engueuler, passer un savon à

►**chew over** *vt sep Fam (think over)* ruminer, retourner dans sa tête; *(discuss)* discuter de

►**chew through** *vt insep* couper à force de ronger; **the mice had chewed through the wood** les souris avaient fait des trous dans le bois; **the rats had chewed through the rope** les rats avaient coupé la corde en la rongeant

►**chew up** *vt sep* (**a**) *(food)* mâchonner, mastiquer (**b**) *(damage)* abîmer à force de ronger

chewing ['tʃuːɪŋ] *n* mastication *f*

►► ***chewing gum*** chewing-gum *m*; ***chewing tobacco*** tabac *m* à chiquer

chewy ['tʃuːɪ] *(compar* **chewier,** *superl* **chewiest)** *adj* (**a**) *Pej (meat)* difficile à mâcher (**b**) *(sweet)* mou (molle), tendre

Cheyenne [ʃaɪ'en] *(pl* **inv** *or* **Cheyennes)** **1** *n* Cheyenne *mf*

2 *adj* cheyenne

Chiang Kai-shek [ˌtʃæŋkaɪ'ʃek] *pr n* Tchang Kaï-Chek

chianti [kɪ'æntɪ] *n* chianti *m*

Chiantishire [kɪ'æntɪʃə(r)] *n Br Hum* = nom humoristique désignant la Toscane, par allusion aux Britanniques qui s'y installent

chiaroscurist [kɪˌɑːrəʊ'skjʊərɪst] *n Art* clair-obscuriste *mf*, peintre *mf* de clair-obscur

chiaroscuro [kɪˌɑːrəʊ'skʊərə] *(pl* **chiaroscuros)** *n Art* clair-obscur *m*

chiasma [kaɪ'æzmə] *(pl* **chiasmata** [ˌkaɪæz'mɑːtə]) *n* (**a**) *Biol* chiasma *m* (**b**) *Anat* **(optic) chiasma** chiasma *m*, chiasme *m*

chiasmus [kaɪ'æzməs] *n Ling* chiasme *m*

chic [ʃiːk] **1** *adj* chic, élégant

2 *n* chic *m*, élégance *f*

Chicago [ʃɪ'kɑːgəʊ] *n* Chicago

►► ***the Chicago Board of Trade, the Chicago Mercantile Exchange*** = les deux plus importantes bourses de marchandises aux États-Unis; ***the Chicago fire*** l'incendie *m* de Chicago

THE CHICAGO FIRE

Ce gigantesque incendie détruisit une bonne partie de la ville en 1871. Selon la légende, ce serait la vache de Madame O'Leary qui, renversant une lanterne dans son étable, amorça le feu. L'incendie ravagea 20 000 habitations et fit 100 000 sans-abri.

chicane [ʃɪ'keɪn] *n* (**a**) *Cards (in bridge)* main *f* à sans atout (**b**) *(barrier)* chicane *f*

chicanery [ʃɪ'keɪnərɪ] *(pl* **chicaneries)** *n (trickery)* ruse *f*, fourberie *f*; *(legal trickery)* chicane *f*

Chicano [tʃɪ'kɑːnəʊ] *(pl* **Chicanos)** *n* Chicano *mf (Américain d'origine mexicaine)*

chichi ['ʃiːʃiː] *adj (affected)* précieux

chick [tʃɪk] *n* (**a**) *(baby bird → gen)* oisillon *m*; *(→ of chicken)* poussin *m* (**b**) *Fam (woman)* poupée *f*, nana *f*

►► *Fam* ***chick flick, chick movie*** = film qui plaît particulièrement aux femmes

chickadee ['tʃɪkədiː] *n Orn* mésange *f (d'Amérique du Nord)*

chicken ['tʃɪkɪn] **1** *n* (**a**) *(bird)* poulet *m*; *(young)* poussin *m*; *Fam* **he's no (spring) chicken** il n'est plus tout jeune ❑; **which came first, the chicken or the egg?** allez savoir quelle est la cause et quel est l'effet, l'œuf ou la poule?; *Fam* **it's a chicken-and-egg situation** c'est le problème de l'œuf et de la poule, on ne sait pas lequel est à l'origine de l'autre

(**b**) *Fam (coward)* poule *f* mouillée, froussard(e) *m,f*

2 *comp (dish, stew)* de poulet; *(sandwich)* au poulet

3 *adj Fam (cowardly)* froussard

►► ***chicken breast*** blanc *m* (de poulet); ***chicken farm*** élevage *m* de poulets, élevage *m* avicole; ***chicken farmer*** éleveur(euse) *m,f* de volailles, aviculteur(trice) *m,f*; ***chicken farming*** élevage *m* avicole *ou* de volailles, aviculture *f*; *Am very Fam* ***chicken hawk*** pédophile ❑ *m*; *Culin* ***chicken Kiev*** poulet *m* Kiev *(blancs de poulet farcis au beurre et à l'ail, panés puis frits ou cuits au four)*; ***chicken leg*** cuisse *f* (de poulet); ***Chicken Licken, Chicken Little*** = conte pour enfants dont le héros croit que le ciel va lui tomber sur la tête; ***chicken liver*** foie *m* de volaille; ***chicken run*** enclos *m (d'un poulailler)*; ***chicken soup*** *(clear)* potage *m* au poulet; *(creamy)* velouté *m ou* crème *f* de volaille; ***chicken wire*** grillage *m*

►**chicken out** *vi Fam* se dégonfler; **he chickened out of the race** il s'est dégonflé et n'a pas pris part à la course

chickenburger ['tʃɪkɪnˌbɜːgə(r)] *n* chickenburger *m*

chickenfeed ['tʃɪkɪnfiːd] *n (UNCOUNT)* (**a**) *(for poultry)* nourriture *f* pour volaille (**b**) *Fam Fig (small amount of money)* cacahuètes *fpl*; **he earns chickenfeed** il gagne des cacahuètes

chicken-fried steak *n Am* steak *m* pané

chicken-hearted [-ˌhɑːtɪd], **chicken-livered** [-ˌlɪvəd] *adj* poltron

chickenpox ['tʃɪkɪnpɒks] *n (UNCOUNT)* varicelle *f*

chickenshit ['tʃɪkɪnʃɪt] *Am very Fam* **1** *n (person)* poule *f* mouillée

2 *adj (cowardly)* dégonflé

chickpea ['tʃɪkpiː] *n* pois *m* chiche

chickweed ['tʃɪkwiːd] *n Bot* mouron *m* blanc *ou* des oiseaux

chicle ['tʃɪkəl] *n* chiclé *m*

chicly ['ʃiːklɪ] *adv* de façon chic, élégamment

chicory ['tʃɪkərɪ] *(pl* **chicories)** *n (for salad)* endive *f*; *(for coffee)* chicorée *f*

chide [tʃaɪd] *(pt* **chided** *or* **chid** [tʃɪd], *pp* **chid** [tʃɪd] *or* **chidden** ['tʃɪdən]) *vt Formal* gronder, réprimander

chief [tʃiːf] **1** *n* (**a**) *(leader → of tribe, group)* chef *m*; **in chief** en chef; **editor in chief** rédacteur(trice) *m,f* en chef; **too many chiefs and not enough Indians** trop de chefs et pas assez d'hommes de troupe *(pour exécuter les ordres et faire le travail)*

(**b**) *Fam (boss)* patron(onne) *m,f*, boss *m*; **he's the big white chief** c'est lui le grand patron

(**c**) *Her* chef *m*

2 *adj* (**a**) *(most important)* principal, premier; **one of the chief conflicts** un des principaux conflits; **the chief reason for doing sth** la raison majeure *ou* principale pour faire qch

(**b**) *(head)* premier, en chef

3 in chief *adv* principalement, surtout

►► *Br* ***chief accountant*** chef *m* comptable, chef *m* de la comptabilité; ***Chief Constable*** = en Grande-Bretagne, chef de la police d'un comté ou d'une région, ≃ commissaire *m* divisionnaire; ***Chief Education Officer*** ≃ recteur *m* d'académie; *Admin* ***chief executive*** directeur(trice) *m,f*; *Am Pol* ***the Chief Executive*** le président des États-Unis, le chef de l'exécutif; *Com & Ind* ***chief executive officer*** président(e)-directeur(trice) général(e) *m,f*; *Am* ***Chief Financial Officer*** chef *m* comptable, chef *m* de la comptabilité; ***chief inspector*** *(gen)* inspecteur(trice) *m,f* principal(e), inspecteur(trice) *m,f* en chef; *Br (of police)* ≃ commissaire *m* de police; *Br Sch* ≃ inspecteur(trice) *m,f* général(e); *Law* ***chief justice*** président(e) *m,f* de la Haute Cour de justice; *Am* juge *m* à la Cour suprême; ***chief librarian*** bibliothécaire *mf* en chef; *Am Mil* ***chief master sergeant*** major *m*; *Naut* ***chief petty officer*** ≃ maître *m*; ***chief of police*** ≃ préfet *m* de police; *Mil* ***chief of staff*** chef *m* d'état-major; *Am (at White House)* secrétaire *m* général de la Maison Blanche; *Br* ***chief superintendent*** *(in police)* ≃ commissaire *m* principal; *Mil Br* ***chief technician*** *(in Air Force)* officier *m* technicien; *Mil* ***chief warrant officer*** adjudant *m* chef; *Pol* ***Chief Whip*** = responsable du maintien de la discipline à l'intérieur d'un parti à la Chambre des communes

chiefly ['tʃiːflɪ] *adv* principalement, surtout

chieftain ['tʃiːftən] *n* chef *m (de tribu)*

chieftaincy ['tʃiːftənsɪ], **chieftainship** ['tʃiːftənʃɪp] *n* chefferie *f*

chiffchaff ['tʃɪftʃæf] *n Orn* pouillot *m* véloce

chiffon ['ʃɪfɒn] **1** *n Tex* mousseline *f* de soie

2 *adj* (**a**) *Tex (dress, scarf)* en mousseline (de soie) (**b**) *Culin* à la mousse; **lemon chiffon pie** ≃ tarte *f* à la mousse de citron

chiffonade [ˌʃɪfə'neɪd] *n Am* chiffonnade *f*

chiffonier, chiffonnier [ˌʃɪfə'nɪə(r)] *n* chiffonnier *m*

chigger ['tʃɪgə(r)] *n Entom* (**a**) *(flea)* chique *f* (**b**) *Am (parasitic larva)* aoûtat *m*

chignon ['ʃiːnjɒn] *n* chignon *m*

chigoe ['tʃɪgəʊ] *n Entom* (**a**) *(flea)* chique *f* (**b**) *Am (parasitic larva)* aoûtat *m*

chihuahua [tʃɪ'wɑːwə] *n* chihuahua *m*

chilblain ['tʃɪlbleɪn] *n* engelure *f*

child [tʃaɪld] *(pl* **children** ['tʃɪldrən]) **1** *n* (**a**) *(boy or girl)* enfant *mf*; **ever since I was a child** depuis mon enfance; **while still a child** tout enfant; **children of the 60s** des enfants des années 60; **don't be such a child!** ne fais pas l'enfant!; **stop treating me like a child!** arrête de me traiter comme un enfant!; *Arch or Literary* **to be with child** attendre un enfant, être enceinte; *Arch or Literary* **to get a woman with child** faire un enfant à une femme; *Bible* **the children of Israel** les enfants d'Israël; **he's like a child with a new toy** il est comme un enfant avec un nouveau jouet; *Fam* **it's child's play for** *or* **to him** c'est un jeu d'enfant pour lui

(**b**) *Literary (result)* fruit *m*

2 *comp (psychology)* de l'enfant, infantile; *(psychologist)* pour enfants; *(lock)* ne pouvant pas être ouvert par les enfants, de sécurité; *(not breakable)* ne pouvant être cassé par les enfants

►► ***child abuse*** mauvais traitements *mpl* à enfant; *(sexual)* sévices *mpl* sexuels infligés à un enfant; ***child abuser*** personne *f* coupable de mauvais traitements à enfant; *(sexual)* personne coupable de sévices sexuels infligés à un enfant; *Br Admin* ***child benefit*** *(UNCOUNT)* allocation *f* familiale *ou* allocations *fpl* familiales (pour un enfant); ***child bride*** femme *f* enfant; **she was his child bride** c'était une enfant quand il l'a épousée; ***child guidance*** psychopédagogie *f* pour enfants caractériels; ***child guidance centre*** centre *m* psychopédagogique pour enfants; ***child labour*** travail *m* des enfants; ***child molester*** auteur *m* de sévices sexuels sur des enfants; ***child pornography*** pornographie *f* pédophile; ***child prodigy*** enfant *mf* prodige; ***child psychiatrist*** pédopsychiatre *mf*; ***child psychiatry*** pédopsychiatrie *f*; ***child seat*** siège-auto *m (pour enfant)*; *Br Admin* ***Child Support Agency*** = organisme gouvernemental qui décide du montant des pensions alimentaires et les prélève au besoin; ***child welfare*** protection *f* de l'enfance

childbearing ['tʃaɪld,beərɪŋ] **1** *n* grossesse *f*

2 *adj (complications, problems)* de grossesse; **of childbearing age** en âge d'avoir des enfants; **she's past childbearing age** elle est trop âgée pour avoir des enfants; **she's got childbearing hips** elle est large des hanches

childbed ['tʃaɪldbed] *n Arch or Literary* **in childbed** en couches

childbirth ['tʃaɪldbɜːθ] *n (UNCOUNT)* accouchement *m*; **to die in childbirth** mourir en couches

childcare ['tʃaɪldkeə(r)] *n* (**a**) *(day care)* garde *f* d'enfants; **we haven't decided on childcare arrangements yet** nous n'avons pas encore pris de décision quant à la garde des enfants (**b**) *Br Admin* protection *f* de l'enfance

►► ***childcare centre*** crèche *f*, garderie *f*

childfree ['tʃaɪldfriː] *adj Am (couple, household)* sans enfants

child-friendly *adj (area, city)* aménagé pour les enfants; *(house, furniture)* conçu pour les enfants; *(restaurant)* pour les familles

childhood ['tʃaɪldhʊd] **1** *n* enfance *f*; **to be in one's second childhood** être retombé en enfance

2 *comp (friend, memories)* d'enfance

►► ***childhood sweetheart*** amour *m* d'enfance

childish ['tʃaɪldɪʃ] *adj* (**a**) *(of children, childlike → face, fears, voice)* d'enfant; *(→ laughter, curiosity, innocence)* enfantin (**b**) *(immature)* enfantin, puéril; **don't be so childish** ne fais pas l'enfant, ne sois pas aussi puéril

childishly ['tʃaɪldɪʃlɪ] *adv* comme un enfant, en enfant

childishness ['tʃaɪldɪʃnɪs] *n (UNCOUNT) (of person)* enfantillage *m*, puérilité *f*; *(of behaviour, remark)* puérilité *f*; **that's just childishness!** ce sont des enfantillages!

childless ['tʃaɪldlɪs] *adj* sans enfants

childlessness ['tʃaɪldlɪsnɪs] *n* fait *m* de ne pas avoir d'enfants

childlike ['tʃaɪldlaɪk] *adj* enfantin; *(question)* naïf; *(smile)* d'enfant; **he was childlike in his curiosity** il avait une curiosité enfantine *ou* d'enfant

Childline ['tʃaɪld,laɪn] *n Br* = numéro de téléphone mis à la disposition des enfants maltraités, ≃ SOS enfants battus

childminder ['tʃaɪld,maɪndə(r)] *n Br (for very young children)* nourrice *f*; *(for older children)* assistante *f* maternelle

childminding ['tʃaɪld,maɪndɪŋ] *n* garde *f* d'enfants

childproof ['tʃaɪldpruːf] *adj (door)* ne pouvant pas être ouvert par les enfants, de sécurité; *(not breakable)* ne pouvant pas être cassé par les enfants

►► ***childproof lock*** serrure *f* de sécurité pour enfants

children [illegible]

►► ***children's home*** foyer *m* d'enfants; ***Children In Need*** = association caritative britannique de soutien aux enfants du monde entier, créée par la BBC, qui organise chaque année une grande soirée télévisée pour collecter des fonds

Chile ['tʃɪlɪ] *n* Chili *m*; **in Chile** au Chili

►► *Bot* ***Chile pine*** araucaria *m*, désespoir *m* des singes

Chilean ['tʃɪlɪən] **1** *n* Chilien(enne) *m,f*

2 *adj* chilien

3 *comp (embassy, history)* du Chili

chili = **chilli**

chill [tʃɪl] **1** *vt* (**a**) *(make cold → food, wine, champagne)* mettre au frais; *(→ glass, person)* glacer; **to be chilled to the bone/to the marrow** être glacé jusqu'aux os/jusqu'à la moelle

(**b**) *Fig (enthusiasm)* refroidir

(**c**) *Tech (metal)* tremper

2 *vi* (**a**) *(become cold)* se refroidir, rafraîchir (**b**) *Fam (relax)* décompresser; **chill!** relax!, calmos!

3 *n* (**a**) *(coldness)* fraîcheur *f*, froideur *f*; **there's a chill in the air** il fait assez frais *ou* un peu froid; **to take the chill off** *(room)* réchauffer un peu; *(wine)* chambrer; *Fig* **his remark cast a chill over the meeting** son observation a jeté un froid dans l'assemblée; *Fig* **I sensed a certain chill in his welcome** j'ai senti une certaine froideur dans son accueil

(**b**) *(feeling of fear)* frisson *m*; **the story sent chills down her spine** l'histoire lui a fait froid dans le dos

(**c**) *(illness)* coup *m* de froid, refroidissement *m*; **to catch a chill** attraper *ou* prendre froid

4 *adj (air, weather)* frais (fraîche), froid; *(glance, response)* froid, glacial

►**chill out** *vi Fam* décompresser; **I wish he'd chill out a bit** ça serait bien qu'il soit un peu plus cool; **he likes chilling out at home** il aime bien rester chez lui, peinard; **chill out!** relax!, calmos!

chilled [tʃɪld] *adj* (**a**) *(refrigerated)* **chilled white wine** vin *m* blanc frais; **chilled champagne** champagne *m* frappé; **chilled meat** viande *f* réfrigérée *ou* frigorifiée; **chilled products** produits *mpl* frigorifiés; **best served chilled** *(on label)* servir glacé *ou* très frais (**b**) *Fam (relaxed)* cool

chiller ['tʃɪlə(r)] *n Fam (film)* film *m* d'épouvante; *(book)* roman *m* d'épouvante

chilli ['tʃɪlɪ] *n (vegetable)* piment *m* (rouge); *(dish)* chili *m*

►► ***chilli con carne*** chili *m* con carne; ***chilli dog*** hot dog *m* au chili; ***chilli flakes*** piment *f* râpé, *Can* flocons *mpl* de piment; ***chilli powder*** chili *m*; ***chilli sauce*** sauce *f* aux tomates et piments

chillin ['tʃɪlɪn] *adj Am Fam* génial, cool

chilliness ['tʃɪlɪnɪs] *n (of air, wind)* fraîcheur *f*; *Fig (of greeting, manner)* froideur *f*

chilling ['tʃɪlɪŋ] *adj (wind)* frais (fraîche), froid; *Fig (look, smile)* froid, glacial; *(news, story, thought)* qui donne des frissons

chill-out room *n (in nightclub)* espace *m* chill-out

chilly ['tʃɪlɪ] (*compar* **chillier,** *superl* **chilliest**) *adj* (**a**) *(air, room)* (très) frais (fraîche), froid; **I feel chilly** j'ai froid; **it's rather chilly this morning** il fait plutôt frais *ou* frisquet ce matin (**b**) *Fig (greeting, look)* froid, glacial

Chiltern Hundreds ['tʃɪltən-] *n Pol & Fig* **to apply for the Chiltern Hundreds** démissionner *(du Parlement britannique)*

> **THE CHILTERN HUNDREDS**
>
> Ce nom désigne une circonscription administrative du Buckinghamshire (Grande-Bretagne); il désigne aussi un titre honorifique, "Stewardship of the Chiltern Hundreds", auquel postule un parlementaire qui souhaite démissionner ou prendre sa retraite.

chimaera [kaɪ'mɪərə] *n* (**a**) = **chimera** (**b**) *Ich* chimère *f*

chime [tʃaɪm] **1** *n (bell)* carillon *m*; **the chimes of St Mary's** le carillon de St Mary; **to ring the chimes** carillonner; **(door) chimes** carillon *m* de porte

2 *vi* (**a**) *(bell, voices)* carillonner; *(clock)* sonner

(**b**) *(agree)* s'accorder; **his view chimes with mine** il est d'accord avec moi

3 *vt* sonner; **the clock chimed six** l'horloge a sonné six heures

4 chimes *npl (for door)* carillon *m*, sonnette *f*

►**chime in** *vi Fam* (**a**) *(say)* intervenir; **all the children chimed in** tous les enfants ont fait chorus; **"yes, please do stay!" the children chimed in** "oui, restez donc!" ajoutèrent les enfants; **he chimed in with some silly remark** il est intervenu pour dire une bêtise

(**b**) *(agree)* s'accorder; **his explanation chimes in with the facts** son explication s'accorde avec les faits

chimera [kaɪ'mɪərə] *n Myth & Fig* chimère *f*

chimeric [kaɪ'merɪk], **chimerical** [kaɪ'merɪkəl] *adj Myth & Fig* chimérique

chimerically [kaɪ'merɪkəlɪ] *adv Myth & Fig* chimériquement

chimichanga [,tʃɪmɪ'tʃæŋgə] *n Culin* chimichanga *f (tortilla frite à la viande et/ou aux haricots)*

chiming ['tʃaɪmɪŋ] **1** *adj* carillonnant; *(clock)* à carillon

2 *n* carillonnement *m*, carillon *m*

chimney ['tʃɪmnɪ] *n* (**a**) *(in building)* cheminée *f*; *Fam* **to smoke like a chimney** *(of person)* fumer comme un sapeur *ou* un pompier (**b**) *(of lamp)* verre *m* (**c**) *Geol* cheminée *f*

►► ***chimney corner*** coin *m* du feu

chimneybreast ['tʃɪmnɪbrest] *n Br* manteau *m (de cheminée)*

chimneypiece ['tʃɪmnɪpiːs] *n Br* dessus *m ou* tablette *f* de cheminée

chimneypot ['tʃɪmnɪpɒt] *n* tuyau *m* de cheminée

chimneystack ['tʃɪmnɪstæk] *n (of one chimney)* tuyau *m* de cheminée; *(group of chimneys)* souche *f* de cheminée

chimneysweep ['tʃɪmnɪswiːp] *n* ramoneur *m*

chimp [tʃɪmp], **chimpanzee** [,tʃɪmpən'ziː] *n Zool* chimpanzé *m*

chin [tʃɪn] (*pt & pp* **chinned,** *cont* **chinning**) **1** *n* menton *m*; **(keep your) chin up!** courage!; *Fam* **he took the news on the chin** il a encaissé la nouvelle (sans broncher)

2 *vt Sport* **to chin the bar** faire une traction à la barre fixe

China ['tʃaɪnə] *n* Chine *f*; **in China** en Chine; **the People's Republic of China** la République populaire de Chine

►► ***China Syndrome*** syndrome *m* chinois

china ['tʃaɪnə] **1** *n* (**a**) *(material)* porcelaine *f*; **a piece of china** une porcelaine

(**b**) *(porcelain objects)* porcelaine *f*; *(porcelain dishes)* porcelaine *f*, vaisselle *f* (de porcelaine); *(crockery)* vaisselle *f*

(**c**) *Br Fam (friend)* pote *m*; **my old china!** mon vieux!

2 *comp (cup, plate, doll)* de *ou* en porcelaine; *(shop)* de porcelaine

►► ***china cabinet*** dressoir *m*; ***china clay*** kaolin *m*; *Bot* ***China rose*** rose *f* de Chine; ***the China Sea*** la mer de Chine; ***China tea*** thé *m* de Chine

chinaberry ['tʃaɪnə,berɪ] *n Bot (berry)* baie *f* de l'arbre à chapelet; *(tree)* arbre *m* à chapelet

Chinagraph® ['tʃaɪnəgrɑːf] *n (pencil)* crayon *m* gras

Chinaman ['tʃaɪnəmən] (*pl* **Chinamen** [-mən]) *n Old-fashioned* Chinois *m*

Chinatown ['tʃaɪnətaʊn] *n* le quartier chinois

chinaware ['tʃaɪnəweə(r)] *n (porcelain objects)* porcelaine *f*; *(porcelain dishes)* porcelaine *f*, vaisselle *f* (en porcelaine)

chinch [tʃɪntʃ] *n Am* punaise *f*

chincherinchee [,tʃɪntʃə'rɪntʃɪ] *n Bot* ornithogale *m*

chinchilla [,tʃɪn'tʃɪlə] **1** *n Zool & (fur)* chinchilla *m*

2 *comp (coat, wrap)* de chinchilla

chin-chin *exclam Br Fam Old-fashioned (hello, goodbye)* salut!; *(in toast)* tchin-tchin!

chine [tʃaɪn] *n Anat & Culin* échine *f*

Chinese [,tʃaɪ'niːz] (*pl* **inv**) **1** *npl* **the Chinese** les Chinois *mpl*

2 *n* (**a**) *(person)* Chinois(e) *m,f*

(**b**) *(language)* chinois *m*

(**c**) *Br Fam (meal)* repas *m* chinois ❑; **I feel like a Chinese tonight** j'ai envie de manger chinois ce soir

[illegible]

4 *comp (embassy)* de Chine; *(history)* de la Chine; *(teacher)* de chinois

►► ***Chinese boxes*** boîtes *fpl* gigognes; *Br* ***Chinese burn*** torture *f* indienne; *Bot & Culin* ***Chinese cabbage*** chou *m* chinois; ***Chinese chequers*** *(UNCOUNT)* dames *fpl* chinoises; ***Chinese Chippendale*** Chippendale *m* de style chinois; *Bot & Culin* ***Chinese gooseberry*** kiwi *m (fruit)*; ***Chinese lantern*** lanterne *f* vénitienne; *Br Bot & Culin* ***Chinese leaves*** chou *m* chinois; ***Chinese medecine*** médecine *f* chinoise; ***Chinese noodles*** vermicelles *mpl* chinois; ***Chinese puzzle*** casse-tête *m inv* chinois; *Fin* ***Chinese walls*** = murs imaginaires qui symbolisent la confidentialité indispensable dans certains milieux financiers et séparent des services qui, par ailleurs, travaillent côte à côte; *Zool* ***Chinese water deer*** hydropote *m*; ***Chinese water torture*** supplice *m* chinois; *Br* ***Chinese whispers*** téléphone *m* arabe

Chink [tʃɪŋk] *n Fam* Chinetoque *mf*, = terme injurieux désignant un Chinois

chink [tʃɪŋk] **1** *n* (**a**) *(hole)* fente *f*, fissure *f*; *(of light)* rayon *m*; *Fig* **we found a chink in her armour** nous avons trouvé son point faible *ou* sensible (**b**) *(sound)* tintement *m (de pièces de monnaie, de verres)*

2 *vi (jingle)* tinter

3 *vt* (**a**) *(jingle)* faire tinter (**b**) *Am (wall)* boucher les fentes dans

Chinky ['tʃɪŋkɪ] *n Fam* (**a**) *(restaurant)* (restaurant *m*) chinois❑ *m*; *(meal)* repas *m* chinois❑; **to go for a Chinky** manger chinois❑ (**b**) *(person)* Chinetoque *mf*, = terme injurieux désignant un Chinois

chinless ['tʃɪnlɪs] *adj (with receding chin)* au menton fuyant; *Fig (cowardly)* mou (molle)

▸▸ *Br Fam Hum* ***chinless wonder*** = individu de bonne famille dépourvu de volonté et d'intelligence

chinning bar ['tʃɪnɪŋ-] *n Sport* barre *f* fixe

chino ['tʃiːnəʊ] *n Tex* chino *m*; **chinos** *(trousers)* chinos *mpl*; **a pair of chinos** une paire de chinos

Chinook [tʃɪ'nuːk] (*pl* **inv** *or* **Chinooks**) **1** *n* (**a**) *(person)* Chinook *mf* (**b**) *(language)* langue *f* des Chinooks, langue *f* chinook

2 *adj* chinook *(inv)*

chinook [tʃɪ'nuːk] *n Met (wind)* chinook *m*

chinstrap ['tʃɪnstræp] *n* jugulaire *f (de casque)*

chintz [tʃɪnts] *Tex* **1** *n* chintz *m*

2 *comp (curtain)* de chintz; *(chair)* recouvert de chintz

chintzy ['tʃɪntsɪ] (*compar* **chintzier**, *superl* **chintziest**) *adj* (**a**) *Br Pej (decor)* = typique des intérieurs anglais coquets abondamment ornés de tissus imprimés (**b**) *Am Fam (miserly → person)* mesquin; *(→ amount)* misérable, insuffisant (**c**) *Am Fam (of poor quality)* toc et tape-à-l'œil

chin-up *n Sport* traction *f* (à la barre fixe); **to do chin-ups** faire des tractions (à la barre fixe)

chinwag ['tʃɪnwæg] (*pt & pp* **chinwagged**, *cont* **chinwagging**) *Fam* **1** *n* causette *f*; **to have a chinwag (with sb)** tailler une bavette (avec qn)

2 *vi* bavarder

chinwagging ['tʃɪn,wægɪŋ] *n Fam* bavardage *m*

chip [tʃɪp] (*pt & pp* **chipped**, *cont* **chipping**) **1** *n* (**a**) *(piece)* éclat *m*; *(of wood)* copeau *m*, éclat *m*; *Fam* **she's a chip off the old block** elle est bien la fille de son père/de sa mère❑; *Fam* **to have a chip on one's shoulder** en vouloir à tout le monde❑; **he's got a chip on his shoulder about not having been to college** il n'a pas fait d'études et il en veut à tout le monde à cause de ça

(**b**) *(flaw → in dish, glass)* ébréchure *f*; *(→ in chair, wardrobe)* écornure *f*; **this glass has a chip (in it)** ce verre est ébréché

(**c**) *Br (French fry)* (pomme de terre *f*) frite *f*; *Am (crisp)* chips *f inv*, *Can* croustille *f*

(**d**) *(for games, gambling)* jeton *m*, fiche *f*; **to cash in one's chips** se faire payer; *Fam Fig* casser sa pipe; *Fam* **when the chips are down** dans les moments difficiles❑; *Br Fam* **to have had one's chips** être fichu *ou* cuit

(**e**) *Comput* **(silicon) chip** puce *f*

(**f**) *Golf* coup *m* coché

2 *vt* (**a**) *(dish, glass)* ébrécher; *(furniture)* écorner; *(paint, enamel)* écailler; *(tooth)* casser

(**b**) *(cut into pieces)* piler; **to chip wood** faire des copeaux

(**c**) *(shape by cutting)* tailler

(**d**) *Br (potatoes)* couper en lamelles

(**e**) *Sport (ball)* prendre en dessous, donner une pichenette à; **he chipped the ball over the net** d'une pichenette, il a envoyé la balle au-dessus du filet; *Golf* **to chip the ball** cocher

3 *vi (dish, glass)* s'ébrécher; *(furniture)* s'écorner; *(paint, enamel)* s'écailler

▸▸ *Br* ***chip basket*** panier *m* à frites; *Br* ***chip cutter*** coupe-frites *m inv*; ***chip pan*** friteuse *f*; *Br* ***chip shop*** = boutique où l'on vend des frites ainsi que du poisson frit, des saucisses etc; *Golf* ***chip shot*** coup *m* d'approche roulé; *Br* ***chip van*** friterie *f (camionnette)*

▸**chip at** *vt insep* enlever des éclats de

▸**chip away 1** *vt sep (plaster)* décaper, enlever petit à petit

2 *vi (plaster)* s'écailler

▸**chip away at** *vt insep* **to chip away at the old paintwork** enlever la vieille peinture petit à petit; **to chip away at sb's authority** grignoter l'autorité de qn; **just keep chipping away at him until he changes his mind** continuez à le travailler au corps jusqu'à ce qu'il change d'avis

▸**chip in** *Fam* **1** *vi* (**a**) *(contribute)* contribuer❑; **we all chipped in with £5** nous avons tous donné 5 livres❑

(**b**) *(speak)* mettre son grain de sel; **he chipped in with a suggestion** il est intervenu pour faire une suggestion❑

(**c**) *Cards* miser❑

2 *vt insep* (**a**) *(contribute)* contribuer❑, donner❑

(**b**) *(say)* dire❑

▸**chip off 1** *vi (fall off, break off → paint etc)* s'écailler

2 *vt sep (break off)* enlever; **somebody had chipped the nose off the statue** quelqu'un avait cassé le nez de la statue; **to chip a piece off a plate** ébrécher une assiette

chip-based *adj Comput* à puce

chipboard ['tʃɪpbɔːd] *n (UNCOUNT) Br Constr* (panneau *m* d')aggloméré *m*, panneau *m* de particules

chipmunk ['tʃɪpmʌŋk] *n Zool* tamia *m*, *Can* suisse *m*

chipolata [,tʃɪpə'lɑːtə] *n Br* chipolata *f*

chipotle [tʃɪ'pəʊtəl] *n Culin* chipotle *m*, piment *m* chipotle

chipped [tʃɪpt] *adj (dish, glass)* ébréché; *(furniture)* écorné; *(paint, enamel)* écaillé; *(tooth)* cassé

▸▸ *Culin Am* ***chipped beef*** ≃ émincé *m* de bœuf; *Br* ***chipped potatoes*** (pommes de terre *fpl*) frites *fpl*

Chippendale ['tʃɪpən,deɪl] *n* (**a**) *(style of furniture)* Chippendale *m (style de mobilier anglais du XVIIIème siècle)* (**b**) **the Chippendales** *(male strippers)* les Chippendales *mpl*

chipper ['tʃɪpə(r)] *adj Fam* (**a**) *(lively)* vif❑, fringant❑; **I'm feeling very chipper** j'ai la pêche (**b**) *(smartly dressed)* chic❑, élégant❑

chippie = **chippy**

chippings ['tʃɪpɪŋz] *npl (gen)* éclats *mpl*, fragments *mpl*; *(of wood)* copeaux *mpl*, éclats *mpl*; *(in roadwork)* gravillons *mpl*; *Can* gravelle *f*; **slow, loose chippings** *(sign)* attention gravillons

chippy ['tʃɪpɪ] (*pl* **chippies**) *n* (**a**) *Br Fam* = boutique où l'on vend des frites ainsi que du poisson frit, des saucisses etc (**b**) *Br & NZ Fam (carpenter)* charpentier❑ *m* (**c**) *Am very Fam Pej (woman)* femme *f* légère❑

CHIPS [tʃɪps] *n Am Banking* (*abbr* **Clearing House Interbank Payment System**) SIT *m*

chipset ['tʃɪpset] *n Comput* ensemble *m* de puces

chirography [kaɪərɒgrəfɪ] *n* calligraphie *f*

chiromancer ['kaɪərəʊ,mænsə(r)] *n* chiromancien(enne) *m,f*

chiromancy ['kaɪərəʊ,mænsɪ] *n* chiromancie *f*

chiropodist [kɪ'rɒpədɪst] *n Br* pédicure *mf*

chiropody [kɪ'rɒpədɪ] *n (UNCOUNT) Br (treatment)* soins *mpl* du pied; *(science)* podologie *f*

chiropractic [,kaɪrə'præktɪk] *n* chiropraxie *f*, chiropractie *f*

chiropractor ['kaɪrə,præktə(r)] *n* chiropracteur *m*, chiropracticien(enne) *m,f*

chirp [tʃɜːp] **1** *vi (bird)* pépier, gazouiller; *(insect)* chanter, striduler; *(person)* parler d'une voix flûtée

2 *n (of bird)* pépiement *m*, gazouillement *m*; *(of insect)* chant *m*, stridulation *f*; **chirp-chirp** *(sound of bird)* cri-cri

chirpily ['tʃɜːpɪlɪ] *adv Fam* gaiement❑

chirpiness ['tʃɜːpɪnɪs] *n Fam* humeur *f* joyeuse❑, gaieté❑ *f*

chirpy ['tʃɜːpɪ] (*compar* **chirpier**, *superl* **chirpiest**) *adj Fam (person, voice)* gai❑, plein d'entrain❑; *(mood)* gai, enjoué❑, joyeux❑

chirrup ['tʃɪrəp] **1** *vi (bird)* pépier, gazouiller; *(insect)* chanter, striduler; *(person)* parler d'une voix flûtée

2 *n (of bird)* pépiement *m*, gazouillement *m*; *(of insect)* chant *m*, stridulation *f*

chisel ['tʃɪzəl] (*Br pt & pp* **chiselled**, *cont* **chiselling**, *Am pt & pp* **chiseled**, *cont* **chiseling**) **1** *n (gen)* ciseau *m*; *(for engraving)* burin *m*

2 *vt* (**a**) *(carve)* ciseler; **to chisel a piece out of sth** enlever un morceau de qch au ciseau; **to chisel sth from** *or* **in** *or* **out of marble** ciseler qch dans du marbre; *Fig* **chiselled features** visage délicatement ciselé

(**b**) *(engrave → form, name)* graver au burin; *(→ plate)* buriner

(**c**) *esp Am Fam (cheat)* **to chisel sb out of sth** carotter qch à qn

chiseller, *Am* **chiseler** ['tʃɪzələ(r)] *n Fam* (**a**) *esp Am (cheat)* carotteur(euse) *m,f* (**b**) *Ir (child)* gosse *mf*, môme *mf*

chit [tʃɪt] *n* (**a**) *(memo, note)* note *f*; *(voucher)* bon *m*; *(receipt)* reçu *m*, récépissé *m* (**b**) *Fam Old-fashioned Pej (girl)* **a chit (of a girl)** une gamine

chital ['tʃɪtəl] *n Zool* **chital (deer)** chital *m*

chitchat ['tʃɪttʃæt] **1** *n (UNCOUNT)* bavardage *m*, papotage *m*

2 *vi* bavarder, papoter

chitin ['kaɪtɪn] *n Biol* chitine *f*

chitlings ['tʃɪtlɪŋz], **chitlins** ['tʃɪtlɪnz] *npl Culin* tripes *fpl*

chiton ['kaɪtɒn] *n Zool* chiton *m*

chitterlings ['tʃɪtəlɪŋz] *npl Culin* tripes *fpl*

chitty ['tʃɪtɪ] (*pl* **chitties**) *n Br* note *f*

chivalrous ['ʃɪvəlrəs] *adj* (**a**) *(courteous)* chevaleresque, courtois; *(gallant)* galant (**b**) *(exploit, tournament)* chevaleresque

chivalrously ['ʃɪvəlrəslɪ] *adv (courteously)* de façon chevaleresque, courtoisement; *(gallantly)* galamment

chivalrousness ['ʃɪvəlrəsnɪs] *n (courtesy)* conduite *f* chevaleresque, courtoisie *f*; *(gallantry)* galanterie *f*

chivalry ['ʃɪvəlrɪ] *n* (**a**) *(courtesy)* conduite *f* chevaleresque, courtoisie *f*; *(gallantry)* galanterie *f*; *Hum* **the age of chivalry is not dead** la galanterie existe encore (**b**) *(knights, system)* chevalerie *f*

chives [tʃaɪvz] *npl* ciboulette *f*, civette *f*; **add some chives** ajoutez de la ciboulette *ou* civette

chivy, chivvy ['tʃɪvɪ] (*pt & pp* **chivvied** *or* **chivied**) *vt* (**a**) *Fam (nag)* harceler❑; **to chivy sb into doing sth** harceler qn jusqu'à ce qu'il fasse qch; **you'll have to chivy them along** il faudra que tu les fasses se grouiller; **stop chivying me!** laisse-moi tranquille!❑ (**b**) *(hunt → game)* chasser; *(→ criminal)* pourchasser

▸**chivvy up** *vt sep Fam* faire activer❑

chlamydia [klə'mɪdɪə] *n Med* chlamydia *f*

chloasma [kləʊ'æzmə] *n Med* chloasme *m*, chloasma *m*

Chloe ['kləʊɪ] *pr n Austr Fam* **as drunk as Chloe** bourré comme un coing

chloral ['klɔːrəl] *n Chem* chloral *m*

chloramphenicol [,klɔːræm'fenɪkɒl] *n Chem* chloramphénicol *m*

chlorate ['klɔːreɪt] *n Chem* chlorate *m*

chlorella [klɔː'relə] *n Bot* chlorate *m*

chloric ['klɔːrɪk] *adj Chem* chlorique

▸▸ ***chloric acid*** acide *m* chlorique

chloride ['klɔːraɪd] *n Chem* chlorure *m*

▸▸ ***chloride of silver*** chlorure *m* d'argent

chlorinate ['klɔːrɪneɪt] *vt (water)* javelliser; *Chem* chlorurer, chlorer

chlorinated ['klɔːrɪneɪtɪd] *adj (water)* chloré

chlorination [,klɔːrɪn'eɪʃən] *n (of water)* javellisation *f*, chloration *f*; *Chem* chloration *f*

chlorine ['klɔːriːn] *n Chem* chlore *m*

▸▸ ***chlorine bleach*** eau *f* de Javel

chlorite ['klɔːraɪt] *n Chem* chlorite *m*

chlorofluorocarbon [,klɔːrə,flɔːrəʊ'kɑːbən] *n Chem* chlorofluorocarbure *m*

chloroform ['klɒrəfɔːm] *Chem* **1** *n* chloroforme *m*

2 *vt* chloroformer

chlorophyll, *Am* **chlorophyl** ['klɒrəfɪl] *n Bot* chlorophylle *f*

chlorophytum [,klɔːrəʊ'faɪtəm] *n Bot* chlorophytum *m*

chloroplast ['klɔːrəʊplæst] *n Biol* chloroplaste *m*

chloroprene ['klɔːrəʊpriːn] *n Chem* chloroprène *m*, chlorobutadiène *f*

chloroquine ['klɔːrəʊkwiːn] *n Pharm* chloroquine *f*

chlorosis [klɔː'rəʊsɪs] *n Med* chlorose *f*

chlorotic [klɔː'rɒtɪk] *Med* **1** *n* chlorotique *mf*

2 *adj* chlorotique

choc [tʃɒk] *n Fam* chocolat❑ *m*; **a box of chocs** une boîte de chocolats❑

chocaholic = **chocoholic**
choccy [tʃɒkɪ] *(pl* **choccies**) *n Fam* chocolat❑ *m*
choc-ice *n Br* = glace individuelle rectangulaire enrobée de chocolat
chock [tʃɒk] **1** *n Tech (for door, wheel)* cale *f*; *(for barrel)* cale *f*, chantier *m*; *Naut* chantier *m*, cale *f*
2 *vt Tech (barrel, door, wheel)* caler; *Naut* mettre sur un chantier *ou* sur cales
chocka ['tʃɒkə], **chock-a-block, chock-full** *adj Br Fam (room, theatre)* plein à craquer; *(container)* bourré, plein à ras bord; **the town is chock-a-block with tourists** la ville est archipleine de touristes
chocoholic [ˌtʃɒkə'hɒlɪk] *n Fam* accro *mf* au chocolat, chocophile *mf*
chocolate ['tʃɒkələt] **1** *n (drink, sweet)* chocolat *m*; **a piece of chocolate** un morceau de chocolat; **a box of chocolates** une boîte de chocolats; **a cup of (hot) chocolate** une tasse de chocolat (chaud)
2 *comp (biscuit, cake)* au chocolat, chocolaté
3 *adj* chocolat *(inv)*
►► ***chocolate bar*** barre *f* chocolatée; ***chocolate brown*** **1** *n* (couleur *f*) chocolat *m inv* **2** *adj* chocolat *(inv)*; ***chocolate chip cookie*** biscuit *m* aux pépites de chocolat; ***chocolate factory*** chocolaterie *f*; ***chocolate manufacturer*** chocolatier-confiseur *m*

'Charlie and the Chocolate Factory' *Dahl, Stuart* 'Charlie et la chocolaterie'

chocolate-box *adj Fam* **a chocolate-box landscape** un paysage très carte postale
choice [tʃɔɪs] **1** *n* (**a**) *(act of choosing)* choix *m*; **to make a choice** faire un choix; **you'll have to make a choice** il faudra que tu choisisses *ou* que tu fasses un choix; **to make one's choice** faire son choix; **to have first choice** pouvoir choisir en premier; **it's your choice** c'est à vous de choisir *ou* décider; **by** *or* **from choice** de *ou* par préférence; **the profession of her choice** la profession de son choix; **the holiday destination of choice** la destination de prédilection de bien des vacanciers
(**b**) *(option)* choix *m*, option *f*; **they were given a choice between basketball and soccer** ils ont eu le choix entre le basket et le foot; **this is the drug of choice used to treat such ailments** on considère que c'est le meilleur médicament pour le traitement de ce genre de maladie; **you have no choice (in the matter)** vous n'avez pas le choix; **I had no choice but to leave** je ne pouvais que partir
(**c**) *(selection)* choix *m*, assortiment *m*; **a wide choice of goods** un grand choix de marchandises; **available in a choice of colours** disponible en plusieurs couleurs
(**d**) *(thing, person chosen)* choix *m*; **he would be a good choice for president** il ferait un bon président; **the red wine was her choice** c'est elle qui avait choisi le vin rouge; **Spain would be my choice** je choisirais l'Espagne; **you made the right/wrong choice** vous avez fait le bon/mauvais choix
2 *adj* (**a**) *(fruit, meat)* de choix, de première qualité; *(wine)* fin
(**b**) *(well chosen → phrase, words)* bien choisi; **in a few choice words** en quelques mots bien choisis
(**c**) *(coarse → language)* grossier
choiceness ['tʃɔɪsnɪs] *n (of fruit, meat)* excellence *f*, supériorité *f*; *(of wine)* finesse *f*
choir ['kwaɪə(r)] **1** *n* (**a**) *(group of singers)* chœur *m*, chorale *f*; *(in church)* chœur *m*, maîtrise *f*; **male voice choir** chœur *m ou* chorale *f* d'hommes; **we sing in the choir** *(gen)* nous faisons partie du chœur *ou* de la chorale; *(in church)* nous faisons partie du chœur, nous chantons dans la maîtrise
(**b**) *Archit* chœur *m*
(**c**) *(group of instruments)* chœur *m*
►► ***choir practice*** répétition *f* de la chorale; **we have choir practice tonight** nous avons chorale ce soir; ***choir school*** maîtrise *f*
choirboy ['kwaɪəbɔɪ] *n* jeune choriste *m*
choirmaster ['kwaɪəˌmɑːstə(r)] *n (gen)* chef *m* de chœur; *(in church)* maître *m* de chapelle
choirstall ['kwaɪəstɔːl] *n* stalle *f* du chœur

choke [tʃəʊk] **1** *vi* étouffer, s'étouffer, s'étrangler; **to choke on sth** s'étouffer *ou* s'étrangler en avalant qch de travers; **to choke to death** mourir étouffé; **to choke with laughter** s'étouffer *ou* s'étrangler de rire; **to choke with rage** s'étouffer *ou* s'étrangler de rage
2 *vt* (**a**) *(asphyxiate)* étrangler, étouffer; **in a voice choked with emotion** d'une voix étranglée par l'émotion
(**b**) *(strangle)* étrangler; **to choke sb to death** étrangler qn
(**c**) *(clog)* boucher, obstruer; **choked with traffic** embouteillé, bouché; **choked with weeds** étouffé par les mauvaises herbes
(**d**) *Tech (engine, fire)* étouffer
3 *n* (**a**) *Aut* starter *m*; *Tech (in pipe)* buse *f*; *Aut* **to pull out the choke** mettre le starter
(**b**) *(of artichoke)* foin *m*
►► ***choke chain*** *(for dog)* collier *m* étrangleur
►**choke back, choke down** *vt sep (anger)* refouler, étouffer; *(tears)* refouler, contenir; *(complaint, cry)* retenir
►**choke off** *vt sep (objection, opposition)* étouffer (dans l'œuf); *(discussion)* empêcher; *(person)* envoyer promener *ou* paître
►**choke up** *vt sep* (**a**) *(block → road)* boucher, embouteiller; *(→ pipe)* boucher, obstruer; **the drain is all choked up with leaves** la bouche d'égout est complètement obstruée par les feuilles
(**b**) *Fam (emotionally)* émouvoir❑, toucher profondément❑; **she was all choked up** elle était bouleversée❑ *ou* toute émue
choked [tʃəʊkt] *adj* (**a**) *(cry, voice)* étranglé (**b**) *Br Fam (person → moved)* secoué; *(→ sad)* peiné, attristé; *(→ annoyed)* énervé, fâché
choker ['tʃəʊkə(r)] *n (necklace)* collier *m* (court); *(neckband)* tour *m* de cou
chokey ['tʃəʊkɪ] *n Br Old-fashioned (prison)* taule *f*; **to be in chokey** être en taule
choking ['tʃəʊkɪŋ] **1** *n* étouffement *m*, suffocation *f*
2 *adj* étouffant, suffocant; **he made a choking sound** il a fait un bruit comme quelqu'un qui s'étouffe
cholecystectomy [ˌkɒlɪsɪs'tektəmɪ] *n Med* cholécystectomie *f*
cholecystitis [ˌkɒlɪsɪs'taɪtɪs] *n Med* cholécystite *f*
cholecystography [ˌkɒlɪsɪs'tɒgrəfɪ] *n Med* cholécystographie *f*
cholecystostomy [ˌkɒlɪsɪs'tɒstəmɪ] *n Med* cholécystostomie *f*
choler ['kɒlə(r)] *n Arch or Literary* (**a**) *Med* bile *f* (**b**) *Fig (ill humour)* irascibilité *f*
cholera ['kɒlərə] *n Med* choléra *m*
choleric ['kɒlərɪk] *adj Med* colérique, coléreux
cholesteraemia, *Am* **cholesteremia** [ˌkɒlestə'riːmɪə] *n Med* cholestérinémie *f*
cholesterol [kə'lestərɒl] *n Chem* cholestérol *m*
►► ***cholesterol level*** taux *m* de cholestérol
cholesterolaemia, *Am* **cholesterolemia** [ˌkɒlestərə'liːmɪə] *n Med* cholestérolémie *f*
cholic acid ['kəʊlɪk-] *n Chem* acide *m* cholique
choline ['kəʊliːn] *n Biol & Chem* choline *f*
cholinesterase [ˌkəʊlɪ'nestəreɪs] *n Chem* cholinestérase *f*
chomp ['tʃɒmp] *Fam* **1** *vt* mastiquer bruyamment
2 *vi* mastiquer bruyamment❑
3 *n* mastication *f* bruyante❑
Chomskyan ['tʃɒmskɪən] *adj* de Chomsky
chondriosome ['kɒndrɪəʊsəʊm] *n Biol* élément *m* du chondriome, chondriosome *m*
choo-choo ['tʃuːˌtʃuː] *n (in children's language)* train❑ *m*
chook [tʃuːk] *n Austr Fam (chicken)* poulet❑ *m*
choose [tʃuːz] *(pt* **chose** [tʃəʊz], *pp* **chosen** ['tʃəʊzən]) **1** *vt* (**a**) *(select)* choisir, prendre; **I don't know what to choose** je ne sais pas quoi choisir; **she chose a man as her assistant** elle a pris un homme pour assistant; **choose your words carefully** pesez bien vos mots; **there's little** *or* **not much to choose between the two parties** les deux partis se valent
(**b**) *(elect)* élire
(**c**) *(decide)* décider, juger bon; **they chose to ignore his rudeness** ils ont préféré ignorer sa grossièreté; **I didn't choose to invite her** *(invited unwillingly)* je l'ai invitée contre mon gré
2 *vi* choisir; **do as you choose** faites comme bon vous semble *ou* comme vous l'entendez *ou* comme vous voulez; **you can come if you so choose** vous pouvez venir si cela vous dit *ou* si vous le voulez; **she'll finish it when she so chooses** elle le terminera quand bon lui semblera; **to choose from** *or* **between several people** choisir entre *ou* parmi plusieurs personnes; **there's not a lot to choose from** il n'y a pas beaucoup de choix
►**choose up** *Am Sport* **1** *vt sep (players)* sélectionner
2 *vi* sélectionner les joueurs
chooser ['tʃuːzə(r)] *n Comput* sélecteur *m*
choosing ['tʃuːzɪŋ] *n* choix *m*; **it was none of my choosing** ce n'est pas moi qui l'ai choisi; **the circumstances were not of his choosing** les circonstances n'étaient pas de son fait
choosey, choosy ['tʃuːzɪ] *(compar* **choosier,** *superl* **choosiest**) *adj Fam* difficile❑; **she's very choosey about what she eats** elle ne mange pas n'importe quoi❑, elle est très difficile sur la nourriture❑; **you decide, I'm not choosey** décide, cela m'est égal; **he can't afford to be choosey** il ne peut pas se permettre de faire le difficile
chop [tʃɒp] *(pt & pp* **chopped,** *cont* **chopping**) **1** *vt* (**a**) *(cut → gen)* couper; *(→ wood)* couper; *Culin* hacher; **to chop sth into pieces** couper qch en morceaux; **to chop sth finely** hacher qch menu; **to chop logic** couper les cheveux en quatre
(**b**) *(hit)* donner un coup à, frapper
(**c**) *Fam (reduce → budget, funding)* réduire❑, diminuer❑; *(→ project)* mettre au rancart
(**d**) *Sport (ball)* couper
2 *vi (change direction)* varier; **to chop and change** changer constamment d'avis; **he's always chopping and changing** *(changing his mind)* il change d'opinion à tout bout de champ
3 *n* (**a**) *(blow → with axe)* coup *m* de hache; *(→ with hand)* coup *m*; *Fam* **to get** *or* **to be given the chop** *Br (employee)* être viré; *(project)* être mis au rancart; *(chapter, part of text, film etc)* être supprimé❑; *Br Fam* **the welfare programmes are for the chop** les programmes d'assistance sociale vont être supprimés; **he's for the chop** il va y passer
(**b**) *Culin (of pork, lamb)* côtelette *f*
(**c**) *Golf* coup *m* piqué
(**d**) *(in tennis)* volée *f* coupée *ou* arrêtée
4 chops *npl (jowls → of person)* joue *f*; *(→ of animal)* bajoues *fpl*; **to lick one's chops** se pourlécher les babines
►**chop at** *vt insep* (**a**) *(try to cut → gen)* tenter de couper; *(→ with axe)* donner des coups de hache à, tailler (à la hache)
(**b**) *(try to hit)* essayer de frapper
►**chop down** *vt sep* abattre
►**chop off** *vt sep* trancher, couper; **they chopped off the king's head** ils ont coupé la tête au roi
►**chop up** *vt sep* couper en morceaux, hacher; *Culin* hacher
chop-chop *Fam* **1** *adv* rapidement, vite; **get to work, chop-chop!** au travail, et que ça saute!
2 *exclam* allez, et que ça saute!
chophouse ['tʃɒphaʊs, *pl* -haʊzɪz] *n Old-fashioned* restaurant *m* spécialisé dans les grillades
Chopin ['ʃəʊpæn] *pr n* Chopin
chopper ['tʃɒpə(r)] *n* (**a**) *Br (axe)* petite hache *f*; *Culin (cleaver)* couperet *m*, hachoir *m* (**b**) *Fam (helicopter)* hélico *m* (**c**) *Fam (motorcycle)* chopper *m*; *(bicycle)* vélo *m (à haut guidon)* (**d**) *Br Vulg (penis)* bite *f*
choppers ['tʃɒpəz] *npl Fam (false teeth)* râtelier *m*; *(teeth)* ratiches *fpl*
choppiness ['tʃɒpɪnɪs] *n (of lake, sea)* agitation *f*
chopping ['tʃɒpɪŋ] *n (of wood)* coupe *f*
►► ***chopping block*** billot *m*; ***chopping board*** planche *f* à découper; ***chopping knife*** couperet *m*, hachoir *m*
choppy ['tʃɒpɪ] *(compar* **choppier,** *superl* **choppiest**) *adj* (**a**) *(lake, sea)* un peu agité; *(waves)* clapotant (**b**) *(wind)* variable
chopstick ['tʃɒpstɪk] *n* baguette *f (pour manger)*
chop suey [-'suːɪ] *n* chop suey *m*
choral ['kɔːrəl] **1** *adj* choral

cho–cho

2 *n* (**a**) *(hymn)* chœur *m*, choral *m* (**b**) *Am (choir)* chœur *m*, chorale *f*

►► ***choral society*** chorale *f*; ***choral symphony*** symphonie *f* avec chœur

chorale [kɒ'rɑːl] *n* (**a**) *(hymn)* chœur *m*, choral *m* (**b**) *Am (choir)* chœur *m*, chorale *f*

choralist ['kɔːrəlɪst] *n* choriste *mf*

chord [kɔːd] *n* (**a**) *Anat & Geom* corde *f* (**b**) *Mus (group of notes)* accord *m*; *Fig* **to strike** *or* **to touch a chord, to strike the right chord** toucher la corde sensible; **his words struck a chord with the audience** ses paroles ont trouvé un écho auprès du public

chore [tʃɔː(r)] *n (task → routine)* travail *m* de routine; *(→ unpleasant)* corvée *f*; **household chores** travaux *mpl* ménagers; *Am* **I have to do the chores** il faut que je fasse le ménage

chorea [kɒ'rɪə] *n Med* chorée *f*

choreodrama [ˌkɒrɪəʊ'drɑːmə] *n* chorédrame *m*

choreograph ['kɒrɪəgrɑːf] *vt (ballet, dance)* chorégraphier, faire la chorégraphie de; *Fig (meeting, party)* organiser

choreographer [ˌkɒrɪ'ɒgrəfə(r)] *n* chorégraphe *mf*

choreographic [ˌkɒrɪə'græfɪk] *adj* chorégraphique

choreography [ˌkɒrɪ'ɒgrəfɪ] *n* chorégraphie *f*

chorion ['kɔːrɪɒn] *n Zool* chorion *m*

chorister ['kɒrɪstə(r)] *n* choriste *mf*

chorizo [tʃəʊ'riːzəʊ] *n* chorizo *m*

choroid ['kɒrɔɪd] *n Zool* choroïde *f*

chortle ['tʃɔːtəl] **1** *vi* glousser; **to chortle with delight at** *or* **over sth** glousser de plaisir à propos de qch; **he chortled to himself** il riait discrètement dans son coin

2 *n* gloussement *m*, petit rire *m*

chorus ['kɔːrəs] **1** *n* (**a**) *(choir)* chœur *m*, chorale *f*; **to sing in chorus** chanter en chœur; **"no!", they shouted in chorus** "non!", se sont-ils exclamés en chœur

(**b**) *(piece of music)* chœur *m*, choral *m*

(**c**) *(refrain)* refrain *m*; **to join in the chorus** *(several people)* chanter le refrain en chœur; *(one person)* se joindre aux autres pour le refrain

(**d**) *Theat & Mus (dancers, singers)* troupe *f*; *(speakers)* chœur *m*; **he started his career in the chorus** il a débuté dans la troupe; **I'm part of the chorus** je fais partie de la troupe

(**e**) *(of complaints, groans)* concert *m*; **a chorus of praise** un concert de louanges; **a chorus of criticism** une avalanche de critiques

2 *vt (song)* chanter en chœur; *(poem)* réciter en chœur; *(approval, discontent)* dire *ou* exprimer en chœur; **"yes please!", they chorused** "oui s'il vous plaît!", ont-ils répondu en chœur

►► *Theat & Mus* ***chorus girl*** girl *f*; *Theat & Mus* ***chorus line*** troupe *f*

chorusmaster ['kɔːrəsˌmɑːstə(r)] *n Theat & Mus* maître *m* de chant

chose [tʃəʊz] *pt of* **choose**

chosen ['tʃəʊzən] **1** *pp of* **choose**

2 *adj* choisi; **the chosen few who were invited to the wedding** les quelques privilégiés qui ont été invités au mariage; **she told only a chosen few** elle ne s'est confiée qu'à quelques privilégiés; **a few well chosen words** quelques termes (bien) choisis; **the chosen people** les élus *mpl*

3 *npl* **the chosen** les élus *mpl*

chough [tʃʌf] *n Orn* crave *m*

choux [ʃuː] *n (pastry)* pâte *f* à choux

►► *Culin* ***choux bun*** chou *m* à la crème; ***choux pastry*** pâte *f* à choux

chow [tʃaʊ] *n* (**a**) *(dog)* chow-chow *m* (**b**) *Fam (food)* bouffe *f*

►**chow down** *Am Fam* **1** *vt insep* bouffer

2 *vi* bouffer

chow-chow *n (dog)* chow-chow *m*

chowder ['tʃaʊdə(r)] *n Culin* = potage épais contenant du poisson ou des fruits de mer

chowderhead ['tʃaʊdəhed] *n Am Fam* crétin(e) *m,f*, imbécile *mf*

chow mein [-'meɪn] *n Culin* chow mein *m*

chrism, chrisom ['krɪzəm] *n Rel* chrême *m*

Christ [kraɪst] **1** *pr n* le Christ, Jésus-Christ *m*; **the Christ child** l'enfant *m* Jésus

2 *exclam very Fam* Bon Dieu (de Bon Dieu)!; **Christ Almighty!** nom de Dieu!; **for Christ's sake!** bon sang!

Christadelphian [ˌkrɪstə'delfɪən] *Rel* **1** *n* christadelphe *mf*

2 *adj* christadelphe

Christchurch ['kraɪsˌtʃɜːtʃ] *n* Christchurch

christen ['krɪsən] *vt* (**a**) *(gen)* appeler, nommer; *(nickname)* baptiser, surnommer; *Naut & Rel* baptiser; **to christen a child George** baptiser un enfant Georges; **she was christened Victoria but is known as Vicky** son nom de baptême est Victoria mais tout le monde l'appelle Vicky; **he was christened after his grandfather** on lui a donné le nom de son grand-père; **we christened the car "the Crate"** nous avons baptisé la voiture "le Tacot"

(**b**) *Fam (use for first time)* étrenner

Christendom ['krɪsəndəm] *n* chrétienté *f*; **throughout Christendom** dans toute la chrétienté; **he's the biggest fool in Christendom** c'est l'homme le plus bête du monde

christening ['krɪsənɪŋ] **1** *n* baptême *m*

2 *comp (ceremony, robe)* de baptême

Christian ['krɪstʃən] **1** *n* chrétien(enne) *m,f*; **to become a Christian** se convertir au christianisme

2 *adj* chrétien; *Fig (charitable)* charitable, bon; **Christian burial** sépulture *f* en terre sainte; **Christian charity** charité *f* chrétienne; **the Christian era** l'ère *f* chrétienne; **early Christian** paléochrétien; **that wasn't very Christian of you** ce n'était pas très charitable de ta part; **that's not a very Christian attitude** ce n'est pas une attitude très charitable

►► ***Christian Aid*** = association humanitaire britannique; ***the Christian Coalition*** = groupe de pression américain chrétien de droite, opposé notamment à l'avortement et à l'égalité des droits pour les homosexuels; *Pol* ***Christian Democrat*** **1** *n* démocrate-chrétien(enne) *m,f* **2** *adj* démocrate-chrétien; ***Christian name*** nom *m* de baptême, prénom *m*; **his Christian name is Frank** il s'appelle Frank; ***Christian Science*** la Science chrétienne; ***Christian Scientist*** scientiste *mf* chrétien(enne)

Christianity [ˌkrɪstɪ'ænətɪ] *n* christianisme *m*

christianization [ˌkrɪstʃənaɪ'zeɪʃən] *n* christianisation *f*

christianize, -ise ['krɪstʃənaɪz] *vt* christianiser, convertir au christianisme

Christlike ['kraɪstlaɪk] *adj* semblable *ou* qui ressemble au Christ

Christmas ['krɪsməs] **1** *n* Noël *m*; **where are you celebrating Christmas?** où fêtez-vous Noël?; **I'm staying with my parents over Christmas** je vais passer Noël chez mes parents; **at Christmas** à Noël; **for Christmas** pour Noël; **Merry Christmas!** joyeux Noël!; **I thought all my Christmases had come at once!** je n'en pouvais plus de joie!

2 *comp (party, present)* de Noël

►► ***Christmas bonus*** prime *f* de fin d'année; *Br* ***Christmas box*** étrennes *fpl (offertes à Noël)*; *Bot* ***Christmas cactus*** cactus *m* de Noël; ***Christmas cake*** gâteau *m* de Noël *(cake décoré au sucre glace)*; ***Christmas card*** carte *f* de Noël; *Hum* **I don't think he will be on her Christmas card list** on ne peut pas dire qu'il ait la cote avec elle; ***Christmas carol*** chant *m* de Noël, noël *m*; *Rel* cantique *m* de Noël; ***Christmas club*** = caisse de contributions pour les cadeaux de Noël; ***Christmas cracker*** = papillote contenant un pétard et une surprise traditionnelle au moment des fêtes; ***Christmas Day*** le jour de Noël; ***Christmas decorations*** décorations *fpl* de Noël; ***Christmas dinner*** repas *m* de Noël; ***Christmas Eve*** la veille de Noël; ***Christmas Island*** l'île *f* Christmas; **on Christmas Island** à l'île Christmas; *Br* ***Christmas pudding*** pudding *m*, plum-pudding *m*; ***Christmas rose*** rose *f* de Noël; ***Christmas stocking*** = chaussette que les enfants suspendent à la cheminée pour que le père Noël y dépose les cadeaux; ***Christmas tree*** sapin *m ou* arbre *m* de Noël

'A Christmas Carol' *Dickens* 'Les Contes de Noël' *ou* 'Un Chant de Noël'

It will (all) be over by Christmas

Il s'agit de la célèbre formule qui avait cours au tout début de la Première Guerre mondiale en Grande-Bretagne lorsque nombreux étaient ceux qui croyaient que la victoire contre les Allemands serait acquise avant Noël 1914.

Aujourd'hui on utilise cette phrase de manière allusive lorsqu'on estime que quelqu'un fait preuve d'un excès d'optimisme en s'imaginant que telle ou telle chose sera terminée dans les temps. On pourra dire par exemple **This project is a nightmare – Don't worry, it will all be over by Christmas** ("ce projet est un vrai cauchemar – ne t'en fais pas, on aura fini d'ici Noël").

CHRISTMAS CARDS

Les Britanniques envoient (ou donnent en main propre) une carte de Noël à toutes leurs connaissances. C'est l'occasion de reprendre ou de maintenir le contact avec des gens avec qui on ne correspond qu'épisodiquement. Pendant cette période des fêtes, les services postaux sont souvent saturés. Les dates limites d'envoi sont affichées par les bureaux de poste pour assurer la réception des cartes avant Noël.

Christmassy ['krɪsməsɪ] *adj* typique de Noël, qui rappelle la fête de Noël; **the town looks so Christmassy** la ville a un tel air de fête

Christmastide ['krɪsməsˌtaɪd] *n Literary* la période de Noël *ou* des fêtes (de fin d'année) *(du 24 décembre au 6 janvier)*

Christmastime ['krɪsməsˌtaɪm] *n* la période de Noël *ou* des fêtes (de fin d'année) *(du 24 décembre au 6 janvier)*

Christology [krɪs'tɒlədʒɪ] *n Rel* christologie *f*

Christopher ['krɪstəfə(r)] *pr n* **Christopher Columbus** Christophe Colomb

chroma key ['krəʊmə-] *n TV* incrustation *f*, effet *m* d'incrustation

chromatic [krə'mætɪk] *adj* chromatique

►► *Phys* ***chromatic colour*** couleur *f* chromatique; *Typ* ***chromatic printing*** impression *f* polychrome; *Mus* ***chromatic scale*** gamme *f* chromatique

chromaticism [krə'mætɪsɪzəm] *n Mus* chromatisme *m*

chromatid ['krəʊmətɪd] *n Biol* chromatide *f*

chromatin ['krəʊmətɪn] *n Biol* chromatine *f*

chromatographic [ˌkrəʊmətəʊ'græfɪk] *adj Chem* chromatographique

chromatography [ˌkrəʊmə'tɒgrəfɪ] *n Chem* chromatographie *f*

chrome [krəʊm] **1** *n* chrome *m*

2 *comp (fittings, taps)* chromé

►► ***chrome green*** **1** *n* vert *m* de chrome **2** *adj* vert de chrome; ***chrome nickel*** nickel-chrome *m*; ***chrome red*** **1** *n* rouge *m* de chrome **2** *adj* rouge de chrome; ***chrome steel*** acier *m* chromé, chromé *m*; ***chrome tape*** bande *f* magnétique chromée; ***chrome yellow*** **1** *n* jaune *m* de chrome **2** *adj* jaune de chrome

chromic ['krəʊmɪk] *adj Chem* chromique

►► *Miner* ***chromic signal*** picotite *f*

chrominance ['krəʊmɪnəns] *n TV* chrominance *f*

chromite ['krəʊmaɪt] *n Miner* chromite *f*

chromium ['krəʊmɪəm] *n Chem* chrome *m*

chromium-plated [-'pleɪtɪd] *adj* chromé

chromium-plating [-'pleɪtɪŋ] *n* chromage *m*

chromogen ['krəʊmədʒen] *n Chem* chromogène *m*

chromogenic [ˌkrəʊmə'dʒenɪk], **chromogenous** [krəʊ'mɒdʒɪnəs] *adj Chem* chromogène

chromolithograph [ˌkrəʊməʊ'lɪθəgrɑːf] *n* chromolithographie *f*

chromolithography [ˌkrəʊməʊlɪ'θɒgrəfɪ] *n* chromolithographie *f*

chromomere ['krəʊməmɪə(r)] *n Biol* chromomère *m*

chromophore ['krəʊməfɔː(r)] *n Chem* chromophore *m*

chromoplast ['krəʊməplæst] *n Bot* chromoplaste *m*

chromoprotein [ˌkrəʊmə'prəʊtiːn] *n Biol* chromoprotéine *f*

chromosomal [ˌkrəʊmə'səʊməl] *adj Biol* chromosomique

chromosome ['krəʊməsəʊm] *n Biol* chromosome *m*
▸▸ *Biol* ***chromosome number*** nombre *m* chromosomique

chromosomic [,krəʊmə'səʊmɪk] *adj Biol* chromosomique

chromosphere ['krəʊməsfɪə(r)] *n Astron* chromosphère *f*

chronic ['krɒnɪk] *adj* (**a**) *(long-lasting → illness, unemployment)* chronique; **chronic invalid** invalide *mf* chronique; **to suffer from chronic ill health** être de santé fragile
(**b**) *(habitual → smoker, gambler)* invétéré
(**c**) *(serious → problem, situation)* difficile, grave
(**d**) *Br Fam (very bad)* atroce □, affreux □; **my back's hurting something chronic** mon dos me fait un mal de chien
▸▸ *Med* ***chronic fatigue syndrome*** encéphalomyélite *f* myalgique, syndrome *m* de fatigue chronique

chronically ['krɒnɪkəlɪ] *adv* (**a**) *(habitually)* chroniquement (**b**) *(severely)* gravement, sérieusement

chronicity [krɒ'nɪsɪtɪ] *n Med* chronicité *f*

chronicle ['krɒnɪkəl] **1** *n* chronique *f*; **their holiday was a chronicle of misadventures** leurs vacances furent une succession de mésaventures
2 *vt* faire la chronique de
3 Chronicles *n Bible* **the (Book of) Chronicles** le livre des Chroniques

'Chronicle of a Death Foretold' *Garcia Márquez*
'Chronique d'une mort annoncée'

chronicler ['krɒnɪklə(r)] *n* chroniqueur(euse) *m,f*

chronobiology [,krɒnəbaɪ'ɒlədʒɪ] *n* chronobiologie *f*

chronogram ['krɒnəgræm] *n* chronogramme *m*

chronograph ['krɒnəgrɑːf] *n* chronographe *m*

chronographic [,krɒnə'græfɪk] *adj* chronographique

chronological [,krɒnə'lɒdʒɪkəl] *adj* chronologique; **in chronological order** par ordre *ou* dans un ordre chronologique

chronologically [,krɒnə'lɒdʒɪkəlɪ] *adv* chronologiquement, par ordre chronologique

chronology [krə'nɒlədʒɪ] *n* chronologie *f*

chronometer [krə'nɒmɪtə(r)] *n* chronomètre *m*

chronometric [,krɒnə'metrɪk], **chronometrical** [krɒnə'metrɪkəl] *adj* chronométrique
▸▸ ***chronometric measurement*** chronométrage *m*

chronometry [krə'nɒmɪtrɪ] *n* chronométrie *f*

chrysalid ['krɪsəlɪd] *(pl* **chrysalides** [-'sælɪdiːz]*) n Entom* chrysalide *f*

chrysalis ['krɪsəlɪs] *(pl* **chrysalises** [-siːz]*) n Entom* chrysalide *f*

chrysanthemum [krɪ'sænθəməm] *n* chrysanthème *m*

chryselephantine [,krɪselɪ'fæntaɪn] *adj* chryséléphantin

chrysoberyl ['krɪsəʊberɪl] *n Miner* chrysobéryl *m*
▸▸ ***chrysoberyl cat's eye*** cymophane *f*

chrysoidine [krɪ'sɔɪdɪn] *n Chem* chrysoïdine *f*

chrysolite ['krɪsəlaɪt] *n Miner* chrysolit(h)e *f*, péridot *m*

chrysoprase ['krɪsəʊpreɪz] *n Miner* chrysoprase *f*

chub [tʃʌb] *(pl* **inv** *or* **chubs***) n Ich* chevaine *m*

chubbiness ['tʃʌbɪnɪs] *n* rondeur *f*

Chubb lock® [tʃʌb-] *n* = type de serrure réputé incrochetable

chubby ['tʃʌbɪ] *(compar* **chubbier,** *superl* **chubbiest***) adj (fingers, person)* potelé; *(baby)* dodu; *(face)* joufflu; **chubby-cheeked** joufflu

chuck [tʃʌk] **1** *vt* (**a**) *Fam (toss)* jeter □, lancer □; **she chucked him the ball** elle lui a lancé *ou* envoyé le ballon □; **chuck me that hammer** balance-moi le marteau; **they chucked him off the bus** ils l'ont vidé du bus
(**b**) *Fam (give up → activity, job)* laisser tomber □, lâcher □
(**c**) *Fam (jilt → boyfriend, girlfriend)* plaquer □
(**d**) *(tap)* tapoter; **she chucked the child under the chin** elle a tapoté le menton de l'enfant
(**e**) *Scot Fam* **chuck it!** *(stop it!)* arrête! □
2 *n Br* (**a**) *(tap)* petite tape *f*; **he gave her a chuck under the chin** il lui a tapoté le menton
(**b**) *Tech* mandrin *m*
(**c**) *Culin (steak)* morceau *m* de bœuf dans le paleron
(**d**) *Fam (idiom)* **to give sb the chuck** *(employee)* virer *ou* vider qn; *(boyfriend, girlfriend)* plaquer qn
▸▸ *Culin* ***chuck steak*** morceau *m* de bœuf dans le paleron; ***chuck wagon*** cantine *f* ambulante *(pour les cow-boys)*
▸**chuck away** *vt sep Fam (old clothing, papers)* balancer; *(chance, opportunity)* laisser passer □; *(money)* jeter par les fenêtres
▸**chuck down** *vt sep Br Fam* **it's chucking it down** *(raining)* il tombe des cordes
▸**chuck in** *vt sep Br Fam (give up → activity, job)* lâcher; *(→ attempt)* renoncer à; **he chucked it all in and bought a farm** il a tout plaqué pour acheter une ferme; **to chuck one's hand in** *Cards* jeter ses cartes sur la table; *Fig (admit defeat)* s'avouer vaincu
▸**chuck off** *vt sep Fam* virer; **he was chucked off the team** il s'est fait virer de l'équipe
▸**chuck out** *vt sep Fam (old clothing, papers)* balancer; *(person)* vider, sortir □; **he chucked the troublemakers out** il a flanqué les provocateurs à la porte
▸**chuck up** *very Fam* **1** *vt sep (give up)* laisser tomber □
2 *vi Fam (vomit)* dégueuler

chucker-out [,tʃʌkər-] *n Br Fam* videur *m*

chucking-out time [,tʃʌkɪŋ-] *n Br Fam (in pub)* heure *f* de la fermeture □

chuckle ['tʃʌkəl] **1** *vi* glousser, rire; **to chuckle with delight** rire avec jubilation; **he chuckled to himself** il riait tout seul
2 *n* gloussement *m*, petit rire *m*; **they had a good chuckle over her mishap** sa mésaventure les a bien fait rire

chucklehead ['tʃʌkəlhed] *n Br Fam* balourd(e) □ *m,f*

chuckwalla ['tʃʌk,wɒlə] *n Zool* chuckwalla *m*

chuff [tʃʌf] *vi* souffler, haleter; **the train chuffed up the hill** le train a monté la pente en haletant

chuffed [tʃʌft] *adj Br Fam* vachement *ou* super content, ravi □; **to be chuffed about** *or* **at sth** être ravi de qch; **I was chuffed to bits** j'étais vachement content; **I'm really chuffed with myself** je suis vachement content de moi

chug [tʃʌg] **1** *n* (**a**) *(of engine, car, train)* halètement *m* (**b**) *Br very Fam* **to have a chug** *(masturbate)* se branler
2 *vt Fam (drink quickly)* descendre
3 *vi* (**a**) *(make noise → engine, car, train)* s'essouffler, haleter (**b**) *(move)* avancer en soufflant *ou* en haletant (**c**) *Br very Fam (masturbate)* se branler
▸**chug along** *vi Fam (move slowly)* se traîner □; **the guy in front was chugging along at 30 km/h** le type devant moi se traînait à 30km à l'heure
▸**chug down** *vt sep (drink) Fam* **to chug sth down** descendre qch

chug-a-lug *Am* **1** *n* cul *m* sec
2 *vt (drink)* descendre

chukka ['tʃʌkə], *Am* **chukker** ['tʃʌkə(r)] *n Sport (in polo)* période *f* de jeu *(de sept minutes et demie)*
▸▸ *Sport* ***chukka boot,*** *Am* ***chukker boot*** bottine *f (portée par les joueurs de polo)*

chum [tʃʌm] *Fam* **1** *n* copain (copine) *m,f*; **the game's up, chum** c'est fichu, mon vieux
2 *vt Scot (in Edinburgh, Fife)* accompagner □
▸**chum up** *vi Fam* **to chum up with sb** devenir copain (copine) avec qn

chummy ['tʃʌmɪ] *(compar* **chummier,** *superl* **chummiest***) adj Fam* amical □; **to be chummy with sb** être copain (copine) avec qn; **she's very chummy with the boss** elle est très copine avec le patron

chump [tʃʌmp] *n Fam Old-fashioned* (**a**) *(dolt → boy)* ballot *m*; *(→ girl)* gourde *f* (**b**) *Br (head)* boule *f*; **to go off one's chump** perdre la boule, disjoncter; **you're off your chump!** tu as perdu la boule!
▸▸ *Am Fam* ***chump change*** *(small amount of money)* cacahuètes *fpl*; *Br Culin* ***chump chop*** côtelette *f* d'agneau *(coupée dans le gigot)*

chunder ['tʃʌndə(r)] *Fam* **1** *n* vomi □ *m*
2 *vi* dégueuler

chunk [tʃʌŋk] *n (of meat, wood)* gros morceau *m*; *(of budget, time)* grande partie *f*

chunky ['tʃʌŋkɪ] *(compar* **chunkier,** *superl* **chunkiest***) adj* (**a**) *(person → stocky)* trapu; *(→ chubby)* potelé, enrobé; *(food, stew)* avec des morceaux (**b**) *Br (clothing, sweater)* de grosse laine; *(jewellery)* gros (grosse)

Chunnel ['tʃʌnəl] *n Br Fam* **the Chunnel** le tunnel sous la Manche □, l'Eurotunnel □ *m*

chunter ['tʃʌntə(r)] *vi Br* râler, rouspéter; **what's he chuntering on about now?** qu'est-ce qu'il a encore à râler *ou* rouspéter?

church [tʃɜːtʃ] **1** *n* (**a**) *(building → gen)* église *f*; *(→ Protestant)* église *f*, temple *m*; **I saw her in church on Sunday** je l'ai vue à l'église dimanche
(**b**) *(services → Protestant)* office *m*; *(→ Catholic)* messe *f*; **to be at** *or* **in church** *(Protestants)* être à l'office *ou* au temple; *(Catholics)* être à la messe; **to go to church** *(Protestants)* aller au temple *ou* à l'office; *(Catholics)* aller à la messe *ou* à l'église; **do you go to church?** êtes-vous pratiquant?
(**c**) *(denomination)* Église *f*; **churches all over the world have condemned this decision** toutes les Églises du monde ont condamné cette décision
(**d**) *(UNCOUNT) (clergy)* **the church** les ordres *mpl*; **to go into the church** entrer dans les ordres; **to leave the church** quitter les ordres
2 *comp (bell, roof)* d'église
3 *vt Br (gen)* faire assister à la messe; *(woman after childbirth)* faire assister à la messe de relevailles
4 Church *n (institution)* **the Church** l'Église *f*; **the Anglican Church** l'Église *f* anglicane, **the (Roman) Catholic Church** l'Église *f* catholique; **Church and State** l'Église *f* et l'État *m*; **Church of Christian Science** Église *f* de la Science chrétienne; **Church of England** Église *f* anglicane; **Church of Scotland/Ireland** Église *f* d'Écosse/d'Irlande; **Church of Rome** Église *f* catholique
▸▸ ***the Church Commissioners*** = commission nommée par le gouvernement pour gérer les finances de l'Église d'Angleterre; ***Church Fathers*** Pères *mpl* de l'Église; ***church hall*** salle *f* paroissiale; ***Church House*** = siège du synode général de l'Église d'Angleterre; *Am Fam* ***church key*** *(bottle opener)* décapsuleur □ *m*; ***church leader*** chef *m* de l'église; *Br* ***church school*** = école primaire gérée par l'Eglise; ***church service*** office *m*, culte *m*; ***church wedding*** mariage *m* religieux

CHURCHES OF ENGLAND, SCOTLAND AND IRELAND

L'Église d'Angleterre (anglicane) est l'Église officielle d'Angleterre; son chef laïc est le souverain, son chef spirituel l'archevêque de Cantorbéry. Par contre, la "Church of Scotland", en Écosse, est une église presbytérienne de tendance calviniste. C'est l'église officielle en Écosse depuis 1690: elle est régie par le "Moderator" qui est élu tous les ans par les membres de l'assemblée générale de l'Église. Les membres de son clergé s'appellent des "ministers", et la hiérarchie ne compte pas d'évêques. La branche écossaise de l'Église d'Angleterre se nomme "Episcopal Church in Scotland"; elle fut fondée au XVIème siècle et dispose d'un nombre de fidèles moins important que l'Église d'Écosse. Une troisième Église, la "Free Church of Scotland" fut établie par des protestants écossais dissidents au XIXème siècle. En Irlande il existe aussi la "Church of Ireland", qui est la branche irlandaise de l'Église d'Angleterre.

churchgoer ['tʃɜːtʃ,gəʊə(r)] *n* pratiquant(e) *m,f*

churchgoing ['tʃɜːtʃ,gəʊɪŋ] **1** *adj* pratiquant; **the churchgoing public** les gens qui vont à l'église
2 *n* fréquentation *f* des églises; **churchgoing is not regarded as essential** aller à l'église n'est pas considéré comme essentiel

Churchillian [tʃɜː'tʃɪlɪən] *adj* churchillien

churchiness ['tʃɜːtʃɪnɪs] *n Fam Pej* bondieuserie *f*

churching ['tʃɜːtʃɪŋ] *n (UNCOUNT) Br* relevailles *fpl*

churchman ['tʃɜːtʃmən] (*pl* **churchmen** [-mən]) *n (clergyman)* ecclésiastique *m*; *(churchgoer)* pratiquant *m*

churchwarden [,tʃɜːtʃ'wɔːdən] *n* bedeau *m*, marguillier *m*

churchwoman ['tʃɜːtʃ,wʊmən] (*pl* **churchwomen** [-,wɪmɪn]) *n* (**a**) *(clergywoman)* femme *f* d'église (**b**) pratiquante *f*

churchy ['tʃɜːtʃɪ] (*compar* **churchier,** *superl* **churchiest**) *adj* (**a**) *(atmosphere, song)* qui rappelle l'église (**b**) *Fam Pej (person)* bigot; **she's very churchy** c'est une grenouille de bénitier

churchyard ['tʃɜːtʃ,jɑːd] *n (grounds)* terrain *m* autour de l'église; *(graveyard)* cimetière *m (autour d'une église)*

churl [tʃɜːl] *n Literary (ill-bred person)* rustre *mf*, malotru(e) *m,f*; *(surly person)* ronchon(onne) *m,f*

churlish ['tʃɜːlɪʃ] *adj (rude)* fruste, grossier; *(bad-tempered → person)* qui a mauvais caractère, revêche; *(→ attitude, behaviour)* revêche, désagréable; **it would be churlish not to acknowledge the invitation** ce serait grossier *ou* impoli de ne pas répondre à l'invitation

churlishly ['tʃɜːlɪʃlɪ] *adv (rudely)* grossièrement; *(in bad-tempered manner)* hargneusement, de façon revêche

churlishness ['tʃɜːlɪʃnɪs] *n (rudeness)* grossièreté *f*; *(bad temper → habitual)* mauvais caractère *m*; *(→ temporary)* mauvaise humeur *f*

churn [tʃɜːn] **1** *vt* (**a**) *(cream)* baratter (**b**) *(mud)* remuer; *(water)* faire bouillonner (**c**) *Fam St Exch (portfolio)* faire tourner ❏

2 *vi (sea, water)* bouillonner; *Fig* **the thought made my stomach churn** j'ai eu l'estomac tout retourné à cette idée

3 *n* (**a**) *(for butter)* baratte *f* (**b**) *Br (milk can)* bidon *m* (**c**) *Mktg* perte *f* de clients passés à la concurrence

▸**churn out** *vt sep Fam* (**a**) *(produce rapidly → gen)* produire rapidement ❏; *(→ novels, reports)* pondre à la chaîne *ou* en série (**b**) *(produce mechanically)* débiter

▸**churn up** *vt sep (mud)* remuer; *(sea, water)* faire bouillonner; *Fig* **I felt all churned up** *(nervous)* j'étais tout retourné; *(excited)* j'étais tout excité ❏

churning ['tʃɜːnɪŋ] *n* (**a**) *(of cream)* barattage *m* (**b**) *Fam St Exch* rotation *f* de portefeuille ❏

chute [ʃuːt] *n* (**a**) *(for parcels)* glissière *f*; *(for rubbish)* vide-ordures *m inv* (**b**) *(for sledding, in swimming pool)* toboggan *m* (**c**) *(in river)* rapide *m* (**d**) *Fam (parachute)* parachute ❏ *m* (**e**) *Am (idiom)* **out of the chute** *(at the beginning)* d'entrée de jeu

chutney ['tʃʌtnɪ] *n* chutney *m (condiment à base de fruits)*

chutzpah ['hʊtspə] *n esp Am Fam* culot *m*

chyluria [kaɪ'luːrɪə] *n Med* chylurie *f*

chyme [kaɪm] *n Physiol* chyme *m*

chymotrypsin [,kaɪməʊ'trɪpsɪn] *n Biol & Chem* chymotrypsine *f*

CI[1] *(written abbr* **Channel Islands**) îles *fpl* Anglo-Normandes

CI[2] [,siː'aɪ] *n* (**a**) *Am (abbr* **counter-intelligence**) contre-espionnage *m* (**b**) *Math (abbr* **confidence interval**) IC *m*

CIA [,siːaɪ'eɪ] *n Am (abbr* **Central Intelligence Agency**) CIA *f*

ciabatta [tʃə'bɑːtə] *n Culin* ciabatta *f*

ciao [tʃaʊ] *exclam* ciao!

ciborium [sɪ'bɔːrɪəm] (*pl* **ciboria**) [-rɪə] *n Rel* (**a**) *(canopy)* ciborium *m* (**b**) *(vessel)* ciboire *m*

CIC *Mil (written abbr* **commander-in-chief**) commandant *m* en chef, généralissime *m*

cicada [sɪ'kɑːdə] (*pl* **cicadas** *or* **cicadae** [-diː]) *n Entom* cigale *f*

cicatrice ['sɪkətrɪs], **cicatrix** ['sɪkətrɪks] (*pl* **cicatrices** [-'traɪsiːz]) *n Med* cicatrice *f*

cicatrization [,sɪkətraɪ'zeɪʃən] *n Med* cicatrisation *f*

cicatrize, -ise ['sɪkətraɪz] *Med* **1** *vt* (**a**) *(heal)* cicatriser (**b**) *(scar)* marquer de cicatrices

2 *vi* se cicatriser

CICB [,siːaɪ,siː'biː] *n Br (abbr* **Criminal Injuries Compensation Board**) = organisme gouvernemental dont le rôle est de dédommager les victimes d'actes criminels

cicely ['sɪsəlɪ] *n Bot* cerfeuil *m* musqué

Cicero ['sɪsərəʊ] *pr n* Cicéron

cicerone [,tʃɪtʃə'rəʊnɪ] (*pl* **cicerones** *or* **ciceroni** [-niː]) *n* cicérone *m*, guide *m*

Ciceronian [,sɪsə'rəʊnɪən] *adj* cicéronien

cichlid ['sɪklɪd] *n Ich* cichlide *m*

CID [,siːaɪ'diː] *n (abbr* **Criminal Investigation Department**) = police judiciaire britannique, ≃ PJ *f*

Cid [sɪd] *pr n* **El Cid** le Cid

cider ['saɪdə(r)] *n* (**a**) *Br (alcoholic drink)* cidre *m* (**b**) *Am (apple juice)* jus *m* de pommes

▸▸ ***cider apple*** pomme *f* à cidre; ***cider press*** pressoir *m* à cidre; ***cider vinegar*** vinaigre *m* de cidre

cif, CIF [,siːaɪ'ef] *n Com (abbr* **cost, insurance and freight**) CAF, caf

cig [sɪg] *n Fam* clope *m or f*, sèche *f*

cigar [sɪ'gɑː(r)] **1** *n* cigare *m*; *Fam* **close, but no cigar!** c'est presque ça, mais pas tout à fait!

2 *comp (box, tobacco)* à cigares; *(ash, smoke)* de cigare

▸▸ ***cigar case*** étui *m* à cigares; ***cigar cutter*** coupe-cigares *m inv*; ***cigar holder*** fume-cigare *m inv*; ***cigar lighter*** allume-cigare *m inv*

cigarette, *Am* **cigaret** [,sɪgə'ret] **1** *n* cigarette *f*; **cigarette smoking is a major cause of lung cancer** la cigarette est une des causes principales du cancer du poumon

2 *comp (ash, burn)* de cigarette; *(packet, smoke)* de cigarettes; *(paper, tobacco)* à cigarettes

▸▸ ***cigarette card*** = image offerte autrefois avec chaque paquet de cigarettes; ***cigarette case*** étui *m* à cigarettes, porte-cigarettes *m inv*; ***cigarette end*** mégot *m*; ***cigarette holder*** fume-cigarette *m inv*; ***cigarette lighter*** briquet *m*; ***cigarette machine*** *(vending machine)* distributeur *m* automatique de cigarettes; *(for rolling cigarettes)* rouleuse *f*; ***cigarette manufacturer*** fabricant(e) *m,f* de cigarettes, cigarettier(ère) *m,f*; ***cigarette smoker*** fumeur(euse) *m,f* (de cigarettes)

cigarillo [,sɪgə'rɪləʊ] (*pl* **cigarillos**) *n* petit cigare *m*, cigarillo *m*

cigar-shaped *adj* en forme de cigare

ciggie, ciggy ['sɪgɪ] *n Fam* clope *m or f*, sèche *f*

cilantro [sɪ'læntrəʊ] *n Am Bot & Culin* coriandre *f*

ciliary muscle ['sɪlɪərɪ-] *n Anat* muscle *m* ciliaire

ciliate ['sɪlɪeɪt], **ciliated** ['sɪlɪeɪtɪd] *adj Biol & Zool* cilié, cilifère

cilium ['sɪlɪəm] (*pl* **cilia** [-lɪə]) *n Anat & Biol* cil *m*

CIM [,siːaɪ'em] *n* (**a**) *Comput (abbr* **computer-integrated manufacturing**) CFAO *f* (**b**) *(abbr* **Chartered Institute of Marketing**) = institut britannique de marketing

cimbalom ['sɪmbələm] *n Mus* cymbalum *m*

Cimmerian [sɪ'mɪərɪən] *Hist* **1** *n* Cimmérien(enne) *m,f*

2 *adj* cimmérien; *Fig* **Cimmerian darkness** ténèbres *fpl* cimmériennes

CIM waybill *n Com* lettre *f* de voiture CIM

C-in-C *Mil (written abbr* **Commander-in-Chief**) commandant *m* en chef, généralissime *m*

cinch [sɪntʃ] **1** *n* (**a**) *Fam* **it's a cinch** *(easy to do)* c'est simple comme bonjour, c'est du gâteau; *(certainty)* c'est du tout cuit (**b**) *Am (for saddle)* sous-ventrière *f*, sangle *f*

2 *vt Am (horse)* sangler; *(saddle)* attacher par une sangle

cinchona [sɪŋ'kəʊnə] *n Bot* quinquina *m*

Cincinnati [,sɪnsɪ'nætɪ] *n* Cincinnati

cincture ['sɪŋktjə(r)] *n* (**a**) *Arch or Literary (girdle, belt)* enceinte *f*; **the town is enclosed in a cincture of walls** la ville est entourée d'une enceinte *ou* d'une ceinture de murailles (**b**) *Archit* ceinture *f*, filet *m*

cinder ['sɪndə(r)] *n* cendre *f*; **cinders** *(in fireplace)* cendres *fpl*; *(from furnace, volcano)* scories *fpl*; **burnt to a cinder** réduit en cendres

▸▸ *Am* ***cinder block*** parpaing *m*; ***cinder track*** (piste *f*) cendrée *f*

Cinderella [,sɪndə'relə] **1** *pr n* Cendrillon

2 *n Fig* parent *m* pauvre ❏

'Cinderella' *Perrault* 'Cendrillon'

Cinders ['sɪndəz] *n Fam* Cendrillon ❏ *f*

cineaste, cineast ['sɪnɪæst] *n* cinéphile *mf*

cine camera ['sɪnɪ-] *n Br* caméra *f*

cine-film *n Br* film *m*

cinema ['sɪnəmə] *n Br (building)* cinéma *m*; *esp Br (industry)* (industrie *f* du) cinéma *m*; **to go to the cinema** aller au cinéma

▸▸ *Mktg* ***cinema advertising*** publicité *f* au cinéma; *TV* ***cinema channel*** chaîne *f* de cinéma

cinema-goer *n Br* personne *f* qui fréquente les cinémas

cinema-going *Br* **1** *n* fréquentation *f* des salles de cinéma

2 *adj* **the cinema-going public** les cinéphiles *mfpl*

Cinemascope® ['sɪnəməskəʊp] *n* Cinémascope® *m*

cinematic [,sɪnɪ'mætɪk] *adj (tradition, style, technique)* cinématographique; **the novel has a very cinematic quality** le roman utilise des effets qui rappellent le cinéma

cinematograph [,sɪnə'mætəgrɑːf] *n Br* cinématographe *m*

cinematographer [,sɪnəmə'tɒgrəfə(r)] *n* directeur(trice) *m,f* de la photographie, chef opérateur *m*

cinematographic [,sɪnəmætə'græfɪk] *adj* cinématographique

cinematographically [,sɪnəmætə'græfɪkəlɪ] *adv* cinématographiquement

cinematography [,sɪnəmə'tɒgrəfɪ] *n Br* cinématographie *f*

cinephile ['sɪnɪfaɪl] *n Am* cinéphile *mf*

cineplex ['sɪnɪpleks] *n Am* multiplexe *m*

cine-projector *n Br* projecteur *m* de cinéma

Cinerama® [,sɪnə'rɑːmə] *n* Cinérama® *m*

cineraria [,sɪnə'reərɪə] **1** *pl of* **cinerarium**

2 *n Bot* cinéraire *f*

cinerarium [,sɪnə'reərɪəm] (*pl* **cineraria** [-rɪə]) *n* cinéraire *m*

cinerary ['sɪnərərɪ] *adj* cinéraire

cinnabar ['sɪnəbɑː(r)] *n Miner* cinabre *m*

cinnamon ['sɪnəmən] **1** *n* (**a**) *(spice)* cannelle *f* (**b**) *(tree)* cannelier *m* (**c**) *(colour)* cannelle *f*

2 *comp (flavour, tea)* à la cannelle

3 *adj* cannelle *(inv)*

▸▸ ***cinnamon stick*** bâton *m* de cannelle

cinqfoil, cinquefoil ['sɪŋkfɔɪl] *n* (**a**) *Bot* potentille *f* rampante, quintefeuille *f* (**b**) *Archit* quintefeuille *m*

Cinque Ports ['sɪŋkpɔːts] *npl* Cinq ports *mpl (ancienne confédération réunissant les cinq ports de la côte sud-est de l'Angleterre)*

cipher ['saɪfə(r)] **1** *n* (**a**) *(code)* chiffre *m*, code *m* secret; **written in cipher** crypté, codé (**b**) *(monogram)* chiffre *m*, monogramme *m* (**c**) *(Arabic numeral)* chiffre *m* (**d**) *Literary (zero)* zéro *m*; *Fig* **they're mere ciphers** ce sont des moins que rien

2 *vt* (**a**) *(encode)* crypter, chiffrer, coder (**b**) *(calculate)* chiffrer

circa ['sɜːkə] *prep* circa, vers

circadian [sɜː'keɪdɪən] *adj Biol* circadien

▸▸ ***circadian rhythm*** rhythme *m* circadien

Circassian [sɜː'kæsɪən] **1** *n* (**a**) *Geog* Circassien(enne) *m,f* (**b**) *(language)* circassien *m*

2 *adj Geog* circassien

circassian [sɜː'kæsɪən] *n Tex* circassienne *f*

Circe ['sɜːsɪ] *pr n Myth* Circé

circle ['sɜːkəl] **1** *n* (**a**) *(gen) & Geom* cercle *m*; *(around eyes)* cerne *m*; **we stood in a circle around him** nous formions (un) cercle *ou* nous nous tenions en cercle autour de lui; **she had dark circles under her eyes** elle avait les yeux cernés, elle avait des cernes sous les yeux; **he had us going** *or* **running round in circles trying to find the information** il nous a fait tourner en rond à chercher les renseignements; **to come full circle** revenir au point de départ, boucler la boucle

(**b**) *(group of people)* cercle *m*, groupe *m*; **the family circle** le cercle familial; **she has a wide circle of friends** elle a beaucoup d'amis *ou* un grand cercle d'amis; **his circle of advisors** son groupe de conseillers; **in artistic/political circles** dans les milieux artistiques/politiques

(**c**) *Theat* balcon *m*

(**d**) *Archeol* **stone circle** cromlech *m*

2 *vt* (**a**) *(draw circle round)* entourer (d'un cercle), encercler

(**b**) *(move round)* tourner autour de; **the moon**

circles the earth la lune est en orbite autour *ou* tourne autour de la terre
(**c**) *(surround)* encercler, entourer
(**d**) *Am (idiom)* **to circle the wagons** se préparer à se défendre
3 *vi* (**a**) *(bird, plane)* faire *ou* décrire des cercles; **the plane circled overhead** l'avion a décrit des cercles dans le ciel; *Fig* **she circled round the issue** elle tournait autour du pot
(**b**) *(planet)* tourner

circlet ['sɜːklɪt] *n (on head → crown)* couronne *f*; *(→ for hair)* bandeau *m*; *(on arm)* brassard *m*; *(on finger)* anneau *m*

circlip ['sɜːklɪp] *n Tech* circlip *m*
►► ***circlip pliers*** pince *f* à circlip

circuit ['sɜːkɪt] *n* (**a**) *(series of events, venues, places)* circuit *m*; **the tennis circuit** le circuit des matches de tennis
(**b**) *(periodical journey)* tournée *f*; *Law* tournée *f (d'un juge d'assises)*; **to be on the western circuit** faire la tournée de l'ouest
(**c**) *(journey around)* circuit *m*, tour *m*; **we made a circuit of the grounds** nous avons fait le tour des terrains; **the Earth's circuit around the Sun** l'orbite de la terre autour du soleil
(**d**) *Elec* circuit *m*
(**e**) *Sport (track)* circuit *m*, parcours *m*; **to make one circuit of the track** faire un tour de circuit
►► *Elec* ***circuit board*** plaquette *f* (de circuits imprimés); *Elec* ***circuit breaker*** disjoncteur *m*; *Law* ***circuit court*** = tribunal en service dans les principales villes de province lors du passage du "circuit judge"; *Am Hist* ***Circuit Court of Appeals*** = cour d'appel du système judiciaire des États-Unis avant 1948; *Law* ***circuit judge*** = juge itinérant; *Sport* ***circuit training*** programme *m* d'exercices en salle

circuitous [sə'kjuːɪtəs] *adj (route)* qui fait un détour, détourné; *(journey)* compliqué; *Fig (reasoning, thinking)* contourné, compliqué; **by circuitous means** par des moyens détournés *ou* indirects

circuitously [sə'kjuːɪtəslɪ] *adv (reach destination)* par le chemin le plus long; *(reason, argue)* avec beaucoup de circonvolutions; **the path winds circuitously to the summit** le chemin monte en lacets jusqu'au sommet

circuitry ['sɜːkɪtrɪ] *n* système *m* de circuits

circular ['sɜːkjʊlə(r)] **1** *adj* (**a**) *(movement, shape, ticket)* circulaire; **circular journey** voyage *m* circulaire, circuit *m*
(**b**) *(reasoning)* faux (fausse), mal fondé
2 *n (letter, memo)* circulaire *f*; *(publicity material)* prospectus *m*
►► ***circular argument*** pétition *f* de principe; ***circular letter*** circulaire *f*; *Fin* ***circular letter of credit*** lettre *f* de crédit circulaire; ***circular memo*** circulaire *f*; *Tech* ***circular saw*** scie *f* circulaire

circularity [ˌsɜːkjʊ'lærətɪ] *n* (**a**) *(of movement, shape)* forme *f* circulaire (**b**) *(of reasoning, argument)* circularité *f*

circularization [ˌsɜːkjʊləraɪ'zeɪʃən] *n (sending of letters)* envoi *m* de circulaires; *(sending of publicity material)* envoi *m* de prospectus

circularize, -ise ['sɜːkjʊləraɪz] *vt (send letters to)* envoyer des circulaires à; *(send publicity material to)* envoyer des prospectus à

circulate ['sɜːkjʊleɪt] **1** *vt* (**a**) *(book, bottle)* faire circuler; *(document → from person to person)* faire circuler; *(→ in mass mailing)* diffuser; *(news, rumour)* propager; **the memo was circulated to all members of staff** on a fait circuler le document parmi tout le personnel (**b**) *(banknotes)* mettre en circulation, émettre
2 *vi* circuler; *(at a party)* aller de groupe en groupe

circulating ['sɜːkjʊleɪtɪŋ] *adj* circulant
►► *Acct* ***circulating assets*** actif *m* circulant; *Fin* ***circulating capital*** capitaux *mpl* circulants; *Math* ***circulating decimal*** fraction *f* périodique; ***circulating library*** *(mobile library)* bibliothèque *f* ambulante *ou* mobile; *Am (lending library)* bibliothèque *f* de prêt

circulation [ˌsɜːkjʊ'leɪʃən] *n* (**a**) *(gen)* circulation *f*; **to be in circulation** *(book, money)* être en circulation; *(person)* être dans le circuit; **to put forged notes into circulation** mettre de faux billets en circulation; **the memo was for internal circulation only** c'était une note de service à usage interne uniquement; **she's out of circulation at the moment** elle a disparu de la circulation pour l'instant
(**b**) *(of magazine, newspaper)* tirage *m*; **a newspaper with a large circulation** un journal à grand tirage; **the Times has a circulation of 200,000** le Times tire à 200 000 exemplaires
(**c**) *Anat & Bot* circulation *f*; **to have good/poor circulation** avoir une bonne/une mauvaise circulation
(**d**) *(of traffic)* circulation *f*
►► *Press* ***circulation figures*** chiffres *mpl* de diffusion

circulatory [ˌsɜːkjʊ'leɪtərɪ] *adj Anat & Bot* circulatoire

circumambiency [ˌsɜːkəm'æmbɪənsɪ] *n Literary* ambiance *f*

circumambient [ˌsɜːkəm'æmbɪənt] *adj Literary* ambiant

circumambulate [ˌsɜːkəm'æmbjʊleɪt] *Literary* **1** *vt (walk round)* faire le tour de
2 *vi* se promener çà et là

circumambulation [ˌsɜːkəmˌæmbjʊ'leɪʃən] *n Literary* promenades *fpl* sans but

circumcise ['sɜːkəmˌsaɪz] *vt (boy)* circoncire; *(girl)* exciser

circumcised ['sɜːkəmˌsaɪzd] *adj (boy, man)* circoncis

circumcision [ˌsɜːkəm'sɪʒən] *n (act)* circoncision *f*; *Rel* **the Circumcision** la (fête de la) Circoncision; **female circumcision** excision *f*
►► ***circumcision ritual*** rituel *m* de la circoncision

circumference [sə'kʌmfərəns] *n* circonférence *f*; **to be 30 metres in circumference** avoir 30 mètres de circonférence

circumferential [ˌsɜːkʌmfə'renʃəl] *adj* circonférentiel

circumflex ['sɜːkəmfleks] *Ling* **1** *n* accent *m* circonflexe
2 *adj* circonflexe

circumfuse [ˌsɜːkəm'fjuːz] *vt Literary* répandre; **to circumfuse sth with air/light, to circumfuse air/light about sth** répandre de l'air/de la lumière autour de qch

circumjacent [ˌsɜːkəm'dʒeɪsənt] *adj Literary* circonjacent, circonvoisin

circumlocution [ˌsɜːkəmlə'kjuːʃən] *n* circonlocution *f*, périphrase *f*; **without circumlocution** sans ambages

circumlocutory [ˌsɜːkəm'lɒkjʊtərɪ] *adj* qui procède par circonlocutions, périphrastique

circumlunar [ˌsɜːkəm'luːnə(r)] *adj Astron* circumlunaire

circumnavigate [ˌsɜːkəm'nævɪgeɪt] *vt (iceberg, island)* contourner; **to circumnavigate the world** faire le tour du monde

circumnavigation [ˌsɜːkəmˌnævɪ'geɪʃən] *n* circumnavigation *f*

circumnavigator [ˌsɜːkəm'nævɪgeɪtə(r)] *n* = personne qui fait le tour du monde

circumpolar [ˌsɜːkəm'pəʊlə(r)] **1** *n* étoile *f* circumpolaire
2 *adj* circumpolaire

circumscribe ['sɜːkəmskraɪb] *vt* (**a**) *(limit)* restreindre, limiter (**b**) *Math* circonscrire

circumscribed ['sɜːkəmskraɪbd] *adj* (**a**) *(limited)* restreint, limité (**b**) *Math* circonscrit

circumscription [ˌsɜːkəm'skrɪpʃən] *n* (**a**) *(limitation)* restriction *f*, limitation *f* (**b**) *Math* circonscription *f*

circumsolar [ˌsɜːkəm'səʊlə(r)] *adj Astron* autour du soleil

circumspect ['sɜːkəmspekt] *adj* circonspect

circumspection [ˌsɜːkəm'spekʃən] *n* circonspection *f*

circumspectly ['sɜːkəmˌspektlɪ] *adv* avec circonspection

circumspectness [ˌsɜːkəm'spektnɪs] *n* circonspection *f*

circumstance ['sɜːkəmstəns] **1** *n (UNCOUNT)* (**a**) *(events)* **force of circumstance** contrainte *f ou* force *f* des circonstances; **I am a victim of circumstance** je suis victime des circonstances
(**b**) *Formal (ceremony)* **pomp and circumstance** grand apparat *m*, pompe *f*
2 circumstances *npl* (**a**) *(conditions)* circonstance *f*, situation *f*; **in** *or* **under these circumstances** dans les circonstances actuelles, vu la situation actuelle *ou* l'état actuel des choses; **in** *or* **under exceptional circumstances** dans des circonstances exceptionnelles; **in** *or* **under normal circumstances** en temps normal; **under no circumstances** en aucun cas; **under similar circumstances** en pareil cas; **due to circumstances beyond our control** en raison de circonstances indépendantes de notre volonté
(**b**) *(facts)* circonstance *f*, détail *m*; **the circumstances of her death** les circonstances de sa mort; **you have to take into account the circumstances** il faut tenir compte des circonstances
(**c**) *(financial situation)* **if his circumstances allowed** si ses moyens le permettaient; **in easy circumstances** à l'aise

circumstantial [ˌsɜːkəm'stænʃəl] *adj* (**a**) *(incidental)* accidentel, fortuit (**b**) *Formal (description, report)* circonstancié, détaillé
►► *Law* ***circumstantial evidence*** preuves *fpl* indirectes

circumstantiality [ˌsɜːkəmstænʃɪ'ælɪtɪ] *n Formal* (**a**) *(minuteness in details)* abondance *f* de détails (**b**) *(detail)* circonstance *f*, détail *m*

circumstantiate [ˌsɜːkəm'stænʃɪeɪt] *vt (event, report)* donner des détails circonstanciés sur; *Law (evidence)* confirmer en donnant des détails sur

circumvent [ˌsɜːkəm'vent] *vt* (**a**) *(law, rule)* tourner, contourner (**b**) *(outwit → person)* circonvenir, manipuler; *(→ plan)* faire échouer (**c**) *(enemy)* encercler, entourer

circumvention [ˌsɜːkəm'venʃən] *n (of law, rule)* fait *m* de tourner *ou* contourner

circus ['sɜːkəs] **1** *n* (**a**) *(gen) & Antiq* cirque *m*; **to join a circus** entrer dans un cirque (**b**) *Br (roundabout)* rond-point *m*
2 *comp* de cirque

cirque [sɜːk] *n Geol* cirque *m*

cirrhosis [sɪ'rəʊsɪs] *n (UNCOUNT) Med* cirrhose *f*; **cirrhosis of the liver** cirrhose *f* du foie; **to have cirrhosis** avoir une cirrhose

cirriped ['sɪrɪped] *n Zool* cirripède *m*, cirrhipède *m*

cirrocumulus [ˌsɪrəʊ'kjuːmjʊləs] *(pl* **cirrocumuli** [-laɪ]*) n Met* cirrocumulus *m*

cirrostratus [ˌsɪrəʊ'strɑːtəs] *(pl* **cirrostrati** [-taɪ]*) n Met* cirrostratus *m*

cirrus ['sɪrəs] *(pl* **cirri** [-raɪ]*) n* (**a**) *Met* cirrus *m* (**b**) *Bot* vrille *f*

CIS [ˌsiːaɪ'es] *n (abbr* **Commonwealth of Independent States***)* CEI *f*

cisalpine [sɪs'ælpaɪn] *adj* cisalpin
►► ***Cisalpine Gaul*** Gaule *f* cisalpine

CISC [ˌsiːaɪˌes'siː] *n (abbr* **complex instruction set computer***)* CISC *m*

cissy = **sissy**

Cistercian [sɪ'stɜːʃən] *Rel* **1** *n* cistercien(enne) *m,f*
2 *adj* cistercien
►► ***Cistercian monk*** cistercien *m*; ***Cistercian nun*** cistercienne *f*; ***the Cistercian Order*** l'ordre *m* de Cîteaux

cistern ['sɪstən] *n (tank)* citerne *f*; *(for toilet)* réservoir *m* de chasse d'eau

cistron ['sɪstrɒn] *n Biol* cistron *m*

citable ['saɪtəbəl] *adj* citable

citadel ['sɪtədəl] *n also Fig* citadelle *f*

citation [saɪ'teɪʃən] *n* (**a**) *(quotation)* citation *f* (**b**) *Am Law (summons)* citation *f*
►► ***citation file*** corpus *m*

cite [saɪt] *vt* (**a**) *(quote)* citer; **he cited it as an example** il l'a cité en exemple (**b**) *(commend)* citer; **she was cited for bravery** elle a été citée pour sa bravoure (**c**) *Law* citer; **they were cited to appear as witnesses** ils étaient cités comme témoins

CITES [ˌsaɪ'tiːz] *n (abbr* **Convention on International Trade in Endangered Species***)* CITES *f*

citizen ['sɪtɪzən] *n* (**a**) *(of nation, state)* citoyen(enne) *m,f*; *Admin (national)* ressortissant(e) *m,f*; **to become a French citizen** prendre la nationalité française; **citizen of the world** citoyen(enne) *m,f* du monde
(**b**) *(of town)* habitant(e) *m,f*; **the citizens of Rome** les habitants de Rome, les Romains
(**c**) *(civilian)* civil(e) *m,f (opposé à militaire)*
►► *Admin* ***Citizens' Advice Bureau*** = en Grande-Bretagne, bureau où les citoyens peuvent

obtenir des conseils d'ordre juridique, social etc; ***citizen army*** armée *f* de citoyens; ***citizen's arrest*** = arrestation par un citoyen d'une personne soupçonnée d'avoir commis un délit; *Rad* ***citizens' band*** citizen band *f*; ***citizens' band radio*** CB *f*; ***citizens' band user*** cibiste *mf*; *Admin* ***Citizens' Charter*** = programme lancé par le gouvernement britannique en 1991 et qui vise à améliorer la qualité des services publics; ***citizen rights*** droits *mpl* civiques

citizenry ['sɪtɪzənrɪ] *n (of nation)* (ensemble *m* des) citoyens *mpl*; *(of town)* (ensemble *m* des) habitants *mpl*

citizenship ['sɪtɪzənʃɪp] *n* citoyenneté *f*, nationalité *f*; **to apply for French citizenship** demander la citoyenneté *ou* nationalité française; **to be granted full citizenship of a country** se voir accorder la citoyenneté d'un pays; **citizenship papers** déclaration *f* de naturalisation; **good citizenship** civisme *m*

citrate ['sɪtreɪt] *n Chem* citrate *m*

citric ['sɪtrɪk] *adj Chem* citrique
►► ***citric acid*** acide *m* citrique

citril finch ['sɪtrɪl-] *n Orn* venturon *m* montagnard

citrine ['sɪtrɪn] **1** *n* (**a**) *Miner* citrine *f*, fausse topaze *f* (**b**) *(colour)* jaune *m* verdâtre
2 *adj (colour)* jaune verdâtre
►► *Pharm* ***citrine ointment*** onguent *m* citrin

citron ['sɪtrən] *n Bot (fruit)* cédrat *m*; *(tree)* cédratier *m*

citronella [ˌsɪtrə'nelə] *n Bot* citronnelle *f*
►► ***citronella oil*** citronnelle *f*

citrus fruit ['sɪtrəs-] *n* **a citrus fruit** un agrume; **citrus fruit** *or* **fruits** agrumes *mpl*

city ['sɪtɪ] *(pl* **cities**) **1** *n (town)* (grande) ville *f*; **the City of Brotherly Love** = surnom de Philadelphie; **life in the city** la vie en ville, la vie citadine; **the whole city turned out** toute la ville était présente, tous les habitants de la ville étaient présents
2 *comp (lights, limits, streets)* de la ville; *(officers, police, services)* municipal; *(life)* en ville, citadin
3 City 1 *n Fin (of London)* = centre d'affaires de Londres; **the City** la City (de Londres); **he's something in the City** il travaille à la City (de Londres); **the City Companies** les corporations *fpl* de la City de Londres **2** *comp Br Press (news, page, press)* financier
►► ***city break*** *(holiday)* court séjour *m* en ville; *Br* ***city centre*** centre *m* de la ville, centre-ville *m*; *Am Fam* ***city cop*** flic *m*; *Press* ***city desk*** *Br* service *m* financier; *Am* service *m* des nouvelles locales; *Press* ***city editor*** *Br* rédacteur(trice) *m,f* en chef pour les nouvelles financières; *Am* rédacteur(trice) *m,f* en chef pour les nouvelles locales; ***city farm*** = ferme située en ville dans le but de permettre aux jeunes citadins de se familiariser avec le monde campagnard tout en restant en ville; ***city fathers*** édiles *mpl* locaux; *Br* ***city gent*** homme *m* d'affaires de la City *(souvent représenté en costume rayé et chapeau melon)*; ***city hall*** (**a**) *(building)* mairie *f*, hôtel *m* de ville (**b**) *Am (municipal government)* administration *f* (municipale); **you can't fight city hall** on ne peut rien contre l'administration; *Acct* ***city ledger*** *(in hotels, business)* débiteurs *mpl* divers; *Am Admin* ***city manager*** administrateur(trice) *m,f (payé par la municipalité pour gérer ses affaires)*; ***city planner*** urbaniste *mf*; ***city planning*** urbanisme *m*; *Fam Pej* ***city slicker*** = citadin sophistiqué; ***city technology college*** = collège technique britannique, généralement établi dans des quartiers défavorisés

THE CITY

La City, quartier financier de la capitale, est une circonscription administrative autonome de Londres ayant sa propre police.

City and Guilds *n* = diplôme britannique d'enseignement technique

city-dweller *n Br* citadin(e) *m,f*

cityscape ['sɪtɪˌskeɪp] *n* paysage *m* urbain

city-state *n Hist* cité *f*

civet ['sɪvɪt] *n Zool (mammal, secretion)* civette *f*
►► ***civet cat*** civette *f*

civic ['sɪvɪk] *adj (authority, building)* municipal; *(duty, right)* civique
►► ***civic centre*** = centre administratif d'une ville, parfois complété par des équipements de loisirs, ≃ cité *f* administrative; ***civic event*** événement *m* officiel local; ***Civic Trust*** = groupement de bénévoles animant des actions de mise en valeur du patrimoine en Grande-Bretagne; ***civic university*** = université de ville, en Grande-Bretagne

civically ['sɪvɪkəlɪ] *adv* (**a**) *(gen)* du point de vue civique (**b**) *(behave)* en citoyen

civics ['sɪvɪks] *n (UNCOUNT)* instruction *f* civique

civies = **civvies**

civil ['sɪvəl] *adj* (**a**) *(of community)* civil (**b**) *(non-military)* civil (**c**) *(polite)* poli, courtois, civil; **she was very civil to me** elle s'est montrée très aimable avec moi; **keep a civil tongue in your head!** restez poli!
►► *Am Formerly* ***Civil Aeronautics Authority*** = organisme américain de contrôle des compagnies aériennes; *Am Formerly* ***Civil Aeronautics Board*** = organisme américain de réglementation de l'aviation civile; ***civil aircraft*** appareil *m* de l'aviation civile; ***civil aviation*** aviation *f* civile; ***Civil Aviation Authority*** = organisme de contrôle des compagnies aériennes; *Law* ***civil court*** tribunal *m* civil; *Law* ***civil death*** mort *f* civile; *Mil* ***civil defence*** protection *f* civile; ***civil disobedience*** résistance *f* passive (à la loi); ***civil disturbance*** émeute *f*; ***civil engineer*** ingénieur *m* des travaux publics; ***civil engineering*** génie *m* civil; ***civil engineering firm*** entreprise *f* de travaux publics; ***civil law*** droit *m* civil; ***civil libertarian*** défenseur *m* des droits du citoyen; ***civil liberties*** libertés *fpl* civiques; *Br* ***Civil List*** liste *f* civile *(allouée à la famille royale britannique)*; ***civil marriage*** mariage *m* civil; ***Civil and Public Services Association*** = syndicat de la fonction publique; ***civil rights*** droits *mpl* civils *ou* civiques; *Am* ***Civil Rights Commission*** = organisme gouvernemental qui veille au respect des droits civiques; ***the civil rights movement*** la lutte pour les droits civils *ou* civiques; *Admin* ***civil servant*** fonctionnaire *mf*; *Admin* ***civil service*** fonction *f* publique, administration *f*; **to be in the civil service** être fonctionnaire *ou* dans l'administration *ou* dans la fonction publique; ***civil service exam*** concours *m* administratif; ***Civil Service Union*** = syndicat britannique de la fonction publique; ***civil strife*** conflit *m* interne *ou* intestin; ***civil war*** guerre *f* civile; ***the American Civil War*** la guerre de Sécession; ***the English Civil War*** la guerre civile anglaise; ***civil wedding*** mariage *m* civil; **we had a civil wedding** nous nous sommes mariés à la mairie

THE AMERICAN CIVIL WAR

Déclenchée par l'élection d'Abraham Lincoln, attisée par les différences sociales et économiques, la guerre de Sécession opposa, de 1861 à 1865, le sud esclavagiste (les "Confédérés", qui voulaient faire sécession) au nord abolitionniste (les "Fédéraux", qui voulaient préserver l'union). Le conflit se termina par la victoire du camp nordiste, supérieur en hommes et en moyens.

THE ENGLISH CIVIL WAR

Ce conflit (1642–51) fut provoqué par la révolte du Parlement contre le roi Charles Ier. La victoire fut remportée par l'armée de Cromwell, qui fit exécuter le roi en 1649.

civilian [sɪ'vɪljən] **1** *adj* civil *(opposé à militaire)*; **in civilian clothes** en civil; **in civilian life** dans le civil
2 *n* civil(e) *m,f (opposé à militaire)*

civilianize, -ise [sɪ'vɪljənaɪz] *vt* **to civilianize a military establishment** remplacer le personnel d'un établissement militaire par des civils

civility [sɪ'vɪlətɪ] *(pl* **civilities**) *n* (**a**) *(quality)* courtoisie *f*, civilité *f* (**b**) *(act)* civilité *f*, politesse *f*; **exchange of civilities** échange *m* d'amabilités

civilization [ˌsɪvɪlaɪ'zeɪʃən] *n* civilisation *f*; *Fam* **it's miles from civilization** c'est à des kilomètres du monde civilisé

civilize, -ise ['sɪvɪlaɪz] *vt* civiliser

civilized ['sɪvɪlaɪzd] *adj (person, society)* civilisé; **they have real coffee in their office – very civilized!** ils ont du vrai café dans leur bureau – la classe!; **their divorce was a very civilized affair** ils ont divorcé comme des gens civilisés; **let's be civilized about this** tâchons d'être conciliants

civilizing ['sɪvɪlaɪzɪŋ] *adj* **the civilizing influence of...** l'influence civilisatrice de...; **the new teacher has had a civilizing influence on them** le nouveau professeur semble les avoir calmés

civilly ['sɪvəlɪ] *adv* poliment, courtoisement

civvy ['sɪvɪ] *(pl* **civies** *or* **civvies**) *Br Fam* **1** *n (civilian)* civil(e) ❑ *m,f (opposé à militaire)*
2 *adj* civil ❑
3 civvies *npl (dress)* vêtements *mpl* civils ❑; **in civvies** (habillé) en civil
►► *Br Fam* ***civvy street*** vie *f* civile ❑; **in civvy street** dans le civil ❑, dans la vie civile ❑

CJD [ˌsiːdʒeɪ'diː] *n Med (abbr* **Creutzfeld-Jakob disease**) MCJ *f*; **new variant CJD** nouveau variant *m* de MCJ

Cl *Chem (written abbr* **chlorine**) Cl

cl *(written abbr* **centilitre**) cl

clabbered milk ['klæbəd-] *n* lait *m* fermenté

clack [klæk] **1** *vi (make noise)* claquer; *(jabber)* jacasser, papoter; **their friendship set tongues clacking** leur amitié a fait jaser
2 *vt* faire claquer
3 *n* (**a**) *(sound)* claquement *m* (**b**) *Tech (valve)* clapet *m*

clacking ['klækɪŋ] *n (noise)* claquement *m*

clad [klæd] **1** *pt & pp of* **clothe**
2 *adj Literary* habillé, vêtu; **clad in rags** habillé *ou* vêtu de haillons
3 *vt Tech* revêtir

cladding ['klædɪŋ] *n Tech* revêtement *m*, parement *m*

clade [kleɪd] *n Biol* clade *m*

CLAIM [kleɪm]

prétendre	► **1 (a)**
revendiquer	► **1 (b)**
réclamer	► **1 (b), (d), (e)**
demander	► **1 (c), (d)**
récupérer	► **1 (e)**
affirmation	► **3 (a)**
droit	► **3 (b)**
demande	► **3 (c), (d)**

1 *vt* (**a**) *(assert, maintain)* prétendre, déclarer; **it is claimed that...** on dit *ou* prétend que...; **to claim to be sth** se faire passer pour qch, prétendre être qch; **to claim acquaintance with sb** prétendre connaître qn
(**b**) *(assert one's right to)* revendiquer, réclamer; *(responsibility, right)* revendiquer; **he claims all the credit** il s'attribue tout le mérite; **to claim damages/one's due** réclamer des dommages et intérêts/son dû; **no one has yet claimed responsibility for the hijacking** le détournement n'a pas encore été revendiqué; **workers are claiming the right to strike** les ouvriers revendiquent le droit de (faire) grève
(**c**) *(apply for → money)* demander; *(→ expenses)* demander le remboursement de; **to claim financial assistance from the government** demander une aide financière à l'administration
(**d**) *(call for → attention)* réclamer, demander; *(→ respect, sympathy)* solliciter
(**e**) *(collect, take → baggage)* récupérer; *(→ lost property)* réclamer; **has anyone arrived to claim her?** *(lost child)* est-ce que quelqu'un est venu la chercher?; **the storm claimed five lives** *or* **five victims** l'orage a fait cinq victimes
2 *vi* **to claim for** *or* **on sth** *(insurance)* demander le paiement de qch; *(travel expenses)* demander le remboursement de qch
3 *n* (**a**) *(assertion)* affirmation *f*, prétention *f*; **they have been making all sorts of claims about their new product** ils ont paré leur nouveau produit de toutes sortes de qualités; **I make no claims to understand why** je ne prétends pas comprendre pourquoi; **the town lays**

claim to being the place where golf was invented les gens de cette ville prétendent que c'est ici que le golf fut inventé

(**b**) *(right)* droit *m*, titre *m*; *(by trade unions)* demande *f* d'augmentation, revendication *f* salariale; **claim to property** droit *m* à la propriété; **what is her claim to the throne?** quel est son titre à la couronne?; **his only claim to fame is that he once appeared on TV** c'est à une apparition à la télévision qu'il doit d'être célèbre

(**c**) *(demand)* demande *f*; **he has no claims on me** je ne lui suis redevable de rien; **he made too many claims on their generosity** il a abusé de leur générosité; **she has many claims on her time** elle est très prise; **to have many claims on one's purse** avoir beaucoup de frais; **to lay claim to** *(property etc)* prétendre à, revendiquer son droit à; *(skills)* s'attribuer; **we put in a claim for better working conditions** nous avons demandé de meilleures conditions de travail; **pay claim** revendications *fpl* salariales

(**d**) *Ins* demande *f* d'indemnité, déclaration *f* de sinistre; **to put in a claim for sth** demander une indemnité pour qch, faire une déclaration de sinistre pour qch; **the company pays 65 percent of all claims** la société satisfait 65 pour cent de toutes les demandes de dédommagement

(**e**) *(piece of land)* concession *f*

►► *Ins* ***claims adjuster*** répartiteur(trice) *m,f*; *Ins* ***claim form*** *(for insurance)* formulaire *m* de déclaration de sinistre; *(for expenses)* note *f* de frais

►**claim back** *vt sep (expenses, cost)* se faire rembourser; *(VAT)* récupérer

claimable ['kleɪməbəl] *adj* revendicable, réclamable

claimant ['kleɪmənt] *n* (**a**) *Admin & Ins* demandeur(eresse) *m,f*; *Law* demandeur(eresse) *m,f*, requérant(e) *m,f* (**b**) *(to throne)* prétendant(e) *m,f*

clairvoyance [kleə'vɔɪəns] *n* voyance *f*, don *m* de seconde vue

clairvoyant [kleə'vɔɪənt] **1** *n* voyant(e) *m,f*, extralucide *mf*

2 *adj* doué de seconde vue

clam [klæm] **1** *n* (**a**) *Zool* palourde *f*, clam *m*; *Fam* **to shut up like a clam** refuser de parler❑ (**b**) *Am Fam (dollar)* dollar❑ *m*

2 *vi Am* **to go clamming** aller ramasser des clams

►► *Culin* ***clam chowder*** = potage épais aux palourdes

►**clam up** *vi Fam* ne plus piper mot

clamant ['klæmənt] *adj Literary (voice)* criard; *(crowd)* bruyant

clambake ['klæmbeɪk] *n Am* = repas de fruits de mer sur la plage; *Fig* fête *f*

clamber ['klæmbə(r)] **1** *vi* grimper (en s'aidant des mains); **to clamber aboard a train** se hisser à bord d'un train; **we clambered up the hill** nous avons gravi la colline avec difficulté; **he clambered over the rocks** il a escaladé les rochers

2 *n* escalade *f*

clamminess ['klæmɪnɪs] *n (of hands, skin)* moiteur *f* froide; *(of air)* humidité *f* froide

clammy ['klæmɪ] (*compar* **clammier,** *superl* **clammiest**) *adj (hands, skin)* moite (et froid); *(weather)* humide, lourd; *(walls)* suintant, humide

clamor *Am* = **clamour**

clamorous ['klæmərəs] *adj* (**a**) *(noisy)* bruyant (**b**) *(demands)* insistant

clamorously ['klæmərəslɪ] *adv* bruyamment

clamour, *Am* **clamor** ['klæmə(r)] **1** *n* (**a**) *(noise)* clameur *f*, vociférations *fpl*, cri *m*, cris *mpl* (**b**) *(demand)* revendication *f* bruyante; *(protest)* tollé *m*; **there was a great clamour** ça a été un tollé général

2 *vi* vociférer, crier; **to clamour for sth** demander *ou* réclamer qch à grands cris *ou* à cor et à cri; **the children clamoured to go out** les enfants ont demandé à sortir à grands cris

clamp [klæmp] **1** *n* (**a**) *(fastener)* pince *f*; *Med* clamp *m*; *Tech* crampon *m*; *(on worktable)* valet *m* (d'établi)

(**b**) *Tech (for joint)* serre-joint *m inv*, serre-joints *m inv*

(**c**) *Naut* serre-câbles *m inv*

(**d**) *Agr* = tas de navets ou de pommes de terre couvert de paille

(**e**) *(of bricks)* tas *m*, pile *f*

(**f**) *Aut* sabot *m* de Denver

2 *vt* (**a**) *(fasten)* attacher, fixer; *Med (wound)* clamper; *Tech* serrer, cramponner; **to clamp sth to sth** fixer qch sur qch (à l'aide d'une pince)

(**b**) *(curfew, restrictions)* imposer; **the authorities clamped a curfew on the town** les autorités ont imposé le couvre-feu à la ville

(**c**) *Agr* entasser (**d**) *(vehicle)* mettre un sabot à; **my car has been clamped** on a mis un sabot à ma voiture

►**clamp down** *vi* donner un coup de frein; **to clamp down on** *(expenses, inflation)* mettre un frein à; *(crime, demonstrations)* stopper; *(information)* censurer; *(the press)* bâillonner; *(person)* serrer la vis à; **the police are clamping down on illegal parking** la police sévit contre *ou* devient plus sévère avec les automobilistes en stationnement interdit

clampdown ['klæmpdaʊn] *n* mesures *fpl* répressives, répression *f*; **there has been a clampdown on credit** il y a eu un resserrement du crédit; **a clampdown on crime** un plan de lutte contre la criminalité; **a clampdown on demonstrations** une interdiction de manifester

clamping ['klæmpɪŋ] *n (of cars)* immobilisation *f* des voitures au moyen de sabots de Denver

clamshell ['klæmʃel] *n (packaging)* coque *f* plastique

clan [klæn] *n* clan *m*

clandestine [klæn'destɪn] *adj* clandestin

clandestinely [klæn'destɪnlɪ] *adv* clandestinement

clandestineness [klæn'destɪnnɪs], **clandestinity** [ˌklændes'tɪnɪtɪ] *n* clandestinité *f*

clang [klæŋ] **1** *vi* retentir *ou* résonner (d'un bruit métallique); **the gate clanged shut** le portail s'est fermé avec un bruit métallique

2 *vt* faire retentir *ou* résonner; **she clanged the gate shut** elle ferma le portail bruyamment

3 *n* bruit *m* métallique

clanger ['klæŋə(r)] *n Br Fam* gaffe *f*; **to drop a clanger** faire une gaffe

clangour, *Am* **clangor** ['klæŋgə(r)] *n Formal* bruits *mpl* métalliques

clank [klæŋk] **1** *n* cliquetis *m*, bruit *m* sec et métallique

2 *vi* cliqueter, faire un bruit sec

3 *vt* faire cliqueter

clannish ['klænɪʃ] *adj Pej (group)* fermé, exclusif; *(person)* qui a l'esprit de clan *ou* de corps

clannishness ['klænɪʃnɪs] *n Pej (of group)* esprit *m* de corps; *(of person)* esprit *m* de clan *ou* de corps

clanship ['klænʃɪp] *n* système *m* du clan

clansman ['klænzmən] (*pl* **clansmen** [-mən]) *n* membre *m* d'un clan

clanswoman ['klænzˌwʊmən] (*pl* **clanswomen** [-ˌwɪmɪn]) *n* membre *m* d'un clan

clap [klæp] (*pt & pp* **clapped,** *cont* **clapping**) **1** *vt* (**a**) **to clap one's hands** *(to get attention, to mark rhythm)* frapper dans ses mains, taper des mains; *(in applause)* applaudir

(**b**) *(pat)* taper, frapper; **the boss clapped her on the back** le patron lui a donné une tape dans le dos

(**c**) *(put)* mettre, poser; **she clapped her hand to her forehead** elle s'est frappé le front; *Fam* **the judge clapped them into jail** le juge les a flanqués en prison; **he clapped his hat on his head** il a enfoncé son chapeau sur sa tête; *Fam* **to clap hold of sth** saisir qch; *Fam* **the minute she clapped eyes on him** dès qu'elle eut posé les yeux sur lui; **I've never clapped eyes on her before** je ne l'ai jamais vue de ma vie

2 *vi (to get attention, to mark rhythm)* frapper dans ses mains; *(in applause)* applaudir

3 *n* (**a**) *(sound → gen)* claquement *m*; *(→ of hands)* battement *m*; *(→ of applause)* applaudissements *mpl*; **let's give them a clap!** on les applaudit (bien fort)!; **clap of thunder** coup *m* de tonnerre

(**b**) *(pat)* tape *f*; **she gave him a clap on the back** elle lui a donné une tape dans le dos

(**c**) *very Fam* **the clap** *(venereal disease)* la chaude-pisse; **to have (a dose of) the clap** avoir la chaude-pisse

clapboard ['klæpbɔːd] *n Constr* planche *f* à clin; **clapboard (house)** maison *f* à clins

clapboarding ['klæpbɔːdɪŋ] *n Constr* revêtement *m* de planches à clin

Clapham ['klæpəm] *n* = quartier dans le sud de Londres; **the man on the Clapham omnibus** Monsieur Tout-le-Monde

►► ***Clapham Junction*** = important échangeur ferroviaire au sud de Londres

clapometer [klæ'pɒmɪtə(r)] *n* applaudimètre *m*

clapped-out [klæpt-] *adj Br Fam (machine, TV)* fichu; *(person)* crevé

clapper ['klæpə(r)] **1** *n (of bell)* battant *m*

2 clappers *npl Br Fam* **to go** *or* **to move like the clappers** aller à toute pompe; **he ran like the clappers** il a couru à toutes jambes, il a pris ses jambes à son cou

clapperboard ['klæpəbɔːd] *n Cin* claquette *f*, claquoir *m*, clap *m*

clapping ['klæpɪŋ] *n (UNCOUNT) (to get attention, to mark rhythm)* battements *mpl* de mains; *(applause)* applaudissements *mpl*

claptrap ['klæptræp] *n (UNCOUNT) Fam (nonsense)* âneries❑ *fpl*; **to talk claptrap** raconter des âneries❑

claque [klæk] *n* (**a**) *Theat (for applause)* claque *f* (**b**) *(group of admirers)* admirateurs(trices) *mpl,fpl*

Clare [kleə(r)] *n* le comté de Clare, = comté dans l'ouest de la République d'Irlande; **in Clare** dans le comté de Clare

Clarence House ['klærəns-] *n* = résidence de la Reine Mère, à Londres

claret ['klærət] **1** *n* (**a**) *Br* (vin *m* de) bordeaux *m* (rouge) (**b**) *(colour)* bordeaux *m inv*

2 *adj* bordeaux *(inv)*

Claridge's ['klærɪdʒɪz] *n* = hôtel de luxe à Londres

clarification [ˌklærɪfɪ'keɪʃən] *n* (**a**) *(explanation)* clarification *f*, éclaircissement *m*; **to ask for clarification** demander des éclaircissements (**b**) *(of butter)* clarification *f*; *(of wine)* collage *m*

clarify ['klærɪfaɪ] (*pt & pp* **clarified**) **1** *vt* (**a**) *(explain)* clarifier, éclaircir; **to clarify sb's mind on sth** expliquer qch à qn, éclaircir les idées de qn sur qch (**b**) *(butter)* clarifier; *(wine)* coller

2 *vi* (**a**) *(matter, situation)* s'éclaircir (**b**) *(butter)* se clarifier

clarifying ['klærɪfaɪɪŋ] *adj* clarificateur

clarinet [ˌklærə'net] *n* clarinette *f*

►► ***clarinet case*** étui *m* à clarinette; ***clarinet player*** clarinettiste *mf*

clarinetist, clarinettist [ˌklærə'netɪst] *n* clarinettiste *mf*

clarion ['klærɪən] **1** *n* clairon *m*

2 *vt Literary* claironner

►► ***clarion call*** appel *m* de clairon; **a clarion call to action** un appel à l'action

clarity ['klærətɪ] *n* (**a**) *(of explanation, of text)* clarté *f*, précision *f*; **clarity of mind** lucidité *f*, clarté *f* d'esprit (**b**) *(of liquid)* clarté *f*

clash [klæʃ] **1** *n* (**a**) *(sound → gen)* choc *m* métallique, fracas *m*; *(→ of cymbals)* retentissement *m*

(**b**) *(between people → fight)* affrontement *m*, bagarre *f*; *(→ disagreement)* dispute *f*, différend *m*; **clash of personalities, personality clash** incompatibilité *f* de caractères; **clashes on the border** des affrontements *mpl* à la frontière

(**c**) *(incompatibility → of ideas, opinions)* incompatibilité *f*; *(→ of interests)* conflit *m*; *(→ of colours)* discordance *f*

(**d**) *(of appointments, events)* coïncidence *f* fâcheuse

2 *vi* (**a**) *(swords, metallic objects)* s'entrechoquer, se heurter; *(cymbals)* résonner

(**b**) *(people → fight)* se battre; *(→ disagree)* se heurter; **to clash with sb over sth** avoir un différend avec qn à propos de qch; **police clashed with protestors** il y a eu des heurts entre la police et les manifestants

(**c**) *(be incompatible → ideas, opinions)* se heurter, être incompatible *ou* en contradiction; *(→ interests)* se heurter, être en conflit; *(→ colours)* jurer, détonner; **that shirt clashes with your trousers** cette chemise jure avec ton pantalon

(**d**) *(appointments, events)* tomber en même temps

3 *vt (metallic objects)* heurter *ou* entrechoquer bruyamment; *(cymbals)* faire résonner

clashing [ˈklæʃɪŋ] *adj* (**a**) *(sound)* bruyant, retentissant (**b**) *(opinions)* opposé; *(colours, styles)* discordant

clasp [klɑːsp] **1** *vt (hold)* serrer, étreindre; *(grasp)* saisir; **to clasp sb/sth in one's arms** serrer qn/qch dans ses bras; **to clasp sb/sth to one's breast** serrer qn/qch sur son cœur; **he clasped her hand** il lui a serré la main

2 *vi* s'attacher, se fermer

3 *n* (**a**) *(fastening → on handbag, dress, necklace)* fermoir *m*; *(→ on belt)* boucle *f* (**b**) *(hold)* prise *f*, étreinte *f*; **hand clasp** poignée *f* de mains

►► ***clasp knife*** couteau *m* pliant

class [klɑːs] **1** *n* (**a**) *(category, division)* classe *f*, catégorie *f*; **what class are you travelling in?** en quelle classe voyagez-vous?; **class A eggs** œufs de catégorie A; **he's just not in the same class as his brother** il n'arrive pas à la cheville de son frère; **to be in a class by oneself** *or* **in a class of one's own** être unique, former une classe à part

(**b**) *Biol, Bot & Zool* classe *f*

(**c**) *(social division)* classe *f*

(**d**) *Sch & Univ (group of students)* classe *f*; *(course)* cours *m*, classe *f*; **he used to give a class in history** il donnait des cours d'histoire; **she's attending** *or* **taking a psychology class** elle suit un cours de psychologie; *Am* **the class of 1972** la promotion de 1972

(**e**) *Br Univ (grade)* **what class (of) degree did you get?** quelle mention est-ce que tu as eu (à ton diplôme)?; **first class honours** licence *f* avec mention très bien

(**f**) *(elegance)* classe *f*; **to have class** avoir de la classe

2 *adj Fam (excellent)* classe *(inv)*; **a class car/hi-fi** une voiture/chaîne classe; **she's a real class act** elle est vraiment classe

3 *vt* classer, classifier; **classed first** classé premier; **to class sb/sth with sb/sth** assimiler qn/qch à qn/qch

►► *Am Law* ***class action*** recours *m* collectif en justice; ***class distinctions*** distinctions *fpl* entre les classes; ***class prejudice*** préjugés *mpl* sociaux; *Am* ***class reunion*** réunion *f* d'anciens élèves de la même classe; ***class struggle*** lutte *f* des classes; ***class system*** système *m* de classes; ***class traitor*** personne *f* qui renie ses origines sociales; ***class war(fare)*** lutte *f* des classes

classable [ˈklɑːsəbəl] *adj* que l'on peut classer

class-conscious *adj (person → aware)* conscient des distinctions sociales; *(→ snobbish)* snob; *(attitude, manners)* snob

class-consciousness *n (awareness)* conscience *f* des distinctions sociales; *(snobbishness)* snobisme *m*

classic [ˈklæsɪk] **1** *adj also Fig* classique; **it was a classic case of xenophobia** c'était un cas typique de xénophobie; *Fam* **it was classic!** *(joke, situation, event)* ça payait!

2 *n* (**a**) *(gen)* classique *m*; **it's a classic of modern cinema** c'est un classique du cinéma moderne; **the game wasn't exactly a classic** le match n'avait rien d'extraordinaire; *Fam* **it was a classic!** *(joke, situation, event)* ça payait!

(**b**) *Sport* classique *f*; *Horseracing* **the Classics** = les cinq courses de plat les plus importantes, en Grande-Bretagne

(**c**) *Sch & Univ* **classics** les lettres *fpl* classiques

►► ***classic car*** voiture *f* ancienne; ***classics degree*** licence *f* de lettres classiques; ***Classics Illustrated*** = bandes dessinées américaines reprenant les grands classiques de la littérature; *Mus* ***classic rock*** rock *m* classique

classical [ˈklæsɪkəl] *adj* (**a**) *(gen)* classique (**b**) *(civilization)* de l'antiquité; *Sch & Univ* **classical education** études *fpl* de lettres; **classical Greece** la Grèce antique; **classical scholar** humaniste *mf*; **in classical times** dans l'antiquité; **the classical world** le monde de l'antiquité

►► ***classical music*** musique *f* classique

classicalism [ˈklæsɪkəlɪzəm] *n* classicisme *m*

classically [ˈklæsɪkəlɪ] *adv* classiquement, de façon classique; **a classically trained musician** un musicien de formation classique; **she's not classically beautiful** elle n'a pas une beauté classique

classicism [ˈklæsɪsɪzəm] *n* classicisme *m*

classicist [ˈklæsɪsɪst] *n* humaniste *mf*; *(advocate of classical studies)* partisan(e) *m,f* des études classiques

classifiable [ˈklæsɪfaɪəbəl] *adj* qui peut être classifié, classable

classification [ˌklæsɪfɪˈkeɪʃən] *n* (**a**) *(action → of plants, animals)* classification *f*; *(→ of papers, competitors, books etc)* classement *m* (**b**) *(category)* classification *f*, classe *f*

classified [ˈklæsɪfaɪd] **1** *adj* (**a**) *(arranged)* classifié, classé (**b**) *(secret → document)* (classé) secret

2 *n* petite annonce *f*; **the classifieds** les petites annonces *fpl*

►► ***classified ad, classified advertisement*** petite annonce *f*; ***classified information*** renseignements *mpl* (classés) secrets

classifier [ˈklæsɪfaɪə(r)] *n* classeur *m*

classify [ˈklæsɪfaɪ] *vt* (**a**) *(categorize)* classer; **their music is classified as jazz** leur musique est classée comme étant du jazz (**b**) *(make secret → document)* classer secret

classless [ˈklɑːslɪs] *adj (society)* sans classes; *(person, accent)* qui n'appartient à aucune classe (sociale)

classmate [ˈklɑːsmeɪt] *n* camarade *mf* de classe

classroom [ˈklɑːsrʊm] *n* (salle *f* de) classe *f*

►► ***classroom teaching*** enseignement *m* en classe

classy [ˈklɑːsɪ] *(compar* **classier**, *superl* **classiest**) *adj Fam (hotel, restaurant)* chic[□] *(inv)*, de luxe[□] *(inv)*, classe *(inv)*; *(person)* chic[□] *(inv)*, classe *(inv)*

clatter [ˈklætə(r)] **1** *n (rattle)* cliquetis *m*; *(commotion)* fracas *m*; **she banged her cup down with a clatter** elle a posé sa tasse bruyamment; **the clatter of dishes** le bruit d'assiettes entrechoquées

2 *vt* heurter *ou* entrechoquer bruyamment

3 *vi (typewriter)* cliqueter; *(dishes)* s'entrechoquer bruyamment; *(falling object)* faire du bruit; **the old cart clattered by** le vieux chariot est passé dans un bruit de ferraille

claudication [ˌklɔːdɪˈkeɪʃən] *n Med* claudication *f*; **intermittent claudication** claudication *f* intermittente

Claudius [ˈklɔːdɪəs] *pr n (emperor)* Claude

'I, Claudius' *Graves* 'Moi, Claude'

---

clausal [ˈklɔːzəl] *adj* (**a**) *Gram* propositionnel (**b**) *Law* relatif aux clauses

clause [klɔːz] *n* (**a**) *Gram* proposition *f*

(**b**) *Law (of treaty, law)* clause *f*, article *m*; *(of will)* disposition *f*; *Ins (of policy)* avenant *m*; *Pol* **Clause 4** = article de la constitution du Parti travailliste britannique affirmant son attachement au principe de propriété publique des grands secteurs industriels (abrogé en 1995); **Clause 28** = disposition juridique en Grande-Bretagne interdisant aux enseignants du secondaire d'aborder le thème de l'homosexualité en classe; *see also box at* **Section 28**

claused bill [klɔːzd-] *n Com* connaissement *m* clausé

claustral [ˈklɔːstrəl] *adj* claustral

claustrophobia [ˌklɔːstrəˈfəʊbjə] *n* claustrophobie *f*

claustrophobic [ˌklɔːstrəˈfəʊbɪk] *adj (person)* claustrophobe; *(feeling)* de claustrophobie; *(place, situation)* où l'on se sent claustrophobe; **I feel claustrophobic** j'ai un sentiment de claustrophobie

clavichord [ˈklævɪkɔːd] *n* clavicorde *m*

clavicle [ˈklævɪkəl] *n Anat* clavicule *f*

clavicular [kləˈvɪkjʊlə(r)] *adj Anat* claviculaire

clavier [ˈklævɪə(r)] *n Mus (keyboard)* clavier *m*; *(instrument)* instrument *m* à clavier

claw [klɔː] **1** *n* (**a**) *(of bird, cat, dog)* griffe *f*; *(of bird of prey)* serre *f*; *(of crab, lobster)* pince *f*; *Fam (hand)* patte *f*; *also Fig* **to draw in/to show one's claws** rentrer/sortir ses griffes; *Fam* **to get one's claws into sb** mettre le grappin sur qn

(**b**) *(of hammer)* pied-de-biche *m*

2 *vt (scratch)* griffer; *(grip)* agripper *ou* serrer (avec ses griffes); *(tear)* déchirer (avec ses griffes); *Fig* **he clawed his way to the top** il a employé tous les moyens nécessaires pour arriver en haut de l'échelle

►► ***claw hammer*** marteau *m* à pied-de-biche, marteau *m* fendu

►**claw at** *vt insep* **to claw at sth** *(of cat)* saisir qch avec ses griffes, s'accrocher à qch; *(grip)* s'accrocher à qch, agripper qch; *(try to grip)* essayer de s'accrocher à qch *ou* d'agripper qch; **she clawed at my face** *(scratched me)* elle a essayé de me griffer au visage

►**claw back** *vt sep Br* (**a**) *Fin (expenditure)* récupérer

(**b**) *(regain)* regagner péniblement; **she clawed her way back to a prominent position** à force de persévérance, elle a réussi à regagner une position influente

clawback [ˈklɔːbæk] *n Fin (recovery)* récupération *f*; *(sum)* somme *f* récupérée

claw-footed *adj (table, chair)* à pied de griffon

clawmark [ˈklɔːmɑːk] *n* griffure *f*

clay [kleɪ] **1** *n* (**a**) *(gen)* argile *f*, (terre *f*) glaise *f*; *(for pottery)* argile *f*; **(modelling) clay** pâte *f* à modeler; *Fig* **to have feet of clay** avoir des pieds d'argile; *Literary* **mortal clay** le corps humain

(**b**) *Sport (in tennis)* **to play on clay** jouer sur terre battue; **to be good on clay** jouer bien sur la terre battue

2 *comp (brick, pot)* en argile, en terre; *(pipe)* en terre

►► *Sport* ***clay court*** court *m* en terre battue; ***clay pigeon*** pigeon *m* d'argile *ou* de ball-trap; *Am Fam Fig (sitting duck)* cible *f* facile[□]; ***clay pigeon shooting*** ball-trap *m*; ***clay pit*** glaisière *f*; ***clay soil*** terre *f* glaise

claybank [ˈkleɪbæŋk] *adj Am (horse)* isabelle *(inv)*

clayey [ˈkleɪɪ] *adj* argileux, glaiseux

claymation [kleɪˈmeɪʃən] *n Br Cin & TV* = animation de figurines en pâte à modeler

claymore [ˈkleɪmɔː(r)] *n Hist* claymore *f*

CLEAN [kliːn]

propre	► **1 (a)**
net	► **1 (a) – (e)**
pur	► **1 (b)**
adroit	► **1 (f)**
habile	► **1 (f)**
nettoyer	► **2 (a); 3 (a)**
vider	► **2 (b)**
se nettoyer	► **3 (b)**
carrément	► **4 (a)**
nettoyage	► **5**

1 *adj* (**a**) *(free from dirt → hands, shirt, room)* propre, net; *(→ animal, person)* propre; *(→ piece of paper)* vierge, blanc (blanche); **my hands are clean** j'ai les mains propres, mes mains sont propres; *Fig* j'ai la conscience nette *ou* tranquille; **he made a clean breast of it** il a dit tout ce qu'il avait sur la conscience, il a déchargé sa conscience; **he made a clean sweep of the medals/prizes** il a raflé toutes les médailles/tous les prix; **the new government made a clean sweep of the legislation introduced by their predecessors** *(did away with)* le nouveau gouvernement a fait table rase des lois votées par le gouvernement précédent

(**b**) *(free from impurities → air)* pur, frais (fraîche); *(→ water)* pur, clair; *(→ sound)* net, clair

(**c**) *(morally pure → conscience)* net, tranquille; *(→ joke)* qui n'a rien de choquant; **it was all good clean fun** c'était une façon innocente de nous amuser; **keep it clean!** pas de grossièretés!; **clean living** une vie saine

(**d**) *(honourable → fight)* loyal; *(→ reputation)* net, sans tache; **he's got a clean driving licence** il n'a jamais eu de contraventions graves; **to have a clean record** avoir un casier (judiciaire) vierge; **the doctor gave him a clean bill of health** le docteur l'a trouvé en parfaite santé

(**e**) *(smooth → curve, line)* bien dessiné, net; *(→ shape)* fin, élégant; *(→ cut)* net, franc (franche); **the building has clean lines** le bâtiment a de belles lignes; **to make a clean break** en finir une bonne fois pour toutes; **we made a clean break with the past** nous avons rompu avec le passé, nous avons tourné la page

(**f**) *(throw)* adroit, habile

(**g**) *Fam* **to be clean** *(innocent)* n'avoir rien à se reprocher❑; *(without incriminating material)* n'avoir rien sur soi❑; *(not carrying drugs)* ne pas avoir de drogue sur soi❑; *(not carrying weapons)* ne pas être armé❑; *(no longer addicted to drugs)* avoir décroché

(**h**) *Nucl (not radioactive)* non radioactif; **a clean bomb** une bombe propre *ou* sans retombées radioactives

2 *vt* (**a**) *(room, cooker)* nettoyer; *(clothing)* laver; **I cleaned the mud from my shoes** j'ai enlevé la boue de mes chaussures; **to clean one's teeth** se laver *ou* se brosser les dents; **to have one's teeth cleaned** se faire faire un détartrage; **to clean the windows** faire les vitres *ou* les carreaux; *Am* **to clean house** *(do housework)* faire du ménage; *Fig (restructure system, organization)* restructurer

(**b**) *(chicken, fish)* vider

3 *vi* (**a**) *(person)* nettoyer; **she spends her day cleaning** elle passe sa journée à faire le ménage

(**b**) *(carpet, paintbrush)* se nettoyer; **this cooker cleans easily** ce four est facile à nettoyer *ou* se nettoie facilement

4 *adv Fam* (**a**) *(completely)* carrément❑; **the handle broke clean off** l'anse a cassé net; **the match burnt a hole clean through the rug** l'allumette a fait un trou dans la moquette; **he cut clean through the bone** il a coupé l'os de part en part; **the bullet went clean through his chest** la balle lui a carrément traversé la poitrine; **the robbers got clean away** les voleurs se sont enfuis sans laisser de trace; **we clean forgot about the appointment** nous avions complètement oublié le rendez-vous

(**b**) *(idiom)* **to come clean about sth** révéler qch❑; **the murderer finally came clean** l'assassin a fini par avouer❑

5 *n* nettoyage *m*; **the carpet needs a good clean** la moquette a grand besoin d'être nettoyée; **I gave my shoes a clean** j'ai nettoyé mes chaussures

▸▸ *Fin* ***clean bill*** effet *m* libre, traite *f* libre; *St Exch* ***clean float*** taux *mpl* de change libres *ou* flottants; *Typ* ***clean proof*** *(with few corrections)* épreuve *f* peu chargée; *(final)* épreuve *f* pour bon à tirer; ***clean room*** *Med* pièce *f* aseptisée; *Comput* salle *f* blanche

▸**clean down** *vt sep (wall)* laver

▸**clean off** *vt sep* (**a**) *(mud, stain)* enlever

(**b**) *(sofa, table)* débarrasser

▸**clean out** *vt sep* (**a**) *(tidy)* nettoyer à fond; *(empty)* vider

(**b**) *Fam (person)* nettoyer, plumer; **we're completely cleaned out** nous sommes totalement fauchés; **he cleaned me out** il m'a plumé

▸**clean up 1** *vt sep* (**a**) *(make clean)* nettoyer à fond; **I cleaned the children up as best I could** j'ai fait de mon mieux pour débarbouiller les enfants; **clean this mess up!** nettoyez-moi ce fouillis!

(**b**) *(make orderly → cupboard, room)* ranger; *(→ affairs, papers)* ranger, mettre de l'ordre dans; **the police intend to clean up the city** la police a l'intention d'épurer [illegible] cette ville

2 *vi* (**a**) *(tidy room)* nettoyer; *(tidy cupboard, desk)* ranger; *(wash oneself)* faire un brin de toilette

(**b**) *Fam (make profit)* gagner gros❑; **we cleaned up on the deal** nous avons touché un gros paquet sur cette affaire, cette affaire nous a rapporté gros

---

clean-and-jerk *n Sport (in weightlifting)* épaulé-jeté *m*

clean-burning *adj (fuel)* = brûlant sans résidu de combustible

clean-cut *adj* (**a**) *(lines)* net; *(shape)* bien délimité, net (**b**) *(person)* propre (sur soi), à l'apparence très soignée

cleaner ['kliːnə(r)] *n* (**a**) *(cleaning lady)* femme *f* de ménage; *(man)* (ouvrier *m*) nettoyeur *m* (**b**) *(product → gen)* produit *m* d'entretien; *(→ stain remover)* détachant *m*; *(device)* appareil *m* de nettoyage (**c**) *(dry cleaner)* teinturier(ère) *m,f*; **I took the clothes to the cleaner's** j'ai donné les vêtements à nettoyer *ou* au teinturier; *Fam* **to take sb to the cleaners** nettoyer *ou* plumer qn

clean-handed *adj Am* **he got out of the inquiry clean-handed** l'enquête l'a lavé de tout soupçon

cleaning ['kliːnɪŋ] **1** *n* (**a**) *(activity → gen)* nettoyage *m*; *(→ household)* ménage *m*; **to do the cleaning** faire le ménage

(**b**) *(clothes)* vêtements *mpl* à faire nettoyer

2 *comp (staff)* de nettoyage

▸▸ ***cleaning fluid*** produit *m* nettoyant; ***cleaning lady*** femme *f* de ménage; ***cleaning materials*** produits *mpl* d'entretien; ***cleaning up*** *(of room)* & *Fig (of neighbourhood)* nettoyage *m*; *(of exhaust gases)* dépollution *f*; ***cleaning woman*** femme *f* de ménage

clean-limbed *adj* bien proportionné *ou* bâti

cleanliness ['klenlɪnɪs] *n* propreté *f*; *Prov* **cleanliness is next to godliness** = la pureté de l'âme passe d'abord par celle du corps

clean-living *adj* qui mène une vie saine

cleanly[1] ['kliːnlɪ] *adv* (**a**) *(smoothly)* net; **the handle snapped off cleanly** l'anse s'est cassée net; **she cut it cleanly in two** elle l'a coupé en deux parties égales (**b**) *(fight, play)* loyalement

cleanly[2] ['klenlɪ] *(compar* **cleanlier,** *superl* **cleanliest**) *adj Literary* propre

cleanness ['kliːnnɪs] *n (of hands, habits, language, apartment etc)* propreté *f*; *(of water)* pureté *f*; *(of lines)* netteté *f*, pureté

clean-out *n* nettoyage *m* à fond; **to give a room a clean-out** nettoyer une pièce

clean-room clothing *n Comput* vêtements *mpl* de salle blanche

cleanse [klenz] *vt* (**a**) *(clean → gen)* nettoyer; *(→ with water)* laver; *Med (→ blood)* dépurer; *(→ wound)* nettoyer (**b**) *Fig (purify)* purifier; **to cleanse sb of their sins** laver qn de ses péchés

cleanser ['klenzə(r)] *n* (**a**) *(detergent)* détergent *m*, détersif *m* (**b**) *(for skin)* (lait *m*) démaquillant *m*

clean-shaven *adj (face, man)* rasé de près

cleansing ['klenzɪŋ] **1** *n* nettoyage *m*

2 *adj (lotion)* démaquillant; *(power, property)* de nettoyage

▸▸ ***cleansing cream*** crème *f* démaquillante; *Br Admin* ***cleansing department*** service *m* du nettoyage; ***cleansing lotion, cleansing milk*** *(for skin)* lait *m* démaquillant; ***cleansing pads*** disques *mpl* démaquillants

clean-up *n* nettoyage *m* à fond; **the house needs a good clean-up** la maison a besoin d'être nettoyée à fond; **to give sth a clean-up** nettoyer qch à fond

---

CLEAR [klɪə(r)]

transparent	▸ **1 (a)**
clair	▸ **1 (a) – (f)**
vif	▸ **1 (c)**
net	▸ **1 (d), (h), (l)**
évident	▸ **1 (f)**
certain	▸ **1 (g)**
libre	▸ **1 (i), (k)**
tranquille	▸ **1 (j)**
distinctement	▸ **2 (a)**
entièrement	▸ **2 (c)**
débarrasser	▸ **4 (a), (b)**
clarifier	▸ **4 (c)**
autoriser	▸ **4 (d)**
innocenter	▸ **4 (e)**
franchir	▸ **4 (f)**
finir	▸ **4 (h)**
s'éclaircir	▸ **5 (a), (b)**

1 *adj* (**a**) *(transparent → glass, plastic)* transparent; *(→ water)* clair, limpide; *(→ river)* limpide, transparent; *(→ air)* pur; **clear honey** miel *m* liquide; **clear soup** *(plain stock)* bouillon *m*; *(with meat)* consommé *m*

(**b**) *(cloudless → sky)* clair, dégagé; *(→ weather)* clair, beau (belle); **on a clear day** par temps clair; **the sky grew clearer** le ciel se dégagea; **as clear as day(light)** clair comme le jour *ou* comme de l'eau de roche

(**c**) *(not dull → colour)* vif; *(→ light)* éclatant, radieux; *(untainted → complexion)* clair, frais (fraîche); **clear blue** bleu vif; **to have (a) clear skin** avoir la peau nette

(**d**) *(distinct → outline)* net, clair; *(→ photograph)* net; *(→ sound)* clair, distinct; *(→ voice)* clair, argentin; *TV* **the picture was very clear** l'image était très nette; **make sure your writing is clear** efforcez-vous d'écrire distinctement *ou* proprement; **the lyrics are not very clear** je ne distingue pas très bien les paroles de la chanson; **the sound was as clear as a bell** on entendait un son aussi clair que celui d'une cloche

(**e**) *(not confused → mind)* pénétrant, lucide; *(→ thinking, argument, style)* clair; *(→ explanation, report)* clair, intelligible; *(→ instructions)* clair, explicite; *(→ message)* en clair; **I want to keep a clear head** je veux rester lucide *ou* garder tous mes esprits; **a clear thinker** un esprit lucide; **clear thinking is essential** il est essentiel de garder un esprit lucide; **he is quite clear about what has to be done** il sait parfaitement ce qu'il y a à faire; **I've got the problem clear in my head** je comprends *ou* saisis le problème; **to make one's meaning** *or* **oneself clear** se faire comprendre; **now let's get this clear – I want no nonsense** comprenons-nous bien *ou* soyons clairs – je ne supporterai pas de sottises

(**f**) *(obvious, unmistakable)* évident, clair; **a clear indication of a forthcoming storm** un signe certain qu'il va y avoir de l'orage; **it is a clear case of favouritism** c'est manifestement du favoritisme, c'est un cas de favoritisme manifeste; **it's clear that he's lying** il est évident *ou* clair qu'il ment; **it's clear from her letter that she's unhappy** sa lettre montre clairement qu'elle est malheureuse; **it becomes clearer every day** cela devient plus évident chaque jour; **it's far from clear who will win the election** on ne peut vraiment pas dire qui va gagner les élections; **it was not clear who had won** on ne savait pas exactement qui avait gagné; **it is clear to me that he is telling the truth** pour moi, il est clair qu'il dit la vérité; **he was unable to make his meaning clear** il n'arrivait pas à s'expliquer; **we want to make it clear that…** nous tenons à préciser que…; **to make it clear to sb that…** bien faire comprendre à qn que…; **she made it quite clear to them what she wanted** elle leur a bien fait comprendre ce qu'elle voulait; **it is important to make clear exactly what our aims are** il est important de bien préciser quels sont nos objectifs; **is that clear?** est-ce que c'est clair?; **do I make myself clear?** est-ce que je me fais bien comprendre?, est-ce que c'est bien clair?; *Hum* **as clear as mud** clair comme l'encre

(**g**) *(free from doubt, certain)* certain; **she seems quite clear about what she wants** elle sait très bien ce qu'elle veut; **I want to be clear in my mind about it** je veux en avoir le cœur net

(**h**) *(unqualified)* net, sensible; **it's a clear improvement over the other** c'est nettement mieux que l'autre, il y a un net progrès par rapport à l'autre; **they won by a clear majority** ils ont gagné avec une large majorité

(**i**) *(unobstructed, free → floor, path)* libre, dégagé; *(→ route)* sans obstacles, sans danger; *(→ view)* dégagé; **the roads are clear of snow** les routes sont déblayées *ou* déneigées; **clear of obstacles** sans obstacles; **I left the desk clear** j'ai débarrassé le bureau; **his latest X-rays are clear** ses dernières radios ne montrent rien d'anormal; **clear space** espace *m* libre; **we had a clear view of the sea** nous avions une très belle vue sur la mer; **to be clear of sth** être débarrassé de qch; **we're clear of the traffic** nous sommes sortis des encombrements; **we were clear of the last checkpoint** nous avions passé le dernier poste de contrôle; **once the plane was clear of the trees** une fois que l'avion eut franchi les arbres; **to be clear of debts** être libre de dettes; *Fig* **can you see your way clear to lending me £5?** auriez-vous la possibilité de me prêter 5 livres?; **all clear!** *(there's no traffic, no one is watching)* vous pouvez y aller, la voie est libre; *Mil* fin d'alerte!

(**j**) *(free from guilt → conscience)* tranquille; **is your conscience clear?** as-tu la conscience tranquille?; **I can go home with a clear conscience** je peux rentrer la conscience tranquille

(**k**) *(time)* libre; **his schedule is clear** il n'a rien

cle–cle

de prévu sur son emploi du temps; **I have Wednesday clear** je n'ai rien de prévu pour mercredi; **we have four clear days to finish** nous avons quatre jours pleins *ou* entiers pour finir

(**l**) *(net → money, wages)* net; **he brings home £300 clear** il gagne 300 livres net; **a clear profit** un bénéfice net; **a clear loss** une perte sèche; **clear of taxes** net d'impôts

(**m**) *Ling* antérieur

2 *adv* (**a**) *(distinctly)* distinctement, nettement; *Rad* **reading you loud and clear** je te reçois cinq sur cinq; **I can hear you as clear as a bell** je t'entends très clairement

(**b**) *(away from, out of the way)* **to get clear of sb** échapper à qn; **when we got clear of the town** quand nous nous sommes éloignés de la ville; **when I get clear of my debts** quand je serai débarrassé de mes dettes; **we pulled him clear of the wrecked car/of the water** nous l'avons sorti de la carcasse de la voiture/de l'eau; **she was thrown clear of the car** elle a été éjectée de la voiture; **stand clear!** écartez-vous!; **stand clear of the entrance!** dégagez l'entrée!; **stand clear of the doors!** attention à la fermeture automatique des portes!; **to keep** *or* **steer clear of sth** éviter qch; *Naut* **to steer clear of a rock** passer au large d'un écueil

(**c**) *(all the way)* entièrement, complètement; **you can see clear to the mountain** on peut voir jusqu'à la montagne; **they went clear around the world** ils ont fait le tour du monde; **the thieves got clear away** les voleurs ont disparu sans laisser de trace

3 *n (idiom)* **to be in the clear** *(out of danger)* être hors de danger; *(out of trouble)* être tiré d'affaire; *(free of blame)* être blanc comme neige; *(above suspicion)* être au-dessus de tout soupçon; *(no longer suspected)* être blanchi (de tout soupçon); *Sport* être démarqué

4 *vt* (**a**) *(remove → object)* débarrasser, enlever; *(→ obstacle)* écarter; *(→ weeds)* arracher, enlever; **clear the papers off the desk** enlevez ces papiers du bureau, débarrassez le bureau de ces papiers; **she cleared the plates from the table** elle a débarrassé la table

(**b**) *(remove obstruction from → gen)* débarrasser; *(→ entrance, road)* dégager, déblayer; *(→ forest, land)* défricher; *(→ streets, room)* faire évacuer; *(→ pipe)* déboucher; **it's your turn to clear the table** c'est à ton tour de débarrasser la table *ou* de desservir; **to clear one's desk** *(tidy)* débarrasser son bureau; *(complete pending tasks)* régler les affaires en suspens; **to clear one's throat** se racler la gorge; **this land has been cleared of trees** ce terrain a été déboisé; **clear the room!** évacuez la salle!; **the judge cleared the court** le juge a fait évacuer la salle; **the police cleared the way for the procession** la police a ouvert un passage au cortège; *Fig* **the talks cleared the way for a ceasefire** les pourparlers ont préparé le terrain *ou* ont ouvert la voie pour un cessez-le-feu; *also Fig* **to clear the ground** déblayer le terrain; **to clear the decks** *(prepare for action)* se mettre en branle-bas de combat; *(make space)* faire de la place, faire le ménage

(**c**) *(clarify → liquid)* clarifier; *(→ wine)* coller, clarifier; *(→ skin)* purifier; *(→ complexion)* éclaircir; **open the windows to clear the air** ouvrez les fenêtres pour aérer; *Fig* **his apology cleared the air** ses excuses ont détendu l'atmosphère; **I went for a walk to clear my head** *(from hangover)* j'ai fait un tour pour m'éclaircir les idées; *(from confusion)* j'ai fait un tour pour me rafraîchir les idées *ou* pour me remettre les idées en place

(**d**) *(authorize)* autoriser, approuver; **the plane was cleared for take-off** l'avion a reçu l'autorisation de décoller; **the editor cleared the article for publication** le rédacteur en chef a donné son accord *ou* le feu vert pour publier l'article; **the investigators cleared him for top secret work** après enquête, il a été autorisé à mener des activités top secret; **you'll have to clear it with the boss** il faut demander l'autorisation *ou* l'accord *ou* le feu vert du patron

(**e**) *(vindicate, find innocent)* innocenter, disculper; **to clear sb of a charge** disculper qn d'une accusation; **he was cleared of having been drunk in charge of a ship** accusé d'avoir tenu les commandes (d'un navire) en état d'ivresse, il a été disculpé; **the court cleared him of all blame** la cour l'a totalement disculpé *ou* innocenté; **give him a chance to clear himself** donnez-lui la possibilité de se justifier *ou* de prouver son innocence; **to clear one's name** se justifier, défendre son honneur

(**f**) *(avoid touching)* franchir; *(obstacle)* éviter; **to clear a ditch** sauter *ou* franchir un fossé; **the horse cleared the fence with ease** le cheval a sauté sans peine par-dessus *ou* a franchi sans peine la barrière; **the plane barely cleared the trees** l'avion a franchi les arbres de justesse; **hang the curtains so that they just clear the floor** accrochez les rideaux de façon à ce qu'ils touchent à peine le parquet

(**g**) *(make a profit of)* **she cleared 10 percent on the deal** l'affaire lui a rapporté 10 pour cent net *ou* 10 pour cent tous frais payés; **I clear a thousand pounds monthly** je fais un bénéfice net de mille livres par mois

(**h**) *(dispatch → work)* finir, terminer; *Com (→ stock)* liquider; **he cleared the backlog of work** il a rattrapé le travail en retard; **we must clear this report by Friday** il faut que nous nous débarrassions de ce rapport avant vendredi

(**i**) *(settle → account)* liquider, solder; *(→ cheque)* compenser; *(→ debt)* s'acquitter de; *(→ dues)* acquitter

(**j**) *(of customs officer → goods)* dédouaner; *(→ ship)* expédier

(**k**) *(pass through)* **to clear customs** *(person)* passer la douane; *(shipment)* être dédouané; **the bill cleared the Senate** le projet de loi a été voté par le Sénat

(**l**) *Med (blood)* dépurer, purifier; *(bowels)* purger, dégager

(**m**) *Sport* **to clear the ball** dégager le ballon

(**n**) *Tech (decode)* déchiffrer

(**o**) *Comput* **to clear the screen** vider l'écran

5 *vi* (**a**) *(weather)* s'éclaircir, se lever; *(sky)* se dégager; *(fog)* se lever, se dissiper; **it's clearing** le temps se lève, le ciel se dégage

(**b**) *(liquid)* s'éclaircir; *(skin)* devenir plus sain; *(complexion)* s'éclaircir; *(expression)* s'éclairer; **her face cleared** son visage s'est éclairé

(**c**) *(cheque)* être encaissé; **it takes three days for the cheque to clear** il y a trois jours de délai d'encaissement

(**d**) *(obtain clearance)* recevoir l'autorisation

►**clear away 1** *vt sep (remove)* enlever, ôter; *(one's things)* ranger; **we cleared away the dishes** nous avons débarrassé (la table) *ou* desservi

2 *vi* (**a**) *(tidy up)* débarrasser, desservir (**b**) *(disappear → fog, mist)* se dissiper

►**clear off 1** *vi Fam* filer; **clear off!** dégage!, fiche le camp!

2 *vt sep* (**a**) *(get rid of → debt)* s'acquitter de; *Com (→ stock)* liquider (**b**) *(remove)* retirer, enlever

►**clear out 1** *vt sep* (**a**) *(tidy)* nettoyer, ranger; *(empty → cupboard)* vider; *(→ room)* débarrasser

(**b**) *(throw out → rubbish, old clothes)* jeter; **he cleared everything out of the house** il a fait le vide dans la maison; **to clear everyone out of a room** faire évacuer une pièce

(**c**) *Fam (leave without money)* nettoyer, plumer; **that last game cleared me out** je me suis fait plumer dans cette dernière partie; **I'm cleared out** je suis fauché *ou* à sec

(**d**) *Fam (goods, stock)* épuiser

2 *vi Fam (leave building, room etc)* filer, déguerpir; *(leave home → spouse, partner)* se tirer; **he was clearing out when I arrived** il faisait ses valises quand je suis arrivé; **he told us to clear out** il nous a ordonné de disparaître; **clear out (of here)!** dégage!, fiche le camp!

►**clear up 1** *vt sep* (**a**) *(settle → problem)* résoudre; *(→ misunderstanding)* dissiper; *(→ mystery)* éclaircir, résoudre; **can you clear up this point?** pouvez-vous éclaircir ce point?; **let's clear this matter up** tirons cette affaire au clair

(**b**) *(tidy up)* ranger, faire du rangement dans; **clear up that mess in the garden, will you?** range-moi ce fouillis dans le jardin, d'accord?; **I have a lot of work to clear up** j'ai beaucoup de travail à rattraper

2 *vi* (**a**) *(weather)* s'éclaircir, se lever; *(fog, mist)* se dissiper, se lever; **it's clearing up** le temps se lève

(**b**) *(spots, rash)* disparaître; **his cold is clearing up** son rhume tire à sa fin

(**c**) *(tidy up)* ranger, faire le ménage; **I'm fed up with clearing up after you** j'en ai assez de faire le ménage derrière toi

---

clearance ['klɪərəns] *n* (**a**) *(removal → of buildings, litter)* enlèvement *m*; *(→ of obstacles)* déblaiement *m*; *(→ of people)* évacuation *f*; *Com (→ of merchandise)* liquidation *f*; **land clearance** *(clearing of vegetation)* défrichement *m*; *(removal of debris)* déblaiement *m ou* dégagement *m* de terrain; **slum clearance** assainissement *m* des taudis; *Hist* **the (Highland) Clearances** = expulsion des habitants des Highlands d'Écosse par les grands propriétaires terriens aux XVIIIème et XIXème siècles, pour faire de la place pour l'élevage des moutons

(**b**) *(space)* jeu *m*, dégagement *m*; **there was a 10-centimetre clearance between the lorry and the bridge** il y avait un espace de 10 centimètres entre le camion et le pont; **how much clearance is there?** que reste-t-il comme place?

(**c**) *(permission)* autorisation *f*, permis *m*; *(from customs)* dédouanement *m*; **we have to get clearance to leave** il nous faut l'autorisation de *ou* pour partir; **the plane was given clearance to land** l'avion a reçu l'autorisation d'atterrir; **they sent the order to headquarters for clearance** ils ont envoyé la commande au siège pour contrôle; **clearance inward(s)** déclaration *f* d'entrée; **clearance outward(s)** déclaration *f* de sortie

(**d**) *Banking (of cheque)* compensation *f*

(**e**) *Sport* dégagement *m*

►► *Com* ***clearance sale*** liquidation *f*, soldes *mpl*

clear-cut *adj* (**a**) *(lines, shape)* nettement défini, net (**b**) *(decision, situation)* clair; *(difference)* clair, net; *(opinion, plan)* bien défini, précis

clearer ['klɪərə(r)] *n Br Banking* banque *f (appartenant à une chambre de compensation)*

clear-eyed *adj* qui a de bons yeux, clairvoyant; *Fig* réaliste, lucide

clear-headed *adj (person)* lucide, perspicace; *(decision)* lucide, rationnel

clear-headedness [-'hedɪdnɪs] *n (of person)* lucidité *f*, perspicacité *f*; *(of decision)* lucidité *f*

clearing ['klɪərɪŋ] *n* (**a**) *(in forest)* clairière *f*; *(in clouds)* éclaircie *f*

(**b**) *(of land)* déblaiement *m*, défrichement *m*; *(of passage)* dégagement *m*, déblaiement *m*; *(of pipe)* débouchage *m*

(**c**) *(removal → of objects)* enlèvement *m*; *(→ of people)* évacuation *f*

(**d**) *(of name, reputation)* réhabilitation *f*; *Law (of accused)* disculpation *f*

(**e**) *Banking & Fin (of cheque)* compensation *f*; *(of account)* liquidation *f*, solde *m*; *(of debt)* acquittement *m*; **general clearing** compensation *f* de chèques en dehors de Londres; **under the clearing procedure** par voie de compensation

(**f**) *(of debt)* acquittement *m*

(**g**) *Br Univ* = système selon lequel les places restantes dans les universités sont attribuées aux étudiants qui n'ont pas été acceptés lors d'une première sélection

►► *Banking & Fin* ***clearing account*** compte *m* de compensation; *Banking & Fin* ***clearing agreement*** accord *m* de clearing; *Br* ***clearing bank*** banque *f* de compensation; ***clearing house*** *Banking & Fin* chambre *f* de compensation; *(for information, materials)* bureau *m* central; **to pass a cheque through the clearing house** compenser un chèque; *Mil* ***clearing station*** *(for wounded)* centre *m* de triage *ou* d'évacuation; *Banking & Fin* ***clearing system*** système *m* de compensation; *Banking & Fin* ***clearing transaction*** opération *f* de clearing

clearing-up *n* nettoyage *m*

clearly ['klɪəlɪ] *adv* (**a**) *(distinctly → see)* clair, bien; *(→ understand)* clairement, bien; *(→ hear, speak)* distinctement; *(→ describe, explain)* clairement, précisément; *(→ think)* clairement, lucidement; **clearly legible** bien lisible (**b**) *(obviously)* manifestement, à l'évidence; **they**

clearly didn't expect us il était clair *ou* évident qu'ils ne nous attendaient pas

clearness ['klɪənɪs] *n* (**a**) *(of air, glass)* transparence *f*; *(of water)* limpidité *f* (**b**) *(of speech, thought)* clarté *f*, précision *f*

clear-out *n Br Fam* rangement *m*; **to have a clear-out** faire du rangement

clear-sighted *adj Fig (person)* perspicace, lucide, clairvoyant; *(decision, plan)* réaliste

clear-sightedness [-'saɪtɪdnɪs] *n Fig (of person)* perspicacité *f*, lucidité *f*, clairvoyance *f*; *(of plan)* réalisme *m*

clearway ['klɪəweɪ] *n Br Aut* route *f* à stationnement interdit

cleat [kli:t] *n* (**a**) *(on shoe)* clou *m* (**b**) *Carp (block of wood)* tasseau *m* (**c**) *Naut (for fastening ropes)* taquet *m*

cleavage ['kli:vɪdʒ] *n* (**a**) *(of woman)* décolleté *m*; **to show a lot of cleavage** *(woman)* avoir un décolleté plongeant; *(dress)* être très décolleté (**b**) *Biol (of cell)* division *f* (**c**) *Chem & Geol* clivage *m*

cleave [kli:v] (*pt* **cleaved** *or* **clove** [kləʊv] *or* **cleft** [kleft], *pp* **cleaved** *or* **cloven** ['kləʊvən] *or* **cleft** [kleft]) *vt* (**a**) *Literary (split)* fendre; *Fig* diviser, séparer (**b**) *Biol (cell)* diviser (**c**) *Chem & Geol (mineral)* cliver

►**cleave through** *vt insep* **to cleave through the waves** fendre les vagues

►**cleave to** (*pt* **cleaved** *or* **clove** [kləʊv] *or* **cleft** [kleft], *pp* **cleaved** *or* **clove** [kləʊv]) *vt insep Literary (person, party, principle)* être fidèle à; **they cleave to traditional values** ils sont très attachés aux valeurs traditionnelles

cleaver ['kli:və(r)] *n* couperet *m*

clef [klef] *n Mus* clef *f*, clé *f*

cleft [kleft] **1** *pt & pp of* **cleave**

2 *adj (split → gen)* fendu; *(→ branch)* fourchu

3 *n (opening → gen)* fissure *f*; *(→ in rock)* fissure *f*, crevasse *f*

►► *Med* ***cleft palate*** palais *m* fendu; ***cleft stick*** branche *f* fourchue; *Br Fam* **to be in a cleft stick** être *ou* se trouver entre le marteau et l'enclume[❑]

cleg [kleg] *n Entom* taon *m*

clematis ['klemətɪs] *n Bot* clématite *f*

clemency ['klemənsɪ] (*pl* **clemencies**) *n* (**a**) *(mercy)* clémence *f*, indulgence *f* (**to** envers); **to show clemency** faire preuve de clémence (**b**) *(of weather)* douceur *f*, clémence *f*

clement ['klemənt] *adj* (**a**) *(person)* clément, magnanime (**b**) *(weather)* doux (douce), clément

clementine ['kleməntaɪn] *n* clémentine *f*

clench [klentʃ] **1** *vt (fist, jaw, buttocks)* serrer; *(grasp firmly)* empoigner, agripper; *(hold tightly)* serrer

2 *n* (**a**) *(grip)* prise *f*, étreinte *f* (**b**) *Tech (clamp)* crampon *m*

Cleopatra [ˌkli:ə'pætrə] *pr n* Cléopâtre

►► ***Cleopatra's Needle*** l'obélisque *m* de Cléopâtre

CLEP [ˌsi:elˌi:'pi:] *n Am* (*abbr* **College Level Examination Program**) = examen d'entrée à l'université aux États-Unis

clepsydra ['klepsɪdrə] *n* clepsydre *f*

clerestory ['klɪəstɔ:rɪ] (*pl* **clerestories**) *n Archit* claire-voie *f (dans une église)*

clergy ['klɜ:dʒɪ] *n (collectively)* (membres *mpl* du) clergé *m*

clergyman ['klɜ:dʒɪmən] (*pl* **clergymen** [-mən]) *n* *(gen)* ecclésiastique *m*; *(Catholic)* curé *m*, prêtre *m*; *(Protestant)* pasteur *m*

clergywoman ['klɜ:dʒɪˌwʊmən] (*pl* **clergywomen** [-ˌwɪmɪn]) *n* (femme *f*) pasteur *m*

cleric ['klerɪk] *n* ecclésiastique *m*

clerical ['klerɪkəl] *adj* (**a**) *(office → staff, work)* de bureau; *(→ position)* de commis; **to do clerical work** travailler dans un bureau (**b**) *Rel* clérical, du clergé

►► ***clerical collar*** col *m* d'ecclésiastique; ***clerical error*** *(in document)* faute *f* de copiste; *(in accounting)* erreur *f* d'écriture

clericalism ['klerɪkəlɪzəm] *n Rel* cléricalisme *m*

clericalize, -ise ['klerɪkəlaɪz] *vt* cléricaliser

clerically ['klerɪkəlɪ] *adv* cléricalement

clerihew ['klerɪhju:] *n* petit poème *m* humoristique *(qui concerne une personnalité connue)*

clerk [*Br* klɑ:k, *Am* klɜ:k] **1** *n* (**a**) *Admin & Com (in office)* employé(e) *m,f* (de bureau), commis *m*; *(in bank)* employé(e) *m,f* de banque

(**b**) *Law* clerc *m*

(**c**) *Am (sales assistant)* vendeur(euse) *m,f*

(**d**) *Am (receptionist)* réceptionniste *mf*

(**e**) *Rel* **clerk in holy orders** ecclésiastique *m*

(**f**) *Arch (scholar)* savant(e) *m,f*, clerc *m*

2 *vi Am* (**a**) *(as assistant)* **to clerk for sb** être assistant(e) de qn

(**b**) *(as sales assistant)* travailler comme vendeur(euse)

►► ***Clerk of the Court*** greffier(ère) *m,f* (du tribunal); *Br Constr* ***clerk of works*** conducteur(trice) *m,f* de travaux

clerkship [*Br* 'klɑ:kʃɪp, *Am* 'klɜ:kʃɪp] *n* (**a**) *Admin & Com* emploi *m* de commis (**b**) *Law* emploi *m* de clerc; **clerkship to the Court** fonctions *fpl* de greffier

Cleveland ['kli:vlənd] *n Formerly* le Cleveland, = comté dans le nord-est de l'Angleterre; **in Cleveland** dans le Cleveland

clever ['klevə(r)] *adj* (**a**) *(intelligent)* intelligent, astucieux; **he has a clever face** il a l'air intelligent *ou* astucieux

(**b**) *(skilful → person)* adroit, habile; *(→ work)* bien fait; **to be clever with one's hands** être adroit *ou* habile de ses mains; **to be clever at sth/at doing sth** être doué pour qch/pour faire qch; **to be clever at maths** être fort en maths

(**c**) *(cunning)* malin(igne), astucieux; *Pej* rusé; **he was too clever for us** il s'est montré plus malin que nous

(**d**) *(ingenious → book)* intelligemment *ou* bien écrit, ingénieux; *(→ film)* ingénieux, intelligent; *(→ idea, plan)* ingénieux, astucieux; *(→ story)* fin, astucieux; **there's a clever way of getting around the problem** il y a une astuce pour contourner le problème

►► *Br Fam* ***clever clogs, clever Dick*** petit(e) malin(igne)[❑] *m,f*; **OK, clever clogs, show me how to do it** vas-y, petit malin, montre-moi comment on fait

clever-clever *adj Br Fam* trop malin(igne)[❑]

cleverly ['klevəlɪ] *adv (intelligently)* intelligemment, astucieusement; *(skilfully)* adroitement, habilement; *(cunningly)* avec ruse; *(ingeniously)* ingénieusement; **she cleverly managed to avoid paying the fine** elle s'est débrouillée pour ne pas payer l'amende

cleverness ['klevənɪs] *n (intelligence)* intelligence *f*, astuce *f*; *(skilfulness)* habileté *f*, adresse *f*; *(cunning)* ruse *f*; *(ingenuity)* ingéniosité *f*

clew = **clue**

CLI [ˌsi:el'aɪ] *n Fin* (*abbr* **cost-of-living index**) indice *m* du coût de la vie

cliché [*Br* 'kli:ʃeɪ, *Am* kli:'ʃeɪ] *n* (**a**) *(idea)* cliché *m*; *(phrase)* cliché *m*, lieu *m* commun, banalité *f* (**b**) *Typ* cliché *m*

clichéd [*Br* 'kli:ʃeɪd, *Am* kli:'ʃeɪd] *adj* banal; **a clichéd phrase** un cliché, une banalité, un lieu commun; **the end of the film is very clichéd** la fin du film est très conventionnelle

cliché-ridden *adj* bourré *ou* truffé de clichés

click [klɪk] **1** *n* (**a**) *(sound)* petit bruit *m* sec; *(of tongue)* claquement *m*; *Ling* clic *m*, click *m*

(**b**) *(of ratchet, wheel)* cliquet *m*

(**c**) *Am Fam Mil slang (kilometre)* borne *f*, kilomètre *m*

2 *vt* (**a**) *(fingers, tongue)* faire claquer; **he clicked his heels (together)** il a claqué les talons

(**b**) *Comput* cliquer (sur)

3 *vi* (**a**) *(make sound)* faire un bruit sec; **she clicked along the pavement in her high heels** ses hauts talons faisaient de petits bruits secs sur le trottoir; **cameras were clicking** on entendait le déclic des appareils; **the lamp clicked on** la lampe s'alluma avec un déclic; **to click shut** *(door etc)* se refermer avec un bruit sec; **the lock clicked into place** la serrure s'est enclenchée avec un déclic

(**b**) *Fam (become clear)* **it suddenly clicked** tout à coup ça a fait tilt

(**c**) *Fam (be a success)* bien marcher[❑]; **they clicked from the beginning** *(got on well)* ils se sont bien entendus dès le début[❑], ça a tout de suite collé entre eux; **to click with the public** *(play, film)* avoir du succès auprès du public[❑]

(**d**) *Comput* cliquer; **to click on sth** cliquer sur qch; **to click and drag** cliquer et glisser

►► *Entom* ***click beetle*** taupin *m*; ***click language*** langue *f* à clics

►**click on** *vi Br Fam (understand)* piger

clickable ['klɪkəbəl] *adj Comput* que l'on peut cliquer

►► ***clickable image*** image *f* cliquable; ***clickable image map*** image *f* cliquable

clickety-click [ˌklɪkətɪ-] *onomat* clic-clic *m*

clicking ['klɪkɪŋ] *n (sound)* cliquetis *m*

client ['klaɪənt] *n* (**a**) *(customer)* client(e) *m,f*

(**b**) *Comput* client *m*

►► *Banking* ***client account*** compte *m* client; *Com & Mktg* ***client base*** clientèle *f*; *Com & Mktg* ***client confidence*** confiance *f* de la clientèle, confiance *f* du client; *Com & Mktg* ***client file*** dossier *m* client, fichier *m* client; *Pej* ***client government*** gouvernement *m* à la solde d'un autre; *Com & Mktg* ***client list*** liste *f* de clients; *Pej* ***client state*** état *m* à la solde d'un autre

clientele [ˌkli:ɒn'tel] *n Com* clientèle *f*; *Theat* clientèle *f*, public *m* (habituel)

clientelism [klaɪ'entɪlɪzəm] *n Formal Pol* clientélisme *m*

clientelist [klaɪ'entɪlɪst] *adj Formal Pol* clientéliste

clientilism, clientilist = **clientelism, clientelist**

client-server *adj Comput* client-serveur

►► ***client-server database*** base *f* de données client-serveur; ***client-server model*** modèle *m* client-serveur

cliff [klɪf] *n* escarpement *m*; *(on coast)* falaise *f*; *(in mountaineering)* à-pic *m inv*

cliffhanger ['klɪfˌhæŋə(r)] *n Fam (situation in film, story)* situation *f* à suspense[❑]; *(moment of suspense)* moment *m* d'angoisse[❑]; **it was a real cliffhanger** ça m'a/nous a/*etc* tenu en haleine jusqu'à la fin; **the election was a real cliffhanger** le résultat des élections est resté incertain jusqu'au dernier moment

Clifton Suspension Bridge ['klɪftən-] *n* = pont suspendu à Bristol (Angleterre)

climacteric [klaɪ'mæktərɪk] **1** *n (gen)* climatère *m*; *(women's)* ménopause *f*, *(men's)* andropause *f*

2 *adj* climatérique; *Fig* crucial, critique

climactic [klaɪ'mæktɪk] *adj* à son apogée, à son point culminant; **the climactic love scene towards the end of the play** la scène d'amour finale qui constitue le point culminant de la pièce; **the climactic moment of the film** le paroxysme du film

climate ['klaɪmɪt] *n Met* climat *m*; *Fig* climat *m*, ambiance *f*; **the climate of opinion** (les courants *mpl* de) l'opinion *f*; **the economic climate** la conjoncture économique

►► *Am Aut* ***climate control*** climatiseur *m*

climatic [klaɪ'mætɪk] *adj Met* climatique

climatological [ˌklaɪmətə'lɒdʒɪkəl] *adj Met* climatologique; **climatological conditions** climature *f*

climatologist [ˌklaɪmə'tɒlədʒɪst] *n Met* climatologue *mf*

climatology [ˌklaɪmə'tɒlədʒɪ] *n Met* climatologie *f*

climax ['klaɪmæks] **1** *n* (**a**) *(highest point)* paroxysme *m*; *(of film, play, piece of music)* point *m* culminant; *(of career)* apogée *f*, point *m* culminant; **the directorship was the climax of her business career** son poste d'administratrice marqua l'apogée de sa carrière dans les affaires; **this brought matters to a climax** ceci a porté l'affaire à son point culminant; **as the battle reached its climax** lorsque la bataille fut à son paroxysme; **he worked up to the climax of his story** il amena le récit à son point culminant

(**b**) *(sexual)* orgasme *m*

(**c**) *(in rhetoric)* gradation *f*

2 *vi* (**a**) *(film, story)* atteindre son paroxysme *ou* point culminant; **a tough election campaign climaxing in victory on polling day** une campagne électorale acharnée qui a été couronnée de succès le jour du scrutin

(**b**) *(sexually)* atteindre l'orgasme

3 *vt* amener *ou* porter à son point culminant

climb [klaɪm] **1** *vi* (**a**) *(road, sun)* monter; *(plane)* monter, prendre de l'altitude; *(prices)* monter, augmenter; *(plant)* grimper; **the plane climbed**

200 feet ≃ l'avion a pris 60 mètres d'altitude

(**b**) *(person)* grimper; **I climbed into bed/into the boat** j'ai grimpé dans mon lit/à bord du bateau; **to climb over an obstacle** escalader un obstacle; **he climbed (up) out of the hole/through the opening** il s'est hissé hors du trou/par l'ouverture; *Fam* **he climbed into his jeans** il a enfilé son jean, il a sauté dans son jean; **to climb to power** se hisser au pouvoir; *Fam Fig* **he climbed to power on the backs of his former colleagues** il s'est servi de ses anciens collègues pour accéder au pouvoir❑; **to climb (socially** *or* **in the world)** s'élever (au-dessus de sa condition)

(**c**) *Sport* faire de l'escalade; *(on rocks)* varapper; **to go climbing** faire de l'escalade

2 *vt* (**a**) *(ascend → stairs, steps)* monter, grimper; *(→ hill)* escalader, grimper; *(→ mountain)* gravir, faire l'ascension de; *(→ cliff, wall)* escalader; *(→ ladder, tree)* monter sur; *(→ rope)* monter à

(**b**) *Sport (rockface)* escalader, grimper sur

3 *n* (**a**) *(of hill, slope)* montée *f*, côte *f*; *(in mountaineering)* ascension *f*, escalade *f*; **it's quite a climb** ça monte dur; **it was an easy climb to the top (of the hill)** ça montait en pente douce jusqu'au sommet (de la colline); **there were several steep climbs along the route** il y avait plusieurs bonnes côtes sur le trajet

(**b**) *(of plane)* montée *f*, ascension *f*; **rate of climb** vitesse *f* ascensionnelle *ou* de montée

▸**climb aboard 1** *vt insep* (**a**) *(boat)* monter à bord de

(**b**) *(campaign, bandwagon)* se joindre à

2 *vi* (**a**) *(get on boat)* monter à bord, embarquer

(**b**) *(join campaign, bandwagon)* **they've been campaigning for years but few people have climbed aboard** ça fait des années qu'ils font campagne, mais ils ont fait peu d'adeptes; **the anti-gun lobby received a boost when the State Governor climbed aboard** le lobby qui fait campagne contre les armes à feu a été très aidé par l'adhésion du gouverneur

▸**climb down** *vi* (**a**) *(descend)* descendre; *Sport* descendre, effectuer une descente

(**b**) *(back down)* en rabattre, céder

▸**climb up** *vt insep* (**a**) *(ascend → stairs, steps)* monter, grimper; *(→ hill)* escalader, grimper; *(→ mountain)* gravir, faire l'ascension de; *(→ cliff, wall)* escalader; *(→ ladder, tree)* monter sur; *(→ rope)* monter à

(**b**) *Sport (rockface)* escalader, grimper sur

climb-down *n* dérobade *f*, reculade *f*

climber ['klaɪmə(r)] *n* (**a**) *(person)* grimpeur(euse) *m,f*; *(mountaineer)* alpiniste *mf*; *Sport (rock climber)* varappeur(euse) *m,f*; *Fig Pej* **(social) climber** arriviste *mf* (**b**) *(plant)* plante *f* grimpante (**c**) *(bird)* grimpeur *m*

climbing ['klaɪmɪŋ] **1** *n* (**a**) *(action)* montée *f*, escalade *f*; **the climbing of Everest** l'escalade *f* de l'Everest (**b**) *(mountaineering)* alpinisme *m*; *Sport (rock climbing)* varappe *f*, escalade *f*

2 *adj* (**a**) *(plant)* grimpant (**b**) *(bird)* grimpeur (**c**) *(plane, star)* ascendant

►► *Br* ***climbing frame*** cage *f* à poules *(jeu)*; ***climbing irons*** *(for mountaineer)* grappins *mpl*; *(on boots)* crampons *mpl*; *(for climbing trees, poles)* étriers *mpl*; *Ich* ***climbing perch*** perche *f* grimpeuse; ***climbing shoes*** chaussons *mpl* d'escalade; *Sport* ***climbing wall*** mur *m* d'escalade

climes [klaɪmz] *npl Literary or Hum* régions *fpl*, contrées *fpl*; **he's gone to sunnier climes** il est allé sous des climats plus souriants

clinch [klɪntʃ] **1** *vt* (**a**) *(settle → deal)* conclure; *(→ argument)* régler, résoudre; *(→ agreement)* sceller; **the clinching argument** l'argument *m* décisif; **that clinches it!** comme ça, c'est réglé!; **that was what clinched it for me** c'est ce qui m'a décidé

(**b**) *Tech (nail)* river; *Naut* étalinguer

2 *vi Boxing* combattre corps à corps

3 *n* (**a**) *Tech* rivetage *m*; *Naut* étalingure *f*

(**b**) *Boxing* corps à corps *m*; **they went into a clinch** ils ont lutté corps à corps

(**c**) *Fam (embrace)* étreinte❑ *f*, enlacement❑ *m*; **they were in a clinch** ils étaient enlacés

clincher ['klɪntʃə(r)] *n Fam* argument *m* décisif❑, argument *m* massue❑

cline [klaɪn] *n Biol* cline *m*

cling [klɪŋ] *(pt & pp* **clung** [klʌŋ]*)* *vi* (**a**) *(hold on tightly)* s'accrocher, se cramponner; **they clung to one another** ils se sont enlacés, ils se sont cramponnés l'un à l'autre; *Fig* **to cling to a hope/to a belief/to the past** se raccrocher à un espoir/à une croyance/au passé; **we can't afford to cling to the past** il est dangereux de se raccrocher au passé; **she clings to her children even though they are now grown up** elle s'accroche à ses enfants bien qu'ils soient maintenant adultes

(**b**) *(stick)* adhérer, coller; **a dress that clings to the body** une robe très près du corps *ou* très ajustée

(**c**) *(smell)* persister

clingfilm ['klɪŋfɪlm] *n Br* film *m* alimentaire (transparent)

clinging ['klɪŋɪŋ] *adj (clothing)* collant, qui moule le corps; *Pej (person)* collant

►► *Am Fam Fig* ***clinging vine*** pot *m* de colle

clingstone ['klɪŋstəʊn] *n* **clingstone (peach)** (pavie *f*) alberge *f*

clingy ['klɪŋɪ] *(compar* **clingier**, *superl* **clingiest**) *adj (clothing)* moulant; *Pej (person)* collant; **she's so clingy** *(child)* elle est toujours dans mes jupes; **he's the clingy type** c'est le genre collant

clinic ['klɪnɪk] *n* (**a**) *(part of hospital)* service *m*; **eye clinic** clinique *f* ophtalmologique

(**b**) *(treatment session)* consultation *f*; **the doctor holds his clinic twice a week** le docteur consulte deux fois par semaine

(**c**) *Br (private hospital)* clinique *f*

(**d**) *(consultant's teaching session)* clinique *f*

(**e**) *(health centre)* centre *m* médico-social *ou* d'hygiène sociale

(**f**) *Br (of MP)* permanence *f*

(**g**) *Am Sport* séance *f* d'entraînement *(avec un spécialiste)*

clinical ['klɪnɪkəl] *adj* (**a**) *Med (lecture, tests)* clinique (**b**) *Fig (attitude, tone)* froid, aseptisé

►► ***clinical linguistics*** linguistique *f* clinique; *Med* ***clinical psychologist*** spécialiste *mf* en psychologie clinique; *Med* ***clinical psychology*** psychologie *f* clinique; *Med* ***clinical thermometer*** thermomètre *m* médical; ***clinical trials*** tests *mpl* cliniques

clinically ['klɪnɪkəlɪ] *adv* (**a**) *Med* cliniquement (**b**) *Fig (act, speak)* objectivement, froidement

clinician [klɪ'nɪʃən] *n Med* clinicien(enne) *m,f*

clink [klɪŋk] **1** *vt* faire tinter *ou* résonner; **they clinked (their) glasses** ils ont trinqué

2 *vi* tinter, résonner

3 *n* (**a**) *(sound)* tintement *m* (de verres) (**b**) *Fam (jail)* taule *f*; **in the clink** en taule

clinker ['klɪŋkə(r)] *n* (**a**) *(UNCOUNT) (ash)* mâchefer *m*, scories *fpl* (**b**) *Constr (brick)* brique *f* vitrifiée (**c**) *Am Fam (mistake)* gaffe *f*; *Mus* couac❑ *m*; **I pulled a real clinker** j'ai fait une énorme gaffe; **the orchestra hit some clinkers** l'orchestre a fait des canards❑ (**d**) *Am Fam (film, play)* bide *m*

clinker-built *adj Naut (boat)* (bordé) à clin

clinometer [klaɪ'nɒmɪtə(r)] *n Tech* clinomètre *m*

clint [klɪnt] *n Scot Geol* lapié *m*, lapiaz *m*

Clio ['klaɪəʊ] *pr n Myth* Clio

clip [klɪp] *(pt & pp* **clipped**, *cont* **clipping**) **1** *vt* (**a**) *(cut)* couper (avec des ciseaux), rogner; *(hedge)* tailler; *(animal)* tondre; **clip the coupon out of the magazine** découpez le bon dans le magazine; **I clipped five seconds off my personal best** j'ai amélioré mon record de cinq secondes; **to clip a bird's wings** rogner les ailes d'un oiseau; *Fig* **to clip sb's wings** laisser moins de liberté à qn

(**b**) *Br (ticket)* poinçonner

(**c**) *(attach)* attacher; *(papers)* attacher (avec un trombone); *(brooch)* fixer; **to clip a microphone to sb's tie** attacher *ou* fixer un micro à la cravate de qn

(**d**) *Br Fam (hit)* frapper❑, cogner; **to clip sb round the ear** flanquer une taloche à qn

(**e**) *Br (skim, graze)* effleurer; **I clipped the gate as I drove in** j'ai effleuré la barrière en rentrant la voiture; **the bullet clipped his arm** la balle lui a effleuré le bras

(**f**) *Am Fam (cheat)* escroquer, rouler

2 *n* (**a**) *(snip)* petit coup *m* de ciseaux; **to give sth a clip** donner un coup de ciseaux à qch

(**b**) *(from film, TV programme)* court extrait *m*; *Am (from newspaper)* coupure *f*

(**c**) *(clasp)* pince *f*; *(for paper)* trombone *m*, pince *f*; *(for pipe)* collier *m*, bague *f*; **bicycle** *or* **trouser clip** pince *f* à pantalon, pince-pantalon *m inv*

(**d**) *(for bullets)* chargeur *m*

(**e**) *(brooch)* clip *m*; *(for hair)* barrette *f*; *(for tie)* fixe-cravate *m*

(**f**) *Br Fam (blow)* gifle❑ *f*, taloche *f*; **he got a clip round the ear** il s'est pris une taloche; *Am Fig* **at one clip** d'un seul coup

(**g**) *Fam (speed)* **at a (good) clip** à vive allure❑, à toute vitesse❑

►► *Comput* ***clip art*** clipart *m*; *Fam* ***clip joint*** = boîte de nuit où l'on pratique des prix excessifs

▸**clip on 1** *vt sep* (**a**) *(document)* attacher (avec un trombone)

(**b**) *(brooch, earrings)* mettre

2 *vi* s'attacher *ou* se fixer avec une pince

▸**clip together** *vt sep* attacher

clipboard ['klɪpbɔːd] *n* (**a**) *(writing board)* écritoire *f* à pince, clipboard *m* (**b**) *Comput* bloc-notes *m*

►► ***clipboard file*** fichier *m* presse-papiers

clip-clop [-klɒp] *(pt & pp* **clip-clopped**, *cont* **clip-clopping**) **1** *n* clip-clop *m*; **we heard the clip-clop of horses' hooves** nous avons entendu les chevaux passer et le clip-clop de leurs sabots

2 *onomat* clip-clop

3 *vi* faire clip-clop

clip-on 1 *adj* amovible

2 clip-ons *npl (sunglasses)* = verres teintés amovibles; *(earrings)* clips *mpl (d'oreilles)*

►► ***clip-on earrings*** clips *mpl (d'oreilles)*; ***clip-on microphone*** micro-cravate *m*

clipped [klɪpt] *adj (speech, style)* heurté, saccadé; **a clipped manner of speaking** un débit heurté

clipper ['klɪpə(r)] **1** *n* (**a**) *Naut (ship)* clipper *m* (**b**) *(horse)* cheval *m* qui court vite

2 clippers *npl (for nails)* pince *f* à ongles; *(for hair)* tondeuse *f*; *(for hedge)* sécateur *m* à haie

clippety-clop [ˌklɪpətɪ'klɒp] **1** *n* clic-clac *m*

2 *onomat* clic-clac

clippie ['klɪpɪ] *n Br Fam* receveuse❑ *f (de bus)*

clipping ['klɪpɪŋ] *n* (**a**) *(from newspaper)* coupure *f* de presse (**b**) **clippings** *(from nails)* rognures *fpl*; *(from hair)* mèches *fpl (de cheveux coupés)*; *(from hedge)* bouts *mpl* de branches; **grass clippings** herbe *f* coupée

clique [kliːk] *n Pej* clique *f*, coterie *f*

cliquey ['kliːkɪ], **cliquish** ['kliːkɪʃ] *adj Pej* exclusif, qui a l'esprit de clan

cliquishness ['kliːkɪʃnɪs] *n Pej* esprit *m* de clan

clitic ['klɪtɪk] *adj Ling (enclitic)* enclitique; *(proclitic)* proclitique

clitoral ['klɪtərəl] *adj* clitoridien; *Physiol* **clitoral orgasm** orgasme *m* clitoridien; **clitoral stimulation** stimulation *f* clitoridienne

clitoridectomy [ˌklɪtərɪ'dektəmɪ] *n Med* clitoridectomie *f*

clitoris ['klɪtərɪs] *n* clitoris *m*

Cllr *(written abbr* **Councillor**) conseiller(ère) *m,f*

cloaca [kləʊ'ɑːkə] *n* (**a**) *Zool* cloaque *m* (**b**) *Formal (sewer)* cloaque *m*

cloacal [kləʊ'ɑːkəl] *adj* (**a**) *Zool* cloacal (**b**) *Formal (filthy)* infecte

►► *Zool* ***cloacal sac*** poche *f* cloacale

cloak [kləʊk] **1** *n (cape)* grande cape *f*; *Fig* **under the cloak of darkness** sous le couvert de la nuit, à la faveur de l'obscurité; **as a cloak for his illegal activities** pour cacher *ou* masquer ses activités illégales

2 *vt* (**a**) *(cover with cloak)* revêtir d'un manteau (**b**) *Fig* masquer, cacher; **cloaked with** *or* **in secrecy/mystery** empreint de secret/mystère

cloak-and-dagger *adj (affair, goings-on)* clandestin; **a cloak-and-dagger story** un roman d'espionnage; **the cloak-and-dagger brigade** les services *mpl* secrets

cloakroom ['kləʊkrʊm] *n* (**a**) *(for coats)* vestiaire *m*; **I left my coat in the cloakroom** j'ai laissé mon manteau au vestiaire (**b**) *Br Euph (toilet → public)* toilettes *fpl*; *(→ in home)* cabinets *mpl*

►► ***cloakroom attendant*** préposé(e) *m,f* au vestiaire; ***cloakroom ticket*** numéro *m* de vestiaire

clobber ['klɒbə(r)] *Fam* **1** *vt* (**a**) *(hit)* mettre une raclée à, tabasser, dérouiller (**b**) *(defeat)* battre à plate couture (**c**) *(penalize)* écraser ᵒ, accabler ᵒ; **the new tax legislation will clobber small businesses** les nouvelles lois fiscales vont saigner à blanc les petites entreprises

2 *n Br (UNCOUNT) (clothes)* frusques *fpl*; *(belongings)* effets ᵒ *mpl*, barda *m*

clobbering ['klɒbərɪŋ] *n Fam* **to get a clobbering** *(be beaten up)* prendre une dérouillée *ou* une raclée, se faire tabasser; *(be defeated)* se prendre une pâtée, être battu à plate couture; *(get penalized)* être écrasé ᵒ; **to give sb a clobbering** *(beat up)* tabasser qn, flanquer une raclée à qn; *(defeat)* flanquer une raclée à qn

cloche [klɒʃ] *n* (**a**) **cloche (hat)** chapeau *m* cloche, cloche *f* (**b**) *Agr & Hort* cloche *f*

clock [klɒk] **1** *n* (**a**) *(gen)* horloge *f*; *(small)* pendule *f*; **the church clock chimed four** l'horloge de l'église sonna quatre heures; **it took us fifteen minutes by the clock** il nous a fallu quinze minutes montre en main; *Fig* **the clock is ticking** le temps passe; **to put a clock back/forward** retarder/avancer une horloge; **to put** *or* **turn the clocks back/forward** retarder/avancer les pendules; *Fig* **you can't turn the clock back** ce qui est fait est fait; **this law will put the clock back a hundred years** cette loi va nous ramener cent ans en arrière; **a race against the clock** une course contre la montre; **they worked against** *or* **to beat the clock** ils ont travaillé dur pour finir à temps; *Horseriding* **the jump-off was against the clock** il y a eu un barrage contre la montre; **to work round the clock** travailler vingt-quatre heures sur vingt-quatre; **to sleep round the clock** faire le tour du cadran; *Fig* **to watch the clock** *(employee)* avoir les yeux rivés sur l'horloge, ne penser qu'à l'heure de la sortie; **I don't pay you to come in here and watch the clock** je ne vous paie pas pour que vous passiez votre temps à ne rien faire; *Am Fam Sport* **to kill the clock** jouer la montre

(**b**) *(taximeter)* compteur *m*, taximètre *m*

(**c**) *Fam (mileometer)* ≃ compteur *m* kilométrique; **a car with 30,000 miles on the clock** une voiture qui a 30 000 miles au compteur

(**d**) *Comput* horloge *f*

2 *vt* (**a**) *(measure speed of)* enregistrer; *Sport (runner, driver)* chronométrer; **winds clocked at 50 miles per hour** des vents qui ont atteint 50 miles à l'heure; **he was clocked at 185 mph** ≃ il a atteint les 300 km/h chrono; **she's clocked five minutes for the mile** elle court le mile en cinq minutes; **the fastest time he's clocked this year** son meilleur temps cette année

(**b**) *Fam (hit)* flanquer un marron à

(**c**) *Fam (notice)* repérer ᵒ; **she clocked him as soon as he walked in** elle l'a repéré dès qu'il est entré

▸▸ ***clock golf*** jeu *m* de l'horloge; ***clock radio*** radio-réveil *m*; *Comput* ***clock speed*** fréquence *f* d'horloge; *Comput* ***clock speed doubler*** doubleur *m* de fréquence (d'horloge); ***clock tower*** tour *f* (de l'horloge)

▸**clock in** *vi* (**a**) *Ind (employee)* pointer (à l'arrivée); **I clocked in at seven o'clock** j'ai pointé à sept heures

(**b**) *Sport (have a time of)* **for the 100 metres she clocked in at nine seconds** elle a fait neuf secondes aux 100 mètres; **the last of the marathon runners clocked in at six hours** le dernier marathonien a effectué le parcours en six heures

▸**clock off** *vi Ind* pointer (à la sortie), dépointer

▸**clock on** *vi Ind (employee)* pointer (à l'arrivée)

▸**clock out** *vi Ind* pointer (à la sortie), dépointer

▸**clock up** *vt sep (work)* effectuer, accomplir; *(victory)* remporter; *Aut* **she clocked up 300 miles** elle a fait 300 miles au compteur

clock-doubled [-dʌbəld] *adj Comput* à fréquence d'horloge doublée

clockface ['klɒkfeɪs] *n* cadran *m*

clocking ['klɒkɪŋ] *n Ind*

▸▸ ***clocking in*** pointage *m* à l'arrivée; ***clocking in card*** fiche *f* de pointage; ***clocking off*** pointage *m* à la sortie; ***clocking on*** pointage *m* à l'arrivée; ***clocking out*** pointage *m* à la sortie

clocklike ['klɒklaɪk] *adj (regularity)* d'horloge

clockmaker ['klɒkˌmeɪkə(r)] *n* horloger(ère) *m,f*

clock-watch *vi* **the job is so boring that they are constantly clock-watching** leur travail est tellement ennuyeux qu'ils passent leur temps à surveiller l'heure

clock-watcher *n* **they're terrible clock-watchers** ils passent leur temps à guetter l'heure (de sortie)

clockwise ['klɒkwaɪz] **1** *adv* dans le sens des aiguilles d'une montre

2 *adj* **in a clockwise direction** dans le sens des aiguilles d'une montre

clockwork ['klɒkwɜːk] **1** *n (of clock, watch)* mouvement *m* (d'horloge); *(of toy)* mécanisme *m*, rouages *mpl*; **to go** *or* **to run like clockwork** marcher comme sur des roulettes; **the office runs like clockwork** le travail au bureau est réglé comme du papier à musique

2 *adj (toy)* mécanique; *(mechanism)* qui se remonte; **everything is done with clockwork precision** tout est réglé comme du papier à musique

'A Clockwork Orange' *Burgess, Kubrick* 'Orange mécanique'

'A Clockwork Testament' *Burgess* 'Le Testament de l'orange'

clod [klɒd] *n* (**a**) *(of earth)* motte *f* (de terre) (**b**) *Fam (idiot)* imbécile ᵒ *m,f*, crétin(e) *m,f*

clodhopper ['klɒdˌhɒpə(r)] *n Fam* (**a**) *(clumsy person)* balourd(e) ᵒ *m,f* (**b**) *Hum (shoe)* godillot *m*

clodhopping ['klɒdˌhɒpɪŋ] *adj Fam* gauche ᵒ, maladroit ᵒ

clog [klɒg] *(pt & pp* **clogged**, *cont* **clogging**) **1** *n (wooden)* sabot *m*; *(leather)* sabot *m*; *Br Fam* **to pop one's clogs** *(die)* casser sa pipe

2 *vt* (**a**) *(pipe)* boucher, encrasser; *(street)* boucher, bloquer; *(wheel)* bloquer

(**b**) *Fig (hinder)* entraver, gêner

3 *vi (pipe)* se boucher; *(firearm, machine)* s'encrasser

▸▸ ***clog dance*** = danse où les participants marquent le rythme avec leurs sabots

▸**clog up 1** *vt sep* (**a**) *(pipe)* boucher, encrasser; *(street)* boucher, bloquer; *(wheel)* bloquer

2 *vi (pipe)* se boucher; *(firearm, machine)* s'encrasser

cloisonné ['klwazəˌneɪ] *Art* **1** *n* cloisonné *m*

2 *adj* en cloisonné

cloister ['klɔɪstə(r)] **1** *n Archit & Rel* cloître *m*; **cloisters** *(of convent, church)* cloître *m*

2 *vt Rel* cloîtrer; *Fig* éloigner *ou* isoler (du monde)

cloistered ['klɔɪstəd] *adj Fig (life)* de reclus; **she leads a cloistered life** elle mène une vie de recluse; **a cloistered childhood** une enfance protégée

cloistral ['klɔɪstrəl] *adj* claustral

clone [kləʊn] **1** *n* clone *m*; **a Tom Cruise/Marilyn Monroe clone** un clone de Tom Cruise/Marilyn Monroe

2 *vt* cloner

cloner ['kləʊnə(r)] *n Mktg* cloneur *m*

cloning ['kləʊnɪŋ] *n* clonage *m*

clonk [klɒŋk] **1** *vi* faire un bruit sourd

2 *vt* cogner, frapper

3 *n* bruit *m* sourd

CLOSE[1] [kləʊs]

proche	▸ **1 (a), (b), (f)**
serré	▸ **1 (d), (g)**
attentif	▸ **1 (e)**
mal aéré	▸ **1 (h)**
près	▸ **1 (a); 2 (a)**
étroitement	▸ **2 (b)**

(compar **closer**, *superl* **closest**) **1** *adj* (**a**) *(near in space or time)* proche; **the library is close to the school** la bibliothèque est près *ou* proche de l'école; **in close proximity to sth** dans le voisinage immédiat de *ou* tout près de qch; **they're very close in age** ils ont presque le même âge; **his death brought the war closer to home** c'est avec sa mort que nous avons vraiment pris conscience de la guerre; **we are close to an agreement** nous sommes presque arrivés à un accord; **at close intervals** à intervalles rapprochés; **I saw him at close quarters** je l'ai vu de près; **at close range** à bout portant; **to be close at** *or* **to hand** *(shop, cinema etc)* être tout près; *(book, pencil etc)* être à portée de main; **to be close to tears** être au bord des larmes; **to be (very) close to victory** être (tout) près de la victoire; *Fam* **I came close to thumping him one** j'ai bien failli lui en coller une; **he keeps things close to his chest** il ne fait guère de confidences; **to see sth at close quarters** voir qch de près; **to give sb a close shave** raser qn de près; *Fam* **that was a close shave** *or Am* **call!** on l'a échappé belle!, on a eu chaud!; **the bill was passed but it was a close thing** la loi a été votée de justesse; **he managed to get elected but it was a close run thing** il a été élu de justesse

(**b**) *(in relationship)* proche; **they're very close (friends)** ils sont très proches; **he's a close friend of mine** c'est un ami intime; **a close relative** un parent proche; **I'm very close to my sister** je suis très proche de ma sœur; **he has close ties with Israel** il a des rapports étroits avec Israël; **there's a close connection between the two things** il y a un rapport étroit entre les deux; **the President consulted his closest advisers** le président consulta ses conseillers les plus proches; **sources close to the royal family** des sources proches de la famille royale; **a subject close to my heart** un sujet qui me tient à cœur; **to keep sth a close secret** garder le secret absolu sur qch

(**c**) *(continuous)* **they stay in close contact** ils restent en contact en permanence

(**d**) *(in competition, race etc)* serré; *(election)* vivement serré; **it was a close contest** ce fut une lutte serrée; **to play a close game** jouer serré; **close finish** arrivée *f* serrée

(**e**) *(thorough, careful)* attentif, rigoureux; **pay close attention to what she says** faites très attention *ou* prêtez une grande attention à ce qu'elle dit; **have a close look at these figures** examinez ces chiffres de près; **upon close examination** après un examen détaillé *ou* minutieux; **to keep (a) close watch** *or* **eye on sb/sth** surveiller qn/qch de près; **I keep close control of the expenses** je contrôle étroitement les dépenses; **in close confinement** en détention surveillée

(**f**) *(roughly similar)* proche; **his version of events was close to the truth** sa version des faits était très proche de la réalité; **he bears a close resemblance to his father** il ressemble beaucoup à son père; **it's the closest thing we've got to an operating theatre** voilà à quoi se réduit notre salle d'opération

(**g**) *(compact → handwriting, print)* serré; *(→ grain)* dense, compact; *Mil* **in close formation** en ordre serré

(**h**) *Br (stuffy → room)* mal aéré, qui manque de ventilation *ou* d'air; **it's very close in here** on manque vraiment d'air ici; **it's terribly close today** il fait très lourd aujourd'hui

(**i**) *(secretive)* renfermé, peu communicatif; **he's very close about his private life** il est très discret sur sa vie privée

(**j**) *Fam (miserly)* pingre, radin

(**k**) [illegible]

2 *adv* (**a**) *(near)* près; **don't come too close** n'approche pas *ou* ne t'approche pas trop; **I live close to the river** j'habite près de la rivière; **did you win? – no, we didn't even come close** avez-vous gagné? – non, loin de là; **she came close to losing her job** elle a failli perdre son emploi; **to come close to death** frôler la mort; **to come close to the world record** frôler le record du monde; **they walked close behind us** ils nous suivaient de près; **she lives close by** elle habite tout près; **I looked at it close to** *or* **up** je l'ai regardé de près; **close together** serrés les uns contre les autres; **sit closer together!** serrez-vous!; **it's brought us closer** ça nous a rapprochés

(**b**) *(tight)* étroitement, de près; **he held me close** il m'a serré dans ses bras

3 *n* (**a**) *(field)* clos *m*

(**b**) *Br (street)* impasse *f*

(**c**) *Br (of cathedral)* enceinte *f*

(**d**) *Scot* = passage conduisant de la rue à une cour ou à un immeuble en retrait

4 close on *prep* **it's close on nine o'clock** il est presque neuf heures; **she must be close on fifty** elle doit friser la cinquantaine *ou* doit avoir près de cinquante ans

5 close to *prep (almost, nearly)* presque; **the baby weighs close to 7 pounds** ≃ le bébé pèse presque 3 kilos et demi

►► *Mil* ***close combat*** corps à corps *m*; *Mus* ***close harmony*** tessiture *f* limitée

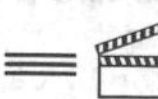

'Close Encounters of the Third Kind' *Spielberg* 'Rencontres du troisième type'

CLOSE² [kləʊz]

fermer	► 1 (a) – (d), (j); 2 (a)
conclure	► 1 (e), (h)
arrêter	► 1 (f)
liquider	► 1 (g)
se refermer	► 2 (b)
se terminer	► 2 (d)
clôturer	► 2 (e)
fin, conclusion	► 3

1 *vt* (**a**) *(shut → door, window, shop, book)* fermer; **he closed his eyes and went to sleep** il ferma les yeux et s'endormit; *Fig* **the committee had not closed the books on the inquiry** le comité n'avait pas refermé le dossier de l'affaire; **to close one's eyes to sth** fermer les yeux sur qch; **to close one's mind to sth** refuser de penser à qch; **she closed her mind to anything new** elle s'est fermée à tout ce qui était neuf

(**b**) *(opening, bottle)* fermer, boucher; *Fig* **we must close the gap between the rich and the poor** nous devons combler le fossé entre riches et pauvres

(**c**) *(block → border, road)* fermer; **they've closed the airport** ils ont fermé l'aéroport; **a road closed to motor traffic** une route interdite à la circulation automobile

(**d**) *(shut down → factory)* fermer; **they plan to close more rural stations** ils ont l'intention de fermer d'autres petites gares de campagne

(**e**) *(conclude → matter)* conclure, terminer; *(→ meeting, session)* lever, clore; *(→ debate)* fermer; **she closed the conference with a rallying call to the party faithful** elle termina la conférence en lançant un appel de solidarité aux fidèles du parti; **a neat way of closing the discussion** un habile moyen de clore la discussion; **the subject is now closed** l'affaire est close

(**f**) *Com & Fin (account)* arrêter, clore; **to close the books** balancer les comptes, régler les livres; **to close the yearly accounts** arrêter les comptes de l'exercice

(**g**) *St Exch (operation)* liquider; *(position)* couvrir

(**h**) *(settle → deal)* conclure; **we closed a deal with them last week** nous avons conclu un accord avec eux la semaine dernière

(**i**) *(move closer together)* serrer, rapprocher; *Mil* **close ranks!** serrez les rangs!; *Fig* **the party closed ranks behind their leader** le parti a serré les rangs derrière le leader

(**j**) *Elec (circuit)* fermer

2 *vi* (**a**) *(shut → gate, window)* fermer, se fermer; *(→ shop)* fermer; *(→ cinema, theatre)* faire relâche; **this window doesn't close properly** cette fenêtre ne ferme pas bien *ou* ferme mal; **the door closed quietly behind them** la porte s'est refermée sans bruit derrière eux; **the bakery closes on Fridays** la boulangerie ferme le vendredi

(**b**) *(wound, opening)* se refermer; **the gap was closing fast** l'écart diminuait rapidement

(**c**) *(cover, surround)* **the waves closed over him** les vagues se refermèrent sur lui; **the onlookers closed around us** un cercle de curieux se forma autour de nous; **my fingers closed around the gun** mes doigts se resserrèrent sur le revolver

(**d**) *(meeting)* se terminer, prendre fin; *(speaker)* terminer, finir; **I closed with a reference to Rimbaud** j'ai terminé par une référence à Rimbaud

(**e**) *St Exch* clôturer; **the shares closed at 420p** les actions ont clôturé *ou* terminé à 420 pence; **the share index closed two points down** l'indice (boursier) a clôturé en baisse de deux points

3 *n* fin *f*, conclusion *f*; *(of day)* tombée *f*; *St Exch (on financial futures market)* clôture *f*; *(closing price)* cours *m* de clôture; **at close of business** à la *ou* en clôture; **the concert came to a close** le concert s'acheva; **the year drew to a close** l'année s'acheva; **it's time to draw the meeting to a close** il est temps de mettre fin à cette réunion; **towards the close of the century** vers la fin du siècle; **at close of play** *(in cricket)* à la fin du match

►► *Comput* ***close box*** case *f* de fermeture; *Br* ***close season*** *Hunt* fermeture *f* de la chasse; *Fishing* fermeture *f* de la pêche; *Ftbl* intersaison *f*

►**close down 1** *vi* (**a**) *(business, factory)* fermer; **the shop had to close down** le magasin a dû fermer

(**b**) *Br TV & Rad* terminer les émissions

2 *vt sep (business, factory)* fermer; **they had to close down their shop** ils ont dû fermer leur magasin

►**close in** *vi* (**a**) *(approach)* approcher, se rapprocher; *(encircle)* cerner de près; **to close in on** *or* **upon** se rapprocher de; **the hunters closed in on their prey** les chasseurs se rapprochèrent de leur proie; **the police/his creditors are closing in** l'étau de la police/de ses créanciers se resserre

(**b**) *(evening, night)* approcher, descendre; *(day)* raccourcir; *(darkness, fog)* descendre; **darkness closed in on us** la nuit nous enveloppa

►**close off** *vt sep* isoler, fermer; **the area was closed off to the public** le quartier était fermé au public; **some of the rooms in the house have been closed off** certaines pièces de la maison ont été fermées; *Acct* **to close off an account** arrêter un compte

►**close on** *vt insep* se rapprocher de; **we were closing on them fast** nous nous rapprochions d'eux rapidement

►**close out** *vt sep* (**a**) *Am (factory, shop, business)* liquider *(avant fermeture)*

(**b**) *(complete successfully → game, competition)* remporter; **to close it out** l'emporter

(**c**) *St Exch* **to close a position** boucler *ou* clore *ou* fermer une position

►**close up 1** *vt sep* (**a**) *(seal)* fermer; *(opening, pipe)* obturer, boucher; *(wound)* refermer, recoudre

(**b**) *Typ (characters)* rapprocher; *Mil etc (ranks)* serrer

(**c**) *(shop, house)* fermer

2 *vi* (**a**) *(wound)* se refermer

(**b**) *(shopkeeper)* fermer

►**close with** *vt insep* (**a**) *(finalize deal with)* conclure un marché avec (**b**) *Literary (fight with)* engager la lutte *ou* le combat avec

close-clipped [ˌkləʊs-] *adj (dog, sheep)* tondu de près; *(moustache)* très court

close-cropped [ˌkləʊs-] *adj (hair)* (coupé) ras; *(grass)* ras

closed [kləʊzd] *adj* (**a**) *(shut → shop, museum etc)* fermé; *(→ eyes)* fermé, clos; *(→ opening, pipe)* obturé, bouché; *(→ road)* barré; *(→ economy, mind)* fermé; **road closed to traffic** *(sign)* route interdite à la circulation; **closed on Tuesdays** *(sign)* fermé le mardi; *Theat* relâche le mardi; *Fig* **we found the door closed** nous avons trouvé porte close; *Law* **in closed session** à huis clos; **to do sth behind closed doors** faire qch en cachette; **economics is a closed book to me** je ne comprends rien à l'économie

(**b**) *(restricted)* exclusif; **a closed society** un cercle fermé

(**c**) *Ling (sound, syllable)* fermé

(**d**) *Elec (circuit, switch)* fermé

►► ***closed circuit television*** télévision *f* en circuit fermé; *Pol* ***closed primary*** = aux États-Unis, élection primaire réservée aux membres d'un parti; *Br Hunt* ***closed season*** fermeture *f* de la chasse; ***closed set*** ensemble *m* fermé; *Ind* ***closed shop*** *(practice)* = système selon lequel une entreprise n'embauche que des travailleurs syndiqués; *(establishment)* = entreprise qui n'embauche que des travailleurs syndiqués

closed-door *adj* privé; **they held a closed-door meeting** ils ont tenu une réunion privée *ou* à huis clos

closed-end *adj*

►► ***closed-end (investment) fund*** société *f* d'investissement à capital fixe; ***closed-end mortgage*** prêt *m* hypothécaire à montant fixe

closedown ['kləʊzdaʊn] *n* (**a**) *(of shop)* fermeture *f* (définitive) (**b**) *Br TV & Rad* fin *f* des émissions

close-fisted [ˌkləʊs'fɪstɪd] *adj* avare

close-fitting [ˌkləʊs-] *adj* ajusté, près du corps

close-grained [ˌkləʊs-] *adj* (**a**) *(wood)* à grain fin *ou* serré (**b**) *Metal* à grains fins, à fine cristallisation

close-knit [ˌkləʊs-] *adj Fig (community, family)* très uni

closely ['kləʊslɪ] *adv* (**a**) *(near)* de près; *(tightly)* en serrant fort; **I held her closely** je l'ai serrée fort *ou* (tout) contre moi

(**b**) *(carefully → watch)* de près; *(→ study)* minutieusement, de près; *(→ listen)* attentivement

(**c**) *(connected, guarded)* étroitement; **he's closely related to him** il est l'un de ses proches parents; **closely connected with sth** étroitement lié à qch; **to work closely with sb** travailler en collaboration étroite avec qn

(**d**) *(resemble)* beaucoup

(**e**) *(evenly)* **closely contested elections** élections *fpl* très serrées *ou* très disputées

closeness ['kləʊsnɪs] *n* (**a**) *(nearness)* proximité *f* (**b**) *(intimacy → of relationship, friendship, family)* intimité *f* (**c**) *(compactness → of weave)* texture *f ou* contexture *f* serrée; *(→ of print)* resserrement *m (des caractères)* (**d**) *(similarity → of copy, translation)* fidélité *f* (**e**) *(thoroughness → of examination)* minutie *f*, rigueur *f* (**f**) *(of weather)* lourdeur *f*; *(of room)* manque *m* d'air (**g**) *(miserliness)* avarice *f*

closeout ['kləʊzaʊt] *n Am Com & Fin* liquidation *f*

close-range [ˌkləʊs-] *adj (weapon)* à courte portée

close-run [ˌkləʊs-] *adj (competition, race etc)* serré; **it was a close-run contest** ce fut une lutte serrée

close-set [ˌkləʊs-] *adj (eyes)* rapproché

close-shaven [ˌkləʊs-] *adj* rasé de près

closet ['klɒzɪt] **1** *n* (**a**) *esp Am (cupboard)* placard *m*, armoire *f*; *(for hanging clothes)* penderie *f*; *Fam Fig* **to come out of the closet** *(homosexual)* révéler (publiquement) son homosexualité ☐, faire son come-out; *Fam* **many economists are coming out of the closet as Keynesians** beaucoup d'économistes se révèlent keynésiens; *Fam* **many country music fans are now coming out of the closet** bien des fans de country avouent maintenant leur passion

(**b**) *Arch (small room)* cabinet *m*

(**c**) *Old-fashioned* **(water) closet** waters *mpl*, cabinets *mpl*

2 *adj* secret(ète); **she's a closet gambler** elle n'ose pas avouer qu'elle joue; **closet homosexual** = personne qui cache son homosexualité

3 *vt* enfermer *(pour discuter)*; **to be closeted with sb** être en tête à tête avec qn

closetful ['klɒzɪtˌfʊl] *n* **a closetful of dresses** une armoire pleine de robes

close-up [kləʊs-] **1** *n (photograph, in movie)* gros plan *m*; *(programme)* portrait *m*, portrait-interview *m*; **in close-up** en gros plan; *Fig* **the programme gives us a close-up of life in prison** l'émission nous donne une vision en gros plan de la vie carcérale

2 *adj (shot, photograph, picture)* en gros plan

►► ***close-up lens*** bonnette *f*

closing ['kləʊzɪŋ] **1** *n* (**a**) *(shutting → of factory, shop, business, theatre)* fermeture *f*

(**b**) *(ending → of meeting, session)* levée *f*; *(→ of conference)* clôture *f*

(**c**) *Fin & Admin (of account)* arrêté *m*, règlement *m*; *(of bank account)* fermeture *f*; *St Exch (of position)* clôture *f*

2 *adj* (**a**) *(concluding)* final, dernier

(**b**) *(last)* de fermeture

►► ***closing date*** *(for applications)* date *f* limite de dépôt; *(for project)* date *f* de réalisation *(d'une opération)*; ***closing down*** *(of factory, shop, business)* fermeture *f* (définitive); *Acct* ***closing entry*** écriture *f* d'inventaire *ou* de clôture; ***closing headlines*** *(in news programme)* rappel *m* des titres; ***closing off*** *Acct (of accounts)* arrêté *m*; *Comput (of bad sector)* fermeture *f*; *Am* ***closing out*** *(of factory, shop, business)* fermeture *f* (définitive); *St Exch* ***closing price*** cours *m* à la clôture; *St Exch* ***closing quotation*** cotes *fpl* en clôture; ***closing remarks*** observations *fpl* finales; *St Exch* ***closing session*** séance *f* de clôture; ***closing speech*** discours *m* de clôture; ***closing stock*** stock *m* final; *Comput* ***closing tag*** balise *f* de fin; ***closing time*** heure *f* de fermeture; **when is closing time?** à quelle heure ça ferme?; **it's closing time!** on ferme!; *St Exch* ***closing trade*** transactions *fpl* de clôture

closing-down sale, *Am* **closing-out sale** *n* solde *m* de fermeture

closure ['kləʊʒə(r)] *n* (**a**) *(gen)* fermeture *f*; *(of factory, shop, business)* fermeture *f* définitive; *St Exch* **closure by repurchase** clôture *f* par rachat (**b**) *(of meeting)* clôture *f*; *Parl* **to move the closure** demander la clôture (**c**) *(for container)* fermeture *f* (**d**) *Ling* fermeture *f (d'une voyelle)*

►► *Pol* ***closure rule*** = règle du Sénat américain limitant le temps de parole

clot [klɒt] *(pt & pp* **clotted,** *cont* **clotting)** **1** *vt* cailler, coaguler

2 *vi* (se) cailler, (se) coaguler

3 *n* (**a**) *(of blood)* caillot *m*; *Med* **a clot on the lung/on the brain** une embolie pulmonaire/cérébrale; **a blood clot, a clot of blood** un caillot de sang (**b**) *Br Fam (fool)* cruche *f*

cloth [klɒθ] **1** *n* (**a**) *(material)* tissu *m*, étoffe *f*; *Naut (sail)* toile *f*, voile *f*; *(for bookbinding)* toile *f*; **cloth of gold** drap *m* d'or (**b**) *(individual piece)* linge *m*; *(for cleaning)* chiffon *m*, linge *m*; *(tablecloth)* nappe *f*; *Theat* toile *f* (de décor) (**c**) *Rel* **the cloth** *(the clergy)* le clergé; **a man of the cloth** un membre du clergé

2 *comp (clothing)* de *ou* en tissu, de *ou* en étoffe

►► ***cloth binding*** reliure *f* en toile; ***cloth cap*** casquette *f (symbole de la classe ouvrière britannique)*; **the Labour Party wants to get rid of its cloth cap image** les travaillistes veulent se débarrasser de leur image prolétaire

clothbound ['klɒθbaʊnd] *adj (book)* relié toile

clothe [kləʊð] *(pt & pp* **clothed** *or Literary* **clad** [klæd]) *vt* habiller, vêtir; *Fig* revêtir, couvrir; **three children to feed and clothe** trois enfants à nourrir et à habiller; **clothed in furs** vêtu de fourrures; *Fig* **the countryside was clothed in snow** la campagne était recouverte de neige

cloth-eared *adj Br Fam* dur de la feuille, sourdingue

cloth-ears *n Br Fam* sourdingue *mf*; **hey, cloth-ears, didn't you hear me?** espèce de sourdingue, tu n'as pas entendu ce que j'ai dit?

clothes [kləʊðz] *npl* (**a**) *(garments)* vêtements *mpl*, habits *mpl*; **to put one's clothes on** s'habiller; **to take one's clothes off** se déshabiller; **with one's clothes on** (tout) habillé; **with one's clothes off** déshabillé, (tout) nu; **dressed in one's best clothes** sur son trente et un, endimanché (**b**) *Br (bedclothes)* draps *mpl*

►► ***clothes basket*** panier *m* à linge; ***clothes brush*** brosse *f* à habits; *Am* ***clothes closet*** penderie *f*; ***clothes hanger*** cintre *m*; ***clothes hook*** patère *f*; ***clothes moth*** mite *f*; *Br* ***clothes peg,*** *Am* ***clothes pin*** pince *f* à linge; ***clothes prop*** perche *f* de corde à linge; *Am* ***clothes rack*** séchoir *m*

clotheshorse ['kləʊðzhɔːs, *pl* -hɔːsɪz] *n* (**a**) *(for laundry)* séchoir *m* à linge (**b**) *Fig (model)* mannequin *m*; *Pej* **she's such a clotheshorse** elle ne pense qu'à ses toilettes

clothesline ['kləʊðzlaɪn] *n* corde *f* à linge

clothespole ['kləʊðzpəʊl], **clothesprop** ['kləʊðzprɒp] *n* support *m* pour corde à linge

clothier ['kləʊðɪə(r)] *n* (**a**) *(cloth dealer, maker)* drapier(ère) *m,f* (**b**) *(clothes seller)* marchand(e) *m,f* de vêtements *ou* de confection

clothing ['kləʊðɪŋ] **1** *n (UNCOUNT)* (**a**) *(garments)* vêtements *mpl*, habits *mpl*; **an article of clothing** un vêtement; **articles of clothing** vêtements *mpl*; **warm clothing** vêtements *mpl* chauds

(**b**) *(act of dressing)* habillage *m*; *(providing with garments)* habillement *m*; *Rel (of monk, nun)* prise *f* d'habit

2 *comp (industry, trade)* du vêtement, de l'habillement; *(shop)* de vêtements

►► ***clothing allowance*** indemnité *f* vestimentaire; ***clothing manufacturer*** confectionneur(euse) *m,f*

clotted cream ['klɒtɪd-] *n* = crème fraîche très épaisse typique du sud-ouest de l'Angleterre

clotting ['klɒtɪŋ] *n (of blood)* caillement *m*, coagulation *f*

►► ***clotting factor*** facteur *m* de coagulation

cloture ['kləʊtʃə(r)] *Pol* **1** *n* clôture *f*

2 *vt* clôturer

►► ***cloture rule*** = règle limitant le temps de parole au Sénat américain

cloud [klaʊd] **1** *n* (**a**) *Met* nuage *m*, *Literary* nuée *f*; **he resigned under a cloud** *(of suspicion)* en butte aux soupçons, il a dû démissionner; *(in disgrace)* tombé en disgrâce, il a dû démissionner; **to be on cloud nine** être aux anges *ou* au septième ciel; **to come down from the clouds** revenir sur terre; **to have one's head in the clouds** être dans les nuages *ou* la lune; *Prov* **every cloud has a silver lining** à quelque chose malheur est bon

(**b**) *(of dust, smoke)* nuage *m*; *(of gas)* nappe *f*; *(of insects)* nuée *f*

(**c**) *(haze → on mirror)* buée *f*; *(→ in liquid)* nuage *m*; *(→ in marble)* tache *f* noire

2 *vt* (**a**) *(make hazy → mirror)* embuer; *(→ liquid)* rendre trouble; **a clouded sky** un ciel couvert *ou* nuageux

(**b**) *(confuse)* obscurcir; **don't cloud the issue** ne brouillez pas les cartes

(**c**) *(spoil → career, future)* assombrir; *(→ reputation)* ternir; *(→ happiness)* troubler

3 *vi* (**a**) *(sky)* se couvrir (de nuages), s'obscurcir

(**b**) *(face)* s'assombrir

►► *Met* ***cloud bank*** banc *m* de nuages; *Nucl* ***cloud chamber*** chambre *f* de détente *ou* d'ionisation; ***cloud formation*** formation *f* de nuages; ***cloud mass*** masse *f* nuageuse; *Met* ***cloud seeding*** ensemencement *m* des nuages

►**cloud over** *vi (sky)* se couvrir *ou* se voiler (de nuages); *Fig (face)* s'assombrir; **it clouded over in the afternoon** ça s'est couvert dans l'après-midi

cloudbase ['klaʊdbeɪs] *n Met* plafond *m* de nuages

cloudberry ['klaʊd,berɪ] *(pl* **cloudberries)** *n Bot* ronce *f*, faux mûrier *m*

cloudburst ['klaʊdbɜːst] *n* grosse averse *f*

cloud-capped [-kæpt] *adj* couronné de nuages

cloud-cuckoo-land *n Br Fam* **they're living in cloud-cuckoo-land** ils planent complètement, ils n'ont pas les pieds sur terre ❑

clouded ['klaʊdɪd] *adj* (**a**) *(sky)* couvert (de nuages); *(liquid)* trouble; **to become clouded** *(sky)* se couvrir; *(mind)* s'obscurcir (**b**) *Fig (expression)* sombre, attristé; *(reputation)* terni; *(judgement)* altéré

cloudiness ['klaʊdɪnɪs] *n (of sky)* nébulosité *f*; *(of liquid)* aspect *m* trouble; *(of mirror)* fait *m* d'être embué

cloudless ['klaʊdlɪs] *adj (sky)* sans nuages; *Fig (days, future)* sans nuages, serein

cloudlet ['klaʊdlɪt] *n* petit nuage *m*

cloudscape ['klaʊdskeɪp] *n Art* étude *f* de nuages

cloudy ['klaʊdɪ] *(compar* **cloudier,** *superl* **cloudiest)** *adj* (**a**) *Met* nuageux, couvert; **it will be cloudy today** le temps sera couvert aujourd'hui (**b**) *(liquid)* trouble; *(mirror)* embué; *(gem)* taché, nuageux; *(urine)* chargé (**c**) *Fig (confused)* obscur, nébuleux; *(gloomy)* sombre, attristé

clough [klʌf] *n Geog* ravin *m*, gorge *f*

clout [klaʊt] *Fam* **1** *n* (**a**) *(blow)* calotte *f*; **to give sb a clout** flanquer une calotte à qn; **to give sth a clout** flanquer un coup dans qch

(**b**) *Fig (influence)* influence *f*, poids *m*; **to have** *or* **to carry a lot of clout** avoir le bras long

(**c**) *NEng & Scot (cloth)* chiffon *m*; *(garment)* vêtement *m*; *Prov* **ne'er cast a clout till May be out** ≃ en avril, ne te découvre pas d'un fil

2 *vt (hit → person)* flanquer une calotte à; *(→ thing)* flanquer un coup dans

clove [kləʊv] **1** *pt of* **cleave**

2 *n* (**a**) *(spice)* clou *m* de girofle; *(tree)* giroflier *m*; **oil of cloves** essence *f* de girofle (**b**) *(of garlic)* gousse *f*

►► ***clove hitch*** demi-clef *f*, nœud *m* de cabestan; *Bot* ***clove pink*** œillet-giroflée *m*

cloven ['kləʊvən] **1** *pp of* **cleave**

2 *adj* fendu, fourchu; **cloven foot** *or* **hoof** *(of animal)* sabot *m* fendu; *(of devil)* pied *m* fourchu

cloven-footed, cloven-hoofed [-huːft] *adj (animal)* aux sabots fendus; *(devil)* aux pieds fourchus

clover ['kləʊvə(r)] *n Bot* trèfle *m*; *Fig* **to be in clover** être comme un coq en pâte

►► ***clover honey*** miel *m* de trèfle

cloverleaf ['kləʊvəliːf] *(pl* **cloverleaves** [-liːvz]) *n Bot* feuille *f* de trèfle

Clovis ['kləʊvɪs] *pr n* Clovis

clown [klaʊn] **1** *n (entertainer)* clown *m*; *Theat* bouffon *m*; *Fig (fool)* pitre *m*, imbécile *mf*; **to act the clown** faire le clown; **to make a clown of oneself** se rendre ridicule

2 *vi (joke)* faire le clown; *(act foolishly)* faire le pitre *ou* l'imbécile

►**clown about, clown around** *vi (joke)* faire le clown; *(act foolishly)* faire le pitre *ou* l'imbécile

clownery ['klaʊnərɪ], **clowning** ['klaʊnɪŋ] *n (UNCOUNT)* clowneries *fpl*, pitreries *fpl*

clownish ['klaʊnɪʃ] *adj* clownesque

cloy [klɔɪ] *also Fig* **1** *vt* écœurer

2 *vi* devenir écœurant

cloying ['klɔɪɪŋ] *adj* écœurant

cloze test [kləʊz-] *n* ≃ exercice *m* à trous

CLU [,siːel'juː] *n Am (abbr* **Civil Liberties Union)** = ligue américaine des droits du citoyen

club [klʌb] *(pt & pp* **clubbed,** *cont* **clubbing)** **1** *n* (**a**) *(association)* club *m*, cercle *m*; **a tennis/football club** un club de tennis/football; *Hum* **join the club!** bienvenue au club!, tu n'es pas le seul!; **I've got a cold – join the club!** j'ai un rhume – on est deux!; *Fam* **to be in the (pudding) club** *(pregnant)* être en cloque

(**b**) *(nightclub)* boîte *f* (de nuit); **the club scene** = milieux branchés fréquentant les boîtes de nuit

(**c**) *(weapon)* matraque *f*, massue *f*; *Sport* **(Indian) club** massue *f* de gymnastique

(**d**) *Golf* club *m* (de golf)

(**e**) *Cards* trèfle *m*; **clubs** trèfles *mpl*; **the nine of clubs** le neuf de trèfle; **clubs are trumps** atout trèfle; **to play a club** jouer (un *ou* du) trèfle

2 *vt* matraquer, frapper avec une massue; **he was clubbed to death** il a été matraqué à mort

►► *Am Rail* ***club car*** wagon-restaurant *m*; ***club chair*** club *m*; *Aviat* ***club class*** classe *f* club, classe *f* affaires; ***club sandwich*** sandwich *m* mixte *(à trois étages)*; *Am* ***club soda*** eau *f* de Seltz; ***club tie*** = cravate aux couleurs d'une association sportive

►**club together** *vi (share cost)* se cotiser; **to club together to buy sth** se cotiser pour acheter qch

CLUBS

Les clubs britanniques sont des lieux de rencontre et de détente très fermés, qui jouent un rôle important dans la vie sociale des milieux aisés en Grande-Bretagne. Traditionnellement ces institutions (notamment les "gentlemen's clubs" londoniens, tels que l'Athenaeum ou le Reform Club) étaient interdites aux femmes, mais récemment cette tendance a commencé à changer.

clubbable ['klʌbəbəl] *adj Old-fashioned* sociable

clubber ['klʌbə(r)] *n Fam* **he's a real clubber** il adore aller en boîte

clubbing ['klʌbɪŋ] *n Fam* **to go clubbing** aller en boîte

clubby ['klʌbɪ] *(compar* **clubbier,** *superl* **clubbiest)** *adj (sociable)* sociable; *(cliquey)* qui a l'esprit de club

clubfoot [,klʌb'fʊt] *(pl* **clubfeet** [-'fiːt]) *n* pied *m* bot

clubfooted [,klʌb'fʊtɪd] *adj* **to be clubfooted** avoir un pied bot

clubhead ['klʌbhed] *n Golf* tête *f* de club

clubhouse ['klʌbhaʊs, *pl* -haʊzɪz] *n Sport* pavillon *m*

clubland ['klʌblənd] *n Br* (**a**) *(area of gentlemen's* *clubs)* = quartier des alentours de Saint James's où se trouvent la plupart des clubs sélects de Londres (**b**) *(nightclub area)* = quartier des boîtes de nuit

clubman ['klʌbmən] (*pl* **clubmen** [-mən]) *n (member of club)* membre *m* d'un club; *(man about town)* homme *m* du monde, mondain *m*

clubroom ['klʌbrʊm] *n* salle *f* de club *ou* de réunion

clubroot ['klʌbru:t] *n Bot* hernie *f* du chou

cluck [klʌk] **1** *vi (hen, person)* glousser; *Fig* **to cluck over sb** être aux petits soins pour *ou* avec qn; **she clucked in disapproval** elle a claqué sa langue de désapprobation

2 *n* (**a**) *(of hen)* gloussement *m*; *(of person → in pleasure)* gloussement *m*; *(→ in disapproval)* claquement *m* de langue (**b**) *Fam (fool)* andouille *f*; **you dumb cluck!** c'est malin!

clucking ['klʌkɪŋ] *n (of hen, person)* gloussement *m*

clue [klu:] *n* (**a**) *(gen)* indice *m*, indication *f*; *(to crime)* indice *m*; **give me a clue** mettez-moi sur la piste; **her hat provides a clue to her profession** on devine sa profession à son chapeau; **where's John? – I haven't a clue!** où est John? – je n'en ai pas la moindre idée *ou* je n'en ai aucune idée!; *Fam* **he's useless at cooking, he hasn't got a clue!** il est nul en cuisine, il n'y connaît absolument rien!; *Fam* **he hasn't got a clue what he's doing** il fait n'importe quoi

(**b**) *(in crosswords)* définition *f*; **what's the clue to 13 down?** quelle est la définition du 13 vertical?

(**c**) *Naut* point *m* d'écoute

►**clue in** *vt sep Fam (person)* mettre au courant ❑

►**clue up** *vt sep Fam (person)* renseigner ❑, mettre au courant ❑

clued-up [klu:d-] *adj Fam* informé ❑; **to be clued-up on sth** s'y connaître en qch; **she's really clued-up on computers** elle s'y connaît en informatique

clueless ['klu:lɪs] *adj Br Fam Pej* qui ne sait rien de rien

clump [klʌmp] **1** *n* (**a**) *(cluster → of bushes)* massif *m*; *(→ of trees)* bouquet *m*; *(→ of hair, grass)* touffe *f*

(**b**) *(mass → of earth)* motte *f*

(**c**) *(sound)* bruit *m* sourd

2 *vi (walk)* **to clump (about** *or* **around)** marcher d'un pas lourd; **with the neighbours clumping about upstairs** avec les voisins qui font du potin en haut

3 *vt (gather)* **to clump (together)** grouper; *(bushes, flowers)* planter en massif

clumpy ['klʌmpɪ] *adj (shoes)* gros (grosse)

clumsily ['klʌmzɪlɪ] *adv* (**a**) *(awkwardly)* maladroitement, gauchement (**b**) *(tactlessly)* sans tact (**c**) *(drawn)* grossièrement; **clumsily built** mal bâti

clumsiness ['klʌmzɪnɪs] *n* (**a**) *(of person, movement)* maladresse *f*, gaucherie *f* (**b**) *(tactlessness)* gaucherie *f*, manque *m* de tact (**c**) *(awkwardness → of tool)* caractère *m* peu pratique; *(→ of design)* lourdeur *f*; *(→ of shape)* grossièreté *f*, lourdeur *f*; *(→ of sentence)* lourdeur *f*, maladresse *f*

clumsy ['klʌmzɪ] *adj* (**a**) *(uncoordinated → person, movement)* maladroit, gauche (**b**) *(tactless)* gauche, malhabile; **he made a clumsy apology** il s'est excusé de façon gauche (**c**) *(awkward → tool)* peu commode *ou* pratique; *(→ design)* lourd, disgracieux; *(→ painting)* maladroit; *(→ style)* lourd, maladroit

clung [klʌŋ] *pt & pp of* **cling**

clunk [klʌŋk] **1** *n (sound)* bruit *m* sourd

2 *vi* faire un bruit sourd

clunker ['klʌŋkə(r)] *n Am Fam (car)* tas *m* de ferraille

clunky ['klʌŋkɪ] *adj (shoes)* gros (grosse); *(furniture)* encombrant

cluster ['klʌstə(r)] **1** *n* (**a**) *(of fruit)* grappe *f*; *(of dates)* régime *m*; *(of flowers)* touffe *f*; *(of trees)* bouquet *m*; *(of stars)* amas *m*; *(of diamonds)* entourage *m* (**b**) *(group → of houses, people)* groupe *m*; *(→ of bees)* essaim *m* (**c**) *Ling* groupe *m*, agglomérat *m* (**d**) *Comput (of terminals)* grappe *f*

2 *vi* (**a**) *(people)* **to cluster around sb/sth** se grouper autour de qn/qch

(**b**) *(things)* former un groupe; **pretty cottages clustered around the church** l'église était entourée de petites maisons coquettes; **to cluster together** se grouper

►► *Mktg* ***cluster analysis*** analyse *f* par segments; ***cluster bomb*** bombe *f* à fragmentation; *Med* ***cluster headache*** migraine *f* ophtalmique; *Mktg* ***cluster sample*** échantillon *m* aréolaire, échantillon *m* par grappes; *Mktg* ***cluster sampling*** échantillonnage *m* aréolaire, échantillonnage *m* par grappes

clutch [klʌtʃ] **1** *vt* (**a**) *(hold tightly)* serrer fortement, étreindre

(**b**) *(seize)* empoigner, se saisir de; **to clutch hold of sth** s'agripper *ou* se cramponner à qch

2 *vi* **to clutch at sth** se cramponner à qch, s'agripper à qch; *Fig* se cramponner à qch, se raccrocher à qch

3 *n* (**a**) *(grasp)* étreinte *f*, prise *f*

(**b**) *Aut (mechanism)* embrayage *m*; *(pedal)* pédale *f* d'embrayage; **to let in the clutch** embrayer; **to let out the clutch** débrayer

(**c**) *(of eggs, chicks)* couvée *f*; *Fig (group)* série *f*, ensemble *m*

(**d**) *Am Fam (crisis)* crise ❑ *f*; **to be in a clutch** être dans le pétrin

(**e**) *Am (bag)* pochette *f (sac à main)*

4 clutches *npl Fig (control)* influence *f*; **to have sb in one's clutches** tenir qn en son pouvoir; **to fall into sb's clutches** tomber dans les griffes de qn; **he escaped the clutches of the law** il a échappé aux griffes de la justice

►► ***clutch bag*** *(handbag)* pochette *f (sac à main)*; *Aut* ***clutch cable*** câble *m* de commande d'embrayage; *Aut* ***clutch disc*** disque *m* d'embrayage; *Aut* ***clutch fluid*** fluide *m* d'embrayage; *Aut* ***clutch housing*** carter *m* d'embrayage; *Aut* ***clutch pedal*** pédale *f* d'embrayage *ou* de débrayage; *Aut* ***clutch plate*** disque *m* d'embrayage

clutter ['klʌtə(r)] **1** *n* (**a**) *(mess)* désordre *m*; **the house is in a bit of a clutter** la maison est plutôt en désordre (**b**) *(disordered objects)* désordre *m*, fouillis *m*; **among the clutter on her desk** au milieu du désordre qu'il y a sur son bureau

2 *vt (room)* mettre en désordre; **a desk cluttered with papers** un bureau encombré de papiers; **his mind was cluttered with useless facts** son esprit était encombré d'informations inutiles

►**clutter up** *vt sep (room)* mettre en désordre; **don't clutter up the worktop** n'encombre pas le plan de travail

cluttered ['klʌtəd] *adj* encombré (**with** de); **the cluttered appearance of the room** l'impression d'encombrement qui se dégageait de la pièce

Clwyd ['klu:ɪd] *n* le Clwyd, = comté du nord-est du pays de Galles; **in Clwyd** dans le Clwyd

Clydesdale ['klaɪdzdeɪl] *n (horse)* (cheval *m* de trait) clydesdale *m*

Clydeside ['klaɪdsaɪd] *n* = ancienne zone de construction navale s'étendant entre Greenock et Glasgow

clypeus ['klɪpɪəs] (*pl* **clypei** [-aɪ]) *n Zool* clypeus *m*, chaperon *m*, épistome *m*

Clytemnestra [ˌklaɪtɪm'nestrə] *pr n Myth* Clytemnestre

cm (*written abbr* **centimetre**) cm

Cmdr *Mil* (*written abbr* **Commander**) Cdt

CMI [ˌsi:em'aɪ] *n Med & Vet* (*abbr* **cell-mediated immunity**) immunité *f* cellulaire

CMO [ˌsi:em'əʊ] *n Am Fin* (*abbr* **collateralized mortgage obligation**) obligation *f* garantie par une hypothèque

CMOS ['si:mɒs] *n Comput* (*abbr* **complementary metal oxide silicon**) CMOS

CMR waybill [ˌsi:em'ɑ:-] *n Com* lettre *f* de voiture CMR

CMV [ˌsi:em'vi:] *n Med* (*abbr* **cytomegalovirus**) CMV *m*

CMYK [ˌsi:emˌwaɪ'keɪ] *n Comput* (*abbr* **cyan, magenta, yellow, black**) CMJN

CNAA [ˌsi:enˌeɪ'eɪ] *n Br* (*abbr* **Council for National Academic Awards**) = organisme non universitaire délivrant des diplômes en Grande-Bretagne

CND [ˌsi:en'di:] *n Br* (*abbr* **Campaign for Nuclear Disarmament**) = en Grande-Bretagne, mouvement pour le désarmement nucléaire

CNN [ˌsi:en'en] *n TV* (*abbr* **Cable News Network**) réseau *m* d'informations américain diffusé par câble et satellite

CNS [ˌsi:en'es] *n Biol* (*abbr* **central nervous system**) système *m* nerveux central

Cnut = **Canute**

CO[1] [ˌsi:'əʊ] *n Mil* (**a**) (*abbr* **commanding officer**) commandant *m* (**b**) (*abbr* **conscientious objector**) objecteur *m* de conscience

CO[2] (*written abbr* **Colorado**) Colorado *m*

Co.[1] [kəʊ] *n* (*abbr* **company**) Cie; *Fig* **Jane and co** Jane et compagnie

Co.[2] (*written abbr* **county**) comté *m*

.co [kəʊ] *Comput* = abréviation désignant les entreprises commerciales dans les adresses électroniques britanniques

c/o [ˌsi:'əʊ] (*abbr* **care of**) chez

co- [kəʊ] *pref* co-; **co-worker** collègue *mf*; **he's her co-star** il partage l'affiche avec elle

coacervate [kəʊ'æsəveɪt] *n Chem* coacervat *m*

coacervation [kəʊˌæsə'veɪʃən] *n Chem* coacervation *f*

coach [kəʊtʃ] **1** *n* (**a**) *(tutor)* répétiteur(trice) *m,f*; *Sport (trainer)* entraîneur(euse) *m,f*; *Ski (instructor)* moniteur(trice) *m,f* (**b**) *Br (bus)* car *m*, autocar *m* (**c**) *Br Rail* voiture *f*, wagon *m* (**d**) *(carriage)* carrosse *m*; **(stage) coach** diligence *f*, coche *m*; *Fig* **to drive a coach and horses through sth** démolir *ou* torpiller qch

2 *comp (driver)* de car; *(tour, trip)* en car

3 *vt (tutor)* donner des leçons particulières à; *Sport* entraîner; **to coach sb in maths/in English** donner des leçons de math/d'anglais à qn; **they employed a tutor to coach him for the exam** ils ont fait appel à un professeur particulier pour le préparer à l'examen; *Theat* **to coach sb for a part** faire répéter son rôle à qn; **the police coached the witness** la police a préparé le témoin à la déclaration; **he had been carefully coached in what to say** on lui avait bien expliqué quoi dire

4 *vi (tutor)* donner des leçons particulières; *Sport* être entraîneur(euse)

►► *Tech* ***coach bolt*** boulon *m* d'ancrage; *Am Aviat* ***coach class*** classe *f* économique; *Am Aviat* ***coach fare*** tarif *m* économique; ***coach house*** remise *f (pour carrosse ou voiture)*; ***coach park*** emplacement *m* (de parking) réservé aux autocars; ***coach party*** groupe *m* voyageant en autocar; **we have three coach parties coming tomorrow** il y a trois cars qui arrivent demain; *Br* ***coach station*** gare *f* routière; ***coach tour operator*** autocariste *m*

coach-and-four *n* carrosse *m* à quatre chevaux

coachbuilder ['kəʊtʃˌbɪldə(r)] *n* carrossier *m*

coachbuilt ['kəʊtʃbɪlt] *adj* construit sur mesure

coaching ['kəʊtʃɪŋ] *n (tutoring)* leçons *fpl* particulières; *Sport (training)* entraînement *m*

►► *Hist* ***coaching inn*** relais *m*

coachload ['kəʊtʃləʊd] *n* **a coachload of tourists** un autocar *ou* car plein de touristes

coachman ['kəʊtʃmən] (*pl* **coachmen** [-mən]) *n* cocher *m*

coachwork ['kəʊtʃwɜ:k] *n* carrosserie *f*

coadjutant [kəʊ'ædʒʊtənt] *n* assistant(e) *m,f*, aide *mf*

co-administration *n* cogérance *f*

coagulant [kəʊ'ægjʊlənt] *n* coagulant *m*

coagulate [kəʊ'ægjʊleɪt] **1** *vi* (se) coaguler

2 *vt* coaguler

coagulation [kəʊˌægjʊ'leɪʃən] *n* coagulation *f*

coagulative [kəʊ'ægjʊlətɪv] *adj* de coagulation

coal [kəʊl] **1** *n* (**a**) *(gen)* charbon *m*; **a piece** *or* **lump of coal** un morceau de charbon; *Fig* **he was treading on hot coals** il était sur des charbons ardents; *Fig* **to carry coals to Newcastle** porter de l'eau à la rivière

(**b**) *Ind (ore)* houille *f*; **soft coal** houille *f* grasse

2 *comp (chute)* à charbon; *(depot, fire)* de charbon

3 *vt (supply with coal)* fournir *ou* ravitailler en charbon; *Naut* charbonner

4 *vi Naut* charbonner

►► ***coal basin*** bassin *m* houiller; ***coal black*** noir *m*; *Br* ***coal bunker*** coffre *m* à charbon; *Naut* soute *f* à charbon; ***coal cellar*** cave *f* à charbon; ***coal gas*** gaz *m* de houille; ***coal industry*** industrie *f* houillère; ***coal merchant*** charbonnier(ère) *m,f*, marchand(e) *m,f* de charbon;

Am **coal oil** kérosène *m*, pétrole *m* (lampant); **coal scuttle** seau *m* à charbon; **coal seam** couche *f* houillère, gisement *m* houiller; **coal tar** coaltar *m*, goudron *m* de houille; **coal tar soap** savon *m* au coaltar; **coal tit** mésange *f* noire

coal-black *adj* noir comme du charbon

coal-burning *adj* à charbon, qui marche au charbon

coaldust ['kəʊldʌst] *n* poussier *m ou* poussière *f* de charbon

coaler ['kəʊlə(r)] *n* charbonnier *m (navire ou train)*

coalesce [ˌkəʊə'les] *vi* s'unir (en un groupe), se fondre (ensemble)

coalescence [ˌkəʊə'lesəns] *n* fusion *f*, union *f*

coalface ['kəʊlfeɪs] *n* front *m* de taille

coalfield ['kəʊlfiːld] *n* bassin *m* houiller, gisement *m* de houille

coal-fired *adj* à charbon, qui marche au charbon

coalfish ['kəʊlfɪʃ] (*pl* **inv** *or* **coalfishes**) *n Ich* lieu *m* noir, colin *m*

coalhole ['kəʊlhəʊl] *n* petite cave *f* à charbon

coaling station ['kəʊlɪŋ-] *n* dépôt *m* de charbon

Coalite® ['kəʊlaɪt] *n* = combustible domestique produisant peu de fumée

coalition [ˌkəʊə'lɪʃən] *n* coalition *f*; *Pol* **to form a coalition** former une coalition, se coaliser

►► *Pol* **coalition government** gouvernement *m* de coalition

coalitionist [kəʊə'lɪʃənɪst] *n Pol* coalitionniste *mf*

coalman ['kəʊlmən] (*pl* **coalmen** [-men]) *n* charbonnier *m*, marchand *m* de charbon

coalmine ['kəʊlmaɪn] *n* mine *f* de charbon, houillère *f*

coalminer ['kəʊlˌmaɪnə(r)] *n* mineur *m*

coalmining ['kəʊlˌmaɪnɪŋ] *n* charbonnage *m*; **coalmining area** région *f* houillère

coalpit ['kəʊlpɪt] *n* mine *f* de charbon, houillère *f*

coalshed ['kəʊlʃed] *n* hangar *m* à charbon

co-anchor *Am* **1** *n* co-présentateur(trice) *m,f*

2 *vt* co-présenter; **the show will be co-anchored by Elizabeth Lewis and Steve Warwick** Elizabeth Lewis co-présentera l'émission avec Steve Warwick

coaptation [ˌkəʊæp'teɪʃən] *n* coaptation *f*

coarse [kɔːs] *adj* (**a**) *(rough in texture, appearance)* gros (grosse), grossier; *(skin, hands)* rugueux, rêche; *(hair)* rêche; *(sandpaper)* épais(aisse); *(salt)* gros (grosse); *(features)* grossier, lourd

(**b**) *(vulgar → person, behaviour, remark, joke)* grossier, vulgaire; *(→ laugh)* gros (grosse), gras; *(→ accent)* commun, vulgaire

(**c**) *(inferior → food, drink)* ordinaire, commun; **this is a fairly coarse wine** ce vin n'est pas très fin

►► **coarse cloth** drap *m* grossier; **coarse fish** poisson *m* d'eau douce *(sauf truite et saumon)*; **coarse fishing** pêche *f* à la ligne en eau douce; **coarse grain** gros grain *m*; **coarse linen** grosse toile *f*; **coarse weave** texture *f* grossière

coarse-cut marmalade *n* marmelade *f* avec des écorces d'orange

coarse-featured *adj* aux traits grossiers *ou* épais

coarse-grained *adj* à gros grain

coarsely ['kɔːslɪ] *adv* (**a**) *(roughly)* grossièrement; **coarsely chopped** grossièrement haché; **coarsely ground** grossièrement moulu; **coarsely woven** de texture grossière (**b**) *(uncouthly → speak)* vulgairement, grossièrement; *(→ laugh)* grassement; *(vulgarly)* indécemment, crûment

coarsen ['kɔːsən] **1** *vi* (**a**) *(texture, appearance)* devenir rude *ou* grossier; *(features)* s'épaissir (**b**) *(person)* devenir grossier *ou* vulgaire

2 *vt* (**a**) *(texture, appearance)* rendre rude *ou* grossier; *(features)* épaissir (**b**) *(person, speech)* rendre grossier *ou* vulgaire

coarseness ['kɔːsnɪs] *n* (**a**) *(of skin)* rugosité *f*; *(of hair)* caractère *m* rêche; *(of fabric)* grossièreté *f*; *(of features)* grossièreté *f*, lourdeur *f* (**b**) *(uncouthness)* manque *m* de savoir-vivre; *(vulgarity)* grossièreté *f*, vulgarité *f*

coast [kəʊst] **1** *n* (**a**) *(of sea)* côte *f*; *(extensive)* littoral *m*; *Br* **the coast** *(seaside)* la côte; **coast path** chemin *m* côtier; **we took the coast road** nous avons pris la route qui longe la mer; **off the coast of Ireland** *or* **the Irish coast** au large des côtes irlandaises; **from coast to coast** d'un bout à l'autre du pays, *Can* d'un océan à l'autre; **broadcast from coast to coast** diffusé dans tout le pays; *Fig* **the coast is clear** la voie est libre

(**b**) *Am (act of coasting)* descente *f* en roue libre

2 *vi (vehicle)* avancer en roue libre; *(downhill)* descendre en roue libre; *Naut* caboter; **the car coasted along/down the street** la voiture avançait le long de la rue/descendait la rue en roue libre; *Fam Fig* **he coasted through the exam** il a eu l'examen les doigts dans le nez; *Fig* **you're coasting** *(not working hard)* tu te la coules douce

coastal ['kəʊstəl] *adj* littoral, côtier

►► **coastal traffic** navigation *f* côtière, cabotage *m*; **coastal waters** eaux *fpl* littorales

coaster ['kəʊstə(r)] *n* (**a**) *(protective mat → for glass)* dessous *m* de verre; *(→ for bottle)* dessous *m* de bouteille; *(stand, tray)* présentoir *m* à bouteilles (**b**) *Naut (ship)* caboteur *m*

coastguard ['kəʊstgɑːd] *n* (**a**) *(organization)* ≃ gendarmerie *f* maritime, *Can* ≃ Garde *f* côtière (**b**) *Br (person)* membre *m* de la gendarmerie maritime; *Hist* garde-côte *m*

►► **coastguard station** bureau *m* de la gendarmerie maritime; **coastguard vessel** garde-côte *m*

coasting ['kəʊstɪŋ] *n Naut* navigation *f* côtière; **coasting vessel** caboteur *m*

coastline ['kəʊstlaɪn] *n* littoral *m*

coast-to-coast *adj* à l'échelle nationale, *Can* d'un océan à l'autre

coat [kəʊt] **1** *n* (**a**) *(overcoat → gen)* manteau *m*; *(→ man's)* manteau *m*, pardessus *m*; *(jacket)* veste *f*; *esp Am (of man's suit)* veston *m*

(**b**) *(of animal)* pelage *m*, poil *m*; *(of horse)* robe *f*

(**c**) *(covering → of dust)* couche *f*; *(→ of snow)* manteau *m*, couche *f*; *(→ of paint, varnish, tar)* couche *f*, application *f*

2 *vt* (**a**) *(cover)* couvrir, revêtir; *(with paint, varnish, tar)* enduire; *(cable)* revêtir, armer; *(paper)* coucher; **the shelves were coated with dust** les étagères étaient recouvertes de poussière; **my shoes were coated with mud** mes chaussures étaient couvertes de boue; **a coated tongue** une langue chargée

(**b**) *Culin* **to coat sth with flour/sugar** saupoudrer qch de farine/de sucre; **to coat sth with chocolate** enrober qch de chocolat; **to coat sth with egg** dorer qch à l'œuf

►► *Her* **coat of arms** blason *m*, armoiries *fpl*; **coat button** bouton *m* pour manteau; **coat hanger** cintre *m*; **coat hook** patère *f*; *Hist* **coat of mail** cotte *f* de mailles; **coat rack, coat stand** portemanteau *m*; **coat tails** queue *f* de pie *(costume)*; **to ride on sb's coat tails** profiter de l'influence *ou* de la position de qn; **she hangs on his coat tails** elle est pendue à ses basques

coat-dress *n* robe-manteau *f*

-coated ['kəʊtɪd] *suff* recouvert de; **chocolate-coated** enrobé de chocolat; **sugar-coated almonds** dragées *fpl*

coati [kəʊ'ɑːtɪ] *n Zool* coati *m*

coating ['kəʊtɪŋ] *n* couche *f*; *(on pan)* revêtement *m*

co-author **1** *n* coauteur *m*

2 *vt (book)* écrire en collaboration; **a book co-authored by Marsh and Brown** un livre écrit conjointement par Marsh et Brown

coax [kəʊks] *vt* cajoler, enjôler; **he coaxed us into going** à force de nous cajoler, il nous a persuadés d'y aller; **I coaxed the money out of him** j'ai obtenu l'argent de lui par des cajoleries; **he coaxed the box open with a screwdriver** il est parvenu à ouvrir la boîte en faisant levier avec un tournevis

coaxial [ˌkəʊ'æksɪəl] *adj Geom & Elec* coaxial

►► *Comput* **coaxial cable** câble *m* coaxial

coaxing ['kəʊksɪŋ] **1** *n (UNCOUNT)* cajolerie *f*, cajoleries *fpl*; **after a lot of coaxing, he agreed** il s'est fait prier avant d'accepter; **no amount of coaxing would get him to agree** malgré les efforts pour l'enjôler, on n'a pas réussi à le faire accepter

2 *adj* enjôleur, cajoleur

coaxingly ['kəʊksɪŋlɪ] *adv* d'un ton câlin *ou* cajoleur

cob [kɒb] *n* (**a**) *(horse)* cob *m* (**b**) *(swan)* cygne *m* mâle (**c**) *(of corn)* épi *m* (**d**) *(of coal)* briquette *f* de charbon (**e**) *Br (bread)* pain *m* rond, miche *f* de pain (**f**) *Br (nut)* noisette *f* (**g**) *Constr* torchis *m*, pisé *m*

►► *Br* **cob loaf** pain *m* rond, miche *f* de pain; *Am Culin* **cob salad** = salade à base d'œufs durs, de bacon et de poulet

cobalt ['kəʊbɔːlt] **1** *n* (**a**) *Chem* cobalt *m* (**b**) *(colour)* bleu *m* de cobalt

2 *adj (colour)* bleu de cobalt

►► **cobalt blue** **1** *n* bleu *m* de cobalt **2** *adj* bleu de cobalt; *Chem* **cobalt bomb** bombe *f* au cobalt; **cobalt 60** cobalt *m* 60, cobalt *m* radioactif

cobber ['kɒbə(r)] *n Austr Fam* copain *m*, pote *m*

cobble ['kɒbəl] **1** *n (stone)* pavé *m*

2 *vt* (**a**) *(road)* paver (**b**) *Br Old-fashioned (shoes)* réparer❑

►**cobble together** *vt sep* bricoler, concocter; **they cobbled a compromise together** ils ont bricolé un compromis

cobbled ['kɒbəld] *adj (path, street)* pavé

cobbler ['kɒblə(r)] **1** *n* (**a**) *(shoe repairer)* cordonnier(ère) *m,f*; *(shoemaker)* bottier *m* (**b**) *Am Culin (cake)* = dessert composé de fruits recouverts d'une couche de pâte; *(drink)* punch *m*

2 **cobblers** *Br very Fam* **1** *npl* (**a**) *(testicles)* balloches *fpl*, boules *fpl* (**b**) *(nonsense)* foutaises *fpl* **2** *exclam* n'importe quoi!, des foutaises, tout ça!

cobblestone ['kɒbəlˌstəʊn] *n* pavé *m (rond)*

cobb salad [kɒb-] *n Am Culin* = salade à base d'œufs durs, de bacon et de poulet

cobelligerent [ˌkəʊbə'lɪdʒərənt] **1** *n* cobelligérant(e) *m,f*

2 *adj* cobelligérant

cobnut ['kɒbnʌt] *n* noisette *f*, aveline *f*

COBOL ['kəʊbɒl] *n Comput (abbr* **Common Business-Oriented Language***)* cobol *m*

cobra ['kəʊbrə] *n* cobra *m*

co-branding *n Mktg* alliance *f* de marque, co-branding *m*

cobweb ['kɒbweb] *n* toile *f* d'araignée; *(single thread)* fil *m* d'araignée; *Fig* **I'm going for a walk to clear away the cobwebs** *or* **to blow the cobwebs away** je vais faire un tour pour me rafraîchir les idées; *Fig* **to brush the cobwebs off sth** ressortir qch

cobwebbed ['kɒbwebd] *adj* couvert de toiles d'araignée

coca ['kəʊkə] *n Bot (shrub)* coca *m*; *(leaf substance)* coca *f*

Coca-Cola® [ˌkəʊkə'kəʊlə] *n* Coca® *m*, Coca-Cola® *m*

cocaine [kəʊ'keɪn] *n* cocaïne *f*

►► **cocaine addict** cocaïnomane *mf*; **cocaine addiction** cocaïnomanie *f*

cocainism [kəʊ'keɪnɪzəm] *n* cocaïnisme *m*, cocaïsme *m*

coccidiosis [ˌkɒksɪdɪ'əʊsɪs] *n Vet* coccidiose *f*

coccus ['kɒkəs] (*pl* **cocci** [-saɪ]) *n Biol* coque *f*

coccyx ['kɒksɪks] (*pl* **coccyges** [ˌkɒk'saɪdʒiːz]) *n Anat* coccyx *m*

Cochin China ['kɒˌtʃɪn-] *n* Cochinchine *f*; **in Cochin China** en Cochinchine

cochineal ['kɒtʃɪniːl] *n* (**a**) *Entom* cochenille *f* (**b**) *(dye)* carmin *m*, cochenille *f* des teinturiers

cochlea ['kɒklɪə] (*pl* **cochleae** [-lɪiː] *or* **cochleas**) *n Anat* cochlée *f*, limaçon *m*

cock [kɒk] **1** *n* (**a**) *(rooster)* coq *m*; *(male bird)* (oiseau *m*) mâle *m*; *Fam Fig* **he thinks he's cock of the walk** il se prend pour le grand chef❑

(**b**) *(tap)* robinet *m*

(**c**) *(of gun)* chien *m*; **at full cock** armé

(**d**) *Vulg (penis)* bite *f*, bitte *f*

(**e**) *Br very Fam (nonsense)* conneries *fpl*

(**f**) *(tilt)* inclinaison *f*, aspect *m* penché; **a cock of the head** une inclinaison de la tête

(**g**) *Br Fam (term of address)* pote *m*; **all right, cock?** ça va, mon pote?

(**h**) *Agr (of hay)* meulon *m*

2 *vt* (**a**) *(gun)* armer

(**b**) *(raise)* **the dog cocked its ears** le chien a dressé les oreilles; *Fig* **she cocked an ear towards the door** elle a tendu une oreille du côté de la porte; **keep an eye cocked on the kids** tenez les enfants à l'œil; **the dog cocked its leg** le chien a levé la patte; *Br Fam* **to cock a snook at sb** faire un pied de nez à qn (**c**) *(head, hat)* pencher, incliner; *(thumb)* tendre

(**d**) *(hay)* mettre en meulons

►► ***cock lobster*** homard *m* mâle; ***cock pheasant*** coq faisan *m*; ***cock sparrow*** moineau *m* mâle

►**cock up** *Br very Fam* **1** *vt sep* **to cock sth up** *(interview, exam)* foirer qch, se planter à qch; *(plan, arrangement)* faire foirer qch

2 *vi* **he's cocked up again** il a encore tout fait foirer

cockade [kɒ'keɪd] *n Hist* cocarde *f*

cock-a-doodle-doo [ˌkɒkəduːdəl'duː] **1** *n* cocorico *m*

2 *exclam* cocorico!

cock-a-hoop *adj Fam* fier comme Artaban □

Cockaigne, Cockayne [kɒ'keɪn] *n Literature* le pays *m* de Cocagne

cock-a-leekie [-'liːkɪ] *n Culin* **cock-a-leekie (soup)** = potage au poulet et aux poireaux

cockamamie [ˌkɒkə'meɪmɪ] *adj Am Fam (ridiculous, incredible)* abracadabrant; **what cockamamie story did he tell you this time?** qu'est-ce qu'il t'a encore raconté comme histoire abracadabrante?

cock-and-bull story *n* histoire *f* à dormir debout

cockatoo [ˌkɒkə'tuː] *n Orn* cacatoès *m*

cockatrice [ˌkɒkə'triːs] *n* (**a**) *Myth* basilic *m (monstre)* (**b**) *Bible* vipère *f*

cockchafer ['kɒkˌtʃeɪfə(r)] *n Entom* hanneton *m*

cockcrow ['kɒkkrəʊ] *n* aube *f*; **at cockcrow** au chant du coq

cocked hat [kɒkt-] *n* tricorne *m*; *Fig* **to knock sb into a cocked hat** *(defeat)* battre qn à plate(s) couture(s), démolir qn; *(be better than)* dépasser qn de très loin

cockerel ['kɒkərəl] *n* jeune coq *m*

cocker ['kɒkə(r)] *n* cocker *m*

►► ***cocker spaniel*** cocker *m*

cock-eyed [-aɪd] *adj Fam* (**a**) *(cross-eyed)* qui louche □ (**b**) *(crooked)* de travers □ (**c**) *(absurd → idea, plan)* absurde □; *(→ story)* qui ne tient pas debout □ (**d**) *(drunk)* pompette

cockfight ['kɒkfaɪt] *n* combat *m* de coqs

cockfighting ['kɒkˌfaɪtɪŋ] *n (UNCOUNT)* combats *mpl* de coqs

cockily ['kɒkɪlɪ] *adv Fam* effrontément □, avec suffisance □

cockiness ['kɒkɪnɪs] *n* impertinence *f*

cockle ['kɒkəl] **1** *n* (**a**) *Zool* coque *f* (**b**) *(in paper)* froissure *f*, pliure *f*; *(in cloth)* faux pli *m*

2 *vt (paper)* froisser; *(cloth)* chiffonner

3 *vi (paper)* se froisser; *(cloth)* se chiffonner

cocklebur ['kɒkəlˌbɜː(r)] *n Bot* lampourde *f*

cockleshell ['kɒkəlˌʃel] *n (shell)* coquille *f*; *(boat)* coque *f*

Cockney ['kɒknɪ] **1** *n* (**a**) *(person)* cockney *mf (Londonien né dans le "East End")* (**b**) *Ling* cockney *m*

2 *adj* cockney; **Cockney accent** accent *m* cockney

►► *Fam Hum* ***Cockney sparrow*** = jeune femme de l'Est de Londres

cock-of-the-rock *n Orn* coq *m* de roche, *Spec* rupiciole *m*

cockpit ['kɒkpɪt] *n* (**a**) *(of plane)* cabine *f* de pilotage, cockpit *m*; *(of racing car)* poste *m* du pilote; *(of yacht)* cockpit *m* (**b**) *(in cockfighting)* arène *f*; *Fig* arènes *fpl*

cockroach ['kɒkrəʊtʃ] *n Entom* cafard *m*, blatte *f*

cockscomb ['kɒkskəʊm] *n* (**a**) *(of rooster)* crête *f* (**b**) *Bot* crête-de-coq *f*

cocksucker ['kɒkˌsʌkə(r)] *n Vulg* suceur(euse) *m,f*; *Fig (despicable person)* enculé(e) *m,f*

cocksure [ˌkɒk'ʃʊə(r)] *adj Pej* suffisant, outrecuidant

cocksureness [ˌkɒk'ʃjʊənɪs] *n Pej* suffisance *f*, outrecuidance *f*

cocktail ['kɒkteɪl] *n* (**a**) *(mixed drink)* cocktail *m (boisson)*

(**b**) *(gen → mixture of things)* mélange *m*, cocktail *m*

►► ***cocktail bar*** bar *m*; ***cocktail cabinet*** bar *m (meuble)*; ***cocktail dress*** robe *f* de cocktail; ***cocktail lounge*** bar *m*; ***cocktail onion*** petit oignon *m* (à apéritif); ***cocktail party*** cocktail *m (fête)*; ***cocktail sausage*** petite saucisse *f* (à apéritif); ***cocktail shaker*** shaker *m*; ***cocktail stick*** pique *f* à apéritif

cocktease ['kɒkˌtiːz], **cockteaser** ['kɒkˌtiːzə(r)] *n Vulg Pej* allumeuse *f*

cock-up *n Br very Fam* foirade *f*; **it was a cock-up** ça a foiré; **to make a cock-up of sth** *(interview, exam)* foirer qch, se planter à qch; *(plan, arrangement)* faire foirer qch; **he made a cock-up of his exam** il s'est planté à l'examen

cocky ['kɒkɪ] *(compar* **cockier**, *superl* **cockiest**) *Fam* **1** *adj (smug)* suffisant; **don't get cocky!** ne prends pas ton air supérieur!

2 *n Austr* (**a**) *(cockatoo)* cacatoès *m* (**b**) *(small-scale farmer)* petit agriculteur *m*

coco ['kəʊkəʊ] *n Br Fam* **I should coco!** tu l'as dit!

cocoa ['kəʊkəʊ] *n* (**a**) *(powder, drink)* cacao *m* (**b**) *(colour)* marron *m* clair

►► ***cocoa bean*** graine *f* de cacao; ***cocoa butter*** beurre *m* de cacao

coconut ['kəʊkənʌt] *n* noix *f* de coco

►► ***coconut fibre*** fibre *f* de coco, coir *m*; ***coconut ice*** = friandise à base de noix de coco; ***coconut matting*** tapis *m* en fibres de noix de coco; ***coconut milk*** lait *m* de coco; ***coconut oil*** huile *f* de coco; ***coconut palm*** cocotier *m*; ***coconut shy*** jeu *m* de massacre *(où l'on essaie d'abattre des noix de coco)*

cocoon [kə'kuːn] **1** *n* cocon *m*; *Fig* **wrapped in a cocoon of blankets** emmitouflé dans des couvertures; **he felt safe in his cocoon of solitude** enveloppé dans sa solitude, il se sentait à l'abri

2 *vt (wrap)* envelopper avec soin; *Fig (overprotect → child)* couver; **workers in the public sector have been cocooned from unemployment** les travailleurs du secteur public ont été protégés du chômage

cocooned [kə'kuːnd] *adj* enfermé, cloîtré

cocooning [kə'kuːnɪŋ] *n* cocooning *m*

Coco the Clown ['kəʊkəʊ-] *pr n* = clown célèbre en Grande-Bretagne dans les années 50

co-creditor *n Law* cocréancier(ère) *m,f*

COD [ˌsiːəʊ'diː] *adv Com (abbr Br* **cash on delivery**, *Am* **collect on delivery**) **to send sth COD** envoyer qch contre remboursement; **all goods are sent COD** toutes les marchandises doivent être payées à la livraison

cod [kɒd] *(pl* **inv** *or* **cods**) *n* (**a**) *(fish)* morue *f*; *Culin* **dried cod** merluche *f*, morue *f* séchée; *Culin* **fresh cod** morue *f* fraîche, cabillaud *m* (**b**) *Br Fam (nonsense)* foutaises *fpl*

►► *Culin* ***cod fillet*** filet *m* de cabillaud; *Culin* ***cod roe*** œufs *mpl* de morue; ***the cod war*** la guerre de la morue *(série de conflits ayant opposé la Grande-Bretagne et l'Islande au sujet de zones de pêche islandaises)*

coda ['kəʊdə] *n Mus* coda *f*

coddle ['kɒdəl] *vt* (**a**) *(pamper → child)* dorloter, choyer (**b**) *Culin* (faire) cuire à feu doux; **a coddled egg** un œuf à la coque

code [kəʊd] **1** *n* (**a**) *(cipher)* code *m*, chiffre *m*; *Biol & Comput* code *m*; **a message in code** un message chiffré *ou* codé; **the letter was in code** la lettre était codée

(**b**) *(statement of rules)* code *m*; **code of conduct** code *m* de conduite; **code of ethics** *(gen)* sens *m* des valeurs morales, moralité *f*; *(professional)* code *m* de déontologie *f*; **code of honour** code *m* de l'honneur; **code of practice** *(gen)* code *m* de déontologie *f*; *(rules)* règlements *mpl* et usages *mpl*

(**c**) *(postcode)* code *m* postal

(**d**) *(dialling code)* code *m*, indicatif *m*

2 *vt (message)* coder, chiffrer

►► *Am Med* ***code blue*** urgence *f*; ***code book*** *(for encoding)* code *m ou* carnet *m* de chiffrement; *(for decoding)* code *m ou* carnet *m* de déchiffrement; ***code name*** nom *m* de code; *Ling* ***code switching*** changement *m* de code

►**code up** *vt sep Typ (text)* insérer les codes dans

coded ['kəʊdɪd] *adj* (**a**) *(message)* codé, chiffré (**b**) *Comput* codé

►► *Aut* ***coded engine immobilizer*** antidémarrage *m* codé, ADC *m*; ***coded signal*** *(video)* signal *m* codé

co-defendant *n Law* coaccusé(e) *m,f*, *(in civil law)* codéfendeur(eresse) *m,f*

codeine ['kəʊdiːn] *n* codéine *f*

code-named *adj* qui porte le nom de code de

co-dependant *n Psy* codépendant(e) *m,f*

co-dependency *n Psy* codépendance *f*

coder ['kəʊdə(r)] *n (device)* codeur *m*

codeword ['kəʊdwɜːd] *n (password)* mot *m* de passe; *(name)* mot *m* codé

codex ['kəʊdeks] *(pl* **codices** [-dɪsiːz]) *n* volume *m* de manuscrits anciens

codfish ['kɒdfɪʃ] *(pl* **inv** *or* **codfishes**) *n Ich* morue *f*

codger ['kɒdʒə(r)] *n Fam* bonhomme *m*; **he's a bad-tempered old codger** c'est un vieux bonhomme bourru

codices ['kəʊdɪsiːz] *pl of* **codex**

codicil ['kɒdɪsɪl] *n Law* codicille *m*

codicology [ˌkəʊdɪ'kɒlədʒɪ] *n* codicologie *f*

codification [ˌkəʊdɪfɪ'keɪʃən] *n* codification *f*

codify ['kəʊdɪfaɪ] *(pt & pp* **codified**) *vt* codifier

coding ['kəʊdɪŋ] *n* (**a**) *(of message)* chiffrage *m* (**b**) *Comput* codage *m*

►► *Comput* ***coding error*** erreur *f* de codage; *Comput* ***coding line*** ligne *f* de programmation; *Comput* ***coding sequence*** séquence *f* programmée

co-director *n* codirecteur(trice) *m,f*

cod-liver oil *n* huile *f* de foie de morue

codon ['kəʊdɒn] *n Biol* codon *m*

codpiece ['kɒdpiːs] *n Hist* braguette *f*

co-driver *n (in rally, race)* copilote *m*; *(of bus, coach)* deuxième chauffeur *m*

codswallop ['kɒdzˌwɒləp] *n (UNCOUNT) Br Fam* bêtises □ *fpl*, âneries □ *fpl*

co-ed *Fam Sch* **1** *adj (school)* mixte □; **to go co-ed** *(school)* devenir mixte □

2 *n* (**a**) *Br (school)* école *f* mixte □ (**b**) *Am (student)* étudiante □ *f (dans un établissement scolaire mixte)*

co-edit *vt* coéditer

co-edition *n* coédition *f*

co-editor *n* coéditeur(trice) *m,f*

coeducation [ˌkəʊedʒʊ'keɪʃən] *n* éducation *f* mixte

coeducational [ˌkəʊedʒʊ'keɪʃənəl] *adj* mixte

coefficient [ˌkəʊɪ'fɪʃənt] *n Math & Phys* coefficient *m*

►► *Phys* ***coefficient of expansion*** coefficient *m* de dilatation; *Fin* ***coefficient tax*** impôt *m* de quotité

coelacanth ['siːləkænθ] *n Ich* cœlacanthe *m*

coelenterate [siː'lentəreɪt] *n Zool* cœlentéré *m*

coeliac, *Am* **celiac** ['siːlɪæk] *Med* **1** *n* = personne atteinte de maladie cœliaque

2 *adj* cœliaque

►► ***coeliac disease*** maladie *f* cœliaque

coelioscopy [ˌsiːlɪ'ɒskəpɪ] *n Med* cœlioscopie *f*

coelom ['siːləʊm] *n Zool* cœlome *m*

coenobite ['siːnəbaɪt] *n Rel* cénobite *m*

co-enzyme *n Biol* coenzyme *f*

coequal [ˌkəʊ'iːkwəl] **1** *adj* égal

2 *n* égal(e) *m,f*

coerce [kəʊ'ɜːs] *vt* contraindre, forcer; **we coerced them into confessing** nous les avons contraints à avouer

coercion [kəʊ'ɜːʃən] *n (UNCOUNT)* coercition *f*, contrainte *f*; *Law* coaction *f*; **to act under coercion** agir sous la contrainte

coercive [kəʊ'ɜːsɪv] *adj* coercitif; *Phys* **coercive force** force *f* coercitive

coercively [kəʊ'ɜːsɪvlɪ] *adv* par la force *ou* par contrainte

coerciveness [kəʊ'ɜːsɪvnɪs] *n* caractère *m* coercitif

coercivity [kəʊɜː'sɪvɪtɪ] *n Phys* coercitivité *f*

coeval [kəʊ'iːvəl] *Formal* **1** *adj* contemporain

2 *n* contemporain(e) *m,f*

coexist [ˌkəʊɪg'zɪst] *vi* coexister

coexistence [ˌkəʊɪg'zɪstəns] *n* coexistence *f*

coexistent [ˌkəʊɪg'zɪstənt] *adj* coexistant

coextensive [ˌkəʊɪk'stensɪv] *adj* **coextensive with** *(in space)* de même étendue que; *(in time)* de même durée que

co-factor *n Med (risk factor)* facteur *m* prédisposant, cofacteur *m*; *Biol & Chem* cofacteur *m*

C of C [ˌsiːəv'siː] *n (abbr* **Chamber of Commerce**) chambre *f* de commerce

C of E [ˌsiːəv'iː] *(abbr* **Church of England**) **1** *n* Église *f* anglicane

2 *adj* anglican; **he's C of E** il appartient à l'Église anglicane

coffee ['kɒfɪ] **1** *n* (**a**) *(drink)* café *m*; **a cup of coffee** une tasse de café; **would you like a coffee?** voulez-vous un café?; **we talked over**

coffee nous avons bavardé en prenant un café; **black coffee** café *m* noir; *Br* **white coffee,** *Am* **coffee with cream** *or* **milk** *(gen)* café *m* au lait; *(in café)* café *m* crème, crème *m* (**b**) *(colour)* café au lait *m inv*
2 *adj (colour)* café au lait *(inv)*
3 *comp (filter, jar, service)* à café; *(ice cream, icing)* au café
►► *Br* ***coffee bar*** café *m*, caféteria *f*; ***coffee bean*** grain *m* de café; ***coffee break*** pause-café *f*; ***coffee cake*** *Br (coffee-flavoured)* moka *m*; *Am (served with coffee)* gâteau *m (que l'on sert avec le café)*; ***coffee cream*** *(chocolate)* chocolat *m* fourré au café; ***coffee cup*** tasse *f* à café; ***coffee grinder*** moulin *m* à café; ***coffee grounds*** marc *m* de café; ***coffee house*** *(on the continent)* café *m*; *Br Hist* = café de type français ou viennois, qui était, au XVIIIème siècle, le lieu de rendez-vous des gens à la mode; *Am Fam* ***coffee klatch, coffee klatsch*** = réunion d'amis autour d'une tasse de café; **he's probably in the coffee klatch** il est sans doute en train de prendre un café et de papoter avec les autres; ***coffee machine*** *(gen)* cafetière *f* électrique; *(in café)* percolateur *m*; *(drinks dispenser)* machine *f* à café; ***coffee mill*** moulin *m* à café; *Br* ***coffee morning*** = rencontre amicale autour d'un café, destinée souvent à réunir de l'argent au profit d'œuvres de bienfaisance; ***coffee mug*** = petite chope en faïence; ***coffee pot*** cafetière *f*; ***coffee shop*** *(small restaurant)* ≃ café-restaurant *m*; *(shop selling coffee)* magasin *m* spécialisé dans le café; ***coffee spoon*** cuillère *f ou* cuiller *f* à café, petite cuillère *f ou* cuiller *f*; *(smaller)* cuillère *f ou* cuiller *f* à moka; ***coffee table*** table *f* basse; ***coffee tree*** caféier *m*

coffee-coloured *adj* café au lait *(inv)*

coffee-maker *n* cafetière *f* électrique

coffee-table book *n* = livre de grand format abondamment illustré (destiné à être feuilleté plutôt que véritablement lu)

coffer ['kɒfə(r)] **1** *n* (**a**) *(strongbox)* coffre *m*, caisse *f* (**b**) *(watertight chamber)* caisson *m* (**c**) *Archit* caisson *m (de plafond)*
2 *vt* (**a**) *Mines & Constr (well)* coffrer (**b**) *Archit (ceiling)* diviser en caissons
3 coffers *npl Fin (funds → of nation)* coffres *mpl*; *(→ of organization)* caisses *fpl*, coffres *mpl*; **the Government hasn't got much left in the coffers** le gouvernement n'a plus grand-chose dans ses coffres

cofferdam ['kɒfədæm] *n Constr* batardeau *m*

coffered ['kɒfəd] *adj Archit* à caissons

coffering ['kɒfərɪŋ] *n Mining & Constr* coffrage *m*

coffin ['kɒfɪn] **1** *n* (**a**) *(box)* cercueil *m*, bière *f* (**b**) *Zool (of hoof)* cavité *f* du sabot
2 *vt (put in coffin)* mettre en bière; *Fig* **to live coffined in a dark basement** vivre enterré dans un sous-sol mal éclairé
►► *Br Fam Pej* ***coffin dodger*** *(old person)* croulant(e) *m,f*; *Fam Hum* ***coffin nail*** *(cigarette)* clope *m or f*, tige *f*

C of I [ˌsiːəv'aɪ] *n (abbr* **Church of Ireland**) Église *f* d'Irlande *(branche de l'Église anglicane)*

cofounder [ˌkəʊ'faʊndə(r)] *n* cofondateur(trice) *m,f*

C of S [ˌsiːəv'es] *n* (**a**) *(abbr* **Church of Scotland**) Église *f* d'Écosse (**b**) *Am (abbr* **Chief of Staff**) [illegible]

cog [kɒg] *n* (**a**) *(gearwheel)* roue *f* dentée; *Am Fam Fig* **to slip a cog** *(go insane)* perdre la boule; **his memory has slipped a cog** il a eu un trou de mémoire (**b**) *(tooth)* dent *f (d'engrenage)*; *Fig* **you're only a (small) cog in the machine** *or* **the wheel** vous n'êtes qu'un simple rouage (dans *ou* de la machine)
►► ***cog rail*** crémaillère *f*; *Am* ***cog railroad,*** *Br* ***cog railway*** chemin *m* de fer à crémaillère

cogency ['kəʊdʒənsɪ] *n* force *f*, puissance *f*

cogent ['kəʊdʒənt] *adj Formal (argument, reasons → convincing)* convaincant, puissant; *(→ pertinent)* pertinent; *(→ compelling)* irrésistible

cogently ['kəʊdʒəntlɪ] *adv Formal (argue → convincingly)* puissamment; *(→ pertinently)* pertinemment, avec à-propos; *(→ compellingly)* irrésistiblement

cogitate ['kɒdʒɪteɪt] *vi Formal* méditer, réfléchir; **to cogitate about** *or* **on sth** méditer sur qch, réfléchir à qch

cogitation [ˌkɒdʒɪ'teɪʃən] *n* réflexion *f*, méditation *f*; *Hum* cogitations *fpl*

cognac ['kɒnjæk] *n* cognac *m*

cognate ['kɒgneɪt] **1** *n* (**a**) *Ling* mot *m* apparenté (**b**) *Law (person)* parent *m* proche, cognat *m*
2 *adj* (**a**) *Ling* apparenté, de même origine; **English is cognate with German** l'anglais est apparenté à *ou* de même origine que l'allemand (**b**) *Law* parent

cognition [kɒg'nɪʃən] *n (gen)* connaissance *f*; *Phil* cognition *f*

cognitive ['kɒgnɪtɪv] *adj Psy* cognitif
►► ***cognitive psychology*** psychologie *f* cognitive; ***cognitive science*** les sciences cognitives; ***cognitive therapy*** thérapie *f* cognitive

cognizance ['kɒgnɪzəns] *n* (**a**) *Formal (knowledge)* connaissance *f*; **to take cognizance of sth** prendre connaissance de qch (**b**) *Formal (range, scope)* compétence *f*; **the matter is outside our cognizance** l'affaire n'est pas de notre compétence; *Law* **within the cognizance of this court** de la compétence de ce tribunal (**c**) *Her (badge)* emblème *m*

cognizant ['kɒgnɪzənt] *adj* (**a**) *Formal (aware)* ayant connaissance, conscient; **to be cognizant of a fact** être instruit d'un fait (**b**) *Law* compétent; **court cognizant of an offence** tribunal *m* compétent pour juger un délit

cognomen [kɒg'nəʊmen] *(pl* **cognomens** *or* **cognomina** [-mɪnə]) *n (surname)* nom *m* de famille; *(nickname)* surnom *m*

cognoscenti [ˌkɒnjə'ʃentiː] *npl* connaisseurs *mpl*

COGS [ˌsiːəʊˌdʒiː'es] *n Acct (abbr* **cost of goods sold**) coût *m* des produits vendus

cogwheel ['kɒgwiːl] *n* roue *f* dentée, roue *f* d'engrenage

cohabit [ˌkəʊ'hæbɪt] *vi* vivre maritalement (**with** avec)

cohabitant [ˌkəʊ'hæbɪtənt] *n* (**a**) *(fellow member)* **the cohabitants of the new Europe** les pays qui constituent la nouvelle Europe (**b**) *Admin & Law* concubin(e) *m,f*

cohabitation [ˌkəʊhæbɪ'teɪʃən] *n* vie *f* maritale, union *f* libre (**with** avec)

cohabitee [kəʊˌhæbɪ'tiː] *n* concubin(e) *m,f*

coheir [ˌkəʊ'eə(r)] *n* cohéritier(ère) *m,f*

coheiress [ˌkəʊ'eərɪs] *n* cohéritière *f*

cohere [kəʊ'hɪə(r)] *vi* (**a**) *(stick together)* adhérer, coller (**b**) *(be logically consistent)* être cohérent; *(reasoning, argument)* (se) tenir

coherence [kəʊ'hɪərəns] *n* (**a**) *(cohesion)* adhérence *f* (**b**) *(logical consistency)* cohérence *f*
►► *Phil* ***coherence theory*** théorie *f* de la cohérence

coherent [kəʊ'hɪərənt] *adj (logical → person, structure)* cohérent, logique; *(→ story, speech)* facile à suivre *ou* comprendre; *Fam* **the man wasn't coherent** il racontait n'importe quoi, il était incohérent

coherently [kəʊ'hɪərəntlɪ] *adv* de façon cohérente

cohesion [kəʊ'hiːʒən] *n* cohésion *f*

cohesive [kəʊ'hiːsɪv] *adj* cohésif; *Phys (force)* de cohésion

cohesively [kəʊ'hiːsɪvlɪ] *adv* cohésivement

cohesiveness [kəʊ'hiːsɪvnɪs] *n* cohésion *f*

cohort ['kəʊhɔːt] *n* (**a**) *(group, band)* cohorte *f* (**b**) [illegible] *mf*, compère *m* (**d**) *(follower)* acolyte *m*; *(supporter)* partisan *m* (**e**) *Biol* ordre *m* (**f**) *(in statistics)* cohorte *f*

co-host 1 *n* co-présentateur(trice) *m,f*
2 *vt* co-présenter; **he co-hosted the Eurovision Song Contest** il a co-présenté le concours de l'Eurovison; **the Oscars were co-hosted by Whoopi Goldberg and Billy Crystal** les Oscars ont été présentés par Whoopi Goldberg et Billy Crystal

COHSE ['kəʊzɪ] *n Br Admin (abbr* **Confederation of Health Service Employees**) = ancien syndicat des employés des services de santé en Grande-Bretagne

COI [ˌsiːəʊ'aɪ] *n Admin (abbr* **Central Office of Information**) = service public d'information en Grande-Bretagne

coif [kɔɪf] *n (headdress)* coiffe *f*; *(skullcap)* calotte *f*

coiffure [kwɑː'fjʊə(r)] *n Formal* coiffure *f*

coil [kɔɪl] **1** *n* (**a**) *(spiral → of rope, wire)* rouleau *m*; *(→ of hair)* rouleau *m*; *(in bun)* chignon *m* (**b**) *(single loop → of rope, wire)* tour *m*; *(→ of hair)* boucle *f*; *(→ of smoke, snake)* anneau *m* (**c**) *Elec* bobine *f* (**d**) *(contraceptive device)* stérilet *m* (**e**) *Naut* glène *f*
2 *vt* (**a**) *(rope)* enrouler; *(hair)* enrouler, torsader; **the snake coiled itself up** le serpent s'est lové *ou* enroulé (**b**) *Elec* bobiner
3 *vi* (**a**) *(river, smoke, procession)* onduler, serpenter (**b**) *(rope)* s'enrouler; *(snake)* se lover, s'enrouler; **the python coiled around its prey** le python s'est enroulé autour de sa proie
►► *Aut* ***coil ignition system*** circuit *m* d'allumage par bobine; *Tech* ***coil spring*** ressort *m* hélicoïdal

►**coil up** *vt sep (rope, hose)* enrouler

coiled [kɔɪld] *adj (rope)* enroulé, en spirale; *(spring)* en spirale; *(snake)* lové; *Fig* **like a coiled spring** tendu, prêt à l'action

coin [kɔɪn] **1** *n* (**a**) *(item of metal currency)* pièce *f* (de monnaie); **a 5p coin** une pièce de 5 pence; *Fig* **that's the other side of the coin** c'est le revers de la médaille (**b**) *(UNCOUNT) (metal currency)* monnaie *f*; **£50 in coin** 50 livres en espèces; *Fig* **to pay sb back in his own coin** rendre à qn la monnaie de sa pièce
2 *vt* (**a**) *(money)* **to coin money** battre monnaie; *Fam* **she's coining it (in)** elle se fait du fric (**b**) *(word)* fabriquer, inventer; *Ironic* **to coin a phrase** comme on dit
►► *Br Tel* ***coin box*** cabine *f* téléphonique (à pièces)

coinage ['kɔɪnɪdʒ] *n* (**a**) *(creation → of money)* frappe *f*; *Fig (→ of word)* invention *f* (**b**) *(coins)* monnaie *f* (**c**) *(currency system)* système *m* monétaire (**d**) *(invented word, phrase)* invention *f*, création *f*; **the word is a recent coinage** c'est un mot nouveau, c'est un néologisme

coincide [ˌkəʊɪn'saɪd] *vi* (**a**) *(in space, time)* coïncider (**b**) *(correspond)* coïncider, s'accorder; **our views coincide** nous sommes d'accord, nos opinions coïncident

coincidence [kəʊ'ɪnsɪdəns] *n* (**a**) *(accident)* coïncidence *f*, hasard *m*; **what a coincidence!** quelle coïncidence! (**b**) *(correspondence)* coïncidence *f*

coincidental [kəʊˌɪnsɪ'dentəl] *adj* (**a**) *(accidental)* de coïncidence; **our meeting was entirely coincidental** notre rencontre était une pure coïncidence; **this had the coincidental effect of...** par coïncidence, cela a eu le résultat de... (**b**) *(having same position)* coïncident

coincidentally [kəʊˌɪnsɪ'dentəlɪ] *adv* par hasard

coiner ['kɔɪnə(r)] *n (of word, expression)* inventeur(trice) *m,f*

coin-op *n Fam* laverie *f* automatique

coin-operated [-'ɒpəˌreɪtɪd] *adj* automatique

co-insurance *n* coassurance *f*

co-insurer *n* coassureur *m*

coir [kɔɪə(r)] *n* coir *m*
►► ***coir matting*** tapis *m* en coco

coitus ['kɔɪtəs] *n* coït *m*
►► ***coitus interruptus*** coït *m* interrompu

Coke® [kəʊk] *n (cola)* Coca® *m*; **a can of Coke**® une boîte ou cannette de Coca®

coke [kəʊk] **1** *n* (**a**) *(fuel)* coke *m* (**b**) *Fam Drugs slang (cocaine)* cocaïne ❑ *f*, coke *f*
2 *vt (coal)* cokéfier, convertir en coke
3 *vi (coal)* se cokéfier, se convertir en coke

coked up [kəʊkt-] *adj Fam Drugs slang* défoncé à la coke

coke-fired *adj* à coke

cokehead ['kəʊkhed] *n Fam Drugs slang* **to be a cokehead** marcher à la coke

coke-oven *n* four *m* à coke

coking ['kəʊkɪŋ] **1** *n* cokéfaction *f*, coké(i)fication *f*
2 *adj (coal)* cokéfiable

COL [ˌsiːəʊ'el] *n (abbr* **cost of living**) coût *m* de la vie

Col. *Mil (written abbr* **colonel**) Col

col[1] [kɒl] *n* (**a**) *Geol (pass)* col *m (d'une montagne)* (**b**) *Met* col *m* barométrique

col[2] *(written abbr* **column**) col

COLA ['kəʊlə] *n Am Fin (abbr* **cost-of-living**

adjustment) augmentation *f* de salaire indexée sur le coût de la vie

cola ['kəʊlə] *n Bot* cola *m*
►► ***cola nut*** noix *f* de cola

colander ['kʌləndə(r)] *n* passoire *f*

colcannon [kəl'kænən] *n Culin* = purée de pommes de terre et de chou

cold [kəʊld] **1** *adj* (**a**) *(body, object, food etc)* froid; **I'm cold** j'ai froid; **her hands are cold** elle a les mains froides; **my feet are cold** j'ai froid aux pieds; **he's getting cold** il commence à avoir froid; **eat it before it gets cold** mangez avant que cela refroidisse; *Fig* **the trail was cold** toute trace avait disparu; **her answer was cold comfort to us** sa réponse ne nous a pas réconfortés; **is it over here? – no, you're getting colder** *(in children's game)* est-ce par ici? – non, tu refroidis; *Fig* **she poured cold water on our plans** sa réaction à l'égard de nos projets nous a refroidis; **to be as cold as ice** *(thing)* être froid comme de la glace; *(room)* être glacial; *(person)* être glacé jusqu'aux os; *Fig* **to get** *or* **to have cold feet** avoir la trouille; *Fam* **he's a cold fish** c'est un pisse-froid; *Fam* **to give sb the cold shoulder** snober qn; *Prov* **cold hands, warm heart** mains froides, cœur chaud
(**b**) *(weather)* froid; **it's cold** il fait froid; **it will be cold today** il va faire froid aujourd'hui; **it's freezing cold** il fait un froid de loup *ou* de canard; **it's getting colder** la température baisse
(**c**) *(unfeeling)* froid, indifférent; *(objective)* froid, objectif; *(unfriendly)* froid, peu aimable; **to be cold towards sb** se montrer froid envers qn; **the play left me cold** la pièce ne m'a fait ni chaud ni froid, la pièce m'a laissé froid; **to have a cold heart** avoir un cœur de pierre; **in cold blood** de sang-froid; **he murdered them in cold blood** il les a assassinés de sang-froid
(**d**) *(unconscious)* **she was out cold** elle était sans connaissance; **he knocked him (out) cold** il l'a mis KO
(**e**) *(colour)* froid
2 *n* (**a**) *(cold weather, lack of heat)* froid *m*; **in this bitter cold** par ce froid intense; **the cold doesn't bother him** il ne craint pas le froid, il n'est pas frileux; **to feel the cold** être frileux; **come in out of the cold** entrez vous mettre au chaud; *Fig* **to come in from the cold** rentrer en grâce; *Fig* **the newcomer was left out in the cold** personne ne s'est occupé du nouveau venu
(**b**) *Med* rhume *m*; **to have a** *or Scot* **the cold** être enrhumé; **to catch a** *or Scot* **the cold** s'enrhumer, attraper un rhume; **a cold in the chest/in the head** un rhume de poitrine/de cerveau; **a bad cold** un mauvais rhume
3 *adv* (**a**) *(without preparation)* à froid; **she had to play the piece cold** elle a dû jouer le morceau sans avoir répété; *Med* **to operate cold** opérer à froid
(**b**) *Am Fam (absolutely)* **she turned me down cold** elle m'a dit non carrément❑; **he knows his subject cold** il connaît son sujet à fond❑
►► ***cold buffet*** buffet *m* froid; *Mktg* ***cold call*** visite *f* à froid; *(on phone)* appel *m* à froid; *Tech* ***cold chisel*** ciseau *m* à froid; ***cold cream*** crème *f* de beauté, cold-cream *m*; *Am Culin* ***cold cuts*** *(gen)* viandes *fpl* froides; *(on menu)* assiette *f* anglaise; ***cold drink*** boisson *f* fraîche; *Hort* ***cold frame*** châssis *m* de couches *(pour plantes)*; *Met* ***cold front*** front *m* froid; *Phys* ***cold fusion*** fusion *f* à froid; *Tech* ***cold riveting*** rivure *f* à froid; ***cold room*** chambre *f* froide *ou* frigorifique; *Mktg* ***cold selling*** vente *f* à froid; ***cold snap*** vague *f* de froid; ***cold sore*** bouton *m* de fièvre, *Can* feu *m* sauvage; *Aut & Comput* ***cold start, cold starting*** démarrage *m* à froid; *Aut* ***cold start protection*** protection *f* de démarrage à froid; ***cold steel*** arme *f* blanche; ***cold storage*** conservation *f* par le froid; **to put sth into cold storage** *(food)* mettre qch en chambre froide; *(furs)* mettre qch en garde; *Fig* mettre qch en attente; ***cold storage dock*** dock *m* frigorifique; ***cold store*** *(room)* chambre *f* froide *ou* frigorifique; *(warehouse)* entrepôt *m* frigorifique; ***cold supper*** dîner *m* froid; ***cold sweat*** sueur *f* froide; **to be in a cold sweat about sth** avoir des sueurs froides au sujet de qch; *Fam* **just thinking about my exams brings me out in a cold sweat** rien que de penser à mes examens, j'en ai des sueurs froides; ***cold tap*** robinet *m* d'eau froide; *Fam Drugs slang* ***cold turkey*** *(drugs withdrawal)* manque *m*; **to go cold turkey** décrocher d'un seul coup; **to be cold turkey** être en manque; *Pol* ***cold war*** guerre *f* froide; *Pol* ***cold warrior*** partisan *m* de la guerre froide; ***cold wave*** vague *f* de froid

'In Cold Blood' *Capote, Kaplan* 'De sang-froid'

cold-blooded *adj* (**a**) *(animal)* à sang froid; **reptiles are cold-blooded** les reptiles sont des animaux à sang froid (**b**) *Fig (unfeeling)* insensible; *(ruthless)* sans pitié; **a cold-blooded murder** un meurtre commis de sang-froid; **a cold-blooded murderer** un meurtrier sans pitié

cold-bloodedly [-'blʌdɪdlɪ] *adv* de sang-froid

cold-bloodedness [-'blʌdɪdnɪs] *n (of person)* manque *m* de sensibilité, dureté *f*; *(of crime)* cruauté *f*

cold-calling *n Mktg* démarchage *m*; *(on phone)* démarchage *m* par téléphone

coldcock ['kəʊldkɒk] *vt Am Fam (knock out)* assommer❑, estourbir

cold-hearted *adj* sans pitié, insensible

cold-heartedly [-'hɑːtɪdlɪ] *adv* sans pitié

coldish ['kəʊldɪʃ] *adj (gen)* un peu froid, plutôt *ou* assez froid; *(weather)* frais, frisquet

coldly ['kəʊldlɪ] *adv* froidement, avec froideur

coldness ['kəʊldnɪs] *n also Fig* froideur *f*; **there is a coldness between them** il y a un froid entre eux

cold-pressed [-prest] *adj (olive oil)* pressé à froid

cold-rivet *vt Tech* riveter à froid

cold-shoulder *vt Fam* snober; **we cold-shouldered them** nous leur avons battu froid *ou* les avons snobés; **the party continues to be cold-shouldered by the electorate** le parti est toujours boudé par les électeurs

Coldstream Guards ['kəʊld,striːm-] *npl Mil* **the Coldstream Guards** = régiment d'infanterie de la Garde Royale britannique

cold-weather payment *n Formerly Admin* = en Grande-Bretagne, allocation complémentaire versée aux personnes âgées en période de grand froid pour les aider à payer le chauffage

cold-work *vt Metal* écrouir

cold-working *n Metal* écrouissage *m*

colectomy [kə'lektəmɪ] *n Med* colectomie *f*

Colemanballs ['kəʊlmən,bɔːlz] *n Br Press* = rubrique du magazine satirique 'Private Eye' qui répertorie les âneries proférées par des célébrités

coleopteran [,kɒlɪ'ɒptərən] *n Entom* coléoptère *m*

coleslaw ['kəʊlslɔː] *n* salade *f* de chou cru

coley ['kəʊlɪ] *n Br* colin *m*, lieu *m* noir

colibacillum [,kəʊlɪ'bæsɪləm] *n Biol* colibacille *m*

colic ['kɒlɪk] *n (UNCOUNT)* coliques *fpl*

colicky ['kɒlɪkɪ] *adj* qui souffre de coliques

colie ['kəʊlɪ] *n Orn* coliou *m*, oiseau-souris *m*

coliform bacteria ['kɒlɪfɔːm-] *npl Biol* colibacilles *mpl*

Coliseum [,kɒlɪ'sɪəm] *n* Colisée *m*

colitis [kɒ'laɪtɪs] *n (UNCOUNT) Med* colite *f*

collaborate [kə'læbəreɪt] *vi* collaborer; **she collaborated with us on the project** elle a collaboré avec nous au projet; **to collaborate with the enemy** collaborer avec l'ennemi

collaboration [kə,læbə'reɪʃən] *n* collaboration *f* (**with sb** avec qn; **on sth** à qch); **in collaboration with** en collaboration avec

collaborationist [kə,læbə'reɪʃənɪst] *n Pej* collaborateur(trice) *m,f*, collaborationniste *mf*

collaborative [kə'læbərətɪv] *adj* conjugué, combiné

collaborator [kə'læbəreɪtə(r)] *n* collaborateur(trice) *m,f*

collage ['kɒlɑːʒ] *n* (**a**) *Art (picture, method)* collage *m* (**b**) *(gen → combination of things)* mélange *m*

collagen ['kɒlədʒən] *n Biol* collagène *m*

collapse [kə'læps] **1** *vi* (**a**) *(building, roof)* s'écrouler, s'effondrer; *(beam)* fléchir; *(land)* s'ébouler
(**b**) *Fig (institution, plan)* s'effondrer, s'écrouler; *(government)* tomber, chuter; *(country, market, defence, economy, currency, prices)* s'effondrer
(**c**) *(person)* s'écrouler, s'effondrer; *(health)* se délabrer, se dégrader; **he collapsed and died** il a eu un malaise et il est mort; **he collapsed onto the bed and slept for hours** il s'est écroulé sur son lit et a dormi pendant des heures; **to collapse with laughter** se tordre de rire; **I collapsed from the heat** je me suis évanoui tellement il faisait chaud; **he collapsed into an armchair** il s'effondra dans un fauteuil; **I feel like I'm about to collapse** j'ai l'impression que je vais m'effondrer; *Med* **her lung has collapsed** elle a eu *ou* fait un collapsus pulmonaire
(**d**) *(fold up)* se plier; **the bicycle collapses so it can be stored away easily** la bicyclette se plie et peut ainsi être rangée facilement
2 *vt* (**a**) *(fold up → table, chair)* plier
(**b**) *(merge → paragraphs, entries)* mettre ensemble, fusionner
(**c**) *Comput (subdirectories)* réduire
3 *n* (**a**) *(of building, roof)* écroulement *m*, effondrement *m*; *(of beam)* rupture *f*; *(of land)* éboulement *m*
(**b**) *Fig (of institution, plan)* effondrement *m*, écroulement *m*; *(of government)* chute *f*; *(of country)* effondrement *m*, débâcle *f*; *(of market, defence, economy, currency)* effondrement *m*; *(of prices)* effondrement *m*, chute *f* subite
(**c**) *(of person)* écroulement *m*, effondrement *m*; *(of health)* délabrement *m*; *(of lung)* collapsus *m*

collapsed [kə'læpst] *adj Med* **collapsed lung** collapsus *m* pulmonaire; **to have a collapsed lung** avoir fait un collapsus pulmonaire

collapsible [kə'læpsəbəl] *adj (chair, boat)* pliant; *(handle etc)* rabattable; *Aut (steering column)* rétractile, rétractable
►► *Aut* ***collapsible hood*** capote *f* pliante *ou* rabattable

collar ['kɒlə(r)] **1** *n* (**a**) *(on clothing)* col *m*; *(detachable → for men)* faux col *m*; *(→ for women)* col *m*, collerette *f*; **he seized me by the collar** il m'a attrapé par le col
(**b**) *(for animal)* collier *m*; *(neck of animal)* collier *m*; *Culin (of beef)* collier *m*; *Culin (of mutton, veal)* collet *m*
(**c**) *Tech (on pipe)* bague *f*
(**d**) *Zool (marking → on bird, animal)* collier *m*
2 *vt* (**a**) *Fam (seize)* prendre *ou* saisir au collet, colleter; *(criminal)* arrêter; *(detain)* intercepter, harponner
(**b**) *Tech (pipe)* baguer
►► ***collar button*** bouton *m* de col; ***collar size*** encolure *f*; ***collar stud*** bouton *m* de col

collarbone ['kɒləbəʊn] *n* clavicule *f*

collard greens ['kɒləd-] *npl Culin* chou *m* frisé

collared dove ['kɒləd-] *n Orn* tourterelle *f* turque

collate [kə'leɪt] *vt* (**a**) *(assemble → information, texts)* collationner; *(in bookbinding → sheets, signatures)* collationner (**b**) *(compare → text)* collationner (**with** avec) (**c**) *Rel* nommer *(à un bénéfice ecclésiastique)*

collateral [kɒ'lætərəl] **1** *n Fin (guarantee)* nantissement *m*; **what can you provide as collateral?** qu'est-ce que vous pouvez fournir en nantissement?; **offered as collateral** remis en nantissement
2 *adj* (**a**) *(secondary)* subsidiaire, accessoire; *Fin* subsidiaire (**b**) *(parallel)* parallèle; *(fact)* concomitant; *Law* collatéral (**c**) *(branch, family) & Med (artery)* collatéral
►► *Mil* ***collateral damage*** dégâts *mpl* collatéraux; *Fin* ***collateral loan*** prêt *m* avec garantie; *Fin* ***collateral security*** nantissement *m*

collateralize, -ise [kə'lætərəlaɪz] *vt Fin* garantir
►► *Am* ***collateralized mortgage obligation*** obligation *f* garantie par une hypothèque

collation [kə'leɪʃən] *n* (**a**) *(of information, texts)* collation *f*; *(in bookbinding → of sheets, signatures)* collationnure *f* (**b**) *(comparison → of texts)* collation *f* (**c**) *Formal (light meal)* collation *f*

collator [kə'leɪtə(r)] *n* (**a**) *(person)* collationneur(euse) *m,f*; *(machine)* assembleuse *f* (**b**) *Rel* collateur *m*

colleague ['kɒliːg] *n (in office, school)* collègue *mf*

collect[1] [kə'lekt] **1** *vt* (**a**) *(gather → objects)* ramasser; *(→ information, documents)* recueillir, rassembler; *(→ evidence)* rassembler; *(→ people)* réunir, rassembler; *(→ wealth)* accumuler, amasser; **a water butt collects rainwater for use in the garden** une citerne recueille l'eau de pluie pour le jardin; **to collect dust** prendre la poussière; **solar panels collect the heat** des panneaux solaires captent la chaleur

(**b**) *Fig* **to collect oneself** *(calm down)* se reprendre, se calmer; *(reflect)* se recueillir; **let me collect my thoughts** laissez-moi réfléchir *ou* me concentrer; **to collect one's wits** rassembler ses esprits

(**c**) *(as hobby)* collectionner, faire collection de; **she has collected more than 2,000 records** elle a une collection de plus de 2000 disques

(**d**) *(money)* recueillir; *(taxes, fines, dues)* percevoir; *(pension, salary)* toucher; *(homework)* ramasser, relever; *(debt)* recouvrer

(**e**) *Br (take away)* ramasser; **the council collects the rubbish** la commune se charge du ramassage des ordures; **when is the mail collected?** à quelle heure est la levée du courrier?; *Com* **to collect an order** retirer une commande

(**f**) *(pick up → people)* aller chercher, (passer) prendre; *(→ luggage, ticket, car)* aller chercher, aller prendre; *(→ goods)* enlever; **he'll collect us in his car** il viendra nous chercher *ou* passera nous prendre en voiture; **the bus collects the children at eight o'clock** le bus ramasse les enfants à huit heures; **I'll collect you at midday** je passerai vous prendre à midi

2 *vi* (**a**) *(accumulate → people)* se rassembler, se réunir; *(→ things)* s'accumuler, s'amasser; *(→ water, dirt)* s'accumuler

(**b**) *(raise money)* **to collect for charity** faire la quête *ou* quêter pour une œuvre de bienfaisance

(**c**) *Am Com* **collect on delivery** paiement *m* à la livraison, (livraison *f*) contre remboursement

3 *adv Am Tel* **to call (sb) collect** téléphoner (à qn) en PCV, *Can* faire un appel à frais virés (à qn); *Com* **to send a parcel collect** envoyer un colis en port dû *ou* payable à destination

►► *Am Tel* ***collect call*** appel *m* en PCV, *Can* appel *m* à frais virés; **to make a collect call** faire un appel *ou* téléphoner en PCV, *Can* faire un appel à frais virés

►**collect up** *vt sep* ramasser; **they collected up their belongings and left** ils ont ramassé leurs affaires et sont partis

collect[2] ['kɒlekt] *n Rel (prayer)* collecte *f*

collectable [kə'lektəbəl] **1** *adj* (**a**) *(sought-after)* très recherché; *(valued by collectors)* prisé par les collectionneurs (**b**) *(debt)* recouvrable

2 *n* objet *m* de collection

collected [kə'lektɪd] *adj* (**a**) *(calm, composed)* maître de soi, calme (**b**) *(complete)* complet(ète); **the collected works of Whitman** les œuvres complètes de Whitman

collectedly [kə'lektɪdlɪ] *adv* avec calme, avec sang-froid

collectible = **collectable**

collecting [kə'lektɪŋ] *n* collection *f*; **he does a lot of collecting for the blind** il quête beaucoup *ou* il fait de nombreuses quêtes pour les aveugles

►► *Banking & Fin* ***collecting agency, collecting bank*** banque *f* de recouvrement; *Banking & Fin* ***collecting banker*** banquier(ère) *m,f* encaisseur(euse); *Banking & Fin* ***collecting department*** service *m* de recouvrement; ***collecting tin*** = boîte de collecte au profit d'une association caritative

collection [kə'lekʃən] *n* (**a**) *(UNCOUNT) (collecting → objects)* ramassage *m*; *(→ information)* rassemblement *m*; *(→ wealth)* accumulation *f*; *(→ rent, money)* encaissement *m*; *(→ debts)* recouvrement *m*; *(→ taxes)* perception *f*; *(→ data)* collecte *f*

(**b**) *(things collected)* collection *f*; **a coin collection** une collection de monnaies; **Armani's winter collection** la collection d'hiver d'Armani

(**c**) *(picking up → of rubbish)* ramassage *m*; *Br (→ of mail)* levée *f*; **your order is ready for collection** votre commande est prête; **collection times are 8.45 and 17.30** *(from letterbox)* les levées sont à 8h45 et 17h30

(**d**) *(sum of money)* collecte *f*, quête *f*; **to take** *or* **to make a collection (for)** faire une quête *ou* collecte (pour)

(**e**) *(group → of people, things)* rassemblement *m*, groupe *m*; *(ordered)* assemblage *m*; **a collection of rubbish had built up outside the door** des ordures s'étaient amassées devant la porte; **a motley collection** un rassemblement hétéroclite

(**f**) *(anthology)* recueil *m*

(**g**) *Fin (of bill)* encaissement *m*; **to hand sth in for collection** donner qch à l'encaissement; **a bill for collection** un effet à l'encaissement

►► *Banking & Fin* ***collection bank*** banque *f* d'encaissement; ***collection box*** *(gen)* caisse *f*; *(in church)* tronc *m*; *Fin* ***collection charges, collection fees*** frais *mpl* d'encaissement; ***collection plate*** *(in church)* corbeille *f*; *Fin* ***collection rate*** tarif *m* d'encaissement; ***collection tin*** = boîte de collecte au profit d'une association caritative

collective [kə'lektɪv] **1** *adj* collectif

2 *n* coopérative *f*

►► *Ind* ***collective agreement*** convention *f* collective; *Ind* ***collective bargaining*** = négociations pour une convention collective; *Agr* ***collective farm*** ferme *f* collective; *Ling* ***collective noun*** collectif *m*; *Law* ***collective ownership*** propriété *f* collective; *(of building)* copropriété *f*; *Mktg* ***collective promotion*** communication *f* collective; *Psy* ***the collective unconscious*** l'inconscient *m* collectif

collectively [kə'lektɪvlɪ] *adv* collectivement

collectivism [kə'lektɪvɪzəm] *n Econ* collectivisme *m*

collectivist [kə'lektɪvɪst] *Econ* **1** *adj* collectiviste

2 *n* collectiviste *mf*

collectivity [ˌkɒlek'tɪvɪtɪ] *n Econ* collectivité *f*

collectivization [kəˌlektɪvaɪ'zeɪʃən] *n Econ* collectivisation *f*

collectivize, -ise [kə'lektɪvaɪz] *vt Econ* collectiviser

collector [kə'lektə(r)] *n* (**a**) *(as a hobby)* collectionneur(euse) *m,f* (**b**) *(of money)* encaisseur *m*; *(for charity)* quêteur(euse) *m,f*; *(of taxes)* percepteur *m*; *(of debts)* receveur *m* (**c**) *Tech (for oil, steam)* collecteur *m*; *(of overflow)* récepteur *m*

►► ***collector's item, collector's piece*** pièce *f* de collection, collector *m*

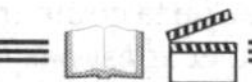

'The Collector' *Fowles, Wyler* 'Le Collectionneur'

collectorship [kə'lektəʃɪp] *n (referring to tax collector)* fonctions *fpl* de percepteur; *(referring to debt collector)* fonctions *fpl* de receveur

colleen ['kɒliːn, kɒ'liːn] *n Ir* jeune fille *f*; *(Irish girl)* jeune Irlandaise *f*

college ['kɒlɪdʒ] *n* (**a**) *Br (institution of higher education)* établissement *m* d'enseignement supérieur; **I go to college** je suis étudiant; **when you were at college** ≃ quand tu étais à l'université; *Am* **to be college bound** se destiner aux études supérieures; **college of agriculture** ≃ lycée *m* agricole; **college of art** école *f* des beaux-arts; **college of music** conservatoire *m* de musique; **a college chum** un (une) copain (copine) de fac; **college days** années *fpl* de fac

(**b**) *Br (within university)* collège *m (dans les universités traditionnelles, communauté d'enseignants et d'étudiants disposant d'une semi-autonomie administrative)*

(**c**) *(for professional training)* école *f* professionnelle, collège *m* technique

(**d**) *(organization)* société *f*, académie *f*; **the Royal College of Physicians/Surgeons** ≃ l'Académie *f* de médecine/de chirurgie

►► *Br* ***College of Advanced Technology*** ≃ institut *m* universitaire de technologie, IUT *m*; ***the College of Arms*** = organisation statuant sur les armoiries en Grande-Bretagne; ***the College of Cardinals*** le Sacré Collège; *Am* ***college degree*** diplôme *m* universitaire; ***college education*** études *fpl* supérieures; *Br* ***College of Education*** ≃ institut *m* de formation des maîtres; *Am Univ* ***College Entry Examination Board*** = commission d'admission dans l'enseignement supérieur aux États-Unis; *Br* ***College of Further Education*** ≃ institut *m* d'éducation permanente; ***the College of Heralds*** = organisation statuant sur les armoiries en Grande-Bretagne; ***college student*** étudiant(e) *m,f*

collegiate [kə'liːdʒɪət] *adj (life)* universitaire; *(university)* composé de collèges semi-autonomes

►► *Rel* ***collegiate church*** collégiale *f*; *Can* ***Collegiate Institute*** école *f* secondaire

Colles' fracture ['kɒlɪs-] *n Med* fracture *f* de Pouteau-Colles

collide [kə'laɪd] *vi* (**a**) *(crash)* entrer en collision, se heurter; **to collide with** *(of vehicle)* heurter, tamponner, entrer en collision avec; **to collide with sb** *(of person)* se heurter à *ou* contre qn; **the bus collided with the lorry** le bus est entré en collision avec *ou* a heurté le camion

(**b**) *Fig (clash)* entrer en conflit, se heurter; **I can see that we are going to collide on this issue** je sens qu'on va être en désaccord sur cette question; **the two countries have collided over the issue of human rights** les deux pays se sont heurtés sur la question des droits de l'homme

collie ['kɒlɪ] *n (dog)* colley *m*

collier ['kɒlɪə(r)] *n Br* (**a**) *Mining* mineur *m* (**b**) *Naut* charbonnier *m*

colliery ['kɒljərɪ] (*pl* **collieries**) *n Br Mining* houillère *f*, mine *f* (de charbon)

colligative [ˌkə'lɪgətɪv] *adj Biol & Chem* colligatif

collimate ['kɒlɪmeɪt] *vt* (**a**) *(make parallel)* rendre parallèle (**b**) *Opt (adjust line of sight of)* collimater

collimator ['kɒlɪmeɪtə(r)] *n Phys* collimateur *m*

►► *Phot* ***collimator viewfinder*** viseur *m* à cadre lumineux

collinear [ˌkəʊ'lɪnɪə(r)] *adj Math* colinéaire

collinearity [kəʊˌlɪnɪ'ærɪtɪ] *n Math* colinéarité *f*

collision [kə'lɪʒən] *n* (**a**) *(crash)* collision *f*, choc *m*; *Rail* collision *f*, tamponnement *m*; **to come into collision with sth** entrer en collision avec *ou* tamponner qch; *Naut* **to be on a collision course** être sur un cap de collision; **the two planes were on a collision course** les deux avions risquaient d'entrer en collision; *Fig* **the government is on a collision course with the unions** le gouvernement va au-devant d'un conflit avec les syndicats

(**b**) *Fig (clash)* conflit *m*, opposition *f*; **a collision of interests** un conflit d'intérêts

(**c**) *Phys (of particles)* choc *m*, collision *f*

►► *Ins* ***collision damage waiver*** = suppression de franchise pour les dommages causés aux véhicules

collocate *Ling* **1** *vi* ['kɒləkeɪt] être cooccurrent; **to collocate with sth** être cooccurrent de qch

2 *n* ['kɒləkət] cooccurrent *m*

collocation [ˌkɒlə'keɪʃən] *n Ling* cooccurrence *f*, collocation *f*

collocutor [kə'lɒkjʊtə(r)] *n Formal* interlocuteur(trice) *m,f*

collodion [kə'ləʊdɪən] *n Med & Phot* collodion *m*

collodion-coated *adj Phot* colloïdin

colloid ['kɒlɔɪd] *Chem* **1** *adj* colloïdal

2 *n* colloïde *m*

colloidal [kə'lɔɪdəl] *adj Chem* colloïdal

colloquia [kə'ləʊkwɪə] *pl of* **colloquium**

colloquial [kə'ləʊkwɪəl] *adj Ling (language, expression)* familier, parlé; *(style)* familier

colloquialism [kə'ləʊkwɪəˌlɪzəm] *n Ling* expression *f* familière

colloquially [kə'ləʊkwɪəlɪ] *adv Ling* familièrement, dans la langue parlée; **known colloquially as…** communément appelé…

colloquist ['kɒləkwɪst] *n Formal* interlocuteur(-trice) *m,f*

colloquium [kə'ləʊkwɪəm] (*pl* **colloquiums** *or* **colloquia** [-kwɪə]) *n* colloque *m*

colloquy ['kɒləkwɪ] (*pl* **colloquies**) *n Formal (conversation)* colloque *m*, conversation *f*; *(meeting)* colloque *m*

collude [kə'luːd] *vi* être de connivence *ou* de mèche (**with sb** avec qn); **to collude with sb in sth** être de connivence avec qn dans *ou* pour qch; **they accused the oil companies of colluding to raise prices** ils ont accusé les compagnies pétrolières de s'entendre pour augmenter les prix

collusion [kə'luːʒən] *n* collusion *f*; **to act in collusion with sb** agir de connivence avec qn;

to do sth in collusion with sb faire qch de connivence avec qn; **to be in collusion with sb** être d'intelligence *ou* de connivence avec qn

collusive [kə'lu:sɪv] *adj (agreement)* collusoire; **a collusive relationship between the police and paramilitary groups** une collusion entre la police et des groupes paramilitaires; **their collusive behaviour finally aroused suspicion** leur air conspirateur a fini par les rendre suspects

►► *Com* ***collusive bidding*** offre *f* collusoire

collusively [kə'lu:sɪvlɪ] *adv* **to smile at sb collusively** faire un sourire de connivence à qn

collywobbles ['kɒlɪˌwɒbəlz] *npl Br Fam (stomach ache)* mal *m* au ventre; *(nervousness)* trouille *f*; **I always get the collywobbles before an exam** j'ai toujours la trouille avant un examen

Colo *(written abbr* **Colorado***)* Colorado *m*

colobus ['kɒləbəs] *n Zool* **colobus (monkey)** colobe *m*

co-location *n Comput & Tel* colocalisation *f*

Cologne [kə'ləʊn] *n* Cologne

cologne [kə'ləʊn] *n* eau *f* de Cologne

Colombia [kə'lɒmbɪə] *n* Colombie *f*; **in Colombia** en Colombie

Colombian [kə'lɒmbɪən] **1** *n* Colombien(enne) *m,f*

2 *adj* colombien

3 *comp (embassy)* de Colombie; *(history)* de la Colombie

Colombo [kə'lʌmbəʊ] *n* Colombo

colon ['kəʊlən] *n* **(a)** *(in punctuation)* deux-points *m inv* **(b)** *Anat* côlon *m*

colonel ['kɜ:nəl] *n Mil* colonel *m*; **Colonel Jones** le colonel Jones

►► ***Colonel Blimp*** vieux réac *m*; ***Colonel Bogey*** = titre d'une célèbre marche militaire

COLONEL BLIMP

"Colonel Blimp" est un personnage de vieil officier, réfractaire à tout ce qui est nouveau, créé par le dessinateur britannique David Low; on utilise ce nom, parfois réduit à "Blimp", pour désigner une personne ayant ce même trait de caractère.

colonelcy ['kɜ:nəlsɪ] *n Mil* grade *m* de colonel

colonel-in-chief *n Br Mil* = titre honorifique souvent décerné à un membre de la famille royale britannique

colonelship ['kɜ:nəlʃɪp] *n Mil* grade *m* de colonel

colonial [kə'ləʊnɪəl] **1** *adj* **(a)** *(power, life)* colonial; *Pej (attitude)* colonialiste; **colonial days** époque *f* coloniale **(b)** *Archit* de style colonial; *(in America)* de style colonial *(du XVIIIème siècle)* **(c)** *(animals, insects)* qui vit en colonie

2 *n* colonial(e) *m,f*

►► *Br* ***the Colonial Office*** le ministère des Colonies

colonialism [kə'ləʊnɪəlɪzəm] *n* colonialisme *m*

colonialist [kə'ləʊnɪəlɪst] **1** *adj* colonialiste

2 *n* colonialiste *mf*

colonic [kə'lɒnɪk] *Med* **1** *adj* du côlon

2 *n* lavement *m*

►► ***colonic irrigation*** lavement *m*

colonist ['kɒlənɪst] *n* colon *m*

colonization [ˌkɒlənaɪ'zeɪʃən] *n* colonisation *f*

colonize, -ise ['kɒlənaɪz] *vt* coloniser

colonizer ['kɒlənaɪzə(r)] *n* colonisateur(trice) *m,f*

colonnade [ˌkɒlə'neɪd] *n Archit* colonnade *f*

colonoscopy [ˌkɒlən'ɒskəpɪ] *n Med* coloscopie *f*

colony ['kɒlənɪ] *(pl* **colonies***) n (of people, animals, plants, bacteria)* colonie *f*; **to live in the colonies** vivre aux colonies; *Hist* **the Colonies** les Colonies *fpl*; **the English colony in Paris** la colonie anglaise de Paris

colophon ['kɒləfən] *n* **(a)** *(logo)* logo *m*, colophon *m* **(b)** *(end text in book)* achevé *m* d'imprimer; *(end text in manuscript)* colophon *m*

color, colored *etc Am* = **colour, coloured** *etc*

Colorado [ˌkɒlə'rɑ:dəʊ] *n (state, river)* le Colorado; **in Colorado** au Colorado

►► *Entom* ***Colorado beetle*** doryphore *m*, *Can* bête *f* à patates; ***the Colorado River*** le Colorado

colorant ['kʌlərənt] *n* colorant *m*

coloration [ˌkʌlə'reɪʃən] *n (colouring)* coloration *f*; *(choice of colours)* coloris *m*

coloratura [ˌkɒlərə'tʊərə] *n Mus* colorature *f*

►► ***coloratura aria*** air *m* de colorature; ***coloratura soprano*** (soprano *f*) colorature *f*

colossal [kə'lɒsəl] *adj* colossal

Colosseum [ˌkɒlə'sɪəm] *n* Colisée *m*

Colossian [kə'lɒʃən] *n Bible* **the Epistle of Paul to the Colossians** l'Épître de saint Paul aux Colossiens

colossus [kə'lɒsəs] *(pl* **colossuses** *or* **colossi** [-saɪ]*) n* colosse *m*

►► ***the Colossus of Rhodes*** le colosse de Rhodes

colostomy [kə'lɒstəmɪ] *(pl* **colostomies***) n Med* colostomie *f*; **to have a colostomy** subir une colostomie

►► ***colostomy bag*** poche *f*

colour, *Am* **color** ['kʌlə(r)] **1** *n* **(a)** *(hue)* couleur *f*; **what colour is it?** de quelle couleur est-ce?; **what colour are his eyes?** de quelle couleur sont ses yeux?; **a dark grey colour** une couleur gris foncé; **it's a sort of greenish colour** c'est d'une couleur un peu verdâtre; **the bleach took the colour out of it** l'eau de Javel l'a décoloré; **the movie is in colour** le film est en couleur *ou* couleurs; **he painted the room in bright/dark colours** il a peint la pièce de couleurs vives/sombres; **the paint comes in a wide range of colours** cette peinture est disponible dans un grand choix de couleurs *ou* se décline dans de nombreuses couleurs; *Fam* **we've yet to see the colour of his money** nous n'avons pas encore vu la couleur de son argent

(b) *Fig* **the political colour of a newspaper** la couleur politique d'un journal; **under the colour of patriotism** sous prétexte *ou* couleur de patriotisme

(c) *Art (shade)* coloris *m*, ton *m*; *(paint)* peinture *f*; *(dye)* teinture *f*, matière *f* colorante; **box of colours** boîte *f* de couleurs

(d) *(pigment)* matière *f* colorante, couleur *f*

(e) *(complexion)* teint *m*, couleur *f (du visage)*; **her colour isn't good** elle a mauvaise mine; **he changed colour** il a changé de couleur *ou* de visage; **to lose one's colour** pâlir, perdre ses couleurs; **to get one's colour back** reprendre des couleurs; **she had a lot of colour in her cheeks** ses joues avaient de belles couleurs; **to have a high colour** avoir le visage rouge; *Br* **to be off colour** ne pas être dans son assiette; *Fig* **the joke was a bit off colour** la plaisanterie était d'un goût douteux

(f) *(race)* couleur *f*; **to discriminate against sb on grounds of colour** établir une discrimination à l'encontre de qn à cause de la couleur de sa peau; **colour isn't an issue** ce n'est pas une question de couleur (de peau); **person of colour** personne *f* de couleur

(g) *(interest)* couleur *f*; **to add colour to a story** colorer un récit; **a play full of colour** une pièce haute en couleur

2 *comp (photography, picture, slide, magazine)* en couleur, en couleurs

3 *vt* **(a)** *(give colour to → with chemical, dye)* colorer; *(→ with paint)* peindre; *(→ with crayons, felt-tips)* colorier; **he coloured it blue** il l'a colorié en bleu; **to colour one's hair** se faire une couleur

(b) *(distort → judgement)* fausser; *(→ fact)* influencer

(c) *(exaggerate → story, facts)* exagérer; *(enliven)* rendre plus vivant

4 *vi (person)* rougir; *(thing)* se colorer; *(fruit)* mûrir

5 colours *npl* **(a)** *(of team)* couleurs *fpl*; **to get** *or* **to win one's colours** être sélectionné pour faire partie d'une équipe; *Fig* **to show one's true colours** se montrer sous son vrai jour; **to see sb in his/her true colours** voir qn sous son vrai jour

(b) *(of school)* couleurs *fpl*

(c) *Mil (flag)* couleurs *fpl*, drapeau *m*; *Naut* couleurs *fpl*, pavillon *m*; **to serve with the colours** servir sous les drapeaux; **to be called to the colours** être appelé sous les drapeaux; **salute the colours!** saluez le drapeau *ou* les couleurs!; **to sail under false colours** naviguer sous un faux pavillon

(d) *(clothes for washing)* couleurs *fpl*

►► *Phot* ***colour balance*** équilibre *m* des couleurs; *Br* ***colour bar*** discrimination *f* raciale; ***colour bearer*** porte-drapeau *m*; ***colour blindness*** daltonisme *m*; ***colour chart*** nuancier *m*; ***colour code*** code *m* coloré; *Comput* ***colour display*** affichage *m* couleur; ***colour film*** *(for camera)* pellicule *f* (en) couleur; *(movie)* film *m* en couleur; *Phot* ***colour filter*** filtre *m* coloré; *Comput* ***colour graphics*** graphisme *m* en couleur; *Phot* ***colour graphics adapter*** adaptateur *m* graphique couleur, CGA *m*; ***colour line*** discrimination *f ou* ségrégation *f* raciale; **to cross the colour line** faire fi de la ségrégation raciale; *Comput* ***colour monitor*** moniteur *m* couleur; *Mil* ***colour party*** garde *f* du drapeau; ***colour photocopying*** photocopie *f* en couleurs; *Typ & Phot* ***colour positive*** positif *m* (en) couleur; *Typ* ***colour print*** reproduction *f* en couleurs; *Typ* ***colour printer*** imprimante *f* couleur; *Typ* ***colour printing*** impression *f* couleur; ***colour scheme*** palette *f ou* combinaison *f* de couleurs; **to choose a colour scheme** assortir les couleurs *ou* les tons; *Typ* ***colour separation*** séparation *f* des couleurs, séparation *f* quadrichromique; *Br Mil* ***colour sergeant*** ≃ sergent-chef *m (de la garde du drapeau)*; *Br Press* ***colour supplement*** supplément *m* illustré; ***colour television*** télévision *f* couleur; ***colour television set*** téléviseur *m* couleur; ***colour therapy*** chromothérapie *f*; *Art* ***colour value*** valeur *f* chromatique

►**colour in,** *Am* **color in** *vt sep* colorier; **colour it in in blue** colorie-le en bleu

►**colour up,** *Am* **color up** *vi (blush)* rougir

'The Color Purple' *Walker, Spielberg* 'La Couleur pourpre'

colour-blind, *Am* **color-blind** *adj* daltonien

colour-code, *Am* **color-code** *vt* **to colour-code sth** coder qch avec des couleurs

colour-coded, *Am* **color-coded** *adj* dont la couleur correspond à un code; **the wires are colour-coded** la couleur des fils correspond à un code

colour-coding, *Am* **color-coding** *n* système *m* de classement par couleurs; **what's their colour-coding?** de quelle couleur sont-elles dans le classement?

coloured, *Am* **colored** ['kʌləd] **1** *adj* **(a)** *(having colour)* coloré; *(drawing)* colorié; *(pencils)* de couleur **(b)** *(person → gen)* de couleur; *(→ in South Africa)* métis

2 coloureds *npl* **(a)** *(clothes for washing)* couleurs *fpl* **(b)** *(people → gen)* gens *mpl* de couleur; *(→ in South Africa)* métis *mpl*

-coloured, *Am* **-colored** ['kʌləd] *suff* **rust-coloured** couleur *f* de rouille; **dark-coloured** foncé; **light-coloured** clair; **brightly-coloured** aux couleurs *fpl* vives

colourfast, *Am* **colorfast** ['kʌləfɑ:st] *adj* grand teint, qui ne déteint pas

colourful, *Am* **colorful** ['kʌləfʊl] *adj* **(a)** *(brightly coloured)* coloré, vif **(b)** *Fig (person)* original, pittoresque; *(story)* coloré; **a colourful character** un original; **colourful language** langage *m* coloré

colourfully, *Am* **colorfully** ['kʌləfʊlɪ] *adv* **a colourfully dressed woman** une femme vêtue de couleurs vives; **colourfully portrayed characters** des personnages décrits de façon pittoresque

colouring, *Am* **coloring** ['kʌlərɪŋ] *n* **(a)** *(act)* coloration *f*; *(of drawing)* coloriage *m*; **go and do some colouring** *(to child)* va faire du coloriage **(b)** *(hue)* coloration *f*, coloris *m* **(c)** *(complexion)* teint *m*; **high colouring** teint *m* coloré; **fair/dark colouring** teint *m* clair/mat **(d)** *Fig (exaggeration)* travestissement *m*, dénaturation *f* **(e)** *(for food)* colorant *m*

►► ***colouring book*** album *m* à colorier

colouring-in, *Am* **coloring-in** *n* coloriage *m*

►► ***colouring-in book*** album *m* à colorier

colourist, *Am* **colorist** ['kʌlərɪst] *n Art* coloriste *mf*

colourization, *Am* **colorization** [ˌkʌləraɪ'zeɪʃən] *n Cin* colorisation *f*

colourize, -ise, *Am* **colorize** ['kʌləraɪz] *vt Cin* coloriser

colourless, *Am* **colorless** ['kʌləlɪs] *adj* **(a)** *(clear)* sans couleur, incolore **(b)** *(pale)* terne, incolore; *(face)* blême; *(complexion)* pâle, délavé; *(light)* pâle, falot **(c)** *Fig (style)* sans intérêt, fade; *(voice)* terne; *(person)* insignifiant, falot

colourlessness, *Am* **colorlessness** ['kʌləlɪsnɪs] *n* (**a**) *(paleness, transparency)* absence *f* de couleur; *(of complexion)* pâleur *f* (**b**) *Fig (of style)* fadeur *f*; *(of person)* manque *m* de personnalité

colourwash, *Am* **colorwash** ['kʌləwɒʃ] *Art* **1** *n* badigeon *m*

2 *vt* badigeonner

colourway, *Am* **colorway** ['kʌləweɪ] *n* coloris *m*

colposcope ['kɒlpəskəʊp] *n Med* colposcope *m*

colposcopy ['kɒlpə,skəʊpɪ] *n Med* colposcopie *f*

Colt® [kəʊlt] *n (revolver)* colt *m*, pistolet *m* (automatique)

colt [kəʊlt] *n* (**a**) *(horse)* poulain *m* (**b**) *Fig (young person)* petit jeune *m*; *(inexperienced person)* novice *m*

coltish ['kəʊltɪʃ] *adj (gait, figure)* dégingandé; *(movement)* gauche

coltishly ['kəʊltɪʃlɪ] *adv* gauchement

coltsfoot ['kəʊltsfʊt] *n Bot* pas-d'âne *m inv*, tussilage *m*

colugo [kɒ'lu:gəʊ] *n Zool* galéopithèque *m*, lémur *m* volant

Columba [kə'lʌmbə] *n Astron* la Colombe

columbarium [,kɒləm'beərɪəm] *(pl* **columbaria** [-rɪə]) *n* (**a**) *(vault for funeral urns)* columbarium *m* (**b**) *(dovecote)* colombier *m*, pigeonnier *m*

Columbia [kə'lʌmbɪə] *n* **the District of Columbia** le district fédéral de Columbia

►► ***Columbia Broadcasting System*** = chaîne de télévision américaine; ***the Columbia River*** la Columbia; ***Columbia University*** = université de la ville de New York, célèbre pour son école de journalisme

columbine ['kɒləm,baɪn] *n Bot* ancolie *f*

Columbus [kə'lʌmbəs] *pr n* **Christopher Columbus** Christophe Colomb

►► ***Columbus Day*** = aux États-Unis, jour commémorant l'arrivée de Christophe Colomb en Amérique (deuxième lundi d'octobre)

column ['kɒləm] *n* (**a**) *(gen) & Archit* colonne *f*

(**b**) *Press (section of print)* colonne *f*; *(regular article)* rubrique *f*; **he writes the sports column** il tient la rubrique des sports

(**c**) *Comput & Typ* colonne *f*

(**d**) *Mil & Naut (formation)* colonne *f*; **to march in column/in two columns** marcher en colonne/en deux colonnes; **supply/relief column** colonne *f* de ravitaillement/de secours

►► *Aut* ***column change*** levier *m* de vitesses sur colonne de direction; *Comput & Typ* ***column graph*** histogramme *m*; *Comput & Typ* ***column header*** en-tête *m* de colonnes; *Press* ***column inch*** = unité de mesure des espaces publicitaires équivalant à une colonne sur un pouce, ≃ centimètre-colonne *m*; **it got a lot of column inches** *(story)* on y a consacré beaucoup d'espace dans le journal; ***column mode*** mode *m* colonne; *Comput & Typ* ***column printing*** impression *f* en colonnes; ***column space*** colonnage *m*; *Comput & Typ* ***column spacing*** espacement *m* des colonnes

columnar [kə'lʌmnə(r)] *adj* colomnaire, en forme de colonne

columned ['kɒləmd] *adj Archit* à colonnes

columnist ['kɒləmnɪst] *n Press & Journ* chroniqueur(euse) *m,f*, échotier(ère) *m,f*; **sports columnist** chroniqueur(euse) *m,f* sportif(ive)

colza ['kɒlzə] *n Bot & Culin* colza *m*

►► ***colza oil*** huile *f* de colza

.com *Comput* = abréviation désignant les entreprises commerciales dans les adresses électroniques

coma¹ ['kəʊmə] *n Med* coma *m*; **in a coma** dans le coma

coma² *n* (**a**) *Bot* barbe *f* (**b**) *Astron* chevelure *f* (**c**) *Opt* coma *f*, comète *f*

Coma Berenices [,kəʊmə,berə'naɪsi:z] *n Astron* la chevelure de Bérénice

co-management *n* cogérance *f*

Comanche [kə'mæntʃɪ] *(pl* **inv** *or* **Comanches**) *n* (**a**) *(person)* Comanche *mf*; **the Comanche** les Comanches (**b**) *(language)* comanche *m*

comatose ['kəʊmətəʊs] *adj Med* comateux; **to be comatose** être dans le coma; *Fam (fast asleep)* en écraser; *(drunk)* être ivre mort ❑

comb [kəʊm] **1** *n* (**a**) *(for hair)* peigne *m*; *(large-toothed)* démêloir *m*; **to run a comb through one's hair, to give one's hair a comb** se donner un coup de peigne, se peigner

(**b**) *(for horses)* étrille *f*

(**c**) *Tex (for cotton, wool)* peigne *m*, carde *f*; *Elec* balai *m*

(**d**) *(of fowl)* crête *f*; *(on helmet)* cimier *m*

(**e**) *(honeycomb)* rayon *m* de miel

2 *vt* (**a**) *(hair)* peigner; **he combed his hair** il s'est peigné; **I combed the girl's hair** j'ai peigné la fille

(**b**) *(horse)* étriller

(**c**) *Tex (cotton, wool)* peigner, carder; **combed cotton** coton *m* peigné

(**d**) *Fig (search)* fouiller, ratisser; **the police combed the area for clues** la police a passé le quartier au peigne fin *ou* a ratissé le quartier à la recherche d'indices; **she combed the book for references to the crisis** elle a passé le livre au peigne fin *ou* au crible pour trouver des références à la crise

►**comb out** *vt sep* (**a**) *(hair)* peigner; *(untangle)* démêler

(**b**) *Tex (cotton, wool)* peigner

(**c**) *(fleas)* retirer avec un peigne

(**d**) *Fig (remove)* éliminer

combat ['kɒmbæt] *(pt & pp* **combated,** *cont* **combating**) *Mil* **1** *n* combat *m*; **killed/lost in combat** tué/perdu au combat; **women are now used in a combat role** on envoie maintenant les femmes dans des situations de combat

2 *comp (troops, mission)* de combat

3 *vt* combattre, lutter contre

4 *vi* combattre, lutter; **the need to combat against racism** la nécessité de lutter contre le racisme

►► ***combat dress*** tenue *f* de combat; ***combat duty*** service *m* commandé; **on combat duty** en service commandé; *Psy* ***combat fatigue*** psychose *f* traumatique, syndrome *m* commotionnel; ***combat gear*** tenue *f* de combat; ***combat jacket*** veste *f* de treillis; ***combat trousers*** battledress *m*, pantalon *m* multi-poches; ***combat zone*** zone *f* de combat

combatant ['kɒmbətənt] *Mil* **1** *n* combattant(e) *m,f*

2 *adj* combattant

combative ['kɒmbətɪv] *adj* combatif

combatively ['kɒmbətɪvlɪ] *adv* de manière combative

combativeness ['kɒmbətɪvnɪs], **combativity** [,kɒmbə'tɪvɪtɪ] *n* combativité *f*

combe = **coomb**

comber ['kəʊmə(r)] *n* (**a**) *Tex (person)* peigneur(euse) *m,f*; *(machine)* peigneuse *f* (**b**) *(wave)* grande vague *f*

combi ['kɒmbɪ] *n Austr Fam* **combi (van)** camping-car ❑ *m*

combination [,kɒmbɪ'neɪʃən] **1** *n* (**a**) *(gen) & Chem & Math* combinaison *f*; *(of circumstances)* concours *m*; **nitrogen in combination with oxygen** l'azote combiné avec l'oxygène; **an attractive colour combination** une combinaison de couleurs attrayante; **an interesting combination of flavours** un mélange intéressant de parfums

(**b**) *(of lock)* combinaison *f*

(**c**) *(association, team)* association *f*, coalition *f*; **together they formed a winning combination** ensemble ils formaient une équipe gagnante

(**d**) *Br Aut* side-car *m*

2 combinations *npl Br Old-fashioned (under-clothing)* combinaison-culotte *f*

►► ***combination lock*** serrure *f* à combinaison; *Am Culin* ***combination sandwich*** = très gros sandwich contenant au minimum cinq ingrédients; ***combination skin*** peau *f* mixte; *Tech* ***combination spanner*** clé *f* mixte; *Med* ***combination therapy*** trithérapie *f*

combinative ['kɒmbɪnətɪv], **combinatory** [kɒmbɪ'neɪtərɪ] *adj* combinatoire

combine 1 *vt* [kəm'baɪn] *(gen)* combiner, joindre; *Chem* combiner; **to combine work and studying** combiner le travail et les études; **let's combine forces** unissons *ou* joignons nos forces; **to combine business and** *or* **with pleasure** joindre l'utile à l'agréable; **the event was organized by all the groups combined** la réunion a été organisée par tous les groupes réunis; **this, combined with her other problems, made her ill** ceci, conjugué à ses autres problèmes, l'a rendue malade; **this furniture combines comfort with style** ces meubles allient confort et style

2 *vi* [kəm'baɪn] *(unite)* s'unir, s'associer; *(workers)* se syndiquer; *Pol (parties)* fusionner; *Chem* se combiner; **events combined to leave her penniless** les événements ont concouru à la laisser sans le sou

3 *n* ['kɒmbaɪn] (**a**) *(association)* association *f*; *Fin* trust *m*, cartel *m*; *Law* corporation *f* (**b**) *Agr* moissonneuse-batteuse *f*

►► *Agr* ***combine harvester*** moissonneuse-batteuse *f*

combined [kəm'baɪnd] *adj* combiné, conjugué; **the combined sound of a pneumatic drill and the traffic** le bruit d'un marteau piqueur ajouté à celui de la circulation; **a combined effort** un effort conjugué; **combined operation** *(by several nations)* opération *f* alliée; *(by forces of one nation)* opération *f* interarmées

►► *Naut* ***combined fleets*** flottes *fpl* combinées; *Mil* ***combined forces*** forces *fpl* alliées; *Com* ***combined transport bill of lading*** connaissement *m* de transport combiné; ***combined transport company*** entrepreneur *m* de transport combiné, ETC *m*

combining form [kəm'baɪnɪŋ-] *n Ling* affixe *m*

combo ['kɒmbəʊ] *(pl* **combos**) *n* (**a**) *Mus* combo *m* (**b**) *Fam (combination)* combinaison ❑ *f*; *(mixture)* mélange ❑ *m*

combust [kəm'bʌst] *vi* brûler

combustible [kəm'bʌstəbəl] **1** *adj* combustible

2 *n* matière *f* inflammable; *(fuel)* combustible *m*

combustion [kəm'bʌstʃən] *n* combustion *f*

►► ***combustion chamber*** chambre *f* de combustion; ***combustion engine*** moteur *m* à combustion; ***combustion gases*** gaz *mpl* de combustion

COME [kʌm]

venir	► **1 (a) – (d)**
se produire	► **1 (e)**
exister	► **1 (h)**
devenir	► **1 (i)**
en venir à	► **1 (j)**

(pt **came** [keɪm], *pp* **come** [kʌm]) **1** *vi* (**a**) *(move in direction of speaker)* venir; **she won't come when she's called** elle ne vient pas quand on l'appelle; **here come the children** voici les enfants qui arrivent; **here he comes!** le voilà qui arrive!; **it's stuck – ah, no, it's coming!** c'est coincé – ah, non, ça vient!; **coming!** j'arrive!; **come here!** venez ici!; *(to dog)* au pied!; **come to the office tomorrow** passez *ou* venez au bureau demain; **he came to me for advice** il est venu me demander conseil; **you've come to the wrong person** vous vous adressez à la mauvaise personne; **you've come to the wrong place** vous vous êtes trompé de chemin, vous faites fausse route; **if you're looking for sun, you've come to the wrong place** si c'est le soleil que vous cherchez, il ne fallait pas venir ici; **come with me** *(accompany)* venez avec moi, accompagnez-moi; *(follow)* suivez-moi; **please come this way** par ici *ou* suivez-moi s'il vous plaît; **I come this way every week** je passe par ici toutes les semaines; *Am* **come and look, come look** venez voir; *Fam* **come and get it!** à la soupe!; **he came whistling up the stairs** il a monté l'escalier en sifflant; **a car came hurtling round the corner** une voiture a pris le virage à toute vitesse; **to come and go** *(gen)* aller et venir; *Fig (pains, cramps etc)* être intermittent; **people are constantly coming and going** il y a un va-et-vient continuel; **fashions come and go** la mode change tout le temps; **after many years had come and gone** après bien des années; *Fam* **I don't know whether I'm coming or going** je ne sais pas où j'en suis; **you have come a long way** vous êtes venu de loin; *Fig (made progress)* vous avez fait du chemin; **the computer industry has come a very long way since then** l'informatique a fait énormément de progrès depuis ce temps-là; *also Fig* **to come running** arriver en courant; **we could see him coming a mile off** on l'a vu venir avec ses gros sabots; *Fig* **you could see it coming** on l'a vu venir de loin, c'était prévisible; *Prov* **everything comes to him who waits** tout vient à point à qui sait attendre

(**b**) *(as guest, visitor)* venir; **can you come to**

my party on Saturday night? est-ce que tu peux venir à ma soirée samedi?; **I'm sorry, I can't come** (je suis) désolé, je ne peux pas venir; **would you like to come for lunch/dinner?** voulez-vous venir déjeuner/dîner?; **I can only come for an hour or so** je ne pourrai venir que pour une heure environ; **come for a ride in the car** viens faire un tour en voiture; **she's come for her money** elle est venue prendre son argent; **I've got people coming** *(short stay)* j'ai des invités; *(long stay)* il y a des gens qui viennent; **Angela came and we had a chat** Angela est venue et on a bavardé; **they came for a week and stayed a month** ils sont venus pour une semaine et ils sont restés un mois; **he couldn't have come at a worse time** il n'aurait pas pu tomber plus mal

(**c**) *(arrive)* venir, arriver; **to come in time/late** arriver à temps/en retard; **I've just come from the post office** j'arrive de la poste à l'instant; **we came to a small town** nous sommes arrivés dans une petite ville; **the time has come to tell the truth** le moment est venu de dire la vérité; **to come to the end of sth** arriver à la fin de qch; **I was coming to the end of my stay** mon séjour touchait à sa fin; **there will come a point when...** il viendra un moment où...; **when you come to the last coat of paint...** quand tu en seras à la dernière couche de peinture...; *(reach)* **her hair comes (down) to her waist** ses cheveux lui arrivent à la taille; **the mud came (up) to our knees** la boue nous arrivait *ou* venait (jusqu') aux genoux

(**d**) *(occupy specific place, position)* venir, se trouver; **the address comes above the date** l'adresse se met au-dessus de la date; **my birthday comes before yours** mon anniversaire vient avant *ou* précède le tien; **a colonel comes before a lieutenant** un colonel a la préséance sur un lieutenant; **Friday comes after Thursday** vendredi vient après *ou* suit jeudi; **that speech comes in Act 3/on page 10** on trouve ce discours dans l'acte 3/à la page 10; **the fireworks come next** le feu d'artifice est après; **what comes after the performance?** qu'est-ce qu'il y a après la représentation?

(**e**) *(occur, happen)* arriver, se produire; **when my turn comes, when it comes to my turn** quand ce sera (à) mon tour, quand mon tour viendra; **such an opportunity only comes once in your life** une telle occasion ne se présente qu'une fois dans la vie; **he has a birthday coming** son anniversaire approche; **there's a storm coming** un orage se prépare; **success was a long time coming** la réussite s'est fait attendre; **take life as it comes** prenez la vie comme elle vient; **Christmas comes but once a year** il n'y a qu'un Noël par an; *Bible* **it came to pass that...** il advint que...; **come what may** advienne que pourra, quoi qu'il arrive *ou* advienne

(**f**) *(occur to the mind)* **the idea just came to me one day** l'idée m'est soudain venue un jour; **suddenly it came to me** *(I remembered)* tout d'un coup, je m'en suis souvenu; *(I had an idea)* tout d'un coup, j'ai eu une idée; **I said the first thing that came into my head** *or* **that came to mind** j'ai dit la première chose qui m'est venue à l'esprit; **the answer came to her** elle a trouvé la réponse

(**g**) *(be experienced in a specified way)* **writing comes naturally to her** écrire lui est facile, elle est douée pour l'écriture; **a house doesn't come cheap** une maison coûte *ou* revient cher; **the news came as a shock to her** la nouvelle lui a fait un choc; **her visit came as a surprise** sa visite nous a beaucoup surpris; **it comes as no surprise to learn he's gone** (le fait) qu'il soit parti n'a rien de surprenant; **he's as silly as they come** il est sot comme pas un; **they don't come any tougher than Big Al** on ne fait pas plus fort que Big Al; **it'll all come right in the end** tout cela va finir par s'arranger; **the harder they come the harder they fall** plus dure sera la chute

(**h**) *(be available)* exister; **this table comes in two sizes** cette table existe *ou* se fait en deux dimensions; **the dictionary comes with a magnifying glass** le dictionnaire est livré avec une loupe

(**i**) *(become)* devenir; **it was a dream come true** c'était un rêve devenu réalité; **to come unhooked** se décrocher; **to come unravelled** se défaire; **the buttons on my coat keep coming undone** mon manteau se déboutonne toujours

(**j**) *(+ infinitive) (indicating gradual action)* en venir à, finir par; *(indicating chance)* arriver; **she came to trust him** elle en est venue à *ou* elle a fini par lui faire confiance; **we have come to expect this kind of thing** nous nous attendons à ce genre de chose maintenant; **how did you come to lose your umbrella?** comment as-tu fait pour perdre ton parapluie?; **how did the door come to be open?** comment se fait-il que la porte soit ouverte?; **(now that I) come to think of it** maintenant que j'y songe, réflexion faite; **it's not much money when you come to think of it** ce n'est pas beaucoup d'argent quand vous y réfléchissez

(**k**) *(be owing, payable)* **I still have £5 coming (to me)** on me doit encore 5 livres; **there'll be money coming from her uncle's will** elle va toucher l'argent du testament de son oncle; **he got all the credit coming to him** il a eu tous les honneurs qu'il méritait; *Fam* **you'll get what's coming to you** tu l'auras cherché *ou* voulu; *Fam* **he had it coming (to him)** il ne l'a pas volé

(**l**) *(appear)* **a smile came to her lips** un sourire parut sur ses lèvres *ou* lui vint aux lèvres

(**m**) *very Fam (have orgasm)* jouir

(**n**) *(idioms)* **how come?** comment ça?; *Fam* **come again?** quoi?; *Am* **how's it coming?** comment ça va?; **come to that** à propos, au fait; **I haven't seen her in weeks, or her husband, come to that** ça fait des semaines que je ne l'ai pas vue, son mari non plus d'ailleurs; **if it comes to that, I'd rather stay home** à ce moment-là *ou* à ce compte-là, je préfère rester à la maison; **don't come the fine lady with me!** ne fais pas la grande dame *ou* ne joue pas à la grande dame avec moi!; **don't come the innocent!** ne fais pas l'innocent!; *Br Fam* **you're coming it a bit strong!** tu y vas un peu fort!; *Br Fam* **don't come it with me!** *(try to impress)* n'essaie pas de m'en mettre plein la vue!; *(lord it over)* pas la peine d'être si hautain avec moi!; **the days to come** les prochains jours, les jours qui viennent; **the battle to come** la bataille qui va avoir lieu; *Rel* **the life to come** l'autre vie; **in times to come** à l'avenir; **for some time to come** pendant quelque temps; **that will not be for some time to come** ce ne sera pas avant quelque temps

2 *prep (by)* **come tomorrow/Tuesday you'll feel better** vous vous sentirez mieux demain/mardi; **I'll have been here two years come April** ça fera deux ans en avril que je suis là; **come the revolution you'll all be out of a job** avec la révolution, vous vous retrouverez tous au chômage

3 *exclam* **come, come!, come now!** allons!, voyons!

4 *n Vulg (semen)* foutre *m*

►**come about** *vi* (**a**) *(occur)* arriver, se produire; **it came about that...** il arriva *ou* il advint que...; **how could such a mistake come about?** comment une telle erreur a-t-elle pu se produire?; **the discovery of penicillin came about quite by accident** la pénicilline a été découverte tout à fait par hasard

(**b**) *Naut (wind)* tourner, changer de direction; *(ship)* virer de bord

►**come across 1** *vi* (**a**) *(walk, travel across → field, street)* traverser; **as we stood talking she came across to join us** pendant que nous discutions, elle est venue se joindre à nous

(**b**) *(create specified impression)* **to come across well/badly** *(at interview)* faire une bonne/mauvaise impression, bien/mal passer; *(on TV)* bien/mal passer; **he never comes across as well on film as in the theatre** il passe mieux au théâtre qu'à l'écran; **he came across as a total idiot** il donnait l'impression d'être complètement idiot

(**c**) *(be communicated effectively)* **the author's message comes across well** le message de l'auteur passe bien; **her disdain for his work came across** le mépris qu'elle avait pour son travail transparaissait

(**d**) *Fam (do as promised)* s'exécuter❑, tenir parole❑

2 *vt insep (person)* rencontrer par hasard, tomber sur; *(thing)* trouver par hasard, tomber sur; **we came across an interesting problem** on a été confrontés à *ou* on est tombés sur un problème intéressant; **she reads everything she comes across** elle lit tout ce qui lui tombe sous la main

►**come across with** *vt insep Fam (give → information)* donner❑, fournir❑; *(→ help)* offrir❑; *(→ money)* raquer, se fendre de; **he came across with the money he owed me** il m'a filé le fric qu'il me devait; **the crook came across with the names of his accomplices** l'escroc a vendu ses complices

►**come after** *vt insep (pursue)* poursuivre; **he came after me with a stick** il m'a poursuivi avec un bâton

►**come along** *vi* (**a**) *(encouraging, urging)* **come along, drink your medicine!** allez, prends *ou* bois ton médicament!; **come along, we're late!** dépêche-toi, nous sommes en retard!

(**b**) *(accompany)* venir, accompagner; **she asked me to come along (with them)** elle m'a invité à aller avec eux *ou* à les accompagner

(**c**) *(occur, happen)* arriver, se présenter; **an opportunity like this doesn't come along often** une telle occasion ne se présente pas souvent; **don't accept the first job that comes along** ne prenez pas le premier travail qui se présente; **he married the first woman that came along** il a épousé la première venue

(**d**) *(progress)* avancer, faire des progrès; *(grow)* pousser; **the patient is coming along well** le patient se remet bien; **the work isn't coming along as expected** le travail n'avance pas comme prévu; **how's your computer class coming along?** comment va ton cours d'informatique?

►**come apart** *vi (object → come to pieces)* se démonter; *(→ break)* se casser; *(project, policy)* échouer; **to come apart at the seams** *(garment)* se défaire aux coutures; **the book came apart in my hands** le livre est tombé en morceaux quand je l'ai pris; *Fig* **under pressure he came apart** sous la pression il a craqué

►**come around** = **come round**

►**come at** *vt insep (attack)* attaquer, se jeter sur; **he came at me with a knife** il s'est jeté sur moi avec un couteau; *Fig* **questions came at me from all sides** j'ai été assailli de questions

►**come away** *vi* (**a**) *(leave)* partir, s'en aller; **come away from that door!** écartez-vous de cette porte!; **I came away with the distinct impression that all was not well** je suis reparti avec la forte impression que quelque chose n'allait pas; **he asked her to come away with him** *(elope)* il lui a demandé de s'enfuir avec lui; *Br (go on holiday)* il lui a demandé de partir avec lui

(**b**) *(separate)* partir, se détacher; **the page came away in my hands** la page m'est restée dans les mains

►**come back** *vi* (**a**) *(return)* revenir; **he came back with me** il est revenu avec moi; **to come back home** rentrer (à la maison); *Fig* **the colour came back to her cheeks** elle reprit des couleurs; **we'll come back to that question later** nous reviendrons à cette question plus tard; **to come back to what we were saying** pour en revenir à ce que nous disions

(**b**) *(to memory)* **it's all coming back to me** tout cela me revient (à l'esprit *ou* à la mémoire); **her name will come back to me later** son nom me reviendra plus tard

(**c**) *(reply)* répondre; *Am (retort)* rétorquer, répliquer; **they came back with an argument in favour of the project** ils ont répondu par un argument en faveur du projet

(**d**) *(recover)* remonter; **he came back strongly in the second set** il a bien remonté au deuxième set; **they came back from 3–0 down** ils ont remonté de 3 à 0

(**e**) *(become fashionable again)* revenir à la mode; *(make comeback)* faire un come-back

►**come before** *vt insep Law (of person)* comparaître devant; *(of case)* être entendu par

►**come between** *vt insep* brouiller, éloigner; **he**

came between her and her friend il l'a brouillée avec son amie, il l'a éloignée de son amie; **we mustn't let a small disagreement come between us** nous n'allons pas nous disputer à cause d'un petit malentendu

▶**come by** 1 *vi (stop by)* passer, venir

2 *vt insep (acquire → work, money)* obtenir, se procurer; *(→ idea)* se faire; **jobs are hard to come by** il est difficile de trouver du travail; **how did you come by this camera/those bruises?** comment as-tu fait pour avoir cet appareil-photo/ces bleus?; **how did she come by all that money?** comment s'est-elle procuré tout cet argent?; **how on earth did he come by that idea?** où est-il allé chercher cette idée?

▶**come down** 1 *vt insep (descend → ladder, stairs)* descendre; *(→ mountain)* descendre, faire la descente de

2 *vi* (**a**) *(descend → from ladder, stairs)* descendre; *(→ from mountain etc)* descendre, faire la descente; *(plane → crash)* s'écraser; *(→ land)* atterrir; **to come down to breakfast** descendre déjeuner *ou* prendre le petit déjeuner; **come down from that tree!** descends de cet arbre!; **they came down to Paris** ils sont descendus à Paris; **hem-lines are coming down this year** les jupes rallongent cette année; **he's come down in the world** il a déchu; **you'd better come down to earth** tu ferais bien de revenir sur terre *ou* de descendre des nues

(**b**) *(fall)* tomber; **rain was coming down in sheets** il pleuvait des cordes; **the ceiling came down** le plafond s'est effondré

(**c**) *(reach)* descendre; **the dress comes down to my ankles** la robe descend jusqu'à mes chevilles; **her hair came down to her waist** les cheveux lui tombaient *ou* descendaient jusqu'à la taille

(**d**) *(decrease)* baisser; **he's ready to come down 10 percent on the price** il est prêt à rabattre *ou* baisser le prix de 10 pour cent

(**e**) *(be passed down)* être transmis (de père en fils); **this custom comes down from the Romans** cette coutume nous vient des Romains; **the necklace came down to her from her great-aunt** elle tient ce collier de sa grand-tante

(**f**) *(reach a decision)* se prononcer; **the majority came down in favour of/against abortion** la majorité s'est prononcée en faveur de/contre l'avortement; **to come down on sb's side** décider en faveur de qn

(**g**) *(be removed)* être défait *ou* décroché; **that wallpaper will have to come down** il va falloir enlever ce papier peint; **the Christmas decorations are coming down today** aujourd'hui, on enlève les décorations de Noël; **the tree will have to come down** *(be felled)* il faut abattre cet arbre; **these houses are coming down soon** on va bientôt démolir ces maisons

(**h**) *Br Univ* obtenir son diplôme

(**i**) *Fam Drugs slang* redescendre

▶**come down on** *vt insep* (**a**) *(rebuke)* s'en prendre à; **the boss came down hard on him** le patron lui a passé un de ces savons; **one mistake and he'll come down on you like a ton of bricks** si tu fais la moindre erreur, il te tombera sur le dos

(**b**) *Fam (pressurize)* **they came down on me to sell the land** ils ont essayé de me faire vendre le terrain ❑

▶**come down to** *vt insep (amount)* se réduire à, se résumer à; **it all comes down to what you want to do** tout cela dépend de ce que vous souhaitez faire; **it all comes down to the same thing** tout cela revient au même; **that's what his argument comes down to** voici à quoi se réduit son raisonnement

▶**come down with** *vt insep (become ill)* attraper; **he came down with a cold** il s'est enrhumé, il a attrapé un rhume

▶**come forward** *vi (present oneself)* se présenter; **more women are coming forward as candidates** davantage de femmes présentent leur candidature; **the police have appealed for witnesses to come forward** la police a demandé aux témoins de se faire connaître

▶**come forward with** *vt insep (offer)* **the townspeople came forward with supplies** les habitants de la ville ont offert des provisions; **he came forward with a new proposal** il a fait une nouvelle proposition; *Law* **to come forward with evidence** présenter des preuves

▶**come from** *vt insep* venir; **she comes from China** elle vient *ou* elle est originaire de Chine; **to come from a good family** être issu *ou* venir d'une bonne famille; **this word comes from Latin** ce mot vient du latin; **this wine comes from the south of France** ce vin vient du sud de la France; **this passage comes from one of his novels** ce passage est extrait *ou* provient d'un de ses romans; **that's surprising coming from him** c'est étonnant de sa part; **a sob came from his throat** un sanglot s'est échappé de sa gorge; *Fam* **I'm not sure where he's coming from** je ne sais pas très bien ce qui le motive ❑

▶**come in** *vi* (**a**) *(enter)* entrer; *(come inside)* rentrer; **come in!** entrez!; **they came in through the window** ils sont entrés par la fenêtre; **come in now, children, it's getting dark** rentrez maintenant, les enfants, il commence à faire nuit; *Br Fam* **Mrs Brown comes in twice a week** *(to clean)* Madame Brown vient (faire le ménage) deux fois par semaine

(**b**) *(plane, train)* arriver

(**c**) *(in competition)* arriver; **she came in second** elle est arrivée deuxième

(**d**) *(be received → money, contributions)* rentrer; **there isn't enough money coming in to cover expenditure** l'argent qui rentre ne suffit pas à couvrir les dépenses; **how much do you have coming in every week?** combien touchez-vous *ou* encaissez-vous chaque semaine?

(**e**) *Press (news, report)* être reçu; **news is just coming in of a riot in Red Square** on nous annonce à l'instant des émeutes sur la place Rouge

(**f**) *Rad & TV (begin to speak)* parler; **come in car number 1, over** j'appelle voiture 1, à vous; **come in Barry Stewart from New York** à vous, Barry Stewart à New York

(**g**) *(become seasonable)* être de saison; *(become fashionable)* entrer en vogue; **when do endives come in?** quand commence la saison des endives?; **leather has come in** le cuir est à la mode *ou* en vogue

(**h**) *(prove to be)* **to come in handy** *or* **useful** *(tool, gadget)* être utile *ou* commode; *(contribution)* arriver à point; **these gloves come in handy** *or* **useful for driving** ces gants sont bien commodes *ou* utiles pour conduire

(**i**) *(be involved)* être impliqué; *(participate)* participer, intervenir; **where do I come in?** quel est mon rôle là-dedans?; **this is where the law comes in** c'est là que la loi intervient; **he should come in on the deal** il devrait participer à l'opération; **I'd like to come in on this** *(conversation)* j'aimerais dire quelques mots là-dessus *ou* à ce sujet

(**j**) *(tide)* monter

▶**come in for** *vt insep (be object of → abuse, reproach)* subir; **to come in for criticism** être critiqué, être l'objet de critiques; **the government came in for a lot of criticism over its handling of the crisis** le gouvernement a été très critiqué pour la façon dont il gérait la crise; **to come in for praise** être félicité

▶**come in on** *vt insep (be given a part in)* prendre part à; **they let him come in on the deal** ils l'ont laissé prendre part à l'affaire

▶**come into** *vt insep* (**a**) *(inherit)* hériter de; *(acquire)* entrer en possession de; **to come into some money** *(inherit it)* faire un héritage; *(win it)* gagner le gros lot; **they came into a fortune** *(won)* ils ont gagné une fortune; *(inherited)* ils ont hérité d'une fortune

(**b**) *(play a role in)* jouer un rôle; **it's not simply a matter of pride, though pride does come into it** ce n'est pas une simple question de fierté, bien que la fierté joue un certain rôle; **money doesn't come into it!** l'argent n'a rien à voir là-dedans!

▶**come of** *vt insep* résulter de; **what will come of it?** qu'en adviendra-t-il?, qu'en résultera-t-il?; **no good will come from** *or* **of it** ça ne mènera à rien de bon, il n'en résultera rien de bon; **let me know what comes of the meeting** faites-moi savoir ce qui ressortira de la réunion; **that's what comes from listening to you!** voilà ce qui arrive quand on vous écoute!

▶**come off** 1 *vt insep* (**a**) *(fall off → of rider)* tomber de; *(→ of button)* se détacher de, se découdre de; *(→ of handle, label)* se détacher de; *(of tape, wallpaper)* se détacher de, se décoller de; *(be removed → of stain, mark)* partir de, s'enlever de

(**b**) *(stop taking → drug, medicine)* arrêter de prendre; *(→ drink)* arrêter de boire; **to come off the pill** arrêter (de prendre) la pilule

(**c**) *(climb down from, leave → wall, ladder etc)* descendre de; **to come off a ship/plane** débarquer d'un navire/d'un avion; **I've just come off the night shift** *(finished work)* je viens de quitter l'équipe de nuit; *(finished working nights)* je viens de finir le travail de nuit

(**d**) *Ftbl (field)* sortir de

(**e**) *Fam (idiom)* **oh, come off it!** allez, arrête ton char!

2 *vi* (**a**) *(rider)* tomber; *(button)* se détacher, se découdre; *(handle, label)* se détacher; *(stain, mark)* partir, s'enlever; *(tape, wallpaper)* se détacher, se décoller; **the handle came off in his hand** la poignée lui est restée dans la main

(**b**) *Ftbl (leave the field)* sortir

(**c**) *(fare, manage)* s'en sortir, se tirer de; **you came off well in the competition** tu t'en es bien tiré au concours; **to come off best** gagner

(**d**) *Fam (happen)* avoir lieu ❑, se passer ❑; *(be carried through)* se réaliser ❑; *(succeed)* réussir ❑; **did the game come off all right?** le match s'est bien passé?; **my trip to China didn't come off** mon voyage en Chine n'a pas eu lieu; **his plan didn't come off** son projet est tombé à l'eau

(**e**) *Cin & Theat (film, play)* fermer

(**f**) *very Fam (have orgasm)* décharger

▶**come on** *vi* (**a**) *(follow)* suivre; **I'll come on after (you)** je vous suivrai

(**b**) *(in imperative)* **come on!** *(with motion, encouraging, challenging)* vas-y!, allez!; *(hurry)* allez!; *Fam (expressing incredulity)* tu rigoles!; **come on Scotland!** allez l'Écosse!; **come on in/up!** entre/monte donc!; **oh, come on, for goodness sake!** allez, arrête!

(**c**) *(progress)* avancer, faire des progrès; *(grow)* pousser, venir bien; **how is your work coming on?** où en est votre travail?; **my roses are coming on nicely** mes rosiers se portent bien; **her new book is coming on quite well** son nouveau livre avance bien; **he's coming on in physics** il fait des progrès en physique

(**d**) *(begin → illness)* se déclarer; *(→ storm)* survenir, éclater; *(→ season)* arriver; **as night came on** quand la nuit a commencé à tomber; **it's coming on to rain** il va pleuvoir; **I feel a headache/cold coming on** je sens un mal de tête qui commence/que je m'enrhume

(**e**) *(start functioning → electricity, gas, heater, lights, radio)* s'allumer; *(→ motor)* se mettre en marche; *(→ utilities at main)* être mis en service; **has the water come on?** y a-t-il de l'eau?

(**f**) *(behave, act)* **don't come on all macho with me!** ne joue pas les machos avec moi!; *Fam* **you came on a bit strong** tu y es allé un peu fort

(**g**) *Theat (actor)* entrer en scène; *(play)* être joué *ou* représenté; **his new play is coming on** on va donner sa nouvelle pièce

(**h**) *Br Fam (start menstruating)* avoir ses ragnagnas

▶**come on to** *vt insep* (**a**) *(proceed to consider)* aborder, passer à; **I want to come on to the issue of epidemics** je veux passer à la question des épidémies

(**b**) *Fam (flirt with)* draguer; **she was coming on to me in a big way** elle me draguait à fond

▶**come out** *vi* (**a**) *(exit, go out socially)* sortir; **as we came out of the theatre** au moment où nous sommes sortis du théâtre; **would you like to come out with me tonight?** est-ce que tu veux sortir avec moi ce soir?; *Fig* **if he'd only come out of himself** *or* **out of his shell** si seulement il sortait de sa coquille

(**b**) *(make appearance → stars, sun)* paraître, se montrer; *(→ flowers)* sortir, éclore; *Fig (→ book)* paraître, être publié; *(→ film)* paraître, sortir; *(→ new product)* sortir; **to come out in a rash** *(person)* se couvrir de boutons, avoir une éruption; **his nasty side came out** sa méchanceté s'est manifestée; **I didn't mean it the way it came out** ce n'est pas ce que je voulais dire

(**c**) *(be revealed → news, secret)* être divulgué *ou* révélé; *(→ facts, truth)* émerger, se faire jour; **as soon as the news came out** dès qu'on a su la nouvelle, dès que la nouvelle a été annoncée

(**d**) *(be removed → stain)* s'enlever, partir; *(colour → fade)* passer, se faner; *(→ run)* déteindre; **when do your stitches come out?** quand est-ce qu'on t'enlève tes fils?

(**e**) *(declare oneself publicly)* se déclarer; **to come out strongly (for/against)** se prononcer avec vigueur (pour/contre); **the governor came out against/for abortion** le gouverneur s'est prononcé (ouvertement) contre/pour l'avortement; *Fam* **to come out (of the closet)** *(homosexual)* révéler (publiquement) son homosexualité ❑, faire son come-out

(**f**) *Br (on strike)* se mettre en *ou* faire grève

(**g**) *(emerge, finish up)* se tirer d'affaire, s'en sortir; *(in competition)* se classer; **the government came out of the deal badly** le gouvernement s'est mal sorti de l'affaire; **everything will come out fine** tout va s'arranger; **I came out top in maths** j'étais premier en maths; **to come out on top** gagner

(**h**) *(go into society)* faire ses débuts *ou* débuter dans le monde

(**i**) *Math (yield solution)* **this sum won't come out** je n'arrive pas à résoudre cette opération

(**j**) *Phot* **the pictures came out well/badly** les photos étaient très bonnes/n'ont rien donné; **the house didn't come out well** la maison n'est pas très bien sur les photos

(**k**) *Comput (exit)* sortir; **to come out of a document** sortir d'un document

►**come out at** *vt insep (amount to)* s'élever à

►**come out in** *vt insep* **to come out in spots** *or* **a rash** avoir une éruption de boutons

►**come out with** *vt insep (say)* dire, sortir; **what will he come out with next?** qu'est-ce qu'il va nous sortir encore?; **he finally came out with it** il a fini par le sortir

►**come over 1** *vi* (**a**) *(move, travel in direction of speaker)* venir; **at the party she came over to talk to me** pendant la soirée, elle est venue me parler; **do you want to come over this evening?** tu veux venir à la maison ce soir?; **his family came over with the early settlers** sa famille est arrivée *ou* venue avec les premiers pionniers; **I met him in the plane coming over** je l'ai rencontré dans l'avion en venant

(**b**) *(stop by)* venir, passer

(**c**) *(change sides)* **they came over to our side** ils sont passés de notre côté; **he finally came over to their way of thinking** il a fini par se ranger à leur avis

(**d**) *(make specified impression)* **her speech came over well** son discours a fait bon effet *ou* bonne impression; **he came over as honest** il a donné l'impression d'être honnête; **he doesn't come over well on television** il ne passe pas bien à la télévision; **her voice comes over well** sa voix passe *ou* rend bien

(**e**) *Fam (feel)* devenir ❑; **he came over all funny** *(felt ill)* il s'est senti mal tout d'un coup, il a eu un malaise; *(behaved oddly)* il est devenu tout bizarre; **to come over dizzy** être pris de vertige; **to come over faint** être pris d'une faiblesse

2 *vt insep* affecter, envahir; **a change came over him** un changement se produisit en lui; **a feeling of fear came over him** il a été saisi de peur, la peur s'est emparée de lui; **what has come over him?** qu'est-ce qui lui prend?

►**come round** *vi* (**a**) *(make a detour)* faire le détour; **we came round by the factory** nous sommes passés par *ou* nous avons fait le détour par l'usine

(**b**) *(stop by)* passer, venir

(**c**) *(occur → regular event)* **don't wait for Christmas to come round** n'attendez pas Noël; **when the championships/elections come round** au moment des championnats/élections; **the summer holidays will soon be coming round again** bientôt, ce sera de nouveau les grandes vacances

(**d**) *(change mind)* changer d'avis; **he finally came round to our way of thinking** il a fini par se ranger à notre avis; **they soon came round to the idea** ils se sont faits à cette idée; *(change to better mood)* **don't worry, she'll soon come round** ne t'en fais pas, elle sera bientôt de meilleure humeur

(**e**) *(recover consciousness)* reprendre connaissance, revenir à soi; *(get better)* se remettre, se rétablir; **she's coming round after a bout of pneumonia** elle se remet d'une pneumonie

(**f**) *Naut* venir au vent

►**come through 1** *vi* (**a**) *(be communicated)* **his sense of conviction came through** on voyait qu'il était convaincu; **her enthusiasm comes through in her letters** son enthousiasme se lit dans ses lettres; **your call is coming through** je vous passe votre communication; **you're coming through loud and clear** je vous reçois cinq sur cinq; *Fig* **his message came through loud and clear** son message a été reçu cinq sur cinq

(**b**) *(be granted, approved)* se réaliser; **did your visa come through?** avez-vous obtenu votre visa?; **my request for a transfer came through** ma demande de mutation a été acceptée

(**c**) *(survive)* survivre, s'en tirer

(**d**) *Am Fam (do what is expected)* **he came through for us** il a fait ce qu'on attendait de lui ❑; **did he come through on his promise?** a-t-il tenu parole? ❑; **they came through with the documents** ils ont fourni les documents ❑; **he came through with the money** il a rendu l'argent comme prévu ❑

2 *vt insep* (**a**) *(cross)* traverser; *Fig (penetrate)* traverser; **we came through marshland** nous sommes passés par *ou* avons traversé des marais; **the rain came through my coat** la pluie a traversé mon manteau; **water is coming through the roof** l'eau s'infiltre par le toit

(**b**) *(survive)* **they came through the accident without a scratch** ils sont sortis de l'accident indemnes; **I'm sure you will come through this crisis** je suis sûr que tu te sortiras de cette crise; **she came through the exam with flying colours** elle a réussi l'examen avec brio

►**come to 1** *vi* (**a**) *(recover consciousness)* reprendre connaissance, revenir à soi

(**b**) *Naut (change course)* venir au vent, lofer; *(stop)* s'arrêter

2 *vt insep* (**a**) *(concern)* **when it comes to physics, she's a genius** pour ce qui est de la physique, c'est un génie; **when it comes to paying you can't see anyone for dust** quand il faut payer, il n'y a plus personne

(**b**) *(amount to)* s'élever à, se monter à; **how much did dinner come to?** à combien s'élevait le dîner?; **her salary comes to £750 a month** elle gagne 750 livres par mois; **the plan never came to anything** le projet n'a abouti à rien; **that nephew of yours will never come to anything** ton neveu n'arrivera jamais à rien

(**c**) *Fig (arrive at, reach)* **now we come to questions of health** nous en venons maintenant aux questions de santé; **he got what was coming to him** il n'a eu que ce qu'il méritait; **to come to a conclusion** arriver à une conclusion; **to come to power** accéder au pouvoir; **what is the world** *or* **what are things coming to?** où va-t-on ?; **what are things coming to when there aren't even enough hospital beds available?** où va-t-on s'il n'y a pas assez de lits dans les hôpitaux?; **I never thought it would come to this** je ne me doutais pas qu'on en arriverait là; **let's hope it won't come to that** espérons que nous n'en arrivions pas là

►**come together** *vi* (**a**) *(assemble)* se réunir, se rassembler; *(meet)* se rencontrer; **the two roads come together at this point** les deux routes se rejoignent à cet endroit

(**b**) *Fam (combine successfully)* **everything came together at the final performance** tout s'est passé à merveille pour la dernière représentation ❑

►**come under** *vt insep* (**a**) *(be subjected to → authority, control)* dépendre de; *(→ influence)* tomber sous, être soumis à; **the government is coming under pressure to lower taxes** le gouvernement subit des pressions visant à réduire les impôts

(**b**) *(be classified under)* être classé sous; **that subject comes under "current events"** ce sujet est classé *ou* se trouve sous la rubrique "actualités"

►**come up** *vi* (**a**) *(move upwards)* monter; *(moon, sun)* se lever

(**b**) *(travel in direction of speaker)* **I come up to town every Monday** je viens en ville tous les lundis; **they came up to Chicago** ils sont venus à Chicago; **to come up for air** *(diver)* remonter à la surface; *Fig (take break)* faire une pause; **she came up the hard way** elle a réussi à la force du poignet; *Mil* **an officer who came up through the ranks** un officier sorti du rang

(**c**) *(approach)* s'approcher; **to come up to sb** s'approcher de qn, aborder qn; **the students came up to him with their questions** les étudiants sont venus le voir avec leurs questions; **it's coming up to five o'clock** il est presque cinq heures; **coming up now on Channel 4, the seven o'clock news** et maintenant, sur Channel 4, le journal de sept heures; *Fam* **one coffee, coming up!** et un café, un!

(**d**) *(plant)* sortir, germer; **my beans are coming up nicely** mes haricots poussent bien

(**e**) *(come under consideration → matter)* être soulevé, être mis sur le tapis; *(→ question, problem)* se poser, être soulevé; *Law (→ accused)* comparaître; *(→ case)* être entendu; **that problem has never come up** ce problème ne s'est jamais posé; **the question of financing always comes up** la question du financement se pose toujours; **the subject came up twice in the conversation** le sujet est revenu deux fois dans la conversation; **your name came up twice** on a mentionné votre nom deux fois; **she comes up for re-election this year** son mandat prend fin cette année; **my contract is coming up for review** mon contrat doit être révisé; **to come up before the judge** *or* **the court** *(accused)* comparaître devant le juge; *(case)* être entendu par la cour; **her case comes up next Wednesday** elle passe au tribunal mercredi prochain

(**f**) *(happen unexpectedly → event)* survenir, surgir; *(→ opportunity)* se présenter; **to deal with problems as they come up** traiter les problèmes au fur et à mesure; **she's ready for anything that might come up** elle est prête à faire face à toute éventualité; **I can't make it, something has come up** je ne peux pas venir, j'ai un empêchement; **I'll let you know if anything comes up** *(if I find further information)* s'il y a du nouveau, je vous tiendrai au courant; *(anything that is suitable)* je vous tiendrai au courant si je vois quelque chose qui vous convienne

(**g**) *(intensify → wind)* se lever; *(→ light)* s'allumer; *(→ sound)* s'intensifier; **when the lights came up at the interval** lorsque les lumières se rallumèrent à l'entracte

(**h**) *(be vomited)* **everything she eats comes up (again)** elle vomit *ou* rejette tout ce qu'elle mange

(**i**) *(colour, wood etc)* **the colour comes up well when it's cleaned** la couleur revient bien au nettoyage

(**j**) *Fam (win)* gagner ❑; **did their number come up?** *(in lottery)* ont-ils gagné au loto?; *Fig* est-ce qu'ils ont touché le gros lot?

(**k**) *Fam Drugs slang (after taking drugs)* décoller

►**come up against** *vt insep (be confronted with)* rencontrer; **they came up against some tough competition** ils se sont heurtés à des concurrents redoutables

►**come upon** *vt insep (find unexpectedly → person)* rencontrer par hasard, tomber sur; *(→ object)* trouver par hasard, tomber sur; **we came upon the couple just as they were kissing** nous avons surpris le couple en train de s'embrasser

►**come up to** *vt insep* (**a**) *(reach)* arriver à; **the mud came up to their knees** la boue leur montait *ou* arrivait jusqu'aux genoux; **she comes up to his shoulder** elle lui arrive à l'épaule; **we're coming up to the halfway mark** nous atteindrons bientôt la moitié

(**b**) *(equal)* **his last book doesn't come up to**

the others son dernier livre ne vaut pas les autres; **to come up to sb's expectations** répondre à l'attente de qn; **the play didn't come up to our expectations** la pièce nous a déçus

▸**come up with** *vt insep (offer, propose → money, loan)* fournir; *(think of → plan, suggestion)* suggérer, proposer; *(→ answer)* trouver; *(→ excuse)* trouver, inventer; **they came up with a wonderful idea** ils ont eu une idée géniale; **what will she come up with next?** qu'est-ce qu'elle va encore inventer?

Come on down!
Il s'agit de la formule consacrée du jeu télévisé *The Price is Right* (dont l'équivalent français est *Le Juste prix*) qui débuta en 1957 aux États-Unis, et dans les années 80 en Grande-Bretagne. L'animateur de l'émission prononçait ces paroles ("Descendez!") pour inviter les membres du public sélectionnés pour participer au jeu à venir le rejoindre sur la scène.
Aujourd'hui on utilise cette formule plaisamment pour dire à quelqu'un d'approcher ou bien pour indiquer à quelqu'un qui doit prononcer un discours ou se produire sur scène qu'il est temps de prendre place.

Come up and see me sometime...
Cette formule fut utilisée pour la première fois par Mae West dans le film de 1933 *She Done Him Wrong* (dont le titre français est *Lady Lou*); la citation exacte était en fait **Why don't you come up sometime, see me?** ("Pourquoi est-ce que tu ne monterais pas un de ces jours, pour me voir?"). Il s'agit de l'archétype de l'invitation au badinage. Encore aujourd'hui on utilise cette formule en imitant l'air canaille de Mae West.

comeback ['kʌmbæk] *n Fam* (**a**) *(return → of person)* retour *m*, come-back *m*; *Theat* rentrée *f*; **to make** *or* **to stage a comeback** faire une rentrée *ou* un come-back; **70s fashions are making a comeback** la mode des années 70 revient (**b**) *(retort)* réplique *f* (**c**) *(justification for complaint)* **to have no comeback** n'avoir aucun recours

Comecon ['kɒmɪkɒn] *n (abbr* **Council for Mutual Economic Assistance**) le Comecon

comedian [kə'miːdɪən] *n* (**a**) *(comic)* comique *m*; *Fig (funny person)* clown *m*, pitre *m* (**b**) *Theat (comic actor)* comédien *m*

comedienne [kəˌmiːdɪ'en] *n* (**a**) *(comic)* actrice *f* comique (**b**) *Theat (comic actress)* comédienne *f*

comedo ['kɒmɪdəʊ] *(pl* **comedones** [-'dəʊniːz]) *n Med* comédon *m*

comedogenic [ˌkɒmɪdəʊ'dʒenɪk] *adj Med* comédogène

comedown ['kʌmdaʊn] *n Fam* déchéance□ *f*, dégringolade *f*; **he finds working in sales a bit of a comedown** il trouve plutôt humiliant de travailler comme vendeur

comedy ['kɒmədɪ] *(pl* **comedies**) **1** *n* (**a**) *(genre)* comédie *f*; *Theat* genre *m* comique, comédie *f* (**b**) *(play, film)* comédie *f*; *(situation comedy)* sitcom *m*; **the whole affair has been a comedy of errors** toute cette affaire n'a été qu'une farce (**c**) *(of situation)* comique *m*

2 *comp (act, duo)* comique

▸▸ ***comedy of manners*** comédie *f* de mœurs; ***comedy show*** spectacle *m* comique

'The Comedy of Errors' *Shakespeare* 'La Comédie des erreurs'

come-hither *adj Fam* aguichant□; **a come-hither look** un regard aguichant

comeliness ['kʌmlɪnɪs] *n Literary* beauté *f*, charme *m*

comely ['kʌmlɪ] *(compar* **comelier**, *superl* **comeliest**) *adj Literary* charmant, beau (belle)

come-on *n Fam (enticement)* incitation□ *f*; **it was a come-on to get buyers interested** c'était pour attirer les clients□; **to give sb the come-on** *(sexually)* faire du gringue à qn

comer ['kʌmə(r)] *n* (**a**) *(arrival)* arrivant(e) *m,f*; **the first comers** les premiers venus; **open to all comers** ouvert à tous *ou* au tout-venant (**b**) *Am Fam (potential success)* **she's a real comer!** elle a un bel avenir devant elle!□

comestible [kə'mestɪbəl] **1** *adj Formal* comestible

2 comestibles *npl* comestibles *fpl*, denrées *mpl* comestibles

comet ['kɒmɪt] *n* comète *f*

come-to-bed *adj* **come-to-bed eyes** regard *m* aguichant *ou* suggestif

comeuppance [ˌkʌm'ʌpəns] *n Fam* **she got her comeuppance** elle n'a eu que ce qu'elle méritait□; **you'll get your comeuppance** tu auras ce que tu mérites□

comfort ['kʌmfət] **1** *n* (**a**) *(well-being)* confort *m*, bien-être *m*; **to live in comfort** vivre dans l'aisance *ou* à l'aise; **she's used to comfort** elle a toujours eu tout le *ou* son confort; **the boots are fur-lined for extra comfort** les bottes sont fourrées pour plus de confort; **to do sth in the comfort of one's own home** faire qch confortablement chez soi; *Fig* **the explosion was too close for comfort** l'explosion a eu lieu un peu trop près à mon goût; **the deadline's getting a bit too close for comfort** la date limite est un peu trop proche à mon goût

(**b**) *(usu pl) (amenities)* aises *fpl*, commodités *fpl*; **every modern comfort** tout le confort moderne; **I like my comfort** *or* **comforts** j'aime bien mes aises *ou* mon confort

(**c**) *(consolation)* réconfort *m*, consolation *f*; **to take comfort in sth** trouver un réconfort dans qch; **she took comfort from his words** elle a trouvé un réconfort dans ses paroles; **I took comfort from** *or* **in the knowledge that it would soon be over** je me suis consolé en me disant que ce serait bientôt fini; **it's a comfort to know** c'est un soulagement de savoir; **if it's any comfort to you** si cela peut vous consoler; **you've been a great comfort to me** vous avez été pour moi un grand réconfort; **some comfort you are/that is!** tu parles d'une consolation!

2 *vt* (**a**) *(console)* consoler; *(relieve)* soulager; **they comforted the wounded** ils ont réconforté les blessés; **it comforted him to know she had had a decent burial** ça l'a réconforté de savoir qu'elle avait eu un enterrement décent

(**b**) *(cheer)* réconforter, encourager

▸▸ ***comfort eating*** = fait de manger pour se remonter le moral; ***comfort food*** = chose que l'on mange pour se remonter le moral; *Am* ***comfort station*** toilettes *fpl* publiques *(sur le bord d'une route)*

comfortable ['kʌmfətəbəl] *adj* (**a**) *(chair, shoes, bed, room)* confortable; *(temperature)* agréable

(**b**) *(person)* à l'aise; **are you comfortable?** êtes-vous bien installé?; **make yourself comfortable** *(sit down)* installez-vous confortablement; *(feel at ease)* mettez-vous à l'aise, faites comme chez vous; **he couldn't get comfortable in bed** il ne savait pas comment se mettre dans le lit pour être à l'aise; **I'm not very comfortable about** *or* **I don't feel comfortable with the idea** l'idée ne me plaît pas particulièrement; **I wouldn't feel comfortable accepting that money** ça me mettrait mal à l'aise d'accepter cet argent

(**c**) *(financially secure)* aisé, riche; *(easy → job)* tranquille; **they're very comfortable** ils ont une vie aisée; **comfortable income** revenu *m* suffisant; **he makes a comfortable living** il gagne bien sa vie

(**d**) *(not in pain)* **to be comfortable** *(after illness, operation, accident)* ne pas souffrir; **he had a comfortable night** il a passé une bonne nuit

(**e**) *Fig (lead, win)* confortable; **that leaves us a comfortable margin** ça nous laisse une marge confortable

comfortably ['kʌmfətəblɪ] *adv* (**a**) *(in a relaxed position → sit, sleep)* confortablement, agréablement

(**b**) *(in financial comfort)* à l'aise; **they live comfortably** ils vivent dans l'aisance *ou* à l'aise; **to be comfortably off** être à l'aise

(**c**) *(easily)* facilement, à l'aise; **we can fit five people in the car comfortably** la voiture contient bien cinq personnes, on tient à l'aise à cinq dans la voiture; **we should manage it comfortably in two hours** deux heures suffiront largement

comforter ['kʌmfətə(r)] *n* (**a**) *(person)* consolateur(trice) *m,f* (**b**) *Br Old-fashioned (scarf)* cache-nez *m* (**c**) *(for baby)* tétine *f*, sucette *f* (**d**) *Am (quilt)* édredon *m*, *Can* confortable *m*; *(duvet)* couette *f*

comforting ['kʌmfətɪŋ] **1** *adj (consoling → remark, thought)* consolant, réconfortant, rassurant; *(encouraging)* encourageant

2 *n (consolation)* réconfort *m*, consolation *f*; *(encouragement)* encouragement *m*

comfortless ['kʌmfətlɪs] *adj* (**a**) *(room)* sans confort (**b**) *(dismal → person)* triste, désolé; *(→ thought)* peu rassurant, triste

comfrey ['kʌmfrɪ] *n Bot* consoude *f*

comfy ['kʌmfɪ] *(compar* **comfier**, *superl* **comfiest**) *adj Fam (chair, place, bed)* confortable□; **are you comfy?** vous êtes bien installés?□

comic ['kɒmɪk] **1** *adj* comique, humoristique

2 *n* (**a**) *(entertainer)* (acteur *m*) comique *m*, actrice *f* comique (**b**) *(magazine)* BD *f*, bande *f* dessinée

3 comics *npl Am (in newspaper)* bandes *fpl* dessinées

▸▸ ***comic book*** magazine *m* de bandes dessinées; ***comic opera*** opéra *m* comique; ***Comic Relief*** = association caritative britannique qui collecte des fonds en organisant chaque année un "téléthon" auquel participent de nombreux comiques, et en vendant des petits nez rouges en plastique que les gens portent en signe de solidarité; ***comic relief*** *Theat* intervalle *m* comique; *Fig* moment *m* de détente (comique); ***comic strip*** bande *f* dessinée

comical ['kɒmɪkəl] *adj* drôle, comique

comically ['kɒmɪkəlɪ] *adv* drôlement, comiquement

coming ['kʌmɪŋ] **1** *adj* (**a**) *(time, events)* à venir, futur; *(in near future)* prochain; **this coming Tuesday** mardi prochain; **the coming storm** l'orage qui approche

(**b**) *Fam (promising → person)* qui a de l'avenir□

2 *n* (**a**) *(gen)* arrivée *f*, venue *f*; **coming and going** va-et-vient *m*; **comings and goings** allées *fpl* et venues

(**b**) *Rel* avènement *m*; **the Second Coming** le second avènement

▸▸ ***coming of age*** majorité *f*; **on his coming of age** à sa majorité; ***coming away*** départ *m*; ***coming back*** retour *m*; ***coming in*** entrée *f*; ***coming out*** *(exit)* sortie *f*; *(of debutante)* entrée *f* dans la société; *(of homosexual)* = fait de déclarer son homosexualité

COMING OF AGE
À sa majorité, c'est-à-dire à 18 ans, un(e) jeune Britannique acquiert le droit de voter, de faire partie d'un jury, de boire de l'alcool dans les pubs et de se marier sans le consentement de ses parents.

Comintern ['kɒmɪntɜːn] *n Pol (abbr* **Communist International**) Komintern *m*

comity ['kɒmɪtɪ] *n Literary* courtoisie *f*, politesse *f*; **comity of nations** courtoisie *f* internationale

comma ['kɒmə] *n* (**a**) *Gram* virgule *f* (**b**) *Mus* comma *m*

command [kə'mɑːnd] **1** *n* (**a**) *(order)* ordre *m*; *Mil* ordre *m*, commandement *m*; **to give a command** donner un ordre; **the troops were withdrawn at** *or* **on his command** les troupes ont été retirées sur ses ordres; **they are at your command** ils sont à vos ordres; **at the word of command** au commandement

(**b**) *(authority)* commandement *m*; **who is in command here?** qui est-ce qui commande ici?; **to be in command of sth** avoir qch sous ses ordres, être à la tête de qch; **to be first/second in command** commander en premier/en second; **he had/took command of the situation** il avait/a pris la situation en main; **they are under her command** ils sont sous ses ordres *ou* son commandement

(**c**) *(control, mastery)* maîtrise *f*; **command of the seas** maîtrise *f* des mers; **he's in full command of his faculties** il est en pleine possession de ses moyens; **she has a good command of two foreign languages** elle possède bien deux langues étrangères; **her command of Spanish** sa maîtrise de l'espagnol; **all the resources at my command** toutes les ressources à ma disposition *ou* dont je dispose; **I'm at your command** je suis à votre disposition; **command of the market** domination *f* sur le marché

(**d**) *Mil (group of officers)* commandement *m*; *(troops)* troupes *fpl*; **to be responsible for one's command** être responsable de ses troupes; **they were my first command** c'est la première section que j'ai commandée

(**e**) *Mil (area)* région *f* militaire; **Scottish/Northern command** région *f* militaire d'Écosse/du Nord

(**f**) *Comput* commande *f*

2 *vt* (**a**) *(order)* ordonner, commander; **she commanded that we leave immediately** elle nous a ordonné *ou* nous a donné l'ordre de partir immédiatement; **the general commanded his men to attack** le général a donné l'ordre à ses hommes d'attaquer

(**b**) *(have control over → army, ship, regiment)* commander; *(→ emotions)* maîtriser, dominer

(**c**) *(receive as due)* commander, imposer; **to command respect** inspirer le respect, en imposer; **to command the attention of one's audience** tenir son public en haleine; **the translator commands a high fee** les services du traducteur valent cher; **this painting will command a high price** ce tableau se vendra à un prix élevé

(**d**) *(have use of)* disposer de; **all the skill he could command** toute l'habileté qu'il possédait; **all the resources that the country can command** toutes les ressources dont le pays peut disposer

(**e**) *(of building, statue → overlook)* dominer; **to command a view of** avoir vue sur, donner sur

3 *vi* (**a**) *(order)* commander, donner des ordres

(**b**) *(be in control)* commander; *Mil* commander, avoir le commandement

►► *Comput* ***command button*** case *f* de commande; *Comput* ***command code*** code *m* de commande; ***command economy*** économie *f* planifiée; *Comput* ***command file*** fichier *m* de commande; *Comput* ***command key*** touche *f* de commande; *Comput* ***command language*** langage *m* de commande; *Comput* ***command line*** ligne *f* de commande; ***command module*** *(of spacecraft)* module *m* de commande; *Br Theat* ***command performance*** = représentation (d'un spectacle) à la requête du monarque; *Mil* ***command post*** poste *m* de commandement; *Comput* ***command sequence*** séquence *f* de commandes

commandant [ˌkɒmən'dænt] *n Mil* commandant *m*

commandeer [ˌkɒmən'dɪə(r)] *vt* (**a**) *Mil* réquisitionner (**b**) *(take for one's own use)* accaparer; **the boss commandeered our photocopier** le patron a fait main basse sur notre photocopieuse *ou* a réquisitionné notre photocopieuse

commandeering [ˌkɒmən'dɪərɪŋ] *n Mil* réquisitionnement *m*, réquisition *f*

commander [kə'mɑːndə(r)] *n* (**a**) *(person in charge)* chef *m*; *Mil* commandant *m*; *Naut (rank)* ≃ capitaine *m* de frégate; *Aviat* chef *m* de bord (**b**) *Br (of police)* ≃ commissaire *m* divisionnaire, ≃ divisionnaire *m*

commander-in-chief *n Mil* commandant *m* en chef, généralissime *m*

commanding [kə'mɑːndɪŋ] *adj* (**a**) *(in command)* qui commande

(**b**) *(overlooking → view)* élevé; *(overlooking and dominant → position)* dominant, important; **to have a commanding lead** avoir une solide avance; **to be in a commanding position** avoir une position dominante

(**c**) *(tone, voice)* impérieux, de commandement; *(look)* impérieux; *(air)* imposant; *(beauty)* majestueux

►► *Mil* ***commanding officer*** commandant *m*

commandment [kə'mɑːndmənt] *n* commandement *m*; **to keep the commandments** observer les commandements; *Bible* **the Ten Commandments** les dix commandements, le décalogue

commando [kə'mɑːndəʊ] (*pl* **commandos** *or* **commandoes**) *Mil* **1** *n* commando *m*

2 *comp (raid, unit)* de commando

command-orientated *adj Comput (program)* orienté commande

commemorate [kə'meməˌreɪt] *vt* commémorer

commemoration [kəˌmemə'reɪʃən] *n* commémoration *f*; *Rel* commémoraison *f*; **in commemoration of** en commémoration de

commemorative [kə'memərətɪv] *adj* commémoratif

commence [kə'mens] *Formal* **1** *vi* commencer

2 *vt* commencer; **the date on which you commenced employment** la date à laquelle vous avez commencé à travailler; **she commenced speaking at 2 o'clock** elle a commencé à parler à 2 heures; *Law* **to commence proceedings against sb** former un recours contre qn *(devant une juridiction)*

commencement [kə'mensmənt] **1** *n* (**a**) *Formal (beginning)* commencement *m*, début *m*; *Law (of law)* date *f* d'entrée en vigueur (**b**) *Univ (in US, Canada, at Cambridge, in Trinity College, Dublin)* remise *f* des diplômes

2 commencements *n Ir Univ (in Trinity College, Dublin)* jour *m* de la remise des diplômes

►► *Univ* ***Commencement Day*** *(in US, at Cambridge)* jour *m* de la remise des diplômes

commend [kə'mend] *vt* (**a**) *(recommend)* recommander, conseiller; **he commended the proposal to the committee** il a recommandé le projet au comité; **if this policy commends itself to the public…** si cette politique est du goût du public…; **the report has little to commend it** il n'y a pas grand-chose d'intéressant dans ce rapport; **the hotel has little to commend it apart from the cooking** il n'y a pas grand chose de bien à dire sur cet hôtel à part la cuisine

(**b**) *(praise)* louer, faire l'éloge de; **to commend sb for bravery** louer qn pour sa bravoure; **you are to be commended for your hard work** on doit vous féliciter pour votre dur labeur

(**c**) *(entrust)* confier; **to commend sth to sb** confier qch à qn, remettre qch aux bons soins de qn; *Rel* **we commend our souls to God** nous recommandons notre âme à Dieu

(**d**) *Arch or Formal (remember)* **commend me to Dr Smith** rappelez-moi au bon souvenir du Docteur Smith

commendable [kə'mendəbəl] *adj* louable; **with commendable promptness** avec une rapidité digne d'éloges

commendably [kə'mendəblɪ] *adv* de façon louable; **his speech was commendably brief** son discours avait le mérite de la brièveté

commendation [ˌkɒmən'deɪʃən] *n* (**a**) *(praise)* éloge *f*, louange *f* (**b**) *(recommendation)* recommendation *f*; *(award in competition)* mention *f* spéciale (**c**) *(award for bravery)* décoration *f* (**d**) *(entrusting)* remise *f*

commensurable [kə'menʃərəbəl] *adj Math* commensurable (**with** *or* **to** avec)

commensurate [kə'menʃərət] *adj Formal* (**a**) *(of equal measure)* de même mesure, commensurable; *Math* **the side is commensurate with the diagonal** on peut mesurer le côté en fonction de la diagonale

(**b**) *(proportionate)* proportionné (**with** *or* **to** à); **the salary will be commensurate with your experience** le salaire sera en fonction de votre expérience; **there was no post commensurate with his abilities** aucun poste ne correspondait à ses compétences; **of commensurate value** d'une valeur équivalente

commensurately [kə'menʃərətlɪ] *adv* proportionnellement (**to** *or* **with** à)

comment ['kɒment] **1** *n* (**a**) *(remark)* commentaire *m*, observation *f*; **to make a comment about sth** faire des observations sur qch; **she let it pass without comment** elle n'a pas relevé; **to refrain from comment** s'abstenir de faire des commentaires; *Fig* **it's a comment on our society** c'est une réflexion sur notre société; **no comment!** je n'ai rien à dire!; **(it's a) fair comment** c'est juste

(**b**) *(UNCOUNT) (gossip, criticism)* **the decision provoked much comment** la décision a suscité de nombreux commentaires

(**c**) *(note)* commentaire *m*, annotation *f*; *(critical)* critique *f*; *Sch* **teacher's comments** appréciations *fpl* du professeur

2 *vt* **to comment that…** faire remarquer *ou* observer que…

3 *vi* (**a**) *(remark)* faire une remarque *ou* des remarques; **she commented on his age** elle a fait des remarques *ou* commentaires sur son âge; **nobody commented on it** personne n'a fait de commentaire à ce sujet

(**b**) *(give opinion)* **to comment on a text** commenter un texte, faire le commentaire d'un texte

►► ***comment card*** fiche *f* d'observations

commentary ['kɒməntrɪ] (*pl* **commentaries**) *n* (**a**) *(remarks)* commentaire *m*, observations *fpl* (**b**) *Rad & TV* commentaire *m*; **with commentary by Des Lynam** commenté par Des Lynam (**c**) *(on text)* commentaire *m*

►► *Rad & TV* ***commentary box*** tribune *f* des journalistes

commentate ['kɒmənteɪt] *Rad & TV* **1** *vt* commenter

2 *vi* faire le commentaire; **to commentate on an event** faire le commentaire d'un *ou* commenter un événement

commentator ['kɒmənˌteɪtə(r)] *n* (**a**) *Rad & TV* commentateur(trice) *m,f* (**b**) *Journ* journaliste *mf (de la presse écrite)*; **political commentator** journaliste *mf* politique (**c**) *(analyst → of text)* commentateur(trice) *m,f*

commerce ['kɒmɜːs] *n (UNCOUNT)* (**a**) *(trade)* commerce *m*, affaires *fpl*; *Am* **Secretary/Department of Commerce** ministre *m*/ministère *m* du Commerce (**b**) *Fig Literary (of ideas, opinions)* relations *fpl*, commerce *m*

commercial [kə'mɜːʃəl] **1** *adj* (**a**) *(economic)* commercial; *(port, tribunal etc)* de commerce; **a commercial venture** une entreprise commerciale

(**b**) *(profitable)* commercial, marchand; **a commercial success** un succès commercial

(**c**) *Pej (profit-seeking → record, book, pop group, film)* commercial; **their motives are purely commercial** ils ont des motivations purement commerciales

(**d**) *(television, radio)* commercial

2 *n TV & Rad* publicité *f*, spot *m* publicitaire

►► ***commercial agency*** agence *f* commerciale; ***commercial art*** graphisme *m*; ***commercial artist*** graphiste *mf*; ***commercial attaché*** attaché *m* commercial; ***commercial bank*** banque *f* commerciale; *Fin* ***commercial bill*** effet *m* de commerce; *TV & Rad* ***commercial break*** page *f* de publicité; ***commercial broker*** courtier *m* de marchandises; ***commercial channel*** circuit *m* commercial; ***commercial college*** école *f* de commerce; ***commercial contract*** contrat *m* commercial; *Br Law* ***Commercial Court*** tribunal *m* de commerce; ***commercial directory*** annuaire *m* du commerce; ***commercial district*** quartier *m* commerçant; ***commercial documents*** papiers *mpl* d'affaires; ***commercial law*** droit *m* commercial; ***commercial loan*** prêt *m* commercial; *Fin* ***commercial paper*** billet *m* de trésorerie; ***commercial port*** port *m* de commerce; *Old-fashioned* ***commercial traveller*** voyageur *m ou* représentant *m* de commerce, VRP *m*; ***commercial value*** valeur *f* marchande; *Br* ***commercial vehicle*** véhicule *m* utilitaire, commerciale *f*

commercialism [kə'mɜːʃəlɪzəm] *n* (**a**) *(practice of business)* (pratique *f* du) commerce *m*, (pratique *f* des) affaires *fpl* (**b**) *Pej (profit-seeking)* mercantilisme *m*, esprit *m* commercial; *(on large scale)* affairisme *m*

commercialization [kəˌmɜːʃəlaɪ'zeɪʃən] *n* commercialisation *f*

commercialize, -ise [kə'mɜːʃəlaɪz] *vt* commercialiser

commercialized [kə'mɜːʃəlaɪzd] *adj Pej (profit-seeking)* commercialisé

commercially [kə'mɜːʃəlɪ] *adv* commercialement; **commercially available** disponible dans le commerce

commercial-use *adj* à usage commercial

commie ['kɒmɪ] *Fam Pej* **1** *adj* coco

2 *n* coco *mf*

commination [ˌkɒmɪ'neɪʃən] *n* (**a**) *Rel* commination *f* (**b**) *Literary* menaces *fpl*

commingle [kɒ'mɪŋgəl] **1** *vt* emmêler, entremêler

2 *vi* se mêler (**with** avec), se mélanger (**with** avec)

commis ['kɒmɪ] *n*

►► ***commis chef*** commis *m*, commis *m* cuisinier, commis *m* de cuisine; ***commis waiter*** commis *m*

commiserate [kə'mɪzəreɪt] *vi* **to commiserate with sb** *(feel sympathy)* éprouver de la compassion pour qn; *(show sympathy)* témoigner de la sympathie à qn; **we commiserated with him on his misfortune** nous avons compati à sa malchance

commiseration [kə,mɪzə'reɪʃən] *n* commisération *f*

commissar ['kɒmɪsɑː(r)] *n Pol* commissaire *m* (du peuple)

commissarial [,kɒmɪ'seərɪəl] *adj* (**a**) *Am Mil* d'intendance (**b**) *Rel (duties)* de délégué

commissariat [,kɒmɪ'seərɪət] *n* (**a**) *Pol* commissariat *m* (**b**) *Mil (department)* intendance *f*; *(food supply)* ravitaillement *m*

commissary ['kɒmɪsərɪ] (*pl* **commissaries**) *n* (**a**) *Am Mil (shop)* intendance *f*; *(officer)* intendant *m* (**b**) *Am Cin (cafeteria)* restaurant *m* (du studio) (**c**) *Rel* délégué *m (d'un évêque)*

commission [kə'mɪʃən] **1** *n* (**a**) *(authority for special job)* mission *f*; *Art* commande *f*; **to give a commission to an artist** passer une commande à un artiste; **work done on commission** travail *m* fait sur commande

(**b**) *(delegation of authority)* délégation *f* de pouvoir *ou* d'autorité, mandat *m*; *(formal warrant)* mandat *m*, pouvoir *m*; *Mil* brevet *m*; **to resign one's commission** démissionner; **when he received his commission** quand il a été élevé *ou* promu au grade d'officier

(**c**) *(committee)* commission *f*, comité *m*;

(**d**) *Com (fee)* commission *f*, courtage *m*; **to work on a commission basis** travailler à la commission; **I get (a) 5 percent commission** je reçois une commission de 5 pour cent; **commission only** rémunération *f* à la commission

(**e**) *Law (of crime)* perpétration *f*

(**f**) *Naut (of ship)* armement *m*; **to put a ship into commission** armer un navire

2 *vt* (**a**) *(work of art, book)* commander; *(artist)* passer commande à; **we commissioned the architect to design a new house** nous avons engagé un architecte pour faire les plans d'une nouvelle maison; **we'll have to commission some freelance illustrators** nous allons faire appel à des illustrateurs extérieurs

(**b**) *(grant authority to)* donner pouvoir *ou* mission à, déléguer, charger; **to commission sb to do sth** charger qn de faire qch; **I was commissioned to investigate** j'ai reçu la *ou* pour mission d'enquêter

(**c**) *Mil (make officer)* nommer à un commandement; **he was commissioned general** il a été promu au grade de *ou* nommé général

(**d**) *(make operative)* mettre en service; *Naut (ship)* mettre en service, armer

3 in commission *adj (gen)* en service; *Naut (ship)* en armement, en service

4 out of commission 1 *adj (gen)* hors service; *(car)* en panne; *Naut (not working)* hors service; *(in reserve)* en réserve; **you'll be out of commission for six weeks** vous serez obligé de suspendre vos activités pendant six semaines **2** *adv Naut* **to take a ship out of commission** désarmer un navire

►► *Com* ***commission agent*** commissionaire *mf*; ***commission of inquiry*** commission *f* d'enquête; *Acct* ***commission note*** note *f* de commission; *Admin* ***Commission for Racial Equality*** = organisme britannique qui intervient auprès des établissements scolaires et les entreprises pour enrayer la discrimination raciale

commissionaire [kə,mɪʃə'neə(r)] *n Br* portier *m (d'un hôtel etc)*

commissioned [kə'mɪʃənd] *adj (operative)* en service; *Naut (ship)* armé

►► *Mil* ***commissioned officer*** officier *m*

commissioner [kə'mɪʃənə(r)] *n* (**a**) *(member of commission)* membre *m* d'une commission, commissaire *m*

(**b**) *(of police) Br* ≃ préfet *m* de police, *Am* ≃ (commissaire *m*) divisionnaire *m*; *(of government department)* haut fonctionnaire *m*

►► *Am Sch & Univ* ***commissioner of education*** ≃ recteur *m*, ≃ doyen *m*; *Br Fin* ***Commissioner of the Inland Revenue*** ≃ Inspecteur *m* des impôts; *Law* ***commissioner for oaths*** = officier ayant qualité pour recevoir les déclarations sous serment

commissioning [kə'mɪʃənɪŋ] *n* (**a**) *Mil (of officer)* nomination *f* à un commandement (**b**) *Naut (of ship)* armement *m*; *(of new power plant)* mise *f* en service *ou* en exploitation;

►► ***commissioning editor*** directeur(trice) *m,f* éditorial(e) *(chargé(e) notamment de commander de nouveaux ouvrages aux auteurs)*

commit [kə'mɪt] (*pt & pp* **committed**, *cont* **committing**) **1** *vt* (**a**) *(crime)* commettre, perpétrer; *(mistake)* faire, commettre; **to commit suicide** se suicider; **committing perjury is a crime** se parjurer *ou* faire un faux serment est un délit

(**b**) *(entrust → thing)* confier, remettre; *(→ person)* confier; **to commit sth to sb's care** confier qch aux soins de qn *ou* à la garde de qn; **to commit a body to the earth** porter un corps en terre; **to commit a body to the deep** confier un corps aux flots; *Rel* **to commit one's soul to God** rendre son âme à Dieu; **to commit sth to memory** apprendre qch par cœur; **to commit sth to paper** *or* **writing** coucher *ou* consigner qch par écrit

(**c**) *(confine)* **to commit sb (to a mental hospital)** interner qn; **to commit sb to prison** incarcérer qn

(**d**) *(promise)* engager; **to commit oneself** s'engager; **to commit oneself to sth/to doing sth** s'engager à qch/à faire qch; **he refused to commit himself** il s'est tenu sur la réserve, il a refusé de prendre parti *ou* de s'engager; *Mil* **to commit troops (to a region)** engager des troupes (dans une région); *Mil* **he had committed 2,000 troops to the defence of the village** il avait assigné 2000 soldats à la défense du village

(**e**) *Pol (legislative bill)* renvoyer en commission

(**f**) *Law* **to commit sb for trial** mettre qn en accusation

2 *vi (emotionally)* s'engager, s'investir; **he can't commit** il ne peut pas s'engager

commitment [kə'mɪtmənt] *n* (**a**) *(promise, loyalty)* engagement *m*; **to make a commitment** *(emotionally, intellectually)* s'engager; **his commitment to the proposed reform of the tax system** son soutien pour la réforme du système fiscal qui a été proposée; **so many men avoid commitment in relationships** il y a tellement d'hommes qui refusent de s'investir dans les relations amoureuses

(**b**) *(obligation)* obligations *fpl*, responsabilités *fpl*; **I cannot do it because of other commitments** d'autres obligations m'empêchent de le faire; **he has family commitments** il a des obligations familiales; **teaching commitments** charge *f* d'enseignement, enseignement *m*

(**c**) *Com & Fin* engagement *m* financier; **with no commitment** sans obligation d'achat

(**d**) *(to mental hospital)* internement *m*; *(to prison)* incarcération *f*, emprisonnement *m*

(**e**) *(of crime)* perpétration *f*

(**f**) *Pol (of legislative bill)* renvoi *m* en commission

(**g**) *Law (order)* mandat *m* de dépôt

►► *Banking* ***commitment fee*** commission *f* d'engagement

committal [kə'mɪtəl] *n* (**a**) *(sending → gen)* remise *f*; *(→ to mental hospital)* internement *m*; *(→ to prison)* incarcération *f*, emprisonnement *m* (**b**) *(of body to grave)* mise *f* en terre (**b**) *(of crime)* perpétration *f*

►► *Law* ***committal order*** mandat *m* de dépôt; *Law* ***committal proceedings, committal for trial*** ≃ mise *f* en accusation

committed [kə'mɪtɪd] *adj (writer, artist)* engagé; **a committed Socialist/Christian** un socialiste/chrétien convaincu; **he didn't seem very committed** son engagement ne semblait pas être très ferme; **to be committed to an idea** être attaché à une idée

►► *Acct* ***committed costs*** coûts *mpl* engagés

committee [kə'mɪtɪ] **1** *n* commission *f*, comité *m*; *(in government)* commission *f*; **to be** *or* **to sit on a committee** faire partie d'une commission *ou* d'un comité; *Br Parl* **the House went into committee** la Chambre s'est constituée en comité

2 *comp (member)* d'une commission, d'un comité

►► ***committee meeting*** réunion *f* de comité; *Br* ***Committee of Ways and Means*** commission *f* du budget; *Br Parl* ***Committee of the Whole House*** = séance de commission étendue à la chambre entière; *Br Parl* ***committee stage*** = stade de discussion d'un projet de loi par une commission

committeeman [kə'mɪtɪmən] (*pl* **committeemen** [-mən]) *n* membre *m* d'une commission *ou* d'un comité

committeeperson [kə'mɪtɪ,pɜːsən] *n* membre *m* d'une commission *ou* d'un comité

committeewoman [kə'mɪtɪ,wʊmən] (*pl* **committeewomen** [-,wɪmɪn]) *n* membre *m* d'une commission *ou* d'un comité

committing magistrate [kə'mɪtɪŋ-] *n Am Law* juge *m* d'instruction

commode [kə'məʊd] *n* (**a**) *(chest of drawers)* commode *f* (**b**) *(for chamber pot)* chaise *f* percée

commodious [kə'məʊdjəs] *adj Formal (building, room)* spacieux, vaste; *(armchair)* grand et confortable

commodiousness [kə'məʊdɪəs,nɪs] *n Formal (of building, room)* amples dimensions *fpl*

commodity [kə'mɒdətɪ] (*pl* **commodities**) *n* (**a**) *(product)* marchandise *f*; *(consumer good)* produit *m*, article *m*; *(food item)* denrée *f*; **a basic** *or* **staple commodity** un produit de base; **household commodities** articles *mpl* ménagers

(**b**) *Econ (raw material)* produit *m* de base, matière *f* première; *St Exch* **to trade in commodities** faire le négoce de matières premières

►► *St Exch* ***commodity broker, commodity dealer*** courtier(ère) *m,f* en matières premières; *St Exch* ***commodity exchange*** échange *m* des marchandises; *St Exch* ***commodity futures*** opérations *fpl* à terme sur matières premières; *St Exch* ***commodity market, commodities market*** marché *m* des matières premières; ***commodity money*** monnaie *f* de marchandise; *Econ* ***commodity terms of trade*** termes *mpl* de l'échange

commodore ['kɒmədɔː(r)] *n* (**a**) *(navy rank)* ≃ contre-amiral *m*, *Belg* ≃ amiral *m* de flotille, *Can* ≃ commodore *m* (**b**) *Naut (of merchant ships)* chef *m* de convoi; *(of shipping line)* doyen *m* (des capitaines); *(of yacht club)* président *m*

common ['kɒmən] **1** *adj* (**a**) *(ordinary)* courant, commun; *(plant, species)* commun; **it's quite common** c'est courant *ou* tout à fait banal; **it's a common experience** cela arrive à beaucoup de gens *ou* à tout le monde; **he's nothing but a common criminal** ce n'est qu'un vulgaire criminel; **a common expression** une expression courante; **common name** *(of plant)* nom *m* vulgaire; **a common occurrence** une chose fréquente *ou* qui arrive souvent; **a common sight** un spectacle familier; **in common parlance** dans le langage courant; *Br Pej* **the common horde** la plèbe, la populace; **the common man** l'homme du peuple; **the common people** le peuple, les gens du commun; **common prostitute** vulgaire prostituée *f*; **common salt** sel *m* (ordinaire); **a common soldier** un simple soldat; **common thief** vulgaire voleur *m*; **it's only common courtesy to reply** ce serait la moindre des politesses de répondre; *Br* **to have the common touch** savoir parler aux gens simples

(**b**) *(shared, public)* commun; **by common consent** d'un commun accord; **the common good** le bien public; **common land** terrain *m* communal *ou* banal; **common ownership** copropriété *f*; **the common parts** *(in building)* les parties communes; **common staircase** escalier *m* commun; **common wall** mur *m* commun *ou* mitoyen; **common ground** *(in interests)* intérêt *m* commun; *(for discussion)* terrain *m* d'entente; **there is no common ground between the two groups** il n'y a pas de terrain d'entente entre les deux groupes; *Br* **to make common cause with sb** faire cause commune avec qn; *Com* **common carrier** transporteur *m* (public); **common interest group** groupe *m* d'intérêt commun; *Aviat* **common rated fare** tarif *m* commun; *Aviat* **common rated points** = destinations pour lesquelles les tarifs sont identiques à partir d'un même point de départ

(**c**) *(widespread)* général, universel; **the common belief** la croyance universelle; **in common use** d'usage courant; **it's common knowledge that...** tout le monde sait que... + *indicative*, il est de notoriété publique que...+ *indicative*; **the agreement is common knowledge** l'accord est connu de tous; **it's common practice to thank your host** il est d'usage de remercier son hôte; *Br* **it's common talk that...** on entend souvent dire que... + *indicative*

(**d**) *Pej (vulgar)* commun, vulgaire; **a common little man** un petit homme vulgaire

(**e**) *Gram (gender)* non marqué

(**f**) *Mus* **common time** *or* **measure** mesure *f* à quatre temps

2 *n* (**a**) *(land)* terrain *m* communal; *Br Law* **right of common** *(of land)* communauté *f* de jouissance; *(of pasture)* droit *m* de (vaine) pâture; *(of property)* droit *m* de servitude

(**b**) *Br (idiom)* **nothing out of the common** rien d'extraordinaire

3 commons *npl* (**a**) *Arch or Literary* **the commons** *(common people)* le peuple

(**b**) *Old-fashioned (food)* chère *f*; **to be on short common** faire maigre chère

4 Commons *npl Br & Can Pol* **the Commons** les Communes *fpl*

5 in common *adv* en commun; **to have sth in common with sb** avoir qch en commun avec qn; **we have nothing in common** nous n'avons rien en commun; **they have certain ideas in common** ils partagent certaines idées

►► *EU* ***Common Agricultural Policy*** politique *f* agricole commune; ***common cold*** rhume *m*; ***common crab*** crabe *m* vert; ***common currency*** *Fin* monnaie *f* commune; *Fig* **to be common currency** être monnaie courante; *Math & Fig* ***common denominator*** dénominateur *m* commun; *Math* ***common divisor*** commun diviseur *m*; *Br Sch* ***Common Entrance*** = examen de fin d'études primaires permettant d'entrer dans une "public school"; *Am St Exch* ***common equities*** actions *fpl* ordinaires; *Rel* ***Common Era*** ère *f* chrétienne; *EU* ***common external tariff*** tarif *m* externe commun; *Math* ***common factor*** facteur *m* commun; *EU* ***Common Fisheries Policy*** politique *f* commune de la pêche; *Acct* ***common fixed costs*** coûts *mpl* fixes communs; *Am Math* ***common fraction*** fraction *f* ordinaire; *EU* ***Common Foreign and Security Policy*** politique *f* étrangère et de sécurité commune; *Comput* ***common gateway interface*** interface *f* commune de passerelle; *Orn* ***common gull*** goéland *m* cendré; ***common law*** droit *m* coutumier, common law *f*; *Math* ***common logarithm*** logarithme *m* vulgaire *ou* décimal; *EU* ***the Common Market*** le marché commun; *Math* ***common multiple*** commun multiple *m*; *Gram* ***common noun*** nom *m* commun; ***common ownership*** copropriété *f*; ***the Common Riding*** = festival se déroulant dans plusieurs villes des Borders, en Écosse, au cours duquel ont lieu des proclamations, des processions, des cavalcades, des manifestations sportives et des reconstitutions historiques; *Br Sch & Univ* ***common room*** *(for students)* salle *f* commune; *(for staff)* salle *f* des professeurs; ***common sense*** bon sens *m*, sens *m* commun; **she has a great deal of common sense** elle a beaucoup de bon sens; **it's only common sense** ça tombe sous le sens; *Orn* ***common snipe*** bécassine *f* des marais; *Am St Exch* ***common stock*** actions *fpl* ordinaires; *Orn* ***common tern*** sterne *f* pierregarin

COMMON LAW

On désigne ainsi l'ensemble des règles de droit qui constituent la base du système juridique des pays de langue anglaise. À l'opposé des systèmes issus du droit romain, qui s'appuie sur la loi telle qu'elle est fixée dans des Codes, ces règles, non écrites, sont établies par la jurisprudence.

commonality [,kɒmə'nælɪtɪ] *n* (**a**) *(fact of having aspects in common)* points *mpl* communs (**b**) *(common people)* peuple *m*

commonalty ['kɒmənəltɪ] *(pl* **commonalties***) n Formal (common people)* peuple *m*

commoner ['kɒmənə(r)] *n* (**a**) *(not noble)* roturier(ère) *m,f* (**b**) *Br Law (with joint land rights)* = personne qui a droit de vaine pâture (**c**) *Br Univ* = étudiant ne bénéficiant pas de bourse (particulièrement à Oxford ou à Cambridge)

commonhold ['kɒmən,həʊld] *Br* **1** *n* copropriété *f*

2 *adj (system)* de copropriété

►► ***commonhold association*** syndicat *m* de copropriétaires

common-law *adj* **common-law wife** concubine *f* (reconnue juridiquement); **common-law marriage** concubinage *m*

commonly ['kɒmənlɪ] *adv* (**a**) *(usually)* généralement, communément; **what is commonly known as...** ce que l'on appelle dans le langage courant... (**b**) *Pej (vulgarly)* vulgairement

commonness ['kɒmənnɪs] *n* (**a**) *(usualness)* caractère *m* commun *ou* ordinaire (**b**) *(frequency)* fréquence *f* (**c**) *(universality)* généralité *f*, universalité *f* (**d**) *Pej (vulgarness)* vulgarité *f*

common-or-garden *adj Br* **the common-or-garden variety** le modèle standard *ou* ordinaire; *Hum* **I'm just a common-or-garden journalist** je ne suis qu'un journaliste ordinaire *ou* un journaliste parmi tant d'autres; **you may think this just a common-or-garden wristwatch but...** tu as peut-être l'impression que c'est une montre ordinaire *ou* comme les autres mais...

commonplace ['kɒmən,pleɪs] **1** *adj* banal, ordinaire; **compact discs have become commonplace** les disques compacts sont devenus courants *ou* sont maintenant monnaie courante

2 *n (thing)* banalité *f*; *(saying)* lieu *m* commun, platitude *f*

►► *Old-fashioned* ***commonplace book*** recueil *m* de pensées

commonsense ['kɒmən,sens], **commonsensical** [,kɒmən'sensɪkəl] *adj (attitude, approach, decision)* sensé, plein de bon sens

commonweal ['kɒmənwi:l] *n Literary* bien *m* commun

commonwealth ['kɒmənwelθ] **1** *n* (**a**) *(country)* pays *m*; *(state)* État *m*; *(republic)* république *f*

(**b**) *(body politic)* corps *m* politique

2 Commonwealth 1 *n* (**a**) **the (British) Commonwealth (of Nations)** le Commonwealth; **Minister** *or* **Secretary of State for Commonwealth Affairs** ministre *m* du Commonwealth (**b**) *Hist* **the Commonwealth** = période de l'histoire britannique de 1649 (mort de Charles I) à 1660 (rétablissement de la monarchie) **2** *comp (country)* du Commonwealth

►► ***Commonwealth Day*** = commémoration de la naissance de la reine Victoria, jour férié dans de nombreux pays du Commonwealth (deuxième lundi de mars); ***the Commonwealth Games*** les jeux *mpl* du Commonwealth; ***the Commonwealth of Australia*** le Commonwealth d'Australie; ***the Commonwealth of Independent States*** la Communauté d'États indépendants; ***the Commonwealth of Massachusetts*** l'état *m* du Massachusetts; ***the Commonwealth of Pennsylvania*** l'état *m* de Pennsylvanie

COMMONWEALTH

Le Commonwealth comprend cinquante états souverains qui, à un moment ou à un autre, firent partie de l'Empire britannique. C'est en 1931 que le statut du Commonwealth – fondé sur les principes d'autonomie, d'égalité et d'allégeance à la Couronne parmi les colonies et dépendances britanniques – fut adopté. Malgré l'effondrement de l'Empire, le monarque britannique est toujours à la tête du Commonwealth et les dirigeants de tous les États membres se réunissent bisannuellement lors de la "Commonwealth Conference". Les jeux du Commonwealth, ou "Commonwealth Games", permettent aux États membres de se mesurer dans la majorité des disciplines olympiques et ont lieu tous les quatre ans dans un pays différent.

commotion [kə'məʊʃən] *n* (**a**) *(noise)* brouhaha *m*; **what's all the commotion (about)?** qu'est-ce que c'est que ce brouhaha *ou* vacarme?; **who's making all this commotion?** qui est-ce qui fait tout ce tapage?

(**b**) *(disturbance)* agitation *f*; **what a commotion!** quel cirque!; **to be in a (state of) commotion** *(person)* être vivement ému; *(crowd)* être agité; *(city)* être en émoi; **the news caused a real commotion** la nouvelle a causé un véritable désordre

(**c**) *(civil unrest)* insurrection *f*, troubles *mpl*

comms [kɒmz] *adj Br* de communication

►► *Comput* ***comms package*** logiciel *m* de communication; *Comput* ***comms port*** port *m* de communication

communal ['kɒmjʊnəl] *adj* (**a**) *(shared → bathroom, changing room)* commun; **communal property** biens *mpl* en commun *ou* en copropriété; **communal room** pièce *f* commune (**b**) *(of community)* communautaire, collectif; **a communal activity** une activité collective; **communal violence** violence *f* entre communautés

communalism ['kɒmjʊnəlɪzəm] *n* = théorie confiant la plus grande partie du pouvoir aux communes

communally ['kɒmjʊnəlɪ] *adv* collectivement, en commun; **communally owned** en copropriété

commune 1 *n* ['kɒmju:n] (**a**) *(group of people)* communauté *f*; **to live in a commune** vivre en communauté (**b**) *Admin (district)* commune *f*

2 *vi* [kə'mju:n] (**a**) *(communicate)* communier; **to commune with nature** communier avec la nature (**b**) *Rel* communier

3 Commune *n* ['kɒmju:n] *Hist* **the (Paris) Commune** la Commune

communicability [kə,mju:nɪkə'bɪlɪtɪ], **communicableness** [kə'mju:nɪkəbəlnɪs] *n* communicabilité *f*

communicable [kə'mju:nɪkəbəl] *adj* communicable; *Med (disease)* contagieux, transmissible

communicant [kə'mju:nɪkənt] **1** *n* (**a**) *Rel* communiant(e) *m,f* (**b**) *(informant)* informateur(trice) *m,f*

2 *adj* (**a**) *(communicating)* qui communique, communicant (**b**) *Rel* pratiquant

communicate [kə'mju:nɪkeɪt] **1** *vi* (**a**) *(be in touch)* communiquer; *(contact)* prendre contact, se mettre en contact; **they communicate with each other by phone** ils communiquent par téléphone; **I find it difficult to communicate (with others)** j'ai du mal à entrer en relation avec les autres; **they communicate well (with one another)** ils s'entendent bien; **she no longer communicates with him** elle n'est plus en contact avec lui; **we can't seem to communicate** on ne se comprend pas; **we've stopped communicating** on a cessé de communiquer, on ne se parle plus

(**b**) *(rooms → connect)* communiquer

(**c**) *Rel* communier, recevoir la communion

2 *vt* (**a**) *(impart → news)* communiquer, transmettre; *(→ feelings)* communiquer, faire partager; **she communicated the news to them** elle leur a fait part de la nouvelle

(**b**) *(disease)* transmettre

communicating [kə'mju:nɪkeɪtɪŋ] *adj (room)* communicant; **a hotel suite with communicating rooms** une suite avec chambres communicantes

►► ***communicating door*** porte *f* de communication

communication [kə,mju:nɪ'keɪʃən] **1** *n* (**a**) *(contact)* communication *f*; **are you in communication with her?** êtes-vous en contact *ou* en relation avec elle?; **to be in close communication with one another** être en relation constante; **we haven't had any communication for six months** nous ne sommes plus en relation(s) depuis six mois; **we broke off all communication with him** nous avons rompu tout contact avec lui; **to be in radio communication with sb** communiquer avec qn par radio, être en communication radio avec qn

(**b**) *(of thoughts, feelings)* communication *f*; **to be good at communication, to have good communication skills** avoir des talents de communicateur, être un bon communicateur; **communication gap** manque *m* de communication; **communication problem** problème *m* de communication (**c**) *(message)* communication *f*, message *m*; **no official communication of his death has yet been received** on n'a encore reçu aucune communication officielle de sa mort

2 communications *npl (technology)* communications *fpl*; *(roads, telegraph lines etc)* communications *fpl*; *Mil* liaison *f*, communications *fpl*

►► *Com* ***communications channel*** canal *m* de communication; *Com* ***communications conglomerate*** groupe *m* multimédia; *Br* ***communication cord*** sonnette *f* d'alarme *(dans les trains)*; ***communications director*** directeur *m* de la communication, dircom *m*; *Comput* ***communication interface*** interface *f* de communication; ***communications link*** liaison *f* de communications; ***communications manager*** directeur(trice) *m,f* de la communication, dircom *m*; ***communications officer*** responsable *mf* de la communication; *Astron* ***communications satellite*** satellite *m* de télécommunication; ***communications sector*** secteur *m* des communications; *Comput* ***communications software*** logiciel *m* de communication; *Mil* ***communication trench*** boyau *m*

communications-intensive *adj* = utilisant intensivement les moyens de communication

communicative [kə'mju:nɪkətɪv] *adj* (**a**) *(talkative)* communicatif, expansif; **he's not very communicative** il est peu communicatif (**b**) *(ability, difficulty)* de communication

►► *Ling* ***communicative competence*** compétence *f* de communication

communicatively [kə'mju:nɪkətɪvlɪ] *adv* du point de vue *ou* sur le plan de la communication; **to be communicatively disposed** être d'humeur expansive; *Ling* **to be communicatively competent** avoir atteint une compétence de communication

communicativeness [kə'mju:nɪkətɪvnɪs] *n* caractère *m* communicatif *ou* expansif

communicator [kə'mju:nɪˌkeɪtə(r)] *n* = personne douée pour la communication; **she's a good/bad communicator** elle est douée/n'est pas douée pour la communication

communion [kə'mju:njən] **1** *n* (**a**) *(sharing)* communion *f*; **a communion of interests** une communauté d'intérêts; **communion with nature** communion *f* avec la nature (**b**) *Rel (group)* communion *f*; *(denomination)* confession *f*

2 Communion *n Rel (sacrament)* communion *f*; **to give Communion** donner la communion; **to take** *or* **to receive Communion** recevoir la communion; **they go to Communion every Sunday** ils communient tous les dimanches; **she made her Communion** elle a fait sa communion; **to make one's Easter Communion** faire ses pâques

►► *Rel* ***communion cup*** calice *m*; *Rel* ***communion service*** célébration *f* de la communion; *Rel* ***communion wafer*** hostie *f*; *Rel* ***communion wine*** vin *m* de messe

communiqué [kə'mju:nɪkeɪ] *n* communiqué *m*

Communism ['kɒmjʊnɪzəm] *n* communisme *m*

Communist ['kɒmjʊnɪst] **1** *n* communiste *mf*

2 *adj* communiste

►► ***Communist cell*** cellule *f* communiste; ***Communist International*** Komintern *m*; ***Communist Party*** parti *m* communiste

---

'The Communist Manifesto' *Marx & Engels* 'Le Manifeste du parti communiste'

---

community [kə'mju:nətɪ] *(pl* **communities***)* **1** *n* (**a**) *(group of people, animals)* communauté *f*, groupement *m*; **the American community in Paris** la communauté américaine de Paris; **the business community** le monde des affaires; **the international community** la communauté internationale; **for the good of the community** pour le bien public *ou* le bien de la communauté; **a sense of community** un sens communautaire *ou* de la solidarité

(**b**) *(locality)* communauté *f*; **a small mining community** une petite communauté minière; **a community of 2,000** une communauté de 2000 habitants

(**c**) *Rel* communauté *f*

(**d**) *(sharing)* propriété *f* collective; *Law* communauté *f*; **community of goods/interests** communauté *f* de biens/d'intérêts

2 Community *n EU* **the (European) Community** la Communauté (européenne)

►► ***community antenna*** antenne *f* communautaire; ***community association*** = en Grande-Bretagne, association socioculturelle locale; *Admin* ***community care*** = système britannique de soins et d'aide au niveau local; ***community centre*** foyer *m* municipal, centre *m* social; *Am TV* ***community channel*** = chaîne du réseau câblé sur laquelle des particuliers peuvent diffuser leurs propres émissions; *Br Formerly Admin* ***community charge*** = impôt aboli en 1993, regroupant taxe d'habitation et impôts locaux, payable par chaque occupant adulte d'une même habitation; *Am Fin* ***community chest*** fonds *m* commun *(à des fins sociales)*; *Am* ***community college*** centre *m* universitaire (de premier cycle); *Br* ***community home*** *(for deprived children)* assistance *f* publique; *(for young offenders)* centre *m* d'éducation surveillée; ***community leader*** = personne qui joue un rôle actif dans la vie d'une communauté; ***community policing*** ≃ îlotage *m*, *Can* services *mpl* de police communautaires, patrouille *f* pédestre de quartier; *Am Law* ***community property*** biens *mpl* soumis au régime de la communauté; ***community radio*** radio *f* communautaire; ***community relations*** relations *fpl* publiques; *Br* ***community school*** = école servant de maison de la culture; *Law* ***community service*** ≃ travail *m* d'intérêt général; ***community singing*** *(UNCOUNT)* chansons *fpl* populaires *(reprises en chœur)*; ***community spirit*** esprit *m* de groupe; ***community worker*** animateur(trice) *m,f* socioculturel(elle)

commutable [kə'mju:təbəl] *adj* (**a**) *(exchangeable)* interchangeable, permutable (**b**) *Law (sentence)* commuable; **a death sentence commutable to life imprisonment** une peine capitale commuable en emprisonnement à perpétuité

commutate ['kɒmju:teɪt] *vt Elec (current)* redresser

commutation [ˌkɒmju:'teɪʃən] *n* (**a**) *Law (of penalty)* commutation *f*; **commutation of sentence** commutation *f* de peine (**b**) *(UNCOUNT) (exchange)* échange *m*, substitution *f* (**c**) *(payment)* échange *m* (**d**) *Elec (of current)* redressement *m* (**e**) *Am (commuting)* migration *f* journalière

►► *Am Transp* ***commutation ticket*** carte *f* d'abonnement

commutative [kə'mju:tətɪv] *adj (gen) & Math* commutatif

commutator ['kɒmju:ˌteɪtə(r)] *n Elec* commutateur *m*

commute [kə'mju:t] **1** *n* trajet *m (entre travail et domicile)*; **it's an easy commute** c'est un trajet commode

2 *vi* faire un trajet régulier, faire la navette; **I commute from the suburbs** je viens tous les jours de banlieue; **to commute by train/car** se rendre à son travail en train/voiture

3 *vt* (**a**) *(exchange)* substituer, échanger; **to commute one thing for another** substituer une chose à une autre, échanger une chose pour *ou* contre une autre

(**b**) *(convert)* convertir; **Midas commuted metal into gold** Midas changeait le métal en or; *Fin* **to commute an annuity into a lump sum** racheter une rente en un seul versement

(**c**) *Law (sentence)* commuer; **a sentence commuted to life imprisonment** une peine commuée en emprisonnement à vie

commuter [kə'mju:tə(r)] **1** *n* banlieusard(e) *m,f (qui fait un trajet journalier pour se rendre au travail)*, *Belg* navetteur(euse) *m,f*, *Suisse* pendulaire *mf*; **I've been a commuter for fifteen years** ça fait quinze ans que je fais la navette (entre chez moi et le travail); **the problems caused by commuter traffic** les problèmes provoqués par l'utilisation de la voiture pour se rendre au travail; **commuter traffic is very heavy this evening** la circulation en direction de la banlieue est très dense ce soir

2 *comp (line, train)* de banlieue

►► ***commuter airline*** compagnie *f* d'aviation court-courrier; *Br* ***the commuter belt*** la grande banlieue; ***commuter plane*** commuter *m*

commuterland [kə'mju:təlænd] *n* = grande banlieue considérée comme un pays à part, où l'on ne fait rien d'autre que dormir

commuting [kə'mju:tɪŋ] *n (UNCOUNT)* trajets *mpl* réguliers, migrations *fpl* quotidiennes *(entre le domicile, généralement en banlieue, et le lieu de travail)*

Como ['kəʊməʊ] *n* Côme; **Lake Como** le lac de Côme

Comoran ['kɒmərən], **Comorian** [kə'mɒrjən] **1** *n* Comorien(enne) *m,f*

2 *adj* comorien

Comoro Islands ['kɒmərəʊ-] *npl* **the Comoro Islands** les îles *fpl* Comores; **in the Comoro Islands** aux îles Comores

comp [kɒmp] *n* (**a**) *Typ (compositor)* metteur *m* (en pages) (**b**) *(ticket)* exonéré *m*

.comp *Comput (written abbr* **computers***) (in newsgroups)* = abréviation désignant les forums de discussion qui ont pour thème l'informatique

compact 1 *adj* [kəm'pækt] (**a**) *(small)* compact, petit; *(person)* trapu; **the gadget is compact and easy to use** ce gadget ne prend pas de place et est facile à utiliser

(**b**) *(dense)* dense, serré

(**c**) *(concise)* concis, condensé

2 *vt* [kəm'pækt] *(compress)* compacter, tasser; *Comput (file)* comprimer

3 *n* ['kɒmpækt] (**a**) *(for powder)* poudrier *m*

(**b**) *Am (car)* (voiture *f*) compacte *f*, petite voiture *f*

(**c**) *Formal (agreement)* convention *f*, contrat *m*; *(informal)* accord *m*, entente *f*

►► ***compact camera*** (appareil photo *m*) compact *m*; *Am* ***compact car*** (voiture *f*) compacte *f*, petite voiture *f*; ***compact disc*** (disque *m*) compact *m*, CD *m*; ***compact disc interactive*** CDI *m*; ***compact disc player*** platine *f* CD; ***compact disc recorder*** graveur *m* de disque compact; ***compact disc rewritable*** CD *m* réinscriptible; ***compact disc video*** CD vidéo *m*

compacting [kəm'pæktɪŋ] *n Comput* compression *f*

compactly [kəm'pæktlɪ] *adv* (**a**) *(made)* de manière compacte; **compactly designed** conçu sans perte de place (**b**) *(concisely)* de manière concise

compactness [kəm'pæktnɪs] *n* (**a**) *(smallness)* compacité *f*; **the compactness of the design** la compacité de la conception (**b**) *(denseness)* compacité *f*, densité *f* (**c**) *(conciseness)* concision *f*

Companies ['kʌmpənɪz] *npl*

►► *Law* ***Companies Act*** Loi *f* sur les sociétés; *Br Com* ***Companies House, Companies Registration Office*** = institut où sont enregistrées toutes les informations concernant les entreprises du pays

companion [kəm'pænjən] *n* (**a**) *(friend)* compagnon (compagne) *m,f*; *(employee)* dame *f* de compagnie; **to be employed as a companion to sb** être employé pour tenir compagnie à qn; **a travelling companion** un compagnon de voyage; **a drinking companion** un compagnon de bistrot; **companions in arms/distress** compagnons *mpl* d'armes/d'infortune

(**b**) *(one of pair)* pendant *m*; **to be a companion to sth** faire pendant à qch

(**c**) *(handbook)* manuel *m*

(**d**) *(in titles)* compagnon *m*; **Companion to English Literature** *(title of book)* guide *m* de la littérature anglaise

(**e**) *Naut* capot *m* (d'escalier)

►► ***Companion of (the Order of) the Bath*** = distinction honorifique britannique; ***Companion of (the Order of) the British Empire*** = distinction honorifique britannique; ***Companion of Honour*** = décoration britannique remise aux citoyens qui ont rendu des services à l'État, ≃ chevalier *m* de la Légion d'honneur; *Naut* ***companion ladder*** échelle *f* de commandement; ***companion volume*** *(book)* volume *m* qui va de pair

companionable [kəm'pænjənəbəl] *adj (person)* sociable, d'une compagnie agréable; **they sat in companionable silence** ils étaient assis tranquillement sans éprouver le besoin de parler

companionably [kəm'pænjənəblɪ] *adv* amicalement, sociablement

companionship [kəm'pænjənʃɪp] *n (UNCOUNT) (fellowship)* compagnie *f*; *(friendship)* amitié *f*, camaraderie *f*; **she longs for companionship** la compagnie *ou* la société (des autres) lui manque; **he enjoys the companionship of the football team** il aime la camaraderie qui règne au sein de l'équipe de football; **the dog provides companionship for her** le chien lui fait de la compagnie *ou* lui tient compagnie

companionway [kəm'pænjənweɪ] *n Naut* escalier *m* de descente; *(on smaller boat)* montée *f*, descente *f*

company ['kʌmpənɪ] *(pl* **companies***)* **1** *n* (**a**) *(companionship)* compagnie *f*; **we enjoy one another's company** nous aimons être ensemble; **I like his company** j'aime sa compagnie, j'aime être avec lui; **she's good company** elle est d'agréable compagnie; **to keep sb company** tenir compagnie à qn; **it's nice to have company** c'est agréable d'avoir de la compagnie; **she needs the company of children of her own age** elle a besoin d'être avec des enfants de son âge; **to be fond of one's own company** aimer être seul; **in company with others** en compagnie d'autres; **we request the pleasure of your company at dinner** nous ferez-vous le plaisir de venir dîner?; **here's where we part company** voilà où nos chemins se séparent; *Fig* là, je ne suis plus d'accord avec vous; **they parted company last year** ils ont rompu l'année dernière; *Hum* **the handle finally parted company with the door** la poignée a fini par fausser compagnie à la porte

(**b**) *(companions)* compagnie *f*, fréquentation *f*; **I don't like the company he keeps** je n'aime pas ses fréquentations; **she has got into** *or* **she's keeping bad company** elle a de mauvaises fréquentations; **to be in good company** être en bonne compagnie; *Fig* **if I'm wrong, I'm in good company** si j'ai tort, je ne suis pas le seul; *Prov* **a man is known by the company he keeps** dis-moi qui tu fréquentes, je te dirai qui tu es

(**c**) *(people present)* assemblée *f*, personnes *fpl* présentes; **to do sth in company** faire qch en public; **you mustn't speak like that in company** on ne dit pas ces choses-là en société; **present company excepted** à part les personnes ici présentes; **the most intelligent of the company were in agreement** les plus intelligentes des personnes présentes étaient d'accord

(**d**) *(UNCOUNT) (guests)* invités *mpl*, compagnie *f*; **are you expecting company?** attendez-vous de la visite?; *Fam* **we've got company!** *(there's someone else here, we're being followed)* nous avons de la compagnie

(**e**) *Com (firm)* société *f*, compagnie *f*; **to form** *or* **incorporate a company** constituer une société; **Jones & Company** Jones et Compagnie; **to do sth on** *or* **in company time** faire qch pendant les heures de travail

(**f**) *(group of people)* compagnie *f*, assemblée *f*

(**g**) *Theat (of actors)* troupe *f*, compagnie *f*

(**h**) *Mil* compagnie *f*; *Naut (crew)* équipage *m*

(**i**) *(of girl guides)* compagnie *f*

(**j**) *(guild)* corporation *f* de marchands

2 *comp (policy)* d'entreprise

3 Company *n Am Fam* **the Company** la CIA

►► ***company accounts*** comptes *mpl* sociaux; ***company car*** voiture *f* de fonction; ***company credit card*** carte *f* de crédit professionnelle; ***company director*** directeur(trice) *m,f*; ***company doctor*** *(medical)* médecin *m* du travail; *(businessperson)* redresseur *m* d'entreprises; ***company funds*** fonds *m* social; ***company law*** droit *m* des sociétés; ***company lawyer*** avocat(e) *m,f* d'une entreprise *ou* société; *Mil* ***company officer*** officier *m* de compagnie; ***company reserves*** épargne *f* des entreprises; ***company savings scheme*** plan *m* d'épargne entreprise; ***company secretary*** secrétaire *mf* général(e) *(d'une entreprise)*; *Mil* ***company sergeant-major*** adjudant *m*

comparability [ˌkɒmpərə'bɪlətɪ] *n* comparabilité *f*

comparable ['kɒmprəbəl] *adj* comparable; **to be comparable to sth** être comparable à qch; **the salaries aren't at all comparable** il n'y a pas de comparaison possible entre les salaires

comparably ['kɒmpərəblɪ] *adv* comparablement; **the two items are comparably priced** les deux articles coûtent à peu près le même prix

comparative [kəm'pærətɪv] **1** *adj* (**a**) *(relative)* relatif; **the comparative wealth of the two countries** la fortune relative des deux pays; **she's a comparative stranger to me** je la connais relativement peu (**b**) *(study)* comparatif; *(field of study)* comparé (**c**) *Gram* comparatif

2 *n Gram* comparatif *m*; **in the comparative** au comparatif

►► ***comparative adverb*** adverbe *m* de comparaison *ou* comparatif; *Am* ***comparative advertising*** publicité *f* comparative; *Gram* ***the comparative degree*** le comparatif; ***comparative history*** histoire *f* comparée; ***comparative law*** droit *m* comparé; ***comparative linguistics*** linguistique *f* comparée; ***comparative literature*** littérature *f* comparée

comparatively [kəm'pærətɪvlɪ] *adv* (**a**) *(quite)* relativement (**b**) *(study)* comparativement

compare [kəm'peə(r)] **1** *vt* (**a**) *(contrast)* comparer, mettre en comparaison; **let's compare Fitzgerald with Hemingway** comparons Fitzgerald à *ou* avec Hemingway; **compared with** *or* **to sth** en comparaison de *ou* par comparaison avec qch; **compared with the others she's brilliant** elle est brillante par rapport aux autres; **compared with last year's figures** par rapport aux chiffres de l'année dernière; **to compare notes** échanger ses impressions

(**b**) *(liken)* comparer, assimiler; **to compare sth to sth** comparer qch à qch; **his paintings have been compared to those of Manet** on a comparé ses tableaux à ceux de Manet; **it's impossible to compare the two systems** il n'y a pas de comparaison possible entre les deux systèmes

(**c**) *Gram* former les degrés de comparaison de

2 *vi* être comparable (**with** à); **to compare well** *or* **favourably (with sth)** soutenir la comparaison (avec qch); **how do the two candidates compare?** quelles sont les qualités respectives des deux candidats?; **how do the brands compare in (terms of) price?** les marques sont-elles comparables du point de vue prix?; **other kinds of washing powder just can't compare** les autres marques de lessive ne sont pas à la hauteur de celle-ci; **her cooking doesn't** *or* **can't compare with yours** il n'y a aucune comparaison entre sa cuisine et la tienne

3 *n Literary* **he's intelligent beyond compare** il est incomparablement intelligent; **beauty beyond compare** beauté *f* sans pareille

comparison [kəm'pærɪsən] **1** *n* (**a**) *(gen)* comparaison *f*; **there's no comparison** il n'y a aucune comparaison (possible); **to draw** *or* **to make a comparison between sth and sth** faire la comparaison de qch avec qch *ou* entre qch et qch; **this book stands** *or* **bears comparison with the classics** ce livre soutient la comparaison avec les classiques; **without comparison, beyond all comparison** sans comparaison

(**b**) *Gram* comparaison *f*; **degrees of comparison** degrés *mpl* de comparaison

2 by comparison *adv* par comparaison

3 in comparison *adv* par comparaison

4 in comparison with *prep* en comparaison de, par rapport à

compartment [kəm'pɑːtmənt] *n* (**a**) *(section)* compartiment *m* (**b**) *Naut & Rail* compartiment *m*

compartmental [ˌkɒmpɑːt'mentəl] *adj* compartimenté

compartmentalization [ˌkɒmpɑːtˌmentəlaɪ'zeɪʃən] *n* compartimentage *m*

compartmentalize, -ise [ˌkɒmpɑːt'mentəlaɪz] *vt* compartimenter

compass ['kʌmpəs] **1** *n* (**a**) *(for direction)* boussole *f*; *Naut* compas *m*; **to take a compass bearing** prendre un relèvement au compas

(**b**) *Geom* compas *m*

(**c**) *(limits)* étendue *f*; *(range)* portée *f*; **within the narrow compass of this book** dans les limites restreintes de ce livre; **that does not lie within the compass of this committee** ce n'est pas du ressort de ce comité; **beyond the compass of the human mind** au-delà de la portée de l'esprit humain

(**d**) *Mus (of voice)* étendue *f*, portée *f*

2 *comp (error)* du compas

3 *vt* (**a**) *(go round)* faire le tour de; *(surround)* encercler, entourer

(**b**) *Literary (accomplish → goal)* atteindre; *(→ ends)* en venir à; *(→ task)* accomplir

4 compasses *npl Geom* **(a pair of) compasses** un compas

►► *Naut* ***compass card*** rose *f* des vents; ***compass course*** route *f* magnétique; ***compass point*** aire *f* de vent; *Naut* ***compass rose*** rose *f* des vents; *Tech* ***compass saw*** scie *f* à guichet; *Archit* ***compass window*** fenêtre *f* en saillie ronde

compassion [kəm'pæʃən] *n* compassion *f*, pitié *f*; **to arouse compassion** faire pitié, exciter la compassion; **to show compassion** montrer de la compassion; **you have no compassion** tu n'as pas de pitié

►► ***compassion fatigue*** = lassitude du public à l'égard des nécessiteux

compassionate [kəm'pæʃənət] *adj* compatissant; **on compassionate grounds** pour des raisons personnelles *ou* familiales

►► ***compassionate leave*** congé *m* exceptionnel; *Mil* permission *f* exceptionnelle *(pour raisons personnelles)*

compassionately [kəm'pæʃənətlɪ] *adv* avec compassion

compatibility [kəmˌpætə'bɪlətɪ] *n* compatibilité *f*

compatible [kəm'pætəbəl] *adj* compatible (**with** avec); *Comput* **IBM-compatible** compatible IBM

compatibly [kəm'pætəblɪ] *adv* d'une manière compatible (**with** avec)

compatriot [kəm'pætrɪət] *n* compatriote *mf*

compeer [kəm'pɪə(r)] *n Formal* (**a**) *(equal)* pair *m* (**b**) *(companion)* camarade *m*

compel [kəm'pel] *(pt & pp* **compelled,** *cont* **compelling***)* *vt* (**a**) *(force)* contraindre, obliger; **to compel sb to do sth** contraindre *ou* forcer qn à faire qch; **ill health compelled her to retire** pour des raisons de santé, elle a été obligée de prendre sa retraite

(**b**) *(demand)* imposer, forcer; **the sort of woman who compels admiration** le genre de femme qu'on ne peut s'empêcher d'admirer *ou* qui force l'admiration; **a tone of voice that compels attention** un ton de voix qui retient l'attention

compelling [kəm'pelɪŋ] *adj* (**a**) *(reason, desire, urge)* convaincant, irrésistible (**b**) *(book, film, performance)* envoûtant; **her book makes compelling reading** son livre est captivant *ou* prenant; **a compelling speaker** un orateur qui subjugue *ou* captive son auditoire

compellingly [kəm'pelɪŋlɪ] *adv* irrésistiblement, d'une façon irrésistible

compendious [kəm'pendɪəs] *adj Formal* concis

compendium [kəm'pendɪəm] *(pl* **compendiums** *or* **compendia** [-dɪə]*)* *n* (**a**) *(summary)* abrégé *m*, précis *m* (**b**) *Br (collection)* collection *f*

►► ***compendium of games*** boîte *f* de jeux

compensable [kəm'pensəbəl] *adj* indemnisable; *Acct* **compensable loss** perte *f* indemnisable

compensate ['kɒmpenseɪt] **1** *vt* (**a**) *(make amends to → person)* dédommager, indemniser; **to compensate sb for sth** *(for loss)* dédommager qn de qch; *(for injury)* dédommager qn pour qch; **the firm compensated the workman for his injuries** l'entreprise a dédommagé l'ouvrier pour ses blessures

(**b**) *(offset)* compenser, contrebalancer; *Tech* compenser, neutraliser

2 *vi* (**a**) *(make up)* être une *ou* servir de compensation, compenser; **she compensates for her short stature by wearing high heels** elle porte des talons hauts pour compenser sa petite taille

(**b**) *(with money)* dédommager, indemniser

(**c**) *Psy* compenser

compensating ['kɒmpenseɪtɪŋ] *adj* compensateur

►► *Tech* ***compensating arm*** bras *m* de rappel; ***compensating coil*** bobine *f* compensatrice *ou* de compensation; ***compensating coupling*** manchon *m* élastique; ***compensating gear*** engrenage *m* différentiel; ***compensating magnet*** aimant *m* correcteur *ou* de correction; ***compensating network*** circuit *m* compensateur; *Fin* ***compensating payment*** règlement *m* en compensation; ***compensating spring*** ressort *m* compensateur; ***compensating valve*** soupape *f* de compensation; ***compensating winding*** enroulement *m* compensateur *ou* de compensation

compensation [ˌkɒmpen'seɪʃən] *n* (**a**) *(recompense)* indemnité *f*, dédommagement *m*; *(payment)* rémunération *f*; **all of the victims will receive compensation** toutes les victimes recevront une indemnité; **working for oneself has its compensations** travailler à son compte a ses avantages; **in compensation for** en compensation de; **by way of compensation for your wasted time** pour compenser le temps perdu
(**b**) *(adaptation)* compensation *f*; *(in weight)* contrepoids *m*; *Tech* compensation *f*, neutralisation *f*
▸▸ *Br Law* ***compensation order*** = obligation de la part de l'accusé de réparer ses actions; *Br* ***compensation package*** *(for redundancy)* prime *f* de licenciement; *Am (when starting new job)* avantages *mpl* sociaux; *Com* ***compensation plan*** mode *m* de rémunération

compensator ['kɒmpenseɪtə(r)] *n*
▸▸ *Tech* ***compensator arm*** bras *m* compensateur; ***compensator valve*** valve *f* de compensation

compensatory [ˌkɒmpen'seɪtərɪ] *adj* compensateur, compensatoire
▸▸ *EU* ***compensatory amounts*** montants *mpl* compensatoires; *EU* ***compensatory levy*** prélèvement *m* compensatoire

comper ['kɒmpə(r)] *n Fam* = personne qui participe à de nombreux jeux-concours et qui en fait parfois son activité principale

compere ['kɒmpeə(r)] *Br* **1** *n* animateur(trice) *m,f*, présentateur(trice) *m,f*
2 *vi* animer, présenter
3 *vt* animer, présenter

compete [kəm'piːt] *vi* (**a**) *(vie)* rivaliser; **to compete with sb for sth** rivaliser avec qn pour qch, disputer qch à qn; **seven candidates are competing for the position** sept candidats se disputent le poste; *Fig* **her cooking can't compete with yours** sa cuisine n'a rien de commun *ou* ne peut pas rivaliser avec la vôtre; **children here aren't encouraged to compete** ici, les enfants ne sont pas encouragés à la compétition
(**b**) *Com (one company)* faire de la concurrence (**with** à); *(two or more companies)* se faire concurrence; **they compete with foreign companies for contracts** ils sont en concurrence avec des entreprises étrangères pour obtenir des contrats; **we have to compete on an international level** nous devons être à la hauteur de la concurrence sur le plan international
(**c**) *Sport (take part)* participer; *(contend)* concourir; **ten women are competing in the race** dix femmes participent à la course; **to compete against sb for sth** concourir *ou* être en compétition avec qn pour qch; **the player had competed for every point** le joueur s'était battu sur chaque point; **we're competing against the Japanese** nous concourons *ou* sommes en compétition avec les Japonais; **there are only three teams competing** il n'y a que trois équipes sur les rangs

competence ['kɒmpɪtəns] *n* (**a**) *(ability)* compétence *f* (**in** pour *ou* en), aptitude *f* (**in** à *ou* pour); **to have the competence to do sth** avoir les moyens *ou* la capacité de faire qch; **that's beyond my competence** c'est au-delà de mes moyens, ça dépasse mes compétences
(**b**) *Law (of court)* compétence *f*; *(of evidence)* admissibilité *f*; **to be within the competence of the court** être de la compétence du tribunal
(**c**) *Ling* compétence *f*
(**d**) *Literary (income)* aisance *f*, moyens *mpl*

competency ['kɒmpɪtənsɪ] *(pl* **competencies***)* *n* (**a**) *Law (of witness)* habileté *f* (**b**) *(ability)* compétence *f* (**in** pour *ou* en), aptitude *f* (**in** à *ou* pour) (**c**) *Literary (income)* aisance *f*, moyens *mpl*

competent ['kɒmpɪtənt] *adj* (**a**) *(capable)* compétent, capable; *(qualified)* qualifié; **is she competent to handle the accounts?** est-elle compétente *ou* qualifiée pour tenir la comptabilité?; **he's quite competent at French** il a un bon niveau de français; **a competent piece of work** du bon travail
(**b**) *(sufficient)* suffisant
(**c**) *Law (witness)* habile; *(court)* compétent; *(evidence)* admissible, recevable; **competent to inherit** habilité à succéder

competently ['kɒmpɪtəntlɪ] *adv* (**a**) *(capably)* avec compétence (**b**) *(sufficiently)* suffisamment

competing [kəm'piːtɪŋ] *adj* en concurrence

competition [ˌkɒmpɪ'tɪʃən] *n* (**a**) *(rivalry)* compétition *f*, rivalité *f*; **competition for the position is fierce** il y a beaucoup de concurrence pour le poste, on se dispute âprement le poste; **to be in competition (with sb)** être en compétition *ou* concurrence (avec qn); **to enter into competition with sb** concurrencer *ou* faire concurrence à qn
(**b**) *Com & Econ* concurrence *f*; **unfair competition** concurrence *f* déloyale; **what's the competition doing?** que fait la concurrence?, que font nos rivaux *ou* concurrents?; **the company has to stay ahead of the competition** l'entreprise doit rester plus compétitive que les autres
(**c**) *(opposition)* **you're up against some tough competition** *(in race)* vous êtes en face d'adversaires de taille; *(for job, university)* la concurrence est rude
(**d**) *(contest)* concours *m*; *Sport* compétition *f*; *(race)* course *f*; **beauty/fishing competition** concours *m* de beauté/de pêche; **competition winner** gagnant(e) *m,f*; **to enter a competition** se présenter à un concours; **the candidate will be chosen by competition** le candidat sera choisi par concours; **that's him out of the competition** le voilà hors compétition; **competition car** voiture *f* de compétition
(**e**) *Biol* concurrence *f*

competitive [kəm'petətɪv] *adj* (**a**) *(involving competition)* de compétition
(**b**) *(person)* qui a l'esprit de compétition; *(atmosphere, environment)* de compétition; **he's so competitive** il a vraiment l'esprit de compétition
(**c**) *Com & Econ (product, price)* concurrentiel, compétitif; *(company, industry)* compétitif; **in a competitive marketplace** dans un marché de concurrence; **to offer competitive terms** proposer des prix très compétitifs
▸▸ *Com & Mktg* ***competitive advantage*** avantage *m* concurrentiel; ***competitive advertising*** publicité *f* concurrentielle; ***competitive analysis*** analyse *f* des concurrents; *Com & Mktg* ***competitive awareness*** sensibilité *f* compétitive; ***competitive bidding*** appel *m* d'offres; ***competitive edge*** (léger) avantage *m* concurrentiel; ***competitive examination*** concours *m*; ***competitive game*** jeu *m* de compétition; ***competitive scope*** domaine *m* concurrentiel, champ *m* concurrentiel; ***competitive society*** société *f* de compétition; ***competitive sports*** sports *mpl* de compétition; ***competitive strategy*** stratégie *f* concurrentielle

competitively [kəm'petətɪvlɪ] *adv* avec un esprit de compétition; *Com* **competitively priced goods** produits *mpl* au prix compétitif

competitiveness [kəm'petətɪvnɪs] *n (of product)* concurrence *f*; *(of company, price)* compétitivité *f*; *(of person)* esprit *m* de compétition

competitor [kəm'petɪtə(r)] *n (gen) & Com & Sport* concurrent(e) *m,f*; *(participant)* participant(e) *m,f*

compilation [ˌkɒmpɪ'leɪʃən] *n* compilation *f*
▸▸ ***compilation album*** compilation *f*

compile [kəm'paɪl] *vt* (**a**) *(gather → facts, material)* compiler (**b**) *(compose → list)* dresser; *(→ dictionary)* rédiger *(par compilation)* (**c**) *Comput* compiler

compiler [kəm'paɪlə(r)] *n* (**a**) *(gen)* compilateur(trice) *m,f* (**b**) *(of dictionary)* rédacteur(trice) *m,f* (**c**) *Comput* compilateur *m*

comping ['kɒmpɪŋ] *n Fam* = participation à de nombreux jeux-concours

complacence [kəm'pleɪsəns], **complacency** [kəm'pleɪsənsɪ] *n* autosatisfaction *f*, complaisance *f*

complacent [kəm'pleɪsənt] *adj (person)* satisfait *ou* content de soi, suffisant, complaisant; *(look, remark)* très satisfait; **to be complacent about sth** faire de l'autosatisfaction à propos de qch

complacently [kəm'pleɪsəntlɪ] *adv (act, smile, reply)* d'un air suffisant, avec suffisance *ou* complaisance; *(speak)* d'un ton suffisant, avec suffisance

complain [kəm'pleɪn] **1** *vi* (**a**) *(grumble)* se plaindre; **he's always complaining** il n'arrête pas de se plaindre; **he complained of a headache** il s'est plaint d'un mal de tête; *Fam* **how's it going? – can't complain** comment ça va? – je n'ai pas à me plaindre *ou* ça peut aller
(**b**) *(make formal protest)* formuler une plainte *ou* une réclamation, se plaindre; **to complain to sb (about sth)** se plaindre à *ou* auprès de qn (au sujet de qch)
2 *vt* **to complain that...** se plaindre que... + *indicative*; **she complained that he was always late** elle s'est plainte qu'il était toujours en retard

complainant [kəm'pleɪnənt] *n Law* demandeur(eresse) *m,f*, plaignant(e) *m,f*

complainer [kəm'pleɪnə(r)] *n* (**a**) *(grumbler)* grondeur(euse) *m,f* (**b**) *Law* demandeur(eresse) *m,f*, plaignant(e) *m,f* (**c**) *(person who makes formal complaint)* réclamant(e) *m,f*

complaint [kəm'pleɪnt] *n* (**a**) *(official protest)* plainte *f*, récrimination *f*; *Com* réclamation *f*; *Law* plainte *f*; **to make** *or* **lodge a complaint** se plaindre; **to lodge a complaint against sb** porter plainte contre qn
(**b**) *(grievance)* sujet *m ou* motif *m* de plainte, grief *m*; **I have no complaint** *or* **no cause for complaint** je n'ai aucune raison de me plaindre; **do you have any complaints about the company?** est-ce que vous avez à vous plaindre de l'entreprise?; **this is her latest complaint** c'est la dernière chose dont elle s'est plaint
(**c**) *(illness)* maladie *f*, affection *f*; **she has a liver complaint** elle souffre du foie; **a heart complaint** une maladie de cœur
▸▸ ***complaints book*** cahier *m* de réclamations; ***complaints department*** service *m* des réclamations; ***complaints office*** bureau *m* des réclamations

---

'Portnoy's Complaint' *Roth* 'Portnoy et son complexe'

---

complaisance [kəm'pleɪzəns] *n Formal* complaisance *f*, obligeance *f*

complaisant [kəm'pleɪzənt] *adj Formal* complaisant, obligeant

-complected [kəm'plektɪd] *suff Am* **dark-complected** au teint mat, *Can* au teint foncé; **fair-complected, light-complected** au teint clair

complement 1 *n* ['kɒmplɪmənt] (**a**) *(gen)* complément *m*; **with a full complement** au grand complet; **the English department now has a full complement of staff** tous les postes du département d'anglais sont pourvus; **have we got a full complement?** *(in office, team etc)* est-ce que nous sommes au complet?
(**b**) *Math* complément *m*
(**c**) *Gram (of verb)* complément *m*; *(of subject)* attribut *m*
(**d**) *Naut (ship's crew, staff)* personnel *m*, effectif *m* (complet)
(**e**) *Mus* complément *m*
2 *vt* ['kɒmplɪˌment] compléter, être le complément de; **they complement each other well** *(of two people)* ils se complètent parfaitement

complementarity [ˌkɒmplɪmen'tærətɪ] *(pl* **complementarities***)* *n* complémentarité *f*

complementary [ˌkɒmplɪ'mentərɪ] *adj* (**a**) *(gen)* complémentaire; **the two pieces are complementary** les deux morceaux se complètent (**b**) *Math* complémentaire
▸▸ *Geom* ***complementary angle*** angle *m* complémentaire; ***complementary colour*** couleur *f* complémentaire; ***complementary DNA*** ADN *m* complémentaire; ***complementary medicine*** médecine *f* douce

complementizer ['kɒmplɪmənˌtaɪzə(r)] *n Gram* conjonction *f* de subordination

complete [kəm'pliːt] **1** *adj* (**a**) *(entire)* complet(ète), total; **a complete set of golf clubs** un jeu complet de clubs; **Christmas wouldn't be complete without the traditional dinner** Noël ne serait pas Noël sans le repas traditionnel; **he didn't tell you the complete story** il ne vous a pas tout dit; **my happiness is complete** mon bonheur est total, rien ne manque à mon bonheur; **the complete works of Shakespeare** les œuvres complètes de Shakespeare
(**b**) *(finished)* achevé, terminé

(**c**) *(as intensifier)* complet(ète), absolu; **if the job is not done to your complete satisfaction** si vous n'êtes pas entièrement satisfait du travail effectué; **I need a complete break from teaching** j'ai besoin de vraies vacances où je ne penserai plus du tout à mes cours; **he's a complete fool** c'est un crétin fini *ou* un parfait imbécile; **he's a complete stranger** c'est un total inconnu; **a complete (and utter) failure** un échec total *ou* sur toute la ligne; **the project was a complete success** le projet a pleinement réussi

2 *vt* (**a**) *(make whole)* compléter; **to complete her happiness** pour combler son bonheur; **I just need one more card to complete my collection** il me manque une seule carte pour compléter ma collection; *Com* **to complete an order** exécuter une commande

(**b**) *(finish)* achever, finir; *(training, apprenticeship)* accomplir

(**c**) *(form, questionnaire)* remplir

3 complete with *prep* avec, doté *ou* pourvu de; **complete with instructions** comprenant des instructions; **a flat complete with furniture** un appartement meublé

▸▸ *Med* ***complete blood count*** hémogramme *m*

completely [kəm'pli:tlɪ] *adv* complètement; **I completely understand your frustration** je comprends tout à fait ta frustration

completeness [kəm'pli:tnɪs] *n* état *m* complet; **there's a completeness to it** *(to novel, film etc)* il a un caractère abouti; **they added a final volume for completeness** ils ont ajouté un dernier volume pour que l'ensemble soit complet

completion [kəm'pli:ʃən] *n* (**a**) *(of work)* achèvement *m*; **the bridge is due for completion in January** le pont doit être fini en janvier; **in the process of completion** en (cours d')achèvement; **near completion** près d'être achevé; **the project is nearing completion** le projet est près de son terme *ou* s'achève

(**b**) *Law (of sale)* exécution *f*; **payment on completion of contract** paiement *m* à l'exécution du contrat

(**c**) *(of happiness, misfortune)* comble *m*

▸▸ ***completion date*** *(for building, repair work)* date *f* d'achèvement; *Com (for sale)* date *f* d'exécution; ***completion guarantee*** caution *f* de bonne fin

completist [kəm'pli:tɪst] *n* complétiste *mf (personne qui collectionne l'intégralité de l'œuvre d'un écrivain ou d'un musicien)*

complex ['kɒmpleks] **1** *adj (gen)* complexe

2 *n* (**a**) *(system)* complexe *m*, ensemble *m*; **housing complex** grand ensemble *m*; **shopping/industrial complex** complexe *m* commercial/industriel

(**b**) *Psy* complexe *m*; **she has a complex about her weight** elle est complexée par son poids; **you'll give her a complex** tu vas lui donner un complexe

▸▸ *Math* ***complex number*** nombre *m* complexe; *Gram* ***complex sentence*** phrase *f* complexe

complexion [kəm'plekʃən] *n* (**a**) *(of face)* teint *m*; **to have a dark/fair complexion** avoir le teint mat/clair; **to have a good** *or* **clear complexion** avoir une belle peau (**b**) *(aspect)* aspect *m*; **that puts a different complexion on things** voilà qui change la situation

-complexioned [kəm'plekʃənd] *suff* **dark-complexioned** au teint mat, *Can* au teint foncé; **fair-complexioned, light-complexioned** au teint clair

complexity [kəm'pleksətɪ] *n* complexité *f*

compliance [kəm'plaɪəns] **1** *n* (**a**) *(conformity)* conformité *f* (**b**) *(agreement)* acquiescement *m*; *(submission)* complaisance *f* (**c**) *Tech (flexibility)* élasticité *f*

2 in compliance with *prep* conformément à; **in compliance with the law** conformément à la loi; **she acted in compliance with the terms of the contract** elle a agi en accord avec les stipulations du contrat

▸▸ *Com* ***compliance test*** test *m* de conformité

compliant [kəm'plaɪənt] *adj* (**a**) *(person)* accommodant, docile (**b**) *Comput* conforme (**with** à); **year 2000 compliant** conforme à l'an 2000

compliantly [kəm'plaɪəntlɪ] *adv* docilement

complicacy ['kɒmplɪkəsɪ] *n Literary* complexité *f*

complicate ['kɒmplɪkeɪt] *vt* compliquer, embrouiller; **don't complicate the situation any further** ne compliquez pas davantage la situation; **that complicates matters** cela complique les choses; **why complicate things?** pourquoi se compliquer la vie?; **her illness was complicated by an infection** sa maladie s'est compliquée d'une infection

complicated ['kɒmplɪkeɪtɪd] *adj (complex)* compliqué, complexe; *(muddled)* embrouillé; **to become** *or* **to get complicated** se compliquer

complication [ˌkɒmplɪ'keɪʃən] *n (gen)* complication *f*; *Med* **if no complications set in** s'il ne survient pas de complications; **you're always creating complications!** tu compliques toujours les choses!

complicity [kəm'plɪsətɪ] *n* complicité *f*; **his complicity in the murder** sa complicité dans le meurtre

compliment 1 *n* ['kɒmplɪmənt] *(expression of praise)* compliment *m*; **to pay sb a compliment** faire *ou* adresser un compliment à qn; *Ironic* **she returned the compliment** elle lui a retourné le compliment

2 *vt* ['kɒmplɪment] faire des compliments à, complimenter; **to compliment sb on sth** féliciter qn de qch, faire des compliments à qn sur qch; **she complimented him on his English/haircut** elle l'a félicité *ou* elle lui a fait des compliments pour son anglais/sa coupe de cheveux; **she complimented him on his calm handling of the situation** elle l'a félicité du calme avec lequel il a arrangé les choses

3 compliments *npl* ['kɒmplɪmənts] *Formal (respects)* compliments *mpl*, respects *mpl*; **to convey** *or* **present one's compliments to sb** présenter ses compliments *ou* hommages à qn; **give him my compliments** faites-lui mes compliments; **compliments of the season** *(greeting, on card)* meilleurs vœux; **with compliments** *(on compliments slip, card)* avec nos compliments; **with the compliments of Mr Smith** avec les hommages *ou* compliments de M. Smith; **my compliments to the chef** mes compliments au chef; *Com* **to send sth with one's compliments** envoyer qch à titre gratuit *ou* gracieux (avec ses compliments)

▸▸ *Com* ***compliments slip*** papillon *m (joint à un envoi)*

complimentary [ˌkɒmplɪ'mentərɪ] *adj* (**a**) *(approving)* flatteur; **they weren't very complimentary about my paintings** ils ne se sont pas montrés très flatteurs à l'égard de mes tableaux; **complimentary remarks** compliments *mpl*, félicitations *fpl* (**b**) *(given free)* gratuit, gracieux

▸▸ ***complimentary copy*** *(of book)* exemplaire *m* offert à titre gracieux; ***complimentary ticket*** billet *m* de faveur

compline, Compline ['kɒmplɪn] *n (UNCOUNT) Rel* complies *fpl*

comply [kəm'plaɪ] (*pt & pp* **complied**) *vi* (**a**) *(agree, consent)* accepter, consentir; **he complied gracefully** il s'exécuta avec grâce; **to comply with sth** *(obey → code, specifications)* se conformer à qch; *(→ contract)* respecter qch; *(→ request)* accepter qch; *(→ order)* obéir à qch; **to comply with the law** se soumettre à la loi; **to comply with the rules** observer *ou* respecter les règlements; **I will comply with your wishes** je me conformerai à vos désirs; **she complied with our request** elle a accédé à notre demande; **your request has been complied with** votre demande a reçu satisfaction

(**b**) *(machinery)* être conforme; **cars must comply with existing regulations** les voitures doivent être conformes aux normes en vigueur

compo ['kɒmpəʊ] *n Austr & Ir Fam (worker's compensation → unemployment benefit)* allocation *f* chômage ◻; *(→ disability allowance)* prestation *f* d'invalidité ◻

component [kəm'pəʊnənt] **1** *n (of program, education, system)* élément *m*; *Elec, Phys & Chem* composant *m*; *Aut & Tech* pièce *f*

2 *adj* composant, constituant

▸▸ ***component part*** *(of machine)* pièce *f* détachée; *(of theory)* composante *f*

componential [ˌkɒmpə'nenʃəl] *adj* componentiel

▸▸ *Ling* ***componential analysis*** analyse *f* componentielle

comport [kəm'pɔ:t] *Formal* **1** *vt* **to comport oneself** se comporter, se conduire

2 *vi (suit, be appropriate)* concorder (**with** avec)

comportment [kəm'pɔ:tmənt] *n Formal* comportement *m*, conduite *f*

compose [kəm'pəʊz] **1** *vt* (**a**) *(make up)* **to be composed of sth** se composer *ou* être composé de qch

(**b**) *(letter, musical or literary work)* composer; **to compose a poem/a symphony** composer un poème/une symphonie; **the way the artist composes a painting** la façon dont l'artiste compose un tableau; **I composed a reply to his letter** j'ai formulé une réponse à sa lettre

(**c**) *Typ (set)* composer

(**d**) *(make calm)* **compose yourself!** calmez-vous!; **she composed her features** elle a composé son visage; **I need to compose my thoughts** j'ai besoin de mettre de l'ordre dans mes idées

(**e**) *Formal (settle → quarrel)* arranger, régler

2 *vi (create music)* composer

composed [kəm'pəʊzd] *adj* calme, posé

composedly [kəm'pəʊzɪdlɪ] *adv* calmement, posément

composer [kəm'pəʊzə(r)] *n Mus* compositeur(trice) *m,f*

composing [kəm'pəʊzɪŋ] *n* (**a**) *(of letter, musical or literary work)* composition *f*, création *f* (**b**) *Typ* composition *f*

▸▸ *Typ* ***composing room*** (salle *f* de) composition *f*

composite ['kɒmpəzɪt] **1** *adj* (**a**) *(gen) & Archit & Phot* composite

(**b**) *Bot & Math* composé

2 *n* (**a**) *(compound)* composite *m*; *Archit* (ordre *m*) composite *m*

(**b**) *Bot* composée *f*, composacée *f*

(**c**) *Pol* = proposition discutée au niveau national

3 *vt Pol* **to composite proposals** = établir une liste de propositions à discuter au niveau national, à partir des propositions émises au niveau régional

▸▸ *St Exch* ***composite index*** indice *m* composé *ou* composite; *Can* ***composite school*** école *f* polyvalente

composition [ˌkɒmpə'zɪʃən] *n* (**a**) *(of letter, musical or literary work)* composition *f*, création *f*; **she struggled with the composition of the letter** elle a eu du mal à rédiger la lettre; **poetry of his own composition** poésie de sa composition

(**b**) *(musical or literary work)* composition *f*, œuvre *f*; **one of Mozart's finest compositions** une des plus belles œuvres de Mozart

(**c**) *Sch (essay)* dissertation *f*

(**d**) *(constitution → parts)* composition *f*, constitution *f*; *(→ mixture)* mélange *m*, composition *f*; *Constr* stuc *m*; **the chemical composition of water** la composition chimique de l'eau

(**e**) *Art (distribution of elements)* composition *f*

(**f**) *Ling (of sentence)* construction *f*; *(of word)* composition *f*

(**g**) *Typ* composition *f*

(**h**) *Law (agreement → with creditors)* arrangement *m*, accommodement *m*; *(on bankruptcy)* concordat *m* préventif

compositor [kəm'pɒzɪtə(r)] *n Typ* compositeur(trice) *m,f*

compos mentis [ˌkɒmpəs'mentɪs] *adj Law* sain d'esprit; *Fam* **to be compos mentis** *(not drunk, not half asleep)* être en possession de toutes ses facultés ◻; **I'm not compos mentis yet** je suis encore à moitié endormi ◻

compost [*Br* 'kɒmpɒst, *Am* 'kɒmpəʊst] **1** *n* compost *m*

2 *vt* (**a**) *(treat with compost)* composter *(une terre)* (**b**) *(convert into compost)* faire du compost à partir de

▸▸ ***compost heap*** tas *m* de compost

composure [kəm'pəʊʒə(r)] *n* calme *m*, sang-froid *m*; **to lose one's composure** perdre son calme; **to recover** *or* **regain one's composure** se ressaisir

compote [ˈkɒmpɒt] *n Culin (dessert)* compote *f*; *Am (dish)* compotier *m*

compound 1 *adj* [ˈkɒmpaʊnd] (**a**) *(gen)* composé; *Chem* composé, combiné; *Tech (engine)* compound *(inv)*

(**b**) *Gram (sentence)* complexe; *(tense, word)* composé

(**c**) *Mus* composé

(**d**) *Math (number)* complexe

2 *n* [ˈkɒmpaʊnd] (**a**) *(enclosed area)* enceinte *f*, enclos *m*; *(for prisoners of war)* camp *m*

(**b**) *(in South Africa → for workers)* quartier *m* des noirs; *(→ for livestock)* parc *m* à bétail

(**c**) *(mixture)* composé *m*, mélange *m*; *Chem* composé *m*; *Tech* compound *m*

(**d**) *Gram* mot *m* composé

3 *vt* [kəmˈpaʊnd] (**a**) *Chem (combine)* combiner, mélanger; *(form by combining)* composer

(**b**) *(make worse → difficulties, mistake)* aggraver

(**c**) *Law (settle)* régler à l'amiable; **to compound an offence** composer *ou* pactiser avec un criminel; **to compound a debt** faire une transaction pour le règlement d'une dette

4 *vi* [kəmˈpaʊnd] *Law* composer, transiger; *(with one's creditors)* arriver à un concordat; **to compound with sb for sth** transiger avec qn au sujet de *ou* pour qch; **the neighbours compounded for the damages** les voisins se sont arrangés au sujet des dommages

►► *Acct & Fin* ***compound annual return*** annuités *fpl* composées; *Acct* ***compound entry*** *(in bookkeeping)* article *m* composé; *Biol* ***compound eye*** œil *m* composé *ou* à facettes; *Math* ***compound fraction*** fraction *f* composée; ***compound fracture*** fracture *f* multiple; *Fin* ***compound interest*** *(UNCOUNT)* intérêts *mpl* composés; *Mus* ***compound time*** mesure *f* composée

comprehend [ˌkɒmprɪˈhend] **1** *vt* (**a**) *(understand)* comprendre, saisir (**b**) *(include)* comprendre, inclure

2 *vi (understand)* comprendre, saisir

comprehending [ˌkɒmprɪˈhendɪŋ] *adj (understanding)* qui comprend

comprehensibility [ˌkɒmprɪhensəˈbɪlɪtɪ] *n* compréhensibilité *f*, intelligibilité *f*

comprehensible [ˌkɒmprɪˈhensəbəl] *adj* compréhensible, intelligible

comprehensibly [ˌkɒmprɪˈhensəblɪ] *adv* d'une manière compréhensible *ou* intelligible

comprehension [ˌkɒmprɪˈhenʃən] *n* (**a**) *(understanding)* compréhension *f*; **things that are beyond our comprehension** des choses qui nous dépassent (**b**) *Sch (exercise)* exercice *m* de compréhension; **a reading/listening comprehension** un exercice de compréhension écrite/orale (**c**) *(inclusion)* inclusion *f*

comprehensive [ˌkɒmprɪˈhensɪv] **1** *adj* (**a**) *(thorough)* complet(ète), exhaustif; *(detailed)* détaillé, complet(ète); *(defeat, victory)* écrasant; *(knowledge)* vaste, étendu; **comprehensive measures** mesures *fpl* d'ensemble

(**b**) *Br Sch* polyvalent; **the schools went comprehensive** les écoles ont abandonné les critères sélectifs d'entrée

2 *n Br Sch (school)* = établissement secondaire d'enseignement général

►► *Am* ***comprehensive assurance*** assurance *f* tous risques; *Am Sch* ***comprehensive examination*** examen *m* de synthèse; *Br* ***comprehensive insurance*** assurance *f* tous risques; ***comprehensive policy*** police *f* tous risques, police *f* multirisque; ***comprehensive school*** = établissement secondaire d'enseignement général; ***comprehensive site insurance*** assurance *f* tous-risques chantiers

COMPREHENSIVE SCHOOLS

Les "comprehensive schools" ont été introduites en Grande-Bretagne en 1965 par les travaillistes dans le but de démocratiser l'enseignement et d'assurer l'égalité des chances pour tous les enfants, quels que soient les revenus de leurs parents et leur origine sociale. En 1975 une série de lois fut votée pour promouvoir ce type d'éducation. Mais le changement est lent et les progrès sont entravés par des poches de résistance en faveur des traditionnelles "grammar schools" et "public schools", ainsi que par le niveau insuffisant de certaines "comprehensives" situées dans des quartiers déshérités. Aujourd'hui 90 pour cent des élèves du secondaire fréquentent les "comprehensive schools". Bien qu'il n'y ait pas de sélection, la qualité de l'enseignement varie énormément suivant les établissements.

comprehensively [ˌkɒmprɪˈhensɪvlɪ] *adv (thoroughly)* complètement, exhaustivement; *(in detail)* en détail

comprehensiveness [ˌkɒmprɪˈhensɪvnɪs] *n (of answer, treatment of subject)* caractère *m* complet

compress 1 *vt* [kəmˈpres] (**a**) *(squeeze together)* comprimer; **to compress one's lips** serrer *ou* pincer les lèvres

(**b**) *Fig (condense → ideas, facts, writing)* condenser, concentrer; **three centuries are compressed into two chapters** trois siècles sont concentrés en deux chapitres

(**c**) *Tech (air)* refouler, comprimer

(**d**) *Comput (file)* compresser

2 *vi* [kəmˈpres] (**a**) *Tech (material)* se comprimer

(**b**) *Fig (be condensed)* se condenser, se concentrer

3 *n* [ˈkɒmpres] *Med* compresse *f*

compressed [kəmˈprest] *adj* (**a**) *(lips)* serré, pincé (**b**) *(style)* condensé

►► *Tech* ***compressed air*** air *m* comprimé

compressibility [kəmˌpresɪˈbɪlɪtɪ] *n* compressibilité *f*

compressible [kəmˈpresɪbəl] *adj* compressible

compression [kəmˈpreʃən] *n* (**a**) *(of material)* compression *f*; *Tech* **in compression** comprimé (**b**) *Fig (condensing)* réduction *f* (**c**) *Comput (of file)* compression *f*

►► *Tech* ***compression chamber*** chambre *f* de compression; *Aut* ***compression ignition*** allumage *m* par compression; ***compression period*** période *f* de compression; ***compression pump*** pompe *f* de compression; *Tech* ***compression ratio*** taux *m* de compression; *Tech* ***compression stroke*** *(in engine)* (temps *m* de) compression *f*

compressive [kəmˈpresɪv] *adj* qui peut être comprimé, compressible

►► *Tech* ***compressive strain*** déformation *f* occasionnée par la compression; *Tech* ***compressive strength*** résistance *f* à la compression; *Tech* ***compressive stress*** contrainte *f* de compression

compressor [kəmˈpresə(r)] *n Anat & Tech* compresseur *m*

►► *Tech* ***compressor unit*** groupe *m* compresseur

comprise [kəmˈpraɪz] *vt* (**a**) *(consist of)* comprendre, consister en; **the group comprises** *or* **is comprised of four women and two men** il y a quatre femmes et deux hommes dans le groupe, le groupe est formé de quatre femmes et deux hommes (**b**) *(constitute)* constituer; **women comprise 60 percent of the population** les femmes représentent 60 pour cent de la population

compromise [ˈkɒmprəmaɪz] **1** *n* compromis *m*; **to agree to a compromise** accepter un compromis; **to reach** *or* **arrive at a compromise** aboutir *ou* parvenir à un compromis; **there must be no compromise** il ne faut pas faire de compromis

2 *comp (decision, solution)* de compromis

3 *vi* transiger, aboutir à *ou* accepter un compromis; **to compromise with sb (on sth)** transiger avec qn *ou* aboutir à un compromis avec qn (sur qch)

4 *vt* (**a**) *(principles, reputation)* compromettre; **don't say anything to compromise yourself** ne dites rien qui puisse vous compromettre; **the minister was compromised by the allegations of improper conduct** les allégations selon lesquelles il se serait conduit de façon indécente ont compromis le ministre

(**b**) *(jeopardize)* mettre en péril, risquer; **the party's chances of electoral success were severely compromised by the character of their leader** la personnalité du leader a sérieusement compromis les chances de victoire du parti aux élections

compromising [ˈkɒmprəˌmaɪzɪŋ] *adj* compromettant

comptroller [kənˈtrəʊlə(r)] *n Admin* administrateur(trice) *m,f*, intendant(e) *m,f*; *Fin* contrôleur(euse) *m,f*

►► *Am* ***Comptroller General*** ≃ président *m* de la Cour des comptes, *Can* Contrôleur *m* général

compulsion [kəmˈpʌlʃən] *n* (**a**) *(force)* contrainte *f*, coercition *f*; **to act under compulsion** agir sous la contrainte; **there's no compulsion to do it** il n'y a pas d'obligation à le faire; **he is under no compulsion to sell** il n'est nullement obligé de vendre, rien ne l'oblige à vendre (**b**) *Psy (impulse)* compulsion *f*; **I felt a sudden compulsion to visit my grandmother** j'ai soudain ressenti un besoin urgent de rendre visite à ma grand-mère

compulsive [kəmˈpʌlsɪv] *adj* (**a**) *Psy (behaviour)* compulsif; *(smoker, gambler)* invétéré; **he's a compulsive liar** il ne peut pas s'empêcher de mentir, mentir est un besoin chez lui (**b**) *(reason)* coercitif (**c**) *Fig (absorbing)* passionnant; **this TV series is compulsive viewing** quand on commence à regarder ce feuilleton, on ne peut plus s'en passer

►► ***compulsive eating disorder*** boulimie *f*

compulsively [kəmˈpʌlsɪvlɪ] *adv* (**a**) *Psy (drink, steal, smoke)* d'une façon compulsive (**b**) *Fig* irrésistiblement; **it's compulsively readable/watchable** c'est passionnant

compulsorily [kəmˈpʌlsərəlɪ] *adv* d'office; *Admin* **to be retired compulsorily** être mis à la retraite d'office

compulsory [kəmˈpʌlsərɪ] **1** *adj* (**a**) *(obligatory)* obligatoire; **military service/Latin is compulsory** le service militaire/le latin est obligatoire; (**b**) *(compelling)* irrésistible (**c**) *(law)* obligatoire (**d**) *(coercive)* coercitif;

2 *n Sport (in ice-skating)* **the compulsories** les figures *fpl* imposées

►► ***compulsory education*** enseignement *m* obligatoire; *Fin* ***compulsory liquidation*** liquidation *f* forcée; ***compulsory powers*** pouvoirs *mpl* coercitifs; *Br Admin* ***compulsory purchase*** expropriation *f* pour cause d'utilité publique; ***compulsory purchase order*** ordre *m* d'expropriation; *Ind* ***compulsory redundancy*** licenciement *m* sec; ***compulsory retirement*** mise *f* à la retraite d'office; *Law* ***compulsory sale*** adjudication *f* forcée; ***compulsory schooling*** scolarisation *f* obligatoire

compunction [kəmˈpʌŋkʃən] *n (remorse)* remords *m*; *(misgiving)* scrupule *m*; *Rel* componction *f*; **he has no compunction about stealing** il n'a aucun scrupule *ou* il n'hésite pas à voler; **without the slightest compunction** sans le moindre scrupule

computation [ˌkɒmpjuːˈteɪʃən] *n* (**a**) *(calculation)* calcul *m* (**b**) *(reckoning)* estimation *f*

computational [ˌkɒmpjuːˈteɪʃənəl] *adj* quantitatif, statistique

►► ***computational linguistics*** linguistique *f* computationnelle

compute [kəmˈpjuːt] **1** *vt* calculer

2 *vi* calculer; *Fam* **it doesn't compute** ça ne tient pas debout

computer [kəmˈpjuːtə(r)] *n (electronic)* ordinateur *m*; **he's good at/he works in computers** il est bon en/il travaille dans l'informatique; **to have sth on computer** avoir qch sur ordinateur

►► ***the computer age*** l'ère *f* des ordinateurs *ou* de l'informatique; ***computer analyst*** analyste *mf*; ***computer animation*** animation *f* par ordinateur; ***computer art*** dessin *m* par ordinateur; *Am* ***computer camp*** colonie *f* de vacances centrée sur l'informatique; ***computer centre*** centre *m* informatique, infocentre *m*; ***computer code*** code *m* d'ordinateur; ***computer course*** cours *m* d'informatique; ***computer crime*** fraude *f* informatique; ***computer dating*** = rencontres sélectionnées par ordinateur; ***computer dealer*** revendeur *m* informatique; ***computer diagram*** diagramme *m* réalisé par *ou* sur ordinateur; ***computer engineer*** ingénieur-informaticien(enne) *m,f*; ***computer equipment*** équipment *m* informatique; ***computer expert*** informaticien(enne) *m,f*; ***computer fraud*** fraude *f* informatique; *Fam* ***computer freak*** *(enthusiast)* dingue *mf* d'informatique; ***computer game*** jeu *m* informatique; *Fam* ***computer geek*** allumé(e) *m,f* de l'informatique; ***computer generation*** génération *f* d'ordinateur; ***computer genius*** génie *m* de l'informatique; ***computer graphics*** **1** *npl (function)* graphiques *mpl* **2** *n (field)* infographie *f*; ***computer hacker*** pirate *mf* informatique; ***computer hardware*** matériel *m* informatique; ***computer instruction*** instruction *f* machine; ***computer keyboard*** clavier *m* d'ordinateur; ***computer language*** langage *m* de programmation; ***computer link-up*** liaison *f* informatique; ***computer literacy*** compétence *f* informatique; ***computer manager*** directeur(trice) *m,f* informatique; ***computer manufacturer*** constructeur *m* informatique; ***computer model*** modèle *m* informatique; ***computer network*** réseau *m* informatique; ***computer operator*** opérateur(trice) *m,f* (sur ordinateur); ***computer output*** sortie *f* d'ordinateur; ***computer printout*** sortie *f* papier; *(continuous)* listing *m*, listage *m*; ***computer processing*** traitement *m* sur ordinateur; ***computer program*** programme *m* informatique; ***computer programmer*** programmeur(euse) *m,f*; ***computer programming*** programmation *f*; ***computer rage*** = manifestations d'agressivité à l'égard de son ordinateur; ***computer room*** salle *f* des ordinateurs; ***computer science*** informatique *f*; ***computer scientist*** informaticien(enne) *m,f*; ***computer simulation*** simulation *f* par ordinateur; ***computer stationery*** papier *m* listing ***computer supplier*** fournisseur *m* informatique; ***computer system*** système *m* informatique; ***computer technician*** technicien(enne) *m,f* en informatique; ***computer terminal*** terminal *m* informatique; ***computer translation*** traduction *f* par ordinateur; ***computer typesetting*** composition *f* par ordinateur; ***computer vaccine*** vaccin *m* informatique; ***computer virus*** virus *m* informatique

computer-aided, computer-assisted *adj* assisté par ordinateur

►► ***computer-aided audit techniques*** techniques *fpl* d'audit assistées par ordinateur; ***computer-aided design*** conception *f* assistée par ordinateur; ***computer-aided engineering*** ingénierie *f* assistée par ordinateur; ***computer-aided instruction*** enseignement *m* assisté par ordinateur; ***computer-aided learning*** enseignement *m* assisté par ordinateur; ***computer-aided manufacturing*** fabrication *f* assistée par ordinateur; ***computer-aided presentation*** presentation *f* assistée par ordinateur; ***computer-aided sales and marketing*** vente *f* et marketing *m* assistés par ordinateur; ***computer-aided trading*** commerce *m* assisté par ordinateur; ***computer-aided translation*** traduction *f* assistée par ordinateur

computer-based *adj (training)* assisté par ordinateur

computer-controlled *adj* contrôlé par ordinateur

►► ***computer-controlled lock*** serrure *f* électronique

computer-enhanced *adj (graphics etc)* amélioré par ordinateur

computerese [kəm,pjuːtə'riːz] *n* jargon *m* informatique

computer-generated *adj* généré par ordinateur

►► ***computer-generated image*** image *f* de synthèse

computer-integrated manufacturing *n* fabrication *f* intégrée par ordinateur

computerizable [kəm,pjuːtə'raɪzəbəl] *adj* informatisable

computerization [kəm,pjuːtəraɪ'zeɪʃən] *n* **(a)** *(of system, of work)* automatisation *f*, informatisation *f* **(b)** *(of information → inputting)* saisie *f* sur ordinateur; *(→ processing)* traitement *m* (électronique)

computerize, -ise [kəm'pjuːtəraɪz] *vt (data → put on computer)* saisir sur ordinateur; *(→ process by computer)* traiter par ordinateur; *(company)* informatiser

computerized [kəm'pjuːtəraɪzd] *adj* informatisé

►► ***computerized accounts*** compatabilité *f* informatisée; ***computerized banking*** informatique *f* bancaire; ***computerized data*** données *fpl* informatiques; ***computerized key*** clé *f* magnétique; *Med* ***computerized tomography*** tomodensitométrie *f*; *St Exch* ***computerized trading system*** système *m* informatique de cotation; ***computerized typesetting*** composition *f* par ordinateur

computer-literate *adj* **to be computer-literate** avoir des connaissances en informatique

computernik [kəm'pjuːtənɪk] *n Am Fam* fada *mf* d'informatique

computer-to-computer *adj (transmission)* d'ordinateur à ordinateur

computer-typeset **1** *vt* composer sur ordinateur
2 *vi* composer sur ordinateur

computing [kəm'pjuːtɪŋ] *n* **(a)** *(field)* informatique *f*; **she works in computing** elle travaille dans l'informatique **(b)** *(calculation)* calcul *m*; *(reckoning)* estimation *f*

►► ***computing centre*** centre *m* de calcul; ***computing course*** stage *m* d'informatique; ***computing machine*** machine *f* à calcul; ***computing power*** puissance *f* de calcul

comrade ['kɒmreɪd] *n* camarade *mf*

comrade-in-arms *n* compagnon *m* d'armes

comradeship ['kɒmreɪdʃɪp] *n* camaraderie *f*

comsat ['kɒmsæt] *n (abbr* **communications satellite***)* satellite *m* de communication

Con. **(a)** *(written abbr* **constable***)* agent *m (de police)* **(b)** *Pol (written abbr* **conservative***)* conservateur

con [kɒn] *(pt & pp* **conned**, *cont* **conning***)* **1** *vt* **(a)** *Fam (swindle)* arnaquer; *(trick)* duper[❑]; **don't try to con me!** n'essayez pas de me faire marcher!; **I've been conned!** je me suis fait avoir!, on m'a eu!; **he conned us into buying it** il nous a persuadés de l'acheter et nous nous sommes fait avoir; **they were conned out of £500** ils se sont fait arnaquer de 500 livres
(b) *Arch (study)* étudier en détail; *(learn by heart)* apprendre par cœur
(c) *Naut (steer)* gouverner, piloter
2 *n* **(a)** *Fam (swindle)* arnaque *f*; *(trick)* duperie[❑] *f*
(b) *Fam (convict)* taulard(e) *m,f*
(c) *(disadvantage)* contre *m*; **the pros and cons** le pour et le contre

►► *Fam* ***con artist*** arnaqueur *m*; *Am Fam* ***con job*** *(swindle)* arnaque *f*; *(trick)* duperie[❑] *f*

concatenate [kɒn'kætəneɪt] *vt* **(a)** *(link up)* enchaîner, lier **(b)** *Comput & Ling* concaténer

concatenated [kɒn'kætəneɪtɪd] *adj* **(a)** *(linked)* enchaîné, lié **(b)** *Comput & Ling* concaténé

concatenation [kɒn,kætə'neɪʃən] *n* **(a)** *(series)* série *f*, chaîne *f*; *(of circumstances)* enchaînement *m* **(b)** *Comput & Ling* concaténation *f*

concave [kɒn'keɪv] *adj Phys & Opt* concave

concavity [kɒn'kævətɪ] *n Phys & Opt* concavité *f*

conceal [kən'siːl] *vt (hide → object)* cacher, dissimuler; *(→ emotion, truth)* cacher, dissimuler; *(→ news)* tenir secret(ète); *Fin & Law (→ assets)* dissimuler; **to conceal sth from sb** cacher qch à qn; **he concealed the truth from her** il lui a caché la vérité; **to conceal oneself** se cacher; **to conceal one's intentions** cacher *ou* déguiser ses intentions *ou* son jeu; **in order to conceal the fact that...** pour dissimuler le fait que...

concealed [kən'siːld] *adj (lighting)* indirect; *(driveway, entrance, microphone)* caché; **danger! concealed entrance** *(sign)* danger! sortie de véhicules

concealer [kən'siːlə(r)] *n (make-up)* correcteur *m* de teint

concealment [kən'siːlmənt] *n (act of hiding)* dissimulation *f*; *Law (of criminal)* recel *m*; *(of facts, truth)* non-divulgation *f*; *Fin & Law* **concealment of assets** dissimulation *f* d'actif

concede [kən'siːd] **1** *vt* **(a)** *(admit)* concéder, admettre; **to concede a point** concéder un point (important); **he conceded (that) he was wrong** il a admis *ou* reconnu qu'il avait tort; **to concede defeat** s'avouer vaincu
(b) *(give up)* concéder, accorder; *Sport* concéder; **he refused to concede any ground** il n'a voulu céder sur rien; *Ftbl* **they conceded a free kick/a goal** ils ont concédé un coup franc/un but
(c) *(grant → privileges)* concéder
2 *vi* céder

conceit [kən'siːt] *n* **(a)** *(vanity)* vanité *f*, suffisance *f* **(b)** *Literary (witty expression)* trait *m* d'esprit

conceited [kən'siːtɪd] *adj* vaniteux, suffisant; **I don't want to sound conceited but...** je ne veux pas avoir l'air prétentieux mais...

conceitedly [kən'siːtɪdlɪ] *adv* avec vanité *ou* suffisance; **he conceitedly imagined that...** il a eu la prétention d'imaginer que...

conceitedness [kən'siːtɪdnɪs] *n* vanité *f*, prétention *f*, suffisance *f*

conceivable [kən'siːvəbəl] *adj* concevable, imaginable; **every conceivable means** tous les moyens possibles et imaginables; **it's quite conceivable that it was an accident** il est tout à fait concevable que ç'ait été un accident; **what conceivable reason could I have?** quelle raison pourrais-je bien avoir?

conceivably [kən'siːvəblɪ] *adv* **I don't see how it's conceivably possible** ce n'est pas concevable; **this might conceivably start a war** il est concevable que *ou* il se peut que cela déclenche une guerre; **she could conceivably have done it, it's conceivably possible that she did it** il n'est pas exclu qu'elle l'ait fait; **it couldn't conceivably have been him** il n'est pas possible que ç'ait été lui; **is he capable of it? – conceivably** en est-il capable? – c'est fort possible

conceive [kən'siːv] **1** *vt* **(a)** *(idea, plan)* concevoir; **I can't conceive why they did it** je ne comprends vraiment pas pourquoi ils l'ont fait **(b)** *(child)* concevoir; *Fig* **she conceived a passion for jazz** elle conçut une passion pour le jazz
2 *vi* **(a)** *(think)* concevoir; **I can conceive of him having done it** je peux très bien imaginer qu'il l'ait fait; **can't you conceive of a better plan?** ne pouvez-vous rien concevoir de mieux? **(b)** *(become pregnant)* concevoir

concentrate ['kɒnsəntreɪt] **1** *vi* **(a)** *(pay attention)* se concentrer, concentrer *ou* fixer son attention; **I can't concentrate with all that noise** tout ce bruit m'empêche de me concentrer; **to concentrate on sth** se concentrer sur qch; **concentrate on your work!** appliquez-vous à votre travail!
(b) *(focus)* **the government should concentrate on improving the economy** le gouvernement devrait s'attacher à améliorer la situation économique; **just concentrate on getting the suitcases ready!** occupe-toi seulement des valises!; **the speaker concentrated on the Luddite movement** le conférencier a surtout traité du luddisme
(c) *(gather)* se concentrer, converger; **the population tends to concentrate in cities** la population tend à se concentrer dans les villes; **the crowd concentrated in the square** la foule s'est rassemblée sur la place
2 *vt* **(a)** *(focus)* concentrer; **to concentrate one's attention on sth** concentrer son attention sur qch; **it concentrates the mind** cela aide à se concentrer; **our hopes are concentrated on her success** tous nos espoirs sont concentrés sur son succès
(b) *(bring together)* concentrer, rassembler; *Chem* concentrer; **Conservative support is concentrated in the South** le soutien du parti conservateur est concentré dans le Sud
3 *n (of tomatoes, fruit juice etc)* concentré *m*; *(mineral)* minerai *m* concentré; **made from concentrate** *(fruit juice)* fait à base de concentré

concentrated ['kɒnsən,treɪtɪd] *adj* **(a)** *(liquid)* concentré; **concentrated fruit juice** jus *m* de fruit concentré **(b)** *(intense)* intense; **a period of concentrated activity** une période d'activité intense

►► ***concentrated marketing*** marketing *m* concentré

concentration [,kɒnsən'treɪʃən] *n* **(a)** *(mental)* concentration *f*, application *f*; **to lose one's concentration** se déconcentrer; **the work requires concentration** le travail demande de la concentration; **concentration span** concentration *f*; **he has a poor concentration span** il n'arrive pas à se concentrer très longtemps
(b) *(specializing)* spécialisation *f*; **in view of their recent concentration on other areas of the market** étant donné qu'ils se sont récemment concentrés sur d'autres secteurs du marché
(c) *(grouping → of troops etc)* concentration *f*; **there was a concentration of cases of food**

poisoning in the area il y a eu plusieurs cas d'intoxication alimentaire dans le quartier; **concentration of effort** convergence *f* des efforts; *Chem* **(degree of) concentration** *(of acid)* titre *m*; **the large urban concentrations** les grandes agglomérations *fpl* urbaines
►► ***concentration camp*** camp *m* de concentration; ***concentration camp victim*** victime *f* des camps de concentration

concentre [kən'sentə(r)] **1** *vt* concentrer
2 *vi* se concentrer

concentric [kən'sentrɪk] *adj* concentrique

concept ['kɒnsept] *n* concept *m*
►► ***concept car*** concept-car *m*; *Mktg* ***concept test*** test *m* de concept

conception [kən'sepʃən] *n* **(a)** *(idea)* conception *f*; **to have a clear conception of sth** se représenter clairement qch; **she has no conception of time** elle n'a aucune notion du temps **(b)** *(of child)* conception *f*

concept-testing *n Mktg* tests *mpl* de concept

conceptual [kən'septʃʊəl] *adj* conceptuel
►► ***conceptual art*** art *m* conceptuel

conceptualism [kən'septʃʊə,lɪzəm] *n* conceptualisme *m*

conceptualize, -ise [kən'septʃʊəlaɪz] *vt* concevoir, conceptualiser

conceptually [kən'septʃʊəlɪ] *adv* comme concept

CONCERN [kən'sɜːn]

inquiétude	► **1 (a)**
souci	► **1 (a), (b)**
affaire	► **1 (c), (d)**
intérêt	► **1 (e)**
inquiéter	► **2 (a)**
concerner	► **2 (b)**
intéresser	► **2 (c)**
traiter	► **2 (d)**

1 *n* **(a)** *(worry)* inquiétude *f*, souci *m*; **his condition is giving cause for concern** son état est inquiétant; **there's no cause for concern** il n'y a pas de raison de s'inquiéter; **to express concern about sth** exprimer de l'inquiétude au sujet de qch; **there is growing concern for her safety** on est de plus en plus inquiet à son sujet *ou* sur son sort; **there is growing concern that...** on craint de plus en plus que... + *subjunctive*; **she showed great concern for their welfare** elle s'est montrée très soucieuse de leur bien-être; **a look of concern** un regard inquiet; **this is a matter of great concern** c'est un sujet très inquiétant

(b) *(source of worry)* souci *m*, préoccupation *f*; **my main concern is the price** ce qui m'inquiète surtout, c'est le prix

(c) *(affair, business)* affaire *f*; **what concern is it of yours?** en quoi est-ce que cela vous regarde?; **it's none of my concern** cela ne me regarde pas, ce n'est pas mon affaire

(d) *Com (firm)* **a (business) concern** une affaire, une firme

(e) *(share)* intérêt *m*; **we have a concern in the restaurant** nous avons des intérêts dans le restaurant

(f) *Fam (object)* truc *m*, machin *m*

2 *vt* **(a)** *(worry)* inquiéter; **your health concerns me** je m'inquiète *ou* je suis inquiet pour votre santé; **they're concerned about her** ils s'inquiètent *ou* se font du souci à son sujet; **we were concerned to learn that...** nous avons appris avec inquiétude que...; **I'm only concerned with the facts** je ne m'intéresse qu'aux faits

(b) *(involve)* concerner; **where** *or* **as far as the budget is concerned** en ce qui concerne le budget; **as far as this matter is concerned** en ce qui concerne cette question; **to concern oneself in** *or* **with sth** s'occuper de *ou* s'intéresser à qch; **there is no need for you to concern yourself with my affairs** vous n'avez pas à vous occuper de mes affaires; **this doesn't concern you** cela ne vous regarde pas; **it concerns your mother** c'est au sujet de votre mère; **as far as I'm concerned** en ce qui me concerne, quant à moi; **where you are concerned** en ce qui vous concerne; **to whom it may concern** à qui de droit

(c) *(be important to)* intéresser, importer; **the outcome concerns us all** les résultats nous importent à tous

(d) *(of book, report)* traiter de

concerned [kən'sɜːnd] *adj* **(a)** *(worried)* inquiet(ète), soucieux; **we were concerned for** *or* **about his health** nous étions inquiets pour sa santé; **he didn't seem at all concerned** il n'avait pas du tout l'air inquiet *ou* de s'inquiéter

(b) *(involved)* intéressé; **pass this request on to the department concerned** transmettez cette demande au service compétent; **notify the person concerned** avisez qui de droit; **the people concerned** *(in question)* les personnes *fpl* en question *ou* dont il s'agit; *(involved)* les intéressés *mpl*

concernedly [kən'sɜːnɪdlɪ] *adv* avec inquiétude

concerning [kən'sɜːnɪŋ] *prep* au sujet de, à propos de; **I wrote to her concerning the lease** je lui ai écrit au sujet du bail; **any news concerning the accident?** y a-t-il du nouveau au sujet de *ou* concernant l'accident?

concert 1 *n* ['kɒnsət] **(a)** *(performance)* concert *m*; **to give a concert** donner un concert; **Miles Davis in concert** Miles Davis en concert; **to sing in concert** chanter à l'unisson *ou* en chœur **(b)** *Br Fig Formal (agreement)* accord *m*, entente *f*

2 *comp* ['kɒnsət] *(performer, pianist)* de concert

3 *vt* [kən'sɜːt] concerter, arranger

4 in concert with *prep* ['kɒnsət] *Br Formal* de concert avec; **we acted in concert with the police** nous avons agi de concert avec la police
►► ***concert grand*** piano *m* de concert; ***concert hall*** salle *f* de concert; *St Exch* ***concert party*** action *f* de concert; *Mus* ***concert pitch*** diapason *m* (de concert); *Fig* **to be at concert pitch** être en pleine forme; *Mus* ***concert tour*** tournée *f*; *Br* ***concert venue*** salle *f* de concert

concerted [kən'sɜːtɪd] *adj* concerté; **a concerted effort** un effort concerté; **concerted action** action *f* d'ensemble *ou* concertée

concertgoer ['kɒnsət,gəʊə(r)] *n* amateur *m* de concerts

concertina [,kɒnsə'tiːnə] **1** *n* concertina *m*
2 *vi* se plier en accordéon; **the front of the car concertinaed** le devant de la voiture s'est plié en accordéon

concertmaster ['kɒnsət,mɑːstə(r)] *n Am Mus* premier violon *m*

concerto [kən'tʃeətəʊ] *(pl* **concertos** *or* **concerti** [-tiː]) *n Mus* concerto *m*; **piano/violin concerto** concerto *m* pour piano/violon

concession [kən'seʃən] *n* **(a)** *(gen) & Law* concession *f*; **to make a concession (to sb)** faire une concession (à qn); **to make concessions** faire des concessions; **as a concession to sb/sth** comme concession à qn/qch; **the only concession the film makes to reality is...** la seule concession que le film fasse à la réalité est...

(b) *Com (within store)* concession *f*; **she has a concession in a department store** elle a une concession dans un grand magasin

(c) *Com (reduction)* réduction *f*; **price: £5 (concessions £3)** prix des billets: 5 livres (tarif réduit 3 livres); **we offer a 10 percent concession to retailers** nous accordons une remise de 10 pour cent aux détaillants

(d) *Mining & Petr* concession *f*; **an oil concession** une concession pétrolière
►► *Com* ***concession close*** conclusion *f* par concession; *Am* ***concession stand*** buvette *f* *(dans un cinéma, un stade etc)*; *Br* ***concession ticket*** *(for theatre, cinema)* billet *m* à prix réduit

concessionaire [kən,seʃə'neə(r)] *n Com* concessionnaire *mf*

concessionary [kən'seʃənərɪ] *(pl* **concessionaries**) **1** *adj* **(a)** *(gen) & Fin & Law* concessionnaire **(b)** *Com (fare, ticket)* à prix réduit
2 *n* concessionnaire *mf*

concessive [kən'sesɪv] *adj* concessif
►► *Gram* ***concessive clause*** proposition *f* concessive; *Gram* ***concessive conjunction*** conjonction *f* concessive

conch [kɒntʃ, kɒŋk] *(pl* **conches** ['kɒntʃɪz] *or* **conchs** [kɒŋks]) *n* **(a)** *Zool* conque *f* **(b)** *Archit* (voûte *f* d') abside *f*

conchie = **conchy**

conchoid ['kɒŋkɔɪd] *Math* **1** *n* conchoïde *f*
2 *adj* conchoïde

conchologist [kɒŋ'kɒlədʒɪst] *n* conchyliologiste *mf*

conchology [kɒŋ'kɒlədʒɪ] *n* conchyliologie *f*

conchy ['kɒnʃɪ] *(pl* **conchies**) *n Br Fam Pej (abbr* **conscientious objector**) objecteur *m* de conscience[□]

concierge ['kɒnsɪerʒ] *n Am* concierge *mf*

conciliate [kən'sɪlɪeɪt] **1** *vt* **(a)** *(appease)* apaiser; *(win over)* se concilier (l'appui de); **she managed to conciliate my mother** elle a réussi à se concilier les bonnes grâces de ma mère **(b)** *(reconcile)* concilier
2 *vi Formal* **to conciliate between two people/countries** réconcilier deux peuples/pays

conciliation [kən,sɪlɪ'eɪʃən] *n* **(a)** *(appeasement)* apaisement *m* **(b)** *(reconciliation)* conciliation *f* **(c)** *Ind (in dispute)* conciliation *f*, arbitrage *m*
►► *Ind* ***conciliation board*** conseil *m* d'arbitrage; *Ind* ***conciliation service*** service *m* de conciliation

conciliator [kən'sɪlɪeɪtə(r)] *n* **(a)** *(appeaser)* conciliateur(trice) *m,f* **(b)** *Ind (in dispute)* médiateur *m*

conciliatory [kən'sɪlɪətrɪ] *adj* **(a)** *(manner, words)* conciliant; *(person)* conciliateur, conciliant; **in a conciliatory spirit** dans un esprit de conciliation **(b)** *Law & Pol (procedure)* conciliatoire

concise [kən'saɪs] *adj (succinct)* concis; *(abridged)* abrégé; *(dictionary)* abrégé

concisely [kən'saɪslɪ] *adv* avec concision

conciseness [kən'saɪsnɪs], **concision** [kən'sɪʒən] *n* concision *f*

conclave ['kɒŋkleɪv] *n* **(a)** *(private meeting)* assemblée *f ou* réunion *f* à huis clos; **in conclave** en réunion privée **(b)** *Rel* conclave *m*

conclude [kən'kluːd] **1** *vt* **(a)** *(finish)* conclure, terminer; *(meeting, session)* clore, clôturer; **to be concluded** *(serialized story)* suite et fin au prochain numéro; *(TV serial)* suite et fin au prochain épisode

(b) *(settle – deal, treaty)* conclure

(c) *(deduce)* conclure, déduire; **may I conclude from your statement that...** dois-je conclure *ou* déduire de votre remarque que... + *indicative*

(d) *(decide)* décider; **she concluded she would wait** elle a décidé d'attendre

2 *vi* **(a)** *(person)* conclure; **to conclude, I would just like to say...** en conclusion *ou* pour conclure, je voudrais simplement dire...

(b) *(event)* se terminer, s'achever; **the meeting concluded with the chairman's summary** la réunion s'est achevée avec la récapitulation du président

concluding [kən'kluːdɪŋ] *adj* de conclusion, final; **he made a few concluding remarks** il a fait quelques remarques finales

conclusion [kən'kluːʒən] **1** *n* **(a)** *(end)* conclusion *f*, fin *f*; *(of meeting, session)* clôture *f*; **to bring sth to a conclusion** mener qch à sa conclusion *ou* à terme; **she brought the matter to a successful conclusion** elle a mené l'affaire à (bon) terme

(b) *(decision, judgement)* conclusion *f*, décision *f*; **to come to** *or* **reach the conclusion that...** conclure que... + *indicative*; (en) arriver à la conclusion que... + *indicative*; **the conclusion to be drawn from this matter** la conclusion à tirer de cette affaire; **it's up to you to draw your own conclusions** c'est à vous d'en juger; **the facts lead me to the conclusion that...** les faits m'amènent à conclure que... + *indicative*

(c) *(settling – of deal, treaty)* conclusion *f*

(d) *Phil* conclusion *f*

2 in conclusion *adv* en conclusion, pour conclure

conclusive [kən'kluːsɪv] *adj (decisive – proof, argument)* concluant, décisif; *(final)* final

conclusively [kən'kluːsɪvlɪ] *adv (prove, argue, show)* de façon concluante *ou* décisive, définitivement

conclusiveness [kən'kluːsɪvnɪs] *n (decisiveness – of proof, argument)* caractère *m* décisif

concoct [kən'kɒkt] *vt* **(a)** *(prepare – meal, dish)* confectionner **(b)** *Fig (invent – excuse, scheme)* combiner, concocter; *(– plot)* machiner

concoction [kən'kɒkʃən] *n* (**a**) *(action)* confection *f*, préparation *f* (**b**) *(meal, dish, drink)* mélange *m* (**c**) *Fig (scheme)* combinaison *f*

concomitant [kən'kɒmɪtənt] *Formal* **1** *adj* concomitant; **adolescence with all its concomitant anxieties** l'adolescence et les angoisses qui l'accompagnent

2 *n* accessoire *m*; **ill health is a common concomitant of poverty** la mauvaise santé va souvent de pair avec la misère

concomitantly [kən'kɒmɪtəntlɪ] *adv* de façon concomitante, simultanément

concord ['kɒŋkɔːd] *n* (**a**) *Formal (harmony)* concorde *f*, harmonie *f*; **to live in concord** vivre en bon accord *ou* en harmonie (**b**) *(treaty)* accord *m*, entente *f* (**c**) *Gram* accord *m*; **to be in concord with sth** s'accorder avec qch (**d**) *Mus* accord *m*

concordance [kən'kɔːdəns] **1** *n* (**a**) *Formal (agreement)* accord *m* (**b**) *(index)* index *m*; *(of Bible, of author's works)* concordance *f*

2 in concordance with *prep* en accord avec; **the policy is in concordance with our declared aims** cette politique s'accorde *ou* est en accord avec les objectifs que nous nous sommes fixés

concordant [kən'kɔːdənt] *adj Formal* concordant, s'accordant; **concordant with** s'accordant avec

concordat [kɒn'kɔːdæt] *n* concordat *m*

Concorde ['kɒnkɔːd] *n Aviat* Concorde *m*

concourse ['kɒŋkɔːs] *n* (**a**) *(of people, things)* multitude *f*, rassemblement *m*; *(crowd)* foule *f* (**b**) *(of circumstances, events)* concours *m* (**c**) *(meeting place)* lieu *m* de rassemblement; *(in building)* hall *m* (**d**) *Am (street)* boulevard *m*; *(crossroads)* carrefour *m*

concrete ['kɒŋkriːt] **1** *n* (**a**) *Constr* béton *m* (**b**) *Phil* **the concrete** le concret

2 *adj* (**a**) *(specific → advantage)* concret(ète), réel; *(→ example, proposal, term)* concret(ète); **he made us a concrete offer** il nous a fait une offre précise *ou* concrète; **we need concrete proof** il nous faut des preuves concrètes *ou* matérielles; **in concrete terms** concrètement

(**b**) *Gram, Math & Mus* concret(ète)

(**c**) *Constr* en *ou* de béton; **concrete monstrosity** horreur *f* architecturale; **concrete slab** dalle *f* de béton

3 *vt Constr* bétonner

►► *Fig* ***concrete jungle*** univers *m* de béton; *Constr* ***concrete mixer*** bétonnière *f*; ***concrete music*** musique *f* concrète; *Gram* ***concrete noun*** nom *m* concret; ***concrete poem*** calligramme *m*; ***concrete poetry*** calligrammes *mpl*

►**concrete over** *vt sep (garden, field etc)* bétonner

concretely ['kɒŋkriːtlɪ] *adv* d'une manière concrète

concreteness ['kɒŋkriːtnɪs] *n* caractère *m* concret

concreting ['kɒnkriːtɪŋ] *n Constr* bétonnage *m*

concretion [kən'kriːʃən] *n* concrétion *f*

concretization [ˌkɒŋkriːtaɪ'zeɪʃən] *n* concrétisation *f*

concretize, -ise ['kɒŋkriːtaɪz] *vt* concrétiser

concubinage [kɒn'kjuːbɪnɪdʒ] *n* concubinage *m*

concubine ['kɒŋkjʊbaɪn] *n* concubine *f*

concupiscence [kən'kjuːpɪsəns] *n* concupiscence *f*

concur [kən'kɜː(r)] (*pt & pp* **concurred,** *cont* **concurring**) *vi* (**a**) *(agree)* être d'accord, s'entendre; **to concur with sb/sth** être d'accord avec qn/qch; **I concur with you in your decision** je suis d'accord avec vous sur *ou* au sujet de cette décision; **she concurs with the proposals** elle est d'accord avec le projet; **the experts' opinions concur** les avis des experts convergent; **he proposed a different approach and she concurred** il a proposé une approche différente et elle a approuvé

(**b**) *(occur together)* coïncider, arriver en même temps; **events concurred to make it a miserable Christmas** tout a concouru à gâcher les fêtes de Noël

(**c**) *(findings, results of experiment)* concorder (**with** avec)

concurrence [kən'kʌrəns] *n* (**a**) *(agreement)* accord *m*, concordance *f* de vues (**b**) *(assent)* assentiment *m*, consentement *m* (**in** à) (**c**) *(simultaneous occurrence)* coïncidence *f*, concomitance *f*, simultanéité *f*; **concurrence of events** concours *m* de circonstances

concurrent [kən'kʌrənt] *adj* (**a**) *(simultaneous)* concomitant, simultané; *Law* **two concurrent sentences** deux peines *fpl* confondues (**b**) *(acting together)* concerté (**c**) *(agreeing)* concordant, d'accord (**d**) *Math & Tech (intersecting)* concourant

►► *Law* ***concurrent cause*** cause *f* contribuante

concurrently [kən'kʌrəntlɪ] *adv* simultanément; *Law* **the two sentences to run concurrently** avec confusion des deux peines

concuss [kən'kʌs] *vt* (**a**) *Med (injure → brain)* commotionner; **to be concussed** être commotionné (**b**) *(shake)* ébranler, secouer violemment

concussion [kən'kʌʃən] *n* (**a**) *(UNCOUNT) Med (brain injury)* commotion *f* cérébrale (**b**) *(shaking)* ébranlement *m*, secousse *f* violente

condemn [kən'dem] *vt* (**a**) *Law (sentence)* condamner; **condemned to death** condamné à mort; *Fig* **people who are condemned to live in poverty** les gens qui sont condamnés à vivre dans la misère

(**b**) *(disapprove of)* condamner, censurer; **she condemned the remarks as pure prejudice** elle a condamné les remarques comme étant de purs préjugés

(**c**) *(declare unsafe → building)* déclarer inhabitable, condamner; **this meat has been condemned** cette viande a été jugée impropre à la consommation

(**d**) *Am Law (property)* exproprier pour cause d'utilité publique

condemnable [kən'demnəbəl] *adj* condamnable

condemnation [ˌkɒndem'neɪʃən] *n* (**a**) *Law (sentence)* condamnation *f* (**b**) *(criticism)* condamnation *f*, censure *f* (**c**) *(of building)* condamnation *f*; *(of meat)* fait *m* de juger impropre à la consommation (**d**) *Am Law (of property)* expropriation *f* pour cause d'utilité publique

condemnatory [kən'demnətrɪ] *adj* condamnatoire

condemned [kən'demd] *adj* (**a**) *Law (sentenced)* condamné; **the condemned man** le condamné (**b**) *(building)* condamné; *(meat)* jugé impropre à la consommation

►► ***condemned cell*** cellule *f* des condamnés

condensation [ˌkɒnden'seɪʃən] *n* (**a**) *(of gas, liquid, vapour)* condensation *f* (**b**) *(on glass)* buée *f*, condensation *f* (**c**) *Phys (of beam)* concentration *f*

►► *Phys* ***condensation reaction*** réaction *f* de condensation

condense [kən'dens] **1** *vt* (**a**) *(make denser)* condenser, concentrer; *(gas, liquid, vapour)* condenser (**b**) *(report, book, text)* condenser, résumer (**c**) *Phys (beam)* concentrer

2 *vi (become liquid)* se condenser; *(become concentrated)* se concentrer

condensed [kən'denst] *adj* condensé, concentré; *Typ* **in condensed print** en petits caractères

►► ***condensed book*** livre *m* condensé; ***condensed milk*** lait *m* concentré

condenser [kən'densə(r)] *n* (**a**) *Elec & Tech* condensateur *m* (**b**) *(of gas)* condenseur *m* (**c**) *Phys (of beam, light source)* condensateur *m*

►► ***condenser microphone*** microphone *m* électrostatique

condensing [kən'densɪŋ] *n* condensation *f*

condescend [ˌkɒndɪ'send] *vi* (**a**) *(behave patronizingly)* **to condescend (to sb)** se montrer condescendant (envers qn *ou* à l'égard de qn) (**b**) *(lower oneself)* **to condescend to do sth** condescendre à *ou* daigner faire qch; **she condescended to speak to me** elle a condescendu à *ou* a daigné me parler; **he does condescend to set the table occasionally** il condescend à mettre le couvert de temps en temps

condescending [ˌkɒndɪ'sendɪŋ] *adj* condescendant

condescendingly [ˌkɒndɪ'sendɪŋlɪ] *adv* avec condescendance; *(speak)* d'un ton condescendant; **he treated me very condescendingly** il m'a traité de haut, il m'a pris de très haut

condescension [ˌkɒndɪ'senʃən] *n* condescendance *f* (**to** envers *ou* pour)

condign [kən'daɪn] *adj Formal (appropriate)* adéquat, idoine; *(deserved)* mérité

condiment ['kɒndɪmənt] *n* condiment *m*

►► ***condiment set*** poivrier *m* et salière *f*

condition [kən'dɪʃən] **1** *n* (**a**) *(state → mental, physical)* état *m*; **the human condition** la condition humaine; **the financial condition of a company** l'état *m* financier d'une entreprise; **in your condition** *(to pregnant woman)* dans ton état; **you're in no condition to drive** vous n'êtes pas en état de conduire; **books in good/poor condition** livres en bon/mauvais état; **I'm out of condition** je ne suis pas en forme; **you should get yourself into condition** vous devriez faire des exercices pour retrouver la forme; **he's in excellent condition** sa condition physique est excellente; **in working condition** en état de marche

(**b**) *(stipulation)* condition *f*; **to make a condition that...** stipuler que... + *indicative*; **you can borrow the book, on one condition** tu peux emprunter le livre, à une condition; **it was a condition of the lease that...** l'une des stipulations du bail était que...+ *subjunctive*; *Com* **conditions of sale** conditions *fpl* de vente; *Law* **the conditions of a contract** les conditions *fpl* *ou* stipulations *fpl* d'un contrat

(**c**) *(illness)* maladie *f*, affection *f*; **he has a heart condition** il a une maladie de cœur

(**d**) *Formal (social status)* situation *f*, position *f*

2 *vt* (**a**) *(train)* conditionner; *Psy* provoquer un réflexe conditionné chez, conditionner; **her upbringing conditioned her to believe in God** son éducation l'a automatiquement portée à croire en Dieu

(**b**) *(make fit → animal, person)* mettre en forme; *(→ thing)* mettre en bon état; **to condition one's hair** mettre de l'après-shampoing

(**c**) *(determine)* conditionner, déterminer; **the market is conditioned by the economic situation** le marché dépend de la conjoncture économique

3 conditions *npl (circumstances)* conditions *fpl*, circonstances *fpl*; **living/working conditions** conditions *fpl* de vie/de travail; **under these conditions** dans ces conditions; **road** *or* **driving conditions** état *m* des routes; **drive with particular care as conditions on the roads are hazardous** soyez prudents sur les routes: le mauvais temps rend la circulation très dangereuse; **the weather conditions** les conditions *fpl* météorologiques

4 on condition that *conj* à condition que + *subjunctive*; **I'll tell you on condition that you keep it secret** je vais vous le dire à condition que vous gardiez le secret; **he'll do it on condition that he's well paid** il le fera à condition d'être bien payé

conditional [kən'dɪʃənəl] **1** *adj* (**a**) *(dependent on other factors)* conditionnel; **to be conditional on** *or* **upon sth** dépendre de qch; **negotiations are conditional upon withdrawal of enemy forces** les négociations dépendent du retrait des troupes ennemies; **a conditional promise** une promesse conditionnelle *ou* sous condition (**b**) *Gram* conditionnel

2 *n Gram* conditionnel *m*; **in the conditional** au conditionnel

►► ***conditional acceptance*** acceptation *f* sous réserve; ***conditional access television*** télévision *f* à accès conditionnel; *Law* ***conditional discharge*** mise *f* en liberté conditionnelle

conditionality [kənˌdɪʃə'nælɪtɪ] *n* état *m* conditionnel

conditionally [kən'dɪʃənəlɪ] *adv* conditionnellement

conditioned [kən'dɪʃənd] *adj* conditionné

►► *Psy* ***conditioned reflex*** réflexe *m* conditionné; *Psy* ***conditioned response*** réaction *f* conditionnée; *Psy* ***conditioned stimulus*** stimulus *m* conditionnel

conditioner [kən'dɪʃənə(r)] *n (for hair)* après-shampo(o)ing *m*; *(for fabric)* assouplisseur *m*

conditioning [kən'dɪʃənɪŋ] **1** *n (gen)* conditionnement *m*; *(fitness)* mise *f* en forme

2 *adj* traitant

►► ***conditioning shampoo*** shampo(o)ing *m* démêlant

condo ['kɒndəʊ] *n Am Fam (ownership)* copropriété ❑ *f*; *(building)* immeuble *m* (en copropriété) ❑; *(flat)* appartement *m* en copropriété ❑

condole [kən'dəʊl] *vi Literary* exprimer ses condoléances *ou* sa sympathie (**with** à)
condolence [kən'dəʊləns] *n* condoléances *fpl*; **a letter of condolence** une lettre de condoléances; **to offer one's condolences to sb** présenter ses condoléances à qn
condom ['kɒndəm] *n* préservatif *m (masculin)*
condominium [ˌkɒndə'mɪnɪəm] *n* (**a**) *(government)* condominium *m* (**b**) *(country)* condominium *m* (**c**) *Am (ownership)* copropriété *f*; *(building)* immeuble *m* (en copropriété); *(flat)* appartement *m* en copropriété
condone [kən'dəʊn] *vt (overlook)* fermer les yeux sur; *(forgive)* pardonner, excuser; **we cannot condone such immoral behaviour** nous ne pouvons excuser un comportement aussi immoral; *Law* **to condone adultery** pardonner un adultère
condor ['kɒndɔː(r)] *n* condor *m*
conduce [kən'djuːs] *vi Formal (action, thing)* contribuer (**to** à)
conducive [kən'djuːsɪv] *adj* favorable; **this weather is not conducive to studying** ce temps n'incite pas à étudier
conduct 1 *n* ['kɒndʌkt] (**a**) *(behaviour)* conduite *f*, comportement *m* (**towards sb** à l'égard de *ou* avec *ou* envers qn); **bad/good conduct** mauvaise/bonne conduite *f*; **her conduct towards me** son comportement envers moi *ou* à mon égard
(**b**) *(handling → of business, negotiations)* conduite *f*; **the lawyer's conduct of the case** la manière dont l'avocat a mené l'affaire
2 *vt* [kən'dʌkt] (**a**) *(manage, carry out → business, operations, religious service)* diriger; *(→ campaign, survey)* mener; *(→ inquiry)* conduire, mener; *(→ experiment)* effectuer; **this is not the way to conduct negotiations** ce n'est pas ainsi qu'on négocie; *Law* **who is conducting your case?** qui assure votre défense?; *Law* **to conduct one's own case** plaider soi-même sa cause
(**b**) *(guide)* conduire, mener; **the director conducted us through the factory** le directeur nous a fait visiter l'usine
(**c**) *(behave)* **to conduct oneself** se conduire, se comporter
(**d**) *(musicians, music)* diriger; **Bernstein will be conducting the orchestra** l'orchestre sera (placé) sous la direction de Bernstein
(**e**) *Elec & Phys (transmit)* conduire, être conducteur de; **water conducts electricity** l'eau est conductrice d'électricité
3 *vi* [kən'dʌkt] *Mus* diriger; *(work as conductor)* être chef d'orchestre; **who's conducting?** qui est le chef d'orchestre?, qui dirige?
►► *Sch* ***conduct report*** rapport *m (sur la conduite d'un élève)*; *Mil* ***conduct sheet*** feuille *f ou* certificat *m* de conduite
conductance [kən'dʌktəns] *n Elec & Phys* conductance *f*
conducted tour [kən'dʌktɪd-] *n Br (short)* visite *f* guidée; *(longer)* voyage *m* organisé; **a conducted tour of the museum** une visite guidée du musée; **he runs conducted tours of the region** il dirige des voyages organisés *ou* des excursions accompagnées dans la région
conducting [kən'dʌktɪŋ] *n* (**a**) *(of business, people)* [illegible] (**b**) [illegible] diriger
conduction [kən'dʌkʃən] *n Elec & Phys* conduction *f*
conductive [kən'dʌktɪv] *adj Elec & Phys* conducteur
►► ***conductive education*** = enseignement adapté aux besoins des handicapés moteurs
conductivity [ˌkɒndʌk'tɪvətɪ] *n Elec & Phys* conductivité *f*
conductor [kən'dʌktə(r)] *n* (**a**) *(of musicians, music)* chef *m* d'orchestre (**b**) *Transp (railway official)* chef *m* de train; *Br (on bus)* receveur *m* (**c**) *Elec & Phys* (corps *m*) conducteur *m*
conductress [kən'dʌktrɪs] *n Br (on bus)* receveuse *f*
conduit ['kɒndɪt] *n Tech (for fluid)* conduit *m*, canalisation *f*; *Elec* tube *m*; *Fig (for money)* intermédiaire *mf*
condylar ['kɒndɪlə(r)] *adj Anat* condylien
condyle ['kɒndɪl] *n Anat* condyle *m*
condyloma [ˌkɒndɪ'ləʊmə] *n Med* condylome *m*
cone [kəʊn] *n* (**a**) *(gen) & Math* cône *m* (**b**) **(traffic) cone** cône *m* de signalisation (**c**) *(for ice cream)* cornet *m* (**d**) *Anat (in retina)* cône *m* (**e**) *Bot (of pine, fir)* pomme *f*, cône *m*
►► *Aut* ***cone clutch*** embrayage *m* à cône
►**cone off** *vt sep Br* mettre des cônes de signalisation sur
cone-bearing *adj Bot* conifère
conehead ['kəʊnhed] *n Am Fam* imbécile; **you conehead!** (espèce d')imbécile!
cone-shaped [-ʃeɪpt] *adj* en forme de cône, conique
Conestoga wagon [ˌkɒnɪ'stəʊgə-] *n Am Hist* = grosse voiture couverte des pionniers américains, au XIXème siècle
coney = **cony**
Coney Island ['kəʊnɪ-] *n* Coney Island *(île située au large de New York et où se trouve un grand parc d'attractions)*
confab ['kɒnfæb] *(pt & pp* **confabbed,** *cont* **confabbing)** *Fam* **1** *n* causette *f*; **to have a confab (about sth)** causer (de qch)
2 *vi* causer, bavarder
confabulate [kən'fæbjʊleɪt] *vi* (**a**) *Fam (chat)* causer, bavarder (**b**) *Psy* fabuler
confabulation [kənˌfæbjʊ'leɪʃən] *n* (**a**) *Fam (chat)* causette *f* (**b**) *Psy* fabulation *f*
confection [kən'fekʃən] *n* (**a**) *(act)* confection *f* (**b**) *(sweet)* sucrerie *f*, friandise *f*; *(pastry)* pâtisserie *f*; *(cake)* gâteau *m*
confectioner [kən'fekʃənə(r)] *n (of sweets)* confiseur(euse) *m,f*; *(of pastry, cakes)* pâtissier(ère) *m,f*; **confectioner's** *(shop → for sweets)* confiserie *f*; *(→ for pastry, cakes)* pâtisserie *f*
►► ***confectioner's custard*** crème *f* pâtissière, *Can* costarde *f*; ***confectioner's shop*** *(for sweets)* confiserie *f*; *(for pastry, cakes)* pâtisserie *f*; *Am* ***confectioner's sugar*** sucre *m* glace
confectionery [kən'fekʃənərɪ] *(pl* **confectioneries**) *n (sweets)* confiserie *f*; *(pastry)* pâtisserie *f*
confederacy [kən'fedərəsɪ] *(pl* **confederacies**) **1** *n* (**a**) *(alliance)* confédération *f* (**b**) *(conspiracy)* conspiration *f*
2 Confederacy *n Hist* **the Confederacy** les États *mpl* confédérés *(pendant la guerre de Sécession américaine)*
confederate 1 *n* [kən'fedərət] (**a**) *(member of confederacy)* confédéré(e) *m,f* (**b**) *(accomplice)* complice *mf*
2 *adj* [kən'fedərət] confédéré
3 *vt* [kən'fedəreɪt] confédérer
4 *vi* [kən'fedəreɪt] se confédérer
5 Confederate [kən'fedərət] *n Hist* sudiste *mf (pendant la guerre de Sécession américaine)*; **the Confederates** les Confédérés *mpl*
►► ***the Confederate flag*** = drapeau des sudistes américains, considéré aujourd'hui comme un symbole raciste; *Hist* ***the Confederate States (of America)*** les États *mpl* confédérés *(pendant la guerre de Sécession américaine)*
confederation [kənˌfedə'reɪʃən] *n* confédération *f*
►► ***Confederation of Australian Industry*** = confédération du patronat australien; ***Confederation of British Industry*** = patronat britannique, ≃ Medef *m*; *Br* ***Confederation of Health Service Employees*** = ancien syndicat des employés des services de santé; *Br* ***Confederation of Shipbuilding and Engineering Unions*** = confédération des syndicats de la construction navale et de la mécanique
confer [kən'fɜː(r)] *(pt & pp* **conferred,** *cont* **conferring)** **1** *vi* conférer, s'entretenir; **to confer with sb (about sth)** s'entretenir avec qn (de qch); **he conferred with her about the guest list** il s'est entretenu avec elle de la liste des invités; **contestants are not allowed to confer** les concurrents n'ont pas le droit de se consulter
2 *vt (title, rank, powers)* conférer, accorder (**on** à); *(degree, diploma)* remettre (**on** à); **the Queen conferred a title on him** la Reine lui a conféré un titre; **to confer an award on sb** remettre une récompense *ou* un prix à qn; **degrees were conferred on thirty students** des diplômes ont été remis à trente étudiants
conferee [ˌkɒnfɜː'riː] *n* (**a**) *(conference member)* participant(e) *m,f*, congressiste *mf* (**b**) *(recipient → of title, rank, powers)* anobli(e) *m,f*; *(→ of scholarship)* récipiendaire *mf*; *(→ of degree, diploma)* diplômé(e) *m,f*, récipiendaire *mf*
conference ['kɒnfərəns] *n* (**a**) *(meeting)* conférence *f*; *(consultation)* conférence *f*, consultation *f*; **to be in conference (with)** *(with several people)* être en conférence (avec); *(with one or two people)* être en réunion (avec); **we hope to get management to the conference table** nous espérons réunir la direction en table ronde
(**b**) *(convention)* congrès *m*, colloque *m*; *Pol* congrès *m*, assemblée *f*; **the Labour Party conference** le congrès du parti travailliste
(**c**) *Am Sport (association)* association *f*, ligue *f*
►► ***conference call*** téléconférence *f*; ***conference centre*** *(building)* centre *m* de congrès; *(town)* = ville pouvant accueillir des congrès; ***conference coordinator*** responsable *mf* des congrès; ***conference delegate*** congressiste *mf*; ***conference hall*** salle *f* de conférence; *Naut & Com* ***conference line*** ligne *f* maritime de conférence; ***conference organizer*** organisateur(-trice) *m,f* de conférences *ou* de congrès; ***conference pack*** = dossier offert aux conférenciers avec informations générales sur la conférence, petits cadeaux etc; ***conference room*** salle *f* de conférence; *Naut & Com* ***conference ship*** navire *m* de conférence
conference-goer *n* participant(e) *m,f* à une conférence
Conference pear ['kɒnfərəns-] *n* poire *f* conférence
conferencing ['kɒnfərənsɪŋ] *n (UNCOUNT)* téléconférence *f*
conferment [kən'fɜːmənt], **conferral** [kən'fɜːrəl] *n* action *f* de conférer; *(of degree, diploma)* remise *f* (de diplôme); *(of favour, title)* octroi *m*; **the conferment of a title on sb** l'anoblissement *m* de qn
conferree = **conferee**
confess [kən'fes] **1** *vt* (**a**) *(admit → fault, crime)* avouer, confesser; **to confess one's guilt** *or* **that one is guilty** avouer sa culpabilité, s'avouer coupable; **I must** *or* **I have to confess I was wrong** je dois reconnaître *ou* admettre que j'avais tort; **I don't understand either, I must confess** je dois avouer que je ne comprends pas non plus; **medical experts confess themselves helpless** les médecins s'avouent impuissants
(**b**) *Rel (sins)* confesser, se confesser de; *(of priest)* confesser
2 *vi* (**a**) *(criminal)* avouer, faire des aveux; **to confess to a crime** avouer un crime; **the thief confessed** le voleur est passé aux aveux; **she confessed to five murders** elle a avoué *ou* confessé cinq meurtres
(**b**) *(admit)* faire des aveux; **he confessed to having lied** il a reconnu *ou* avoué avoir menti; **I confess to not liking her** j'avoue que je ne l'aime pas; **I confess to a weakness for sweets** j'avoue *ou* je reconnais que j'ai un faible pour les sucreries
(**c**) *Rel* se confesser
confessant [kən'fesənt] *n Rel* pénitent(e) *m,f*
confessed [kən'fest] *adj* de son propre aveu; **he was a confessed liar** il reconnaissait lui-même être menteur
confessedly [kən'fesɪdlɪ] *adv* de son propre aveu
confession [kən'feʃən] *n* (**a**) *(of guilt)* aveu *m*, confession *f*; **to make a full confession** faire des aveux complets; **I have a confession to make** j'ai un aveu à faire; **on my own confession** de mon propre aveu
(**b**) *Rel* confession *f*; *(sect)* confession *f*; **do you go to confession?** allez-vous vous confesser?; **she made her confession** elle s'est confessée; **the priest heard our confession** le prêtre nous a confessés; **the seal of confession** le secret de la confession *ou* du confessionnal; **a confession of faith** une confession de foi

'Confessions of an English Opium-Eater' *De Quincey* 'Les Confessions d'un mangeur d'opium anglais'

con–con

confessional [kən'feʃənəl] *Rel* **1** *n* confessionnal *m*; **the secrets of the confessional** les secrets du confessionnal

2 *adj* confessionnel

confessor [kən'fesə(r)] *n Rel* confesseur *m*

confetti [kən'fetɪ] *n (UNCOUNT)* confettis *mpl*

confidant [,kɒnfɪ'dænt] *n* confident *m*

confidante [,kɒnfɪ'dænt] *n* confidente *f*

confide [kən'faɪd] *vt* (**a**) *(reveal)* avouer en confidence, confier; **to confide a secret to sb** confier un secret à qn; **she confided her fear to them** elle leur a avoué en confidence sa peur; **I didn't confide my thoughts to anyone** je n'ai révélé mes pensées à personne

(**b**) *(entrust)* confier; **they confided their daughter to her** ils ont confié leur fille à sa garde *ou* à ses soins; **to confide sth to sb's care** confier qch à la garde de qn

▸**confide in** *vt insep* (**a**) *(talk freely to)* se confier à; **there's nobody I can confide in** il n'y a personne à qui je puisse me confier

(**b**) *(trust)* avoir confiance en, se fier à; **you can confide in me!** vous pouvez me faire confiance!, fiez-vous à moi!

confidence ['kɒnfɪdəns] *n* (**a**) *(faith)* confiance *f*; **we have confidence in her ability** nous avons confiance en ses capacités; **she has no confidence in her own ability** elle n'a aucune confiance en elle; **I have every confidence that you'll succeed** je suis absolument certain que vous réussirez; **to put one's confidence in sb/sth** faire confiance à qn/qch; **the confidence placed in me** la confiance qui m'a été témoignée; **with complete confidence** en toute confiance

(**b**) *(self-assurance)* confiance *f* (en soi), assurance *f*; **he spoke with confidence** il a parlé avec assurance; **he lacks confidence** il n'est pas très sûr de lui; **full of confidence** *(person)* plein d'assurance *ou* de confiance en soi; *(performance)* plein d'assurance

(**c**) *(certainty)* confiance *f*, certitude *f*; **to win sb's confidence** gagner la confiance de qn; **she has every confidence that they'll win** elle est certaine qu'ils vont gagner; **I can say with confidence** je peux dire avec confiance *ou* assurance

(**d**) *(trust)* confiance *f*; **I was told in confidence** on me l'a dit confidentiellement *ou* en confiance; **she told me in the strictest confidence** elle me l'a dit dans la plus stricte confidence; **to take sb into one's confidence** se confier à qn, faire des confidences à qn; **to be in sb's confidence** partager les secrets de qn

(**e**) *(private message)* confidence *f*; **to exchange confidences** échanger des confidences; **to repeat a confidence** répéter quelque chose dit en confidence, répéter un secret

▸▸ *Math* ***confidence interval*** intervalle *m* de confiance; ***confidence man*** escroc *m*; ***confidence trick*** escroquerie *f*, abus *m* de confiance; ***confidence trickster*** escroc *m*

confidence-building *adj (exercise, activity)* = qui vise à stimuler la confiance en soi

confident ['kɒnfɪdənt] *adj* (**a**) *(self-assured)* sûr (de soi), assuré (**b**) *(certain)* assuré, confiant; **confident of success** sûr de réussir; **in a confident tone** d'un ton assuré *ou* plein d'assurance; **we are confident that the plan will work** nous sommes persuadés que le projet va réussir

confidential [,kɒnfɪ'denʃəl] *adj* (**a**) *(private)* confidentiel; *(on envelope)* confidentiel; **I would like you to treat this conversation as confidential** j'aimerais que vous considériez cette conversation comme étant confidentielle; **it's confidential, of course** c'est confidentiel *ou* vous le gardez pour vous, bien entendu; **his voice became confidential** il prit le ton de la confidence (**b**) *(attached to one person → position)* de confiance

▸▸ ***confidential agent*** homme *m* de confiance; ***confidential secretary*** secrétaire *mf* particulier(ère)

confidentiality ['kɒnfɪ,denʃɪ'ælətɪ] *n* confidentialité *f*; **all inquiries treated with complete confidentiality** *(in advertisement)* les demandes de renseignements sont traitées en toute discrétion

confidentially [,kɒnfɪ'denʃəlɪ] *adv* confidentiellement; **confidentially, I don't trust him** entre nous, je ne lui fais pas confiance

confidently ['kɒnfɪdəntlɪ] *adv* (**a**) *(with certainty)* avec confiance; **I can confidently predict (that)...** je peux prédire avec assurance (que)... (**b**) *(assuredly)* avec assurance

confiding [kən'faɪdɪŋ] *adj* confiant, sans méfiance

confidingly [kən'faɪdɪŋlɪ] *adv (act)* d'un air confiant; *(speak)* en confidence

config. sys [,kɒnfɪg'sɪs] *n Comput* **config. sys (file)** fichier *m* config. sys

configurable [kən'fɪgjʊrəbəl] *adj (gen) & Comput* configurable, paramétrable

configuration [kən,fɪgə'reɪʃən] *n (gen) & Comput* configuration *f*, paramétrage *m*

configure [kən'fɪgə(r)] *vt (gen) & Comput* configurer

confine [kən'faɪn] *vt* (**a**) *(restrict)* limiter, borner; **to confine oneself to sth** se borner *ou* s'en tenir à qch; **we confined ourselves to (discussing) the financial arrangements** nous nous en sommes tenus à discuter des dispositions financières, nous nous en sommes tenus aux dispositions financières; **the report confines itself to single women** le rapport ne traite que des femmes célibataires; **please confine your remarks to the subject under consideration** veuillez vous limiter au sujet en question

(**b**) *(shut up)* confiner, enfermer; *(imprison)* incarcérer, enfermer; **her illness confined her to the house/to bed** sa maladie l'a obligée à rester à la maison/à garder le lit; *Mil* **to confine sb to barracks** consigner qn

(**c**) *Old-fashioned (pregnant woman)* **to be confined** accoucher, être en couches

confined [kən'faɪnd] *adj* (**a**) *(area, atmosphere)* confiné; **in a confined space** dans un espace restreint *ou* réduit (**b**) *(shut up)* renfermé; *(imprisoned)* emprisonné, incarcéré; *Mil* **to be confined to barracks** être consigné; **confined to bed** alité

confinement [kən'faɪnmənt] *n* (**a**) *(detention)* détention *f*, réclusion *f*; *(imprisonment)* emprisonnement *m*, incarcération *f*; **confinement to bed** alitement *m*; **confinement to the house/to one's room** obligation *f* de rester à la maison/de garder la chambre; *Mil* **confinement to barracks** consigne *f* (au quartier); **six months' confinement** six mois de prison

(**b**) *Old-fashioned (in childbirth)* couches *fpl*, accouchement *m*

confines ['kɒnfaɪnz] *npl* confins *mpl*, limites *fpl*; **within the confines of reason** dans les limites de la raison; **within/beyond the confines of human knowledge** dans/au delà des limites de la connaissance humaine

confirm [kən'fɜːm] **1** *vt* (**a**) *(verify)* confirmer, corroborer; **I can confirm that story** je peux confirmer cette histoire; **to confirm that...** confirmer que... + *indicative*; *Com* **we confirm receipt of** *or* **that we have received your letter** nous accusons réception de votre lettre

(**b**) *(finalize → arrangement, booking)* confirmer; **confirm our reservation with the restaurant** confirmez notre réservation auprès du restaurant; **to be confirmed** *(sign for concert, film etc)* à confirmer

(**c**) *(strengthen → position)* assurer, consolider; *(→ belief, doubts, resolve)* confirmer, raffermir; **that confirms her in her opinion** cela la conforte dans son opinion

(**d**) *(make valid → treaty)* ratifier; *(→ result)* confirmer; *(→ election)* valider; *(→ nomination)* approuver; *(→ decision)* entériner; *Law* entériner, homologuer

(**e**) *Rel* confirmer

2 *vi* confirmer; **please confirm in writing** veuillez confirmer par écrit

confirmation [,kɒnfə'meɪʃən] *n* (**a**) *(verification)* confirmation *f*; **the report is still awaiting confirmation** cette nouvelle n'a pas encore été confirmée; **in confirmation of** en confirmation de

(**b**) *(finalization → of arrangements)* confirmation *f*; **all bookings subject to confirmation** *(in brochure, on form, Web site)* toute réservation doit être confirmée

(**c**) *(strengthening → of position)* consolidation *f*, raffermissement *m*; *(→ of belief, doubts, resolve)* confirmation *f*

(**d**) *(validation → of treaty)* ratification *f*; *(→ of result)* confirmation *f*; *(→ of election)* validation *f*; *(→ of nomination)* approbation *f*; *(→ of decision)* entérinement *m*; *Law* entérinement *m*, homologation *f*

(**e**) *Rel* confirmation *f*

▸▸ *Am Pol* ***confirmation hearing*** = entretien à l'issue duquel un comité de sénateurs décide si un haut fonctionnaire nommé par le président est un candidat valable; *Com* ***confirmation of receipt*** accusé *m* de réception

confirmed [kən'fɜːmd] *adj* (**a**) *(long-established)* invétéré; **he's a confirmed bachelor** c'est un célibataire endurci; **he's a confirmed smoker** c'est un fumeur invétéré (**b**) *Rel* confirmé (**c**) *Fin (letter of credit)* irrévocable

▸▸ *Aviat* ***confirmed seat*** place *f* confirmée

confirming [kən'fɜːmɪŋ] *n*

▸▸ ***confirming bank*** banque *f* confirmatrice; *Banking* ***confirming house*** organisme *m* confirmateur

confiscate ['kɒnfɪskeɪt] *vt* confisquer; **to confiscate sth from sb** confisquer qch à qn

confiscation [,kɒnfɪ'skeɪʃən] *n* confiscation *f*

confiscator ['kɒnfɪ,skeɪtə(r)] *n* confiscateur(trice) *m,f*

confiscatory [,kɒnfɪ'skeɪtərɪ] *adj (power)* de confiscation

conflagration [,kɒnflə'greɪʃən] *n Formal* incendie *m*

conflate [kən'fleɪt] *vt Formal* réunir, regrouper

conflation [kən'fleɪʃən] *n Formal* fusion *f*

conflict 1 *n* ['kɒnflɪkt] (**a**) *(clash)* conflit *m*, lutte *f*; *Mil* conflit *m*, guerre *f*; **she often comes into conflict with her mother** elle entre souvent en conflit *ou* se heurte souvent avec sa mère; **this was in conflict with her principles** c'était en conflit *ou* en contradiction avec ses principes

(**b**) *(disagreement)* dispute *f*; *Law* conflit *m*; **to be in conflict (with)** être en conflit (avec); **the parties are often in conflict** les partis sont souvent en désaccord; **our differing beliefs brought us into conflict** nos croyances divergentes nous ont opposés; **the unions are in conflict with the management** les syndicats sont en conflit avec la direction; **there is a conflict between the two statements** les deux déclarations ne concordent pas

(**c**) *Psy (turmoil)* conflit *m*

2 *vi* [kən'flɪkt] (**a**) *(ideas, interests)* s'opposer, se heurter; **the research findings conflict with this view** les résultats des recherches sont en contradiction avec *ou* contredisent cette idée; **the policies conflict (with one another)** ces politiques sont incompatibles

(**b**) *(fight)* être en conflit *ou* en lutte

▸▸ ***a conflict of interests*** un conflit d'intérêts

conflicting [kən'flɪktɪŋ] *adj (opinions)* incompatible; *(advice, evidence, reports)* contradictoire

▸▸ ***conflicting interests*** des intérêts *mpl* qui s'opposent

confliction [kən'flɪkʃən] *n Literary* incompatibilité *f*

conflictual [kən'flɪktʃəl] *adj* conflictuel

confluence ['kɒnflʊəns] *n* (**a**) *(of rivers, glaciers → place)* confluent *m*; *(→ action)* confluence *f* (**b**) *(gathering together)* confluence *f*; *Fig (crowd)* rassemblement *m*

confluent ['kɒnflʊənt] **1** *adj* confluent

2 *n* confluent *m*

conform [kən'fɔːm] **1** *vi* (**a**) *(comply → person)* se conformer, s'adapter; **to conform to** *or* **with sth** se conformer *ou* s'adapter à qch; **to conform to the law** obéir aux lois; **you are expected to conform** tu es supposé te conformer

(**b**) *(action, thing)* être en conformité; **all cars must conform to** *or* **with the regulations** toute voiture doit être conforme aux normes

(**c**) *(correspond)* correspondre, répondre; **she conforms to** *or* **with my idea of a president** elle correspond *ou* répond à ma conception d'un président; **this conforms with what we were told/we expected** ceci est conforme à ce que l'on nous avait dit/nos attentes

(**d**) *Rel* être conformiste

2 *vt (ideas, actions)* conformer, rendre conforme

conformable [kən'fɔːməbəl] *adj Formal* (**a**) *(alike)* conforme (**b**) *(in agreement with)* adapté, compatible; **to be conformable to sth** être adapté à *ou* compatible avec qch (**c**) *(obedient)* accommodant

conformation [ˌkɒnfɔː'meɪʃən] *n* (**a**) *(configuration)* conformation *f*, structure *f* (**b**) *(act of forming)* conformation *f*

conformism [kən'fɔːmɪzəm] *n* conformisme *m*

conformist [kən'fɔːmɪst] **1** *adj* conformiste
 2 *n (gen) & Rel* conformiste *mf*

conformity [kən'fɔːmətɪ] *(pl* **conformities***)* **1** *n* (**a**) *(with rules, regulations)* conformité *f* (**b**) *(in behaviour, dress, attitude)* conformisme *m* (**c**) *Rel* conformisme *m*
 2 in conformity with *prep* en accord avec, conformément à; **their action was in conformity with the law** ce qu'ils ont fait était en conformité avec la loi

confound [kən'faʊnd] *vt* (**a**) *(perplex)* déconcerter; **to be confounded** être confondu; **he confounded his critics** il a fait mentir les gens qui le critiquaient (**b**) *(bring to nothing → plans)* renverser; *(→ hopes)* réduire à néant (**c**) *Formal (mix up)* confondre (**d**) *Fam Old-fashioned (curse)* **confound him!** qu'il aille au diable!; **confound it!** quelle barbe! (**e**) *Arch (defeat → enemy)* confondre

confounded [kən'faʊndɪd] *adj Fam Old-fashioned (wretched)* maudit; **it's a confounded nuisance!** c'est la barbe!, quelle barbe!; **that man is a confounded nuisance!** ce type est une vraie plaie!; **this confounded thing has broken again!** ce satané truc est encore cassé!

confoundedly [kən'faʊndɪdlɪ] *adv Fam Old-fashioned* furieusement, diablement; **confoundedly cold** bigrement froid

confraternity [ˌkɒnfrə'tɜːnɪtɪ] *n* association *f*

confront [kən'frʌnt] *vt* (**a**) *(face)* affronter, faire face à; **the obstacles confronting us** les obstacles auxquels nous devons faire face; **the headmaster confronted him in the corridor** le directeur l'affronta dans le couloir; **he had to confront a crowd of hecklers** il a dû affronter un groupe de perturbateurs; **the two groups of demonstrators confronted each other** les deux groupes de manifestants se sont affrontés; **to be confronted by** *or* **with sth** *(problem, risk)* se trouver en face de qch
 (**b**) *(present)* confronter; **she confronted him with the facts** elle l'a confronté avec les faits; **she confronted him with his responsibilities** elle l'a mis face à ses responsabilités

confrontation [ˌkɒnfrʌn'teɪʃən] *n* (**a**) *(conflict)* conflit *m*, affrontement *m*; *Mil* affrontement *m*; **he hates confrontation** il a horreur des situations de conflit (**b**) *(act of confronting)* confrontation *f*; **the confrontation of the defendant with the evidence** la confrontation de l'accusé aux *ou* avec les preuves

confrontational [ˌkɒnfrʌn'teɪʃənəl] *adj (situation)* d'affrontement; *(policy)* de confrontation; **to be confrontational** *(person)* aimer les conflits

Confucian [kən'fjuːʃən] **1** *adj* confucéen
 2 *n* confucéen(enne) *m,f*

Confucianism [kən'fjuːʃəˌnɪzəm] *n* confucianisme *m*

[illegible]

confusable [kən'fjuːzəbəl] **1** *n* = terme qui est souvent confondu avec un autre
 2 *adj (term, word)* qui est souvent confondu avec un autre

confuse [kən'fjuːz] *vt* (**a**) *(muddle → person)* embrouiller; *(→ thoughts)* embrouiller, brouiller; *(→ memory)* brouiller; **don't confuse me!** ne m'embrouillez pas (les idées)!; **to confuse the issue, to confuse matters** embrouiller *ou* compliquer les choses
 (**b**) *(perplex)* déconcerter, rendre perplexe; *(fluster)* troubler; *(embarrass)* embarrasser
 (**c**) *(mix up)* confondre; **you're confusing me with my brother** vous me confondez avec mon frère; **don't confuse the two issues** ne confondez pas les deux problèmes
 (**d**) *(disconcert → opponent)* confondre

confused [kən'fjuːzd] *adj* (**a**) *(muddled → person)* désorienté; *(→ sounds)* confus, indistinct; *(→ thoughts)* confus, embrouillé; *(→ memory)* confus, vague; **wait a minute, I'm getting confused** attends, là, je ne suis plus; **very old people often get confused** les personnes très âgées ont souvent les idées confuses
 (**b**) *(perplexed)* perplexe; *(flustered)* troublé; *(embarrassed)* confus; **I'm still a little confused as to why he did it** je ne comprends toujours pas très bien pourquoi il a fait cela
 (**c**) *(disordered)* en désordre; *(opponent)* confus

confusedly [kən'fjuːzɪdlɪ] *adv* confusément

confusible = **confusable**

confusing [kən'fjuːzɪŋ] *adj* embrouillé, déroutant; **it's very confusing** on s'y perd; **the plot is confusing** on se perd dans l'intrigue; **it's too confusing for the user** l'utilisateur s'y perdra; **I hope my explanation wasn't too confusing** j'espère que mon explication ne vous a pas trop embrouillé; **there's a confusing number of different makes** il y a tant de marques différentes qu'on s'y perd

confusingly [kən'fjuːzɪŋlɪ] *adv* de façon embrouillée; **confusingly, they both had the same name** ils avaient le même nom, ce qui provoquait souvent des confusions

confusion [kən'fjuːʒən] *n* (**a**) *(bewilderment)* confusion *f*; *(embarrassment)* déconfiture *f*, trouble *m*, embarras *m*; **he stared at it in confusion** il le fixa d'un regard perplexe; **she's in a state of confusion** elle a l'esprit troublé; **this news added to her confusion** cette nouvelle a ajouté à sa confusion; **in my confusion I said yes** dans mon embarras, j'ai dit oui; **it will only lead to confusion** ce ne va faire qu'embrouiller les choses
 (**b**) *(mixing up)* confusion *f*; **to avoid confusion** pour éviter toute confusion; **there is some confusion as to who won** il y a incertitude sur le vainqueur
 (**c**) *(disorder)* désordre *m*; *(of enemy)* désordre *m*, désarroi *m*; **everything was in confusion** tout était en désordre *ou* sens dessus dessous; **to add to the confusion...** pour ajouter à la confusion...

confute [kən'fjuːt] *vt Formal (argument)* réfuter; *(person)* réfuter les arguments de

conga ['kɒŋgə] *Mus* **1** *n* conga *f*
 2 *vi* danser la conga
 ►► ***conga drum*** conga *f*

congeal [kən'dʒiːl] **1** *vi (fat, oil)* (se) figer; *(blood)* (se) coaguler; *(milk)* (se) cailler
 2 *vt (fat, oil)* (faire) figer; *(blood)* (faire) coaguler; *(milk)* (faire) cailler

congener ['kɒndʒɪnə(r)] *n Bot & Zool* congénère *m*

congeneric [kɒndʒɪ'nerɪk] *Bot & Zool* **1** *n* congénère *m*
 2 *adj* congénère

congenial [kən'dʒiːnjəl] *adj (pleasant)* sympathique, agréable; **in congenial surroundings** dans un cadre agréable; **to spend an afternoon in congenial company** passer un après-midi en agréable compagnie

congeniality [kənˌdʒiːnɪ'ælɪtɪ] *n* caractère *m* agréable

congenially [kən'dʒiːnɪəlɪ] *adv* agréablement

congenital [kən'dʒenɪtəl] *adj Med* congénital, de naissance; *Fig* **he's a congenital liar** c'est un [illegible]
 ►► ***congenital defect*** vice *m* de conformation

congenitally [kən'dʒenɪtəlɪ] *adv* de manière congénitale, congénitalement

conger ['kɒŋgə(r)] *n Zool* congre *m*, anguille *f* de mer
 ►► ***conger eel*** congre *m*, anguille *f* de mer

congeries [kɒn'dʒɪəriːz] *n Arch or Literary* amas *m*, accumulation *f*

congest [kən'dʒest] **1** *vt* (**a**) *(crowd)* encombrer (**b**) *Med (clog)* congestionner
 2 *vi* (**a**) *(become crowded)* s'encombrer (**b**) *Med (become clogged → organ)* se congestionner; *(→ nose)* se boucher

congested [kən'dʒestɪd] *adj* (**a**) *(area, town)* surpeuplé; *(road)* encombré, embouteillé; *(airport, communication lines)* encombré; **the roads are congested with traffic** il y a des embouteillages *ou* des encombrements sur les routes (**b**) *Med (clogged → organ)* congestionné; *(→ nose)* bouché; **I'm feeling really congested** j'ai les bronches très prises

congestion [kən'dʒestʃən] *n* (**a**) *(of area)* surpeuplement *m*; *(of road, traffic)* encombrement *m*, embouteillage *m*; **the new road will relieve the congestion in the town** la nouvelle route va décongestionner la ville (**b**) *Med (blockage → in organ, nose)* congestion *f*

conglomerate 1 *n* [kən'glɒmərət] (**a**) *(mass)* conglomérat *m* (**b**) *Fin & Econ* conglomérat *m* (**c**) *Geol* conglomérat *m*
 2 *adj* [kən'glɒmərət] (**a**) *(composed of various things)* congloméré, aggloméré (**b**) *Geol* congloméré
 3 *vt* [kən'glɒməreɪt] agglomérer, conglomérer
 4 *vi* [kən'glɒməreɪt] s'agglomérer

conglomeration [kənˌglɒmə'reɪʃən] *n* (**a**) *(mass)* groupement *m*, rassemblement *m*; *(of buildings)* agglomération *f*; *Fig* **a conglomeration of ideas** un mélange d'idées (**b**) *(act, state)* agglomération *f*, conglomération *f*

Congo ['kɒŋgəʊ] *n* (**a**) *(country)* **the Congo** le Congo; **in the Congo** au Congo; *Hist* **the Belgian Congo** le Congo belge (**b**) *(river)* **the Congo** le Congo

Congolese [ˌkɒŋgə'liːz] **1** *n* Congolais(e) *m,f*
 2 *adj* congolais
 3 *comp (embassy, history)* du Congo

congrats [kən'græts] *exclam Fam* chapeau!

congratulate [kən'grætʃʊleɪt] *vt* féliciter, complimenter; **I congratulate you** je vous félicite, (je vous fais) mes compliments; **her parents congratulated her on passing her exams** ses parents l'ont félicitée d'avoir réussi à ses examens; **she congratulated them on their engagement** elle leur a présenté ses félicitations à l'occasion de leurs fiançailles; **I congratulated myself for having kept my temper** je me suis félicité d'avoir gardé mon sang-froid

congratulation [kənˌgrætʃʊ'leɪʃən] **1** *n* félicitation *f*
 2 congratulations 1 *exclam* (toutes mes) félicitations!, je vous félicite! **2** *npl* félicitations *fpl*; **congratulations on the new job/your engagement/passing your exams** félicitations pour votre nouveau poste/vos fiançailles/vos examens; **I hear congratulations are in order** il paraît qu'il faut vous féliciter; **give her my congratulations** transmets-lui mes félicitations, félicite-la de ma part; **a letter of congratulations** une lettre de félicitations

congratulatory [kən'grætʃʊlətərɪ] *adj* de félicitations

congregate ['kɒŋgrɪgeɪt] **1** *vt* rassembler, réunir
 2 *vi* se rassembler, se réunir; **the demonstrators congregated in the park** les manifestants se sont rassemblés dans le parc
 ►► *Am* ***congregate housing*** = résidence aménagée pour personnes âgées

congregation [ˌkɒŋgrɪ'geɪʃən] *n* (**a**) *(group)* assemblée *f*, rassemblement *m* (**b**) *Rel (of worshippers)* assemblée *f* (de fidèles), assistance *f*; *(of priests)* congrégation *f*; **I'm not a member of your congregation** je ne fais pas partie de votre paroisse, je ne viens pas à l'église ici (**b**) *Br Univ* assemblée *f* générale

congregational [ˌkɒŋgrɪ'geɪʃənəl] **1** *adj* (**a**) *(relating to a group)* d'une assemblée (**b**) *Rel* de l'assemblée (des fidèles); *(priests)* de *ou* d'une congrégation
 [illegible]
 the Congregational Church l'Église *f* congrégationaliste

congress ['kɒŋgres] **1** *n* (**a**) *(association, meeting)* congrès *m* (**b**) *(UNCOUNT) Formal (sexual intercourse)* rapports *mpl* sexuels; **to have congress with sb** avoir des rapports sexuels avec qn
 2 Congress *n Pol* Congrès *m*; *(session)* = session du Congrès américain
 ►► *Am* ***Congress On Racial Equality*** = ligue américaine contre le racisme

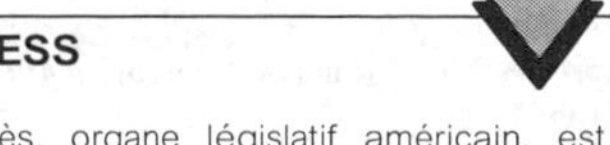

CONGRESS

Le Congrès, organe législatif américain, est constitué du Sénat et de la Chambre des représentants. Une proposition de loi doit obligatoirement être approuvée séparément par ces deux Chambres.

congressional [kəŋ'greʃənəl] **1** *adj (gen)* d'un congrès

2 Congressional *adj Pol* du Congrès

►► ***Congressional district*** = circonscription d'un représentant du Congrès américain; ***Congressional Medal of Honor*** = la plus haute distinction militaire américaine; ***Congressional Record*** = journal officiel du Congrès américain

congressman ['kɒŋgresmən] *(pl* **congressmen** [-mən]) *n Pol* membre *m* du Congrès américain; **Mr Congressman, do you believe that...** Monsieur le Député, croyez-vous que...; **congressman-at-large** = représentant du Congrès américain non attaché à une circonscription électorale

congresswoman ['kɒŋgres,wʊmən] *(pl* **congresswomen** [-,wɪmɪn]) *n Pol* membre *m* du Congrès américain; **Miss/Ms/Mrs Congresswoman** Madame le *ou* la député

congruence ['kɒŋgrʊəns], **congruency** ['kɒŋgruənsɪ] *n* (**a**) *Formal (similarity)* conformité *f* (**b**) *Formal (correspondence)* correspondance *f*; *(suitability)* convenance *f* (**c**) *Math* congruence *f*

congruent ['kɒŋgrʊənt] *adj* (**a**) *Formal (similar)* conforme; **congruent with** *or* **to** conforme à (**b**) *Formal (corresponding)* en harmonie; *(suitable)* convenable; **to be congruent with sth** être en harmonie avec qch; **the sentence is congruent with the crime** la peine correspond au crime (**c**) *Math (number)* congru, congruent; *(triangle)* congruent

congruity [kɒŋ'gruːətɪ] *(pl* **congruities**) *n Formal* convenance *f*

congruous ['kɒŋgrʊəs] *adj Formal* (**a**) *(corresponding)* qui s'accorde; **to be congruous with sth** s'accorder avec qch (**b**) *(suitable)* convenable, qui convient

conic ['kɒnɪk] *adj Geom* conique; **a conic paper hat** un chapeau pointu en papier

►► ***conic projection*** *(in mapmaking)* projection *f* conique; *Geom* ***conic section*** section *f* conique

conical ['kɒnɪkəl] *adj* conique

conifer ['kɒnɪfə(r)] *n* conifère *m*

coniferous [kə'nɪfərəs] *adj* conifère; **a coniferous forest** une forêt de conifères

conjectural [kən'dʒektʃərəl] *adj* conjectural

conjecture [kən'dʒektʃə(r)] **1** *n* conjecture *f*; **whether he knew or not is a matter for conjecture** savoir s'il était au courant ou pas relève de la conjecture; **it's sheer conjecture** ce ne sont que des conjectures

2 *vt* conjecturer, présumer

3 *vi* conjecturer, faire des conjectures

conjoin [kən'dʒɔɪn] *Formal* **1** *vt* joindre, unir

2 *vi* s'unir

conjoint ['kɒndʒɔɪnt] *adj Formal* conjoint, uni

conjointly ['kɒndʒɔɪntlɪ] *adv Formal* conjointement

conjugal ['kɒndʒʊgəl] *adj* conjugal

►► ***conjugal rights*** droits *mpl* conjugaux

conjugality [,kɒndʒʊ'gælɪtɪ] *n* état *m* conjugal

conjugally ['kɒndʒʊgəlɪ] *adv* conjugalement

conjugate 1 *vt* ['kɒndʒʊ,geɪt] *Gram (verb)* conjuguer

2 *vi* ['kɒndʒʊ,geɪt] *Gram & Biol* se conjuguer

3 *adj* ['kɒndʒʊgɪt] (**a**) *(joined, connected)* conjoint, uni (**b**) *Chem* conjugué

conjugation [,kɒndʒʊ'geɪʃən] *n Gram & Biol* conjugaison *f*

conjunct [kən'dʒʌŋkt] *adj* conjoint

conjunction [kən'dʒʌŋkʃən] **1** *n* (**a**) *(combination)* conjonction *f*, union *f* **conjunction tickets** billets *mpl* complémentaires

(**b**) *Astron & Gram* conjonction *f*; *Astron* **in conjunction** *(planets)* en conjonction

2 in conjunction with *prep* conjointement avec; **to work in conjunction with sb** travailler conjointement avec qn; **these factors, in conjunction with others, were responsible for...** ces facteurs combinés à d'autres furent responsables de...

conjunctiva [,kɒndʒʌŋk'taɪvə] *n Anat* conjonctive *f*

conjunctive [kən'dʒʌŋktɪv] *adj (gen) & Anat & Gram* conjonctif

conjunctivitis [kən,dʒʌŋktɪ'vaɪtɪs] *n Med* conjonctivite *f*; **to have conjunctivitis** avoir de la conjonctivite

conjuncture [kən'dʒʌŋktʃə(r)] *n Formal (combination of events)* conjoncture *f*; *(resulting crisis)* moment *m* critique

conjure 1 *vt* (**a**) ['kʌndʒə(r)] *(produce → gen)* faire apparaître, produire; *(→ by magic)* faire apparaître *(par prestidigitation)*; **to conjure a rabbit from a hat** faire sortir un lapin d'un chapeau; **they conjured a bottle of wine out of nowhere** *or* **thin air** ils ont fait apparaître une bouteille de vin comme par enchantement

(**b**) [kən'dʒʊə(r)] *Arch (appeal to)* conjurer, implorer

2 *vi* ['kʌndʒə(r)] faire des tours de passe-passe; *Br Fig* **his is a name to conjure with** c'est quelqu'un d'important

►► *Am* ***conjure man*** *(witch doctor)* guérisseur *m*

►**conjure away** *vt sep* faire disparaître

►**conjure up** *vt sep* (**a**) *(call to mind → images, memories)* évoquer

(**b**) *(call up → spirit etc)* faire apparaître

(**c**) *(produce)* **they conjured up some armchairs** ils ont déniché des fauteuils d'on ne sait où; **she conjured up an incredible meal out of almost nothing** elle a réussi à préparer un repas fantastique avec presque rien; **I'll conjure something up** *(to eat)* je vais me débrouiller pour préparer quelque chose avec ce que j'ai; **I can't just conjure extra staff up out of thin air!** je ne peux pas sortir du personnel supplémentaire de mon chapeau!

conjurer ['kʌndʒərə(r)] *n (magician)* prestidigitateur(trice) *m,f*; *(sorcerer)* sorcier(ère) *m,f*

conjuring ['kʌndʒərɪŋ] *n* prestidigitation *f*

►► ***conjuring trick*** tour *m* de passe-passe *ou* de prestidigitation

conjuror = **conjurer**

conk [kɒŋk] *Fam* **1** *vt* (**a**) *(hit)* cogner; **he conked me** il m'a cogné *ou* frappé (sur la caboche) (**b**) *Am (hair)* défriser□ *(au moyen d'un produit coiffant)*

2 *n* (**a**) *(blow)* gnon *m*; **he gave me a conk on the nose** il m'a flanqué un gnon sur le nez (**b**) *Br (head)* caboche *f* (**c**) *Br (nose)* pif *m* (**d**) *Am (hairstyle)* coiffure *f* défrisée□

►**conk out** *vi Fam* (**a**) *(machine, television etc)* tomber en panne□ (**b**) *(lose consciousness)* tomber dans les pommes (**c**) *(go to sleep)* s'endormir□, s'écrouler (**d**) *Am (die)* clamser, clamecer

conker ['kɒŋkə(r)] **1** *n Br Fam* marron□ *m*

2 conkers *n* = jeu d'enfant qui consiste à tenter de casser un marron tenu au bout d'un fil par son adversaire

conman ['kɒnmæn] *(pl* **conmen** [-men]) *n Fam* arnaqueur *m*

Conn *(written abbr* **Connecticut**) Connecticut *m*

connect [kə'nekt] **1** *vt* (**a**) *(join → pipes, wires)* raccorder; *(→ pinions, shafts, wheels)* engrener, coupler; *Elec (→ circuits)* interconnecter; *Elec (→ wires)* connecter; **to connect sth to sth** joindre *ou* relier *ou* raccorder qch à qch; **connect this wire to the other terminal** connectez ce fil à l'autre borne

(**b**) *(join to supply → machine, house, telephone)* brancher, raccorder; **to connect sth to sth** raccorder qch à qch, brancher qch sur qch; **to be connected (up) to sth** être branché sur qch

(**c**) *Tel* mettre en communication, relier; **to connect sb to sb** mettre qn en communication avec qn; **will you connect me with reservations, please?** est-ce que vous pouvez me passer votre service des réservations?; **I'm trying to connect you** j'essaie d'obtenir votre communication

(**d**) *(link → of path, railway, road, airline)* relier; **to connect with** *or* **to** relier à; **the new rail link connects Terminal 3 with** *or* **to the train station** la nouvelle liaison ferroviaire relie l'aérogare 3 à la gare; **a corridor connects the room to the library** il y a un couloir qui relie la pièce à la bibliothèque

(**e**) *(associate → person, place, event)* associer; **to connect sb/sth with sb/sth** associer qn/qch avec qn/à qch, faire le rapprochement entre qn/qch et qn/qch; **I'd never connected the two things before** je n'avais (encore) jamais fait le rapprochement entre les deux; **there is nothing to connect the two crimes** il n'y a aucun lien entre les deux crimes; **at first I didn't connect the name with the face** au début je n'ai pas fait le lien *ou* le rapprochement entre le nom et le visage; **to be connected with** *(of person)* avoir des relations *ou* un lien avec; *(of thing)* se rattacher *ou* se rapporter à; **the questions were connected with another subject** les questions étaient relatives *ou* se rapportaient à un autre sujet

2 *vi* (**a**) *(bus, plane, train)* assurer la correspondance; **to connect with** assurer la correspondance avec

(**b**) *(blow)* atteindre son but; *(boxer)* frapper *ou* atteindre son adversaire; *(tennis player, cricketer, racket, bat)* frapper la balle; *Fam* **my fist connected with his chin** je l'ai touché au menton□

(**c**) *(wires)* être reliés (**with** à); *(roads)* se rejoindre; *(rooms)* communiquer (**with** avec); **this road connects with the motorway** cette route rejoint l'autoroute; **the tunnels don't connect** les deux tunnels ne sont pas reliés *ou* ne communiquent pas

(**d**) *Am Fam Drugs slang (buy drugs)* s'approvisionner en drogue□

3 *n Comput* connexion *f*

►► ***connect time*** durée *f* (d'établissement) de la connexion

►**connect up** *vt sep (pipes)* raccorder; *Elec (wires)* connecter

connected [kə'nektɪd] *adj* (**a**) *(linked → subjects, species)* connexe (**b**) *(coherent → speech, sentences)* cohérent, suivi (**c**) *(associated)* **to be connected with** avoir un lien *ou* rapport avec (**d**) *(related)* **to be connected with** *or* **to** avoir un lien de parenté avec; **to be well connected** *(person)* avoir des relations

Connecticut [kə'netɪkət] *n* le Connecticut; **in Connecticut** dans le Connecticut

connecting [kə'nektɪŋ] *adj Elec (cable, wire)* de connexion

►► *Elec* ***connecting block*** domino *m*; ***connecting door*** porte *f* de communication; ***connecting flight*** correspondance *f*; *Tech* ***connecting piece*** pièce *f* de raccordement; *Tech* ***connecting pipe*** tuyau *m* de raccordement *ou* de jonction; *Tech* ***connecting rod*** bielle *f*; ***connecting rooms*** *(in hotel)* pièces *fpl* communicantes; ***connecting train*** correspondance *f*

connection [kə'nekʃən] **1** *n* (**a**) *(link, association)* lien *m*, rapport *m*, connexion *f*; **to make a connection between** *or* **to** *or* **with sth** faire le lien avec qch; **does this have any connection with what happened yesterday?** ceci a-t-il un rapport quelconque avec ce qui s'est passé hier?; **in this** *or* **that connection** à ce propos, à ce sujet

(**b**) *Tech* connexion *f*; *(of pipes, wires)* assemblage *m*, raccordement *m*; *(of machine parts)* accouplement *m*, engrenage *m*; *Elec* prise *f*, raccord *m*; *Comput* connexion *f*, liaison *f*

(**c**) *Tel* communication *f*, ligne *f*; **a bad connection** une mauvaise communication *ou* ligne

(**d**) *(transfer → between buses, planes, trains)* correspondance *f*; **to miss one's connection** rater sa correspondance

(**e**) *(transport)* liaison *f*; **the town enjoys excellent road and rail connections** la ville dispose d'excellentes liaisons routières et ferroviaires

(**f**) *(personal relationship)* rapport *m*, relation *f*; **to form/to break a connection with sb** établir/rompre des relations avec qn; **he has CIA connections** il a des liens avec la CIA; **family connections** parenté *f*; **to establish a business connection with a firm** établir des relations commerciales avec une entreprise

(**g**) *(family relationship)* parenté *f*; **to form a connection by marriage with a good family** s'allier à *ou* avec une bonne famille; **there's no connection with the Yorkshire Smythes** il n'y a pas de lien de parenté avec les Smythe du Yorkshire; **my family has Scottish connections** il y a des Écossais dans ma famille

(**h**) *(colleague, business contact)* relation *f* (d'affaires); **she has important connections** elle a des relations en haut lieu; **she has some useful connections in the publishing world** elle a des relations utiles dans le monde de l'édition

(**i**) *Am Fam Drugs slang (dealer)* dealer *m*

2 in connection with *prep* à propos de

►► *Tech* ***connection kit*** kit *m* d'accès *ou* de connexion

connective [kə'nektɪv] **1** *adj Gram (word, phrase)* conjonctif

2 *n* conjonction *f*

►► *Anat* ***connective tissue*** tissu *m* conjonctif

connectivity [ˌkɒnek'tɪvɪtɪ] *n Comput* connectivité *f*

connector [kə'nektə(r)] *n Elec* connecteur *m*; *Tech* raccord *m*

►► *Tech* ***connector kit*** kit *m* d'accès *ou* de connexion

connect-the-dots *n (UNCOUNT) Am* = jeu qui consiste à relier des points numérotés pour découvrir un dessin

connexion = **connection**

conning tower ['kɒnɪŋ-] *n Naut (on submarine)* kiosque *m*; *(on warship)* centre *m* opérationnel

conniption [kə'nɪpʃən] *n (often pl) Am Fam* crise *f* d'hystérie; **to be in a conniption, to have conniptions** piquer une crise

connivance [kə'naɪvəns] *n Pej* connivence *f*; **with the connivance of, in connivance with** de connivence avec; **he acted with the connivance of** *or* **in connivance with government officials** il a agi de connivence avec des membres du gouvernement

connive [kə'naɪv] *vi Pej (plot)* être de connivence; **they connived together to undermine government policy** ils étaient de connivence pour déstabiliser la politique du gouvernement

►**connive at** *vt insep* (**a**) *(ignore)* fermer les yeux sur (**b**) *(abet)* être complice de

conniving [kə'naɪvɪŋ] *adj Pej* malhonnête, rusé, sournois

connoisseur [ˌkɒnə'sɜː(r)] *n* connaisseur(euse) *m,f*; **a connoisseur of fine wine/good literature** un connaisseur en vins/littérature

connotation [ˌkɒnə'teɪʃən] *n* (**a**) *(association)* connotation *f*; **for me the word has very sad connotations** ce mot a pour moi des connotations très tristes; **the name has connotations of quality and expertise** ce nom évoque la qualité et la compétence (**b**) *Ling* connotation *f* (**c**) *(in logic)* implication *f*

connote [kə'nəʊt] *vt* (**a**) *Formal (imply → of word, phrase, name)* évoquer (**b**) *Ling* connoter (**c**) *(in logic)* impliquer

connubial [kə'njuːbjəl] *adj Formal or Hum* conjugal, matrimonial; **connubial bliss** bonheur *m* conjugal

conquer ['kɒŋkə(r)] *vt* (**a**) *(defeat → person, enemy)* vaincre

(**b**) *(take control of → city, nation)* conquérir; *Com & Mktg (→ market, market share)* conquérir; **the latest British group to conquer America** le dernier groupe britannique à conquérir l'Amérique

(**c**) *(succeed in climbing, reaching etc)* conquérir; **Everest was conquered in 1953** l'Everest a été conquis en 1953

(**d**) *(master → feelings, habits)* surmonter; *(→ disease, disability, fears)* vaincre, surmonter

(**e**) *(win over → someone's heart)* conquérir; *(→ audience, public)* conquérir, subjuguer

conquering ['kɒŋkərɪŋ] *adj* victorieux; *Literary* **hail the conquering hero!** vive le vainqueur!

conqueror ['kɒŋkərə(r)] *n* (**a**) *(of country)* conquérant *m*; *Hist* **(William) the Conqueror** Guillaume le Conquérant (**b**) *(victor)* vainqueur *m*

conquest ['kɒŋkwest] *n* (**a**) *(of land, person)* conquête *f*; *Com & Mktg (of market, market share)* conquête *f*; **our men faced conquest by enemy forces** nos hommes allaient être vaincus par les forces ennemies; **the conquest of space** la conquête de l'espace; *Hist* **the (Norman) Conquest** la conquête de l'Angleterre

(**b**) *(land, person conquered)* conquête *f*; **he boasted of his conquests** il se vantait de ses conquêtes; **he's her latest conquest** c'est sa dernière conquête; **to make a conquest** faire une conquête; **to make a conquest of sb** faire la conquête de qn

Conrail®, **ConRail**® ['kɒnreɪl] *n* = transport urbain new-yorkais

conrod ['kɒnrɒd] *n Aut* bielle *f*

Cons *Pol (written abbr* **Conservative**) conservateur(trice) *m,f*

consanguine [kɒn'sæŋgwɪn] *adj* consanguin

consanguinity [ˌkɒnsæŋ'gwɪnətɪ] *n* consanguinité *f*

conscience ['kɒnʃəns] *n* (**a**) *(moral sense)* conscience *f*; **always let your conscience be your guide** laissez-vous toujours guider par votre conscience; **a matter of conscience** un cas de conscience; **to have a clear** *or* **an easy conscience** avoir la conscience tranquille; **my conscience is clear** j'ai la conscience tranquille; **to have a bad** *or* **guilty conscience** avoir mauvaise conscience; **to have sth on one's conscience** avoir qch sur la conscience; **it's on my conscience that I left him alone** je l'ai laissé tout seul et j'ai mauvaise conscience; **I can't sleep with that on my conscience** je ne peux pas dormir avec ça sur la conscience; **in all conscience** en toute conscience

(**b**) *(UNCOUNT) (scruples)* mauvaise conscience *f*, remords *m*, scrupule *m*; **to have no conscience (about doing sth)** ne pas avoir de scrupules (à faire qch)

►► ***conscience clause*** clause *f* de conscience; ***conscience money*** argent *m* restitué *(pour soulager sa conscience)*

conscience-stricken *adj* pris de remords; **to be conscience-stricken** être pris de remords, être la proie des remords; **conscience-stricken faces** des visages tourmentés par le remords

conscientious [ˌkɒnʃɪ'enʃəs] *adj* consciencieux; **she was her usual conscientious self** elle était consciencieuse comme toujours

►► ***conscientious objection*** objection *f* de conscience; ***conscientious objector*** objecteur *m* de conscience

conscientiously [ˌkɒnʃɪ'enʃəslɪ] *adv* consciencieusement

conscientiousness [ˌkɒnʃɪ'enʃəsnɪs] *n* conscience *f*

conscious ['kɒnʃəs] **1** *adj* (**a**) *(aware)* conscient; **to be conscious of sth/of doing sth** être conscient de qch/de faire qch; **he's all too conscious of his shortcomings as a writer** il n'est que trop conscient de ses défauts en tant qu'écrivain; **I wasn't conscious of having annoyed you** je ne m'étais pas rendu compte que je t'avais énervé; **to become conscious of sth** prendre conscience de qch; **politically conscious** politisé

(**b**) *(awake)* conscient; **to become conscious** reprendre connaissance; **he's not conscious yet** il n'a pas encore repris connaissance; *Fam Hum (he's still in bed)* il n'a pas encore fait surface

(**c**) *(deliberate → attempt)* conscient; *(→ cruelty, rudeness)* intentionnel, délibéré; **it was not a conscious decision** ce n'était pas une décision prise de façon consciente; **it required a conscious effort to...** il fallait se forcer pour...

(**d**) *(able to think → being, mind)* conscient

2 *n Psy* **the conscious** le conscient

-conscious ['kɒnʃəs] *suff* conscient de; **clothes-conscious** qui fait attention à sa tenue; **fashion-conscious** qui suit la mode; **safety-conscious** soucieux de sécurité; **health-conscious** soucieux de sa santé

consciously ['kɒnʃəslɪ] *adv* consciemment, délibérément; **he would never consciously do such a cruel thing** il ne ferait jamais une chose aussi cruelle délibérément

consciousness ['kɒnʃəsnɪs] *n* (**a**) *(awareness)* conscience *f*; **political consciousness** conscience *f* politique; **the organization aims to raise people's consciousness of these problems** l'organisme a pour objet de sensibiliser les gens à ces problèmes

(**b**) *(state of being awake)* connaissance *f*; **to lose consciousness** perdre connaissance; **to regain consciousness** reprendre connaissance

(**c**) *(mentality)* conscience *f*; **the national consciousness** la conscience nationale

►► ***consciousness raising*** sensibilisation *f*

consciousness-raising *adj* (**a**) *(activity, campaign)* de sensibilisation (**b**) *Psy (group, session)* d'aide psychologique

conscript 1 *vt* [kən'skrɪpt] *(men, troops)* enrôler, recruter; *(workers, labourers)* recruter d'office; **to be conscripted** être appelé (sous les drapeaux); *Fig* **I've been conscripted to do the dishes** on m'a enrôlé *ou* réquisitionné pour faire la vaisselle

2 *n* ['kɒnskrɪpt] conscrit *m*, appelé *m*

3 *adj* ['kɒnskrɪpt] *(army)* de conscrits

conscripted [kən'skrɪptɪd] *adj (labour)* recruté d'office; **conscripted men, conscripted troops** conscrits *mpl*

conscription [kən'skrɪpʃən] *n* conscription *f*

consecrate ['kɒnsɪkreɪt] *vt* (**a**) *Rel (sanctify → church, building, bread, wine)* consacrer

(**b**) *Rel (ordain → bishop)* consacrer, sacrer

(**c**) *(dedicate)* consacrer, dédier; **to consecrate one's life to sth** consacrer sa vie à qch; **the day was consecrated to the memory of the country's dead** la journée a été dédiée à la mémoire des morts du pays

(**d**) *(make venerable)* consacrer; **a custom consecrated by time** une coutume consacrée par l'usage

consecrated ['kɒnsɪkreɪtɪd] *adj Rel* consacré

►► ***consecrated ground*** terre *f* sainte *ou* bénite

consecration [ˌkɒnsɪ'kreɪʃən] *n* (**a**) *Rel (sanctification)* consécration *f* (**b**) *Rel (ordination)* sacre *m* (**c**) *(dedication)* consécration *f*; **the consecration of her life to helping the poor** le fait de consacrer sa vie à aider les pauvres (**d**) *(veneration)* consécration *f*

consecutive [kən'sekjʊtɪv] *adj* (**a**) *(successive → days, weeks)* consécutif; **for the third consecutive day** pour le troisième jour consécutif; **they have had five consecutive home wins** ils ont remporté cinq victoires consécutives sur leur terrain; **consecutive interpreting** interprétation *f* consécutive (**b**) *Gram (clause)* consécutif

consecutively [kən'sekjʊtɪvlɪ] *adv* consécutivement; **for five years consecutively** pendant cinq années consécutives; *Law* **the sentences to be served consecutively** avec cumul de peines

consensual [kən'sensjʊəl] *adj* (**a**) *Law (contract, agreement)* consensuel (**b**) *Physiol* consensuel

consensus [kən'sensəs] **1** *n* consensus *m*; **to reach a consensus** arriver à un consensus; **there was a consensus of opinion to reject the board's offer** il y avait un consensus en faveur du rejet de la proposition du conseil d'administration; **they failed to reach a consensus (of opinion)** ils n'ont pas obtenu de consensus (d'opinion); **the general consensus was that the new road was unnecessary** l'opinion générale était que la nouvelle route n'était pas nécessaire; **what is the scientific consensus on the matter?** quelle est l'opinion des scientifiques sur ce sujet?

2 *comp (politics)* de consensus; *(management)* par consensus

consent [kən'sent] **1** *vi* consentir; **to consent to sth/to do sth** consentir à qch/à faire qch; **they consented to my request for compassionate leave** ils ont consenti à ma demande de congé exceptionnel

2 *n* consentement *m*, accord *m*; **to give/withhold one's consent to sth** donner/ne pas donner son consentement à qch; **we got married without my parents' consent** nous nous sommes mariés sans le consentement de mes parents; **he refused his consent to a divorce** il a refusé son consentement pour le divorce; **by common consent** d'un commun accord; **by mutual consent** par consentement mutuel

►► *Am Law* ***consent decree*** = accord à l'amiable entre un contrevenant (le plus souvent une entreprise) et le gouvernement afin d'éviter un procès

consenting [kən'sentɪŋ] *adj Law (adult)* consentant; *Fam Hum* **she is a consenting adult, after all** elle est majeure et vaccinée après tout

consequence ['kɒnsɪkwəns] **1** *n* (**a**) *(result)* conséquence *f*, suite *f*; **as a consequence of** à la suite de; **it all came about as a consequence of that one brief meeting** tout est arrivé à la suite de cette courte réunion; **she acted regardless of the consequences** elle a agi sans se soucier des conséquences; **the policy had terrible consequences for the poor** cette mesure a eu des conséquences terribles pour les pauvres

(**b**) *(importance)* conséquence *f*, importance *f*;

con–con

a person of no *or* **little consequence** une personne sans importance; **it is of some consequence to me** ça a de l'importance pour moi; **a man of consequence** un homme important; **it's of no consequence** c'est sans conséquence, cela n'a pas d'importance

2 consequences 1 *npl (results)* conséquences *fpl*; **to take** *or* **to suffer the consequences** accepter *ou* subir les conséquences; **to face the consequences** faire face aux conséquences **2** *n Br (game)* ≃ cadavres *mpl* exquis

3 in consequence *adv* par conséquent

4 in consequence of *prep* **in consequence of which, we have made the following decision** à la suite de quoi nous avons pris la décision suivante

consequent [ˈkɒnsɪkwənt] *adj* (**a**) *(resulting)* résultant; **consequent upon sth** qui est la conséquence de qch, qui résulte de qch; **a glut and the consequent drop in prices** un surplus et la baisse des prix qui en résulte (**b**) *(in logic)* conséquent

consequential [ˌkɒnsɪˈkwenʃəl] *adj* (**a**) *(resulting)* conséquent, consécutif (**to** à); **consequential effects** *(of action)* répercussions *fpl* (**b**) *(self-important)* vaniteux, suffisant (**c**) *(significant, important)* important

▸▸ *Law* ***consequential damages*** dommages *mpl* indirects

consequently [ˈkɒnsɪkwəntlɪ] *adv* par conséquent, donc

conservancy [kənˈsɜːvənsɪ] (*pl* **conservancies**) *n Ecol* (**a**) *Br (commission)* administration *f* (**b**) *(of natural resources)* préservation *f* (**c**) *(protected area)* zone *f* protégée *(d'un point de vue écologique)*

conservation [ˌkɒnsəˈveɪʃən] *n* (**a**) *(of works of art)* préservation *f* (**b**) *Ecol (of natural resources)* préservation *f*; **nature conservation** défense *f* de l'environnement (**c**) *Phys* conservation *f*; **the conservation of energy/mass/momentum** le principe de conservation de l'énergie/de la masse/du moment

▸▸ *Ecol* ***conservation area*** zone *f* protégée *(d'un point de vue architectural ou historique)*; ***conservation law*** loi *f* de conservation

conservationist [ˌkɒnsəˈveɪʃənɪst] *n Ecol* défenseur *m* de l'environnement

conservatism [kənˈsɜːvəˌtɪzəm] **1** *n (traditionalism)* conservatisme *m*

2 Conservatism *n Pol (policy of Conservative Party)* conservatisme *m*

▸▸ *Acct* ***conservatism concept*** principe *m* de prudence

conservative [kənˈsɜːvətɪv] **1** *n (traditionalist)* traditionaliste *mf*, conformiste *mf*

2 *adj* (**a**) *(traditionalist → views)* conformiste (**b**) *(conventional → suit, clothes)* classique (**c**) *(modest → estimate)* prudent; **at a conservative estimate** au minimum, au bas mot (**d**) *Phys* conservateur

3 Conservative *Pol* **1** *n* conservateur(trice) *m,f* **2** *adj (policy, government, MP)* conservateur

▸▸ ***the Conservative Party*** le parti conservateur

conservatively [kənˈsɜːvətɪvlɪ] *adv (dress)* de façon conventionnelle; **it was conservatively estimated at £5,000** selon des estimations prudentes, cela devrait coûter 5000 livres

conservatoire [kənˈsɜːvəˌtwɑː(r)] *n* conservatoire *m*

conservator [kənˈsɜːvətə(r)] *n* gardien(enne) *m,f*

conservatory [kənˈsɜːvətrɪ] (*pl* **conservatories**) *n* (**a**) *(greenhouse)* jardin *m* d'hiver (**b**) *(attached to house)* véranda *f* (**c**) *(school)* conservatoire *m*

conserve 1 *vt* [kənˈsɜːv] (**a**) *(save → energy, resources, battery)* économiser; **to conserve one's strength** ménager ses forces (**b**) *(building, monument)* conserver, préserver (**c**) *Literary (preserve → privilege, freedom)* protéger, préserver

2 *n* [ˈkɒnsɜːv, kənˈsɜːv] confiture *f*; **strawberry conserve** confiture *f* de fraises

consider [kənˈsɪdə(r)] **1** *vt* (**a**) *(believe)* considérer, estimer, penser; **I've always considered her (to be) a good friend** je l'ai toujours considérée comme une bonne amie; **she considers it wrong to say such things** elle pense qu'il est mauvais de dire de telles choses; **consider it done** considérez cela comme fait; **consider yourself dismissed** tenez-vous pour congédié; **I consider myself lucky** je m'estime heureux; **I would consider it an honour** je m'estimerais honoré; **I consider it my duty to...** j'estime qu'il est de mon devoir de...; **we consider it likely that...** nous estimons qu'il est probable que... + *indicative*

(**b**) *(ponder → problem, offer, possibility)* considérer, examiner; *(→ issue, question)* réfléchir à; **have you ever considered becoming an actress?** avez-vous jamais songé à devenir actrice?; **have you considered (buying) a larger model?** est-ce que vous avez envisagé d'acheter un modèle plus grand?; **he was considering whether to go out when...** il se demandait s'il allait sortir quand...; **I'm willing to consider your offer** je suis prêt à examiner votre proposition; **I'll consider it** je verrai, je réfléchirai; **the jury retired to consider its verdict** le jury se retira pour délibérer

(**c**) *(bear in mind → points, facts)* prendre en considération; *(→ costs, difficulties, dangers)* tenir compte de; **we got off lightly, when you consider what might have happened** nous nous en sommes bien tirés, quand on pense à ce qui aurait pu arriver; **all things considered** tout bien considéré

(**d**) *(show regard for → feelings, wishes)* tenir compte de; **he has a wife and family to consider** il a une femme et une famille à prendre en considération; **she never considers anybody but herself** elle ne fait jamais attention aux autres

(**e**) *(discuss → report, case)* examiner, considérer; **she's being considered for the post of manager** on pense à elle pour le poste de directeur

(**f**) *(contemplate → picture, scene)* examiner, observer

2 *vi* réfléchir; **I need time to consider** j'ai besoin de temps pour réfléchir

considerable [kənˈsɪdərəbəl] *adj* (**a**) *(great)* considérable; **she showed considerable courage** elle a fait preuve de beaucoup de courage; **a considerable number (of)** un nombre considérable (of); **to a considerable extent** dans une (très) large mesure; **she only found the house after considerable difficulty** elle n'a trouvé la maison qu'avec beaucoup de difficulté

(**b**) *(worthy of attention)* digne d'attention; *(person)* notable, important

considerably [kənˈsɪdərəblɪ] *adv* considérablement

considerate [kənˈsɪdərət] *adj (person)* prévenant (**with** envers), plein d'égards (**with** envers *ou* pour), aimable (**with** envers); **that's very considerate of you** c'est très aimable à vous; **try to be more considerate** essaie d'être un peu plus prévenant; **he's always so considerate of** *or* **towards others** il est toujours si prévenant envers les autres

considerately [kənˈsɪdərətlɪ] *adv* avec des égards

considerateness [kənˈsɪdərətnɪs] *n (thoughtfulness)* égard *m*

consideration [kənˌsɪdəˈreɪʃən] *n* (**a**) *(thought)* considération *f*; **I'll give it some consideration** j'y penserai; **the matter needs careful consideration** le sujet demande une attention particulière; **to take sth into consideration** prendre qch en considération, tenir compte de qch; **taking everything** *or* **all things into consideration** tout bien considéré; **after due consideration** après mûre réflexion

(**b**) *(factor)* considération *f*, préoccupation *f*; **time is our main consideration** le temps est notre principale préoccupation; **there is another consideration** il y a autre chose dont il faut tenir compte; **money is always the first consideration** la question d'argent vient toujours en premier; **on no consideration** à aucun prix; **money is no consideration** l'argent n'entre pas en ligne de compte

(**c**) *(thoughtfulness)* égard *m*; **to show consideration for sb/sb's feelings** ménager qn/la sensibilité de qn; **show some consideration!** fais preuve d'un peu de considération!; **have you no consideration for other people?** n'as-tu donc aucun égard pour les autres?; **she remained silent out of consideration for his family** elle se tut par égard pour sa famille

(**d**) *(discussion)* étude *f*; **under consideration** *(question, candidate etc)* à l'étude

(**e**) *(importance)* **of no consideration** sans importance

(**f**) *Formal (payment)* rémunération *f*, finance *f*; **for a small consideration** moyennant rémunération *ou* finance; **he'll do it for a consideration** il le fera si vous le payez; **in consideration of your services** en récompense de vos services

considered [kənˈsɪdəd] *adj* (**a**) *(reasoned → opinion, manner)* bien pesé, mûrement réfléchi; **it's my considered opinion that...** après mûre réflexion, je pense que... + *indicative*; **is that your considered opinion?** est-ce ainsi que vous voyez les choses? (**b**) *Formal (respected → artist, writer)* considéré, respecté

considering [kənˈsɪdərɪŋ] **1** *conj* étant donné que, vu que; **considering she'd never played the part before, she did very well** pour quelqu'un qui n'avait jamais tenu ce rôle, elle s'est très bien débrouillée

2 *prep* étant donné, vu; **considering his age/the circumstances** étant donné *ou* vu son âge/les circonstances; **considering how hard he tried, he did rather poorly** vu tout le mal qu'il s'est donné, c'était plutôt médiocre

3 *adv Fam* tout compte fait ❑, finalement ❑; **it's not so bad, considering** ce n'est pas si mauvais après tout ❑ *ou* malgré tout ❑; **she writes quite well, considering** elle écrit assez bien, finalement

consign [kənˈsaɪn] *vt* (**a**) *Com (send → goods)* envoyer, expédier; **to consign sth to sb** envoyer qch à qn

(**b**) *(relegate → thing)* reléguer; **I consigned all my clutter to the attic** j'ai relégué tout mon fourbi au grenier; **I consigned his last letter to the rubbish bin** sa dernière lettre s'est retrouvée à la poubelle

(**c**) *(entrust → person)* confier; **to consign sb to sb** confier qn à *ou* aux soins de qn; **as a child I was consigned to the care of my grandmother** enfant je fus confié aux soins de ma grand-mère

consignee [ˌkɒnsaɪˈniː] *n Com* consignataire *mf*

consigner [kənˈsaɪnə(r)] *n Com* expéditeur(trice) *m,f*

Consignia [kɒnˈsɪgnɪə] *n Br* ≃ la Poste;

consignment [ˌkənˈsaɪnmənt] *n Com* (**a**) *(despatch)* envoi *m*, expédition *f*; **goods for consignment** marchandise *f* à expédier; **consignment note** bordereau *m* d'expédition (**b**) *(batch of goods)* arrivage *m*, lot *m*; **a consignment of heavy machinery** un arrivage de machines lourdes

consignor = **consigner**

▸**consist in** [kənˈsɪst-] *vt insep Formal* **to consist in sth/in doing sth** consister dans qch/à faire qch; **his "genius" consists in a mere talent for mimicry** son "génie" se résume à son talent d'imitateur; **the book's success consists largely in its simplicity** le succès du livre réside en grande partie dans sa simplicité

▸**consist of** *vt insep* consister en, se composer de; **the panel consists of five senior lecturers** le jury se compose de cinq maîtres de conférence; **the book consists largely of photos of his family** le livre est constitué surtout de photos de sa famille

consistence [kənˈsɪstəns], **consistency** [kənˈsɪstənsɪ] (*pl* **consistences** *or* **consistencies**) *n* (**a**) *(texture)* consistance *f*; **keep stirring until you get the right consistence** remuez jusqu'à ce que vous obteniez la consistance souhaitée; **consistencies can vary** la consistance peut changer

(**b**) *(coherence → of behaviour, argument, ideas etc)* cohérence *f*, logique *f*; **their policies lack consistence** leur politique manque de cohérence

(**c**) *(constancy → of quality of work, ideas)* constance *f*; *(→ of athlete, performances)* régularité *f*; **consistence check** contrôle *m* d'uniformité

(**d**) *(compatibility → of result with theory)* concordance *f*

▸▸ *Acct* ***consistency concept*** principe *m* de la permanence (des méthodes)

consistent [kənˈsɪstənt] *adj* (**a**) *(having internal* *logic → reasoning, behaviour, person)* conséquent, cohérent, logique; **she was consistent in her choice of partners** elle a toujours fait preuve de cohérence dans le choix de ses partenaires

(**b**) *(constant → quality of work, ideas)* constant; *(→ refusal, failure)* persistant; *(athlete, performer)* régulier; **because of her consistent denial of the accusation** du fait qu'elle a toujours nié être coupable

(**c**) *(compatible)* compatible (**with** avec); **the results are consistent with the theory** les résultats concordent avec la théorie; **this action is not consistent with his character** cette action n'est pas en harmonie avec son caractère; **her behaviour is consistent with a diagnosis of...** son comportement est caractéristique d'un diagnostic de...

consistently [kən'sɪstəntlɪ] *adv* (**a**) *(with logic)* de manière cohérente *ou* conséquente (**b**) *(with regularity → play, perform, work)* avec régularité; *(→ fail, maintain)* constamment; **she has consistently denied the accusation** elle a toujours nié cette accusation; **he has been consistently better than the others** il a constamment été meilleur que les autres

consistory [kən'sɪstərɪ] *n Rel (pontifical)* consistoire *m*

▸▸ ***Consistory Court*** tribunal *m* ecclésiastique

consolation [ˌkɒnsə'leɪʃən] *n* consolation *f*, réconfort *m*; **that's one consolation** c'est déjà une consolation; **if it's any consolation, the same thing happened to me** si cela peut te consoler, il m'est arrivé la même chose; **words of consolation** mots *mpl* de réconfort; **she sought consolation in music** elle cherchait le réconfort dans la musique; **her children were a great consolation to her** ses enfants étaient une grande consolation pour elle

▸▸ *also Fig* ***consolation prize*** prix *m* de consolation

consolatory [kən'sɒlətrɪ] *adj (message, words)* consolant, réconfortant

console 1 *vt* [kən'səʊl] consoler; **he consoled me in my grief** il m'a consolé de ma peine; **console yourself with the thought that it's Friday tomorrow** console-toi en pensant que demain c'est vendredi

2 *n* ['kɒnsəʊl] (**a**) *(control panel)* console *f*, pupitre *m*; *Aviat* tableau *m* de bord (**b**) *(cabinet)* meuble *m (pour téléviseur, chaîne hi-fi)* (**c**) *Mus (on organ)* console *f* (**d**) *Archit* console *f*

▸▸ ***console table*** console *f*

consolidate [kən'sɒlɪdeɪt] **1** *vt* (**a**) *(reinforce → forces, power)* consolider; *(→ knowledge)* consolider, renforcer; *Mil (position)* raffermir; **the company has consolidated its position as the market leader** la société a conforté *ou* renforcé sa position de leader sur le marché

(**b**) *(combine → companies, states)* réunir, fusionner; *Fin (→ funds, loans, debt)* consolider; *St Exch (→ shares)* regrouper; *Com (→ orders, deliveries, consignments)* grouper

2 *vi* se consolider

consolidated [kən'sɒlɪdeɪtɪd] *adj* (**a**) *Fin (funds, loan, debt)* consolidé; *St Exch (shares)* regroupé; *Com (orders, deliveries, consignments)* groupé

(**b**) *(in name of company)* = désigne une association née de la fusion de deux entreprises

▸▸ *Acct* ***consolidated accounts*** comptes *mpl* consolidés; *Fin* ***consolidated annuities*** fonds *mpl* consolidés; *Acct* ***consolidated balance sheet*** bilan *m* consolidé; *Acct* ***consolidated entry*** écriture *f* de consolidation; *Br Fin* ***consolidated funds*** fonds *mpl* consolidés; ***consolidated loan*** emprunt *m* consolidé; ***consolidated profit and loss account*** bilan *m* consolidé; ***consolidated statement of net income*** résultat *m* net consolidé; ***consolidated stock*** fonds *mpl* consolidés

consolidation [kənˌsɒlɪ'deɪʃən] *n* (**a**) *(reinforcement → of power)* consolidation *f*; *(→ of knowledge)* consolidation *f*, renforcement *m* (**b**) *(amalgamation → of companies, states)* fusion *f*; *Fin (→ of funds, loan, debt)* consolidation *f*; *St Exch (→ of shares)* regroupement *m*; *Com (→ of orders, deliveries, consignments)* groupage *m*

consolidator [kən'sɒlɪdeɪtə(r)] *n Com* groupeur *m*

consoling [kən'səʊlɪŋ] *adj (idea, thought)* réconfortant

consols ['kɒnsɒlz] *npl Br Fin* (fonds *mpl*) consolidés *mpl*

consommé [*Br* kən'sɒmeɪ, *Am* ˌkɒnsə'meɪ] *n Culin* consommé *m*

consonance ['kɒnsənəns] *n* (**a**) *Formal (of ideas)* accord *m*; **in consonance with** en accord avec (**b**) *Literature, Ling & Mus* consonance *f*

consonant ['kɒnsənənt] **1** *n Ling* consonne *f*

2 *adj Formal* en accord; **to be consonant with** *or* **to sth** être en accord avec qch

▸▸ *Ling* ***consonant shift*** mutation *f* des consonnes

consonantal [ˌkɒnsə'næntəl] *adj Ling* consonantique

consort 1 *n* ['kɒnsɔːt] (**a**) *(spouse)* époux *m*, épouse *f*; *(of monarch)* consort *m* (**b**) *Naut (ship)* escorteur *m*

2 *vi* [kən'sɔːt] **to consort with sb** fréquenter qn, frayer avec qn

consortium [kən'sɔːtjəm] (*pl* **consortiums** *or* **consortia** [-tjə]) *n Com, Fin & Law* consortium *m*

conspectus [kən'spektəs] *n Formal* (**a**) *(overview)* vue *f* d'ensemble (**b**) *(summary)* résumé *m*, synopsis *m*

conspicuous [kən'spɪkjʊəs] *adj* (**a**) *(visible)* bien visible; *(behaviour, hat, person)* voyant; **he felt conspicuous in his new hat** il avait l'impression que son nouveau chapeau ne passait pas inaperçu; **to make oneself conspicuous** se faire remarquer (**b**) *(obvious → failure, lack)* manifeste, évident; *(→ bravery, gallantry)* insigne; **to be conspicuous by one's absence** briller par son absence

▸▸ ***conspicuous consumption*** consommation *f* ostentatoire

conspicuously [kən'spɪkjʊəslɪ] *adv* (**a**) *(visibly → dressed)* de façon à se faire remarquer (**b**) *(obviously → successful)* de façon remarquable *ou* évidente

conspicuousness [kən'spɪkjʊəsnɪs] *n* (**a**) *(visibility)* caractère *m* bien visible; *(of behaviour, hat, person)* caractère *m* voyant (**b**) *(obvious nature → of action)* caractère *m* insigne *ou* remarquable

conspiracy [kən'spɪrəsɪ] (*pl* **conspiracies**) *n* (**a**) *(plotting)* conspiration *f*, complot *m*; *(plot)* complot *m*; **he's been charged with conspiracy** on l'a accusé de conspiration; **there's a conspiracy against me** il y a un complot contre moi; **it's a conspiracy** c'est un complot; **a conspiracy of silence** une conspiration du silence (**b**) *Law (group of conspirators)* association *f* de malfaiteurs

▸▸ ***conspiracy theorist*** partisan *m* de la thèse *ou* théorie du complot; ***conspiracy theory*** thèse *f ou* théorie *f* du complot

conspirator [kən'spɪrətə(r)] *n* conspirateur(trice) *m,f*, comploteur(euse) *m,f*, conjuré(e) *m,f*

conspiratorial [kənˌspɪrə'tɔːrɪəl] *adj (smile, whisper, wink)* de conspirateur; *(group)* de conspirateurs

conspiratorially [kənˌspɪrə'tɔːrɪəlɪ] *adv (smile, whisper, wink)* d'un air de conspiration

conspire [kən'spaɪə(r)] *vi* (**a**) *(plot)* conspirer; **to conspire (with sb) to do sth** comploter *ou* s'entendre (avec qn) pour faire qch; **to conspire against sb** conspirer contre qn (**b**) *(combine → events, the elements)* concourir, se conjurer; **to conspire to do sth** concourir à faire qch; **everything conspired to make him late** tout a contribué à le mettre en retard; **circumstances conspired against me** les circonstances se sont liguées contre moi

constable ['kʌnstəbəl] *n Br* **(police) constable** agent *m* de police; **excuse me, Constable** excusez-moi, monsieur l'agent

constabulary [kən'stæbjʊlərɪ] (*pl* **constabularies**) **1** *n* **the constabulary** la police

2 *adj (duties)* de policier

constancy ['kɒnstənsɪ] *n* (**a**) *(steadfastness)* constance *f*; *(of feelings)* constance *f*, fidélité *f* (**b**) *(stability → of temperature, light)* constance *f*; *(→ of wind)* régularité *f*

constant ['kɒnstənt] **1** *adj* (**a**) *(continuous → interruptions, noise, pain)* constant, continuel, perpétuel; *(→ doubts, questions, complaining)* incessant; *(→ care)* continuel, assidu, soutenu; **the entrance is in constant use** il y a un mouvement continuel à l'entrée; **through constant repetition** à force de répéter; **there was constant pressure for reform** il y avait une pression continuelle pour qu'une réforme soit mise en œuvre

(**b**) *(unchanging → pressure, temperature, light)* constant; *(wind)* régulier

(**c**) *(faithful → affection, friend)* fidèle, loyal; **he was her constant companion** il était son fidèle compagnon

2 *n Math & Phys* constante *f*

constant-choke carburettor *n Aut* carburateur *m* à orifice constant

Constantine ['kɒnstəntaɪn] **1** *pr n Hist (emperor)* Constantin

2 *n Geog* Constantine

Constantinople [ˌkɒnstæntɪ'nəʊpəl] *n Hist* Constantinople

constantly ['kɒnstəntlɪ] *adv* constamment, sans cesse

constant-velocity joint *n Aut* joint *m* de cardan, joint *m* homocinétique

constellate ['kɒnstəleɪt] **1** *vt* consteller (**with** de)

2 *vi* (**a**) *(gather in constellations)* se former en constellations (**b**) *Fig Literary (group together)* se grouper (**into** en)

constellation [ˌkɒnstə'leɪʃən] *n* (**a**) *Astron (of stars)* constellation *f* (**b**) *Fig (of celebrities)* constellation *f*

consternation [ˌkɒnstə'neɪʃən] *n* consternation *f*; **I watched in consternation** je regardais avec consternation; **a look of consternation** un air consterné; **the meeting ended amidst general consternation** la réunion s'acheva dans la consternation générale; **the prospect filled me with consternation** cette perspective m'a plongé dans la consternation

constipate ['kɒnstɪpeɪt] *vt* constiper

constipated ['kɒnstɪpeɪtɪd] *adj also Fig* constipé; *Fig* **his rather constipated prose style** son style plutôt empesé *ou* guindé

constipation [ˌkɒnstɪ'peɪʃən] *n* constipation *f*

constituency [kən'stɪtjʊənsɪ] (*pl* **constituencies**) *Pol* **1** *n (area)* circonscription *f* électorale; *(people)* = habitants d'une circonscription électorale

2 *comp (meeting, organization)* local; *Br* **the constituency party** la section locale du parti

constituent [kən'stɪtjʊənt] **1** *adj* (**a**) *(component → part, element)* constituant, composant (**b**) *Pol (assembly, power)* constituant

2 *n* (**a**) *Pol* administré(e) *m,f* (**b**) *(element)* élément *m* constitutif

▸▸ *Ling* ***constituent analysis*** analyse *f* en constituants

constitute ['kɒnstɪtjuːt] *vt* (**a**) *(represent)* constituer; **what constitutes a state of emergency?** qu'est-ce que c'est qu'un état d'urgence?; **they constitute a threat to the government** ils représentent une menace pour le gouvernement

(**b**) *(make up)* constituer; **women constitute a large section of the workforce** les femmes constituent une grande partie de la main d'œuvre; **the countries that constitute the EU** les pays qui constituent l'UE

(**c**) *(set up → committee)* constituer

(**d**) *Formal (appoint → chairman)* désigner; **to constitute sb arbitrator** constituer qn arbitre

constitution [ˌkɒnstɪ'tjuːʃən] *n* (**a**) *Pol (statute)* constitution *f*; *Am Pol* **the (United States) Constitution** la Constitution (**b**) *(health)* constitution *f*; **to have a strong/weak constitution** avoir une constitution robuste/chétive (**c**) *(structure)* composition *f*

▸▸ ***the Constitution State*** = surnom donné au Connecticut

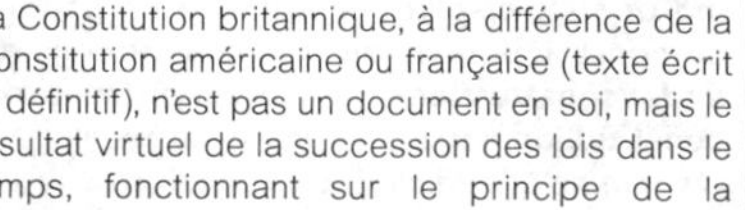

CONSTITUTION

La Constitution britannique, à la différence de la Constitution américaine ou française (texte écrit et définitif), n'est pas un document en soi, mais le résultat virtuel de la succession des lois dans le temps, fonctionnant sur le principe de la jurisprudence.

constitutional [ˌkɒnstɪ'tjuːʃənəl] **1** *adj* (**a**) *Pol*

con–con

(regime, reform) constitutionnel; **the president's actions are not constitutional** les actions du président sont anticonstitutionnelles (**b**) *(official → head, privilege)* constitutionnel (**c**) *(inherent → weakness)* constitutionnel

2 *n Old-fashioned or Hum* **to go for a constitutional** aller faire un petit tour; **he's gone for his morning constitutional** il est allé faire sa petite promenade matinale

►► ***constitutional law*** droit *m* constitutionnel; ***constitutional lawyer*** constitutionnaliste *mf*; ***constitutional monarchy*** monarchie *f* constitutionnelle

constitutionalism [ˌkɒnstɪ'tjuːʃənəlɪzəm] *n Pol* constitutionnalisme *m*

constitutionalist [ˌkɒnstɪ'tjuːʃənəlɪst] *n* (**a**) *Pol* constitutionnel *m* (**b**) *(specialist)* spécialiste *mf* des constitutions politiques

constitutionality ['kɒnstɪˌtjuːʃə'nælətɪ] *n Pol* constitutionnalité *f*

constitutionally [ˌkɒnstɪ'tjuːʃənəlɪ] *adv* (**a**) *Pol (act)* constitutionnellement; **constitutionally, the government is within its rights** constitutionnellement, le gouvernement est dans ses droits (**b**) *(inherently → strong, weak, lazy)* de *ou* par nature

constitutive [kən'stɪtjʊtɪv] *adj* (**a**) *(body, organization)* constitutif (**b**) *Chem* constitutif (**c**) *(component → part, element)* constituant, composant

constrain [kən'streɪn] *vt* (**a**) *(force)* contraindre, forcer; **to constrain sb to do sth** contraindre qn à faire qch (**b**) *(limit → feelings, freedom)* contraindre, restreindre; *(of clothing)* gêner

constrained [kən'streɪnd] *adj* (**a**) *(inhibited)* contraint; **to feel constrained to do sth** se sentir contraint *ou* obligé de faire qch; **he felt constrained by his clothes** il se sentait à l'étroit dans ses vêtements (**b**) *(tense → manner, speech)* contraint; *(→ atmosphere, smile)* contraint, gêné

constrainedly [kən'streɪnɪdlɪ] *adv* (**a**) *(by force)* par contrainte (**b**) *(inhibitedly, tensely)* d'un air gêné; **to smile constrainedly** sourire d'un air contraint

constraint [kən'streɪnt] *n* (**a**) *(restriction)* contrainte *f*; **they are subject to the constraints of time and money** ils sont sujets aux contraintes du temps et de l'argent; **there are certain constraints on their activities** ils subissent certaines contraintes dans leurs activités; **social constraints** contraintes *fpl* sociales; **to speak without constraint** parler librement *ou* sans contrainte

(**b**) *(pressure)* contrainte *f*; **to do sth under constraint** agir *ou* faire qch sous la contrainte

constrict [kən'strɪkt] *vt* (**a**) *(make narrower → blood vessels, throat)* resserrer, serrer (**b**) *(hamper → breathing, movement)* gêner

constricted [kən'strɪktɪd] *adj (opening, passage)* étroit; *(breathing, movement)* gêné, restreint; *also Fig* **to feel constricted by sth** se sentir limité par qch

constricting [kən'strɪktɪŋ] *adj (clothes)* étroit; *Fig (beliefs, ideology)* limité

constriction [kən'strɪkʃən] *n* (**a**) *(→ in chest, throat)* constriction *f* (**b**) *(restriction)* restriction *f*; **social constrictions** restrictions *fpl* sociales

constrictor [kən'strɪktə(r)] *n* (**a**) *Anat* (muscle *m*) constricteur *m* (**b**) *Zool (snake)* constricteur *m*

construct 1 *vt* [kən'strʌkt] (**a**) *(build → building, bridge, dam, house, road)* construire; *(→ nest, raft)* construire, bâtir; **to construct sth (out) of sth** construire qch à partir de qch (**b**) *(formulate → sentence, play)* construire; *(→ system, theory)* bâtir; **a beautifully constructed play** une pièce magnifiquement construite *ou* composée

2 *n* ['kɒnstrʌkt] (**a**) *Formal (thing constructed)* construction *f* (**b**) *Psy (idea)* concept *m*

construction [kən'strʌkʃən] **1** *n* (**a**) *(act of building → of road, bridge, house)* construction *f*; *(→ of machine)* construction *f*, réalisation *f*; **a building of simple/solid construction** un bâtiment de construction simple/solidement construit; **under construction** en construction; **to work in construction** travailler dans le bâtiment

(**b**) *(thing constructed)* construction *f*

(**c**) *(formulation → of sentence, play)* construction *f*; *(→ of system, theory)* construction *f*, élaboration *f*

(**d**) *(interpretation)* interprétation *f*; **to put a wrong construction on sb's words** mal interpréter les paroles de qn; **to put a sympathetic construction on sb's words** interpréter les paroles de qn avec indulgence

(**e**) *Gram* construction *f*

(**f**) *Geom* construction *f*

(**g**) *Art* sculpture *f* constructiviste

2 *comp (site, work)* de construction; *(worker)* du bâtiment;

►► ***the construction industry*** le bâtiment; ***construction set*** jeu *m* de construction

constructional [kən'strʌkʃənəl] *adj* de construction; *(technique)* mécanique

►► *Tech* ***constructional engineering*** construction *f* mécanique

constructive [kən'strʌktɪv] *adj* (**a**) *(criticism, remark)* constructif (**b**) *Law* implicite (**c**) *(relating to construction)* de construction

►► *Ind* ***constructive dismissal*** = démission provoquée par la conduite de l'employeur

constructively [kən'strʌktɪvlɪ] *adv* de manière constructive

constructivism [kən'strʌktɪˌvɪzəm] *n Art* constructivisme *m*

constructivist [kən'strʌktɪvɪst] *n Art* constructiviste *mf*

constructor [kən'strʌktə(r)] *n* (**a**) *(of building, road, machine)* constructeur *m* (**b**) *(of system, theory)* créateur *m*

construe [kən'struː] *vt* (**a**) *(interpret, understand → attitude, statement)* interpréter, expliquer; **the phrase can be construed to mean two things** on peut interpréter l'expression de deux manières différentes (**b**) *Gram (parse)* analyser, décomposer (**c**) *Old-fashioned Gram (translate)* traduire oralement

consubstantial [ˌkɒnsəb'stænʃəl] *adj Rel* consubstantiel

consubstantiation ['kɒnsəbˌstænʃɪ'eɪʃən] *n Rel* consubstantiation *f*

consul ['kɒnsəl] *n* consul *m*

►► ***consul general*** consul *m* général

consular ['kɒnsjʊlə(r)] *adj* consulaire

►► *Com* ***consular fees*** frais *mpl* consulaires; *Com* ***consular invoice*** facture *f* consulaire

consulate ['kɒnsjʊlət] *n* consulat *m*

consulship ['kɒnsəlʃɪp] *n* fonctions *fpl ou* charge *f* de consul

consult 1 *vt* [kən'sʌlt] (**a**) *(ask → doctor, expert)* consulter; **to consult sb about sth** consulter qn sur *ou* au sujet de qch (**b**) *(consider → person's feelings)* prendre en considération (**c**) *(refer to → book, map, watch)* consulter

2 *vi* [kən'sʌlt] consulter, être en consultation; **to consult together over sth** se consulter sur *ou* au sujet de qch; **to consult with sb** conférer avec qn

3 *n* ['kɒnsʌlt] *Fam* consultation ❑ *f*

consultancy [kən'sʌltənsɪ] (*pl* **consultancies**) *n* (**a**) *(company)* cabinet *m* d'expert-conseil (**b**) *(advice)* assistance *f* technique; **to do consultancy work** être consultant (**c**) *Med (hospital post)* poste *m* de médecin/chirurgien consultant

►► ***consultancy fees*** frais *mpl* de conseil; ***consultancy service*** service *m* d'assistance technique

consultant [kən'sʌltənt] **1** *n* (**a**) *Med (doctor → specialist)* médecin *m* spécialiste, consultant *m*; *(→ in charge of department)* consultant *m* (**b**) *(expert)* expert-conseil *m*, consultant *m*

2 *comp (engineer)* conseil *(inv)*; *Med (doctor)* consultant

consultation [ˌkɒnsəl'teɪʃən] *n* (**a**) *(discussion)* consultation *f*, délibération *f*; **a matter for consultation** un sujet à débattre; **in consultation with** en consultation *ou* en concertation avec; **the matter will be decided in consultation with our colleagues** la décision sera prise en consultation *ou* en concertation avec nos collègues; **to hold consultations about sth** avoir des consultations sur qch

(**b**) *(reference)* consultation *f*; **the dictionary is designed for easy consultation** le dictionnaire a été conçu pour être consulté facilement

consultative [kən'sʌltətɪv] *adj* consultatif; **I'm here in a purely consultative capacity** je ne suis ici qu'à titre consultatif

consulting [kən'sʌltɪŋ] *adj (engineer)* conseil *(inv)*

►► *Med* ***consulting room*** cabinet *m* de consultation

consumable [kən'sjuːməbəl] **1** *adj (substance → by fire)* consumable; *(foodstuffs)* consommable, de consommation

2 **consumables** *npl (food)* denrées *fpl* alimentaires, comestibles *mpl*; *(hardware)* consommables *mpl*

►► *Com & Econ* ***consumable goods*** produits *mpl* de consommation

consume [kən'sjuːm] *vt* (**a**) *(eat or drink)* consommer (**b**) *(use up → energy, fuel)* consommer; *(→ time)* dépenser (**c**) *(burn up → of fire, flames)* consumer; **the city was consumed by fire** la ville a brûlé; *Fig* **to be consumed with desire/love** brûler de désir/d'amour; *Fig* **to be consumed with grief** être miné par le chagrin; *Fig* **to be consumed with hatred/jealousy** être dévoré par la haine/jalousie

consumer [kən'sjuːmə(r)] **1** *n (purchaser, user)* consommateur(trice) *m,f*; **gas/electricity consumer** abonné *m* au gaz/à l'électricité

2 *comp* du consommateur, des consommateurs

►► *Com* ***Consumers' Association*** = association britannique des consommateurs; *Mktg* ***consumer behaviour*** comportement *m* du consommateur; *Mktg* ***consumer benefit*** bénéfice *m* consommateur; *Com & Mktg* ***consumer brand*** marque *f* grand public; *Com & Mktg* ***consumer credit*** crédit *m* à la consommation; *Com & Econ* ***consumer debt*** endettement *m* des consommateurs; *Com & Mktg* ***consumer demand*** demande *f* des consommateurs; *Com & Econ* ***consumer durables*** biens *mpl* de consommation durables; ***consumer expenditure*** dépenses *fpl* de consommation; ***consumer goods*** biens *mpl* de consommation durables; *Com & Econ* ***consumer industry*** industrie *f* de consommation; ***consumer loan*** prêt *m* à la consommation; ***consumer magazine*** magazine *m* pour les consommateurs; *Com & Econ* ***consumer market*** marché *m* de la consommation; *Com* ***consumer organization*** organisme *m* de défense des consommateurs; *Mktg* ***consumer panel*** groupe-témoin *m*, panel *m* de consommateurs; *Com & Econ* ***consumer price index*** indice *m* des prix à la consommation; *Com & Econ* ***consumer protection*** défense *f* des consommateurs; ***consumer protection agency*** bureau *m* d'accueil des consommateurs; *Am Press* ***Consumer Reports*** = magazine américain de défense des consommateurs; *Mktg* ***consumer research*** étude *f* de marché; *Mktg* ***consumer resistance*** résistance *f ou* réticence *f* des consommateurs; *Com & Econ* ***consumer society*** société *f* de consommation; *Econ* ***consumer sovereignty*** souveraineté *f* du consommateur; *Com & Econ* ***consumer spending*** dépenses *fpl* de consommation; *Mktg* ***consumer survey*** étude *f* auprès des consommateurs finaux; ***consumer terrorism*** = actes de terrorisme perpétrés contre une entreprise par un client mécontent; *Mktg* ***consumer welfare*** intérêt *m* du consommateur

consumerism [kən'sjuːmərɪzəm] *n Com & Econ* (**a**) *(consumer protection)* consumérisme *m* (**b**) *Pej (consumption)* consommation *f* à outrance

consuming [kən'sjuːmɪŋ] *adj (desire, interest)* dévorant

consummate 1 *adj* ['kɒnsjʊmət, kən'sʌmət] *Formal* (**a**) *(very skilful → artist, musician)* consommé, accompli; **she was consummate in the art of concealing her feelings** elle était maître dans l'art de cacher ses sentiments (**b**) *(utter → coward, fool, liar, snob)* accompli, parfait, fini

2 *vt* ['kɒnsəmeɪt] *(marriage, relationship)* consommer

consummately ['kɒnsjʊmətlɪ, kən'sʌmətlɪ] *adv Formal* (**a**) *(skilfully)* avec une grande maîtrise; **he lied consummately to achieve what he wanted** il a menti avec beaucoup d'adresse pour obtenir ce qu'il voulait (**b**) *(utterly)* complètement, parfaitement; **a consummately successful businesswoman** une femme d'affaires qui réussit tout ce qu'elle entreprend

consummation [ˌkɒnsə'meɪʃən] *n* (**a**) *(of*

marriage, relationship) consommation *f* (**b**) *(culmination → of career, life's work)* couronnement *m* (**c**) *(achievement → of ambitions, desires)* achèvement *m*

consumption [kən'sʌmpʃən] *n* (**a**) *(eating, drinking)* consommation *f*; **unfit for human consumption** non comestible; *Fig* **his words were not intended for public consumption** ses paroles n'étaient pas destinées au public
(**b**) *Com & Econ (purchasing)* consommation *f*
(**c**) *(using up, amount used → of gas, energy, oil)* consommation *f*, dépense *f*
(**d**) *Old-fashioned Med (tuberculosis)* consomption *f* (pulmonaire), phtisie *f*

consumptive [kən'sʌmptɪv] *Old-fashioned Med* **1** *adj (disease, illness)* consomptif, destructif
2 *n* phtisique *mf*, tuberculeux(euse) *m,f*

cont. (**a**) (*written abbr* **contents**) contenu *m*; *(in book)* table *f* des matières (**b**) (*written abbr* **continued**) suite

contact ['kɒntækt] **1** *n* (**a**) *(communication)* contact *m*, rapport *m*; **we don't have much contact with our neighbours** nous n'avons pas beaucoup de contacts avec nos voisins; **to be in contact with sb** être en contact *ou* en rapport avec qn; **are you still in contact?** *(of two people)* est-ce que vous êtes toujours en contact?; **the two leaders are in close contact** les deux dirigeants sont en contact étroit; **to come into contact with sb** entrer *ou* se mettre en contact *ou* en rapport avec qn; **anyone who has come into contact with the sick man** quiconque s'est trouvé au contact du malade; **she hadn't come into contact with poverty** elle ne s'était pas trouvée au contact de la pauvreté; **to make contact with sb** prendre contact avec qn; **to stay in contact with sb** garder le contact *ou* rester en contact avec qn; **to lose contact with sb** *(lose touch)* perdre contact avec qn; **shall I give you a contact address/number?** voulez-vous que je vous donne l'adresse/le numéro où vous pouvez me joindre?
(**b**) *(touch)* contact *m*; **to come into contact with** entrer en contact avec, toucher; **the substance must not come into contact with the air** la substance ne doit pas être exposée à l'air; **always keep one foot in contact with the ground** gardez toujours un pied au sol; **physical contact** contact *m* physique; **eye contact** contact *m* visuel
(**c**) *(person)* relation *f*; **she has some useful business contacts** elle a quelques bons contacts (professionnels); **I have a contact who may be able to help you** je connais quelqu'un qui pourrait vous aider; **who's our contact in Paris?** qui est notre contact à Paris?
(**d**) *Elec (connector, connection)* contact *m*; **to make/break (the) contact** mettre/couper le contact
(**e**) *Med* = personne ayant approché un malade contagieux
(**f**) *Phot (contact print)* planche *f* contact, épreuve *f* par contact
(**g**) *(contact lens)* verre *m ou* lentille *f* de contact; **to wear contacts** porter des lentilles de contact
2 *comp* (**a**) *Med (contagious → dermatitis)* par contact
(**b**) *(killing on contact → herbicide, insecticide)* par contact
3 *vt* prendre contact avec, contacter; **we'll contact you later on this week** nous vous contacterons cette semaine
►► *Elec* ***contact breaker*** disjoncteur *m*; ***contact breaker plate*** plateau *m* porte-rupteur; ***contact breaker points*** contacts *mpl* rupteur; *Aviat* ***contact flight*** *(flight)* vol *m* à basse altitude; *(navigation)* navigation *f* à vue; ***contact lens*** verre *m ou* lentille *f* de contact; ***contact man*** contact *m*, agent *m* de liaison; *Phot* ***contact print*** planche *f* contact, épreuve *f* par contact; ***contact sport*** sport *m* de contact

contactable [kɒn'tæktəbəl] *adj* que l'on peut joindre *ou* contacter, joignable; **I'm contactable at this number** on peut me contacter *ou* m'appeler à ce numéro

contagion [kən'teɪdʒən] *n* (**a**) *(contamination)* contagion *f* (**b**) *(disease)* contagion *f*, maladie *f* contagieuse (**c**) *Literary (moral corruption)* contamination *f*

contagious [kən'teɪdʒəs] *adj also Fig* contagieux; **he's no longer contagious** il n'est plus contagieux

contagiously [kən'teɪdʒəslɪ] *adv* par contagion; *Fig (laugh)* d'une façon contagieuse

contagiousness [kən'teɪdʒəsnɪs] *n* contagion *f*, contagiosité *f*

contain [kən'teɪn] *vt* (**a**) *(hold → of bag, house, city)* contenir
(**b**) *(include → of pill, substance)* contenir; *(→ of book, speech)* contenir, comporter; **her story does contain some truth** il y a du vrai dans son histoire; **the ore contains a high percentage of iron** le minerai a une forte teneur en fer; **the document contains a reference to...** le document contient une référence à...
(**c**) *(restrain → feelings)* contenir, cacher; **to contain one's anger** contenir sa colère; **to contain one's disappointment** cacher sa déception; **he was unable to contain his laughter** il ne pouvait pas s'empêcher de rire; **I could barely contain myself** j'avais du mal à me contenir
(**d**) *(curb → enemy, growth, riot, inflation)* contenir, maîtriser
(**e**) *(hold back → fire, epidemic)* circonscrire; *(→ flood waters)* contenir, endiguer
(**f**) *(limit → damage)* limiter
(**g**) *Math* être divisible par

contained [kən'teɪnd] *adj (person)* maître de soi

container [kən'teɪnə(r)] **1** *n* (**a**) *(bottle, box, tin etc)* récipient *m* (**b**) *Com (for transporting cargo)* conteneur *m*, container *m*
2 *comp Com (port, ship, terminal)* porte-conteneurs; *(dock, line, transport)* pour porte-conteneurs
►► *Com* ***container depot*** entrepôt *m* de conteneurs, dépôt *m* pour conteneurs; *Br Com* ***container lorry*** camion *m* adapté au transport des conteneurs; *Com* ***container premium*** prime *f* contenant; *Com* ***container truck*** camion *m* adapté au transport des conteneurs

containerization [kən,teɪnəraɪ'zeɪʃən] *n Com* (**a**) *(of cargo)* conteneurisation *f*, transport *m* par conteneurs (**b**) *(of port)* conteneurisation *f*

containerize, -ise [kən'teɪnəraɪz] *vt Com (cargo)* conteneuriser, transporter par conteneurs, *(port)* convertir à la conteneurisation

containerized freight [kən'teɪnəraɪzd-] *n Com* fret *m* par conteneur

containment [kən'teɪnmənt] *n* (**a**) *Pol* endiguement *m*, freinage *m*, retenue *f*; **a policy of containment** une politique d'endiguement (**b**) *Phys* confinement *m*
►► ***containment building*** enceinte *f* de confinement

contaminate [kən'tæmɪneɪt] *vt* (**a**) *(pollute → food, river, water)* contaminer; *Fig (corrupt)* contaminer, souiller (**b**) *(irradiate → land, person, soil)* contaminer

contaminated [kən'tæmɪ,neɪtɪd] *adj* (**a**) *(polluted → food, river, water)* contaminé; *(→ air)* contaminé, vicié; *Fig (corrupted)* contaminé, corrompu (**b**) *(irradiated → land, person, soil)* contaminé

contaminating [kən'tæmɪ,neɪtɪŋ] *adj* contaminant

contamination [kən,tæmɪ'neɪʃən] *n* (**a**) *(pollution → of food, river, water)* contamination *f*; *Fig* contamination *f*, corruption *f* (**b**) *(irradiation → of land, person, soil)* contamination *f*; **high levels of contamination** de hauts niveaux de contamination

contango [kən'tæŋgəʊ] (*pl* **contangos,** *pt & pp* **contangoed,** *cont* **contangoing**) *Br St Exch* **1** *n* (**a**) *(postponement of payment)* report *m* (**b**) *(fee)* taux *m* de report
2 *vt (shares)* reporter
3 *vi* reporter une position
►► ***contango day*** jour *m* des reports; ***contango rate*** taux *m* de report

cont'd, contd (*written abbr* **continued**) suite *f*; **cont'd on p14** suite à la page 14; **to be cont'd** à suivre

contemn [kən'tem] *vt Literary* mépriser

contemner [kən'temnə(r)] *n* (**a**) *Literary (scornful person)* contempteur(trice) *m,f* (**b**) *Law* = personne qui s'est rendu coupable d'un outrage à magistrat

contemplate ['kɒntempleɪt] **1** *vt* (**a**) *(ponder)* considérer, réfléchir sur
(**b**) *(consider)* considérer, envisager; **it's too awful to contemplate** c'est insupportable rien que d'y penser; **to contemplate suicide** songer au suicide; **he's contemplating marriage** il envisage de *ou* songe à se marier; **to contemplate doing sth** envisager de *ou* songer à faire qch
(**c**) *(observe)* contempler; **she sat contemplating the scene** elle était assise à contempler la scène
2 *vi* (**a**) *(ponder)* méditer, se recueillir
(**b**) *(consider)* réfléchir

contemplation [,kɒntem'pleɪʃən] *n* (**a**) *(thought)* réflexion *f*; **deep in contemplation** en pleine réflexion; **his contemplations were rudely interrupted by the doorbell** la sonnette le tira brusquement de ses réflexions
(**b**) *(observation)* contemplation *f*; **she returned to her contemplation of the sea** elle se remit à contempler la mer
(**c**) *(meditation)* contemplation *f*, recueillement *m*, méditation *f*; **a period of contemplation** une période de recueillement

contemplative [kən'templətɪv] **1** *adj (look, mood)* songeur, pensif; *(life)* contemplatif; *Rel (order, prayer)* contemplatif
2 *n Rel* contemplatif(ive) *m,f*

contemplatively [kən'templətɪvlɪ] *adv (live)* contemplativement; **he looked at me contemplatively** il m'a regardé pensivement *ou* d'un air songeur

contemporaneity [kən,tempərə'niːɪtɪ] *n* contemporanéité *f*

contemporaneous [kən,tempə'reɪnɪəs] *adj Formal* contemporain; **to be contemporaneous (with sb/sth)** être contemporain (de qn/ qch)

contemporaneously [kən,tempə'reɪnɪəslɪ] *adv Formal (exist, live)* à la même époque; **contemporaneously with** à la même époque que

contemporaneousness [kən,tempə'reɪnɪəsnɪs] *n* contemporanéité *f*

contemporary [kən'tempərərɪ] (*pl* **contemporaries**) **1** *adj* (**a**) *(modern → art, writer)* contemporain, d'aujourd'hui; *(→ design, style)* moderne; **a study of contemporary Britain** une étude de la Grande-Bretagne d'aujourd'hui
(**b**) *(of the same period → account, report)* contemporain; **he was contemporary with Thackeray** il vivait à la même époque que *ou* il était contemporain de Thackeray
2 *n* contemporain(e) *m,f*; **she and I are contemporaries** elle et moi sommes de la même génération; **he was a contemporary of mine at university** nous étions ensemble *ou* en même temps à l'université

contempt [kən'tempt] *n* (**a**) *(scorn)* mépris *m*; **to feel contempt for sb/sth, to hold sb/sth in contempt** mépriser qn/qch, avoir du mépris pour qn/qch; **to treat sb/sth with contempt** traiter qn/qch avec dédain *ou* mépris; **I feel nothing but contempt for him** je n'ai que du mépris pour lui; **to be beneath contempt** être tout ce qu'il y a de plus méprisable
(**b**) *Law* outrage *m*; **to charge sb with contempt (of court)** accuser qn d'outrage (à magistrat *ou* à la Cour)

contemptible [kən'temptəbəl] *adj (action, attitude, person)* méprisable

contemptibly [kən'temptəblɪ] *adv* dérisoirement; **a contemptibly small sum** une somme dérisoire

contemptuous [kən'temptʃʊəs] *adj Formal (look, manner, remark)* méprisant, dédaigneux; **to be contemptuous of sb/sth** dédaigner qn/ qch, faire peu de cas de qn/qch

contemptuously [kən'temptʃʊəslɪ] *adv (laugh, reject, smile)* avec mépris, avec dédain

contend [kən'tend] **1** *vi* (**a**) *(deal)* **to contend with sb** avoir affaire à qn; **to contend with sth** être aux prises avec qch; **this is just one of the difficulties we have to contend with** ce n'est que l'une des difficultés auxquelles nous devons faire face; **they still had the perimeter fence to contend with** il leur restait encore à régler le problème de la clôture d'enceinte; **if you do that again, you'll have me to contend with** si tu recommences, tu auras affaire à moi (**b**) *(compete)* combattre, lutter; **to contend with sb for** *or* **over sth** disputer *ou* contester qch à qn; **several candidates were contending for the job** plusieurs candidats étaient en compétition pour le poste

2 *vt Formal (maintain, argue)* **to contend that...** soutenir que...

contender [kən'tendə(r)] *n (in boxing match)* adversaire *mf*; *(in race)* concurrent(e) *m,f*; *(for title)* prétendant(e) *m,f* (**for** à); *(for political office)* candidat(e) *m,f*

> **I could have been a contender**
> Il s'agit d'une formule extraite du film d'Elia Kazan de 1954 *On the Waterfront* (*Sur les quais*). C'est Terry Malloy, le personnage interprété par Marlon Brando, qui déclare en s'adressant à son frère, interprété par Rod Steiger, **I could have been a contender** ("j'aurais pu devenir quelqu'un"). On utilise cette phrase pour exprimer une certaine mélancolie et les regrets que l'on éprouve en pensant aux occasions que l'on n'a pas su saisir.

contending [kən'tendɪŋ] *adj* opposé

content 1 *n* (**a**) ['kɒntent] *(amount contained)* teneur *f*; **gold/moisture content** teneur *f* en or/humidité; **with a high iron content** avec une forte teneur en fer, riche en fer; **peanut butter has a high protein content** le beurre de cacahuètes est riche en protéines

(**b**) ['kɒntent] *(substance → of book, film, speech)* contenu *m*; *(meaning)* teneur *f*, fond *m*; **his films are all style and no content** dans ses films, il y a la forme mais pas le fond

(**c**) [kən'tent] *(satisfaction)* contentement *m*, satisfaction *f*

(**d**) ['kɒntent] *Ling* contenu *m*

2 *adj* [kən'tent] content, satisfait (**with** de); **to be content to do sth** ne pas demander mieux que de faire qch; **he seems quite content with his lot in life** il semble assez content de son sort; **not content with having ruined our evening, he came round next day** non content d'avoir gâché notre soirée, il revint le lendemain

3 *vt* [kən'tent] **to content oneself with sth/doing sth** se contenter de *ou* se borner à qch/à faire qch; **my reply seemed to content them** ils semblaient satisfaits de ma réponse

4 contents *npl* ['kɒntents] (**a**) *(of bag, bottle, house etc)* contenu *m*

(**b**) *(of book, letter)* contenu *m*; **the contents (list), the list of contents** la table des matières

►► ***content analysis*** analyse *f* de contenu; ***contents insurance*** assurance *f* mobilier; *Comput* ***content provider*** fournisseur *m* de contenu; *Ling* ***content word*** mot *m* à contenu lexical

contented [kən'tentɪd] *adj (person)* content, satisfait (**with** de); *(smile)* de contentement, de satisfaction; **she seems very contented with life** elle semble très contente de son sort

contentedly [kən'tentɪdlɪ] *adv* avec contentement; **to live contentedly** vivre heureux

contentedness [kən'tentɪdnɪs] *n* contentement *m*, satisfaction *f*

contention [kən'tenʃən] *n* (**a**) *Formal (belief)* affirmation *f*; **it is my contention that...** je soutiens que... (**b**) *(disagreement)* dispute *f*; **his morals are not in contention** sa moralité n'est pas ici mise en doute (**c**) *(competition)* **to be in contention for sth** être en compétition pour qch; **the teams in contention** les équipes concurrentes *ou* rivales

contentious [kən'tenʃəs] *adj* (**a**) *(controversial → issue, subject)* controversé (**b**) *(argumentative → family, group, person)* querelleur, chicanier (**c**) *Law* contentieux

contentiously [kən'tenʃəslɪ] *adv* (**a**) *(controversially)* **he declared contentiously that a woman's place is in the kitchen** il a dit que la place des femmes est aux fourneaux, ce qui a provoqué une polémique (**b**) *(argumentatively)* en chicanant (**c**) *Law* contentieusement

contentiousness [kən'tenʃəsnɪs] *n* (**a**) *(controversial nature)* nature *f* litigieuse (**b**) *(argumentativeness)* humeur *f* querelleuse (**c**) *Law* contentieux *m*

contentment [kən'tentmənt] *n* contentement *m*, satisfaction *f*; **she beamed with contentment** elle rayonnait de satisfaction; **a look of contentment** un regard de satisfaction

conterminous [kɒn'tɜːmɪnəs] *adj Formal* (**a**) *(sharing the same border → country, land)* limitrophe; *(→ estate, garden)* adjacent, attenant, contigu; **to be conterminous with sth** être adjacent à qch (**b**) *(uninterrupted)* bout à bout (**c**) *(coincident → in range, scope, time)* de même étendue

contest 1 *n* ['kɒntest] (**a**) *(competition)* concours *m*; **beauty contest** concours *m* de beauté

(**b**) *(struggle)* combat *m*, lutte *f*; **a contest for/between** un combat pour/entre

(**c**) *Sport* rencontre *f*; *Boxing* combat *m*, rencontre *f*; **a contest with/between** un combat contre/entre

(**d**) *Am Law* **no contest** pas de témoins à charge

2 *vt* [kən'test] (**a**) *(dispute → idea, statement)* contester, discuter; **he contested my right to be at the meeting** il m'a contesté le droit d'assister à la réunion; **to contest a will** contester un testament

(**b**) *Pol (fight for → election, seat)* disputer; *Sport (→ match, title)* disputer; **a keenly contested game** une partie très disputée

►► *Fin* ***contested debt*** créance *f* litigieuse

contestant [kən'testənt] *n* concurrent(e) *m,f*, adversaire *mf*; *Boxing* combattant *m*

contestation [ˌkɒntes'teɪʃən] *n* contestation *f*

context ['kɒntekst] *n* contexte *m*; **out of/in context** hors/en contexte; **the book places the writer in his social context** le livre replace l'écrivain dans son contexte social; **her comments had been taken out of context** ses commentaires avaient été retirés de leur contexte; **she was quoted out of context** on a cité ses paroles hors de leur contexte

context-dependent *adj* **to be context-dependent** dépendre du contexte

context-sensitive *adj Comput (spellchecker, help)* contextuel

contextual [kɒn'tekstjʊəl] *adj* contextuel

contextualization [kɒnˌtekstjʊəlaɪ'zeɪʃən] *n* contextualisation *f*

contextualize, -ise [kɒn'tekstjʊəlaɪz] *vt (events, facts)* contextualiser, remettre dans son contexte; *(word, expression)* contextualiser, utiliser en contexte

contextually [kɒn'tekstjʊəlɪ] *adv (examine)* dans son contexte; **to be contextually dependent** dépendre du contexte

contexture [kən'tekstjə(r)] *n Literary* contexture *f*

contiguity [ˌkɒntɪ'gjuːətɪ] *n* contiguïté *f*

contiguous [kən'tɪgjʊəs] *adj Formal* contigu(uë); **to be contiguous to** *or* **with sth** être contigu à qch

continence ['kɒntɪnəns] *n* (**a**) *Med* continence *f* (**b**) *Formal (chastity)* continence *f*, chasteté *f*

continent ['kɒntɪnənt] **1** *n Geog* continent *m*

2 *adj* (**a**) *Med* continent, qui n'est pas incontinent (**b**) *Formal (chaste)* continent, chaste

3 Continent *n Br* **the Continent** l'Europe *f* continentale; **on the Continent** en Europe (continentale), outre-Manche

continental [ˌkɒntɪ'nentəl] **1** *adj* (**a**) *Br (European)* d'outre-Manche, européen, d'Europe continentale (**b**) *Geog (crust, divide)* continental

2 *n Br* continental(e) *m,f*, habitant(e) *m,f* de l'Europe continentale

►► ***continental breakfast*** petit déjeuner *m* à la française; *Met* ***continental climate*** climat *m* continental; *Am Hist* ***Continental Congress*** = corps législatif qui gouverna les treize colonies américaines jusqu'à la proclamation de l'indépendance en 1776; *Am Geog* ***Continental Divide*** = ligne de partage des eaux entre l'Atlantique et le Pacifique; *Geol* ***continental drift*** dérive *f* des continents; ***continental Latin America*** l'Amérique *f* latine continentale; *Am* ***continental plan*** *(at hotel)* tarif *m* chambre avec petit déjeuner continental; ***continental quilt*** couette *f*, duvet *m*; *Geol* ***continental shelf*** plateau *m* continental, plate-forme *f* continentale; *Am* ***continental United States*** = désigne les 48 États des États-Unis qui forment un bloc géographique (excluant Hawaii et l'Alaska)

> **CONTINENTAL BREAKFAST**
> Ce terme désigne un petit déjeuner léger, par opposition au breakfast anglais, beaucoup plus copieux et comportant un plat chaud.

contingency [kən'tɪndʒənsɪ] (*pl* **contingencies**) **1** *n Formal* (**a**) *(possibility)* éventualité *f*, contingence *f*; **to provide for all contingencies** parer à toute éventualité (**b**) *(chance)* événement *m* inattendu; *(uncertainty)* (cas *m*) imprévu *m*, éventualité *f* (**c**) *(in statistics)* contingence *f*

2 *comp (plan)* d'urgence; *(table, coefficient)* des imprévus

3 contingencies *npl Fin* frais *mpl* divers

►► *Law* ***contingency fee*** = aux États-Unis, principe permettant à un avocat de recevoir une part des sommes attribuées à son client si ce dernier gagne son procès; *Fin* ***contingency fund*** fonds *mpl* de prévoyance; *Fin* ***contingency and loss provision*** provision *f* pour risques et charges; *Acct* ***contingency theory*** théorie *f* de la contingence

contingent [kən'tɪndʒənt] **1** *adj Formal* (**a**) *(dependent)* contingent; **to be contingent on** *or* **upon sth** dépendre de qch (**b**) *(accidental)* accidentel, fortuit (**c**) *(uncertain)* éventuel (**d**) *Phil* contingent

2 *n* (**a**) *Mil* contingent *m* (**b**) *(representative group)* groupe *m* représentatif

►► *Acct* ***contingent liability*** passif *m* éventuel *ou* exigible; *St Exch* ***contingent order*** ordre *m* conditionnel; *Acct* ***contingent profit*** profit *m* aléatoire; *St Exch* ***contingent value right*** certificat *m* de valeur garantie

contingently [kən'tɪndʒəntlɪ] *adv Formal* (**a**) *(accidentally)* accidentellement, fortuitement (**b**) *(uncertainly)* éventuellement

continual [kən'tɪnjʊəl] *adj* (**a**) *(continuous → pain, pleasure, struggle)* continuel (**b**) *(repeated → nagging, warnings)* incessant, continuel

continually [kən'tɪnjʊəlɪ] *adv* (**a**) *(continuously → change, evolve)* continuellement (**b**) *(repeatedly → complain, nag, warn)* sans cesse

continuance [kən'tɪnjʊəns] *n* (**a**) *(continuation)* continuation *f*, persistance *f*, durée *f* (**b**) *Am Law* ajournement *m (d'un procès)*

continuant [kən'tɪnjʊənt] **1** *n Ling* (consonne *f*) continue *f*

2 *adj* continu

continuation [kənˌtɪnjʊ'eɪʃən] *n* (**a**) *(sequel)* continuation *f*, suite *f* (**b**) *(resumption)* reprise *f* (**c**) *(prolongation)* prolongement *m*, suite *f*; *(of road)* prolongement *m*

continue [kən'tɪnjuː] **1** *vi* (**a**) *(carry on)* continuer; **the situation cannot continue** la situation ne peut pas durer; **the situation continued into the 1960s** la situation s'est prolongée jusque dans le courant des années 60; **she will continue as director until December** elle gardera les fonctions de directrice jusqu'en décembre; **his bad luck continues** ses malheurs se poursuivent; **we continued on our way** nous avons poursuivi notre chemin, nous nous sommes remis en route; **the path continues on down to the river** le chemin continue jusqu'à la rivière; **to continue with a treatment** continuer un traitement

(**b**) *(resume)* reprendre; **the talks will continue today** les entretiens reprendront aujourd'hui

2 *vt* (**a**) *(carry on → education, work, activity)* poursuivre, continuer; *(→ tradition)* perpétuer, continuer; *(→ journey)* poursuivre; *(→ conversation, treatment)* continuer; **to continue to do sth** *or* **doing sth** continuer à faire qch

(**b**) *(resume → conversation, performance, talks)* reprendre, continuer; **"furthermore", he continued...** "de plus", continua-t-il...; **to be continued** *(TV programme, serialized story)* à suivre; **continued on the next page** suite à la page suivante

continuing [kən'tɪnjuːɪŋ] *adj* continu; *(interest)* soutenu; **the continuing story of a small American town** *(TV serial)* l'histoire *f* d'une petite ville américaine

►► ***continuing education*** formation *f* permanente *ou* continue; ***continuing education class*** cours *mpl* de formation permanente *ou* continue

continuity [ˌkɒntɪ'nju:ətɪ] (*pl* **continuities**) **1** *n* (**a**) *(cohesion)* continuité *f* (**b**) *Cin & TV* continuité *f*
2 *comp Cin & TV (department, studio)* pour raccords
►► *TV & Rad* ***continuity announcement*** annonce *f* de continuité; *TV & Rad* ***continuity announcer*** speaker(ine) *m,f* (de transition); *Cin & TV* ***continuity girl*** scripte *f*; *Cin & TV* ***continuity man*** scripte *m*

continuo [kən'tɪnjʊəʊ] (*pl* **continuos**) *n Mus* continuo *m*

continuous [kən'tɪnjʊəs] *adj* (**a**) *(uninterrupted → noise, process)* continu, ininterrompu
(**b**) *(unbroken → line)* continu
(**c**) *Gram (tense)* continu
►► *Sch & Univ* ***continuous assessment*** contrôle *m* continu; *Acct* ***continuous budget*** budget *m* renouvelable; *Comput* ***continuous mode*** mode *m* continu; *Comput* ***continuous paper*** papier *m* en continu; *Cin* ***continuous performances*** spectacle *m* permanent; *Art* ***continuous representation*** = représentation des différentes étapes d'une histoire en un seul tableau; *Comput* ***continuous stationery*** papier *m* en continu

continuously [kən'tɪnjʊəslɪ] *adv* continuellement, sans arrêt
►► *Aut* ***continuously variable transmission*** transmission *f* à réglage continu, transmission *f* CVT

continuum [kən'tɪnjʊəm] (*pl* **continuums** *or* **continua** [-njʊə]) *n* continuum *m*

contort [kən'tɔ:t] **1** *vt (body, features)* tordre; **face contorted by pain** visage tordu par la douleur
2 *vi* **his face contorted with rage/pain** il grimaçait de rage/de douleur

contorted [kən'tɔ:tɪd] *adj (body, features)* tordu, crispé

contortion [kən'tɔ:ʃən] *n (of body)* contorsion *f*; *(of features)* crispation *f*; *Fig* **he went through all sorts of contortions to justify this decision** il a fait des pieds et des mains pour justifier cette décision

contortionist [kən'tɔ:ʃənɪst] *n* contorsionniste *mf*, homme *m* caoutchouc; *Fam* **you have to be a contortionist to get into this car!** il faut faire toute une gymnastique *ou* tout un tas de contorsions pour monter dans cette voiture; *Fig* **verbal contortionist** virtuose *mf* de la rhétorique

contour ['kɒntʊə(r)] **1** *n* (**a**) *(line)* contour *m* (**b**) *(contour line)* courbe *f* de niveau (**c**) *(shape → of body, car)* contour *m*; **the contours of the hill** les contours *mpl* de la colline
2 *vt* (**a**) *(map)* tracer les courbes de niveaux sur (**b**) *(shape → dress, car)* tracer les contours de
►► ***contour line*** courbe *f* de niveau; ***contour map*** carte *f* topographique

Contra ['kɒntrə] *n Pol (Nicaraguan)* contra *mf*

contra ['kɒntrə] *Acct* **1** *n* **per contra** par contre; **as per contra** en contrepartie, porté ci-contre
2 *vt* contrepasser
►► ***contra account*** compte *m* de contrepartie *ou* d'autre part; ***contra entry*** article *m ou* écriture *f* inverse, contre-passation *f*

contra- ['kɒntrə] *pref* (**a**) *(opposing)* contre-, contra- (**b**) *Mus* contra-

contraband ['kɒntrəbænd] **1** *n (UNCOUNT)* (**a**) *(smuggling)* contrebande *f* (**b**) *(smuggled goods)* (marchandises *fpl* de) contrebande *f*
2 *adj (activities, goods)* de contrebande

contrabass ['kɒntrəbeɪs] *n Mus* contrebasse *f*

contrabassoon [ˌkɒntrəbə'su:n] *n Mus* contrebasson *m*

contraception [ˌkɒntrə'sepʃən] *n* contraception *f*

contraceptive [ˌkɒntrə'septɪv] **1** *n* contraceptif *m*
2 *adj (device, method)* contraceptif
►► ***contraceptive advice*** conseils *mpl* sur la contraception; ***contraceptive pill*** pilule *f* contraceptive; ***contraceptive sponge*** éponge *f* contraceptive

contract 1 *n* ['kɒntrækt] (**a**) *Com & Fin (agreement)* contrat *m*, convention *f*; *(to supply goods, services)* soumission *f*, adjudication *f*; *(document)* contrat *m*; **to draw up a contract** dresser *ou* rédiger un contrat; **to sign a contract** signer un contrat; **to be under contract** être sous contrat, avoir un contrat; **to put work out to contract** sous-traiter du travail; **they were given the contract to build the new road** ils se sont vu attribuer le contrat pour construire la nouvelle route; *Fam* **to put out a contract on sb** mettre la tête de qn à prix; **contract of employment** contrat *m* de travail; **the police suspect it was a contract killing** la police soupçonne que c'est le travail d'un tueur à gages
(**b**) *Cards (contract bridge)* bridge *m* contrat
2 *comp* ['kɒntrækt] *(work)* à forfait, contractuel
3 *vt* [kən'trækt] (**a**) *Formal (agree)* **to contract (with sb) to do sth** s'engager par contrat à faire qch; **she has contracted to make two films** elle a signé un contrat pour faire deux films
(**b**) *Formal (agree to → alliance, marriage)* contracter
(**c**) *(acquire → disease, illness, debt)* contracter
(**d**) *(make tense → features)* crisper; *Physiol (→ muscle)* contracter; *(→ tissues)* resserrer
(**e**) *Ling (vowel, word)* contracter
4 *vi* [kən'trækt] (**a**) *(metal)* se contracter; *(opening, material)* rétrécir, se contracter; **the pupil contracts in bright light** la pupille se contracte à la lumière intense
(**b**) *Physiol (muscle, pupil)* se contracter; *(tissues)* se resserrer
(**c**) *Ling (vowel, word)* se contracter; **"cannot" contracts into "can't"** "cannot" se contracte en "can't"
(**d**) *Com* **to contract for a supply of sth** s'engager à fournir qch; **to contract for work** entreprendre des travaux à forfait
►► *St Exch* ***contract bond*** garantie *f* d'exécution; *Cards* ***contract bridge*** bridge *m* contrat; ***contract killer*** tueur *m* à gages; ***contract labour*** main-d'œuvre *f* contractuelle; ***contract law*** droit *m* des contrats; *St Exch* ***contract note*** avis *m* d'exécution, avis *m* d'opération sur titre; ***contract staff*** personnel *m* en contrat à durée déterminée *ou* en CDD; *(in public sector)* contractuels *mpl*

►**contract in** *vi Br Com* s'engager (par contrat préalable)

►**contract out 1** *vt sep Com (work)* sous-traiter
2 *vi Br* **to contract out of sth** cesser de cotiser à qch

contract-awarding party *n Com* adjudicateur *m*

contractile [kən'træktaɪl] *adj* contractile, de contraction

contracting [kən'træktɪŋ] *adj*
►► ***contracting company*** *(party to a contract)* contractant *m*; *(sub-contractor)* sous-traitant *m*; *Com & Fin* ***contracting parties*** contractants *mpl*

contraction [kən'trækʃən] *n* (**a**) *(shrinkage → of metal)* contraction *f*; *(→ of opening, material)* rétrécissement *m*
(**b**) *Physiol (of muscle, pupil)* contraction; *(of tissues)* resserrement *m*
(**c**) *Ling (of vowel, word)* contraction *f*; *(word)* mot *m* contracté; *(short form of word)* contraction *f*, forme *f* contractée; **"haven't" is a contraction of "have not"** "haven't" est une forme contractée de "have not"
(**d**) *Obst (in childbirth)* contraction *f*

contractor [kən'træktə(r)] *n* (**a**) *(firm of builders)* entrepreneur *m* (en bâtiment); *(building worker)* ouvrier *m* en bâtiment; **the contractors haven't finished yet** les ouvriers n'ont pas encore fini (**b**) *Com (company, supplier)* **haulage contractor** entreprise *f* de transports; **arms contractor** fournisseur *m* d'armement (**c**) *Law (party to a contract)* entrepreneur *m*

contractual [kən'træktʃʊəl] *adj Com & Fin (agreement, obligation)* contractuel; **on the present contractual basis** selon les stipulations actuelles du contrat
►► *Acct* ***contractual allowance*** indemnité *f* conventionnelle; *Ins* ***contractual cover*** garantie *f* conventionnelle; *Com & Fin* ***contractual date*** date *f* contractuelle; *Com & Fin* ***contractual guarantee*** garantie *f* contractuelle; *Com & Fin* ***contractual liability*** responsabilité *f* contractuelle; *Com & Fin* ***contractual price*** prix *m* contractuel

contractually [kən'træktʃʊəlɪ] *adv (binding, obliged)* par contrat; **I'm contractually forbidden to...** le contrat m'interdit de...

contradict [ˌkɒntrə'dɪkt] *vt* (**a**) *(challenge → person, statement)* contredire; **she hates being contradicted** elle déteste qu'on la contredise; **to contradict oneself** se contredire; **don't contradict me!** ne me contredisez pas! (**b**) *(conflict with → of facts, stories)* contredire; **the statements of the witnesses contradict each other** les dépositions des témoins se contredisent

contradiction [ˌkɒntrə'dɪkʃən] *n* (**a**) *(inconsistency)* contradiction *f*; **he's full of contradictions** il est plein de contradictions; **in contradiction with** en désaccord avec (**b**) *(conflicting statement)* démenti *m*, contradiction *f*; **this was a contradiction of what they had previously said** c'était un démenti de ce qu'ils avaient dit auparavant; **a contradiction in terms** une contradiction dans les termes

contradictorily [ˌkɒntrə'dɪktərəlɪ] *adv* contradictoirement; *(say, remark)* d'un ton de contradiction

contradictoriness [ˌkɒntrə'dɪktərɪnɪs] *n* (**a**) *(of statements, stories)* contradiction *f* (**b**) *(of person)* esprit *m* de contradiction

contradictory [ˌkɒntrə'dɪktərɪ] *adj* (**a**) *(statements, stories)* contradictoire, opposé (**b**) *(person)* qui a l'esprit de contradiction

contradistinction [ˌkɒntrədɪ'stɪŋkʃən] *n Formal* opposition *f*, contraste *m*; **in contradistinction to** par opposition à, par contraste avec

contradistinguish [ˌkɒntrədɪs'tɪŋgwɪʃ] *vt Literary* distinguer (**from** de)

contraflow ['kɒntrəˌfləʊ] *n Br Transp* circulation *f* à contre-courant
►► ***contraflow system*** système *m* de circulation à contre-sens

contrail ['kɒntreɪl] *n Phys* traînée *f* de condensation

contra-indicate *vt Med* contre-indiquer

contra-indication *n Med* contre-indication *f*

contralto [kən'træltəʊ] (*pl* **contraltos**) *Mus* **1** *n (voice)* contralto *m*; *(singer)* contralto *mf*
2 *adj (part, voice)* de contralto

contraposition [ˌkɒntrəpə'zɪʃən] *n* opposition *f*, antithèse *f*

contraption [kən'træpʃən] *n Fam* engin *m*, truc *m*

contrapuntal [ˌkɒntrə'pʌntəl] *adj Mus* en contrepoint, contrapuntique

contrarily *adv* (**a**) [*Br* kən'treərɪlɪ, *Am* kɒn'trerəlɪ] *(obstinately)* par esprit de contradiction (**b**) [*Br* 'kɒntrərɪlɪ, *Am* kɒn'trerəlɪ] *(on the other hand)* contrairement

contrariness [kən'treərɪnɪs] *n (obstinacy)* esprit *m* de contradiction

contrariwise *adv* (**a**) ['kɒntrərɪˌwaɪz] *(on the other hand)* d'autre part, en revanche (**b**) ['kɒntrərɪˌwaɪz] *(in the opposite direction)* en sens opposé (**c**) [kən'treərɪwaɪz] *(perversely)* par esprit de contradiction

contrary 1 *n* ['kɒntrərɪ] contraire *m*
2 *adj* (**a**) ['kɒntrərɪ] *(opposed → attitudes, ideas, opinions)* contraire, en opposition (**to** à)
(**b**) [kən'treərɪ] *(obstinate → attitude, person)* contrariant
(**c**) ['kɒntrərɪ] *Formal (winds)* contraire
3 contrary to *prep* ['kɒntrərɪ] contrairement à; **contrary to nature** contre nature; **contrary to reason** contraire à la raison; **contrary to the terms of the contract** contraire aux termes du contrat; **contrary to popular belief** contrairement à ce que l'on croit généralement; **contrary to what I had been told** contrairement à ce qu'on m'avait dit
4 on the contrary *adv* ['kɒntrərɪ] au contraire
5 to the contrary *adv* ['kɒntrərɪ] **the meeting will be at six, unless you hear to the contrary** la réunion sera à six heures, sauf contrordre *ou* avis contraire

contrast 1 *vt* [kən'trɑ:st] contraster, mettre en contraste; **to contrast sb/sth with, to contrast sb/sth to** mettre qn/qch en contraste avec
2 *vi* [kən'trɑ:st] contraster, trancher; **to contrast with sth** contraster avec qch
3 *n* ['kɒntrɑ:st] (**a**) *(difference)* contraste *m*; *(person, thing)* contraste *m*; **as a contrast to...** comme contraste à...; **there is a marked contrast between his public and his private life** il y a un contraste frappant entre sa vie d'homme public et sa vie privée; **life in Africa was a complete contrast to life in Europe** la vie en Afrique présentait un contraste total avec la vie en Europe; **her response was in stark contrast**

to the government's sa réponse était en contraste absolu avec celle du gouvernement

(**b**) *Art, Phot & TV* contraste *m*

4 by contrast, in contrast ['kɒntrɑːst] *adv* par contraste

5 in contrast with, in contrast to ['kɒntrɑːst] *prep* par opposition à, par contraste avec

►► *Phot & TV* ***contrast button*** bouton *m* de contraste

contrasting [kən'trɑːstɪŋ], **contrastive** [kən'trɑːstɪv] *adj (attitudes, lifestyles, responses)* qui fait contraste; *(colours)* opposé, contrasté

contrasty ['kɒntrɑːstɪ] *adj Phot* contrasté

contravene [,kɒntrə'viːn] *vt* (**a**) *(infringe → law, rule)* transgresser, enfreindre, violer (**b**) *(dispute → statement)* nier, opposer un démenti à

contravention [,kɒntrə'venʃən] *n* infraction *f*, violation *f*; **what he did was in contravention of the law/regulations** ce qu'il a fait constitue une infraction par rapport à la loi/au règlement

contretemps ['kɒntrətɑ̃] *n (slight disagreement)* malentendu *m*; *(mishap)* contretemps *m*

contribute [kən'trɪbjuːt] **1** *vt (give → money)* donner; *(→ article, poem)* écrire; *(→ ideas)* apporter (**to** à); **the government will contribute a further two million pounds** le gouvernement ajoutera deux millions de livres à sa contribution; *Fin* **she contributes 10 percent of her salary to the pension scheme** elle verse 10 pour cent de son salaire dans son plan de retraite; **they contributed their ideas and enthusiasm to the project** ils ont apporté leurs idées et leur enthousiasme au projet

2 *vi* (**a**) *(donate money)* contribuer; **we ask everyone to contribute generously** nous demandons à chacun de contribuer généreusement; **to contribute to a charity** donner à une association caritative

(**b**) *(give)* donner; **she still has a lot to contribute to her family** elle a encore beaucoup à apporter à sa famille; **he rarely contributes to discussions** il contribue rarement aux discussions

(**c**) *(influence)* **to contribute to sth** contribuer à qch; **to contribute to the success of sth** contribuer au succès de qch

(**d**) *(journalist, author)* **to contribute to a newspaper/magazine** écrire pour un journal/un magazine; **she contributes to various literary magazines** elle écrit pour divers magazines littéraires

(**e**) *Fin (to pension scheme)* cotiser (**to** à)

contributing [kən'trɪbjuːtɪŋ] *adj* **to be a contributing factor in** *or* **to** contribuer à; **alcohol abuse was a contributing factor to his death/dismissal** son alcoolisme a contribué à sa mort/à le faire licencier

contribution [,kɒntrɪ'bjuːʃən] *n* (**a**) *(of money, goods)* contribution *f*, cotisation *f*; *(of ideas, enthusiasm)* apport *m*; **I've already made a contribution** j'ai déjà donné; **he made a valuable contribution to the project** il a apporté une collaboration précieuse au projet; **we encourage the contribution of regular sums of money to charity** nous encourageons les versements d'argent réguliers à des œuvres de charité; **the chocolate mousse was David's contribution** c'est David qu'il faut remercier pour la mousse au chocolat

(**b**) *(article)* article *m (écrit pour un journal)*

(**c**) *Fin (to pension scheme, National Insurance)* cotisation *f*; **employer's and employee's contributions** cotisations *fpl* patronales et ouvrières

(**d**) *Acct (in management accounting)* marge *f* (brute); **contribution in kind** apport *m* en nature

(**e**) *St Exch (to share capital)* apport *m*

►► *Acct* ***contribution margin*** marge *f* sur les coûts variables

contributor [kən'trɪbjʊtə(r)] *n* (**a**) *(of money, goods)* donateur(trice) *m,f* (**b**) *(to magazine)* collaborateur(trice) *m,f* (**c**) *(factor)* facteur *m*

contributory [kən'trɪbjʊtərɪ] (*pl* **contributories**) **1** *adj (cause, factor)* contribuant, qui contribue; **to be a contributory factor in sth** contribuer à qch; **the weather may have had a contributory effect, but...** le temps a peut-être joué un rôle mais...

2 *n St Exch* = actionnaire qui doit contribuer au paiement des dettes

►► *Law* ***contributory negligence*** imprudence *f*, faute *f (avant un accident)*; *Fin* ***contributory pension plan, contributory pension scheme*** système *m* de retraite par répartition

contrite [kən'traɪt] *adj (face, look)* contrit, repentant; **to look/be contrite** avoir un air/être contrit

contritely [kən'traɪtlɪ] *adv* d'un air contrit, avec contrition

contrition [kən'trɪʃən] *n* contrition *f*, pénitence *f*

contrivance [kən'traɪvəns] *n* (**a**) *(contraption)* dispositif *m*, mécanisme *m* (**b**) *(scheme)* manigance *f* (**c**) *(invention → of scheme)* invention *f*; **I was fairly sure the scheme was of George's contrivance** j'étais presque certain que c'était un stratagème de George

contrive [kən'traɪv] **1** *vt* (**a**) *(engineer → meeting)* combiner (**b**) *(invent → device, machine)* inventer, imaginer

2 *vi* **to contrive to do sth** trouver le moyen de faire qch; **she contrived to confuse matters still further** elle a réussi à embrouiller encore plus les choses

contrived [kən'traɪvd] *adj* (**a**) *(deliberate)* délibéré, arrangé (**b**) *(artificial)* forcé, peu naturel

CONTROL [kən'trəʊl]

direction	► **1 (a)**
contrôle	► **1 (a), (b), (e), (f)**
maîtrise	► **1 (a)**
témoin	► **1 (d)**
douane	► **1 (e)**
diriger	► **3 (a)**
contrôler	► **3 (a), (c), (d)**
régler	► **3 (b)**
maîtriser	► **3 (c)**

1 *n* (**a**) *(of country, organization)* direction *f*; *(of car, machine)* contrôle *m*; *(of one's life)* maîtrise *f*; *(of oneself)* maîtrise *f* (de soi); *Sport (of ball)* contrôle *m*; **to have control of** *or* **over sb** avoir de l'autorité sur qn; **to have control of** *or* **over sth** avoir le contrôle de qch; **to gain control of sth** prendre le contrôle de qch; **the rebels have gained control of the capital** les rebelles ont pris le contrôle de la capitale; **to be in control of sth** être maître de qch; **to lose control of** *(car)* perdre le contrôle de; *(situation)* ne plus être maître de; **to lose control (of oneself)** ne plus être maître de soi; **to regain control of oneself** se ressaisir; **the situation is under control** nous maîtrisons la situation; **everything's under control** *(organized, in hand)* tout est en bonne voie; *(there's no need to panic)* tout va bien; **to keep sth under control** maîtriser qch; **dogs must be kept under control** les chiens doivent être tenus en laisse; **the fire was finally brought under control** l'incendie fut finalement maîtrisé; **public spending is under the control of our department** le budget national relève de notre département; **the country is no longer under British/government control** le pays n'est plus sous contrôle britannique/gouvernemental; **beyond** *or* **outside one's control** indépendant de sa volonté; **due to circumstances beyond our control** en raison de circonstances indépendantes de notre volonté; **the fire was out of control** on n'arrivait pas à maîtriser l'incendie; **the car went out of control** le chauffeur a perdu le contrôle de sa voiture; **things/the situation had got out of control** la situation était devenue incontrôlable; **the crowd got out of control** la foule s'est déchaînée; **her children are completely out of control** ses enfants sont intenables

(**b**) *(check)* contrôle *m*

(**c**) *(device)* **volume control** réglage *m* du volume; **controls** *(on car, aircraft, machine)* commandes *fpl*; **the pilot was at the controls/took over the controls** le pilote était aux commandes/a pris les commandes

(**d**) *(in experiment)* témoin *m*

(**e**) *(checkpoint → at border)* douane *f*; *(→ in car rally)* contrôle *m*; **passport and custom controls** formalités *fpl* de douane

(**f**) *(restraint)* contrôle *m*; **price/wage controls** contrôle *m* des prix/des salaires; **immigration controls** contrôle *m* de l'immigration; **there are to be new government controls on financial practices** il y aura de nouvelles réglementations gouvernementales sur les pratiques financières

2 *comp (button, switch)* de commande, de réglage

3 *vt* (**a**) *(be in charge of, direct → government, organization)* diriger; *Mil (→ area)* contrôler

(**b**) *(regulate → machine, system)* régler; *(→ traffic)* régler; **this switch controls the central heating** ce commutateur règle *ou* commande le chauffage central

(**c**) *(curb → inflation, prices, spending, fire)* maîtriser; *(→ imports)* limiter; *(→ disease)* enrayer, juguler; *(master, restrain → activities, emotions)* maîtriser; *(→ one's passions)* dompter; *(→ one's reactions)* contrôler, maîtriser; *(→ animal, pupil)* tenir, se faire obéir de; *(→ crowd)* contenir; **try to control yourself** essaie de te contrôler *ou* maîtriser; **she could barely control her anger** elle avait du mal à maîtriser sa colère; **he can't control his pupils** il ne tient pas ses élèves, il manque d'autorité sur ses élèves

(**d**) *(verify → accounts)* contrôler; *(→ experiment)* vérifier

►► *Fin* ***control account*** compte *m* collectif; *Comput* ***control bit*** bit *m* de contrôle; *Aut* ***control box*** régulateur *m* de charge; *Comput* ***control bus*** bus *m* de contrôle; *Comput* ***control character*** caractère *m* de contrôle; *Comput* ***control code*** code *m* de commande; ***control column*** manche *m* à balai; ***control commands*** commandes *fpl*; *Fin* ***control commission*** commission *f* de contrôle; ***control desk*** bureau *m* de contrôle; ***control experiment*** expérience *f* de contrôle; ***control freak*** personne *f* qui veut tout contrôler; ***control freakery*** manie *f* de vouloir tout contrôler; *Tech* ***control gear*** appareils *mpl ou* organes *mpl* de commande; ***control group*** groupe *m* témoin; *Comput* ***control key*** touche *f* contrôle; *Comput* ***control knob*** molette *f* de réglage; *Mktg* ***control market*** marché *m* témoin; ***control panel*** *Aviat* tableau *m* de bord; *Comput* panneau *m* de configuration; *Sport & Aut* ***control point*** contrôle *m*; *Comput* ***control program*** programme *m* de contrôle; *Mktg* ***control question*** *(in market research)* question *f* de contrôle; *Nucl* ***control rod*** barre *f* de commande; ***control room*** salle *f* des commandes; *Naut* poste *m* de commande; *Rad & TV* (cabine *f* de) régie *f*; ***control tower*** tour *f* de contrôle

controllable [kən'trəʊləbəl] *adj (animal, person, crowd)* discipliné; *(emotions, situation)* maîtrisable; *(expenditure, inflation, costs, mechanism)* contrôlable; *(speed, heat, brightness)* réglable; **if you find that the class is just not controllable** si vous trouvez que la classe est vraiment intenable; **the spread of the disease is controllable** la progression de la maladie peut être maîtrisée *ou* enrayée; **the more easily controllable aspects of the project** les aspects du projet les plus faciles à contrôler

►► *Acct* ***controllable costs*** coûts *mpl* maîtrisables

controlled [kən'trəʊld] *adj (emotions, voice)* contenu; *(person)* calme; *(market)* réglementé; *(experiment)* contrôlé; *Med (diabetes etc)* équilibré; **she remained very controlled** elle est restée très calme

►► *Econ* ***controlled economy*** économie *f* dirigée *ou* planifiée; ***controlled explosion*** neutralisation *f (d'un explosif)*; **the bomb was let off in a controlled explosion** la bombe a été neutralisée; *Econ* ***controlled price*** taxe *f*; **to sell goods at the controlled price** vendre des marchandises à la taxe; *Br* ***controlled school*** = école privée financée par l'État et qui n'a aucun pouvoir de décision quant aux cours d'instruction religieuse; ***controlled substance*** substance *f* réglementée

controller [kən'trəʊlə(r)] *n* (**a**) *(person in charge)* responsable *m*; **the new Controller of BBC1** le nouveau responsable de BBC1 (**b**) *(accountant)* contrôleur *m*; *Fin* **controller in bankruptcy** contrôleur *m* aux liquidations (**c**) *Comput* contrôleur *m*

controlling [kən'trəʊlɪŋ] *adj (power)* dirigeant; *(factor)* déterminant

►► *Fin* ***controlling interest*** participation *f*

majoritaire; **they now have a controlling interest in the company** à présent, ils ont une participation majoritaire dans cette société

controversial [ˌkɒntrə'vɜːʃəl] *adj (book, film, issue, subject)* controversé; *(decision, speech)* sujet à controverse; *(person)* controversé; **he's trying to be controversial** il cherche la controverse; **I only said that to be controversial** je n'ai dit cela que pour provoquer la controverse

controversially [ˌkɒntrə'vɜːʃəlɪ] *adv* **Owen has been controversially omitted from the England team** Owen n'a pas été sélectionné pour l'équipe d'Angleterre, ce qui a donné lieu à une controverse; **even more controversially, it is now forbidden to receive personal phone calls** plus discutable encore, il est maintenant interdit de recevoir des appels personnels

controversy ['kɒntrəˌvɜːsɪ, *Br* kən'trɒvəsɪ] *n* controverse *f*, polémique *f*; **to be the subject of controversy** être sujet à controverse; **her speech caused a lot of controversy** son discours a provoqué beaucoup de controverses; **a major controversy is brewing over unemployment** un grand scandale se prépare autour du chômage

controvert ['kɒntrəˌvɜːt] *vt Formal* controverser

contumacious [ˌkɒntjuː'meɪʃəs] *adj Literary* insubordonné

contumacy ['kɒntjʊməsɪ] *n* (**a**) *Literary (disobedience)* insubordination *f* (**b**) *Law* contumace *f*

contumelious [ˌkɒntjuː'miːljəs] *adj Literary* insolant, méprisant

contumely ['kɒntjuːmlɪ] *n Literary (language)* insolence *f*; *(insult)* offense *f*

contuse [kən'tjuːz] *vt Med* contusionner; **contused wound** plaie *f* contuse

contusion [kən'tjuːʒən] *n Med* contusion *f*

conundrum [kə'nʌndrəm] *n* (**a**) *(riddle)* devinette *f*, énigme *f* (**b**) *(problem)* énigme *f*

conurbation [ˌkɒnɜː'beɪʃən] *n* conurbation *f*

convalesce [ˌkɒnvə'les] *vi* se remettre *(d'une maladie)*; **she's convalescing from a bad bout of flu** elle se remet d'une mauvaise grippe

convalescence [ˌkɒnvə'lesəns] *n (return to health)* rétablissement *m*; *(period of recovery)* convalescence *f*

convalescent [ˌkɒnvə'lesənt] **1** *n* convalescent(e) *m,f*

2 *adj* convalescent

►► ***convalescent home*** maison *f* de convalescence *ou* de repos

convection [kən'vekʃən] *Geol, Met & Phys* **1** *n* convection *f*

2 *comp (heating)* à convection; *(current)* de convection

convector [kən'vektə(r)] *n* radiateur *m* à convection, convecteur *m*

►► ***convector heater*** radiateur *m* à convection, convecteur *m*

convene [kən'viːn] **1** *vt (conference, meeting)* convoquer

2 *vi (board, jury, members)* se réunir

convener [kən'viːnə(r)] *n* (**a**) *Br Ind (in trade union)* = secrétaire des délégués syndicaux (**b**) *(of meeting)* président(e) *m,f*

convenience [kən'viːnjəns] *n* (**a**) *(ease of use)* commodité *f*; *(benefit)* avantage *m*; **for convenience, for convenience's sake** par commodité; **a bus service is provided for our customers' convenience** un service d'autobus est à la disposition de nos clients; **our customers can now enjoy the convenience of on-site parking** nous offrons désormais à notre clientèle la commodité d'un parking attenant; *Formal* **at your earliest convenience** dans les meilleurs délais; **at your convenience** quand cela vous conviendra

(**b**) *(facility)* commodités *fpl*, confort *m*; **the house has every modern convenience** la maison a tout le confort moderne

(**c**) *Br Formal Euph (lavatory)* toilettes *fpl*; **public conveniences** toilettes *fpl* publiques

►► *Com* ***convenience brand*** marque *f* pratique; ***convenience food*** aliment *m* prêt à consommer, plat *m* cuisiné; *Com* ***convenience goods*** produits *mpl* d'achat courant, produits *mpl* de consommation courante; *Am* ***convenience store*** = supérette de quartier qui reste ouverte tard le soir, *Can* dépanneur *m*

convenient [kən'viːnjənt] *adj* (**a**) *(suitable)* commode; **when would be convenient for you?** quand cela vous arrangerait-il?; **this isn't a very convenient moment to talk** le moment n'est pas bien choisi pour parler

(**b**) *(handy)* pratique; **the house is very convenient for local shops and schools** la maison est très bien située pour les magasins et les écoles; **the bus stop's just round the corner – how convenient!** l'arrêt de bus se trouve juste au coin de la rue – c'est bien pratique!

(**c**) *(nearby)* **I grabbed a convenient chair and sat down** j'ai saisi la chaise la plus proche et me suis assis

conveniently [kən'viːnjəntlɪ] *adv* commodément; **the cottage is conveniently situated for the beach** le cottage est bien situé pour la plage; *Ironic* **they very conveniently forgot to enclose the cheque** comme par hasard, ils ont oublié de joindre le chèque

convening [kən'viːnɪŋ] **1** *adj (authority)* habilité à convoquer; *(country)* hôte

2 *n* convocation *f*

convenor = **convener**

convent ['kɒnvənt] **1** *n* (**a**) *Rel* couvent *m*; **to enter a convent** entrer au couvent (**b**) *(convent school)* école *f* tenue par des religieuses; **to have had a convent education** avoir été (à l'école) chez les religieuses

►► ***convent school*** école *f* tenue par des religieuses

convent-educated *adj* **she was convent-educated** elle a fait ses études chez les religieuses

convention [kən'venʃən] *n* (**a**) *(customs)* usage *m*, convenances *fpl*; **to defy convention** braver les usages; **according to convention** selon l'usage

(**b**) *(accepted usage)* convention *f*, usage *m*; **to observe the conventions** respecter les convenances; **social conventions** conventions *fpl* sociales; **there is a convention that Ministers do not answer such questions** l'usage est que les ministres ne répondent pas à ce genre de questions; **it's a common convention in the nineteenth-century novel** c'est une convention courante dans les romans du dix-neuvième siècle

(**c**) *(agreement)* convention *f*; **to sign a convention on sth** signer une convention sur qch

(**d**) *(meeting)* convention *f*, congrès *m*; *Am Pol* convention *f*; **medical convention** congrès *m* médical

►► ***convention centre*** palais *m* des congrès; ***Convention on International Trade in Endangered Species*** Convention *f* sur le commerce international des espèces de faune et de flora sauvages menacées d'extinction

conventional [kən'venʃənəl] *adj* (**a**) *(customary → behaviour, ideas, upbringing)* conventionnel; *(→ person)* conformiste; *(→ beauty, good looks)* classique; **conventional wisdom** sagesse *f* populaire; **conventional wisdom has it that...** d'aucuns disent que... (**b**) *(traditional → medicine, methods, art)* classique, traditionnel (**c**) *Mil (non-nuclear)* conventionnel

►► *Constr* ***conventional material*** matériau *m* traditionnel; *Comput* ***conventional memory*** mémoire *f* conventionnelle; ***conventional oven*** four *m* traditionnel *ou* classique; *Mil* ***conventional weapons*** armes *fpl* conventionnelles

conventionality [kənˌvenʃə'nælətɪ] *n* conformisme *m*

conventionally [kən'venʃənəlɪ] *adv* (**a**) *(in accepted fashion)* conventionnellement; **she's not conventionally beautiful** elle n'est pas d'une beauté classique (**b**) *(traditionally)* d'une manière classique

conventioneer [kənˌvenʃə'nɪə(r)] *n Am* participant(e) *m,f (à un congrès)*

converge [kən'vɜːdʒ] *vi* (**a**) *(merge → paths, lines)* converger; *(→ ideas, tendencies)* converger (**b**) *(groups, people)* se rassembler; **thousands of fans converged on the stadium** des milliers de fans se sont rassemblés sur le stade (**c**) *Math* converger

convergence [kən'vɜːdʒəns] *n* (**a**) *(of paths, lines)* convergence *f*; *(of ideas, tendencies)* convergence *f* (**b**) *Math* convergence *f*

convergent [kən'vɜːdʒənt], **converging** [kən'vɜːdʒɪŋ] *adj* (**a**) *(paths, tendencies)* convergent (**b**) *Math* convergent

►► *Opt* ***convergent lens*** lentille *f* convexe *ou* convergente; ***convergent thinking*** raisonnement *m* convergent

conversable [kən'vɜːsəbəl] *adj Literary (inclined to converse)* de bonne conversation; *(pleasant to talk to)* sociable

conversance [kən'vɜːsəns], **conversancy** [kən'vɜːsənsɪ] *n Literary* connaissance *f* (**with** de)

conversant [kən'vɜːsənt] *adj* **to be conversant with** *(language, regulations)* connaître; *(machinery, computers)* s'y connaître en; *(facts)* être au courant de; **we were expected to be fully conversant with colloquial French** nous étions censés avoir une connaissance parfaite du français familier

conversation [ˌkɒnvə'seɪʃən] *n* conversation *f*; **the art of conversation** l'art *m* de la conversation; **to hold** *or* **have a conversation with sb** avoir une conversation avec qn; **we had a long conversation about fishing** nous avons eu une longue conversation sur la pêche; **she was deep in conversation with my sister** elle était en grande conversation avec ma sœur; **a telephone conversation** une conversation téléphonique; **to get into conversation with sb** engager la conversation avec qn; **to make conversation** faire la conversation; **I'm not good at (making) conversation** je ne suis pas très doué pour faire la conversation; **she was just making conversation** elle parlait par politesse; **to run out of conversation** n'avoir plus rien à dire; *Fam* **conversation stopper** *or* **killer** remarque *f*/sujet *m* qui arrête net les conversations ❑; *Fam* **that was a real conversation stopper!** cela a arrêté net la conversation! ❑

►► ***conversation piece*** (**a**) *(unusual object)* = objet qui suscite bien des commentaires; **the vase is quite a conversation piece** le vase suscite bien des commentaires (**b**) *Theat (play)* = pièce au dialogue brillant; ***conversation skills*** l'art *m* de la conversation; **he has good/no conversation skills** il est doué/n'est pas doué pour la conversation

conversational [ˌkɒnvə'seɪʃənəl] *adj (tone, voice)* de la conversation; *(style)* familier; *Comput (mode)* dialogue; **conversational Spanish** espagnol *m* courant

conversationalist [ˌkɒnvə'seɪʃənəlɪst] *n* causeur(euse) *m,f*; **he's a brilliant conversationalist** il brille dans la conversation

conversationally [ˌkɒnvə'seɪʃənəlɪ] *adv (mention, say)* sur le ton de la conversation

converse **1** *vi* [kən'vɜːs] *Formal* converser; **to converse with sb** s'entretenir avec qn

2 *adj* ['kɒnvɜːs] *(opinion, statement, results)* contraire; *Math* réciproque

3 *n* ['kɒnvɜːs] (**a**) *(gen)* contraire *m*, inverse *m*; **I believe the converse to be true** je crois que l'inverse est vrai

(**b**) *Phil* (proposition *f*) converse *f*

(**c**) *Math* (proposition *f*) réciproque *f*

(**d**) *Formal or Literary* conversation *f*, entretien *m*; **to hold converse with sb** s'entretenir avec qn

conversely [kən'vɜːslɪ] *adv* inversement, réciproquement; **conversely, you can use the paint directly on the wood** inversement, vous pouvez utiliser la peinture directement sur le bois

conversion [kən'vɜːʃən] *n* (**a**) *(process)* conversion *f*, transformation *f*; **the conversion of water into wine** la transformation de l'eau en vin; **the conversion of a house into flats** l'aménagement *m ou* la transformation d'une maison en appartements

(**b**) *Math & Comput* conversion *f*

(**c**) *Rel (change of beliefs)* conversion *f*

(**d**) *Rugby* transformation *f*

(**e**) *(in converted building)* = appartement aménagé dans un ancien hôtel particulier, entrepôt, atelier etc

(**f**) *Law* conversion *f*

(**g**) *Fin (of bonds, securities, loan stock)* conversion *f*

►► *Acct* ***conversion cost*** coût *m* de transformation; *Fin* ***conversion issue*** émission *f* de conversion; *Fin* ***conversion loan*** emprunt *m* de conversion; *Fin* **conversion premium** prime *f* de conversion; *Fin* **conversion price** prix *m* de conversion; *Comput* **conversion program** programme *m* de conversion; *Fin* **conversion rate** taux *m* de conversion; *Comput* **conversion software** logiciel *m* de conversion; **conversion table** table *f* de conversion

convert 1 *vt* [kən'vɜːt] (**a**) *(building, car)* aménager, convertir; *(machine)* transformer; **to convert sth to** *or* **into sth** transformer *ou* convertir qch en qch; **the school was converted to house several workshops** l'école a été aménagée de façon à avoir plusieurs ateliers

(**b**) *Math & Comput* convertir; **how do you convert pints into litres?** comment convertir des pintes en litres?; **to convert pesetas into pounds** *(as calculation)* convertir des pesetas en livres; *(by exchanging money)* changer des pesetas en livres

(**c**) *Rel* convertir; **to convert sb to sth** convertir qn à qch; **to be converted to Christianity** se convertir au christianisme; *Fig* **she converted them to her way of thinking** elle les a amenés à voir les choses à sa manière

(**d**) *Sport* **to convert a try** *(in rugby)* transformer un essai

(**e**) *Law* convertir; **to convert funds to another purpose** affecter des fonds à un autre usage

(**f**) *Fin (bonds, securities, loan stock)* convertir

2 *vi* [kən'vɜːt] (**a**) *(vehicle, machine)* se convertir; **the settee converts into a bed** le canapé se transforme en lit

(**b**) *Rel* se convertir (**to** à); *Fig* **she converted to a belief in capitalism** elle s'est mise à croire au capitalisme

(**c**) *Sport (in rugby)* transformer l'essai/un essai

3 *n* ['kɒnvɜːt] (**a**) *(person)* converti(e) *m,f*; **to become a convert to sth** se convertir à qch; **to make a convert of sb** convertir qn; **she's made another convert** elle a encore converti quelqu'un; *Rel* **she's a convert to Catholicism** c'est une catholique convertie

(**b**) *Am Fin* obligation *f* convertible (en actions)

converted [kən'vɜːtɪd] *adj (factory, farmhouse, school etc)* aménagé, transformé

converter [kən'vɜːtə(r)] *n* (**a**) *Metal & Phys* convertisseur *m*; *Rad* modulateur *m* de fréquence; *Comput* convertisseur *m*; **steel converter** convertisseur *m* Bessemer (**b**) *Nucl (converter reactor)* réacteur *m* convertisseur

►► *Nucl* ***converter reactor*** réacteur *m* convertisseur

convertibility [kən,vɜːtə'bɪlətɪ] *n* (**a**) *(of money, currency)* convertibilité *f* (**b**) *(of building, machine)* convertibilité *f*

convertible [kən'vɜːtəbəl] **1** *adj* (**a**) *(money, currency)* convertible (**b**) *(machine, couch)* convertible (**c**) *(car)* décapotable (**d**) *Fin (bonds, securities, loan stock)* convertible

2 *n* (**a**) *(car)* décapotable *f* (**b**) *(money, currency)* monnaie *f* convertible

convertor = **converter**

convex [kɒn'veks] *adj Phys & Opt* convexe

convexity [kən'veksətɪ] *n Phys & Opt* convexité *f*

convey [kən'veɪ] *vt* (**a**) *Formal (transport)* transporter

(**b**) *(communicate)* transmettre; **to convey one's meaning** communiquer sa pensée; **I tried to convey to him the importance of the decision** j'ai essayé de lui faire comprendre l'importance de la décision; **no words can convey my gratitude** aucun mot ne peut traduire ma gratitude; **his writing conveys the mood of the country** sa manière d'écrire évoque l'atmosphère du pays; **please convey my thanks (to them)** veuillez leur transmettre mes remerciements

(**c**) *(of air → sound, smell)* transmettre

(**d**) *Law* transférer (**to** à)

conveyance [kən'veɪəns] *n* (**a**) *(transport)* transport *m* (**b**) *Old-fashioned (vehicle)* véhicule *m* (**c**) *Law (transfer of property)* cession *f*, transfert *m*; *(document)* acte *m* de cession

conveyancing [kən'veɪənsɪŋ] *n Law* (**a**) *(procedure)* procédure *f* translative de propriété (**b**) *(drawing up documents)* rédaction *f* des actes de cession *ou* des actes translatifs de propriété

conveyor [kən'veɪə(r)] *n* (**a**) *(transporter)* transporteur *m*; *Mining* convoyeur *m* (**b**) *(belt)* tapis *m* roulant; **bucket conveyor** transporteur *m* à godets (**c**) *Formal (person → of letter, parcel)* porteur(euse) *m,f*

►► ***conveyor belt*** tapis *m* roulant

convict 1 *vt* [kən'vɪkt] déclarer *ou* reconnaître coupable; **she was convicted** elle a été déclarée *ou* reconnue coupable; **to convict sb of** *or* **for sth** déclarer *ou* reconnaître qn coupable de qch; **you stand convicted by your own words** vos propres paroles vous condamnent

2 *n* ['kɒnvɪkt] *(convicted person)* détenu(e) *m,f*; *Old-fashioned (prisoner)* forçat *m*, bagnard *m*

3 *vi* [kən'vɪkt] rendre un verdict de culpabilité; **the jury is unlikely to convict** il est peu probable que le jury rende un verdict de culpabilité

convicted [kən'vɪktɪd] *adj (criminal)* reconnu coupable

conviction [kən'vɪkʃən] *n* (**a**) *(belief)* conviction *f*

(**b**) *(certainty)* certitude *f*, conviction *f*; **he lacks conviction** il manque de conviction; **"I suppose so", I said without much conviction** "je suppose", dis-je sans grande conviction

(**c**) *(plausibility)* **to carry conviction** *(voice, manner)* être convaincant; **the theory carries little conviction** la théorie est peu convaincante

(**d**) *Law* condamnation *f*; **the prosecution called for his conviction** la partie plaignante a demandé sa condamnation; **she has several previous convictions** elle a déjà été condamnée plusieurs fois

convince [kən'vɪns] *vt* convaincre, persuader; **to allow oneself to be convinced** se laisser convaincre; **his arguments don't convince me** ses arguments ne me convainquent pas; **to convince sb of sth** convaincre *ou* persuader qn de qch; **to convince sb to do sth** convaincre *ou* persuader qn de faire qch

convinced [kən'vɪnst] *adj* convaincu; **to be convinced of sth** être convaincu de qch; **to be convinced (that)...** être convaincu que... + *indicative*

convincing [kən'vɪnsɪŋ] *adj (argument, person, performance)* convaincant; *(victory, win)* décisif, éclatant; **she wasn't very convincing as Juliet** elle n'était pas convaincante dans le rôle de Juliette; **the battle scenes were very convincing** les scènes de bataille étaient très réalistes

convincingly [kən'vɪnsɪŋlɪ] *adv (argue, speak, pretend)* de façon convaincante; *(beat, win)* haut la main

convivial [kən'vɪvɪəl] *adj (atmosphere, lunch)* convivial, joyeux; *(manner, person)* joyeux, plein d'entrain

conviviality [kən,vɪvɪ'ælətɪ] *n* convivialité *f*, gaieté *f*, jovialité *f*

convivially [kən'vɪvɪəlɪ] *adv* convivialement, joyeusement

convocation [,kɒnvə'keɪʃən] *n* (**a**) *(summoning)* convocation *f* (**b**) *(meeting)* assemblée *f*, réunion *f*; *Br Rel* synode *m*

convoke [kən'vəʊk] *vt (assembly, meeting)* convoquer

convoluted ['kɒnvə,luːtɪd] *adj (shape)* convoluté; *(prose, reasoning, argument)* alambiqué

convolution [,kɒnvə'luːʃən] *n Formal* (**a**) *(complication → of prose, reasoning, argument)* méandre *f* (**b**) *(twist)* circonvolution *f* (**c**) *Anat (of brain)* circonvolution *f*

convolvulus [kən'vɒlvjʊləs] *(pl* **convolvuluses** *or* **convolvuli** [-laɪ]) *n Bot* liseron *m*

convoy ['kɒnvɔɪ] **1** *n* convoi *m*; **to travel in convoy** voyager en convoi

2 *vt* convoyer, escorter

convulsant [kən'vʌlsənt] *Med* **1** *adj (drug)* convulsivant

2 *n* convulsivant *m*

convulse [kən'vʌls] **1** *vt* (**a**) *(person)* secouer; *Fig (someone's life)* bouleverser; **the scene convulsed the audience** la scène a fait tordre de rire toute la salle (**b**) *Med (muscle)* convulsionner

2 *vi Med (person)* avoir des convulsions; *(face, lungs, muscle)* se convulser, se contracter, se crisper

convulsed [kən'vʌlst] *adj* **he was convulsed with pain** il se tordait de douleur; **the audience were convulsed with laughter** l'auditoire se tordait de rire

convulsion [kən'vʌlʃən] *n* (**a**) *Med* convulsion *f*; **to have convulsions** avoir des convulsions; *Fam* **to be in convulsions** *(laughing)* se tordre de rire (**b**) *(revolution, war)* bouleversement *m*; *(earthquake)* secousse *f*; *Fig* **political convulsions** bouleversements *mpl* politiques

convulsive [kən'vʌlsɪv] *adj* (**a**) *Med (movement)* convulsif (**b**) *(transition)* brutal; **the most convulsive years in the country's history** les années les plus agitées dans l'histoire du pays

convulsively [kən'vʌlsɪvlɪ] *adv Med* convulsivement

cony ['kəʊnɪ] *(pl* **conies**) **1** *n (rabbit)* lapin *m*; *(rabbit fur)* lapin *m*

2 *comp (skin)* de lapin

coo [kuː] *(pl* **coos**) **1** *n* roucoulement *m*

2 *vi (dove, pigeon)* roucouler; *(baby, person)* babiller, gazouiller; **the neighbours came to coo over the baby** les voisins sont venus s'extasier sur le bébé

3 *vt (endearments, sweet nothings)* roucouler

4 *exclam Fam Old-fashioned* ça alors!

cooee, cooey ['kuːɪ] **1** *exclam Br Fam* coucou!

2 *n Austr & NZ* **to be within cooee of** être à portée de voix de

cooing ['kuːɪŋ] *n (of dove, pigeon)* roucoulement *m*; *(of baby, person)* gazouillement *m*

cook [kʊk] **1** *n* cuisinier(ère) *m,f*; **she's an excellent cook** c'est une excellente cuisinière; *Fam* **chief** *or* **head cook and bottle-washer** bonne *f* à tout faire; *Prov* **too many cooks spoil the broth** = si tout le monde met son grain de sel, on n'arrive à rien

2 *vt* (**a**) *(meal)* faire, préparer; *(food, meat)* (faire) cuire; **the meat should be cooked all the way through** la viande doit être bien cuite; *Fam* **to cook sb's goose** mettre qn dans le pétrin; *Fam* **this time, your goose is cooked!** cette fois-ci, tu ne t'en sortira pas!

(**b**) *Br Fam* **to cook the accounts** *or* **the books** falsifier *ou* truquer les comptes

(**c**) *Fam Drugs slang* **to cook a shot** préparer un shoot d'héroïne

3 *vi (person)* cuisiner, faire la cuisine; *(food)* cuire; **can you cook?** est-ce que tu sais faire la cuisine?; **he cooks well** il cuisine bien; **it cooks in five minutes** ça cuit en cinq minutes; *Fam* **what's cooking?** qu'est-ce qui se mijote?; *Fam Fig* **now we're cooking**, *Br* **now we're cooking with gas!** maintenant tout marche comme sur des roulettes!

►**cook out** *vi Am Fam* faire un barbecue

►**cook up 1** *vt sep* (**a**) *Fam (plan)* mijoter; *(excuse, story)* inventer ❑ (**b**) *Fam Drugs slang (heroin)* préparer un shoot de

2 *vi Fam Drugs slang (heat heroin)* préparer un shoot d'héroïne

cookbook ['kʊkbʊk] *n* livre *m* de cuisine

cook-chill *adj* cuisiné (et réfrigéré)

cooked [kʊkt] *adj (food, meat)* cuit; **I always have a cooked meal in the evening** je mange toujours un repas chaud le soir; *Br* **cooked breakfast** petit déjeuner *m* anglais

cooker ['kʊkə(r)] *n Br* (**a**) *(stove)* cuisinière *f*; **gas/electric cooker** cuisinière *f* à gaz/électrique (**b**) *Br Fam (apple)* pomme *f* à cuire ❑

cookery ['kʊkərɪ] *n* cuisine *f*

►► ***cookery book*** livre *m* de cuisine; ***cookery course*** stage *m* de cuisine; ***cookery programme*** émission *f* de cuisine

cookhouse ['kʊkhaʊs, *pl* -haʊzɪz] *n* cuisine *f*

cookie ['kʊkɪ] *n* (**a**) *Am (biscuit)* biscuit *m* (**b**) *Fam (person)* **a tough cookie** un dur à cuire; **a smart cookie** un petit malin (**c**) *Comput* cookie *m*, cafteur *m*, *Can* témoin *m* (**d**) *(idioms)* **that's the way the cookie crumbles!** c'est la vie!; *Fam* **to toss** *or* *Am* **shoot one's cookies** *(vomit)* gerber, dégueuler

►► ***cookie cutter*** emporte-pièce *m*; ***cookie jar*** bocal *m* à biscuits; *Fig* **to be caught with one's hand in the cookie jar** être pris en flagrant délit; *Comput* ***cookie file*** fichier *m* de cookies *ou Can* témoins

cooking ['kʊkɪŋ] **1** *n* (**a**) *(activity)* cuisine *f*; **to do the cooking** faire la cuisine (**b**) *(food)* cuisine *f*; **French/home cooking** cuisine *f* française/maison

2 *comp (oil, sherry)* de cuisine

►► ***cooking apple*** pomme *f* à cuire; ***cooking chocolate*** chocolat *m* à cuire; ***cooking fat*** matière *f* grasse pour la cuisine; ***cooking foil*** papier *m* d'aluminium; ***cooking time*** temps *m* de cuisson; ***cooking utensils*** batterie *f* de cuisine

cookout ['kʊkaʊt] *n Am* barbecue *m*

Cook Strait [kʊk-] *n* le détroit de Cook

cooky ['kʊkɪ] *(pl* **cookies***)* = **cookie (a)**

cool [ku:l] **1** *adj* (**a**) *(in temperature → breeze, room, weather, drink)* frais (fraîche); *(→ clothes, material)* léger; **it's cool** *(weather)* il fait frais; **it's getting cooler in the evenings** *(weather)* les soirées sont plus fraîches; **keep in a cool place** tenir au frais

(**b**) *(colour → blue, green)* clair

(**c**) *(calm → person, manner, voice)* calme; *Fam* **keep cool!** du calme!❑; **to keep a cool head** garder la tête froide, garder son sang-froid; *Fam* **she's a cool customer!** *(cheeky)* elle a du culot!, elle en prend à son aise!; *(self-possessed)* elle a beaucoup de sang-froid!; **to be cool, calm and collected** être d'un calme olympien; **to be/look as cool as a cucumber** garder son sang-froid *ou* calme

(**d**) *(unfriendly → person, greeting, welcome)* froid

(**e**) *Fam (sum of money)* **she earned a cool million dollars last year** elle a gagné la coquette somme d'un million de dollars l'année dernière; **I lost a cool thousand** j'ai perdu mille livres bien comptées

(**f**) *Fam (fashionable, sophisticated)* branché; **Glasgow's a really cool city** Glasgow est une ville hyper-branchée; **he still thinks it's cool to smoke** il pense encore que ça fait bien de fumer

(**g**) *Fam (great)* génial, super; **we had a really cool weekend** on a passé un super week-end; **that's a cool jacket** elle est cool *ou* super, cette veste; **that's cool!** c'est génial!; **I'll be there at eight – cool!** je serai là à huit heures – super!

(**h**) *Fam (allowed, acceptable)* **is it cool to skin up in here?** on peut se rouler un joint ici?; **it's not cool to wear jeans in that restaurant** on ne peut pas entrer dans ce restaurant si on porte un jean

(**i**) *Fam (accepting, not upset)* **are you cool with that?** ça te va?; **they're not cool about me smoking at home** ils n'aiment pas que je fume à la maison; **I thought she'd be angry, but she was really cool about it** je pensais qu'elle se fâcherait, mais en fait elle a été très cool

2 *adv Fam* **to play it cool** *(act calm)* jouer décontracté; *(be calm)* être décontracté❑; **play it cool!** ne nous énervons pas!❑

3 *n* (**a**) *(coolness)* fraîcheur *f*; **the cool of the evening** la fraîcheur du soir

(**b**) *(calm)* calme *m*, sang-froid *m*; **to keep/to lose one's cool** garder/perdre son calme

4 *vt (air, liquid, room)* rafraîchir, refroidir; *(brow, feet)* rafraîchir; **to cool sb's ardour** refroidir l'ardeur de qn; *Fig* **to cool one's heels** faire le pied de grue; **they left him to cool his heels in jail** ils l'ont laissé mijoter en prison; *Fam* **cool it!** du calme!❑

5 *vi (food, liquid)* (se) refroidir; *(friendship etc)* se refroidir; *(enthusiasm, passion, temper)* s'apaiser, se calmer

►► ***cool bag*** glacière *f*; *Fam* ***Cool Britannia*** = formule qui tend à véhiculer l'image d'une Grande-Bretagne jeune, dynamique et tournée vers l'avenir; il s'agit d'un jeu de mots avec Rule Britannia, chant patriotique britannique; *Mus* ***cool jazz*** cool *m*

►**cool down 1** *vi* (**a**) *(weather)* se rafraîchir; *(liquid)* (se) refroidir, se rafraîchir; *(machine)* se refroidir

(**b**) *(person)* se calmer; **give him time to cool down** donne-lui le temps de se calmer

(**c**) *Fig (situation)* se détendre; **things have cooled down between them** les relations se sont refroidies entre eux

2 *vt sep* (**a**) *(person)* calmer; *(situation)* calmer, détendre

(**b**) *(of cold drink)* rafraîchir

►**cool off** *vi* (**a**) *(person → become less hot)* se rafraîchir; *(→ become calmer)* se calmer

(**b**) *Fig (affection, enthusiasm)* se refroidir

coolant ['ku:lənt] *n Tech* liquide *m* de refroidissement

►► *Tech* ***coolant inlet*** arrivée *f* de liquide de refroidissement; *Tech* ***coolant outlet*** sortie *f* de liquide de refroidissement

coolbox ['ku:lbɒks] *n* glacière *f*

cooler ['ku:lə(r)] *n* (**a**) *(for food)* glacière *f* (**b**) *Tech (device for cooling)* (appareil *m*) refroidisseur *m* (**c**) *Fam (prison)* taule *f*; **in the cooler** en taule (**d**) *(drink)* **(wine) cooler** = mélange de vin, de jus de fruit et d'eau gazeuse

cool-headed *adj* calme, imperturbable

coolie ['ku:lɪ] *n* coolie *m*

cooling ['ku:lɪŋ] **1** *n (in temperature)* rafraîchissement *m*, refroidissement *m*; *(in relationships)* refroidissement *m*; **there had been a cooling in their relationship** leurs relations s'étaient refroidies

2 *adj (breeze, drink)* rafraîchissant; *Ind & Tech* réfrigérant

►► *Tech* ***cooling fan*** ventilateur *m* de refroidissement; *Aut* ***cooling fin*** ailette *f* de refroidissement; *Tech* ***cooling jacket*** chemise *f* d'eau; *Tech* ***cooling system*** système *m* de refroidissement; *Tech* ***cooling tower*** refroidisseur *m*; *Aut & Nucl* ***cooling water*** eau *f* de refroidissement

cooling-off period *n* (**a**) *(in dispute)* moment *m* de répit (**b**) *(after signing contract)* délai *m* de résiliation; *(after purchase)* délai *m* de réflexion

coolish ['ku:lɪʃ] *adj* un peu frais (fraîche)

coolly ['ku:lɪ] *adv* (**a**) *(calmly → react, respond)* calmement; **she walked coolly out of the room** elle a calmement quitté la pièce (**b**) *(without enthusiasm → greet, welcome)* froidement, fraîchement (**c**) *(impertinently → behave, say)* avec impertinence

coolness ['ku:lnɪs] *n* (**a**) *(in temperature → of air, water, weather)* fraîcheur *f*; *(→ of clothes)* légèreté *f* (**b**) *(calmness)* calme *m*, sang-froid *m* (**c**) *(of welcome, manner)* froideur *f* (**d**) *(impertinence)* culot *m*, toupet *m*

cooly *(pl* **coolies***)* = **coolie**

coomb, coombe [ku:m] *n Geog* combe *f*

coon [ku:n] *n* (**a**) *Fam (raccoon)* raton *m* laveur❑ (**b**) *very Fam* nègre (négresse) *m,f*, = terme raciste désignant un Noir

coonskin ['ku:nskɪn] **1** *n* (**a**) *(skin)* peau *f* de raton laveur (**b**) *(hat)* chapeau *m* en peau de raton laveur (**c**) *(coat)* manteau *m* en peau de raton laveur

2 *comp* en peau de raton laveur

coop [ku:p] *n* poulailler *m*

►**coop up** *vt sep (animal, person, prisoner)* enfermer; **we were cooped up for hours in a tiny room** nous sommes restés enfermés pendant des heures dans une pièce minuscule; **to feel cooped up** se sentir à l'étroit; **I've been cooped up at home all day** j'ai été cloîtré chez moi toute la journée

co-op ['kəʊ,ɒp] *(abbr* **co-operative society***)* **1** *n* coopérative *f*, coop *f*

2 Co-op *n Br* **the Co-op** la Coop

cooper ['ku:pə(r)] *n* tonnelier *m*

cooperage ['ku:pərɪdʒ] *n* tonnellerie *f*

cooperate [kəʊ'ɒpə,reɪt] *vi* (**a**) *(work together)* [illegible] collaborer avec qn (**b**) *(be willing to help)* se montrer coopératif

cooperation [kəʊ,ɒpə'reɪʃən] *n* (**a**) *(collaboration)* coopération *f*, concours *m*; **in cooperation with** *or* **with the cooperation of sb** avec la coopération *ou* le concours de qn (**b**) *(willingness to help)* coopération *f*

cooperative [kəʊ'ɒpərətɪv] **1** *adj* (**a**) *(joint → activity, work)* coopératif (**b**) *(helpful → attitude, person)* coopératif; **he has been most cooperative** il a été très coopératif

2 *n Com* coopérative *f*

►► ***cooperative advertising*** publicité *f* coopérative *ou* associée; ***Cooperative for American Relief Everywhere*** = organisation humanitaire américaine; *Fin* ***cooperative credit society*** coopérative *f* de crédit; *Agr* ***cooperative dairy*** coopérative *f* laitière; *Com* ***cooperative exporting*** exportation *f* collective; *Com* ***cooperative group*** coopérative *f* (de consommateurs); *Com* ***cooperative selling*** vente *f* en coopération; *Com* ***cooperative society*** société *f* coopérative

cooperatively [kəʊ'ɒpərətɪvlɪ] *adv* coopérativement

Cooperstown ['ku:pəz,taʊn] *n* = ville de l'État de New York où se trouve le musée du baseball

co-opt *vt* (**a**) *(onto committee)* coopter, admettre; **I was co-opted as a member of the committee** on m'a coopté *ou* admis comme membre du comité; **to be co-opted into/onto sth** être coopté à qch (**b**) *Fam (commandeer)* réquisitionner❑; **I've been co-opted to help with the spring cleaning** j'ai été réquisitionné pour le nettoyage de printemps

co-option [kəʊ'ɒpʃən] *n* cooptation *f*

coordinate 1 *vt* [kəʊ'ɔ:dɪneɪt] coordonner

2 *n* [kəʊ'ɔ:dɪnət] *Geom* coordonnée *f*

3 *adj* [kəʊ'ɔ:dɪnət] *Gram & Geom* coordonné

4 coordinates *npl* [kəʊ'ɔ:dɪnəts] *(clothes)* coordonnés *mpl*

►► *Chem* ***coordinate bond*** liaison *f* de coordination; *Gram* ***coordinate clause*** proposition *f* coordonnée; *Geom* ***coordinate geometry*** géométrie *f* analytique

coordinated [kəʊ'ɔ:dɪ,neɪtɪd] *adj (physically, in movements)* coordonné; **I'm not very coordinated** je ne suis pas très coordonné; **to give sth a more coordinated appearance** donner à qch une apparence plus harmonieuse

coordinating [kəʊ'ɔ:dɪ,neɪtɪŋ] *adj (body, officer)* de coordination

►► *Gram* ***coordinating conjunction*** conjonction *f* de coordination

coordination [kəʊ,ɔ:dɪ'neɪʃən] *n* (**a**) *(harmonious combination)* coordination *f*; **we need greater coordination between doctors and nurses** il nous faut une plus grande coordination entre médecins et infirmières (**b**) *(ease of movement)* coordination *f*; **she lacks coordination** elle manque de coordination; **to have a coordination problem** avoir des problèmes de coordination

coordinator [kəʊ'ɔ:dɪ,neɪtə(r)] *n* coordinateur(trice) *m,f*, coordonnateur(trice) *m,f*

coot [ku:t] *n* (**a**) *(bird)* foulque *f* (macroule) (**b**) *Fam Old-fashioned (fool)* bêta *m*; **silly old coot!** gros bêta!

cooties ['ku:tɪz] *npl Am Fam* poux❑ *mpl*; **don't sit beside her, she's got cooties!** ne t'assieds pas à côté d'elle, elle a des poux!

co-owner *n* copropriétaire *mf*

co-ownership *n* copropriété *f*

cop [kɒp] *(pt & pp* **copped**, *cont* **copping***)* *Fam* **1** *n* (**a**) *(policeman)* flic *m*; **to play cops and robbers** jouer aux gendarmes et aux voleurs (**b**) *Br (arrest)* arrestation❑ *f*; **it's a fair cop!** je suis fait! (**c**) *Br (idiom)* **it's not much cop** ça ne vaut pas grand-chose, c'est pas terrible

2 *vt Fam (catch)* attraper❑, pincer; **to get copped** *(by police)* se faire pincer; *Br* **to cop it** *(be caught and punished)* se faire pincer; *(get injured)* être blessé❑; *(die)* clamser; **you'll cop it if he finds out!** qu'est-ce que tu vas prendre s'il s'en rend compte!; **to cop hold of sth** attraper qch; **cop hold of that rope!** attrape cette corde!; **cop this!** *(listen)* écoute-moi ça!; *(look)* regarde-moi ça!; *Law* **to cop a plea** plaider coupable❑ *(pour éviter une charge plus grave)*; [illegible]

►► *Fam TV* ***cop show*** série *f* policière❑; *Fam* ***cop shop*** *(police station)* poste *m* de police❑

►**cop out** *vi Fam (avoid responsibility)* se défiler; *(choose easy solution)* choisir la solution de facilité❑; **to cop out of doing sth** ne pas avoir le cran de faire qch

copacetic [,kəʊpə'setɪk] *adj Am Fam* super, génial; **everything's copacetic** ça gaze

copal ['kəʊpəl] *n Bot* copal *m*

copartner [kəʊ'pɑ:tnə(r)] *n* coassocié(e) *m,f*

copartnership [kəʊ'pɑ:tnəʃɪp] *n* partenariat *m*

cope [kəʊp] **1** *vi (person)* se débrouiller, s'en sortir; **I can't cope any more** je n'en peux plus; **she's coping very well on her own** elle s'en sort très bien toute seule; **to cope with** *(situation, danger, job, debt)* faire face à; *(difficulty)* venir à bout de; *(troublemaker)* se charger de; *(look after → children, noise)* s'occuper de; *(put up with → children, noise)* supporter; **we cope with more than 5,000 visitors a week** nous recevons plus

de 5000 visiteurs par semaine; **I can't cope with her when she gets angry** je ne sais pas comment la prendre quand elle se met en colère; **the system can't cope with this volume of work** le système ne peut pas supporter ce volume de travail; **the engine couldn't cope with the extra weight** le moteur n'était pas assez puissant pour supporter cette charge supplémentaire; **I'll just have to cope with the problems as they arise** il faudra que je m'occupe des problèmes au fur et à mesure qu'ils se présenteront
2 *n* (**a**) *Rel* chape *f*
(**b**) *Literary (covering)* **the cope of heaven** la voûte céleste, la calotte des cieux; **under the cope of night** sous le voile *ou* le manteau de la nuit
3 *vt Constr* (**a**) *(provide with coping → wall)* chaperonner
(**b**) *(join → timbers)* assembler

Copenhagen [ˌkəʊpən'heɪgən] *n* Copenhague

Copernican [kə'pɜːnɪkən] *adj Astron* copernicien
►► ***the Copernican revolution*** la révolution copernicienne; ***the Copernican system, the Copernican theory*** le système de Copernic

Copernicus [kə'pɜːnɪkəs] *pr n* Copernic

copestone ['kəʊpstəʊn] *n* (**a**) *Constr (coping stone)* couronnement *m*, chaperon *m* (**b**) *Archit (capstone)* pierre *f* de faîte; *Fig* sommet *m*

copiable ['kɒpɪəbəl] *adj Comput* copiable

copier ['kɒpɪə(r)] *n* photocopieuse *f*, copieur *m*

co-pilot *n* copilote *mf*

coping ['kəʊpɪŋ] *n Constr (of wall)* chaperon *m*
►► *Psy* ***coping mechanism*** stratégie *f* d'adaptation; *Tech* ***coping saw*** scie *f* à découper *ou* à chantourner; *Constr* ***coping stone*** couronnement *m*, chaperon *m*

copious ['kəʊpjəs] *adj (amount, food)* copieux; *(sunshine)* abondant; *(notes)* abondant; **they wept copious tears** ils ont pleuré à chaudes larmes; **we drank copious amounts of beer** nous avons bu des quantités de bière

copiously ['kəʊpjəslɪ] *adv (cry, produce, write)* en abondance, abondamment

copiousness ['kəʊpjəsnɪs] *n (of food, notes)* abondance *f*; *(of detail)* abondance *f*, profusion *f*

cop-killer bullet *n Am Fam Crime slang* = balle capable de traverser un gilet pare-balles

co-plaintiff *n Law* codemandeur(eresse) *m,f*

copolymer [ˌkəʊ'pɒlɪmə(r)] *n Chem* copolymère *m*

cop-out *n Fam* dérobade *f*; **what a cop-out!** belle façon de se défiler!

copper ['kɒpə(r)] **1** *n* (**a**) *(colour, metal)* cuivre *m* (**b**) *Fam* **coppers** *(coins)* monnaie ❑*f*; **to give a beggar a few coppers** donner quelques sous à un mendiant (**c**) *Fam (policeman)* flic *m* (**d**) *(container)* lessiveuse *f*
2 *comp (coin, kettle, wire)* en cuivre
3 *adj (colour, hair)* cuivré
4 *vt (in metalwork)* cuivrer
►► *Bot* ***copper beech*** hêtre *m* pourpre; *Geol* ***copper pyrites*** pyrite *f* de cuivre; *Chem* ***copper sulphate*** sulfate *m* de cuivre

copper-bottomed [-'bɒtəmd] *adj (saucepan)* à fond de cuivre; *Fig (deal, guarantee)* en béton

copper-coloured *adj* cuivré

copperhead ['kɒpəhed] *n Zool* trigonocéphale *m*

copperplate ['kɒpəpleɪt] **1** *n* (**a**) *Typ (plate)* cuivre *m* (**b**) *(print)* plaque *f* (de cuivre) (**c**) *(handwriting)* écriture *f* moulée
2 *comp (handwriting)* moulé
►► ***copperplate engraving*** taille *f* douce

copperplated [ˌkɒpə'pleɪtɪd] *adj* cuivré

coppersmith ['kɒpəsmɪθ] *n* chaudronnier(ère) *m,f*

copperware ['kɒpəweə(r)] *n* ustensiles *mpl* en cuivre

coppery ['kɒpərɪ] *adj (colour)* cuivré

coppice ['kɒpɪs] *Agr* **1** *n* taillis *m*
2 *vt* couper en taillis
3 *vi* couper des arbres en taillis

copra ['kɒprə] *n Bot* coprah *m*

co-present *vt* coprésenter

co-presenter *n* coprésentateur(trice) *m,f*

co-processor *n Comput* coprocesseur *m*

coproduce [ˌkəʊprə'djuːs] *vt (film, play)* coproduire

coproduction [ˌkəʊprə'dʌkʃən] *n* coproduction *f*

coprolalia [ˌkɒprəʊ'leɪlɪə] *n Psy* coprolalie *f*

coprophagous [kɒ'prɒfəgəs] *adj Zool & Psy* coprophage

coprophagy [kɒ'prɒfədʒɪ] *n Zool & Psy* coprophagie *f*

coprophilia [ˌkɒprəʊ'fɪlɪə] *n Psy* coprophilie *f*

coprophiliac [ˌkɒprəʊ'fɪlɪæk] *Psy* **1** *n* coprophile *m*
2 *adj* coprophile

coprophilous [kə'prɒfɪləs] *adj Zool* coprophile

copse [kɒps] *n Bot* taillis *m*

Copt [kɒpt] *n* Copte *mf*

copter ['kɒptə(r)] *n Fam* hélico *m*

Coptic ['kɒptɪk] **1** *adj* copte
2 *n Ling* copte *m*
►► ***the Coptic church*** l'Église *f* copte

copula ['kɒpjʊlə] (*pl* **copulas** *or* **copulae** [-liː]) *n Gram* copule *f*

copulate ['kɒpjʊleɪt] *vi* copuler

copulation [ˌkɒpjʊ'leɪʃən] *n* copulation *f*

copulative ['kɒpjʊlətɪv] *adj* (**a**) *Gram* copulatif (**b**) *Physiol* copulateur

copy ['kɒpɪ] (*pl* **copies**, *pt & pp* **copied**) **1** *n* (**a**) *(duplicate → of painting, statue)* copie *f*, reproduction *f*; *(→ of document, letter, photograph)* copie *f*; **to make a copy of sth** faire une copie de qch
(**b**) *(of book, magazine, record)* exemplaire *m*; *(of newspaper)* numéro *m*; **500 copies of the book were printed** le livre a été tiré à 500 exemplaires
(**c**) *(UNCOUNT) Typ, Press & Journ (written material)* copie *f*; *(in advertisement)* texte *m*; **his story made good copy** son histoire a fait un bon papier; **he wrote some brilliant copy** *(one article)* il a écrit un article excellent; *(several articles)* il a écrit d'excellents articles
(**d**) *Comput* **copy and paste** copier-coller *m*
2 *vt* (**a**) *(work of art, drawing etc)* copier, imiter
(**b**) *(write out → letter, notes)* copier
(**c**) *(imitate → person, movements, gestures)* copier, imiter; *(→ style, system)* copier
(**d**) *(in order to cheat)* copier (**from sb** sur qn; **from sth** dans qch)
(**e**) *(photocopy)* photocopier
(**f**) *Comput* copier; **to copy sth to disk** copier qch sur disquette; **to copy and paste sth** faire un copier-coller sur qch
(**g**) *(send copy to)* envoyer une copie à; **to copy sb with sth** faire parvenir une copie de qch à qn
3 *vi* (**a**) *(cheat)* copier (**from sb** sur qn; **from sth** dans qch); **no copying!** on ne copie pas!
(**b**) *Am Tel (hear)* **do you copy?** vous me recevez?
►► *Comput* ***copy block*** copie *f* de bloc; *Comput* ***copy check*** contrôle *m* par duplication; *Comput* ***copy command*** commande *f* de copie; *Press* ***copy deadline*** tombée *f*, dernière heure *f*; *Am Press* ***copy desk*** secrétariat *m* de rédaction; *Comput* ***copy disk*** disquette *f* de copie; ***copy editor*** *Press* secrétaire *mf* de rédaction; *(in publishing)* préparateur(trice) *m,f* de copie; *Comput* ***copy protection*** protection *f* contre la copie; ***copy taster*** premier lecteur *m*; *Mktg* ***copy test*** pré-test *m* publicitaire; *Mktg* ***copy testing*** pré-tests *mpl* publicitaires; ***copy typing*** dactylographie *f*, dactylo *f*; ***copy typist*** dactylographe *mf*, dactylo *mf*

►**copy down** *vt sep* noter

►**copy out** *vt sep* recopier; **to copy out a passage from a book** transcrire *ou* recopier un passage d'un livre

copybook ['kɒpɪbʊk] **1** *n* cahier *m*
2 *adj (sentiments)* commun; **a copybook example** un exemple classique

copycat ['kɒpɪkæt] **1** *n Fam* copieur(euse)❑ *m,f*
2 *comp (killing, murder, crime)* inspiré par un autre

copy-edit **1** *vt (manuscript)* corriger
2 *vi* préparer la copie

copy-editing *n* préparation *f* de copie

copyholder ['kɒpɪˌhəʊldə(r)] *n* (**a**) *Typ (reader)* lecteur(trice) *m,f*, teneur(euse) *m,f* de copie (**b**) *(device)* porte-copie *m*

copying ['kɒpɪɪŋ] *n (imitation)* imitation *f*; *Sch (cheating)* copiage *m*
►► ***copying machine*** duplicateur *m*; *(photocopier)* photocopieuse *f*; *Comput* ***copying program*** programme *m* de copie

copyist ['kɒpɪɪst] *n* copiste *mf*

copy-protect *vt Comput* protéger (contre la copie)

copy-protected *adj Comput* protégé (contre la copie)

copyread ['kɒpɪriːd] (*pt & pp* **copyread** [-red]) *Am Typ* **1** *vt* corriger, préparer pour l'impression
2 *vi* travailler comme secrétaire de rédaction

copyreader ['kɒpɪˌriːdə(r)] *n Am Typ* secrétaire *mf* de rédaction

copyright ['kɒpɪraɪt] **1** *n* copyright *m*, droit *m* d'auteur; **she has copyright on the book** elle a des droits d'auteur sur le livre; **it's still subject to copyright** c'est toujours soumis au droit d'auteur; **breach** *or* **infringement of copyright** violation *f* du droit d'auteur; **copyright Lawrence Durrell** copyright, Lawrence Durrell; **out of copyright** dans le domaine public
2 *vt* obtenir les droits exclusifs *ou* le copyright de
3 *adj (book)* qui est protégé par des droits d'auteur; *(article)* dont le droit de reproduction est réservé
►► ***copyright (deposit) library*** bibliothèque *f* de dépôt légal; ***copyright notice*** mention *f* de réserve

copyrighted ['kɒpɪˌraɪtɪd] *adj (book)* déposé

copytaker ['kɒpɪˌteɪkə(r)] *n Journ* opérateur *m*

copywriter ['kɒpɪˌraɪtə(r)] *n Journ* rédacteur(trice) *m,f* publicitaire

copywriting ['kɒpɪˌraɪtɪŋ] *n Journ* rédaction *f* publicitaire

coquetry ['kəʊkɪtrɪ, 'kɒkɪtrɪ] (*pl* **coquetries**) *n* coquetterie *f*

coquette [kəʊ'ket, kɒ'ket] *Literary* **1** *n* coquette *f*
2 *vi* faire la coquette

coquettish [kəʊ'ketɪʃ, kɒ'ketɪʃ] *adj (woman)* coquet; *(look, smile, behaviour)* charmeur, aguichant

coquettishly [kəʊ'ketɪʃlɪ, kɒ'ketɪʃlɪ] *adv* de façon aguichante

cor [kɔː(r)] *exclam Br Fam* **cor (blimey)!** ça alors!

coracle ['kɒrəkəl] *n* coracle *m*

coral ['kɒrəl] **1** *n* (**a**) *(substance)* corail *m* (**b**) *(colour)* corail *m inv*
2 *adj* (**a**) *(pink, red, lipstick)* corail *(inv)*; *Literary (lips)* de corail (**b**) *(colour)* corail *(inv)*
3 *comp (earrings, necklace)* de corail; *(island)* coralien
►► ***coral reef*** récif *m* de corail; ***the Coral Sea*** la mer de Corail; *Zool* ***coral snake*** serpent *m* corail

coral-coloured *adj* (couleur) corail *(inv)*

coralline ['kɒrəlaɪn] **1** *n* (**a**) *Miner* coralline *f* (**b**) *Biol* bryozoaire *m*
2 *adj* (**a**) *Miner* corallien, corailleux (**b**) *(pinkish-red)* corallin
►► ***coralline limestone*** calcaire *m* corallien; *Biol* ***coralline zone*** *(in the ocean)* zone *f* des bryozoaires *(30 à 100 m)*

cor anglais [-'ɒŋgleɪ] *n Mus* cor *m* anglais

corbel ['kɔːbəl] *n Archit* corbeau *m*

corbelled, *Am* **corbeled** ['kɔːbəld] *adj Archit* en encorbellement

corbelling, *Am* **corbeling** ['kɔːbəlɪŋ] *n Archit* encorbellement *m*

cord [kɔːd] **1** *n* (**a**) *(string)* cordon *m*; *(for climbing)* cordelette *f* (**b**) *(cable)* câble *m* (**c**) *(corduroy)* velours *m* côtelé (**d**) *Anat* **(umbilical) cord** cordon *m* (ombilical) (**e**) *Literary (tie, connection)* lien *m*; **cords of affection** liens *mpl* d'amitié
2 *comp (skirt, trousers)* en velours côtelé
3 *vt* corder
4 **cords** *npl Fam* **(pair of) cords** pantalon *m* en velours côtelé❑

cordage ['kɔːdɪdʒ] *n Naut* cordage *m*

corded ['kɔːdɪd] *adj (material)* côtelé

cordial ['kɔːdɪəl] **1** *adj* (**a**) *(warm → greeting, welcome)* chaleureux (**b**) *(strong → hatred)* cordial; **to have a cordial dislike for sb** détester qn cordialement
2 *n (drink)* cordial *m*

cordiality [ˌkɔːdɪ'ælətɪ] (*pl* **cordialities**) *n* cordialité *f*

cordially ['kɔːdɪəlɪ] *adv* (**a**) *(warmly → greet etc)* cordialement; *Am* **cordially yours** *(at end of* *letter)* salutations amicales (**b**) *(completely → hate, detest)* cordialement

cordillera [ˌkɔːdɪl'jeərə] *n Geog* cordillère *f*

cordite ['kɔːdaɪt] *n* cordite *f*

cordless ['kɔːdlɪs] *adj (telephone, iron, kettle, mouse)* sans fil

Cordoba ['kɔːdəbə] *n* Cordoue

cordon ['kɔːdən] **1** *n* (**a**) *(barrier)* cordon *m*; **police cordon** cordon *m* de police; **the police put a cordon round the building** la police a encerclé le bâtiment (**b**) *Hort* cordon *m* (**c**) *(decoration)* cordon *m*

2 *vt* barrer, interdire l'accès à, isoler

►**cordon off** *vt sep* barrer, interdire l'accès à, isoler

cordon bleu [-blɜː] **1** *adj* de cordon bleu; **cordon bleu cook** cordon bleu *m*

2 *n (cookery, chef)* cordon bleu *m*

corduroy ['kɔːdərɔɪ] **1** *n* velours *m* côtelé; **(pair of) corduroys** pantalon *m* de *ou* en velours côtelé

2 *adj* de velours côtelé

►► ***corduroy road*** chemin *m* de rondins

CORE [kɔː(r)] *n Am (abbr* **Congress On Racial Equality**) = ligue américaine contre le racisme

core [kɔː(r)] **1** *n* (**a**) *(of mass)* centre *m*, partie *f* centrale; *(of apple, pear)* trognon *m*, cœur *m*; *(of organization)* noyau *m*; *(of argument)* essentiel *m*, centre *m*; *Fig* **to be French/a socialist to the core** être français/socialiste jusqu'à la moelle; *Fig* **rotten to the core** pourri jusqu'à l'os

(**b**) *Geol (of earth)* noyau *m*

(**c**) *Tech (of electric cable)* âme *f*, noyau *m*; *(of nuclear reactor)* cœur *m*; *(of magnet)* noyau *m*

2 *vt (apple, pear)* enlever le trognon de

►► *Mining* ***core boring*** carottage *m*; *Com & Mktg* ***core brand*** marque *f* phare; *Com* ***core business*** activité *f* principale; *Am* ***core city*** centre-ville *m*; ***core competence*** principale compétence *f*; *Sch* ***core curriculum*** tronc *m* commun; *Mining* ***core drill*** carotteuse *f*; *Comput* ***core dump*** vidage *m* de mémoire; *Fin* ***core holding*** investissement *m* de base *(dans le portefeuille des investisseurs institutionnels)*; *Tech* ***core hole*** *(in engine block)* trou *m* de coulée *ou* d'usinage; *Mktg* ***core market*** marché *m* principal, marché *m* de référence; *Comput* ***core memory*** mémoire *f* à tores (magnétiques); *Com & Mktg* ***core message*** *(in advertising)* message *m* principal; *Aut* ***core plug*** obturateur *m* de trou de coulée *ou* de trou d'usinage; *Geol* ***core sample*** carotte *f*; *Sch* ***core subject*** matière *f* principale; *Ind* ***core time*** *(in flexitime)* plage *f* fixe; ***core values*** valeurs *fpl* principales; *Ling* ***core vocabulary*** vocabulaire *m* de base

coreligionist [ˌkəʊrɪ'lɪdʒənɪst] *n* coreligionnaire *mf*

corer ['kɔːrə(r)] *n* **(apple) corer** vide-pomme *m inv*

co-respondent [ˌkəʊrɪ'spɒndənt] **1** *adj (shoes)* bicolore *(style années quarante)*

2 *n Law (in divorce suit)* complice *mf* de l'adultère

Corfu [kɔː'fuː] *n* Corfou; **in Corfu** à Corfou

corgi ['kɔːgɪ] *n* corgi *m*

coriander [ˌkɒrɪ'ændə(r)] *n* coriandre *f*

►► ***coriander seeds*** graines *fpl* de coriandre

Corinth ['kɒrɪnθ] *n Geog* Corinthe

Corinthian [kə'rɪnθɪən] **1** *n* Corinthien(enne) *m,f*; *Bible* **the Epistle of Paul to the Corinthians** l'Épître de saint Paul aux Corinthiens

2 *adj* (**a**) *Geog* corinthien (**b**) *Archit (column etc)* corinthien

Coriolanus [ˌkɒrɪə'leɪnəs] *pr n* Coriolan

Coriolis effect [kɒrɪ'əʊlɪs-] *n Phys* force *f* de Coriolis

Cork [kɔːk] *n* (**a**) *(town)* Cork (**b**) *(county)* le comté de Cork, = comté dans le sud-ouest de la République d'Irlande; **in Cork** dans le comté de Cork

cork [kɔːk] **1** *n* (**a**) *(substance)* liège *m* (**b**) *(stopper)* bouchon *m*; **he took** *or* **pulled the cork out of the bottle** il a débouché la bouteille; *Fam* **put a cork in it!** la ferme! (**c**) *Fishing (float)* flotteur *m*, bouchon *m*

2 *comp (sole, tile, bathmat etc)* de *ou* en liège

3 *vt* (**a**) *(seal → bottle)* boucher (**b**) *(blacken)* **to cork one's face** se noircir le visage avec un bouchon brûlé

►► *Bot* ***cork oak*** chêne-liège *m*

►**cork up** *vt sep* (**a**) *(seal → bottle)* boucher (**b**) *(suppress → emotions, feelings)* réprimer

corkage ['kɔːkɪdʒ] *n (UNCOUNT)* droit *m* de bouchon

corkboard ['kɔːkbɔːd] *n* liège *m* aggloméré

corked [kɔːkt] *adj (wine)* qui sent le bouchon

corker ['kɔːkə(r)] *n Br Fam Old-fashioned* **he's/she's a real corker** *(good-looking)* c'est un beau gars/un beau brin de fille; **that was a corker of a goal** c'était un super but; **that was a corker of a joke** c'était une plaisanterie à vous faire mourir de rire; **it's a corker** *(car, bike etc)* c'est un (vrai) bijou

corking ['kɔːkɪŋ] *adj Br Fam Old-fashioned* épatant, fameux

corkscrew ['kɔːkskruː] **1** *n* tire-bouchon *m*

2 *vi (staircase)* tourner en vrille; *(plane)* vriller; **the plane corkscrewed out of the sky** l'avion est tombé en vrille

►► ***corkscrew curl*** mèche *f* en tire-bouchon

cork-tipped [-tɪpt] *adj (cigarette)* (à bout) filtre

corkwood ['kɔːkwʊd] *n Bot* liège *m*

corm [kɔːm] *n Bot* bulbe *m*

cormorant ['kɔːmərənt] *n Orn* cormoran *m*

Corn *(written abbr* **Cornwall**) Cornouailles *f*

corn [kɔːn] *n* (**a**) *Br (cereal)* blé *m*

(**b**) *esp Am (maize)* maïs *m*; **corn on the cob** épi *m* de maïs; **grains of corn** grains *mpl* de maïs

(**c**) *(seed)* grain *m (de plante céréalière)*

(**d**) *(UNCOUNT) Fam (banality)* banalité ❑ *f*; *(sentimentality)* sentimentalité *f* bébête; **the book/film is pure corn** le livre/film est d'un gnan-gnan!

(**e**) *(on foot)* cor *m*; *Fam Fig* **to tread on sb's corns** *Br (upset)* toucher qn à l'endroit sensible; *(trespass)* marcher sur les plates-bandes de qn

►► *Geog* ***corn belt*** plaines *fpl* du centre des Etats-Unis *(où est cultivé le maïs)*; ***corn bread*** pain *m* à la farine de maïs; *Orn* ***corn bunting*** bruant *m*; ***corn chandler*** marchand *m* de blé *ou* de grains; ***corn chip*** *Am* tortilla *f (chips)*; *Am Culin* ***corn dog*** = saucisse de Francfort enrobée de farine de maïs, frite et servie sur un bâtonnet; ***corn dolly*** figurine *f* en paille tressée; ***corn exchange*** halle *f* au blé; *Br Hist* ***the Corn Laws*** les lois *fpl* sur le blé; *Am* ***corn liquor*** whisky *m* à base de maïs; *Bot* ***corn marigold*** marguerite *f* dorée; ***corn merchant*** marchand *m* de blé *ou* de grains; *Bot* ***corn mignonette*** réséda *m* raiponce; ***corn oil*** huile *f* de maïs; ***corn plaster*** pansement *m* (pour cors); *Am Culin* ***corn pone*** pain *m* de maïs; ***corn poppy*** coquelicot *m*; ***corn rows*** = coiffure féminine de style africain ou antillais consistant en rangées de nattes; *Bot & Culin* ***corn salad*** mâche *f*; *Bot* ***corn silk*** barbe *f*; ***corn syrup*** sirop *m* de maïs; *Am* ***corn whiskey*** whisky *m* de maïs

THE CORN LAWS

Cette mesure protectionniste, prise par le Parlement britannique en 1815 pour pallier l'effet des mauvaises récoltes, consistait à augmenter le tarif du grain importé. Très impopulaire, cette loi provoqua la naissance de la "Anti-Corn Law League", dont la liberté du commerce devint le slogan.

cornball ['kɔːnbɔːl] *Am Fam* **1** *n* sentimental(e) ❑ *m,f*

2 *adj (trite)* bateau, banal ❑; *(sentimental)* sentimental ❑, à l'eau de rose ❑

corncob ['kɔːnkɒb] *n* épi *m* de maïs; *(pipe)* pipe *f* en épi de maïs

►► ***corncob pipe*** pipe *f* en épi de maïs

corncockle ['kɔːnˌkɒkəl] *n Bot* nielle *f*

corncrake ['kɔːnkreɪk] *n Orn* râle *m* des genêts

cornea ['kɔːnɪə] *n* cornée *f*

corneal ['kɔːnɪəl] *adj* cornéen

►► *Med* ***corneal graft*** greffe *f* de la cornée

corned beef [kɔːnd-] *n* corned beef *m*

Cornelian [kɔː'niːlɪən] *adj* cornélien

cornelian [kɔː'niːlɪən] *n Miner* cornaline *f*

Cornell [kɔː'nel] *n* = université dans l'État de New York

CORNER ['kɔːnə(r)]

coin	►1 (a) – (d), (f)
virage	►1 (c)
situation difficile	►1 (e)
corner	►1 (g)
coincer	►3 (a)
accaparer	►3 (b)
prendre un virage	►4

1 *n* (**a**) *(of page, painting, table etc)* coin *m*; **to turn down the corner of a page** faire une corne à une page

(**b**) *(inside room, house etc)* coin *m*; **to search every corner of the house** chercher dans tous les coins et recoins de la maison; **to put a child in the corner** mettre un enfant au coin; *Br* **to fight one's corner** *(argue one's case)* défendre sa position; **the Minister fought his corner well and got an increase in his budget** le ministre a bien défendu son point de vue et a obtenu une augmentation de son budget; **to be in sb's corner** être du côté de qn, soutenir qn; **with someone as powerful as her in your corner, you can't lose** avec quelqu'un d'aussi puissant qu'elle derrière toi, tu ne peux pas perdre

(**c**) *(of street)* coin *m*; *(bend in the road)* tournant *m*, virage *m*; **on** *or* **at the corner** au coin; **the house on** *or* **at the corner** la maison qui fait l'angle; **at the corner of Regent Street and Oxford Street** à l'intersection *ou* à l'angle de Regent Street et d'Oxford Street; **to hang around street corners** traîner dans les rues; **he/the car took the corner at high speed** il/la voiture a pris le tournant à toute allure; **to overtake on a corner** doubler dans un virage; **the car takes corners well** la voiture prend bien les virages; **it's just around** *or Br* **round the corner** *(house, shop etc)* c'est à deux pas d'ici; *Fig (Christmas, economic recovery etc)* c'est tout proche; **it's literally just round the corner** c'est juste au coin de la rue; *Fig* **a cure is just round the corner** on est sur le point de découvrir un remède; *Fig* **you never know what's round the corner** on ne sait jamais ce qui peut arriver; **to turn the corner** *(car)* prendre le tournant; *Fig (patient)* passer le moment *ou* stade critique; *(business, economy, relationship)* passer un cap critique; **to cut the corner** *(in car, on bike)* couper le virage, prendre le virage à la corde; *(on foot)* couper au plus court, prendre le plus court

(**d**) *(of eye)* coin *m*; *(of mouth)* coin *m*, commissure *f*; **with a cigarette hanging from the corner of his mouth** une cigarette au coin de la bouche; **to look at sb/sth out of the corner of one's eye** regarder qn/qch du coin de l'œil

(**e**) *Fam (difficulty)* situation *f* difficile ❑, mauvaise passe ❑ *f*; **to drive sb into a tight corner** acculer qn, mettre qn dans une situation difficile

(**f**) *(remote place)* coin *m*; **the four corners of the earth** les quatre coins du monde; **they had created a little corner of France in Edinburgh** ils avaient recréé un petit coin de France à Édimbourg

(**g**) *Ftbl* corner *m*

(**h**) *Com* **to make a corner in sth** avoir le monopole de qch, accaparer qch

[illegible]

3 *vt* (**a**) *(animal, prey etc)* coincer, acculer; **she cornered me at the party** elle m'a coincé à la soirée

(**b**) *Com (market)* accaparer; **to corner the market in sth** accaparer le marché de qch

4 *vi Aut* prendre un virage; **the car corners well** la voiture tient bien la route dans les virages

►► *Sport* ***corner flag*** drapeau *m* de corner; *Ftbl* ***corner kick*** corner *m*; *Ftbl* ***corner post*** piquet *m* de corner; *Br* ***corner shop***, *Am* ***corner store*** magasin *m* du coin, *Can* dépanneur *m*

cornered ['kɔːnəd] *adj (animal, prey)* acculé, coincé; **we've got him cornered** on l'a acculé *ou* coincé; **his opponent in the debate had him cornered** son adversaire dans le débat l'avait acculé

cornering ['kɔːnərɪŋ] *n* (**a**) *Br Aut (of driver)* façon *f* de prendre les virages; *(of car)* stabilité *f* dans les virages; **your cornering has improved** tu prends mieux les virages (**b**) *Com (of market)* accaparement *m*

cornerstone ['kɔːnəstəʊn] *n Archit* pierre *f* d'angle *ou* angulaire; *Fig* pierre *f* angulaire, fondement *m*

cornerways ['kɔːnəweɪz], **cornerwise** ['kɔːnəwaɪz] **1** *adj* en diagonale, en coin

2 *adv* en diagonale, en coin

cornet ['kɔːnɪt] *n* (**a**) *Mus (instrument)* cornet *m* à pistons; *(player)* cornettiste *mf* (**b**) *Br* (**ice-cream) cornet** cornet *m* (de glace)

cornetist, cornettist [kɔː'netɪst] *n Mus* cornettiste *mf*

corn-fed *adj (chicken)* nourri au grain

cornfield ['kɔːnfiːld] *n Br* champ *m* de blé; *Am* champ *m* de maïs

cornflakes ['kɔːnfleɪks] *npl* cornflakes *mpl*

cornflour ['kɔːnflaʊə(r)] *n Br* fécule *f* de maïs, Maïzena® *f*

cornflower ['kɔːnflaʊə(r)] **1** *n* (**a**) *(plant)* bleuet *m*, bluet *m*, barbeau *m* (**b**) *(colour)* bleu *m* centaurée

2 *adj (colour)* bleu centaurée

▸▸ ***cornflower blue*** **1** *n* bleu *m* centaurée **2** *adj* bleu centaurée

Cornhusker State ['kɔːnˌhʌskə-] *n* **the Cornhusker State** = surnom donné au Nebraska

cornice ['kɔːnɪs] *n* (**a**) *Archit* corniche *f* (**b**) *(snow)* corniche *f*

corniced ['kɔːnɪst] *adj* à corniche

corniche [kɔː'niːʃ] *n (road)* corniche *f*

Cornish ['kɔːnɪʃ] **1** *npl (people)* **the Cornish** les Cornouaillais *mpl*

2 *n (language)* cornique *m*

3 *adj* cornouaillais

▸▸ *Br Culin* ***Cornish pasty*** = chausson à la viande et aux légumes

Cornishman ['kɔːnɪʃmən] *(pl* **Cornishmen** [-mən]) *n* Cornouaillais *m*

Cornishwoman ['kɔːnɪʃˌwʊmən] *(pl* **Cornishwomen** [-ˌwɪmɪn]) *n* Cornouaillaise *f*

cornmeal ['kɔːnmiːl] *n* farine *f* de maïs

cornstarch ['kɔːnstɑːtʃ] *n Am* fécule *f* de maïs, Maïzena® *f*

cornucopia [ˌkɔːnjʊ'kəʊpjə] *n Myth & Fig* corne *f* d'abondance

Cornwall ['kɔːnwɔːl] *n* la Cornouailles, = comté dans le sud-ouest de l'Angleterre; **in Cornwall** en Cornouailles

corny ['kɔːnɪ] *(compar* **cornier**, *superl* **corniest**) *adj (trite)* bateau, banal; *(sentimental)* sentimental, à l'eau de rose; **he's so corny** il est vraiment lourd; **a corny joke** une blague éculée, *Can* une farce plate

corolla [kə'rɒlə] *n Bot* corolle *f*

corollary [kə'rɒlərɪ] *(pl* **corollaries**) *n Formal* corollaire *m*; **the corollary of that is...** le corollaire de ceci, c'est..., ceci a pour corollaire...; **as a corollary to this** en corollaire à ceci

Coromandel Coast [ˌkɒrə'mændəl-] *n* **the Coromandel Coast** la côte de Coromandel

corona [kə'rəʊnə] *(pl* **coronas** *or* **coronae** [-niː]) *n* (**a**) *Anat, Astron, Bot & Phys* couronne *f* (**b**) *Archit* larmier *m* (**c**) *(cigar)* corona *m*

▸▸ *Phys* ***corona discharge*** effluve *f* électrique; *Phys* ***corona shielding*** dispositif *m* anti-effluves

coronary ['kɒrənərɪ] *Med* **1** *adj* coronaire; **the country has a high incidence of coronary heart disease** il y a de nombreux cas de maladies coronariennes dans ce pays

2 *n* infarctus *m* (du myocarde); **to have a coronary** avoir un infarctus du (myocarde); *Fam* **I just about had a coronary when I saw the bill** j'ai failli avoir une attaque quand j'ai vu l'addition

▸▸ *Med* ***coronary artery*** artère *f* coronaire; *Med* ***coronary bypass*** pontage *m* coronaire; *Med* ***coronary care unit*** unité *f* de soins coronariens; *Med* ***coronary thrombosis*** infarctus *m* du myocarde, thrombose *f* coronarienne

coronation [ˌkɒrə'neɪʃən] **1** *n (of monarch)* couronnement *m*, sacre *m*

2 *comp (robes, day)* du couronnement, du sacre

▸▸ *Culin* ***coronation chicken*** = morceaux de poulet froid à la mayonnaise parfumée au curry; *Br* ***coronation mug*** = tasse haute fabriquée spécialement à l'occasion d'un couronnement et décorée sur ce thème; ***'Coronation Street'*** = feuilleton télévisé britannique

CORONATION STREET

Ce feuilleton à succès, le plus ancien des "soap operas" britanniques encore à l'écran, évoque la vie quotidienne de plusieurs familles ouvrières vivant dans la même rue d'une ville du nord de l'Angleterre.

coroner ['kɒrənə(r)] *n Law* coroner *m*

▸▸ ***coroner's inquest*** enquête *f* judiciaire *(menée par le coroner)*; ***coroner's jury*** jury *m* du coroner

coronet ['kɒrənɪt] *n (of prince, duke)* couronne *f*; *(for woman)* diadème *m*

Corp. (**a**) *Com (written abbr* **corporation**) Cie (**b**) *Mil (written abbr* **corporal**) caporal *m*

corpora ['kɔːpərə] *pl of* **corpus**

corporal ['kɔːpərəl] **1** *n* (**a**) *Mil (in infantry, air force)* caporal-chef *m*; *(in artillery)* brigadier-chef *m* (**b**) *Rel* corporal *m*

2 *adj* corporel

▸▸ ***corporal punishment*** châtiment *m* corporel

corporate ['kɔːpərət] *adj* (**a**) *Law (forming a single body)* constitué (en corps), formant (un) corps

(**b**) *(of a specific company)* d'une société, de la société; *(of companies in general)* d'entreprise; *(taxation)* sur les sociétés; **to make one's way up the corporate ladder** faire carrière dans l'entreprise; **if we are to be regarded as a good corporate citizen** si nous voulons être considérés comme une entreprise qui assume ses responsabilités dans la société; **he's a good corporate man** il est dévoué à l'entreprise; **the restaurant is hoping for good corporate business** le restaurant espère attirer une nombreuse clientèle d'affaires; **Britain's largest corporate donors** les entreprises donatrices les plus généreuses de Grande-Bretagne; **we have a number of corporate customers** certains de nos clients sont des entreprises; **corporate customers provide the bulk of our profits** la plus grande partie de nos bénéfices provient des entreprises; **one of our largest corporate sponsors** un de nos plus importants sponsors

(**c**) *(collective → decision, responsibility)* collectif

▸▸ ***corporate advertising*** publicité *f* institutionnelle, publicité *f* d'entreprise; ***corporate assets*** biens *mpl* sociaux; ***corporate banking*** banque *f* d'entreprise; ***corporate body*** personne *f* morale; ***corporate bond*** obligation *f* de sociétés; ***corporate budget*** budget *m* de l'entreprise; *Fin* ***corporate buy-out*** rachat *m* d'une entreprise par les salariés; ***corporate culture*** culture *f* d'entreprise; ***corporate entertainment*** divertissement *m* fourni par la société; ***corporate finance*** finance *f* d'entreprise; ***corporate hospitality*** = réceptions, déjeuners, billets de spectacles etc offerts par une entreprise à ses clients; ***corporate identity, corporate image*** image *f* de marque; **the company cares about its corporate image** la société se préoccupe de son image; **the company's corporate image** l'image *f* de la société; **our corporate image demands that...** notre image en tant que société exige que...; ***corporate income*** revenu *m* de société; ***corporate income tax*** impôt *m* sur les bénéfices des sociétés; ***corporate institution*** personne *f* morale; ***corporate law*** droit *m* des sociétés *ou* des entreprises; ***corporate lawyer*** juriste *m* spécialisé en droit des sociétés; *Fin* ***corporate lending*** crédit *m* aux entreprises; *Am Com* ***corporate licensing*** marchandisage *m*; ***corporate literature*** brochures *fpl* décrivant une société; ***corporate member*** *(of association)* société-membre *f*; ***corporate name*** raison *f* sociale; *St Exch* ***corporate raider*** attaquant *m*; ***corporate sector*** secteur *m* des grandes entreprises; ***corporate sponsorship*** sponsoring *m*, parrainage *m* d'entreprises; ***corporate strategy*** stratégie *f* de l'entreprise; ***corporate structure*** structure *f* de l'entreprise; *Fin* ***corporate tax*** impôt *m* sur les sociétés

corporately ['kɔːpərətlɪ] *adv* (**a**) *(as a corporation)* **I don't think we should involve ourselves corporately** je ne pense pas que nous devrions nous impliquer en tant que société (**b**) *(as a group)* collectivement

corporation [ˌkɔːpə'reɪʃən] **1** *n* (**a**) *(company)* compagnie *f*, société *f*; *Law* personne *f* morale (**b**) *(municipal authorities)* municipalité *f* (**c**) *Fam (paunch)* bedaine *f*, brioche *f*; **to develop a corporation** prendre de la bedaine *ou* de la brioche

2 *comp Br (bus, worker)* municipal, de la ville

▸▸ *Am Fin* ***corporation income tax*** impôt *m* sur les sociétés; *Br Fin* ***corporation tax*** impôt *m* sur les sociétés

corporatism ['kɔːpərətɪzəm] *n* corporatisme *m*

corporeal [kɔː'pɔːrɪəl] *adj* corporel, matériel

corporeality [kɔːˌpɔːrɪ'ælɪtɪ] *n* matérialité *f*

corps [kɔː(r)] *(pl* **inv** [kɔːz]) *n* (**a**) *Mil* corps *m*; *Admin* service *m*; **medical/intelligence corps** service *m* de santé/de renseignements; **pay corps** service *m* de la solde; **tank corps** blindés *mpl* (**b**) *(trained team of people)* corps *m*

▸▸ ***corps de ballet*** corps *m* de ballet

corpse [kɔːps] **1** *n* cadavre *m*, corps *m*

2 *vi Fam (actor)* avoir une crise de fou rire ❑

corpulence ['kɔːpjʊləns] *n* corpulence *f*, embonpoint *m*

corpulent ['kɔːpjʊlənt] *adj* corpulent

corpus ['kɔːpəs] *(pl* **corpuses** *or* **corpora** [-pərə]) *n* (**a**) *(collection of writings → by author)* recueil *m*; *(→ on specific subject)* corpus *m* (**b**) *(main body)* corpus *m*

Corpus Christi [ˌkɔːpəs'krɪstɪ] *n Rel* la Fête-Dieu

corpuscle ['kɔːpʌsəl] *n Anat* corpuscule *m*; **red/white blood corpuscles** globules *mpl* rouges/blancs

corpuscular [kɔː'pʌskjʊlə(r)] *adj Anat* corpusculaire

corral [kɒ'rɑːl] *(pt & pp* **corralled**, *cont* **corralling**) *Am* **1** *n* corral *m*

2 *vt (cattle, horses)* enfermer dans un corral; *Fig* encercler; *Fam Fig* **she corralled me** elle m'a mis le grappin dessus; **to corral sb into doing sth** amener qn à faire qch

correct [kə'rekt] **1** *adj* (**a**) *(right → answer, spelling etc)* correct; **do you have the correct time?** avez-vous l'heure exacte?; **that is correct** c'est exact; **to prove (to be) correct** s'avérer juste; **correct to four decimal places** exact à quatre chiffres après la virgule; **am I correct in thinking that...?** ai-je raison de penser que...?; **you must be Mr Jones – that's correct** vous devez être M. Jones – c'est exact; **she was quite correct** elle avait tout à fait raison; **she was quite correct in her assumptions** ses suppositions étaient parfaitement justes; **if my memory is correct** si j'ai bonne mémoire; **figures correct at time of going to press** chiffres exacts au moment de la publication

(**b**) *(suitable, proper → behaviour, manners etc)* correct, convenable, bienséant; *(→ person)* correct, convenable; **the correct thing for him to do in the circumstances is to resign** dans ces circonstances la bienséance veut qu'il démissionne; **she was quite correct to do what she did** elle a fait ce qu'il convenait de faire; **the correct procedure** la procédure d'usage; **as is only correct** comme il se doit, comme il convient; **correct dress must be worn** une tenue correcte est de rigueur

2 *vt* (**a**) *(rectify → mistake, spelling etc)* corriger, rectifier; *(→ squint, bad posture, imbalance)* corriger; *(→ situation)* rectifier; *(→ instrument setting)* modifier

(**b**) *(mark errors in → exam, proofs, homework)* corriger

(**c**) *(indicate error to → person)* corriger, reprendre; **please correct me whenever I make a mistake** veuillez me corriger *ou* me reprendre si je fais des erreurs; **to correct sb on** *or* **about sth** corriger *ou* reprendre qn sur qch; **to correct sb's French** corriger le français de qn, reprendre qn sur son français; **if I may correct you** si vous permettez que je vous reprenne; **correct me if I'm wrong, but...** corrigez-moi si je me trompe, mais...; **I stand corrected** je reconnais mon erreur; **to correct oneself** se reprendre, se corriger

(**d**) *Arch (punish)* punir; *(physically)* corriger, infliger une correction à

corrected entry [kə'rektɪd-] *n Acct* écriture *f* d'ajustement, écriture *f* rectificative

correcting fluid [kə'rektɪŋ-] *n* liquide *m* correcteur

correction [kə'rekʃən] *n* (**a**) *(action → of exam paper, proofs, homework etc)* correction *f*; *(of error)* correction *f*, rectification *f*
(**b**) *(alteration)* correction *f*; **to make corrections** faire des corrections; **to make corrections to sth** apporter des corrections à qch
(**c**) *Arch (punishment)* correction *f*, punition *f*, châtiment *m*; **house of correction** maison *f* de correction *ou* de redressement
►► ***correction fluid*** liquide *m* correcteur; ***correction paper*** *(for typewriter)* papier *m* correcteur; ***correction tape*** *(for typewriter)* ruban *m* correcteur

correctional [kə'rekʃənəl] *adj* correctionnel
►► *Am* ***correctional facility*** établissement *m* pénitentiaire

corrective [kə'rektɪv] **1** *adj (action, measure)* rectificatif, correctif; *(exercises, treatment)* correctif; *(lens, make-up)* correcteur
2 *n* correctif *m* (**to** de); *Med (for teeth)* appareil *m* dentaire; *(for deformed limb)* appareil *m* orthopédique

correctly [kə'rektlɪ] *adv* (**a**) *(in the right way → answer, pronounce, report)* correctement; **he correctly predicted that...** il a prédit avec raison que...; **the XYZ, more correctly known as...** XYZ, ou selon son appellation plus correcte...
(**b**) *(properly → behave, dress, speak)* correctement

correctness [kə'rektnɪs] *n* (**a**) *(of answer, prediction etc)* exactitude *f*, justesse *f* (**b**) *(of behaviour, dress etc)* correction *f*

Correggio [kɒ'redʒjəʊ] *pr n* le Corrège; **a painting by Correggio** un tableau du Corrège

correlate ['kɒrəleɪt] **1** *vi* **to correlate (with sth)** *(gen)* être en corrélation *ou* rapport (avec qch), correspondre (à qch); *(in statistics)* être en corrélation (avec qch)
2 *vt (gen)* mettre en corrélation *ou* en rapport, faire correspondre; *(in statistics)* corréler; **to correlate sth with sth** *(gen)* mettre qch en corrélation *ou* rapport avec qch; *(in statistics)* corréler qch avec qch; **these two trends are closely correlated** ces deux tendances sont en rapport étroit

correlation [ˌkɒrə'leɪʃən] *n* corrélation *f*
►► ***correlation coefficient*** *(in statistics)* coefficient *m* de corrélation

correlational [ˌkɒrə'leɪʃənəl] *adj* corrélationnel

correlative [kɒ'relətɪv] **1** *n* corrélatif *m*
2 *adj* corrélatif

correspond [ˌkɒrɪ'spɒnd] *vi* (**a**) *(tally → dates, statements)* correspondre; **to correspond with** *or* **to sth** correspondre à qch
(**b**) *(be equivalent)* correspondre, équivaloir (**with** *ou* **to** à); **this animal corresponds roughly with** *or* **to our own domestic cat** cet animal correspond à peu près à notre *ou* est à peu près l'équivalent de notre chat domestique
(**c**) *(exchange letters)* correspondre; **we have been corresponding (with each other) for years** cela fait des années que nous correspondons; **we don't often correspond** nous ne correspondons *ou* nous ne nous écrivons pas souvent; **we only correspond at Christmas** nous ne nous écrivons qu'à Noël

correspondence [ˌkɒrɪ'spɒndəns] **1** *n* (**a**) *(relationship, similarity)* correspondance *f*, rapport *m*, relation *f*
(**b**) *(letter-writing)* correspondance *f*; **to be in correspondence with sb** être en correspondance avec qn; **to enter into (a) correspondence with sb** établir une *ou* entrer en correspondance avec qn; **no correspondence will be entered into** *(in competition)* il ne sera répondu à aucun courrier; **to keep up a correspondence with sb** rester en correspondance avec qn
(**c**) *(letters)* correspondance *f*, courrier *m*; **to read/to do one's correspondence** lire/faire son courrier *ou* sa correspondance; **she doesn't get much correspondence** elle ne reçoit pas beaucoup de courrier
2 *comp* par correspondance; *(school)* d'enseignement par correspondance
►► *Press* ***correspondence column*** courrier *m* des lecteurs; ***correspondence course*** cours *m* par correspondance; ***correspondence tray*** bac *m* à correspondance

correspondent [ˌkɒrɪ'spɒndənt] **1** *n* (**a**) *(reporter)* correspondant(e) *m,f*; **special correspondent** envoyé(e) *m,f* spécial(e); **sports correspondent** correspondant *m* sportif; **war/environment correspondent** correspondant *m* de guerre/pour les questions d'environnement; **our Moscow correspondent** notre correspondant à Moscou
(**b**) *(letter-writer)* correspondant(e) *m,f*; **I am a very bad correspondent** j'écris très peu
2 *adj* correspondant
►► ***correspondent bank account*** compte *m* de correspondant

corresponding [ˌkɒrɪ'spɒndɪŋ] *adj* correspondant; **unemployment/inflation is higher than in the corresponding period last year** le chômage/l'inflation a augmenté par rapport à la période correspondante de l'année dernière *ou* à la même période l'année dernière
►► *Acct* ***corresponding entry*** écriture *f* conforme; ***corresponding member*** *(of society, club)* membre *m* correspondant

correspondingly [ˌkɒrɪ'spɒndɪŋlɪ] *adv* (**a**) *(proportionally)* proportionnellement; **prices are correspondingly more expensive** les prix sont proportionnellement plus élevés
(**b**) *(related to this, in line with this)* **the translation should be correspondingly informal in register** la traduction devrait être d'un niveau de familiarité correspondant; **we got a lot of negative press and our election results were correspondingly poor** nous avons eu beaucoup de commentaires négatifs dans la presse, ce qui nous a valu de mauvais résultats aux élections

corridor ['kɒrɪˌdɔː(r)] *n (in building)* corridor *m*, couloir *m*; *(in train)* couloir *m*; *Fig* **the corridors of power** les allées *fpl* du pouvoir; *(behind the scenes)* les coulisses *fpl* du pouvoir; *Hist* **the Polish Corridor** le couloir de Dantzig
►► *Rail* ***corridor train*** train *m* à couloir

corrie ['kɒrɪ] *n Scot Geog* cirque *m*

corrie-fisted [-fɪstɪd] *adj Scot Fam* gaucher ❑

corrigendum [kɒrɪ'dʒendəm] *(pl* **corrigenda** [-də]*) n* erratum *m*

corroborate [kə'rɒbəreɪt] *vt* confirmer, corroborer; **for lack of corroborating evidence** faute de preuves à l'appui

corroboration [kəˌrɒbə'reɪʃən] *n* confirmation *f*, corroboration *f*; **to provide corroboration of sth** confirmer *ou* corroborer qch; **evidence produced in corroboration of sb's testimony** des preuves fournies à l'appui du témoignage de qn

corroborative [kə'rɒbərətɪv] *adj (evidence, statement)* à l'appui

corroboree [kəˌrɒbə'riː] *n Austr (tribal gathering)* = réunion d'Aborigènes; *Fam (get-together)* petite fête ❑ *f*

corrode [kə'rəʊd] **1** *vt (of acid, rust)* corroder, ronger, attaquer; *Fig (happiness)* entamer, miner; **it's very badly corroded** *(by acid, rust)* c'est très corrodé
2 *vi (due to acid, rust)* se corroder

corroded [kə'rəʊdɪd] *adj* corrodé, attaqué; **badly corroded metal** métal très corrodé *ou* attaqué

corrosion [kə'rəʊʒən] *n (of metal)* corrosion *f*

corrosion-resistant *adj* anti-corrosion

corrosive [kə'rəʊsɪv] **1** *adj* corrosif; *Fig* **the corrosive effects of long term unemployment** les effets destructeurs du chômage de longue durée
2 *n* corrosif *m*

corrosiveness [kə'rəʊsɪvnɪs] *n (of acid, chemical)* action *f* corrosive; *Fig (of effect)* caractère *m* destructeur

corrugated ['kɒrəˌgeɪtɪd] *adj (cardboard, paper)* ondulé
►► ***corrugated iron*** tôle *f* ondulée; **a corrugated iron hut** une cabane en tôle ondulée

corrugation [kɒrə'geɪʃən] *n* ondulation *f*

corrupt [kə'rʌpt] **1** *adj* (**a**) *(dishonest → person, society)* corrompu; **corrupt practices** pratiques *fpl* malhonnêtes
(**b**) *(depraved, immoral)* dépravé, corrompu
(**c**) *(containing alterations → text)* altéré
(**d**) *Comput (containing errors → disk, file)* altéré
2 *vt* (**a**) *(make dishonest)* corrompre; **corrupted by power** corrompu par le pouvoir
(**b**) *(deprave, debase → person, society)* dépraver, corrompre; *(→ language)* corrompre
(**c**) *(alter → text)* altérer, corrompre
(**d**) *Comput (disk, file)* altérer

corrupter [kə'rʌptə(r)] *n* corrupteur(trice) *m,f*

corruptible [kə'rʌptəbəl] *adj* corruptible

corrupting [kə'rʌptɪŋ] *adj* dépravant, corrupteur; **corrupting influence** influence *f* corruptrice

corruption [kə'rʌpʃən] *n* (**a**) *(of official, politician etc → action, state)* corruption *f* (**b**) *(depravity, debasement → action, state)* dépravation *f*, corruption *f*; *Law* **the corruption of minors** le détournement de mineurs (**c**) *(of text → action)* altération *f*, corruption *f*; *(→ state)* version *f* corrompue; *(of word → action)* corruption *f*; *(→ state)* forme *f* corrompue (**d**) *Comput (of disk, file)* altération *f* (**e**) *Formal (putrefaction)* corruption *f*

corruptive [kə'rʌptɪv] *adj* corrupteur

corruptly [kə'rʌptlɪ] *adv* (**a**) *(dishonestly)* de manière corrompue; **he had corruptly accepted bribes** il s'est corrompu en acceptant des pots-de-vin (**b**) *(in a depraved way)* d'une manière dépravée *ou* corrompue

corsage [kɔː'sɑːʒ] *n* (**a**) *(flowers)* = petit bouquet de fleurs à accrocher au corsage ou au poignet (**b**) *(bodice)* corsage *m*

corsair [kɔː'seə(r)] *n Naut* corsaire *m*

corse [kɔːs] *n Arch or Literary* cadavre *m*

corset ['kɔːsɪt] *n* corset *m*; **surgical corset** corset *m* orthopédique
►► ***corset stay*** baleine *f* de corset

Corsica ['kɔːsɪkə] *n* Corse *f*; **in Corsica** en Corse

Corsican ['kɔːsɪkən] **1** *n* (**a**) *(person)* Corse *mf* (**b**) *(language)* corse *m*
2 *adj* corse

cortège [kɔː'teɪʒ] *n* cortège *m*; **funeral cortège** cortège *m* funèbre

cortex ['kɔːteks] *(pl* **cortices** [-tɪsiːz]*) n Anat & Bot* cortex *m*

cortical ['kɔːtɪkəl] *adj Anat & Bot* cortical

corticoid ['kɔːtɪkɔɪd] *n Med* corticoïde *m*

corticosteroid [ˌkɔːtɪkəʊ'stɪərɔɪd] *n Med* corticoïde *m*

cortisone ['kɔːtɪzəʊn] *n Biol & Chem* cortisone *f*
►► ***cortisone injection*** piqûre *f* de cortisone

corundum [kə'rʌndəm] *n Miner* corindon *m*

Corus ['kɔːrəs] *n* = principale entreprise productrice de fer et d'acier en Grande-Bretagne

coruscate [ˌkɒrə'skeɪt] *vi Formal* briller, scintiller

coruscating [ˌkɒrə'skeɪtɪŋ] *adj Formal* brillant, scintillant; *Fig (wit)* brillant, étincelant

coruscation [ˌkɒrə'skeɪʃən] *n Formal* lueur *f* brillante, vif éclat *m*; *Fig* **coruscation of wit** paillettes *fpl* d'esprit

corvette [kɔː'vet] *n Naut* corvette *f*

corvine ['kɔːvaɪn] *adj Zool* corvin

COS [ˌsiːəʊ'es] *n Com (abbr* **cash on shipment***)* = paiement à l'expédition

cos[1] [kɒs] *n Br* **cos (lettuce)** (laitue *f*) romaine *f*

cos[2] [kɒs] *n Math (abbr* **cosine***)* cos

cos[3] [kɒz] *conj Fam (abbr* **because***)* parce que ❑

Cosa Nostra [ˌkəʊzə'nɒstrə] *n* Cosa Nostra *f*

cosecant [kəʊ'siːkənt] *n Math* cosécante *f*

cosh [kɒʃ] **1** *n* gourdin *m*, matraque *f*
2 *vt* assommer, matraquer

cosign ['kəʊsaɪn] *vt* cosigner

cosignatory [ˌkəʊ'sɪgnətərɪ] *(pl* **cosignatories***) n Formal* cosignataire *mf*; **the cosignatories to the agreement** les cosignataires de l'accord

cosily, *Am* **cozily** ['kəʊzɪlɪ] *adv (warmly)* confortablement; **they were sitting cosily by the fire** ils étaient assis confortablement près du feu; **cosily wrapped up** bien emmitouflé

cosine ['kəʊsaɪn] *n Math* cosinus *m*

cosiness, *Am* **coziness** ['kəʊzɪnɪs] *n* (**a**) *(warmness, comfort)* confort *m*; **there's nothing I like better than the cosiness of a big comfy sofa** il n'y a rien de mieux qu'un grand canapé bien confortable (**b**) *Fig (intimacy)* **the cosiness of her novels** l'atmosphère douce qui règne dans ses romans; **given the cosiness of their relationship** vu les rapports copain-copain qu'ils entretiennent

cosmetic [kɒz'metɪk] **1** *adj* (**a**) *(for beautifying)* cosmétique; **that type of dental surgery would**

be regarded as purely cosmetic ce type de chirurgie dentaire serait considéré comme purement esthétique

(**b**) *Fig (superficial → change, measure)* superficiel, symbolique; **it's purely cosmetic** c'est purement symbolique, c'est uniquement pour la forme; **the policy change is cosmetic rather than real** le changement de politique est plutôt un changement de forme que de fond; **the alterations they made to the translation are purely cosmetic** les changements qu'ils ont apportés à la traduction sont très superficiels

2 *n* cosmétique *m*, produit *m* de beauté; **to wear a lot of cosmetics** se maquiller beaucoup; **she's in cosmetics** elle est dans les cosmétiques

►► ***cosmetics counter*** rayon *m* des cosmétiques; ***cosmetics industry*** industrie *f* des cosmétiques; ***cosmetic surgery*** chirurgie *f* esthétique; **to have cosmetic surgery** se faire faire de la chirurgie esthétique

cosmetician [ˌkɒzmə'tɪʃən] *n (specialist)* esthéticien(enne) *m,f*

cosmetologist [ˌkɒzmə'tɒlədʒɪst] *n* cosmétologue *mf*

cosmetology [ˌkɒzmə'tɒlədʒɪ] *n* cosmétologie *f*

cosmic ['kɒzmɪk] *adj* (**a**) *(relating to the universe)* cosmique (**b**) *(large, significant)* gigantesque; **of cosmic proportions** aux proportions gigantesques

►► ***cosmic dust*** poussières *fpl* cosmiques; ***cosmic ray*** rayon *m* cosmique

cosmodrome ['kɒzmədrəʊm] *n* cosmodrome *m*

cosmogony [kɒz'mɒgənɪ] *n* cosmogonie *f*

cosmographer [kɒz'mɒgrəfə(r)] *n* cosmographe *mf*

cosmography [kɒz'mɒgrəfɪ] *n* cosmographie *f*

cosmologist [kɒz'mɒlədʒɪst] *n* cosmologue *mf*, cosmologiste *mf*

cosmology [kɒz'mɒlədʒɪ] *n* cosmologie *f*

cosmonaut ['kɒzmənɔːt] *n* cosmonaute *mf*

cosmopolitan [ˌkɒzmə'pɒlɪtən] **1** *adj (city, person, restaurant)* cosmopolite

2 *n* (**a**) *(person)* cosmopolite *mf* (**b**) *(cocktail)* cosmopolitan *m*

cosmopolitanism [ˌkɒzmə'pɒlɪtənɪzəm] *n* cosmopolitisme *m*

cosmos ['kɒzmɒs] *n* cosmos *m*; *Fig* univers *m*

co-sponsor 1 *n* = entreprise ou personne contribuant à un sponsoring; **we need at least one more co-sponsor** il nous faut encore au moins un autre sponsor; **I agreed to act as (a) co-sponsor** j'ai accepté d'être le deuxième sponsor *ou* l'un des sponsors

2 *vt* **the company has been approached to co-sponsor the exhibition** l'entreprise a été sollicitée pour participer au sponsoring *ou* pour être l'un des sponsors de l'exposition

Cossack ['kɒsæk] **1** *adj* cosaque

2 *n* Cosaque *m*

cosset ['kɒsɪt] *vt (person)* dorloter, choyer, câliner; **to cosset oneself** se dorloter

cossie ['kɒzɪ] *n Br & Austr Fam* maillot *m* de bain ❑

COST [kɒst]

coût	►**1 (a)**
prix	►**1 (a), (b)**
coûter	►**2 (a)**
évaluer le coût de	►**2 (b)**
coûter cher	►**3**
frais	►**4**

(*pt & pp vt sense* (**a**) & *vi* **cost**, *pt & pp vt sense* (**b**) **costed**) **1** *n* (**a**) *(amount charged or paid)* coût *m*; **the car was repaired at a cost of £50** la réparation de la voiture a coûté 50 livres; **the cost of petrol has gone up** le prix de l'essence a augmenté; **the cost of money** le loyer de l'argent; **think of the cost (involved)!** imagine un peu le prix que ça coûte!; **to bear the cost of sth** payer qch; *(with difficulty)* faire face aux frais *ou* aux dépenses de qch; **to buy/to sell sth at cost** *(cost price)* acheter/vendre qch au prix coûtant; **at little/great cost** à peu de/à grands frais; **at no extra cost** sans frais supplémentaires; **the firm cut its costs by 30 percent** l'entreprise a réduit ses frais de 30 pour cent; *Com* **cost, insurance and freight** coût, assurance et fret; *Acct* **cost of goods purchased** coût *m* d'achat; *Acct* **cost of goods sold** coût *m* des ventes, coût *m* des marchandises vendues; *Mktg* **cost per thousand** coût *m* par mille, CPM *m*

(**b**) *Fig* prix *m*; **whatever the cost** à tout prix, à n'importe quel prix; **whatever the cost to his health** quoi qu'il en coûte à sa santé, quel qu'en soit le prix pour sa santé; **whatever the cost to myself** quoi qu'il m'en coûte; **he was always helping people, whatever the cost to himself** il était toujours à aider les autres, quoi qu'il lui en coûte; **at the cost of her job/reputation/marriage** au prix de son travail/sa réputation/son mariage; **he saved them at the cost of his (own) life** il les a sauvés au prix de sa vie; **to find out** *or* **to learn** *or* **to discover to one's cost** apprendre *ou* découvrir à ses dépens; **as I discovered to my cost** comme je l'ai appris *ou* découvert à mes dépens; **as I know to my cost** comme j'en ai fait la dure expérience; **to count the cost of sth** faire le bilan de qch; **no-one stopped to count the cost** *(in advance)* personne n'a pensé au prix à payer; **what will be the cost in terms of human suffering?** quel sera le prix à payer en termes de souffrances humaines?; **the cost in human life** le prix en vies humaines; **the cost in human terms** *(of unemployment, closure)* le coût humain

2 *vt* (**a**) coûter; **how much** *or* **what does it cost?** combien ça coûte?; **how much is it going to cost me?** combien est-ce que ça va me coûter?, à combien est-ce que ça va me revenir?; **how much will it cost the taxpayer?** combien cela coûtera-t-il au contribuable?; **it costs £10** cela coûte 10 livres; **it cost me £200** cela m'est revenu à *ou* m'a coûté 200 livres; **did it cost much?** est-ce que cela a coûté cher?; **it costs nothing to join** l'inscription est gratuite; **it's a hobby that doesn't cost anything** c'est un passe-temps qui ne coûte rien; **it didn't cost me a penny** ça ne m'a rien coûté du tout, ça ne m'a pas coûté un sou; *Fam* **it'll cost you!** *(purchase)* tu vas le sentir passer!; *(help, favour)* ce ne sera pas gratuit! ❑; **electricity costs money, you know!** l'électricité, ce n'est pas gratuit!; **it cost her a lot of time and effort** cela lui a demandé beaucoup de temps et d'efforts; **the puncture cost us a bit of time** la crevaison nous a fait perdre pas mal de temps; **it cost him his job** cela lui a coûté son travail, cela lui a fait perdre son travail; **it cost her her life** cela lui a coûté la vie; **drinking and driving costs lives** la conduite en état d'ivresse coûte des vies humaines; **it doesn't cost anything to be polite** ça ne coûte rien d'être poli; **it must have cost him to say sorry** cela a dû lui coûter de s'excuser; **whatever it costs** *(purchase)* quel qu'en soit le prix; **whatever it costs, I'm not going to give up** quoi qu'il m'en coûte, je n'abandonnerai pas; *Fam* **to cost an arm and a leg, to cost the earth** coûter les yeux de la tête *ou* la peau des fesses

(**b**) *(work out price of → trip)* évaluer le coût de; *(→ job, repairs)* établir un devis pour; *Com (→ product)* établir le prix de revient de; **how much was it costed at?** *(job)* à combien est-ce que le coût a été évalué?; **he costed the repairs to the car at £150** il a établi un devis de 150 livres pour les réparations de la voiture, il a évalué les réparations de la voiture à 150 livres; **a carefully costed budget** un budget calculé avec soin

3 *vi Fam (be expensive)* coûter cher ❑, ne pas être donné ❑; **we can do it but it will cost** on peut le faire mais ça ne sera pas donné

4 costs *npl Law* frais *mpl* (d'instance) et dépens *mpl*; **to be awarded costs** se voir accorder des frais et dépens; **to be ordered to pay costs** être condamné aux dépens

5 at all costs *adv* à tout prix

6 at any cost *adv* en aucun cas; **he should not be approached at any cost** en aucun cas il ne doit être approché

►► ***cost accountant*** comptable *mf* spécialisé(e) en comptabilité analytique *ou* en comptabilité d'exploitation; ***cost accounting*** comptabilité *f* analytique *ou* d'exploitation; *Acct* ***cost allocation*** imputation *f* des charges; *Fin* ***cost analysis*** analyse *f* des coûts, analyse *f* du prix de revient; *Fin* ***cost base*** prix *m* de base; *Acct* ***cost centre*** centre *m* d'analyse; *Fin* ***cost curve*** courbe *f* des coûts; ***cost equation*** équation *f* de coût; ***cost factor*** facteur *m* coût; ***cost of living*** coût *m* de la vie; **the cost of living keeps going up** le coût de la vie ne cesse d'augmenter; **in order to keep up with the cost of living** afin de suivre le coût de la vie; *Fin* ***cost management*** gestion *f* des coûts; *Fin* ***cost price*** prix *m* coûtant *ou* de revient; **to buy/to sell sth at cost price** acheter/vendre qch à prix coûtant; *Acct* ***cost pricing*** méthode *f* des coûts marginaux; *Fin* ***cost unit*** unité *f* de coût; *Fin* ***cost variance*** écart *m* des coûts

►**cost out** *vt sep (work out price of → trip)* évaluer le coût de; *(→ job, repairs)* établir un devis pour; *Com (→ product)* établir le prix de revient de

costa ['kɒstə] *n Anat* côte *f*

Costa Brava [ˌkɒstə'brɑːvə] *n* Costa Brava *f*

Costa del Crime *n Br Hum* = appellation humoristique de la Costa del Sol, par allusion au grand nombre d'anciens criminels britanniques qui y résident

Costa del Sol *n* Costa del Sol *f*

costal ['kɒstəl] *adj Anat* costal

co-star (*pt & pp* **co-starred**, *cont* **co-starring**) **1** *n (of actor, actress)* partenaire *mf*

2 *vi (in film, TV programme)* être l'une des vedettes principales; **to co-star with sb** partager la vedette *ou* l'affiche avec qn; **they have co-starred in several films** ils ont partagé la vedette *ou* l'affiche de plusieurs films; **she has co-starred in three films** elle a joué l'un des rôles principaux dans trois films; **this is his first co-starring role** c'est la première fois qu'il a un des rôles principaux

3 *vt* **the film co-stars Tom Cruise and Nicole Kidman** le film met en scène Tom Cruise et Nicole Kidman dans les rôles principaux *ou* vedettes; **the film co-stars Harvey Keitel** le film met en scène Harvey Keitel dans l'un des rôles principaux *ou* vedettes; **co-starring Gwyneth Paltrow** *(in credits)* avec Gwyneth Paltrow

Costa Rica [-'riːkə] *n* Costa Rica *m*; **in Costa Rica** au Costa Rica

Costa Rican [-'riːkən] **1** *n* Costaricien(enne) *m,f*

2 *adj* costaricien

3 *comp (embassy, history)* du Costa Rica

cost-benefit *adj Fin*

►► ***cost-benefit analysis*** analyse *f* des coûts et rendements; ***cost-benefit ratio*** rapport *m* coût/profit

cost-competitive *adj Com (product)* à prix compétitif; **we're not cost-competitive** nos prix ne sont pas compétitifs

cost-conscious *adj* **to be cost-conscious** contrôler ses dépenses; **in these cost-conscious days** par les temps qui courent où tout le monde fait attention à *ou* surveille ses dépenses

cost-cutting 1 *n* compression *f ou* réduction *f* des coûts; **further cost-cutting may be necessary** d'autres compressions *ou* réductions des coûts pourraient s'avérer nécessaires

2 *adj* de compression *ou* de réduction des coûts; **this is only part of a larger cost-cutting exercise** ce n'est qu'un élément d'une opération plus vaste de compression *ou* de réduction des coûts; **a cost-cutting drive** une opération de réduction des dépenses

cost-effective *adj* rentable; **the project must be made cost-effective** il faut rentabiliser le projet

cost-effectiveness *n* rentabilité *f*

costermonger ['kɒstəˌmʌŋgə(r)] *n Br Old-fashioned* marchand(e) *m,f* de quatre-saisons

costing ['kɒstɪŋ] *n Com* (**a**) *(of product)* estimation *f* du prix de revient; *(of job, repairs)* établissement *m* d'un devis; **based on detailed costings** basé sur des calculs détaillés (**b**) *(form, document → of job, repairs)* devis *m*; *(→ of product)* estimation *f* du prix de revient

costive ['kɒstɪv] *adj Med* constipé

costiveness ['kɒstɪvnɪs] *n Med* constipation *f*

costliness ['kɒstlɪnɪs] *n (high price)* cherté *f*; *Fig* **we didn't realize the costliness of our mistake** nous ne nous sommes pas rendu compte combien notre erreur allait nous coûter cher

costly ['kɒstlɪ] (*compar* **costlier**, *superl* **costliest**) *adj* (**a**) *(expensive)* coûteux, cher; **this may be a costly mistake** cette erreur pourrait me/vous/

etc coûter cher; **the costliest war this country has ever known in terms of human suffering** la guerre la plus meurtrière et traumatisante que le pays ait jamais connue (**b**) *(of high quality)* somptueux, riche

cost-of-living *adj*

►► *Fin* ***cost-of-living adjustment*** *(in salary)* augmentation *f* de salaire indexée sur le coût de la vie; *Fin* ***cost-of-living allowance*** indemnité *f* de vie chère; *Fin* ***cost-of-living increase*** *(in salary)* augmentation *f* de salaire indexée sur le coût de la vie; *Fin* ***cost-of-living index*** indice *m* du coût de la vie

cost-plus *adj Fin* à coût majoré; **on a cost-plus basis** sur la base du prix de revient majoré; *Fin* **cost-plus pricing** fixation *f* du prix en fonction du coût

cost-push inflation *n Fin* inflation *f* par les coûts

cost-reduce *vt Com* réduire le coût de

costume ['kɒstjuːm] **1** *n* (**a**) *(in cinema, theatre, TV)* costume *m*; **to be (dressed) in costume** porter un costume (de scène); **did you make your own costume?** est-ce que vous avez fait votre costume vous-même?; **I hate wearing costume** je déteste porter des costumes; **costumes by...** *(in credits)* costumes réalisés par...

(**b**) *(fancy dress)* costume *m*, déguisement *m*; **to be (dressed) in costume** être costumé *ou* déguisé; **are you going to the party in costume?** serez-vous déguisé à la soirée?

(**c**) *(traditional dress)* **national costume** costume *m* national; **to wear national costume** porter le costume national

(**d**) *(for swimming)* maillot *m* de bain

(**e**) *Br Old-fashioned (woman's suit)* tailleur *m*

2 *vt (film, play)* réaliser les costumes pour

►► ***costume ball*** bal *m* costumé; *Theat* ***costume(s) department*** service *m* des costumes; ***costume designer*** costumier(ère) *m,f*; ***costume drama*** dramatique *f* en costumes d'époque; ***costume hire*** location *f* de costumes; ***costume jewellery*** *(UNCOUNT)* bijoux *mpl* fantaisie; **a piece of costume jewellery** un bijou fantaisie; ***costume party*** bal *m* costumé; ***costume piece, costume play*** pièce *f* en costumes d'époque

costumier [kɒ'stjuːmɪə(r)], **costumer** ['kɒstjuːmə(r)] *n* costumier(ère) *m,f*

cost-volume-profit analysis *n Acct* étude *f* de coût-efficacité

cosy, *Am* **cozy** ['kəʊzɪ] (*Br compar* **cosier**, *superl* **cosiest**, *Am compar* **cozier**, *superl* **coziest**) **1** *adj* (**a**) *(warm, snug → flat, room, atmosphere)* douillet, confortable; **it's nice and cosy in here** on est bien ici; **to be snug and cosy in one's bed** être bien confortablement installé dans son lit; **to look cosy** avoir l'air bien confortable; **to feel cosy** se sentir bien; **isn't this cosy?** on n'est pas bien ici?

(**b**) *(intimate → chat, evening etc)* intime; *(→ novel)* à l'atmosphère douce; *Pej* **they've got a very cosy relationship** ils sont très copain-copain; **a cosy little job** *(undemanding)* un travail pépère; *Pej* **a cosy deal** une combine

2 *n (for teapot)* couvre-théière *m*; *(for egg)* couvre-œuf *m*

►**cosy up to**, *Am* **cozy up to** *vt insep Fam* se mettre dans les petits papiers de; **he's always cosying up to the boss** il essaie tout le temps de se mettre dans les petits papiers du patron

cot [kɒt] *n Br (for baby)* lit *m* d'enfant; *Am (camp bed)* lit *m* de camp; *Naut* cadre *m* à l'anglaise

►► *Br* ***cot death*** mort *f* subite du nourrisson; **she lost her first child through cot death** son premier enfant est mort de la mort subite du nourrisson

cotangent [kəʊ'tændʒənt] *n Math* cotangente *f*

cote [kəʊt] *n (for doves)* colombier *m*, pigeonnier *m*; *(for sheep)* abri *m*, bergerie *f*

cotel ['kɒtel] *n Am* auberge *f* de jeunesse

cotenant [ˌkəʊ'tenənt] *n* colocataire *mf*

coterie ['kəʊtərɪ] *n* cercle *m*, cénacle *m*; *Pej* coterie *f*, clique *f*

coterminous [ˌkəʊ'tɜːmɪnəs] *adj Formal* limitrophe, frontalier; **France is coterminous with Spain and Switzerland** la France a des frontières communes avec l'Espagne et la Suisse

cotillion, cotillon [kə'tɪljən] *n* cotillon *m*

cotinga [kəʊ'tɪŋgə] *n Orn* cotinga *m*

co-trustee *n Law* co-administrateur(trice) *m,f*

Cotswolds ['kɒtswəʊldz] *npl* **the Cotswolds** = région touristique du sud-ouest de l'Angleterre, connue pour ses pittoresques villages en pierre locale

cottage ['kɒtɪdʒ] *n* (**a**) *(in country)* petite maison *f* (à la campagne), cottage *m*; **thatched cottage** chaumière *f*

(**b**) *Am (holiday home)* maison *f* de campagne, *Can* chalet *m*

(**c**) *Br very Fam* = toilettes publiques servant aux rencontres des homosexuels

►► ***cottage cheese*** fromage *m* blanc (égoutté), cottage cheese *m*; *Br* ***cottage flat*** = appartement situé dans un pavillon; *Br* ***cottage hospital*** petit hôpital *m* de campagne; ***cottage industry*** industrie *f* artisanale; *(small-scale, at home)* industrie *f* familiale; *Br* ***cottage loaf*** = miche de pain en forme de brioche; *Br* ***cottage pie*** hachis *m* parmentier

cottager ['kɒtɪdʒə(r)] *n Br* habitant(e) *m,f* d'un cottage; *Am (owner)* propriétaire *mf* d'une maison de campagne; *(tenant)* locataire *mf* d'une maison de campagne

cottaging ['kɒtɪdʒɪŋ] *n (UNCOUNT) Br very Fam* = rencontres homosexuelles dans les toilettes publiques

cotter ['kɒtə(r)] *n Tech (wedge)* goupille *f*; *(pin)* clavette *f*

►► ***cotter pin*** clavette *f*

cotton ['kɒtən] **1** *n* (**a**) *(material, plant)* coton *m*; **to pick cotton** cueillir le coton; **put it with the rest of the cottons** *(garments made of cotton)* mets-le avec le reste du (linge en) coton; **is this dress cotton?** *(made of cotton)* cette robe est-elle en coton?

(**b**) *Br (thread for sewing)* fil *m*

2 *comp (garment)* en coton; *(industry, trade)* du coton; *(culture, field, grower, plantation)* de coton

►► *Am* ***cotton batting*** bourre *f* de coton; *Geog* ***Cotton Belt*** = région du coton dans le sud des États-Unis; *Br* ***cotton bud*** coton-tige® *m*; *Bot* ***cotton bush*** cotonnier *m*; *Am* ***cotton candy*** barbe *f* à papa; *Tech* ***cotton gin*** égreneuse *f* de coton; ***cotton grass*** linaigrette *f*, lin *m* des marais; ***cotton mill*** filature *f* de coton; ***cotton picker*** *(person)* cueilleur(euse) *m,f* de coton; ***cotton plant*** cotonnier *m*; ***the Cotton State*** = surnom donné à l'Alabama; *Am* ***cotton swab*** coton-tige® *m*; ***cotton waste*** *(UNCOUNT)* déchets *mpl* de coton; *Br* ***cotton wool*** coton *m* hydrophile, ouate *f*; *Fam* **my legs feel like cotton wool** j'ai les jambes en coton; *Fig* **to wrap sb in cotton wool** être aux petits soins pour qn; **to bring a child up in cotton wool** élever un enfant dans du coton; ***cotton wool balls*** boules *fpl* de coton; *Fig* ***cotton wool clouds*** nuages *mpl* cotonneux; ***cotton wool pads*** rondelles *fpl* de coton *ou* d'ouate; ***cotton wool swab*** coton-tige® *m*

►**cotton on** *vi Fam* piger; **to cotton on to sth** piger qch; **one of the first companies to cotton on to the advantages of the system** l'une des premières sociétés à piger les avantages du système

►**cotton to** *vt insep Am Fam* (**a**) *(take a liking to → person)* se prendre d'amitié pour□; **I didn't cotton to her at first** ça n'a pas accroché avec elle au début (**b**) *(approve of → person)* avoir à la bonne; *(→ behaviour, suggestion)* voir d'un bon œil; **I don't cotton to that kind of behaviour** je n'approuve pas ce genre de comportement□

cottonmouth ['kɒtənˌmaʊθ, *pl* -maʊðz] *n* (**a**) *Zool* mocassin *m* d'eau (**b**) *Am (dry mouth)* **to have cottonmouth** avoir la bouche pâteuse

cotton-picking *adj Am very Fam* sale, sacré; **that's a cotton-picking lie!** ce n'est qu'un sale mensonge!; **get your cotton-picking hands off me!** enlève tes sales pattes!

cottonseed ['kɒtənˌsiːd] *n* graine *f* de coton

►► ***cottonseed oil*** huile *f* de coton

cottontail ['kɒtənˌteɪl] *n Zool* lapin *m* (de garenne)

cotyledon [ˌkɒtɪ'liːdən] *n Bot* cotylédon *m*

couch [kaʊtʃ] **1** *n (sofa)* canapé *m*, divan *m*, sofa *m*; *(in psychiatrist's office)* divan *m*; *Fam* **to be on the couch** faire une psychanalyse□, voir un psy; *Fam Pej* **he's a real couch potato** il passe son temps affalé devant la télé

2 *vt (express → phrase, comment)* formuler; **to be couched in very polite terms/in jargon** *(letter, document)* être formulé en termes très polis/en jargon

►► *Bot* ***couch grass*** chiendent *m*

couchant ['kaʊtʃənt] *adj Her* couché, accroupi

couchette [kuː'ʃet] *n Rail & Naut* couchette *f*

►► *Rail* ***couchette car*** voiture-couchette *f*

couching ['kaʊtʃɪŋ] *n* (**a**) *Med* cataractopièse *f* (**b**) *(in embroidery)* broderie *f* sur fils couchés

cougar ['kuːgə(r)] *n Zool* couguar *m*, cougouar *m*, puma *m*

cough [kɒf] **1** *n* toux *f*; **to have a cough** tousser; **her cough doesn't seem to be getting any better** sa toux n'a pas l'air de s'arranger, elle tousse toujours autant; **you want to get that cough seen to** avec cette toux, tu devrais te faire examiner; **I can't get rid of this cough** cette toux ne me passe pas; **can you do something for this cough, doctor?** pouvez-vous faire quelque chose pour soigner ma toux, docteur?; **that's a nasty cough (you've got)** tu as une mauvaise toux; **she gave a loud cough** elle a toussé fort; **to give a warning cough** tousser *ou* toussoter en guise d'avertissement; **she gave me a warning cough that they were coming** elle a toussé *ou* toussoté pour m'avertir qu'ils arrivaient; **he cleared his throat with a loud cough** il s'est éclairci la voix en toussant bruyamment; *Fig* **there's a cough in the engine** le moteur tousse, le moteur a des ratés

2 *comp* pour *ou* contre la toux, *Spec* antitussif

3 *vi* tousser; *Fig* **the engine coughed into life** le moteur a toussé puis s'est mis en marche

4 *vt (blood)* cracher; *Fig* **the old car coughed its way down the street** la vieille voiture a descendu la rue en faisant des ratés

►► ***cough drop*** pastille *f* contre la toux *ou* antitussive; ***cough lozenge*** pastille *f* contre *ou* pour la toux; ***cough mixture*** sirop *m* antitussif *ou* contre la toux; ***cough sweet*** pastille *f* contre la toux *ou* antitussive; ***cough syrup*** sirop *m* antitussif *ou* contre la toux

►**cough up 1** *vt sep* (**a**) *(blood)* cracher (en toussant) (**b**) *Fam (money)* cracher, raquer; **cough up what you owe me** crache ce que tu me dois

2 *vi Fam (pay up)* banquer, raquer; **come on then, cough up!** allez, banque!

coughing ['kɒfɪŋ] *n* toux *f*; **I can't stand his coughing** je ne supporte pas de l'entendre tousser; **your coughing woke me up** tu m'as réveillé en toussant; **fit of coughing, coughing fit** quinte *f* de toux

COULD [kʊd]

> La forme négative est **couldn't**. Dans les contextes où il est nécessaire d'utiliser une forme plus soignée, on écrit **could not**.

modal aux v (**a**) *(be able to)* **I'd come if I could** je viendrais si je (le) pouvais; **she could no longer walk** elle ne pouvait plus marcher; **they couldn't very well refuse** il leur aurait été difficile de refuser; **five years ago I could run a mile in four minutes but I couldn't anymore** il y a cinq ans, je courais un mile en quatre minutes mais je ne pourrais plus maintenant; **she could have had the job if she'd wanted it** elle aurait pu obtenir cet emploi si elle l'avait voulu

(**b**) *(with verbs of perception or understanding)* **he could see her talking to her boss** il la voyait qui parlait avec son patron; **I could see his point of view** je comprenais son point de vue

(**c**) *(indicating ability or skill)* **she could read and write** elle savait lire et écrire; **she could speak three languages** elle parlait trois langues

(**d**) *(in polite requests)* **could I borrow your sweater?** est-ce que je pourrais t'emprunter ton pull?; **could I join you?** est-ce que je pourrais me joindre à vous?; **couldn't I come too?** est-ce que je ne pourrais pas venir moi aussi?; **could you help me please?** pourriez-vous *ou* est-ce que vous pourriez m'aider, s'il vous plaît?; **could you bring the bill, please?** pourriez-vous apporter l'addition, s'il vous plaît?

(**e**) *(indicating supposition or speculation)* **they could give up at any time** ils pourraient abandonner n'importe quand; **could he be lying?** se pourrait-il qu'il mente?; **the stock market could crash tomorrow** le marché pourrait s'effondrer demain; **you could well be right** tu pourrais bien avoir raison; **don't touch it, it could be dangerous** n'y touchez pas, ça pourrait être dangereux; **they could have changed their plans** ils ont peut-être changé leurs plans

(**f**) *(indicating possibility)* **you could have told me the truth** tu aurais pu me dire la vérité; **they could easily have got here earlier** ils auraient facilement pu arriver ici plus tôt; **you could have warned me!** tu aurais pu me prévenir!; **what could I have done with the keys?** qu'est-ce que j'ai bien pu faire des clés?; **I could kill him!** je pourrais le tuer!; **he could have jumped for joy** il en aurait presque sauté de joie; **I'm as happy as could be** je suis on ne peut plus heureux; **she was as kind as could be** elle était on ne peut plus gentille

(**g**) *(indicating unwillingness)* **I couldn't just leave him there, could I?** je ne pouvais vraiment pas le laisser là; **I couldn't possibly do it before tomorrow** je ne pourrai vraiment pas le faire avant demain

(**h**) *(in polite suggestions)* **you could always complain to the director** tu pourrais toujours te plaindre au directeur; **couldn't you just apologize?** tu ne pourrais pas simplement présenter tes excuses?; **couldn't we at least talk about it?** est-ce que nous ne pourrions pas au moins en discuter?

(**i**) *(introducing comments or opinions)* **if I could just intervene here** est-ce que je peux me permettre d'intervenir ici?; **you could argue it's a waste of resources** tu pourrais argumenter que c'est un gaspillage de ressources

(**j**) *(indicating surprise or disbelief)* **the house couldn't have been THAT expensive** la maison n'a pas dû coûter si cher que ça; **how could she have done such a thing?** comment a-t-elle pu faire une chose pareille?; **how could you say that?** comment avez-vous pu dire ça *ou* une chose pareille?; **who on earth could that be?** qui diable cela peut-il bien être?

(**k**) *(inviting agreement)* **he left and you couldn't blame him** il est parti et on ne peut pas lui en vouloir

---

couldn't ['kʊdənt] = **could not**

couldn't-care-less *adj Fam (attitude)* je-m'en-foutiste

couldst [kʊdst] *Arch 2nd pers sing of* **could**

could've ['kʊdəv] = **could have**

coulee ['ku:lɪ] *n Am Geol* ravin *m*

coulis ['ku:li:] *n Culin* coulis *m*

couloir ['ku:lwɑ:(r)] *n Geol* couloir *m*

coulomb ['ku:lɒm] *n Elec* coulomb *m*

council ['kaʊnsəl] **1** *n* (**a**) *(group of people)* conseil *m*; **the UN Security Council** le Conseil de sécurité des Nations unies

(**b**) *Br (elected local body → people)* conseil *m*; *(→ government)* municipalité *f*; **she's standing for election to the council** elle se présente aux élections du conseil; **to be on the council** être au conseil; **the council are improving services** la municipalité est en train d'améliorer les services; **county** *or Scot* **regional council** conseil *m* régional

(**c**) *(meeting)* conseil *m*; **to hold a council of war** tenir un conseil de guerre

(**d**) *Rel* concile *m*

2 *comp* (**a**) *(meeting)* du conseil

(**b**) *Br (election, service, worker)* municipal; *(leader, meeting)* du conseil municipal

►► ***council estate*** cité *f*; **to live on a council estate** habiter dans une cité; ***Council of Europe*** Conseil *m* de l'Europe; ***council flat/house*** ≃ habitation *f* à loyer modéré, ≃ HLM *f or m*; ***council housing*** ≃ habitations *fpl* à loyer modéré, ≃ HLM *fpl or mpl*; ***Council of the Isles*** Conseil *m* des Îles, = conseil mis en place pour permettre aux parlementaires d'Angleterre, du pays de Galles, d'Écosse, d'Irlande et d'Irlande du Nord de se réunir pour débattre de questions d'intérêt commun; ***Council for Mutual Economic Aid*** Comecon *m*; *Br* ***Council for National Academic Awards*** = organisme non universitaire délivrant des diplômes en Grande-Bretagne; *EU* ***Council for Security and Cooperation in Europe*** Conférence *f* sur la sécurité et la coopération en Europe; *Br Fin* ***council tax*** *(UNCOUNT)* impôts *mpl* locaux; ***council tenants*** = locataires d'un appartement ou d'une maison appartenant à la municipalité

councillor, *Am* **councilor** ['kaʊnsələ(r)] *n* conseiller(ère) *m,f*; **Councillor (John) Murray** Monsieur le Conseiller Murray; **town/county councillor** conseiller(ère) *m,f* municipal(e)/régional(e)

councillorship, *Am* **councilorship** ['kaʊnsələʃɪp] *n* (**a**) *(rank)* dignité *f* de conseiller (**b**) *(period in office)* période *f* d'exercice des fonctions de conseiller

councilman ['kaʊnsəlmæn] *(pl* **councilmen** [-men]) *n Am* conseiller *m*

councilor, councilorship *Am* = **councillor, councillorship**

councilwoman ['kaʊnsəl,wʊmən] *(pl* **councilwomen** [-,wɪmɪn]) *n Am* conseillère *f*

counsel ['kaʊnsəl] *(Br pt & pp* **counselled,** *cont* **counselling,** *Am pt & pp* **counseled,** *cont* **counseling**) **1** *n* (**a**) *Formal (advice)* conseil *m*; **to take counsel with sb about sth** prendre conseil auprès de qn sur qch; **to take counsel (together)** tenir conseil; **to keep one's own counsel** garder ses opinions *ou* intentions pour soi

(**b**) *Law* avocat(e) *m,f*; **counsel for the defence** avocat(e) *m,f* de la défense; **counsel for the prosecution** procureur *m*; **to seek the advice of counsel** se faire conseiller par un avocat; **both parties contacted their counsel** les deux parties ont contacté leurs avocats; **if counsel would approach the bench** si vous voulez bien vous approcher, maître; *Br* **King's counsel, Queen's counsel** avocat(e) *m,f* de la Couronne

2 *vt* (**a**) *Formal* conseiller; **to counsel sb to do sth** conseiller à qn de faire qch; **to counsel caution** recommander la prudence

(**b**) *(in therapy)* conseiller

counselling, *Am* **counseling** ['kaʊnsəlɪŋ] *n (gen)* assistance *f*, *Can* counseling *m*; *(psychological)* aide *f* psychologique; **you need counselling** tu as besoin de voir un psychologue; **she does counselling at the university** elle est conseillère auprès des étudiants à l'université

counsellor, *Am* **counselor** ['kaʊnsələ(r)] *n* (**a**) *(gen)* conseiller(ère) *m,f*; *(in therapy)* psychologue *mf* (**b**) *Am Law* avocat(e) *m,f*; **that's enough, counsellor!** cela suffit, maître!

COUNT [kaʊnt]

compte	►**1 (a)**
chef d'accusation	►**1 (c)**
taux	►**1 (d)**
comte	►**1 (e)**
compter	►**2 (a), (b); 3**
considérer	►**2 (c)**

1 *n* (**a**) *(gen)* compte *m*, comptage *m*; *(of ballot papers)* dépouillement *m*; **to have a count** faire le compte, compter; **it took three/several counts** il a fallu faire trois/plusieurs fois le compte, il a fallu compter trois/plusieurs fois; **to have a second count** refaire le compte, recompter; **to lose count** perdre le compte; **I've lost count of the number of times he's been late** je ne compte plus le nombre de fois où il est arrivé en retard; **to keep count (of sth)** tenir le compte (de qch); **I have a job keeping count of all your boyfriends** j'ai du mal à tenir le compte de tous tes petits amis; **at the last count** *(gen)* la dernière fois qu'on a compté; *Admin (of people)* au dernier recensement; **on the count of three, begin** à trois, vous commencez

(**b**) *Boxing* **he took a count of nine** il est resté à terre jusqu'à neuf; **to take the count** être mis K-O; **to be out for the count** *(boxer, person in fight)* être K-O; *(fast asleep)* dormir comme une souche

(**c**) *Law* chef *m* d'accusation; **guilty on three counts of murder** coupable de meurtre sur trois chefs d'accusation; **the judge found him guilty on the first count, but cleared him of the second** le juge l'a déclaré coupable sur le *ou* quant au premier chef, mais l'a acquitté pour le second; *Fig* **the argument is flawed on both counts** l'argumentation est défectueuse sur les deux points; **I'm annoyed with you on a number of counts** je suis fâché contre toi pour un certain nombre de raisons *ou* à plus d'un titre

(**d**) *Med* taux *m*; **blood (cell) count** numération *f* globulaire

(**e**) *(nobleman)* comte *m*

2 *vt* (**a**) *(add up)* compter; **I counted ten people in the room** j'ai compté dix personnes dans la pièce; **to count the votes** dépouiller le scrutin; *Fig* **to count sheep** *(when sleepless)* compter les moutons; **to count the pennies** faire attention à ses sous; **you can count his good points on the fingers of one hand** ses qualités se comptent sur les doigts de la main; **count your blessings** pense à tout ce que tu as pour être heureux; **count your blessings that there was someone around** tu peux t'estimer heureux qu'il y ait eu quelqu'un dans les parages; *Prov* **don't count your chickens (before they're hatched)** il ne faut pas vendre la peau de l'ours (avant de l'avoir tué)

(**b**) *(include)* compter; **have you counted yourself?** est-ce que tu t'es compté?; **counting Alan, there were ten of us** en comptant Alan, nous étions dix; **not counting public holidays** sans compter les jours fériés

(**c**) *(consider)* considérer, estimer; **to count sb among one's friends** compter qn parmi ses amis; **do you count her as a friend?** la considères-tu comme une amie?; **student grants are not counted as taxable income** les bourses d'études ne sont pas considérées comme revenu imposable; **count yourself lucky you've got good friends** estime-toi heureux d'avoir des amis sur qui compter; **I count myself as very lucky** je considère *ou* j'estime que j'ai beaucoup de chance; **I count myself happy** je m'estime heureux; **to be counted a success** *(person)* être considéré comme quelqu'un qui a réussi; *(project)* être considéré comme un succès

3 *vi* (**a**) *(add up)* compter; **to learn to count** apprendre à compter; **to count to twenty/fifty/a hundred** compter jusqu'à vingt/cinquante/cent; **to count on one's fingers** compter sur ses doigts; **counting from tomorrow** à partir *ou* à compter de demain

(**b**) *(be considered, qualify)* compter; **two children count as one adult** deux enfants comptent pour un adulte; **anyone over fourteen counts as an adult** toutes les personnes âgées de plus de quatorze ans comptent pour des adultes; **unemployment benefit counts as taxable income** les allocations (de) chômage comptent comme revenu imposable; **this exam counts towards the final mark** cet examen compte dans la note finale; **that/he doesn't count** ça/il ne compte pas; **she counts among my very best friends** elle compte parmi mes meilleurs amis; **his record counted in his favour/against him** son casier judiciaire a joué en sa faveur/l'a desservi

(**c**) *(be important)* compter; **every second/minute counts** chaque seconde/minute compte; **experience counts more than qualifications** l'expérience compte davantage que les diplômes; **he counts for nothing** il n'est pas important, il ne compte pas; **a private education doesn't count for much now** avoir reçu une éducation privée n'est plus un grand avantage de nos jours; **what counts around here is enthusiasm** ce qui compte ici c'est l'enthousiasme; **he's the one who counts around here** c'est lui qui décide ici

►► *Gram* ***count noun*** nom *m* comptable

►**count against** *vt insep* jouer contre

►**count down** *vi* faire le compte à rebours

►**count in** *vt sep (include)* compter, inclure; **to count sb in on sth** inclure *ou* compter qn dans qch; **will we count you in for the weekend or not?** on te compte pour le week-end ou pas?; **count me in!** je suis partant!, j'en suis!

►**count off** *vt sep Am* compter

►**count on** *vt insep* (**a**) *(rely on)* compter sur; **we're counting on you** nous comptons sur toi; **I wouldn't count on him turning up, if I were you** si j'étais vous, je ne m'attendrais pas à ce qu'il vienne; **you can always count on him to be late** tu peux compter sur lui pour être en retard, tu

peux être sûr qu'il sera en retard; **can we count on your vote?** pouvons-nous compter sur votre voix?; **you can count on it/me** vous pouvez compter dessus/sur moi; **I wouldn't count on it** je n'y compterais pas
(**b**) *(expect)* compter; **I wasn't counting on getting here so early** je ne comptais pas arriver si tôt; **I wasn't counting on my husband being here** je ne comptais *ou* pensais pas que mon mari serait ici
►**count out** *vt sep* (**a**) *(money, objects)* compter (**b**) *(exclude)* **(you can) count me out** ne compte surtout pas sur moi (**c**) *(in boxing)* **to be counted out** être déclaré K-O
►**count up 1** *vt sep* compter, additionner; *Fig* **when you count it all up** en fin de compte
2 *vi* compter, additionner
►**count upon** *vt insep* = **count on**

---

countability [ˌkaʊntə'bɪlətɪ] *n Gram* aspect *m* comptable
countable ['kaʊntəbəl] *adj Gram (noun)* comptable, dénombrable
countdown ['kaʊntdaʊn] *n Astron* compte *m* à rebours; *Fig* **the countdown to the wedding/Christmas has begun** la date du mariage/de Noël se rapproche
countenance ['kaʊntənəns] **1** *n* (**a**) *Formal or Literary (face)* visage *m*; *(facial expression)* expression *f*, mine *f*; **to keep one's countenance** faire bonne contenance; **to lose countenance** *(person)* perdre contenance; *(government)* perdre la face
(**b**) *Formal (support, approval)* **to give** *or* **to lend countenance to sth** approuver qch
2 *vt Formal (support, approve of → terrorism, violence, lying)* approuver; *(→ idea, proposal)* approuver, accepter; **the government will never countenance (doing) a deal with the terrorists** le gouvernement n'approuvera *ou* n'acceptera jamais l'idée d'un marché avec les terroristes
counter ['kaʊntə(r)] **1** *n* (**a**) *(in shop)* comptoir *m*; *(in supermarket)* rayon *m*, *Can* comptoir *m*; *(in bank, post office)* guichet *m*; **ask at the counter** *(in bank, post office)* demandez au guichet; **it's available over the counter** *(medication)* on peut l'acheter sans ordonnance; *St Exch* **to buy shares over the counter** acheter des actions sur le marché hors cote; *Br Fam* **to sell sth under the counter** vendre qch en douce *ou* sous le manteau
(**b**) *(device, on Web page)* compteur *m*; **set the counter to zero** mettre *ou* remettre le compteur à zéro
(**c**) *(in board game → round)* jeton *m*; *(→ square)* fiche *f*
(**d**) *Am (in kitchen)* plan *m* de travail
(**e**) *Fencing & Boxing* contre *m*
2 *vt (respond to → increase in crime, proposal)* contrecarrer; *(→ accusation, criticism)* contrer; *(→ threat)* contrer; **in order to counter the threat from the enemy tanks** pour contrer la menace que constituent les tanks ennemis; **he countered that the project couldn't go ahead without him** il a répliqué *ou* rétorqué que le projet ne pouvait pas continuer sans lui; *Boxing* **to counter a blow** contrer un coup; *(ward off)* parer un coup
3 *vi* riposter, contre-attaquer; *Fencing & Boxing* contrer; **then he countered with his left** puis il a contré du gauche *ou* fait un contre du gauche; **she countered with a suggestion that/by asking whether...** elle a riposté en suggérant que/en demandant si...
4 *adv* **to go** *or* **to run counter to sth** aller à l'encontre de qch; **to act counter to sb's advice/wishes** agir à l'encontre des conseils/des souhaits de qn
►► *Acct* ***counter cash book*** main *f* courante de caisse; *Br* ***counter hand*** vendeur(euse) *m,f*; *Med* ***counter indication*** contre-indication *f*; *Austr* ***counter meal*** = repas pris dans un pub ou un hôtel; *Banking* ***counter services*** services *mpl* de caisse; *Banking* ***counter staff*** employé(e)s *mpl,fpl* du guichet, guichetiers(ères) *mpl,fpl*; *Banking* ***counter transactions*** opérations *fpl* de caisse
counteract [ˌkaʊntə'rækt] *vt (person)* contrebalancer l'influence de; *(influence)* contrebalancer; *(effects of drug, taste of something)* neutraliser; *(rising crime)* lutter contre
counter-appraisal *n Am Com* contre-expertise *f*
counterargument [ˌkaʊntə'rɑːgjʊmənt] *n* argument *m* contraire
counterattack [ˌkaʊntərə'tæk] **1** *n Mil & Sport* contre-attaque *f*, contre-offensive *f*; *Fig (in business, election etc)* contre-offensive *f*
2 *vi Mil & Sport* contre-attaquer; *Fig* riposter, contrer; **the company counterattacked with claims that...** la compagnie a riposté *ou* contré en affirmant que...
counterattraction [ˌkaʊntərə'trækʃən] *n* spectacle *m* rival; **TV is a counterattraction to live theatre** la télévision fait de la concurrence au théâtre
counterbalance [ˌkaʊntə'bæləns] **1** *n* contrepoids *m*
2 *vt* contrebalancer, faire contrepoids à; *Fig* contrebalancer, compenser
counterbid ['kaʊntəbɪd] *n Fin* suroffre *f*, surenchère *f*; *(during takeover)* contre-OPA *f*
counterbidder [ˌkaʊntə'bɪdə(r)] *n* surenchérisseur(euse) *m,f*
counterblast ['kaʊntəˌblɑːst] *n Fam* vive riposte ❑ *f*
countercharge ['kaʊntəˌtʃɑːdʒ] *Law* **1** *n* contre-accusation *f*
2 *vi* faire une contre-accusation
3 *vt* **to countercharge that...** riposter que...
countercheck ['kaʊntətʃek] *vt* vérifier (une seconde fois)
counterclaim ['kaʊntəˌkleɪm] *Law* **1** *n* demande *f* reconventionnelle *(en dommages-intérêts)*
2 *vi* faire une demande reconventionnelle *(en dommages-intérêts)*
counterclaimant ['kaʊntəˌkleɪmənt] *n Law* demandeur(eresse) *m,f* reconventionnel(elle)
counterclockwise [ˌkaʊntə'klɒkwaɪz] *Am* **1** *adj* dans le sens inverse *ou* contraire des aiguilles d'une montre
2 *adv* dans le sens inverse *ou* contraire des aiguilles d'une montre
counterculture ['kaʊntəˌkʌltʃə(r)] *n* culture *f* alternative
counterdemonstration [ˌkaʊntədemən'streɪʃən] *n* contre-manifestation *f*
counterespionage [ˌkaʊntər'espɪənɑːʒ] *n* contre-espionnage *m*
counterfeit ['kaʊntəfɪt] **1** *n (banknote, document)* faux *m*, contrefaçon *f*; *(piece of jewellery)* faux *m*
2 *adj (banknote, document)* faux (fausse); *(piece of jewellery)* contrefait; *Fig (sympathy, affection)* feint
3 *vt (banknote, passport, document, piece of jewellery)* contrefaire; *Fig (sympathy, affection)* feindre
4 *vi* **he's been counterfeiting for years** ça fait des années qu'il est faussaire
counterfeiter ['kaʊntəˌfɪtə(r)] *n (of banknote)* faux-monnayeur *m*; *(of document, jewellery)* faussaire *mf*
counterfoil ['kaʊntəfɔɪl] *n Br (of cheque, ticket)* talon *m*, souche *f*
►► ***counterfoil book*** carnet *m* à souches
counter-guarantee *n St Exch* contre-garantie *f*
counterinsurgency [ˌkaʊntərɪn'sɜːdʒənsɪ] **1** *n* contre-insurrection *f*
2 *adj (activities, tactics etc)* de contre-insurrection
counterintelligence [ˌkaʊntərɪn'telɪdʒəns] *n* contre-espionnage *m*; *(information)* renseignements *mpl* (provenant du contre-espionnage)
counterintuitive [ˌkaʊntərɪn'tjuːɪtɪv] *adj* qui va contre l'intuition
counterirritant [ˌkaʊntər'ɪrɪtənt] *n Med* révulsif *m*
counterman ['kaʊntəmæn] *(pl* **countermen** [-men]*) n Am* barman *m*
countermand [ˌkaʊntə'mɑːnd] *vt (order)* annuler
countermarketing ['kaʊntəˌmɑːkətɪŋ] *n* contre-marketing *m*
countermeasure [ˌkaʊntə'meʒə(r)] *n* contre-mesure *f*
countermove ['kaʊntəmuːv] *n* contre-mesure *f*; **in a countermove** en guise de contre-mesure
countermovement ['kaʊntəˌmuːvmənt] *n* mouvement *m* contraire
counteroffensive [ˌkaʊntərə'fensɪv] *n Mil* contre-offensive *f*
counteroffer ['kaʊntəˌrɒfə(r)] *n Com & Fin* offre *f*; *(higher)* surenchère *f*; **I'm waiting for a counter-offer from the other party** j'attends l'offre de l'autre partie
counterorder ['kaʊntəˌrɔːdə(r)] *n* contrordre *m*
counterpane ['kaʊntəpeɪn] *n Br* dessus-de-lit *m inv*, couvre-lit *m*
counterpart ['kaʊntəpɑːt] *n* homologue *mf*; *(thing, system)* équivalent *m*; *(piece that corresponds)* pièce *f* qui va de pair
counterparty risk ['kaʊntəˌpɑːtɪ-] *n Banking* risque *m* de contrepartie
counterplot ['kaʊntəplɒt] *n* contre-ruse *f*
counterpoint ['kaʊntəpɔɪnt] *n Mus* contrepoint *m*
counterpoise ['kaʊntəpɔɪz] **1** *n* contrepoids *m*; *Fig* **to be in counterpoise** être en équilibre
2 *vt* contrebalancer, faire contrepoids à; *Fig* contrebalancer, compenser
counterproductive [ˌkaʊntəprə'dʌktɪv] *adj* qui va à l'encontre du but recherché, qui a des effets contraires, contre-productif
counterproposal ['kaʊntəprəˌpəʊzəl] *n* contre-proposition *f*
counterpurchase ['kaʊntəˌpɜːtʃɪs] *n* contre-achat *m*
Counter-Reformation *n Hist* Contre-Réforme *f*
counter-revolution *n* contre-révolution *f*
counter-revolutionary 1 *n* contre-révolutionnaire *mf*
2 *adj* contre-révolutionnaire
countersank ['kaʊntəsæŋk] *pt of* **countersink**
countersegmentation [ˌkaʊntəsegmen'teɪʃən] *n Mktg* contre-segmentation *f*, stratégie *f* d'indifférenciation
countershaft ['kaʊntəʃɑːft] *n Tech (layshaft)* arbre *m* intermédiaire
countersign ['kaʊntəsaɪn] *vt* contresigner
countersignature ['kaʊntəˌsɪgnətjə(r)] *n* contreseing *m*
countersink ['kaʊntəsɪŋk] *(pt* **countersank** [-sæŋk], *pp* **countersunk** [-sʌŋk]*) Tech* **1** *vt (screw)* noyer; *(hole)* fraiser
2 *n (tool)* **countersink (bit)** fraise *f*
counterstroke ['kaʊntəstrəʊk] *n Mil & Fig* contre-offensive *f*
countersunk ['kaʊntəsʌŋk] **1** *pp of* **countersink**
2 *adj Tech (screw)* noyé; *(hole)* fraisé
countertenor [ˌkaʊntə'tenə(r)] *n Mus (singer)* haute-contre *m*; *(voice)* haute-contre *f*
counterterrorism [ˌkaʊntə'terərɪzəm] *n* contre-terrorisme *m*
counterterrorist [ˌkaʊntə'terərɪst] *adj* contre-terroriste
countertop ['kaʊntəˌtɒp] *n Am* plan *m* de travail
countertrade ['kaʊntətreɪd] *n Com* commerce *m* d'échange, troc *m*
countertrading [kaʊntə'treɪdɪŋ] *n Com* troc *m*
countertransference [ˌkaʊntə'trænsfərəns] *n Psy* contre-transfert *m*
countervail ['kaʊntəveɪl] *vt Literary* contrebalancer, compenser
countervailing ['kaʊntəveɪlɪŋ] *adj Literary* compensatoire, compensateur
countervaluation [ˌkaʊntəvæljʊ'eɪʃən] *n* contre-expertise *f*
counterweight [illegible]
countess ['kaʊntɪs] *n* comtesse *f*
counting ['kaʊntɪŋ] *n (gen)* calcul *m*, compte *m*; *(of votes)* dépouillement *m*; *(of people)* compte *m*, dénombrement *m*
►► *Arch Com* ***counting house*** salle *f* du trésor
countless ['kaʊntlɪs] *adj* innombrable; **countless letters/people** un nombre incalculable de lettres/personnes; **I've told you countless times not to do that** je t'ai répété des centaines de fois *ou* je ne sais combien de fois de ne pas faire ça
countrified ['kʌntrɪfaɪd] *adj* (**a**) *Pej* campagnard, provincial (**b**) *(rural)* **it's quite countrified round here** c'est vraiment la campagne ici
country ['kʌntrɪ] *(pl* **countries**) **1** *n* (**a**) *(land, nation)* pays *m*; *(homeland)* patrie *f*; **in this country** dans ce pays; **the Prime Minister isn't in the country** le Premier ministre est à l'étranger; **the country is in mourning** le pays est en deuil; **I have the support of the country** tout le

pays me soutient; **to fight/to die for one's country** se battre/mourir pour sa patrie; **to love one's country** aimer son pays *ou* sa patrie; **in my country** dans mon pays, chez moi; **my country right or wrong** = expression typique du patriotisme forcené; **'My Country 'Tis of Thee'** = chant patriotique que l'on apprend souvent aux enfants américains; *Br Pol* **to go to the country** appeler le pays aux urnes

(**b**) *(as opposed to the city)* campagne *f*; **to live in the country** vivre à la campagne; **to spend a day in the country** passer une journée à la campagne; **to travel** *Br* **across** *or Am* **cross country** *(in car, on bike)* prendre *ou* emprunter les petites routes (de campagne); *(on foot)* aller à travers champs

(**c**) *(area of land, region)* région *f*; **the country around Gloucester** la région autour de Gloucester; **we passed through some beautiful country** nous avons traversé de beaux paysages; **this is good farming country** c'est une bonne région agricole; **Wordsworth/Constable country** le pays de Wordsworth/Constable; **this is bear country** il y a beaucoup d'ours par ici; *Br* **it's not my line of country** ce n'est pas mon domaine

(**d**) *Mus* country *f*

2 *comp (house, road, town, bus)* de campagne; *(people)* de la campagne; *(life)* à la campagne

►► ***country boy*** gars *m* de la campagne; *Fam Pej* ***country bumpkin*** péquenaud(e) *m,f*, plouc *mf*; **I felt like a country bumpkin** j'ai eu l'impression de débarquer de ma campagne; ***country club*** = club sportif ou de loisirs situé à la campagne; ***the country code*** = code de conduite à respecter lorsqu'on se promène dans la campagne, qu'on y pique-nique etc; *Pej* ***country cousin*** cousin(e) *m,f* de province; ***country dance*** danse *f* folklorique; ***country dancing*** danse *f* folklorique; **to go country dancing** aller danser des danses folkloriques; ***country gentleman*** gentilhomme *m* campagnard; ***country house*** = grande maison de campagne, souvent historique; *Comput* ***country keyboard*** clavier *m* national; ***country music*** country *f*; *Br* ***country park*** parc *m* naturel; ***country seat*** *(of noble family)* manoir *m*

'The Country Wife' *Wycherley* 'La Provinciale' *ou* 'L'Épouse campagnarde'

Your country needs you

Cette phrase ("la patrie vous réclame") figurait sur les affiches qui appelaient les Britanniques à s'engager dans l'armée, au début de la Première Guerre mondiale. On y voyait Lord Kitchener, ministre de la Guerre, l'index pointé vers la personne regardant l'affiche. L'idée fut reprise par les Américains avec l'Oncle Sam à la place de Lord Kitchener et le slogan **I want you** ("J'ai besoin de vous").

Aujourd'hui on utilise l'expression dans tout appel à la nation, comme dans l'exemple suivant: **Thinking about becoming a nurse? Call this number now, your country needs you** ("La carrière d'infirmière vous intéresse? Composez ce numéro dès maintenant, le pays a besoin de vous.").

country and western *Mus* **1** *n* country *f*

2 *comp (band, music, singer)* country; *(fan)* de country

country-dweller *n* campagnard(e) *m,f*, habitant(e) *m,f* de la campagne

countryfolk ['kʌntrɪfəʊk] *npl* gens *mpl* de la campagne

countryman ['kʌntrɪmən] (*pl* **countrymen** [-mən]) *n* (**a**) *(who lives in the country)* campagnard *m*, habitant *m* de la campagne (**b**) *(compatriot)* compatriote *m*

countryside ['kʌntrɪsaɪd] *n* campagne *f*; *(scenery)* paysage *m*; **in the countryside** à la campagne; **there is some magnificent countryside around here** il y a des paysages magnifiques par ici

►► ***the Countryside Alliance*** = association britannique qui milite contre l'interdiction de la chasse à courre; ***the Countryside Commission*** = organisme britannique indépendant chargé de la protection du milieu rural et de la gestion des parcs nationaux

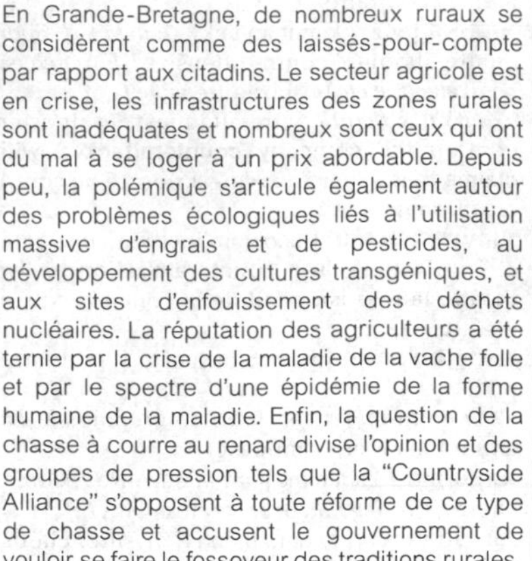

COUNTRYSIDE DEBATE

En Grande-Bretagne, de nombreux ruraux se considèrent comme des laissés-pour-compte par rapport aux citadins. Le secteur agricole est en crise, les infrastructures des zones rurales sont inadéquates et nombreux sont ceux qui ont du mal à se loger à un prix abordable. Depuis peu, la polémique s'articule également autour des problèmes écologiques liés à l'utilisation massive d'engrais et de pesticides, au développement des cultures transgéniques, et aux sites d'enfouissement des déchets nucléaires. La réputation des agriculteurs a été ternie par la crise de la maladie de la vache folle et par le spectre d'une épidémie de la forme humaine de la maladie. Enfin, la question de la chasse à courre au renard divise l'opinion et des groupes de pression tels que la "Countryside Alliance" s'opposent à toute réforme de ce type de chasse et accusent le gouvernement de vouloir se faire le fossoyeur des traditions rurales.

country-specific *adj Comput (keyboard)* particulier à un pays

countrywoman ['kʌntrɪ,wʊmən] (*pl* **countrywomen** [-,wɪmɪn]) *n* (**a**) *(who lives in the country)* campagnarde *f*, habitante *f* de la campagne (**b**) *(compatriot)* compatriote *f*

county ['kaʊntɪ] (*pl* **counties**) **1** *n* comté *m*; *Br* **the county of Kent** le comté du Kent; *Am* **New York County** le comté de New York

2 *comp (boundary)* de comté

3 *adj Br Pej* **she's very county** elle est de la haute; **the horse sale was full of county types** le marché aux chevaux grouillait de petits hobereaux

►► *Br* ***county council*** ≃ conseil *m* général; *Br* ***county councillor*** ≃ conseiller(ère) *m,f* général(e); *Eng Law* ***county court*** tribunal *m* d'instance; *Br* ***county cricket*** = grands matches de cricket disputés par les équipes du comté; *Am* ***county fair*** fête *f* du comté; *Br* ***County Hall*** hôtel *m* du comté, siège *m* du conseil de comté; *Am* ***county line*** frontière *f* délimitant un comté; ***county seat*** *(in US)* chef-lieu *m* de comté; ***county town*** *(in England)* chef-lieu *m* de comté

coup [ku:] *n* (**a**) *(feat)* (beau) coup *m*; **to pull off a coup** réussir un beau coup (**b**) *(overthrow of government)* coup *m* d'État

►► ***coup d'état*** coup *m* d'État

coupé ['ku:peɪ] *n Aut* coupé *m*

couple ['kʌpəl] **1** *n* (**a**) *(pair)* couple *m*; **an engaged couple** un couple de fiancés; **they make a lovely couple** ils forment un beau couple; **the happy couple** les jeunes mariés; **the couples on the dance floor** les couples sur la piste de danse; **everyone came in couples** tout le monde est venu en couple; **I'm not going if it's all couples** je n'y vais pas s'il n'y a que des couples; **they go everywhere as a couple** ils vont partout ensemble *ou* en couple

(**b**) *(as quantifier)* **a couple** *(a few)* quelques-uns (quelques-unes); **were there many mistakes? – only a couple** est-ce qu'il y avait beaucoup de fautes? – seulement quelques-unes; **a couple of** *(a few)* quelques; *(two)* deux; **a couple of drinks** un verre ou deux, quelques verres; *Am* **he's a couple years older** il a deux ou trois ans de plus

(**c**) *Phys* couple *m*

2 *vi (animals, birds, humans)* s'accoupler

3 *vt* (**a**) *(join → oxen)* (ac)coupler; *(two engines, batteries)* accoupler

(**b**) *(tie up → horse)* atteler; *Rail (→ carriage)* atteler, accrocher

(**c**) *Fig (associate)* associer; **to couple sth with sth** associer qch à qch; **the name of Freud is coupled with that of Vienna** le nom de Freud est associé à Vienne; **she coupled her announcement with a plea for increased funding** elle a profité de son annonce pour demander davantage de fonds; **her name has been coupled with his** *(romantically)* son nom a été uni au sien

(**d**) **to be coupled with sth** *(accompanied by)* être associé à qch; **coupled with that,...** en plus de cela,..., venant s'ajouter à cela,...

coupler ['kʌplə(r)] *n Tech* coupleur *m*

couplet ['kʌplɪt] *n Literature* distique *m*; **rhyming couplets** distiques *mpl* qui riment

coupling ['kʌplɪŋ] *n* (**a**) *(mating → of animals, birds, humans)* accouplement *m* (**b**) *Tech (static device)* raccord *m*, joint *m*; *(device for transmitting motion)* accouplement *m*, embrayage *m*; *Rail (for carriages)* attelage *m* (**c**) *(joining) Rail (of carriages)* attelage *m*; *Tech (of batteries)* couplage *m* (**d**) *(bringing together)* accouplement *m*; *(of ideas, names)* association *f*

►► *Aut* ***coupling bar*** barre *f* d'accouplement

coupon ['ku:pɒn] *n (to be filled in)* coupon *m*; *Com (exchangeable voucher)* bon *m*; *Fin (on bearer bond)* coupon *m*; *Com* **(money-off) coupon** bon *m* de réduction

►► *Fin* ***coupon bond*** obligation *f* au porteur; *Com* ***coupon offer*** offre *f* de bon de réduction; *Fin* ***coupon yield*** rendement *m* coupon

couponing ['ku:pɒnɪŋ] *n Mktg* couponing *m*, couponnage *m*

courage ['kʌrɪdʒ] *n* courage *m*; **to have the courage to do sth** avoir le courage de faire qch; **he has to be told – I know, but I don't have the courage** il faut le lui dire – je (le) sais, mais je n'en ai pas le courage; **a woman of great courage** une femme d'un grand courage, une femme très courageuse; **people with courage** des gens courageux; **to take one's courage in both hands** prendre son courage à deux mains; **to take courage from the fact that...** être encouragé par le fait que...; **to have the courage of one's convictions** avoir le courage de ses opinions

courageous [kə'reɪdʒəs] *adj* courageux

courageously [kə'reɪdʒəslɪ] *adv* courageusement

courante [kʊ'rɑ:nt] *n Mus* courante *f*

courgette [kɔ:'ʒet] *n Br* courgette *f*

courier ['kʊrɪə(r)] *n* (**a**) *(messenger)* coursier(ère) *m,f*, messager(ère) *m,f*; *(company)* messagerie *f*; **to send sth by courier** *(locally)* envoyer qch par coursier; *(long-distance)* envoyer qch par messagerie; **she was a courier for drug dealers** elle transportait de la drogue pour le compte de trafiquants (**b**) *(in tourism)* accompagnateur(trice) *m,f*

COURSE [kɔ:s]

route	►1 (a)
ligne de conduite	►1 (b)
cours	►1 (c), (d)
plat	►1 (f)
terrain	►1 (g)
au cours de	►4
bien sûr	►5

1 *n* (**a**) *(path, route → of ship, plane)* route *f*; *(→ of river)* cours *m*; **what is our course?** quelle est notre route?; **to change course** *(ship, plane)* changer de cap; *Fig (argument, discussion)* changer de direction, dévier; *(company)* changer de cap; **to be on course** *(ship, plane)* suivre le cap fixé; *Fig* être en bonne voie; *Fig* **the company is on course to achieve a record profit** la société est bien partie pour atteindre des bénéfices record; **to be off course** *(ship, plane)* dévier de son cap; **you're a long way off course** *(walking, driving)* vous n'êtes pas du tout dans la bonne direction *ou* sur la bonne route; *(with project, workflow)* vous êtes en mauvaise voie; **to set a course for Marseilles** *(ship, plane)* mettre le cap sur Marseille

(**b**) *Fig (approach)* **course (of action)** ligne *f* (de conduite); **what is the recommended course of action in such cases?** quelle est la ligne de conduite conseillée dans de tels cas?; **what other course is open to us?** quelle autre solution avons-nous?; **your best course of action is to sue** la meilleure chose que vous ayez à faire est d'intenter un procès; *Prov* **the course of true love never runs smooth** les grandes amours sont toujours orageuses

(**c**) *(development, progress → of history, war)* cours *m*; **the law must take its course** la loi doit suivre son cours; **the illness takes** *or* **runs its course** la maladie suit son cours; **in the course of time** avec le temps; **in the course of time he became a very wealthy man** il a fini par devenir très riche; **you will forget him in the course of time** tu finiras par l'oublier, avec le temps tu l'oublieras; **in the normal** *or* **ordinary course of events** normalement, en temps normal; **a building in the course of construction/demolition** un bâtiment en cours de construction/démolition

(**d**) *Sch & Univ* cours *mpl*; **a geography/music course** des cours *mpl* de géographie/musique; **he's giving a course of lectures on romanticism this term** ce trimestre il fait un cours sur le romantisme; **it's a five-year course** c'est un enseignement sur cinq ans; **we offer courses in a number of subjects** nous offrons *ou* proposons des cours dans plusieurs domaines; **he has published a French course** il a publié une méthode de français; **to go on a (training) course** faire un stage; **I'm taking** *or* **doing a computer course** je suis des cours *ou* un stage d'informatique; **what are the other people on the course like?** comment sont les autres personnes qui suivent les cours?

(**e**) *Med* **a course of injections** une série de piqûres; **a course of pills** un traitement à base de comprimés; **course of treatment** *(for an illness)* traitement *m*

(**f**) *(in meal)* plat *m*; **first course** entrée *f*; **they were halfway through the second course when the telephone rang** ils en étaient au plat principal lorsque le téléphone sonna; **there's a cheese course as well** il y a aussi du fromage

(**g**) *Golf* terrain *m*; *Horseracing* champ *m* de courses; *(in athletics)* parcours *m*; *Fig* **to stay the course** tenir le coup

(**h**) *Constr (of bricks)* assise *f*

2 *vi* (**a**) *(flow)* **tears coursed down his cheeks** les larmes ruisselaient sur ses joues; **I could feel the blood coursing through my veins** je sentais le sang bouillonner dans mes veines

(**b**) *Hunt (hunt rabbits, hares)* chasser *(surtout le lièvre)*

3 *adv Fam (of course)* bien sûr[□]; **course I believe you** bien sûr que je te crois

4 in the course of *prep* au cours de; **in the course of the next few weeks** dans le courant des semaines qui viennent

5 of course *adv* bien sûr; **of course I believe you/she loves you** bien sûr que je te crois/qu'elle t'aime; **no one believed me, of course** évidemment *ou* bien sûr, personne ne m'a cru; *Ironic* **I don't matter, of course** évidemment *ou* naturellement, moi, je ne compte pas; **of course I'll tell you** il va de soi que je vous le dirai; **may I use your phone? – of course!** puis-je utiliser votre téléphone? – mais bien sûr!; **was there much damage? – of course!** y a-t-il eu beaucoup de dégâts? – tu parles!; **of course not!** bien sûr que non!

-course [kɔːs] *suff* **a three/five-course meal** un repas comprenant trois/cinq plats; **she served a four-course dinner** elle a servi quatre plats au dîner

coursebook ['kɔːsbʊk] *n* livre *m* de classe

courser ['kɔːsə(r)] *n* (**a**) *Hunt* chasseur(euse) *m,f* de lièvres (**b**) *Literary (swift horse)* coursier *m* (**c**) *Orn* courvite *m*; **cream-coloured courser** courvite *m* isabelle *ou* gaulois

courseware ['kɔːsweə(r)] *n Comput* didacticiel *m*

coursework ['kɔːswɜːk] *n Sch & Univ* travail *m* de l'année *(qui permet d'exercer le contrôle continu)*

coursing ['kɔːsɪŋ] *n Hunt* chasse *f* à courre au lièvre

court [kɔːt] **1** *n* (**a**) *Law (institution)* cour *f*, tribunal *m*; *(court room, people in room)* cour *f*; **the court rose** la cour s'est levée; **silence in court!** silence dans la salle!; **to clear the court** évacuer la salle; **to appear in court** *(accused, witness)* comparaître au tribunal; **to come before a court** *(person)* comparaître devant un tribunal; *(case)* être jugé; **to take sb to court** poursuivre qn en justice, intenter un procès contre qn; **to go to court** faire appel à la justice, aller en justice; **to go to court over sth** faire appel à la justice pour régler qch; **are you prepared to say that in court?** est-ce que vous seriez prêt à le jurer devant le tribunal?; **tell the court what you saw** veuillez dire à la cour ce que vous avez vu; **I'll see you in court then!** alors nous réglerons cela au tribunal!; **to settle sth out of court** régler qch à l'amiable; **it won't stand up in court** *or* **in a court of law** cela n'aura aucun poids au tribunal; *Fig* **to put** *or* **to rule sth out of court** exclure qch

(**b**) *(of monarch → people)* cour *f*; *(→ building)* palais *m*; *Br* **to be presented at court** être introduit à la cour; **to pay court to the king** faire sa cour au roi; **it is said in court circles that...** on dit à la cour que...; *Fig* **to hold court** avoir une cour d'adorateurs

(**c**) *Sport (for tennis, badminton)* court *m*, terrain *m*; *(for squash)* court *m*; **to come on court** entrer sur le court *ou* terrain; **he was on court for three hours** il a été sur le court pendant trois heures; **on court and off, on and off court** sur le court et dans la vie

(**d**) *(courtyard)* cour *f*; *(in names of blocks of flats)* ≃ résidence *f*; *(in names of palaces)* château *m*, palais *m*

(**e**) *Old-fashioned* **to pay court to a woman** faire la cour à une femme

2 *vt* (**a**) *Old-fashioned (seek in marriage)* faire la cour à, courtiser; **they had been courting one another for nearly a year** ils se fréquentaient depuis presque un an

(**b**) *Fig (voters)* courtiser, chercher à séduire; **she's courting the director** elle essaie de gagner la faveur du metteur en scène; **to court popularity** chercher à se rendre populaire; **to court sb's approval/support** chercher à gagner l'approbation/le soutien de qn; **to court danger/disaster** aller au devant du danger/désastre; **I told him he was courting arrest** je lui ai dit qu'il risquait de se faire arrêter

3 *vi Old-fashioned (one person)* fréquenter; *(two people)* se fréquenter

▸▸ *Law* ***Court of Appeal*** cour *f* d'appel; *Am Law* ***court of appeals*** cour *f* d'appel; *Law* ***court appearance*** *(of accused)* comparution *f* en justice; *Br Cards* ***court card*** figure *f*; *Law* ***court case*** procès *m*, affaire *f*; **the whole court case was seen on TV** le procès a été retransmis à la télévision dans son intégralité; *Br Journ* ***court circular*** = rubrique d'un journal indiquant les engagements officiels de la famille royale; *Journ* ***court correspondent*** correspondant(e) *m,f* à la cour royale; *Law* ***court of first instance*** juridiction *f* de première instance; *Br* ***court of inquiry*** *(body of people)* commission *f* d'enquête; *(investigation)* enquête *f*; ***court jester*** bouffon *m* de cour; *EU & Law* ***Court of Justice of the European Communities*** Cour *f* de Justice des Communautés européennes; ***court of law*** tribunal *m*; **would you be prepared to say that in a court of law?** est-ce que vous seriez prêt à le jurer devant le tribunal?; *Law* ***court order*** ordonnance *f* du tribunal; *Law* ***court reporter*** chroniqueur(euse) *m,f* judiciaire; *Law* ***court ruling*** décision *f* de justice; *Law* ***Court of Session*** = tribunal civil en Écosse; *Br* ***court shoe*** escarpin *m*; ***Court of St James*** = cour du roi ou de la reine d'Angleterre (l'expression désigne métaphoriquement la Grande-Bretagne); *Am* ***court tennis*** jeu *m* de paume; *Law* ***court usher*** huissier *m* de justice

Courtauld Institute ['kɔːtəʊld-] *n* = musée des beaux-arts à Londres connu pour sa collection [illegible]

court-bouillon [ˌkɔːt'buːjɒn] *n Culin* court-bouillon *m*

courteous ['kɜːtjəs] *adj (person, gesture, treatment)* courtois (**to** *or* **towards** envers)

courteously ['kɜːtjəslɪ] *adv (speak, reply etc)* avec courtoisie, courtoisement

courtesan [ˌkɔːtɪ'zæn] *n* courtisane *f*

courtesy ['kɜːtɪsɪ] (*pl* **courtesies**) **1** *n* (**a**) *(politeness)* courtoisie *f*; **at least have the courtesy to apologize** aie au moins la courtoisie de t'excuser; **it would only have been common courtesy to apologize** la moindre des courtoisies *ou* politesses aurait été de s'excuser; **common courtesy dictates that you should thank her** la moindre des courtoisies *ou* des politesses serait que tu la remercies; **do her the courtesy of hearing what she has to say** aie l'obligeance d'écouter ce qu'elle a à dire

(**b**) *(polite action, remark)* politesse *f*; **after a brief exchange of courtesies** après un bref échange de politesses; **to show sb every courtesy** faire montre d'une extrême courtoisie envers qn

2 *comp (visit)* de politesse

3 (by) courtesy of *prep* avec l'aimable autorisation de; **by courtesy of an agreement with the management** grâce à un accord avec la direction; **the following footage is brought to you courtesy of French TV** la séquence qui suit vous est présentée avec l'aimable permission *ou* autorisation de la télévision française

▸▸ ***courtesy call*** visite *f* de politesse; **to pay a courtesy call on sb, to pay sb a courtesy call** faire une visite de politesse à qn; ***courtesy car*** *(from hotel)* voiture *f* de courtoisie; *(from garage)* véhicule *m* de remplacement; ***courtesy coach*** *(at airport)* navette *f* gratuite; ***courtesy light*** plafonnier *m*, éclairage *m* intérieur; ***courtesy shuttle*** navette *f* gratuite; *Am* ***courtesy telephone*** = téléphone mis à la disposition des usagers d'un aéroport et permettant de diffuser une annonce personnelle ou de se mettre en contact avec un appel; *Br* ***courtesy title*** titre *m* de courtoisie

courthouse ['kɔːthaʊs, *pl* -haʊzɪz] *n Am Law* palais *m* de justice, tribunal *m*

courtier ['kɔːtjə(r)] *n* courtisan *m*

courting ['kɔːtɪŋ] *n Old-fashioned* **this is where we did our courting** c'est ici que nous venions à l'époque où nous nous fréquentions

▸▸ ***courting couple*** couple *m* d'amoureux

courtliness ['kɔːtlɪnɪs] *n* (**a**) *(politeness, refinement → of person, style)* courtoisie *f* (**b**) *(regal splendour)* majesté *f*

courtly ['kɔːtlɪ] *adj* (**a**) *(polite, refined → person, manners)* plein de style et de courtoisie (**b**) *(of a royal court → life, ritual, pursuits)* de la cour; *(→ splendour)* majestueux

▸▸ *Hist* ***courtly love*** amour *m* courtois

court-martial (*pl* **courts-martial**, *Br pt & pp* **court-martialled**, *cont* **court-martialling**, *Am pt & pp* **court-martialed**, *cont* **court-martialing**) *Mil* **1** *n* tribunal *m* militaire; **to be tried by court-martial** être jugé par un tribunal militaire; **your court-martial has been postponed** la date de votre comparution devant le tribunal militaire a été reportée

2 *vt* faire comparaître devant un tribunal militaire; **he was court-martialled** il est passé au tribunal militaire

court-ordered *adj Law (sale)* judiciaire

courtroom ['kɔːtrʊm] *n* salle *f* d'audience; *(people)* auditoire *m* d'un/du tribunal

▸▸ *Cin & TV* ***courtroom drama*** drame *m* judiciaire

courtship ['kɔːtʃɪp] **1** *n* (**a**) *(of couple)* **their courtship lasted six years** ils se sont fréquentés pendant six ans; **they married after a brief courtship** ils se sont mariés peu de temps après avoir commencé à se fréquenter; *Fig* **his courtship of new financial backers was unsuccessful** ses tentatives pour attirer de nouveaux commanditaires n'ont rien donné

(**b**) *(of animals)* période *f* nuptiale, période *f* des amours

2 *adj (dance, display)* nuptial

▸▸ ***courtship ritual*** rituel *m* nuptial

courtyard ['kɔːtjɑːd] *n (of building)* cour *f*

[illegible]

▸▸ ***couscous steamer*** couscousière *f*

co-user *n Comput* co-utilisateur(trice) *m,f*

cousin ['kʌzən] *n* cousin(e) *m,f*; **a distant cousin** un cousin éloigné, une cousine éloignée; *Fig* **a distant cousin of the sparrow** un cousin éloigné du moineau; *Fig* **our American cousins** nos cousins américains

couth [kuːθ] *adj Br Hum* **he's not very couth** il n'est pas très raffiné

couture [kuː'tʊə(r)] *n* couture *f*

couturier [kuː'tʊərɪeɪ] *n* couturier(ère) *m,f*; *(head of company)* directeur(trice) *m,f* d'une maison de haute couture

covalence [kəʊ'veɪləns], **covalency** [kəʊ'veɪlənsɪ] *n Chem* covalence *f*

covalent [ˌkəʊ'veɪlənt] *adj Chem* covalent

▸▸ ***covalent bond*** liaison *f* covalente

covariance [kəʊ'veərɪəns] *n Math* covariance *f*

cove [kəʊv] *n* (**a**) *(bay)* crique *f* (**b**) *Br Old-fashioned* gars *m*; **a rum cove** un drôle de gars

coven ['kʌvən] *n* ordre *m ou* réunion *f* de sorcières

covenant ['kʌvənənt] **1** *n* (**a**) *Fin (promise of money)* convention *f*, engagement *m*; **(deed of) covenant** contrat *m*
(**b**) *(agreement)* engagement *m*
(**c**) *Bible (of Jews)* alliance *f*
2 *vt Fin (promise payment of)* s'engager (par contrat) à payer
3 *vi Fin* **to covenant for a sum** s'engager (par contrat) à payer une somme; **to covenant with sb for sth** convenir (par contrat) de qch avec qn

covenanter ['kʌvənəntə(r)] **1** *n (person who makes a covenant)* partie *f* contractante
2 Covenanter *n Scot Hist* Covenanter *mf (presbytérien écossais qui s'opposa à l'introduction de l'anglicanisme au XVIIème siècle)*

Covent Garden ['kɒvənt-] *n* Covent Garden

COVENT GARDEN

"Covent Garden", jadis le marché aux fruits, légumes et fleurs du centre de Londres, est aujourd'hui une importante galerie marchande. Ce nom désigne également la "Royal Opera House", située près de l'ancien marché.

Coventry ['kɒvəntrɪ] *n* Coventry; *Br Fig* **to send sb to Coventry** *(ostracize)* mettre qn en quarantaine

COVER ['kʌvə(r)]

housse	► **1 (a)**
couvre-lit	► **1 (b)**
couvercle	► **1 (c)**
couverture	► **1 (d), (f), (g)**
abri	► **1 (e)**
remplacement	► **1 (h)**
couvrir	► **2 (a), (d), (f) – (k)**
recouvrir	► **2 (b)**
parcourir	► **2 (d)**
traiter	► **2 (e)**
avoir sous surveillance	► **2 (l)**
marquer	► **2 (m)**

1 *n* (**a**) *(protective → for cushion, typewriter)* housse *f*; *(→ for umbrella)* fourreau *m*; **loose cover** *(for chair, sofa)* housse *f*
(**b**) *(on bed → bedspread)* couvre-lit *m*; **the covers** *(blankets)* les couvertures *fpl*
(**c**) *(lid)* couvercle *m*
(**d**) *(of book, magazine)* couverture *f*; **(front) cover** couverture *f*; **to read a book (from) cover to cover** lire un livre de la première à la dernière page *ou* d'un bout à l'autre
(**e**) *(shelter, protection)* abri *m*; *Hunt (for birds, animals)* couvert *m*; *Mil (from gunfire etc)* couvert *m*, abri *m*; *(firing)* tir *m* de couverture *ou* de protection; **to take cover** se mettre à l'abri; **to take cover from the rain** s'abriter de la pluie; **to run for cover** courir se mettre à l'abri; **that tree will provide cover** cet arbre va nous permettre de nous abriter *ou* nous offrir un abri; **we'll give you cover** *(by shooting)* nous vous couvrirons; **to keep sth under cover** garder qch à l'abri; **to do sth under cover of darkness** faire qch à la faveur de la nuit; **under cover of the riot/noise** profitant de l'émeute/du bruit; **they escaped under cover of the riot/noise** ils ont profité de l'émeute/du bruit pour s'échapper; **to work under cover** travailler clandestinement; **to break cover** *(animal, person in hiding)* sortir à découvert
(**f**) *Ins* couverture *f*; **to have cover against sth** être couvert *ou* assuré contre qch; **I've taken out cover for medical costs** j'ai pris une assurance pour les frais médicaux
(**g**) *(disguise, front → for criminal enterprise)* couverture *f*; *(→ for spy)* fausse identité *f*, identité *f* d'emprunt; *Fam* **your cover has been blown** vous avez été démasqué; **to be a cover for sth** servir de couverture à qch; **it's just a cover for her shyness** c'est juste pour cacher *ou* masquer sa timidité
(**h**) *(during a person's absence)* remplacement *m*; **to provide cover for sb** remplacer qn; **I provide emergency cover** je fais des remplacements d'urgence
(**i**) *Fin* marge *f* de sécurité; **to operate with/without cover** opérer avec couverture/à découvert
(**j**) *Mus (new version of song)* reprise *f*
(**k**) *(in restaurant)* couvert *m*
(**l**) *(envelope)* enveloppe *f*; **under plain/separate cover** sous pli discret/séparé
2 *vt* (**a**) *(in order to protect)* couvrir; *(in order to hide)* cacher, dissimuler; *(cushion, chair, settee)* recouvrir; *(in bookbinding → book)* couvrir; **to cover sth with a sheet/blanket** recouvrir qch d'un drap/d'une couverture; **to cover one's eyes** se couvrir les yeux; **to cover one's ears** se boucher les oreilles; **to cover one's face with one's hands** *(in shame, embarrassment)* se couvrir le visage de ses mains; **to cover one's shyness/nervousness** dissimuler *ou* masquer sa timidité/nervosité
(**b**) *(coat → of dust, snow)* recouvrir; **to be covered in dust/snow** être recouvert de poussière/neige; **his face was covered in spots** son visage était couvert de boutons; **you're covering everything in dust/paint** tu mets de la poussière/peinture partout; *Fig* **I was covered in** *or* **with shame** j'étais mort de honte; *Fig* **to cover oneself in glory** se couvrir de gloire; **our team didn't exactly cover itself in glory** notre équipe n'est pas rentrée très glorieuse
(**c**) *(extend over, occupy → of city, desert etc)* couvrir une surface de; **water covers most of the earth's surface** l'eau recouvre la plus grande partie de la surface de la terre; **his interests cover a wide field** il a des intérêts très variés; **does this translation cover the figurative meaning of the word?** cette traduction couvre-t-elle bien le sens figuré du mot?
(**d**) *(travel over)* parcourir, couvrir; **we've covered every square inch of the park looking for it** nous avons ratissé chaque centimètre carré du parc pour essayer de le retrouver; **we covered 100 kilometres before breakfast** nous avons fait 100 kilomètres avant le petit déjeuner; **to cover a lot of ground** *(travel great distance)* faire beaucoup de chemin; *(search etc over a wide area)* parcourir un champ très vaste; *Fig (book, author etc)* couvrir de nombreux domaines; *(meeting etc)* traiter bien des problèmes
(**e**) *(deal with)* traiter; **there's one point we haven't covered** il y a un point que nous n'avons pas traité *ou* vu; **is that everything covered?** *(in discussion)* tout a été vu?; **the course covers the first half of the century** le cours couvre la première moitié du siècle; **to cover all eventualites** parer à toute éventualité; **the law doesn't cover that kind of situation** la loi ne prévoit pas ce genre de situation
(**f**) *(report on)* couvrir, faire la couverture de
(**g**) *(of salesman, representative)* couvrir
(**h**) *(be enough money for → damage, expenses)* couvrir; *(→ meal)* suffire à payer; **£30 should cover it** 30 livres devraient suffire; **to cover a deficit** combler un déficit; *Acct* **to cover a loss** couvrir un déficit; **to cover one's costs** *(company)* rentrer dans ses frais
(**i**) *Ins* couvrir, garantir; **to be covered against** *or* **for sth** être couvert *ou* assuré contre qch
(**j**) *Fin* **to cover a bill** faire la provision d'une lettre de change; *St Exch* **to cover a position** couvrir une position
(**k**) *(with gun → colleague)* couvrir; **I've got you covered** *(to criminal)* j'ai mon arme braquée sur toi; *Fig* **the president covered himself by saying that...** le président s'est couvert en disant que...
(**l**) *(monitor permanently → exit, port etc)* avoir sous surveillance; **I want all exits covered immediately** je veux que toutes les sorties soient mises sous surveillance immédiatement
(**m**) *Sport* marquer
(**n**) *Mus (song)* faire une reprise de
(**o**) *(of male animal)* couvrir, s'accoupler avec
3 covers *npl Sport (in cricket)* = partie du terrain située sur l'avant et sur la droite du batteur, à mi-distance de la limite du terrain
►► ***cover charge*** *(in restaurant)* couvert *m*; *Am (in bar)* entrée *f*, prix *m* d'entrée; ***cover girl*** cover-girl *f*; *Am* ***cover letter*** lettre *f* explicative *ou* de couverture; ***cover mount*** = cadeau offert avec un magazine; *Br Ins* ***cover note*** attestation *f* provisoire; ***cover page*** *(of fax)* page *f* de garde; *Sport* ***cover point*** *(in cricket)* = joueur qui double celui qui est situé à droite du guichet; ***cover price*** *(of magazine)* prix *m*; ***cover sheet*** *(of fax)* page *f* de garde; *Press* ***cover story*** article *m* principal (faisant la couverture)
►**cover for** *vt insep (replace)* remplacer; *(provide excuses for)* couvrir; **I refuse to cover for you with the boss** je refuse de te couvrir auprès du patron
►**cover in** *vt sep (hole)* remplir
►**cover up 1** *vt sep* (**a**) *(hide, conceal)* cacher, dissimuler; *(in order to protect)* recouvrir; *Pej (involvement, report etc)* dissimuler, garder secret(ète); *(affair)* étouffer; **they covered up the body with a sheet** ils ont recouvert le cadavre d'un drap; **cover yourself up!** *(for decency)* couvre-toi!
(**b**) *(in order to keep warm)* couvrir
2 *vi (hide something)* **the government is covering up again** le gouvernement est encore en train d'étouffer une affaire; **to cover up for sb** couvrir qn, protéger qn; **they're covering up for each other** ils se couvrent l'un l'autre

coverage ['kʌvərɪdʒ] *n* (**a**) *(UNCOUNT) (reporting)* couverture *f*; **his coverage of the coup** le reportage qu'il a fait du coup d'État; **the coverage given to the elections was biased** le compte-rendu des élections était partial; **the newspaper gave good coverage of the event** le journal a bien couvert cet événement; **royal weddings always get a lot of coverage** les mariages de la famille royale bénéficient toujours d'une importante couverture médiatique; **radio/television coverage of the tournament** la retransmission radiophonique/télévisée du tournoi
(**b**) *(in book, dictionary)* traitement *m*; **the author's coverage of the years 1789 to 1815 is sketchy** l'auteur traite les années 1789 à 1815 de manière sommaire
(**c**) *Ins* couverture *f*

coveralls ['kʌvərɔːlz] *npl Am* bleu *m ou* bleus *mpl* (de travail)

covered ['kʌvəd] *adj (walkway, bridge, market)* couvert
►► *St Exch* ***covered position*** position *f* couverte; *St Exch* ***covered short position*** position *f* courte couverte; ***covered wagon*** chariot *m* (à bâche)

covering ['kʌvərɪŋ] **1** *n* (**a**) *(of snow, dust, chocolate)* couche *f* (**b**) *(protective → for floor)* revêtement *m*; *(for plants, object in trailer)* bâche *f*; *(on furniture)* housse *f*
2 *adj* (**a**) *Mil (forces, troops)* de couverture
►► *Mil* ***covering fire*** tir *m* de couverture; *Br* ***covering letter*** lettre *f* explicative *ou* de couverture; *St Exch* ***covering purchases*** rachats *mpl*

coverlet ['kʌvəlɪt] *n (for bed)* dessus-de-lit *m inv*, couvre-lit *m*

coverline ['kʌvəlaɪn] *n Journ* titraille *f*, titre *m* de rappel

covert ['kəʊvɜːt, 'kʌvət] **1** *adj (operation, payments, contacts)* secret(ète); *(threats)* voilé; *(glance, look)* furtif; **she had a covert dislike of him** sans le laisser paraître, elle ne pouvait pas le souffrir; **he stole a covert glance at her** il lui a jeté un regard furtif
2 *n* (**a**) *(hiding place for animals)* fourré *m*, couvert *m* (**b**) *(of bird)* tectrice *f*, plume *f* de couverture

covertly ['kəʊvɜːtlɪ, 'kʌvətlɪ] *adv (sold, paid)* secrètement; *(threaten)* de manière voilée; *(signal)* furtivement; **he glanced at her covertly** il l'a regardée à la dérobée, il lui a jeté un regard furtif

coverture ['kəʊvɜːtʃə(r), 'kʌvətʃə(r)] *n Literary* refuge *m*, abri *m*

cover-up *n* **the government has been accused of a cover-up** le gouvernement a été accusé d'avoir étouffé l'affaire; **the government denied that there had been any cover-up** le gouvernement a nié avoir étouffé l'affaire; **in a cover-up attempt that went wrong** dans une tentative ratée pour étouffer l'affaire; **it's a cover-up** c'est un complot

covet ['kʌvɪt] *vt (crave, long for)* convoiter; *(wish for)* avoir très envie de; **the much-coveted prix Goncourt** le prix Goncourt, objet de tant de convoitise; **I've always coveted a house like**

this j'ai toujours eu très envie d'une maison comme celle-ci

covetous [ˈkʌvɪtəs] *adj (person)* avide; *(look)* de convoitise; **to be covetous of sth** convoiter qch

covetously [ˈkʌvɪtəslɪ] *adv* avec convoitise

covetousness [ˈkʌvɪtəsnɪs] *n* convoitise *f*, avidité *f*

covey [ˈkʌvɪ] *n (of partridge, grouse)* compagnie *f ou* vol *m*

cow [kaʊ] **1** *n* (**a**) *(farm animal)* vache *f*; *Fig* **we'll be here until the cows come home!** on y sera encore dans dix ans!, on en a pour jusqu'à la Saint-Glinglin!; **I could eat chocolate ice cream until the cows come home** de la glace au chocolat, je pourrais en manger des kilos et des kilos

(**b**) *(female elephant)* éléphant *m* femelle, éléphante *f*; *(female seal)* phoque *m* femelle; *(female whale)* baleine *f* femelle

(**c**) *Br very Fam Pej (woman)* vache *f*, chameau *m*; **that old cow next door** la vieille bique d'à côté; **you cow!** espèce de conasse!; **you silly cow!** espèce d'abrutie!; **poor cow!** la pauvre!; **lucky cow!** la veinarde!

2 *vt* effrayer, intimider; **to cow sb into submission** intimider qn jusqu'à ce qu'il/elle se soumette; **a cowed look** un air de chien battu

▸▸ *Bot* **cow parsley** cerfeuil *m* sauvage

cowabunga [kaʊəˈbʌŋɡɑː] *exclam Am Fam* = cri de joie ou de victoire

coward [ˈkaʊəd] *n* lâche *mf*, poltron(onne) *m,f*; **don't be such a coward** ne sois pas aussi lâche; **I'm an awful coward when it comes to physical pain** j'ai très peur de *ou* je redoute beaucoup la douleur physique; **he's a moral coward** il n'a aucune force morale

cowardice [ˈkaʊədɪs] *n* lâcheté *f*; **an act of cowardice** un acte de lâcheté; **moral cowardice** manque *m* de force morale

cowardliness [ˈkaʊədlɪnɪs] *n* lâcheté *f*

cowardly [ˈkaʊədlɪ] *adj* lâche; **it was cowardly of him** c'était lâche de sa part

cowbell [ˈkaʊbel] *n* clochette *f*, sonnaille *f*

cowberry [ˈkaʊberɪ] *n Bot* airelle *f* rouge

cowbird [ˈkaʊbɜːd] *n Orn* carouge *m*

cowboy [ˈkaʊbɔɪ] **1** *n* (**a**) *(in American West)* cowboy *m*; **to play cowboys and Indians** jouer aux cow-boys et aux Indiens

(**b**) *Br Fam Pej (workman)* petit rigolo *m*; **what cowboy did this plumbing?** quel est le petit rigolo qui s'est occupé de la plomberie?; **a bunch of cowboys** une bande de petits rigolos; **some cowboy builder/plumber** un petit rigolo d'entrepreneur/de plombier, un soi-disant entrepreneur/plombier; **there are too many cowboy plumbers around here** il y a trop de petits rigolos dans la plomberie

(**c**) *Am Fam Pej (driver)* chauffard *m*

2 *comp* de cow-boy

▸▸ ***cowboy boots*** bottes *fpl* de cow-boy, santiags *fpl*; ***cowboy film, cowboy movie*** film *m* de cow-boys; ***the Cowboy State*** = surnom donné au Wyoming

cowcatcher [ˈkaʊˌkætʃə(r)] *n Am Rail* chasse-pierres *m inv*

cower [ˈkaʊə(r)] *vi (person)* se recroqueviller; *(animal)* se tapir; **I cowered** *or* **was cowering in my seat** j'étais recroquevillé sur ma chaise; **she cowered away from him** tremblante de peur, elle s'est écartée de lui; **the dog was cowering in a corner** tout tremblant, le chien était tapi dans un coin; **he stood cowering before the boss** il tremblait devant le patron

Cowes [kaʊz] *n* **Cowes (Week)** = régate et événement mondain se tenant chaque année à Cowes, sur l'île de Wight

cowgirl [ˈkaʊɡɜːl] *n* fille *f* de l'ouest, *Can* cow-girl *f*

cowhand [ˈkaʊhænd] *n* vacher(ère) *m,f*; *(in Western)* cow-boy *m*

cowherd [ˈkaʊhɜːd] *n* vacher(ère) *m,f*, bouvier(ère) *m,f*

cowhide [ˈkaʊhaɪd] *n* peau *f* de vache; *(leather)* cuir *m ou* peau *f* de vache

cowl [kaʊl] *n* (**a**) *(of chimney)* capuchon *m* (**b**) *Rel (hood)* capuchon *m*; *(habit)* habit *m* à capuchon (**c**) *Tech (cowling)* capot *m*

▸▸ ***cowl neck, cowl neckline*** *(on sweater, dress)* col *m* boule

cowlick [ˈkaʊlɪk] *n* mèche *f* rebelle

cowling [ˈkaʊlɪŋ] *n Tech* capot *m*

cowman [ˈkaʊmən] *(pl* **cowmen** [-mən]*) n* (**a**) *(who looks after cattle)* vacher *m*, bouvier *m* (**b**) *(who owns cattle ranch)* propriétaire *m* d'un ranch

cowmuck [ˈkaʊmʌk] *n* bouse *f* de vache

co-worker *n esp Am* collègue *mf*

cowpat [ˈkaʊpæt] *n* bouse *f* de vache

cowpea [ˈkaʊpiː] *n Bot* dolique *m*, dolic *m*, niébé *m*

cowpoke [ˈkaʊpəʊk] *n Am Fam* cowboy ❑ *m*

cowpox [ˈkaʊpɒks] *n Vet* vaccine *f*

cowpuncher [ˈkaʊpʌntʃə(r)] *n Am Fam Old-fashioned* cow-boy ❑ *m*

cowrie, cowry [ˈkaʊrɪ] *(pl* **cowries**) *n Zool (mollusc)* porcelaine *f*; *(shell)* cauri *m*

cowshed [ˈkaʊʃed] *n* étable *f*

cowshit [ˈkaʊʃɪt] *n very Fam* merde *f* de vache

cowslip [ˈkaʊslɪp] *n Bot* primevère *f*, coucou *m*

cox [kɒks] *Sport* **1** *n (of rowing team)* barreur(euse) *m,f*

2 *vt* barrer

3 *vi* barrer; **he has coxed for Cambridge** il a été barreur dans l'équipe de Cambridge

coxcomb [ˈkɒkskəʊm] *n* (**a**) *(of rooster)* crête *f* (**b**) *Bot* crête-de-coq *f* (**c**) *Arch (fop)* fat *m*, poseur *m*

coxed [kɒkst] *adj Br Sport (in rowing)*

▸▸ ***coxed four*** quatre *m* de pointe avec barreur; ***coxed pair*** deux *m* de pointe avec barreur

coxless [ˈkɒkslɪs] *adj Br Sport (in rowing)*

▸▸ ***coxless four*** quatre *m* de pointe sans barreur; ***coxless pair*** deux *m* de pointe sans barreur

Cox's (orange pippin) [ˈkɒksɪz-] *n* = variété de pomme à couteau, proche de la reinette, très répandue en Grande-Bretagne

coxswain [ˈkɒksən] *n Br* (**a**) *Sport (of rowing team)* barreur(euse) *m,f* (**b**) *(of lifeboat)* timonier *m*, homme *m* de barre

coy [kɔɪ] *adj* (**a**) *(shy → person)* qui fait le/la timide; *(→ answer, smile)* faussement timide; **why be so coy about accepting?** pourquoi faire semblant d'hésiter?

(**b**) *Pej (affectedly shy)* qui fait la sainte-nitouche; **a coy look** un air de sainte-nitouche

(**c**) *(provocative, playful)* coquet; **with a coy little smile** avec un petit sourire séducteur

(**d**) *(evasive)* évasif; **he was rather coy about the price** il était plutôt évasif quant au prix

coyly [ˈkɔɪlɪ] *adv (timidly)* avec une timidité affectée *ou* feinte; *(provocatively)* coquettement

coyness [ˈkɔɪnɪs] *n (timidity)* timidité *f* affectée *ou* feinte; *(provocativeness)* coquetteries *fpl*

coyote [kɔɪˈəʊtɪ] *n Zool* coyote *m*

▸▸ ***the Coyote State*** = surnom donné au Dakota du Sud

coypu [ˈkɔɪpuː] *n Zool* ragondin *m*

cozen [ˈkʌzən] *vt Arch* duper, tromper

cozy *Am* = **cosy**

CP [ˌsiːˈpiː] *n (abbr* **Communist Party**) PC *m*

c/p *Com (written abbr* **carriage paid**) pp

cp. *(written abbr* **compare**) cf

CPA [ˌsiːpiːˈeɪ] *n Am (abbr* **certified public accountant**) ≃ expert-comptable *m*

cpa [ˌsiːpiːˈeɪ] *n (abbr* **critical path analysis**) analyse *f* du chemin critique

CPI [ˌsiːpiːˈaɪ] *n Com & Econ (abbr* **Consumer Price Index**) IPC *m*

cpi [ˌsiːpiːˈaɪ] *Comput (abbr* **characters per inch**) cpp

Cpl *Mil (written abbr* **corporal**) caporal *m*

cpm *(written abbr* **copies per minute**) cpm

CP/M [ˌsiːpiːˈem] *n (abbr* **control program for microcomputers**) CP/M *m*

CPR [ˌsiːpiːˈɑː(r)] *n Med (abbr* **cardiopulmonary resuscitation**) réanimation *f* cardiorespiratoire

CPS [ˌsiːpiːˈes] *n Law (abbr* **Crown Prosecution Service**) ≃ ministère *m* public

cps [ˌsiːpiːˈes] *Comput (abbr* **characters per second**) cps

CPSA [ˌsiːpiːˌesˈeɪ] *n Admin (abbr* **Civil and Public Services Association**) = syndicat de la fonction publique

CPU [ˌsiːpiːˈjuː] *n Comput (abbr* **central processing unit**) unité *f* centrale (de traitement)

CPVE [ˌsiːpiːˌviːˈiː] *n Br Sch (abbr* **Certificate of pre-vocational education**) = examen d'accès à une formation professionnelle pour les élèves désirant poursuivre leurs études après le GCSE mais ne souhaitant pas passer les "A levels"

CR [ˌsiːˈɑː(r)] *n Typ & Comput (abbr* **carriage return**) retour *m* chariot

cr. (**a**) *(written abbr* **credit**) crédit *m* (**b**) *(written abbr* **creditor**) créancier(ère) *m,f*

crab [kræb] *(pt & pp* **crabbed**, *cont* **crabbing**) **1** *n* (**a**) *(crustacean)* crabe *m* (**b**) *Sport (in rowing)* **to catch a crab** faire (une) fausse pelle (**c**) *Astron* **the Crab** le Cancer (**d**) *(irritable person)* grincheux(euse) *m,f*

2 *vt Am* **to crab sb's act** casser la baraque *ou* la cabane à qn

3 *vi* (**a**) *(grumble)* maugréer, rouspéter (**b**) *(hunt crabs)* pêcher des crabes

4 crabs *npl Fam (pubic lice)* morpions *mpl*; **to have crabs** avoir des morpions

▸▸ ***crab apple*** *(fruit)* pomme *f* sauvage; *(tree)* pommier *m* sauvage; ***crab apple jelly*** gelée *f* de pommes sauvages; *Entom* ***crab louse*** morpion *m*; *Astron* ***Crab Nebula*** nébuleuse *f* du Crabe; *Culin* ***crab paste*** beurre *m* de crabe; *Orn* ***crab plover*** drome *m* ardéole; *Entom* ***crab spider*** araignée-crabe *f*

crabbed [kræbd] *adj* (**a**) *(handwriting)* en pattes de mouche (**b**) *Fam Old-fashioned* grognon, ronchon

crabby [ˈkræbɪ] *(compar* **crabbier**, *superl* **crabbiest**) *adj Fam* grognon, ronchon

crabgrass [ˈkræbɡrɑːs] *n Bot* digitaria *m*

CRACK [kræk]

fêlure	▸ **1 (a)**
fissure	▸ **1 (a)**
crevasse	▸ **1 (a)**
fente	▸ **1 (b)**
craquement	▸ **1 (c)**
claquement	▸ **1 (c)**
coup	▸ **1 (c), (d)**
tentative	▸ **1 (e)**
blague	▸ **1 (f)**
fêler	▸ **3 (a)**
fissurer	▸ **3 (a)**
crevasser	▸ **3 (a)**
casser	▸ **3 (b)**
cogner	▸ **3 (c)**
faire craquer	▸ **3 (d)**
faire claquer	▸ **3 (d)**
se fêler	▸ **4 (a)**
se fissurer	▸ **4 (a)**
se crevasser	▸ **4 (a)**
claquer	▸ **4 (b)**
craquer	▸ **4 (b), (c)**

1 *n* (**a**) *(in cup, glass, egg)* fêlure *f*; *(in ceiling, wall)* lézarde *f*, fissure *f*; *(in rock)* fissure *f*; *(in ground)* crevasse *f*; *(in varnish, enamel)* craquelure *f*; *(in skin)* gerçure *f*, crevasse *f*; *(in bone)* fêlure *f*; *Fig (fault → in policy, argument etc)* fissure *f*, faiblesse *f*; **did you know there was a crack in this glass?** avais-tu remarqué que ce verre était fêlé?; *Fig* **the cracks are beginning to show in their marriage** leur mariage commence à battre de l'aile

(**b**) *(small opening or gap → in floorboards, door etc)* fente *f*; *(→ in wall)* fissure *f*; **there were some cracks in the wall** le mur était fissuré

(**c**) *(noise → of branches, ice etc)* craquement *m*; *(→ of whip)* claquement *m*; *(→ of thunder)* coup *m*

(**d**) *(blow → on head, knee etc)* coup *m*; **that was a nasty crack you got** tu as pris un drôle de mauvais coup; **I gave myself a crack on the head** je me suis cogné la tête

(**e**) *Fam (attempt)* tentative ❑ *f*; **I'll have a crack (at it), I'll give it a crack** je vais tenter le coup, je vais essayer (un coup); **do you want another crack (at it)?** tu veux réessayer? ❑, tu veux retenter le coup?; **this is her fourth crack at (winning) the title** c'est sa quatrième tentative pour gagner le titre ❑, c'est la quatrième fois qu'elle tente de gagner le titre ❑; **to give sb a fair crack of the whip** donner sa chance à qn ❑; **to get a fair crack of the whip** avoir l'occasion de montrer de quoi on est capable ❑

(**f**) *(joke, witticism)* blague *f*, plaisanterie *f*; **to make a crack** faire une plaisanterie, lancer une vanne; **a cheap crack about short people** une plaisanterie facile sur les gens de petite taille

(g) *(drug)* crack *m*

(h) *Comput (program)* = programme permettant de forcer un système informatique

(i) *Vulg (woman's genitals)* chatte *f*, con *m*

(j) *Vulg (anus)* troufignon *m*, trou *m* du cul

(k) *(idiom)* **at the crack of dawn** au point du jour; **I've been up since the crack of dawn** je suis debout *ou* levé depuis l'aube; *Old-fashioned Hum* **we'll be here until the crack of doom** on va être ici jusqu'aux calendes grecques

2 *adj (regiment, team etc)* d'élite; **one of their crack players** un de leurs meilleurs joueurs

3 *vt* (a) *(damage → cup, glass, egg)* fêler; *(→ ice)* fendre; *(→ ceiling, wall)* lézarder, fissurer; *(→ ground)* crevasser; *(→ varnish, enamel)* craqueler; *(→ skin)* gercer, crevasser; *(→ bone)* fêler

(b) *(open → eggs, nuts)* casser; **to crack a safe** fracturer un coffre-fort; *Fam* **to crack (open) a bottle** ouvrir *ou* déboucher une bouteille❑; *Fam* **she never cracked a smile the entire evening** elle n'a pas souri une seule fois de la soirée❑; *Am* **I didn't crack a book all term** je n'ai pas ouvert un livre du trimestre❑

(c) *(bang, hit → head, knee)* **to crack one's head/knee on sth** se cogner la tête/le genou contre qch

(d) *(make noise with → whip)* faire claquer; *(→ knuckles)* faire craquer; **to crack the whip** faire le gendarme; **he's very good at cracking the whip** il est très doué pour donner des ordres

(e) *(solve)* **to crack a code** déchiffrer un code; **the police think they have cracked the case** la police pense qu'elle a résolu l'affaire; **I think we've cracked it** je pense que nous y sommes arrivés

(f) *(market)* percer sur

(g) *Chem* craquer

(h) *Comput* craquer, déplomber

(i) *Fam (idiom)* **to crack a joke** sortir une blague; **"got a half-day today?" she cracked** "tu t'es pris une demi-journée de congé?" dit-elle en blaguant *ou* plaisantant

4 *vi* (a) *(cup, glass, ice)* se fissurer, se fêler; *(ceiling, wall)* se lézarder, se fissurer; *(ground)* se crevasser; *(varnish, enamel)* se craqueler; *(skin)* se gercer, se crevasser; *(bone)* se fêler

(b) *(make noise → whip)* claquer; *(→ twigs)* craquer; **a rifle cracked and he dropped to the ground** un coup de fusil a retenti et il s'est effondré; **the sound of submachine-guns cracking** le crépitement des mitraillettes

(c) *(give way, collapse → through nervous exhaustion)* s'effondrer, craquer; *(→ under questioning, surveillance)* craquer; **their marriage cracked under the strain** leur mariage s'est détérioré sous l'effet du stress; **his voice cracked with emotion** sa voix se brisa sous le coup de l'émotion

(d) *Fam (idiom)* **to get cracking** *(start work)* s'y mettre❑, se mettre au boulot; *(get ready, get going)* se mettre en route❑; **I'll get cracking on dinner/cleaning the windows** je vais me mettre à préparer le dîner/nettoyer les vitres❑; **get cracking!, let's get cracking!** au boulot!

►► ***crack baby*** = bébé né dépendant du crack; ***crack cocaine*** crack *m*; ***crack shot*** tireur(euse) *m,f* d'élite; ***crack troops*** soldats *mpl* d'élite

►**crack down** *vi* sévir; **to crack down on sb/sth** sévir contre qn/qch

►**crack open** *vt sep (eggs, nuts)* casser; *Fam (bottle)* ouvrir❑, déboucher❑

►**crack up 1** *vi* (a) *(ice)* se fissurer; *(paint, enamel, make-up)* se craqueler; *(ground)* se crevasser; *(skin)* se gercer, se crevasser

(b) *Fam (through nervous exhaustion)* s'effondrer❑, craquer❑; **I must be cracking up** *(going mad)* je débloque

(c) *Br Fam (get angry)* péter les plombs

(d) *Fam (with laughter)* se tordre de rire

2 *vt sep* (a) *(make laugh)* **it really cracked me up when I heard about it** je me suis vraiment écroulé de rire quand j'ai entendu parler de ça

(b) *(always passive) (say good things about)* **he's not what he's cracked up to be** il n'est pas aussi fantastique qu'on le dit *ou* prétend; **the play is everything it's cracked up to be** la pièce a toutes les qualités qu'on lui vante

(c) *Fam (destroy)* bousiller

crackbrain ['krækbreɪn] *n Fam* fêlé(e) *m,f*, taré(e) *m,f*

crackbrained ['krækbreɪnd] *adj Fam* débile, dingue

crackdown ['krækdaʊn] *n* **we're going to have a crackdown on petty theft** on va sévir contre les petits larcins; **the annual Christmas crackdown on drink driving** les mesures prises tous les ans à Noël contre la conduite en état d'ivresse; **the crackdown on dissidents** la répression contre les dissidents; **the government crackdown on reporting** les restrictions *fpl* gouvernementales concernant les reportages

cracked [krækt] *adj* (a) *(damaged → cup, glass)* fêlé; *(→ ice)* fendu; *(→ ceiling, wall)* lézardé; *(→ ground)* crevassé; *(→ varnish)* craquelé; *(→ skin)* gercé, crevassé (b) *Fam (mad → person)* fêlé, taré

►► ***cracked pepper*** poivre *m* concassé

cracker ['krækə(r)] *n* (a) *(savoury biscuit)* biscuit *m* salé, cracker *m*

(b) *Br (for pulling)* = papillote contenant un pétard, une blague, un chapeau en papier et une surprise, traditionnelle en Grande-Bretagne au moment des fêtes

(c) *(firework)* pétard *m*

(d) *Br Fam (good-looking person)* canon *m*

(e) *Br Fam (excellent thing)* merveille❑ *f*; **that was a cracker of a goal** c'était un but magnifique❑

(f) *Am Fam Pej (redneck)* = Blanc pauvre du sud des États-Unis

(g) *Comput* pirate *m* informatique

►► *Am* ***cracker barrel*** boîte *f* à biscuits

CRACKER

Les "crackers" décorent la table à Noël en Grande-Bretagne. Un "cracker" est un tube en carton enveloppé d'un papier cadeau, contenant généralement un petit jouet, une blague et un chapeau en papier. On se met à deux pour l'ouvrir, chacun tirant sur un bout du "cracker", dans lequel il y a un petit pétard.

cracker-barrel *adj Am Fam (wisdom, philosophy etc)* de quatre sous

crackerjack ['krækə,dʒæk] *Am Fam* **1** *n* **to be a crackerjack** *(person)* être un crack *ou* un as; *(thing)* être génial

2 *adj (excellent)* génial, du tonnerre

crackers ['krækəz] *adj Br Fam* cinglé, fêlé, taré; **to drive sb crackers** faire tourner qn en bourrique

crackhead ['krækhed] *n Fam Drugs slang* accro *mf* au crack

crackhouse ['krækhaʊs, *pl* -haʊzɪz] *n Fam Drugs slang* = lieu où l'on achète, vend et consomme du crack

cracking ['krækɪŋ] **1** *adj* (a) *Br Fam (excellent)* génial, épatant (b) *(fast)* **to keep up a cracking pace** aller à fond de train

2 *adv Br Fam Old-fashioned* **cracking good** *(match, meal)* de première

3 *n* (a) *(sound)* craquement *m*; *(of whip)* claquement *m* (b) *(of paint)* craquelure *f*, craquelage *m* (c) *Chem* craquage *m*

►► *Chem* ***cracking plant*** usine *f* de craquage

crackle ['krækəl] **1** *n* (a) *(of paper, twigs, dry leaves)* craquement *m*; *(of fire)* crépitement *m*, craquement *m*; *(of radio)* grésillement *m*; *(on telephone)* friture *f*; *(of something frying)* grésillement *m*; *(of machine-gun fire)* crépitement *m*

(b) *(finish → of paint, porcelain)* craquelure *f*

2 *vt Cer (glaze)* craqueler

3 *vi (paper, twigs, dry leaves)* craquer; *(fire)* crépiter, craquer; *(radio)* grésiller; *(something frying)* grésiller; *(machine-gun fire)* crépiter; *Fig* **to crackle with energy** pétiller d'énergie

►► *Cer* ***crackle finish*** craquelage *m*

crackleware ['krækəl,weə(r)] *n Cer* poterie *f* craquelée

crackling ['kræklɪŋ] *n* (a) *(of paper, twigs, dry leaves)* craquement *m*; *(of fire)* crépitement *m*, craquement *m*; *(of radio)* grésillement *m*; *(on telephone)* friture *f*; *(of something frying)* grésillement *m*; *(of machine-gun fire)* crépitement *m*

(b) *Culin (of roast pork)* couenne *f* rôtie

crackly ['kræklɪ] *(compar* **cracklier**, *superl* **crackliest**) *adj* **the line is a bit crackly** *(on phone)* il y a de la friture sur la ligne; **the radio's a bit crackly** la radio grésille un peu

cracknel ['kræknəl] *n (biscuit)* craquelin *m*; *(filling for chocolate)* nougatine *f*

crackpot ['krækpɒt] *Fam* **1** *n (person)* cinglé(e) *m,f*

2 *adj (idea, scheme)* tordu; *(person)* cinglé

cracksman ['kræksmən] *(pl* **cracksmen** [-mən]) *n Fam Old-fashioned* casseur *m* (de coffres)

crack-up *n Fam* (a) *(of person)* dépression *f* (nerveuse)❑ (b) *(of country, economy)* effondrement❑ *m*

Cracow ['krækaʊ] *n* Cracovie

cradle ['kreɪdəl] **1** *n* (a) *(for baby) & Fig* berceau *m*; **the cradle of democracy/the trade union movement** le berceau de la démocratie/du mouvement syndical; **from the cradle to the grave** du berceau au tombeau; **to provide comprehensive health cover from cradle to grave** assurer une couverture santé complète tout au long de la vie d'un individu; **they've known each other since they were in their cradles** ils se connaissent depuis qu'ils sont tout petits; *Am Hum* **to rob the cradle** les prendre au berceau *ou* biberon

(b) *(frame → for painter, window cleaner)* pont *m* volant, échafaudage *m* volant; *(→ in hospital bed)* arceau *m*

(c) *(for telephone receiver)* support *m*

2 *vt (hold carefully → baby, kitten)* tenir tendrement (dans ses bras); *(→ delicate object)* tenir précieusement *ou* délicatement (dans ses bras); *Fig* **cradled in luxury** bercé dans le luxe; **the village was cradled in a valley** le village était blotti au fond d'une vallée

►► ***cradle cap*** dermite *f* séborrhéique; **to have cradle cap** *(of baby)* avoir des croûtes de lait; *Archit* ***cradle vault*** (voûte *f* en) tonnelle *f*, (voûte en) berceau *m*

cradle-snatcher *n Br Fam* **he's/she's a cradle-snatcher** il/elle les prend au berceau; **I'm no cradle-snatcher** je ne les prends pas au berceau; **you cradle-snatcher!** tu les prends au berceau!

cradle-snatching [-'snætʃɪŋ] *n Fam* **I don't go in for cradle-snatching** je ne les prends pas au berceau

cradle-song *n* berceuse *f*

cradle-to-grave *adj* (a) *(health cover, welfare system)* qui prend l'individu en charge tout au long de sa vie (b) *(gen) & Comput (service, support)* de bout en bout; *Ecol* **cradle-to-grave management** *or* **control of toxic waste** gestion *f* de bout en bout des déchets dangereux

►► *Mktg* ***cradle-to-grave marketing*** = type de marketing qui vise les enfants dès le plus jeune âge

craft [krɑːft] *(pl sense* (c) **inv**) **1** *n* (a) *(art)* art *m*; *(occupation)* métier *m* (manuel); **crafts** *(activity)* activités *fpl* manuelles

(b) *(guile, cunning)* ruse *f*; **to use craft** employer la ruse; **to obtain sth by craft** obtenir qch par la ruse

(c) *(boat, ship)* bateau *m*; *(aircraft)* avion *m*; *(spacecraft)* engin *m ou* vaisseau *m* spatial; **all the small craft in the harbour** tous les petits bateaux *ou* toutes les embarcations dans le port

2 *vt (usu passive)* travailler; *Fig* **a beautifully crafted film** un film magnifiquement travaillé

►► *Br Sch* ***craft, design and technology*** = matière enseignée dans le secondaire qui incorpore travaux manuels et technologie; ***craft(s) fair*** foire *f* d'artisanat; ***craft guild*** corporation *f* artisanale *ou* d'artisans; ***craft shop*** boutique *f* d'artisanat; ***craft union*** syndicat *m* d'artisans

craftily ['krɑːftɪlɪ] *adv* astucieusement; **to behave craftily** agir astucieusement *ou* habilement; *Pej (with cunning)* agir avec ruse

craftiness ['krɑːftɪnɪs] *n* habileté *f*; *Pej* ruse *f*, roublardise *f*

craftsman ['krɑːftsmən] *(pl* **craftsmen** [-mən]) *n* artisan *m*, homme *m* de métier; *(writer, actor)* homme *m* de métier; **he's not much of a craftsman** ce n'est pas un très bon artisan; *(amateur)* il n'est pas très doué de ses mains

craftsmanship ['krɑːftsmənʃɪp] *n* connaissance *f* d'un *ou* du métier; **a fine example of craftsmanship** un bel ouvrage, un vrai travail d'artiste;

this is French craftsmanship at its best voici l'artisanat français au sommet de sa qualité; **the craftsmanship is superb** cela a été superbement travaillé; **you have to pay for good craftsmanship** il faut payer si on veut du bon travail; **there's no craftsmanship these days** il n'y a plus de travail bien fait de nos jours

craftswoman ['krɑːfts,wʊmən] *(pl* **craftswomen** [-,wɪmɪn]) *n* artisane *f*

craftwork ['krɑːftwɜːk] *n* artisanat *m*

crafty ['krɑːftɪ] *(compar* **craftier,** *superl* **craftiest**) *adj (person, idea, scheme)* malin(igne), astucieux; *Pej (person)* rusé, roublard; *(idea, scheme)* rusé; **you crafty old devil!** espèce de vieux renard!

crag [kræg] *n (steep rock)* rocher *m* escarpé *ou* à pic

►► *Orn* ***crag martin*** hirondelle *f* des rochers

craggedness ['krægɪdnɪs], **cragginess** ['krægɪnɪs] *n (of mountain, landscape)* aspect *m* escarpé; *Fig* **the craggedness of his features** son visage anguleux

craggy ['krægɪ] *(compar* **craggier,** *superl* **craggiest**) *adj (hill)* escarpé, à pic; *Fig (features)* anguleux, taillé à la serpe

crake [kreɪk] *n* (**a**) *Orn* râle *m*, marouette *f* (**b**) *(call)* cri *m* du râle

cram [kræm] *(pt & pp* **crammed,** *cont* **cramming**) **1** *vt* (**a**) *(objects)* fourrer; *(people)* entasser; **to cram sth into a drawer** fourrer qch dans un tiroir; **there were ten of us crammed into a tiny office** nous étions dix entassés dans un bureau minuscule; **to cram clothes into a suitcase** bourrer des vêtements dans une valise, bourrer une valise de vêtements; **you can't cram anything else in** tu ne peux plus rien y mettre, même en forçant; **could you cram one more person in?** y aurait-il encore une petite place?; **to cram food into one's mouth** se bourrer de nourriture, se gaver; **I crammed a lot of quotations into my essay** j'ai bourré ma dissertation de citations; **we crammed a lot into one day** on en a fait beaucoup en une seule journée; **could you cram one more visit into your schedule?** pourriez-vous trouver une petite place pour ajouter une visite à votre programme chargé?

(**b**) *Fam (facts)* apprendre à toute vitesse ❑; *(students)* faire bachoter

(**c**) *Agr (poultry)* appâter, gaver

2 *vi* (**a**) *Fam (study hard)* bachoter

(**b**) *(into small space)* **100 people crammed in** 100 personnes se *ou* s'y sont entassées; **people crammed into the streets to watch the parade** les gens se sont entassés dans les rues pour regarder le défilé; **we all crammed into his office** nous nous sommes tous entassés dans son bureau

cram-full *adj Br* **to be cram-full (of sth)** être plein à craquer *ou* bourré (de qch)

crammed ['kræmd] *adj (full → bus, train, room, suitcase)* bourré, bondé; **to be crammed with people** être bondé; **to be crammed with sth** être plein à craquer *ou* bourré de qch; **the encyclopedia is crammed with useful information** l'encyclopédie regorge d'informations utiles

crammer ['kræmə(r)] *n Br Fam (teacher)* répétiteur(trice) ❑ *m,f*; *(student)* bachoteur(euse) *m,f*; *(school)* boîte *f* à bac

cramming ['kræmɪŋ] *n* [illegible] bachotage *m*; *(intensive teaching)* bourrage *m* de crâne

cramp [kræmp] **1** *n* (**a**) *(muscle pain)* crampe *f*; **to have cramp** *or Am* **a cramp** avoir une crampe; **I've got cramp in my leg** j'ai une crampe à la jambe; **she dropped out (of the race) with cramp** elle a abandonné (la course) parce qu'elle avait une crampe; *Am* **to have stomach cramp, to have cramps** avoir des crampes d'estomac

(**b**) *Carp* serre-joint *m*

(**c**) *Constr (cramp iron)* crampon *m*, happe *f*, clameau *m*

2 *vt* (**a**) *(hamper → person)* gêner; *(→ project)* entraver, contrarier; *Fam* **to cramp sb's style** faire perdre tous ses moyens à qn ❑, priver qn de ses moyens ❑

(**b**) *Carp (secure with a cramp)* maintenir à l'aide d'un serre-joint

(**c**) *Constr (stones etc)* cramponner, agrafer

►► *Constr* ***cramp iron*** crampon *m*, happe *f*, clameau *m*

cramped [kræmpt] *adj* (**a**) *(room, flat)* exigu; **they live in very cramped conditions** ils vivent très à l'étroit; **we're a bit cramped for space** nous sommes un peu à l'étroit (**b**) *(position)* inconfortable (**c**) *(handwriting)* en pattes de mouche, serré

crampon ['kræmpən] *n* crampon *m* (à glace)

cranachan ['krænəχən] *n Culin* = dessert d'origine écossaise à base d'avoine grillée, de whisky, de crème fouettée et de framboises

cranberry ['krænbərɪ] *(pl* **cranberries**) *n* canneberge *f*

►► ***cranberry juice*** jus *m* de canneberge; ***cranberry sauce*** sauce *f* à la canneberge

crane [kreɪn] **1** *n* (**a**) *Orn* grue *f* (**b**) *Tech & Cin* grue *f*

2 *vt* **to crane one's neck** tendre le cou

3 *vi* **to crane (forward)** tendre le cou

►► *Bot* ***crane's bill*** géranium *m*; ***crane driver*** grutier(ère) *m,f*; *Entom* ***crane fly*** tipule *f*; ***crane jib*** potence *f*; ***crane operator*** grutier(ère) *m,f*

crania ['kreɪnjə] *pl of* **cranium**

cranial ['kreɪnjəl] *adj Anat* crânien; *(fracture)* du crâne

►► *Med* ***cranial index*** indice *m* de volume crânien; *Anat* ***cranial nerve*** nerf *m* crânien

craniology [,kreɪnɪ'ɒlədʒɪ] *n Med* craniologie *f*

craniometry [,kreɪnɪ'ɒmɪtrɪ] *n* craniométrie *f*, céphalométrie *f*

craniosacral therapy [,kreɪnɪəʊ'seɪkrəl-] *n Med* osthéopathie *f* crânienne

craniotomy [,kreɪnɪ'ɒtəmɪ] *n Med* craniotomie *f*

cranium ['kreɪnɪəm] *(pl* **craniums** *or* **crania** [-njə]) *n Anat (skull → gen)* crâne *m*; *(→ part enclosing brain)* boîte *f* crânienne

crank [kræŋk] **1** *n* (**a**) *Fam (eccentric)* allumé(e) *m,f*; **a religious crank** un (une) fanatique; **she's a bit of a crank** elle est un peu allumée; **what a crank!** quel allumé!

(**b**) *Am Fam (bad-tempered person)* grognon(onne) *m,f*

(**c**) *Tech* manivelle *f*

2 *vt (engine)* démarrer à la manivelle; *(gramophone)* remonter à la manivelle; **to crank the shutters up/down** remonter/baisser les volets (à la manivelle)

►► *Tech* ***crank handle*** manivelle *f*

►**crank out** *vt sep Am Fam (books, plays etc)* produire en quantités industrielles ❑; **this is the fourth novel he's cranked out this year** c'est le quatrième roman d'affilée qu'il sort cette année

►**crank up 1** *vt sep* (**a**) *(engine)* démarrer à la manivelle; *(gramophone)* remonter à la manivelle

(**b**) *Fig (increase)* augmenter; **crank up the volume** monte le son

(**c**) *(idiom)* **to get things cranked up** mettre tout en place

2 *vi Fam Drugs slang* se shooter

crankcase ['kræŋkkeɪs] *n Tech* carter *m*

crankily ['kræŋkɪlɪ] *adv* (**a**) *Am & Ir (say, reply)* d'un ton grognon, avec humeur (**b**) *(of machine → start operating)* par à-coups, en geignant

crankiness ['kræŋkɪnɪs] *n Fam* (**a**) *(eccentricity)* bizarrerie ❑ *f* (**b**) *Am, Austr & Ir (bad temper)* caractère *m* de cochon [illegible] mauvaise humeur *f*

cranking ['kræŋkɪŋ]

►► *Tech* ***cranking handle*** manivelle *f*; *Aut* ***cranking speed*** vitesse *f* du démarreur, régime *m* de démarrage; *Aut* ***cranking torque*** couple *m* de démarrage

crankpin ['kræŋkpɪn] *n Tech* maneton *m*

crankshaft ['kræŋkʃɑːft] *n Tech* vilebrequin *m*

cranky ['kræŋkɪ] *(compar* **crankier,** *superl* **crankiest**) *adj Fam* (**a**) *Br (eccentric → person, behaviour, ideas)* bizarre ❑, loufoque ❑ (**b**) *Am, Austr & Ir (bad-tempered)* grognon (**c**) *(unreliable → machine)* capricieux

cranny ['krænɪ] *(pl* **crannies**) *n (crack)* fente *f*

crap [kræp] *(pt & pp* **crapped,** *cont* **crapping**) **1** *n (UNCOUNT)* (**a**) *very Fam (faeces)* merde *f*; **to have** *or* **take a crap** chier, couler un bronze

(**b**) *very Fam (nonsense)* conneries *fpl*; **to talk crap** raconter *ou* dire des conneries; **that's crap, I never said that!** c'est des conneries, je n'ai jamais dit ça!; **don't give me that crap!** arrête de me raconter des conneries!; **he's full of crap** il raconte n'importe quoi; **what a load of crap!** quelles conneries!; **cut the crap!** arrête tes conneries!, arrête de dire n'importe quoi!

(**c**) *very Fam (rubbish)* merde *f*; **get all this crap off the table** enlève tout ce bordel *ou* toute cette merde de la table; **he writes absolute crap** ce qu'il écrit c'est de la merde; **she eats crap out of fast-food places** elle bouffe la saloperie *ou* la merde qu'on vend dans les fast-foods; **his cooking is crap** sa cuisine, c'est de la merde; **to feel like crap** *(ill)* se sentir vraiment patraque

(**d**) *very Fam (unfair treatment)* **I'm not taking that crap from you!** si tu crois que je vais supporter tes conneries sans réagir, tu te goures!; **I don't need this crap!** je me passerais bien de ce genre de conneries!

(**e**) *Am (dice game)* = jeu de dés similaire au quatre-cent-vingt-et-un et où on parie sur le résultat; **crap game** partie *f* de dés

2 *vi very Fam (defecate)* chier, couler un bronze

3 *vt very Fam* **to crap oneself** *(defecate, be scared)* faire dans son froc

4 *adj Br very Fam (of poor quality)* de merde, merdique; *(nasty)* dégueulasse; **that was a crap thing to do!** c'est vraiment dégueulasse d'avoir fait ça!; **what a crap book** quel livre merdique *ou* de merde *ou* à la con; **she's a crap cook** sa cuisine, c'est de la merde; **to feel crap** *(ill)* se sentir vraiment mal fichu; *(guilty)* se sentir coupable ❑

5 craps *n Am (dice game)* = jeu de dés similaire au quatre-cent-vingt-et-un et où on parie sur le résultat; **to shoot craps** *(play game)* jouer aux dés, faire une partie de dés; *(throw dice)* lancer les dés

►**crap out** *vi* (**a**) *Am (in game)* = ne pas obtenir le résultat sur lequel on a parié dans un jeu de dés

(**b**) *very Fam (back out)* se dégonfler; **he crapped out of the fight** il s'est dégonflé au dernier moment et a refusé de se battre; **he crapped out of asking her for a date** il allait lui demander de sortir avec lui mais il s'est dégonflé

crape [kreɪp] *n* (**a**) *(fabric)* crêpe *m* (**b**) *(for people in mourning)* crêpe *m* noir (de deuil)

crapper ['kræpə(r)] *n very Fam (toilet)* chiottes *fpl*, gogues *mpl*

crappy ['kræpɪ] *(compar* **crappier,** *superl* **crappiest**) *adj very Fam (of poor quality)* de merde, merdique, à la con; *(nasty)* dégueulasse; **to feel crappy** *(ill)* se sentir vraiment mal fichu; *(guilty)* se sentir coupable ❑

crapshooter ['kræp,ʃuːtə(r)] *n Am* joueur(euse) *m,f* de dés

crapulous ['kræpjʊləs], **crapulent** ['kræpjʊlənt] *adj Literary* intempérant

CRASH [kræʃ]

accident	►1 (a)
fracas	►1 (b)
krach	►1 (c)
panne	►1 (d)
patatras	►4
avoir un accident	►5 (a)
s'écraser	►5 (a), (b)
retentir	►5 (b)
s'effondrer	►5 (d)
tomber en panne	►5 (e)

1 *n* (**a**) *(collision)* accident *m*; **car/plane/train crash** accident *m* de voiture/d'avion/ferroviaire; **we were in a crash** *(car accident)* nous avons eu un accident de voiture; **the car looks as though it has been in a crash** la voiture semble avoir été accidentée; **the force of the crash** la force de l'impact; *Rugby* **to do a crash tackle** plaquer violemment

(**b**) *(loud noise)* fracas *m*; **a crash of thunder** un coup de tonnerre; **there was a loud crash as the plate hit the ground** cela a fait un bruit fracassant quand l'assiette est tombée par terre; **there was a loud crash from the kitchen** un grand fracas a retenti dans la cuisine; **he closed the lid with a crash** il a fermé le couvercle avec fracas; **he fell to the floor with a crash** il est tombé par terre dans un grand fracas

(c) *Fin (slump)* krach *m*, débâcle *f*

(d) *Comput* panne *f*

2 *comp (diet, programme)* intensif, de choc

3 *adv* **he ran crash into a wall** il est rentré en plein dans le mur; **it went crash** ça a fait boum; **something went crash in the attic** quelque chose est tombé dans le grenier

4 *onomat* patatras!

5 *vi* (a) *(car, train, driver)* avoir un accident; *(plane)* s'écraser, se crasher; **we're going to crash** *(plane)* on va s'écraser; *(car)* on va lui rentrer dedans/rentrer dans le mur/*etc*; *(train)* on va avoir un accident; **the car hit a patch of ice and crashed** la voiture a eu un accident après avoir glissé sur une plaque de verglas; **a detailed study of what actually happens when a car crashes** une étude détaillée de ce qui se passe vraiment lors des accidents de voiture; **the French car crashed at the first bend** la voiture française a eu un accident dans le premier virage; **the cars crashed (head on)** les voitures se sont percutées (de plein fouet); **to crash into sth** percuter qch, rentrer dans qch; **the car crashed through the fence** la voiture est passée à travers la clôture; **to crash into sb** *(person)* rentrer dans qn; **I crashed into him** je lui suis rentré dedans

(b) *(make loud noise → thunder)* retentir; *(→ waves)* s'écraser; **the thunder crashed** *(once)* il y eut un violent coup de tonnerre; *(repeatedly)* le tonnerre retentit; **what are you crashing about at this hour for?** pourquoi fais-tu autant de vacarme *ou* boucan à cette heure?; **the elephants crashed through the undergrowth** les éléphants ont traversé le sous-bois dans un vacarme terrible

(c) *(fall, hit with loud noise or violently)* **the tree came crashing down** l'arbre s'est abattu avec fracas; **the bookcase came crashing down** la bibliothèque s'est écroulée avec fracas; **her world came crashing down (about) her** *or* **her ears** tout son monde s'est écroulé; **the vase crashed to the ground** le vase s'est fracassé au sol; **his fist crashed into the other man's face** son poing a percuté avec force *ou* violence le visage de l'autre

(d) *St Exch* s'effondrer; **shares crashed from 750p to 110p** le cours des actions s'est effondré: de 750 pence il est passé à 110 pence

(e) *Comput (computer network, system)* sauter; *(computer)* tomber en panne, planter

(f) *Fam (spend night, sleep)* pieuter, pioncer; *(fall asleep)* s'endormir□; **can I crash at your place?** je peux pieuter chez toi?; **I need somewhere to crash for the next week** j'ai besoin d'un endroit où crécher la semaine prochaine

6 *vt* (a) *(vehicle)* **to crash a car** avoir un accident avec une voiture; *(on purpose)* démolir une voiture; **to crash a plane** s'écraser en avion; **he crashed the car through the fence/shop-window** il a traversé la clôture/la vitrine avec la voiture; **she crashed the car into a wall** elle est rentrée dans *ou* a percuté un mur (avec la voiture)

(b) *Fam (party)* s'inviter à□, taper l'incruste à

(c) *Comput* faire tomber en panne

►► ***crash barrier*** glissière *f* de sécurité; ***crash course*** cours *m* intensif; **a crash course in French** un cours intensif de français; ***crash dive*** *(of submarine)* plongée *f* raide; *(of plane)* plongeon *m*; ***crash helmet*** casque *m* (de protection); ***crash landing*** atterrissage *m* forcé *ou* en catastrophe; *Fam* ***crash pad*** piaule *f* de dépannage; **he let me use his place as a crash pad** il m'a laissé crécher chez lui pour me dépanner; ***crash test dummy*** mannequin-test *m*; ***crash victim*** victime *f* d'un accident

►**crash out** *vi Fam (fall asleep)* s'endormir□; *(spend the night, sleep)* pieuter, pioncer; **I found him crashed out in the corner** je l'ai trouvé endormi□ *ou* qui roupillait dans le coin; **she's absolutely crashed out** elle dort comme une souche□, elle en écrase

---

crash-dive *vi (submarine)* plonger; *(plane)* faire un plongeon

crashing ['kræʃɪŋ] *adj Br Fam* **a crashing bore** *(person)* une personne assommante; *(task)* une besogne assommante; *(party)* une soirée assommante; **to be a crashing bore** être assommant

crashingly ['kræʃɪŋlɪ] *adv Br Fam (boring)* incroyablement, terriblement

crash-land 1 *vi (aircraft)* faire un atterrissage forcé, atterrir en catastrophe

2 *vt (aircraft)* poser *ou* faire atterrir en catastrophe

crash-test *vt* **to crash-test a car** tester une voiture en situation d'accident

crashworthiness ['kræʃˌwɜːðɪnɪs] *n (of vehicle, helicopter)* résistance *f* aux chocs

crashworthy ['kræʃˌwɜːðɪ] (*compar* **crashworthier**, *superl* **crashworthiest**) *adj* qui a une bonne résistance aux collisions

crass [kræs] *adj (comment, person)* lourd; *(behaviour, stupidity)* grossier; *(ignorance)* grossier, crasse

crassly ['kræslɪ] *adv (behave, comment)* lourdement

crassness ['kræsnɪs] *n (of comment, person)* lourdeur *f*, manque *m* de finesse; **the crassness of his ignorance** son ignorance crasse; **the crassness of his behaviour** son manque de finesse

crate [kreɪt] 1 *n* (a) *(for storage, transport)* caisse *f*; *(for fruit, vegetables)* cageot *m*, cagette *f*; *(for glass, china)* harasse *f*; *(for bottles)* casier *m* (b) *Fam (old car)* caisse *f*; *(plane)* coucou *m*

2 *vt (goods)* mettre dans une caisse *ou* en caisses; *(fruit, vegetables)* mettre dans un cageot *ou* en cageots

crater ['kreɪtə(r)] 1 *n (of volcano, moon etc)* cratère *m*; *(from bomb)* entonnoir *m*; **the explosion had left a crater 20 feet wide** l'explosion avait laissé un cratère de 6 mètres de large; **bomb crater** entonnoir *m*; **shell crater** entonnoir *m*, trou *m* d'obus

2 *vt* creuser; **a street cratered by shellfire** une rue défoncée par des éclats d'obus

cratered ['kreɪtəd] *adj (landscape)* couvert de cratères; *Mil (road)* défoncé; *Fig (face)* crevassé

craton ['kreɪtɒn] *n Geol* craton *m*

cravat [krə'væt] *n Br* foulard *m*

crave [kreɪv] *vt* (a) *(long for → cigarette, drink)* avoir terriblement envie de; *(→ affection, love)* avoir soif *ou* terriblement besoin de; *(→ stardom)* avoir soif de; *(→ luxury, wealth)* avoir soif *ou* être avide de; *Med & Psy* éprouver un besoin impérieux de

(b) *Formal (beg)* implorer; **to crave sb's permission to do sth** implorer qn pour obtenir la permission de faire qch; **to crave sb's pardon** implorer le pardon de qn; **to crave sb's indulgence** faire appel à l'indulgence de qn; **may I crave your attention?** puis-je me permettre de solliciter votre attention?

►**crave for** *vt insep (long for → cigarette, drink)* avoir terriblement envie de; *(→ affection, love)* avoir soif *ou* terriblement besoin de; *(→ stardom)* avoir soif de; *(→ luxury, wealth)* avoir soif *ou* être avide de; *(in medical, psychological context)* éprouver un besoin impérieux de

craveable ['kreɪvəbəl] *adj Am Fam (desirable)* appétissant□

craven ['kreɪvən] *adj Literary (person, attitude)* lâche, veule; **a craven coward** un (une) lâche

cravenly ['kreɪvənlɪ] *adv Literary* avec lâcheté, lâchement

cravenness ['kreɪvənnɪs] *n Literary* lâcheté *f*

craving ['kreɪvɪŋ] *n (longing)* envie *f* impérieuse *ou* irrésistible; *(physiological need)* besoin *m* impérieux; **pregnant women often get cravings** les femmes enceintes éprouvent souvent des envies irrésistibles; **to have a craving for sth** *(chocolate, sweets, cigarette)* avoir terriblement envie de qch; *(of alcoholic, drug addict)* avoir un besoin impérieux de qch

craw [krɔː] *n (of bird)* jabot *m*; *(of animal)* estomac *m*; *Fam* **it sticks in my craw** cela me reste en travers de la gorge, j'ai du mal à l'avaler

crawfish ['krɔːfɪʃ] (*pl* **inv** *or* **crawfishes**) *n Ich* écrevisse *f*

crawl [krɔːl] 1 *n* (a) *(of person)* **it involved a laborious crawl through the undergrowth** il a fallu ramper tant bien que mal à travers le sous-bois

(b) *(of vehicle)* ralenti *m*; **to move at a crawl** avancer au ralenti *ou* au pas; **the traffic/train has slowed to a crawl** les voitures avancent/le train avance maintenant au pas *ou* au ralenti; **I had to slow to a crawl** *(in car)* j'ai dû ralentir jusqu'à rouler au pas

(c) *(swimming stroke)* crawl *m*; **to do the crawl** nager le crawl

2 *vi* (a) *(move on all fours → person)* ramper; *(→ baby)* marcher à quatre pattes; **she tried to crawl away from danger** elle a essayé de s'éloigner du danger en rampant *ou* en se traînant sur les genoux; **he crawled out of/into bed** il se traîna hors du/au lit; **to crawl on one's hands and knees** marcher *ou* se traîner à quatre pattes; **she crawled under the desk** elle s'est mise à quatre pattes sous le bureau; **what are you crawling about on the floor for?** qu'est-ce que tu fais à quatre pattes?

(b) *(move slowly → traffic, train)* avancer au ralenti *ou* au pas; *(→ insect, snake)* ramper; **the train crawled out of the station** le train est sorti de la gare au ralenti *ou* au pas; **there's a caterpillar crawling up your arm** il y a une chenille qui te grimpe sur le bras

(c) *(be infested)* **to be crawling with** être infesté de, grouiller de; **the kitchen was crawling with ants** la cuisine grouillait *ou* était infestée de fourmis; *Fam Fig* **the streets were crawling with police/tourists** les rues grouillaient de policiers/touristes

(d) *(come out in goose pimples)* **to make sb's flesh crawl** donner la chair de poule à qn; **just the thought of it makes my skin crawl** j'ai la chair de poule rien que d'y penser

(e) *Fam (grovel)* **I'll crawl if I have to** je me mettrai à genoux s'il le faut; **to crawl to sb** ramper *ou* s'aplatir devant qn, lécher les bottes de qn; **he got promoted by crawling to the boss** il a été promu à force de ramper *ou* de s'aplatir devant le patron; **he'll come crawling back** il reviendra te supplier à genoux

(f) *(in swimming)* nager le crawl

3 *vt Am Fam* **to crawl the bars** faire la tournée des bars

►► *Am Constr* ***crawl space*** vide *m* sanitaire

crawler ['krɔːlə(r)] 1 *n* (a) *Fam Pej (groveller)* lèche-bottes *mf inv* (b) *Comput (on Internet)* araignée *f*

2 **crawlers** *npl (for baby)* grenouillère *f*

►► *Br Aut* ***crawler lane*** file *f* *ou* voie *f* pour véhicules lents

crawling ['krɔːlɪŋ] 1 *adj* (a) *Fam Pej (grovelling)* rampant, de lèche-bottes

(b) *(on all fours)* **she's reached the crawling stage** *(baby)* elle commence à marcher à quatre pattes; *Fig* **compared with the Japanese, we're still at the crawling stage** comparés aux Japonais, nous en sommes encore aux balbutiements

(c) *(infested)* grouillant (**with** de); **the kitchen was absolutely crawling** la cuisine était d'une saleté repoussante

2 *n Fam Pej (grovelling)* **if there's one thing I hate, it's crawling to the teacher** s'il y a bien quelque chose que je déteste, c'est qu'on lèche les bottes du prof; **that's just crawling** c'est du lèche-botte

►► *St Exch* ***crawling peg*** parité *f* rampante

crawlway ['krɔːlweɪ] *n* passage *m* souterrain, galerie *f* d'accès *(que l'on ne peut suivre qu'en rampant)*

crayfish ['kreɪfɪʃ] (*pl* **inv** *or* **crayfishes**) *n Ich* écrevisse *f*

crayon ['kreɪɒn] 1 *n (coloured pencil)* crayon *m* de couleur; *(pastel)* pastel *m*; *(made of wax)* pastel *m*; **eye/lip crayon** crayon *m* pour les yeux/à lèvres

2 *vt (draw)* dessiner avec des crayons de couleurs; *(colour)* colorier *(avec des crayons)*

craze [kreɪz] 1 *n* engouement *m*, folie *f*; **it's the latest craze** c'est la dernière folie *ou* lubie; **the latest dance/music craze** la nouvelle danse/musique à la mode; **it's becoming a craze** ça devient une vraie folie; **a craze for sth** un engouement pour qch; **this craze for video games** cet engouement pour les jeux vidéo; **the latest craze is wearing baggy jeans** la dernière mode, c'est de porter des jeans larges; **to have a craze for sth** être fou de

2 *vt* (a) *Literary (send mad)* rendre fou (folle)

(**b**) *(damage → windscreen, glass)* étoiler; *Cer (→ glazed, varnished surface)* craqueler

3 *vi (windscreen, glass)* s'étoiler; *Cer (glazed, varnished surface)* se craqueler

crazed [kreɪzd] *adj* (**a**) *(mad → look, expression)* fou (folle); **crazed with fear/grief** fou (folle) de peur/douleur (**b**) *Cer (glazed, varnished surface)* craquelé

-crazed [kreɪzd] *suff* rendu fou (folle) par; **drug-crazed** rendu fou (folle) par la drogue; **power-crazed dictators** des dictateurs fous de pouvoir; **he was half-crazed with fear** il était à moitié fou de peur

crazily ['kreɪzɪlɪ] *adv (behave)* comme un fou (folle); **crazily, she walked home on her own** cette inconsciente est rentrée à pied toute seule

craziness ['kreɪzɪnɪs] *n* folie *f*; **it's sheer craziness** c'est de la folie

crazy ['kreɪzɪ] (*compar* **crazier,** *superl* **craziest**) **1** *adj* (**a**) *(insane → person, dream)* fou (folle); **to have crazy eyes** avoir des yeux de fou; **that's a crazy idea!, that's crazy!** c'est de la folie!; **this is crazy** c'est fou; **he was crazy to do it** il a été fou de le faire; **that's the craziest thing I've ever heard** c'est la chose la plus insensée que j'aie jamais entendue; **to drive** *or* **to send sb crazy** rendre qn fou; **it's enough to drive you crazy** c'est à vous rendre fou; **he went crazy** *(insane)* il est devenu fou; *(angry)* il est devenu fou (de colère *ou* de rage); *Fam* **the fans went crazy** les fans ne se sont plus sentis; **to be/to go crazy with fear/grief** être/devenir fou de peur/douleur; **power crazy** avide de pouvoir; **you must be crazy!** mais tu es fou!; **like crazy** *(work, drive, run, spend money)* comme un fou; *Hum* **a crazy mixed-up kid** un jeune qui ne sait pas où il en est

(**b**) *Fam (very fond)* **to be crazy about sb/sth** être fou (folle) *ou* dingue de qn/qch; **I'm not crazy about the idea** l'idée ne m'emballe pas vraiment; **he's football crazy** c'est un fana *ou* un cinglé de foot; **to go crazy over sth** flasher sur qch

(**c**) *(strange, fantastic)* bizarre, fou (folle)

(**d**) *Am (very good)* formidable, génial

2 *n esp Am (person)* original(e) *m,f*

►► *Am* ***crazy bone*** petit juif *m*; ***crazy golf*** mini-golf *m*; *Hist* ***Crazy Horse*** Crazy Horse; *Br* ***crazy paving*** = dallage irrégulier en pierres plates; *Am* ***crazy quilt*** couette *f* en patchwork

CRC [ˌsiːɑːˈsiː] *n* (**a**) *Typ (abbr* **camera-ready copy**) copie *f* prête pour la reproduction (**b**) *Am (abbr* **Civil Rights Commission**) = organisme gouvernemental qui veille au respect des droits civiques

CRE [ˌsiːɑːˈriː] *n (abbr* **Commission for Racial Equality**) = commission contre la discrimination raciale

creak [kriːk] **1** *vi (chair, floorboard, person's joints)* craquer; *(door hinge)* grincer; *(shoes)* crisser; *Fig (plot etc)* être boiteux; **the chair creaked under his weight** la chaise a craqué sous son poids; *Fig* **to creak with age** donner des signes de vieillesse; *Fig* **the legal system is creaking under the weight of untried cases** le système juridique craque sous le poids des affaires en suspens

2 *n (of chair, floorboard, person's joints)* craquement *m*; *(of door hinge)* grincement *m*; *(of shoes)* crissement *m*; **to give a creak** *(of chair, floorboard, person's joints)* craquer; *(of door hinge)* grincer; *(of shoes)* crisser

creakily ['kriːkɪlɪ] *adv* en grinçant

creaking ['kriːkɪŋ] **1** *adj (chair, floorboard, person's joints)* qui craque; *(door hinge)* grinçant; *(shoes)* qui crisse

2 *n (of chair, floorboard, person's joints)* craquement *m*; *(of door hinge)* grincement *m*; *(of shoes)* crissement *m*

creaky ['kriːkɪ] (*compar* **creakier,** *superl* **creakiest**) *adj (chair, floorboard, person's joints)* qui craque; *(door hinge)* grinçant; *(shoes)* qui crisse; *Fig (dialogue, plot etc)* boiteux; **a creaky noise** un craquement, un grincement, un crissement

cream [kriːm] **1** *n* (**a**) *(of milk)* crème *f*; **do you like cream in your coffee?** vous prenez de la crème dans votre café?; **strawberries and cream** des fraises *fpl* à la crème; **cream of tomato/asparagus soup** velouté *m* de tomates/d'asperges

(**b**) *(filling for biscuits, chocolates)* fondant *m*; *(individual chocolate)* chocolat *m* fourré; **vanilla cream** *(biscuit)* biscuit *m* fourré à la vanille; *(dessert)* crème *f* à la vanille; *(individual chocolate)* chocolat *m* fourré à la crème

(**c**) *(mixture)* mélange *m* crémeux

(**d**) *Fig (best, pick)* crème *f*; **the cream of society** la crème *ou* le gratin de la société; **they were the cream of their year at university** ils formaient l'élite de leur promotion à l'université; **the cream of the crop** le dessus du panier

(**e**) *(for face, shoes etc)* crème *f*

(**f**) *(colour)* crème *m*

2 *comp (cake)* à la crème; *(jug)* à crème

3 *adj (colour)* crème *(inv)*

4 *vt* (**a**) *(skim → milk)* écrémer

(**b**) *Culin (beat)* écraser, travailler; **cream the butter and sugar** travailler le beurre et le sucre en crème

(**c**) *(hands, face)* mettre de la crème sur

(**d**) *(add cream to → coffee)* mettre de la crème dans

(**e**) *Fam (defeat)* battre à plate couture, mettre la pâtée à; *Am (beat up)* casser la figure à; **we got creamed 4–0** on s'est fait écraser 4–0

(**f**) *Am* **to cream the market** écrémer le marché

(**g**) *Vulg* **to cream one's jeans** prendre son pied

5 *vi* (**a**) *Vulg (man → ejaculate)* décharger, balancer la sauce; *(woman → be aroused)* mouiller

(**b**) *(milk)* crémer

►► ***cream bun*** = petit pain au lait servi avec de la crème chantilly; ***cream cheese*** ≃ fromage *m* frais; *Br* ***cream cracker*** biscuit *m* sec; ***cream eyeshadow*** ombre *f* à paupières en crème; ***cream puff*** chou *m* à la crème; ***cream sherry*** sherry *m ou* xérès *m* doux; ***cream slice*** = sorte de mille-feuille; ***cream soda*** = boisson gazeuse aromatisée à la vanille; ***cream soup*** velouté *m*; *Culin* ***cream of tartar*** crème *f* de tartre; *Br* ***cream tea*** = goûter composé de thé et de scones servis avec de la confiture et de la crème; *Am Culin* ***cream of wheat*** farine *f* de blé *(pour bouillies)*

►**cream off** *vt sep (profits)* accaparer; **to cream off the best students** sélectionner les meilleurs étudiants; **they have creamed off the elite** ils se sont accaparé l'élite

cream-coloured *adj* crème *(inv)*

creamed [kriːmd] *adj Culin (chicken etc)* à la crème

►► *Culin* ***creamed coconut*** lait *m* de coco solidifié; ***creamed potatoes*** purée *f* de pommes de terre

creamer ['kriːmə(r)] *n* (**a**) *(machine)* écrémeuse *f* (**b**) *(for coffee)* succédané *m* de crème (**c**) *Am (jug)* pot *m* à crème

creamery ['kriːmərɪ] *n* (**a**) *(dairy)* laiterie *f* (**b**) *(shop)* crémerie *f*

creaminess ['kriːmɪnɪs] *n* (**a**) *(of sauce, soup)* abondance *f* en crème; *(of texture)* consistance *f* crémeuse (**b**) *(of complexion, skin, voice)* velouté *m*

creamy ['kriːmɪ] (*compar* **creamier,** *superl* **creamiest**) *adj* (**a**) *(containing cream → coffee, sauce)* à la crème; *(→ milk)* qui contient de la crème; **it's too creamy** il y a trop de crème (**b**) *(smooth → drink, sauce etc)* crémeux; *(→ complexion, voice)* velouté (**c**) *(colour)* **creamy white** blanc *m* cassé

crease [kriːs] **1** *n* (**a**) *(in material, paper → made on purpose)* pli *m*; *(→ accidental)* faux pli *m*; *(in skin, on face)* pli *m*; **to put a crease in a pair of trousers** faire le pli d'un pantalon; **in order to get rid of the creases** *(in shirt, blouse etc)* pour le/la défroisser

(**b**) *(in cricket)* limite *f* du batteur

2 *vt* (**a**) *(on purpose)* faire les plis de; *(accidentally)* froisser, chiffonner; **this shirt is all creased** cette chemise est toute froissée; **to crease one's brow** froncer les sourcils

(**b**) *(amuse)* **this one'll crease you** celle-là va te faire mourir de rire

(**c**) *(of bullet → scalp etc)* érafler

3 *vi (clothes)* se froisser, se chiffonner; **his face creased with laughter** son visage s'est plissé de rire

►**crease up** *Fam* **1** *vi* se tordre de rire

2 *vt sep* faire mourir *ou* se tordre de rire; **you just have to look at him and he creases you up** il suffit de le regarder pour se tordre de rire

creased [kriːst] *adj* (**a**) *(fabric)* froissé (**b**) *(face)* plissé

crease-resistant *adj* infroissable

create [kriːˈeɪt] **1** *vt* (**a**) *(employment, problem, difficulties, the world)* créer; *(fuss, noise, impression, draught)* faire; **to create a stir** *or* **a sensation** faire sensation; **to create a scene** *(fuss)* faire une scène; *Law* **to create a disturbance** porter atteinte à l'ordre public

(**b**) *(appoint)* **he was created (a) baron** il a été fait baron

2 *vi* (**a**) *(be creative)* créer; **the instinct to create is strong in all of us** il y a un puissant instinct de création en chacun d'entre nous

(**b**) *Br Fam (cause a fuss)* faire des histoires

creatin [krɪətɪn], **creatine** [krɪətaɪn] *n Biol & Chem* créatine *f*

creatinine [kriːˈætɪniːn] *n Biol & Chem* créatinine *f*

creation [krɪˈeɪʃən] *n* (**a**) *(process of creating)* création *f*; *Bible* **the Creation** la Création

(**b**) *(something created)* création *f*; **the latest creations** *(fashions)* les dernières créations

(**c**) *(universe)* création *f*; **the most beautiful woman in all creation** *or* **the whole of creation** la plus belle femme de la terre; *Fam* **where in creation did you get that hat!** où diable as-tu trouvé ce chapeau!

►► *Rel* ***creation science*** créationnisme *m*

creationism [krɪˈeɪʃənɪzəm] *n Rel & Biol* créationisme *m*

creationist [krɪˈeɪʃənɪst] *n Rel & Biol* créationiste *mf*

creative [krɪˈeɪtɪv] **1** *n (department, work)* création *f*; *(person)* créatif(ive) *m,f*; **we prefer creative to be handled out of house** nous préférons que tout ce qui est création artistique soit réalisé à l'extérieur

2 *adj (person, mind, skill)* créatif; **to encourage sb to be creative** encourager la créativité chez qn; **we need some creative thinking** nous avons besoin d'idées originales

►► *Euph* ***creative accounting*** *(manipulation of accounts)* comptabilité *f* fantaisiste; ***creative brief*** *(in advertising)* plan *m* de travail créatif, PTC *m*; ***creative department*** service *m* de création; ***creative director*** directeur(trice) *m,f* de la création; ***the creative instinct*** l'instinct *m* de création; ***creative team*** équipe *f* de création; ***creative writing*** techniques *fpl* de l'écriture; **he's good at creative writing** il est doué pour l'écriture; ***creative writing class*** atelier *m* d'écriture

creatively [krɪˈeɪtɪvlɪ] *adv* de manière créative; **you're not thinking very creatively about your future** tu n'as pas d'idées très originales pour ton avenir

creativeness [krɪˈeɪtɪvnɪs], **creativity** [ˌkrɪeɪˈtɪvətɪ] *n* créativité *f*

creator [krɪˈeɪtə(r)] *n* créateur(trice) *m,f*; *Rel* **the Creator** le Créateur

creature ['kriːtʃə(r)] *n* (**a**) *(living being)* créature *f*, être *m* (vivant); **we are all God's creatures** nous sommes tous les créatures de Dieu; **creatures from outer space** des créatures *fpl* de l'espace

(**b**) *(person)* créature *f*; **poor creature!** le/la pauvre!; **he's a creature of habit** il est esclave de ses habitudes; **she's a creature of impulse** elle est très impulsive de nature

(**c**) *(animal)* bête *f*; **dumb creatures** les bêtes *fpl*

(**d**) *Literary Pej (dependent person)* créature *f*; **man is the creature of circumstances** l'homme dépend des circonstances

►► ***creature comforts*** confort *m* matériel; **I like my creature comforts** j'aime *ou* je suis attaché à mon (petit) confort

crèche [kreʃ] *n Br (nursery)* crèche *f*; *(in shopping centre, leisure complex)* garderie *f*

►► ***crèche facilities*** garderie *f*

cred [kred] *n Br Fam (credibility)* **to have (street) cred** être branché *ou* dans le coup; **he wants to get some (street) cred** il veut faire branché *ou* dans le coup

credal ['kriːdəl] *adj Rel* provenant d'une croyance religieuse

credence ['kri:dəns] *n* (**a**) *(faith, belief)* croyance *f*, foi *f*; **to give** *or* **to attach credence to sth** ajouter foi à qch; **to give** *or* **to lend credence to sth** rendre qch crédible (**b**) *Rel* crédence *f* *(meuble)*

credentials [krɪ'denʃəlz] *npl* (**a**) *(references, proof of ability)* références *fpl*; **what are your credentials?** quelles sont vos références?; *Fig* **a film director with excellent credentials** un metteur en scène aux excellents antécédents (**b**) *(identity papers)* papiers *mpl* d'identité; **to ask to see sb's credentials** demander ses papiers (d'identité) à qn, demander une pièce d'identité à qn (**c**) *(of diplomat)* lettres *fpl* de créance

credenza [krɪ'denzə] *n Rel* crédence *f (meuble)*

credibility [,kredə'bɪlətɪ] *n* (**a**) *(trustworthiness)* crédibilité *f*; **the party has lost credibility with the electorate** le parti a perdu de sa crédibilité auprès de l'électorat; **there are doubts about its credibility as a deterrent** on doute de son efficacité en tant que moyen de dissuasion; **he has a credibility problem** il manque de crédibilité

(**b**) *(belief)* **it's beyond credibility** c'est invraisemblable, c'est difficile à croire

▸▸ ***credibility gap*** manque *m* de crédibilité; **the party has a major credibility gap** le parti souffre d'un énorme manque de crédibilité, le parti manque énormément de crédibilité; **to narrow the credibility gap** regagner de sa crédibilité; ***credibility rating*** crédibilité *f*

credible ['kredəbəl] *adj (person)* crédible; *(evidence, statement)* crédible, plausible; **I don't find his reassurances very credible** j'ai du mal à croire ce qu'il dit pour me rassurer

credibly ['kredəblɪ] *adv (argue)* de manière crédible

CREDIT ['kredɪt]

crédit	▸ **1 (a)**
mérite	▸ **1 (b)**
croyance	▸ **1 (c)**
unité de valeur	▸ **1 (d)**
créditer	▸ **3 (a)**
supposer	▸ **3 (b)**
croire	▸ **3 (c)**
générique	▸ **4**

1 *n* (**a**) *Fin* crédit *m*; *(in an account)* avoir *m*; **to be in credit** *(person)* avoir de l'argent sur son compte; *(account)* être créditeur; **he has £50 to his credit** il a 50 livres sur son compte, il a un avoir de 50 livres; **to get back into credit** *(person)* rembourser un découvert; *(account)* redevenir créditeur; **to enter** *or* **to place a sum to sb's credit** créditer le compte de qn d'une somme, porter une somme à l'actif de qn; **debit and credit** débit *m* et crédit *m*; **to give sb credit, to give credit to sb** *(of bank)* accorder un découvert à qn; *(of shop, pub)* faire crédit à qn; **to run a credit check on sb** *(to ensure enough money in account)* vérifier la solvabilité de qn, vérifier que le compte de qn est approvisionné; *(to ensure no record of bad debts)* vérifier le passé bancaire de qn; **we do not give credit** *(sign)* la maison ne fait pas crédit; **to sell/to buy/to live on credit** vendre/acheter/vivre à crédit; **her credit is good** elle a une bonne réputation de solvabilité; *Fig (she is trustworthy)* elle est digne de confiance; *Fig* **isn't my credit good any more?** on ne me fait plus confiance?

(**b**) *(merit, honour)* mérite *m*; **all the credit should go to the team** tout le mérite doit revenir à l'équipe; **to take the credit for sth/doing sth** s'attribuer le mérite de qch/d'avoir fait qch; **I can't take all the credit for it** tout le mérite ne me revient pas; **to give sb the credit for sth/doing sth** attribuer à qn le mérite de qch/d'avoir fait qch; **management got all the credit** tout le mérite est revenu à la direction; **give her credit for what she has achieved** reconnais ce qu'elle a accompli; **with credit** *(perform)* honorablement; **nobody emerged with any credit except him** c'est le seul qui s'en soit sorti à son honneur; **it must be said to his credit that...** il faut dire en sa faveur que...; **to her credit she did finish the exam** il faut lui accorder qu'elle a fini l'examen; **she has five novels to her credit** elle a cinq romans à son actif; **to be a credit to one's family/school, to do one's family/school credit** faire honneur à sa famille/son école, être l'honneur de sa famille/son école; **it does her (great) credit** c'est tout à son honneur; **it does you credit that you gave the money back** c'est tout à votre honneur d'avoir rendu l'argent; **give me SOME credit!** je ne suis quand même pas si bête!; **credit where credit is due** il faut reconnaître ce qui est

(**c**) *(credence)* croyance *f*; **to give credit to sb/sth** ajouter foi à qn/qch; **to lend credit to sth** accréditer qch, rendre qch plausible; **to lose credit** *(partially)* perdre de son crédit; *(totally)* perdre son crédit; **the theory is gaining credit** cette théorie est de plus en plus acceptée; **he's cleverer than I gave him credit for** il est plus intelligent que je le pensais *ou* supposais; **I gave you credit for more sense** je vous supposais plus de bon sens; **I gave him credit for more sense than I perhaps should have done** j'ai peut-être surestimé son bon sens

(**d**) *Univ* unité *f* de valeur, UV *f*; **how many credits do you need?** combien d'UV faut-il que tu aies?

2 *comp (boom)* du crédit; *(purchase, sale, transaction)* à crédit; *(balance)* créditeur

3 *vt* (**a**) *Fin (account)* créditer; **to credit an account with £200, to credit £200 to an account** créditer un compte de 200 livres

(**b**) *(accord)* **to credit sb with intelligence/tact/sense** supposer de l'intelligence/du tact/du bon sens à qn; **I credited her with more sense** je lui supposais plus de bon sens; **credit me with a bit more intelligence!** tu serais gentil de ne pas sous-estimer mon intelligence!; **she is credited with being the first woman to attend medical school** elle est considérée comme la première femme à avoir fait des études de médecine; **he is credited with the discovery of DNA** on lui attribue la découverte de l'ADN

(**c**) *(believe)* croire; **would you credit it!** tu te rends compte!; **you wouldn't credit some of the things he's done** tu n'en reviendrais pas si tu savais les choses qu'il a faites; **I could hardly credit it** j'avais du mal à le croire

4 credits *npl Cin & TV* générique *m*

▸▸ ***credit account*** *Banking* compte *m* créditeur; *Br Com (with shop)* compte *m* client; ***credit advice*** avis *m* de crédit; ***credit agency*** institution *f* de crédit; ***credit agreement*** accord *m ou* convention *f* de crédit; ***credit bank*** banque *f* de crédit; ***credit broker*** courtier(ère) *m,f* en crédits *ou* en prêts; *Am* ***credit bureau*** institution *f* de crédit; ***credit card*** carte *f* de crédit; **to pay by credit card** payer avec une *ou* régler par carte de crédit; ***credit card fraud*** usage *m* frauduleux de cartes de crédit; ***credit card number*** numéro *m* de carte de crédit; ***credit card reader*** lecteur *m* de cartes; ***credit card transactions*** transactions *fpl* effectuées par carte de crédit; ***credit ceiling*** plafond *m* de crédit; *Acct* ***credit column*** colonne *f* créditrice; ***credit control*** *(government restrictions)* resserrement *m ou* encadrement *m* du crédit; *(monitoring)* surveillance *m* des crédits; ***credit controller*** contrôleur(euse) *m,f* du crédit; ***credit enquiry*** renseignements *mpl* de crédit, enquête *f* de solvabilité; ***credit entry*** *Banking* article *m* porté au crédit d'un compte; *Acct* écriture *f* au crédit; ***credit facilities*** facilités *fpl* de crédit; ***credit freeze*** blocage *m* du crédit; ***credit history*** profil *m* crédit; **to obtain information on sb's credit history** établir des renseignements de solvabilité sur qn; ***credit institution*** établissement *m* de crédit; ***credit insurance*** assurance-crédit *f*; *Acct* ***credit item*** poste *m* créditeur; ***credit limit*** limite *f ou* plafond *m* de crédit; ***credit line*** *Br (loan)* autorisation *f* de crédit; *Am (limit)* limite *f ou* plafond *m* de crédit; ***credit management*** direction *f* des crédits; ***credit manager*** directeur(trice) *m,f* du crédit; ***credit margin*** marge *f* de crédit; ***credit memo*** bulletin *m* de versement; *Br* ***credit note*** *(in business)* facture *f ou* note *f* d'avoir; *(in shop)* avoir *m*; ***credit period*** délai *m* de crédit; ***credit rating*** *(of person, company)* degré *m* de solvabilité; *(awarded by credit reference agency)* notation *f*; ***credit rating agency*** agence *f* de notation; ***credit risk*** risque *m* de crédit; **to be a good/bad credit risk** représenter un risque peu important/important; ***credit scoring*** = méthode d'évaluation de la solvabilité, crédit-scoring *m*; *Acct* ***credit side*** crédit *m*, avoir *m*; *Fig* **on the credit side, the proposed changes will cut costs** les changements projetés auront l'avantage de réduire les coûts; *Fig* **on the credit side, he's a good cook** il faut lui accorder qu'il cuisine bien; ***credit squeeze*** restriction *f ou* encadrement *m* du crédit; **there's a credit squeeze** le crédit est restreint *ou* encadré; ***credit terms*** modalités *fpl* de crédit; *Banking* ***credit transfer*** virement *m*, transfert *m* (de compte à compte); *Am* ***credit union*** société *f ou* caisse *f* de crédit; ***credit voucher*** chèque *m* de caisse

creditable ['kredɪtəbəl] *adj* honorable, estimable

creditably ['kredɪtəblɪ] *adv* honorablement

creditor ['kredɪtə(r)] *n Fin* créancier(ère) *m,f*

▸▸ ***creditor countries*** nations *fpl* créancières; *Acct* ***creditor's turnover*** rotation *f* des fournisseurs

creditworthiness ['kredɪt,wɜ:ðɪnɪs] *n Com & Fin* solvabilité *f*

creditworthy ['kredɪt,wɜ:ðɪ] *adj Com & Fin* solvable

credo ['kreɪdəʊ] (*pl* **credos**) *n* credo *m inv*

credulity [krɪ'dju:lətɪ] *n* crédulité *f*

credulous ['kredjʊləs] *adj* crédule, naïf

credulously ['kredjʊləslɪ] *adv* naïvement

credulousness ['kredjʊləsnɪs] *n* crédulité *f*

Cree [kri:] *n* (**a**) **the Cree** *(Native American tribe)* les Cree *mpl*, *Can* les Cri *mpl* (**b**) *(member of tribe)* Cree *mf*, *Can* Cri *mf* (**c**) *(language)* cree *m*, *Can* cri *m*

creed [kri:d] *n (religious)* credo *m*, croyance *f*; *(political)* credo *m*; **people of every colour and creed** des gens de toutes races et de toutes croyances; *Rel* **the (Apostles') Creed** le Credo

Creek [kri:k] *n* (**a**) **the Creek** *(Native American tribe)* les Creeks *mpl* (**b**) *(member of tribe)* Creek *mf*

creek [kri:k] *n Br (of sea)* crique *f*, anse *f*; *Am, Austr & NZ (stream)* ruisseau *m*; *(river)* rivière *f*; *Fam* **to be up the creek** être dans de beaux draps *ou* dans le pétrin; *very Fam* **to be up shit creek (without a paddle)** être dans la merde (jusqu'au cou)

creel [kri:l] *n (for fish)* panier *m* à poisson; *(for catching lobsters)* casier *m*

CREEP [kri:p] (*pt & pp* **crept** [krept]) **1** *n Fam (unpleasant person)* sale type *m*; *Br (obsequious person)* lèche-bottes *mf inv*; **I can't stand that creep she's married to** je ne peux pas sentir ce sale type avec qui elle est mariée

2 *vi* (**a**) *(person, animal)* se glisser; **to creep into a room** entrer sans bruit *ou* se glisser dans une pièce; **I crept upstairs** je suis monté sans bruit; **to creep into bed** se glisser dans le lit; **I was creeping about so as not to waken you** je ne faisais pas de bruit pour ne pas te réveiller; **I can hear somebody creeping about downstairs** j'entends quelqu'un bouger en bas; **the dog crept under the chair** le chien s'est tapi sous la chaise; **the shadows crept across the lawn** l'ombre a peu à peu envahi la pelouse; **the hours crept slowly by** les heures se sont écoulées lentement; *Fig* **fear began to creep into his heart** *or* **over him** la peur a commencé à le gagner *ou* à s'insinuer en lui; *Fig* **a moralizing tone has crept into her writing** un ton moralisateur s'est insidieusement glissé dans ses écrits; **a feeling of uneasiness crept over me** un sentiment de gêne commençait à me gagner

(**b**) *(plant → along the ground)* ramper; *(→ upwards)* grimper

(**c**) *(be obsequious)* **she's always creeping to the teacher** elle est toujours en train de ramper devant le professeur

(**d**) *(idiom)* **to make sb's flesh creep** donner la chair de poule à qn, faire froid dans le dos à qn

3 creeps *npl Fam* **he gives me the creeps** *(is frightening)* il me fait froid dans le dos[❑], il me donne la chair de poule[❑]; *(is repulsive)* il me dégoûte[❑] *ou* répugne[❑]

▸**creep along** *vi (stealthily)* s'avancer

furtivement, marcher à pas de loup; *(move slowly, in car etc)* se traîner

▸**creep away** *vi* s'éloigner à pas de loup

▸**creep in** *vi (person)* entrer sans bruit; *Fig (mistakes)* se glisser; *(doubts, fears)* s'insinuer; **the use of the word as a verb is beginning to creep in** l'usage de ce mot en tant que verbe commence à se répandre *ou* gagner du terrain

▸**creep out** *vi* sortir sans bruit

▸**creep up** *vi* (**a**) *(approach)* s'approcher sans bruit; **old age is creeping up** la vieillesse s'approche doucement; **to creep up to sth** s'approcher sans bruit de qch; **to creep up behind sb** s'approcher doucement *ou* discrètement de qn par derrière

(**b**) *(increase → water, prices)* monter lentement; *(→ sales)* monter *ou* progresser petit à petit; **sales have crept up to the million mark** les ventes ont progressé lentement jusqu'à la barre du million

▸**creep up on** *vt insep* (**a**) *(in order to attack, surprise)* s'approcher discrètement de, s'approcher à pas de loup de; **don't creep up on me like that!** ne t'approche pas de moi sans faire de bruit comme ça!; **darkness crept up on us** l'obscurité est arrivée sans que nous nous en rendions compte, nous avons été surpris par l'obscurité; **old age crept up on me** je suis devenu vieux sans m'en rendre compte

(**b**) *(catch up with → in competition, business etc)* rattraper peu à peu; **the deadline is creeping up on us** la date limite se rapproche

creeper ['kri:pə(r)] *n* (**a**) *(climbing plant)* plante *f* grimpante; *(that creeps along the ground)* plante *f* rampante (**b**) *Br Fam (shoe)* chaussure *f* à semelles de crêpe❑ (**c**) *Am* **creepers** *(crampons)* crampons *mpl* à verglas (**d**) *Am* **creepers** *(child's garment)* barboteuse *f*

creeping ['kri:pɪŋ] **1** *adj* (**a**) *(plant → upwards)* grimpant; *(→ along the ground)* rampant (**b**) *(animal, insect)* rampant (**c**) *Fig (inflation)* rampant; *(change)* graduel (**d**) *Fam (obsequious)* servile❑, rampant❑

2 *n Fam (obsequiousness)* servilité❑ *f*

▸▸ *Bot* ***creeping Jenny*** lysimaque *f*; *Bot* ***creeping lady's tresses*** goodyère *f* rampante; *Med* ***creeping paralysis*** paralysie *f* progressive

creepy ['kri:pɪ] *(compar* **creepier**, *superl* **creepiest**) *adj Fam* qui donne la chair de poule❑, qui fait froid dans le dos❑; **he's/it's creepy** il/ça vous donne la chair de poule

creepy-crawly [-'krɔ:lɪ] *(pl* **creepy-crawlies**) *Fam*

1 *n* petite bestiole *f*

2 *adj* **a horrible creepy-crawly feeling** une très désagréable sensation de fourmillement❑

cremate [krɪ'meɪt] *vt* incinérer

cremation [krɪ'meɪʃən] *n* incinération *f*, crémation *f*

cremationist [krɪ'meɪʃənɪst] *n* crématiste *mf*

crematorium [ˌkremə'tɔ:rɪəm] *(pl* **crematoria** [-rɪə] *or* **crematoriums**) *n (establishment)* crématorium *m*; *(furnace)* four *m* crématoire

crematory ['kreməˌtəʊrɪ] *(pl* **crematories**) *n Am (establishment)* crématorium *m*; *(furnace)* four *m* crématoire

crème [krem] *n* **the crème de la crème** le gratin, le dessus du panier

▸▸ *Culin* ***crème caramel*** crème *f* (au) caramel; *Culin* ***crème fraîche*** crème *f* fraîche; ***crème de menthe*** crème *f* de menthe

The crème de la crème

Cette expression hyperbolique et faussement française fut popularisée par l'ouvrage de la romancière écossaise Muriel Spark *The Prime of Miss Jean Brodie* ("Le Bel Âge de Miss Brodie") (1961). Dans ce roman, Miss Brodie est institutrice à Édimbourg et elle utilise cette expression à propos de ses élèves préférées. Aujourd'hui on utilise cette formule pour parler de ce qui se fait de mieux dans un domaine donné. On dira par exemple **the company only recruits the crème de la crème of recent graduates** ("cette entreprise ne recrute que le gratin des diplômés").

crenellated, *Am* **crenelated** ['krenəˌleɪtɪd] *adj Archit* crénelé, à créneaux

crenellation, *Am* **crenelation** [ˌkrenə'leɪʃən] *n (usu pl) Archit* créneau *m*

Creole ['kri:əʊl] **1** *n* (**a**) *(person)* Créole *mf* (**b**) *(language)* créole *m*

2 *adj* créole

creosote ['krɪəsəʊt] **1** *n* créosote *f*

2 *vt* traiter à la créosote

crepe [kreɪp, krep] **1** *n* (**a**) *Tex (fabric)* crêpe *m*; (**b**) *(crape rubber)* crêpe *m* (**c**) *(crepe paper)* papier *m* crépon (**d**) *Culin (pancake)* crêpe *f*

2 *comp (skirt, blouse etc)* de *ou* en crêpe

▸▸ ***crepe bandage*** bande *f* Velpeau®; ***crepe de Chine*** crêpe de Chine; ***crepe paper*** papier *m* crépon; ***crepe rubber*** crêpe *m*; ***crepe soles*** semelles *fpl* de crêpe

crepe-soled *adj* à semelle(s) de crêpe

crept [krept] *pt & pp of* **creep**

crepuscular [krɪ'pʌskjʊlə(r)] *adj* (**a**) *Literary (dim)* crépusculaire (**b**) *(animal)* crépusculaire

Cres. *Br (written abbr* **Crescent**) rue *f*

crescendo [krɪ'ʃendəʊ] *(pl* **crescendos** *or* **crescendoes**) **1** *n Mus & Fig* crescendo *m*; *Mus* **to build up to a crescendo** aller crescendo; *Fig* **to reach a crescendo** atteindre son paroxysme

2 *vi (gen)* augmenter; *Mus* faire un crescendo

3 *adv Mus* crescendo, en augmentant

crescent ['kresənt] **1** *n* (**a**) *(shape)* croissant *m*; *Rel* **the Crescent** *(Islamic emblem)* le Croissant (**b**) *Br (street)* rue *f* (en arc de cercle)

2 *adj (shaped)* en (forme de) croissant

▸▸ ***the Crescent City*** = surnom de La Nouvelle-Orléans; ***crescent moon*** croissant *m* de lune; *Am Culin* ***crescent roll*** croissant *m*; *Am Tech* ***crescent wrench*** clé *f* anglaise *ou* à molette

cresol ['kri:sɒl] *n Chem* crésol *m*

cress [kres] *n* cresson *m*

Cressida ['kresɪdə] *pr n Myth* Cressida

crest [krest] **1** *n* (**a**) *(peak → of hill, wave)* crête *f*; *(→ of ridge)* arête *f*; *(→ of road)* haut *m ou* sommet *m* de côte; *Fig* **she's (riding) on the crest of a wave just now** tout lui réussit *ou* elle a le vent en poupe en ce moment

(**b**) *(on chicken, lizard)* crête *f*; *(of bird)* huppe *f*; *(of peacock)* aigrette *f*

(**c**) *(on helmet)* cimier *m*

(**d**) *Her (coat of arms)* timbre *m*; *(emblem)* armoiries *fpl*; **a family crest** des armoiries *fpl* familiales

(**e**) *Anat (of bone)* crête *f*, arête *f*

2 *vt* (**a**) *(reach the top of)* franchir la crête de (**b**) *Her (provide with emblem)* armorier

3 *vi* monter en crête

Cresta Run ['krestə-] *n Br Sport* **the Cresta Run** le Cresta Run

crested ['krestɪd] *adj* (**a**) *(chicken, lizard)* orné d'une crête; *(bird)* huppé (**b**) *(helmet)* orné d'un cimier; *(plumed)* panaché (**c**) *Her (with emblem)* armorié

▸▸ *Orn* ***crested lark*** cochevis *m*; *Orn* ***crested tit*** mésange *f* huppée

crestfallen ['krestˌfɔ:lən] *adj* découragé, déconfit; **the loser looked crestfallen** le perdant avait l'air abattu *ou* déconfit

cretaceous [krɪ'teɪʃəs] *Geol* **1** *n* **the Cretaceous** le crétacé

2 *adj* crétacé

▸▸ ***the Cretaceous period*** le crétacé

Cretan ['kri:tən] **1** *n* Crétois(e) *m,f*

2 *adj* crétois

Crete [kri:t] *n* Crète *f*; **in Crete** en Crète

cretin ['kretɪn] *n* (**a**) *Med* crétin(e) *m,f* (**b**) *Fam (idiot)* crétin(e)❑ *m,f*, imbécile❑ *mf*

cretinism ['kretɪnɪzəm] *n Med* crétinisme *m*

cretinous ['kretɪnəs] *adj Med & Fig* crétin

cretonne ['kretɒn] *n Tex* cretonne *f*

Creutzfeldt-Jacob disease ['krɔɪtsfelt'jækɒb-] *n Med* maladie *f* de Creutzfeldt-Jacob

crevasse [krɪ'væs] *n Geol* crevasse *f*; *Am (in dam)* crevasse *f*, fissure *f*

crevice ['krevɪs] *n* fissure *f*, fente *f*

crew [kru:] **1** *Br pt of* **crow**

2 *n* (**a**) *(in rowing)* équipe *f*; *(on plane, ship)* équipage *m*; **ambulance/camera crew** équipe *f* d'ambulanciers/de cameramen

(**b**) *Fam (crowd, gang)* bande *f*, équipe❑ *f*; **what a crew!** (quelle) drôle d'équipe!; **they're a good crew to work with** c'est une bonne équipe avec qui travailler

(**c**) *Cin & TV* équipe *f*

3 *vi* **to crew for sb** être l'équipier de qn

4 *vt (ship)* armer d'un équipage; *(plane)* fournir un équipage à; **this yacht can't be crewed by fewer than six** ce yacht exige un équipage de six au moins; *Naut* **crewed charter** location *f* de bateau avec équipage

▸▸ ***crew cut*** coupe *f* de cheveux en brosse; **crew cuts are in fashion again** les cheveux en brosse reviennent à la mode; ***crew member*** membre *mf* d'équipage; ***crew neck*** col *m* ras le *ou* du cou, ras-le-cou *m*

crewel ['kru:əl] *n (yarn)* laine *f* à broder *ou* à tapisserie

▸▸ ***crewel work*** tapisserie *f* sur canevas

crewman ['kru:mən] *(pl* **crewmen** [-mən]) *n* membre *m* de l'équipage

crew-neck, crew-necked *adj* **a crew-neck(ed) sweater** un pull ras le *ou* du cou

crib [krɪb] *(pt & pp* **cribbed**, *cont* **cribbing**) **1** *n* (**a**) *esp Am (cot)* lit *m* d'enfant

(**b**) *(bin)* grenier *m* (à blé); *(stall)* stalle *f*

(**c**) *(manger)* mangeoire *f*, râtelier *m*; *Rel* crèche *f*

(**d**) *Fam (plagiarism)* plagiat❑ *m*; *Br Sch (list of answers)* antisèche *f*

(**e**) *Cards (cribbage)* = jeu de cartes où l'on marque les points à l'aide de fiches que l'on enfonce sur une planche de bois

2 *vt* (**a**) *Fam (plagiarize)* plagier❑, copier❑; *Sch* **he cribbed the answers from his friend** il a copié les réponses sur son ami, il a pompé sur son ami

(**b**) *Tech (line with planks)* boiser

3 *vi* copier; **the author had cribbed from Shaw** l'auteur avait plagié Shaw; *Sch* **don't crib off me!** ne copie pas sur moi!

▸▸ *Am* ***crib death*** mort *f* subite (du nourrisson)

cribbage ['krɪbɪdʒ] *n (UNCOUNT)* = jeu de cartes où l'on marque les points à l'aide de fiches que l'on enfonce sur une planche de bois

crick [krɪk] **1** *n* (**a**) **to have a crick in one's neck** avoir un torticolis; **a crick in one's back** un tour de reins (**b**) *Am Fam (stream)* ruisseau❑ *m*

2 *vt* **to crick one's neck** attraper un torticolis; **to crick one's back** se faire un tour de reins

cricket ['krɪkɪt] **1** *n* (**a**) *Entom* grillon *m* (**b**) *(game)* cricket *m*; **to play cricket** jouer au cricket; *Br Fam* **that's not cricket** ça ne se fait pas❑, ce n'est pas fair-play❑

2 *comp (ball, bat, match)* de cricket

▸▸ ***cricket field, cricket pitch*** terrain *m* de cricket

CRICKET

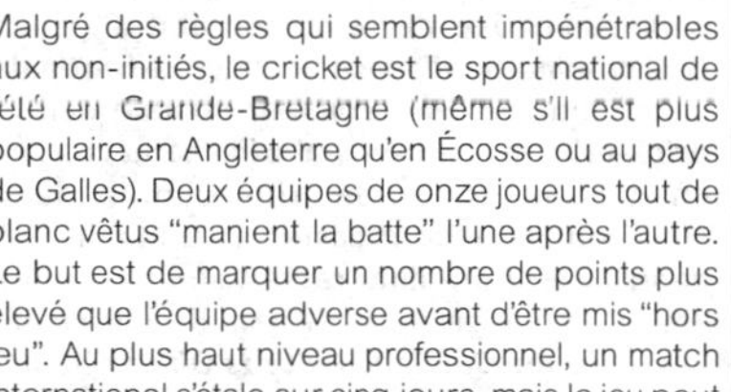

Malgré des règles qui semblent impénétrables aux non-initiés, le cricket est le sport national de l'été en Grande-Bretagne (même s'il est plus populaire en Angleterre qu'en Écosse ou au pays de Galles). Deux équipes de onze joueurs tout de blanc vêtus "manient la batte" l'une après l'autre. Le but est de marquer un nombre de points plus élevé que l'équipe adverse avant d'être mis "hors jeu". Au plus haut niveau professionnel, un match international s'étale sur cinq jours, mais le jeu peut se limiter à une demi-journée lors d'une rencontre amateur entre deux villages.

cricketer ['krɪkɪtə(r)] *n* joueur(euse) *m,f* de cricket

cri de coeur [kridəkɜ:(r)] *(pl* **cris de coeur** [kridəkɜ:(r)]) *n Literary* cri *m* du cœur

cried [kraɪd] *pt & pp of* **cry**

crier ['kraɪə(r)] *n Hist* crieur(euse) *m,f*; *(in court)* huissier *m*

crikey ['kraɪkɪ] *exclam Br Fam Old-fashioned* mince alors!

crime [kraɪm] *n* (**a**) *(act)* crime *m*; *(phenomenon)* criminalité *f*; **crime is on the decline** il y a une baisse de la criminalité; **a life of crime** une vie de criminel; **crime doesn't pay** le crime ne paie pas; **a minor** *or* **petty crime** un délit mineur; **a crime against humanity** un crime contre l'humanité; *Law* **a crime of passion** un crime passionnel; *Fig* **it's a crime that she died so young** c'est vraiment injuste qu'elle soit morte si jeune; *Fig* **it's not a crime to...** ce n'est pas un crime de...

(**b**) *Mil* manquement *m* à la discipline, infraction *f* cri–cri

▸▸ ***crime fiction*** romans *mpl* policiers; ***crime figures*** chiffres *mpl* de la criminalité; ***crime prevention*** lutte *f* contre la criminalité; ***crime prevention officer*** = agent de police chargé d'informer le public sur les moyens de lutter efficacement contre la délinquance; ***crime rate*** taux *m* de (la) criminalité; *Journ* ***crime reporter*** journaliste *mf* qui couvre les affaires criminelles; ***crime scene*** lieu *m* du crime; ***crime series*** série *f* policière; ***crime story*** *(novel)* roman *m* noir; *(detective novel)* roman *m* policier; ***crime wave*** vague *f* de criminalité; ***crime writer*** auteur *m* de romans policiers

'Crimes and Misdemeanors' *Allen* 'Crimes et délits'

'Crime and Punishment' *Dostoyevsky* 'Crime et châtiment'

Crimea [kraɪˈmɪə] *n Hist* **the Crimea** la Crimée; **in the Crimea** en Crimée

Crimean [kraɪˈmɪən] *Hist* **1** *n* Criméen(enne) *m,f*
2 *adj* criméen
▸▸ ***the Crimean War*** la guerre de Crimée

crimebuster [ˈkraɪmˌbʌstə(r)] *n* superflic *m*

criminal [ˈkrɪmɪnəl] **1** *n* criminel(elle) *m,f*
2 *adj* criminel; *Law* **to take criminal proceedings against sb** poursuivre qn au pénal; *Fig* **it would be criminal to cut down these trees** ce serait un crime d'abattre ces arbres; *Fig* **it's criminal the way he treats her** il ne devrait pas avoir le droit de la traiter comme ça
▸▸ *Law* ***criminal assault*** agression *f* criminelle, voie *f* de fait; *Law* ***criminal case*** affaire *f* criminelle; *Law* ***criminal conversation*** adultère *m*; *Law* ***criminal court*** ≃ cour *f* d'assises; *Law* ***criminal damage*** = délit consistant à causer volontairement des dégâts matériels; *Br* ***Criminal Injuries Compensation Board*** = organisme gouvernemental dont le rôle est de dédommager les victimes d'actes criminels; ***criminal investigation*** enquête *f* criminelle; *Br* ***Criminal Investigation Department*** = police judiciaire britannique, ≃ PJ *f*; *Br Law* ***Criminal Justice Bill*** = loi très controversée adoptée en 1995, limitant certains droits civils (droit au silence devant un tribunal, droits des squatters etc); ***criminal law*** droit *m* pénal *ou* criminel; ***criminal lawyer*** avocat(e) *m,f* au criminel, pénaliste *mf*; *Law* ***criminal liability*** responsabilité *f* pénale, majorité *f* pénale; **to be under the age of criminal liability** ne pas avoir atteint la majorité pénale *ou* l'âge de la responsabilité pénale; *Law* ***criminal negligence*** négligence *f* coupable *ou* criminelle; *Law* ***criminal offence*** délit *m*; **drink-driving is a criminal offence** la conduite en état d'ivresse est un crime puni par la loi; *Law* ***criminal record*** casier *m* judiciaire; **she hasn't got a criminal record** son casier judiciaire est vierge, elle n'a pas de casier judiciaire; *Br* ***the Criminal Records Office*** l'identité *f* judiciaire

criminality [ˌkrɪməˈnælətɪ] *n* criminalité *f*

criminalization [ˌkrɪmɪnəlaɪˈzeɪʃən] *n* criminalisation *f*

criminalize, -ise [ˈkrɪmɪnəlaɪz] *vt* criminaliser

criminally [ˈkrɪmɪnəlɪ] *adv* criminellement; **to be criminally insane** être dément; **the criminally insane** les fous dangereux; **he's been criminally negligent** sa négligence est criminelle; *Fig* **it's criminally wasteful** c'est un crime de gaspiller comme ça

criminogenic [ˌkrɪmɪnəʊˈdʒenɪk] *adj* criminogène

criminological [ˌkrɪmɪnəˈlɒdʒɪkəl] *adj* criminologique

criminologist [ˌkrɪmɪˈnɒlədʒɪst] *n* criminologiste *mf*

criminology [ˌkrɪmɪˈnɒlədʒɪ] *n* criminologie *f*

criminy [ˈkrɪmənɪ] *exclam Fam Old-fashioned* mince!

crimp [krɪmp] **1** *vt* **(a)** *(hair)* friser; *(pie crust)* pincer; *(metal)* onduler **(b)** *Fam (pinch together)* pincer❑, sertir❑ **(c)** *Am Fam (hinder)* gêner❑, entraver❑
2 *n* **(a)** *(wave in hair)* cran *m*, ondulation *f*; *(fold in metal)* ondulation *f* **(b)** *Am Fam (obstacle)* obstacle❑ *m*, entrave❑ *f* **(c)** *(in cloth)* pli *m*

crimpers [ˈkrɪmpəz], **crimping irons** [ˈkrɪmpɪŋ-] *npl* fer *m* à friser

Crimplene® [ˈkrɪmpliːn] *n Br* ≃ crêpe *m* acrylique

crimson [ˈkrɪmzən] **1** *adj* cramoisi; **she turned crimson with** *or* **in embarrassment** elle a rougi *ou* est devenue cramoisie de confusion; **the evening sky turned crimson** le ciel nocturne est devenu pourpre *ou* s'est empourpré
2 *n* cramoisi *m*

cringe [krɪndʒ] **1** *n Pej* **the lyrics of these sentimental songs have a high cringe factor** les paroles de ces chansons à l'eau-de-rose sont d'une mièvrerie désolante; *Pej* **the cringe factor usually associated with that type of Hollywood film** le côté insupportablement mélo de ce genre de production hollywoodienne
2 *vi* **(a)** *(shrink back)* avoir un mouvement de recul, reculer; *(cower)* se recroqueviller; **to cringe in terror** reculer de peur; **the dog cringed in the corner** le chien se blottit dans le coin
(b) *Fam (wince)* avoir envie de rentrer sous terre❑; **to cringe with embarrassment** être mort de honte; **it's so sentimental, it makes me cringe** un tel mélo, ça me fait fuir!; **I cringe at the very thought** j'ai envie de rentrer sous terre rien que d'y penser
(c) *(be servile)* s'humilier, ramper, s'aplatir (**before sb** devant qn)

cringe-making *adj Br Fam* embarrassant❑, gênant❑

cringing [ˈkrɪndʒɪŋ] *adj (fearful)* craintif; *(servile)* servile, obséquieux

cringingly [ˈkrɪndʒɪŋlɪ] *adv* **(a)** *(fearfully)* craintivement **(b)** *(obsequiously)* servilement, obséquieusement

crinkle [ˈkrɪŋkəl] **1** *vt* froisser, chiffonner; **to crinkle one's nose** froncer le nez
2 *vi* se froisser, se chiffonner; **his nose crinkled at the smell** l'odeur lui fit froncer le nez
3 *n* **(a)** *(wrinkle)* fronce *f*, pli *m*; *(on face)* ride *f* **(b)** *(noise)* froissement *m*

crinkle-cut *adj (chips, crisps)* dentelé

crinkly [ˈkrɪŋklɪ] *(compar* **crinklier**, *superl* **crinkliest**) *adj (material, paper)* gaufré; *(hair)* crépu, crêpelé; **my fingers have gone all crinkly** la peau de mes doigts est toute fripée

crinoline [ˈkrɪnəliːn] *n* crinoline *f*

cripes [kraɪps] *exclam Br Fam Old-fashioned* sapristi!, mince!

Crippen [ˈkrɪpɪn] *pr n* **(Doctor) Crippen** = médecin américain condamné à mort en Angleterre en 1910 pour avoir assassiné sa femme

cripple [ˈkrɪpəl] **1** *vt* **(a)** *(person)* estropier **(b)** *Fig (damage → industry, country, system)* paralyser; *(→ plane, ship)* désemparer; *(→ machine)* empêcher de fonctionner; *(→ tank)* mettre hors de combat
2 *n* **(a)** *Fam (lame person)* estropié(e) *m,f*; *(invalid)* invalide *mf*; *(maimed person)* mutilé(e) *m,f* **(b)** *Fig* **he's an emotional cripple** il est incapable d'exprimer ses émotions

crippled [ˈkrɪpəld] *adj* **(a)** *(person)* estropié, infirme; **to be crippled with rheumatism** être perclus de rhumatismes **(b)** *Fig (industry, country, system)* paralysé; *(plane, ship)* désemparé; *(machine)* hors d'usage; *(tank)* hors de combat; **the country is crippled with debt** le pays est paralysé par les dettes

crippling [ˈkrɪpəlɪŋ] *adj* **(a)** *(disease)* invalidant **(b)** *Fig (strikes)* paralysant; *(prices, taxes)* écrasant; **the crippling effect of the blockade** l'effet *m* paralysant du blocus

Crisco® [ˈkrɪskəʊ] *n Am Culin* = graisse végétale, ≃ Végétaline® *f*

crisis [ˈkraɪsɪs] *(pl* **crises** [-siːz]) *n* crise *f*; **things have come to a crisis** la situation est à un point critique; **a minor family crisis** un petit problème familial; **the government has a crisis on its hands** le gouvernement se trouve face à une crise; **to settle** *or* **to resolve a crisis** dénouer *ou* résoudre une crise; **the oil crisis** le choc pétrolier; **an emotional crisis** un passage difficile *(nerveusement)*
▸▸ ***crisis centre*** *(for disasters)* cellule *f* de crise; *(for personal help)* centre *m* d'aide; *(for battered women)* association *f* d'aide d'urgence; ***Crisis at Christmas*** = organisation britannique d'aide aux sans-abri pendant la période de Noël; ***crisis of confidence*** crise *f* de confiance; *Am* ***crisis line*** ligne *f* d'assistance téléphonique; ***crisis management*** gestion *f* des crises; ***crisis point*** point *m* critique

crisp [krɪsp] **1** *adj* **(a)** *(crunchy → vegetable, apple, lettuce)* croquant; *(→ cracker, biscuit, pastry)* croquant, croustillant; *(→ bread, bacon)* croustillant; *(→ snow)* craquant; **the snow was crisp underfoot** la neige craquait sous mes/nos/*etc* pas
(b) *(fresh → clothing)* pimpant; *(→ linen)* apprêté; *(→ paper)* craquant, raide; **a crisp five pound note** un billet de cinq livres tout neuf
(c) *(air, weather)* vif, tonifiant
(d) *(concise → style)* précis, clair et net
(e) *(brusque)* tranchant, brusque; *(manner)* brusque; *(tone)* acerbe
2 *n* **(a)** *Br* **(potato) crisp** (pomme *f*) chips *f*, *Can* croustille *f*
(b) *Fam* **to be burnt to a crisp** être carbonisé
3 *vt* faire chauffer pour rendre croustillant
4 *vi* devenir croustillant

crispbread [ˈkrɪspbred] *n Culin* pain *m* suédois

crisper [ˈkrɪspə(r)] *n (in refrigerator)* bac *m* à légumes

crispiness [ˈkrɪspɪnɪs] *n (of vegetable)* croquant *m*; *(of biscuit)* croquant *m*, croustillant *m*; *(of bacon)* croustillant *m*

crisply [ˈkrɪsplɪ] *adv* **(a)** *(succinctly)* avec concision **(b)** *(sharply)* d'un ton acerbe *ou* cassant

crispness [ˈkrɪspnɪs] *n* **(a)** *(of vegetable, apple, lettuce)* croquant *m*; *(of cracker, biscuit, pastry)* croquant *m*, croustillant *m*; *(of bread, bacon)* croustillant *m*; *(of snow)* caractère *m* craquant **(b)** *(of clothing, linen)* fraîcheur *f*; *(of paper)* raideur *f* **(c)** *(of air, weather)* fraîcheur *f* vivifiante **(d)** *(of reasoning)* clarté *f*, rigueur *f* **(e)** *(of style)* précision *f* **(f)** *(brusqueness)* tranchant *m*, brusquerie *f*

crispy [ˈkrɪspɪ] *(compar* **crispier**, *superl* **crispiest**) *adj (vegetable)* croquant; *(biscuit)* croquant, croustillant; *(bacon)* croustillant

crisscross [ˈkrɪsˌkrɒs] **1** *vt* entrecroiser; **footpaths crisscrossed the hillside** des chemins s'entrecroisaient sur le flanc de la colline; **a network of streets criss-crosses the town** un réseau de rues quadrille la ville; **a brow criss-crossed with wrinkles** un front sillonné de rides
2 *vi* s'entrecroiser
3 *adj (lines)* entrecroisé; *(in disorder)* enchevêtré; **in a crisscross pattern** en croisillons
4 *n* entrecroisement *m*; **a crisscross of paths** un réseau de chemins
5 *adv* en réseau

crit [krɪt] *n Fam (criticism)* critique❑ *f*

criterion [kraɪˈtɪərɪən] *(pl* **criteria** [-rɪə]) *n* critère *m*; **what criteria do you apply** *or* **what are your criteria when selecting candidates?** sur quels critères vous fondez-vous *ou* quels sont vos critères lorsque vous sélectionnez des candidats?

criterium [kraɪˈtɪərɪəm] *n Br Cycling* critérium *m*

critic [ˈkrɪtɪk] *n (reviewer)* critique *mf*; *(fault-finder)* critique *mf*, détracteur(trice) *m,f*; **film/art/theatre critic** critique *mf* de cinéma/d'art/de théâtre; **she has her critics** il y en a qui la critiquent; **there are few critics of the policy** peu de gens critiquent la politique

critical [ˈkrɪtɪkəl] *adj* **(a)** *(crucial)* critique, crucial; *(situation)* critique; **at a critical time** à un moment critique *ou* crucial; **he's in a critical condition** *or* **on the critical list** il est dans un état critique; **the next few days will be critical** les prochains jours seront décisifs
(b) *(analytical)* critique; *(disparaging)* critique, négatif; **to be critical of sb/sth** *(person)* se montrer *ou* être critique à l'égard de qn/qch; *(report, article etc)* être critique à l'égard de qn/qch; **he's very critical of others** il critique beaucoup les autres, il est très critique vis-à-vis des autres; **to look at sth with a critical eye** regarder qch d'un œil critique; **don't be so critical** ne soyez pas si négatif
(c) *(analysis, edition)* critique; *(essay, study)*

critique, de critique; *(from the critics)* des critiques; **the play met with critical acclaim** la pièce fut applaudie par la critique

(**d**) *Phys* critique; **the nuclear reactor went critical** le réacteur a atteint le seuil critique

►► *Phys* ***critical angle*** angle *m* critique; *Phys* ***critical mass*** masse *f* critique; *Com & Tech* ***critical path*** chemin *m* critique; *Com & Tech* ***critical path analysis*** analyse *f* du chemin critique; *Com & Tech* ***critical path method*** méthode *f* du chemin critique; *Com & Tech* ***critical path model*** modèle *m* du chemin critique; *Phys* ***critical temperature*** température *f* critique

critically ['krɪtɪkəlɪ] *adj* (**a**) *(analytically)* d'un œil critique, en critique; *(disparagingly)* sévèrement (**b**) *(seriously)* gravement; **she is critically ill** elle est gravement malade, elle est dans un état critique (**c**) *(crucially)* **critically important** d'une importance vitale

criticism ['krɪtɪsɪzəm] *n* (**a**) *(action, act of criticizing)* critique *f*; **to come in for criticism** se faire *ou* se voir critiquer; **to lay oneself open to criticism** s'exposer à la critique; **this isn't meant as a criticism but…** ce n'est pas une critique mais…, ce n'est pas pour critiquer mais…; **the report contained strong criticism of this department** le rapport contenait de graves critiques de ce service

(**b**) *(of film, book, work of art etc)* critique *f*

criticize, -ise ['krɪtɪsaɪz] **1** *vt* (**a**) *(find fault with)* critiquer, réprouver; **to criticize sb for sth** critiquer qn pour qch; **to criticize sb for doing sth** critiquer qn d'avoir fait qch; **they have been criticized for not trying** on leur a reproché de ne pas avoir essayé; **his report has been criticized for being too…** on a reproché à son rapport d'être trop…

(**b**) *(film, book, work of art etc)* critiquer, faire la critique de

2 *vi* critiquer; **stop criticizing** arrête de critiquer *ou* de faire des critiques

critique [krɪ'ti:k] **1** *n* critique *f*

2 *vt* faire une critique de

critter ['krɪtə(r)] *n Am Fam (creature)* créature❑ *f*; *(animal)* bête❑ *f*, bestiole *f*

CRN [ˌsi:ɑ:'ren] *n Com (abbr* **customs registered number**) numéro *m* d'enregistrement douanier

CRO [ˌsi:ɑ:'rəʊ] *n Br Com (abbr* **Companies Registration Office**) = institut britannique où sont enregistrées toutes les informations concernant les entreprises du pays

croak [krəʊk] **1** *vi* (**a**) *(frog)* coasser; *(crow)* croasser (**b**) *(person)* parler d'une voix rauque; *(grumble)* ronchonner (**c**) *Fam (die)* crever

2 *vt (utter)* dire d'une voix rauque *ou* éraillée

3 *n (of frog)* coassement *m*; *(of crow)* croassement *m*; *(of person)* ton *m* rauque

croakily ['krəʊkɪlɪ] *adv* d'une voix rauque *ou* éraillée

croaking ['krəʊkɪŋ] *n (of frog)* coassement *m*; *(of crow)* croassement *m*

croaky ['krəʊkɪ] *adj* enroué

Croat ['krəʊæt] **1** *adj* croate

2 *n* (**a**) *(person)* Croate *mf* (**b**) *(language)* croate *m*

Croatia [krəʊ'eɪʃə] *n* Croatie *f*; **in Croatia** en Croatie

Croatian [krəʊ'eɪʃən] **1** *n* (**a**) *(person)* Croate *mf* (**b**) *(language)* croate *m*

2 *adj* croate

3 *comp (embassy)* de Croatie; *(history)* de la Croatie; *(teacher)* de croate

crochet ['krəʊʃeɪ] **1** *n* **crochet (work)** (travail *m* au) crochet *m*

2 *vt* faire au crochet

3 *vi* faire du crochet

crochet-hook *n* crochet *m*

crocheting ['krəʊʃeɪɪŋ] *n* (travail *m* au) crochet *m*

crock [krɒk] **1** *n* (**a**) *(jar, pot)* cruche *f*, pot *m* de terre; *(broken earthenware)* morceau *m* de faïence, tesson *m*; *Am very Fam* **that's a crock (of shit)!** tout ça, c'est des conneries! (**b**) *Br Fam* **old crock** *(car)* tacot *m*, guimbarde *f*; *(person)* croulant(e) *m,f*

2 crocks *npl Fam* vaisselle❑ *f*

crockery ['krɒkərɪ] *n (pottery)* poterie *f*, faïence *f*; *(plates, cups, bowls etc)* vaisselle *f*

crocodile ['krɒkədaɪl] **1** *n* (**a**) *(reptile)* crocodile *m* (**b**) *Br Sch* cortège *m* en rangs *(par deux)*; **to walk in a crocodile** marcher deux par deux

2 *comp (shoes, handbag)* en crocodile

►► ***crocodile clip*** pince *f* crocodile; ***crocodile skin*** peau *f* de crocodile; ***crocodile tears*** larmes *fpl* de crocodile

crocus ['krəʊkəs] *n* crocus *m*

►► ***crocus corm*** bulbe *m* de crocus

Croesus ['kri:səs] *pr n Myth* Crésus; **as rich as Croesus** riche comme Crésus

croft [krɒft] *n* petite ferme *f*

crofter ['krɒftə(r)] *n (farmer)* petit fermier *m*

crofting ['krɒftɪŋ] *n* (exploitation *f* en) affermage *m*

Crohn's disease ['krəʊnz-] *n Med* maladie *f* de Crohn

Cro-Magnon [ˌkrəʊ'mægnɒn] *n Hist* **Cro-Magnon man** homme *m* de Cro-Magnon

Cromalin® ['krəʊməlɪn] *n Typ* Cromalin® *m*

cromlech ['krɒmlek] *n (circle of stones)* cromlech *m*; *(tomb)* tombeau *m ou* tombe *f* mégalithique

Cromwellian [krɒm'welɪən] *adj* cromwellien

crone [krəʊn] *n Fam* vieille bique *f*

Cronos ['krəʊnɒs] *pr n Myth* Cronos

crony ['krəʊnɪ] *(pl* **cronies**) *n Fam* pote *m*, copain (copine) *m,f*

cronyism ['krəʊnɪɪzəm] *n Pej* copinage *m*

crook [krʊk] **1** *n* (**a**) *Fam (thief)* escroc *m*, filou *m* (**b**) *(bend → in road)* courbe *f*, coude *m*; *(→ in river)* coude *m*, détour *m*; *(→ in arm)* creux *m*; *(→ in leg)* flexion *f*; **in the crook of her arm** dans le creux de son bras (**c**) *(staff → of shepherd)* houlette *f*; *(→ of bishop)* crosse *f*

2 *adj Austr & NZ Fam (ill)* mal fichu; *(not working)* détraqué

3 *vt (finger)* courber, recourber; *(arm)* plier

crooked ['krʊkɪd] **1** *adj* (**a**) *(not straight, bent → stick)* courbé, crochu, *Can* croche; *(→ path)* tortueux; *(→ person)* courbé; **his hat was on crooked** son chapeau était de travers; **a crooked smile** un sourire en coin (**b**) *Fam (dishonest)* malhonnête❑, *Can* croche

2 *adv* de travers

crookedly ['krʊkɪdlɪ] *adv* (**a**) *(walk, stand)* de travers (**b**) *(smile)* **to smile crookedly** avoir un sourire en coin

crookedness ['krʊkɪdnɪs] *n* (**a**) *(of outlines etc)* irrégularité *f*; *(curvature)* courbure *f* (**b**) *Fam (dishonesty)* malhonnêteté❑ *f*, fausseté❑ *f*

croon [kru:n] **1** *vi & vt* (**a**) *(sing softly)* fredonner, chantonner; *(professionally)* chanter *(en crooner)* (**b**) *(speak softly, sentimentally)* susurrer

2 *n* fredonnement *m*

crooner ['kru:nə(r)] *n* crooner *m*, chanteur(euse) *m,f* de charme

crop [krɒp] *(pt & pp* **cropped**, *cont* **cropping**) **1** *n* (**a**) *(produce)* produit *m* agricole, culture *f*; *(harvest)* récolte *f*; *(of fruit)* récolte *f*, cueillette *f*; *(of grain)* moisson *f*; **food crops** cultures *fpl* vivrières; **to get in** *or* **to harvest the crops** faire la récolte, rentrer les récoltes; **a poor/good crop** une mauvaise/bonne récolte; **we had a good wheat crop** *or* **crop of wheat** le blé a bien donné

(**b**) *Fig* fournée *f*; **what do you think of this year's crop of students?** que pensez-vous des étudiants de cette année?

(**c**) *(of whip)* manche *m*; *(riding whip)* cravache *f*

(**d**) *(of bird)* jabot *m*

(**e**) *(haircut → for man)* coupe *f* rase *ou* courte; *(→ for woman)* coupe courte *ou* à la garçonne; **the barber gave me a (close) crop** le coiffeur m'a coupé les cheveux ras

2 *vt* (**a**) *(cut → hedge)* tailler, tondre; *(→ hair)* tondre; *(→ tail)* écourter

(**b**) *Phot* recadrer; *Comput & Typ (graphic)* rogner

(**c**) *(of animal)* brouter, paître

(**d**) *(farm)* cultiver; *(harvest)* récolter

3 *vi (land, vegetables)* donner *ou* fournir une récolte; **to crop well** donner une bonne récolte

►► ***crop circle*** = motif circulaire tracé dans un champ, attribué par certains à l'intervention d'extraterrestres; *Agr* ***crop dusting*** pulvérisation *f* des cultures; *Comput* ***crop mark*** trait *m* de coupe; *Agr* ***crop rotation*** assolement *m*, rotation *f* des cultures; *Agr* ***crop spraying*** pulvérisation *f* des cultures

►**crop up** *vi* survenir, se présenter; **his name cropped up in the conversation** son nom a surgi dans la conversation; **we'll deal with anything that crops up while you're away** on s'occupera de tout pendant votre absence; **something has cropped up** j'ai un empêchement

crop-eared *adj Hist (Puritan)* aux cheveux coupés ras

cropper ['krɒpə(r)] *n Br Fam* **to come a cropper** *(fall)* se casser la figure; *(fail)* se planter; **I came a cropper in the exams** je me suis ramassé *ou* planté aux examens

cropping ['krɒpɪŋ] *n Comput & Typ (of graphic)* rognage *m*, recadrage *m*

croquet ['krəʊkeɪ] **1** *n* croquet *m*; **to play croquet** jouer au croquet

2 *comp (hoop, lawn, mallet)* de croquet

croquette [krɒ'ket] *n Culin* croquette *f*; **potato croquette** croquette *f* de pomme de terre

crosier ['krəʊʒjə(r)] *n Rel* crosse *f (d'évêque)*

CROSS [krɒs]

croix	►**1 (a), (b)**
hybride	►**1 (c)**
biais	►**1 (d)**
traverser	►**2 (a); 3 (a)**
croiser	►**2 (b), (d)**
faire une croix	►**2 (c)**
contrarier	►**2 (e)**
se croiser	►**3 (b)**
de mauvaise humeur	►**4 (a)**
diagonal	►**4 (b)**

1 *n* (**a**) *(mark, symbol)* croix *f*; **he signed with a cross** il a signé d'une croix; **the Iron Cross** la Croix de fer

(**b**) *Rel & Fig (burden)* croix *f*; **the Cross** la Croix; **to make the sign of the cross** faire le signe de (la) croix; **we each have our cross to bear** chacun porte sa croix

(**c**) *(hybrid)* hybride *m*, croisement *m*; **a cross between a horse and a donkey** un croisement *ou* hybride du cheval et de l'ânesse; *Fig* **the novel is a cross between a thriller and a comedy** ce roman est un mélange de policier et de comédie

(**d**) *(in sewing)* **on the cross** en biais; **to cut sth on the cross** couper qch dans le biais; **a sleeve cut on the cross** une manche coupée en biais

2 *vt* (**a**) *(go across → road, room, sea)* traverser; *(→ bridge, river)* traverser, passer; *(→ fence, threshold)* franchir; **the bridge crosses the river at Orléans** le pont franchit *ou* enjambe le fleuve à Orléans; **she crossed the Atlantic** elle a fait la traversée de l'Atlantique; **to cross a picket line** franchir un piquet de grève; **a look of distaste crossed her face** une expression de dégoût passa sur son visage; **it crossed my mind that…** j'ai pensé *ou* l'idée m'a effleuré que…; **didn't it cross your mind that she might have been lying?** est-ce qu'il ne t'est pas venu à l'idée qu'elle ait pu mentir? **he crossed my path again a few years later** nos chemins se sont à nouveau croisés quelques années plus tard; *Br Fig Parl* **to cross the floor (of the House)** changer de parti politique; *Fig* **I'll cross that bridge when I come to it** je m'occuperai de ce problème en temps voulu; *Naut* **to cross the line** passer l'équateur

(**b**) *(place one across the other)* croiser; **to cross one's arms/one's legs** croiser les bras/les jambes; **cross your fingers** *or* **keep your fingers crossed for me** pense à moi et croise les doigts; **let's keep our fingers crossed** croisons les doigts; *also Fig* **to cross swords with sb** croiser le fer avec qn; **cross my palm (with silver)!** donnez-moi une petite pièce!

(**c**) *(mark with cross)* faire une croix; *Rel* **to cross oneself** faire le signe de (la) croix, se signer; **cross your "t"s** barrez *ou* mettez des barres à vos "t"; *Am Fig* **we'll send you the contract as soon as we've crossed the ts** nous vous enverrons le contrat dès que nous aurons réglé les derniers détails; *Br* **to cross a cheque** barrer un chèque; *Fam* **cross my heart (and hope to die)** croix de bois croix de fer(, si je mens je vais en enfer) (**d**) *(animals, plants)* croiser; *Fig (two styles)* mélanger, marier

(**e**) *(oppose)* contrarier, contrecarrer; **to be crossed in love** avoir une déception amoureuse

(**f**) *Tel* **we've got a crossed line** il y a des interférences sur la ligne

3 *vi* (**a**) *(go across)* traverser; **she crossed (over) to the door** elle est allée à la porte; **she crossed (over) to the other side of the road** elle a traversé la route; **we crossed from Belgium into France** nous sommes passés de Belgique en France; **they crossed from Dover to Boulogne** ils ont fait la traversée de Douvres à Boulogne

(**b**) *(intersect → lines, paths, roads)* se croiser, se rencontrer; **our letters crossed in the post** nos lettres se sont croisées

4 *adj* (**a**) *(angry)* de mauvaise humeur, en colère; **she's cross with me** elle est fâchée contre moi; **don't be cross with me** il ne faut pas m'en vouloir; **he makes me so cross!** qu'est-ce qu'il peut m'agacer!; **I got cross with them** je me suis fâché contre eux; **I never heard her utter a cross word** elle ne dit jamais un mot plus haut que l'autre; **we've never had a cross word** nous ne nous sommes jamais disputés; *Fam* **to be as cross as a bear** *or Ir* **as a bag of cats** être dans une colère noire

(**b**) *(diagonal)* diagonal

►► *Opt* ***cross hairs*** = fils croisés d'une lunette qui déterminent la ligne de visée; *Constr* ***cross member*** traverse *f*, entremise *f*; *Am* ***cross street*** rue *f* transversale; ***cross wires*** = fils croisés d'une lunette qui déterminent la ligne de visée

►**cross off** *vt sep (item)* barrer, rayer; *(person)* radier; **to cross sb off the list** radier qn

►**cross out** *vt sep* barrer, rayer

---

crossbar ['krɒsbɑː(r)] *n (on bike)* barre *f*; *(on goalposts)* barre *f* traversale

crossbeam ['krɒsbiːm] *n Constr* traverse *f*, sommier *m*

crossbench ['krɒsbentʃ] *n (usu pl) Br Parl* = banc où s'assoient les députés non inscrits à un parti; **on the crossbenches** du côté des non-inscrits

crossbencher [,krɒs'bentʃə(r)] *n Br Parl* = au Parlement britannique, membre non inscrit, assis sur les bancs transversaux

crossbill ['krɒsbɪl] *n Orn* bec-croisé *m*

crossbones ['krɒsbəʊnz] *npl* os *mpl* en croix *ou* de mort

cross-border *adj* transfrontalier

crossbow ['krɒsbəʊ] *n* arbalète *f*

►► ***crossbow slit (window)*** arbalétrière *f*

crossbred ['krɒsbred] **1** *adj* hybride, métis

2 *n* hybride *m*, métis(isse) *m,f*

crossbreed ['krɒsbriːd] *(pt & pp* **crossbred** [-bred]) **1** *vt (animals)* croiser; *(humans)* métisser; *(plants)* hybrider

2 *n (animal, plant)* hybride *m*, métis(isse) *m,f*; *Pej (person)* métis(isse) *m,f*, sang-mêlé *mf inv*

crossbreeding [,krɒs'briːdɪŋ] *n (of animals)* croisement *m* de races; *(of humans)* métissage *m*; *(of plants)* hybridation *f*

cross-Channel *adj Br (ferry, route)* trans-Manche

cross-check 1 *vt* contrôler (par contre-épreuve *ou* par recoupement)

2 *vi* vérifier par recoupement

3 *n* contre-épreuve *f*, recoupement *m*

cross-checking *n* contrôle *m* (par contre-épreuve *ou* par recoupement), contre-épreuve *f*, recoupement *m*

cross-claim *Law* **1** *n* demande *f* reconventionnelle

2 *vt* faire une demande reconventionnelle contre

3 *vi* faire une demande reconventionnelle

cross-compiler *n Comput* compilateur *m* croisé

cross-country 1 *n* cross-country *m*, cross *m*

2 *adv* à travers champs

►► ***cross-country runner*** coureur(euse) *m,f* de cross; ***cross-country skier*** fondeur(euse) *m,f*; ***cross-country skiing*** ski *m* de fond

cross-cultural *adj* interculturel

cross-currency *adj*

►► *Fin* ***cross-currency interest rate*** taux *m* d'intérêt croisé; *St Exch* ***cross-currency swap*** crédit *m* croisé

cross-current *n* contre-courant *m*

crosscut ['krɒskʌt] *Carp* **1** *adj (incision)* coupé en travers; *(tool)* qui coupe en travers

2 *vt* couper en travers

►► ***crosscut chisel*** bédane *m*; ***crosscut saw*** scie *f* passe-partout

cross-dresser *n* travesti(e) *m,f*

cross-dressing *n* travestisme *m*, transvestisme *m*

crosse [krɒs] *n* crosse *f (au jeu de la crosse)*

crossed [krɒst] *adj* croisé

►► ***crossed cheque*** chèque *m* barré

cross-examination *n* contre-interrogatoire *m*

cross-examine *vt (gen)* soumettre à un interrogatoire serré; *Law* faire subir un contre-interrogatoire à

cross-eyed *adj* qui louche; **she's cross-eyed** elle louche

cross-fertilization *n Bot* croisement *m*; *Fig* osmose *f*, enrichissement *m* croisé

cross-fertilize, -ise 1 *vt Bot* hybrider; *Fig (ideas)* échanger

2 *vi Bot* s'hybrider; *Fig (teams, people at conference etc)* échanger des idées

crossfire ['krɒs,faɪə(r)] *n* feux *mpl* croisés; *Mil & Fig* **to be caught in the crossfire** être pris entre deux feux

cross-flow radiator *n Aut* radiateur *m* à flux transversal

cross-grained *adj* (**a**) *(wood)* à fibres torses (**b**) *(person)* revêche, acariâtre

crosshair pointer ['krɒsheə-] *n Comput* pointeur-croix *m*

cross-hatch *vt Art* hachurer en croisillons

cross-hatching *n Art* hachures *fpl* croisées

crosshead ['krɒshed] *n* (**a**) *Typ* sous-titre *m* (**b**) *Tech (block → gen)* palier *m*; *(→ in engine)* crosse *f* (**c**) *Naut* (barre *f* de) traverse *f*

crossheaded ['krɒshedɪd] *adj Tech (screwdriver)* cruciforme

cross-hedge *n St Exch* couverture *f* croisée

cross-holding *n Fin* participation *f* croisée

cross-impact analysis *n Mktg* analyse *f* d'interférence

cross-index 1 *vi* renvoyer à

2 *vt* établir les renvois de

3 *n* renvoi *m*, référence *f*

crossing ['krɒsɪŋ] *n* (**a**) *(sea journey)* traversée *f*; *Mil (of river)* franchissement *m*; **we had a good crossing** nous avons eu *ou* fait une belle traversée (**b**) *(intersection)* croisement *m*; *(of roads)* croisement *m*, carrefour *m* (**c**) *(inter-breeding)* croisement *m*

cross-kick *Sport* **1** *n* = coup de pied qui envoie le ballon à travers le terrain

2 *vi* = envoyer le ballon à l'autre bout du terrain

cross-leaved heath *n Bot* bruyère *f* des marais

cross-legged *adj* en tailleur

crossly ['krɒslɪ] *adv (with annoyance)* avec mauvaise humeur; *(angrily)* d'un air/d'un ton fâché

cross-member *n Aut* traverse *f*

crossness ['krɒsnɪs] *n* mauvaise humeur *f*

crossover ['krɒs,əʊvə(r)] **1** *n* (**a**) *(of roads)* (croisement *m* par) pont *m* routier; *(for pedestrians)* passage *m* clouté; *Rail* voie *f* de croisement (**b**) *Biol* croisement *m*

2 *adj Mus (style)* hybride

►► *Mus* ***crossover album*** album *m* hybride

cross-party *adj*

►► *Pol* ***cross-party agreement*** accord *m* entre partis

crosspatch ['krɒspætʃ] *n Fam* grincheux(euse) *m,f*

crosspiece ['krɒspiːs] *n Tech* traverse *f*

cross-platform *adj Comput* multiplateforme

crossply ['krɒsplaɪ] *adj (tyre)* à carcasse biaise *ou* croisée

cross-pollinate *Bot* **1** *vi* se reproduire par pollinisation croisée

2 *vt* féconder par pollinisation croisée

cross-pollination *n Bot* pollinisation *f* croisée

cross-post *vt Comput* faire un envoi multiple de

cross-posting *n Comput* envoi *m* multiple

cross-pricing *n Com* fixation *f* de prix croisés

cross-purposes *npl* **to be at cross-purposes with sb** *(misunderstand)* comprendre qn de travers; *(oppose)* être en désaccord avec qn; **we were at cross-purposes** il y a eu un malentendu entre nous; **they were talking at cross-purposes** ils ne parlaient pas de la même chose

cross-question *vt (gen)* soumettre à un interrogatoire serré; *Law* faire subir un contre-interrogatoire à

cross-refer 1 *vi* **to cross-refer to sth** renvoyer à qch

2 *vt* renvoyer; **the reader is cross-referred to page 332** il y a un renvoi à la page 332

cross-reference 1 *n* renvoi *m*, référence *f*

2 *vt (provide with cross-references)* introduire des renvois dans

crossroad ['krɒsrəʊd] *n Am (across a road)* = route qui en coupe une autre; *(between main roads)* route *f* secondaire, route *f* départementale

crossroads ['krɒsrəʊdz] *(pl* **inv**) *n* croisement *m*, carrefour *m*; *Fig* **the city is at the crossroads of Europe** la ville est au carrefour de l'Europe; **her career is at a crossroads** sa carrière va maintenant prendre un tournant décisif

cross-section *n* (**a**) *(gen) & Biol* coupe *f* transversale; **in cross-section** en coupe transversale

(**b**) *(sample)* échantillon *m*; **a cross-section of the population** un groupe représentatif de la population

cross-stitch *Sewing* **1** *n* point *m* de croix

2 *vt* coudre au point de croix

crosstalk ['krɒs,tɔːk] *n* (**a**) *Rad & Tel* diaphonie *f* (**b**) *Br (witty exchange)* joutes *fpl* oratoires; *Am (trivial conversation)* banalités *fpl*, bavardages *mpl*

crosstie ['krɒstaɪ] *n Am Constr* traverse *f*

crosstown ['krɒstaʊn] *Am* **1** *adj* qui traverse la ville

2 *adv* à travers la ville

►► ***crosstown artery*** voie *f* qui traverse la ville; ***crosstown bus*** bus *m* qui traverse la ville

cross-training *n Sport* = entraînement dans d'autres disciplines afin d'améliorer ses performances dans sa discipline principale

crosstree ['krɒstriː] *n Constr* traverse *f*

crosswalk ['krɒswɔːk] *n Am* passage *m* clouté

crossway ['krɒsweɪ] *n Am (across a road)* = route qui en coupe une autre; *(between main roads)* route *f* secondaire, route *f* départementale

crossways ['krɒsweɪz] *(pl* **inv**) **1** *n Am* croisement *m*, carrefour *m*

2 *adj (shaped like a cross)* en croix; *(across)* en travers; *(diagonally)* en travers, en diagonale

3 *adv (into the shape of a cross)* en croix; *(across)* en travers; *(diagonally)* en travers, en diagonale

crosswind ['krɒswɪnd] *n* vent *m* de travers

crosswise ['krɒswaɪz] **1** *adj (shaped like a cross)* en croix; *(across)* en travers; *(diagonally)* en travers, en diagonale

2 *(into the shape of a cross)* en croix; *(across)* en travers; *(diagonally)* en travers, en diagonale

crossword (puzzle) ['krɒswɜːd-] *n* mots *mpl* croisés; **to do a crossword (puzzle)** faire des mots croisés

crotch [krɒtʃ] *n (of tree)* fourche *f*; *(of trousers)* entre-jambes *m inv*; **she kicked him in the crotch** elle lui a donné un coup de pied entre les jambes

crotchet ['krɒtʃɪt] *n Br Mus* noire *f*

crotchety ['krɒtʃɪtɪ] *adj Fam* grognon, bougon

croton ['krəʊtən] *n Bot* croton *m*

crouch [kraʊtʃ] **1** *vi* **to crouch (down)** *(person)* s'accroupir; *(animal)* se tapir

2 *n (posture)* **to go into a crouch** s'accroupir; **to be in a crouch** être accroupi

croup [kruːp] *n* (**a**) *(of animal)* croupe *f* (**b**) *Med* croup *m*

croupier ['kruːpɪə(r)] *n* croupier *m*

crouton ['kruːtɒn] *n Culin* croûton *m*

crow [krəʊ] *(Br pt* **crowed** *or* **crew** [kruː], *pp* **crowed** *or* **crown** [krəʊn], *Am pt* **crowed**) **1** *n* (**a**) *(bird)* corbeau *m*; *(smaller)* corneille *f*; **it's 3 miles as the crow flies** c'est à 3 miles à vol d'oiseau; *Am Fam* **he had to eat crow** il a dû admettre qu'il avait tort □

(**b**) *(sound of cock)* chant *m* du coq, cocorico *m*

(**c**) *(of baby)* gazouillis *m*

2 *vi* (**a**) *(cock)* chanter

(**b**) *(baby)* gazouiller

(**c**) *(boast)* fanfaronner; **it's nothing to crow about** il n'y a pas de quoi être fier; **to crow over sth** se vanter de qch

►► *Am Orn* ***crow blackbird*** quiscale *m*; ***crow's feet*** *(wrinkles)* pattes *fpl* d'oie; *Naut* ***crow's nest*** nid *m* de pie

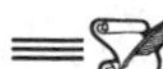

'Crow' *Hughes* 'Corbeau'

crowbar ['krəʊbɑː(r)] *n* (pince *f* à) levier *m*

crowd [kraʊd] **1** *n* (**a**) *(throng)* foule *f*, masse *f*; **a crowd of noisy children** une bande d'enfants bruyants; **don't get lost in the crowd** ne vous perdez pas dans la foule; **a disorderly crowd** une cohue; **there were crowds of people in town** il y avait foule en ville; **there was quite a crowd at the match** il y avait beaucoup de monde au match; **the concert drew a good crowd** le concert a attiré beaucoup de monde; **she stands out in a crowd** elle se distingue de la masse; *Fig* **to follow the crowd** suivre le mouvement

(**b**) *Fam (social group)* bande *f*; **to be in with the wrong crowd** avoir de mauvaises fréquentations; **they stick to their own crowd** ils font bande à part

(**c**) *Fig Pej (people as a whole)* **the crowd** la foule, la masse du peuple; **she always goes with** *or* **follows the crowd** elle suit toujours le mouvement; **she doesn't like to be one of the crowd** elle n'aime pas faire comme tout le monde

2 *vi* se presser; **to crowd round sb/sth** se presser autour de qn/qch; **they crowded round to read the poster** ils se sont attroupés pour lire l'affiche; **the reporters crowded into the room** les journalistes se sont entassés dans la pièce; **don't all crowd together!** ne vous serrez pas comme ça!; **they came crowding through the door** ils se sont bousculés pour entrer; **we crowded up/down the stairs** tout le monde a monté/descendu l'escalier

3 *vt* (**a**) *(cram)* serrer, entasser; **people crowded the streets/the shops** des gens se pressaient dans les rues/les magasins; **the tables are crowded together** les tables sont collées les unes aux autres; **the park was crowded with sunbathers** le parc était plein de gens qui prenaient des bains de soleil

(**b**) *Fam (jostle)* bousculer; **stop crowding me!** arrêtez de me bousculer!, ne me poussez pas!; **I was crowded off the bus** la foule m'a éjecté du bus

(**c**) *Naut* **to crowd on sail** mettre toutes les voiles dehors

(**d**) *Am Fam (idiom)* **to crowd one's luck** exagérer, forcer la chance

►► *Cin & TV* ***crowd scene*** scène *f* de foule; ***crowd surfing*** = pratique courante dans les concerts pop ou rock, qui consiste à se laisser transporter, allongé, au-dessus de la foule

►**crowd in** *vi* (**a**) *(enter)* entrer en foule, affluer (**b**) *Fig (flood in)* submerger; **gloomy thoughts kept crowding in on me** de sombres pensées m'assaillaient

►**crowd out 1** *vi* sortir en foule

2 *vt sep* **we were crowded out by a bunch of students** un groupe d'étudiants nous a poussés vers la sortie; **independent traders are being crowded out by bigger stores** les petits commerçants sont étouffés par les grands magasins

crowded ['kraʊdɪd] *adj* (**a**) *(busy → room, building, bus etc)* bondé, plein; *(→ street)* plein (de monde); *(→ town)* encombré (de monde), surpeuplé; **the crowded streets of Bombay** les rues pleines de monde de Bombay; **a room crowded with furniture/with people** une pièce encombrée de meubles/pleine de monde; **the shops are too crowded** il y a trop de monde dans les magasins; **he has a crowded schedule** son emploi du temps est surchargé

(**b**) *(overpopulated)* surpeuplé; **crowded inner-city areas** les quartiers surpeuplés du centre-ville

crowdpleaser ['kraʊd,pliːzə(r)] *n* **to be a crowd-pleaser** plaire aux foules

crowdpuller ['kraʊd,pʊlə(r)] *n Br Fam* **his play is a real crowdpuller** sa pièce attire les foules ❑

crowfoot ['krəʊfʊt] *(pl sense* (**a**) **crowfoots**, *pl sense* (**b**) **crowfeet** [-fiːt]) *n* (**a**) *Bot* renoncule *f* (**b**) *Naut* araignée *f*

crowing ['krəʊɪŋ] *n (of cock)* chant *m*; *Fig* fanfaronnades *fpl*

crown [kraʊn] **1** *n* (**a**) *(of monarch, martyr, made of flowers etc)* couronne *f*; **to succeed to the crown** accéder au trône; **she wears the crown** c'est elle qui règne; **crown of thorns** couronne *f* d'épines

(**b**) *(award)* prix *m*; **she won the Wimbledon crown for the second year running** elle a remporté le tournoi de Wimbledon pour la seconde année consécutive

(**c**) *(top → of hill, tree)* sommet *m*, cime *f*; *(→ of roof)* faîte *m*; *(→ of hat)* fond *m*; *(→ of road)* bombement *m*; *(→ of tooth)* couronne *f*; *Archit (→ of arch)* clef *f*; **the crown (of the head)** le sommet de la tête

(**d**) *(coin)* couronne *f*

(**e**) *(outstanding achievement)* couronnement *m*; **it was the crown of his career** ce fut le couronnement de sa carrière

(**f**) *(paper size)* couronne *f*

(**g**) *Naut (of anchor)* diamant *m*

2 *vt* (**a**) *(confer a title on)* couronner, sacrer; **she was crowned queen/champion** elle fut couronnée reine/championne; **the crowned heads of Europe** les têtes couronnées de l'Europe

(**b**) *(top)* couronner; *Fig (person's happiness)* combler, couronner; *(person's efforts)* récompenser; **to crown a tooth** couronner une dent; **the woods that crown the hill** les bois qui couronnent la colline; **her election success crowned her career** son succès aux élections a couronné sa carrière; *Fig* **and to crown it all, it started to rain** et pour couronner le tout, il s'est mis à pleuvoir

(**c**) *(in draughts)* damer; **to be crowned** aller à dame

(**d**) *Br Fam (hit)* flanquer un coup (sur la tête) à; **I'll crown you!** *(hit you)* je vais te flanquer un de ces coups sur la tête!

3 Crown *n* **the Crown** la Couronne, l'État *m* (monarchique); *Br Law* **Counsel for the Crown** conseiller *m* juridique de la Couronne

►► *Pol* ***Crown Agent*** = fonctionnaire du ministère britannique du développement outre-mer chargé des pays étrangers et des organisations internationales; *Br* ***crown cap*** capsule *f* (de bouteille); *Br* ***crown colony*** colonie *f* de la Couronne; *Can* ***Crown corporation*** société *f* d'État; *Law* ***Crown Court*** ≃ Cour *f* d'assises *(en Angleterre et au pays de Galles)*; *Cer* ***Crown Derby*** = vaisselle de porcelaine fabriquée à Derby en Angleterre; ***crown estates*** terres *fpl* domaniales *ou* appartenant à la Couronne; ***crown green*** terrain *m* (de boules) bombé; *Bot* ***crown imperial*** couronne *f* impériale; ***crown jewels*** *(crown, sceptre etc)* joyaux *mpl* de la Couronne; *very Fam Hum (man's genitals)* bijoux *mpl* de famille; ***crown land*** terres *fpl* domaniales; *Mining* ***crown pillar*** stot *m*; ***crown prince*** prince *m* héritier; ***crown princess*** *(heir to throne)* princesse *f* héritière; *(wife of crown prince)* princesse *f* royale; *Br Law* **Crown Prosecution Service** ≃ ministère *m* public; **Crown rating system** *(for hotels)* système *m* de classement (des hôtels britanniques); *Culin* ***crown roast*** rôti *m* en couronne; ***crown wheel*** *(gen)* couronne *f*; *Aut* grande couronne *f*; *Tech* ***crown wheel and pinion*** couronne *f* d'entraînement; *Law* ***crown witness*** témoin *m* à charge

crowning ['kraʊnɪŋ] **1** *n* couronnement *m*

2 *adj Fig* suprême

►► *Hum* ***crowning glory*** *(hair)* chevelure *f*; **the red hair that was her crowning glory** la belle crinière rousse qui faisait l'admiration de tout le monde; **the crowning glory of her career** *(peak)* le plus grand triomphe de sa carrière

crozier = **crosier**

CRT [,siːɑː'tiː] *n* (*abbr* **cathode-ray tube**) (**a**) *(in TV set)* tube *m* cathodique (**b**) *Am (work station)* poste *m* de travail

cruces ['kruːsiːz] *pl of* **crux**

crucial ['kruːʃəl] *adj* (**a**) *(critical)* critique, crucial; *Med & Phil* crucial (**b**) *Br Fam (excellent)* d'enfer; **those jeans are crucial** il est d'enfer, ce jean!

crucially ['kruːʃəlɪ] *adv* fondamentalement

crucible ['kruːsɪbəl] *n (vessel)* creuset *m*; *Fig (test)* (dure) épreuve *f*; *Literary* **to be tested in the crucible of adversity** passer par le creuset de l'adversité

►► ***crucible steel*** acier *m* fondu au creuset

'The Crucible' *Miller, Hytner* 'Les Sorcières de Salem'

crucifix ['kruːsɪfɪks] *n* christ *m*, crucifix *m*; **(roadside) crucifix** calvaire *m*

crucifixion [,kruːsɪ'fɪkʃən] **1** *n* crucifiement *m*

2 Crucifixion *n Rel* **the Crucifixion** la crucifixion, la mise en croix

cruciform ['kruːsɪfɔːm] *adj Tech* cruciforme, en croix

crucify ['kruːsɪfaɪ] *(pt & pp* **crucified**) *vt* (**a**) *(execute)* crucifier, mettre en croix; *Rel* **Christ Crucified** le Crucifié (**b**) *Fig (treat harshly)* mettre au pilori; *(defeat)* démolir; **he was crucified in the courtroom when he tried to defend himself** il a été mis au pilori lorsqu'il a essayé de se défendre au tribunal; **my mum will crucify us if she finds out!** ma mère va nous étriper si elle découvre ça!

crud [krʌd] *n Fam* (**a**) *(dirt)* crasse *f* (**b**) *(nonsense)* conneries *fpl*; **he was talking some crud about the dangers of drugs** il était en train de raconter des conneries sur les dangers de la drogue (**c**) *(person)* ordure *f*, saloperie *f*; **you crud!** espèce de minable! (**d**) *(disease)* **the crud** la crève

cruddy ['krʌdɪ] *(compar* **cruddier**, *superl* **cruddiest**) *adj Fam* (**a**) *(dirty)* crado (**b**) *(of poor quality)* dégueulasse (**c**) *(unwell)* **I feel cruddy** je ne me sens pas bien ❑, je ne suis pas dans mon assiette

crude [kruːd] **1** *adj* (**a**) *(vulgar → person, behaviour)* vulgaire, grossier; *(→ manners)* fruste, grossier; **a crude remark** une grossièreté; **crude jokes** des plaisanteries *fpl* grossières

(**b**) *(raw)* brut; *(sugar)* non raffiné

(**c**) *(unsophisticated → tool)* grossier, rudimentaire; *(→ piece of work)* mal fini, sommaire; *(→ drawing)* grossier; **it was a crude attempt at self-promotion** c'était une tentative grossière pour se mettre en avant

(**d**) *(stark → colour, light)* cru, vif

2 *n Petr (crude oil)* brut *m*

►► *Petr* ***crude oil*** (pétrole *m*) brut *m*; **crude ore** tout-venant *m inv*

crudely ['kruːdlɪ] *adv* (**a**) *(vulgarly)* grossièrement; *(bluntly)* crûment, brutalement; **to put it crudely** *(bluntly)* pour être tout à fait franc (**b**) *(unsophisticatedly)* grossièrement, sommairement; **a crudely built hut** une cabane grossière

crudeness ['kruːdnɪs] *n* (**a**) *(vulgarity)* grossièreté *f* (**b**) *(rawness → of material)* état *m* brut (**c**) *(lack of sophistication → of tool)* caractère *m* rudimentaire; *(→ of drawing, work)* manque *m* de fini, caractère *m* sommaire

crudités ['kruːdɪteɪz] *npl Culin* crudités *fpl*

crudity ['kruːdɪtɪ] *n* (**a**) *(vulgarity)* grossièreté *f* (**b**) *(rawness → of material)* état *m* brut (**c**) *(lack of sophistication → of tool)* caractère *m* rudimentaire; *(→ of drawing, work)* manque *m* de fini, caractère *m* sommaire

cruel [krʊəl] *adj* (**a**) *(unkind)* cruel; **to be cruel to sb** être cruel envers qn; **you've got to be cruel to be kind** qui aime bien châtie bien (**b**) *(painful)* douloureux, cruel; **it was a cruel disappointment** ce fut une cruelle déception; **a cruel wind** un vent mauvais *ou* cinglant

cruelly ['krʊəlɪ] *adv* cruellement

cruelty ['krʊəltɪ] *(pl* **cruelties**) *n* (**a**) *(gen)* cruauté *f*; **cruelty to animals** la cruauté envers les animaux (**b**) *Law* sévices *mpl*; **indicted for cruelty to her children** inculpée pour sévices sur ses enfants; **divorce on the grounds of cruelty** divorce pour sévices (**c**) *(cruel act)* cruauté *f*; **he had to suffer the cruelties of his classmates** il lui a fallu endurer les cruautés de ses camarades de classe

cruelty-free *adj (make-up, toiletries)* non testé sur les animaux

cruet ['kruːɪt] *n* (**a**) *(for oil, vinegar)* petit flacon *m* (**b**) *(set of condiments)* service *m* à condiments (**c**) *Rel* burette *f*

Cruft's [krʌfts] *n* = le plus important concours canin de Grande-Bretagne, qui se tient chaque année à Londres

cruise [kruːz] **1** *n* (**a**) *(sea trip)* croisière *f*; **they went on a cruise** ils sont partis en *ou* ont fait une croisière; **to be on a cruise** être en croisière
(**b**) *(missile)* missile *m* de croisière
2 *vi* (**a**) *(ship)* croiser; *(tourists)* être en croisière
(**b**) *(car → gen)* rouler; *(→ police car, taxi)* marauder, être en maraude; *(plane)* voler; **we cruised along at 70 km/h** nous roulions tranquillement à 70 km/h; **I cruised through the exam** j'ai trouvé l'examen super facile; **a cruising taxi** un taxi en maraude; *Hum* **you're cruising for a bruising!** toi, tu cherches les emmerdes!
(**c**) *Fam (for sexual partner)* draguer
(**d**) *Am Fam (leave)* mettre les bouts, se casser, s'arracher; **ready to cruise?** on y va?
3 *vt* (**a**) *(ocean)* croiser dans
(**b**) *Fam (sexual partner)* draguer; *(place)* aller draguer dans
►► *Aut* ***cruise control*** régulateur *m* d'allure; ***cruise liner*** paquebot *m* de croisière; ***cruise missile*** missile *m* de croisière; ***cruise ship*** bateau *m* de croisière

cruiser ['kruːzə(r)] *n* (**a**) *(warship)* croiseur *m*; *(pleasure boat)* yacht *m* de croisière (**b**) *Am (police patrol car)* voiture *f* de police (en patrouille)

cruiserweight ['kruːzəweɪt] *n Br Boxing* poids *m* mi-lourd

cruising ['kruːzɪŋ] *n (in boat)* croisière(s) *f(pl)*
►► ***cruising altitude*** altitude *f* de croisière; ***cruising holiday*** croisière *f*; *Aviat* ***cruising range*** autonomie *f* à vitesse de croisière; ***cruising speed*** vitesse *f* de croisière

cruller ['krʌlə(r)] *n Am Culin* beignet *m*

crumb [krʌm] *n* (**a**) *(of bread)* miette *f*; *(inside loaf)* mie *f*; *Fig (small piece)* miette *f*, brin *m*; **crumb of comfort** brin *m* de consolation; **a few crumbs of information** des bribes *fpl* d'information; *Fig* **they make the profit and we get the crumbs from their table** ils réalisent les bénéfices et nous récupérons les miettes (**b**) *Fam Pej (person)* nul (nulle) *m,f*

crumble ['krʌmbəl] **1** *vt (bread, stock cube)* émietter; *(earth, plaster)* effriter
2 *vi (bread, stock cube)* s'émietter; *(plaster)* s'effriter; *(building)* tomber en ruines, se désagréger; *(earth, stone)* s'ébouler; *Fig (hopes, society)* s'effondrer, s'écrouler; **everything is crumbling to dust** tout tombe en poussière; *Fig* **his world was crumbling around him** tout son petit monde s'écroulait *ou* s'effondrait
3 *n Br Culin (dessert)* crumble *m (dessert composé d'une couche de compote de fruits recouverte de pâte)*

crumbling ['krʌmblɪŋ] **1** *adj (stone, earth)* qui s'effrite; *(wall etc)* qui s'écroule, croulant; *Fig (empire, opposition, resistance)* qui s'effondre
2 *n (of stone, earth)* effritement *m*; *Fig (of empire, opposition, resistance, prices etc)* effondrement *m*

crumbly ['krʌmblɪ] *(compar* **crumblier,** *superl* **crumbliest)** **1** *adj* friable
2 *n Br Fam (old person)* croulant(e) *m,f*

crumbs [krʌmz] *exclam Br Fam Old-fashioned* mince!, zut!

crumhorn ['krʌm,hɔːn] *n Mus* cromorne *m*

crummy ['krʌmɪ] *(compar* **crummier,** *superl* **crummiest)** *adj Fam* (**a**) *(bad)* minable, nul (**b**) *(unwell)* patraque; **I feel crummy** je me sens patraque

crump [krʌmp] *Fam Mil slang* **1** *vi* éclater ❑
2 *vt* bombarder ❑
3 *n* (**a**) *(noise)* éclatement ❑ *m* (**b**) *(shell)* obus ❑ *m*

crumpet ['krʌmpɪt] *n Br* (**a**) *Culin (cake)* = galette épaisse qu'on mange chaude et beurrée (**b**) *very Fam (women)* jolies nanas *fpl*, pépées *fpl*; *(men)* beaux mecs *mpl*; **a nice bit of crumpet** une jolie nana, une belle pépée; *(man)* un beau gars *ou* garçon ❑

crumple ['krʌmpəl] **1** *vt* froisser, friper; **be careful not to crumple your dress** fais attention de ne pas froisser *ou* chiffonner ta robe; **to crumple a piece of paper** chiffonner *ou* froisser du papier; *(make into a ball)* mettre un papier en boule; **to get crumpled** se froisser
2 *vi* (**a**) *(crease)* se froisser, se chiffonner (**b**) *(collapse)* s'effondrer, s'écrouler; *Fig* **his face crumpled and tears came to his eyes** son visage se contracta et ses yeux se remplirent de larmes
►► *Aut* ***crumple zone*** zone *f* d'absorption

crumpled ['krʌmpəld] *adj* froissé; **his clothes were lying in a crumpled heap** ses vêtements étaient jetés en boule; **she was lying in a crumpled heap** elle était recroquevillée par terre

crunch [krʌntʃ] **1** *n* (**a**) *(sound → of teeth)* coup *m* de dents; *(→ of food)* craquement *m*; *(→ of gravel, snow)* craquement *m*, crissement *m*
(**b**) *Fam (critical moment)* moment *m* critique ❑; **when it comes to the crunch** dans une situation critique ❑, au moment critique; **if it comes to the crunch** en cas de besoin ❑
(**c**) *Fam (busy time)* **to have a crunch on** être surchargé ❑
2 *adj Fam* critique ❑, décisif ❑; **a crunch match** un match décisif ❑
3 *vt* (**a**) *(chew)* croquer; **the dog was crunching a bone** le chien mordait bruyamment un os
(**b**) *(crush underfoot)* faire craquer *ou* crisser, écraser
(**c**) *(process → data, numbers)* traiter à grande vitesse
4 *vi* (**a**) *(gravel, snow)* craquer, crisser; **the snow crunched beneath my feet** la neige crissait sous mes pieds
(**b**) *(chew)* croquer; **to crunch on sth** croquer qch

►**crunch up** *vt sep* broyer

crunched [krʌntʃt] *adj Fam (busy)* très occupé ❑; **how crunched are you?** tu as beaucoup de travail? ❑

crunching ['krʌntʃɪŋ] *n (sound → of teeth)* coup *m* de dents; *(→ of food)* craquement *m*; *(→ of gravel, snow)* craquement *m*, crissement *m*

crunchy ['krʌntʃɪ] *(compar* **crunchier,** *superl* **crunchiest)** *adj* (**a**) *(food)* croquant; *(snow, gravel)* qui craque *ou* crisse (**b**) *Am Fam (interested in health foods)* bio

crupper ['krʌpə(r)] *n Horseriding (on saddle)* croupière *f*; *Zool (of horse)* croupe *f (de cheval)*

crusade [kruː'seɪd] **1** *n Hist & Fig* croisade *f*; *Hist* **to go on (a) crusade** partir en croisade; *Fig* faire une croisade; **to start a crusade (against)** lancer une croisade (contre); *Hist* **the Crusades** les Croisades *fpl*
2 *vi Hist* partir en croisade, être à la croisade; *Fig* faire une croisade; **to crusade for/against sth** mener une croisade pour/contre qch; **she spent her life crusading against injustice** elle a passé sa vie à lutter contre l'injustice

crusader [kruː'seɪdə(r)] *n Hist* croisé *m*; *Fig* champion(onne) *m,f*, militant(e) *m,f*; **a crusader against injustice** un (une) champion(onne) de la lutte contre l'injustice; **the crusaders for/against nuclear power** ceux qui militent pour/contre l'énergie nucléaire

Cruse [kruːz] *n* = association de soutien aux personnes ayant perdu un proche

crush [krʌʃ] **1** *vt* (**a**) *(smash → gen)* écraser, broyer; *(grapes etc)* exprimer le jus de; *(of boa constrictor → victim)* comprimer; **crushed ice** glace *f* pilée; **his leg/arm had been crushed in the accident** sa jambe a été écrasée/son bras a été écrasé dans l'accident; **they were crushed to death** ils sont morts écrasés
(**b**) *(crease)* froisser, chiffonner; **crushed velvet** velours *m* frappé
(**c**) *(defeat → enemy)* écraser; *(suppress → revolt)* écraser, réprimer; *Fig (→ hopes)* écraser; **she felt crushed by the news** elle a été accablée *ou* atterrée par la nouvelle; **he crushed any attempt at reconciliation** il a fait échouer toutes les tentatives de réconciliation
(**d**) *(squash, press)* serrer; **to be crushed together** être tassés *ou* serrés les uns contre les autres; **too many things had been crushed into the box** on avait entassé trop de choses dans la boîte; **we were crushed in the race for the door** nous avons été écrasés dans la ruée vers la porte
2 *vi* (**a**) *(throng)* se serrer, s'écraser; **we all crushed into the lift** nous nous sommes tous entassés dans l'ascenseur
(**b**) *(crease)* se froisser
3 *n* (**a**) *(crowd)* foule *f*, cohue *f*; **there was a terrible crush** il y avait un monde fou; **in the crush to enter the stadium** dans la bousculade pour entrer dans le stade
(**b**) *Fam (infatuation)* béguin *m*; **to have a crush on sb** en pincer *ou* avoir le béguin pour qn
(**c**) *Br (drink)* jus *m* de fruit; **lemon crush** citron *m* pressé
►► *Theat* ***crush bar*** bar *m* des spectateurs; ***crush barrier*** barrière *f* de sécurité

crusher ['krʌʃə(r)] *n* broyeur *m*, concasseur *m*

crushing ['krʌʃɪŋ] **1** *adj (defeat)* écrasant; *(remark)* cinglant, percutant; **to be dealt a crushing blow** *(army, hopes etc)* en prendre un sacré coup
2 *n (of grapes)* pressage *m*; *(of ore)* broyage *m*, concassage *m*; *(of rebellion, uprising)* écrasement *m*; *(of hopes)* anéantissement *m*

crushingly ['krʌʃɪŋlɪ] *adv* d'un ton écrasant

crush-resistant *adj* solide, résistant (au choc)

crust [krʌst] **1** *n* (**a**) *(of bread, pie)* croûte *f*; *(of snow, ice)* couche *f*; **a crust of bread** un croûton, une croûte; *Geol* **the earth's crust** la croûte *ou* l'écorce *f* terrestre; *Fam* **to earn a** *or* **one's crust** gagner sa croûte
(**b**) *(on wound)* croûte *f*, escarre *f*
(**c**) *(on wine)* dépôt *m*
2 *vt* couvrir d'une croûte
3 *vi* former une croûte

►**crust over** *vi (become covered with a crust)* se couvrir d'une croûte; *(wound etc)* former une croûte

crustacean [krʌ'steɪʃən] *Zool* **1** *adj* crustacé
2 *n* crustacé *m*

crusted ['krʌstɪd] *adj* **to be crusted with ice** être couvert d'une croûte de glace

crustie ['krʌstɪ] *n Br Fam* jeune hippie *mf* crado

crusty ['krʌstɪ] *(pl* **crusties,** *compar* **crustier,** *superl* **crustiest)** **1** *n* = **crustie**
2 *adj* (**a**) *(bread)* croustillant (**b**) *(bad-tempered → person)* hargneux, bourru; *(→ remark)* brusque, sec (sèche)

crutch [krʌtʃ] *n* (**a**) *(support)* support *m*, soutien *m*; *(for walking)* béquille *f*; *Archit* étançon *m*; *Naut* support *m*; **she uses crutches** elle marche avec des béquilles (**b**) *Fig* soutien *m*; **he uses notes as a mental crutch** il se sert de ses notes comme aide-mémoire (**c**) *Br (of tree)* fourche *f*; *(of trousers)* entre-jambes *m inv*; **she kicked him in the crutch** elle lui a donné un coup de pied entre les jambes

crux [krʌks] *(pl* **cruxes** *or* **cruces** ['kruːsiːz]) *n* (**a**) *(vital point)* point *m* crucial *ou* capital; *(of problem)* cœur *m*; **the crux of the matter** le nœud de l'affaire (**b**) *(in climbing)* passage-clef *m*

cry [kraɪ] *(pt & pp* **cried,** *pl* **cries)** **1** *vi* (**a**) *(weep)* pleurer; **she cried in** *or* **with frustration** elle pleurait d'impuissance; **we laughed until we cried** nous avons pleuré de rire *ou* avons ri aux larmes; **the film made them cry** ils ont pleuré pendant le film; **to cry loudly/bitterly** pleurer à chaudes larmes/amèrement; *Prov* **it's no use crying over spilt milk** = ce qui est fait est fait
(**b**) *(call out)* crier, pousser un cri; **to cry (out) in pain** pousser un cri de douleur; **to cry for help** crier au secours; **to cry for mercy** demander grâce, implorer la pitié; **to cry for the moon** demander la lune *ou* l'impossible
(**c**) *(bird, animal)* pousser un cri *ou* des cris; *(hounds)* donner de la voix, aboyer
2 *vt* (**a**) *(weep)* pleurer; **she cried herself to sleep** elle s'est endormie en pleurant; **he cried tears of joy** il versa des larmes de joie; **he was crying his heart** *or* **eyes out** il pleurait toutes les larmes de son corps
(**b**) *(shout)* crier; **"look," she cried** "regardez," s'écria-t-elle; **he cried quits** *or* **mercy** il s'est avoué vaincu; *Old-fashioned* **to cry one's wares** vendre sa marchandise à la criée; **to cry wolf** crier au loup
3 *n* (**a**) *(exclamation)* cri *m*; **to give** *or* **utter a cry** pousser un cri; **a cry of pain** un cri de douleur; *also Fig* **a cry for help** un appel au secours; **he heard a cry for help** il a entendu

crier au secours; **there were cries of "down with the king!"** on criait "à bas le roi!"; **it's a far cry from what they promised us** cela n'a rien à voir avec ce qu'ils nous avaient promis; **it's still a far cry from what I asked for** cela reste loin de ce que j'avais demandé
(**b**) *(of birds, animals)* cri *m*; *(of hounds)* aboiements *mpl*, voix *f*; **to be in full cry** donner de la voix
(**c**) *(weep)* **to have a good cry** pleurer un bon coup

►**cry down** *vt sep* décrier

►**cry off** *vi (from meeting)* se décommander; *(from promise)* se rétracter, se dédire; **she's crying off from the project** elle se retire du *ou* renonce au projet

►**cry out 1** *vi* pousser un cri; **I cried out to them** je les ai appelés; *Fig* **to cry out against** protester contre; **the country is crying out against high taxation** tout le pays proteste contre les impôts élevés; **to cry out for sth** demander *ou* réclamer qch; *Fig* **the system is crying out for revision** *or* **to be revised** le système a grand besoin d'être révisé; *Fam* **for crying out loud!** bon sang!
2 *vt sep* s'écrier; **"listen," she cried out** "écoutez," s'écria-t-elle

►**cry up** *vt sep* prôner, exalter

'Cry, the Beloved Country' *Paton* 'Pleure, ô pays bien-aimé'

crybaby ['kraɪ,beɪbɪ] *(pl* **crybabies**) *n Fam* pleurnichard(e) *m,f*

crying ['kraɪɪŋ] **1** *adj* (**a**) *(person)* qui pleure, pleurant (**b**) *Fam (as intensifier)* criant, flagrant; **there is a crying need for more teachers** on a un besoin urgent d'enseignants ❑; **it's a crying shame** c'est un scandale ❑
2 *n (UNCOUNT)* (**a**) *(shouting)* cri *m*, cris *mpl*; **we could hear the crying of the baby** on entendait les cris du bébé (**b**) *(weeping)* pleurs *mpl*; **stop your crying** arrête de pleurer

cryobiology [,kraɪəʊbaɪ'ɒlədʒɪ] *n* cryobiologie *f*

cryogen ['kraɪəʊdʒen] *n Phys* cryogène *m*

cryogenic [,kraɪə'dʒenɪk] *adj Phys* cryogène

cryogenics [,kraɪə'dʒenɪks] *n (UNCOUNT) Phys (science)* cryologie *f*; *(production)* cryogénie *f*

cryohydrate [,kraɪəʊ'haɪdreɪt] *n Chem* cryohydrate *m*

cryolite ['kraɪəlaɪt] *n Geol* cryolithe *f*

cryonics [kraɪ'ɒnɪks] *n (UNCOUNT) Biol* cryogénisation *f*

cryoscopic [,kraɪəʊ'skɒpɪk] *adj Phys* cryoscopique

cryoscopy [kraɪ'ɒskəpɪ] *n Phys* cryoscopie *f*

cryostat ['kraɪəʊstæt] *n Phys* cryostat *m*

cryosurgery [,kraɪəʊ'sɜːdʒərɪ] *n Med* cryo-chirurgie *f*

cryotherapy [,kraɪəʊ'θerəpɪ] *n Med* cryothérapie *f*

crypt [krɪpt] *n* crypte *f*

cryptanalysis [,krɪptə'næləsɪs] *n* cryptographie *f*

cryptic ['krɪptɪk] *adj (secret)* secret(ète); *(obscure)* énigmatique, sibyllin; **he was very cryptic about his future plans** il a été très mystérieux sur ses projets d'avenir
►► ***cryptic crossword*** = mots croisés dont les définitions sont des énigmes qu'il faut résoudre

cryptically ['krɪptɪkəlɪ] *adv (secretly)* secrètement; *(obscurely)* énigmatiquement

crypto ['krɪptəʊ] *n Fam Med* cryptosporidiose ❑ *f*

crypto- ['krɪptəʊ] *pref* crypto-; **crypto-fascist** cryptofasciste *mf*

cryptococcosis [,krɪptəʊkɒ'kəʊsɪs] *n Med* cryptococcose *f*

cryptogam ['krɪptəʊgæm] *n Bot* cryptogame *m or f*

cryptogamic [,krɪptəʊ'gæmɪk], **cryptogamous** [krɪp'tɒgəməs] *adj Bot* cryptogamique

cryptogenetic [,krɪptəʊdʒə'netɪk], **cryptogenic** [,krɪptəʊ'dʒenɪk] *adj Med* cryptogénétique, cryptogénique

cryptogram ['krɪptəʊgræm] *n* cryptogramme *m*

cryptographer [krɪp'tɒgrəfə(r)] *n* cryptographe *mf*

cryptographic [,krɪptə'græfɪk] *adj* cryptographique
►► *Comput* ***cryptographic key*** *(on Internet)* clé *f* de chiffrement

cryptography [krɪp'tɒgrəfɪ], **cryptology** [krɪp'tɒlədʒɪ] *n* cryptographie *f*

cryptosporidiosis [,krɪptəʊspə,rɪdɪ'əʊsɪs] *n Med* cryptosporidiose *f*

cryptosporidium [,krɪptəʊspə'rɪdɪəm] *(pl* **cryptosporidia** [-ɪə]) *n Biol* cryptosporidium *m*

crystal ['krɪstəl] **1** *n* (**a**) *(gen) & Miner* cristal *m*; **as clear as crystal** clair comme le jour *ou* comme de l'eau de roche
(**b**) *(chip)* cristal *m*; **salt/snow crystals** cristaux *mpl* de sel/de neige
(**c**) *Am (of watch)* verre *m* (de montre)
(**d**) *Electron* galène *f*
2 *adj (vase, glass, water)* de cristal
►► ***crystal ball*** boule *f* de cristal; ***crystal factory*** cristallerie *f*; ***crystal healing*** = utilisation de cristaux à des fins curatives; ***Crystal Palace*** = édifice de verre et d'acier construit à Londres en 1851 et détruit en 1936 par un incendie, qui a donné son nom à un terrain de football; *Rad* ***crystal set*** poste *m* à galène

crystal-clear *adj* clair comme le jour *ou* comme de l'eau de roche; *(voice)* cristalline; **it's all crystal-clear to me now** ça me paraît clair comme de l'eau de roche maintenant; **to make sth crystal-clear** rendre qch bien clair

crystal-gazer *n* voyant(e) *m,f (qui lit dans une boule de cristal)*

crystal-gazing *n (UNCOUNT) (in ball)* (art *m* de la) voyance *f*; *Fig* prédictions *fpl*, prophéties *fpl*

crystalline ['krɪstəlaɪn] *n Chem & Miner* cristallin
►► *Opt* ***crystalline lens*** cristallin *m*

crystallinity [krɪstə'lɪnɪtɪ] *n Miner* cristallinité *f*

crystallite ['krɪstəlaɪt] *n Miner* cristallite *f*

crystallization [,krɪstəlaɪ'zeɪʃən] *n (gen) & Chem* cristallisation *f*

crystallize, -ise ['krɪstəlaɪz] **1** *vi also Fig* se cristalliser
2 *vt* cristalliser; *(sugar)* (faire) candir
►► ***crystallized fruit*** fruits *mpl* confits

crystallographer [,krɪstə'lɒgrəfə(r)] *n Miner* cristallographe *mf*

crystallographic [,krɪstələʊ'græfɪk], **crystallographical** [,krɪstələʊ'græfɪkəl] *adj Miner* cristallographique

crystallography [,krɪstə'lɒgrəfɪ] *n Miner* cristallographie *f*

crystalloid ['krɪstəlɔɪd] *Chem* **1** *adj* cristalloïde
2 *n* cristalloïde *m*

CSA [,siːes'eɪ] *n* (**a**) *Hist (abbr* **Confederate States of America**) États *mpl* confédérés d'Amérique (**b**) *Br Admin (abbr* **Child Support Agency**) = en Grande-Bretagne, organisme gouvernemental qui décide du montant des pensions alimentaires et les prélève au besoin

CSC [,siːes'siː] *n Admin (abbr* **Civil Service Commission**) = commission de recrutement des fonctionnaires

CSCE [,siːessiː'iː] *n EU (abbr* **Council for Security and Cooperation in Europe**) CSCE *f*

CSD [,siːes'diː] *n Banking & St Exch (abbr* **Central Securities Depository**) depositaire *m* national de titres

CSE [,siːes'iː] *n Formerly Sch (abbr* **Certificate of Secondary Education**) = ancien brevet de l'enseignement secondaire en Grande-Bretagne, aujourd'hui remplacé par le GCSE

C-section *n Obst* césarienne *f*

CSEU [,siːes,iː'juː] *n Br (abbr* **Confederation of Shipbuilding and Engineering Unions**) = confédération britannique des syndicats de la construction navale et de la mécanique

CS gas [siː,es-] *n Br Chem* gaz *m* CS *ou* lacrymogène

CSM [,siːes'em] *n Mil (abbr* **Company Sergeant-Major**) adjudant *m*

CST [,siːes'tiː] *n Am (abbr* **Central Standard Time**) heure *f* d'hiver du centre des États-Unis

CSU [,siːes'juː] *n Br (abbr* **Civil Service Union**) = syndicat britannique de la fonction publique

CSV [,siːes'viː] *npl Comput (abbr* **comma-separated values**) valeurs *fpl* séparées par des virgules

CSYS [,siːes,waɪ'es] *n Scot Sch (abbr* **Certificate of Sixth Year Studies**) = certificat sanctionnant une année d'étude supplémentaire facultative avant l'entrée à l'université, en Écosse

CT[1] [,siː'tiː] *n Med (abbr* **computerized tomography**) TDM *f*; **a CT (scan)** une scanographie

CT[2] *(written abbr* **Connecticut**) Connecticut *m*

ct *(written abbr* **carat**) ct

CTC [,siːtiː'siː] *n (abbr* **city technology college**) = collège technique britannique, généralement établi dans des quartiers défavorisés

cu. *(written abbr* **cubic**) **cu. cm** cm^3; **cu. metre** m^3

cub [kʌb] *n* (**a**) *(animal → gen)* petit(e) *m,f*; *(→ of fox)* renardeau *m*; *(→ of bear)* ourson *m*; *(→ of lion)* lionceau *m*; *(→ of wolf)* louveteau *m*; **a lioness and her cubs** une lionne et ses petits
(**b**) *(youngster)* **young cub** jeune blanc-bec *m*
(**c**) *(scout)* louveteau *m (scout)*; **he goes to Cubs on Fridays** il va à la réunion des louveteaux le vendredi
►► ***cub master*** chef *m (des scouts)*; ***cub mistress*** cheftaine *f (des scouts)*; ***cub reporter*** jeune journaliste *mf*; ***cub scout, Cub Scout*** louveteau *m (scout)*

Cuba ['kjuːbə] *n* Cuba; **in Cuba** à Cuba
►► ***Cuba libre*** *(cocktail)* = cocktail contenant du Coca®, du rhum et du jus de citron vert

Cuban ['kjuːbən] **1** *n* Cubain(e) *m,f*
2 *adj* cubain
3 *comp (embassy, history)* de Cuba
►► ***Cuban heel*** talon *m* cubain; ***the Cuban missile crisis*** la crise de Cuba *(conflit américano-soviétique dû à la présence de missiles soviétiques à Cuba en 1962)*

cubbyhole ['kʌbɪhəʊl] *n* (**a**) *(cupboard)* débarras *m*, remise *f*; *(small room)* cagibi *m*, réduit *m* (**b**) *(in desk)* case *f*; *Aut* vide-poches *m inv*

cube [kjuːb] **1** *n (gen) & Math* cube *m*
2 *vt* (**a**) *(cut into cubes)* couper en cubes *ou* en dés (**b**) *Math* cuber; *Tech (measure)* cuber
►► *Math* ***cube root*** racine *f* cubique

cubic ['kjuːbɪk] *adj Math (shape, volume)* cubique; *(measurement)* cube
►► ***cubic capacity*** volume *m*; ***cubic centimetre*** centimètre cube; ***cubic content*** capacité *f* cubique; ***cubic equation*** équation *f* du troisième degré; ***cubic inch*** pouce *m* cube; ***cubic metre*** mètre *m* cube

cubical ['kjuːbɪkəl] *adj Math* cubique, en (forme de) cube

cubicle ['kjuːbɪkəl] *n (in dormitory, hospital ward)* alcôve *f*, box *m*; *(in swimming baths)* cabine *f*; *(in public toilets)* W-C *mpl*; *(for trying on clothes)* cabine *f* d'essayage

cubiform ['kjuːbɪfɔːm] *adj Math* cubique, en (forme de) cube

cubism, Cubism ['kjuːbɪzəm] *n Art* cubisme *m*

cubist, Cubist ['kjuːbɪst] *Art* **1** *adj* cubiste
2 *n* cubiste *mf*

cubit ['kjuːbɪt] *n (measurement)* coudée *f (unité de mesure)*

cuboid ['kjuːbɔɪd] **1** *n* (**a**) *Anat (bone)* cuboïde *m* (**b**) *Math (figure)* parallélépipède *m* rectangle
2 *adj* (**a**) *Anat* cuboïde (**b**) *Math* cuboïde

cuckold ['kʌkəʊld] **1** *n* (mari *m*) cocu *m*
2 *vt* faire cocu, cocufier

cuckoldry ['kʌkəʊldrɪ] *n* cocuage *m*

cuckoo ['kʊkuː] *(pl* **cuckoos**) **1** *n* (**a**) *(bird, sound)* coucou *m* (**b**) *Fam (mad person)* imbécile ❑ *mf*, idiot(e) ❑ *m,f*
2 *adj Fam (mad)* loufoque, toqué; **to go cuckoo** perdre la boule
►► ***cuckoo clock*** coucou *m (pendule)*; *Bot* ***cuckoo flower*** cardamine *f* des prés; *Bot* ***cuckoo spit*** crachat *m* de coucou; *Ich* ***cuckoo wrasse*** vieille *f* coquette

cuckoopint ['kʊkuːpaɪnt] *n Bot* pied-de-veau *m*

cucumber ['kjuːkʌmbə(r)] *n* concombre *m*
►► ***cucumber sandwich*** = petit sandwich au pain de mie et au concombre *(l'expression est parfois utilisée pour évoquer certains milieux bourgeois)*

cud [kʌd] *n* bol *m* alimentaire *(d'un ruminant)*; **to chew the cud** *(of cow etc)* ruminer; *Fig (of person)* ruminer une idée, méditer

cuddle ['kʌdəl] **1** *vi* se faire un câlin, se câliner; **they were cuddling on the sofa** ils se faisaient un câlin sur le divan
2 *vt* câliner; *(child)* bercer *(dans ses bras)*
3 *n* câlin *m*; **they were having a cuddle** ils se faisaient un câlin; **she gave the child a cuddle** elle a fait un câlin à l'enfant

►**cuddle up** *vi* se blottir, se pelotonner; **she**

cuddled up close to him elle se blottit contre lui; **they cuddled up to each other for warmth** ils se sont pelotonnés *ou* blottis l'un contre l'autre pour se tenir chaud

cuddlesome ['kʌdəlsəm] *adj (child, animal)* mignon à croquer; *(soft toy)* tout doux, *f* toute douce

cuddly ['kʌdlɪ] *(compar* **cuddlier,** *superl* **cuddliest)** *adj (child, animal)* mignon à croquer; *(soft toy)* tout(e) doux (douce); *Euph (plump)* rond
▸▸ ***cuddly toy*** peluche *f*

cudgel ['kʌdʒəl] *(Br pt & pp* **cudgelled,** *cont* **cudgelling,** *Am pt & pp* **cudgeled,** *cont* **cudgeling)**
1 *n* gourdin *m*, trique *f*; *Fig* **to take up** *or* **to carry the cudgels for sb/sth** prendre fait et cause pour qn/qch
2 *vt* battre à coups de gourdin; **to cudgel sb to death** tuer qn à coups de gourdin; *Fam Fig* **he cudgelled his brains** il s'est creusé la tête *ou* le cerveau

cue [kju:] **1** *n* **(a)** *Theat (verbal)* réplique *f*; *Cin & TV (action)* signal *m*; *Mus* signal *m* d'entrée; *Theat* **to give sb their cue** donner la réplique à qn; *Theat* **to miss one's cue** manquer la réplique; *Cin & TV* rater le signal; **he took his cue** il a entamé sa réplique
(b) *Fig (signal)* signal *m*; **on cue** au bon moment; **to take one's cue from sb** prendre exemple sur qn; **her cough was my cue to enter** elle devait tousser pour signaler que je pouvais entrer; **her yawn was our cue to leave** nous avons compris qu'il fallait partir quand elle s'est mise à bâiller; **right on cue, the door opened** la porte s'est ouverte juste au bon moment *ou* à point nommé
(c) *(for snooker, pool)* queue *f (de billard)*; **cue rack** porte-queue *m*
(d) *(of hair)* queue *f (de cheval)*
2 *vi (in snooker, pool)* queuter
3 *vt (prompt)* donner le signal à; *Theat* donner la réplique à
▸▸ ***cue ball*** *(ball)* bille *f* de joueur; *Am Fam (bald person)* chauve[□] *mf*; *Cards* ***cue bid*** = annonce qui montre un as ou un vide
▸**cue in** *vt sep Theat* donner la réplique à; *Cin & TV* donner le signal à

cuesta ['kwestə] *n Geol* cuesta *f*

cuff [kʌf] **1** *n* **(a)** *(of sleeve)* poignet *m*; *(that takes cuff links)* manchette *f*; *(of glove)* poignet *m*; *(of coat)* parement *m*; *Am (of trousers)* revers *m*; **off the cuff** à l'improviste; **she was speaking off the cuff** elle improvisait son discours, elle faisait un discours improvisé; **I can't tell you off the cuff** je ne peux pas te le dire comme ça *ou* tout de suite; *Am* **he bought it on the cuff** il l'a acheté à crédit
(b) *(blow)* gifle *f*, claque *f*; **I got a cuff round the ear** j'ai reçu une claque *ou* une gifle
2 *vt* **(a)** *(hit)* gifler, donner une gifle *ou* une claque à
(b) *Fam (handcuff)* mettre *ou* passer les menottes à
(c) *Am (trousers)* faire un revers à
3 cuffs *npl Fam (handcuffs)* menottes *fpl*[□], bracelets *mpl*
▸▸ ***cuff link*** bouton *m* de manchette

cu.in. *(written abbr* **cubic inch(es)**) pouce *m* cube

cuirass [kwɪ'ræs] *n* cuirasse *f*

Cuisinart® ['kwɪzɪnɑ:t] *n Am* robot *m* ménager

cuisine [kwɪ'zi:n] *n* cuisine *f*

culchie ['kʌltʃɪ] *n Ir Fam Pej* plouc *mf*, péquenaud(e) *m,f*

cul-de-sac ['kʌldəsæk] *n* cul-de-sac *m*, impasse *f*; *Fig* impasse *f*; **cul-de-sac** *(sign)* voie sans issue

culinary ['kʌlɪnərɪ] *adj* culinaire

cull [kʌl] **1** *vt* **(a)** *(sample)* sélectionner **(b)** *(remove from herd → animal)* éliminer, supprimer; **to cull a herd of deer** = abattre une partie d'un troupeau de daims pour en réduire la taille **(c)** *(gather → flowers, fruit)* cueillir
2 *n* **(a)** *(killing)* élimination *f* **(b)** *(animal)* animal *m* à éliminer

cullender ['kʌlɪndə(r)] *n* passoire *f*

cullen skink [ˌkʌlən'skɪŋk] *n Scot Culin* = potage au haddock fumé, aux pommes de terre et à la crème

culling ['kʌlɪŋ] *n (of herd)* élimination *f (pour éviter la prolifération)*

Culloden Moor [kə'lɒdən-] *n* = site de la bataille de Culloden, près d'Inverness

> **CULLODEN**
>
> 
>
> C'est à l'issue de cette bataille, en 1746, que les partisans écossais de Charles-Édouard Stuart (surnommé "Bonnie Prince Charlie"), prétendant catholique au trône, furent vaincus par l'armée anglaise aux ordres du roi George II, monarque protestant de la maison de Hanovre. À la suite de cette bataille les Anglais entreprirent une campagne de répression féroce en Écosse, principalement dans les Highlands. Cette défaite sonna le glas de la culture gaélique des Highlands.

culminate ['kʌlmɪˌneɪt] *vi Astron* culminer
▸**culminate in** *vt insep* **to culminate in sth** *(undesirable)* se terminer en *ou* par qch; *(desirable)* aboutir à qch; **the demonstration culminated in a riot** la manifestation s'est terminée en émeute; **the excavations culminated in the discovery of a temple** les fouilles ont abouti à la découverte d'un temple; **the disagreement culminated in the end of their friendship** le différend a mis fin à leur amitié

culminating ['kʌlmɪneɪtɪŋ] *adj* culminant

culmination [ˌkʌlmɪ'neɪʃən] *n* **(a)** *(climax → of career)* apogée *m*; *(→ of efforts)* maximum *m*; *(→ of disagreement)* point *m* culminant **(b)** *Astron* culmination *f*

culottes [kju:'lɒts] *npl* jupe-culotte *f*

culpability [ˌkʌlpə'bɪlətɪ] *n* culpabilité *f*

culpable ['kʌlpəbəl] *adj Formal* coupable
▸▸ *Scot Law* ***culpable homicide*** homicide *m* involontaire; ***culpable negligence*** négligence *f* coupable

culpably ['kʌlpəblɪ] *adv* coupablement, d'une manière coupable

culprit ['kʌlprɪt] *n (guilty person)* coupable *mf*; **I'm the culprit** c'est moi le coupable; **poor housing is the main culprit** ce sont les mauvaises conditions de logement qui sont principalement responsables

cult [kʌlt] **1** *n Fig or Rel* culte *m*; **personality cult** culte *m* de la personnalité; **it's become something of a minor cult** cela a suscité un véritable engouement; **the film has a cult following** c'est un film culte
2 *comp (book, film)* culte
▸▸ ***cult figure*** idole *f*

cultism ['kʌltɪzəm] *n* cultisme *m*

cultist ['kʌltɪst] *n* cultiste *mf*

cultivar ['kʌltɪˌvɑ:(r)] *n Bot* cultivar *m*

cultivate ['kʌltɪveɪt] *vt* **(a)** *(land)* cultiver, exploiter; *(crop)* cultiver **(b)** *Biol (bacillus)* faire une culture de **(c)** *Fig (idea, person, friendship)* cultiver; **reading is the best way to cultivate the mind** la lecture est le meilleur moyen de se cultiver (l'esprit)

cultivated ['kʌltɪveɪtɪd] *adj (land)* cultivé, exploité; *(person)* cultivé; *(voice)* distingué

cultivation [ˌkʌltɪ'veɪʃən] *n* **(a)** *(of land, crops)* culture *f*; **fields under cultivation** cultures *fpl* **(b)** *Fig (of taste)* éducation *f*; *(of relations)* entretien *m*

cultivator ['kʌltɪveɪtə(r)] *n (person)* cultivateur(-trice) *m,f*; *(tool)* cultivateur *m*; *(power-driven)* motoculteur *m*

cultural ['kʌltʃərəl] *adj* **(a)** *(background, institute)* culturel; **the cultural environment** le milieu culturel **(b)** *Agr* de culture, cultural
▸▸ ***cultural anthropology*** culturologie *f*; *Fig* ***a cultural desert*** un désert culturel; ***cultural event*** manifestation *f* culturelle; ***cultural integration*** acculturation *f*; ***cultural literacy*** culture *f* générale; ***the Cultural Revolution*** la Révolution culturelle

culturally ['kʌltʃərəlɪ] *adv* culturellement

culture ['kʌltʃə(r)] **1** *n* **(a)** *(civilization, learning)* culture *f*; **popular/youth culture** culture *f* populaire/des jeunes; **a man of culture** un homme cultivé *ou* qui a de la culture; **to have no culture** être inculte
(b) *(ethos, environment)* **the system breeds a culture of nepotism** ce système favorise le copinage à tous les niveaux; **the culture of violence inherent in some forms of nationalism** la violence inhérente à certaines formes de nationalisme; **a society characterized by a culture of individualism** une société où l'individualisme règne en maître
(c) *Sport* **physical culture** culture *f* physique
(d) *Agr (of land, crops)* culture *f*; *(of animals)* élevage *m*; *(of fowl)* aviculture *f*
(e) *Biol* culture *f*
2 *vt (plants)* cultiver; *(animals)* élever; *(bacteria)* faire une culture de
▸▸ ***culture gap*** fossé *m* culturel; *Biol* ***culture medium*** milieu *m* de culture; ***culture shock*** choc *m* culturel; *Fam Hum* ***culture vulture*** fana *mf* de culture, culturophage *mf*

cultured ['kʌltʃəd] *adj* **(a)** *(refined → person)* cultivé, lettré; *Fig* **the fullback has a cultured left foot** l'arrière a un très bon pied gauche **(b)** *(grown artificially)* cultivé
▸▸ ***cultured pearls*** perles *fpl* de culture

culvert ['kʌlvət] *n Tech (for water)* caniveau *m*; *(for cable)* conduit *m*

cum [kʌm] **1** *prep* avec; **a kitchen-cum-dining area** une cuisine avec coin-repas; **he's a teacher-cum-philosopher** il est philosophe et enseignant
2 *n Vulg (semen)* foutre *m*

Cumberland ['kʌmbələnd]
▸▸ *Culin* ***Cumberland sauce*** = sauce servie avec le canard ou l'oie, à base de gelée de groseille, de porto et de jus d'orange; *Culin* ***Cumberland sausage*** = type de saucisse produite dans le nord-ouest de l'Angleterre

cumbersome ['kʌmbəsəm] *adj (bulky)* encombrant, embarrassant; *Fig (process, system, style)* lourd, pesant

cumbersomeness ['kʌmbəsəmnɪs] *n (bulkiness)* incommodité *f*; *Fig (of process, system, style)* lourdeur *f*

Cumbria ['kʌmbrɪə] *n* le Cumbria, = comté dans le nord-ouest de l'Angleterre; **in Cumbria** dans le Cumbria

cumin ['kju:mɪn] *n* cumin *m*

cum laude [kʌm'lɔ:dɪ] *adv Univ* avec distinction

cummerbund ['kʌməbʌnd] *n* large ceinture *f (de smoking)*

cumulative ['kju:mjʊlətɪv] *adj* cumulatif
▸▸ *Fin* ***cumulative balance*** solde *m* cumulé; *Law* ***cumulative evidence*** preuve *f* par accumulation de témoignages; *Fin* ***cumulative interest*** intérêts *mpl* cumulatifs; *St Exch* ***cumulative preference share*** action *f* privilégiée; *Fin* ***cumulative profit*** bénéfice *m* cumulé; *Pol* ***cumulative voting*** vote *m* plural

cumulatively ['kju:mjʊlətɪvlɪ] *adv* de façon cumulée

cumuli ['kju:mjʊlaɪ] *pl of* **cumulus**

cumulonimbus [ˌkju:mjʊləʊ'nɪmbəs] *(pl* **cumulonimbi** [-baɪ] *or* **cumulonimbuses)** *n Met* cumulo-nimbus *m*

cumulus ['kju:mjʊləs] *(pl* **cumuli** [-laɪ]) *n Met* cumulus *m*

cuneiform ['kju:nɪfɔ:m] **1** *adj* cunéiforme
2 *n* écriture *f* cunéiforme

cunnilingus [ˌkʌnɪ'lɪŋgəs] *n* cunnilingus *m*

cunning ['kʌnɪŋ] **1** *adj* **(a)** *(shrewd)* astucieux, malin(igne); *Pej* rusé, fourbe; **he's as cunning as a fox** il est rusé comme un renard **(b)** *(skilful)* habile, astucieux **(c)** *Am (cute)* mignon, charmant
2 *n* **(a)** *(guile)* finesse *f*, astuce *f*; *Pej* ruse *f*, fourberie *f* **(b)** *(skill)* habileté *f*, adresse *f*

> **I have a cunning plan**
>
> La série télévisée comique *Blackadder* a été diffusée pendant de nombreuses années en Grande-Bretagne. Baldrick, qui en était l'un des personnages principaux et qui était particulièrement stupide, inventait toujours des stratagèmes qu'il présentait à son maître précédés de la formule **I have a cunning plan** ("J'ai un plan des plus ingénieux").
> Aujourd'hui on utilise cette phrase sur le mode humoristique en référence à la série télévisée ou bien lorsque quelqu'un est sur le point d'expliquer un projet qu'il a conçu.

cunningly ['kʌnɪŋlɪ] *adv* **(a)** *(shrewdly)* astucieusement, finement; *Pej* avec ruse *ou* fourberie **(b)** *(skilfully)* habilement, astucieusement

cunt [kʌnt] *n Vulg* (**a**) *(vagina)* con *m*, chatte *f* (**b**) *Pej (man)* enculé *m*; *(woman)* salope *f*

cup [kʌp] (*pt & pp* **cupped,** *cont* **cupping**) **1** *n* (**a**) *(for drinking, cupful)* tasse *f*; *Rel* calice *m*; **a cup of coffee** une tasse de café; **would you like another cup?** en voulez-vous encore une tasse?; **add two cups of sugar** ajoutez deux tasses de sucre; *Literary* **my cup runneth over** mon bonheur est complet *ou* parfait; *Literary* **he drained the cup of sorrow** il a bu la coupe jusqu'à la lie; **that's just her cup of tea** c'est tout à fait à son goût; *Fam* **he's not (really) my cup of tea** il n'est pas (tout à fait) mon genre; *Fam* **rap isn't everyone's cup of tea** tout le monde n'aime pas le rap; *Fam Old-fashioned* **he was in his cups** il avait du vent dans les voiles
(**b**) *Sport (trophy, competition)* coupe *f*
(**c**) *(shape → of plant)* corolle *f*; *(→ of bone)* cavité *f* articulaire, glène *f*; *(→ of bra)* bonnet *m*
(**d**) *(drink)* **champagne/cider cup** cocktail *m* au champagne/cidre; **fruit cup** cocktail *m* aux fruits *(pouvant contenir de l'alcool)*
(**e**) *Tech* godet *m*, cuvette *f*
(**f**) *Golf* trou *m*
2 *comp* (**a**) *Sport (winners, holders, match)* de coupe
(**b**) *(handle)* de tasse; *(rack)* pour tasses
3 *vt* (**a**) *(hands)* mettre en coupe; *(hold)* **to cup one's hands around sth** mettre ses mains autour de qch; **he cupped a hand to his ear** il mit sa main derrière son oreille; **she cupped her hands around her mouth and shouted** elle mit ses mains en porte-voix et cria; **he sat with his chin cupped in his hand** il était assis, le menton dans le creux de sa main
(**b**) *Med (with cupping glass)* appliquer des ventouses sur
►► *Sport* ***cup final*** finale *f* de la coupe; *Br Ftbl* ***the Cup Final*** la finale de la Coupe de Football; *Sport* ***cup finalist*** finaliste *mf* de la coupe; ***cup size*** *(of bra)* profondeur *f* de bonnet; *Sport* ***cup tie*** match *m* de coupe

> **The cup that cheers**
> "Le breuvage qui réconforte"; il s'agit du slogan d'une vieille publicité pour une marque de thé. Aujourd'hui, on utilise cette expression pour parler du thé en général; on pourra dire par exemple **this café makes the best cup that cheers for miles around** ("ce café sert le meilleur thé à des lieux à la ronde").

cup-and-ball joint *n Tech* joint *m* à rotule

cupbearer ['kʌpˌbeərə(r)] *n Hist* échanson *m*

cupboard ['kʌbəd] *n (on wall)* placard *m*; *(free-standing → for dishes, pans)* buffet *m*, placard *m*; *(→ for clothes)* placard *m*, armoire *f*; *Fig* **the cupboard is bare** il n'y a rien à se mettre sous la dent
►► *Br* ***cupboard love*** amour *m* intéressé

cupcake ['kʌpkeɪk] *n* (**a**) *(cake)* petit gâteau *m (dans une caissette en papier)* (**b**) *(term of affection)* mon chou, ma puce (**c**) *Am Fam (eccentric person)* allumé(e) *m,f* (**d**) *Am (homosexual)* pédale *f*, tantouze *f*, = terme injurieux désignant un homosexuel

cupful ['kʌpfʊl] *n* tasse *f*; **a cupful of sugar** une tasse de sucre

Cupid ['kju:pɪd] **1** *pr n Myth* Cupidon *m*; *Fig* **to play Cupid** jouer les entremetteurs(euses)
2 cupid *n Art (cherub)* chérubin *m*, amour *m*
►► ***Cupid's arrow*** les flèches *fpl* de Cupidon; ***Cupid's bow*** bouche *f* en forme de cœur; ***Cupid's dart*** les flèches *fpl* de Cupidon

cupidity [kju:'pɪdɪtɪ] *n* cupidité *f*

cupola ['kju:pələ] *n* (**a**) *Archit (ceiling, roof)* coupole *f*, dôme *m*; *(tower)* belvédère *m* (**b**) *Naut* coupole *f* (**c**) *Metal (furnace)* cubilot *m*

cuppa ['kʌpə] *n Br Fam* tasse *f* de thé ❑

cupping glass ['kʌpɪŋ-] *n Med* ventouse *f*

cupreous ['kju:prɪəs] *adj Chem* cuivreux

cupric ['kju:prɪk] *adj Chem* cuprique
►► ***cupric oxide*** oxyde *m* de cuivre

cuprite ['kju:praɪt] *n Miner* cuprite *f*

cupro-nickel [ˌkju:prəʊ-] *n* cupronickel *m*

cuprous ['kju:prəs] *adj Chem* cuivreux

cup-shaped *adj Bot* cupulaire

cup-tied *adj Sport (player)* disqualifié pour un match de coupe

cur [kɜ:(r)] *n Old-fashioned or Literary* (**a**) *(dog)* (chien *m*) bâtard *m*, sale chien *m* (**b**) *(person)* malotru(e) *m,f*, roquet *m*

curability [kjʊərə'bɪlɪtɪ] *n* curabilité *f*

curable ['kjʊərəbəl] *adj* guérissable, curable

curaçao ['kjʊərəsəʊ] *n* curaçao *m*

curacy ['kjʊərəsɪ] (*pl* **curacies**) *n Rel* vicariat *m*

curare, curari [kjʊ'rɑ:rɪ] *n Bot* curare *m*

curassow [kjʊərə'səʊ] *n Orn* hocco *m*

curate ['kjʊərət] *n Rel* vicaire *m (de l'Église anglicane)*; *Br* **it's a curate's egg** il y a du bon et du mauvais

curative ['kjʊərətɪv] *adj* curatif

curator [ˌkjʊə'reɪtə(r)] *n* (**a**) *(of museum)* conservateur(trice) *m,f* (**b**) *Scot (guardian)* curateur(-trice) *m,f*

curatorship [ˌkjʊə'reɪtəʃɪp] *n* (**a**) *(of museum)* fonction *f* de conservateur (**b**) *Scot (of child)* fonction *f* de curateur

curb [kɜ:b] **1** *n* (**a**) *(restraint)* frein *m*; **a curb on trade** une restriction au commerce; **to put a curb on sb's enthusiasm** mettre un frein à l'enthousiasme de qn; **she put a curb on her anger** elle a refréné sa colère
(**b**) *(of well)* margelle *f*
(**c**) *Am* = **kerb**
2 *vt* (**a**) *(restrain → emotion)* refréner, maîtriser; *(→ expenses)* restreindre, mettre un frein à; *(→ child)* modérer, freiner; **curb your tongue!** mesure tes paroles!
(**b**) *(horse)* mettre un mors à
(**c**) *Am* **curb your dog** *(sign)* votre chien doit faire ses besoins dans le caniveau
►► ***curb bit*** *(on harness)* mors *m*; ***curb chain*** gourmette *f*; ***curb reins*** rênes *fpl* de filet; *Archit* ***curb roof*** comble *m* brisé; *Am* ***curb service*** service *m* au volant *(dans un restaurant drive-in)*

curb-side service *n Am* service *m* au volant *(dans un restaurant drive-in)*

curbstone *Am* = **kerbstone**

curd [kɜ:d] *n (usu pl) (of milk)* caillot *m*, grumeau *m*; **curds** lait *m* caillé, caillebotte *f*; **curds and whey** lait *m* caillé sucré
►► ***curd cheese*** fromage *m* blanc battu

curdle ['kɜ:dəl] **1** *vi (milk)* cailler; *(sauce)* tourner; *(mayonnaise)* tomber; *Fig* **his screams made my blood curdle** ses cris m'ont glacé le sang
2 *vt (milk)* cailler; *(sauce)* faire tourner; *(mayonnaise)* faire tomber; *Fig* **the thought's enough to curdle one's blood** c'est une idée à vous glacer le sang

cure [kjʊə(r)] **1** *vt* (**a**) *(disease, person)* guérir; *Fig (problem)* éliminer, remédier à; **he was cured of cancer** il a été guéri du cancer; **the nap seems to have cured my headache** on dirait que la sieste m'a fait passer mon mal de tête; **he cured himself of nailbiting** il a réussi à arrêter de se ronger les ongles; *Fig* **his experiences in politics cured him of all his illusions** son expérience de la politique lui a fait perdre toutes ses illusions; *Prov* **what can't be cured must be endured** il faut prendre son mal en patience
(**b**) *(tobacco, meat, fish → gen)* traiter; *(→ with salt)* saler; *(→ by smoking)* fumer; *(→ by drying)* sécher
2 *n* (**a**) *(remedy)* remède *m*, cure *f*; **a cure for the common cold** un remède contre le rhume de cerveau; **there's no known cure** on ne connaît pas de remède; **to take** *or* **to follow a cure** faire une cure; *Fig* **a cure for all ills** la panacée
(**b**) *(recovery)* guérison *f*; **to be beyond** *or* **past cure** *(person)* être incurable *Fig (problem, situation)* être irrémédiable
(**c**) *Rel* **the cure of souls** la charge d'âmes

cure-all *n* panacée *f*

curettage [ˌkjʊərɪ'tɑ:ʒ, ˌkjʊə'retɪdʒ] *n Med* curetage *m*

curfew ['kɜ:fju:] *n* couvre-feu *m*; **the authorities imposed a/lifted the curfew** les autorités ont imposé/levé le couvre-feu; *Am Fig* **to be under curfew** *(teenager)* devoir rentrer à une heure précise

curia ['kjʊərɪə] *n* (**a**) *Antiq & Rel* curie *f* (**b**) *Hist* cour *f* de justice

curie ['kjʊərɪ] *n Phys* curie *m*

curing ['kjʊərɪŋ] *n* (**a**) *(of disease, patient)* guérison *f* (**b**) *(of meat, tobacco, fish → gen)* traitement *m*; *(→ by salting)* salaison *f*; *(→ by smoking)* fumaison *f*; *(→ by drying)* séchage *m*

curio ['kjʊərɪəʊ] (*pl* **curios**) *n* curiosité *f*, bibelot *m*

curiosity [kjʊərɪ'ɒsətɪ] (*pl* **curiosities**) *n* (**a**) *(interest)* curiosité *f*; **out of curiosity** par curiosité; *Prov* **curiosity killed the cat** la curiosité est un vilain défaut (**b**) *(novelty → object)* curiosité *f*; *(→ person)* bête *f* curieuse; **they considered me to be something of a curiosity** on me regardait un peu comme une bête curieuse

curious ['kjʊərɪəs] *adj* (**a**) *(inquisitive)* curieux; **I'm curious to see/know** je suis curieux de voir/savoir; **I'm curious as to what happened next** je serais curieux de savoir ce qui s'est passé après (**b**) *(strange)* curieux, singulier; **the curious thing (about it) is...** ce qui est curieux là-dedans *ou* dans tout ça, c'est...; **a curious looking object** un objet bizarre

> **Curiouser and curiouser**
> Cette expression trouve son origine dans *Alice in Wonderland* ("Alice au pays des merveilles") de Lewis Carroll (1865), lorsqu'Alice prend conscience de l'étrangeté du pays où elle a échoué.
> On utilise cette expression ("de plus en plus étrange") pour exprimer sa surprise ou sa perplexité, parfois de façon ironique comme dans l'exemple suivant: **hmmm, curiouser and curiouser, first she goes away for the weekend unexpectedly, then she gets a new hairstyle, then she keeps mentioning her "friend" Lawrence** ("tiens, c'est de plus en plus étrange, d'abord elle part en week-end sans prévenir, ensuite elle change de coiffure, et en plus elle n'arrête pas de parler de son 'ami' Lawrence"). C'est sans doute parce que cette formule est grammaticalement incorrecte qu'elle a marqué les esprits (la forme correcte serait en effet **more and more curious**).

curiously ['kjʊərɪəslɪ] *adv* (**a**) *(inquisitively)* avec curiosité (**b**) *(strangely)* curieusement, singulièrement; **curiously enough** chose bizarre *ou* curieuse

curl [kɜ:l] **1** *vi* (**a**) *(hair)* friser; *(loosely)* boucler
(**b**) *(paper, leaf)* se recroqueviller, se racornir; *(lip)* se retrousser; **her lip curled in contempt** elle fit une moue de mépris
(**c**) *(road)* serpenter; *(smoke)* monter en spirale; *(waves)* onduler, déferler; **to curl round sth** *(plant etc)* s'enrouler autour de qch
(**d**) *Sport* jouer au curling
2 *vt* (**a**) *(hair)* friser; *(loosely)* (faire) boucler
(**b**) *(paper)* enrouler; *(ribbon)* faire boucler; *(lip)* retrousser; **he curled his lip in scorn** il a fait une moue de mépris
(**c**) *Sport (ball)* donner une trajectoire courbe à
3 *n* (**a**) *(of hair)* boucle *f* (de cheveux); **her hair hung over her shoulders in curls** ses cheveux lui tombaient en boucles sur les épaules
(**b**) *(spiral)* courbe *f*; *(of smoke)* spirale *f*; *(of wave)* ondulation *f*; *Fig* **with a scornful curl of the lip** avec une moue méprisante

►**curl up 1** *vi* (**a**) *(leaf, paper)* s'enrouler, se recroqueviller; *(bread)* se racornir
(**b**) *(person)* se pelotonner; *(cat)* se mettre en boule, se pelotonner; *(dog)* se coucher en rond; **curled up in bed** pelotonné dans son lit; **the cat was sleeping curled up in a ball** le chat dormait roulé en boule; **she curled up in front of the fire with a book** elle s'est pelotonnée devant le feu avec un livre; **to curl up with laughter** se tordre de rire; *Fig* **I just wanted to curl up and die** *(in shame)* j'aurais voulu rentrer sous terre
2 *vt sep* enrouler; **to curl oneself up** *(person)* se pelotonner; *(cat)* se mettre en boule, se pelotonner; *(dog)* se coucher en rond

curler ['kɜ:lə(r)] *n* (**a**) *(for hair)* bigoudi *m*; **in her curlers** en bigoudis (**b**) *Sport* joueur(euse) *m,f* de curling

curlew ['kɜ:lju:] *n Orn* courlis *m*

curlicue ['kɜ:lɪkju:] *n (in design, handwriting)* enjolivure *f*; *(in skating)* figure *f* (compliquée)

curliness ['kɜ:lɪnɪs] *n (of hair → loose)* boucles *fpl*; *(→ tight)* frisure *f*

curling ['kɜ:lɪŋ] *n Sport* curling *m*
►► ***curling irons*** *(for hair)* fer *m* à friser; *Sport*

curling stone pierre *f* de curling; ***curling tongs*** *(for hair)* fer *m* à friser

curlpaper ['kɜːl,peɪpə(r)] *n* papillote *f*

curly ['kɜːlɪ] **1** *adj (compar* **curlier**, *superl* **curliest***)* *(hair → tight)* frisé; *(→ loose)* bouclé; *(long piece of paper etc)* en spirale; *(eyelashes)* recourbé

2 *n Fam* **(a) to have sb by the short and curlies** pouvoir faire ce qu'on veut de qn; **they've got us by the short and curlies** ils nous tiennent

(b) *(person with curly hair)* **hi there, curly** salut, le/la frisé(e)

►► *Typ* ***curly bracket*** accolade *f*; ***curly endive*** frisée *f*; ***curly kale*** chou *m* frisé; ***curly lettuce*** (laitue *f*) frisée *f*; *Br Typ* ***curly quotes*** guillemets *mpl* anglais

curly-headed, curly-haired *adj (with loose curls)* à la tête bouclée, aux cheveux bouclés; *(with tight curls)* aux cheveux frisés

curmudgeon [kɜː'mʌdʒən] *n (grouch)* rouspéteur(euse) *m,f*; *(miser)* avare *mf*, grippe-sou *m*

curmudgeonly [kɜː'mʌdʒənlɪ] *adj (grouchy)* grincheux

currach ['kʌrəχ] *n Ir & Scot* coracle *m*

currant ['kʌrənt] *n* **(a)** *(fruit)* groseille *f* **(b)** *(dried grape)* raisin *m* de Corinthe

►► ***currant bun*** petit pain *m* aux raisins; ***currant bush*** groseiller *m*

currency ['kʌrənsɪ] *(pl* **currencies***)* *n* **(a)** *Econ & Fin* monnaie *f*, devise *f*; **he has no Spanish currency** il n'a pas d'argent espagnol; **this coin is no longer legal currency** cette pièce n'a plus cours (légal) *ou* n'est plus en circulation

(b) *Fig (prevalence)* cours *m*, circulation *f*; **to gain currency** *(of news)* s'accréditer; *(of expression, habit)* devenir de plus en plus courant; *(of ideas)* se répandre; **I give no currency to that idea** je n'accrédite pas cette idée; **ideas which had currency in the 1960s** des idées qui avaient cours dans les années 60

►► *Fin* ***currency conversion*** conversion *f* de monnaies; *Fin* ***currency dealer*** cambiste *mf*; *Fin* ***currency exposure*** risque *m* de change; *Fin* ***currency interest-rate swap*** échange *m* d'intérêts et de monnaies; *Econ & Fin* ***currency market*** marché *m* monétaire; *Fin* ***currency note*** billet *m* de banque; *Fin* ***currency risk*** risque *m* de change; *Econ & Fin* ***currency snake*** serpent *m* monétaire; *Fin & St Exch* ***currency speculation*** spéculation *f* sur les devises; *Fin & St Exch* ***currency speculator*** spéculateur(trice) *m,f* sur devises; *Fin & St Exch* ***currency swap*** échange *m* de devises; *Fin* ***currency transfer*** transfert *m* de devises; ***currency unit*** unité *f* monétaire

current ['kʌrənt] **1** *n (gen) & Elec* courant *m*; *Fig (trend)* cours *m*, tendance *f*; **the boat drifts with the current** le courant fait dériver le bateau; **the currents of opinion** les tendances *fpl* de l'opinion; *also Fig* **to go with the current** suivre le courant; *Fig* **to go against the current** aller à contre-courant; **to swim against the current** nager contre le courant *ou* à contre-courant

2 *adj* **(a)** *(widespread)* courant, commun; **the current theory** la théorie actuelle; **to be current** *(word, expression)* être courant; *(theory, fashion)* avoir cours; **it's in current use** c'est d'usage courant; **words that are in current use** des mots courants *ou* qui s'emploient couramment; **as current rumour has it, she...** on dit qu'elle..., si l'on en croit les rumeurs, elle...

(b) *(most recent → fashion, trend)* actuel; *(→ price)* courant; **the current issue of this magazine** le dernier numéro de cette revue; **the current month** le mois courant *ou* en cours; **the current week** la semaine en cours; **the current projects** les projets en cours; **the current exhibition at the Louvre** l'exposition qui a lieu en ce moment au Louvre; **his current girlfriend** la fille avec qui il est en ce moment, sa copine du moment

►► *Br* ***current account*** *Banking* compte *m* courant; *St Exch* liquidation *f* courante; ***current affairs* 1** *npl* l'actualité *f*, les questions *fpl* d'actualité **2** *comp (programme, magazine)* d'actualités; *Acct* ***current assets*** actif *m* de roulement; *Com & Fin* ***current cost*** prix *m* courant *ou* du marché; *St Exch* cours *m* instantané; *Acct* ***current cost accounting*** comptabilité *f* en coûts actuels; *Acct* ***current earnings*** bénéfices *mpl* de l'exercice, revenus *mpl* actuels; ***current events*** les événements *mpl* actuels, l'actualité *f*; *Acct & Fin* ***current expenses*** dépenses *fpl* de fonctionnement *ou* d'exploitation; *Acct* ***current financial*** *or Am* ***fiscal year*** exercice *m* en cours; *Acct* ***current liabilities*** passif *m* exigible à court terme; *Fin* ***current rate of exchange*** cours *m* actuel du change; *Acct* ***current ratio*** coefficient *m* de liquidité; *Acct* ***current value*** valeur *f* actuelle; *Acct* ***current value accounting*** comptabilité *f* en valeur actuelle; *Acct* ***current year*** exercice *m* en cours; *Fin* ***current yield*** taux *m* de rendement courant

currently ['kʌrəntlɪ] *adv* actuellement, à présent; **currently showing** *(at cinema)* à l'affiche

curricular [kə'rɪkjələ(r)] *adj* au programme

curriculum [kə'rɪkjələm] *(pl* **curricula** [-lə] *or* **curriculums***)* *n* programme *m* d'enseignement; **on the curriculum** au programme; **the maths curriculum** le programme de maths

►► ***curriculum vitae*** *Br* curriculum *m* (vitae)

curried ['kʌrɪd] *adj Culin* au curry *ou* cari; **curried eggs** des œufs *mpl* au curry *ou* à l'indienne

Currier and Ives [,kʌrɪərən'aɪvz] *pr n* = nom de deux artistes dont l'œuvre représente des scènes de la vie quotidienne aux États-Unis au XIXème siècle

curry ['kʌrɪ] *(pl* **curries**, *pt & pp* **curried***)* **1** *n Culin* curry *m*, cari *m*; **chicken curry** curry *m ou* cari *m* de poulet

2 *vt* **(a)** *Culin* accommoder au curry **(b)** *(horse)* étriller; *(leather)* corroyer; **to curry favour with sb** s'insinuer dans les bonnes grâces de qn

►► *Culin* ***curry powder*** curry *m*, cari *m*; *Culin* ***curry sauce*** sauce *f* au curry *ou* cari

currycomb ['kʌrɪ,kəʊm] *n* étrille *f*

curse [kɜːs] **1** *n* **(a)** *(evil spell)* malédiction *f*; **to call down** *or* **to put a curse on sb** maudire qn; **a curse on the day I met you!** maudit soit le jour où je vous ai connu!; **the town is under a curse** la ville est sous le coup d'une malédiction

(b) *(swearword)* juron *m*, imprécation *f*; *Fam* **curses!** zut!, mince alors!

(c) *Fig (bane)* fléau *m*, calamité *f*; **the curse of loneliness** le fléau de la solitude

(d) *Fam Old-fashioned or Euph (menstruation)* **the curse** les règles *fpl*; **she's got the curse** elle a ses règles

2 *vt* **(a)** *(damn)* maudire; **curse him!** maudit soit-il!; **curse it!** le diable l'emporte!

(b) *(swear at)* injurier

(c) *(afflict)* affliger; **he's cursed with a bad temper** il est affligé d'un mauvais caractère

3 *vi (swear)* jurer, blasphémer

►► *Am* ***curse word*** juron *m*

cursed ['kɜːsɪd] *adj* maudit

cursing ['kɜːsɪŋ] *n* jurons *mpl*

cursive ['kɜːsɪv] **1** *adj* cursif

2 *n* (écriture *f*) cursive *f*

cursor ['kɜːsə(r)] *n Comput* curseur *m*; **move the cursor to the right/left** déplacez le curseur vers la droite/gauche; **the word where the cursor is** le mot pointé

►► ***cursor blink rate*** vitesse *f* de clignotement du curseur; ***cursor control*** contrôle *m* du curseur; ***cursor key*** touche *f* de curseur; ***cursor movement*** déplacement *m* du curseur; ***cursor position*** position *f* du curseur

cursorily ['kɜːsərəlɪ] *adv (superficially)* superficiellement; *(hastily)* hâtivement, à la hâte

cursoriness ['kɜːsərɪnɪs] *n* caractère *m* sommaire

cursory ['kɜːsərɪ] *adj (superficial)* superficiel; *(hasty)* hâtif; **she gave the painting only a cursory glance** elle n'a jeté qu'un bref coup d'œil au tableau; **after a cursory examination of the document** après avoir lu le document en diagonale

curt [kɜːt] *adj (person, reply, manner)* brusque, sec (sèche); **in a curt tone** d'un ton cassant *ou* sec; **with a curt nod** avec un bref signe de tête

curtail [kɜː'teɪl] *vt* **(a)** *(cut short → story, visit, studies)* écourter **(b)** *(reduce → expenses)* réduire, rogner; *(→ power, freedom)* limiter, réduire

curtailment [kɜː'teɪlmənt] *n* **(a)** *(of studies, visit)* raccourcissement *m* **(b)** *(of expenses)* réduction *f*; *(of power, freedom)* limitation *f*, réduction *f*

curtain ['kɜːtən] **1** *n* **(a)** *(gen)* rideau *m*; *Fig* rideau *m*, voile *m*; **to draw the curtains** *(open)* ouvrir les rideaux; *(close)* tirer *ou* fermer les rideaux; *Fig* **a curtain of smoke** un rideau de fumée; *Fam* **if she finds out, it's curtains for us** si elle apprend ça, on est fichus

(b) *Theat (for actor)* rappel *m*; **the singer took four curtains** le chanteur a été rappelé quatre fois

2 *vt* garnir de rideaux

►► *Theat* ***curtain call*** rappel *m*; **she took four curtain calls** elle a été rappelée quatre fois; ***curtain hook*** crochet *m* de rideau; ***curtain material*** tissu *m* à rideaux; ***curtain rail*** tringle *f* à rideau *ou* à rideaux; *Theat* ***curtain raiser*** lever *m* de rideau; *Fig* événement *m* avant-coureur, prélude *m*; ***curtain ring*** anneau *m* de rideau; ***curtain rod*** tringle *f* à rideau *ou* à rideaux; *Archit* ***curtain wall*** mur-rideau *m*

►**curtain off** *vt sep* séparer par un rideau

curtained ['kɜːtənd] *adj (window, door)* garni d'un rideau *ou* de rideaux

curtainsider ['kɜːtən,saɪdə(r)] *n Aut* camion *m* bâché

curtly ['kɜːtlɪ] *adv (bluntly → say, reply)* avec brusquerie, sèchement, sans ménagement

curtness ['kɜːtnɪs] *n (bluntness → of tone, reply, manner, person)* brusquerie *f*, sécheresse *f*

curtsey, curtsy ['kɜːtsɪ] *(pl* **curtseys** *or* **curtsies**, *pt & pp* **curtseyed** *or* **curtsied***)* **1** *n* révérence *f*; **she made** *or* **gave a curtsey** elle a fait une révérence

2 *vi* faire une révérence

curvaceous [kɜː'veɪʃəs] *adj Hum (woman)* bien fait, plantureux

curvature ['kɜːvətjə(r)] *n (gen)* courbure *f*; *Med* déviation *f*; **curvature of the spine** *(abnormal)* déviation *f* de la colonne vertébrale, scoliose *f*; **the curvature of space** la courbure de l'espace

curve [kɜːv] **1** *n* **(a)** *(gen)* courbe *f*; *(in road)* tournant *m*, virage *m*; *Archit (of arch)* voussure *f*; *(of beam)* cambrure *f*; **the curve of the bay** la courbe de la baie; **a woman's curves** les rondeurs *fpl* d'une femme

(b) *Math* courbe *f*

(c) *Am Sport* balle *f* coupée; *Fig* **to throw sb a curve** prendre qn de court

2 *vi (gen)* se courber; *(road)* être en courbe, faire une courbe; **the road curves up the mountainside** la route monte en lacets le long de la montagne; **the path curved round to the left** le chemin tournait vers la gauche; **the river curves through the valley** la rivière serpente dans la vallée

3 *vt (gen)* courber; *Tech* cintrer

curveball ['kɜːvbɔːl] *n Am Sport* balle *f* à effet

curved [kɜːvd] *adj (gen)* courbe; *(edge)* arrondi; *(road)* en courbe; *(nose)* busqué; *(convex)* convexe; *Tech* cintré

curvet [kɜː'vet] *(Br pt & pp* **curvetted**, *cont* **curvetting**, *Am pt & pp* **curveted**, *cont* **curveting***)* **1** *n* courbette *f*

2 *vi* faire une courbette *ou* des courbettes

curvilinear [,kɜːvɪ'lɪnɪə(r)] *adj Math* curviligne

curvy ['kɜːvɪ] *(compar* **curvier**, *superl* **curviest***)* *adj* **(a)** *(road, line)* sinueux **(b)** *Fam (woman)* bien roulé

cuscus ['kʊskʊs] *n Zool* couscous *m*

Cushing's syndrome ['kuːʃɪŋz-] *n Med* syndrome *m* de Cushing

cushion ['kʊʃən] **1** *n* **(a)** *(pillow)* coussin *m*; *Fig* tampon *m*; **on a cushion of air** sur un coussin d'air; *Fig* **the annual increase in salary acts as a cushion against inflation** l'augmentation annuelle des salaires amortit les effets de l'inflation

(b) *(in snooker, billiards etc)* bande *f*; **to play off the cushion** jouer par la bande; **stroke off the cushion** doublé *m*

2 *vt* **(a)** *(sofa)* mettre des coussins à; *(seat)* rembourrer; *Tech* matelasser

(b) *Fig (shock, blow)* amortir; **to cushion a fall** amortir une chute; **these tax cuts will cushion price rises** ces réductions d'impôts amortiront la hausse des prix; **they have been cushioned against unemployment** ils ont été protégés contre le chômage

cushioning ['kʊʃənɪŋ] *n Tech* matelassage *m*

Cushitic [kʊ'ʃɪtɪk] *adj Ling* couchitique

cushti ['kʊʃtɪ] *adj Br Fam* super, génial

cushy ['kʊʃɪ] *(compar* **cushier**, *superl* **cushiest***)* *adj Fam* peinard, pépère; **a cushy job** *or* **number** une bonne planque, un boulot peinard; **he has a cushy life** il a une petite vie peinarde

cusp [kʌsp] *n Anat & Bot* cuspide *f*; *Astron (of moon)* cuspide *f*; *Astrol* corne *f*; **on the cusp of the 20th century** au tout début du XXème siècle; **on the cusp between the 19th and 20th centuries** à la charnière du XIXème et du XXème siècle

cuspate ['kʌspeɪt] *adj Archit* redenté

cusped [kʌspt] *adj Astron (moon)* à cornes; *Archit (arch)* redenté

cuspidor ['kʌspɪdɔː(r)] *n Am* crachoir *m*

cuss [kʌs] *Fam* **1** *vi* jurer❑, blasphémer❑

2 *vt* injurier❑

3 *n* (**a**) *(oath)* juron❑ *m* (**b**) *Pej (person)* type *m*; **an awkward cuss** un mauvais coucheur

►**cuss out** *vt sep Am Fam* **to cuss sb out** traiter qn de tous les noms❑

cussed ['kʌsɪd] *adj Fam* (**a**) *(obstinate)* têtu❑, entêté❑ (**b**) *(cursed)* sacré; **it's a cussed nuisance** c'est bigrement embêtant

cussedness ['kʌsɪdnɪs] *n Fam* esprit *m* de contradiction❑; **out of sheer cussedness** rien que pour embêter le monde

custard ['kʌstəd] *n* (**a**) *(sauce)* crème *f* anglaise épaisse (**b**) *(dessert)* crème *f* renversée, flan *m*

►► ***custard apple*** anone *f*; ***custard cream*** biscuit *m* fourré à la vanille; ***custard pie*** tarte *f* à la crème; ***custard powder*** ≃ crème *f* anglaise instantanée; ***custard tart*** tarte *f* à la crème

Custer ['kʌstə(r)] *pr n Hist* Custer; **Custer's Last Stand** = expression désignant la bataille de Little Bighorn

custodial [kʌ'stəʊdɪəl] *adj Law* de prison

►► ***custodial sentence*** peine *f* de prison *ou* de détention; ***custodial staff*** personnel *m* de surveillance

custodian [kʌ'stəʊdɪən] *n* (**a**) *(of building)* gardien(enne) *m,f*; *(of museum)* conservateur(trice) *m,f*; *(of prisoner)* gardien(enne) *m,f*, surveillant(e) *m,f* (**b**) *Am St Exch* dépositaire *mf*, conservateur(trice) *m,f* de titres (**c**) *Fig (of morals, tradition)* gardien(enne) *m,f*, protecteur(trice) *m,f*

custodianship [kʌ'stəʊdɪənʃɪp] *n* (**a**) *(guarding)* surveillance *f* (**b**) *Br Law* = garde d'un enfant à long terme sans obligation d'adoption

custody ['kʌstədɪ] (*pl* **custodies**) *n* (**a**) *(care)* garde *f*; **the son is in the custody of his mother** le fils est sous la garde de sa mère; **to be given** *or* **awarded custody of a child** obtenir la garde d'un enfant; **the court awarded custody (of the children) to the father** le tribunal a confié la garde des enfants au père; **in safe custody** sous bonne garde

(**b**) *Law (detention)* garde *f* à vue; *(imprisonment)* emprisonnement *m*; *(before trial)* détention *f* préventive; **the police held her in custody** la police l'a mise en garde à vue; **he was taken into (police) custody** il a été mis en état d'arrestation

►► *Am Fin* ***custody account*** compte *m* de garde

custom ['kʌstəm] *n* (**a**) *(tradition)* coutume *f*, usage *m*; **it is the custom to eat fish on Friday** l'usage veut qu'on mange du poisson le vendredi; **as custom has it** selon la coutume *ou* les us et coutumes; **it's her custom to read before going to sleep** elle a l'habitude de lire avant de s'endormir

(**b**) *Com (trade)* clientèle *f*; **they have a lot of foreign custom** ils ont beaucoup de clients étrangers; **he has lost all his custom** il a perdu toute sa clientèle; **I'll take my custom elsewhere** je vais me fournir ailleurs

(**c**) *Law* coutume *f*, droit *m* coutumier

►► ***custom car*** voiture *f* customisée, custom *m*; *Customs* ***custom house*** douane *f*; ***custom order*** commande *f* à façon

customarily [,kʌstə'merəlɪ] *adv* d'habitude

customary ['kʌstəmərɪ] *adj Formal* (**a**) *(traditional)* coutumier, habituel; *(usual)* habituel; **as is customary** comme le veut l'usage; **it is customary to tip taxi drivers** l'usage *ou* la coutume veut que l'on donne un pourboire aux chauffeurs de taxi; **at the customary time** à l'heure habituelle (**b**) *Law* coutumier

►► ***customary tenant*** tenancier *m* censitaire

custom-built *adj* (fait) sur commande

customer ['kʌstəmə(r)] *n* (**a**) *(client)* client(e) *m,f*; **regular customer** *(of restaurant etc)* habitué(e) *m,f*; *Prov* **the customer is always right** le client a toujours raison, le client est roi

(**b**) *Fam (character)* type *m*; **he's an awkward customer** il n'est pas commode; **a queer customer** un drôle de type

►► *Com & Mktg* ***customer base*** base *f* de clientèle; *Com & Mktg* ***customer care*** = qualité du service fourni à la clientèle; *Com & Mktg* ***customer database*** base *f* de données de consommateurs; *Com & Mktg* ***customer loyalty*** fidélité *f* de la clientèle; *Com & Mktg* ***customer profile*** profil *m* de la clientèle; *Com & Mktg* ***customer relations*** relations *fpl* clientèle; *Com & Mktg* ***customer satisfaction*** satisfaction *f* de la clientèle; *Com & Mktg* ***customer service*** service *m* clientèle; *Com & Mktg* ***customer service department*** service *m* clientèle, service *m* clients

customizable ['kʌstəmaɪzəbəl] *adj* qui peut être personnalisé

customization [,kʌstəmaɪ'zeɪʃən] *n* personnalisation *f*

customize, -ise ['kʌstəmaɪz] *vt (make to order)* faire *ou* fabriquer *ou* construire sur commande; *(personalize)* personnaliser; *Comput* **customized software** logiciel *m* sur mesure

custom-made *adj (clothing)* (fait) sur mesure; *(other articles)* (fait) sur commande

customs ['kʌstəmz] *npl* (**a**) *(authorities, checkpoint)* douane *f*; **to clear** *or* **go through customs** passer la douane; **at customs** à la douane; *Br* **Customs and Excise** ≃ la Régie (**b**) *(duty)* droits *mpl* de douane

►► ***customs agent*** commissionnaire *mf* en douane; ***customs allowance*** tolérance *f ou* franchise *f* douanière; ***customs barriers*** barrières *fpl* douanières; ***customs clearance*** dédouanement *m*; ***customs declaration*** déclaration *f* de *ou* en douane; ***customs duty*** droit *m ou* droits *mpl* de douane; ***customs house*** (poste *m ou* bureau *m* de) douane *f*; ***customs inspector*** inspecteur(trice) *m,f* des douanes; ***customs officer*** douanier(ère) *m,f*; ***customs registered number*** numéro *m* d'enregistrement douanier; ***customs regulations*** réglementation *f* douanière; ***customs union*** union *f* douanière

CUT [kʌt]

couper	► 1 (a) – (f), (h), (j), (o), (q), (t); 2 (a), (d) – (g)
découper	► 1 (b)
tondre	► 1 (c)
interrompre	► 1 (f)
arrêter	► 1 (g)
réduire	► 1 (i), (j)
blesser	► 1 (k)
manquer	► 1 (m)
percer	► 1 (n)
graver	► 1 (p)
monter	► 1 (r)
se couper	► 2 (b)
faire mal	► 2 (c)
coupure	► 3 (a), (b), (f)
coup	► 3 (c), (g)
morceau	► 3 (d)
réduction	► 3 (e)
coupe	► 3 (h), (k)
part	► 3 (i)
coupé	► 4 (a), (c)
réduit	► 4 (b)

(*pt & pp* **cut**, *cont* **cutting**) **1** *vt* (**a**) *(incise, slash, sever)* couper; **cut the box open with the knife** ouvrez la boîte avec le couteau; **he fell and cut his knee (open)** il s'est ouvert le genou en tombant; **she cut her hand** elle s'est coupé la main *ou* à la main; **he cut his wrists** il s'est ouvert *ou* taillé les veines; **to cut one's throat** se trancher la gorge; **they cut his throat** ils lui ont coupé *ou* tranché la gorge, ils l'ont égorgé; **they cut the prisoners free** *or* **loose** ils ont détaché les prisonniers; *Fig* **to cut oneself loose from sth** se libérer de qch; **they cut our supply line** ils nous ont coupé notre approvisionnement; *Fig* **the fog's so thick you could cut it with a knife** il y a un brouillard à couper au couteau; **the atmosphere was so tense, you could cut it with a knife** l'atmosphère était extrêmement tendue; **you're cutting your own throat** c'est du suicide

(**b**) *(divide into parts)* couper, découper; *(meat)* découper; *(slice)* découper en tranches; **she cut articles from the paper** elle découpait des articles dans le journal; **cut the cake in half/in three pieces** coupez le gâteau en deux/en trois; **to cut sth to shreds** *or* **to ribbons** mettre qch en pièces; *Fig* **the enemy cut the army to pieces** l'ennemi a taillé l'armée en pièces; *Fig* **the critics cut the play to pieces** les critiques ont esquinté la pièce

(**c**) *(trim → grass, lawn)* tondre; *(→ bush, tree)* tailler; *(reap → crop)* couper, faucher; **I'll have to cut the grass this weekend** il faudra que je tonde la pelouse ce week-end; **I cut my nails/my hair** je me suis coupé les ongles/les cheveux; **you've had your hair cut** vous vous êtes fait couper les cheveux

(**d**) *(shape → dress, suit)* couper; *(→ diamond, glass, key)* tailler; *(→ screw)* fileter; *(dig → channel, tunnel)* creuser, percer; *(engrave)* graver; *(sculpt)* sculpter; **steps had been cut in the rock** on avait taillé des marches dans le rocher; **we cut our way through the crowd** nous nous sommes frayé *ou* ouvert un chemin à travers la foule; **the advance cut a swath through the enemy's defences** l'avance des troupes ouvrit une brèche dans la défense ennemie; *Prov* **cut your coat according to your cloth** = il ne faut pas vivre au-dessus de ses moyens

(**e**) *(cross, traverse)* couper, croiser; *Math* couper; **where the path cuts the road** à l'endroit où le chemin coupe la route

(**f**) *(interrupt)* interrompre, couper; **to cut sb short** couper la parole à qn; **we had to cut our visit short** nous avons dû écourter notre visite; **his career was tragically cut short by illness** sa carrière a été tragiquement interrompue par la maladie; **to cut a long story short, I left** bref *ou* en deux mots, je suis parti

(**g**) *(stop)* arrêter, cesser; **he cut working weekends** il a arrêté de travailler le weekend; **cut the** *very Fam* **crap** *or Vulg* **shit!** arrête tes conneries!

(**h**) *(switch off)* couper; **cut the lights!** coupez la lumière!, éteignez!; **he cut the engine** il a coupé *ou* arrêté le moteur

(**i**) *(reduce → numbers, spending)* réduire; *(→ production)* diminuer; *(→ speech)* abréger, raccourcir; **we cut our costs by half** nous avons réduit les frais de moitié; **they cut taxes in the run-up to the election** ils ont réduit les impôts juste avant les élections; **to cut prices** casser les prix; **the athlete cut five seconds off the world record** *or* **cut the world record by five seconds** l'athlète a amélioré le record mondial de cinq secondes

(**j**) *Cin & TV (edit out)* faire des coupures dans, réduire; *(drop)* couper; **the censors cut all scenes of violence** la censure a coupé *ou* supprimé toutes les scènes de violence; **the film was cut to 100 minutes** le film a été ramené à 100 minutes

(**k**) *(hurt feelings of)* blesser profondément; **her remark cut me deeply** sa remarque m'a profondément blessé

(**l**) *Fam (ignore, snub)* **they cut me (dead) in the street** dans la rue ils ont fait comme s'ils ne me voyaient pas❑; **he cut me dead for days after our argument** il m'a battu froid pendant des jours après notre dispute❑

(**m**) *Fam (absent oneself from → meeting, appointment etc)* manquer (volontairement)❑, sauter❑; **I had to cut lunch in order to get there on time** j'ai dû me passer de déjeuner pour arriver à l'heure; **the students cut class** les étudiants ont séché le cours; **to cut school** sécher les cours

(**n**) *(tooth)* percer; **the baby is cutting his first tooth** le bébé perce sa première dent; *Fam Fig* **a pianist who cut her teeth on Bach** une pianiste qui s'est fait la main sur du Bach

(**o**) *(dilute)* couper

(**p**) *(record, track)* graver, faire

(**q**) *Cards* **to cut the cards** couper

(**r**) *Cin (edit → film)* monter

(**s**) *Med (incise)* inciser; *Vet (castrate)* châtrer

(**t**) *Sport (ball)* couper

(**u**) *(idioms)* **to cut the ground from under sb's feet** couper l'herbe sous le pied de qn; **her promotion cut the ground from under his feet** sa promotion lui a coupé l'herbe sous le pied; *Fam* **he couldn't cut it, he couldn't cut the mustard** il n'était pas à la hauteur❑; **to cut sth fine** compter un peu juste, ne pas se laisser de marge; **you're cutting it a bit fine** vous comptez un peu juste; **an hour is cutting it too fine** une heure, ce n'est pas suffisant; *Fam* **that argument cuts no ice with me** cet argument ne m'impressionne pas❑; **to cut a fine figure** avoir fière allure; **to cut one's losses** sauver les meubles; **we decided to cut our losses** nous avons décidé de sauver les meubles; **to cut a caper** *or* **capers** *(skip)* faire des cabrioles, gambader; *(fool around)* faire l'idiot; *Aut* **to cut a corner** prendre un virage à la corde, couper un virage; *Fig* sauter des étapes; *Fig* **to cut corners** *(economize excessively)* faire des économies exagérées; *(not follow rules)* contourner les règlements; **if you cut corners now you'll just have more work to do later on** si tu fais les choses trop vite maintenant, tu auras plus à faire plus tard; *Fig* **she doesn't believe in cutting corners** elle fait toujours les choses à fond; *Fig* **they cut corners to finish on time** ils ont brûlé les étapes pour finir à temps; *Old-fashioned* **to cut a rug** danser

2 *vi* (**a**) *(incise, slash)* couper, trancher; **this knife doesn't cut** ce couteau ne coupe pas bien; **cut around the edge** découpez *ou* coupez en suivant le bord; **she cut into the bread** elle a entamé le pain; **the rope cut into my wrists** la corde m'a coupé *ou* cisaillé les poignets; **the string is cutting into me** le cordon me coupe la chair; *Fig* **he cut through all the red tape** il s'est dispensé de toutes les formalités administratives; *Fig* **the whip cut through the air** le fouet fendit l'air; *Fig* **the yacht cut through the waves** le yacht fendait les vagues; *Naut* **the boat cut loose** le bateau a rompu les amarres; *Fig* **to cut loose** se libérer; **to cut and run** se sauver, filer; **that argument cuts both** *or* **two ways** c'est un argument à double tranchant

(**b**) *(cloth, paper)* se couper; **this meat cuts easily** cette viande se coupe facilement; **the cake will cut into six pieces** ce gâteau peut se couper en six

(**c**) *(hurtfully)* faire mal

(**d**) *(take shorter route)* couper, passer; **cut through the back way and you'll get there first** coupez par derrière et vous arriverez (là-bas) les premiers; **we cut across the fields** nous avons coupé par les champs

(**e**) *(cross)* traverser, couper; *Math (lines)* se couper; **this path cuts across** *or* **through the swamp** ce sentier traverse *ou* coupe à travers le marécage

(**f**) *(in cards)* couper; **they cut for the deal** ils ont coupé avant de donner

(**g**) *Cin & TV (stop filming)* couper; **the film cuts straight from the love scene to the funeral** l'image passe directement de la scène d'amour à l'enterrement; **cut!** coupez!

3 *n* (**a**) *(slit)* coupure *f*; *(deeper)* entaille *f*; *(wound)* balafre *f*; *Med* incision *f*; **a cut on the arm** une coupure *ou* une entaille au bras; **she had a nasty cut on her leg from the fall** elle s'était fait une vilaine entaille à la jambe en tombant; **to be a cut above (the rest)** être nettement mieux que les autres *ou* le reste; **that film is a cut above the others** ce film est nettement mieux que les autres

(**b**) *(act of cutting)* coupure *f*, entaille *f*; **to make a cut in sth** *(with knife, scissors etc)* faire une entaille dans qch

(**c**) *(blow, stroke)* coup *m*; **a knife/sword cut** un coup de couteau/d'épée; **a saw cut** un trait de scie; *Fig* **his treachery was the unkindest cut of all** sa trahison était le coup le plus perfide

(**d**) *(meat → piece)* morceau *m*; *(→ slice)* tranche *f*; **a cut off the joint** un morceau de rôti; **prime cut** morceau *m* de (premier) choix; **cheap cuts** bas morceaux *mpl*

(**e**) *(reduction → in price, taxes)* réduction *f*, diminution *f*; *(→ in staff)* compression *f*; **a cut in government spending** une réduction *ou* diminution des dépenses publiques; **the cuts in the Health Service** la réduction *ou* diminution du budget de la santé; **she took a cut in pay** elle a subi une diminution *ou* réduction de salaire; *Fin* **the cuts** les compressions *fpl* budgétaires; **power** *or* **electricity cut** coupure *f* de courant

(**f**) *(deletion)* coupure *f*; **they made several cuts in the film** ils ont fait plusieurs coupures dans le film

(**g**) *(gibe, nasty remark)* trait *m*, coup *m*

(**h**) *(shape, style → of clothes, hair)* coupe *f*; *(→ of jewel)* taille *f*; **the cut of a suit** la coupe d'un costume

(**i**) *Fam (portion, share)* part❑ *f*; **what's his cut (of the profits)?** à combien s'élève sa part?

(**j**) *Am Fam (absence)* absence❑ *f*

(**k**) *Cards* coupe *f*

(**l**) *Fam (on record)* plage❑ *f*

(**m**) *Cin & TV* coupe *f*; **the cut from the love scene to the funeral** le changement de séquence de la scène d'amour à l'enterrement

(**n**) *Sport (in tennis → backspin)* effet *m*; *(in cricket)* coup *m* tranchant

(**o**) *Am Typ (block)* cliché *m*

(**p**) *Br (body of water)* étendue *f* d'eau; *(canal)* canal *m*

(**q**) *(of tobacco)* **I prefer a finer/coarser cut of tobacco** je préfère le tabac plus fin/grossier

(**r**) *(idioms)* **the cut and thrust of parliamentary debate** les joutes oratoires des débats parlementaires; **the cut and thrust of the business world** la concurrence féroce qui règne dans le monde des affaires; **it's cut and thrust** la lutte est acharnée

4 *adj* (**a**) *(hand, flowers)* coupé; *(tobacco)* découpé

(**b**) *(reduced)* réduit; *(shortened)* raccourci; **to sell sth at cut prices** vendre qch au rabais; **the cut version of the film** la version raccourcie du film

(**c**) *(shaped → clothing)* coupé; *(faceted → gem)* taillé; **a well-cut suit** un costume bien coupé *ou* de bonne coupe

(**d**) *Br Fam (drunk)* soûl, plein

▶▶ ***cut glass*** cristal *m* taillé; *Comput* ***cut sheet feed*** dispositif *m* d'alimentation feuille à feuille; *(act)* alimentation *f* feuille à feuille; *Comput* ***cut sheet feeder*** dispositif *m* d'alimentation feuille à feuille

▶**cut across** *vt insep* (**a**) *(cross, traverse)* traverser, couper à travers; **it's quicker if you cut across the fields** c'est plus rapide si tu coupes à travers (les) champs; **they cut across country** ils ont coupé à travers champs

(**b**) *(go beyond)* surpasser, transcender; **the issue cuts across party lines** la question transcende le clivage des partis

(**c**) *(contradict)* contredire, aller à l'encontre de; **it cuts across all my principles** ça va à l'encontre de tous mes principes

▶**cut along** *vi Br Fam Old-fashioned* filer

▶**cut away** *vt sep (remove)* enlever *ou* ôter (en coupant); *(branch)* élaguer, émonder; **they had to cut away the wreckage to reach the victim** ils ont dû découper l'épave pour atteindre la victime

▶**cut back 1** *vi* (**a**) *(return)* rebrousser chemin, revenir sur ses pas; **we cut back to the car** nous sommes revenus à la voiture

(**b**) *Cin & TV* revenir en arrière

(**c**) *(financially)* économiser, réduire les dépenses

2 *vt sep* (**a**) *(reduce)* réduire, diminuer; **arms spending has been cut right back** les dépenses d'armement ont été nettement réduites

(**b**) *(prune, trim)* tailler; *(shrub, tree)* élaguer, tailler

▶**cut back on** *vt insep (financially)* économiser sur; *(time)* réduire; **the factory cut back on production** la fabrique a réduit la production

▶**cut down** *vt sep* (**a**) *(tree)* couper, abattre; *(person → in battle)* abattre; *Fig* **he was cut down by malaria** *(killed)* il est mort de la malaria; *(incapacitated)* il était terrassé par la malaria; *Literary* **to be cut down in one's prime** être fauché à la fleur de l'âge

(**b**) *(make smaller → article, speech)* abréger; *(→ clothing)* rendre plus petit; **to cut sth down to about 150,000 words** réduire qch à environ 150 000 mots; **she cuts down her dresses for her daughter** elle ajuste ses robes pour sa fille; **to cut sb down to size** remettre qn à sa place

(**c**) *(curtail)* réduire, diminuer; *(expenses)* réduire, rogner; **we've been asked to cut down the amount of time we devote to sports** on nous a demandé de consacrer moins de temps au sport; **he cut his smoking down to ten a day** il ne fume plus que dix cigarettes par jour

▶**cut down on** *vt insep (expenditure)* réduire; **I'm going to cut down on drinking/smoking** je vais boire/fumer moins; **they have cut down on eating out in restaurants** ils vont moins souvent au restaurant; **to cut down on the amount of time spent doing sth** passer moins de temps à faire qch

▶**cut in 1** *vi* (**a**) *(interrupt)* interrompre; **she cut in on their conversation** elle est intervenue dans leur conversation; **he cut in on me to ask a question** il m'a coupé la parole pour poser une question; *Fig* **the new store is cutting in on our business** le nouveau magasin nous fait perdre de la clientèle

(**b**) *Aut* faire une queue de poisson; **the taxi cut in on them** le taxi leur a fait une queue de poisson

(**c**) *(at a dance)* **mind if I cut in?** vous permettez que je vous emprunte votre partenaire?

2 *vt sep (include)* **we should cut him in on the deal** nous devrions l'intéresser à l'affaire

▶**cut into** *vt insep* (**a**) *(interrupt)* **to cut into a conversation** intervenir dans *ou* interrompre brusquement la conversation (**b**) *(use)* **to cut into one's savings** entamer ses économies; **this work cuts into my free time** ce travail empiète sur mes heures de loisir

▶**cut off** *vt sep* (**a**) *(hair, piece of meat, bread)* couper; *(arm, leg)* amputer, couper; **they cut off the king's head** ils ont décapité le roi; **he was cut off in his prime** il a été emporté à la fleur de l'âge; **she cut off her nose to spite her face** elle s'est fait du tort en voulant se venger

(**b**) *(interrupt → speaker)* interrompre, couper; **he was cut off in mid sentence** il a été interrompu au milieu de sa phrase

(**c**) *(disconnect, discontinue)* couper; *Tel* **he's been cut off** *(during conversation)* il a été coupé; *(disconnected)* on lui a coupé le téléphone; **they cut off the electricity** *or* **power** ils ont coupé le courant; **they cut off his allowance** ils lui ont coupé les vivres; **her family cut her off without a penny** sa famille l'a déshéritée; **it cut off the supply of blood to the brain** cela a empêché l'irrigation du cerveau

(**d**) *(separate, isolate)* isoler; **the house was cut off by snow drifts** la maison était isolée par des congères; **he cut himself off from his family** il a rompu avec sa famille; **housewives often feel cut off** les femmes au foyer se sentent souvent isolées

(**e**) *(bar passage of)* couper la route à; **the police cut off the thief** la police a barré le passage au voleur; **the battalion cut off the enemy's retreat** le bataillon a coupé la retraite à l'ennemi

▶**cut out 1** *vt sep* (**a**) *(make by cutting → coat, dress)* couper, tailler; *(→ statue)* sculpter, tailler; **a valley cut out by the river** une vallée creusée par le fleuve; *Fig* **to be cut out for sth** être fait pour qch, avoir des dispositions pour qch; **I'm not cut out for living abroad** je ne suis pas fait pour vivre à l'étranger; **he's not cut out to be a politician** il n'a pas l'étoffe d'un homme politique; **you have your work cut out for you** vous avez du pain sur la planche *ou* de quoi vous occuper; **she'll have her work cut out to finish the report on time** elle va avoir du mal à finir le rapport à temps

(**b**) *(remove by cutting → article, picture)* découper; *Med (→ tumour etc)* enlever; **advertisements cut out from** *or* **of the paper** des annonces découpées dans le journal

(**c**) *(eliminate)* supprimer; *(stop)* arrêter; **unnecessary expense must be cut out** il faut éliminer *ou* supprimer les frais superflus; **they cut out all references to the president** ils ont supprimé toute référence au président; **try and cut out all unnecessary details** essayez de supprimer tous les détails superflus; **he cut out smoking** il a arrêté de fumer; **cut out the screaming!** arrête de crier!, assez crié!; *Fam*

cut it out! ça suffit!, ça va comme ça!
(**d**) *Fam (rival)* supplanter ❑
(**e**) *(deprive)* priver; **his father cut him out of his will** son père l'a rayé de son testament; **they cut him out of his share** ils lui ont escroqué sa part
(**f**) *Phot & Typ* détourer
2 *vi* (**a**) *(machine, engine → stop operating)* caler; *(→ switch off)* s'éteindre
(**b**) *Am Fam (leave)* mettre les bouts, calter

▸**cut up 1** *vt sep* (**a**) *(food, wood)* couper; *(meat → carve)* découper; *(→ chop up)* hacher; *(body)* couper en morceaux
(**b**) *(usu passive) Fam (affect deeply)* **she's really cut up about her dog's death** la mort de son chien a été un coup pour elle ❑; **he's very cut up about it** ça l'a beaucoup affecté ❑
(**c**) *Am Fam (amuse)* **that really cut me up!** ça m'a fait rire! ❑
(**d**) *Br Aut* faire une queue de poisson de
2 *vi Fam* (**a**) *Am (fool around)* faire le pitre
(**b**) *Br (idiom)* **to cut up rough** se mettre en rogne *ou* en boule

---

cut-and-dried *adj* **a cut-and-dried formula** une formule toute faite; **it's all cut-and-dried** *(prearranged)* tout est déjà décidé; *(inevitable)* il n'y a rien à (y) faire

cut-and-paste *Comput* **1** *vt* couper-coller
2 *vi* couper-coller
3 *n* couper-coller *m*

cutaneous [kju'teɪnjəs] *adj Anat* cutané

cutaway ['kʌtəweɪ] *n* (**a**) *(coat)* jaquette *f (d'homme)* (**b**) *(drawing, model)* écorché *m* (**c**) *Cin & TV* changement *m* de plan

cutback ['kʌtbæk] *n* (**a**) *(reduction → in costs)* réduction *f*, diminution *f*; *(→ in staff)* compression *f*; **a cutback in production** une réduction de production (**b**) *Am Cin & TV* retour *m* en arrière, flash-back *m*

cute [kju:t] *adj Fam* (**a**) *(attractive)* mignon ❑; *Am Pej* affecté ❑ (**b**) *(clever)* malin(igne) ❑; *Pej* **don't get cute with me** ne fais pas le malin avec moi

cutely ['kju:tlɪ] *adv Fam* (**a**) *(attractively)* d'une manière charmante ❑ (**b**) *(cleverly)* avec ruse ❑

cuteness ['kju:tnɪs] *n Fam* (**a**) *(attractiveness)* charme ❑ *m* (**b**) *(cleverness)* ruse ❑ *f*

cutesy ['kju:tsɪ] *adj Fam Pej* mièvre ❑

cut-glass *adj* **a cut-glass vase** un vase *m* en cristal taillé; *Br Fig* **a cut-glass accent** un accent distingué

cuticle ['kju:tɪkəl] *n* (**a**) *Anat (skin)* épiderme *m*; *(on nails)* petites peaux *fpl*, envie *f* (**b**) *Bot* cuticule *f*
▸▸ ***cuticle remover*** repousse-peaux *m*

cuticular [kjʊ'tɪkjʊlə(r)] *adj Bot* cuticuleux

cutie ['kju:tɪ] *n Fam* (**a**) *(child, baby)* mignon(onne) ❑ *m,f*; *(term of endearment)* mon chou (**b**) *(shrewd person)* malin(igne) ❑

cutie-pie *n Fam* mon chou, mon lapin

cutlass ['kʌtləs] *n Hist* coutelas *m*

cut-leaved *adj Bot*
▸▸ ***cut-leaved crane's bill*** géranium *m* découpé; ***cut-leaved dead nettle*** lamier *m* hybride

cutler ['kʌtlə(r)] *n* coutelier(ère) *m,f*

cutlery ['kʌtlərɪ] *n (UNCOUNT)* (**a**) *(eating utensils)* couverts *mpl* (**b**) *(knives, trade)* coutellerie *f*

cutlet ['kʌtlɪt] *n Culin* (**a**) *(gen)* côtelette *f*; *(of veal)* escalope *f* (**b**) *Br (croquette)* croquette *f*; **vegetable cutlets** croquettes *fpl* de légumes

cutoff ['kʌtɒf] **1** *n* (**a**) *(stopping point)* limite *f*; **$100 is our cutoff (point)** nous nous arrêtons à 100 dollars, nous n'irons pas au-delà de 100 dollars; **we've taken a score of 370 as the cut-off point in deciding who to interview** *(no less than)* les candidats doivent avoir au minimum 370 points pour pouvoir passer l'entretien; **the cutoff point for remedial lessons is 150** *(no more than)* seuls les élèves qui obtiennent 150 points ou en deçà pourront bénéficier de cours de rattrapage
(**b**) *Am (shortcut)* raccourci *m*
2 cutoffs *npl* **(a pair of) cutoffs** = un jean coupé pour en faire un short
▸▸ ***cutoff date*** date *f* limite; *Tech* ***cutoff device*** système *m* d'arrêt; *Tech* ***cutoff switch*** interrupteur *m*

cutout ['kʌtaʊt] *n* (**a**) *(figure)* découpage *m* (**b**) *Elec* disjoncteur *m*, coupe-circuit *m*; *Aut* échappement *m* libre
▸▸ ***cutout book*** livre *m* de découpages; *Astron* ***cutout point*** *(of rocket)* point *m* de largage

cut-price 1 *adj (articles)* à prix réduit, au rabais; *(shop)* à prix réduits; *(manufacturer)* qui vend à prix réduits
2 *adv* à prix réduit

cut-rate *adj* en promotion, à prix réduit

cutter ['kʌtə(r)] *n* (**a**) *(person → of clothes)* coupeur(euse) *m,f*; *(→ of jewels)* tailleur *m*; *(→ of film)* monteur(euse) *m,f* (**b**) *(tool)* coupoir *m* (**c**) *(sailing boat)* cotre *m*, cutter *m*; *(motorboat)* vedette *f*; *(of coastguard)* garde-côte *m*; *(warship)* canot *m*

cut-throat ['kʌtθrəʊt] **1** *n* (**a**) *(murderer)* assassin *m* (**b**) *(razor)* rasoir *m* à main
2 *adj* féroce; *(competition)* acharné; *(prices)* très compétitif; **publishing is a cut-throat business** le milieu de l'édition est un panier de crabes
▸▸ *Cards* ***cut-throat game*** partie *f* à trois; ***cut-throat razor*** rasoir *m* à main

cutting ['kʌtɪŋ] **1** *n* (**a**) *(act)* coupe *f*; *(of jewel, stone)* taille *f*; *(of film)* montage *m*; *(of trees)* coupe *f*, abattage *m*
(**b**) *(piece → of cloth)* coupon *m*; *(→ from newspaper)* coupure *f*; *Agr (→ of shrub, vine)* marcotte *f*; *Hort (→ of plant)* bouture *f*; **to take a cutting** faire une bouture; **to grow a plant from a cutting** faire pousser une plante à partir d'une bouture
(**c**) *(for railway, road)* tranchée *f*
2 *adj* (**a**) *(tool)* tranchant, coupant
(**b**) *(wind)* glacial, cinglant; *(rain)* cinglant
(**c**) *(hurtful → remark)* mordant, tranchant; *(→ word)* cinglant, blessant; **she was rather cutting about them** elle a dit des choses un peu dures sur eux
▸▸ ***cutting back*** *(of tree)* élagage *m*; *(of production, budget)* réduction *f*; ***cutting edge*** tranchant *m*; *Fig* **to be at the cutting edge of technological progress** être à la pointe du progrès en technologie; ***cutting pliers*** pinces *fpl* coupantes; *Cin* ***cutting room*** salle *f* de montage; **my best scenes ended up on the cutting room floor** mes meilleures scènes ont été coupées (au montage)

cutting-edge *adj (technology)* de pointe

cuttingly ['kʌtɪŋlɪ] *adv (say)* d'un ton caustique

cuttlebone ['kʌtəlbəʊn] *n* os *m* de seiche

cuttlefish ['kʌtəlfɪʃ] *(pl* **inv***) n Ich* seiche *f*
▸▸ ***cuttlefish ink*** sépia *f*

cutup ['kʌtʌp] *n Am Fam* farceur(euse) ❑ *m,f*, rigolo(ote) *m,f*

cutwater ['kʌt,wɔ:tə(r)] *n Naut (of boat)* guibre *f*

cuvette [kjʊ'vet] *n* (**a**) *(shallow dish)* cuvette *f* (**b**) *Geol* cuvette *f* (**c**) *(in fortifications)* cunette *f*

CV [,si:'vi:] **1** *n (abbr* **curriculum vitae***)* CV *m*
2 *adj (abbr* **cardio-vascular***)* cardio-vasculaire; **a CV workout** une séance de cardio-training

CV joint [,si:'vi:-] *n Aut (abbr* **constant velocity joint***)* joint *m* de cardan

CVP [,si:vi:'pi:] *n Fin (abbr* **cost-volume-profit***)* étude *f* de coût-efficacité

CVR [,si:vi:'ɑ:(r)] *n Fin (abbr* **contingent value rights***)* CVR *m*

CVS [,si:vi:'es] *n Med (abbr* **chorionic villus sampling***)* prélèvement *m* des villosités choriales

CW [,si:'dʌbəlju:] *Rad & Tech (abbr* **continuous waves***)* **1** *npl* ondes *fpl* entretenues
2 *n (Morse code)* morse *m*

cwm [ku:m] *n Geol* cirque *m* (glaciaire); *(in Wales)* vallée *f*

cwo, CWO *Com (written abbr* **cash with order***)* payable à la commande

cwt *(written abbr* **hundredweight***) Br* = 50,8 kg, (poids *m* de) 112 livres *fpl*; *Am* = 45,36 kg, (poids *m* de) 100 livres *fpl*

cyan ['saɪən] *Comput & Typ* **1** *adj* cyan *(inv)*
2 *n* cyan *m*

cyanide ['saɪənaɪd] *n Chem* cyanure *m*
▸▸ ***cyanide poisoning*** empoisonnement *m* au cyanure

cyanogen [saɪ'ænədʒɪn] *n Chem* cyanogène *m*

cyanogenesis [,saɪənəʊ'dʒenɪsɪs] *n Chem* cyanogénèse *f*

cyanosis [,saɪə'nəʊsɪs] *n (UNCOUNT) Med* cyanose *f*

Cybele ['sɪbəlɪ] *pr n Myth* Cybèle

cyber ['saɪbə(r)] *n Comput* cyber *m*

cyberbanking ['saɪbə,bæŋkɪŋ] *n Comput* transactions *fpl* bancaires en ligne

cybercafé ['saɪbə,kæfeɪ] *n Comput* cybercafé *m*

cybercrime ['saɪbəkraɪm] *n Comput* cybercrime *m*

cyberculture ['saɪbə,kʌltʃə(r)] *n Comput* cyberculture *f*

cybernaut ['saɪbənɔ:t] *n Comput* cybernaute *m*

cybernetic [,saɪbə'netɪk] *adj Biol & Comput* cybernétique

cybernetician [,saɪbənə'tɪʃən], **cyberneticist** [,saɪbə'netɪsɪst] *n Biol & Comput* cybernéticien(enne) *m,f*

cybernetics [,saɪbə'netɪks] *n (UNCOUNT) Biol & Comput* cybernétique *f*

cyberporn ['saɪbə,pɔ:n] *n Comput* cyberporno *m*

cyberpunk ['saɪbə,pʌŋk] *n Literature* cyberpunk *m*

cybersex ['saɪbə,seks] *n Comput* cybersexe *m*

cyberspace ['saɪbə,speɪs] *n Comput* cyberespace *m*; **in cyberspace** dans le cyberespace

cybersquatter ['saɪbə,skwɒtə(r)] *n Comput* cybersquatteur *m*

cybersquatting ['saɪbə,skwɒtɪŋ] *n Comput* cybersquatting *m*, *Offic* cybersquattage *m*

cycad ['saɪkæd] *n Bot* cycas *m*

Cyclades ['sɪklədi:z] *npl Geog* **the Cyclades** les Cyclades *fpl*; **in the Cyclades** dans les Cyclades

Cycladic [sɪ'klædɪk] *adj Geog* cycladique

cyclamate ['saɪkləmeɪt] *n Chem* cyclamate *m*

cyclamen ['sɪkləmən] *(pl* **inv***) n Bot* cyclamen *m*

cycle ['saɪkəl] **1** *n* (**a**) *(gen)* cycle *m*; **the cycle of the seasons** le cycle des saisons
(**b**) *(bicycle)* bicyclette *f*, vélo *m*; *(tricycle)* tricycle *m*; *(motorcycle)* motocyclette *f*, moto *f*
2 *comp (track)* cyclable
3 *vi* faire de la bicyclette *ou* du vélo; **she cycled into town everyday** elle allait en ville à bicyclette *ou* à vélo chaque jour
▸▸ ***cycle lane*** piste *f* cyclable; ***cycle path*** piste *f ou* bande *f* cyclable; ***cycle racing track*** vélodrome *m*; ***cycle rack*** *(on pavement)* râtelier *m* à bicyclettes *ou* à vélos; *(on car)* porte-vélos *m inv*

cycler ['saɪklə(r)] *n Am* cycliste *mf*

cycleway ['saɪkəlweɪ] *n Br* piste *f ou* bande *f* cyclable

cyclic ['saɪklɪk], **cyclical** ['saɪklɪkəl] *adj* cyclique; **cyclic unemployment** chômage *m* conjoncturel
▸▸ *St Exch* ***cyclical stocks*** valeurs *fpl* cycliques

cycling ['saɪklɪŋ] **1** *n* cyclisme *m*; **I go cycling every weekend** *(gen)* je fais du vélo tous les week-ends; *Sport* tous les week-ends, je fais du cyclisme; **we went on a cycling holiday** nous avons fait du cyclotourisme
2 *comp (magazine, shoes)* de cyclisme
▸▸ ***cycling clothes*** tenue *f* cycliste; ***cycling shorts*** cuissard *m*; ***cycling tour*** circuit *m* à bicyclette *ou* à vélo

cyclist ['saɪklɪst] *n* cycliste *mf*

cyclo-cross ['saɪkləʊ-] *n* cyclo-cross *m*

cyclohexane [,saɪkləʊ'heksem] *n Chem* cyclohexane *m*

cycloid ['saɪklɔɪd] **1** *n* (**a**) *Math* cycloïde *f*; **curtate cycloid** cycloïde *f* raccourcie; **prolate cycloid** cycloïde *f* allongée (**b**) *Med* cycloïde *mf*
2 *adj* (**a**) *Math* cycloïdal (**b**) *Med* cycloïdique (**c**) *Zool (scales)* cycloïde

cycloidal [saɪ'klɔɪdəl] *adj Math* cycloïdal
▸▸ ***cycloidal curve*** anse *f*, cycloïde *f*; ***cycloidal pendulum*** pendule *f* cycloïdale

cyclometer [saɪ'klɒmɪtə(r)] *n* odomètre *m*, compteur *m* kilométrique *(sur vélo)*

cyclone ['saɪkləʊn] *n Met* cyclone *m*
▸▸ *Met* ***cyclone cellar*** abri *m* anticyclone

cyclonic [saɪ'klɒnɪk] *adj Met* cyclonique, cyclonal

cycloplegia [,saɪkləʊ'pli:dʒɪə] *n Med* cycloplégie *f*

cyclopropane [,saɪkləʊ'prəʊpeɪn] *n Chem* cyclopropane *m*

cyclops ['saɪklɒps] **1** *n* cyclope *m*
2 Cyclops *n Myth* **(the) Cyclops** le Cyclope

cyclorama [ˌsaɪkləʊ'rɑːmə] *n Art & Theat* cyclorama *m*

cyclosporin-A [ˌsaɪkləʊ'spɔːrɪn-] *n Pharm* cyclosporine-A *f*

cyclostome ['saɪkləʊˌstəʊm] *n Zool* cyclostome *m*

cyclostyle ['saɪkləʊˌstaɪl] *Old-fashioned* **1** *n* machine *f* à polycopier
2 *vt* polycopier

cyclothymia [ˌsaɪkləʊ'θaɪmɪə] *n Med* cyclothymie *f*

cyclothymic [ˌsaɪkləʊ'θaɪmɪk] *adj Med* cyclothymique

cyclotron ['saɪklətrɒn] *n Phys* cyclotron *m*

cygnet ['sɪgnɪt] *n* jeune cygne *m*

cylinder ['sɪlɪndə(r)] *n* (**a**) *Aut, Math & Tech* cylindre *m*; **four-cylinder engine** moteur *m* à quatre cylindres; **six-cylinder car** six-cylindres *f*; **oxygen/gas cylinder** bouteille *f* d'oxygène/de gaz (**b**) *(of typewriter)* rouleau *m*; *(of gun)* barillet *m*
►► *Tech* ***cylinder block*** bloc-cylindres *m*; *Tech* ***cylinder head*** culasse *f (d'un moteur)*; ***cylinder hoover*** aspirateur-traîneau *m*; *Tech* ***cylinder press*** presse *f* à cylindres; *Antiq* ***cylinder seal*** cylindre-sceau *m*; ***cylinder vacuum cleaner*** aspirateur-traîneau *m*

cylindrical [sɪ'lɪndrɪkəl] *adj* cylindrique

cymbal ['sɪmbəl] *n* cymbale *f*

cymbalo ['sɪmbələʊ], **cymbalum** ['sɪmbələm] *n Mus* cymbalum *m*, tympanon *m*

cymbidium [sɪm'bɪdɪəm] *n Bot* cymbidium *m*

Cymru ['kʊmrɪ] *n* = nom gallois du pays de Galles

cynic ['sɪnɪk] *(gen) & Phil* **1** *adj* cynique
2 *n* cynique *mf*

cynical ['sɪnɪkəl] *adj (gen) & Phil* cynique

cynically ['sɪnɪklɪ] *adv (gen) & Phil* cyniquement, avec cynisme

cynicism ['sɪnɪsɪzəm] *n (gen) & Phil* (**a**) *(attitude)* cynisme *m* (**b**) *(cynical remark)* remarque *f* cynique

cynosure ['sɪnəˌzjʊə(r)] *n* centre *m* d'attraction, point *m* de mire

CYO [ˌsiːwaɪ'əʊ] *n Am (abbr* **Catholic Youth Organization**) = association de jeunes catholiques aux États-Unis

cypher = **cipher**

cypress ['saɪprəs] *n Bot* cyprès *m*

cyprina [sɪ'praɪnə] *n Zool* cyprine *f*

Cypriot ['sɪprɪət] **1** *n* Chypriote *mf*, Cypriote *mf*; **Greek Cypriot** Chypriote grec *m*, Chypriote grecque *f*; **Turkish Cypriot** Chypriote turc *m*, Chypriote turque *f*
2 *adj* chypriote, cypriote
3 *(embassy, history)* de Chypre

Cyprus ['saɪprəs] *n* Chypre; **in Cyprus** à Chypre

Cyrillic [sɪ'rɪlɪk] **1** *adj* cyrillique
2 *n* alphabet *m* cyrillique

cyst [sɪst] *n* (**a**) *Med* kyste *m* (**b**) *Biol* sac *m* (membraneux)

cystalgia [sɪs'tældʒə] *n Med* cystalgie *f*

cystectomy [sɪs'tektəmɪ] *n Med* cystectomie *f*

cysteine ['sɪstiːn] *n Biol & Chem* cystéine *f*

cystic ['sɪstɪk] *adj Med* kystique
►► ***cystic fibrosis*** mucoviscidose *f*

cystitis [sɪs'taɪtɪs] *n Med* cystite *f*; **to have cystitis** avoir une cystite

cystogram ['sɪstəgræm] *n Med* cystogramme *m*

cystoscope ['sɪstəskəʊp] *n Med* cystoscope *m*

cystoscopy [sɪs'tɒskəpɪ] *n Med* cystoscopie *f*

cytochrome ['saɪtəʊkrəʊm] *n Biol* cytochrome *m*

cytogenetic [ˌsaɪtəʊdʒə'netɪk] *Biol* **1** *adj* cytogénétique
2 cytogenetics *n (UNCOUNT)* cytogénétique *f*

cytokinesis [ˌsaɪtəʊkɪ'niːsɪs] *n Biol* cytokinèse *f*

cytological [saɪtə'lɒdʒɪkəl] *adj Med* cytologique

cytologist [saɪ'tɒlədʒɪst] *n Med* cytologiste *mf*

cytology [saɪ'tɒlədʒɪ] *n Med* cytologie *f*

cytomegalovirus [ˌsaɪtəʊ'megələʊˌvaɪrəs] *n Med* cytomégalovirus *m*

cytoplasm ['saɪtəʊplæzəm] *n Biol* cytoplasme *m*

cytoplasmic [ˌsaɪtəʊ'plæzmɪk] *adj Biol* cytoplasmique
►► ***cytoplasmic heredity, cytoplasmic inheritance*** hérédité *f* cytoplasmique

cytosine ['saɪtəʊsiːn] *n Biol & Chem* cytosine *f*

cytoskeleton ['saɪtəʊˌskelətən] *n Biol* cytosquelette *m*

cytosol ['saɪtəsɒl] *n Biol* cytosol *m*

cytotoxic [ˌsaɪtəʊ'tɒksɪk] *adj Biol & Chem* cytotoxique

cytotoxin, cytotoxine [ˌsaɪtəʊ'tɒksɪn] *n Biol & Chem* cytotoxine *f*

CZ [*Br* ˌsiː'zed, *Am* ˌsiː'ziː] *n Am Geog (abbr* **Canal Zone**) zone *f* du canal de Panama

czar [zɑː(r)] *n (monarch)* tsar *m*; *(top person)* éminence *f* grise, ponte *m*

czarevitch ['zɑːrəvɪtʃ] *n* tsarévitch *m*

czarina [zɑː'riːnə] *n* tsarine *f*

czarism ['zɑːrɪzəm] *n* tsarisme *m*

czarist ['zɑːrɪst] **1** *n* tsariste *mf*
2 *adj* tsariste

Czech [tʃek] **1** *n* (**a**) *(person)* Tchèque *mf* (**b**) *(language)* tchèque *m*
2 *adj* tchèque
3 *comp (embassy, history)* de la République tchèque; *(teacher)* de tchèque
►► ***the Czech Republic*** la République tchèque

Czechoslovak [ˌtʃekə'sləʊvæk] **1** *n* Tchécoslovaque *mf*
2 *adj* tchécoslovaque

Czechoslovakia [ˌtʃekəslə'vækɪə] *n Formerly* Tchécoslovaquie *f*; **in Czechoslovakia** en Tchécoslovaquie

Czechoslovakian [ˌtʃekəslə'vækɪən] **1** *n* Tchécoslovaque *mf*
2 *adj* tchécoslovaque

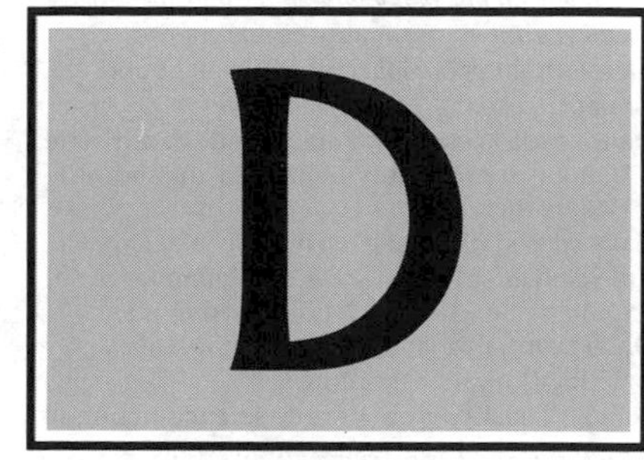

D[1], **d**[1] [diː] **1** *n* (**a**) *(letter)* D, d *m inv*; **D for dog** ≃ D comme Désiré; **in 3-D** en trois dimensions, en 3-D (**b**) *Sch* **to get a D** avoir une mauvaise note, ≃ avoir entre 7 et 9 sur 20 (**c**) *Mus* ré *m* (**d**) *Sport* **the D** *(on soccer field)* l'arc *m* de cercle pour coup de réparation
2 *adj Mus (string)* de ré

D[2] *Am (written abbr* **democrat, democratic**) démocrate

d[2] (**a**) *(written abbr* **penny**) = symbole du penny anglais jusqu'en 1971 (**b**) *(written abbr* **died**) **d 1913** mort en 1913

DA [ˌdiːˈeɪ] *n* (**a**) *Am Law (abbr* **District Attorney**) ≃ Procureur *m* de la République; **the DA's office** le parquet (**b**) *(abbr* **duck's arse**) = coiffure masculine populaire dans les années cinquante (cheveux courts plaqués vers l'arrière)

D/A *Com (written abbr* **documents against acceptance**) documents *mpl* contre acceptation

dab [dæb] *(pt & pp* **dabbed**, *cont* **dabbing**) **1** *n* (**a**) *(small amount)* **a dab** un petit peu; **a dab of perfume** une goutte de parfum; **a dab of powder** un peu de poudre; **a dab of butter** une noisette de beurre; **just give it a dab of paint** mets-y un coup de peinture
(**b**) *Ich* limande *f*
(**c**) *Br Fam (idiom)* **to be a dab hand at sth** être doué en *ou* pour qch❑; **to be a dab hand at doing sth** être doué pour faire qch❑
2 *vt* (**a**) *(touch lightly)* tamponner; **to dab one's eyes (with a handkerchief)** se tamponner les yeux; **she dabbed the graze with cotton wool** elle tamponna l'écorchure avec du coton
(**b**) *(daub)* **he dabbed the canvas with paint** il posait la peinture sur la toile par petites touches
3 dabs *npl Br very Fam (fingerprints)* empreintes *fpl* digitales❑

▸**dab at** *vt insep* tamponner; **she dabbed at the stain with a sponge** elle a tamponné la tache avec une éponge

▸**dab off** *vt sep* ôter en tamponnant

▸**dab on** *vt sep (paint, antiseptic etc)* appliquer par petites touches

dabble [ˈdæbəl] **1** *vt* mouiller; **they dabbled their feet in the water** ils trempaient les pieds dans l'eau
2 *vi Fig* **he dabbles at painting** il fait un peu de peinture; **she dabbles in politics** elle fait un peu de politique; **to dabble in art/music** être un peu artiste/musicien; **to dabble on the Stock Market** boursicoter

dabbler [ˈdæblə(r)] *n* dilettante *mf*

dabbling [ˈdæblɪŋ] *n* dilettantisme *m*

dabchick [ˈdæbtʃɪk] *n Orn* petit grèbe *m*, grèbe *m* castagneux

DAC [ˌdiːeɪˈsiː] *n (abbr* **Development Assistance Committee**) CAD *m*

Dacca [ˈdækə] *n* Dacca

dace [deɪs] *n Ich* dard *m*, vandoise *f*

dacha [ˈdætʃə] *n* dacha *f*

dachshund [ˈdækshʊnd] *n* teckel *m*

Dacia [ˈdeɪsɪə] *n Hist* Dacie *f*

Dacian [ˈdeɪsɪən] *Hist* **1** *n* Dace *mf*
2 *adj* dace, dacique

dacoit [dəˈkɔɪt] *n Hist* dacoït *m*

Dacron® [ˈdækrɒn] *n Am Tex* Dacron® *m*, ≃ Tergal® *m*

dactyl [ˈdæktɪl] *n Literature* dactyle *m*

dactylic [dækˈtɪlɪk] *Literature* **1** *n* dactyle *m*; **written in dactylics** composé en vers dactyliques
2 *adj* dactylique

dactylography [ˌdæktɪˈlɒgrəfɪ] *n esp Am* dactyloscopie *f*

dad [dæd] *n Fam (father)* papa *m*; *(old man)* pépé *m*

Dada [ˈdɑːdɑː] *Art & Literature* **1** *n* dada *m*
2 *adj* dada *(inv)*, dadaïste

Dadaism [ˈdɑːdɑːɪzəm] *n Art & Literature* dadaïsme *m*

Dadaist [ˈdɑːdɑːɪst] *Art & Literature* **1** *adj* dadaïste
2 *n* dadaïste *mf*

daddy [ˈdædɪ] *(pl* **daddies**) *n Fam* papa *m*; *Am* **the daddy of them all** le meilleur de tous❑

daddy-long-legs *n Br, Austr & NZ (cranefly)* tipule *f*; *Am (harvestman)* faucheur *m*, faucheux *m*

Daddy Warbucks [-ˈwɔːbʌks] *pr n* = personnage de bande dessinée américaine: riche homme d'affaires, protecteur de l'orpheline "Little Orphan Annie"

dado [ˈdeɪdəʊ] *(pl* **dadoes**) *n Constr (of wall)* lambris *m* d'appui; *Archit (of pedestal)* dé *m*
▸▸ ***dado rail*** cimaise *f*

Daedalus [ˈdaɪdələs] *pr n Myth* Dédale

daemon [ˈdiːmən] *n* (**a**) *(demigod)* demi-dieu *m* (**b**) *(devil, evil spirit)* démon *m*

daff [dæf] *n Br Fam (daffodil)* jonquille❑ *f*

daffodil [ˈdæfədɪl] *n* jonquille *f*
▸▸ ***daffodil bulb*** bulbe *m* de jonquille; ***daffodil yellow*** jaune *m* d'or

DAFFODIL

La jonquille est le symbole du pays de Galles. Le jour de la Saint David, les Galloises en portent une épinglée à la boutonnière.

daffodil-yellow *adj* jaune d'or

daffy [ˈdæfɪ] *(compar* **daffier**, *superl* **daffiest**) *Fam*
1 *adj (person, idea)* loufoque, timbré
2 *n (daffodil)* jonquille❑ *f*

daft [dɑːft] *Fam* **1** *adj Br (foolish)* idiot❑, bête❑; **don't be daft!** (ne) fais pas l'idiot!; **he's daft about her** il est fou d'elle
2 *adv* **don't talk daft** ne dites pas de bêtises

daftie [ˈdɑːftɪ] *n Br Fam* toqué(e) *m,f*

daftness [ˈdɑːftnɪs] *n Br Fam* stupidité❑ *f*

dag [dæg] *n Austr Fam* (**a**) *(unfashionable person)* ringard(e) *m,f* (**b**) *(untidy man)* type *m* négligé; *(untidy woman)* bonne femme *f* négligée

dagger [ˈdægə(r)] *n* (**a**) *(weapon)* poignard *m*; *(smaller)* dague *f*; **to be at daggers drawn with sb** être à couteaux tirés avec qn; **to** *Br* **look** *or Am* **shoot daggers at sb** foudroyer qn du regard (**b**) *Typ* croix *f*

daggy [ˈdægɪ] *adj Austr Fam* (**a**) *(unfashionable)* ringard (**b**) *(untidy)* négligé❑

dago [ˈdeɪgəʊ] *(pl* **dagos** *or* **dagoes**) *n* métèque *mf*, = terme injurieux désignant une personne d'origine espagnole, italienne ou portugaise

daguerreotype [dəˈgerətaɪp] *n Phot* daguerréotype *m*

Dagwood sandwich [ˈdægwʊd-] *n Am* = gros sandwich avec viande, fromage etc

dahabiyah, dahabiyeh [ˌdɑːhəˈbiːə] *n Naut* dahabieh *f*

dahlia [ˈdeɪljə] *n* dahlia *m*
▸▸ ***dahlia corm*** bulbe *m* de dahlia

Dahomey [dəˈhəʊmɪ] *n Geog* Dahomey *m*

Dáil (Éireann) [dɔɪl(ˈeərən)] *n Ir Parl* = chambre des députés de la république d'Irlande

daily [ˈdeɪlɪ] *(pl* **dailies**) **1** *adj (routine, task)* quotidien, de tous les jours; *(output, wage)* journalier; **to be paid on a daily basis** être payé à la journée; **(to earn) one's daily bread** (gagner) son pain quotidien; *Bible* **give us this day our daily bread** donne-nous aujourd'hui notre pain de ce jour
2 *adv* tous les jours, quotidiennement; **twice daily** deux fois par jour
3 *n* (**a**) *(newspaper)* quotidien *m*
(**b**) *Br Fam (servant)* femme *f* de ménage *(qui vient tous les jours)*
(**c**) *Cin & TV* **dailies** rushes *mpl*
▸▸ *Horseracing* ***daily double*** = pari unique portant sur le gagnant de deux courses de chevaux ayant lieu le même jour; *Br Fam Old-fashioned* ***daily dozen*** gym *f* quotidienne❑; *Press* ***the Daily Express*** = quotidien britannique populaire de droite; *Fam* ***the daily grind*** le train-train quotidien; *Br* ***daily help, daily maid*** femme *f* de ménage *(qui vient tous les jours)*; *Press* ***the Daily Mail*** = quotidien britannique de droite; *Press* ***the Daily Mirror*** = quotidien britannique populaire centriste; *St Exch* ***Daily Official List*** cours *mpl* de clôture quotidiens; ***daily paper*** quotidien *m*; ***the daily round*** la tournée quotidienne; *Fam* ***the daily routine*** le train-train quotidien; *Press* ***the Daily Sport*** = quotidien britannique traitant de l'actualité sportive et publiant de nombreuses photos de pin-ups; *Press* ***the Daily Star*** = quotidien britannique populaire de droite; *Press* ***the Daily Telegraph*** = quotidien britannique de tendance conservatrice; *Fin* ***daily trading report*** rapport *m* de situation journalière

daimon = **daemon**

daintily [ˈdeɪntɪlɪ] *adv* (**a**) *(eat, hold)* délicatement; *(walk)* avec grâce (**b**) *(dress)* coquettement

daintiness [ˈdeɪntɪnɪs] *n* (**a**) *(of manner)* délicatesse *f*, raffinement *m* (**b**) *(of dress)* coquetterie *f*

dainty [ˈdeɪntɪ] *(pl* **dainties**, *compar* **daintier**, *superl* **daintiest**) **1** *n (food)* mets *m* délicat; *(sweet)* friandise *f*
2 *adj* (**a**) *(small)* menu, petit; *(delicate → features, porcelain, ornament)* délicat; **to walk with dainty steps** marcher à petits pas délicats (**b**) *(food)* de choix, délicat; **dainty morsels** mets *mpl* de choix (**c**) *(fussy)* **she's a dainty eater** elle est difficile pour *ou* sur la nourriture

daiquiri [ˈdaɪkɪrɪ] *n* daiquiri *m*

dairy [ˈdeərɪ] *(pl* **dairies**) **1** *n (building on farm)* laiterie *f*; *(shop)* crémerie *f*, laiterie *f*
2 *comp (cow, farm, products)* laitier; *(butter, cream)* fermier
▸▸ ***dairy cattle*** vaches *fpl* laitières; ***dairy farmer*** producteur(trice) *m,f* de lait *ou* laitier(ère); ***dairy farming*** industrie *f* laitière; ***dairy herd*** troupeau *m* de vaches laitières; ***dairy ice cream*** glace *f* à la crème; ***dairy produce*** produits *mpl* laitiers; ***Dairy Queen***® = chaîne de fast-food américaine

dairying [ˈdeərɪɪŋ] *n* industrie *f* laitière

dairymaid [ˈdeərɪmeɪd] *n* fille *f* de ferme *(qui s'occupe de la laiterie)*

dairyman [ˈdeərɪmən] *(pl* **dairymen** [-mən]) *n (on farm)* employé *m* de laiterie; *(in shop)* crémier *m*, laitier *m*

dais [ˈdeɪɪs] *n* estrade *f*

daisied [ˈdeɪzɪd] *adj Literary* émaillé de pâquerettes

daisy [ˈdeɪzɪ] *(pl* **daisies**) *n (smaller)* pâquerette *f*; *(bigger)* marguerite *f*; **as fresh as a daisy** frais (fraîche) comme une rose; *Fam* **he's pushing up the daisies** il mange les pissenlits par les racines
▸▸ ***daisy chain*** guirlande *f* de pâquerettes; *Comput* ***daisy chaining*** connexion *f* en boucle;

Typ & Comput ***daisy wheel*** marguerite *f*; ***daisy wheel printer*** imprimante *f* à marguerite

daisy-chain *vt Comput* connecter en boucle

Dakar ['dækɑː(r)] *n* Dakar

Dakota [də'kəʊtə] *n* Dakota *m*; **in Dakota** dans le Dakota; **the Dakotas** le Dakota du sud et le Dakota du nord

daks [dæks] *npl Austr Fam* futal *m*, falzar *m*

dal [dɑːl] *n* (**a**) *Bot* = sorte de légumineuse (**b**) *Culin* = plat à base de lentilles et d'épices

Dalai Lama [ˌdælaɪ'lɑːmə] *pr n* dalaï-lama *m*

dale [deɪl] *n* vallée *f*, vallon *m*

Dalek ['dɑːlek] *n* = créature de science-fiction au comportement agressif et impitoyable

Dallas ['dæləs] *n* Dallas; **the Dallas shooting** = l'assassinat de J.F. Kennedy

►► *Sport* ***Dallas Cowboys*** = équipe de football américain de Dallas

dalliance ['dælɪəns] *n Literary* badinage *m*

dally ['dælɪ] (*pt & pp* **dallied**) *vi* (**a**) *(dawdle)* lanterner, lambiner; **to dally over sth** s'attarder sur qch (**b**) *(toy)* badiner; *(→ with idea)* caresser; *(→ with affections)* jouer (**c**) *Arch (flirt)* flirter

Dalmatia [dæl'meɪʃə] *n Geog* Dalmatie *f*; **in Dalmatia** en Dalmatie

Dalmatian [dæl'meɪʃən] **1** *n* (**a**) *(dog)* dalmatien(enne) *m,f* (**b**) *(person)* habitant(e) *m,f* de la Dalmatie

2 *adj* dalmate

dalmatic [dæl'mætɪk] *n Rel* dalmatique *f*

dalton ['dɔːltən] *n Chem* dalton *m*

daltonism ['dɔːltəˌnɪzəm] *n* daltonisme *m*

dam [dæm] (*pt & pp* **dammed,** *cont* **damming**) **1** *n* (**a**) *(barrier)* barrage *m* (de retenue) (**b**) *(reservoir)* réservoir *m* (**c**) *(animal)* mère *f*

2 *vt (river, lake)* construire un barrage sur; *(valley)* construire un barrage dans

►► *Mil & Hist* ***Dam Busters*** = aviateurs de la RAF ayant bombardé des barrages dans la région de la Ruhr en 1943

►**dam up** *vt sep* (**a**) construire un barrage sur (**b**) *Fig (feelings)* refouler, ravaler; *(words)* endiguer

damage ['dæmɪdʒ] **1** *n* (**a**) *(UNCOUNT) (harm)* dommage *m*, dommages *mpl*; *(visible effects)* dégâts *mpl*, dommages *mpl*; *(to ship, shipment)* avarie *f*, avaries *fpl*; **damage to property** dégâts *mpl* matériels; **the storm did a lot of damage** l'orage a causé des dégâts importants; **he said he would make good the damage** il a dit qu'il allait réparer les dégâts; **smoking can cause serious damage to your health** le tabac nuit gravement à la santé

(**b**) *Fig* tort *m*, préjudice *m*; **the scandal has done the government serious damage** le scandale a fait énormément de tort *ou* a énormément porté préjudice au gouvernement; **the damage is done** le mal est fait; *Fam* **what's the damage?** *(how much do I owe?)* ça fait combien? ❑

2 *vt (harm → crop, object)* endommager, causer des dégâts à; *(→ food)* abîmer, gâter; *(→ eyes, health)* abîmer; *(→ ship, shipment)* avarier; *(→ reputation)* porter atteinte à, nuire à; *(→ cause)* faire du tort à, porter préjudice à; **the storm damaged a lot of trees** de nombreux arbres ont été endommagés par la tempête; **damaged goods** marchandises *fpl* avariées; *Fig (person)* personne *f* au passé chargé

3 damages *npl Law* dommages *mpl* et intérêts *mpl*, dommages-intérêts *mpl*; **to award damages to sb for sth** accorder des dommages et intérêts à qn pour qch; **to sue sb for damages** poursuivre qn en dommages et intérêts; **liable for damages** civilement responsable; **war damages** dommages *mpl ou* indemnités *fpl* de guerre

►► ***damage limitation*** effort *m* pour limiter les dégâts

damaging ['dæmɪdʒɪŋ] *adj* dommageable, nuisible; *Law* préjudiciable; **psychologically damaging** dommageable sur le plan psychologique; **it's a damaging blow to his re-election prospects/career** cela compromet sérieusement ses chances d'être réélu/sa carrière

Damascene ['dæməˌsiːn] *Geog* **1** *n* Damascène *mf*

2 *adj* de Damas

damascene ['dæməˌsiːn] *vt Metal* damasquiner

Damascus [də'mæskəs] *n* Damas

damask ['dæməsk] **1** *n* (**a**) *(silk)* damas *m*, soie *f* damassée; *(linen)* damassé *m* (**b**) *Metal (steel)* (acier *m*) damasquiné *m* (**c**) *(colour)* vieux rose *m inv*

2 *adj* (**a**) *(cloth)* damassé (**b**) *(colour)* vieux rose *(inv)*; *Literary* **her damask cheeks** l'incarnat de ses joues

►► ***damask rose*** rose *f* de Damas

dame [deɪm] **1** *n* (**a**) *Arch or Literary (noble)* dame *f*; **Dame Fortune** Dame *f* Fortune; *Br Theat* **(pantomime) dame** vieille femme *f* comique *(dont le rôle est joué par un homme)*

(**b**) *Am Fam Old-fashioned (woman)* pépée *f*

2 Dame *n Br (title)* = titre donné à une femme ayant reçu certaines distinctions honorifiques

►► *Br* ***Dame Commander of the Order of the British Empire*** = distinction honorifique britannique pour les femmes; *Hist* ***dame school*** = école dirigée par une vieille dame, souvent dans sa propre maison; *Bot* ***dame's violet*** julienne *f*

damfool [dæm'fuːl] *adj Fam* débile

dammit ['dæmɪt] *exclam Fam* mince!; *Br* **as near as dammit** à un cheveu près

damn [dæm] **1** *exclam Fam* mince!

2 *n Fam* **I don't give a damn** j'en ai rien à cirer, je m'en balance; **I don't give a damn about the money** je me fiche pas mal de l'argent; **it's not worth a damn** ça ne vaut pas un pet de lapin *ou* un clou

3 *vt* (**a**) *Rel* damner

(**b**) *(condemn)* condamner; **they damned him with faint praise** ils l'ont éreinté sous couleur d'éloge; **you're damned if you do and damned if you don't** quoique tu fasses tu es perdant

(**c**) *Fam* **damn you!** va te faire voir!; **he found out, damn him!** il s'en est rendu compte, le salaud!; **damn the expense/the consequences** au diable l'avarice/tant pis pour les conséquences; **well I'll be damned!** ça, c'est le comble!; **I'll be damned if I'll apologize!** m'excuser? plutôt mourir!

4 *adj Fam* fichu, sacré; **you damn fool!** espèce d'idiot!; **he's a damn nuisance** il est vraiment casse-pied; **it's a damn nuisance!** ce que c'est casse-pied!, quelle barbe!; **it's one damn thing after another** quand ce n'est pas une chose c'est l'autre

5 *adv Fam* (**a**) *(as intensifier)* vachement; **a damn good idea** une super bonne idée; **you're damn right** t'as parfaitement raison; **he's so damn slow** il est hyper lent; **he knows damn well what I mean** il sait exactement *ou* très bien ce que je veux dire ❑

(**b**) *Br (idiom)* **damn all** que dalle; **damn all money/thanks** pas un sou/merci; **there's damn all in the fridge** il y a que dalle dans le frigo; **it's got damn all to do with you** ça n'a absolument rien à voir avec toi ❑; **what can you see? damn all!** tu vois quelque chose? que dalle!; **she did damn all** elle n'a rien fichu; **he knows damn all about it** il n'en sait fichtre rien

damnable ['dæmnəbəl] *adj* (**a**) *Rel* damnable (**b**) *Fam Old-fashioned (awful)* exécrable, odieux

damnably ['dæmnəblɪ] *adv Fam Old-fashioned* rudement

damnation [dæm'neɪʃən] **1** *n Rel* damnation *f*

2 *exclam Fam* enfer et damnation!

damned [dæmd] **1** *adj* (**a**) *Rel* damné, maudit (**b**) *Fam* fichu, sacré; **he's a damn nuisance** il est vraiment casse-pied

2 *adv Fam* rudement, vachement; **you know damned well what I mean** tu sais très bien ce que je veux dire ❑; **do what you damned well like!** fais ce que tu veux, je m'en fiche

3 *npl Rel or Literary* **the damned** les damnés *mpl*

damnedest ['dæmdəst] *Fam* **1** *n (utmost)* **to do one's damnedest (to do sth)** faire tout son possible (pour faire qch) ❑; **he did his damnedest to ruin the party** il a vraiment fait tout ce qu'il pouvait pour gâcher la soirée ❑

2 *adj Am* incroyable ❑; **it was the damnedest thing!** il fallait voir ça!

damn-fool *adj Fam* débile

damning ['dæmɪŋ] *adj (evidence, statement)* accablant; **the report was a damning indictment of the government** le rapport constituait un témoignage accablant contre le gouvernement

Damocles ['dæməˌkliːz] *pr n Myth* Damoclès; **the sword of Damocles** l'épée *f* de Damoclès

damp [dæmp] **1** *adj (air, clothes, heat)* humide; *(skin, hand)* moite

2 *n* (**a**) *(moisture)* humidité *f*

(**b**) *Mining (air)* mofette *f*; *(gas)* grisou *m*

3 *vt* (**a**) *(wet)* humecter

(**b**) *Aut, Elec & Tech* amortir; *Mus* étouffer; *Fig (spirits)* décourager, refroidir

(**c**) *(fire)* couvrir

►► ***damp course*** revêtement *m* d'étanchéité; *Br Fam* **damp squib** déception *f*, *Br Fam* **to be a damp squib** faire l'effet d'un pétard mouillé

►**damp down** *vt sep (fire)* couvrir; *Fig (enthusiasm)* refroidir; *(crisis)* atténuer, rendre moins violent

dampen ['dæmpən] *vt* (**a**) *(wet)* humecter (**b**) *(ardour, courage)* refroidir; **don't dampen their spirits** ne les découragez pas

damper[1] ['dæmpə(r)], *Am* **dampener** ['dæmpənə(r)] *n* (**a**) *(in furnace)* registre *m* (**b**) *Fig* **that put a damper on things** ça a fait l'effet d'une douche froide; **the news put a damper on the party/his enthusiasm** la nouvelle a jeté un froid sur la fête/a refroidi son enthousiasme (**c**) *Aut, Elec & Tech* amortisseur *m*; *Mus* étouffoir *m* (**d**) *(for linen, stamps)* mouilleur *m*

damper[2] *n Austr* = sorte de pain cuit au feu de bois

damping ['dæmpɪŋ] *n* (**a**) *(wetting)* mouillage *m* (**b**) *Aut, Elec & Tech* amortissement *m*

dampish ['dæmpɪʃ] *adj* un peu humide

dampness ['dæmpnɪs] *n* humidité *f*; *(of skin)* moiteur *f*

damp-proof *adj Constr* protégé contre l'humidité, hydrofuge

►► ***damp-proof course*** revêtement *m* d'étanchéité

damp-proofing *n Constr* isolation *f* contre l'humidité

damsel ['dæmzəl] *n Arch or Literary* damoiselle *f*; *Hum* **a damsel in distress** une belle éplorée

damselfish ['dæmzəlfɪʃ] *n Ich* poisson-ange *m*

damselfly ['dæmzəlflaɪ] (*pl* **damselflies**) *n Entom* demoiselle *f*, libellule *f*

damson ['dæmzən] **1** *n (tree)* prunier *m* de Damas; *(fruit)* prune *f* de Damas

2 *comp (jam, wine)* de prunes (de Damas)

Dan [dæn] *pr n* **Dan Dare** = jeune capitaine d'un vaisseau spatial dans une bande dessinée

dan [dæn] *n Sport (in martial arts)* dan *m*

dance [dɑːns] **1** *n* (**a**) *(gen)* danse *f*; **may I have the next dance?** voulez-vous m'accorder la prochaine danse?; **shall we have one more dance?** dansons-nous encore une fois?; **to do a dance** *(in exultation)* sauter de joie; **dance of death** danse *f* macabre; **to lead sb a (merry** *or* **pretty) dance** *(exasperate)* donner du fil à retordre à qn; *(deceive)* faire marcher qn; *(in romantic context)* mener qn en bateau; **the dance of the seven veils** la danse des sept voiles

(**b**) *(piece of music)* morceau *m* (de musique)

(**c**) *(art)* danse *f*; **the world of dance** le milieu de la danse

(**d**) *(social occasion)* soirée *f* dansante; *(larger)* bal *m*; **to hold a dance** donner une soirée dansante *ou* un bal

2 *comp (class, school, step, studio)* de danse

3 *vi (person)* danser; *Fig (leaves, light, words)* danser; *(eyes)* scintiller; **do you want to dance?** tu veux danser?; **to dance with sb** danser avec qn; **to ask sb to dance** inviter qn à danser; **it's not the type of music you can dance to** ce n'est pas le genre de musique sur lequel on peut danser; **to dance for joy** sauter de joie; **she danced along the street** elle descendit la rue d'un pas joyeux; *Fig* **to dance to sb's tune** obéir à qn au doigt et à l'œil

4 *vt (waltz, polka)* danser; **to dance a step** faire *ou* exécuter un pas de danse; **we danced every dance** nous n'avons pas arrêté de danser; **they danced every dance together** ils n'ont pas arrêté de danser ensemble; **to dance a baby on one's knee** faire sauter un bébé sur ses genoux; *Br* **to dance attendance on sb** s'empresser auprès de qn

►► ***dance band*** orchestre *m* de bal; ***dance card***

carnet *m* de bal; ***dance floor*** piste *f* de danse; ***dance hall*** salle *f* de bal; ***dance music*** musique *f* dansante; *(modern)* dance *f*

'A Dance to the Music of Time' *Powell* 'La Ronde de la musique du temps'

---

dancer ['dɑːnsə(r)] *n* danseur(euse) *m,f*

dancing ['dɑːnsɪŋ] **1** *n* danse *f*; **to go dancing** aller danser; **a book on dancing** un livre sur la danse

2 *comp (class, teacher, school)* de danse

3 *adj (eyes)* scintillant

►► ***dancing dervish*** derviche *m* tourneur; ***dancing girl*** danseuse *f*; ***dancing partner*** cavalier (ère) *m,f*; ***dancing shoe*** *(for dance)* chaussure *f* de bal; *(for ballet)* chausson *m* de danse

D and C, D & C [ˌdiːən'siː] *n Med (abbr* **dilation and curettage**) (dilation *f* et) curetage *m*

dandelion ['dændɪlaɪən] *n* pissenlit *m*, dent-de-lion *f*; **dandelion and burdock** = boisson gazeuse à base d'extraits de plantes

►► ***dandelion clock*** aigrettes *fpl* de pissenlits; *Br* **to play dandelion clocks** *(children's game)* = souffler sur les aigrettes de pissenlits pour savoir l'heure

dander ['dændə(r)] *n Fam* **to get one's/sb's dander up** se mettre/mettre qn en rogne

dandified ['dændɪfaɪd] *adj (person)* à l'allure de dandy; *(appearance)* de dandy

dandle ['dændəl] *vt Br (small child → on knee)* faire sauter; *(→ in arms)* bercer

dandruff ['dændrʌf] *n (UNCOUNT)* pellicules *fpl*; **to have dandruff** avoir des pellicules; **he has very bad dandruff** il a beaucoup de pellicules

►► ***dandruff shampoo*** shampooing *m* antipelliculaire

dandy ['dændɪ] (*pl* **dandies**) **1** *n* dandy *m*

2 *adj Fam* extra, épatant; **everything's fine and dandy** tout va très bien[❑]; *Ironic* **that's just dandy!** c'est vraiment génial!

dandyish ['dændɪɪʃ] *adj* élégant

dandyism ['dændɪɪzəm] *n* dandysme *m*

Dane [deɪn] *n* Danois(e) *m,f*

dang [dæŋ] *Am Fam* = **damn** *exclam & adv*

danger ['deɪndʒə(r)] *n* danger *m*; **is there any danger of fire?** y a-t-il un danger *ou* risque d'incendie?; **the dangers of smoking/making rash judgements** les dangers du tabac/des jugements hâtifs; **danger, keep out!** *(sign)* danger, entrée interdite!; **danger of death** *(sign)* danger de mort; **fraught with danger** extrêmement dangereux; **to be out of/in danger** être hors de/en danger; **to put sb/sth in danger** mettre qn/qch en danger; **he was in no danger** il n'était pas en danger, il ne courait aucun danger; **she was in little danger** elle ne courait pas un grand danger; **her life is in danger** sa vie est en danger, elle est en danger de mort; **to be in danger of doing sth** courir le risque *ou* risquer de faire qch; **to be a danger to sb/sth** être un danger pour qn/qch; **he's a danger to society** c'est un danger public; **it's a danger to my health** c'est dangereux pour ma santé; **there is some danger of that** il y a un certain risque que cela se produise; **there is no danger of that happening** il n'y a pas de danger *ou* de risque que cela se produise; **that's the danger in this case** voilà le danger *ou* le risque qui menace ici; *Med* **to be on the danger list** être dans un état critique; *Med* **to be off the danger list** être hors de danger; *Fam* **no danger!** ça ne risque pas!; **there's no danger of him doing that!** il n'y a pas de danger *ou* de risque qu'il le fasse!; **there's no danger of that!** il n'y a pas de danger!

►► ***danger area*** zone *f* dangereuse; *Br* ***danger money*** prime *f* de risque; ***danger point*** cote *f* d'alerte; ***danger signal*** *Rail* signal *m* d'arrêt; *Fig* signal *m* d'alerte *ou* d'alarme; ***danger zone*** zone *f* dangereuse

dangerous ['deɪndʒərəs] *adj (job, sport, criminal, animal)* dangereux; *(illness)* dangereux, grave; *(operation)* délicat, périlleux; *(assumption)* risqué; *Fig* **to be on dangerous ground** être sur un terrain glissant

►► *Law* ***dangerous driving*** conduite *f* dangereuse

dangerously ['deɪndʒərəslɪ] *adv* dangereusement; *(ill)* gravement; **to live dangerously** vivre dangereusement; **the car was dangerously near the edge of the cliff** la voiture était dangereusement près du bord de la falaise; **you're coming dangerously close to being fired/spanked** continue comme ça et tu es viré/tu as une fessée; **this firm is dangerously close to collapse/bankruptcy** cette entreprise est au bord de l'effondrement/la faillite

dangle ['dæŋgəl] **1** *vt (legs, arms, hands)* laisser pendre; *(object on chain, string)* balancer; **to dangle sth in front of sb** balancer qch devant qn; *Fig* faire miroiter qch aux yeux de qn; **they dangled promotion in front of her** ils lui ont fait miroiter un avancement

2 *vi (legs, arms, hands)* pendre; *(keys, earrings)* se balancer; **with his legs dangling** les jambes pendant dans le vide *ou* ballantes; **with his arms dangling** les bras ballants; **the climber was dangling at the end of the rope** l'alpiniste se balançait *ou* était suspendu au bout de la corde; *Fig* **to keep sb dangling** laisser qn dans le vague

dangling ['dæŋglɪŋ] *adj* pendillant, pendu

►► *Gram* ***dangling participle*** anacoluthe *f*

Daniel ['dænjəl] *pr n Bible* Daniel

Danish ['deɪnɪʃ] **1** *npl* **the Danish** les Danois *mpl*

2 *n* (**a**) *(language)* danois *m* (**b**) *Culin (pastry)* = sorte de pâtisserie fourrée

3 *adj* danois

4 *comp (embassy, history)* du Danemark; *(teacher)* de danois

►► ***Danish blue*** *(cheese)* bleu *m* du Danemark; *Culin* ***Danish pastry*** = sorte de pâtisserie fourrée

dank [dæŋk] *adj (weather, dungeon)* humide et froid

Dante ['dæntɪ] *pr n* Dante; **Dante's Inferno** l'Enfer de Dante

Dantean ['dæntɪən], **Dantesque** [dæn'tesk] *adj Literature* dantesque

Danube ['dænjuːb] *n* **the Danube** le Danube

Daphne ['dæfnɪ] *pr n Myth* Daphné

daphne ['dæfnɪ] *n Bot* daphné *m*

daphnia ['dæfnɪə] *n Entom* daphnie *f*

dapper ['dæpə(r)] *adj* propre sur soi, soigné; **he was looking very dapper** il était tiré à quatre épingles

dapple ['dæpəl] *vt* tacheter; **sunlight dappled the wall/water** le soleil faisait des taches sur le mur/l'eau

dappled ['dæpəld] *adj (animal)* tacheté; **dappled shade** ombre *f* mouchetée de lumière

dapple-grey **1** *adj* gris pommelé *(inv)*

2 *n* (**a**) *(colour)* gris *m* pommelé *(inv)* (**b**) *(horse)* cheval *m* gris pommelé; *(mare)* jument *f* gris pommelé

DAR [ˌdiːeɪ'ɑː(r)] *n (abbr* **Daughters of the American Revolution**) = organisme à tendance nationaliste et conservatrice regroupant des femmes descendant des patriotes de la guerre d'Indépendance aux États-Unis

Darby and Joan [ˌdɑːbɪən'dʒəʊn] *n* = couple uni de personnes âgées

►► ***Darby and Joan club*** club *m* du troisième âge *(en Grande-Bretagne)*

Dardanelles [ˌdɑːdə'nelz] *npl* **the Dardanelles** les Dardanelles *fpl*

dare [deə(r)] **1** *modal vb (venture)* oser; **to dare (to) do sth** oser faire qch; **I daren't think** *or* **don't dare (to) think about it** je n'ose (pas) y penser; **nobody would dare (to) contradict her** personne n'oserait la contredire; **she didn't dare (to)** *or* **dared not say a word** elle n'a pas osé dire un mot; **I lay there hardly daring to breathe** j'étais couché là, osant à peine respirer; **let them try it if they dare!** qu'ils essaient s'ils osent!; **dare I interrupt?** puis-je me permettre de vous interrompre?; **don't you dare tell me what to do!** ne t'avise surtout pas de me dire ce que j'ai à faire!; **don't you dare!** je te le déconseille!; **how dare you speak to me in that tone of voice!** comment oses-tu me parler sur ce ton!; **dare I say it** si j'ose m'exprimer ainsi; **I dare say you're hungry after your journey** je suppose que vous êtes affamés après ce voyage; **I dare say she's right** elle a probablement raison; **he was most apologetic – I dare say!** il s'est confondu en excuses – j'imagine!

2 *vt* (**a**) *(challenge)* défier; **to dare sb to do sth** défier qn de faire qch; **I dare you!** chiche!

(**b**) *Literary (death, dishonour)* braver, défier; *(displeasure)* braver

3 *n (challenge)* défi *m*; **to do sth for a dare** faire qch pour relever un défi

daredevil ['deəˌdevəl] **1** *n* casse-cou *m inv*

2 *adj* casse-cou *(inv)*

daren't [deənt] = **dare not**

daresay [ˌdeə'seɪ] *vi Br* **I daresay** *(probably, I suppose)* j'imagine, je suppose; **she's telling the truth – I daresay (she is)** elle dit la vérité – je veux bien le croire

Dar es-Salaam [ˌdɑːressə'lɑːm] *n* Dar es-Salaam

daring ['deərɪŋ] **1** *n (of person)* audace *f*, hardiesse *f*; *(of feat)* hardiesse *f*; **of great daring** très audacieux

2 *adj (audacious)* audacieux, hardi; *(provocative)* audacieux, provocant

daringly ['deərɪŋlɪ] *adv* audacieusement, hardiment; **a daringly low neckline** un décolleté audacieux *ou* provocant; **to be daringly different** afficher sa différence avec audace

dariole ['dærɪəʊl] *n Culin (mould, prepared dish)* dariole *f*

dark [dɑːk] **1** *n* noir *m*; **to see in the dark** voir dans le noir; **before/after dark** avant/après la tombée de la nuit; **to be afraid of the dark** avoir peur du noir *ou* dans le noir; **I can't work in the dark!** je ne peux pas travailler sans savoir où je vais!; **to keep sb in the dark about sth** maintenir qn dans l'ignorance à propos de qch; **to be in the dark about sth** être dans l'ignorance à propos de qch; **she left us in the dark** elle nous a laissés dans l'ignorance

2 *adj* (**a**) *(without light → night, room, street)* sombre, obscur; *Fig (thoughts)* sombre; *(ideas)* noir; **it's very dark in here** il fait très sombre ici; **it's too dark to see what I'm doing** il fait *ou* c'est trop sombre pour que je voie ce que je suis en train de faire; **it's getting dark** il commence à faire nuit, la nuit tombe; **it's getting darker** il fait de plus en plus nuit; **it gets dark early** il fait nuit de bonne heure; **to get dark** *(sky)* s'assombrir; **it won't be dark for another hour yet** il ne fera pas nuit avant une heure; **it's still dark (outside)** il fait encore nuit; **the dark days of the war** la sombre période de la guerre; **to look on the dark side** voir tout en noir

(**b**) *(colour)* foncé; *(dress, suit)* sombre; **she always wears dark colours** elle porte toujours des couleurs sombres; **I'd like some dark meat** *(of poultry)* je voudrais une aile ou une cuisse

(**c**) *(hair, eyes)* foncé; *(skin, complexion)* foncé, brun; **a dark man** un brun; **a dark woman** une brune; **to be dark** être brun; **to have dark hair** avoir les cheveux bruns, être brun; **to get darker** *(hair)* foncer; **his dark good looks** sa beauté ténébreuse

(**d**) *(hidden, mysterious)* mystérieux, secret(ète); *(secret)* bien gardé; *(hint)* mystérieux, énigmatique; **the dark side of the moon** la face cachée de la lune; **to keep sth dark** tenir qch secret; **keep it dark!** garde-le pour toi!; **you kept it very dark!** tu nous avais caché ça!

(**e**) *(sinister)* noir; **to give sb a dark look** lancer un regard noir à qn; **there's a dark side to her** il y a une part d'ombre en elle; **a dark chapter in the country's history** un chapitre peu glorieux de l'histoire du pays

►► *Hist* ***Dark Ages*** Haut Moyen Âge *m*; *Fig* **he's still in the Dark Ages** il est resté au Moyen Âge; ***dark chocolate*** chocolat *m* noir; *Old-fashioned* ***the Dark Continent*** le Continent noir; ***dark glasses*** lunettes *fpl* noires; ***dark horse*** *(competitor, horse)* participant(e) *m,f* inconnu(e); *Am Pol* candidat(e) *m,f* surprise; *Fig* **to be a dark horse** *(secretive person)* être très secret; **you're a dark horse!** tu caches bien ton jeu!

Dark Satanic mills

Cette formule ("Les sombres et diaboliques usines") est tirée du cantique *Jerusalem*, inspiré d'un poème de William Blake de 1804 (le poème est connu sous le titre *Jerusalem* mais son titre diffère en réalité de celui du cantique). Ces mots évoquent la transformation du paysage du nord d'Angleterre survenue avec la révolution industrielle. Aujourd'hui on les cite volontiers pour parler de cette période de l'histoire d'Angleterre ou bien pour évoquer tout paysage industriel hideux et oppressant.

darken ['dɑːkən] **1** *vt (sky)* assombrir; *(colour)* foncer; **to darken a room** *(make look darker)* assombrir *ou* obscurcir une pièce; *(plunge into darkness)* faire l'obscurité dans une pièce; **a darkened building** un immeuble dans le noir; **a darkened room** une pièce sombre; **never darken my door again!** et que je ne te revoie plus ici!

2 *vi (sky, room)* s'assombrir, s'obscurcir; *(hair, wood)* foncer; *(face, brow)* s'assombrir; *(painting)* s'obscurcir

darkening ['dɑːkənɪŋ] **1** *adj (sky, face)* qui s'assombrit; **he looked up at the darkening sky** il regarda le ciel qui s'assombrissait

2 *n (of sky, painting)* assombrissement *m*; *Literary* **at the darkening** à la tombée de la nuit

dark-eyed *adj* aux yeux sombres *ou* foncés

dark-haired *adj* aux cheveux foncés

darkie ['dɑːkɪ] *n Fam Old-fashioned* moricaud(e) *m,f*, = terme raciste désignant un Noir

darkish ['dɑːkɪʃ] *adj (colour, sky, wood)* plutôt *ou* assez sombre; *(hair, skin)* plutôt brun *ou* foncé; *(person)* plutôt brun

darkle ['dɑːkəl] *vi Literary* (**a**) *(get dark)* s'assombrir (**b**) *(appear indistinct)* se dissimuler à l'ombre

darkling ['dɑːklɪŋ] *Literary* **1** *adj (dark)* sombre, obscur

2 *adv* dans l'obscurité

darkly ['dɑːklɪ] *adv (hint)* énigmatiquement; *(say)* sur un ton sinistre

darkness ['dɑːknɪs] *n* (**a**) *(of night, room, street)* obscurité *f*; **darkness had fallen** il faisait nuit; **to be in darkness** être plongé dans l'obscurité (**b**) *(of hair, skin)* couleur *f* foncée; **I don't like the darkness of the colours** je n'aime pas toutes ces couleurs foncées

'Darkness at Noon' *Koestler* 'Le Zéro et l'infini'

darkroom ['dɑːkrʊm] *n Phot* chambre *f* noire

dark-skinned *adj (having a dark complexion)* au teint mat; *(black)* à la peau noire

darksome ['dɑːksəm] *adj Arch or Literary* sombre

darky (*pl* **darkies**) = **darkie**

darling ['dɑːlɪŋ] **1** *n* (**a**) *(term of affection)* chéri(e) *m,f*; **yes darling?** oui (mon) chéri?; **Kate darling** Kate chérie; **she's a darling** c'est un amour; **you darling!** tu es un amour!; **he was an absolute darling about it** il a été absolument charmant; **be a darling and...** sois gentil *ou* un amour... (**b**) *(favourite → of teacher, parents)* favori(ite) *m,f*, chouchou(oute) *m,f*; (→ *of media, high society)* coqueluche *f*

2 *adj (beloved)* chéri; *(delightful)* charmant, adorable; **you darling man!** tu es un amour!, tu es adorable!

darn [dɑːn] **1** *n* (**a**) *(in garment)* reprise *f*; **there was a darn in the elbow of his sweater** son pull était reprisé au coude

(**b**) *Fam (idioms)* **I couldn't** *or* **I don't give a darn** je m'en fiche

2 *vt* (**a**) *(garment)* repriser, raccommoder

(**b**) *Fam (damn)* **darn it!** bon sang!; **he's late, darn him!** il est en retard, il fait vraiment chier!; **darn that cat/man!** saleté de chat/de bonhomme!; **I'll be darned!** ça alors!, oh, la vache!

3 *exclam Fam* bon sang!

4 *adj Fam* sacré; **the darn car won't start** cette sacrée bagnole ne veut pas démarrer; **you're a darn fool** t'es vraiment idiot

5 *adv Fam* vachement; **it's darn late** il est vachement tard; **it's too darn late** bon sang, il est trop tard; **we were darn lucky** on a eu une sacrée veine; **don't be so darn stupid!** ce que tu peux être bête!; **that's just too darn bad** tant pis; **to have a darn good try** faire un sacré effort; **you know darn well what I mean!** tu comprends parfaitement ce que je veux dire!

darned [dɑːnd] *Am Fam* = **darn** *adj & adv*

darning ['dɑːnɪŋ] *adj (action)* reprise *f*, raccommodage *m*; *(items to be darned)* linge *m* à repriser *ou* raccommoder

►► ***darning egg*** œuf *m* à repriser; ***darning needle*** aiguille *f* à repriser; ***darning wool*** laine *f* à repriser

dart [dɑːt] **1** *n* (**a**) *(weapon)* flèche *f*; *(for playing darts)* fléchette *f* (**b**) *Sewing* pince *f* (**c**) *(sudden movement)* **to make a dart for the door/telephone** se précipiter vers la porte/sur le téléphone; **to make a dart at sb/sth** se précipiter sur qn/qch

2 *vt* (**a**) *(glance, look → quickly)* lancer, jeter; (→ *angrily)* darder (**b**) *(tranquilize)* **to dart an animal** = administrer un produit anesthésiant à un animal à l'aide d'une carabine

3 *vi* **to dart away** *or* **off** partir en *ou* comme une flèche; **to dart for the door/telephone** se précipiter vers la porte/sur le téléphone; **to dart at sb/sth** se précipiter sur qn/qch; **to dart in/out** entrer/sortir comme une flèche; **her eyes darted from one face in the crowd to another** son regard passait rapidement d'un visage à l'autre dans la foule

4 darts *n (game)* fléchettes *fpl*; **to play darts** jouer aux fléchettes

►► ***darts champion*** champion(onne) *m,f* de fléchettes; ***darts match*** match *m* de fléchettes; *Entom* ***dart moth*** agrotide *f ou* agrotis *f* des moissons

dartboard ['dɑːtˌbɔːd] *n* cible *f* (de jeu de fléchettes)

Dartford ['dɑːtfəd] *pr n* Dartford

►► ***Dartford Tunnel*** = tunnel passant sous la Tamise à Dartford; *Orn* ***Dartford warbler*** fauvette *f* pitchou

Dartmoor ['dɑːtmɔː(r)] *n* = lande dans le sud-ouest de l'Angleterre

Dartmouth ['dɑːtməθ] *n* = port du sud-ouest de l'Angleterre où sont formés les officiers de la marine

Darwinian [dɑː'wɪnɪən] *adj (of Darwin → theory)* darwinien; *(in favour of Darwinism → thinker)* darwiniste

Darwinism ['dɑːwɪnɪzəm] *n* darwinisme *m*

Darwinist ['dɑːwɪnɪst] *n* darwiniste *mf*

dash [dæʃ] **1** *n* (**a**) *(quick movement)* mouvement *m* précipité; **to make a dash for freedom** s'enfuir vers la liberté; **to make a dash for it** *(rush)* se précipiter; *(escape)* saisir l'occasion de s'enfuir; **it was a headlong dash to the station** ça n'a été qu'une course effrénée jusqu'à la gare; **a quick dash across to Paris** un petit saut à Paris

(**b**) *Am Sport* sprint *m*; **the 100 meter dash** le 100 mètres plat

(**c**) *(small amount → of water, soda)* goutte *f*, trait *m*; (→ *of cream, milk)* nuage *m*; (→ *of lemon juice, vinegar)* filet *m*; (→ *of salt, pepper)* soupçon *m*; (→ *of colour, humour)* pointe *f*

(**d**) *Typ (punctuation mark)* tiret *m*; *(in Morse code)* trait *m*

(**e**) *(style)* panache *m*; **to cut a dash** avoir fière allure

(**f**) *Aut (dashboard)* tableau *m* de bord

2 *vt* (**a**) *(throw)* jeter (avec violence); **to dash sth to the ground** jeter qch par terre avec violence; **to dash sth to pieces** fracasser qch; **several boats were dashed against the cliffs** plusieurs bateaux ont été projetés *ou* précipités contre les falaises; *Fig* **to dash sb's hopes** réduire les espoirs de qn à néant; *Fig* **to dash sb's spirits** démoraliser *ou* abattre qn

(**b**) *Fam Old-fashioned (damn)* **dash it!** bon sang!; **I'll be dashed!** ça alors!, oh, la vache!

3 *vi* (**a**) *(rush)* se précipiter; *Br* **I must dash** je dois filer; **he dashed back to his room** il est retourné à sa chambre en vitesse, il s'est dépêché de retourner à sa chambre; **to come dashing in** entrer comme un bolide, entrer en trombe; *Br* **I'll just dash out to the shops** je vais faire quelques courses en vitesse; *Br* **I'll just dash out to the post office/library** je vais juste faire un saut à la poste/bibliothèque; *Br* **dash upstairs and fetch it, will you?** monte vite le chercher, s'il te plaît; **the dog dashed across the road in front of us** le chien a traversé la route à toute vitesse devant nous

(**b**) *(waves)* se jeter

4 *exclam Br Fam Old-fashioned* bon sang!

►**dash off 1** *vi* partir en flèche

2 *vt sep (letter, memo)* écrire en vitesse; *(drawing)* faire en vitesse

dashboard ['dæʃbɔːd] *n Aut* tableau *m* de bord

dashed [dæʃt] *Br Fam Old-fashioned* **1** *adj* de malheur; **he really is a dashed nuisance** c'est vraiment enquiquinant

2 *adv* rudement, drôlement; **it's dashed annoying** c'est rudement embêtant

dashing ['dæʃɪŋ] *adj* pimpant, fringant; **a dashing young man** un beau jeune homme

dashingly ['dæʃɪŋlɪ] *adv (behave)* avec allant; *(be dressed)* dans un style fringuant

dashpot ['dæʃpɒt] *n Aut* dash-pot *m*

dastard ['dæstəd] *n Literary* personne *f* ignoble

dastardliness ['dæstədlɪnɪs] *n Literary* caractère *m* odieux *ou* infâme

dastardly ['dæstədlɪ] *adj Literary (act, person)* odieux, infâme

dasyure ['dæsɪjʊə(r)] *n Zool* dasyure *m*

DAT [ˌdiːeɪ'tiː, dæt] *n (abbr* **digital audio tape***)* DAT *m*

►► ***DAT cartridge*** cartouche *f* DAT; ***DAT drive*** lecteur *m* DAT, lecteur *m* de bande audionumérique

data ['deɪtə] (*pl of* **datum**, *usu with sing vb)* **1** *n* informations *fpl*, données *fpl*; *Comput* données *fpl*; **a piece** *or* **an item of data** une donnée, une information; *Comput* une donnée; **what little data we do have suggests that...** le peu d'informations que nous avons semble montrer que...; **to collect data on sb/sth** recueillir des informations sur qn/qch

2 *comp Comput* de données

►► ***data acquisition*** collecte *f* de données, saisie *f* de données; ***data bank*** banque *f* de données; ***data bus*** bus *m* de données; ***data capture*** saisie *f* de données; ***data carrier*** support *m* de données; ***data collection*** recueil *m* de données, collecte *f* de données; ***data compression*** compression *f* de données; ***data encryption*** cryptage *m* ou codage *m* de données; ***data exchange*** échange *m* de données; ***data management*** gestion *f* de données; ***data path*** chemin *m* d'accès aux données; ***data privacy*** secret *m ou* protection *f* des données; ***data processing*** **1** *n* traitement *m* de l'infoumation **2** *comp (department, service)* de traitement des données *ou* de l'information, informatique; ***data processor*** *(machine)* ordinateur *m*; *(person)* informaticien(enne) *m,f*; ***data protection*** protection *f* de l'information; ***Data Protection Act*** loi *f* sur la protection de l'information *(en Grande-Bretagne)*; ***data security*** sécurité *f* des données; ***data set*** ensemble *m* de données; ***data storage*** stockage *m* de données; ***data stream*** flot *m* de données; ***data switch*** commutateur *m* de données; ***data transfer*** transfert *m ou* transmission *f* de données; ***data transmission*** transmission *f* de données

database ['deɪtəbeɪs] *Comput* **1** *n* base *f* de données; **to enter sth into a database** mettre qch dans une base de données

2 *vt* mettre sous forme de base de données

►► ***database integration*** intégration *f* de bases de données; ***database management*** gestion *f* de base de données; ***database management system*** système *m* de gestion de bases de données

datacomms ['deɪtəkɒms], **datacommunications** [ˌdeɪtəkəˌmjuːnɪ'keɪʃənz] *n Br Comput* communication *f ou* transmission *f* de données, télématique *f*

►► ***datacomms linkup*** liaison *f* télématique; ***datacomms network*** réseau *m* de communication de données; ***datacomms software*** logiciel *m* de communication

dataglove ['deɪtəglʌv] *n Comput* gant *m* de données

Datapost® ['deɪtəpəʊst] *n* = service postal britannique pour paquets urgents

DATE[1] [deɪt]

date	► **1 (a)**
rendez-vous	► **1 (b)**
ami	► **1 (c)**
terme	► **1 (d)**
dater	► **2 (a), (b)**
sortir avec	► **2 (c); 3 (b)**
se démoder	► **3 (a)**

1 *n* (**a**) *(of letter, day of the week)* date *f*; *(on coins, books etc)* millésime *m*; **what's the date today?, what's today's date?** quelle est la date aujourd'hui?, le combien sommes-nous aujourd'hui?; **today's date is the 20th of January** nous sommes le 20 janvier; **what's the date of**

the coin/building? de quelle année est cette pièce/ce bâtiment?; **would you be free on that date?** est-ce que vous seriez libre ce jour-là *ou* à cette date?; **at a later** *or* **some future date** plus tard, ultérieurement; **of an earlier/a later date** plus ancien/récent; **to set** *or* **fix a date** fixer une date; *(engaged couple)* fixer la date de son mariage; **shall we fix a date now?** est-ce que nous prenons date *ou* fixons une date maintenant?; **to put a date to sth** *(remember when it happened)* se souvenir de la date de qch; *(estimate when built, established etc)* attribuer une date à qch, dater qch; **date of birth** date *f* de naissance

(**b**) *(meeting)* rendez-vous *m*; **let's make a date for lunch** prenons rendez-vous pour déjeuner ensemble; **to have a date** avoir rendez-vous; **I already have a date on Saturday night** j'ai déjà un rendez-vous samedi soir; **to go out on a date** sortir en compagnie de quelqu'un; **her parents don't let her go out on dates** ses parents ne la laissent pas sortir avec des garçons; **I went out on a date with him once** je suis sortie avec lui une fois; **on our first date** la première fois que nous sommes sortis ensemble

(**c**) *(person)* ami(e) *m,f*; **who's your date tonight?** avec qui sors-tu ce soir?; **do you have a date for the dance?** as-tu un cavalier pour le bal?; **can I bring a date?** puis-je amener un ami?; **my date didn't show up** on m'a posé un lapin

(**d**) *Fin (of bill)* terme *m*, échéance *f*; **date of maturity, due date** (date *f* d')échéance; **three months after date, at three months' date** à trois mois de date *ou* d'échéance

2 *vt* (**a**) *(write date on → cheque, letter, memo)* dater; **a fax dated 6 May** un fax daté du 6 mai

(**b**) *(attribute date to → building, settlement etc)* dater; *(→ bottle of wine etc)* millésimer; **to date sb** *(show age of)* donner une idée de l'âge de qn; **gosh, that dates him!** eh bien, ça montre qu'il n'est plus tout jeune *ou* ça ne le rajeunit pas!

(**c**) *esp Am (go out with)* sortir avec; **they're dating each other** ils sortent ensemble

3 *vi* (**a**) *(clothes, style)* se démoder; *(novel)* vieillir

(**b**) *esp Am (go out on dates)* sortir avec des garçons/filles; **how long have you two been dating?** ça fait combien de temps que vous sortez ensemble *ou* que vous vous voyez?

4 out of date *adj* **to be out of date** *(dress, style, concept, slang)* être démodé *ou* dépassé; *(magazine, newspaper)* être vieux (vieille); *(dictionary)* ne pas être à jour *ou* à la page; *(passport, season ticket etc)* être périmé; **it's the kind of dress that will never go out of date** c'est le genre de robe indémodable *ou* qui ne se démodera jamais

5 to date *adv* à ce jour, jusqu'à maintenant

6 up to date *adj* **to be up to date** *(dress, style, person)* être à la mode *ou* à la page; *(newspaper, magazine)* être du jour/de la semaine/*etc*; *(dictionary)* être à la page *ou* à jour; *(passport)* être valide *ou* valable; *(list)* être à jour; **I'm not up to date on what's been happening** je ne suis pas au courant de ce qui s'est passé dernièrement; **to keep up to date with the news/scientific developments** se tenir au courant de l'actualité/des progrès de la science; **to keep sb up to date on sth** tenir qn au courant de qch; **to bring sb up to date on sth** mettre qn au courant de qch; **to bring one's diary up to date** mettre à jour son journal

►► ***date rape*** = viol commis par une connaissance, un ami etc; **date rape frequently goes unreported** peu de femmes violées par une connaissance ou un ami portent plainte

►**date back to, date from** *vt insep* dater de; **this church dates back to** *or* **from the 13th century** cette église date du XIIIème siècle; **a friendship dating back to** *or* **from the days of their youth** une amitié qui remonte à leur jeunesse

DATE

Pour donner une date en anglais, on n'emploie pas l'article à l'écrit. En anglais britannique, on écrira donc "Monday 25th December 2000" ou, de plus en plus souvent, "Monday 25 December 2000", et, en abrégé, "25.12.00". Notez cependant qu'à l'oral, on prononce "Monday the twenty-fifth of December...". En anglais américain, le mois est indiqué avant le jour. On écrira ainsi "Monday December 25 2000" et, en abrégé, "12.25.00", et on prononcera "December twenty-five".

date² *n (fruit)* datte *f*

►► *Bot* ***date palm*** palmier *m* dattier

datebook ['deɪtbʊk] *n Am* agenda *m*

dated ['deɪtɪd] *adj (clothes, style)* démodé; *(term, expression, concept)* vieilli, désuet(ète); *(novel)* qui a mal vieilli

dateless ['deɪtlɪs] *adj* (**a**) *(timeless)* indémodable (**b**) *(not dated → document, letter)* non daté

dateline ['deɪt,laɪn] *n* (**a**) *Press* date *f* de rédaction (**b**) *(on world map)* ligne *f* de changement de date

datestamp ['deɪtstæmp] **1** *n* tampon *m* dateur; *(used for cancelling)* oblitérateur *m*, timbre *m* à date; *(postmark)* cachet *m* de la poste

2 *vt (book)* tamponner, mettre le cachet de la date sur; *(letter)* oblitérer

date-stamping *n* compostage *m*

dating ['deɪtɪŋ] *n (of building, settlement etc)* datation *f*

►► ***dating agency*** agence *f* matrimoniale; *Am* ***dating bar*** bar *m* pour célibataires

dative ['deɪtɪv] *Gram* **1** *n* datif *m*; **in the dative** au datif

2 *adj* datif

datum ['deɪtəm] *(pl* **data**) *n Formal* donnée *f*, information *f*; *Comput* donnée *f*

daub [dɔːb] **1** *n* (**a**) *(of paint)* tache *f*, barbouillage *m*; *(done on purpose)* barbouillage *m* (**b**) *Pej (painting)* croûte *f* (**c**) *(for walls)* torchis *m*

2 *vt* enduire; *(with mud)* couvrir; **a wall daubed with slogans** un mur couvert de slogans

3 *vi Pej (paint badly)* peinturlurer, barbouiller

Daubenton's bat [daʊ'bentənz-] *n Zool* vespertilion *m* de Daubenton

dauber ['dɔːbə(r)] *n Pej* barbouilleur(euse) *m,f*

daughter ['dɔːtə(r)] *n* fille *f*

►► ***Daughters of the American Revolution*** = organisme à tendance nationaliste et conservatrice regroupant des femmes descendant des patriotes de la guerre d'Indépendance aux États-Unis; *Comput* ***daughter board*** carte *f* fille; *Biol* ***daughter cell*** cellule *f* fille; *Phys* ***daughter element*** élément *m* engendré

'Ryan's Daughter' *Lean* 'La Fille de Ryan'

daughter-in-law *n* bru *f*, belle-fille *f*

daughterly ['dɔːtəlɪ] *adj* filial

daunt [dɔːnt] *vt* intimider; **nothing daunted** nullement découragé

daunting ['dɔːntɪŋ] *adj* intimidant

dauntless ['dɔːntlɪs] *adj* déterminé

dauntlessly ['dɔːntlɪslɪ] *adv* sans se décourager

dauntlessness ['dɔːntlɪsnɪs] *n* intrépidité *f*

dauphin ['dɔːfɪn] *n Hist* dauphin *m*

dauphine ['dɔːfiːn] *n Hist* dauphine *f*

davenport ['dævənpɔːt] *n* (**a**) *Br (desk)* secrétaire *m* (**b**) *Am (sofa)* canapé(-lit) *m*

David ['deɪvɪd] *pr n Bible* David

Davis Strait ['deɪvɪs-] *n* **the Davis Strait** le détroit de Davis

davit ['dævɪt] *n Naut* bossoir *m*, portemanteau *m*

Davy ['deɪvɪ] *pr n* **Davy Crockett** = pionnier américain rendu célèbre par sa participation héroïque à la bataille de Fort Alamo; **in Davy Jones's locker** *(person, ship)* au fond de la mer

►► *Mining* ***Davy lamp*** lampe *f* de sécurité de mineur

dawdle ['dɔːdəl] *vi Pej* traîner, lambiner, traînasser; **to dawdle over sth** traînasser *ou* traîner en faisant qch

►**dawdle about** *vi Pej* traîner, lambiner, traînasser

dawdler ['dɔːdlə(r)] *n* lambin(e) *m,f*, traînard(e) *m,f*

dawdling ['dɔːdlɪŋ] **1** *n* **stop all this dawdling!** arrête de traînasser!

2 *adj* traînard

Dawes plan [dɔːz-] *n Hist* **the Dawes plan** le plan Dawes

dawn [dɔːn] **1** *n* (**a**) *(part of day)* aube *f*; **at dawn** à l'aube; **from dawn till dusk** du matin au soir; **at the crack of dawn** au point du jour; **(just) as dawn was breaking** alors que l'aube pointait; **to watch the dawn** regarder le jour se lever

(**b**) *Fig (of civilization, era)* aube *f*; *(of hope)* naissance *f*, éclosion *f*; **since the dawn of time** depuis la nuit des temps

2 *vi* (**a**) *(day)* se lever

(**b**) *Fig (new era, hope)* naître

►► ***dawn chorus*** chant *m* des oiseaux à l'aube; ***dawn raid*** descente *f* à l'aube; *(by police)* descente *f ou* rafle *f* à l'aube; *St Exch* raid *m (mené dès l'ouverture de la Bourse)*; *St Exch* ***dawn raider*** raider *m (qui opère dès l'ouverture de la Bourse)*

►**dawn on** *vt insep* **the truth dawned on** *or* **upon him** la vérité lui apparut; **it dawned on me that...** j'ai commencé à me rendre compte que...; **that's just dawned on you, has it?** voilà seulement *ou* c'est seulement maintenant que tu t'en rends compte?

dawning ['dɔːnɪŋ] **1** *adj* naissant

2 *n Fig (of civilization, era)* aube *f*; *(of hope)* naissance *f*, éclosion *f*

Dax [dæks] *n St Exch* **the Dax (index)** l'indice *m* Dax

DAY [deɪ]

jour	► **1 (a), (b)**
journée	► **1 (a) – (c)**
époque	► **1 (d)**

1 *n* (**a**) *(period of twenty-four hours)* jour *m*; *(emphasizing duration)* journée *f*; **it's a nice** *or* **fine day** c'est une belle journée, il fait beau aujourd'hui; **on a clear day** par temps clair; **a summer's/winter's day** un jour d'été/d'hiver; **to have a day out** aller passer une journée quelque part; **a day at the seaside/the races** une journée au bord de la mer/aux courses; **we went to the country for the day** nous sommes allés passer la journée à la campagne; **to have a lazy day** passer une journée à paresser; *Literary* **when day is done** quand le jour s'achève; **what day is it (today)?** quel jour sommes-nous (aujourd'hui)?; **what day is she arriving (on)?** quel jour arrive-t-elle?; **(on) that day** ce jour-là; **(on) the day (that** *or* **when) she was born** le jour où elle est née; **on the first/last day of the holidays** le premier/dernier jour des vacances; **on a day like this/today** un jour comme celui-là/aujourd'hui; **the day after, (on) the next** *or* **following day** le lendemain, le jour suivant; **the day after the party** le lendemain de *ou* le jour d'après la fête; **two days after the party** le surlendemain de *ou* deux jours après la fête; **the day after tomorrow** après-demain; **the day before, (on) the previous day** la veille, le jour d'avant; **I had first met him two days before** je l'avais rencontré l'avant-veille pour la première fois; **the day before yesterday** avant-hier; **four days before/later** quatre jours plus tôt/tard; **in four days, in four days' time** dans quatre jours; **it took me four days to do it** ça m'a pris quatre jours pour le faire; **once/twice a day** une fois/deux fois par jour; **good day!** bonjour!; **have a nice day!** bonne journée!; **the other day** l'autre jour; *Rel* **Day of Judgement** (jour du) jugement dernier; *Rel* **day of atonement** jour *m* du Grand Pardon; **dish of the day** plat *m* du jour; **day of reckoning** jour de vérité; **any day now** d'un jour à l'autre; **day after day, day in day out** jour après jour; **for days on end** *or* **at a time** pendant des jours et des jours; **from day to day** de jour en jour; **to live from day to day** vivre au jour le jour; **from one day to the next** d'un jour à l'autre; **from that day on** *or* **onwards** à partir de ce jour-là; **from that day to this** depuis ce jour-là; *Literary* **from this day forth** à partir *ou* à compter d'aujourd'hui; **to the day I die** *or* **my dying day** jusqu'à mon dernier jour; **I'd rather work in Madrid any day (of the week)** je préférerais largement *ou* de loin travailler à Madrid; **you've done enough mischief for one day** tu as fait assez de bêtises pour une seule journée; *Hum* **another day, another dollar** ≃ c'est le train-train quotidien; **from day one** depuis le premier jour; **one day** un jour; **one of these days** un de ces jours; **some day** un jour; **she's**

seventy if she's a day elle a soixante-dix ans bien sonnés; **he doesn't look a day older than 40/you** il n'a pas l'air d'avoir plus de 40 ans/ d'être plus vieux que toi; **he doesn't look a day older than when I last saw him** il n'a pas vieilli d'un poil depuis la dernière fois que je l'ai vu; **it's been one of those days!** tu parles d'une journée!; **on this (day) of all days!** justement aujourd'hui!; **of all (the) days to choose for a conference!** quelle idée d'avoir choisi de faire une conférence justement aujourd'hui!; **let's make a day of it** passons-y la journée; **that really made my day!** ça m'a fait très plaisir; **it's not my (lucky) day** ce n'est pas mon jour (de chance); *Fam* **that'll be the day!** *(it's highly unlikely)* il n'y a pas de danger que ça arrive de sitôt!; **at the end of the day** à la fin de la journée; *Fig* en fin de compte, au bout du compte; **to carry** *or* **win the day** gagner la journée *ou* la bataille

(**b**) *(hours of daylight)* jour *m*, journée *f*; **all day (long)** toute la journée; **we haven't got all day** nous n'avons pas que ça à faire; **to travel during the** *or* **by day** voyager pendant la journée *ou* de jour; **to sleep during the** *or* **by day** dormir le jour; **day and night, night and day** jour et nuit, nuit et jour; **in the cold light of day the plan seemed unfeasible** avec un peu de distance critique, le projet semblait infaisable

(**c**) *(working hours)* journée *f*; **paid by the day** payé à la journée; **to work a seven-hour day** travailler sept heures par jour, faire des journées de sept heures; **how was your day?, what kind of day have you had?** comment s'est passée ta journée?; **did you have a good day?** tu as passé une bonne journée?; **it's been a hard/long day** la journée a été dure/longue; **day off** jour *m* de congé; **day of rest** jour *m* de repos; **let's call it a day** *(stop work)* arrêtons-nous pour aujourd'hui; *(end relationship)* finissons-en; **it's all in a day's work!** ça fait partie du travail!

(**d**) *(often pl) (lifetime, era)* époque *f*; **in Caesar's day** du temps de César; **in the days of King Arthur, in King Arthur's day** du temps du Roi Arthur; **in days to come** à l'avenir; **in days gone by** par le passé; **in those days** à l'époque; **what are you up to these days?** qu'est-ce que tu fais de beau ces temps-ci?; **honestly, teenagers these days!** vraiment, les adolescents d'aujourd'hui!; *Literary or Hum* **in days of old** *or* **yore** il y a fort longtemps; **in the good old days** dans le temps; **in my/our day** de mon/notre temps; **in this day and age** de nos jours, aujourd'hui; **he was well-known in his day** il était connu de son temps *ou* à son époque; **in his working/married days** du temps où il travaillait/était marié; **in his younger days** dans son jeune temps, dans sa jeunesse; **the happiest/worst days of my life** les plus beaux/les pires jours de ma vie; **during the early days of the strike/my childhood** au tout début de la grève/de mon enfance; **he ended his days in poverty** il a fini ses jours dans la misère; **her day will come** son heure viendra; **to have had its day** *(theory, fashion etc)* être démodé; *(car, TV)* avoir fait son temps; **he's had his day** il a eu son heure; **he's/this chair has seen better days** il/cette chaise a connu des jours meilleurs; **those were the days** c'était le bon temps

(**e**) *(battle, game)* **to win** *or* **to carry the day** l'emporter; **to lose the day** perdre la partie

2 days *adv* **to work days** travailler de jour

3 this day week *adv* dans huit jours aujourd'hui

4 to the day *adv* jour pour jour; **it's a year ago to the day** il y a un an jour pour jour *ou* aujourd'hui

5 to this day *adv* à ce jour, aujourd'hui encore

►► ***day bed*** lit *m* de repos; *Am* ***day camp*** centre *m* aéré; ***day care*** *(for elderly, disabled)* service *m* d'accueil de jour; *(for children)* service *m* de garderie; **the children go to day care** les enfants vont à la garderie; ***day centre*** = centre d'animation et d'aide sociale; ***day cream*** crème *f* de jour; ***day job*** travail *m* principal; *Fam Hum* **don't give up the day job** *(to aspiring artist etc)* je ne crois pas que tu es prêt pour une carrière professionnelle; ***day labourer*** journalier(ère) *m,f*; ***day nurse*** infirmier(ère) *m,f* qui est de service de jour; ***day nursery*** garderie *f*; *St Exch* ***day order*** ordre *m* valable pour la journée; ***day pass*** *(for skiing)* forfait *m* journalier; *Sch* ***day pupil*** (élève *mf*) externe *mf*; *Br Ind* ***day release*** formation *f* continue en alternance; **to be on day release** être en formation continue en alternance; *Rail* ***day return*** aller-retour *m* valable pour la journée; ***day room*** salle *f* commune; ***day school*** externat *m*; ***day shift*** *(period worked)* service *m* de jour; *(workers)* équipe *f* de jour; **to work the day shift** travailler de jour, être (dans l'équipe) de jour; **when do you go on day shift?** quand est-ce que tu prends le service de jour?; *St Exch* ***day trade*** opération *f* de journée; *St Exch* ***day trader*** spéculateur(trice) *m,f* à la journée; ***day trip*** excursion *f*; ***day tripper*** excursionniste *mf*; ***day work*** travail *m* de jour

'The Day of the Jackal' *Forsyth, Zimmermann* 'Le Chacal'

day-after recall *n Mktg* mémorisation *f* un jour après

day-blind *adj* nyctalope

daybook ['deɪbʊk] *n Acct* brouillard *m*

dayboy ['deɪbɔɪ] *n Br Sch* = demi-pensionnaire, dans une école où de nombreux élèves sont internes

daybreak ['deɪbreɪk] *n* point *m* du jour; **at daybreak** au point du jour

day-care *adj (facilities → for elderly, disabled)* d'accueil de jour; *(→ for children)* de garderie

►► ***day-care centre*** = centre d'animation et d'aide sociale; *Am (for children)* garderie *f*

daydream ['deɪdri:m] **1** *n* rêverie *f*; *Pej* rêvasserie *f*; **to have a daydream** rêver, rêvasser; **to be in the middle of a daydream** être en pleine rêverie

2 *vi* rêver; *Pej* rêvasser; **to daydream about sth** rêver *ou* rêvasser à qch; **daydreaming again?** encore en train de rêvasser *ou* de rêver tout éveillé?

daydreamer ['deɪdri:mə(r)] *n* rêveur(euse) *m,f*

daydreaming ['deɪdri:mɪŋ] *n (UNCOUNT)* rêveries *fpl*, rêvasseries *fpl*

day-for-night *n Cin* nuit *f* américaine

daygirl ['deɪgɜ:l] *n Br Sch* = demi-pensionnaire, dans une école où de nombreux élèves sont internes

Day-Glo® ['deɪgləʊ] **1** *n* tissu *m* fluorescent

2 *adj* fluorescent; **Day-Glo**® **cycling shorts** cuissard *m* de cycliste fluorescent

daylight ['deɪlaɪt] *n* (**a**) *(dawn)* aube *f*, point *m* du jour; **before daylight** avant l'aube

(**b**) *(light of day)* jour *m*, lumière *f* du jour; **it was still daylight** il faisait encore jour; **in daylight** de jour; **in broad daylight** en plein jour; **daylight hours** heures durant lesquelles il fait jour; *Fig* **to put daylight between oneself and sb** distancer qn; **to put daylight between two teams** creuser l'écart entre deux équipes; *Fig* **to begin to see daylight** *(approach end of task)* commencer à voir le bout (du tunnel); *(begin to understand)* commencer à voir clair; *Fam* **it's daylight robbery** c'est du vol pur et simple

(**c**) *Fam* **to beat** *or* **to thrash** *or* **to knock the living daylights out of sb** tabasser qn; *Fam* **to scare** *or* **to frighten the living daylights out of sb** flanquer une trouille bleue à qn

►► ***daylight saving (time)*** heure *f* d'été

daylong ['deɪlɒŋ] *adj (meeting, journey)* d'une journée

day-old *adj (chick, baby)* d'un jour

daytime ['deɪtaɪm] **1** *n* journée *f*; **in the daytime** le jour, pendant la journée

2 *adj* de jour

►► ***daytime TV*** émissions *fpl* télévisées pendant la journée

day-to-day *adj (life, running of business)* quotidien; *(chores, tasks)* journalier, quotidien; **to lead a day-to-day existence** vivre au jour le jour; *(with difficulty)* vivre péniblement jour après jour; **the day-to-day management of a company** l'administration courante d'une entreprise; **on a day-to-day basis** au jour le jour

Daytona Beach [deɪ'təʊnə-] *n* Daytona Beach

Dayton Agreement ['deɪtən-] *n* accords *mpl* de Dayton

daze [deɪz] **1** *n (caused by blow)* étourdissement *m*; *(caused by emotional shock, surprise)* ahurissement *m*; *(caused by medication)* abrutissement *m*; **to be in a daze** *(because of blow)* être étourdi; *(because of emotional shock, surprise)* être abasourdi *ou* ahuri; *(because of medication)* être abruti

2 *vt (of blow)* étourdir; *(of emotional shock, surprise)* abasourdir, ahurir; *(of medication)* abrutir

dazed [deɪzd] *adj (by blow)* étourdi, hébété; *(by emotional shock, surprise)* abasourdi, ahuri, hébété; *(by medication)* abruti

dazedly ['deɪzɪdlɪ] *adv (by blow, emotional shock, surprise)* d'un air hébété; *(by medication)* d'un air abruti

dazzle ['dæzəl] **1** *n (of headlights)* lueur *f* éblouissante *ou* aveuglante; *Fig* éclat *m*

2 *vt also Fig* éblouir; **she was quite dazzled by him** il l'a complètement éblouie

dazzling ['dæzlɪŋ] *adj* éblouissant

dazzlingly ['dæzlɪŋlɪ] *adv* **a dazzlingly bright day** une journée d'une clarté éblouissante; **he is dazzlingly successful** il réussit brillamment dans la vie; **dazzlingly beautiful** d'une beauté éblouissante

dB *Phys (written abbr* **decibel**) dB

DBA [ˌdi:bi:'eɪ] *n (abbr* **Doctor of Business Administration**) docteur *m* en gestion

dbase *n Comput (written abbr* **database**) BD *f*

DBE [ˌdi:bi:'i:] *n Br (abbr* **Dame Commander of the Order of the British Empire**) = distinction honorifique britannique pour les femmes

DBMS [ˌdi:bi:ˌem'es] *n Comput (abbr* **database management system**) SGBD *m*

DBS [ˌdi:bi:'es] *n (abbr* **direct broadcasting by satellite**) télédiffusion *f* directe par satellite

DC [ˌdi:'si:] *n* (**a**) *Elec (abbr* **direct current**) CC (**b**) *Am Fam (abbr* **District of Columbia**) DC (**c**) *(abbr* **Detective Constable**) ≃ inspecteur(trice) *m,f* de police

DCC [ˌdi:si:'si:] *(abbr* **digital compact cassette**) DCC *f*

DCF [ˌdi:si:'ef] *n Fin (abbr* **discounted cash flow**) cash-flow *m* actualisé, flux *mpl* de trésorerie actualisés

DD [ˌdi:'di:] *n* (**a**) *Univ (abbr* **Doctor of Divinity**) *(person)* = titulaire d'un doctorat en théologie; *(qualification)* doctorat *m* en théologie (**b**) *Comput (abbr* **double density**) double densité *f* (**c**) *Am Mil (abbr* **dishonorable discharge**) = exclusion de l'armée pour manquement à l'honneur

D/D *Fin (written abbr* **direct debit**) prélèvement *m* automatique

dd. *(written abbr* **delivered**) livré

D-day *n* le jour J

DDE [ˌdi:di:'i:] *n Comput (abbr* **dynamic data exchange**) DDE *m*

DDS [ˌdi:di:'es] *n Univ (abbr* **Doctor of Dental Science**) *(person)* = titulaire d'un doctorat en dentisterie; *(qualification)* doctorat *m* en dentisterie

DDT [ˌdi:di:'ti:] *n Chem (abbr* **dichlorodiphenyltrichloroethane**) DDT *m*

DE *(written abbr* **Delaware**) Delaware *m*

DEA [ˌdi:i:'eɪ] *n Am (abbr* **Drug Enforcement Administration**) = agence américaine de lutte contre la drogue

deacon ['di:kən] *n Rel* diacre *m*

deaconess [ˌdi:kə'nes] *n Rel* diaconesse *f*

deactivate [ˌdi:'æktɪveɪt] *vt* désamorcer

deactivation [ˌdi:ˌæktɪ'veɪʃən] *n* désamorçage *m*

DEAD [ded]

mort	► **1 (a), (c) – (e), (g), (i); 3**
engourdi	► **1 (b)**
éteint	► **1 (c)**
hors jeu	► **1 (f)**
terne	► **1 (h)**
exactement	► **2 (a)**
complètement	► **2 (b)**

1 *adj* (**a**) *(not alive → person, animal, plant)* mort; *(→ flower)* fané; **dead man** *(person)* mort *m*; *Br Fam (empty bottle)* cadavre *m*; **dead woman** morte *f*; **the dead woman's husband** le mari de la défunte; **he has been dead for five years** il est mort *ou* décédé il y a cinq ans, cela fait cinq ans qu'il est mort; **to be dead on arrival** être mort *ou* décédé avant l'arrivée à l'hôpital; **dead or alive** mort ou vif; **more dead than alive** plus mort que vif; **half dead with hunger/exhaustion/fear** à demi mort de faim/d'épuisement/de peur; *also Fig* **dead and buried** mort et enterré; **they are all dead and gone now** ils sont tous morts maintenant; **stone dead** raide mort; **to drop (down)** *or* **to fall down dead** tomber raide mort; **to shoot sb dead** tuer qn (avec une arme à feu), abattre qn; **to leave sb for dead** laisser qn pour mort; *Fam* **we're just** *Br* **flogging** *or Am* **beating a dead horse** nous nous dépensons en pure perte□, nous nous acharnons inutilement□; *Fam* **you're a dead man** tu es un homme mort; *Fam Fig* **you're dead** *or* **dead meat if he finds out** s'il l'apprend, tu es mort; *Fam* **drop dead!** va te faire voir!; *Fam* **dead as a doornail** *or* **a dodo** on ne peut plus mort; **to step into a dead man's shoes** être promu à la suite du décès de son supérieur; *Fam* **I wouldn't be seen dead in that restaurant** je ne mettrai jamais les pieds dans ce restaurant□; *Fam* **I wouldn't be seen dead wearing something like that** jamais de la vie je ne mettrai quelque chose comme ça□; *Fam* **I wouldn't be seen dead with him** plutôt mourir que de me montrer en sa compagnie□; *Prov* **dead men tell no tales** les morts ne parlent pas; **dead in the water** mort dans l'œuf

(**b**) *(lacking in sensation → fingers, toes etc)* engourdi; **to go dead** s'engourdir; **dead to all sense of honour** insensible à tout sentiment d'honneur; **he is dead to reason** il ne veut pas entendre raison; *Fam* **she's dead from the neck up** elle n'a rien dans la tête; *Fam* **to be dead to the world** dormir d'un sommeil de plomb

(**c**) *(not alight → fire)* mort, éteint; *(→ coals)* éteint; *(→ match)* usé

(**d**) *(lacking activity → town)* mort; *(→ business, market)* très calme; *Banking & Fin (→ account)* inactif; **this place is dead in winter** cet endroit est mort l'hiver

(**e**) *(language)* mort

(**f**) *Sport (out of play → ball)* hors jeu *(inv)*

(**g**) *Elec (battery)* mort, à plat; *(wire)* hors *ou* sans tension; *Tel (phone, line)* coupé; **the line went dead** la ligne a été coupée; **the phone is** *or* **has gone dead** il n'y a pas de tonalité

(**h**) *(dull → colour)* terne, fade; *(→ sound)* sourd

(**i**) *Fam (tired out)* mort, crevé

(**j**) *(finished with → cigar)* entièrement fumé; *Fam* **are these glasses dead?** est-ce que vous avez fini avec ces verres□?

(**k**) *Fam (no longer working → TV, fridge etc)* foutu

(**l**) *(idioms)* **in dead earnest** *(be)* très sérieux; *(speak)* très sérieusement; *Fam* **he's the dead spit of his father** c'est son père tout craché; **she fell to the floor in a dead faint** elle tomba à terre, inconsciente; **on a dead level with sth** exactement au même niveau que qch; *Br Old-fashioned* **to make a dead set at sb** *(romantically)* jeter son dévolu sur qn

2 *adv* (**a**) *(precisely)* **dead ahead** tout droit; **dead in the middle** juste au milieu, au beau milieu; *Br* **to be dead level (with sth)** être exactement au même niveau (que qch); *Br* **dead on time** juste à l'heure; *Br* **to arrive dead on the hour** arriver à l'heure pile *ou* juste à l'heure; **dead on target** *Br (hit something)* en plein dans le mille; *Br Fam* **you're dead right** tu as entièrement raison□; *Br Fam* **you're dead on** c'est exactement ça□

(**b**) *Fam (very)* super; **dead beat** crevé, mort; **dead broke** complètement fauché; **dead drunk** ivre mort; **dead easy** super facile, fastoche; *Br* **dead good** super bon; *Br* **it was dead lucky** c'était un super coup de bol *ou* de pot; **dead tired** mort, crevé

(**c**) *(completely)* **the sea was dead calm** la mer était parfaitement calme; **to be dead against sb/sth** être absolument contre qn/qch; **to be dead set on doing sth** être fermement décidé à faire qch; **to be dead set on sth** tenir absolument *ou* à tout prix à qch; **to be dead set against sb/sth** être résolument opposé à qn/qch; *Naut* **wind dead ahead** vent droit debout

(**d**) *Aut* **dead slow** *(sign)* au pas; *Hum* **he has two speeds – dead slow and stop** il est d'une lenteur!

(**e**) *(idioms)* **to play dead** faire le mort; **to stop dead** s'arrêter net; **to stop sb dead** arrêter qn net

3 *npl* **the dead** les morts; *Rel* **to rise from the dead** ressusciter d'entre les morts

4 *n (depth)* **in the dead of winter** au cœur de l'hiver; **in the** *or* **at dead of night** au milieu *ou* au plus profond de la nuit

►► ***dead body*** cadavre *m*, corps *m*; *Fam* **(it'll be) over my dead body!** il faudra me tuer d'abord!; *Fam* **you'll marry him over my dead body!** moi vivant, tu ne l'épouseras pas!; *Naut* ***dead calm*** calme *m* plat; *Tech* ***dead centre*** point *m* mort; *(of lathe)* centre *m* fixe; *Br Fam* ***dead cert*** *(in race, competition)* valeur *f* sûre□; **it's a dead cert that he'll be there** il sera là à coup sûr; *Typ* ***dead copy*** vieille épreuve *f*; *Fig* ***dead duck*** *(plan, proposal → which will fail)* désastre *m* assuré□, plan *m* foireux; *(→ which has failed)* désastre *m*, fiasco *m*; **he's a dead duck** c'en est fini de lui; ***dead end*** *(road)* cul *m* de sac, voie *f* sans issue, impasse *f*; **it's a dead end** *(job)* il n'y a aucune perspective d'avenir; *(line of investigation, research)* cela ne mènera *ou* conduira à rien; **to come to a dead end** *(street)* se terminer en cul de sac; *Fig* **to come to** *or* **to reach a dead end** aboutir à une impasse; ***dead hand*** (**a**) *(influence)* mainmise *f*, emprise *f*; **the dead hand of tradition** le poids de la tradition (**b**) *Law* mainmorte *f*; ***dead heat*** = course dont les vainqueurs sont déclarés ex aequo; *(horse race)* dead-heat *m*; **it was a dead heat** *(athletics race)* les coureurs sont arrivés ex aequo; ***dead letter*** *Admin (letter that cannot be delivered)* lettre *f* non distribuée, (lettre *f* passée au) rebut *m*; *(law, rule)* loi *f ou* règle *f* caduque *ou* tombée en désuétude; **to become a dead letter** *(law, rule)* tomber en désuétude; *Fig* **it's a dead letter** c'est mort et enterré; *Br Com* ***dead loss*** perte *f* sèche; *Br Fam* **to be a dead loss** *(person, thing)* être complètement nul; *Am Admin* ***dead mail*** courrier *m* non distribuée; ***dead man's fingers*** *(coral)* alcyon *m*; *Rail* ***dead man's handle*** manette *f* d'homme-mort; ***dead march*** marche *f* funèbre; *Naut* ***dead reckoning*** estime *f*; **to navigate by dead reckoning** naviguer à l'estime; *Fam* ***dead ringer*** sosie□ *m*; **to be a dead ringer for sb** être le sosie de qn; ***the Dead Sea*** la mer Morte; ***the Dead Sea Scrolls*** les manuscrits *mpl* de la mer Morte; ***dead silence*** silence *m* complet *ou* de mort; ***dead stock*** *(UNCOUNT) Agr* machines *fpl* agricoles; ***dead stop*** arrêt *m* brutal; **to come to a dead stop** s'arrêter net; ***dead weight*** poids *m* mort; *Aut* poids *m* utile; *Fig* **he's a dead weight** c'est un poids mort; ***dead white European male*** = écrivain, musicien etc européen blanc mort depuis longtemps; *Br* ***dead wood*** *(trees, branches)* bois *m* mort; *Fig (people)* personnel *m* inutile; **there is too much dead wood in this office** il y a trop de gens payés à ne rien faire dans ce bureau

'Dead of Night' *Hamer, Dearden et al* 'Au cœur de la nuit'

'The Dead' *Joyce, Huston* 'Les Morts' (nouvelle), 'Les Gens de Dublin' (film)

dead-and-alive *adj Br* mort, triste; **it's a dead-and-alive sort of place** c'est un vrai trou

dead-ball line *n Rugby* ligne *f* de ballon mort

deadbeat ['dedbi:t] *n Fam (good-for-nothing)* bon (bonne) *m,f* à rien; *(tramp)* épave *f*, loque *f*; *(parasite)* pique-assiette *mf*

►► *Am* ***deadbeat dad*** = père qui refuse de payer la pension alimentaire de ses enfants

dead-cat bounce *n Fam St Exch* = reprise de courte durée lors de l'effondrement des cours de la Bourse

deaden ['dedən] *vt (sound)* assourdir; *(sense, nerve, hunger pangs)* calmer; *(pain)* endormir, calmer; *(blow)* amortir

dead-end *adj (street)* sans issue; *Fig* **a dead-end job** un travail qui n'offre aucune perspective d'avenir

deadening ['dedənɪŋ] *adj (boredom, task)* abrutissant; **the deadening effects of alcohol** les effets insensibilisants *ou* anesthésiants de l'alcool

deadfall [ded'fɔ:l] *n* = piège consistant à faire tomber un objet pesant sur la proie

Deadhead ['dedhed] *n* = fan du groupe de rock américain The Grateful Dead

deadhead ['dedhed] **1** *n* (**a**) *Fam (dull person)* nullité *f* (**b**) *(person using free ticket → in theatre)* spectateur(trice) *m,f* ayant un billet de faveur; *(→ on train)* voyageur(euse) *m,f* muni(e) d'un billet gratuit (**c**) *Am (empty vehicle)* = train, avion, camion etc circulant à vide

2 *vt (plants)* enlever les fleurs fanées de

3 *vi Am (train)* circuler à vide

dead-letter *adj*

►► ***dead-letter box, dead-letter drop*** cachette *f (pour le courrier)*; ***dead-letter office*** = bureau où est entreposé le courrier dont les destinataires sont introuvables

deadline ['dedlaɪn] *n (day)* date *f* limite; *(time)* heure *f* limite; **Monday is the absolute deadline** c'est pour lundi dernier délai *ou* dernière limite; **the deadline for returning your essays** la date limite *ou* la dernière limite pour rendre vos dissertations; **to meet/to miss a deadline** respecter/laisser passer une date limite; **I'm working to a deadline** j'ai un délai à respecter; **must be able to work to deadlines** *(in job advertisement)* doit être capable de travailler en fonction de délais précis

deadliness ['dedlɪnɪs] *n (of poison, snake)* caractère *m* mortel; *(of weapon)* caractère *m* meurtrier; *Fig (of wit, repartee)* mordant *m*, causticité *f*

deadlock ['dedlɒk] *n* (**a**) *(situation)* impasse *f*; **to reach (a) deadlock** arriver à une impasse; **to break the deadlock** *(negotiators)* sortir de l'impasse; *(concession)* apporter une solution à l'impasse (**b**) *Tech* serrure *f* à pêne dormant; *Aut* serrure passive

deadlocked ['dedlɒkt] *adj* **to be deadlocked** *(of talks, negotiations)* être dans une impasse

deadly ['dedlɪ] *(compar* **deadlier**, *superl* **deadliest**) **1** *adj* (**a**) *(lethal → poison, blow)* mortel; *(→ snake)* au venin mortel; *(→ weapon)* meurtrier; *Fig (hatred)* mortel; *(wit, satire)* mordant, caustique; *(silence, pallor)* de mort, mortel; *Fig* **they are deadly enemies** ce sont des ennemis mortels; **the seven deadly sins** les sept péchés *mpl* capitaux

(**b**) *(precise)* **his aim is deadly** il a un tir excellent; **with deadly accuracy** avec une extrême précision; **to deadly effect** de façon dévastatrice

(**c**) *(extreme)* **in deadly earnest** *(say)* avec le plus grand sérieux

(**d**) *Fam (boring)* mortel, barbant

(**e**) *Ir Fam (excellent)* d'enfer, super *(inv)*

2 *adv* extrêmement, terriblement; **deadly accurate** extrêmement précis; **to be deadly serious** être tout à fait sérieux; **deadly pale** pâle comme la mort, d'une pâleur de mort *ou* mortelle; **it was deadly boring** *or* **dull** c'était mortellement ennuyeux

►► *Bot* ***deadly nightshade*** belladone *f*

deadman ['dedmæn] *(pl* **deadmen** [-men]) *n Tech* ancrage *m*; *(in mountaineering)* piton *m* à neige

[illegible]ment *m* (**b**) *(of sound)* caractère *m* sourd (**c**) *(of colour)* caractère *m* terne (**d**) *(of place)* caractère *m* ennuyeux *ou* mortel

dead-nettle *n Bot* ortie *f* blanche

deadpan ['dedpæn] **1** *adj (face, expression)* impassible; *(humour)* pince-sans-rire *(inv)*

2 *adv* d'un air impassible

deadwood ['dedwʊd] *n Am (trees, branches)* bois *m* mort; *Fig (people)* personnel *m* inutile

deaf [def] **1** *adj* sourd; **to go deaf** devenir sourd; **deaf in one ear** sourd d'une oreille; **deaf people** les sourds *mpl*; **are you deaf?** tu es sourd?; *Fig* **to turn a deaf ear to sb/sth** faire la sourde oreille à qn/qch; *Fig* **our complaints fell on deaf ears** nos protestations n'ont pas été entendues; **(as) deaf as a post** sourd comme un pot; *Prov* **there are none so deaf as those who will not hear** il n'est pire sourd que celui qui ne veut entendre

2 *npl* **the deaf** les sourds *mpl*

deaf-aid *n Br* appareil *m* acoustique

dea–dea

deaf-and-dumb *adj* sourd-muet

deafen ['defən] *vt* rendre sourd; *Fig* casser les oreilles à; **you're deafening me** vous me cassez les oreilles

deafening ['defənɪŋ] *adj (music, noise, roar)* assourdissant; *(applause)* retentissant; *Hum* **the silence was deafening** il y avait un grand silence *ou* un silence impressionnant

deafeningly ['defənɪŋlɪ] *adv* **deafeningly loud** assourdissant

deaf-mute 1 *n* sourd-muet (sourde-muette) *m,f*
2 *adj* sourd-muet

deafness ['defnɪs] *n* surdité *f*

DEAL [di:l]

affaire	▸ **1 (a)**
donne	▸ **1 (c)**
donner	▸ **2 (a)**
revendre	▸ **2 (c); 3 (a), (c)**
négocier	▸ **3 (b)**

(pt & pp **dealt** [delt]) **1** *n* (**a**) *(agreement)* affaire *f*, marché *m*; *St Exch* opération *f*, transaction *f*; **business deal** affaire *f*, marché *m*, transaction *f*; **to do** *or* **to make a deal with sb** conclure une affaire *ou* un marché avec qn; **I'll make a deal with you** je te propose un marché; **the deal is off** l'affaire est annulée, le marché est rompu; **the government does not do deals with terrorists** le gouvernement ne traite pas avec les terroristes; **no deals!** pas de marchandage!; **no deal!** je ne marche pas!; **it's a deal!** marché conclu!; *Fam* **you've got (yourself) a deal!** ça marche!, ça roule!; **that wasn't the deal** ce n'est pas ce qui était convenu; **a good/bad deal** une bonne/mauvaise affaire; **to get a good deal** faire une bonne affaire; *esp Am Fam* **what's the deal?** qu'est-ce qui se passe? ❑

(**b**) *(treatment)* **to give sb a fair deal** être juste avec qn; **the government promised (to give) teachers a better deal** le gouvernement a promis d'améliorer la condition des enseignants; **to get a rotten deal out of life** ne pas être gâté par la vie; *Pol* **the New Deal** le New Deal, la Nouvelle Donne

(**c**) *Cards* donne *f*, distribution *f*; **it's my deal** c'est à moi de donner

(**d**) *(quantity)* **a (good) deal of, a great deal of** *(money, time etc)* beaucoup de; **he thinks a good/great deal of her** il l'estime beaucoup/énormément; **I didn't enjoy it a great deal** je n'ai pas trop *ou* pas tellement aimé; **there's a good** *or* **great deal of truth in what you say** il y a beaucoup de vrai dans ce que vous dites; **I didn't do a great deal last night** je n'ai pas fait grand-chose hier soir; **a good/great deal faster** beaucoup plus vite; *Fam Ironic* **big deal!** la belle affaire!; *Fam* **no big deal** ça ne fait rien; *Fam* **he made a big deal out of it** il en a fait tout un plat *ou* tout un cinéma; *Fam* **what's the big deal?** et alors?, et puis quoi?; *Fam* **that's not such a big deal** ça ne vaut pas la peine qu'on en fasse tout un plat *ou* tout un cinéma

(**e**) *Carp (timber)* planche *f*; **a deal table** une table en bois

2 *vt* (**a**) *Cards* donner, distribuer

(**b**) *(strike)* **to deal sb a blow** assener un coup à qn; *Fig* **the news of her death dealt him a heavy blow** ce fut pour lui un coup terrible que d'apprendre sa mort; *Fig* **to deal sth a blow, to deal a blow to sth** porter un coup à qch

(**c**) *(drugs)* revendre

3 *vi* (**a**) *Cards* faire la donne, donner; **it's your turn** *or* **it's you to deal** c'est à toi de distribuer *ou* de donner

(**b**) *Com* négocier, traiter; **the firm has been dealing for over 50 years** cette société est en activité depuis plus de 50 ans; **to deal on the Stock Exchange** faire des opérations *ou* des transactions en bourse; **to deal in leather/in options** faire le commerce des cuirs/des primes; **to deal in drugs** revendre de la drogue; *Fig* **to deal in death/human misery** être un marchand de mort/de misère humaine

(**c**) *(in drugs)* revendre de la drogue, dealer

▸**deal in** *vt sep Cards (player)* donner *ou* distribuer des cartes à, servir; *Fig* **deal me in** tu peux compter sur moi

▸**deal off** *vt sep Am (company)* se débarrasser de

▸**deal out** *vt sep (cards, gifts)* donner, distribuer; *(justice)* rendre; *(punishment)* distribuer; *Fig* **deal me out** ne compte pas sur moi

▸**deal with** *vt insep* (**a**) *(handle → problem, situation, query, complaint)* traiter; *(→ customer, member of the public)* traiter avec; *(→ difficult situation, child)* s'occuper de; **a difficult child to deal with** un enfant difficile; **a job that involves dealing with the public** un travail qui implique un contact avec le public; **the author deals with the question very sensitively** l'auteur traite *ou* aborde ce sujet avec beaucoup de délicatesse; **I'll deal with it** *(problem, situation etc)* je m'en occupe, je m'en charge; **I know how to deal with him** je sais m'y prendre avec lui; **I'll deal with you later** *(to naughty child)* je vais m'occuper de toi *ou* de ton cas plus tard; **I can't deal with all the work I've got** je ne me sors pas de tout le travail que j'ai; **the management dealt with the situation promptly** la direction a réagi immédiatement; **the culprits were dealt with severely** les coupables ont été sévèrement punis; **the switchboard deals with over 1,000 calls a day** le standard traite *ou* reçoit plus de 1000 appels par jour; **that's that dealt with** voilà qui est fait

(**b**) *(do business with)* traiter *ou* négocier avec; *(get supplies from → grocer etc)* se fournir chez; **she's not an easy woman to deal with** ce n'est pas facile de traiter *ou* négocier avec elle

(**c**) *(be concerned with)* traiter de; **in my lecture, I shall deal with...** dans mon cours, je traiterai de...

de-alcoholize, -ise [ˌdi:'ælkəhəlaɪz] *vt (beer, wine)* désalcooliser

dealer ['di:lə(r)] *n* (**a**) *Com* marchand(e) *m,f*, négociant(e) *m,f* (**in** en); *(supplier)* fournisseur *m* (**in** de); *St Exch* courtier(ère) *m,f*; *(in foreign exchange)* cambiste *mf*; *Aut* concessionnaire *mf* (**b**) *(in drugs)* dealer *m* (**c**) *Cards* donneur(euse) *m,f*

▸▸ *Com* ***dealer brand*** marque *f* de revendeur; *Mktg* ***dealer test*** test *m* auprès des distributeurs

dealership ['di:ləʃɪp] *n Aut & Com* concession *f*

dealing ['di:lɪŋ] *n* (**a**) *(UNCOUNT) St Exch* opérations *fpl*, transactions *fpl*; *(trading)* commerce *m* (**b**) *(UNCOUNT) Cards* donne *f*, distribution *f* (**c**) **dealings** *(business)* affaires *fpl*, transactions *fpl*; *(personal)* relations *fpl*; **to have dealings with sb** *(in business)* traiter avec qn, avoir affaire à qn; *(personal)* avoir affaire à qn (**d**) *(in drugs)* vente *f*

▸▸ *St Exch* ***dealing room*** salle *f* de marchés

dealt [delt] *pt & pp of* **deal**

deambulation [di:ˌæmbjʊ'leɪʃən] *n Literary* déambulation *f*, promenade *f*

deambulatory [di:'æmbjʊlətərɪ] *adj Literary* déambulatoire

deamination [ˌdi:æmɪ'neɪʃən] *n Biol & Chem* désamination *f*

dean [di:n] *n Rel & Univ* doyen(enne) *m,f*

▸▸ *Am Univ* ***Dean's List*** = tableau d'honneur dans les universités américaines

deanery ['di:nərɪ] *n Rel* doyenné *m*; *Univ* résidence *f* du doyen

deanship ['di:nʃɪp] *n Rel* doyenné *m*, décanat *m*; *Univ* doyennat *m*

dear [dɪə(r)] **1** *adj* (**a**) *(loved)* cher; *(precious)* cher, précieux; *(appealing)* adorable, charmant; **he is a dear friend of mine** c'est un ami très cher; **she's such a dear girl** elle est tellement gentille; **Margot dearest** ma chère Margot; **he/the memory is very dear to me** il/ce souvenir m'est très cher; *Formal or Literary* **to hold sb/sth dear** chérir qn/qch; **all that I hold dear (in life)** tout ce qui m'est cher; **my dearest wish is that...** mon vœu le plus cher est que...; **to run for dear life** courir à toute vitesse; **to hang on for dear life** s'accrocher désespérément; **my dear fellow** mon cher ami; **my dear girl** ma chère; **my dear Mrs Stevens** chère madame Stevens; **what a dear little child/cottage/frock!** quel enfant/quel cottage/quelle robe adorable!

(**b**) *(in letter)* **Dear Sir** Monsieur; **Dear Madam** Madame; **Dear Sir or Madam** Madame, Monsieur; **Dear Sirs** Messieurs; **Dear Mrs Baker** Madame; *(less formal)* Chère Madame; *(informal)* Chère Madame Baker; **Dear John Smith** Cher Monsieur Smith; **Dear Henry** Cher Henry; **Dear Mum and Dad** Chers Maman et Papa; **Dear Alan and Avril** Chers Alan et Avril; **My dear Clare** Ma chère Clare; **Dearest Richard** Très cher Richard

(**c**) *(expensive → item, shop)* cher; *(→ price)* haut, élevé; *esp Br* **things are getting dearer** la vie augmente

2 *exclam* **dear!, dear, dear, dear me!, oh dear!** *(surprise)* oh mon Dieu!; *(regret)* oh là là!; **oh dear!** *(worry)* mon Dieu!; **oh dear no!** (oh) que non!

3 *n* **my dear** *(to child, spouse, lover)* mon (ma) chéri(e); *(to friend)* mon (ma) cher (chère); **my dearest** mon (ma) chéri(e); **she's such a dear** elle est tellement gentille; *Br Fam* **I gave the old dear my seat** j'ai laissé ma place à la vieille dame; **poor dear** pauvre chéri(e); **be a dear and answer the phone, answer the phone, there's a dear** sois gentil *ou* un amour, réponds au téléphone; *Fam* **dear knows!** va savoir!

4 *adv (sell, pay, cost)* cher

▸▸ *Am Press* ***dear Abby*** = la rubrique courrier du cœur d'Abigail Van Buren, publiée dans de nombreux journaux américains; *Fam* ***Dear John (letter)*** lettre *f* de rupture; *Fin* ***dear money*** argent *m* cher

dearie ['dɪərɪ] *Fam* **1** *n* chéri(e) *m,f*
2 *exclam* **(oh) dearie me!** oh mon Dieu!

dearly ['dɪəlɪ] *adv* (**a**) *(very much)* beaucoup, énormément; **I love him dearly** je l'aime tendrement *ou* de tout mon cœur; **I would dearly love to live in the country** j'aimerais beaucoup *ou* j'adorerais vivre à la campagne; **dearly beloved son of...** *(on gravestone)* fils bien-aimé de...; **dearly beloved, we are gathered here today...** mes biens chers frères, nous sommes aujourd'hui rassemblés...

(**b**) *(at high cost)* **to pay dearly for sth** payer cher qch; **you shall pay dearly for this** cela vous coûtera cher

dearness ['dɪənɪs] *n* (**a**) *(costliness)* cherté *f* (**b**) *(of loved one)* **her dearness to him grew with every day that passed** l'affection qu'il avait pour elle croissait de jour en jour

dearth [dɜ:θ] *n* pénurie *f*

deary ['dɪərɪ] *n Fam* chéri(e) *m,f*

DEATH [deθ] *n* mort *f*; *Admin & Law* décès *m*; *Press* **deaths (column)** rubrique *f* nécrologique; **his death came as a shock to me** sa mort a été un choc pour moi; **I was with him at the time of his death** j'étais auprès de lui quand il est mort; **how many deaths were there?** combien y a-t-il eu de morts?; **their deaths were caused by smoke inhalation** leur mort a été causée *ou* provoquée par l'inhalation de fumée; **a death in the family** un décès dans la famille; **police are treating the death as suspicious** la police n'écarte pas l'hypothèse du meurtre; **to fall/to jump to one's death** se tuer en tombant/se jetant dans le vide; **to freeze/to starve to death** mourir de froid/de faim; **to be beaten to death** être battu à mort; **to be burnt to death** *(accidentally)* périr dans les flammes; *(as form of martyrdom)* périr sur le bûcher; **to bleed to death** perdre tout son sang; **to fight to the death** se battre à mort; **to meet one's death** trouver la mort; **to meet an early death** mourir jeune; **to die a violent death** mourir de mort violente; **he died an easy death** il n'a pas souffert; **a quick death is preferable to days of agony** mieux vaut mourir rapidement que d'agoniser pendant des jours; **condemned to** *or* **under sentence of death** condamné à mort; **to sentence/to put sb to death** condamner/mettre qn à mort; **to send sb to his/her death** envoyer qn à la mort; **to smoke/to drink oneself to death** se tuer à force de fumer/boire; **to stab sb to death** tuer qn à coups de couteau; **to work sb to death** tuer qn à force de surmenage; **death to the Czar!** mort au Tsar!; **till death do us part** *(in marriage ceremony)* jusqu'à ce que la mort nous sépare; **one false move could mean death** *(for trapeze artist etc)* un faux mouvement pourrait entraîner la mort; **this means the death of the steel industry** cela sonne le glas de la sidérurgie; *Fig* **it's been done to death** *(play, subject for novel etc)* ça a été fait et refait; *Fig* **to**

discuss sth to death discuter de qch jusqu'à l'épuisement du sujet; *Fam* **to look like death (warmed up)** avoir une mine de déterré; *Fam* **to feel like death (warmed up)** être en piteux état[❑]; *Fam* **to catch one's death (of cold)** attraper la mort *ou* la crève; **to be in at the death** être là pour voir aboutir l'affaire, assister au dénouement; *Hunt* être à l'hallali; **to die a horrible death** avoir une mort atroce; *Fam* **to be sick** *or* **tired to death of sb/sth** en avoir ras le bol de qn/qch; *Fam* **to be bored to death** s'ennuyer à mourir; *Fam* **to be worried/scared to death** être mort d'inquiétude/de frousse; *Fam* **you'll be the death of me!** *(with amusement)* tu me feras mourir (de rire)!; *(with irritation)* tu es tuant!; **that job will be the death of her** ce travail la tuera; **to be at death's door** *(patient)* être à l'article de la mort; **to die a thousand deaths** *(worry about somebody)* mourir d'inquiétude; *(worry about oneself)* être mort de peur; *(be embarrassed)* mourir de honte; *Fam* **to die a death** *(actor, film)* faire un bide; *(joke)* tomber à plat; *(idea, plan, hope)* tomber à l'eau; **death by misadventure** mort *f* accidentelle; **to hang** *or* **to hold** *or* **to cling on like grim death** s'accrocher désespérément

►► *Zool* ***death adder*** acanthopis *m*, serpent *m* de la mort; ***death camp*** camp *m* de la mort; *Bot* ***death cap*** amanite *f* phalloïde; ***death cell*** cellule *f* de condamné à mort; ***death certificate*** acte *m ou* certificat *m* de décès; *Am* ***death chamber*** *(in prison)* = local où l'on procède aux éxécutions capitales; *(in home)* chambre *f* du défunt; *Br Formerly Fin* ***death duty*** droits *mpl* de succession; *Fin* ***death in service benefit*** capital-décès *m*; ***death knell*** glas *m*; *Fig* **to sound the death knell for** *or* **of sth** sonner le glas de qch; ***death march*** marche *f* funèbre; ***death mask*** masque *m* mortuaire; ***death penalty*** peine *f* de mort, peine *f* capitale; ***death rate*** taux *m* de mortalité; ***death rattle*** râle *m* d'agonie; ***death row*** quartier *m* des condamnés à mort; **he's been on death row for ten years** cela fait dix ans qu'il est au quartier des condamnés à mort; *Am & Austr Fam* ***death seat*** *(in a vehicle)* place *f* du mort; ***death sentence*** condamnation *f* à mort; ***death squad*** escadron *m* de la mort; ***death star*** = arme métallique en forme d'étoile utilisée comme projectile; *Am Fin* ***death tax*** droits *mpl* de succession; ***death throes*** agonie *f*; *(painful)* affres *fpl* de la mort; *Fig* agonie *f*; **to be in one's death throes** agoniser, être agonisant; *(suffering)* connaître les affres de la mort; *Fig* **to be in its death throes** *(project, business etc)* agoniser, être agonisant; ***death toll*** nombre *m* de morts; **the death toll stands at 567** il y a 567 morts, le bilan est de 567 morts; ***death trap*** = véhicule ou endroit extrêmement dangereux; **the building is a death trap** l'édifice est extrêmement dangereux; ***Death Valley*** la Vallée de la Mort; ***death warrant*** ordre *m* d'exécution; *Fig* **to sign one's own death warrant** signer son propre arrêt de mort; *Psy* ***death wish*** désir *m* de mort; *Fig* **he seems to have a death wish** il faut croire qu'il est suicidaire

'Death in Venice' *Mann, Visconti* 'Mort à Venise'

'Death of a Salesman' *Miller, Schlöndorff* 'Mort d'un commis voyageur'

'Death and the Maiden' *Schubert, Dorfmann, Polanski* 'La Jeune fille et la mort'

DEATH ROW

"Death Row" est le surnom donné aux quartiers réservés aux condamnés à mort dans les prisons américaines. La peine de mort est l'objet d'une vive polémique aux États-Unis, où elle est autorisée dans 38 États. Dans les années soixante-dix, la constitutionnalité de la peine de mort fut remise en question; la Cour Suprême jugea qu'elle était souvent appliquée de façon arbitraire et plus de 600 détenus virent leur peine commuée. Par conséquent les condamnés à mort furent de plus en plus nombreux à demander à ce que leur cas soit réexaminé, ce qui aboutit au surpeuplement des quartiers réservés aux condamnés à mort. Au cours des dernières années, le nombre d'exécutions capitales a augmenté de façon spectaculaire dans certains États, notamment au Texas.

deathbed ['deθbed] **1** *n* lit *m* de mort; **on one's deathbed** sur son lit de mort

2 *adj (confession)* fait à l'article de la mort; *(repentance)* exprimé à l'article de la mort

►► *Theat* ***deathbed scene*** scène *f* du lit de mort

deathblow ['deθbləʊ] *n* coup *m* fatal *ou* mortel; *Fig* coup *m* fatal; **to be the deathblow for sth** porter un coup fatal à qch

death-dealing *adj* mortel, fatal

deathless ['deθlɪs] *adj* immortel; *Hum* inimitable

deathlike ['deθlaɪk] *adj* de mort, mortel

deathly ['deθlɪ] **1** *adj (silence, pallor)* de mort, mortel

2 *adv* **deathly pale** pâle comme la mort; **deathly cold** glacial; **the house was deathly quiet** *(silent)* la maison était plongée dans un profond silence; *(sinister)* la maison était plongée dans un silence de mort

death's-head *n* tête *f* de mort

►► *Entom* ***death's-head moth*** sphinx *m* tête-de-mort

deathwatch ['deθwɒtʃ] *n* veillée *f* mortuaire

►► *Entom* ***deathwatch beetle*** grande *ou* grosse vrillette *f*, horloger *m* de la mort

deb [deb] *n Br Fam* débutante[❑] *f*; **deb's delight** beau parti *m*

debacle [de'bɑːkəl] *n* débâcle *f*

debag [ˌdiː'bæg] *(pt & pp* **debagged,** *cont* **debagging)** *vt Fam* déculotter de force

debar [ˌdiː'bɑː(r)] *(pt & pp* **debarred,** *cont* **debarring)** *vt* interdire à; **to debar sb from sth/doing sth** interdire qch à qn/à qn de faire qch

debark[1] [ˌdiː'bɑːk] **1** *vt (passengers, cargo)* débarquer

2 *vi* débarquer

debark[2] *vt (tree)* écorcer

debarkation [ˌdiːbɑː'keɪʃən] *n* débarquement *m*

debarment [dɪ'bɑːmənt] *n* interdiction *f*

debase [dɪ'beɪs] *vt* (**a**) *(degrade → person, sport)* avilir, abaisser; *(→ reputation)* ternir; *(→ tradition, profession, politics)* dévaloriser (**b**) *(make less valuable → object)* dégrader, altérer; *(→ metal, currency, coinage)* déprécier

debasement [dɪ'beɪsmənt] *n* (**a**) *(degradation → of person, sport)* avilissement *m*, abaissement *m*; *(of tradition, profession, politics)* dévalorisation *f* (**b**) *(of object)* dégradation *f*, altération *f*; *(of metal, currency, coinage)* dépréciation *f*

debasing [dɪ'beɪsɪŋ] *adj (degrading)* avilissant, abaissant

debatable [dɪ'beɪtəbəl] *adj* discutable, contestable; **it is debatable whether...** on peut se demander si..., on peut se poser la question de savoir si...

debate [dɪ'beɪt] **1** *vt (question etc)* débattre, discuter, agiter; [illegible] **A much debated question** une question très débattue; **we don't have time to debate the issue now** on n'a plus le temps de discuter le problème; **to debate (with oneself) whether to do sth or not** se demander si on doit faire qch

2 *vi* discuter (**with sb** avec qn; **on sth** sur qch); *(take part in a debate)* prendre part à un débat; **she frequently debated for her university** elle prenait souvent part à des débats pour son université

3 *n (gen)* discussion *f*; *(organized)* débat *m*; **to have** *or* **to hold a debate about** *or* **on sth** tenir un débat *ou* avoir une discussion sur *ou* à propos de qch; **there's been a lot of debate about it** cela a été très *ou* longuement débattu; **there has been some debate over the effectiveness of the treatment** l'efficacité du traitement a été mise en doute; **the subject under debate** le sujet des débats; **open to debate** discutable, contestable; **after much** *or* **lengthy debate** *(between two or more people)* après de longs débats; *(with oneself)* après de longs débats intérieurs; **to be the subject of debate** faire le thème de débats

debater [dɪ'beɪtə(r)] *n* débatteur *m*; **to be a skilled debater** exceller dans les débats

debating [dɪ'beɪtɪŋ] *n* art *m* du débat; **she took up debating at university** elle a pris part à des débats formels à l'université

►► ***debating society*** société *f* de débats contradictoires

debauch [dɪ'bɔːtʃ] **1** *vt* débaucher; *Arch or Literary (woman)* séduire

2 *n Arch or Literary* partie *f* de débauche

debauched [dɪ'bɔːtʃt] *adj (person)* débauché; *(tastes)* dépravé; *(life)* de débauche

debauchee [dɪbɔː'tʃiː] *n* débauché(e) *m,f*

debauchery [dɪ'bɔːtʃərɪ] *n* débauche *f*

debeak [ˌdiː'biːk] *vt (chicken)* débecquer

debeaking [ˌdiː'biːkɪŋ] *n (of chicken)* débecquage *m*

debeard [ˌdiː'bɪəd] *vt Culin (seafood)* nettoyer

debenture [dɪ'bentʃə(r)] *n Fin* obligation *f*

►► ***debenture bond*** titre *m* d'obligation, *Can* débenture *f*; ***debenture holder*** obligataire *mf*, détenteur(trice) *m,f* d'obligations; ***debenture issue*** émission *f* d'obligations; ***debenture loan*** emprunt *m* obligataire; ***debenture stock*** obligation *f* sans garantie

debilitate [dɪ'bɪlɪteɪt] *vt* débiliter

debilitating [dɪ'bɪlɪteɪtɪŋ] *adj (illness)* débilitant; *(climate)* anémiant; **it had a debilitating effect on her concentration** cela a provoqué une baisse de sa concentration

debilitation [dɪˌbɪlɪ'teɪʃən] *n* débilitation *f*

debility [dɪ'bɪlətɪ] *n* débilité *f*; *Literary* **debility of purpose** faiblesse *f* de caractère

debit ['debɪt] *Acct, Banking & Fin* **1** *n* débit *m*; *Br* **your account is in debit** votre compte est déficitaire *ou* débiteur

2 *comp (balance, account)* débiteur

3 *vt (account)* débiter; *(person)* porter au débit de qn; **to debit £50 from sb's account, to debit sb's account with £50** débiter 50 livres du compte de qn, débiter le compte de qn de 50 livres; **has this cheque been debited to my account?** est-ce que ce chèque a été débité de mon compte?

►► *Fin* ***debit advice*** avis *m* de débit; *Banking* ***debit card*** = carte de paiement à débit immédiat; *Acct* ***debit column*** colonne *f* débitrice *ou* des débits; ***debit entry*** *Acct* écriture *f* passée au débit; *Banking* article *m* porté au débit d'un compte; *Fin* ***debit interest*** intérêts *mpl* débiteurs; *Acct* ***debit item*** poste *m* débiteur; *Fin* ***debit note*** note *f* de débit; *Acct* ***debit side*** débit *m*; *Fig* **on the debit side, he is not very presentable** ce qui le dessert, c'est qu'il n'est pas très présentable; *Fig* **on the debit side, it means we won't see her** l'inconvénient, c'est que nous ne la verrons pas

debonair [ˌdebə'neə(r)] *adj (person)* d'une élégance nonchalante; *(smile, charm)* nonchalant

Deborah ['debərə] *pr n Bible* Déborah

debouch [dɪ'baʊtʃ] *vi Geog & Mil* déboucher

Debrett's [də'brets] *n* **Debrett's (peerage)** = annuaire de l'aristocratie britannique

debride [deɪ'briːd] *vt Med* débrider

debridement [deɪ'briːdmənt] *n Med* débridement *m*

debrief [ˌdiː'briːf] *vt* faire faire un compte rendu verbal de mission à, débriefer; **pilots are debriefed after every flight** on fait faire un compte rendu verbal de mission aux pilotes *ou* on débriefe les pilotes après chaque vol

debriefing [ˌdiː'briːfɪŋ] *n* compte rendu *m* verbal de mission

►► ***debriefing officer*** officier *m* chargé de recevoir le compte rendu verbal des pilotes; ***debriefing room*** salle *f* de compte rendu de mission

debris ['deɪbriː] *n (UNCOUNT)* débris *mpl*; *Fig (after party etc)* détritus *mpl*; *Fig* **to salvage something from the debris of one's marriage** sauver quelque chose des restes de son mariage

debt [det] **1** *n Fin (gen)* dette *f*; *Admin (to be recovered)* créance *f*; **to be in debt, to have debts** avoir des dettes, être endetté; **to be out of debt** s'être acquitté de ses dettes; **to get** *or* **to**

dea–deb

run into debt s'endetter; **to get out of debt** s'acquitter de ses dettes; **to pay one's debts** régler ses dettes; **he has paid his debt to society** il s'est acquitté de sa dette envers la société; **to reschedule** *or* **restructure a debt** rééchelonner une dette; **to be in debt to sb** être endetté auprès de qn; *Fig* avoir une dette envers qn, être redevable à qn; **debt of honour** dette *f* d'honneur; **outstanding debt** dette *f ou* créance *f* à recouvrer

2 *comp* de la dette

►► ***debt burden*** surendettement *m*, fardeau *m* de la dette; ***debt capacity*** capacité *f* d'endettement; *Fin* ***debt collection*** recouvrement *m ou* récupération *f* des créances; ***debt collection agency*** bureau *m* de recouvrement *ou* récupération des créances; ***debt collector*** agent *m* de recouvrement; ***debt due*** créance *f* exigible; ***debt financing*** financement *m* par endettement; ***debt instrument*** titre *m* de créance; ***debt ratio*** ratio *m* d'endettement; ***debt rescheduling, debt restructuring*** rééchelonnement *m* des dettes; *Am* ***debt service,*** *Br* ***debt servicing*** service *m* de la dette; ***debt swap*** échange *m* de créances

debt-equity *adj*

►► ***debt-equity ratio*** rapport *m* dettes-actions; ***debt-equity swap*** échange *m* de créances contre actifs

debtor ['detə(r)] *n Fin* débiteur(trice) *m,f*

►► *Acct* ***debtor account*** compte *m* débiteur; ***debtor nation*** pays *m* débiteur; ***debtor's prison*** prison *f* pour dettes; *Acct* ***debtor side*** débit *m*, doit *m*; *Acct* ***debtors' turnover*** rotation *f* des clients

debt-ridden *adj* criblé de dettes

debug [ˌdiːˈbʌg] (*pt & pp* **debugged,** *cont* **debugging**) *vt* (**a**) *Comput (program)* déboguer; *(machine)* mettre au point (**b**) *(remove hidden microphones from)* débarrasser des micros (cachés) (**c**) *(remove insects from)* débarrasser des insectes, désinsectiser

debugger [ˌdiːˈbʌgə(r)] *n Comput* (programme *m*) débogueur *m*

debugging [ˌdiːˈbʌgɪŋ] **1** *n* (**a**) *Comput (of program)* débogage *m*; *(of machine)* mise *f* au point (**b**) *(removal of microphones)* élimination *f* des micros (cachés) (**c**) *(removal of insects)* désinsectisation *f*

2 *comp* (**a**) *Comput* de débogage (**b**) *(to remove microphones → operation)* d'élimination des micros (cachés); *(→ team)* chargé d'éliminer les micros (cachés); *(→ expert)* dans l'élimination de micros (cachés) (**c**) *(to remove insects)* de désinsectisation

debunk [ˌdiːˈbʌŋk] *vt Fam* (**a**) *(ridicule)* tourner en ridicule (**b**) *(show to be false)* démystifier

debunking [ˌdiːˈbʌŋkɪŋ] *n Fam* (**a**) *(ridiculing)* = fait de tourner en ridicule; **he's famous for his relentless debunking of the British class system** il est connu pour la façon dont il se moque continuellement du système de classes britannique (**b**) *(showing to be false)* démystification *f*

debus [ˌdiːˈbʌs] (*pt & pp* **bused** *or* **bussed,** *cont* **busing** *or* **bussing**) **1** *vt* (faire) débarquer de l'autobus/des autobus

2 *vi* débarquer de l'autobus/des autobus

debut ['deɪbjuː] (*pt & pp* **debut'd** [-bjuːd]) **1** *n* début *m*; **to make one's debut** faire ses débuts

2 *vi* débuter; **to debut as** débuter dans le rôle de

►► ***debut performance*** première apparition *f*

debutante ['debjʊˌtɑːnt] *n* débutante *f*

Dec. (*written abbr* **December**) déc

decade ['dekeɪd] *n* (**a**) *(ten years)* décennie *f*; **before the end of the decade** avant la fin de cette décennie; **over a decade ago** il y a plus de dix ans (**b**) *Rel (of rosary)* dizaine *f*

decadence ['dekədəns] *n* (**a**) *(of person, life, society etc)* décadence *f* (**b**) *Art & Literature* décadentisme *m*

decadent ['dekədənt] **1** *adj* décadent; **to become decadent** tomber dans la décadence; *Hum* **how decadent!** quelle décadence!

2 *n* (**a**) *(person)* personne *f* décadente (**b**) *Art & Literature* décadent(e) *m,f*

decadentism ['dekədəntɪzəm] *n Art & Literature* décadentisme *m*

decadently ['dekədəntlɪ] *adv* de manière décadente

decaf, decaff ['diːkæf] *n Fam (coffee)* déca *m*

decaffeinate [ˌdiːˈkæfɪneɪt] *vt* décaféiner

decaffeinated [ˌdiːˈkæfɪneɪtɪd] *adj* décaféiné

decagon ['dekəgən] *n Geom* décagone *m*

decagonal [dɪˈkægənəl] *adj Geom* décagonal

decagramme, *Am* **decagram** ['dekəgræm] *n* décagramme *m*

decahedral [ˌdekəˈhedrəl, ˌdekəˈhiːdrəl] *adj Geom* décaèdre

decahedron [ˌdekəˈhedrən, ˌdekəˈhiːdrən] *n Geom* décaèdre *m*

decal ['diːkæl] *n Am Fam* décalcomanie ❑ *f*

decalcification [ˈdiːˌkælsɪfɪˈkeɪʃən] *n* décalcification *f*

decalcify [ˌdiːˈkælsɪfaɪ] *vt* décalcifier

decalcomania [dɪˌkælkəˈmeɪnjə] *n* décalcomanie *f*

decalitre, *Am* **decaliter** ['dekəˌliːtə(r)] *n* décalitre *m*

Decalogue ['dekəlɒg] *n Bible* décalogue *m*

Decameron [dɪˈkæmərən] *n Literature* **the Decameron** le Décaméron

decametre, *Am* **decameter** ['dekəˌmiːtə(r)] *n* décamètre *m*

decamp [dɪˈkæmp] *vi* (**a**) *Mil* lever le camp (**b**) *Fam (abscond)* décamper, ficher le camp; **to decamp to another room** aller s'installer dans une autre pièce

decanal [dɪˈkeɪnəl] *adj Rel* (**a**) *(relating to a dean)* décanal (**b**) *(of choir)* côté *m* sud du chœur *(où se trouve la stalle du doyen)*

decant [dɪˈkænt] *vt* (**a**) *(liquid)* transvaser; *(wine, brandy etc)* décanter dans une carafe (**b**) *Fam (move, transfer → people)* transférer

decanter [dɪˈkæntə(r)] *n* carafe *f*

decapitate [dɪˈkæpɪteɪt] *vt* décapiter

decapitation [dɪˌkæpɪˈteɪʃən] *n* décapitation *f*

decapod ['dekəpɒd] *n Zool* décapode *m*

Decapolis [dɪˈkæpəlɪs] *n* **the Decapolis** la Décapole

decarbonate [diːˈkɑːbəneɪt] *vt Chem* décarbonater

decarbonation [diːˌkɑːbəˈneɪʃən] *n Chem* décarbonatation *f*

decarbonization [diːˌkɑːbənaɪˈzeɪʃən] *n* (**a**) *Tech* décalaminage *m* (**b**) *Metal* décarburation *f*

decarbonize, -ise [ˌdiːˈkɑːbənaɪz] *vt* (**a**) *Tech* décalaminer (**b**) *Metal* décarburer

decasualization [diːˌkæʒʊəlaɪˈzeɪʃən] *n Ind* **the decasualization of labour** la régularisation du travail

decasualize, -ise [diːˈkæʒʊəlaɪz] *vt Ind (workers)* régulariser le travail de

decasyllabic [ˌdekəsɪˈlæbɪk] *adj Ling* décasyllabe, décasyllabique

decasyllable ['dekəˌsɪləbəl] *Ling* **1** *n* décasyllabe *m*

2 *adj* décasyllabe

decathlete [dɪˈkæθliːt] *n Sport* décathlonien(enne) *m,f*

decathlon [dɪˈkæθlɒn] *n Sport* décathlon *m*

decatholicize, -ise [diːkəˈθɒlɪsaɪz] *vt Rel* décatholiciser

decay [dɪˈkeɪ] **1** *vi* (**a**) *(rot → food, wood, flowers)* pourrir; *(→ meat)* s'avarier, pourrir; *(→ corpse)* se décomposer; *(→ tooth)* se carier; *(→ building)* se délabrer; *(→ stone)* s'effriter, se désagréger

(**b**) *Fig (beauty, civilization, faculties)* décliner; *(family, country)* tomber en décadence

(**c**) *Phys* dépérir, se dégrader, se désintégrer

2 *vt (wood)* pourrir; *(stone)* désagréger; *(tooth)* carier

3 *n* (**a**) *(of food, wood, flowers)* pourriture *f*; *(of corpse)* décomposition *f*; *(of teeth)* carie *f*; *(of building)* délabrement *m*; *(of stone)* effritement *m*, désagrégation *f*; **area of decay** *(in tooth)* zone *f* cariée

(**b**) *Fig (of beauty, faculties)* délabrement *m*; *(of family, country)* décadence *f*, déchéance *f*; *(of civilization)* déclin *m*; *also Fig* **to fall into decay** se délabrer; **in an advanced state of decay** *(building)* dans un état de délabrement avancé; *(corpse)* dans un état de putréfaction avancé; **moral decay** déchéance *f* morale

(**c**) *Phys* désintégration *f*, dégradation *f*

decayed [dɪˈkeɪd] *adj* (**a**) *(food, wood, flowers)* pourri; *(meat)* avarié, pourri; *(corpse)* décomposé; *(tooth)* carié; *(building)* délabré, en ruines; *(stone)* effrité, désagrégé (**b**) *Fig (beauty)* fané; *(civilization)* délabré, en ruines

decaying [dɪˈkeɪɪŋ] *adj* (**a**) *(food, wood, flowers)* pourrissant; *(meat)* en train de s'avarier; *(corpse)* en décomposition; *(tooth)* en train de se carier; *(building)* qui se délabre; *(stone)* en désagrégation (**b**) *Fig (beauty)* qui se fane; *(civilization)* sur le déclin

Deccan ['dekən] *n Geog* Deccan *m*

decease [dɪˈsiːs] *Law & Admin* **1** *n* décès *m*

2 *vi* décéder

deceased [dɪˈsiːst] (*pl* **inv**) *Law & Admin* **1** *n* **the deceased** le défunt (la défunte)

2 *adj* décédé, défunt; **son of Robert Martin, deceased** fils de feu M. Robert Martin

decedent [dɪˈsiːdənt] *n Am Law* défunt(e) *m,f*

deceit [dɪˈsiːt] *n* (**a**) *(quality)* duplicité *f* (**b**) *(trick)* supercherie *f*, tromperie *f* (**c**) *Law* fraude *f*; **by deceit** frauduleusement

deceitful [dɪˈsiːtfʊl] *adj* trompeur; *(behaviour)* trompeur, sournois; **it was very deceitful of her** c'était très malhonnête de sa part

deceitfully [dɪˈsiːtfʊlɪ] *adv* trompeusement, avec duplicité; **to obtain sth deceitfully** obtenir qch en usant de duplicité; **deceitfully, she omitted to mention the fact** par duplicité, elle s'est gardée de mentionner ce fait

deceitfulness [dɪˈsiːtfʊlnɪs] *n* tromperie *f*, duplicité *f*

deceive [dɪˈsiːv] **1** *vt* tromper; **to deceive sb into doing sth** amener qn à faire qch en le trompant; **she deceived me into believing that...** elle m'a fait croire que...; **don't be deceived** ne vous y fiez pas; **to be deceived by appearances** se laisser tromper par les apparences; **to deceive oneself** se mentir à soi-même; **don't deceive yourself that it will be easy** ne croyez pas que ce sera facile; **unless my eyes deceive me** à moins que mes yeux ne me jouent des tours *ou* que ma vue ne me joue des tours; **I thought my eyes were deceiving me** je ne pouvais pas en croire mes yeux

2 *vi* tromper; **it was not done with intent to deceive** cela n'a pas été fait dans l'intention de tromper

deceiver [dɪˈsiːvə(r)] *n* trompeur(euse) *m,f*

decelerate [ˌdiːˈseləreɪt] **1** *vt* ralentir

2 *vi* ralentir

deceleration [ˈdiːˌseləˈreɪʃən] *n* ralentissement *m*

December [dɪˈsembə(r)] *n* décembre; *see also* **February**

Decembrist [dɪˈsembrɪst] *n Hist* décembriste *m*, décabriste *m*

decency ['diːsnsɪ] (*pl* **decencies**) *n* décence *f*; **for decency's sake** pour respecter les convenances; **for decency's sake!** un peu de décence!; *Br* **an offence against public decency** un outrage à la pudeur; **to have the (common) decency to do sth** avoir la décence de faire qch; **the decencies** les convenances; **to observe the decencies** observer les convenances

decennial [dɪˈsenɪəl] **1** *n Am* dixième anniversaire *m*

2 *adj* décennal

decent ['diːsənt] *adj* (**a**) *(proper, morally correct)* décent, convenable; **decent, church-going folk** des gens comme il faut, qui vont à la messe tous les dimanches; **after a decent length of time** après une période de temps convenable; **to do the decent thing** se comporter *ou* agir dans les règles; *(marry woman one has made pregnant)* faire son devoir, réparer; **are you decent?** *(dressed)* es-tu habillé?

(**b**) *(satisfactory, reasonable → housing, wage)* décent, convenable; *(→ price)* convenable, raisonnable; **I earn a decent wage** je gagne un salaire décent; **wait until you have a decent amount of money** attends d'avoir suffisamment d'argent; **a decent meal** un bon repas; **a decent night's sleep** une bonne nuit de sommeil; **the rooms are a decent size** les pièces sont de bonne taille; **to speak decent French** parler assez bien *ou* parler convenablement le français

(**c**) *Fam (kind, good)* bien ❑, sympa; *Br* **he's a decent sort (of chap)** c'est un type bien; **that's very decent of you** c'est très sympa de ta part

(**d**) *Am Fam (excellent)* super, dément

decently ['diːsəntlɪ] *adv* (**a**) *(properly)* décemment, convenablement; **you can't decently**

ask her to do that tu ne peux pas décemment lui demander de faire cela (**b**) *(reasonably)* pas trop mal; **the job pays decently** le travail paie raisonnablement bien (**c**) *Fam (kindly)* de manière sympa

decentralist [diːˈsentrəlɪst] *n Pol* décentraliste *mf*, décentralisateur(trice) *m,f*

decentralization [diːˌsentrəlaɪˈzeɪʃən] *n Pol* décentralisation *f*

decentralize, -ise [ˌdiːˈsentrəlaɪz] *vt Pol* décentraliser

decentralizing [ˌdiːˈsentrəlaɪzɪŋ] *adj Pol* décentralisateur

decentre [ˌdiːˈsentə(r)] *vt Opt* décentrer

decent-sized *adj (house, room)* de bonnes dimensions

deception [dɪˈsepʃən] *n* (**a**) *(act of deceiving)* tromperie *f*, duperie *f*; **by deception** en usant de tromperie (**b**) *(trick)* subterfuge *m*, tromperie *f* (**c**) *(state of being deceived)* duperie *f*

deceptive [dɪˈseptɪv] *adj* trompeur; **appearances can be deceptive** il ne faut pas se fier aux apparences, les apparences sont trompeuses; **he appears to be gentle but his manner is deceptive** il a l'air doux, mais il ne faut pas se fier aux apparences

deceptively [dɪˈseptɪvlɪ] *adv* **deceptively worded/written** trompeur; **it looks deceptively easy/near** cela donne l'illusion d'être facile/tout près, on a l'impression que c'est facile/tout près; **he has a deceptively calm exterior** il paraît calme mais il ne faut pas s'y tromper

deceptiveness [dɪˈseptɪvnɪs] *n* caractère *m* trompeur

decerebrate [ˌdiːˈserɪbreɪt] *vt* décérébrer

decerebration [ˌdiːserɪˈbreɪʃən] *n* décérébration *f*

dechristianization [ˈdiːˌkrɪstʃənaɪˈzeɪʃən] *n Rel* déchristianisation *f*

dechristianize, -ise [ˌdiːˈkrɪstʃənaɪz] *vt Rel* déchristianiser

decibel [ˈdesɪbel] *n* décibel *m*; **decibel level** niveau *m* en décibels; **to measure the decibel level of sth** mesurer le niveau en décibels de qch; **the decibel level was quite overpowering** le bruit était assourdissant

decide [dɪˈsaɪd] **1** *vt* (**a**) *(resolve)* décider; **to decide to do sth** décider de faire qch; **it was decided to alter our strategy** il a été décidé que nous devions modifier notre stratégie; **nothing has been decided** rien n'a été décidé; **what have you decided?** qu'avez-vous décidé?; **the weather hasn't decided what it's doing yet** le temps n'arrive pas à se décider

(**b**) *(determine → outcome, someone's fate, career)* décider de, déterminer; *(→ person)* décider; **that was what decided me to leave him** c'est ce qui m'a décidé à le quitter

(**c**) *(settle → debate, war)* décider de l'issue de

2 *vi* (**a**) *(make up one's mind)* décider, se décider; **I can't decide** je n'arrive pas à me décider; **you decide** c'est toi qui décides; **I haven't decided yet** je n'ai pas encore décidé; **he'll need time to decide** il lui faudra du temps pour décider; **you'll have to decide for yourself** c'est toi qui devras décider; **we've decided against a holiday this year** nous avons décidé de ne pas prendre de vacances cette année; **to decide against/in favour of doing sth** décider de ne pas/de faire qch; *Law* **to decide in favour of sb/sth** décider en faveur de qn/qch; *Law* **to decide against sb/sth** décider contre qn/qch

(**b**) *(determine)* **but circumstances decided otherwise** mais les circonstances en ont décidé autrement

(**c**) *(choose)* choisir; **you'll have to decide between me and him** il va falloir choisir entre moi et lui

▸**decide on** *vt insep* décider de, se décider pour; **what plan of action have you decided on?** pour quel plan d'action vous êtes-vous décidé?, quel plan d'action avez-vous décidé de suivre?; **have you decided on a date/a name?** vous êtes-vous décidés sur une date/un nom?; **I've decided on Greece for my holiday** j'ai décidé d'aller passer mes vacances en Grèce

decided [dɪˈsaɪdɪd] *adj* (**a**) *(distinct → improvement, difference)* net, incontestable; *(→ success)* éclatant (**b**) *(resolute → person, look)* décidé, résolu; *(→ opinion, stance)* ferme; *(→ effort)* résolu; *(→ refusal)* ferme, catégorique; **I'm quite decided about leaving** je suis fermement décidé à partir

decidedly [dɪˈsaɪdɪdlɪ] *adv* (**a**) *(distinctly → better, different)* vraiment; **I feel decidedly unwell today** je ne me sens vraiment pas bien aujourd'hui; **so she's better? – yes, decidedly so** alors, elle va mieux? – beaucoup *ou* nettement mieux, oui; **was the weather unpleasant? – yes, decidedly so** avez-vous eu du mauvais temps? – extrêmement mauvais, oui (**b**) *(resolutely)* résolument, fermement

decider [dɪˈsaɪdə(r)] *n (goal)* but *m* décisif; *(point)* point *m* décisif; *(match)* match *m* décisif, rencontre *f* décisive; *(factor)* facteur *m* décisif; **the decider** *(to determine winner)* la belle

deciding [dɪˈsaɪdɪŋ] *adj* décisif, déterminant; **the chairperson has the deciding vote** la voix du président est prépondérante

deciduous [dɪˈsɪdjʊəs] *adj Bot & Biol (tree)* à feuilles caduques; *(leaves, antlers, teeth)* caduc

decilitre, *Am* **deciliter** [ˈdesɪˌliːtə(r)] *n* décilitre *m*

decimal [ˈdesɪməl] **1** *n* chiffre *m* décimal; **we haven't done decimals yet** on n'a pas encore vu les chiffres décimaux

2 *adj* décimal; **to go decimal** adopter le système décimal

▸▸ ***decimal coding*** codification *f* décimale; ***decimal currency*** monnaie *f* décimale; *Math* ***decimal fraction*** chiffre *m* décimal; *Math* ***decimal place*** décimale *f*; **correct to four decimal places** exact jusqu'à la quatrième décimale *ou* jusqu'au quatrième chiffre après la virgule *ou* au dix millième près; *Math* ***decimal point*** virgule *f*; ***decimal system*** système *m* décimal

decimalization [ˌdesɪməlaɪˈzeɪʃən] *n* décimalisation *f*

decimalize, -ise [ˈdesɪməlaɪz] **1** *vt* décimaliser

2 *vi* adopter le système décimal

decimate [ˈdesɪmeɪt] *vt* décimer

decimation [ˌdesɪˈmeɪʃən] *n* décimation *f*

decimetre, *Am* **decimeter** [ˈdesɪˌmiːtə(r)] *n* décimètre *m*

decipher [dɪˈsaɪfə(r)] *vt (code, handwriting)* déchiffrer

decipherable [dɪˈsaɪfərəbəl] *adj* déchiffrable

deciphering [dɪˈsaɪfərɪŋ], **decipherment** [dɪˈsaɪfəmənt] *n* déchiffrement *m*

decision [dɪˈsɪʒən] *n* (**a**) *(choice, judgement)* décision *f*; **to make** *or* **to take a decision** prendre une décision, se décider; *Law & Admin* prendre une décision; **to come to** *or* **to arrive at** *or* **to reach a decision** parvenir à une décision; **to make the right/wrong decision** faire le bon/mauvais choix; **it's your decision** c'est toi qui décides; **is that your decision?** ta décision est prise?; **the referee's decision is final** la décision de l'arbitre est irrévocable *ou* sans appel

(**b**) *Formal (decisiveness)* décision *f*, résolution *f*, fermeté *f*

(**c**) *(decision-making)* **it's a matter for personal decision** c'est une affaire de choix personnel

▸▸ ***decision model*** modèle *m* décisionnel *ou* déterministe *ou* de décision; *Comput* ***decision table*** table *f* de décision; ***decision theory*** théorie *f* de la décision; ***decision tree*** modèle *m* de décision en arborescence

decision-maker *n* décideur(euse) *m,f*, décisionnaire *mf*; **to be a good decision-maker** savoir prendre des décisions; **to be a bad decision-maker** ne pas savoir prendre de décisions

decision-making *n* prise *f* de décision; **the decision-making process** le processus de (prise de) décision; **he's no good at decision-making** il ne sait pas prendre des décisions; **a job which calls for a lot of decision-making** un travail qui demande qu'on prenne beaucoup de décisions

▸▸ ***decision-making tool*** outil *m* d'aide à la décision; ***decision-making unit*** unité *f* de prise de décision(s)

decision-tree analysis *n* analyse *f* d'arbre décisionnel *ou* de décision

decisive [dɪˈsaɪsɪv] *adj* (**a**) *(manner, person, tone)* décidé, résolu; **be decisive!** montre-toi décidé *ou* résolu! (**b**) *(factor, battle, argument, question)* décisif, déterminant

decisively [dɪˈsaɪsɪvlɪ] *adv* (**a**) *(resolutely)* résolument, sans hésitation (**b**) *(conclusively)* de manière décisive

decisiveness [dɪˈsaɪsɪvnɪs] *n* (**a**) *(of manner, person, tone)* décision *f*; **to say sth with decisiveness** dire qch d'un air décidé *ou* résolu (**b**) *(of factor, battle, argument, question)* caractère *m* décisif *ou* déterminant

dec–dec

deck [dek] **1** *n* (**a**) *Naut* pont *m*; **upper/lower deck** pont *m* supérieur/inférieur; **on deck** sur le pont; **to go (up) on deck** monter sur le pont; **below deck** *or* **decks** sous le pont; *Fig* **to clear the decks** mettre de l'ordre avant de passer à l'action; *Fam* **to hit the deck** *(fall)* se foutre la gueule par terre; *(to avoid injury)* tomber à plat ventre; *(get out of bed)* se lever; **hit the deck!** *(fall to the ground)* tout le monde à plat ventre!; *(get out of bed)* debout!; *also Fig* **all hands on deck!** tous sur le pont!; **it's all hands on deck at the moment as the project enters its final phase** tout le monde doit mettre la main à la pâte maintenant que le projet est entré dans sa phase finale

(**b**) *(of plane, bus)* étage *m*; **top** *or* **upper deck** *(of bus)* impériale *f*

(**c**) *(of cards)* jeu *m*; **to shuffle the deck** battre les cartes; **there are only 51 cards in this deck** il n'y a que 51 cartes dans ce jeu; *Fam Fig* **he's not playing with a full deck** *(is not very bright)* c'est pas une lumière, il n'a pas inventé l'eau chaude

(**d**) *(in hi-fi system)* platine *f*

(**e**) *Constr* tablier *m*; *(of bridge)* plancher *m*; *Am (terrace)* ponton *m*

2 *comp Naut (officer, cabin, crane)* de pont

3 *vt* (**a**) *(decorate)* parer, orner (**with** de)

(**b**) *Fam (knock to the ground)* envoyer au tapis

(**c**) *Naut (ship)* ponter

▸▸ ***deck cargo, deck load*** pontée *f*; ***deck tennis*** = sorte de tennis joué sur le pont d'un navire

▸**deck out** *vt sep* parer, orner; **to deck oneself out in one's best clothes** se mettre sur son trente et un

deckchair [ˈdektʃeə(r)] *n* chaise *f* longue, transat *m*

▸▸ ***deckchair attendant*** *(male)* garçon *m* de plage; *(female)* fille *f* de plage

deckel = **deckle**

-decker [ˈdekə(r)] *suff* **double-decker bus** bus *m* à impériale; **double-decker sandwich** sandwich *m* double

deckhand [ˈdekhænd] *n Naut* matelot *m*

deckhouse [ˈdekhaʊs, *pl* -haʊzɪz] *n Naut* rouf *m*

deckle [ˈdekəl] *n* cadre *m* volant *(utilisé dans la fabrication artisanale du papier)*

▸▸ ***deckle edge*** *(on paper)* bord *m* frangeux, barbes *fpl*

deckle-edged *adj (paper)* à bord frangeux, à barbes

declaim [dɪˈkleɪm] *Formal* **1** *vi* déclamer; **to declaim against sth** récriminer *ou* se récrier contre qch

2 *vt* déclamer

declamation [ˌdekləˈmeɪʃən] *n Formal* déclamation *f*

declamatory [dɪˈklæmətrɪ] *adj Formal (style)* déclamatoire

declarant [dɪˈkleərənt] *n Law* déclarant(e) *m,f*

declaration [ˌdekləˈreɪʃən] *n* (**a**) *(gen)* déclaration *f*; **to make a declaration that...** déclarer que...; **declaration of love/war/income** déclaration *f* d'amour/de guerre/de revenu (**b**) *Cards* annonce *f*

▸▸ *Law & Fin* ***declaration of bankruptcy*** jugement *m* déclaratif de faillite, déclaration *f* de faillite; *St Exch* ***declaration of dividend*** déclaration *f* de dividende; *Fin* ***declaration of income*** déclaration *f* de revenu; *Am Hist* ***the Declaration of Independence*** la Déclaration d'indépendance (américaine); ***declaration of intent*** déclaration *f* d'intention; *St Exch* ***declaration of options*** réponse *f* des primes; *Law & Fin* ***declaration of solvency*** déclaration *f* de solvabilité; ***declaration of value*** déclaration *f* de valeur

THE DECLARATION OF INDEPENDENCE

C'est par ce document, rédigé par Thomas Jefferson, que fut proclamée, le 4 juillet 1776, l'indépendance des treize colonies composant la Nouvelle-Angleterre. Cette déclaration d'indépendance est considérée comme l'acte de naissance des États-Unis d'Amérique.

declarative [dɪ'klærətɪv] *adj Gram* déclaratif

declaratory [dɪ'klærətrɪ] *adj Law* déclaratoire

▸▸ ***declaratory judgement*** jugement *m* déclaratoire

declare [dɪ'kleə(r)] **1** *vt* (**a**) *(proclaim → independence, war etc)* déclarer; **the two countries have declared war** *(on each other)* les deux pays se sont déclaré la guerre; **to declare a moratorium** décréter un moratoire; **to declare a strike** proclamer la grève; **she was declared the winner** elle a été déclarée vainqueur; *Law & Fin* **to declare sb bankrupt** constater *ou* prononcer l'état de faillite *ou* la faillite de qn; *Fin* **to declare a dividend of ten per cent** déclarer un dividende de dix pour cent; *Customs* **have you anything to declare?** avez-vous quelque chose à déclarer?; **I declare this meeting officially open** je déclare la séance ouverte

(**b**) *(announce)* déclarer; **to declare oneself** *(proclaim one's love)* se déclarer; *Pol* se présenter, présenter sa candidature; **to declare oneself for/against sth** se déclarer pour/contre qch

(**c**) *Cards (trumps, suit)* appeler; **to declare one's hand** annoncer son jeu; *Fig* avouer ses intentions

2 *vi* (**a**) **to declare for/against sth** faire une déclaration en faveur de/contre qch; **well, I (do) declare!** eh bien ça alors!

(**b**) *Cards* faire l'annonce, annoncer; *Sport (in cricket)* déclarer la tournée terminée *(avant sa fin normale)*

declared [dɪ'kleəd] *adj (intention, opponent)* déclaré, ouvert

declarer [dɪ'kleərə(r)] *n Cards* demandeur *m*

declassification [diː,klæsɪfɪ'keɪʃən] *n (of information)* déclassement *m*

declassified [,diː'klæsɪfaɪd] *adj (information)* déclassifié

declassify [,diː'klæsɪfaɪ] *(pt & pp* **declassified***) vt (information)* déclassifier

declension [dɪ'klenʃən] *n Gram* déclinaison *f*

declinable [dɪ'klaɪnəbəl] *adj Gram* déclinable

declination [,deklɪ'neɪʃən] *n* (**a**) *Astron* déclinaison *f* (**b**) *Am (refusal)* refus *m* poli

decline [dɪ'klaɪn] **1** *n (decrease → in prices, standards, crime, profits)* baisse *f*; *Fig (of civilization, empire)* déclin *m*; **there has been a decline in child mortality** il y a eu une baisse de la mortalité infantile; **sales have shown a rapid decline over the last six months** on a observé une forte chute des ventes au cours des six derniers mois; **to be in decline** être en déclin; **to be on the decline** *(prices, sales)* être en baisse; *(civilization, influence)* être sur le déclin; *Fig* **to fall into decline** dépérir; *Old-fashioned* **to fall into a decline** *(person)* dépérir

2 *vt* (**a**) *(refuse → invitation, honour, offer of help)* décliner, refuser; *(→ food, drink)* refuser; *(→ responsibility)* décliner; **to decline to do sth** refuser de faire qch

(**b**) *Gram* décliner

3 *vi* (**a**) *(decrease, diminish → empire, health)* décliner; *(→ prices, sales, population)* baisser, être en baisse, diminuer; *(→ influence, enthusiasm, fame)* baisser, diminuer; **to decline in importance/value/significance** perdre de son importance/de sa valeur/de sa signification

(**b**) *(refuse)* refuser; **she declined with thanks** elle a refusé avec ses remerciements

(**c**) *(slope downwards)* être en pente, descendre

(**d**) *Gram* se décliner

▸▸ *Mktg* ***decline stage*** *(of product)* phase *f* de déclin

'(History of the) Decline and Fall of the Roman Empire' *Gibbon* 'Histoire de la décadence et de la chute de l'Empire romain'

'Decline and Fall' *Waugh* 'Grandeur et décadence'

declining [dɪ'klaɪnɪŋ] *adj (health, industry, market)* sur le déclin; **he is in declining health** sa santé décline *ou* faiblit; **she was in her declining years** elle était au déclin de sa vie; **he wants to spend his declining years in Britain** il veut passer les dernières années de sa vie en Grande-Bretagne; *Literary* **the declining day** le jour à son déclin

▸▸ *Acct* ***declining balance depreciation*** amortissement *m* dégressif; *Acct* ***declining balance method*** méthode *f* de l'amortissement dégressif

declivitous [dɪ'klɪvɪtəs] *adj Literary* déclive

declivity [dɪ'klɪvətɪ] *n* déclivité *f*

declutch [dɪ'klʌtʃ] *vi Aut* débrayer

declutching [dɪ'klʌtʃɪŋ] *n Aut* débrayage *m*

decoct [dɪ'kɒkt] *vt* obtenir par décoction

decoction [dɪ'kɒkʃən] *n* décoction *f*

decode [,diː'kəʊd] *vt* décoder, déchiffrer; *Comput & TV* décoder; **the file is automatically decoded when it is received** le fichier est décodé automatiquement à la réception

decoder [,diː'kəʊdə(r)] *n* décodeur *m*

decoding [,diː'kəʊdɪŋ] *n* décodage *m*

decoke [,diː'kəʊk] *Br Tech* **1** *vt* décalaminer

2 *n* décalaminage *m*; **the car needs a decoke** la voiture a besoin d'un décalaminage *ou* d'être décalaminée

▸▸ ***decoke machine*** machine *f* de décalaminage

decollate [,diː'kɒleɪt] *vt* (**a**) *Arch (decapitate)* décoller, décapiter (**b**) *Comput (stationery)* déliasser

decollation [,diːkɒ'leɪʃən] *n* (**a**) *Arch (decapitation)* décollation *f* (**b**) *Comput (of stationery)* déliassage *m*

décolletage [,deɪkɒl'tɑːʒ] *n* décolleté *m*

décolleté [deɪ'kɒlteɪ] **1** *adj* décolleté

2 *n* décolleté *m*

decolonization [diː,kɒlənaɪ'zeɪʃən] *n* décolonisation *f*

decolonize, -ise [diː'kɒlənaɪz] *vt* décoloniser

decolourization, decolorization [diː,kʌlərаɪ'zeɪʃən] *n* décoloration *f*

decolourize, -ise, decolorize, -ise [,diː'kʌləraɪz] *vt* décolorer

decommission [,diːkə'mɪʃən] *vt* (**a**) *Nucl (shut down → nuclear power station)* déclasser (**b**) *Mil (remove from active service → warship, aircraft)* mettre hors service

decommissioning [,diːkə'mɪʃənɪŋ] *n* (**a**) *Nucl (of nuclear power station)* déclassement *m* (**b**) *Mil (of warship, aircraft)* mise *f* hors service

decompartmentalize, -ise [,diːkɒmpɑːt'mentəlaɪz] *vt* décompartementaliser

decompensated [,diː'kɒmpenseɪtɪd] *adj Med* décompensé

decompensation [,diː,kɒmpen'seɪʃən] *n Med* décompensation *f*; **cardiac decompensation** décompensation *f* cardiaque

decomposable [,diːkəm'pəʊzəbəl] *adj Chem & Phys* décomposable (**into** en)

decompose [,diːkəm'pəʊz] *Chem & Phys* **1** *vi* se décomposer

2 *vt* décomposer

decomposing [,diːkəm'pəʊzɪŋ] *adj Chem & Phys* (**a**) *(force, agent)* décomposant (**b**) *(matter, substance)* en décomposition

decomposition [,diːkɒmpə'zɪʃən] *n Chem & Phys* décomposition *f*

decompress [,diːkəm'pres] *vt (gas, air)* décomprimer; *(diver)* faire passer en chambre de décompression; *Comput* décompresser

decompression [,diːkəm'preʃən] *n* décompression *f*

▸▸ ***decompression chamber*** chambre *f* de décompression; ***decompression sickness*** maladie *f* des caissons; *Comput* ***decompression software*** logiciel *m* de décompression

decompressor [,diːkəm'presə(r)] *n Comput* logiciel *m* de décompression

decondition [,diːkən'dɪʃən] *vt Psy* déconditionner

decongest [,diːkən'dʒest] *vt Med* décongestionner

decongestant [,diːkən'dʒestənt] *Med* **1** *n* décongestif *m*

2 *adj* décongestif

decongestion [,diːkən'dʒestʃən] *n Med* décongestion *f*

deconsecrate [,diː'kɒnsɪkreɪt] *vt Rel* désaffecter

deconsecration [,diːkɒnsɪ'kreɪʃən] *n Rel* désaffectation *f*

deconsignment [,diːkən'saɪnmənt] *n Com* déconsignation *f*

deconstruct [,diːkən'strʌkt] *vt* déconstruire

'Deconstructing Harry' *Allen* 'Harry dans tous ses états'

deconstruction [,diːkən'strʌkʃən] *n* déconstruction *f*

deconstructive criticism [diːkən'strʌktɪv-] *n Phil & Literature* déconstruction *f*

decontaminate [,diːkən'tæmɪneɪt] *vt* décontaminer

decontamination ['diːkən,tæmɪ'neɪʃən] **1** *n* décontamination *f*

2 *comp (equipment, team, measures)* de décontamination; *(expert)* en décontamination

decontrol [,diːkən'trəʊl] *Com & Econ* **1** *vt (trade)* lever le contrôle gouvernemental sur; **to decontrol prices** libérer les prix

2 *n (of prices)* libération *f*

decontrolled road [,diːkən'trəʊld-] *n Transp* route *f* sans limitation de vitesse

decor ['deɪkɔː(r)] *n* décor *m*; *Fam* **he's part of the decor** *(has been here for a long time)* il fait partie des meubles

decorate ['dekəreɪt] **1** *vt* (**a**) *(house, room → paint)* peindre; *(→ wallpaper)* tapisser (**b**) *(dress, hat)* garnir, orner; *(cake, tree, street)* décorer (**c**) *(give medal to)* décorer, médailler; **to be decorated for bravery** être décoré pour son courage

2 *vi (paint)* peindre; *(wallpaper)* tapisser

decorating ['dekəreɪtɪŋ] *n* (**a**) *(of house, room)* décoration *f*; **to do the decorating** faire les travaux (de décoration); *Br* **painting and decorating** peinture *f* et décoration *f* (**b**) *(of dress, hat)* garnissage *m*, ornementation *f*; *(of cake, tree, street)* décoration *f*

decoration [,dekə'reɪʃən] *n* (**a**) *(action → of house, street, cake, tree)* décoration *f*; *(→ of dress, hat)* ornementation *f*; **interior decoration** décoration *f* intérieure (**b**) *(ornament → for house, street, cake, tree)* décoration *f*; *(→ for dress, hat)* garniture *f*, ornements *mpl* (**c**) *(with medal)* remise *f* d'une décoration (**of sb** à qn); *(medal)* décoration *f*, médaille *f*

▸▸ ***Decoration Day*** = fête nationale américaine en souvenir des soldats morts à la guerre, appelée aussi "Memorial Day" (dernier lundi de mai)

decorative ['dekərətɪv] *adj* décoratif, ornemental; **the house is in excellent decorative order** la décoration de la maison est en excellent état

▸▸ ***decorative arts*** arts *mpl* décoratifs

decoratively ['dekərətɪvlɪ] *adv* décorativement

decorator ['dekəreɪtə(r)] *n* décorateur(trice) *m,f*; *Br* **(painter and) decorator** peintre *mf* décorateur(trice); *Br* **we're having the decorators in next week** les peintres viennent la semaine prochaine

decorous ['dekərəs] *adj Formal (behaviour)* bienséant, séant, convenable; *(person)* convenable, comme il faut

decorously ['dekərəslɪ] *adv Formal (dressed)* convenablement, comme il faut; **to behave decorously** se conduire convenablement *ou* comme il faut, respecter les convenances

decorticate [,diː'kɔːtɪkeɪt] *vt Formal* décortiquer

decortication [,diːkɔːtɪ'keɪʃən] *n Formal* décortication *f*

decorum [dɪ'kɔːrəm] *n* bienséance *f*, décorum *m*; **to behave with decorum** se comporter comme il faut *ou* avec bienséance; **to have a sense of decorum** avoir le sens des convenances; **to have no sense of decorum** ne pas avoir le sens des convenances; **his sense of decorum was offended** il a été choqué dans son sens des convenances

decoupage [,deɪkuː'pɑːʒ] *n Art (craft, picture)* découpage *m*

decouple [dɪ'kʌpəl] *vt Elec* découpler

decoupling [dɪ'kʌplɪŋ] *n Elec* découplage *m*

decoy 1 *n* ['di:kɔɪ] (**a**) *(for catching birds → live bird)* appeau *m*, chanterelle *f*; *(→ artificial device)* leurre *m*

(**b**) *Fig (person)* appât *m*; *(message, tactic, phone call)* piège *m*; **we want you to act as a decoy** nous voulons que vous serviez d'appât

2 *vt* [dɪ'kɔɪ] *(bird → using live bird)* attirer à l'appeau *ou* à la chanterelle; *(→ using artificial means)* attirer au leurre; *(person)* appâter, attirer; **they decoyed him into leaving his house** ils l'ont appâté *ou* attiré hors de chez lui; **the phone call decoyed her away from the office** le coup de téléphone était un piège pour la faire sortir du bureau

►► ***decoy duck*** *(live)* appeau *m*, chanterelle *f*; *(wooden)* leurre *m*

decrease 1 *vi* [dɪ'kri:s] *(number, enthusiasm, population, speed)* décroître, diminuer; *(value, price, crime. inflation)* diminuer, baisser; *(in knitting)* diminuer, faire des diminutions

2 *vt* [dɪ'kri:s] réduire, diminuer; *(prices → of government)* baisser; *(→ of economic forces)* faire baisser; *Knitting* **decrease three stitches** diminuer de trois mailles, faire trois diminutions

3 *n* ['di:kri:s] *(in size)* réduction *f*, diminution *f*; *(in popularity)* baisse *f*; *(in price)* réduction *f*, baisse *f*; **a decrease in numbers** une baisse des effectifs; **to be on the decrease** être en diminution *ou* en baisse

decreasing [di:'kri:sɪŋ] *adj (amount, energy, population)* décroissant; *(value, price, popularity)* en baisse; **in decreasing order of importance** par ordre d'importance décroissant; **a decreasing number of students are going into industry** de moins en moins d'étudiants se dirigent vers l'industrie

►► *Fin* ***decreasing costs*** frais *mpl* dégressifs; *Acct* ***decreasing rate*** taux *m* dégressif

decreasingly [di:'kri:sɪŋlɪ] *adv* de moins en moins

decree [dɪ'kri:] **1** *n Pol* décret *m*, arrêté *m*; *Rel* décret *m*; *Law* jugement *m*, arrêt *m*; **by royal decree** par décret du roi/de la reine; **by presidential decree** par décret présidentiel; *Hum* **we've received a decree from management that...** la direction a décrété que...

2 *vt* décréter; *Pol* décréter, arrêter; *Rel* décréter; *Law* ordonner (par jugement); **fate decreed that...** le sort avait voulu que...

►► *Law* ***decree absolute*** jugement *m* définitif (de divorce); *Law* ***decree nisi*** jugement *m* provisoire (de divorce)

decrement ['dekrɪmənt] *n* (**a**) *(decrease)* décroissement *m*, décroissance *f*; *Her* **moon in decrement** croissant *m* contourné (**b**) *Math* décrément *m*; **logarithmic decrement** décrément *m* logarithmique

decrepit [dɪ'krepɪt] *adj (building, furniture)* délabré; *(person, animal)* décrépit

decrepitate [ˌdi:'krepɪteɪt] *Phys* **1** *vt* faire décrépiter

2 *vi* décrépiter

decrepitude [dɪ'krepɪtju:d] *n (of building, furniture)* délabrement *m*; *(of person)* décrépitude *f*

decrescendo [ˌdi:krɪ'ʃendəʊ] *Mus* **1** *n* decrescendo *m*

2 *adv* decrescendo

decretal [dɪ'kri:təl] *n Rel* décrétale *f*; **the Gregorian Decretals** les Décrétales *fpl* de Grégoire

decriminalization [ˌdi:ˌkrɪmɪnəlaɪ'zeɪʃən] *n* dépénalisation *f*

decriminalize, -ise [ˌdi:'krɪmɪnəˌlaɪz] *vt* dépénaliser

decry [dɪ'kraɪ] *(pt & pp* **decried**) *vt* décrier, dénigrer; **the union has decried the suggested increase as an insult** le syndicat a qualifié l'augmentation proposée d'insulte; **his intervention has been decried as worsening the problem** on l'a accusé, en intervenant, d'avoir aggravé le problème

decrypt [dɪ'krɪpt] *vt* décrypter

decryption [dɪ'krɪpʃən] *n* déchiffrement *m*

decubitus [di:'kju:bɪtəs] *n Med* décubitus *m*

►► ***decubitus ulcer*** escarre *f* décubitus

decumbent [di:'kʌmbənt] *adj* (**a**) *(lying down)* couché, allongé (**b**) *Bot* décombant

DEd [ˌdi:'ed] *n Univ (abbr* **Doctor of Education**) *(person)* = titulaire d'un doctorat en sciences de l'éducation; *(qualification)* doctorat *m* en sciences de l'education

dedicate ['dedɪkeɪt] *vt* (**a**) *(devote)* consacrer; **to dedicate oneself to sb/sth** se consacrer à qn/qch (**b**) *(book, record etc)* dédier; **to dedicate sth to sb** dédier qch à qn (**c**) *Rel (consecrate → church, shrine)* consacrer

dedicated ['dedɪkeɪtɪd] *adj* (**a**) *(devoted)* dévoué; **to be dedicated to one's work** être dévoué à son travail; **she is dedicated to her family/to helping the poor** elle se dévoue pour sa famille/pour aider les pauvres; **she is a dedicated teacher/doctor** c'est un professeur/médecin dévoué à son travail; **you've got to be dedicated (to do this job)** il faut pouvoir tout donner (pour faire ce travail); **he is dedicated** il se donne à fond

(**b**) *(assigned for particular purpose)* dédié, spécialisé; **the Saturday edition has a dedicated travel section** l'édition du samedi contient un supplément voyage

►► ***dedicated circuit*** circuit *m* dédié; *Tel* ***dedicated line*** ligne *f* spécialisée; *Comput* ***dedicated terminal*** terminal *m* dédié; *Comput* ***dedicated word processor*** machine *f* exclusivement destinée au traitement de texte

dedicatee [ˌdedɪkə'ti:] *n* dédicataire *mf*

dedication [ˌdedɪ'keɪʃən] *n* (**a**) *(devotion)* dévouement *m*; **a life of dedication** une vie de dévouement; **his dedication to his job** son dévouement à son travail; **dedication is what is needed** il est essentiel de pouvoir tout donner

(**b**) *(in book, on photograph etc)* dédicace *f*; **I asked the author for a dedication** j'ai demandé à l'auteur qu'il me dédicace mon livre, j'ai demandé une dédicace à l'auteur; **I've got a few dedications to play** *(records)* j'ai quelques dédicaces à passer

(**c**) *Rel (of church, shrine)* consécration *f*; *Am (of building)* inauguration *f*

dedicatory [ˌdedɪ'keɪtərɪ] *adj* dédicatoire

dedifferentiation ['di:ˌdɪfərensʃ'eɪʃən] *n Biol* différenciation *f*

deduce [dɪ'dju:s] *vt* déduire; **to deduce sth from sth** déduire qch de qch; **what do you deduce from that?** qu'en déduisez-vous?; **I deduced that she was lying** j'en ai déduit qu'elle mentait

deducible [dɪ'dju:səbəl] *adj* qui peut se déduire

deduct [dɪ'dʌkt] *vt* déduire, retrancher; *(tax)* prélever; **to deduct £10 from the price** déduire *ou* retrancher 10 livres du prix; **to deduct 25 percent from a salary** prélever 25 pour cent d'un salaire; **to be deducted at source** *(tax)* être prélevé à la source; **after deducting expenses** après déduction des frais

deductibility [dɪˌdʌktə'bɪlɪtɪ] *n* déductibilité *f*

deductible [dɪ'dʌktəbəl] *adj* déductible

deduction [dɪ'dʌkʃən] *n* (**a**) *(inference)* déduction *f*; **your deduction is correct** vous avez fait une bonne déduction; **by (a process of) deduction** par déduction (**b**) *(subtraction)* déduction *f*; *(from pay)* retenue *f*, prélèvement *m*; **how much is that after deductions?** combien reste-t-il après déductions?; **after deductions, I'm left with a salary of £20,000** une fois les prélèvements décomptés, il me reste un salaire de 20 000 livres; **deduction at source** retenue *f* à la source; **tax deductions** prélèvements *mpl* fiscaux

deductive [dɪ'dʌktɪv] *adj* déductif

deductively [dɪ'dʌktɪvlɪ] *adv* déductivement, par déduction

deed [di:d] **1** *n* (**a**) *(action)* action *f*; **in word and deed** en parole et en fait *ou* action; **brave deed** acte *m* de bravoure; *Literary* **deed of valour** haut fait *m*; **to do one's good deed for the day** faire sa bonne action *ou* sa BA de la journée; **we want deeds not words** nous voulons du concret *ou* des actions, pas des discours (**b**) *Law* acte *m* notarié

2 *vt Am Law* transférer par acte notarié; **the house was deeded to his daughter** la maison a été transférée à sa fille par acte notarié

►► *Law* ***deed of acknowledgment*** acte *m* récognitif; ***deed of arrangement, deed of assignment*** acte *m* de transfert; ***deed box*** classeur *m* à documents; ***deed of covenant*** = déclaration par laquelle on s'engage à verser régulièrement une certaine somme à un particulier, une association caritative, etc; ***deed of partnership*** acte *m* constitutif *ou* de société; ***deed poll*** contrat *m* unilatéral; **to change one's name by deed poll** changer de nom par contrat unilatéral, changer de nom officiellement; ***deed of sale*** acte *m* de vente; ***deed of transfer*** acte *m* de cession

deejay ['di:dʒeɪ] *n Fam* DJ *mf*

deem [di:m] *vt Formal* juger, considérer, estimer; **it was deemed necessary/advisable to call an enquiry** on a jugé qu'il était nécessaire/opportun d'ordonner une enquête; **if you deem it necessary** si vous le jugez nécessaire; **he deemed it a great honour** il considéra cela comme un grand honneur, il estima que c'était un grand honneur; **she was deemed (to be) the rightful owner** elle était considérée comme la propriétaire de droit

de-emphasize, -ise [ˌdi:-] *vt (need, claim, feature)* moins insister sur, se montrer moins insistant sur

de-energization ['di:ˌenədʒaɪ'zeɪʃən] *n Elec* désexcitation *f*

de-energize, -ise [ˌdi:-] *vt Elec* désexciter

DEEP [di:p]

profond	►1
profondément	►2
océan	►3 (a)

1 *adj* (**a**) *(going far down → water, hole, wound etc)* profond; **deep snow lay round about** une épaisse couche de neige recouvrait les alentours; **the water/hole is five metres deep** l'eau/le trou a cinq mètres de profondeur; **the road was a foot deep in snow** ≃ la route était sous *ou* recouverte de trente centimètres de neige; **to inflict a deep wound** *(weapon)* pénétrer très profondément; **a hole ten feet deep** un trou de dix pieds de profondeur; **the deep blue sea** le vaste océan; **to be in a deep sleep** être profondément endormi; **deep in thought/study** plongé dans ses pensées/l'étude; **deep in debt** criblé de dettes; **to get deeper and deeper into debt** s'endetter de plus en plus; **a deep breath** une inspiration profonde; *Fig* **take a deep breath and just do it** respire un bon coup et vas-y; **deep breathing** *(action, noise)* respiration *f* profonde; *(exercices)* exercices *mpl* respiratoires; **we're in deep trouble** nous sommes dans de sales draps; **the deep end** *(of swimming pool)* le côté le plus profond; **to plunge** *or* **to jump in at the deep end** y aller carrément; *Fam* **to go off the deep end** *(lose one's temper)* piquer une crise *ou* une colère; *(panic)* perdre tous ses moyens, paniquer à mort; *Fig* **to be thrown in at the deep end** être mis dans le bain tout de suite; **to be in deep water** être dans le pétrin, avoir des problèmes; **I think we're getting into deep water here** je crois que nous sommes en train de nous engager sur un terrain dangereux

(**b**) *(going far back → forest, cupboard, serve)* profond; **deep in the forest** au (fin) fond de la forêt; **the crowd stood 15 deep** la foule se tenait sur 15 rangs; *Hum* **deep in Buckinghamshire, in deepest Buckinghamshire** dans le Buckinghamshire profond; **deep space** profondeurs *fpl* de l'espace

(**c**) *(strong → feelings)* profond; **with deepest sympathy** avec mes plus sincères condoléances

(**d**) *(profound → thinker)* profond

(**e**) *(mysterious, difficult to understand → book)* profond; **a deep mystery** un mystère profond *ou* épais; **a deep dark secret** un sinistre secret; **he's a deep one** on ne peut jamais savoir ce qu'il pense

(**f**) *(dark, vivid → colour)* profond; **deep blue eyes** des yeux d'un bleu profond; **to be in deep mourning** être en grand deuil

(**g**) *(low → sound, note)* grave; *(→ voice)* grave, profond

(**h**) *Fin* **deep discount** forte remise *f*

2 *adv* profondément; **they went deep into the forest** ils se sont enfoncés dans la forêt; **the**

dec–dee

snow lay deep on the ground il y avait une épaisse couche de neige sur le sol; **he dug (down) deep into the ground** il a creusé profond *ou* profondément dans la terre; **he looked deep into her eyes** *(romantically)* il a plongé ses yeux dans les siens; *(probingly)* il l'a regardée droit dans les yeux; **the goalkeeper kicked the ball deep into the opposition's half** le gardien de but a shooté loin dans le camp adverse; **to go** *or* **to run deep** *(emotions)* être profond; **deep down she knew she was right** au fond *ou* dans son for intérieur elle savait qu'elle avait raison; **he thrust his hands deep into his pockets** il plongea les mains au fond de ses poches; **deep into the night** tard dans la nuit; **don't go in too deep** *(in water)* n'allez pas où c'est profond, n'allez pas trop loin; **don't get in too deep** *(involved)* ne t'implique pas trop; *Fam* **she's in it pretty deep** elle est dedans jusqu'au cou

3 *n Literary* (**a**) *(ocean)* **the deep** l'océan *m*

(**b**) *(depth)* **in the deep of winter** au plus profond *ou* au cœur de l'hiver

►► ***deep freeze*** *(in home, shop)* congélateur *m*; *(industrial)* surgélateur *m*; ***the Deep South*** *(of the USA)* le Sud profond; *Ling* ***deep structure*** structure *f* profonde; *Med* ***deep therapy*** radiothérapie *f* profonde *ou* pénétrante; *Fam* ***deep throat*** *(informer)* informateur *m*, indicateur *m*

-deep [diːp] *suff* **she was knee-/waist-deep in water** elle avait de l'eau jusqu'aux genoux/ jusqu'à la taille; **the water is only ankle-deep** l'eau ne monte *ou* n'arrive qu'aux chevilles; **a ten-foot-deep hole** un trou de dix pieds de profondeur

deep-chested *adj* à forte poitrine

deep-discount bond *n Fin* obligation *f* à forte remise

deep-dish pie *n Am Culin* tourte *f*

deepen ['diːpən] **1** *vt* (**a**) *(hole, river bed, knowledge)* approfondir; *(mystery)* épaissir; *(love, friendship)* faire grandir, intensifier

(**b**) *(sound, voice)* rendre plus grave; *(colour)* rendre plus profond, intensifier

2 *vi* (**a**) *(sea, river)* devenir plus profond; *(silence, mystery)* s'épaissir; *(crisis)* s'aggraver, s'intensifier; *(knowledge)* s'approfondir; *(love, friendship)* s'intensifier, grandir

(**b**) *(colour)* devenir plus profond, s'intensifier; *(sound)* devenir plus grave

deepening ['diːpənɪŋ] **1** *adj (silence, shadows, emotion)* de plus en plus profond; *(crisis)* qui s'aggrave *ou* s'intensifie; *(love, friendship)* de plus en plus profond

2 *n (of hole, channel)* approfondissement *m*; *(of silence, love)* intensification *f*

deep-fat fryer *n* friteuse *f*

deep-fat frying *n* cuisson *f* en bain de friture

deep-freeze *vt (at home)* congeler; *(industrially)* surgeler

deep-fried *adj* frit

deep-frozen *adj (at home)* congelé; *(industrially)* surgelé

deep-fry *vt* faire frire

deep-fryer *n* friteuse *f*

deep-heat treatment *n Med* thermothérapie *f*

deep-laid *adj (plan, scheme)* secret(ète), machiné dans le secret

deeply ['diːplɪ] *adv* (**a**) *(dig, breathe, sleep, admire, regret, think)* profondément; *(drink)* à grands traits; **to sigh deeply** pousser un profond soupir; **they gazed deeply into each other's eyes** leurs regards étaient plongés dans les yeux l'un de l'autre; **to fall deeply in love with sb** tomber profondément amoureux de qn; **to care deeply about sb** être profondément attaché à qn; **I care deeply about your happiness/this country's future** ton bonheur/l'avenir de ce pays est très important pour moi; **to go deeply into sth** approfondir qch; **she can't have looked into it very deeply** elle n'a pas dû s'en occuper très sérieusement; **his forehead was deeply lined** son front était creusé de rides profondes

(**b**) *(offended, relieved, grateful, religious)* profondément, extrêmement

deepness ['diːpnɪs] *n (of ocean, voice, writer, remark)* profondeur *f*; *(of note, sound)* gravité *f*

deep-pan pizza *n Culin* pizza *f* à pâte épaisse

deep-rooted *adj (tree)* dont les racines sont profondes; *Fig (ideas, belief, prejudice)* profondément ancré *ou* enraciné; *(feeling)* profond

deep-sea *adj (creatures, exploration)* des grands fonds

►► ***deep-sea diver*** plongeur(euse) *m,f* sous-marin(e); ***deep-sea diving*** plongée *f* sous-marine; ***deep-sea fisherman*** pêcheur *m* hauturier *ou* en haute mer; ***deep-sea fishing*** pêche *f* hauturière *ou* en haute mer

deep-seated [-'siːtɪd] *adj (sorrow, dislike)* profond; *(idea, belief, complex, prejudice)* profondément ancré *ou* enraciné

deep-set *adj* enfoncé

deep-six *vt Am Fam (throw away)* balancer; **we deep-sixed the project** on a balancé cette idée de projet

deep-throated [-'θrəʊtɪd] *adj (cough, laugh)* caverneux

deep-vein thrombosis *n Med* thrombose *f* veineuse profonde

deepwater ['diːpwɔːtə(r)] *adj* (**a**) *(vessel)* hauturier (**b**) *(port)* en eau profonde, de toute marée

deer [dɪə(r)] *(pl* **inv***)* **1** *n (male)* cerf *m*; *(female)* biche *f*; **(red) deer** cerf *m* commun; **(fallow) deer** daim *m*; **(roe) deer** chevreuil *m*; **a herd of deer** un troupeau *ou* une harde de cerfs/de daims/de chevreuils; **the different species of deer** les différents types de cervidés

2 *comp (hunter)* de cerf *ou* cerfs

►► ***deer fence*** = clôture haute conçue pour empêcher les daims de s'échapper; ***deer park*** chasse *f* gardée pour le cerf

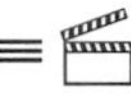

'The Deer Hunter' *Cimino* 'Voyage au bout de l'enfer'

---

deerhound ['dɪəhaʊnd] *n* limier *m*, lévrier *m* d'Écosse

deerskin ['dɪəskɪn] **1** *n* peau *f* de daim

2 *comp (coat, gloves)* en daim

deerstalker ['dɪə,stɔːkə(r)] *n* (**a**) *(hunter)* chasseur(euse) *m,f* de cerf (**b**) *(hat)* chapeau *m* à la Sherlock Holmes

deerstalking ['dɪə,stɔːkɪŋ] *n* chasse *f* au cerf

de-escalate [,diː-] **1** *vt (crisis)* désamorcer; *(tension)* faire baisser

2 *vi (crisis)* se désamorcer; *(tension)* baisser

de-escalation [,diː-] *n (of crisis)* désescalade *f*, désamorçage *m*; *(of tension)* baisse *f*

def [def] *adj Fam (excellent)* super, génial

deface [dɪ'feɪs] *vt (statue, painting* → *with paint, aerosol spray)* barbouiller; *(*→ *by writing slogans)* dégrader par des inscriptions; *(book)* abîmer *ou* endommager par des gribouillages *ou* des inscriptions

defacement [dɪ'feɪsmənt] *n* (**a**) *(of statue, painting* → *with paint, aerosol spray)* barbouillage *m*; *(*→ *with slogans)* dégradation *f (par des inscriptions)*; *(of book)* dégradation *f (par des notes, des incriptions)*

de facto [deɪ'fæktəʊ] **1** *adj* de facto, de fait; *Law* **de facto possession** possession *f* de fait

2 *adv Law* **de facto and de jure** de droit et de fait

3 *n Austr (partner)* concubin(e) *m,f*

defalcate ['diːfælkeɪt] *vi Law* commettre des détournements de fonds

defalcation [,diːfæl'keɪʃən] *n Law* détournement *m* de fonds

defamation [,defə'meɪʃən] *n Law* diffamation *f*; **to sue sb for defamation of character** poursuivre qn en justice pour diffamation

defamatory [dɪ'fæmətrɪ] *adj Law* diffamatoire

defame [dɪ'feɪm] *vt Law* diffamer, calomnier

default [dɪ'fɔːlt] **1** *n* (**a**) *Law (non-appearance* → *in civil court)* défaut *m*, non-comparution *f*; *(*→ *in criminal court)* contumace *f*

(**b**) *Formal (absence)* **in default of** à défaut de

(**c**) *Comput* défaut *m*; **drive C is the default** C est l'unité de disque par défaut

(**d**) *Fin & St Exch* défaut *m* de paiement, manquement *m* à payer

2 *vi* (**a**) *Law (fail to appear* → *in civil court)* ne pas comparaître; *(*→ *in criminal court)* être en état de contumace

(**b**) *Fin & St Exch* manquer *ou* faillir à ses engagements; **to default on a payment** ne pas honorer un paiement; **to default on alimony payments** manquer aux versements de pension alimentaire

(**c**) *Sport* déclarer forfait

(**d**) *Comput & Tech* **to default to sth** sélectionner qch par défaut; **the computer automatically defaults to drive C** l'ordinateur sélectionne l'unité de disque C par défaut

3 by default *adv* (**a**) *(through lack of action)* **you are responsible by default** tu es responsable pour n'avoir rien fait

(**b**) *Law* **judgement by default** jugement *m* par défaut *ou* contumace

(**c**) *Sport* par forfait; **to win/to lose by default** gagner/perdre par forfait

(**d**) *Comput & Tech* par défaut; **the machine sets itself to 1 by default** la machine se réglera sur 1 par défaut

►► *Comput* ***default drive*** lecteur *m* par défaut; *Comput* ***default font*** police *f* par défaut; *Fin* ***default interest*** intérêts *mpl* moratoires; *Comput* ***default setting*** configuration *f* par défaut; *Comput* ***default value*** valeur *f* par défaut

defaulter [dɪ'fɔːltə(r)] *n* (**a**) *Law (defendant)* inculpé(e) *m,f* contumace *ou* défaillant(e); *(witness)* témoin *m* défaillant (**b**) *Fin & St Exch* débiteur(trice) *m,f* défaillant(e) (**c**) *Br Mil & Naut* = soldat ou marin qui a transgressé la discipline

defaulting [dɪ'fɔːltɪŋ] *adj* (**a**) *Law (defendant)* contumace; *(witness)* défaillant (**b**) *Fin & St Exch* défaillant

defeasance [dɪ'fiːzəns] *n Law* defeasance *m*

defeat [dɪ'fiːt] **1** *n* (**a**) *(of army, opposition, team, government)* défaite *f*; **to suffer a defeat** connaître une défaite, échouer; **to admit defeat** s'avouer vaincu

(**b**) *(of project, bill)* échec *m*; *Parl (of measure)* rejet *m*

2 *vt* (**a**) *(army, opposition)* vaincre; *(team, government)* battre; **they were defeated by one goal to nil** ils ont été battus par un but à zéro; **it defeats me** *(I don't understand)* cela me dépasse

(**b**) *(attempts, project, bill)* faire échouer; **we were defeated by the weather** nous avons échoué à cause du temps; **to defeat the ends of justice** contrarier la justice; **that defeats the object** ça va à l'encontre du but recherché

defeatism [dɪ'fiːtɪzəm] *n* défaitisme *m*; **an air/mood of defeatism** un air/une atmosphère défaitiste *ou* de défaite

defeatist [dɪ'fiːtɪst] **1** *adj* défaitiste

2 *n* défaitiste *mf*

defecate ['defəkeɪt] *vi* déféquer

defecation [,defə'keɪʃən] *n* défécation *f*

defect 1 *n* ['diːfekt] défaut *m*; **physical defect** malformation *f*; **hearing/speech defect** défaut de l'ouïe/de prononciation

2 *vi* [dɪ'fekt] *Pol (to another country)* passer à l'étranger; *(to another party)* quitter son parti pour un autre; **to defect to the West** passer à l'Ouest; **to defect to the enemy** passer à l'ennemi; **yet another dissident has defected** un nouveau dissident est passé à l'étranger; **he defected from his native Poland** il s'est enfui de sa Pologne natale; **she defected to the Labour Party** elle a rejoint le parti travailliste; *Fig* **she's defected to our main competitor** elle est passée chez notre concurrent principal

defection [dɪ'fekʃən] *n Pol (to another country)* passage *m* à un pays ennemi; *(to another party)* passage *m* à un parti adverse; **there were many successful defections by East Germans** beaucoup d'Allemands de l'Est ont réussi à passer à l'Ouest; **the country was shocked by his defection** le pays a été choqué quand il est passé à l'étranger; **after his defection from his native Poland** après qu'il se fut enfui de sa Pologne natale

defective [dɪ'fektɪv] **1** *adj* (**a**) *(machine, reasoning)* défectueux; *(hearing, sight, organ)* déficient; *(memory)* infidèle; *(brakes)* en mauvais état; **to be mentally defective** souffrir de débilité mentale; *Ind* **defective part** pièce *f* défectueuse (**b**) *Gram* défectif

2 *n* **mental defective** débile *mf* mental(e)

defectively [dɪ'fektɪvlɪ] *adv* défectueusement

defectiveness [dɪ'fektɪvnɪs] *n* (**a**) *(defective*

dee–def

state) état *m* défectueux, défectuosité *f* (**b**) *Gram* défectivité *f*

defector [dɪ'fektə(r)] *n Pol & Fig* transfuge *mf*

defence, *Am* **defense** [dɪ'fens] **1** *n* (**a**) *(protection)* défense *f*; **how much is spent on defence?** combien dépense-t-on pour la défense?; **to carry a weapon for defence** porter une arme pour se défendre; **to come to sb's defence** venir à la défense de qn; **he killed the man in defence of his wife** il a tué l'homme pour défendre sa femme; **to act/to speak in defence of sth** *(following attack)* agir/parler en défense de qch; *(in support of)* agir/parler en faveur de qch; **to speak in defence of sb, to speak in sb's defence** *(following attack)* parler en défense de qn; *(in support of)* parler en faveur de qn; **the best form of defence is attack** la meilleure forme de défense, c'est l'attaque

(**b**) *(thing providing protection)* protection *f*, défense *f*; *(argument)* défense *f*; **defences** *(weapons)* moyens *mpl* de défense; *(fortifications)* défenses *fpl*, fortifications *fpl*; **Holland's defences against the flood waters** les défenses *fpl* dont dispose la Hollande contre les inondations; **to use sth as a defence against sth** se servir de qch comme défense *ou* protection contre qch, se servir de qch pour se défendre *ou* se protéger de qch; **the body's natural defences against infection** les défenses naturelles de l'organisme contre l'infection; **to put up a stubborn defence** se défendre avec entêtement; **to catch sb when his/her defences are down** prendre qn quand il/elle n'est pas en position de se défendre *ou* de faire face; **to draw up a defence of sth** préparer la défense de qch

(**c**) *Law* défense *f*; **the defence** *(lawyers)* la défense; **who have we got for the defence?** qui assurera la défense?; **counsel for the defence** avocat *m* de la défense; **witness for the defence** témoin *m* à décharge, témoin de la défense; **to appear for the defence** comparaître pour la défense; **the case for the defence** la défense; **what is our defence going to be?** quelle ligne de défense allons-nous adopter?; **to conduct one's own defence** assurer sa propre défense; **do you have anything to say in your defence?** avez-vous quelque chose à dire pour votre défense?; **it must be said in her defence that...** il faut dire à sa décharge *ou* pour sa défense que...

(**d**) *Sport* défense *f*; **the defence** *(players)* la défense; **to turn defence into attack** faire *ou* lancer une contre-attaque

2 *comp* (**a**) *(forces)* de défense; *(cuts, minister, spending)* de la défense

(**b**) *Law (lawyer)* de la défense

►► *Law* ***defence counsel*** défenseur *m*; *(in civil law)* avocat(e) *m,f* de la défense; *Med* ***defence mechanism*** défenses *fpl* immunitaires; *Psy* mécanisme *m* de défense; ***defence plant*** usine *f* d'armements; *Law* ***defence witness*** témoin *m* à décharge

defenceless, *Am* **defenseless** [dɪ'fenslɪs] *adj* sans défense, vulnérable

defencelessness, *Am* **defenselessness** [dɪ'fenslɪsnɪs] *n* vulnérabilité *f*

defend [dɪ'fend] *vt* (**a**) *(protect)* défendre; **to defend sb/sth from** *or* **against attack** défendre qn/qch contre une attaque; **to defend oneself** se défendre (**b**) *(justify → opinion)* justifier (**c**) *Sport (goalmouth, title)* défendre (**d**) *Law* défendre

defendant [dɪ'fendənt] *n Law (in civil court)* défendeur(eresse) *m,f*; *(in criminal court)* inculpé(e) *m,f*; *(accused of serious crimes)* accusé(e) *m,f*

defender [dɪ'fendə(r)] *n* (**a**) *(of a cause, rights)* défenseur *m*, avocat(e) *m,f* (**b**) *Sport (player)* défenseur *m*; *(of title, record)* détenteur(trice) *m,f* (**c**) *Am Law* **public defender** avocat(e) *m,f* commis d'office

►► ***Defender of the Faith*** Défenseur *m* de la foi

defending [dɪ'fendɪŋ] *adj* (**a**) *Sport (champion)* en titre (**b**) *Law* de la défense

►► *Law* ***defending counsel*** défenseur *m*

defenestration [ˌdiːfenɪ'streɪʃən] *n* défenestration *f*

defense, defenseless *etc Am* = **defence, defenceless** *etc*

defensible [dɪ'fensəbəl] *adj (idea, opinion etc)* défendable

defensive [dɪ'fensɪv] **1** *adj (strategy, weapon, game etc)* défensif; **to get defensive** se mettre sur la défensive; **don't be so defensive!** ne te mets pas sur la défensive comme ça!; **she's very defensive about it** elle est très susceptible quand on parle de cela

2 *n Mil & Fig* défensive *f*; **to be on the defensive** être *ou* se tenir sur la défensive; **to go on the defensive** se mettre sur la défensive

►► *Mil* ***defensive action*** action *f* défensive; *Sport* ***defensive end*** *(in American football)* defensive end *m*; ***defensive position*** position *f* de défense; *St Exch* ***defensive stocks*** titres *mpl* de placement, valeurs *fpl* d'investissement

defensively [dɪ'fensɪvlɪ] *adv (say)* d'un ton défensif; *(react)* d'une manière défensive; **they played very defensively** ils ont eu un jeu très défensif; *Mil* **used defensively** utilisé pour la défense; **"it's not my fault", she said, defensively** "ce n'est pas de ma faute", dit-elle, sur la défensive

defensiveness [dɪ'fensɪvnɪs] *n* **when she reacted/spoke with such defensiveness** quand elle a réagi/parlé d'une manière aussi défensive; **I get really tired of his defensiveness** j'en ai vraiment assez qu'il soit toujours sur la défensive; **her defensiveness in the face of criticism** la façon qu'elle a de se mettre sur la défensive quand on la critique

defer [dɪ'fɜː(r)] *(pt & pp* **deferred**, *cont* **deferring**) **1** *vt* (**a**) *(question, case)* différer, ajourner, remettre; *(decision, meeting)* remettre, reporter; *(payment, business, judgment)* différer, retarder; *(verdict)* suspendre; **to defer sth to a later date** remettre *ou* reporter qch à plus tard; **to defer doing sth** différer de faire qch; *Law* **to defer sentencing** suspendre le prononcé du jugement

(**b**) *Mil (person)* mettre en sursis (d'appel); **to defer sb on medical grounds** réformer qn temporairement pour raisons médicales

2 *vi (give way)* **to defer to sb** s'en remettre à qn; **to defer to sb's judgement/knowledge** s'en remettre au jugement/aux connaissances de qn; **to defer to sb's wishes** agir conformément aux souhaits de qn, se soumettre à la volonté de qn

deference ['defərəns] *n* déférence *f*, égard *m*, considération *f*; **out of** *or* **in deference to sb/sb's wishes** par égard *ou* considération pour qn/les souhaits de qn; **to treat sb with deference, to pay** *or* **to show deference to sb** traiter qn avec déférence *ou* égards

deferential [ˌdefə'renʃəl] *adj (air, tone)* de déférence, respectueux; *(behaviour)* respectueux; *(person)* déférent, respectueux; **to be deferential to sb** faire montre de déférence *ou* d'égards envers qn

deferentially [ˌdefə'renʃəlɪ] *adv* avec déférence

deferment [dɪ'fɜːmənt], **deferral** [dɪ'fɜːrəl] *n* (**a**) *(of decision, meeting, payment, sentence)* report *m*, ajournement *m* (**b**) *Mil (for health reasons)* réforme *f*; **to apply for deferment** demander à être réformé

deferred [dɪ'fɜːd] *adj (gen)* ajourné, retardé; *Fin (payment, shares)* différé; *Fin (annuity)* à paiement différé, à jouissance différée

►► *Fin* ***deferred annuity*** annuité *f* différée; *Fin* ***deferred asset*** actif *m* différé; *Fin* ***deferred charges*** frais *mpl* différés; *Fin* ***deferred credit*** paiement *m* différé; *Fin* ***deferred debit*** débit *m* différé; *Fin* ***deferred income*** produit *m* constaté d'avance; *Fin* ***deferred liabilities*** passif *m* reporté; *Fin* ***deferred pay*** rappel *m* de traitement; *Fin* ***deferred payment*** paiement *m* différé; *Fin* ***deferred rebate*** rabais *m* différé; *Law* ***deferred sentence*** jugement *m* dont le prononcé est suspendu, jugement *m* ajourné; *Fin* ***deferred taxation*** impôts *mpl* différés

deffo ['defəʊ] *adv Br Fam* absolument ❑; **are you coming tonight? – deffo!** tu viens ce soir? – je veux!

defiance [dɪ'faɪəns] **1** *n* défi *m*; **I will not tolerate any further defiance** je ne tolérerai plus qu'on me défie ainsi; **your defiance of my orders meant that people's lives were put at risk** en défiant mes ordres vous avez mis la vie d'autrui en danger; **gesture/act of defiance** geste *m*/acte *m* de défi

2 in defiance of *prep* **in defiance of sb/sth** au mépris de qn/qch

defiant [dɪ'faɪənt] *adj (gesture, remark, look)* de défi; *(person, reply)* provocateur

defiantly [dɪ'faɪəntlɪ] *adv (act)* avec une attitude de défi; *(reply, look at)* d'un air de défi

defibrillation ['diːˌfɪbrɪ'leɪʃən] *n Med* défibrillation *f*

defibrillator [ˌdiː'fɪbrɪleɪtə(r)] *n Med* défibrillateur *m*

deficiency [dɪ'fɪʃənsɪ] *(pl* **deficiencies**) *n* (**a**) *(lack)* manque *m*, insuffisance *f* (**of** de); *Med (shortage)* carence *f*; **a deficiency in** *or* **of calcium, a calcium deficiency** une carence en calcium; **mental deficiency** déficience *f* mentale (**b**) *(flaw → in character, system)* défaut *m* (**c**) *(deficit)* manquant *m*, déficit *m*; *Com* découvert *m*; *Pol* déficit *m* budgétaire

►► *Med* ***deficiency disease*** maladie *f* de carence

deficient [dɪ'fɪʃənt] *adj* (**a**) *(insufficient)* insuffisant; **to be deficient in sth** manquer de qch (**b**) *(defective)* défectueux; **to be mentally deficient** avoir une déficience mentale

deficit ['defɪsɪt] *n Com & Fin* déficit *m*; **to be in deficit** être en déficit, être déficitaire; **to make up the deficit** combler le déficit; **the balance of payments shows a deficit of £800 million** la balance des paiements indique un déficit de 800 millions de livres

defile 1 *vt* [dɪ'faɪl] *(grave, memory)* profaner; **they've defiled my home** *(entered uninvited)* ils ont violé l'intimité de ma maison

2 *vi* [dɪ'faɪl] *Mil* défiler

3 *n* ['diːfaɪl] *(valley, passage)* défilé *m*

defilement [dɪ'faɪlmənt] *n (of grave, memory)* profanation *f*

definable [dɪ'faɪnəbəl] *adj* définissable

define [dɪ'faɪn] *vt* (**a**) *(term, word)* définir

(**b**) *(boundary, role, subject)* définir, délimiter; *(concept, idea, feeling)* définir, préciser; *(objectives)* formuler; *(scope, extent)* déterminer; *(powers)* délimiter; **he defines politics as being the art of the possible** il définit la politique comme l'art du possible

(**c**) *(object, shape)* définir; **the figures in the painting are not clearly defined** les formes humaines du tableau ne sont pas bien définies

(**d**) *Comput (value)* déclarer

defining [dɪ'faɪnɪŋ] *adj* restrictif

definite ['defɪnɪt] *adj* (**a**) *(precise, clear)* précis; *(advantage, improvement, opinion)* net; *(answer)* définitif; *(orders, proof)* formel; *(price)* fixe; **their plans to marry are still not definite** leurs projets de mariage sont encore vagues; **it's a definite advantage being a woman** c'est décidément un avantage d'être une femme; **the boss was very definite about the need for punctuality** le patron a été très ferme en ce qui concerne la ponctualité; **he has very definite ideas on the subject** il a des idées bien arrêtées sur la question

(**b**) *(certain)* certain, sûr; *(date)* définitif, certain; **it's not definite yet** ce n'est pas encore définitif *ou* sûr; **is it definite that the Pope is coming to England?** est-il certain *ou* sûr que le pape vienne en Angleterre?; **I've heard rumours of a merger, but nothing definite** j'ai entendu dire qu'il allait y avoir une fusion, mais rien de sûr pour l'instant; **and that's definite!** et c'est sûr!

►► *Gram* ***definite article*** article *m* défini; *Math* ***definite integral*** intégrale *f* définie

definitely ['defɪnɪtlɪ] *adv* (**a**) *(certainly)* certainement, sans aucun doute; **he has definitely decided to resign** il ne fait aucun doute qu'il a décidé de démissionner; **she's definitely innocent** elle est innocente, c'est sûr *ou* certain; **I'll definitely call you** je te téléphonerai sans faute; **she's definitely leaving, but I don't know when** je sais qu'elle part, mais je ne sais pas quand; **are you definitely giving up your flat?** allez-vous vraiment quitter votre appartement?; **that's definitely not the man I saw** je suis sûr que ce n'est pas l'homme que j'ai vu; **are you going to the show? – definitely!** est-ce que tu vas au spectacle? – absolument!; **definitely not!** certainement pas!

(**b**) *(clearly, without ambiguity)* **he told me very definitely that he didn't want to come** il m'a dit très clairement qu'il ne voulait pas venir

definition [defɪ'nɪʃən] *n* (**a**) *(of term, word)* définition *f*; **by definition** par définition; **to give a definition of sth** donner une définition de qch, définir qch (**b**) *(of duties, powers, territory)* définition *f*, délimitation *f*; *(of objectives)* formulation *f* (**c**) *(of photograph, sound)* netteté *f*; *TV* définition *f*

definitional [ˌdefɪ'nɪʃənəl] *adj* définitionnel

definitive [dɪ'fɪnɪtɪv] *adj* (**a**) *(conclusive)* définitif; *(battle, victory)* définitif, décisif; *(result)* définitif, qui fait autorité (**b**) *(authoritative → biography, edition)* qui fait autorité; **the definitive book on the subject** le livre qui fait autorité *ou* décisif en la matière; **she was, for me, the definitive Juliet** pour moi, c'est une Juliette inégalable (**c**) *Zool (fully developed)* définitif

definitively [dɪ'fɪnɪtɪvlɪ] *adv* définitivement

deflagrate [deflə'greɪt] *Chem & Phys* **1** *vt* faire déflagrer

2 *vi* déflagrer

deflagration [deflə'greɪʃən] *n Chem & Phys* déflagration *f*

deflate [dɪ'fleɪt] **1** *vt* (**a**) *(ball, balloon, tyre)* dégonfler; *Fig (person)* démonter; **to deflate sb's ego** porter un coup à l'orgueil de qn; **I felt rather deflated** *(disappointed)* j'étais assez déçu (**b**) *Fin & Econ (prices)* faire baisser, faire tomber; **to deflate the currency** provoquer la déflation de la monnaie; **the measure is intended to deflate the economy** cette mesure est destinée à faire de la déflation

2 *vi* (**a**) *(ball, balloon, tyre)* se dégonfler (**b**) *Fin & Econ* provoquer la déflation de la monnaie

deflation [dɪ'fleɪʃən] *n* (**a**) *(of ball, balloon, tyre)* dégonflement *m* (**b**) *Fin & Econ* déflation *f* (**c**) *Geog* déflation *f* (**d**) *(anti-climax)* abattement *m*; **...which resulted in the deflation of his ego** ...ce qui l'a complètement abattu

deflationary [dɪ'fleɪʃənərɪ], **deflationist** [dɪ'fleɪʃənɪst] *adj Fin & Econ* déflationniste

deflator [diː'fleɪtə(r)] *n* dégonfleur *m*

deflect [dɪ'flekt] **1** *vt (ball, bullet)* (faire) dévier; *Phys (light)* défléchir; *(sound)* renvoyer; *Fig (person, attention, criticism)* détourner; **he would not be deflected from his purpose** rien ne l'aurait détourné de son but; **the ball was deflected into the net** le ballon a rebondi dans le filet

2 *vi (projectile)* dévier; *Phys (light)* être défléchi; *(magnetic needle)* décliner; **the ball deflected off the post** le ballon a rebondi contre le poteau

deflection [dɪ'flekʃən] *n* déviation *f*; *(of magnetic needle)* déclinaison *f*; *Phys (of light)* déflexion *f*; **it was a lucky deflection off the post** heureusement la balle a été déviée par le montant du but

deflector [dɪ'flektə(r)] *n* déflecteur *m*

deflexion = **deflection**

defloration [ˌdiːflɔː'reɪʃən] *n Literary* défloration *f*

deflower [ˌdiː'flaʊə(r)] *vt* (**a**) *Literary or Hum (woman)* déflorer (**b**) *Bot* défleurir

deflowering [ˌdiː'flaʊərɪŋ] *n Literary or Hum (of virgin)* défloration *f*

defocus [ˌdiː'fəʊkəs] *vi Opt* passer au flou

defog [ˌdiː'fɒg] *vt Am Aut* désembuer

defogger [ˌdiː'fɒgə(r)] *n Am Aut* dispositif *m* antibuée *(inv)*

defoliant [ˌdiː'fəʊlɪənt] *n Bot* défoliant *m*

defoliate [ˌdiː'fəʊlɪeɪt] *vt Bot* défolier

defoliation [ˌdiːfəʊlɪ'eɪʃən] *n Bot* défoliation *f*

deforest [ˌdiː'fɒrɪst] *vt Agr* déboiser

deforestation ['diːˌfɒrɪ'steɪʃən] *n Agr* déboisement *m*, déforestation *f*

deform [dɪ'fɔːm] *vt* déformer; *Fig (distort, ruin)* défigurer

deformation [ˌdiːfɔː'meɪʃən] *n* déformation *f*

deformed [dɪ'fɔːmd] *adj (person)* malformé; *(limb)* difforme, malformé; **the baby was born deformed** le bébé est né avec une malformation

deformity [dɪ'fɔːmətɪ] *n* difformité *f*

defragment [ˌdiːfræg'ment] *vt Comput* défragmenter

defragmentation ['diːˌfrægmen'teɪʃən] *n Comput* défragmentation *f*

defragmenter [ˌdiːfræg'mentə(r)] *n Comput* défragmenteur *m*

defraud [dɪ'frɔːd] **1** *vt (the state)* frauder; *(company, person)* escroquer, *Spec* frustrer; **to defraud sb of sth** escroquer qch à qn, frustrer qn de qch; **he defrauded the government of £15,000 in unemployment benefits** il a frauduleusement perçu 15 000 livres d'allocations chômage

2 *vi Law* **conspiracy to defraud** entente *f* délictueuse dans le but de frauder

defrauder [dɪ'frɔːdə(r)] *n* fraudeur(euse) *m,f*

defray [dɪ'freɪ] *vt Formal* rembourser, prendre en charge; **all charges to be defrayed by the purchaser** tous les frais sont à la charge de l'acheteur; **we will defray the cost of your air fare** nous vous rembourserons le prix de votre billet d'avion

defrayal [dɪ'freɪəl], **defrayment** [dɪ'freɪmənt] *n Formal* remboursement *m*

defrock [ˌdiː'frɒk] *vt Rel* défroquer

defrost [ˌdiː'frɒst] **1** *vt* (**a**) *(food)* décongeler; *(refrigerator)* dégivrer (**b**) *Am Aut (demist)* désembuer; *(de-ice)* dégivrer

2 *vi (food)* se décongeler; *(refrigerator)* se dégivrer

defroster [ˌdiː'frɒstə(r)] *n* dégivreur *m*

deft [deft] *adj* adroit, habile; *(fingers)* habile

deftly ['deftlɪ] *adv* adroitement, habilement

deftness ['deftnɪs] *n* adresse *f*, habileté *f*

defuel [diː'fjuːl] *vt Aviat* vidanger

defunct [dɪ'fʌŋkt] *adj (person)* défunt, décédé; *Fig (industry, company)* disparu; *(project, practice, law)* révolu

defuse [ˌdiː'fjuːz] *vt also Fig* désamorcer

defy [dɪ'faɪ] (*pt & pp* **defied**) *vt* (**a**) *(disobey)* s'opposer à; *(law, rule)* braver; **the union defied the court order** le syndicat n'a pas tenu compte de la décision judiciaire (**b**) *(challenge, dare)* défier; **she defied him to justify his claims** elle l'a défié *ou* mis au défi de justifier ses revendications; **a death-defying feat** un exploit téméraire (**c**) *Fig (make impossible)* défier; **his behaviour defies explanation** son comportement défie toute explication

degas [ˌdiː'gæs] (*pt & pp* **degassed** *or* **degased**, *cont* **degassing** *or* **degasing**) *vt Chem* dégazer

degauss [ˌdiː'gaʊs] *vt Phys* dégausser, démagnétiser

degaussing [ˌdiː'gaʊsɪŋ] *adj Phys (material, equipment)* de dégaussage, de dégaussement

►► ***degaussing girdle*** ceinture *f* de démagnétisation; ***degaussing lane*** parcours *m* de démagnétisation

degearing [ˌdiː'gɪərɪŋ] *n Fin* désendettement *m*

degeneracy [dɪ'dʒenərəsɪ] *n (process)* dégénérescence *f*; *(state)* décadence *f*, corruption *f*

degenerate **1** *vi* [dɪ'dʒenəreɪt] dégénérer (**from/into** en/de); *Fig* **the discussion degenerated into an argument** la discussion dégénéra en dispute

2 *adj* [dɪ'dʒenərət] *Literary* dégénéré; *(person)* dépravé

3 *n* [dɪ'dʒenərət] *Literary (person)* dépravé(e) *m,f*

degeneration [dɪˌdʒenə'reɪʃən] *n (process, state)* dégénérescence *f*

degenerative [dɪ'dʒenərətɪv] *adj* dégénératif

deglaciation [ˌdiːgleɪsɪ'eɪʃən] *n Geol* déglaciation *f*

deglaze [ˌdiː'gleɪz] *vt Culin* déglacer

degradable [dɪ'greɪdəbəl] *adj* dégradable

degradation [ˌdegrə'deɪʃən] *n* (**a**) *(deterioration)* dégradation *f*; *Geol* érosion f (**b**) *(debasement)* avilissement *m*, dégradation *f* (**c**) *(poverty)* misère *f* abjecte (**d**) *Mil* dégradation *f*

degrade [dɪ'greɪd] *vt* (**a**) *(deteriorate)* dégrader; *Geol* éroder (**b**) *(debase)* avilir, dégrader; **to degrade oneself** s'avilir; **I refuse to degrade myself by playing these silly games** je refuse de m'abaisser à ces jeux idiots (**c**) *Mil (officer)* dégrader, casser (**d**) *Euph Mil (destroy)* détruire; *(kill)* tuer

degrading [dɪ'greɪdɪŋ] *adj* avilissant, dégradant

degrease [ˌdiː'griːs] *vt* dégraisser

degree [dɪ'griː] **1** *n* (**a**) *(unit of measurement)* degré *m*; **the temperature is 28 degrees in New York** la température est de 28 degrés à New York; **we can expect temperatures of 15 to 20 degrees** nous pouvons nous attendre à des températures de 15 à 20 degrés; **10 degrees below zero** 10 degrés au-dessous de zéro; **he had to work in 32 degrees of heat** il a dû travailler par une chaleur de 32 degrés; **it's 3 degrees outside** il fait 3 degrés dehors; *Geog* **Paris is about 2 degrees east of Greenwich** Paris est environ à 2 degrés de longitude est de Greenwich; *Geom* **a 90-degree angle** un angle de 90 degrés

(**b**) *(extent, amount)* degré *m*; **to feel a degree of optimism** ressentir un certain optimisme; **there was a certain degree of mistrust between them** il y avait un certain degré de méfiance entre eux; **there are varying degrees of opposition to the new law** il y a une opposition plus ou moins forte à la nouvelle loi; **his allergy affected him to such a degree that he had to stop working** son allergie était un tel handicap pour lui qu'il a dû s'arrêter de travailler

(**c**) *(stage, step)* degré *m*; **an honour of the highest degree** un honneur du plus haut degré; **a degree of precision never before thought possible** un niveau de précision jusqu'à présent considéré comme inaccessible

(**d**) *(academic qualification)* diplôme *m* universitaire; *(undergraduate)* ≃ licence *f*; **she has a degree in economics** elle a une licence en sciences économiques; **he's taking** *or* **doing a degree in biology** il fait une licence de biologie; **I'd like to go on and do a further degree** je voudrais continuer après la licence; **it took me five years to get my degree** j'ai mis cinq ans pour avoir ma licence

(**e**) *Gram & Mus* degré *m*

(**f**) *Arch or Literary (rank, status)* rang *m*; **a man of high degree** un homme de haut rang

(**g**) *Am Law* **murder in the first degree** ≃ homicide *m* volontaire

2 by degrees *adv* par degrés, au fur et à mesure; **he realized, by degrees, that his wife no longer loved him** petit à petit il s'est rendu compte que sa femme ne l'aimait plus

3 to a degree *adv (to an extent)* jusqu'à un certain point; **the Prime Minister does accept criticism to a degree** le Premier ministre accepte les critiques, mais jusqu'à un certain point

►► *Univ* ***degree ceremony*** cérémonie *f* de remise des diplômes; *Gram* ***degree of comparison*** degré *m* de comparaison

-degree [dɪ'griː] *suff* **first/second/third-degree burns** brûlures *fpl* au premier/deuxième/troisième degré; *Am Law* **first-degree murder** ≃ homicide *m* volontaire

degression [dɪ'greʃən] *n* dégression *f*

degressive [dɪ'gresɪv] *adj* dégressif

►► *Fin* ***degressive taxation*** impôt *m* dégressif

dehire [ˌdiː'haɪə(r)] *vt Am Euph (dismiss)* remercier

dehorn [ˌdiː'hɔːn] *vt* décorner

dehumanization ['diːˌhjuːmənaɪ'zeɪʃən] *n* déshumanisation *f*

dehumanize, -ise [ˌdiː'hjuːmənaɪz] *vt* déshumaniser

dehumidification ['diːhjuːˌmɪdɪfɪ'keɪʃən] *n* déshumidification *f*

dehumidifier [ˌdiːhjuː'mɪdɪfaɪə(r)] *n* déshumidificateur *m*

dehumidify [ˌdiːhjuː'mɪdɪfaɪ] *vt* déshumidifier

dehydrate [ˌdiːhaɪ'dreɪt] **1** *vt* déshydrater; **to become dehydrated** se déshydrater

2 *vi (person)* se déshydrater

dehydrated [ˌdiːhaɪ'dreɪtɪd] *adj (person, foodstuffs)* déshydraté; *(milk, eggs)* en poudre

dehydration [ˌdiːhaɪ'dreɪʃən] *n* déshydratation *f*

dehydrator [ˌdiːhaɪ'dreɪtə(r)] *n* déshydrateur *m*

dehydrogenase [ˌdiːhaɪ'drɒdʒəneɪs] *n Chem* déshydrogénase *m*

dehydrogenate [ˌdiːhaɪ'drɒdʒəneɪt] *vt Chem* déshydrogéner

dehydrogenated [ˌdiːhaɪ'drɒdʒəneɪtɪd] *adj Chem* déshydrogéné

dehydrogenation ['diːhaɪˌdrɒdʒə'neɪʃən] *n Chem* déshydrogénation *f*

de-ice [diː-] *vt* dégivrer

de-icer [diː'aɪsə(r)] *n* dégivreur *m*

de-icing [diː-] *n* dégivrage *m*

deictic ['daɪktɪk] *adj Gram* déictique

deification [ˌdiːɪfɪˈkeɪʃən] *n Rel* déification *f*
deify [ˈdiːɪfaɪ] *vt Rel* déifier
deign [deɪn] *vt* daigner; *Formal or Hum* **he didn't deign to reply** il n'a pas daigné répondre
deindex [ˌdiːˈɪndeks] *vt Fin* désindexer
deindexation [ˈdiːˌɪndeksˈeɪʃən] *n Fin* désindexation *f*
deindustrialization [ˈdiːɪnˌdʌstrɪəlaɪˈzeɪʃən] *n* désindustrialisation *f*
deindustrialize, -ise [ˌdiːɪnˈdʌstrɪəlaɪz] *vt* désindustrialiser
deinstall [ˌdiːɪnˈstɔːl] *vt Br Comput* désinstaller
deinstallation [ˌdiːɪnstɔˈleɪʃən] *n Br Comput* désinstallation *f*
deinstaller [ˌdiːɪnˈstɔːlə(r)] *n Br Comput* désinstallateur *m*
deionization [ˈdiːˌaɪənaɪˈzeɪʃən] *n Chem* déionisation *f*
deionize, -ise [ˌdiːˈaɪənaɪz] *vt Chem* déioniser
deionized water [ˌdiːˈaɪənaɪzd-] *n Chem* eau *f* déminéralisée
deionizer [ˌdiːˈaɪənaɪzə(r)] *n Chem* dispositif *m* de désionisation
deism [ˈdiːɪzəm] *n Rel* déisme *m*
deist [ˈdiːɪst] *n Rel* déiste *mf*
deity [ˈdiːɪtɪ] (*pl* **deities**) **1** *n* (**a**) *Myth (god)* dieu (déesse) *m,f* (**b**) *Rel (divinity)* divinité *f*
2 Deity *n Rel* **the Deity** Dieu *m*, la Divinité
deixis [ˈdaɪksɪs] *n Gram* déixis *f*
déjà vu [ˌdeʒɑːˈvuː] *n* déjà-vu *m inv*; **to have a feeling of déjà vu** avoir une impression de déjà-vu
dejected [dɪˈdʒektɪd] *adj* abattu, découragé; **he looked sad and dejected** il avait l'air triste et abattu; **the dejected loser left the court** le perdant quitta le court d'un air abattu
dejectedly [dɪˈdʒektɪdlɪ] *adv (speak)* d'un ton abattu; *(look)* d'un air abattu
dejection [dɪˈdʒekʃən] *n* abattement *m*, découragement *m*
de jure [deɪˈdʒʊəreɪ] *adv Law* de jure, en droit
dekko [ˈdekəʊ] (*pl* **dekkos**) *n Fam Br* **to have** *or* **to take a dekko at sth** jeter un coup d'œil *ou* un œil à qch
Del (*written abbr* **Delete**) *(on keyboard)* Suppr
Del. (*written abbr* **Delaware**) Delaware *m*
Delaware [ˈdeləweə(r)] *n* le Delaware; **in Delaware** dans le Delaware
delay [dɪˈleɪ] **1** *vt* (**a**) *(cause to be late)* retarder; *(person)* retarder, retenir; **the flight was delayed (for) three hours** le vol a été retardé de trois heures; **they've been delayed by fog** ils ont été retardés par le brouillard
(**b**) *(postpone, defer)* reporter, remettre; **she delayed handing in her resignation** elle a tardé à donner sa démission; **the publication of the book has been delayed** la publication du livre a été différée *ou* reportée; **she delayed leaving until the last possible moment** elle a repoussé *ou* retardé son départ jusqu'au dernier moment; **the poison had a delayed effect** le poison a agi avec retard; **he had a delayed reaction to the news of his mother's death** il a mis un certain temps à réagir à la nouvelle de la mort de sa mère; **she's suffering from delayed shock** elle souffre d'un choc après coup *ou* a posteriori
2 *exclam* **don't delay, write off today for your free sample** demandez aujourd'hui même votre échantillon gratuit
3 *n* (**a**) *(lateness)* retard *m*; **there are long delays on the M25** la circulation est très ralentie *ou* est très perturbée sur la M25; **all flights are subject to delay** tous les vols ont du retard; **there's a three to four hour delay on all international flights** il y a trois à quatre heures de retard sur tous les vols internationaux
(**b**) *(waiting period)* **without delay** sans tarder *ou* délai; **without (any) further delay** sans plus tarder; **after much delay** après un long moment; **the defence lawyer requested a delay in the hearing** l'avocat de la défense demanda un report de (la) séance; **there's no time for delay** il n'y a pas de temps à perdre
delayed-action [dɪˈleɪd-] *adj (fuse, shutter)* à retardement
delayed cut-off [dɪˈleɪd-] *n (of courtesy light)* extinction *f* retardée
delayering [ˌdiːˈleɪərɪŋ] *n* suppression *f* d'échelons; **middle management has been cut back through delayering** la suppression d'échelons a réduit la hiérarchie intermédiaire
delaying [dɪˈleɪɪŋ] *adj* dilatoire; **delaying action** *or* **tactics** manœuvres *fpl* dilatoires
del credere [delˈkreɪdərɪ] *n Com* ducroire *m*
►► ***del credere agent*** commissionnaire *m* ducroire; ***del credere clause*** clause *f* ducroire
delectable [dɪˈlektəbəl] *adj* délectable
delectably [dɪˈlektəblɪ] *adv* délectablement
delectation [ˌdiːlekˈteɪʃən] *n Literary or Hum* délectation *f*; **for your delectation** pour votre plus grand plaisir
delegate 1 *n* [ˈdelɪgət] délégué(e) *m,f*
2 *vt* [ˈdelɪgeɪt] (**a**) *(person)* déléguer; **the parents delegated Mrs Parker to represent them at the meeting** les parents déléguèrent *ou* désignèrent Mme Parker pour les représenter à la réunion (**b**) *(work, powers)* déléguer
3 *vi* [ˈdelɪgeɪt] déléguer; **she's not very good at delegating** elle ne sait pas déléguer
delegation [ˌdelɪˈgeɪʃən] *n* (**a**) *(group of delegates)* délégation *f* (**b**) *(of work, power)* délégation *f*
delegator [ˈdelɪgeɪtə(r)] *n* délégateur(trice) *m,f*
delete [dɪˈliːt] **1** *vt* (**a**) *(remove)* supprimer; *(erase)* effacer; *(cross out)* barrer, biffer; *Comput* effacer, supprimer; **delete where applicable, delete as appropriate** *(on form)* rayer les mentions inutiles (**b**) *Com (from stock, catalogue)* supprimer
2 *vi Comput* effacer
►► *Comput* ***delete key*** touche *f* d'effacement
deleterious [ˌdelɪˈtɪərɪəs] *adj Formal (effect)* nuisible; *(influence, substance)* nuisible, délétère
deletion [dɪˈliːʃən] *n* (**a**) *(action)* suppression *f*; *Comput* effacement *m*, suppression *f*; **the editor circled certain words for deletion** l'éditeur a entouré certains mots à supprimer; **I made a lot of deletions in the text** j'ai supprimé beaucoup de choses *ou* j'ai fait beaucoup de coupes dans le texte (**b**) *(passage)* passage *m* effacé *ou* supprimé; *(word)* mot *m* effacé *ou* supprimé
delft [delft] *n Cer* faïence *f* (de Delft)
►► ***delft blue* 1** *n* bleu *m* de faïence **2** *adj* bleu de faïence
Delhi [ˈdelɪ] *n* Delhi
►► *Hum* ***Delhi belly*** turista *f*
deli [ˈdelɪ] *n Fam* (*abbr* **delicatessen**) (**a**) *(fine foods shop)* épicerie *f* fine; *(food shop)* ≃ traiteur *m* (**b**) *Am (restaurant)* ≃ restaurant *m* traiteur
►► ***deli counter*** *(in supermarket)* rayon *m* traiteur
deliberate 1 *adj* [dɪˈlɪbərət] (**a**) *(intentional)* délibéré, volontaire, voulu; **it was a deliberate attempt to embarrass the minister** cela visait délibérément à embarrasser le ministre; **it was quite deliberate!** c'était voulu, c'était fait exprès! (**b**) *(unhurried, careful)* mesuré, posé; **her speech was slow and deliberate** elle parlait lentement et posément
2 *vi* [dɪˈlɪbəreɪt] délibérer; **to deliberate on** *or* **upon sth** délibérer sur qch; **they deliberated whether or not to expel him** ils ont délibéré pour savoir s'ils allaient l'expulser
3 *vt* [dɪˈlɪbəreɪt] délibérer sur *ou* de
deliberately [dɪˈlɪbərətlɪ] *adv* (**a**) *(intentionally)* volontairement; **I deliberately didn't invite her** c'est intentionnellement que je ne l'ai pas invitée; **I didn't hurt him deliberately** je n'ai pas fait exprès de le blesser; **you have deliberately lied to the court** vous avez menti délibérément *ou* sciemment à la cour (**b**) *(unhurriedly, carefully)* de façon mesurée, avec mesure; *(walk)* d'un pas ferme
deliberateness [dɪˈlɪbərətnɪs] *n* (**a**) *(of insult, lie)* intention *f* marquée (**b**) *(unhurriedness, carefulness)* mesure *f*
deliberation [dɪˌlɪbəˈreɪʃən] **1** *n* (**a**) *(consideration, reflection)* délibération *f*, réflexion *f*; **after much deliberation we have decided to accept your application** après délibération *ou* mûre réflexion, nous avons décidé d'accepter votre demande (**b**) *(care, caution)* attention *f*, soin *m*; **with deliberation** *(say)* posément; *(do sth)* de façon réfléchie; *(walk)* d'un pas mesuré; *(act)* avec circonspection
2 deliberations *npl* délibérations *fpl*
deliberative [dɪˈlɪbərətɪv] *adj* (**a**) *(group, assembly)* délibérant (**b**) *(conclusion)* mûrement réfléchi
delicacy [ˈdelɪkəsɪ] (*pl* **delicacies**) *n* (**a**) *(fineness → of lace, china, features, fingers)* délicatesse *f*, finesse *f*
(**b**) *(fragility → of person, health)* délicatesse *f*, fragilité *f*; *(difficulty)* délicatesse *f*
(**c**) *(sensitivity → of mechanism, situation, question)* délicatesse *f*; *(→ of feelings)* sensibilité *f*; **it's a matter of great delicacy** c'est une affaire très délicate; **the question must be handled with delicacy** la question doit être traitée avec délicatesse
(**d**) *(gentleness, lightness → of touch)* légèreté *f*
(**e**) *(of smell, colour, flavour)* délicatesse *f*
(**f**) *(fine food)* mets *m* délicat; **it's considered a great delicacy in China** c'est considéré comme un mets très délicat *ou* fin en Chine
delicate [ˈdelɪkət] **1** *adj* (**a**) *(fine → lace, china, features, fingers)* délicat, fin
(**b**) *(fragile → person, health)* délicat, fragile
(**c**) *(sensitive → mechanism, situation, question)* délicat, difficile; *(feelings)* sensible; *(person → over-refined, easily shocked)* précieux; **a delicate international situation** une situation internationale délicate; **it's a matter that needs delicate handling** c'est une affaire qui doit être traitée avec délicatesse; **we're at a very delicate stage in our negotiations** nous en sommes à une étape très délicate de nos négociations; **to tread on delicate ground** toucher à des questions délicates
(**d**) *(gentle, light → touch)* délicat
(**e**) *(smell, colour, flavour)* délicat
(**f**) *(instrument)* sensible
2 delicates *npl* linge *m* délicat
delicately [ˈdelɪkətlɪ] *adv* (**a**) *(finely → carved, embroidered etc)* délicatement, finement (**b**) *(sensitively → deal with, approach)* avec délicatesse; **the mechanism is very delicately balanced** le réglage du mécanisme est très sensible (**c**) *(gently, lightly → touch, hold, pick up etc)* délicatement (**d**) *(subtly → coloured, flavoured)* délicatement
delicatessen [ˌdelɪkəˈtesən] *n* (**a**) *Br (fine foods shop)* épicerie fine *f*; *(food shop)* ≃ traiteur *m*; (**b**) *Am (restaurant)* ≃ restaurant *m* traiteur
►► ***delicatessen counter*** *(in supermarket)* rayon *m* traiteur
delicious [dɪˈlɪʃəs] *adj* délicieux
deliciously [dɪˈlɪʃəslɪ] *adv* délicieusement
deliciousness [dɪˈlɪʃəsnɪs] *n* goût *m* délicieux
delict [ˈdiːlɪkt] *n Law* délit *m*
delight [dɪˈlaɪt] **1** *n* (**a**) *(pleasure)* joie *f*, (grand) plaisir *m*; **she listened with delight** elle écoutait avec délectation; **to the delight of the audience** à la plus grande joie *ou* pour le plus grand plaisir de l'auditoire; **her brother took (great) delight in teasing her** son frère prenait (un malin) plaisir à la taquiner (**b**) *(source of pleasure)* délice *m*; **the film is a delight** le film est un délice; **the delights of gardening** les charmes *mpl ou* délices *fpl* du jardinage; **the child was a delight to teach** c'était un plaisir d'enseigner à cet enfant
2 *vt* ravir, réjouir; **to delight the ear** charmer les oreilles; **to delight the eye** enchanter la vue; **her show has delighted audiences everywhere** son spectacle a partout conquis *ou* ravi le public
►**delight in** *vt insep* se délecter de, aimer beaucoup; **to delight in doing sth** se délecter à *ou* aimer beaucoup faire qch; **he delights in publicity** il adore faire parler de lui; **she delights in irritating people** elle prend plaisir *ou* se complaît à énerver les gens; **she delights in her grandchildren** elle adore ses petits-enfants
delighted [dɪˈlaɪtɪd] *adj* ravi; **I'm delighted to see you again** je suis ravi de vous revoir; **we are delighted that you were able to accept our invitation** nous sommes ravis que vous ayez pu accepter notre invitation; **a delighted smile** un sourire ravi; **I was delighted at the news** la nouvelle m'a fait très plaisir; **to be delighted with sth** être ravi de qch; **could you come to dinner on Saturday? – I'd be delighted (to)** pourriez-vous venir dîner samedi? – avec (grand) plaisir

delightedly [dɪ'laɪtɪdlɪ] *adv* avec joie, joyeusement

delightful [dɪ'laɪtfʊl] *adj (person, place)* charmant; *(book, experience, film)* merveilleux; **the garden was simply delightful** le jardin était tout simplement merveilleux; **this rose has a delightful perfume** cette rose a un parfum délicieux; **she looked delightful in her new dress** sa nouvelle robe lui allait à ravir

delightfully [dɪ'laɪtfʊlɪ] *adv (dance, perform, sing)* merveilleusement, à ravir; **the evenings were delightfully cool** les soirées étaient merveilleusement fraîches; **he was delightfully unpretentious** il était merveilleusement simple

Delilah [dɪ'laɪlə] *pr n Bible* Dalila

delimit [ˌdiː'lɪmɪt] *vt Comput* délimiter

delimitation ['diːˌlɪmɪ'teɪʃən] *n Comput* délimitation *f*

delimiter [ˌdiː'lɪmɪtə(r)] *n Comput* délimiteur *m*

delineate [dɪ'lɪnɪeɪt] *vt Formal* **(a)** *(outline, sketch)* tracer **(b)** *Fig (define, describe)* définir, décrire; *(character in novel)* faire le portrait de

delineation [dɪˌlɪnɪ'eɪʃən] *n* **(a)** *(outline, sketch)* tracé *m* **(b)** *(definition, description)* définition *f*, description *f*; *(of character in novel)* portrait *m*

delinquency [dɪ'lɪŋkwənsɪ] (*pl* **delinquencies**) *n* **(a)** *Law (criminal behaviour)* délinquance *f*; *(negligence)* faute *f* **(b)** *Fin* défaillance *f*, défaut *m* de paiement

delinquent [dɪ'lɪŋkwənt] **1** *n* **(a)** *Law (lawbreaker)* délinquant(e) *m,f* **(b)** *Fin (bad debtor)* mauvais payeur *m*

2 *adj* **(a)** *Law (law-breaking)* délinquant; *(negligent)* fautif **(b)** *Fin (person)* défaillant; *(taxes, bill)* impayé; *(account, debt, loan)* en souffrance

deliquesce [delɪ'kwes] *vi Chem* tomber en déliquescence

deliquescence [ˌdelɪ'kwesəns] *n Chem* déliquescence *f*

deliquescent [ˌdelɪ'kwesənt] *adj Chem* déliquescent

delirious [dɪ'lɪrɪəs] *adj* **(a)** *Med* en délire; **the fever made him delirious** la fièvre l'a fait délirer; **to become delirious** se mettre à délirer, être pris de délire **(b)** *Fig (excited, wild)* délirant, en délire; **he was delirious with joy** il était fou de joie; **she's delirious about being pregnant** elle est ravie d'être enceinte; **I'm not exactly delirious at the prospect** cette perspective ne m'enchante guère

deliriously [dɪ'lɪrɪəslɪ] *adv* de façon délirante, frénétiquement; **deliriously happy** follement heureux

delirium [dɪ'lɪrɪəm] *n* **(a)** *Med* délire *m*; **to be in a delirium** être en plein délire **(b)** *Fig (state of excitement)* délire *m*; *Literary* **to be in a delirium of joy** être transporté de joie

►► *Med* ***delirium tremens*** delirium tremens *m*

delish [dɪ'lɪʃ] *adj Br Fam (delicious)* extra *(inv)*

delist [diː'lɪst] *vt Com & Mktg (product)* déréférencer; *St Exch (company)* radier de la cote

delisting [ˌdiː'lɪstɪŋ] *n Com & Mktg (of product)* déréférencement *m*; *St Exch (of company)* radiation *f* de la cote

deliver [dɪ'lɪvə(r)] **1** *vt* **(a)** *(letter, parcel, telegram)* remettre, apporter (**to** à); *(mail)* distribuer (**to** à); *(goods)* livrer (**to** à); **what time is the mail delivered?** le courrier est distribué à quelle heure?; **was my message delivered to you?** est-ce qu'on t'a remis mon message?; **the letter was delivered by hand** on m'a/lui/*etc* remis la lettre en main propre; **I delivered the books to the library** j'ai remis les livres à la bibliothèque; **the train delivered us safely home** nous sommes rentrés en train sains; *Fig* **to deliver the goods** *(of person)* remplir ses engagements; *(of new product)* tenir ses promesses

(b) *Formal or Literary (save, rescue)* délivrer; **to deliver sb from death** sauver qn de la mort; *Bible* **deliver us from evil** délivre-nous du mal

(c) *Obst* **to deliver a baby** faire un accouchement; *Formal or Literary* **she was delivered of a daughter** elle accoucha d'une fille; **he delivered the mare of her foal** il aida la jument à mettre bas

(d) *(pronounce, utter)* **to deliver a sermon/speech** prononcer un sermon/discours; *Formal* **to deliver oneself of an opinion** faire part de *ou* émettre son opinion; *Law* **the jury delivered a verdict of not guilty** le jury a rendu un verdict de non-culpabilité

(e) *(provide → service)* assurer; *Tech (of machine, dynamo → power)* débiter, fournir; *Aut (horsepower)* développer; *Fin* **to deliver a profit** rapporter *ou* faire un profit; *St Exch* **to deliver shares** délivrer des valeurs

(f) *Am Pol* **can he deliver the Black vote?** est-ce qu'il peut nous assurer les voix des Noirs?

(g) *(strike)* **to deliver a blow (to the head/stomach)** porter *ou* asséner un coup (à la tête/à l'estomac); *Ftbl* **to deliver a pass** faire une passe

(h) *Mil (of rocket)* lancer

2 *vi* **(a)** *(make delivery)* livrer

(b) *Fam (do as promised)* tenir parole❑, tenir bon❑; **it/he just doesn't deliver** il n'est pas à la hauteur❑

►**deliver over** *vt sep* remettre; **he delivered himself over to the police** il s'est livré *ou* rendu à la police

►**deliver up** *vt sep (fugitive, town)* livrer

deliverance [dɪ'lɪvərəns] *n* **(a)** *Formal or Literary (release, rescue)* délivrance *f* **(b)** *(pronouncement)* déclaration *f*; *Law* prononcé *m*

delivered [dɪ'lɪvəd] *adj Com* **delivered free** livraison franco; **delivered at** *or* **to domicile** livré à domicile; **delivered at frontier** rendu à la frontière; **delivered free at** *or* **to domicile** livré franco domicile; **delivered free on board** rendu franco bord

deliverer [dɪ'lɪvərə(r)] *n* **(a)** *Formal or Literary (saviour)* sauveur *m* **(b)** *Com (of goods)* livreur *m*

delivery [dɪ'lɪvərɪ] (*pl* **deliveries**) **1** *n* **(a)** *(of goods)* livraison *f*; *(of letter, parcel, telegram)* remise *f*; *(of mail)* distribution *f*; **post** *or* **mail deliveries are rather irregular** la distribution du courrier est assez irrégulière; **I was entrusted with (the) delivery of the documents** on m'a confié la remise des documents; **to take delivery of sth** prendre livraison de qch; **allow two weeks for delivery** *(on sign, in advertisement)* délai de livraison: deux semaines; **payment on delivery** règlement *m ou* paiement *m* à la livraison; **to pay on delivery** payer à *ou* sur livraison;

(b) *Formal or Literary (release, rescue)* délivrance *f*; *(of prisoner)* reddition *f*

(c) *Obst* accouchement *m*; **it was an easy delivery** l'accouchement a été facile

(d) *(of speech)* prononciation *f*; *(of speaker)* débit *m*, élocution *f*; **to have a good delivery** avoir un bon débit

(e) *(of water, power etc)* débit *m*; *(of pump)* refoulement *m*

(f) *Sport (in ball games)* = manière de passer la balle; *(in cricket, baseball)* lancer *m*; **that was an excellent delivery** c'était une très belle passe

(g) *Law (of property)* tradition *f*; *(of bequest etc)* délivrance *f* (**to** à)

(h) *Mil (of rocket)* lancement *m*

(i) *St Exch (of shares)* livraison *f*

2 *comp Com* de livraison

►► ***delivery address*** adresse *f* de livraison; ***delivery boy*** livreur *m*; ***delivery charges*** frais *mpl* de livraison; ***delivery conditions*** conditions *fpl* de livraison; ***delivery date*** date *f* de livraison; ***delivery girl*** livreuse *f*; ***delivery man*** livreur *m*; ***delivery note*** bon *m ou* bordereau *m ou* bulletin *m* de livraison; ***delivery point*** lieu *m* de livraison; *Obst* ***the delivery room*** la salle de travail *ou* d'accouchement; ***delivery schedule*** planning *m* de livraison; ***delivery time*** délai *m* de livraison; ***delivery van*** camion *m* de livraison; *(smaller)* camionnette *f* de livraison

dell [del] *n* vallon *m*

delocalization ['diːˌləʊkəlaɪ'zeɪʃən] *n* délocalisation *f*

delocalize, -ise [ˌdiː'ləʊkəlaɪz] *vt* délocaliser

Delos ['diːlɒs] *n Geog* Délos; **in Delos** à Délos

delouse [ˌdiː'laʊs] *vt (animal, person)* épouiller; *(clothing, furniture)* enlever les poux de

delousing [ˌdiː'laʊsɪŋ] *n* épouillage *m*

►► *Mil* ***delousing station*** poste *m* d'épouillage

Delphi ['delfaɪ] *n Antiq* Delphes; **at Delphi** à Delphes

Delphic ['delfɪk] *adj Antiq* delphique, de Delphes; *Fig Literary (obscure)* obscur

delphinium [del'fɪnɪəm] (*pl* **delphiniums** *or* **delphinia** [-nɪə]) *n Bot* delphinium *m*

delta ['deltə] **1** *n* **(a)** *(in Greek alphabet)* delta *m* **(b)** *(of river)* delta *m*

2 *comp* en delta

►► *Mil* ***Delta Force*** = force militaire américaine spécialisée notamment dans les opérations de sauvetage; *Phys* ***delta ray*** rayon *m* delta; *Physiol* ***delta rhythm*** rythme *m* delta; *Astron* ***Delta rocket*** fusée *f* Delta; ***delta wave*** rythme *m* delta; *Aviat* ***delta wing*** aile *f* (en) delta; ***delta wing aircraft*** avion *m* à ailes delta

deltiology [ˌdeltɪ'ɒlədʒɪ] *n* = étude et collecte des cartes postales

deltoid ['deltɔɪd] **1** *n* deltoïde *m*

2 *adj* deltoïde

►► *Anat* ***deltoid muscle*** muscle *m* deltoïde

delts [delts] *npl Fam (deltoid muscles)* muscles *mpl* deltoïdes❑

delude [dɪ'luːd] *vt* tromper, duper; **he deluded investors into thinking that the company was doing well** il a fait croire aux investisseurs que la société se portait bien; **to delude oneself** se faire des illusions; **he's deluding himself if he thinks his wife will forgive him** il se fait des illusions *ou* il se leurre s'il pense que sa femme va lui pardonner; **let's not delude ourselves about his motives** ne nous leurrons pas sur ses motivations

deluded [dɪ'luːdɪd] *adj* **(a)** *(mistaken, foolish)* **a poor deluded young man** un pauvre jeune homme qu'on a trompé *ou* induit en erreur **(b)** *Psy* sujet à des délires

deluge ['deljuːdʒ] **1** *n also Fig* déluge *m*; **a deluge of rain** une pluie diluvienne

2 *vt also Fig* inonder; **we have been deluged with letters** nous avons été submergés *ou* inondés de lettres

delusion [dɪ'luːʒən] *n* **(a)** *(illusion, mistaken idea)* illusion *f*; **she's under the delusion that her illness isn't serious** elle s'imagine à tort que sa maladie n'est pas grave **(b)** *Psy* délire *m*; **to suffer from delusions** être sujet à des hallucinations; *Fig* **he has delusions of grandeur** il a la folie des grandeurs

delusive [dɪ'luːsɪv] *adj* trompeur, illusoire

delusiveness [dɪ'luːsɪvnɪs] *n* caractère *m* trompeur *ou* illusoire

delusory [dɪ'luːsərɪ] *adj* trompeur, illusoire

deluxe [də'lʌks] *adj* de luxe; *(apartment)* (de) grand standing

delve [delv] *vi* **(a)** *(investigate)* fouiller; **she preferred not to delve too deeply into the past** elle préférait ne pas fouiller trop profondément (dans) le passé **(b)** *(search)* fouiller; **to delve in(to) one's pocket** fouiller dans sa poche; **he delved into the bag** il a fouillé dans le sac **(c)** *(dig, burrow)* creuser; *(animal)* fouiller

Dem. *Am (written abbr* **Democrat(ic)**) démocrate

demagnetization ['diːˌmægnɪtaɪ'zeɪʃən] *n Phys* démagnétisation *f*

demagnetize, -ise [ˌdiː'mægnɪtaɪz] *vt Phys* démagnétiser

demagog *Am* = **demagogue**

demagogic [ˌdemə'gɒgɪk] *adj* démagogique

demagogue ['deməgɒg] *n* démagogue *mf*

demagoguery [ˌdemə'gɒgərɪ] *n* démagogie *f*

demagogy ['deməgɒgɪ] *n* démagogie *f*

de-man ['diːmæn] (*pt & pp* **de-manned,** *cont* **de-manning**) *vt Br Ind* réduire les effectifs de

demand [dɪ'mɑːnd] **1** *vt* **(a)** *(request firmly)* exiger; *(money)* réclamer; **to demand an apology/explanation** exiger des excuses/une explication; **I demand to see the manager** appelez-moi le gérant; **they're demanding payment** ils réclament le paiement; **the terrorists demanded to be flown to Tehran** les terroristes exigeaient d'être emmenés en avion à Téhéran; **to demand that...** exiger que... + *subjunctive*; **pressure groups are demanding that fuller information be released** les groupes de pression exigent la publication de plus amples informations; **to demand one's rights** revendiquer ses droits; **she demanded nothing of** *or* **from her children** elle n'exigeait rien de ses enfants; **he demanded to know/to be told the truth** il exigeait de connaître/qu'on lui dise la vérité (**b**) *(require, necessitate)* exiger, réclamer; **he doesn't have the imagination demanded of a good writer** il n'a pas l'imagination que l'on attend d'un bon écrivain

2 *n* (**a**) *(obligation, requirement)* exigence *f*; **the demands of motherhood** les exigences de la maternité; **to make demands on sb** exiger beaucoup de qn; **his work makes great demands on his time** son travail lui prend beaucoup de temps; **he makes a lot of emotional demands** il a une très grande demande affective; **there are many demands on her at work** elle est très prise au travail

(**b**) *(firm request)* demande *f*, réclamation *f*; **demand for payment** demande de paiement; **payable on demand** payable sur demande; **wage demands** revendications *fpl* salariales; **there have been many demands for the minister's resignation** beaucoup de voix se sont élevées pour exiger la démission du ministre; **to give in to sb's demands** céder aux exigences de qn; **you make too many demands on her** tu exiges trop d'elle; **I have many demands on my time** je suis très pris

(**c**) *Com & Econ* demande *f*; **to be in (great) demand** être (très) demandé *ou* recherché; **American jeans were in great demand in Eastern Europe** les jeans américains étaient très demandés *ou* recherchés dans les pays de l'Est; **due to public demand** à la demande du public; **there is not much demand for books on the subject** les livres sur ce sujet ne sont pas très demandés; **qualified maths teachers are in increasing demand** les professeurs de mathématiques diplômés sont de plus en plus demandés

3 on demand *adv* sur demande; **she's in favour of abortion on demand** elle est pour l'avortement libre

►► *Com & Mktg* ***demand analysis*** analyse *f* de la demande; *Fin* ***demand bill*** bon *m* à vue; ***demand curve*** courbe *f* (d'évolution) de la demande; *Am Banking* ***demand deposit*** dépôt *m* à vue; *Am Banking* ***demand deposit account*** compte *m* à vue; ***demand driver*** dynamisant *m* de la demande; ***demand feeding*** *(of baby)* allaitement *m* à la demande; ***demand forecasting*** prévision *f* de la demande; ***demand function*** fonction *f* de demande; *Com* ***demand management*** contrôle *m* de la demande; *Fin* ***demand note*** bon *m* à vue

demander [dɪ'mɑːndə(r)] *n Law* demandeur(eresse) *m,f*

demanding [dɪ'mɑːndɪŋ] *adj (person)* exigeant; *(job, profession, task)* difficile, astreignant; **the work is not physically demanding** ce travail ne demande pas beaucoup de force physique; **children are at their most demanding between the ages of two and four** les enfants demandent le plus d'attention entre deux et quatre ans

demand-led *adj Econ* tiré par la demande

demand-pull inflation *n Econ* inflation *f* par la demande

demand-side economics *n Econ* économie *f* de la demande

de-manning [ˌdiː'mænɪŋ] *n Br Ind* réduction *f* des effectifs

demarcate ['diːmɑːkeɪt] *vt Formal (boundary)* établir; *(territories)* délimiter

demarcation [ˌdiːmɑː'keɪʃən] *n* (**a**) *(of boundary, border)* établissement *f*; *(of two pieces of land)* démarcation *f*; *(of several territories)* délimitation *f*; **a line of demarcation** une ligne de démarcation (**b**) *Ind* attributions *fpl*

►► ***demarcation dispute*** conflit *m* d'attributions; ***demarcation line*** ligne *f* de démarcation

demarket [ˌdiː'mɑːkɪt] *vt Com & Mktg* retirer du marché

demarketing [ˌdiː'mɑːkɪtɪŋ] *n Com & Mktg* démarketing *m*

dematerialization ['diːməˌtɪərɪəlaɪ'zeɪʃən] *n* dématérialisation *f*

dematerialize, -ise [ˌdiːmə'tɪərɪəlaɪz] *vi* se volatiliser

demean [dɪ'miːn] *vt Formal* avilir, rabaisser; **she wouldn't demean herself by marrying him** elle refusait de se rabaisser en l'épousant; **your behaviour demeans the office you hold** votre comportement déshonore la charge que vous occupez

demeaning [dɪ'miːnɪŋ] *adj* avilissant, déshonorant

demeanour, *Am* **demeanor** [dɪ'miːnə(r)] *n Formal (behaviour)* comportement *m*; *(manner)* allure *f*, maintien *m*; **he had the demeanour of a gentleman** il avait des allures d'homme raffiné *ou* de gentleman

demented [dɪ'mentɪd] *adj* dément; *Fig* fou (folle); **to be demented with grief/anger/worry** être fou de douleur/de colère/d'inquiétude; **to drive sb demented** rendre qn fou

dementedly [dɪ'mentɪdlɪ] *adv* comme un fou (une folle)

dementia [dɪ'menʃə] *n* démence *f*

►► *Old-fashioned Med* ***dementia praecox*** démence *f* précoce

demerara [ˌdemə'reərə] *n (sugar)* cassonade *f*

►► ***demerara sugar*** cassonade *f*

demerge [ˌdiː'mɜːdʒ] *vi Com (companies)* se scinder

demerger [ˌdiː'mɜːdʒə(r)] *n Br Com* scission *f*; **several new companies were formed after the demerger of the holding group** plusieurs entreprises nouvelles ont été créées à la suite de la scission du holding

demerit [diː'merɪt] *n* (**a**) *Formal (flaw)* démérite *m*, faute *f* (**b**) *Am Sch & Mil* blâme *m*

demersal [diː'mɜːsəl] *adj Zool* démersal

demesne [dɪ'meɪn] *n* (**a**) *Formal (land, estate)* domaine *m* (**b**) *Law (possession)* possession *f*; **land held in demesne** terrain *m* possédé en toute propriété

Demeter [dɪ'miːtə(r)] *pr n Myth* Déméter

Demetrius [dɪ'miːtrɪəs] *pr n Myth* Démétrios

demigod ['demɪgɒd] *n* demi-dieu *m*

demijohn ['demɪdʒɒn] *n* dame-jeanne *f*, bonbonne *f*

demilitarization ['diːˌmɪlɪtəraɪ'zeɪʃən] *n* démilitarisation *f*

demilitarize, -ise [ˌdiː'mɪlɪtəraɪz] *vt* démilitariser; **a demilitarized zone** une zone démilitarisée

demi-monde [ˌdemɪ'mɒnd] *n* demi-monde *m*

demineralization ['diːˌmɪnərəlaɪ'zeɪʃən] *n* déminéralisation *f*

demineralize, -ise [ˌdiː'mɪnərəlaɪz] *vt* déminéraliser

demise [dɪ'maɪz] **1** *n* (**a**) *Formal (death)* mort *f*, disparition *f*; *(end – of newspaper, empire etc)* fin *f*, mort *f* (**b**) *Law (transfer)* cession *f* (**c**) *Hist* **the demise of the Crown** la transmission de la Couronne

2 *vt* (**a**) *Law (lease)* louer à bail; *(bequeath)* léguer (**b**) *Hist (transfer)* transmettre

demisemiquaver ['demɪsemɪˌkweɪvə(r)] *n Br Mus* triple croche *f*

demist [ˌdiː'mɪst] *vt Br Aut* désembuer

demister [ˌdiː'mɪstə(r)] *n Br Aut* dispositif *m* antibuée

demisting [ˌdiː'mɪstɪŋ] *n Br Aut* désembuage *m*

demitasse ['demɪtæs] *n (cup)* tasse *f* à café; *(coffee)* café *m* serré

demiurge ['demɪɜːdʒ] *n Rel* démiurge *m*

demo ['deməʊ] *n Fam* (*pl* **demos**) *n Fam* (*abbr* **demonstration**) (**a**) *(protest)* manif *f*

(**b**) *(of band, singer)* disque *m*/cassette *f*/vidéo *f* de démonstration ❑

(**c**) *(of device, system)* démonstration *f*; **we received a demo of the new software system** quelqu'un est venu nous faire une démonstration du nouveau logiciel

►► *Comput* ***demo disk*** disquette *f* de démonstration *ou* d'évaluation; ***demo tape*** bande *f* démo; *Comput* ***demo version*** version *f* de démonstration *ou* d'évaluation

demob [ˌdiː'mɒb] (*pt & pp* **demobbed**, *cont* **demobbing**) *Br Fam Mil* **1** *vt* démobiliser ❑

2 *n* (**a**) *(demobilization)* démobilisation ❑ *f* (**b**) *(soldier)* soldat *m* démobilisé ❑

►► ***demob suit*** ≃ tenue *f* civile ❑

demobilization [diːˌməʊbɪlaɪ'zeɪʃən] *n Mil* démobilisation *f*

demobilize, -ise [ˌdiː'məʊbɪlaɪz] *vt Mil* démobiliser

democracy [dɪ'mɒkrəsɪ] (*pl* **democracies**) *n* démocratie *f*

democrat ['deməkræt] **1** *n* démocrate *mf*

2 Democrat *n* (**a**) *(in US)* démocrate *mf* (**b**) *(in UK)* = membre des "Liberal Democrats"

democratic [ˌdemə'krætɪk] *adj (country, organization, principle)* démocratique; *(person)* démocrate

►► ***the Democratic Convention*** la convention démocrate; ***the Democratic Party*** le parti démocrate (américain)

democratically [ˌdemə'krætɪkəlɪ] *adv* démocratiquement

democratization [dɪˌmɒkrətaɪ'zeɪʃən] *n* démocratisation *f*

democratize, -ise [dɪ'mɒkrətaɪz] **1** *vt* démocratiser

2 *vi* se démocratiser

Democritus [dɪ'mɒkrɪtəs] *pr n* Démocrite

demodulate [ˌdiː'mɒdjʊleɪt] *vt Phys & Rad* démoduler

demodulation ['diːˌmɒdjʊ'leɪʃən] *n Phys & Rad* démodulation *f*

demodulator [ˌdiː'mɒdjʊleɪtə(r)] *n Comput* démodulateur *m*

demographer [dɪ'mɒgrəfə(r)] *n* démographe *mf*

demographic [ˌdemə'græfɪk] *adj* démographique

►► ***demographic analysis*** analyse *f* démographique; ***demographic profile*** profil *m* démographique; ***demographic segment*** segment *m* démographique; ***demographic segmentation*** segmentation *f* démographique

demographics [ˌdemə'græfɪks] **1** *n (UNCOUNT) (science)* (étude *f* de la) démographie *f*

2 *npl (statistics)* statistiques *fpl* démographiques

demography [dɪ'mɒgrəfɪ] *n* démographie *f*

demoiselle crane [ˌdəmwæ'zel-] *n Orn* demoiselle *f* de Numidie

demolish [dɪ'mɒlɪʃ] *vt* (**a**) *also Fig (destroy)* démolir; **to demolish sb** *(in argument)* démolir qn; *(in competition, fight)* mettre la pâtée à qn (**b**) *Fam (devour)* dévorer ❑

demolisher [dɪ'mɒlɪʃə(r)] *n also Fig* démolisseur *m*

demolition [ˌdemə'lɪʃən] **1** *n also Fig* démolition *f*

2 demolitions *npl Mil* explosifs *mpl*

►► ***demolition contractor*** démolisseur *m*; *Sport* ***demolition derby*** = course de voitures dans laquelle celles-ci sont délibérément détruites; *Br* ***demolitions expert*** expert *m* en explosifs; ***demolition squad*** équipe *f* de démolition

demon ['diːmən] *n* (**a**) *(devil, evil spirit)* démon *m* (**b**) *Fig* diable *m*; **that child's a little demon** cet enfant est un petit démon; **she works like a demon** c'est un bourreau de travail; **he's a demon tennis player** il joue au tennis comme un dieu; **the demon drink** le démon de la boisson

demonetarize, -ise [ˌdiː'mʌnətəraɪz] *vt Fin* démonétiser

demonetization ['diːˌmʌnɪtaɪ'zeɪʃən] *n Fin* démonétisation *f*

demonetize, -ise [ˌdiː'mʌnɪtaɪz] *vt Fin* démonétiser

demoniac [dɪ'məʊnɪæk] **1** *adj* démoniaque

2 *n* démoniaque *mf*

demoniacal [ˌdiːmə'naɪəkəl] *adj* démoniaque

demonic [diː'mɒnɪk] *adj* diabolique

demonism ['diːmənɪzəm] *n* (**a**) *(belief)* démonisme *m* (**b**) *(study)* démonologie *f*

demonization [ˌdiːmənaɪ'zeɪʃən] *n* diabolisation *f*

demonize, -ise ['diːmənaɪz] *vt* diaboliser

demonologist [ˌdiːmə'nɒlədʒɪst] *n* démonologue *mf*

demonology [ˌdiːmə'nɒlədʒɪ] *n* démonologie *f*

demonstrable [dɪ'mɒnstrəbəl] *adj* démontrable

demonstrably [dɪ'mɒnstrəblɪ] *adv* manifestement

demonstrate ['demənstreɪt] **1** *vt* (**a**) *(prove, establish)* démontrer; **that just demonstrates how stupid he is** ça ne fait que démontrer à quel point il est stupide

(**b**) *(appliance, machine)* faire une démonstration de; **he demonstrated how to use a sewing machine** il a montré comment se servir d'une machine à coudre

(**c**) *(ability, quality)* faire preuve de; **she demonstrated great musical ability** elle a fait preuve de grandes prédispositions pour la musique

2 *vi* manifester; **to demonstrate for/against sth** manifester pour/contre qch; **the students are**

dem–dem

demonstrating against higher fees les étudiants manifestent contre l'augmentation des frais de scolarité

demonstration [ˌdemən'streɪʃən] **1** *n* (**a**) *(proof)* démonstration *f*
(**b**) *(of appliance, machine, skills)* démonstration *f*; **the salesman gave a demonstration of the word processor** le vendeur a fait une démonstration du traitement de texte
(**c**) *(protest)* manifestation *f*; **to hold** *or* **stage a demonstration** faire une manifestation
(**d**) *(of emotion)* démonstration *f*, manifestation *f*
(**e**) *Mil* démonstration *f*
2 *comp (car, copy, lesson, model)* de démonstration

demonstrative [dɪ'mɒnstrətɪv] **1** *adj* (**a**) *(person)* démonstratif (**b**) *(argument, proof)* démonstratif (**c**) *Gram (adjective, pronoun)* démonstratif
2 *n Gram* démonstratif *m*

demonstratively [dɪ'mɒnstrətɪvlɪ] *adv* (**a**) *(expansively)* avec effusion (**b**) *(argue, prove)* démonstrativement

demonstrativeness [dɪ'mɒnstrətɪvnɪs] *n (expansiveness)* caractère *m* démonstratif

demonstrator ['demənˌstreɪtə(r)] *n* (**a**) *(of appliance, machine)* démonstrateur(trice) *m,f* (**b**) *(protester)* manifestant(e) *m,f* (**c**) *Br Univ* ≃ préparateur(trice) *m,f* (**d**) *Am (appliance, machine)* modèle *m* de démonstration; *(car)* voiture *f* de démonstration

demoralization [dɪˌmɒrəlaɪ'zeɪʃən] *n* démoralisation *f*

demoralize, -ise [dɪ'mɒrəlaɪz] *vt* démoraliser

demoralized [dɪ'mɒrəlaɪzd] *adj* démoralisé; **to become demoralized** perdre courage *ou* le moral

demoralizing [dɪ'mɒrəˌlaɪzɪŋ] *adj* démoralisant

demoralizingly [dɪ'mɒrəˌlaɪzɪŋlɪ] *adv* **our results were demoralizingly poor** nos résultats étaient si médiocres que c'en était démoralisant

demos ['diːmɒs] *n Formal* peuple *m*

Demosthenes [dɪ'mɒsθəˌniːz] *pr n* Démosthène

demote [ˌdiː'məʊt] *vt* rétrograder; **she's been demoted to assistant manager** elle a été rétrogradée au poste de directeur-adjoint

demotic [dɪ'mɒtɪk] **1** *adj* (**a**) *(of the people)* populaire (**b**) *Ling* démotique
2 *n Antiq* démotique *m*
3 Demotic *n Antiq* grec *m* démotique

demotion [ˌdiː'məʊʃən] *n* rétrogradation *f*

demotivate [ˌdiː'məʊtɪveɪt] *vt* démotiver

demotivation [diːˌməʊtɪ'veɪʃən] *n* démotivation *f*

demount [ˌdiː'maʊnt] *vt* démonter

demulcent [dɪ'mʌlsənt] *Med* **1** *adj* lénifiant
2 *n* onguent *m*

demur [dɪ'mɜː(r)] (*pt & pp* **demurred,** *cont* **demurring**) **1** *vi* (**a**) *Formal* soulever une objection; **he demurred at the idea of accepting a reward** il s'est opposé à l'idée de recevoir une récompense; **I suggested she join us but she demurred** j'ai proposé qu'elle se joigne à nous mais elle s'y est opposée (**b**) *Law* opposer une exception
2 *n* objection *f*; **without demur** sans sourciller *ou* faire d'objection

demure [dɪ'mjʊə(r)] *adj* (**a**) *(modest)* modeste, pudique; *(well-behaved)* sage; *(reserved)* retenu (**b**) *Pej (coy)* d'une modestie affectée

demurely [dɪ'mjʊəlɪ] *adv* (**a**) *(modestly)* modestement; *(reservedly)* avec retenue; **she sipped her tea demurely** elle buvait son thé à petites gorgées *ou* avec délicatesse (**b**) *Pej (coyly)* avec une modestie affectée

demureness [dɪ'mjʊənɪs] *n* (**a**) *(modesty)* modestie *f*, pudeur *f*; *(reserve)* retenue *f* (**b**) *Pej (coyness)* modestie *f* affectée

demurrage [dɪ'mʌrɪdʒ] *n Com* surestarie *f*

demurrer [dɪ'mʌrə(r)] *n Law* fin *f* de non-recevoir

demutualization ['diːˌmjuːtʃʊəlaɪ'zeɪʃən] *n Fin* = transformation d'une société mutuelle en société par actions

demutualize, -ise [ˌdiː'mjuːtʃʊəlaɪz] *vi Fin* = passer d'un statut de société mutuelle à un statut de société par actions

demy [dɪ'maɪ] (*pl* **demies**) *n Typ* coquille *f*, format *m* carré

demystification ['diːˌmɪstɪfɪ'keɪʃən] *n* démystification *f*

demystify [ˌdiː'mɪstɪfaɪ] (*pt & pp* **demystified**) *vt* démystifier

demythologization ['diːmɪˌθɒlədʒaɪ'zeɪʃən] *n* démythification *f*

demythologize, -ise [ˌdiːmɪ'θɒlədʒaɪz] *vt* démythifier

den [den] *n* (**a**) *(of animal)* repaire *m*, tanière *f*; *Fig (hideout)* repaire *m*, nid *m*; **a den of thieves** un repaire de voleurs; **a den of iniquity** un lieu de perdition (**b**) *(room, study)* ≃ bureau *m*, ≃ cabinet *m* de travail; **he uses the study as his den** quand il veut se détendre, il va dans le bureau
▸▸ *Am* **den mother** *(in scout group)* cheftaine *f*

Denali [dɪ'nælɪ] *n* = nom d'origine du Mont McKinley
▸▸ ***Denali National Park*** = parc national en Alaska

denar [dɪ'neə(r)] *n* denar *m*

denarius [dɪ'neərɪəs] *n Antiq* denier *m (romain)*

denary ['diːnərɪ] *adj* décimal

denationalization ['diːˌnæʃənəlaɪ'zeɪʃən] *n* dénationalisation *f*

denationalize, -ise [ˌdiː'næʃənəlaɪz] *vt* dénationaliser

denaturalize, -ise [ˌdiː'nætʃrəlaɪz] *vt* (**a**) *(deprive of nationality)* dénaturaliser (**b**) *(make unnatural)* dénaturer

denaturation [ˌdiːneɪtʃə'reɪʃən] *n Biol & Chem* dénaturation *f*

denature [ˌdiː'neɪtʃə(r)], **denaturize, -ise** [ˌdiː'neɪtʃəraɪz] *vt Biol & Chem* dénaturer

denazification ['diːˌnɑːtsɪfɪ'keɪʃən] *n* dénazification *f*

denazify [ˌdiː'nɑːtsɪfaɪ] *vt* dénazifier

dendrite ['dendraɪt] *n Miner* arborisation *f*, dendrite *f*

dendritic [den'drɪtɪk] *adj Miner* dendritique, arborisé
▸▸ ***dendritic agate*** agate *f* arborisée; ***dendritic markings*** arborisations *fpl*

dendrochronology [ˌdendrəʊkrə'nɒlədʒɪ] *n Ecol* dendrochronologie *f*

dendroclimatology ['dendrəʊˌklaɪmə'tɒlədʒɪ] *n Ecol* dendroclimatologie *f*

dendroid ['dendrɔɪd] *adj Bot* dendroïde

dendrologist [den'drɒlədʒɪst] *n Bot* dendrologue *mf*, dendrologiste *mf*

dendrology [den'drɒlədʒɪ] *n Bot* dendrologie *f*

dene [diːn] *n Br (valley)* val *m*, vallée *f*

denervate [ˌdiː'nɜːveɪt] *vt Med* énerver

denervation [ˌdiːnɜː'veɪʃən] *n Med* énervation *f*

dengue ['deŋgɪ] *n Med (fever)* dengue *f*
▸▸ *Med* ***dengue fever*** dengue *f*

deniable [dɪ'naɪəbəl] *adj* niable

denial [dɪ'naɪəl] *n* (**a**) *(of story, rumour)* démenti *m*; *(of wrongdoing)* dénégation *f*; **to issue a denial** publier un démenti; **the minister's denial of responsibility was greeted with outrage** c'est avec indignation qu'on a appris que le ministre rejetait toute responsabilité
(**b**) *(of request, right)* refus *m*; *Law* **denial of justice** déni *m* de justice
(**c**) *(disavowal, repudiation)* reniement *m*; *Bible* **Peter's denial of Christ** le reniement du Christ par Pierre
(**d**) *(abstinence)* abnégation *f*; **the monks led a life of denial** les moines menaient une vie d'abnégation
(**e**) *Psy* **to be in denial** refuser de se rendre à l'évidence

denier ['denɪə(r), də'nɪə(r)] *n* (**a**) *Br (measure)* denier *m*; **15-denier stockings** bas *m* de 15 deniers (**b**) *Hist (coin)* denier *m*

denigrate ['denɪgreɪt] *vt* dénigrer

denigration [ˌdenɪ'greɪʃən] *n* dénigrement *m*

denigrator ['denɪgreɪtə(r)] *n* dénigreur(euse) *m,f*

denim ['denɪm] **1** *n* (toile *f* de) jean *m*, denim *m*
2 *comp (garment)* en jean
3 denims *npl* blue-jean *m*, jean *m*; **all the students were wearing denims** tous les étudiants portaient des jeans
▸▸ ***denim jacket*** veste *f* en jean

denitrate [ˌdiː'naɪtreɪt] *vt Chem* dénitrifier

denitration ['diːˌnaɪ'treɪʃən], **denitrification** ['diːˌnaɪtrɪfɪ'keɪʃən] *n Chem* dénitrification *f*

denitrify [ˌdiː'naɪtrɪfaɪ] (*pt & pp* **denitrified**) *vt Chem* dénitrifier

denizen ['denɪzən] *n* (**a**) *Literary or Hum (inhabitant)* habitant(e) *m,f*, hôte *mf*; *(regular visitor)* habitué(e) *m,f*; *Fig* **the denizens of the deep** *(fish)* les poissons *mpl*; **the denizens of the forest** les hôtes *mpl* des bois (**b**) *Br (permanent resident)* ≃ résident(e) *m,f* (**c**) *Bot (non-native plant)* plante *f* allogène; *Zool (non-native animal)* animal *m* allogène

Denmark ['denmɑːk] *n* Danemark *m*; **in Denmark** au Danemark

> **Something is rotten in the state of Denmark**
> Cette célèbre formule ("Il y a quelque chose de pourri au royaume du Danemark") provient de *Hamlet* (Acte I, scène 4) de William Shakespeare où elle est prononcée par Marcellus, qui s'inquiète des intrigues qui se nouent au sein du royaume.
> Aujourd'hui cette phrase est souvent utilisée, notamment dans la presse, pour parler d'une situation où règne la corruption, dans le monde politique ou bien dans une organisation par exemple. Le terme **the state of Denmark** est alors remplacé par le terme approprié comme dans l'exemple suivant: **the recent revelations have shown that there is something rotten at the heart of the British civil service** ("les dernières révélations prouvent qu'il y a quelque chose de pourri au cœur de l'administration britannique").

Dennis the Menace ['denɪs-] *pr n* = petit garçon bagarreur et insolent dans une bande dessinée britannique

denominate [dɪ'nɒmɪneɪt] *vt* (**a**) *Formal (name)* dénommer (**b**) *Fin* libeller; **denominated in dollars** libellé en dollars

denomination [dɪˌnɒmɪ'neɪʃən] *n* (**a**) *Fin* valeur *f*; *(of share, banknote)* coupure *f*; **small/large denomination notes** petites/grosses coupures *fpl*; **coins of different denominations** des pièces de différentes valeurs (**b**) *Rel* confession *f*, culte *m* (**c**) *Formal (designation, specification)* dénomination *f*

denominational [dɪˌnɒmɪ'neɪʃənəl] *adj Rel* confessionnel
▸▸ ***denominational school*** école *f* confessionnelle

denominationalism [dɪˌnɒmɪ'neɪʃənəlɪzəm] *n Rel* appartenance *f* à une confession

denominative [dɪ'nɒmɪnətɪv] **1** *n* dénominatif *m*
2 *adj* dénominatif

denominator [dɪ'nɒmɪneɪtə(r)] *n Math* dénominateur *m*

denotation [ˌdiːnəʊ'teɪʃən] *n (UNCOUNT)* (**a**) *(indication)* dénotation *f*; *(representation, symbol)* signes *mpl*, symboles *mpl*; *Literary* **the denotations of an uneasy conscience** les signes d'une conscience troublée (**b**) *(specific meaning)* signification *f*

denotative [dɪ'nəʊtətɪv] *adj* dénotatif

denote [dɪ'nəʊt] *vt* (**a**) *(indicate)* dénoter (**b**) *(mean)* signifier

denouement [deɪ'nuːmɑ̃] *n (of play, situation)* dénouement *m*

denounce [dɪ'naʊns] *vt* (**a**) *(inform against → criminal, crime)* dénoncer; **to denounce sb to the authorities** signaler qn à la justice; **to denounce sb as an impostor** taxer qn d'imposture
(**b**) *(protest about → abuse, government action, drug-taking)* dénoncer, s'élever contre; *(modern art, exhibition)* dénigrer; **they have been denounced as nothing more than murderers** ils ont été accusés de n'être que de vulgaires assassins
(**c**) *(declare termination of → treaty, agreement)* dénoncer

denouncement [dɪ'naʊnsmənt] *n* dénonciation *f*

denouncer [dɪ'naʊnsə(r)] *n* dénonciateur(trice) *m,f*

dense [dens] *adj* (**a**) *(body, metal etc)* dense (**b**) *(thick → fog, smoke)* épais(aisse); *(→ undergrowth, vegetation, population, traffic)* dense; *(→ crowd)* compact, dense; *Phot* opaque (**c**) *(prose, text)* dense, ramassé (**d**) *Fam (stupid)* bouché, stupide ❑

densely ['denslɪ] *adv* **to be densely packed together** être serrés les uns contre les autres; **a densely-populated area** une région très peuplée *ou* à forte densité de population; **the book**

is very densely written le livre est écrit d'une manière dense *ou* ramassée; **a densely-wooded valley** une vallée très boisée

denseness ['densnɪs] *n* (**a**) *(of undergrowth, vegetation, crowd, traffic)* densité *f* (**b**) *Fam (stupidity)* stupidité □ *f*

densimeter [den'sɪmɪtə(r)], **densitometer** [ˌdensɪ'tɒmɪtə(r)] *n Opt & Phys* densitomètre *m*

density ['densɪtɪ] *n* (**a**) *(of body, metal etc)* densité *f*; *Tech* masse *f* volumique; *Phys* **ion/neutron density** densité *f* ionique/neutronique (**b**) *(of population)* densité *f*

►► ***density chart*** *(in hotel)* feuille *f* d'occupation journalière

dent [dent] **1** *n* (**a**) *(in metal, wall)* bosse *f*; *(in bed, pillow)* creux *m*; **he made a dent in his car** il a cabossé sa voiture; **the car has a dent in the bumper** la voiture a le pare-chocs cabossé (**b**) *Fig (reduction)* **to make a dent in one's savings** faire un trou dans ses économies; *Fig* **to make a dent in sb's self-confidence** entamer la confiance en soi *ou* l'assurance de qn

2 *vt* (**a**) *(metal, wall)* cabosser, bosseler (**b**) *Fig (pride)* froisser; *(self-confidence)* entamer

dental ['dentəl] **1** *adj* (**a**) *(concerned with dentistry)* dentaire (**b**) *Ling* dental

2 *n Ling* dentale *f*

►► ***dental appointment*** rendez-vous *m* chez le dentiste; ***dental care*** soins *mpl* dentaires; *Ling* ***dental consonant*** (consonne *f*) dentale *f*; ***dental floss*** fil *m* dentaire; ***dental hygiene*** hygiène *f* dentaire; ***dental hygienist*** ≃ assistant(e) *m,f*, de dentiste *(qui s'occupe du détartrage etc)*; ***dental mechanic*** mécanicien-dentiste (mécanicienne dentiste) *m,f*; ***dental nurse*** assistant(e) *m,f* dentaire; *Am* ***dental office*** cabinet *m* dentaire; *Br* ***dental orthopaedics,*** *Am* ***dental orthopedics*** *(UNCOUNT)* orthodontie *f*; ***dental plate*** dentier *m*; ***dental record*** dossier *m* médical *(chez le dentiste)*; *Br* ***dental surgeon*** chirurgien-dentiste (chirugienne-dentiste) *m,f*; ***dental surgery*** *(activity)* chirurgie *f* dentaire; *Br (office)* cabinet *m* dentaire; ***dental technician*** prothésiste *mf* (dentaire); ***dental treatment*** traitement *m* dentaire

dentate ['denteɪt] *adj* denté, dentelé

dented ['dentɪd] *adj (metal)* cabossé

dentifrice ['dentɪfrɪs] *n (paste)* pâte *f* dentifrice; *(powder)* poudre *f* dentifrice

dentine ['denti:n], *Am* **dentin** ['dentɪn] *n Anat & Zool* dentine *f*

dentist ['dentɪst] *n* dentiste *mf*; **to go to the dentist('s)** aller chez le dentiste

►► ***dentist's chair*** fauteuil *m* de dentiste; *Am* ***dentist's office,*** *Br* ***dentist's surgery*** cabinet *m* dentaire

dentistry ['dentɪstrɪ] *n* dentisterie *f*

dentition [den'tɪʃən] *n Anat & Zool* dentition *f*

denture ['dentʃə(r)] **1** *n (artificial tooth)* prothèse *f* dentaire

2 dentures *npl* dentier *m*; **to wear dentures** porter un dentier

denturist ['dentʃərɪst] *n* denturologiste *mf*

denuclearization ['di:ˌnju:klɪəraɪ'zeɪʃən] *n* dénucléarisation *f*

denuclearize, -ise [ˌdi:'nju:klɪəraɪz] *vt* dénucléariser

denude [dɪ'nju:d] *vt* dénuder; **a landscape denuded of trees** un paysage sans arbres

denumerable [dɪ'nju:mərəbəl] *adj Math* dénombrable

denunciation [dɪˌnʌnsɪ'eɪʃən] *n* dénonciation *f*

denunciative [dɪ'nʌnsɪətɪv] *adj* dénonciateur

denunciator [dɪ'nʌnsɪeɪtə(r)] *n* dénonciateur(trice) *m,f*

denunciatory [dɪˌnʌnsɪ'eɪtərɪ, dɪ'nʌnsɪətərɪ] *adj* dénonciateur

Denver boot ['denvə-] *n Fam Aut* sabot *m* de Denver □

deny [dɪ'naɪ] *(pt & pp* **denied**) *vt* (**a**) *(declare untrue)* nier; *(report, rumour)* démentir; **the prisoner denied having conspired** *or* **conspiring against the government** le prisonnier nia avoir conspiré contre le gouvernement; **the accused denies the charge** l'accusé nie; **he denied that he had been involved** il nia avoir été impliqué; **there's no denying that we have a problem** il est indéniable que nous avons un problème; **he denied all knowledge of the incident** il a nié être au courant de l'incident

(**b**) *(refuse)* refuser, *Literary* dénier; **to deny sb sth** *or* **sth to sb** refuser qch à qn; **to be denied access to sb/sth** se voir refuser l'accès à qn/qch; **in many countries people are denied even basic human rights** dans beaucoup de pays les gens sont privés des droits les plus fondamentaux

(**c**) *(deprive)* priver; **she thought that by denying herself she could help others** elle pensait qu'en se privant elle pourrait aider les autres

(**d**) *Arch or Literary (disavow, repudiate)* renier; *Bible* **before the cock crow, thou shalt deny me thrice** avant que le coq chante, tu m'auras renié trois fois

deodorant [di:'əʊdərənt] *n* déodorant *m*

deodorization [di:ˌəʊdəraɪ'zeɪʃən] *n* désodorisation *f*

deodorize, -ise [di:'əʊdəraɪz] *vt* désodoriser

deodorizer [di:'əʊdəˌraɪzə(r)] *n (for home)* désodorisant *m*

deontological [dɪˌɒntə'lɒdʒɪkəl] *adj* déontologique

deontology [ˌdi:ɒn'tɒlədʒɪ] *n* déontologie *f*

deoxidation [di:ɒksɪ'deɪʃən], **deoxidisation** [di:ˌɒksɪdaɪ'zeɪʃən] *n Chem* désoxydation *f*

deoxidize, -ise [di:'ɒksɪdaɪz] *vt Chem* désoxyder

deoxygenate [ˌdi:'ɒksɪdʒəneɪt] *vt Chem* désoxygéner

deoxygenation [ˌdi:ɒksɪdʒən'eɪʃən] *n Chem* désoxygénation *f*

deoxyribonuclease ['di:ɒksɪˌraɪbəʊ'nju:klɪeɪs] *n Biol & Chem* désoxyribonucléase *f*

deoxyribonucleic acid ['di:ɒksɪˌraɪbəʊnju:'kli:ɪk-] *n Biol & Chem* acide *m* désoxyribonucléique

deoxyribonucleotid ['di:ɒksɪˌraɪbəʊnju:kli:'əʊtɪd] *n Biol & Chem* désoxyribonucléotide *m*

deoxyribose [ˌdi:ɒksɪ'raɪbəʊs] *n Biol & Chem* désoxyribose *m*

dep *(written abbr* **departure/departs**) dép

depart [dɪ'pɑ:t] **1** *vi Formal* (**a**) *(leave)* partir; **the train now departing from platform two is the express to Liverpool** le train en partance au quai numéro deux est l'express de Liverpool; **they departed for Canada from Portsmouth** ils sont partis pour le Canada depuis Portsmouth

(**b**) *(deviate, vary)* s'écarter; **to depart from tradition** s'écarter de la tradition; **to depart from sb's wishes** ne pas respecter la volonté de qn

2 *vt* quitter; *Euph* **to depart this life** quitter ce monde

departed [dɪ'pɑ:tɪd] *Euph Formal* **1** *adj (dead)* défunt, disparu

2 *n* **the departed** le (la) défunt(e), le (la) disparu(e)

department [dɪ'pɑ:tmənt] *n* (**a**) *Admin & Pol (division)* département *m*; *(ministry)* ministère *m*; **she works in the housing department** elle travaille au ministère du Logement

(**b**) *(in company, organization)* service *m*; **the sales/personnel department** le service commercial/du personnel; **the complaints department** le service des réclamations

(**c**) *(field, responsibility)* domaine *m*; **recruiting staff is not my department** le recrutement du personnel n'est pas mon domaine *ou* de mon ressort; *Fig* **cooking's not really my department** la cuisine n'est pas vraiment mon domaine *ou* ma spécialité

(**d**) *(in shop)* rayon *m*; **the toy department** le rayon des jouets

(**e**) *(in university)* département *m*; **the French/maths department** *(at school)* = ensemble des professeurs de français/de mathématique d'un établissement d'enseignement secondaire sous la responsabilité de l'un d'entre eux

(**f**) *Geog* département *m*

►► *Br* ***Department of Culture, Media and Sport*** ministère *m* de la culture, de la communication et des sports; *Am* ***Department of Defense*** ministère *m* de la Défense; *Br* ***Department of Education and Employment*** = ministère britannique de l'Éducation et de l'Emploi; *Am* ***Department of Education*** ministère *m* de l'Éducation nationale; *Am* ***Department of Energy*** = ministère américain de l'Énergie; *Br Formerly* ***Department of the Environment*** ministère *m* de l'environnement; *Br* ***Department of the Environment, Transport and the Regions*** = Ministère britannique de l'Environnement, des Transports et des Régions; *Br* ***Department of Health*** ministère *m* de la Santé; *Am Formerly* ***Department of Health, Education and Welfare*** = ancien ministère américain de l'Éducation et de la Santé publique; *Am* ***Department of Health and Human Services*** ministère *m* de la Santé; *Am Formerly* ***Department of Housing and Urban Development*** ministère *m* du logement et de la ville; *Br* ***Department for International Development*** = secrétariat d'État à la Coopération; *Am* ***Department of the Interior*** = ministère de l'Intérieur; *Am* ***Department of Justice*** ministère *m* de la Justice; *Am* ***Department of Labor*** = ministère de l'Emploi et de la Solidarité; *Am* ***Department of Motor Vehicles*** = service des immatriculations et des permis de conduire aux États-Unis; *Br* ***Department of National Heritage*** ≃ ministère *m* du patrimoine national; *Br* ***Department of Public Works*** ≃ ministère *m* de l'Équipement; *Br* ***Department of Social Security*** ≃ ministère *m* des Affaires sociales; *Am* ***Department of State*** Département *m* d'État, ≃ ministère *m* des Affaires étrangères; ***department store*** grand magasin *m*; *Am* ***Department of Trade*** ministère *m* du commerce; *Br* ***Department of Trade and Industry*** ministère *m* du commerce et de l'industrie; *Br* ***Department of Transport,*** *Am* ***Department of Transportation*** ministère *m* des Transports

departmental [ˌdi:pɑ:t'mentəl] *adj* (**a**) *Admin & Pol* du département (**b**) *(in company, organization)* du service (**c**) *(in shop)* du rayon (**d**) *(in university)* du département (**e**) *Geog* du département, départemental

►► ***departmental manager*** chef *m* de service; ***departmental meeting*** réunion *f* de service

departmentalization [ˌdi:pɑ:tmentəlaɪ'zeɪʃən] *n* (**a**) *Admin & Pol* division *f* en départements (**b**) *(in company, organization)* division *f* en services (**c**) *(in shop)* division *f* en rayons (**d**) *(in university)* division *f* en départements

departmentalize, -ise [ˌdi:pɑ:t'mentəlaɪz] *vt* (**a**) *Admin & Pol* diviser en départements (**b**) *(company, organization)* diviser en services (**c**) *(shop)* diviser en rayons (**d**) *(university)* diviser en départements

departure [dɪ'pɑ:tʃə(r)] *n* (**a**) *(leaving)* départ *m*; **the crew were preparing for departure** l'équipage se préparait au départ; **our departure was delayed for three hours** notre départ a été retardé de trois heures; **her unexpected departure from politics** son départ inattendu de la scène politique; *Formal* **to take one's departure** prendre congé

(**b**) *(variation, deviation)* modification *f*; **a departure from standard company policy** une entorse à la politique habituelle de l'entreprise; **a departure from his usual habits** une action contraire à ses habitudes

(**c**) *(orientation)* orientation *f*; **farming was an entirely new departure for him** l'agriculture était une voie *ou* orientation tout à fait nouvelle pour lui

(**d**) *Arch (death)* disparition *f*, trépas *m*

►► ***departure date*** date *f* de départ; ***departure gate*** *(in airport)* porte *f* (d'embarquement); ***departure list*** liste *f* des départs; ***departure lounge*** salle *f* d'embarquement; ***departure quay*** quai *m* de départ; ***departure tax*** taxe *f* de départ; ***departure time*** heure *f* de départ

depend [dɪ'pend] *vi* dépendre; **that depends, it all depends** ça dépend

►**depend on, depend upon 1** *vt sep* (**a**) *(be determined by)* dépendre de; **the outcome of the war will depend on** *or* **upon a number of factors** l'issue de la guerre dépendra d'un certain nombre de facteurs; **his job depends on his** *or* **him getting the contract** il ne gardera son emploi que s'il obtient le contrat; **survival depended on their finding enough water** pour survivre, il leur fallait trouver suffisamment d'eau; **her future may depend on it** son avenir en dépend peut-être

(**b**) *(rely on)* dépendre de; **the firm depends heavily on orders from abroad** l'entreprise dépend beaucoup des commandes de l'étranger; **she depends on the money her children give her** l'argent qu'elle reçoit de ses enfants est sa seule ressource; *Ironic* **you can**

depend on him to be late on peut être sûr qu'il arrive en retard

(**c**) *(trust, be sure of)* compter sur; **he's a friend you can depend on** c'est un ami sur qui vous pouvez compter; **I'm depending on you to help me** je compte sur vous pour m'aider; **we need somebody who can be depended on to be discreet** il nous faut quelqu'un sur la discrétion de qui on puisse compter; **you can depend on it!** vous pouvez en être sûr *ou* compter là-dessus!

2 depending on *prep* selon; **a degree takes three or four years of study, depending on the subject chosen** un diplôme demande trois ou quatre ans d'études, selon la matière choisie

dependability [dɪˌpendəˈbɪlətɪ] *n (of machine, information)* fiabilité *f*; *(of person)* fiabilité *f*, sérieux *m*; *(of organization)* sérieux *m*

dependable [dɪˈpendəbəl] *adj (machine, information)* fiable; *(person)* fiable, sérieux; *(organization)* sérieux

dependably [dɪˈpendəblɪ] *adv* d'une manière sûre

dependant [dɪˈpendənt] *n Admin* personne *f* à charge; **do you have any dependants?** avez-vous des personnes à charge?

dependence [dɪˈpendəns] *n* (**a**) *(reliance)* dépendance *f* (**on** de); **the government hopes to reduce our dependence on oil** le gouvernement espère diminuer notre dépendance vis-à-vis du pétrole; **her dependence on her children increased with the years** elle devenait de plus en plus dépendante de ses enfants au fil des années

(**b**) *(trust)* confiance *f* (**on** en); **to place a lot of dependence on sth** accorder un grand crédit à qch

dependency [dɪˈpendənsɪ] *(pl* **dependencies***)* *n* (**a**) *(country)* dépendance *f* (**b**) *esp Am* = **dependence**

►► ***dependency culture*** = situation d'une société dont les membres ont une mentalité d'assistés

dependent [dɪˈpendənt] **1** *adj* (**a**) *(reliant)* dépendant; **to be dependent on sb/sth** dépendre de qn/qch; **he became increasingly dependent on his children** il devenait de plus en plus dépendant de ses enfants; **she's financially dependent on her parents** elle dépend financièrement *ou* elle est à la charge de ses parents; *Admin* **he has two dependent children** il a deux enfants à charge; **to be dependent on heroin/drugs** être héroïnomane/toxicomane; **she's heavily dependent on sleeping pills** elle ne peut se passer de somnifères

(**b**) *(contingent)* **to be dependent on sth** dépendre de qch; **their economy is highly dependent on foreign investment** leur économie dépend énormément des investissements étrangers; **the prosperity of his business was dependent on the continuation of the war** la prospérité de son entreprise dépendait *ou* était tributaire de la poursuite de la guerre; **her father's consent to the wedding was dependent on the young man's success** son père a donné son assentiment au mariage à condition que le jeune homme réussisse

(**c**) *Gram (clause)* subordonné

(**d**) *Math (variable)* dépendant

2 *n Gram* subordonnée *f*

depersonalization [diːˌpɜːsənəlaɪˈzeɪʃən] *n Psy* dépersonnalisation *f*

depersonalize, -ise [ˌdiːˈpɜːsənəlaɪz] *vt Psy* dépersonnaliser

depict [dɪˈpɪkt] *vt* (**a**) *(describe)* dépeindre; **Shakespeare depicts Richard III as cruel and calculating** Shakespeare dépeint Richard III comme un homme cruel et calculateur (**b**) *(paint, draw)* représenter

depiction [dɪˈpɪkʃən] *n* (**a**) *(description)* description *f* (**b**) *(picture)* représentation *f*

depilate [ˈdepɪleɪt] *vt* épiler

depilation [ˌdepɪˈleɪʃən] *n* épilation *f*

depilator [dɪˈpɪlətə(r)] *n* épileur(euse) *m,f*

depilatory [dɪˈpɪlətrɪ] *(pl* **depilatories***)* **1** *n* épilatoire *m*, dépilatoire *m*

2 *adj* épilatoire, dépilatoire

►► ***depilatory cream*** crème *f* dépilatoire

deplane [ˌdiːˈpleɪn] *vi* descendre d'avion

deplete [dɪˈpliːt] *vt* (**a**) *(reduce)* diminuer, réduire; **the illness depleted her strength** la maladie amoindrissait ses forces; **our stocks have become depleted** nos stocks ont beaucoup diminué (**b**) *(impoverish, exhaust)* épuiser; **overproduction has depleted the soil** la surproduction a épuisé *ou* appauvri la terre; **the stream is depleted of fish** la rivière est beaucoup moins poissonneuse qu'avant

depleted uranium [dɪˈpliːtɪd-] *n Chem* uranium *m* appauvri

depletion [dɪˈpliːʃən] *n* (**a**) *(reduction)* diminution *f*, réduction *f* (**b**) *(exhaustion)* épuisement *m*; *(of soil)* appauvrissement *m*

deplorable [dɪˈplɔːrəbəl] *adj* déplorable, lamentable

deplorably [dɪˈplɔːrəblɪ] *adv* d'une manière déplorable, lamentablement

deplore [dɪˈplɔː(r)] *vt* (**a**) *(regret)* déplorer, regretter; **we all deplored the loss of life** nous avons tous déploré la perte de vies humaines (**b**) *(condemn, disapprove of)* désapprouver, condamner; **the President deplored the use of force against unarmed civilians** le Président a condamné l'usage de la force envers des civils non armés

deploy [dɪˈplɔɪ] **1** *vt* déployer; **I think your talents would be better deployed elsewhere** je pense que vos talents seraient mieux utilisés ailleurs

2 *vi* se déployer

deployment [dɪˈplɔɪmənt] *n* déploiement *m*

depolarization [diːˌpəʊləraɪˈzeɪʃən] *n Electron* dépolarisation *f*

depolarize, -ise [ˌdiːˈpəʊləraɪz] *vt Electron* dépolariser

depoliticization [ˈdiːpəˌlɪtɪsaɪˈzeɪʃən] *n* dépolitisation *f*

depoliticize, -ise [ˌdiːpəˈlɪtɪsaɪz] *vt* dépolitiser

depolymerize, -ise [ˌdiːˈpɒlɪməraɪz] *vt Chem* dépolymériser

deponent [dɪˈpəʊnənt] **1** *n* (**a**) *Gram* déponent *m* (**b**) *Law* déposant(e) *m,f*

2 *adj Gram* déponent

depopulate [ˌdiːˈpɒpjʊleɪt] *vt* dépeupler

depopulated [ˌdiːˈpɒpjʊleɪtɪd] *adj* dépeuplé; **to become depopulated** se dépeupler

depopulation [diːˌpɒpjʊˈleɪʃən] *n* dépeuplement *m*

deport [dɪˈpɔːt] *vt* (**a**) *(expel)* expulser; *Hist (to colonies, camp)* déporter; **they were deported to Mexico** ils furent expulsés vers le Mexique (**b**) *Formal (behave)* **to deport oneself** se comporter, se conduire

deportation [ˌdiːpɔːˈteɪʃən] *n* expulsion *f*; *Hist (to colonies, camp)* déportation *f*; **many refugees were threatened with deportation** beaucoup de réfugiés furent menacés d'expulsion; **resistance fighters risked deportation or death** les combattants de la résistance risquaient la déportation ou la mort

►► ***deportation order*** arrêt *m* d'expulsion

deportee [ˌdiːpɔːˈtiː] *n* expulsé(e) *m,f*; *Hist (prisoner)* déporté(e) *m,f*

deportment [dɪˈpɔːtmənt] *n Formal (behaviour)* comportement *m*; *(carriage, posture)* maintien *m*

depose [dɪˈpəʊz] **1** *vt* (**a**) *(remove)* destituer; *(sovereign)* déposer, destituer (**b**) *Law* déposer

2 *vi Law* faire une déposition

deposit [dɪˈpɒzɪt] **1** *vt* (**a**) *(leave, place)* déposer; **she deposited her belongings in a locker at Victoria Station** elle déposa *ou* laissa ses affaires dans une consigne à la gare Victoria; **the bus deposited me in front of my house** le bus m'a déposé devant ma maison

(**b**) *(document → with a bank)* mettre en dépôt (**with** dans); *(→ with a solicitor)* confier (**with** à)

(**c**) *(of liquid, river)* déposer; **the river had deposited silt along its banks** le fleuve avait laissé un dépôt de vase le long de ses rives

(**d**) *Banking* déposer, remettre; **I'd like to deposit £500** j'aimerais faire un versement de 500 livres; **to deposit a cheque** déposer *ou* remettre un chèque (à la banque)

(**e**) *(pay)* verser; **you must deposit 10 percent of the value of the house** vous devez faire un premier versement correspondant à 10 pour cent de la valeur de la maison; *Fin* **to deposit sth as security** nantir qch, gager qch; *Fin* **to deposit security** déposer une caution

(**f**) *Am (insert)* mettre; **please deposit one dollar for your call** veuillez introduire un dollar pour votre appel

2 *vi Geol* se déposer

3 *n* (**a**) *Banking* dépôt *m*; **to make a deposit** déposer de l'argent; **to make a deposit of £200** faire un versement de 200 livres; **on deposit** en dépôt

(**b**) *Com & Fin (down payment)* acompte *m*; *(not returnable, for contract)* arrhes *fpl*; **she put down a deposit on a house** elle a versé un acompte *ou* a fait un premier versement pour une maison; **a £50 deposit** 50 livres d'acompte/d'arrhes

(**c**) *(guarantee against loss or damage)* caution *f*; *(on bottle)* consigne *f*; **is there a deposit on the bottle?** est-ce que la bouteille est consignée?; **the landlord asked for two months' deposit** le propriétaire a demandé une caution de deux mois

(**d**) *Br Parl* cautionnement *m*; **to lose one's deposit** perdre son cautionnement

(**e**) *Geol* gisement *m*; **oil deposits** gisements *mpl* de pétrole

(**f**) *(sediment, silt)* dépôt *m*; *(in wine)* dépôt *m*

►► *Br Banking* ***deposit account*** compte *m* livret, compte *m* de dépôt; *(when notice has to be given before withdrawal)* compte *m* à terme; *Banking* ***deposit bank*** banque *f* de dépôt; *Banking* ***deposit book*** livret *m ou* carnet *m* de dépôt; *Banking* ***deposit money*** monnaie *f* de banque, monnaie *f* scripturale; *Banking* ***deposit slip*** bulletin *m* de versement

depositary [dɪˈpɒzɪtrɪ] *(pl* **depositaries***)* *n* dépositaire *mf*

deposition[1] [ˌdepəˈzɪʃən] *n* (**a**) *Law* déposition *f* (**b**) *(sediment, silt)* dépôt *m* (**c**) *(removal of leader)* déposition *f*

deposition[2] [ˌdiːpəˈzɪʃən] *vt Mktg (product)* dépositionner

depositor [dəˈpɒzɪtə(r)] *n* déposant(e) *m,f*

depository [*Br* dəˈpɒzɪtrɪ, *Am* dəˈpɒzɪtəʊrɪ] *(pl* **depositories***)* *n* dépôt *m*

depot *n* (**a**) [ˈdepəʊ] *(warehouse)* dépôt *m* (**b**) [ˈdepəʊ] *Br (garage)* dépôt *m*, garage *m* (**c**) [ˈdepəʊ] *Br Mil* ≃ caserne *f* (**d**) [ˈdiːpəʊ] *Am (bus station)* gare *f* routière; *(railway station)* gare *f*

depravation [ˌdeprəˈveɪʃən] *n* dépravation *f*

deprave [dɪˈpreɪv] *vt* dépraver

depraved [dɪˈpreɪvd] *adj* dépravé, perverti

depravity [dɪˈprævətɪ] *(pl* **depravities***)* *n* dépravation *f*, corruption *f*

deprecate [ˈdeprɪkeɪt] *vt* (**a**) *Formal (disapprove of, deplore)* désapprouver; **any renunciation of sovereignty over the territory is to be deprecated** il faut condamner toute renonciation de souveraineté sur le territoire (**b**) *(denigrate, disparage)* dénigrer

deprecating [ˈdeprɪkeɪtɪŋ] *adj* (**a**) *(disapproving)* désapprobateur; *(derogatory)* dénigrant; **to be deprecatory about sb/sth** désapprouver qn/qch (**b**) *(apologetic)* navré

deprecatingly [ˈdeprɪkeɪtɪŋlɪ] *adv* (**a**) *(disapprovingly → say, speak)* d'un ton désapprobateur; *(→ look)* avec désapprobation (**b**) *(apologetically)* avec remords

deprecation [ˌdeprɪˈkeɪʃən] *n* (**a**) *(disapproval)* désapprobation *f* (**b**) *Rel* déprécation *f*

deprecatory [ˈdeprɪkətrɪ] *adj* (**a**) *(disapproving)* désapprobateur; *(derogatory)* dénigrant; **to be deprecatory about sb/sth** désapprouver qn/qch (**b**) *(apologetic)* navré

depreciable [dɪˈpriːʃəbəl] *adj* (**a**) *Am Fin* amortissable (**b**) *Com (liable to depreciation)* dépréciable

►► *Am Fin* ***depreciable base*** assiette *f* de l'amortissement

depreciate [dɪˈpriːʃɪeɪt] **1** *vt* (**a**) *Com (value of something)* déprécier, rabaisser; *Acct (property, equipment)* amortir; *Fin (currency)* dévaloriser, déprécier (**b**) *(denigrate)* dénigrer, déprécier

2 *vi Com (value of something)* diminuer de valeur; *Com & Ind (machinery)* se déprécier; *Fin (currency)* se dévaloriser, se déprécier; *(prices, shares etc)* baisser; **the pound has depreciated against the dollar** la livre a reculé par rapport au dollar; **the tractor depreciated by**

£2,000 la valeur du tracteur a baissé de 2000 livres

depreciated [dɪ'pri:ʃɪeɪtɪd] *adj Com & Ind* amorti; *Fin (currency)* déprécié

depreciation [dɪ,pri:ʃɪ'eɪʃən] *n* (**a**) *Com (of goods)* dépréciation *f*; *Acct (of property, equipment)* amortissement *m*; *Fin (of currency)* dévalorisation *f*, dépréciation; *(amount)* moins-value *f*

(**b**) *(disparagement)* dénigrement *m*, dépréciation *f*

►► ***depreciation accounting*** comptabilité *f* de la dépréciation; ***depreciation charges*** frais *mpl* d'amortissement; ***depreciation period*** période *f* d'amortissement; ***depreciation provision*** dotation *f* aux amortissements; *Acct* ***depreciation rate*** taux *m* d'amortissement; *Acct* ***depreciation schedule*** tableau *m ou* plan *m* d'amortissement

depreciative [dɪ'pri:ʃɪətɪv], **depreciatory** [dɪ'pri:ʃɪətərɪ] *adj (remark)* de dénigrement, critique

►► *Ling* ***depreciatory suffix*** suffixe *m* dépréciatif

depredation [,deprɪ'deɪʃən] *n* déprédation *f*

depress [dɪ'pres] *vt* (**a**) *(deject, sadden)* déprimer; **it depressed her to talk about her father** le fait de parler de son père la déprimait *ou* lui donnait le cafard (**b**) *Econ (price)* (faire) baisser; *(trade)* faire languir; *(economy, market)* affaiblir (**c**) *Formal (push down on → button, lever)* appuyer sur

depressant [dɪ'presənt] *Med* **1** *adj* dépresseur

2 *n* dépresseur *m*

depressed [dɪ'prest] *adj* (**a**) *(dejected, sad)* déprimé, abattu; *Med* déprimé; **you mustn't get depressed about your exam results** tu ne dois pas te laisser abattre *ou* perdre le moral à cause de tes résultats d'examen; **it's nothing to get depressed about** il n'y a pas de quoi se laisser abattre; **visiting her grandparents made her feel depressed** le fait de rendre visite à ses grands-parents la déprimait *ou* lui donnait le cafard

(**b**) *Econ (area, industry)* en déclin, touché par la crise, déprimé; *(prices, profits, wages)* en baisse; *St Exch* **the market is depressed** les cours sont en baisse; **one of the most depressed sectors of the economy** un des secteurs économiques les plus touchés par la crise; **the economy has been in a depressed state for nearly three years** l'économie est dans un état de marasme depuis bientôt trois ans

(**c**) *(sunken, hollow)* creux

depressing [dɪ'presɪŋ] *adj* déprimant; *(idea, place)* triste, sinistre; **what a depressing thought!** quelle triste idée!; **the unemployment figures make for depressing reading** les chiffres du chômage sont plutôt déprimants; **the failure of the talks was depressing news** l'échec des pourparlers fut une nouvelle déprimante *ou* décourageante

depressingly [dɪ'presɪŋlɪ] *adv (say, speak)* d'un ton abattu; **unemployment is depressingly high** le taux de chômage est déprimant; **his meaning was depressingly clear** la signification de ses paroles était d'une clarté déprimante

depression [dɪ'preʃən] *n* (**a**) *(dejection, sadness)* dépression *f*; *Med* dépression *f* (nerveuse); **she suffers from depression** elle fait de la dépression; **he's in a state of depression** il est dans un état dépressif

(**b**) *Econ (slump)* dépression *f*, crise *f* économique; **the country's economy is in a state of depression** l'économie du pays est en crise; *Am Hist* **the Great Depression** la grande dépression

(**c**) *Tech (pressing down)* abaissement *m*; *Aut (of pedal)* enfoncement *m*

(**d**) *(hollow, indentation)* creux *m*; *Geog (in landscape)* dépression *f*

(**e**) *Met* dépression *f*

THE GREAT DEPRESSION

C'est la plus grave crise économique qu'aient connue les États-Unis, qui, de 1929 (date du krach de Wall Street) au début des années 40, plongea de nombreux Américains dans le chômage et la misère.

depressive [dɪ'presɪv] *Med* **1** *adj* dépressif

2 *n* dépressif(ive) *m,f*

depressor [dɪ'presə(r)] *n Anat* abaisseur *m*; *Med* **a tongue depressor** un abaisse-langue

depressurization ['di:,preʃəraɪ'zeɪʃən] *n* dépressurisation *f*

depressurize, -ise [,di:'preʃəraɪz] **1** *vt* dépressuriser

2 *vi* se dépressuriser

deprivation [,deprɪ'veɪʃən] *n (UNCOUNT)* privation *f*; **a life of deprivation and misery** une vie de souffrances et de privations; **emotional deprivation** carence *f* affective

deprive [dɪ'praɪv] *vt* priver; **to deprive sb of sth** priver qn de qch; **the prisoners were deprived of letters for a month** les prisonniers furent privés de lettres pendant un mois; **he was deprived of his rank** il fut déchu de son grade; **she deprives herself of nothing** elle ne se prive de rien; **the legitimate heir was deprived of his inheritance** l'héritier légitime fut frustré *ou* dépossédé de son héritage; **I won't deprive you of the pleasure of telling him about it** je ne te priverai pas du plaisir de le lui dire

deprived [dɪ'praɪvd] *adj (area, child)* défavorisé; **the boy is emotionally deprived** le garçon souffre d'une carence affective; **many of these young offenders come from deprived backgrounds** beaucoup de ces jeunes délinquants viennent de milieux défavorisés

deprogram [,di:'prəʊgræm] *vt* déprogrammer

dept. *(written abbr* **department***)* service *m*

depth [depθ] **1** *n* (**a**) *(distance downwards)* profondeur *f*; **the wreck was located at a depth of 200 metres** l'épave a été repérée à 200 mètres de profondeur *ou* par 200 mètres de fond; **the canal is about 12 metres in depth** le canal a environ 12 mètres de profondeur; **this submarine could dive to a depth of 500 feet** ce sous-marin pouvait descendre jusqu'à une profondeur de 500 pieds

(**b**) *(in deep water)* **the child was warned not to go out of his depth** l'enfant a été averti de ne pas aller où il n'avait pas pied; **she swam too far and got out of her depth** elle a nagé trop loin et a perdu pied; **to be out of one's depth** ne plus avoir pied; *Fig* avoir perdu pied, ne plus être sur son terrain; **I think she's a bit out of her depth in the new job** je crois qu'elle est un peu dépassée dans son nouveau travail

(**c**) *Phot* **depth of field/focus** profondeur *f* de champ/foyer

(**d**) *(of voice, sound)* registre *m* grave

(**e**) *(extent, intensity)* profondeur *f*; *(of colour)* intensité *f*; **the depth of his knowledge of the subject was impressive** sa connaissance approfondie du sujet était impressionnante; **he had not realized her depth of feeling on the matter** il ne s'était pas rendu compte à quel point ce sujet lui tenait à cœur; **we must study the proposal in depth** nous devons étudier à fond *ou* en profondeur cette proposition

2 depths *npl* **the ocean depths** les grands fonds *mpl*; **the depths of the earth** les profondeurs *fpl ou* entrailles *fpl* de la terre; **in the depths of the forest** au (fin) fond de la forêt; *Fig* **in the depths of his soul** au plus profond de son âme; **in the depths of despair** dans le plus profond désespoir; **in the depths of winter** au cœur de l'hiver

►► ***depth bomb, depth charge*** grenade *f* sous-marine; *Tech* ***depth finder*** sondeur *m*; *Tech* ***depth gauge*** hydromètre *m*; *Mktg* ***depth interview*** *(in market research)* entretien *m* en profondeur; ***depth psychology*** psychologie *f* des profondeurs; *Tech* ***depth recorder*** sondeur *m*

deputation [,depjʊ'teɪʃən] *n* (**a**) *(representatives)* députation *f*, délégation *f* (**b**) *(action)* députation *f*, délégation *f*

depute 1 *vt* [dɪ'pju:t] *Formal (person)* députer; *(authority, power)* déléguer; **she deputed the running of the business to her eldest son** elle délégua la gestion de l'entreprise à son fils aîné

2 ['depju:t] *n Scot* = **deputy**

deputize, -ise ['depjʊtaɪz] **1** *vt* députer

2 *vi* **to deputize for sb** représenter qn; **the First Secretary deputized for the Ambassador at the reception** le premier secrétaire représentait l'ambassadeur à la réception

deputy ['depjʊtɪ] *(pl* **deputies***)* *n* (**a**) *(assistant)* adjoint(e) *m,f* (**b**) *(substitute)* remplaçant(e) *m,f*, suppléant(e) *m,f*; **to act as sb's deputy** remplacer qn, suppléer qn (**c**) *Pol (elected representative)* député *m* (**d**) *Am (law enforcement agent)* shérif *m* adjoint

►► ***deputy chairman*** vice-président *m*; ***deputy governor*** sous-gouverneur *m*; *Br* ***deputy head teacher, deputy head*** directeur(trice) *m,f* adjoint(e); ***deputy manager*** directeur(trice) *m,f* adjoint(e); ***deputy mayor*** adjoint(e) *m,f* au maire; ***Deputy Prime Minister*** vice-Premier-Ministre *m*; ***deputy sheriff*** shérif *m* adjoint

DEQ [,di:i:'kju:] *adj Com (abbr* **delivered ex quay***)* DEQ

deracialize, -ise [di:'reɪʃəlaɪz] *vt* déracialiser

deracinate [,di:'ræsɪneɪt] *vt* déraciner, extirper

deracination [,di:ræsɪ'neɪʃən] *n* déracinement *m*, extirpation *f*

derail [dɪ'reɪl] **1** *vt (train)* faire dérailler; *Fig (project, negotiations)* faire avorter; **to be derailed** *(train)* dérailler; *Fig* avorter

2 *vi* dérailler

derailleur [dɪ'reɪljə(r)] *n Br Tech* dérailleur *m*

derailment [dɪ'reɪlmənt] *n (of train)* déraillement *m*; *Fig (of plans, negotiations etc)* échec *m*

derange [dɪ'reɪndʒ] *vt* (**a**) *(disarrange, disorder)* déranger (**b**) *(drive insane)* rendre fou (folle)

deranged [dɪ'reɪndʒd] *adj* dérangé, déséquilibré; **the killer must have been deranged** le tueur devait être fou *ou* déséquilibré; **the old woman seemed slightly deranged** la vieille femme semblait un peu dérangée *ou* avoir l'esprit un peu dérangé; **it's the work of a deranged mind** c'est l'œuvre d'un esprit dérangé *ou* détraqué

derangement [dɪ'reɪndʒmənt] *n* (**a**) *(disorder, disarray)* désordre *m* (**b**) *(mental illness)* démence *f*

derate [,di:'reɪt] *vt Br (property)* dégrever

deration [,di:'ræʃən] *vt* cesser le rationnement de

derby [*Br* 'dɑ:bɪ, *Am* 'dɜ:bɪ] **1** *n* (**a**) *(match)* **(local) derby** derby *m* (**b**) *Am (race)* derby *m* (**c**) *Am (hat)* chapeau *m* melon

2 Derby *n Horseracing* **the Derby** = grande course annuelle de chevaux à Epsom, en Grande-Bretagne

Derbyshire ['dɑ:bɪ,ʃɪə] *n* le Derbyshire, = comté dans le nord de l'Angleterre; **in Derbyshire** dans le Derbyshire

derecognition [di:,rekəg'nɪʃən] *n* **the derecognition of a state/a trade union** le fait de ne plus reconnaître un état/un syndicat

derecognize, -ise [di:'rekəgnaɪz] *vt (state, trade union)* cesser de reconnaître

deregister [,di:'redʒɪstə(r)] *vt (person, political party, organization)* radier

deregistration [,di:redʒɪs'treɪʃən] *n (of person, political party, organization)* radiation *f*

deregulate [,di:'regjʊleɪt] *vt* (**a**) *Econ (prices, wages)* libérer, déréguler (**b**) *(relax restrictions on)* assouplir les règlements de, déréglementer; **he's in favour of deregulating the economy** il est partisan de la déréglementation de l'économie

deregulation [,di:regjʊ'leɪʃən] *n* (**a**) *Econ (of prices, wages)* libération *f*, dérégulation *f* (**b**) *(relaxation of restrictions)* assouplissement *m* des règlements, déréglementation *f*

derelict ['derəlɪkt] **1** *adj* (**a**) *(abandoned)* abandonné, délaissé; **a derelict old building** un vieux bâtiment à l'abandon (**b**) *Formal (negligent, neglectful)* négligent

2 *n* (**a**) *(vagrant)* clochard(e) *m,f*, vagabond(e) *m,f* (**b**) *Naut* navire *m* abandonné

dereliction [,derə'lɪkʃən] *n* (**a**) *(abandonment)* abandon *m* (**b**) *Br (negligence)* négligence *f*; **dereliction of duty** manquement *m* au devoir

derestrict [,di:rɪ'strɪkt] *vt Br* **to derestrict a road** supprimer une limitation de vitesse sur une route

derestricted [,di:rɪ'strɪktɪd] *adj Br (road)* sans limitation de vitesse

derestriction [,di:rɪ'strɪkʃən] *n* exemption *f*

►► *Br* ***derestriction sign*** fin *f* de limitation de vitesse

deride [dɪ'raɪd] *vt* tourner en ridicule, railler

derision [dɪ'rɪʒən] *n* dérision *f*

derisive [dɪ'raɪsɪv] *adj* moqueur

derisively [dɪ'raɪsɪvlɪ] *adv* avec dérision; *(say, speak)* d'un ton moqueur
derisory [də'raɪzərɪ] *adj* (**a**) *(ridiculous)* dérisoire (**b**) *(mocking, scornful)* moqueur
derivation [ˌderɪ'veɪʃən] *n* dérivation *f*; **what is the derivation of...?** quelle est l'origine de...?
derivative [dɪ'rɪvətɪv] **1** *adj* (**a**) *(gen)* dérivé (**b**) *Pej (unoriginal)* peu original, banal; **his work is very derivative** il n'a pas encore trouvé son style propre, il emprunte beaucoup aux autres; **I find his paintings rather derivative** je trouve que ses peintures ne sont pas très originales
 2 *n (gen)* dérivé *m*; *Math* dérivée *f*; *St Exch* produit *m* dérivé
 ►► *St Exch* ***derivative market*** marché *m* à terme des instruments financiers
derive [dɪ'raɪv] **1** *vt* (**a**) *(gain, obtain → origin, income, profit)* tirer (**from** de); *(→ satisfaction)* trouver, tirer; *(→ ideas)* trouver, puiser; **she derives great pleasure from her garden** elle tire beaucoup de plaisir de son jardin; **the young man derived little benefit from his expensive education** le jeune homme n'a guère tiré profit de ses études coûteuses; **to derive courage/strength from sth** trouver du courage/des forces dans qch
 (**b**) *(deduce)* dériver de
 2 *vi* **to derive from** provenir de, venir de; **the word "coward" derives originally from French** le mot "coward" vient du français
derived unit [dɪ'raɪvd-] *n Phys* unité *f* dérivée
dermabrasion ['dɜːməˌbreɪʒən] *n Med* dermabrasion *f*
dermal ['dɜːməl] *adj Anat* dermique
dermatitis [ˌdɜːmə'taɪtɪs] *n (UNCOUNT) Med* dermite *f*, dermatite *f*
dermatological [ˌdɜːmətə'lɒdʒɪkəl] *adj Med* dermatologique
dermatologist [ˌdɜːmə'tɒlədʒɪst] *n Med* dermatologiste *mf*, dermatologue *mf*
dermatology [ˌdɜːmə'tɒlədʒɪ] *n Med* dermatologie *f*
dermatoplasty [ˌdɜːmətəʊ'plæstɪ] *n Med* dermatoplastie *f*
dermatosis [ˌdɜːmə'təʊsɪs] *(pl* **dermatoses** [-siːz]) *n (UNCOUNT) Med* dermatose *f*
dermis ['dɜːmɪs] *n Anat* derme *m*
derogate ['derəgeɪt] **1** *vt Formal (disparage)* dénigrer, déprécier
 2 *vi* **to derogate from sth** porter atteinte à qch; **the claims in no way derogate from her reputation as an artist** ces affirmations n'ont en aucune manière altéré sa réputation d'artiste
derogation [ˌderə'geɪʃən] *n Formal* (**a**) *(of law, rule)* dérogation *f* (**of** à) (**b**) **derogation from a right** atteinte *f* portée à un droit
derogatorily [dɪ'rɒgətrəlɪ] *adv* de façon péjorative
derogatory [dɪ'rɒgətrɪ] *adj (comment, remark)* désobligeant, critique; *(word)* péjoratif
derrick ['derɪk] *n* (**a**) *Tech (crane)* mât *m* de charge (**b**) *Petr* derrick *m*, tour *f* de forage
derrière [ˌderɪ'eə(r)] *n Euph* derrière *m*
derring-do [ˌderɪŋ'duː] *n Literary or Hum* bravoure *f*; **deeds of derring-do** prouesses *fpl*
derringer ['derɪndʒə(r)] *n Am* pistolet *m* (à gros calibre)
Derry ['derɪ] *n* (**a**) *(town)* Derry (**b**) *(county)* le comté de Derry, = comté dans l'Irlande du Nord; **in Derry** dans le comté de Derry
derv [dɜːv] *n Br* gas-oil *m*
dervish ['dɜːvɪʃ] *n Rel* derviche *m*; **a whirling dervish** un derviche tourneur
DES [ˌdiːiː'es] *n Formerly Admin (abbr* **Department of Education and Science**) = ancien ministère britannique de l'Éducation et de la Recherche scientifique
desalinate [ˌdiː'sælɪneɪt] *vt* dessaler
desalination [diːˌsælɪ'neɪʃən] *n* dessalement *m*
 ►► ***desalination plant*** usine *f* de dessalement
desalinize, -ise [ˌdiː'sælɪnaɪz] *vt* dessaler
desalt [ˌdiː'sɔːlt] *vt* dessaler
desaturate [ˌdiː'sætʃəreɪt] *vt* désaturer
descale [ˌdiː'skeɪl] *vt* détartrer
descaling [ˌdiː'skeɪlɪŋ] *n* détartrage *m*
descant ['deskænt] **1** *n Mus* déchant *m*
 2 *vi* (**a**) *Mus* déchanter (**b**) *Literary Pej (comment, ramble)* discourir, pérorer; **to descant on** *or* **upon sth** pérorer au sujet de qch
 ►► *Mus* ***descant recorder*** flûte *f* à bec soprano
Descartes [deɪ'kɑːt] *pr n* Descartes
descend [dɪ'send] *vi* (**a**) *Formal (go, move down)* descendre; **she descended from the train** elle est descendue du train; **the path descends to the sea** le sentier descend jusqu'à la mer
 (**b**) *(fall)* tomber, s'abattre; **a thick blanket of fog descended on the valley** une couche épaisse de brouillard tomba sur la vallée; *Fig* **despair descended upon the families of the missing men** le désespoir gagna *ou* envahit les familles des disparus
 (**c**) *(pass on by ancestry)* descendre; *(pass on by inheritance)* revenir; **dogs and wolves probably descend from a common ancestor** les chiens et les loups descendent probablement d'un ancêtre commun; **Lord Grey's title descended to his grandson** le titre de Lord Grey est revenu à son petit-fils
 (**d**) **to descend on** *(attack → group of people)* s'abattre *ou* tomber sur; *(invade → village, town)* faire une descente sur; **Henry's army descended on the French coast** l'armée de Henri s'abattit sur la côte française; *Hum* **my in-laws descended on us last weekend** ma belle-famille a débarqué chez nous le week-end dernier
 (**e**) *(sink, stoop)* s'abaisser, descendre; **I never thought she would descend to malicious gossip** je n'aurais jamais pensé qu'elle s'abaisserait à cancaner; **you don't want to descend to their level** tu ne vas quand même pas te rabaisser à leur niveau
descendant [dɪ'sendənt] *n* descendant(e) *m,f*
descended [dɪ'sendɪd] *adj* **she is descended from the Russian aristocracy** elle descend *ou* est issue de l'aristocratie russe; **man is descended from the apes** l'homme descend du singe
descender [dɪ'sendə(r)] *n* (**a**) *Typ (of character)* jambage *m* (**b**) *(in mountaineering)* descendeur *m*
descending [dɪ'sendɪŋ] *adj* descendant
 ►► ***descending order*** ordre *m* décroissant; **in descending order of importance** par ordre décroissant d'importance; *Comput* ***descending sort*** tri *m* en ordre décroissant
descent [dɪ'sent] *n* (**a**) *(move downward)* descente *f*; **the aircraft made a sudden descent** l'avion a fait une descente subite; **the stream makes a gentle descent** le lit du ruisseau est en pente douce
 (**b**) *Fig Literary (decline)* chute *f*; **a descent into hell** une descente aux enfers
 (**c**) *(origin)* origine *f*; **of Irish descent** d'origine irlandaise; **I've traced my descent back to a sixteenth-century noble family** j'ai retrouvé la trace de mes ascendants dans une famille noble du seizième siècle
 (**d**) *(succession, transmission)* transmission *f*
 (**e**) *(invasion)* descente *f*; **we're braced for the descent on the town of thousands of football fans** nous sommes prêts pour la venue des milliers de fans de football qui vont s'abattre sur la ville
deschool [ˌdiː'skuːl] *vt (child)* retirer du système scolaire
deschooling [ˌdiː'skuːlɪŋ] *n* = fait d'élargir l'enseignement au-delà du seul cadre scolaire
descramble [ˌdiː'skræmbəl] *vt Tel, Electron & TV* décrypter; *Comput* désembrouiller
descrambler [ˌdiː'skræmblə(r)] *n TV* décodeur *m*
descrambling [ˌdiː'skræmblɪŋ] *n TV* décryptage *m*; *Comput* désembrouillage *m*
describable [dɪs'kraɪbəbəl] *adj* descriptible
describe [dɪ'skraɪb] *vt* (**a**) *(recount, represent)* décrire; **how would you describe yourself?** comment vous décririez-vous?; **witnesses described the man as tall and dark-haired** des témoins ont décrit l'homme comme étant grand et brun; **she described her attacker to the police** elle a fait une description *ou* un portrait de son agresseur à la police; **he described her to them in great detail** il la leur a décrite de façon très détaillée; **the book describes how they escaped** le livre décrit la façon dont ils se sont évadés
 (**b**) *(characterize)* définir, qualifier; **the general described himself as a simple man** le général s'est défini comme un homme simple; **the Chancellor's methods have been described as unorthodox** on a qualifié les méthodes du Chancelier de pas très orthodoxes; **our relations with them could best be described as strained** nos relations avec eux pourraient être qualifiées de *ou* sont pour le moins tendues
 (**c**) *(outline, draw → circle, line)* décrire; *(→ triangle)* tracer
description [dɪ'skrɪpʃən] *n* (**a**) *(account, representation)* description *f*; *(physical)* portrait *m*; *Admin (for police purposes, on passport)* signalement *m*; **the brochure gives a detailed description of the hotel** la brochure donne une description détaillée de l'hôtel; **can you give us a description of the man?** pouvez-vous nous faire un portrait de l'homme?; **a man answering the police description** un homme correspondant au signalement donné par la police; **the food at the reception was beyond** *or* **past description** le repas servi à la réception était indescriptible; **her father was angry beyond description** son père était dans une colère indescriptible
 (**b**) *(kind)* sorte *f*, genre *m*; **the police seized weapons of every description** la police a saisi toutes sortes d'armes; **we were unable to find a vehicle of any description** nous étions incapables de trouver un quelconque véhicule
descriptive [dɪ'skrɪptɪv] *adj* descriptif
 ►► ***descriptive geometry*** géométrie *f* descriptive; ***descriptive linguistics*** linguistique *f* descriptive
descriptively [dɪ'skrɪptɪvlɪ] *adv* de façon descriptive; **he gave a descriptively accurate account of events** il nous a fait une description très fidèle des faits
descriptivism [dɪ'skrɪptɪvɪzəm] *n Gram & Phil* descriptivisme *m*
descriptor [dɪ'skrɪptə(r)] *n Comput* descripteur *m*
descry [dɪ'skraɪ] *(pt & pp* **descried**) *vt Literary* apercevoir, distinguer
Desdemona [dezdɪ'məʊnə] *pr n* Desdémone
desecrate ['desɪkreɪt] *vt* profaner, souiller
desecration [ˌdesɪ'kreɪʃən] *n* profanation *f*
desecrator ['desɪkreɪtə(r)] *n* profanateur(trice) *m,f*
deseed ['diːˌsiːd] *vt (fruit)* épépiner
desegregate [ˌdiː'segrɪgeɪt] *vt* abolir la ségrégation raciale dans; **desegregated schools** = écoles qui ne sont plus soumises à la ségrégation raciale
desegregation [ˌdiːsegrɪ'geɪʃən] *n* déségrégation *f*
deselect [ˌdiːsɪ'lekt] *vt* (**a**) *Br Pol (candidate)* ne pas resélectionner (**b**) *Comput* désactiver
desensitization [ˌdiːsensɪtaɪ'zeɪʃən] *n* désensibilisation *f*
desensitize, -ise [ˌdiː'sensɪtaɪz] *vt* désensibiliser
desert[1] ['dezət] **1** *n (wilderness)* désert *m*
 2 *comp (area, plant, sand)* désertique
 ►► ***desert boots*** = chaussures en daim à lacets; ***desert island*** île *f* déserte; ***Desert Island Discs*** = émission de radio hebdomadaire britannique; ***desert rat*** *Zool* gerboise *f*; *Br Mil* = soldat britannique combattant en Afrique du Nord (pendant la Seconde Guerre mondiale)

DESERT ISLAND DISCS

"Desert Island Discs" est une émission radiophonique de la BBC au cours de laquelle une personnalité invitée doit choisir les disques qu'elle emporterait sur une île déserte. Ponctuée par des extraits des morceaux de musique choisis par l'invité pour les souvenirs qu'ils évoquent, l'émission donne l'occasion aux personnes interviewées de parler de leur vie et de leur carrière.

desert[2] [dɪ'zɜːt] **1** *vt (person)* abandonner, délaisser; *(place)* abandonner, déserter; *(organization, principle)* déserter; **the soldier deserted his post** le soldat déserta son poste; *Fig* **his wits deserted him** il a perdu son sang-froid
 2 *vi Mil* déserter; **to desert from the army** déserter l'armée; **one of the officers deserted to the enemy** un des officiers est passé à l'ennemi

deserted [dɪ'zɜːtɪd] *adj* désert; **the streets were deserted** les rues étaient désertes

deserter [dɪ'zɜːtə(r)] *n Mil* déserteur *m*; **to be shot as a deserter** être fusillé pour désertion

desertification [dɪˌzɜːtɪfɪ'keɪʃən] *n Ecol* désertification *f*

desertion [dɪ'zɜːʃən] *n Mil* désertion *f*; *Law (of spouse)* abandon *m* (du domicile conjugal); *(of cause, organization)* défection *f*, désertion *f*

deserts [dɪ'zɜːts] *npl (reward)* **to get one's just deserts** avoir ce que l'on mérite

deserve [dɪ'zɜːv] **1** *vt* mériter; **the book, though controversial, didn't deserve to be banned** le livre, bien que controversé, ne méritait pas d'être interdit *ou* qu'on l'interdise; **he deserves to die** il mérite la mort; **she deserves wider recognition** elle mérite d'être plus largement reconnue; **she's taking a much deserved holiday** elle prend des vacances bien méritées; **I think he got what he deserved** je pense qu'il a eu ce qu'il méritait; **frankly, they deserve each other** franchement ils se valent l'un l'autre *ou* ils sont dignes l'un de l'autre

2 *vi* mériter; *Formal* **to deserve well of sth** bien mériter de qch

deservedly [dɪ'zɜːvɪdlɪ] *adv* à juste titre, à bon droit; **Mozart has been described as a genius, and deservedly so** on a décrit Mozart comme un génie, à juste titre

deserving [dɪ'zɜːvɪŋ] *adj (person)* méritant; *(cause, organization)* méritoire; *Br Old-fashioned Hum* **the deserving poor** les pauvres méritants *mpl*; *Formal* **a musician deserving of greater recognition** un musicien qui mérite d'être davantage reconnu du public

desex [ˌdiː'seks], **desexualize, -ise** [ˌdiː'seksjʊəlaɪz] *vt* désexualiser

deshabille ['dezæbiːl] *n* **in deshabille** en déshabillé, en négligé

desiccant ['desɪkənt] *n* dessiccatif *m*

desiccate ['desɪkeɪt] *vt* dessécher, sécher

desiccated ['desɪkeɪtɪd] *adj* (**a**) *(dehydrated)* séché (**b**) *(dull → style)* aride; *(→ person)* desséché

►► ***desiccated coconut*** noix *f* de coco séchée

desiccation [ˌdesɪ'keɪʃən] *n* dessication *f*

desiccator ['desɪkeɪtə(r)] *n Chem* dessicateur *m*

desiderate [ˌdiː'zɪdəreɪt] *vt Literary* soupirer après, sentir le besoin de; **the reforms desiderated by the public** les réformes que réclame le public

desideratum [dɪˌzɪdə'rɑːtəm] (*pl* **desiderata** [-tə]) *n (usu pl) Formal* desideratum *m*

design [dɪ'zaɪn] **1** *n* (**a**) *(drawing, sketch)* dessin *m*; *Ind* dessin *m*, plan *m*; *Archit* plan *m*, projet *m*; *Tex* modèle *m*; *(of book, magazine)* maquette *f*; **the design for the new museum has been severely criticized** les projets *ou* plans du nouveau musée ont été sévèrement critiqués

(**b**) *Ind (composition, structure → of car, computer etc)* conception *f*; **the problems were all due to poor design** tous les problèmes viennent de ce que la conception est mauvaise

(**c**) *(subject for study)* design *m*; **book design** conception *f* graphique; **fashion design** stylisme *m*; **industrial design** design *m*

(**d**) *(pattern → on sweater, carpet, wallpaper etc)* motif *m*; **a geometric design** un motif géométrique

(**e**) *(purpose, intent)* dessein *m*; **to do sth by design** faire qch à dessein *ou* exprès; **to have designs on sb/sth** avoir des vues sur qn/qch

2 *comp (course)* de dessin

3 *vt (plan)* concevoir; *(on paper)* dessiner; *Archit* faire les plans de; *(clothes)* concevoir, créer; *(syllabus)* concevoir, mettre au point; **the system is designed to favour the landowners** le système est conçu pour *ou* vise à favoriser les propriétaires terriens; **it's specially designed for very low temperatures** c'est spécialement conçu pour les très basses températures; **she designs jewellery** elle dessine des bijoux

►► ***design award*** prix *m* du meilleur design; ***design department*** bureau *m* d'études; ***design engineer*** ingénieur *m* d'études; ***design fault*** défaut *m* de conception; ***design stage*** phase *f* de conception; ***design studio*** cabinet *m* de design; ***design team*** équipe *f* des concepteurs

designate *Formal* **1** *vt* ['dezɪgneɪt] (**a**) *(appoint, name)* désigner, nommer; **he has been designated as the new Foreign Minister** il a été désigné pour être le nouveau ministre des Affaires étrangères; **a special prosecutor was designated to investigate the charges** un procureur spécial fut désigné pour enquêter sur les accusations; **the theatre should rightfully be designated a national monument** il serait légitime que le théâtre soit classé monument historique; **the school was designated as a civil defence training centre** l'école fut choisie comme centre de défense civile

(**b**) *(indicate, signify)* indiquer, montrer; **the flags on the map designate enemy positions** les drapeaux sur la carte indiquent *ou* signalent les positions ennemies

2 *adj* ['dezɪgnət] désigné; **the Prime Minister designate** le Premier ministre désigné

►► ***designated driver*** = personne qui s'engage à ne pas boire pour pouvoir reconduire d'autres personnes en voiture

designation [ˌdezɪg'neɪʃən] *n* désignation *f*

►► *Com & Law* ***designation of origin*** appellation *f* d'origine

designedly [dɪ'zaɪnɪdlɪ] *adv* à dessein

designer [dɪ'zaɪnə(r)] **1** *n Art & Ind* dessinateur(trice) *m,f*; *Tex* modéliste *mf*, styliste *mf*; *Cin & Theat* décorateur(trice) *m,f*; *(of haute couture)* couturier(ère) *m,f*; *(of books, magazines)* maquettiste *mf*; *(of furniture)* designer *m*; **she's a jewellery designer** elle est dessinatrice en bijouterie

2 *comp (jeans)* haute couture; *(glasses, handbag)* de marque; *(furniture)* design

►► ***designer drug*** = drogue de synthèse conçue spécialement pour contourner la loi sur les stupéfiants; ***designer label*** griffe *f* de grande marque; *Hum* ***designer stubble*** barbe *f* de deux jours *(faisant partie d'un look étudié, faussement négligé)*

designing [dɪ'zaɪnɪŋ] **1** *adj (cunning)* rusé; *(scheming)* intrigant

2 *n (design work)* conception *f*, dessin *m*, design *m*

desinence ['desɪnəns] *n Formal* désinence *f*

desirability [dɪˌzaɪərə'bɪlətɪ] *n (UNCOUNT)* (**a**) *(benefits)* intérêt *m*, avantage *m*, opportunité *f*; **no one questions the desirability of lowering interest rates** personne ne conteste les avantages d'une baisse des taux d'intérêts (**b**) *(attractiveness)* charmes *mpl*, attraits *mpl*

desirable [dɪ'zaɪərəbəl] *adj* (**a**) *(advisable)* souhaitable, *Formal* désirable; **some knowledge of languages is desirable** connaissances en langues étrangères souhaitées (**b**) *(attractive)* à désirer, tentant; **a desirable residence** une belle propriété (**c**) *(sexually appealing)* désirable, séduisant

desirably [dɪ'zaɪərəblɪ] *adv* d'une manière désirable

desire [dɪ'zaɪə(r)] **1** *n* (**a**) *(wish)* désir *m*, envie *f*; **she had no desire to go back** elle n'avait aucune envie d'y retourner; **he had not the least** *or* **slightest desire to find a job** il n'avait nullement *ou* pas la moindre envie de trouver un emploi; **my one desire is that you should be happy** mon seul désir *ou* tout ce que je souhaite, c'est que vous soyez heureux; **it is your father's desire that you should become an officer** c'est le désir de votre père que vous deveniez officier

(**b**) *(sexual)* désir *m*; **to feel desire for sb** désirer *ou* avoir envie de qn

2 *vt* (**a**) *(want, wish)* désirer; **you may spend the night here, if you so desire** vous pouvez passer la nuit ici, si vous le désirez; *Formal* **your presence is desired at the palace** votre présence est requise au palais; *Formal* **the Prince desires that you should be his guest tonight** le Prince désire que vous soyez son invité ce soir; **it leaves much** *or* **a lot to be desired** cela laisse beaucoup à désirer; **it leaves nothing to be desired** cela ne laisse rien à redire; **his words had the desired effect** ses paroles eurent l'effet désiré *ou* escompté

(**b**) *(want sexually)* désirer; **she no longer desired him** elle ne le désirait plus, elle n'avait plus envie de lui

desirous [dɪ'zaɪərəs] *adj Formal* désireux; **he was desirous of re-establishing friendly relations** il était désireux de rétablir des relations amicales

desist [dɪ'zɪst] *vi Formal* cesser; **he was asked to desist from his political activities** on lui a demandé de cesser ses activités politiques

desistance [dɪ'zɪstəns] *n Formal* désistement *m* (**from** de)

desk [desk] **1** *n* (**a**) *(in home, office)* bureau *m*; *(with folding top)* secrétaire *m*; *(for pupil)* pupitre *m*; *(for teacher)* bureau *m*

(**b**) *(reception counter)* réception *f*; *(cashier)* caisse *f*; **please leave your keys at the desk** *(in hotel)* prière de laisser les clefs à la réception

(**c**) *Press (section)* service *m*; **the sports desk** le service des informations sportives; *Br* **Latin America desk** direction *f* des affaires latino-américaines

2 *comp (diary, job, lamp)* de bureau

►► ***desk accessory*** accessoire *m* de bureau; *Br* ***desk blotter*** sous-main *m inv*; *Am* ***desk clerk*** réceptionniste *mf*; *Journ* ***desk editor*** rédacteur(trice) *m,f*; ***desk research*** recherche *f* documentaire; ***desk tidy*** accessoire *m* de rangement pour bureau

deskbound ['deskbaʊnd] *adj* sédentaire; **she hates being deskbound** elle déteste faire un travail sédentaire

deskill [ˌdiː'skɪl] *vt Ind (workforce)* déqualifier; *(process, job)* automatiser

deskilling [ˌdiː'skɪlɪŋ] *n Ind (of workforce)* déqualification *f*; *(of process, job)* automatisation *f*

deskman ['deskmæn] *n Journ* deskman *m*

desktop ['desktɒp] **1** *n Comput (screen area)* bureau *m*; **you will find the icon on your desktop** l'icône se trouve sur le bureau

2 *adj (computer, model)* de bureau

►► ***desktop calculator*** calculatrice *f*; *Comput* ***desktop publishing*** publication *f* assistée par ordinateur, microédition *f*; *Comput* ***desktop publishing operator*** opérateur(trice) *m,f* de publication assistée par ordinateur; *Comput* ***desktop publishing package*** logiciel *m* de mise en page

desolate 1 *adj* ['desələt] (**a**) *(area, place → empty)* désert; *(→ barren, lifeless)* désolé; *Fig (gloomy, bleak)* morne, sombre (**b**) *(person → sorrowful)* consterné, abattu; *(→ friendless)* délaissé

2 *vt* ['desəleɪt] (**a**) *(area, place → devastate)* dévaster, saccager; *(→ depopulate)* dépeupler (**b**) *(person)* désoler, navrer; **he was desolated at** *or* **by the loss of his job** il était désolé *ou* navré d'avoir perdu son emploi

desolately ['desələtlɪ] *adv (say)* d'un ton désolé; *(look at)* d'un air désolé

desolateness ['desələtnɪs] *n* désolation *f*, aspect *m* vide *ou* déshérité

desolation [ˌdesə'leɪʃən] *n* (**a**) *(barrenness, emptiness)* caractère *m* désert, désolation *f*; *(devastation, ruin)* dévastation *f*, ravages *mpl* (**b**) *(despair, sorrow)* désolation *f*, consternation *f*; *(loneliness)* solitude *f*

desorption [dɪ'sɔːpʃən] *n* désorption *f*

despair [dɪ'speə(r)] **1** *n* (**a**) *(hopelessness)* désespoir *m*; **to be in despair** être au désespoir; **..., she said in despair** ..., dit-elle, désespérée; **in despair, she took her own life** de désespoir elle a mis fin à ses jours; **his despair at ever finding a job made him turn to crime** parce qu'il désespérait de trouver un emploi, il est tombé dans la délinquance; **the people are in despair at** *or* **over the prospect of war** les gens sont désespérés à cause des perspectives de guerre; **to drive sb to despair** réduire qn au désespoir, désespérer qn

(**b**) *(cause of distress)* désespoir *m*; **William was the despair of his teachers** William faisait *ou* était le désespoir de tous ses professeurs

2 *vi* désespérer; **she began to despair of ever finding her brother alive** elle commençait à désespérer de retrouver un jour son frère vivant; **he despaired at the thought of all the work he had to do** il était désespéré à l'idée de tout le travail qu'il avait à faire; **don't despair, help is on the way** ne désespérez pas, les secours arrivent; **I despair of you** tu me désespères; *Formal* **they despair of his life** ils craignent pour sa vie

despairing [dɪ'speərɪŋ] *adj (cry, look)* de désespoir, désespéré; *(person)* abattu, consterné

despairingly [dɪ'speərɪŋlɪ] *adv (look, speak)* avec désespoir

despatch = **dispatch**

despecialization [ˌdiːspeʃəlaɪ'zeɪʃən] *n* déspécialisation *f*

despecialize, -ise [ˌdiː'speʃəlaɪz] *vt* déspécialiser

desperado [ˌdespə'rɑːdəʊ] *(pl* **desperadoes** *or* **desperados**) *n Literary or Hum* desperado *m*, hors-la-loi *m inv*

desperate ['desprət] *adj* (**a**) *(hopeless, serious)* désespéré; **we were in a desperate state** nous étions dans une situation désespérée; **the refugees are in desperate need of help** les réfugiés ont désespérément besoin d'assistance

(**b**) *(reckless)* désespéré; **he died in a desperate attempt to escape** il est mort en essayant désespérément de s'évader; **we heard desperate screams** nous avons entendu des cris désespérés *ou* de désespoir; **I'm afraid she'll do something desperate** j'ai bien peur qu'elle ne tente un acte désespéré; **a desperate criminal/man** un criminel/homme prêt à tout

(**c**) *(intent, eager)* **to be desperate for money** avoir un besoin urgent d'argent; **she was desperate to leave home** elle voulait à tout prix partir de chez elle; *Fam Hum* **I'm desperate to go to the loo** je ne tiens plus, ça urge

▸▸ ***Desperate Dan*** = cowboy dans une bande dessinée britannique, connu pour sa grande taille et son énorme appétit

desperately ['desprətlɪ] *adv* (**a**) *(hopelessly, seriously)* désespérément; **their country is desperately poor** leur pays est d'une pauvreté désespérante; **he was desperately ill with malaria** il était gravement atteint par le paludisme; **they're desperately in love** ils s'aiment éperdument

(**b**) *(recklessly)* désespérément; **the soldiers fought desperately** les soldats se battaient désespérément *ou* avec acharnement

(**c**) *(as intensifier)* terriblement; **he desperately wanted to become an actor** il voulait à tout prix devenir acteur; **we're desperately busy at the moment** nous sommes terriblement occupés en ce moment; **he's desperately sorry** il est affreusement désolé; **do you want to go? – not desperately** tu veux y aller? – pas vraiment

desperation [ˌdespə'reɪʃən] *n* désespoir *m*; **an act of desperation** un acte de désespoir; **he agreed in desperation** en désespoir de cause, il a accepté

despicable [dɪ'spɪkəbəl] *adj (person)* méprisable, détestable; *(action, behaviour)* méprisable, ignoble; **it was a despicable thing to do** c'était un acte indigne

despicably [dɪ'spɪkəblɪ] *adv (behave)* bassement, d'une façon indigne

despise [dɪ'spaɪz] *vt (feel contempt for)* mépriser; **he despised himself for his cowardice** il se méprisait d'avoir été lâche; **these things are not to be despised** cela n'est pas à dédaigner

despite [dɪ'spaɪt] **1** *prep* malgré, en dépit de; **despite leaving early, I still missed the train** bien que je sois parti de bonne heure, j'ai manqué mon train; **despite having a degree she's still unemployed** bien que diplômée *ou* malgré son diplôme, elle est toujours au chômage; **he laughed despite himself** il n'a pas pu s'empêcher de rire; **despite the fact that...** malgré le fait que...

2 *n Arch (malice, spite)* dépit *m*

despoil [dɪ'spɔɪl] *vt Formal or Literary (person)* spolier, dépouiller; *(land, town)* piller

despoiler [dɪ'spɔɪlə(r)] *n* spoliateur(trice) *m,f*

despoiling [dɪ'spɔɪlɪŋ] *n* spoliation *f*

despoilment [dɪs'pɔɪlmənt], **despoliation** [dɪspəʊlɪ'eɪʃən] *n* spoliation *f*

despondence [dɪ'spɒndəns], **despondency** [dɪ'spɒndənsɪ] *n* découragement *m*, abattement *m*

despondent [dɪ'spɒndənt] *adj* découragé, abattu; **to become despondent** se laisser abattre; **try not to be too despondent about losing** ne te laisse pas trop abattre *ou* décourager par cette défaite

despondently [dɪ'spɒndəntlɪ] *adv* d'un air découragé *ou* abattu; *(say, speak)* d'un ton découragé *ou* abattu; **he wrote despondently of his failure to find work** il écrivit une lettre découragée où il disait qu'il ne trouvait pas de travail

despot ['despɒt] *n also Fig* despote *m*

despotic [de'spɒtɪk] *adj also Fig* despotique

despotically [de'spɒtɪkəlɪ] *adv also Fig* despotiquement; **to govern/to rule despotically** gouverner/régner en despote

despotism ['despətɪzəm] *n* despotisme *m*

desquamate ['deskwəmeɪt] **1** *vi* se desquamer, s'exfolier

2 *vt* desquamer

desquamation [ˌdeskwə'meɪʃən] *n* desquamation *f*, exfoliation *f*

des res [ˌdez'rez] *n Br Fam (abbr* **desirable residence**) *(flat)* bel appartement ◻ *m*; *(house)* belle maison ◻ *f*

dessert [dɪ'zɜːt] **1** *n* dessert *m*; **what's for dessert?** qu'est-ce qu'il y a comme dessert?; **we had ice cream for dessert** nous avons eu de la glace en dessert

2 *comp (knife, dish, plate)* à dessert

▸▸ ***dessert apple*** pomme *f* à couteau; ***dessert menu*** carte *f* des desserts; ***dessert trolley*** chariot *m* de desserts; ***dessert wine*** vin *m* doux

dessertspoon [dɪ'zɜːtspuːn] *n* cuiller *f ou* cuillère *f* à dessert

dessertspoonful [dɪ'zɜːtˌspuːnfʊl] *n* cuillerée *f* à dessert

destabilization [diːˌsteɪbɪlaɪ'zeɪʃən] *n* déstabilisation *f*

destabilize, -ise [ˌdiː'steɪbɪlaɪz] *vt* déstabiliser

de-Stalinization ['diːˌstɑːlɪnaɪ'zeɪʃən] *n Pol* déstalinisation *f*

de-Stalinize, -ise [ˌdiː'stɑːlɪnaɪz] *vt Pol* déstaliniser

destination [ˌdestɪ'neɪʃən] *n* destination *f*; **to reach one's destination** arriver à sa destination

▸▸ *Comput* ***destination disk*** *(hard disk)* disque *m*; *(floppy disk)* disquette *f* cible; *Comput* ***destination drive*** lecteur *m* de destination; *Mktg* ***destination purchase*** achat *m* prévu

destine ['destɪn] *vt* destiner (**for** à; **to do** de faire)

destined ['destɪnd] *adj* (**a**) *(intended)* **she felt she was destined for an acting career** elle sentait qu'elle était destinée à une carrière d'actrice; **she was destined for greater things** elle était promise à un plus grand avenir; **their plan was destined to fail** *or* **for failure** leur projet était voué à l'échec; **she was destined never to have children** le destin a voulu qu'elle n'ait jamais d'enfant; **De Gaulle felt he was destined to lead France** De Gaulle sentait que son destin était de diriger la France; **he was destined never to see her again** il ne devait plus la revoir

(**b**) *(bound)* **the flight was destined for Sydney** le vol était à destination de Sydney

destiny ['destɪnɪ] *n (fate)* destin *m*; *(personal fate)* destinée *f*, destin *m*; **she felt it was her destiny to become a writer** elle avait le sentiment que c'était son destin de devenir écrivain

destitute ['destɪtjuːt] **1** *adj* (**a**) *(extremely poor)* dans la misère, sans ressources; **to be utterly destitute** être dans la misère; **the drought has left many farmers destitute** la sécheresse a réduit beaucoup d'agriculteurs à la misère (**b**) *Formal (lacking)* **destitute of** dépourvu de; *Fig* **destitute of talent** dépourvu *ou* démuni de talent

2 *npl* **the destitute** les indigents *mpl ou* démunis *mpl*

destitution [ˌdestɪ'tjuːʃən] *n* misère *f*, indigence *f*; **the old woman lived in utter destitution** la vieille femme vivait dans une misère noire

destock [ˌdiː'stɒk] *vt Com (goods)* déstocker

destocking [ˌdiː'stɒkɪŋ] *n Com (of goods)* déstockage *m*

destrier ['destrɪə(r)] *n Arch or Literary* destrier *m*, cheval *m* de bataille

destroy [dɪ'strɔɪ] *vt* (**a**) *(demolish, wreck)* détruire; **an explosion has completely destroyed the railway station** une explosion a dévasté *ou* complètement détruit la gare; **they threaten to destroy our democratic way of life** ils menacent d'anéantir *ou* de détruire nos institutions démocratiques

(**b**) *(ruin, spoil* → *efforts)* réduire à néant; *(*→ *hope, love)* détruire; *(*→ *career, friendship, marriage)* briser; *(*→ *health)* ruiner, détruire; **his wartime experiences destroyed his faith in humanity** ses expériences de guerre ont brisé sa foi en l'humanité; **to destroy sb's life** briser la vie de qn; **to destroy one's health** se ruiner *ou* se détruire la santé

(**c**) *(kill* → *farm animal)* abattre; *(*→ *pet)* supprimer, (faire) piquer; **we had to have the dog destroyed** nous avons dû faire piquer le chien

destroyer [dɪ'strɔɪə(r)] *n* (**a**) *Mil* destroyer *m*, contre-torpilleur *m* (**b**) *(person)* destructeur(trice) *m,f*

▸▸ *Mil* ***destroyer escort*** escorteur *m*

destruct [dɪ'strʌkt] **1** *vt* détruire

2 *vi* s'auto-détruire

3 *n* destruction *f*

4 *comp (button, mechanism)* de destruction

destructible [dɪ'strʌktəbəl] *adj* destructible

destruction [dɪ'strʌkʃən] *n* (**a**) *(demolition, devastation)* destruction *f*; **the earthquake brought about the destruction of whole villages** le tremblement de terre a entraîné la disparition de villages entiers; **a nuclear war would result in total destruction** une guerre nucléaire mènerait à une destruction totale; **the destruction caused by the fire/storm** les ravages du feu/de la tempête

(**b**) *(elimination* → *of evidence)* suppression *f*; *(*→ *of life, hope)* anéantissement *m*

(**c**) *Fig (ruin)* ruine *f*; **drink and drugs proved to be his destruction** l'alcool et la drogue l'ont détruit *ou* mené à sa perte

destructive [dɪ'strʌktɪv] *adj* destructeur; **the destructive power of a bomb** le pouvoir destructif d'une bombe; **she's a destructive child** c'est une enfant qui aime casser; **destructive criticism** critique négative

destructively [dɪ'strʌktɪvlɪ] *adv* de façon destructrice

destructiveness [dɪ'strʌktɪvnɪs] *n (of bomb, weapon)* capacité *f* destructrice; *(of criticism)* caractère *m* destructeur; *(of person)* penchant *m* destructeur

destructor [dɪ'strʌktə(r)] *n Br (incinerator)* incinérateur *m*; *Aviat* bouton *m* explosif

desuetude [dɪ'sjuːɪtjuːd] *n Literary* désuétude *f*

desulphurization [ˌdiːsʌlfəraɪ'zeɪʃən] *n Chem & Ind* désulfuration *f*, désoufrage *m*

desulphurize, -ise [ˌdiː'sʌlfəraɪz] *vt Chem & Ind* désulfurer, désoufrer, dessoufrer

desultorily ['desəltrɪlɪ] *adv (converse)* d'une manière décousue; *(wander, stroll)* sans but; *(recite, perform)* sans conviction

desultoriness ['desəltrɪnɪs] *n Formal (of conversation, attempt)* manque *m* de suite; **the desultoriness of my reading** le décousu de mes lectures

desultory ['desəltrɪ] *adj Formal (conversation)* décousu, sans suite; *(attempt)* peu suivi, peu soutenu, sans suite; **he made only a desultory attempt to learn Italian** il a essayé d'apprendre l'italien, mais sans conviction; **she wandered about the town in a desultory fashion** elle errait sans but dans la ville

Det. (*written abbr* **detective**) **Det. Jenkins** l'inspecteur Jenkins

detach [dɪ'tætʃ] *vt* (**a**) *(handle, hood)* détacher; *(trailer)* décrocher; *(stamp etc)* décoller

(**b**) *(person)* **she managed to detach herself from the rest of the group** elle a réussi à s'éloigner du reste du groupe; **he can't detach himself sufficiently from the conflict** il n'a pas assez de recul par rapport au conflit; **he detached himself from the surrealists** il a pris ses distances par rapport aux surréalistes; **he became detached from his group and got lost** il s'est retrouvé séparé de son groupe et s'est perdu

(**c**) *Mil (troops)* détacher

detachable [dɪ'tætʃəbəl] *adj (gen)* détachable; *(collar, lining, strap, handle, lens)* amovible

detached [dɪ'tætʃt] *adj* (**a**) *(separate)* détaché, séparé; **to become detached** *(stamp, retina)* se décoller; *(price tag, carriage)* se détacher; *(trailer)* se décrocher (**b**) *(objective)* objectif; *(unemotional)* détaché

▸▸ *Br* ***detached house*** maison *f* individuelle, pavillon *m*; *Med* ***detached retina*** rétine *f* décollée

detachedly [dɪ'tætʃɪdlɪ] *adv (say, observe)* d'un air détaché

detachment [dɪ'tætʃmənt] *n* (**a**) *(separation)* séparation *f* (**b**) *(indifference)* détachement *m*; *(objectivity)* objectivité *f*; **with an air of detachment** avec un air distancié *ou* détaché (**c**) *Mil* détachement *m*

detail [*Br* 'diːteɪl, *Am* dɪ'teɪl] **1** *n* (**a**) *(item, element)* détail *m*; **there's no need to go into detail** *or* **details** ça ne sert à rien d'entrer dans les détails; **down to the last detail** jusqu'au moindre détail; **the author recounts his childhood in great detail** l'auteur raconte son enfance dans les moindres détails; **attention to detail is important** il faut être minutieux *ou* méticuleux; **that's just a minor detail** ça n'a pas d'importance; **the detail of the carving** le détail *ou* les détails de la sculpture
(**b**) *Mil (group of soldiers)* détachement *m*
2 *vt* (**a**) *(enumerate, specify)* raconter en détail, détailler, énumérer; **operating instructions are fully detailed in the booklet** le mode d'emploi détaillé se trouve dans le livret
(**b**) *Mil* détacher, affecter
3 details *npl (particulars)* renseignements *mpl*, précisions *fpl*; *(name, address etc)* coordonnées *fpl*; **for further details please contact...** pour plus de renseignements, veuillez contacter...; **let me take down your details** laissez-moi vos coordonnées; **I'll send you the details of the property** je vous enverrai les informations *ou* renseignements concernant la propriété
►► *Constr* ***detail drawing*** épure *f*

detailed [*Br* 'diːteɪld, *Am* dɪ'teɪld] *adj* détaillé; **a detailed account** un compte rendu détaillé *ou* très précis

detailing ['diːteɪlɪŋ] *n Am (thorough cleaning)* nettoyage *m* complet

detain [dɪ'teɪn] *vt* (**a**) *Formal (delay)* retenir; *(in hospital)* garder; *Sch (pupil)* consigner; **I won't detain you any longer than is necessary** je ne vous retiendrai pas plus longtemps que nécessaire *ou* qu'il n'est nécessaire; **I'm afraid I've been detained** *(when cancelling appointment)* je suis désolé, je suis retenu; **this question need not detain us** cette question ne nous retiendra pas
(**b**) *Law (keep in custody)* détenir, garder à vue; **to detain sb for questioning** mettre *ou* placer qn en garde à vue

detainee [ˌdiːteɪ'niː] *n Law* détenu(e) *m,f*

detect [dɪ'tekt] *vt (change, emotion, trace of substance)* déceler; *(error, pattern)* découvrir; *Mil & Mining* détecter; *Med (disease)* dépister; **the aircraft cannot be detected by radar** l'avion ne peut pas être détecté *ou* repéré par radar; **do I detect a certain lack of enthusiasm on your part?** je crois déceler un certain manque d'enthousiasme de ta part; **the thieves managed to enter the building without being detected** les cambrioleurs ont pénétré dans le bâtiment sans éveiller l'attention *ou* sans qu'on s'en aperçoive; **she could barely detect his pulse** elle sentait à peine son pouls

detectable [dɪ'tektəbəl] *adj Mil & Mining* détectable; *Med (disease)* que l'on peut dépister; **the poison is not detectable in the bloodstream** on [illegible] le sang

detection [dɪ'tekʃən] **1** *n* (**a**) *(discovery)* découverte *f*; *Mil & Mining* détection *f*; *Med (of disease)* dépistage *m*; **to escape detection** *(mistake)* passer inaperçu; *(killer)* échapper aux recherches; **athletes who have used banned drugs have so far escaped detection** on n'a pas encore repéré les athlètes qui se sont dopés avec des substances interdites; **crime detection** la recherche des criminels
2 *adj Mil & Mining (device)* de détection; *Med* de dépistage

detective [dɪ'tektɪv] **1** *n (on a police force)* ≃ inspecteur(trice) *m,f* de police; *(private)* détective *m* (privé)
2 *comp (film, novel)* policier
►► ***detective agency*** agence *f* de détectives privés; *Br* ***detective constable*** ≃ inspecteur(trice) *m,f* de police; *Br* ***detective inspector*** ≃ inspecteur(trice) *m,f* de police principal(e); *Br* ***detective sergeant*** ≃ inspecteur(trice) *m,f* de police; ***detective story*** roman *m* policier, polar *m*

detector [dɪ'tektə(r)] *n* détecteur *m*
►► *Br* ***detector van*** = voiture-radar utilisée pour la détection des postes de télévision non déclarés

détente [deɪ'tɒnt] *n Pol* détente *f*

detention [dɪ'tenʃən] *n* (**a**) *(captivity)* détention *f*; **in detention** *(gen)* en détention; *Mil* aux arrêts
(**b**) *Sch* retenue *f*, consigne *f*; **the entire class was given an hour's detention** toute la classe a eu une heure de retenue; **to put a pupil in detention** consigner un élève, mettre un élève en retenue
►► *Br Law* ***detention centre*** = jusqu'en 1988, centre de détention pour jeunes délinquants (aujourd'hui appelé "young offenders' institution")

deter [dɪ'tɜː(r)] *(pt & pp* **deterred**, *cont* **deterring**) *vt* (**a**) *(discourage → person)* dissuader; **to deter sb from doing sth** dissuader qn de faire qch; **he was not to be deterred from his purpose** il n'allait pas se laisser détourner de son but; **why should that deter you from going?** pourquoi est-ce que ça t'empêche d'y aller? (**b**) *(prevent → attack)* prévenir

detergent [dɪ'tɜːdʒənt] **1** *n* détergent *m*, détersif *m*; *Am (washing powder)* lessive *f*
2 *adj* détersif, détergent

deteriorate [dɪ'tɪərɪəreɪt] *vi (weather, economy, building, health)* se détériorer; *(work, situation, relations)* se dégrader; **her health has deteriorated rapidly over the past few months** sa santé s'est détériorée rapidement au cours des derniers mois; **the situation has deteriorated even further** la situation a encore empiré *ou* s'est encore dégradée; **the patient's condition deteriorated overnight** l'état du malade s'est aggravé pendant la nuit

deterioration [dɪˌtɪərɪə'reɪʃən] *n (in economy, building, health)* détérioration *f*; *(in work, situation, relations)* dégradation *f*, détérioration *f*; **there has been a deterioration in living standards** le niveau de vie a baissé; **there has been a deterioration in the weather** le temps s'est dégradé *ou* gâté; **despite the continuing deterioration of the situation** bien que la situation continue à empirer

determinable [dɪ'tɜːmɪnəbəl] *adj* (**a**) *(quantity)* déterminable (**b**) *(cause, conditions, factors)* que l'on peut déterminer *ou* préciser; *(price)* que l'on peut fixer (**c**) *Law (contract, lease)* résoluble

determinant [dɪ'tɜːmɪnənt] *Math* **1** *n* déterminant *m*
2 *adj* déterminant

determinate [dɪ'tɜːmɪnɪt] *adj (distinct, fixed)* déterminé

determination [dɪˌtɜːmɪ'neɪʃən] *n* (**a**) *(resolve)* détermination *f*, résolution *f*; **an air of determination** un air résolu *ou* décidé; **she showed a dogged determination to find her natural mother** elle était plus que déterminée *ou* résolue à retrouver sa vraie mère (**b**) *(establishment, fixing → of prices, wages etc)* détermination *f*, fixation *f*; *(→ of boundaries)* délimitation *f*, établissement *m* (**c**) *Law (termination → of contract etc)* résiliation *f*, résolution *f*

determinative [dɪ'tɜːmɪnətɪv] **1** *n* élément *m* déterminant; *Gram* déterminant *m*, déterminatif *m*
2 *adj* déterminant; *Gram* déterminatif

determine [dɪ'tɜːmɪn] *vt* (**a**) *(control, govern)* déterminer, décider de; **the commanding officer determined the fate of the prisoners** le commandant décida du sort des prisonniers
(**b**) *(establish, find out)* déterminer, établir; **the police were unable to determine the cause of death** la police n'a pas pu déterminer *ou* établir la cause du décès
(**c**) *(settle → date, price)* déterminer, fixer; *(→ boundary)* délimiter, établir
(**d**) *(resolve)* **she determined to prove her innocence** elle a décidé de prouver son innocence
(**e**) *Law (terminate → contract, lease)* résoudre, résilier

determined [dɪ'tɜːmɪnd] *adj* (**a**) *(decided, resolved)* déterminé, décidé; **to be determined to do sth** être déterminé *ou* résolu à faire qch; **she was determined (that) her son would go to university** elle était bien décidée *ou* déterminée à ce que son fils fasse des études supérieures; **he's a very determined young man** c'est un jeune homme très décidé *ou* qui a de la suite dans les idées
(**b**) *(resolute)* **they made determined efforts to find all survivors** ils ont fait tout ce qu'ils ont pu pour retrouver tous les survivants

determinedly [dɪ'tɜːmɪndlɪ] *adv* avec détermination

determiner [dɪ'tɜːmɪnə(r)] *n Gram* déterminant *m*

determining [dɪ'tɜːmɪnɪŋ] *adj (factor)* déterminant

determinism [dɪ'tɜːmɪnɪzəm] *n Phil* déterminisme *m*

determinist [dɪ'tɜːmɪnɪst] *Phil* **1** *n* déterministe *mf*
2 *adj* déterministe

deterministic [dɪˌtɜːmɪ'nɪstɪk] *adj Phil* déterministe

deterrence [dɪ'terəns] *n (gen)* dissuasion *f*; *Mil* force *f* de dissuasion

deterrent [dɪ'terənt] **1** *n* (**a**) *(gen)* agent *m* de dissuasion; **to act as** *or* **be a deterrent (to)** exercer un effet dissuasif (contre); **nuclear weapons act as a deterrent** les armes nucléaires ont un rôle dissuasif (**b**) *Mil* arme *f* de dissuasion
2 *adj* dissuasif, de dissuasion

detest [dɪ'test] *vt* détester; **I detest housework** j'ai horreur de *ou* je déteste faire le ménage; **she detests having to make small talk** elle a horreur de *ou* elle déteste papoter

detestable [dɪ'testəbəl] *adj* détestable, exécrable

detestably [dɪ'testəblɪ] *adv* détestablement

detestation [ˌdiːte'steɪʃən] *n* haine *f*, horreur *f*

dethrone [dɪ'θrəʊn] *vt* détrôner, déposer

dethronement [dɪ'θrəʊnmənt] *n* déposition *f* *(d'un souverain)*

detonate ['detəneɪt] **1** *vt* faire détoner *ou* exploser
2 *vi* détoner, exploser

detonation [ˌdetə'neɪʃən] *n* détonation *f*, explosion *f*

detonator ['detəneɪtə(r)] *n* (**a**) *(for explosive)* détonateur *m*, amorce *f* (**b**) *Rail (fog signal)* pétard *m*

detour ['diːtʊə(r)] **1** *n (in road, stream)* détour *m*; *(for traffic)* déviation *f*; **to make a detour** faire un détour
2 *vi* faire un détour
3 *vt (faire)* dévier

detox ['diːtɒks] *n Fam* désintoxication *f*
►► *Fam* ***detox centre*** centre *m* de désintoxication

detoxicate [ˌdiː'tɒksɪkeɪt] *vt* (**a**) *(person)* désintoxiquer (**b**) *(poison)* détoxiquer

detoxication ['diːˌtɒksɪ'keɪʃən] *n* (**a**) *(of person)* désintoxication *f* (**b**) *(of poison)* détoxication *f*
►► ***detoxication centre*** centre *m* de désintoxication; ***detoxication programme*** cure *f* de désintoxication

detoxification ['diːˌtɒksɪfɪ'keɪʃən] *n (of person)* désintoxication *f*
►► ***detoxification centre*** centre *m* de désintoxication; ***detoxification programme*** cure *f* de désintoxication

detoxify [ˌdiː'tɒksɪfaɪ] *(pt & pp* **detoxified**) *vt (person)* désintoxiquer

DETR [ˌdiːiːˌtiː'ɑː(r)] *n Br (abbr* **Department of the Environment, Transport and the Regions**) = ministère britannique de l'Environnement, des Transports et des Régions

detract [dɪ'trækt] *vi* **to detract from** *(someone's pleasure, beauty of something)* diminuer, porter atteinte à; *(someone's worth, achievements)* déprécier; **the bad weather did not in the least detract from our enjoyment of the holiday** le mauvais temps ne nous a pas le moins du monde empêchés d'apprécier nos vacances; **the criticism in no way detracts from her achievements** la critique ne réduit en rien la portée de *ou* n'enlève rien à ce qu'elle a accompli

detraction [dɪ'trækʃən] *n* critique *f*, dénigrement *m*

detractor [dɪ'træktə(r)] *n* détracteur(trice) *m,f*

det–det

detrain [ˌdiːˈtreɪn] *Formal* **1** *vi* descendre *(d'un train)*

2 *vt* débarquer *(d'un train)*

detribalization [ˈdiːˌtraɪbəlaɪˈzeɪʃən] *n* détribalisation *f*

detribalize, -ise [ˌdiːˈtraɪbəlaɪz] *vt* détribaliser

detriment [ˈdetrɪmənt] *n* **to the detriment of** au détriment de; **without detriment to the truth** sans porter atteinte *ou* sans nuire à la vérité

detrimental [ˌdetrɪˈmentəl] *adj* nuisible; **to be detrimental to, to have a detrimental effect on** *(health, reputation)* être nuisible à, être préjudiciable à, nuire à; **pollution has a detrimental effect on** *or* **is detrimental to plant life** la pollution nuit à la flore; **it would be detrimental to my interests** cela desservirait mes intérêts

detrimentally [ˌdetrɪˈmentəlɪ] *adv (affect)* d'une manière préjudiciable *ou* nuisible

detrition [dɪˈtrɪʃən] *n Geol* détrition *f*

detritus [dɪˈtraɪtəs] *n (UNCOUNT) Formal (debris)* détritus *m*; *Geol* roches *fpl* détritiques, pierrailles *fpl*

Detroit [dɪˈtrɔɪt] *n* Detroit

Dettol® [ˈdetɒl] *n* = solution antiseptique

detumescence [ˌdiːtjuːˈmesəns] *n* détumescence *f*

detumescent [ˌdiːtjuːˈmesənt] *adj* détumescent

deuce [djuːs] *n* **(a)** *(on card, dice)* deux *m* **(b)** *Sport (in tennis)* égalité *f* **(c)** *Fam Old-fashioned (as expletive)* **where the deuce is it?** où diable peut-il bien être?; **what the deuce!** bon sang!; **how the deuce should I know?** comment voulez-vous que je sache? ❑; **we're in a deuce of a mess** nous sommes dans un sacré *ou* satané pétrin

deuced [djuːst] *Fam Old-fashioned* **1** *adj* sacré, satané, fichu

2 *adv* diablement, bigrement

deus ex machina [ˌdeɪəseksˈmækɪnə] *n Literature & Theat* deus ex machina *m*

deuterium [djuːˈtɪərɪəm] *n Chem* deutérium *m*

►► *Chem* ***deuterium oxide*** eau *f* lourde

deuteron [ˈdjuːtərɒn] *n Chem* deutéron *m*, deuton *m*

Deuteronomy [ˌdjuːtəˈrɒnəmɪ] *n Bible* Deutéronome

Deutsche [ˈdɔɪtʃə] *adj*

►► ***Deutsche Mark*** (Deutsche) Mark *m*; *St Exch* ***Deutsche Industrie Norm*** (indice *m*) DIN *f*

Deutschmark [ˈdɔɪtʃmɑːk] *n* (Deutsche) Mark *m*

devaluation [ˈdiːˌvæljʊˈeɪʃən] *n Econ* dévaluation *f*

devalue [ˌdiːˈvæljuː] *vt Econ* dévaluer; *Fig (person, achievements, efforts)* dévaloriser; **the franc has been devalued by 3 percent** le franc a été dévalué de 3 pour cent

devastate [ˈdevəsteɪt] *vt* **(a)** *(country, town)* dévaster, ravager; *(enemy)* anéantir **(b)** *(overwhelm)* foudroyer, accabler, anéantir; **he was devastated by his mother's death** la mort de sa mère l'a complètement anéanti

devastated [ˈdevəsteɪtɪd] *adj* **(a)** *(area, city)* dévasté **(b)** *(person)* accablé

devastating [ˈdevəsteɪtɪŋ] *adj* **(a)** *(disastrous → passion, storm)* dévastateur, ravageur; *(→ news)* accablant; *(→ argument, effect)* accablant, écrasant; **to deal a devastating blow to sb/sth** porter un rude coup à qn/qch **(b)** *(highly effective → person, charm)* irrésistible; **he has a devastating wit** son (sens de l') humour est irrésistible

devastatingly [ˈdevəsteɪtɪŋlɪ] *adv* **(a)** *(disastrously)* de manière dévastatrice **(b)** *(as intensifier)* **devastatingly beautiful** d'une beauté irrésistible; **devastatingly funny** d'une drôlerie irrésistible

devastation [ˌdevəˈsteɪʃən] *n (disaster)* dévastation *f*; **scenes of utter devastation** des scènes de dévastation

devein [ˌdiːˈveɪn] *vt Culin (prawn, lobster)* déveiner

develop [dɪˈveləp] **1** *vi* **(a)** *(evolve → country, person)* se développer, évoluer; *(→ feeling)* se former, grandir; *(→ plot)* se développer, se dérouler; **to develop into sth** devenir qch; **let's see how things develop** attendons de voir comment les choses évoluent *ou* tournent

(b) *(become apparent → disease)* se manifester, se déclarer; *(→ talent, trend)* se manifester; *(→ event)* se produire

(c) *Phot* se développer

2 *vt* **(a)** *(form → body, mind)* développer, former; *(→ story)* développer; *(→ feeling)* former; **to develop one's muscles** développer ses muscles, se muscler

(b) *(expand → business, market)* développer; *(→ idea, argument)* développer, expliquer (en détail), exposer (en détail)

(c) *(improve → skill)* développer, travailler; *(→ machine, process)* mettre au point

(d) *(acquire → disease)* contracter; *(→ cold, tic)* attraper; *(→ symptoms)* présenter; **she developed a habit of biting her nails** elle a pris l'habitude de se ronger les ongles; **he has developed cancer** il est atteint de cancer; **to develop a temperature** *or* **a fever** (se mettre à) avoir *ou* faire de la température; **I've developed a taste for opera** je me suis mis à aimer l'opéra; **she's developed a tendency to stutter** elle s'est plus ou moins mise à bégayer

(e) *(land, resources)* exploiter, mettre en valeur, aménager; **the site is to be developed** on va construire sur ce terrain, on va aménager le site

(f) *Math, Mus & Phot* développer

developed [dɪˈveləpt] *adj (film)* développé; *(land)* mis en valeur, aménagé; *(country)* développé; **this coast is highly developed** on a beaucoup construit le long de cette côte

developer [dɪˈveləpə(r)] *n* **(a)** *(of land)* promoteur *m* (de construction) **(b)** *(person)* **to be a late developer** se développer sur le tard **(c)** *Phot* révélateur *m*, développateur *m*

developing [dɪˈveləpɪŋ] **1** *adj (crisis, storm)* qui se prépare, qui s'annonce; *(industry)* en expansion; **a developing interest in...** un intérêt grandissant pour...

2 *n Phot* développement *m*; **developing and printing** *(sign)* travaux photographiques, développement et tirage

►► ***developing bath*** (bain *m*) révélateur *m*; *Econ* ***developing country, developing nation*** pays *m ou* nation *f* en voie de développement; ***developing tank*** cuve *f* à développement

development [dɪˈveləpmənt] *n* **(a)** *(of body, person, mind)* développement *m*, formation *f*; *(of ideas, language)* développement *m*, évolution *f*; *(of argument, theme)* développement *m*, exposé *m*; *(of plot, situation)* déroulement *m*, développement *m*; *(of business)* développement *m*, expansion *f*; *(of invention, process)* mise *f* au point; *(of region)* mise *f* en valeur, exploitation *f*; **they propose the development of this land as a residential area** ils suggèrent d'aménager ce terrain en zone résidentielle;

(b) *(incident, event)* fait *m* nouveau; **we're awaiting further developments** nous attendons la suite des événements *ou* les derniers développements; **a surprise development** un rebondissement; **there has been an unexpected development** l'affaire a pris une tournure inattendue; **there are no new developments** il n'y a rien de nouveau; **the latest developments in the former Soviet Union** les derniers événements survenus dans l'ex-Union Soviétique; **the latest developments in medical research** les dernières découvertes médicales

(c) *(tract of land)* **housing development** cité *f* (ouvrière); **industrial development** zone *f* industrielle

(d) *Math, Mus & Phot* développement *m*

►► *Br* ***development area*** = zone économiquement sinistrée bénéficiant d'aides publiques en vue de sa reconversion; *Fin* ***development capital*** capital-développement *m*; ***development grant*** subvention *f* pour le développement; ***development loans*** crédits *mpl* de développement; *Mktg* ***development stage*** *(of product)* phase *f* de développement; ***development system*** = système informatique conçu pour le développement de logiciels

developmental [dɪˌveləpˈmentəl] *adj* de développement

deviance [ˈdiːvɪəns], **deviancy** [ˈdiːvɪənsɪ] *n* déviance *f*; **deviance from the norm** écart *m* par rapport à la norme

deviant [ˈdiːvɪənt] **1** *adj* **(a)** *(behaviour)* déviant, qui s'écarte de la norme; *(growth)* anormal; **sexually deviant** perverti **(b)** *Ling* déviant

2 *n* déviant(e) *m,f*; **sexual deviant** pervers(e) *m,f*

deviate [ˈdiːvɪeɪt] *vi* **(a)** *(differ)* dévier, s'écarter; **those who deviate from the norm** ceux qui s'écartent de la norme **(b)** *(plane, ship)* dévier, dériver; *(missile)* dévier

deviation [ˌdiːvɪˈeɪʃən] *n* **(a)** *(from custom, principle)* déviation *f*; *(from social norm)* déviance *f*; **there must be no deviation from the party line** on ne doit en aucun cas s'écarter de la ligne du parti **(b)** *(in statistics)* écart *m* **(c)** *(of plane, ship)* déviation *f*, dérive *f*; *(of missile)* déviation *f*, dérivation *f* **(d)** *Math, Med & Phil* déviation *f*

deviationism [ˌdiːvɪˈeɪʃənɪzəm] *n* déviationnisme *m*

deviationist [ˌdiːvɪˈeɪʃənɪst] *Pol* **1** *adj* déviationniste

2 *n* déviationniste *mf*

device [dɪˈvaɪs] *n* **(a)** *(gadget)* appareil *m*, engin *m*; *(mechanism)* mécanisme *m*, dispositif *m*; **a clever device** un gadget astucieux; **safety device** dispositif *m* de sécurité; **nuclear device** engin *m* nucléaire

(b) *Comput* (unité *f*) périphérique *m*

(c) *(scheme)* ruse *f*, stratagème *m*; **it was just a device to get attention** ce n'était qu'une ruse pour *ou* c'était juste un moyen de se faire remarquer; **to leave sb to their own devices** *(alone)* laisser qn s'occuper comme bon lui semble; *(without help)* laisser qn se débrouiller

(d) *Literary (figure of speech)* formule *f*

(e) *Her* emblème *m*

►► *Comput* ***device driver*** pilote *m* de périphérique

devil [ˈdevəl] *(Br pt & pp* **devilled,** *cont* **devilling,** *Am pt & pp* **deviled,** *cont* **deviling)** **1** *n* **(a)** *(demon)* diable *m*, démon *m*; *Rel* **the Devil** le Diable, Satan *m*; *Old-fashioned* **the devil take him!** qu'il aille au diable!, que le diable l'emporte!; *Fam Old-fashioned* **go to the devil!** va te faire voir!, va au diable!

(b) *Fam Fig (person)* **you little devil!** petit monstre!; **you lucky devil!** veinard!; *Br* **poor devil!** pauvre diable! *Br Hum* **go on, be a devil!** allez, laisse-toi faire *ou* tenter!

(c) *Fam (as intensifier)* **what the devil are you doing?** mais enfin, qu'est-ce que tu fabriques?; **where the devil is it?** où diable peut-il bien être?, mais où est-ce que ça pourrait bien être?; **how the devil should I know?** comment voulez-vous que je sache? ❑; **who the devil are you?** qui diable êtes-vous?, et d'où est-ce que vous sortez, vous?; **this house is the very devil to keep clean** c'est vraiment la galère de nettoyer cette maison; **they worked/ran like the devil** ils ont travaillé/couru comme des fous *ou* des malades; **he has a devil of a temper** il a un fichu caractère, il a un caractère de cochon; **I had a devil of a time getting here** j'ai eu un mal fou *ou* un mal de chien à arriver jusqu'ici; **there'll be the devil to pay when your father finds out** ça va barder quand ton père apprendra ça; **we had the devil of a job** *or* **the devil's own job finding the house** on a eu un mal fou à trouver la maison; **to be (caught) between the devil and the deep blue sea** être pris entre deux feux, être entre le marteau et l'enclume; **to give the devil his due...** en toute honnêteté, il faut dire que..., rendons *ou* rendons-lui justice...; **he has the luck of the devil** *or* **the devil's own luck** il a une veine de pendu *ou* de cocu; **speak** *or* **talk of the devil (and he's sure to appear)!** quand on parle du loup (on en voit la queue)!; *Prov* **better the devil you know (than the devil you don't)** mieux vaut se contenter de ce qu'on a que de risquer de trouver pire; *Prov* **the devil finds** *or* **makes work for idle hands (to do)** l'oisiveté est (la) mère de tous les vices; *Prov* **(every man for himself and) let the devil take the hindmost** chacun pour soi et Dieu pour tous

(d) *Tech (brazier)* brasero *m*

(e) *(ghostwriter)* nègre *m (d'un écrivain)*; *Law (assistant)* avocat(e) *m,f* stagiaire; *Typ* **printer's devil** apprenti(e) *m,f* imprimeur

2 *vt* **(a)** *Culin* accommoder à la moutarde et au poivre; **devilled egg** œuf *m* à la diable

(b) *Am Fam (harass)* harceler ❑

3 *vi Br* **to devil for sb** *(author)* servir de nègre à qn; *(lawyer)* être avocat stagiaire auprès de qn; *Typ (printer)* être apprenti imprimeur chez qn

►► ***devil's advocate*** avocat *m* du diable; **to play devil's advocate** se faire l'avocat du diable; *Am*

devil's food cake gâteau *m* au chocolat noir; *Culin* **devils on horseback** pruneaux *mpl* au bacon; ***Devil's Island*** l'île *f* du Diable; ***devil worship*** culte *m* du diable

devilfish ['devəlfɪʃ] *n Ich* mante *f*, diable *m* de mer

devilish ['devəlɪʃ] **1** *adj* (**a**) *(fiendish)* diabolique, infernal; *(mischievous)* espiègle (**b**) *Fam Old-fashioned (extreme)* sacré, satané

2 *adv Fam Old-fashioned* sacrément, rudement; **this work is devilish hard** ce travail est sacrément *ou* rudement dur

devilishly ['devəlɪʃlɪ] *adv* (**a**) *(fiendishly)* diaboliquement; *(mischievously)* par espièglerie (**b**) *Fam Old-fashioned (as intensifier)* rudement, sacrément

devilishness ['devəlɪʃnɪs] *n* (**a**) *(fiendishness)* caractère *m* diabolique (**b**) *(mischievousness)* espièglerie *f*

devil-may-care *adj (careless)* insouciant; *(reckless)* casse-cou

devilment ['devəlmənt] *n (mischief)* espièglerie *f*; *(malice)* méchanceté *f*, malice *f*; **a piece of devilment** une espièglerie, une diablerie; **out of sheer devilment** par pure méchanceté

devilry ['devəlrɪ] *n (UNCOUNT)* (**a**) *(mischief)* espièglerie *f*; *(recklessness)* témérité *f* (**b**) *(black magic)* magie *f* noire, maléfices *mpl*

devil-worshipper *n* adorateur(trice) *m,f* du diable

devious ['di:vɪəs] *adj* (**a**) *(cunning → person)* retors, sournois; *(→ means, method)* détourné; *(→ mind)* tortueux; **she can be very devious** elle est parfois très retorse *ou* sournoise (**b**) *(winding → route)* sinueux

deviously ['di:vɪəslɪ] *adv* sournoisement

deviousness ['di:vɪəsnɪs] *n (of person)* sournoiserie *f*; *(of plan)* complexité *f*

devise [dɪ'vaɪz] **1** *vt* (**a**) *(plan)* imaginer, inventer, concevoir, élaborer; *(plot)* combiner, manigancer (**b**) *Law (property)* léguer

2 *n* legs *m* (de biens immobiliers)

deviser [dɪ'vaɪzə(r)] *n (of plan)* inventeur(trice) *m,f*; *(of scheme)* auteur *m*

devising [dɪ'vaɪzɪŋ] *n* **a scheme of his own devising** un plan de son invention

devitalize, -ise [,di:'vaɪtəlaɪz] *vt* affaiblir

devitrification ['di:,vɪtrɪfɪ'keɪʃən] *n* dévitrification *f*

devitrify [,di:'vɪtrɪfaɪ] *(pt & pp* **devitrified**) **1** *vt* dévitrifier

2 *vi* se dévitrifier

devocalize, -ise [,di:'vəʊkəlaɪz] *vt* assourdir

devoice [,di:'vɔɪs] *vt* assourdir

devoid [dɪ'vɔɪd] *adj* **devoid of** dépourvu de, dénué de; **devoid of interest** dépourvu d'intérêt, sans intérêt

devolution [,di:və'lu:ʃən] *n* (**a**) *(of duty, power)* délégation *f*; *Law (of property)* transmission *f*, dévolution *f* (**b**) *Pol* décentralisation *f* (**c**) *Biol* dégénérescence *f*

DEVOLUTION

Le projet de décentralisation pour l'Écosse et le pays de Galles ("devolution"), soumis à référendum dans les années soixante-dix, fut [illegible] à la tête de la Grande-Bretagne de 1979 à 1997. Cependant, à la suite de la victoire des travaillistes en 1997, Tony Blair honora sa promesse électorale et organisa un nouveau référendum dans les deux régions. Les Écossais se déclarèrent en faveur de la décentralisation à une écrasante majorité. Le "oui" l'emporta également au Pays de Galles mais de façon moins convaincante. Moins de deux ans plus tard, le 6 mai 1999, l'Écosse retrouvait un parlement après 300 ans d'interruption et les Gallois disposaient d'une assemblée pour la première fois en 500 ans (voir aussi encadrés sous **Scottish Parliament** et **Welsh Assembly**).

devolutionary [,di:və'lu:ʃənərɪ] *adj* (**a**) *Law* dévolutif (**b**) *Pol* décentralisateur

devolutionist [,di:və'lu:ʃənɪst] *Pol* **1** *adj* décentralisateur

2 *n* partisan *m* de la décentralisation

devolve [dɪ'vɒlv] **1** *vi* (**a**) *(duty, job)* incomber; *(by chance)* incomber, échoir; **it devolves on** *or* **upon me to decide** c'est à moi (qu'il incombe) de décider; **the responsibility devolves on** *or* **upon him** la responsabilité lui incombe *ou* lui échoit

(**b**) *Law (estate)* passer; **the property devolves on** *or* **upon the son** les biens passent *ou* sont transmis au fils

2 *vt* déléguer; **to devolve sth on** *or* **upon** *or* **to sb** déléguer qch à qn, transmettre qch à qn

►► *Pol* ***devolved parliament*** ≃ parlement *m* régional

Devon ['devən] *n* le Devon, = comté dans le sud-ouest de l'Angleterre; **in Devon** dans le Devon

Devonian [de'vəʊnɪən] *Geol* **1** *adj* dévonien

2 *n* dévonien *m*

Devonshire cream ['devənʃə(r)-] *n Culin* crème *f* caillée

devote [dɪ'vəʊt] *vt* consacrer; **to devote oneself to** *(study, work)* se consacrer *ou* s'adonner à; *(a cause)* se vouer *ou* se consacrer à; *(pleasure)* se livrer à; **she devotes all her energies to writing** elle se consacre entièrement à l'écriture; **all funds are devoted entirely to research** tous les crédits sont entièrement consacrés *ou* affectés à la recherche

devoted [dɪ'vəʊtɪd] *adj* (**a**) *(friend, servant, service)* dévoué, fidèle; *(husband, wife, mother, father)* dévoué; *(admirer)* fervent; **they are devoted to each other** ils sont dévoués l'un à l'autre; **I'm devoted to my children** je ferais tout pour mes enfants (**b**) *Arch or Literary (doomed)* voué au malheur; **blows fell thick and fast upon his devoted head** il courbait la tête sous les coups du malheur

devotedly [dɪ'vəʊtɪdlɪ] *adv* avec dévouement

devotee [,devə'ti:] *n (of opera, sport etc)* passionné(e) *m,f*; *(of doctrine)* adepte *mf*, partisan(e) *m,f*; *(of religion)* adepte *mf*; **a devotee of Haydn** un fervent *ou* un grand amateur de Haydn; **a devotee of classical music** un passionné de musique classique

devotion [dɪ'vəʊʃən] **1** *n* (**a**) *(to person)* dévouement *m*, attachement *m*; *(to cause)* dévouement *m*; **no one doubts her devotion to her work** personne ne met en doute *ou* ne doute de son dévouement professionnel; **he showed great devotion to duty** il a prouvé son sens du devoir (**b**) *Rel* dévotion *f*, piété *f*

2 devotions *npl Rel* dévotions *fpl*, prières *fpl*

devotional [dɪ'vəʊʃənəl] *Rel* **1** *adj (book, work)* de dévotion *ou* piété; *(attitude)* de prière, pieux

2 *n* service *m* (religieux)

devour [dɪ'vaʊə(r)] *vt* (**a**) *(food)* dévorer, engloutir; *Fig (book)* dévorer; **he devoured her with his eyes** il l'a dévorée des yeux (**b**) *(of fire)* dévorer, consumer; *Fig* **devoured by hatred** dévoré par la haine

devourer [dɪ'vaʊərə(r)] *n* dévorateur(trice) *m,f* (**of** de)

devouring [dɪ'vaʊərɪŋ] *adj (hunger, jealousy)* dévorant; *(interest)* ardent; *(need)* urgent

devout [dɪ'vaʊt] *adj (person)* pieux, dévot; *(hope, prayer)* fervent; **a devout Catholic/Muslim** un catholique/musulman fervent

devoutly [dɪ'vaʊtlɪ] *adv* (**a**) *(pray)* avec dévotion, dévotement (**b**) *Formal (earnestly)* sincèrement; **I devoutly hope that some good comes of this war** j'espère vivement *ou* profondément [illegible]

devoutness [dɪ'vaʊtnɪs] *n* dévotion *f*

dew [dju:] *n* rosée *f*

►► *Met* ***dew point*** point *m* de rosée

dewberry ['dju:berɪ] *n* ronce *f* arctique; **European dewberry** ronce *f* bleue

dewclaw ['dju:klɔ:] *n Zool* ergot *m*

dewdrop ['dju:drɒp] *n* goutte *f* de rosée; *Fam Fig* **he had a dewdrop on the end of his nose** il avait la goutte au nez

Dewey Decimal System ['dju:ɪ-] *n* classification *f* décimale de Dewey

dewfall ['dju:fɔ:l] *n* formation *f* de la rosée, *Literary* serein *m*; *Literary (evening)* tombée *f* de la nuit

dewlap ['dju:læp] *n also Hum* fanon *m*

deworm [,di:'wɜ:m] *vt* administrer un vermifuge à

dewpond ['dju:pɒnd] *n Br* mare *f* artificielle *(alimentée par les eaux de condensation)*

dewy ['dju:ɪ] *(compar* **dewier**, *superl* **dewiest**) *adj* couvert *ou* humide de rosée; *Fig* **dewy complexion** teint *m* frais

dewy-eyed *adj (innocent)* innocent; *(trusting)* naïf, ingénu; **she looked at him dewy-eyed** elle l'a regardé d'un air ingénu; **she gets all dewy-eyed about her husband/France** elle est tout émue quand elle parle de son mari/la France

dexamphetamine [,deksæm'fetəmi:n] *n Pharm* dexamphétamine *f*

Dexedrine® ['deksɪdri:n] *n Pharm* Dexédrine® *f*

dexter ['dekstə(r)] *adj Her* dextre

dexterity [dek'sterətɪ] *n* adresse *f*, dextérité *f*; **the job requires great dexterity** ce travail nécessite beaucoup d'adresse

dexterous ['dekstrəs] *adj* (**a**) *(person)* adroit, habile; *(movement)* adroit, habile, agile (**b**) *Formal (right-handed)* droitier

dexterously ['dekstrəslɪ] *adv* adroitement, habilement

dextral ['dekstrəl] *adj* (**a**) *Her* dextre (**b**) *(person)* droitier (**b**) *(located on the right hand side)* situé à droite

dextran ['dekstrən] *n Chem & Med* dextran *m*

dextrin ['dekstrɪn] *n Biol & Chem* dextrine *f*

dextrorotatory [,dekstrəʊrəʊ'teɪtərɪ] *adj Formal* dextrorsum

dextrose ['dekstrəʊs] *n Chem* dextrose *m*

dextrous = **dexterous**

dextrously = **dexterously**

dexy ['deksɪ] *n Fam Drugs slang (dexamphetamine)* amphé *f*, amphet *f*

DF [,di:'ef] *n (abbr* **Direction Finder**) radiogoniomètre *m*

DFC [,di:ef'si:] *n Mil (abbr* **Distinguished Flying Cross**) = distinction honorifique des armées de l'air américaine et britannique

DFE [,di:ef'i:] *n Admin (abbr* **Department for Education**) ministère *m* de l'Éducation

DFM [,di:ef'em] *n Mil (abbr* **Distinguished Flying Medal**) = médaille des armées de l'air américaine et britannique

DG [,di:'dʒi:] **1** *n (abbr* **director-general**) directeur(trice) *m,f* général(e)

2 *adv (written abbr* **Deo Gratias**) Dieu merci

DH [,di:'eɪtʃ] *n Br Admin (abbr* **Department of Health**) ministère *m* de la Santé

dhal [dɑ:l] *n Bot* = sorte de légumineuse; *Culin* = plat à base de lentilles et d'épices

dhoti ['dəʊtɪ] *n* pagne *m*

dhow [daʊ] *n Naut* = petit bateau arabe à une voile

DHSS [,di:eɪtʃ,es'es] *n* (**a**) *Br Formerly Admin (abbr* **Department of Health and Social Security**) = ancien nom du ministère britannique de la Santé et de la Sécurité sociale (**b**) *Am Admin (abbr* **Department of Health and Social Services**) ≃ ministère *m* de la Santé

diabetes [,daɪə'bi:ti:z] *n* diabète *m*; **to have diabetes** avoir du diabète; **diabetes sufferer** diabétique *mf*

diabetic [,daɪə'betɪk] **1** *adj* diabétique; **to be in a diabetic coma** faire un *ou* être en coma diabétique

2 *n* diabétique *mf*

3 *comp (biscuits, jam)* pour diabétiques

diabolic [,daɪə'bɒlɪk] *adj (action, plan)* diabolique, infernal; *(look, smile)* diabolique, satanique

diabolical [,daɪə'bɒlɪkəl] *adj* (**a**) *(fiendish → action, plan)* diabolique, infernal; *(→ look, smile)* diabolique, satanique (**b**) *Br Fam (terrible)* nul; **the food was diabolical** la nourriture était infecte; **she speaks diabolical French** elle parle français comme une vache espagnole; **I think it's a diabolical liberty** il faut un toupet monstre *ou* un sacré culot pour faire une chose pareille

diabolically [,daɪə'bɒlɪklɪ] *adv* (**a**) *(fiendishly)* diaboliquement, de manière diabolique (**b**) *Br Fam (for emphasis)* vachement, sacrément

diabolism [daɪ'æbəlɪzəm] *n (black magic)* diablerie *f*, magie *f* noire; *(witchcraft)* sorcellerie *f*; *(satanism)* satanisme *m*, diabolisme *m*

diabolist [daɪ'æbəlɪst] *n* démoniste *mf*

diabolize, -ise [daɪ'æbəlaɪz] *vt (demonize)* rendre démoniaque; *(cast spell on)* soumettre à une influence démoniaque

diabolo [dɪ'æbələʊ] *n (game)* diabolo *m*

diachronic [,daɪə'krɒnɪk] *adj Ling* diachronique

diachronism [daɪ'ækrənɪzəm], **diachrony** [daɪ'ækrənɪ] *n Ling* diachronie *f*

diacid [daɪˈæsɪd] *Chem* **1** *adj* biacide, diacide
 2 *n* biacide *m*, diacide *m*
diaconal [daɪˈækənəl] *adj Rel* diaconal
diaconate [daɪˈækəneɪt] *n Rel* diaconat *m*
diacritic [ˌdaɪəˈkrɪtɪk] *Ling* **1** *adj* diacritique
 2 *n* signe *m* diacritique
diacritical [ˌdaɪəˈkrɪtɪkəl] *adj Ling* diacritique
diactinic [ˌdaɪækˈtɪnɪk] *adj Phys & Opt* capable de transmettre des rayons actiniques
diadem [ˈdaɪədem] *n* diadème *m*; *Literary* **to assume the diadem** ceindre le diadème
diaeresis, *Am* **dieresis** [daɪˈerɪsɪs] (*Br pl* **diaereses,** *Am* **diereses** [-ˌsiːz]) (**a**) *Ling & Literature* diérèse *f* (**b**) *Comput & Typ* tréma *m*
diagenesis [ˌdaɪəˈdʒenɪsɪs] *n Geol* diagénèse *f*
diagnosable [ˌdaɪəgˈnəʊzəbəl] *adj* susceptible d'être diagnostiqué, décelable
diagnose [ˈdaɪəgnəʊz] *vt* (**a**) *Med (illness)* diagnostiquer; **they diagnosed her illness as cancer** ils ont diagnostiqué un cancer; **she has been diagnosed as a schizophrenic** d'après le diagnostic, elle est schizophrène (**b**) *Fig (fault, problem)* déceler, discerner
diagnosis [ˌdaɪəgˈnəʊsɪs] (*pl* **diagnoses** [-siːz]) *n Med & Fig* diagnostic *m*; *Biol & Bot* diagnose *f*; **to make** *or* **give a diagnosis** faire un diagnostic
diagnostic [ˌdaɪəgˈnɒstɪk] *adj* diagnostique; **diagnostic skill/ability** talent *m*/capacité *f* à diagnostiquer
 ►► *Com* ***diagnostic audit*** audit *m* de diagnostic; *Comput* ***diagnostic disk*** disquette *f* de diagnostic; *Comput* ***diagnostic program*** programme *m* de diagnostic
diagnostician [ˌdaɪəgnɒsˈtɪʃən] *n* diagnostiqueur *m*; **she's an excellent diagnostician** elle fait de très bons diagnostics
diagnostics [ˌdaɪəgˈnɒstɪks] *n (UNCOUNT) Comput & Med* diagnostic *m*
diagonal [daɪˈægənəl] **1** *adj* diagonal
 2 *n* diagonale *f*
diagonally [daɪˈægənəlɪ] *adv* en diagonale, diagonalement, obliquement; **we cut diagonally across the field** nous avons traversé le champ en diagonale *ou* en biais; **his desk is diagonally across from mine** son bureau est en diagonale par rapport au mien; **a ribbon worn diagonally across the chest** un ruban porté en écharpe sur la poitrine
diagonal-ply tyre *n* pneu *m* à carcasse diagonale
diagram [ˈdaɪəgræm] (*Br pt & pp* **diagrammed,** *cont* **diagramming**, *Am pt & pp* **diagramed** *or* **diagrammed,** *cont* **diagraming** *or* **diagramming**) **1** *n (gen)* diagramme *m*, schéma *m*; *Geom & Math* diagramme *m*, figure *f*; **to draw** *or* **make a diagram of sth** faire un schéma *ou* un dessin de qch; *Fig* **do I need to draw you a diagram?** est-ce que je dois te faire un dessin?
 2 *vt* donner une représentation graphique de
diagrammatic [ˌdaɪəgrəˈmætɪk] *adj* schématique
dial [ˈdaɪəl] (*Br pt & pp* **dialled,** *cont* **dialling**, *Am pt & pp* **dialed,** *cont* **dialing**) **1** *n* (**a**) *(of clock, telephone)* cadran *m*; *(of radio, TV)* bouton *m* (de réglage); **tune in to 98 on the FM dial** réglez vos postes sur 98 sur la bande FM
 (**b**) *Br Fam Old-fashioned (face)* tronche *f*
 2 *vt (number)* faire, composer; **to dial a wrong number** faire *ou* composer un mauvais *ou* faux numéro; **the number you have dialled has not been recognized** ≃ il n'y a pas d'abonné au numéro que vous avez demandé; **to dial Spain direct** appeler l'Espagne par l'automatique; **dial the operator** appelez l'opératrice; **to dial** *Br* **999** *or Am* **911** ≃ appeler Police Secours; **dial-a-joke/-disc** la plaisanterie/le disque du jour par téléphone
 ►► *Am* ***dial code*** indicatif *m*; *Am* ***dial tone*** tonalité *f*

'Dial M for Murder' *Hitchcock* 'Le Crime était presque parfait'

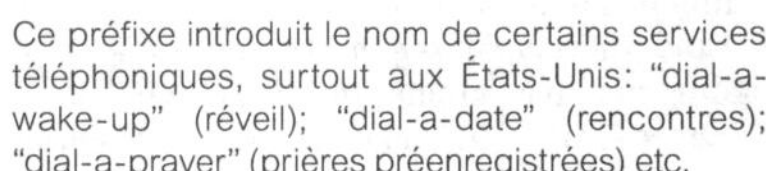

DIAL-A-...

Ce préfixe introduit le nom de certains services téléphoniques, surtout aux États-Unis: "dial-a-wake-up" (réveil); "dial-a-date" (rencontres); "dial-a-prayer" (prières préenregistrées) etc.

dial. (*written abbr* **dialect**) dial.
dialect [ˈdaɪəlekt] *n Ling (regional)* dialecte *m*, parler *m*; *(local, rural)* patois *m*
dialectal [ˌdaɪəˈlektəl] *adj Ling* dialectal, de dialecte
dialectic [ˌdaɪəˈlektɪk] *Ling* **1** *adj* dialectique
 2 *n* dialectique *f*
dialectical [ˌdaɪəˈlektɪkəl] *adj Phil* dialectique
 ►► *Phil* ***dialectical materialism*** matérialisme *m* dialectique
dialectically [ˌdaɪəˈlektɪkəlɪ] *adv Phil* dialectiquement
dialectician [ˌdaɪəlekˈtɪʃən] *n Phil* dialecticien(enne) *m,f*
dialectics [ˌdaɪəˈlektɪks] *n (UNCOUNT) Phil* dialectique *f*
dialectologist [ˌdaɪəlekˈtɒlədʒɪst] *n Ling* dialectologue *mf*
dialectology [ˌdaɪəlekˈtɒlədʒɪ] *n Ling* dialectologie *f*
dialler [ˈdaɪələ(r)] *n* composeur *m* de numéros
dialling, *Am* **dialing** [ˈdaɪəlɪŋ] *n* composition *f* du numéro, numérotation *f*
 ►► ***dialling code*** indicatif *m*; ***dialling tone*** tonalité *f*; **I can't get a dialling tone** je n'arrive pas à avoir la tonalité
dialogue, *Am* **dialog** [ˈdaɪəlɒg] *n* dialogue *m*
 ►► *Comput* ***dialogue box*** zone *f ou* boîte *f* de dialogue; ***dialogue mode*** mode *m* dialogue
dial-up *n Comput & Tel*
 ►► ***dial-up access*** accès *m* commuté; *Br* ***dial-up account*** compte *m* d'accès par ligne commutée; ***dial-up line*** ligne *f* commutée; ***dial-up modem*** modem *m* réseau commuté; ***dial-up service*** service *m* de télétraitement
dialyse, *Am* **dialyze** [ˈdaɪəlaɪz] *vt Chem* dialyser
dialysis [daɪˈælɪsɪs] (*pl* **dialyses** [-siːz]) *n Chem & Med* dialyse *f*; **to be on dialysis** être sous dialyse
 ►► ***dialysis machine*** dialyseur *m*
diamanté [dɪəˈmɒnteɪ] *n* tissu *m* diamanté
diamantine [ˌdaɪəˈmæntaɪn] *adj* diamantin
diameter [daɪˈæmɪtə(r)] *n* (**a**) *(gen) & Geom* diamètre *m*; **the tree is two metres in diameter** l'arbre fait deux mètres de diamètre (**b**) *(of microscope)* unité *f* de grossissement
diametric [ˌdaɪəˈmetrɪk], **diametrical** [ˌdaɪəˈmetrɪkəl] *adj Geom & Fig* diamétral
diametrically [ˌdaɪəˈmetrɪklɪ] *adv Geom & Fig* diamétralement; **diametrically opposed** diamétralement opposé
diamond [ˈdaɪəmənd] **1** *n* (**a**) *(gem)* diamant *m*; *esp Am* **he's a diamond in the rough** il a un cœur d'or sous ses dehors frustes
 (**b**) *(shape)* losange *m*
 (**c**) *Cards* carreau *m*; **the ace/jack of diamonds** l'as/le valet de carreau; **do you have any diamonds?** avez-vous du carreau?; **diamonds are trumps** atout carreau
 (**d**) *Sport (in baseball)* terrain *m* (de baseball)
 2 *comp (brooch, ring etc)* de diamant *ou* diamants
 ►► ***diamond anniversary*** noces *fpl* de diamant; ***diamond drill*** foreuse *f* à pointe de diamant; ***diamond jubilee*** (célébration *f* du) soixantième anniversaire *m*; *Am Aut* ***diamond lane*** = voie réservée, les jours de grande circulation, aux voitures à deux passagers ou plus; ***diamond merchant*** diamantaire *m*; ***diamond mine*** mine *f* de diamants; ***diamond necklace*** collier *m ou* rivière *f* de diamants; ***the Diamond State*** = surnom donné au Delaware; ***diamond wedding*** noces *fpl* de diamant

'A Diamond as big as the Ritz' *Fitzgerald* 'Un Diamant gros comme le Ritz'

diamondback [ˈdaɪəməndbæk] *n Zool (snake)* = sorte de crotale; *(turtle)* = sorte de tortue d'eau douce
diamond-shaped *adj* en forme de losange
diamorphine [ˌdaɪəˈmɔːfiːn] *n Chem* diamorphine *f*, diacétylmorphine *f*
Diana [daɪˈænə] *pr n Myth* Diane
dianthus [daɪˈænθəs] *n Bot* dianthus *m*
diapason [ˌdaɪəˈpeɪsən] *n Mus* diapason *m*; *(of organ)* principaux jeux *mpl* de fond
diaper [ˈdaɪəpə(r)] *n* (**a**) *Am (nappy)* couche *f* (*de bébé*) (**b**) *(fabric)* damassé *m*

diaphanous [daɪˈæfənəs] *adj* diaphane
diaphone [ˈdaɪəfəʊn] *n* (**a**) *Ling* = série complète des phonèmes d'une langue (**b**) *(foghorn)* sirène *f* de brume à deux tons
diaphony [daɪˈæfənɪ] *n Mus* diaphonie *f*
diaphoretic [ˌdaɪəfəˈretɪk] *Med* **1** *n* diaphorétique *m*
 2 *adj* diaphorétique
diaphragm [ˈdaɪəfræm] *n* (**a**) *Anat* diaphragme *m* (**b**) *Phot* diaphragme (**c**) *(contraceptive)* diaphragme *m*
diaphragmatic [ˈdaɪəˌfrægˈmætɪk] *adj Anat* diaphragmatique
diaphysis [daɪˈæfɪsɪs] *n Anat & Bot* diaphyse *f*
diapositive [ˌdaɪəˈpɒzɪtɪv] *n Phot* diapositive *f*
diarchy [ˈdaɪɑːkɪ] *n* (**a**) *Pol* dyarchie *f* (**b**) *Bot* structure *f* diarche
diarist [ˈdaɪərɪst] *n (private)* auteur *m* d'un journal intime; *(of public affairs)* chroniqueur *m*
diarrhoea, *Am* **diarrhea** [ˌdaɪəˈrɪə] *n* diarrhée *f*; **to have diarrhoea** avoir la diarrhée
diarrhoeal, *Am* **diarrheal** [daɪəˈrɪəl], **diarrhoeic,** *Am* **diarrheic** [daɪəˈriːɪk] *adj* diarrhéique
diary [ˈdaɪərɪ] (*pl* **diaries**) *n* (**a**) *(personal)* journal *m* (intime); **to keep a diary** tenir un journal (**b**) *Br (for business)* agenda *m*; **I've written it down in my diary** je l'ai noté dans mon agenda
diascope [ˈdaɪəskəʊp] *n Opt & Phot* diascope *m*
Diaspora [daɪˈæspərə] *n Hist & Fig* diaspora *f*
diastema [ˌdaɪəˈstiːmə] (*pl* **diastemata** [daɪəˈstiːmətə]) *n Anat & Zool* diastème *f*
diastole [daɪˈæstəlɪ] *n Physiol* diastole *f*
diastolic [ˌdaɪəˈstɒlɪk] *adj Physiol* diastolique
diathermy [ˈdaɪəθɜːmɪ] *n Med* diathermie *f*
diathesis [daɪˈæθɪsɪs] *n Med* diathèse *f*
diatom [ˈdaɪətɒm] *n Bot & Geol* diatomée *f*
diatomaceous [ˌdaɪətəˈmeɪʃəs] *adj Bot & Geol* **diatomaceous earth** diatomite *f*, terre *f* d'infusoires
diatomic [ˌdaɪəˈtɒmɪk] *adj Chem* diatomique
diatomite [daɪˈætəmaɪt] *n Geol* diatomite *f*
diatonic [ˌdaɪəˈtɒnɪk] *adj Mus* diatonique
 ►► ***diatonic scale*** gamme *f* diatonique
diatribe [ˈdaɪətraɪb] *n* diatribe *f*
diazepam [daɪˈæzɪpæm] *n Pharm* diazépam *m*
diazo [daɪˈæzəʊ, daɪˈeɪzəʊ] *adj Chem*
 ►► ***diazo compound*** diazoïque *m*; ***diazo reaction*** diazo-réaction *f*
dib [dɪb] (*pt & pp* **dibbed,** *cont* **dibbing**) *vi Fishing* pêcher à la ligne flottante
dibasic [daɪˈbeɪsɪk] *adj Chem* dibasique
dibber [ˈdɪbə(r)] *n Br Hort* plantoir *m*
dibble [ˈdɪbəl] **1** *n Hort* plantoir *m*
 2 *vt* (**a**) *Hort (plant)* repiquer au plantoir; *(seeds)* semer au plantoir (**b**) *(dabble)* **they dibbled their feet in the water** ils ont trempé les pieds dans l'eau
 3 *vi Hort* semer/repiquer au plantoir
dibs [dɪbz] *npl* (**a**) *(jacks)* osselets *mpl* (**b**) *Fam (claim)* **to have dibs on sth** avoir des droits sur qch ▫ (**c**) *Br Fam (money)* fric *m*, pognon *m*
dice [daɪs] (*pl* **inv**) **1** *n* (**a**) *(game)* dé *m*; **to throw the dice** lancer le(s) dé(s); **to play dice** jouer aux dés; *Am Fam* **no dice!** des clous! (**b**) *Culin* dé *m*, cube *m*
 2 *vt Culin* couper en dés *ou* en cubes
 3 *vi Br* jouer aux dés; **to dice with death** jouer avec sa vie
dicey [ˈdaɪsɪ] *Br* (*compar* **dicier,** *superl* **diciest**) *adj Fam* risqué
dichotomize, -ise [daɪˈkɒtəmaɪz] **1** *vi* (se) dichotomiser
 2 *vt* dichotomiser
dichotomous [daɪˈkɒtəməs] *adj* dichotomique
 ►► *Mktg* ***dichotomous question*** *(in survey)* question *f* dichotomique
dichotomy [daɪˈkɒtəmɪ] (*pl* **dichotomies**) *n* dichotomie *f*
dichroism [ˈdaɪkrəʊɪzəm] *n Phys* dichroïsme *m*
dichromatic [ˌdaɪkrəʊˈmætɪk] *adj Med & Zool* dichromatique
Dick [dɪk] *pr n* **Dick and Jane** = personnages de livres scolaires américains des années 50–60
 ►► ***Dick Turpin*** = bandit de grand chemin devenu héros populaire; ***Dick Whittington*** = personnage de conte de fées et de pantomime, toujours accompagné d'un chat
dick [dɪk] *n* (**a**) *Vulg (penis)* bite *f*, queue *f* (**b**) *Am*

Fam (detective) privé *m* (**c**) *very Fam (idiot)* con *m*

dickens [ˈdɪkɪnz] *n Fam* **what the dickens are you doing?** mais qu'est-ce que tu fabriques?; **a dickens of a noise** un bruit d'enfer; **we had a dickens of a job getting a babysitter** ça a été la galère *ou* la croix et la bannière pour trouver une baby-sitter

Dickensian [dɪˈkenzɪən] *adj (scene, Christmas etc)* à la Dickens; *(conditions)* qui sort d'un roman de Dickens

dicker [ˈdɪkə(r)] *vi* marchander; **to dicker with sb (for sth)** marchander avec qn (pour obtenir qch)

dickey [ˈdɪkɪ] *n* (**a**) *(shirt)* faux plastron *m* (de chemise) (**b**) *Br (in carriage)* siège *m* du cocher; *Aut* spider *m*, strapontin *m* (**c**) *Br Fam (bow tie)* nœud *m* pap (**d**) *Br Fam (donkey)* âne ❑ *m*

▸▸ *Br Fam* ***dickey bow*** nœud *m* pap

dickhead [ˈdɪkhed] *n very Fam* con *m*

dicky [ˈdɪkɪ] (*pl* **dickies**, *compar* **dickier**, *superl* **dickiest**) **1** *n* = **dickey**

2 *adj Br Fam (ladder)* peu solide ❑, branlant; *(situation)* peu sûr ❑; **to have a dicky heart** avoir le palpitant fragile

dickybird [ˈdɪkɪbɜːd] *n Br Fam* (**a**) *(in children's language)* petit oiseau *m* (**b**) *(rhyming slang* **word***)* mot ❑ *m*; **not a dickybird!** motus et bouche cousue!; **did you hear anything? – not a dickybird** tu as entendu quelque chose? – non, que dalle

dicotyledon [ˌdaɪkɒtɪˈliːdən] *n Bot* dicotylédone *f*

dicta [ˈdɪktə] *pl of* **dictum**

Dictaphone® [ˈdɪktəfəʊn] *n* Dictaphone® *m*, machine *f* à dicter

dictate 1 *vt* [dɪkˈteɪt] (**a**) *(letter)* dicter; **to dictate sth to sb** dicter qch à qn

(**b**) *(determine → terms, conditions)* dicter, imposer; **he dictates how we run the business** c'est lui qui décide de la marche de l'entreprise; **our budget will dictate the type of computer we buy** le type d'ordinateur que nous achèterons dépendra de notre budget

2 *vi* [dɪkˈteɪt] *(give dictation)* dicter

3 *n* [ˈdɪkteɪt] (**a**) *(order)* ordre *m*

(**b**) *(usu pl) (principle)* précepte *m*; **the dictates of conscience/reason** la voix de la conscience/raison

▸**dictate to** *vt insep* donner des ordres à; **I won't be dictated to** je n'ai pas d'ordres à recevoir!

dictating machine [dɪkˈteɪtɪŋ-] *n* machine *f* à dicter

dictation [dɪkˈteɪʃən] *n (of letter, story)* dictée *f*; **to take dictation** écrire sous la dictée; **at dictation speed** à la vitesse d'une dictée; *Sch* **to do dictation** faire la dictée; **French dictation** dictée *f* de français

dictator [dɪkˈteɪtə(r)] *n* dictateur *m*

dictatorial [ˌdɪktəˈtɔːrɪəl] *adj* (**a**) *(power)* dictatorial (**b**) *(tone)* impérieux, autoritaire; *(person)* tyrannique

dictatorially [ˌdɪktəˈtɔːrɪəlɪ] *adv* dictatorialement, en dictateur

dictatorship [dɪkˈteɪtəʃɪp] *n* dictature *f*

diction [ˈdɪkʃən] *n* (**a**) *(pronunciation)* diction *f*, élocution *f*; **to have good diction** avoir une bonne diction (**b**) *(phrasing)* style *m*, langage *m*

dictionary [ˈdɪkʃənərɪ] (*pl* **dictionaries**) **1** *n* dictionnaire *m*; **a French-English dictionary** un dictionnaire français-anglais; **look it up in the dictionary** cherchez dans le dictionnaire

2 *comp (entry)* de dictionnaire

▸▸ ***dictionary definition*** définition *f* de dictionnaire; **the dictionary definition of love** l'amour tel que le définit le dictionnaire

Dictograph® [ˈdɪktəgrɑːf] *n* appareil *m* enregistreur (pour écoutes téléphoniques)

dictum [ˈdɪktəm] (*pl* **dicta** [-tə] *or* **dictums**) *n Formal* (**a**) *(statement)* affirmation *f*; *Law* remarque *f* superfétatoire (**b**) *(maxim)* dicton *m*, maxime *f*

dicty [ˈdɪktɪ] *n Am Fam (snob)* snob ❑ *mf*

did [dɪd] *pt of* **do**

didactic [dɪˈdæktɪk] **1** *adj* didactique

2 didactics *n (UNCOUNT)* didactique *f*

didactically [dɪˈdæktɪklɪ] *adv* didactiquement

didacticism [dɪˈdæktɪsɪzəm] *n* le didactique

diddle [ˈdɪdəl] **1** *vt Br Fam* duper, rouler; **to diddle sb out of sth** carotter qch à qn; **I've been diddled** je me suis fait avoir

2 *vi Am very Fam (have sex)* baiser

diddler [ˈdɪdlə(r)] *n Br Fam* escroqueur(euse) *m,f*

diddly [ˈdɪdlɪ] *n Am Fam* que dalle; **that's not worth diddly** ça ne vaut pas un clou; **I don't know diddly about computers** l'informatique, j'y pige que dalle

diddlyshit [ˈdɪdəlɪʃɪt] *n Am very Fam* **I don't give a diddlyshit** je m'en balance, je m'en fous complètement

diddly-squat *n Am Fam* que dalle; **that's not worth diddly-squat** ça ne vaut pas un clou; **I don't know diddly-squat about computers** l'informatique, j'y pige que dalle

diddums [ˈdɪdəmz] *n Fam* pauvre petit(e) *m,f*

didgeridoo [ˌdɪdʒərɪˈduː] *n* didgeridoo *m (instrument à vent des Aborigènes d'Australie)*

didn't [ˈdɪdənt] = **did not**

Dido [ˈdaɪdəʊ] *pr n Myth* Didon

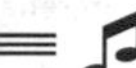

'Dido and Aeneas' *Purcell* 'Didon et Énée'

didst [dɪdst] *Arch 2nd pers sing of* **did**

DIE[1] [daɪ]

mourir	▸ **1 (a), (b), (d); 2**
caler	▸ **1 (c)**
s'éteindre	▸ **1 (d)**
avoir envie	▸ **1 (e)**

1 *vi* (**a**) *(person)* mourir, décéder; **she's dying** *(has incurable illness)* elle est condamnée; *(is in her death throes)* elle est mourante *ou* à l'agonie; **she died of cancer** elle est morte du *ou* d'un cancer; **he died from his wounds** il est mort des suites de ses blessures; **thousands are dying of hunger** des milliers de gens meurent de faim; *Literary* **she died by her own hand** elle s'est suicidée *ou* donné la mort, elle a mis fin à ses jours; **to die a hero** mourir en héros; **he left us to die** il nous a abandonnés à la mort; **to die in one's bed** mourir dans son lit; *Fam Fig* **to die laughing** mourir de rire; *Fam* **I nearly died, I could have died** *(from fear)* j'étais mort de trouille; *(from embarrassment)* j'aurais voulu rentrer sous terre, je ne savais plus où me mettre; **he'll do it or die in the attempt** il y arrivera coûte que coûte; **to die with one's boots on** *or* **in harness** mourir debout *ou* en pleine activité; **never say die!** *(don't give up)* il ne faut jamais désespérer!; *(stay cheerful)* courage!, tenez bon!

(**b**) *(animal, plant)* mourir

(**c**) *(engine)* caler, s'arrêter; *(battery)* se mettre à plat

(**d**) *(fire, love, memory)* s'éteindre, mourir; *(tradition)* s'éteindre, disparaître, mourir; *(smile)* disparaître, s'évanouir; **old habits die hard** les mauvaises habitudes ne se perdent pas facilement; **her secret died with her** elle a emporté son secret dans la tombe

(**e**) *Fam* **to be dying for sth** *(want very much)* avoir une envie folle de qch; **I'm dying for a drink** j'ai une envie folle de boire qch; **to be dying to do sth** mourir d'envie de faire qch; **she's dying to see him** elle meurt d'envie de le voir

2 *vt* **to die a natural/violent death** mourir de sa belle mort/de mort violente

▸**die away** *vi* s'affaiblir, s'éteindre, mourir

▸**die back** *vi (plant)* dépérir

▸**die down** *vi* (**a**) *(wind)* tomber, se calmer; *(fire → in chimney)* baisser; *(→ in building, forest)* s'apaiser, diminuer; *(noise)* diminuer; *(anger, protest)* se calmer, s'apaiser

(**b**) *(plant)* se flétrir, perdre ses feuilles et sa tige

▸**die off** *vi* mourir les uns après les autres

▸**die out** *vi (family, tribe, tradition)* disparaître, s'éteindre; *(fire)* s'éteindre; **the panda is in danger of dying out** le panda est menacé d'extinction

die[2] *n* (*pl sense* (**a**) **dice** [daɪs], *pl sense* (**b**) **dies**) (**a**) *(dice)* dé *m* (à jouer); *Fig* **the die is cast** les dés sont jetés (**b**) *Archit (dado)* dé *m (d'un piédestal)*; *Tech (stamp)* matrice *f*; *(in minting)* coin *m*; **stamping die** étampe *f*; **as straight as a die** franc comme l'or

dieback [ˈdaɪbæk] *n Bot* = maladie des plantes se traduisant par un dépérissement des pousses

die-cast *Tech* **1** *vt* mouler sous pression *ou* en matrice

2 *adj* moulé sous pression *ou* en matrice

die-casting *n Tech* moulage *m* en matrice

dieffenbachia [ˌdiːfənˈbækɪə] *n Bot* dieffenbachia *f*

diehard [ˈdaɪhɑːd] **1** *n* conservateur(trice) *m,f*, réactionnaire *mf*; **the party diehards** les durs *mpl* du parti

2 *adj* intransigeant; *Pol* réactionnaire; **a diehard liberal** un libéral pur et dur

dielectric [ˌdaɪɪˈlektrɪk] *Phys* **1** *adj* diélectrique

2 *n* diélectrique *m*

Dien Bien Phu [ˌdjenbjenˈfuː] *n* Diên Biên Phu

diencephalic [ˌdaɪensəˈfælɪk] *adj Anat* diencéphalique

diencephalon [ˌdaɪenˈsefəlɒn] *n Anat* diencéphale *m*

dieresis (*pl* **diereses** [-siːz]) *Am* = **diaeresis**

diesel [ˈdiːzəl] *n* (**a**) *(vehicle)* diesel *m*; *(fuel)* gasoil *m*, gazole *m* (**b**) *very Fam Pej* **diesel (dyke)** gouine *f (à l'allure masculine)*

▸▸ ***diesel engine*** *Aut* moteur *m* diesel; *Rail* motrice *f*; ***diesel fuel, diesel oil*** gas-oil *m*, gazole *m*; ***diesel train*** autorail *m*

diesel-electric 1 *adj* diesel-électrique

2 *n* diesel-électrique *m*

dieses [ˈdaɪɪsiːz] *pl of* **diesis**

diesinker [ˈdaɪˌsɪŋkə(r)] *n Tech* = personne ou machine qui fabrique des matrices industrielles

diesis [ˈdaɪəsɪs] (*pl* **dieses** [-siːz]) *n Mus* dièse *m*; *Typ* double croix *f*

diestock [ˈdaɪstɒk] *n Tech* porte-filière *m*

diet [ˈdaɪət] **1** *n* (**a**) *(regular food)* alimentation *f*, nourriture *f*; **they live on a diet of rice and fish** ils se nourrissent de riz et de poisson; **a balanced diet** un régime équilibré; **a poor diet** un régime mal équilibré, une alimentation mal équilibrée

(**b**) *(for medical reasons)* régime *m*, diète *f*; *(to lose weight)* régime *m*; **to be on a diet** être au régime; **to go on a diet** faire *ou* suivre un régime; **to put sb on a diet** mettre qn au régime; **to be put on a starvation diet** être mis à la diète; **a low-fat diet** un régime à faible teneur en matières grasses

(**c**) *Hist (assembly)* diète *f*

2 *comp (drink, food)* de régime, basses calories

3 *vi* suivre un régime

▸▸ ***diet pill*** pilule *f* pour maigrir; ***diet sheet*** programme *m* de régime *ou* nutritionnel

dietary [ˈdaɪətrɪ] (*pl* **dietaries**) **1** *adj (supplement)* alimentaire; *(of special food)* de régime, diététique

2 *n Formal* régime *m* alimentaire *(d'un malade, d'une prison)*

▸▸ ***dietary fibre*** cellulose *f* végétale; ***dietary laws*** règles *fpl* diététiques

diet-conscious *adj* **she is very diet-conscious** elle fait très attention à ce qu'elle mange

dieter [ˈdaɪətə(r)] *n* personne *f* au régime

dietetic [ˌdaɪəˈtetɪk] *adj* diététique

[illegible]

dietetics [ˌdaɪəˈtetɪks] *n (UNCOUNT)* diététique *f*

diethyl [daɪˈeθɪl] *adj Chem (ether)* diéthylique

dietician, dietitian [daɪəˈtɪʃən] *n* diététicien(enne) *m,f*

differ [ˈdɪfə(r)] *vi* (**a**) *(vary)* différer, être différent (**from** de); **in what way does this text differ from the first?** en quoi ce texte diffère-t-il du premier?; **the two approaches differ quite considerably** les deux approches n'ont pas grand-chose à voir l'une avec l'autre; **to differ in size/shape/colour** être de tailles/de formes/de couleurs différentes; **to differ in price** avoir des prix différents

(**b**) *(disagree)* être en désaccord, ne pas être d'accord; **I beg to differ** permettez-moi d'être d'un autre avis; **to agree to differ** garder chacun son opinion; **the authorities differ on the dates** les experts ne sont pas d'accord sur les dates; **he differs with me about the best solution to apply** il n'est pas d'accord avec moi *ou* il ne partage pas mon avis sur la meilleure solution à adopter

difference ['dɪfrəns] *n* (**a**) *(dissimilarity)* différence *f*; *(in age, size, weight)* écart *m*, différence *f*; **there's a big difference between living with someone and marrying them** il y a une grande différence entre vivre ensemble et être mariés; **there are many differences between the two cultures** les deux cultures sont très différentes l'une de l'autre; **I can't tell the difference between the two** je ne vois pas la différence entre les deux; **there's a difference in height of six inches** ≃ il y a une différence de hauteur de quinze centimètres; **she says the age difference doesn't matter** elle dit que la différence d'âge n'a pas d'importance; **it makes no difference, it doesn't make the slightest difference** ça n'a aucune importance, ça revient au même, ça ne change absolument rien; **it makes no difference to me (one way or the other)** (d'une manière ou d'une autre), cela m'est (parfaitement) égal; **to make a difference** *(improve society)* faire avancer les choses; **it made a big difference to him** cela a beaucoup compté *ou* a tout changé pour lui; **does it make any difference whether he comes or not?** est-ce que ça change quelque chose qu'il vienne ou pas?; **that makes all the difference** voilà qui change tout; **a lick of paint makes all the difference** un petit coup de peinture et ça n'a plus du tout la même allure; **the difference in you is amazing** c'est incroyable à quel point tu as changé; **to notice a (big) difference in sb** trouver que qn a (énormément) changé; **a computer/a skiing holiday with a difference** un ordinateur/des vacances de ski pas comme les autres

(**b**) *(disagreement)* différend *m*; **we have our differences** nous ne sommes pas toujours d'accord; **a difference of opinion** une différence *ou* divergence d'opinion; **to have a difference of opinion with sb** se disputer avec qn

(**c**) *(in numbers, quantity)* différence *f*; **I'll pay the difference** je paierai la différence *ou* le reste; *Fam* **(it's the) same difference!** cela revient au même!

►► *Physiol* ***difference threshold*** seuil *m* différentiel

different ['dɪfrənt] **1** *adj* (**a**) *(not identical)* différent, autre; **different from** *or* **to** *or esp Am* **than** différent de; **this book is very different from her first** ce livre est très différent de *ou* n'a rien à voir avec son premier; **it's very different from any other city I've visited** ça ne ressemble en rien aux autres villes que j'ai visitées; **he reads a different paper every day** il lit chaque jour un journal différent; **you look different today** tu n'es pas comme d'habitude aujourd'hui; **that dress makes you look different** cette robe vous change; **he put on a different shirt** il a mis une autre chemise; **she's a different person since their wedding** elle a beaucoup changé depuis leur mariage; **I feel like a different person since my holiday** j'ai l'impression d'avoir fait peau neuve depuis mes vacances; **what's different about it?** qu'est-ce qu'il y a de différent *ou* de changé?; **let's do something different** faisons quelque chose de nouveau *ou* de différent; **I now see things in a different light** je vois désormais les choses sous un autre jour *ou* angle; **that's quite a different matter** ça, c'est une autre affaire *ou* histoire

(**b**) *(various)* divers, différents, plusieurs; **she visited different schools** elle a visité diverses *ou* différentes écoles; **at different times** à différentes *ou* diverses reprises; **I talked to different people about it** j'en ai parlé à plusieurs personnes; **different people say different things** les avis diffèrent

(**c**) *(unusual)* original; **I'm looking for something different** je cherche quelque chose d'original *ou* qui sorte de l'ordinaire; **she always has to be different** elle veut toujours se singulariser, elle ne peut jamais faire comme tout le monde; **I've been out with a lot of men before, but he's different** je suis sortie avec beaucoup d'hommes, mais celui-là n'est pas comme les autres; **it's certainly different** c'est original

2 *adv Fam* **she thinks he's a saint but I know different** elle le prend pour un petit saint mais moi je sais que ce n'est pas vrai; **you can pretend it's your house, they won't know any different** tu peux faire comme si c'était ta maison, ils ne s'en rendront pas compte

> **And now for something completely different**
> Cette expression ("Et maintenant passons à tout autre chose") était souvent utilisée pour assurer la transition entre les sketches dans l'émission de télévision *Monty Python's Flying Circus*, de la célèbre troupe de comiques britanniques. Ces paroles étaient prononcées avec un accent aristocratique sur un ton qui évoquait celui des anciens présentateurs de la BBC.
> Aujourd'hui on utilise cette expression sur le mode humoristique lorsque l'on change de sujet de conversation.

differential [ˌdɪfə'renʃəl] **1** *adj* (**a**) *(gen)* différentiel (**b**) *Math* différentiel (**c**) *Aut* différentiel *m*

2 *n* (**a**) *(in salary)* écart *m* salarial (**b**) *Math* différentielle *f* (**c**) *Aut* différentiel *m*, engrenage *m* différentiel

►► *Math* ***differential calculus*** calcul *m* différentiel; *Biol & Chem* ***differential centrifugation*** centrifugation *f* différentielle; *Math* ***differential coefficient*** dérivée *f*; *Math* ***differential equation*** équation *f* différentielle; *Aut* ***differential gear*** différentiel *m*, engrenage *m* différentiel; *Aut* ***differential housing*** boîtier *m* de différentiel; *Math* ***differential operator*** opérateur *m* différentiel; ***differential pricing*** établissement *m* des prix différentiels, tarification *f* différentielle; ***differential tariff*** tarif *m* différentiel

differentially [ˌdɪfə'renʃəlɪ] *adv (pay)* à des taux différentiels

differentiate [ˌdɪfə'renʃɪeɪt] **1** *vt* (**a**) *(distinguish)* différencier, distinguer; **what differentiates this product from its competitors?** qu'est-ce qui différencie *ou* distingue ce produit de ses concurrents?

(**b**) *Math* différencier, calculer la différentielle de

2 *vi* faire la différence *ou* distinction; **I'm unable to differentiate between the two** je ne vois pas de différence entre les deux; **she differentiates between morality and religion** elle fait une distinction entre moralité et religion

►► ***differentiated marketing*** marketing *m* de différenciation, marketing *m* différencié

differentiation [ˌdɪfərenʃɪ'eɪʃən] *n (gen)* différenciation *f*; *Math* différentiation *f*

differentiator [ˌdɪfə'renʃɪeɪtə(r)] *n Comput* différentiateur *m*; *(circuit)* circuit *m* différentiateur

differently ['dɪfrəntlɪ] *adv* différemment, autrement; **if things had turned out differently** si les choses s'étaient passé autrement; **I do it differently from** *or esp Am* **than you** je le fais différemment de *ou* autrement que vous, je ne fais pas ça comme vous; **she acts differently from** *or esp Am* **than the others** elle n'a pas le même comportement que *ou* elle ne se comporte pas comme les autres

differently-abled *adj (in politically correct usage)* handicapé

difficult ['dɪfɪkəlt] *adj* (**a**) *(problem, task)* difficile, dur; *(book, question)* difficile; **it was a difficult decision to make** ce n'était pas une décision facile à prendre; **he's had a difficult life** il a eu une vie difficile; **that's not so difficult** ce n'est pas si difficile que ça; **I find it difficult to believe she's gone** j'ai du mal à *ou* il m'est difficile de croire qu'elle est partie; **the most difficult part is over** le plus difficile *ou* le plus dur est fait

(**b**) *(awkward)* difficile, peu commode; **don't be so difficult!** ne fais pas le difficile!, ne fais pas la fine bouche!; **he's difficult to get along with** il n'est pas commode, il a un caractère difficile; **we could make life/things very difficult for you** on pourrait sérieusement vous compliquer la vie/les choses; **she's at a difficult age** elle est à l'âge ingrat

difficulty ['dɪfɪkəltɪ] (*pl* **difficulties**) *n* (**a**) *(UNCOUNT) (trouble)* difficulté *f*, difficultés *fpl*; **to have** *or* **experience difficulty (in) doing sth** avoir du mal *ou* de la peine *ou* des difficultés à faire qch; **I had difficulty (in) climbing the stairs** j'ai eu du mal *ou* de la peine *ou* des difficultés à monter l'escalier; **she experienced difficulty breathing** elle avait du mal *ou* de la peine *ou* des difficultés à respirer, elle respirait difficilement; **degree of difficulty** niveau *m* de difficulté; **with difficulty** avec difficulté *ou* peine; **without difficulty** sans difficulté *ou* peine; **it can be done, but with difficulty** cela peut se faire, mais difficilement

(**b**) *(obstacle, problem)* difficulté *f*, problème *m*; **the main difficulty is getting the staff** le plus difficile, c'est de trouver le personnel; **I don't foresee any difficulties** je ne prévois aucun problème *ou* aucune difficulté

(**c**) *(predicament)* difficulté *f*, embarras *m*; **to get into difficulties** être en difficulté; **to be in financial difficulties** avoir des ennuis d'argent, être dans l'embarras; **he's always getting into all kinds of difficulty** il se crée *ou* s'attire toujours toutes sortes d'ennuis

diffidence ['dɪfɪdəns] *n* manque *m* d'assurance *ou* de confiance en soi, timidité *f*

diffident ['dɪfɪdənt] *adj (person)* qui manque de confiance en soi *ou* d'assurance; *(remark, smile)* timide; *(tone)* hésitant; **he was diffident about speaking out** il hésitait à parler (par timidité)

diffidently ['dɪfɪdəntlɪ] *adv (smile)* timidement, d'un air peu assuré; *(express oneself, say something)* sur un ton peu assuré

diffract [dɪ'frækt] *vt Phys* diffracter

diffraction [dɪ'frækʃən] *n Phys* diffraction *f*

►► ***diffraction grating*** réseau *m* de diffraction

diffractive [dɪ'fræktɪv] *adj Phys* diffractif

diffractometer [ˌdɪfræk'tɒmɪtə(r)] *n Phys* diffractomètre *m*

diffuse 1 *vt* [dɪ'fju:z] diffuser, répandre

2 *vi* [dɪ'fju:z] se diffuser, se répandre

3 *adj* [dɪ'fju:s] (**a**) *(light)* diffus; *(thought)* diffus, vague (**b**) *(wordy)* diffus, prolixe

diffused [dɪ'fju:zd] *adj* diffus

►► ***diffused lighting*** éclairage *m* diffus *ou* indirect

diffusely [dɪ'fju:slɪ] *adv* (**a**) *(of light → fall)* diffusément (**b**) *(speak, write)* d'une manière diffuse, avec prolixité

diffuseness [dɪ'fju:snɪs] *n (of style)* prolixité *f*, caractère *m* diffus

diffuser [dɪ'fju:zə(r)] *n (gen) & Elec* diffuseur *m*

diffusion [dɪ'fju:ʒən] *n* (**a**) *(of light, news)* diffusion *f* (**b**) *(of style)* prolixité *f* (**c**) *Phys* diffusion *f*

diffusive [dɪ'fju:sɪv] *adj* (**a**) *(property, characteristic)* diffusif (**b**) *(style)* diffus, prolixe

diffusor = **diffuser**

dig [dɪg] (*pt & pp* **dug** [dʌg], *cont* **digging**) **1** *vt* (**a**) *(in ground → hole)* creuser; *(→ tunnel)* creuser, percer; *(with spade)* bêcher; **he dug his way under the fence** il s'est creusé un passage sous la clôture; **he's been out digging the garden** il a bêché le jardin; **to dig potatoes** arracher des pommes de terre; *Fig* **to dig one's own grave** creuser sa propre tombe

(**b**) *(jab)* enfoncer; **she dug me in the ribs (with her elbow)** elle m'a donné un coup de coude dans les côtes

(**c**) *Fam Old-fashioned (understand)* piger; *(appreciate, like)* aimer[□]; *(look at)* viser; **dig that music!** écoute-moi (un peu) cette musique!; **I dig that** *(like it)* ça me plaît *ou* me botte, j'aime bien ça; **she really digs you** *(likes you)* elle en pince vraiment pour toi

2 *vi* (**a**) *(person)* creuser; *(animal)* fouiller, fouir; **to dig for gold** creuser pour trouver de l'or; *Fig* **he spends hours digging about in old junk shops** il passe des heures à fouiller dans les magasins de brocante; *Fig* **if you dig a bit deeper** si on creuse un peu

(**b**) *Fam Old-fashioned (understand)* piger

3 *n* (**a**) *(in ground)* coup *m* de bêche

(**b**) *Archeol* fouilles *fpl*; **to go on a dig** faire des fouilles

(**c**) *(jab)* coup *m*; **to give sb a dig in the ribs** donner un coup de coude dans les côtes de qn

(**d**) *Fam (snide remark)* pique[□] *f*; **he made a nasty dig at the government** il a lancé une pique au gouvernement; **that was a dig at you** cette pique était pour toi

►**dig in 1** *vi* (**a**) *Mil (dig trenches)* se retrancher; *Fig* tenir bon (**b**) *Fam (eat)* commencer à manger[□]; **dig in!** allez-y, mangez!, attaquez!

2 *vt sep* (**a**) *(mix with ground)* enterrer (**b**) *(jab)* enfoncer; **he dug in his spurs** il a éperonné son cheval; **to dig in one's heels** se braquer, se buter; **to dig oneself in** se retrancher; *Fig* camper sur ses positions; **he's really dug himself in** il s'est encroûté

▸**dig into** *vt insep* (**a**) *(delve into)* fouiller dans; *Fig* **don't dig into your savings** n'entame pas tes économies, ne pioche pas dans tes économies (**b**) *(start eating)* attaquer (**c**) *(jab)* **your elbow is digging into me** ton coude me rentre dans les côtes

▸**dig out** *vt sep* (**a**) *(remove)* extraire; *(from ground)* déterrer; **they had to dig the car out of the snow** il a fallu qu'ils dégagent la voiture de la neige (à la pelle) (**b**) *Fam (find)* dénicher

▸**dig up** *vt sep* (**a**) *(ground → gen)* retourner; *(→ with spade)* bêcher (**b**) *(plant)* arracher (**c**) *(unearth)* déterrer; *Fam Fig (find)* dénicher; **where did you dig him up?** où est-ce que tu l'as pêché *ou* dégoté?

digest **1** *vt* [dɪ'dʒest] (**a**) *(food)* digérer; **I find cheese difficult to digest** je digère mal le fromage

(**b**) *(idea)* assimiler, digérer; *(information)* assimiler, comprendre

(**c**) *(classify)* classer; *(sum up)* résumer

2 *vi* [dɪ'dʒest] digérer

3 *n* ['daɪdʒest] (**a**) *(of book, facts)* résumé *m*; **in digest form** en abrégé

(**b**) *Law* digeste *m*

(**c**) *(magazine)* digest *m*

(**d**) *Comput (of newsgroup, mailing list)* synthèse *f*

digestibility [dɪˌdʒestə'bɪlɪtɪ] *n* digestibilité *f*

digestible [dɪ'dʒestəbəl] *adj also Fig* digeste, facile à digérer

digestion [dɪ'dʒestʃən] *n* digestion *f*

digestive [dɪ'dʒestɪv] **1** *adj* digestif; **digestive troubles** troubles *mpl* de la digestion

2 *n (drink)* digestif *m*; *Br (biscuit)* = sorte de sablé

►► *Br* ***digestive biscuit*** = sorte de sablé; ***digestive system*** système *m* digestif; ***digestive tract*** tube *m* digestif

digger ['dɪgə(r)] **1** *n* (**a**) *(miner)* mineur *m*; *Br Fam* terrassier❑ *m* (**b**) *(machine)* excavatrice *f*, pelleteuse *f* (**c**) *Fam (Australian)* Australien(-enne)❑ *m,f*; *(New Zealander)* Néo-Zélandais(e)❑ *m,f* (**d**) *Austr Fam (soldier)* = soldat qui a participé à la Première Guerre mondiale; *(old-timer)* vieux *m*

2 Digger *n Hist* **the Diggers** = mouvement mené par Gerrard Winstanley, qui prêchait un communisme agraire et chrétien en Angleterre, en 1649 et 1650

digging ['dɪgɪŋ] *n (of soil)* bêchage *m*, labour *m* à la bêche; *(of well, ditches etc)* creusement *m*; *Archeol* fouilles *fpl*

diggings ['dɪgɪŋz] *npl* (**a**) *Archeol* fouilles *fpl* (**b**) *Mining (dirt)* terrassement *m*; *(pit)* creusement *m*, excavation *f*; *(of gold)* placer *m* (**c**) *Br Fam Old-fashioned* chambre *f* meublée❑; **to live in diggings** loger dans une chambre meublée; **I'm in diggings in Wimbledon** j'habite une chambre meublée à Wimbledon

digicash ['dɪdʒɪkæʃ] *n Br Comput* monnaie *f* électronique

digit ['dɪdʒɪt] *n* (**a**) *(number)* chiffre *m*; **three-digit number** nombre *m* à trois chiffres; **double digit inflation** taux *m* d'inflation à deux chiffres (**b**) *Anat (finger)* doigt *m*; *(toe)* orteil *m*; *Br Hum* **extract the digit!** grouille-toi! (**c**) *Astron* doigt *m*

digital ['dɪdʒɪtəl] *adj* (**a**) *Comput* numérique; *(clock, watch)* à affichage numérique; *(display, readout)* numérique (**b**) *Anat* digital

►► *Comput* ***digital analog converter*** convertisseur *m* analogique numérique; ***digital audio broadcasting*** diffusion *f* audio numérique; ***digital audio tape*** cassette *f* numérique; ***digital camera*** appareil *m* photo numérique; ***digital compact cassette*** cassette *f* compacte numérique; ***digital compact disc*** disque *m* compact audionumérique; ***digital computer*** calculateur *m* numérique; ***digital recording*** enregistrement *m* numérique; ***digital signal*** signal *m* numérique; *Comput* ***digital signature*** signature *f* électronique; ***digital television*** *(technique)* télévision *f* numérique; *(appliance)* téléviseur *m* numérique; ***digital terrestrial television*** télévision *f* numérique terrestre; *Comput* ***digital versatile disk*** disque *m* vidéo numérique; ***digital video*** vidéo *f* numérique; ***digital video camera*** caméra *f* vidéo numérique; *Comput* ***digital wallet*** porte-monnaie *m* électronique

digitalin [ˌdɪdʒɪ'teɪlɪn] *n Chem* digitaline *f*

digitalis [ˌdɪdʒɪ'teɪlɪs] *n Bot* digitale *f*; *Pharm* digitaline *f*

digitalization [ˌdɪdʒɪtəlaɪ'zeɪʃən] *n Math & Comput* numérisation *f*; *Med* digitalisation *f*

digitalize, -ise ['dɪdʒɪtəlaɪz] *vt Med* administrer de la digitoxine à

digitally ['dɪdʒɪtəlɪ] *adv* numériquement, sous forme digitale; **digitally controlled** à commande numérique; **digitally programmed machine tool** machine-outil *m* à commande numérique; **digitally recorded** enregistré en numérique; **digitally remastered** remixé en numérique

digitigrade ['dɪdʒɪtɪgreɪd] *Zool* **1** *adj* digitigrade

2 *n* digitigrade *m*

digitization [ˌdɪdʒɪtaɪ'zeɪʃən] *n Math & Comput* numérisation *f*

digitize, -ise ['dɪdʒɪtaɪz] *vt Math & Comput* numériser

digitizer ['dɪdʒɪtaɪzə(r)] *n Math & Comput* numériseur *m*

digitoxin [ˌdɪdʒɪ'tɒksɪn] *n Med* digitoxine *f*

diglossia [daɪ'glɒsɪə] *n Ling* diglossie *f*

dignified ['dɪgnɪfaɪd] *adj (person)* plein de dignité, digne; *(silence)* digne; **she is very dignified** elle a beaucoup de dignité; **she wasn't very dignified** elle manquait de dignité *ou* de tenue

dignify ['dɪgnɪfaɪ] (*pt & pp* **dignified**) *vt* donner de la dignité à; **to dignify sb with the name of...** honorer qn du nom de...; **I refuse to even dignify that question with an answer** cette question n'est même pas digne de réponse *ou* ne mérite même pas une réponse

dignitary ['dɪgnɪtrɪ] (*pl* **dignitaries**) *n* dignitaire *m*

dignity ['dɪgnətɪ] (*pl* **dignities**) *n* (**a**) *(importance, poise)* dignité *f*; **it would be beneath my dignity to accept** accepter serait indigne de moi *ou* serait m'abaisser; **she considered it beneath her dignity** elle s'estimait au-dessus de ça; **to stand on one's dignity** se draper dans sa dignité; **with dignity** avec dignité, dignement (**b**) *(rank)* dignité *f*, haut rang *m*; *(title)* titre *m*, dignité *f*

digraph ['daɪgrɑːf] *n Ling* digramme *m*

digress [daɪ'gres] *vi* s'éloigner, s'écarter; **you're digressing from the subject** vous vous éloignez du sujet; **but I digress** mais je m'égare, revenons à nos moutons

digression [daɪ'greʃən] *n* digression *f*

digressive [daɪ'gresɪv] *adj* qui s'écarte *ou* s'éloigne du sujet

digs [dɪgz] *npl Br Fam Old-fashioned* chambre *f* meublée❑; **to live in digs** loger dans une chambre meublée; **I'm in digs in Wimbledon** j'habite une chambre meublée à Wimbledon

dihedral [daɪ'hiːdrəl] *Geom* **1** *adj* dièdre

2 *n* dièdre *m*

dihydrogen [daɪ'haɪdrədʒən] *n Chem* dihydrogène *m*

►► ***dihydrogen monoxide*** oxyde *m* d'hydrogène

dik-dik ['dɪkdɪk] *n Zool* dik-dik *m*

dike = **dyke**

diktat ['dɪktæt] *n* (**a**) *Pol (decree)* diktat *m* (**b**) *(statement)* affirmation *f* catégorique

dilapidated [dɪ'læpɪdeɪtɪd] *adj (house)* délabré; *(car)* déglingué; **in a dilapidated state** dans un état de délabrement *ou* de dégradation avancé

dilapidation [dɪˌlæpɪ'deɪʃən] *n* (**a**) *(of building)* délabrement *m*, dégradation *f*; **in a state of dilapidation** dans un état de délabrement *ou* de dégradation avancé (**b**) *(usu pl) Law* détérioration *f (causée par un locataire)*

dilate [daɪ'leɪt] **1** *vi* (**a**) *(eyes)* se dilater (**b**) *Formal (talk)* **to dilate on** *or* **upon a topic** s'étendre sur un sujet

2 *vt* dilater

dilation [daɪ'leɪʃən] *n* (**a**) *(gen) & Med* dilatation *f*; (**b**) *Formal (talk)* exposition *f* en détail

►► ***dilation and curettage*** (dilatation *f* et) curetage *m*

dilatometer [ˌdaɪlə'tɒmɪtə(r)] *n Phys* dilatomètre *m*

dilatometry [ˌdaɪlə'tɒmɪtrɪ] *n Phys* dilatométrie *f*

dilator [daɪ'leɪtə(r)] *n (instrument)* dilatateur *m*; *(muscle)* muscle *m* dilatateur

dilatoriness ['dɪlətrɪnɪs] *n Formal* lenteur *f*

dilatory ['dɪlətrɪ] *adj Formal (action, method)* dilatoire; *(person)* lent; **forgive me for being so dilatory in coming to a decision** veuillez m'excuser pour avoir mis tant de temps à me décider

dildo ['dɪldəʊ] (*pl* **dildos**) *n* (**a**) *(device)* godemiché *m* (**b**) *very Fam (person)* trou *m* du cul, trouduc *m*

dilemma [dɪ'lemə] *n* dilemme *m*; **to be in a dilemma** être pris dans un dilemme; **her decision leaves me in something of a dilemma** sa décision me pose un dilemme

dilettante [ˌdɪlɪ'tæntɪ] (*pl* **dilettantes** *or* **dilettanti** [-tɪ]) **1** *n* dilettante *mf*

2 *adj* dilettante

dilettantish [ˌdɪlɪ'tæntɪʃ] *adj* de dilettante

dilettantism [ˌdɪlɪ'tæntɪzəm] *n* dilettantisme *m*

dilettantist [ˌdɪlɪ'tæntɪst] *adj* de dilettante

diligence ['dɪlɪdʒəns] *n* (**a**) *(effort)* assiduité *f*, application *f*, zèle *m*; **she shows great diligence in her work** elle fait preuve de beaucoup de zèle *ou* d'assiduité dans son travail (**b**) *(carriage)* diligence *f*

diligent ['dɪlɪdʒənt] *adj (person)* assidu, appliqué; *(work)* appliqué, diligent; **he is very diligent in his work** *or* **carrying out his work** il fait son travail avec beaucoup d'assiduité *ou* beaucoup de zèle

diligently ['dɪlɪdʒəntlɪ] *adv* avec assiduité *ou* soin *ou* application, assidûment

dill[1] [dɪl] *n (herb)* aneth *m*

►► ***dill pickle*** cornichon *m* à l'aneth

dill[2] *n Austr & NZ Fam (fool)* andouille *f*

dilly ['dɪlɪ] (*pl* **dillies**) *n Am Fam Old-fashioned* **she's a real dilly!** elle est formidable *ou* sensationnelle!; **a dilly of a joke** une blague vachement marrante; **a dilly of a storm** un sacré orage

dilly-dally (*pt & pp* **dilly-dallied**) *vi Fam (dawdle)* lanterner❑, lambiner; *(hesitate)* hésiter❑, tergiverser❑

dilly-dallying [-'dælɪɪŋ] *n (UNCOUNT) Fam (dawdling)* flânerie❑ *f*; *(hesitation)* hésitations❑ *fpl*, tergiversations❑ *fpl*

diluent ['dɪljʊənt] *n Chem* diluant *m*

dilute [daɪ'luːt] **1** *vt* (**a**) *(liquid)* diluer, étendre; *(milk, wine)* mouiller, couper d'eau; *(sauce)* délayer, allonger; *(colour)* délayer; **dilute to taste** *(on bottle)* diluer selon votre goût (**b**) *Chem & Pharm* diluer (**c**) *Fig (weaken)* diluer, édulcorer; **diluted socialism** socialisme *m* édulcoré

2 *adj (liquid)* dilué, coupé *ou* étendu (d'eau); *(colour)* délayé, adouci; *Fig* dilué, édulcoré

dilution [daɪ'luːʃən] *n* (**a**) *(act, product)* dilution *f*; *(of milk, wine)* coupage *m*, mouillage *m*; *Fig* édulcoration *f* (**b**) *Fin & St Exch (of shareholding)* dilution *f*; **dilution of equity** dilution *f* du bénéfice par action

diluvial [daɪ'luːvɪəl], **diluvian** [daɪ'luːvɪən] *adj* diluvien

dim [dɪm] (*pt & pp* **dimmed**, *cont* **dimming**) **1** *adj* (**a**) *(light)* faible, pâle; *(lamp)* faible; *(room)* sombre; *(colour)* terne, sans éclat; **to grow dim** *(light)* baisser; *(room)* devenir sombre; *(colour)* devenir terne; **her eyes grew dim with tears** ses yeux se voilèrent de larmes

(**b**) *(indistinct → shape)* vague, imprécis; *(→ sight)* faible, trouble; *(→ sound)* vague, indistinct; **she has only a dim memory of it** elle n'en a qu'un vague souvenir; *Hum* **in the dim and distant past** au temps jadis; **to grow dim** *(shape, memory)* s'estomper, s'effacer; *(sight)* baisser, se troubler; *(sound)* s'affaiblir

(**c**) *(gloomy)* sombre, morne; **to take a dim view of sth** ne pas beaucoup apprécier qch, voir qch d'un mauvais œil; **she takes a pretty dim view of him going out with other women** elle n'apprécie guère qu'il sorte avec d'autres femmes

(**d**) *Fam (stupid)* gourde

2 *vt* (**a**) *(light)* baisser; **I'll dim the lamp** je vais mettre la lampe en veilleuse; *Aut* **to dim one's headlights** se mettre en codes *ou* en feux de croisement; **to drive with dimmed headlights** conduire en codes *ou* en feux de croisement

(**b**) *(beauty, colour, hope, metal)* ternir; *(memory)* estomper, effacer; *(mind, senses)* affaiblir, troubler; *(sound)* affaiblir; *(sight)* baisser, troubler; **his eyes were dimmed with tears** ses yeux étaient voilés de larmes

3 *vi (light)* baisser, s'affaiblir; *(beauty, glory, hope)* se ternir; *(colour)* devenir terne *ou* mat; *(memory)* s'estomper, s'effacer; *(sound)* s'affaiblir; *(sight)* baisser, se troubler

▸**dim out** *vt sep Am* plonger dans un black-out partiel

dimbo ['dɪmbəʊ] *n Fam* ballot *m*, nigaud *m*

dim-dip *n Aut* veilleuses-codes *fpl*

dime [daɪm] *n Am* pièce *f* de dix cents; **I did it on my own dime** j'ai payé de ma poche; *Fam* **guys like that are a dime a dozen** des types comme lui, on en trouve à la pelle; *Fam* **it's not worth a dime** *or* **one thin dime** ça ne vaut pas un clou

►► *Fam Drugs slang* ***dime bag*** = sachet de drogue; *Am* ***dime novel*** roman *m* à quatre sous; *Am* ***dime store*** supérette *f* de quartier

dimension [dɪ'menʃən] **1** *n* (**a**) *(measurement, size)* dimension *f*; *Archit & Geom* dimension *f*, cote *f*; *Math & Phys* dimension *f* (**b**) *Fig (scope)* étendue *f*; *(aspect)* dimension *f*; **the book opens up a whole new dimension of thought** ce livre ouvre un nouveau champ de réflexion

2 dimensions *npl Tech (of bulky object)* encombrement *m*

-dimensional [dɪ'menʃənəl] *suff* **two/four-dimensional** à deux/quatre dimensions

dimer ['daɪmə(r)] *n Chem* dimère *m*

dimeric [daɪ'merɪk] *adj Chem* dimère

dimeter ['dɪmɪtə(r)] *n Literature* dimètre *m*

dimethyl [daɪ'meθɪl] *n Chem* diméthyle *m*

diminish [dɪ'mɪnɪʃ] **1** *vt* (**a**) *(number)* diminuer, réduire; *(effect, power)* diminuer, amoindrir; *(value)* réduire (**b**) *(person)* déprécier, rabaisser (**c**) *Archit (column)* amincir, diminuer; *Mus* diminuer

2 *vi* diminuer, se réduire; **their profits have diminished** leurs bénéfices ont diminué; **the number of homeless has diminished** le nombre des sans-abri a diminué

diminished [dɪ'mɪnɪʃt] *adj* (**a**) *(number, power, speed)* diminué, amoindri; *(reputation)* diminué, terni; *(value)* réduit (**b**) *Mus* diminué

►► *Law* ***diminished responsibility*** responsabilité *f* atténuée

diminishing [dɪ'mɪnɪʃɪŋ] **1** *adj (influence, number, speed)* décroissant, qui va en diminuant; *(price, quality)* qui baisse, en baisse

2 *n* diminution *f*, baisse *f*

►► *Acct* ***diminishing balance*** amortissement *m* linéaire; *Econ* ***diminishing marginal product*** produit *m* marginal décroissant; ***diminishing returns*** rendements *mpl* décroissants; *Econ & Fig* **the law of diminishing returns** la loi des rendements décroissants

diminuendo [dɪˌmɪnjʊ'endəʊ] (*pl* **diminuendos**) *Mus* **1** *n* diminuendo *m*

2 *adv* diminuendo

diminution [ˌdɪmɪ'njuːʃən] *n* (**a**) *(in number, value)* diminution *f*, baisse *f*; *(in speed)* réduction *f*; *(in intensity, importance, strength)* diminution *f*, affaiblissement *m*; *(in temperature)* baisse *f*, abaissement *m*; *(in authority, price)* baisse *f*; **there has been no diminution in** *or* **of our enthusiasm** notre enthousiasme n'a en rien faibli (**b**) *Mus* diminution *f*

diminutive [dɪ'mɪnjʊtɪv] **1** *adj (tiny)* minuscule, tout petit; *Ling* diminutif

2 *n Ling* diminutif *m*

diminutiveness [dɪ'mɪnjʊtɪvnɪs] *n* petitesse *f*

dimity ['dɪmɪtɪ] *n Tex* futaine *f* croisée

dimly ['dɪmlɪ] *adv (shine)* faiblement, sans éclat; *(see)* indistinctement, à peine; *(remember)* vaguement, à peine; **the room was dimly lit** la pièce était mal *ou* faiblement éclairée

dimmed [dɪmd] *adj Comput (command)* en grisé, estompé

►► *Aut* ***dimmed headlights*** feux *mpl* de croisement, codes *mpl*; *Comput* ***dimmed icon*** icône *f* estompée

dimmer ['dɪmə(r)] **1** *n* (**a**) *(on lamp)* variateur *m* (de lumière) (**b**) *Am Aut (switch)* basculeur *m* (de phares)

2 dimmers *npl Aut (headlights)* phares *mpl* code; *(parking lights)* feux *mpl* de position

►► ***dimmer switch*** variateur *m* (de lumière)

dimming ['dɪmɪŋ] *n (of light)* affaiblissement *m*, obscurcissement *m*; *(of colour, metal, reputation)* ternissement *m*; *(of memory)* affaiblissement *m*; *Am Aut (of headlights)* mise *f* en codes

dimness ['dɪmnɪs] *n* (**a**) *(of light, sight)* affaiblissement *m*; *(of room)* obscurité *f*; *(of colour, metal)* aspect *m* terne; *(of memory, shape)* imprécision *f* (**b**) *Fam (stupidity)* sottise ❑ *f*

dimorphic [daɪ'mɔːfɪk] *adj* dimorphe

dimorphism [daɪ'mɔːfɪzəm] *n* dimorphisme *m*, dimorphie *f*

dimorphous [daɪ'mɔːfəs] *adj* dimorphe

dimout ['dɪmaʊt] *n Am* black-out *m* partiel

dimple ['dɪmpəl] **1** *n (in cheek, chin)* fossette *f*; *(in surface of ground, water)* ride *f*, ondulation *f*

2 *vt* (**a**) *(of smile → somebody's cheeks)* creuser des fossettes dans (**b**) *(of wind → surface of water)* rider

3 *vi (cheek)* se creuser de fossettes; *(surface of ground)* onduler, former des rides; *(surface of water)* onduler, se rider

dimpled ['dɪmpəld] *adj (cheek, chin)* à fossettes; *(arm, knee)* potelé; *(surface)* ridé, ondulé

dim sum [dɪm'sʌm] *n Culin* dim sum *m*

dimwit ['dɪmwɪt] *n Fam* crétin(e) *m,f*

dimwitted ['dɪmˌwɪtɪd] *adj Fam* crétin, gourde; **my dimwitted brother** mon crétin de frère

DIN [dɪn] *n* (*abbr* **Deutsche Industrie Norm**) (indice *m*) DIN *f*

din [dɪn] (*pt & pp* **dinned**, *cont* **dinning**) **1** *n (of people)* tapage *m*, tumulte *m*; *(in classroom)* chahut *m*; *(of industry, traffic)* vacarme *m*; *Fam* **they were kicking up** *or* **making a real din** ils faisaient un boucan d'enfer *ou* monstre

2 *vt Fam* **to din sth into sb** faire (bien) comprendre qch à qn ❑, enfoncer qch dans le crâne à qn; **to din manners/the rules of the road into sb** inculquer les bonnes manières/le code de la route à qn ❑

dinar ['diːnɑː(r)] *n* dinar *m*

dindins ['dɪndɪnz] *n (in children's language)* dîner ❑ *m*

dine [daɪn] **1** *vi* dîner, *Belg, Can & Suisse* souper; **to dine off** *or* **on sth** dîner de qch; **she dined off** *or* **on trout and fresh strawberries** elle a dîné d'une truite et de fraises fraîches; **we're dining in tonight** nous dînons à la maison ce soir

2 *vt* offrir à dîner à

▸**dine out** *vi* dîner dehors *ou* en ville; *Fig* **I dined out on that story for weeks** ça m'a fait une bonne histoire à raconter pendant des semaines

diner ['daɪnə(r)] *n* (**a**) *(person)* dîneur(euse) *m,f*; **there were only a few late diners left in the restaurant** il n'y avait plus que quelques clients attardés dans le restaurant (**b**) *Am* petit restaurant *m*; *Rail* wagon-restaurant *m*

dinette [daɪ'net] *n* coin-repas *m*

ding [dɪŋ] **1** *n* tintement *m*

2 *vt* **to ding sth into sb** faire (bien) comprendre qch à qn ❑, enfoncer qch dans le crâne à qn; **to ding manners/the rules of the road into sb** inculquer les bonnes manières/le code de la route à qn ❑

3 *vi* tinter

ding-a-ling ['dɪŋəˌlɪŋ] *n* (**a**) *(ring)* dring dring *m*, tintement *m* (**b**) *Am Fam (fool)* cloche *f*, andouille *f*

dingbat ['dɪŋbæt] *n* (**a**) *Am Fam (thing)* truc *m*, machin *m* (**b**) *Fam (fool)* crétin(e) *m,f*, gourde *f* (**c**) *Comput* symbole *m* Dingbat

ding-dong **1** *n* (**a**) *(of bells)* tintement *m*, sonnerie *f*; *(of doorbell)* sonnerie *f*; **to go ding-dong** faire ding-ding-dong (**b**) *Fam (fight)* bagarre *f*

2 *adj Fam* **to have a ding-dong argument** *(of two people)* se disputer violemment ❑; **ding-dong match** partie *f* vivement disputée

dinge [dɪndʒ] *n (shabbiness)* aspect *m* miteux *ou* douteux; *(drabness)* couleur *f* terne

dinger ['dɪŋə(r)] *n Am Fam (person)* crétin(e) *m,f*

dinghy ['dɪŋgɪ] (*pl* **dinghies**) *n (rowing boat)* petit canot *m*, youyou *m*; *(sailboat)* dériveur *m*; *(made of rubber)* canot *m* pneumatique, dinghy *m*

dinginess ['dɪndʒɪnɪs] *n (shabbiness)* aspect *m* miteux *ou* douteux; *(drabness)* couleur *f* terne

dingle ['dɪŋgəl] *n* vallon *m* boisé

dingo ['dɪŋgəʊ] (*pl* **dingoes**) *n Zool* dingo *m*

dingus ['dɪŋʌs] *n Am Fam* truc *m*, machin *m*

dingy ['dɪndʒɪ] (*compar* **dingier**, *superl* **dingiest**) *adj (shabby)* miteux; *(dirty)* douteux; *(colour)* terne

dining ['daɪnɪŋ-]

►► *Rail* ***dining car*** wagon-restaurant *m*; ***dining club*** club-restaurant *m* pour étudiants; ***dining hall*** réfectoire *m*, salle *f* à manger; ***dining room*** **1** *n* salle *f* à manger **2** *comp (curtains, furniture)* de (la) salle à manger; ***dining room suite*** salle *f* à manger *(meubles)*; ***dining table*** table *f* de salle à manger

dink [dɪŋk] *n* (**a**) *Fam (person)* crétin(e) *m,f* (**b**) *very Fam (penis)* queue *f*

dinkum ['dɪŋkəm] *Austr Fam* **1** *adj (person)* franc (franche) ❑, sincère ❑; *(thing)* authentique ❑; **fair dinkum** régulier, vrai de vrai; **dinkum?** sans blague?; **he's a dinkum Aussie** c'est un vrai Australien ❑; **dinkum oil** la vérité ❑

2 *n* Australien(enne) *m,f* de naissance ❑

3 *adv* franchement ❑, vraiment ❑

Dinky® ['dɪŋkɪ] *n* = marque de petites voitures

dinky[1] ['dɪŋkɪ] (*compar* **dinkier**, *superl* **dinkiest**) *adj Fam* (**a**) *Br (small, neat)* mignon, coquet (**b**) *Am Pej (insignificant)* de rien du tout

dinky[2] (*abbr* **double income no kids yet**) *Fam Hum*

1 *n* = membre d'un couple à deux revenus sans enfants

2 *comp (lifestyle etc)* de couple sans enfants à deux revenus

dinky-di *adj Austr Fam* authentique ❑

dinner ['dɪnə(r)] **1** *n* (**a**) *(evening meal)* dîner *m*; *Belg, Can & Suisse* souper *m*; *(very late)* souper *m*; **to be at dinner** être en train de dîner; **they were just getting up from dinner** ils sortaient à peine de table; **ask her round for dinner next week** invite-la à venir dîner la semaine prochaine; **she's having guests to dinner** elle a des invités à dîner; **they went out to dinner** *(in restaurant)* ils ont dîné au restaurant *ou* en ville; *(at friends)* ils ont dîné chez des amis; **dinner's on the table** *or* **ready!** le dîner est prêt!, c'est prêt!, à table!; **she rang the dinner bell** elle a sonné pour annoncer le dîner; **did you have a good dinner?** avez-vous bien mangé *ou* dîné?; **did you give the cat its dinner?** avez-vous donné à manger au chat?; **a formal dinner** un grand dîner *ou* dîner officiel; *Br Fam* **he's had more girlfriends than I've had hot dinners** il a eu je ne sais combien de petites amies ❑

(**b**) *Ir, Scot & NEng (lunch)* déjeuner *m*

2 *comp (fork, knife)* de table

►► ***dinner dance*** dîner *m* dansant; *Sch* ***dinner duty*** service *m* de réfectoire; ***dinner hour*** *(at work)* heure *f* du déjeuner; *(at school)* pause *f* de midi; ***dinner jacket*** smoking *m*; *Br* ***dinner lady*** = employée d'une cantine scolaire; *Br* ***dinner money*** argent *m* pour la cantine; ***dinner party*** dîner *m (sur invitation)*; **we're having** *or* **giving a dinner party** nous avons du monde à dîner, nous donnons un dîner; ***dinner plate*** (grande) assiette *f*; ***dinner roll*** petit pain *m*; ***dinner service, dinner set*** service *m* de table; ***dinner table*** table *f* de salle à manger; **at** *or* **over the dinner table** pendant le dîner, au dîner; ***dinner trolley*** chariot *m* à repas

dinnertime ['dɪnətaɪm] *n* heure *f* du dîner

dinnerware ['dɪnəweə(r)] *n Am* vaisselle *f*

dinosaur ['daɪnəsɔː(r)] *n (animal)* dinosaure *m*; *Mktg (product)* poids *m* mort, produit *m* dodo; *Fig* **the institute's become a bit of a dinosaur** l'institut est le survivant d'une époque révolue *ou* a fait son temps

dint [dɪnt] **1** *n Arch (blow)* coup *m*; *(mark of blow → in metal, wall)* bosse *f*; *(→ in bed, pillow)* creux *m*

2 by dint of *prep* à force de; **she succeeded by dint of sheer hard work** elle a réussi à force de travailler dur

dinucleotide [ˌdaɪ'njuːklɪəʊˌtaɪd] *n Biol & Chem* dinucléotide *m*

diocesan [daɪ'ɒsɪsən] *Rel* **1** *adj* diocésain

2 *n* (évêque *m*) diocésain *m*

diocese ['daɪəsɪs] *n Rel* diocèse *m*

diode ['daɪəʊd] *n Electron* diode *f*

dioecious [daɪ'iːʃəs] *adj Bot & Biol* doïque

Diogenes [daɪ'ɒdʒɪniːz] *pr n* Diogène

Dionysiac [ˌdaɪəˈnɪzɪæk], **Dionysian** [ˌdaɪəˈnɪzɪən] *adj Antiq* dionysiaque

Dionysus [ˌdaɪəˈnaɪsəs] *pr n Myth* Dionysos

diopside [daɪˈɒpsaɪd] *n Miner* diopside *m*

dioptase [daɪˈɒpteɪz] *n Miner* dioptase *f*

diopter *Am* = **dioptre**

dioptometer [ˌdaɪɒpˈtɒmɪtə(r)] *n Opt* instrument *m* de mesure dioptrique

dioptre, *Am* **diopter** [daɪˈɒptə(r)] *n Opt* dioptrie *f*

dioptric [daɪˈɒptrɪk] **1** *adj* dioptrique
2 *n* dioptrie *f*

dioptrics [daɪˈɒptrɪks] *n* dioptrique *f*

diorama [ˌdaɪəˈrɑːmə] *n* diorama *m*

dioxide [daɪˈɒksaɪd] *n Chem* dioxyde *m*

dioxin [daɪˈɒksɪn] *n Chem* dioxine *f*

dioxygen [daɪˈɒksɪdʒən] *n* dioxygène *m*

dip [dɪp] (*pt & pp* **dipped**, *cont* **dipping**) **1** *vi* (**a**) *(incline → ground)* descendre, s'incliner; *(→ road)* descendre, plonger; *(→ head)* pencher, s'incliner; **the road dips sharply** la route descend brusquement
(**b**) *(drop → sun)* baisser, descendre à l'horizon; *(→ price)* diminuer, baisser; *(→ temperature)* baisser; *(→ plane)* piquer; *(→ boat)* tanguer, piquer; **the sun dipped below the horizon** le soleil est descendu derrière l'horizon; **shares dipped on the London Stock Market yesterday** les actions ont baissé à la Bourse des valeurs de Londres hier
(**c**) *(during dance)* se renverser
2 *vt* (**a**) *(immerse)* tremper, plonger; *Tech* tremper; *(clean)* décaper; *(dye)* teindre; *Agr (sheep)* baigner *(dans un bain parasiticide)*
(**b**) *(plunge)* plonger; *Fig* **to dip one's hand in one's pocket** mettre la main à la poche
(**c**) *Br Aut* **to dip one's headlights** se mettre en codes; **dipped headlights** codes *mpl*, feux *mpl* de croisement; **to drive on** *or* **with dipped headlights** rouler en codes
(**d**) *(flag)* baisser; *Naut* **to dip a flag** (faire) marquer un pavillon; **to dip one's flag to a ship** saluer un navire avec son pavillon
3 *n* (**a**) *Fam (swim)* baignade [❑] *f*, bain [❑] *m (en mer, en piscine)*; **to go for a dip** aller se baigner, aller faire trempette; *Fig* **a brief dip into Homer** un survol rapide d'Homère
(**b**) *(liquid)* bain *m*; *Agr (for sheep)* bain *m* parasiticide
(**c**) *(slope → in ground)* déclivité *f*; *(→ in road)* descente *f*; *Geol* pendage *m*
(**d**) *(bob)* inclinaison *f*; *(of head)* hochement *m*
(**e**) *(drop → in temperature)* baisse *f*; *(→ in price)* fléchissement *m*, baisse *f*; **the winter months saw a sharp dip in profits** les bénéfices ont fortement baissé pendant l'hiver
(**f**) *Culin* = sauce dans laquelle on trempe les crudités etc; **avocado dip** purée *f* d'avocat; **cheese dip** hors d'œuvre *m* au fromage
(**g**) *Am Fam (idiot)* andouille *f*, cruche *f*
(**h**) *Br Fam Crime slang (pickpocket)* pickpocket [❑] *m*
(**i**) *(in dance)* tombé *m*
▸▸ ***dip needle*** aiguille *f* aimantée *(de boussole)*; *Br Aut* ***dip switch*** basculeur *m* de phares

▸**dip into** *vt insep* (**a**) *(dabble)* **I've only really dipped into Shakespeare** j'ai seulement survolé *ou* feuilleté Shakespeare (**b**) *(draw upon)* puiser dans; **we've had to dip into our** [illegible] économies; **I'm always dipping into my pocket** je suis toujours à débourser

Dip. (*written abbr* **diploma**) diplôme *m*

DipEd [ˌdɪpˈed] *n Br Univ* (*abbr* **Diploma in Education**) ≃ CAPES *m*

diphase [ˈdaɪfeɪz] *adj Electron* diphasé

diphenyl [daɪˈfenɪl] *n Chem* diphényle *m*

diphosgene [daɪˈfɒsdʒiːn] *n Chem* = composé toxique de la phosgène et du méthanol

diphtheria [dɪfˈθɪərɪə] *n* diphtérie *f*; **to have diphtheria** être atteint de la diphtérie, avoir la diphtérie
▸▸ ***diphtheria vaccine*** vaccin *m* antidiphtérique

diphthong [ˈdɪfθɒŋ] *n Ling* diphtongue *f*

diphthongism [ˈdɪfθɒŋɪzəm], **diphthongization** [ˌdɪfθɒŋaɪˈzeɪʃən] *n Ling* diphtongaison *f*

diphthongize, -ise [ˈdɪfθɒŋgaɪz] *Ling* **1** *vt* diphtonguer
2 *vi* se diphtonguer

diplex [ˈdaɪpleks] *adj Tel* duplex

diplococcus [ˌdɪpləʊˈkɒkəs] (*pl* **diplococci** [-saɪ]) *n* diplocoque *m*

diplodocus [dɪˈplɒdəkəs] *n* diplodocus *m*

diploid [ˈdɪplɔɪd] *adj Biol* diploïde

diploma [dɪˈpləʊmə] *n* diplôme *m*; **she has a diploma in business studies** elle est diplômée de *ou* en commerce; **teaching diploma** diplôme *m* d'enseignement
▸▸ *Br Univ* ***Diploma in Education*** ≃ CAPES *m*; *Univ* ***Diploma in Public Health*** diplôme *m* de santé publique

diplomacy [dɪˈpləʊməsɪ] *n Pol & Fig* diplomatie *f*; **you have to use a bit of diplomacy** vous devez user d'un peu de diplomatie, il faut être un peu diplomate

diplomat [ˈdɪpləmæt] *n Pol & Fig* diplomate *mf*

diplomate [ˈdɪpləmeɪt] *n (gen)* diplômé(e) *m,f*; *Med* diplômé(e) *m,f* spécialiste

diplomatic [ˌdɪpləˈmætɪk] *adj* (**a**) *Pol* diplomatique (**b**) *Fig (person)* diplomate; *(action, remark)* diplomatique; **you have to be diplomatic when dealing with these people** il faut faire preuve de tact *ou* user de diplomatie pour traiter avec ces gens-là; **that wasn't very diplomatic** ça manquait un peu de tact *ou* de diplomatie
▸▸ *Pol* ***diplomatic bag*** valise *f* diplomatique; *Pol* ***diplomatic corps*** corps *m* diplomatique; *Pol* ***diplomatic immunity*** immunité *f* diplomatique; **to claim diplomatic immunity** faire valoir l'immunité diplomatique; *Am Pol* ***diplomatic pouch*** valise *f* diplomatique; *Pol* ***diplomatic relations*** relations *fpl* diplomatiques; *Pol* ***the Diplomatic Service*** la diplomatie, le service diplomatique; **to enter the Diplomatic Service** entrer dans la diplomatie

diplomatically [ˌdɪpləˈmætɪkəlɪ] *adv Pol* diplomatiquement; *Fig* avec diplomatie, diplomatiquement

diplomatist [dɪˈpləʊmətɪst] *n Pol & Fig* diplomate *mf*

diplopia [dɪˈpləʊpɪə] *n Med* diplopie *f*

dipolar [daɪˈpəʊlə(r)] *adj* (**a**) *(magnet)* bipolaire (**b**) *Elec* dipolaire

dipole [ˈdaɪpəʊl] *n Phys* dipôle *m*

dipped [dɪpt] *adj (sloping)* incliné
▸▸ *Br Aut* ***dipped headlights*** codes *mpl*, feux *mpl* de croisement

dipper [ˈdɪpə(r)] *n* (**a**) *(ladle)* louche *f* (**b**) *(of machine)* godet *m* (de pelleteuse); *(for lake, river)* benne *f* (de drague), hotte *f* à draguer (**c**) *Br Aut* basculeur *m* (de phares) (**d**) *Orn* cincle *m* (plongeur) (**e**) *Br Fam Crime slang (pickpocket)* pickpocket [❑] *m*

dipping [ˈdɪpɪŋ] *n* (**a**) *(plunging)* plongée *f*, immersion *f*; *Metal* décapage *m*; *Agr (of sheep)* baignage *m* (**b**) *Br Aut (of headlights)* mise *f* en code

dippy [ˈdɪpɪ] (*compar* **dippier**, *superl* **dippiest**) *adj Fam* loufoque, loufedingue; **to be dippy about sb/sth** être dingue de qn/qch

diprod [ˈdɪprɒd] *n Am Aut* jauge *f* (de niveau d'huile)

dipshit [ˈdɪpʃɪt] *n Am Vulg* con (conne) *m,f*

dipso [ˈdɪpsəʊ] *n Fam* alcoolo *mf*

dipsomania [ˌdɪpsəˈmeɪnjə] *n* dipsomanie *f*

dipsomaniac [ˌdɪpsəˈmeɪnɪæk] **1** *adj* dipsomane
2 *n* dipsomane *mf*

dipstick [ˈdɪpstɪk] *n* (**a**) *Aut* jauge *f* (de niveau d'huile) (**b**) *Fam (idiot)* empoté(e) *m,f*

DIP switch [ˈdɪp-] *n Comput* interrupteur *m* DIP

diptera [ˈdɪptərə] *npl Entom* diptères *mpl*

dipteran [ˈdɪptərən] *n Entom* diptère *m*

dipterous [ˈdɪptərəs] *adj Entom* diptère

diptych [ˈdɪptɪk] *n Art* diptyque *m*

dir (**a**) *Admin* (*written abbr* **director**) directeur(trice) *m,f* (**b**) *Comput* (*written abbr* **directory**) répertoire *m*

dire [ˈdaɪə(r)] *adj* (**a**) *(fearful)* affreux, terrible; *(ominous)* sinistre; **dire warnings** avertissements *mpl* sinistres
(**b**) *Fam (very bad)* **the film was pretty dire** le film était vraiment mauvais [❑] *ou* nul
(**c**) *(extreme)* extrême; **he's in dire need of sleep** il a absolument besoin de sommeil; **only in cases of dire necessity** seulement en cas de necessité absolue; **he sold the family seat out of dire necessity** il a vendu la demeure familiale parce qu'il ne pouvait pas faire autrement; **dire poverty** misère *f* noire; **to be in dire straits** être dans une situation désespérée

DIRECT [dɪˈrekt]

diriger	▸ **1 (a), (d), (g); 2 (a), (b)**
réaliser	▸ **1 (b)**
adresser	▸ **1 (c)**
ordonner	▸ **1 (e)**
instruire	▸ **1 (f)**
faire de la réalisation	▸ **2 (c)**
direct	▸ **3 (a) – (c), (e)**
exact	▸ **3 (d)**
directement	▸ **4**

1 *vt* (**a**) *(supervise → business)* diriger, gérer, mener; *(→ office, work)* diriger; *(→ movements)* guider; *(→ traffic)* régler
(**b**) *Cin, Rad & TV (film, programme)* réaliser; *(actors)* diriger; *Theat (play)* mettre en scène; **directed by Danny Boyle** *Cin, Rad & TV* réalisation Danny Boyle; *Theat* mise *f* en scène Danny Boyle
(**c**) *(address)* adresser; **please direct your remarks to the chairperson** veuillez adresser vos observations au président; **the accusation was directed at him** l'accusation le visait; **he directed my attention to the map** il a attiré mon attention sur la carte; **we should direct all our efforts towards improving our education service** nous devrions consacrer tous nos efforts à améliorer notre système scolaire
(**d**) *(point)* diriger; **I directed my steps homewards** je me suis dirigé vers la maison; **can you direct me to the train station?** pourriez-vous m'indiquer le chemin de la gare?
(**e**) *(instruct)* ordonner; **he directed them to leave at once** il leur a donné l'ordre de partir immédiatement; **she directed him to take control of the project** elle l'a chargé de prendre en main le projet; **I did as I was directed** j'ai fait comme on m'avait dit *ou* comme on m'en avait donné l'ordre; **take as directed** *(on drugs packaging)* se conformer à la prescription du médecin
(**f**) *Law* **to direct the jury** instruire le jury; **the judge directed the jury to bring in a verdict of guilty** le juge incita le jury à rendre un verdict de culpabilité; *Am* **directed verdict** = verdict rendu par le jury sur la recommandation du juge
(**g**) *Am Mus* diriger
2 *vi* (**a**) *(command)* diriger, commander
(**b**) *Am Mus* diriger
(**c**) *Cin, Rad & TV* faire de la réalisation; *Theat* faire de la mise en scène; **it's her first chance to direct** *Cin, Rad & TV* c'est la première fois qu'elle a l'occasion de faire de la réalisation; *Theat* c'est la première fois qu'elle a l'occasion de faire de la mise en scène; **he's never directed before** il n'a jamais fait de mise en scène
3 *adj* (**a**) *(straight)* direct; **direct flight/route** vol *m*/chemin *m* direct; **direct heating/lighting** chauffage *m*/éclairage *m* direct
(**b**) *(immediate → cause, effect)* direct, immédiat; **she has direct control over the finances** [illegible] de sa responsabilité; **he's a direct descendant of the King** il descend du roi en ligne directe; **keep out of direct sunlight** *(on packaging)* évitez l'exposition directe au soleil; **you're not in direct danger of catching the disease** vous ne courez pas de risque immédiat d'attraper cette maladie
(**c**) *(frank)* franc (franche), direct; *(denial, refusal)* catégorique, absolu; **he was always very direct with us** il nous a toujours parlé très franchement; **she asked some very direct questions** elle a posé des questions parfois très directes
(**d**) *(exact)* exact, précis; **direct quotation** citation *f* exacte; **it's the direct opposite of what I said** c'est exactement le contraire de ce que j'ai dit
(**e**) *Astron & Gram* direct
4 *adv (go)* directement, tout droit; **to travel direct from London to Edinburgh** prendre un train/un vol/*etc* direct de Londres à Edimbourg;

to dispatch goods direct to sb expédier des marchandises directement à qn; **the concert will be broadcast direct from Paris** ce concert sera transmis en direct de Paris

►► *Comput* ***direct access*** accès *m* direct; ***direct action*** action *f* directe; ***direct advertising*** publicité *f* directe; ***direct banking*** banque *f* à distance; *Tel* ***direct broadcast satellite*** satellite *m* de télédiffusion directe; ***direct costs*** charges *fpl* directes, frais *mpl* directs; ***direct cost accounting*** (méthode *f* de) comptabilité *f* des coûts variables; ***direct costing*** méthode *f* des coûts variables *ou* proportionnels; *Elec* ***direct current*** courant *m* continu; *Br Banking & Fin* ***direct debit*** prélèvement *m* automatique; **to pay by direct debit** payer par prélèvement automatique; *Br Banking & Fin* ***direct debit advice*** avis *m* de prélèvement; *Br Banking & Fin* ***direct debit mandate*** autorisation *f* de prélèvement; *Tel* ***direct dialling*** automatique *m*; *Am Gram* ***direct discourse*** discours *m ou* style *m* direct; ***direct fixed costs*** coûts *mpl* fixes directs *ou* attribuables; ***direct hit*** coup *m* au but; **to score a direct hit on sth** *(of bomber)* toucher qch en plein dans le mille; *(of bomb)* tomber en plein dans qch; **the missile made a direct hit** le missile a atteint son objectif; **the palace is built to withstand a direct hit** le palais a été construit pour résister à une bombe lâché d'un avion ou à un missile; **the ship suffered two direct hits from missiles** le bateau a été touché par deux missiles; ***direct investment*** investissement *m* direct; ***direct labour*** main-d'œuvre *f* directe; ***direct labour cost*** prix *m* de la main-d'œuvre directe; *Tel* ***direct line*** ligne *f* directe; *Com & Mktg* ***direct mail*** publipostage *m*; ***direct mail advertising*** publicité *f* directe, publicité *f* par publipostage; ***direct mail campaign*** campagne *f* de publicité directe; ***direct marketing*** marketing *m* direct; *Comput* ***direct memory access*** accès *m* direct à la mémoire; *Gram* ***direct object*** complément *m* (d'objet) direct; *Am Pol* ***direct primary*** élections *fpl* primaires directes, primaires *fpl* directes; ***direct purchasing*** achats *mpl* directs; *Gram* ***direct question*** question *f* au style direct; *Pol* ***direct rule*** = contrôle direct du maintien de l'ordre par le gouvernement britannique en Irlande du Nord imposé en 1972; ***direct selling*** vente *f* directe; *Br Gram* ***direct speech*** discours *m ou* style *m* direct; *Fin* ***direct tax*** impôt *m* direct; *Fin* ***direct taxation*** imposition *f* directe

---

direct-dial *adj Tel*

►► ***direct-dial number*** numéro *m* direct; ***direct-dial telephone*** ligne *f* téléphonique directe, téléphone *m* direct

direct-grant school *n Br* = établissement scolaire privé subventionné par l'État si l'établissement accepte un certain nombre d'élèves qui ne paient pas

direction [dɪ'rekʃən] **1** *n* (**a**) *(way)* direction *f*, sens *m*; **in every direction** en tous sens, dans tous les sens; **in the opposite direction** dans la direction opposée, en sens inverse; **in the right/wrong direction** dans le bon/mauvais sens, dans la bonne/mauvaise direction; **in the (general) direction of Chicago** dans la direction de Chicago; **we were travelling in the direction of Paris** nous allions dans la *ou* en direction de Paris; **which direction are you going (in)?** vers où allez-vous?, quelle direction prenez-vous?; *Fig* **a step in the right direction** un pas dans la bonne voie *ou* direction; *Fig* **she lacks direction** elle ne sait pas très bien où elle va; **to have a good/bad sense of direction** avoir un bon/mauvais sens de l'orientation; **to lose one's sense of direction** perdre le sens de l'orientation

(**b**) *(control, management)* direction *f*; **the investigation was carried out under the direction of an independent body** l'enquête a été menée sous la direction *ou* conduite d'un organisme indépendant

(**c**) *Cin, Rad & TV* réalisation *f*; *Theat* mise *f* en scène; *Cin, Rad & TV* **under the direction of...** réalisation de..., réalisé par...; *Theat* mise en scène de...

2 directions *npl* (**a**) *(instructions)* indications *fpl*, instructions *fpl*, mode *m* d'emploi; **read the directions** lisez le mode d'emploi; *Theat* **stage directions** indications *fpl* scéniques

(**b**) *(to find location)* **I asked for directions to the station** j'ai demandé le chemin de la gare; **you've been given the wrong directions** on vous a mal renseigné

►► ***direction finder*** radiogoniomètre *m*; *Aut* ***direction indicator*** clignotant *m*

directional [dɪ'rekʃənəl] *adj (gen) & Electron* directionnel

directive [dɪ'rektɪv] **1** *n* directive *f*, instruction *f*

2 *adj* directeur

directly [dɪ'rektlɪ] **1** *adv* (**a**) *(straight)* directement; **go directly to the police station** allez directement *ou* tout droit au poste de police; **to be directly descended from sb** descendre en droite ligne *ou* en ligne directe de qn; **the affair concerns me directly** cette affaire me concerne directement; **to come directly to the point** aller droit au fait

(**b**) *(promptly)* immédiatement; **directly after lunch** tout de suite après le déjeuner; **directly before the film** juste avant le film; **I'll be there directly** j'arrive tout de suite

(**c**) *(frankly)* franchement

(**d**) *(exactly)* exactement; **directly opposite the station** juste en face de la gare

2 *conj Br* aussitôt que + *indicative*, dès que + *indicative*; **we'll leave directly the money arrives** nous partirons dès que l'argent sera arrivé

directness [dɪ'rektnɪs] *n* (**a**) *(of person, reply)* franchise *f*; *(of remark)* absence *f* d'ambiguïté (**b**) *(of attack)* caractère *m* direct

director [dɪ'rektə(r)] *n* (**a**) *(person → of business)* directeur(trice) *m,f*, chef *m*; *(→ of organization)* directeur(trice) *m,f*; *(board member)* administrateur(trice) *m,f*

(**b**) *Am Mus* chef *m* d'orchestre

(**c**) *Cin, Rad & TV* réalisateur(trice) *m,f*; *Theat* metteur *m* en scène

(**d**) *(device)* guide *m*

►► *Cin & TV* ***director's chair*** régisseur *m*; *Cin* ***director's cut*** version *f* du réalisateur, director's cut *f*; *Br* ***Director of Education*** ≃ recteur *m* d'académie; ***director of programmes*** directeur(trice) *m,f* des programmes; *Br Law* ***Director of Public Prosecutions*** ≃ procureur *m* général; ***directors' report*** rapport *m* annuel; *Br Univ* ***director of studies*** = enseignant qui suit la scolarité d'un étudiant tout au long de son cursus universitaire

directorate [dɪ'rektərət] *n* (**a**) *(board)* conseil *m* d'administration (**b**) *(position)* direction *f*, poste *m* de directeur

director-general *n* directeur(trice) *m,f* général(e)

directorial [ˌdaɪrek'tɔːrɪəl] *adj* de mise en scène; *Cin* **his directorial début** son premier film derrière le caméra

directorship [dɪ'rektəʃɪp] *n* direction *f*, poste *m ou* fonctions *fpl* de directeur; **she holds directorships in several companies** elle fait partie du conseil d'administration de plusieurs entreprises

directory [dɪ'rektərɪ] (*pl* **directories**) **1** *n* (**a**) *(of addresses)* répertoire *m* (d'adresses); *Tel* annuaire *m* (des téléphones), bottin *m*; *Comput* répertoire *m* (**b**) *(of instructions)* mode *m* d'emploi; *Rel* directoire *m*

2 *adj* directeur

3 Directory *n Hist* **the Directory** le Directoire

►► *Tel Am* ***directory assistance,*** *Br* ***directory enquiries*** (service *m* des) renseignements *mpl* téléphoniques; *Comput* ***directory structure*** structure *f* arborescente, structure *f* du répertoire

directrix [dɪ'rektrɪks] *n (gen) & Geom* directrice *f*

direfully ['daɪəfʊlɪ], **direly** ['daɪəlɪ] *adv Literary (gen)* désastreusement, affreusement; *(say)* lugubrement

direness ['daɪənɪs] *n Literary (gen)* caractère *m* affreux; *(of prediction)* caractère *m* funeste

dirge [dɜːdʒ] *n Mus* hymne *m ou* chant *m* funèbre; *Fig* chant *m* lugubre

dirham ['dɪəræm] *n* dirham *m*, dirhem *m*

dirigible ['dɪrɪdʒəbəl] **1** *adj* dirigeable

2 *n* dirigeable *m*

dirigisme ['dɪrɪʒɪzəm] *n Econ & Pol* dirigisme *m*

dirk [dɜːk] *n Scot* dague *f*, poignard *m*

dirndl ['dɜːndəl] *n (skirt)* jupe *f* paysanne froncée; *(dress)* robe *f* paysanne froncée

►► ***dirndl skirt*** jupe *f* paysanne froncée

dirt [dɜːt] *n (UNCOUNT)* (**a**) *(grime)* saleté *f*, crasse *f*; *(mud)* boue *f*; *(excrement)* crotte *f*, ordure *f*; **don't tread dirt into the carpet** ne ramène pas de boue sur la moquette; **she was covered in dirt** elle était toute sale *ou* couverte de crasse; **this dress really shows the dirt** cette robe fait vite sale *ou* est très salissante

(**b**) *(soil)* terre *f*; **stop scrabbling in the dirt** arrête de gratter la terre; **to be as common as dirt** *(person)* avoir mauvais genre; **to treat sb like dirt** traiter qn comme un chien; *Am Fam Fig* **to eat dirt** ramper ❑

(**c**) *(obscenity)* obscénité *f*

(**d**) *Fam (scandal)* ragots *mpl*, cancans *mpl*; **to dig the dirt on sb** dénicher des ragots sur qn; **to dish the dirt on sb** colporter des ragots sur qn

(**e**) *Ind (in material, solution)* impuretés *fpl*, corps *mpl* étrangers; *(in machine)* encrassement *m*; **the wheel is full of dirt** la roue est encrassée

►► *Am* ***dirt bike*** moto *f* tout-terrain; ***dirt farmer*** petit fermier *m*; ***dirt road*** chemin *m* de terre *ou* non goudronné; ***dirt track*** *(gen)* chemin *m* de terre; *Sport* (piste *f*) cendrée *f*; ***dirt track racing*** courses *fpl* sur cendrée

dirt-cheap *Fam* **1** *adv* pour rien ❑; **I bought it dirt-cheap** je l'ai payé trois fois rien

2 *adj* très bon marché ❑

dirtily ['dɜːtɪlɪ] *adv* (**a**) *(eat)* salement (**b**) *(speak)* grossièrement (**c**) *(play, fight)* déloyalement

dirtiness ['dɜːtɪnɪs] *n* malpropreté *f*

dirt-poor *adj esp Am Fam* **to be dirt-poor** vivre dans une misère noire

dirt-proof *adj* insalissable

dirty ['dɜːtɪ] (*compar* **dirtier**, *superl* **dirtiest**, *pt & pp* **dirtied**) **1** *adj* (**a**) *(not clean → clothes, hands, person)* sale, malpropre, crasseux; *(→ machine)* encrassé; *(→ wound)* infecté; *(muddy)* plein de boue, crotté; **don't get dirty!** ne vous salissez pas!; **to get one's hands dirty** se salir les mains; **he got his shirt dirty** il a sali sa chemise; **this rug gets dirty easily** ce tapis est salissant; *Fam* **he's one of the dirty mac brigade** c'est un vieux cochon

(**b**) *(colour)* sale; **a dirty green** un vert sale

(**c**) *(nasty)* sale; **it was a dirty business** c'était une sale affaire; **politics is a dirty business** il est difficile de garder les mains propres quand on fait de la politique; **a dirty campaign** une campagne sordide; *Fam* **no dirty cracks!** pas de vacheries!; **that's a dirty lie** ce n'est absolument pas vrai; **he's a dirty fighter** il se bat en traître; **to give sb a dirty look** regarder qn de travers *ou* d'un sale œil; *Am* **that's dirty pool!** c'est un tour de cochon!; *Fam* **you dirty rat!** espèce de salaud!

(**d**) *(weather)* sale, vilain

(**e**) *(obscene)* grossier, obscène; **to have a dirty mind** avoir l'esprit mal tourné; **to have a dirty mouth** être mal embouché; **dirty magazines** revues *fpl* pornographiques; *Fam* **a dirty old man** un vieux cochon *ou* vicelard; **a dirty joke/story** une blague/histoire cochonne; **a dirty word** une grossièreté, un gros mot; **"middle class" is a dirty word around here** le terme "classe moyenne" est une insulte par ici

2 *adv Fam* (**a**) *(fight, play)* déloyalement; **to talk dirty** *(swearing)* dire des gros mots; *(sexually)* dire des trucs cochons

(**b**) *Br (as intensifier)* vachement; **a dirty great skyscraper** un gratte-ciel énorme

3 *vt (soil)* salir; *(machine)* encrasser; *also Fig* **to dirty one's hands** se salir les mains; *Fig* **to dirty one's reputation** entacher *ou* salir sa réputation

4 *vi* se salir, se souiller; **to dirty easily** *(material, car etc)* se salir facilement, être salissant

5 *n Br Fam* **to do the dirty on sb** jouer un sale tour *ou* faire une vacherie à qn

►► *St Exch* ***dirty float*** taux *mpl* de change concertés; *Fin* ***dirty money*** argent *m* sale *ou* mal acquis; *Br Fam Hum* ***dirty stop-out*** débauché(e) *m,f (qui découche)*; ***dirty trick*** *(malicious act)* sale tour *m*; **to play a dirty trick on sb** jouer un sale tour *ou* un tour de cochon à qn; **they've been up to their dirty tricks again** ils ont encore fait des leurs; *Pol* ***dirty tricks campaign*** = manœuvres déloyales visant à discréditer un adversaire politique; *Fam* ***dirty weekend*** week-end *m* coquin; ***dirty work*** *(UNCOUNT) (unpleasant)* travail *m* salissant; *Fam (dishonest)* sale boulot *m*; **to do sb's dirty work** faire le sale boulot pour qn

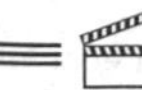

'The Dirty Dozen' *Aldrich* 'Douze salopards'

dirty-minded *adj* qui a l'esprit mal tourné

dis [dɪs] *vt esp Am Fam (disparage)* débiner

disability [ˌdɪsəˈbɪlətɪ] *(pl* **disabilities***) n* (**a**) *(state → physical)* incapacité *f*, invalidité *f*; **partial/total disability** incapacité *f* partielle/totale

(**b**) *(handicap)* infirmité *f*, handicap *m*; **her disability makes her eligible for a pension** son infirmité lui donne droit à une pension

(**c**) *Law* **disability to do sth** incapacité *f ou* inhabilité *f* à faire qch

►► *Admin* ***disability allowance*** pension *f* d'invalidité; *Ins* ***disability clause*** = clause d'une police d'assurance-vie permettant à l'assuré de cesser tout paiement et de recevoir une pension en cas d'invalidité; *Admin* ***disability pension*** pension *f* d'invalidité

disable [dɪsˈeɪbəl] *vt* (**a**) *(accident, illness)* rendre infirme; *(maim)* mutiler, estropier; **a disabling disease** une maladie invalidante (**b**) *Mil (army, battalion)* mettre hors de combat (**c**) *(machine)* mettre hors service; *(ship)* faire subir une avarie à, désemparer; *(gun, tank)* mettre hors d'action; *(propeller)* immobiliser; *Comput (option)* désactiver (**d**) *Law* **to disable sb from doing sth** rendre qn inhabile à faire qch; *(pronounce)* prononcer qn inhabile à faire qch

disabled [dɪsˈeɪbəld] **1** *adj* (**a**) *(handicapped)* infirme, handicapé; *(maimed)* mutilé, estropié; **disabled ex-servicemen** invalides *mpl ou* mutilés *mpl* de guerre

(**b**) *Mil (army, battalion)* mis hors de combat

(**c**) *(machine)* hors service; *(ship)* avarié, désemparé; *(gun, tank)* mis hors d'action; *(propeller)* immobilisé; *Comput (option)* désactivé

(**d**) *Law* **to be disabled from doing sth** être incapable de *ou* inhabile à faire qch

2 *npl* **the disabled** *(handicapped)* les handicapés *mpl*; *(maimed)* les mutilés *mpl ou* estropiés *mpl*; **the war disabled** les mutilés *mpl ou* invalides *mpl* de guerre

►► ***disabled access*** facilité *f* d'accès pour personnes handicapées

disablement [dɪsˈeɪbəlmənt] *n* invalidité *f*, infirmité *f*

►► *Admin* ***disablement benefit*** allocation *f* d'invalidité; ***disablement insurance*** assurance *f* invalidité; *Admin* ***disablement pension*** pension *f* d'invalidité

disabuse [ˌdɪsəˈbjuːz] *vt Formal* détromper, ôter ses illusions à; **to disabuse sb of sth** détromper qn de qch

disaccharide [daɪˈsækəraɪd] *n Chem* disaccharide *m*, diholoside *m*

disadvantage [ˌdɪsədˈvɑːntɪdʒ] **1** *n* (**a**) *(condition)* désavantage *m*, inconvénient *m*; **to be at a disadvantage** être désavantagé *ou* dans une position désavantageuse; **she's at a big disadvantage being the oldest** le fait qu'elle soit la plus vieille la désavantage nettement; **to put sb at a disadvantage** désavantager *ou* défavoriser qn; **the situation works** *or* **is to her disadvantage** la situation est un handicap *ou* un désavantage pour elle; **it would be to his disadvantage to sue** cela lui porterait préjudice *ou* lui ferait du tort d'intenter un procès

(**b**) *Com (loss)* perte *f*

2 *vt* désavantager, défavoriser

disadvantaged [ˌdɪsədˈvɑːntɪdʒd] **1** *adj (gen)* défavorisé; *(economically)* déshérité; **socially disadvantaged** défavorisé sur le plan social

2 *npl* **the disadvantaged** les défavorisés *mpl*

disadvantageous [ˌdɪsædvɑːnˈteɪdʒəs] *adj* désavantageux, défavorable; **to be disadvantageous to sb** être désavantageux *ou* défavorable à qn

disadvantageously [ˌdɪsædvɑːnˈteɪdʒəslɪ] *adv* d'une manière désavantageuse, désavantageusement

disaffected [ˌdɪsəˈfektɪd] *adj (discontented)* mécontent; *(rebellious)* rebelle; **disaffected youth** jeunesse *f* révoltée

disaffectedly [ˌdɪsəˈfektɪdlɪ] *adv (discontentedly)* avec mécontentement; *(rebelliously)* de manière rebelle

disaffection [ˌdɪsəˈfekʃən] *n (discontent)* mécontentement *m* (**from** à l'égard de); **there is widespread disaffection in the country** *(rebelliousness)* le pays est au bord de la rébellion

disaffiliate [ˌdɪsəˈfɪlɪeɪt] *vt* désaffilier

disaffiliation [ˌdɪsəfɪlɪˈeɪʃən] *n* désaffiliation *f*

disafforest [ˌdɪsəˈfɒrɪst] *vt (land → gen)* déboiser; *Law* déclarer hors du régime forestier

disafforestation [ˌdɪsəfɒrɪsˈteɪʃən] *n* déboisement *m*

disagree [ˌdɪsəˈgriː] *vi* (**a**) *(person, people)* ne pas être d'accord, être en désaccord; **she disagrees** elle n'est pas d'accord, elle n'est pas de cet avis; **to disagree with sb about** *or* **on sth** ne pas être d'accord avec *ou* ne pas être du même avis que qn sur qch; **I disagree with everything they've done** je suis contre *ou* je désapprouve tout ce qu'ils ont fait; **we disagree on everything** *(differ)* nous ne sommes jamais d'accord; **I can't say I disagree with her** *(in opinion etc)* je ne peux pas dire que je ne suis pas de son avis; *(as regards an action)* je ne peux pas dire que je la désapprouve

(**b**) *(figures, records)* ne pas concorder; **the two men's accounts of events disagree** les récits des deux hommes sur ce qui s'est passé ne concordent pas

(**c**) *(food, weather)* ne pas convenir; **spicy food disagrees with him** les plats épicés ne lui réussissent pas, il digère mal les plats épicés; **I must have eaten something that disagreed with me** j'ai dû manger quelque chose qui n'est pas bien passé

disagreeable [ˌdɪsəˈgrɪəbəl] *adj (person, remark)* désagréable, désobligeant; *(experience, job)* désagréable, pénible; *(smell)* désagréable, déplaisant; **don't be so disagreeable!** ne soyez pas si désagréable!

disagreeableness [ˌdɪsəˈgrɪəbəlnɪs] *n (of situation, job, experience, smell)* caractère *m* désagréable; *(of person)* mauvaise humeur *f*, *(of remark)* désobligeance *f* (**to** envers)

disagreeably [ˌdɪsəˈgrɪəblɪ] *adv* désagréablement, d'une façon désagréable *ou* désobligeante; **he behaved so disagreeably!** il a été tellement insupportable!

disagreement [ˌdɪsəˈgriːmənt] *n* (**a**) *(of opinions, records)* désaccord *m*, conflit *m*; **I'm in complete disagreement with you about** *or* **on this** je ne partage pas du tout votre avis là-dessus; **they are in disagreement about** *or* **on what action to take** ils ne sont pas d'accord sur les mesures à prendre (**b**) *(quarrel)* différend *m*, querelle *f*; **they've had a disagreement over** *or* **about money** ils se sont disputés à propos d'argent, ils ont eu une querelle d'argent

disallow [ˌdɪsəˈlaʊ] *vt (argument, opinion)* rejeter; *Sport (goal, try)* refuser; *Law* débouter, rejeter

disambiguate [ˌdɪsæmˈbɪgjʊeɪt] *vt* désambiguïser

disambiguation [ˈdɪsæmˌbɪgjʊˈeɪʃən] *n* désambiguïsation *f*

disappear [ˌdɪsəˈpɪə(r)] *vi* (**a**) *(vanish → person, snow)* disparaître; *(→ object)* disparaître, s'égarer; *Ling* s'amuïr; **she disappeared from sight** on l'a perdue de vue; **he disappeared into the crowd** il s'est perdu dans la foule; **to disappear over the horizon** disparaître à l'horizon; **to make sth disappear** *(gen)* faire disparaître qch; *(magician)* escamoter qch

(**b**) *(cease to exist → pain, tribe)* disparaître; *(→ problem)* disparaître, s'aplanir; *(→ memory)* s'effacer, s'estomper; *(→ tradition)* disparaître, tomber en désuétude; **as a species, the turtle is fast disappearing** les tortues sont une espèce en voie de disparition

disappearance [ˌdɪsəˈpɪərəns] *n (gen)* disparition *f*, *Ling* amuïssement *m*

disappearing act [ˌdɪsəˈpɪərɪŋ-] *n* **to do a disappearing act** *(conjurer → make someone or something disappear)* faire disparaître quelqu'un/quelque chose; *(→ make self disappear)* disparaître; *Fam Fig (→ sneak away)* s'esquiver❏, s'éclipser❏; *Fam* **the scissors have done a disappearing act** les ciseaux ont disparu❏; **he's done his famous disappearing act again** il s'est encore éclipsé

disappoint [ˌdɪsəˈpɔɪnt] *vt* (**a**) *(person)* décevoir, désappointer; **you promised to come, so don't disappoint him** vous avez promis de venir, alors ne lui faites pas faux bond (**b**) *(hope)* décevoir; *(plan)* contrarier, contrecarrer

disappointed [ˌdɪsəˈpɔɪntɪd] *adj* (**a**) *(person)* déçu, désappointé; **disappointed customers** clients *mpl* insatisfaits; **I'm very disappointed in him** il m'a beaucoup déçu; **I was disappointed to hear you won't be coming** j'ai été déçu d'apprendre que vous ne viendrez pas; **are you disappointed at** *or* **with the results?** les résultats vous ont-ils déçu?, avez-vous été déçu par les résultats?; **to be disappointed in love** être malheureux en amour

(**b**) *(ambition, hope)* déçu; *(plan)* contrarié, contrecarré

disappointedly [ˌdɪsəˈpɔɪntɪdlɪ] *adv* d'un air déçu; *(say)* d'un ton déçu

disappointing [ˌdɪsəˈpɔɪntɪŋ] *adj* décevant; **how disappointing!** quelle déception!, comme c'est décevant!; **I found the film very disappointing** j'ai trouvé le film vraiment décevant, j'ai été vraiment déçu par le film

disappointingly [ˌdɪsəˈpɔɪntɪŋlɪ] *adv* **disappointingly low grades** des notes *fpl* d'une faiblesse décourageante *ou* décevante; **he did disappointingly badly in the exam** ses résultats à l'examen ont été très décevants; **the unemployment figures are still disappointingly high** il est décevant de constater que les chiffres du chômage restent élevés

disappointment [ˌdɪsəˈpɔɪntmənt] *n* (**a**) *(state)* déception *f*, désappointement *m*, déconvenue *f*; **to her great disappointment she failed** à sa grande déception *ou* déconvenue, elle a échoué; **book early to avoid disappointment** réservez bien à l'avance pour ne pas être déçu

(**b**) *(letdown)* déception *f*, désillusion *f*; **she has suffered many disappointments** elle a essuyé bien des déboires; **he has been a great disappointment to me** il m'a beaucoup déçu

disapprobation [ˌdɪsæprəˈbeɪʃən] *n Formal* désapprobation *f*; *(strong)* réprobation *f*; **a murmur of disapprobation** un murmure désapprobateur *ou* de désapprobation

disapproval [ˌdɪsəˈpruːvəl] *n* désapprobation *f*; *(strong)* réprobation *f*; **a look of disapproval** un regard désapprobateur *ou* de désapprobation; **to shake one's head in disapproval** faire un signe désapprobateur de la tête; **she showed/expressed her disapproval of his decision** elle a montré/exprimé sa désapprobation à l'égard de sa décision; **much to my disapproval she decided to get married** elle a décidé de se marier, ce que je désapprouve entièrement

disapprove [ˌdɪsəˈpruːv] **1** *vi* désapprouver; **to disapprove of sth** désapprouver qch; **she disapproves of smoking** elle désapprouve *ou* elle est contre le tabac; **your mother disapproves of your going** votre mère n'est pas d'accord pour que vous y alliez; **he disapproves of everything I do** il trouve à redire à tout ce que je fais; **her father disapproves of me** son père ne me trouve pas à son goût

2 *vt* désapprouver

disapproving [ˌdɪsəˈpruːvɪŋ] *adj* désapprobateur, de désapprobation; **don't look so disapproving** ne prends pas cet air désapprobateur; **he was a stern, rather disapproving man** c'était un homme sévère, qui portait sur toutes choses un œil désapprobateur

disapprovingly [ˌdɪsəˈpruːvɪŋlɪ] *adv (look)* d'un air désapprobateur; *(speak)* d'un ton désapprobateur, avec désapprobation

disarm [dɪsˈɑːm] **1** *vt* (**a**) *(country, enemy, critic)* désarmer (**b**) *(charm)* désarmer, toucher

2 *vi* désarmer

disarmament [dɪsˈɑːməmənt] **1** *n* désarmement *m*

2 *comp (conference, negotiations, talks)* sur le désarmement

disarming [dɪsˈɑːmɪŋ] **1** *adj* désarmant

2 *n* désarmement *m*

disarmingly [dɪsˈɑːmɪŋlɪ] *adv* de façon désarmante; **disarmingly honest/friendly** d'une honnêteté/amabilité désarmante

disarrange [ˌdɪsəˈreɪndʒ] *vt (order, room)* déranger, mettre en désordre; *(plans)* déranger, bouleverser; *(hair)* défaire

disarray [ˌdɪsəˈreɪ] **1** *n (of person)* confusion *f*, désordre *m*; *(of clothing)* désordre *m*; **in total disarray** *(person, political party)* en plein désarroi; *(objects, room, life)* en désordre; *(troops)* en déroute; **the group was thrown into disarray** la confusion *ou* le désordre régnait dans le groupe; **her thoughts were in disarray** ses pensées étaient très confuses; **her clothes were in disarray** elle était débraillée

2 *vt* (**a**) *Literary (throw into confusion → person, political party)* mettre en désarroi; *(→ objects, room, life)* metter en désordre; *(→ troops)* mettre en déroute

(**b**) *Arch (undress)* dévêtir

disarticulate [ˌdɪsɑːˈtɪkjʊleɪt] *vt* (**a**) *(carcass, skeleton)* désarticuler (**b**) *(mechanism, machine)* disjoindre, démonter

disarticulation [ˌdɪsɑːtɪkjʊˈleɪʃən] *n* (**a**) *(of carcass, skeleton)* désarticulation *f* (**b**) *(of mechanism, machine)* démontage *m*

disassemble [ˌdɪsəˈsembəl] *vt* démonter, désassembler

disassembly [ˌdɪsəˈsemblɪ] *n* démontage *m*, désassemblage *m*

disassociate [ˌdɪsəˈsəʊʃɪeɪt] **1** *vt* (**a**) *(gen)* dissocier, séparer; **to disassociate oneself from sb/sth** se dissocier *ou* désolidariser de qn/qch (**b**) *Chem* dissocier

2 *vi Chem (chemist)* opérer une dissociation; *(molecules)* se dissocier

disassociated [ˌdɪsəˈsəʊʃɪeɪtɪd] *adj*

▸▸ *Psy* ***disassociated personality*** personnalité *f* simultanée

disassociation [dɪsəˌsəʊsɪˈeɪʃən] *n* dissociation *f*

disassociative [dɪsəˈsəʊsɪətɪv] *adj Psy* dissociatif

disaster [dɪˈzɑːstə(r)] *n* désastre *m*, catastrophe *f*; *(natural)* catastrophe *f*, sinistre *m*; **air disaster** catastrophe *f* aérienne; **financial disaster** désastre *m* financier; **a series of disasters** une suite de désastres *ou* de malheurs; **at the scene of the disaster** sur les lieux de la catastrophe *ou* du sinistre; **the town has suffered one disaster after another** la ville a subi désastre après désastre; **the project is heading for disaster** le projet est voué à l'échec *ou* à la catastrophe; **she's heading for** *or* **courting disaster** elle court à sa perte *ou* à la catastrophe; **they were near the summit when disaster struck** ils avaient presque atteint le sommet quand la catastrophe s'est produite; **we were going along quite happily then disaster struck** nous suivions notre petit bonhomme de chemin, quand soudain, catastrophe!; **as a manager, he's a disaster!** en tant que directeur, ce n'est pas une réussite!; **my hair's a disaster this morning!** mes cheveux sont dans un état épouvantable ce matin!

▸▸ ***disaster area*** région *f* sinistrée; *Fig* champ *m* de bataille; **to declare a town a disaster area** déclarer une ville zone sinistrée; **your sister's a walking disaster area!** ta sœur est une vraie catastrophe ambulante!; ***disaster fund*** fonds *m* de secours; ***disaster movie*** film *m* catastrophe

disastrous [dɪˈzɑːstrəs] *adj* désastreux, catastrophique

disastrously [dɪˈzɑːstrəslɪ] *adv* désastreusement; **the performance went disastrously wrong** la représentation a tourné au désastre; **the estimates were disastrously inaccurate** l'inexactitude des prévisions s'est révélée désastreuse

disattribution [ˌdɪsætrɪˈbjuːʃən] *n (of work of art, book)* désattribution *f*

disavow [ˌdɪsəˈvaʊ] *vt Formal (child, opinion)* désavouer; *(responsibility, faith)* renier

disavowal [ˌdɪsəˈvaʊəl] *n Formal (of child, opinion)* désaveu *m*; *(of responsibility, faith)* reniement *m*

disband [dɪsˈbænd] **1** *vt (army, club)* disperser; *(organization)* disperser, dissoudre

2 *vi (army, club)* se disperser; *(organization)* se dissoudre

disbandment [dɪsˈbændmənt] *n (of army, club)* dispersion *f*; *(of organization)* dissolution *f*

disbar [dɪsˈbɑː(r)] *(pt & pp* **disbarred,** *cont* **disbarring**) *vt Law* rayer du barreau *ou* du tableau de l'ordre *(des avocats)*; **he was disbarred for malpractice** il s'est fait rayer du barreau pour faute professionnelle

disbarment [dɪsˈbɑːmənt] *n Law* radiation *f* (du barreau)

disbelief [ˌdɪsbɪˈliːf] *n* incrédulité *f*; **she looked at him in disbelief** elle l'a regardé avec incrédulité

disbelieve [ˌdɪsbɪˈliːv] **1** *vt (person)* ne pas croire; *(news, story)* ne pas croire à; **I see no reason to disbelieve his story** je ne vois pas pourquoi on ne croirait pas à ce qu'il dit

2 *vi Rel* ne pas croire (**in** à)

disbeliever [ˌdɪsbɪˈliːvə(r)] *n (gen)* incrédule *mf*; *Rel* incroyant(e) *m,f*, incrédule *mf*

disbelieving [ˌdɪsbɪˈliːvɪŋ] *adj* incrédule

disbud [ˌdɪsˈbʌd] *vt Bot (fruit tree)* ébourgeonner

disburden [ˌdɪsˈbɜːdən] *vt Literary* décharger, soulager (**of** de); **to disburden one's mind of a secret** décharger sa conscience d'un secret

disburse [dɪsˈbɜːs] *vt Fin* débourser

disbursement [dɪsˈbɜːsmənt] *n Fin* (**a**) *(payment)* débours *m*, dépense *f* (**b**) *(action)* déboursement *m*

disc [dɪsk] *n* (**a**) *(flat circular object)* disque *m*; **the disc of the moon** le disque de la lune (**b**) *(record)* disque *m* (**c**) *Anat* disque *m* (intervertébral); **to slip a disc** se faire une hernie discale (**d**) *(identity tag)* plaque *f* d'identité; *Aut* **parking disc** disque *m* de stationnement;

▸▸ *Aut* ***disc brake*** frein *m* à disque; *Phot* ***disc camera*** appareil *m* photo à disque; *Phot* ***disc film*** disque *m*; *Agr* ***disc harrow*** pulvériseur *m*; ***disc jockey*** animateur(trice) *m,f*, *(on radio, at disco)* disc-jockey *m*; ***disc parking*** stationnement *m* à disque

disc. *(written abbr* **discount**) esc.

discard 1 *vt* [dɪˈskɑːd] (**a**) *(get rid of)* se débarrasser de, mettre au rebut; *(idea, system)* renoncer, abandonner; *(friend)* abandonner; **his discarded coat still lay on the sofa** son manteau était toujours sur le canapé, tel qu'il l'y avait jeté

(**b**) *Cards* se défausser de, défausser; *(in cribbage)* écarter

2 *vi* [dɪˈskɑːd] *Cards* se défausser; *(in cribbage)* écarter

3 *n* [ˈdɪskɑːd] (**a**) *Com & Ind (reject)* pièce *f* de rebut

(**b**) *Cards* défausse *f*; *(in cribbage)* écart *m*

discarded [dɪˈskɑːdɪd] *adj (small object)* jeté; *(larger)* abandonné

discarnate [dɪsˈkɑːneɪt] *adj Arch or Literary* **discarnate bones** os *mpl* décharnés; **discarnate soul** âme *f* libérée du corps

discern [dɪˈsɜːn] *vt (see)* discerner, distinguer; *(understand)* discerner

discernible [dɪˈsɜːnəbəl] *adj (visible)* visible; *(detectable)* discernable, perceptible; **he left for no discernible reason** il est parti sans raison apparente

discernibly [dɪˈsɜːnəblɪ] *adv (visibly)* visiblement; *(perceptibly)* perceptiblement, sensiblement

discerning [dɪˈsɜːnɪŋ] *adj (person)* judicieux, sagace; *(taste)* fin, délicat; *(look)* perspicace; **with a discerning eye** d'un œil averti; **a house/car for the discerning buyer** une maison/voiture pour l'acheteur avisé; **for the discerning reader** pour le lecteur averti

discernment [dɪˈsɜːnmənt] *n* discernement *m*, perspicacité *f*

discharge 1 *vt* [ˈdɪstʃɑːdʒ] (**a**) *(release → patient)* laisser sortir, libérer; *(→ prisoner)* libérer, mettre en liberté; **he was discharged from hospital yesterday** il est sorti de l'hôpital hier; **the patient discharged herself** la malade a signé une décharge et est partie

(**b**) *(dismiss → employee)* renvoyer, congédier; *(→ official)* destituer; *Law (→ jury)* dessaisir; *(→ accused)* acquitter, relaxer; *Mil (from service)* renvoyer à la vie civile; *(from active duty)* démobiliser; *(for lack of fitness)* réformer; *Fin* **discharged bankrupt** failli *m* réhabilité

(**c**) *(unload → cargo)* décharger; *(→ passengers)* débarquer

(**d**) *(emit → liquid)* dégorger, déverser; *(→ gas)* dégager, émettre; *(of gland → hormones)* sécréter; *Elec* décharger; *Med* **to discharge pus** *(abscess)* suppurer

(**e**) *(perform → duty)* remplir, s'acquitter de; *(→ function)* remplir

(**f**) *Fin (debt)* s'acquitter de, régler

(**g**) *(gun)* décharger, tirer; *(arrow)* décocher

2 *vi* [ˈdɪstʃɑːdʒ] (**a**) *(ship)* décharger

(**b**) *Med (wound)* suinter

(**c**) *Elec* être en décharge

3 *n* [dɪsˈtʃɑːdʒ] (**a**) *(release → of patient)* sortie *f* *(of prisoner)* libération *f*, mise *f* en liberté

(**b**) *(dismissal → of employee)* renvoi *m*; *(→ of soldier)* libération *f*; *(after active duty)* démobilisation *f*; *Law (acquittal)* acquittement *m*

(**c**) *(of cargo)* déchargement *m*

(**d**) *(emission)* émission *f*; *(of liquid)* écoulement *m*; *Med (of wound)* suintement *m*; *(vaginal)* pertes *fpl* (blanches); *(of pus)* suppuration *f*

(**e**) *Elec* décharge *f*

(**f**) *(of duty)* exécution *f*, accomplissement *m*

(**g**) *(of debt)* acquittement *m*

(**h**) *(of gun)* décharge *f*

▸▸ *Tech* ***discharge pipe*** tuyau *m* de décharge *ou* de débit

disciple [dɪˈsaɪpəl] *n (gen) & Rel* disciple *m*

disciplinarian [ˌdɪsɪplɪˈneərɪən] **1** *n* partisan *m* de la manière forte; **he is a strict disciplinarian** il est strict en matière de discipline

2 *adj* disciplinaire

disciplinary [ˈdɪsɪplɪnərɪ] *adj* (**a**) *(corrective → measure)* disciplinaire *(→ committee)* de discipline; **to take disciplinary action** *(of employer)* prendre des mesures disciplinaires (**b**) *(relating to field)* relatif à une discipline

▸▸ ***disciplinary board*** conseil *m* de discipline; ***disciplinary hearing*** séance *f* du conseil de discipline; ***disciplinary procedure*** procédure *f* disciplinaire

discipline [ˈdɪsɪplɪn] **1** *n* (**a**) *(training, control)* discipline *f*; **to keep discipline** *(of teacher)* maintenir la discipline; **with iron discipline** avec une discipline de fer (**b**) *(area of study)* discipline *f*, matière *f*

2 *vt* (**a**) *(train → person)* discipliner; *(→ mind)* discipliner, former (**b**) *(punish)* punir

disciplined [ˈdɪsɪplɪnd] *adj* discipliné

disclaim [dɪsˈkleɪm] *vt* (**a**) *(deny → responsibility)* rejeter, décliner; *(→ knowledge)* nier; *(→ news, remark)* démentir; *(→ paternity)* désavouer (**b**) *Law* se désister de, renoncer à

disclaimer [dɪsˈkleɪmə(r)] *n* (**a**) *(denial)* démenti *m*, désaveu *m*; **the president issued a disclaimer denying all knowledge of the affair** le président a publié un démenti où il nie être au courant de cette affaire (**b**) *Law* désistement *m*, renonciation *f*

disclose [dɪsˈkləʊz] *vt* (**a**) *(reveal → secret)* divulguer, dévoiler; *(→ news)* divulguer; *(→ feelings)* révéler (**b**) *(uncover)* exposer, montrer

disclosing tablet [dɪsˈkləʊzɪŋ-] *n* comprimé *m* révélateur de plaque (dentaire)

disclosure [dɪsˈkləʊʒə(r)] *n* (**a**) *(revelation)* divulgation *f*, révélation *f* (**b**) *(fact revealed)* révélation *f* (**c**) *St Exch* information *f* aux actionnaires

▸▸ *Acct* ***disclosure of accounts*** publication *f* des comptes; *St Exch* ***disclosure threshold*** seuil *m* d'annonce obligatoire

disco [ˈdɪskəʊ] *(pl* **discos**) **1** *n* (**a**) *(place)* discothèque *f*, boîte *f* (**b**) *(music)* disco *m or f*

2 *comp (dancing, music)* disco

discography [dɪsˈkɒgrəfɪ] *n* discographie *f*

discoid [ˈdɪskɔɪd] *adj* discoïde, discoïdal

discolour, *Am* **discolor** [dɪsˈkʌlə(r)] **1** *vt (change colour of, fade)* décolorer; *(turn yellow)* jaunir

2 *vi (change colour, fade)* se décolorer; *(turn yellow)* jaunir

discolouration, *Am* **discoloration** [dɪsˌkʌləˈreɪʃən] *n (fading)* décoloration *f*, *(yellowing)* jaunissement *m*; *(dulling)* ternissement *m*

discoloured, *Am* **discolored** [dɪsˈkʌləd] *adj (faded)* décoloré; *(yellowed)* jauni

discombobulate [ˌdɪskəmˈbɒbjʊleɪt] *vt Am Fam Hum (plans)* chambarder; *(person)* déconcerter[❑], confondre[❑]

discomfit [dɪsˈkʌmfɪt] *vt Formal* (**a**) *(confuse, embarrass)* déconcerter, gêner (**b**) *(thwart → plan, project)* contrecarrer, contrarier

discomfiture [dɪs'kʌmfɪtʃə(r)] *n Formal (embarrassment)* embarras *m*, gêne *f*
discomfort [dɪs'kʌmfət] **1** *n* (**a**) *(pain)* malaise *m*; *(unease)* gêne *f*; **she's in some discomfort** elle a assez mal; **you may experience some discomfort** il se peut que vous ressentiez une gêne; **her letter caused him some discomfort** sa lettre l'a mis un peu mal à l'aise (**b**) *(cause of pain, unease)* incommodité *f*, inconfort *m*
2 *vt* incommoder, gêner
discommode [ˌdɪskə'məʊd] *vt Formal* importuner
discompose [ˌdɪskəm'pəʊz] *vt Formal* déconcerter, décontenancer
discomposure [ˌdɪskəm'pəʊʒə(r)] *n Formal* embarras *m*, gêne *f*
disconcert [ˌdɪskən'sɜːt] *vt* (**a**) *(fluster)* déconcerter, décontenancer (**b**) *(upset)* troubler, gêner
disconcerted [ˌdɪskən'sɜːtɪd] *adj (air)* déconcerté
disconcertedly [ˌdɪskən'sɜːtɪdlɪ] *adv* d'un air déconcerté
disconcerting [ˌdɪskən'sɜːtɪŋ] *adj* (**a**) *(unnerving)* déconcertant, déroutant (**b**) *(upsetting)* gênant
disconcertingly [ˌdɪskən'sɜːtɪŋlɪ] *adv* de façon déconcertante *ou* déroutante; **she had a disconcertingly abrupt manner** elle était d'une brusquerie déconcertante
disconnect [ˌdɪskə'nekt] *vt* (**a**) *(detach → plug, pipe, radio, TV)* débrancher; *(→ wire, battery)* déconnecter; *(→ gas, electricity, telephone, water)* couper (**b**) *Rail (carriages)* décrocher
disconnected [ˌdɪskə'nektɪd] *adj* (**a**) *(remarks, thoughts)* décousu, sans suite; *(facts)* sans rapport (**b**) *(detached → wire, battery)* déconnecté; *(→ plug, appliance)* débranché; *(→ gas, electricity, telephone, water)* coupé; *Tel* **I've been disconnected** *(for non-payment of bill)* ils m'ont coupé le téléphone; **to get the gas/electricity/telephone disconnected** faire couper le gaz/l'électricité/le téléphone
disconnectedness [ˌdɪskə'nektɪdnɪs] *n (of remarks)* manque *m* de suite, caractère *m* décousu; *(of ideas, thoughts)* incohérence *f*
disconnection, disconnexion [ˌdɪskə'nekʃən] *n* (**a**) *(action → of phone, gas, water, in phone call)* coupure *f*; *(→ of wire, battery)* déconnexion *f*; *(→ of appliance)* débranchement *m* (**b**) *Rail (of carriage)* décrochage *m*
disconsolate [dɪs'kɒnsələt] *adj* triste, inconsolable
disconsolately [dɪs'kɒnsələtlɪ] *adv* tristement, inconsolablement
discontent [ˌdɪskən'tent] **1** *n* (**a**) *(dissatisfaction)* mécontentement *m*; **general** *or* **public discontent** malaise *m*; **a cause of discontent** un grief (**b**) *(person)* mécontent(e) *m,f*
2 *adj* mécontent
3 *vt* mécontenter
discontented [ˌdɪskən'tentɪd] *adj* mécontent
discontentedly [ˌdɪskən'tentɪdlɪ] *adv* avec mécontentement; **to work discontentedly** travailler en rechignant
discontinue [ˌdɪskən'tɪnjuː] *vt* (**a**) *(gen)* cesser, interrompre; **I've discontinued my subscription** j'ai arrêté mon abonnement (**b**) *Com & Ind (production)* abandonner; *(product)* interrompre; *(publication)* interrompre la publication de; **this item/model has been discontinued** cet article/ce modèle ne se fait plus; **discontinued** *(on label)* fin de série (**c**) *Law (action, suit)* abandonner
►► *Com & Ind* ***discontinued line*** fin *f* de série
discontinuity [ˌdɪskɒntɪ'njuːətɪ] (*pl* **discontinuities**) *n* (**a**) *(gen) & Math* discontinuité *f* (**b**) *Geol* zone *f* de discontinuité
discontinuous [ˌdɪskən'tɪnjʊəs] *adj (gen) & Ling & Math* discontinu
discophile ['dɪskəʊfaɪl] *n* discophile *mf*
discord ['dɪskɔːd] *n* (**a**) *(UNCOUNT) (conflict)* désaccord *m*, discorde *f*; **civil discord** dissensions *fpl* sociales (**b**) *Mus* dissonance *f*
discordant [dɪ'skɔːdənt] *adj* (**a**) *(opinions)* incompatible, opposé; *(colours, sounds)* discordant (**b**) *Mus* dissonant
discordantly [dɪs'kɔːdəntlɪ] *adv (sound, ring)* d'une manière discordante

discotheque ['dɪskəʊtek] *n* discothèque *f*
discount 1 *n* ['dɪskaʊnt] (**a**) *Com (price reduction)* remise *f*, rabais *m*; **I bought it at a discount** je l'ai acheté au rabais; **she got a discount** on lui a fait une remise; **the store is currently offering a 5 percent discount on radios** le magasin fait (une réduction de) 5 pour cent sur les radios en ce moment
(**b**) *Fin & St Exch (deduction)* escompte *m*; **discount for cash** escompte *m* au comptant; **discounts and allowances** remise *f*, rabais *m*, ristourne *f*; **to be at a discount** *(shares)* être en perte, se trouver en moins-value; *Fig (politeness etc)* être en défaveur; **shares offered at a discount** des actions *fpl* offertes en dessous du pair
2 *comp* ['dɪskaʊnt] *Com (price, tariff)* réduit
3 *vt* ['dɪskaʊnt, dɪs'kaʊnt] (**a**) *(disregard)* ne pas tenir compte de; **you have to discount half of what she says** il ne faut pas croire la moitié de ce qu'elle raconte; **they did not discount the possibility** ils n'ont pas écarté cette possibilité
(**b**) *Com (article)* faire une remise *ou* un rabais sur
(**c**) *Fin (sum of money)* faire une remise de, escompter; *(bill, banknote)* prendre à l'escompte, escompter
►► ***discount bank*** banque *f* d'escompte; *St Exch* ***discount bond*** obligation *f* émise au dessous du pair; *Com* ***discount card*** carte *f* de réduction; ***discount house*** *Br Fin (bank)* banque *f* d'escompte; *(organization)* = organisme qui escompte des traites ou des effets; *Am Com (shop)* solderie *f*, magasin *m* de vente au rabais; *Fin* ***discount loan*** prêt *m* escompté; *Fin* ***discount market*** marché *m* de l'escompte; *Fin* ***discount mechanism*** mécanisme *m* de l'escompte; *Fin* ***discount rate*** taux *m* d'escompte; *Com* ***discount store*** solderie *f*, magasin *m* de vente au rabais; *Com* ***discount voucher*** bon *m* de réduction
discountable [dɪs'kaʊntəbəl] *adj Fin* escomptable
discounted *adj* [dɪs'kaʊntɪd]
►► *Fin* ***discounted bill*** effet *m* escompté; *Acct* ***discounted cashflow*** valeur *f* actualisée nette; *Fin* ***discounted rate*** taux *m* d'escompte; *Acct* ***discounted value*** valeur *f* actualisée
discountenance [dɪs'kaʊntənəns] *vt* (**a**) *(disapprove of)* désapprouver (**b**) *(embarrass)* décontenancer
discounter [dɪs'kaʊntə(r)] *n Com (shop)* solderie *f*, magasin *m* de vente au rabais; *(person)* bradeur(euse) *m,f*; *Fin* escompteur *m*
discounting [dɪs'kaʊntɪŋ] *n Com* remise *f*; *Fin (of bill)* escompte *m*
►► ***discounting bank*** banque *f* ou maison *f* d'escompte
discourage [dɪ'skʌrɪdʒ] *vt* (**a**) *(dishearten)* décourager, abattre; **to become discouraged** se laisser décourager; **the art school discouraged his ideas** l'école des beaux-arts a tenté de le faire changer d'idées
(**b**) *(dissuade)* décourager, dissuader; **to discourage sb from doing sth** dissuader qn de faire qch; **we are trying to discourage smoking** nous essayons de dissuader les gens de fumer; **in order to discourage burglars** pour décourager les voleurs; **a type of diet which should be discouraged** un type de régime qui devrait être déconseillé; **her parents tried to discourage this friendship** ses parents ont essayé d'empêcher cette amitié
discouraged [dɪs'kʌrɪdʒd] *adj* découragé; **don't be discouraged** ne te laisse pas abattre *ou* décourager
discouragement [dɪ'skʌrɪdʒmənt] *n* (**a**) *(depressed state)* découragement *m* (**b**) *(attempt to discourage)* **I met with discouragement on all sides** tout le monde a essayé de me décourager; **my plans met with discouragement** on a essayé de me dissuader de poursuivre mes projets (**c**) *(deterrent)* **I hope this won't be a discouragement to you** j'espère que ceci ne te découragera pas; **to act as a discouragement** avoir un effet dissuasif
discouraging [dɪ'skʌrɪdʒɪŋ] *adj* décourageant
discouragingly [dɪ'skʌrɪdʒɪŋlɪ] *adv (speak)* d'une manière décourageante; **discouragingly, the government has refused to finance the research** ce qui est décourageant, c'est que le gouvernement a refusé de financer la recherche
discourse 1 *n* ['dɪskɔːs] (**a**) *Formal (sermon)* discours *m*; *(dissertation)* discours *m*, traité *m* (**b**) *Ling* discours *m* (**c**) *(UNCOUNT) Literary (conversation)* conversation *f*, débat *m*; **to be engaged in discourse with sb** s'entretenir avec qn
2 *vi* [dɪ'skɔːs] (**a**) *Formal (speak)* **to discourse on** *or* **upon sth** traiter de *ou* parler de qch; **to discourse at great length on sth** discourir longuement sur qch (**b**) *Literary (converse)* s'entretenir; **to discourse with sb** s'entretenir avec qn
►► *Ling* ***discourse analysis*** analyse *f* du discours

'Discourse on Method' *Descartes* 'Le Discours de la méthode'

---

discourteous [dɪs'kɜːtɪəs] *adj* discourtois, impoli; **to be discourteous to** *or* **towards sb** être discourtois *ou* impoli avec *ou* envers qn
discourteously [dɪs'kɜːtɪəslɪ] *adv* d'une façon discourtoise *ou* impolie; **to behave discourteously towards sb** manquer de politesse envers qn, se montrer impoli *ou* discourtois avec qn
discourtesy [dɪs'kɜːtɪsɪ] (*pl* **discourtesies**) *n* manque *m* de courtoisie, impolitesse *f*; **to behave with great discourtesy** se comporter de façon très discourtoise; **to treat sb with discourtesy** manquer de courtoisie envers qn; **I meant no discourtesy** je ne voulais pas me montrer discourtois
discover [dɪ'skʌvə(r)] *vt* (**a**) *(country, answer, reason)* découvrir; **the police discovered who the guilty party was** la police a découvert qui était coupable; **I finally discovered my glasses in my desk** j'ai fini par trouver mes lunettes dans mon bureau
(**b**) *(realize)* se rendre compte; **I discovered that he had been lying** je me suis rendu compte qu'il avait menti; **when did you discover that your wallet had been stolen?** quand vous êtes-vous rendu compte qu'on vous avait volé votre portefeuille?
(**c**) *(actor, singer etc)* découvrir; **to be discovered** être découvert
discoverable [dɪs'kʌvərəbəl] *adj* que l'on peut découvrir, décelable
discoverer [dɪ'skʌvərə(r)] *n* découvreur *m*; **Christopher Columbus was the discoverer of America** Christophe Colomb a découvert l'Amérique; **the discoverer of penicillin** la personne qui a découvert la pénicilline
discovery [dɪ'skʌvərɪ] (*pl* **discoveries**) *n* (**a**) *(act, event)* découverte *f*; **voyage of discovery** voyage *m* d'exploration (**b**) *(actor, singer, place, thing)* révélation *f*; **he's quite a discovery** *(of new actor, soccer player etc)* c'est une vraie révélation (**c**) *Law (of documents)* divulgation *f*
►► ***discovery well*** puits *m* de découverte
discredit [dɪs'kredɪt] **1** *vt* (**a**) *(person)* discréditer (**b**) *(report, theory → cast doubt on)* discréditer, mettre en doute; *(→ show to be false)* montrer l'inexactitude de; **this theory is now considered discredited by most linguists** cette théorie est maintenant en discrédit auprès de la majorité des linguistes
2 *n (loss of good reputation)* discrédit *m*; **to bring discredit on** *or* **upon** jeter le discrédit sur; **it is very much to his discredit** ce n'est pas du tout à son honneur; **to his great discredit, he told a lie** à sa grand honte, il a menti; **to be a discredit to one's family/school** déshonorer sa famille/son école
discreditable [dɪs'kredɪtəbəl] *adj* peu honorable, indigne
discredited [dɪs'kredɪtɪd] *adj* discrédité
discreet [dɪ'skriːt] *adj* discret(ète); **can you trust him to be discreet?** peut-on compter sur sa discrétion?; **to follow sb at a discreet distance** suivre qn à une distance respectueuse
discreetly [dɪ'skriːtlɪ] *adv* discrètement, de manière discrète
discrepancy [dɪ'skrepənsɪ] (*pl* **discrepancies**) *n*

(in figures) contradiction *f*; *(in statements)* contradiction *f*, désaccord *m*, divergence *f*; **there's a discrepancy between these reports** ces rapports se contredisent *ou* divergent (sur un point); **there's a discrepancy in the accounts** les comptes ne concordent pas

discrete [dɪ'skriːt] *adj (gen) & Tech & Math* discret(ète)

discretion [dɪ'skreʃən] *n* (**a**) *(tact, prudence)* discrétion *f*; **to be the soul of discretion** être la discrétion même; *Prov* **discretion is the better part of valour** prudence est mère de sûreté (**b**) *(judgment, taste)* jugement *m*; **I'll leave it to your discretion** je laisse cela à votre discrétion *ou* jugement; **use your own discretion** jugez par vous-même; **a woman of discretion** une femme de raison; **you have reached the age of discretion** tu as atteint l'âge de raison; **at the manager's discretion** à la discrétion du directeur; **the committee has discretion to award more than one prize** à la discrétion du comité, plus d'un prix peut être accordé

discretionary [dɪs'kreʃənərɪ] *adj Law* discrétionnaire

►► *Banking* ***discretionary account*** compte *m* sous mandat de gestion; *Fin* ***discretionary costs*** coûts *mpl* discrétionnaires; *Fin* ***discretionary fund*** compte *m* sous mandat de gestion; *St Exch* ***discretionary order*** ordre *m* à appréciation; *Fin* ***discretionary portfolio*** portefeuille *f* avec mandat

discriminate [dɪs'krɪmɪneɪt] **1** *vi* (**a**) *(on grounds of race, sex etc)* **to discriminate in favour of** favoriser; **she was discriminated against** elle faisait l'objet *ou* était victime de discrimination; **there are many people being sexually/racially discriminated against** nombreux sont ceux qui sont victimes de discrimination sexuelle/raciale

(**b**) *(distinguish)* établir *ou* faire une distinction, faire une différence; **to discriminate between right and wrong** distinguer le bien du mal

2 *vt* distinguer; **to discriminate right from wrong** distinguer le bien du mal

discriminating [dɪs'krɪmɪneɪtɪŋ] *adj* (**a**) *(showing discernment)* judicieux; *(in matters of taste)* qui a un goût sûr; *(audience, eye)* averti; *(ear, judgement)* fin; **he is not very discriminating in his choice of friends** il n'est pas très difficile dans le choix de ses amis; **the company was very discriminating in its choice of employees** l'entreprise était très sélective dans le choix de ses employés; **a car for the discriminating motorist** une voiture pour l'automobiliste averti

(**b**) *(tax, tariff)* différentiel

discriminatingly [dɪs'krɪmɪneɪtɪŋlɪ] *adv (discerningly)* judicieusement

discrimination [dɪsˌkrɪmɪ'neɪʃən] *n* (**a**) *(on grounds of race, sex etc)* discrimination *f*; **sexual discrimination** discrimination *f* sexuelle

(**b**) *(good judgment)* discernement *m*; *(in matters of taste)* goût *m*; **he shows no discrimination in his choice of clothes/friends** il ne fait preuve d'aucun discernement dans le choix de ses vêtements/amis; **he is a man of great discrimination** c'est un homme qui a énormément de goût

(**c**) *(ability to distinguish)* **powers of discrimination** capacités *fpl* de distinction, discernement *m*

discriminative [dɪs'krɪmɪneɪtɪv] = **discriminating**

discriminator [dɪs'krɪmɪneɪtə(r)] *n Elec* discriminateur *m*; **pulse amplitude discriminator** discriminateur *m* d'amplitude

►► *Elec* ***discriminator curve*** courbe *f* de discrimination; ***discriminator threshold value*** seuil *m* de discrimination

discriminatory [dɪs'krɪmɪnətrɪ] *adj (treatment, proposals)* discriminatoire; **the company is being discriminatory** la société pratique la discrimination

discursive [dɪs'kɜːsɪv] *adj Formal (essay, report, person etc)* discursif

discursively [dɪs'kɜːsɪvlɪ] *adv Formal* (**a**) *(write, speak, argue)* en passant d'un sujet à un autre (**b**) *(in logic)* par déduction

discursiveness [dɪs'kɜːsɪvnɪs] *n Formal* tendance *f* à s'écarter du sujet

discus ['dɪskəs] *(pl* **discuses** *or* **disci** [-kaɪ]) *n* (**a**) *Sport* disque *m*; **to come first in the discus** être premier au lancer du disque (**b**) *(in Ancient Greece)* discobole *m*

►► *Sport* ***discus thrower*** lanceur(euse) *m,f* de disque

discuss [dɪs'kʌs] *vt (talk about → problem, price, subject etc)* discuter de, parler de; *(→ person)* parler de; *(debate)* discuter de; *(examine → of author, book, report etc)* examiner, parler de, traiter de; **I'll discuss it with you later** nous en parlerons *ou* discuterons plus tard; **I'll discuss it with him** j'en parlerai *ou* discuterai avec lui; **it is being discussed** c'est en cours de discussion; **I don't want to discuss it** je ne veux pas en parler; **I refuse to discuss rumours** je refuse de commenter des rumeurs; **discuss** *(in exam questions)* discutez

discussion [dɪs'kʌʃən] *n (talk)* discussion *f*; *(debate)* débat *m*; *(examination → by author in report)* traitement *m*; *(→ of report)* examen *m*; **the report contained a discussion of the recent findings** le rapport parlait *ou* traitait des découvertes récentes; **there's been a lot of discussion about it** on en a beaucoup parlé; *(in parliament, on board etc)* cela a été beaucoup débattu; *(in press, in media)* cela a été largement traité; **an ideal subject for discussion** un sujet de discussion idéal; **to come up for discussion** *(report, proposal etc)* être discuté; **the subject under discussion was highly controversial** le sujet dont il était question prêtait à controverse; **it is still under discussion** c'est encore en cours de discussion

►► *Comput* ***discussion list*** *(on Internet)* liste *f* de diffusion; *TV & Rad* ***discussion programme*** table *f* ronde; ***discussion table*** table *f* ronde

disdain [dɪs'deɪn] **1** *vt Formal* dédaigner; **he disdained to reply to her letter/remark** il n'a pas daigné répondre à sa lettre/remarque

2 *n* dédain *m*, mépris *m*; **she was an object of disdain to him** il la dédaignait *ou* la méprisait; **with** *or* **in disdain** avec dédain, dédaigneusement; **a look of disdain** un regard dédaigneux

disdainful [dɪs'deɪnfʊl] *adj* dédaigneux; **to be disdainful of sb/sth** se montrer dédaigneux envers qn/qch, dédaigner qn/qch

disdainfully [dɪs'deɪnfʊlɪ] *adv* avec dédain, dédaigneusement

disease [dɪ'ziːz] *n* (**a**) *(illness)* maladie *f*; **he's suffering from a kidney disease** il a une maladie des reins, il est malade des reins; **the elimination of disease** l'élimination *f ou* l'éradication *f* des maladies; **to combat disease** combattre la maladie (**b**) *Fig* mal *m*, maladie *f*; **boredom is a disease of the rich** l'ennui est une maladie *ou* un mal de riches

diseased [dɪ'ziːzd] *adj* (**a**) *(body)* malade (**b**) *Fig (mind)* malade, dérangé; *(imagination)* malade

diseconomy [dɪsɪ'kɒnəmɪ] *n Econ* déséconomie *f*

disembark [ˌdɪsem'bɑːk] **1** *vi* débarquer; **to disembark from the ferry** débarquer du ferry

2 *vt (passengers, cargo)* débarquer

disembarkation [ˌdɪsembɑː'keɪʃən], **disembarkment** [ˌdɪsɪm'bɑːkmənt] *n (of passengers, cargo)* débarquement *m*

disembodied [ˌdɪsɪm'bɒdɪd] *adj (voice, spirit)* désincarné

disembowel [ˌdɪsɪm'baʊəl] *vt* éviscérer, éventrer

disempower [ˌdɪsɪm'paʊə(r)] *vt* (**a**) **to disempower sb** *(emotionally, psychologically)* priver qn des moyens de se prendre en charge *ou* de s'assumer (**b**) *(employee)* donner moins d'autonomie à

disenchant [ˌdɪsɪn'tʃɑːnt] *vt* désillusionner; **a disenchanting experience/encounter** une expérience/rencontre décevante

disenchanted [ˌdɪsɪn'tʃɑːntɪd] *adj* désillusionné; **to be disenchanted with sb/sth** avoir perdu ses illusions sur qn/qch, être désillusionné par qn/qch; **to become disenchanted with sb/sth** perdre ses illusions sur qn/qch

disenchantment [ˌdɪsɪn'tʃɑːntmənt] *n* désillusion *f*; **disenchantment with the government has been growing** de plus en plus de gens sont déçus par le gouvernement

disencumber [ˌdɪsɪn'kʌmbə(r)] *vt Formal* **to disencumber oneself of sth** *(of coat etc)* se débarrasser de qch; *(of one's responsibilities, burdens)* s'affranchir de qch

disenfranchise [ˌdɪsɪn'fræntʃaɪz] *vt* priver du droit de vote

disenfranchisement [ˌdɪsɪn'fræntʃɪzmənt] *n (of person)* déchéance *f* de ses droits civiques; *(of borough)* déchéance *f* de ses droits de représentation

disengage [ˌdɪsɪn'geɪdʒ] **1** *vt* (**a**) *Tech* désenclencher; *(cogwheel)* désengrener; *(part, component)* débrayer, désembrayer; *(lever, catch)* dégager; *Aut (handbrake)* desserrer; *Aut* **to disengage the clutch** débrayer

(**b**) *(release)* dégager; **to disengage oneself from sb's embrace** se dégager de l'étreinte de qn; **I tried to disengage my hand from his** j'ai essayé de dégager ma main de la sienne

(**c**) *Mil* **the order came through to disengage the troops** l'ordre arriva de cesser le combat

2 *vi* (**a**) *(disconnect)* **to disengage from** *(process)* se désintéresser de; *(society, group)* se détacher de (**b**) *Mil* cesser le combat (**c**) *Tech* se désenclencher; *Aut* **the clutch won't disengage** impossible de débrayer

disengagement [ˌdɪsɪn'geɪdʒmənt] *n* (**a**) *(from political group, organization)* désengagement *m* (**b**) *Mil* cessez-le-feu *m inv*

disentangle [ˌdɪsɪn'tæŋgəl] *vt (string, plot, mystery)* démêler; **I tried to disentangle myself from the net** j'ai essayé de me dépêtrer du filet; **to disentangle oneself from a difficult situation** se sortir à grand-peine d'une situation difficile

disequilibrium [ˌdɪsekwɪ'lɪbrɪəm] *n Formal* déséquilibre *m*

disestablish [ˌdɪsɪ'stæblɪʃ] *vt* séparer; **to disestablish the Church** séparer l'Église de l'État

disestablishment [ˌdɪsɪ'stæblɪʃmənt] *n* séparation *f*

disfavour, *Am* **disfavor** [dɪs'feɪvə(r)] *n* désapprobation *f*, défaveur *f*; **to regard sb/sth with disfavour** considérer qn/qch avec désapprobation, voir qn/qch d'un mauvais œil; **to fall into disfavour with sb** tomber en défaveur auprès de qn; **at the risk of incurring sb's disfavour** au risque de déplaire à qn

disfigure [dɪs'fɪgə(r)] *vt (person, statue etc)* défigurer; *(landscape)* gâter, enlaidir; **a disfiguring disease** une maladie qui défigure

disfigured [dɪs'fɪgəd] *adj (person, statue etc)* défiguré; *(landscape)* enlaidi

disfigurement [dɪs'fɪgəmənt] *n (of person, statue etc)* défiguration *f*; *(of landscape)* enlaidissement *m*

disfranchise [ˌdɪs'fræntʃaɪz] *vt* priver du droit de vote

disfranchisement [ˌdɪs'fræntʃɪzmənt] *n (of person)* déchéance *f* de ses droits civiques; *(of borough)* déchéance *f* de ses droits de représentation

disgorge [dɪs'gɔːdʒ] **1** *vt* (**a**) *(food)* régurgiter, rendre; *Fig (contents, passengers, pollutants)* déverser; **chimneys disgorging smoke** des cheminées *fpl* crachant de la fumée

(**b**) *(give unwillingly → information)* donner avec répugnance *ou* à contrecœur

2 *vi (river)* se jeter, se dégorger

disgrace [dɪs'greɪs] **1** *n* (**a**) *(dishonour)* disgrâce *f*; **it will bring disgrace on** *or* **to the family** cela fera tomber la famille dans la disgrâce, cela déshonorera la famille; **there's no disgrace in not knowing** il n'y a pas de honte à ne pas savoir; **it's no disgrace to be poor** il n'y a pas de honte à être pauvre

(**b**) *(disfavour)* disgrâce *f*, défaveur *f*; **to be in disgrace (with sb)** être en disgrâce (auprès de qn)

(**c**) *(shameful example or thing)* honte *f*; **it's a disgrace** c'est une honte, c'est honteux; **it's a disgrace that they weren't allowed into the country** il est honteux *ou* c'est une honte qu'on leur ait interdit l'entrée dans le pays; **these streets are a disgrace** ces rues sont une honte; **house prices are a disgrace** c'est une honte de vendre les maisons si cher; **look at you, you're a disgrace!** regarde-toi, tu fais honte (à voir)!; **that jacket is a disgrace!** cette veste est une vraie guenille!; **look at you, your hair's a disgrace** regarde-toi, tu es coiffé n'importe comment; **he's a disgrace to his profession** il déshonore sa profession; **you're a disgrace to your family** tu déshonores ta famille, tu es la honte de ta famille

2 *vt* (**a**) *(bring shame on)* faire honte à, couvrir de honte, déshonorer; **to disgrace oneself** se couvrir de honte; **you disgraced me in front of all those people** tu m'as couvert de honte devant tous ces gens

(**b**) *(usu passive) (discredit)* disgracier; **to be disgraced** être disgrâcié

disgraceful [dɪs'greɪsfʊl] *adj (behaviour)* honteux, scandaleux; *Fam (hat, jacket etc)* miteux; **look at you, you're disgraceful!** regarde-toi, tu fais honte (à voir)!; **it's disgraceful** c'est honteux; **it's disgraceful that he wasn't there** il est honteux qu'il ne soit pas venu

disgracefully [dɪs'greɪsfʊlɪ] *adv* honteusement; **a disgracefully untidy room** une pièce honteusement mal rangée; *Hum* **to grow old disgracefully** ne pas s'assagir avec les ans

disgracefulness [dɪs'greɪsfʊlnɪs] *n* honte *f*, ignominie *f*, infamie *f*; **the disgracefulness of the whole proceedings** la façon indigne dont a été menée toute l'affaire

disgruntled [dɪs'grʌntəld] *adj (discontented)* mécontent; *(sulky)* maussade; **to be disgruntled at** *or* **about sth/doing sth** être mécontent de qch/faire qch

disguise [dɪs'gaɪz] **1** *n* déguisement *m*; **in disguise** déguisé; **to put on a disguise** se déguiser; *Fig* **it was all a disguise** ce n'était qu'un masque; **to be a master of disguise** être un roi du déguisement

2 *vt* (**a**) *(voice, handwriting, person)* déguiser; **to be disguised as sb/sth, to disguise oneself as sb/sth** être déguisé en qn/qch

(**b**) *(feelings, disappointment etc)* dissimuler, masquer; *(truth, facts)* dissimuler, cacher; *(unsightly feature)* cacher; *(bad taste of food, cough mixture etc)* couvrir; **there's no disguising the fact that business is bad** on ne peut pas cacher le fait que les affaires vont mal; **there's no disguising the fact that I'm in love with you** je dois avouer que je vous aime

disgust [dɪs'gʌst] **1** *n (sick feeling)* dégoût *m*, aversion *f*, répugnance *f*; *(displeasure)* écœurement *m*, dégoût *m*; **to be filled with disgust at sth** être écœuré par qch; **in order to express our disgust with the decision** pour montrer que nous sommes écœurés par cette décision; **I resigned in disgust** dégoûté *ou* écœuré, j'ai démissionné; **much to my disgust** à mon grand dégoût

2 *vt (sicken)* dégoûter; *(displease)* écœurer; **I am disgusted with him/this government/his behaviour** il/ce gouvernement/son comportement m'écœure; **I was disgusted by the accounts of torture** *(sickened)* les récits de torture m'ont écœuré *ou* m'ont donné la nausée; **to be disgusted with oneself** *(displeased)* s'en vouloir; **I am disgusted with** *or* **at my own stupidity** *(displeased)* je m'en veux d'être aussi stupide

disgusted [dɪs'gʌstɪd] *adj (displeased)* écœuré; *(sick)* écœuré, dégoûté

> **Disgusted of Tunbridge Wells**
> Tunbridge Wells est une ville très bourgeoise située dans le Kent, au sud de Londres. Un anglais britannique cette phrase (que l'on pourrait traduire par "signé: un habitant dégoûté de Tunbridge Wells") fait référence à un certain type d'Anglais aisé et généralement réactionnaire qui envoie volontiers des lettres rageuses aux journaux pour se plaindre de tel ou tel aspect de la société dans laquelle nous vivons.

disgustedly [dɪs'gʌstɪdlɪ] *adv* d'un air écœuré

disgusting [dɪs'gʌstɪŋ] *adj* (**a**) *(sickening → person, behaviour, smell)* écœurant, dégoûtant; *(→ habit, language)* dégoûtant; **how disgusting!** c'est écœurant!, c'est dégoûtant! (**b**) *(very bad)* écœurant, déplorable; **you disgusting little boy!** espèce de petit dégoûtant!

disgustingly [dɪs'gʌstɪŋlɪ] *adv* (**a**) *(sickeningly)* **a disgustingly bad meal** un repas épouvantable

(**b**) *Fam (for emphasis)* **to be disgustingly rich** être scandaleusement riche❑; **she is disgustingly clever/successful** ça me rend malade de voir comme elle est intelligente/comme elle réussit; **you look disgustingly fit** vous avez l'air vachement en forme; **he makes it look disgustingly easy** ça a l'air ridiculement facile quand c'est lui qui le fait❑

dish [dɪʃ] **1** *n* (**a**) *(for food)* plat *m*; **the dishes** la vaisselle; **to wash** *or* **to do the dishes** faire la vaisselle; **to wash dishes** *(in restaurant)* faire la plonge

(**b**) *(food)* plat *m*; **it's not a dish I often make** ce n'est pas une recette *ou* un plat que je prépare souvent

(**c**) *(amount of food)* plat *m*; **we ate two whole dishes of lasagne** nous avons mangé deux plats entiers de lasagnes

(**d**) *Fam Old-fashioned (good looking woman)* belle plante *f*, belle fille❑ *f*; *(good looking man)* beau type *m*

(**e**) *(of telescope)* miroir *m* concave *(de télescope)*

(**f**) *(container)* récipient *m*; *Phot* cuvette *f*

2 *vt Fam* (**a**) *Br (chances, hopes)* ruiner

(**b**) *Am (criticize)* **to dish sb** critiquer qn

(**c**) *(idiom)* **to dish the dirt (on sb)** *(gossip)* colporter des ragots (sur qn)

►► *TV Br* ***dish aerial,*** *Am* ***dish antenna*** antenne *f* parabolique; ***dish mop*** lavette *f*; ***dish rack*** égouttoir *m* (à vaisselle); *Am* ***dish soap*** liquide *m* vaisselle

►**dish out 1** *vt sep* (**a**) *(food)* servir (**b**) *Fam Fig (money, leaflets etc)* distribuer❑; *(advice)* prodiguer❑; **you can dish it out but you can't take it** *(criticism)* tu es bon pour critiquer mais pour ce qui est d'accepter la critique, c'est un autre problème!; **you're going to have to take whatever they dish out** *(punishment, discipline)* il va te falloir accepter ce qu'ils te réservent; **he's really dishing it out** *(boxer)* il frappe vraiment à coups redoublés

2 *vi (serve food)* faire le service

►**dish up 1** *vt sep (food)* servir *ou* verser *ou* mettre dans un plat; *Fam (arguments, excuses etc)* ressortir

2 *vi (serve food)* servir; **shall I dish up?** je sers?

disharmonious [ˌdɪshɑː'məʊnjəs] *adj* peu harmonieux

disharmony [ˌdɪs'hɑːmənɪ] *n* manque *m* d'harmonie

dishcloth ['dɪʃklɒθ] *n (for washing)* lavette *f*; *(for drying)* torchon *m* (à vaisselle)

dishearten [dɪs'hɑːtən] *vt* décourager, abattre, démoraliser; **don't get disheartened** ne te décourage pas, ne te laisse pas abattre

disheartened [dɪs'hɑːtənd] *adj* découragé

disheartening [dɪs'hɑːtənɪŋ] *adj* décourageant

dishearteningly [dɪs'hɑːtənɪŋlɪ] *adv* de façon décourageante; **dishearteningly brief** d'une brièveté décourageante; **dishearteningly few people turned up** peu de monde est venu, ce qui était décourageant

dished [dɪʃt] *adj (angled)* non parallèle; *(convex)* lenticulaire

dishevelled, *Am* **disheveled** [dɪ'ʃevəld] *adj (hair)* ébouriffé, dépeigné; *(clothes)* débraillé, en désordre; *(person, appearance)* débraillé

dishful ['dɪʃfʊl] *n (of food)* plat *m*

dishonest [dɪs'ɒnɪst] *adj* malhonnête; **you're being dishonest not telling him how you feel** c'est malhonnête de ne pas lui dire ce que tu ressens

dishonestly [dɪs'ɒnɪstlɪ] *adv* de manière malhonnête, malhonnêtement

dishonesty [dɪs'ɒnɪstɪ] *n* malhonnêteté *f*

dishonour, *Am* **dishonor** [dɪs'ɒnə(r)] **1** *n* déshonneur *m*; **to bring dishonour on sb/one's country** déshonorer qn/son pays; **death before dishonour!** plutôt mourir qu'être déshonoré!

2 *vt* (**a**) *(family, country, profession etc)* déshonorer (**b**) *Fin (cheque)* refuser d'honorer; **dishonoured cheque** chèque impayé *ou* non honoré

dishonourable, *Am* **dishonorable** [dɪs'ɒnərəbəl] *adj (person)* sans honneur; *(conduct)* déshonorant; **there's nothing dishonourable about losing** perdre n'a rien de honteux; *Mil* **he was given a dishonourable discharge** il a été renvoyé pour manquement à l'honneur

dishonourably, *Am* **dishonourably** [dɪs'ɒnərəblɪ] *adv (behave)* de façon *ou* manière déshonorante; *Mil* **to be dishonourably discharged** être renvoyé de l'armée pour manquement à l'honneur

dishpan ['dɪʃpæn] *n Am* bassine *f*; **to have dishpan hands** avoir les mains abîmées par la vaisselle

dishrag ['dɪʃræg] *n (for washing)* lavette *f*; *(for drying)* torchon *m* (à vaisselle)

dishtowel ['dɪʃtaʊəl] *n (for washing)* lavette *f*; *(for drying)* torchon *m* (à vaisselle)

dishwasher ['dɪʃˌwɒʃə(r)] *n* (**a**) *(machine)* lave-vaisselle *m*; **dishwasher safe** *(glass, plate etc)* garanti lave-vaisselle (**b**) *(person)* plongeur(euse) *m,f*

dishwashing liquid ['dɪʃˌwɒʃɪŋ-] *n* produit *m* à vaisselle

dishwater ['dɪʃˌwɔːtə(r)] *n* eau *f* de vaisselle; *Fam* **this coffee is like dishwater!** c'est du jus de chaussettes, ce café!; *Fam Pej* **dishwater blonde** *(hair)* (blond) filasse

dishy ['dɪʃɪ] (*compar* **dishier,** *superl* **dishiest**) *adj Br Fam* sexy *(inv)*, séduisant❑; **what a dishy guy!** il est canon, ce mec!

disillusion [ˌdɪsɪ'luːʒən] **1** *vt* faire perdre ses illusions à, désillusionner; **I hate to disillusion you but he's really after your money** je suis désolé de devoir t'ôter tes illusions mais c'est après ton argent qu'il en a; **he has been disillusioned by his experiences** ses expériences lui ont fait perdre ses illusions *ou* l'ont désillusionné

2 *n* désillusion *f*, désabusement *m*

disillusioned [ˌdɪsɪ'luːʒənd] *adj* désillusionné, désabusé; **to be disillusioned with sb/sth** avoir perdu ses illusions sur qn/qch

disillusionment [ˌdɪsɪ'luːʒənmənt] *n* désillusion *f*, désabusement *m*; **the fans' increasing disillusionment with club management** la désillusion grandissante des fans envers la direction du club; **disillusionment was not long in coming** il ne m'a/lui a/*etc* pas fallu beaucoup de temps pour perdre mes/ses/*etc* illusions; **her disillusionment was complete** elle était complètement désillusionnée *ou* désabusée

disincentive [ˌdɪsɪn'sentɪv] *n* facteur *m* décourageant; **taxes are a disincentive to expansion** les impôts découragent l'expansion; **this will act as a disincentive** ceci aura un effet dissuasif *ou* de dissuasion; **are social security payments a disincentive to work?** est-ce que les prestations sociales dissuadent les gens de travailler?

disinclination [ˌdɪsɪnklɪ'neɪʃən] *n (of person)* manque *m* d'inclination; **her disinclination to believe him** sa tendance à ne pas le croire; **the West's disinclination to go on lending** le peu d'enthousiasme dont fait preuve l'Occident pour continuer à prêter de l'argent; **he showed a marked disinclination to take part** il a mis une mauvaise volonté évidente à participer; **to show a disinclination for work** montrer *ou* manifester peu d'inclination au travail

disinclined [ˌdɪsɪn'klaɪnd] *adj* **to be disinclined to do sth** être peu disposé *ou* enclin à faire qch; **because I feel disinclined to do so** parce que je ne me sens pas disposé à le faire

disinfect [ˌdɪsɪn'fekt] *vt* désinfecter

disinfectant [ˌdɪsɪn'fektənt] *n* désinfectant *m*

disinfection [ˌdɪsɪn'fekʃən] *n* désinfection *f*

disinflation [ˌdɪsɪn'fleɪʃən] *n Econ* désinflation *f*

disinflationary [ˌdɪsɪn'fleɪʃənərɪ] *adj Econ* désinflationniste

disinformation [ˌdɪsɪnfə'meɪʃən] *n* désinformation *f*

disingenuous [ˌdɪsɪn'dʒenjʊəs] *adj* peu sincère

disingenuously [ˌdɪsɪn'dʒenjʊəslɪ] *adv* avec peu de sincérité

disingenuousness [ˌdɪsɪn'dʒenjʊəsnɪs] *n* manque *m* de sincérité

disinherit [ˌdɪsɪn'herɪt] *vt* déshériter

disinheritance [ˌdɪsɪn'herɪtəns] *n* déshéritement *m*

disinherited [ˌdɪsɪn'herɪtɪd] **1** *adj* déshérité

2 *npl Fig* **the disinherited of the earth** les déshérités *mpl* de la terre

disintegrate [dɪs'ɪntɪgreɪt] *vi* (**a**) *(break into pieces → stone, wet paper)* se désagréger; *(→ plane, rocket)* se désintégrer (**b**) *Fig (break down → coalition, the family)* se désagréger; *(→ calm, confidence)* s'effriter; *(→ health)* se dégrader, s'effriter (**c**) *Nucl* se désintégrer

disintegration [dɪsˌɪntɪ'greɪʃən] *n* (**a**) *(of stone, wet paper)* désagrégation *f*; *(of plane, rocket)* désintégration *f* (**b**) *Fig (of coalition, the family)* désagrégation *f* (**c**) *Nucl* désintégration *f*

disinter [ˌdɪsɪn'tɜː(r)] *(pt & pp* **disinterred,** *cont* **disinterring)** *vt* (**a**) *(body)* déterrer, exhumer (**b**) *Fig (scandal, information)* déterrer

disinterest [ˌdɪs'ɪntərest] *n* (**a**) *(objectivity)* désintéressement *m*; **his disinterest was the reason we chose him** on l'a choisi parce qu'il n'avait aucun intérêt dans l'affaire (**b**) *(lack of interest)* manque *m* d'intérêt

disinterested [ˌdɪs'ɪntərestɪd] *adj* (**a**) *(objective)* désintéressé (**b**) *Fam (uninterested)* indifférent ❑

disinterestedly [ˌdɪs'ɪnterestɪdlɪ] *adv* (**a**) *(objectively)* avec désintéressement (**b**) *Fam (with a lack of interest)* avec indifférence

disinterestedness [ˌdɪs'ɪntərestɪdnɪs] *n* (**a**) *(objectivity)* désintéressement *m* (**b**) *(lack of interest)* manque *m* d'intérêt

disintermediation ['dɪsɪntəˌmiːdɪ'eɪʃən] *n Fin* désintermédiation *f*

disinterment [ˌdɪsɪn'tɜːmənt] *n* déterrement *m*, exhumation *f*

disinvest [ˌdɪsɪn'vest] *vi* désinvestir

disinvestment [ˌdɪsɪn'vestmənt] *n* désinvestissement *m*

disjointed [dɪs'dʒɔɪntɪd] *adj (conversation, film, speech)* décousu, incohérent; *(movements)* désordonné

disjointedly [dɪs'dʒɔɪntɪdlɪ] *adv (speak)* de manière décousue *ou* incohérente; *(move)* de manière désordonnée

disjointedness [dɪs'dʒɔɪntɪdnɪs] *n (of conversation, film, speech)* incohérence *f*; *(of movements)* caractère *m* désordonné

disjunctive [dɪs'dʒʌŋktɪv] *adj Gram* disjonctif

disk [dɪsk] *n* (**a**) *Comput (hard)* disque *m*; *(soft)* disquette *f*; **on disk** sur disque, sur disquette; **to write sth to disk** sauvegarder qch sur disque *ou* disquette (**b**) *Am* = **disc**

▸▸ ***disk access time*** temps *m* d'accès disque; ***disk box*** boîte *f* à disquettes; ***disk capacity*** capacité *f* de disque/disquette; ***disk controller*** contrôleur *m* de disque; ***disk controller card*** carte *f* contrôleur de disque; ***disk copy*** copie *f* de disquette; ***disk crash*** atterrissage *m* de tête; ***disk drive*** lecteur *m* de disquettes; ***disk file*** fichier *m* disque; ***disk fragmentation*** fragmentation *f* de disque; ***disk mailer*** pochette *f* d'expédition de disquette; ***disk memory*** mémoire *f* à disque; ***disk operating system*** système *m* d'exploitation de disques; ***disk space*** espace *m* disque

disk-based *adj Comput* conçu pour disque; *(for floppy)* conçu pour disquettes

diskette [dɪs'ket] *n Comput* disquette *f*; **on diskette** sur disquette

▸▸ ***diskette box*** boîte *f* à disquettes; *Am Comput* ***diskette drive*** lecteur *m* de disquettes

diskless ['dɪsklɪs] *adj Comput* sans disque, sans unité de disque

▸▸ *Comput* ***diskless workstation*** station *f* de travail sans unité de disque

dislikable [dɪs'laɪkəbəl] *adj* antipathique

dislike [dɪs'laɪk] **1** *vt* ne pas aimer; **I dislike flying** je n'aime pas prendre l'avion; **why do you dislike him so much?** pourquoi le détestes-tu autant?; **he is much disliked** il est loin d'être apprécié; **I don't dislike him** je n'ai rien contre lui

2 *n (for person)* aversion *f*, antipathie *f*; *(for thing)* aversion *f*; **to have a dislike for** *or* **of sth** détester qch; **mutual dislike** antipathie *f* mutuelle; **to take a dislike to sb/sth** prendre qn/qch en grippe; **they have the same likes and dislikes** ils ont les mêmes goûts et dégoûts; **we all have our likes and dislikes** on est tous pareils, il y a des choses qu'on aime et des choses qu'on n'aime pas

dislocate ['dɪsləkeɪt] *vt* (**a**) *(shoulder, knee etc* → *of person)* se démettre, se déboîter, se luxer; *(*→ *of accident, fall)* démettre, déboîter, luxer; **he has dislocated his shoulder** il s'est démis *ou* déboîté *ou* luxé l'épaule; **a dislocated shoulder** une épaule démise *ou* déboîtée *ou* luxée (**b**) *(disrupt* → *plans)* désorganiser, perturber

dislocation [ˌdɪslə'keɪʃən] *n* (**a**) *(of shoulder, knee etc)* luxation *f*, déboîtement *m* (**b**) *(disruption* → *of plans)* perturbation *f*

dislodge [dɪs'lɒdʒ] *vt (fish bone, piece of apple etc)* dégager; *(large rock)* déplacer; *Fig (enemy, prey)* déloger; *(leader, title holder)* prendre la place de; **several bricks had become dislodged** plusieurs briques s'étaient détachées; *Fig* **now he's been made manager nobody is ever going to dislodge him** maintenant qu'il a été nommé au poste de directeur, personne ne l'en fera jamais sortir; *Fig* **nothing would dislodge him from his position on arms control** rien ne pouvait ébranler sa conviction sur le contrôle des armements

disloyal [ˌdɪs'lɔɪəl] *adj* déloyal; **to be disloyal to sb/sth** être déloyal envers qn/qch

disloyally [ˌdɪs'lɔɪəlɪ] *adv* déloyalement

disloyalty [ˌdɪs'lɔɪəltɪ] *n* déloyauté *f*; **your disloyalty to the company** votre déloyauté envers la compagnie; **an act of disloyalty** un acte déloyal

dismal ['dɪzməl] *adj (face, person)* lugubre, sombre, triste; *(day, weather)* horrible; *(streets, countryside)* lugubre; *(song)* mélancolique, triste; *Fig (result, performance)* lamentable; *(future, prospect)* sombre; **what are you looking so dismal about?** pourquoi as-tu l'air aussi lugubre?; **to be a dismal failure** *(person)* être un zéro sur toute la ligne; *(film, project)* échouer lamentablement; *Hum* **the dismal science** l'économie *f*

dismally ['dɪzməlɪ] *adv* lugubrement; *(fail)* lamentablement

dismantle [dɪs'mæntəl] **1** *vt (object, scenery, exhibition)* démonter; *Fig (system, reforms, arrangement)* démanteler

2 *vi* se démonter

dismantling [dɪs'mæntlɪŋ] *n (of object, scenery, exhibition)* démontage *m*; *Fig (of system, reforms, arrangement)* démantèlement *m*

dismast [ˌdɪs'mɑːst] *vt Naut (ship)* démâter

dismay [dɪs'meɪ] **1** *n* consternation *f*; *(stronger)* désarroi *m*; **there was a look of dismay on his face** la consternation *ou* le désarroi se lisait sur son visage; **in** *or* **with dismay** avec consternation *ou* désarroi; **in her dismay at the news** dans la consternation *ou* le désarroi où l'avaient mise les nouvelles; **to be filled with dismay by sth** être consterné par *ou* rempli de désarroi à cause de qch; **(much) to my dismay** à ma grande consternation, à mon grand désarroi

2 *vt* consterner; *(stronger)* emplir de désarroi, effondrer; **we were dismayed by the news** nous avons été effondrés par la nouvelle, la nouvelle nous a remplis de désarroi

dismayed [dɪs'meɪd] *adj* consterné, effondré; **don't look so dismayed** n'aie pas l'air si consterné *ou* effondré

dismember [dɪs'membə(r)] *vt* démembrer

dismemberment [dɪs'membəmənt] *n* démembrement *m*

dismiss [dɪs'mɪs] **1** *vt* (**a**) *(from job* → *employee)* licencier, congédier, renvoyer; *(*→ *magistrate, official)* destituer, révoquer, relever de ses fonctions; *Mil* **to dismiss sb from the army** rayer qn des cadres de l'armée

(**b**) *(not take seriously* → *proposal, theory, explanation)* rejeter; *(*→ *objection, warning, rumours)* ne pas tenir compte de, ne pas prendre au sérieux; *(*→ *danger)* mépriser; *(*→ *problem)* écarter, refuser de considérer; **you cannot go on dismissing the threats/evidence** vous ne pouvez pas continuer à ignorer ces menaces/preuves; **he dismissed him as a crank** il a déclaré que c'était un excentrique à ne pas prendre au sérieux; **he was long dismissed as a crank** on l'a longtemps pris pour un excentrique; **it has been dismissed as a rumour** on a rejeté cette information en n'y voyant qu'une simple rumeur; **police dismissed the warning as a hoax** la police n'a pas tenu compte de l'avertissement et l'a pris pour une mauvaise plaisanterie; **the incident was dismissed as a mere schoolboy prank** on n'a vu dans cet incident qu'une simple farce d'écolier; **she is dismissed as an intellectual lightweight** on la considère comme une non-valeur sur le plan intellectuel

(**c**) *(send away)* congédier; *Fig (thought, possibility)* écarter; *(memory)* effacer; *(suggestion, idea)* rejeter; *Sch (class)* laisser partir; **dismiss him from your thoughts** chasse-le de tes pensées; **you can dismiss that idea from your thoughts!** tu peux t'ôter cette idée de la tête!; *Sch* **class dismissed!** vous pouvez sortir!; *Mil* **dismissed!** rompez!

(**d**) *Law (hung jury)* dissoudre; **to dismiss a charge** *(judge)* rendre une ordonnance de non-lieu; **all charges against her have been dismissed** toutes les accusations qui pesaient sur elle ont été levées; **to dismiss a case** classer une affaire; **the judge dismissed the case** le juge a rendu une fin de non-recevoir; **case dismissed!** affaire classée!

(**e**) *Sport (in cricket* → *batsman, team)* éliminer; **England were dismissed for 127** l'équipe d'Angleterre a été éliminée avec 127 points

2 *vi Mil* **dismiss!** rompez (les rangs)!

dismissal [dɪs'mɪsəl] *n* (**a**) *(from work* → *of employee)* licenciement *m*, renvoi *m*; *(*→ *of magistrate, official)* destitution *f*, révocation *f*; **dismissal with/without notice** licenciement *m* avec/sans préavis

(**b**) *(of proposal, theory, explanation)* rejet *m*; *(of danger)* mépris *m*; **the police's dismissal of the telephone call** le fait que la police n'ait pas pris le coup de téléphone au sérieux

(**c**) *Law (of case)* fin *f* de non-recevoir; *(of request, appeal)* rejet *m*; **the judge's dismissal of the case met with widespread approval** la fin de non-recevoir rendue par le juge a été accueillie avec satisfaction; **dismissal of the charge** non-lieu *m*; **the dismissal of the charges against you** le non-lieu qui a été prononcé en votre faveur

dismissive [dɪs'mɪsɪv] *adj (tone of voice, gesture)* dédaigneux; **to be dismissive of sb/sth** ne faire aucun cas de qn/qch; **you're always so dismissive of my efforts** tu fais toujours si peu de cas de mes efforts

dismissively [dɪs'mɪsɪvlɪ] *adv (offhandedly)* d'un ton dédaigneux; *(in final tone of voice)* d'un ton sans appel

dismount [ˌdɪs'maʊnt] **1** *vi* descendre; **she dismounted from her horse/bike** elle est descendue de son cheval/vélo

2 *vt* (**a**) *(cause to fall* → *from horse)* désarçonner, démonter; *(*→ *from bicycle, motorcycle)* faire tomber (**b**) *(gun, device)* démonter

disobedience [ˌdɪsə'biːdjəns] *n* désobéissance *f*; **she was punished for (her) disobedience** elle a été punie pour avoir désobéi; **an act of disobedience** un acte de désobéissance

disobedient [ˌdɪsə'biːdjənt] *adj* désobéissant; **to be disobedient to sb** désobéir à qn; **don't be disobedient to your father!** ne désobéis pas à ton père!; **that was very disobedient of you** c'était très désobéissant de ta part

disobediently [ˌdɪsə'biːdjəntlɪ] *adv* de manière désobéissante

disobey [ˌdɪsə'beɪ] *vt* désobéir à

disobliging [ˌdɪsə'blaɪdʒɪŋ] *adj Formal* (**a**) *(unhelpful)* **I'm sorry to be disobliging** je suis désolé de ne pouvoir vous rendre service (**b**) *(unpleasant)* désobligeant

disobligingly [ˌdɪsə'blaɪdʒɪŋlɪ] *adv (unpleasantly)* avec désobligeance

disorder [dɪs'ɔːdə(r)] **1** *n* (**a**) *(untidiness* → *of house, room, desk)* désordre *m*; **to be in (a state of) disorder** être en désordre; **his financial affairs were in total disorder** le désordre le plus total régnait dans ses finances; **the meeting broke up in disorder** la réunion s'est achevée dans le désordre *ou* la confusion; **the army is retreating in disorder** l'armée se retire en désordre

(**b**) *(unrest)* trouble *m*; **serious disorders have broken out** de graves désordres ont éclaté; **public disorder** atteinte *f* à *ou* trouble *m* de l'ordre public

(**c**) *Med* trouble *m*, troubles *mpl*; **nervous/blood disorder** troubles *mpl* nerveux/de la circulation

2 *vt (make untidy* → *files, papers)* mettre en désordre

disordered [dɪs'ɔːdəd] *adj (room)* en désordre; *(mind)* malade; **to lead a disordered life** mener une vie désordonnée; *Br* **to be mentally disordered** souffrir de troubles mentaux

disorderliness [dɪs'ɔːdəlɪnɪs] *n* (**a**) *(untidiness)* désordre *m*; **the disorderliness of the room** le désordre dans lequel se trouvait la pièce; **the disorderliness of their life** leur vie désordonnée (**b**) *(of mob)* turbulence *f*

disorderly [dɪs'ɔːdəlɪ] *adj* (**a**) *(untidy → room, house)* en désordre, désordonné
(**b**) *(unruly → crowd, mob)* désordonné, agité; *(→ person,conduct)* désordonné; *(→ meeting, demonstration)* désordonné, confus; **to lead a disorderly life** mener une vie désordonnée *ou* déréglée; *Law* **to charge sb with being drunk and disorderly** inculper qn pour ivresse et atteinte à l'ordre public; *Law* **to keep a disorderly house** tenir une maison close
►► *Law* ***disorderly conduct*** conduite *f* portant atteinte à l'ordre public

disorganization [dɪsˌɔːgənaɪ'zeɪʃən] *n* désorganisation *f*; **in a state of disorganization** désorganisé

disorganize, -ise [dɪs'ɔːgənaɪz] *vt (disrupt → plans, schedule)* déranger

disorganized [dɪs'ɔːgənaɪzd] *adj (person)* désorganisé; *(room)* désordonné; *(memories, ideas)* confus, désordonné

disorient [dɪs'ɔːrɪənt], **disorientate** [dɪs'ɔːrɪənteɪt] *vt* désorienter; **to be disoriented** être désorienté; **it's easy to become disoriented** c'est facile de perdre son sens de l'orientation; *Fig* on a vite fait d'être désorienté

disorientation [dɪsˌɔːrɪən'teɪʃən] *n* désorientation *f*

disorienting [dɪs'ɔːrɪəntɪŋ] *adj* déroutant

disown [dɪs'əʊn] *vt (child, opinion, statement)* renier, désavouer; *(country)* renier; *Fam* **if you go out looking like that I'll disown you!** si tu sors habillé comme ça, je ne te connais plus!

disparage [dɪ'spærɪdʒ] *vt* dénigrer, décrier

disparagement [dɪ'spærɪdʒmənt] *n* dénigrement *m*

disparaging [dɪ'spærɪdʒɪŋ] *adj (person, newspaper report → about person)* désobligeant, malveillant; *(→ about proposals, ideas)* critique; **to make disparaging remarks about sb** faire des remarques désobligeantes à propos de *ou* sur qn; **she made disparaging remarks about his project** elle a fait des remarques qui dénigraient son projet; **why are you so disparaging about him?** pourquoi est-ce que tu es si désobligeant à son égard?; **the critics were very disparaging about his latest play** les critiques ont beaucoup dénigré sa dernière pièce

disparagingly [dɪ'spærɪdʒɪŋlɪ] *adv (say)* d'un ton désobligeant; *(look at)* d'un air désobligeant; **you have written very disparagingly about him in the past** vous avez écrit des propos fort désobligeants à son égard dans le passé; **to speak disparagingly of sb** parler de qn en termes de mépris, faire des remarques désobligeantes à l'égard de qn

disparate ['dɪspərət] *adj Formal* disparate

disparity [dɪ'spærətɪ] (*pl* **disparities**) *n (in ages)* disparité *f*; *(in report, statement, story)* contradiction *f*; *(of wealth, status)* disparité *f*, écart *m*

dispassionate [dɪ'spæʃənət] *adj* (**a**) *(calm)* sans passion, dépassionné, calme (**b**) *(impartial)* impartial; **to take a dispassionate view of things** juger impartialement les choses

dispassionately [dɪ'spæʃənətlɪ] *adv* (**a**) *(calmly)* sans émotion, calmement (**b**) *(impartially)* objectivement, impartialement

dispatch [dɪ'spætʃ] **1** *vt* (**a**) *(send → letter, merchandise, telegram)* envoyer, expédier; *(→ messenger)* envoyer, dépêcher; *(→ troops, envoy)* envoyer
(**b**) *(complete → task, work)* expédier, en finir avec
(**c**) *Euph (kill → person)* tuer; *(→ animal)* achever
(**d**) *Fam (food)* s'envoyer
2 *n* (**a**) *(of letter, merchandise, telegram)* envoi *m*, expédition *f*; *(of messenger, troops, envoy)* envoi *m*
(**b**) *Mil & Press (report)* dépêche *f*; *Mil* **to be mentioned in dispatches** être cité à l'ordre du jour
(**c**) *Old-fashioned (swiftness)* promptitude *f*; **with dispatch** avec promptitude, rapidement
(**d**) *(completion → of task, work)* expédition *f*
(**e**) *(execution)* exécution *f*
►► ***dispatch box*** *(for documents)* boîte *f* à documents; *Br Pol* ***the dispatch box*** = tribune de d'où parlent les membres du gouvernement et leurs homologues du cabinet fantôme; ***dispatch case*** serviette *f*, porte-documents *m inv*; ***dispatch clerk*** expéditionnaire *mf*; ***dispatch department*** service *m* des expéditions; ***dispatch note*** bordereau *m* d'expédition; ***dispatch rider*** estafette *f*

dispatcher [dɪ'spætʃə(r)] *n* expéditeur(trice) *m,f*

dispel [dɪ'spel] (*pt & pp* **dispelled**, *cont* **dispelling**) *vt (clouds, mist → of sun)* dissiper; *(→ of wind)* chasser; *(doubts, fears, anxiety)* dissiper

dispensable [dɪ'spensəbəl] *adj* dont on peut se passer, superflu; **the rest of the employees were dispensable** les autres employés n'étaient pas indispensables; **the rest is dispensable** le reste est superflu; **do you think this is dispensable?** penses-tu qu'on puisse se débarrasser de cela?

dispensary [dɪ'spensərɪ] (*pl* **dispensaries**) *n Pharm* pharmacie *f*; *(for free distribution of medicine)* dispensaire *m*

dispensation [ˌdɪspen'seɪʃən] *n* (**a**) *(handing out)* distribution *f*
(**b**) *(administration → of charity, justice)* exercice *m*
(**c**) *Admin, Law & Rel (exemption)* dispense *f*; **to receive dispensation from military service** être exempté du service militaire; **she was granted dispensation from the exam** elle a été dispensée de l'examen; **special dispensation** permission *f* exceptionnelle; **as a special dispensation the prisoner was allowed to attend the funeral** le prisonnier a reçu une permission exceptionnelle pour assister à l'enterrement
(**d**) *Pol & Rel (system)* régime *m*

dispense [dɪ'spens] *vt* (**a**) *(of vending machine)* distribuer (**b**) *(administer → justice, charity)* exercer; **to dispense advice** donner des conseils (**c**) *Pharm* préparer (**d**) *Formal (exempt)* dispenser; **to dispense sb from sth/doing sth** dispenser qn de qch/de faire qch

►**dispense with** *vt insep (do without)* se passer de; *(get rid of)* se débarrasser de; **to dispense with the formalities** couper court aux *ou* se dispenser des formalités; **let's dispense with that idea for a start** commençons par éliminer cette idée; **to dispense with the need for sth** rendre qch superflu; **credit cards dispense with the need for cash** avec les cartes de crédit, on n'a plus besoin d'avoir de l'argent liquide

dispenser [dɪ'spensə(r)] *n* (**a**) *Pharm* pharmacien(enne) *m,f* (**b**) *(machine)* distributeur *m*; **soap/coffee dispenser** distributeur *m* de savon/café (**c**) *Rel (of alms)* dispensateur(trice) *m,f*, distributeur(trice) *m,f*

dispensing [dɪ'spensɪŋ] *adj*
►► *Br Pharm* ***dispensing chemist*** *(person)* préparateur(trice) *m,f* en pharmacie; *(establishment)* pharmacie *f*; ***dispensing machine*** distributeur *m*; ***dispensing optician*** opticien(enne) *m,f*

dispersal [dɪ'spɜːsəl] *n (of crowd, seeds)* dispersion *f*; *(of gas → disappearance)* dissipation *f*; *(→ spread)* dispersion *f*; *(of light → by prism)* dispersion *f*, décomposition *f*
►► *Br* ***dispersal prison*** = établissement pénitentiaire accueillant entre autres des détenus dangereux

dispersant [dɪ'spɜːsənt] *n Chem* dispersant *m*

disperse [dɪ'spɜːs] **1** *vt* (**a**) *(crowd, seeds)* disperser; *(clouds, mist, smoke → of sun)* dissiper; *(→ of wind)* chasser; *(gas, chemical → cause to spread)* propager; *(→ cause to vanish)* disperser; *(light → of prism)* disperser, décomposer
(**b**) *(place at intervals)* répartir; **policemen were dispersed along the length of the road** des agents de police étaient répartis *ou* disséminés le long de la route
2 *vi (crowds, seeds)* se disperser; *(clouds, mist, smoke → with sun)* se dissiper; *(→ with wind)* être chassé; *(gas, chemicals → spread)* se propager; *(→ vanish)* se dissiper; *(light → with prism)* se décomposer

dispersing agent [dɪ'spɜːsɪŋ-] *n* agent *m* dispersant

dispersion [dɪ'spɜːʃən] *n* (**a**) *(of crowd, seeds)* dispersion *f*; *(of gas → disappearance)* dissipation *f*; *(→ spread)* dispersion *f*; *(of light → by prism)* dispersion *f*, décomposition *f* (**b**) *Rel* **the Dispersion** la Diaspora

dispirit [dɪ'spɪrɪt] *vt* décourager, abattre

dispirited [dɪ'spɪrɪtɪd] *adj* abattu

dispiritedly [dɪ'spɪrɪtɪdlɪ] *adv (say)* d'un ton découragé *ou* abattu; *(look)* d'un air découragé *ou* abattu; *(play, do something)* sans enthousiasme

dispiritedness [dɪs'pɪrɪtɪdnɪs] *n* découragement *m*, abattement *m*

dispiriting [dɪ'spɪrɪtɪŋ] *adj* décourageant

dispiritingly [dɪ'spɪrɪtɪŋlɪ] *adv* de façon décourageante *ou* démoralisante; **their reply was dispiritingly unenthusiastic** le manque d'enthousiasme de leur réponse était décourageant *ou* démoralisant; **dispiritingly, no one had come to meet them** personne n'était venu à leur rencontre, ce qui les démoralisait

displace [dɪs'pleɪs] *vt* (**a**) *(refugees, population)* déplacer (**b**) *Med* **to displace a bone** se déplacer un os (**c**) *(supplant)* supplanter, remplacer (**d**) *Chem & Phys (water, air)* déplacer

displaced [dɪs'pleɪst] *adj*
►► *Admin & Pol* ***displaced person*** personne *f* déplacée

displacement [dɪs'pleɪsmənt] *n* (**a**) *(of refugees, population)* déplacement *m* (**b**) *Med (of bone)* déplacement *m* (**c**) *(supplanting)* remplacement *m* (**d**) *Chem & Phys (of water, air)* déplacement *m* (**e**) *Naut* déplacement *m*; **a ship of 10,000 tons displacement** un bateau de 10 000 tonnes de déplacement (**f**) *Psy* déplacement *m*
►► *Psy* ***displacement activity*** activité *f* de déplacement; *Naut* ***displacement ton*** tonne *f*

displacer unit [dɪs'pleɪsə-] *n Aut* amortisseur *m* à déplacement de fluide

display [dɪ'spleɪ] **1** *vt* (**a**) *(gifts, medals, ornaments etc)* exposer; *Pej* exhiber; *(items in exhibition)* mettre en exposition, exposer; *Com (goods for sale)* mettre en étalage, exposer
(**b**) *(notice, poster, exam results, prices)* afficher
(**c**) *(courage, determination, skill)* faire preuve de, montrer; *(anger, affection, friendship, interest)* manifester; **the country displayed its military might** le pays a montré sa puissance militaire; **to display one's ignorance/talent** faire la preuve de son ignorance/talent
(**d**) *Press & Typ* mettre en vedette
(**e**) *Comput (of screen)* afficher; *(of user)* visualiser
2 *vi (animal, bird, fish)* faire la parade
3 *n* (**a**) *(of gifts, medals, ornaments)* exposition *f*; *Pej* exhibition *f*; *Com (of goods for sale)* mise *f* en étalage; *(goods for sale)* étalage *m*, exposition *f*; **to be on display** être exposé; **to put sth on display** exposer qch; **to be on public display** être présenté au public; **for display (only)** *(on book)* exemplaire de démonstration; **you'll have a fine display of flowers** vous aurez un beau déploiement de fleurs
(**b**) *(of notice, poster, exam results, prices)* affichage *m*; **the exam results were on display** les résultats des examens étaient affichés
(**c**) *(of courage, determination, skill)* démonstration *f*; *(of anger, affection, friendship, interest)* manifestation *f*; **an air display** un meeting aérien; **a military display** une parade militaire; **a fireworks display** un feu d'artifice; **a display of force** une démonstration de force; **he gave us a display of his juggling skills** il nous a fait une démonstration de ses talents de jongleur; **I have never seen such a display of incompetence** je n'ai jamais vu un tel déploiement *ou* étalage d'incompétence; **to make a great display of sth** faire parade de qch; **he made a great display of being injured** il a joué les grands blessés
(**d**) *(event → of works of art)* exposition *f*; *(→ of dancing, handicraft)* démonstration *f*
(**e**) *Comput (screen, device)* écran *m*; *(visual information)* affichage *m*, visualisation *f*; *(of calculator)* viseur *m*
(**f**) *(by animal, bird, fish)* parade *f*
(**g**) *Press & Typ* lignes *fpl* en vedette

►► *Press & Typ* **display advertisement** encadré *m*; *Press & Typ* **display advertising** étalage *m* publicitaire; *Comput* **display area** surface *f* d'affichage, zone *f* d'affichage; *(in store)* espace *m* d'exposition; **display cabinet** *(in shop)* étalage *m*, vitrine *f*; *(in home)* vitrine *f*; **display card** carte *f* d'affichage; **display case** *(in shop)* étalage *m*, vitrine *f*; *(in home)* vitrine *f*; **display copy** *(of book)* exemplaire *m* de démonstration; **display furniture** mobilier *m* de présentation; **display lighting** éclairage *m* de l'étalage *ou* de la vitrine; **display material** matériel *m* de présentation; *Com & Mktg* **display pack** emballage *m* de présentation, emballage *m* présentoir; **display panel** tableau *m ou* panneau *m* d'affichage; **display rack** présentoir *m*; **display screen** écran *m* de visualisation; **display shelf** présentoir *m*; **display space** surface *f* d'exposition; **display stand** présentoir *m*; *Comput* **display unit** unité *f* de visualisation *ou* d'affichage; *(for goods)* présentoir *m*; **display window** *(of shop)* vitrine *f*, étalage *m*; *(of calculator)* viseur *m*

displease [dɪs'pliːz] *vt* mécontenter

displeased [dɪs'pliːzd] *adj* mécontent; **to be displeased with** *or* **at** être mécontent de

displeasing [dɪs'pliːzɪŋ] *adj* déplaisant, désagréable (**to** à)

displeasure [dɪs'pleʒə(r)] *n* mécontentement *m*; **to incur sb's displeasure** encourir *ou* s'attirer le mécontentement de qn

disport [dɪ'spɔːt] *vt Formal* **to disport oneself** s'ébattre, folâtrer

disposable [dɪ'spəʊzəbəl] **1** *adj* (**a**) *(throwaway → lighter, nappy, cup)* jetable; *(→ bottle)* non consigné; *(→ wrapping)* perdu (**b**) *(available → money)* disponible

2 *n (nappy)* couche *f* jetable; *(lighter)* briquet *m* jetable

3 disposables *n Com* biens *mpl* de consommation non durables

►► *Fin* **disposable assets** fonds *mpl* disponibles; *Fin* **disposable funds** disponibilités *fpl*, fonds *mpl* disponibles; *Com* **disposable goods** biens *mpl* de consommation non durables; *Fin* **disposable income** revenus *mpl* disponibles (après impôts); **people with high disposable incomes** personnes disposant de hauts revenus

disposal [dɪ'spəʊzəl] *n* (**a**) *(taking away)* enlèvement *m*; *(of rubbish, by authority)* enlèvement *m*, ramassage *m*; **they arranged for the disposal of the body** ils ont pris les dispositions nécessaires pour se débarrasser du corps; **waste** *or* **refuse disposal** traitement *m* des ordures

(**b**) *(sale)* vente *f*; *Law (of property)* cession *f*; **she left no instructions for the disposal of her property** elle n'a laissé aucune instruction quant à ce qui devait être fait de ses biens

(**c**) *(resolution → of problem, question)* résolution *f*; *(→ of business)* exécution *f*, expédition *f*

(**d**) *Am (disposal unit)* broyeur *m* d'ordures *(dans un évier)*

(**e**) *(availability)* **to be at sb's disposal** être à la disposition de qn; **I am entirely at your disposal** je suis à votre entière disposition; **to have sth at one's disposal** avoir qch à sa disposition; **to put sb/sth at sb's disposal** mettre qn/qch à la disposition de qn; **in the time at your disposal** dans le temps dont tu disposes

(**f**) *Formal (arrangement)* disposition *f*, arrangement *m*; *(of troops)* déploiement *m*

dispose [dɪ'spəʊz] **1** *vt* (**a**) *Formal (arrange → ornaments, books)* disposer, arranger; *(→ troops, forces)* déployer

(**b**) *(incline)* disposer, porter; **I am not disposed to help him** je ne suis pas disposé à l'aider; **his moving testimonial disposed the jury to leniency** son témoignage émouvant a disposé le jury à l'indulgence

2 *vi Prov* **man proposes, God disposes** l'homme propose et Dieu dispose

►**dispose of** *vt insep* (**a**) *(get rid of → waste, rubbish, problem)* se débarrasser de; *(by taking away → refuse)* enlever, ramasser; *(by selling)* vendre; *(by throwing away)* jeter; *(workers)* congédier, renvoyer; **I'll dispose of it as I like** j'en ferai ce que je voudrai; **I can dispose of this old table for you** je peux te débarrasser de cette vieille table

(**b**) *(deal with → problem, question)* résoudre, régler; *(→ task, matter under discussion)* expédier, régler; **to dispose of an argument** détruire un argument

(**c**) *Fam (food)* s'envoyer

(**d**) *(have at one's disposal)* disposer de, avoir à sa disposition

(**e**) *Fam (kill → person, animal)* liquider; *Fig (team, competitor)* se débarrasser de ❑

disposed [dɪ'spəʊzd] *adj* **to be disposed to do sth** être disposé à faire qch; **I am disposed to be lenient** je suis disposé à me montrer indulgent; **to be well/ill disposed towards sb** être bien/mal disposé envers qn

disposition [ˌdɪspə'zɪʃən] *n* (**a**) *(temperament, nature)* naturel *m*; **to have** *or* **to be of a cheerful disposition** être d'un naturel enjoué; **she is of** *or* **has a kindly disposition** c'est une bonne nature (**b**) *Formal (arrangement → of ornaments, books)* disposition *f*, arrangement *m*; *(→ of troops, forces)* disposition *f* (**c**) *(inclination, tendency)* disposition *f* (**d**) *Law* aliénation *f*

dispossess [ˌdɪspə'zes] *vt (person)* déposséder; *Law (of house, land)* exproprier; **to dispossess sb of sth** déposséder qn de qch

dispossessed [ˌdɪspə'zest] **1** *npl* **the dispossessed** les dépossédés *mpl*

2 *adj* dépossédé

dispossession [ˌdɪspə'zeʃən] *n* dépossession *f*; *Law* expropriation *f*

Disprin® ['dɪsprɪn] *n* = marque d'analgésique

disproof [dɪs'pruːf] *n* (**a**) *(action)* réfutation *f* (**b**) *(evidence, fact)* **this is (a) disproof of his theory** c'est la preuve que sa théorie est fausse

disproportion [ˌdɪsprə'pɔːʃən] *n* disproportion *f*

disproportionally [ˌdɪsprə'pɔːʃənəlɪ] *adv* disproportionnellement

disproportionate [ˌdɪsprə'pɔːʃənət] *adj (excessive)* disproportionné; **to be disproportionate to sth** être disproportionné à *ou* avec qch; **we spent a disproportionate amount of time on it** on a passé plus de temps dessus que cela ne le méritait

disproportionately [ˌdɪsprə'pɔːʃənətlɪ] *adv* d'une façon disproportionnée; **disproportionately long/expensive** d'une longueur/d'un prix disproportionné(e); **a disproportionately large sum** une somme disproportionnée

disprove [ˌdɪs'pruːv] *(pp* **disproved** *or* **disproven** [-'pruːvən]) *vt (theory)* réfuter; **you can't disprove it** tu ne peux pas prouver que ce n'est pas vrai

disputable [dɪ'spjuːtəbəl] *adj* discutable, contestable

disputant [dɪs'pjuːtənt] *n* (**a**) *Formal* personne *f* participant à un débat (**b**) *Am Law* partie *f* en litige

disputation [ˌdɪspjuː'teɪʃən] *n Formal* (**a**) *(debate)* discussion *f* (**b**) *(argument)* controverse *f*, débat *m*

disputatious [ˌdɪspjuː'teɪʃəs] *adj Formal* raisonneur

dispute [dɪ'spjuːt] **1** *vt* (**a**) *(question → claim, theory, statement etc)* contester, mettre en doute; *Law (will)* contester; **I'm not disputing that** je ne conteste pas cela, je ne mets pas cela en doute; **I would dispute that** je ne suis pas d'accord

(**b**) *(debate → subject, motion)* discuter, débattre

(**c**) *(fight for → territory, championship, title)* disputer

2 *vi (argue)* se disputer; *(debate)* discuter, débattre; **to dispute over** *or* **about sth** débattre qch *ou* de qch

3 *n* (**a**) *(debate)* discussion *f*, débat *m*; **there's some dispute about the veracity of his statement** la véracité de sa déclaration fait l'objet de discussions *ou* est sujette à controverse; **your honesty is not in dispute** votre honnêteté n'est pas mise en doute *ou* contestée; **the matter is beyond (all) dispute** la question est tout à fait incontestable; **he is beyond (all) dispute** *or* **without dispute the best player the team has got** c'est incontestablement *ou* indiscutablement le meilleur joueur de l'équipe; **open to dispute** contestable

(**b**) *(argument → between individuals)* dispute *f*, différend *m*; *(→ between management and workers)* conflit *m*; *Law* litige *m*; **these are the main areas of dispute** ce sont là les questions les plus conflictuelles *ou* litigieuses; **there has been much dispute over the new proposals** les nouvelles propositions ont fait l'objet d'un conflit; **in dispute is the right of employees to strike** l'enjeu des discussions est le droit des employés à faire grève; **to be in dispute with sb over sth** être en conflit avec qn sur qch; **to be in dispute** *(proposals, territory, ownership)* faire l'objet d'un conflit; **a border dispute** un litige portant sur une question de frontière

disputed [dɪ'spjuːtɪd] *adj* (**a**) *(decision, fact, claim)* contesté (**b**) *(fought over)* **this is a much disputed territory** ce territoire fait l'objet de beaucoup de conflits, c'est un territoire très contesté

disqualification [dɪsˌkwɒlɪfɪ'keɪʃən] *n* (**a**) *(from standing for election)* exclusion *f*; *(from sporting event)* disqualification *f*; *(from exam)* exclusion *f*; **your disqualification from driving will last for four years** vous aurez un retrait de permis (de conduire) de quatre ans

(**b**) *Law (of witness)* inhabilité *f*, incapacité *f*; *(of testimony)* exclusion *f*; **reasons for the disqualification of jurors include the following...** parmi les motifs donnant lieu à une exclusion du jury on peut citer...

(**c**) *(disqualifying factor)* cause *f* d'incapacité (**for** à); **it's not necessarily a disqualification** cela ne vous exclut pas forcément

disqualify [ˌdɪs'kwɒlɪfaɪ] *(pt & pp* **disqualified**) *vt* (**a**) *(from standing for election, from exam)* exclure; *Sport* disqualifier; **her youth disqualifies her from participating** son jeune âge ne l'autorise pas à participer; **being a woman doesn't disqualify me from expressing an opinion** le fait que je suis une femme ne m'interdit pas de donner mon avis; **to disqualify sb from driving** retirer son permis (de conduire) *ou* infliger un retrait de permis (de conduire) à qn; **he's been disqualified for speeding** on lui a retiré son permis *ou* il a eu un retrait de permis pour excès de vitesse; **she was fined for driving while disqualified** on lui a mis une amende pour avoir conduit alors qu'on lui avait retiré son permis

(**b**) *Law (witness)* rendre inhabile *ou* incapable; *(testimony)* exclure; *(juror)* empêcher de faire partie du jury

disqualifying [ˌdɪs'kwɒlɪfaɪɪŋ] *adj (conditions)* qui entraîne l'exclusion; *Sport* disqualificatif

disquiet [dɪs'kwaɪət] *Formal* **1** *n* inquiétude *f*

2 *vt* inquiéter, troubler; **to be disquieted by sth** être inquiet *ou* s'inquiéter de qch

disquieting [dɪs'kwaɪətɪŋ] *adj Formal* inquiétant, troublant

disquietingly [dɪs'kwaɪətɪŋlɪ] *adv Formal* **a disquietingly high number of errors have been made** un nombre inquiétant d'erreurs a été commis; **we seem to have made disquietingly little progress** il est inquiétant de voir à quel point nous avons peu avancé; **they have remained disquietingly silent ever since** il n'ont pas donné signe de vie depuis, ce qui est assez inquiétant

disquisition [ˌdɪskwɪ'zɪʃən] *n Formal (in writing)* dissertation *f*, étude *f*; *(in speech)* discours *m*

disregard [ˌdɪsrɪ'gɑːd] **1** *vt (person, order, law, rules)* ne tenir aucun compte de; *(feelings, instructions, remark, warning)* ne tenir aucun compte de, négliger; *(danger)* ne tenir aucun compte de, ignorer; **I'll disregard what you just said** je ne tiendrai pas compte de ce que tu viens de dire

2 *n (for person, feelings)* manque *m* de considération; *(of order, warning, danger etc)* mépris *m*; *(of the law, convention)* inobservation *f*; **he showed a flagrant disregard for the rules** il a fait preuve d'un mépris flagrant pour le règlement; **to show complete disregard for the feelings of others** ne pas du tout prendre les sentiments des autres en considération; **with complete disregard for her own safety** au mépris total de sa vie

disremember [ˌdɪsrɪ'membə(r)] *vt Am Fam* ne pas se rappeler ❑, ne pas se souvenir de ❑

disrepair [ˌdɪsrɪ'peə(r)] *n (of building)* mauvais état *m*, délabrement *m*; *(of road)* mauvais état *m*; **in (a state of) disrepair** en mauvais état; **to fall into disrepair** *(building)* se délabrer; *(road)* se dégrader, s'abîmer

disreputable [dɪs'repjʊtəbəl] *adj* (**a**) *(dishonourable → behaviour)* honteux; *(→ action, methods)* déshonorant, peu honorable; *(→ life)* peu honorable (**b**) *(not respectable → person)* de mauvaise réputation, louche; *(→ area, club)* mal famé, de mauvaise réputation; *Hum (→ clothing)* miteux; **she has some disreputable friends** elle a des amis pas très fréquentables

disreputably [dɪs'repjʊtəblɪ] *adv (behave)* d'une manière honteuse; **he was dressed rather disreputably** il avait l'air d'un vrai loqueteux

disrepute [ˌdɪsrɪ'pjuːt] *n* discrédit *m*; **to bring sth into disrepute** discréditer qch; **to fall into disrepute** *(acquire bad reputation)* tomber en discrédit; *(become unpopular)* tomber en défaveur

disrespect [ˌdɪsrɪ'spekt] *n* irrespect *m*, irrévérence *f*; **she has a healthy disrespect for authority** elle porte un irrespect *ou* une irrévérence salutaire à toute forme d'autorité; **I meant no disrespect (to your family)** je ne voulais pas me montrer irrespectueux *ou* irrévérencieux (envers votre famille); **to show disrespect towards sb/sth** manquer de respect à qn/qch; **to treat sb/sth with disrespect** traiter qn/qch irrespectueusement; **no disrespect, but isn't that a bit stupid?** sans vouloir te vexer, est-ce que ce n'est pas un peu bête?

disrespectful [ˌdɪsrɪ'spektfʊl] *adj* irrespectueux, irrévérencieux; **to be disrespectful to sb** manquer de respect à qn; **it would be disrespectful not to go to the funeral** ce serait manquer de respect que de ne pas assister à l'enterrement

disrespectfully [ˌdɪsrɪ'spektfʊlɪ] *adv* irrespectueusement

disrobe [ˌdɪs'rəʊb] *Formal* **1** *vi (judge, priest)* enlever sa robe; *(undress)* se déshabiller

2 *vt (judge, priest)* aider à enlever sa robe; *(undress)* déshabiller

disrupt [dɪs'rʌpt] *vt (lesson, meeting, transport services)* perturber; *(conversation)* interrompre; *(plans)* déranger, perturber

disruption [dɪs'rʌpʃən] *n (of lesson, meeting, transport service, plans)* perturbation *f*; *(of conversation)* interruption *f*; **there were several disruptions to the meeting** la réunion a été perturbée à plusieurs reprises; **all the disruptions to everyday life caused by the earthquake** tous les bouleversements de la vie quotidienne provoqués par le tremblement de terre; **we apologize to viewers for the disruption to this evening's programmes** nous prions les téléspectateurs de bien vouloir nous excuser pour les changements intervenus dans les programmes de la soirée

disruptive [dɪs'rʌptɪv] *adj (factor, person, behaviour)* perturbateur; **he is** *or* **has a disruptive influence** il a une influence perturbatrice; **the disruptive element** l'élément perturbateur; **your presence would be disruptive** votre présence aurait un effet perturbateur

diss = **dis**

dissatisfaction ['dɪsˌsætɪs'fækʃən] *n* mécontentement *m*; **there is growing dissatisfaction with his policies** le mécontentement grandit à l'égard de sa politique

dissatisfied [ˌdɪs'sætɪsfaɪd] *adj* mécontent; **to be dissatisfied with sb/sth** être mécontent de qn/qch; **I am very dissatisfied with the service I received** je suis très mécontent *ou* je ne suis pas du tout satisfait du service que j'ai reçu; **the meal/explanation left me dissatisfied** le repas/l'explication m'a laissé sur ma faim

dissatisfy [ˌdɪs'sætɪsfaɪ] *(pt & pp* **dissatisfied***) vt* mécontenter

dissect [dɪ'sekt] *vt (animal, plant)* disséquer; *Fig (argument, theory)* disséquer; *(book, report)* éplucher

dissected [dɪ'sektɪd] *adj (body)* disséqué; *Bot (leaf)* découpé; *Geol (landscape)* découpé

dissecting [dɪ'sektɪŋ] *adj (table, room)* de dissection

▸▸ ***dissecting knife*** scalpel *m*; ***dissecting microscope*** microscope *m* à dissection

dissection [dɪ'sekʃən] *n (of animal, plant)* dissection *f*; *Fig (of argument, theory)* dissection *f*; *(of book, report)* épluchage *m*

dissemble [dɪ'sembəl] *Literary* **1** *vi* dissimuler

2 *vt (feelings, motives)* dissimuler

dissembler [dɪ'semblə(r)] *n Literary* dissimulateur(trice) *m,f*

disseminate [dɪ'semɪneɪt] *vt (knowledge, ideas)* disséminer, propager; *(information, news)* diffuser, propager

disseminated [dɪ'semɪneɪtɪd] *adj*

▸▸ *Med* ***disseminated sclerosis*** sclérose *f* en plaques

dissemination [dɪˌsemɪ'neɪʃən] *n (of knowledge, ideas)* propagation *f*, dissémination *f*; *(of information, news)* diffusion *f*, propagation *f*

disseminator [dɪ'semɪneɪtə(r)] *n (of knowledge, ideas)* disséminateur(trice) *m,f*, propagateur(trice) *m,f*; *(of information, news)* propagateur(trice) *m,f*

dissension [dɪ'senʃən] *n* dissension *f*, discorde *f*; **there is dissension in the ranks** il y a de la dissension *ou* discorde dans les rangs

dissent [dɪ'sent] **1** *vi* (**a**) *(person)* différer; *(opinion)* diverger; **to dissent from an opinion** être en désaccord avec une opinion; **two members of the enquiry dissented from the findings** deux membres de l'enquête ont exprimé une opinion divergente sur les conclusions

(**b**) *Rel* être dissident *ou* en dissidence

2 *n* (**a**) *(UNCOUNT) (gen)* désaccord *m*; **to voice** *or* **to express one's dissent** exprimer son désaccord; **voices of dissent** voix discordantes; *Ftbl* **he has been booked for dissent** l'arbitre a pris son nom après qu'il eut refusé d'obtempérer

(**b**) *Rel* dissidence *f*

(**c**) *Am Law* avis *m* contraire *(d'un juge)*

dissenter [dɪ'sentə(r)] *n* (**a**) *(gen)* dissident(e) *m,f* (**b**) *Rel* = dissident de l'Église anglicane

dissenting [dɪ'sentɪŋ] *adj (opinion)* divergent; **mine was the only dissenting voice** j'étais le seul à ne pas être d'accord

▸▸ *Am Law* ***dissenting opinion*** = déclaration d'un juge dont l'opinion ne coïncide pas avec celle du jury au cours d'un procès

dissert [dɪ'sɜːt], **dissertate** ['dɪsəteɪt] *vi Formal* disserter (**on** sur)

dissertation [ˌdɪsə'teɪʃən] *n* (**a**) *Univ Br* mémoire *m*, *Am* thèse *f* (**b**) *Formal (essay)* dissertation *f*; *(speech)* exposé *m*

disservice [ˌdɪs'sɜːvɪs] *n* mauvais service *m*; **to do sb a disservice** faire du tort à qn, rendre un mauvais service à qn; **to do oneself a disservice** se faire du tort

dissidence ['dɪsɪdəns] *n (disagreement)* désaccord *m*; *Pol* dissidence *f*

dissident ['dɪsɪdənt] **1** *n* dissident(e) *m,f*

2 *adj* dissident

dissimilar [ˌdɪ'sɪmɪlə(r)] *adj* dissemblable; **they are not dissimilar** ils se ressemblent; **the situation now is not dissimilar to what was going on 20 years ago** la situation actuelle n'est pas sans rappeler ce qui s'est passé il y a 20 ans

dissimilarity [ˌdɪsɪmɪ'lærətɪ] *(pl* **dissimilarities***) n* différence *f*

dissimulate [dɪ'sɪmjʊleɪt] *Formal* **1** *vt* dissimuler, cacher

2 *vi* dissimuler

dissimulation [dɪˌsɪmjʊ'leɪʃən] *n Formal* dissimulation *f*

dissipate ['dɪsɪpeɪt] **1** *vt* (**a**) *(disperse → cloud,* [illegible] *fortune)* dilapider, gaspiller; *(→ energy)* disperser, gaspiller (**c**) *Phys (heat, energy)* dissiper

2 *vi* (**a**) *(cloud, crowd, fears)* se disperser; *(hopes)* s'évanouir (**b**) *Phys (heat, energy)* se dissiper

dissipated ['dɪsɪpeɪtɪd] *adj (person)* débauché; *(habit, life)* de débauche; *(society)* décadent; **to lead** *or* **to live a dissipated life** mener une vie de débauche

dissipation [ˌdɪsɪ'peɪʃən] *n* (**a**) *(of cloud, fears, hopes)* dissipation *f* (**b**) *(of fortune)* dilapidation *f*; *(of energy)* dispersion *f*, gaspillage *m* (**c**) *Phys (of heat, energy)* dissipation *f* (**d**) *(debauchery)* débauche *f*; **to lead** *or* **to live a life of dissipation** mener une vie de débauche

dissipative ['dɪsɪpeɪtɪv] *adj* dispersif

dissociate [dɪ'səʊʃɪeɪt] **1** *vt* (**a**) *(gen)* dissocier, séparer; **to dissociate oneself from sb/sth** se dissocier *ou* désolidariser de qn/qch (**b**) *Chem* dissocier

2 *vi Chem (chemist)* opérer une dissociation; *(molecules)* se dissocier

dissociated [dɪ'səʊsɪeɪtɪd] *adj*

▸▸ *Psy* ***dissociated personality*** personnalité *f* simultanée

dissociation [dɪˌsəʊsɪ'eɪʃən] *n* dissociation *f*

dissociative [dɪ'səʊsɪeɪtɪv] *adj Psy* dissociatif

dissolubility [dɪˌsɒljʊ'bɪlɪtɪ] *n Chem* dissolubilité *f*

dissoluble [dɪ'sɒljʊbəl] *adj Chem* soluble

dissolute ['dɪsəluːt] *adj (person)* débauché; *(life)* de débauche, dissolu

dissolutely ['dɪsəluːtlɪ] *adv* dissolument; *(live)* dans la débauche

dissoluteness ['dɪsəluːtnɪs] *n* débauche *f*

dissolution [ˌdɪsə'luːʃən] *n* (**a**) *(gen)* dissolution *f* (**b**) *Am Law (divorce)* divorce *m* (**c**) *Hist* **the Dissolution of the Monasteries** = destruction des monastères en 1539 après la proclamation de Henri VIII comme chef suprême de l'Église d'Angleterre

dissolvable [dɪ'zɒlvəbəl] *adj* soluble

dissolve [dɪ'zɒlv] **1** *vt* (**a**) *(salt, sugar)* dissoudre (**b**) *(empire, marriage, Parliament)* dissoudre (**c**) *(cloud, illusion)* dissiper

2 *vi* (**a**) *(salt, sugar)* se dissoudre; *Fig (fear, hopes)* s'évanouir, s'envoler; *(apparition)* s'évanouir; *(crowd)* se disperser; *(clouds)* disparaître; **to dissolve into tears** fondre en larmes; **to dissolve into laughter** être pris de rire

(**b**) *(marriage, Parliament)* être dissout; *(empire)* se dissoudre

(**c**) *Cin & TV* faire un fondu enchaîné

3 *n Cin & TV* fondu *m* enchaîné

dissolvent [dɪ'zɒlvənt] **1** *n* dissolvant *m*

2 *adj* dissolvant

dissonance ['dɪsənəns] *n Mus* dissonance *f*; *Fig (of colours, opinions)* discordance *f*

dissonant ['dɪsənənt] *adj Mus* dissonant; *Fig (colours, opinions)* discordant

dissuade [dɪ'sweɪd] *vt (person)* dissuader; **to dissuade sb from doing sth** dissuader qn de faire qch; **to dissuade sb from sth** détourner qn de qch

dissuasion [dɪ'sweɪʒən] *n* dissuasion *f*

dissuasive [dɪ'sweɪsɪv] *adj (person, effect)* dissuasif; **it had a dissuasive effect on them** cela les a dissuadés

dissyllabic [dɪsɪ'læbɪk] *adj Ling* dissyllabique

dissyllable [dɪ'sɪləbəl] *n Ling* dissyllabe *m*

distaff ['dɪstɑːf] *n (for spinning)* quenouille *f*; *Fig* **on the distaff side** du côté maternel

distance ['dɪstəns] **1** *n* (**a**) *(between two places)* distance *f*; **distance is measured in miles/kilometres** on mesure la distance en miles/kilomètres; **modern technology makes distance irrelevant** avec la technologie moderne, les distances ne veulent plus rien dire; **at a distance of 50 metres** à (une distance de) 50 mètres; **within walking/cycling distance from the station** à quelques minutes de marche/en vélo de la gare; **is it within walking distance?** peut-on y aller à pied?; **the house is some distance from the village** la maison est assez loin du village; **it's some** *or* **quite a** *or* **a good distance from here** c'est assez loin d'ici; **a short distance away** tout près; **it's no distance (at all)** c'est tout près *ou* à deux pas; **we covered the distance in ten hours** nous avons fait le trajet en dix heures; **to cover great distances on foot** couvrir de grandes distances à pied; **distance (is) no object** *(in advertisement)* toutes distances couvertes, toutes destinations; **to keep at a safe distance (from)** se tenir à une distance prudente (de); *Fig* **to keep sb at a distance** tenir qn à distance (respectueuse); **to keep one's distance (from sb)** garder ses distances (par rapport à qn); **we keep our distance from each other** nous gardons nos distances (l'un par rapport à l'autre); **to go** *or* **stay the distance** *(boxer, political campaigner)* tenir la distance; **the fight went the distance** le combat est allé jusqu'à la limite

(**b**) *(distant point, place)* **to see/to hear sth in the distance** voir/entendre qch au loin; **in the middle distance** au second plan; **to see sth from a distance** voir qch de loin; **you can't see it from** *or* **at this distance** on ne peut pas le voir à cette distance; *Fig* **to admire sb from** *or* **at a distance** admirer qn de loin (**c**) *(separation in time)* **at a distance of 200 years, it's very difficult to know** 200 ans plus tard, il est très difficile de savoir; **it's very hard for me to remember at this distance in time** c'est très difficile de m'en souvenir après tout ce temps

(**d**) *Fig (gap)* **there's a great distance between us** il y a un grand fossé entre nous

(**e**) *(aloofness, reserve)* froideur *f*

2 *vt* distancer; **she is distancing herself from the other runners** elle est en train de distancer les autres coureurs *ou* de se détacher des autres coureurs; *Fig* **to distance oneself (from sb/sth)** prendre ses distances (par rapport à qn/qch)

►► ***distance banking*** banque *f* à distance; ***distance education*** enseignement *m* à distance *ou* par correspondance; ***distance learning*** enseignement *m* à distance *ou* par correspondance; *Sport* ***distance race*** épreuve *f* de fond; *Sport* ***distance runner*** coureur(euse) *m,f* de fond; ***distance teaching*** enseignement *m* à distance

distant ['dɪstənt] **1** *adj* (**a**) *(faraway → country, galaxy, place)* lointain, éloigné; **in the most distant corner of the universe** dans le coin le plus éloigné *ou* reculé de l'univers; **we had a distant view of the sea from the hotel** on pouvait voir la mer au loin depuis l'hôtel; **the distant sound of the sea** le bruit de la mer au loin

(**b**) *(in past → times)* lointain, reculé; *(→ memory)* lointain; **in the (dim and) distant past** il y a bien *ou* très longtemps, dans le temps

(**c**) *(in future → prospect)* lointain; **in the distant future** dans un avenir lointain; **in the not too distant future** dans un avenir proche, prochainement; **in the (dim and) distant past** dans le temps, il y a bien longtemps

(**d**) *(relation)* éloigné; *(resemblance)* vague

(**e**) *(remote → person, look)* distant; *(aloof)* froid; **to have a distant manner** être distant *ou* froid

2 *adv* **three miles distant from here** à trois miles d'ici; **not far distant** pas très loin

►► *Rail* ***distant signal*** signal *m* à distance

distantly ['dɪstəntlɪ] *adv* (**a**) *(in the distance)* au loin (**b**) *(resemble)* vaguement; **to be distantly related** *(people)* avoir un lien de parenté éloigné; *(ideas, concepts etc)* avoir un rapport éloigné (**c**) *(speak, behave, look)* froidement, d'un air distant *ou* froid

distaste [dɪs'teɪst] *n* dégoût *m* (**for** de), répugnance *f* (**for** pour); **to feel distaste for sth** ne pas aimer qch; *(stronger)* éprouver du dégoût *ou* de la répugnance pour qch; **if you could only overcome your initial distaste for opera** si seulement tu parvenais à surmonter ta répugnance pour l'opéra

distasteful [dɪs'teɪstfʊl] *adj (unpleasant → task, thought)* désagréable; *(in bad taste → joke, remark etc)* de mauvais goût; **to be distasteful to sb** déplaire à qn; **I find it extremely distasteful** je trouve ça tout à fait déplaisant

distastefully [dɪs'teɪstfʊlɪ] *adv (with repugnance → look)* d'un air dégoûté; *(with bad taste → presented, portrayed)* avec mauvais goût

distastefulness [dɪs'teɪstfʊlnɪs] *n (repugnance)* caractère *m* désagréable; *(bad taste)* mauvais goût *m*

Dist. Atty *Am (written abbr* **district attorney**) ≃ procureur *m* de la République

distemper[1] [dɪ'stempə(r)] **1** *n (paint)* détrempe *f*

2 *vt* peindre à la *ou* en détrempe

distemper[2] *n Vet* maladie *f* de Carré

distend [dɪ'stend] **1** *vt (cheeks)* gonfler; *(nostrils)* dilater; *(stomach)* distendre, ballonner

2 *vi (cheeks)* se gonfler; *(nostrils)* se dilater; *(stomach)* se ballonner, se distendre; *(sails)* se gonfler

distended [dɪ'stendɪd] *adj (cheeks)* gonflé; *(nostrils)* dilaté; *(stomach)* gonflé, ballonné; *(sails)* gonflé

distension [dɪ'stenʃən] *n (of cheeks)* gonflement *m*; *(of nostrils)* dilatation *f*; *(of stomach)* ballonnement *m*; *(sails)* gonflement *m*

distich ['dɪstɪk] *n Literature (couplet)* distique *m*

distil, *Am* **distill** [dɪ'stɪl] *(pt & pp* **distilled,** *cont* **distilling**) **1** *vt* (**a**) *Chem (liquid)* distiller (**b**) *Fig* condenser

2 *vi* se distiller

►► ***distilled water*** eau *f* distillée

►**distil off, distil out** *vt sep Chem* chasser par la distillation

distillate ['dɪstɪlət] *n Chem* distillat *m*

distillation [ˌdɪstɪ'leɪʃən] *n* (**a**) *Chem (process)* distillation *f*; *(product)* produit *m* de la distillation (**b**) *Fig* condensé *m*

distiller [dɪ'stɪlə(r)] *n Chem* distillateur *m*

distillery [dɪ'stɪlərɪ] *(pl* **distilleries**) *n* distillerie *f*; **whisky distillery** distillerie *f* de whisky

distinct [dɪ'stɪŋkt] **1** *adj* (**a**) *(different)* distinct; **to be distinct from** se distinguer de; **the two poems are quite distinct from each other** les deux poèmes sont tout à fait différents l'un de l'autre

(**b**) *(clear → memory)* clair, net; *(→ voice, announcement, place, object)* distinct

(**c**) *(decided, evident → accent)* prononcé; *(→ difference)* net, clair; *(→ preference)* marqué; *(→ lack of respect, interest)* évident; *(→ likeness)* clair, net, prononcé; *(→ advantage, improvement, impression)* net; **to make distinct progress** progresser nettement; **she had a distinct feeling that something would go wrong** elle avait le sentiment très net que quelque chose allait mal tourner; **I have the distinct impression you're trying to avoid me** j'ai la nette impression que tu essaies de m'éviter; **there's a distinct smell of smoke in here** cela sent vraiment la fumée ici; **a distinct possibility** une forte possibilité; **there is a distinct possibility of rain tomorrow** il est fort possible qu'il pleuve demain; **it is a distinct possibility** *(in answer to question)* c'est fort possible

2 as distinct from *prep* par opposition à

distinction [dɪ'stɪŋkʃən] *n* (**a**) *(difference)* distinction *f*; **her distinction between the two things** la distinction qu'elle fait entre les deux choses; **to make** *or* **to draw a distinction between two things** faire *ou* établir une distinction entre deux choses

(**b**) *(excellence)* distinction *f*; **a writer/artist of great distinction** un écrivain/artiste très réputé; **to win** *or* **to gain distinction (as)** se distinguer (en tant que); **she has the distinction of being the only woman to become Prime Minister** elle se distingue pour être la seule femme à avoir été nommée Premier ministre

(**c**) *Sch & Univ (mark)* mention *f*; **he got a distinction in maths** il a été reçu en maths avec mention; **to pass with distinction** réussir un examen avec mention très bien

(**d**) *(honour, award)* honneur *m*

distinctive [dɪ'stɪŋktɪv] *adj (colour, feature, style)* distinctif; **to be distinctive of sth** être caractéristique de qch; **her car is quite distinctive** sa voiture se remarque facilement

►► *Ling* ***distinctive feature*** trait *m* pertinent

distinctively [dɪ'stɪŋktɪvlɪ] *adv* de manière distinctive

distinctiveness [dɪ'stɪŋktɪvnɪs] *n* caractère *m* distinctif

distinctly [dɪ'stɪŋktlɪ] *adv* (**a**) *(clearly → speak, hear)* distinctement, clairement; *(→ remember)* clairement; **I distinctly told you not to do that** je t'ai bien dit de ne pas faire cela (**b**) *(very)* vraiment, franchement; **he was distinctly rude to the old lady** il a été vraiment grossier avec la vieille dame; **by now the weather was distinctly cold** à présent il faisait vraiment froid

distinctness [dɪ'stɪŋktnɪs] *n* (**a**) *(clearness)* clarté *f*, netteté *f* (**b**) *(separate nature)* spécificité *f*

distinguish [dɪ'stɪŋgwɪʃ] **1** *vt* (**a**) *(set apart)* distinguer; **to distinguish oneself** se distinguer; **to distinguish sth from sth** distinguer qch de qch; **reason distinguishes man from the other animals** la raison sépare l'homme des autres animaux

(**b**) *(tell apart)* distinguer

(**c**) *(discern)* distinguer

2 *vi* faire *ou* établir une distinction; **to distinguish between two things/people** faire la distinction entre deux choses/personnes

distinguishable [dɪ'stɪŋgwɪʃəbəl] *adj* (**a**) *(visible)* visible; **the horizon was hardly distinguishable** on distinguait à peine l'horizon

(**b**) *(recognizable)* reconnaissable; *(sound, difference)* perceptible; *(improvement)* sensible; **the coast was hardly distinguishable** c'est à peine si l'on distinguait la côte

(**c**) *(that can be differentiated)* que l'on peut distinguer, qui se distingue (**from** de); **to be easily distinguishable from sb/sth** se distinguer facilement de qn/qch, être facile à distinguer de qn/qch; **the male is distinguishable by his red legs** le mâle est reconnaissable à *ou* se distingue par ses pattes rouges; **the two ideas are barely distinguishable** les deux idées diffèrent à peine

distinguished [dɪ'stɪŋgwɪʃt] *adj* (**a**) *(eminent)* distingué (**b**) *(refined → manners, voice)* distingué; **to look distinguished** avoir l'air distingué; **distinguished-looking** distingué; **distinguished-sounding** *(voice)* distingué; *(person)* à la voix distinguée

►► *Mil* ***Distinguished Flying Cross*** = distinction honorifique des armées de l'air américaine et britannique; *Mil* ***Distinguished Flying Medal*** = médaille des armées de l'air américaine et britannique; *Br Mil* ***Distinguished Service Cross*** = décoration de l'armée britannique; *Br Mil* ***Distinguished Service Medal*** = décoration de l'armée britannique; *Br Mil* ***Distinguished Service Order*** = décoration de l'armée britannique

distinguishing [dɪ'stɪŋgwɪʃɪŋ] *adj (feature, mark, characteristic)* distinctif

►► ***distinguishing features, distinguishing marks*** *(on passport)* signes *mpl* particuliers

distort [dɪ'stɔːt] **1** *vt* (**a**) *(face, image, structure, limbs)* déformer (**b**) *Fig (facts, truth, account)* déformer, dénaturer; *(judgment)* fausser; **his upbringing distorted his view of life** son éducation a déformé *ou* faussé son image de la vie (**c**) *Electron, Rad & TV* déformer

2 *vi* (**a**) *(face, image, structure, limbs)* se déformer (**b**) *Electron, Rad & TV* se déformer

distorted [dɪ'stɔːtɪd] *adj* (**a**) *(face, image, structure, limbs)* déformé (**b**) *Fig (facts, truth, account)* déformé, dénaturé; *(view of life)* déformé, faussé; *(judgment)* faussé (**c**) *Electron, Rad & TV* déformé

distorting [dɪ'stɔːtɪŋ] *adj* déformant

►► ***distorting mirror*** glace *f* déformante

distortion [dɪ'stɔːʃən] *n* (**a**) *(of face, image, structure, limbs)* déformation *f* (**b**) *Fig (of facts, truth, account)* déformation *f* (**c**) *Electron & Rad* distorsion *f*; *TV* déformation *f*

distract [dɪ'strækt] *vt* (**a**) *(break concentration of)* distraire; *(disturb)* déranger; **to distract sb from his/her work** distraire qn de son travail; **to distract sb from his/her objective** détourner qn de son but; **to distract sb** *or* **sb's attention** *(accidentally)* distraire l'attention de qn; *(on purpose)* détourner l'attention de qn; **distract her for a couple of minutes** détourne son attention pendant quelques minutes

(**b**) *(amuse)* distraire

(**c**) *(preoccupy)* préoccuper

distracted [dɪ'stræktɪd] *adj* (**a**) *(with thoughts elsewhere)* distrait (**b**) *(upset)* affolé, bouleversé; **distracted with worry/with grief** fou (folle) d'inquiétude/de chagrin

distractedly [dɪ'stræktɪdlɪ] *adv* (**a**) *(with thoughts elsewhere)* distraitement, d'un air absent (**b**) *(anxiously)* d'un air affolé *ou* bouleversé; **she was sobbing distractedly** elle sanglotait, éperdue de douleur

distracting [dɪ'stræktɪŋ] *adj* (**a**) *(disruptive)* gênant; **I find it distracting** ça m'empêche de me concentrer; **it's very distracting having so many people in the office** c'est très difficile de se concentrer (sur son travail) avec autant de gens dans le bureau (**b**) *(amusing)* distrayant

distractingly [dɪ'stræktɪŋlɪ] *adv (disruptively)* **his leg ached dully but distractingly** la douleur sourde qu'il ressentait dans la jambe ne lui laissait aucun répit; **the music was distractingly intrusive** la musique l'empêchait de se concentrer; **she was distractingly beautiful** elle était d'une beauté envoûtante

distraction [dɪ'strækʃən] *n* (**a**) *(interruption → of attention, from objective)* distraction *f*; **taking on another job now would just be an unwelcome distraction for us** entreprendre un nouveau travail maintenant nous détournerait de notre objet; **I need a place where I can work without**

distraction il me faut un endroit où je pourrais travailler sans être dérangé
(**b**) *(amusement)* distraction *f*; **to do sth for distraction** faire qch pour se distraire
(**c**) *(anxiety)* affolement *m*; *(absent-mindedness)* distraction *f*
(**d**) *(madness)* affolement *m*; **to drive sb to distraction** rendre qn fou (folle); **I'm being driven to distraction** je deviens fou; **to love sb to distraction** aimer qn éperdument *ou* à la folie

distrain [dɪ'streɪn] *vi Law* **to distrain on sb's goods** saisir les biens de qn
►► *Law* ***distraining order*** ordre *m* de saisie

distraint [dɪ'streɪnt] *n Law* saisie *f*

distraught [dɪ'strɔ:t] *adj (with worry)* angoissé, fou (folle) d'angoisse; *(after death)* fou (folle) *ou* éperdu de douleur, désespéré; **the distraught mother made a plea to the kidnappers** folle d'angoisse, la mère a imploré les kidnappeurs; **he sounds distraught** il a l'air affolé; **to be distraught with grief** être fou (folle) de douleur; **to be distraught over sth** être angoissé à cause de *ou* désespéré par qch

distress [dɪ'stres] **1** *n* (**a**) *(suffering → mental)* angoisse *f*; *(→ physical)* souffrance *f*; *(hardship)* détresse *f*; **to cause sb distress** causer du tourment à qn; **to be in distress** *(horse, athlete)* souffrir; *(mentally)* être angoissé; *(ship)* être en détresse *ou* perdition; *(aircraft)* être en détresse; **to be in financial distress** avoir de sérieux problèmes financiers (**b**) *Law (action)* saisie *f*; *(goods)* biens *mpl* saisis
2 *vt* (**a**) *(upset)* faire de la peine à, tourmenter; **he was distressed by the animal's suffering** les souffrances de la bête lui faisaient de la peine (**b**) *(furniture, leather, clothing)* vieillir
►► *Am* ***distress call*** appel *m* de détresse; *Am Com* ***distress merchandise*** = marchandises écoulées à bas prix parce qu'elles sont endommagées ou pour permettre de régler des dettes importantes; *Am Com* ***distress sale*** soldes *fpl* avant fermeture; ***distress signal*** signal *m* de détresse; **to send out a distress signal** *(ship, aircraft)* envoyer un signal de détresse; *Fig* **to send out distress signals** envoyer des signaux de détresse; *Law* ***distress warrant*** mandat *m* de saisie

distressed [dɪ'strest] *adj* (**a**) *(mentally)* tourmenté; *(very sorry)* affligé; *(physically)* souffrant; *(financially)* dans le besoin; **there's no need to get distressed** ce n'est pas la peine de vous tourmenter; **we were distressed to hear of his death** nous avons été affligés d'apprendre sa mort; **to be distressed by** *or* **about sth** être affligé par qch; *Euph* **they are in distressed circumstances** ils sont dans le besoin; *Old-fashioned Euph* **distressed gentlewoman** = dame de bonne famille dans le besoin (**b**) *(furniture, leather, clothing)* vieilli (**c**) *Law* saisi
►► ***distressed area*** *(underprivileged)* quartier *m* défavorisé; *(after disaster)* zone *f* sinistrée

distressing [dɪ'stresɪŋ] *adj* pénible

distressingly [dɪ'stresɪŋlɪ] *adv* désespérément

distributable [dɪ'strɪbjʊtəbəl] *adj* (**a**) *(money, leaflets, gifts etc)* distribuable (**b**) *(wealth, weight)* répartissable (**c**) *Fin (dividend)* répartissable (**d**) *Cin & Com* distribuable

distribute [dɪ'strɪbju:t] *vt* (**a**) [illegible] *leaflets, gifts etc)* distribuer (**b**) *(share out, allocate → wealth, weight)* répartir; *(→ paint)* répandre (**c**) *Fin (dividend)* répartir (**d**) *Cin & Com (supply)* distribuer

distributed database [dɪ'strɪbju:tɪd-] *n Comput* base *f* de données répartie

distribution [ˌdɪstrɪ'bju:ʃən] *n* (**a**) *(of money, leaflets, gifts etc)* distribution *f*
(**b**) *Cin & Com (delivery, supply)* distribution *f*; *(of books)* diffusion *f*; *Com* **to have a wide distribution** être largement distribué
(**c**) *(of wealth)* répartition *f*, distribution *f*; *(of load, population)* répartition *f*
(**d**) *Math (in statistics)* distribution *f*
►► *Elec* ***distribution box*** boîte *f* de dérivation *ou* de jonction; *Com* ***distribution centre*** centre *m* de distribution; *Com* ***distribution chain*** chaîne *f* de distribution; *Com* ***distribution channel*** canal *m* de distribution; ***distribution contract*** contrat *m* de distribution; ***distribution costs*** frais *mpl* de distribution, coût *m* de la distribution; ***distribution depot*** dépôt *m* de distributeur; ***distribution market*** marché *m* de la distribution; ***distribution method*** mode *m* de distribution; *Com* ***distribution network*** réseau *m* de distribution, circuit *m* de distribution; ***distribution outlet*** point *m* de distribution; ***distribution ratio*** ratio *m* de distribution; *Cin* ***distribution rights*** droits *mpl* de distribution; ***distribution system*** système *m* de distribution

distributional [ˌdɪstrɪ'bju:ʃənəl] *adj* distributionnel
►► ***distributional effect*** effet *m* sur la répartition

distributive [dɪ'strɪbjʊtɪv] **1** *adj Gram* distributif
2 *n Gram (pronoun)* pronom *m* distributif; *(adjective)* adjectif *m* distributif
►► *Com* ***the distributive trades*** le secteur de la distribution

distributor [dɪ'strɪbjʊtə(r)] *n* (**a**) *Cin & Com* distributeur *m*; *(of particular make of car, product)* concessionnaire *m*
(**b**) *Aut* distributeur *m*
►► *Com* ***distributor brand*** marque *f* de distributeur; *Aut* ***distributor cap*** tête *f* de Delco® *ou* d'allumeur; *Com* ***distributor discount*** remise *f* au distributeur; *Com* ***distributor's margin*** marge *f* du distributeur; *Com* ***distributor panel*** panel *m* de distributeurs

distributorship [dɪ'strɪbjʊtəʃɪp] *n Com* **to have the distributorship for sth** distribuer qch

district ['dɪstrɪkt] *n (of country)* région *f*; *(of town)* quartier *m*; *(administrative area → of country)* district *m*; *(→ of city)* ≃ arrondissement *m*; *(surrounding area)* région *f*
►► *Am Law* ***district attorney*** ≃ procureur *m* de la République; ***the District of Columbia*** le district fédéral de Columbia; **in the District of Columbia** dans le district fédéral de Columbia; *Br Admin* ***district council*** conseil *m* municipal; *Am Law* ***district court*** ≃ tribunal *m* d'instance (fédéral); *Com* ***district manager*** directeur (trice) *m,f* régional(e); *Br* ***district nurse*** infirmière *f* visiteuse; *Admin* ***district surveyor*** cadastreur *m*; *Br* ***district visitor*** = membre d'une paroisse qui rend visite aux personnes en difficulté

distrust [dɪs'trʌst] **1** *vt* se méfier de
2 *n* méfiance *f*; **my distrust of her** la méfiance que j'éprouve pour elle *ou* à son égard; **to have a deep distrust of sb/sth** éprouver une profonde méfiance à l'égard de qn/qch

distrustful [dɪs'trʌstfʊl] *adj* méfiant; **to be deeply distrustful of sb/sth** éprouver une extrême méfiance pour *ou* à l'égard de qn/qch

distrustfully [dɪs'trʌstfʊlɪ] *adv* avec méfiance

disturb [dɪ'stɜ:b] *vt* (**a**) *(interrupt → person)* déranger; *(→ silence, sleep)* troubler; *(→ criminal)* surprendre; **(please) do not disturb** *(sign)* (prière de) ne pas déranger; *Law* **to disturb the peace** troubler l'ordre public
(**b**) *(distress, upset)* troubler, perturber; *(alarm)* inquiéter
(**c**) *(alter condition of → water)* troubler; *(→ mud, sediment)* agiter, remuer; *(→ papers)* déranger
(**d**) *Phys (magnetic field)* perturber
(**e**) *Law (interfere with the rights of)* inquiéter *ou* troubler dans la jouissance d'un droit

disturbance [dɪ'stɜ:bəns] *n* (**a**) [illegible] *ruption)* dérangement *m*
(**b**) *Pol* **disturbances** *(unrest)* troubles *mpl*, émeute *f*
(**c**) *(noise)* bruit *m*, vacarme *m*; *Law* **to cause a disturbance** troubler l'ordre public; **you're creating a disturbance** vous dérangez tout le monde; **they create such a disturbance when they leave the disco** ils font tant de chahut *ou* de tapage lorsqu'ils sortent de la discothèque; **police were called to a disturbance in the early hours of the morning** la police a été appelée au petit matin pour mettre fin à un tapage nocturne
(**d**) *(distress, alarm)* trouble *m*, perturbation *f*
(**e**) *Law (interference with rights)* trouble *m* de jouissance

disturbed [dɪ'stɜ:bd] *adj* (**a**) *(distressed, upset)* troublé, perturbé; *(alarmed)* inquiet; *(as a characteristic)* perturbé; *St Exch (market)* agité; **to be disturbed at** *or* **by sth** être troublé par *ou* perturbé par *ou* inquiet de qch; **I am disturbed by it** cela me dérange *ou* perturbe, cela m'inquiète; **mentally disturbed** qui souffre de troubles mentaux; **emotionally disturbed children** enfants *mpl* souffrant de troubles émotionnels *ou* affectifs (**b**) *(interrupted → sleep)* troublé; **we had a disturbed night** notre sommeil a été troublé

disturber [dɪ'stɜ:bə(r)] *n (gen)* dérangeur(euse) *m,f*; *Law* perturbateur(trice) *m,f*

disturbing [dɪ'stɜ:bɪŋ] *adj (alarming)* inquiétant; *(distressing, upsetting)* troublant, perturbant; **some viewers may find the programme disturbing** cette émission pourrait troubler *ou* perturber certains spectateurs

disturbingly [dɪ'stɜ:bɪŋlɪ] *adv* **the level of pollution is disturbingly high** la pollution a atteint un niveau inquiétant; **it is disturbingly evident that the cease-fire will not hold** il est inquiétant de voir que le cessez-le-feu n'a aucune chance d'être respecté

disulphide, *Am* **disulfide** [daɪ'sʌlfaɪd] *n Chem* bisulfure *m*, disulfure *m*; **carbon disulphide** carbosulfure *m*, sulfure *m* de carbone
►► ***disulphide of tin*** or *m* mussif

disunite [ˌdɪsju:'naɪt] *vt* désunir

disunited [ˌdɪsju:'naɪtɪd] *adj* désuni

disunity [ˌdɪs'ju:nətɪ] *n* désunion *f*

disuse [ˌdɪs'ju:s] *n (of term)* désuétude *f*; *(of machine)* abandon *m*, mise *f* au rancart; **the machine has rusted from disuse** la machine a rouillé à force de ne pas être utilisée; **to fall into disuse** *(word, custom, law)* tomber en désuétude

disused [ˌdɪs'ju:zd] *adj (machine)* mis au rancart; *(public building)* désaffecté; *(mine, well, railway line)* abandonné

disyllabic [ˌdɪsɪ'læbɪk] *adj Ling* dissyllabe, dissyllabique

disyllable [daɪ'sɪləbɪl] *n Ling* dissyllabe *m*

ditch [dɪtʃ] **1** *n* (**a**) *(by roadside)* fossé *m*; *(for irrigation, drainage)* rigole *f*; **he drove the car into the ditch** il est tombé dans le fossé avec la voiture (**b**) *Fam Aviat* **the ditch** la baille, la flotte
2 *vt* (**a**) *Fam (abandon → car)* abandonner ❑; *(→ plan, idea)* abandonner ❑, laisser tomber ❑; *(→ boyfriend, girlfriend)* plaquer, laisser tomber ❑; *(throw out)* se débarrasser de ❑; **the lorry driver ditched us** le chauffeur du camion nous a laissés en rade (**b**) *Aviat* **to ditch a plane** faire un amerrissage forcé
3 *vi* (**a**) *Aviat* faire un amerrissage forcé (**b**) *Agr* creuser un fossé

ditching ['dɪtʃɪŋ] *n* (**a**) *Agr* creusement *m* de fossés (**b**) *Fam (dumping → of car, plan, idea)* abandon ❑ *m* (**c**) *Aviat* amerrissage *m* forcé

ditchwater ['dɪtʃˌwɔ:tə(r)] *n Fam (idiom)* **to be as dull as ditchwater** être ennuyeux comme la pluie

dither ['dɪðə(r)] *Fam* **1** *vi (be indecisive)* hésiter ❑, tergiverser ❑, se tâter ❑; **to dither about** *or* **over whether to do sth** hésiter à *ou* se tâter pour faire qch; **stop dithering (about)!** *(decide)* décide-toi!; *(make a start)* arrête de tourner en rond!
2 *n* **to be in a dither** hésiter ❑, tergiverser ❑, se tâter ❑; **I'm in a dither about what to do** je n'arrive pas à me décider sur ce que je dois faire ❑; **he was in** *or* **all of a dither about his exams** il était dans tous ses états à cause de ses examens

ditherer ['dɪðərə(r)] *n Fam* **he's such a terrible ditherer** il est toujours à hésiter sur tout ❑

dithery ['dɪðərɪ] *adj Fam* (**a**) *(indecisive)* hésitant ❑, indécis ❑ (**b**) *(agitated)* nerveux ❑, agité ❑

dithyramb ['dɪθɪræm] *n Literature* dithyrambe *m*

dithyrambic [ˌdɪθɪ'ræmbɪk] *adj Literature* dithyrambique

ditransitive [daɪ'trænsɪtɪv] *adj Gram* à deux compléments d'objet

ditsy ['dɪtsɪ] (*compar* **ditsier**, *superl* **ditsiest**) *adj esp Am Fam* écervelé

ditto ['dɪtəʊ] *adv* idem, de même; *Fam* **I feel like a drink – ditto** j'ai bien envie de prendre un verre – idem; **I don't like her – ditto** je ne l'aime pas – moi non plus
►► *Ling* ***ditto mark*** guillemets *mpl* itératifs, signes *mpl* d'itération

ditty ['dɪtɪ] (*pl* **ditties**) *n Fam* chanson ❑ *f*

diuresis [ˌdaɪjʊ'ri:sɪs] *n Med* diurèse *f*

dis–diu

diuretic [ˌdaɪjʊ'retɪk] *Med* **1** *adj* diurétique
2 *n* diurétique *m*

diurnal [daɪ'ɜːnəl] **1** *adj Bot, Zool & Astron* diurne
2 *n Rel* diurnal *m*

div [dɪv] *n Br Fam (idiot)* abruti(e) *m,f*

diva ['diːvə] *n* diva *f*; *Fig* **she's a bit of a diva** elle est un peu comédienne

divan [dɪ'væn] *n (couch)* divan *m*
►► ***divan bed*** divan-lit *m*

dive [daɪv] *(Br pt & pp* **dived**, *Am pt* **dove** [dəʊv] or **dived**, *pp* **dived**) **1** *vi* (**a**) *(person, bird, submarine)* plonger; *(aircraft)* plonger, piquer, descendre en piqué; **to dive for clams/pearls** pêcher la palourde/des perles *(en plongée)*; **the bird dived on its prey** l'oiseau a plongé *ou* fondu sur sa proie; **she dived off the side of the boat** elle a plongé depuis le bord du bateau; **to dive for the ball** *(goalkeeper)* plonger (pour attraper le ballon)
(**b**) *(as sport)* faire de la plongée
(**c**) *(rush)* **they dived for the exit** ils se sont précipités *ou* ils ont foncé vers la sortie; **he dived for his camera** il s'est rué sur son appareil photo; **the soldiers dived into the doorway** les soldats se sont engouffrés dans l'entrée; **the rabbit dived down its hole** le lapin s'est enfoui *ou* a plongé dans son trou; **he dived into the car** il s'engouffra dans la voiture; **he dived into his pocket/the bag** il a plongé la main dans sa poche/le sac; *Fig* **she always dives headlong into a task** elle fonce toujours tête baissée pour faire quelque chose; **she dived out of sight** elle s'est cachée précipitamment; **to dive under the table** plonger *ou* se jeter sous la table; **he dived under the covers and shut his eyes** il s'est enfoui *ou* il a plongé sous les couvertures et a fermé les yeux
2 *n* (**a**) *(of swimmer, bird)* plongeon *m*; *(of submarine, diver)* plongée *f*; *(by aircraft)* piqué *m*; **to go into a dive** *(aircraft)* piquer, descendre en piqué; **to pull out of a dive** *(aircraft)* se redresser d'un piqué, effectuer un rétablissement; **to make a dive for the ball** plonger (pour attraper le ballon); *Fam Boxing* **to take a dive** feindre le K-O; *Ftbl* **he took a dive in the box** il a fait exprès de s'effondrer dans la surface de réparation
(**b**) *(sudden movement)* **to make a dive for the exit** se précipiter vers la sortie; **to make a dive for shelter** se précipiter pour se mettre à l'abri; **I made a dive for the vase** *(to stop it breaking)* je me suis précipité vers le vase
(**c**) *Fam Pej (bar, café)* bouge *m*; *(hotel)* hôtel *m* borgne

►**dive in** *vi* (**a**) *(swimmer)* plonger (**b**) *Fam* **dive in!** *(eat)* attaquez!; **we're just going to have to dive in** *(set to work)* il va falloir qu'on s'y mette; **we can't just dive in without any preparation** nous ne pouvons pas nous lancer comme ça sans aucune préparation

dive-bomb *vt (of aircraft)* bombarder *ou* attaquer en piqué; *(of bird)* attaquer en piqué

dive-bomber *n (aircraft)* chasseur *m* bombardier

dive-bombing *n (by aircraft)* bombardement *m* en piqué

diver ['daɪvə(r)] *n* (**a**) *(from diving board, underwater)* plongeur(euse) *m,f*; *(deep-sea)* scaphandrier *m*; **pearl/clam diver** pêcheur(euse) *m,f* de perles/de palourdes *(en plongée)* (**b**) *Orn* plongeon *m*

diverge [daɪ'vɜːdʒ] **1** *vi* (**a**) *(paths, roads)* se séparer, diverger; *(rays, lines)* diverger (**b**) *Fig (people, opinions)* diverger; **to diverge from the truth** s'écarter de la vérité; **our paths diverged** nos chemins se sont séparés
2 *vt (rays, lines)* faire diverger

divergence [daɪ'vɜːdʒəns] *n* (**a**) *(of paths, roads)* séparation *f*, divergence *f*; *(of rays, lines)* divergence *f* (**b**) *Fig (of people, opinions)* divergence *f*; **this divergence in our opinions** cette divergence d'opinion entre nous

divergent [daɪ'vɜːdʒənt] *adj (opinions)* divergent; **we take divergent views on certain points** nos opinions divergent *ou* diffèrent sur certains points

diverging beam [daɪ'vɜːdʒɪŋ-] *n Aut* faisceau *m* divergent

divers ['daɪvəz] *adj Arch or Literary (several)* divers, plusieurs

diverse [daɪ'vɜːs] *adj* (**a**) *(different from each other)* divers, différent; **they are very diverse in their approach** ils ont une approche très différente (**b**) *(varied)* divers, varié

diversely [daɪ'vɜːslɪ] *adv* diversement

diverseness [daɪ'vɜːsnɪs] *n* diversité *f*

diversification [daɪˌvɜːsɪfɪ'keɪʃən] *n* diversification *f*; **the company's recent diversification into cosmetics** la diversification qu'a récemment entreprise la société en pénétrant le marché des cosmétiques

diversify [daɪ'vɜːsɪfaɪ] *(pt & pp* **diversified**) **1** *vi (company)* se diversifier; **to diversify into a new market** se diversifier en pénétrant un nouveau marché; **to diversify into a new product** se diversifier en fabriquant un nouveau produit; **to diversify into software/banking** se diversifier en pénétrant le secteur du logiciel/le secteur bancaire
2 *vt* diversifier; **we must aim to diversify our product portfolio** il nous faut essayer de diversifier notre portefeuille de produits

diversion [daɪ'vɜːʃən] *n* (**a**) *(of traffic)* déviation *f*; *(of river)* dérivation *f*, détournement *m* (**b**) *(distraction)* diversion *f*; **it was a welcome diversion** cela a été une diversion agréable; **to create a diversion** *(distract attention)* faire (une) diversion; *Mil* opérer une diversion (**c**) *(amusement)* distraction *f*; **to seek diversion from sth** chercher à se distraire de qch

diversionary [daɪ'vɜːʃənrɪ] *adj* (**a**) *(remark, proposal)* destiné à faire diversion; **diversionary tactics** tactique *f* de diversion (**b**) *Mil (manoeuvre)* de diversion

diversity [daɪ'vɜːsətɪ] *n* diversité *f*

divert [daɪ'vɜːt] *vt* (**a**) *(reroute → traffic)* dévier; *(→ train, plane, ship)* dévier (la route de); *(→ river, attention, conversation, blow)* détourner; *Elec (current)* dévier; **I managed to divert his attention from the problem** j'ai réussi à détourner son attention de ce problème; **the train was diverted via Birmingham** le train a été dévié par Birmingham; **the plane was diverted to London** l'avion a été dévié *ou* détourné sur Londres; **to divert water from a river** détourner de l'eau d'une rivière
(**b**) *(money)* transférer; *(illegally)* détourner
(**c**) *(amuse)* distraire; **to divert oneself by doing sth** faire qch pour se distraire

diverticulitis [ˌdaɪvəˌtɪkjʊ'laɪtɪs] *n (UNCOUNT) Med* diverticulite *f*

diverticulosis [ˌdaɪvəˌtɪkjʊ'ləʊsɪs] *n (UNCOUNT) Med* diverticulose *f*

diverticulum [daɪvə'tɪkjʊləm] *n Anat* diverticule *m*

divertimento [dɪvɜːtɪ'mentəʊ] *(pl* **divertimenti** [dɪvɜːtɪ'mentiː]) *n Mus* divertissement *m*

diverting [daɪ'vɜːtɪŋ] *adj* divertissant

divest [daɪ'vest] *vt Formal* (**a**) *(take away from)* priver; **to divest sb of sth** priver qn de qch (**b**) *(rid)* **to divest oneself of** *(opinion, belief)* se défaire de; *(coat)* enlever; *(luggage)* se débarrasser de; *(authority)* se dévêtir de; *(duty)* se désinvestir de; *(right)* renoncer à

divestiture [daɪ'vestɪtʃə(r)] *n Am* désinvestissement *m*

divestment [daɪ'vestmənt] *n Am* désinvestissement *m*; *Fin* **divestment of assets** scission *f* d'actifs

divide [dɪ'vaɪd] **1** *vt* (**a**) *(split up → territory, property, work, inheritance)* diviser; *(→ kingdom)* démembrer; *(→ land)* morceler; *(→ family)* diviser, désunir; *(→ party)* diviser, scinder; **to divide sth in** *or* **into two** couper *ou* diviser qch en deux; **she divided the cake into six equal portions** elle a partagé *ou* coupé le gâteau en six parts égales
(**b**) *(share out)* partager, répartir; **she divided the cake equally among the children** elle a partagé le gâteau en parts égales entre les enfants; **they divided the work between them** ils se sont partagé *ou* réparti le travail; **he divides his time between the office and home** il partage son temps entre le bureau et la maison
(**c**) *(separate)* séparer; **to divide sth from sth** séparer qch de qch; **the Berlin Wall used to divide East and West** le mur de Berlin séparait l'Est de l'Ouest
(**d**) *Math* diviser; **to divide 10 by 2** diviser 10 par 2; **40 divided by 5 equals 8** 40 divisé par 5 égale 8
(**e**) *(disunite → family, party)* diviser
(**f**) *Br Pol* **to divide the House** faire voter la Chambre
2 *vi* (**a**) *(cells, group of people, novel)* se diviser; *Pol* **a policy of divide and rule** une politique consistant à diviser pour régner; **the class divided into groups** la classe s'est divisée *ou* répartie en groupes
(**b**) *(river, road)* se séparer
(**c**) *Math* diviser; **we're learning to divide** nous apprenons à faire des divisions; **10 divides by 2** 10 est divisible par 2, 10 est un multiple de 2
(**d**) *Br Pol* aller aux voix; **the House divided on the question** la Chambre a voté sur la question
3 *n* (**a**) *(gap)* fossé *m*; **the North-South divide** la division Nord-Sud
(**b**) *Am Geog (watershed)* ligne *f* de partage des eaux; **the Great** *or* **Continental Divide** la ligne de partage des eaux des Rocheuses; **to cross the Great Divide** *(die)* passer de vie à trépas

►**divide off** *vt sep* séparer; **to divide sth off from sth** séparer qch de qch

►**divide out** *vt sep* partager, répartir; **to divide sth out between** *or* **among people** partager qch entre des gens

►**divide up 1** *vi* se diviser
2 *vt sep* diviser; **they divided the area/work up between them** ils se sont partagés le secteur/travail

divided [dɪ'vaɪdɪd] *adj* (**a**) *(property, territory)* divisé; *(work)* partagé; *Bot* découpé (**b**) *(disunited → family, party)* divisé; **the party is divided on the issue** le parti est divisé sur ce problème; **opinion is divided on the matter** les avis sont partagés sur ce problème; **I feel divided (in my mind)** *or* **my mind is divided on the issue** je suis partagé sur la question; **a political party divided against itself** un parti divisé; **to have divided loyalties** être déchiré; **my loyalties are divided** je suis déchiré
►► *Am* ***divided highway*** route *f* à quatre voies; ***divided skirt*** jupe-culotte *f*

dividend ['dɪvɪdend] *n Fin, Math & St Exch* dividende *m*; *(from cooperative society)* ristourne *f*; *Fin* **to pay a dividend** *(company)* verser un dividende; *St Exch (shares)* rapporter un dividende; *Fig* **to pay dividends** porter ses fruits; **the company has declared a dividend of 10 percent** la société a déclaré un dividende de 10 pour cent; **cum dividend,** *Am* **dividend on** avec le dividende attaché; **ex dividend,** *Am* **dividend off** ex-dividende; **dividend per share** dividende *f* par action
►► ***dividend announcement*** déclaration *f* de dividende; ***dividend cover*** taux *m* de couverture du dividende; ***dividend mandate*** ordonnance *f* de paiement; ***dividend share*** action *f* de jouissance; *Fin* ***dividend tax*** impôt *m* sur les dividendes; ***dividend warrant*** chèque-dividende *m*, coupon *m* d'arrérages; ***dividend yield*** taux *m* de rendement des actions

dividend-price ratio *n Am St Exch* ratio *m* cours-bénéfice

divider [dɪ'vaɪdə(r)] **1** *n* (**a**) *(in room → partition)* cloison *f* amovible; *(→ piece of furniture)* meuble *m* de séparation (**b**) *(for files)* intercalaire *m*
2 dividers *npl Math* **(a pair of) dividers** un compas à pointes sèches

dividing [dɪ'vaɪdɪŋ] *adj (fence)* de séparation; **dividing line** limite *f*; *Fig* distinction *f*; *Fig* **it's a very thin dividing line** c'est une distinction très subtile; **she has crossed the dividing line between confidence and arrogance** elle a franchi la limite entre confiance en soi et arrogance
►► *Elec* ***dividing box*** boîte *f* de dérivation; ***dividing wall*** mur *m* de séparation, cloison *f*

divination [ˌdɪvɪ'neɪʃən] *n* divination *f*

divine [dɪ'vaɪn] **1** *adj* (**a**) *Rel* divin; **it was divine retribution** c'était le châtiment de Dieu; *Formal* **to attend divine service** aller à l'église
(**b**) *Fam (delightful)* divin; **you look simply divine!** tu es absolument divine!
2 *n Rel (priest)* théologien *m*
3 *vt* (**a**) *Literary (foretell → the future)* présager, prédire

(**b**) *Literary (conjecture, guess)* deviner
(**c**) *Literary (perceive by intuition)* pressentir
(**d**) *(locate → water)* détecter *ou* découvrir par la radiesthésie
4 *vi* **to divine for water** détecter *ou* découvrir de l'eau par la radiesthésie
▸▸ *also Fig* ***divine inspiration*** inspiration *f* divine; ***divine intervention*** intervention *f* divine; ***divine office*** office *m* divin; *Hist* ***the divine right of kings*** la monarchie de droit divin

'The Divine Comedy' *Dante* 'La Divine Comédie'

divinely [dɪ'vaɪnlɪ] *adv* divinement
diviner [dɪ'vaɪnə(r)] *n* (**a**) *(of future)* devin *m*, devineresse *f* (**b**) *(for water)* sourcier *m*, radiesthésiste *mf*
diving ['daɪvɪŋ] *n (underwater)* plongée *f* sous-marine; *(from board)* plongeon *m*
▸▸ ***diving bell*** cloche *f* à plongeur *ou* de plongée; ***diving board*** plongeoir *m*; *Naut* ***diving rudder*** *(of submarine)* gouvernail *m* de profondeur; ***diving suit*** scaphandre *m*
divining [dɪ'vaɪnɪŋ] *n* divination *f*; *(for water)* radiesthésie *f*
▸▸ ***divining rod*** baguette *f* de sourcier
divinity [dɪ'vɪnətɪ] *(pl* **divinities**) *Rel n* (**a**) *(quality, state)* divinité *f* (**b**) *(god, goddess)* divinité *f*; **the Divinity** la Divinité (**c**) *(theology)* théologie *f*; *Sch* instruction *f* religieuse; **Faculty/Doctor of Divinity** faculté *f* de/docteur *m* en théologie
▸▸ *Am* ***divinity school*** faculté *f* (libre) de théologie; ***divinity student*** étudiant(e) *m,f* en théologie
divisibility [dɪ,vɪzɪ'bɪlɪtɪ] *n* divisibilité *f*
divisible [dɪ'vɪzəbəl] *adj* divisible; **divisible by** divisible par
division [dɪ'vɪʒən] *n* (**a**) *(splitting up → of territory, property, family, work, inheritance)* division *f*; *(→ of kingdom)* démembrement *m*; *(→ of land)* morcellement *m*; *(→ of party)* division *f*, scission *f*
(**b**) *(sharing out)* partage *m*; **the division of labour** la division du travail; **the division of responsibility** le partage des responsabilités
(**c**) *(section → of company, organization)* division *f*; *(→ of scale, thermometer)* graduation *f*; *Law (→ of court)* section *f*; *(compartment → in box, bag)* compartiment *m*
(**d**) *Biol, Mil & Sport* embranchement *m*
(**e**) *Math* division *f*
(**f**) *(that which separates)* division *f*; *(dividing line)* division *f*, scission *f*; *(in room)* cloison *f*; **class divisions** divisions *fpl* entre les classes, divisions *fpl* sociales; **the motorway forms a division between the two halves of the city** l'autoroute sépare la ville en deux
(**g**) *(dissension)* division *f*
(**h**) *Br Pol* = vote officiel à la Chambre des communes (pour lequel les députés se répartissent dans les deux "division lobbies"); **a division will be necessary** il faudra procéder à un vote; **the bill was passed without division** le projet de loi a été adopté sans qu'on ait procédé à un vote; **to carry a division** avoir *ou* remporter la majorité des voix; **to come to a division** procéder à un vote; **to call a division** [illegible] un vote; **to call for a division on sth** demander que qch soit soumis à un vote
▸▸ *Br Pol* ***division bell*** = sonnerie à la Chambre des communes prévenant les députés qu'il faut venir voter; *Br Pol* ***division lobby*** = nom des deux salles dans lesquelles les députés britanniques se répartissent pour voter; *Math* ***division sign*** symbole *m* de division
divisional [dɪ'vɪʒənəl] *adj* de la division, de division; **divisional manager** directeur(trice) *m,f* de la division; **there were six divisional managers there** il y avait six directeurs de division
▸▸ *Br Law* ***Divisional Court*** = juridiction d'appel rattachée à chacune des divisions de la "High Court"
divisionism [dɪ'vɪʒənɪzəm] *n Art* divisionnisme *m*
divisionist [dɪ'vɪʒənɪst] *Art* **1** *n* divisionniste *mf*
2 *adj* divisionniste
divisive [dɪ'vaɪsɪv] *adj (policy, issue)* qui crée des divisions
divisiveness [dɪ'vaɪsɪvnɪs] *n* **the divisiveness of this policy is evident to everyone** il apparaît clairement à tout le monde que cette politique crée des *ou* est source de divisions
divisor [dɪ'vaɪzə(r)] *n Math* diviseur *m*
divorce [dɪ'vɔːs] **1** *n* (**a**) *(of married couple)* divorce *m*; **I want a divorce** je veux divorcer, je veux le divorce; **he asked his wife for a divorce** il a demandé à sa femme de divorcer, il a demandé le divorce à sa femme; **one in three marriages ends in divorce** un couple sur trois divorce; **a lawyer who specializes in divorce** un avocat spécialisé dans les affaires *ou* cas de divorce; **her first marriage ended in divorce** son premier mariage s'est soldé par un divorce; **to file** *or* **to sue for (a) divorce** demander le divorce; **to get** *or* **to obtain a divorce** obtenir le divorce; **Hannah's getting a divorce from Luke** Hannah divorce d'avec Luke; **they're getting a divorce** ils divorcent; **why don't you get a divorce?** pourquoi ne divorces-tu pas?
(**b**) *Fig* séparation *f*, divorce *m*
2 *comp (case, proceedings)* de divorce
3 *vt* (**a**) *(of husband, wife)* divorcer d'avec; *(of judge)* prononcer le divorce de; **you should divorce him** tu devrais divorcer (d'avec lui); **they got divorced a few years ago** ils ont divorcé il y a quelques années
(**b**) *Fig* séparer; **to divorce sth from sth** séparer qch de qch
4 *vi* divorcer
▸▸ ***divorce court*** = chambre spécialisée dans les affaires familiales au tribunal de grande instance; ***divorce lawyer*** avocat(e) *m,f* spécialisé(e) dans les affaires *ou* cas de divorce
divorced [dɪ'vɔːst] *adj* (**a**) *(person, couple)* divorcé; **a divorced woman** une (femme) divorcée (**b**) *Fig* **to be divorced from reality** *(person)* être coupé de la réalité, ne pas avoir les pieds sur terre; *(suggestion, plan)* être irréaliste; **divorced from commonsense** dénué de bon sens
divorcee [dɪvɔː'siː] *n (man)* divorcé *m*; *(woman)* divorcée *f*
divot ['dɪvət] *n* motte *f* de terre
divulgation [,daɪvʌl'geɪʃən] *n* divulgation *f*
divulge [daɪ'vʌldʒ] *vt* divulguer, révéler
divulgement [daɪ'vʌldʒmənt], **divulgence** [daɪ'vʌldʒəns] *n* divulgation *f*
divvy ['dɪvɪ] *(pl* **divvies**, *pt & pp* **divvied**, *cont* **divvying**) *n Br Fam* (**a**) *Fin* dividende *m* (**b**) *(idiot)* abruti(e) *m,f*
▸ **divvy up** *Fam* **1** *vt sep* partager; **they divvied up the money between them** ils se sont partagé l'argent
2 *vi* faire le partage
Dixie ['dɪksɪ] *n Am Fam* le Sud *(terme désignant le sud-est des États-Unis, particulièrement les anciens États esclavagistes)*
dixie ['dɪksɪ] *n Br Fam Mil slang* gamelle ❑ *f*
Dixieland ['dɪksɪlænd] *n Mus* jazz *m* dixieland
▸▸ ***Dixieland jazz*** le (jazz) dixieland
DIY [,diːaɪ'waɪ] *Br (abbr* **do-it-yourself**) **1** *n* bricolage *m*
2 *comp* de bricolage
▸▸ ***DIY expert*** spécialiste *m* du bricolage; ***DIY shop*** magasin *m* de bricolage; ***DIY superstore*** grande surface *f* de bricolage
dizygotic [daɪzaɪ'gɒtɪk] *adj Biol* dizygote
dizzily ['dɪzɪlɪ] *adv* (**a**) *(walk)* avec une sensation de vertige (**b**) *(rise → of cliffs, prices etc)* vertigineusement (**c**) *(behave, laugh)* étourdiment
dizziness ['dɪzɪnɪs] *n (UNCOUNT)* vertiges *mpl*
dizzy ['dɪzɪ] *(compar* **dizzier**, *superl* **dizziest**) *adj* (**a**) *(giddy)* **to feel dizzy** avoir le vertige, avoir la tête qui tourne; **you'll make yourself dizzy** tu vas avoir la tête qui tourne; **it makes me (feel) dizzy** cela me donne le vertige; **a dizzy spell** *or* **turn** un éblouissement (**b**) *(height, speed)* vertigineux; **the dizzy heights of fame** les sommets grisants de la célébrité *ou* gloire (**c**) *Fam (scatterbrained)* étourdi; **a dizzy blonde** une blonde évaporée
DJ [,diː'dʒeɪ] **1** *n* (**a**) *(abbr* **disc jockey**) DJ *m* (**b**) *Fam (abbr* **dinner jacket**) smoking ❑ *m*
2 *vi (work as DJ)* travailler comme DJ; **he DJ's every Friday night at the Volcano** il travaille comme DJ au Volcano tous les vendredis soir
Djakarta [dʒə'kɑːtə] *n* Djakarta, Jakarta
djembe drum ['dʒembə-] *n Mus* djembé *m*
Djerba ['dʒɜːbə] *n* Djerba; **in Djerba** à Djerba
DJIA [,diːdʒeɪ,aɪ'eɪ] *n Am St Exch (abbr* **Dow Jones Industrial Average**) DJIA *m*
Djibouti [dʒɪ'buːtɪ] *n* (République *f* de) Djibouti; **in Djibouti** à Djibouti; **Djibouti City** Djibouti; **in Djibouti City** à Djibouti
djinn [dʒɪn] *n* djinn *m*
dl *(written abbr* **decilitre**) dl
DLit [,diː'lɪt] *n Univ (abbr* **Doctor of Literature**) *(person)* = titulaire d'un doctorat ès lettres; *(qualification)* doctorat *m* ès lettres
DLitt [,diː'lɪt] *n Univ (abbr* **Doctor of Letters**) *(person)* = titulaire d'un doctorat ès lettres; *(qualification)* doctorat *m* ès lettres
DLO [,diːel'əʊ] *n (abbr* **dead-letter office**) = bureau où est entreposé le courrier dont les destinataires sont introuvables
DM[1] *(written abbr* **Deutsche Mark**) DM
DM[2] [,diː'em] *n (abbr* **direct mail**) publipostage *m*
dm *(written abbr* **decimetre**) dm
DMA [,diːem'eɪ] *n Comput (abbr* **direct memory access**) accès *m* direct à la mémoire
DMs [,diː'emz] *npl Br Fam (abbr* **Doc Martens**®) Docs *fpl*, Doc Martens® *fpl*
DMus [,diː'mjuːz] *n Univ (abbr* **Doctor of Music**) *(person)* = titulaire d'un doctorat en musique; *(qualification)* doctorat *m* en musique
DMV [,diːem'viː] *n Am Admin (abbr* **Department of Motor Vehicles**) = service des immatriculations et des permis de conduire aux États-Unis
DMZ [,diːem'zed] *n (abbr* **demilitarized zone**) zone *f* démilitarisée
DNA [,diːen'eɪ] *n Biol (abbr* **deoxyribonucleic acid**) ADN *m*
▸▸ ***DNA fingerprinting*** analyse *f* de l'empreinte génétique; ***DNA profiling*** séquençage *m* de l'ADN
Dnieper [d'niːpə(r)] *n* **the (River) Dnieper** le Dniepr
D-notice *n Press* = consigne donnée par le gouvernement britannique à la presse pour empêcher la diffusion d'informations touchant à la sécurité du pays
DNR [,diːen'ɑː(r)] *n Med (abbr* **do not resuscitate**) ne pas réanimer *(mention figurant sur le dossier de patients ne souhaitant pas être réanimés)*
DNS [,diːen'es] *n Comput (abbr* **Domain Name System**) système *m* de nom de domaine, DNS *m*
do. *(written abbr* **ditto**) do

DO[1] [duː]

à la forme interrogative	▸ **1 (a)**
dans les question tags	▸ **2 (b)**
à la forme négative	▸ **1 (c)**
usage emphatique	▸ **1 (d)**
usage elliptique	▸ **1 (e)**
faire	▸ **2 (a), (b), (d), (f) – (j), (m), (q); 3 (c)**
s'occuper de	▸ **2 (c)**
étudier	▸ **2 (e)**
suffire	▸ **2 (k); 3 (d)**
s'en tirer	▸ **3 (a)**
aller	▸ **3 (b), (e)**

(3rd person singular **does** [dʌz], *pt* **did** [dɪd], *pp* **done** [dʌn])

Les formes négatives sont **don't/doesn't** et **didn't,** qui deviennent **do not/does not** et **did** [illegible]

1 *v aux* (**a**) *(in questions)* **do you know her?** est-ce que tu la connais?, la connais-tu?; **don't/didn't you know?** vous ne le savez/saviez pas?; **did I understand you correctly?** vous ai-je bien compris?, est-ce que je vous ai bien compris?; **why don't you tell her?** pourquoi est-ce que tu ne (le) lui dis pas?, pourquoi ne (le) lui dis-tu pas?; **do I know London!** si je connais Londres?; **boy, do I hate paperwork!** nom d'un chien, qu'est-ce que je peux avoir horreur des paperasses!
(**b**) *(in tag questions)* **he takes you out a lot, doesn't he?** il te sort souvent, n'est-ce pas *ou* hein?; **he doesn't take you out very often, does he?** il ne te sort pas souvent, n'est-ce pas *ou* hein?; **so you want to be an actress, do you?** alors tu veux devenir actrice?; **you didn't sign it, did you?** *(in disbelief, horror)* tu ne l'as pas signé, quand même?; **you surely don't want any more, do you?** tu ne veux quand même

pas en reprendre, si?; **look, we don't want any trouble, do we?** *(encouraging, threatening)* écoute, nous ne voulons pas d'histoires, hein?

(**c**) *(with the negative)* **I don't believe you** je ne te crois pas; **please don't tell her** s'il te plaît, ne (le) lui dis pas; *Br* **don't let's go out** ne sortons pas

(**d**) *(for emphasis)* **I DO believe you** sincèrement, je vous crois; **do you mind if I smoke? – yes I DO mind** cela vous dérange-t-il que je fume? – justement, oui, ça me dérange; **he DOES know where it is** il sait bien où c'est; **we DO like it here** *(refuting accusation)* mais si, nous nous plaisons ici, bien sûr que nous nous plaisons ici; *(like it very much)* nous nous plaisons vraiment ici; **I DID tell you** *(refuting someone's denial)* mais si, je te l'ai dit, bien sûr que je te l'ai dit; *(emphasizing earlier warning)* je te l'avais bien dit; **if you DO decide to buy it** si tu décides finalement de l'acheter; **let me know when you DO decide** dis-moi quand tu auras décidé; **DO sit down** asseyez-vous donc; **DO let us know how your mother is** surtout dites-nous comment va votre mère; **DO stop crying** mais arrête de pleurer, enfin

(**e**) *(elliptically)* **you know as much as/more than I do** tu en sais autant que/plus que moi; **so do I/does she** moi/elle aussi; **neither do I/does she** moi/elle non plus; **he didn't know and neither did I** il ne savait pas et moi non plus; **do you smoke? – I do/don't** est-ce que vous fumez? – oui/non; **may I sit down? – please do** puis-je m'asseoir? – je vous en prie; **I'll talk to her about it – please do/don't!** je lui en parlerai – oh, oui/non s'il vous plaît!; **don't, you'll make me blush!** arrête, tu vas me faire rougir!; **will you tell her? – I may do** (le) lui diras-tu? – peut-être; **I may come to Paris next month – let me know if you do** il se peut que je vienne à Paris le mois prochain – préviens-moi si tu viens; **you said eight o'clock – oh, so I did** tu as dit huit heures – oh, c'est vrai; **I liked her – you didn't!** *(surprised)* elle m'a plu – non! vraiment?; **I wear a toupee – you do?** *(astonished)* je porte une perruque – vraiment? *ou* non! *ou* pas possible!; **it belongs/it doesn't belong to me – does/doesn't it?** cela m'appartient/ne m'appartient pas – vraiment?; **yes you do – no I don't** mais si – mais non; **yes it does – no it doesn't** mais si – mais non; **you know her, I don't** tu la connais, moi pas; **you don't know her – I do!** tu ne la connais pas – si (je la connais)!; **I do** *(marriage service)* ≃ oui

(**f**) *(in sentences beginning with adverbial phrase)* **not only did you lie...** non seulement tu as menti...; **little did I realize...** j'étais bien loin de m'imaginer...

2 *vt* (**a**) *(be busy or occupied with)* faire; *(carry out → task, work)* faire; **what are you doing?** qu'est-ce que tu fais?, que fais-tu?, qu'es-tu en train de faire?; **are you doing anything next Saturday?** est-ce que tu fais quelque chose samedi prochain?; **what do you do for a living?** qu'est-ce que vous faites dans la vie?; **what are these files doing here?** qu'est-ce que ces dossiers font ici?; **somebody DO something!** que quelqu'un fasse quelque chose!; **there's nothing more to be done** il n'y a plus rien à faire; **he does nothing but sleep, all he does is sleep** il ne fait que dormir; **you'll have to do it again** il va falloir que tu le refasses; **he did a good job** il a fait du bon travail; **what do I do to start the machine?** comment est-ce que je fais pour mettre la machine en marche?; **what do I have to do to make you understand?** mais qu'est-ce que je dois faire pour que tu comprennes?; **have I done the right thing?** ai-je fait ce qu'il fallait?; **what are you going to do about the noise?** qu'est-ce que tu vas faire au sujet du bruit?; **what can I do for you?** que puis-je (faire) pour vous?; **the doctors can't do anything more for him** la médecine ne peut plus rien pour lui; **that dress really does something/nothing for you** cette robe te va vraiment très bien/ne te va vraiment pas du tout; **the new wallpaper does a lot for the room** le nouveau papier peint transforme la pièce; **what do you do for entertainment?** quelles sont vos distractions?, comment est-ce que vous vous distrayez?; **what shall we do for water to wash in?** où est-ce qu'on va trouver de l'eau pour se laver?; **who did this to you?** qui est-ce qui t'a fait ça?; **what have you done to your hair?** qu'est-ce que tu as fait à tes cheveux?; **I hate what your job is doing to you** je n'aime pas du tout l'effet que ton travail a sur toi; **it does something to me** ça me fait quelque chose; *Hum* **don't do anything I wouldn't do** ne fais pas de bêtises; **that does it!** cette fois c'en est trop!; **that's done it, the battery's flat** et voilà, la batterie est à plat

(**b**) *(produce, provide → copy, report)* faire; **I don't do portraits** je ne fais pas les portraits; *Br* **the pub does a good lunch** on sert un bon déjeuner dans ce pub; **could you do me a quick translation of this?** pourriez-vous me traduire ceci rapidement?; **do you do day trips to France?** *(to travel agent)* est-ce que vous avez des excursions d'une journée en France?

(**c**) *(work on, attend to)* s'occuper de; **he's doing your car now** il est en train de s'occuper de votre voiture; **can you do Mrs Baker first?** *(in hairdresser's)* peux-tu t'occuper de Mme Baker d'abord?; **to do the garden** s'occuper du jardin; **he's doing the garden** il est en train de jardiner; **they do you very well in this hotel** on est très bien dans cet hôtel; **this old car has done me well over the years** cette voiture m'a bien servi au cours des années

(**d**) *(clean, tidy → room, cupboard)* faire; *(decorate → room)* faire la décoration de; *(arrange → flowers)* arranger; **to do one's teeth** se brosser les dents

(**e**) *Sch & Univ (subject)* étudier; *Br (course)* suivre; **to do medicine/law** étudier la médecine/le droit, faire sa médecine/son droit; **we're doing Tartuffe** nous étudions Tartuffe

(**f**) *(solve → sums, crossword, equation)* faire

(**g**) *Aut & Transp (speed, distance)* faire; **the car will do over 100** ≃ la voiture peut faire du 160; **it does thirty-five miles to the gallon** ≃ elle fait sept litres aux cents (kilomètres); **we did the trip in under two hours** nous avons fait le voyage en moins de deux heures

(**h**) *Cin, Theat & TV (produce → play, film)* faire; *(appear in)* être dans; *(play part of)* faire; *Mus (perform)* jouer

(**i**) *Culin (cook)* faire; *(prepare → vegetables, salad)* préparer; **to do sth in the oven** faire (cuire) qch au four; **how would you like your steak done?** comment voulez-vous votre steak?

(**j**) *Fam (spend time → working, in prison)* faire ❑; **she's doing three years for robbery** elle fait trois ans pour vol

(**k**) *(be enough or suitable for)* suffire; **will £10 do you?** 10 livres, ça te suffira?; **those shoes will have to do the children for another year** les enfants devront encore faire un an avec ces chaussures

(**l**) *(finish)* **well that's that done, thank goodness** bon, voilà qui est fait, dieu merci; **once I've done what I'm doing** dès que j'aurai fini ce que je suis en train de faire; **have you done eating/crying?** tu as fini de manger/pleurer?; **it will never be done in time** ce ne sera jamais fini à temps; **done!** *(in bargain)* marché conclu!

(**m**) *(imitate)* imiter, faire; **he does you very well** il t'imite très bien

(**n**) *Br Fam (prosecute)* **she was done for speeding** elle s'est fait pincer pour excès de vitesse; **we could do you for dangerous driving** nous pourrions vous arrêter pour conduite dangereuse ❑

(**o**) *Fam (rob, burgle → bank, shop)* cambrioler ❑, se faire

(**p**) *Fam (cheat)* rouler, avoir; **you've been done** tu t'es fait rouler *ou* avoir

(**q**) *Fam (visit)* faire; **to do London/the sights** faire Londres/les monuments

(**r**) *Fam (take)* **to do drugs** se camer; **let's do lunch** il faudrait qu'on déjeune ensemble un de ces jours

(**s**) *Br Fam (beat up)* s'occuper de, en mettre une à; **I'll do you!** je vais m'occuper de toi, moi!

(**t**) *Fam (kill)* zigouiller, buter

3 *vi* (**a**) *(perform → in exam, competition etc)* s'en tirer, s'en sortir; **you did very well** tu t'en es très bien tiré *ou* sorti; **his team didn't do well in the match** son équipe ne s'en est pas très bien tirée pendant le match; **the company's not doing too badly** l'entreprise ne se débrouille pas trop mal; **how are you doing in the new job/at school?** comment te débrouilles-tu dans ton nouveau travail/à l'école?; **try to do better in future** essaie de mieux faire à l'avenir; **how are we doing with the corrections?** *(checking progress)* où en sommes-nous avec les corrections?; **well done!** bien joué!, bravo!

(**b**) *(referring to health)* aller; **how is she doing, doctor?** comment va-t-elle, docteur?; **he's not doing too well** il ne va pas trop bien; **mother and baby are both doing well** la maman et le bébé se portent tous les deux à merveille; **how is your eldest boy doing?** comment va votre aîné?

(**c**) *(act, behave)* faire; **do as you please** fais ce qui te plaît, fais ce que tu veux; **do as you're told!** fais ce qu'on te dit!; **you would do well to listen to your mother** tu ferais bien d'écouter ta mère; **to do well by sb** bien traiter qn; *Br* **to be/to feel hard done by** être/se sentir lésé; *Br* **he'll feel very hard done by if you don't at least send him a birthday card** il se sentira vraiment blessé si tu ne lui envoies même pas de carte d'anniversaire; *Prov* **do as you would be done by** = traite les autres comme tu voudrais être traité

(**d**) *(be enough)* suffire; **will £20 do?** 20 livres, ça ira *ou* suffira?; **that will do!** *(stop it)* ça suffit comme ça!

(**e**) *(be suitable)* aller; **that will do (nicely)** ça ira *ou* conviendra parfaitement, cela fera très bien l'affaire; **this won't do** ça ne peut pas continuer comme ça; **it wouldn't do to be late** ce ne serait pas bien d'arriver en retard; **will that do?** *(as alternative)* est-ce que ça ira?; **will Sunday do instead?** et dimanche, ça irait?

(**f**) *(always in continuous form) (happen)* **is there anything doing at the club tonight?** est-ce qu'il y a quelque chose au club ce soir?; **there's nothing doing here at weekends** il n'y a rien à faire ici le week-end; *Fam* **nothing doing** *(rejection, refusal)* rien à faire

(**g**) *(always in perfect tense) (finish)* **have you done?** tu as fini?

(**h**) *(be connected with)* **it has to do with your missing car** c'est au sujet de votre voiture volée; **that's got nothing to do with it!** *(is irrelevant)* cela n'a rien à voir!; **I want nothing to do with it/you** je ne veux rien avoir à faire là-dedans/avec toi; **I had nothing at all to do with it** je n'avais rien à voir là-dedans, je n'y étais pour rien; **it's nothing to do with me** je n'y suis pour rien; **we don't have much to do with the people next door** nous n'avons pas beaucoup de contacts avec les gens d'à côté; **what I said to him has got nothing to do with you** *(it's none of your business)* ce que je lui ai dit ne te regarde pas; *(it's not about you)* ce que je lui ai dit n'a rien à voir avec toi; **that has a lot to do with it** cela joue un rôle très important; **he is** *or* **has something to do with printing** il est dans l'imprimerie

(**i**) *Br Fam (work as cleaner)* faire le ménage ❑; **to do for sb** faire le ménage chez qn

4 *n* (**a**) *(tip)* **the do's and don'ts of car maintenance** les choses à faire et à ne pas faire dans l'entretien des voitures

(**b**) *Br Fam (party, celebration)* fête ❑ *f*; **he's having a do to celebrate his promotion** il donne une fête pour célébrer sa promotion; **leaving do** pot *m* de départ

(**c**) *Fam (excrement)* **dog do** crotte *f* de chien ❑

►**do away with** *vt insep* (**a**) *(abolish → institution, rule, restriction)* abolir; *(get rid of → object)* se débarrasser de

(**b**) *(kill)* se débarrasser de, faire disparaître; **to do away with oneself** mettre fin à ses jours

►**do down** *vt sep Br Fam* (**a**) *(criticize, disparage)* rabaisser ❑, médire sur ❑, dire du mal de ❑; **to do oneself down** se rabaisser ❑

(**b**) *(cheat)* avoir, rouler

►**do for** *vt insep Fam* (**a**) *Br (murder)* zigouiller; *(cause death of)* tuer ❑

(**b**) *(ruin → object, engine)* bousiller; *(cause failure of → plan)* ruiner ❑; *(→ company)* couler ❑; **I'm done for** je suis cuit; **the project is done for** le projet est tombé à l'eau *ou* foutu; **the industry is done for** l'industrie est fichue

(**c**) *Br (exhaust)* tuer, crever; **shopping always**

does for me je suis toujours crevé après les courses; **I'm done for** je suis mort *ou* crevé; **it was that last hill that did for me** c'est la dernière colline qui m'a épuisé ❑

(**d**) *Br Fam (do housework for)* faire le ménage chez ❑; **who does for you?** qui fait votre ménage?

▸**do in** *vt sep Br Fam* (**a**) *(murder, kill)* zigouiller, buter, butter

(**b**) *(exhaust)* tuer, crever; **I'm completely done in** je suis complètement crevé

(**c**) *(injure)* **to do one's back/one's knee in** se bousiller le dos/le genou; **you'll do your lungs in** tu vas te bousiller les poumons

▸**do out** *vt sep Br Fam (clean thoroughly)* nettoyer à fond ❑; *(decorate)* refaire ❑

▸**do out of** *vt sep Fam (cheat)* **to do sb out of sth** soutirer ❑ *ou* carotter qch à qn; *(money)* refaire *ou* escroquer ❑ qn de qch; **to do sb out of a job** *(of person)* faire perdre son travail à qn ❑; **all this automation is doing people out of jobs** toute cette automatisation supprime des emplois ❑; **the new structure did him out of his job** la nouvelle structure lui a fait perdre son travail; **she's been done out of her share of the money** elle s'est fait escroquer de sa part de l'argent

▸**do over** *vt sep* (**a**) *(room)* refaire; **the whole house needs doing over** toute la maison a besoin d'être refaite

(**b**) *Am (do again)* refaire

(**c**) *Br Fam (beat up)* casser la gueule *ou* la tête à

(**d**) *Br Fam (rob → person)* dépouiller; *(→ house, bank etc)* cambrioler ❑

▸**do up 1** *vt sep* (**a**) *(fasten → dress, jacket)* fermer; *(→ zip)* fermer, remonter; *(→ buttons)* boutonner; *(→ shoelaces)* attacher; **do me up will you?** tu peux fermer ma robe?

(**b**) *(wrap, bundle up)* emballer; **envelopes done up in bundles of 20** des enveloppes en paquets de 20; **a parcel done up in brown paper** un paquet emballé dans du papier kraft

(**c**) *Fam (renovate → house, cottage etc)* refaire ❑, retaper; *(old dress, hat)* arranger; **the house needs a bit of doing up** la maison a besoin d'être un peu refaite *ou* retapée; **to do oneself up** *(make more glamorous)* se faire beau/belle; **I didn't recognize you all done up like that** je ne t'ai pas reconnu tout beau comme ça; **to be done up to the nines** être sur son trente et un

2 *vi (skirt, dress)* se fermer; *(zip)* se fermer, se remonter; *(buttons)* se fermer, se boutonner; **it does up at the side** cela se ferme sur le côté

▸**do with** *vt insep* (**a**) *Br Fam (after "could") (need, want)* avoir besoin de ❑; **I could have done with some help** j'aurais eu bien besoin d'aide; **I could do with a drink** je prendrais bien un verre, j'ai bien envie de prendre un verre

(**b**) *Br Fam (after "can't") (tolerate)* supporter ❑; **I can't do** *or* **be doing with all this noise** je ne supporte pas ce vacarme; **he couldn't be doing with living in London** il ne pouvait pas supporter de vivre à Londres

(**c**) *(after "what") (act with regard to)* faire de; **she didn't know what to do with herself** *(to keep busy)* elle ne savait que faire *ou* à quoi s'occuper; *(for joy)* elle ne se tenait pas de joie; *(for awkwardness)* elle était gênée, elle ne savait plus où se mettre; **what are we going to do with your father for two whole weeks!** qu'allons-nous faire de ton père pendant deux semaines entières?; **what do you want me to do with this?** que veux-tu que je fasse de ça?; **what have you done with the hammer?** qu'as-tu fait du marteau?

(**d**) *(with past participle) (finish with)* finir avec; **I'm done with men for ever** j'en ai fini pour toujours avec les hommes; **I haven't done with him yet!** *(haven't finished scolding him)* je n'en ai pas encore fini avec lui!; **I'm done with trying to be nice to her** je n'essaierai plus jamais d'être gentil avec elle; **can I borrow the ashtray if you've done with it?** puis-je emprunter le cendrier si tu n'en as plus besoin?

▸**do without 1** *vi* faire sans; **he'll have to do without** il devra s'en passer *ou* faire sans

2 *vt insep* se passer de; **I could have done without this long wait** j'aurais bien pu me passer de cette longue attente; **we can do without the sarcasm** on n'a pas besoin de ces sarcasmes

---

do² [dəʊ] *n Mus (fixed)* do *m inv*, ut *m inv*; *Scot Fam* **to be up to high do** être dans tous ses états

DOA [ˌdiːəʊ'eɪ] *Med (abbr* **dead on arrival**) **1** *n* personne *f* morte *ou* décédée avant l'arrivée à l'hôpital

2 *adj* mort *ou* décédé avant l'arrivée à l'hôpital

doable ['duːəbəl] *adj Fam* faisable ❑

do-all *n Am Fam* larbin *m*

d.o.b., DOB *(written abbr* **date of birth**) date *f* de naissance

▸**dob in** [dɒb-] *vt sep Austr Fam* moucharder

Dobbin ['dɒbɪn] *n* = surnom donné à un cheval, spécialement dans les contes pour enfants

Dobermann (pinscher) ['dəʊbəmən('pɪnʃə(r)] *n* doberman *m*

doc [dɒk] *n Fam (doctor)* toubib *m*; **morning, doc** bonjour docteur ❑

docent [dəʊ'sent] *n Am (guide)* guide *mf (souvent bénévole)*

docile [*Br* 'dəʊsaɪl, *Am* 'dɒsəl] *adj* docile

docilely [*Br* 'dəʊsaɪllɪ, *Am* 'dɒsəllɪ] *adv* docilement

docility [də'sɪlətɪ] *n* docilité *f*

dock [dɒk] **1** *vi* (**a**) *(ship)* se mettre à quai; **when do we dock?** quand arrivons-nous à quai?; **we'll be docking at New York** nous entrerons à quai à New York

(**b**) *(two spacecraft)* s'amarrer, s'arrimer

2 *vt* (**a**) *(ship)* mettre à quai; *(spacecraft)* amarrer, arrimer

(**b**) *(money)* **to dock sb's pay/pocket money** faire une retenue sur la paye/réduire l'argent de poche de qn; **you'll be docked £20** on retiendra 20 livres sur votre salaire; **they docked me for being late** ils ont fait une retenue sur mon salaire à cause de mon retard

(**c**) *(animal's tail)* couper

3 *n* (**a**) *Naut* dock *m*, docks *mpl*; **the docks** les docks *mpl*; **to be in dry dock** *(ship)* être en cale sèche; *Fig* **to be in dock** *(car, plane)* être en réparation

(**b**) *Br Law* banc *m* des accusés; **the prisoner in the dock** l'accusé(e) *m,f*; **prisoner in the dock, have you anything to say in your defence?** accusé, avez-vous quelque chose à dire pour votre défense?; *Fig* **to be in the dock** être sur la sellette

(**c**) *Br Bot* patience *f*

4 *comp (manager)* des docks

▸▸ ***dock strike*** grève *f* des dockers; *Br* ***dock worker*** docker *m*

docker ['dɒkə(r)] *n Br* docker *m*

▸▸ ***dockers' strike*** grève *f* des dockers

docket ['dɒkɪt] **1** *n* (**a**) *Br (on file, package)* fiche *f* (de renseignements) (**b**) *Law Br (summary)* compte-rendu *m* des jugements; *Am (list of cases)* liste *f* des affaires en instance (**c**) *Br Customs (document)* récépissé *m* de douane

2 *vt* (**a**) *(file, package)* mettre une fiche (indiquant le contenu) sur; **the parcel has been docketed** le colis porte une fiche indiquant son contenu (**b**) *Law Br (make summary of)* résumer; *Am (register)* enregistrer

docking ['dɒkɪŋ] *n* (**a**) *(of ship)* mise *f* à quai (**b**) [illegible]

▸▸ ***docking manoeuvre*** accostage *m*; *Comput* ***docking station*** *(for notebook)* station *f* d'accueil

dockland ['dɒklənd] **1** *n* quartier *m* des docks

2 Docklands *n* = quartier d'affaires très moderne à Londres sur les bords de la Tamise

dockmaster ['dɒkˌmɑːstə(r)] *n Am* = directeur d'une marina

dockside ['dɒksaɪd] *n* **on the dockside** sur le quai

dockyard ['dɒkjɑːd] *n* chantier *m* naval *ou* de constructions navales; **naval dockyard** arsenal *m* maritime *ou* de la marine

Doc Martens® [-'mɑːtənz] *npl* Doc Martens® *fpl*

doctor ['dɒktə(r)] **1** *n* (**a**) *(of medicine)* docteur *m*, médecin *m*; **good morning, doctor** bonjour docteur; **dear Doctor Cameron** *(in letter)* docteur; **I've an appointment with Doctor Cameron** j'ai rendez-vous avec le docteur Cameron; **thank you, doctor** merci, docteur; **he/she is a doctor** il/elle est docteur *ou* médecin; **to go to the doctor** *or* **doctor's** aller chez le docteur *ou* médecin; **you should see a doctor** tu devrais consulter un docteur *ou* médecin; *Fam* **to be under the doctor** être sous traitement médical ❑; **woman doctor, female doctor** femme *f* médecin; **army doctor** médecin militaire; *Fam* **that's just what the doctor ordered!** c'est exactement ce qu'il me faut *ou* fallait!

(**b**) *Univ* docteur *m*; **Doctor of Science** docteur *m* ès *ou* en sciences; **to do a** *or* **to take one's doctor's degree** faire un doctorat

2 *vt* (**a**) *(tamper with → results, figures)* falsifier, trafiquer; *(→ accounts, evidence)* falsifier, fausser; *(→ dice, cards)* piper; *(→ wine)* frelater; **we'll need to doctor the figures a little** il va falloir un peu arranger ces chiffres

(**b**) *(drug → drink, food)* mettre de la drogue dans; *(→ racehorse)* doper

(**c**) *Br (castrate, sterilize → cat, dog)* châtrer

(**d**) *(treat)* soigner

▸▸ *Univ* ***Doctor of Dental Science*** *(person)* = titulaire d'un doctorat en dentisterie; *(qualification)* doctorat *m* en dentisterie; *Univ* ***Doctor of Divinity*** *(person)* = titulaire d'un doctorat en théologie; *(qualification)* doctorat *m* en théologie; *Univ* ***Doctor of Education*** *(person)* = titulaire d'un doctorat en sciences de l'éducation; *(qualification)* doctorat *m* en sciences de l'éducation; *Am Univ* ***Doctor of Jurisprudence*** *(person)* = titulaire d'un doctorat en droit; *(qualification)* doctorat *m* en droit; ***doctor's line*** certificat *m* médical; *Univ* ***Doctor of Literature, Doctor of Letters*** *(person)* = titulaire d'un doctorat ès lettres; *(qualification)* doctorat *m* ès lettres; *Univ* ***Doctor of Music*** *(person)* = titulaire d'un doctorat en musique; *(qualification)* doctorat *m* en musique; ***doctor's note*** certificat *m* médical; *Univ* ***Doctor of Philosophy*** *(person)* = titulaire d'un doctorat de 3ème cycle; *(qualification)* doctorat *m* de 3ème cycle; *Am Univ* ***Doctor of Veterinary Medicine*** = docteur vétérinaire; *TV* ***Doctor Who*** = série télévisée britannique de science-fiction, dont le héros dispose d'une machine à voyager dans le temps

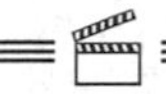

'Doctor Strangelove' *Kubrick* 'Docteur Folamour'

'(The Tragical History of) Doctor Faustus' *Marlowe* 'La Tragique histoire du docteur Faust'

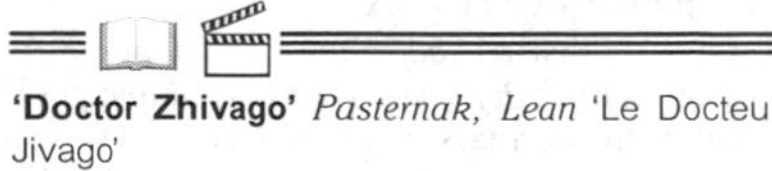

'Doctor Zhivago' *Pasternak, Lean* 'Le Docteur Jivago'

---

doctoral ['dɒktərəl] *adj Univ (thesis, degree)* de doctorat

doctorate ['dɒktərət] *n Univ* doctorat *m*; **to have/to do a doctorate in sth** avoir/faire un doctorat en qch

doctoring ['dɒktərɪŋ] *n* (**a**) *(of results, figures, accounts, evidence etc)* falsification *f* (**b**) *(drugging → of drink, food)* adjonction *f* de drogue (**of** à); *(of racehorse)* doping *m* (**c**) *Fam (profession)* profession *f* de médecin ❑ (**d**) *Br (of cat, dog)* castration *f* (**e**) *(treatment)* soins *mpl* (**of sb** donnés à qn)

doctrinaire [ˌdɒktrɪ'neə(r)] **1** *n* doctrinaire *mf*

2 *adj* doctrinaire

doctrinairism [ˌdɒktrɪ'neərɪzəm] *n* doctrinarisme *m*

doctrinarian [ˌdɒktrɪ'neərɪən] **1** *n* doctrinaire *mf*

2 *adj* doctrinaire

doctrinarianism [ˌdɒktrɪ'neərɪənɪzəm] *n* doctrinarisme *m*

doctrinal [dɒk'traɪnəl] *adj* doctrinal

doctrinally [dɒk'traɪnəlɪ] *adv* doctrinalement

doctrine ['dɒktrɪn] *n* doctrine *f*

docudrama [ˌdɒkjʊ'drɑːmə] *n TV* docudrame *m*

document 1 *n* ['dɒkjʊmənt] document *m*; *Law* acte *m*; **to draw up a document** rédiger un document; **may I have a look at your travel documents, sir?** pourrais-je voir votre titre de transport, monsieur?; *Law* **the documents in the case** le dossier de l'affaire; *Com* **documents against acceptance/payment** documents *mpl* contre acceptation/paiement

2 *vt* ['dɒkjʊment] (**a**) *(write about in detail)* décrire (de façon détaillée); *(record on film → of film)* montrer (en détail), présenter (de façon détaillée); *(→ of photographer)* faire un reportage sur; **the book documents life in the 1920s** le livre décrit la vie dans les années 20; **it is well documented** c'est bien documenté; **the first documented case of smallpox** le premier cas de variole qu'on ait enregistré

(**b**) *(support → with evidence or proof)* fournir des preuves à l'appui de, attester; *(→ with citations, references)* documenter

►► ***document case*** porte-documents *m inv*; ***document collator*** unité *f* de classement de documents; ***document cover*** pochette *f*; *Comput* ***document file*** fichier *m* document; ***document handling*** manipulation *f* de documents; ***document holder*** *(for keyboarder)* bras *m* porte-copies; *Comput* ***document reader*** lecteur *m* de documents; *Law* ***document of title*** acte *m* de propriété

documentarist [dɒkjʊ'mentərɪst] *n Cin & TV* documentariste *mf*

documentary [ˌdɒkjʊ'mentərɪ] (*pl* **documentaries**) **1** *adj (factual → film, programme)* documentaire

2 *n Cin & TV* documentaire *m*

►► *Com & Fin* ***documentary bill*** traite *f* documentaire; ***documentary charges*** frais *mpl* de crédit documentaire; ***documentary credit*** crédit *m* documentaire; ***documentary credit application*** demande *f* d'ouverture de crédit documentaire; ***documentary credit department*** service *m* des crédits documentaires; ***documentary evidence*** preuve *f* littérale; ***documentary letter of credit*** lettre *f* de crédit documentaire; ***documentary remittance*** remise *f* documentaire

documentation [ˌdɒkjʊmen'teɪʃən] *n* documentation *f*

docusoap ['dɒkjʊsəʊp] *n TV* docu-soap *m*

DOD [ˌdiːəʊ'diː] *n Am Admin* (*abbr* **Department of Defense**) = ministère américain de la Défense

dodder[1] ['dɒdə(r)] *vi (walk)* marcher d'un pas hésitant

dodder[2] *n Bot* cuscute *f*, *Fam* cheveux *mpl* du diable

dodderer ['dɒdərə(r)] *n Fam Pej* croulant(e) *m,f*, gâteux(euse) *m,f*

doddering ['dɒdərɪŋ] *adj (walk)* hésitant, chancelant; *Pej (elderly person)* gâteux; **a doddering old fool** un vieux gâteux

doddery ['dɒdərɪ] *adj Fam (walk)* hésitant ❑, chancelant ❑; *Pej (elderly person)* gâteux; **I still feel a bit doddery** *(after illness)* je me sens encore un peu faible ❑ *ou* flagada; **a doddery old fool** un vieux gâteux

doddle ['dɒdəl] *n Br Fam* **it's a doddle** c'est simple comme bonjour, c'est du gâteau

dodecagon [dəʊ'dekəgən] *n Geom* dodécagone *m*

dodecagonal [ˌdəʊdə'kægənəl] *adj Geom* dodécagonal

dodecahedral [ˌdəʊdekə'hiːdrəl] *adj Geom* dodécaèdre, dodécaédrique

dodecahedron [ˌdəʊdekə'hiːdrən] *n Geom* dodécaèdre *m*

Dodecanese [ˌdəʊdekə'niːz] *npl* **the Dodecanese** le Dodécanèse; **in the Dodecanese** dans le Dodécanèse

dodecaphonic [ˌdəʊdekə'fɒnɪk] *adj Mus* dodécaphonique

dodecaphony [ˌdəʊdə'kæfənɪ] *n Mus* dodécaphonie *f*

dodecasyllable [ˌdəʊdekə'sɪləbəl] *n Literature* dodécasyllabe *m*

dodge [dɒdʒ] **1** *n* (**a**) *(evasive movement)* écart *m*; *(by footballer, boxer)* esquive *f*; **to make a dodge** faire un écart *ou* une esquive

(**b**) *Br Fam (trick)* truc *m*, combine *f*; **to be up to all the dodges** connaître toutes les combines

2 *vi (make evasive movement)* s'écarter vivement; *(footballer, boxer)* faire une esquive; **he dodged into the doorway** il s'est esquivé *ou* il a disparu dans l'entrée; **she dodged to the side** elle a fait un bond de côté; **to dodge in and out of the crowd** faire du slalom dans la foule; **to dodge out of the way** s'écarter vivement; *Fig* **to dodge out of doing sth** se défiler pour ne pas faire qch

3 *vt (blow)* esquiver; *(falling rock, ball)* éviter; *(bullets)* passer entre, éviter; *(pursuer, police)* échapper à; *(creditor, landlord etc)* éviter; *(question)* éluder; **he has dodged the taxman** *or* **paying tax all his life** il a échappé au fisc toute sa vie; **to dodge military service** échapper au service militaire; **to dodge the issue** éluder *ou* esquiver le problème; **you dodged doing the dishes last night!** tu t'es défilé pour la vaisselle hier soir!; **to dodge school** sécher l'école

Dodgem® ['dɒdʒəm] *n Br* auto *f* tamponneuse, *Belg* auto-scooter *m ou f*; **to have a ride on the Dodgems**® faire un tour d'autos tamponneuses

dodger ['dɒdʒə(r)] *n Fam (workshy)* tire-au-flanc *m inv*; *(dishonest)* combinard(e) *m,f*, roublard(e) *m,f*; *Old-fashioned* **an artful dodger** un fin matois; **fare dodger** resquilleur(euse) *m,f*; **they're after tax dodgers** ils cherchent à coincer ceux qui fraudent le fisc

dodgy ['dɒdʒɪ] (*compar* **dodgier**, *superl* **dodgiest**) *adj Br Fam* (**a**) *(risky, dangerous → plan, idea)* risqué ❑; **the house is nice, but it's in a really dodgy area** la maison est bien mais elle est dans un quartier vraiment craignos; **investing money in a scheme like that is just too dodgy** c'est vraiment trop risqué d'investir dans ce genre de truc; **the weather looks pretty dodgy** *(unreliable)* le temps a l'air plutôt douteux ❑ *ou* menaçant ❑

(**b**) *(untrustworthy → person)* louche; *(→ scheme)* douteux ❑, suspect ❑; **he's OK, but all his friends are well dodgy** lui, ça va, mais ses amis craignent vraiment; **they were involved in a couple of dodgy business deals** ils ont été impliqués dans des transactions plutôt louches

(**c**) *(not working properly, unstable)* merdique; **the brakes are really dodgy** les freins sont très douteux; **the engine sounds a bit dodgy** le moteur fait un bruit suspect; **don't sit on that chair, it's a bit dodgy** ne t'assieds pas sur cette chaise, elle est un peu branlante ❑; **the ceiling looks a bit dodgy** le plafond n'a pas l'air en très bon état ❑; **my stomach's been a bit dodgy for the last couple of days** ça fait deux jours que j'ai l'estomac un peu dérangé ❑

dodo ['dəʊdəʊ] (*pl* **dodos** *or* **dodoes**) *n* (**a**) *(extinct bird)* dronte *m*, dodo *m* (**b**) *Fam (fool)* andouille *f*; **what a dodo!** quelle andouille! (**c**) *Mktg (product)* poids *m* mort, produit *m* dodo

DOE [ˌdiːəʊ'iː] *n Am Admin* (*abbr* **Department of Energy**) = ministère américain de l'Énergie

DoE [ˌdiːəʊ'iː] *n Br Formerly Admin* (*abbr* **Department of the Environment**) = ministère britannique de l'Environnement

doe [dəʊ] *n (deer)* biche *f*; *(fallow deer)* daine *f*; *(rabbit)* lapine *f*; *(wild rabbit, hare)* hase *f*; *(rat)* rate *f*, ratte *f*

doe-eyed *adj (person)* aux yeux de biche; **her doe-eyed gaze** son regard de biche

doer ['duːə(r)] *n (dynamic person)* personne *f* dynamique; **she's a real doer** c'est une femme très active; **she is more (of) a doer than a talker** elle préfère l'action à la parole

does [dəz, *stressed* dʌz] *3rd pers sing of* **do**

doeskin ['dəʊskɪn] **1** *n* peau *f* de daim; **made of doeskin** en daim

2 *comp (gloves, shoes etc)* en daim

doesn't ['dʌzənt] = **does not**

doff [dɒf] *vt (hat)* ôter; **to doff one's cap to sb** ôter son chapeau *ou* se découvrir devant qn; *Fig* faire preuve de respect envers qn

dog [dɒg] (*pt & pp* **dogged**, *cont* **dogging**) **1** *n* (**a**) *(animal)* chien *m*; **to treat sb like a dog** traiter qn comme un chien; **to follow sb about like a dog** suivre qn comme un petit chien; **she's like a dog with a bone** elle est toute contente *ou* joyeuse; *Br* **this is a real dog's dinner** *or* **breakfast** *(mess)* c'est un vrai torchon *ou* gâchis; *Br* **you've made a real dog's dinner** *or* **breakfast of this** ton travail est un vrai torchon; *Br Fam* **to be dressed** *or* **done up like a dog's dinner** *(gaudy, showy)* être habillé de façon extravagante ❑; **to lead sb a dog's life** mener la vie dure à qn; **it's a dog's life being a teacher** c'est une vie de chien que d'être professeur; *Am Fam* **a dog and pony show** = spectacle fait pour en mettre plein la vue au public; *Br Fam* **he doesn't have** *or* **stand a dog's chance** il n'a pas la moindre chance ❑, il n'a aucune chance ❑; *Br Fam* **to give sb dog's abuse** traiter qn de tous les noms; **a dog in the manger** un empêcheur de danser *ou* tourner en rond; *Fam* **I'm going to see a man about a dog** = façon humoristique d'éviter de dire où l'on va; **it's (a case of) dog eat dog** c'est la loi de la jungle; *Am Fam* **to put on the dog** se donner de grands airs ❑; *Prov* **every dog has its** *or* **his day** = tout le monde a son heure de gloire; *Prov* **give a dog a bad name (and hang him)** qui veut noyer son chien l'accuse de la rage; *Prov* **let sleeping dogs lie** n'éveillez pas le chat qui dort; *Prov* **you can't teach an old dog new tricks** = les vieilles habitudes ont la vie dure; *Br Fam* **the dogs** les courses *fpl* de lévriers ❑; **to go to the dogs** aller aux courses de lévriers; *Fam* **he's gone to the dogs** il a mal tourné; *Fam* **this country's going to the dogs** le pays va à sa ruine ❑; *Fam* **this restaurant has gone to the dogs since he took over** ce restaurant ne vaut plus rien du tout depuis qu'il l'a racheté ❑; *Fam* **to have dog breath** puer de la gueule

(**b**) *(male fox, wolf etc)* mâle *m*

(**c**) *Fam (person)* **you lucky dog!** sacré veinard!; **dirty dog** sale type *m*; **sly dog** (vieux) malin *m*; *Old-fashioned* **gay dog** joyeux luron *m*; **there's life in the old dog yet!** je ne suis/ce n'est pas encore un vieux croulant!

(**d**) *very Fam Pej (ugly woman)* cageot *m*

(**e**) *Am Fam (hopeless thing)* catastrophe ❑ *f*

(**f**) *Mktg (product)* poids *m* mort, gouffre *m* financier

(**g**) *Fam (foot)* panard *m*

(**h**) *(firedog)* chenet *m*

(**i**) *Tech (pawl)* cliquet *m*; *(cramp)* crampon *m*

(**j**) *Am (hot dog)* hot dog *m*

(**k**) *SEng Fam (rhyming slang* **dog and bone** = **phone**) bigophone *m*

2 *comp (bowl, basket)* pour chien

3 *vt* (**a**) *(follow closely)* suivre de près; **to dog sb's footsteps** ne pas lâcher qn d'une semelle

(**b**) *(plague)* **to be dogged by bad health/problems** ne pas arrêter d'avoir des ennuis de santé/des problèmes; **to be dogged by scandal** être poursuivi par le scandale; **the team has been dogged by injury** l'équipe n'a pas arrêté d'avoir des blessés; **she is dogged by misfortune** elle est poursuivie par la malchance

(**c**) *Am Fam (get rid of)* se débarrasser de ❑

►► ***dog biscuit*** biscuit *m* pour chien; ***dog breeder*** éleveur(euse) *m,f* de chiens; ***dog breeding*** élevage *m* de chiens; *Tech* ***dog clutch*** embrayage *m* à crabot, crabot *m*; ***dog collar*** *(for dog)* collier *m* pour *ou* de chien; *Fam (of clergyman)* col *m* d'ecclésiastique ❑; ***dog days*** canicule *f*; ***the dog family*** la famille des chiens; ***dog food*** *(UNCOUNT)* nourriture *f* pour chiens; ***dog fox*** renard *m* mâle; ***dog hairs*** poils *mpl* de chien; ***dog handler*** maître-chien *m*; ***dog iron*** chenet *m*; ***dog Latin*** latin *m* de cuisine; *Br* ***dog licence*** = permis de posséder un chien; ***dog musher*** *(person)* conducteur *m* de traîneau à chiens; *(competition)* course *f* de traîneaux à chiens; ***dog mushing*** *(racing)* courses *fpl* de traîneaux à chiens; ***dog paddle*** nage *f* du petit chien; ***dog racing*** courses *fpl* de lévriers; ***dog rose*** églantine *f*; ***dog show*** exposition *f* canine; ***Dog Star*** Sirius *f*; ***dog tag*** *(for dog, soldier)* plaque *f* d'identification; ***dog team*** attelage *m* de chiens; ***dog track*** cynodrome *m*

'Dog Day Afternoon' *Lumet* 'Un après-midi de chien'

dogberry ['dɒgbərɪ] *n Bot (fruit)* cornouille *f*; *(tree)* cornouiller *m*

dogcart ['dɒgkɑːt] *n* dog-cart *m*

dog-catcher *n* employé(e) *m,f* de la fourrière

dog-cheap *adj Am Fam* donné, qui coûte une misère

doge [dəʊdʒ] *n Hist* doge *m*

dog-ear 1 *n* corne *f*

2 *vt (page)* corner

dog-eared *adj (page)* corné; *(book)* aux pages cornées

dog-eat-dog *adj (business)* impitoyable, sans pitié; **it's a dog-eat-dog world** c'est un monde sans pitié

dog-end *n Br Fam (of cigarette)* mégot ❑ *m*

dogfight ['dɒgfaɪt] *n (between dogs)* combat *m* de chiens; *Mil (between aircraft)* combat *m* rapproché

dogfish ['dɒgfɪʃ] *n Ich* roussette *f*, chien *m* de mer

dogged ['dɒgɪd] *adj (courage, perseverance, pursuit)* tenace; *(person, character)* tenace, déterminé, persévérant; *(refusal)* obstiné; *(attachment)* fidèle

doggedly ['dɒgɪdlɪ] *adv (fight, persist)* avec ténacité *ou* persévérance; *(refuse)* obstinément; **to be doggedly intent on doing sth** avoir la ferme intention de faire qch

doggedness ['dɒgɪdnɪs] *n (of person)* ténacité *f*, persévérance *f*; *(of courage)* ténacité *f*; **the doggedness of his refusal** l'obstination avec laquelle il a refusé

doggerel ['dɒgərəl] **1** *n (silly and comical)* poésie *f* burlesque; *(mediocre)* vers *mpl* de mirliton

2 *adj (rhyme, verse → silly and comical)* burlesque; *(→ mediocre)* de mirliton

doggie = **doggy**

doggo ['dɒgəʊ] *adv Br Fam* **to lie doggo** se tenir coi ❑

doggone ['dɒgɒn] *Am Fam* **1** *exclam* **doggone (it)!** zut!, nom d'une pipe!

2 *adj* fichu; **I've lost the doggone car keys** j'ai perdu ces saletés de clés de bagnole

3 *adv* vachement; **it's so doggone hot!** il fait une chaleur à crever!

doggoned ['dɒgɒnd] *Am Fam* **1** *adj* fichu; **well, I'll be doggoned!** ça, c'est trop fort!; **it's a doggoned shame!** c'est vraiment honteux!

2 *adv* vachement; **he's so doggoned slow!** il est vachement lent!

doggy ['dɒgɪ] (*pl* **doggies**) *Fam* **1** *n (in children's language)* toutou *m*

2 *adj (smell)* de chien; **he's a doggy person** il adore les chiens

►► ***doggy bag*** = sachet ou boîte que l'on propose aux clients dans les restaurants pour qu'ils emportent ce qu'ils n'ont pas consommé; *very Fam* ***doggy position*** levrette *f*

doggy-fashion *adv very Fam* en levrette; **to do it doggy-fashion** faire l'amour en levrette

doggy-paddle **1** *n* nage *f* du petit chien

2 *vi* faire la nage du petit chien

doggy-style *adv very Fam* en levrette; **to do it doggy-style** faire l'amour en levrette

doghouse ['dɒghaʊs, *pl* -haʊzɪz] *n* (**a**) *Am (kennel)* chenil *m*, niche *f* (**b**) *Fam (idiom)* **to be in the doghouse (with sb)** ne pas être en odeur de sainteté *ou* être en disgrâce (auprès de qn) ❑; **am I in the doghouse again?** est-ce que je suis de nouveau en disgrâce?

dogie ['dəʊgɪ] *n Am* veau *m* sans mère

dogleg ['dɒgleg] **1** *n (in pipe, road, on golf course)* coude *m*

2 *vi (pipe, road, golf course)* faire un coude

3 *adj (pipe, road, golf course)* qui fait un coude

doglike ['dɒglaɪk] *adj (devotion)* aveugle

dogma ['dɒgmə] *n* dogme *m*

dogmatic [dɒg'mætɪk] *adj* dogmatique; **to be dogmatic about sth** être dogmatique au sujet de qch

dogmatically [dɒg'mætɪklɪ] *adv* dogmatiquement

dogmatism ['dɒgmətɪzəm] *n* dogmatisme *m*

dogmatist ['dɒgmətɪst] *n* personne *f* dogmatique

do-gooder [-'gʊdə(r)] *n Pej* âme *f* charitable, bonne âme *f*

dogsbody ['dɒgzˌbɒdɪ] (*pl* **dogsbodies**) *n Br Fam* bonne *f* à tout faire ❑; **I'm not your dogsbody** je ne suis pas ton chien *ou* ta bonne

dogsled ['dɒgsled] *n* luge *f* tirée par des chiens

dog's-tooth check *n Br Tex* pied-de-poule *m*

dog-tired *adj Fam* épuisé

dogtooth ['dɒgtu:θ] *n (tooth)* canine *f*

►► *Tex* ***dogtooth check*** pied *m* de poule; *Bot* ***dogtooth violet*** érythrone *m*, dent-de-chien *f*

dogtrot ['dɒgtrɒt] *n* petit trot *m*; **at a dogtrot** au petit trot

dogwarden ['dɒgwɔ:dən] *n* = employé municipal chargé de recueillir les chiens errants

dogwatch ['dɒgwɒtʃ] *n Naut* petit quart *m*

dogwood ['dɒgwʊd] *n Bot* cornouiller *m*

dogy ['dəʊgɪ] (*pl* **dogies** [-gi:z]) = **dogie**

doh = **do²**

Doha ['dəʊə] *n* (al-) Dawha, (al-) Doha

DOI [ˌdi:əʊ'aɪ] *n Am Admin (abbr* **Department of the Interior**) = ministère américain de l'Intérieur

doily ['dɔɪlɪ] (*pl* **doilies**) *n* napperon *m*

doing ['du:ɪŋ] *n* (**a**) *(work, activity)* **it's all your doing** tout cela, c'est de ta faute; **is this your doing?** *(have you done this?)* c'est toi qui as fait cela?; *(are you behind this?)* c'est toi qui es derrière cela?; **it's none of my doing** je n'y suis pour rien; **that'll take some doing** cela ne va pas être facile; **it will take some doing to persuade him** cela ne va pas être facile de le persuader; **a job like this is going to take a lot of doing** un tel travail ne se fera pas en un tour de main *ou* en un tournemain; **he told them all about his doings on holiday** il leur a raconté tout ce qu'il avait fait en vacances

(**b**) *Fam (beating)* **to give sb a doing (over)** passer qn à tabac, tabasser qn

doings ['du:ɪŋz] **1** *n Br Fam (thing)* machin *m*, truc *m*

2 *npl* (**a**) *(of person)* ce qu'on fait, *Pej* agissements *mpl*; **to be informed of sb's doings** être au courant des faits et gestes de qn (**b**) *Fam (events)* événements ❑ *mpl*; **there have been great doings at their house** il y a eu bien du mouvement chez eux

do-it-yourself **1** *n* bricolage *m*

2 *comp (manual, shop)* de bricolage; **a do-it-yourself enthusiast** un bricoleur; **the do-it-yourself craze** l'engouement pour le bricolage

►► ***do-it-yourself kit*** des éléments en kit

do-it-yourselfer [-jə'selfə(r)] *n Fam* bricoleur(euse) *m,f*

DOJ [ˌdi:əʊ'dʒeɪ] *n Am Admin (abbr* **Department of Justice**) = ministère américain de la Justice

dojo ['dəʊdʒəʊ] *n Sport* dojo *m*

dol *(written abbr* **dollar**) dol(l)

Dolby® ['dɒlbɪ] *n* Dolby® *m*; **in Dolby® stereo** en Dolby® stéréo

►► ***Dolby® system*** système *m* Dolby® stéréo

doldrums ['dɒldrəmz] *npl* (**a**) *Geog (zone)* zones *fpl* des calmes équatoriaux, pot *m* au noir; *(weather)* calme *m* équatorial (**b**) *(idiom)* **to be in the doldrums** *(person)* avoir le cafard, broyer du noir; *(activity, trade)* être en plein marasme

dole [dəʊl] *n (UNCOUNT) Br Fam Admin* (indemnités *fpl* de) chômage ❑ *m*; **how much is the dole nowadays?** combien est-ce qu'on touche au chômage maintenant?; **there was no dole in those days** on ne touchait pas de chômage à cette époque; **to be/to go on the dole** être/s'inscrire au chômage; **the dole queues are getting longer** de plus en plus de gens pointent au chômage

►► *Austr Fam* ***dole bludger*** parasite ❑ *m (qui touche le chômage et ne cherche pas de travail)*; *Br Fam* ***dole money*** (indemnités *fpl* de) chômage ❑ *m*

►**dole out** *vt sep (distribute)* distribuer; *(in small amounts)* distribuer au compte-gouttes

doleful ['dəʊlfʊl] *adj (mournful → look, voice)* malheureux; *(→ person, song)* triste

dolefully ['dəʊlfʊlɪ] *adv* d'un air malheureux

dolefulness ['dəʊlfʊlnɪs] *n* tristesse *f*

dolichocephalism [ˌdɒlɪkəʊ'sefəlɪzəm], **dolichocephaly** [ˌdɒlɪkəʊ'sefəlɪ] *n Anat* dolichocéphalie *f*

dolichocranial [ˌdɒlɪkəʊ'kreɪnɪəl] *adj Anat* dolichocrâne

doll [dɒl] *n* (**a**) *(for child)* poupée *f*; *(for ventriloquist)* marionnette *f* (de ventriloque); **to play with dolls** jouer à la poupée (**b**) *Fam (girl)* nana *f*, souris *f*; *(attractive woman)* poupée *f* (**c**) *Fam (term of address)* poupée *f*; **hi doll!** salut poupée! (**d**) *Am Fam (nice person)* trésor *m*, chou *m*; **you're a doll** tu es un amour

►► ***doll's hospital*** atelier *m* de réparation de jouets; *also Fig Br* ***doll's house,*** *Am* ***doll house*** maison *f* de poupée; ***doll's pram*** poussette *f* de poupée

►**doll up** *vt sep* **to get dolled up, to doll oneself up** se faire beau (belle), se pomponner; **she was all dolled up** elle s'était faite toute belle, elle était toute pomponnée; **to doll sb up** pomponner qn

'A Doll's House' *Ibsen* 'Maison de poupée'

dollar ['dɒlə(r)] *n* (**a**) *(currency)* dollar *m*; **you can bet your bottom dollar** *or* **dollars to doughnuts that he'll be there** tu peux être sûr qu'il sera là; **I feel like a million dollars** je me sens merveilleusement bien; *Fam* **you look like a million dollars in that dress!** tu es magnifique dans cette robe!; **that's the sixty-four thousand dollar question** c'est la question à mille francs

(**b**) *Br Fam Old-fashioned* = cinq shillings

►► *Fin & Econ* ***dollar area*** zone *f* dollar; ***dollar balances*** soldes *mpl* en dollars; ***dollar bill*** billet *m* d'un dollar; ***dollar cost averaging*** = calcul du coût moyen en dollars; *St Exch* coût *m* moyen des actions achetées par sommes fixes; ***dollar crisis*** crise *f* du dollar; ***dollar diplomacy*** diplomatie *f* du dollar; *Fin* ***dollar premium*** prime *f* sur le dollar; *Fin* ***dollar rate*** cours *m* du dollar; ***dollar sign*** (signe *m* du) dollar *m*

dollarization [dɒləraɪ'zeɪʃən] *n Fin & Econ* dollarisation *f*

dollars-and-cents *adj Am Fam (approach, attitude)* purement commercial

dollop ['dɒləp] *Fam* **1** *n (of mashed potatoes, cream etc)* (bonne) cuillerée ❑ *f*; *(of mud, plaster, clay)* (petit) tas ❑ *m*; *(of butter, margarine)* (gros *ou* bon) morceau ❑ *m*

2 *vt* **to dollop food out onto plates** balancer de la nourriture dans des assiettes

dolly ['dɒlɪ] (*pl* **dollies,** *pt & pp* **dollied**) **1** *n* (**a**) *Fam (for child)* poupée *f*

(**b**) *Cin & TV (for camera)* chariot *m*, dolly *m*

(**c**) *Br Fam Old-fashioned (woman)* poupée *f*

(**d**) *Sport (in cricket)* prise *f* au vol facile; *(in tennis)* coup *m* facile

(**e**) *(for clothes)* agitateur *m*

2 *vt Cin & TV* **to dolly a camera in/out** faire un travelling avant/arrière

3 *vi Cin & TV* **to dolly in/out** faire un travelling avant/arrière

►► *Br Fam Old-fashioned* ***dolly bird*** poupée *f* *(femme)*; *Cin & TV* ***dolly grip*** perchiste *mf*; *Br* ***dolly mixtures*** *(sweets)* petits bonbons *mpl* assortis; *Cin & TV* ***dolly shot*** travelling *m*; ***dolly tub*** *(for laundry)* baquet *m* à lessive

dolmades [dɒl'mɑ:di:z] *npl Culin* feuilles *fpl* de vigne farcies

dolman ['dɒlmən] *n* (**a**) *(Turkish robe)* dolman *m* (**b**) *(hussar's jacket)* dolman *m* (**c**) *(woman's mantle)* pelisse *f*

►► ***dolman sleeve*** manche *f* chauve-souris

dolmen ['dɒlmən] *n Archeol* dolmen *m*

dolomite ['dɒləmaɪt] *n Miner* dolomite *f*; *Geol (rock)* dolomie *f*, dolomite *f*

Dolomites ['dɒləmaɪts] *npl* **the Dolomites** les Dolomites *fpl*, les Alpes *fpl* dolomitiques

dolomitic [dɒlə'mɪtɪk] *adj Miner* dolomitique

dolomitization [ˌdɒləmaɪtɪ'zeɪʃən] *n Miner* dolomitisation *f*

dolorous ['dɒlərəs] *n Literary* (**a**) *(pained)* douloureux (**b**) *(sad)* triste, plaintif

dolorously ['dɒlərəslɪ] *adv Literary* (**a**) *(painfully)* douloureusement (**b**) *(sadly)* tristement, plaintivement

dolphin ['dɒlfɪn] *n* (**a**) *Zool* dauphin *m* (**b**) *Ich (Coryphena hippurus)* dorade *f*, coryphène *m*

dolphinarium [ˌdɒlfɪ'neərɪəm] *n* aquarium *m* à dauphins

dolphin-friendly *adj (tuna)* = pêché sans dommages pour les dauphins

dolt [dəʊlt] *n (stupid person)* lourdaud *m*, gourde *f*

doltish ['dəʊltɪʃ] *adj (person)* lourdaud; *(behaviour)* idiot

doltishness ['dəʊltɪʃnɪs] *n* stupidité *f*

domain [də'meɪn] *n* (**a**) *(territory, sphere of interest)* domaine *m*; *Fig* **that's your domain** c'est ton domaine; **to be in the public domain** *(information)* être dans le domaine public (**b**) *Math, Biol, Chem & Phys* domaine *m* (**c**) *Comput* domaine *m*

►► *Comput* ***domain name*** nom *m* de domaine; ***Domain Name System*** système *m* de nom de domaine

dome [dəʊm] *n* (**a**) *Archit* dôme *m*, coupole *f* (**b**) *(of head, skull)* calotte *f*; *(of hill)* dôme *m*; *(of heavens, sky)* voûte *f*; **the dome of his bald head** le sommet de son crâne chauve (**c**) *Fam (head)* tête ❑ *f* (**d**) *Metal (of furnace)* dôme *m*, voûte *f*

►► *Am* ***dome fastener*** bouton-pression *m*, pression *f*

domed [dəʊmd] *adj* **(a)** *Archit (building)* à coupole, à dôme **(b)** *(shaped like a dome → roof)* en forme de dôme *ou* de coupole; *(→ forehead)* bombé

Domesday Book ['du:mzdeɪ-] *n Hist* **the Domesday Book** = recueil cadastral établi à la fin du XIème siècle à l'initiative de Guillaume le Conquérant afin de permettre l'évaluation des droits fiscaux sur les terres d'Angleterre

domestic [də'mestɪk] **1** *adj* **(a)** *(household → duty, chore)* ménager; **for domestic use only** *(on packaging)* réservé à l'usage domestique
(b) *(of the family → duties, problems)* familial; *(→ life)* familial, de famille; **they lived in domestic bliss for many years** ça a été un ménage très heureux pendant de nombreuses années; **a minor domestic crisis** un petit problème à la maison; **a domestic sort of person** *(woman)* une femme d'intérieur; *(man)* un homme d'intérieur; **this is all very domestic** tout ceci donne une ambiance très familiale
(c) *(not foreign → affairs, flight, trade, policy)* intérieur; *(→ currency, economy, news, produce)* national
(d) *(not wild → animal)* domestique
2 *n Br Formal* domestique *mf*; *Am* femme *f* de ménage
►► ***domestic airline*** ligne *f* intérieure; ***domestic appliance*** appareil *m* ménager; ***domestic excursionist*** excursionniste *mf* (dans son propre pays); ***domestic fowl*** volaille *f*; ***domestic help*** aide *f* ménagère; *Am* ***domestic mail*** correspondance *f* à destination de l'intérieur; *Com & Econ* ***domestic market*** marché *m* intérieur; ***domestic product*** produit *m* ménager; *Com & Econ* ***domestic products*** denrées *fpl* du pays; ***domestic refuse*** ordures *fpl* ménagères; *Aviat* ***domestic route*** ligne *f* intérieure; ***domestic sales*** ventes *fpl* domestiques; *Br Formerly Sch* ***domestic science*** enseignement *m* ménager; ***domestic servant*** domestique *m*; ***domestic service*** domesticité *f*; **she was in domestic service** elle était domestique; ***domestic staff*** employés *mpl* de maison, domestiques *mpl*; ***domestic tourism*** tourisme *m* national; ***domestic tourist*** touriste *m* national; ***domestic travel*** voyages *mpl* domestiques; ***domestic visitor*** touriste *m* national

domestically [də'mestɪklɪ] *adv* **(a) to be domestically inclined** être une personne d'intérieur **(b) to be produced domestically** être produit à l'intérieur du pays *ou* au niveau national

domesticate [də'mestɪkeɪt] *vt (animal)* domestiquer, apprivoiser; *Hum (person)* habituer aux tâches ménagères

domesticated [də'mestɪkeɪtɪd] *adj (animal)* domestiqué, apprivoisé; **she's very domesticated** c'est une vraie femme d'intérieur; **her husband is quite domesticated** son mari est un vrai petit homme d'intérieur

domestication [də,mestɪ'keɪʃən] *n (of animal)* domestication *f*, apprivoisement *m*

domesticity [,dəʊme'stɪsətɪ] *n* **(a)** *(liking for home)* attachement *m* au foyer **(b)** *(home life)* vie *f* de famille; **the cosy domesticity of their life** leur petite vie tranquille

domicile ['dɒmɪsaɪl] **1** *n Admin, Fin & Law* domicile *m*
2 *vt* **(a)** *Admin & Law (usu passive) (person)* **domiciled at Leeds** domicilié *ou* demeurant à Leeds **(b)** *Fin* domicilier; **bills domiciled in France** traites *fpl* payables en France
►► ***domiciled bill*** effet *m* domicilié

domiciliary [,dɒmɪ'sɪljərɪ] *adj Admin (visit)* domiciliaire; *(care, services)* à domicile

domiciliation [,dɒmɪsɪlɪ'eɪʃən] *n Fin* domiciliation *f*
►► ***domiciliation papers*** dossier *m* de domiciliation

dominance ['dɒmɪnəns] *n* **(a)** *(command, influence → of race, person, football team, political party)* prédominance *f* **(b)** *Biol (→ of animal, gene, disease)* dominance *f* **(c)** *(importance)* importance *f*

dominant ['dɒmɪnənt] **1** *adj* **(a)** *(most important)* dominant; *(race, team, political party etc)* prédominant
(b) *Biol (animal, gene, disease)* dominant
(c) *(person, personality)* dominateur
(d) *(building, geographical feature → most elevated)* dominant; *(→ most striking)* le plus frappant
(e) *Mus* de dominante
2 *n* **(a)** *Mus (note)* dominante *f*
(b) *Biol (gene)* dominance *f*
►► *Mus* ***dominant chord*** accord *m* de dominante; *Biol* ***the dominant female*** la femelle dominante; *Biol* ***the dominant male*** le mâle dominant; *Mus* ***dominant seventh*** septième *f* de dominante

dominantly ['dɒmɪnəntlɪ] *adv* d'une manière dominante

dominate ['dɒmɪneɪt] **1** *vt* **(a)** *(person, a people)* dominer (sur); **to dominate a match/game** *(of player, team)* dominer un match/un jeu; **to be dominated by sb** être dominé par qn; **the wedding dominated his thoughts to the exclusion of everything else** le mariage prédominait sur toute autre chose dans ses pensées
(b) *(of mountain etc → landscape)* dominer; **the fortress dominates the town** la forteresse domine *ou* commande la ville
2 *vi* dominer

dominating ['dɒmɪneɪtɪŋ] *adj (feature, colour)* dominant; *(personality)* dominateur

domination [,dɒmɪ'neɪʃən] *n* domination *f*; *(of organization)* contrôle *m*; *(of conversation)* monopolisation *f*; **Spain was under Roman domination at the time** à cette époque, l'Espagne était sous la domination romaine; **Manchester United's domination of English football** la suprématie exercée par Manchester United sur le football anglais

dominator ['dɒmɪneɪtə(r)] *n* dominateur(trice) *m,f*

domineer [,dɒmɪ'nɪə(r)] *vi* se montrer autoritaire; **to domineer over sb** se montrer autoritaire avec qn

domineering [,dɒmɪ'nɪərɪŋ] *adj* autoritaire

domineeringly [,dɒmɪ'nɪərɪŋlɪ] *adv* autoritairement

Dominica [də'mɪnɪkə] *n* Dominique *f*; **in Dominica** à la Dominique

dominical [də'mɪnɪkəl] *adj Rel* dominical

Dominican [də'mɪnɪkən] **1** *n* **(a)** *(person from the Dominican Republic)* Dominicain(e) *m,f* **(b)** *(person from Dominica)* Dominiquais(e) *m,f* **(c)** *Rel* dominicain(e) *m,f*
2 *adj* **(a)** *(from the Dominican Republic)* dominicain **(b)** *(from Dominica)* dominiquais **(c)** *Rel* dominicain
►► ***the Dominican Republic*** la République Dominicaine; **in the Dominican Republic** en République Dominicaine

dominion [də'mɪnjən] *n* **(a)** *(rule, authority)* domination *f*, empire *m*; **to have dominion over a country** avoir un pays sous sa domination; **under foreign dominion** sous domination étrangère **(b)** *(territory)* territoire *m*; *(in British Commonwealth)* dominion *m*
►► *Can* ***Dominion Day*** Fête *f* du Canada *(anniversaire de l'indépendance canadienne, le 1 juillet)*

domino ['dɒmɪnəʊ] *(pl* **dominoes***)* *n* **(a)** *(for game)* domino *m*; **to play dominoes** jouer aux dominos **(b)** *(cloak, mask)* domino *m*
►► ***domino effect*** effet *m* d'entraînement; ***domino theory*** théorie *f* des dominos

Don [dɒn] *n* **the (River) Don** le Don

don¹ [dɒn] *(pt & pp* **donned,** *cont* **donning***)* *vt Formal (put on)* mettre

don² *n* **(a)** *Br Univ* = professeur d'université (en particulier à Oxford et Cambridge) **(b)** *(Spanish title)* don *m* **(c)** *Am* chef *m* de la Mafia

Donald Duck ['dɒnəld-] *pr n* Donald

donate [də'neɪt] **1** *vt (money, goods)* faire un don de; *(specific amount)* faire (un) don de; **to donate blood** donner son *ou* du sang; **the strips were donated to the team by a local sports shop** les tenues ont été données à l'équipe par un magasin de sport local; **would you care to donate something?** voudriez-vous faire un don *ou* donner quelque chose?
2 *vi (give money, goods)* faire un don, faire des dons; **I've been donating for ten years** *(blood)* je donne mon sang depuis dix ans

donation [də'neɪʃən] *n (action)* don *m*, donation *f*; *(money, goods or blood given)* don *m*; **all donations are tax-deductible** tous les dons sont déductibles des impôts; **would you care to make a donation?** voudriez-vous faire un don *ou* faire une donation *ou* donner quelque chose?; **to make a donation to a charity** faire un don *ou* une donation à une œuvre (de charité)

donator [də'neɪtə(r)] *n* donateur(trice) *m,f*

done [dʌn] **1** *pp of* **do**
2 *adj* **(a)** *(finished)* fini; **are you done yet?** est-ce que tu as fini?; **aren't you done yet?** tu n'as pas encore fini?; **to get sth done** *(completed)* finir qch; **everything should be done and dusted by the end of the month** tout doit être bouclé pour la fin du mois
(b) *(cooked → food)* cuit
(c) *Fam (exhausted)* crevé, claqué
(d) *Fam (used up)* **that's the milk done** il n'y a plus de lait ❑; **when the ammunition was done** quand ils ont été à court de munitions ❑
(e) *(fitting)* **it's not the done thing, it's not done** ça ne se fait pas; **speaking with your mouth full is not done** *or* **the done thing** ça ne se fait pas de parler la bouche pleine; **it used to be the done thing to send your hostess flowers** ça se faisait d'envoyer des fleurs à son hôtesse
►► *Com* ***done deal*** = transaction dans laquelle les invendus ne peuvent être retournés au fournisseur; *Fig* **the peace agreement/merger is not a done deal yet** l'accord de paix/la fusion n'est pas encore chose faite

Donegal [dɒnɪ'gɔ:l] *n* **(a)** *(town)* Donegal **(b)** *(county)* le Donegal, = comté dans le nord-ouest de la république d'Irlande; **in Donegal** dans le Donegal
►► *Tex* ***Donegal tweed*** = tweed fabriqué dans le Donegal

doner kebab ['dɒnə-, 'dəʊnə-] *n* sandwich *m* grec

dong [dɒŋ] *n* **(a)** *(noise of bell)* ding-dong *m* **(b)** *Vulg (penis)* queue *f*, bite *f*

dongle ['dɒŋgəl] *n Comput* fiche *f* gigogne, clé *f* gigogne

donjon ['dɒndʒən] *n* donjon *m*

Don Juan [-'dʒu:ən] *n also Fig* don Juan *m*; **he's a bit of a Don Juan** il est un peu du genre don Juan

donkey ['dɒŋkɪ] *n* **(a)** *(animal)* âne *m*, ânesse *f*; *Fam* **he could talk the hind legs off a donkey** il est bavard comme une pie; **I haven't seen her for donkey's years** je ne l'ai pas vue depuis une éternité; **he's worked in the same place for donkey's years** ça fait une éternité qu'il travaille au même endroit
(b) *Fam (idiot)* âne *m*, imbécile ❑ *mf*
(c) *Br Fam Pej (sportsman)* incapable ❑ *m*
►► *Naut* ***donkey boiler*** chaudière *f* auxiliaire; *Br* ***donkey derby*** course *f* d'ânes; *Tech* ***donkey engine*** moteur *m* auxiliaire; *Br* ***donkey jacket*** = veste longue en tissu épais, généralement bleu foncé; ***donkey ride*** promenade *f* à dos d'âne; *Austr* ***donkey vote*** = situation, lors d'un scrutin avec vote préférentiel, où un votant laisse inchangé l'ordre des candidats tel qu'il apparaît sur le bulletin de vote

donkey-work *n (UNCOUNT) Fam* **to do the donkey-work** *(drudgery)* faire le sale boulot; *(difficult part)* faire le gros du travail ❑

donnish ['dɒnɪʃ] *adj Br (person)* érudit, savant; *(look, speech)* d'érudit, cultivé; *Pej* pédant; **he's a bit donnish** il a un petit air professoral

donnishly ['dɒnɪʃlɪ] *adv Br* de façon érudite *ou* savante, savamment; *Pej* doctoralement, doctement

donnybrook ['dɒnɪbrʊk] *n Am Fam (fight)* bagarre *f* de poivrots

donor ['dəʊnə(r)] *n* **(a)** *(to charity)* donateur(trice) *m,f* **(b)** *(of blood, organ)* donneur(euse) *m,f*
►► ***donor card*** carte *f* de don d'organe; ***donor insemination*** insémination *f* avec sperme de donneur, IAD *f*

don't [dəʊnt] **1** = **do not**
2 *n (usu pl)* chose *f* à ne pas faire; **a list of do's and don'ts** une liste de choses à faire et à ne pas faire

dontcha, dontcher ['dəʊntʃə] *Br Fam* = **don't you**

don't know *n (on survey)* sans opinion *mf inv*; *(voter)* indécis(e) *m,f*

donut ['dəʊnʌt] *n Am* beignet *m*, *Can* beigne *m*

doobie ['du:bɪ] *n Fam (cannabis cigarette)* joint ❑ *m*

doodah ['du:dɑ:] *n Fam* truc *m*, bidule *m*

doodle ['du:dəl] **1** *vi & vt* gribouiller, griffonner
2 *n* gribouillage *m*, griffonnage *m*

doodlebug ['du:dəl,bʌg] *n* (**a**) *Fam (bomb)* V1 ❑ *m*, bombe *f* volante ❑ (**b**) *Am (insect)* larve *f* de cincindèle

doofer ['du:fə(r)] *n Br Fam* truc *m*, machin *m*

doofus ['du:fəs] *n Am Fam* andouille *f*

doohickey ['du:,hɪkɪ] *n Am Fam* truc *m*, machin *m*

doo-lally [,du:'lælɪ] *adj Fam* timbré

doom [du:m] **1** *n (UNCOUNT) (terrible fate)* destin *m* (malheureux), sort *m* (tragique); *(ruin)* perte *f*, ruine *f*; *(death)* mort *f*; **to meet one's doom** trouver la mort; **thousands were sent to their doom** on envoya des milliers de gens à la mort; **an air/a feeling of doom** un air/sentiment funeste; *Fig* **to be full of** *or* **all doom and gloom** voir tout en noir; **the situation's not all doom and gloom** la situation n'est pas aussi sombre qu'il y paraît
2 *vt* condamner

doomed [du:md] *adj (town)* condamné; *(person)* perdu; *(ship, aircraft)* marqué par le destin; **to be doomed (to failure)** être voué à l'échec; **she is doomed to a life of poverty** elle est condamnée à une vie de misère; **the doomed ship set sail that day** le navire condamné à sombrer prit la mer ce jour-là

doom-laden *adj* de mauvais augure, sinistre

doomsayer ['du:mseɪə(r)] *n Formal* prophète *m* de malheur

Doomsday ['du:mzdeɪ] *n* jour *m* du Jugement dernier; **till Doomsday** jusqu'à la fin du monde *ou* des temps; **to put sth off till doomsday** renvoyer qch aux calendes grecques
►► *Hist* ***the Doomsday Book*** = recueil cadastral établi à la fin du XIème siècle à l'initiative de Guillaume le Conquérant afin de permettre l'évaluation des droits fiscaux sur les terres d'Angleterre

doomster ['du:mstə(r)] *n Br Fam* prophète *m* de malheur ❑

doomwatch ['du:mwɒtʃ] *n Ecol (of environment)* surveillance *f* de l'environnement

doona ['du:nə] *n Austr (duvet)* couette *f (de lit)*

door [dɔ:(r)] *n* (**a**) *(of building, room, refrigerator, wardrobe)* porte *f*; **she walked through the door** elle franchit la porte; **they shut the door in my face** ils m'ont fermé la porte au nez; **he lives two doors down** *or* **away** il habite deux portes plus loin; **I found the door closed** j'ai trouvé porte close; **out of doors** dehors, en plein air; **to go from door to door** aller de porte en porte; **can someone answer the door?** est-ce que quelqu'un peut aller ouvrir?; **it was Tricia who answered the door (to me)** c'est Tricia qui m'a ouvert (la porte); **I'll see you to the door** je vous reconduis jusqu'à la porte; **the bank closes its doors at 3:30** la banque ferme à 15 heures 30; **the business finally closes its doors tomorrow** l'entreprise ferme définitivement demain; **tickets available at the door** *(in advertisement, on sign)* billets en vente à l'entrée; **the agreement leaves the door open for further discussion** l'accord laisse la porte ouverte à des discussions ultérieures; **the discovery opens the door to medical advances** la découverte ouvre la voie à des progrès médicaux; **having a famous name certainly helps to open doors** avoir un nom célèbre permet sans aucun doute de voir s'ouvrir des portes; *Fig* **to lay sth at sb's door** imputer qch à qn, reprocher qch à qn; **to shut the door in sb's face** fermer la porte au nez de qn; *Fig* **doors kept being closed in our faces** tout le monde nous a fermé la porte au nez; **she closed** *or* **shut the door on any further negotiations** elle a rendu toute nouvelle négociation impossible; *Fig* **as one door closes, another opens** chaque fois qu'une porte se ferme, une autre s'ouvre; **to show sb to the door** conduire qn à la porte, reconduire qn; *Fig* **to show sb the door** montrer la porte à qn; **the foot in the door technique** *(of salesman)* = la vente (en porte-à-porte) forcée
(**b**) *(of car)* porte *f*, portière *f*; *(of train)* portière *f*
►► ***door chain*** chaînette *f* de sûreté; *Mktg* ***door drop*** distribution *f* à domicile; ***door handle*** poignée *f* de porte; *Aut* poignée *f* de portière; ***door viewer*** judas *m* (optique)

doorbell ['dɔ:bel] *n* sonnette *f*; **to ring the doorbell** sonner à la porte; **the doorbell rang** on sonna à la porte

do-or-die *adj (chance, effort)* désespéré, ultime; *(attitude, person)* jusqu'au-boutiste

doorframe ['dɔ:freɪm] *n* chambranle *m*, châssis *m* de porte

doorjamb ['dɔ:dʒæm] *n* montant *m* de porte, jambage *m*

doorkeeper ['dɔ:,ki:pə(r)] *n (at hotel)* portier *m*; *(at apartment building)* concierge *mf*

doorknob ['dɔ:nɒb] *n* poignée *f* de porte

doorknocker ['dɔ:,nɒkə(r)] *n Br* heurtoir *m*, marteau *m (de porte)*

doorman ['dɔ:mən] *(pl* **doormen** [-mən]*) n (at hotel)* portier *m*; *(at apartment building)* concierge *m*; *(at pub, nightclub)* videur *m*

doormat ['dɔ:mæt] *n* (**a**) *(for door)* paillasson *m*, essuie-pieds *m inv* (**b**) *Fig (person)* chiffe *f* molle; **don't be such a doormat** ne te laisse pas marcher sur les pieds comme ça; **to treat sb like a doormat** traiter qn comme un moins que rien

doornail ['dɔ:neɪl] *n* clou *m* de porte

doorplate ['dɔ:pleɪt] *n* plaque *f*

doorpost ['dɔ:pəʊst] *n* montant *m* de porte, jambage *m*

doorsill ['dɔ:sɪl] *n* seuil *m* de porte

doorstep ['dɔ:step] **1** *n* (**a**) *(step)* pas *m* de la porte, seuil *m* de porte; **leave the milk on the doorstep** laissez le lait devant la porte; **don't leave him standing on the doorstep, ask him to come in!** ne le laisse pas à la porte, fais-le entrer!; *Fig* **there are shops and a library on your doorstep** tu as des boutiques et une bibliothèque à ta porte; **they're building a huge factory practically on my doorstep** ils construisent une immense usine presque à ma porte
(**b**) *Br Hum (thick slice of bread)* grosse tranche *f* de pain
2 *vt Br (of politician)* démarcher; *(of journalists)* harceler jusque devant sa porte
►► *Br* ***doorstep salesman*** vendeur *m* à domicile, démarcheur *m*; ***doorstep selling*** vente *f* à domicile, porte-à-porte *m inv*, démarchage *m*

doorstepping ['dɔ:stepɪŋ] *Br* **1** *n (by politician)* démarchage *m* électoral; *(by journalists)* = pratique journalistique qui consiste à harceler les gens jusque devant leur porte
2 *adj (politician)* qui fait du démarchage électoral; *(journalist)* qui harcèle les gens jusque devant leur porte

doorstop ['dɔ:stɒp] *n (fixed)* butoir *m*; *(wedge)* cale-porte *m*

door-to-door *adv* **a two-hour trip door-to-door** un trajet de deux heures de porte à porte; **the journey takes twenty-five minutes door-to-door** le voyage prend vingt-cinq minutes de porte à porte
►► ***door-to-door enquiries*** enquête *f* de voisinage; ***door-to-door salesman*** vendeur *m* à domicile, démarcheur *m*; **he's a door-to-door salesman** il fait du porte-à-porte; ***door-to-door selling*** vente *f* à domicile, porte-à-porte *m inv*; ***door-to-door service*** service *m* à domicile

doorway ['dɔ:weɪ] *n* porte *f*, *(frame)* encadrement *m* de la porte; **standing in the doorway** debout dans l'embrasure de la porte

doozie, doozy ['du:zɪ] *n Am Fam* **that was a total doozie!** *(good)* c'était vraiment super!; *(bad)* c'était vraiment nul!

dopamine ['dəʊpəmɪn] *n Physiol* dopamine *f*

dope [dəʊp] **1** *n* (**a**) *(UNCOUNT) Fam (illegal drug)* drogue ❑ *f*, dope *f*; *(cannabis)* shit ❑ *m*
(**b**) *(for athlete, horse)* dopant *m*
(**c**) *Fam (idiot)* crétin(e) *m,f*, andouille *f*
(**d**) *(UNCOUNT) Fam Old-fashioned (news, information)* tuyau *m*, renseignement ❑ *m*; **to give sb the dope on sth** rencarder qn sur qch; **have you got any dope on the murder?** avez-vous des tuyaux *ou* renseignements sur le meurtre?
(**e**) *Chem & Tech (varnish)* enduit *m*; *(for fuel)* dopant *m*
(**f**) *(for dynamite)* absorbant *m*
2 *adj Am Fam (excellent)* génial, super *(inv)*
3 *vt* (**a**) *(drug → horse, person) (to prevent from winning)* droguer; *(to increase chances)* doper; *(→ drink, food)* mettre une drogue *ou* un dopant dans; *Fam* **she was all doped up** *or Am* **out** elle planait complètement
(**b**) *Chem & Tech (varnish)* enduire; *(fuel)* doper
►► *Fam* ***dope addict*** toxicomane ❑ *mf*, drogué(e) ❑ *m,f*; *Fam* ***dope dealer, dope pusher*** revendeur(euse) ❑ *m,f* de drogue, dealer *m*; *Br Fam Horseracing* ***dope sheet*** = journal des courses; ***dope test*** test *m* antidopage *ou* antidoping; **to fail/take a dope test** être déclaré positif à/subir un test antidopage *ou* antidoping

▶**dope out** *vt sep Am Fam (devise)* combiner, bidouiller; *(solve)* deviner ❑, piger

dopehead ['dəʊphed] *n Fam* (**a**) *(drug user)* camé(e) *m,f* (**b**) *(heavy cannabis user)* = personne qui fume beaucoup de cannabis

doper ['dəʊpə(r)] *n Am Fam (drug pusher)* pusher *m*

dopey *(compar* **dopier**, *superl* **dopiest***)* = **dopy**

dopiness ['dəʊpɪnɪs] *n* (**a**) *(sleepiness)* torpeur *f*, somnolence *f* (**b**) *(silliness)* stupidité *f*

doping ['dəʊpɪŋ] *n* (**a**) *(to prevent from winning)* administration *f* d'un narcotique (**of** à); *(to increase chances of winning)* dopage *m*, doping *m* (**b**) *Chem & Tech (varnishing)* enduisage *m*; *(of fuel)* dopage *m*

doppelgänger ['dɒpəl,gæŋə(r)] *n* double *m* *(d'une personne vivante)*, sosie *m*

Doppler effect ['dɒplə(r)-] *n Phys* effet *m* Doppler

dopy ['dəʊpɪ] *(compar* **dopier**, *superl* **dopiest***) adj* (**a**) *(sleepy)* (à moitié) endormi; *(drugged)* drogué, dopé (**b**) *Fam (silly)* idiot ❑, abruti

do-re-mi [dəʊreɪ'mi:] *n Am Fam (money)* fric *m*, blé *m*

Dorian ['dɔ:rɪən] **1** *n* Dorien(enne) *m,f*
2 *adj Ling & Mus* dorien

Doric ['dɒrɪk] **1** *adj Archit* dorique
2 *n* (**a**) *Archit* dorique *m* (**b**) *Ling (in Ancient Greece)* dorien *m*; *(in Scotland)* = dialecte de l'anglais parlé dans le nord-est de l'Écosse

dork [dɔ:k] *n Am Fam (idiot)* niais(e) ❑ *m,f*; *(studious person)* ringard(e) *m,f*

dorky ['dɔ:kɪ] *adj Am Fam (idiotic)* niais ❑; *(studious)* ringard

dorm [dɔ:m] *n Fam (abbr* **dormitory***)* (**a**) *(room)* dortoir ❑ *m* (**b**) *Am Univ* résidence *f* universitaire ❑
►► *Am Univ* ***dorm mother*** surveillante ❑ *f*

dormancy ['dɔ:mənsɪ] *n Formal* (**a**) *(of animal)* état *m* endormi; *(of plant)* dormance *f* (**b**) *(of volcano)* état *m* inactif

dormant ['dɔ:mənt] *adj* (**a**) *(idea, passion)* qui sommeille; *(energy, reserves)* inexploité; *(disease)* à l'état latent; *(law)* inappliqué; **to lie dormant** sommeiller (**b**) *(animal)* endormi; *(plant)* dormant (**c**) *(volcano)* en repos, en sommeil (**d**) *Banking (account)* sans mouvement (**e**) *Her* dormant

dormer ['dɔ:mə(r)] *n (window)* lucarne *f*
►► ***dormer window*** lucarne *f*

dormice ['dɔ:maɪs] *pl of* **dormouse**

dormie ['dɔ:mɪ] *adj Golf* dormie

dormitory ['dɔ:mətrɪ] *(pl* **dormitories***) n* (**a**) *(room)* dortoir *m* (**b**) *Am Univ* résidence *f* universitaire
►► *Am* ***dormitory suburb***, *Br* ***dormitory town*** cité-dortoir *f*

Dormobile® ['dɔ:mə,bi:l] *n Br* camping-car *m*

dormouse ['dɔ:maʊs] *(pl* **dormice** [-maɪs]*) n Zool* loir *m*

Dorothy Dixer [,dɒrəθɪ'dɪksə(r)] *n Austr Fam* = question que l'on pose à son interlocuteur de façon à lui permettre de donner une réponse préparée à l'avance

Dors *(written abbr* **Dorset***)* Dorset *m*

dorsal ['dɔ:səl] **1** *adj* dorsal
2 *n* dorsale *f*
►► ***dorsal fin*** nageoire *f* dorsale

dorsally ['dɔ:səlɪ] *adv (located, situated)* sur le dos

Dorset ['dɔ:sɪt] *n* le Dorset, = comté dans le sud-ouest de l'Angleterre; **in Dorset** dans le Dorset

dory ['dɔ:rɪ] *(pl* **dories***) n* (**a**) *(saltwater fish)* saint-pierre *m inv*, dorée *f*; *(freshwater fish)* dorée *f* (**b**) *Am (boat)* doris *m*

DOS [dɒs] *n Comput (abbr* **disk operating system***)* DOS *m*

►► ***DOS command*** commande *f* du DOS; ***DOS prompt*** indicatif *m* (du) DOS, invite *f* du DOS; ***DOS switch*** clé *f ou* paramètre *m* du DOS

dosage ['dəʊsɪdʒ] *n (giving of dose)* dosage *m*; *(amount)* dose *f*; *(directions)* posologie *f*

dose [dəʊs] **1** *n* (**a**) *(amount)* dose *f*; **she took her daily dose of medicine** elle a pris son médicament quotidien; **in small/large doses** à faible/haute dose; **I can only take him in small doses** je ne peux le supporter qu'à petites doses; **with a strong dose of humour** avec beaucoup d'humour

(**b**) *(of illness)* attaque *f*; **a bad dose of flu** une mauvaise grippe

(**c**) *very Fam (venereal disease)* bléno *f*; **to catch a dose** attraper une bléno

2 *vt* (**a**) *(of pharmacist)* doser

(**b**) *(person)* administrer un médicament à; **she dosed herself (up) with pills** elle s'est bourrée de médicaments

dosh [dɒʃ] *n Br Fam* fric *m*

do-si-do [ˌdəʊsɪ'dəʊ] *n* = figure de quadrille où les danseurs sont dos à dos

dosimeter [dəʊ'sɪmɪtə(r)] *n* dosimètre *m*

dosimetric [ˌdəʊsɪ'metrɪk] *adj* dosimétrique

dosimetry [dəʊ'sɪmɪtrɪ] *n* dosimétrie *f*

doss [dɒs] *Br Fam* **1** *n* (**a**) *(bed)* lit ❑ *m*, pieu *m* (**b**) *(nap)* somme *m*, roupillon *m*; **to have a doss** faire un somme (**c**) *(easy thing)* **it was a real doss** c'était fastoche

2 *vi (sleep)* pieuter; *(in doss house)* coucher à l'asile de nuit

►**doss about, doss around** *vi Br Fam* glander

►**doss down** *vi Br Fam* coucher, crécher ❑; **do you mind dossing down on the floor?** est-ce que ça t'embête de coucher par terre?; **I need somewhere to doss down for the night** j'ai besoin d'un endroit où coucher cette nuit ❑

dosser ['dɒsə(r)] *n Br Fam* (**a**) *(homeless person)* sans-abri ❑ *mf inv*, clochard(e) *m,f* (**b**) *(house)* foyer *m* de sans-abri (**c**) *Ir Fam Pej (lazy person)* fainéant(e) *m,f*, glandeur(euse) *m,f*

dosshouse ['dɒshaʊs, *pl* -haʊzɪz] *n Br Fam* foyer *m* de sans-abri ❑

dossier ['dɒsɪeɪ] *n* dossier *m*; **to keep a dossier on sb** avoir un dossier sur qn

Dostoievsky [ˌdɒstɔɪ'efskɪ] *pr n* Dostoïevski

DOT [ˌdiːəʊ'tiː] *n Am Admin (abbr* **Department of Transportation**) = ministère des Transports

dot [dɒt] *(pt & pp* **dotted**, *cont* **dotting**) **1** *n* point *m*; *(on material)* pois *m*; *Mus* point *m* d'augmentation; **"www dot harrap dot com"** *(in URL)* "www point harrap point com"; **dot, dot, dot** *(in punctuation)* points *mpl* de suspension; **dots and dashes** *(Morse code)* points *mpl* et traits *mpl*; *Fam* **since the year dot** depuis des siècles; *Fam* **that was in the year dot** c'était il y a une éternité

2 *vt* (**a**) *(mark)* marquer avec des points, pointiller; *(an "i")* mettre un point sur; *Fig* **to dot one's i's and cross one's t's** mettre les points sur les i

(**b**) *(spot)* parsemer; **the lake was dotted with boats** des bateaux étaient dispersés sur le lac; **his shirt was dotted with flecks of tomato sauce** sa chemise était tachetée de sauce tomate; **the islands are dotted all round the coast** les îles sont éparpillées tout autour de la côte; *Culin* **dot the surface with butter** mettez des morceaux de beurre sur le dessus

(**c**) *Mus (note)* pointer

(**d**) *Fam* **to dot sb one** *(hit)* flanquer un gnon à qn

3 on the dot *adv (arrive)* à l'heure tapante; **at 3 o'clock on the dot** à 3 heures pile *ou* tapantes; **he always pays right on the dot** il paye toujours recta

►► *Comput* ***dot com*** *(company)* start-up *f*

dotage ['dəʊtɪdʒ] *n* gâtisme *m*; **to be in one's dotage** être gâteux, être retombé en enfance

dotard ['dəʊtəd] *n* gâteux(euse) *m,f*

dote [dəʊt] *vi* être gâteux

►**dote on, dote upon** *vt insep* **to dote on** *or* **upon sb** être fou (folle) de qn, aimer qn à la folie

doth [dəθ, *stressed* dʌθ] *Arch 3rd pers sing of* **do**

doting ['dəʊtɪŋ] *adj (parents, grandparents)* qui montre une tendresse *ou* une indulgence exagérée; **he has a doting mother** sa mère l'aime à la folie

dotingly ['dəʊtɪŋlɪ] *adv* avec une tendresse *ou* une indulgence exagérée

dot-matrix printer *n Comput* imprimante *f* matricielle

dotted ['dɒtɪd] *adj* (**a**) *(shirt, tie)* à pois (**b**) *Mus* pointé

►► ***dotted line*** *(on form)* ligne *f* en pointillés; *Aut* ligne *f* discontinue; **to sign on the dotted line** *(on form)* signer à l'endroit indiqué; *Fig* donner son consentement; **tear along the dotted line** détachez suivant le pointillé; *Mus* ***dotted note*** note *f* pointée; *Comput* ***dotted quad*** adresse *f* IP; *Mus* ***dotted rest*** silence *m* pointé; *Mus* ***dotted rhythm*** notes *fpl* pointées

dottel = **dottle**

dotterel ['dɒtərəl] *n* (**a**) *Orn* pluvier *m* (guignard) (**b**) *Br (foolish person)* gourde *f*

dottiness ['dɒtɪnɪs] *n Br Fam* folie ❑ *f*

dottle ['dɒtəl] *n* culot *m (dans une pipe)*

dotty ['dɒtɪ] *(compar* **dottier**, *superl* **dottiest**) *adj Br Fam (crazy)* fou (folle) ❑, dingue; **she's slightly dotty** elle travaille du chapeau, elle est toquée; **he's absolutely dotty about her** il est fou d'elle; **he's dotty about steam trains** c'est un fana *ou* un mordu des trains à vapeur

Douay Bible ['daʊeɪ-] *n Cathol* Bible *f* de Douai

DOUBLE ['dʌbəl]

double	►**1 (a) – (c), (g); 3 (a), (b), (d)**
deux fois	►**1 (d)**
en double	►**1 (e)**
pour deux personnes	►**1 (f)**
deux fois plus	►**2**
demi-tour	►**3 (c)**
en deux	►**4**
doubler	►**5 (a), (c); 6**
plier en deux	►**5 (b)**
contrer	►**5 (d); 6 (c)**
tourner	►**6 (b)**

1 *adj* (**a**) *(twice as large → quantity, portion)* double; **a double whisky** un double whisky

(**b**) *Bot* double

(**c**) *(line, row)* double; **to go into** *or* **reach double figures** *(of inflation, unemployment etc)* atteindre la barre des dix pour cent; **an egg with a double yolk** un œuf à deux jaunes

(**d**) *(with figures, letters)* deux fois; **double five two one** *(figure)* deux fois cinq deux un; *(phone number)* cinquante-cinq, vingt et un; **"letter" is spelt with a double "t"** "letter" s'écrit avec deux "t"; **to throw a double six/three** faire un double six/trois

(**e**) *(folded in two)* en double, replié; **double thickness** double épaisseur *f*

(**f**) *(for two people)* pour *ou* à deux personnes

(**g**) *(dual → purpose, advantage)* double; *(ambiguous)* double, ambigu(uë); **a word with a double meaning** un mot à double sens; **to lead a double life** mener une double vie; **to have double standards** faire deux poids, deux mesures; *Fam* **to do a double take** marquer un temps d'arrêt ❑ *(par surprise)*; **he did a double take when I told him** lorsque je le lui ai dit, il a marqué un temps d'arrêt; **the brothers had a double wedding** les deux frères se sont mariés au cours de la même cérémonie

2 *predet (twice)* deux fois plus; **she earns double my salary** elle gagne deux fois plus que moi *ou* le double de moi; **we ordered double the usual quantity** nous avons commandé le double de la quantité habituelle; **it took me double the time I expected** ça m'a pris le double du temps que je pensais; **food here costs nearly double what it does at home** la nourriture ici coûte presque le double de chez moi

3 *n* (**a**) *(twice the amount)* double *m*; *(of alcohol)* double *m*; **he charged us double** il nous a fait payer le double; **they pay him double if he works nights** on le paye (au tarif) double s'il travaille la nuit; **at** *or* **on the double** au pas de course; *also Fig* **on the double!** magnez-vous!; **double or quits** quitte ou double

(**b**) *(duplicate)* double *m*, réplique *f*; *(of person)* double *m*, sosie *m*; *Cin & TV (stand-in)* doublure *f*; *Theat (actor with two parts)* acteur(trice) *m,f* qui tient deux rôles; **she's your double!** c'est ton sosie!

(**c**) *(turn)* demi-tour *m*

(**d**) *Horseracing* pari *m* couplé; *Cards* contre *m*; *(in darts)* double *m*; *(in billiards)* doublé *m*

4 *adv (in two)* en deux; **to fold sth double** plier qch en deux; **I was bent double with pain** j'étais plié en deux de douleur; **to see double** *(two of the same)* voir double

5 *vt* (**a**) *(increase)* doubler; **he doubled my salary** il a doublé mon salaire; **to double the stakes** doubler la mise

(**b**) *(fold)* plier en deux, replier

(**c**) *Cin & TV* doubler

(**d**) *Cards (bid, opponent)* contrer

6 *vi* (**a**) *(increase)* doubler

(**b**) *(turn)* tourner, faire un crochet

(**c**) *Cards* contrer; **double!** *(in bridge)* contre!

(**d**) *(serve two purposes)* **the dining room doubles as a study** la salle à manger sert également de bureau; *Theat* **he doubles as the priest and the servant** il joue les rôles du prêtre et du domestique

►► ***double act*** duo *m* comique; ***double agent*** agent *m* double; *Mus* ***double bar*** double barre *f*; *Mus* ***double bass*** contrebasse *f*; *Mus* ***double bassoon*** contrebasson *m*; ***double bed*** grand lit *m*, lit *m* à deux places; ***double bill*** *Cin* = séance avec deux longs métrages à la suite; *TV* = programmation de deux longs métrages à la suite; *Psy* ***double bind*** double contrainte *f*; **to be caught in a double bind** se trouver dans une situation insoluble, être dans une impasse; *Br* ***double bluff*** = technique consistant à faire croire qu'on bluffe alors qu'on dit la vérité; **it was a double bluff on her part** elle voulait lui/nous/*etc* faire croire qu'elle bluffait; *Golf* ***double bogey*** bogey *m* double; *Am* ***double boiler*** casserole *f* à double fond; **to heat sth in a double boiler** faire chauffer qch au bain-marie; ***double check*** revérification *f*; ***double chin*** double menton *m*; *Br* ***double cream*** crème *f* épaisse, *Can* crème *f* à fouetter; ***double cross*** trahison *f*, traîtrise *f*; *Typ* ***double dagger*** diésis *m*; *Am* ***double date*** sortie *f* à quatre *(deux couples)*; *Am* ***double digit*** nombre *m* à deux chiffres; ***double doors, a double door*** une porte à deux battants; *Sport* ***double dribble*** *(in basketball)* reprise *f* de dribble; ***double Dutch*** *Br Fam* charabia *m*, baragouin *m*; *Am (game)* double dutch *m*; **to talk double Dutch** baragouiner; **it's all double Dutch to me!** c'est de l'hébreu pour moi!; ***double entendre*** mot *m ou* expression *f* à double sens; *Acct* ***double entry*** comptabilité *f* en partie double; *Phot* ***double exposure*** surimpression *f*; *Sport* ***double fault*** double faute *f*; *Cin* ***double feature*** = séance avec deux longs métrages à la suite; *Br Univ* ***double first*** ≃ mention *f* très bien *(dans deux disciplines à la fois)*; *Mus* ***double flat*** double bémol *m*; ***double Gloucester*** = fromage à pâte pressée; ***double helix*** double hélice *f*; *Br Univ* ***double honours*** = licence portant sur deux matières; *Am Ins* ***double indemnity*** = clause d'une assurance-vie qui stipule qu'en cas de mort accidentelle de l'assuré la prime est doublée; *Am Law* ***double jeopardy*** double incrimination *f*; ***double knit*** tricot *m* double face, double face *f*; ***double knitting*** = laine assez épaisse utilisée en tricot; ***double knot*** double nœud *m*; *Gram* ***double negative*** double négation *f*; ***double occupancy*** *(of hotel room)* occupation *f* double; *St Exch* ***double option*** stellage *m*; ***double parking*** stationnement *m* en double file; ***double play*** *(in baseball)* double retrait *m*; *Am Fig* **to do a double play** faire d'une pierre deux coups; *Med* ***double pneumonia*** pneumonie *f* double; *Comput* ***double precision*** double précision *f*; *Sport* ***double pump*** *(in basketball)* = smash en deux temps; ***double room*** chambre *f* pour deux personnes; *Sport* ***double Salchow*** *(in figure skating)* double Salchow *m*; *Br* ***double saucepan*** casserole *f* à double fond; **to cook in a double saucepan** faire cuire au bain-marie; ***double scull*** *(in rowing)* deux *m* de couple; *Mus* ***double sharp*** double dièse *m*; *Typ* ***double spacing*** double interligne *m*; **in double spacing** à double interligne; *Astron* ***double star*** étoile *f* double; *Mus* ***double stopping*** *(on violin)* double-corde *f*; *Fin* ***double taxation*** double imposition *f*; *Sport*

double team = bloc de deux défenseurs contre un attaquant; ***double time*** *(pay)* salaire *m* double; *Mil* pas *m* redoublé; *Mus* mesure *f* double; **I get double time on Sundays** je suis payé le double le dimanche; **to march in double time** marcher à pas redoublés; *Mus* **in double time** en mesure double; *Med* ***double vision*** double vision *f*; **to have double vision** voir double; *Fam* ***double whammy*** double coup *m* de malchance; **it was a double whammy: he was attacked by the opposition and by his own party at the same time** il était pris entre deux feux, assailli d'un côté par l'opposition, de l'autre par son propre parti; *Br* ***double white line*** *(on road)* double ligne *f* blanche *(d'interdiction de doubler)*; *Am Mus* ***double whole note*** double ronde *f*; ***double yellow line*** *(on road)* double ligne *f* jaune *(qui indique une zone de stationnement interdit)*; **to be parked on a double yellow line** être en stationnement interdit

▸**double back 1** *vi (animal, person, road)* tourner brusquement; **he doubled back down a side road** il a rebroussé chemin par une petite route; **the path doubles back on itself** le sentier te ramène sur tes pas

2 *vt sep (sheet)* mettre en double

▸**double for** *vt insep Cin & Theat* doubler

▸**double over** *vi (bend over)* se plier, se courber; **he doubled over in pain** il se plia en deux de douleur

▸**double up 1** *vi* (**a**) *(bend over)* se plier, se courber; **he doubled up in pain** il se plia en deux de douleur; **to double up with laughter** se tordre de rire (**b**) *(share)* partager; **there weren't enough rooms so we doubled up** il n'y avait pas assez de place, alors nous nous sommes mis à deux par chambre

2 *vt sep* plier en deux, replier

'Double Indemnity' *Wilder* 'Assurance sur la mort'

double-acting, double-action *adj* à double effet

double-A rating *n St Exch* notation *f* AA

double-barrelled, *Am* **double-barreled** [-'bærəld] *adj (gun)* à deux coups; *Fig (question, remark)* équivoque

▸▸ *Br* ***double-barrelled name*** = nom de famille composé (p.ex. Burnes-Jones) indiquant souvent une origine noble

double-blind *adj (experiment, test)* en double aveugle; *(method)* à double insu, à double anonymat

double-book 1 *vt (seat, room)* réserver pour deux personnes différentes, sur-réserver; **we've been double-booked again** nous sommes encore en double réservation; **I've double-booked myself for next Friday** je me suis engagé à faire deux choses différentes vendredi prochain

2 *vi (of hotel, airline)* faire une/des double(s) réservation(s)

double-booking *n* double réservation *f*

double-bottomed *adj (saucepan, suitcase)* à double fond; *(dinghy)* à double coque

double-breasted [-'brestɪd] *adj* croisé

double-check 1 *vt* revérifier

2 *vi* revérifier

double-click *Comput* **1** *n* double-clic *m*

2 *vt* cliquer deux fois sur, double-cliquer

3 *vi* cliquer deux fois, faire un double-clic

double-clutch *vi Am Aut* faire un double débrayage

double-cross *vt* trahir, doubler; **he double-crossed them** il les a doublés

double-crosser [-'krɒsə(r)] *n* traître(esse) *m,f*, faux jeton *m*

double-date *vi Am* sortir à quatre *(deux couples)*

double-dealer *n* fourbe *m*

double-dealing 1 *n (UNCOUNT)* fourberie *f*, double jeu *m*

2 *adj* fourbe, faux (fausse) comme un jeton

double-decker [-'dekə(r)] *n* (**a**) *Br (bus)* autobus *m* à impériale (**b**) *Am (aircraft)* deux-ponts *m* (**c**) *Fam (sandwich)* club sandwich *m*

double-declutch *vi Br Aut* faire un double débrayage

double-declutching *n Br Aut* double débrayage *m*

double-density *adj Comput (disk)* (à) double densité

double-digit *adj* à deux chiffres; **double-digit inflation** = inflation qui a atteint ou dépassé les 10 pour cent

double-dyed *adj Literary* invétéré; *Fig* **a double-dyed villain** une crapule de la pire espèce

double-edged *adj (blade, knife, sword)* à double tranchant, à deux tranchants; *Fig (compliment, remark)* à double tranchant

double-entry bookkeeping *n Acct* digraphie *f*, comptabilité *f* en partie double

double-faced *adj* (**a**) *(reversible)* réversible, à double face (**b**) *Am (hypocritical)* hypocrite

double-fault *vi* faire une double faute

double-fronted *adj (house)* à deux pignons en façade

double-glaze *vt Br* isoler *(par système de double vitrage)*; **to double-glaze a window** poser un double vitrage

double-glazed *adj Br* à double vitrage

double-glazing *Br* **1** *n (UNCOUNT)* double vitrage *m*; **to put in** *or* **to install double-glazing** installer un double vitrage

2 *comp (salesman)* de double vitrage

double-headed *adj* à deux têtes, *Spec* bicéphale; *TV (programme)* animé par deux présentateurs

▸▸ ***double-headed coin*** pièce *f* de monnaie à deux faces; *Her* ***double-headed eagle*** aigle *f* à deux têtes

double-header *n Am Fam* = deux matchs disputés l'un après l'autre

double-jointed *adj* désarticulé

double-lock *vt* fermer à double tour

double-minded *adj Am (undecided)* hésitant

double-park 1 *vi* se garer *ou* stationner en double file

2 *vt* garer en double file

double-pointed *adj Knitting (needle)* à double pointe

double-quick 1 *adj* très rapide; **in double-quick time** *(move)* au pas de course *ou* de gymnastique; *(finish, work)* en un rien de temps

2 *adv* en un rien de temps

doubles ['dʌbəlz] *(pl* **inv**) *n Sport* double *m*; **to play doubles** jouer un double; **a doubles player** un joueur de double; **ladies'/men's/mixed doubles** double *m* dames/messieurs/mixte

double-sided *adj*

▸▸ *Comput* ***double-sided disk*** disque *m* double face; ***double-sided tape*** bande *f* adhésive double-face

double-space *vt Typ* taper à double interligne; **the text is double-spaced** le texte est à double interligne

double-speak *n* propos *mpl* ambigus *ou* équivoques; **rationalization is just double-speak for more unemployment** rationalisation n'est qu'un euphémisme pour plus de chômage

double-speed *adj Comput (CD-ROM)* double vitesse

double-stitched [-stɪtʃt] *adj* à double couture

double-stop *(pt & pp* **double-stopped,** *cont* **double-stopping**) *vi Mus (on violin)* faire des doubles-cordes

doublet ['dʌblɪt] *n* (**a**) *Hist (jacket)* pourpoint *m*, justaucorps *m*; **doublet and hose** pourpoint *m* et haut-de-chausse *m* (**b**) *(of words)* doublet *m* (**c**) *Typ* doublon *m* (**d**) *(of dice)* doublet *m*

double-talk *n (UNCOUNT) Fam (ambiguous)* = propos ambigus et contournés; *(gibberish)* charabia *m*

doublethink ['dʌbəlˌθɪŋk] *n (UNCOUNT)* = raisonnement de mauvaise foi qui contient des contradictions flagrantes; **it's another case of doublethink** c'est encore un raisonnement pervers

doubleton ['dʌbəltən] *n Cards* doublette *f*

double-tongue *vi Mus* faire des doubles coups de langue *(sur un instrument à vent)*

doubling ['dʌbəlɪŋ] *n (of letter, number)* redoublement *m*, doublement *m*

doubloon [dʌ'bluːn] *n Hist* doublon *m*

doubly ['dʌbəlɪ] *adv (twice as much)* doublement, deux fois plus; *(in two ways)* doublement; **she's doubly careful now** elle redouble de prudence maintenant; *Med* **doubly incontinent** incontinent

doubt [daʊt] **1** *n* (**a**) *(uncertainty → about fact)* doute *m*, incertitude *f*; **there is now considerable doubt about the convictions** on a maintenant de sérieux doutes au sujet des condamnations; **beyond all reasonable doubt** à n'en pas douter, sans le moindre doute; **to raise doubts in sb's mind** soulever des doutes dans l'esprit de qn; **the whole thing raised doubts about his abilities** toute cette affaire a mis ses capacités en question; **to cast doubt on sth** mettre en doute *ou* jeter le doute sur qch; **the report casts doubt on the police evidence** les auteurs du rapport émettent des doutes sur les preuves fournies par la police; **to be in doubt** *(person)* être en *ou* dans le doute; *(future, event)* être douteux *ou* incertain; **her honesty is in doubt** *or* **open to doubt** *(generally)* on a des doutes sur son honnêteté, son honnêteté est sujette à caution; *(this time)* son honnêteté est mise en doute; **we are in no doubt as to his competence** nous n'avons aucun doute sur ses compétences; **the future of the company is in some doubt** l'avenir de l'entreprise est incertain; **if** *or* **when in doubt** s'il y a un doute, en cas de doute; **when in doubt, do nothing** dans le doute, abstiens-toi; **there is some doubt as to whether they paid** on n'est pas certain qu'ils aient payé; **there is no doubt about it** cela ne fait pas de doute; **there's no doubt (but) that it will be a difficult journey** il n'y a pas de doute que le voyage sera pénible; **no doubt** sans doute; **he'll no doubt be late** il sera sûrement en retard; **there is room for doubt** il est permis de douter; **without (any) doubt** sans aucun *ou* le moindre doute

(**b**) *(feeling of distrust)* doute *m*; **I have my doubts about him** j'ai des doutes sur lui *ou* à son sujet; **she has her doubts (about) whether it's true** elle doute que cela soit vrai; **I have no doubt** *or* **doubts about it** je n'en doute pas

2 *vt* (**a**) *(consider unlikely)* **I doubt (whether) she'll be there** je doute qu'elle soit là; **she'll be there – I don't doubt it** elle sera là – je n'en doute pas *ou* j'en suis certain; **I doubt it** j'en doute; **I never once doubted that they would succeed** je n'ai pas douté une seule fois qu'ils réussiraient; **I doubt if it makes him happy** je doute que cela le rende heureux

(**b**) *(distrust)* douter de; **there was no doubting their sincerity** on ne pouvait pas mettre en doute leur sincérité; **she began to doubt the evidence of her own eyes** elle n'en croyait pas ses yeux

3 *vi (have doubts)* douter, avoir des doutes

doubter ['daʊtə(r)] *n* incrédule *mf*, sceptique *mf*

doubtful ['daʊtfʊl] *adj* (**a**) *(unlikely)* improbable, douteux

(**b**) *(uncertain → person)* incertain, indécis; **to be doubtful of** *or* **about sth** avoir des doutes sur qch; **I'm doubtful about his chances** je doute de *ou* j'ai des doutes sur ses chances; **we're doubtful about accepting** nous hésitons à accepter; **it's doubtful whether they're really serious** il est douteux qu'ils soient vraiment sérieux, on ne sait pas s'ils sont vraiment sérieux; **she looked doubtful** elle avait l'air peu convaincu

(**c**) *(questionable → answer, results)* douteux, discutable

(**d**) *(dubious → person)* louche, suspect; *(affair)* douteux, louche; **a joke in doubtful taste** une plaisanterie d'un goût douteux

▸▸ *Fin* ***doubtful debt*** client *m* douteux, créance *f* douteuse; ***doubtful loan*** prêt *m* douteux

doubtfully ['daʊtfʊlɪ] *adv (uncertainly)* avec doute, d'un air de doute; *(indecisively)* avec hésitation, de façon indécise

doubtfulness ['daʊtfʊlnɪs] *n* (**a**) *(uncertainty)* incertitude *f*; *(hesitation)* indécision *f* (**b**) *(dubiousness)* caractère *m* équivoque *ou* douteux

doubting ['daʊtɪŋ] *adj* sceptique, incrédule

▸▸ ***doubting Thomas*** Thomas *m* l'incrédule; **don't be such a doubting Thomas** ne fais pas l'incrédule, ne fais pas comme saint Thomas

doubtless ['daʊtlɪs], **doubtlessly** ['daʊtlɪslɪ] *adv (certainly)* sans aucun *ou* le moindre doute; *(probably)* (très) probablement

douche [duːʃ] *Med* **1** *n* lavage *m* interne, douche *f*; *(instrument)* poire *f* à injections

2 *vt* doucher

dou-dou

dough [dəʊ] *n* (**a**) *Culin* pâte *f*; **bread dough** pâte *f* à pain (**b**) *Fam (money)* blé *m*

doughboy ['dəʊ,bɔɪ] *n* (**a**) *Culin* boulette *f* (de pâte) (**b**) *Am Fam Mil slang* sammy *m (soldat américain de la Première Guerre mondiale)*

doughiness ['dəʊɪnɪs] *n* (**a**) *(consistency)* consistance *f* pâteuse; *(of bread)* mauvaise cuisson *f* (**b**) *(of complexion)* aspect *m* terreux; **the doughiness of her complexion suggested an unhealthy diet** son teint terreux était le signe d'une mauvaise hygiène alimentaire

doughnut ['dəʊnʌt] **1** *n* beignet *m*, *Can* beigne *m*; **jam doughnut** beignet *m* à la confiture

2 *vi Br Parl (surround speaker)* = à la Chambre des communes ou des lords, faire bloc autour d'un orateur lors d'une session filmée, pour créer l'illusion soit d'une solidarité, soit d'une fréquentation assidue

doughtily ['daʊtɪlɪ] *adv Literary* vaillamment

doughtiness ['daʊtɪnɪs] *n Literary* vaillance *f*

doughty ['daʊtɪ] *(compar* **doughtier,** *superl* **doughtiest**) *adj Literary* vaillant

doughy ['dəʊɪ] *(compar* **doughier,** *superl* **doughiest**) *adj* (**a**) *(consistency)* pâteux; *(bread)* mal cuit (**b**) *(complexion)* terreux

dour [dʊə(r)] *adj (sullen)* renfrogné; *(stern)* austère, dur

dourly ['dʊəlɪ] *adv (look)* d'un air renfrogné; *(say)* d'un ton maussade

dourness ['dʊənɪs] *n* maussaderie *f*; **the dourness of his expression** son air renfrogné

douse [daʊs] *vt* (**a**) *(extinguish → light, fire)* éteindre (**b**) *(drench)* tremper, inonder; *(plunge)* plonger, tremper; **he doused himself with** *or* **in aftershave** il s'est aspergé d'après-rasage

dove¹ [dʌv] *n* (**a**) *(bird)* colombe *f*; **ring dove** (pigeon *m*) ramier *m*, palombe *f*; **dove of peace** colombe *f* de la paix (**b**) *Pol* colombe *f*; **the doves and the hawks** les colombes *fpl* et les faucons *mpl*

►► *Bot* ***dove's foot crane's bill*** géranium *m* mou

dove² [dəʊv] *Am pt of* **dive**

dovecot, dovecote ['dʌvkɒt] *n* colombier *m*, pigeonnier *m*

dove-grey *adj* gris perle *(inv)*

Dover ['dəʊvə(r)] *n* Douvres; **the Strait of Dover** le pas de Calais

►► ***Dover sole*** sole *f*

dovetail ['dʌvteɪl] **1** *vt* (**a**) *Tech* assembler à queue d'aronde

(**b**) *Fig (combine)* faire concorder, raccorder; **he managed to dovetail his plans with hers** il s'est débrouillé pour accorder *ou* faire concorder ses projets avec les siens

2 *vi* (**a**) *Tech* se raccorder; **to dovetail into** se raccorder à

(**b**) *Fig (combine)* bien cadrer, concorder; **the two projects dovetail nicely** les deux projets se rejoignent parfaitement

3 *n Tech* queue-d'aronde *f*

►► *Tech* ***dovetail joint*** assemblage *m* à queue-d'aronde

dovish ['dʌvɪʃ] *adj esp Am Pol (person)* partisan de la manière douce; *(speech)* conciliateur

dowager ['daʊədʒə(r)] *n* douairière *f*; **the dowager duchess** la duchesse douairière

►► ***dowager's hump*** déformation *f* ostéoporotique postménopausique, bosse *f* de sorcière

dowdily ['daʊdɪlɪ] *adv* de façon démodée

dowdiness ['daʊdɪnɪs] *n* manque *m* d'élégance *ou* de distinction

dowdy ['daʊdɪ] *(compar* **dowdier,** *superl* **dowdiest,** *pl* **dowdies**) **1** *adj (person)* sans chic, inélégant; *(dress)* peu flatteur, sans chic

2 *n Old-fashioned* femme *f* sans chic

dowel ['daʊəl] *vt Carp* assembler avec des goujons, goujonner

►► ***dowel pin*** cheville *f* en bois, goujon *m*

dowelling ['daʊəlɪŋ] *n Carp* (**a**) *(act)* assemblage *m* à goujons, goujonnage *m* (**b**) *(wood)* tourillon *m*

dower ['daʊə(r)] **1** *n* (**a**) *(of widow)* douaire *m* (**b**) *Arch or Literary (dowry)* dot *f* (**c**) *Literary (gift, talent)* don *m*, apanage *m*

2 *vt* (**a**) *(widow)* assigner un douaire à (**b**) *Arch or Literary (give a dowry to)* doter (**c**) *Literary (gifted, talented)* doué; **dowered with the most brilliant talents** doué des plus brillantes qualités

►► *Br* ***dower house*** petit manoir *m* (de douairière)

dowerless ['daʊəlɪs] *adj* (**a**) *(widow)* sans douaire (**b**) *Arch or Literary (without a dowry)* sans dot

Dow-Jones [,daʊ'dʒəʊnz] *n Am St Exch* l'indice *m* Dow Jones

►► ***the Dow-Jones average, the Dow Jones index*** l'indice *m* Dow Jones

DOWN¹ [daʊn]

en bas de	► 1 (b)
le long de	► 1 (c)
à travers	► 1 (d)
en bas	► 2 (a), (b)
vers le bas	► 2 (a), (c)
en panne	► 2 (h)
déprimé	► 3 (a)
mettre à terre	► 4 (a)
descendre	► 4 (b)

1 *prep* (**a**) *(towards lower level of)* **a line down the middle of the page** une ligne verticale au milieu de la page; **to go down the steps/the escalator/the mountain** descendre l'escalier/l'escalier mécanique/la montagne; **she fell down the stairs** elle est tombée dans l'escalier; **tears ran down her face** des larmes coulaient le long de son visage; **her hair hung down her back** les cheveux lui tombaient dans le dos; **to go down the plughole** passer par le trou (de l'évier/de la baignoire/*etc*); **the rabbit disappeared back down its hole** le lapin a redisparu dans son trou

(**b**) *(at lower level of)* en bas de; **it's down the stairs** c'est en bas de l'escalier; **to work down a mine** travailler au fond d'une mine; **they live down the street** ils habitent plus loin *ou* plus bas dans la rue

(**c**) *(along)* le long de; **he walked down the street** il a descendu la rue; **look down the corridor** regardez le long du couloir; **down the side of his trousers/the box** le long de son pantalon/de la boîte

(**d**) *(through)* à travers; **down (through) the ages** à travers les âges

(**e**) *Br Fam (to)* à ❑; **they went down the shops** ils sont partis faire des courses

2 *adv* (**a**) *(downwards)* vers le bas, en bas; **down!** *(to dog)* couché!, bas les pattes!; **down and down** de plus en plus bas; **to come** *or* **go down** descendre; **my trousers keep slipping down** mon pantalon n'arrête pas de descendre *ou* tomber

(**b**) *(on lower level)* en bas; **down at the bottom of the hill/page** en bas de la colline/de la page; **down there** là-bas; **I'm down here** je suis ici en bas; **she lives three floors down** elle habite trois étages plus bas; **his office is three doors down on the left** *(along passage)* son bureau est trois portes plus loin sur la gauche; **the blinds are down** les stores sont baissés; **the river is down** la rivière est basse; **I'll be down in a minute** *(downstairs)* je descends dans un instant; **they aren't down yet** ils ne sont pas encore descendus; *(on the ground or floor)* à terre; **he was down for a count of eight** il est resté à terre le temps de compter jusqu'à huit

(**c**) *(facing downwards)* vers le bas, dessous; **he was lying face down** il était couché sur le ventre; **smooth side down** le côté lisse dessous

(**d**) *(reduced, lower)* **prices are down** les prix ont baissé; *Fin* **the pound is down two cents against the dollar** la livre a baissé de deux cents par rapport au dollar

(**e**) *(below expected, desired level)* **the tyres are down** *(underinflated)* les pneus sont dégonflés; *(flat)* les pneus sont à plat; **the cashier is £10 down** il manque 10 livres au caissier; **bookings are down on last week's** les réservations sont en baisse par rapport à la semaine dernière; *Ftbl* **we were two goals down at half-time** on avait deux buts de retard à la mi-temps

(**f**) *(on paper)* **get it down in writing** *or* **on paper** mettez-le par écrit; **it's down in my diary/on the calendar** c'est dans mon agenda/sur le calendrier; **he's down to speak at the conference** il est inscrit en tant qu'intervenant à la conférence

(**g**) *(from city, the north)* **she came down from Berlin** elle est arrivée de Berlin; **we're going down south** nous descendons vers le sud; **they're going down to the coast** ils descendent sur la côte; *Am* **to go down East** aller au nord-est de la Nouvelle-Angleterre; *Br Univ* **she came down from Oxford** *(on vacation)* elle est descendue d'Oxford; *(graduated)* elle est sortie d'Oxford; *Fam* **to go/to live down under** *(gen)* aller/vivre aux antipodes ❑; *(to Australia)* aller/vivre en Australie ❑; *(to New Zealand)* aller/vivre en Nouvelle-Zélande ❑

(**h**) *(out of action → machine, computer)* en panne; **the wires are down** les lignes sont coupées; **the computer has gone down** l'ordinateur est tombé en panne

(**i**) *(paid)* **he paid** *or* **put £5 down** *(whole amount)* il a payé 5 livres comptant; *(as deposit)* il a versé (un acompte de) 5 livres; **5 down and 3 to go** ça fait 5, il en reste 3

(**j**) *(ill)* **he's (gone) down with flu** il est au lit avec la grippe

(**k**) *(idioms) Fam* **to be down on sb** être monté contre qn ❑; **down with...!** à bas...!; **down with the system!** à bas le système!; **down with it!** *(of medicine etc)* avalez!

3 *adj* (**a**) *(depressed)* déprimé, malheureux; **to feel down** avoir le cafard

(**b**) *Br (train)* = en provenance d'une grande ville

(**c**) *(elevator)* qui descend

(**d**) *(critical)* **to be down on sb** être dur *ou* sévère avec qn

4 *vt* (**a**) *(knock down → opponent)* mettre à terre; *(→ object, target)* faire tomber; **the pilot downed two enemy aircraft** le pilote a descendu deux avions ennemis

(**b**) *(drink)* descendre; *(eat)* avaler; **he downed three beers** il a descendu trois bières

5 *n* (**a**) *(setback)* revers *m*, bas *m*

(**b**) *(in American football)* = chacune des quatre tentatives pour avancer d'au moins 10 yards, au football américain; **first down** premier "down"

(**c**) *Fam (idiom)* **to have a down on sb** avoir une dent contre qn

6 down for *prep* **she's down for physics** elle est inscrite au cours de physique; **they've got me down for the 200m hurdles** ils m'ont inscrit au 200m haies; **the meeting is down for today** la réunion est prévue pour aujourd'hui

7 down to *prep* (**a**) *(through to and including)* jusqu'à; **down to the smallest details** jusqu'aux moindres détails; **she sold everything right down to the house** elle a tout vendu, y compris la maison; **from the richest down to the poorest** du plus riche (jusqu') au plus pauvre; **from the boss down to the office boy** depuis le patron jusqu'au garçon de bureau; **from the Middle Ages down to the present** du *ou* depuis le Moyen Âge jusqu'à nos jours

(**b**) *(reduced to)* **I'm down to my last pound** il ne me reste qu'une livre; **the team was down to 10 men** l'équipe était réduite à 10 hommes

(**c**) *(indicating responsibility)* **it's down to you now** c'est à toi de jouer maintenant; **any breakages will be down to you** si vous cassez quelque chose, c'est vous qui paierez les dégâts

►► *Comput* ***down arrow*** flèche *f* vers le bas; *Comput* ***down arrow key*** touche *f* de déplacement vers le bas; *Fin* ***down payment*** acompte *m*; **to make a down payment on sth** verser un acompte pour qch; **he made a down payment of £500** il a versé un acompte de 500 livres

'Down by Law' *Jarmusch* 'Sous le coup de la loi'

down² *n* (**a**) *(on bird, person, plant, fruit)* duvet *m* (**b**) *(hill)* colline *f* dénudée; *(sand dune)* dune *f*

down-and-out 1 *adj* indigent, sans ressources

2 *n* clochard(e) *m,f*; **the down-and-out** *or* **down-and-outs** les sans-abri *mpl*

'Down and Out in Paris and London' *Orwell* 'Dans la dèche à Paris et à Londres'

down-at-heel *adj* (**a**) *(person)* miteux (**b**) *(shoe)* éculé

downbeat ['daʊnbiːt] **1** *n Mus* temps *m* frappé
 2 *adj* (**a**) *(gloomy → person)* abattu, triste; *(→ story)* pessimiste (**b**) *(relaxed → person)* décontracté, flegmatique; *(→ situation)* décontracté

downcast ['daʊnkɑːst] **1** *adj* (**a**) *(person)* abattu, démoralisé (**b**) *(eyes, look)* baissé
 2 *n Mining* puits *m* d'aérage

downcourt [ˌdaʊn'kɔːt] *adv Sport (in basketball, netball)* dans/vers son camp; **to move the ball downcourt** faire passer la balle dans son camp

downdraught, *Am* **downdraft** ['daʊndrɑːft] *n Met* courant *m* d'air descendant
 ►► *Aut* ***downdraught carburettor*** carburateur *m* inversé

downer ['daʊnə(r)] *n* (**a**) *Fam (experience)* expérience *f* déprimante ☐; **to be on a downer** avoir le cafard, être déprimé ☐; **that film's a real downer** ce film est à vous donner le cafard; **it was a real downer to find out I hadn't even got an interview** ça m'a mis le moral complètement à zéro de savoir que je n'avais même pas obtenu d'entretien (**b**) *Fam (drug)* tranquillisant ☐ *m*, sédatif ☐ *m*

downfall ['daʊnfɔːl] *n* (**a**) *(of person, institution)* chute *f*, ruine *f*; *(of dream, hopes)* effondrement *m*; *(of government)* écroulement *m*, effondrement *m*; **drink was his downfall** la boisson l'a perdu (**b**) *(of rain, snow)* chute *f*

downgrade ['daʊngreɪd] **1** *vt* (**a**) *(job)* déclasser; *(employee)* rétrograder; *(hotel)* déclasser; *(goods)* classer dans une catégorie inférieure; **he was downgraded to area manager** il a été rétrogradé au rang de responsable régional; **the hurricane has been downgraded to a storm** l'ouragan n'est maintenant plus qu'une tempête
 (**b**) *(devalue → role, status, significance)* dévaloriser
 (**c**) *(belittle)* rabaisser
 2 *n* descente *f*

downgrading [ˌdaʊnˌgreɪdɪŋ] *n* (**a**) *(of job)* déclassement *m*; *(of employee)* déclassement *m* à une échelle de salaire inférieure, rétrogradation *f*; *(of hotel)* déclassement *m*; *(of goods)* classement *m* dans une catégorie inférieure (**b**) *(devaluing → of role, status, significance)* dévalorisation *f*

downhearted [ˌdaʊn'hɑːtɪd] *adj* abattu, découragé; **don't be downhearted!** ne te décourage pas!, ne te laisse pas abattre!

downheartedly [ˌdaʊn'hɑːtɪdlɪ] *adv* avec découragement

downheartedness [ˌdaʊn'hɑːtɪdnɪs] *n* abattement *m*, découragement *m*

downhill [ˌdaʊn'hɪl] **1** *adv* **to go downhill** *(car, road)* descendre, aller en descendant; *(business)* péricliter; *Fig* se dégrader; **television is going rapidly downhill** la télévision baisse *ou* se dégrade de plus en plus; **he let himself go downhill after he lost his job** il a dégringolé *ou* il s'est laissé aller après avoir perdu son travail; **her health went rapidly downhill** sa santé déclina *ou* baissa rapidement
 2 *adj (road)* en pente, incliné; *(walk)* en descente; **once you get to 40, it's downhill all the way** passé la quarantaine, vous ne faites plus que décliner; **it should all be downhill from now on** *(be easy)* maintenant ça devrait aller comme sur des roulettes
 3 *n* (**a**) *(of road)* descente *f*
 (**b**) *Ski* descente *f*
 ►► *Ski* ***downhill race*** descente *f*; ***downhill racer, downhill skier*** descendeur(euse) *m,f*; ***downhill skiing*** ski *m* alpin

down-home *adj Am Fam* (des États) du Sud ☐; *Pej* plouc

downie ['daʊnɪ] *n (duvet)* couette *f*

downiness ['daʊnɪnɪs] *n (of leaf, skin)* duveté *m*; *(of fruit)* duveté *m*, velouté *m*

Downing Street ['daʊnɪŋ-] *n* Downing Street, = rue de Londres où se trouve la résidence officielle du Premier ministre britannique; **there has been no confirmation from Downing Street** le Premier ministre n'a pas apporté de confirmation

DOWNING STREET

C'est à Downing Street à Londres que se trouvent les résidences officielles du Premier ministre, au n° 10, et du ministre des Finances, au n° 11. Le terme "Downing Street" est souvent employé pour désigner le gouvernement.

DOWNING STREET DECLARATION

La déclaration de Downing Street est une déclaration faite conjointement en 1993 par le Premier ministre britannique John Major et son homologue irlandais Albert Reynolds. Les deux chefs d'État s'engagèrent à négocier avec les différents groupes impliqués dans le conflit d'Irlande du Nord à condition que ces derniers déposent les armes. La déclaration fut suivie d'un cessez-le-feu entre les groupes paramilitaires protestants et catholiques et a été déterminante dans le processus de paix qui aboutit au **Good Friday Agreement** (voir encadré) de 1998.

down-in-the-mouth *adj Br* **to be down-in-the-mouth** être abattu; **she looks down-in-the-mouth** elle a l'air plutôt abattue

downland ['daʊnlænd] *n (UNCOUNT)* collines *fpl* herbeuses

download ['daʊnləʊd] *Comput* **1** *n* téléchargement *m*
 2 *vt* télécharger
 3 *vi* effectuer un téléchargement; **graphic files take a long time to download** le téléchargement de fichiers graphiques est très lent

downloadable [ˌdaʊn'ləʊdəbəl] *adj Comput* téléchargeable; **downloadable font** police *f* téléchargeable

downloading [ˌdaʊn'ləʊdɪŋ] *n Comput* téléchargement *m*

down-low *n Am Fam* **on the down-low** *(confidential)* confidentiel ☐; **I'm telling you this on the down-low** je te dis ça, mais c'est entre nous

downmarket ['daʊnˌmɑːkɪt] **1** *adj (product, car)* bas de gamme; *(book)* grande diffusion *(inv)*; **it's a rather downmarket area** ce n'est pas un quartier très chic
 2 *adv* **to move downmarket** passer au bas de gamme

downpipe ['daʊnpaɪp] *n Br Constr* (tuyau *m* de) descente *f*

downplay ['daʊnpleɪ] *vt (event, person)* minimiser l'importance de; *(situation)* dédramatiser

downpour ['daʊnpɔː(r)] *n* averse *f*, déluge *m*

downright ['daʊnraɪt] **1** *adj* (**a**) *(complete → lie)* effronté, flagrant; *(→ refusal)* catégorique; **downright stupidity** bêtise crasse; **a downright fool** un crétin achevé (**b**) *(blunt, frank → person, speech)* franc (franche), direct
 2 *adv (as intensifier)* franchement, carrément; **the sales assistant was downright rude** la vendeuse a été franchement grossière

downriver [ˌdaʊn'rɪvə(r)] **1** *adj* (situé) en aval
 2 *adv (move)* vers l'aval; *(live)* en aval

Downs [daʊnz] *npl Br* **the Downs** les Downs *fpl*; **the South/North Downs** les Downs du Sud/du Nord

Down's [daʊnz] *Fam* = **Down's Syndrome**

downshift [ˌdaʊn'ʃɪft] *vi* (**a**) *Am Aut (change gear)* rétrograder (**b**) *(change lifestyle)* travailler moins pour mieux profiter de la vie

downshifting [ˌdaʊn'ʃɪftɪŋ] *n* = adoption d'un style de vie où le travail et l'argent passent après le temps libre

downside ['daʊnsaɪd] *n* (**a**) *(underside)* dessous *m*; *Am* **downside up** sens dessous dessus
 (**b**) *(trend)* **prices have tended to be on the downside** la tendance des prix est plutôt à la baisse
 (**c**) *(disadvantage)* inconvénient *m*; **there's a downside to everything** toute médaille a son revers; **on the downside, however, the situation has worsened in the South** mais par contre la situation a empiré dans le sud; **on the downside, we'll have to sleep in the train** le désavantage, c'est que nous devrons dormir dans le train
 ►► *St Exch* ***downside potential*** potentiel *m* de baisse; *St Exch* ***downside risk*** risque *m* de baisse

downsize ['daʊnsaɪz] **1** *vi (of company)* réduire ses effectifs
 2 *vt* (**a**) *(company)* réduire les effectifs de; *Suisse* redimensionner; *(project)* réduire l'envergure de (**b**) *(of designers → car)* réduire les dimensions de (**c**) *Comput* micromiser

downsizing ['daʊnsaɪzɪŋ] *n* (**a**) *(of company)* réduction *f* d'effectifs; *Suisse* redimensionnement *m* (**b**) *Comput* micromisation *f*

downslope 1 *n* ['daʊnsləʊp] pente *f* descendante
 2 *adv* [ˌdaʊn'sləʊp] en descendant

downspout ['daʊnspaʊt] *n Am* (tuyau *m* de) descente *f*

Down's syndrome [daʊnz-] *n* trisomie 21 *f*; **Down's syndrome baby** bébé *m* trisomique

downstage [ˌdaʊn'steɪdʒ] **1** *adj* du devant de la scène
 2 *adv* vers le devant de la scène; **downstage from her** vers le devant de la scène par rapport à elle; **to stand downstage of sb** se tenir plus en avant que qn sur la scène
 3 *n* avant-scène *f*

downstairs 1 *adv* [ˌdaʊn'steəz] (**a**) *(gen)* en bas (de l'escalier); **to come** *or* **to go downstairs** descendre (les escaliers); **she ran downstairs** elle a descendu l'escalier *ou* elle est descendue en courant; **he fell downstairs** il a dégringolé l'escalier
 (**b**) *(on lower floor)* à l'étage en dessous *ou* inférieur; *(on ground floor)* au rez-de-chaussée; **the family downstairs** la famille du dessous
 (**c**) *(in the servants' quarters)* chez les domestiques
 2 *adj* ['daʊnˌsteəz] (**a**) *(gen)* en bas; **I'm using the downstairs phone** j'utilise le téléphone d'en bas
 (**b**) *(of lower floor)* de l'étage au-dessous *ou* inférieur; *(of ground floor)* du rez-de-chaussée
 3 *n* ['daʊnˌsteəz] (**a**) **the downstairs** *(ground floor)* le rez-de-chaussée; *(lower floors)* les étages *fpl* inférieures
 (**b**) *(servants)* les domestiques *mpl*

downstate ['daʊnsteɪt] *Am* **1** *adj (in the country)* de la campagne; *(in the south)* du sud de l'État; **in downstate New York** dans le sud de l'État de New York
 2 *adv (go)* vers le sud; *(be)* dans le sud
 3 *n* campagne *f*, sud *m* de l'État

downstream 1 *adv* [ˌdaʊn'striːm] (**a**) *(live)* en aval; *(move)* vers l'aval; **the boat drifted downstream** le bateau était poussé par le courant (**b**) *Econ* en aval
 2 *adj* ['daʊnˌstriːm] (**a**) *(gen)* (situé) en aval (**b**) *Econ* en aval
 ►► *Petr* ***downstream operations*** opérations *fpl* en aval

downstroke ['daʊnstrəʊk] *n* (**a**) *Tech (of piston)* course *f* descendante (**b**) *(in handwriting)* plein *m* (**c**) *Orn (of wing)* abaissée *f*

downswept ['daʊnswept] *adj* surbaissé

downswing ['daʊnswɪŋ] *n* (**a**) *(trend)* tendance *f* à la baisse, baisse *f* (**b**) *Golf* mouvement *m* descendant

down-the-line 1 *adj (ballerina)* qui n'occupe qu'une place secondaire dans le corps de ballet
 2 *adv (in tennis)* **to go down-the-line** renvoyer la balle dans un axe perpendiculaire au filet

downtime ['daʊntaɪm] *n (UNCOUNT) Ind* période *f* de non-fonctionnement *(d'une machine, d'une usine)*; *Comput* période *f* de non-productivité

down-to-earth *adj (direct)* direct; *(unpretentious)* simple; **he's very down-to-earth** *(practical)* il a les pieds sur terre

downtown *Am* **1** *n* [ˌdaʊn'taʊn] centre-ville *m*
 2 *adj* ['daʊnˌtaʊn] **downtown New York** le centre *ou* centre-ville de New York; **downtown theatres** théâtres *mpl* du centre-ville
 3 *adv* [ˌdaʊn'taʊn] en ville; **to live downtown** habiter en ville; **he gave me a lift downtown** il m'a descendu en ville

downtrend ['daʊntrend] *n* baisse *f*

downtrodden ['daʊnˌtrɒdən] *adj* (**a**) *(person)* opprimé (**b**) *(grass)* piétiné

downturn ['daʊntɜːn] *n (in inflation, unemployment figures)* baisse *f*; *(in economy)* ralentissement *m*

downward ['daʊnwəd] **1** *adj (movement)* vers le bas; *(path)* descendant; **to take a downward**

dow–dow

glance *or* **look at sth** jeter un coup d'œil par en dessous à qch; *Fig* **a downward trend** une tendance à la baisse; **the economy is on a downward path** l'économie est sur une mauvaise pente

2 *adv* = **downwards**

downward-compatible *adj Comput* compatible vers le bas

downwards ['daʊnwədz] *adv* vers le bas, de haut en bas; *(on river)* en aval; *(look)* en bas; **she put the letter face downwards** elle a posé la lettre à l'envers; **the garden slopes downwards away from the house** le jardin descend en pente depuis la maison; **the road drops sharply downwards** la route descend brusquement; *Fig* **everyone from the president downwards** tout le monde depuis le président jusqu'en bas de la hiérarchie; **from the Middle Ages downwards** depuis le Moyen Âge; **we will have to revise our estimates downwards** il faudra que nous revoyions nos estimations à la baisse; **prices started to spiral downwards** les prix commencèrent à dégringoler

downwash ['daʊnwɒʃ] *n* déflexion *f* vers le bas

downwind [ˌdaʊn'wɪnd] *adv* sous le vent; **to sail downwind** naviguer sous le vent; **to be downwind of sth** être sous le vent de qch

downy ['daʊnɪ] *(compar* **downier,** *superl* **downiest)** *adj* **(a)** *(leaf, skin)* couvert de duvet, duveté; *(fruit)* duveté, velouté **(b)** *(fluffy)* duveteux **(c)** *(filled with down)* garni de duvet

dowry ['daʊərɪ] *(pl* **dowries)** *n* **(a)** *(money, property)* dot *f* **(b)** *Literary (gift, talent)* don *m*, apanage *m*

dowse [daʊz] **1** *vt* **(a)** *(extinguish → light, fire)* éteindre **(b)** *(drench)* tremper, inonder; *(plunge)* plonger, tremper; **he dowsed himself with** *or* **in aftershave** il s'est aspergé d'après-rasage

2 *vi (for water, for minerals)* faire de la radiesthésie, prospecter à la baguette

dowser ['daʊzə(r)] *n (for water)* sourcier *m*, radiesthésiste *mf*; *(for minerals)* radiesthésiste *mf*

dowsing ['daʊzɪŋ] *n* radiesthésie *f*

►► ***dowsing rod*** baguette *f* (de sourcier)

doxographer [dɒk'sɒgrəfə(r)] *n* doxographe *m*

doxographic [ˌdɒksə'græfɪk], **doxographical** [ˌdɒksə'græfɪkəl] *adj* doxographique

doxography [dɒk'sɒgrəfɪ] *n* doxographie *f*

doxological [ˌdɒksə'lɒdʒɪkəl] *adj* doxologique

doxology [dɒk'sɒlədʒɪ] *n Rel* doxologie *f*

doxy ['dɒksɪ] *(pl* **doxies)** *n* **(a)** *(doctrine)* doctrine *f* **(b)** *Fam Arch (prostitute)* catin *f*; *(mistress)* maîtresse ❑ *f*

doyen ['dɔɪən] *n* doyen *m* (d'âge)

doyenne ['dɔɪen] *n* doyenne *f* (d'âge)

doyly *(pl* **doylies)** = **doily**

doz. *(written abbr* **dozen)** douz

doze [dəʊz] **1** *vi* sommeiller

2 *n* somme *m*; **to have a doze** faire un petit somme

►**doze off** *vi* s'assoupir

dozen ['dʌzən] *n* douzaine *f*; **a dozen eggs** une douzaine d'œufs; **30 pence a dozen** 30 pence la douzaine; **half a dozen** une demi-douzaine; **have some more, there are dozens of them** reprenez-en, il y en a beaucoup *ou* des tas; **I've told you a dozen times!** je te l'ai déjà dit vingt fois!; **dozens and dozens of times** maintes et maintes fois; **there are dozens of men like him** des hommes comme lui, on en trouve à la douzaine

dozenth ['dʌzənθ] *adj* douzième; **for the dozenth time** pour la douzième fois

dozer ['dəʊzə(r)] *n Br Fam* bulldozer *m*, *Offic* bouteur *m*

dozily ['dəʊzɪlɪ] *adv (watch)* d'un œil somnolent; *(say, answer)* d'une voix endormie

doziness ['dəʊzɪnɪs] *n* **(a)** *(drowsiness)* somnolence *f* **(b)** *Br Fam (stupidity)* bêtise ❑ *f*

dozy ['dəʊzɪ] *(compar* **dozier,** *superl* **doziest)** *adj* **(a)** *(drowsy)* à moitié endormi, assoupi; **to feel dozy** avoir envie de dormir **(b)** *Br Fam (stupid)* lent ❑, engourdi

DP [ˌdiː'piː] *n* **(a)** *Comput (abbr* **data processing)** TD *m* **(b)** *(abbr* **disabled person)** handicapé(e) *m,f*

DPH [ˌdiːpiː'eɪtʃ] *n (abbr* **Diploma in Public Health)** diplôme *m* de santé publique

DPh [ˌdiːpiː'eɪtʃ] *n (abbr* **Doctor of Philosophy)** *(person)* = titulaire d'un doctorat de 3ème cycle; *(qualification)* = doctorat de 3ème cycle

DPhil [ˌdiː'fɪl] *n (abbr* **Doctor of Philosophy)** *(person)* = titulaire d'un doctorat de 3ème cycle; *(qualification)* = doctorat de 3ème cycle

dpi [ˌdiːpiː'aɪ] *Comput (abbr* **dots per inch)** dpi, ppp

DPP [ˌdiːpiː'piː] *n Br Law (abbr* **Director of Public Prosecutions)** ≃ procureur *m* général

DPT [ˌdiːpiː'tiː] *n Med (abbr* **diphtheria, pertussis, tetanus)** DCT *m*

dpt *(written abbr* **department)** service *m*

DPW [ˌdiːpiː'dʌbəljuː] *n Br Admin (abbr* **Department of Public Works)** ≃ ministère *m* de l'Équipement

Dr **(a)** *(written abbr* **Doctor) Dr Jones** *(on envelope)* Dr Jones; **Dear Dr Jones** *(in letter)* Monsieur, Madame; *(less formal)* Cher Monsieur, Chère Madame; *(if acquainted)* Cher Docteur **(b)** *(written abbr* **drive)** allée *f*

dr **(a)** *(written abbr* **debtor)** débiteur(trice) *m,f* **(b)** *(written abbr* **dram)** drachme *m* **(c)** *(written abbr* **drachma)** drachme *f*

drab [dræb] *(compar* **drabber,** *superl* **drabbest) 1** *adj* **(a)** *(colour)* terne, fade; *(surroundings)* morne, triste; *(existence)* terne, monotone; *(person)* insignifiant **(b)** *(shabby)* miteux

2 *n* **(a)** *(colour)* gris-vert *m*, gris-beige *m* **(b)** *(cloth)* grosse toile *f* bise **(c)** *Arch Pej (woman)* souillon *f*

drabble ['dræbəl] **1** *vt* salir, crotter

2 *vi* devenir sale, se salir, se crotter

drably ['dræblɪ] *adv* de façon terne; **drably coloured** aux couleurs ternes *ou* mornes

drabness ['dræbnɪs] *n (of colour)* caractère *m ou* aspect *m* terne, fadeur *f*; *(of surroundings)* caractère *m ou* aspect *m* morne, tristesse *f*, grisaille *f*

drachm [dræm] *n* **(a)** *(gen) & Pharm* drachme *m* **(b)** *(currency)* drachme *f*

drachma ['drækmə] *(pl* **drachmas** *or* **drachmae** [-miː]) *n (currency)* drachme *f*

draconian [drə'kəʊnɪən] *adj* draconien

Dracula ['drækjʊlə] *pr n* Dracula

'Dracula, Prince of Darkness' *Fisher* 'Dracula, prince des ténèbres'

draft¹ [drɑːft] **1** *n* **(a)** *(of letter)* brouillon *m*; *(of novel, speech)* premier jet *m*, ébauche *f*; *(of plan, treaty)* avant-projet *m*; **this is only the first draft** ceci n'est qu'une ébauche; **the first draft of a novel** le premier jet d'un roman

(b) *Com & Fin* traite *f*, effet *m*; **a draft on my bank in England for £500** une traite de 500 livres sur ma banque en Angleterre

(c) *Mil (detachment → of troops)* détachement *m*; *(→ of recruits)* contingent *m*

(d) *Am Mil* conscription *f*; **he left in order to avoid the draft** il est parti pour éviter de faire son service

(e) *Am (beer)* pression *f*

2 *vt* **(a)** *(draw up → first version)* faire le brouillon de, rédiger; *(→ diagram)* dresser; *(→ plan)* esquisser, dresser; *Law (→ contract, will)* rédiger, dresser; *(→ bill)* préparer

(b) *(recruit)* détacher, désigner; **to draft sb to sth/to do sth** détacher qn à qch/pour faire qch

(c) *Am Mil (enlist)* appeler (sous les drapeaux), incorporer; **he was drafted into the army** il fut appelé sous les drapeaux

(d) *Austr & NZ (cattle, sheep)* trier

(e) *(in stonework)* appareiller

3 *comp (agreement)* préliminaire

►► *Am Mil* ***draft board*** conseil *m* de révision; ***draft budget*** projet *m* de budget; *Am Mil* ***draft card*** ordre *m* d'incorporation; *Am Mil* ***draft dodger*** réfractaire *m*; *Am Mil* ***draft dodging*** insoumission *f*; ***draft letter*** *(gen)* brouillon *m* de lettre; *(formal)* projet *m* de lettre; *Br Comput* ***draft mode*** mode *m* rapide *ou* brouillon; *Comput* ***draft printout*** brouillon *m*; *Br Comput* ***draft quality*** qualité *f* brouillon; *Comput* ***draft quality printing*** impression *f* en qualité brouillon; *Am Mil* ***draft resister*** réfractaire *m*; ***draft treaty*** projet *m* de convention; *Comput* ***draft version*** version *f* brouillon

►**draft in** *vt sep (experts, police)* faire venir, faire appel à; *(employees)* recruter; **could we draft in some outside help?** est-ce que nous pourrions obtenir de l'aide à l'extérieur?

draft² *Am* = **draught**

draftee [ˌdrɑːf'tiː] *n Am Mil* recrue *f*

drafter ['drɑːftə(r)] *n (of document)* rédacteur (trice) *m,f*

drafting ['drɑːftɪŋ] *n* **(a)** *(of letter, document)* rédaction *f* **(b)** *Austr & NZ (of cattle)* triage *m* du bétail; *(of sheep)* triage *m* des moutons **(c)** *(in stonework)* appareillage *m*

►► ***drafting committee*** comité *m* de rédaction

draftsman, draftsmanship *etc Am* = **draughtsman, draughtsmanship** *etc*

drafty *(compar* **draftier,** *superl* **draftiest)** *Am* = **draughty**

drag [dræg] *(pt & pp* **dragged,** *cont* **dragging) 1** *vt* **(a)** *(pull)* traîner, tirer; **to drag sth on** *or* **along the ground** traîner qch par terre; **he dragged me to a concert** il m'a traîné *ou* entraîné à un concert; **to drag sb out of bed** tirer qn de son lit; **to drag sb through the courts** traîner qn devant les tribunaux; **don't drag me into this!** ne me mêlez pas à vos histoires!; **I had to drag the truth out of her** il m'a fallu lui arracher la vérité; *Naut* **to drag anchor** chasser sur ses ancres; **to drag one's feet** traîner les pieds; *Fig* **to drag one's feet** *or* **heels (over doing sth)** tarder (à faire qch); **she dragged her feet over the decision** elle a tardé à se décider; **the government has been accused of dragging its feet** *or* **heels over the issue** on a accusé le gouvernement de montrer peu d'empressement à s'occuper de la question; **to drag sb's name through the mud** traîner qn dans la boue

(b) *(search → pond, river)* draguer; **they dragged the lake for the body** ils ont dragué le lac à la recherche du corps

(c) *Comput (with mouse)* faire glisser

2 *vi* **(a)** *(trail → skirt, coat)* traîner (par terre); *Naut (→ anchor)* chasser

(b) *(hang behind)* traîner, rester à l'arrière

(c) *(search)* draguer

(d) *(go on and on)* traîner, s'éterniser; *(conversation)* languir; **the minutes dragged by** les minutes s'étiraient; **the second act dragged** le deuxième acte n'en finissait plus

(e) *(smoker)* **to drag on** *or* **at a cigarette** tirer des bouffées d'une cigarette

(f) *Comput* **to drag and drop** faire un glisser-lâcher

(g) *Aut (brakes)* frotter, gripper, se gripper

3 *n* **(a)** *(pull)* tirage *m*; *Aviat, Aut & Naut* résistance *f*, traînée *f*

(b) *(dredge)* drague *f*; *(sledge)* traîneau *m*; *Agr (harrow)* herse *f*; *Naut* araignée *f*

(c) *(brake)* sabot *m ou* patin *m* de frein

(d) *(handicap)* entrave *f*, frein *m*; **unemployment is a drag on the economy** le chômage est un frein pour l'économie

(e) *(trail of fox)* piste *f*

(f) *Fam (bore)* **he's a real drag!** quel raseur!; **the exams are a real drag!** quelle barbe ces examens!; **what a drag!** quelle barbe!, c'est la barbe!

(g) *Fam (puff on cigarette)* bouffée *f*, taffe *f*; **I had a drag on** *or* **of his cigarette** j'ai tiré une bouffée de sa cigarette

(h) *Fam (women's clothing)* **in drag** en travesti ❑

(i) *Am Fam (street)* **the main drag** la rue principale ❑

(j) *Am Fam (influence)* piston *m*; **she has a lot of drag** elle a le bras long; **use your drag** usez de votre influence ❑

4 *comp Fam (disco, show)* de travestis ❑

►► ***drag act*** numéro *m* de travesti(s); ***drag artist*** travesti *m*; *Aviat & Aut* ***drag coefficient, drag factor*** coefficient *m* de traînée; ***drag hunt*** drag *m*; *Fam* ***drag queen*** travelo *m*; *Aut* ***drag race*** course *f* de dragsters; *Aut* ***drag racer*** = participant à des courses de dragsters; *Aut* ***drag racing*** course *f* de dragsters

►**drag along** *vt sep (chair, toy)* tirer, traîner; *(person)* traîner, entraîner; **to drag oneself along** se traîner

►**drag apart** *vt sep* séparer de force

►**drag away** *vt sep* emmener de force; **I couldn't**

drag him away from his work je ne pouvais pas l'arracher à son travail; **I couldn't drag myself away** j'étais cloué sur place

►**drag down** *vt sep* (**a**) *(lower)* entraîner (en bas); **being rude only drags you down to his level** être grossier ne fait que vous rabaisser à son niveau (**b**) *(weaken)* affaiblir; *(depress)* déprimer, décourager

►**drag in** *vt sep* apporter (de force); **he insisted on dragging in the issue of housing** il voulait à tout prix mettre la question du logement sur le tapis

►**drag on 1** *vi* se prolonger, s'éterniser; **don't let the matter drag on** ne laissez pas traîner l'affaire; **the day dragged on** la journée s'éternisait *ou* n'en finissait pas

2 *vt insep* **to drag on a cigarette** tirer sur une cigarette

►**drag out** *vt sep* (**a**) *(prolong)* faire traîner; **to drag out talks** faire traîner des négociations (**b**) *(extract)* **to drag the truth/a confession out of sb** arracher la vérité/des aveux à qn; **I finally managed to drag out of him the reason why he was so upset** j'ai finalement réussi à lui faire dire pourquoi il était si retourné

►**drag up** *vt sep* (**a**) *(affair, story)* remettre sur le tapis, ressortir (**b**) *Br Fam (child)* élever à la diable *ou* tant bien que mal ❑; *Hum* **where were you dragged up?** où donc as-tu été élevé?

drag-and-drop *n Comput* glisser-lâcher *m*

dragging ['drægɪŋ] *n* (**a**) *(pulling)* traînement *m*; *Naut* **dragging of the anchor** dérapage *m*; **dragging step** pas *m* traînant (**b**) *(of pond, river)* dragage *m*

draggy ['drægɪ] (*compar* **draggier**, *superl* **draggiest**) *adj Br Fam (boring)* ennuyeux ❑, assommant; *(listless)* mou (molle) ❑, avachi ❑

draglift ['dræglɪft] *n Ski* tire-fesses *m*

dragnet ['drægnet] *n* (**a**) *(for fish)* seine *f*, drège *f*; *(for game)* tirasse *f* (**b**) *(for criminals)* rafle *f*

dragoman ['drægəʊmən] (*pl* **dragomen** [-mən]) *n* drogman *m*

dragon ['drægən] *n Myth, Zool & Fig* dragon *m*; *Fam Drugs slang* **to chase the dragon** chasser le dragon

►► *Fam* ***dragon's teeth*** = obstacles antichars en béton; *Fig* **to sow** *or* **plant dragon's teeth** jeter de l'huile sur le feu tout en pensant arranger les choses

dragonfly ['drægənflaɪ] (*pl* **dragonflies**) *n* libellule *f*

dragonnade [drægə'nɑːd] *n Hist* dragonnade *f*

dragoon [drə'guːn] **1** *n Mil* dragon *m*

2 *vt (force)* contraindre, forcer; **he dragooned us into going** il nous a contraints *ou* forcés à y aller

dragrope ['drægrəʊp] *n Aviat* guiderope *m*

dragster ['drægstə(r)] *n Aut* voiture *f* à moteur gonflé, dragster *m*

dragsville ['drægzvɪl] *n Am Fam Old-fashioned* **it was dragsville** c'était casse-pieds *ou* la barbe

drain [dreɪn] **1** *n* (**a**) *(in house)* canalisation *f ou* tuyau *m* d'évacuation; *(of dishwasher)* tuyau *m* de vidange; *(outside house)* puisard *m*; *(sewer)* égout *m*; *(grid in street)* bouche *f* d'égout; *(in field, marshland)* fossé *m* de drainage; **a smell of drains** [illegible]; **the drains are overflowing** les égouts débordent; *Fig* **the family business went down the drain** l'entreprise familiale a fait faillite; **all our plans went down the drain** tous nos projets sont tombés à l'eau; **that's five years' work down the drain** voilà cinq années de travail perdues; **to throw money down the drain** jeter son argent par les fenêtres; **to laugh like a drain** rire comme une baleine

(**b**) *Agr & Med* drain *m*

(**c**) *(depletion)* perte *f*, épuisement *m*; **a drain on resources** une ponction sur les ressources; **the upkeep of the house is a continual drain on their resources** l'entretien de la maison entraîne constamment des dépenses; **all that travelling was a terrible drain on him** tous ces voyages l'ont terriblement épuisé

2 *vt* (**a**) *(dry → dishes, vegetables)* égoutter; *(→ land)* drainer, assécher; *(→ reservoir)* vider, mettre à sec; *(→ mine)* drainer; *(→ oil tank)* vider, vidanger; **she drained her glass** elle a vidé son verre *ou* a tout bu jusqu'à la dernière goutte; *Com* **drained weight** poids *m* net égoutté

(**b**) *Agr & Med* drainer; **well drained soil** sol *m* bien drainé

(**c**) *(deplete)* épuiser; **to drain sb of his/her strength** épuiser qn; **the war drained the country of its resources** la guerre a saigné le pays

3 *vi* (**a**) *(colour)* disparaître; *(blood)* s'écouler; **the colour drained from her face** son visage a blêmi

(**b**) *(dishes, vegetables)* s'égoutter; **leave the dishes to drain** laisse égoutter la vaisselle

►**drain away 1** *vi (liquid)* s'écouler; *(hope, strength)* s'épuiser

2 *vt sep* faire écouler

►**drain off 1** *vt sep* (**a**) *(liquid)* faire écouler; *(dishes, vegetables)* égoutter (**b**) *Agr & Med* drainer

2 *vi* s'écouler

drainage ['dreɪnɪdʒ] *n (UNCOUNT)* (**a**) *(process)* drainage *m*, assèchement *m*; **soil with good drainage** sol *m* perméable (**b**) *(system → in house)* système *m* d'évacuation des eaux; *(→ in town)* système *m* d'égouts; *(→ of land)* système *m* de drainage; *Geol* système *m* hydrographique (**c**) *(sewage)* eaux *fpl* usées, vidanges *fpl*

►► *Geol* ***drainage area, drainage basin*** bassin *m* hydrographique; *Agr* ***drainage ditch*** fossé *m* d'écoulement

drainboard ['dreɪnbɔːrd] *n Am* égouttoir *m*

drained [dreɪnd] *adj* épuisé, éreinté; **he looked tired and drained** il avait l'air fatigué et à bout de forces; **the incident left me emotionally drained** l'incident m'a épuisé nerveusement

drainer ['dreɪnə(r)] *n* égouttoir *m*

draining ['dreɪnɪŋ] *adj (person, task)* épuisant

►► ***draining board, draining rack*** égouttoir *m*

drainpipe ['dreɪnpaɪp] *n (from roof)* (tuyau *m* de) descente *f*; *(from sink)* tuyau *m* d'écoulement; *Agr (on land)* drain *m*

►► *Br* ***drainpipe trousers*** pantalon *m* étroit

drake [dreɪk] *n* canard *m* (mâle)

Dralon® ['dreɪlɒn] *n* Dralon® *m*

DRAM ['diːræm] *n Comput* (*abbr* **dynamic random access memory**) DRAM *f*

dram [dræm] *n* (**a**) *(gen) & Pharm* drachme *m* (**b**) *Fam (drop)* goutte ❑ *f*; **a dram (of whisky)** un petit verre (de whisky)

drama ['drɑːmə] *n* (**a**) *(theatre)* théâtre *m*; **she teaches drama** elle enseigne l'art dramatique; **Spanish drama** le théâtre espagnol

(**b**) *(play)* pièce *f* (de théâtre), drame *m*

(**c**) *(situation)* drame *m*; *Fig* **to make a drama out of sth** faire un drame de qch

(**d**) *(excitement)* intensité *f*; **the drama of the situation is heightened by the fact that...** l'intensité de la situation est renforcée par le fait que...; **a moment of high drama** un moment d'émotion intense; **full of drama** *(film etc)* plein de rebondissements

►► ***drama critic*** critique *mf* dramatique *ou* de théâtre; *TV* ***drama documentary*** docudrame *m*; *Fam Pej* ***drama queen*** comédien(enne) ❑ *m,f*; **she's such a drama queen!** quelle comédienne, celle-là!; **don't be such a drama queen!** arrête ton cinéma!; ***drama school*** école *f* d'art dramatique, école *f* de théâtre; *TV* ***drama series*** [illegible]; ***drama student*** étudiant(e) *m,f* en art dramatique

dramadoc ['drɑːmədɒk] *n TV* docudrame *m*

dramatic [drə'mætɪk] *adj* (**a**) *Literature, Mus & Theat* dramatique; **the dramatic works of Racine** le théâtre de Racine

(**b**) *Fig (theatrical) (effect, entry)* théâtral, dramatique; *(gesture, effect)* théâtral; *(spectacular) (change)* remarquable, spectaculaire; *(rise in prices)* spectaculaire, vertigineux; *(scenery)* spectaculaire, grandiose; **there's no need to be so dramatic about it** ce n'est pas la peine d'en faire un drame *ou* toute une histoire; **the story took a dramatic turn** l'histoire prit un tour dramatique

dramatically [drə'mætɪklɪ] *adv* (**a**) *Literature, Mus & Theat* du point de vue théâtral (**b**) *Fig (act, speak)* de manière dramatique, dramatiquement; *(change, increase, drop)* de manière spectaculaire

dramatics [drə'mætɪks] **1** *n (UNCOUNT) Theat* art *m* dramatique, dramaturgie *f*

2 *npl Fig (behaviour)* comédie *f*, cirque *m*; *Pej* **this is no time for dramatics** ce n'est pas le moment de jouer la comédie *ou* de faire ton cinéma

dramatis personae [,drəmætɪs,pɜː'səʊnaɪ] *npl Literature & Theat* personnages *mpl (d'une pièce ou d'un roman)*

dramatist ['dræmətɪst] *n* auteur *m* dramatique, dramaturge *mf*

dramatization [,dræmətaɪ'zeɪʃən] *n* (**a**) *(for theatre)* adaptation *f* pour la scène; *(for film)* adaptation *f* pour l'écran; *(for television)* adaptation *f* pour la télévision (**b**) *(exaggeration)* dramatisation *f*

dramatize, -ise ['dræmətaɪz] **1** *vt* (**a**) *(for theatre)* adapter pour la scène; *(for film)* adapter pour l'écran; *(for television)* adapter pour la télévision (**b**) *(exaggerate)* faire un drame de, dramatiser; *(make dramatic)* rendre dramatique

2 *vi* dramatiser; **he tends to dramatize** il a tendance à dramatiser

dramaturge ['dræmətɜːdʒ], **dramaturgist** ['dræmətɜːdʒɪst] *n Theat* dramaturge *mf*, auteur *m* de théâtre

dramaturgy ['dræmətɜːdʒɪ] *n Theat* dramaturgie *f*

Drambuie® [dræm'bjuːɪ] *n* Drambuie® *m*

drank [dræŋk] *pt of* **drink**

drape [dreɪp] **1** *n (way something hangs)* drapé *m*

2 *vt* (**a**) *(adorn → person, window)* draper; *(→ altar, room)* tendre; **the stage was draped with** *or* **in black** la scène était tendue de noir (**b**) *(hang)* étendre; **she draped a leg over the chair arm** elle a étendu sa jambe sur l'accoudoir; **he draped himself over the sofa** il s'est allongé langoureusement sur le canapé

3 drapes *npl Br (drapery)* tentures *fpl*; *Am (curtains)* rideaux *mpl*

draper ['dreɪpə(r)] *n Br* marchand(e) *m,f* de tissus

drapery ['dreɪpərɪ] (*pl* **draperies**) *n* (**a**) *(UNCOUNT) (material)* étoffes *fpl*; *(arrangement of material)* draperie *f* (**b**) *(usu pl) (hangings)* tentures *fpl*; *(curtains)* rideaux *mpl* (**c**) *Br (shop)* magasin *m* de tissus

drastic ['dræstɪk] *adj (measures)* sévère, draconien; *(change, effect)* radical; *(remedy)* énergique; *(decline, rise, improvement)* dramatique; **drastic cutbacks** coupes *fpl* sombres; *Com* **drastic reductions** réductions *fpl* massives; **to take drastic steps** trancher dans le vif, prendre des mesures draconiennes *ou* énergiques

drastically ['dræstɪklɪ] *adv* radicalement; *(cut, reduce)* radicalement, sévèrement; **prices rose drastically** les prix ont augmenté considérablement

drat [dræt] *exclam Fam* diable!, bon sang!; **oh, drat!** bon sang!, nom de nom!

dratted ['drætɪd] *adj Fam* sacré, fichu; **where's that dratted brother of mine?** mais où est passé mon frangin?

draught, *Am* **draft** [drɑːft] **1** *n* (**a**) *(breeze)* courant *m* d'air; **I can feel a draught** je suis dans un courant d'air; **there's a terrific draught in here** il y a un courant d'air terrible ici

(**b**) *(in fireplace)* tirage *m*

(**c**) *(drink → swallow)* trait *m*, gorgée *f*; **a draught of water** une gorgée d'eau; **in one draught** d'un seul trait *ou* coup

(**d**) *(medicine)* potion *f*, breuvage *m*

(**e**) **on draught** *(beer)* à la pression

(**f**) *(in game)* pion *m (de jeu de dames)*

(**g**) *(pulling)* traction *f*, tirage *m*; *Naut (of ship)* tirant *m* (d'eau)

2 *adj (horse)* de trait

►► ***draught beer*** bière *f* pression; *Br* ***draught excluder*** bourrelet *m* (de porte)

draughtboard ['drɑːftbɔːd] *n Br* damier *m*

draughtiness, *Am* **draftiness** ['drɑːftɪnɪs] *n* courants *mpl* d'air

draught-proof 1 *vt* calfeutrer

2 *adj* calfeutré

draught-proofing [-,pruːfɪŋ] *n* calfeutrage *m*

draughts [drɑːfts] *n Br (game)* (jeu *m* de) dames *fpl*; **a game of draughts** un jeu de dames; **to play draughts** jouer aux dames

draughtsman, *Am* **draftsman** ['drɑːftsmən] (*Br pl* **draughtsmen** [-mən], *Am pl* **draftsmen** [-mən]) *n* (**a**) *(artist)* dessinateur(trice) *m,f*; *Archit & Ind* dessinateur(trice) *m,f* industriel(elle) (**b**) *Br (in game)* pion *m (de jeu de dames)*

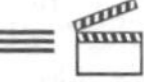

'The Draughtsman's Contract' *Greenaway*
'Meutre dans un jardin anglais'

draughtsmanship, *Am* **draftsmanship** ['drɑːftsmənʃɪp] *n (of artist)* talent *m* de dessinateur, coup *m* de crayon; *(of work)* art *m* du dessin

draughtswoman, *Am* **draftswoman** ['drɑːfts,wʊmən] *(Br pl* **draughtswomen** [-wɪmɪn], *Am pl* **draftswomen** [-wɪmɪn]) *n* dessinatrice *f*; *Archit & Ind* dessinatrice *f* industrielle

draughty, *Am* **drafty** ['drɑːftɪ] *(Br compar* **draughtier,** *superl* **draughtiest**, *Am compar* **draftier,** *superl* **draftiest**) *adj (house, room)* plein de courants d'air; *(street, corner)* exposé à tous les vents *ou* aux quatre vents

Dravidian [drə'vɪdɪən] **1** *adj* dravidien
2 *n* dravidien *m*

DRAW [drɔː]

tirer	▶ 1 (a) – (c), (f), (h), (k); 2 (b), (e)
conduire	▶ 1 (d)
attirer	▶ 1 (e)
gagner	▶ 1 (i)
dessiner	▶ 1 (j)
établir	▶ 1 (k)
tirer au hasard	▶ 2 (c)
dessiner	▶ 2 (d)
être ex aequo	▶ 2 (g)
faire match nul	▶ 2 (g)
loterie	▶ 3 (c)
attraction	▶ 3 (d)
match nul	▶ 3 (e)

(pt **drew** [druː], *pp* **drawn** [drɔːn]) **1** *vt* (**a**) *(pull)* tirer; **to draw the curtains** *(open)* tirer *ou* ouvrir les rideaux; *(shut)* tirer *ou* fermer les rideaux; **he drew the blankets round him** il a tiré les couvertures autour de lui; **I drew my coat closer around me** je me suis enveloppé dans mon manteau; **he drew his hand wearily across his forehead** il se passa la main sur le front avec lassitude; **she drew his hand towards her** elle approcha sa main de la sienne; **to draw a bow** *(in archery)* tirer à l'arc

(**b**) *(haul, pull behind → car)* tirer, traîner, remorquer; *(→ trailer)* remorquer; **a carriage drawn by two horses** un équipage attelé à *ou* tiré par deux chevaux; **drawn by a locomotive** remorqué par une locomotive

(**c**) *(take out)* tirer, retirer; *(remove)* retirer, enlever; *(tooth)* arracher, extraire; **he drew his knife from** *or* **out of his pocket** il a tiré son couteau de sa poche; **the thief drew a gun on us** le voleur a sorti un pistolet et l'a braqué sur nous; **to draw a sword** dégainer une épée

(**d**) *(lead)* conduire, entraîner; **she drew me towards the door** elle m'a entraîné vers la porte; *Fig* **I was drawn into the controversy** j'ai été mêlé à *ou* entraîné dans la dispute; **the senator refused to be drawn** *(refused to answer)* le sénateur refusa de répondre; *(refused to be provoked)* le sénateur refusa de réagir; **to draw a meeting to a close** mettre fin à une réunion

(**e**) *(attract, elicit)* attirer; **to be drawn to sb** être attiré par qn; **his remarks drew a lot of criticism** ses observations lui ont attiré de nombreuses critiques; **to draw sb's attention to sth** faire remarquer qch à qn; *Fig* **to draw the enemy's fire** attirer le feu de l'ennemi sur soi; **to draw blood** *(of weapon)* faire couler le sang; *(of dog)* mordre jusqu'au sang; *(of cat)* griffer jusqu'au sang; *Fig (of remark, criticism)* avoir un effet dévastateur; **to draw a crowd** *(of incident)* créer un attroupement; *(of play)* attirer le public

(**f**) *(take from source)* tirer, puiser; **to draw water from a well** puiser de l'eau dans un puits; **to draw wine (from a barrel)** tirer du vin (d'un tonneau); **to draw (out) money from the bank** retirer de l'argent à la banque; **the university draws its students from all social backgrounds** l'université recrute ses étudiants dans toutes les couches sociales; **her performance drew an ovation from the audience** son interprétation lui a valu l'ovation du public; **our members are drawn from all walks of life** nos membres appartiennent à tous les milieux; **his confession drew tears from his mother** son aveu a arraché des larmes à sa mère; **I draw comfort from the fact that he didn't suffer** je me console en me disant qu'il n'a pas souffert; **Cézanne drew inspiration from the French countryside** Cézanne s'est inspiré de *ou* a tiré inspiration de la campagne française; *Cards* **to draw trumps** faire tomber les atouts

(**g**) *(breathe in)* **we barely had time to draw (a) breath** nous avons à peine eu le temps de souffler

(**h**) *(choose at random)* tirer; **he drew the winning number** il a tiré le numéro gagnant; **to draw lots** tirer au sort

(**i**) *(earn → amount, salary)* gagner, toucher; *(→ pension)* toucher; *Fin (→ interest)* rapporter

(**j**) *(sketch)* dessiner; *(line, triangle)* tracer; *(map)* faire; **to draw a picture of sb** faire le portrait de qn; **he drew us a map of the village** il nous a fait un plan du village; *Hum* **do you want me to draw you a map?** tu veux que je te fasse un dessin?; *Fig* **she drew a vivid picture of village life** elle (nous) a fait une description vivante de la vie de village; *Fig* **the author has drawn his characters well** l'auteur a bien dépeint ses personnages; **to draw the line at sth** ne pas admettre qch, se refuser à qch; **you have to draw the line somewhere** il faut fixer des limites, il y a des limites; **he doesn't know where to draw the line** il ne sait pas où s'arrêter; **I draw the line at lying** je refuse de mentir; *(referring to other people)* je ne tolère pas le mensonge

(**k**) *(formulate → comparison, parallel, distinction)* établir, faire; *(→ conclusion)* tirer; **she drew a direct comparison between our situation and her own** elle a établi une comparaison explicite entre notre situation et la sienne

(**l**) *Fin* **to draw a cheque on one's account** tirer un chèque sur son compte

(**m**) *(disembowel)* vider

(**n**) *(tie)* **the game was drawn** *Sport* ils ont fait match nul; *Cards* ils ont fait partie nulle

(**o**) *Hunt (game)* débusquer; *(covert)* battre

(**p**) *Med (abscess)* crever, percer

(**q**) *Naut* **the ocean liner draws 8 metres** le paquebot a un tirant d'eau de 8 mètres

(**r**) *Tech (metal)* étirer; *(wire)* tréfiler

2 *vi* (**a**) *(move)* **the crowd drew to one side** la foule s'est rangée sur le côté *ou* s'est écartée; **the bus drew into the coach station** l'autocar est arrivé *ou* entré dans la gare routière; **to draw ahead of sb** prendre de l'avance sur qn; **one cyclist drew ahead of the others** un cycliste s'est détaché du peloton; **to draw to a halt** s'arrêter; **they drew level with** *or* **alongside the window** ils sont arrivés à la hauteur de la fenêtre; **to draw near** *(elections, Christmas)* approcher; **to draw near (to sb)** *(person)* se rapprocher (de qn), s'approcher (de qn); **they drew nearer to us** ils se sont approchés un peu plus de nous; **night draws near** la nuit approche; **to draw to an end** *or* **to a close** tirer *ou* toucher à sa fin

(**b**) *(pull out gun)* tirer; **the policeman drew and fired** le policier a dégainé *ou* sorti son pistolet et a tiré

(**c**) *(choose at random)* tirer au hasard; **they drew for partners** ils ont tiré au sort leurs partenaires

(**d**) *(sketch)* dessiner; **she draws well** elle dessine bien

(**e**) *(fireplace, pipe)* tirer; *(pump, vacuum cleaner)* aspirer

(**f**) *(tea)* infuser

(**g**) *Sport (be equal → two competitors)* être ex aequo *(inv)*; *(→ two teams)* faire match nul; **Italy drew against Spain** l'Italie et l'Espagne ont fait match nul; **they drew two all** ils ont fait deux partout; **the two contestants drew for third prize** les deux concurrents ont remporté le troisième prix ex aequo *ou* sont arrivés troisièmes ex aequo

3 *n* (**a**) *(act of pulling)* **to be quick on the draw** dégainer vite, avoir la détente rapide; *Fig* avoir de la repartie; **to beat sb to the draw** dégainer plus vite que qn; *Fig* devancer qn

(**b**) *(card)* carte *f* tirée; **it's your draw** c'est à vous de tirer une carte

(**c**) *(raffle, lottery)* loterie *f*, tombola *f*; *(selection of winners, competitors)* tirage *m* (au sort); **the draw will take place tonight** le tirage aura lieu ce soir

(**d**) *(attraction)* attraction *f*; **the polar bears are the main draw at the zoo** les ours polaires sont la grande attraction du zoo; **the show proved to be a big draw** le spectacle s'est révélé être un grand succès

(**e**) *Sport* match *m* nul; *Cards* partie *f* nulle; **the chess tournament ended in a draw** le tournoi d'échecs s'est terminé par une partie nulle; **two wins and three draws** deux matches gagnés et trois matchs nuls

(**f**) *Am (gully)* ravine *f*; *(drain)* rigole *f*

(**g**) *Am (sum of money)* avance *f*

(**h**) *Br Fam Drugs slang (cannabis)* shit *m*

▶▶ ***draw curtains*** doubles rideaux *mpl*

▶**draw along** *vt sep (cart, caravan)* tirer, traîner; *(person)* entraîner

▶**draw apart** **1** *vi* se séparer; **they drew apart when I entered the room** ils se sont éloignés *ou* écartés l'un de l'autre quand je suis entré dans la pièce

2 *vt sep* prendre à l'écart

▶**draw aside** **1** *vi* s'écarter, se ranger; **I drew aside to let them pass** je me suis écarté (du chemin) *ou* je me suis rangé pour les laisser passer

2 *vt sep (person)* prendre *ou* tirer à l'écart; *(thing)* écarter

▶**draw away** *vi* (**a**) *(move away → person)* s'éloigner, s'écarter; *(→ vehicle)* s'éloigner, démarrer; **she drew away from the crowd** elle s'est éloignée *ou* écartée de la foule

(**b**) *(move ahead)* prendre de l'avance; **the leading runner drew away from the others** le coureur de tête a pris de l'avance sur les *ou* s'est détaché des autres

▶**draw back** **1** *vi* (**a**) *(move backwards)* reculer, se reculer, avoir un mouvement de recul; **the child drew back in fear** l'enfant a reculé de peur

(**b**) *(avoid commitment)* se retirer

2 *vt sep* (**a**) *(pull back → person)* faire reculer; *(→ one's hand, thing)* retirer; **to draw back the curtains** ouvrir les rideaux

(**b**) *(attract back)* **what drew you back to your home town?** qu'est-ce qui t'a poussé à revenir dans ta ville natale?; **I'm increasingly being drawn back to folk music** je reviens de plus en plus à la musique folk

▶**draw down** *vt sep* (**a**) *(lower → blinds)* baisser, descendre

(**b**) *(provoke)* attirer; **their policy drew down a storm of protest** leur politique a soulevé une vague de protestations

▶**draw in** **1** *vi* (**a**) *(move)* **the train drew in** le train est entré en gare; **the bus drew in to the kerb** *(pulled over)* le bus s'est rapproché du trottoir; *(stopped)* le bus s'est arrêté le long du trottoir

(**b**) *(day, evening)* diminuer, raccourcir; **the nights are drawing in** les nuits raccourcissent *ou* diminuent

2 *vt sep* (**a**) *(pull in)* rentrer; **to draw in the reins** tirer sur les rênes, serrer la bride; **the cat drew in its claws** le chat fit patte de velours *ou* rentra ses griffes

(**b**) *(involve)* impliquer, mêler; **he drew me into the conversation** il m'a mêlé à la conversation; **I got drawn into the project** je me suis laissé impliquer dans le projet; **he listened to the debate but refused to be drawn in** il a écouté le débat mais a refusé d'y participer *ou* de s'y joindre

(**c**) *(attract)* attirer; **the film is drawing in huge crowds** le film fait de grosses recettes

(**d**) *(sketch)* ébaucher

(**e**) *(air)* aspirer, respirer; **to draw in a deep breath** respirer profondément

▶**draw off** *vt sep* (**a**) *Br (remove → clothing)* enlever, ôter; *(→ gloves)* retirer, ôter

(**b**) *(liquid)* tirer; **he drew off some wine from the cask** il a tiré du vin du fût; **to draw off blood** faire une prise de sang

▶**draw on** **1** *vt sep Br* (**a**) *(put on → gloves, trousers, socks)* enfiler

(**b**) *(entice, encourage)* encourager, entraîner; **the thought of success drew him on** la perspective de la réussite l'encourageait à continuer

2 *vt insep* (**a**) *(as source)* faire appel à; **the campaigners drew on the community's support** les militants ont fait appel au soutien de la communauté locale; **I drew on my own experiences for the novel** je me suis inspiré *ou* servi de mes propres expériences pour mon roman; **I had to draw on my savings** j'ai dû prendre *ou* tirer sur mes économies

(**b**) *(suck)* tirer sur; **to draw on a pipe** tirer sur une pipe

3 *vi (time → come near)* approcher; *(→ get late)* avancer; **as the day drew on** au fur et à mesure que la journée avançait; **the winter drew on** l'hiver approchait

►**draw out 1** *vt sep* (**a**) *(remove)* sortir, retirer, tirer; *(money)* retirer; **she drew some papers out of her pocket** elle a sorti des papiers de sa poche; **how much money did you draw out (of the bank)?** combien d'argent as-tu retiré (de la banque)?

(**b**) *(extend → sound, visit)* prolonger; *(→ meeting, speech)* prolonger, faire traîner; *Tech (→ metal)* étirer; *(→ wire)* tréfiler

(**c**) *(cause to speak freely)* faire parler; **she has a way of drawing people out** elle sait faire parler les gens, elle sait faire sortir les gens de leur coquille

(**d**) *(information, secret)* soutirer; **to draw sth out of sb** soutirer qch de qn; **the police managed to draw the names out of him** la police est arrivée à lui soutirer les noms

2 *vi (vehicle)* sortir, s'éloigner; **the train drew out (of the station)** le train est sorti de la gare

►**draw together 1** *vt sep (people, objects)* rassembler, réunir; **the child's illness had drawn them together** la maladie de l'enfant les avait rapprochés

2 *vi* se rassembler

►**draw up 1** *vt sep* (**a**) *Br (pull up)* tirer; **I drew the covers up around my neck** j'ai ramené les couvertures autour de mon cou; **to draw a boat up (on the beach)** tirer un bateau à sec; **she drew herself up (to her full height)** elle s'est redressée (de toute sa hauteur)

(**b**) *Br (move closer → chair)* approcher; *Mil (troops)* aligner, ranger; **draw your chair up to the table** approche ta chaise de la table

(**c**) *(formulate → deed, document, will)* dresser, rédiger; *(→ bill, list)* dresser, établir; *(→ plan)* préparer, établir; *(→ budget, itinerary)* établir

2 *vi Br* (**a**) *(move)* se diriger; **the other boat drew up alongside us** l'autre bateau est arrivé à notre hauteur *ou* à côté de nous

(**b**) *(stop → vehicle)* s'arrêter, stopper; *(→ person)* s'arrêter

►**draw upon** *vt insep* **they had to draw upon their emergency funds** ils ont dû tirer sur *ou* prendre sur leur caisse de réserve; **you have to draw upon your previous experience** il faut faire appel à votre expérience antérieure

---

drawback ['drɔːbæk] *n* (**a**) *(disadvantage)* inconvénient *m*, désavantage *m*; **there are drawbacks to the scheme** ce projet présente des inconvénients; **the main drawback to the plan is its cost** le principal inconvénient du projet est son coût (**b**) *Admin* drawback *m*

drawbar ['drɔːbɑː(r)] *n Aut* barre *f* d'attelage

drawbridge ['drɔːbrɪdʒ] *n* pont-levis *m*, pont *m* basculant *ou* à bascule

drawcard ['drɔːkɑːd] *n Am (of festival, show)* attraction *f*, clou *m*

drawcord ['drɔːkɔːd] *n (of curtains)* cordon *m*

drawdown ['drɔːdaʊn] *n* (**a**) *Fin* tirage *m* (**b**) *(in a reservoir)* abaissement *m* du niveau

drawee [drɔː'iː] *n Banking & Fin* tiré *m*

drawer *n* (**a**) [drɔː(r)] *(in chest, desk)* tiroir *m* (**b**) [drɔː(r)] *Banking & Fin (of cheque)* tireur *m*; *(of bill)* souscripteur *m*; **to refer a cheque to drawer** refuser d'honorer un chèque (**c**) ['drɔːə(r)] *(of pictures)* dessinateur(trice) *m,f*; **she's a good drawer** *(of child, amateur)* elle dessine bien

►► ***drawer liner*** = feuille de papier servant à tapisser les fonds de tiroirs

drawers [drɔːz] *npl Old-fashioned (for men)* caleçon *m*; *(for women)* culotte *f*

drawing ['drɔːɪŋ] **1** *n* (**a**) *(picture)* dessin *m*; **to make a drawing of sth** dessiner qch; **to study drawing** étudier le dessin; **a pen drawing** un dessin à la plume

(**b**) *Metal (shaping, tapering)* étirage *m*

(**c**) *Culin (of poultry)* vidage *m*

2 *comp (paper, table)* à dessin; *(lesson, teacher)* de dessin

►► *Am Banking* ***drawing account*** compte *m* courant *(pour frais professionnels)*; ***drawing board*** planche *f* à dessin; *Fig* **still on the drawing board** *(plan, project)* encore à l'étude; **it's back to the drawing board** il faudra tout recommencer; ***drawing book*** cahier *m* de dessin; *Com* ***drawing card*** valeur *f* sûre; *Am Fig (of festival etc)* attraction *f*, clou *m*; **she's always a big drawing card** elle attire toujours beaucoup de monde; ***drawing off*** *(of liquid)* soutirage *m*; ***drawing pen*** tire-ligne *m*; *Br* ***drawing pin*** punaise *f (à papier)*; *Comput* ***drawing program*** programme *m* de dessin, logiciel *m* de dessin; *Fin* ***drawing rights*** droits *mpl* de tirage; ***drawing room*** *(living room)* salon *m*; *(reception room)* salle *f ou* salon *m* de réception; *Am Rail* compartiment *m* privé; ***drawing up*** *(of deed, document, will)* rédaction *f*; *(of constitution, plan)* élaboration *f*; *(of bill, list, budget, plan, itinerary)* établissement *m*

drawl [drɔːl] **1** *n* débit *m* traînant, voix *f* traînante; **a Southern drawl** un accent du sud des États-Unis; **"sure I do", he said with a drawl** "bien sûr", dit-il d'une voix traînante

2 *vi* parler d'une voix traînante

3 *vt* dire d'une voix traînante

drawling ['drɔːlɪŋ] **1** *adj (voice, tone)* traînant

2 *n* = affectation de langueur dans le débit; **his drawling gets on my nerves** sa voix traînante me porte sur les nerfs

drawn [drɔːn] **1** *pp of* **draw**

2 *adj* (**a**) *(blind, curtain)* fermé, tiré (**b**) *(face, features)* tiré; **he looked tired and drawn** il avait l'air fatigué et avait les traits tirés (**c**) *Sport & Cards (match, game)* nul

►► *Culin* ***drawn butter*** beurre *m* fondu; *Sewing* ***drawn (thread) work*** ouvrage *m* à jours

drawn-out *adj* prolongé, qui traîne; **a long drawn-out dispute** un conflit qui traîne en longueur *ou* qui n'en finit pas

drawsheet ['drɔːʃiːt] *n* alaise *f*

drawstring ['drɔːstrɪŋ] *n* cordon *m*; **drawstring hood** capuche *f* à lien coulissant; **drawstring trousers, trousers with a drawstring waist** pantalon *m* à taille coulissante

dray [dreɪ] *n (for barrels)* haquet *m*; *(for stones, wood)* binard *m*, fardier *m*

drayhorse ['dreɪhɔːs, *pl* -hɔːsɪz] *n* cheval *m* de roulage

drayman ['dreɪmən] *(pl* **draymen** [-mən]) *n* conducteur *m* de haquet

dread [dred] **1** *n* terreur *f*, effroi *m*; **I have a dread of dentists** j'ai la hantise des dentistes; **she has a terrible dread of heights** elle a effroyablement peur du vide; **she lives in dread of her ex-husband** elle vit dans la crainte de son ex-mari; **she waited in dread for the phone to ring** angoissée, elle attendait que le téléphone sonne

2 *vt* craindre, redouter; **I'm dreading Monday** je redoute la journée de lundi; **she's dreading the journey** elle redoute *ou* elle appréhende le voyage; **I dread to think of what might happen** je n'ose pas imaginer ce qui pourrait arriver

3 *adj* redoutable, effrayant

dreaded ['dredɪd] *adj (news, event)* tant redouté; *(person)* redoutable, terrible; **she said the dreaded words** elle prononça les mots tant redoutés

dreadful ['dredfʊl] *adj* (**a**) *(terrible → crime, pain)* affreux, épouvantable; *(→ enemy, weapon)* redoutable; **how dreadful!** quelle horreur!; **I'm a dreadful dancer** je danse atrocement mal; **to be dreadful at maths** être nul en maths

(**b**) *(unpleasant)* atroce, affreux; **what a dreadful child!** cet enfant est insupportable!; **they said some dreadful things about her** ils ont raconté des horreurs sur son compte; **I feel dreadful** *(ill)* je ne me sens pas du tout bien; *(embarrassed)* je suis vraiment gêné

(**c**) *(as intensifier)* **he's a dreadful bore!** c'est un casse-pieds insupportable!, c'est un horrible casse-pieds!; **what a dreadful waste!** quel affreux gaspillage!

dreadfully ['dredfʊlɪ] *adv* (**a**) *(very)* terriblement; **dreadfully ugly** affreusement laid; **he was dreadfully afraid** il avait horriblement peur *ou* une peur atroce; **I'm dreadfully sorry** je regrette infiniment *ou* énormément; **his handwriting is dreadfully untidy** son écriture est terriblement mauvaise, il écrit horriblement mal (**b**) *(badly)* affreusement; **the children behaved dreadfully** les enfants se sont affreusement mal comportés

dreadfulness ['dredfʊlnɪs] *n (of crime, deed)* horreur *f*, atrocité *f*; *(of weapon)* caractère *m* redoutable; *(of sound, scream)* horreur *f*

dreadlocks ['dredlɒks] *npl* dreadlocks *fpl*

dreadnought ['drednɔːt] *n Naut* cuirassé *m*

dreads [dredz] *npl* dreadlocks *fpl*

dream [driːm] *(pt & pp* **dreamt** [dremt] or **dreamed**) **1** *vi* (**a**) *(in sleep)* rêver; **to dream of** *or* **about sb/sth** rêver de qn/qch; **it can't be true, I must be dreaming** ce n'est pas vrai, je rêve

(**b**) *(daydream)* rêvasser, rêver; **he's always dreaming** il est toujours dans la lune; **stop dreaming and get on with your work!** arrête de rêver *ou* de rêvasser et remets-toi au travail!; **for years she'd dreamt of having a cottage in the country** elle rêvait depuis des années d'avoir un cottage à la campagne; **I know it'll never happen but there's nothing to stop me dreaming!** je sais que ça n'arrivera jamais, mais je ne peux pas m'empêcher de rêver!; *Fam* **dream on!** tu peux toujours rêver!

(**c**) *(imagine)* **to dream of doing sth** songer à faire qch; **nobody dreamt of suspecting her** personne n'a songé à *ou* il n'est venu à l'idée de personne de la soupçonner; **I never dreamt you would take me seriously** je n'aurais jamais pensé que tu me prendrais au sérieux; **don't tell anyone – I wouldn't dream of it!** ne le dis à personne – jamais je ne songerais à faire une chose pareille!; **she'd never dream of complaining** jamais elle ne songerait à se plaindre

2 *vt* (**a**) *(in sleep)* rêver; **he dreamt a dream** il a fait un rêve; **she dreamt we were in Spain** elle a rêvé que nous étions en Espagne; **you must have dreamt it** vous avez dû le rêver

(**b**) *(daydream)* rêvasser; **to dream idle dreams** se nourrir d'illusions, rêver creux

(**c**) *(imagine)* songer, imaginer; **I never dreamt that he would actually accept the offer!** j'étais à mille lieues de supposer qu'il accepterait effectivement la proposition!

3 *n* (**a**) *(during sleep)* rêve *m*; **to have a dream** faire un rêve; **to have a dream about sb/sth** rêver de qn/qch; **to see sth in a dream** voir qch en rêve; **the child had a bad dream** l'enfant a fait un mauvais rêve *ou* un cauchemar; **the meeting was like a bad dream** la réunion était un cauchemar; **sweet dreams!** faites de beaux rêves!; *Literary* **life is but a dream** la vie n'est qu'un songe; *Austr* **in the dream time** *(of native people)* au temps où l'homme n'était pas encore arrivé sur la terre; *Fam Fig* il y a des siècles

(**b**) *(wish, fantasy)* rêve *m*, désir *m*; **the woman of his dreams** la femme de ses rêves; **her dream was to become a pilot** elle rêvait de devenir pilote; **a job beyond my wildest dreams** un travail comme je n'ai jamais osé imaginer *ou* qui dépasse tous mes rêves; **even in her wildest dreams she never thought she'd win first prize** même dans ses rêves les plus fous, elle n'avait jamais pensé remporter le premier prix; **the American dream** le rêve américain; **may all your dreams come true** que tous vos rêves se réalisent; **the holiday was like a dream come true** les vacances étaient comme un rêve devenu réalité; **this boat is a sailor's dream come true** ce bateau est la matérialisation du rêve d'un marin; *Fam* **in your dreams!** tu peux toujours rêver!

(**c**) *(marvel)* merveille *f*; **it's a dream come true** c'est un rêve devenu réalité, mon/son/*etc* rêve s'est réalisé; **it worked like a dream** cela a réussi à merveille; **my interview went like a dream** mon entretien s'est passé à merveille; **this car goes like a dream** cette voiture marche à merveille; *Fam* **a dream of a house** une maison de rêve ❑; *Fam* **she's a real dream** c'est un amour, elle est vraiment adorable ❑

(**d**) *(daydream)* rêverie *f*, rêve *m*; **he's always in a dream** il est toujours dans les nuages *ou* en train de rêver

4 *comp (car, person, house)* de rêve

▸▸ *Cin* ***dream sequence*** séquence *f* onirique; *Pol* ***the dream ticket*** *(policies)* le programme utopique *ou* à faire rêver; *(candidates)* le couple idéal; ***a dream world*** *(ideal)* un monde utopique; *(imaginary)* un monde imaginaire; **she lives in a dream world** elle vit dans les nuages

▸**dream away** *vt sep* passer *ou* perdre en rêveries; **she would dream away the hours watching the clouds float by** elle passait des heures à rêver en regardant passer les nuages

▸**dream up** *vt sep* imaginer, inventer, concocter; **some wonderful new scheme that the government has dreamt up** encore un de ces merveilleux projets concoctés par le gouvernement; **where did you dream that up?** où es-tu allé pêcher ça?

'The Dream of Gerontius' *Newman, Elgar* 'Le Songe de Gerontius'

I have a dream

Cette célèbre formule est extraite d'un discours que prononça Martin Luther King à Washington au cours d'un rassemblement du mouvement pour les droits civiques en 1963. Dans son discours il parlait de l'Amérique dont il rêvait, où tous les citoyens seraient égaux et vivraient ensemble dans l'harmonie.

Aujourd'hui on utilise cette phrase pour parler de tout projet, toute idée nouvelle qui nous tient particulièrement à cœur. On pourra dire par exemple **I have a dream that one day everyone will have access to a computer** ("je rêve qu'un jour chacun puisse avoir accès à un ordinateur").

dreamboat ['dri:mbəʊt] *n Fam Old-fashioned (man)* beau gosse *m*

dreamer ['dri:mə(r)] *n* rêveur(euse) *m,f*; *(idealist)* rêveur(euse) *m,f*, utopiste *mf*; *Pej* songe-creux *m inv*

dreamily ['dri:mɪlɪ] *adv (act)* d'un air rêveur *ou* songeur; *(speak)* d'un ton rêveur *ou* songeur; *(to wander)* comme dans un rêve; *(absent-mindedly)* d'un air absent

dreaminess ['dri:mɪnɪs] *n* (état *m* de) rêverie *f*, (état *m* d') esprit *m* songeur; **the dreaminess of her eyes** ses yeux *mpl* rêveurs

dreamland ['dri:mlænd] *n* pays *m* imaginaire *ou* des rêves *ou* des songes; **she's in dreamland** elle est au pays des rêves

dreamless ['dri:mlɪs] *adj* sans rêves

dreamlessly ['dri:mlɪslɪ] *adv (sleep)* d'un sommeil sans rêves

dreamlike ['dri:mlaɪk] *adj* irréel, onirique; **the music/the play has a dreamlike quality** la musique/la pièce a quelque chose d'irréel

dreamt [dremt] *pt & pp of* **dream**

dreamy ['dri:mɪ] *(compar* **dreamier,** *superl* **dreamiest)** *adj* (**a**) *(vague → person)* rêveur, songeur; *(→ expression)* rêveur; *(absent-minded)* rêveur, distrait; **the dreamy look in her eye** son regard rêveur (**b**) *(impractical → person)* utopique, rêveur; *(→ idea)* chimérique, utopique (**c**) *(music, voice)* langoureux (**d**) *Fam (wonderful)* magnifique ❑, ravissant ❑

drear [drɪə(r)] *adj Literary* morne, triste

drearily ['drɪərəlɪ] *adv* tristement; **drearily dressed** tristement vêtu; **drearily furnished** tristement meublé; **the storyline is drearily predictable** l'intrigue n'est que trop prévisible

dreariness ['drɪərɪnɪs] *n (of surroundings)* aspect *m* morne *ou* terne, monotonie *f*; *(of life)* monotonie *f*, tristesse *f*; **the dreariness of the weather** la grisaille

dreary ['drɪərɪ] *(compar* **drearier,** *superl* **dreariest)** *adj (surroundings)* morne, triste; *(life)* morne, monotone; *(work, job)* monotone, ennuyeux; *(person)* ennuyeux (comme la pluie); *(weather)* maussade, morne

dreck [drek] *n (UNCOUNT) Am very Fam (rubbish)* ordures ❑ *fpl*; *(excrement)* merde *f*

drecky ['drekɪ] *(compar* **dreckier,** *superl* **dreckiest)** *adj Am very Fam* merdique

dredge [dredʒ] **1** *vt* (**a**) *(river)* draguer; **they dredged the river for the body** ils ont dragué le fleuve à la recherche du corps (**b**) *Culin (with flour, sugar)* saupoudrer; *(with breadcrumbs)* paner

2 *n Naut* drague *f*

▸**dredge up** *vt sep* draguer; *Fig (scandal, unpleasant news)* déterrer, ressortir; **to dredge sth up out of one's memory** ressortir qch de sa mémoire; **where did you dredge these old photographs up from?** où as-tu été repêcher ces vieilles photos?

dredger ['dredʒə(r)] *n* (**a**) *Naut (ship)* dragueur *m*; *(machine)* drague *f* (**b**) *Culin* saupoudreuse *f*, saupoudroir *m*

dredging ['dredʒɪŋ] *n Naut (of river)* dragage *m*

Dred Scott [ˌdred'skɒt] *n* **the Dred Scott case** = procès de 1857 par lequel la Cour suprême des États-Unis refusait d'accorder la citoyenneté aux Noirs et leur interdisait ainsi de mener des actions en justice

dregs [dregz] *npl also Fig* lie *f*; **she drank the tea down to the dregs** elle a bu le thé jusqu'à la dernière goutte; **the dregs of society** la lie *ou* les bas-fonds *mpl* de la société

dreich [dri:χ] *adj Scot* lugubre

drench [drentʃ] **1** *vt* (**a**) *(soak)* tremper, mouiller; **to get drenched (with rain)** se faire tremper, *Fam* se faire saucer; **drenched to the skin** trempé jusqu'aux os; **to be drenched with sweat** être en nage; **by the time we got home we were absolutely drenched** le temps d'arriver à la maison, nous étions complètement trempés; *Fig* **she had drenched herself with perfume** elle s'était aspergée de parfum

(**b**) *Vet* donner *ou* faire avaler un médicament à

2 *n Vet* (dose *f* de) médicament *m*

drenching ['drentʃɪŋ] **1** *n* trempage *m*

2 *adj* **drenching rain** pluie *f* battante *ou* diluvienne

Dresden ['drezdən] *n* (**a**) *(city)* Dresde (**b**) *(china)* porcelaine *f* de Saxe, saxe *m*; **a piece of Dresden china** un saxe

dress [dres] **1** *n* (**a**) *(frock)* robe *f*; **a cotton/summer dress** une robe de coton/d'été

(**b**) *(clothing)* habillement *m*, tenue *f*

(**c**) *(style of dress)* tenue *f*, toilette *f*; **formal/informal dress** tenue *f* de cérémonie/de ville; **in Indian dress** en tenue indienne; **to wear Western dress** s'habiller à l'occidentale; **in full dress** *(of men)* en grande tenue; *(of women)* en grande toilette; *Mil* en grande tenue, en uniforme de parade; **to have good dress sense** savoir s'habiller; **she's got no dress sense** elle ne sait pas s'habiller

2 *vt* (**a**) *(clothe)* habiller; **she dressed herself** *or* **got dressed** elle s'est habillée; **to be dressed in black/silk** être vêtu de noir/soie; **dressed in rags** vêtu *ou* couvert de haillons; **dressed as a clown/a witch** *(for a party)* déguisé en clown/en sorcière

(**b**) *(arrange → gen)* orner, parer; *(→ shop window)* faire la vitrine de; *(→ ship)* pavoiser; *(groom → horse)* panser; *(→ hair)* coiffer

(**c**) *(wound)* panser; **he dressed my wound** il a fait mon pansement

(**d**) *Culin (salad)* assaisonner, garnir; *(meat, fish)* parer; **dressed chicken** poulet *m* prêt à cuire; **dressed crab** crabe *m* tout préparé pour la table

(**e**) *(treat → cloth, skins)* préparer, apprêter; *(→ leather)* corroyer; *(→ stone)* tailler, dresser; *(→ metal)* polir; *(→ timber)* dégrossir

(**f**) *(bush, tree)* tailler; *(woods)* dégrossir

(**g**) *Agr (field)* façonner

(**h**) *Mil (troops)* aligner; **to dress ranks** se mettre en rangs

(**i**) *(neuter → animal)* dresser

3 *vi* (**a**) *(get dressed, wear clothes)* s'habiller; **she always dresses very smartly** elle s'habille toujours avec beaucoup d'élégance; **to dress for dinner** *(gen)* se mettre en tenue de soirée; *(man)* se mettre en smoking; *(woman)* se mettre en robe du soir; **do we have to dress for dinner?** est-ce qu'il faut s'habiller pour le dîner?

(**b**) *Mil (soldiers)* s'aligner

▸▸ ***dress coat*** habit *m*, queue-de-pie *f*; ***dress code*** code *m* vestimentaire; *Theat* ***dress circle*** premier balcon *m*, corbeille *f*; ***dress designer*** modéliste *mf*, dessinateur(trice) *m,f* de mode; *(famous)* couturier *m*; *Theat* ***dress rehearsal*** (répétition *f*) générale *f*; *Fig (practice)* répétition *f* générale; ***dress shield*** dessous-de-bras *m inv*; ***dress shirt*** chemise *f* de soirée; ***dress suit*** habit *m*, tenue *f* de soirée; *Mil* ***dress uniform*** tenue *f* de cérémonie

▸**dress down** *Br* **1** *vi* s'habiller simplement

2 *vt sep Fam (scold)* passer un savon à

▸**dress up** **1** *vi* (**a**) *(put on best clothes)* s'habiller, se mettre sur son trente et un; **he was all dressed up** il était tout endimanché

(**b**) *(put on disguise)* se déguiser, se costumer; **she dressed up as a clown** elle s'est déguisée en clown; **children love dressing up** les enfants adorent se déguiser

2 *vt sep* (**a**) *(put on best clothes)* habiller; **to be all dressed up, to be dressed up to the nines** être sur son trente et un; *Fam Hum* **she's all dressed up with nowhere to go** elle s'est mise sur son trente et un mais elle n'a personne avec qui sortir

(**b**) *(disguise)* déguiser; **his mother had dressed him up as a soldier** sa mère l'avait déguisé en soldat

(**c**) *(smarten)* rendre plus habillé

(**d**) *(embellish)* orner; **you could dress up the outfit with a nice scarf** tu pourrais rendre la tenue plus habillée avec un joli foulard; **it's the same old clichés dressed up as new ideas** c'est toujours les mêmes clichés, mais présentés comme des idées novatrices

dressage ['dresɑ:ʒ] *n Horseriding* dressage *m*

dressed ['drest] *adj* habillé; **a well-dressed/smartly-dressed man** un homme bien habillé/élégant; **dressed in blue chiffon** vêtu de mousseline de soie bleue; **I'm not dressed yet** je ne suis pas encore habillé; **she was not appropriately dressed for the country/for gardening** elle n'avait pas la tenue appropriée *ou* qui convenait pour la campagne/pour jardiner; **she was dressed as a man** elle était habillée en homme; *Fam* **she was dressed to kill** elle s'était mise sur son trente et un

dresser ['dresə(r)] *n* (**a**) *(person)* **he's a smart/sloppy dresser** il s'habille avec beaucoup de goût/avec négligence (**b**) *Theat* habilleur(euse) *m,f* (**c**) *(tool → for wood)* raboteuse *f*; *(→ for stone)* rabotin *m* (**d**) *(for dishes)* buffet *m*, dressoir *m* (**e**) *Am (for clothing)* commode *f*

dressiness ['dresɪnɪs] *n (of clothes, person)* élégance *f*, chic *m*

dressing ['dresɪŋ] **1** *n* (**a**) *(act of getting dressed)* habillement *m*, habillage *m*

(**b**) *Culin (sauce)* sauce *f*, assaisonnement *m*; *Am (stuffing)* farce *f*; **an oil and vinegar dressing** une vinaigrette

(**c**) *(for wound)* pansement *m*; **to apply a dressing** mettre *ou* faire un pansement

(**d**) *Agr (fertilizer)* engrais *m*

(**e**) *(for cloth, leather)* apprêt *m*

2 dressings *npl Constr* moulures *fpl*, parement *m*

▸▸ *Old-fashioned* ***dressing case*** trousse *f* de toilette, nécessaire *m* de toilette; ***dressing gown*** robe *f* de chambre, peignoir *m*; ***dressing room*** *(at home)* dressing-room *m*, dressing *m*, vestiaire *m*; *(at gymnasium, sports ground)* vestiaire *m*; *Theat* loge *f* (d'acteur); *Am (in shop)* cabine *f* d'essayage; *Mil* ***dressing station*** poste *m* de secours; ***dressing table*** coiffeuse *f*, (table *f* de) toilette *f*; ***dressing up*** *(children's activity)* déguisement *m*

dressing-down *n Br Fam* réprimande ❑ *f*, semonce ❑ *f*; **to give sb a dressing-down** passer un savon à qn; **his boss gave him a real** *or* **severe dressing-down** son patron lui a passé un sacré *ou* sérieux savon; **he got a dressing-down** il s'est fait passer un savon

dressing-table set *n* accessoires *mpl* pour coiffeuse

dressmaker ['dresˌmeɪkə(r)] *n* couturier(ère) *m,f*

dressmaking ['dresˌmeɪkɪŋ] *n* couture *f*, confection *f* des robes

dressy ['dresɪ] *(compar* **dressier,** *superl* **dressiest)** *adj (clothes)* (qui fait) habillé, élégant;

(person) élégant, chic; *(event)* habillé; **the charity ball is always a very dressy occasion** le bal de charité est toujours un événement très habillé

drew [druː] *pt of* **draw**

drey [dreɪ] *n* nid *m* d'écureuil

drib [drɪb] *n (idiom)* **in dribs and drabs** petit à petit

dribble ['drɪbəl] **1** *vi* (**a**) *(liquid → drop by drop)* dégoutter, tomber goutte à goutte; *(→ in a trickle)* dégouliner; **the wine dribbled down his chin** le vin lui dégoulina le long du menton; *Fig* **the strikers slowly dribbled back to work** les grévistes reprenaient le travail par petits groupes

(**b**) *(baby)* baver

(**c**) *Sport* dribbler

2 *vt* (**a**) *(trickle)* laisser couler *ou* tomber lentement; **he was dribbling milk from his mouth** du lait dégoulinait de sa bouche; **you're dribbling water everywhere!** tu fais dégouliner de l'eau partout!

(**b**) *Sport (ball, puck)* dribbler

3 *n* (**a**) *(of person, dog)* bave *f*

(**b**) *(trickle)* filet *m*

(**c**) *Fig (small amount)* **a dribble of** un petit peu de

(**d**) *Sport* dribble *m*

dribbler ['drɪblə(r)] *n Sport* dribbleur *m*

dribbling ['drɪblɪŋ] *n* (**a**) *(of baby)* écoulement *m* de bave; **people were disgusted by his dribbling** les gens étaient dégoûtés de le voir baver comme ça (**b**) *Sport* dribbling *m*

driblet ['drɪblɪt] *n (of liquid)* gouttelette *f*, petite goutte *f*; **in driblets** goutte à goutte, au compte-gouttes; *Fig* au compte-gouttes

dried [draɪd] *adj (fruit)* sec (sèche); *(meat)* séché; *(milk, eggs)* déshydraté

dried-up *adj (river bed, lake)* asséché; *(apple, person)* ratatiné, desséché; *(talent, well)* tari; *(beauty, love)* fané

drier ['draɪə(r)] **1** *compar of* **dry**

2 *n (for clothes)* séchoir *m* (à linge); *(for hair → hand-held)* séchoir *m* (à cheveux), sèche-cheveux *m inv*; *(→ helmet)* casque *m* (sèche-cheveux); **under the drier** sous le casque

driest ['draɪɪst] *superl of* **dry**

drift [drɪft] **1** *vi* (**a**) *(float → on water)* aller à la dérive, dériver; *(→ in current, wind)* être emporté; *Aviat* dériver; *Naut* **to drift off course** dévier de son cap; **the boat drifted downstream** le bateau descendait le fleuve à la dérive *ou* à vau-l'eau; **the clouds drifted** les nuages étaient poussés par le vent; **mist drifted in from the sea** il y avait de la brume qui venait de la mer; **the smell of cooking drifted up from the restaurant** des odeurs de cuisine montaient du restaurant; **the sound of music drifted up from the garden** on entendait de la musique qui montait du jardin

(**b**) *(sand, snow)* s'amonceler, s'entasser; **some snow had drifted in through the open door** de la neige s'était infiltrée par la porte ouverte

(**c**) *(move aimlessly)* marcher nonchalamment; **people began to drift in/out** les gens commençaient à entrer/sortir d'un pas nonchalant; **the audience started to drift towards the exit** les spectateurs se dirigeaient lentement vers la sortie; *Fig* **the conversation drifted from one topic to another** la conversation passait d'un sujet à un autre; **he just drifts along, he drifts through life** il se laisse porter par les événements; **to drift apart** *(friends)* se perdre de vue; *(couple)* se séparer petit à petit; **he drifted into a life of crime** il a sombré dans la délinquance

(**d**) *Electron* se décaler

2 *vt* (**a**) *(of current)* entraîner, charrier; *(of wind)* emporter, pousser

(**b**) *(of sand, snow)* amonceler, entasser

3 *n* (**a**) *(flow)* mouvement *m*, force *f*; *(of air, water)* poussée *f*; **the drift of the current took us southwards** le courant nous a emportés vers le sud; **the drift of the tide** *(speed)* la vitesse de la marée; *(direction)* le sens de la marée; *Fig* **the drift from the land** l'exode *m* rural, la migration vers la ville; **population drift** mouvement *m* de population; **the drift towards war** la dérive vers la guerre; *Geog* **the North Atlantic Drift** le courant nord-atlantique

(**b**) *(of leaves, sand)* amoncellement *m*, entassement *m*; *(of fallen snow)* amoncellement *m*, congère *f*; *(of falling snow)* rafale *f*, bourrasque *f*; *(of clouds)* traînée *f*; *(of dust, mist)* nuage *m*; *Geol (deposits)* apports *mpl*

(**c**) *Aviat & Naut (of plane, ship)* dérivation *f*; *(of missile)* déviation *f*; *(deviation from course)* dérive *f*

(**d**) *Electron* déviation *f*

(**e**) *(trend)* tendance *f*; **the drift back towards the classics** le retour aux classiques

(**f**) *(meaning)* sens *m*, portée *f*; **do you get my drift?** voyez-vous où je veux en venir?; *Fam* **I get the/your drift** je pige

(**g**) *Ling* évolution *f (d'une langue)*

(**h**) *Mining* galerie *f* chassante

►► *Naut* ***drift anchor*** ancre *f* flottante; ***drift ice*** *(UNCOUNT)* glaces *fpl* flottantes *ou* en dérive; *Fishing* ***drift net*** filet *m* dérivant

►**drift off** *vi (fall asleep)* s'assoupir; **I drifted off for a while** je me suis assoupi quelques instants

drifter ['drɪftə(r)] *n* (**a**) *(person)* = personne qui n'a pas de but dans la vie; **he's a bit of a drifter** il n'arrive pas à se fixer (**b**) *Naut (boat)* drifter *m*

drifting ['drɪftɪŋ] **1** *adj (ship)* à la dérive; *(cloud)* traînant; **drifting snow** neige *f* soulevée par le vent; **drifting banks of fog/cloud** des traînées *fpl* de brouillard/de nuages

2 *n (caused by current)* entraînement *m* par le courant; *(caused by wind)* entraînement *m* par le vent; *(formation of drifts → of snow)* amoncellement *m*; **caused by the drifting of the snow across the road** causé par la neige soulevée par le vent en travers de la route

driftwood ['drɪftwʊd] *n (UNCOUNT)* bois *mpl* flottants

drill [drɪl] **1** *n* (**a**) *(manual)* porte-foret *m*; *(electric)* perceuse *f*; *(of dentist)* fraise *f (de dentiste)*, roulette *f*; *Petr (for oil well)* trépan *m*; *(pneumatic)* marteau *m* piqueur; *Mining* perforatrice *f*

(**b**) *(bit)* **drill (bit)** foret *m*, mèche *f*

(**c**) *(exercises)* exercice(s) *m(pl)*; *Mil* manœuvre(s) *f(pl)*, drill *m*; *Sch* **verb drill** exercices *mpl* oraux sur les verbes; *Mil* **firing drill** instruction *f* du tir; *Br Fam Fig* **I know the drill** je sais ce qu'il faut faire ❑, je connais la marche à suivre ❑; *Br Fam* **what's the drill?** *(what do you want me to do?)* qu'est-ce qu'il y a à faire?; *(for working the photocopier etc)* comment on fait?

(**d**) *Tex* treillis *m*

(**e**) *Agr (machine)* semoir *m*; *(furrow)* sillon *m*

2 *vt* (**a**) *(metal, wood)* forer, percer; *(hole)* percer; *(dentist)* fraiser; *Petr* **to drill an oil well** forer un puits de pétrole

(**b**) *(train)* faire faire des exercices à; *Mil* faire faire l'exercice à; **I drilled him in what to say** je lui ai fait la leçon sur ce qu'il fallait dire; **the troops are well drilled** les troupes sont bien entraînées; **to drill good manners into sb** apprendre les bonnes manières à qn; **it was drilled into them from an early age not to accept lifts from strangers** depuis leur plus jeune âge, on leur avait enfoncé dans la tête qu'il ne fallait pas accepter de monter en voiture avec des inconnus; *Sch* **to drill pupils in French verbs** faire faire aux élèves des exercices sur les verbes français

(**c**) *Agr (seeds)* semer en sillon; *(field)* tracer des sillons dans

(**d**) *Fam (ball)* **he drilled the ball into the back of the net** il envoya la balle droit au fond du filet ❑

3 *vi* (**a**) *(bore)* forer; **they are drilling for oil** ils forent *ou* effectuent des forages pour trouver du pétrole

(**b**) *(train)* faire de l'exercice, s'entraîner; *Mil* être à l'exercice, manœuvrer

►► *Mil* ***drill sergeant*** sergent *m* instructeur

drilling ['drɪlɪŋ] *n (UNCOUNT) (in metal, wood)* forage *m*, perçage *m*; *(by dentist)* fraisage *m*; **drilling for oil** forage *m* pétrolier

►► *Petr* ***drilling platform*** plate-forme *f* (de forage); *Petr* ***drilling rig*** *(on land)* derrick *m*, tour *f* de forage; *(at sea)* plate-forme *f* (de forage); *Petr* ***drilling ship*** navire *m* de forage

drillmaster ['drɪlˌmɑːstə(r)] *n Am* (**a**) *Mil* sergent *m* instructeur (**b**) *Fam Fig* garde-chiourme *m*

drily ['draɪlɪ] *adv (wryly)* d'un air pince-sans-rire; *(coldly)* sèchement, d'un ton sec

DRINK [drɪŋk]

boire	► **1; 2**
boisson	► **3 (a)**
verre	► **3 (b)**
gorgée	► **3 (c)**
alcool	► **3 (d)**

(*pt* **drank** [dræŋk], *pp* **drunk** [drʌŋk]) **1** *vt* boire, prendre; **would you like something to drink?** voulez-vous boire quelque chose?; **I never drink coffee** je ne prends jamais de café; **what are you drinking tonight?** que voulez-vous boire ce soir?; **the water is not fit to drink** l'eau n'est pas potable; **this coffee isn't fit to drink** ce café est imbuvable; **the wine is best drunk at room temperature** ce vin se boit chambré; **drink your soup** mange ta soupe; **to drink one's fill** boire à sa soif; **to drink sb's health, to drink a toast to sb** boire à la santé de qn; **he drank himself into a stupor** il s'est soûlé jusqu'à l'hébétude; **I could drink the well dry** je boirais la mer et ses poissons; **he's drinking himself to death** l'alcool le tue peu à peu; **to drink sb under the table** faire rouler qn sous la table; **he drank us under the table** il était encore debout alors que nous roulions sous la table; **I could drink you under the table any day!** je te parie que je peux boire plus que toi!

2 *vi* (**a**) *(gen)* boire; **I don't drink** je ne bois pas; **to drink heavily** boire beaucoup; **she drank out of** *or* **(straight) from the bottle** elle a bu à la bouteille; **I only drink socially** je ne bois jamais seul; **don't drink and drive** ≃ boire ou conduire, il faut choisir; **he drinks like a fish** il boit comme un trou; **I'll drink to that!** je suis pour!; **we drank to their success** nous avons bu *ou* porté un toast à leur succès

(**b**) *(of wine)* **it won't drink quite as well in two years' time** dans deux ans il aura perdu de sa saveur

3 *n* (**a**) *(non-alcoholic)* boisson *f*; **may I have a drink?** puis-je boire quelque chose?; **a drink of water** un verre d'eau; **to give sb a drink** donner à boire à qn; **there's plenty of food and drink** il y a tout ce qu'on veut à boire et à manger; **you can get drinks from the machine** vous pouvez prendre des boissons à la machine; **hot drinks** boissons chaudes

(**b**) *(alcoholic)* verre *m*; *(before dinner)* apéritif *m*; *(after dinner)* digestif *m*; **we invited them in for a drink** nous les avons invités à prendre un verre; *Fam* **fancy a drink?** que diriez-vous d'un verre? ❑; **I need a drink!** vite, donnez-moi à boire!; **I haven't had a drink in six months** je n'ai pas bu d'alcool depuis six mois; **he likes** *or* **enjoys a drink** il aime bien boire un verre; **to buy** *or* **to stand a round of drinks** payer une tournée; **to pay for the drinks** payer les consommations; **drinks are on the house!** la maison offre à boire!; **he'd had one drink too many** il avait bu un verre de trop, il avait un verre dans le nez

(**c**) *(mouthful)* gorgée *f*; **have another little drink** prends encore une petite gorgée

(**d**) *(alcohol)* la boisson, l'alcool *m*; **she's taken to drink** elle s'est mise à boire; **to be the worse for drink** être en état d'ébriété; **he can't hold his drink** il ne tient pas l'alcool; **to drive under the influence of drink** conduire en état d'ivresse *ou* d'ébriété; **to smell of drink** sentir l'alcool; **he has a drink problem** il boit trop, il s'adonne à la boisson

(**e**) *Br Fam (sea)* flotte *f*; **to be in the drink** être dans la flotte *ou* à la baille

►► *Am* ***drinks machine, drink machine*** distributeur *m* de boissons

►**drink away** *vt sep (troubles)* noyer; *(fortune)* boire; **he's trying to drink his troubles away** il essaie de noyer ses ennuis dans l'alcool; **to drink away one's fortune** boire sa fortune

►**drink down** *vt sep* avaler *ou* boire d'un trait

►**drink in** *vt sep* (**a**) *(water)* absorber, boire (**b**) *Fig (story, words)* boire; *(atmosphere, surroundings)* s'imprégner de; **we drank in every word** pas un seul mot ne nous a échappé, nous avons bu ses paroles

▶**drink up** **1** *vt sep* boire (jusqu'à la dernière goutte), finir

2 *vi* vider son verre; **drink up!** finissez vos verres!

---

drinkable ['drɪŋkəbəl] *adj (safe to drink)* potable; *(pleasant to drink)* buvable; **this wine's very drinkable** c'est un vin qui se laisse boire

drink-driver *n Br* conducteur(trice) *m,f* ivre; **he's a notorious drink-driver** tout le monde sait qu'il conduit souvent en état d'ébriété

drink-driving *n Br* conduite *f* en état d'ivresse

drinker ['drɪŋkə(r)] *n* buveur(euse) *m,f*; **I'm not a coffee drinker** je ne suis pas un buveur de café; **he's a hard** *or* **heavy drinker** il boit sec *ou* beaucoup; **we're not really drinkers** nous ne sommes pas des grands buveurs

drinking ['drɪŋkɪŋ] **1** *n* fait *m* de boire; **eating and drinking** manger et boire; **heavy drinking** ivrognerie *f*; **I'm not used to drinking** je n'ai pas l'habitude de boire; **his drinking is becoming a problem** le fait qu'il boive devient un problème; **it was her drinking that destroyed the marriage** c'est son alcoolisme qui a détruit leur mariage; **I'm not a drinking man** je n'ai pas l'habitude de boire

2 *comp (habits)* de buveur; *(bout, companion, session)* de beuverie

▶▶ ***drinking chocolate*** chocolat *m* à boire; *(powder)* chocolat *m* en poudre; *(hot drink)* chocolat *m* chaud; ***drinking fountain*** *(in street)* fontaine *f* publique; *(in corridor, public conveniences)* jet *m* d'eau potable; ***drinking laws*** = lois sur les débits de boissons; ***drinking song*** chanson *f* à boire; ***drinking straw*** paille *f*; ***drinking trough*** abreuvoir *m*; ***drinking water*** eau *f* potable

drinking-up time *n Br* = moment où les clients doivent finir leur verre avant la fermeture du bar

drip [drɪp] *(pt & pp* **dripped**, *cont* **dripping**) **1** *vi* (**a**) *(liquid)* tomber goutte à goutte, dégoutter; **the rain is dripping down my neck** la pluie me dégouline dans le cou; **sweat dripped from his brow** son front ruisselait de sueur; **I was dripping with sweat** j'étais en nage; **her hands dripped with blood** du sang dégoulinait de ses mains; *Fig* **she was dripping with diamonds** elle était couverte de diamants; *Fig* **dripping with sentimentality** dégoulinant de sentimentalité

(**b**) *(tap)* fuir, goutter; *(nose)* couler; *(washing)* s'égoutter; *(walls)* suinter; *(hair, trees)* dégoutter, ruisseler

2 *vt* laisser tomber goutte à goutte; **you're dripping coffee everywhere** tu mets du café partout

3 *n* (**a**) *(falling drops → from tap, gutter, ceiling)* égouttement *m*, dégoulinement *m*; **the drip method of making coffee** la méthode filtre de faire le café

(**b**) *(sound → from trees, roofs)* bruit *m* de l'eau qui goutte; *(→ from tap)* bruit *m* d'un robinet qui fuit *ou* goutte

(**c**) *(drop)* goutte *f*

(**d**) *Fam Pej (person)* nouille *f*, lavette *f*

(**e**) *Med (device)* goutte-à-goutte *m inv*; *(solution)* perfusion *f*; **she's on a drip** elle est sous perfusion

(**f**) *Archit* larmier *m*

▶▶ *Mktg* ***drip advertising*** publicité *f* continue, publicité *f* goutte à goutte; ***drip mat*** dessous-de-verre *m inv*; ***drip pan*** lèchefrite *f*; ***drip tray*** lèchefrite *f*

drip-dry **1** *adj* qui ne nécessite aucun repassage

2 *vi* s'égoutter

3 *vt* (faire) égoutter

drip-feed **1** *n Med (device)* goutte-à-goutte *m inv*; *(solution)* perfusion *f*

2 *vt Med* alimenter par perfusion; *Fig (company)* perfuser

drip-feeding *n Med* alimentation *f* par perfusion; *Fig (of company)* subventions *fpl* données au coup par coup

dripping ['drɪpɪŋ] **1** *n* (**a**) *Culin (of meat)* graisse *f* *(de rôti)*; **bread and dripping** tartine *f* à la graisse (**b**) *(of liquid)* égouttement *m*, égouttage *m*

2 *adj* (**a**) *(tap)* qui fuit *ou* goutte; **dripping with blood/with sweat** ruisselant de sang/de sueur (**b**) *(very wet)* trempé

3 *adv* **his clothes were dripping wet** ses vêtements étaient trempés *ou* étaient à tordre

▶▶ ***dripping pan*** lèchefrite *f*

drip-proof *adj (paint, varnish)* qui ne coule pas

drippy ['drɪpɪ] *(compar* **drippier**, *superl* **drippiest**) *adj* (**a**) *Fam Pej (person)* mou (molle) ▫ (**b**) *(tap)* qui fuit *ou* goutte

dripstone ['drɪpstəʊn] *n Archit* larmier *m*

drivability = **driveability**

DRIVE [draɪv]

conduire	▶ **1 (a); 2 (a)**
chasser	▶ **1 (b)**
pousser	▶ **1 (b), (d)**
surmener	▶ **1 (c)**
percer	▶ **1 (f)**
faire fonctionner	▶ **1 (g)**
aller en voiture	▶ **2 (a)**
rouler	▶ **2 (b)**
se ruer	▶ **2 (c)**
promenade en voiture	▶ **3 (a)**
allée	▶ **3 (b)**
dynamisme	▶ **3 (c)**
campagne	▶ **3 (d)**

(pt **drove** [drəʊv], *pp* **driven** ['drɪvən]) **1** *vt* (**a**) *(bus, car, train)* conduire; *(racing car)* piloter; **can you drive a minibus?** savez-vous conduire un minibus?; **I drive a Volvo** j'ai une Volvo; **he drives a taxi/lorry** il est chauffeur de taxi/camionneur; **she drives racing cars** elle est pilote de course; **he drove her into town** il l'a conduite *ou* emmenée en voiture en ville; **could you drive me home?** pourriez-vous me reconduire chez moi?; **she drove the car into a tree** elle a heurté un arbre avec la voiture; **I haven't driven all this way just to...** je n'ai pas fait tout ce chemin juste pour...

(**b**) *(chase)* chasser, pousser; **to drive sb out of the house/of the country** chasser qn de la maison/du pays; **we drove the cattle back into the shed** nous avons fait rentrer le bétail dans l'étable; **the wind drove the snow up against the wall** le vent chassait la neige contre le mur; **the waves drove the ship against the rocks** les vagues ont jeté le navire contre les rochers; **the strong winds had driven the ship off course** les vents forts avaient dévié le navire de sa route; *Fig* **her words drove all worries from his mind** ses paroles lui ont fait complètement oublier ses soucis; **they have driven us into a corner** ils nous ont mis au pied du mur

(**c**) *(work)* **it doesn't pay to drive your workers too hard** on ne gagne rien à surmener ses employés; **he drives himself too hard** il se surmène

(**d**) *(force)* pousser, inciter; **he was driven to it** on lui a forcé la main; **driven by jealousy, he killed her** il l'a tuée sous l'emprise de la jalousie; **it's enough to drive you to drink!** cela vous pousserait un honnête homme à boire!; **it's driving him to drink** cela le pousse à boire *ou* à la boisson; **the situation is driving me to despair/distraction** la situation me pousse au désespoir/me rend fou (folle); *Fam* **to drive sb crazy** *or* **mad** *or* **up the wall** rendre qn fou (folle); *Fam* **his performance drove the audience wild** son spectacle a mis le public en délire

(**e**) *(hammer)* **to drive a nail home** enfoncer un clou; *Fig* **to drive a point home** faire admettre son point de vue; *Fam* **I can't drive it into his thick head that...** je n'arrive pas à faire comprendre à cet idiot que...; **to drive a hard bargain** avoir toujours le dernier mot en affaires, être dur en affaires

(**f**) *(bore → hole)* percer; *(→ tunnel)* percer, creuser

(**g**) *(operate → machine)* faire fonctionner; *Tech* entraîner; **driven by electricity** marchant à l'électricité; **the pinion is driven in rotation** le pignon est actionné par rotation

(**h**) *Golf* **to drive a ball** driver

(**i**) *Hunt (game)* rabattre; *(area)* battre

2 *vi* (**a**) *(operate a vehicle)* conduire; *(travel in vehicle)* aller en voiture; **do you** *or* **can you drive?** savez-vous conduire?; **I don't drive** *(I never learned)* je n'ai pas mon permis; **I was driving at 100 mph** ≃ je roulais à 160 km/h; **we drove home/down to the coast** nous sommes rentrés/descendus sur la côte en voiture; **they drove all night** ils ont roulé toute la nuit; **are you walking or driving?** êtes-vous à pied ou en voiture?; **who was driving?** qui était au volant?; **how did you get here? – we drove down** comment êtes-vous venus? – nous sommes venus *ou* descendus en voiture; **drive on the right** roulez à droite, tenez votre droite; **they drove straight through the town** ils ont traversé la ville sans s'y arrêter; **to drive while intoxicated** *or* **under the influence of alcohol** conduire en état d'ivresse *ou* d'ébriété

(**b**) *(car)* rouler; *Fam* **this car drives like a dream** c'est un plaisir de conduire cette voiture ▫

(**c**) *(dash)* se ruer; **rain was driving against the window** la pluie fouettait les vitres

3 *n* (**a**) *(trip in car)* promenade *f ou* trajet *m* (en voiture); **we went for a drive** nous avons fait une promenade *ou* un tour en voiture; **it's an hour's drive from here** c'est à une heure d'ici en voiture; **it's a very pleasant drive to the coast** la route est très belle jusqu'à la côte; **a 50-km drive** un parcours *ou* un trajet de 50 km

(**b**) *(leading to house)* allée *f*; **the car was parked in the drive** la voiture était garée dans l'allée

(**c**) *(energy)* dynamisme *m*, énergie *f*; **we need someone with drive** il nous faut quelqu'un de dynamique *ou* d'entreprenant; **to have plenty of drive** être très dynamique; **he lacks drive** il manque d'allant *ou* de dynamisme

(**d**) *Psy (urge)* besoin *m*, instinct *m*; *(sexual)* pulsions *fpl*

(**e**) *(campaign)* campagne *f*; **the company is having a sales drive** la compagnie fait une campagne de vente

(**f**) *Br Cards (for bridge, whist)* tournoi *m*

(**g**) *Sport (in cricket, tennis)* coup *m* droit; *Golf* drive *m*; *Ftbl* tir *m*, shoot *m*

(**h**) *(of animals)* rassemblement *m*; *Hunt* battue *f*; **cattle drive** rassemblement *m* du bétail

(**i**) *Tech (power transmission)* transmission *f*, commande *f*; *Aut* **four-wheel drive** quatre roues motrices *f inv*, quatre-quatre *m inv ou f inv*

(**j**) *Comput (for disk)* unité *f*, lecteur *m*; *(for tape)* dérouleur *m*; **drive a:/b:** unité *f* de disque a:/b:

(**k**) *Mil* poussée *f*, offensive *f*

4 *comp Tech (mechanism, device)* d'entraînement, d'actionnement, de transmission

▶**drive along** **1** *vi (car)* rouler, circuler; *(person)* rouler, conduire

2 *vt sep (of river, wind)* pousser, chasser

▶**drive at** *vt insep* vouloir dire; **she didn't understand what he was driving at** elle ne comprenait pas où il voulait en venir; **I see what you're driving at** je vous vois venir

▶**drive away** **1** *vi (person)* s'en aller *ou* partir (en voiture); *(car)* démarrer

2 *vt sep (car)* démarrer; *(person)* emmener en voiture; *Fig (animal, intruder)* chasser, éloigner; *(friend)* éloigner; *(doubt, suspicion)* écarter; *(fear)* chasser

▶**drive back** **1** *vi (person)* rentrer en voiture; *(car)* retourner

2 *vt sep* (**a**) *(person)* ramener *ou* reconduire en voiture; *(car)* reculer

(**b**) *(repel)* repousser, refouler; **the soldiers were driven back by heavy machine-gun fire** les soldats furent repoussés par un puissant tir de mitrailleuse; **fear drove them back** la peur leur a fait rebrousser chemin

▶**drive by** *vi* passer *(en voiture)*

▶**drive down** *vt sep (prices, inflation etc)* faire baisser

▶**drive in** **1** *vi (person)* entrer (en voiture); *(car)* entrer

2 *vt sep (nail, stake)* enfoncer; *(screw)* visser; *(rivet)* poser

▶**drive off** **1** *vi* (**a**) *(leave → person)* s'en aller *ou* s'éloigner en voiture; *(→ car)* démarrer (**b**) *Golf* driver

2 *vt sep (frighten away)* éloigner, chasser

▶**drive on** **1** *vi (continue trip)* poursuivre sa route; *(after stopping)* reprendre la route

2 *vt sep (push)* pousser, inciter; **she drove him on to work even harder** elle l'a poussé à travailler encore plus

▶**drive out 1** *vi (person)* sortir (en voiture); *(car)* sortir
 2 *vt sep (person)* chasser, faire sortir; *(thought)* chasser; **to drive out evil spirits** *(from a place)* chasser les mauvais esprits; *(from a person)* chasser le mauvais œil

▶**drive over 1** *vi* venir *ou* aller en voiture; **we drove over to visit some friends** nous sommes allés en voiture rendre visite à des amis
 2 *vt insep (crush)* écraser
 3 *vt sep* conduire *ou* emmener en voiture

▶**drive up** *vi (person)* arriver (en voiture); *(car)* arriver; **a car drove up to the door** une voiture vint s'arrêter devant la porte

driveability [ˌdraɪvəˈbɪlɪtɪ] *n* maniabilité *f*, manœuvrabilité *m*

driveaway [ˈdraɪvəweɪ] *n Am (car)* = voiture convoyée jusqu'à son propriétaire par un autre conducteur
 ▶▶ ***driveaway car*** = voiture convoyée jusqu'à son propriétaire par un autre conducteur; ***driveaway company*** = société qui s'occupe du convoyage de véhicules jusqu'à leur propriétaire

drive-by *adj*
 ▶▶ ***drive-by killing, drive-by shooting*** fusillade *f* exécutée d'une voiture en marche

drive-in 1 *n (cinema)* drive-in *m inv*, *Can* ciné-parc *m*; *(restaurant)* = restaurant où l'on est servi dans sa voiture; *(bank)* = banque où l'on est servi dans sa voiture
 2 *adj* où l'on reste dans sa voiture

drivel [ˈdrɪvəl] *(Br pt & pp* **drivelled,** *cont* **drivelling,** *Am pt & pp* **driveled,** *cont* **driveling)** *Fam* **1** *n (UNCOUNT)* (**a**) *(nonsense)* bêtises *fpl*, radotage *m*; **to talk drivel** radoter (**b**) *(saliva)* bave ❑ *f*
 2 *vi* (**a**) *(speak foolishly)* dire des bêtises, radoter; **what's he drivelling on about?** qu'est-ce qu'il radote? (**b**) *(dribble)* baver ❑

driveline [ˈdraɪvlaɪn] *n Aut* chaîne *f* cinématique

drivelling, *Am* **driveling** [ˈdrɪvəlɪŋ] *adj Fam* radoteur; **you drivelling idiot!** espèce d'idiot!

driven [ˈdrɪvən] **1** *pp of* **drive**
 2 *adj (person)* motivé, déterminé
 ▶▶ *Tech* ***driven shaft*** arbre *m* mené *ou* récepteur

-driven [ˈdrɪvən] *suff* (**a**) *Tech* (fonctionnant) à; **electricity-/steam-driven engine** moteur *m* électrique/à vapeur (**b**) *Fig* déterminé par; **market-/consumer-driven** déterminé par les contraintes du marché/les exigences du consommateur; **to adopt a market-driven approach** se mettre dans une logique de marché (**c**) *Comput* contrôlé par; **menu-driven** contrôlé par menu

driver [ˈdraɪvə(r)] *n* (**a**) *(of car)* conducteur(-trice) *m,f*; *(of bus, taxi, lorry)* chauffeur *m*, conducteur(trice) *m,f*; *(of racing car)* pilote *m*; *(of train)* mécanicien *m*, conducteur(trice) *m,f*; *(of cart)* charretier(ère) *m,f*; *Sport (of horse-drawn vehicle)* driver *m*; **she's a good driver** elle conduit bien
 (**b**) *(of animals)* conducteur(trice) *m,f*
 (**c**) *Golf* driver *m*
 (**d**) *Comput (software)* programme *m* de gestion, pilote *m*; *(hardware)* unité *f* de contrôle
 (**e**) *(decisive factor)* facteur *m* prépondérant ou déterminant; **the key drivers of the technology boom** les facteurs déterminants dans le boom technologique
 ▶▶ *Am Sch* ***driver education,*** *Fam* ***driver ed*** cours *mpl* de conduite *(au lycée)*; *Ins* ***driver liability*** responsabilité *f* du conducteur; *Am* ***driver's license*** permis *m* de conduire; ***the driver's seat*** la place du conducteur; *Fig* **to be in the driver's seat** mener l'affaire; *Br* ***Driver and Vehicle Licensing Agency*** = service des immatriculations et des permis de conduire en Grande-Bretagne; *Br Formerly* ***Driver and Vehicle Licensing Centre*** = service des immatriculations et des permis de conduire en Grande-Bretagne

driveshaft [ˈdraɪvʃɑːft] *n Tech* arbre *m* d'entraînement, arbre *m* de transmission, arbre *m* de commande

drive-through 1 *adj* où l'on reste dans sa voiture
 2 *n (restaurant)* drive-in *m inv*; *(bank)* = banque où l'on est servi dans sa voiture

drive-time programme *n Rad* = émission aux heures de grande écoute en voiture

driveway [ˈdraɪvweɪ] *n* voie *f* privée *(menant à une habitation)*

driving [ˈdraɪvɪŋ] **1** *adj* (**a**) *(rain)* battant; **driving snow** neige *f* fouettée par le vent (**b**) *(powerful)* fort; *(ambition)* ferme
 2 *n* conduite *f*; **her driving is good** elle conduit bien; **I like driving** j'aime conduire; **bad driving** conduite *f* imprudente; *Br* **driving under the influence,** *Am* **driving while intoxicated** conduite *f* en état d'ivresse; *Am* **he was stopped for Driving While Black** un policier l'a fait se ranger sur le bord de la route pour contrôler ses papiers pour la seule raison qu'il est noir
 ▶▶ *Tech* ***driving belt*** courroie *f* de commande; *Tech* ***driving force*** force *f* motrice; *Fig* **she's the driving force behind the project** c'est elle le moteur du projet; *Br* ***driving instructor*** moniteur(trice) *m,f* de conduite *ou* d'auto-école; ***driving lesson*** leçon *f* de conduite; *Br* ***driving licence*** permis *m* de conduire; ***driving mirror*** rétroviseur *m*; *Golf* ***driving range*** practice *m*; ***driving school*** auto-école *f*; ***driving seat*** place *f* du conducteur; *Fig* **she's in the driving seat** c'est elle qui mène l'affaire *ou* qui tient les rênes; *Tech* ***driving shaft*** arbre *m* moteur; ***driving test*** examen *m* du permis de conduire; **I passed my driving test today/in 1992** j'ai eu mon permis aujourd'hui/en 1992; **he failed his driving test** il a raté son permis; *Tech* ***driving wheel*** roue *f* motrice

drizzle [ˈdrɪzəl] **1** *n* bruine *f*, crachin *m*; **the rain came down in a steady drizzle** il tombait un crachin persistant
 2 *vi* bruiner, crachiner

drizzly [ˈdrɪzlɪ] *adj* de bruine *ou* crachin, bruineux

drogue [drəʊg] *n* (**a**) *Aviat (parachute)* parachute *m* antivrille; *(windsock)* manche *f* à air (**b**) *Naut* ancre *f* flottante

droll [drəʊl] **1** *n Arch or Literary* bouffon *m*, triboulet *m*
 2 *adj (comical)* drôle, comique; *(odd)* curieux, drôle

drollery [ˈdrəʊlərɪ] *(pl* **drolleries)** *n* (**a**) *(of situation)* caractère *m* drôle, comique *m*; *(of person)* humour *m* (**b**) *(act, story, remark)* drôlerie *f*, bouffonnerie *f*, farce *f*

drollness [ˈdrəʊlnɪs] *n (of situation)* caractère *m* drôle; *(of person)* humour *m*

dromedary [ˈdrɒmədərɪ] *(pl* **dromedaries)** *n* dromadaire *m*

drone [drəʊn] **1** *n* (**a**) *(sound → of bee)* bourdonnement *m*; *(→ of engine, aircraft)* ronronnement *m*; *(louder)* vrombissement *m*; *Fig* **the drone of his voice** le ronronnement de sa voix
 (**b**) *(male bee)* abeille *f* mâle, faux-bourdon *m*; *Pej (person)* fainéant(e) *m,f*
 (**c**) *Mus* bourdon *m*
 (**d**) *(plane)* avion *m* téléguidé, drone *m*
 2 *vi (bee)* bourdonner; *(engine, aircraft)* ronronner; *(more loudly)* vrombir; **to drone on** *(person)* parler d'un ton monotone; **he droned on for hours (about his wife)** il radotait pendant des heures de sa voix monotone (sur sa femme)

drongo [ˈdrɒŋgəʊ] *(pl* **drongos)** *n* (**a**) *Zool* drongo *m* (**b**) *Austr Fam (idiot)* abruti(e) *m,f*

droning [ˈdrəʊnɪŋ] *adj (sound)* bourdonnant; *(voice)* traînant

drool [druːl] *vi* baver; *Fig* **to drool over sth** baver d'admiration *ou* s'extasier devant qch

droop [druːp] **1** *vi (head)* pencher; *(eyelids)* s'abaisser; *(body)* s'affaisser; *(shoulders)* tomber; *(flowers)* commencer à baisser la tête *ou* à se faner; **her spirits drooped** elle s'est démoralisée
 2 *n (of eyelids)* abaissement *m*; *(of head)* attitude *f* penchée; *(of body, shoulders)* affaissement *m*; *(of spirits)* langueur *f*, abattement *m*; **he could tell from the droop of her shoulders/head** il savait à ses épaules tombantes/à la façon dont elle penchait la tête

drooping [ˈdruːpɪŋ] *adj (shoulders, moustache)* tombant; *(eyelids)* abaissé; *(flowers)* qui commence à se faner; *Fig (person)* languissant; **to revive sb's drooping spirits** remonter le moral à qn

droopy [ˈdruːpɪ] *(compar* **droopier,** *superl* **droopiest)** *adj (moustache, shoulders)* tombant; *(flowers)* qui commence à se faner

DROP [drɒp]

laisser tomber	▶ **1 (a), (d)**
baisser	▶ **1 (b)**
déposer	▶ **1 (c)**
laisser échapper	▶ **1 (e)**
écrire	▶ **1 (f)**
omettre	▶ **1 (g)**
perdre	▶ **1 (h)**
tomber	▶ **2 (a), (b)**
s'écrouler	▶ **2 (b)**
baisser	▶ **2 (c)**
goutte	▶ **3 (a)**
baisse	▶ **3 (b)**
chute	▶ **3 (b), (c)**
hauteur de chute	▶ **3 (d)**

(pt & pp **dropped,** *cont* **dropping) 1** *vt* (**a**) *(let fall → accidentally)* laisser tomber; *(→ liquid)* laisser tomber goutte à goutte; *(→ trousers)* laisser tomber; *(→ bomb)* lancer, lâcher; *(→ stitch)* sauter, laisser tomber; *(release)* lâcher; **be careful not to drop it** fais attention à ne pas le laisser tomber; **drop it!** *(to dog)* lâche ça!; **he dropped it from the balcony to his accomplice** il l'a lancé à son complice depuis le balcon; **they dropped soldiers/supplies by parachute** ils ont parachuté des soldats/du ravitaillement; **to drop a curtsy** faire une révérence; *Naut* **to drop anchor** mouiller, jeter l'ancre; *Sport* **to drop a goal** *(in rugby)* marquer un drop; **she dropped the ball over the net** *(in tennis)* elle a placé un amorti juste derrière le filet; *Br Fam* **to drop a brick** *or* **a clanger** faire une gaffe
 (**b**) *(lower → voice)* baisser; *(→ speed)* réduire; *(→ hem)* ressortir
 (**c**) *(deliver)* déposer; **could you drop me at the corner, please?** pouvez-vous me déposer au coin, s'il vous plaît?; **we dropped the parcel at John's on the way home** nous avons déposé le paquet chez John en rentrant
 (**d**) *(abandon → friend)* laisser tomber, lâcher; *(→ discussion, work)* abandonner, laisser tomber; **I've dropped the idea of going** j'ai renoncé à y aller; **to drop everything** laisser tout tomber; **he dropped what he was doing and came round to help us** il a abandonné ce qu'il était en train de faire pour venir nous aider; **let's drop the subject** ne parlons plus de cela, parlons d'autre chose; **she dropped me to go out with the captain of the rugby team** elle m'a laissé tomber pour sortir avec le capitaine de l'équipe de rugby; **just drop it!** laissez tomber!, assez!
 (**e**) *(utter → remark)* laisser échapper; **to drop a hint about sth** faire allusion à qch; **he dropped me a hint that she wanted to come** il m'a fait comprendre qu'elle voulait venir; **she let (it) drop that she had been there** *(accidentally)* elle a laissé échapper qu'elle y était allée; *(deliberately)* elle a fait comprendre qu'elle y était allée
 (**f**) *(send → letter, note)* écrire, envoyer; **I'll drop you a line next week** je t'enverrai un petit mot la semaine prochaine; **I'll drop it in the mail** *or Br* **post** je la mettrai à la poste
 (**g**) *(omit → when speaking)* ne pas prononcer; *(→ when writing)* omettre; *(→ intentionally)* supprimer; **we dropped the love scene** nous avons supprimé la scène d'amour; **he drops his h's** il n'aspire pas les h; **let's drop the formalities, shall we?** oublions les formalités, d'accord?; **to drop a player from a team** écarter un joueur d'une équipe
 (**h**) *Br (lose)* perdre; **he dropped $50 gambling** il a laissé *ou* perdu 50 dollars au jeu; **they dropped one game** ils ont perdu un match
 (**i**) *Comput (icon)* lâcher
 (**j**) *Am Fam (spend)* claquer
 (**k**) *Fam (knock down → with punch)* sonner; *(→ with shot)* descendre ❑
 (**l**) *Fam Drugs slang* **to drop acid** prendre *ou* avaler de l'acide ❑
 2 *vi* (**a**) *(fall → object)* tomber, retomber; *(→ liquid)* tomber goutte à goutte; *(→ ground)* s'abaisser; **the book dropped from** *or* **out of her hands** le livre lui tomba des mains; **the road drops into the valley** la route plonge vers la vallée; *Fig* **it all dropped into place** tout s'est mis en place; *Theat* **the curtain dropped** le rideau tomba

dri–dro

(**b**) *(person → sink down)* se laisser tomber, tomber; *(→ collapse)* s'écrouler, s'affaisser; **she dropped to her knees** elle est tombée à genoux; **I dropped exhausted into a chair** je me suis écroulé exténué sur une chaise; **I'm ready to drop** *(from fatigue)* je tombe de fatigue, je ne tiens plus sur mes jambes; *(from sleepiness)* je tombe de sommeil; **he'll work until he drops** il va travailler jusqu'à épuisement; **she dropped dead** elle est tombée raide morte; *Fam* **drop dead!** va te faire voir!; **I find that I drop back into the local dialect when I go home** je réalise que je retombe dans le dialecte quand je rentre chez moi; **the team dropped to third place** l'équipe est descendue à la troisième position

(**c**) *(decrease → price, speed)* baisser, diminuer; *(→ temperature)* baisser; *(→ wind)* se calmer, tomber; *(→ voice)* baisser; **shares dropped a point** les actions ont reculé d'un point; **the pound dropped three points against the dollar** la livre a reculé de *ou* a perdu trois points par rapport au dollar; **interest rates have dropped by 1 percent** les taux d'intérêt ont baissé de 1 pour cent

(**d**) *(end)* cesser; **there the matter dropped** l'affaire en est restée là

(**e**) *(give birth → animal)* mettre bas

3 *n* (**a**) *(of liquid)* goutte *f*; **the rain fell in huge drops** la pluie tombait à grosses gouttes; **drop by drop** goutte à goutte; **there hasn't been a drop of rain for weeks** il n'y a pas eu une goutte de pluie depuis des semaines; **would you like a drop of wine?** que diriez-vous d'une goutte *ou* d'une larme de vin?; **there's a drop left in the bottle** il reste une goutte dans la bouteille; *Fam* **he's had a drop too much (to drink)** il a bu un verre de trop❑; **I haven't touched a drop since** je n'y ai pas touché depuis; **it's just a drop in the ocean** ce n'est qu'une goutte d'eau dans la mer

(**b**) *(decrease → in price)* baisse *f*, chute *f* (**in** de); *(→ in temperature)* baisse *f* (**in** de); *(→ in voltage)* chute *f* (**in** de)

(**c**) *(fall)* chute *f*; *(in parachuting)* saut *m* (en parachute); **it was a long drop from the top of the wall** ça faisait haut depuis le haut du mur; **at the drop of a hat** sans hésiter, à tout moment; **she'll offer to sing at the drop of a hat** elle propose de chanter pour un oui ou pour un non

(**d**) *(vertical distance)* hauteur *f* de chute; *(slope)* descente *f* brusque; *(abyss)* à-pic *m inv*, précipice *m*; *(in climbing)* vide *m*; **a sudden drop in the ground level** une soudaine dénivellation; **it's a 50-metre drop from the cliff to the sea** il y a (un dénivelé de) *ou* une hauteur de 50 mètres entre le haut de la falaise et la mer; **careful, it's a long drop** attention, c'est haut; *Am* **to have the drop on sb** avoir l'avantage sur qn

(**e**) *(earring)* pendant *m*, pendeloque *f*; *(on necklace)* pendentif *m*; *(on chandelier)* pendeloque *f*

(**f**) *(sweet)* bonbon *m*, pastille *f*; **lemon drops** bonbons *mpl* au citron

(**g**) *(delivery)* livraison *f*; *(from plane)* parachutage *m*, droppage *m*; **to make a drop** déposer un colis

(**h**) *(hiding place)* cachette *f*, dépôt *m* (clandestin)

(**i**) *(place to leave something)* lieu *m* de dépôt

(**j**) *Fam Old-fashioned* **the drop** *(hanging)* la potence❑; **he's for the drop** il est bon pour la potence

4 drops *npl Med* gouttes *fpl*

►► *Aut* ***drop arm*** bielle *f* pendante; *Comput & Typ* ***drop cap*** lettrine *f*; ***drop curtain*** rideau *m* (à la française); *Metal* ***drop forge*** marteau-pilon *m*; *Sport* ***drop goal*** *(in rugby)* drop-goal *m*, drop *m*; *Tech* ***drop hammer*** marteau-pilon *m*; ***drop handlebars*** guidon *m* renversé; *Sport* ***drop kick*** *(in rugby)* coup *m* de pied tombé; *Comput & Typ* ***drop letter*** lettrine *f*; *Br Culin* ***drop scone*** = sorte de crêpe épaisse; ***drop seat*** strapontin *m*; *Com* ***drop shipment*** = envoi commercial facturé à un grossiste mais expédié directement au détaillant; *Sport* ***drop shot*** *(in tennis)* amorti *m*; *Aut* ***drop test*** essai *m* de chute; ***drop zone*** zone *f* de droppage

►**drop away** *vi* (**a**) *(interest, support)* diminuer, baisser

(**b**) *(land)* s'abaisser

►**drop back** *vi* retourner en arrière, se laisser devancer *ou* distancer

►**drop by** *vi* passer

►**drop down** *vi (person)* tomber (par terre); *(table leaf)* se rabattre

►**drop in 1** *vi* passer; **I just dropped in for a chat** je suis seulement passé bavarder un moment; **to drop in on sb** passer voir qn

2 *vt sep (deliver)* déposer; **I'll drop it in on my way to work** je le déposerai demain en allant au travail; *Fam* **you dropped me right in it** tu m'as mis dans le pétrin

►**drop off 1** *vt sep (person)* déposer; *(package, thing)* déposer, laisser

2 *vi* (**a**) *(fall asleep)* s'endormir; *(have a nap)* faire un (petit) somme

(**b**) *(decrease → membership, attendance etc)* diminuer, baisser

(**c**) *(fall off)* tomber; **all the flowers dropped off when I moved the plant** toutes les fleurs sont tombées lorsque j'ai déplacé la plante

►**drop out** *vi* (**a**) *(fall out)* tomber; **my purse must have dropped out of my bag** mon porte-monnaie a dû tomber de mon sac

(**b**) *(withdraw)* renoncer; **she dropped out of the race** elle s'est retirée de la course; **he dropped out of school** il a abandonné ses études; **words that have dropped out of current usage** des mots qui ont disparu de l'usage courant

(**c**) *(person → from society)* vivre en marge de la société

►**drop round** *Br* **1** *vi* passer; **I just dropped round for a chat** je suis seulement passé bavarder un moment

2 *vt sep (deliver)* déposer; **I'll drop that book round for you tomorrow** je déposerai ce livre chez toi demain

---

drop-dead *adj Fam* **the drop-dead date** le dernier délai❑; **he's drop-dead gorgeous** il est hyper canon

►► *Fin* ***drop-dead fee*** commission *f* de désintéressement; *Fin* ***drop-dead rate*** taux *m* de désintéressement

drop-down *adj (door)* qui s'ouvre par le haut

►► *Comput* ***drop-down menu*** menu *m* déroulant

drop-forge *vt Metal* forger au marteau-pilon

drop-forging *n Metal* (**a**) *(process)* estampage *m* (**b**) *(result)* pièce *f* emboutie *ou* étampée

drop-front *adj (bureau)* à abattant

drophead coupé ['drɒphed-] *n Br Aut* coupé *m* décapotable

drop-in centre *n Br* centre *m* d'assistance sociale *(où l'on peut aller sans rendez-vous)*

drop-kick *Sport* **1** *vt* **to drop-kick the ball** donner un coup de pied tombé (au ballon); **to drop-kick a goal** marquer un point par un coup de pied tombé

2 *vi* donner un coup de pied tombé

drop-leaf table *n* table *f* à abattants *ou* à volets

droplet ['drɒplɪt] *n* gouttelette *f*

drop-off *n* (**a**) *(decrease)* baisse *f*, diminution *f*; **a drop-off in sales** une baisse des ventes (**b**) *Am (descent)* à-pic *m inv*; **there's a sharp drop-off in the road** la rue descend en pente très raide

►► *Am* ***drop-off charge*** *(for hired car)* = supplément compté lorsque l'on rend un véhicule de location dans une autre ville que celle où on l'a loué

dropout ['drɒpaʊt] *n Fam (from society)* marginal(e)❑ *m,f*; *(from studies)* étudiant(e) *m,f* qui abandonne ses études❑; *Am* **he's a high school dropout** il a quitté le lycée avant le bac

drop-out *n Sport (in rugby)* renvoi *m* aux vingt-deux mètres

dropped [drɒpt] *adj*

►► ***dropped ceiling*** plafond *m* suspendu; *Sport* ***dropped goal*** *(in rugby)* drop-goal *m*

dropper ['drɒpə(r)] *n* compte-gouttes *m inv*

dropper-in *n* visiteur(euse) *m,f* inattendu(e)

dropping ['drɒpɪŋ] **1** *n* (**a**) *(of object)* descente *f*, chute *f*; *Aviat (of parachutist, package)* largage *m*, droppage *m*

(**b**) *(reduction → of prices)* baisse *f*, chute *f*

(**c**) *(omission → of word)* suppression *f*

(**d**) *(abandonment → of project, course)* abandon *m*

(**e**) *Aut (of chassis)* surbaissement *m*

(**f**) *Vet* **dropping (of young)** mise *f* bas

2 droppings *npl (of animal)* crottes *fpl*; *(of bird)* fiente *f*

►► ***dropping off*** *(of membership, attendance etc)* diminution *f*; *Fam* **dropping out** *(of school, university)* abandon❑ *m*; *(from society)* désinsertion *f* sociale❑; *Aviat* ***dropping zone*** zone *f* de largage *ou* de droppage

dropsical ['drɒpsɪkəl] *adj Med* hydropique

dropsy ['drɒpsɪ] *n Med* hydropisie *f*

droshki ['drɒʃkɪ], **droski** ['drɒskɪ] *n* droschki *m*

drosophila [drɒ'sɒfɪlə] (*pl* **drosophilas** *or* **drosophilae** [-liː]) *n Entom* drosophile *f*

dross [drɒs] *n (UNCOUNT)* (**a**) *Metal* scories *fpl*, crasse *f*; *Ind (of minerals)* schlamm *m* (**b**) *(waste)* déchets *mpl*, impuretés *fpl*; *Fig* **they chose all the nice things and we were left with the dross** ils ont choisi tout ce qu'il y avait de joli et nous ont laissé le rebut; **it's total dross** ça ne vaut rien

drought [draʊt] *n* (**a**) *(lack of rain)* sécheresse *f* (**b**) *(shortage)* disette *f*, manque *m*

drove [drəʊv] **1** *pt of* **drive**

2 *n* (**a**) *(of animals)* troupeau *m* en marche; *(of people)* foule *f*, multitude *f*; **droves of students** des foules *fpl* d'étudiants; **every summer the tourists come in droves** chaque été les touristes arrivent en foule (**b**) *Tech (chisel)* boucharde *f*

3 *vt* (**a**) *(animals)* chasser, conduire (**b**) *Tech (stone)* boucharder

►► ***drove road*** = sentier emprunté par les troupeaux

drover ['drəʊvə(r)] *n* toucheur *m* de bestiaux

drown [draʊn] **1** *vt* (**a**) *(person, animal)* noyer; **to be drowned** se noyer; *(in battle, disaster)* mourir noyé; **to drown oneself** se noyer

(**b**) *(field, village)* noyer; **don't drown it!** *(my drink)* ne mets pas trop d'eau!; **the pie was absolutely drowned in cream** le gâteau baignait dans la crème; **to drown one's sorrows** noyer son chagrin (dans la boisson)

(**c**) *(make inaudible)* noyer, couvrir; **his voice was drowned by the music** sa voix était couverte par la musique

2 *vi* se noyer; *(in battle, disaster)* mourir noyé

►**drown out** *vt sep (make inaudible)* noyer, couvrir

drowned [draʊnd] *adj* noyé; **a drowned man** un noyé; *Fig* **he came home like a drowned rat** il est rentré trempé

'The Drowned World' *Ballard* 'Le Monde englouti'

---

drowning ['draʊnɪŋ] **1** *adj* **a drowning man** un homme en train de se noyer; **the drowning woman was saved just in time** la noyée a été sauvée de justesse; *Prov* **a drowning man will clutch at a straw** = dans une situation désespérée on se raccroche à un rien

2 *n* noyade *f*; **four drownings** *or* **cases of drowning** quatre noyades *fpl*; **to save sb from drowning** sauver qn de la noyade

drowse [draʊz] *vi* somnoler

►**drowse off** *vi* s'assoupir

drowsily ['draʊzɪlɪ] *adv* d'un air somnolent

drowsiness ['draʊzɪnɪs] *n (UNCOUNT)* somnolence *f*; **may cause drowsiness** *(on drugs packaging)* peut provoquer des somnolences

drowsy ['draʊzɪ] (*compar* **drowsier**, *superl* **drowsiest**) *adj (person, voice)* somnolent, engourdi; *(place)* endormi; **to feel drowsy** être tout endormi; **to make sb feel drowsy** *(of atmosphere)* engourdir qn; *(of drug)* endormir qn, provoquer des somnolences chez qn

drub [drʌb] (*pt & pp* **drubbed**, *cont* **drubbing**) *vt* (**a**) *(defeat thoroughly)* anéantir, battre à plate couture (**b**) *Arch (beat with stick)* battre, rosser (**c**) *(instil forcefully)* **to drub sth into sb** faire entrer qch dans la tête de qn

drubbing ['drʌbɪŋ] *n (defeat, punishment)* raclée *f*; **to give sb a real drubbing** mettre une raclée *ou* donner une correction à qn; **to get a good drubbing** se faire battre à plate couture

drudge [drʌdʒ] **1** *n* (**a**) *(person)* bête *f* de somme; **the household drudge** la bonne à tout faire (**b**) *(work)* besogne *f*

2 *vi* trimer

drudgery ['drʌdʒərɪ] *n (UNCOUNT)* travail *m* de bête de somme; **just two more weeks of drudgery** plus que deux semaines à trimer; **the sheer drudgery of it!** quelle corvée!

drug [drʌg] (*pt & pp* **drugged,** *cont* **drugging**) **1** *n* (**a**) *(medication)* médicament *m*; **to be on drugs** prendre des médicaments; **to be put on drugs by the doctor** se voir prescrire des médicaments par le médecin
(**b**) *(illegal substance)* drogue *f*; *Law* stupéfiant *m*; **to be on drugs** se droguer; **to take drugs** se droguer; *(athlete)* se doper; *Fam* **to do** *or* **to use drugs** se droguer❑; **I don't do drugs** je ne touche pas à la drogue; **to be arrested on drugs charges** *(possession)* être arrêté pour détention de drogue *ou* de stupéfiants; *(trafficking)* être arrêté pour trafic de drogue; **the whole question of drugs in sport** tout le problème du dopage dans le sport; **music is (like) a drug for him** la musique est (comme) une drogue pour lui; *Fig* **a drug on the market** un produit invendable *ou* qui ne se vend pas
2 *comp* de drogue
3 *vt* droguer; *(athlete, horse)* doper; **to drug sb's drink** mettre de la drogue dans le verre de qn; *Fam* **he's drugged up to the eyeballs** *(after operation)* il est bourré de médicaments; *Fig* **to be drugged with sleep** être engourdi de sommeil
►► ***drug abuse*** usage *m* de stupéfiants; ***drug addict*** drogué(e) *m,f*, toxicomane *mf*; ***drug addiction*** toxicomanie *f*; ***drug baron*** gros bonnet *m* de la drogue; ***drug courier*** passeur(euse) *m,f* de drogue; ***drug czar*** = haut responsable de la lutte contre la drogue; ***drug dependency*** dépendance *f* à l'égard des drogues, toxicomanie *f*, *Spec* pharmacodépendance *f*; ***Drug Enforcement Administration*** = agence américaine de lutte contre la drogue; ***drug habit*** accoutumance *f* à la drogue; ***drug money*** argent *m* de la drogue; ***drug peddling*** trafic *m* de drogue; ***drug prevention*** prévention *f* de la toxicomanie; ***drug pushing*** trafic *m* de drogue; ***drug rehabilitation*** désintoxication *f*; ***drug rehabilitation centre*** centre *m* de désintoxication; ***drug smuggler*** trafiquant(e) *m,f* de drogue; ***drug smuggling*** trafic *m* de drogue; ***Drug Squad*** *(police)* brigade *f* des stupéfiants; ***drug taker*** *(addict)* drogué(e) *m,f*; *(athlete)* consommateur(trice) *m,f* de produits dopants; ***drug taking*** dopage *m*; ***drugs test*** *(on athlete, horse)* contrôle *m* antidopage; ***drug traffic*** trafic *m* de drogue *ou* stupéfiants; ***drug trafficker*** narcotrafiquant(e) *m,f*; ***drug trafficking*** trafic *m* de drogue; ***drug user*** drogué(e) *m,f*

drugget ['drʌgɪt] *n* = sorte de tapis en toile de jute

druggie ['drʌgɪ] *n Fam* camé(e) *m,f*

druggist ['drʌgɪst] *n Am (person)* pharmacien(enne) *m,f*; **druggist, druggist's** *(shop)* pharmacie *f*

druggy (*pl* **druggies**) = **druggie**

drug-peddler, drug-pusher *n* trafiquant(e) *m,f* de drogue

drug-related *adj (crime, offence)* lié à la drogue

drugstore ['drʌgstɔː(r)] *n Am* drugstore *m*

druid ['druːɪd] *n* druide(esse) *m,f*

druidess ['druːɪdɪs] *n* druidesse *f*

druidical [drʊ'ɪdɪkəl] *adj* druidique

druidism ['druːɪdɪzəm] *n* druidisme *m*

drum [drʌm] (*pt & pp* **drummed,** *cont* **drumming**) **1** *n* (**a**) *(instrument → gen)* tambour *m*; *(→ African)* tam-tam *m*; **to play (the) drums** jouer de la batterie; **John Rae on drums** John Rae à la batterie; **to beat** *or* **to bang a drum** taper *ou* frapper sur un tambour; *Fig* **to beat the drum for sb/sth** faire de la publicité pour qn/qch; *Mus* **drum and bass, drum & bass** drum and bass *m*, drum & bass *m*
(**b**) *(for fuel)* fût *m*, bidon *m*; *(for rope)* cylindre *m*; *Comput (cylinder)* tambour *m*; *Constr* **(concrete) mixing drum** tambour *m* mélangeur (de béton)
(**c**) *Anat (eardrum)* tympan *m*
(**d**) *(noise → of rain, fingers)* tambourinement *m*
2 *vi* (**a**) *(on drum kit)* jouer de la batterie; *(on one drum)* jouer du tambour
(**b**) *(rain, fingers)* tambouriner
3 *vt* (**a**) *(on instrument)* tambouriner
(**b**) **to drum one's fingers on the table** tambouriner de ses doigts sur la table
►► *Aut* ***drum brake*** frein *m* à tambour; ***drum kit*** batterie *f*; *Mus* ***drum machine*** boîte *f* à rythmes; *Mil* ***drum major*** tambour-major *m*; *esp Am* ***drum majorette*** chef-majorette *f*; *Comput* ***drum printer*** imprimante *f* à tambour; ***drum roll*** roulement *m* de tambour; *Comput* ***drum scanner*** scanner *m* à tambour; *Am* ***drum set*** batterie *f*
►**drum in** *vt sep* insister lourdement sur
►**drum into** *vt sep* **to drum sth into sb** enfoncer qch dans la tête de qn; **we had it drummed into us that...** on nous a enfoncé dans la tête que...; **drum it into her that...** mets-lui bien dans la tête que...
►**drum out** *vt sep* expulser; **he was drummed out of the club/the army** il a été expulsé du club/de l'armée
►**drum up** *vt insep (customers, support)* trouver; *(supporters)* battre le rappel de; *(enthusiasm)* chercher à susciter; **to drum up business** rechercher des clients

drumbeat ['drʌmbiːt] *n* battement *m* de tambour

drumfire ['drʌmfaɪə(r)] *n Mil* tir *m* de barrage, feu *m* roulant

drumhead ['drʌmhed] *n Mus* peau *f* de tambour
►► *Mil* ***drumhead court-martial*** conseil *m* de guerre *(tenu sur le champ de bataille)*

drumlin ['drʌmlɪn] *n Geol* drumlin *m*

drummer ['drʌmə(r)] *n (in band)* batteur *m*; *(tribal)* joueur *m* de tambour; *Mil* tambour *m*
►► ***drummer boy*** tambour *m*

drumming ['drʌmɪŋ] *n (UNCOUNT) (sound → of one drum)* son *m* du tambour; *(→ of set of drums)* son *m* de la batterie; *(→ of fingers, rain, woodpecker, in the ears)* tambourinement *m*, tambourinage *m*; **I really like his drumming** j'aime beaucoup sa façon de jouer de la batterie; **some really great drumming** un jeu de batterie superbe

drumstick ['drʌmstɪk] *n* (**a**) *Mus* baguette *f* (**b**) *Culin* pilon *m*

drunk [drʌŋk] **1** *pp of* **drink**
2 *adj* (**a**) *(intoxicated)* soûl, saoul, ivre; **to get drunk (on beer/on wine)** se soûler (à la bière/au vin); **to get sb drunk** soûler qn; **he gets drunk on very little, it doesn't take much to make him drunk** il lui en faut très peu pour être soûl; *Law* **drunk and disorderly** en état d'ivresse publique; **he was arrested for being drunk and disorderly** il s'est fait arrêter pour ivresse publique; **drunk and incapable** en état d'ivresse manifeste; *Fam* **dead** *or* **blind drunk** ivre mort; **as drunk as a lord** soûl comme une grive
(**b**) *Fig* **drunk with power/success** ivre de pouvoir/succès
3 *n (habitual)* ivrogne *mf*; *(on one occasion → man)* homme *m* soûl *ou* ivre; *(→ woman)* femme *f* soûle *ou* ivre; **some old drunk came up to me** un vieil ivrogne s'est approché de moi
►► *Am Fam* ***drunk tank*** cellule *f* de dégrisement

drunkard ['drʌŋkəd] *n* ivrogne *mf*

drunk-driving *n Am* conduite *f* en état d'ivresse

drunken ['drʌŋkən] *adj (person)* ivre; *(laughter, sleep)* d'ivrogne; *(evening, party)* très arrosé; **drunken brawl** querelle *f* d'ivrognes; **drunken debauchery** ivrognerie *f*; **drunken orgy** beuverie *f*, soûlerie *f*

drunkenly ['drʌŋkənlɪ] *adv (speak, sing, shout)* comme un ivrogne; **he slumped drunkenly into an armchair** complètement soûl, il s'affala dans un fauteuil; **he staggered drunkenly down the street/the stairs** il a descendu la rue/l'escalier en titubant

drunkenness ['drʌŋkənnɪs] *n (state)* ivresse *f*; *(habit)* ivrognerie *f*

drunkometer [drʌŋ'kɒmɪtə(r)] *n Am Fam* Alcootest® ❑ *m*

drupe [druːp] *n Bot* drupe *f*

Drury Lane ['drʊərɪ-] *n* = nom courant du Théâtre royal de Londres

DRURY LANE

"Drury Lane" est le plus ancien théâtre de Londres encore en activité; fondé en 1663, il est connu pour ses comédies musicales. Il doit son nom à la rue située derrière le bâtiment.

Druse [druːz] *n Rel* Druze *mf*; **the Druse** les Druzes

Drusean ['druːzɪən] *adj Rel* druze

druthers ['drʌðəz] *npl Am Fam* **if I had my druthers** si j'avais le choix❑

Druze = **Druse**

Druzean = **Drusean**

dry [draɪ] (*compar* **drier,** *superl* **driest,** *pt & pp* **dried**) **1** *adj* (**a**) *(climate, season, clothing, skin)* sec (sèche); **a dry spell** une période sèche; **tomorrow will be dry and bright** demain sera une journée sans pluie et ensoleillée; **to go** *or* **to run dry** *(well, river)* s'assécher, se tarir; **to pump a well dry** épuiser un puits; **to keep sth dry** garder qch au sec; **keep dry** *(on packaging)* conserver à l'abri de l'humidité; **shampoo for dry hair** shampoing *m* (pour) cheveux secs; **her mouth had gone** *or* **turned dry with fear** elle avait la bouche sèche de peur; **to be dry** *(be thirsty)* avoir soif; *(cow)* être tarie *ou* sèche; **to be (as) dry as a bone, to be bone dry** *(washing, earth etc)* être très sec (sèche); *Hum* **there wasn't a dry eye in the house** tout le monde pleurait
(**b**) *(vermouth, wine)* sec (sèche); *(champagne)* brut; **medium dry** *(wine)* demi-sec
(**c**) *(where alcohol is banned)* où l'alcool est prohibé; *(where alcohol is not sold)* où on ne vend pas d'alcool; **to go dry** *(prohibit alcohol)* prohiber la consommation des boissons alcoolisées; **he's been dry for two years** ça fait deux ans qu'il ne boit plus; **we've run dry** *(at party)* il n'y a plus rien à boire
(**d**) *(boring → book, lecture)* aride; **dry as dust** ennuyeux comme la pluie
(**e**) *(wit, sense of humour)* pince-sans-rire *(inv)*
(**f**) *Br Fam Pol (hardline)* = en faveur de la politique extrémiste du Parti Conservateur
2 *n* (**a**) *Br Fam Pol (hardliner)* = conservateur en faveur de la politique extrémiste du Parti
(**b**) *Austr Fam (dry season)* saison *f* sèche❑
(**c**) *(dry place)* **come into the dry** viens te mettre au sec
(**d**) *(with towel, cloth)* **to give sth a dry** essuyer qch; **give your hair a dry** sèche tes cheveux
3 *vt (clothes, fruit, leaves)* (faire) sécher; *(dishes)* essuyer; **to dry one's eyes** se sécher les yeux, sécher ses yeux; **to dry one's tears** sécher ses larmes; **to dry one's hair** se sécher les cheveux; **to dry oneself** se sécher, s'essuyer
4 *vi* (**a**) *(clothes, hair, fruit, leaves)* sécher; **to put sth out to dry** mettre qch à sécher dehors; **you wash, I'll dry** *(dishes)* tu laves et moi j'essuie
(**b**) *(cow)* se tarir
►► ***dry battery*** pile *f* sèche; *Am* ***dry bulk*** vrac *m* sec; ***dry cell*** pile *f* sèche; ***dry cleaner*** *(person)* teinturier(ère) *m,f*; ***dry cleaner's*** *(shop)* teinturerie *f*, pressing *m*; **to be in** *or* **at the dry cleaner's** être chez le teinturier *ou* à la teinturerie *ou* au pressing; **to take sth to the dry cleaner's** porter qch chez le teinturier *ou* à la teinturerie *ou* au pressing; *Naut* ***dry dock*** cale *f* sèche; **in dry dock** en cale sèche; *Agr* ***dry farming*** culture *f* sèche, dry-farming *m*; ***dry ginger*** = boisson gazeuse aux extraits de gingembre; *Com* ***dry goods*** *Br* marchandises *fpl* sèches; *Am* tissus *mpl* et articles *mpl* de bonneterie; ***dry hole*** *(oil well)* puits *m* sec; ***dry ice*** neige *f* carbonique; ***dry ice machine*** machine *f* à neige carbonique; ***dry land*** terre *f* ferme; ***dry martini*** martini *m* dry; ***dry measure*** = unité de mesure des matières sèches; ***dry nurse*** nourrice *f* sèche; ***dry riser*** colonne *f* sèche; ***dry rot*** *(UNCOUNT) (in wood, potatoes)* pourriture *f* sèche; ***dry run*** *(trial, practice)* coup *m* d'essai, test *m*; *Mil* entraînement *m* avec tir à blanc; **to give sth a dry run** tester qch; **to have a dry run** faire un essai; ***dry ski slope*** piste *f* de ski artificielle; *Am* ***dry state*** = État ayant adopté les lois de la prohibition; ***dry suit*** combinaison *f* de plongée
►**dry off 1** *vi (clothes)* sécher; *(person)* se sécher
2 *vt sep* sécher; **to dry oneself off** se sécher
►**dry out 1** *vi* (**a**) *(clothes)* sécher; *(person)* se sécher (**b**) *(alcoholic)* se faire désintoxiquer, faire une cure de désintoxication
2 *vt sep (alcoholic)* désintoxiquer
►**dry up** *vi* (**a**) *(well, river)* s'assécher, se tarir; *(puddle, street)* sécher; *(inspiration)* se tarir; *(cow)* se tarir (**b**) *(dry the dishes)* essuyer la

vaisselle (**c**) *Fam (be quiet)* la fermer, la boucler; **dry up, will you?** ferme-la *ou* boucle-la, tu veux? (**d**) *Fam (actor, speaker)* avoir un trou (de mémoire)❑

dryad ['draɪəd] (*pl* **dryads** *or* **dryades** [-di:z]) *n Myth* dryade *f*

dry-bulb thermometer *n Tech* thermomètre *m* (à réservoir) sec

dry-bulk *adj*
▸▸ ***dry-bulk cargo ship*** vraquier *m*

dry-clean *vt* nettoyer à sec; **to have sth dry-cleaned** faire nettoyer qch (à sec); **to take sth to be dry-cleaned** emmener qch au nettoyage (à sec) *ou* chez le teinturier *ou* à la teinturerie; **dry-clean only** *(on garment label)* nettoyage à sec

dry-cleaning *n (UNCOUNT)* (**a**) *(action)* nettoyage *m* à sec (**b**) *(clothes → being cleaned)* vêtements *mpl* laissés au nettoyage (à sec) *ou* chez le teinturier *ou* à la teinturerie; *(→ to be cleaned)* vêtements *mpl* à emmener au nettoyage (à sec) *ou* chez le teinturier *ou* à la teinturerie
▸▸ ***dry-cleaning fluid*** produit *m* de nettoyage à sec

dryer = **drier**

dry-eyed *adj* **to be dry-eyed** ne pas pleurer

dry-fly fishing *n* pêche *f* à la mouche sèche *ou* artificielle

dry-hump *vi Am very Fam* faire l'amour tout habillé❑

drying ['draɪɪŋ] **1** *n (of clothes, hair)* séchage *m*; *(of skin, flowers, wood)* dessèchement *m*; *(with cloth)* essuyage *m*
2 *adj (wind)* desséchant
▸▸ ***drying cupboard*** armoire *f* sèche-linge; ***drying out*** (**a**) *Fam (of alcoholic)* désintoxication❑ *f* (**b**) *(of skin)* dessèchement *m*; *(of soil, wood, clothes)* séchage *m*; ***drying rack*** séchoir *m*; ***drying room*** séchoir *m*; ***drying shed*** séchoir *m (hangar)*; ***drying up*** *(of stream, river etc)* tarissement *m*; *Br* **to do the drying up** *(dry the dishes)* essuyer la vaisselle

drying-out clinic *n Fam* centre *m* de désintoxication pour alcooliques❑

drying-up cloth *n* torchon *m* (à vaisselle), essuie-verres *m inv*

dryly = **drily**

dryness ['draɪnɪs] *n* (**a**) *(of region, weather, skin)* sécheresse *f* (**b**) *(of humour)* mordant *m*, causticité *f*; **the dryness of her wit** son humour pince-sans-rire

dryopithecine [ˌdraɪəʊ'pɪθəsi:n] *n Zool* dryopithèque *m*

dry-roasted *adj (peanuts)* grillé à sec

drysalter ['draɪˌsɔ:ltə(r)] *n Arch* marchand(e) *m,f* de salaisons et de couleurs

dry-shod *adj Literary* à pied sec

dry-stone *adj (wall)* en pierres sèches

DSC [ˌdi:es'si:] *n Br Mil (abbr* **Distinguished Service Cross**) = décoration de l'armée britannique

DSc [ˌdi:es'si:] *n Univ (abbr* **Doctor of Science**) *(person)* = titulaire d'un doctorat en sciences; *(qualification)* doctorat *m* en sciences

DSL [ˌdi:es'el] *n Comput (abbr* **Digital Subscriber Line**) ligne *f* d'abonné numérique, DSL *m*

DSM [ˌdi:es'em] *n Br Mil (abbr* **Distinguished Service Medal**) = décoration de l'armée britannique

DSO [ˌdi:es'əʊ] *n Br Mil (abbr* **Distinguished Service Order**) = décoration de l'armée britannique

DSS [ˌdi:es'es] *n Br Admin (abbr* **Department of Social Security**) = ministère britannique de la Sécurité sociale

DST [ˌdi:es'ti:] *n Am (abbr* **daylight saving time**) heure *f* d'été

DT [ˌdi:'ti:] *n Comput (abbr* **data transmission**) transmission *f* de données

DTI [ˌdi:ti:'aɪ] *n Br Admin (abbr* **Department of Trade and Industry**) = ministère britannique du Commerce et de l'Industrie

DTP [ˌdi:tɪ'pi:] *n Comput (abbr* **desktop publishing**) PAO *f*
▸▸ ***DTP operator*** opérateur(trice) *m,f* de PAO; ***DTP software*** logiciel *m* de PAO

DTp [ˌdi:ti:'pi:] *n Br Admin (abbr* **Department of Transports**) ≃ ministère *m* des Transports

DT's [ˌdi:'ti:z] *npl Fam (abbr* **delirium tremens**) delirium tremens❑ *m*; **to have the DT's** avoir une crise de delirium tremens

DTT [ˌdi:ti:'ti:] *n (abbr* **digital terrestrial television**) télévision *f* numérique terrestre

DU [ˌdi:'ju:] *n Chem (abbr* **depleted uranium**) uranium *m* appauvri

dual ['dju:əl] *adj (purpose, nationality)* double; **to have dual nationality** avoir la double nationalité; **to have a dual personality** souffrir d'un dédoublement de la personnalité; **to have a dual purpose** *or* **function** avoir une double fonction; **with the dual aim of reducing inflation and stimulating demand** dans le but à la fois de réduire l'inflation et de stimuler la demande
▸▸ *Br Aut* ***dual carriageway*** route *f* à quatre voies; *EU* ***dual circulation*** *(of currencies)* double circulation *f*; *EU* ***dual circulation period*** période *f* de double circulation; *Aviat & Aut* ***dual controls*** double commande *f*; ***dual currency*** deux monnaies *fpl*; *St Exch* ***dual exchange market*** double marché *m* des changes; *St Exch* ***dual listing*** cotation *f* sur deux Bourses; *Br* ***dual ownership*** copropriété *f*; ***dual pricing*** régime *m* du double prix; *(display)* double affichage *m* (des prix)

dual-control *adj Aviat & Aut* à double commande

dual-currency *adj (system)* bi-monétaire

dualism ['dju:əˌlɪzəm] *n Phil & Rel* dualisme *m*

dualist ['dju:əlɪst] *adj Phil & Rel* dualiste

dualistic [dju:ə'lɪstɪk] *adj Phil & Rel* dualiste

duality [dju:'ælɪtɪ] *n* dualité *f*

dual-purpose *adj* à double fonction

dual-venturi *adj Tech* à double venturi

dub [dʌb] (*pt & pp* **dubbed**, *cont* **dubbing**) **1** *n Mus* dub *m*
2 *vt* (**a**) *(nickname)* surnommer (**b**) *Cin & TV (add soundtrack, voice)* sonoriser; *(in foreign language)* doubler; **dubbed into French** doublé en français (**c**) *Arch or Literary* armer *ou* adouber chevalier

Dubai [ˌdu:'baɪ] *n* Dubayy; **in Dubai** à Dubayy

dubbin ['dʌbɪn] **1** *n* graisse *f* à chaussures, dégras *m*
2 *vt* graisser

dubbing ['dʌbɪŋ] *n Cin & TV (addition of soundtrack)* sonorisation *f*; *(in a foreign language)* doublage *m*
▸▸ ***dubbing mixer*** mélangeur *m* de son, ingénieur *m* du son; ***dubbing suite*** studio *m* de doublage

dubiety [dju:'baɪətɪ] *n Formal (uncertainty → in voice, of expression, reply)* incertitude *f*; *(→ of outcome)* nature *f* incertaine

dubious ['dju:bɪəs] *adj* (**a**) *(unsure → reply, voice)* dubitatif; *(→ expression)* dubitatif, d'incertitude; *(→ outcome, value)* incertain; **to look dubious** *(person)* avoir l'air dubitatif; **I'm rather dubious about the whole thing** j'ai des doutes sur toute cette affaire; **I'm a bit dubious about whether it will work** je ne suis pas très sûr que ça marche; **to be dubious about whether to do sth** hésiter à faire qch
(**b**) *(suspect → person, nature, reputation, decision, origin)* douteux; *(→ advantage)* contestable; *(→ compliment)* équivoque; **of dubious character** douteux; **he's a dubious character** c'est un type douteux; **a dubious distinction** *or* **honour** un triste honneur

dubiously ['dju:bɪəslɪ] *adv* (**a**) *(doubtfully)* d'un air de doute (**b**) *(in suspect manner)* d'une manière douteuse

dubiousness ['dju:bɪəsnɪs] *n* (**a**) *(uncertainty → in voice, of expression, reply)* incertitude *f*; *(→ of outcome)* nature *f* incertaine (**b**) *(suspect nature → of person, reputation, decision, origin)* caractère *m* douteux; *(of advantage)* caractère *m* contestable; *(of compliment)* caractère *m* équivoque

dubitable ['dju:bɪtəbəl] *adj Literary* douteux

dubitate ['dju:bɪteɪt] *vi Literary (be uncertain)* rester incertain *ou* indécis; *(hesitate)* hésiter

dubitation [ˌdju:bɪ'teɪʃən] *n Literary* doute *m*, indécision *f*

Dublin ['dʌblɪn] *n* (**a**) *(capital)* Dublin (**b**) *(county)* le comté de Dublin, = comté dans l'est de la république d'Irlande; **in Dublin** dans le comté de Dublin
▸▸ ***Dublin Bay prawn*** grosse crevette *f*

Dubliner ['dʌblɪnə(r)] *n* Dublinois(e) *m,f*

'Dubliners' *Joyce* 'Gens de Dublin'

dubnium ['dʌbnɪəm] *n Chem* dubnium *m*

ducal ['dju:kəl] *adj* ducal

ducat ['dʌkət] **1** *n Hist* ducat *m*
2 ducats *npl Am Fam (money)* fric *m*, blé *m*, oseille *f*

duchess ['dʌtʃɪs] *n* duchesse *f*

'The Duchess of Malfi' *Webster* 'La Duchesse de Malfi'

duchesse potatoes ['djʊʃes-] *npl Culin* pommes *fpl* (de terre) duchesse

duchy ['dʌtʃɪ] (*pl* **duchies**) *n* duché *m*; **the Duchy of Cornwall** le duché de Cornouailles

duck [dʌk] **1** *n* (**a**) *(bird)* canard *m*; **to take to sth like a duck to water** *(become good at)* se mettre à qch comme si on avait fait ça toute sa vie; *(develop a liking for)* prendre tout de suite goût à qch, mordre à qch; **criticism runs off him like water off a duck's back** les critiques glissent sur lui comme de l'eau sur les plumes d'un canard; *Br* **to play ducks and drakes** *(game)* faire des ricochets (dans l'eau); **to play ducks and drakes with** *(money)* gaspiller; *(person, issue)* traiter à la légère; *Am Fam* **it's duck soup** *(easily done)* c'est du gâteau; *Am Fig* **to get one's ducks in a row** se préparer❑
(**b**) *(in cricket)* score *m* nul; **to be out for a duck** ne marquer aucun point, faire un score nul; **to break one's duck** marquer son premier point
(**c**) *Mil* véhicule *m* amphibie
(**d**) *(material)* coutil *m*
2 ducks 1 *n Br Fam (form of address)* mon canard; **what do you want, ducks?** *(to woman)* et pour vous, ma petite dame?; *(to man)* et pour le monsieur, qu'est-ce que ce sera? **2** *npl (trousers)* pantalon *m* de coutil
3 *vt* (**a**) *(dodge → blow)* esquiver; **to duck one's head (out of the way)** baisser vivement la tête
(**b**) *(submerge in water)* faire boire la tasse à
(**c**) *(evade → responsibility, question)* se dérober à, esquiver; **to duck the issue** s'esquiver; *(in reply)* user de faux-fuyants
4 *vi* (**a**) *(drop down quickly)* se baisser vivement; *Boxing* esquiver un coup; **duck!** baisse-toi!; **to duck under the water** plonger sous l'eau; **to duck behind a hedge** se cacher derrière une haie
(**b**) *(move quickly)* **to duck out of a room** s'esquiver d'une pièce
(**c**) *Fam (avoid)* se défiler; **to duck out of doing sth** se défiler pour ne pas faire qch
▸▸ *Br very Fam* ***duck's arse*** *(hairstyle)* = coiffure masculine populaire dans les années cinquante (cheveux courts plaqués vers l'arrière)

duck-billed platypus [-bɪld-] *n* ornithorynque *m*

duckboards ['dʌkbɔ:dz] *npl* caillebotis *m*

duck-egg blue 1 *n* bleu-vert *m* pâle
2 *adj* bleu-vert pâle

duckie = **ducky**

ducking ['dʌkɪŋ] *n* bain *m* forcé; **he got** *or* **took a ducking** on lui a fait boire la tasse; *Br Fam* **ducking and diving** *(trickery)* combines *fpl*; *(prevarication)* faux-fuyants *mpl*
▸▸ *Hist* ***ducking stool*** sellette *f* à plongeon *(appareil servant à punir des personnes présumées coupables de sorcellerie au Moyen Âge)*

duckling ['dʌklɪŋ] *n (male)* caneton *m*; *(female)* canette *f*; *(older)* canardeau *m*

duckpond ['dʌkpɒnd] *n* mare *f* aux canards

duckweed ['dʌkwi:d] *n Bot* lentille *f* d'eau

ducky ['dʌkɪ] *Fam* **1** *n Br (term of endearment)* mon canard; **what can I get you, ducky?** *(to woman)* qu'est-ce qu'elle voulait, la petite dame *ou* demoiselle?; *(to man)* qu'est-ce qu'il voulait, le petit monsieur?
2 *adj Am* (**a**) *(perfect)* impec; **that's just ducky** c'est impec (**b**) *(cute)* joli❑

duct [dʌkt] *n (for gas, liquid, electricity)* conduite *f*, canalisation *f*; *Anat* conduit *m*, canal *m*; *Bot* vaisseau *m*; **tear/hepatic duct** canal *m* lacrymal/hépatique

►► ***duct tape*** ruban *m* adhésif en toile

ductile ['dʌktaɪl] *adj (metal, plastic)* ductile; *Fig (person)* malléable, influençable

ductility [dʌk'tɪlɪtɪ] *n (of metal, plastic)* ductilité *f*; *Fig (of person)* malléabilité *f*

ductless gland ['dʌktlɪs-] *n Anat* glande *f* endocrine

dud [dʌd] *Fam* **1** *adj (false → coin, note)* faux (fausse)❑; *(useless → drill, video)* qui ne marche pas❑; *(→ shell, bomb)* qui a raté❑; *(→ idea)* débile

2 *n (person)* nullité *f*, tache *f*; *(cheque)* chèque *m* en bois; *(coin)* fausse pièce *f* de monnaie❑; *(note)* faux billet *m*❑; *(shell)* obus *m* qui a raté *ou* qui n'a pas explosé❑; **it's a dud** *(firework)* ça a raté, ce n'est pas parti; **to be a dud at maths/sport** être nul en maths/sport

►► ***dud cheque*** chèque *m* en bois; ***dud note*** faux billet❑ *m*

dude [du:d] *n Am Fam* **(a)** *(man)* type *m*, mec *m*; **hi, dude!** salut mon vieux!; **a cool dude** un mec cool **(b)** *Old-fashioned (dandy)* gommeux *m* **(c)** *(city dweller)* citadin(e)❑ *m,f*

►► *Am* ***dude ranch*** = ranch qui propose des activités touristiques

►**dude up** *vi Am Fam* se mettre sur son trente-et-un

dudgeon ['dʌdʒən] *n Formal* **in high dudgeon** fort en colère, fort indigné

duds [dʌdz] *npl Fam (clothes)* fringues *fpl*

DUE [dju:] **1** *n (what one deserves)* **to give him his due, he did apologize** pour lui rendre justice, il faut reconnaître qu'il s'est excusé

2 *adj* **(a)** *(owed, payable → amount, balance, money)* dû; *(debt)* exigible; *(bill)* échu; **when's the next instalment due?** quand le prochain versement doit-il être fait?; **due and payable now** *(on bill)* payable dès maintenant; **he's due some money from me** je lui dois de l'argent; **I'm due some money next week** on doit me verser de l'argent la semaine prochaine; **repayment due on 1 December** remboursement à effectuer le 1 décembre; **to fall due** *(bill)* arriver à échéance, échoir; **to be due an apology** avoir droit à des excuses; **to be due a bit of luck/some good weather** mériter un peu de chance/du beau temps; **I'm due (for) a rise** *(I will receive one)* je vais être augmenté, je vais recevoir une augmentation; *(I deserve one)* je suis en droit d'attendre une augmentation; **(to give) credit where credit's due** pour dire ce qui est, pour être juste

(b) *(expected)* **we're due round there at 7.30** on nous attend à 7 heures 30, nous devons y être à 7 heures 30; **to be due to do sth** devoir faire qch; **we were due to meet at 10 p.m.** nous devions nous retrouver à 22 heures; **the train is due in** *or* **to arrive now** le train devrait arriver d'un instant à l'autre; **when is he/the train due?** quand doit-il/quand le train doit-il arriver?; **she's due back next week** elle doit rentrer la semaine prochaine; **the next issue is due out next week** le prochain numéro doit sortir la semaine prochaine; **her baby is** *or* **she's due any day now** elle doit accoucher d'un jour à l'autre

(c) *(proper)* **to give sth due consideration** accorder mûre réflexion à qch; **after due consideration** après mûre réflexion; **to fail to exercise due care and attention** ne pas prêter l'attention nécessaire; **to give sb due warning** prévenir qn suffisamment tôt; **due process of law** garantie *f* suffisante du droit; **in due course** *(at the proper time)* en temps voulu; *(in the natural course of events)* à un certain moment; *(at a later stage, eventually)* plus tard; **the impostor was unmasked in due course** l'imposteur a finalement été démasqué; **to treat sb with due respect** traiter qn avec le respect qui lui est dû; **with (all) due respect...** avec tout le respect que je vous dois..., sauf votre respect...; **with (all) due respect to the Prime Minister** avec tout le respect qui est dû au Premier ministre

3 *adv (east, west etc)* plein

4 dues *npl* droits *mpl*; *Fig* **he's paid his dues, he deserves his promotion** il a travaillé dur, il a mérité son avancement

5 due to *prep* **(a)** *(owing to)* à cause de, en raison de; **due to bad weather they arrived late** ils sont arrivés en retard à cause du mauvais temps **(b)** *(because of)* grâce à; **it's all due to you** c'est grâce à toi; **her success is due in (large) part to hard work** elle doit sa réussite en grande partie à son travail acharné; **our late arrival was due to the bad weather** notre retard était dû au mauvais temps

►► ***due date*** *(of bill, payment)* échéance *f*; *(of baby)* date *f* prévue pour la naissance; **on the due date** à l'échéance, à terme échu

duel ['dju:əl] *(Br pt & pp* **duelled,** *cont* **duelling,** *Am pt & pp* **dueled,** *cont* **dueling) 1** *n* duel *m*; **to fight a duel** se battre en duel; **to challenge sb to a duel** provoquer qn en duel

2 *vi* se battre en duel

duelling, *Am* **dueling** ['dju:əlɪŋ] *n* le duel

►► ***duelling pistols*** pistolets *mpl* de duel

duellist, *Am* **duelist** ['dju:əlɪst] *n* duelliste *mf*

duenna [dju:'enə] *n* duègne *f*

duet [dju:'et] **1** *n* duo *m*; **to sing/to play a duet** chanter/jouer en duo; **violin duet** duo *m* pour violon; **piano duet** *(performed on different pianos)* duo *m* pour piano; *(performed on one piano)* morceau *m* à quatre mains

2 *vi* **to duet with sb** chanter/jouer en duo avec qn

duettist [dju:'etɪst] *n* duettiste *mf*

duff [dʌf] **1** *adj Fam (useless)* qui ne marche pas❑; *(idea)* débile; **to be duff at sth** être nul en qch

2 *n* **(a)** *Br Fam* **up the duff** *(pregnant)* en cloque; **to get sb up the duff** mettre qn en cloque **(b)** *Am Fam (buttocks)* cul *m*, derche *m*; **get up off your duff!** bouge ton cul! **(c)** *Culin* = variante du plum-pudding

►**duff up** *vt sep Br Fam (beat up)* tabasser, démolir; **to get duffed up** se faire tabasser

duffel ['dʌfəl] *n* **(a)** *(fabric)* tissu *m* de laine **(b)** *Am (bag)* sac *m* marin

►► ***duffel bag*** sac *m* marin; ***duffel coat*** duffel-coat *m*, duffle-coat *m*

duffer ['dʌfə(r)] *n Br Fam* **(a)** *(useless person)* gourde *f*; *(academically)* nullité *f*, cancre *m*; **to be a duffer at sth** être nul en qch **(b)** *(old man)* vieux bonhomme *m*

duffle = **duffel**

dug [dʌg] **1** *pt & pp of* **dig**

2 *n* mamelle *f*; *(of cow, goat)* pis *m*

dugong ['du:gɒŋ] *n* dugon *m*, dugong *m*

dugout ['dʌgaʊt] *n* **(a)** *Mil* tranchée-abri *f*; *Sport* banc *m* abri de touche **(b)** *(canoe)* canoë *m* creusé dans un tronc

DUI [,di:ju:'aɪ] *n (abbr* **driving under the influence***)* conduite *f* en état d'ivresse

duiker ['daɪkə(r)] *n Zool* céphalophe *m*, bichecochon *f*

duke [*Br* dju:k, *Am* du:k] *n (nobleman)* duc *m*; **the Duke of York** le duc d'York; **the Duke of Edinburgh's Award Scheme** ≃ la bourse du duc d'Édimbourg

DUKE OF EDINBURGH'S AWARD SCHEME

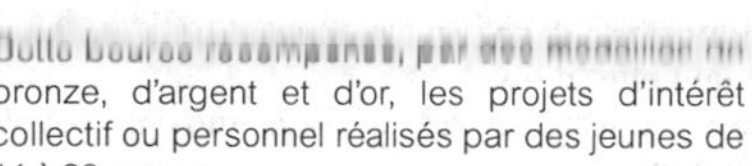

Cette bourse récompense, par des médailles de bronze, d'argent et d'or, les projets d'intérêt collectif ou personnel réalisés par des jeunes de 14 à 23 ans.

►**duke out** *vt sep Am Fam Old-fashioned* **to duke it out (with sb)** se bagarrer (avec qn)

dukedom [*Br* 'dju:kdəm, *Am* 'du:kdəm] *n (territory)* duché *m*; *(title)* titre *m* de duc

dukes [*Br* dju:ks, *Am* du:ks] *npl Fam (fists)* poings❑ *mpl*; **to put up one's dukes** se mettre en garde

dulcet ['dʌlsɪt] *adj Literary* doux (douce), suave; **her dulcet tones** sa douce voix

dulcimer ['dʌlsɪmə(r)] *n Mus* dulcimer *m*, tympanon *m*

dull [dʌl] **1** *adj* **(a)** *(slow-witted → person)* peu intelligent; *(→ reflexes)* ralenti; **she's very dull when it comes to maths** elle est très médiocre en maths; **to grow dull** *(intellectual capacities)* s'affaiblir, décliner

(b) *(boring → book, person, lecture)* ennuyeux, assommant; **there's never a dull moment with him around** on ne s'ennuie jamais avec lui; **deadly dull** mortel, ennuyeux à mourir; **it's deadly dull here** on s'ennuie à mourir ici

(c) *(not bright → colour)* terne, fade; *(→ light, eyes)* terne; *(→ weather, sky)* sombre, maussade

(d) *(not sharp → blade)* émoussé; *(→ pain)* sourd; *(→ sound)* sourd, étouffé; **the knife is dull** le couteau ne coupe plus bien

(e) *(listless → person)* abattu

(f) *Com & Fin (market)* calme, inactif; **business is dull** les affaires ne marchent pas fort

2 *vt (sound)* assourdir; *(colour, metal)* ternir; *(blade, pleasure, senses, impression)* émousser; *(grief)* endormir

3 *vi (colour)* se ternir, perdre son éclat; *(pleasure)* s'émousser; *(pain)* s'atténuer; *(eyes)* s'assombrir, perdre son éclat; *(mind)* s'affaiblir, décliner

dullard ['dʌləd] *n Literary* benêt *m*

dullness ['dʌlnɪs] *n* **(a)** *(slow-wittedness)* lenteur *f* *ou* lourdeur *f* d'esprit **(b)** *(tedium → of book, speech)* caractère *m* ennuyeux **(c)** *(dimness → of light)* faiblesse *f*; *(→ of weather)* caractère *m* maussade **(d)** *(of sound, pain)* caractère *m* sourd; *(of blade)* manque *m* de tranchant **(e)** *(listlessness)* apathie *f* **(f)** *Com & Fin (of business)* stagnation *f*; *(of market)* inactivité *f*

dullsville ['dʌlzvɪl] *n Fam (boring place)* trou *m*; **it's dullsville round here** c'est un vrai trou ici; **his party was dullsville!** sa fête était ennuyeuse à mourir!

dully ['dʌlɪ] *adv* **(a)** *(listlessly)* d'un air déprimé; **..., she said dully** ..., dit-elle d'une voix terne **(b)** *(tediously)* de manière ennuyeuse **(c)** *(dimly)* faiblement **(d)** *(not sharply)* sourdement

dulse [dʌls] *n Bot* algue *f* comestible

Dulux dog ['dju:lʌks-] *n Br Fam* bobtail❑ *m (par allusion au chien qui apparaît dans les publicités des peintures Dulux®)*

duly ['dju:lɪ] *adv* **(a)** *(properly)* comme il convient; *(in accordance with the rules)* dans les règles, dûment; **duly appointed/elected** nommé/élu dans les règles, dûment nommé/élu **(b)** *(as expected → arrive, call)* comme prévu; **I was duly surprised** comme de bien entendu, j'ai été surpris; **and he duly did what he had promised** et il a bien fait ce qu'il avait promis

dumb [dʌm] *adj* **(a)** *(unable or unwilling to speak)* muet; **to be struck dumb (with fear/surprise)** rester muet (de peur/ surprise); **have you been struck dumb?** tu es devenu muet?; **dumb animal** bête *f*, animal *m*; **dumb insolence** silence *m* *ou* mutisme *m* insolent

(b) *Fam (stupid)* bête❑; **that was a dumb thing to do** c'est bête *ou* idiot d'avoir fait ça; **he's really dumb** il est complètement abruti; **to play** *or* **act dumb** jouer les imbéciles; **don't act dumb with me** ne joue pas les imbéciles avec moi; *Am* **dumb as a stump** con comme un balai

►► *Pej* ***dumb blonde*** blonde *f* évaporée; ***dumb show*** = pantomime faisant partie d'une pièce de théâtre; *Fig* **she told us to go in dumb show** elle nous a fait signe de partir; *Br* ***dumb waiter*** *(lift)* monte-plats *m inv*; *(trolley)* table *f* roulante; *(revolving tray)* plateau *m* tournant

►**dumb down** *vt sep (population, youth, electorate)* infantiliser; *(media, programme)* faire baisser le niveau de

dumbass ['dʌmæs] *Am very Fam* **1** *n* taré(e) *m,f*, débile *mf*

2 *adj* débile

dumbbell ['dʌmbel] *n* **(a)** *Sport* haltère *m* **(b)** *Fam (fool)* abruti(e) *m,f*

dumbfound [dʌm'faʊnd] *vt* abasourdir, interloquer

dumbfounded [dʌm'faʊndɪd] *adj (person)* muet de stupeur, abasourdi, interloqué; *(silence)* stupéfait; **to be dumbfounded at** *or* **by sth** être abasourdi *ou* interloqué par qch

dumbfuck ['dʌmfʌk] *n Vulg* connard (connasse) *m,f*

dumbhead ['dʌmhed] *n Am Fam (idiot)* abruti(e) *m,f*

dumbing down ['dʌmɪŋ-] *n (of population, youth, electorate)* infantilisation *f*; *(of media, programme)* baisse *f* de niveau

duc–dum

dumbly ['dʌmlɪ] *adv* silencieusement, sans prononcer un mot

dumbness ['dʌmnɪs] *n* (**a**) *(inability to speak)* mutité *f*; *(unwillingness to speak)* mutisme *m* (**b**) *Fam (stupidity)* bêtise❑ *f*, stupidité❑ *f*, imbécillité❑ *f*

dumbo ['dʌmbəʊ] *n Fam (fool)* abruti(e) *m,f*

dumbstruck ['dʌmstrʌk] *adj (person)* muet de stupeur, abasourdi, interloqué

dumdum ['dʌmdʌm] *n* (**a**) *Mil (bullet)* balle *f* dum-dum (**b**) *Fam (fool)* cloche *f*

Dumfries and Galloway [ˌdʌm'friːsən'gæləˌweɪ] *n* le Dumfries and Galloway, = région du sud-ouest de l'Écosse; **in Dumfries and Galloway** dans le Dumfries and Galloway

dummy ['dʌmɪ] *(pl* **dummies**) **1** *n* (**a**) *(in shop window, for dressmaking)* mannequin *m*; *(of ventriloquist)* marionnette *f*; *Fin (representative)* prête-nom *m*, homme *m* de paille; *Fam* **standing there like a stuffed dummy** planté comme un piquet
(**b**) *(fake object)* objet *m* factice; *(book, model for display)* maquette *f*; **all the bottles are dummies** toutes les bouteilles sont factices
(**c**) *Br (for baby)* tétine *f*
(**d**) *(in bridge → cards)* main *f* du mort; *(→ player)* mort *m*; **he is dummy** c'est lui le mort
(**e**) *Pej (mute)* muet(ette) *m,f*
(**f**) *Fam (fool)* imbécile❑ *mf*
(**g**) *Sport* feinte *f*; **to sell sb a dummy** feinter qn
2 *adj (fake)* factice; **this is just a dummy version** ce n'est qu'un modèle factice
3 *vt Sport* feinter
4 *vi Sport* feinter
►► *Fin* ***dummy buyer*** acheteur(euse) *m,f* prête-nom; ***dummy company*** société *f* fictive; ***dummy issue*** numéro *m* zéro; ***dummy run*** *(trial)* essai *m*; *Aviat & Mil* attaque *f* simulée *ou* d'entraînement; **to give sth a dummy run** faire l'essai de qch

►**dummy up** *vi Am Fam (remain quiet)* la boucler, la fermer; **he decided to dummy up** il a décidé de la boucler

dump [dʌmp] **1** *vt* (**a**) *(rubbish, waste)* déverser, déposer; *(sand, gravel)* déverser; *(car, corpse)* abandonner; *(oil → of ship)* vidanger; **to dump waste at sea** rejeter *ou* immerger des déchets dans la mer; **he just dumped me off at the motorway exit** il m'a déposé à la sortie de l'autoroute
(**b**) *Fam (get rid of → boyfriend, girlfriend)* plaquer; *(→ member of government, board)* se débarrasser de❑; **to dump sb/sth on sb** laisser qn/qch sur les bras de qn❑; **they've dumped the kids on her again** ils lui ont encore refilé les gamins
(**c**) *(set down → bags, shopping, suitcase)* poser; **I'm just going home to dump my suitcase** je vais déposer ma valise chez moi
(**d**) *Com* **to dump goods** faire du dumping
(**e**) *Comput (memory)* vider
(**f**) *Am Fam (kill)* buter, zigouiller
2 *n* (**a**) *(rubbish heap)* tas *m* d'ordures; *(place)* décharge *f*, dépôt *m* d'ordures
(**b**) *Mil* dépôt *m*
(**c**) *Fam Pej (town, village)* trou *m*; *(messy room, flat)* dépotoir *m*; **it's a real dump here** *(town)* c'est vraiment mortel ici; **this dump of a school** cette nullité de bahut
(**d**) *Comput* cliché *m* mémoire; **(memory) dump** vidage *m* (de) mémoire; **(screen) dump** capture *f* d'écran
(**e**) *very Fam* **to have** *or* **take a dump** *(defecate)* chier, couler un bronze
3 *vi very Fam (defecate)* chier, couler un bronze
►► *Mktg* ***dump bin*** panier *m* de présentation en vrac, panier *m* présentoir; *Comput* ***dump tape*** bande *f* de vidage; ***dump truck*** dumper *m*, tombereau *m*

►**dump on** *vt insep Am Fam* (**a**) *(criticize)* s'en prendre à❑ (**b**) *Pej (complain to)* se décharger de ses problèmes sur❑

dumper ['dʌmpə(r)] *n* (**a**) *(vehicle)* dumper *m*, tombereau *m* (**b**) *(of waste → person)* personne *f* qui déverse des ordures; *(→ company)* entreprise *f* déposant des déchets (toxiques) (**c**) *Com (of goods)* entreprise *f* pratiquant le dumping
►► ***dumper truck*** dumper *m*, tombereau *m*

dumpiness ['dʌmpɪnɪs] *n Fam (of person)* apparence *f* boulotte

dumping ['dʌmpɪŋ] *n* (**a**) *(of rubbish, waste)* dépôt *m ou* décharge *f* d'ordures *ou* de déchets; *(of toxic or nuclear waste → at sea)* déversement *m ou* immersion *f* de déchets; *(→ underground)* entreposage *m* sous terre de déchets; *(of oil from ship)* vidange *f*; **no dumping** *(sign)* dépôt d'ordures interdit, décharge interdite
(**b**) *Com* dumping *m*
(**c**) *Comput (of memory)* vidage *m*
►► ***dumping ground*** *(for rubbish)* décharge *f*, dépôt *m* d'ordures; *Fig (for inferior goods)* dépotoir *m*

dumpling ['dʌmplɪŋ] *n* (**a**) *Culin (savoury)* boulette *f* de pâte, knödel *m*; *Scot (sweet)* = variante du plum-pudding; **apple dumpling** pomme *f* en chausson (**b**) *Fam (plump person)* boulot(otte) *m,f*

dumps [dʌmps] *npl Fam* **to be down in the dumps** avoir le cafard

Dumpster® ['dʌmpstə(r)] *n Am* benne *f* à ordures

dumpy ['dʌmpɪ] *adj Fam (person)* courtaud❑, boulot; *(bottle)* pansu
►► *Tech* ***dumpy level*** niveau *m* à lunette

dun [dʌn] *(pt & pp* **dunned**, *cont* **dunning**) **1** *adj* brun gris *(inv)*
2 *n (colour)* brun *m* gris *(inv)*; *(horse)* cheval *m* louvet; *(mare)* jument *f* louvette
3 *vt Com* presser, harceler; **to dun sb for money** *or* **payment** presser *ou* harceler qn pour qu'il paye

dunce [dʌns] *n* âne *m*, cancre *m*; **to be a dunce at sth** être nul en qch
►► ***dunce cap, dunce's cap*** bonnet *m* d'âne

duncish ['dʌnsɪʃ] *adj Am Fam (stupid)* cloche

Dundee cake [dʌn'diː-] *n* = cake épicé aux fruits secs, décoré avec des amandes

dunderhead ['dʌndəhed] *n* âne *m*; **(you) dunderhead!** espèce d'âne!

dune [djuːn] *n* dune *f*
►► ***dune buggy*** buggy *m*

dung [dʌŋ] *n (UNCOUNT)* crotte *f*; *(of cow)* bouse *f*; *(of horse)* crottin *m*; *(of wild animal)* fumées *fpl*; *(manure)* fumier *m*
►► *Entom* ***dung beetle, dung chafer*** bousier *m*

dungarees [ˌdʌŋgə'riːz] *npl Br (with bib)* salopette *f*; *Am (overalls)* bleu *m* de travail; **a pair of dungarees** *Br* une salopette, *Am* un bleu de travail

dungeon ['dʌndʒən] *n (in castle)* cachot *m* souterrain; *(tower)* donjon *m*; **Dungeons and Dragons**® *(game)* Donjons et Dragons *m*

dungheap ['dʌŋhiːp] *n* tas *m* de fumier

dunghill ['dʌŋhɪl] *n* gros tas *m* de fumier

dunk [dʌŋk] **1** *vt* (**a**) *(dip)* tremper; **to dunk one's bread** tremper son pain (**b**) *(in basketball)* **to dunk the ball** faire un lancer coulé
2 *n (basketball)* dunk *m*, lancer *m* coulé

dunny ['dʌnɪ] *n Austr Fam (toilet)* chiottes *mpl*

Dunkirk [dʌn'kɜːk] *n* (**a**) *Geog* Dunkerque (**b**) *Hist* = l'évacuation des troupes alliées de Dunkerque, en mai-juin 1940
►► ***Dunkirk spirit*** esprit *m* de ténacité

dunlin ['dʌnlɪn] *n Orn* bécasseau *m* variable

dunno [də'nəʊ] *exclam Fam (abbr* **I don't know**) j'sais pas!

dunnock ['dʌnək] *n Orn* accenteur *m* mouchet, fauvette *f* d'hiver

duo ['djuːəʊ] *n Mus & Theat* duo *m*; *(couple)* couple *m*

duochrome ['djuːəʊkrəʊm] *n Art & Phot* **1** *n* dichromie *f*
2 *adj* bicolore

duodecimal [ˌdjuːəʊ'desɪməl] *adj* duodécimal

duodenal [ˌdjuːəʊ'diːnəl] *adj Anat* duodénal
►► *Med* ***duodenal ulcer*** ulcère *m* duodénal

duodenitis [ˌdjuːəʊdɪ'naɪtɪs] *n Med* duodénite *f*

duodenum [ˌdjuːəʊ'diːnəm] *(pl* **duodenums** *or* **duodena** [-nə]) *n Anat* duodénum *m*

duologue ['djuːəʊlɒg] *n* dialogue *m*

duopoly [djʊ'ɒpəlɪ] *(pl* **duopolies**) *n* duopole *m*

duotone ['djuːətəʊn] *adj (car)* de deux couleurs, de deux tons; *(photograph, printing)* deux tons

dupe [djuːp] **1** *vt* duper, leurrer; **to dupe sb into doing sth** duper *ou* leurrer qn pour qu'il fasse qch; **she duped him into believing that...** elle lui a fait gober que...
2 *n* dupe *f*

dupery ['djuːpərɪ] *n* duperie *f*

duple ['djuːpəl] *adj* (**a**) *Formal (double)* double (**b**) *Mus* binaire, à deux temps
►► *Mus* ***duple time*** rythme *m* binaire *ou* à deux temps

duplex ['djuːpleks] **1** *adj* (**a**) *(double, twofold)* double (**b**) *Elec & Tel* duplex
2 *n (apartment)* (appartement *m* en) duplex *m*; *Am (house)* = maison convertie en deux appartements
►► ***duplex apartment*** (appartement *m* en) duplex *m*

duplicate 1 *vt* ['djuːplɪkeɪt] (**a**) *(document)* dupliquer, faire un double/des doubles de; *(key)* faire un double *ou* des doubles de
(**b**) *(repeat → work)* refaire; *(→ feat)* reproduire; **that's just duplicating what they've already done** cela revient à refaire ce qu'ils ont déjà fait
2 *n* ['djuːplɪkət] *(of key, document)* double *m*; *Admin & Law* duplicata *m*, copie *f* conforme; **in duplicate** en double, en deux exemplaires
3 *adj* ['djuːplɪkət] *(key, document)* en double; *(receipt, certificate)* en duplicata
►► ***duplicate copy*** *(of key, document)* double *m*; *(of receipt, certificate)* duplicata *m*

duplicating machine ['djuːplɪˌkeɪtɪŋ-] *n* duplicateur *m*

duplication [ˌdjuːplɪ'keɪʃən] *n* (**a**) *(on machine)* reproduction *f*; *(result)* double *m* (**b**) *(repetition → of work, efforts)* répétition *f*; **that would just be a duplication of what we've already done** ce ne serait que répéter *ou* refaire ce que nous avons déjà fait

duplicator ['djuːplɪˌkeɪtə(r)] *n* duplicateur *m*

duplicity [djuː'plɪsɪtɪ] *n* fausseté *f*, duplicité *f*

Dupont's lark ['duːpɒnz-] *n Orn* sirli *m* de Dupont

Dur *(written abbr* **Durham**) comté *m* de Durham

durability [ˌdjʊərə'bɪlɪtɪ] *n (of construction, relationship, peace)* caractère *m* durable, durabilité *f*; *(of fabric, metal)* résistance *f*; *(of politician, athlete)* longévité *f*

durable ['djʊərəbəl] **1** *adj (construction, relationship, peace)* durable; *(fabric, metal)* résistant; *(politician, athlete)* qui jouit d'une grande longévité
2 durables *npl* biens *mpl* durables *ou* non périssables
►► *Com* ***durable goods*** biens *mpl* durables *ou* non périssables

durably ['djʊərəblɪ] *adv* durablement, d'une façon durable

Duralumin® [djʊə'ræljʊmɪn] *n* Duralumin® *m*

dura mater ['djuːrə'meɪtə(r)] *n* dure-mère *f*

durance ['djʊərəns] *n Arch or Literary* captivité *f*

duration [djʊ'reɪʃən] *n* durée *f*; **of short duration** de courte durée; **to be of long duration** durer longtemps; **for the duration of the summer holiday** pendant toute la durée des grandes vacances; **are you here for the duration?** êtes-vous ici jusqu'à la fin?

durative ['djʊərətɪv] *adj Gram* duratif

duress [djʊ'res] *n* contrainte *f*; **under duress** sous la contrainte

Durex® ['djʊəreks] *n* (**a**) *Br (condom)* préservatif *m* (**b**) *Austr* Scotch® *m (ruban adhésif)*

Durham ['dʌrəm] *n* le Durham, = comté dans le nord-est de l'Angleterre; **in Durham** dans le Durham

durian ['djʊərɪən] *n* durion *m*

during ['djʊərɪŋ] *prep* pendant; *(in the course of)* au cours de; **they met during the war** ils se sont rencontrés pendant la guerre; **during the investigation it emerged that...** au cours de l'enquête, il est apparu que...

durst [dɜːst] *Arch or Literary pt of* **dare**

durum ['djʊərəm] *n* blé *m* dur
►► ***durum (wheat) semolina*** semoule *f* de blé dur

dusk [dʌsk] **1** *n* crépuscule *m*; **at dusk** au crépuscule, à la nuit tombante
2 *vt Literary* assombrir, obscurcir
3 *vi Literary* s'assombrir, s'obscurcir

duskiness ['dʌskɪnɪs] *n (of complexion)* matité *f*

dusky ['dʌskɪ] *(compar* **duskier**, *superl* **duskiest**) *adj* (**a**) *(light)* crépusculaire; *(colour)* sombre, foncé; *(room)* sombre (**b**) *(skin)* mat; *Literary* **a dusky maiden** une jeune fille au teint bistre
►► *Bot* ***dusky crane's bill*** géranium *m* brun

dust [dʌst] **1** *n* (**a**) *(UNCOUNT) (on furniture, of* *gold, coal)* poussière *f*; **a speck of dust** une poussière, un grain de poussière; **thick dust covered the furniture** une poussière épaisse couvrait les meubles; **to shake the dust off one's feet** secouer la poussière de ses chaussures; **to gather dust** *(ornaments)* amasser la poussière; *Fig (plans, proposals)* rester en plan; *Fig* **his money is just gathering dust in the bank** il a de l'argent qui dort à la banque; **to lay** *or* **to settle the dust** mouiller la poussière; *Fig* **to allow the dust to** *or* **to let the dust settle** attendre que les choses se calment; *Fig* **once the dust has settled** quand les choses se seront calmées; *Fig* **to trample sb in the dust** fouler qn aux pieds; *Fam* **to raise a dust** faire tout un cinéma *ou* foin; **to throw dust in sb's eyes** tromper qn; **we won't see him for dust** *(he'll leave)* il partira en moins de temps qu'il n'en faut pour le dire

(**b**) *(action)* **to give sth a dust** épousseter qch

(**c**) *(earthly remains)* poussière *f*

2 *vt* (**a**) *(furniture, room)* épousseter; *Fig* **everything should be done and dusted by next Friday** tout doit être bouclé pour vendredi

(**b**) *(with powder, flour)* saupoudrer; **to dust a field with insecticide** répandre de l'insecticide sur un champ

►► ***dust bag*** *(for vacuum cleaner)* sac *m* à poussière; *Am* ***dust ball*** mouton *m (poussière)*; *Geog* ***dust bowl*** zone *f* semi-désertique; ***the Dust Bowl*** *(in US)* le Dust Bowl; *Am* ***dust bunny*** mouton *m (poussière)*; ***dust coat*** cache-poussière *m inv*; ***dust cover*** *(for book)* jaquette *f*; *(for machine)* housse *f* de rangement; *(for furniture)* housse *f* de protection; ***dust devil*** tourbillon *m* de poussière; ***dust jacket*** *(for book)* jaquette *f*; *Am* ***dust kitten*** mouton *m (poussière)*; *Entom* ***dust mite*** acarien *m* de poussière; *Br* ***dust sheet*** housse *f* de protection; ***dust storm*** tempête *f* de poussière; *Am Fam Fig* **to kick up** *or* **raise a dust storm** faire du foin; ***dust trap*** nid *m* à poussière; ***dust wrapper*** *(for book)* jaquette *f*

►**dust down** *(with brush)* brosser; *(with hand)* épousseter

►**dust off** *(dust, crumbs, dandruff)* nettoyer, enlever; *Fig (skill)* se remettre à; *(speech, lecture notes)* ressortir

THE DUST BOWL

On désigne ainsi une région des Grandes Plaines aux États-Unis où sévissaient, dans les années 30, de redoutables tempêtes de poussière provoquées par la sécheresse et l'érosion. Ce phénomène fut la cause de la migration de milliers de paysans vers la Californie, thème du roman "Les Raisins de la colère" de John Steinbeck.

dust-bath *n* **to take a dust-bath** *(bird)* prendre un bain de poussière

dustbin ['dʌstbɪn] *n* (**a**) *Br (for rubbish)* poubelle *f*

(**b**) *SEng Fam* **dustbins** *(rhyming slang* **dustbin lids = kids)** gosses *mpl*, mômes *mpl*

►► ***dustbin lid*** couvercle *m* de poubelle; ***dustbin liner*** sac-poubelle *m*; *Br* ***dustbin man*** éboueur *m*

dustcart ['dʌstkɑːt] *n Br* camion *m* des éboueurs

dustcloth ['dʌstklɒθ] *n Am* chiffon *m* (à poussière)

dustcloud ['dʌstklaʊd] *n* nuage *m* de poussière

duster ['dʌstə(r)] *n* (**a**) *(cloth)* chiffon *m* (à poussière); *(for blackboard)* tampon *m* effaceur (**b**) *Am (garment → for doing housework)* blouse *f*, tablier *m*; *(→ for driving)* cache-poussière *m inv* (**c**) *(lightweight coat)* manteau *m* léger (**d**) *Agr* poudreuse *f*; *(aircraft)* = avion servant à répandre de l'insecticide sur les champs

dust-free *adj (environment)* protégé de la poussière

dustheap ['dʌsthiːp] *n Am (rubbish heap)* tas *m* d'ordures; *Fig* **to be consigned to the dustheap** être mis au rebut

dustiness ['dʌstɪnɪs] *n* état *m* poussiéreux

dusting ['dʌstɪŋ] *n* (**a**) *(of room, furniture)* époussetage *m*, dépoussiérage *m*; **to do the dusting** enlever la poussière, faire la poussière *ou* les poussières; **have you done the dusting?** tu as enlevé la poussière?, tu as fait la poussière *ou* les poussières? (**b**) *(with sugar, insecticide)* saupoudrage *m*; **give the cake a dusting of icing sugar** saupoudrez le gâteau de sucre glace

►► ***dusting powder*** talc *m*

dustman ['dʌstmən] *(pl* **dustmen** [-mən]) *n Br* éboueur *m*

dustpan ['dʌstpæn] *n* pelle *f* à poussière

dustproof ['dʌstpruːf] *adj* imperméable *ou* étanche à la poussière

dust-up *n Fam* accrochage ❑ *m*, prise *f* de bec; **to have a bit of a dust-up with sb** avoir une prise de bec avec qn; **to have a dust-up over** *or* **about sth** avoir une prise de bec à propos de qch

dusty ['dʌstɪ] *(compar* **dustier**, *superl* **dustiest)** *adj* (**a**) *(room, furniture, road)* poussiéreux; **to get dusty** s'empoussiérer, se couvrir de poussière; *Fam Fig Old-fashioned* **not so dusty** pas si mal (**b**) *(colour)* cendré; **dusty pink** vieux rose *m inv* (**c**) *Fam Old-fashioned (idiom)* **to get a dusty answer** se faire envoyer balader *ou* paître, se faire recevoir

Dutch [dʌtʃ] **1** *npl* **the Dutch** les Hollandais *mpl*, les Néerlandais *mpl*

2 *n (language)* néerlandais *m*

3 *adj (cheese)* de Hollande; *(bulbs, city)* hollandais; **to talk (to sb) like a Dutch uncle** faire la morale (à qn)

4 *comp (embassy, history)* des Pays-Bas; *(teacher)* de néerlandais

5 *adv* **to go Dutch (with sb)** *(share cost equally)* partager les frais (avec qn)

►► ***Dutch auction*** vente *f* à la baisse; *Br* ***Dutch barn*** hangar *m* à récoltes; *Br* ***Dutch cap*** diaphragme *m (contraceptif)*; *Fam* ***Dutch courage*** = courage trouvé dans la boisson, **I need some Dutch courage** il faut que je boive un verre pour me donner du courage ❑; *Am* ***Dutch door*** porte *f* à deux vantaux; ***Dutch elm disease*** *(UNCOUNT)* maladie *f* de l'orme, graphiose *f*; ***Dutch oven*** *(casserole)* marmite *f*, fait-tout *m inv*; *Fam* ***Dutch treat*** = sortie où chacun paye son écot; **to go on a Dutch treat** partager les frais

dutch [dʌtʃ] *n Br Fam Old-fashioned* **the old dutch** *(wife)* la patronne

Dutchman ['dʌtʃmən] *(pl* **Dutchmen** [-mən]) *n* Hollandais *m*, Néerlandais *m*; *Fig* **(then) I'm a Dutchman!** je mange mon chapeau!

Dutchwoman ['dʌtʃ,wʊmən] *(pl* **Dutchwomen** [-,wɪmɪn]) *n* Hollandaise *f*, Néerlandaise *f*

duteous ['djuːtɪəs] *adj Literary* soumis, respectueux

duteously ['djuːtɪəslɪ] *adv Literary* avec soumission, respectueusement

dutiable ['djuːtjəbəl] *adj (goods purchased abroad)* soumis aux droits de douane, taxable

dutiful ['djuːtɪfʊl] *adj (child)* obéissant, respectueux; *(husband, wife)* dévoué; *(worker, employee)* consciencieux; *(laughter, applause)* poli

dutifully ['djuːtɪflɪ] *adv (work)* consciencieusement; **they smiled dutifully** ils sourirent poliment; **he kissed his mother dutifully** il embrassa sa mère machinalement

dutifulness ['djuːtɪfʊlnɪs] *n* obéissance *f*, soumission *f*

duty ['djuːtɪ] *n* (**a**) *(moral or legal obligation)* devoir *m*; **to do one's duty** faire *ou* remplir son devoir; **to do one's duty by sb** remplir son devoir envers qn; **to fail in one's duty** manquer à son devoir; **it is my duty to say that...** il est de mon devoir de dire que...; **it is my painful duty to inform you that...** j'ai la douloureuse tâche de vous informer que...; **to make it one's duty to do sth** se faire un devoir de faire qch; *Hum* **I must go, duty calls** je dois y aller, le devoir m'appelle; **to do sth out of a sense of duty** faire qch par sens du devoir

(**b**) *(usu pl) (responsibility)* fonction *f*; **to take up one's duties** entrer en fonction; **to carry out** *or* **perform one's duties** exercer ses fonctions; **to hand over one's duties (to sb)** transmettre ses fonctions (à qn); **in the course of one's duties** dans l'exercice de ses fonctions; **public duties** responsabilités *fpl* publiques *ou* envers la communauté

(**c**) *(tax)* taxe *f*, droit *m*; **customs duty** droit(s) *m(pl)* de douane; **liable to duty** passible de droits; **to pay duty on sth** payer une taxe sur qch

(**d**) *(of employee)* **on duty** *(soldier, doctor)* de garde; *(policeman)* de service; **to go on/off duty** *(soldier)* prendre/laisser la garde; *(doctor)* prendre la/cesser d'être de garde; *(policeman)* prendre/quitter son service; *Mil* **to be off duty** avoir quartier libre; **to do duty for sb** remplacer qn (dans son service); *Fig* **to do duty for sth** faire office de qch

►► ***duty call*** visite *f* de politesse; **to pay a duty call** faire une visite de politesse; ***duty doctor*** médecin *m* de garde; ***duty manager*** directeur(trice) *m,f* de service; ***duty officer*** officier *m* de service; ***duty roster, duty rota*** tableau *m* de service

duty-bound *adj Br* tenu (par son devoir); **you are duty-bound to do it** votre devoir vous y oblige, vous y êtes tenu; **I feel duty-bound to...** je me sens tenu par mon devoir de...

duty-free **1** *adj (goods)* hors taxe, en franchise; *(shop)* hors taxe; **my duty-free allowance** les marchandises hors taxe auxquelles j'ai droit

2 *adv* hors taxe, en franchise; **how much can I bring back duty-free?** combien de marchandises puis-je rapporter hors taxe *ou* en franchise?

3 *n* marchandises *fpl* hors taxe *ou* en franchise

duty-paid *adj (goods)* acquitté, dédouané

duumvir [djuː'ʌmvə(r)] *(pl* **duumvirs** *or* **duumviri** [-'vɪrɪ]) *n* duumvir *m*

duumvirate [djuː'ʌmvɪrət] *n* duumvirat *m*

duvet ['duːveɪ] *n Br* couette *f*

►► ***duvet cover*** housse *f* de couette

dux [dʌks] *n Scot Sch* premier(ère) *m,f* de l'école

duxelle [duːk'sel] *n* **duxelle (of mushrooms), duxelles** duxelles *f*

DV [,diː'viː] *adv (abbr* **Deo volente)** si Dieu le veut

DVD [,diːviː'diː] *n Comput (abbr* **Digital Versatile Disk, Digital Video Disk)** DVD *m*, disque *m* vidéo numérique

DVD-ROM [,diːviː,diː'rɒm] *n (abbr* **Digital Versatile Disk read-only memory)** DVD-ROM *m*, DVD-Rom *m*

DVLA [,diːviː,el'eɪ] *n Br (abbr* **Driver and Vehicle Licensing Agency)** = service des immatriculations et des permis de conduire en Grande-Bretagne

DVLC [,diːviː,el'siː] *n Br Formerly (abbr* **Driver and Vehicle Licensing Centre)** = service des immatriculations et des permis de conduire en Grande-Bretagne

DVM [,diːviː'em] *n Am Univ (abbr* **Doctor of Veterinary Medicine)** = titulaire d'un diplôme en médecine vétérinaire

DVT [,diːviː'tiː] *n Med (abbr* **deep-vein thrombosis)** TVP *f*

dwarf [dwɔːf] *(pl* **dwarfs** *or* **dwarves** [dwɔːvz]) **1** *n* (**a**) *(person)* nain(e) *m,f*

(**b**) *(tree)* arbre *m* nain

(**c**) *Myth* nain(e) *m,f*

2 *adj (plant, animal)* nain; **dwarf variety** variété *f* naine

3 *vt* (**a**) *(building)* écraser; *(achievements)* éclipser; **the tower dwarfs the main building** le bâtiment principal paraît tout petit à côté de la tour; **the church is dwarfed by the skyscraper** l'église est écrasée par le gratte-ciel; **Jack was so tall that he dwarfed his classmates** Jack était tellement grand que ses camarades de classe avaient l'air de nains par rapport à lui

(**b**) [illegible]

►► *Bot* ***dwarf mallow*** mauve *f* négligée, mauve *f* naine; *Astron* ***dwarf star*** étoile *f* naine, naine *f*

dwarfish ['dwɔːfɪʃ] *adj (hands, feet)* de nain; *(person)* de taille très petite

dwarfism ['dwɔːfɪzəm] *n* nanisme *m*

DWB [,diːdʌbəljuː'biː] *n Am (abbr* **Driving While Black)** **he was stopped for DWB** un policier l'a fait se ranger sur le bord de la route pour contrôler ses papiers pour la seule raison qu'il est noir

dweeb [dwiːb] *n Am Fam* ringard(e) *m,f*

dwell [dwel] *(pt & pp* **dwelt** [dwelt] *or* **dwelled)** *vi Literary* demeurer, habiter; **to dwell in sb's mind** *(image, thought)* rester dans l'esprit de qn

►**dwell on, dwell upon** *vt insep (the past → think about)* penser sans cesse à; *(→ talk about)* parler sans cesse de; *(problem, fact, memories)* s'attarder sur; **don't dwell on it** *(in thought)* n'y pense pas trop

dus–dwe

-dweller ['dwelə(r)] *suff* habitant(e) *m,f*; **city-dweller** citadin(e) *m,f*; **cave-dweller** troglodyte *mf*

dwelling ['dwelɪŋ] *n Literary* demeure *f*; *Admin* domicile *m*

►► *Law* ***dwelling house*** maison *f* d'habitation; *Literary* ***dwelling place*** demeure *f*

-dwelling ['dwelɪŋ] *suff* **tree-dwelling** arboricole, qui vit sur les arbres; **ocean-dwelling** qui vit dans l'océan; **cave-dwelling people** troglodytes *mpl*

dwelt [dwelt] *pt & pp of* **dwell**

DWEM [dwem] *n* (*abbr* **dead white European male**) = écrivain, musicien etc européen blanc mort depuis longtemps

DWI [ˌdiːdʌbəljuːˈaɪ] *n Am* (*abbr* **driving while intoxicated**) conduite *f* en état d'ébriété

dwindle ['dwɪndəl] *vi (hopes, savings, population)* se réduire, diminuer; **the island's population has dwindled to 120** la population de l'île est descendue à 120 habitants; **to dwindle (away) to nothing** se réduire à rien

dwindling ['dwɪndlɪŋ] **1** *n (of savings, hopes)* diminution *f*; *(of population, audience, membership)* baisse *f*, diminution *f*; *(of enthusiasm)* baisse *f*

2 *adj (savings, hopes)* décroissant; *(population, audience, membership)* en baisse, décroissant; *(enthusiasm)* faiblissant; **dwindling numbers of pupils** le nombre décroissant d'élèves; **dwindling numbers of people visit the area** de moins en moins de gens visitent cette région

dyad ['daɪæd] *n Biol & Math* dyade *f*; *Chem* radical *m* divalent

dyadic [daɪ'ædɪk] *adj* dyadique; *Comput* **dyadic operation** opération *f* dyadique

dyarchy ['daɪɑːkɪ] *n* dyarchie *f*

dye [daɪ] **1** *n (substance)* teinture *f*; *(colour)* teinte *f*, couleur *f*; **the dye will run in the wash** la couleur partira au lavage; **it's the dye from my shoes** ce sont mes chaussures qui déteignent; **it isn't taking the dye** la teinture ne prend pas; *Literary* **villain of the deepest dye** fieffé coquin *m*

2 *vt (fabric, hair)* teindre; **to dye sth yellow/green** teindre qch en jaune/en vert; **to dye one's hair** se teindre les cheveux

3 *vi (fabric)* se teindre; **nylon doesn't dye well** le nylon est difficile à teindre *ou* se teint difficilement

►► ***dye powder*** poudre *f* de teinture

dyed [daɪd] *adj (fabric, wool, hair)* teint; *(foodstuff)* qui contient des colorants; **she's got dyed blond hair** elle a les cheveux teints en blond

dyed-in-the-wool *adj* bon teint *(inv)*, invétéré; **a dyed-in-the-wool conservative** un conservateur bon teint

dyeing ['daɪɪŋ] *n (action)* teinture *f*

dyer ['daɪə(r)] *n* teinturier(ère) *m,f*; **dyer and cleaner** teinturier(ère) *m,f* dégraisseur(euse)

►► *Bot* ***dyer's rocket*** réséda *m* des teinturiers

dyestuff ['daɪstʌf] *n* teinture *f*, colorant *m*

dyeworks ['daɪwɜːks] (*pl* **inv**) *n* teinturerie *f*

Dyfed ['dʌved] *n* le Dyfed, = comté du sud-ouest du pays de Galles; **in Dyfed** dans le Dyfed

dying ['daɪɪŋ] **1** *adj* (**a**) *(person, animal)* mourant; *Literary* agonisant; *(tree, forest)* mourant; *(species)* en voie de disparition; **the dying man** le mourant; **her dying words** les mots qu'elle a prononcés en mourant, ses derniers mots; **it was her dying wish that...** sa dernière volonté était que...; **to** *or* **till my dying day** jusqu'à ma mort, jusqu'à mon dernier jour; **men like him are a dying breed** des hommes comme lui, on n'en fait plus

(**b**) *Fig (art, craft)* en train de disparaître; *(industry)* en train de disparaître, en voie de disparition

2 *n (death throes)* agonie *f*; *(death)* mort *f*

3 *npl* **the dying** les mourants *mpl*, les agonisants *mpl*; **the dead and the dying** les morts et les mourants *ou* agonisants; **prayers for the dying** prières *fpl* pour les mourants

►► ***dying out*** *(of race, tribe, animal, species, tradition)* disparition *f* progressive

dyke [daɪk] **1** *n* (**a**) *(against flooding)* digue *f*; *(for carrying water away)* fossé *m*; *(embankment)* chaussée *f* surélevée *ou* en remblai; *Scot (wall)* mur *m* (**b**) *very Fam (lesbian)* gouine *f*, = terme injurieux désignant une lesbienne

2 *vt (river)* endiguer; *(land)* protéger par des digues

dynamic [daɪ'næmɪk] **1** *adj* (**a**) *(person)* dynamique (**b**) *Tech* dynamique

2 *n* dynamique *f*

►► *Comput* ***dynamic data exchange*** échange *m* dynamique de données; *Comput* ***dynamic RAM*** mémoire *f* RAM dynamique

dynamically [daɪ'næmɪkəlɪ] *adv* dynamiquement

dynamics [daɪ'næmɪks] **1** *npl (of a situation, group)* dynamique *f*

2 *n (UNCOUNT) (study)* dynamique *f*

dynamism ['daɪnəmɪzəm] *n Phys & Fig* dynamisme *m*

dynamite ['daɪnəmaɪt] **1** *n (explosive)* dynamite *f*; **a stick of dynamite** un bâton de dynamite; *Fig* **this story is dynamite!** cette histoire, c'est de la dynamite!; **a subject that is political dynamite** un sujet explosif sur le plan politique; *Fig* **this band is dynamite!** ce groupe est génial!

2 *vt (blow up)* dynamiter

dynamiting ['daɪnəˌmaɪtɪŋ] *n* dynamitage *m*

dynamo ['daɪnəməʊ] *n Tech* dynamo *f*; *Fig* **he's a human dynamo** il déborde d'énergie

dynamometer [ˌdaɪnə'mɒmɪtə(r)] *n* (**a**) *Tech* dynamomètre *m* (**b**) *Opt* dynamomètre *m*, dynamètre *m*

dynastic [dɪ'næstɪk] *adj* dynastique

dynasty [*Br* 'dɪnəstɪ, *Am* 'daɪnəstɪ] *n* dynastie *f*; **the Romanov/Bourbon dynasty** la dynastie des Romanov/des Bourbon

dyne [daɪn] *n Phys* dyne *f*

dysarthria [dɪs'ɑːθrɪə] *n Med* dysarthrie *f*

dyscrasia [dɪs'kreɪzɪə] *n Med* dyscrasie *f*; **blood dyscrasia** dyscrasie *f* sanguinaire

dysenteric [ˌdɪsən'terɪk] *adj Med* dysentérique

dysentery ['dɪsəntrɪ] *n (UNCOUNT) Med* dysenterie *f*; **to have dysentery** avoir la dysenterie

dysfunction [dɪs'fʌŋkʃən] *n Med* dysfonction *f*, dysfonctionnement *m*

dysfunctional [dɪs'fʌŋkʃənəl] *adj* dysfonctionnel; **a dysfunctional family** une famille à problèmes

dysgraphia [dɪs'grɑːfɪə] *n Med* dysgraphie *f*

dyskinesia [ˌdɪskɪ'niːzɪə] *n Med* dyscinésie *f*, dyskinésie *f*

dyslalia [dɪs'leɪlɪə] *n Med* dyslalie *f*

dyslectic [dɪs'lektɪk] **1** *adj* dyslexique

2 *n* dyslexique *mf*

dyslexia [dɪs'leksɪə] *n* dyslexie *f*; **to suffer from dyslexia** être dyslexique

dyslexic [dɪs'leksɪk] **1** *adj* dyslexique

2 *n* dyslexique *mf*

dyslogistic [ˌdɪslə'dʒɪstɪk] *adj Literary* de désapprobation

dysmenorrhoea, *Am* **dysmenorrhea** [ˌdɪsmenə'rɪə] *n (UNCOUNT) Med* dysménorrhée *f*; **to have dysmenorrhoea** souffrir de dysménorrhée

dysmorphophobia [ˌdɪsmɔːfə'fəʊbɪə] *n (UNCOUNT) Med* dysmorphophobie *f*

dyspepsia [dɪs'pepsɪə] *n (UNCOUNT) Med* dyspepsie *f*; **to have dyspepsia** souffrir de dyspepsie

dyspeptic [dɪs'peptɪk] **1** *adj* (**a**) *Med* dyspeptique, dyspepsique (**b**) *Fig (irritable)* irritable

2 *n Med* dyspeptique *mf*, dyspepsique *mf*

dysphagia [dɪs'feɪdʒɪə] *n Med* dysphagie *f*

dysphasia [dɪs'feɪzɪə] *n Med* dysphasie *f*

dysphasic [dɪs'feɪzɪk] *adj Med* dysphasique

dysplasia [dɪs'pleɪzɪə] *n Med* dysplasie *f*

dysplastic [dɪs'plæstɪk] *adj Med* caractérisé par la dysplasie

dyspnoea, *Am* **dyspnea** [dɪs'niːə] *n Med* dyspnée *f*

dyspraxia [dɪs'præksɪə] *n Med* dyspraxie *f*

dysprosium [dɪs'prəʊzɪʌm] *n Chem* dysprosium *m*

dystrophin ['dɪstrəfɪn] *n Biol* dystrophine *f*

dysuria [dɪs'jʊrɪə], **dysury** ['dɪsjʊrɪ] *n Med* dysurie *f*

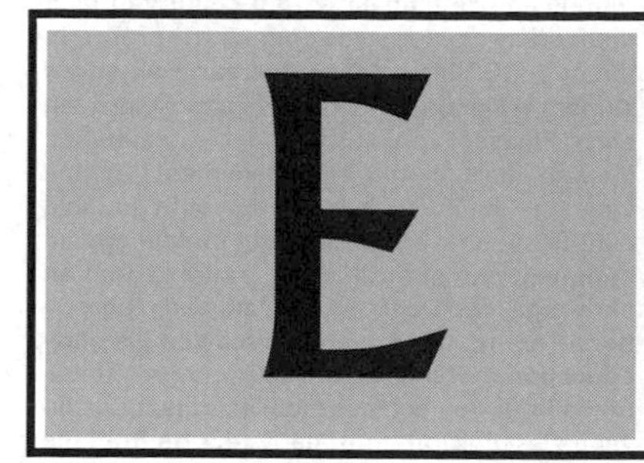

E¹, e [iː] **1** *n* (**a**) *(letter)* E, e *m inv*; **two e's** deux e; **E for Eric** ≃ E comme Eugène; *Fam* **to give sb the big E** *(partner)* plaquer qn; *(employee)* virer qn (**b**) *Sch* **to get an E** avoir une très mauvaise note, ≃ avoir une note inférieure à 7 sur 20 (**c**) *Mus* mi *m*; **in E flat** en mi bémol

2 *adj Mus (string)* de mi

E² *n Fam Drugs slang* (*abbr* **ecstasy**) *(drug, pill)* ecsta *f*

E³ (**a**) (*written abbr* **East**) E (**b**) (*written abbr* **English**) anglais

EA [ˌiː'eɪ] *n Am Sch* (*abbr* **educational age**) âge *m* pédagogique

ea. (*written abbr* **each**) **£3.00 ea.** 3 livres pièce

each [iːtʃ] **1** *adj* chaque; **each child has a different name** chaque enfant a un nom différent; **each day** chaque jour, tous les jours; **each (and every) one of us/you/them** chacun/chacune d'entre nous/vous/eux (sans exception); **you're mad, each and every one of you!** vous êtes fous, tous autant que vous êtes!

2 *pron (every one)* chacun, chacune; **each of his six children** chacun de ses six enfants; **a number of suggestions, each more crazy than the last** un certain nombre de suggestions toutes plus folles les unes que les autres; **or would you like some of each?** ou bien voudriez-vous un peu de chaque?; **to each his own, each to his own** à chacun ses goûts

3 *adv (apiece)* **we have a book/a room each** nous avons chacun un livre/une pièce; **the tickets cost £20 each** les billets coûtent 20 livres chacun

4 each other *pron* **to hate each other** se détester (l'un l'autre); *(more than two people)* se détester (les uns les autres); **do you two know each other?** est-ce que vous vous connaissez?; **the children took each other's hand** les enfants se sont pris par la main; **the two sisters wear each other's clothes** les deux sœurs échangent leurs vêtements; **they walked towards each other** ils ont marché l'un vers l'autre; **we get on each other's nerves** nous nous portons mutuellement sur les nerfs; **we get on very well with each other's parents** nous nous entendons très bien avec les parents l'un de l'autre

5 each way 1 *adj* **each way bet** pari sur un cheval gagnant, premier ou placé **2** *adv (in betting)* placé; **to put money each way on a horse** jouer un cheval placé; **French Silk, £50 each way** French Silk, 50 livres placé

eager ['iːgə(r)] *adj (impatient, keen)* impatient; *(learner, helper)* enthousiaste, fervent; *(crowd, face, look)* passionné, enfiévré; **to be eager to do sth** *(impatient)* avoir hâte de faire qch; *(very willing)* faire preuve d'enthousiasme *ou* de ferveur pour faire qch; **I am eager to help in any way I can** je tiens absolument à apporter mon aide; **to be eager to please** avoir envie de faire plaisir; **to be eager for affection/for success** être avide d'affection/de succès; **to be eager for acceptance** tenir beaucoup à être accepté; **he's eager for me to see his work** il a très envie que je voie son travail; **don't be too eager** *(in relationship etc)* ne te montre pas trop empressé

►► *Fam* **eager beaver** travailleur(euse) *m,f* acharné(e)[□], mordu(e) *m,f* du travail; **I've never seen such an eager beaver** je n'ai jamais vu quelqu'un d'aussi zélé

eagerly ['iːgəlɪ] *adv (wait)* impatiemment; *(help, ask)* avec empressement; *(say, look at, study)* avec passion; **her eagerly awaited second album** son deuxième album impatiemment attendu

eagerness ['iːgənɪs] *n (to know, see, find out)* impatience *f*; *(to help)* empressement *m*; *(in eyes, voice)* excitation *f*, enthousiasme *m*; **to show** *or* **have no eagerness for sth** n'avoir aucunement envie de qch; **his eagerness to please** sa volonté de plaire; **her eagerness to succeed** son ardent désir de réussir

eagle ['iːgəl] *n* (**a**) *(bird)* aigle *m*; **to have an eagle eye** avoir un œil d'aigle (**b**) *(standard, seal)* aigle *f* (**c**) *(lectern)* aigle *m* (**d**) *Am Mil* aigle *m (insigne de grade de colonel)* (**e**) *Golf* eagle *m*

►► *Orn* ***eagle owl*** grand-duc *m*

eagle-eyed 1 *adj* aux yeux d'aigle

2 *adv (watch)* avec une grande attention

eaglet ['iːglɪt] *n Orn* aiglon(onne) *m,f*

eaglewood ['iːgəlwʊd] *n* calambac *m*, calambour *m*, calambouc *m*

Ealing comedy ['iːlɪŋ-] *n* = genre de film comique britannique produit dans les studios d'Ealing (Londres) vers 1950

E and OE, E&OE [ˌiːənd'əʊiː] *n Com* (*abbr* **errors and omissions excepted**) SEO

ear [ɪə(r)] *n* (**a**) *(of person, animal)* oreille *f*; **to have a good ear** avoir de l'oreille; **to have an ear for music** avoir l'oreille musicale; **to have an ear for poetry** être sensible à la poésie; **to keep an ear** *or* **one's ears open** ouvrir les oreilles, tendre l'oreille; **keep an ear open for the baby** ouvre l'oreille au cas où le bébé pleurerait; **to reach sb's ears** *(news)* arriver aux oreilles de qn; **it has reached my ears that...** j'ai entendu dire que...; **he closed his ears to her request for help** elle lui a demandé de l'aide mais il a fait la sourde oreille; *Fam* **I've heard that until it's coming out of my ears** je l'ai tellement entendu que ça me sort par les oreilles; **to have the ear of sb** *(have influence with)* avoir l'oreille de qn; **to be grinning from ear to ear** sourire jusqu'aux oreilles; *Fam* **to be all ears** être tout oreilles *ou* tout ouïe; *Fam* **to be out on one's ear** *(from job, school)* être viré; **he's out on his ear** *(been dismissed)* il s'est fait virer; *(from family home)* il s'est fait flanquer dehors; *Fam* **to throw sb out on his/her ear** *(from job, school)* virer qn; *(from family home)* flanquer qn dehors; *Fam* **to be up to one's ears in work** *or* **in it** être débordé (de travail); **to be up to one's ears in debt** être endetté jusqu'au cou; **his ears are flapping** *(he's listening closely)* ses oreilles sont grandes ouvertes; **it just goes in one ear and out the other** ça entre par une oreille et ça ressort par l'autre; **to keep one's ear to the ground** ouvrir l'oreille, être à l'écoute; **my ears are burning!** j'ai les oreilles qui (me) sifflent!; *Mus* **to play by ear** jouer à l'oreille; *Fig* **to play it by ear** improviser

(**b**) *Tech (of vase)* anse *f*, oreille *f*; *(of bell)* anse

(**c**) *(of seashell)* oreillette *f*

(**d**) *(of grain)* épi *m*

►► ***ear flap*** *(on cap)* oreillette *f*; ***ear infection*** otite *f*; ***ear, nose and throat department*** service *m* d'oto-rhino-laryngologie; ***ear, nose and throat specialist*** oto-rhino *mf*, oto-rhino-laryngologiste *mf*; ***ear protector*** *(against cold)* protège-tympan *m inv*; *(against noise)* casque *m* anti-bruit; *Zool* ***ear shell*** ormeau *m*; ***ear trumpet*** cornet *m* acoustique

earache ['ɪəreɪk] *n* mal *m* d'oreille; **to have** *Br* **earache** *or Am* **an earache** avoir mal aux oreilles

earbashing [ˌɪəbæʃɪŋ] *n Br Fam* **to give sb an earbashing** passer un savon à qn, souffler dans les bronches à qn; **to get an earbashing** se faire passer un savon, se faire souffler dans les bronches

eardrops ['ɪədrɒps] *npl* gouttes *fpl* pour les oreilles

eardrum ['ɪədrʌm] *n* tympan *m*

-eared [ɪəd] *suff* **long/short-eared** à oreilles longues/courtes; *Fam* **pointy-eared** aux oreilles en pointe[□]

earful ['ɪəfʊl] *n* **to get an earful of water** prendre de l'eau plein l'oreille; *Fam* **to get an earful** *(be told off)* se faire passer un savon; *Fam* **get an earful of this!** écoute un peu ça!; *Fam* **to give sb an earful** *(tell off)* passer un savon à qn; *Am Fam* **to give sb an earful about sth** *(say a lot to)* raconter qch à qn en long, en large et en travers

earhole ['ɪəhəʊl] *n Br Fam (ear)* esgourde *f*

earing ['ɪərɪŋ] *n Naut* raban *m ou* cosse *f* d'empointure

earl [ɜːl] *n* comte *m*

►► ***Earl's Court*** = grand centre d'expositions à Londres; ***Earl Grey*** *(tea)* Earl Grey *m*

earldom ['ɜːldəm] *n (title)* titre *m* de comte; *(estates, land)* comté *m*

earlier ['ɜːlɪə(r)] *compar of* **early**

earliest ['ɜːlɪəst] *superl of* **early**

earliness ['ɜːlɪnɪs] *n* (**a**) *(of day)* heure *f* peu avancée (**b**) *(prematurity)* précocité *f*; *(prematurity of death)* heure *f* prématurée

earlobe ['ɪələʊb] *n* lobe *m* de l'oreille

EARLY ['ɜːlɪ]

matinal	► **1 (a)**
premier	► **1 (b)**
en avance	► **1 (c); 2 (c)**
de bonne heure	► **1 (c); 2 (a), (c)**
précoce	► **1 (d)**

(*compar* **earlier**, *superl* **earliest**) **1** *adj* (**a**) *(morning)* matinal; **I had an early breakfast** j'ai déjeuné de bonne heure; **to get off to an early start** partir de bonne heure; **the early shuttle to London** le premier avion pour Londres; **it's too early to get up** il est trop tôt pour se lever; **it's earlier than I thought** il est plus tôt que je ne pensais; **to be an early riser** être matinal *ou* un lève-tôt; **very early in the morning** très tôt; **early morning call** appel *m* matinal; **could you give me an early call at 6:30?** pouvez-vous me réveiller à 6 heures 30?; **early morning tea** thé *m* du matin; **early morning walk** promenade *f* matinale

(**b**) *(belonging to the beginning of a period of time → machine, film, poem)* premier; *(→ Edwardian,* [illegible]*)* [illegible] de l'[illegible]; **in the early afternoon/spring/fifties** au début de l'après-midi/du printemps/des années cinquante; **in the early nineteenth century** au début du XIXème siècle; **the earlier applicants were better than the later ones** les premiers candidats étaient meilleurs que les derniers; **when was that? – early September** quand était-ce? – début septembre; **from the earliest days of the century** depuis le tout début du siècle; *Br* **it's early days yet** *(difficult to be definite)* il est trop tôt pour se prononcer; *(might yet be worse, better)* il est encore tôt; **from the earliest times** depuis le début des temps; **I need an early night** je dois me coucher de bonne heure; **a couple of early nights wouldn't do you any harm** cela ne te ferait pas de mal de te coucher de bonne heure pendant quelques jours; **it's too early to tell** il est trop tôt pour se prononcer, on ne peut encore rien dire; **the earliest human artefacts** les premiers objets fabriqués par l'homme; **the early Roman Empire** l'Empire romain naissant; **an early 18th-century form of democracy** une forme de démocratie propre au début du XVIIIème siècle; **the early American settlers** les premiers pionniers américains; **an early Picasso** une des premières œuvres de Picasso; **he's in his early twenties** il a une vingtaine d'années; **in his early youth** quand il était très jeune; **a man in early middle age** un homme d'une quarantaine d'années; **from an early age** dès l'enfance; **at an early age** de bonne heure, très jeune; **he received his early education in Paris** il reçut sa première éducation à Paris; **my earliest recollections** mes souvenirs les plus lointains; **early reports from the front indicate that...** les premières nouvelles du front semblent indiquer que...; **in the early stages of the project** dans une phase initiale du projet

(**c**) *(ahead of time)* **to be early** *(person, train, flight, winter)* être en avance; **I am half an hour early** je suis en avance d'une demi-heure; **let's have an early lunch** déjeunons de bonne heure; **you're too early** vous arrivez trop tôt, vous êtes en avance; **Easter is early this year** Pâques est de bonne heure cette année

(**d**) *(premature)* précoce, hâtif; *(death)* prématuré; **early beans** haricots *mpl* de primeur; **early vegetables/fruit/produce** primeurs *fpl*; **we're having an early winter** l'hiver est précoce

(**e**) *(relating to the future → reply)* prochain; **at an early date** de bonne heure; **at an earlier date** plus tôt; **we need an early meeting** il faut que nous nous réunissions bientôt; *Com* **at your earliest convenience** dans les meilleurs délais; **what is your earliest possible delivery date?** quelle est votre première possibilité de livraison?; **give us the earliest possible notice** avertissez-nous le plus tôt possible

2 *adv* (**a**) *(in the morning → rise, leave)* tôt, de bonne heure; **let's set off as early as we can** mettons-nous en route le plus tôt possible; **how early should I get there?** à quelle heure dois-je y être?

(**b**) *(at the beginning of a period of time)* **early in the evening/in the afternoon** tôt le soir/(dans) l'après-midi; **early in the year/winter** au début de l'année/de l'hiver; **as early as the tenth century** dès le dixième siècle; **I can't make it earlier than 2.30** je ne peux pas avant 14 heures 30; **what's the earliest you can make it?** *(be here)* quand pouvez-vous être ici?; **early on** tôt; **early on it was apparent that...** il est vite apparu que...; **early on in June** au début du mois de juin; **earlier on** plus tôt

(**c**) *(ahead of schedule)* en avance; *(earlier than usual)* de bonne heure; **I want to leave early tonight** *(from work)* je veux partir de bonne heure ce soir; **shop/post early for Christmas** faites vos achats/postez votre courrier à l'avance pour Noël

(**d**) *(prematurely)* **to die early** *(young)* mourir jeune; *(sooner than expected)* mourir prématurément; **this flower blooms very early** cette fleur s'épanouit très précocement

(**e**) *(relating to the future)* **at the earliest** au plus tôt; **we can't deliver earlier than Friday** nous ne pouvons pas livrer avant vendredi

►► *Mktg* ***early adopter*** réceptif *m* précoce, adopteur *m* précoce; ***early American*** = style de mobilier et d'architecture du début du XIXème siècle; ***early bird*** *(early riser)* lève-tôt *mf*; *(person who arrives early)* = personne qui arrive tôt; *Prov* **the early bird catches the worm** *(it's good to get up early)* le monde appartient à ceux qui se lèvent tôt; *(it's good to arrive early)* les premiers arrivés sont les mieux servis; *Am Com* ***early bird special*** = dans un restaurant, prix avantageux accordés aux clients qui consomment avant une certaine heure; ***the early Church*** l'Église *f* primitive; *Br Com* ***early closing*** = jour où l'on ferme tôt; **it's early closing today** *(for all shops)* les magasins ferment de bonne heure aujourd'hui; *(for this shop)* on ferme de bonne heure aujourd'hui; *Br Pol* ***Early Day Motion*** = proposition de loi dont la discussion n'est pas à l'ordre du jour, présentée par un député qui recherche l'appui de collègues de façon à attirer l'attention du parlement sur une question; ***early English*** gothique *m* anglais primitif; *Mktg* ***early follower*** suiveur *m* immédiat; ***Early Learning Centre*** = chaîne de magasins de jouets d'éveil, en Grande-Bretagne; *Mktg* ***early majority*** majorité *f* innovatrice; *Art* ***the early masters*** les primitifs *mpl*; ***early music*** *(baroque)* musique *f* ancienne; *Fin* ***early redemption*** amortissement *m* anticipé; ***early retirement*** retraite *f* anticipée; **to take early retirement** prendre sa retraite anticipée, partir en retraite anticipée

Here's one I made earlier
L'émission éducative britannique *Blue Peter*, diffusée sur le petit écran depuis de nombreuses années, comprend souvent des séquences de travaux manuels et de cuisine. Les animateurs présentent toujours le produit fini à la caméra en prononçant les mots **here's one I made earlier** ("en voici un que j'ai confectionné au préalable").
On utilise cette phrase de façon humoristique lorsqu'on montre à quelqu'un une chose que l'on a réalisée.

early-purchase discount *n Mktg* discompte *m* sur achat dans un bref délai

early-warning system *n* système *m* de préalerte

earlywood ['ɜːlɪˌwʊd] *n* bois *m* de printemps

earmark ['ɪəmɑːk] **1** *vt* (**a**) *(assign)* réserver; *(money)* affecter, assigner; **this money has been earmarked for research** cet argent a été affecté à la recherche; **I'll just earmark that for myself** je me le réserve; **this land is earmarked for development** ce terrain est réservé *ou* assigné à l'aménagement

(**b**) *(animal, livestock)* marquer à l'oreille

2 *n* marque *f* à l'oreille; *Fig* **to have all the earmarks of embezzlement/another of her silly ideas** porter tous les signes d'un détournement de fonds/d'une de ses idées stupides

earmuffs ['ɪəmʌfs] *npl* protège-oreille *m*

earn [ɜːn] **1** *vt* (**a**) *(money)* gagner; *(interest)* rapporter; **how much do you earn?** combien gagnez-vous?; **to earn a living** gagner sa vie; **to earn one's living by writing** gagner sa vie de sa plume; **their money is earning a high rate of interest** leur argent est rémunéré à un taux élevé

(**b**) *(respect, punishment → of activities)* valoir; *(→ of person)* mériter; **it earned him ten years in prison** cela lui a valu dix ans de prison; **her attitude has earned her a lot of friends/supporters** son attitude lui a gagné de nombreux amis/partisans; **you've earned it!** tu l'as mérité!

2 *vi (person)* gagner de l'argent; *(investment)* rapporter

earned ['ɜːnd] *adj*

►► *Com* ***earned income*** revenus *mpl* salariaux; *Com* ***earned income allowance*** = déduction au titre de revenus salariaux ou professionnels; *Am Admin* ***earned income credit*** = aide aux foyers à revenu faible, prélevée sur les salaires; *Fin* ***earned interest*** revenu *m* des intérêts; *Acct* ***earned surplus*** bénéfices *mpl* non distribués

earner ['ɜːnə(r)] *n* (**a**) *(person)* salarié(e) *m,f*; **one of the biggest earners in the company** un des plus gros salaires de l'entreprise; **she's not a big earner** elle ne gagne pas beaucoup; **she's the main earner in the family** c'est elle qui fait vivre la famille (**b**) *Br Fam (source of income)* **it's a nice little earner** *(business, shop)* c'est une bonne petite affaire[□]; **interested in a little earner, mate?** ça te dirait de te faire un peu d'argent, mec?

earnest ['ɜːnɪst] **1** *adj* (**a**) *(person, expression, tone)* sérieux (**b**) *(hope, request)* ardent, fervent; *(endeavour)* fervent; *(desire)* profond

2 *n Arch or Formal (guarantee, deposit)* gage *m*, garantie *f*

3 in earnest 1 *adv (seriously)* sérieusement, sincèrement; *(in a determined way)* sérieusement; **it's raining in earnest now** il pleut pour de bon cette fois **2** *adj* **to be in earnest** être sérieux; **are you in earnest?** *(in what you're saying)* parlez-vous sérieusement?

earnestly ['ɜːnɪstlɪ] *adv (behave)* sérieusement; *(study, work)* sérieusement, avec ardeur; *(speak, nod, look at)* gravement; *(desire)* profondément; **we earnestly hope that...** nous espérons sincèrement que...

earnestness ['ɜːnɪstnɪs] *n (of discussion)* caractère *m* sérieux; *(of tone, person)* gravité *f*, sérieux *m*; *(of hope, desire)* sincérité *f*; *(of request)* ferveur *f*

earning ['ɜːnɪŋ] *n (act)* gain *m*

►► *Com* **earning capacity, earning power** *(of business)* rapport *m*; *(of person)* revenu *m* potentiel

earnings ['ɜːnɪŋz] *npl (of person)* salaire *m*, revenus *mpl*; *(of company)* revenus *mpl*; **do you have earnings from any other sources?** avez-vous d'autres sources de revenus?; **to live off immoral earnings** gagner sa vie par des procédés immoraux; *Fin* **earnings before interest and tax** bénéfices *mpl* avant impôts et charges

►► *Fin* ***earnings forecast*** résultats *mpl* prévisionnels; *Fin* ***earnings growth*** accroissement *m ou* augmentation *f* des bénéfices; *Fin* ***earnings per share*** bénéfice *m* par action; *Fin* ***earnings retained*** bénéfices *mpl* non distribués

earnings-related *adj* proportionnel au revenu

►► ***earnings-related pension*** retraite *f* indexée sur le revenu

earnout ['ɜːnaʊt] *n Fin* = supplément de prix payable éventuellement en fonction des bénéfices futurs *(dans le cadre de l'acquisition d'une entreprise)*

earphones ['ɪəfəʊnz] *npl* écouteurs *mpl*, casque *m*

earpiece ['ɪəpiːs] *n (of telephone receiver, personal stereo)* écouteur *m*

ear-piercing ['ɪəpɪəsɪŋ] **1** *adj (scream)* à vous percer les tympans

2 *n (for earrings)* **do you know anywhere in town that does ear-piercing?** connais-tu un endroit en ville où l'on peut se faire percer les oreilles?

earplugs ['ɪəplʌgz] *npl (for sleeping)* bouchons *mpl* d'oreilles; *(made of wax)* boules *fpl* Quiès®; *(for protection against water, noise)* protège-tympans *mpl*

earring ['ɪərɪŋ] *n* boucle *f* d'oreille

earshot ['ɪəʃɒt] *n* **out of/within earshot** hors de/à portée de voix

ear-splitting *adj (noise)* assourdissant

earth [ɜːθ] **1** *n* (**a**) *(the world, the planet)* terre *f*; **the earth** *or* **Earth** *(planet)* la Terre; **the earth's crust/atmosphere** l'écorce *f*/l'atmosphère *f* terrestre; **on earth** sur terre; *Bible* **on earth as it is in heaven** sur la terre comme au ciel; *Fam* **where/why on earth...?** où/pourquoi diable...?; *Fam* **what on earth have you done to your hair?** que diable as-tu fait à tes cheveux?; *Fam* **how on earth should I know?** comment veux-tu que je le sache?; **there's no reason on earth** il n'y a absolument aucune raison; *Fam* **to look like nothing on earth** ne ressembler à rien; *Fam* **to feel like nothing on earth** ne vraiment pas être dans son assiette; **to pay the earth for sth** payer qch les yeux de la tête; **it wouldn't cost the earth** ça ne coûterait pas les yeux de la tête; **he promised people the earth** il a promis la lune aux gens; *Fam Hum* **earth to Jane, earth to Jane, can you hear me?** allô, Jane, est-ce que tu me reçois?

(**b**) *(ground)* sol *m*; *Fig* **to come back to earth (with a bump)** revenir (brutalement) sur terre; **it brought her down to earth with a bit of a bump** ça l'a ramenée sur terre un peu brutalement; **the earth moved** la terre a tremblé; *Hum* **did the earth move for you?** *(after making love)* est-ce que tu as eu le grand frisson?

(**c**) *Agr (soil)* terre *f*; **loose/heavy earth** terre(s) *f(pl)* meuble(s)/lourde(s)

(**d**) *Br Elec* terre *f*, masse *f*; *(terminal)* mise *f* à terre; **dead earth** contact *m* parfait avec le sol; **earth to frame** *(of car etc)* contact *m* à la masse; *Aut* câble *m* de masse

(**e**) *(of fox)* terrier *m*, tanière *f*; **to go to earth** *(fox, fugitive)* se terrer; **I've been trying to get in touch with him but he seems to have gone to earth** j'ai essayé de le joindre mais on dirait qu'il s'est volatilisé; **to run to earth** *(fox)* chasser jusqu'à son terrier; *(fugitive)* dépister; *(person)* dénicher; *(mistake in the figures)* découvrir la source de

2 *vt* (**a**) *Br Elec* mettre à la terre

(**b**) *Hunt* poursuivre jusqu'à son terrier

3 *comp (floor)* en terre battue

►► ***earth cable*** câble *m* de terre; ***earth closet*** fosse *f* d'aisance; ***earth connection*** prise *f* de terre; ***earth creature*** *(in science fiction)* créature *f* terrestre; ***earth mother*** *Myth* déesse *f* de la terre; *Fam Fig* mère *f* nourricière ❑; *Astron* ***earth orbit*** *(of satellite)* orbite *f* terrestre; *Zool* ***earth pig*** oryctérope *m* (du Cap); *Astron* ***earth satellite*** satellite *m* terrestre; ***earth science*** sciences *fpl* de la terre; ***Earth Shoe***® = sandale qui fut à la mode chez les hippies; *Astrol* ***earth sign*** signe *m* de terre; *TV* ***earth station*** station *f* terrestre; ***the Earth Summit*** le Sommet de la Terre; *Br* ***earth tremor*** secousse *f* sismique; *Br Elec* ***earth wire*** fil *m* de terre

►**earth up** *vt sep (plant)* chausser, enchausser, butter

earthborn ['ɜːθbɔːn] *adj Literary* humain, mortel

earthbound ['ɜːθbaʊnd] *adj* (**a**) *(insects)* non volant (**b**) *(spaceship)* progressant en direction de la terre; *(journey)* en direction de la terre (**c**) *(unimaginative)* terre à terre

earthed [ɜːθt] *adj Br Elec* mis à la terre

►► ***earthed conductor*** conducteur *m* au sol

earthen ['ɜːθən] *adj (dish)* en *ou* de terre (cuite); *(floor)* en terre

earthenware ['ɜːθənweə(r)] **1** *n (pottery)* poterie *f*; *(glazed)* faïence *f*

2 *adj* en *ou* de terre (cuite), en *ou* de faïence

earthfall ['ɜːθfɔːl] *n* éboulement *m* de terres

earthiness ['ɜːθɪnɪs] *n* (**a**) *(of humour)* truculence *f*; *(of person, character)* nature *f* directe (**b**) *(of food)* goût *m* de terre

earthing ['ɜːθɪŋ] *n* (**a**) *(of plant)* buttage *m* (**b**) *Br Elec* mise *f* à la terre

►► ***earthing resistance*** résistance *f* de mise à la terre; ***earthing switch*** commutateur *m* de mise à la terre

earthlight ['ɜːθlaɪt] *n Astron (of moon)* lumière *f* cendrée

earthling ['ɜːθlɪŋ] *n* terrien(enne) *m,f*

earthly ['ɜːθlɪ] **1** *adj* (**a**) *(worldly)* terrestre; **earthly possessions** biens *mpl* matériels (**b**) *Fam (possible)* **there's no earthly reason why I should believe you** je n'ai absolument aucune raison de te croire ❑; **she hasn't an earthly chance of succeeding** elle n'a pas la moindre chance *ou* la plus petite chance de réussir ❑

2 *n Br Fam* (**a**) *(chance)* **he doesn't have an earthly of passing the exam** il n'a aucune chance de réussir à l'examen ❑ (**b**) *(idea)* **I haven't an earthly where he is** je ne sais vraiment pas où il se trouve ❑

►► ***the Earthly Paradise*** le Paradis terrestre

'Earthly Powers' *Burgess* 'La Puissance des ténèbres'

earthman ['ɜːθmən] (*pl* **earthmen** [-mən]) *n* terrien *m*

earthmover ['ɜːθˌmuːvə(r)] *n* bulldozer *m*, *Offic* bouteur *m*

earthmoving ['ɜːθˌmuːvɪŋ] *adj*

►► ***earthmoving equipment*** engins *mpl* de terrassement

earthquake ['ɜːθkweɪk] *n* tremblement *m* de terre

earth-shaking [-ˌʃeɪkɪŋ], **earth-shattering** *adj Fam* (**a**) *(discovery, news)* stupéfiant ❑; *(defeat)* accablant ❑ (**b**) *(explosion, crash etc)* assourdissant ❑

earthward ['ɜːθwəd] **1** *adj (journey)* en direction de la Terre; **in an earthward direction** *(travel)* en direction de la Terre, (avec) cap sur la Terre

2 *adv* en direction de la Terre

earthwards ['ɜːθwədz] *adv* en direction de la Terre

earthwoman ['ɜːθwʊmən] (*pl* **earthwomen** [-wɪmɪn]) *n* terrienne *f*

earthworks ['ɜːθwɜːks] *npl Constr* terrassement *m*; *Archeol & Mil* fortification *f* en terre

earthworm ['ɜːθwɜːm] *n* ver *m* de terre, lombric *m*

earthy ['ɜːθɪ] *adj* (**a**) *(taste, smell)* de terre (**b**) *(humour)* truculent; *(person, character)* direct

earwax ['ɪəwæks] *n* cire *f (sécrétée par les oreilles)*, cérumen *m*

earwig ['ɪəwɪg] **1** *n* perce-oreille *m*

2 *vt Fam* écouter de façon indiscrète ❑

3 *vi Fam* écouter aux portes ❑

EAS [ˌiːeɪ'es] *n Br Com (abbr* **Enterprise Allowance Scheme***)* fonds *m* d'aide à la création d'entreprise

ease [iːz] **1** *n* (**a**) *(comfort)* aise *f*; **to be** *or* **to feel at ease** être *ou* se sentir à l'aise; **to be** *or* **to feel ill at ease** être *ou* se sentir mal à l'aise; **we're at ease with each other now** maintenant nous nous sentons à l'aise ensemble; **to be at ease with oneself** être bien dans sa peau; **a nation at ease with itself** une nation qui s'accepte; **to be at ease with one's sexuality** assumer pleinement sa sexualité; **I feel at ease about the new proposals** les nouvelles propositions me conviennent tout à fait; **to set sb's mind at ease** tranquilliser qn; **set your mind at ease** rassurez-vous, soyez tranquille; **now that your mind's at ease** maintenant que tu es tranquillisé; **to put sb at (his** *or* **her) ease** mettre qn à l'aise; *Mil* **(stand) at ease!** repos!; *Old-fashioned* **to take one's ease** prendre ses aises, se mettre à l'aise

(**b**) *(facility)* facilité *f*; *(of movements)* aisance *f*; **to do sth with ease** faire qch facilement *ou* aisément; **to speak with ease** parler avec aisance; **the ease with which they adapted** la facilité avec laquelle ils se sont adaptés; **ease of access** facilité *f* d'accès; **ease of use** facilité *f* d'emploi

(**c**) *(affluence)* **to live a life of ease** avoir la belle vie, mener une vie facile

2 *vt* (**a**) *(alleviate → anxiety, worry)* calmer; *(→ pain)* calmer, soulager; *(→ pressure, tension)* relâcher; *(→ traffic flow)* rendre plus fluide; *(→ workload)* alléger; **to ease sb's mind** rassurer qn; **to ease sb of a burden** décharger qn d'un fardeau, retirer un fardeau des épaules de qn; **to ease sb of their anxiety/pain** calmer l'inquiétude/la douleur de qn

(**b**) *(move gently)* **to ease oneself into a chair** s'installer délicatement dans un fauteuil; *Aut* **to ease in the clutch** embrayer en douceur; **she eased the rucksack from her back** elle fit glisser le sac à dos de ses épaules; **they eased him out of the car** ils l'ont aidé à sortir de la voiture; **to ease sth out** faire sortir qch délicatement; **to ease sb out** *(from position, job)* pousser qn vers la sortie; **they eased him out** ils se sont débarrassés de lui en douceur; **he eased himself through the gap in the hedge** il s'est glissé *ou* faufilé à travers le trou dans la haie

3 *vi (pain)* se calmer, s'atténuer; *(situation, tension, rain)* se calmer; **the awkwardness between them eased** le malaise qu'il y avait entre eux s'est dissipé

►**ease back** *vt sep (throttle, lever)* tirer doucement

►**ease off 1** *vt sep* (**a**) *(lid, bandage)* enlever délicatement (**b**) *Naut (let out) (rigging)* filer, choquer

2 *vi (rain)* se calmer; *(business)* ralentir; *(traffic)* diminuer; *(tension)* se relâcher; **work has eased off** il y a moins de travail

►**ease up** *vi (slow down → in car)* ralentir; *(rain)* se calmer; *(business, work)* ralentir; *(traffic)* diminuer; **to ease up on sb/sth** y aller doucement avec qn/qch

easeful ['iːzfʊl] *adj Literary* tranquille, paisible

easel ['iːzəl] *n* chevalet *m*

easeless ['iːzlɪs] *adj Literary* qui manque d'aise

easement ['iːzmənt] *n* (**a**) *Law* servitude *f* (**b**) *Literary (of pain)* soulagement *m*

easily ['iːzɪlɪ] *adv* (**a**) *(without difficulty)* facilement; **that's easily said/done** c'est facile à dire/faire; **the car holds six people easily** six personnes tiennent à l'aise dans cette voiture; **she is easily pleased** elle n'est pas difficile

(**b**) *(undoubtedly)* sans aucun doute; **she's easily the best** c'est de loin la meilleure; **it's easily two hours from here** c'est facilement à deux heures d'ici

(**c**) *(very possibly)* **he could easily change his mind** il pourrait bien changer d'avis; **the information could easily be wrong** les informations pourraient très bien être fausses

(**d**) *(in a relaxed manner → talk)* de manière décontractée; *(→ smile, answer)* d'un air décontracté

easiness ['iːzɪnɪs] *n* (**a**) *(lack of difficulty)* facilité *f* (**b**) *(relaxed nature)* décontraction *f*

easing ['iːzɪŋ] *n* (**a**) *(of suffering, pressure)* atténuation *f*; *(caused by medication)* soulagement *m*; *(of beam etc)* allègement *m* (**b**) *(relaxation) (of conflict, pressure)* atténuation *f*; *(of restrictions)* allègement *m*; **easing of tension** *(political etc)* détente *f*; *Com* **easing of the market** détente *f* du marché

►► ***easing off*** *(of pain)* atténuation *f*; *(from work)* relâchement *m*; **there had been no easing off of the pain** la douleur ne s'était pas atténuée

east [iːst] **1** *n* (**a**) *Geog* est *m*; **in the east** à l'est, dans l'est; **to the east of the mainland** à l'est *ou* au large de la côte est du continent; **two miles to the east** ≃ trois kilomètres à l'est; **look towards the east** regardez vers l'est; **I was born in the east** je suis né dans l'Est; **in the east of Austria** dans l'est de l'Autriche; **on the east of the island** à l'est de l'île; **the wind is in the east** le vent est à l'est; **the wind is coming from the east** le vent vient *ou* souffle de l'est; **the east of England** l'est de l'Angleterre; **the East** *(the Orient)* l'Orient *m*; *(in US)* l'Est *m (États situés à l'est du Mississippi)*; **Istanbul, where East meets West** Istanbul, où l'Orient et l'Occident se rejoignent *ou* à la confluence de l'Orient et de l'Occident; **East-West relations** relations *fpl* Est-Ouest

(**b**) *Cards* est *m*

2 *adj* (**a**) *Geog* est *(inv)*, de l'est; *(country)* de l'Est; *(wall)* exposé à l'est; **the east coast** la côte est; **in east London** dans l'est de Londres; **on the east side** du côté est

(**b**) *(wind)* d'est

3 *adv* à l'est; *(travel)* vers l'est, en direction de l'est; **the village lies east of Swansea** le village est situé à l'est de Swansea; **the living room faces east** la salle de séjour est exposée à l'est; **the path heads (due) east** le chemin va *ou* mène (droit) vers l'est; **drive east until you come to a main road** roulez vers l'est jusqu'à ce que vous arriviez à une route principale; **I drove east for three hours** j'ai roulé pendant trois heures en direction de l'est; **I travelled east** je suis allé vers l'est; **to sail east** naviguer cap sur l'est; **it's 20 miles east of Manchester** ≃ c'est à 32 kilomètres à l'est de Manchester; **east by north** est quart-nord-est; **east by south** est-quart-sud-est; **further east** plus à l'est; *Am Fam* **back east** dans l'est ❑ *(des États-Unis)*

►► ***East Africa*** Afrique *f* orientale; ***East African*** **1** *n* Africain(e) *m,f* de l'est **2** *adj* d'Afrique orientale; ***East End*** *(of city)* quartiers *mpl* est; **to live in the East End of Glasgow** habiter dans l'est de Glasgow; ***the East End*** = quartier industriel de Londres, connu pour ses docks et, autrefois, pour sa pauvreté; *esp Am* ***East Europe*** Europe *f* de l'Est; ***East European*** **1** *n* Européen(enne) *m,f* de l'Est **2** *adj* d'Europe de l'Est; ***East German*** **1** *n* Allemand(e) *m,f* de l'Est **2** *adj* est-allemand, d'Allemagne de l'Est; ***(the former) East Germany*** (l'ex-)Allemagne *f* de l'Est; **in East Germany** en Allemagne de l'Est; *Hist* ***East India Company*** compagnie *f* des Indes Orientales; *Hist* ***East Indian*** **1** *n* natif(ive) *m,f* des Indes orientales **2** *adj* des Indes orientales; *Hist* ***the East Indies*** les Indes *fpl* orientales; ***the East Side*** l'East Side *m (quartier situé à l'est de Manhattan)*; ***East Sussex*** le Sussex oriental, = comté dans le sud de l'Angleterre; **in East Sussex** dans le Sussex oriental

'East of Eden' *Steinbeck, Kazan* 'À l'Est d'Éden'

eastbound ['iːstbaʊnd] *adj (traffic)* en direction de l'est; *(lane, carriageway)* de l'est; *(road)* vers l'est; **eastbound traffic is subject to delays** la circulation est ralentie dans le sens est; *Br* **the eastbound carriageway of the motorway is closed** l'axe est de l'autoroute est fermé (à la circulation); **there are roadworks on the eastbound carriageway of the motorway** il y a des travaux sur l'autoroute en direction de l'est; **there's a jam on the eastbound carriageway** il y a un bouchon en direction de l'est

Eastender [ˌiːst'endə(r)] **1** *n* habitant(e) *m,f* de l'est de Londres

2 Eastenders *n Br TV* = feuilleton dont l'action se déroule dans un quartier populaire de Londres

Easter ['iːstə(r)] **1** *n* Pâques *fpl*; **Happy Easter!** joyeuses Pâques!; **last/next Easter** à Pâques l'année dernière/l'année prochaine

2 *comp (holiday, weekend)* de Pâques; *(celebrations)* pascal

▸▸ *Am* ***Easter basket*** = panier de friandises dont on raconte aux enfants qu'il s'agit d'un cadeau du "Easter bunny"; ***Easter bunny*** lapin *m* de Pâques; *(in US)* = personnage imaginaire qui distribue des friandises aux enfants; ***Easter Day*** le jour *ou* le dimanche de Pâques; ***Easter egg*** œuf *m* de Pâques; ***Easter Island*** l'île *f* de Pâques; **in** *or* **on Easter Island** à l'île de Pâques; ***Easter Monday*** le lundi de Pâques; *Hist* ***the Easter Rising*** = insurrection irlandaise contre la Grande-Bretagne en 1916; ***Easter Sunday*** le jour *ou* le dimanche de Pâques; ***Easter week*** *(following Easter)* la semaine de Pâques; *(Holy Week)* la semaine sainte

easterly ['iːstəlɪ] *(pl* **easterlies)** **1** *n* vent *m* d'est

2 *adj* **(a)** *Geog* est *(inv)*, de l'est; **to travel in an easterly direction** aller vers l'est; **easterly point** point situé à l'est *ou* vers l'est; **the most easterly point of the island** le point situé le plus à l'est de l'île; **a room with an easterly aspect** une pièce exposée à l'est; *Naut* **to steer an easterly course** faire route vers l'est; *(when setting out)* mettre le cap à l'est **(b)** *(wind)* d'est

3 *adv* vers l'est, en direction de l'est

eastern ['iːstən] *adj* **(a)** *Geog* est *(inv)*, de l'est; *(of Far East)* oriental; **the eastern wing of the castle** l'aile est du château; **in eastern Canada** dans l'est du Canada; **the eastern side of the country** la partie est du pays **(b)** *(wind)* d'est

▸▸ ***the Eastern Bloc*** le bloc de l'Est; *Rel* ***the Eastern Church*** l'Église *f* d'Orient; ***Eastern Daylight Time*** heure *f* d'été de New York; ***Eastern Europe*** Europe *f* de l'Est; ***Eastern European*** **1** *n* Européen(enne) *m,f* de l'Est **2** *adj* d'Europe de l'Est; ***Eastern European Time*** heure *f* d'Europe orientale; *Orn* ***eastern kingbird*** tyran *m* savana; *Rel* ***the Eastern Orthodox Church*** l'Église *f* d'Orient; ***Eastern Standard Time*** heure *f* d'hiver de New York; ***the Eastern Townships*** *(of Canada)* les Cantons *mpl* de l'Est

> **Full of Eastern promise**
>
> Il s'agit du slogan utilisé dans la publicité pour la barre chocolatée Fry's Turkish Delight des années 50 aux années 70, slogan que l'on pourrait traduire librement par "toute la saveur de l'Orient".
>
> Aujourd'hui on utilise cette formule de façon allusive à propos de toute chose considérée comme exotique ou provenant d'Asie; on pourra dire par exemple **the new restaurant offers a menu full of Eastern promise with the emphasis on Chinese-influenced food** ("ce nouveau restaurant propose un menu plein des saveurs de l'Orient avec une forte influence chinoise").

Easterner, easterner ['iːstənə(r)] *n* **(a)** *(in US)* = personne qui vient de l'est des États-Unis **(b)** *(oriental)* Oriental(e) *m,f*

easternmost ['iːstənməʊst] *adj* le plus à l'est; **the easternmost town in Germany** la ville la plus à l'est de l'Allemagne; **the easternmost limits of the Sahara** les limites orientales du Sahara

Eastertide ['iːstətaɪd] *n Literary* (saison *f* de) Pâques *fpl*

east-facing *adj (house, wall)* (exposé) à l'est

easting ['iːstɪŋ] *n Naut* chemin *m* est

eastmost ['iːstməʊst] *adj* le plus à l'est

east-north-east **1** *n* est-nord-est *m*

2 *adj* **(a)** *Geog* est-nord-est *(inv)*, de l'est-nord-est **(b)** *(wind)* d'est-nord-est

3 *adv* à l'est-nord-est; *(travel)* vers l'est-nord-est, en direction de l'est-nord-est

east-south-east **1** *n* est-sud-est *m*

2 *adj* **(a)** *Geog* est-sud-est *(inv)*, de l'est-sud-est **(b)** *(wind)* d'est-sud-est

3 *adv* à l'est-sud-est; *(travel)* vers l'est-sud-est, en direction de l'est-sud-est

eastward ['iːstwəd] **1** *adj* vers l'est, en direction de l'est

2 *adv* vers l'est, en direction de l'est; **to sail eastward** naviguer cap sur l'est

3 *n* est *m*

eastwardly ['iːstwədlɪ] **1** *adj* vers l'est, en direction de l'est

2 *adv* vers l'est, en direction de l'est

eastwards ['iːstwədz] *adv* vers l'est, en direction de l'est; **to sail eastwards** naviguer cap sur l'est

easy ['iːzɪ] *(compar* **easier**, *superl* **easiest)** **1** *adj* **(a)** *(not difficult)* facile; **it's easy to see why/that...** on voit bien pourquoi/que...; **it's easy to say that...** c'est facile de dire que...; **it's easy for her to say that...** c'est facile pour elle de dire que...; **this will make your job easier** ceci vous facilitera la tâche; **it makes life much easier not having to fill in these forms** ça facilite bien les choses de ne pas avoir à remplir ces formulaires; **to be easy to live with** être facile à vivre; **to be easy to get on with** être facile à vivre; **she is easy** *or* **an easy person to please** *(gen)* c'est facile de lui faire plaisir; *(concerning food)* elle n'est pas difficile; **it's an easy mistake to make** c'est une erreur qui est facile à faire; **it's not easy being the eldest child** ce n'est pas facile d'être l'aîné; **it's far from easy, it's none too easy** c'est loin d'être facile, ce n'est pas facile du tout; **in easy stages** *(travel)* par petites étapes; *(learn)* sans peine; **learn Japanese in ten easy stages!** apprenez le japonais en dix petites leçons!; **within easy reach of** près de; **the shop is within easy walking distance of here** d'ici, on peut facilement aller au magasin à pied; **the easy way out** *or* **option** la solution facile *ou* de facilité; **there are no easy answers** c'est un problème qui est loin d'être facile à résoudre; **to have an easy time (of it)** *(a good life)* avoir la belle vie *ou* la vie facile; **she had an easy time of it** *(in exams)* ç'a été facile pour elle; **she hadn't had an easy time of it** elle n'avait pas eu une vie facile; *Fam* **it's easy money** c'est de l'argent gagné facilement *ou* sans se fatiguer❑; **to come in an easy first** *(in a race)* arriver bon premier; **an easy prey** *or* **victim** une proie facile; *Fam* **easy game** *or* **meat** bonne poire *f*; *Fam* **as easy as pie** *or* **ABC** *or* **as falling off a log** simple comme bonjour *ou* tout; *Fam* **to be on easy street** rouler sur l'or

(b) *(at peace)* **to feel easy in one's mind** être tranquille, avoir l'esprit tranquille

(c) *(easygoing → person, atmosphere)* décontracté; *(→ disposition, nature)* facile; *(→ manner)* décontracté, naturel; *(→ style)* coulant, facile; *Fam* **I'm easy** *(I don't mind)* ça m'est égal❑; **they're usually fairly easy about deadlines** d'habitude ils sont assez accommodants sur les délais; **to be on easy terms with sb** avoir des rapports plutôt amicaux avec qn; *Com* **on easy terms** avec facilités de paiement; **to go at an easy pace** aller tranquillement; **to be an easy fit** *(clothes)* être confortable

(d) *(sexually) very Fam Pej* **she's easy** *or* **an easy lay** elle couche avec tout le monde, c'est une Marie-couche-toi-là; *Literary* **a woman of easy virtue** une femme de petite vertu *ou* aux mœurs légères

(e) *(pleasant)* **to be easy on the eye** *(film, painting)* être agréable à regarder; *(person)* être bien fait de sa personne; **to be easy on the ear** *(music)* être agréable à écouter

(f) *St Exch (market)* calme

2 *adv (in a relaxed or sparing way)* doucement; **to go easy** y aller doucement; **to go easy on** *or* **with sb** y aller doucement avec qn; **to go easy on** *or* **with sth** y aller doucement avec *ou* sur qch; **go easy on the cream** vas-y doucement avec la crème; *Fam* **he's got it easy** *(has an easy life)* il se la coule douce, il a la belle vie; **to take things** *or* **it** *or* **life easy** *(lead a life of ease)* mener une vie tranquille; *(not overdo things)* ralentir; **you'll have to take it easy** *or* **go easy for a bit** il va falloir ralentir *ou* freiner un peu; *Fam* **take it easy!** *(gen)* doucement!; *(don't get upset)* ne t'en fais pas!; *Am (on parting)* bon courage!; *Fam* **easy now!, easy does it!** doucement!; **to sleep easy in one's bed** dormir sur ses deux oreilles; *Mil* **stand easy!** repos!; **easier said than done** plus facile à dire qu'à faire; **(it's) easy come easy go** *(money)* l'argent, ça va ça vient; **I hear she's got a new boyfriend – oh well, easy come easy go!** j'ai appris qu'elle avait un nouveau copain – un de perdu, dix de retrouvés!; *Am Fam* **easy over** *(egg)* cuit des deux côtés

▸▸ ***easy chair*** fauteuil *m*; *Mus* ***easy listening*** variété *f*

'Easy Street' *Chaplin* 'Charlot policier'

easy-care *adj* d'entretien facile

easy-clean *adj (garment, surface)* facile à nettoyer, d'entretien facile

easy-come-easy-go *adj Fam (attitude)* insouciant❑

easy-going *adj* **(a)** *(not given to anger)* qui prend les choses tranquillement; *(not worrying)* qui ne se fait pas de bile, décontracté; *(undemanding)* accommodant, coulant, peu exigeant; *(permissive)* qui a la conscience élastique; **the police take an easy-going attitude to such cases** dans de tels cas, la police se montre assez conciliante **(b)** *(horse)* à l'allure douce

easy-peasy [-piːzɪ] *adj (in children's language)* fastoche

easy-to-use *adj* facile à utiliser

eat [iːt] *(pt* **ate** [eɪt], *pp* **eaten** ['iːtən]) **1** *vt* **(a)** manger; **to eat (one's) breakfast/lunch/dinner** prendre son petit déjeuner/déjeuner/dîner; **to eat one's fill** manger tout son soûl *ou* content; **I don't eat meat** je ne mange pas de viande; **there's nothing to eat** il n'y a rien à manger; **would you like something to eat?** voulez-vous manger quelque chose?; **to eat one's way through a whole cake** manger un gâteau en entier; **it looks good enough to eat!** on en mangerait!; **he/she looks good enough to eat** il est beau/elle est belle à croquer; **go on, she's not going to eat you** va, elle ne va pas te manger; **I'll eat my hat if he gets elected** s'il est élu, je veux bien être pendu; **he eats people like you for breakfast** il ne fait qu'une bouchée des gens comme toi; **to eat one's words** ravaler ses mots; **they ate us out of house and home** ils ont dévalisé notre frigo; **she ate her way through six packets of biscuits** elle a réussi à engloutir six paquets de biscuits; *Am Fam Fig* **to eat sb's lunch** *(defeat)* battre qn à plates coutures; *Am Vulg* **eat shit!** va te faire voir!

(b) *(of machine → credit card, ticket)* avaler

(c) *Fam* **what's eating you?** qu'est-ce que tu as?❑

2 *vi* **(a)** *(consume food)* manger; **to eat like a horse** manger comme un ogre; **to eat like a bird** avoir un appétit d'oiseau, manger trois fois rien; **to eat for two** *(pregnant woman)* manger pour deux; **to eat, drink and be merry** faire la fête, s'amuser; **he eats out of my hand** *(bird)* il vient manger dans ma main; *Fig (person)* il fait tout ce que je veux; **treat them right and you'll have them eating out of your hand** traite-les bien et ils te mangeront dans la main

(b) *(have meal)* dîner; **we eat at seven** nous dînons à sept heures; **to eat well** bien manger; **let's eat!** on mange?

3 eats *npl Fam* bouffe *f*; **plenty of eats** plein à bouffer; **let's get some eats** allons chercher de la bouffe

▸**eat away** **1** *vt sep* **(a)** *(of waves)* ronger; *(of mice)* ronger; *(of acid, rust)* ronger, corroder **(b)** *Fig (confidence)* miner; *(support, capital, resources)* entamer

2 *vi (person)* manger

▸**eat away at** *vt insep* **(a)** *(of waves)* ronger; *(of mice)* ronger; *(of acid, rust)* ronger, corroder **(b)** *Fig (confidence)* miner; *(support, capital, resources)* entamer

▸**eat in** *vi* manger chez soi *ou* à la maison

▸**eat into** *vt insep* **(a)** *(destroy)* attaquer **(b)** *(use up → savings)* entamer; *(→ time)* empiéter sur

▸**eat out** **1** *vi* soutir déjeuner *ou* dîner, aller au restaurant

2 *vt sep* **to eat one's heart out** se morfondre; **eat your heart out!** dommage pour toi!

▸**eat up** **1** *vi* manger; **eat up!** *(there's lots more)* vas-y, mange!

2 *vt sep (food)* terminer, finir; *Fig (electricity, gas, petrol)* consommer beaucoup de; **to eat up the miles** dévorer *ou* avaler les kilomètres; *Fam* **this stove eats up the coal** cette poêle mange beaucoup de charbon; **the telephone is really eating up my money** le téléphone avale mes pièces à toute vitesse; **to be eaten up with sth**

(jealousy, hate, ambition) être rongé *ou* dévoré par qch

eatable ['i:təbəl] *adj (fit to eat)* mangeable; *(edible)* comestible

eatables ['i:təbəlz] *npl Hum* vivres *mpl*, victuailles *fpl*

eaten ['i:tən] *pp of* **eat**

eater ['i:tə(r)] *n* (**a**) *(person)* mangeur(euse) *m,f*; **he's a big/small eater** c'est un gros/petit mangeur; **to be a messy eater** manger salement; **to be a fussy eater** être difficile (sur la nourriture) (**b**) *Br Fam (apple)* pomme *f* à couteau ▫

eatery ['i:tərɪ] (*pl* **eateries**) *n Fam* café-restaurant ▫ *m*

eating ['i:tɪŋ] *n* manger *m*; **eating is one of his favourite pastimes** manger constitue un de ses passe-temps favoris; **to make good eating** *(be good to eat)* être bon

▸▸ ***eating apple*** pomme *f* à couteau; ***eating disorder*** trouble *m* du comportement alimentaire; ***eating habits*** habitudes *fpl* alimentaires; ***eating pear*** poire *f* à couteau; ***eating place*** restaurant *m*

eau [əʊ] *n*

▸▸ ***eau de Cologne*** eau *f* de Cologne; ***eau de toilette*** eau *f* de toilette; ***eau de vie*** eau *f* de vie

eau-de-nil [-'ni:l] **1** *adj* vert (de) Nil

2 *n* vert *m* (de) Nil

eaves ['i:vz] *npl* avant-toit *m*, corniche *f*

▸▸ *Am* ***eaves trough*** gouttière *f* pendante

eavesdrop ['i:vzdrɒp] (*pt & pp* **eavesdropped**, *cont* **eavesdropping**) *vi* écouter aux portes; **to eavesdrop on a conversation** tendre l'oreille pour écouter une conversation privée; **I found myself eavesdropping on their conversation** j'ai entendu leur conversation sans le vouloir; **stop eavesdropping!** arrête d'espionner le monde!

eavesdropper ['i:vz,drɒpə(r)] *n* indiscret(ète) *m,f*, personne *f* qui écoute aux portes

eavesdropping ['i:vz,drɒpɪŋ] *n* fait *m* d'écouter aux portes; **eavesdropping is a very bad habit** c'est très mal d'écouter aux portes

e-banking *n Comput* banque *f* en ligne, banque *f* électronique

ebb [eb] **1** *n (of tide)* reflux *m*; *(of public opinion)* variations *fpl*; **ebb and flow** flux *m* et reflux *m*; **the ebb and flow of married life** les hauts et les bas de la vie conjugale; **to be on the ebb** descendre; **to be at a low ebb** *(person)* ne pas avoir le moral; *(patient, enthusiasm, spirits)* être bien bas; *(business)* aller mal, être *ou* tourner au ralenti; *(finances, relations)* aller mal; **to be at one's lowest ebb** *(person)* avoir le moral à zéro; *(patient)* être au plus mal *ou* bas; **to be at its lowest ebb** *(enthusiasm, spirits)* être au plus bas; *(business, finances, relations)* aller au plus mal

2 *vi* (**a**) *(tide)* baisser, descendre; **to ebb and flow** monter et baisser *ou* descendre

(**b**) *Fig (confidence, enthusiasm, strength etc → diminish)* baisser peu à peu; *(→ disappear)* disparaître; *(rage, indignation)* se calmer; *(support)* s'amenuiser; *(time, water)* s'écouler; **his life was ebbing** il baissait d'heure en heure

▸▸ ***ebb tide*** marée *f* descendante

▸ **ebb away** *vi (confidence, enthusiasm, strength etc → diminish)* baisser peu à peu; *(→ disappear)* disparaître; *(rage, indignation)* se calmer; *(support)* s'amenuiser; *(time, water)* s'écouler; **his life was ebbing away** il baissait d'heure en heure

ebbing ['ebɪŋ] *adj* (**a**) *(water)* qui reflue (**b**) *(fortunes etc)* sur le déclin; *(popularity)* en baisse; *(strength, enthusiasm)* faiblissant

Ebionite ['ebɪənaɪt] *n Rel & Hist* ébionite *m*

EBIT [,i:bi:,aɪ'ti:] *npl Fin* (*abbr* **earnings before interest and tax**) bénéfices *mpl* avant impôts et charges

Ebola virus ['ebələ-, ə'bəʊlə-] *n Med* virus *m* Ebola

ebonics [ə'bɒnɪks] *n (UNCOUNT) Ling* = anglais parlé par une partie de la communauté Noire américaine

ebonite ['ebənaɪt] *n Chem* ébonite *f*

ebonize, -ise ['ebənaɪz] *vt* ébéner; **ebonized wood** bois *m* noirci

ebony ['ebənɪ] **1** *n* (**a**) *(tree)* ébénier *m* (**b**) *(wood)* ébène *f* (**c**) *Fig (colour)* ébène *f*

2 *adj* (**a**) *(chair, table, bracelet)* en ébène (**b**) *Fig (eyes, hair)* d'ébène

e-book *n* livre *m* numérique, livre *m* électronique

ebracteate [ɪ'bræktɪət] *adj Bot* ébracté

EBRD [,i:bi:,ɑ:'di:] *n Pol* (*abbr* **European Bank for Reconstruction and Development**) BERD *f*

ebriety [i:'braɪətɪ] *n Formal* ébriété *f*, ivresse *f*

ebrious ['i:brɪəs] *n Formal* en état d'ébriété

e-broker *n St Exch* courtier(ère) *m,f* électronique

e-broking *n St Exch* courtage *m* électronique

EBU [,i:bi:'ju:] *n* (*abbr* **European Broadcasting Union**) Union *f* européenne de radiodiffusion, UER *f*

ebullience [ɪ'bʊlɪəns] *n* exubérance *f*

ebullient [ɪ'bʊlɪənt] *adj* exubérant; **they were in (an) ebullient mood** *or* **in ebullient spirits** ils étaient d'une humeur exubérante

ebulliometer [ɪ,bʊlɪ'ɒmɪtə(r)] *n Phys* ébulliomètre *m*, ébullioscope *m*

ebulliometric [ɪ,bʊlɪə'metrɪk] *adj Phys* ébulliométrique

ebulliometry [ɪ,bʊlɪ'ɒmɪtrɪ] *n Phys* ébulliométrie *f*, ébullioscopie *f*

ebullioscope [ɪ'bʊlɪəʊskəʊp] *n Phys* ébullioscope *m*

ebullioscopic [ɪ,bʊlɪəʊ'skɒpɪk] *adj Phys* ébullioscopique

ebullioscopy [ɪ,bʊlɪ'ɒskəpɪ] *n Phys* ébullioscopie *f*

eburnation [,i:bɜ:'neɪʃən] *n Med* éburnation *f*

eburnean [ɪ'bɜ:nɪən] *adj* éburnéen

e-business *n Comput* commerce *m* électronique

EBV [,i:bi:'vi:] *n Med* (*abbr* **Epstein-Barr Virus**) EBV *m*

EC [,i:'si:] *n Pol* (*abbr* **European Community**) CE *f*

ecad ['i:kæd] *n Biol & Bot* = organisme qui s'est adapté à son environnement

e-card *n Comput* carte *f* électronique

e-cash *n Comput* argent *m* électronique, argent *m* virtuel, e-cash *m*

ECB [,i:si:'bi:] *n Com* (*abbr* **European Central Bank**) BCE *f*

écartelé [eɪ'kɑ:təleɪ] *adj Her* écartelé

ecbolic [ek'bɒlɪk] *Med* **1** *n* abortif *m*

2 *adj* abortif

ecce homo [,ekeɪ'həʊməʊ] *n Art* ecce homo *m*

eccentric [ɪk'sentrɪk] **1** *adj* (**a**) *(person, clothes, behaviour)* excentrique (**b**) *Astron, Math & Tech* excentrique, excentré

2 *n* (**a**) *(person)* excentrique *mf*, original(e) *m,f* (**b**) *Tech* excentrique *m*

eccentrically [ɪk'sentrɪkəlɪ] *adv* (**a**) *(dress, talk)* de manière excentrique (**b**) *Astron, Math & Tech* excentriquement

eccentricity [,eksen'trɪsətɪ] (*pl* **eccentricities**) *n* (**a**) *(of character, behaviour etc)* excentricité *f*; **eccentricities** *(of person)* excentricités *fpl* (**b**) *Math (of ellipse)* excentricité *f*; *Tech* excentricité *f*, désaxage *m*

Eccles cake ['ekəlz-] *n Br* = petit gâteau rond en pâte feuilletée fourré de fruits secs

Ecclesiastes [ɪ,kli:zɪ'æsti:z] *n Bible* **(the book of) Ecclesiastes** l'Ecclésiaste *m*

ecclesiastic [ɪ,kli:zɪ'æstɪk] **1** *adj (robes, traditions, calendar)* ecclésiastique; *(history)* de l'Église; *(music)* d'église

2 *n* ecclésiastique *m*

ecclesiastical [ɪ,kli:zɪ'æstɪkəl] *adj (robes, traditions, calendar)* ecclésiastique; *(history)* de l'Église; *(music)* d'église

ecclesiastically [ɪ,kli:zɪ'æstɪkəlɪ] *adv* ecclésiastiquement

ecclesiasticism [ɪ,kli:zɪ'æstɪsɪzəm] *n (temperament, spirit)* esprit *m* clérical; *(clericalism)* cléricalisme *m*

ecclesiologist [ɪ,kli:zɪ'ɒlədʒɪst] *n* ecclésiologue *mf*

ecclesiology [ɪ,kli:zɪ'ɒlədʒɪ] *n* ecclésiologie *f*

ecdysis ['ekdɪsɪs] *n Zool* ecdysis *f*

ECG [,i:si:'dʒi:] *n Med* (**a**) (*abbr* **electrocardiogram**) ECG *m* (**b**) (*abbr* **electrocardiograph**) ECG *m*

ECGD [,i:si:,dʒi:'di:] *n Com* (*abbr* **Export Credits Guarantee Department**) = organisme d'assurance pour le commerce extérieur, ≃ COFACE *f*

ecgonine ['ekgəni:n] *n Chem* ecgonine *f*

ECH (*written abbr* **electric central heating**) chauffage *m* central électrique

echelon ['eʃəlɒn] *n* (**a**) *(level)* échelon *m*; **the higher** *or* **upper echelons of the Civil Service** les niveaux supérieurs de l'administration (**b**) *Mil* échelon *m*

echeveria [etʃ,i:və'rɪə] *n Bot* écheveria *m*

echidna [ɪ'kɪdnə] *n Zool* échidné *m*

echinite ['ekɪnaɪt] *n Archeol* échinide *m* fossile

echinocactus [e,kaɪnəʊ'kæktəs] *n Bot* échinocactus *m*

echinocaris [e,kaɪnəʊ'kɑ:rɪs] *n Archeol* échinocaris *m*

echinocarpous [e,kaɪnəʊ'kɑ:pəs] *adj Bot* échinocarpe

echinocereus [e,kaɪnəʊ'si:rɪəs] *n Bot* échinocéreus *m*

echinococcosis [e,kaɪnəʊkɒ'kəʊsɪs] *n Vet* échinococcose *f*

echinocystis [e,kaɪnəʊ'sɪstɪs] *n Bot* échinocystis *m*

echinoderm [ɪ'kaɪnəʊdɜ:m] *n Zool* échinoderme *m*

echinoid [ɪ'kaɪnɔɪd] *adj Zool* semblable à l'oursin

echinus [ɪ'kaɪnəs] *n Zool* oursin *m (du genre Echinus)*

Echo ['ekəʊ] *pr n Myth* Écho

echo ['ekəʊ] (*pl* **echoes**) **1** *n* (**a**) *(of sound)* écho *m*; **to cheer sb to the echo** applaudir qn à tout rompre; *Fig* **there are echoes of the 18th century in this novel** il y a des accents du XVIIIème siècle dans ce roman; **there were echoes of Proust in his novel** son roman avait des accents proustiens; **her words found an echo in many hearts** ses mots ont fait vibré la corde sensible dans beaucoup de cœurs

(**b**) *(radio signal)* écho *m*

2 *vt (sound)* répéter; *Fig (colour, theme)* reprendre, rappeler; *(architecture, style)* rappeler, évoquer; **to echo sb's opinions** *(person)* se faire l'écho des opinions de qn; *(editorial)* reprendre les opinions de qn

3 *vi (noise, voice, music)* résonner; *(place)* faire écho, résonner; **the corridor echoed with shouts/footsteps** des cris/bruits de pas résonnèrent dans le couloir, le couloir résonna de cris/bruits de pas

▸▸ ***echo box*** cavité *f* resonnante; ***echo chamber*** chambre *f* de réverbération; ***echo sounder*** échosondeur *m*; ***echo sounding*** sondage *m* par ultrasons; *Med* ***echo virus*** virus *m* ECHO; ***echo wave*** onde *f* d'écho

echocardiogram [,ekəʊ'kɑ:dɪəʊgræm] *n Med* échocardiogramme *m*

echogram ['ekəʊgræm] *n* échogramme *m*

echograph ['ekəʊgrɑ:f] *n* échographe *m*

echoic [e'kəʊɪk] *adj* échoïque

echolalia [,ekəʊ'leɪlɪə] *n Med* écholalie *f*

echolocation [,ekəʊləʊ'keɪʃən] *n* (**a**) *Zool* audio-détection *f*, écholocation *f* (**b**) *Tech* écholocalisation *f*

echopraxia [,ekəʊ'præksɪə], **echopraxis** [,ekəʊ'præksɪs] *n Med* échopraxie *f*

eciton ['esɪtɒn] *n Entom* éciton *m*

éclair [eɪ'kleə(r)] *n Culin* éclair *m*

eclampsia [ɪ'klæmpsɪə] *n Med* éclampsie *f*

éclat [eɪ'klɑ:] *n* éclat *m*

eclectic [ɪ'klektɪk] **1** *n* éclectique *mf*

2 *adj* éclectique; **an eclectic blend** un mélange varié

eclectically [ɪ'klektɪkəlɪ] *adv* éclectiquement

eclecticism [ɪ'klektɪsɪzəm] *n* éclectisme *m*

eclipse [ɪ'klɪps] *Astron & Fig* **1** *n* éclipse *f*; **an eclipse of the sun/moon** une éclipse de soleil/lune; **total/partial eclipse** éclipse *f* totale/partielle; **to be in eclipse** être éclipsé; **to go into eclipse** *(sun, moon)* s'éclipser; *Fig* **his career went into eclipse** il a connu une traversée du désert

2 *vt* éclipser; *Fig* **his performance was only eclipsed in 1998** sa performance n'a été améliorée qu'en 1998

ecliptic [ɪ'klɪptɪk] *Astron* **1** *n* écliptique *m*

2 *adj* écliptique

eclogite ['eklədʒaɪt] *n Miner* éclogite *f*

eclogue ['eklɒg] *n Literature* églogue *f*

eclosion [ɪ'kləʊʒən] *n Zool* éclosion *f*

ECM [,i:si:'em] *n Am* (*abbr* **European Common Market**) = Marché commun européen

ECN [,i:si:'en] *n St Exch* (*abbr* **electronic communications network**) = marché électronique privé

eco- [ˌiːkəʊ] *pref* éco-
ecocide [ˈiːkəʊsaɪd] *n* écocide *m*
ecodevelopment [ˌiːkəʊdɪˈveləpmənt] *n* écodéveloppement *m*
ECOFIN [ˈiːkəʊˌfɪn] *n Fin* (*abbr* **Economic and Financial Council of Ministers**) Conseil *m* Ecofin
ecofreak [ˈiːkəʊfriːk] *n Fam* écologiste *mf* enragé(e)
eco-friendly *adj (product)* qui ne nuit pas à l'environnement; *(lifestyle, person)* qui respecte l'environnement
eco-hazard *n* substance *f* toxique
eco-label *n Br* écolabel *m*
eco-labelling *n Br* attribution *f* d'écolabels
E-coli [ˌiːˈkəʊlaɪ] *n Med* E-coli *f*
ecological [ˌiːkəˈlɒdʒɪkəl] *adj* écologique
ecologically [ˌiːkəˈlɒdʒɪklɪ] *adv* écologiquement; **ecologically (speaking)** du point de vue de l'écologie; **ecologically harmful/sound** qui est nuisible à/qui respecte l'environnement; **to be ecologically conscious** *or* **aware** se préoccuper *ou* se soucier de l'environnement
ecologist [ɪˈkɒlədʒɪst] *n* écologiste *mf*
ecology [ɪˈkɒlədʒɪ] *n* écologie *f*
e-commerce *n Comput* commerce *m* électronique
►► ***e-commerce site*** site *m* marchand
econometric [ɪˌkɒnəˈmetrɪk] *adj* économétrique
econometrician [ɪˌkɒnəmeˈtrɪʃən] *n* économétricien(enne) *m,f*
econometrics [ɪˌkɒnəˈmetrɪks] *n (UNCOUNT)* économétrie *f*
economic [ˌiːkəˈnɒmɪk] *adj* (**a**) *Econ (growth, system, recovery)* économique
(**b**) *(profitable)* rentable; **economic rent** loyer rentable; **it isn't economic, it doesn't make economic sense** ce n'est pas rentable *ou* avantageux; **to make sth economic** rentabiliser qch
(**c**) *Fam (inexpensive)* économique
►► ***economic adviser*** conseiller(ère) *m,f* économique; ***economic aid*** aide *f* économique; ***economic analysis*** analyse *f* économique; ***economic appraisal*** évaluation *f* économique; ***economic climate*** climat *m* économique; ***economic cost*** coût *m* économique; ***economic crisis*** crise *f* économique; ***economic development*** croissance *f* par habitant *ou* per capita; *Fin* ***Economic and Financial Council of Ministers*** Conseil *m* Ecofin; ***economic forecast*** prévisions *fpl* économiques; ***economic growth rate*** taux *m* d'expansion économique; ***economic indicator*** indicateur *m* économique; *Com* ***economic life*** durée *f* de vie utile; *Pol* ***economic migrant*** émigrant *m* de la faim *ou* pour des raisons économiques; ***economic miracle*** miracle *m* économique; *Pol & Fin* ***Economic and Monetary Union*** union *f* économique et monétaire; ***economic performance*** *(of country)* résultats *mpl* économiques; ***economic policy*** politique *f* économique; ***economic prospects*** prévisions *fpl* conjoncturelles *ou* économiques; ***economic rate of return*** taux *f* de rentabilité économique; ***economic recovery*** reprise *f ou* redressement *m* économique; ***economic sanctions*** sanctions *fpl* économiques; ***economic situation*** conjoncture *f* économique; *Br* ***Economic and Social Research Council*** = organisme chargé de distribuer des subventions pour la recherche en sciences sociales; ***economic trend*** tendance *f ou* conjoncture *f* économique; *Acct* ***economic value added*** valeur *f* ajoutée économique; *Mktg* ***economic value to the customer*** valeur *f* économique apportée au consommateur
economical [ˌiːkəˈnɒmɪkəl] *adj* (**a**) *(person)* économe; *(machine, method, approach)* économique; **it's more economical to buy in bulk** c'est plus économique *ou* avantageux d'acheter par grandes quantités; **to be economical to run** *(car, heating)* être économique; **to be economical with sth** économiser qch; *Euph* **to be economical with the truth** dire la vérité avec parcimonie (**b**) *(style)* concis, sobre
economically [ˌiːkəˈnɒmɪklɪ] *adv* (**a**) *Econ* économiquement; **economically viable** *(campaign, project, product)* économiquement viable (**b**) *(live)* de manière économe; *(use)* de manière économe, avec parcimonie (**c**) *(write)* avec sobriété
economics [ˌiːkəˈnɒmɪks] **1** *n (UNCOUNT) (science)* économie *f* (politique), sciences *fpl* économiques
2 *npl (financial aspects)* aspects *mpl* financiers; *(profitability)* rentabilité *f*; **the economics of town planning** les aspects financiers de l'urbanisme; **we must consider the economics of the project before making any decisions** nous devons considérer l'aspect financier du projet avant de prendre une décision
3 *comp (teacher, class)* d'économie
economism [ɪˈkɒnəmɪzəm] *n* économisme *m*
economist [ɪˈkɒnəmɪst] *n* économiste *mf*; *Press* **the Economist** = hebdomadaire britannique politique, économique et financier
economize, -ise [ɪˈkɒnəmaɪz] **1** *vt (time, money etc)* économiser (sur), ménager
2 *vi* économiser, faire des économies; **to economize on sth** économiser sur qch
economy [ɪˈkɒnəmɪ] (*pl* **economies**) **1** *n* (**a**) *(system)* économie *f*; **(centrally) planned economy** économie *f* planifiée; *Old-fashioned* **political economy** économie *f* politique
(**b**) *(saving)* économie *f*; **to practise economy** économiser, épargner; **to make economies** faire des économies; **it's a false economy** ce n'est pas vraiment rentable; **with (an) economy of effort** sans effort inutile; **economy of style** concision *f* de style
2 *comp (pack)* économique
3 *adv (fly, travel)* en classe touriste
►► ***economy brand*** marque *f* économique; *Am* ***economy car*** = voiture de taille moyenne, consommant peu par rapport aux "grosses américaines"; ***economy class*** classe *f* touriste; ***economy drive*** *(of company, government)* politique *f* de réduction des dépenses; **I'm on an economy drive at the moment** j'essaie d'économiser en ce moment; ***economy fare*** tarif *m* économique; ***economy measure*** mesure *f* de réduction des dépenses; **as an economy measure** par mesure d'économie; *Aut* ***economy mode*** *(with automatic gears)* mode *m* économique; ***economies of scale*** économies *fpl* d'échelle
economy-class syndrome *n Fam* syndrome *m* de la classe économique
economy-size(d) *adj (pack, jar)* taille économique *(inv)*
ecopolitics [ˈiːkəʊˌpɒlɪtɪks] *n (UNCOUNT)* politique *f* et environnement *m (sujet d'étude)*
ecosphere [ˈiːkəʊˌsfɪə(r)] *n* écosphère *f*
ecosystem [ˈiːkəʊˌsɪstəm] *n* écosystème *m*
ecotage [ˈiːkəʊtɑːʒ] *n* = actes de sabotage perpétrés par des militants écologistes
ecotax [ˈiːkəʊtæks] *n* taxe *f* écologique, écotaxe *f*
ecoterrorism [ˈiːkəʊˌterərɪzəm] *n* = militantisme écologiste faisant intervenir des actions violentes
ecoterrorist [ˈiːkəʊˌterərɪst] *n* = militant écologiste ayant recours à des actions violentes
ecothermic [ˌiːkəʊˈθɜːmɪk] *adj Physiol* ectotherme
ecotone [ˈiːkətəʊn] *n* écotone *f*
ecotourism [ˌiːkəʊˈtʊərɪzəm] *n* écotourisme *m*
ecotoxic [ˌiːkəʊˈtɒksɪk] *adj* écotoxique
ecotoxicology [ˌiːkəʊtɒksɪˈkɒlədʒɪ] *n* écotoxicologie *f*
ecotype [ˈiːkəʊtaɪp] *n* écotype *m*
ecowarrior [ˌiːkəʊˈwɒrɪə(r)] *n* écoguerrier(ère) *m,f*
ECP [ˌiːsiːˈpiː] *n Fin* (*abbr* **euro-commercial paper**) billet *m* de trésorerie *(émis sur le marché des eurodevises)*
ecru [ˈeɪkruː] **1** *n* écru *m*
2 *adj* écru
ECSC [ˌiːsiːˌesˈsiː] *n Pol* (*abbr* **European Coal & Steel Community**) CECA *f*
ECSDA [ˌiːsiːˌesdiːˈeɪ] *n Fin* (*abbr* **European Central Securities Depositories Association**) association *f* européenne des dépositaires centraux de titres
ecstasy [ˈekstəsɪ] (*pl* **ecstasies**) *n* (**a**) *(pleasure)* extase *f*, ravissement *m*; **to be in an ecstasy of delight** être transporté de joie; **to go into/be in ecstasies over sth** s'extasier/être en extase devant qch; *(critics)* être dithyrambique à propos de qch; **to send sb into ecstasies** faire tomber qn en extase (**b**) *(drug)* ecstasy *f* (**c**) *Rel & Psy* extase *f*
ecstatic [ekˈstætɪk] *adj* ravi; **he got an ecstatic reception from the crowd** il a été accueilli par une foule en délire; **to be ecstatic about sth** *(in admiration → gen)* être en extase devant qch; *(→ with joy)* être ravi de qch; **I'm not ecstatic about it** cela ne m'enchante pas
ecstatically [ekˈstætɪklɪ] *adv* avec extase; **to be ecstatically happy** être dans un bonheur extatique
ECT [ˌiːsiːˈtiː] *n Med* (*abbr* **electroconvulsive therapy**) traitement *m* par électrochocs
ecthyma [ˈekθɪmə] *n Med* ecthyma *m*
ectoblast [ˈektəʊˌblæst] *n Biol* ectoderme *m*
ectoblastic [ˌektəʊˈblæstɪk] *adj Biol* ectodermique
ectocardia [ˌektəʊˈkɑːdɪə] *n Med* ectocardie *f*
ectoderm [ˈektəʊdɜːm] *n Biol* ectoderme *m*
ectodermal [ˌektəʊˈdɜːməl], **ectodermic** [ˌektəʊˈdɜːmɪk] *adj Biol* ectodermique
ectomorph [ˈektəʊmɔːf] *n* ectomorphe *mf*
ectomorphic [ˌektəʊˈmɔːfɪk] *adj* ectomorphe
ectomorphy [ˈektəʊmɔːfɪ] *n* ectomorphisme *m*
ectoparasite [ˌektəʊˈpærəsaɪt] *n Zool* ectoparasite *m*
ectoparasitic [ektəʊˌpærəˈsɪtɪk] *adj Zool* ectoparasite
ectopia [ekˈtəʊpɪə] *n Med* ectopie *f*
ectopic [ekˈtəʊpɪk] *adj Med (pregnancy)* extra-utérin, ectopique
ectoplasm [ˈektəʊplæzəm] *n Biol* ectoplasme *m*
ectoplasmic [ˌektəʊˈplæzmɪk] *adj Biol* ectoplasmique
ectosome [ˈektəʊsəʊm] *n Biol* ectosome *m*
ectotrophic [ˌektəʊˈtrɒfɪk] *adj Biol* ectotrophe
ectropion [ˌekˈtrəʊpjən] *n Med* ectropion *m*
ECU [ˈeɪkjuː] *n* (*abbr* **European Currency Unit**) ECU *m*, écu *m*
Ecuador [ˈekwədɔː(r)] *n* Équateur *m*; **in Ecuador** en Équateur
Ecuadoran [ˌekwəˈdɔːrən], **Ecuadorian** [ˌekwəˈdɔːrɪən] **1** *n* Équatorien(enne) *m,f*
2 *adj* équatorien
3 *comp (embassy)* d'Équateur; *(history)* de l'Équateur
ecumenical [ˌiːkjʊˈmenɪkəl] *adj* œcuménique
ecumenicalism [ˌiːkjʊˈmenɪkəlɪzəm] *n* œcuménisme *m*
ecumenically [ˌiːkjʊˈmenɪkəlɪ] *adv* œcuméniquement
ecumenism [iːˈkjuːmənɪzəm], **ecumenicism** [ˌiːkjuːˈmenɪsɪzəm] *n* œcuménisme *m*
eczema [ˈeksɪmə] *n Med* eczéma *m*; **to have eczema** avoir de l'eczéma; **eczema sufferer** eczémateux(euse) *m,f*
eczematous [ˌekˈsemətəs] *adj Med* eczémateux
ED [ˌiːˈdiː] *n Admin* (*abbr* **Employment Department**) ≃ ministère *m* du Travail
ed.[1] [ed] *n* (**a**) (*abbr* **editor**) éd., édit (**b**) (*abbr* **education**) éducation *f*
ed.[2] (**a**) (*written abbr* **edited**) sous la dir. de, coll (**b**) (*written abbr* **edition**) éd., édit (**c**) (*written abbr* **education**) éduc
Edam [ˈiːdæm] *n (cheese)* édam *m*
edaphic [əˈdæfɪk] *adj Biol & Ecol* édaphique
►► ***edaphic factor*** facteur *m* édaphique
EdD [ˌedˈdiː] *n Am* (*abbr* **Doctor of Education**) *(person)* docteur *m* en sciences de l'éducation; *(qualification)* doctorat *m* en sciences de l'éducation
eddy [ˈedɪ] (*pl* **eddies**) **1** *n (of water, wind)* remous *m*, tourbillon *m*; *(of leaves, dust)* tourbillon
2 *vi (water)* faire des remous; *(wind, smoke, snow)* tourbillonner, tournoyer; *(crowds)* tournoyer
►► *Elec* ***eddy currents*** courants *mpl* de Foucault
eddying [ˈedɪɪŋ] *adj (water, wind)* qui fait des remous; *(leaves, dust)* tourbillonnant
►► ***eddying flow*** remous *m*
edelweiss [ˈeɪdəlvaɪs] *n Bot* edelweiss *m*, immortelle *f* des neiges
edema, edematose *etc Am* = **oedema, oedematose** *etc*
Eden [ˈiːdən] *n Bible* l'Éden *m*, le Paradis terrestre; *Fig* éden *m*
Edenic [iːˈdenɪk] *adj* édénique
edentate [iːˈdenteɪt] *Biol* **1** *n* édenté *m*
2 *adj* édenté
edentulous [iːˈdentjʊləs] *adj Biol* édenté

EDF [ˌiːdiːˈef] *n Pol* (*abbr* **European Development Fund**) FED *m*

EDGAR [ˈedgə(r)] *n Fin* (*abbr* **electronic data gathering, analysis and retrieval**) = banque de données créée par la commission américaine des opérations de Bourse (le SEC), qui contient toutes sortes d'informations sur de nombreux fonds communs de placement et entreprises publiques

edge [edʒ] **1** *n* (**a**) *(of blade)* fil *m*, tranchant *m*; **a knife with a sharp** *or* **keen edge** un couteau à la lame aiguisée *ou* affilée; **to put an edge on** *(knife, blade)* aiguiser, affiler, affûter; **to take the edge off** *(knife, blade)* émousser; *Fig (pleasure)* gâter; *(argument)* couper tout l'effet de; **seeing that film has taken the edge off my appetite** ça m'a coupé l'appétit de voir ce film; **the sandwich took the edge off my hunger** ce sandwich a calmé ma faim; **he smiled to take the edge off his words** il souria pour atténuer l'effet de ses paroles; **the walk gave an edge to his appetite** la promenade lui a ouvert l'appétit; **to have the edge on** *(be better than)* avoir légèrement le dessus *ou* l'avantage sur; *(have an advantage over)* avoir l'avantage sur; *Am Fam* **to have an edge on** *(be drunk)* être éméché *ou* pompette; **to give sb/sth that extra edge** donner un plus à qn/qch; **the performance lacked edge** le spectacle manquait de ressort *ou* d'énergie; **I've lost my edge** *(athlete)* j'ai perdu mon brio; *(writer)* j'ai perdu mon mordant; **with an edge in one's voice** d'un ton légèrement agacé; **to speak with a sarcastic/nervous/contemptuous edge to one's voice** parler avec une pointe de sarcasme/de nervosité/de mépris dans la voix

(**b**) *(outer limit → of table, cliff, road)* bord *m*; *(→ of page)* bord *m*, marge *f*; *(→ of forest)* lisière *f*, orée *f*; *(→ of cube, brick)* arête *f*; *(→ of coin, book)* tranche *f*; *(→ of ski)* carre *f*; **at** *or* **by the water's edge** au bord de l'eau; **to stand sth on its edge** *(coin, book)* mettre qch sur la tranche; *(brick, stone)* poser *ou* mettre qch de *ou* sur chant; **it fell off the edge** il est tombé; **pages with gilt edges** pages aux tranches dorées, pages dorées sur tranches; **to be on the edge of** *(war, disaster, madness)* être au bord de; *Fig* **I was on the edge of my seat** *(waiting for news)* j'étais sur des charbons ardents; *Fig* **this film will have you on the edge of your seat** ce film est d'un suspense à vous faire frémir; **to be close to the edge** être près du bord; *Fig* être au bord du précipice; *Fig* **to push sb over the edge** faire craquer qn; **to live on the edge** prendre des risques

2 *vt* (**a**) *(give a border to)* border; **to edge sth with sth** border qch de qch

(**b**) *(sharpen)* aiguiser, affiler, affûter

(**c**) *(move gradually)* **to edge one's way** avancer *ou* progresser lentement; **she edged her way out onto the window ledge** elle gagna le rebord de la fenêtre avec précaution; **to edge one's way along a ledge** avancer *ou* progresser lentement le long d'une corniche; **to edge one's chair nearer sb/sth** approcher sa chaise de qn/qch

(**d**) *(in skiing)* **to edge one's skis** planter ses carres

3 *vi* avancer *ou* progresser lentement; **to edge through the crowd** se frayer un chemin à travers la foule; **to edge past sb/sth** se faufiler à côté de qn/qch; **to edge into a room** se faufiler dans une pièce; **to edge away (from sb/sth)** s'éloigner doucement *ou* discrètement (de qn/qch); **he edged a little closer** il s'est rapproché un peu; **the car edged forward/backward** la voiture avança/recula doucement

4 on edge 1 *adj* **to be on edge** être énervé *ou* sur les nerfs **2** *adv* **to set sb on edge** crisper qn, énerver qn; **to set sb's teeth on edge** faire grincer les dents à qn; **to set sb's nerves on edge** mettre les nerfs de qn à fleur de peau

►► ***edge cutter*** *(for grass)* coupe-bordure(s) *m*; ***edge tool*** outil *m* tranchant; ***edge trimmer*** *(for grass)* coupe-bordure(s) *m*

►**edge out 1** *vt sep Fig* **she was edged out of her job** elle a été évincée de son poste; **the runner was edged out of second place** le coureur, qui avait longtemps été en deuxième place, a été dépassé peu avant l'arrivée

2 *vi* sortir lentement; **to edge out of a room** se glisser hors d'une pièce; **the driver/car edged out** le conducteur/la voiture se dégagea lentement

►**edge up 1** *vt sep* **to edge prices up** faire monter les prix doucement

2 *vi* (**a**) *(prices)* monter doucement (**b**) *(approach slowly)* **to edge up to sb/sth** s'avancer lentement vers qn/qch

-edged [edʒd] *suff* **double-edged** à double tranchant; **sharp-edged** bien affilé *ou* aiguisé

edger [ˈedʒə(r)] *n (gardening tool)* coupe-bordure(s) *m*

edgeways [ˈedʒweɪz], **edgewise** [ˈedʒwaɪz] *adv* (**a**) *(on its edge)* de chant; **to lay** *or* **set a plank edgeways** placer une planche de chant; *Fam* **I can't get a word in edgeways** je n'arrive pas à placer un mot (dans la conversation) (**b**) *(from side)* latéralement, de côté; **seen edgeways (on)** vu de côté

edgily [ˈedʒɪlɪ] *adv* nerveusement

edginess [ˈedʒɪnɪs] *n* nervosité *f*; **there was an edginess about him** il était assez nerveux

edging [ˈedʒɪŋ] *n (border → on dress, of flowers etc)* bordure *f*

►► *Hort* ***edging shears*** cisaille *f* à gazon; *Hort* ***edging tool*** coupe-gazon *m inv*, molette *f*

edgy [ˈedʒɪ] (*compar* **edgier**, *superl* **edgiest**) *adj* nerveux, sur les nerfs; **to get edgy** s'énerver

EDI [ˌiːdiːˈaɪ] *n* (**a**) *Comput* (*abbr* **Electronic Data Interchange**) EDI *m* (**b**) *Fin* (*abbr* **European Data Interchange**) EED *m*

edibility [edɪˈbɪlɪtɪ] *n* comestibilité *f*

edible [ˈedɪbəl] **1** *adj (mushroom, berry)* comestible; *(fit to eat)* bon à manger, mangeable; **edible crab** tourteau *m*; **is it edible?** c'est bon à manger?; *Fam* **this is very edible!** c'est délicieux![❑]

2 edibles *npl* comestibles *mpl*

edict [ˈiːdɪkt] *n Pol* décret *m*; *Fig* ordre *m*

►► *Hist* ***the Edict of Nantes*** l'édit *m* de Nantes

edification [ˌedɪfɪˈkeɪʃən] *n Formal* édification *f*, instruction *f*; *esp Ironic* **for your edification** pour votre édification

edifice [ˈedɪfɪs] *n also Fig* édifice *m*

edify [ˈedɪfaɪ] (*pt & pp* **edified**) *vt Formal* édifier

edifying [ˈedɪfaɪɪŋ] *adj Formal* édifiant; *Hum* **it was hardly an edifying spectacle/experience** le spectacle/l'expérience était loin d'être édifiant(e)

Edinburgh [ˈedɪnbrə] *n* Édimbourg

►► ***the Edinburgh Festival*** le Festival d'Édimbourg; ***Edinburgh Rock*** *(sweet)* = sorte de confiserie, spécialité d'Édimbourg

EDINBURGH FESTIVAL

Le festival international d'Édimbourg, créé en 1947, est aujourd'hui un des plus grands festivals de théâtre et de musique au monde; il se tient chaque année dans la capitale écossaise en août et en septembre. Le festival "off" (fringe) est une grande rencontre du théâtre expérimental.

edit [ˈedɪt] **1** *n* (**a**) *(of text)* révision *f*, correction *f* (**b**) *Comput (menu heading)* Edition *f*

2 *vt* (**a**) *(correct → article, text, book)* corriger, réviser; *(prepare for publication → book, article)* éditer, préparer pour la publication; *(→ film, TV programme, tape)* monter; **the footnotes were edited from the book** les notes ont été coupées dans le *ou* retranchées du livre; **give me an edited version of what happened** dites-moi brièvement ce qui s'est passé; **edited highlights** *(on television)* résumé *m* en images; *Fig* **there's no need to go into details, just give me the edited highlights** inutile d'entrer dans les détails, fais-moi un résumé

(**b**) *(newspaper, magazine, series)* diriger la rédaction de; **edited by...** *(series, newspaper)* sous la direction de...

(**c**) *Comput (text)* modifier, éditer

►► *Comput* ***edit keys*** touches *fpl* de modification; *Comput* ***edit mode*** mode *m* Edition; *TV* ***edit suite*** régie *f ou* salle *f* de montage

►**edit down** *vt sep* raccourcir

►**edit in** *vt sep* insérer

►**edit out** *vt sep (scene)* couper; *(from text)* supprimer; *(write out of TV series)* faire disparaître; **he was edited out of the film when he broke his contract** on a coupé toutes les scènes du film où il apparaissait quand il a rompu son contrat

editable [ˈedɪtəbəl] *adj* pouvant être édité

editing [ˈedɪtɪŋ] *n* (**a**) *(initial corrections)* révision *f*, correction *f*; *(in preparation for publication)* édition *f*, préparation *f* à la publication; *(of film, tape)* montage *m*

(**b**) *(of newspaper, magazine)* rédaction *f*

(**c**) *Comput (of file, text)* édition *f*

►► *TV* ***editing desk*** table *f ou* banc *m* de montage; *Comput* ***editing function*** fonction *f* d'édition; *TV* ***editing table*** table *f* de montage; *TV* ***editing terminal*** terminal *m* de montage; *Comput* ***editing window*** fenêtre *f* d'édition

edition [ɪˈdɪʃən] *n (of book, newspaper)* édition *f*; **first edition** première édition *f*; **revised/limited edition** édition *f* revue et corrigée/à tirage limité; **in Tuesday's edition of the programme** dans l'émission de mardi

►► ***edition time*** *(for newspaper)* bouclage *m*, heure *f* de l'édition, tombée *f*

editor [ˈedɪtə(r)] *n* (**a**) *(of newspaper, magazine)* rédacteur(trice) *m,f* en chef; *(of author)* éditeur(trice) *m,f*; *(of dictionary)* rédacteur(trice) *m,f*; *(of book, article → who makes corrections)* correcteur(trice) *m,f*; *(→ who writes)* rédacteur(trice) *m,f*; *(of film)* monteur(euse) *m,f*; **series editor** directeur(trice) *m,f* de la publication; *Press* **political editor** rédacteur(trice) *m,f* politique; *Press* **sports editor** rédacteur(trice) *m,f* sportif(ive); *Press* **editor's note** note *f* de la rédaction

(**b**) *Comput (software)* éditeur *m* (de texte)

editorial [ˌedɪˈtɔːrɪəl] **1** *adj (decision, comment)* de la rédaction; *(job, problems, skills)* de rédaction, rédactionnel

2 *n* (**a**) *(article)* éditorial *m* (**b**) *(department)* service *m* de la rédaction, rédaction *f*

►► ***editorial changes*** corrections *fpl*; ***editorial content*** contenu *m* rédactionnel; ***editorial department*** *(in press)* service *m* de la rédaction, rédaction *f*, direction *f* de la rédaction; ***editorial director*** *(of newspaper)* rédacteur(trice) *m,f* en chef, directeur(trice) *m,f* de la rédaction; *(of publishing company)* directeur(trice) *m,f* de la rédaction; ***editorial freedom*** liberté *f* des rédacteurs; ***editorial interference*** ingérence *f* rédactionnelle; ***editorial office*** (salle *f* de) rédaction *f*; ***editorial opinion*** *(in press)* avis *m* éditorial; ***editorial policy*** politique *f* éditoriale; *(in press)* politique *f* de la rédaction; ***the editorial staff*** la rédaction

editorialist [ˌedɪˈtɔːrɪəlɪst] *n Am* éditorialiste *mf*

editorialize, -ise [ˌedɪˈtɔːrɪəlaɪz] *vi* émettre des opinions personnelles, être subjectif; **as the Times editorialized,...** comme l'affirmait l'éditorial du Times,...

editorially [ˌedɪˈtɔːrɪəlɪ] *adv* du point de vue de la rédaction

editor-in-chief *n* rédacteur(trice) *m,f* en chef

editorship [ˈedɪtəʃɪp] *n* rédaction *f*; **during her editorship** quand elle dirigeait la rédaction; **the series was produced under the general editorship of...** la série a été produite sous la direction générale de...

EdM [edˈem] *n Am* (*abbr* **Master of Education**) *(person)* = titulaire d'une maîtrise en sciences de l'éducation; *(qualification)* maîtrise *f* en sciences de l'éducation

EDP [ˌiːdiːˈpiː] *n Comput* (*abbr* **electronic data processing**) traitement *m* électronique de l'information

EDT [ˌiːdiːˈtiː] *n Am* (*abbr* **Eastern Daylight Time**) heure *f* d'été de l'Est

.edu [ˈedjuː] *Comput* (*abbr* **education**) = abréviation désignant les universités et les sites éducatifs dans les adresses électroniques

educable [ˈedʒʊkəbəl] *adj Formal* éducable

educatability [ˌedjʊkətəˈbɪlɪtɪ] *n Formal* éducabilité *f*

educate [ˈedjʊkeɪt] *vt* (**a**) *(pupil)* donner de l'instruction à, instruire; **he was educated in France/at Oxford** il a fait ses études en France/à Oxford; **to have one's child educated** faire faire des études à son enfant; **to be impossible to educate** être inéducable

(**b**) *(train, develop) (person, someone's taste/*

mind) former; **the campaign aims to educate young people about the risks of drugs** la campagne a pour objet de sensibiliser les jeunes aux dangers de la drogue; **she was educated always to think of others before herself** on lui a enseigné à toujours penser aux autres avant elle-même

educated ['edʒʊkeɪtɪd] *adj (person)* instruit; *(voice)* distingué; *(palate)* fin; **to make an educated guess** faire une supposition bien informée; **he was well educated in the ways of the locals** il était bien renseigné sur le mode de vie des gens de la région

education [,edʒʊ'keɪʃən] **1** *n* **(a)** *(teaching)* enseignement *m*; **a classical/scientific education** une formation classique/scientifique; **he has had a good education** il a reçu une bonne instruction; **to get oneself an education** faire des études; **he never completed his education** il n'a jamais fini *ou* terminé ses études; **the education of poor countries in modern farming techniques** la formation des pays pauvres aux techniques agricoles modernes; **to have** *or* **to receive a good education** recevoir une bonne éducation *ou* formation; **she completed her education in Italy** elle a terminé ses études en Italie; **standards of education** niveau *m* scolaire; **it was an education** cela m'a beaucoup appris; *Hum* c'était très édifiant

(b) *(learning)* éducation *f*; **a man without education** un homme sans éducation; **to have gaps in one's education** avoir des lacunes dans son éducation

2 *comp (costs, budget)* de l'éducation

►► ***Education Act*** ≃ réforme *f* (de l'Éducation); *Br* ***education authority*** ≃ académie *f* régionale; *Press* ***education correspondent*** correspondant(e) *m,f* chargé(e) des problèmes d'enseignement; ***education supplement*** supplément *m* éducation; ***the education system*** le système éducatif

educational [,edʒʊ'keɪʃənəl] *adj (programme, system)* éducatif; *(establishment)* d'éducation, d'enseignement; *(books, publisher)* scolaire; *(method, film, visit, TV)* éducatif, pédagogique; **they talked about rising/falling educational standards** ils ont évoqué la hausse/baisse du niveau scolaire; **it was very educational** c'était très instructif; *Hum* c'était très édifiant; **it was an educational experience/visit** c'était une expérience/visite instructive

►► ***educational adviser*** conseiller(ère) *m,f* d'orientation; ***educational age*** niveau *m* scolaire; ***educational channel*** chaîne *f* du savoir; ***educational cruise*** croisière *f* culturelle; ***Educational Institute of Scotland*** = syndicat écossais d'enseignants; ***educational psychologist*** *(practical)* psychologue *mf* scolaire; *(academic)* psychopédagogue *mf*; ***educational qualification*** diplôme *m*; *Comput* ***educational software*** logiciel *m* didactique; *Am* ***Educational Television*** chaîne *f* de télévision éducative et culturelle

educationalist [,edʒʊ'keɪʃənəlɪst] *n* pédagogue *mf*

educationally [,edʒʊ'keɪʃənəlɪ] *adv* d'un point de vue éducatif; **educationally deprived child** = enfant qui n'a pas suivi une scolarité normale; *Br Old-fashioned* **educationally subnormal** en retard sur le plan scolaire

educationist [,edʒʊ'keɪʃənɪst] *n* éducateur(-trice) *m,f*

educative ['edʒʊkətɪv] *adj* éducatif

educator ['edʒʊkeɪtə(r)] *n esp Am* éducateur(-trice) *m,f*

educe [ɪ'dju:s] *vt Formal* dégager, tirer

edutainment [,edju:'teɪnmənt] **1** *n* loisirs *mpl* éducatifs

2 *adj* ludo-éducatif

Edward ['edwəd] *pr n* **Edward the Confessor** Édouard le Confesseur; **Prince Edward** le prince Edward

Edwardian [ed'wɔ:dɪən] **1** *adj (architecture, design)* édouardien, de style Édouard VII, des années 1900; *(society, gentleman)* de l'époque d'Édouard VII, des années 1900; **Edwardian style** style *m* Édouard VII; **the Edwardian era** ≃ la Belle Époque

2 *n* = Britannique qui vivait sous le règne d'Édouard VII

EE [,i:'i:] *n (abbr* **electrical engineer**) ingénieur *m* électricien

EEB [,i:i:'bi:] *n (abbr* **European Environmental Bureau**) BEE *m*

EEA [,i:i:'eɪ] *n Pol (abbr* **European Economic Area**) EEE *m*

EEC [,i:i:'si:] *n Formerly Pol (abbr* **European Economic Community**) CEE *f*

EEG [,i:i:'dʒi:] *n Med* **(a)** *(abbr* **electroencephalogram**) EEG *m* **(b)** *(abbr* **electroencephalograph**) EEG *m*

eejit ['i:dʒɪt] *n Ir & Scot Fam* idiot(e)❑ *m,f*, andouille *f*

eek [i:k] *exclam Fam* hi!

eel [i:l] *n* anguille *f*; *Fig* **to be as slippery as an eel** glisser comme une anguille; *Br Culin* **jellied eels** anguilles *fpl* en gelée

eelgrass ['i:lgrɑ:s] *n Bot* zostère *f*

eelworm ['i:lwɜ:m] *n Zool* anguillule *f*

e'en [i:n] *Arch or Literary* = **even** *adv*

EENT [,i:i:,en'ti:] *n Med (abbr* **eye, ear, nose and throat**) ophtalmologie *f* et ORL *f*

EEOC [,i:i:,əʊ'si:] *n Am Admin (abbr* **Equal Employment Opportunities Commission**) = commission pour l'égalité des chances d'emploi aux États-Unis

EEPROM ['i:prɒm] *n Comput (abbr* **electrically erasable programmable ROM**) EEPROM *f*

e'er [eə(r)] *Arch or Literary* = **ever** *adv*

eerie ['ɪərɪ] *(compar* **eerier**, *superl* **eeriest**) *adj (house, silence, sound)* inquiétant, sinistre; **it gave me an eerie feeling** ça m'a fait froid dans le dos; **an eerie silence** *(after explosion, in empty house etc)* un silence de mort; **it was eerie to think that...** cela donnait des frissons *ou* la chair de poule de penser que...

eerily ['ɪərəlɪ] *adv* sinistrement, d'une manière sinistre; **it was eerily quiet in the house** un calme inquiétant régnait dans la maison; **to fall eerily silent** tomber dans un silence étrange

eeriness ['ɪərɪnɪs] *n* caractère *m* étrange *ou* sinistre

eery ['ɪərɪ] *(compar* **eerier**, *superl* **eeriest**) = **eerie**

EET [,i:i:'ti:] *n (abbr* **Eastern European Time**) heure *f* de l'Europe orientale

eff [ef] *vi Br very Fam Euph* **to eff and blind** jurer à tout va

►**eff off** *vi Br very Fam Euph* **eff off!** va te faire voir!; **I told him to eff off** je lui ai dit d'aller se faire voir

efface [ɪ'feɪs] *vt also Fig* effacer; **to efface oneself** s'effacer

effacement [ɪ'feɪsmənt] *n* effacement *m*

effect [ɪ'fekt] **1** *n* **(a)** *(of action, law)* effet *m*; *(of chemical, drug, weather)* effet *m*, action *f*; **to have an effect on** avoir *ou* produire un effet sur; **to have no effect** ne produire aucun effet; *Fam* **feeling the effects, are you?** *(of over-indulgence)* alors, on se ressent de ses excès?; **the effect of the law will be to...** la loi aura pour effet de...; **the effect of all this is that...** tout cela a pour résultat que...; *Br* **with effect from 1 January** à partir *ou* à compter du 1er janvier; **with immediate effect** à compter d'aujourd'hui; **to no** *or* **little effect** en vain; **to use** *or* **to put sth to good effect** *(technique, talent)* utiliser qch avec succès; *(money, inheritance)* faire bon usage de qch; **to such good effect that...** tellement bien que...; **to put sth into effect** *(plan)* mettre qch à exécution; *(decision)* donner suite à qch; **to come into** *or* **to take effect** *(law)* entrer en vigueur; **to take effect** *(drug)* (commencer à) faire effet

(b) *(meaning)* sens *m*; **to this** *or* **that effect** dans ce sens; **letters to the same effect** des lettres allant dans le même sens; **a rumour to the effect that...** une rumeur selon laquelle...; **a telegram/an announcement to the effect that...** un télégramme/une annonce disant que...; **or words to that effect** ou quelque chose dans le genre

(c) *(impression)* effet *m*; **the combination of colours creates a pleasing effect** le mélange des couleurs laisse une impression agréable; **(just) for effect** (juste) pour faire de l'effet

(d) *(simulation)* **moonlight effect** effet *m* de lune; **clever use of lighting created the effect of a thunderstorm** une utilisation adroite de la lumière donnait l'impression qu'il y avait un orage; **stage effects** jeux *mpl* scéniques; *Cin & TV* **(special) effects** trucage *m*, effets *mpl* spéciaux; **sound effects** bruitage *m*; *TV* **effects microphone** microphone *m* d'ambiance

2 *vt Formal (reform, repair)* effectuer; *(sale, purchase)* réaliser, effectuer; *(improvement)* apporter; *(cure, rescue, reconciliation)* mener à bien; **to effect one's escape** s'échapper; **to effect an entry** entrer de force; **to effect a cure for sth** apporter un remède à qch; **to effect a solution to sth** apporter une solution à qch; *Mil* **to effect a retreat** battre en retraite; **to effect a payment** effectuer un paiement; **to effect a saving in** *or* **of sth** faire *ou* réaliser une économie de qch

3 effects *npl Formal* **household effects** articles *mpl* ménagers; **personal effects** effets *mpl* personnels

4 in effect 1 *adj (law, system)* en vigueur **2** *adv (in fact)* en fait, en réalité; **that is, in effect, a refusal** c'est de fait un refus

effective [ɪ'fektɪv] **1** *adj* **(a)** *(which works well → measure, treatment, advertising etc)* efficace; *(→ worker, manager)* efficace; *(→ argument)* qui porte; *(→ service, system)* qui fonctionne bien; *(→ disguise)* réussi; **an effective way of doing sth** un moyen efficace de faire qch; **the medicine was effective** le médicament a produit son effet

(b) *Admin & Fin* **effective date** date *f* d'entrée en vigueur; **effective as from 1 January** *(law)* en vigueur *ou* applicable à compter du 1er janvier; **effective 1 January** à compter du 1er janvier; **to cease to be effective** *(policy, law)* cesser d'être applicable; **to become effective** entrer en vigueur

(c) *(actual)* véritable; **to assume effective command of a team** assumer la direction réelle d'une équipe; **this resulted in the effective silencing of all opposition** *(was tantamount to)* cela a eu en effet pour résultat de faire taire les opposants

(d) *Fin (yield, return, production)* effectif; *(value)* réel

(e) *(creating effect → colour, illustration)* qui fait de l'effet

2 effectives *npl Mil* effectifs *mpl*

►► *Fin* ***effective annual rate*** taux *m* annuel effectif; *Fin* ***effective income*** revenu *m* réel; *Com* ***effective life*** *(of product, structure)* durée *f* de vie effective; ***effective range*** *(of firearm, missile)* portée *f* utile; *Fin* ***effective tax rate*** taux *m* d'imposition effectif

effectively [ɪ'fektɪvlɪ] *adv* **(a)** *(in fact)* en réalité, en fait; **the country was effectively ruled by the military** en fait *ou* en réalité, le pays était dirigé par les militaires; **the game was effectively over** c'était comme si le match était déjà terminé **(b)** *(efficiently → work, run, manage)* efficacement **(c)** *(successfully)* avec succès **(d)** *(impressively)* d'une manière impressionnante

effectiveness [ɪ'fektɪvnɪs] *n* **(a)** *(efficiency → of treatment, advertising)* efficacité *f*; *(→ of undertaking, attempt)* succès *m* **(b)** *(effect → of entrance, gesture, colour)* effet *m*; **to improve the effectiveness of your backhand** pour améliorer votre revers

effector [ɪ'fektə(r)] *Physiol* **1** *n* effecteur *m*

2 *adj* effecteur

effectual [ɪ'fektʃʊəl] *adj* **(a)** *Formal (action, plan)* efficace **(b)** *Law (contract)* valide; *(ruling)* en vigueur

effectually [ɪ'fektjʊəlɪ] *adv Formal* efficacement

effectuate [ɪ'fektjʊeɪt] *vt Formal* effectuer, réaliser

effectuation [ɪ,fektjʊ'eɪʃən] *n Formal* réalisation *f*

effeminacy [ɪ'femɪnəsɪ] *n (of man)* caractère *m* efféminé; **the effeminacy of his voice** sa voix efféminée

effeminate [ɪ'femɪnət] *adj (man, voice)* efféminé

effeminately [ɪ'femɪnətlɪ] *adv (dress, behave)* de manière efféminée; *(speak)* d'une voix efféminée

efferent ['efərənt] *adj Anat* efférent

effervesce [,efə'ves] *vi (liquid)* être en effervescence; *(wine)* pétiller; *(gas)* s'échapper par effervescence; *Fig (person)* déborder de vie; **when the mixture effervesces** quand le mélange entre en effervescence

effervescence [ˌefə'vesəns] *n (of liquid)* effervescence *f*; *(of wine)* pétillement *m*; *Fig (of person)* vitalité *f*, pétulance *f*; *(of personality)* pétulance *f*

effervescent [ˌefə'vesənt] *adj (liquid)* effervescent; *(wine)* pétillant; *Fig (person)* débordant de vie, pétulant; *(personality)* pétulant

effete [ɪ'fi:t] *adj Formal (weak → person)* mou (molle); *(→ civilization, society)* affaibli; *(decadent)* décadent

effeteness [ɪ'fi:tnɪs] *n Formal (weakness → of person)* mollesse *f*; *(→ of civilization, society)* affaiblissement *m*; *(decadence)* décadence *f*

efficacious [ˌefɪ'keɪʃəs] *adj Formal* efficace

efficaciously [ˌefɪ'keɪʃəslɪ] *adv Formal* efficacement

efficacy ['efɪkəsɪ], **efficaciousness** [efɪ'keɪʃəsnɪs] *n Formal* efficacité *f*

efficiency [ɪ'fɪʃənsɪ] *n* (**a**) *(of company, method)* efficacité *f*; *(of machine → in operation)* fonctionnement *m*; *(→ in output)* rendement *m*; *(of person)* capacité *f*, compétence *f* (**b**) *Am (apartment)* studio *m*

►► *Am* ***efficiency apartment*** studio *m*; ***efficiency expert*** expert *m* en organisation

efficient [ɪ'fɪʃənt] *adj (method, company)* efficace; *(piece of work)* bien fait; *(machine → in operation)* qui fonctionne bien; *(→ in output)* qui a un bon rendement; *(person)* performant, capable, compétent; **to be efficient at sth** faire qch avec compétence; **to be efficient in one's work** se montrer capable dans son travail; **the machine is now at its most efficient** *(functions well)* la machine a maintenant un fonctionnement optimal; *(has high output)* la machine a maintenant un rendement optimal; **to make more efficient use of sth** utiliser qch de manière plus efficace; **it was an efficient performance by the Australian team** ce fut une belle performance de la part de l'équipe australienne

efficiently [ɪ'fɪʃəntlɪ] *adv (effectively)* efficacement; *(competently)* avec compétence; **the machine works efficiently** *(functions well)* la machine fonctionne bien; *(has high output)* la machine a un bon rendement; **to organize one's time efficiently** utiliser son temps de manière rationnelle

effigy ['efɪdʒɪ] (*pl* **effigies**) *n* effigie *f*; **to burn sb in effigy** brûler qn en effigie

effing ['efɪŋ] *Br very Fam Euph* **1** *adj* de merde; **you effing idiot!** espèce de connard!

2 *adv* foutrement; **don't be so effing stupid!** qu'est-ce que tu peux être con!

3 *n* **there was a lot of effing and blinding** on a eu droit à un chapelet de jurons

effleurage [ˌeflɜ:'rɑ:ʒ] *n Med* effleurage *m*

effloresce [ˌeflə'res] *vi* (**a**) *Bot* fleurir (**b**) *Chem* effleurir

efflorescence [ˌeflə'resəns] *n* (**a**) *Bot* floraison *f* (**b**) *Chem* efflorescence *f*

efflorescent [ˌeflə'resənt] *adj Chem* efflorescent

effluence ['eflʊəns] *n Literary* émanation *f*, effluence *f*

effluent ['eflʊənt] **1** *adj* effluent

2 *n* (**a**) *(waste)* effluent *m* (**b**) *(stream)* effluent *m*

effluvium [ɪ'flu:vjəm] (*pl* **effluviums** or **effluvia** [-vjə]) *n* effluve *m*, émanation *f*; *Pej* émanation *f* désagréable *ou* fétide

efflux ['eflʌks] *n* flux *m*; *(of liquid)* écoulement *m*; *(of gas)* dégagement *m*, émanation *f*; *Fin (of capital)* exode *m*

effluxion [ɪ'flʌkʃən] *n* (**a**) *(outflow)* flux *m*; *(of liquid)* écoulement *m*; *(of gas)* dégagement *m*, émanation *f*; *Fin (of capital)* exode *m* (**b**) *Law* **effluxion of time** expiration *f* du terme

effort ['efət] *n* (**a**) *(exertion)* effort *m*; **it will be a bit of an effort** ce sera un peu difficile; **without much effort** sans trop d'effort *ou* de peine; **with an effort** en faisant un effort; **your efforts on our behalf** les efforts que vous avez faits pour nous; **their efforts were rewarded** leurs efforts ont été récompensés; **it was an effort for me to stay awake** j'avais du mal à rester éveillé; *(stronger)* rester éveillé me coûtait; **put some effort into it!** fais un effort!; **I put a lot of effort into that project** je me suis donné beaucoup de mal *ou* de peine pour ce projet; **to make an effort to do sth** faire (un) effort pour faire qch; **he made no effort to contact us** il n'a fait aucun effort pour nous joindre; *Formal* **we make every effort to ensure our products reach you in perfect condition** nous faisons tout ce qui est en notre pouvoir pour que nos produits vous parviennent en bon état; **in an effort to do sth** dans le but de faire qch; **to make no effort to do sth** ne pas essayer de faire qch; **to make every effort to do sth** faire tout son possible pour faire qch; **at least she made the effort** au moins elle a essayé; **it's not worth the effort** ça ne vaut pas la peine de se fatiguer

(**b**) *(attempt)* essai *m*, tentative *f*; **it's only my first effort** ce n'est que la première fois que j'essaie; **it was a good effort** pour un essai, c'était bien; **that's not a bad effort** ce n'est pas mal réussi; *Fam* **what do you think of his latest effort?** qu'est-ce que vous pensez de sa dernière performance?

(**c**) *Phys (of traction etc)* effort *m*, poussée *f*, travail *m*

(**d**) *Fam (thing, gadget)* truc *m*; **there's this sort of lever effort** il y a une espèce de levier ❑

effortless ['efətlɪs] *adj (win)* facile; *(style, movement)* aisé; **it seems so effortless** cela a l'air si facile; **she won with an almost effortless ease** elle a gagné avec une facilité presque absolue

effortlessly ['efətlɪslɪ] *adv* facilement, sans effort *ou* peine; **to be effortlessly graceful/skilful** être naturellement gracieux/talentueux; **her voice soars effortlessly to the high notes** elle peut chanter très haut sans aucun effort

effrontery [ɪ'frʌntərɪ] *n* effronterie *f*; **she had the effrontery to correct me!** elle a eu l'audace de me corriger!

effulgence [ɪ'fʌldʒəns] *n Literary* rayonnement *m*

effulgent [ɪ'fʌldʒənt] *adj Literary* rayonnant

effuse [ɪ'fju:z] *vi Literary (liquid, blood)* s'écouler

effusion [ɪ'fju:ʒən] *n Literary* (**a**) *(of words)* effusion *f* (**b**) *(of liquid)* écoulement *m*; *(of blood)* hémorragie *f*

effusive [ɪ'fju:sɪv] *adj* (**a**) *(person)* expansif; *(welcome, thanks)* chaleureux; *Pej* exagéré; **to be effusive in one's thanks** se confondre en remerciements; **to be effusive in one's praise/congratulations** louer/féliciter qn avec grand enthousiasme (**b**) *Geol* effusif

effusively [ɪ'fju:sɪvlɪ] *adv* avec effusion; *Pej* avec une effusion exagérée; **to thank sb effusively** se confondre en remerciements

effusiveness [ɪ'fju:sɪvnɪs] *n* effusion *f*; *Pej* effusion *f* exagérée; **the effusiveness of his praise** l'enthousiasme *m* de ses louanges

E-fit® ['i:fɪt] *n* portrait-robot *m* électronique

EFL [ˌi:ef'el] *n* (*abbr* **English as a foreign language**) = anglais langue étrangère

EFT [eft] *n Comput* (*abbr* **electronic funds transfer**) transfert *m* de fonds électronique

eft [eft] *n* triton *m*

EFTA ['eftə] *n* (*abbr* **European Free Trade Association**) AELE *f*, AEL-E *f*

EFTPOS ['eftpɒs] *n Comput* (*abbr* **electronic funds transfer at point of sale**) transfert *m* de fonds électronique sur point de vente

EFTS [efts] *n Comput* (*abbr* **electronic funds transfer system**) = système électronique de transfert de fonds

eg [ˌi:'dʒi:] *adv* (*abbr* **exempli gratia**) par exemple

EGA [ˌi:dʒi:'eɪ] *n Comput* (*abbr* **enhanced graphics adapter**) EGA *m*

egad [i:'gæd] *exclam Arch* sacredieu!

egalitarian [ɪˌgælɪ'teərɪən] **1** *n* égalitariste *mf*

2 *adj* égalitaire

egalitarianism [ɪˌgælɪ'teərɪənɪzəm] *n* égalitarisme *m*

egg [eg] *n* (**a**) *(foodstuff)* œuf *m*; **bacon and eggs** œufs *mpl* au bacon; **fried egg** œuf *m* sur le plat; **hard-boiled egg** œuf *m* dur; **soft-boiled egg** œuf *m* à la coque; *Fig* **to be left with** *or* **to get egg on one's face** avoir l'air ridicule; **that's how you get egg on your face** c'est comme ça qu'on se couvre de ridicule; *Fam* **you've got egg on your chin** *(fly is undone)* ta braguette est ouverte ❑

(**b**) *(of bird, insect, fish)* œuf *m*; *(of woman)* ovule *m*; **to lay an egg** *(bird)* pondre un œuf; *Fig (fail)* faire un bide; *Prov* **don't put all your eggs in one basket** il ne faut pas mettre tous ses œufs dans le même panier; *Fam* **as sure as eggs is eggs** aussi sûr que deux et deux font quatre

(**c**) *Br Old-fashioned (person)* **he's/she's a good egg** c'est un brave garçon/une brave fille; **a bad egg** un sale individu

►► *Am* ***Egg Beaters***® = ersatz d'œufs brouillés, sans cholestérol; ***eggs Benedict*** = plat composé d'une tranche de pain grillé surmontée d'une tranche de jambon et d'un œuf poché, le tout recouvert de sauce hollandaise; *Am* ***egg crate*** boîte *f* à œufs; *Br Culin* ***egg custard*** ≃ crème *f* anglaise; ***egg flip*** *(with milk)* lait *m* de poule; *(with alcohol)* lait *m* de poule alcoolisé; ***egg mayonnaise*** œuf *m* mayonnaise; *Am Culin* ***egg roll*** pâté *m* impérial; ***egg slicer*** coupe-œufs *m inv*; ***egg spoon*** cuillère *f* à œufs (à la coque); ***egg timer*** sablier *m*; *Zool* ***egg tooth*** dent *f* d'éclosion; *Br* ***egg whisk*** fouet *m*; ***egg white*** blanc *m* d'œuf; ***egg yolk*** jaune *m* d'œuf

►**egg on** *vt sep* encourager, inciter; **to egg sb on to do sth** encourager *ou* inciter qn à faire qch

egg-and-spoon race *n* = jeu consistant à courir en tenant un œuf dans une cuillère

eggbeater ['egˌbi:tə(r)] *n* (**a**) *(whisk)* fouet *m* (**b**) *Am Fam (helicopter)* hélico *m*

eggbox ['egbɒks] *n Br* boîte *f* à œufs

eggcup ['egkʌp] *n* coquetier *m*

egghead ['eghed] *n Fam* intello *mf*

egg-laying **1** *adj* ovipare

2 *n* ponte *f*

eggnog ['egnɒg] *n* lait *m* de poule alcoolisé

eggplant ['egplɑ:nt] *n Am* aubergine *f*

egg-shaped *adj* en forme d'œuf, ovoïde

eggshell ['egʃel] **1** *n* (**a**) *(of bird's egg)* coquille *f* d'œuf; **we all walk around on eggshells when the boss is in a bad mood** on marche tous sur des œufs quand le patron est de mauvaise humeur (**b**) *(colour)* coquille *f* d'œuf (**c**) *(paint)* peinture *f* coquille d'œuf

2 *adj (finish, paint)* coquille d'œuf *(inv)*

►► ***eggshell blue*** bleu *m* pâle; ***eggshell china, eggshell porcelain*** coquille *f* d'œuf

eggslice ['egslaɪs] *n* spatule *f*

eggwash ['egwɒʃ] *n Culin* dorure *f*

eggy ['egɪ] *adj Fam (stained)* taché *ou* souillé de jaune d'œuf ❑; **an eggy taste/smell** un goût/une odeur d'œuf ❑

►► ***eggy bread*** pain *m* perdu ❑

egis *Am* = **aegis**

eglantine ['egləntaɪn] *n Bot (bush)* églantier *m*; *(flower)* églantine *f*

EGM [ˌi:dʒi:'em] *n Com* (*abbr* **extraordinary general meeting**) AGE *f*

ego ['i:gəʊ] *n* (**a**) *(self-esteem)* amour-propre *m*; **to have an enormous ego** être imbu de soi-même; **it gave my ego a boost** mon ego en est ressorti gonflé; **I need an ego boost** j'ai besoin de quelque chose qui me redonne de l'amour propre; **it's just your ego that's hurt** tu es seulement blessé dans ton amour-propre; *Fam* **she's just on an ego trip** c'est par vanité qu'elle le fait ❑; **he's been on an ego trip since his promotion** il ne se sent plus depuis sa promotion

(**b**) *Psy* le moi, l'ego

►► *Psy* ***ego ideal*** moi *m* idéal

egocentric [ˌi:gəʊ'sentrɪk] *adj* égocentrique

egocentricity [ˌi:gəʊsen'trɪsətɪ], **egocentrism** [ˌi:gəʊ'sentrɪzəm] *n* égocentrisme *m*

egoism ['i:gəʊɪzəm] *n (selfishness)* égoïsme *m*

egoist ['i:gəʊɪst] *n* égoïste *mf*

egoistic [ˌi:gəʊ'ɪstɪk], **egoistical** [ˌi:gəʊ'ɪstɪkəl] *adj* égoïste

egoistically [ˌi:gəʊ'ɪstɪkəlɪ] *adv* égoïstement

egomania [ˌi:gəʊ'meɪnjə] *n* manie *f* égocentrique

egomaniac [ˌi:gəʊ'meɪnɪæk] *n* égocentrique *mf*

egotism ['i:gətɪzəm] *n* égotisme *m*

egotist ['i:gətɪst] *n* égotiste *mf*

egotistic [ˌi:gə'tɪstɪk], **egotistical** [ˌi:gə'tɪstɪkəl] *adj* égotiste

egotistically [ˌi:gə'tɪstɪklɪ] *adv* de manière égotiste

ego-trip *vi Fam* **you're just ego-tripping** tu fais ça par vanité ❑

egregious [ɪ'gri:dʒəs] *adj Formal (blatant → error, mistake)* monumental, énorme; *(→ lie)* énorme; *(→ cowardice, incompetence)* extrême

egress ['i:gres] *n Formal (way out, exit)* sortie *f*,

issue *f*; *(action of going out)* sortie *f*; **means of egress** issue *f*

egression [ɪ'greʃən] *n Formal* sortie *f*

egret ['iːgrɪt] *n Orn* aigrette *f*

Egypt ['iːdʒɪpt] *n* Égypte *f*; **in Egypt** en Égypte; **Lower Egypt** Basse-Égypte *f*; **Upper Egypt** Haute-Égypte *f*

Egyptian [ɪ'dʒɪpʃən] **1** *n* (**a**) *(person)* Égyptien(enne) *m,f* (**b**) *Ling* égyptien *m*
 2 *adj* égyptien
 3 *comp (embassy)* d'Égypte; *(history)* de l'Égypte
 ►► ***Egyptian cotton*** coton *m* égyptien, coton *m* jumel; *Orn* ***Egyptian goose*** oie *f* d'Égypte; *Orn* ***Egyptian vulture*** percnoptère *m* (d'Égypte), néophron *m*

Egyptologist [ˌiːdʒɪp'tɒlədʒɪst] *n* égyptologue *mf*

Egyptology [ˌiːdʒɪp'tɒlədʒɪ] *n* égyptologie *f*

eh [eɪ] *exclam* (**a**) *(what did you say?)* **eh?** hein? (**b**) *(seeking agreement)* **eh?** hein? (**c**) *(in astonishment)* **eh?** quoi? (**d**) *(in doubt, hesitation)* heu

EHO [ˌiːeɪtʃ'əʊ] *n (abbr* **environmental health officer**) inspecteur(trice) *m,f* de la santé publique

EIA [ˌiːaɪ'eɪ] *n (abbr* **environmental impact assessment**) étude *f* d'impact sur l'environnement

EIB [ˌiːaɪ'biː] *n (abbr* **European Investment Bank**) BEI *f*

EID [ˌiːaɪ'diː] *npl Biol & Med (abbr* **emerging infectious diseases**) maladies *fpl* infectieuses émergentes

eider ['aɪdə(r)] *n Orn* eider *m*
 ►► ***eider duck*** eider *m*

eiderdown ['aɪdədaʊn] *n* (**a**) *(feathers)* duvet *m* d'eider (**b**) *(for bed)* édredon *m*

eidetic [aɪ'detɪk] *adj Psy* eidétique

Eiffel Tower ['aɪfəl-] *n* **the Eiffel Tower** la tour Eiffel

Eiger ['eɪgə(r)] *n* **the Eiger** l'Eiger *m*

eight [eɪt] **1** *n* (**a**) *(number, numeral)* huit *m inv*; **to reach the last eight** *(in knockout competition)* être en quart de finale; *Br* **to have had one over the eight** avoir bu plus que son compte (**b**) *(in rowing)* huit *m* (de pointe)
 2 *pron* huit
 3 *adj* huit; **to work an eight-hour day** travailler huit heures par jour, faire des journées de huit heures; *see also* **five**
 ►► *Am* ***eight ball*** *(ball)* bille *f* numéro huit; *(game)* = variante du billard; *Fam Fig* **to be behind the eight ball** être dans la mouise; *Am* ***eight hundred number*** ≃ numéro *m* vert

eight-bit *adj Comput*
 ►► ***eight-bit byte*** octet *m*; ***eight-bit character*** caractère *m* à huit bits

eighteen [ˌeɪ'tiːn] **1** *n* dix-huit *m inv*
 2 *pron* dix-huit
 3 *adj* dix-huit; *see also* **five**

eighteenth [ˌeɪ'tiːnθ] **1** *n* (**a**) *(fraction)* dix-huitième *m* (**b**) *(in series)* dix-huitième *mf* (**c**) *(of month)* dix-huit *m inv*
 2 *adj* dix-huitième
 3 *adv* dix-huitièmement; *(in contest)* en dix-huitième position, à la dix-huitième place; *see also* **fifth**

eighteen-wheeler *n* dix-huit roues *m (très gros camion)*

eightfold ['eɪtfəʊld] **1** *adj* **there's been an eightfold increase in property prices in the past decade** le prix des logements a été multiplié par huit au cours des dix dernières années
 2 *adv* **to increase eightfold** être multiplié par huit

eighth [eɪtθ] **1** *n* (**a**) *(fraction)* huitième *m* (**b**) *(in series)* huitième *mf* (**c**) *(of month)* huit *m inv*
 2 *adj* huitième
 3 *adv* huitièmement; *(in contest)* en huitième position, à la huitième place; *see also* **fifth**
 ►► *Am Sch* ***eighth grade*** = classe de lycée (12–13 ans); *Am Mus* ***eighth note*** croche *f*

eighthly ['eɪtθlɪ] *adv* huitièmement, en huitième lieu

eightieth ['eɪtɪəθ] **1** *n* (**a**) *(fraction)* quatre-vingtième *m* (**b**) *(in series)* quatre-vingtième *mf*
 2 *adj* quatre-vingtième
 3 *adv* quatre-vingtièmement; *(in contest)* en quatre-vingtième position, à la quatre-vingtième place; *see also* **fifth**

eightsome reel ['eɪtsəm-] *n* = danse folklorique écossaise pour huit danseurs

Eights Week [eɪts-] *n* = semaine de la course d'avirons aux universités de Cambridge et d'Oxford

eighty ['eɪtɪ] *(pl* **eighties**) **1** *n* quatre-vingt *m inv*, *Suisse* octante *m inv*
 2 *pron* quatre-vingt, *Suisse* octante
 3 *adj* quatre-vingts, *Suisse* octante; **page eighty** page quatre-vingt; **eighty million** quatre-vingts millions
 4 *comp* **eighty-one** quatre-vingt-un; **eighty-two** quatre-vingt-deux; **eighty-first** quatre-vingt-unième; **eighty-second** quatre-vingt-deuxième; *see also* **fifty**

eighty-six *Am* **1** *adj* **to be eighty-six on sth** *(in restaurant, bar)* être à court de qch ❑; **tell the customer we're eighty-six on the chicken** dis au client qu'il n'y a plus de poulet
 2 *vt* (**a**) *(eject)* vider (**b**) *(kill)* buter, refroidir

eighty/twenty rule, 80/20 rule *n Fin* règle *f* 80/20

Eilat [eɪ'læt] *n* Eilat

Einsteinian [ˌaɪn'staɪnɪən] *adj* einsteinien

einsteinium [ˌaɪn'staɪnɪəm] *n Chem* einsteinium *m*

Eire ['eərə] *n* Eire *f*

EIS [ˌiːaɪ'es] *n (abbr* **Educational Institute of Scotland**) = syndicat écossais d'enseignants

eisteddfod [aɪ'stedfɒd] *n* = festival annuel de musique, littérature et théâtre au pays de Galles

either [*esp Br* 'aɪðə(r), *esp Am* 'iːðə(r)] **1** *adj* (**a**) *(one or the other)* l'un (l'une) ou l'autre; **if you don't agree with either suggestion...** si vous n'approuvez ni l'une ni l'autre *ou* aucune de ces suggestions...; **you can take either route** tu peux prendre l'un ou l'autre de ces chemins; **either bus will get you there** les deux bus y vont; **he can write with either hand** il peut écrire avec la main droite ou avec la main gauche
 (**b**) *(each)* chaque; **there were candles at either end of the table** il y avait des bougies aux deux bouts *ou* à chaque bout de la table; **there were people standing on either side of the road** il y avait des gens de chaque côté *ou* de part et d'autre de la route
 2 *pron (one or the other)* l'un (l'une) ou l'autre; **you can take either** *(bus, train etc)* vous pouvez prendre l'un ou l'autre *ou* n'importe lequel (des deux); **I don't like either of them** je ne les aime ni l'un ni l'autre; **if either of you two makes the slightest noise** si l'un de vous deux fait le moindre bruit; **which would you like? – either** lequel voudriez-vous? – n'importe lequel
 3 *adv* (**a**) *(gen)* non plus; **we can't hear anything either** nous n'entendons rien non plus
 (**b**) *(emphatic use)* **and don't take too long about it either!** et ne traîne pas, surtout!; **he had a suggestion to make and not such a silly one either** il avait une suggestion à faire et qui n'était pas bête en plus
 4 either...or *conj* ou...ou, soit...soit; *(with negative)* ni...ni; **either you stop complaining or I go home!** ou tu arrêtes de te plaindre, ou je rentre chez moi; **they're either very rich or very stupid** ils sont soit très riches soit très bêtes; **she usually goes out with either Ian or Simon** d'habitude elle sort (ou) avec Ian ou avec Simon *ou* soit avec Ian soit avec Simon; **either come in or go out!** entre ou sors!; **either pay up or be taken to court!** tu payes ou sinon c'est le tribunal!; **I've not met either him or his brother** je n'ai rencontré ni lui ni son frère
 5 either way *adv* (**a**) *(in either case)* dans les deux cas; **either way I lose** dans les deux cas je suis perdant; **you can do it either way** tu peux le faire d'une façon comme de l'autre; **there is no evidence either way** les preuves manquent de part et d'autre; **it's fine by me either way** n'importe *ou* ça m'est égal
 (**b**) *(more or less)* en plus ou en moins; **a few days either way could make all the difference** quelques jours en plus ou en moins pourraient changer tout
 (**c**) *(indicating advantage)* **it could go either way** on ne peut rien prévoir; **the match could have gone either way** le match était ouvert

either-or *adj* **it's an either-or situation** il n'y a que deux solutions possibles

ejaculate [ɪ'dʒækjʊleɪt] **1** *vi* (**a**) *Physiol* éjaculer (**b**) *Literary (call out)* s'écrier, s'exclamer
 2 *vt* (**a**) *Physiol* éjaculer (**b**) *Literary (utter)* lancer, pousser

ejaculation [ɪˌdʒækjʊ'leɪʃən] *n* (**a**) *Physiol* éjaculation *f* (**b**) *Literary (exclamation)* cri *m*, exclamation *f*; **an ejaculation of surprise/joy/horror** un cri de surprise/de joie/d'horreur

ejaculatory [ɪ'dʒækjʊlətrɪ] *adj Physiol* éjaculateur

eject [ɪ'dʒekt] **1** *vt* (**a**) *(troublemaker)* expulser (**b**) *(CD, video, pilot)* éjecter; *(lava)* projeter
 2 *vi (pilot)* s'éjecter

ejection [ɪ'dʒekʃən] *n* (**a**) *(of troublemaker)* expulsion *f* (**b**) *(of CD, video, pilot)* éjection *f*; *(of lava)* projection *f*
 ►► *Am* ***ejection seat*** siège *m* éjectable

ejector [ɪ'dʒektə(r)] *n (on gun)* éjecteur *m*
 ►► *Br* ***ejector seat*** siège *m* éjectable

►**eke out** [iːk-] *vt sep* (**a**) *(make last → rations)* faire durer (**b**) *(scrape)* **to eke out a living** gagner tout juste sa vie; **they eked out a miserable existence on the barren land** ils tiraient leur maigre subsistance du sol aride (**c**) *(by adding something)* augmenter

EKG [ˌiːkeɪ'dʒiː] *n Am Med (abbr* **electrocardiogram**) ECG *m*

el [el] *n Am Fam (abbr* **elevated railroad**) métro *m* aérien ❑

elaborate 1 *adj* [ɪ'læbrət] *(system, preparations)* élaboré; *(style, costume)* recherché, travaillé; *(excuse)* alambiqué; *(pattern, design)* compliqué; *(details)* minutieux; *(map, description, plans)* détaillé; **in elaborate detail** de manière très détaillée; **the whole thing was an elaborate joke** c'était une vaste plaisanterie
 2 *vt* [ɪ'læbəreɪt] *(work out in detail → plan, scheme etc)* élaborer; *(describe in detail)* décrire en détail
 3 *vi* [ɪ'læbəreɪt] *(go into detail)* donner des détails; **there's no need to elaborate further** inutile de donner plus de détails; **could you elaborate?** est-ce que vous pouvez être plus précis?

►**elaborate on** *vt insep (idea, statement)* développer

elaborately [ɪ'læbərətlɪ] *adv (decorated, designed etc)* minutieusement, avec recherche; *(planned)* minutieusement; *(packaged)* de manière élaborée

elaborateness [ɪ'læbərətnɪs] *n (of system, preparations)* caractère *m* élaboré, complexité *f*; *(of costume)* caractère *m* élaboré; *(of details, decoration)* minutie *f*; *(of map)* caractère *m* détaillé

elaboration [ɪˌlæbə'reɪʃən] *n (working out → of scheme, plan)* élaboration *f*; *(details)* exposé *m* minutieux

élan [eɪ'læn] *n* vigueur *f*, énergie *f*

eland ['iːlənd] *n Zool* éland *m*

elapse [ɪ'læps] *vi* s'écouler, passer

elapsed time [ɪ'læpst-] *n Comput* temps *m* écoulé

elastic [ɪ'læstɪk] **1** *adj* (**a**) *(material)* élastique (**b**) *Fig (timetable, arrangements, concept)* souple; *(word, moral principles)* élastique, souple; *(working hours, price, demand)* élastique (**c**) *Literary (step)* élastique
 2 *n* (**a**) *(material)* élastique *m* (**b**) *Am (rubber band)* élastique *m*, caoutchouc *m*
 ►► *Br* ***elastic band*** élastique *m*, caoutchouc *m*; ***elastic stockings*** bas *mpl* anti-varices

elasticated [ɪ'læstɪkeɪtɪd] *adj (stockings, waist)* élastique

elasticity [iːlæs'tɪsɪtɪ] *n Phys (of body)* élasticité *f*; *(of wood, metal)* flexibilité *f*; *Med (of muscles)* tonicité *f*; *(of hair)* élasticité *f*; *Mktg (of price, demand)* élasticité *f*; **elasticity of interpretation** *(of law)* élasticité *f*; *Econ* **the elasticity of supply and demand** l'élasticité *f* de l'offre et de la demande

elastin [ɪ'læstɪn] *n Biol* elastine *f*

elastomer [ɪ'læstəmə(r)] *n Chem* élastomère *m*

elastomeric [ɪˌlæstə'merɪk] *adj Chem* élastomère

Elastoplast® [ɪ'læstəplɑːst] *n Br* sparadrap *m*

elate [ɪ'leɪt] *vt* remplir de joie, rendre euphorique

elated [ɪ'leɪtɪd] *adj* fou (folle) de joie, exalté, euphorique; **to feel elated** être fou de joie, exulter

elaterite [ɪ'lætəraɪt] *n Miner* élatérite *f*

elation [ɪ'leɪʃən] *n* allégresse *f*, exaltation *f*, euphorie *f*

Elba ['elbə] *n* l'île *f* d'Elbe; **on Elba** sur l'île d'Elbe

Elbe [elb] *n* **the (River) Elbe** l'Elbe *m*

elbow ['elbəʊ] **1** *n (of arm, jacket, pipe, river)* coude *m*; **out at the elbows** *(jacket)* troué aux coudes; **with his elbows on the bar** les coudes sur le bar, accoudé au bar; *Fig* **to stand elbow to elbow** être coude à coude; **to be at sb's elbow** être *ou* se tenir aux côtés de qn; *Br Fam* **to give sb the elbow** *(employee)* virer qn; *(boyfriend, girlfriend)* larguer *ou* jeter qn; *(tenant)* mettre qn à la porte; *Br Fam* **to get the elbow** *(employee)* se faire virer; *(boyfriend, girlfriend)* se faire larguer *ou* jeter; *(tenant)* se faire mettre à la porte; *Br Fam* **to bend the** *or* **one's elbow** picoler, lever le coude

2 *vt (hit)* donner un coup de coude à; *(push)* pousser du coude; **to elbow one's way through the crowd** se frayer un passage à travers la foule en jouant des coudes; **he just elbowed me aside** il m'a écarté du coude

►► *Fam* ***elbow grease*** huile *f* de coude; ***elbow joint*** *Anat* articulation *f* de coude; *Tech* raccord *m* coudé; ***elbow pad*** coudière *f*; ***elbow patch*** coude *m*

►**elbow out** *vt sep (from job)* se débarrasser de

elbow-length *adj* **elbow-length gloves** gants *mpl* longs (montant jusqu'au coude)

elbow-rest *n* accoudoir *m*

elbow-room *n* **I don't have enough elbow-room** je n'ai pas assez de place (pour me retourner); *Fig* je n'ai pas suffisamment de liberté d'action

El Cheapo [ˌel'tʃiːpəʊ] *Fam Hum* **1** *n* article *m* bas de gamme ❑

2 *adj* bas de gamme ❑

elder[1] ['eldə(r)] **1** *adj (brother, sister)* aîné; **Pitt the Elder** le Premier Pitt; **Pliny the Elder** Pline l'Ancien

2 *n* (**a**) *(of two children)* aîné(e) *m,f* (**b**) *(of tribe, the Church)* ancien *m* (**c**) *(senior)* **you should respect your elders (and betters)** vous devez le respect à vos aînés

►► ***elder statesman*** *(gen)* vétéran *m*; *(politician)* vétéran *m* de la politique

elder[2] *n* sureau *m*

elderberry ['eldəˌberɪ] **1** *n Bot & Culin* baie *f* de sureau

2 *comp (wine)* de sureau

elderflower ['eldəˌflaʊə(r)] *n Bot & Culin* fleur *f* de sureau

elderly ['eldəlɪ] **1** *adj* âgé; **my elderly uncle** mon vieil oncle; **she's getting rather elderly** elle se fait bien vieille

2 *npl* **the elderly** les personnes *fpl* âgées

eldest ['eldɪst] **1** *adj* aîné; **my eldest daughter** ma fille aînée, mon aînée; **their eldest son** leur fils aîné

2 *n* aîné(e) *m,f*

►► *Cards* ***eldest hand*** premier *m* en cartes

Eldorado, El Dorado [ˌeldɒ'rɑːdəʊ] *n* l'Eldorado *m*

Eleanor ['elɪnə(r)] *pr n* **Eleanor of Aquitaine** Aliénor *ou* Éléonore d'Aquitaine

elecampane [elɪ'kæmpeɪn] *n Bot* aunée *f* hélène

elect [ɪ'lekt] **1** *vt* (**a**) *(by voting)* élire; **to elect sb President** élire qn président; **to get elected** être élu; **to elect sb to office** élire qn (**b**) *Formal (choose)* choisir; **to elect to do sth** choisir de faire qch

2 *adj* élu; **the President elect** le président élu

3 *npl Rel* **the elect** les élus *mpl*

elected [ɪ'lektɪd] *adj* élu; **as an elected official of the society** en tant que représentant élu de la société

election [ɪ'lekʃən] **1** *n* élection *f*; **to stand for election** se présenter aux élections; **to hold an election** procéder à une élection; **the elections** les élections

2 *comp (agent, campaign, speech, promise)* électoral; *(day, results)* des élections

electioneer [ɪlekʃə'nɪə(r)] *vi* participer à la campagne électorale; *Pej* faire de la propagande électorale

electioneering [ɪˌlekʃə'nɪərɪŋ] **1** *n* campagne *f* électorale; *Pej* propagande *f* électorale

2 *adj (speech, campaign)* électoral; *Pej* propagandiste

elective [ɪ'lektɪv] **1** *adj* (**a**) *(with power to elect → assembly)* électoral (**b**) *(chosen → official, post)* électif (**c**) *Am & Scot Sch & Univ (optional → course, subject)* optionnel, facultatif

(**b**) *Br Univ (medical student)* qui effectue un stage pratique *(dans un centre hospitalier)*

2 *n* (**a**) *Am & Scot Sch & Univ (subject)* cours *m* optionnel *ou* facultatif; **I'm taking two electives in psychology** je suis deux cours facultatifs en psychologie

(**b**) *Br Univ (of medical student)* stage *m* pratique *(effectué dans un centre hospitalier)*; **she is on elective in Peru** elle est en stage pratique au Pérou

►► ***elective surgery*** chirurgie *f* de confort

elector [ɪ'lektə(r)] **1** *n (with power to elect)* électeur(trice) *m,f*; *(in US electoral system)* grand électeur *m*, membre *m* du collège électoral

2 Elector *n Hist* Électeur *m*

electoral [ɪ'lektərəl] *adj* électoral

►► ***electoral college*** collège *m* électoral *(qui élit le président des États-Unis)*; *Br* ***electoral reform*** réforme *f* électorale; *Br* ***electoral register, electoral roll*** liste *f* électorale; **on the electoral roll** *or* **register** sur la liste électorale

electorate [ɪ'lektərət] *n* électorat *m*

Electra [ɪ'lektrə] *pr n Myth* Électre

►► *Psy* ***Electra complex*** complexe *m* d'Électre

Electress [ɪ'lektrɪs] *n Hist* Électrice *f*

electret [ɪ'lektrət] *n Elec* électret *m*

electric [ɪ'lektrɪk] **1** *adj* (**a**) *(cooker, cable, current, musical instrument)* électrique; *Fig* **the atmosphere of the meeting was electric** l'atmosphère de la réunion était électrique; **the effect of her words was electric** ses mots ont eu un effet électrisant (**b**) *Ich* électrogène

2 *n Br Fam* électricité ❑ *f*

3 electrics *npl Br Fam (of car, machine)* installation *f* électrique ❑

►► *Tech* ***electric arc*** arc *m* électrique; *Br* ***electric blanket*** couverture *f* chauffante; ***electric blue*** bleu *m* électrique; *Ich* ***electric catfish*** silure *m* électrique, malaptérure *m*; ***electric central heating*** chauffage *m* central électrique; ***electric chair*** chaise *f* électrique; **to go to the electric chair** être envoyé à la chaise électrique; ***electric charge*** charge *f* électrique; *Ich* ***electric eel*** anguille *f* électrique; ***electric eye*** œil *m* électrique; ***electric fence*** clôture *f* électrique; ***electric field*** champ *m* électrique; ***electric fire*** appareil *m* de chauffage électrique; ***electric guitar*** guitare *f* électrique; ***electric heater*** appareil *m* de chauffage électrique; ***electric light*** *(individual appliance)* lumière *f* électrique; *(lighting)* éclairage *m ou* lumière *f* électrique; ***electric motor*** moteur *m* électrique; ***electric organ*** *Mus* orgue *f* électrique; *Ich* appareil *m* électrogène; ***electric power station*** centrale *f* électrique; *Ich* ***electric ray*** torpille *f*; ***electric shock*** décharge *f* électrique; **I got an electric shock from the switch** j'ai reçu une décharge en touchant l'interrupteur; *Med* ***electric shock therapy*** *or* ***treatment*** traitement *m* par électrochocs; ***electric storm*** orage *m*; ***electric underblanket*** protège-matelas *m* chauffant; *Aut* ***electric window*** glace *f ou* vitre *f* électrique

electrical [ɪ'lektrɪkəl] *adj* électrique

►► ***electrical appliance*** appareil *m* électrique; ***electrical engineer*** ingénieur *m* électricien; ***electrical engineering*** électrotechnique *f*; ***electrical failure*** panne *f* d'électricité; ***electrical fault*** défaut *m* dans le système électrique; *Am* ***electrical shock*** décharge *f* électrique; ***electrical storm*** orage *m*; *Br* ***Electrical Trades Union*** = syndicat britannique d'électriciens

electrically [ɪ'lektrɪkəlɪ] *adv* électriquement; **electrically operated** *(machine)* fonctionnant à l'électricité; *(windows)* à commande électrique; **electrically charged** chargé d'électricité; *Fig* **an electrically charged atmosphere** une atmosphère électrique

electric-blue *adj* bleu électrique

electrician [ˌɪlek'trɪʃən] *n* électricien(enne) *m,f*

electricity [ˌɪlek'trɪsətɪ] **1** *n* électricité *f*; **to turn** *or* **to switch the electricity off** couper le courant; **to turn** *or* **to switch the electricity on** mettre le courant; **to connect the electricity up to a house** installer *ou* poser l'électricité dans une maison; **to be without electricity** *(because of power cut)* être privé d'électricité; *(not installed)* ne pas avoir l'électricité; *Fig* **there was electricity in the air** il y avait de l'électricité dans l'air

2 *comp (bill)* d'électricité; *(supply)* en électricité

►► *Br Formerly* ***electricity board*** agence *f* régionale de distribution de l'électricité; ***electricity showroom*** magasin d'électro-ménager *(où l'on peut aussi payer ses factures d'électricité)*

electrification [ɪˌlektrɪfɪ'keɪʃən] *n* électrification *f*

electrify [ɪ'lektrɪfaɪ] *vt* (**a**) *(railway line)* électrifier; *(charge with electricity → fence)* électriser (**b**) *Fig (audience)* électriser

electrifying [ɪ'lektrɪfaɪɪŋ] *adj Fig* électrisant

electro- [ɪ'lektrəʊ] *pref* électro-

electroacoustic [ɪˌlektrəʊə'kuːstɪk] *adj* électroacoustique

electroacoustics [ɪˌlektrəʊə'kuːstɪks] *n (UNCOUNT)* électroacoustique *f*

electrobiology [ɪˌlektrəʊbaɪ'ɒlədʒɪ] *n* électrobiologie *f*

electrocapillarity [ɪˌlektrəʊˌkæpɪ'lærətɪ] *n* électrocapillarité

electrocapillary [ɪˌlektrəʊˌkæ'pɪlərɪ] *adj* électrocapillaire

electrocardiogram [ɪˌlektrəʊ'kɑːdɪəgræm] *n Med* électrocardiogramme *m*

electrocardiograph [ɪˌlektrəʊ'kɑːdɪəgrɑːf] *n Med* électrocardiographe *m*

electrocardiography [ɪˌlektrəʊˌkɑːdɪ'ɒgrəfɪ] *n Med* électrocardiographie *f*

electrocardioscope [ɪˌlektrəʊ'kɑːdɪəskəʊp] *n Med* électrocardioscope *m*

electrocautery [ɪˌlektrəʊ'kɔːtərɪ] *n* électrocautère *m*

electrochemical [ɪˌlektrəʊ'kemɪkəl] *adj* électrochimique

electrochemistry [ɪˌlektrəʊ'kemɪstrɪ] *n* électrochimie *f*

electrocoagulation [ɪˌlektrəʊkəʊægjʊ'leɪʃən] *n Med* électrocoagulation *f*

electroconvulsive therapy [ɪˌlektrəʊkən'vʌlsɪv-] *n Med* thérapie *f* par électrochocs

electrocute [ɪ'lektrəkjuːt] *vt* électrocuter; **you'll electrocute yourself** *(give yourself a shock)* tu vas prendre une décharge

electrocution [ɪˌlektrə'kjuːʃən] *n* électrocution *f*

electrode [ɪ'lektrəʊd] *n Chem & Elec* électrode *f*

►► ***electrode gap*** écartement *m* des électrodes; ***electrode holder*** porte-électrodes *m inv*

electrodeposition [ɪˌlektrəʊdiːpə'zɪʃən] *n Chem* électrodéposition *f*

electrodiagnosis [ɪˌlektrəʊdaɪəg'nəʊsɪs] *n Med* électrodiagnostic *m*

electrodialysis [ɪˌlektrəʊdaɪ'ælɪsɪs] *n Chem* électrodialyse *f*

electrodynamic [ɪˌlektrəʊdaɪ'næmɪk] *adj Phys* électrodynamique *f*

electrodynamics [ɪˌlektrəʊdaɪ'næmɪks] *n (UNCOUNT) Phys* électrodynamique *f*

electrodynamometer [ɪˌlektrəʊˌdaɪnə'mɒmɪtə(r)] *n* électrodynamomètre *m*

electroencephalogram [ɪˌlektrəʊen'sefələgræm] *n Med* électro-encéphalogramme *m*

electroencephalograph [ɪˌlektrəʊen'sefələgrɑːf] *n Med* électro-encéphalographe *m*

electroencephalography [ɪˌlektrəʊenˌsefə'lɒgrəfɪ] *n Med* électroencéphalographie *f*

electroendosmosis [ɪˌlektrəʊˌendɒz'məʊsɪs] *n* électro-osmose *f*

electroforming [ɪˌlektrə'fɔːmɪŋ] *n Metal* électroformage *m*

electrokinetics [ɪˌlektrəʊkɪ'netɪks] *n (UNCOUNT) Phys* électrocinétique *f*

electrolocation [ɪˌlektrəʊləʊ'keɪʃən] *n Ich* électrolocation *f*

electrology [ɪˌlek'trɒlədʒɪ] *n* électrologie *f*

electroluminescence [ɪˌlektrəʊˌluːmɪ'nesəns] *n Phys* électroluminescence *f*

electroluminescent [ɪˌlektrəʊˌluːmɪ'nesənt] *adj Phys* électroluminescent

electrolyser [ɪ'lektrəʊˌlaɪzə(r)] *n Chem* électrolyseur *m*

electrolysis [ˌɪlek'trɒləsɪs] *n Chem & Med* électrolyse *f*

electrolyte [ɪ'lektrəʊlaɪt] *n Chem* électrolyte *m*

electrolytic [ɪˌlektrəʊ'lɪtɪk] *adj Chem* électrolytique

electrolyze, -yse [ɪ'lektrəʊlaɪz] *vt Chem* électrolyser

electromagnet [ɪˌlektrəʊ'mægnɪt] *n* électro-aimant *m*

electromagnetic [ɪˌlektrəʊmæg'netɪk] *adj* électromagnétique

electromagnetism [ɪˌlektrəʊ'mægnɪtɪzəm] *n* électromagnétisme *m*

electromechanical [ɪˌlektrəʊmɪ'kænɪkəl] *adj* électromécanique

electrometallurgic [ɪˌlektrəʊˌmetə'lɜːdʒɪk] *adj Tech* électrométallurgique

electrometallurgy [ɪˌlektrəʊme'tælədʒɪ] *n Tech* électrométallurgie *f*

electrometer [ˌɪlek'trɒmɪtə(r)] *n* électromètre *m*

electrometry [ɪlek'trɒmɪtrɪ] *n* électrométrie *f*

electromotive [ɪˌlektrəʊ'məʊtɪv] *adj Phys* électromoteur

►► ***electromotive force*** force *f* électromotrice

electromyography [ɪˌlektrəʊmaɪ'ɒgrəfɪ] *n Med* électromyographie *f*

electron [ɪ'lektrɒn] *n Phys* électron *m*; **positive/negative electron** électron *m* positif/négatif

►► *Electron* ***electron beam*** faisceau *m* d'électrons; *Opt* ***electron camera*** caméra *f* électronique; *Electron* ***electron gun*** canon *m* électronique *ou* à électrons; *Biol* ***electron microscope*** microscope *m* électronique; *Chem* ***electron probe*** sonde *f* électronique; *Astron* ***electron telescope*** télescope *m* électronique; *Elec* ***electron tube*** tube *m* électronique

electronegative [ɪˌlektrəʊ'negətɪv] *adj Chem* électronégatif

electronegativity [ɪˌlektrəʊˌnegə'tɪvɪtɪ] *n Chem* électronégativité *f*

electronic [ˌɪlek'trɒnɪk] **1** *adj* électronique

2 electronics 1 *n (UNCOUNT)* électronique *f*

2 *npl (of machine)* système *m* électronique

3 *comp (company)* d'électronique

►► *Comput* ***electronic banking*** transactions *fpl* bancaires électroniques, bancatique *f*; ***electronic brain*** cerveau *m* électronique; *Comput* ***electronic cash*** argent *m* électronique, argent *m* virtuel; *Comput* ***electronic catalogue*** catalogue *m* en ligne; *Comput* ***electronic commerce*** commerce *m* électronique; *Comput* ***electronic computer*** calculateur *m* électronique; ***electronic crime*** crime *m* informatique; *Comput* ***electronic data interchange*** échange *m* de données informatisé; *Fin* ***electronic data gathering, analysis and retrieval*** = banque de données créée par la commission américaine des opérations de Bourse (le SEC), qui contient toutes sortes d'informations sur de nombreux fonds communs de placement et entreprises publiques; *Comput* ***electronic data processing*** traitement *m* électronique de l'information; ***electronics engineer*** ingénieur *m* électronicien, électronicien(enne) *m,f*; *Phot* ***electronic flash*** flash *m* électronique; *Fin & Comput* ***electronic funds transfer*** transfert *m* de fonds électronique; ***electronic funds transfer at point of sale*** transfert *m* de fonds électronique au point de vente; ***electronic funds transfer system*** = système électronique de transfert de fonds; *Aut* ***electronic ignition*** allumage *m* électronique; ***electronics industry*** industrie *f* électronique; *Comput* ***electronic journal*** journal *m* en ligne; *Comput* ***electronic mail*** courrier *m* électronique; *Comput* ***electronic mailbox*** boîte *f* à *ou* aux lettres électronique; *Comput* ***electronic mall*** galeries *fpl* électroniques; ***electronic monetary systems*** monétique *f*; *Comput* ***electronic money*** argent *m* électronique, argent virtuel; *(concept)* monétique *f*; ***electronic music*** musique *f* électronique; *TV* ***electronic news gathering*** journalisme *m* électronique de télévision; *Com* ***electronic office*** bureau *m* informatisé; *Mus* ***electronic organ*** orgue *m* électronique; *Com* ***electronic payment*** paiement *m* électronique; ***electronic payment terminal*** terminal *m* électronique de paiement; *Comput* ***electronic point of sale*** point *m* de vente électronique; *Comput* ***electronic publishing*** édition *f* électronique, éditique *f*; *Comput* ***electronic purse*** porte-monnaie *m* électronique; *Comput* ***electronic shopping*** téléachat *m*, achats *mpl* en ligne; *Ecol* ***electronic smog*** brouillard *m* électronique; ***electronic surveillance*** surveillance *f* électronique; ***electronic tagging*** étiquetage *m* électronique; *St Exch* ***electronic trading*** transactions *fpl* boursières electroniques; *Fin* ***electronic transfer*** transfert *m* de fonds électronique

electronically [ˌɪlek'trɒnɪklɪ] *adv* électroniquement; *(operated)* par voie électronique

electronvolt [ɪˌlektrɒn'vəʊlt] *n* électronvolt *m*

electro-osmosis *n* électro-osmose *f*

electrophilic [ɪˌlektrəʊ'fɪlɪk] *adj Chem* électrophile

electrophoresis [ɪˌlektrəʊfə'riːsɪs] *n Chem* électrophorèse *f*

electrophysiological [ɪˌlektrəʊˌfɪzɪəʊ'lɒdʒɪkəl] *adj Physiol* électrophysiologique

electrophysiologist [ɪˌlektrəʊˌfɪzɪ'ɒlədʒɪst] *n Physiol* électrophysiologiste *mf*

electrophysiology [ɪˌlektrəʊˌfɪzɪ'ɒlədʒɪ] *n Physiol* électrophysiologie *f*

electroplate [ɪ'lektrəʊpleɪt] **1** *vt* plaquer par galvanoplastie; *(with gold)* dorer par galvanoplastie; *(with silver)* argenter par galvanoplastie

2 *n (UNCOUNT)* articles *mpl* plaqués (par galvanoplastie); *(with silver)* articles *mpl* argentés

electroplated [ɪ'lektrəʊpleɪtɪd] *adj* plaqué *(par galvanoplastie)*

►► ***electroplated nickel silver*** rudz *m*

electropositive [ɪˌlektrəʊ'pɒzɪtɪv] *adj Chem* électropositif

electropositivity [ɪˌlektrəʊˌpɒzɪ'tɪvɪtɪ] *n* électropositivité *f*

electropuncture [ɪˌlektrəʊ'pʌŋktʃə(r)] *n Med* électropuncture *f*

electroradiologist [ɪˌlektrəʊˌreɪdɪ'ɒlədʒɪst] *n Med* électroradiologiste *mf*

electroradiology [ɪˌlektrəʊˌreɪdɪ'ɒlədʒɪ] *n Med* électroradiologie *f*

electroretinogram [ɪˌlektrəʊ'retɪnəʊgræm] *n Med* électrorétinogramme *m*

electroscope [ɪ'lektrəʊskəʊp] *n Elec* électroscope *m*

electrosensitive [ɪˌlektrəʊ'sensɪtɪv] *adj Elec* électrosensible

electroshock [ɪ'lektrəʊʃɒk] *n Elec* électrochoc *m*

►► *Med* ***electroshock therapy*** thérapie *f* par électrochocs

electrostatic [ɪˌlektrəʊ'stætɪk] *adj Elec* électrostatique

electrostatics [ɪˌlektrəʊ'stætɪks] *n (UNCOUNT) Elec* électrostatique *f*

electrostriction [ɪˌlektrəʊ'strɪkʃən] *n Elec & Phys* électrostriction *f*

electrotechnic [ɪˌlektrəʊ'teknɪk], **electrotechnical** [ɪˌlektrəʊ'teknɪkəl] *adj Elec* électrotechnique

electrotechnics [ɪˌlektrəʊ'teknɪks] *n (UNCOUNT) Elec* électrotechnique *f*

electrotherapeutic [ɪˌlektrəʊˌθerə'pjuːtɪk], **electrotherapeutical** [ɪˌlektrəʊˌθerə'pjuːtɪkəl] *adj Med* électrothérapeutique, électrothérapique

electrotherapeutics [ɪˌlektrəʊˌθerə'pjuːtɪks] *n (UNCOUNT) Med* électrothérapie *f*

electrotherapeutist [ɪˌlektrəʊˌθerə'pjuːtɪst], **electrotherapist** [ɪˌlektrəʊ'θerəpɪst] *n Med* électrothérapeute *mf*

electrotherapy [ɪˌlektrəʊ'θerəpɪ] *n Med* électrothérapie *f*

electrothermal [ɪˌlektrəʊ'θɜːməl], **electrothermic** [ɪˌlektrəʊ'θɜːmɪk] *adj Elec, Metal & Phys* électrothermique

electrothermics [ɪˌlektrəʊ'θɜːmɪks] *n (UNCOUNT) Elec, Metal & Phys* électrothermie *f*

electrotropism [ɪˌlektrəʊ'trəʊpɪzəm] *n Elec* électrotropisme *m*

electrotype [ɪ'lektrəʊtaɪp] *Typ* **1** *n* galvanotype *m*

2 *vt* galvanotyper

electrovalence [ɪˌlektrəʊ'veɪləns], **electrovalency** [ɪˌlektrəʊ'veɪlənsɪ] *n Chem* électrovalence *f*

electrovalent [ɪ'lektrəʊ'veɪlənt] *adj Chem* électrovalent

electrum [ɪ'lektrəm] *n Miner* électrum *m*

electuary [ɪ'lektjʊərɪ] *n Pharm* électuaire *m*

eleemosynary [ˌeliiː'mɒsɪnərɪ] *adj Formal* (**a**) *(relating to charity)* charitable, de charité (**b**) *(dependent on charity)* qui vit de charités

►► ***eleemosynary corporation*** société *f* de bienfaisance

elegance ['elɪgəns] *n* élégance *f*

elegant ['elɪgənt] *adj (person, style, solution)* élégant; *(building, furniture)* aux lignes élégantes

elegantly ['elɪgəntlɪ] *adv* élégamment; **elegantly proportioned** aux proportions élégantes

elegiac [elɪ'dʒaɪək] **1** *adj* élégiaque

2 elegiacs *npl* vers *mpl* élégiaques

elegiast [elɪ'dʒaɪəst], **elegist** ['elɪdʒɪst] *n* (poète *m*) élégiaque *m*

elegize, -ise ['elədʒaɪz] **1** *vt* écrire une élégie sur

2 *vi* (**a**) *(write elegies)* écrire des élégies (**b**) *(write in elegiac style)* écrire d'une façon élégiaque

elegy ['elɪdʒɪ] *(pl* **elegies***)* *n* élégie *f*

'Elegy (Written) in a Country Churchyard' *Gray*
'Élégie écrite dans un cimetière de campagne'

element ['elɪmənt] *n* (**a**) *(water, air etc)* élément *m*; **the four elements** les quatre éléments *mpl*; **to be exposed to/to brave the elements** être exposé aux/affronter les éléments; *Fig* **to be in one's element** être dans son élément

(**b**) *(in kettle, electric heater)* résistance *f*

(**c**) *(factor)* facteur *m*; *(small amount)* part *f*; **element of uncertainty/danger/chance** part *f* d'incertitude/de danger/de chance; **there is an element of risk involved** cela comporte un risque; **the element of surprise** l'élément de *ou* le facteur surprise; **disturbing element** élément *m* d'instabilité; **the personal/time element** le facteur humain/temps; **the film has all the elements of a hit movie** le film a tous les ingrédients d'un film à succès; **a key element in selling is...** un des facteurs clés dans la vente est...

(**d**) *(usu pl) (rudiment)* rudiment *m*; **the elements of computing** les rudiments de l'informatique

(**e**) *(in society, group)* élément *m*; **the hooligan element** l'élément hooligan de la société; **a disruptive element** *(in class)* un élément perturbateur; **undesirable elements (in society)** éléments indésirables (de la société)

(**f**) *Chem* élément *m*

(**g**) *Rel* **the elements (of bread and wine)** les espèces *fpl*

elemental [ˌelɪ'mentəl] **1** *adj* (**a**) *(basic)* fondamental, de base; **the elemental needs of man** les besoins fondamentaux de l'homme; **to be elemental to sth** être essentiel à qch (**b**) *(relating to the elements)* propre aux éléments; **the elemental force of the storm** la force des éléments déchaînés dans la tempête (**c**) *(primitive)* élémentaire, primitif (**d**) *Chem* élémentaire

2 *n Literary* esprit *m*

elementary [ˌelɪ'mentərɪ] *adj* élémentaire; **I only speak elementary Russian** mon russe est rudimentaire

►► *Am* ***elementary education*** enseignement *m* primaire; *Chem & Phys* ***elementary particle*** particule *f* élémentaire; *Am* ***elementary school*** école *f* primaire

> **Elementary my dear Watson**
> Cette expression ("élémentaire, mon cher Watson") a pour origine les romans de Conan Doyle où apparaissent le détective Sherlock Holmes et son associé le Docteur Watson. Ce sont les mots que prononcent invariablement Holmes avant d'expliquer à Watson comment il est parvenu à résoudre une énigme. On utilise cette formule de façon humoristique lorsque l'on explique quelque chose à quelqu'un.

elephant ['elɪfənt] *n* éléphant *m*; **African/Indian elephant** éléphant *m* d'Afrique/d'Asie; *Fam* **baby elephant** éléphanteau □ *m*

►► *Zool* ***elephant calf*** éléphanteau *m*; *Bot* ***elephant's ears*** colocase *f*; *Zool* ***elephant seal*** éléphant *m* de mer; *Zool* ***elephant shrew*** macrosélide *m*

elephantiasis [ˌelɪfən'taɪəsɪs] *n Med* éléphantiasis *m*

elephantine [ˌelɪ'fæntaɪn] *adj (proportions, size)* éléphantesque; *(gait)* lourd, pesant; *(movement)* gauche, maladroit; *Fig (humour)* lourd

elevate ['elɪveɪt] *vt* (**a**) *(raise)* élever, hausser; *Mil* *(gun)* pointer en hauteur; *Rel (host, mind)* élever; **to elevate sb to the peerage** élever qn à la pairie (**b**) *(exalt → person)* exalter; *(someone's soul)* élever; **they had elevated their legends into a religion** ils avaient élevé leurs légendes au rang de religion

elevated ['elɪveɪtɪd] *adj* (**a**) *(height, position, rank)* haut, élevé; *(thoughts)* noble, élevé; *(style)* élevé, soutenu; **he has an elevated opinion of himself** il a une haute opinion de lui-même (**b**) *(raised → road, platform)* surélevé
►► *Am* ***elevated railroad, elevated railway*** métro *m* aérien; *TV & Cin* ***elevated shot*** plongée *f*

elevating ['elɪveɪtɪŋ] **1** *adj (edifying)* édifiant; **the experience was far from elevating** l'expérience n'a rien eu de bien inspirant
2 *n* élévation *f*, levage *m*

elevation [ˌelɪ'veɪʃən] *n* (**a**) *(raising → of roof, in rank)* élévation *f*; *Rel (→ of host)* élévation *f*; *(→ of style, language)* caractère *m* élevé *ou* soutenu (**b**) *(height)* **elevation above sea-level** altitude *f ou* hauteur *f* au-dessus du niveau de la mer (**c**) *Astron (of star)* élévation *f* (**d**) *(hill)* élévation *f*, hauteur *f* (**e**) *(of cannon)* hausse *f* (**f**) *Archit* élévation *f*; **front elevation** façade *f*; **side elevation** façade *f* latérale; **rear elevation** derrière *m*

elevator ['elɪveɪtə(r)] *n* (**a**) *Am (lift)* ascenseur *m*; *(for goods)* monte-charge *m inv*; *Fam Hum* **the elevator doesn't go up to the top floor** c'est pas une lumière (**b**) *Aviat* gouvernail *m* de profondeur *ou* d'altitude
►► ***elevator angle*** angle *m* de braquage; ***elevator attendant, elevator operator*** garçon *m* d'ascenseur; ***elevator shaft*** cage *f* d'ascenseur; ***elevator shoes*** chaussures *fpl* à semelles compensées

eleven [ɪ'levən] **1** *n* (**a**) *(number, numeral)* onze *m inv* (**b**) *Sport (team)* onze *m*; **the French eleven** le onze de France
2 *pron* onze
3 *adj* onze; *see also* **five**

eleven-plus *n Br Sch* = examen de sélection pour l'entrée dans le secondaire en Grande-Bretagne

elevenses [ɪ'levənzɪz] *n Br* = boisson ou en-cas pour la pause de onze heures

eleventh [ɪ'levənθ] **1** *n* (**a**) *(fraction)* onzième *m* (**b**) *(in series)* onzième *mf* (**c**) *(of month)* onze *m inv*
2 *adj* onzième; **at the eleventh hour** à la dernière minute
3 *adv* onzièmement; *(in contest)* en onzième position, à la onzième place; *see also* **fifth**
►► *Am Sch* ***eleventh grade*** = classe de lycée (15–16 ans)

eleventh-hour *adj* de dernière minute; **eleventh-hour talks** discussions *fpl* de dernière minute

eleventhly [ɪ'levənθlɪ] *adv* onzièmement, en onzième lieu

elf [elf] (*pl* **elves** [elvz]) *n* elfe *m*, lutin *m*

elfin ['elfɪn] *adj* (**a**) *Fig (face, features)* délicat (**b**) *(music, dance)* féerique

elfish ['elfɪʃ] *adj* (**a**) *Fig (face, features)* délicat (**b**) *(music, dance)* féerique (**c**) *(mischievous)* espiègle

Elgin Marbles ['elgɪn-] *npl* **the Elgin Marbles** les frises *fpl* du Parthénon

El Cîngh [ˌel'giŋə] *n* Cîngh, Cuingòh

elicit [ɪ'lɪsɪt] *vt (information, explanation, response)* obtenir; *(facts, truth)* découvrir, mettre au jour; **to elicit sth from sb** tirer qch de qn; **to elicit a smile from sb** tirer un sourire de qn, arracher un sourire à qn

elide [ɪ'laɪd] *vt Ling* élider

eligibility [ˌelɪdʒə'bɪlətɪ] *n (to vote)* éligibilité *f*; *(for a job)* admissibilité *f*; **there was no doubt as to his eligibility** *(for marriage)* c'était sans aucun doute un bon parti; **to determine sb's eligibility for promotion** décider si qn présente les conditions requises pour bénéficier d'une promotion

eligible ['elɪdʒəbəl] *adj (to vote)* éligible; *(for a job)* admissible; *(for promotion)* pouvant bénéficier d'une promotion; *(for marriage)* mariable; **to be eligible for a pension/a tax rebate** avoir droit à une retraite/un dégrèvement fiscal; **to be eligible** *(as possible husband or boyfriend)* être un bon *ou* beau parti; **there were lots of eligible men at the party** il y avait beaucoup de bons *ou* beaux partis à la fête
►► ***eligible bachelor*** bon *ou* beau parti *m*; *Br Fin* ***eligible bill*** effet *m* escomptable; *Br Fin* ***eligible list*** effet *m* bancable; *Am Fin* ***eligible paper*** effet *m* escomptable

Elijah [ɪ'laɪdʒə] *pr n Bible* Élie

eliminate [ɪ'lɪmɪneɪt] *vt (competitor, alternative)* éliminer; *(stain, mark)* enlever, faire disparaître; *(item from diet)* supprimer, éliminer; *(possibility)* écarter, éliminer; *(kill)* éliminer, supprimer; *Math & Physiol* éliminer; **to eliminate hunger and poverty from the world** éliminer *ou* supprimer la faim et la pauvreté dans le monde; **the police have eliminated him from their enquiries** la police l'a écarté de son enquête; *Sport* **they were eliminated in the first round** ils ont été éliminés au premier round

eliminating [ɪ'lɪmɪneɪtɪŋ] *adj* éliminateur
►► *Sport* ***eliminating heats, eliminating rounds*** épreuves *fpl* éliminatoires

elimination [ɪˌlɪmɪ'neɪʃən] *n* élimination *f*; **by (a process of) elimination** par élimination

eliminator [ɪ'lɪmɪneɪtə(r)] *n Sport* éliminateur *m*; **the next match will be the eliminator** le prochain match décidera de qui sera éliminé

eliminatory [ɪ'lɪmɪnətrɪ] *adj* éliminatoire

Elisha [ɪ'laɪʃə] *pr n Bible* Élisée

elision [ɪ'lɪʒən] *n Ling* élision *f*

elite [ɪ'liːt], **élite** [eɪ'liːt] **1** *n* élite *f*; **the elite of society** l'élite de la société; **to be one of the elite** faire partie de l'élite
2 *adj* d'élite

elitism [ɪ'liːtɪzəm] *n* élitisme *m*

elitist [ɪ'liːtɪst] **1** *n* élitiste *mf*
2 *adj* élitiste

elixir [ɪ'lɪksə(r)] *n* élixir *m*; **elixir of life** élixir *m* de vie

Elizabeth [ɪ'lɪzəbəθ] *pr n* **Queen Elizabeth** la reine Élisabeth
►► ***Elizabeth Regina*** = emblème de la reine Élisabeth

Elizabethan [ɪˌlɪzə'biːθən] **1** *adj* élisabéthain
2 *n* Élisabéthain(e) *m,f*

elk [elk] (*pl* **inv** *or* **elks**) **1** *n Zool* élan *m*; **American elk** wapiti *m*
2 Elk *n Am* (**a**) **the Elks** *(charitable organization)* – organisation américaine à but non lucratif réservée aux hommes, qui s'occupe entre autres choses d'œuvres caritatives (**b**) *(person)* = membre des "Elks"

El Khalil [ˌelkæ'liːl] *n* al-Khalil

elkhound ['elkhaʊnd] *n* chien *m* d'élan

ell [el] *n Arch* aune *f*

Ellesmere Island [ˌelzmɪər-] *n* l'île *f* Ellesmere

ellipse [ɪ'lɪps] **1** *n Math* ellipse *f*
2 Ellipse *n* **the Ellipse** = endroit situé près de la Maison Blanche, à Washington, où ont lieu des cérémonies officielles ainsi que des manifestations

ellipsis [ɪ'lɪpsɪs] (*pl* **ellipses** [-siːz]) *n Gram* ellipse *f*

ellipsoid [ɪ'lɪpsɔɪd] *n Math* ellipsoïde *m*

ellipsoidal [ɪlɪp'sɔɪdəl] *adj Math* ellipsoïdal

elliptic [ɪ'lɪptɪk], **elliptical** [ɪ'lɪptɪkəl] *adj* elliptique

elliptically [ɪ'lɪptɪkəlɪ] *adv* de manière elliptique, par ellipse

Ellis Island ['elɪs-] *n* Ellis Island *(dans la première moitié du XXème siècle, lieu de débarquement des immigrés, situé au large de New York)*

elm [elm] *n* orme *m*
►► ***elm grove*** ormaie *f*

elocution [ˌelə'kjuːʃən] **1** *n* élocution *f*, diction *f*
2 *comp (lesson, teacher)* d'élocution, de diction

elocutionist [ˌelə'kjuːʃənɪst] *n* professeur *m* d'élocution *ou* de diction

elongate ['iːlɒŋgeɪt] **1** *vt* allonger; *(line)* prolonger
2 *vi* s'allonger, s'étendre

elongated ['iːlɒŋgeɪtɪd] *adj (in space)* allongé; *(in time)* prolongé

elongation [ˌiːlɒŋ'geɪʃən] *n* (**a**) *(lengthening)* allongement *m*; *(of line)* prolongement *m* (**b**) *Astron* élongation *f*

elope [ɪ'ləʊp] *vi* s'enfuir pour se marier; **to elope with sb** s'enfuir avec qn pour l'épouser; **they eloped together** ils se sont enfuis pour se marier

elopement [ɪ'ləʊpmənt] *n* fugue *f* amoureuse *(en vue d'un mariage)*

eloquence ['eləkwəns] *n* éloquence *f*

eloquent ['eləkwənt] *adj* éloquent; **to be an eloquent speaker** être éloquent, avoir de l'éloquence; *Fig* **an eloquent gesture** un geste éloquent; **the state of the economy is an eloquent indictment of this policy** la situation économique en dit long sur cette politique

eloquently ['eləkwəntlɪ] *adv* éloquemment, avec éloquence

El Salvador [el'sælvədɔː(r)] *n* Salvador *m*; **in El Salvador** au Salvador

Elsan® ['elsæn] *n* = W-C chimique portable

ELSE [els] *adv* (**a**) *(after indefinite pronoun)* d'autre; **anybody** *or* **anyone else** *(at all)* n'importe qui d'autre, toute autre personne; *(in addition)* quelqu'un d'autre; **anyone else would have phoned the police** n'importe qui d'autre aurait appelé la police; **is there anybody else?** y a-t-il quelqu'un d'autre?; **I couldn't find anyone else to help me** je n'ai pu trouver personne d'autre pour m'aider; **he's no cleverer than anybody else** il n'est pas plus intelligent qu'un autre; **it couldn't be anyone else's** ça ne pouvait être celui de personne d'autre; **anything else** *(at all)* n'importe quoi d'autre; *(in addition)* quelque chose d'autre; **would you like** *or* **will there be anything else?** *(in shop)* vous fallait-il autre chose?; *(in restaurant)* désirez-vous autre chose?; **he wouldn't accept anything else** il n'a rien voulu accepter d'autre; **I couldn't do anything else but** *or* **except apologize** je ne pouvais (rien faire d'autre) que m'excuser; **anywhere else** ailleurs; **I haven't got anywhere else** *or* **I've got nowhere else to go** je n'ai nulle part ailleurs où aller; **everybody else** tous les autres; **everything else** tout le reste; **everywhere else** partout ailleurs; **everywhere else was shut** *(other shops)* tous les autres magasins étaient fermés; **there is little else we can do** nous ne pouvons pas faire grand-chose d'autre; **and much else (besides)** et beaucoup de choses encore; **there isn't much else to be done** il ne reste pas beaucoup à faire; *(we've no choice)* il n'y a pas grand chose d'autre à faire; **nobody** *or* **no one else** personne d'autre; **nothing else** rien d'autre; **we're alive, nothing else matters** nous sommes vivants, c'est tout ce qui compte; **there's nothing else for it** il n'y a rien d'autre à faire; **nowhere else** nulle part ailleurs; **there's nowhere else I'd rather be but here** c'est ici et nulle part ailleurs que je veux être; **somebody** *or* **someone else** quelqu'un d'autre; **this is somebody else's** c'est à quelqu'un d'autre; **something else** autre chose, quelque chose d'autre; **somewhere** *or Am* **someplace else** ailleurs, autre part; **if all else fails** en dernier recours; **it'll teach him a lesson, if nothing else** au moins, ça lui servira de leçon; *Fam* **he's/she's/it's something else!** il est/elle est/c'est incroyable!; *Fam* **the price of petrol is something else!** bonjour le prix de l'essence!
(**b**) *(after interrogative pronoun) (in addition)* d'autre; **what/who else?** quoi/qui d'autre?; **what else can I do?** que puis-je faire d'autre?; **who else but Frank?** qui d'autre que Frank?; **you think they'll give the prize to Jameson? – who else?** tu crois qu'ils attribueront le prix à Jameson? – à qui d'autre veux-tu qu'ils le donnent?; **how/why else would I do it?** comment/pourquoi le ferais-je sinon?; **where else would he be?** où peut-il être à part là?; **so we're all meeting at Cleo's – where else?** alors, on se retrouve tous chez Cleo – où d'autre?
(**c**) *(otherwise)* autrement; *(if not, then)* ou bien; **come tomorrow or else it will be too late** venez demain, autrement il sera trop tard; **he must be joking, or else he's mad** il plaisante, ou bien alors il est fou; **do what I tell you or else!** fais ce que je te dis, sinon!

elsewhere [els'weə(r)] *adv* ailleurs; **to go elsewhere** aller ailleurs; **elsewhere in France** ailleurs en France; **her ambitions lie elsewhere** ses ambitions se situent à un autre niveau

elsewhither ['elswɪðə(r)] *adv Literary* ailleurs

Elstree Studios ['elstrɪ-] *npl* = studios de cinéma londoniens

ELT [ˌiːel'tiː] *n (abbr* **English language teaching***)* = enseignement de l'anglais

elucidate [ɪ'lu:sɪdeɪt] **1** *vt (point, question)* élucider, expliciter; *(reasons)* expliquer
2 *vi* expliquer, être plus clair; **could you elucidate?** pourrais-tu être plus clair?
elucidation [ɪ,lu:sɪ'deɪʃən] *n (of point, question)* élucidation *f*, éclaircissement *m*; *(of reasons)* explication *f*
elucidatory [ɪ,lu:sɪ'deɪtərɪ] *adj* éclaircissant
elude [ɪ'lu:d] *vt (enemy, pursuers)* échapper à; *(question)* éluder; *(blow)* esquiver; *(someone's gaze)* éviter, fuir; *(obligation, responsibility)* se dérober à, se soustraire à; *(justice)* se soustraire à; **his name/that word eludes me** son nom/ce mot m'échappe; **to elude sb's grasp** échapper à (l'emprise de) qn; **success has always eluded him** la réussite lui a toujours échappé
elusive [ɪ'lu:sɪv] *adj (enemy, prey, happiness, thought)* insaisissable; *(word, concept)* difficile à définir; *(answer)* élusif, évasif; **she's being rather elusive** *(difficult to find)* elle se fait plutôt discrète ces derniers temps; *(vague)* elle se montre assez évasive
elusively [ɪ'lu:sɪvlɪ] *adv (answer)* de manière élusive; *(move)* de manière insaisissable
elusiveness [ɪ'lu:sɪvnɪs] *n (of answer)* caractère *m* élusif *ou* évasif; *(of thoughts, happiness)* caractère *m* insaisissable
elute [ɪ'lu:t] *vt Chem* éluer
elution [ɪ'lu:ʃən] *n Chem* élution *f*
elver ['elvə(r)] *n Ich* civelle *f*, pibale *f*
elves [elvz] *pl of* **elf**
elvish ['elvɪʃ] *adj* (**a**) *Fig (face, features)* délicat (**b**) *(music, dance)* féerique (**c**) *(mischievous)* espiègle
Elysian [ɪ'lɪzɪən] *adj Myth* élyséen
►► ***Elysian fields*** champs *mpl* Elysées
Elysium [ɪ'lɪzɪəm] *n Myth* Élysée *m*
em [em] *n Typ* cadratin *m*
►► ***em dash*** tiret *m* cadratin
'em [əm] *Br Fam* = **them**
EMA [,i:em'eɪ] *n Fin (abbr* **European Monetary Agreement**) AME *m*
emaciated [ɪ'meɪʃɪeɪtɪd] *adj* émacié, décharné; **to become emaciated** s'émacier, se décharner
emaciation [ɪ,meɪsɪ'eɪʃən] *n* émaciation *f*; **in a state of emaciation** émacié, décharné
e-mail, email ['i:meɪl] *Comput* **1** *n (UNCOUNT)* courrier *m* électronique, e-mail *m*, mél *m*, *Can* courriel *m*; **to contact sb by e-mail** contacter qn par courrier électronique; **to send sth by e-mail** envoyer qch par courrier électronique; **to check one's e-mail** consulter sa boîte à lettres électronique
2 *vt (message, document)* envoyer par courrier électronique; *(person)* envoyer un courrier électronique à; **can I e-mail you?** est-ce que je peux vous contacter par courrier électronique?; **e-mail us at...** envoyez-nous vos messages à l'adresse suivante...
►► ***e-mail account*** compte *m* de courrier électronique; ***e-mail address*** adresse *f* électronique; ***e-mail client*** client *m* de courrier électronique *ou* de messagerie électronique; ***e-mail program*** programme *m* de courrier électronique; ***e-mail software*** logiciel *m* de courrier électronique
emanate ['emәneɪt] **1** *vi* **to emanate from** émaner de
2 *vt (love)* rayonner de; *(concern)* respirer
emanation [,emə'neɪʃən] *n* émanation *f*
emancipate [ɪ'mænsɪpeɪt] *vt* émanciper; *(slaves)* affranchir
emancipated [ɪ'mænsɪpeɪtɪd] *adj* émancipé; *(slaves)* affranchi
emancipation [ɪ,mænsɪ'peɪʃən] *n* émancipation *f*; *(of slaves)* affranchissement *m*
►► *Am Hist* ***the Emancipation Proclamation*** la proclamation d'émancipation

THE EMANCIPATION PROCLAMATION

Il s'agit de l'allocution prononcée par le président américain Abraham Lincoln en 1863, proclamant les esclaves de la Confédération (États sudistes) "libres à jamais". Bien qu'elle n'ait eu aucun effet concret (ces États échappaient au contrôle fédéral), c'est à cette proclamation que les Américains font référence en parlant de l'émancipation des esclaves par Lincoln.

emancipationist [ɪ,mænsɪ'peɪʃənɪst] *n* (**a**) *Hist (supporting emancipation of slaves)* antiesclavagiste *mf* (**b**) *Rel (supporting emancipation of Catholics)* partisan(e) *m,f* de la réhabilitation des catholiques
emancipator [ɪ'mænsɪ,peɪtə(r)] *n* émancipateur(trice) *m,f*
emancipatory [ɪ,mænsɪ'peɪtərɪ] *adj* émancipateur
emasculate [ɪ'mæskjʊ,leɪt] *vt* émasculer; *Fig* émasculer, affaiblir
emasculated [ɪ'mæskjʊ,leɪtɪd] *adj* émasculé; *Fig* émasculant, affaibli
emasculating [ɪ'mæskjʊ,leɪtɪŋ] *adj* émasculant; *Fig* émasculant, affaiblissant
emasculation [ɪ,mæskjʊ'leɪʃən] *n* émasculation *f*; *Fig* émasculation *f*, affaiblissement *m*
embalm [ɪm'bɑ:m] *vt* (**a**) *(body)* embaumer (**b**) *Literary (memory)* conserver
embalmer [ɪm'bɑ:mə(r)] *n* embaumeur *m*, thanatopracteur *m*
embalming [ɪm'bɑ:mɪŋ] *n* embaumement *m*
►► ***embalming fluid*** fluide *m* de thanatopraxie
embanked [ɪm'bæŋkt] *adj (road)* encaissé en remblai; *(river)* endigué; *(garden)* en terrasse
embankment [ɪm'bæŋkmənt] **1** *n (of concrete)* quai *m*; *(of earth)* berge *f*; *(to contain river)* digue *f*; *(along railway, road)* talus *m*
2 Embankment *n* **the Embankment** = nom abrégé du "Victoria Embankment", rue de la rive nord de la Tamise à Londres
embargo [em'bɑ:gəʊ] *(pl* **embargoes**) **1** *n* (**a**) *Com & Pol* embargo *m*; **to put** *or* **to place** *or* **to lay an embargo on sth** mettre l'embargo sur qch; **to lift/to break an embargo** lever/enfreindre un embargo; **there is still an embargo on arms, arms are still under an embargo** les armes sont encore sous embargo; **oil/arms embargo** embargo *m* pétrolier/sur les armes; **trade embargo** embargo *m* commercial (**b**) *Fig (on spending)* interdiction *f*; **to put an embargo on sth** interdire *ou* bannir qch
2 *vt Com & Pol* mettre l'embargo sur; *Fig* interdire
embark [ɪm'bɑ:k] **1** *vt (passengers, cargo)* embarquer
2 *vi* embarquer, monter à bord
►**embark on, embark upon** *vt insep (journey, career)* commencer, entreprendre; *(explanation, venture)* se lancer dans; *(risky operations)* se lancer dans, s'embarquer dans
embarkation [,embɑ:'keɪʃən], **embarkment** [ɪm'bɑ:kmənt] *n (of passengers, cargo)* embarquement *m*
►► ***embarkation card, embarkation papers*** carte *f* d'embarquement
embarrass [ɪm'bærəs] *vt* embarrasser, gêner; **to embarrass the government/one's family** mettre le gouvernement/sa famille dans l'embarras
embarrassed [ɪm'bærəst] *adj* embarrassé; **to feel embarrassed (about sth)** être embarrassé *ou* se sentir gêné (à propos de qch); **to look embarrassed** avoir l'air embarrassé *ou* gêné; **to be (financially) embarrassed** être gêné, avoir des problèmes d'argent
embarrassing [ɪm'bærəsɪŋ] *adj (experience, person)* embarrassant, gênant; *(situation)* embarrassant, délicat; **how embarrassing!** comme c'est gênant *ou* embarrassant!; **how embarrassing for you!** comme cela a dû être gênant *ou* embarrassant pour toi!; **this is rather embarrassing but...** cela me gêne beaucoup mais...
embarrassingly [ɪm'bærəsɪŋlɪ] *adv* de manière embarrassante; **it was embarrassingly obvious** c'était évident au point d'en être embarrassant; **he gave an embarrassingly bad performance** sa prestation était tellement mauvaise qu'on en était gêné pour lui; **to be embarrassingly candid** être d'une franchise embarrassante; **embarrassingly, we seem to have omitted the principal's name** il semble que nous ayons oublié le nom du directeur, ce qui est plutôt embarrassant
embarrassment [ɪm'bærəsmənt] *n* (**a**) *(feeling)* embarras *m*, gêne *f*; **(much) to my embarrassment** à mon grand embarras; **to cause sb embarrassment** mettre qn dans l'embarras; **to be in a state of financial embarrassment** avoir des problèmes *ou* embarras financiers; **an embarrassment of riches** l'embarras du choix (**b**) *(person, thing)* source *f* d'embarras; **to be an embarrassment to sb** être une source d'embarras pour qn, faire honte à qn
embassy ['embəsɪ] *(pl* **embassies**) **1** *n* ambassade *f*; **the British/French Embassy** l'ambassade *f* de Grande-Bretagne/France
2 *comp (staff, employee)* d'ambassade
embattled [ɪm'bætəld] *adj (army)* engagé dans la bataille; *(town)* ravagé par les combats; *Fig (leader, government)* en difficulté, aux prises avec des difficultés
embayment [ɪm'beɪmənt] *n* (**a**) *(bay)* baie *f* (**b**) *(of coastline)* partie *f* en retrait
embed [ɪm'bed] *(pt & pp* **embedded**, *cont* **embedding**) *vt* (**a**) *(in wood)* enfoncer; *(in rock)* sceller; *(in cement)* sceller, noyer; *(jewels)* enchâsser, incruster; **to be embedded in sth** *(hook, tooth etc)* être enfoncé dans qch; **embedded in concrete** noyé dans le béton; **to be embedded in sb's memory** être gravé dans la mémoire de qn; **to be embedded in sb's mind** être ancré dans l'esprit de qn; **to be embedded in sb's personality** être enraciné dans la personnalité de qn
(**b**) *Comput* intégrer, imbriquer
embedded [ɪm'bedɪd] *adj (in wood)* enfoncé; *(in rock)* scellé; *(in cement)* scellé, noyé; *(jewels)* enchâssé, incrusté; **embedded in my memory** gravé dans ma mémoire; **the event has become embedded in my memory** l'événement s'est gravé dans ma mémoire
►► *Gram* ***embedded clause*** proposition *f* enchâssée; *Comput* ***embedded command*** commande *f* intégrée
embedding [ɪm'bedɪŋ] *n* (**a**) *(in wood)* enfoncement *m*; *(in rock, cement)* scellement *m* (**b**) *Gram* enchâssement *m* (**c**) *Comput* imbrication *f*
embellish [ɪm'belɪʃ] *vt (garment, building)* embellir, décorer, orner; *(account, story etc)* enjoliver, embellir
embellishment [ɪm'belɪʃmənt] *n (of building)* embellissement *m*; *(of garment)* décoration *f*; *(of account, story etc)* enjolivement *m*, embellissement *m*; *(in handwriting)* fioritures *fpl*
ember ['embə(r)] *n* charbon *m* ardent, morceau *m* de braise; **embers** braise *f*; *Literary* **the embers of a dying passion** les cendres d'une passion mourante
►► *Rel* ***the Ember days*** les Quatre-Temps *mpl*
embezzle [ɪm'bezəl] **1** *vt (money)* détourner, escroquer; **to embezzle money from sb** escroquer de l'argent à qn
2 *vi* commettre des détournements de fonds; **to embezzle from a company** détourner les fonds d'une société
embezzlement [ɪm'bezəlmənt] *n (of funds)* détournement *m*; **to be convicted of embezzlement** être reconnu coupable de détournement de fonds
embezzler [ɪm'bezlə(r)] *n* escroc *m*, fraudeur(euse) *m,f*, auteur *m* d'un détournement de fonds
embitter [ɪm'bɪtə(r)] *vt (person)* remplir d'amertume, aigrir; *(relations)* altérer, détériorer
embittered [ɪm'bɪtəd] *adj* aigri
embittering [ɪm'bɪtərɪŋ] *adj (experience)* qui aigrit
embitterment [ɪm'bɪtəmənt] *n (of person)* amertume *f*, aigreur *f*; *(of relations)* détérioration *f*, altération *f*
emblazon [ɪm'bleɪzən] *vt* (**a**) *Her* blasonner; **the shield is emblazoned with dragons** le bouclier porte des dragons (**b**) *(display)* **the team strip had the name of their sponsors emblazoned across the front** le nom de leur sponsor était inscrit sur le devant du maillot de l'équipe; **she didn't want to see her name emblazoned across the front page of the 'Sun'** elle ne voulait pas voir son nom étalé en première page du 'Sun'
emblem ['embləm] *n* emblème *m*; *Her* emblème *m*, devise *f*; *Aut (on radiator)* écusson *m*; **he has become the emblem of defiant youth** il est devenu l'incarnation de la jeunesse révoltée
emblematic [,emblə'mætɪk] *adj* emblématique; **to be emblematic of sth** être emblématique de qch

emblematically [ˌembləˈmætɪkəlɪ] *adv* d'une manière emblématique

embodiment [ɪmˈbɒdɪmənt] *n* (**a**) *(epitome)* incarnation *f*, personnification *f*; **to be the embodiment of goodness/evil** *(person)* être la bonté même/le mal incarné; **the new building is the embodiment of modernity** ce nouveau bâtiment est la modernité même (**b**) *(inclusion)* intégration *f*, incorporation *f*

embody [ɪmˈbɒdɪ] (*pt & pp* **embodied**) *vt* (**a**) *(epitomize → of person)* incarner; **she embodies the archetypal career woman** c'est le type même de la femme qui se consacre entièrement à sa carrière (**b**) *(include)* inclure, intégrer; **the principles embodied in the American Constitution** les principes inscrits dans la constitution américaine

embolden [ɪmˈbəʊldən] *vt* (**a**) *Formal* enhardir, donner du courage à; **to embolden sb to do sth** enhardir qn à faire qch, donner à qn le courage de faire qch; **to feel emboldened to do sth** se sentir le courage de faire qch (**b**) *Typ (characters)* renforcer, graisser

embolic [emˈbɒlɪk] *adj Med* embolique

embolism [ˈembəlɪzəm] *n Med* embolie *f*; **to suffer** *or* **to have an embolism** faire *ou* avoir une embolie

embolus [ˈembələs] (*pl* **emboli** [-laɪ]) *n Med* embole *m*, embolus *m*

embonpoint [ˌɒmbɒnˈpwæn] *n Hum* embonpoint *m*, rondeurs *fpl*

emboss [ɪmˈbɒs] *vt (metal)* repousser, estamper; *(leather)* estamper, gaufrer; *(cloth, paper)* gaufrer

embossed [ɪmˈbɒst] *adj (metal)* repoussé; *(leather)* gaufré; *(cloth, wallpaper)* gaufré, à motifs en relief

embouchure [ˌɑːmbuːˈʃʊə(r)] *n Mus* embouchure *f*

embower [ɪmˈbaʊə(r)] *vt Literary* abriter *(dans un berceau de verdure)*

embrace [ɪmˈbreɪs] **1** *vt* (**a**) *(friend, child)* étreindre; *(lover)* étreindre, enlacer; *(official visitor, statesman)* donner l'accolade à; **to embrace one another tenderly** s'étreindre tendrement

(**b**) *(include)* regrouper, comprendre, embrasser; **the view from the terrace embraces the whole valley** de la terrasse la vue s'étend sur toute la vallée *ou* embrasse toute la vallée

(**c**) *(adopt → religion, cause)* embrasser; *(→ opportunity)* saisir

2 *vi (friends)* s'étreindre; *(lovers)* s'étreindre, s'enlacer; *(statesmen)* se donner l'accolade

3 *n (of friend, child)* étreinte *f*; *(of lover)* étreinte *f*, enlacement *m*; *(of official visitor, statesman)* accolade *f*; **to hold** *or* **to clasp sb in an embrace** étreindre qn; **to greet sb with an embrace** accueillir qn dans une étreinte; *Literary* **winter's iron embrace** l'étreinte *f* glacée de l'hiver

embrasure [ɪmˈbreɪʒə(r)] *n* (**a**) *Archit* embrasure *f*, ébrasement *m* (**b**) *Mil* embrasure *f*, sabord *m*

embrasured [ɪmˈbreɪʒəd] *adj* (**a**) *Archit* à embrasure, ébrasé (**b**) *Mil* muni d'embrasures

embrocation [ˌembrəˈkeɪʃən] *n Old-fashioned* embrocation *f*

embroider [ɪmˈbrɔɪdə(r)] **1** *vt (garment, cloth)* broder; *Fig (story, truth)* embellir, enjoliver

2 *vi (with needle)* broder; *Fig (embellish)* broder, enjoliver

►**embroider on** *vt insep (story, truth)* enjoliver

embroidered [ɪmˈbrɔɪdəd] *adj (garment, cloth)* brodé

embroiderer [ɪmˈbrɔɪdərə(r)] *n* brodeur(euse) *m,f*

embroideress [ɪmˈbrɔɪdəres] *n* brodeuse *f*

embroidering [ɪmˈbrɔɪdərɪŋ] *n (on garment, cloth)* broderie *f*; *Fig (of story, truth)* enjolivement *m*, embellissement *m*

embroidery [ɪmˈbrɔɪdərɪ] (*pl* **embroideries**) *n (on garment, cloth)* broderie *f*; *Fig (of story, truth)* enjolivement *m*, embellissement *m*

►► ***embroidery frame*** métier *m* à broder; ***embroidery silk*** soie *f* à broder; ***embroidery thread*** fil *m* à broder

embroil [ɪmˈbrɔɪl] *vt* mêler, impliquer; **to embroil sb in sth** mêler qn à qch, impliquer qn dans qch; **to get embroiled in sth** se retrouver mêlé à qch; **to get embroiled with sb** *(romantically)* avoir une liaison avec qn; **I wouldn't get embroiled with her if I was you** à ta place je ne me compliquerais pas la vie avec elle

embroilment [ɪmˈbrɔɪlmənt] *n Formal (in matter, situation)* implication *f*; *(with lover)* liaison *f*

embryo [ˈembrɪəʊ] (*pl* **embryos**) *n Biol & Fig* embryon *m*; **I have the embryo of an idea** j'ai un embryon d'idée; **in embryo** *(foetus, idea)* à l'état embryonnaire

►► ***embryo research*** recherche *f* portant sur les embryons; ***embryo transfer*** transfert *f* d'embryon

embryogenesis [ˌembrɪəʊˈdʒenɪsɪs] *n Med* embryogénèse *f*

embryological [ˌembrɪəˈlɒdʒɪkəl] *adj Biol* embryologique

embryologist [ˌembrɪˈɒlədʒɪst] *n Biol* embryologiste *mf*

embryology [ˌembrɪˈɒlədʒɪ] *n Biol* embryologie *f*

embryonic [ˌembrɪˈɒnɪk] *adj Biol* embryonnaire; *Fig (plan, idea)* à l'état embryonnaire; **the plan is still at an embryonic stage** le projet est encore à l'état embryonnaire

embus [ɪmˈbʌs] *Mil* **1** *vt* faire monter à bord d'un autocar

2 *vi* monter à bord d'un autocar

emcee [ˌemˈsiː] *Fam (abbr* **master of ceremonies**)

1 *n* maître *m* de cérémonies ☐; *Rad & TV* animateur(trice) ☐ *m,f*

2 *vt* animer ☐

emend [ɪˈmend], **emendate** [ˈɪmendeɪt] *vt Formal* corriger

emendation [ɪmenˈdeɪʃən] *n Formal* correction *f*

emerald [ˈemərəld] **1** *n* (**a**) *(gemstone)* émeraude *f* (**b**) *(colour)* (vert *m*) émeraude *m*

2 *adj (colour)* émeraude

3 *comp (brooch, ring)* en émeraude; *(necklace)* d'émeraudes

►► ***emerald green*** **1** *n* (vert *m*) émeraude *m* **2** *adj* (vert *m*) émeraude; *Literary* ***the Emerald Isle*** Île *f* d'Émeraude

emerge [ɪˈmɜːdʒ] *vi (person, animal)* sortir; *(sun)* sortir, émerger; *(truth, difficulty)* émerger, apparaître; *(theory, new state)* émerger; *(new leader)* apparaître; **to emerge from the water** *(diver, submarine, island)* émerger; **to emerge from hiding** sortir de sa cachette; **new playwrights have emerged on the scene** de nouveaux dramaturges ont fait leur apparition; **to emerge as favourite** apparaître comme le favori; **it emerges that...** il apparaît *ou* ressort que...; **it later emerged that...** il est apparu par la suite que...; **to emerge victorious** *or* **the winner** sortir vainqueur; **to emerge unscathed** sortir indemne; **he was soon to emerge from his father's shadow** il allait bientôt sortir de l'ombre de son père

emergence [ɪˈmɜːdʒəns] *n (of theory)* émergence *f*; *(of new state, new leader)* apparition *f*

emergency [ɪˈmɜːdʒənsɪ] (*pl* **emergencies**) **1** *n* (**a**) *(situation)* (cas *m* d')urgence *f*; **this is an emergency!** c'est une urgence!; **in case of emergency, in an emergency** en cas d'urgence; **to provide for emergencies** parer à l'imprévu; **to be prepared for any emergency** être prêt à toutes les éventualités; **state of emergency** état *m* d'urgence; **to declare a state of emergency** déclarer l'état d'urgence; **national emergency** catastrophe *f* nationale; **for emergency use only** *(sign)* à n'utiliser qu'en cas d'urgence

(**b**) *Med (department)* (service *m* des) urgences *fpl*

2 *comp (measures, procedure, meeting)* d'urgence

►► ***emergency brake*** frein *m* de secours; *Am Aut (handbrake)* frein *m* à main; *Med* ***emergency case*** urgence *f*; ***emergency exit*** sortie *f ou* issue *f* de secours; ***emergency food aid*** aide *f* alimentaire d'urgence; ***emergency fund*** fonds *m* de secours; *Aviat* ***emergency landing*** atterrissage *m* forcé; *Med* ***emergency medical technician*** = technicien médical des services d'urgence; *Med* ***emergency medicine*** médecine *f* d'urgence; *Med* ***emergency operation*** opération *f* à chaud; *Med* ***emergency patient*** urgence *f*; ***emergency powers*** pouvoirs *mpl* extraordinaires; ***emergency rations*** vivres *mpl* de secours *ou* de réserve; ***emergency regulations*** mesures *fpl* d'exception; ***emergency repairs*** réparations *fpl* d'urgence; *Am Med* ***emergency room*** salle *f* des urgences; ***emergency service*** *Aut* service *m* de dépannage; *Med* service *m* des urgences; ***emergency services*** services *mpl* d'urgence; *Aut* ***emergency stop*** arrêt *m* d'urgence; ***emergency supply*** réserve *f*; *Aviat* ***emergency tank*** réservoir *m* auxiliaire; *Fin* ***emergency tax*** impôt *m* extraordinaire; ***emergency telephone*** téléphone *m* d'urgence, poste *m* d'appel d'urgence; *Br Med* ***emergency ward*** salle *f* des urgences

emergent [ɪˈmɜːdʒənt] *adj (theory, nation)* naissant

emerging [ɪˈmɜːdʒɪŋ] *adj*

►► *Biol & Med* ***emerging infectious diseases*** maladies *fpl* infectieuses émergentes; *Fin* ***emerging market*** marché *m* émergeant

emeritus [ɪˈmerɪtəs] *adj Univ* honoraire

emery [ˈemərɪ] *n Miner* émeri *m*

►► ***emery board*** lime *f* à ongles; ***emery cloth*** toile *f* (d')émeri; ***emery paper*** papier *m* (d')émeri; ***emery powder*** poudre *f* d'émeri; ***emery wheel*** meule *f* (en) émeri

emetic [ɪˈmetɪk] *Med* **1** *adj* émétique

2 *n* émétique *m*, vomitif *m*

emf, EMF [ˌiːemˈef] *n* (**a**) *Elec (abbr* **electromotive force**) force *f* électromotrice (**b**) *(abbr* **European Monetary Fund**) FME *m*

EMI [ˌiːemˈaɪ] *n (abbr* **European Monetary Institute**) IME *m*

emigrant [ˈemɪgrənt] **1** *n* émigrant(e) *m,f*; *(when established abroad)* émigré(e) *m,f*

2 *comp (worker, population)* émigré

emigrate [ˈemɪgreɪt] *vi* émigrer (**to** à)

emigrating [ˈemɪgreɪtɪŋ] *adj* émigrant

emigration [ˌemɪˈgreɪʃən] *n* émigration *f*

émigré [ˈemɪgreɪ] **1** *n* émigré(e) *m,f*

2 *comp (writer)* émigré

eminence [ˈemɪnəns] **1** *n* (**a**) *(prominence)* rang *m* éminent; *(of office)* grandeur *f*, distinction *f*; **to occupy a position of eminence** avoir un rang éminent; **to achieve eminence in one's profession** atteindre un rang éminent dans sa profession (**b**) *(high ground)* éminence *f*, hauteur *f*

2 Eminence *n Rel (title)* Éminence *f*; **Your/His Eminence** Votre/Son Éminence

Eminency [ˈemɪnənsɪ] *n Rel (title)* Éminence *f*; **Your/His Eminency** Votre/Son Éminence

eminent [ˈemɪnənt] *adj* (**a**) *(distinguished)* éminent (**b**) *(conspicuous)* éminent, remarquable, insigne; **in view of his eminent suitability for the job** du fait qu'il convient tout à fait pour le poste; **it makes eminent good sense** cela paraît le bon sens même

►► *Am Law* ***eminent domain*** ≃ droit *m* d'expropriation pour cause d'utilité publique

eminently [ˈemɪnəntlɪ] *adv (very)* éminemment, tout à fait; **an eminently likeable young man** un jeune homme tout à fait aimable; **to be eminently successful** réussir brillamment; **eminently suitable** qui convient parfaitement; **it is eminently desirable that...** il est fort à souhaiter que..., il est éminemment souhaitable que...; **what an eminently sensible idea!** quelle sage idée!; **he was eminently unqualified** il n'était absolument pas qualifié; *Hum* **an eminently forgettable film** un film qui n'a rien d'inoubliable

emir [eˈmɪə(r)] *n* émir *m*

emirate [ˈemərɪt] *n* émirat *m*

emissary [ˈemɪsərɪ] (*pl* **emissaries**) *n* émissaire *m*

emission [ɪˈmɪʃən] *n* (**a**) *(action → of gas, heat)* émission *f*, dégagement *m*; *(→ of pollutant, radiation, light, sound)* émission *f*; *Fin (→ of bank notes)* émission *f* (**b**) *(substance)* émanation *f*; **nocturnal emissions** pollutions *fpl* nocturnes

►► *Aut* ***emission limit*** seuil *m* d'émission

emit [ɪˈmɪt] (*pt & pp* **emitted,** *cont* **emitting**) *vt (sound, radiation, light)* émettre; *(heat)* dégager, émettre; *(smell)* exhaler, dégager; *(gas)* dégager; *(sparks, cry)* lancer

emitter [ɪˈmɪtə(r)] *n Nucl, Phys & Electron* émetteur *m*

Emmanuel [ɪˈmænjʊəl] *pr n Bible* Emmanuel

Emmaus [ɪˈmeɪəs] *n Bible* Emmaüs *m*

Emmental [ˈemənˌtɑːl] *n Culin* Emmental *m*

Emmentaler [ˈemənˌtɑːlə(r)] *n Culin* Emmental *m*

Emmenthal, Emmenthaler = **Emmental, Emmentaler**

Emmy ['emɪ] *n* **Emmy (award)** = distinction récompensant les meilleures émissions télévisées américaines de l'année

emollient [ɪ'mɒlɪənt] **1** *adj* émollient; *Fig* adoucissant, calmant

2 *n* émollient *m*

emolument [ɪ'mɒljʊmənt] *n Formal (usu pl)* **emoluments** émoluments *mpl*, rémunération *f*

e-money *n* argent *m* électronique, argent *m* virtuel

emote [ɪ'məʊt] *vi (on stage)* faire dans le genre tragique; *(in life)* avoir un comportement théâtral

emoticon [ɪ'məʊtɪkɒn] *n Comput (Internet)* émoticon *m*, *Can* binette *f*

emotion [ɪ'məʊʃən] *n (particular feeling)* sentiment *m*; *(faculty)* émotion *f*; **to be in control of one's emotions** contrôler *ou* maîtriser ses émotions; **to show no emotion** ne laisser paraître aucune émotion; **to shake with emotion** *(person, voice)* trembler d'émotion; **to appeal to the emotions** faire appel aux sentiments; **to express one's emotions** exprimer ses sentiments; **don't let your emotions get in the way** ne te laisse pas influencer par tes sentiments; **full of emotion** ému

emotional [ɪ'məʊʃənəl] *adj* (**a**) *(stress)* émotionnel; *(life, problems)* affectif; **to have** *or* **carry a lot of emotional baggage** avoir accumulé les échecs sentimentaux; **to be afraid of emotional commitment** avoir peur de s'engager sur le plan émotionnel; **emotional shock** choc *m* émotif *ou* émotionnel; **she's an emotional wreck** elle a de gros problèmes émotionnels; **he was something of an emotional cripple** il était quelque peu handicapé sur le plan affectif

(**b**) *(person → easily moved)* sensible, qui s'émeut facilement; *(→ stronger)* émotif; *(appealing to the emotions → plea, speech, music)* émouvant; **he got very emotional at the funeral** il était très ému à l'enterrement; **why do you always have to get so emotional?** pourquoi faut-il toujours que tu te mettes dans de tels états?; *Hum Euph* **to be tired and emotional** être ivre mort

(**c**) *(charged with emotion → issue)* passionné, brûlant; *(→ reunion, farewell, scene)* chargé d'émotion

(**d**) *(governed by emotions → person)* passionné, ardent; *(→ reaction, state)* émotionnel; **you shouldn't be so emotional** tu es vraiment trop sensible

►► ***emotional blackmail*** chantage *m* affectif

emotionalism [ɪ'məʊʃənəlɪzəm] *n Pej* sensiblerie *f*; **it's a piece of emotionalism** c'est du sentimentalisme; **the emotionalism of his writing** son style sentimentaliste

emotionality [ɪˌməʊʃə'nælɪtɪ] *n* émotivité *f*

emotionally [ɪ'məʊʃənəlɪ] *adv* (**a**) *(immature, scarred)* sur le plan affectif; **to feel emotionally exhausted** *or* **drained** se sentir vidé (sur le plan émotionnel); **to be emotionally disturbed** souffrir de troubles affectifs; **emotionally, he's not strong enough for the job** sur le plan émotionnel, il n'est pas assez solide pour ce travail; **to be emotionally involved with sb** avoir des liens affectifs avec qn; **I don't want to get emotionally involved** je ne veux pas m'attacher; **I'm too emotionally involved with the whole situation** cette situation me touche de trop près

(**b**) *(react, speak)* avec émotion; **an emotionally charged atmosphere** une atmosphère chargée d'émotion

emotionless [ɪ'məʊʃənlɪs] *adj (person)* indifférent; *(face, look)* impassible; *(style)* sobre

emotionlessness [ɪ'məʊʃənlɪsnɪs] *n (of person)* indifférence *f*; *(of face, look)* impassibilité *f*; *(of style)* sobriété *f*

emotive [ɪ'məʊtɪv] *adj* qui déchaîne les passions; **emotive speech/language** discours *m*/langage *m* sensationnaliste; **racism is a very emotive issue** le racisme est un sujet qui déchaîne les passions; **an emotive word** un mot chargé

emotiveness [ɪ'məʊtɪvnɪs], **emotivity** [ɪməʊ'tɪvɪtɪ] *n* émotivité *f*

empanel [ɪm'pænəl] (*Br pt & pp* **empanelled**, *cont* **empanelling**, *Am pt & pp* **empaneled**, *cont* **empaneling**) *vt (jury)* constituer; *(juror)* inscrire sur la liste *ou* le tableau du jury

empathetic [ˌempə'θetɪk] *adj (person)* compréhensif; *Psy* empathique

empathetically [ˌempə'θetɪkəlɪ] *adv* avec compassion

empathize, -ise ['empəθaɪz] *vi* **to empathize with sb** s'identifier à qn

empathy ['empəθɪ] *n (affinity → gen)* affinité *f*, affinités *fpl*; *Phil & Psy* empathie *f*; *(power, ability)* capacité *f* à s'identifier à autrui; **the part calls for a good deal of empathy** le rôle exige une grande capacité à s'identifier au personnage; **the empathy between them** les affinités qui existent entre eux; **our empathy with her pain** notre sympathie à sa douleur

Empedocles [ɪm'pedəkliːz] *pr n* Empédocle

empennage [em'penɪdʒ] *n Aviat* empennage *m*

emperor ['empərə(r)] *n* empereur *m*

►► ***Emperor Augustus*** l'Empereur Auguste; *Zool* ***emperor moth*** saturnie *f*, paon *m* de nuit; *Orn* ***emperor penguin*** manchot *m* empereur

'The Emperor's New Clothes' *Andersen* 'Les Habits neufs de l'empereur'

emphasis ['emfəsɪs] (*pl* **emphases** [-siːz]) *n* (**a**) *(importance)* accent *m*; **to place** *or* **to lay** *or* **to put emphasis on sth** mettre l'accent sur qch; **there is too much emphasis on materialism in our society** on accorde trop d'importance aux choses matérielles dans notre société; **this year the emphasis is on bright colours/steady growth** cette année, l'accent est mis sur les couleurs vives/sur une croissance régulière; **a change of emphasis** un changement de priorités; **the emphasis now is on winning votes** ce qui est important maintenant c'est de gagner des voix

(**b**) *(stress → in words)* force *f*, accentuation *f*; *Gram* mise *f* en relief; *Ling* accent *m*; **the emphasis comes on the last syllable** l'accent est placé *ou* tombe sur la dernière syllabe; **to say sth with emphasis** dire qch avec emphase *ou* emphatiquement; **he waved his arms around for emphasis** il faisait de grands gestes pour ponctuer son discours; **the word is only used in the sentence for emphasis** dans la phrase, le mot n'a qu'une valeur intensive

emphasize, -ise ['emfəsaɪz] *vt* (**a**) *(detail, need, importance)* insister sur; **she emphasized the need for caution** elle a bien insisté sur la nécessité d'être prudent; **I cannot emphasize this point enough** je ne saurais trop insister sur ce point (**b**) *(physical feature)* accentuer; **to emphasize the waist** *(garment)* marquer *ou* accentuer la taille (**c**) *Ling (syllable)* accentuer; *(word)* accentuer, appuyer sur

emphatic [ɪm'fætɪk] *adj* (**a**) *(refusal)* catégorique; *(speaker, manner, tone)* énergique, vigoureux; *(victory, defeat)* net; **to be emphatic** insister; **she was emphatic that they must not be late** elle a bien insisté sur le fait qu'ils ne devaient pas être en retard; **he was quite emphatic on that point** il s'est montré très catégorique sur ce point; **to be emphatic in one's denials** nier catégoriquement; **an emphatic gesture** un grand geste (**b**) *Ling* emphatique

emphatically [ɪm'fætɪklɪ] *adv* (**a**) *(forcefully)* énergiquement; *(deny)* catégoriquement; **they had been emphatically defeated** ils avaient été largement battus (**b**) *(definitely)* clairement; **I most emphatically do not agree with you** je ne suis absolument pas d'accord avec vous; **emphatically yes!** tout à fait, oui!

emphysema [ˌemfɪ'siːmə] *n Med* emphysème *m*

empire ['empaɪə(r)] **1** *n* empire *m*; *Hist* **the (British) Empire** l'Empire *m* britannique; *Fig* **a shipbuilding empire** un empire dans le monde de la construction navale

2 Empire *comp (costume, furniture, style)* Empire

►► ***the Empire State*** = surnom donné à l'État de New York; ***the Empire State Building*** l'Empire State Building *m*

'The Empire Strikes Back' *Kershner* 'L'Empire contre-attaque'

empire-build *vi Fig* **he's empire-building again** il est encore à jouer les bâtisseurs d'empires

empire-builder *n Fig* bâtisseur *m* d'empires

empire-building *Fig* **1** *adj* de bâtisseur d'empires

2 *n* **there's too much empire-building going on** on joue trop les bâtisseurs d'empires

empiric [ɪm'pɪrɪk] **1** *adj* empirique

2 *n* empiriste *mf*

empirical [ɪm'pɪrɪkəl] *adj* empirique

►► *Chem* ***empirical formula*** formule *f* empirique

empirically [ɪm'pɪrɪklɪ] *adv* empiriquement

empiricism [ɪm'pɪrɪsɪzəm] *n* empirisme *m*

empiricist [ɪm'pɪrɪsɪst] *n* empiriste *mf*

emplacement [ɪm'pleɪsmənt] *n Mil (of cannon)* emplacement *m*

emplane [ɪm'pleɪn] **1** *vt* embarquer (à bord d'un avion)

2 *vi* embarquer (à bord d'un avion)

employ [ɪm'plɔɪ] **1** *vt* (**a**) *(give work to)* employer; **they employ 245 staff** ils ont 245 employés; **to employ sb as a receptionist** employer qn comme réceptionniste; **he has been employed with the firm for twenty years** il travaille pour cette entreprise depuis vingt ans

(**b**) *(use → means, method, word)* employer, utiliser; *(→ skill, diplomacy)* faire usage de, employer; *(→ force)* employer, avoir recours à

(**c**) *(occupy)* **to employ oneself/to be employed in doing sth** s'occuper/être occupé à faire qch; **you'd be better employed doing your homework** tu ferais mieux de faire tes devoirs; **have you no better way of employing your time?** tu n'as rien de mieux à faire?

2 *n Formal* service *m*; **to be in sb's employ** travailler pour qn, être au service de qn; **to have sb in one's employ** employer qn, avoir qn à son service

employability [ɪmˌplɔɪə'bɪlɪtɪ] *n* **this training scheme is designed to increase the students' employability** ce stage a pour but d'accroître les chances des participants sur le marché de l'emploi; **the employability of the graduates is one way of measuring the quality of a university** la facilité avec laquelle les diplômés d'une université parviennent à trouver un emploi est un moyen de mesurer la qualité de son enseignement; **the changing job market has led many people to question their employability** la transformation du marché de l'emploi conduit beaucoup de gens à se demander avec quelle facilité ils trouveraient à s'employer

employable [ɪm'plɔɪəbəl] *adj (person)* susceptible d'être employé; *(method)* utilisable; **a good education makes you more employable** une bonne formation donne plus de chances de trouver du travail

employed [ɪm'plɔɪd] **1** *adj* employé; **I am not employed at the moment** je n'ai pas de travail en ce moment

2 *npl* personnes *fpl* qui ont un emploi; **employers and employed** patronat *m* et salariat *m*

employee [ɪm'plɔɪiː] *n* employé(e) *m,f*, salarié(e) *m,f*; **she is an employee of Company X, she is a Company X employee** c'est une employée de la Société X; **management and employees** la direction et les employés *ou* le personnel; *(in negotiations)* les partenaires *mpl* sociaux

►► *Com* ***employee association*** comité *m* d'entreprise; *Com* ***employee benefits*** avantages *mpl* accordés aux employés; *Com* ***employee buyout*** reprise *f* de l'entreprise par les salariés, RES *f*; *Com* ***employee contributions*** cotisations *fpl* salariales, charges *fpl* sociales salariales; *Com* ***employee incentive scheme*** système *m* de rémunération au rendement; *Com* ***employee profit-sharing scheme*** intéressement *m* aux résultats; **to provide an employee profit-sharing scheme** intéresser les employés aux bénéfices; *Com* ***employee representative*** délégué(e) *m,f* du personnel; *Am* ***Employee Retirement Income Security Act*** = loi américaine sur les pensions de retraite; *Com* ***employee shareholding*** actionnariat *m* ouvrier; *Com Br* ***employee share ownership plan,*** *Am* ***employee stock ownership plan*** plan *m* d'actionnariat des salariés

employer [ɪm'plɔɪə(r)] *n* patron(onne) *m,f*, *Formal* employeur(euse) *m,f*; **they are good**

employers ce sont de bons employeurs *ou* patrons; **who is your employer?** pour qui travaillez-vous?; **this company is the town's largest employer** c'est cette entreprise qui emploie le plus de gens dans la ville; **employers** *(as a body)* patronat *m*

►► ***employers' association*** organisation *f* patronale, syndicat *m* patronal; ***employer's contribution*** *(to employee benefits)* cotisation *f* patronale; ***employer's liability*** responsabilité *f* patronale; ***employers' organization*** syndicat *m* patronal

employment [ɪm'plɔɪmənt] *n* (**a**) *(work)* emploi *m*; **to be without employment** être sans emploi *ou* travail; **to be in employment** avoir un emploi *ou* du travail; **full employment** plein emploi *m*; **conditions of employment** conditions *fpl* de travail; **to look for** *or* **to seek employment** chercher du travail *ou* un emploi, être demandeur d'emploi; **to give** *or* **to provide employment** donner *ou* fournir du travail; **(the) employment figures** les chiffres *mpl* de l'emploi; *Br* **Secretary (of State) for** *or* **Minister of Employment,** *Am* **Secretary for Employment** ≃ ministre *m* du Travail

(**b**) *(recruitment)* embauche *f*; *(providing work)* emploi *m*

(**c**) *(use → of method, word)* emploi *m*; *(→ of force, skill)* usage *m*, emploi *m*

►► *Br Pol* ***Employment Act*** = loi sur l'égalité des chances pour l'emploi; ***employment agency, employment bureau*** agence *f ou* bureau *m* de placement; ***employment exchange*** ≃ ANPE *f*; ***employment law, employment legislation*** code *m ou* législation *f* du travail; *Br Formerly* ***employment office*** ≃ ANPE *f*; ***employment protection*** protection *f* de l'emploi; *Br* ***Employment Training*** = programme gouvernemental en faveur des chômeurs de longue durée

empoison [ɪm'pɔɪzən] *vt Literary* empoisonner; **to empoison sb** *or* **sb's mind against sb** enfieller qn *ou* le coeur de qn contre qn

emporium [em'pɔːrɪəm] *(pl* **emporiums** *or* **emporia** [-rɪə]) *n* grand magasin *m*

empower [ɪm'paʊə(r)] *vt* (**a**) *Formal (give permission to)* habiliter, autoriser; **to empower sb to do sth** habiliter *ou* autoriser qn à faire qch

(**b**) *(give power to)* **to empower sb** *(emotionally, psychologically)* donner à qn les moyens de s'assumer; **this form of psychotherapy aims to empower people in their everyday lives** ce type de psychothérapie a pour but de permettre aux gens de s'assumer dans leur vie de tous les jours; **political involvement can empower minorities** l'action politique peut permettre aux minorités de s'émanciper

(**c**) *(employee)* donner plus d'autonomie à

empowering [ɪm'paʊərɪŋ] *adj (role, effect)* émancipateur

empowerment [ɪm'paʊəmənt] *n* (**a**) *(of individual, community, minority)* émancipation *f* (**b**) *(of employee)* = fait d'accorder davantage d'autonomie

empress ['emprɪs] *n* impératrice *f*; **Empress Josephine** l'Impératrice Joséphine

emptiness ['emptɪnɪs] *n* vide *m*; **a feeling of emptiness** un sentiment de vide; **the emptiness of my life/days** le vide de mon existence/mes journées

empty ['emptɪ] *(compar* **emptier,** *superl* **emptiest,** *pl* **empties**) **1** *adj* (**a**) *(glass, room, box etc)* vide; *(city, street)* désert; *(cinema)* désert, vide; *(job, post)* vacant, à pourvoir; **the house was empty of people** la maison était vide; **my stomach is empty** *(I'm hungry)* j'ai un creux (à l'estomac); **to do sth on an empty stomach** faire qch à jeun; *Med* **to be taken on an empty stomach** *(on packaging)* à prendre à jeun; **to feel empty** *(drained of emotion)* se sentir vidé (sur le plan émotionnel); **the fuel gauge was at** *or* **showing empty** le niveau du réservoir était à zéro; **to be running on empty** *(car)* avoir le réservoir presque vide; *Fig* ne plus avoir d'énergie, être à bout de souffle; *Prov* **empty vessels make most noise** = ce sont souvent les ignorants qui sont les plus bavards

(**b**) *Fig (words, talk)* creux; *(promise)* en l'air, vain; *(gesture)* dénué de sens; *(threat)* en l'air; **empty of meaning** vide *ou* dénué de sens; **to feel empty** *(after bereavement, trauma)* sentir un vide; **life feels empty now that you've gone** ma vie est vide maintenant que tu es partie

2 *n Fam (bottle)* bouteille *f* vide ❑; *(glass)* verre *m* vide ❑; *(crate)* caisse *f* vide ❑

3 *vt (glass, pocket, room)* vider; *(car, lorry)* décharger; *(cesspool, tank, barrel)* vidanger; *Comput (wastebasket, bin)* vider; **he emptied (the contents of) the bucket over her head** il a vidé le seau sur sa tête; **she emptied the cigarette butts into a plant pot** elle a versé les mégots dans un pot de fleurs

4 *vi (building, street, container)* se vider; *(water)* s'écouler; **to empty into the sea** *(river)* se jeter dans la mer; **the crowd emptied onto the streets** la foule s'est répandue dans les rues

►**empty out 1** *vt sep* vider

2 *vi (tank, container)* se vider; *(water, liquid)* s'écouler

empty-handed [-'hændɪd] *adj* les mains vides; **to leave empty-handed** repartir les mains vides; **to return empty-handed** rentrer bredouille *ou* les mains vides

empty-headed *adj* écervelé, sans cervelle

emptying ['emptɪɪŋ] *n (of glass, pocket, room)* vidage *m*; *(of car, lorry)* déchargement *m*; *(of cesspool, tank, barrel)* vidange *f*; *(of streets)* dépeuplement *m*

empurple [ɪm'pɜːpəl] *vt Literary* empourprer

empyema [ˌempaɪ'iːmə] *n Med* empyème *m*, pyothorax *m*

empyrean [ˌempaɪ'rɪən] *n Literary* empyrée *m*

EMS [ˌiːem'es] *n Formerly Fin (abbr* **European Monetary System**) SME *m*

EMT [ˌiːem'tiː] *n Med (abbr* **emergency medical technician**) – technicien médical des services d'urgence

EMU [ˌiːem'juː] *n Pol & Fin (abbr* **economic and monetary union**) UME *f*

emu ['iːmjuː] *n Orn* émeu *m*

emulate ['emjʊleɪt] *vt (person, action)* imiter; *Comput* émuler, simuler

emulation [ˌemjʊ'leɪʃən] *n (gen) & Comput* émulation *f*

emulative ['emjʊlətɪv] *adj* plein d'émulation; **to be emulative of sb/sth** imiter qn/qch

emulator ['emjʊleɪtə(r)] *n Comput* émulateur *m*

emulsification [ɪˌmʌlsɪfɪ'keɪʃən] *n Chem* émulsionnement *m*

emulsifier [ɪ'mʌlsɪfaɪə(r)] *n Chem* émulsifiant *m*

emulsify [ɪ'mʌlsɪfaɪ] *vt Chem* émulsionner, émulsifier

emulsifying agent [ɪ'mʌlsɪfaɪɪŋ-] *n Chem* émulsifiant *m*

emulsion [ɪ'mʌlʃən] **1** *n* (**a**) *Chem & Phot* émulsion *f* (**b**) *(paint)* (peinture *f*) émulsion *f*

2 *vt* appliquer de la peinture émulsion sur

►► ***emulsion paint*** peinture *f* émulsion *f*

EN [ˌiː'en] *n Br (abbr* **enrolled nurse**) = infirmière diplômée

en [en] *n Typ* demi-cadratin *m*

►► ***en dash*** tiret *m* demi-cadratin

enable [ɪ'neɪbəl] *vt* (**a**) **to enable sb to do sth** permettre à qn de faire qch; *Law* habiliter *ou* autoriser qn à faire qch (**b**) *Comput (option)* activer

enabled [ɪ'neɪbəld] *adj Comput (option)* activé

enabler [ɪ'neɪblə(r)] *n* travailleur(euse) *m,f* social(e)

enabling [ɪ'neɪbəlɪŋ] *adj Law* habilitant

►► ***enabling act*** loi *f* d'habilitation; ***enabling legislation*** décret *m* d'application

enact [ɪ'nækt] *vt* (**a**) *Law (bill, law)* promulguer (**b**) *(scene, play)* jouer; **the political drama currently being enacted** le drame politique qui se joue *ou* se déroule actuellement

enactment [ɪ'næktmənt] *n* (**a**) *Law (of bill, law etc)* promulgation *f* (**b**) *(of play)* représentation *f*

enamel [ɪ'næməl] *(Br pt & pp* **enamelled,** *cont* **enamelling,** *Am pt & pp* **enameled,** *cont* **enameling**) **1** *n* (**a**) *Art (on clay, glass etc)* émail *m* (**b**) *(paint)* peinture *f* laquée *ou* vernie (**c**) *(on teeth)* émail *m*

2 *comp (mug, saucepan)* en émail, émaillé

3 *vt* émailler

►► ***enamel paint*** peinture *f* laquée *ou* vernie; ***enamel painting*** peinture *f* sur émail; ***enamel work*** émaillure *f*; *(painting on enamel)* peinture *f* sur émail

enamelled, *Am* **enameled** [ɪ'næməld] *adj* (**a**) *(covered with enamel → brick)* émaillé; *(→ tile)* vernissé; **enamelled saucepan** casserole *f* émaillée (**b**) *(painted)* peint en émail

enamelling, *Am* **enameling** [ɪ'næməlɪŋ] *n* émaillage *m*

enamelware [ɪ'næməlweə(r)] *n* ustensiles *mpl* en émail

enamour, *Am* **enamor** [ɪ'næmə(r)] *vt Literary* **his behaviour did little to enamour me of him** son comportement ne me l'a guère rendu plus sympathique

enamoured, *Am* **enamored** [ɪ'næməd] *adj Literary* **to be enamoured of** *(person)* être amoureux *ou* épris de; *(job, flat)* être enchanté *ou* ravi de; **to become enamoured of sb** s'éprendre de qn; **he wasn't exactly enamoured of our proposal** notre proposition ne l'enchantait guère

enantiomer [ɪ'næntɪəʊmə(r)] *n Biol & Chem* énantiomère *m*

enantiomorph [ɪ'næntɪəʊmɔːf] *n Biol & Chem* énantiomorphe *m*

en bloc [ɑ̃'blɒk] *adv* en bloc

enc. (**a**) *(written abbr* **enclosure**) PJ (**b**) *(written abbr* **enclosed**) ci-joint

encage [ɪn'keɪdʒ] *vt Formal (animal)* encager

encamp [ɪn'kæmp] **1** *vi* camper

2 *vt* faire camper; **to be encamped** camper

encampment [ɪn'kæmpmənt] *n* campement *m*

encapsulate [ɪn'kæpsjʊleɪt] *vt* (**a**) *Pharm* mettre en capsule (**b**) *(summarize)* résumer; **this film encapsulates the atmosphere of the times** ce film contient *ou* renferme l'atmosphère de l'époque

►► *Comput* ***encapsulated PostScript*** EPS *m*

encapsulation [ɪnˌkæpsjʊ'leɪʃən] *n Pharm* capsulage *m*

encase [ɪn'keɪs] *vt* (**a**) *(provide with covering)* envelopper; **encased in concrete** noyé dans le béton; **encased in chocolate** enrobé de chocolat (**b**) *(put in case)* encaisser (**in** dans)

encash [ɪn'kæʃ] *vt Br Fin (cheque)* encaisser

encashable [ɪn'kæʃəbəl] *adj Br Fin* encaissable

encashment [ɪn'kæʃmənt] *n Br Fin* encaissement *m*

encaustic [en'kɔːstɪk] **1** *adj (brick, tile)* émaillé; *Art (painting)* encaustique

2 *n Art* peinture *f* à l'encaustique

Enceladus [en'selədəs] **1** *pr n Myth* Encelade

2 *n Astron* Encelade *m*

encephalic [ˌenkə'fælɪk] *adj Anat* encéphalique

encephalitis [ˌensefə'laɪtɪs] *n Med* encéphalite *f*

►► ***encephalitis lethargica*** encéphalite *f* épidémique

encephalogram [en'sefələʊgræm] *n Med* encéphalogramme *m*

encephalograph [en'sefələʊgrɑːf] *n Med* encéphalographe *m*

encephalography [enˌsefə'lɒgrəfɪ] *n Med* (électro)encéphalographie *f*

encephalomyelitis [enˌsefələʊmaɪə'laɪtɪs] *n Med* encéphalomyélite *f*

encephalopathic [enˌsefələʊ'pæθɪk] *adj Med* encéphalopathique

encephalopathy [enˌsefə'lɒpəθɪ] *n Med* encéphalopathie *f*

enchain [ɪn'tʃeɪn] *vt Literary* enchaîner

enchainment [ɪn'tʃeɪnmənt] *n Literary* enchaînement *m*

enchant [ɪn'tʃɑːnt] *vt* (**a**) *(delight)* enchanter, ravir; **he was less than enchanted by the prospect** l'idée ne l'enchantait guère (**b**) *(put spell on)* enchanter, ensorceler

enchanted [ɪn'tʃɑːntɪd] *adj* (**a**) *(delighted)* enchanté (**with** de) (**b**) *(under a spell, magic)* enchanté, ensorcelé; **an enchanted wood** une forêt enchantée

enchanter [ɪn'tʃɑːntə(r)] *n* enchanteur *m*

►► *Bot* ***enchanter's nightshade*** circée *f*

enchanting [ɪn'tʃɑːntɪŋ] *adj (smile, scenery)* enchanteur; *(voice, person)* ravissant, charmant; *(idea, thought)* délicieux; **an enchanting little cottage** une charmante petite maison de campagne

enchantingly [ɪn'tʃɑːntɪŋlɪ] *adv (sing, play)* merveilleusement bien; **enchantingly pretty** ravissant

enchantment [ɪn'tʃɑːntmənt] *n* (**a**) *(delight)* enchantement *m*, ravissement *m*; **to fill sb with**

enchantment enchanter *ou* ravir qn (**b**) *(casting of spell)* enchantement *m*, ensorcellement *m*

enchantress [ɪn'tʃɑːntrɪs] *n* enchanteresse *f*

encharm [ɪn'tʃɑːm] *vt Literary* mettre sous un charme

enchilada [ˌentʃɪ'lɑːdə] *n Culin* enchilada *f*; *Fam* **big enchilada** *(person)* huile *f*; **the whole enchilada** *(everything)* tout le tremblement

encipher [ɪn'saɪfə(r)] *vt* chiffrer

encircle [ɪn'sɜːkəl] *vt* entourer; *Mil & Hunt* encercler, cerner; *Literary* **a reputation which encircles the world** une réputation qui a fait le tour du monde

encirclement [ɪn'sɜːkəlmənt] *n* encerclement *m*

►► *Mktg* ***encirclement attack*** attaque *f* par encerclement; *Mktg* ***encirclement strategy*** stratégie *f* d'encerclement

encircling [ɪn'sɜːkəlɪŋ] **1** *n* encerclement *m*

2 *adj Mil* **encircling movement** manœuvre *f* d'encerclement

encl. (**a**) *(written abbr* **enclosure**) PJ (**b**) *(written abbr* **enclosed**) ci-joint

enclasp [ɪn'klɑːsp] *vt Literary* embrasser, étreindre

enclave ['enkleɪv] *n* enclave *f*

enclitic [en'klɪtɪk] **1** *adj* (**a**) *Gram* enclitique (**b**) *Obst* se présentant obliquement

2 *n Gram* enclitique *f*

enclose [ɪn'kləʊz] *vt* (**a**) *(surround → with wall)* entourer, ceinturer; *(→ with fence)* clôturer; **a garden enclosed with** *or* **in** *or* **by high walls** un jardin entouré *ou* ceint de hauts murs (**b**) *(in letter)* joindre; **to enclose sth with a letter** joindre qch à une lettre; **I enclose a cheque for £20** je joins un chèque de 20 livres; **a letter enclosing a cheque** une lettre contenant un chèque

enclosed [ɪn'kləʊzd] **1** *adj* (**a**) *(area)* clos; **an enclosed space** un espace clos (**b**) *Com (cheque)* ci-joint, ci-inclus; **please find enclosed my CV** veuillez trouver ci-joint *ou* ci-inclus mon CV

2 *n* **the enclosed** *(in letter → cheque)* le chèque ci-joint; *(→ cash)* la somme ci-jointe

►► *Rel* ***enclosed order*** ordre *m* cloîtré

enclosure [ɪn'kləʊʒə(r)] *n* (**a**) *(enclosed area)* enclos *m*; **the lions' enclosure** *(in zoo)* l'enclos *m* des lions; **public enclosure** aire *f* réservée au public; *(at racecourse)* pesage *m* (**b**) *(in letter)* pièce *f* jointe *ou* annexée *ou* incluse; **enclosures** pièces *fpl* jointes (**c**) *(action)* action *f* de clôturer (**d**) *Br Hist* enclosure *f*

ENCLOSURE

L'apparition de la "clôture des champs", vers la fin du XVème siècle en Angleterre, a accéléré le passage d'une forme communautaire à une forme individualiste d'économie agraire, provoquant une importante crise sociale.

enclothe [ɪn'kləʊð] *vt Literary* revêtir (**with** de)

encloud [ɪn'klaʊd] *vt Literary (cover in clouds)* envelopper de nuages; *(cover, obscure)* voiler, assombrir; **the town was enclouded in smoke** la ville était voilée d'un nuage de fumée

encode [en'kəʊd] *vt* coder, chiffrer; *Comput* encoder

encoder [en'kəʊdə(r)] *n (gen) & Comput* encodeur *m*

encoding [en'kəʊdɪŋ] *n* codage *m*; *Comput* encodage *m*

encoffin [ɪn'kɒfɪn] *vt Literary* mettre en bière

encomiast [en'kəʊmɪæst] *n Literary* panégyriste *mf*, louangeur(euse) *m,f*

encomium [en'kəʊmjəm] *(pl* **encomiums** *or* **encomia** [-mjə]) *n Formal* panégyrique *m*

encompass [ɪn'kʌmpəs] *vt* (**a**) *(include)* englober, comprendre, regrouper; **their repertoire encompasses most musical styles** leur répertoire englobe la plupart des genres musicaux; **the state education system encompasses children of all ability levels** le système d'éducation nationale regroupe des enfants de tous les niveaux d'aptitude (**b**) *Formal (surround)* entourer, encercler

encore ['ɒŋkɔː(r)] **1** *exclam* **encore! encore!** bis! bis!

2 *n* bis *m*; **to call for an encore** bisser; **to give an encore** *(performer)* donner un bis; **to give an encore of a song** rechanter *ou* rejouer une chanson en bis; **how many encores were there?** combien de rappels y a-t-il eu?

3 *vt (singer, performer)* rappeler, bisser; *(song)* bisser

encounter [ɪn'kaʊntə(r)] **1** *vt (person, enemy)* rencontrer; *(difficulty, resistance, danger)* rencontrer, se heurter à

2 *n (gen) & Mil* rencontre *f*

►► *Psy* ***encounter group*** = séance de psychothérapie de groupe

encourage [ɪn'kʌrɪdʒ] *vt* (**a**) *(person)* encourager, inciter; **to encourage sb to do sth** encourager *ou* inciter qn à faire qch; **don't encourage him!** *(in bad behaviour)* ne l'encourage pas!; **to encourage sb in his/her belief that...** renforcer qn dans sa conviction que..., conforter qn dans son idée que...

(**b**) *(support → good works)* appuyer; *(→ the arts, commerce)* favoriser; *(→ belief)* encourager; **they encouraged their daughter's ambition** ils ont encouragé leur fille à réaliser ses ambitions

encouragement [ɪn'kʌrɪdʒmənt] *n* encouragement *m*; **to give sb encouragement, to give encouragement to sb** donner des encouragements à *ou* encourager qn; **to get** *or* **to receive encouragement from sb** recevoir des encouragements de la part de qn; **all he needs is a bit of encouragement** tout ce qu'il lui faut c'est un peu d'encouragement; **without your encouragement** sans vos encouragements; **shouts/words of encouragement** cris *mpl*/mots *mpl* d'encouragement

encouraging [ɪn'kʌrɪdʒɪŋ] *adj* encourageant; *(smile, words)* d'encouragement; **he wasn't very encouraging to me** il ne s'est pas montré très encourageant à mon égard; **it is encouraging to see the progress that has been made** c'est encourageant de constater les progrès qui ont été faits

encouragingly [ɪn'kʌrɪdʒɪŋlɪ] *adv (smile, speak)* de manière encourageante; **encouragingly, a working party has been set up** fait encourageant, un groupe de travail a été mis en place

encrimson [ɪn'krɪmzən] *vt Literary* empourprer

►**encroach on, encroach upon** [ɪn'krəʊtʃ-] *vt insep (land, rights, time)* empiéter sur; **the sea is encroaching on the land** la mer gagne sur les terres; **the new buildings are encroaching on the countryside** les nouveaux bâtiments envahissent la campagne; *Fig* **to encroach on sb's territory** marcher *ou* empiéter sur les plates-bandes de qn

encroaching [ɪn'krəʊtʃɪŋ] *adj (land)* qui empiète; *(sea)* qui gagne sur les terres; *(person)* usurpateur

encroachment [ɪn'krəʊtʃmənt] *n (on land, rights, time)* empiétement *m*; *(by sea, river)* envahissement *m*, *Spec* ingression *f*; *(by buildings)* envahissement *m*

encrust [ɪn'krʌst] *vt (with jewels)* incruster; *(with mud, snow, ice)* couvrir; **to be encrusted with sth** être incrusté *ou* couvert *ou* recouvert de qch

encrustation [ɪnˌkrʌst'eɪʃən] *n* incrustation *f*

encrypt [en'krɪpt] *n Comput* crypter, chiffrer

encryption [en'krɪpʃən] *n Comput* chiffrement *m*

►► ***encryption key*** clé *f* de chiffrement

encumber [ɪn'kʌmbə(r)] *vt Formal (person, room)* encombrer (**with** de); **encumbered with too many clothes** empêtré dans ses vêtements; **the party remains encumbered by the legacy of its Stalinist past** le parti pâtit encore du legs encombrant de son passé stalinien

►► *Law* ***encumbered estate*** *(with debts)* propriété *f* grevée de dettes; *(with mortgage)* propriété *f* hypothéquée

encumbrance [ɪn'kʌmbrəns] *n Formal* (**a**) *(hindrance)* embarras *m*; **to be an encumbrance to sb** *(physically)* encombrer qn; *(financially)* être à la charge de qn; **to be an encumbrance to sb's plans** gêner les projets de qn; **the suitcase was something of an encumbrance** la valise était plutôt encombrante (**b**) *Law (of inheritance)* charges *fpl*; **to free an estate from encumbrances** dégrever une propriété

encyclical [ɪn'sɪklɪkəl] *Rel* **1** *adj* encyclique

2 *n* encyclique *f*

encyclopaedia, encyclopaedic *etc* = **encyclopedia, encyclopedic** *etc*

encyclopedia [ɪnˌsaɪkləʊ'piːdjə] *n* encyclopédie *f*

encyclopedic [ɪnˌsaɪkləʊ'piːdɪk] *adj* encyclopédique

encyclopedist [ɪnˌsaɪkləʊ'piːdɪst] *n* encyclopédiste *mf*

encyst [en'sɪst] *vi Biol* s'enkyster

encystation [ˌensɪs'teɪʃən] *n Biol* enkystement *m*

encysted [en'sɪstəd] *adj Biol* enkysté

encystment [en'sɪstmənt] *n Biol* enkystement *m*

END [end]

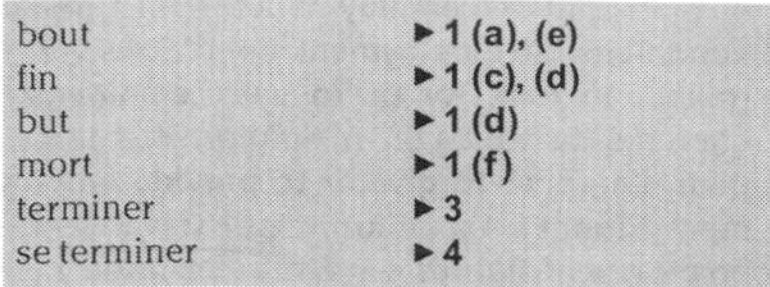

bout	►1 (a), (e)
fin	►1 (c), (d)
but	►1 (d)
mort	►1 (f)
terminer	►3
se terminer	►4

1 *n* (**a**) *(furthermost part, tip, edge)* bout *m*, extrémité *f*; **at the end of the garden** au bout *ou* fond du jardin; **it's at the other end of town** c'est à l'autre bout de la ville; **at the northern end of the park/town/lake** à l'extrémité nord du parc/de la ville/du lac; **the rope is frayed at this end/at that end/at one end** la corde est effilochée à ce bout-ci/à ce bout-là/au bout; **at either end of the political spectrum** aux deux extrémités de l'éventail politique; *Tel* **at the other end of the line** au bout de la ligne; **from one end of the country/of the town to the other** d'un bout à l'autre du pays/de la ville; **they live in the end house** ils habitent la dernière maison, au bout de la rue; **third from the end** troisième en partant de la fin; *Sport* **to change ends** changer de côté

(**b**) *(area, aspect)* côté *m*; **how are things (at) your end?** comment ça va de ton côté *ou* pour toi?; **what's the weather like at your end?** *(in phone conversation)* quel temps fait-il chez vous?, quel temps est-ce que vous avez?; **the marketing/manufacturing end of the operation** le côté marketing/fabrication de l'opération, tout ce qui est marketing/fabrication; **to come to the end of the road** arriver au bout de la route; *Fig (in one's career)* arriver au bout de sa carrière; *(in one's life)* arriver au bout de sa vie; *(be unable to make progress)* être dans une impasse; **this is the end of the road** *or* **line** c'est fini; *Fig* **to get hold of the wrong end of the stick** mal comprendre; *Br very Fam* **to get** *or* **have one's end away** *(have sex)* tirer un *ou* son coup; **to go to the ends of the earth** aller jusqu'au bout du monde; **to keep one's end of the bargain** tenir parole; **to keep one's end up** tenir bon; **he doesn't know** *or* **can't tell one end of a word processor from the other** il ne sait même pas à quoi ressemble un traitement de texte; **to make (both) ends meet** *(financially)* joindre les deux bouts

(**c**) *(conclusion, finish)* fin *f*; **at the end of July/of spring/of the year** à la fin du mois de juillet/du printemps/de l'année; **from beginning to end** du début à la fin, de bout en bout; **to read to the end of a book, to read a book to the end** lire un livre jusqu'au bout *ou* jusqu'à la fin; **I waited until the end of the meeting** j'ai attendu la fin de la réunion; **to be at an end** être terminé *ou* fini; **my patience is at** *or* **has come to an end** ma patience est à bout; **to be at the end of one's resources/one's strength** avoir épuisé ses ressources/ses forces; *Fin* **end of the financial year** clôture *f* de l'exercice; **to bring sth to an end** *(meeting)* clore qch; *(situation)* mettre fin à qch; *(speech)* achever qch; **to come to an end** s'achever, prendre fin; **to draw to an end** arriver *ou* toucher à sa fin; **to put an end to sth** mettre fin à qch; **we want an end to the war** nous voulons que cette guerre cesse *ou* prenne fin; **the end of the world** la fin du monde; *Fam* **it's not the end of the world!** ce n'est pas la fin du monde!; **until the end of time** jusqu'à la fin des temps; **the end is nigh** la fin est proche; **and that was the end of that** et ça s'est terminé comme ça; **let that be an end to the matter!** qu'on en finisse là!, qu'on n'en parle plus!; *Fam* **he's/you're the end!** *(impossible)* il est/tu es incroyable!; *(extremely funny)* il est/tu es trop (drôle)!; **to come to a bad end** mal finir; *Fam* **end of story!** *(stop arguing)* plus de discussions!; *(I don't want to talk about it)* un point, c'est tout!; **we'll never hear the end of it** on n'a pas fini d'en entendre parler; **is there no end to his talents?** a-t-il donc tous les talents?, n'y a-t-il pas de limite à ses talents?

(**d**) *(aim)* but *m*, fin *f*; **to achieve** *or* **to attain one's end** atteindre son but; **with this end in view** *or* **mind, to this end** dans ce but, à cette fin; *Formal* **to what end?** dans quel but?, à quelle fin?; **for political ends** à des fins politiques; **an end in itself** une fin en soi; **the end justifies the means** la fin justifie les moyens

(**e**) *(remnant → of cloth, rope)* bout *m*; *(→ of loaf)* croûton *m*; *(→ of candle)* bout; *(→ of cigarette)* bout, mégot *m*

(**f**) *Euph or Literary (death)* mort *f*; **to meet one's end** trouver la mort; **to be nearing one's end** être à l'article de la mort; **I was with him at the end** j'étais auprès de lui dans ses derniers moments

(**g**) *Sport (in American football)* moitié *f* de terrain

(**h**) *Sport (in bowls, curling)* manche *f*

2 *comp (house, seat, table)* du bout

3 *vt (speech, novel)* terminer, conclure; *(meeting, discussion)* clore; *(day)* terminer, finir; *(war, speculation, relationship)* mettre fin *ou* un terme à; *(work, task)* terminer, finir, achever; **she ended the letter with a promise to write again soon** elle a terminé la lettre en promettant de récrire bientôt; **the war to end all wars** la der des ders; **the joke to end all jokes** la meilleure blague qu'on ait jamais entendue; **he decided to end it all** *(life, relationship)* il décida d'en finir; **she ended her days in a retirement home** elle a fini ses jours dans une maison de retraite

4 *vi (story, film)* finir, se terminer, s'achever; *(path, road etc)* se terminer, s'arrêter; *(season, holiday)* se terminer, toucher à sa fin; **to end happily** *(of story)* avoir une fin heureuse, bien se terminer; **how** *or* **where will it all end?** comment tout cela finira-t-il *ou* se terminera-t-il?; **where does society end and the individual begin?** où s'arrête la société et où commence l'individu?; **to end in a point** se terminer en pointe; **the discussion ended in an argument** la discussion s'est terminée en dispute; **to end in failure/divorce** se solder par un échec/un divorce; **the word ends in -ed** le mot se termine par *ou* en -ed; **the book ends with a quotation** le livre se termine par une citation; **it'll end in tears** ça va mal finir

5 end on *adv* par le bout

6 end to end *adv* (**a**) *(with ends adjacent)* bout à bout

(**b**) *(from one end to another)* d'un bout à l'autre

7 from end to end *adv* d'un bout à l'autre

8 in the end *adv* finalement; **we got there in the end** finalement nous y sommes arrivés, nous avons fini par y arriver; **he always pays me back in the end** il finit toujours par me rendre ce qu'il me doit; **you'll get used to it in the end** tu finiras par t'y habituer

9 no end *adv Fam* **it upset her/cheered her up no end** ça l'a bouleversée/ravie à un point (inimaginable); **it helped me no end** ça m'a énormément aidé

10 no end of *adj Fam* **it'll do you no end of good** cela vous fera un bien fou; **to have no end of trouble doing sth** avoir énormément de mal *ou* un mal fou *ou* un mal de chien à faire qch; **to think no end of sb** porter qn aux nues; **we met no end of interesting people** on a rencontré des tas de gens intéressants

11 on end *adv* (**a**) *(upright)* debout; **to stand sth on end** mettre qch debout; **her hair was standing on end** elle avait les cheveux dressés sur la tête

(**b**) *(in succession)* entier; **for hours/days on end** pendant des heures entières/des jours entiers; **for four hours on end** pendant quatre heures de suite *ou* d'affilée

►► *Rail* ***end carriage*** wagon *m* de queue; *Comput* ***end key*** touche *f* fin; *Am Sport* ***end line*** ligne *f* de fond; *Tech* ***end piece*** embout *m*; ***end product*** *Ind & Com* produit *m* final; *Fig* résultat *m*; ***end result*** résultat *m* final; *Am* ***end run*** faux-fuyant *m*; ***end table*** bout *m* de canapé; *TV & Cin* ***end titles*** générique *m* de fin; ***end zone*** *(in American football)* zone *f* d'en-but

►**end off** *vt sep* terminer; **they ended off the evening with a dance** ils ont terminé la soirée par une danse

►**end up** *vi* finir; **they ended up in Manchester** ils se sont retrouvés à Manchester; **to end up in hospital/in prison** finir à l'hôpital/en prison; **if you keep driving like that, you're going to end up killing yourself** si tu continues à conduire comme ça, tu finiras par te tuer; **to end up doing sth** finir par faire qch; **to end up (as) the boss/on the dole** finir patron/chômeur; **I wonder what he'll end up as/how he'll end up** je me demande ce qu'il deviendra/comment il finira

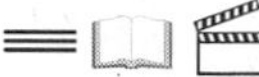

'The End of the Affair' *Greene, Jordan* 'La Fin d'une liaison'

end-all *see* **be-all**

endanger [ɪn'deɪndʒə(r)] *vt (life, country)* mettre en danger; *(health, reputation, future, chances)* compromettre

►► ***endangered species*** espèce *f* en voie de disparition

end-consumer *n Com* utilisateur *m* final; *(of foodstuffs)* consommateur *m* final, utilisateur *m* final

endear [ɪn'dɪə(r)] *vt* faire aimer; **what endears him to me** ce qui le rend cher à mes yeux; **to endear oneself to sb** se faire aimer de qn; **the Chancellor's decision did not endear him to the voters** la décision du Chancelier ne lui a pas gagné la faveur des électeurs

endearing [ɪn'dɪərɪŋ] *adj (personality, person)* attachant; *(smile)* engageant; **it's a very endearing characteristic of his** c'est un trait de caractère qui le rend très attachant

endearingly [ɪn'dɪərɪŋlɪ] *adv* de manière attachante; *(smile)* de manière engageante

endearment [ɪn'dɪəmənt] *n* **endearments, words of endearment** mots *mpl* tendres; **term of endearment** terme *m* affectueux

endeavour, *Am* **endeavor** [ɪn'devə(r)] *Formal* **1** *n* effort *m*; **to wish sb good luck in their endeavours** souhaiter bonne chance à qn dans ses entreprises; **to make every endeavour to obtain sth** faire tout son possible pour obtenir qch; **in an endeavour to stop the strike** en tentant de mettre fin à la grève; **despite her best endeavours** malgré tous ses efforts; **to use one's best endeavours to do sth** employer tous ses efforts à faire qch; **a new field of human endeavour** une nouvelle perspective pour l'homme; **one of the greatest achievements of human endeavour** une des plus belles victoires *ou* conquêtes de l'homme

2 *vi* **to endeavour to do sth** s'efforcer *ou* essayer de faire qch

endemic [en'demɪk] **1** *adj Bot, Med & Fig* endémique; *Fig* **the problem is endemic to the region** c'est un problème endémique dans la région

2 *n Med* endémie *f*

endemically [en'demɪklɪ] *adv Bot, Med & Fig* endémiquement, d'une manière endémique

endemicity [,endə'mɪsɪtɪ] *n Bot, Med & Fig* endémicité *f*

endemism ['endəmɪzəm] *n Bot, Med & Fig* endémisme *m*

endermic [en'dɜ:mɪk] *adj Physiol* transdermique

endgame ['endgeɪm] *n Chess* fin *f* de partie; *Mktg* objectif *m* (marketing)

'Endgame' *Beckett* 'Fin de partie'

ending ['endɪŋ] *n* (**a**) *(of nuclear tests etc)* cessation *f*; *(of restrictions)* levée *f* (**b**) *(of story, book)* fin *f*; **a story with a happy/sad ending** une histoire qui finit bien/mal (**c**) *Ling* terminaison *f*; **accusative/genitive ending** désinence *f* de l'accusatif/du génitif

endive ['endaɪv] *n* (**a**) *(curly-leaved)* (chicorée *f*) frisée *f* (**b**) *esp Am (chicory)* endive *f*

endless ['endlɪs] *adj* (**a**) *(speech, road, journey, list, job)* interminable, sans fin; *(patience)* sans bornes, infini; *(resources)* inépuisable, infini; *(desert)* infini; **it's an endless task, it's endless** cela n'en finit pas; **after what seemed like an endless wait** après une attente qui m'a/lui a/*etc* semblé une éternité; **the possibilities are endless** les possibilités sont innombrables; **to ask endless questions** poser des questions à n'en plus finir (**b**) *Tech (belt, screw)* sans fin

endlessly ['endlɪslɪ] *adv (speak)* continuellement, sans cesse; *(extend)* à perte de vue, interminablement; **to be endlessly patient/generous** être d'une patience/générosité sans bornes

endlessness ['endlɪsnɪs] *n* perpétuité *f*, durée *f* infinie; **the endlessness of her complaints** ses plaintes sans fin

endmost ['endməʊst] *adj* du bout

endnote ['endnəʊt] *n Comput* note *f* de fin de document, NfD *f*

endocardiac [,endəʊ'kɑ:dɪæk], **endocardial** [,endəʊ'kɑ:dɪəl] *adj Med* endocardiaque

endocarditis [,endəʊkɑ:'daɪtɪs] *n Med* endocardite *f*

endocardium [,endəʊ'kɑ:dɪəm] *n Anat* endocarde *m*

endocarp ['endəʊkɑ:p] *n Bot* endocarpe *m*

endocranium [,endəʊ'kreɪnɪəm] (*pl* **endocraniums** *or* **endocrania** [-nɪə]) *n Anat* endocrâne *m*

endocrine ['endəʊkraɪn] *adj Physiol (disorders, system)* endocrinien

►► ***endocrine gland*** glande *f* endocrine

endocrinologist [,endəʊkraɪ'nɒlədʒɪst] *n Med* endocrinologue *mf*, endocrinologiste *mf*

endocrinology [,endəʊkraɪ'nɒlədʒɪ] *n Med* endocrinologie *f*

endoderm ['endəʊdɜ:m] *n Biol* endoderme *m*, endoblaste *m*

endodermal [,endəʊ'dɜ:məl] *adj Biol* endodermique, endoblastique

endodermis [,endəʊ'dɜ:mɪs] *n Bot* endoderme *m*

end-of-month *adj* de fin de mois

►► *Fin* ***end-of-month balance*** solde *m* de fin de mois; *Fin* ***end-of-month payments*** échéances *fpl* de fin de mois; *Fin* ***end-of-month settlement*** liquidation *f* de fin de mois; *Fin* ***end-of-month statement*** relevé *m* de fin de mois

end-of-year *adj* de fin d'année; *Fin* de fin d'exercice

►► *Fin* ***end-of-year balance sheet*** bilan *m* de l'exercice; *Com* ***end-of-year bonus*** gratification *f* de fin d'année

endogamous [en'dɒgəməs] *adj* endogame

endogamy [en'dɒgəmɪ] *n* endogamie *f*

endogenetic [,endəʊdʒə'netɪk] *adj Biol & Bot* endogène

►► *Geol* ***endogenetic rock*** roche *f* endogène

endogenous [en'dɒdʒɪnəs] *adj Biol, Bot & Med* endogène

endometriosis [,endəʊmi:trɪ'əʊsɪs] *n Med* endométriose *f*

endometritis [,endəʊmɪ'traɪtɪs] *n Med* endométrite *f*

endometrium [,endəʊ'mi:trɪəm] (*pl* **endometria** [-trɪə]) *n Anat* endomètre *m*

endomorph ['endəʊmɔ:f] *n* endomorphe *m*

endomorphic [,endəʊ'mɔ:fɪk] *adj* endomorphique

endomorphism [,endəʊ'mɔ:fɪzəm] *n Geol* endomorphisme *m*

endonuclease [,endəʊ'nju:klɪeɪz] *n Biol & Chem* endonucléase *f*

endoparasite [,endəʊ'pærəsaɪt] *n Zool* endoparasite *m*

endoplasm ['endəʊ,plæzəm] *n Biol* endoplasme *m*

endoplasmic [,endəʊ'plæzmɪk] *adj Biol* entoplasmique

►► *Biol* ***endoplasmic reticulum*** ergastoplasme *m*

endorphin [en'dɔ:fɪn] *n Physiol* endorphine *f*

endorse [ɪn'dɔ:s] *vt* (**a**) *(cheque)* endosser; *(document → sign)* apposer sa signature sur; *(→ annotate)* apposer une remarque sur; *(passport)* viser; *Fin (bill of exchange)* avaliser, endosser, donner son aval à

(**b**) *Br Law* **to endorse a driving licence** faire état d'une infraction sur un permis de conduire

(**c**) *(approve → action, decision)* approuver; *(→ opinion)* soutenir, adhérer à; *(→ appeal, candidature)* appuyer, soutenir; **I endorse all you have done** j'approuve tout ce que vous avez fait
(**d**) *(product)* faire de la publicité pour; **sportswear endorsed by top athletes** des vêtements de sport recommandés par des sportifs de haut niveau; **should footballers be seen to endorse alcoholic drinks?** est-il acceptable que les footballeurs fassent de la publicité pour des boissons alcoolisées?

endorsee [ˌendɔːˈsiː] *n Fin* endossataire *mf*

endorsement [ɪnˈdɔːsmənt] *n* (**a**) *(of cheque)* endossement *m*, endos *m*; *(of document → signature)* signature *f*; *(→ annotation)* remarque *f*; *(of bill)* aval *m*; *(on passport)* mention *f* spéciale; *(in insurance)* avenant *m*
(**b**) *Br Law (on driving licence)* = infraction dont il est fait état sur le permis de conduire
(**c**) *(approval → of action, decision)* approbation *f*; *(→ of claim, candidature)* appui *m*; **it was the ultimate endorsement of his ideas** ce fut la reconnaissance ultime *ou* la consécration de sa théorie
(**d**) *(of product)* **the film star has made a fortune from her endorsement of cosmetic products** cette vedette du cinéma a gagné une fortune en faisant de la publicité pour des cosmétiques
►► *Fin* ***endorsement fee*** commission *f* d'endos

endorser [ɪnˈdɔːsə(r)] *n Fin (of document, cheque)* endosseur *m*, cessionnaire *mf*; *(of bill of exchange)* avaliste *mf*, avaliseur *m*

endoscope [ˈendəʊskəʊp] *n Med* endoscope *m*

endoscopic [ˌendəʊˈskɒpɪk] *adj Med* endoscopique

endoscopy [enˈdɒskəpɪ] *n Med* endoscopie *f*

endoskeleton [ˌendəʊˈskelɪtən] *n Zool* endosquelette *m*

endosperm [ˈendəʊspɜːm] *n Bot* endosperme *m*

endothelial [ˌendəʊˈθiːlɪəl] *adj Physiol* endothélial

endothelium [ˌendəʊˈθiːlɪəm] *n Anat* endothélium *m*

endothermic [ˌendəʊˈθɜːmɪk] *adj Chem* endothermique

endotoxin [ˌendəʊˈtɒksɪn] *n Med* endotoxine *f*

endow [ɪnˈdaʊ] *vt* (**a**) *(person, institution)* doter; *(university chair, hospital ward)* fonder; **to endow a hospice with £1 million** doter un hospice d'un million de livres (**b**) *(usu passive)* **to be endowed with sth** être doté de qch; **endowed with great talents** doué de grands talents; **a woman endowed with great beauty** une femme dotée d'une grande beauté; *Fam Hum* **to be well endowed** *(man, woman)* avoir tout ce qu'il faut

endowment [ɪnˈdaʊmənt] *n* (**a**) *Fin (action, money)* dotation *f*
(**b**) *(usu pl) Formal (talent, gift)* don *m*, talent *m*; **man's natural endowments** les qualités naturelles de l'être humain
►► ***endowment assurance*** assurance *f* en cas de vie, assurance *f* à dotation; ***endowment fund*** fonds *m* de dotation; ***endowment insurance*** assurance *f* en cas de vie, assurance *f* à dotation; ***endowment mortgage*** prêt-logement *m* lié à une assurance-vie; ***endowment policy*** assurance *f* en cas de vie, assurance *f* à dotation

endpaper [ˈendˌpeɪpə] *n Typ* garde *f*, page *f* de garde

end-stage *adj Med (disease, patient)* en phase terminale

end-to-end **1** *adj (game, play)* passionnant de bout en bout
2 *adv (arranged, laid, connected)* bout à bout

endue [ɪnˈdjuː] *vt Literary* doter

endurable [ɪnˈdjʊərəbəl] *adj* supportable, endurable

endurance [ɪnˈdjʊərəns] *n* endurance *f*; **to have great powers of endurance** avoir une grande endurance; **it is beyond endurance** c'est insupportable; **she was tried beyond endurance** elle a été éprouvée au-delà des limites du supportable
►► *Sport* ***endurance race*** course *f* d'endurance; ***endurance test*** épreuve *f* d'endurance; *Fig* **this is a real endurance test** c'est une véritable épreuve d'endurance

endure [ɪnˈdjʊə(r)] **1** *vt (bear → hardship)* endurer, subir; *(→ pain)* endurer; *(→ person, stupidity, laziness)* supporter, souffrir; **it was more than she could endure** c'était plus qu'elle ne pouvait supporter; **she can't endure being kept waiting** elle ne supporte *ou* ne souffre pas qu'on la fasse attendre; **he can't endure seeing** *or* **to see children mistreated** il ne supporte pas qu'on maltraite des enfants
2 *vi Formal (relationship, ceasefire, fame)* durer; *(memory)* rester; **he won't be able to endure for long in this weather** il ne résistera *ou* ne tiendra pas longtemps avec un temps pareil; **their names will endure forever in our hearts** leurs noms resteront pour toujours dans nos cœurs

enduring [ɪnˈdjʊərɪŋ] *adj (friendship, fame, peace)* durable; *(democracy, dictatorship)* qui dure; *(epidemic, suffering)* tenace; *(actor, politician)* qui jouit d'une grande longévité *(en tant qu'acteur, homme politique etc)*

'Enduring Love' *McEwan* 'Délire d'amour'

---

enduringly [ɪnˈdjʊərɪŋlɪ] *adv* de manière durable

enduro [ɪnˈdjʊərəʊ] *n Sport* enduro *m*

end-user *n Com* utilisateur *m* final; *(of foodstuffs)* consommateur *m* final, utilisateur *m* final
►► *Mktg* ***end-user specialist*** spécialiste *mf* du marché utilisateur final

endways [ˈendweɪz], **endwise** [ˈendwaɪz] *adv* (**a**) *(end up)* de chant, debout; **endways on** avec le bout en avant; **I could only see the object endways on** je ne voyais que la face latérale de l'objet; **the house stands endways on to the road** la maison est perpendiculaire à la route
(**b**) *(end to end)* bout à bout; **to put things together endways** mettre des choses bout à bout
(**c**) *(lengthways)* longitudinalement; **we'll have to take it through endways** il faudra que nous le passions dans le sens de la longueur

ENE *(written abbr* **east-north-east***)* E-NE

enema [ˈenɪmə] *n Med (act)* lavement *m*; *(liquid)* produit *m* à lavement; **to give sb an enema** administrer un lavement à qn

enemy [ˈenɪmɪ] *(pl* **enemies***)* **1** *n* (**a**) *(foe)* ennemi(e) *m,f*; **to make enemies** se faire des ennemis; **I made an enemy of her** je m'en suis fait une ennemie; **to be one's own worst enemy** se nuire à soi-même (**b**) *Mil* **the enemy** l'ennemi *m*; **the enemy was** *or* **were advancing** l'ennemi avançait; **boredom is the enemy** l'ennui, voilà l'ennemi
2 *comp (forces, attack, missile, country)* ennemi; *(advance, strategy)* de l'ennemi
►► ***enemy alien*** ressortissant(e) *m,f* d'un pays ennemi; ***enemy fire*** feu *m* de l'ennemi

enemy-occupied *adj (territory)* occupé par l'ennemi

energetic [ˌenəˈdʒetɪk] *adj (person, measures)* énergique; *(music)* vif, rapide; *(campaigner, supporter)* enthousiaste; **to feel energetic** se sentir d'attaque *ou* en forme; **after a very energetic day** après une journée très chargée; **do you feel energetic enough for a game of tennis?** te sens-tu d'attaque pour une partie de tennis?; **I don't want to do anything too energetic** je ne veux rien faire qui demande trop d'énergie; **it's a very energetic game** c'est un jeu où l'on se dépense beaucoup

energetically [ˌenəˈdʒetɪkəlɪ] *adv* énergiquement

energetics [ˌenəˈdʒetɪks] *n (UNCOUNT) Phys* énergétique *f*

energize, -ise [ˈenədʒaɪz] *vt (person)* donner de l'énergie à, stimuler; *Elec* alimenter

energizer [ˈenədʒaɪzə(r)] *n Elec* excitateur *m*

energizing [ˈenədʒaɪzɪŋ] *adj (food, effect)* énergisant

energy [ˈenədʒɪ] *(pl* **energies***)* **1** *n* (**a**) *(vitality)* énergie *f*; **to be/to feel full of energy** être/se sentir plein d'énergie; **to have no energy** se sentir sans énergie; **to conserve one's energy** économiser son énergie; **she didn't have the energy for an argument** elle n'avait pas assez d'énergie pour se disputer; **glucose is full of energy** le glucose est très énergétique
(**b**) *(effort)* énergie *f*; **to devote** *or* **to apply (all) one's energy** *or* **energies to sth** consacrer toute son énergie *ou* toutes ses énergies à qch; **to shout/work with all one's energy** crier/travailler de toutes ses forces
(**c**) *Phys* énergie *f*; **kinetic energy** énergie *f* cinétique
(**d**) *(power)* énergie *f*; **to save** *or* **to conserve energy** faire des économies d'énergie; **to consume energy** consommer de l'énergie; **a source of energy** une source d'énergie; **Minister of** *or* **Secretary (of State) for Energy** ministre *m* de l'Énergie
2 *comp (conservation, consumption)* d'énergie; *(supplies, programme, level, resource)* énergétique
►► ***energy audit*** = évaluation de la quantité d'énergie consommée dans un bâtiment; ***energy crisis*** crise *f* énergétique *ou* de l'énergie; ***energy gap*** pénurie *f* d'énergie

energy-giving [-ˌgɪvɪŋ] *adj* énergétique

energy-saving *adj (device)* pour économiser l'énergie

enervate [ˈenəveɪt] *vt* amollir, débiliter

enervating [ˈenəveɪtɪŋ] *adj* amollissant, débilitant

enervation [ˌenəˈveɪʃən] *n (state)* mollesse *f*

enfant terrible [ˌɑ̃fɑ̃teˈriːblə] *n* enfant *mf* terrible; **the enfant terrible of French literature** l'enfant terrible de la littérature française

enfeeble [ɪnˈfiːbəl] *vt* affaiblir

enfeeblement [ɪnˈfiːbəlmənt] *n* affaiblissement *m*

enfilade [ˌenfɪˈleɪd] *Mil* **1** *n* enfilade *f*
2 *vt* prendre en enfilade

enfold [ɪnˈfəʊld] *vt (embrace)* envelopper (**in** dans); **to enfold sb in one's arms** étreindre qn, entourer qn de ses bras

enforce [ɪnˈfɔːs] *vt (policy, decision)* mettre en œuvre, appliquer; *(law)* mettre en vigueur; *(of police)* faire exécuter; *(one's rights)* faire valoir; *(one's will, discipline)* faire respecter; *(contract)* faire exécuter; **such a law would be impossible to enforce** une telle loi serait impossible à appliquer; **to enforce compliance with the law/regulations** faire respecter la loi/les réglementations; **to enforce obedience** se faire obéir

enforceability [ɪnˌfɔːsəˈbɪlɪtɪ] *n* **the enforceability of a law** la possibilité d'appliquer une loi

enforceable [ɪnˈfɔːsəbəl] *adj* exécutoire

enforced [ɪnˈfɔːst] *adj* forcé

enforcement [ɪnˈfɔːsmənt] *n (of policy, decision)* mise *f* en œuvre; *(of law)* mise *f* en vigueur; *(by the police)* mise *f* à exécution; *(of one's rights)* exercice *m*; *(of one's will, discipline)* respect *m*; *(of contract)* exécution *f*

enforcer [ɪnˈfɔːsə(r)] *n Am* agent *m* de police

enfranchise [ɪnˈfræntʃaɪz] *vt* (**a**) *(give vote to)* admettre au suffrage, accorder le droit de vote à (**b**) *(free → slave)* affranchir

enfranchisement [ɪnˈfræntʃɪzmənt] *n* (**a**) *Pol (of citizen)* admission *f* au suffrage (**b**) *(freeing → of slave)* affranchissement *m*

ENG [ˌiːenˈdʒiː] *n (abbr* **electronic news gathering***)* journalisme *m* électronique de télévision

engage [ɪnˈgeɪdʒ] **1** *vt* (**a**) *(occupy, involve)* **to engage sb in conversation** *(talk to)* discuter avec qn; *(begin talking to)* engager la conversation avec qn; **to be engaged in doing sth** être occupé à faire qch; **while we were engaged in conversation** pendant que nous discutions
(**b**) *Formal (employ → staff)* engager; *(→ lawyer)* engager les services de; *(→ workers)* embaucher; **to engage the services of sb** employer les services de qn
(**c**) *Formal (attract, draw → interest, attention)* attirer; *(→ sympathy)* susciter
(**d**) *Aut & Tech* engager; **to engage the clutch** embrayer; **to engage a gear** engager une vitesse; **to engage gear** embrayer
(**e**) *Mil* **to engage the enemy** engager (le combat avec) l'ennemi
2 *vi* (**a**) *(take part)* **to engage in sth** *(game)* prendre part à qch, participer à qch; *(activity)* se livrer à qch; **to be engaged in research** faire de la recherche; **to be engaged in warfare** être en guerre; **to engage in conversation** discuter; **to engage in sex** avoir des relations sexuelles
(**b**) *Mil* **to engage in battle with the enemy** engager le combat avec l'ennemi

(**c**) *Aut & Tech* s'engager; *(cogs)* s'engrener; *(machine part)* s'enclencher
(**d**) *Formal (promise)* **to engage to do sth** s'engager à faire qch

engaged [ɪn'geɪdʒd] *adj* (**a**) *(couple)* fiancé; **to be engaged to be married** être fiancé; **to get engaged** se fiancer; **the engaged couple** les fiancés *mpl*
(**b**) *(busy, occupied)* occupé; **I'm otherwise engaged** je suis déjà pris; **to be engaged in discussions with sb** être engagé dans des discussions avec qn; **to be engaged in a conversation** être en pleine discussion
(**c**) *Br (telephone)* occupé; **the line** *or* **number is engaged** la ligne est occupée; **I got the engaged tone** ça sonnait occupé
(**d**) *(toilet)* occupé

engagement [ɪn'geɪdʒmənt] *n* (**a**) *(betrothal)* fiançailles *fpl*; **they announced their engagement** ils ont annoncé leurs fiançailles
(**b**) *(appointment)* rendez-vous *m*; **dinner engagement** rendez-vous *m* pour dîner; **public engagement** engagement *m* à paraître en public; **she has many social engagements** elle est très demandée; **to have an engagement** être pris, être occupé; **he couldn't come, owing to a prior** *or* **previous engagement** il n'a pas pu venir car il était déjà pris
(**c**) *Mil* engagement *m*
(**d**) *Aut & Tech* engagement *m*
(**e**) *(recruitment)* engagement *m*, embauche *f*
(**f**) *Formal (promise)* obligation *f*, engagement *m*
(**g**) *(for actor, performer)* engagement *m*, contrat *m*
►► ***engagement diary*** agenda *m*; ***engagement party*** (fête *f* de) fiançailles *fpl*; ***engagement ring*** bague *f* de fiançailles

engaging [ɪn'geɪdʒɪŋ] *adj (smile, manner, tone)* engageant; *(person, personality)* aimable, attachant

engagingly [ɪn'geɪdʒɪŋlɪ] *adv* de manière engageante

engarland [ɪn'gɑːlənd] *vt Literary* enguirlander

engender [ɪn'dʒendə(r)] *vt* engendrer, créer; **to engender sth in sb** engendrer qch chez qn

engine ['endʒɪn] **1** *n* (**a**) *(in car, plane)* moteur *m*; *(in ship)* machine *f*; *Fig* **the engine of progress/reform/***etc* le moteur du progrès/de la réforme/*etc*
(**b**) (*Br* **railway** *or Am* **railroad) engine** locomotive *f*; **to sit with one's back to the engine** être assis dans le sens opposé à *ou* inverse de la marche; **to sit facing the engine** être assis dans le sens de la marche
(**c**) *(in computer game)* moteur *m*
2 *comp (failure, trouble)* de moteur *ou* machine
►► *Aut* ***engine block*** bloc-moteur *m*; *Aut* ***engine bulkhead*** pare-feu *m* de moteur; *Aut* ***engine compartment*** compartiment *m* moteur; *Br Rail* ***engine driver*** mécanicien(enne) *m,f*, conducteur(trice) *m,f*; ***engine house*** bâtiment *m* des machines *ou* des moteurs; *(for fire engines)* dépôt *m*; *Aut* ***engine immobilizer*** (dispositif *m*) antidémarrage *m*; *Tech* ***engine mounting*** support *m* moteur; ***engine oil*** huile *f* à *ou* de moteur; *Naut* ***engine room*** salle *f* des machines; *Rail* ***engine shed*** dépôt *m* (des locomotives); *(circular)* rotonde *f*

-engined ['endʒɪnd] *suff* **twin engined** bimoteur

engineer [ˌendʒɪ'nɪə(r)] **1** *n* (**a**) *(for roads, machines, bridges)* ingénieur *m*, femme *f* ingénieur; *(mechanic, repairer)* dépanneur(euse) *m,f*; **civil engineer** ingénieur *m* civil; **marine engineer** ingénieur *m* du génie maritime; **mechanical engineer** ingénieur *m* mécanicien; **mining engineer** ingénieur *m* des mines; **consulting engineer** ingénieur *m* conseil; **production engineer** ingénieur *m* (chargé) de la production; *Tel* **telephone engineer** technicien(enne) *m,f* des télécommunications *ou* du téléphone
(**b**) *Naut* ingénieur *m*, mécanicien *m*; **chief engineer** chef *m* mécanicien; **second engineer** officier *m* mécanicien en second
(**c**) *Aviat* **flight engineer** *(on military aircraft)* mécanicien *m* navigant; *(on civil aircraft)* mécanicien *m* de bord; **aircraft engineer** mécanicien *m* de piste
(**d**) *Mil* soldat *m* du génie, sapeur *m*; **the engineers** le génie, l'arme *f* du génie; *Br* **the Royal Engineers,** *Am* **the Corps of Engineers** ≃ le Génie
(**e**) *Am Rail (driver → of locomotive)* conducteur(trice) *m,f*, mécanicien(enne) *m,f*
(**f**) *Fig Pej (instigator → of plan, plot)* âme *f*, instigateur(trice) *m,f*; **her ex-husband was the engineer of her downfall** son ex-mari a été l'instigateur de sa ruine
2 *vt* (**a**) *(road, bridge, car)* concevoir; **the bridge has been superbly engineered** le pont est un superbe travail d'ingénierie
(**b**) *Fig Pej (bring about → coup, downfall, defeat)* machiner; *(→ event, situation)* manigancer; **she engineered his escape** elle a organisé son évasion; **he had carefully engineered the seating arrangements** il avait disposé les convives avec soin
(**c**) *(work → goal, victory)* amener
►► ***engineer officer*** ingénieur *m* mécanicien

engineering [ˌendʒɪ'nɪərɪŋ] *n* (**a**) *Tech* ingénierie *f*, engineering *m*; **to study engineering** faire des études d'ingénieur; **an incredible feat of engineering** une merveille de la technique; **an intricate piece of engineering** une mécanique très complexe; **agricultural engineering** génie *m* agricole *ou* rural; **civil engineering** génie *m* civil; **industrial engineering** organisation *f* industrielle; **light engineering** petite mécanique *f*; **marine engineering** génie *m* maritime; **mechanical engineering** mécanique *f*; **precision engineering** mécanique *f* de précision; **production engineering** technique *f* de la production
(**b**) *Pej (planning)* machinations *fpl*, manœuvres *fpl*; **he had participated in the engineering of her downfall** il avait participé aux machinations *ou* manœuvres qui ont conduit à sa ruine
►► *Tech* ***engineering consultancy*** *(firm)* compagnie *f* d'ingénieurs-conseils; ***engineering consultant*** ingénieur-conseil *m*; ***engineering department*** service *m* technique; ***engineering and design department*** bureau *m* d'études; ***engineering firm*** entreprise *f* de construction mécanique; *Rail* ***engineering work*** travail *m* d'ingénierie

engineman ['endʒɪnmən] (*pl* **enginemen** [-mən]) *n Am* mécanicien *m*

engird [ɪn'gɜːd] (*pt & pp* **engirded** *or* **engirt** [-gɜːt]) *vt Literary* ceindre, entourer (**with** de)

England ['ɪŋglənd] **1** *n* Angleterre *f*; **to live in England** habiter l'Angleterre *ou* en Angleterre; **to go to England** aller en Angleterre
2 *comp (team)* d'Angleterre; *(player)* anglais; *(victory)* de *ou* pour l'Angleterre

English ['ɪŋglɪʃ] **1** *npl* **the English** les Anglais *mpl*
2 *n (language)* anglais *m*; **do** *or* **can you speak English?** parlez-vous (l')anglais?; **to study English** étudier *ou* apprendre l'anglais; **she speaks excellent English** elle parle très bien (l')anglais; **we spoke (in) English to each other** nous nous sommes parlé en anglais; **that's not good English** ce n'est pas du bon anglais; **in plain** *or* **simple English** clairement; **so what you mean, in plain** *or* **simple English, is that…** autrement dit *ou* en d'autres termes, ce que vous voulez dire, c'est que…; **can you put that in plain** *or* **simple English?** pouvez-vous vous exprimer plus clairement?; **why can't lawyers talk in plain** *or* **simple English?** pourquoi les hommes de loi ne parlent ils pas comme vous et moi?; **American/Australian English** l'anglais *m* américain/australien; **the King's/Queen's English** l'anglais *m* correct; **English as a Foreign Language** anglais *m* langue étrangère; **English Language Teaching** enseignement *m* de l'anglais; **English as a Second Language** anglais *m* deuxième langue
3 *adj* anglais
4 *comp (embassy)* d'Angleterre; *(history)* de l'Angleterre; *(teacher)* d'anglais
►► ***English breakfast*** petit déjeuner *m* anglais *ou* à l'anglaise, breakfast *m*; ***the English Channel*** la Manche; ***the English disease*** *(strikes)* = terme faisant référence à la fréquence des grèves avant les lois anti-syndicales en Grande-Bretagne; *(hooliganism)* = expression qui fait référence aux violences auxquelles se livrent les supporters anglais; ***English English*** l'anglais *m* d'Angleterre; ***English Heritage*** = organisme britannique de protection du patrimoine historique; *Am Mus* ***English horn*** cor *m* anglais; *Am* ***English muffin*** muffin *m*; ***English National Opera*** opéra *m* national d'Angleterre; ***English Riviera*** = surnom donné à Torbay en raison de la douceur de son climat et de la popularité de ses stations balnéaires; ***English rose*** = le type idéal de la femme anglaise; ***English setter*** setter *m* anglais; *Am* ***English sheepdog*** bobtail *m*; ***English speaker*** *(as native speaker)* anglophone *mf*; *(as non-native speaker)* personne *f* parlant anglais; *Am* ***English for Speakers of Other Languages*** = anglais langue étrangère; ***English for special purposes*** = anglais spécialisé

ENGLISH BREAKFAST

Le petit déjeuner traditionnel anglais se compose d'un plat chaud (des œufs au bacon, par exemple), de céréales ou de porridge, et de toasts à la marmelade d'oranges, le tout accompagné de café ou de thé; aujourd'hui il est généralement remplacé par une collation plus légère.

Englishman ['ɪŋglɪʃmən] (*pl* **Englishmen** [-mən]) *n* Anglais *m*; *Prov* **an Englishman's home is his castle** charbonnier est maître dans sa maison

English-speaking *adj (as native language)* anglophone; *(as learned language)* parlant anglais

Englishwoman ['ɪŋglɪʃˌwʊmən] (*pl* **Englishwomen** [-ˌwɪmɪn]) *n* Anglaise *f*

engorged [ɪn'gɔːdʒd] *adj* **engorged (with blood)** gonflé de sang, congestionné; **to become engorged** *(blood vessel)* se congestionner

engrailed [ɪn'greɪld] *adj Her* engrêlé

engrain [ɪn'greɪn] *vt Tex* teindre grand teint

engrave [ɪn'greɪv] *vt* graver; **engraved in her memory** gravé dans sa mémoire

engraver [ɪn'greɪvə(r)] *n* graveur *m*

engraving [ɪn'greɪvɪŋ] *n* gravure *f*

engross [ɪn'grəʊs] *vt* (**a**) *(absorb)* absorber (**b**) *Law (make clear copy of → manuscript, document)* grossoyer

engrossed [ɪn'grəʊst] *adj* **to be engrossed in sth** être absorbé par qch; **to be engrossed in a book** être absorbé *ou* plongé dans un livre; **I was so engrossed in what I was doing** j'étais tellement absorbé par ce que je faisais

engrossing [ɪn'grəʊsɪŋ] *adj* absorbant

engrossment [ɪn'grəʊsmənt] *n* (**a**) *(absorption)* absorption *f* (**in** dans); **her total engrossment in the project meant she had almost no free time** ce projet l'absorbait tellement qu'elle n'avait pour ainsi dire plus une minute à elle (**b**) *Law* rédaction *f* de la grosse

engulf [ɪn'gʌlf] *vt* engloutir; **to be engulfed by the waves** sombrer dans les flots; **engulfed by the flames** englouti par les flammes; **the house was suddenly engulfed in darkness** la maison a été soudain plongée dans l'obscurité; **a feeling of despair engulfed him** le désespoir l'a terrassé

enhance [ɪn'hɑːns] *vt (quality, reputation, performance)* améliorer; *(value, chances, prestige)* augmenter, accroître; *(taste, beauty)* rehausser, mettre en valeur; *Fin (pension)* augmenter; *Comput (image, quality)* améliorer

enhanced [ɪn'hɑːnst] *adj (quality, reputation, performance)* amélioré, meilleur; *(value, chances, prestige)* augmenté, accru; *(taste, beauty)* rehaussé, mis en valeur; *Fin (pension)* augmenté; *Comput (image, quality)* amélioré
►► *Comput* ***enhanced graphics adaptor*** carte *f* EGA; *Comput* ***enhanced keyboard*** clavier *m* étendu; ***enhanced radiation weapon*** arme *f* à rayonnement renforcé

-enhanced [ɪn'hɑːnst] *suff* **computer-enhanced** *(graphics)* optimisé par ordinateur; **protein-enhanced** enrichi en protéines

enhancement [ɪn'hɑːnsmənt] *n (of quality, reputation, performance)* amélioration *f*; *(of value, chances, prestige)* augmentation *f*, accroissement *m*; *(of taste, beauty)* rehaussement *m*, mise *f* en valeur; *Fin (of pension)* augmentation *f*; *Comput (of image, quality)* amélioration *f*

enharmonic [ˌenhɑː'mɒnɪk] *adj Mus* enharmonique

enigma [ɪ'nɪgmə] *n* énigme *f*; **he remains an enigma to us** il est encore une énigme pour nous

enigmatic [ˌenɪg'mætɪk] *adj* énigmatique

enigmatically [ˌenɪg'mætɪkəlɪ] *adv* *(smile, speak)* d'un air énigmatique; *(worded)* énigmatiquement, d'une manière énigmatique

enjambment [ɑ̃n'dʒɑ̃mbmɑ̃n] *n Literature* enjambement *m*

enjoin [ɪn'dʒɔɪn] *vt Formal* (**a**) **to enjoin sb to do sth** *(urge)* exhorter qn à faire qch, recommander fortement *ou* vivement à qn de faire qch; *(command)* enjoindre *ou* ordonner à qn de faire qch; **to enjoin silence on** *or* **upon sb** *(urge)* exhorter qn au silence; *(command)* enjoindre *ou* ordonner le silence à qn; **to enjoin sth on sb** enjoindre qch à qn (**b**) *Am (forbid)* **to enjoin sb from doing sth** interdire à qn de faire qch

enjoy [ɪn'dʒɔɪ] **1** *vt* (**a**) *(like → in general)* aimer; *(→ on particular occasion)* apprécier; **to enjoy sth/doing sth** aimer qch/faire qch; **to enjoy a hot bath** aimer prendre des bains chauds; **to enjoy a glass of wine with one's meal** aimer boire un verre de vin avec son repas; **to enjoy life** aimer la vie; **he enjoys swimming/going to the cinema** il aime la natation/aller au cinéma; **I don't enjoy being made fun of** je n'aime pas qu'on se moque de moi; **enjoy your meal!** bon appétit!; **did you enjoy your meal, sir?** avez-vous bien mangé, monsieur?; **I enjoyed that** *(book, film)* cela m'a plu; *(meal)* je me suis régalé; **I thoroughly enjoyed the weekend/party** j'ai passé un excellent week-end/une excellente soirée; **I enjoy the various advantages the job has to offer** j'apprécie les divers avantages qu'offre ce poste; **I'm really enjoying this fine weather** quel plaisir, ce beau temps; **did you enjoy it?** cela t'a plu?; **what did you enjoy most?** qu'avez-vous préféré?, qu'est-ce qui vous a le plus plu?; **to enjoy oneself** s'amuser; **enjoy yourselves!** amusez-vous bien!; **did you enjoy yourself?** alors, c'était bien?; **to enjoy life** profiter de la vie; **the Duke and Duchess, enjoying a joke with their daughter** *(photograph caption)* le Duc et la Duchesse, riant avec leur fille d'une plaisanterie; **I enjoyed seeing them make fools of themselves** j'ai pris plaisir à les voir se ridiculiser; **I don't enjoy being woken up in the middle of the night** je n'aime pas qu'on me réveille en plein milieu de la nuit

(**b**) *(possess → rights, respect, privilege, income, good health)* jouir de; *(→ profits)* bénéficier de; **to enjoy good health/a high standard of living** jouir d'une bonne santé/d'un haut niveau de vie

2 *exclam esp Am (enjoy yourself)* amusez-vous bien!; *(enjoy your meal)* bon appétit!

enjoyable [ɪn'dʒɔɪəbəl] *adj (book, film, day)* agréable; *(match, contest)* beau (belle); *(meal)* excellent; **we had a most enjoyable evening** nous avons passé une soirée des plus agréables

enjoyably [ɪn'dʒɔɪəblɪ] *adv* de manière agréable, agréablement; **we spent the week most enjoyably** nous avons passé une semaine des plus agréables

enjoyment [ɪn'dʒɔɪmənt] *n* (**a**) *(pleasure)* plaisir *m*; **to get enjoyment from sth/doing sth** tirer du plaisir de qch/à faire qch; **she doesn't get much enjoyment** elle n'a pas beaucoup de distractions; **to get enjoyment out of life** jouir de la vie; **nothing could spoil his enjoyment of the meal** rien ne pouvait gâcher le plaisir que lui procurait ce repas; **I don't do this for enjoyment** je ne fais pas cela pour le *ou* mon plaisir (**b**) *(of privileges, rights etc)* jouissance *f*

enkephalin [eŋ'kefəlɪn] *n Physiol & Chem* enképhaline *f*, encéphaline *f*

enkindle [ɪn'kɪndəl] *vt* (**a**) *Literary (fire)* allumer (**b**) *Fig (emotion, passion)* enflammer, exciter

enlace [ɪn'leɪs] *vt* enlacer; **the tree was enlaced with ivy** l'arbre était enlacé de lierre

enlarge [ɪn'lɑːdʒ] **1** *vt* (**a**) *(expand → territory, house, business)* agrandir; *(→ field of knowledge, group of friends)* étendre, élargir; *(→ hole)* agrandir, élargir; *(→ pores)* dilater; *Med (→ organ)* hypertrophier

(**b**) *Phot* agrandir

2 *vi* (**a**) *(gen)* s'agrandir, se développer; *(pores)* se dilater; *Med (organ)* s'hypertrophier

(**b**) *Phot* **the photo won't enlarge well** la photo ne donnera pas un bon agrandissement *ou* ne rendra pas bien en agrandissement

►**enlarge on, enlarge upon** *vt insep (elaborate on)* s'étendre sur, donner des détails sur; **would you care to enlarge on that point?** est-ce que vous pourriez développer ce point?

enlarged [ɪn'lɑːdʒd] *adj (majority)* accru; *(photograph)* agrandi; *Med (tonsil, liver)* hypertrophié; **enlarged edition** *(of reference book)* édition *f* augmentée

enlargement [ɪn'lɑːdʒmənt] *n* (**a**) *(of territory, house, business)* agrandissement *m*; *(of group of friends, field of knowledge)* élargissement *m*; *(of hole)* agrandissement *m*, élargissement *m*; *(of pore)* dilatation *f*; *Med (of organ)* hypertrophie *f* (**b**) *Phot* agrandissement *m*

enlarger [ɪn'lɑːdʒə(r)] *n Phot* agrandisseur *m*

enlighten [ɪn'laɪtn] *vt* éclairer; **to enlighten sb about sth/as to why…** éclairer qn sur qch/sur la raison pour laquelle…; **can somebody enlighten me as to what is going on?** est-ce que quelqu'un peut m'expliquer ce qui se passe?

enlightened [ɪn'laɪtənd] *adj (person, view, policy)* éclairé; **enlightened self-interest** magnanimité *f* intéressée

►► *Hist* ***enlightened despot*** despote *m* éclairé

enlightening [ɪn'laɪtənɪŋ] *adj (book, experience)* instructif; **the film was very enlightening on the subject** le film en apprenait beaucoup sur le sujet; **that's not very enlightening!** ça ne m'apprend *ou* ne me dit pas grand-chose!

enlightenment [ɪn'laɪtənmənt] **1** *n (explanation, information)* éclaircissements *mpl*; *(state)* édification *f*, instruction *f*; **for your enlightenment** pour votre édification *ou* instruction

2 Enlightenment *n Hist* **the (Age of) Enlightenment** le Siècle des lumières

enlist [ɪn'lɪst] **1** *vt (supporters)* recruter; *Mil (soldier)* enrôler, engager; *(someone's support, help, sympathy)* s'assurer; **to enlist sb's support for a cause** rallier qn à une cause; **she enlisted the help of two bystanders** elle a obtenu de l'aide de la part de deux spectateurs

2 *vi Mil (of soldier)* s'engager

enlisted [ɪn'lɪstɪd] *adj*

►► *Am Mil* ***enlisted man*** (simple) soldat *m*; *Am Mil* ***enlisted woman*** femme *f* soldat de deuxième classe

enlistment [ɪn'lɪstmənt] *n Mil* enrôlement *m*, engagement *m*

enliven [ɪn'laɪvən] *vt (conversation, party)* animer

enlivening [ɪn'laɪvənɪŋ] *adj (music)* entraînant; *(air, climate)* vivifiant

en masse [ɑ̃'mæs] *adv* en masse, massivement

enmesh [ɪn'meʃ] *vt* prendre dans un filet; *Fig* mêler; **to become** *or* **get enmeshed in sth** s'empêtrer dans qch; **he got enmeshed in the plot** il s'est trouvé mêlé au complot

enmity ['enmətɪ] (*pl* **enmities**) *n Formal* inimitié *f*, hostilité *f*; **enmity for/towards sb** inimitié pour/envers qn; **enmity among** *or* **between people** inimitié entre personnes

ennoble [ɪ'nəʊbəl] *vt* (**a**) *(confer title upon)* anoblir (**b**) *Fig (exalt, dignify)* ennoblir, grandir

ennoblement [ɪ'nəʊbəlmənt] *n* (**a**) *(of commoner)* anoblissement *m* (**b**) *Fig (of character)* ennoblissement *m*

ennobling [ɪ'nəʊblɪŋ] *adj Fig (effect, experience)* ennoblissant

ennui [ɒn'wiː] *n Literary* ennui *m*

ENO [ˌiːen'əʊ] *n (abbr* **English National Opera**) opéra *m* national d'Angleterre

enological, enologist *etc Am* = **oenological, oenologist** *etc*

enormity [ɪ'nɔːmətɪ] (*pl* **enormities**) *n* (**a**) *(of action, crime)* énormité *f* (**b**) *Formal (atrocity)* atrocité *f*; *(crime)* crime *m* très grave (**c**) *(great size)* énormité *f*; **they were aware of the enormity of the task ahead of them** ils se rendaient compte de l'énormité de la tâche qui les attendait

enormous [ɪ'nɔːməs] *adj* (**a**) *(very large → thing)* énorme; *(→ amount, number)* énorme, colossal; **they've got an enormous dog** ils ont un chien énorme; **enormous amounts of food** une quantité énorme *ou* énormément de vivres; **an enormous crowd had gathered** un monde fou s'était rassemblé; **he made one last enormous effort** il fit un dernier effort démesuré; **there's an enormous difference between the two estimates** il y a une énorme différence entre les deux estimations; **an enormous number of cars** une énorme quantité de voitures

(**b**) *(as intensifier)* énorme, grand; **the operation was an enormous success** l'opération a été un très grand succès; **it has given me enormous pleasure** cela m'a fait énormément plaisir

enormously [ɪ'nɔːməslɪ] *adv* énormément, extrêmement; **demand has increased enormously** la demande a énormément augmenté; **an enormously big house** une maison terriblement grande; **it was enormously successful** ce fut extrêmement réussi

enosis [e'nəʊsɪs] *n Pol* énosis *f*

ENOUGH [ɪ'nʌf]

assez de	► 1
assez	► 2; 3
suffisamment	► 3 (a)

1 *adj* assez de; **enough money** assez *ou* suffisamment d'argent; **do you have enough money to pay?** avez-vous de quoi payer?; **are there enough copies for all the children?** y a-t-il assez *ou* suffisamment d'exemplaires pour tous les enfants?; **you've had more than enough wine** tu as bu plus qu'assez de vin; **the report is proof enough** le rapport est une preuve suffisante; **she's not fool enough to believe that!** elle n'est pas assez bête pour le croire!

2 *pron* assez; **do you need some money? – I've got enough** avez-vous besoin d'argent? – j'en ai assez *ou* suffisamment; **will this be enough?** est-ce que ça suffira?; **we earn enough to live on** nous gagnons de quoi vivre; **there's enough for everybody** il y en a assez pour tout le monde; **enough/not enough is known for us to be able to make a prediction** on en sait assez/on n'en sait pas assez pour faire une prévision; **not enough of us are here to take a vote** on n'est pas assez nombreux pour voter; **he's had enough to eat** il a assez mangé; **more than enough** plus qu'il n'en faut; **there was more than enough** il y en avait largement; **enough is enough!** ça suffit comme ça!, trop c'est trop!; **after five years he decided that enough was enough and resigned** après cinq ans il en eut assez et donna sa démission; **enough is as good as a feast** mieux vaut assez que trop; *Fam* **enough said!** je vois!; **that's enough!** ça suffit!; **it's enough to drive you mad** c'est à vous rendre fou; **I can't get enough of his films** je ne me lasse jamais de ses films; **to have had enough (of sth)** en avoir assez (de qch); **she's had enough of working late** elle en a assez de travailler tard le soir

3 *adv* (**a**) *(sufficiently)* assez, suffisamment; **he's old enough to understand** il est assez grand pour comprendre; **it's a good enough reason** c'est une raison suffisante; **you know well enough what I mean** vous savez très bien ce que je veux dire; **fair enough!** ça va!, d'accord!

(**b**) *(fairly)* assez; **to do sth well enough** faire qch passablement bien; **she's honest enough** elle est assez honnête; **it's good enough in its own way** ce n'est pas mal dans le genre

(**c**) *(with adverb)* **oddly** *or* **strangely enough, nobody knows her** chose curieuse, personne ne la connaît

en passant [ɑ̃'pæsɑ̃] *adv* en passant

enplane [ɪn'pleɪn] **1** *vt* embarquer (à bord d'un avion)

2 *vi* embarquer (à bord d'un avion)

enprint ['enprɪnt] *n Phot* format *m* normal

enquire = **inquire**

enquiry = **inquiry**

'Enquiry Concerning Human Understanding' *Hume* 'Essais sur l'entendement humain'

enrage [ɪn'reɪdʒ] *vt* rendre furieux, mettre en

rage; **she was enraged by the government's complacency** la complaisance du gouvernement la rendait furieuse

enraged [ɪn'reɪdʒd] *adj (person)* furieux; *(animal)* enragé; **he was enraged to discover that...** il enrageait de découvrir que...; **enraged, I left** furieux, je suis parti

enrapture [ɪn'ræptʃə(r)] *vt* émerveiller, enchanter; **we were enraptured by the beauty of the island** nous étions en extase devant la beauté de l'île

enraptured [ɪn'ræptʃəd] *adj* émerveillé, ébloui

enrobe [ɪn'rəʊb] *vt Literary* vêtir, revêtir (**with** *or* **in** de)

enrich [ɪn'rɪtʃ] *vt (mind, person, life)* enrichir; *(soil)* fertiliser, amender; *Phys* enrichir; **breakfast cereals enriched with vitamins** céréales *fpl* enrichies en vitamines

▸▸ *Phys* ***enriched nuclear fuel*** combustible *m* nucléaire enrichi; *Phys* ***enriched uranium*** uranium *m* enrichi

enriching [ɪn'rɪtʃɪŋ] *adj* enrichissant

enrichment [ɪn'rɪtʃmənt] *n (of mind, person, life)* enrichissement *m*; *(of soil)* fertilisation *f*, amendement *m*; *Phys* enrichissement *m*

enrol, *Am* **enroll** [ɪn'rəʊl] (*Br pt & pp* **enrolled,** *cont* **enrolling,** *Am pt & pp* **enroled,** *cont* **enroling**) **1** *vt* (**a**) *(student)* inscrire, immatriculer; *(member)* inscrire; *Mil (recruit)* enrôler, recruter (**b**) *Am Pol (prepare)* dresser, rédiger; *(register)* enregistrer

2 *vi (student)* s'inscrire; *Mil* s'engager, s'enrôler; **to enrol on** *or* **for a course** s'inscrire à un cours; **to enrol as a student** s'inscrire à la faculté

▸▸ *Am* ***enroled bill*** projet *m* de loi enregistré; *Br* ***enrolled nurse*** = infirmière diplômée

enrolment, *Am* **enrollment** [ɪn'rəʊlmənt] *n (registration → of members)* inscription *f*; *(→ of students)* inscription *f*, immatriculation *f*; *(→ of workers)* embauche *f*; *Mil* enrôlement *m*, recrutement *m*; **the club has an enrolment of 500 members** le club compte 500 membres; **a school with an enrolment of 300 students** une école avec un effectif de 300 élèves

en route [ɒn'ruːt] *adv* en route (**for** pour)

Ens (*written abbr* **Ensign**) (**a**) *Br Mil* (officier *m*) porte-étendard *m* (**b**) *Am Naut* enseigne *m* de vaisseau de deuxième classe

ensanguine [ɪn'sæŋgwɪn] *vt Literary (stain with blood)* tacher de sang; *(cover with blood)* ensanglanter

ensconce [ɪn'skɒns] *vt Formal or Hum* installer; **she ensconced herself/was ensconced in the armchair** elle se cala/était bien calée dans le fauteuil

ensemble [ɒn'sɒmbəl] *n (gen) & Mus* ensemble *m*

ensepulchre [ɪn'sepəlkə(r)] *vt Literary* mettre au tombeau

enshrine [ɪn'ʃraɪn] *vt* enchâsser; *Fig (cherish)* conserver pieusement *ou* religieusement; **our fundamental rights are enshrined in the constitution** nos droits fondamentaux font partie intégrante de la constitution

enshrinement [ɪn'ʃraɪnmənt] *n* enchâssement *m*

enshroud [ɪn'ʃraʊd] *vt Formal* ensevelir; **the countryside was enshrouded in mist** le paysage était enseveli sous la brume; **enshrouded in mystery** enveloppé de mystère

ensign ['ensaɪn] *n* (**a**) *(flag)* drapeau *m*, enseigne *f*; *Naut* pavillon *m* (**b**) *(symbol)* insigne *m*, emblème *m* (**c**) *Br Mil* (officier *m*) porte-étendard *m* (**d**) *Am Naut* enseigne *m* de vaisseau de deuxième classe

ensilage [en'saɪlɪdʒ] *n Agr* ensilage *m*, silotage *m*

ensile [en'saɪl] *vt Agr* ensiler

enslave [ɪn'sleɪv] *vt* réduire en esclavage, asservir; *Fig* asservir; **he was enslaved by his conscience** il était l'esclave de sa conscience

enslavement [ɪn'sleɪvmənt] *n* asservissement *m*, assujettissement *m*; *Fig* sujétion *f*, asservissement *m*, assujettissement *m*

ensnare [ɪn'sneə(r)] *vt also Fig* prendre au piège; **ensnared by her charms** séduit par ses charmes; **she used her beauty to ensnare him into marrying her** elle s'est servi de sa beauté comme d'un appât pour qu'il l'épouse

ensue [ɪn'sjuː] *vi* s'ensuivre, résulter; **a long silence ensued** il se fit un long silence; **the problems that have ensued from government cutbacks** les problèmes qui ont résulté des restrictions gouvernementales

ensuing [ɪn'sjuːɪŋ] *adj (action, event)* qui s'ensuit; *(month, year)* suivant

en suite [ˌɒn'swiːt] **1** *adj* **with en suite bathroom** avec salle de bain particulière

2 *adv* **with bathroom en suite** avec salle de bain particulière

ensure [ɪn'ʃʊə(r)] *vt* (**a**) *(guarantee)* assurer, garantir; **I did everything I could to ensure that he would succeed** *or* **to ensure his success** j'ai fait tout ce que j'ai pu pour m'assurer qu'il réussirait *ou* pour assurer son succès (**b**) *(protect)* protéger, assurer

ENT [ˌiːen'tiː] *Med* (*abbr* **ear, nose & throat**) **1** *n* ORL *f*

2 *adj* ORL

entablature [ɪn'tæblətʃə(r)] *n Archit* entablement *m*

entablement [ɪn'teɪbəlmənt] *n Archit* table *f* supérieure

entail [ɪn'teɪl] **1** *vt* (**a**) *(imply → consequence, expense)* entraîner; *(→ difficulty, risk)* comporter; *(→ delay, expense)* occasionner; *(→ in logic)* entraîner; **it entailed my going to London** cela exigeait que je me rende à Londres; **starting a new job often entails a lot of work** prendre un nouveau poste exige souvent *ou* nécessite souvent beaucoup de travail

(**b**) *Law* **to entail an estate** substituer un héritage; **an entailed estate** un bien grevé

2 *n Law* (**a**) *(act)* substitution *f*

(**b**) *(property)* bien *m* substitué

(**c**) *(inheritance)* héritage *m* inéluctable

entailment [ɪn'teɪlmənt] *n* (**a**) *(of consequences)* entraînement *m*; *(in logic)* enchaînement *m* (**b**) *Law* substitution *f*

entangle [ɪn'tæŋgəl] *vt* (**a**) *(ensnare)* empêtrer, enchevêtrer; **to become** *or* **get entangled in sth** s'empêtrer dans qch; **the bird was entangled in the net** l'oiseau était empêtré dans le filet (**b**) *(snarl → hair)* emmêler; *(→ threads)* emmêler, embrouiller (**c**) *Fig (involve)* entraîner, impliquer; **she got entangled in the dispute** elle s'est retrouvée impliquée dans la dispute; **he became entangled with a group of drug dealers** il s'est retrouvé mêlé à un groupe de dealers

entanglement [ɪn'tæŋgəlmənt] *n* (**a**) *(in net, undergrowth)* enchevêtrement *m* (**b**) *(of hair, thread)* emmêlement *m* (**c**) *Fig (involvement)* implication *f*; **emotional entanglements** complications *fpl* sentimentales; **his entanglement with Marie/with the police** son histoire avec Marie/avec la police

entasis ['entəsɪs] *n Archit* renflement *m* imperceptible

entelechy [en'telɪkɪ] *n Phil* entéléchie *f*

entellus [en'teləs] *n Zool* entelle *m*

entente [ɒn'tɒnt] *n* entente *f*

▸▸ ***entente cordiale*** entente *f* cordiale

ENTER ['entə(r)]

entrer dans	▸ **1 (a), (b)**
s'inscrire à	▸ **1 (b)**
inscrire	▸ **1 (c), (d)**
présenter	▸ **1 (e)**
entrer	▸ **2 (a)**
s'inscrire	▸ **2 (b)**
entrée	▸ **3**

1 *vt* (**a**) *(go into → room)* entrer dans; *(→ building)* entrer dans, pénétrer dans; **as I entered the building** comme j'entrais dans le bâtiment; **the ship entered the harbour** le navire est entré au *ou* dans le port; **where the river enters the sea** à l'embouchure du fleuve; **where the bullet entered the body** l'endroit où la balle a pénétré le corps; **to enter one's sixtieth year** entrer dans sa soixantième année; **as we enter a new decade** alors que nous entrons dans une nouvelle décennie; **the war entered a new phase** la guerre est entrée dans une phase nouvelle; **a note of sadness entered her voice** une note de tristesse s'est glissée dans sa voix; **the thought never entered my head** l'idée ne m'est jamais venue à l'esprit

(**b**) *(join → university)* s'inscrire à, se faire inscrire à; *(→ profession)* entrer dans; *(→ army)* s'engager *ou* entrer dans; *(→ politics)* se lancer dans; **to enter the church/a convent** entrer dans les ordres/dans un couvent; **to enter the war** entrer en guerre

(**c**) *(register)* inscrire; **the school entered the pupils for the exam/in the competition** l'école a présenté les élèves à l'examen/au concours; **to enter a horse for a race** engager *ou* inscrire un cheval dans une course

(**d**) *(record → on list)* inscrire; *(→ in book)* noter; *Comput (→ data)* entrer, introduire; *Acct (→ item)* comptabiliser; **he entered the figures in the ledger** il a porté les chiffres sur le livre de comptes

(**e**) *(submit)* présenter; **to enter a proposal** présenter une proposition; **to enter a protest** protester officiellement; *Law* **to enter an appeal** interjeter appel

2 *vi* (**a**) *(come in)* entrer; *Theat* **enter Juliet** entre Juliette

(**b**) *(register)* s'inscrire; **she entered for the race/for the exam** elle s'est inscrite pour la course/à l'examen

3 *n Comput (key)* touche *f* (d')entrée *f*

▸▸ *Comput* ***enter key*** touche *f* (d')entrée

▸**enter into** *vt insep* (**a**) *(begin → explanation)* se lancer dans; *(→ conversation, relations)* entrer en; *(→ negotiations)* entamer; **I won't enter into details at this stage** je ne vais pas entrer dans les détails à ce stade

(**b**) *(become involved in)* **to enter into an agreement with sb** conclure un accord avec qn; **to enter into partnership with sb** s'associer avec qn; *Fig* **I entered into the spirit of the game** je suis entré dans le jeu

(**c**) *(affect)* entrer dans; **an element of chance enters into every business venture** un facteur hasard entre en jeu dans toute entreprise commerciale; **money doesn't enter into it** l'argent n'entre pas en jeu *ou* en ligne de compte; **my feelings don't enter into my decision** mes sentiments n'ont rien à voir avec *ou* ne sont pour rien dans ma décision

▸**enter up** *vt sep (amount)* inscrire, porter; *Acct* **to enter up an item/figures in the ledger** porter un article/des chiffres sur le livre des comptes

▸**enter upon** *vt insep* (**a**) *(career)* débuter *ou* entrer dans; *(negotiations)* entamer; *(policy)* commencer (**b**) *Law (inheritance)* prendre possession de

enterectomy [entə'rektəmɪ] *n Med* entérectomie *f*

enteric [en'terɪk] *adj Med* entérique

▸▸ ***enteric fever*** (fièvre *f*) typhoïde *f*

entering ['entərɪŋ] *n (of order)* enregistrement *m*; *Comput (of command, character)* entrée *f*; *(of data)* entrée *f*, introduction *f*

enteritis [ˌentə'raɪtɪs] *n (UNCOUNT) Med* entérite *f*

enterobacterium [ˌentərəʊbæk'tɪərɪəm] (*pl* **enterobacteria** [-rɪə]) *n Biol* entérobactérie *f*

enterocolitis [ˌentərəʊkə'laɪtɪs] *n Med* entérocolite *f*

enterocyte ['entərəʊsaɪt] *n* entérocyte *m*

enteroglucagon ['entərəʊ'gluːkəgən] *n Biol* entéroglucagon *m*

[illegible] *n Biol* entérokinase *f*

enterolith ['entərəʊlɪθ] *n Med* entérolithe *m*

enteron ['entərɒn] *n Anat* canal *m* alimentaire

enterotomy [entə'rɒtəmɪ] *n Med* entérotomie *f*

enterovirus [ˌentərəʊ'vaɪrəs] *n Med* entérovirus *m*

enterprise ['entəpraɪz] *n* (**a**) *Com (business, project)* entreprise *f*; **it was an ambitious enterprise** c'était une entreprise ambitieuse; **private enterprise** l'entreprise *f* privée

(**b**) *(initiative)* initiative *f*, esprit *m* entreprenant *ou* d'initiative; **men of enterprise** des hommes *mpl* entreprenants; **she showed great enterprise** elle a fait preuve d'un esprit entreprenant; **to lack enterprise** manquer d'initiative; **to be full of enterprise, to have a lot of enterprise** être très entreprenant

▸▸ *Br Admin & Com* ***enterprise allowance*** aide *f* à la création d'entreprises; *Br Admin & Com* ***Enterprise Allowance Scheme*** fonds *m* d'aide à la création d'entreprise; *Com* ***enterprise culture*** = attitude favorable à l'essor de l'esprit d'entreprise; *Econ* ***enterprise economy*** = type d'économie qui facilite la création d'entreprises; ***enterprise society*** = type de société où l'entreprise privée est valorisée; *Br Com* ***enterprise zone*** = zone d'encouragement à l'implantation d'entreprises dans les régions économiquement défavorisées

enterprising ['entəpraɪzɪŋ] *adj (person)* entreprenant, plein d'initiative; *(project)* audacieux, hardi; *(solution)* imaginatif, ingénieux; **she's very enterprising** elle fait preuve d'initiative

enterprisingly ['entəpraɪzɪŋlɪ] *adv (boldly)* audacieusement, hardiment; *(independently)* de sa propre initiative

entertain [ˌentə'teɪn] **1** *vt* (**a**) *(amuse)* amuser, divertir; **I entertained them with a story** je leur ai raconté une histoire pour les distraire *ou* amuser; **to keep sb entertained** divertir *ou* amuser qn

(**b**) *(show hospitality towards)* recevoir; **he entertained them to dinner** *(at restaurant)* il leur a offert le dîner; *(at home)* il les a reçus à dîner

(**c**) *(idea)* considérer, penser à; *(hope)* caresser, nourrir; *(doubt)* entretenir; *(suggestion)* admettre; **she had never entertained hopes of becoming rich** elle n'avait jamais nourri *ou* caressé l'espoir de devenir riche; **he entertains grave doubts about it** il entretient de sérieux doutes à ce propos; **I refused to entertain such a suggestion** j'ai refusé d'admettre pareille suggestion

2 *vi* recevoir; **we entertain quite often** nous recevons (du monde) assez souvent

entertainer [ˌentə'teɪnə(r)] *n* (**a**) *(comedian)* comique *mf*, amuseur(euse) *m,f*; *(in music hall)* artiste *mf* (de music-hall), fantaisiste *mf*; **a well-known television entertainer** un artiste de télévision bien connu (**b**) *(of guests)* **they never were big entertainers** ils n'ont jamais beaucoup reçu

entertaining [ˌentə'teɪnɪŋ] **1** *n* **she enjoys entertaining** elle aime bien recevoir; **they do a lot of business entertaining** ils donnent pas mal de réceptions d'affaires

2 *adj* amusant, divertissant

entertainingly [ˌentə'teɪnɪŋlɪ] *adv* de façon amusante *ou* divertissante

entertainment [ˌentə'teɪnmənt] *n* (**a**) *(amusement)* amusement *m*, divertissement *m*; **for your entertainment, we have organized...** pour vous distraire *ou* amuser, nous avons organisé...; **much to the entertainment of the crowd** au grand amusement de la foule; **this film is** *or* **provides good family entertainment** ce film est un bon divertissement familial; **her favourite entertainment is reading** la lecture est sa distraction préférée; **we had to make our own entertainment** il a fallu que l'on se divertisse nous-mêmes

(**b**) *(performance)* spectacle *m*, attraction *f*; **musical entertainments will be provided** des attractions musicales sont prévues; **this is a serious job, not an entertainment** c'est un travail sérieux, pas un jeu; **the entertainment business** l'industrie *f* du spectacle; **this show is intended to be an entertainment** ce spectacle est censé être un divertissement

►► *Com* ***entertainment allowance*** frais *mpl* de représentation; ***entertainment centre*** système *m* audio-vidéo; ***entertainments director*** *(at holiday centre etc)* directeur(trice) *m,f* de l'animation; ***entertainment magazine*** guide *m* des spectacles; ***entertainments officer*** *(on ship, in students' union)* responsable *mf* chargé de l'animation; *Comput* ***entertainment software*** logiciel *m* de loisir; ***entertainment system*** système *m* audio-vidéo; ***entertainment tax*** taxe *f* sur les spectacles

'That's Entertainment!' *Jack Haley Jr* 'Il était une fois Hollywood'

enthalpy ['enθəlpɪ] *n Phys* enthalpie *f*

enthral, *Am* **enthrall** [ɪn'θrɔːl] *(pt & pp* **enthralled,** *cont* **enthralling)** *vt* (**a**) *(fascinate)* captiver, passionner; **she was enthralled by the idea** elle était séduite par l'idée (**b**) *Arch or Literary (enslave)* asservir

enthralling [ɪn'θrɔːlɪŋ] *adj (book, film)* captivant, passionnant; *(beauty, charm)* séduisant

enthrallingly [ɪn'θrɔːlɪŋlɪ] *adv* d'une manière captivante; **enthrallingly beautiful** d'une beauté fascinante

enthralment [ɪn'θrɔːlmənt] *n* (**a**) *(fascination)* fascination *f* (**b**) *Arch or Literary (enslavement)* asservissement *m*

enthrone [ɪn'θrəʊn] *vt* (**a**) *(monarch)* mettre sur le trône, introniser; *(bishop)* introniser (**b**) *Literary (idea)* révérer

enthronement [ɪn'θrəʊnmənt] *n* intronisation *f*

enthuse [ɪn'θjuːz] **1** *vi* s'enthousiasmer; **she enthused over the plan** elle parlait du projet avec beaucoup d'enthousiasme

2 *vt* enthousiasmer, emballer; **you don't seem very enthused about it** tu n'as pas l'air emballé par l'idée

enthusiasm [ɪn'θjuːzɪæzəm] *n* (**a**) *(interest)* enthousiasme *m*; **she hasn't much enthusiasm for the project** elle n'a pas beaucoup d'enthousiasme pour le projet; **the discovery has aroused** *or* **stirred up considerable enthusiasm among historians** la découverte a suscité un grand enthousiasme chez les historiens (**b**) *(hobby)* passion *f*; **collecting beer mats is just one of my little enthusiasms** je collectionne les dessous de bock, c'est un de mes passe-temps

enthusiast [ɪn'θjuːzɪæst] *n* enthousiaste *mf*, fervent(e) *m,f*; **she's a jazz enthusiast** elle est passionnée de *ou* elle se passionne pour le jazz; **football enthusiasts** passionnés *mpl* de football

enthusiastic [ɪnˌθjuːzɪ'æstɪk] *adj (person, response)* enthousiaste; *(shout, applause)* enthousiaste, d'enthousiasme; **they gave me an enthusiastic welcome** ils m'ont accueilli chaleureusement; **he's an enthusiastic football player** c'est un footballeur passionné; **she's very enthusiastic about the project** elle est très enthousiaste à l'idée de ce projet; **to be enthusiastic about a suggestion** accueillir une proposition avec enthousiasme; **we're not very enthusiastic about moving** déménager ne nous dit pas grand-chose, nous ne sommes pas enchantés de déménager; *Ironic* **don't sound so enthusiastic!** tu pourrais te montrer un peu plus enthousiaste!

enthusiastically [ɪnˌθjuːzɪ'æstɪkəlɪ] *adv (receive)* avec enthousiasme; *(speak, support)* avec enthousiasme *ou* ferveur; *(work)* avec zèle

entice [ɪn'taɪs] *vt* attirer, séduire; **to entice sb to do sth** convaincre *ou* persuader qn de faire qch; **to entice sb away from sth** éloigner qn de qch; **I managed to entice him away from the television** j'ai réussi à l'arracher à la télévision; **they enticed him into a card game** ils l'ont attiré dans une partie de cartes; **enticed by their offer** alléché *ou* attiré par leur proposition

enticement [ɪn'taɪsmənt] *n* (**a**) *(attraction)* attrait *m*, appât *m*; **the government offered the Japanese company many enticements to locate their factory in Britain** le gouvernement a offert toutes sortes d'avantages à la société japonaise pour l'inciter à installer son usine en Grande-Bretagne (**b**) *(act)* séduction *f*

enticing [ɪn'taɪsɪŋ] *adj (offer)* attrayant, séduisant; *(person)* séduisant; *(food)* alléchant, appétissant; **the water doesn't look very enticing** l'eau n'est pas très tentante

enticingly [ɪn'taɪsɪŋlɪ] *adv* de façon séduisante; **delicious smells wafted enticingly from the kitchen** de délicieuses odeurs de cuisine mettaient l'eau à la bouche

entire [ɪn'taɪə(r)] *adj* (**a**) *(whole)* entier, tout; **my entire life** toute ma vie, ma vie entière; **the entire world** le monde entier; **the entire day** toute la journée; **she read the entire book in an afternoon** elle a lu le livre en entier *ou* tout le livre en l'espace d'un après-midi; **the entire business had proved to be a complete waste of time** toute l'affaire s'est résumée à une pure perte de temps

(**b**) *(total)* entier, complet(ète); *(absolute)* total, absolu; **she has my entire support** elle peut compter sur mon soutien sans réserve; **to enjoy sb's entire confidence** jouir de l'entière confiance de qn

(**c**) *(intact)* entier, intact

(**d**) *Bot* entier

(**e**) *(uncastrated → horse)* cheval *m* entier

entirely [ɪn'taɪəlɪ] *adv* entièrement, totalement; **I agree with you entirely** je suis entièrement d'accord avec vous; **that's entirely unnecessary** c'est absolument inutile; **I'm not entirely satisfied** je ne suis pas complètement satisfait; **they lived their lives entirely in the jungle** ils passèrent toute leur vie dans la jungle; **it's entirely my fault** c'est entièrement ma faute; **that's another matter entirely** c'est une toute autre affaire; **it's not entirely clear what happened** on n'est pas tout à fait sûr de ce qui s'est passé; **the disease has been largely, though not entirely, eliminated** la maladie n'a pas été complètement éradiquée, mais presque; **the news was not entirely unexpected** la nouvelle n'a pas vraiment fait l'effet d'une surprise

entirety [ɪn'taɪrətɪ] *(pl* **entireties)** *n* (**a**) *(completeness)* intégralité *f*; **in its entirety** en (son) entier, intégralement; **the book tells the story in its entirety** le livre raconte l'histoire dans son entier; **the skeleton had been preserved in its entirety** le squelette avait été intégralement conservé (**b**) *(total)* totalité *f*; **the entirety of his estate** la totalité de ses biens

entitle [ɪn'taɪtəl] *vt* (**a**) *(give right to)* autoriser; **the results entitle them to believe that...** les résultats les autorisent à croire que...; **his disability entitles him to a pension** son infirmité lui donne droit à une pension; **this ticket entitles the bearer to free admission** ce billet donne au porteur le droit à une entrée gratuite; **to be entitled to do sth** *(by status)* avoir qualité pour *ou* être habilité à faire qch; *(by rules)* avoir le droit *ou* être en droit de faire qch; **you're entitled to your own opinion but...** vous avez le droit d'avoir votre avis mais...; **we're entitled to some fun!** nous avons bien le droit de nous amuser un peu!; **you're quite entitled to say that...** vous pouvez dire à juste titre que...; **to be entitled to vote** avoir le droit de vote

(**b**) *Law* habiliter; **to be entitled to act** être habilité à agir

(**c**) *(film, book, painting etc)* intituler; **the book is entitled...** le livre s'intitule...

(**d**) *(bestow title on)* donner un titre à

entitlement [ɪn'taɪtəlmənt] *n* droit *m*; **entitlement to social security** droit *m* à la sécurité sociale; *Com* **holiday entitlement** congé *m* annuel *(auquel on a droit)*

entity ['entətɪ] *(pl* **entities)** *n* entité *f*; **legal entity** personne *f* morale; **a separate entity** une entité séparée

entomb [ɪn'tuːm] *vt* mettre au tombeau, ensevelir; *Fig* ensevelir

entombment [ɪn'tuːmmənt] *n* mise *f* au tombeau, ensevelissement *m*; *Fig* ensevelissement *m*

entomological [ˌentəmə'lɒdʒɪkəl] *adj Zool* entomologique

entomologist [ˌentə'mɒlədʒɪst] *n Zool* entomologiste *mf*

entomology [ˌentə'mɒlədʒɪ] *n Zool* entomologie *f*

entopic [en'tɒpɪk] *adj Anat* entopique

entourage [ˌɒntʊ'rɑːʒ] *n* entourage *m*

entozoon ['entəʊzəʊɒn] *n Zool* entozoaire *m*

entr'acte ['ɒntrækt] *n* entracte *m*

entrails ['entreɪlz] *npl also Fig* entrailles *fpl*

entrain [ɪn'treɪn] **1** *vt* (**a**) *Formal (person)* embarquer *(dans un train)* (**b**) *(of liquid, gas)* entraîner

2 *vi Formal* monter *(dans un train)*

entraining [ɪn'treɪnɪŋ], **entrainment** [ɪn'treɪnmənt] *n Formal* embarquement *m (dans un train)*

entrance[1] ['entrəns] *n* (**a**) *(means of entry)* entrée *f*; *(large)* portail *m*; *(foyer)* entrée *f*, vestibule *m*; **the entrance to the store** l'entrée *f* du magasin; **I'll meet you at the entrance** je te retrouverai à l'entrée

(**b**) *(arrival)* entrée *f*; **to make an entrance** *(gen)* faire une entrée; *Theat* entrer en scène

(**c**) *(admission)* admission *f*; **the management reserves the right to refuse entrance** *(sign)* la direction se réserve le droit de refuser l'entrée; **passing this exam does not guarantee you entrance to the school** la réussite à cet examen ne te garantit pas l'admission à l'école; **to gain entrance to** *(club, profession, college etc)* être admis à

(**d**) *(access)* accès *m*, admission *f*; **the police gained entrance to the building from the back** la police a accédé au bâtiment par derrière

►► ***entrance card*** carte *f* d'entrée *ou* d'admission; ***entrance examination*** *(for school)* examen *m* d'entrée; *(for job)* concours *m* de recrutement; ***entrance fee*** *(to exhibition, fair etc)* droit *m* d'entrée; *Br (to club, organization etc)* droit *m* *ou* frais *mpl* d'inscription; ***entrance hall*** *(in house)* vestibule *m*; *(in hotel)* hall *m*; *Am* ***entrance ramp*** bretelle *f* d'accès; ***entrance requirements*** qualifications *fpl* exigées à l'entrée; ***entrance ticket*** billet *m* d'entrée

entrance² [ɪn'trɑːns] *vt* (**a**) *(hypnotize)* hypnotiser, faire entrer en transe (**b**) *Fig (delight)* ravir, enchanter; **she was entranced by the beauty of the place** elle était en extase devant la beauté de l'endroit; **they all sat entranced** ils étaient tous fascinés

entrancing [ɪn'trɑːnsɪŋ] *adj* enchanteur, ravissant

entrancingly [ɪn'trɑːnsɪŋlɪ] *adv (smile)* de façon ravissante *ou* séduisante; *(dance, sing)* à ravir; **entrancingly beautiful** beau (belle) à ravir

entrant ['entrənt] *n* (**a**) *(in exam)* candidat(e) *m,f*; *(in race)* concurrent(e) *m,f*, participant(e) *m,f*; **all entrants for the exam/competition** tous les candidats à l'examen/participants à la compétition

(**b**) *(to profession, society)* débutant(e) *m,f*; *Com (on market)* acteur *m*; **a training course for (new) entrants to the profession** un cours de formation pour ceux qui débutent dans la profession; *Fin* **stocks in two new entrants to the market performed well** les actions de deux sociétés nouvellement introduites en Bourse se sont bien comportées

entrap [ɪn'træp] (*pt & pp* **entrapped**, *cont* **entrapping**) *vt* (**a**) *(animal, bird)* prendre au piège; *Fig* **he felt entrapped** il se sentait pris au piège (**b**) *(trick)* prendre au piège; **she had been entrapped into helping the thieves** elle avait été insidieusement amenée à aider les voleurs; **he claimed that his client had been entrapped into committing a crime** il prétendait que son client avait été piégé et forcé à commettre un crime

entrapment [ɪn'træpmənt] *n* (**a**) *Law* = incitation au délit par un policier afin de justifier une arrestation; *(by journalist)* = fait, pour un journaliste, d'inciter quelqu'un à commettre un délit dans le cadre d'un reportage (**b**) *(confinement)* enfermement *m*; **a sense of entrapment** un sentiment d'enfermement

entreat [ɪn'triːt] *vt Formal* implorer, supplier; **to entreat sb to do sth** supplier qn de faire qch; **I entreat you to help me** je vous supplie de m'aider; **spare his life, I entreat you** épargnez sa vie, je vous en conjure; **I entreated her not to be cross with him** je l'ai priée instamment de ne pas se fâcher contre lui; *Literary* **be merciful, I entreat you** ayez pitié, je vous en implore *ou* supplie

entreating [ɪn'triːtɪŋ] *Formal* **1** *adj* suppliant, implorant

2 *n (UNCOUNT)* supplications *fpl*

entreatingly [ɪn'triːtɪŋlɪ] *adv Formal (look)* d'un air suppliant; *(ask)* d'un ton suppliant, d'une voix suppliante

entreaty [ɪn'triːtɪ] (*pl* **entreaties**) *n Formal* supplication *f*, prière *f*; **a look of entreaty** un regard suppliant; **no one responded to her urgent entreaties** personne ne répondit à ses prières insistantes

entrechat ['ɑ̃trəʃæ] *n (in ballet)* entrechat *m*

entrée ['ɒntreɪ] *n* (**a**) *(right of entry)* entrée *f* (**to** *or* **into** dans) (**b**) *Culin (course preceding main dish)* entrée *f*; *Am (main dish)* plat *m* principal *ou* de résistance

entrench [ɪn'trentʃ] *vt Mil & Fig* retrancher

entrenched [ɪn'trentʃt] *adj* (**a**) *Mil* retranché

(**b**) *Fig (person)* inflexible, inébranlable; *(idea)* arrêté; *(power, tradition)* implanté; **the two neighbours became entrenched in a long-running feud** les deux voisins se retrouvèrent engagés dans une longue querelle; **attitudes that are firmly entrenched in our society** des attitudes qui sont fermement ancrées dans notre société; **he became more and more entrenched in his views** il s'est de plus en plus retranché sur ses positions; **an entrenched position** une position de retranchement

entrenchment [ɪn'trentʃmənt] *n Mil & Fig* retranchement *m*

entrepôt ['ɒntrəpəʊ] *n Com* entrepôt *m*

►► ***entrepôt port*** port *m* franc

entrepreneur [ˌɒntrəprə'nɜː(r)] *n* entrepreneur(euse) *m,f (homme ou femme d'affaires)*

entrepreneurial [ˌɒntrəprə'nɜːrɪəl] *adj (spirit, attitude)* d'entrepreneur; *(society, person)* qui a l'esprit d'entreprise; *(skills)* d'entrepreneur

entrepreneurship [ˌɒntrəprə'nɜːʃɪp] *n* esprit *m* d'entreprise

entropy ['entrəpɪ] *n Phys* entropie *f*

entrust [ɪn'trʌst] *vt* confier; **to entrust sth to sb** confier qch à qn; **she entrusted her children to them** elle leur a confié ses enfants, elle a confié ses enfants à leur garde; **to entrust sb with a job** charger qn d'une tâche, confier une tâche à qn; **she entrusted him with the responsibility of selling it** elle l'a chargé de le vendre, elle lui a confié le soin de le vendre; **to entrust sb with the care of sth** commettre qch à la garde de qn

entry ['entrɪ] (*pl* **entries**) *n* (**a**) *(way in)* entrée *f*; *(larger)* portail *m* (**to** de)

(**b**) *(act)* entrée *f*; **to make an entry** *(gen)* faire une entrée; *Theat* entrer en scène; **Poland's entry into the EU** l'entrée de la Pologne dans l'UE

(**c**) *(admission)* entrée *f*, accès *m*; **this ticket gives you free entry to the exhibition** ce billet te donne le droit d'entrer gratuitement à l'exposition; **she was refused entry to the country** on lui a refusé l'entrée dans le pays; **no entry** *(sign)* défense d'entrer, entrée interdite; *(in street)* sens interdit

(**d**) *(in dictionary)* entrée *f*; *(in diary)* notation *f*; *(in encyclopedia)* article *m*; *(on list)* inscription *f*; *Comput (of data)* entrée *f*; *Acct (in account book, ledger)* écriture *f*, article *m*; *Acct (action)* passation *f* d'écriture, inscription *f*; *Acct* **to make an entry** *(in ledger)* porter un article à compte, passer une écriture; *(in journal etc)* inscrire quelque chose; *Naut* **an entry in the log** un élément du journal de bord

(**e**) *(competitor)* inscription *f*; *(item submitted for competition)* participant(e) *m,f*, concurrent(e) *m,f*; *Sport* **a late entry** un(e) participant(e) de dernière minute

(**f**) *(UNCOUNT) (number of entrants)* taux *m* de participation; **the entry is down this year** *(in competition)* le taux de participation est en baisse cette année; *(in exam)* les candidats sont moins nombreux cette année; *(at school, university)* le nombre d'inscriptions a baissé cette année; **a big/small entry** *(in competition)* une forte/faible participation

►► *Am* ***entry blank*** feuille *f* d'inscription; ***entry card*** *(for entry to a country)* fiche *f* de police *(au débarquement)*; ***entry fee*** *(for show, museum)* prix *m* d'entrée; *(for club, competition)* droit *m* d'inscription; ***entry form*** feuille *f* d'inscription; ***entry permit*** visa *m* d'entrée; ***entry tax*** taxe *f* d'entrée; ***entry visa*** visa *m* d'entrée; ***entry wound*** point *m* d'entrée d'une balle

entryism ['entrɪɪzəm] *n Pol* entrisme *m*, noyautage *m*

entryist ['entrɪɪst] *Pol* **1** *adj* d'entrisme, de noyautage

2 *n* personne *f* qui pratique l'entrisme *ou* le noyautage

entry-level *adj (bottom-of-the-range)* bas de gamme, d'entrée de gamme; **an entry-level computer** un ordinateur d'entrée de gamme

Entryphone® ['entrɪfəʊn] *n Br* Interphone® *m (à l'entrée d'un immeuble ou de bureaux)*

entryway ['entrɪweɪ] *n Am* entrée *f*; *(larger)* portail *m*; *(foyer)* foyer *m*, vestibule *m*

entwine [ɪn'twaɪn] **1** *vt* **to entwine sth round sth** enlacer qch autour de qch; **to become entwined** *(of one thing, ribbon etc)* s'enlacer; *(of two or more things, ribbons etc)* s'entrelacer; **with arms entwined** les bras entrelacés; **her hair was entwined with ribbons** ses cheveux étaient entrelacés de rubans

2 *vi* s'enlacer (**round** autour de); *(two or more things)* s'entrelacer

enucleate [ɪ'njuːklɪeɪt] *vt* (**a**) *Med* énucléer (**b**) *Literary* élucider

enucleation [ɪˌnjuːklɪ'eɪʃən] *n* (**a**) *Med* énucléation *f* (**b**) *Literary* élucidation *f*

E number *n Br* additif *m* code E; **there are a lot of E numbers in this jam** il y a beaucoup d'additifs dans cette confiture

enumerable [ɪ'njuːmərəbəl] *adj* dénombrable

enumerate [ɪ'njuːməreɪt] *vt* énumérer, dénombrer

enumeration [ɪˌnjuːmə'reɪʃən] *n* énumération *f*, dénombrement *m*

enumerative [ɪ'njuːmərətɪv] *adj* énumératif

enumerator [ɪ'njuːməreɪtə(r)] *n Admin* recenseur(euse) *m,f (qui passe à domicile faire remplir le formulaire)*

enunciate [ɪ'nʌnsɪeɪt] **1** *vt* (**a**) *(articulate)* articuler, prononcer (**b**) *Formal (formulate* → *idea, theory, policy)* énoncer, exprimer

2 *vi* articuler

enunciation [ɪˌnʌnsɪ'eɪʃən] *n* (**a**) *(articulation)* articulation *f*, prononciation *f* (**b**) *Formal (of idea, theory, policy)* énonciation *f*, exposition *f*; *(of problem)* énoncé *m*

enure [ɪ'njʊə(r)] **1** *vt* aguerrir; **to become enured to** s'habituer à

2 *vi Law* entrer en vigueur

enuresis [ˌenjʊə'riːsɪs] *n Med* énurésie *f*

enuretic [ˌenjʊə'retɪk] **1** *adj* énurétique

2 *n* énurétique *mf*

envelop [ɪn'veləp] *vt* envelopper (**in** dans *ou* de); **enveloped in a blanket** enveloppé dans une couverture; **enveloped in mystery** entouré *ou* voilé de mystère; **enveloped in mist** voilé de brume

envelope ['envələʊp] *n* (**a**) *(for letter)* enveloppe *f*; **put the letter in an envelope** mettez la lettre sous enveloppe; **in a sealed envelope** sous pli cacheté; **they came in the same envelope** ils sont arrivés sous le même pli; **back of an envelope calculations** calculs *mpl* effectués à la hâte; *Am Fam Fig* **to push the envelope** innover❑; **this company is pushing the envelope in Web design** cette entreprise est à l'avant-garde de la conception de sites Web❑

(**b**) *Biol* enveloppe *f*, tunique *f*; *Math* enveloppe *f*; *Electron* enveloppe *f*

(**c**) *(of balloon)* enveloppe *f*

envelopment [ɪn'veləpmənt] *n* enveloppement *m*

envenom [ɪn'venəm] *vt also Fig* envenimer

enviable ['envɪəbəl] *adj* enviable; **in the enviable position of being offered two jobs** dans la position enviable de se voir proposer deux emplois

enviably ['envɪəblɪ] *adv* d'une manière enviable; **enviably rich/well-read** d'une richesse/culture enviable

envious ['envɪəs] *adj (person)* envieux, jaloux; *(look, tone)* envieux, d'envie; **she's envious of their new house** elle est envieuse de leur nouvelle maison; **my sister's got a big house but I'm not envious** ma sœur a une grande maison, mais je ne l'envie pas; **I am very envious of you!** comme je t'envie!; **her success only made people envious** son succès n'a fait que des envieux *ou* jaloux

[illegible]

enviro [ɪn'vaɪərəʊ] *n Am Fam* écolo *mf*

environment [ɪn'vaɪərənmənt] *n* (**a**) *Ecol & Pol (nature)* environnement *m*; **the Secretary of State for the Environment, the Environment Secretary** ≃ le ministre de l'Environnement

(**b**) *(surroundings* → *physical)* cadre *m*, milieu *m*; (→ *social)* milieu *m*, environnement *m*; (→ *psychological)* milieu *m*, ambiance *f*; *Biol, Bot & Geog* milieu *m*; **an animal in its natural environment** un animal dans son milieu naturel; **a hostile environment** un climat d'hostilité, une ambiance hostile; **the novel examines the effect of environment on character** le roman étudie les effets du milieu ambiant sur le caractère; **a pleasant working environment** des conditions de travail agréables

(**c**) *Comput & Ling* environnement *m*

►► *Br* ***Environment Agency*** agence *f* pour la protection de l'environnement

environmental [ɪnˌvaɪərən'mentəl] *adj* (**a**) *Ecol &*

ent–env

Pol écologique; *(change)* de l'environnement (**b**) *(of surroundings)* du milieu
▸▸ ***environmental audit*** = rapport sur l'impact des activités d'une entreprise sur l'environnement; ***environmental damage*** dégâts *mpl* écologiques; **chemicals that cause environmental damage** produits chimiques nuisibles à l'environnement; ***environmental disaster*** catastrophe *f* écologique; ***environmental economics*** économie *f* de l'environnement; *Br* ***Environmental Health Officer*** inspecteur *m* sanitaire; ***environmental impact*** impact *m* sur l'environnement; ***environmental impact assessment*** étude *f* d'impact sur l'environnement; ***environmental pressure groups*** des groupes de pression pour la défense de l'environnement; *Am* ***Environmental Protection Agency*** = agence américaine pour la protection de l'environnement; ***environmental science*** science *f* de l'environnement; ***environmental stimuli*** stimuli *mpl* provenant du milieu ambiant; ***environmental studies*** science *f* de l'environnement

environmentalism [ɪn,vaɪərən'mentəlɪzəm] *n* (**a**) *Ecol* étude *f* de l'environnement (**b**) *Psy* environnementalisme *m*

environmentalist [ɪn,vaɪərən'mentəlɪst] *n* (**a**) *Ecol* écologiste *mf* (**b**) *Psy* environnementaliste *mf*

environmentally [ɪn,vaɪərən'mentəlɪ] *adv Ecol* écologiquement; **environmentally aware** sensibilisé aux problèmes de l'environnement; **environmentally-friendly** *(policy)* respectueux de l'environnement; *(technology, product)* non polluant; **environmentally sensitive** *(technology)* non polluant; *(site)* écologiquement fragile; **environmentally sound** *(practice, policy)* respectueux de l'environnement
▸▸ ***Environmentally Sensitive Area*** = zone de protection de la nature désignée par l'Union européenne où les agriculteurs doivent utiliser des méthodes traditionnelles

environment-friendly *adj (policy)* respectueux de l'environnement; *(technology, product)* non polluant

environs [ɪn'vaɪərənz] *npl Formal* environs *mpl*, alentours *mpl*; **Paris and its environs** Paris et ses environs

envisage [ɪn'vɪzɪdʒ], *Am* **envision** [ɪn'vɪʒən] *vt (imagine)* envisager; *(predict)* prévoir; **I don't envisage (that there will be) any difficulty** je n'envisage pas (qu'il puisse y avoir) la moindre difficulté

envoy ['envɔɪ] *n* (**a**) *(emissary)* envoyé(e) *m,f*, représentant(e) *m,f*; *Pol* **envoy (extraordinary)** ministre *m* plénipotentiaire (**b**) *Literature* envoi *m*

envy ['envɪ] (*pl* **envies**, *pt & pp* **envied**) **1** *n* (**a**) *(jealousy)* envie *f*, jalousie *f*; **out of envy** par envie *ou* jalousie; **to be green with envy** être dévoré d'envie; **filled with envy** dévoré de jalousie
(**b**) *(object of jealousy)* objet *m* d'envie; **she was the envy of all her friends** elle excitait *ou* faisait l'envie de tous ses amis
2 *vt* envier; **I do envy her** je l'envie vraiment; **I don't envy you!** je ne t'envie pas!; **I can't say I envy you** je ne peux pas dire que je t'envie; **to envy sb sth** envier qch à qn; **I envy him his success** je lui envie son succès; **I don't envy him having to catch such an early train** je ne l'envie pas d'avoir à prendre le train de si bonne heure

enwrap [ɪn'ræp] (*pt & pp* **enwrapped**) *vt Literary* envelopper, enrouler (**in** dans); *Fig* **enwrapped in slumber/thought** plongé dans le sommeil/dans ses pensées

enzootic [,enzəʊ'ɒtɪk] *Vet* **1** *n* enzootie *f*
2 *adj* enzootique

enzymatic [,enzɪ'mætɪk] *adj Biol & Chem* enzymatique

enzyme ['enzaɪm] *n Biol & Chem* enzyme *f*

enzymology [,enzɪ'mɒlədʒɪ] *n Biol & Chem* enzymologie *f*

EOC [,i:əʊ'si:] *n Admin* (*abbr* **Equal Opportunities Commission**) = commission pour l'égalité des chances en matière d'emploi en Grande-Bretagne

Eocene ['i:əʊsi:n] *Geol* **1** *adj* éocène
2 *n* éocène *m*

Eolian *Am* = **Aeolian**

eolith ['i:əʊlɪθ] *n Geol* éolithe *m*

Eolithic [,i:əʊ'lɪθɪk] *adj Geol* éolithique

eon *Am* = **aeon**

EONIA [i:'əʊnɪə] *n St Exch* (*abbr* **Euro Overnight Index Average**) EONIA *m*, TEMPÉ *m*

eonism ['ɪəʊnɪzəm] *n Psy* éonisme *m*

eosin, eosine ['i:əʊsɪn] *n Chem* éosine *f*

eosinophil, eosinophile [,i:əʊ'sɪnəfɪl] *n Biol* éosinophile *m*

eosinophilia [,i:əʊsɪnə'fɪlɪə] *n Med* éosinophilie *f*

eosinophilic [,i:əʊsɪnəʊ'fɪlɪk] *adj Biol* éosinophile

Eozoic [,i:əʊ'zəʊɪk] *adj Geol* précambrien

EP [,i:'pi:] *n* (**a**) (*abbr* **extended play**) super 45 tours *m*, EP *m* (**b**) *Am* (*abbr* **European Plan**) chambre *f* sans pension

EPA [,i:pi:'eɪ] *n* (*abbr* **Environmental Protection Agency**) = agence américaine pour la protection de l'environnement

epanalepsis [e,pænə'lepsɪs] *n Ling* épanalepse *f*

epaulette, *Am* **epaulet** [,epə'let] *n (gen) & Mil* épaulette *f*

épée ['eɪpeɪ] *n Sport (fencing sword)* épée *f*; *(event)* épreuve *f* d'épée

epeirogeny [,epaɪ'rɒdʒənɪ] *n Geol* mouvement *m* épeirogénique

epergne [ɪ'pɜ:n] *n* surtout *m* (de table)

ephedrin, ephedrine [*Br* 'efɪdri:n, *Am* ɪ'fedrən] *n Pharm* éphédrine *f*

ephemera [ɪ'femərə] (*pl* **ephemeras** *or* **ephemerae** [-,ri:]) *n* (**a**) *(short-lived thing)* chose *f* éphémère (**b**) *Zool* éphémère *m*

ephemeral [ɪ'femərəl] *adj* (**a**) *(short-lived)* éphémère, fugitif (**b**) *Zool* éphémère

ephemerid [ɪ'femərɪd] *n Zool* éphémère *m*

ephemeris [ɪ'femərɪs] (*pl* **ephemerides** [,efɪ'merɪ,di:z]) *n Astron* éphéméride *f*

Ephesian [ɪ'fi:ʒən] **1** *n (person)* Éphésien(enne) *m,f*; **the Epistle of Paul to the Ephesians** l'Épître *f* de saint Paul aux Éphésiens
2 *adj* éphésien
3 Ephesians *npl (UNCOUNT) Bible* Éphésiens *mpl*

Ephesus ['efəsəs] *n* Éphèse

Ephraim ['i:freɪm] *pr n Bible* Éphraïm

epiblast ['epɪblɑ:st] *n Biol* épiblaste *m*

epic ['epɪk] **1** *adj* (**a**) *(impressive)* héroïque, épique; *Hum* épique, homérique (**b**) *Literature* épique
2 *n* (**a**) *Literature* épopée *f*, poème *m ou* récit *m* épique (**b**) *(film)* film *m* à grand spectacle

epicalyx [,epɪ'keɪlɪks] *n Bot* épicalice *m*

epicanthus [,epɪ'kænθəs] *n Anat* épicanthus *m*

epicardium [,epɪ'kɑ:dɪəm] *n Anat* épicarde *m*

epicarp ['epɪ,kɑ:p] *n Bot* épicarpe *m*

epicene ['epɪsi:n] *adj* (**a**) *(hermaphrodite)* hermaphrodite; *(sexless)* asexué (**b**) *(effeminate)* efféminé (**c**) *Gram* épicène

epicentre, *Am* **epicenter** ['epɪsentə(r)] *n* épicentre *m*

epichlorhydrin [,epɪklɔ:'haɪdrɪn] *n Chem* épichlorhydrine *f*

epicondylitis [,epɪ,kɒndɪ'laɪtɪs] *n Med* épicondylite *f*

epicontinental [,epɪkɒntɪ'nentəl] *adj Geol* épicontinental

epicranial [,epɪ'kreɪnɪəl] *adj Anat* épicranien

epicranium [,epɪ'kreɪnɪəm] (*pl* **epicraniums** *or* **epicrania** [-nɪə]) *n Anat* épicrâne *m*

epicrisis ['epɪ,kraɪsɪs] *n Med* épicrise *f*

epicure ['epɪ,kjʊə(r)] *n* gourmet *m*, gastronome *mf*

epicurean [,epɪkjʊə'ri:ən] **1** *adj (gen)* épicurien
2 *n* (**a**) *(gen)* épicurien(enne) *m,f* (**b**) *(gourmet)* gourmet *m*, gastronome *mf*
3 Epicurean *Phil* **1** *adj* épicurien **2** *n* épicurien(enne) *m,f*

Epicureanism [,epɪkjʊə'ri:ənɪzəm] *n Phil* épicurisme *m*

Epicurus [,epɪ'kjʊərəs] *pr n* Épicure

epicycle ['epɪsaɪkəl] *n Astron* épicycle *m*

epicyclic [,epɪ'saɪklɪk] *adj Astron & Tech* épicycloïdal
▸▸ ***epicyclic gear, epicyclic train*** train *m* épicycloïdal

epicycloid [,epɪ'saɪklɔɪd] *n Geom* épicycloïde *f*

Epidaurus [,epɪ'dɔ:rəs] *n* Épidaure

epideictic [epɪ'daɪktɪk] *adj Literature* épidictique

epidemic [,epɪ'demɪk] *also Fig* **1** *n* épidémie *f*
2 *adj* épidémique; **of epidemic proportions** qui prend les proportions d'une épidémie

epidemiological [,epɪ,di:mɪə'lɒdʒɪkəl] *adj Med (evidence, research, study)* épidémiologique

epidemiologist [,epɪ,di:mɪ'ɒlədʒɪst] *n Med* épidémiologiste *mf*

epidemiology [,epɪ,di:mɪ'ɒlədʒɪ] *n Med* épidémiologie *f*

epidermal [,epɪ'dɜ:məl], **epidermic** [,epɪ'dɜ:mɪk] *adj Biol & Bot* épidermique

epidermis [,epɪ'dɜ:mɪs] *n Biol & Bot* épiderme *m*

epidermoid [,epɪ'dɜ:mɔɪd], **epidermoidal** [,epɪdɜ:'mɔɪdəl] *adj Med* épidermoïde

epidiascope [,epɪ'daɪəskəʊp] *n Phys* épidiascope *m*

epidiascopic [,epɪdaɪə'skɒpɪk] *adj Phys* épidiascopique

epididymis [,epɪ'dɪdɪmɪs] *n Biol* épididyme *m*

epidiorite [epɪ'daɪəraɪt] *n Miner* épidiorite *f*

epidural [,epɪ'djʊərəl] *Med* **1** *adj* épidural
2 *n* anesthésie *f* épidurale, péridurale *f*; **she had an epidural** on lui a fait une péridurale

epifocal [,epɪ'fəʊkəl] *adj Met* épicentral

epigastric [,epɪ'gæstrɪk] *adj Anat* épigastrique

epigastrium [,epɪ'gæstrɪəm] *n Anat* épigastre *m*

epigenesis [,epɪ'dʒenɪsɪs] *n* (**a**) *Biol* épigenèse *f* (**b**) *Geol* épigénie *f*

epigenetic [epɪdʒə'netɪk] *adj* **1** (**a**) *Biol* épigénétique (**b**) *Geol* épigénique
▸▸ ***epigenetic river*** cours *m* d'eau épigénique; ***epigenetic valley*** vallée *f* épigénique

epiglottis [,epɪ'glɒtɪs] (*pl* **epiglottises** *or* **epiglottides** [-tɪ,di:z]) *n Anat* épiglotte *f*

epigram ['epɪgræm] *n* épigramme *f*

epigrammatic [,epɪgrə'mætɪk] *adj* épigrammatique

epigrammatically [,epɪgrə'mætɪkəlɪ] *adv* épigrammatiquement

epigrammatist [,epɪ'græmətɪst] *n* epigrammatiste *mf*

epigraph ['epɪgrɑ:f] *n* épigraphe *f*

epigraphic [epɪ'grɑ:fɪk] *adj* épigraphique

epilepsy ['epɪlepsɪ] *n* épilepsie *f*

epileptic [,epɪ'leptɪk] **1** *adj* épileptique
2 *n* épileptique *mf*
▸▸ ***epileptic fit*** crise *f* d'épilepsie

epileptiform [,epɪ'leptɪfɔ:m] *adj Med* épileptiforme

epilogue, *Am* **epilog** ['epɪlɒg] *n* épilogue *m*

epinephrine [,epɪ'nefrɪn] *n Am Physiol* adrénaline *f*

Epiphanus [ɪ'pɪfənəs] *adj Antiq* épiphane

Epiphany [ɪ'pɪfənɪ] **1** *n* Épiphanie *f*, fête *f* des rois
2 epiphany *n Literary (revelation)* révélation *f*

epiphenomenon [,epɪfɪ'nɒmɪnən] (*pl* **epiphenomena** [-nə]) *n Phil & Psy* épiphénomène *m*

epiphyllous [epɪ'fɪləs] *adj Bot* épiphylle

epiphyseal, epiphysial [epɪ'fɪzɪəl] *adj Anat* épiphysaire
▸▸ ***epiphyseal cartilage*** cartilage *m* épiphysaire; ***epiphyseal closure*** soudure *f* des épiphyses; ***epiphyseal separation*** décollement *m* épiphysaire

epiphysis [ɪ'pɪfəsɪs] *n Anat* épiphyse *m*

epiphyte ['epɪ,faɪt] *n Bot* épiphyte *m*

epiphytic [,epɪ'fɪtɪk] *adj Bot* épiphyte

epirogenetic [ɪ,paɪrəʊdʒɪ'netɪk], **epirogenic** [ɪ,paɪrəʊ'dʒenɪk] *adj Geol* épirogénique, épeirogénique

Epirus [e'paɪərəs] *n* Épire

episcopacy [ɪ'pɪskəpəsɪ] (*pl* **episcopacies**) *n Rel* (**a**) *(church government)* gouvernement *m* d'une Église par les évêques (**b**) *(bishops collectively)* épiscopat *m*

episcopal [ɪ'pɪskəpəl] *adj Rel* épiscopal
▸▸ *Rel* ***the Episcopal Church*** l'Église *f* épiscopale; ***episcopal palace*** évêché *m*; ***episcopal ring*** anneau *m* pastoral

episcopalian [ɪ,pɪskəʊ'peɪljən] *Rel* **1** *adj* épiscopal, épiscopalien
2 *n* épiscopalien(enne) *m,f*; **the Episcopalians** les épiscopaux *mpl*, les épiscopaliens *mpl*

episcopate [ɪ'pɪskəpət] *n Rel* épiscopat *m*

episcope ['epɪskəʊp] *n Br Phys* épiscope *m*

episiotomy [ɪ,pɪzɪ'ɒtəmɪ] (*pl* **episiotomies**) *n Med* épisiotomie *f*

episode ['epɪsəʊd] *n* (**a**) *(period, event)* épisode m; *(part of story)* épisode *m*; **an unhappy episode in my life** un épisode malheureux de ma vie; **the first episode will be broadcast on Sunday** le premier épisode sera diffusé dimanche (**b**) *Med* crise *f*

episodic [ˌepɪˈsɒdɪk] *adj* épisodique

episodically [ˌepɪˈsɒdɪkəlɪ] *adv* épisodiquement

episome [ˈepɪsəʊm] *n Biol* épisome *m*

epistatic [ˌepɪˈstætɪk] *adj Biol* épistatique

epistaxis [ˌepɪˈstæksɪs] *n Med* épistaxis *f*, saignement *m* du nez

epistemic [ˌepɪˈstiːmɪk] *adj* épistémique

epistemics [ˌepɪˈstiːmɪks] *n (UNCOUNT)* épistémique *f*

epistemological [eˌpɪstɪməˈlɒdʒɪkəl] *adj Phil* épistémologique

epistemology [eˌpɪstiːˈmɒlədʒɪ] *n Phil* épistémologie *f*

episternum [ˌepɪˈstɜːnəm] *n Anat* épisterne *m*, épisternum *m*

epistle [ɪˈpɪsəl] **1** *n* (**a**) *Formal or Hum (letter)* lettre *f*, épître *f*; *Admin* courrier *m* (**b**) *Literature* épître *f*

2 Epistle *n Bible* **the Epistle to the Romans** l'Épître *f* aux Romains

epistolary [ɪˈpɪstələrɪ] *adj Formal* épistolaire

epistyle [ˈepɪstaɪl] *n Archit* épistyle *m*, architrave *f*

epitaph [ˈepɪˌtɑːf] *n* épitaphe *f*; **this, his last and greatest novel, is a fitting epitaph to his genius** ce roman, qui fut son dernier et son meilleur, témoigne de son génie

epitaxial [ˌepɪˈtæksɪəl] *adj Elec* épitaxial

epitaxis [ˌepɪˈtæksɪs], **epitaxy** [ˌepɪˈtæksɪ] *n Elec* épitaxie *f*

epithelial [ˌepɪˈθiːlɪəl] *adj Anat & Bot* épithélial

epithelium [ˌepɪˈθiːljəm] (*pl* **epitheliums** *or* **epithelia** [-ljə]) *n Anat & Bot* épithélium *m*

epithermal [ˌepɪˈθɜːməl] *adj* (**a**) *Geol* épithermal (**b**) *Phys* épithermique

epithet [ˈepɪθet] *n* épithète *f*

epitome [ɪˈpɪtəmɪ] *n* (**a**) *(typical example)* modèle *m*, type *m ou* exemple *m* même; **she's the epitome of generosity** elle est l'exemple même de la générosité *ou* la générosité même; **the house is the epitome of Baroque architecture** la maison est l'exemple même de l'architecture baroque (**b**) *(of book)* abrégé *m*, résumé *m*

epitomize, -ise [ɪˈpɪtəmaɪz] *vt* (**a**) *(typify)* personnifier, incarner; **this latest announcement epitomizes the government's attitude towards education** cette dernière déclaration est caractéristique de l'attitude du gouvernement concernant l'éducation (**b**) *(book)* abréger, résumer

epizoic [ˌepɪˈzəʊɪk] *adj Zool & Bot* épizoïque

epizoon [ˌepɪˈzəʊɒn] (*pl* **epizoa** [-ˈzəʊə]) *n Zool* épizoaire *m*

epizootic [ˌepɪzəʊˈɒtɪk] *Vet* **1** *adj (disease)* épizootique

2 *n* épizootie *f*

EPNS [ˌiːpiːenˈes] *n (abbr* **electroplated nickel silver***)* rudz *m*

EPO [ˌiːpiːˈəʊ] *n Physiol (abbr* **erythropoietin***)* EPO *f*

epoch [ˈiːpɒk] *n* époque *f*; **the discovery marked a new epoch in the history of science** cette découverte a fait date dans l'histoire de la science

epochal [ˈiːpɒkəl] *adj* (**a**) *(historical)* historique (**b**) *(of historical significance)* qui fait date

epoch-making *adj* qui fait date

eponym [ˈepəʊnɪm] *n* éponyme *m*

eponymous [ɪˈpɒnɪməs] *adj* du même nom, éponyme

EPOS [ˈiːpɒs] *n Comput (abbr* **electronic point of sale***)* = point de vente électronique

epoxy [ɪˈpɒksɪ] (*pl* **epoxies**) *Chem* **1** *adj (function, group)* époxy *(inv)*

2 *n* époxyde *m*

►► *Chem* ***epoxy resin*** résine *f* époxyde *ou* époxy

EPROM [ˈiːprɒm] *n Comput (abbr* **erasable programmable read-only memory***)* mémoire *f* morte effaçable

EPS [ˌiːpiːˈes] *n* (**a**) *Fin (abbr* **earnings per share***)* BPA *m* (**b**) *Comput (abbr* **encapsulated PostScript***)* EPS *m*

Epsom [ˈepsəm] *n* = célèbre terrain de courses de chevaux en Angleterre

►► ***Epsom salts*** sel *m* d'Epsom, epsomite *f*

Epstein-Barr virus [ˌepstaɪnˈbɑː-] *n Med* virus *m* d'Epstein-Barr

equability [ˌekwəˈbɪlɪtɪ] *n (of character, person)* placidité *f*, égalité *f* d'humeur; *(of climate)* caractère *m* tempéré; *(of temperature)* constance *f*

equable [ˈekwəbəl] *adj (character, person)* placide; *(climate)* tempéré; *(temperature)* constant

equably [ˈekwəblɪ] *adv* tranquillement, placidement

equal [ˈiːkwəl] *(Br pt & pp* **equalled**, *cont* **equalling**, *Am pt & pp* **equaled**, *cont* **equaling***)* **1** *adj* (**a**) *(of same size, amount, degree, type)* égal; **they are about equal** ils se valent; **equal in number** égal en nombre; **in equal measure** *(elements, ingredients)* en quantité égale; **I was embarrassed and annoyed in equal measure** j'étais aussi gêné qu'agacé; **equal in size to an orange** d'une taille égale à une orange; **to be equal to sth** égaler qch; **mix equal parts of sand and cement** mélangez du sable et du ciment en parts égales; **an equal amount of money** une même somme d'argent; **she speaks French and German with equal ease** elle parle français et allemand avec la même facilité; **to be on an equal footing with sb** être sur un pied d'égalité avec qn; **to meet/to talk to sb on equal terms** rencontrer qn/parler à qn d'égal à égal; **this will allow European businesses to compete on equal terms with their American counterparts** cela permettra aux entreprises européennes de pouvoir rivaliser avec leurs concurrentes américaines sur un pied d'égalité; **other** *or* **all things being equal** toutes choses égales par ailleurs; **equal pay for equal work** à travail égal salaire égal

(**b**) *(adequate)* **he proved equal to the task** il s'est montré à la hauteur de la tâche; **the machine is not equal to such heavy work** la machine n'est pas faite pour fournir un si grand effort; **to feel equal to doing sth** se sentir le courage de faire qch; **I don't feel equal to discussing it today** je ne me sens pas le courage d'en parler aujourd'hui

2 *n* égal(e) *m,f*, pair *m*; **a man who is your intellectual equal** un homme qui est votre égal intellectuellement; **she's easily his equal at tennis/chemistry** elle l'égale facilement au tennis/en chimie; **to talk to sb as an equal** parler à qn d'égal à égal; **we worked together as equals** nous avons travaillé ensemble sur un pied d'égalité; **he has no equal** il est hors pair, il n'a pas son pareil

3 *vt* (**a**) *(gen) & Math* égaler; **2 and 2 equals 4** 2 et 2 égalent *ou* font 4; **let x equal y** si x égale y

(**b**) *(match)* égaler; **no one in parliament could equal his eloquence** personne au parlement ne pouvait égaler son éloquence; **there is nothing to equal it** il n'y a rien de comparable *ou* de tel; **his arrogance is only equalled by his vulgarity** son arrogance n'a d'égale que sa vulgarité

►► *Admin* ***Equal Employment Opportunities Commission*** = commission pour l'égalité des chances en matière d'emploi, aux États-Unis; ***equal opportunities*** chances *fpl* égales, égalité *f* des chances; *Admin* ***Equal Opportunities Commission*** = commission pour l'égalité des chances en matière d'emploi, en Grande-Bretagne; ***equal opportunity employer*** = entreprise s'engageant à respecter la législation sur la non-discrimination dans l'emploi; *Fam* ***equal ops*** chances *fpl* égales❑, égalité *f* des chances❑; ***Equal Pay Act*** = loi garantissant l'égalité des droits des hommes et des femmes en matière d'emploi; ***equal rights*** égalité *f* des droits; ***Equal Rights Amendment*** = projet de loi américain rejeté en 1982 qui posait comme principe l'égalité des individus quels que soient leur sexe, leur religion ou leur race; ***equal sign, equals sign*** signe *m* égal; *Rad & TV* ***equal time*** droit *m* de réponse

equality [iːˈkwɒlətɪ] (*pl* **equalities**) *n* égalité *f*; **equality of opportunity** égalité *f* des chances; **equality in the eyes of the law** égalité *f* devant la loi; **women are still fighting for equality** les femmes se battent encore pour l'égalité

►► ***the Equality State*** = surnom donné au Wyoming

equalization [ˌiːkwəlaɪˈzeɪʃən] *n* (**a**) *(gen)* égalisation *f*; *Electron* régularisation *f* (**b**) *Fin (of taxes, wealth)* péréquation *f*; *(of dividends)* régularisation *f*

►► *Fin* ***equalization fund*** fonds *m* de parité; *Fin* ***equalization payment*** soulte *f*

equalize, -ise [ˈiːkwəlaɪz] **1** *vt (chances)* égaliser; *Fin (taxes, wealth)* faire la péréquation de; *(dividends)* régulariser

2 *vi Sport* égaliser

equalizer [ˈiːkwəlaɪzə(r)] *n* (**a**) *Sport* but *m ou* point *m* égalisateur (**b**) *Electron* égaliseur *m* (**c**) *Am Fam (handgun)* flingue *m*

equalizing [ˈiːkwəlaɪzɪŋ] *adj (current etc)* compensateur; *(pressure)* de compensation; *Sport* **the equalizing goal** le but égalisateur

equally [ˈiːkwəlɪ] *adv* (**a**) *(evenly)* également; **divided equally** divisé en parts *ou* parties égales; **equally spaced** également espacé; **to contribute equally to the expenses** contribuer pour une part égale à la dépense

(**b**) *(to same degree)* également, aussi; **they were equally responsible** ils étaient également responsables *ou* responsables au même degré; **I was equally surprised** j'ai été tout aussi surpris; **it applies equally to both young and old** cela concerne les jeunes comme les personnes âgées; **she worked equally hard** elle a travaillé tout aussi dur; **equally well** tout aussi bien; **equally talented students** élèves également *ou* pareillement doués

(**c**) *(by the same token)* **efficiency is important, but equally we must consider the welfare of the staff** l'efficacité, c'est important, mais nous devons tout autant considérer le bien-être du personnel; **equally, managers have responsibilities towards workers** de même, la direction a des obligations envers le personnel

equanimity [ˌiːkwəˈnɪmɪtɪ] *n Formal* égalité *f* d'âme, équanimité *f*; **to disturb sb's equanimity** troubler la sérénité de qn; **to recover one's equanimity** se ressaisir; **with equanimity** d'une âme égale, avec équanimité

equatable [ɪˈkweɪtəbəl] *adj* comparable, assimilable

equate [ɪˈkweɪt] *vt* (**a**) *(regard as equivalent)* assimiler, mettre sur le même pied; **some people wrongly equate culture with elitism** certaines personnes assimilent à tort culture et élitisme; **you can't equate Joyce with Homer** on ne peut pas mettre Homère et Joyce sur le même pied

(**b**) *(make equal)* égaler, égaliser; **our aim is to equate exports and imports** notre but est d'amener au même niveau les exportations et les importations; *Math* **to equate sth to sth** mettre qch en équation avec qch

equation [ɪˈkweɪʒən] *n* (**a**) *Formal (association)* assimilation *f*; **the equation of fame with success** l'assimilation de la célébrité au succès

(**b**) *Formal (equalization)* égalisation *f*

(**c**) *Chem & Math* équation *f*; *Fig* **money doesn't even come into the equation** les questions d'argent n'entrent même pas en ligne de compte; **after their recent good form, the Bullets must come into the equation too** il va falloir compter avec les Bullets, qui sont très en forme en ce moment

►► *Phys* ***equation of state*** équation *f* d'état; *Astron* ***equation of time*** équation *f* du temps

equator [ɪˈkweɪtə(r)] *n* équateur *m*; **at** *or* **on the equator** sous *ou* à l'équateur

equatorial [ˌekwəˈtɔːrɪəl] *adj* équatorial

Equatorial Guinea *n* Guinée-Équatoriale *f*; **in Equatorial Guinea** en Guinée-Équatoriale

equerry [ˈekwərɪ] (*pl* **equerries**) *n Br (of household)* intendant(e) *m,f (de la maison du roi ou de la reine)*; *(of stable)* écuyer(ère) *m,f*

equestrian [ɪˈkwestrɪən] **1** *adj (event)* hippique; *(skills)* équestre; *(statue)* équestre; *(equipment, clothing)* d'équitation

2 *n (rider)* cavalier(ère) *m,f*; *(in circus) & Mil* écuyer(ère) *m,f*

equestrianism [ɪˈkwestrɪəˌnɪzəm] *n* équitation *f*, hippisme *m*

equiangular [ˌiːkwɪˈæŋgjʊlə(r), ˌekwɪˈæŋgjʊlə(r)] *adj Geom* équiangle

equidistant [ˌiːkwɪˈdɪstənt, ˌekwɪˈdɪstənt] *adj* équidistant, à distance égale (**from** de)

equilateral [ˌiːkwɪˈlætərəl, ˌekwɪˈlætərəl] *adj* équilatéral

►► Geom *equilateral triangle* triangle *m* équilatéral

equilibrate [iː'kwɪlɪbreɪt, e'kwɪlɪbreɪt] *vt* équilibrer

equilibration [ˌiːkwɪlɪ'breɪʃən, eˌkwɪlɪ'breɪʃən] *n (action)* mise *f* en équilibre (**to** *or* **with** avec); *(result)* équilibration *f* (**to** *or* **with** avec)

equilibrium [ˌiːkwɪ'lɪbrɪəm, ˌekwɪ'lɪbrɪəm] *n* équilibre *m*; **in equilibrium** en équilibre; **how does the spinning top maintain its equilibrium?** comment la toupie garde-t-elle l'équilibre?; **she lost her equilibrium** elle a perdu l'équilibre

equine ['ekwaɪn] *adj (disease, family)* équin; *(profile)* chevalin

►► *equine distemper* gourme *f*

equinoctial [ˌiːkwɪ'nɒkʃəl, ˌekwɪ'nɒkʃəl] *adj (flower, line, point)* équinoxial; *(storm, tide)* d'équinoxe

equinox ['ekwɪnɒks] *n* équinoxe *m*; **autumnal equinox** équinoxe *m* d'automne; **spring** *or* **vernal equinox** équinoxe *m* de printemps, point *m* vernal

equip [ɪ'kwɪp] *(pt & pp* **equipped**, *cont* **equipping**) *vt* **(a)** *(fit out → factory)* équiper, outiller; *(→ laboratory, kitchen)* installer, équiper; *(→ army, soldier, ship)* équiper; **the hospital is not equipped to perform heart surgery** l'hôpital n'est pas équipé pour pratiquer la chirurgie du cœur

(b) *Fig (prepare)* **to be well-equipped to do sth** avoir tout ce qu'il faut pour faire qch; **it won't equip her for life's hardships** cela ne la préparera pas à affronter les épreuves de la vie; **he is ill-equipped to handle the situation** il est mal armé pour faire face à la situation

(c) *(supply → person)* équiper, pourvoir; *(→ army, machine, factory)* équiper, munir; **to equip sb with sth** munir *ou* équiper qn de qch; **the fighter plane is equipped with the latest technology** l'avion de combat est doté des équipements les plus modernes; **she equipped herself for the hike with a tent and a sleeping bag** elle s'est munie pour la randonnée d'une tente et d'un sac de couchage; **if your computer is equipped with a DVD drive** si votre ordinateur est pourvu d'un lecteur de DVD

equipage ['ekwɪpɪdʒ] *n (carriage) & Mil* équipage *m*

equipartition [ˌiːkwɪpɑː'tɪʃən] *n Phys* équipartition *f*

equipment [ɪ'kwɪpmənt] *n (UNCOUNT)* **(a)** *(gen)* équipement *m*; *(in laboratory, office, school)* matériel *m*; *Mil & Sport* équipement *m*, matériel *m*; **camping equipment** matériel *m* de camping; **electrical equipment** appareillage *m* électrique; **factory equipment** outillage *m*; **kitchen equipment** ustensiles *mpl* de cuisine; **laboratory/office equipment** matériel *m* de laboratoire/bureau; **lifesaving equipment** matériel *m* de sauvetage; **sports equipment** équipement *m* sportif

(b) *Fig* **intellectual equipment** capacité *f* intellectuelle

(c) *(act)* équipement *m*

(d) *Fam Hum (male genitalia)* service *m* trois pièces

equipoise ['ekwɪpɔɪz] *Formal* **1** *n (equilibrium)* équilibre *m*; *(counterbalance)* contrepoids *m*

2 *vt* contrebalancer, faire contrepoids à

equipotential [ˌiːkwɪpə'tenʃəl, ˌekwɪpə'tenʃəl] *adj Elec* équipotentiel

►► *equipotential surface* (surface *f*) équipotentielle *f*

equitable ['ekwɪtəbəl] *adj* équitable, juste

equitably ['ekwɪtəblɪ] *adv* équitablement, avec justice

equitation [ˌekwɪ'teɪʃən] *n Formal* équitation *f*

equity ['ekwətɪ] *(pl* **equities**) **1** *n* **(a)** *(fairness)* équité *f* **(b)** *Law (system)* équité *f*; *(right)* droit *m* équitable **(c)** *Fin (market value, of shareholders)* fonds *mpl ou* capitaux *mpl* propres; *(share)* action *f* ordinaire; *(of company)* capital *m* actions

2 Equity *n* = principal syndicat britannique des gens du spectacle

►► *equity capital* capital *m* actions; *equity dilution* dilution *f* du capital; *equity financing* financement *m* par actions, financement *m* par capitaux propres; *equity investment* placement *m* en actions; *equity issue* augmentation *f* du capital par émission d'actions; *equity leader* valeur *f* vedette; *Fin* *equity loan* prêt *m ou* titre *m* participatif; *the equities market* le marché des actions ordinaires; *equity risk premium* prime *f* de risque de variation du prix des actions; *equity share capital* capital *m* en actions ordinaires; *equities trader* courtier(ère) *m,f* sur actions; *St Exch* *equity trading* marché *m* des actions, courtage *m* sur actions; *St Exch* *equity unit trust* SICAV *f* actions; *equity warrant* bon *m* de souscription d'actions

equity-based unit trust *adj Fin* SICAV *f* actions

equity-linked *adj Fin & St Exch (policy)* libellé, investi en actions

equivalence [ɪ'kwɪvələns] *n* équivalence *f*; *Fin* **equivalences of exchange** parités *fpl* de change

equivalent [ɪ'kwɪvələnt] **1** *adj* équivalent; **to be equivalent to sth** être équivalent à qch, équivaloir à qch; **is there an equivalent organization in France?** y a-t-il une organisation équivalente en France?; **that would be equivalent to saying that...** cela reviendrait à dire que...

2 *n* équivalent *m*; **the French equivalent for "pound"** l'équivalent français du mot "pound"; **it costs the equivalent of £5 per week** cela coûte l'équivalent de 5 livres par semaine

►► *Chem* *equivalent weight* poids *m* équivalent

equivalve ['ekwɪvælv] *adj Zool* équivalve

equivocal [ɪ'kwɪvəkəl] *adj* **(a)** *(ambiguous → words, attitude)* ambigu(uë), équivoque **(b)** *(dubious → behaviour, person)* suspect, douteux; *(→ outcome)* incertain, douteux

equivocally [ɪ'kwɪvəkəlɪ] *adv* **(a)** *(ambiguously)* de manière équivoque *ou* ambiguë **(b)** *(dubiously)* de manière douteuse

equivocate [ɪ'kwɪvəkeɪt] *vi Formal* user d'équivoques *ou* de faux-fuyants, équivoquer

equivocation [ɪˌkwɪvə'keɪʃən] *n (UNCOUNT) Formal (words)* paroles *fpl* équivoques; *(prevarication)* tergiversation *f*

ER[1] [ˌiː'ɑː(r)] *n Am Med (abbr* **emergency room**) urgences *fpl*

ER[2] *(written abbr* **Elizabeth Regina**) = emblème de la reine Élisabeth

er [ɜː(r)] *exclam* heu

ERA ['ɪərə] *n Am (abbr* **Equal Rights Amendment**) = projet de loi américain rejeté en 1982 qui posait comme principe l'égalité des individus quels que soient leur sexe, leur religion ou leur race

era ['ɪərə] *n (gen)* époque *f*; *Geol & Hist* ère *f*; **the end of an era** la fin d'une époque; **her election marked a new era in politics** son élection a marqué un tournant dans la vie politique; **the era of horse travel** l'époque *ou* le temps des voyages à cheval

eradiate [ɪ'reɪdɪeɪt] *vi Literary* rayonner

eradiation [ɪˌreɪdɪ'eɪʃən] *n Literary* radiation *f*, rayonnement *m*

eradicable [ɪ'rædɪkəbəl] *adj (disease)* qui peut être éradiqué *ou* supprimé; *(poverty, problem, practice, weeds)* que l'on peut éliminer; *(abuse, crime)* extirpable

eradicate [ɪ'rædɪkeɪt] *vt (disease)* éradiquer, faire disparaître; *(poverty, problem)* faire disparaître, supprimer; *(abuse, crime)* extirper, supprimer; *(practice)* bannir, mettre fin à; *(weeds)* détruire, déraciner

eradication [ɪˌrædɪ'keɪʃən] *n (of disease)* éradication *f*; *(of poverty, problem)* suppression *f*; *(of abuse, crime)* extirpation *f*, suppression *f*; *(of practice)* fin *f*; *(of weeds)* destruction *f*, déracinement *m*

erasable [ɪ'reɪzəbəl] *adj* effaçable

erase [*Br* ɪ'reɪz, *Am* ɪ'reɪs] **1** *vt (writing)* effacer, gratter; *(with eraser)* gommer; *(from tape, disk, file)* effacer; *Fig* effacer; **I've erased it from my memory** je l'ai effacé de ma mémoire

2 *vi* s'effacer

►► *erase head* tête *f* d'effacement

eraser [*Br* ɪ'reɪzə(r), *Am* ɪ'reɪsə(r)] *n* gomme *f*

erasing [*Br* ɪ'reɪzɪŋ, *Am* ɪ'reɪsɪŋ] *n* effacement *m*

Erasmus [ɪ'ræzməs] *pr n* Érasme

erasure [ɪ'reɪʒə(r)] *n* **(a)** *(act)* effacement *m*, grattage *m* **(b)** *(mark)* rature *f*, grattage *m*

erbium ['ɜːbɪəm] *n Chem* erbium *m*

ERDF [ˌiːɑːˌdiː'ef] *n Fin (abbr* **European Regional Development Fund**) FEDER *m*

ere [eə(r)] *Arch or Literary* **1** *prep* avant; **ere long** sous peu; **ere now, ere this** déjà, auparavant; **ere then** d'ici là

2 *conj* avant que; **ere I leave** avant que je ne parte

erect [ɪ'rekt] **1** *adj* **(a)** *(upright)* droit; *(standing)* debout; **man walks erect** l'homme marche debout; **she holds herself very erect** elle se tient bien droite; **with head erect** la tête haute; **the dog sat with ears erect** le chien était assis les oreilles dressées **(b)** *Physiol (penis, nipples)* en érection

2 *vt (build → building, wall)* bâtir, construire; *(→ statue, temple)* ériger, élever; *(→ equipment)* installer; *(→ roadblock, tent, mast, scaffolding)* dresser; *Fig (system)* édifier; *(obstacle)* élever

erectile [ɪ'rektaɪl] *adj Anat* érectile

►► *Med* *erectile dysfunction* troubles *mpl* érectiles; *Anat* *erectile tissue* tissu *m* érectile

erection [ɪ'rekʃən] *n* **(a)** *(action → of building, wall)* construction *f*; *(→ of statue, temple)* érection *f*; *(→ of equipment)* installation *f*; *(→ of roadblock, tent, mast, scaffolding)* dressage *m*; *Fig (→ of system, obstacle)* édification *f* **(b)** *(building)* bâtiment *m*, construction *f* **(c)** *Physiol* érection *f*; **to have** *or* **to get an erection** avoir une érection

erectly [ɪ'rektlɪ] *adv (walk)* (tout) droit

erectness [ɪ'rektnɪs] *n* attitude *f* droite; **the erectness of his bearing** sa posture droite

erector [ɪ'rektə(r)] *n* **(a)** *(muscle)* érecteur *m* **(b)** *(builder)* constructeur(trice) *m,f*

►► *Am* *erector set* jeu *m* de construction

eremite ['erɪmaɪt] *n Arch or Literary* ermite *m*

erg [ɜːg] *n Phys & Geog* erg *m*

ergative ['ɜːgətɪv] *Ling* **1** *adj* ergatif

2 *n* ergatif *m*

ergo ['ɜːgəʊ] *adv Formal or Hum* donc, par conséquent

ergometer [ɜː'gɒmɪtə(r)] *n Tech* dynamomètre *m*

ergonomic [ˌɜːgəʊ'nɒmɪk] *adj* ergonomique

ergonomically [ˌɜːgəʊ'nɒmɪkəlɪ] *adv* du point de vue ergonomique; **ergonomically designed** *(chair, car, office)* d'une conception ergonomique

ergonomics [ˌɜːgəʊ'nɒmɪks] *n (UNCOUNT)* ergonomie *f*

ergonomist [ɜː'gɒnəmɪst] *n* ergonomiste *mf*

ergot ['ɜːgət] *n Agr* ergot *m*; *Pharm* ergot *m* de seigle

ergotism ['ɜːgətɪzəm] *n Med* ergotisme *m*

Erhard Seminars Training ['eːrhart-] *n Psy* = méthode de formation psychologique créée par Werner Erhard

ERIC ['erɪk] *n Am (abbr* **Educational Resources Information Center**) = centre d'information américain sur l'éducation

erica ['erɪkə] *n Bot* éricacée *f*

ericaceous [ˌerɪ'keɪʃəs] *adj Bot* éricacé

Erie Canal ['ɪərɪ-] *n* **the Erie Canal** le canal de l'Érié

erigeron [ɪ'rɪdʒərən] *n Bot (plant)* érigéron *m*

Erin ['erɪn] *n Arch or Literary* Irlande *f*

ERISA [ə'riːsə] *n Am (abbr* **Employee Retirement Income Security Act**) = loi américaine sur les pensions de retraite

Eritrea [ˌerɪ'treɪə] *n* Erythrée *f*; **in Eritrea** en Erythrée

Eritrean [ˌerɪ'treɪən] **1** *n* Erythréen(enne) *m,f*

2 *adj* érythréen

ERM [ˌiːɑː'rem] *n Formerly Fin (abbr* **exchange rate mechanism**) mécanisme *m* de change (du SME)

ermine ['ɜːmɪn] *n (fur, robe, stoat)* hermine *f*

Ernie ['ɜːnɪ] *n Br Fam (abbr* **Electronic Random Number Indicator Equipment**) = en Grande-Bretagne, ordinateur qui sert au tirage des numéros gagnants des bons à lots

erode [ɪ'rəʊd] **1** *vt* **(a)** *(of water, wind)* éroder, ronger; *(of acid, rust)* ronger, corroder; **the rock face had been eroded away** la paroi du rocher avait été érodée **(b)** *Fig (courage, power)* ronger, miner; *(confidence)* miner, entamer; **the party's traditional power base has been gradually eroded** la base traditionnelle du parti s'effrite

2 *vi (rock, soil)* s'éroder; **the cliff is slowly eroding (away)** la falaise est lentement en train de s'éroder

erogenous [ɪ'rɒdʒɪnəs] *adj* érogène

►► ***erogenous zone*** zone *f* érogène

Eros ['ɪərɒs] **1** *pr n Myth* Éros

2 *n Br* = surnom donné au monument en l'honneur du comte de Shaftesbury, à Piccadilly Circus

erosion [ɪ'rəʊʒən] *n (of soil, rock)* érosion *f*; *(of metal)* corrosion *f*; *Fig (of courage, power)* érosion *f*, corrosion *f*; *Fig (of confidence, popularity)* détérioration *f*; **wind erosion** érosion *f* éolienne; **soil erosion** érosion *f* du sol; **erosion of prices** effritement *m* des prix

erosive [ɪ'rəʊsɪv] *adj* érosif; *(corrosive)* corrosif

erotic [ɪ'rɒtɪk] *adj* érotique

erotica [ɪ'rɒtɪkə] *npl Art* art *m* érotique; *Literature* littérature *f* érotique

erotically [ɪ'rɒtɪklɪ] *adv* érotiquement; **to be erotically charged** avoir un contenu érotique

eroticism [ɪ'rɒtɪsɪzəm], **erotism** ['erətɪzəm] *n* érotisme *m*

erotogenic [ɪ,rɒtə'dʒenɪk] *adj* érotogène

erotomania [ɪ,rɒtəʊ'meɪnɪə] *n* érotomanie *f*

erotomaniac [ɪ,rɒtəʊ'meɪnɪæk] *n* érotomane *mf*, érotomaniaque *mf*

err [ɜ:(r)] *vi Formal* (**a**) *(make mistake)* se tromper; **to err in one's judgement** faire une erreur de jugement; **I erred on the side of caution** j'ai péché par excès de prudence; *Prov* **to err is human(, to forgive divine)** l'erreur est humaine (, le pardon divin) (**b**) *(sin)* pécher, commettre une faute (**c**) *(stray)* s'égarer, s'écarter (**from** de); *also Hum* **to err from the straight and narrow** s'égarer du droit chemin

errancy ['erənsɪ] *n Literary* état *m* d'erreur

errand ['erənd] *n* commission *f*, course *f*; **to go on** *or* **to do** *or* **to run an errand (for sb)** faire une course (pour qn); **I did** *or* **ran all the errands** j'ai fait toutes les commissions *ou* les courses; **to send sb on an errand** envoyer qn faire une commission *ou* une course; **an errand of mercy** une mission de charité

►► ***errand boy*** garçon *m* de courses

errant ['erənt] *adj* (**a**) *(wayward)* dévoyé; **errant ways** vie *f* dévoyée; **errant husband** mari *m* infidèle (**b**) *(roaming)* errant

errata [e'rɑ:tə] **1** *pl of* **erratum**

2 *npl (list)* errata *m inv*

►► ***errata slip*** liste *f* des errata

erratic [ɪ'rætɪk] **1** *adj* (**a**) *(irregular → results)* irrégulier; *(→ performance)* irrégulier, inégal; *(→ person)* fantasque, excentrique; *(→ mood)* changeant; *(→ movement, course)* mal assuré; **he is a bit erratic** on ne sait jamais comment il va réagir; **erratic driving** conduite *f* déconcertante; **her playing is erratic** *(musician)* son jeu est inégal; **the road/river follows an erratic course** la route/rivière suit un cours irrégulier (**b**) *Geol & Med* erratique

2 *n Geol* bloc *m ou* roche *f* erratique

erratically [ɪ'rætɪkəlɪ] *adv (act, behave)* de manière fantasque *ou* capricieuse; *(move, work)* irrégulièrement, par à-coups; **he drives erratically** il conduit de façon déconcertante; **to play erratically** *(sportsman, musician)* avoir un jeu inégal

erratum [e'rɑ:təm] *(pl* **errata** [e'rɑ:tə]*)* erratum *m*

erring ['ɜ:rɪŋ] *adj (sinning)* dévoyé, égaré; *(mistaken)* tombé dans l'erreur; *(husband, wife)* infidèle; **erring ways** vie *f* dévoyée

erroneous [ɪ'rəʊnjəs] *adj* erroné, inexact

erroneously [ɪ'rəʊnjəslɪ] *adv* erronément, à tort

erroneousness [ɪ'rəʊnjəsnɪs] *n* erreur *f*, fausseté *f*

error ['erə(r)] *n* (**a**) *(mistake)* erreur *f*, faute *f*; **to make** *or* **to commit an error** faire (une) erreur; **an error of judgment** une erreur de jugement; **it would be an error to assume that...** ce serait une erreur *ou* on aurait tort de supposer que...; *Com* **errors and omissions excepted** sauf erreur ou omission

(**b**) *Math (mistake)* faute *f*; *(deviation)* écart *m*; **degree of error** marge *f* d'erreur

(**c**) *(mistakenness)* erreur *f*; **it was done in error** cela a été fait par erreur *ou* méprise; **he was in error over** *or* **on this point of law** il était dans l'erreur *ou* il avait tort sur ce point de loi; **I've seen the error of my ways** je suis revenu de mes erreurs; **to show sb the error of his ways** montrer à qn qu'il est dans le mauvais chemin; *Rel* **to be in/to fall into error** être/tomber dans l'erreur

►► *Comput* ***error code*** code *m* d'erreur; *Comput* ***error correction*** correction *f* d'erreur; *Comput* ***error message*** message *m* d'erreur; *Comput* ***error routine*** sous-programme *m* de correction d'erreurs

ersatz ['eəzæts] **1** *adj* **this is ersatz coffee** c'est de l'ersatz *ou* du succédané de café; **this sugar is ersatz** ce sucre est un ersatz *ou* un succédané

2 *n* ersatz *m*, succédané *m*

Erse [ɜ:s] **1** *adj* gaélique, erse

2 *n* gaélique *m*

erstwhile ['ɜ:stwaɪl] *Literary or Hum* **1** *adj* d'autrefois

2 *adv* autrefois, jadis

eructate ['i:rʌkteɪt] *vi Formal or Med* éructer

eructation [,i:rʌk'teɪʃən] *n Formal or Med* éructation *f*

erudite ['eru:daɪt] *adj (book, person)* érudit, savant; *(word)* savant

eruditely ['eru:daɪtlɪ] *adv* de manière savante, avec érudition

erudition [,eru:'dɪʃən] *n* érudition *f*

erupt [ɪ'rʌpt] *vi* (**a**) *(volcano → start)* entrer en éruption; *(→ continue)* faire éruption; **an erupting volcano** un volcan en éruption

(**b**) *(pimples)* sortir, apparaître; *(tooth)* percer; **her face erupted in spots** elle a eu une éruption de boutons sur le visage

(**c**) *Fig (laughter, war, violence)* éclater; *(fire)* se déclarer; *(anger)* exploser; **the city erupted into violence** il y eut une explosion de violence dans la ville; **the stadium erupted in a huge roar** un énorme rugissement a retenti dans le stade; **he erupted when I told him the news** il est devenu furieux quand je lui ai annoncé la nouvelle

eruption [ɪ'rʌpʃən] *n* (**a**) *(of volcano)* éruption *f* (**b**) *(of pimples)* éruption *f*, poussée *f*; *(of teeth)* percée *f* (**c**) *Fig (of laughter)* éclat *m*, éruption *f*; *(of anger)* accès *m*, éruption *f*; *(of violence)* explosion *f*, accès *m*; **it happened shortly before the eruption of the civil war** cela s'est produit peu avant que la guerre civile n'éclate

eruptive [ɪ'rʌptɪv] *adj Med & Geol* éruptif

ERW [,i:ɑ:'dʌbəlju:] *n Mil* (*abbr* **enhanced radiation weapon**) arme *f* à rayonnement renforcé

erysipelas [,erɪ'sɪpɪləs] *n Med* érysipèle *m*, érésipèle *m*

erythema [,erɪ'θi:mə] *n Med* érythème *m*

erythematous [,erɪθɪ'meɪtəs] *adj Med* érythémateux

erythraemia, *Am* **erythremia** [,erɪ'θri:mɪə] *n Med* érythrémie *f*

erythrasma [,erɪ'θræzmə] *n Med* érythrasma *m*

erythrocyte [ɪ'rɪθrəʊsaɪt] *n Anat* érythrocyte *m*

erythrocytosis [ɪ,rɪθrəʊsaɪ'təʊsɪs] *n Med* érythrocytose *f*

erythromycin [ɪ,rɪθrəʊ'maɪsɪn] *n Pharm* érythromycine *f*

erythropoietin [ɪ,rɪθrəʊpɔɪ'i:tɪn] *n Anat* érythropoïétine *f*

erythrosine [ɪ'rɪθrəʊsɪn] *n Chem* érythrosine *f*

ESA [,i:es'eɪ] *n* (**a**) (*abbr* **European Space Agency**) ESA *f* (**b**) *Ecol* (*abbr* **Environmentally Sensitive Area**) = zone de protection de la nature désignée par l'Union européenne où les agriculteurs doivent utiliser des méthodes traditionnelles

Esau ['i:sɔ:] *pr n Bible* Ésaü

escalate ['eskəleɪt] **1** *vi* (**a**) *(prices etc)* monter (en flèche) (**b**) *(war, situation etc)* s'aggraver; **small incidents can easily escalate into a world war** de simples incidents (militaires) peuvent facilement mener à une guerre mondiale

2 *vt (fighting)* intensifier; *(problem)* aggraver; *(prices)* faire grimper

escalation [eskə'leɪʃən] *n* (**a**) *(of prices etc)* augmentation *f* (rapide), montée *f* en flèche; *(of interest rates)* escalade *f* (**b**) *(of war, situation)* escalade *f*

escalator ['eskəleɪtə(r)] *n* escalier *m* roulant *ou* mécanique, escalator *m*

►► *Law* ***escalator clause*** clause *f* d'indexation *ou* de révision

escalope ['eskə,lɒp] *n Culin* escalope *f*

escapade [,eskə'peɪd] *n (adventure)* équipée *f*; *(scrape)* fredaine *f*, escapade *f*; *(prank)* frasque *f*

escape [ɪ'skeɪp] **1** *vi* (**a**) *(get away → person, animal)* échapper, s'échapper; *(→ prisoner)* s'évader; **they escaped from the enemy/from the hands of their kidnappers** ils ont échappé à l'ennemi/des mains de leurs ravisseurs; **the thieves escaped after a police chase** les voleurs ont pris la fuite après avoir été poursuivis par la police; **the lion escaped from the zoo** le lion s'est échappé du zoo; **she escaped from the camp** elle s'est échappée du camp; *Fig* **to escape from the crowd** fuir la foule; *Fig* **to escape from reality** s'évader *ou* s'échapper de la réalité; **he escaped to Italy** il s'est enfui en Italie

(**b**) *(gas, liquid, steam)* s'échapper, fuir

(**c**) *(survive, avoid injury)* s'en tirer, en réchapper; **she escaped uninjured** elle s'en est tirée sans aucun mal; **they escaped with just a few cuts and bruises** ils en ont été quittes pour quelques coupures et des bleus; **he escaped with a reprimand** il en a été quitte pour une réprimande

2 *vt* (**a**) *(avoid)* échapper à; **to escape doing sth** éviter de faire qch; **I narrowly escaped being killed** j'ai failli *ou* manqué me faire tuer; **they escaped punishment/justice** ils ont échappé à la punition/justice; **he escaped detection** il ne s'est pas fait repérer; **she narrowly escaped death** elle a échappé de justesse à la mort; **there's no escaping the fact that...** il n'y a pas moyen d'échapper au fait que...

(**b**) *(elude notice, memory of)* échapper à; **to escape notice** échapper à l'attention, passer inaperçu; **her name escapes me** son nom m'échappe; **nothing escapes them** rien ne leur échappe

3 *n* (**a**) *(of person)* fuite *f*, évasion *f*; *(of prisoner)* évasion *f*; *(of animal)* fuite *f*; **I made my escape** je me suis échappé *ou* évadé; **to make good one's escape** réussir à s'échapper; **they planned their escape** ils ont combiné leur plan d'évasion; *Fig* **he had a narrow escape** *(from danger)* il l'a échappé belle, il a eu chaud; *(from illness)* il revient de loin

(**b**) *(diversion)* évasion *f*; **an escape from reality** une évasion hors de la réalité; *Fig* **the cinema provided an escape from their daily routine** le cinéma leur offrait un moyen de s'évader de leur routine quotidienne

(**c**) *(of gas, liquid)* fuite *f*; *(of exhaust fumes, steam)* échappement *m*

(**d**) *Comput* échappement *m*; *(key)* touche *f* d'échappement *m*

4 *comp (plot)* d'évasion; *(device)* de sortie, de secours

►► *Law* ***escape clause*** clause *f* échappatoire; ***escape hatch*** trappe *f* de secours; *Comput* ***escape key*** touche *f* d'échappement, touche *f* Echap; ***escape mechanism*** *Tech* mécanisme *m* de secours; *Psy* fuite *f* (devant la réalité); ***escape pipe*** tuyau *m* d'échappement *ou* de refoulement, tuyère *f*; ***escape road*** talus *m* de protection; ***escape route*** *(from fire)* itinéraire *m* de sortie de secours; *(of criminal)* itinéraire *m* ménagé pour s'échapper; *Comput* ***escape routine*** procédure *f* d'échappement; *Tech* ***escape valve*** soupape *f* d'échappement; *Astron* ***escape velocity*** vitesse *f* de libération; *Tech* ***escape wheel*** roue *f* d'échappement

escaped [ɪ'skeɪpt] *adj* échappé; **an escaped prisoner** un(e) évadé(e)

escapee [ɪ,skeɪ'pi:] *n* évadé(e) *m,f*

escapement [ɪ'skeɪpmənt] *n (of clock, piano)* échappement *m*; *Tech* échappement *m*

escaper [ɪs'keɪpə(r)] *n* fugitif(ive) *m,f*

escapism [ɪ'skeɪpɪzəm] *n* évasion *f* hors de la réalité, fuite *f* devant la réalité

escapist [ɪ'skeɪpɪst] **1** *n* = personne cherchant à s'évader du réel

2 *adj* d'évasion

escapologist [,eskə'pɒlədʒɪst] *n* = virtuose de l'évasion dans les spectacles de magie

escapology [,eskə'pɒlədʒɪ] *n* = art de l'évasion dans les spectacles de magie

escarpment [ɪ'skɑ:pmənt] *n Geog* escarpement *m*

esc–est

eschatological [ˌeskətə'lɒdʒɪkəl] *adj* eschatologique

eschatology [ˌeskə'tɒlədʒɪ] *n* eschatologie *f*

escheat [ɪs'tʃiːt] *n Law* dévolution *f* des biens à l'État *(en l'absence des héritiers)*

eschew [ɪs'tʃuː] *vt Formal (duty, work, activity)* éviter; *(alcohol)* s'abstenir de boire; *(publicity, temptation, involvement)* fuir; **they have eschewed the use of new technology in favour of traditional methods** ils ont évité d'employer des techniques nouvelles au profit de méthodes traditionnelles

esc key [esk-] *n Comput* touche *f* d'échappement, touche *f* Echap

escort 1 *n* ['eskɔːt] (**a**) *(guard)* escorte *f*, cortège *m*; *Mil & Naut* escorte *f*; **under the escort of** sous l'escorte de; **under police escort** sous escorte policière; **they were given a police escort** on leur a donné une escorte de police

(**b**) *(from agency → woman)* hôtesse *f*, accompagnatrice *f*, escorte *f*; *(→ man)* accompagnateur *m*, escort *m*

(**c**) *Old-fashioned (for woman)* cavalier *m*; *(for man)* cavalière *f*

2 *comp* ['eskɔːt] d'escorte

3 *vt* [ɪ'skɔːt] (**a**) *Formal (accompany)* accompagner, escorter; **may I escort you home?** permettez-moi de vous raccompagner; **kindly escort these gentlemen to the door** veuillez raccompagner ces messieurs jusqu'à la porte; **her uncle escorted her to the dance** son oncle l'a accompagnée au bal

(**b**) *(of police) & Mil* escorter; *(prisoner)* conduire sous escorte; **they escorted him in/out** ils l'ont fait entrer/sortir sous escorte

►► ***escort agency*** service *m ou* bureau *m* d'hôtesses; *Mil* ***escort duty*** service *m* d'escorte; *Mil & Aviat* ***escort fighter*** chasseur *m* d'escorte; ***escort vessel*** (vaisseau *m*) escorteur *m*

escritoire [ˌeskrɪ'twɑː(r)] *n* secrétaire *m*, bureau *m* (de salon)

escrow ['eskrəʊ] *n Law* dépôt *m* fiduciaire *ou* conditionnel; **in escrow** en dépôt fiduciaire, en main tierce

►► *Law* ***escrow account*** compte *m* bloqué; ***escrow agent*** dépositaire *mf* légal(e)

escudo [es'kuːdəʊ] *n* escudo *m*

esculent ['eskjʊlənt] **1** *n* substance *f* comestible

2 *adj* comestible

escutcheon [ɪ'skʌtʃən] *n* (**a**) *(shield)* écu *m*, écusson *m* (**b**) *(on door, handle, light switch)* écusson *m*

ESE *(written abbr* **east-south-east***)* E-SE

esker ['eskə(r)] *n Geol* os *m*

Eskimo ['eskɪməʊ] *(pl* **inv** *or* **Eskimos***)* **1** *n* (**a**) *(person)* Esquimau(aude) *m,f* (**b**) *Ling* esquimau *m*

2 *adj* esquimau

►► ***Eskimo dog*** chien *m* esquimau; *Sport* ***Eskimo roll*** esquimautage *m*

> **ESKIMO**
>
> Aux États-Unis et au Canada le terme "Eskimo" est souvent considéré comme injurieux; on préfère le terme "Inuit".

Esky, esky ['eskɪ] *n Austr* glacière *f*

ESL [ˌiːes'el] *n (abbr* **English as a Second Language***)* = l'anglais comme deuxième langue

ESN [ˌiːes'en] *adj Old-fashioned (abbr* **educationally subnormal***)* en retard sur le plan scolaire

ESOL [ˌiːesˌəʊ'el] *n Am (abbr* **English for Speakers of Other Languages***)* = anglais langue étrangère

ESOP [ˌiːesˌəʊ'piː] *n (abbr* **employee** *Br* **share** *or Am* **stock ownership plan***)* plan *m* d'actionnariat des salariés

esophagus, esophagitis *etc Am* = **oesophagus, oesphagitis** *etc*

esoteric [ˌesə'terɪk] *adj (obscure)* ésotérique; *(private)* secret(ète)

esoterically [ˌesə'terɪkəlɪ] *adv (obscurely)* d'une façon ésotérique; *(privately)* secrètement

esotericism [ˌesə'terɪsɪzəm], **esoterism** [e'sɒtərɪzəm] *n* ésotérisme *m*

ESP [ˌiːes'piː] *n* (**a**) *(abbr* **extrasensory perception***)* perception *f* extrasensorielle (**b**) *(abbr* **English for special purposes***)* = anglais spécialisé

esp. *(written abbr* **especially***)* particulièrement

espadrille [ˌespə'drɪl] *n* espadrille *f*

espalier [ɪ'spæljə(r)] **1** *n (tree)* arbre *m* en espalier; *(trellis)* espalier *m*; *(method)* culture *f* en espaliers

2 *vt* cultiver en espalier

esparto [e'spɑːtəʊ] *(pl* **espartos***)* *n Bot* **esparto (grass)** alfa *m*

especial [ɪ'speʃəl] *adj Formal (notable)* particulier, exceptionnel; *(specific)* particulier; **of especial importance** d'une importance toute particulière

especially [ɪ'speʃəlɪ] *adv* (**a**) *(to a particular degree)* particulièrement, spécialement; *(particularly)* en particulier, surtout; **the condition usually affects women, especially women over 50** cette maladie touche généralement les femmes, et particulièrement celles de plus de 50 ans; **he likes birds, especially parrots** il aime les oiseaux, spécialement les perroquets; **I can't mention it, especially since** *or* **as I'm not supposed to know anything about it** je ne peux pas en parler d'autant que *ou* surtout que je ne suis pas censé savoir quoi que ce soit à ce sujet; **you especially ought to know better!** vous devriez le savoir mieux que personne!; **the food at this restaurant is especially good** la cuisine de ce restaurant est particulièrement bonne; **be especially careful with this one** faites particulièrement attention à celui-ci; **was it any good? – not especially** est-ce que c'était bien? – pas particulièrement

(**b**) *(for a particular purpose)* exprès; **he went especially to meet her** il est allé exprès pour la rencontrer; **I did it especially for you** je l'ai fait spécialement *ou* exprès pour vous

Esperantist [ˌespə'ræntɪst] **1** *n* espérantiste *mf*

2 *adj* espérantiste

Esperanto [ˌespə'ræntəʊ] **1** *n* espéranto *m*

2 *adj* en espéranto

espial [ɪs'paɪəl] *n Literary* action *f* d'apercevoir

espionage ['espɪəˌnɑːʒ] *n* espionnage *m*

esplanade [ˌesplə'neɪd] *n* esplanade *f*

espousal [ɪ'spaʊzəl] *n* (**a**) *Formal (of belief, cause)* adoption *f* (**b**) *Arch (marriage)* mariage *m*

espouse [ɪ'spaʊz] *vt* (**a**) *Formal (belief, cause)* épouser, adopter (**b**) *Arch (marry)* épouser

espresso [e'spresəʊ] *(pl* **espressos***)* *n* (café *m*) express *m*

►► ***espresso machine*** machine *f* à express

espy [ɪ'spaɪ] *(pt & pp* **espied***)* *vt Literary* apercevoir, distinguer

Esq. *(written abbr* **Esquire***)* **Gregor Clark, Esq.** M.Gregor Clark

esquire [ɪ'skwaɪə(r)] *Br* **1** *n Hist* écuyer *m*

2 Esquire *n* **Gregor Clark, Esquire** M.Gregor Clark

ESRC [ˌiːesˌɑː'siː] *n Br (abbr* **Economic and Social Research Council***)* = organisme chargé de distribuer des subventions pour la recherche en sciences sociales

essay 1 *n* ['eseɪ] (**a**) *Literature* essai *m*; *Sch* composition *f*, dissertation *f*; *Univ* dissertation *f* (**b**) *Formal (attempt)* essai *m*, tentative *f*

2 *vt* [e'seɪ] *Formal* (**a**) *(try)* essayer, tenter; **to essay a smile** tenter de sourire (**b**) *(test)* mettre à l'épreuve

essayist ['eseɪɪst] *n* essayiste *mf*

essence ['esəns] **1** *n* (**a**) *(gen)* essence *f*, essentiel *m*; **the essence of her speech was that...** l'essentiel de son discours tenait en ceci que...; **time is of the essence** il est essentiel de faire vite, la vitesse s'impose; **she's the essence of generosity** elle est la générosité même

(**b**) *Phil* essence *f*, nature *f*; *Rel* essence *f*

(**c**) *Chem* essence *f*; **essence of rosemary** essence *f* de romarin; **peppermint essence** essence *f* de menthe

(**d**) *Culin* extrait *m*; **vanilla essence** extrait *m* de vanille

2 in essence *adv* essentiellement, surtout; **it is in essence a question of...** c'est essentiellement *ou* surtout une question de...

essential [ɪ'senʃəl] **1** *adj* (**a**) *(vital → action, equipment, services)* essentiel, indispensable; *(→ point, role)* essentiel, capital; *(→ question)* essentiel, fondamental; **a well-trained workforce is essential to the success of your business** un personnel qualifié est essentiel au succès de votre entreprise; **it is essential to know whether...** il est essentiel *ou* il importe de savoir si...; **the essential thing** l'essentiel *m*; **the essential thing is to relax** l'essentiel est de rester calme; **a balanced diet is essential for good health** un régime équilibré est essentiel pour être en bonne santé; **essential information** *(on package label)* mentions *fpl* obligatoires

(**b**) *(basic)* essentiel, fondamental; **the essential goodness of man** la bonté essentielle de l'homme; **the essential difference between them is that...** la différence principale entre eux est que...

2 *n* objet *m* indispensable; **the essentials** l'essentiel *m*; **we can only afford to buy the essentials** nous n'avons les moyens d'acheter que l'essentiel; **a dishwasher is an essential of a modern kitchen** un lave-vaisselle est un élément indispensable dans une cuisine moderne; **the essentials of astronomy** les rudiments *mpl* de l'astronomie; **in (all) essentials** essentiellement

►► *Biol* ***essential amino acid*** acide *m* aminé essentiel; ***essential goods*** biens *mpl* de première nécessité; ***essential oil*** huile *f* essentielle

essentialism [ɪ'senʃəlɪzəm] *n Phil* essentialisme

essentialist [ɪ'senʃəlɪst] *Phil* **1** *n* essentialiste **2** *adj* essentialiste

essentially [ɪ'senʃəlɪ] *adv (fundamentally)* essentiellement, fondamentalement; *(mainly)* essentiellement, principalement; **it's essentially a question of taste** c'est avant tout une question de goût; **he was not essentially a bad man** au fond, ce n'était pas quelqu'un de mauvais; **essentially, nothing has changed** pour l'essentiel, rien n'a changé

Essex ['esɪks] *n* l'Essex *m*, = comté dans le sud-est de l'Angleterre; **in Essex** dans l'Essex

►► *Br Fam Pej* ***Essex girl*** minette *f*; *Br Fam Pej* ***Essex man*** = stéréotype du réactionnaire bête et vulgaire, originaire de l'Essex

> **ESSEX**
>
> Il s'aget de stéréotypes sociaux apparus au cours des années 80. L'"Essex Girl" (originaire de l'Essex, comté situé à l'est de Londres) est censée être une jeune femme d'origine modeste aux mœurs légères, vulgaire, bruyante, et peu intelligente. L'"Essex Man" est lui aussi vulgaire et bruyant; de plus, il est réactionnaire et inculte.

EST [ˌiːes'tiː] *n (abbr* **Eastern Standard Time***)* heure *f* normale de l'Est

est [est] *n Psy (abbr* **Erhard Seminars Training***)* = méthode de formation psychologique créée par Werner Erhard

est. (**a**) *(written abbr* **established***)* **est. 1890** fondé en 1890 (**b**) *(written abbr* **estimated***)* **est. cost** coût évalué à

establish [ɪ'stæblɪʃ] *vt* (**a**) *(create, set up → business)* fonder, créer; *(→ government)* constituer, établir; *(→ society, system)* constituer; *(→ factory)* établir, monter; *(→ contact)* établir; *(→ relations)* établir, nouer; *(→ custom, law)* instaurer; *(→ precedent)* créer; *(→ order, peace)* faire régner; **he established a lead of 2 minutes over the field** il devançait le reste des coureurs de 2 minutes; **she has established a 6 percent lead in the polls** elle a une avance de 6 pour cent dans les sondages; **to establish telephone contact with sb** contacter qn par téléphone; *Comput* **to establish a connection** se connecter; **the police have been unable to establish a link between the two murders** la police n'a pas pu établir de lien entre les deux meurtres; **to establish close relations with sb** nouer des relations avec qn; **to establish oneself in business** s'établir dans les affaires

(**b**) *(confirm → authority, power)* affermir; *(→ reputation)* établir; **she has already established her reputation as a physicist** elle s'est déjà fait une réputation de physicienne; **the film established her as an important director** avec ce film, elle s'est affirmée comme un metteur en scène important; **he established himself as a computer consultant** il s'est établi conseiller en informatique (**c**) *(prove → identity, truth)* établir; *(→ cause, nature)* déterminer, établir; *(→ guilt, need)* établir, prouver; *(→ innocence)* établir, démontrer; **it has been established that there is no case against the defendant** il a été démontré qu'il n'y a pas lieu de poursuivre l'accusé

(**d**) *Rel & Pol (Church)* ériger en Église d'État

established [ɪ'stæblɪʃt] *adj* (**a**) *(existing, solid → order, system)* établi; *(→ government)* établi, au pouvoir; *(→ business)* établi, solide; *(→ law)* établi, en vigueur; *(→ tradition)* établi, enraciné; *(→ reputation)* établi, bien assis; **once the company becomes established** quand la société sera bien établie; *Com* **established in 1890** maison fondée en 1890; *Rel* **the established Church** l'Église *f* officielle

(**b**) *(proven → fact)* acquis, reconnu; *(→ truth)* établi, démontré

establishing shot [ɪ'stæblɪʃɪŋ-] *n TV & Cin* plan *m* de situation *ou* de mise en place *ou* d'ensemble

establishment [ɪ'stæblɪʃmənt] **1** *n* (**a**) *(of business)* fondation *f*, création *f*; *(of government)* constitution *f*; *(of society, system)* constitution *f*, création *f*; *(of law)* instauration *f*

(**b**) *(institution)* établissement *m*; **a business establishment** un établissement commercial, une firme; **a research establishment** un établissement de recherche; **a family establishment** *(hotel, restaurant)* un établissement familial

(**c**) *(of fact, guilt, innocence, cause, identity)* établissement *m*

(**d**) *Formal (staff)* personnel *m*; *Mil & Naut* effectif *m*; **to be on the establishment** faire partie du personnel; *Mil* **peacetime establishment** effectifs *mpl* de paix

2 Establishment *n (ruling powers)* **the Establishment** les pouvoirs *mpl* établis, l'ordre *m* établi, l'establishment *m*; **the financial Establishment** ceux qui comptent dans le monde financier; **he's such an Establishment figure** il fait vraiment partie de l'establishment; **to be against the Establishment, to be anti-Establishment** être anticonformiste; **to revolt against the Establishment** se révolter contre l'ordre établi

estate [ɪ'steɪt] *n* (**a**) *(land)* propriété *f*, domaine *m*; **her country estate** ses terres *fpl*; **estate manager** régisseur *m*

(**b**) *Br* **(housing) estate** *(of privately-owned houses)* lotissement *m*; *(of council houses)* grand ensemble *m*; *Br* **(industrial) estate** zone *f* industrielle

(**c**) *Law (property)* biens *mpl*, fortune *f*; *(of deceased)* succession *f*; **she left a large estate** elle a laissé une grosse fortune (en héritage)

(**d**) *Br* **estate (car)** break *m*

(**e**) *Formal (state, position)* état *m*, rang *m*; **men of low/high estate** les hommes d'humble condition/de haut rang; **the estate of matrimony** la condition du mariage; **the three estates** les trois états *mpl*; **the fourth estate** le quatrième pouvoir; *Hist* **the Estates (of the Realm)** les états *mpl ou* les ordres *mpl* (de l'Ancien Régime)

►► *Br* ***estate agency*** agence *f* immobilière; *Br* ***estate agent*** *(salesperson)* agent *m* immobilier; *(manager)* intendant *m*, régisseur *m*; *Br* **estate car** break *m*; *Br* **estate duty**, *Am* **estate tax** droits *mpl* de succession

estate-bottled *adj (wine)* mis en bouteille à la propriété

estd., est'd. (*written abbr* **established**) **estd. 1890** fondé en 1890

esteem [ɪ'sti:m] **1** *vt* (**a**) *(respect → person)* avoir de l'estime pour, estimer; *(→ quality)* estimer, apprécier (**b**) *Formal (consider)* estimer, considérer; **I esteem it a great honour** je m'estime très honoré

2 *n* estime *f*, considération *f*; **to hold sb/sth in high esteem** tenir qn/qch en haute estime; **to go up/down in sb's esteem** monter/baisser dans l'estime *ou* la considération de qn

►► *Mktg* ***esteem needs*** besoin *m* d'estime

esteemed [ɪ'sti:md] *adj Formal* estimé; **our esteemed president** notre (très) estimé président

ester ['estə(r)] *n Chem* ester *m*

esterification [ˌestərɪfɪ'keɪʃən] *n Chem* estérification *f*

esterify [es'terɪfaɪ] *vt Chem* estérifier

Esther ['estə(r)] *pr n Bible* Esther

esthete, esthetic *etc Am* = **aesthete, aesthetic** *etc*

Esthonia, Esthonian *etc* = **Estonia, Estonian**

estimable ['estɪməbəl] *adj* estimable, digne d'estime

estimate 1 *n* ['estɪmət] (**a**) *(evaluation)* évaluation *f*, estimation *f*; **give me an estimate of how much you think it will cost** donnez-moi une idée du prix que cela coûtera, à votre avis; **it's only an estimate** ce n'est qu'une estimation; **his estimate of 500 tonnes is way off the mark** son estimation de 500 tonnes est très éloignée de la réalité; **at a rough estimate** approximativement; **these figures are only a rough estimate** ces chiffres ne sont que très approximatifs; **at the lowest estimate it will take five years** il faudra cinq ans au bas mot; **at an optimistic estimate** dans le meilleur des cas

(**b**) *Com (quote)* devis *m*; **get several estimates before deciding who to employ** faites faire plusieurs devis avant de décider quelle entreprise choisir; **ask the garage to give you an estimate for the repairs** demandez au garage de vous établir un devis pour les réparations

2 *vt* ['estɪmeɪt] (**a**) *(calculate → cost, number)* estimer, évaluer; *(→ distance, speed)* estimer, apprécier; **the cost was estimated at £2,000** le coût était évalué à 2000 livres; **I estimate (that) it will take at least five years** à mon avis cela prendra au moins cinq ans, j'estime que cela prendra au moins cinq ans

(**b**) *(judge)* estimer, juger; **I don't estimate him very highly** je n'ai guère d'estime pour lui

estimated ['estɪmeɪtɪd] *adj* estimé; **an estimated 50,000 people attended the demonstration** environ 50 000 personnes auraient manifesté; **it will cost an estimated £500,000** on estime que cela coûtera 500 000 livres; **it is only an estimated figure** ce n'est qu'une estimation; **estimated time of arrival/of departure** heure *f* probable d'arrivée/de départ

estimation [ˌestɪ'meɪʃən] *n* (**a**) *(calculation)* estimation *f*, évaluation *f* (**b**) *(judgment)* jugement *m*, opinion *f*; **in my estimation** à mon avis, selon moi (**c**) *(esteem)* estime *f*, considération *f*; **he went down/up in my estimation** il a baissé/monté dans mon estime; **to hold sb in estimation** estimer qn

estimator ['estɪmeɪtə(r)] *n Fin* expert *m*

estivate *etc Am* = **aestivate**

Estonia [e'stəʊnjə] *n* Estonie *f*; **in Estonia** en Estonie

Estonian [e'stəʊnjən] **1** *n* (**a**) *(person)* Estonien(enne) *m,f* (**b**) *(language)* estonien *m*

2 *adj* estonien

3 *comp (embassy)* d'Estonie; *(history)* de l'Estonie; *(teacher)* d'estonien

estrade [ɪ'strɑ:d] *n* estrade *f*

estrange [ɪ'streɪndʒ] *vt* aliéner, éloigner

estranged [ɪ'streɪndʒd] *adj (couple)* séparé; **to become estranged from sb** se brouiller avec *ou* se détacher de qn; **he is estranged from his wife** il est séparé de sa femme; **an estranged couple** des époux séparés; **her estranged husband** son mari, dont elle est séparée; **their estranged son** leur fils avec qui ils sont brouillés

estrangement [ɪ'streɪndʒmənt] *n* éloignement *m*; *(from spouse)* séparation *f*

estrogen, estrogenic *Am* = **oestrogen, oestrogenic**

estradiol *Am* = **oestradiol**

estrone, estrous *etc Am* = **oestrone, oestrus** *etc*

estuarine ['estjʊərɪn], **estuarial** [estjʊ'eɪrɪəl] *adj (soil, marshland, regions)* estuarien

►► *Zool* ***estuarine crocodile*** crocodile *m* des estuaires; *Geog* ***estuarine culture*** culture *f* dans les estuaires

estuary ['estjʊərɪ] (*pl* **estuaries**) *n Geog* estuaire *m*; **the Thames estuary** l'estuaire *m* de la Tamise

►► ***estuary English*** = accent standard teinté d'accent Cockney, prédominant à Londres et dans le sud-est de l'Angleterre, ne permettant pas d'identifier l'appartenance sociale du locuteur

esurience [e'sjʊ:rɪəns], **esuriency** [e'sjʊ:rɪənsɪ] *n Arch or Literary* cupidité *f* famélique

esurient [e'sjʊ:rɪənt] *adj Arch or Literary* famélique et cupide

ET [ˌi:'ti:] *n* (**a**) *Br* (*abbr* **Employment Training**) = programme gouvernemental en faveur des chômeurs de longue durée (**b**) (*abbr* **extraterrestrial**) extraterrestre *mf*

ETA [ˌi:ti:'eɪ] *n Aviat* (*abbr* **estimated time of arrival**) HPA *f*; **our ETA is 2300 hours** l'heure d'arrivée prévue est 23 heures

et al. [ˌet'æl] *adv* (*abbr* **et alia**) et autres

etalon ['eɪtəlɒn] *n Phys* étalon *m*

etc. (*written abbr* **et cetera**) etc

et cetera [ɪt'setərə] **1** *adv* et cetera, et cætera

2 *n* **the et ceteras** les et cætera *mpl*

etch [etʃ] **1** *vt* graver; *Art* graver à l'eau-forte; *Fig* **etched on my memory** gravé dans ma mémoire

2 *vi* graver; *Art* graver à l'eau-forte

etcher ['etʃə(r)] *n Art* graveur(euse) *m,f* à l'eau-forte

etching ['etʃɪŋ] *n Art* (**a**) *(print)* (gravure *f* à l')eau-forte *f*; *Hum Euph* **come up and see my etchings** monte, je vais te montrer ma collection d'estampes japonaises (**b**) *(technique)* gravure *f* à l'eau-forte

ETD [ˌi:ti:'di:] *n Aviat* (*abbr* **estimated time of departure**) HPD *f*

eternal [ɪ'tɜ:nəl] **1** *adj* (**a**) *(gen) & Phil & Rel* éternel; **eternal life** la vie éternelle

(**b**) *Pej (perpetual)* continuel, perpétuel; *(arguments, problems)* éternel; *(discussion, wrangling)* continuel, sempiternel; **eternal complaints** perpétuelles récriminations *fpl*; **he's an eternal student** c'est l'étudiant éternel; **to my eternal shame** à ma grande honte

2 *n* **the Eternal** l'Éternel *m*

►► ***the Eternal city*** la Ville éternelle, Rome *f*; *Br* ***the eternal triangle*** l'éternel triangle *m (femme, mari, amant)*

eternally [ɪ'tɜ:nəlɪ] *adv* (**a**) *(forever)* éternellement; **I shall be eternally grateful** je serai infiniment reconnaissant (**b**) *Pej (perpetually)* perpétuellement, continuellement

eternity [ɪ'tɜ:nətɪ] (*pl* **eternities**) *n also Fig* éternité *f*; **it seemed like an eternity** on aurait dit une éternité, **for all eternity** pour l'éternité; **he kept me waiting for an eternity** il m'a fait attendre une éternité *ou* des éternités

►► ***eternity ring*** = bague entièrement sertie de pierres symbolisant l'éternité du mariage

'From Here to Eternity' *Zinnemann* 'Tant qu'il y aura des hommes'

ethanal ['i:θənæl] *n Chem* éthanal *m*

ethane ['i:θeɪn] *n Chem* éthane *m*

ethanol ['eθənɒl] *n Chem* alcool *m* éthylique, éthanol *m*

ether ['i:θə(r)] *n* (**a**) *Chem & Phys* éther *m* (**b**) *Literary (sky)* **the ether** l'éther *m*, la voûte céleste; *Rad* **over** *or* **through the ether** sur les ondes

ethereal [ɪ'θɪərɪəl] *adj (fragile)* éthéré, délicat; *(spiritual)* éthéré, noble; **she had an ethereal beauty** elle était d'une beauté éthérée

ethereality [ɪˌθɪərɪ'ælɪtɪ] *n* légèreté *f* éthérée

ethereally [ɪ'θɪərɪəlɪ] *adv* **ethereally beautiful** d'une beauté éthérée

etherize, -ise ['i:θəraɪz] *vt Med* éthériser

Ethernet® ['i:θənet] *n Comput* Ethernet® *m*

ethic ['eθɪk] **1** *n* éthique *f*, morale *f*

2 *adj* moral, éthique

ethical ['eθɪkəl] *adj* moral, éthique; **it's not ethical** c'est contraire à la morale; **an ethical code** un code déontologique; **the doctor's behaviour was not ethical** *(against professional ethics)* le comportement du médecin n'était pas conforme au code déontologique

►► *Pharm* ***ethical drug*** = remède vendu uniquement sur l'ordonnance d'un médecin; *Fin* ***ethical investment*** investissement *m* éthique; *Fin* ***ethical investment fund*** fonds *m* d'investissement éthique, SICAV *f* éthique

ethically ['eθɪklɪ] *adv* d'un point de vue éthique; **ethically questionable** d'une éthique douteuse; **she has behaved quite ethically** son comportement a été tout à fait éthique *ou* moral

ethics ['eθɪks] **1** *n (UNCOUNT) (study)* éthique *f*, morale *f*

2 *npl (principles)* morale *f*; *(morality)* moralité *f*; **dubious ethics** morale *f* douteuse; **medical ethics** code *m* déontologique *ou* de déontologie

ethionamide [ˌeθɪ'əʊnəmaɪd] *n Med* éthionamide *m*

Ethiopia [ˌi:θɪ'əʊpjə] *n* Éthiopie *f*; **in Ethiopia** en Éthiopie

Ethiopian [ˌi:θɪ'əʊpjən] **1** *n* (**a**) *(person)* Éthiopien(enne) *m,f* (**b**) *Ling* éthiopien *m*

2 *adj* éthiopien

3 *comp (embassy)* d'Éthiopie; *(history)* de l'Éthiopie

Ethiopic [ˌi:θɪ'əʊpɪk] **1** *n Ling* guèze *m*

2 *adj* éthiopien

ethmoid ['eθmɔɪd] *adj Anat* ethmoïde; **the ethmoid bone** l'os *m* ethmoïde

ethmoidal [eθ'mɔɪdəl] *adj Anat* ethmoïdal

ethnic ['eθnɪk] **1** *adj* (**a**) *(of race)* ethnique; **ethnic Albanians/Russians** population *f* d'origine albanaise/russe; **ethnic pride** revendication *f* d'une appartenance ethnique; **ethnic unrest** tensions *fpl* ethniques

(**b**) *(traditional)* folklorique, traditionnel

(**c**) *(exotic → food, furniture, clothes)* exotique

2 *n Am* membre *m* d'une minorité ethnique

►► ***ethnic cleansing*** purification *f* ethnique, nettoyage *f* ethnique; ***ethnic group*** ethnie *f*; ***ethnic minority*** minorité *f* ethnique; ***ethnic origin*** origine *f* ethnique

ethnically ['eθnɪklɪ] *adv* du point de vue ethnique, ethniquement; **an ethnically mixed** *or* **diverse region** une région peuplée de diverses ethnies; **the area has been ethnically cleansed** cette zone a été le théâtre de nettoyages ethniques

ethnicity ['eθnɪsɪtɪ] *n* appartenance *f* ethnique

ethnocentric [ˌeθnəʊ'sentrɪk] *adj* ethnocentrique

ethnocentrism [ˌeθnəʊ'sentrɪzəm] *n* ethnocentrisme *m*

ethnographer [eθ'nɒgrəfə(r)] *n* ethnographe *mf*

ethnographic [ˌeθnə'græfɪk], **ethnographical** [ˌeθnə'græfɪkəl] *adj* ethnographique

ethnography [eθ'nɒgrəfɪ] *n* ethnographie *f*

ethnolinguistics [ˌeθnəʊlɪŋ'gwɪstɪks] *n (UNCOUNT)* ethnolinguistique *f*

ethnological [ˌeθnə'lɒdʒɪkəl] *adj* ethnologique

ethnologically [ˌeθnə'lɒdʒɪklɪ] *adv* ethnologiquement

ethnologist [eθ'nɒlədʒɪst] *n* ethnologue *mf*

ethnology [eθ'nɒlədʒɪ] *n* ethnologie *f*

ethnomusicology [ˌeθnəʊmju:zɪ'kɒlədʒɪ] *n* ethnomusicologie *f*

ethological [i:θə'lɒdʒɪkəl] *adj* éthologique

ethologist [ɪ'θɒlədʒɪst] *n* éthologue *mf*, éthologiste *mf*

ethology [ɪ'θɒlədʒɪ] *n* éthologie *f*, éthographie *f*

ethos ['i:θɒs] *n* philosophie *f*, valeurs *fpl*, esprit *m*

ethyl ['eθɪl, 'i:θaɪl] *n Chem* éthyle *m*

►► ***ethyl acetate*** acétate *m* d'éthyle; ***ethyl alcohol*** alcool *m* éthylique, éthanol *m*

ethylene ['eθɪli:n] *n Chem* éthylène *m*

►► ***ethylene glycol*** éthylène *m* glycol; ***ethylene oxide*** oxyde *m* d'éthylène

etiolate ['i:tɪəʊleɪt] *Bot* **1** *vt* étioler

2 *vi* s'étioler

etiolation [ˌi:tɪəʊ'leɪʃən] *n Bot* étiolement *m*

etiological, etiology *Am* = **aetiological, aetiology**

etiquette ['etɪket] *n (UNCOUNT) (code of practice)* étiquette *f*; *(customs)* bon usage *m*, convenances *fpl*; **according to etiquette** selon l'usage; **it's simply not etiquette** cela ne se fait pas; **etiquette demands that...** l'étiquette veut *ou* exige que...; **court etiquette** cérémonial *m* de cour; **medical etiquette** déontologie *f* médicale; **that's not professional etiquette** c'est contraire à la déontologie *ou* aux usages de la profession

Etna ['etnə] *n* **(Mount) Etna** l'Etna *m*

Eton ['i:tən] *n* **Eton (College)** l'école *f* d'Eton

►► ***Eton crop*** coupe *f* à la garçonne; ***the Eton Wall Game*** = sorte de rugby que l'on joue à Eton, dont le terrain est délimité en partie par un mur d'enceinte

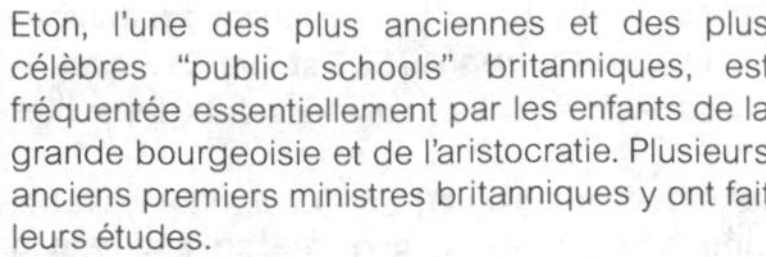

ETON

Eton, l'une des plus anciennes et des plus célèbres "public schools" britanniques, est fréquentée essentiellement par les enfants de la grande bourgeoisie et de l'aristocratie. Plusieurs anciens premiers ministres britanniques y ont fait leurs études.

Etonian [i:'təʊnjən] *n* élève *m* de l'école d'Eton; **Old Etonian** ancien élève *m* d'Eton

Etruria [ɪ'trʊərɪə] *n* Étrurie *f*

Etruscan [ɪ'trʌskən] **1** *n* (**a**) *(person)* Étrusque *mf* (**b**) *Ling* étrusque *m*

2 *adj* étrusque

ETU [ˌi:ti:'ju:] *n Br (abbr* **Electrical Trades Union**) = syndicat britannique d'électriciens

ETV [ˌi:ti:'vi:] *n Am (abbr* **Educational Television**) = chaîne de télévision éducative et culturelle

etymological [ˌetɪmə'lɒdʒɪkəl] *adj* étymologique

etymologically [ˌetɪmə'lɒdʒɪkəlɪ] *adv* étymologiquement

etymologist [ˌetɪ'mɒlədʒɪst] *n* étymologiste *mf*

etymology [ˌetɪ'mɒlədʒɪ] *n* étymologie *f*

etymon ['etɪmɒn] (*pl* **etymons** *or* **etyma** [-mə]) *n Ling* étymon *m*

EU [ˌi:'ju:] *n (abbr* **European Union**) UE *f*; **EU policy** politique *f* communautaire; **the EU member states** les États *mpl* membres de l'UE; **imports to the EU** les importations *fpl* vers l'UE

eucalyptol [ˌju:kə'lɪptɒl] *n Chem* eucalyptol *m*

eucalyptus [ˌju:kə'lɪptəs] (*pl* **eucalyptuses** *or* **eucalypti** [-taɪ]) *n Bot* eucalyptus *m*

►► ***eucalyptus oil*** essence *f* d'eucalyptus

Eucharist ['ju:kərɪst] *n* Eucharistie *f*

euchre ['ju:kə(r)] *Am* **1** *n* euchre *m (jeu de cartes)*

2 *vt* (**a**) *Cards* empêcher de faire trois levées (**b**) *Fam Fig (cheat)* carotter; **he euchred them out of $10** il leur a carotté 10 dollars

euclase ['ju:kleɪz] *n Miner* euclase *f*

Euclid ['ju:klɪd] *pr n Myth* Euclide

Euclidian [ju:'klɪdɪən] *adj Geom* euclidien

►► ***Euclidian geometry*** géométrie *f* euclidienne

eugenic [ju:'dʒenɪk] *adj Biol* eugénique

eugenics [ju:'dʒenɪks] *n (UNCOUNT) Biol* eugénique *f*, eugénisme *m*

eugenist ['ju:dʒənɪst] *n Biol* eugéniste *mf*

eugenol ['ju:dʒənɒl] *n Chem* eugénol *m*

euhedral [ˌju:'hi:drəl] *adj Geol* euhédral, automorphe

eukaryot, eukaryote [ˌju:'kærɪəʊt] *n Biol* eucaryote *m*

eulogist ['ju:lədʒɪst] *n* panégyriste *mf*

eulogistic [ˌju:lə'dʒɪstɪk] *adj* très élogieux, louangeur

eulogistically [ˌju:lə'dʒɪstɪkəlɪ] *adv* élogieusement

eulogize, -ise ['ju:lədʒaɪz] *vt* faire l'éloge *ou* le panégyrique de

eulogy ['ju:lədʒɪ] (*pl* **eulogies**) *n* (**a**) *(commendation)* panégyrique *m* (**b**) *(funeral oration)* éloge *m* funèbre

Eumenides [ju:'menɪˌdi:z] *npl Myth* **the Eumenides** les Euménides *fpl*

eunuch ['ju:nək] *n* eunuque *m*

eupepsia [ju:'pepsɪə] *n Physiol* eupepsie *f*

eupeptic [ju:'peptɪk] *adj Physiol* eupeptique

euphemism ['ju:fəmɪzəm] *n* euphémisme *m*

euphemistic [ˌju:fə'mɪstɪk] *adj* euphémique

euphemistically [ˌju:fə'mɪstɪklɪ] *adv* par euphémisme, *Formal* euphémiquement; **euphemistically known as...** auquel on se réfère par euphémisme sous le terme de...

euphemize, -ise ['ju:fəmaɪz] *vi* parler euphémiquement

euphonic [ju:'fɒnɪk] *adj* euphonique

euphonious [ju:'fəʊnɪəs] *adj* euphonique

euphonium [ju:'fəʊnɪəm] *n Mus* euphonium *m*, saxhorn *m* basse

euphony ['ju:fənɪ] *n* euphonie *f*

euphorbia [ju:'fɔ:bɪə] *n Bot* euphorbe *f*

euphoria [ju:'fɔ:rɪə] *n* euphorie *f*

euphoric [ju:'fɒrɪk] *adj* euphorique

Euphrates [ju:'freɪti:z] *n* **the (River) Euphrates** l'Euphrate *m*

euphuism ['ju:fju:ɪzəm] *n* euphuisme *m*, préciosité *f*

Eurasia [jʊə'reɪʒjə] *n* Eurasie *f*

Eurasian [jʊə'reɪʒjən] **1** *n* Eurasien(enne) *m,f*

2 *adj (person)* eurasien; *(continent)* eurasiatique

Euratom [jʊər'ætəm] *n (abbr* **European Atomic Energy Community**) CEEA *f*

eureka [jʊə'ri:kə] *exclam* eurêka!

eurhythmia [ju:'rɪðmɪə] *n Med* eurythmie *f*

eurhythmic [ju:'rɪðmɪk] *adj Formal* eurythmique

eurhythmics [ju:'rɪðmɪks] *n (UNCOUNT) Formal* gymnastique *f* rythmique

eurhythmy [ju:'rɪðmɪ] *n Formal* eurythmie *f*

EURIBOR ['jʊərɪbɔ:(r)] *n Fin (abbr* **Euro Interbank Offered Rate**) EURIBOR *m*, TIBEUR *m*

Euripidean [jʊəˌrɪpɪ'di:ən] *adj* euripidien

Euripides [jʊə'rɪpɪdi:z] *pr n Myth* Euripide

euro ['jʊərəʊ] *n (currency)* euro *m*

►► *EU* ***Euro area*** zone *f* euro; *St Exch* ***Euro Interbank Offered Rate*** EURIBOR *m*, TIBEUR *m*; *St Exch* ***Euro Overnight Index Average*** EONIA *m*, TEMPÉ *m*; *EU* ***Euro zone*** zone *f* euro

Euro- ['jʊərəʊ] *pref* euro-

Eurobabble ['jʊərəʊˌbæbəl] *n* jargon *m* des eurocrates

Eurobank ['jʊərəʊbæŋk] *n* eurobanque *f*

eurobond ['jʊərəʊbɒnd] *n Fin* euro-obligation *f*

eurocard ['jʊərəʊkɑ:d] *n Banking* eurocarte *f*

Eurocentric ['jʊərəʊˌsentrɪk] *adj* eurocentrique

Eurocentrism ['jʊərəʊˌsentrɪzəm] *n* eurocentrisme *m*

euro-certificate *n St Exch* euro-certificat *m*

Eurocheque ['juərəʊˌtʃek] *n Br Banking* eurochèque *m*

euro-commercial paper *n Fin* billet *m* de trésorerie *(emis sur le marché des eurodevises)*

Eurocommunism [ˌjʊərəʊ'kɒmjʊˌnɪzəm] *n* eurocommunisme *m*

Eurocommunist [ˌjʊərəʊ'kɒmjʊnɪst] **1** *adj* eurocommuniste

2 *n* eurocommuniste *mf*

Eurocorps ['jʊərəʊkɔ:(r)] *n* Eurocorps *m*

Eurocrat ['jʊərəʊkræt] *n* eurocrate *mf*

eurocredit ['jʊərəʊˌkredɪt] *n Com* eurocrédit *m*

eurocurrency ['jʊərəʊˌkʌrənsɪ] *n Banking* eurodevise *f*, euromonnaie *f*

►► ***eurocurrency market*** marché *m* des eurodevises

Eurodisney® ['jʊərəʊˌdɪznɪ] *n* Eurodisney® *m*

eurodollar ['jʊərəʊˌdɒlə(r)] *n Fin* eurodollar *m*

Euro-election *n* **the Euro-elections** les élections *fpl* européennes

Eurofighter ['jʊərəʊˌfaɪtə(r)] *n Aviat* eurofighter *m*

Eurofranc ['jʊərəʊfræŋk] *n Fin* eurofranc *m*

Euroland ['jʊərəʊlænd] *n Pol* Eurolande *f*

Euroloan ['jʊərəʊləʊn] *n Fin* eurocrédit *m*

Euromarket ['jʊərəʊˌmɑ:kɪt] *n Fin* marché *m* des eurodevises, euromarché *m*

euromissile ['jʊərəʊˌmɪsaɪl] *n* euromissile *m*

Euro-MP *n EU (abbr* **European Member of Parliament**) député *m ou* parlementaire *m* européen

Europa [jʊ'rəʊpə] *pr n Myth* Europe

Europe ['jʊərəp] *n* Europe *f*; *Br (continental Europe)* Europe *f* continentale; **in Europe** en Europe; **in Britain, Europe has become a sensitive political subject** en Grande-Bretagne, la question de l'Union européenne est un sujet très délicat; **some MPs want Britain to get out of Europe** certains députés britanniques veulent que la Grande-Bretagne se retire de l'Union européenne; **when Britain went into Europe in 1973** quand la Grande-Bretagne est devenue membre de la CEE en 1973

European [ˌjʊərə'pi:ən] **1** *n (inhabitant of Europe)* Européen(enne) *m,f*; *(pro-Europe)* partisan *m* de l'Europe unie, Européen(enne) *m,f*

2 *adj* européen; **we must adopt a more European outlook** nous devons adopter un point de vue plus européen *ou* plus ouvert sur l'Europe; **the Single European Market** le marché unique (européen)

►► ***European Atomic Energy Community*** Communauté *f* européenne de l'énergie atomique; ***the European Bank for Reconstruction and Development*** la Banque européenne pour la reconstruction et le développement; ***European Broadcasting Union*** Union *f* européenne de radiodiffusion, UER *f*; ***the European Central***

Bank la banque centrale européenne; *Fin* ***European Central Securities Depositories Association*** association *f* européenne des dépositaires centraux de titres; *Pol* ***the European Coal and Steel Community*** la Communauté européenne de charbon et de l'acier; ***the European Commission*** la Commission européenne; ***European Commissioner*** commissaire *m* européen; *Pol* ***the European Community*** la Communauté européenne; ***the European Convention on Human Rights*** la Convention européenne des droits de l'homme; *Am* ***European Common Market*** Marché *m* commun européen; ***the European Court of Justice*** la Cour européenne de justice; *Ftbl* ***European Cup*** Coupe *f* d'Europe; *Formerly Ftbl* ***European Cupwinners' Cup*** Coupe *f* d'Europe des clubs champions; *Fin* ***European currency snake*** serpent *m* monétaire européen; *Formerly Fin* ***European Currency Unit*** Unité *f* monétaire européenne; *Fin* ***European Development Fund*** Fonds *m* européen de développement; *Pol* ***European Economic Area*** Espace *m* économique européen; *Formerly* ***European Economic Community*** Communauté *f* économique européenne; ***European Environmental Bureau*** Bureau *m* européen de l'environnement; *Formerly Fin* ***European Exchange Rate Mechanism*** mécanisme *m* de change européen; ***European Free Trade Association*** Association *f* européenne de libre-échange; ***European Investment Bank*** Banque *f* européenne d'investissement; *Fin* ***European monetary agreement*** accord *m* monétaire européen; *Formerly* ***the European Monetary Cooperation Fund*** le Fonds européen de coopération monétaire; *Fin* ***European Monetary Fund*** Fonds *m* monétaire européen; *Fin* ***the European Monetary Institute*** l'Institut *m* monétaire européen; *Formerly Fin* ***the European Monetary System*** le Système monétaire européen; ***European Parliament*** Parlement *m* européen; *Am* ***European plan*** *(in hotel)* chambre *f* sans pension; ***the European Regional Development Fund*** le fonds européen de développement régional; *Fin* ***European Social Fund*** Fonds *m* social européen; ***European Space Agency*** Agence *f* spatiale européenne; ***European Standards Commission*** comité *m* européen de normalisation; ***the European Union*** l'Union *f* européenne

'The Europeans' *James, Ivory* 'Des Européens'

Europeanism [ˌjʊərə'piːənɪzəm] *n* européanisme *m*

Europeanization [jʊərəˌpiːənaɪ'zeɪʃən] *n* européanisation *f*, européisation *f*

Europeanize, -ise [jʊərə'piːənaɪz] *vt* européaniser

European-style option *n St Exch* option *f* européenne

Europhile ['jʊərəʊfaɪl] *n* europhile *mf*, partisan *m* de l'Europe unie

EUROPHILES AND EUROSCEPTICS

Avec l'avènement de l'euro, le débat sur l'Europe a pris une ampleur toute particulière en Grande-Bretagne. Les [illegible] passionnément la souveraineté nationale dont la livre sterling est devenu le symbole, et s'opposent avec acharnement à une plus grande intégration de la Grande-Bretagne au sein de l'Europe, tandis que les europhiles sont persuadés que la monnaie unique apporterait beaucoup au pays.

europium [jʊə'rəʊpɪəm] *n Chem & Metal* europium *m*

Europol ['jʊərəʊpɒl] *n* Europol *m*

Euro-rebel *n Br* = politicien qui s'oppose à la ligne pro-européenne de son parti

Eurosceptic ['jʊərəʊˌskeptɪk] *n Br* eurosceptique *mf*

Euroscepticism ['jʊərəʊˌskeptɪsɪzəm] *n Br* euroscepticisme *m*

Eurospeak ['jʊərəʊspiːk] *n* jargon *m* communautaire

Eurostar® ['jʊərəʊstɑː(r)] *n* Eurostar® *m*

Eurosterling ['jʊərəʊˌstɜːlɪŋ] *n Fin* eurosterling *m*

Eurostrategic ['jʊərəʊˌstræ'tiːdʒɪk] *adj Mil* eurostratégique

Eurotourism ['jʊərəʊˌtʊərɪzəm] *n* eurotourisme *m*

Eurotunnel® ['jʊərəʊˌtʌnəl] *n* Eurotunnel® *m*

Eurovision® ['jʊərəʊˌvɪʒən] *n* Eurovision® *f*; **who won Eurovision this year?** qui a gagné le concours de l'Eurovision l'année dernière?

►► ***the Eurovision® Song Contest*** le concours Eurovision® de la chanson

euroyen ['jʊərəʊjen] *n Fin* euroyen *m*

Eurydice [jʊ'rɪdɪsɪ] *pr n Myth* Eurydice

euryhaline [ˌjʊərɪ'heɪliːn] *adj Ecol* euryhalin

eurythermal [ˌjʊərɪ'θɜːməl], **eurythermic** [ˌjʊərɪ'θɜːmɪk], **eurythermous** [ˌjʊərɪ'θɜːməs] *adj* eurytherme

eurythermy [ˌjʊərɪ'θɜːmɪ] *n* eurythermie *f*

eurythmia, eurythmic *etc* = **eurhythmia, eurhythmic** *etc*

Euskara [juː'skɑːrə] *n (language)* euskara *m*, euskera *m*

Eustachian tube [juː'steɪʃən-] *n Anat* trompe *f* d'Eustache

eustasy ['juːstəsɪ] *n Geol* eustasie *f*

eustatic [juː'stætɪk] *adj Geol* eustatique

Eusthenopteron [ˌjuːsθə'nɒptərən] *n Ich* eusthenopteron *m*

eutectic [juː'tektɪk] *adj Phys* eutectique

eutexia [juː'teksjə] *n Phys* eutexie *f*

euthanasia [ˌjuːθə'neɪzjə] *n* euthanasie *f*; **voluntary euthanasia** euthanasie *f* volontaire *ou* active

euthanasic [ˌjuːθə'neɪzɪk] *adj* euthanasique

eutherian [juː'θɪərɪən] *n Zool* euthérien *m*

eutocia [juː'tɒsjə] *n Obst* eutocie *f*

eutocic [juː'tɒsɪk] *adj Obst* eutocique

eutrophic [juː'trɒfɪk] *adj Ecol* eutrophique

eutrophication [juːˌtrɒfɪ'keɪʃən] *n Ecol* eutrophisation *f*

EVA [ˌiːviː'eɪ] *n* (**a**) *Astron* (*abbr* **extravehicular activity**) = activité qui a lieu en dehors d'un engin spatial (**b**) (*abbr* **economic value added**) VAE *f*

evacuate [ɪ'vækjʊeɪt] *vt (place, population)* évacuer; *Tech (exhaust gases)* refouler; *Phys (create vacuum in)* faire le vide dans; **children were evacuated to the countryside** les enfants ont été évacués vers la campagne; *Physiol* **to evacuate the bowels** vider les intestins

evacuation [ɪˌvækjʊ'eɪʃən] *n (of place, people, bowels)* évacuation *f*; *Tech (of exhaust gases)* refoulement *m*; *Phys (creation of vacuum)* production *f* du vide

evacuee [ɪˌvækjuː'iː] *n* évacué(e) *m,f*

evade [ɪ'veɪd] *vt* (**a**) *(escape from → pursuers)* échapper à; *(→ punishment)* échapper à, se soustraire à

(**b**) *(avoid → blow, responsibility)* éviter, esquiver; *(→ question)* esquiver, éluder; *(→ eyes, glance)* éviter; **he has so far evaded arrest/detection** jusqu'à présent il a échappé à toute arrestation/détection; **to evade the issue** éluder le problème; **to evade tax** frauder le fisc; **success evades him** le succès lui échappe; **to evade military service** se dérober à ses obligations militaires

evader [ɪ'veɪdə(r)] *n* **tax evader** fraudeur(euse) *m,f* du fisc

evaginate [ɪ'vædʒɪneɪt] *vt Med* évaginer

evagination [ɪˌvædʒɪ'neɪʃən] *n Med* évagination *f*

evaluate [ɪ'væljʊeɪt] *vt* (**a**) *(damages, worth)* évaluer, déterminer le montant de

(**b**) *(assess → situation, success, work)* évaluer, former un jugement sur la valeur de; *(→ evidence, reasons)* peser, évaluer; *(→ quality)* évaluer; *(→ importance, effect)* mesurer (**c**) *Math* évaluer

evaluation [ɪˌvæljʊ'eɪʃən] *n* (**a**) *(of damages, worth)* évaluation *f* (**b**) *(of situation, work)* évaluation *f*, jugement *m*; *(of evidence, reasons, quality, importance, effect)* évaluation *f*

evanesce [ˌiːvə'nes] *vi Literary* disparaître

evanescence [ˌiːvə'nesəns] *n Literary* évanescence *f*, nature *f* éphémère

evanescent [ˌiːvə'nesənt] *adj Literary* évanescent, fugitif

evangelical [ˌiːvæn'dʒelɪkəl] *Rel* **1** *adj (relating to Gospels)* évangélique; **evangelical preacher** évangéliste *mf*; **an evangelical Christian/church/sect** un chrétien/une église/une secte évangélique; **he's one of these evangelical Christians** c'est un de ces évangélistes; **evangelical zeal** zèle *m* religieux; *Fig* **an evangelical vegetarian/communist** un végétarien/communiste à tout crin

2 *n* évangélique *m*

evangelicalism [ˌiːvæn'dʒelɪkəlɪzəm] *n Rel* évangélisme *m*

evangelism [ɪ'vændʒɪlɪzəm] *n Rel* évangélisme *m*

evangelist [ɪ'vændʒɪlɪst] **1** *n* (**a**) *(preacher)* évangélisateur(trice) *m,f* (**b**) *Fig (zealous advocate)* prêcheur(euse) *m,f*

2 Evangelist *n Bible* évangéliste *m*

evangelization [ɪˌvændʒɪlaɪ'zeɪʃən] *n Rel* évangélisation *f*

evangelize, -ise [ɪ'vændʒɪlaɪz] **1** *vt Rel* évangéliser, prêcher l'Évangile à

2 *vi* (**a**) *Rel* prêcher l'Évangile (**b**) *Fig (advocate)* prêcher; **he has been evangelizing about jazz for years** il prêche les mérites du jazz depuis des années

evangelizer [ɪ'vændʒɪˌlaɪzə(r)] *n Rel* évangélisateur(trice) *mf*

evaporable [ɪ'væpərəbəl] *adj Phys* évaporable

evaporate [ɪ'væpəreɪt] **1** *vi (liquid)* s'évaporer; *Fig (hopes, enthusiasm)* s'envoler, se volatiliser; *(doubts, fears)* se dissiper

2 *vt* faire évaporer

evaporated milk [ɪ'væpəreɪtɪd-] *n* lait *m* condensé

evaporation [ɪˌvæpə'reɪʃən] *n (of liquid)* évaporation *f*; *Fig* **this meant the evaporation of their hopes** ceci marqua la fin de leurs espoirs

evaporative [ɪ'væpərətɪv] *adj (method)* évaporatif

evaporativity [ɪˌvæpərə'tɪvɪtɪ] *n* évaporativité *f*

evaporator [ɪ'væpəˌreɪtə(r)] *n Ind* évaporateur *m*

evaporite [ɪ'væpəreɪt] *n Geol* évaporite *f*

evapotranspiration [ɪˌvæpəʊˌtrænspɪ'reɪʃən] *n Ecol* évapotranspiration *f*

evasion [ɪ'veɪʒən] *n* (**a**) *(avoidance → of duty, responsibility, question)* dérobade *f* (**of** devant) (**b**) *(deception, trickery)* détour *m*, faux-fuyant *m*, échappatoire *f*; **to answer without evasion** répondre sans détours *ou* sans biaiser

evasive [ɪ'veɪsɪv] *adj* évasif; **an evasive answer** une réponse évasive *ou* de Normand; **to take evasive action** *(gen)* louvoyer; *Mil* effectuer une manœuvre dilatoire

evasively [ɪ'veɪsɪvlɪ] *adv* évasivement; **he replied evasively** il a répondu en termes évasifs

evasiveness [ɪ'veɪsɪvnɪs] *n* caractère *m* évasif; **her evasiveness increased our suspicions** ses propos évasifs ont renforcé nos soupçons

EVC [ˌiːviː'siː] *n Mktg* (*abbr* **economic value to the customer**) valeur *f* économique apportée au consommateur

Eve [iːv] *pr n Bible* Ève

eve [iːv] *n* (**a**) *(day before)* veille *f*; *Rel* vigile *f*; **on the eve of the election** à la veille des élections (**b**) *Arch or Literary (evening)* soir *m*; **on a summer's eve** un soir d'été

evection [ɪ'vekʃən] *n Astron* évection *f*

EVEN[1] ['iːvən]

plat	► 1 (a)
égal	► 1 (b) – (d)
pair	► 1 (e)
même	► 2 (a)
encore	► 2 (b)
égaliser	► 3
s'égaliser	► 4

1 *adj* (**a**) *(level)* plat, plan; *(smooth)* uni, égal; **to make sth even** égaliser *ou* aplanir qch; **it's even with the desk** c'est au même niveau que le bureau

(**b**) *(steady → breathing, temperature)* égal; *(→ rate, rhythm)* régulier

(**c**) *(equal → distribution, spread)* égal; **the score is** *or* **the scores are even** ils sont à égalité; **it's an even game** la partie est égale; **now we're even** nous voilà quittes, nous sommes quittes maintenant; **there's an even chance he'll lose** il y a une chance sur deux qu'il perde; **the odds** *or* **chances are about**

eur–eve

even les chances sont à peu près égales; *Am* **to lay even odds** donner à égalité; *Am* **the bookmakers are offering even odds** les bookmakers offrent un enjeu égal; **they are an even match** ils sont à partie égale; **to bet even money** *(gen)* donner chances égales; *(in betting)* parier le même enjeu; *Horseracing* **even money favourite** cheval *m* coté à égalité; **to get even with sb** se venger de qn; **I'll get even with you for that!** je vous revaudrai ça!; *Fam* **to be even Stevens** être quitte

(**d**) *(calm → temper)* égal; *(→ voice)* égal, calme; **to have an even disposition** être d'un naturel calme

(**e**) *(number)* pair

2 *adv* (**a**) *(indicating surprise)* même; **he even works on Sundays** il travaille même le dimanche; **even the teacher laughed** même le professeur a ri, le professeur lui-même a ri; **she's even forgotten his name** elle a oublié jusqu'à son nom; **he even said so** il a été jusqu'à le dire, il l'a même dit; **without even apologizing** sans même *ou* sans seulement s'excuser; **this would be sad, tragic even** ça serait triste, tragique même; **he can't even walk** il ne peut même pas marcher; **not even** même pas; **even supposing that...** même en supposant que...

(**b**) *(with comparative) (still)* encore; **even better** encore mieux; **even more tired** encore plus fatigué; **even less** encore moins

(**c**) *(qualifying)* **he seemed indifferent, even hostile** il avait l'air indifférent, hostile même

3 *vt* égaliser, aplanir; **to even the odds** égaliser les chances

4 *vi* s'égaliser, s'aplanir

5 **even as** *conj* (**a**) *Formal (at the very moment that)* au moment même où; **even as we speak** au moment même où nous parlons

(**b**) *Arch or Literary (just as)* comme; **it came to pass even as he had foretold** tout arriva comme il l'avait prédit

6 **even if** *conj* même si; **even if I say so myself** sans fausse modestie; **even if he did say that, what does it matter?** et même s'il a dit ça, quelle importance est-ce que ça a?

7 **even now** *adv* (**a**) *(despite what happened before)* même maintenant; **even now, four years later, I still haven't got over it** aujourd'hui encore, quatre ans plus tard, je ne m'en suis pas encore remis

(**b**) *Literary (at this very moment)* en ce moment même

8 **even so** *adv (nevertheless)* quand même, pourtant; **yes, but even so** oui, mais quand même

9 **even then** *adv* (**a**) *(in that case also)* quand même; **but even then we wouldn't be able to afford it** mais nous ne pourrions quand même pas nous le permettre

(**b**) *(at that time also)* même à ce moment-là; **things were difficult enough even then** les choses étaient assez difficiles même à ce moment-là; **even then she wouldn't believe me** elle ne m'a pas cru pour autant

10 **even though** *conj* **even though he tries** malgré ses efforts; **even though she explained it in detail** bien qu'elle l'ait expliqué en détail

11 **even with** *prep* même avec, malgré

▸**even out** 1 *vt sep (surface)* égaliser, aplanir; *(prices)* égaliser; *(supply)* répartir *ou* distribuer plus également

2 *vi (surface)* s'égaliser, s'aplanir; *(prices)* s'égaliser; *(supply)* être réparti plus également

▸**even up** *vt sep* (**a**) *(make equal → score etc)* égaliser; **to even things up** rétablir l'équilibre (**b**) *(sum)* arrondir au chiffre supérieur; **let's even it up to a pound** arrondissons la somme à une livre

---

even² *n Arch or Literary (evening)* soir *m*

even-handed *adj* équitable, impartial

even-handedly [-'hændɪdlɪ] *adv* équitablement, impartialement

evening ['iːvnɪŋ] 1 *n* (**a**) *(part of day)* soir *m*; **(good) evening!** bonsoir!; **in the evening** le soir; **we went out in the evening** nous sommes sortis le soir; **it is 8 o'clock in the evening** il est 8 heures du soir; **I'm hardly ever at home** *Br* **in the evening** *or Am* **evenings** je suis rarement chez moi le soir; **this evening** ce soir; **that evening** ce soir-là; **yesterday evening** hier soir; **tomorrow evening** demain soir; **on the evening of the next day, on the following evening** le lendemain soir, le soir suivant; **(on) the previous evening** la veille au soir; **on the evening of the fifteenth** le quinze au soir; **on the evening of her departure** le soir de son départ; **one fine spring evening** (par) un beau soir de printemps; **every evening** tous les soirs, chaque soir; **every Friday evening** tous les vendredis soir *ou* soirs; **on the evening of Monday, 29 March** dans la soirée du lundi 29 mars; **the long winter evenings** les longues soirées *ou* veillées d'hiver; **I work evenings** je travaille le soir; **we've had several evenings out this week** nous sommes sortis plusieurs soirs cette semaine; **the evening performance starts at 7.30** en soirée la représentation débute à 19 heures 30; **she's going to an evening performance of the ballet** elle va voir le ballet en soirée; *Sport* **an evening match** une nocturne; *Fig* **in the evening of her life** au soir *ou* au déclin de sa vie

(**b**) *(length of time)* soirée *f*; **all evening** toute la soirée; **we spent the evening playing cards** nous avons passé la soirée à jouer aux cartes; **thank you for a lovely evening** merci pour cette charmante soirée

(**c**) *(entertainment)* soirée *f*; **a musical evening** une soirée musicale

2 *comp (newspaper, train)* du soir

►► ***evening bag*** sac *m* à main de soirée; ***evening class*** cours *m* du soir; ***evening dress*** *(for men)* tenue *f* de soirée, habit *m*; *(for women)* robe *f* du soir; **in evening dress** *(man)* en tenue de soirée; *(woman)* en robe du soir, en toilette de soirée; ***evening fixture*** rencontre *f* sportive en nocturne; ***evening gown*** robe *f* de soirée *ou* du soir; ***evening meal*** dîner *m*; *Rel* ***evening prayers*** office *m ou* service *m* du soir; *Bot* ***evening primrose*** onagre *f*, herbe *f* aux ânes; ***evening primrose oil*** huile *f* d'onagre; *Rel* ***evening service*** office *m ou* service *m* du soir; *Press* ***the Evening Standard*** = quotidien populaire londonien de tendance conservatrice; *Astron* ***evening star*** étoile *f* du berger; ***evening wear*** *(UNCOUNT) (for men)* tenue *f* de soirée, habit *m*; *(for women)* robe *f* du soir

> **Evenin' all!**
> Cette expression ("bonsoir à tous!") était la formule que prononçait l'acteur Jack Warner au début de chaque épisode de la série policière britannique *Dixon of Dock Green* qui fut diffusée à la télévision de 1955 à 1976. Aujourd'hui, on utilise cette phrase en référence aux policiers de la vieille école ou bien simplement en guise de salut.

evenly ['iːvənlɪ] *adv* (**a**) *(breathe, move)* régulièrement; *(talk)* calmement, posément (**b**) *(equally → divide)* également, de façon égale; *(→ spread)* de façon égale, régulièrement; **they are evenly matched** ils sont de force égale; **it was an evenly contested game** c'est une partie qui a opposé des adversaires de force égale

evenness ['iːvənnɪs] *n* (**a**) *(of surface)* égalité *f*, caractère *m* lisse (**b**) *(of competition, movement)* régularité *f*

even-numbered *adj* (portant un nombre) pair

evens ['iːvənz] *npl Br* **to lay evens** donner à égalité; **the bookmakers are offering evens** les bookmakers offrent un enjeu égal

►► ***evens favorite*** favori(ite) *m,f* à égalité

evensong ['iːvənsɒŋ] *n Rel (Anglican)* office *m* du soir; *(Roman Catholic)* vêpres *fpl*

event [ɪ'vent] 1 *n* (**a**) *(happening)* événement *m*; **a historical event** un événement historique; **the course of events** la suite des événements, le déroulement des faits; **in the course of events** par la suite, au cours des événements; **in the normal course of events** normalement; **as recent events have shown** comme l'ont montré de récents événements; **I realized after the event** j'ai réalisé après coup; **the party was quite an event** la soirée était un véritable événement; **a happy event** *(birth)* un heureux événement; **when's the happy event?** quand l'heureux événement doit-il avoir lieu?

(**b**) *(organized activity)* manifestation *f*; **the society organizes a number of social events** l'association organise un certain nombre de soirées *ou* de rencontres

(**c**) *Sport (meeting)* manifestation *f*; *(competition)* épreuve *f*; *(in horseracing)* course *f*; **field events** épreuves *fpl* d'athlétisme; **track events** épreuves *fpl* sur piste; **the sponsoring of sports events** la sponsorisation des manifestations sportives; **what was your best event?** quelle a été ta meilleure discipline?

2 **at all events, in any event** *adv* en tout cas, de toute façon

3 **in either event** *adv* dans l'un ou l'autre cas

4 **in the event** *adv* en fait, en l'occurence; **a result that in the event was most satisfying** un résultat qui était en fait très satisfaisant

5 **in the event of** *prep* **in the event of rain** en cas de pluie; **in the event of her refusing** au cas où *ou* dans le cas où elle refuserait

6 **in the event that** *conj* au cas où; **in the unlikely event that he comes** au cas *ou* dans le cas fort improbable où il viendrait

►► *Mktg* ***event advertising*** publicité *f* par l'événement; *Astron* ***event horizon*** horizon *m* des événements; ***event management*** organisation *f* de manifestations; *Mktg* ***event promotion*** communication *f* événementielle

even-tempered *adj* d'humeur égale; **of an even-tempered disposition** d'humeur égale

eventer [ɪ'ventə(r)] *n Horseriding* participant(e) *m,f* au concours complet

eventful [ɪ'ventfʊl] *adj* (**a**) *(busy → day, holiday, life)* mouvementé, fertile en événements (**b**) *(important)* mémorable, très important

eventfulness [ɪ'ventfʊlnɪs] *n (of day, holiday, life)* abondance *f* d'événements

eventide ['iːvəntaɪd] *n Literary* soir *m*, tombée *f* du jour

►► *Br* ***eventide home*** maison *f* de retraite

eventing [ɪ'ventɪŋ] *n Horseriding* participation *f* au concours complet

eventual [ɪ'ventʃʊəl] *adj (final)* final, ultime; *(resulting)* qui s'ensuit; **bad management led to the eventual collapse of the company** une mauvaise gestion a finalement provoqué la faillite de l'entreprise; **the disease causes deterioration of the muscles and eventual paralysis** la maladie entraîne la dégénérescence des muscles et la paralysie qui en résulte *ou* qui s'ensuit

eventuality [ɪˌventʃʊ'ælətɪ] *(pl* **eventualities***) n* éventualité *f*

eventually [ɪ'ventʃʊəlɪ] *adv* finalement, en fin de compte; **I'll get around to it eventually** je le ferai un jour ou l'autre; **he'll get tired of it eventually** il s'en lassera à la longue, il finira par s'en lasser; **she eventually became a lawyer** elle a fini par devenir avocat; **the people who will eventually benefit from these changes** les personnes qui, en fin de compte *ou* en définitive, bénéficieront de ces changements; **our arguments eventually persuaded him** nos arguments ont fini par le convaincre *ou* l'ont finalement convaincu; **eventually, I decided to give up** pour finir *ou* en fin de compte, j'ai décidé d'abandonner, j'ai finalement décidé d'abandonner

eventuate [ɪ'ventʃʊeɪt] *vi Formal* arriver, se produire; **his illness eventuated in death** sa maladie a fini par l'emporter

---

EVER ['evə(r)]

toujours	▸ **1 (a)**
jamais	▸ **1 (b), (c)**
vraiment	▸ **3; 4**

1 *adv* (**a**) *(always)* toujours; **ever more important** de plus en plus important; **ever-increasing influence** influence toujours croissante *ou* qui croît de jour en jour; **an ever-present fear** une peur constante; **ever hopeful/the pessimist, he...** toujours plein d'espoir/pessimiste, il...; *Old-fashioned* **yours ever, ever yours** *(in letter)* amicalement vôtre

(**b**) *(at any time)* jamais; **have you ever met him?** l'avez-vous jamais rencontré?; **do you ever meet him?** est-ce qu'il vous arrive (jamais) de le rencontrer?; **nothing ever happens** il n'arrive *ou* ne se passe jamais rien; **all they ever do is work** ils ne font que travailler; **he**

hardly *or* **scarcely ever smokes** il ne fume presque jamais; **don't ever come in here again!** ne mettez plus jamais les pieds ici!; **she was as cheerful as ever** elle était aussi gaie qu'à l'habitude; *Am* **ever and again** de temps à autres, de temps en temps

(**c**) *(with comparatives, superlatives)* **lovelier/more slowly than ever** plus joli/plus lentement que jamais; **he's as sarcastic as ever** il est toujours aussi sarcastique; **the first/biggest ever** le tout premier/plus grand qu'on ait jamais vu; **she's my best friend ever** c'est la meilleure amie que j'aie jamais eue; **the worst earthquake ever** le pire tremblement de terre qu'on ait jamais connu; **the best vacation we've ever had** les meilleures vacances qu'on ait jamais eues

(**d**) *Fam (in exclamations) Am* **is it ever big!** comme c'est grand!❑; *Am* **was he ever angry!** qu'est-ce qu'il était furax!; *Am* **do you enjoy dancing? – do I ever!** aimez-vous danser? – et comment!; *Am* **was I ever grateful for your help!** je te suis vraiment reconnaissant de m'avoir donné un coup de main!; **well, did you ever!** ça, par exemple!

(**e**) *(as intensifier)* **as quickly as ever you can** aussi vite que vous pourrez; **as soon as ever she comes** aussitôt *ou* dès qu'elle sera là; **before ever they** *or* **before they ever set out** avant même qu'ils partent

(**f**) *(in questions)* **how ever did you manage that?** comment donc y êtes-vous parvenu?; **what ever is the matter with you?** mais qu'est-ce que vous avez donc?; **when will they ever stop?** quand donc arrêteront-ils?; **where ever can it be?** où diable peut-il être?; **where ever have you been?** d'où venez-vous donc?; **who ever told you that?** qui est-ce qui a bien pu vous dire cela?; **who ever can it be?** qui est-ce que ça peut bien être?; **why ever not?** mais enfin, pourquoi pas?

2 ever after *adv* pour toujours; **they lived happily ever after** ils vécurent heureux jusqu'à la fin de leurs jours

3 ever so *adv* (**a**) *Fam (extremely)* vraiment❑; **she's ever so clever** elle est vraiment intelligente; **she's ever so pretty** elle est jolie comme tout; **it's ever so kind of you** c'est vraiment aimable à vous; **ever so slightly off-centre** un tout petit peu décentré; **thanks ever so (much)** merci vraiment

(**b**) *Formal (however)* **no teacher, be he ever so patient...** aucun enseignant, aussi patient soit-il...

4 ever such *adj Fam* vraiment❑; **they've got ever such pretty curtains in the shop** ils ont vraiment de jolis rideaux dans ce magasin; **it's ever such a shame** c'est vraiment dommage

Everest ['evərɪst] *n* **(Mount) Everest** le mont Everest, l'Everest *m*; **it was his Everest** *(goal)* c'était son but ultime; *(achievement)* c'était sa plus grande réussite

Everglades ['evə,gleɪdz] *npl* **the Everglades** les Everglades *mpl*

▸▸ ***the Everglades National Park*** le Parc national des Everglades

evergreen ['evəgriːn] **1** *n* (**a**) *(tree)* arbre *m* à feuilles persistantes; *(conifer)* conifère *m*; *(bush)* arbuste *m* à feuilles persistantes (**b**) *Fig (song, story)* chanson *f ou* histoire *f* qui ne vieillit jamais

2 *adj* (**a**) *(bush, tree)* à feuilles persistantes (**b**) *Fig (song, story)* qui ne vieillit pas; **an evergreen topic** une question toujours d'actualité

▸▸ *Fin* ***evergreen facility*** possibilité *f* de crédit permanent; *Fin* ***evergreen fund*** fonds *m* de crédit permanent non confirmé; *Am* ***the Evergreen State*** = surnom donné à l'État de Washington

everlasting [,evə'lɑːstɪŋ] **1** *adj* (**a**) *(eternal → hope, mercy)* éternel, infini; *(→ fame)* éternel, immortel; *(→ God, life)* éternel; **Henry, to his everlasting credit, said nothing** Henry n'a rien dit, ce qui est tout à son honneur (**b**) *(incessant)* perpétuel, éternel; **a life of everlasting misery** une vie de misère

2 *n Bot* immortelle *f*

▸▸ *Bot* ***everlasting flower*** immortelle *f*

everlastingly [,evə'lɑːstɪŋlɪ] *adv* (**a**) *(eternally)* éternellement (**b**) *(incessantly)* sans cesse, perpétuellement

evermore [,evə'mɔː(r)] *adv* toujours; **for evermore** pour toujours, à jamais

eversion [ɪ'vɜːʃən] *n Med* éversion *f*; **eversion of the eyelid** ectropion *m*

evert [ɪ'vɜːt] *vt Med* renverser, retourner

EVERY ['evrɪ]

tout	▸ **1 (a) – (c)**
chaque	▸ **1 (a)**
chacun	▸ **1 (d)**

1 *adj* (**a**) *(each)* tout, chaque; **every room has a view of the sea** les chambres ont toutes vue *ou* toutes les chambres ont vue sur la mer; **not every room is as big as this** toutes les chambres ne sont pas aussi grandes que celle-ci; **every word he says** tout ce qu'il dit; **he drank every drop** il a bu jusqu'à la dernière goutte; **every one of these apples** chacune de *ou* toutes ces pommes; **I've read every one** je les ai lus tous; **every one of them arrived late** ils sont tous arrivés en retard; **every (single) one of us was there** nous étions tous là (au grand complet); **every (single) one of these pencils is broken** tous ces crayons (sans exception) sont cassés; **every (single) person in the room** tous ceux qui étaient dans la pièce (sans exception); **every day** tous les jours, chaque jour; **she's feeling a little better every day** elle se sent un peu mieux chaque jour; **at every opportunity** chaque fois que c'est/c'était possible; **from every side** de tous (les) côtés; **every time I go out** chaque fois que je sors; **that's what fools them every time** c'est ce qui les trompe à tous les coups *ou* à chaque fois; **of every age/every sort/every colour** de tout âge/toute sorte/toutes les couleurs; **in every way** *(by any means)* par tous les moyens; *(from any viewpoint)* à tous (les) égards, sous tous les rapports; *Prov* **every little helps** les petits ruisseaux font les grandes rivières; **I can only give you half an hour – every little helps** je ne peux t'accorder qu'une demi-heure – c'est mieux que rien; **every man for himself** chacun pour soi; *(in danger)* sauve qui peut!; **every person has this right** chacun a ce droit; **every man Jack of them** tous sans exception

(**b**) *(with units of time, measurement etc)* tout; **every two days, every second day, every other day** tous les deux jours, un jour sur deux; **every quarter of an hour** tous les quarts d'heure; **every few days** tous les deux ou trois jours; **every few minutes** toutes les cinq minutes; **once every month** une fois par mois; **every ten miles** tous les dix miles; **every third man** un homme sur trois; **three women out of** *or* **in every ten, three out of every ten women** trois femmes sur dix; **every other Sunday** un dimanche sur deux; **write on every other line** écrivez en sautant une ligne sur deux

(**c**) *(indicating confidence, optimism)* tout; **I have every confidence that...** je ne doute pas un instant que...; **there's every chance that we'll succeed** nous avons toutes les chances de réussir; **you have every reason to be happy** vous avez toutes les raisons *ou* tout lieu d'être heureux; **you have every right to be angry** tu as tout à fait le droit d'être en colère; **we wish you every success** nous vous souhaitons très bonne chance

(**d**) *(with possessive adj)* chacun, moindre; **his every action bears witness to it** chacun de ses gestes *ou* tout ce qu'il fait en témoigne; **they hung on his every word** ils ne perdaient pas un seul mot de ce qu'il disait; **her every wish** son moindre désir, tous ses désirs

2 every now and again, every once in a while, every so often *adv* de temps en temps, de temps à autre

3 every which way *adv Am (everywhere)* partout; *(from all sides)* de toutes parts; **he came home with his hair every which way** il est rentré les cheveux en bataille

'Every Man for himself and God against all' *Herzog* 'Chacun pour soi et Dieu contre tous'

everybody ['evrɪ,bɒdɪ] = **everyone**

everyday ['evrɪdeɪ] *adj (daily)* de tous les jours, quotidien; *(ordinary)* banal, ordinaire; **my everyday routine** mon train-train quotidien; **everyday life** la vie quotidienne, la vie de tous les jours; **everyday occurrence** *(happening every day)* fait *m* journalier; *(ordinary)* fait *m* banal; **it's an everyday occurrence** cela arrive tous les jours; **an everyday expression** une expression courante; **in everyday use** d'usage courant; **for everyday wear** pour porter tous les jours

An everyday story of ... folk

À l'origine, le sous-titre du feuilleton radiophonique britannique *The Archers*, diffusé depuis 1951, était la formule **an everyday story of farming folk** ("la chronique d'une famille d'agriculteurs").

Aujourd'hui on utilise cette formule en anglais britannique de façon allusive et souvent sur le mode ironique en parlant du sujet d'un livre ou d'un film. On dira par exemple **NYPD Blue is more than just an everyday story of New York police folk** ("New York Police Blues est plus que la simple chronique de policiers new-yorkais").

Everyman ['evrɪmæn] *n* l'homme *m* de la rue

everyone ['evrɪwʌn] *pron* tout le monde, chacun; **as everyone knows** comme chacun *ou* tout le monde le sait; **everyone knows that!** tout le monde *ou* n'importe qui sait cela!; **not everyone can do it** ce n'est pas tout le monde qui pourrait le faire; **everyone here/in this room** tout le monde ici/dans cette pièce; **everyone else** tous les autres; **in a small town where everyone knows everyone (else)** dans une petite ville où tout le monde se connaît; **everyone who was anyone was there** tous les gens qui comptent étaient là

everyplace ['evrɪ,pleɪs] *Am* = **everywhere** *adv*

everything ['evrɪθɪŋ] *pron* (**a**) *(all things)* tout; **everything he says** tout ce qu'il dit; **they sell everything** ils vendent de tout; **she means everything to me** elle est tout pour moi, je ne vis que pour elle; **don't believe everything you hear** il ne faut pas croire tout ce que tu entends; **you can have everything you ever wanted** tu peux avoir tout ce que tu as toujours voulu; **he's got everything going for him** il a tout pour lui; *Fam* **a party with clowns, cakes and everything** une fête avec des clowns, des gâteaux et tout; *Fam* **I like her and everything, but I wouldn't want to live with her** je l'aime bien, ce n'est pas la question, mais je n'aimerais pas vivre avec elle❑

(**b**) *(the most important thing)* l'essentiel *m*; **winning is everything** l'essentiel, c'est de gagner; **money/beauty isn't everything** il n'y a pas que l'argent/la beauté qui compte

everywhere ['evrɪweə(r)] **1** *adv* partout; **I looked for it everywhere** je l'ai cherché partout; **everywhere she went** partout où elle allait; **cash dispensers are everywhere these days** on trouve des distributeurs (de billets) partout de nos jours; **he's been everywhere** il est allé partout; **everywhere you look there is poverty** de quelque côté que l'on se tourne, on voit la pauvreté; *Fam* **the files were everywhere** *(in disorder)* les dossiers étaient rangés n'importe comment

2 *pron Fam* tout❑; **everywhere's in such a mess** tout est sens dessus dessous

evict [ɪ'vɪkt] *vt* (**a**) *(person)* expulser, chasser (**b**) *(property)* récupérer par moyens juridiques

eviction [ɪ'vɪkʃən] *n* expulsion *f*

▸▸ ***eviction notice*** mandat *m* d'expulsion; ***eviction order*** ordre *m* d'expulsion

evidence ['evɪdəns] **1** *n* (**a**) *(reason for belief)* preuve *f*; *(testimony)* témoignage *m*; **we have clear evidence that...** on a la preuve manifeste que...; **there is no evidence to suggest a link between the two diseases** il n'y a aucune preuve suggérant qu'il y ait un lien entre les deux maladies; **on the evidence of eye witnesses** à en croire les témoins; **on the evidence of their past performances** à en juger par leurs performances passées

(**b**) *Law (proof)* preuves *fpl*; *(testimony)* témoignage *m*; **a piece of evidence** une preuve; **to**

give evidence against/for sb témoigner contre/en faveur de qn; **oral/written evidence** preuve *f* orale/littérale *ou* par écrit; **her statement is being held in evidence** sa déposition fait partie des témoignages; **whatever you say may be held in evidence against you** tout ce que vous direz pourra être retenu contre vous; **the evidence is against him** les preuves pèsent contre lui; *Br* **to turn King's** *or* **Queen's evidence,** *Am* **to turn State's evidence** témoigner contre ses complices *(sous promesse de pardon)*

(**c**) *(indication)* signe *m*, marque *f*; **to bear evidence of sth** porter la marque de qch; **the building bears evidence of recent habitation** il apparaît clairement que l'immeuble était encore occupé récemment; **to show evidence of sth** laisser voir qch; **her face showed no evidence of her anger** son visage ne témoignait pas de *ou* ne trahissait pas sa colère; **this problem is very much in evidence in Scotland** c'est un problème réel en Écosse; **his daughter was nowhere in evidence** sa fille n'était pas là *ou* n'était pas présente; **a politician very much in evidence these days** un homme politique très en vue ces temps-ci

2 *vt Formal* manifester, montrer; **as evidenced by the report that's just been published** comme en témoigne le rapport qui vient d'être publié

evident ['evɪdənt] *adj* évident, manifeste; **with evident pleasure** avec un plaisir manifeste; **it is evident from the way she talks** cela se voit à sa manière de parler; **it is quite evident that he's not interested** on voit bien qu'il ne s'y intéresse pas, il ne s'y intéresse pas, c'est évident; **he's lying, that's evident** il ment, c'est évident

evidential [evɪ'denʃəl] *adj* (**a**) *(based on evidence)* fondé sur les preuves (**b**) *(serving as evidence)* **to be evidential of sth** être indicateur de qch

evidently ['evɪdəntlɪ] *adv* (**a**) *(apparently)* apparemment; **did he refuse? – evidently not** a-t-il refusé? – non apparemment *ou* à ce qu'il paraît; **unemployment is evidently rising again** de toute évidence le chômage est à nouveau en hausse (**b**) *(clearly)* de toute évidence, manifestement; **evidently worried** manifestement inquiet; **he was evidently in pain** il était évident *ou* clair qu'il souffrait

evil ['iːvəl] *(Br compar* **eviller,** *superl* **evillest,** *Am compar* **eviler,** *superl* **evilest)** **1** *adj* (**a**) *(wicked → person)* malveillant, méchant; *(→ deed, plan, reputation)* mauvais; *(→ influence)* néfaste; *(→ doctrine, spell, spirit)* maléfique; **he's in an evil mood** il est d'une humeur massacrante; **she has an evil temper** elle a un sale caractère *ou* un caractère de chien; **to have an evil tongue** être mauvaise langue; **he had his evil way with her** il est arrivé à ses fins avec elle; **to put off the evil day** *or* **hour** repousser le moment fatidique; **of evil repute** *(place)* mal famé; *(person)* tristement célèbre; **the Evil One** le Malin

(**b**) *(smell, taste)* infect, infâme

2 *n* mal *m*; **to speak evil of sb** dire du mal de qn; **I wish her no evil** je ne lui veux pas de mal; **social evils** plaies *fpl* sociales, maux *mpl* sociaux; **the evils of drink** les conséquences *fpl* funestes de la boisson; **a necessary evil** un mal nécessaire; **pollution is one of the evils of our era** la pollution est un fléau de notre époque; **it's the lesser evil** *or* **of two evils** c'est le moindre mal; *Prov* **hear no evil, see no evil(, speak no evil)** = formule qui fait référence aux trois singes dont l'un se couvre la bouche, l'autre les yeux et le troisième les oreilles, et qui symbolise la lâcheté devant l'injustice

►► ***the evil eye*** le mauvais œil; **to give sb the evil eye** jeter le mauvais œil à qn; **to ward off the evil eye** se protéger du mauvais œil

evil-boding [-'bəʊdɪŋ] *adj Arch or Literary* de mauvais présage, de mauvais augure

evildoer ['iːvəl,duːə(r)] *n* méchant(e) *m,f*, scélérat(e) *m,f*

evildoing ['iːvəl,duːɪŋ] *n* méfaits *mpl*

evil-looking *adj (person)* qui a l'air mauvais; *(weapon)* menaçant

evilly ['iːvəllɪ] *adv (smile, say)* avec malveillance; *(look)* d'un mauvais œil, d'un air méchant

evil-minded *adj* malveillant, mal intentionné

evil-smelling *adj Br* nauséabond

evince [ɪ'vɪns] *vt Formal (show → interest, surprise)* manifester, montrer; *(→ quality)* faire preuve de, manifester

evirate ['evɪreɪt] *vt Arch or Literary* émasculer, châtrer, évirer

eviration [,evɪ'reɪʃən] *n Arch or Literary* émasculation *f*, castration *f*, éviration *f*

eviscerate [ɪ'vɪsəreɪt] *vt Formal* éventrer, étriper; *Med* éviscérer

evisceration [ɪ,vɪsə'reɪʃən] *n Formal & Med* éviscération *f*

evocation [,evəʊ'keɪʃən] *n* évocation *f*

evocative [ɪ'vɒkətɪv] *adj* (**a**) *(picture, scent)* évocateur; **to be evocative of sth** évoquer qch (**b**) *(magic)* évocatoire

evoke [ɪ'vəʊk] *vt* (**a**) *(summon up → memory, spirit)* évoquer (**b**) *(elicit → admiration)* susciter; *(→ response, smile)* susciter, provoquer

evoked set [ɪ'vəʊkt-] *n Mktg* ensemble *m* évoqué

evolute ['iːvəluːt] *n Math* développée *f*

evolution [,iːvə'luːʃən] *n* (**a**) *(of language, situation)* évolution *f*; *(of art, society, technology)* développement *m*, évolution *f*; *(of events)* développement *m*, déroulement *m* (**b**) *Biol, Bot & Zool* évolution *f*; **the theory of evolution** la théorie de l'évolution des espèces (**c**) *(of dancers, troops)* évolution *f* (**d**) *Math* extraction *f* (de la racine)

evolutionary [,iːvə'luːʃənərɪ] *adj* (**a**) *Biol* évolutionniste (**b**) *(process)* évolutif

evolutionism [,iːvə'luːʃənɪzəm] *n* évolutionnisme *m*

evolutionist [,iːvə'luːʃənɪst] **1** *adj* évolutionniste

2 *n* évolutionniste *mf*

evolve [ɪ'vɒlv] **1** *vi (events)* se dérouler; *(situation, race)* évoluer, se développer; *Biol, Bot & Zool* évoluer; **to evolve from sth** se développer à partir de qch; **the theory has evolved over the years** la théorie a évolué au fil des années; **medicine has evolved into a sophisticated science** la médecine est devenue une science sophistiquée

2 *vt (system, theory)* développer, élaborer

evzone ['evzəʊn] *n Mil* evzone *m*

ewe [juː] *n* brebis *f*; **a ewe lamb** une agnelle

ewer ['juːə(r)] *n* aiguière *f*

ex [eks] **1** *prep* (**a**) *Com* départ, sortie; **ex quay** à quai; **ex ship** à bord; **ex warehouse** à (prendre à) l'entrepôt, en entrepôt; **ex wharf** à quai; **ex works** départ usine, sortie d'usine; **price ex works** prix *m* départ *ou* sortie usine

(**b**) *Fin* sans; **ex all, ex allotment** ex-répartition *f*; **ex bonus** ex-capitalisation *f*; **ex cap, ex capitalisation** ex-capitalisation *f*; **ex coupon** ex-coupon *m*, coupon *m* détaché; **this stock goes ex coupon on 1 August** le coupon de cette action se détache le 1 août; **ex dividend** ex-dividende *m*, dividende *m* détaché; **ex interest** sans *ou* exonéré d'intérêts; **ex new, ex rights** ex-droit *m*; **ex scrip** ex-répartition *f*

2 *n Fam (former partner, spouse)* ex *mf*

ex- [eks] *pref* ex-, ancien; **his ex-wife** son ex-femme; **he's an ex-teacher** c'est un ancien enseignant; **the ex-president** l'ancien(enne) président(e) *m,f*, l'ex-président(e) *m,f*

exacerbate [ɪg'zæsəbeɪt] *vt Formal* (**a**) *(make worse)* exacerber, aggraver (**b**) *(annoy)* énerver, exaspérer

exacerbation [ɪgzæsə'beɪʃən] *n Formal (worsening)* exacerbation *f*, aggravation *f*

exact [ɪg'zækt] **1** *adj* (**a**) *(accurate, correct)* exact, juste; **it's an exact copy** *(picture)* c'est fidèle à l'original; *(document)* c'est une copie conforme *ou* textuelle; **she told me the exact opposite** elle m'a dit exactement le contraire; **that's the exact problem** c'est précisément le problème; **those were her exact words** ce furent ses propres paroles, voilà ce qu'elle a dit textuellement

(**b**) *(precise → amount, idea, value)* exact, précis; *(→ directions, place, time)* précis; **is it 5 o'clock? – 5:03 to be exact** est-il 5 heures? – 5 heures 03 plus exactement *ou* précisément; **I'm 35 and 2 days to be exact** j'ai exactement 35 ans et 2 jours; **she likes music, or to be exact, classical music** elle aime la musique, ou plus précisément la musique classique; **can you be more exact?** pouvez-vous préciser?; **we need exact details** il nous faut des précisions; *Fam* **the exact same dress** exactement la même robe❑

(**c**) *(meticulous → work)* rigoureux, précis; *(→ mind)* rigoureux; *(→ instrument)* de précision

2 *vt* (**a**) *(demand → money)* extorquer

(**b**) *(insist upon → obedience, discipline)* exiger

►► ***exact sciences*** sciences *fpl* exactes; *Fig* **it's not an exact science** ce n'est pas une science exacte

exacting [ɪg'zæktɪŋ] *adj (person)* exigeant; *(activity, job)* astreignant, exigeant

exaction [ɪg'zækʃən] *n* (**a**) *(act)* exaction *f*, extorsion *f* (**b**) *(money)* paiement *m* (**c**) *(demand)* extorsion *f*, exigence *f*

exactitude [ɪg'zæktɪtjuːd] *n* exactitude *f*

exactly [ɪg'zæktlɪ] *adv* (**a**) *(accurately)* précisément, avec précision; **I followed her instructions exactly** j'ai suivi ses instructions à la lettre *ou* avec précision; **the computer can reproduce this sound exactly** l'ordinateur peut reproduire exactement ce son

(**b**) *(entirely, precisely)* exactement, justement; **I don't remember exactly** je ne me rappelle pas au juste; **but that's exactly what I mean!** mais c'est précisément ce que je veux dire!; **that's not exactly what I meant** ce n'est pas exactement ce que je voulais dire; **I'm not exactly sure what you mean** je ne suis pas tout à fait sûr de ce que tu veux dire; **he did exactly the opposite of what I told him** il a fait exactement le contraire de ce que je lui ai dit; **it's exactly the same thing** c'est exactement la même chose; **it's exactly 5 o'clock** il est 5 heures juste; **it's been six months exactly** cela fait six mois jour pour jour; **the journey took exactly three hours** le voyage a duré très exactement trois heures; **are you ill? – not exactly** êtes-vous malade? – pas exactement *ou* pas vraiment; **she didn't exactly agree, but...** elle n'était pas vraiment d'accord, mais...; **he's not exactly poor** il n'est pas exactement (ce que l'on appelle) pauvre; **exactly!** exactement!, parfaitement!

exactness [ɪg'zæktnɪs] *n* exactitude *f*, soin *m*

exaggerate [ɪg'zædʒəreɪt] **1** *vi* exagérer; **don't exaggerate!** n'exagère pas!; **she always exaggerates** elle exagère toujours

2 *vt* (**a**) *(overstate → quality, situation, size)* exagérer; *(→ facts)* amplifier; *(→ importance)* s'exagérer; **he is exaggerating the seriousness of the problem** il exagère la gravité du problème

(**b**) *(emphasize)* accentuer; **she exaggerates her weakness to gain sympathy** elle se prétend plus faible qu'elle ne l'est réellement pour s'attirer la compassion; **tight trousers will exaggerate your thinness** des pantalons serrés accentueront ta minceur *ou* te feront paraître encore plus mince

exaggerated [ɪg'zædʒəreɪtɪd] *adj* (**a**) *(number, story)* exagéré; *(fashion, style)* outré; **to have an exaggerated opinion of oneself** *or* **of one's own worth** avoir une trop haute opinion de soi-même (**b**) *Med* exagéré

exaggeratedly [ɪg'zædʒəreɪtɪdlɪ] *adv* d'une manière exagérée, exagérément

exaggeration [ɪg,zædʒə'reɪʃən] *n* exagération *f*; **that's an exaggeration!** vous exagérez!/ils exagèrent!/*etc*; **it would be no exaggeration to say that...** on pourrait dire sans exagérer *ou* sans exagération que...

exalt [ɪg'zɔːlt] *vt* (**a**) *(praise highly)* exalter, chanter les louanges de (**b**) *(in rank)* élever (à un rang plus important)

exaltation [,egzɔːl'teɪʃən] *n (UNCOUNT)* (**a**) *(praise)* louange *f*, louanges *fpl*, exaltation *f* (**b**) *(elation)* exultation *f*, exaltation *f*

exalted [ɪg'zɔːltɪd] *adj* (**a**) *(prominent → person)* de haut rang, haut placé; *(→ position, rank)* élevé (**b**) *(elated)* exalté

exam [ɪg'zæm] **1** *n Sch & Univ* examen *m*; **to sit** *or* **to take an exam** passer un examen; **to pass/to fail an exam** réussir à/échouer à un examen; **to have exam nerves** avoir le trac avant les examens; **when do the exam results come out?** quand les résultats de l'examen seront-ils connus?

2 *comp (question)* d'examen

►► ***exam board*** commission *f* d'examen; ***exam conditions*** conditions *fpl* de l'examen; **they wrote the essay under exam conditions** ils ont fait la dissertation dans les conditions de l'examen; ***exam paper*** *(set of questions)* sujet *m* d'examen; *(written answer)* copie *f* (d'examen)

examinable [ɪg'zæmɪnəbəl] *adj Law (witness, suspect)* que l'on peut interroger

examination [ɪg,zæmɪ'neɪʃən] **1** *n* (**a**) *(of records, files, proposal etc)* examen *m*; *(of building → by official)* inspection *f*; *(→ by potential buyer)* visite *f*; **it doesn't stand up to examination** *(argument, theory)* cela ne résiste pas à l'examen; *(alibi)* cela ne tient pas; **to carry out** *or* **to make an examination of sth** procéder à l'examen de qch; **her latest novel is an examination of the generation gap** son dernier roman est une analyse du fossé entre les générations; **the device was removed for examination** on a enlevé le mécanisme afin de l'examiner; **on examination** après examen; **the proposal is still under examination** la proposition est encore à l'étude

(**b**) *Med* examen *m* médical; *(at school, work)* visite *f* médicale; *(regular)* bilan *m* de santé; **I'm just going in for an examination** j'y vais juste pour passer un examen médical

(**c**) *Formal Sch & Univ* examen *m*; **to sit** *or* **to take an examination** passer un examen

(**d**) *Law (of witness)* audition *f*; *(of suspect)* interrogatoire *m*

2 *comp (question, results)* d'examen

►► ***examination board*** commission *f* d'examen; ***examination conditions*** conditions *fpl* de l'examen; **they wrote the essay under examination conditions** ils ont fait la dissertation dans les conditions de l'examen; ***examination paper*** *(set of questions)* sujet *m* d'examen; *(written answer)* copie *f* (d'examen)

examination-in-chief *n Law* interrogatoire *m* principal

examine [ɪg'zæmɪn] *vt* (**a**) *(inspect → records, files, proposal etc)* examiner, étudier; *(→ building)* inspecter; *(→ baggage)* fouiller, examiner; **the weapon is being examined for fingerprints** on est en train d'examiner l'arme pour voir si elle porte des empreintes digitales; **to examine one's conscience** faire son examen de conscience

(**b**) *Med* examiner; *Fam Hum* **he needs his head examined** il est complètement fou *ou* cinglé

(**c**) *Sch & Univ* faire passer un examen à; *(orally)* interroger, faire passer l'épreuve orale à; **you'll be examined in French/in all six subjects/on your knowledge of the subject** vous aurez à passer un examen de français/dans ces six matières/pour évaluer vos connaissances sur le sujet

(**d**) *Law (witness)* entendre; *(suspect)* interroger; *(case)* instruire

examinee [ɪg,zæmɪ'ni:] *n* candidat(e) *m,f (à un examen)*

examiner [ɪg'zæmɪnə(r)] *n (in school, driving test)* examinateur(trice) *m,f*; *Sch & Univ* **the examiners** les examinateurs *mpl*, le jury

examining [ɪg'zæmɪnɪŋ] *adj*

►► ***examining body*** jury *m* d'examen; *Br Law* ***examining magistrate*** juge *m* d'instruction

example [ɪg'zɑ:mpəl] **1** *n* (**a**) *(illustration)* exemple *m*; **can you give me an example?** pouvez-vous me donner un exemple?; **to give just one example,...** pour ne donner *ou* citer qu'un exemple,...; **this is an excellent example of what I meant** ceci illustre parfaitement ce que je voulais dire; **it's a classic example of 1960s architecture** c'est un exemple classique de l'architecture des années 60

(**b**) *(person or action to be imitated)* exemple *m*, modèle *m*; **you're an example to us all** vous êtes un modèle pour nous tous; **to follow sb's example** suivre l'exemple de qn; **I followed your example and complained about the poor service** j'ai fait comme vous et me suis plaint de la médiocrité du service; **following France's example, Britain has introduced sanctions** à l'exemple *ou* à l'instar de la France, la Grande-Bretagne a pris des sanctions; **to set an example** montrer l'exemple; **she sets us all an example** elle nous montre l'exemple à tous; **to set a good/bad example** montrer le bon/mauvais exemple; **you're setting your little brother a bad example** tu montres le mauvais exemple à ton petit frère; **to hold sb up as an example** citer qn en exemple

(**c**) *(sample, specimen)* exemple *m*, spécimen *m*; *(of work)* échantillon *m*

(**d**) *(warning)* exemple *m*; **let this be an example to you** que ça te serve d'exemple; **to make an example of sb** punir qn pour l'exemple

2 for example *adv* par exemple; **large cities, (as) for example London** les grandes villes, telles que Londres (par exemple)

ex ante ['eksæntɪ] *adj* ex ante

exanimate [ek'sænɪmeɪt] *adj Literary* inanimé, mort

exanthema [,eksæn'θi:mə] *(pl* **exanthemata** [-mətə]) *n Med* exanthème *m*

exanthematic [,eksæn'θi:mətɪk], **exanthematous** [,eksæn'θi:mətəs] *adj Med* exanthématique

exarch ['eksɑ:k] *n Rel* exarque *m*

exarchate ['eksɑ:,keɪt] *n Rel* exarchat *m*

exasperate [ɪg'zɑ:spəreɪt] *vt* exaspérer

exasperated [ɪg'zɑ:spəreɪtəd] *adj (person, look, voice)* exaspéré; *(gesture)* d'exaspération; **her father was so exasperated with her that he lost his temper** elle a tellement exaspéré son père que celui-ci s'est mis en colère

exasperating [ɪg'zɑ:spəreɪtɪŋ] *adj* exaspérant; **I've had an exasperating day** j'ai passé une journée exaspérante

exasperatingly [ɪg'zɑ:spəreɪtɪŋlɪ] *adv* **the service is exasperatingly slow in this restaurant** le service est d'une lenteur exaspérante *ou* désespérante dans ce restaurant; **he's exasperatingly arrogant** son arrogance est exaspérante

exasperation [ɪg,zɑ:spə'reɪʃən] *n (irritation, frustration)* exaspération *f*; **to look at sb in exasperation** regarder qn avec exaspération *ou* un air exaspéré; **"shut up!", she screamed in exasperation** "tais-toi!", cria-t-elle, exaspérée; **she was nearly weeping with** *or* **from exasperation** elle pleurait presque d'exaspération; **I did it out of sheer exasperation** j'ai fait cela parce que j'étais exaspéré *ou* je n'en pouvais plus

ex cathedra [,ekskə'θi:drə] *Rel* **1** *adj* ex cathedra

2 *adv* ex cathedra

excavate ['ekskəveɪt] **1** *vt* (**a**) *(hole, trench)* creuser, excaver (**b**) *Archeol (temple, building)* mettre au jour; **to excavate a site** faire des fouilles

2 *vi Archeol* faire des fouilles; *Constr* procéder à une/des excavation(s)

excavation [,ekskə'veɪʃən] *n* (**a**) *(of hole, trench)* excavation *f*, creusement *m* (**b**) *Archeol (of temple, building)* mise *f* au jour; **the excavations at Knossos** les fouilles *fpl* de Knossos

excavator ['ekskə,veɪtə(r)] *n* (**a**) *(machine)* excavateur *m*, excavatrice *f* (**b**) *(archaeologist)* = personne qui conduit des fouilles

exceed [ɪk'si:d] *vt* (**a**) *(be more than)* dépasser, excéder; **demand exceeded supply** la demande a excédé l'offre; **her salary exceeds mine by £5,000 a year** son salaire annuel dépasse le mien de 5000 livres

(**b**) *(go beyond → expectations, hopes, fears)* dépasser; *(→ budget)* excéder, déborder; **to exceed one's authority** outrepasser ses pouvoirs; **to exceed one's instructions** aller au-delà des instructions reçues; **to exceed the speed limit** dépasser la limite de vitesse, faire un excès de vitesse; **to be fined for exceeding the speed limit** avoir une amende pour excès de vitesse; **do not exceed the stated dose** *(on medication)* ne pas dépasser la dose prescrite

exceeding [ɪk'si:dɪŋ] *adv Arch or Literary (extremely)* extrêmement

exceedingly [ɪk'si:dɪŋlɪ] *adv (extremely)* extrêmement

excel [ɪk'sel] *(pt & pp* **excelled**) **1** *vi* exceller; **this is a field where Scots excel** c'est un domaine où les Écossais excellent; **to excel at** *or* **in music** exceller en musique; **I've never excelled at games** je n'ai jamais été très fort en sport; **the company excels in the export field** la société excelle dans l'exportation; **the company doesn't exactly excel at after-sales service** le service après-vente n'est pas vraiment le point fort de la société

2 *vt* surpasser; *also Ironic* **to excel oneself** se surpasser; *Ironic* **you've really excelled yourself this time!** tu t'es vraiment surpassé cette fois-ci!

excellence ['eksələns] *n (high quality)* qualité *f* excellente; *(commercially)* excellence *f*; *Sch* **a prize for general excellence** un prix d'excellence; **to strive for excellence** s'efforcer d'atteindre une qualité excellente; **excellence is our hallmark** l'excellence est notre signe distinctif; **awards for excellence** prix *mpl* d'excellence; **centre of excellence** centre *m* d'excellence

Excellency ['eksələnsɪ] *(pl* **Excellencies**) *n* Excellence *f*; **Your/His Excellency** Votre/Son Excellence

excellent ['eksələnt] *adj* excellent; *(weather)* magnifique; **excellent!** formidable!, parfait!

excellently ['eksələntlɪ] *adv* de façon excellente, superbement; **she had done excellently in her exams** elle avait obtenu d'excellents résultats à ses examens; **it was excellently done** cela a été fait de main de maître

Excelsior® [ek'selsɪɔ:(r)] *n (UNCOUNT) Am* copeaux *mpl* de bois

except [ɪk'sept] **1** *prep (apart from)* à part, excepté, sauf; **everybody was there except him, everybody except him was there** tout le monde était là à part *ou* excepté *ou* sauf lui; **except weekends** à part *ou* excepté *ou* sauf le week-end; **any day except Saturday and anywhere except here** n'importe quel jour sauf le samedi et n'importe où sauf ici; **I know nothing about it except what he told me** je ne sais rien d'autre que ce qu'il m'a raconté; **I remember nothing except that I was scared** je ne me souviens de rien sauf que *ou* excepté que j'avais peur

2 *conj* (**a**) *(apart from)* **I'll do anything except sell the car** je ferai tout sauf vendre la voiture; **except if** sauf *ou* à part si; **except when** sauf *ou* à part quand

(**b**) *(only)* seulement, mais; **I would tell her except she wouldn't believe me** je le lui dirais bien, mais *ou* seulement elle ne me croirait pas; **we would stay longer except (that) we have no more money** nous resterions bien plus long temps, mais *ou* seulement nous n'avons plus d'argent

(**c**) *Arch or Bible (unless)* à moins que

3 *vt (exclude)* excepter, exclure; **all countries, France excepted** tous les pays, la France exceptée *ou* à l'exception de la France; **present company excepted** à l'exception des personnes présentes, les personnes présentes exceptées

4 except for *prep* sauf, à part; **the typing's finished except for the last page** il ne reste plus que la dernière page à taper; **the office will be empty over Christmas except for the boss and me** il n'y aura que le patron et moi au bureau au moment de Noël; **he would have got away with it except for that one mistake** sans cette erreur il s'en serait tiré

excepting [ɪk'septɪŋ] **1** *prep* à part, excepté, sauf; **not excepting...** y compris...; **always excepting really outstanding candidates** à l'exception *ou* en dehors des candidats vraiment brillants

2 *conj Arch (unless)* à moins que + *subjunctive*

exception [ɪk'sepʃən] *n* (**a**) *(deviation, exemption)* exception *f*; **the exception proves the rule** l'exception confirme la règle; **to make an exception (of sth/for sb)** faire une exception (pour qch/qn); **without exception** sans exception; **but she's an exception** mais elle n'est pas comme les autres; **the only exception being Britain, Britain being the only exception** la seule exception étant la Grande-Bretagne; **with the exception of Daniel** à l'exception de Daniel; **and you're no exception** et cela te concerne aussi; **most Western countries were feeling the effects of the recession, and Britain was no exception** la plupart des pays occidentaux ressentaient les effets de la crise, et la Grande-Bretagne n'était pas épargnée

(**b**) *(idiom)* **to take exception to sth** *(object to)* trouver à redire à qch; *(be offended by)* s'offusquer de qch; **I take exception to that remark** je n'apprécie pas du tout ce commentaire

exceptionable [ɪk'sepʃənəbəl] *adj (objectionable)* offensant, outrageant

exceptional [ɪk'sepʃənəl] *adj* exceptionnel; **in**

exa–exc

exceptional circumstances dans des circonstances exceptionnelles; **these are exceptional times we live in** nous vivons une époque exceptionnelle

►► *Am Sch* ***exceptional child*** *(gifted child)* enfant *m* surdoué; *(child with learning difficulties)* = enfant qui a des difficultés d'apprentissage; *Acct* ***exceptional item*** poste *m* extraordinaire

exceptionally [ɪk'sepʃənəlɪ] *adv* exceptionnellement; **that's exceptionally kind of you** c'est extrêmement gentil de votre part; **exceptionally, no bail was granted** à titre exceptionnel, il n'a pas été accordé de remise en liberté sous caution; **she's an exceptionally bright child** c'est une enfant d'une intelligence exceptionnelle

exc–exc

excerpt ['eksɜːpt] *n (extract)* extrait *m* (**from** de)

excess 1 *n* [ɪk'ses] (**a**) *(unreasonable amount)* excès *m*; **an excess of salt/fat in the diet** un excès de sel/de graisses dans l'alimentation

(**b**) *(difference between two amounts)* supplément *m*, surplus *m*; **an excess of supply over demand** un excès de l'offre sur la demande; **there has been an excess of expenditure over revenue** les dépenses ont excédé les recettes

(**c**) *(over-indulgence)* excès *m*; **a life of excess** une vie d'excès

(**d**) *(usu pl) (unacceptable action)* excès *m*, abus *m*; **the excesses of the occupying troops** les excès *ou* abus commis par les soldats pendant l'occupation; **he is famous for his excesses** il est réputé pour ses excès

(**e**) *Br Ins* franchise *f*

2 *adj* ['ekses] *(extra)* en trop, excédentaire; **you're carrying a lot of excess weight** tu as beaucoup de kilos en trop *ou* à perdre

3 in excess of *prep (a stated percentage, weight)* au-dessus de; **she earns in excess of £25,000 a year** elle gagne plus de 25 000 livres par an

4 to excess [ɪk'ses] *adv* **to carry sth to excess** pousser qch trop loin; **he does** *or* **carries it to excess** il exagère, il dépasse les bornes; **to eat/to drink to excess** manger/boire à l'excès

►► ***excess baggage*** *(UNCOUNT) (on plane)* excédent *m* de bagages; **I had 10 kilos of excess baggage** j'avais 10 kilos d'excédent de bagages; *Br* ***excess fare*** supplément *m* de prix; ***excess luggage*** *(UNCOUNT) (on plane)* excédent *m* de bagages; *Fin* ***excess profits*** surplus *m* des bénéfices; *(unexpected)* bénéfices *mpl* exceptionnels, bénéfices *mpl* extraordinaires; *Fin* ***excess profits tax*** impôt *f* sur les bénéfices exceptionnels; *Banking* ***excess reserves*** réserves *fpl* excédentaires; *St Exch* ***excess shares*** actions *fpl* détenues en surnombre; ***excess supply*** suroffre *f*

excessive [ɪk'sesɪv] *adj (unreasonable)* excessif; *(demand)* excessif, démesuré; **excessive drinking** excès *mpl* de boisson; **that's a bit excessive** c'est un peu excessif; **to show excessive interest in sb/sth** s'intéresser de trop près à qn/qch; **in excessive detail** avec trop de détails

excessively [ɪk'sesɪvlɪ] *adv* excessivement; **to eat/drink excessively** manger/boire à l'excès; **it was hot/damaged, but not excessively so** il faisait chaud/il était endommagé, mais pas trop

excessiveness [ɪk'sesɪvnɪs] *n* excessiveté *f*

exchange [ɪks'tʃeɪndʒ] **1** *vt* échanger; **to exchange glances** échanger des regards; **to exchange views** échanger des vues; **we didn't exchange more than a couple of words all evening** nous n'avons pas échangé plus de quelques mots de toute la soirée; *Euph* **to exchange words** *(quarrel)* se disputer; **shots were exchanged** il y a eu un échange de coups de feu; **to exchange sth with sb** échanger qch avec qn; **to exchange places with sb** changer de place avec qn; **we exchanged places (with each other)** nous avons échangé nos places; **would you like to exchange places?** voulez-vous changer de place avec moi?; **we exchanged addresses** nous avons échangé nos adresses; **to exchange sth for sth** échanger qch contre qch; **to exchange sterling for dollars** changer des livres contre des dollars; **I would not exchange my happiness for anything** je n'échangerais *ou* ne donnerais mon bonheur contre rien au monde

2 *n* (**a**) *(swap)* échange *m*; **his old car for my new one didn't seem a fair exchange** échanger sa vieille voiture contre ma neuve ne me semblait pas équitable; **exchange of contracts** échange *m* de contrats à la signature; *Br Prov* **fair exchange is no robbery** = donnant donnant; *Press* **Exchange and Mart** = hebdomadaire britannique de petites annonces

(**b**) *(discussion)* échange *m*; **we had a heated exchange** nous avons eu des mots

(**c**) *(cultural, educational)* échange *m*; **as part of an exchange** dans le cadre d'un échange; **he took part in an exchange with a school in France** il a participé à un échange avec une école française; **the Spanish students are here on an exchange visit** les étudiants espagnols sont en visite ici dans le cadre d'un échange

(**d**) *Fin (of currency)* change *m*; *(of goods, shares, commodities)* échange *m*

(**e**) *Tel* central *m* téléphonique

(**f**) *Com* bourse *f*

3 exchanges *npl Am Fin (bills)* lettres *fpl* de change, traites *fpl*

4 in exchange *adv* en échange

5 in exchange for *prep* en échange de; **in exchange for helping with the housework she was given food and lodging** elle aidait aux travaux ménagers et en échange *ou* en contrepartie elle était nourrie et logée

►► *Fin* ***exchange broker*** cambiste *mf*, agent *m* de change, courtier(ère) *m,f* de change; *Br Fin* ***exchange control*** contrôle *m* des changes; *Fin* ***exchange cross rate*** taux *m* de change entre devises tierces; *Fin* ***exchange dealer*** cambiste *mf*, agent *m* de change, courtier(ère) *m,f* de change; *Fin* ***exchange equalization account*** fonds *m* de stabilisation des changes; *Fin* ***exchange gain*** gain *m* de change; *Fin* ***exchange index*** indice *m* boursier; *Fin* ***exchange loss*** perte *f* de change; *Fin* ***exchange market*** marché *m* des changes; *Fin* ***exchange offer*** offre *f* publique d'échange; *Fin* ***exchange premium*** prime *f* de change; *Sch & Univ* ***exchange programme*** programme *m* d'échange; *Fin* ***exchange rate*** taux *m* de change, cours *m* de change; **at the current exchange rate** au cours du jour; *Formerly Fin* ***Exchange Rate Mechanism*** mécanisme *m* (des taux) de change (du SME); ***exchange rate parity*** parité *f* du change; ***exchange rate stability*** stabilité *f* des changes; *Fin* ***exchange reserves*** réserves *fpl* en devises (étrangères); *Fin* ***exchange restrictions*** contrôle *m* des changes; *Sch & Univ* ***exchange student*** = étudiant qui participe à un échange; *Fin* ***exchange transaction*** opération *f* de change; *Fin* ***exchange value*** contre-valeur *f*, valeur *f* d'échange; *Sch* ***exchange visit*** échange *m*

exchangeable [ɪks'tʃeɪndʒəbəl] *adj* échangeable, qui peut être échangé; **goods are exchangeable only when accompanied by a valid receipt** les articles ne peuvent être échangés que s'ils sont accompagnés du ticket de caisse

exchequer [ɪks'tʃekə(r)] **1** *n Pol & Fin (finances)* finances *fpl*

2 Exchequer *n Admin* **the Exchequer** *(department)* l'Échiquier *m*, le Ministère des Finances *(en Grande-Bretagne)*; *(money)* le Trésor public

►► *Fin* ***exchequer bill*** bon *m* du Trésor

excipient [ɪk'sɪpɪənt] *n Pharm* excipient *m*

excisable [ek'saɪzəbəl] *adj Com* taxable, imposable

excise[1] ['eksaɪz] *n* (**a**) *Com (tax)* taxe *f*, contribution *f* indirecte (**b**) *Br (government office)* régie *f*, service *m* des contributions indirectes; **men from the excise** *(customs officers)* officiers *mpl* des douanes; *(VAT inspectors)* inspecteurs *mpl* de la TVA

►► ***excise bond*** acquit-à-caution *m*; *Com* ***excise duty, excise tax*** contribution *f* indirecte

excise[2] [ek'saɪz] *vt* (**a**) *Formal (remove from a text)* retrancher, supprimer (**b**) *Med* exciser

exciseman ['eksaɪz,mæn] *(pl* **excisemen** [-men]*)* *n Br* employé *m* de la régie *ou* des contributions indirectes

excision [ek'sɪʒən] *n* (**a**) *Formal (of piece of text)* coupure *f*, retranchement *m* (**b**) *Med* excision *f*

excisionist [ek'sɪʒənɪst], **excisor** [ek'saɪzə(r)] *n Med* exciseur(euse) *m,f*

excitability [ɪk,saɪtə'bɪlətɪ] *n* nervosité *f*, émotivité *f*

excitable [ɪk'saɪtəbəl] *adj (gen) & Med & Physiol* excitable

excitant ['eksɪtənt, ek'saɪtənt] **1** *n* excitant *m*, stimulant *m*; **coffee is an excitant** le café est agitant

2 *adj* excitant, stimulant

excitation [,eksɪ'teɪʃən] *n* (**a**) *(process, state)* excitation *f* (**b**) *Phys, Physiol & Elec* excitation *f*

excite [ɪk'saɪt] *vt* (**a**) *(agitate)* exciter, énerver; **the doctor said you weren't to excite yourself** le docteur a dit qu'il ne te fallait pas d'excitation *ou* qu'il ne fallait pas que tu t'énerves; **the sight of the rabbit had excited the dogs** la vue du lapin avait excité les chiens; **excited by the gunfire, the horses bolted** excités *ou* énervés par les coups de feu, les chevaux se sont emballés

(**b**) *(fill with enthusiasm)* enthousiasmer; **it takes a lot to excite her** il en faut beaucoup pour l'enthousiasmer; **I'm very excited by this latest development** ce fait nouveau me remplit d'enthousiasme

(**c**) *(sexually)* exciter

(**d**) *(arouse → interest, curiosity)* susciter

(**e**) *Phys, Physiol & Elec* exciter

excited [ɪk'saɪtɪd] *adj* (**a**) *(enthusiastic, eager)* excité; **to be excited about** *or* **at sth** être excité par qch; **the children were excited at the prospect of going to the seaside** les enfants étaient tout excités à l'idée d'aller au bord de la mer; **you must be very excited at being chosen to play for your country** vous devez être fou de joie d'avoir été choisi pour jouer pour votre pays; **the medical world is very excited** *(by discovery etc)* le monde médical est très enthousiaste; **doctors are excited by this discovery** les médecins sont enthousiasmés par cette découverte; **it's nothing to get excited about** il n'y a pas de quoi en faire un plat, ça n'a rien d'extraordinaire; **don't get too excited** ne t'excite *ou* t'emballe pas trop; **you don't seem very excited** ça n'a pas l'air de t'emballer; *Ironic* **well, don't sound too excited!** eh bien, quel enthousiasme!

(**b**) *(agitated)* **don't go getting excited, don't get excited** ne va pas t'énerver; **it doesn't do him any good getting excited at his age** cela ne lui vaut rien de s'énerver *ou* s'agiter à son âge

(**c**) *(sexually)* excité

(**d**) *Phys, Physiol & Elec* excité

excitedly [ɪk'saɪtɪdlɪ] *adv (behave, watch)* avec agitation; *(say)* sur un ton animé; *(wait)* fébrilement; **she was jumping up and down excitedly** elle sautait dans tous les sens, tout excitée

excitement [ɪk'saɪtmənt] *n* (**a**) *(enthusiasm)* excitation *f*, animation *f*, enthousiasme *m*; **in her excitement at the news she knocked over a vase** les nouvelles l'ont mise dans un tel état d'excitation *ou* d'enthousiasme qu'elle a renversé un vase; **her excitement at the news was obvious** elle était de toute évidence très excitée *ou* enthousiasmée par les nouvelles; **there was a look of excitement on the child's face** l'excitation *ou* l'enthousiasme se lisait sur le visage de l'enfant; **an atmosphere of intense excitement** une grande effervescence *ou* animation; **when the excitement had died down** quand l'agitation *ou* l'effervescence fut retombée

(**b**) *(agitation)* excitation *f*, agitation *f*; **the doctor advised her to avoid excitement** le médecin lui a déconseillé toute agitation *ou* toute surexcitation *ou* tout énervement; **the excitement of departure** l'émoi *m* du départ; **to cause great excitement** faire sensation; *Hum Ironic* **I don't think I could stand the excitement** je ne crois pas que je supporterais des sensations *ou* émotions aussi fortes; **the excitement would kill her** une telle émotion lui serait fatale; **I've had quite enough excitement for one day** j'ai eu assez de sensations fortes pour une seule journée

(**c**) *(sexual)* excitation *f*

(**d**) *(exciting events)* animation *f*; **there should be plenty of excitement in today's match** le match d'aujourd'hui devrait être très animé; **we don't get much excitement round here** il n'y a pas beaucoup d'animation par ici; **all the**

excitement seemed to have gone out of their marriage leur mariage semblait maintenant totalement dénué de passion; **he needs a bit of excitement in his life** il lui faudrait ajouter un peu de piquant à son existence; **what's all the excitement about?** mais que se passe-t-il?; **you shouldn't have had yesterday off, you missed all the excitement** c'est dommage que tu n'aies pas travaillé hier, il y a eu beaucoup d'animation *ou* c'était très animé; **I don't want to miss the excitement** je ne veux pas rater ça

exciter [ɪk'saɪtə(r)] *n Phys* excitatrice *f*

exciting [ɪk'saɪtɪŋ] *adj* (**a**) *(day, life, events, match, novel, film)* passionnant, palpitant; *(prospect)* palpitant; *(news)* sensationnel; **we've had an exciting time (of it) recently** ces derniers temps ont été mouvementés; **nothing exciting ever happens around here** il ne se passe jamais rien d'excitant *ou* de palpitant par ici; **it was exciting to think that we'd soon be in New York** c'était excitant de penser que nous serions bientôt à New York; **it was an exciting place to live** c'était passionnant de vivre là-bas

(**b**) *(sexually)* excitant

►► *Elec* ***exciting coil*** bobine *f* inductrice; *Elec* ***exciting current*** courant *m* d'excitation

excitingly [ɪk'saɪtɪŋlɪ] *adv* d'une manière sensationnelle; *(dress)* avec originalité; **excitingly different** d'une originalité enthousiasmante *ou* électrisante; **the most excitingly dangerous thing she had ever done** la chose la plus follement dangereuse qu'elle ait jamais faite; **the match finished as excitingly as it had started** le match s'est terminé de façon aussi palpitante qu'il avait commencé

excitor = **exciter**

excl. *(written abbr* **excluding***)* non compris; **excl. taxes** HT

exclaim [ɪk'skleɪm] **1** *vi* s'écrier, s'exclamer

2 *vt* **"but why?" he exclaimed** "mais pourquoi?" s'écria-t-il

exclamation [ˌekskləˈmeɪʃən] *n* exclamation *f*

►► *Br* ***exclamation mark,*** *Am* ***exclamation point*** point *m* d'exclamation

exclamatory [ek'sklæmətrɪ] *adj* exclamatif

exclave ['eksklerv] *n* enclave *f*

exclude [ɪk'skluːd] *vt* (**a**) *(bar)* exclure; **to exclude sb from sth** exclure qn de qch; **women were excluded from power** les femmes étaient exclues du pouvoir; **I felt that I was being excluded from the conversation** je sentais qu'on m'excluait de la conversation; **his disability excluded him from many leisure pursuits** son infirmité l'empêchait de pratiquer de nombreux loisirs

(**b**) *(not take into consideration)* exclure; **to exclude sb/sth from sth** exclure qn/qch de qch; **the figures exclude deaths from other causes** ces chiffres ne tiennent pas compte des morts provoquées par d'autres causes; **submarine-launched missiles were excluded from the arms talks** les missiles sous-marins n'entraient pas dans le cadre des négociations sur les armements

excluding [ɪk'skluːdɪŋ] *prep* à l'exclusion *ou* l'exception de, sauf, à part; **not excluding...** y compris...

exclusion [ɪk'skluːʒən] *n* (**a**) *(barring)* exclusion *f*; **the exclusion of sb from a society/conversation** l'exclusion de qn d'une société/conversation; **the exclusion of women from voting** le fait que les femmes n'aient pas le droit de vote

(**b**) *(omission)* exclusion *f*; **the exclusion of her name from the list** l'exclusion de son nom de la liste; **to the exclusion of everything** *or* **all else** à l'exclusion de toute autre chose

►► ***exclusion clause*** clause *f* d'exclusion; ***exclusion order*** ordre *m* d'exclusion; **to serve an exclusion order on sb** frapper qn d'un ordre d'exclusion; *Mil* ***exclusion zone*** zone *f* d'exclusion

exclusionist [ɪk'skluːʒənɪst] *Pol* **1** *adj (action, measure)* relevant d'une politique d'exclusion; *(person)* partisan d'une politique d'exclusion

2 *n* partisan(e) *m,f* d'une politique d'exclusion

exclusive [ɪk'skluːsɪv] **1** *adj* (**a**) *(select → restaurant, neighbourhood)* chic; *(→ club)* fermé; *(→ shop)* de luxe; *(→ school)* élitiste; **they live at a very exclusive address** ils vivent dans un quartier très chic

(**b**) *(deal, contract)* exclusif; **to have exclusive rights in a production** avoir l'exclusivité d'une production; **exclusive to** réservé (exclusivement) à; **an interview exclusive to this magazine** une interview exclusive accordée à notre magazine

(**c**) *(not including)* **exclusive of VAT** TVA non comprise; **exclusive of tax** hors taxe(s); **the rent is £200 a week exclusive** le loyer est de 200 livres par semaine sans les charges; **from 14 to 19 October, exclusive** du 14 au 19 octobre exclu; **all prices are exclusive of postage and packing** les prix indiqués ne tiennent pas compte des frais d'envoi et d'emballage

(**d**) *(incompatible)* exclusif; **the two propositions are/are not mutually exclusive** les deux propositions sont/ne sont pas incompatibles; **they are mutually exclusive** *(propositions)* l'une exclut l'autre, elles sont incompatibles

(**e**) *(sole)* unique; **their exclusive concern** leur seul souci; **the exclusive use of gold** l'emploi exclusif d'or

2 *n Press* exclusivité *f*; *(interview)* interview *f* exclusive; **a Tribune exclusive** une exclusivité de la Tribune

►► *Com* ***exclusive distribution*** distribution *f* exclusive; *Com* ***exclusive economic zone*** zone *f* économique exclusive; *Com* ***exclusive licence*** licence *f* exclusive

exclusively [ɪk'skluːsɪvlɪ] *adv (only)* exclusivement; **published exclusively in the Times** publié en exclusivité dans le Times

exclusiveness [ɪk'skluːsɪvnɪs], **exclusivity** [ˌeksklu:'sɪvətɪ] *n* (**a**) *(of restaurant, district)* caractère *m* huppé; *(of club, social circle)* caractère *m* fermé (**b**) *(of contract)* nature *f* exclusive

exclusivism [ɪk'skluːsɪvɪzəm] *n* exclusivisme *m*

exclusivist [ɪk'skluːsɪvɪst] *n* exclusiviste *mf*

exclusivity [ˌeksklu:'sɪvətɪ] *n* (**a**) *(of restaurant, district)* caractère *m* huppé; *(of club, social circle)* caractère *m* fermé (**b**) *(of contract)* exclusivité *f*

►► ***exclusivity agreement*** accord *m* d'exclusivité; ***exclusivity clause*** clause *f* d'exclusivité

excogitate [eks'kɒdʒɪteɪt] *vt Literary* (**a**) *(devise)* imaginer, combiner (**b**) *(think out)* considérer, approfondir

excommunicate *Rel* **1** *vt* [ˌekskə'mjuːnɪkeɪt] excommunier

2 *n* [ekskə'mjuːnɪkət] excommunié(e) *m,f*

3 *adj* [ekskə'mjuːnɪkət] excommunié

excommunication ['ekskəˌmjuːnɪ'keɪʃən] *n Rel* excommunication *f*

ex-con *n Fam* ancien(enne) taulard(e) *m,f*

excoriate [eks'kɔːrɪeɪt] *vt Formal* (**a**) *(strip skin from)* écorcher (**b**) *Fig (censure, reprimand)* condamner

excoriation [eksˌkɔːrɪ'eɪʃən] *n Formal* (**a**) *(of skin)* excoriation *f*, écorchure *f* (**b**) *Fig (censure, reprimand)* condamnation *f*

excrement ['ekskrɪmənt] *n (UNCOUNT) Formal* excréments *mpl*

excremental [ekskrɪ'mentəl] *adj Formal* excrémentiel

excrescence [ɪk'skresəns] *n Formal (growth)* excroissance *f*

excrescent [ɪk'skresənt] *adj Formal* (**a**) *(outward-growing)* qui forme une excroissance (**b**) *(superfluous)* superflu, redondant

excreta [ek'skriːtə] *npl Formal (faeces)* excréments *mpl*; *(waste matter)* excrétions *fpl*

excrete [ek'skriːt] *vt* excréter; *(of plant)* sécréter

excretion [ek'skriːʃən] *n* (**a**) *(action)* excrétion *f* (**b**) *(substance)* sécrétion *f*

excretory [ek'skriːtərɪ] *adj* excréteur

excruciate [ɪks'kruːʃɪeɪt] *vt Arch or Literary* mettre au supplice, torturer

excruciating [ɪk'skruːʃɪeɪtɪŋ] *adj* (**a**) *(pain, sight)* atroce, insoutenable; *(death)* atroce; *(noise)* infernal; **the pain was excruciating** la douleur était atroce (**b**) *Fam (extremely bad)* atroce, abominable; **it was excruciating** *(embarrassing)* c'était affreux; *(boring)* c'était atroce

excruciatingly [ɪk'skruːʃɪeɪtɪŋlɪ] *adv (painful)* atrocement, affreusement; *Fam* **it was excruciatingly funny/boring** c'était à mourir de rire/d'ennui

exculpate ['ekskʌlpeɪt] *vt Formal* disculper; **to exculpate sb from sth** disculper qn de qch

exculpation [ˌekskʌl'peɪʃən] *n Formal* disculpation *f*

exculpatory [eks'kʌlpətərɪ] *adj Formal* justificatif; qui disculpe

excursion [ɪk'skɜːʃən] *n* (**a**) *(organized trip)* excursion *f*; **to make** *or* **go on an excursion** faire une excursion (**b**) *(short local journey)* expédition *f*; **a shopping excursion** un tour dans les magasins (**c**) *(into a different field)* incursion *f*; **after a brief excursion into politics** après une brève incursion dans la politique

►► *Br Formerly Rail* ***excursion ticket*** billet *m* circulaire *(bénéficiant de tarifs réduits)*; ***excursion train*** train *m* spécial

excursionist [ɪk'skɜːʃənɪst] *n* excursionniste *mf*

excursive [ɪk'skɜːsɪv] *adj Formal (person)* qui a tendance à faire des digressions; *(style)* décousu

excusable [ɪk'skjuːzəbəl] *adj* excusable, pardonnable

excusably [ɪk'skjuːzəblɪ] *adv* **excusably, perhaps, she refused to speak to them** elle a refusé de leur parler, ce qui est peut-être excusable *ou* pardonnable

excuse 1 *n* [ɪk'skjuːs] (**a**) *(explanation, justification)* excuse *f*; **a feeble excuse** une mauvaise excuse; **her excuse for not coming** *(in the past)* son excuse pour n'être pas venue; *(in the future)* son excuse pour ne pas venir; **to give sth as one's excuse** donner qch comme excuse; **that's no excuse** ce n'est pas une excuse *ou* une raison; **that's no excuse for being rude** ce n'est pas une raison *ou* une excuse pour être grossier; **there's no excuse for that kind of behaviour** ce genre de comportement est sans excuse *ou* inexcusable; **there's no excuse for it** c'est sans excuse, c'est inexcusable; **he has no excuse for not finishing the job on time** il n'a pas d'excuse pour ne pas avoir terminé le travail à temps; **I don't want (to hear) any excuses!** je ne veux pas d'excuse!; **well, what's your excuse this time?** alors, quelle excuse as-tu trouvé cette fois?; **you'd better have a good excuse!** tu as intérêt à avoir une bonne excuse!; **excuses, excuses!** des excuses, toujours des excuses!; **he's always finding excuses for them/for their behaviour** il est tout le temps en train de leur trouver des excuses/d'excuser leur comportement; **stop making excuses for him** arrête de lui trouver des excuses; **I'm not making excuses for them** je ne les excuse pas; **to make one's excuses** s'excuser, présenter ses excuses; **make my excuses to them** présente-leur mes excuses; **ignorance of the law is no excuse** nul n'est censé ignorer la loi; **you've all been issued with a copy of the regulations, so from now on ignorance is no excuse** vous disposez tous d'un exemplaire du règlement, vous êtes donc censés le connaître à partir de maintenant; **by way of (an) excuse** en guise d'excuse

(**b**) *(example)* **a poor excuse for a father** un père lamentable; **this is a poor excuse for a bus service** ce service d'autobus est lamentable

(**c**) *(pretext)* excuse *f*, prétexte *m*; **an excuse to do** *or* **for doing sth** une excuse *ou* un prétexte pour faire qch; **it's only an excuse** ce n'est qu'un prétexte; **any excuse will do** n'importe quelle excuse *ou* n'importe quel prétexte fera l'affaire; **the government keeps finding excuses for not introducing reforms** le gouvernement n'arrête pas de trouver des excuses pour retarder l'introduction de réformes; **he's looking for an excuse not to go to the party** il cherche une excuse pour ne pas aller à la soirée; **to look for an excuse to celebrate** chercher un prétexte pour faire la fête; **any excuse for a drink!** toutes les excuses sont bonnes pour boire un verre!

2 *vt* [ɪk'skjuːz] (**a**) *(justify → bad behaviour)* excuser; **his youth excuses him** sa jeunesse l'excuse *ou* peut lui servir d'excuse; **he tried to excuse himself by saying that...** il a essayé de se justifier en disant que...

(**b**) *(forgive → bad behaviour, person)* excuser, pardonner; **you can excuse that in someone of his age** c'est pardonnable chez quelqu'un de son âge; **I'll excuse your lateness (just) this once** je te pardonne ton retard pour cette fois; **to excuse sb's absence** excuser l'absence de qn; **he is unable to attend the meeting and asks to be excused** il lui est impossible d'assister à la réunion et vous prie de bien vouloir l'en excuser; **now, if you will excuse me** maintenant, si vous voulez bien m'excuser; **one could be excused for thinking that he was much younger** on dirait *ou* croirait qu'il est beaucoup plus jeune; **excuse my interrupting, but...** excusez-moi *ou* pardon de vous interrompre, mais...; **excuse me** *(to get past)* pardon; *(as interruption, to attract someone's attention)* pardon, excusez-moi; *Am (as apology)* pardon, excusez-moi; **excuse me, (but) aren't you...?** excusez-moi, vous ne seriez pas...?; *Ironic* **excuse me for asking!** oh, ça va, je ne faisais que demander!, ce n'était qu'une question!; *Ironic* **well, excuse me for mentioning it!** oh, ça va, je n'en parlerai plus!; **to excuse oneself** s'excuser; **if you'll excuse the expression** si vous voulez me pardonner l'expression

(**c**) *(exempt)* dispenser; **to excuse sb from sth/doing sth** dispenser qn de qch/de faire qch; **he is excused gym** il est dispensé de gymnastique

(**d**) *(allow to go)* excuser; **please may I be excused?** *(to go to lavatory)* puis-je sortir, s'il vous plaît?; *(from table)* puis-je sortir de table, s'il vous plaît?

excuse-me [ɪk'skjuːz-] *n* = danse pendant laquelle on peut prendre le ou la partenaire de quelqu'un d'autre

ex-directory *Br* **1** *adj* sur la liste rouge; **an ex-directory number** un numéro ne figurant pas dans l'annuaire *ou* figurant sur la liste rouge

2 *adv* **to go ex-directory** se mettre sur la liste rouge

exeat ['eksɪæt] *n Br* (**a**) *Univ or Formal* permission *f* de sortie (**b**) *Rel* exeat *m*

exec [ɪg'zek] *n (abbr* **executive***)* cadre *m*

execrable ['eksɪkrəbəl] *adj Formal* exécrable

execrably ['eksɪkrəblɪ] *adv Formal* exécrablement

execrate ['eksɪkreɪt] *vt Formal* (**a**) *(loathe)* exécrer (**b**) *(denounce)* condamner, s'élever contre (**c**) *(curse)* maudire

execration [,eksɪ'kreɪʃən] *n Formal* (**a**) *(loathing)* exécration *f* (**b**) *(denunciation)* condamnation *f*, accusation *f*

executable file ['eksɪkjuːtəbəl-] *n Comput* fichier *m* exécutable

executant [ɪg'zekjʊtənt] *n* (**a**) *Formal (of an order)* exécutant(e) *m,f* (**b**) *Mus* exécutant(e) *m,f*

execute ['eksɪkjuːt] *vt* (**a**) *(put to death)* exécuter; **executed for murder/treason** exécuté pour meurtre/trahison (**b**) *Formal (carry out → task)* exécuter; *(→ plan)* metter à exécution; *Mus (→ piece)* exécuter; **a superbly executed carving** une sculpture superbement exécutée (**c**) *Law (will, sentence, law)* exécuter; *(deed)* signer, souscrire (**d**) *Comput* exécuter

►► *Comput* ***execute cycle*** cycle *m* d'exécution; *Comput* ***execute file*** fichier *m* exécutable

execution [,eksɪ'kjuːʃən] *n* (**a**) *(of person)* exécution *f* (**b**) *Formal (of task, plan)* exécution *f*; *Mus (of piece)* exécution *f*; *(by musician)* interprétation *f*; **in the execution of one's duty** dans l'exercice de ses fonctions; **to put sth into execution** mettre qch à exécution (**c**) *Law (of will, sentence, law)* exécution *f*; *(of deed)* signature *f*, souscription *f* (**d**) *Comput* exécution *f*

executioner [,eksɪ'kjuːʃənə(r)] *n* bourreau *m*

executive [ɪg'zekjʊtɪv] **1** *n* (**a**) *(person)* cadre *m*; **a business executive** un cadre commercial; **she looked the executive type** elle avait l'allure d'un cadre

(**b**) *(body)* corps *m* exécutif; *Pol (branch of government)* exécutif *m*; *Am Pol* **the executive** l'exécutif *m*, le pouvoir exécutif

(**c**) *(of political party, union)* bureau *m*, comité *m* central; **the union's national executive** le bureau national du syndicat

2 *adj* (**a**) *(dining room, washroom etc)* des cadres, de la direction; *(desk, chair)* de luxe; **executive model** *or* **version** *(of car)* modèle *m* grand luxe

(**b**) *(function, role)* exécutif; **an executive officer in the civil service** un cadre de l'administration; **he's not good at making executive decisions** il n'est pas doué pour prendre des décisions importantes; **we need an executive decision** il faut trancher; *Hum* **you'll have to make an executive decision** il va falloir que tu prennes une décision capitale *ou* déterminante

►► *Com* ***executive board*** directoire *m*; ***executive briefcase*** attaché-case *m*; *Aviat* ***executive class*** classe *f* affaires; *Com* ***executive director*** cadre *m* supérieur; ***executive jet*** jet *m* privé; ***executive lounge*** salon *m* classe affaires; *Com* ***executive officer*** cadre *m* supérieur; *Am Pol* ***executive privilege*** privilège *m* de l'exécutif *(droit dont bénéficie l'exécutif de limiter l'accès du Congrès, des tribunaux et du public à l'information, pour des raisons d'intérêt national)*; *Cin* ***executive producer*** producteur *m* délégué; *Comput* ***executive program*** programme *m* d'exécution; *Com* ***executive secretary*** secrétaire *mf* de direction; *Am* ***executive session*** *(of Senate)* séance *f* à huis clos; ***executive suite*** *(in hotel)* suite *f* de luxe; *(in company)* bureaux *mpl* de la direction; ***executive toy*** gadget *m* pour cadres

executor [ɪg'zekjʊtə(r)] *n Law (of will)* exécuteur(trice) *m,f* testamentaire; **to make sb one's executor** désigner qn comme son exécuteur testamentaire

executory [ɪg'zekjʊtərɪ] *adj Law* (**a**) *(ruling, sentence)* exécutoire; *(law)* en vigueur (**b**) *(function, role)* exécutif

►► ***executory formula*** formule *f* exécutoire

executrix [ɪg'zekjʊtrɪks] *n Law (of will)* exécutrice *f* testamentaire

exegesis [,eksɪ'dʒiːsɪs] *n* exégèse *f*

exegete ['eksɪdʒiːt] *n* exégète *mf*

exegetic [,eksɪ'dʒetɪk], **exegetical** [,eksɪ'dʒetɪkəl] *adj* exégétique

exegetics [,eksɪ'dʒetɪk] *n (UNCOUNT)* théologie *f* exégétique

exemplar [ɪg'zemplɑː(r)] *n Formal* (**a**) *(model)* modèle *m* (**b**) *(typical example)* exemple *m* typique

exemplariness [ɪg'zemplərɪnɪs], **exemplarity** [,ɪgzem'plærɪtɪ] *n Formal* qualité *f* exemplaire

exemplary [ɪg'zemplərɪ] *adj* (**a**) *(very good → behaviour, pupil)* exemplaire; **he's an exemplary student/husband** c'est un étudiant/mari modèle (**b**) *(serving as a warning)* exemplaire; **exemplary punishment** châtiment *m* exemplaire

►► *Law* ***exemplary damages*** dommages-intérêts *mpl* exemplaires *ou* à titre exemplaire

exemplification [ɪg,zemplɪfɪ'keɪʃən] *n* illustration *f*, illustrations *fpl*, exemplification *f*; **this chapter could do with more exemplification** ce chapitre aurait besoin d'un peu plus d'illustrations *ou* d'une illustration plus riche; **in exemplification of his remarks** pour exemplifier ses remarques

exemplify [ɪg'zemplɪfaɪ] *vt* (**a**) *(give example of)* illustrer, exemplifier (**b**) *(be example of)* illustrer

exempt [ɪg'zempt] **1** *adj* exempt, exempté, dispensé (**from** de); **to be exempt from sth** être exempt de qch; **he was declared exempt from any blame** il a été établi qu'il n'était en aucun responsable de ce qui s'était passé; **exempt from taxes** exonéré d'impôt, exempt d'impôt

2 *vt (gen)* exempter, dispenser (**from** de); *(from tax)* exonérer, exempter (**from** de); *(from military service)* exempter; **to exempt sb/sth from sth** exempter qn/qch de qch; **to exempt sb from blame** n'avoir rien à reprocher à qn

exemption [ɪg'zempʃən] *n (action, state)* exemption *f*, dispense *f*; *(from tax)* exonération *f*, exemption *f*; **tax exemption** exonération *f* fiscale

►► *Law* ***exemption clause*** clause *f* de non-responsabilité

exequies ['eksɪkwɪz] *npl Literary* obsèques *fpl*

exercisable ['eksə,saɪzəbəl] *adj* (**a**) *(right, authority, power)* que l'on peut exercer (**b**) *St Exch (option)* exerçable

exercise ['eksəsaɪz] **1** *n* (**a**) *(physical)* exercice *m*; **to take exercise** prendre de l'exercice; **the doctor has told him to take more exercise** le docteur lui a dit de faire plus d'exercice; **it's good exercise** c'est un bon exercice; **I don't get much exercise** je ne fais pas beaucoup d'exercice; **I'll walk, I need the exercise** j'y vais à pied, j'ai besoin d'exercice; **this is a good exercise for the calf muscles** c'est un bon exercice pour les muscles des mollets; **physical exercises** exercices *mpl* physiques; **he does (physical) exercises every morning** il fait de la gymnastique tous les matins; **breathing exercises** gymnastique *f* respiratoire, exercices *mpl* respiratoires

(**b**) *(mental, in education)* exercice *m*; **grammar exercises** exercices *mpl* de grammaire; **piano exercises** exercices *mpl* de piano

(**c**) *(use)* exercice *m*; **in the exercise of one's duties** dans l'exercice de ses fonctions; **by the exercise of a little imagination** en usant d'un peu d'imagination, avec un peu d'imagination

(**d**) *Mil* exercice *m*; **they're on exercises** ils sont à l'exercice

(**e**) *(activity, operation)* **a fact-finding exercise** une mission d'enquête; **it was an interesting exercise** cela a été une expérience intéressante; **this is more than just a PR exercise** ce n'est pas seulement de la poudre aux yeux; **it was a pointless exercise** cela n'a servi absolument à rien

(**f**) *St Exch (of option)* levée *f*

(**g**) *Am (ceremony)* cérémonie *f*; **graduation exercises** cérémonie *f* de remise des diplômes

2 *vt* (**a**) *(body, muscle)* exercer, faire travailler; *(horse)* faire faire de l'exercice à; **to exercise a dog** *(take for a walk)* promener un chien; **if you were to exercise your brain on the problem** si tu faisais travailler tes méninges pour régler ce problème

(**b**) *(troops)* entraîner

(**c**) *(use, put into practice → right, authority, power)* exercer; **we must exercise caution/restraint** nous devons user de prudence/de retenue

(**d**) *St Exch (option)* lever

(**e**) *Formal (preoccupy)* préoccuper

3 *vi* (**a**) *(take exercise)* faire de l'exercice

(**b**) *(train → in gymnasium etc)* s'exercer, s'entraîner; **he was exercising on the rings** il s'exerçait *ou* s'entraînait aux anneaux

►► ***exercise bike*** vélo *m* d'appartement; ***exercise book*** *(for writing in)* cahier *m* d'exercices; *(containing exercises)* livre *m* d'exercices; ***exercise class*** cours *m* de gymnastique; *St Exch* ***exercise date*** date *f* d'échéance; *St Exch* ***exercise notion*** assignation *f*; *St Exch* ***exercise price*** *(of share)* prix *m* d'exercice, cours *m* de base; ***exercise yard*** *(in prison)* cour *f*, préau *m*

exerciser ['eksə,saɪzə(r)] *n* (**a**) *(piece of equipment)* appareil *m* de gymnastique; *(bike)* vélo *m* d'appartement (**b**) *(person)* personne *f* qui fait de l'exercice

exercitation [ɪg,zɜːsɪ'teɪʃən] *n Arch or Literary (use, putting into practice)* exercice *m*

exert [ɪg'zɜːt] *vt* (**a**) *(pressure, force)* exercer; **they were willing to exert their influence on behalf of our campaign** ils étaient d'accord pour mettre leur influence au service de notre campagne (**b**) **to exert oneself** *(make effort)* se donner de la peine *ou* du mal; *Ironic* **don't exert yourself!** ne te donne pas trop de mal, surtout!

exertion [ɪg'zɜːʃən] *n* (**a**) *(of force)* exercice *m*; **the exertion of pressure on sb/sth** la pression exercée sur qn/qch; **the exertion of influence on political figures by powerful industrialists** la manière dont certains puissants industriels utilisent leur influence sur les personnalités politiques (**b**) *(effort)* effort *m*; **after the day's exertions** après les efforts de la journée; **by one's own exertions** par ses propres moyens

exes ['eksɪz] *npl Fam (expenses)* **to put sth on exes** faire passer qch en note de frais ☐

exeunt ['eksɪʌnt] *vi Theat (in stage directions)* **exeunt the Queen and her attendants** la reine et sa suite sortent

exfoliant [eks'fəʊlɪənt] *n* exfoliant *m*

exfoliate [eks'fəʊlɪeɪt] **1** *vi* s'exfolier

2 *vt* exfolier

exfoliating [eks'fəʊlɪeɪtɪŋ] *adj Biol & Geol* exfoliant

►► ***exfoliating cream*** crème *f* exfoliante; ***exfoliating scrub*** crème *f* exfoliante, gommage *m* exfoliant

exfoliation [eks,fəʊlɪ'eɪʃən] *n Biol & Geol* exfoliation *f*

ex gratia [eks'greɪʃə] *adj Com (payment)* à titre gracieux, à titre de faveur

ex-growth *n Com (decline)* baisse *f*; **to go ex-growth** être en déclin

exhalation [,eksə'leɪʃən] *n* (**a**) *(breathing out → of air)* expiration *f*; *(→ of smoke, fumes)* exhalation *f* (**b**) *(air breathed out)* exhalaison *f*

exhale [eks'heɪl] **1** *vt (air)* expirer; *(gas, fumes)* exhaler

2 *vi (breathe out)* expirer

exhaust [ɪg'zɔːst] **1** *n* (**a**) *Aut (on vehicle → system)* échappement *m*; *(→ pipe)* pot *m ou* tuyau *m* d'échappement

(**b**) *(UNCOUNT) (fumes)* gaz *mpl* d'échappement

2 *vt* (**a**) *(use up → supplies, possibilities)* épuiser; **you're exhausting my patience** tu mets ma patience à bout

(**b**) *(tire out)* épuiser, exténuer; **to exhaust oneself (doing sth)** s'épuiser (en faisant qch)

▸▸ ***exhaust fumes*** gaz *mpl* d'échappement; *Aut* ***exhaust manifold*** collecteur *m* d'échappement; *Br Aut* ***exhaust pipe*** pot *m ou* tuyau *m* d'échappement; *Aut* ***exhaust stroke*** *(in internal combustion engine)* temps *m* d'échappement; *Aut* ***exhaust system*** échappement *m*; *Aut* ***exhaust valve*** soupape *f* d'échappement

exhausted [ɪg'zɔːstɪd] *adj* (**a**) *(person, smile)* épuisé, exténué; **I'm exhausted** je n'en peux plus, je suis épuisé *ou* exténué (**b**) *(used up → mine, land)* épuisé; **my patience is exhausted** je suis à bout de patience

exhaustedly [ɪg'zɔːstɪdlɪ] *adv (move, smile, sigh)* d'un air épuisé *ou* exténué

exhaustible [ɪg'zɔːstɪbəl] *adj* limité; **her patience is easily exhaustible** elle est vite à bout de patience

exhausting [ɪg'zɔːstɪŋ] *adj (job, climb, climate)* épuisant, exténuant, éreintant; *(person)* fatigant, excédant

exhaustion [ɪg'zɔːstʃən] *n* (**a**) *(tiredness)* épuisement *m*, éreintement *m*, grande fatigue *f*; **to be suffering from exhaustion** être dans un état d'épuisement; **to be in a state of total exhaustion** être dans un état d'épuisement total *ou* complet; **they worked to the point of exhaustion** ils ont travaillé jusqu'à épuisement (**b**) *(of supplies, resources, topic)* épuisement *m*

exhaustive [ɪg'zɔːstɪv] *adj (analysis, treatment)* exhaustif; *(investigation, enquiry)* approfondi, poussé; **the list is not exhaustive** cette liste n'est pas exhaustive; **to make an exhaustive study of a subject** traiter un sujet à fond

exhaustively [ɪg'zɔːstɪvlɪ] *adv* exhaustivement

exhaustiveness [ɪg'zɔːstɪvnɪs] *n (of analysis, treatment)* caractère *m* exhaustif, exhaustivité *f*; *(of investigation, enquiry)* caractère *m* approfondi *ou* poussé

exhibit [ɪg'zɪbɪt] **1** *vt* (**a**) *(of artist)* exposer

(**b**) *(show, display → identity card, passport)* montrer; *(→ in shop window)* exposer; *Law (→ items of supporting evidence)* exhiber, produire

(**c**) *(manifest → courage, self-control)* montrer, faire preuve de

2 *vi (artist)* exposer; **he has exhibited all over Europe** il a exposé dans toute l'Europe

3 *n* (**a**) *(in an exhibition)* objet *m* (exposé); **one of the most interesting exhibits at the fair** l'une des pièces les plus intéressantes en exposition à la foire

(**b**) *Law (in criminal proceedings)* pièce *f* à conviction; **exhibit A** première pièce *f* à conviction

(**c**) *Am (exhibition)* exposition *f*

exhibition [,eksɪ'bɪʃən] *n* (**a**) *(of paintings, products)* exposition *f*; *(of film)* présentation *f*; **he's having an exhibition at the new gallery** il expose à la nouvelle galerie; **the Klee exhibition** l'exposition *f* Klee; **trade exhibition** exposition *f* commerciale

(**b**) *(of bad manners, ingenuity)* démonstration *f*; **to give sb an exhibition of sth** faire une démonstration de qch à qn; **to make an exhibition of oneself** se donner en spectacle

(**c**) *Br Univ (award)* bourse *f* d'études

▸▸ ***exhibition centre*** centre *m* d'expositions; ***exhibition hall*** salle *f ou* hall *m* d'exposition; *Sport* ***exhibition match*** match-exhibition *m*; ***exhibition stand*** stand *m* (d'exposition)

exhibitioner [,eksɪ'bɪʃənə(r)] *n Br Univ* boursier(ère) *m,f*

exhibitionism [,eksɪ'bɪʃənɪzəm] *n* (**a**) *(gen)* besoin *m ou* volonté *f* de se faire remarquer (**b**) *Psy* exhibitionnisme *m*

exhibitionist [,eksɪ'bɪʃənɪst] *n* (**a**) *(gen)* = personne qui cherche toujours à se faire remarquer; **he's a terrible exhibitionist** il faut toujours qu'il cherche à se faire remarquer (**b**) *Psy* exhibitionniste *mf*

exhibitionistic [,eksɪ,bɪʃə'nɪstɪk] *adj* (**a**) *(gen → behaviour, person)* démonstratif, exubérant (**b**) *Psy* exhibitionniste

exhibitor [ɪg'zɪbɪtə(r)] *n* (**a**) *(at gallery, trade fair)* exposant(e) *m,f* (**b**) *Am (cinema owner)* exploitant(e) *m,f*

exhilarant [ɪg'zɪlərənt] **1** *n Arch Pharm* exhilarant *m*

2 *adj* exaltant, grisant

exhilarate [ɪg'zɪləreɪt] *vt (experience)* griser, exalter; *(mountain air)* vivifier

exhilarated [ɪg'zɪləreɪtɪd] *adj (mood, laugh)* exalté; **to feel exhilarated** se sentir exalté; **to be exhilarated at the idea of doing sth** être exalté à l'idée de faire qch

exhilarating [ɪg'zɪləreɪtɪŋ] *adj (experience)* exaltant, grisant; *(mountain air)* vivifiant

exhilaration [ɪg,zɪlə'reɪʃən] *n* exaltation *f*, griserie *f*

exhort [ɪg'zɔːt] *vt Formal* exhorter; **to exhort sb to do sth** exhorter qn à faire qch

exhortation [,egzɔː'teɪʃən] *n Formal (act, words)* exhortation *f*

exhumation [,ekshjuː'meɪʃən] *n Formal* exhumation *f*

▸▸ ***exhumation order*** permis *m* d'exhumer

exhume [eks'hjuːm] *vt Formal* exhumer

ex-husband *n* ex-mari *m*

exigency ['eksɪdʒənsɪ] (*pl* **exigencies**), **exigence** ['eksɪdʒəns] *n Formal* (**a**) *(usu pl) (demand)* exigence *f*; **the exigencies of the situation** les exigences *fpl* de la situation (**b**) *(urgent situation)* situation *f* urgente (**c**) *(urgency)* urgence *f*; **a matter of some exigency** une affaire assez urgente *ou* pressante

exigent ['eksɪdʒənt] *adj Formal* (**a**) *(urgent)* urgent, pressant (**b**) *(demanding, exacting)* exigeant

exigible ['eksɪdʒəbəl] *adj* exigible (**from** de)

exiguity [eksɪ'gjuːətɪ] (*pl* **exiguities**) *n Formal* exiguïté *f*

exiguous [eg'zɪgjʊəs] *adj Formal (means, income, quarters)* exigu(uë)

exile ['eksaɪl] **1** *n* (**a**) *(banishment)* exil *m*; **his self-imposed exile** son exil volontaire; **to live in exile** vivre en exil; **to send sb into exile** envoyer qn en exil; **to go into exile** partir en exil; **government in exile** gouvernement en exil; **to return from exile** rentrer d'exil (**b**) *(person)* exilé(e) *m,f*

2 *vt* exiler, expatrier; **he was exiled from his native Poland** il a été exilé *ou* expatrié de sa Pologne natale

exiled ['eksaɪld] *adj* exilé; **the exiled government** le gouvernement en exil

exist [ɪg'zɪst] *vi* exister; **do ghosts exist?** les fantômes existent-ils?; **the half litre pack doesn't exist any more** le carton d'un demi-litre n'existe *ou* ne se fait plus; **they exist in three sizes** elles existent en trois tailles; **the species now only exists in zoos** cette espèce n'existe que dans les zoos; **there exists an ancient tradition which...** il existe une tradition ancienne qui...; **she treats me as if I don't exist** elle fait comme si je n'existais pas; **that's not living, that's just existing!** je n'appelle pas ça vivre, j'appelle ça subsister *ou* survivre; **can life exist under these conditions?** la vie est-elle possible dans ces conditions?; **he earns enough to exist on** il gagne suffisamment pour vivre; **the conditions that are necessary for life to exist** les conditions qui sont nécessaires à la vie; **we can't exist without oxygen** nous ne pouvons pas vivre sans oxygène

existence [ɪg'zɪstəns] *n* (**a**) *(being)* existence *f*; **ever since the existence of man** depuis que l'homme existe; **the continued existence of life on this planet/of these old-fashioned procedures** la survivance de la vie sur la planète/de ces procédures arriérées; **to come into existence** *(species)* apparaître; *(the earth)* se former; *(law, institution)* naître, être créé; **it didn't come into existence until quite recently** cela n'existait pas il y a encore peu de temps; **to be in existence** exister; **the oldest manuscript in existence** le plus ancien manuscrit existant; **it's the only one still in existence** c'est le seul qui existe encore; **the only whale left in existence** la dernière baleine encore en vie; **to go out of existence** cesser d'exister

(**b**) *(life)* existence *f*; **to lead a pleasant/wretched existence** mener une existence agréable/misérable

existent [ɪg'zɪstənt] *adj Formal* existant

existential [,egzɪ'stenʃəl] *adj Phil* existentiel

existentialism [,egzɪ'stenʃəlɪzəm] *n Phil* existentialisme *m*

existentialist [,egzɪ'stenʃəlɪst] *Phil* **1** *n* existentialiste *mf*

2 *adj* existentialiste

existing [ɪg'zɪstɪŋ] *adj (gen)* actuel; *(law, legislation)* en vigueur; **most of the existing building dates from the 18th century** la plus grande partie du bâtiment date du XVIIIème siècle; **under the existing circumstances** dans les circonstances actuelles *ou* présentes

exit ['eksɪt] **1** *n* (**a**) *(way out → from room, building, motorway)* sortie *f*; **let's turn off at the next exit** prenons la prochaine sortie; **exit ramp** bretelle *f* de sortie; **exit only** *(sign)* réservé à la sortie

(**b**) *(act of going out → from a room)* sortie *f*; *Theat* sortie *f*, exit *m inv*; **to make a hurried exit** sortir en vitesse; *Theat or Fig* **to make one's exit** faire sa sortie; **the bullet made its exit through the shoulder** la balle est ressortie par l'épaule

(**c**) *Comput* sortie *f*

2 *vi* (**a**) *Theat* sortir; **he then exits stage left** puis il sort côté jardin; **exit Ophelia** *(as stage direction)* exit Ophélie, Ophélie sort

(**b**) *(go out, leave)* sortir; *(bullet)* ressortir; **he exited through the rear door** il est sorti *ou* parti par la porte de derrière

(**c**) *Comput* sortir

3 *vt Comput* sortir de; *(leave)* quitter, sortir de

▸▸ *Fin* ***exit charges*** frais *mpl* de sortie; *Com* ***exit interview*** = entretien entre un employeur et son employé lors du départ de ce dernier; *Br* ***exit permit*** permis *m* de sortie; *Pol* ***exit poll,*** *Am* ***exit survey*** = sondage réalisé auprès des votants à la sortie du bureau de vote; ***exit visa*** visa *m* de sortie; ***exit wound*** point *m* de sortie d'une balle

ex libris [eks'liːbrɪs] *n (bookplate)* ex-libris *m inv*

Exmoor ['eksmʊə(r)] *n* Exmoor

▸▸ ***Exmoor pony*** exmoor *m*, poney *m* exmoor

exobiologist [eksəʊbaɪ'ɒlədʒɪst] *n Astron & Biol* exobiologiste *m,f*

exobiology [eksəʊbaɪ'ɒlədʒɪ] *n Astron & Biol* exobiologie *f*

Exocet® ['eksəʊset] *n* **Exocet**® **(missile)** (missile *m*) Exocet® *m*

exocrine ['eksəʊkraɪn] *adj Physiol* exocrine

exoderm ['eksəʊdɜːm] *n Biol & Bot* exoderme *m*

exodus ['eksədəs] **1** *n* exode *m*; **the exodus of capital** la fuite des capitaux; **there was a general exodus to the bar** il y a eu un mouvement de masse en direction du bar; **a mass exodus towards the beaches** un exode en direction des plages

2 Exodus *n* (**a**) *Bible* **(the Book of) Exodus** l'Exode (**b**) *(journey)* exode *m*

ex officio [eksə'fɪʃɪəʊ] **1** *adj (member)* de droit

2 *adv (act, decide etc)* de droit

exogamic [,eksəʊ'gæmɪk], **exogamous** [ek'sɒgəməs] *adj* exogame

exogamy [ek'sɒgəmɪ] *n* exogamie *f*

exogenous [ek'sɒdʒənəs] *adj (gen) & Biol & Geol* exogène

exon ['eksɒn] *n Biol* exon *m*

exonerate [ɪg'zɒnəreɪt] *vt* (**a**) *(absolve)* disculper, innocenter; **to exonerate oneself** se disculper (**b**) *(exempt)* exonérer, décharger (**from** de)

exoneration [ɪg,zɒnə'reɪʃən] *n* (**a**) disculpation *f* (**b**) *(exemption)* exonération *f*, décharge *f* (**from** de)

exonuclease [,eksəʊ'njuːklɪeɪz] *n Biol & Chem* exonucléase *m*

exophthalmic [ˌeksɒf'θælmɪk] *adj Med* exophtalmique

exophthalmos, exophthalmus [ˌeksɒf'θælməs] *n Med* exophtalmie *f*

exopodite [ek'sɒpədaɪt] *n Zool* exopodite *m*

exorbitance [ɪg'zɔːbɪtəns] *n (of price, demands, claims)* énormité *f*, démesure *f*

exorbitant [ɪg'zɔːbɪtənt] *adj (price, demands, claims)* exorbitant, démesuré, excessif; **£85 for that? that's exorbitant!** 85 livres pour ça? c'est exorbitant!

exorbitantly [ɪg'zɔːbɪtəntlɪ] *adv (priced)* excessivement, démesurément; **it's so exorbitantly expensive** c'est excessivement *ou* démesurément cher

exorcism ['eksɔːsɪzəm] *n* exorcisme *m*; **to carry out** *or* **to perform an exorcism** pratiquer un exorcisme

exorcist ['eksɔːsɪst] *n* exorciste *m*

exorcize, -ise ['eksɔːsaɪz] *vt (evil spirits, place, fears)* exorciser

exoskeleton ['eksəʊˌskelɪtən] *n Zool* exosquelette *m*, cuticule *f*

exosphere ['eksəʊˌsfɪə(r)] *n Astron* exosphère *f*

exospore ['eksəʊspɔː(r)] *n Bot* exospore *m*

exostosis [ˌeksɒ'stəʊsɪs] *n Med* exostose *f*

exoteric [ˌeksəʊ'terɪk] *adj Formal* exotérique

exothermia [ˌeksəʊ'θɜːmɪə] *n Chem* exothermie *f*

exothermic [ˌeksəʊ'θɜːmɪk] *adj Chem* exothermique

exotic [ɪg'zɒtɪk] **1** *adj* exotique; **an exotic-sounding name** un nom à consonance exotique; **exotic-looking** exotique

2 *n Bot* plante *f* exotique

exotica [ɪg'zɒtɪkə] *npl* objets *mpl* exotiques; **a collection of literary exotica** une collection de pièces littéraires rares

exotically [ɪg'zɒtɪkəlɪ] *adv (dressed, decorated)* avec exotisme; **exotically perfumed** *(flower)* aux senteurs exotiques; *(person)* au parfum exotique

exoticism [ɪg'zɒtɪsɪzəm] *n* exotisme *m*

exotoxin ['eksəʊˌtɒksɪn] *n Biol* exotoxine *f*

expand [ɪk'spænd] **1** *vt* (**a**) *(empire, army, staff)* agrandir; *(company, business)* agrandir, développer; *(chest, muscles, ideas)* développer; *(knowledge, influence)* élargir, étendre; *Phys & Constr* dilater; **it's an idea that could easily be expanded into a novel** c'est une idée qu'on pourrait facilement développer pour en faire un roman; **the police force is to be expanded** les effectifs de la police doivent être augmentés; **to expand a company into a multinational** agrandir une société pour en faire une multinationale

(**b**) *Math (equation)* développer

(**c**) *Comput (memory)* étendre

2 *vi* (**a**) *(empire, army, staff)* s'agrandir; *(company, business)* s'agrandir, se développer; *(chest, muscles, market)* se développer; *(knowledge, influence)* s'étendre, s'élargir; *(gas, metal)* se dilater; *(volume of traffic)* augmenter; *(in business)* se développer, s'agrandir; **we are looking to expand into the cosmetics industry** nous envisageons de nous diversifier en nous lançant dans l'industrie des cosmétiques

(**b**) *(talk, write at greater length)* préciser sa pensée; **could you expand?** est-ce que vous pourriez préciser ce que vous voulez dire par là?

▸**expand on** *vt insep (talk, write at greater length about)* développer; **in the next chapter I shall expand further on these ideas** je développerai ces idées *ou* je m'étendrai davantage sur ces idées au chapitre suivant

expandable [ɪk'spændɪbəl] *adj* (**a**) *(gas, material)* expansible; *(idea, theory)* qui peut être développé; *(basic set)* qui peut être complété (**b**) *Comput (memory)* extensible; **4MB expandable to 64MB** 4 Mo extensible à 64 Mo

expanded [ɪk'spændɪd] *adj Phys & Constr* expansé

▸▸ *Comput* ***expanded keyboard*** clavier *m* étendu; ***expanded memory*** mémoire *f* paginée *ou* expansée; ***expanded polystyrene*** polystyrène *m* expansé

expander [ɪk'spændə(r)] *n* (**a**) *Gym* **(chest) expander** extenseur *m* (**b**) *Aut (in brake drum)* came *f* de frein

expanding [ɪk'spændɪŋ] *adj* (**a**) *(company, empire, gas, metal)* en expansion; *(influence)* grandissant; *(industry, market)* en expansion, qui se développe; *(interests, circle of friends)* qui s'élargit; **the expanding universe** l'univers *m* en expansion; **the expanding universe theory** la théorie de l'expansion de l'univers (**b**) *(extendable → watchstrap, briefcase, suitcase)* extensible

▸▸ *Aut* ***expanding brake*** frein *m* à extension

expanse [ɪk'spæns] *n* étendue *f*; **a vast expanse** *(of water, snow etc)* une vaste étendue; **the vast expanse of the plain** l'immensité *f* de la plaine; **she was showing a large expanse of thigh** on lui voyait une bonne partie des cuisses

expansible [ɪk'spænsɪbəl] *adj* expansible

expansion [ɪk'spænʃən] *n (of empire)* expansion *f*, élargissement *m*; *(of army, staff)* augmentation *f*, accroissement *m*; *(of chest, muscles, ideas)* développement *m*; *(of knowledge, influence)* élargissement *m*; *(of gas, metal)* expansion *f*, dilatation *f*; *Comput (of memory)* extension *f*; *(of business)* développement *m*, agrandissement *m*, extension *f*; **colonial/territorial expansion** expansion *f* coloniale/territoriale

▸▸ *Comput* ***expansion board*** carte *f* d'extension; ***expansion bolt*** *Constr* boulon *m* de scellement *ou* d'expansion; *(in mountaineering)* cheville *f ou* piton *m* d'expansion; *Comput* ***expansion card*** carte *f* d'extension; *Tech* ***expansion curve*** courbe *f* de détente; *Tech* ***expansion joint*** joint *m* de dilatation; *Comput* ***expansion slot*** emplacement *m ou* logement *m* pour carte d'extension; *Aut* ***expansion stroke*** course *f* de détente; *Constr* ***expansion tank*** réservoir *m* d'expansion; *Am Sport* ***expansion team*** nouvelle équipe *f*

expansionary [ɪk'spænʃənərɪ] *adj* qui tend vers *ou* vise à l'expansion

expansionism [ɪk'spænʃəˌnɪzəm] *n* expansionnisme *m*

expansionist [ɪk'spænʃənɪst] **1** *adj* expansionniste

2 *n* expansionniste *mf*

expansive [ɪk'spænsɪv] *adj (person, mood, gesture)* expansif; **in an expansive mood** d'humeur loquace

expansively [ɪk'spænsɪvlɪ] *adv (talk)* de manière expansive; **she gestured expansively towards the skyline/paintings** elle a désigné l'horizon/les tableaux d'un grand geste

expansiveness [ɪk'spænsɪvnɪs] *n (of person)* expansivité *f*

ex parte [eks'pɑːtɪ] *adj Law (injunction, testimony)* émanant d'une seule partie, unilatéral

expat [ˌeks'pæt] *Fam (abbr* **expatriate***)* **1** *n* expatrié(e)[□] *m,f*

2 *adj (Briton, American etc)* expatrié[□]; *(bar, community)* d'expatriés[□]

expatiate [eks'peɪʃɪeɪt] *vi Formal* s'étendre, discourir (longuement); **to expatiate on sth** s'étendre *ou* discourir (longuement) sur qch

expatriate 1 *n* [eks'pætrɪət] expatrié(e) *m,f*

2 *adj* [eks'pætrɪət] *(Briton, American etc)* expatrié; *(bar, community)* d'expatriés

3 *vt* [eks'pætrɪeɪt] expatrier, exiler

expatriation [eksˌpætrɪ'eɪʃən] *n* expatriation *f*

expect [ɪk'spekt] **1** *vt* (**a**) *(anticipate)* s'attendre à; **they are expecting an increase in prices** ils s'attendent à une hausse des prix; **we expect rain/bad weather** nous nous attendons à de la pluie/du mauvais temps; **we expected that it would be much bigger** nous nous attendions à ce qu'il soit beaucoup plus gros, nous pensions qu'il allait être beaucoup plus gros; **we expected you to bring your own** nous pensions que vous alliez apporter le vôtre; **to expect sb to do sth** s'attendre à ce que qn fasse qch; **she knew more Russian than I expected her to** elle était meilleure en russe que je ne m'y attendais; **I hadn't expected them to be French** je ne m'attendais pas à ce qu'ils soient français; **to expect the worst** s'attendre au pire; **I expected as much!** je m'en doutais!, c'est bien ce que je pensais!; **some slight initial difficulty is to be expected** il faut s'attendre à rencontrer quelques légères difficultés initiales; **that's only to be expected** ce n'est pas du tout surprenant; **it was better/worse than I expected** c'était mieux/pire que je ne m'y attendais; **she is as well as can be expected** elle va aussi bien que sa condition le permet; **I had expected better of** *or* **from you** je n'aurais pas cru ça de vous; **she played with the brilliance (which) we have come to expect (from her)** elle a joué avec le brio auquel elle nous a maintenant habitués; **what can you expect?** que voulez-vous?; **what can you expect from a government like that?** que voulez-vous, avec un gouvernement pareil!; **she was angry – well, what did you expect?** elle était en colère – et alors, ça t'étonne?; **as might have been expected, as was to be expected** comme on pouvait s'y attendre; **I knew what to expect** je savais à quoi m'attendre; **I never know what to expect with you** je ne sais jamais à quoi m'attendre *ou* m'en tenir avec vous

(**b**) *(count on)* **we're expecting you to help us** nous comptons sur votre aide; **don't expect me to be there!** ne t'attends pas à ce que j'y sois!

(**c**) *(demand)* **to expect sb to do sth** demander à qn de faire qch; **I expect you to be punctual** je vous demande d'arriver à l'heure; **I expect complete obedience** je demande une obéissance totale; **I expect something to be done** j'exige qu'on fasse quelque chose à ce sujet; **you expect too much of him** tu lui en demandes trop; **it's too much to expect of a child** c'est trop attendre d'un enfant, c'est trop demander à un enfant; **it's no less than I would have expected from my own family** je ne me serais pas attendu à moins de la part de ma propre famille; **it is expected that the candidate will be willing to undertake some travel** on attend du candidat qu'il soit disposé à voyager; **I'm expected to write all his speeches** je suis censé *ou* supposé rédiger tous ses discours

(**d**) *(suppose, imagine)* imaginer, penser, supposer; **I expect so** je pense, j'imagine; **I don't expect so** je ne pense pas, j'imagine que non; **I expect you're right** tu dois avoir raison; **I expect it's where you left it** il doit être là où tu l'as laissé; **I expect you'll be wanting something to drink** vous boirez bien quelque chose; *(grudgingly)* j'imagine que vous voulez quelque chose à boire

(**e**) *(baby)* attendre

(**f**) *(await → guest, letter, phone call)* attendre; **I'm expecting friends for dinner** j'attends des amis à dîner; **(at) what time should we expect you then?** à quelle heure devons-nous vous attendre alors?; *Br Fam* **I'll expect you when I see you then** bon, alors tu rentreras quand tu rentreras; *Br Fam* **you'll just have to expect me when you see me** tu verras bien quand j'arriverai; **we're expecting them back any minute now** nous attendons leur retour d'une minute à l'autre

2 *vi* **to be expecting** *(be pregnant)* être enceinte, attendre un enfant

expectancy [ɪk'spektənsɪ], **expectance** [ɪk'spektəns] *n (anticipation)* **the look of expectancy on his face** l'attente qui se lisait sur son visage; **in a tone of eager expectancy** sur un ton plein d'espérance *ou* d'espoir

expectant [ɪk'spektənt] *adj (full of anticipation)* impatient; **the expectant look on the children's faces** l'attente qui se lisait sur le visage des enfants; **with an expectant look in his eye** avec dans son regard l'air d'attendre quelque chose; **in an expectant tone of voice** la voix chargée d'espoir

▸▸ ***expectant mother*** future maman *f*

expectantly [ɪk'spektəntlɪ] *adv (enquire, glance)* avec l'air d'attendre quelque chose; *(wait)* impatiemment; **fans waiting expectantly at the stage door** des fans qui attendent à la sortie des artistes, pleins d'espoir

expectation [ˌekspek'teɪʃən] *n* (**a**) *(UNCOUNT) (anticipation)* **with eager expectation** avec l'air d'espérer quelque chose; **to live in expectation** vivre dans l'expectative *ou* l'attente; **beyond all expectation** au-delà de toute espérance; **in a tone of gloomy expectation** avec appréhension; **there is every expectation that we shall be seeing them again soon** il y a de grandes chances pour que nous les revoyions bientôt; **in expectation of** dans l'attente de; *Rel* **in the**

sure expectation of life everlasting dans la certitude d'une vie éternelle

(**b**) *(usu pl) (hope, aspiration)* attente *f*; **to come up to sb's expectations** remplir *ou* répondre à l'attente de qn; **his performance fell short of** *or* **did not live up to their expectations** il n'a pas été à la hauteur de leurs espérances, il n'a pas répondu à leur attente; **to exceed sb's expectations** dépasser l'attente *ou* les espérances de qn; **my expectations for its success were not that high** je ne pensais pas vraiment que ça réussirait; **their expectations that he would fail were not fulfilled** ils s'attendaient à ce qu'il échoue, mais finalement ils se sont trompés; **the performance did not confirm the City expectations** les résultats n'ont pas répondu à l'attente de la City; **these unrealistically high profit expectations** ces prévisions de bénéfices totalement fantaisistes; **this merely confirms our worst expectations** cela ne fait que confirmer nos prévisions les plus noires; **contrary to expectations** contrairement à *ou* contre toute attente; **to have high expectations of sb/sth** attendre beaucoup de qn/qch

(**c**) *(usu pl) (requirement)* exigence *f*; **we have certain expectations of our employees** nous avons certaines exigences envers nos employés; **what are your expectations?** *(for salary, job prospects)* quelles sont vos conditions *ou* exigences?

(**d**) *Formal (prospects)* **to have great expectations** avoir de grandes espérances; **uncle from whom one has expectations** oncle *m* à héritage

expected [ɪk'spektɪd] *adj* attendu; *(hoped for)* espéré; **please state expected salary** indiquez vos prétentions

►► *Fin* ***expected monetary value*** valeur *f* monétaire escomptée; *Fin* ***expected value*** valeur *f* attendue

expectorant [ɪk'spektərənt] *n Med* expectorant *m*

expectorate [ɪk'spektəreɪt] *Med or Formal* **1** *vi* rejeter des expectorations

2 *vt* expectorer

expectoration [ɪk,spektə'reɪʃən] *n Med & Formal* expectoration *f*

expediency [ɪk'spiːdjənsɪ] *(pl* **expediencies**), **expedience** [ɪk'spiːdjəns] *n* (**a**) *(advisability → of measure, policy etc)* opportunité *f*; **on grounds of expediency** pour des raisons de convenance (**b**) *(self-interest)* opportunisme *m*; **a measure that smacks of political expediency** une mesure politique opportuniste

expedient [ɪk'spiːdɪənt] **1** *adj* (**a**) *(advisable)* indiqué, convenable, opportun (**b**) *(involving self-interest)* commode; **a politically expedient measure** une mesure politique opportuniste

2 *n* expédient *m*

expediently [ɪk'spiːdɪəntlɪ] *adv* convenablement

expedite ['ekspɪdaɪt] *vt Formal (work, legal process)* hâter, activer, accélérer; *(completion of contract, deal)* hâter; **to expedite matters** accélérer *ou* activer les choses

expediter ['ekspɪ,daɪtə(r)] *n Formal* **the expediter of the work** celui qui a fait accélérer l'exécution du travail

expedition [,ekspɪ'dɪʃən] *n* (**a**) *(journey)* expédition *f*; **one (member) of the expedition** un des membres de l'expédition; **to go on an expedition** aller *ou* partir en expédition, aller faire une expédition; **getting here was quite an expedition!** ça a été toute une expédition pour arriver jusqu'ici!; **expedition leader** chef *m* d'expédition

(**b**) *Arch or Literary (speed)* diligence *f*; **with all possible expedition** avec la plus grande diligence

expeditionary [,ekspɪ'dɪʃənərɪ] *adj*

►► *Mil* ***expeditionary force*** force *f* expéditionnaire; ***expeditionary mission*** mission *f* d'expédition

expeditious [,ekspɪ'dɪʃəs] *adj Formal* diligent

expeditiously [,ekspɪ'dɪʃəslɪ] *adv Formal* diligemment

expel [ɪk'spel] *vt* (**a**) *(from school)* renvoyer; *(from party, country, club)* expulser (**b**) *(gas, liquid)* expulser; *(breath)* exhaler

expend [ɪk'spend] *vt* (**a**) *(time, energy)* consacrer (**on** à); *(money)* dépenser (**on** sur); *(resources)* utiliser, employer (**b**) *(use up → ammunition, supply)* épuiser

expendability [ɪk,spendə'bɪlətɪ] *n (of people, workforce, equipment)* superfluité *f*; *(of troops, spies)* caractère *m* sacrifiable

expendable [ɪk'spendəbəl] *adj (person, workforce, equipment)* superflu; *(troops, spies)* qui peut être sacrifié; **they decided I'm expendable** ils ont décidé qu'ils pouvaient se passer de moi; **none of them was expendable** toutes étaient indispensables; **he thinks people are expendable** il pense qu'il peut se débarrasser des gens comme bon lui semble

expenditure [ɪk'spendɪtʃə(r)] *n* (**a**) *(act of spending → money, energy etc)* dépense *f*; *(→ resources, ammunition)* consommation *f* (**b**) *(UNCOUNT) (money spent)* dépenses *fpl* (**on** en); **arms/defence expenditure** dépenses *fpl* en armes/liées à la défense; **this will involve us in fairly heavy expenditure** cela va nous entraîner dans des dépenses assez considérables

expense [ɪk'spens] **1** *n* (**a**) *(cost)* dépense *f*, frais *mpl*; **at great/little expense** à grands/peu de frais; **at no extra expense** sans supplément de frais; **regardless of expense** sans regarder à la dépense; **anything we can do to offset the expense** tout ce que nous pouvons faire pour compenser le coût *ou* les coûts *ou* les frais; **it's not so much the expense I'm worried about** ce n'est pas tant le coût que cela représente qui m'inquiète; **that's an expense I hadn't reckoned with** c'est une dépense que je n'avais pas prévue; **if it can really be done with such little expense** si cela peut vraiment se faire à si peu de frais; **the huge expense of moving house** le coût énorme qu'entraîne un déménagement; **to go to considerable expense to do sth** faire beaucoup de frais pour faire qch; **don't go to any expense over it** ne vous mettez pas en frais pour cela; **they didn't want to go to the expense of hiring a car** ils ne voulaient pas faire les frais de louer une voiture; **I don't want to put you to any expense** je ne veux pas vous faire faire des dépenses; **no expense was spared** on n'a pas regardé à la dépense; **without any thought for the expense** sans penser au coût que cela représentait; **to do sth at great personal expense** faire qch à grands frais personnels; **at (one's) own expense** à (ses) propres frais; **she had the book published at her own expense** elle a publié le livre à ses frais *ou* à compte d'auteur; **it's not worth the expense** c'est trop cher pour ce que c'est

(**b**) *(expensiveness)* cherté *f*, coût *m* élevé

(**c**) *Fig* **a joke at somebody else's expense** une plaisanterie aux dépens de quelqu'un d'autre; **at the expense of sth** au détriment de qch; **to succeed at other people's expense** réussir aux dépens des autres; **not at my expense, you won't** pas à mes dépens, il n'en est pas question

(**d**) *Com* **no, that's my expense** non, c'est sur mon compte

2 expenses *npl Com* frais *mpl*; **to meet/cover sb's expenses** rembourser/couvrir les frais de qn; **it's on expenses** c'est l'entreprise qui paie, cela passe dans les notes de frais; **to live on expenses** vivre sur ses notes de frais, vivre aux frais de son entreprise; **to incur expenses** faire des dépenses; **to put sth on expenses** mettre qch dans les notes de frais; **to cut down on expenses** réduire les frais; **to get expenses** *(be paid expenses)* être indemnisé de ses frais; **to have all expenses paid** être défrayé de tout; **travelling expenses** frais *mpl* de déplacement; **accommodation expenses** frais *mpl* d'hôtel *ou* de séjour; **entertainment expenses** frais *mpl* de représentation; **incidental expenses** faux frais *mpl*; **all expenses paid** tous frais payés

►► *Com* ***expense account*** **1** *n* note *f* de frais **2** *comp (lunch, dinner)* qui passe dans les notes de frais; **the firm gives him an expense account for basic entertaining** l'entreprise lui attribue une allocation pour ses frais de représentation; **to put sth on the expense account** mettre qch sur la note de frais; ***expenses budget*** budget *m* des dépenses; ***expenses claim form*** note *f* de frais

expenses-paid *adj (trip, holiday)* tous frais payés

expensive [ɪk'spensɪv] *adj* cher; **it's an expensive hobby** c'est un passe-temps coûteux *ou* qui coûte cher; **the central heating became too expensive to run** le chauffage central a commencé à revenir trop cher; **to have expensive tastes** avoir des goûts de luxe; **London is an expensive place to live** la vie est chère à Londres; **exactly how expensive was it?** combien cela a-t-il coûté exactement?; *also Fig* **that could be an expensive mistake** c'est une erreur qui pourrait coûter cher

expensively [ɪk'pensɪvlɪ] *adv (educated, trained, redecorated)* à grands frais; *(furnished)* luxueusement; **to be expensively dressed** porter des vêtements chers; **if we could all try to live less expensively** si nous essayions tous de vivre à moindres frais; **try not to have it done too expensively** essaie de ne pas le faire faire à trop grands frais

expensiveness [ɪk'spensɪvnɪs] *n* cherté *f*; *(of mistake)* coût *m*; **the expensiveness of her tastes** ses goûts de luxe

experience [ɪk'spɪərɪəns] **1** *n* (**a**) *(in life, in a subject)* expérience *f*; **he has lots of experience** il a beaucoup d'expérience *ou* une grande expérience; **I had no previous experience** je n'avais aucune expérience préalable; **I had no experience of looking after disabled people** je ne m'étais jamais occupé de personnes handicapées; **do you have any experience of working with animals?** avez-vous déjà travaillé avec des animaux?; **she has considerable management experience** elle a une expérience considérable de *ou* dans la gestion; **to lack experience** manquer d'expérience *ou* de pratique; **to gain experience of life** faire l'apprentissage de la vie; **experience shows** *or* **proves that...** l'expérience démontre *ou* montre *ou* prouve que...; **I know from experience that he's not to be trusted** je sais par expérience qu'il ne faut pas lui faire confiance; **to know from bitter experience** savoir pour en avoir fait la cruelle expérience; **to speak from experience** parler en connaissance de cause; **in** *or* **from my (own) experience, (speaking) from personal experience** d'après mon expérience personnelle; **my experience has been** *or* **it has been my experience that...** d'après mon expérience...; **has that been your experience?** *(do you agree?)* avez-vous remarqué la même chose?; **to put sth down to experience** tirer un enseignement *ou* une leçon de qch; **it's all good experience** *(as consolation)* à quelque chose malheur est bon; **experience is the best teacher** l'expérience est le meilleur des enseignements; **the black experience in America** la condition des Noirs en Amérique

(**b**) *(event)* expérience *f*; **I had so many exciting experiences** j'ai vécu tant d'aventures passionnantes; **after this stressful experience** après cette expérience stressante; **how did you enjoy the American experience?** comment as-tu trouvé l'Amérique?; *Hum* **bad weather is all part of the Scottish experience** le mauvais temps fait partie intégrante des joies de l'Écosse; **my first experience of French cooking/of a real Scottish New Year** la première fois que j'ai goûté à la cuisine française/que j'ai assisté à un vrai réveillon écossais; **it was his first experience of love** c'était la première fois qu'il tombait amoureux; **the crossing promises to be quite an experience** la traversée promet d'être une expérience mémorable; **I hope it wasn't a nasty experience for you** j'espère que cela n'a pas été trop désagréable pour toi; **a transatlantic cruise: the experience of a lifetime!** une croisière à travers l'Atlantique: une expérience inoubliable!; **it was not an experience I would care to repeat** je ne voudrais pas renouveler l'expérience

2 *vt* (**a**) *(undergo → hunger, hardship, recession)* connaître; **to experience military combat** faire l'expérience du combat militaire; **he experienced great difficulty in raising the money** il a eu beaucoup de mal à trouver l'argent nécessaire

(**b**) *(feel → thrill, emotion, despair)* sentir, ressentir; **she experienced a certain feeling of fear** elle a ressenti une certaine frayeur; **he is experiencing a great deal of anxiety at the**

exp–exp

moment il est très angoissé en ce moment
(**c**) *(have personal knowledge of)* **come and experience Manhattan** venez découvrir Manhattan; **if you've never experienced French cooking** si vous n'avez jamais goûté à la cuisine française; **to experience a real Scottish New Year** assister à un vrai réveillon écossais
►► *Com* ***experience curve*** courbe *f* d'expérience

experience-curve pricing *n Com* tarification *f* en fonction de la courbe d'expérience

experienced [ɪk'spɪərɪənst] *adj (person)* expérimenté; *(observer)* averti; *(eye)* exercé; **we're looking for someone a bit more experienced** nous recherchons quelqu'un qui ait un peu plus d'expérience; **to be experienced in sth** avoir l'expérience de qch; **to be experienced at doing sth** avoir l'habitude de faire qch; **at fifteen he was already sexually experienced** à quinze ans, il avait déjà couché avec plusieurs filles

experiential [ɪk,spɪərɪ'enʃəl] *adj Formal* empirique, expérientiel

experiment [ɪk'sperɪmənt] **1** *n also Fig* expérience *f*; **to carry out** *or* **to conduct an experiment** réaliser *ou* effectuer une expérience; **an experiment in sth** une expérience de qch; **experiments on animals** des expériences *fpl* sur les animaux; **as an experiment, by way of experiment** à titre d'expérience *ou* d'essai; **it's a bit of an experiment actually** *(as modest apology)* je vous préviens, c'est une innovation
2 *vi* faire une expérience *ou* des expériences; **to experiment with a new technique** expérimenter une nouvelle technique; **to experiment with drugs** essayer la drogue; **to experiment on animals** faire des expériences sur les animaux

'The Quatermass Experiment' *Kneale, Guest* 'Le Monstre'

experimental [ɪk,sperɪ'mentəl] *adj* expérimental; **this programme is still at the experimental stage** ce programme est à l'essai *ou* en cours d'expérimentation

experimentalism [ɪk,sperɪ'mentəlɪzəm] *n* expérimentalisme *m*

experimentalist [ɪk,sperɪ'mentəlɪst] *n* expérimentaliste *mf*

experimentally [ɪk,sperɪ'mentəlɪ] *adv (by experimenting)* expérimentalement; *(as an experiment)* à titre expérimental *ou* d'essai; **he dipped his arm into the bathwater experimentally** il plongea son bras dans l'eau du bain pour vérifier la température

experimentation [ɪk,sperɪmen'teɪʃən] *n* expérimentation *f*; **recent experimentation has shown that...** des expériences récentes ont montré que...

experimenter [ɪk'sperɪmentə(r)] *n* expérimentateur(trice) *m,f*; **I've always been a bit of an experimenter** j'ai toujours aimé faire des expériences

expert ['ekspɜːt] **1** *n* expert *m*, spécialiste *mf*; **to be an expert in one's field** être un expert dans son domaine; **he's an expert at archery** c'est un expert au tir à l'arc; **to ask an expert** consulter un spécialiste; **to look at sth with the eye of an expert** regarder qch avec l'œil d'un expert; **I'm no expert, but...** je ne suis pas expert *ou* spécialiste en la matière, mais...; **do it yourself, you're the expert!** fais-le toi-même, c'est toi l'expert!
2 *adj (person)* expert; *(advice, opinion)* autorisé, d'expert; **to be expert at doing sth** être expert à faire qch; **to be expert at sth** être expert en qch; **to run** *or* **to cast an expert eye over sth** jeter un œil expert sur qch
►► ***expert panel*** commission *f* d'experts; *Comput* ***expert system*** système *m* expert; *Law* ***expert testimony*** témoignage *m* d'expert; *Law* ***expert witness*** expert *m (appelé comme témoin)*; **to appear** *or* **to be called as an expert witness** paraître *ou* être appelé à la cour comme expert

expertise [,ekspɜː'tiːz] *n* compétence *f*, savoir-faire *m*; **to do sth with great expertise** faire qch avec beaucoup de compétence

expertize ['ekspɜːtaɪz] *vi Am* donner un point de vue d'expert

expertly ['ekspɜːtlɪ] *adv* d'une manière experte, expertement

expertness ['ekspɜːtnɪs] *n* compétence *f*, savoir-faire *m*

expiate ['ekspɪeɪt] *vt Formal* expier

expiation [,ekspɪ'eɪʃən] *n Formal* expiation *f*; **in expiation of one's sins** pour expier *ou* en expiation de ses péchés

expiatory ['ekspɪətərɪ] *adj Formal* expiatoire

expiration [,ekspɪ'reɪʃən] *n* (**a**) *Formal (of contract, lease, visa)* expiration *f*, échéance *f*; *(of insurance policy, passport)* expiration *f* (**b**) *Formal (exhalation)* expiration *f* (**c**) *Arch or Literary (death)* mort *f*
►► *Am* ***expiration date*** *(of product)* date *f* limite de validité

expire [ɪk'spaɪə(r)] *vi* (**a**) *(contract, lease, insurance policy)* expirer, arriver à terme; *(visa, passport)* expirer (**b**) *(exhale)* expirer (**c**) *Arch or Literary (die)* expirer

expired [ɪk'spaɪəd] *adj (contract, lease, insurance policy)* expiré; *(passport)* périmé; *(visa)* périmé, arrivée à expiration

expiring [ɪk'spaɪərɪŋ] *adj* (**a**) *(contract, lease, insurance policy)* qui expire, qui est à son terme; *(visa, passport)* sur le point d'expirer (**b**) *Arch or Literary (dying)* expirant, qui se meurt; **with an expiring voice** d'une voix mourante

expiry [ɪk'spaɪərɪ] *n (of contract, lease, insurance policy)* expiration *f*, échéance *f*; *(of visa, passport)* expiration *f*
►► ***expiry date*** *(of contract, lease, insurance policy)* date *f* d'expiration *ou* d'échéance; *(of visa, passport)* date *f* d'expiration; *(on food labels)* date *f* limite de consommation; *(on ticket, on voucher)* à utiliser avant le, valable jusqu'au; *(on bank card)* valable jusqu'au

explain [ɪk'spleɪn] **1** *vt* (**a**) *(clarify)* expliquer; **he explained to us how the machine worked** il nous a expliqué comment la machine marchait; **to explain sth in full** expliquer qch en détail; **she explained that she was a tourist in the city** elle a expliqué qu'elle était dans la ville en touriste; **that is easily explained, that is easy to explain** c'est facile à expliquer, cela s'explique facilement; **that explains everything** voilà qui explique tout
(**b**) *(account for)* expliquer; **she's got a cold, which explains** *or* **will explain why she's off work today** elle a un rhume, ce qui explique pourquoi elle ne travaille pas aujourd'hui; **to explain oneself** s'expliquer; **I think you'd better explain yourself** je crois que tu ferais mieux de t'expliquer
2 *vi (clarify)* expliquer; **I don't understand, you'll need to explain** je ne comprends pas, il va falloir que tu m'expliques; **you've got a bit of** *or* **a little** *or* **some explaining to do** il va falloir que tu t'expliques

►**explain away** *vt sep (justify, excuse)* justifier; **explain that away if you can!** essayez donc de justifier cela!; **how did he manage to explain away the broken vase?** quelle raison a-t-il trouvée pour expliquer que le vase soit cassé?

explainable [ɪk'spleɪnəbəl] *adj (explicable)* **it's easily explainable** cela s'explique facilement, c'est facilement explicable

explanation [,eksplə'neɪʃən] *n* explication *f*; **to give** *or* **to offer an explanation for sth** donner une explication à qch; **to find an explanation for sth** trouver une explication à qch; **the instructions for this new video need a bit of explanation** les instructions de ce nouveau magnétoscope nécessitent des explications; **the lecturer gave an explanation of the term** le professeur a donné une explication de ce terme; **one explanation is that...** l'une des explications est que...; **the minister is demanding a full explanation** le ministre exige une explication; **I want an explanation!** je veux une explication!; **you'd better have a good explanation!** j'espère que tu as une bonne excuse *ou* une explication valable!

explanatory [ɪk'splænətrɪ] *adj* explicatif

explant [eks'plɑːnt] *Biol* **1** *vt* explanter *(prélever en vue d'une culture in vitro)*
2 *n* explant *m*

explantation [eksplɑːn'teɪʃən] *n Biol* explantation *f*

expletive [ɪk'spliːtɪv] **1** *n* (**a**) *(swearword)* juron *m*; **a string of expletives** un chapelet de jurons (**b**) *Gram* explétif *m*
2 *adj Gram* explétif

explicable [ɪk'splɪkəbəl] *adj* explicable; **this phenomenon is not explicable by sociological factors alone** ce phénomène ne peut s'expliquer par les seuls facteurs sociologiques

explicate ['eksplɪkeɪt] *vt Formal* (**a**) *(explain)* expliquer (**b**) *(clarify)* éclaircir, clarifier

explication [,eksplɪ'keɪʃən] *n Formal* (**a**) *(explanation)* explication *f* (**b**) *(clarification)* éclaircissement *m*, clarification *f*

explicit [ɪk'splɪsɪt] *adj (denial, meaning, support)* explicite; *(instructions)* explicite, clair; *(details)* clair; **he was explicit on this point** il a été très clair à ce sujet; **I can't be more explicit at this stage** je ne peux pas en dire plus pour l'instant; **explicit sex and violence on the television** le sexe et la violence montrés ouvertement à la télévision; **sexually explicit** cru

explicitly [ɪk'splɪsɪtlɪ] *adv* explicitement

explicitness [ɪk'splɪsɪtnɪs] *n* (**a**) *(clarity* → *of instructions, details)* clarté *f* (**b**) *(sexual* → *of language, scene, film)* caractère *m* cru

explode [ɪk'spləʊd] **1** *vt (detonate)* faire exploser *ou* sauter; *Fig (theory, myth etc)* détruire, anéantir
2 *vi (bomb, mine etc)* exploser, éclater, sauter; *Fig (person)* exploser; **to explode with laughter** éclater de rire; **to explode into fits of giggles** partir dans des fous rires; **to explode with anger** exploser de colère; **the game exploded into life** le match s'est animé d'un seul coup; **the boxer exploded into action** le boxeur est entré en action d'une manière fulgurante; **when the punk movement exploded onto the scene in the 1970s** quand le mouvement punk a pris la scène musicale d'assaut dans les années 70; **the population exploded with the advent of the industrial revolution** l'avènement de la révolution industrielle a provoqué une explosion démographique

exploded [ɪk'spləʊdɪd] *adj (bomb, mine etc)* qu'on a fait exploser; *Fig (theory, myth etc)* détruit, anéanti
►► *Tech* ***exploded diagram, exploded view*** éclaté *m*

exploding star [ɪk'spləʊdɪŋ-] *n Astron* étoile *f* variable

exploit 1 *n* ['eksplɔɪt] exploit *m*
2 *vt* [ɪk'splɔɪt] (**a**) *(workers)* exploiter (**b**) *(natural resources)* exploiter

exploitable [ɪk'splɔɪtəbəl] *adj (resource)* exploitable

exploitation [,eksplɔɪ'teɪʃən] *n (of workers, of natural resources)* exploitation *f*

exploitative [ɪk'splɔɪtətɪv] *adj (practices)* relevant de l'exploitation; **the company's exploitative attitude towards the workforce** la manière dont l'entreprise exploite la main-d'œuvre; **an exploitative employer** un(e) exploiteur(euse)

exploiter [ɪk'splɔɪtə(r)] *n* (**a**) *(of workers)* exploiteur(euse) *m,f* (**b**) *(of natural resources)* exploitant(e) *m,f*

exploration [,eksplə'reɪʃən] *n* (**a**) *(of place, problem)* exploration *f*; **to set off on an exploration of the world** partir explorer le monde, se lancer à la découverte du monde; **voyage of exploration** voyage *m* d'exploration (**b**) *Med* exploration *f*

explorative [ɪk'splɒrətɪv] *adj* explorateur

exploratory [ɪk'splɒrətrɪ] *adj (journey)* d'exploration; *(talks, discussions)* exploratoire; **exploratory drilling** forage *m* d'exploration; *Med* **to have exploratory surgery** subir une exploration

explore [ɪk'splɔː(r)] **1** *vt* (**a**) *(country)* explorer; *(town)* découvrir, explorer; **she explored her new filling with the tip of her tongue** elle a tâté son nouveau plombage du bout de la langue
(**b**) *(issue, possibility, problem)* étudier, examiner; *(market)* prospecter; *Fig* **to explore every avenue** explorer toutes les voies *ou* solutions possibles; *Fig* **to explore the ground** tâter le terrain
(**c**) *Med* explorer, sonder
2 *vi* faire une exploration; **let's go exploring** *(in the woods, countryside etc)* partons en exploration; *(in a city)* allons découvrir la ville

explorer [ɪk'splɔːrə(r)] *n* (**a**) *(person)* explorateur(trice) *m,f*
(**b**) *(instrument)* sonde *f*

explosion [ɪk'spləʊʒən] *n* (**a**) *(of bomb, gas)* explosion *f*; **an explosion ripped through the building** une explosion a ébranlé le bâtiment; *Fig* **an explosion of anger** une explosion de colère; **there was an explosion of laughter from the dining room** une explosion *ou* une tempête de rires est arrivée de la salle à manger
(**b**) *(act of exploding)* explosion *f*

explosive [ɪk'spləʊsɪv] **1** *adj* (**a**) *(causing an explosion)* explosif; *(gas)* explosible; *Fig* **an explosive situation** une situation explosive; *Fig* **an explosive combination** un mélange explosif (**b**) *Ling* explosif
2 *n* (**a**) *(in bomb)* explosif *m*; **high explosive** explosif *m* puissant (**b**) *Ling* explosive *f*
►► ***explosive device*** dispositif *m* explosif; ***explosives expert*** expert(e) *m,f* en explosifs

explosiveness [ɪk'spləʊsɪvnɪs] *n* nature *f* explosive

expo ['ekspəʊ] (*pl* **expos**) *n (exhibition)* expo *f*

exponent [ɪk'spəʊnənt] *n* (**a**) *(of idea, theory)* apôtre *m*, avocat(e) *m,f*; *(of skill)* représentant(e) *m,f*; **he is a leading exponent of this theory** il est l'un des plus fervents apôtres de cette théorie (**b**) *Math* exposant *m*

exponential [ˌekspə'nenʃəl] *adj* exponentiel
►► *Math* ***exponential curve*** courbe *f* exponentielle

exponentially [ˌekspə'nenʃəlɪ] *adv* de manière exponentielle

export 1 *n* ['ekspɔːt] *Com* (**a**) *(action)* exportation *f*; **for export only** réservé à l'exportation
(**b**) *(product)* exportation *f*; **visible/invisible exports** exportations *fpl* visibles/invisibles
2 *comp* ['ekspɔːt] *Com (goods, price)* à l'export
3 *vt* [ɪk'spɔːt] (**a**) *Com & Fig* exporter; **to export goods to other countries** exporter des marchandises vers d'autres pays
(**b**) *Comput* exporter (**to** vers)
4 *vi* [ɪk'spɔːt] *Com* exporter; **the firm exports all over the world** l'entreprise exporte dans le monde entier; **exporting company** société *f* exportatrice; **exporting country** pays *m* exportateur
►► ***export agent*** commissionnaire *m* exportateur; ***export ban*** interdiction *f* d'exporter; **to impose an export ban on sth** interdire qch d'exportation; ***export credit*** crédit *m* à l'exportation; ***Export Credits Guarantee Department*** = organisme d'assurance pour le commerce extérieur, ≃ COFACE *f*; ***export drive*** campagne *f* visant à stimuler l'exportation; ***export duty*** droit *m* de sortie *ou* d'exportation; ***export earnings*** revenus *mpl ou* recettes *fpl* de l'exportation; ***export licence*** permis *m* d'exportation; ***export quotas*** contingents *mpl* d'exportation; ***export reject*** produit *m* impropre à l'exportation; ***export sales*** ventes *fpl* export *ou* à l'exportation; ***export tax*** taxe *f* à l'exportation; ***export trade*** commerce *m* d'exportation

exportable [ɪk'spɔːtəbəl] *adj Com & Comput* exportable

exportation [ˌekspɔː'teɪʃən] *n Com & Fig* exportation *f*

export-driven *adj (expansion, recovery)* basé *ou* [illegible]

exporter [ek'spɔːtə(r)] *n Com* exportateur(trice) *m,f*

export-intensive *adj (country)* fortement exportateur

expose [ɪk'spəʊz] *vt* (**a**) *(uncover)* découvrir; *Phot* exposer; **her low-cut dress leaves her shoulders exposed** sa robe décolletée découvre *ou* laisse voir ses épaules; **to expose sb/sth to sth** exposer qn/qch à qch; **to be exposed to attack** être exposé aux attaques; **to be exposed to the elements** être exposé aux intempéries; **he was exposed to German from the age of five** il a été au contact de l'allemand depuis l'âge de cinq ans; **to expose sth to view** exposer qch à la vue; **to expose oneself** *(exhibitionist)* s'exhiber; *Law* commettre un outrage à la pudeur; **to expose oneself is an offence** l'exhibitionnisme est un délit; **to expose oneself to sth** *(to criticism, ridicule, risk)* s'exposer à qch
(**b**) *(reveal, unmask → plot)* découvrir; *(→ spy)* découvrir, démasquer; **they're trying to expose him as...** ils essaient de démontrer que c'est...; **he feared being exposed as a homosexual** il craignait que son homosexualité ne soit découverte *ou* mise à jour
(**c**) *Rel (the Blessed Sacrament)* exposer
(**d**) *(abandon → baby)* abandonner, exposer

exposé [eks'pəʊzeɪ] *n Press* révélations *fpl*; **the newspaper's exposé of the MP's activities** les révélations du journal sur les activités du parlementaire

exposed [ɪk'spəʊzd] *adj (location, house, position etc)* exposé; *Tech (parts, gears)* apparent, à découvert; *(wires)* à nu; *Archit (beam)* apparent; **the house is in an exposed position** la maison est très exposée; **the troops are in an exposed position** les soldats sont à découvert; *Fig* **the government is in an exposed position** le gouvernement est dans une position précaire

exposition [ˌekspə'zɪʃən] *n* (**a**) *(explanation)* exposé *m* (**b**) *(exhibition)* exposition *f* (**c**) *Rel* exposition *f*; **exposition of the Blessed Sacrament** exposition *f* du Saint Sacrement

expostulate [ɪk'spɒstjʊleɪt] *vi Formal* vitupérer; **to expostulate with sb about sth** faire des remontrances à qn à propos de qch

expostulation [ɪkˌspɒstjʊ'leɪʃən] *n Formal* vitupérations *fpl*, remontrances *fpl*

expostulatory [ɪk'spɒstjʊlətərɪ, ɪkˌspɒstjʊ'leɪtərɪ] *adj Formal* de remontrance

exposure [ɪk'spəʊʒə(r)] *n* (**a**) *(to harm, radiation)* exposition *f*; *Fin* risque *m*; **exposure to danger is something he encounters daily** il est quotidiennement exposé au danger
(**b**) *(to cold)* **to suffer from the effects of exposure** souffrir des effets d'une exposition au froid; **to die of exposure** mourir de froid
(**c**) *(unmasking, revealing → of crime, scandal)* révélation *f*, divulgation *f*
(**d**) *Phot* pose *f*; **a 36-exposure film** une pellicule (de) 36 poses; **time exposure** pose *f*
(**e**) *(position of house)* exposition *f*; **the building has a southern exposure** le bâtiment est exposé au sud
(**f**) *(media coverage)* couverture *f*; **to receive a lot of exposure** *(book, person)* faire l'objet d'une couverture médiatique importante; **pop stars suffer from too much media exposure** les stars de la musique pop sont l'objet d'une attention excessive des média
(**g**) *(abandonment → of baby)* abandon *m*, exposition *f*
►► *Phot* ***exposure counter*** compteur *m* de prises de vue; *Phot* ***exposure meter*** exposimètre *m*, posemètre *m*; *Phot* ***exposure time*** temps *m* de pose

expound [ɪk'spaʊnd] *Formal* **1** *vt* exposer
2 *vi* **to expound on sth** disserter sur qch

express [ɪk'spres] **1** *n* (**a**) *Rail* express *m*; **to travel by express** voyager en express
(**b**) *(system of delivery)* exprès *m*
(**c**) *Press* **the Express** = nom abrégé du "Daily Express"
2 *adj* (**a**) *(clear → instructions)* clair; **with the express purpose of** dans le seul but de
(**b**) *(fast → delivery, messenger)* express
3 *adv (send)* en exprès
4 *vt* (**a**) *(voice, convey)* exprimer; **to express an interest in sth** manifester de l'intérêt pour qch; **to express a wish** formuler un souhait; **to express an opinion** exprimer *ou* émettre une opinion; **the two men expressed optimism that a peaceful solution would be found** les deux hommes se sont montrés optimistes quant à un règlement pacifique; **to express oneself** s'exprimer; **to express oneself through sth** s'exprimer par *ou* à travers qch
(**b**) *(render in a different form)* exprimer; **it's difficult to express this idea in Russian** cette idée est difficile à exprimer en russe; *Math* **to express sth as a fraction** exprimer qch sous la forme d'une fraction
(**c**) *Formal (juice)* extraire, exprimer; *(milk)* tirer
(**d**) *(send)* envoyer en exprès
►► *Am* ***express company*** entreprise *f* de livraison exprès; ***express delivery*** envoi *m* par exprès; ***express freight*** fret *m* express; ***express letter*** lettre *f* exprès; *Am* ***Express Mail*** = service de distribution exprès du courrier, ≃ Chronopost *m*; ***express messenger*** messager *m* exprès; **by express messenger** par exprès; *Rail* ***express train*** train *m* express, express *m*

expressible [ɪk'spresɪbəl] *adj* exprimable; *Math* **x is easily expressible in terms of y** x s'exprime facilement en fonction de *y*

expression [ɪk'spreʃən] *n* (**a**) *(of feelings, thoughts, friendship)* expression *f*; **to give expression to sth** exprimer qch; **her feelings found expression in music** ses sentiments trouvèrent leur expression dans la musique; **we'd like you to have it as an expression of our gratitude** nous vous l'offrons en témoignage de notre reconnaissance; **freedom of expression** liberté *f* d'expression
(**b**) *(feeling → in art, music)* expression *f*; **to play/to paint with expression** jouer/peindre avec expression; **he puts a lot of expression into what he plays** il met beaucoup d'expression dans ce qu'il joue
(**c**) *(phrase)* expression *f*; *Ling* **set** *or* **fixed expression** expression *f ou* locution *f* figée *ou* toute faite; *Math* **algebraic expression** expression *f* algébrique
(**d**) *(facial)* expression *f*; **I could tell by her expression** je voyais bien à son expression
►► *Mus* ***expression mark*** signe *f* d'expression

expressionism, Expressionism [ɪk'spreʃənɪzəm] *n Art & Literature* expressionnisme *m*

expressionist, Expressionist [ɪk'spreʃənɪst] *Art & Literature* **1** *adj* expressionniste
2 *n* expressionniste *mf*

expressionistic, Expressionistic [ɪkˌspreʃə'nɪstɪk] *adj Art & Literature* expressionniste

expressionless [ɪk'spreʃənlɪs] *adj (face, person)* inexpressif, sans expression; *(voice)* inexpressif, éteint, terne; **the accused sat expressionless in the dock** l'inculpé était assis sans expression au banc des accusés

expressive [ɪk'spresɪv] *adj (face, gesture, smile)* expressif; **to be expressive of sth** être indicatif de qch

expressively [ɪk'spresɪvlɪ] *adv (gesture, smile)* avec expression

expressiveness [ɪk'spresɪvnɪs] *n (of face, gesture, smile)* expressivité *f*

expressly [ɪk'spreslɪ] *adv* expressément; **I expressly forbid you to leave** je vous interdis formellement de partir

expressman [ɪk'spresmæn] (*pl* **expressmen** [-men]) *n Am* messager *m* d'une entreprise de livraison exprès

expresso [ɪk'spresəʊ] *n (coffee)* expresso *m*

expressway [ɪk'spresweɪ] *n Am* autoroute *f*

expropriate [eks'prəʊprɪeɪt] *vt* exproprier

expropriation [eksˌprəʊprɪ'eɪʃən] *n* expropriation *f*

expropriator [eks'prəʊprɪˌeɪtə(r)] *n* expropriateur(trice) *m,f*

expulsion [ɪk'spʌlʃən] *n* (**a**) *(from school)* renvoi *m*; *(from party, country, club)* expulsion *f* (**b**) *(of breath)* expulsion *f*

expulsive [ɪk'spʌlsɪv] *adj* expulsif

expunction [ɪk'spʌŋkʃən] *n Formal* suppression *f*; *(from memory)* effacement *m*, suppression *f*

expunge [ɪk'spʌndʒ] *vt Formal (delete)* supprimer, effacer; *(from memory)* effacer

expurgate ['ekspəgeɪt] *vt (book, play, text)* expurger; **expurgated edition** édition *f* expurgée

expurgation [ˌekspə'geɪʃən] *n (of book, play, text)* expurgation *f*

exquisite [ɪk'skwɪzɪt] *adj* (**a**) *(food, beauty, manners)* exquis; *(jewellery, craftsmanship)* raffiné; **a face of exquisite beauty** un visage d'une beauté exquise; **to have exquisite taste** avoir un goût exquis (**b**) *(intense → pleasure, pain, thrill)* intense

exquisitely [ɪk'skwɪzɪtlɪ] *adv* (**a**) *(delightfully)* de façon exquise; **exquisitely polite** d'une exquise courtoisie; **an exquisitely warm afternoon** un après-midi délicieusement chaud; **an exquisitely timed interjection** une exclamation tout à fait opportune (**b**) *(intensely)* intensément

exquisiteness [ɪk'skwɪzɪtnɪs] *n* (**a**) *(delicacy, subtlety → of work of art)* raffinement *m*, finesse *f*; *(→ of hearing)* finesse *f* (**b**) *(intense degree → of pleasure)* intensité *f*; *(→ of pain)* acuité *f*

exsanguination [ɪkˌsæŋgwɪˈneɪʃən] *n Med* exsanguination *f*

ex-service *adj Br* retraité de l'armée

ex-serviceman (*pl* **ex-servicemen** [-men]) *n Br Mil* retraité *m* de l'armée

ex-servicewoman (*pl* **ex-servicewomen** [-wɪmɪn]) *n Br Mil* retraitée *f* de l'armée

ext. (*written abbr* **extension**) poste *m*; **ext. 4174** poste 4174

extant [ekˈstænt] *adj Formal* encore existant; **only one of these manuscripts/buildings is still extant** seul l'un des manuscrits/bâtiments existe toujours

extemporaneous [ɪkˌstempəˈreɪnɪəs], **extemporary** [ɪkˈstempərərɪ] *adj Formal* improvisé, impromptu

extemporaneously [ɪkˌstempəˈreɪnɪəslɪ] *adv Formal* impromptu

extempore [ɪkˈstempərɪ] *Formal* **1** *adj* improvisé, impromptu

2 *adv (speak)* impromptu

extemporization [ɪkˌstempəraɪˈzeɪʃən] *n Formal* improvisation *f*

extemporize, -ise [ɪkˈstempəraɪz] *Formal* **1** *vt (speech, piece of music)* improviser

2 *vi (speaker, musician)* improviser

extend [ɪkˈstend] **1** *vt* (**a**) *(stretch out → arm, leg)* étendre, allonger; *(→ wings)* ouvrir, déployer; *(→ aerial)* déplier, déployer; **to extend one's hand to sb** tendre la main à qn

(**b**) *(in length, duration → guarantee, visa, news programme)* prolonger; *(→ road, runway)* prolonger, allonger; **they extended his visa by six months** on a prolongé son visa de six mois; **the deadline has been extended until 25 May** la date limite a été repoussée au 25 mai

(**c**) *(make larger, widen → frontiers, law, enquiry, search)* étendre; *(→ building)* agrandir; *(→ vocabulary)* enrichir, élargir; **the company decided to extend its activities into the export market** la société a décidé d'étendre ses activités au marché de l'exportation

(**d**) *(offer → friendship, hospitality)* offrir; *(→ thanks, condolences, congratulations)* présenter; *(→ credit)* accorder; **to extend an invitation to sb** faire une invitation à qn; **to extend a welcome to sb** souhaiter la bienvenue à qn; **to extend one's sympathy to sb** présenter ses condoléances à qn

(**e**) *(stretch → horse, person)* pousser au bout de ses capacités *ou* à son maximum; **to extend oneself in a race** se donner à fond dans une course

2 *vi* (**a**) *(protrude → wall, cliff)* avancer, former une avancée

(**b**) *(stretch → country, forest, hills etc)* s'étendre; *(→ period of time)* se prolonger; **the queue extended all the way down the street** il y avait la queue jusqu'au bout de la rue; **the parliamentary recess extends into October** les vacances parlementaires se prolongent jusqu'en octobre; **the laughter extended to the others in the room** le rire a gagné le reste de la salle; **the legislation does not extend to single mothers** la législation ne concerne pas les mères célibataires

extendable [ɪkˈstendəbəl] *adj* (**a**) *(aerial, pole)* télescopique; **extendable ladder** échelle *f* à coulisse (**b**) *(in time → contract, visa)* renouvelable; **the tenancy is extendable by one year** le contrat de location peut être prolongé d'un an

extended [ɪkˈstendɪd] *adj* (**a**) *(in time → contract, visit)* prolongé; **extended holiday** des vacances *fpl* prolongées; **the firm gave him an extended contract** la société a reconduit son contrat; **to be on extended leave** être en arrêt prolongé; **owing to the extended news bulletin** en raison de la prolongation du bulletin d'informations

(**b**) *(larger, wider → frontiers, enquiry, search)* étendu; **the bank granted him extended credit** la banque lui a accordé un crédit à long terme

(**c**) *(in space → body, arm)* étendu, allongé; *(building)* agrandi; *Mil* **in extended order** en ordre dispersé

►► *Am Med* **extended care** soins *mpl* prolongés; **extended coverage** *Ins* couverture *f* multirisque; *Rad & TV* = informations détaillées sur un événement; **extended family** famille *f* élargie; *Am Met* **extended forecast** = prévisions météorologiques sur plus de deux jours; *Comput* **extended keyboard** clavier *m* étendu; *Comput* **extended memory** mémoire *f* étendue; *Horseriding* **extended trot** trot *m* allongé; **extended warranty** garantie *f* prolongée

extender lens [ɪkˈstendə-] *n* bague *f* rallonge

extendible = **extendable**

extending [ɪkˈstendɪŋ] **1** *adj (table)* à rallonge *ou* rallonges; *(ladder)* à coulisse

2 *n* (**a**) *(of arm, leg, freedom)* extension *f* (**b**) *(of motorway)* prolongement *m* (**c**) *(of contract, visa)* prolongation *f*

extensibility [ɪkˌstensəˈbɪlɪtɪ] *n* extensibilité *f*

extensible [ɪkˈstensəbəl] *adj* extensible

extensification [ɪkstensɪfɪˈkeɪʃən] *n Agr* extensification *f*

extension [ɪkˈstenʃən] **1** *n* (**a**) *(of arm, legislation, frontiers)* extension *f*

(**b**) *(of house, building)* **to build an extension onto sth** agrandir qch; **do you like the new extension?** *(to the house)* la nouvelle partie de la maison vous plaît-elle?; *(of library, museum etc)* la nouvelle aile vous plaît-elle?

(**c**) *(of motorway)* prolongement *m*

(**d**) *(of contract, visa, time period)* prolongation *f*; **to ask for/to get an extension** *(to pay, hand in work)* demander/obtenir un délai; **the bar's been granted an extension** le bar a obtenu une prolongation de ses heures d'ouverture

(**e**) *(telephone → in office building)* poste *m*; *(→ in house)* poste *m* supplémentaire; **can I have extension 946?** pouvez-vous me passer le poste 946?; **you can reach me on extension 231** vous pouvez me joindre au poste 231

(**f**) *Elec* prolongateur *m*, rallonge *f*

(**g**) *Comput (of file)* extension *f*

(**h**) *Acct (of balance)* transport *m*, report *m*

2 by extension *adv* par extension

►► **extension cable** câble *m* de raccordement; **extension college** institut *m* de formation permanente; **extension cord** prolongateur *m*, rallonge *f*; **extension course** cours *m* de formation permanente; **extension ladder** échelle *f* à coulisse; *Br* **extension lead** prolongateur *m*, rallonge *f*; *Tel* **extension number** numéro *m* de poste

extensive [ɪkˈstensɪv] *adj* (**a**) *(desert, powers, knowledge)* étendu, vaste; *(damage, repairs)* important, considérable; *(tests, research, investigation)* approfondi; **the area is remarkable for its extensive tree cover** cette région se distingue par l'étendue considérable de ses bois; **the issue has been given extensive coverage in the media** ce problème a été largement traité dans les médias; **to make extensive use of sth** beaucoup utiliser qch, faire un usage considérable de qch

(**b**) *Agr (farming)* extensif

extensively [ɪkˈstensɪvlɪ] *adv (damaged, altered, revised)* considérablement; *(quote)* abondamment; *(travel, read)* beaucoup; *(discuss)* en profondeur; **the car has been extensively tested** la voiture a subi des tests approfondis *ou* poussés; **to research sth extensively** faire des recherches approfondies sur qch; **to use sth extensively** beaucoup utiliser qch, faire un usage considérable de qch

extensiveness [ɪkˈstensɪvnɪs] *n (of powers, knowledge, damage, research)* étendue *f*

extensor [ɪkˈstensə(r)] *n Anat* extenseur *m*

extent [ɪkˈstent] **1** *n* (**a**) *(size, range → of ground, knowledge, influence)* étendue *f*; *(→ of debts, damage)* importance *f*; **trees ran along the entire extent of the boulevard** des arbres longeaient le boulevard sur toute sa longueur; **he has debts to the extent of £1,000** il a des dettes d'une valeur *ou* d'un montant de 1000 livres

(**b**) *(degree)* mesure *f*, degré *m*; **these figures show the extent to which tourism has been affected** ces chiffres montrent à quel point le tourisme a été affecté; **to what extent?** dans quelle mesure?; **to that extent** sur ce point, à cet égard; **to the extent that..., to such an extent that...** à tel point que...

(**c**) *(in publishing → of book)* nombre *m* de pages

2 to a large extent, to a great extent *adv* dans une grande mesure, à un haut point *ou* degré

3 to an extent, to some extent, to a certain extent *adv* dans une certaine mesure, jusqu'à un certain point *ou* degré

extenuate [ɪkˈstenjʊeɪt] *vt* atténuer

extenuating [ɪkˈstenjʊeɪtɪŋ] *adj* **extenuating circumstances** circonstances *fpl* atténuantes

extenuation [ɪkˌstenjʊˈeɪʃən] *n* atténuation *f*; **to say sth in extenuation of an offence/an act** dire qch pour atténuer la gravité d'un délit/d'un acte

exterior [ɪkˈstɪərɪə(r)] **1** *adj* extérieur; **exterior to** extérieur à

2 *n (of house, building)* extérieur *m*; *(of person)* apparence *f*, dehors *m*; **on the exterior** à l'extérieur; **a house with an imposing exterior** une maison aux dehors imposants; **the house had a whitewashed exterior** la maison avait une façade blanchie à la chaux; **underneath his stern exterior he is very sensitive** sous des dehors sévères, c'est un sensible

►► *Math* **exterior angle** angle *m* externe

exteriorization [ɪkˌstɪərɪəraɪˈzeɪʃən] *n* extériorisation *f*

exteriorize, -ise [ɪkˈstɪərɪəraɪz] *vt* extérioriser

exterminate [ɪkˈstɜːmɪneɪt] *vt (pests)* exterminer; *(race, people)* exterminer, anéantir

extermination [ɪkˌstɜːmɪˈneɪʃən] *n (of pests)* extermination *f*; *(of race, people)* extermination *f*, anéantissement *m*

exterminator [ɪkˈstɜːmɪneɪtə(r)] *n (person → gen)* exterminateur(trice) *m,f*; *(→ of vermin)* dératiseur *m*; *(poison)* mort-aux-rats *f inv*

extern [ˈekstɜːn] *n Am Med* externe *mf*

external [ɪkˈstɜːnəl] **1** *adj (events, relations, trade, wall, reality)* extérieur; *(injury)* externe; *(interference, pressure)* du dehors, de l'extérieur; *Comput* externe; *Pharm* **for external use only** *(on packaging)* à usage externe uniquement

2 *n (usu pl)* **externals** extérieur *m*, formes *fpl* extérieures, dehors *mpl*; **to judge by externals** juger les choses selon les apparences

►► *Banking* **external account** compte *m* d'étranger, *Can* compte *m* de non-résident; *Fin* **external audit** audit *m* externe; *Fin* **external auditing** vérification *f* externe, audit *m* externe; *Fin* **external auditor** audit *ou* auditeur(trice) *m,f* externe; *Fin* **external deficit** déficit *m* extérieur; *Univ* **external degree** = diplôme obtenu en examen final, sans que l'étudiant ait assisté aux cours; *Comput* **external device** dispositif *m* externe, périphérique *m*; *Comput* **external drive** unité *f* (de disque) externe; *Anat* **external ear** oreille *f* externe; *Univ* **external examiner** examinateur(trice) *m,f* venant de l'extérieur; *Fin* **external financing** financement *m* externe, fonds *mpl* extérieurs; *Comput* **external modem** modem *m* externe; **external pressure** *(on person)* pression *f* de l'extérieur; *(on device)* pression *f* extérieure *ou* du dehors; *Univ* **external student** = étudiant qui passe un examen dans un établissement où il n'a pas étudié

externality [ˌekstɜːˈnælɪtɪ] *n* extériorité *f*

externalization [ɪkˌstɜːnəlaɪˈzeɪʃən] *n* extériorisation *f*

externalize, -ise [ɪkˈstɜːnəlaɪz] *vt* extérioriser

externally [ɪkˈstɜːnəlɪ] *adv* à l'extérieur; *Pharm* **to be used externally** *(on packaging)* à usage externe

externe = **extern**

extinct [ɪkˈstɪŋkt] *adj (species, race)* disparu, qui n'existe plus; **the horse and plough are nearly extinct** le cheval et la charrue sont en voie d'extinction; **to become extinct** *(species, tradition)* s'éteindre, disparaître; *(method)* disparaître

►► **extinct volcano** volcan *m* éteint

extinction [ɪkˈstɪŋkʃən] *n (of species, race)* extinction *f*, disparition *f*; *(of fire, candle)* extinction *f*; **to be threatened with extinction** être menacé d'extinction, être en voie de disparition; **to threaten sth with extinction** menacer qch d'extinction; **to hunt an animal to extinction** chasser un animal jusqu'à extinction de l'espèce

extinguish [ɪkˈstɪŋgwɪʃ] *vt (fire, candle)* éteindre; *Fig (memory)* effacer

extinguisher [ɪkˈstɪŋgwɪʃə(r)] *n* extincteur *m*

extirpate [ˈekstəpeɪt] *vt Formal* extirper

extirpation [ˌekstəˈpeɪʃən] *n Formal* extirpation *f*

extn. (*written abbr* **extension**) poste *m*; **extn. 421** poste 421

extol, *Am* **extoll** [ɪk'stəʊl] *(pt & pp* **extolled,** *cont* **extolling)** *vt Formal (person, deed, talents)* faire l'éloge de; **to extol the virtues of the system** vanter les mérites du système, faire l'éloge du système; **to extol the beauty of nature** chanter les louanges de la nature

extort [ɪk'stɔːt] *vt (money)* extorquer, soutirer; *(confession, promise)* extorquer, arracher; **to extort money from sb** extorquer *ou* soutirer de l'argent à qn

extortion [ɪk'stɔːʃən] *n (of money, promise, confession)* extorsion *f*; **that's sheer extortion!** *(very expensive)* c'est du vol pur et simple!

extortionate [ɪk'stɔːʃənət] *adj (price, demand)* exorbitant, démesuré; **that's extortionate!** *(very expensive)* c'est exorbitant *ou* du vol!

extortionately [ɪk'stɔːʃənətlɪ] *adv* démesurément, excessivement

extortioner [ɪk'stɔːʃənə(r)], **extortionist** [ɪk'stɔːʃənɪst] *n* extorqueur(euse) *m,f*

extra ['ekstrə] **1** *adj* (**a**) *(additional)* supplémentaire; **there are some extra questions overleaf** il y a des questions supplémentaires au dos; **I put an extra jumper on** j'ai mis un pull en plus; **he takes extra revision classes** il prend des cours de révision supplémentaires *ou* en plus; **he made an extra effort to get there on time** il a redoublé d'efforts pour y arriver à l'heure; **as an extra precaution** pour plus de précaution; **an extra helping of cake** une autre part de gâteau; **no extra charge/cost** aucun supplément de prix/frais supplémentaire; **service/VAT is extra** le service/la TVA est en supplément; **extra pay** supplément *m* de salaire; **she asked for an extra £50** elle a demandé 50 livres de plus; **at no extra charge** sans supplément de prix

(**b**) *(spare)* en plus; **an extra sheet of paper** une feuille en plus

2 *adv* (**a**) *(extremely → polite, kind)* extrêmement; *(→ strong, white)* super-; **to work extra hard** travailler d'arrache-pied; **extra smart** *(dress, outfit)* superchic, ultrachic; **for an extra white wash** pour un linge extra-blanc

(**b**) *(in addition)* plus, davantage; **to pay extra for a double room** payer plus *ou* un supplément pour une chambre double

3 *n* (**a**) *(addition)* supplément *m*; **the paper comes with a business extra** le journal est vendu avec un supplément affaires; **a car with many extras** une voiture avec de nombreux accessoires en option

(**b**) *Cin & TV* figurant(e) *m,f*

(**c**) *(additional charge)* supplément *m*

(**d**) *(luxury)* **little extras** petits extras *mpl ou* luxes *mpl*

►► ***extra point*** *(in American football)* transformation *f*; ***extra time*** *(to pay, finish)* délai *m*; *Sport* prolongations *fpl*; **the game has gone into extra time** on joue les prolongations

extra- ['ekstrə] *pref* extra-; **extra-large** grande taille; **extra-strong** extra-solide

extra-budgetary *adj* extrabudgétaire

extracellular [ˌekstrə'seljələ(r)] *adj Biol* extracellulaire

extracranial [ˌekstrə'kreɪnɪəl] *adj Anat* extracrânien

extract 1 *vt* [ɪk'strækt] (**a**) *(take out → juice, oil, bullet)* extraire; *(→ tooth)* arracher, extraire; *(→ cork)* ôter, enlever; *(→ letter from pocket etc)* tirer (**from** de); **to extract a quotation from a passage** extraire *ou* tirer une citation d'un passage

(**b**) *(obtain → information)* soutirer, arracher; *(→ money)* soutirer; **to extract a confession from sb** soutirer *ou* arracher un aveu à qn

(**c**) *Math* **to extract the square root of a number** extraire la racine carrée d'un nombre

(**d**) *Comput (zipped file)* décompresser

2 *n* ['ekstrækt] (**a**) *(from book, piece of music)* extrait *m*; **selected extracts** *(from author, works)* morceaux *mpl* choisis

(**b**) *(substance)* extrait *m*, concentré *m*; *Pharm* extrait *m*, essence *f*; *Culin* **beef/malt/vegetable extract** extrait *m* de bœuf/de malt/de légumes

extraction [ɪk'strækʃən] *n* (**a**) *(removal → of juice, oil, bullet)* extraction *f*; *(→ of tooth)* extraction *f*, arrachage *m*; **the extraction of stone from the quarry** l'extraction de la pierre de la carrière; **she needs two extractions and three fillings** il faut lui arracher deux dents et en plomber trois

(**b**) *(descent)* extraction *f*; **of noble/humble extraction** de noble/modeste extraction; **he is of Scottish extraction** il est d'origine écossaise

extractor [ɪk'stræktə(r)] *n (machine, tool)* extracteur *m*; *(fan)* ventilateur *m*, aérateur *m*

►► ***extractor fan*** ventilateur *m*, aérateur *m*; ***extractor hood*** *(on stove)* hotte *f* aspirante

extracurricular [ˌekstrəkə'rɪkjʊlə(r)] *adj Sch* hors programme, extrascolaire; *Univ* hors programme

►► ***extracurricular activities*** activités *fpl* extrascolaires; *Fig Hum* frasques *fpl*

extraditable ['ekstrəˌdaɪtəbəl] *adj (person)* passible d'extradition; *(crime, offence)* qui justifie l'extradition

extradite ['ekstrədaɪt] *vt (send back)* extrader; *(procure extradition of)* obtenir l'extradition de; **the authorities were unable to extradite him from the USA** les autorités n'ont pas réussi à obtenir son extradition des États-Unis

extradition [ˌekstrə'dɪʃən] **1** *n* extradition *f*; **to request/to obtain the extradition of sb** demander/obtenir l'extradition de qn

2 *comp (order, warrant)* d'extradition

►► ***extradition treaty*** accord *m* d'extradition

extrados [ek'streɪdɒs] *n Archit* extrados *m*

extra-dry *adj (wine)* très sec (sèche); *(champagne, vermouth)* extra-dry *(inv)*

extra-fine *adj (flour, sugar)* extrafin, surfin

extragalactic [ˌekstrəgə'læktɪk] *adj* extragalactique

extrajudicial [ˌekstrədʒuː'dɪʃəl] *adj Law* extrajudiciaire

extralinguistic [ˌekstrəlɪŋ'gwɪstɪk] *adj* extralinguistique

extramarital [ˌekstrə'mærɪtəl] *adj* extraconjugal

►► ***extramarital relations*** relations *fpl* extraconjugales; ***extramarital sex*** rapports *mpl* extraconjugaux

extramural [ˌekstrə'mjʊərəl] *adj* (**a**) *Br Univ* **extramural lecturer** = enseignant qui donne des cours d'éducation permanente; **extramural course** = cours donné dans le cadre de l'éducation permanente; **Department of Extramural Studies** = service d'une université qui s'occupe de l'éducation permanente, ≃ Institut *m* d'éducation permanente

(**b**) *Am Univ (agency, funding)* extérieur à l'université; *(match, tournament)* interuniversitaire

(**c**) *Formal (district)* extra-muros

extraneous [ɪk'streɪnjəs] *adj* (**a**) *(irrelevant → idea, point, consideration, issue)* étranger, extérieur; **to be extraneous to sth** *(idea, point, issue)* être étranger à qch; *(detail)* être sans rapport avec qch (**b**) *(from outside → noise, force)* extérieur

Extranet ['ekstrənet] *n Comput* Extranet *m*

extraordinarily [ɪk'strɔːdənrəlɪ] *adv* (**a**) *(as intensifier)* extraordinairement, incroyablement; **that play was extraordinarily badly acted** cette pièce était incroyablement mal jouée; **it took an extraordinarily long time to get there** nous avons mis un temps incroyable pour arriver

(**b**) *(unusually)* extraordinairement, d'une manière inhabituelle; **extraordinarily, they escaped unscathed/he made no reference to the event in his speech** fait extraordinaire, ils s'en sont sortis sans une égratignure/il n'a pas fait référence à l'événement dans son discours

extraordinariness [ɪk'strɔːdənrɪnɪs] *n* caractère *m ou* nature *f* extraordinaire

extraordinary [ɪk'strɔːdənrɪ] *adj* (**a**) *(remarkable)* extraordinaire; **quite extraordinary!** absolument extraordinaire!; **(why,) that's** *or* **how extraordinary!** c'est extraordinaire *ou* incroyable!; **I find it extraordinary that you did not inform the police** je trouve incroyable *ou* extraordinaire que vous n'ayez pas prévenu la police

(**b**) *(surprising, unusual → person)* bizarre, singulier; *(→ house)* bizarre, curieux; *(→ appearance, outfit)* insolite, singulier; *(→ event)* bizarre, invraisemblable; *(→ behaviour, speech)* étonnant, surprenant

(**c**) *(additional → meeting, session)* extraordinaire

►► *Acct* ***extraordinary expenses*** frais *mpl* extraordinaires, dépenses *fpl* extraordinaires; *Com* ***extraordinary general meeting*** assemblée *f* générale extraordinaire; *Com* **to call an extraordinary general meeting of the shareholders** convoquer d'urgence les actionnaires; *Acct* ***extraordinary income*** produits *mpl* exceptionnels; *Acct* ***extraordinary item*** poste *m* extraordinaire; *Acct* ***extraordinary loss*** résultats *mpl* exceptionnels *(pertes)*; ***extraordinary profit*** résultats *mpl* exceptionnels *(profits)*

extraparliamentary [ˌekstrəˌpɑːlə'mentərɪ] *adj* extraparlementaire

extrapatrimonial [ˌekstrəpætrɪ'məʊnɪəl] *adj Law* extrapatrimonial

extrapolate [ɪk'stræpəleɪt] **1** *vt (infer from facts)* déduire par extrapolation; *Math* établir par extrapolation; **if we extrapolate these figures** *(use them as a basis)* si nous extrapolons à partir de ces chiffres; *(arrive at by extrapolation)* si nous déduisons ces chiffres par extrapolation; **to extrapolate a curve on a graph** tracer une courbe par extrapolation

2 *vi* extrapoler; **to extrapolate from sth** extrapoler à partir de qch

extrapolation [ɪkˌstræpə'leɪʃən] *n (gen) & Math* extrapolation *f*

extrapyramidal [ˌekstrəpɪ'ræmɪdəl] *adj Med* extrapyramidal

extrarenal [ˌekstrə'riːnəl] *adj Med* extrarénal

extrasensory [ˌekstrə'sensərɪ] *adj* extrasensoriel

►► ***extrasensory perception*** perception *f* extrasensorielle

extra-special 1 *n Journ (evening newspaper)* deuxième édition *f* spéciale

2 *adj* **you'll have to take extra-special care over it** il faudra que tu y fasses particulièrement attention; **an extra-special wine for those extra-special occasions** un grand vin pour les grandes occasions; **I've bought an extra-special bottle of wine for your birthday** j'ai acheté une très bonne bouteille de vin spécialement pour ton anniversaire

►► *Journ* ***extra-special edition*** *(of evening newspaper)* deuxième édition *f* spéciale

extra-statutory *adj* extrastatutaire

extrasystole [ˌekstrə'sɪstələ] *n Med* extrasystole *f*

extraterrestrial [ˌekstrətə'restrɪəl] **1** *adj* extraterrestre

2 *n* extraterrestre *mf*

extraterritorial ['ekstrəˌterɪ'tɔːrɪəl] *adj (possessions)* situé hors du territoire national; *(rights)* d'exterritorialité, d'extra-territorialité

extraterritoriality ['ekstrəterɪˌtɔːrɪ'ælətɪ] *n* exterritorialité *f*, extraterritorialité *f*

extrauterine [ˌekstrə'juːtəraɪn] *adj Med* extra-utérin

extravagance [ɪk'strævəgəns] *n* (**a**) *(wasteful spending)* folles dépenses *fpl*, prodigalités *fpl*; **she accused the government of extravagance** elle a accusé le gouvernement de dilapider le trésor public; **the extravagance of his tastes** ses goûts dispendieux *ou* de luxe (**b**) *(extravagant purchase)* folie *f*; **to allow oneself little extravagances** se permettre des petites folies (**c**) *(exaggerated nature → of behaviour, comparison)* extravagance *f*

extravagant [ɪk'strævəgənt] *adj* (**a**) *(wasteful, profligate → person)* dépensier, prodigue; *(→ tastes)* de luxe, dispendieux; *(→ lifestyle)* dispendieux; **that was much too extravagant of you** tu as fait des folies; **I think you're being a bit extravagant, having the central heating on all the time** je trouve que c'est du gaspillage de laisser le chauffage central allumé en permanence comme tu le fais; **to be extravagant with one's money** être gaspilleur *ou* dépensier, gaspiller son argent

(**b**) *(exaggerated → idea, opinion)* extravagant; *(→ claim, comparison)* exagéré; *(→ behaviour, prices)* extravagant, excessif; *(→ praise)* outré; **to make extravagant claims** avoir des prétentions exagérées; **extravagant claims have been made for the drug** certaines propriétés ont été attribuées abusivement à ce médicament; **his extravagant prose style** le style excessif de sa prose

extravagantly [ɪk'strævəgəntlɪ] *adv* (**a**) *(lavishly)* **to spend money extravagantly** jeter l'argent par les fenêtres; **to live extravagantly** mener grand train; **to entertain extravagantly** recevoir sans regarder à la dépense; **an extravagantly furnished room** une pièce meublée à grands frais *ou* luxueusement meublée; **extravagantly overpriced goods** marchandises à des prix excessifs

(**b**) *(exaggeratedly → behave, act, talk)* de manière extravagante; *(→ praise)* avec excès; **extravagantly worded claims** des affirmations *fpl* exagérées *ou* excessives

extravaganza [ɪkˌstrævəˈgænzə] *n (lavish production)* grand spectacle *m*; *(literary work, piece of music)* œuvre *f* fantaisiste; **jazz extravaganza** grand festival *m* de jazz; **the castle is a Baroque/Gothic extravaganza** le château est construit dans un style baroque/gothique fantaisie

extravasate [ekˈstrævəseɪt] *Med* **1** *vt* épancher

2 *vi* s'épancher

extravasation [ekˌstrævəˈseɪʃən] *n Med* épanchement *m*

extravehicular [ˌekstrəvɪˈhɪkjʊlə(r)] *adj Astron* extravéhiculaire

►► ***extravehicular activity*** = activité qui a lieu en dehors d'un engin spatial

extraversion, extravert *etc* = **extroversion, extrovert** *etc*

extra-virgin *adj (olive oil)* extra vierge

extreme [ɪkˈstriːm] **1** *adj* (**a**) *(heat, pain, views, measures)* extrême; **they live in extreme poverty** ils vivent dans une misère extrême; **to be in extreme pain** souffrir terriblement *ou* atrocement; **to be extreme in one's beliefs** être extrême dans ses convictions; **the extreme left wing of the party** l'aile d'extrême gauche du parti; **extreme old age** grand âge *m*; **an extreme case** un cas exceptionnel

(**b**) *(furthest away)* extrême; **at the extreme end of the platform** à l'extrémité du quai; **on the extreme right of the screen** à l'extrême droite de l'écran; **they are extreme opposites of the political spectrum** ils sont aux deux extrémités de l'éventail politique

2 *n* extrême *m*; **extremes of temperature** extrêmes *mpl* de température; **to go to extremes** exagérer; **to take** *or* **to carry sth to extremes, to go to extremes with sth** pousser qch à l'extrême; **to be driven to extremes** être poussé à bout; **to go from one extreme to the other** aller *ou* passer d'un extrême à l'autre; **don't go to the opposite extreme** ne tombe pas dans l'extrême inverse

3 in the extreme *adv* à l'extrême; **polite/careful in the extreme** poli/soigneux à l'extrême

►► *Cin & TV* ***extreme close-up*** plan *m* très rapproché; *Formal* ***the extreme penalty*** le dernier supplice; ***extreme sports*** sports *mpl* extrêmes; *Rel* ***extreme unction*** extrême-onction *f*

extremely [ɪkˈstriːmlɪ] *adv (very)* extrêmement

extremis [ɪkˈstriːmɪs] **in extremis** *adv Formal* à l'article de la mort; *Fig (as a last resort)* en dernier recours, au pire

extremism [ɪkˈstriːmɪzəm] *n Pol* extrémisme *m*

extremist [ɪkˈstriːmɪst] *Pol* **1** *adj* extrémiste

2 *n* extrémiste *mf*

extremity [ɪkˈstremətɪ] *(pl* **extremities***)* *n* (**a**) *(furthermost tip)* extrémité *f*; **at the southernmost extremity of the peninsula** à l'extrémité sud de la péninsule

(**b**) *(usu pl) (hand, foot)* **the extremities** les extrémités *fpl*

(**c**) *(extreme nature → of belief, view etc)* extrémité *f*

(**d**) *(adversity, danger)* extrémité *f*; **to be reduced to the last extremity** en être réduit à la dernière extrémité; **to help sb in his/her extremity** aider qn dans son malheur

(**e**) *(usu pl) (extreme measure)* extrémité *f*; **to resort to extremities** en venir à des extrêmes; **to drive sb to extremities** pousser *ou* conduire qn à des extrêmes

extremum [ɪkˈstriːməm] *n Math* extremum *m*

extricate [ˈekstrɪkeɪt] *vt (thing)* extirper, dégager; *(person)* dégager; **to extricate oneself from a tricky situation** se sortir *ou* se tirer d'une situation délicate; **to extricate oneself from a boring conversation** s'échapper d'une conversation ennuyeuse

extrication [ˌekstrɪˈkeɪʃən] *n* dégagement *m*

extrinsic [ekˈstrɪnsɪk] *adj* extrinsèque

►► *Fin* ***extrinsic value*** valeur *f* extrinsèque

extrinsically [ekˈstrɪnsɪkəlɪ] *adv* extrinsèquement

extrorse [ekˈstrɔːs] *adj Bot* extrorse

extroversion [ˌekstrəˈvɜːʃən] *n* extraversion *f*, extroversion *f*

extrovert [ˈekstrəvɜːt] **1** *adj* extraverti, extroverti

2 *n* extraverti(e) *m,f*, extroverti(e) *m,f*; **he's an extrovert** c'est un extraverti

extroverted [ˈekstrəvɜːtɪd] *adj* extraverti, extroverti

extrude [ɪkˈstruːd] **1** *vt* (**a**) *Tech (metals, plastics)* extruder (**b**) *Formal (force out → lava)* extruder

2 *vi (protrude)* déborder, s'avancer

extruded [ɪkˈstruːdɪd] *adj Tech* extrudé

extrusion [ɪkˈstruːʒən] *n* (**a**) *Tech (of metal, plastic)* extrusion *f* (**b**) *Formal (action)* extraction *f* (**c**) *(protrusion)* extrusion *f*

extrusive [ɪkˈstruːsɪv] *adj Geol* effusif

exuberance [ɪgˈzjuːbərəns] *n* (**a**) *(of person, writing)* exubérance *f*; **to be full of exuberance** être plein d'exubérance; **youthful/natural exuberance** exubérance *f* juvénile/naturelle (**b**) *(of vegetation)* exubérance *f*, luxuriance *f*

exuberant [ɪgˈzjuːbərənt] *adj* (**a**) *(person, mood, style)* exubérant; *(health, vitality)* débordant; **she felt exuberant at the news** la nouvelle la remplit d'une joie exubérante (**b**) *(vegetation)* exubérant, luxuriant

exuberantly [ɪgˈzjuːbərəntlɪ] *adv* avec exubérance; **exuberantly cheerful** d'une gaieté exubérante; **exuberantly healthy** débordant de santé

exudate [ˈeksjʊdeɪt] *n Biol & Bot* exsudat *m*

exudation [eksjuˈdeɪʃən] *n (gen) & Biol & Bot* exsudation *f*

exude [ɪgˈzjuːd] **1** *vi (gen) & Biol & Bot* exsuder

2 *vt Biol & Bot (blood, sap)* exsuder; *Fig (confidence, love)* déborder de; **she exudes health** elle respire la santé; **he exudes (an air of) confidence/well-being/charm** un halo de confiance en soi/de bien-être/de charme se dégage de tout son être

exult [ɪgˈzʌlt] *vi (rejoice)* exulter, jubiler; *(triumph)* exulter; **to exult at** *or* **in one's success** *(rejoice)* se réjouir de son succès; **to exult over defeated opponents** *(triumph)* exulter de la défaite de ses adversaires

exultant [ɪgˈzʌltənt] *adj (feeling, shout, look)* d'exultation; *(mood, crowd)* jubilant; **to look exultant** avoir l'air d'exulter; **to be** *or* **to feel exultant (at)** exulter (de)

exultantly [ɪgˈzʌltəntlɪ] *adv* avec exultation

exultation [ˌegzʌlˈteɪʃən] *n* exultation *f*

exurban [eksˈɜːbən] *adj Am (in the outer suburbs)* de la grande banlieue; *(rural)* rural

exurbia [eksˈɜːbɪə] *n Am* grande banlieue *f* résidentielle

exuviae [ɪgˈzjuːvɪˌiː] *n Zool* exuvie *f*

ex vivo [-ˈvaɪvəʊ] *Med* **1** *adj* ex vivo

2 *adv* ex vivo

ex-voto [-ˈvəʊtəʊ] *Rel* **1** *n* ex-voto *m inv*

2 *adj* **an ex-voto offering** un ex-voto

ex-wife *n* ex-femme *f*

EYE [aɪ] *(cont* **eyeing** *or* **eying***)* **1** *n* (**a**) *(organ)* œil *m*; **to have green eyes** avoir les yeux verts; **a girl with green eyes** une fille aux yeux verts; **before your very eyes!** sous vos yeux!; **look me in the eye and say that** regarde-moi bien dans les yeux et dis-le moi; **I saw it with my own eyes** je l'ai vu de mes yeux vu *ou* de mes propres yeux; **to open/close one's eyes** ouvrir/fermer les yeux; **with one's eyes closed/open** les yeux fermés/ouverts; *Fig* **she can't keep her eyes open** elle dort debout; **I could do it with my eyes closed** je pourrais le faire les yeux fermés; **he went into it with his eyes open** il s'y est lancé en toute connaissance de cause; **to have the sun/the light in one's eyes** avoir le soleil/la lumière dans les yeux; **to look sb straight in the eye** regarder qn droit dans les yeux; **at eye level** au niveau des yeux

(**b**) *(gaze)* regard *m*; **her eyes fell on the letter** son regard est tombé sur la lettre; **the film looks at the world through the eyes of a child** dans ce film, on voit le monde à travers les yeux d'un enfant; **with a critical eye** d'un œil critique; **I couldn't believe my eyes** je n'en croyais pas mes yeux; **all eyes were upon her** elle était au centre de tous les regards, tous les regards étaient posés sur elle

(**c**) *Mil* **eyes left/right!** tête à gauche/à droite!; **eyes front!** fixe!

(**d**) *Sewing (of needle)* chas *m*, œil *m*; *(eyelet)* œillet *m*

(**e**) *(of potato, twig)* œil *m*

(**f**) *(of hurricane)* œil *m*, centre *m*; **the eye of the storm** l'œil du cyclone; *Fig* **at the eye of the storm** dans l'œil du cyclone

(**g**) *(photocell)* œil *m* électrique

(**h**) *(for hammer handle)* emmanchure *f*; *(for axe blade)* toyère *f*

(**i**) *(idioms)* **as far as the eye can see** à perte de vue; **to keep one's eyes and ears open** avoir l'œil et l'oreille aux aguets; **to open sb's eyes (to sth)** ouvrir les yeux à qn (sur qch), dessiller les yeux à qn (sur qch); **the incident opened his eyes to the truth about her** l'incident lui ouvrit les yeux sur ce qu'elle était vraiment; **we can't close** *or* **shut our eyes to the problem** on ne peut pas fermer les yeux sur ce problème; **to close one's eyes to the evidence** se refuser à l'évidence; **they can't close their eyes to the fact that the company's at fault** ils sont bien obligés d'admettre que la société est en faute; **I could do it with my eyes shut** je pourrais le faire les yeux fermés; **for your eyes only** ultra-confidentiel; **in this job you need to have a good eye for detail** dans ce métier il faut être très méticuleux; **to have an eye for a bargain** savoir reconnaître une bonne affaire; *Br* **to get one's eye in** prendre ses repères; **he only has eyes for her** il n'a d'yeux que pour elle; **the boss has his eye on Smith for the job** le patron a Smith en vue pour le poste; **he has his eye on the gold medal** il vise la médaille d'or; **she has her eye on the mayor's position** elle vise la mairie; **the police have had their eye on him for some time** cela fait un certain temps que la police l'a à l'œil; **he wants to buy an apartment, in fact he's already got his eye on one** il veut acheter un appartement, et d'ailleurs il en a déjà un en vue; **he always has an eye for** *or* **to the main chance** il ne perd jamais de vue ses propres intérêts; **in my/her eyes** à mes/ses yeux; **in the eyes of the law/of the Church** aux yeux *ou* au regard de la loi/de l'Église; **to run** *or* **to cast one's eye over sth** jeter un coup d'œil à qch; **she ran an eye over the contract** elle a parcouru le contrat; **to try to catch sb's eye** essayer d'attirer le regard de qn; **keep your eye on the ball** fixez *ou* regardez bien la balle; **could you keep your eye on the children/the house?** pourriez-vous surveiller les enfants/la maison?; **I have to keep an eye on him** il faut que je l'aie à l'œil; **I couldn't keep my eyes off him/it** je ne pouvais pas en détacher mes yeux; **she keeps an eye on things** elle a l'œil à tout; **to keep a close eye on sth** surveiller qch de près; **keep an eye on the situation** suivez de près la situation; **to keep one's eye on the ball** *(gen)* ne pas quitter la balle des yeux; *Golf* fixer la balle; *Fig* être vigilant; **keep your eyes on the road** regarde la route; **to keep one's eyes open for sth** être attentif à qch; **keep your eyes open** *or* **an eye out for a filling station** essayez de repérer une station service; **keep an eye out for anyone trying to sell it** soyez à l'affût au cas où quelqu'un essaierait de le vendre; *Fam* **keep your eyes skinned** *or* **peeled** restez vigilant❑; **you can see that with half an eye** cela saute aux yeux; **anyone with half an eye can see it's a fake** du premier coup d'œil n'importe qui verrait que c'est un faux; **with half an eye on the weather** sans quitter le ciel des yeux; **the children were all eyes** les enfants n'en perdaient pas une miette; **an eye for an eye (and a tooth for a tooth)** œil pour œil, (dent pour dent); **his eyes are too big for his stomach** il a les yeux plus grands que le ventre; *Fam* **to give sb the eye** *(flirt)* faire de l'œil à qn; *(give signal)* faire signe à qn (d'un clin d'œil)❑; **he has eyes in the back of his head** il a des yeux derrière la tête; **to set** *or* **lay eyes on sth** poser les yeux sur qch, apercevoir qch; **it was the biggest fish I'd ever laid eyes on** c'était le plus gros poisson que j'aie jamais vu; **I've never set** *or* **laid** *or Fam* **clapped eyes on her** je ne l'ai jamais vue de ma vie; **to make eyes at sb** faire de l'œil à qn; *Fam* **my eye!** mon œil!; **she and I don't see eye to eye** *(disagree)* elle ne voit pas les choses du même œil que moi, elle n'est pas de mon avis; *(dislike one another)* elle et moi, nous ne nous entendons pas; *Fam* **that's one in the eye for him!** ça lui fera les pieds!; **there's more to this than meets the eye** *(suspicious)* on ne connaît pas les dessous de l'affaire; *(difficult)* c'est moins simple que cela n'en a l'air; **there's more to her than meets the eye** elle gagne à être connue; **we're up to our eyes in it!** *(overworked)* on a du travail jusque là!; *(in deep trouble)* on est dans les ennuis jusqu'au cou!

2 *vt* regarder, mesurer du regard; **the child eyed the man warily** l'enfant dévisagea l'homme avec circonspection; **she stood eyeing the sweets counter** elle restait là à lorgner les bonbons; **to eye sth hungrily** dévorer qch du regard; **to eye sb up and down** regarder qn de la tête aux pieds

3 with an eye to *prep* **with an eye to sth/to doing sth** en vue de qch/de faire qch; **with an eye to the future** en vue *ou* en prévision de l'avenir

►► ***eye bank*** banque *f* des yeux; ***eye camera*** caméra *f* oculaire; ***eye contact*** croisement *m* des regards; **to establish eye contact (with sb)** croiser le regard (de qn); **to maintain eye contact (with sb)** regarder (qn) dans les yeux; **she always avoids eye contact (with me)** elle évite tout le temps mon regard; *Am* ***eye doctor*** ophtalmologue *mf*; ***eye drops*** gouttes *fpl* pour les yeux; ***eye hospital*** centre *m* hospitalier d'ophtalmologie; ***eye makeup*** maquillage *m* pour les yeux; ***eye makeup remover*** démaquillant *m* pour les yeux; ***eye movement camera*** caméra *f* oculaire; ***eye rhyme*** rime *f* pour l'œil; ***eye socket*** orbite *f*; ***eye specialist*** ophtalmologue *mf*; ***eye test*** examen *m* de la vue

►**eye up** *vt sep Fam* (**a**) *(with sexual interest)* **to eye up the girls/boys** reluquer les filles/les garçons; **he eyed her up** il la regardée de la tête aux pieds (**b**) *(estimate strength of → opponent)* jauger (d'un coup d'œil)

'For Your Eyes Only' *Fleming, Glen* 'Rien que pour vos yeux'

Eyes on the prize
Il s'agit d'une phrase extraite d'une chanson du mouvement pour les droits civils, aux États-Unis: "I know one thing we did right/Was the day we started to fight/Keep your eyes on the prize/Hold on, hold on" ("je sais que l'on a eu raison d'entamer la lutte, ne perdez jamais votre objectif de vue, tenez bon, tenez bon"). Cette phrase symbolise la lutte menée par le mouvement pour les droits civils en Amérique et figure dans de nombreux titres de livres et de films. On l'utilise également dans toute situation où des gens luttent pour l'obtention de droits civils, quel que soit le pays.
En anglais américain, on utilise aussi cette expression de façon allusive lorsque quelqu'un doit se concentrer sur l'objectif à atteindre; on dira par exemple **this year the Pistons need to keep their eyes firmly on the prize of the championship** ("cette année les Pistons doivent faire tout leur possible pour gagner le championnat").

eyeball ['aɪbɔːl] **1** *n* globe *m* oculaire; *Fig* **doped** *or* **drugged (up) to the eyeballs** drogué à mort; **eyeball to eyeball (with)** nez à nez (avec)
2 *vt Fam* regarder fixement❑, reluquer

eyeball-to-eyeball *adj Fam* nez à nez❑; **an eyeball-to-eyeball confrontation** une confrontation entre quatre yeux *ou* quat'z'yeux, un face-à-face *inv*

eyebath ['aɪbɑːθ, *pl* -bɑːðz] *n Br Med* œillère *f*

eyebolt ['aɪbɒlt] *n Tech* tire-fond *m*

eyebright ['aɪbraɪt] *n Bot* euphraise *f*

eyebrow ['aɪbraʊ] *n* sourcil *m*; **to raise one's eyebrows** lever les sourcils; *Fig* **(some) eyebrows were raised at this suggestion** *(in disapproval)* cette proposition a suscité des grimaces de désapprobation; *(in astonishment)* cette proposition a suscité de l'étonnement; **her behaviour raised a few eyebrows** son comportement en a fait tiquer quelques-uns; **to be up to one's eyebrows in sth** être dans qch jusqu'au cou

►► ***eyebrow pencil*** crayon *m* à sourcils; ***eyebrow tweezers*** pince *f* à épiler

eye-catcher *n* tire-l'œil *mf*

eye-catching *adj (colour, dress)* qui attire l'œil; *(poster, title)* accrocheur, tapageur

eyecup ['aɪkʌp] *n Am Med* œillère *f*

-eyed [aɪd] *suff* aux yeux...; **blue-eyed** aux yeux bleus; **she stared at him, wide-eyed** elle le regardait, les yeux écarquillés; **one-eyed** borgne, qui n'a qu'un œil

eyeful ['aɪfʊl] *n* (**a**) *(of dirt, dust)* **I got an eyeful of sand** j'ai reçu du sable plein les yeux (**b**) *Fam* **to get an eyeful (of sb/sth)** mater (qn/qch); **get an eyeful of that!** mate un peu ça!; **she's quite an eyeful!** elle est vachement bien foutue!

eyeglass ['aɪglɑːs] **1** *n (monocle)* monocle *m*
2 eyeglasses *npl Am (spectacles)* lunettes *fpl*

eyehole ['aɪhəʊl] *n* (**a**) *(peephole → in mask)* trou *m* pour les yeux; *(→ in door, wall)* judas *m* (**b**) *(eyelet)* œillet *m* (**c**) *Fam (eye socket)* orbite❑ *f*

eyelash ['aɪlæʃ] *n* cil *m*

►► ***eyelash curlers*** recourbe-cils *m inv*

eyeless ['aɪlɪs] *adj (without eyes)* sans yeux; *(blind)* aveugle

'Eyeless in Gaza' *Huxley* 'La Paix des profondeurs'

eyelet ['aɪlɪt] *n* (**a**) *(gen)* & *Sewing* œillet *m* (**b**) *(peephole → in mask)* trou *m* pour les yeux; *(→ in door, wall)* judas *m*

eye-level *adj* qui est au niveau des yeux

►► ***eye-level grill*** gril *m* surélevé

eyelid ['aɪlɪd] *n* paupière *f*

eye-line *n TV & Cin* direction *f* du regard

eyeliner ['aɪˌlaɪnə(r)] *n* eye-liner *m*

eye-opener *n Fam* (**a**) *(surprise)* révélation❑ *f*, surprise❑ *f*; **her behaviour was a real eye-opener for him** son comportement lui a ouvert les yeux; **the experience proved a bit of an eye-opener!** l'expérience a été assez révélatrice! (**b**) *Am (drink)* = petit verre pris au réveil

eye-opening *adj Fam* qui ouvre les yeux❑, révélateur❑; **it was very eye-opening** ça a été très révélateur

eyepatch ['aɪpætʃ] *n (after operation)* cache *m*, pansement *m (sur l'œil)*; *(permanent)* bandeau *m*

eyepiece ['aɪpiːs] *n* oculaire *m*

eye-popper *n Am Fam* **to be an eye-popper** valoir vraiment le coup d'œil

eye-popping *adj Am Fam* sensationnel

eyeshade ['aɪʃeɪd] *n* visière *f*

eyeshadow ['aɪʃædəʊ] *n* fard *m* à paupières

►► ***eyeshadow brush*** pinceau *m* pour fard à paupières

eyesight ['aɪsaɪt] *n* vue *f*; **to have good eyesight** avoir une bonne vue *ou* de bons yeux; **his eyesight is failing** sa vue baisse; **to lose one's eyesight** perdre la vue

eyesore ['aɪsɔː(r)] *n* horreur *f*; **the building is an eyesore** le bâtiment est une horreur

eyespot ['aɪspɒt] *n Bot* stigmate *m*

eyestrain ['aɪstreɪn] *n* fatigue *f* des yeux; **computer screens can cause eyestrain** les ordinateurs fatiguent les yeux; **to suffer from eyestrain** avoir la vue fatiguée

Eyetie ['aɪtaɪ] *n Br Fam* Rital(e) *m,f*, = terme injurieux désignant un Italien

eyetooth ['aɪtuːθ] (*pl* **eyeteeth** [-tiːθ]) *n* canine *f* supérieure; *Fam* **I'd give my eyeteeth for a bike like that** je donnerais n'importe quoi pour avoir un vélo comme ça

eyewash ['aɪwɒʃ] *n Med* collyre *m*; *Br Fam Fig* **that's a load of eyewash!** *(nonsense)* c'est de la foutaise!; *(boasting)* ce n'est que de la frime!

eyewear ['aɪweə(r)] *n (UNCOUNT)* lunettes *fpl*

eyewink ['aɪwɪŋk] *n Am* coup *m* d'œil; **to take an eyewink at sb/sth** jeter un coup d'œil à qn/sur qch

eyewitness [ˌaɪ'wɪtnɪs] **1** *n* témoin *m* oculaire
2 *comp (description)* d'un témoin oculaire

►► ***eyewitness account*** récit *m* de témoin oculaire

eyot [eɪt] *n Br Arch* îlot *m*

eyra ['aɪərə] *n Zool* eyra *m*

eyrie ['ɪərɪ] *n* aire *f (d'aigle)*

Ezekiel [ɪ'ziːkɪəl] *pr n Bible* Ézéchiel

e-zine, ezine ['iːziːn] *n Comput* ezine *m*, e-zine *m*, magazine *m* électronique

Ezra ['ezrə] *pr n Bible* Ezra

F

F[1], f[1] [ef] **1** *n* (**a**) *(letter)* F, f *m inv*; **two f's** deux f; **F for Freddie** ≃ F comme François (**b**) *Sch* **to get an F** être recalé (**c**) *Mus* fa *m*; **in F** en fa
2 *adj Mus (string)* de fa
►► *Br Euph* ***the F word*** = le mot "fuck", ≃ le mot de Cambronne

F[2] (**a**) (*written abbr* **Fahrenheit**) F (**b**) (*written abbr* **franc**) F (**c**) *Chem* (*written abbr* **fluorine**) F (**d**) *Phys* (*written abbr* **farad**) F (**e**) *Phys* (*written abbr* **force**) F (**f**) *Phys* (*written abbr* **frequency**) F (**g**) (*written abbr* **false**) F

f[2] (**a**) (*written abbr* **fathom**) brasse *f (mesure)* (**b**) (*written abbr* **female**) f (**c**) (*written abbr* **feminine**) f, fém (**d**) *Math* (*written abbr* **function of**) f de (**e**) *Mus* (*written abbr* **forte**) f

f.a., FA[1] [e'feɪ] *n* (*abbr* **fanny adams**) *Br Fam* **sweet f.a.** que dalle

FA[2] [e'feɪ] *n* (*abbr* **Football Association**) **the FA** = la Fédération britannique de football
►► ***the FA cup*** = championnat de football

fa = **fah**

FAA [ˌefeɪ'eɪ] *n Am* (*abbr* **Federal Aviation Administration**) = direction fédérale de l'aviation civile américaine

faa [ˌefeɪ'eɪ] *adj Com* (*abbr* **free of all average**) franc de toute avarie

fab [fæb] *adj Fam* super, génial

Fabian ['feɪbjən] **1** *adj* temporisateur; *Pol* Fabien
2 *n Pol* Fabien(enne) *m,f*
►► *Pol* ***the Fabian Society*** = groupe socialiste de la fin du XIXème siècle en Grande-Bretagne

> **THE FABIAN SOCIETY**
>
> Cette association, fondée en 1883 dans le cadre de l'émergence du socialisme en Grande-Bretagne, était composée en grande partie d'intellectuels. Elle avait pour but de parvenir à un "changement graduel et pacifique" de la société capitaliste. Son influence se fit sentir jusque dans les années 30.

Fabianism ['feɪbjənɪzəm] *n Pol* fabianisme *m*

Fabianist ['feɪbjənɪst] *n Pol* = partisan des Fabiens

fable ['feɪbəl] *n* (**a**) *(legend)* fable *f*, légende *f*; *Literature* fable *f* (**b**) *(false account)* fable *f*

fabled ['feɪbəld] *adj (famous)* légendaire, célèbre; *(fictitious)* légendaire, fabuleux

fabliau ['fæblɪˌəʊ] (*pl* **fabliaux** [-ˌəʊz]) *n Literature* fabliau *m*

fabric ['fæbrɪk] *n* (**a**) *(cloth)* tissu *m*, étoffe *f*; **silk, woollen and cotton fabrics** soieries *fpl*, lainages *mpl* et cotonnades *fpl* (**b**) *(framework, structure)* structure *f*; *Fig* **the fabric of society** le tissu social
►► ***fabric conditioner, fabric softener*** assouplissant *m* (textile)

fabricate ['fæbrɪkeɪt] *vt* (**a**) *(manufacture)* fabriquer; *(produce)* produire (**b**) *(story)* inventer, fabriquer; *(document)* faire un faux de, contrefaire

fabrication [ˌfæbrɪ'keɪʃən] *n* (**a**) *(manufacture)* fabrication *f*; *(production)* production *f* (**b**) *(falsehood)* fabrication *f*; **it's pure fabrication** c'est de la pure invention; **a pure fabrication** *(lie)* une histoire inventée de toutes pièces

fabricator ['fæbrɪˌkeɪtə(r)] *n* (**a**) *(manufacturer)* constructeur(trice) *m,f*, fabricant(e) *m,f* (**b**) *(of story, lie)* fabricateur(trice) *m,f*; *(of document)* contrefacteur(trice) *m,f*

fabulation [ˌfæbjʊ'leɪʃən] *n Literary* fabulation *f*

fabulist ['fæbjʊlɪst] *n Literary (storyteller)* fabuliste *mf*; *(liar)* fabulateur(trice) *m,f*, menteur(euse) *m,f*

fabulous ['fæbjʊləs] *adj* (**a**) *(astounding)* fabuleux, incroyable; **fabulous wealth** une fortune fabuleuse *ou* incroyable (**b**) *Fam (marvellous)* génial; **we had a fabulous time** on s'est amusés comme des fous; **it's fabulous!** c'est super! (**c**) *(mythical → beast, character, city)* fabuleux

fabulously ['fæbjʊləslɪ] *adv* fabuleusement; **a fabulously successful actor** un acteur qui a un succès fabuleux *ou* fou; **fabulously rich** fabuleusement riche

facade, façade [fə'sɑːd] *n Archit & Fig* façade *f*

FACE [feɪs]

visage	► **1 (a), (c)**
figure	► **1 (a)**
expression	► **1 (b)**
apparence	► **1 (c)**
façade	► **1 (d)**
face	► **1 (d) – (f)**
surface	► **1 (f)**
faire face à	► **2 (a) – (d)**
être menacé de	► **2 (e)**
se présenter à	► **2 (f)**
revêtir	► **2 (g)**
se tourner	► **3 (a)**
être orienté	► **3 (b)**

1 *n* (**a**) *(part of body)* visage *m*, figure *f*; **a handsome face** un beau visage; **injuries to the face** blessures *fpl* à la face *ou* au visage; **I know that face** je connais cette tête-là, cette tête me dit quelque chose; **I have a good memory for faces** j'ai une bonne mémoire des visages, je suis très physionomiste; **she was lying face down** *or* **downwards** elle était étendue à plat ventre *ou* face contre terre; **she was lying face up** *or* **upwards** elle était étendue sur le dos; **he told her to her face what he thought of her** il lui a dit en face *ou* sans ambages ce qu'il pensait d'elle; **to look sb in the face** regarder qn en face *ou* dans les yeux; *Fig* **I'll never be able to look him in the face again!** je n'oserai plus jamais le regarder en face!; *Fam* **to put on one's face** *(put make-up on)* se maquiller❑; *Fam Hum* **he has a face only a mother could love** ce n'est pas une beauté

(**b**) *(expression)* mine *f*, expression *f*; **to make** *or* **to pull a face at sb** faire une grimace à qn; **to pull a funny face** faire des simagrées, faire le singe; **what a grumpy face!** quel air renfrogné!; **she put on a brave** *or* **bold face** elle a fait bon visage *ou* bonne contenance; **put a good** *or* **brave face on it** vous n'avez qu'à faire *ou* faites contre mauvaise fortune bon cœur

(**c**) *(appearance)* apparence *f*, aspect *m*; **it changed the face of the town** cela a changé la physionomie de la ville; **this is the ugly face of capitalism** voici l'autre visage *ou* le mauvais côté du capitalisme; **the face of Britain is changing** le visage de la Grande-Bretagne est en train de changer; **Communism with a human face** le communisme à visage humain

(**d**) *(front → of building)* façade *f*, devant *m*; *(→ of cliff)* paroi *f*; *(→ of mountain)* face *f*

(**e**) *Geom* face *f*

(**f**) *(of clock, watch)* cadran *m*; *(of coin)* face *f*; *(of page)* recto *m*; *(of playing card)* face *f*, dessous *m*; *(of the earth)* surface *f*; *(of bat, golf club, tennis raquet)* surface *f* de frappe; *(of crystal)* facette *f*, plan *m*; *(of hammer)* plat *m*; **it fell face down/up** *(gen)* c'est tombé du mauvais/bon côté; *(card, coin)* c'est tombé face en dessous/en dessus; *Fig* **she has vanished off the face of the earth** elle a complètement disparu de la circulation; **my keys can't just have disappeared off the face of the earth!** mes clés n'ont pas pu se volatiliser tout de même!

(**g**) *Br Fam (impudence)* culot *m*, toupet *m*

(**h**) *Mining* front *m* de taille

(**i**) *Typ (typeface)* œil *m*; *(font)* fonte *f*

(**j**) *(idioms)* **she laughed/shut the door in his face** elle lui a ri/fermé la porte au nez; **to lose/to save face** perdre/sauver la face; **to suffer a loss of face** subir une humiliation; **he set his face against our marriage** il s'est élevé contre notre mariage; **he won't show his face here again!** il ne risque pas de remettre les pieds ici!; **her plans blew up in her face** tous ses projets se sont retournés contre elle; *Br Fam* **to be off one's face** *(drunk)* être pété *ou* bourré; *(on drugs)* être défoncé

2 *vt* (**a**) *(turn towards)* faire face à; **I turned and faced him** je me retournai et lui fis face; **face the wall** tournez-vous vers le mur

(**b**) *(be turned towards)* faire face à, être en face de; **he faced the blackboard** il était face au *ou* faisait face au tableau; **she was facing him** elle était en face de lui; **facing one another** l'un en face de l'autre, en vis-à-vis; **we were facing one another** nous étions face à face, nous nous faisions face; **to face the front** regarder devant soi; **a room facing the courtyard** une chambre sur cour *ou* donnant sur la cour; **the house faces south** la maison est orientée *ou* exposée au sud; **my chair faced the window** ma chaise était *ou* faisait face à la fenêtre; **two rows of seats facing one another** deux rangées de sièges en vis-à-vis; **facing page 9** en regard *ou* en face de la page 9

(**c**) *(confront)* faire face *ou* front à, affronter; **he dared not face me** il n'a pas osé me rencontrer face à face; **to face sb with sth** confronter qn à qch; **to be faced with sth** être obligé de faire face à *ou* être confronté à qch; **I was faced with having to pay for the damage** j'ai été obligé *ou* dans l'obligation de payer les dégâts; **he was faced with a difficult choice** il était confronté à un choix difficile; **to be faced with a decision** être confronté à une décision; **faced with the evidence** devant l'évidence, confronté à l'évidence; **we'll just have to face the music** il va falloir affronter la tempête *ou* faire front

(**d**) *(deal with)* faire face à; **to face a problem** faire face à *ou* s'attaquer à un problème; **I can't face telling her** je n'ai pas le courage de le lui dire; **we must face facts** il faut voir les choses comme elles sont; **they won't face the fact that it's too late** ils ne veulent pas se rendre à l'évidence et admettre qu'il est trop tard; **let's face it, we're lost** admettons-le, nous sommes perdus; **face it, she's not coming back** accepte-le, elle ne reviendra pas

(**e**) *(risk → disaster)* être menacé de; *(→ defeat, fine, prison)* encourir, risquer; **she faces the possibility of having to move** elle risque d'être obligée de déménager; **faced with eviction, he paid his rent** face à *ou* devant la perspective d'une expulsion, il a payé son loyer; **thousands face unemployment** des milliers de personnes sont menacés de chômage

(**f**) *(of problem, situation)* se présenter à; **the problem facing us** le problème qui se pose (à nous) *ou* devant lequel on se trouve; **the difficulties facing the EC** les difficultés que rencontre la CEE *ou* auxquelles la CEE doit faire face

(**g**) *(cover)* revêtir (**with** de)

3 *vi* (**a**) *(turn)* se tourner; *(be turned)* être tourné; **she was facing towards the camera** elle était tournée vers *ou* elle faisait face à l'appareil photo; *Am Mil* **right face!** à droite, droite!; *Am Mil* **about face!** demi-tour!

(**b**) *(house, window)* être orienté; *(look over)* faire face à, donner sur; **a terrace facing south** une terrasse orientée au sud; **the terrace faces towards the mountain** la terrasse donne sur la montagne; **facing forwards** *(in bus, train)* dans le sens de la marche; **facing backwards** dans le mauvais sens

4 in the face of *prep* **she succeeded in the face of fierce opposition** elle a réussi malgré une opposition farouche; **in the face of danger** devant le danger; **in the face of adversity** face à l'adversité

5 on the face of it *adv* à première vue

6 face to face *adv* face à face; **she brought him face to face with her father** elle l'a confronté avec son père; **it brought us face to face with the problem** cela nous a mis directement devant le problème

►► *Am* ***face amount*** *(of bank note, traveller's cheque)* valeur *f* nominale; *(of stamp)* valeur *f* faciale; ***face card*** figure *f (de jeu de cartes)*; ***face cream*** crème *f* pour le visage; *Br* ***face flannel*** ≃ gant *m* de toilette; *Fam Hum* ***face fungus*** poils *mpl* du visage ❑; *Metal* ***face hardening*** trempe *f* superficielle; ***face mask*** *(cosmetic)* masque *m* (de beauté); *Sport* masque *m*; ***face pack*** masque *m* (de beauté); ***face powder*** poudre *f*; ***face scrub*** *(cosmetic)* exfoliant *m*; *TV & Cin* ***face shot*** plan *m* de visage; *Am* ***face time*** *(meeting)* = rencontre en face à face entre deux personnes *(par opposition aux contacts par téléphone ou courrier électronique)*; *(on TV)* temps *m* de présence à l'écran; **we need some face time to solve this** il faut qu'on se voie pour régler ça; ***face towel*** serviette *f* de toilette; ***face value*** *(of bank note, traveller's cheque)* valeur *f* nominale; *(of stamp)* valeur *f* faciale; *Fig* **I took her remark at face value** j'ai pris sa remarque au pied de la lettre *ou* pour argent comptant; **don't take him at face value** ne le jugez pas sur les apparences

►**face about** *vi Mil* faire demi-tour

►**face down** *vt sep* tenir tête à

►**face off** *vi Am Sport (teams)* se rencontrer

►**face on to** *vt insep (garden, street)* donner sur

►**face out** *vt sep Br (problems, difficult situation)* surmonter; *(person)* résister à; **to face it out** ne pas broncher

►**face up to** *vt insep* faire face à, affronter; **he won't face up to the fact that he's getting older** il ne veut pas admettre qu'il vieillit

---

faceache [feɪseɪk] *n* (**a**) *(pain)* névralgie *f* faciale (**b**) *Br Fam* **to be a faceache** *(ugly)* être une mocheté; *(miserable)* toujours faire la gueule

facecloth ['feɪsklɒθ] *n Br* ≃ gant *m* de toilette

-faced [feɪst] *suff* au visage...; **round-faced** au visage rond; **white-faced** blême

faceguard ['feɪsgɑːd] *n* ≃ visière *f* de protection

face-harden *vt Metal* aciérer, cémenter

faceless ['feɪslɪs] *adj* anonyme

face lift *n* (**a**) *(surgery)* lifting *m*; **to have a face lift** se faire faire un lifting (**b**) *Fam (renovation)* restauration ❑ *f*; **the house could do with a face-lift** la maison a besoin d'être ravalée *ou* retapée; **the school has had a face-lift** l'école a été remise à neuf ❑

face-off *n Sport* remise *f* en jeu; *Fig* confrontation *f*

faceplate ['feɪspleɪt] *n Tech (on lathe)* plateau *m* de tour

facer ['feɪsə(r)] *n* (**a**) *Tech (tool)* planeuse *f* (**b**) *Br Fam (problem)* os *m*, tuile *f*; **that's a facer!** quelle tuile!

face-saver *n* = quelque chose qui sauve la face; **the new legislation is just a face-saver** le gouvernement passe ces nouvelles lois simplement pour sauver la face

face-saving *adj* qui sauve la face; **a face-saving measure** une mesure qui sauve la face

facet ['fæsɪt] *(Br pt & pp* **facetted,** *cont* **facetting,** *Am pt & pp* **faceted,** *cont* **faceting)** **1** *n* (**a**) *(gen) & Entom* facette *f* (**b**) *(aspect)* aspect *m*, facette *f*

2 *vt (precious stone)* facetter

faceted ['fæsɪtɪd] *adj* à facettes

facetiae [fə'siːʃɪ,iː] *npl* (**a**) *(witticisms)* facéties *fpl* (**b**) *(in booksellers' catalogues → obscene books)* livres *mpl* obscènes; *(→ coarse books)* livres *mpl* grivois

facetious [fə'siːʃəs] *adj (person)* facétieux, moqueur; *(remark)* facétieux, comique; **I was being facetious** je plaisantais; **there's no need to be so facetious** il n'y a pas de quoi se moquer

facetiously [fə'siːʃəslɪ] *adv* de manière facétieuse, facétieusement

facetiousness [fə'siːʃəsnɪs] *n* caractère *m* facétieux *ou* comique

face-to-face *adj (discussion, confrontation)* face à face; **a face-to-face meeting** un face-à-face

facetted ['fæsɪtɪd] *adj* à facettes

facework ['feɪswɜːk] *n Constr* façade *f*

facia = **fascia**

facial ['feɪʃəl] **1** *adj* facial

2 *n* soin *m* du visage; **to have a facial** se faire faire un soin du visage

►► ***facial hair*** poils *mpl* du visage; **to remove facial hair** enlever les poils disgracieux (du visage); ***facial sauna*** sauna *m* facial; ***facial scrub*** exfoliant *m*; ***facial tissues*** tissus *mpl* du visage

facially ['feɪʃəlɪ] *adv* de visage

facies ['feɪʃɪiːz] *(pl* **inv)** *n Geol* faciès *m*

facile [*Br* 'fæsaɪl, *Am* 'fæsəl] *adj Pej (simplistic → remark, argument)* facile, simpliste; *(solution, victory)* trop facile; *(person)* superficiel, complaisant

facilely [*Br* 'fæsaɪlɪ, *Am* 'fæsəllɪ] *adv Pej* avec trop de facilité, d'une façon trop facile

facilitate [fə'sɪlɪteɪt] *vt* faciliter

facilitation [fə,sɪlɪ'teɪʃən] *n* facilitation *f*

facilitator [fə'sɪlɪteɪtə(r)] *n* animateur(trice) *m,f* de groupe

facility [fə'sɪlətɪ] *(pl* **facilities)** **1** *n* (**a**) *(area, building)* installation *f*; **training/research facility** établissement *m* de formation/recherche; **nuclear facility** *(power station)* centrale *f* nucléaire; *(weapons plant)* installations *fpl* nucléaires

(**b**) *(device)* mécanisme *m*; *Comput* fonction *f*; **the clock also has a radio facility** ce réveil fait aussi radio; **an automatic timing facility** un minuteur automatique; **the computer has a spellcheck facility** l'ordinateur est équipé d'un correcteur orthographique

(**c**) *(service)* service *m*; **we offer easy credit facilities** nous offrons des facilités de paiement *ou* crédit; *Br* **an overdraft facility** une autorisation de découvert

(**d**) *(skill)* facilité *f*, aptitude *f*; **to have a facility for** *or* **with languages** avoir beaucoup de facilité pour les langues

(**e**) *(ease)* facilité *f*; **with great facility** avec beaucoup de facilité

2 facilities *npl (equipment)* équipements *mpl*; *(place, building)* installations *fpl*, aménagements *mpl*; *(means)* moyens *mpl*; **play/sports/educational facilities** équipements *mpl* récréatifs/sportifs/scolaires; **military/port facilities** installations *fpl* militaires/portuaires; **storage/cooking facilities** installations *fpl* de stockage/cuisine; **a house/kitchen with no proper storage facilities** une cuisine/maison dépourvue de rangements *ou* d'espaces de rangement; **there are facilities for cooking** il y a la possibilité de *ou* il y a ce qu'il faut pour faire la cuisine; **the lack of sanitary facilities** le manque d'installations sanitaires; **the area has inadequate transport facilities** le quartier est mal desservi; **the university has excellent research facilities** l'université est très bien équipé pour la recherche; **books and other facilities for study** des livres et autres instruments de travail; **there are no facilities for the disabled** il n'y a pas d'aménagements spéciaux prévus pour les handicapés; **the area has excellent housing, shopping and school facilities** c'est un quartier où il est facile de se loger, avec de nombreux magasins et de bonnes écoles à proximité; **feel free to use the facilities** n'hésitez pas à utiliser toutes les installations; **we don't have the facilities to hold a conference here** nous ne sommes pas équipés pour organiser une conférence ici; *Euph* **the facilities** les toilettes *fpl*

facing ['feɪsɪŋ] **1** *n Constr* revêtement *m*; *Sewing* revers *m*

2 *adj (page)* ci-contre

►► ***facing pages*** pages *fpl* en regard

-facing ['feɪsɪŋ] *suff* orienté vers...; **north-facing** orienté *ou* exposé au nord

facsimile [fæk'sɪmɪlɪ] *n* fac-similé *m*; **in facsimile** en fac-similé

►► ***facsimile edition*** *(of book)* fac-similé *m*; ***facsimile machine*** télécopieur *m*; ***facsimile transmission*** télécopie *f*

FACT [fækt] **1** *n* (**a**) *(gen)* fait *m*; **it's a (well-known) fact that...** tout le monde sait (bien) que...; **just stick to the facts** tenez-vous en aux faits; **let's get the facts straight** mettons les choses au clair; **ten facts about whales** dix choses à savoir sur les baleines; **I'll give you all the facts and figures** je vous donnerai tous les détails voulus; **the fact that he left is in itself incriminating** le fait qu'il soit parti est compromettant en soi; **he broke his promise, there's no getting away from the fact** disons les choses comme elles sont, il n'a pas tenu sa promesse; **I'm her friend, a fact you seem to have overlooked** vous semblez ne pas tenir compte du fait que je suis son ami; **I know for a fact that they're friends** je sais pertinemment qu'ils sont amis; **I know it for a fact** je le sais de source sûre, c'est un fait certain; **it's a fact of life** c'est une réalité; **to teach sb the facts of life** *(sex)* apprendre à qn comment les enfants viennent au monde; *(hard reality)* apprendre à qn la réalité des choses, mettre qn devant la réalité de la vie; **there's something strange going on, (and) that's a fact** il se passe quelque chose de bizarre, c'est sûr; **is that a fact?** c'est pas vrai?; **owing to the fact that...** du fait que...

(**b**) *(UNCOUNT) (reality)* faits *mpl*, réalité *f*; **based on fact** *(argument)* basé sur des faits; *(book, film)* basé sur des faits réels; **fact and fiction** le réel et l'imaginaire; **the fact (of the matter) is that I forgot all about it** la vérité, c'est que j'ai complètement oublié; **the fact remains he's my brother** il n'en est pas moins mon frère

(**c**) *Law (act)* fait *m*, action *f*; **the jury only decides issues of fact** les jurés ne sont juges que du fait

2 in fact *adv* (**a**) *(giving extra information)* **he asked us, in fact ordered us, to be quiet** il nous a demandé, ou plutôt ordonné, de nous taire

(**b**) *(correcting)* en fait; **he claims to be a writer, but in (actual) fact he's a journalist** il prétend être écrivain mais en fait c'est un journaliste

(**c**) *(emphasizing, reinforcing)* **did she in fact say when she was going to arrive?** est-ce qu'elle a dit quand elle arriverait en fait?; **he said it'd take two days and he was in fact correct** il a dit que cela mettrait deux jours et en fait, il avait raison

►► ***fact sheet*** fiche *f* d'informations

---

fact-finding *adj* d'information; **a fact-finding mission** une mission d'information; **he's on a fact-finding tour of the disaster area** il enquête sur la région sinistrée

faction¹ ['fækʃən] *n* (**a**) *(group)* faction *f* (**b**) *(strife)* dissension *f*, discorde *f*

faction² *n (book, programme)* docudrame *m*

factional ['fækʃənəl] *adj* de faction; **factional strife** luttes *fpl* intestines

factionalism ['fækʃənəlɪzəm] *n* esprit *m* de discorde *ou* de dissension

factionary ['fækʃənərɪ], **factionist** ['fækʃənɪst] *n* factieux(euse) *m,f*, partisan(e) *m,f*

factious ['fækʃəs] *adj* factieux

factiously ['fækʃəslɪ] *adv* factieusement

factiousness ['fækʃəsnɪs] *n* esprit *m* factieux *ou* de faction

factitious [fæk'tɪʃəs] *adj Literary* factice, artificiel

factitiously [fæk'tɪʃəslɪ] *adv Literary* facticement, d'une manière factice

factitive [ˈfæktɪtɪv] *adj Gram* factitif

factoid [ˈfæktɔɪd] *n* = idée fausse colportée par la presse

factor [ˈfæktə(r)] *n* (**a**) *(element)* facteur *m*, élément *m*; **age is an important factor** l'âge joue un rôle important; **a determining factor** un facteur décisif *ou* déterminant; **the human factor** le facteur humain; **the safety factor** le facteur de sécurité; **the chill factor** le coefficient de froid

(**b**) *Biol & Math* facteur *m*; **sales increased by a factor of ten** les ventes sont dix fois plus élevées, l'indice des ventes est dix fois plus haut; *Econ* **factor of production** facteur *m* de production

(**c**) *(in suntan cream)* indice *m*; **factor 6** indice 6

(**d**) *(agent)* agent *m*

(**e**) *Scot (building manager)* syndic *m*

(**f**) *Fin (factoring company)* société *f* d'affacturage

►► ***factor analysis*** analyse *f* factorielle; *Biol* ***factor 8*** facteur *m* VIII

►**factor in** *vt sep (add to calculation)* inclure

factorage [ˈfæktərɪdʒ] *n Fin* courtage *m*, commission *f* (d'affacturage)

factorial [fækˈtɔːrɪəl] *Math* **1** *adj* factoriel

2 *n* factorielle *f*

factoring [ˈfæktərɪŋ] *n* (**a**) *Fin* affacturage *m* (**b**) *Scot (management of building)* = administration d'un immeuble par l'association de copropriétaires

►► ***factoring agent*** agent *m* d'affacturage; ***factoring charges*** commission *f* d'affacturage; ***factoring company*** société *f* d'affacturage

factorization [ˌfæktəraɪˈzeɪʃən] *n* mise *f* en facteurs

factorize, -ise [ˈfæktəraɪz] *vt* mettre en facteurs

factorship [ˈfæktəʃɪp] *n* (**a**) *Com* office *m* de courtier (**b**) *Scot (management of building)* = administration d'un immeuble par l'association de copropriétaires

factory [ˈfæktərɪ] (*pl* **factories**) **1** *n* usine *f*; *(smaller)* fabrique *f*; **a car factory** une usine d'automobiles; **an arms/munitions factory** une fabrique d'armes/de munitions; **a porcelain factory** une manufacture de porcelaine; **a biscuit factory** une biscuiterie *f*; **on the factory floor** dans les ateliers, parmi les ouvriers; **prices at the factory gate** prix *mpl* départ usine

2 *comp (chimney, manager)* d'usine

►► *Br* ***Factory Acts*** = ensemble de lois régissant les conditions de travail des ouvriers au XIXème siècle; ***factory farm*** ferme *f* industrielle; ***factory farming*** élevage *m* industriel; ***factory inspection*** inspection *f* du travail; ***factory inspector*** inspecteur(trice) *m,f* du travail; ***factory outlet*** magasin *m* d'usine; ***factory overheads*** frais *mpl* généraux de fabrication; ***factory price*** prix *m* usine, prix *m* sortie usine; ***factory ship*** navire-usine *m*; ***factory shop*** magasin *m* d'usine; ***factory unit*** unité *f* de fabrication; ***factory work*** travail *m* en usine *ou* d'usine; ***factory worker*** ouvrier(ère) *m,f* d'usine

factotum [fækˈtəʊtəm] *n* factotum *m*; **general factotum** *(man)* homme *m* à tout faire; *(woman)* femme *f* à tout faire

factual [ˈfæktʃʊəl] *adj (account, speech)* factuel, basé sur les *ou* des faits; *(event)* réel

factuality [ˌfæktʃʊˈælɪtɪ] *n* caractère *m* factuel

factually [ˈfæktʃʊəlɪ] *adv* en se tenant aux faits; **factually inaccurate** inexact dans les faits

factum [ˈfæktəm] *n Law* factum *m*, exposé *m* des faits

facula [ˈfækjʊlə] (*pl* **faculae** [-liː]) *n Astron* facule *f*

facultative [ˈfækəltətɪv] *adj* (**a**) *(optional)* facultatif (**b**) *Phil* casuel, contingent

faculty [ˈfækəltɪ] (*pl* **faculties**) **1** *n* (**a**) *(of mind, body)* faculté *f*; **she's in full command of her faculties** elle a *ou* elle jouit de toutes ses facultés; **his critical faculties** son sens critique; **the faculty of reason** la raison; **the faculty of speech** le don de la parole

(**b**) *Univ (section)* faculté *f*; *(staff)* corps *m* enseignant; **the Faculty of Arts/of Medicine** la faculté de lettres/de médecine

2 *comp Univ (member, staff)* de faculté

fad [fæd] *n Fam (craze)* mode❑ *f*, vogue❑ *f*; *(personal)* lubie❑ *f*, (petite) manie❑ *f*; **it's just a (passing) fad** ce n'est qu'une lubie, ce n'est qu'un engouement passager

faddiness [ˈfædɪnɪs] *n Fam* goûts *mpl* difficiles❑

faddish [ˈfædɪʃ] *adj Fam (idea, taste)* capricieux❑; *(person)* maniaque❑, capricieux❑

faddy [ˈfædɪ] (*compar* **faddier**, *superl* **faddiest**) *adj Fam (idea, taste)* capricieux❑; *(person)* maniaque❑, capricieux❑; **he's faddy about his food, he's a faddy eater** il est difficile sur la nourriture

fade [feɪd] **1** *vi* (**a**) *(colour)* pâlir, passer; *(material)* se décolorer, passer; *(light)* baisser, diminuer; **the light faded from the sky** le jour baissa peu à peu; *Tex* **guaranteed not to fade** garanti bon teint

(**b**) *(wither → flower)* se faner, se flétrir *Fig (→ beauty)* se faner

(**c**) *(disappear → figure)* disparaître; *(→ memory, sight)* baisser; *(→ thing remembered, writing)* s'effacer; *(→ sound)* baisser, s'éteindre; *(→ anger, interest)* diminuer; *(→ hope, smile)* s'éteindre; **to fade from memory** s'effacer de la mémoire; **the light is fading** *(daylight)* le jour baisse; **to fade from sight** disparaître aux regards; **the sound keeps fading** *(of radio, TV)* il y a du fading, le son s'en va

(**d**) *Literary (die)* dépérir, s'éteindre; **he's fading fast** il dépérit à vue d'œil

(**e**) *Am Fam (leave)* s'esbigner, calter

2 *vt* (**a**) *(discolour → material, curtains)* décolorer; *(→ colour)* faner

(**b**) *(reduce)* baisser; *Cin & TV* faire disparaître en fondu

(**c**) *Golf (ball)* faire dévier légèrement à droite

3 *n* (**a**) *Cin & TV* disparition *f* en fondu

(**b**) *Golf* = coup qui fait dévier la balle légèrement à droite

►**fade away** *vi (gen)* disparaître; *(memory, sight)* baisser; *(thing remembered, writing)* s'effacer; *(sound)* s'éteindre; *(anger, interest)* diminuer; *(hope, smile)* s'éteindre; **he faded away** il a peu à peu dépéri

►**fade in** **1** *vt sep Cin & TV (picture)* faire apparaître en fondu; *Rad (sound)* monter

2 *vi Cin & TV (picture)* apparaître en fondu

►**fade out** **1** *vi* (**a**) *(sound)* disparaître, s'éteindre; *Fig (interest)* diminuer, tomber; *(fashion)* passer

(**b**) *Cin & TV (picture)* disparaître en fondu; *Rad (music, dialogue)* être coupé par un fondu sonore

2 *vt sep Cin & TV (picture)* faire disparaître en fondu; *Rad (music, dialogue)* couper par un fondu sonore

fade-away *n Cin* fondu *m* en fermeture; *TV* disparition *f* graduelle; *Rad* évanouissement *m*, fading *m*

faded [ˈfeɪdɪd] *adj (material)* décoloré, déteint; *(jeans)* délavé; *(flower)* fané, flétri; *(beauty)* défraîchi, fané

fade-in *n Cin* fondu *m* en ouverture; *TV* apparition *f* graduelle; *Rad* fondu *m* sonore

fade-out *n Cin* fondu *m* en fermeture; *TV* disparition *f* graduelle; *Rad* fondu *m* sonore

fader [ˈfeɪdə(r)] *n Cin & TV* potentiomètre *m*

fading [ˈfeɪdɪŋ] **1** *n* (**a**) *(of plant)* flétrissure *f*; *(of material)* décoloration *f* (**b**) *Rad* fading *m* (**c**) *Cin & TV* fondu *m*

2 *adj (flower)* qui se fane; *(light)* pâlissant

faecal, *Am* **fecal** [ˈfiːkəl] *adj Biol* fécal; **faecal matter** matières *fpl* fécales, déjections *fpl*

faeces, *Am* **feces** [ˈfiːsiːz] *npl Biol* fèces *fpl*

faerie [ˈfeərɪ] *Old-fashioned or Literary* **1** *n* féerie *f*, monde *m* des fées

2 *adj* féerique

'The Faerie Queene' *Spenser, Purcell* 'la Reine des fées'

Faeroe [ˈfeərəʊ] *n* **the Faeroe Islands, the Faeroes** les îles *fpl* Féroé; **in the Faeroe Islands** aux îles Féroé

Faeroese [ˌfeərəʊˈiːz] (*pl* **inv**) **1** *n* (**a**) *(person)* Féroïen(enne) *m,f*, Féringien(enne) *m,f* (**b**) *Ling* féroïen *m*, féringien *m*

2 *adj* féroïen, féringien

faery = **faerie**

faff [fæf] *Br Fam* **1** *vi* (**a**) *(waste time)* **to faff (about** *or* **around)** glander; **stop faffing (about** *or* **around)!** arrêtez de tourner en rond! (**b**) *(potter)* s'occuper❑, bricoler

2 *n* (**a**) *(panic)* panique❑ *f* (**b**) *(effort)* **it's too much of a faff** c'est trop compliqué❑

fag [fæg] (*pt & pp* **fagged**, *cont* **fagging**) **1** *n* (**a**) *Br Fam (cigarette)* clope *f*

(**b**) *Am very Fam (homosexual)* pédé *m*, = terme injurieux désignant un homosexuel

(**c**) *Br (at school)* = jeune élève d'une "public school" assujetti à un "ancien"

(**d**) *Br Fam (task)* corvée *f*, barbe *f*

2 *vi Br* (**a**) *(at public school)* **to fag for sb** faire les corvées de qn

(**b**) *Fam Old-fashioned (work hard)* travailler dur❑, s'échiner

3 *vt Fam (exhaust)* crever

►► *Br Fam* ***fag end*** *(of cigarette)* mégot *m*; *Fig (remainder)* reste❑ *m*; *(of material, winter)* bout❑ *m*; *(of conversation)* dernières bribes❑ *fpl*; *very Fam* ***fag hag*** fille *f* à pédés

►**fag out** *vt sep Br Fam (of work, task)* crever

fagged [fægd] *adj Br Fam* (**a**) *(exhausted)* crevé, claqué; **we all ended up completely fagged (out)** nous étions tous complètement crevés *ou* claqués à la fin (**b**) *(bothered)* **I can't be fagged** j'ai trop la flemme; **I don't know how he can be fagged doing that** je ne sais pas comment il peut s'embêter à faire ça

fagging [ˈfægɪŋ] *n Br* = sujétion d'un jeune élève à un "ancien" dans une "public school"

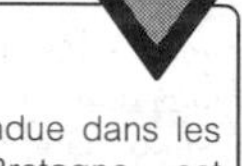

FAGGING

Cette pratique, jadis assez répandue dans les "public schools" en Grande-Bretagne, est maintenant interdite. Les "grands" avaient le droit de donner des ordres aux "petits", qui devaient porter leurs affaires, leur faire à manger etc.

faggot [ˈfægət] *n* (**a**) *Br (of sticks)* fagot *m* (**b**) *Br Culin* boulette *f* de viande (**c**) *Am very Fam (homosexual)* pédé *m*, = terme injurieux désignant un homosexuel

faggy [ˈfægɪ] *adj Am very Fam Pej* qui fait pédé

fagot [ˈfægət] *n Am (of sticks)* fagot *m*

fah [fɑː] *n Br Mus* fa *m*

Fahrenheit [ˈfærənhaɪt] *adj* Fahrenheit *(inv)*; **it's 6° Centigrade – what's that in Fahrenheit?** il fait 6° Centigrade – ça fait combien en Fahrenheit?

►► ***Fahrenheit scale*** échelle *f* Fahrenheit

faience [faɪˈjɑːns] *n* faïence *f*

FAIL [feɪl]

échouer à	► 1 (a), (b)
recaler	► 1 (b)
décevoir	► 1 (c)
négliger	► 1 (d)
échouer	► 2 (a), (b)
être recalé	► 2 (b)
tomber en panne	► 2 (c)
baisser	► 2 (d)
manquer	► 2 (e)
échec	► 3

1 *vt* (**a**) *(not succeed in)* échouer à, ne pas réussir à; **he failed his driving test** il n'a pas eu son permis; **to fail a drugs test** être positif au contrôle anti-dopage; **to fail to do sth** ne pas arriver à faire qch

(**b**) *Sch & Univ (exam)* échouer à, être recalé à; *(candidate)* refuser, recaler; **he failed the exam/history** il a échoué à l'examen/en histoire; **she failed ten students** elle a refusé *ou* recalé dix étudiants

(**c**) *(let down)* décevoir, laisser tomber; **I won't fail you** je ne vous laisserai pas tomber, vous pouvez compter sur moi; **his heart failed him** le cœur lui a manqué; **my memory fails me** la mémoire me fait défaut, ma mémoire me trahit; **her courage failed her** le courage lui a fait défaut *ou* lui a manqué; **words fail me** je ne sais pas quoi dire

(**d**) *(neglect)* **to fail to do sth** négliger de faire qch; **he failed to mention he was married** il a omis de signaler qu'il était marié; **the discussions have failed to bring any progress** les discussions n'ont pas réussi à produire le moindre progrès; **they never fail to call** ils ne manquent jamais d'appeler; **he failed to keep his word** il a manqué à sa parole; **she failed to answer his letter** elle n'a pas répondu à sa lettre; **I fail to see how I can help** je ne vois pas comment je peux aider; **I fail to understand why she came** je n'arrive pas à comprendre pourquoi elle est venue; **such success never fails to arouse jealousy** une telle réussite ne va jamais sans provoquer des jalousies; *Law* **to fail to appear** faire défaut

2 *vi* (**a**) *(not succeed → attempt, plan)* échouer, ne pas réussir; *(→ negotiations)* échouer, ne pas aboutir; *(→ play)* faire fiasco; *(→ person)* échouer; **he failed in his efforts to convince us** il n'a pas réussi *ou* il n'est pas arrivé à nous convaincre; **her attempt was bound to fail** sa tentative était vouée à l'échec; **to fail by three votes/five minutes** échouer à trois voix près/cinq minutes près; **it never fails** ça ne rate jamais; **if all else fails** en désespoir de cause

(**b**) *Sch & Univ* échouer, être recalé; **I failed in maths** j'ai été collé *ou* recalé en maths

(**c**) *(stop working)* tomber en panne, céder; *(brakes)* lâcher; *(engine)* caler; **his heart failed** son cœur s'est arrêté; **the power failed** il y a eu une panne d'électricité; **his parachute failed** son parachute ne s'est pas ouvert

(**d**) *(grow weak → eyesight, health, memory)* baisser, faiblir; *(→ person, voice)* s'affaiblir; *(→ light, strength)* baisser

(**e**) *(be insufficient)* manquer, faire défaut; **their crops failed because of the drought** ils ont perdu les récoltes à cause de la sécheresse; **she failed in her duty** elle a manqué *ou* failli à son devoir

(**f**) *(go bankrupt)* faire faillite

3 *n Sch & Univ* échec *m*; **he only had one fail and that was in maths** il n'a échoué *ou* été recalé qu'en maths; **out of a class of 25, I had 23 passes and 2 fails** sur une classe de 25, 23 ont été reçus et 2 ont été recalés

4 without fail *adv (for certain)* sans faute, à coup sûr; *(always)* inévitablement, immanquablement

---

failed [feɪld] *adj* qui n'a pas réussi, raté; **she's a failed artist** c'est une artiste manquée; **a failed marriage** un mariage manqué *ou* raté

failing ['feɪlɪŋ] **1** *n* défaut *m*

2 *prep* à défaut de; **failing this** à défaut; **failing which** faute *ou* à défaut de quoi, **failing any advice/evidence to the contrary** sauf avis contraire, sauf preuve du contraire

3 *adj (strength)* défaillant; *(business)* qui fait faillite; *(marriage)* qui va à la dérive; *(school)* en état d'échec; *Am (student)* faible, mauvais; **to be in failing health** avoir une santé défaillante

fail-safe 1 *adj (device, machine)* à sûreté intégrée; *(plan)* infaillible

2 *n* dispositif *m* de sécurité *ou* de sûreté (intégrée)

failure ['feɪljə(r)] *n* (**a**) *(lack of success)* échec *m*, insuccès *m*; **to end in failure** se solder *ou* se terminer par un échec; **doomed to failure** voué à l'échec *ou* l'insuccès; **the failure of his new film** l'échec de son nouveau film

(**b**) *Sch & Univ* échec *m*; **failure in an exam/in maths** échec à un examen/en maths; **there are too many failures** trop de candidats ont été recalés

(**c**) *(fiasco)* échec *m*, fiasco *m*; *(plan)* échec *m*, avortement *m*; **the party was a total failure** la soirée a été un fiasco complet; **their plan was a complete failure** leur projet a été un échec total *ou* a échoué sur toute la ligne; **the play was a dismal failure** la pièce a été *ou* a fait un four noir

(**d**) *(person)* raté(e) *m,f*; **he's a failure as a father** il fait un mauvais père, il n'est pas doué pour la paternité; **I feel a complete failure** je me sens vraiment nulle, j'ai l'impression d'être complètement nulle; **I'm a complete failure at maths** je suis totalement nul en maths

(**e**) *(breakdown)* panne *f*; **a power failure** une panne d'électricité

(**f**) *(lack)* manque *m*; **a failure of nerve** un manque de courage; **crop failure** perte *f* des récoltes

(**g**) *(neglect, omission)* manquement *m*, défaut *m*; **his failure to keep his word** son manquement à sa parole; **failure to pay a bill** défaut *m* de paiement d'un effet; **his failure to arrive on time** le fait qu'il soit arrivé en retard; **his failure to appear meant I had to take charge** du fait qu'il ne s'est pas montré, j'ai dû me charger de tout; **the press criticized the government's failure to act** la presse a critiqué l'immobilisme du gouvernement; **failure to observe the rules will result in a fine** le manquement au règlement est passible d'une amende; *Law* **failure to appear** défaut *m* de comparution

(**h**) *(bankruptcy)* faillite *f*

►► *Am Com* ***failure investment*** investissement *m* en valeurs de redressement *ou* de retournement

fain [feɪn] *adv Arch* volontiers; **I would fain be a father to your children** je serais trop heureux d'être un père pour vos enfants; **I would fain have stayed at home** j'aurais bien voulu rester à la maison

faint [feɪnt] **1** *adj* (**a**) *(slight → breeze, feeling, sound, smell)* faible, léger; *(→ idea)* flou, vague; *(→ hope)* léger, faible; *(→ possibility)* vague; *(→ breathing, light)* faible; *(→ voice)* faible, éteint; **there was a faint glow on the horizon** il y avait une faible lueur à l'horizon; **he hasn't the faintest chance of winning** il n'a pas la moindre chance de gagner; **I haven't the faintest idea** je n'en ai pas la moindre idée; **the sound of the footsteps grew fainter** le bruit des pas s'affaiblit; **her cries grew fainter** ses cris s'estompaient *ou* diminuaient

(**b**) *(colour)* pâle, délavé

(**c**) *(half-hearted)* faible, sans conviction; **a faint smile** *(feeble)* un vague sourire; *(sad)* un pauvre *ou* triste sourire; **faint praise** éloges *mpl* tièdes; **to damn sb/sth with faint praise** ne pas se montrer très élogieux envers qn/à propos de qch

(**d**) *(dizzy)* prêt à s'évanouir, défaillant; **to feel faint** se sentir mal, être pris d'un malaise; **he was faint with exhaustion** la tête lui tournait de fatigue

(**e**) *Br Prov* **faint heart never won fair lady** = la pusillanimité n'a jamais conquis de cœur féminin

2 *vi* s'évanouir; **he fainted from the pain** il s'est évanoui de douleur; **a fainting fit** un évanouissement; **to be fainting from** *or* **with hunger** défaillir de faim; *Fig* **I almost fainted when they told me I'd got the job** j'ai failli m'évanouir quand on m'a dit que j'avais le poste

3 *n* évanouissement *m*, syncope *f*; **she fell to the floor in a (dead) faint** elle s'est évanouie *ou* est tombée en syncope

faint-hearted [-'hɑːtɪd] **1** *adj (person)* timoré, pusillanime; *(attempt)* timide, sans conviction

2 *npl* **not for the faint-hearted** à déconseiller aux âmes sensibles

faint-heartedly [-'hɑːtɪdlɪ] *adv* avec pusillanimité

faint-heartedness [-'hɑːtɪdnɪs] *n* pusillanimité *f*

fainting ['feɪntɪŋ] *n* évanouissement *m*

►► ***fainting fit*** évanouissement *m*

faintly ['feɪntlɪ] *adv* (**a**) *(breathe, shine)* faiblement; *(mark, write)* légèrement; *(say, speak)* d'une voix éteinte, faiblement; **faintly visible** à peine visible; **she smiled faintly** elle esquissa un sourire (**b**) *(slightly)* légèrement, vaguement; **the taste is faintly reminiscent of cinnamon** cela rappelle vaguement la cannelle; **faintly absurd/ridiculous** quelque peu absurde/ridicule

faintness ['feɪntnɪs] *n* (**a**) *(of light, sound, voice)* faiblesse *f*; *(of breeze)* légèreté *f*; *(of image, writing)* manque *m* de clarté (**b**) *(dizziness)* malaise *m*, défaillance *f*

faints [feɪnts] *npl (in distilling)* alcools *mpl* de tête *ou* de queue, repasse *f*

FAIR [feə(r)]

juste	► 1 (a)
équitable	► 1 (a)
correct	► 1 (a)
blond	► 1 (b)
beau	► 1 (c), (d)
passable	► 1 (e)
considérable	► 1 (f)
véritable	► 1 (g)
équitablement	► 2 (a)
foire	► 3

1 *adj* (**a**) *(just → person, decision)* juste, équitable; *(→ wage)* équitable; *(→ contest, match, player)* loyal, correct; *(→ deal, exchange)* équitable, honnête; *(→ price)* correct, convenable; *(→ criticism, profit)* justifié, mérité; **it's not fair** ce n'est pas juste; **it's not fair to the others** ce n'est pas juste *ou* honnête vis-à-vis des autres; **it isn't fair to expect children to...** ce n'est pas raisonnable de demander à des enfants de...; **that's a fair point** c'est une remarque pertinente; **she's strict but fair** elle est sévère mais juste; **to be fair (to them), they did contribute their time** rendons-leur cette justice, ils ont donné de leur temps; **it's only fair to let him speak** ce n'est que justice de le laisser parler; **it is only fair to say that...** il faut dire que...; **as is only fair** ce n'est que justice, comme de juste; **I gave him fair warning** je l'ai prévenu à temps; **to get a fair trial** être jugé de façon équitable; **a fair sample** un échantillon représentatif; **he got his fair share of the property** il a eu tous les biens qui lui revenaient (de droit); **she's had more than her fair share of problems** elle a largement eu sa part de problèmes; *Br* **to have a fair crack of the whip** avoir toutes ses chances; *Br* **to give sb a fair crack of the whip** donner toutes ses chances à qn; *Fam* **the boss gave her a fair shake (of the dice)** *or* **a fair deal** *or Am & Austr* **a fair go** le patron l'a traitée équitablement *ou* a été fair-play avec elle ❏; *Austr Fam* **fair go!** donne-moi/nous/*etc* une chance! ❏; **it's all fair and above board, it's all fair and square** tout est régulier *ou* correct; *Prov* **all's fair in love and war** = en amour comme à la guerre, tous les coups sont permis; *Prov* **fair exchange is no robbery** = tout le monde est content; **by fair means or foul** par tous les moyens, d'une manière ou d'une autre; *Br Fam* **fair do's (for all!)** à chacun son dû! ❏; **fair enough!** très bien!, d'accord!; **that's fair enough but don't you think that...** très bien *ou* d'accord, mais est-ce que vous ne pensez pas que...; **fair's fair, it's her turn now** il faut être juste, c'est son tour maintenant

(**b**) *(light → hair)* blond; *(→ skin)* clair, blanc (blanche); **he's very fair** il est très blond

(**c**) *Literary (lovely)* beau (belle); **his fair lady** sa belle; *Hum* **written in her own fair hand** écrit de sa main blanche

(**d**) *(weather)* beau (belle); *(tide, wind)* favorable, propice; **the wind's set fair for France** le temps est au beau fixe sur la France

(**e**) *(adequate)* passable, assez bon; **in fair condition** en assez bon état; **you have a fair chance of winning** vous avez des chances de gagner; **a fair standard** un assez bon niveau; **fair to middling** passable, pas mal; **how are you? – fair to middling** comment allez-vous? – comme çi comme ça; **in a fair way to recovering** en bonne voie de rétablissement

(**f**) *(substantial)* considérable; **he makes a fair amount of money** il gagne pas mal d'argent; **she reads a fair amount** elle lit pas mal; **I have a fair idea (of) why** je crois bien savoir pourquoi; **a fair number** un nombre respectable; **at a fair pace** à une bonne allure

(**g**) *Br Fam (real)* véritable ❏; **I had a fair old time getting here** j'ai eu pas mal de difficultés à arriver jusqu'ici

2 *adv* (**a**) *(act)* équitablement, loyalement; **to play fair** jouer franc jeu; **he told us fair and square** il nous l'a dit sans détours *ou* carrément; **you can't say fairer than that** il n'y a pas plus équitable

(**b**) *Br Fam (completely)* tout à fait ❏, vraiment ❏; **you fair scared me to death** tu m'as vraiment fait une peur atroce

(**c**) *(idiom)* **the play bids fair to being a success** cette pièce a de grandes chances d'être *ou* sera probablement un succès

3 *n* (**a**) *(entertainment)* foire *f*, fête *f* foraine; *(for charity)* kermesse *f*, fête *f*

(**b**) *Com* foire *f*; **the Book Fair** la Foire du livre

►► *Am Sport* ***fair catch*** arrêt *m* de volée; ***fair competition codes*** règles *fpl* de concurrence loyale *(établies aux États-Unis en 1933 pendant le New Deal entre les patrons et les salariés)*; *Br* ***fair copy*** copie *f* au propre *ou* au net; **I made a fair copy of the report** j'ai recopié le rapport au propre; ***fair game*** proie *f* idéale; *Fig* **after such**

behaviour he was fair game for an attack après s'être comporté de cette façon, il méritait bien qu'on s'en prenne à lui; ***Fair Isle*** **1** *n Geog* Fair Isle *(dans les îles Shetland)*; *(sweater)* = pull avec des motifs de couleurs vives **2** *adj* tricoté avec des motifs de couleurs vives; *Fin* ***fair market value*** valeur *f* vénale; ***fair play*** fair-play *m inv*, *Offic* franc-jeu *m*; *Fam* **fair play to you!** chapeau!; *Br* ***fair rent*** = loyer fixé après un examen officiel du logement par l'administration; ***the fair sex*** le beau sexe; *Com* ***fair trade*** commerce *m* équitable

fairground ['feəgraʊnd] *n* champ *m* de foire
►► ***fairground ride*** attraction *f (de fête foraine)*

fair-haired *adj (blond)* blond, aux cheveux blonds; **the fair-haired girl** la blonde; *Am Fam* **the boss's fair-haired boy** le chouchou du patron

fairing ['feərɪŋ] *n (on vehicle)* carénage *m*

fairish ['feərɪʃ] *adj* **(a)** *(chances, salary, weather)* assez bon; *(number)* respectable; **there's a fairish amount of work still to do** il y a encore pas mal de travail **(b)** *(blondish)* plutôt blond

Fairisle, fairisle ['feəraɪl] **1** *n (sweater)* = pull avec des motifs de couleurs vives
2 *adj* tricoté avec des motifs de couleurs vives

fairly ['feəlɪ] *adv* **(a)** *(justly → treat)* équitablement, avec justice; *(→ compare, judge)* impartialement, avec impartialité
(b) *(honestly)* honnêtement, loyalement; **to fight/to play fairly** se battre/jouer loyalement; **fairly priced goods** articles à un prix honnête *ou* raisonnable; **to come by sth fairly (and squarely)** obtenir qch par des moyens honnêtes; **to win fairly and squarely** *(clearly, easily)* remporter une nette victoire; *(without dishonest means)* vaincre honnêtement
(c) *(moderately)* assez, passablement; **a fairly good book** un assez bon livre; **I'm fairly certain** je suis à peu près certain; **she sings fairly well** elle chante passablement bien; **he works fairly hard** il travaille plutôt dur
(d) *Br (positively)* absolument, vraiment; **he was fairly beside himself with worry** il était dans tous ses états; **we fairly raced through the work** nous avons fait notre travail à bonne allure

fair-minded *adj* équitable, impartial

fair-mindedness [-'maɪndɪdnɪs] *n* impartialité *f*

fairness ['feənɪs] *n* **(a)** *(justice)* justice *f*, honnêteté *f*; **the report questions the fairness of the decision** le rapport met en cause l'honnêteté *ou* l'impartialité de cette décision; **in all fairness** en toute justice; **in fairness** *or* **out of fairness to you** pour être juste envers *ou* avec vous, pour vous rendre justice **(b)** *(of hair)* blondeur *f*, blond *m*; *(of skin)* blancheur *f*

fair-sized *adj* assez grand

fair-skinned *adj* blanc (blanche) de peau

fair-spoken *adj Literary* qui parle courtoisement

fairway ['feəweɪ] *n* **(a)** *(in golf)* fairway *m* **(b)** *Naut* chenal *m*, passe *f*

fair-weather *adj (clothing, vessel)* qui convient seulement au beau temps; **a fair-weather friend** un ami des beaux *ou* bons jours

fairy ['feərɪ] *(pl* **fairies***)* **1** *n* **(a)** *(sprite)* fée *f*; **the bad fairy** la fée Carabosse; *Fam* **to be away with the fairies** *(senile)* être complètement gaga; *(eccentric)* être farfelu; *(daydreaming)* être dans les nuages
(b) *very Fam (homosexual)* pédé *m*, tapette *f*, = terme injurieux désignant un homosexuel
2 *adj (enchanted)* magique; *(fairylike)* féerique, de fée; **fairy voices** des voix *fpl* de fées; **fairy footsteps** des pas *mpl* légers
►► *Br* ***fairy cycle*** bicyclette *f* d'enfant; *Austr* ***fairy floss*** barbe *f* à papa; *Literature & Fig* ***fairy godmother*** bonne fée *f*; ***fairy lights*** guirlande *f* électrique; ***fairy queen*** reine *f* des fées; ***fairy ring*** cercle *m ou* rond *m* des sorcières; *Zool* ***fairy shrimp*** artémia *m*; ***fairy story*** conte *m* de fées; *(untruth)* histoire *f* à dormir debout; ***fairy tale*** conte *m* de fées; *(untruth)* histoire *f* à dormir debout

fairyland ['feərɪlænd] *n Literature* royaume *m* des fées, féerie *f*; *Fig* féerie *f*

fairylike ['feərɪlaɪk] *adj* féerique, comme une fée; **fairylike work** ouvrage *m* de fée

fairy-tale *adj* **fairy-tale castle** château *m* de conte de fées; **a fairy-tale ending** une fin digne d'un conte de fées; **a fairy-tale romance** une histoire d'amour digne d'un conte de fées

fait accompli [ˌfeɪtə'kɒmplɪ] *n* fait *m* accompli; **to be presented with a fait accompli** être mis devant un fait accompli

faith [feɪθ] *n* **(a)** *(trust)* confiance *f*; **I have faith in him** je lui fais confiance; **she has lost (all) faith in the doctors** elle n'a plus aucune confiance dans les médecins; **he's lost faith in their promises** il ne croit plus à leurs promesses; **to put one's faith in sth** mettres ses espoirs dans qch
(b) *Rel (belief)* foi *f*; **faith in God** foi en Dieu; **to lose one's faith** perdre la foi; **Faith, Hope and Charity** la foi, l'espérance et la charité
(c) *(particular religion)* foi *f*, religion *f*; **the Buddhist faith** la religion bouddhiste
(d) *(honesty)* **he did it in good faith** il l'a fait en toute bonne foi; **he acted in bad faith** il a agi de mauvaise foi
(e) *(loyalty)* fidélité *f*; **you must keep faith with the movement** il faut tenir vos engagements envers le mouvement; *Fam* **keep the faith!** bon courage!ᑫ; **to break faith with sb** manquer à sa parole envers qn
►► *Am* ***faith cure*** guérison *f* par la prière; ***faith healer*** guérisseur(euse) *m,f* spirituel(elle); ***faith healing*** guérison *f* par la foi

faithful ['feɪθfʊl] **1** *adj* **(a)** *(believer, friend, lover)* fidèle (**to** à) **(b)** *(reliable)* sûr, solide; **he's a faithful employee** c'est quelqu'un de sérieux *ou* sur qui on peut compter **(c)** *(accurate → account, translation)* fidèle, exact; *(→ copy)* conforme
2 *npl* **the faithful** *(supporters)* les fidèles *mpl*; *Rel* les fidèles *mpl*, les croyants *mpl*; *Pol* **the party faithful** les fidèles *mpl* du parti

faithfully ['feɪθfʊlɪ] *adv* **(a)** *(loyally)* fidèlement, loyalement; **she promised faithfully to come** elle a donné sa parole qu'elle viendrait; **yours faithfully** *(in letter)* veuillez agréer mes salutations distinguées **(b)** *(accurately)* exactement, fidèlement

faithfulness ['feɪθfʊlnɪs] *n* **(a)** *(loyalty)* fidélité *f*, loyauté *f*; **faithfulness to the cause** fidélité *f* à *ou* loyauté envers la cause **(b)** *(of report, translation)* fidélité *f*, exactitude *f*; *(of copy)* conformité *f*

faithless ['feɪθlɪs] *adj* **(a)** *(dishonest, unreliable)* déloyal, perfide; *(to spouse, partner)* infidèle **(b)** *Rel* infidèle, non-croyant

faithlessly ['feɪθlɪslɪ] *adv* déloyalement, perfidement

faithlessness ['feɪθlɪsnɪs] *n* **(a)** *(dishonesty, unreliability)* déloyauté *f*, perfidie *f*; *(to spouse, partner)* infidélité *f* **(b)** *Rel* manque *m* de foi

fajitas [fɑː'hiːtəz] *npl Culin* fajitas *mpl*

fake [feɪk] **1** *vt* **(a)** *(make → document, painting)* faire un faux de, contrefaire; *(→ style, furniture)* imiter
(b) *(alter → document)* falsifier, maquiller; *(→ account)* falsifier; *(→ election, interview, photograph)* truquer; **it's all faked** *(in cinema etc)* c'est du trucage
(c) *(simulate)* feindre; **he faked a headache/sadness** il a fait semblant d'avoir mal à la tête/d'être triste; **she faked her own death** elle a fait croire à sa propre mort; *Sport* **to fake a pass** feinter la passe
(d) *(ad-lib)* improviser
2 *vi* faire semblant; *Sport* feinter
3 *n* **(a)** *(thing)* article *m ou* objet *m* truqué; *(antique, painting)* faux *m*
(b) *(person)* imposteur *m*; **she's a fake** elle essaie de se faire passer pour ce qu'elle n'est pas
4 *adj (antique, painting)* faux (fausse); *(account, document)* falsifié, faux (fausse); *(elections, interview, photograph)* truqué; **the pearls are fake** les perles sont fausses
►► ***fake tan*** *(product)* autobronzant *m*

faker ['feɪkə(r)] *n Fam* comédien(enne)ᑫ *m,f*

faking ['feɪkɪŋ] *n* **it's just faking** c'est de la comédie

fakir ['feɪˌkɪə(r)] *n* fakir *m*

falafel = **felafel**

Falangist [fæ'lændʒɪst] *Pol* **1** *adj* phalangiste
2 *n* phalangiste *mf*

falcate ['fælkeɪt] *adj Biol* falciforme, falqué

falchion ['fɔːlʃən] *n* **(a)** *Hist (curved sword)* cimeterre *m*, badelaire *m* **(b)** *Arch (any sword)* glaive *m*

falciform ['fælsɪfɔːm] *adj Biol* falciforme

falcon ['fɔːlkən] *n Orn* faucon *m*

falconer ['fɔːlkənə(r)] *n* fauconnier *m*

falconet ['fɔːlkəˌnet] *n* **(a)** *Hist (cannon)* fauconneau *m* **(b)** *Orn* fauconnet *m*, falconelle *f*, faucon-moineau *m*

falconry ['fɔːlkənrɪ] *n* fauconnerie *f*

falderal ['fældəræl], **falderol** = **folderol**

faldstool ['fɔːldˌstuːl] *n Rel* **(a)** *(bishop's seat)* siège *m* d'évêque (sans accoudoirs) **(b)** *(prayer stool)* prie-dieu *m inv*

Falkland ['fɔːlklənd] *n* **the Falkland Islands, the Falklands** les (îles *fpl*) Falkland *fpl*, les (îles *fpl*) Malouines *fpl*; **in the Falkland Islands** aux (îles) Falkland, aux (îles) Malouines
►► ***the Falklands War*** la guerre des Malouines

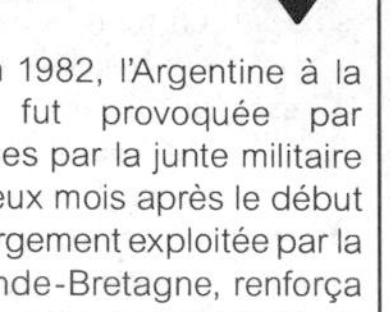

THE FALKLANDS WAR

Cette guerre opposa, en 1982, l'Argentine à la Grande-Bretagne. Elle fut provoquée par l'attaque des îles Malouines par la junte militaire argentine, qui se rendit deux mois après le début du conflit. Cette victoire, largement exploitée par la presse populaire en Grande-Bretagne, renforça de manière significative la cote de popularité de son Premier ministre, Margaret Thatcher, qui en profita pour organiser des élections anticipées qu'elle gagna haut la main.

Falklander ['fɔːlkləndə(r)] *n* habitant(e) *m,f* des îles Malouines *ou* îles Falkland

FALL [fɔːl]

chute	► **1 (a), (b), (d), (e), (k)**
baisse	► **1 (f), (g)**
automne	► **1 (j)**
tomber	► **2 (a), (f) – (h), (j) – (m)**
se laisser tomber	► **2 (b)**
s'écrouler	► **2 (c)**
s'assombrir	► **2 (i)**
cascade	► **4**

(pt **fell** [fel], *pp* **fallen** ['fɔːln]*)* **1** *n* **(a)** *(tumble)* chute *f*; **have you had a fall?** êtes-vous tombé?, avez-vous fait une chute?; **a fall from a horse** une chute de cheval; **a forty-metre fall** une chute de quarante mètres; *Literary* **the fall of night** la tombée de la nuit; **to be heading** *or* **riding for a fall** courir à l'échec; **the government is riding for a fall** le gouvernement va au-devant de la défaite
(b) *(of rain, snow)* chute *f*; **there was a heavy fall of snow overnight** il y a eu de fortes chutes de neige dans la nuit
(c) *Theat (of curtain)* baisser *m*
(d) *(collapse → of building, wall)* chute *f*, effondrement *m*; *(→ of dirt, rock)* éboulement *m*, chute *f*; *(→ of city, country)* chute *f*, capitulation *f*; *(→ of regime)* chute *f*, renversement *m*; **the fall of the Roman Empire** la chute de l'Empire romain; **the fall of the Bastille** la prise de la Bastille
(e) *(ruin → of person)* perte *f*, ruine *f*; *Rel* **the Fall (of Man)** la chute (de l'homme)
(f) *(decrease → in price, income, shares, temperature)* baisse *f* (**in** de); *(→ in currency)* dépréciation *f*, baisse *f* (**in** de); *(more marked)* chute *f* (**in** de); *(→ of barometer, in pressure)* chute *f* (**in** de)
(g) *(lowering → of water)* décrue *f*, baisse *f*; *(→ of voice)* cadence *f*
(h) *(drape)* **the fall of her gown** le drapé de sa robe, la façon dont tombe sa robe
(i) *(slope)* pente *f*, inclinaison *f*
(j) *Am (autumn)* automne *m*; **in the fall** en automne
(k) *Sport (in judo)* chute *f*; *(in wrestling)* chute *f*
2 *vi* **(a)** *(barrier, cup, napkin, water, person)* tomber; **the napkin fell to the floor** la serviette est tombée par terre; **I slipped and fell on the ice** j'ai dérapé sur la glace et je suis tombé; **the child fell into the pond** l'enfant est tombé dans la mare; **she fell off the stool/out of the window**

elle est tombée du tabouret/par la fenêtre; **to fall 20 feet** tomber de 20 pieds; **he fell over the pile of books** il est tombé en butant contre le tas de livres; **just let your arms fall to your sides** laissez simplement vos bras pendre *ou* tomber sur les côtés; **he fell in a heap on the floor** il s'est affaissé *ou* il est tombé comme une masse; **he fell full length** il est tombé de tout son long; **the crowd fell on** *or* **to their knees** la foule est tombée à genoux; **he fell at her feet to ask forgiveness** il est tombé à genoux devant elle pour lui demander pardon; **she did let fall a few hints** elle a fait effectivement quelques allusions; **the book fell open at page 20** le livre s'est ouvert à la page 20; *also Fig* **to fall on one's feet** retomber sur ses pieds; **a cat always falls on its feet** un chat retombe toujours sur ses pattes; **I fell flat on my face** je suis tombé à plat ventre *ou* face contre terre; *Fam Fig* je me suis planté; *Am very Fam also Fig* **he fell flat on his ass** il s'est cassé la gueule; **his only joke fell flat** la seule plaisanterie qu'il a faite est tombée à plat; **the scheme fell flat** le projet est tombé à l'eau; **despite all their efforts, the party fell flat** en dépit de leurs efforts, la soirée a fait un flop; **to fall to bits** *or* **to pieces** tomber en morceaux; **all her good intentions fell by the wayside** toutes ses bonnes intentions sont tombées à l'eau; **the job fell short of her expectations** le poste ne répondait pas à ses attentes

(**b**) *(move deliberately)* se laisser tomber; **I fell into the armchair** je me suis laissé tomber dans le fauteuil; **they fell into one another's arms** ils sont tombés dans les bras l'un de l'autre

(**c**) *(bridge, building)* s'écrouler, s'effondrer

(**d**) *(err, go astray)* s'écarter du droit chemin; *Rel (sin)* pécher; *Rel* **to fall from grace** perdre la grâce; *Fig* tomber en disgrâce

(**e**) *(ground)* descendre, aller en pente

(**f**) *(government)* tomber, être renversé; *(city, country)* tomber; **after a long siege the city fell** après un long siège, la ville a capitulé; **Constantinople fell to the Turks** Constantinople est tombée aux mains des Turcs

(**g**) *(darkness, light, night, rain, snow)* tomber; **as night fell** à la tombée de la nuit; **the tree's shadow fell across the lawn** l'arbre projetait son ombre sur la pelouse

(**h**) *(land → eyes, blow, weapon)* tomber; **my eyes fell on the letter** mon regard est tombé sur la lettre

(**i**) *(face, spirits)* s'assombrir; **at the sight of her, his face fell** quand il l'a vue, son visage s'est assombri *ou* s'est allongé; **my spirits fell** tout d'un coup, j'ai perdu le moral

(**j**) *(hang down)* tomber, descendre; **the curtains fall right to the floor** les rideaux tombent *ou* descendent jusqu'au sol; **the fabric falls in gentle folds** ce tissu retombe en faisant de jolis plis; **his hair fell to his shoulders** ses cheveux lui descendaient *ou* tombaient jusqu'aux épaules; **his hair keeps falling into his eyes** ses cheveux n'arrêtent pas de lui tomber dans les yeux

(**k**) *(decrease in level, value → price, temperature)* baisser, tomber; *(→ pressure)* baisser, diminuer; *(→ wind)* tomber; **the thermometer/temperature has fallen ten degrees** le thermomètre/la température a baissé de dix degrés; **their voices fell to a whisper** ils se sont mis à chuchoter; **the boss fell in our esteem** le patron a baissé dans notre estime

(**l**) *(issue forth)* tomber, s'échapper; **curses fell from her lips** elle laissa échapper des jurons; **the tears started to fall** il/elle se mit à pleurer

(**m**) *(occur)* tomber; **May Day falls on a Tuesday this year** le Premier Mai tombe un mardi cette année; **the accent falls on the third syllable** l'accent tombe sur la troisième syllabe

(**n**) *(descend)* **a great sadness fell over the town** une grande tristesse s'abattit sur la ville; **a hush fell among** *or* **over the crowd** tout d'un coup, la foule s'est tue

(**o**) *(become)* **to fall asleep** s'endormir; **the child fell fast asleep** l'enfant est tombé dans un profond sommeil; **the bill falls due on the 6th** la facture arrive à échéance le 6; **he will fall heir to a vast fortune** il va hériter d'une grande fortune; **to fall ill** *or* **sick** tomber malade; **to fall pregnant** tomber enceinte; **to fall in love (with sb)** tomber amoureux (de qn); **to fall silent** se taire; **it falls vacant in February** *(job)* il se trouvera vacant au mois de février; *(apartment)* il se trouvera libre *ou* il se libérera au mois de février; **to fall victim to sth** être victime de qch; **she fell victim to depression** elle a fait une dépression

(**p**) *(die)* mourir; **the young men who fell in battle** les jeunes tombés au champ d'honneur

(**q**) *(be classified)* **the athletes fall into two categories** les sportifs se divisent en deux catégories; **these facts fall under another category** ces faits entrent dans une autre catégorie; **that falls outside my area of responsibility** cela ne relève pas de ma responsabilité; **that does not fall within the scope of our agreement** ceci n'entre pas dans le cadre de *ou* ne fait pas partie de notre accord

(**r**) *(inheritance)* **the fortune fell to his niece** c'est sa nièce qui a hérité de sa fortune

(**s**) *Sport (in cricket)* **two English wickets fell on the first day** deux batteurs anglais ont été éliminés le premier jour

3 *comp Am (colours, weather)* d'automne, automnal

4 falls *npl (waterfall)* cascade *f*, chute *f* d'eau; **Niagara Falls** les chutes *fpl* du Niagara

▸▸ *Fam* **fall guy** *(dupe)* pigeon *m*; *(scapegoat)* bouc *m* émissaire ❑; *Hunt* **fall trap** assommoir *m*

▸**fall about** *vi Br Fam* se tordre de rire; **they fell about (laughing)** ils se tordaient de rire

▸**fall apart** *vi* (**a**) *(book, furniture)* tomber en morceaux; *Fig (nation)* se désagréger; *(conference)* échouer; *(system)* s'écrouler, s'effondrer; **her plans fell apart at the seams** ses projets sont tombés à l'eau; **her life was falling apart** toute sa vie s'écroulait; **their marriage is falling apart** leur mariage est en train de se briser *ou* va à vau-l'eau

(**b**) *(person)* s'effondrer; **he more or less fell apart after his wife's death** il a plus ou moins craqué après la mort de sa femme

▸**fall away** *vi* (**a**) *(paint, plaster)* s'écailler (**b**) *(diminish in size → attendance, figures)* diminuer; *(→ fears)* se dissiper, fondre (**c**) *(defect)* déserter; **support for his policies is beginning to fall away** dans la politique qu'il mène il commence à perdre ses appuis (**d**) *(land, slope)* s'affaisser

▸**fall back** *vi* (**a**) *(fall)* tomber à la renverse *ou* en arrière (**b**) *(retreat, recede)* reculer, se retirer; *Mil* se replier, battre en retraite (**c**) *(lag, trail)* se laisser distancer, être à la traîne (**d**) *St Exch & Fin* **to fall back two points** se replier de deux points

▸**fall back on** *vt insep* **to fall back on sth** avoir recours à qch; **it's good to have something to fall back on** *(skill)* c'est bien de pouvoir se raccrocher à quelque chose; *(money)* il vaut mieux avoir d'autres ressources; **he knew he could always fall back on his parents** il savait qu'il pouvait compter sur ses parents

▸**fall behind 1** *vi* se laisser distancer, être à la traîne; *Sport* se laisser distancer; *(in cycling)* décrocher; **she fell behind in** *or* **with her work** elle a pris du retard dans son travail; **they've fallen behind with their reading** ils ont pris du retard dans leurs lectures; **we can't fall behind in** *or* **with the rent** nous ne pouvons pas [illegible] retard pour le loyer

2 *vt insep* prendre du retard sur; **he's fallen behind the rest of the class** il a pris du retard sur le reste de la classe

▸**fall down** *vi* (**a**) *(book, person, picture)* tomber (par terre); *(bridge, building)* s'effondrer, s'écrouler; **that house looks as if it's about to fall down** on dirait que cette maison va s'écrouler (**b**) *(argument, comparison)* s'écrouler, s'effondrer; **where the whole thing falls down is...** là où plus rien ne tient debout *ou* où tout s'écroule c'est...

▸**fall down on** *vt insep* **to fall down on sth** échouer à qch; **he's been falling down on the job lately** il n'était pas *ou* ne s'est pas montré à la hauteur dernièrement

▸**fall for** *vt insep Fam* (**a**) *(become infatuated with)* tomber amoureux de ❑; **they fell for each other** ils sont tombés amoureux l'un de l'autre; **they really fell for Spain in a big way** ils ont vraiment été emballés par l'Espagne

(**b**) *(be deceived by)* se laisser prendre par ❑; **they really fell for it!** ils ont vraiment mordu!, ils se sont vraiment fait avoir!; **don't fall for that hard luck story of his** ne te fais pas avoir quand il te raconte qu'il a la poisse; **I'm not falling for that one!** ça ne prend pas!, à d'autres!

▸**fall in** *vi* (**a**) *(tumble)* tomber; **you'll fall in!** tu vas tomber dedans!; **he leant too far over the side of the boat and fell in** il s'est trop penché hors du bateau et il est tombé (**b**) *(roof)* s'effondrer, s'écrouler (**c**) *(line up)* se mettre en rang, s'aligner; *Mil (troops)* former les rangs; *(one soldier)* rentrer dans les rangs; **fall in!** à vos rangs!

▸**fall into** *vt insep* (**a**) *(tumble into)* tomber dans; **they fell into the trap** ils sont tombés dans le piège; **to fall into sb's clutches** *or* **sb's hands** tomber dans les griffes de qn, tomber entre les mains de qn; *Fig* **the pieces began to fall into place** les éléments ont commencé à se mettre en place (**b**) *(begin)* **she fell into conversation with the stranger** elle est entrée en conversation avec l'étranger

▸**fall in with** *vt insep* (**a**) *(frequent)* **to fall in with sb** se mettre à fréquenter qn; **she fell in with a bad crowd** elle s'est mise à fréquenter des gens louches (**b**) *Br (agree with → suggestion)* accepter; *(→ request)* accéder à; **I'll fall in with whatever you decide to do** je me rangerai à ce que tu décideras

▸**fall off** *vi* (**a**) *(drop off)* tomber; *(in mountain climbing)* dévisser; **the leaves of this plant are falling off** les feuilles de cette plante tombent, cette plante perd ses feuilles; **she fell off the bicycle/horse** elle est tombée du vélo/de cheval (**b**) *(diminish → attendance, exports, numbers, sales)* diminuer, baisser; *(→ profits)* diminuer; *(→ enthusiasm, production)* baisser, tomber; *(→ population, rate)* baisser, décroître; *(→ speed)* ralentir; *(→ interest, zeal)* se relâcher; *(→ popularity)* baisser; *(→ wind)* tomber

▸**fall on** *vt insep* (**a**) *(drop on)* tomber sur; **something fell on my head** j'ai reçu quelque chose sur la tête

(**b**) *(attack)* attaquer, se jeter sur; **the starving children fell on the food** les enfants, affamés, se sont jetés sur la nourriture; *Mil* **the guerrillas fell on the unsuspecting troops** les guérilleros ont fondu sur *ou* attaqué les troupes sans qu'elles s'y attendent

(**c**) *(meet with)* tomber sur, trouver; **they fell on hard times** ils sont tombés dans la misère, ils ont subi des revers de fortune

(**d**) *(of responsibility)* revenir à, incomber à; **suspicion falls on them** c'est eux que l'on soupçonne; **responsibility for looking after them falls on me** c'est à moi qu'il incombe de prendre soin d'eux

▸**fall out** *vi* (**a**) *(drop out)* tomber; **the keys must have fallen out of my pocket** les clés ont dû tomber de ma poche; **his hair is falling out** ses cheveux tombent, il perd ses cheveux (**b**) *(quarrel)* se brouiller, se disputer; **she's fallen out with her boyfriend** elle est *ou* s'est brouillée avec son petit ami (**c**) *(happen)* se passer, advenir; **as things fell out** en fin de compte (**d**) *Mil* rompre les rangs; **fall out!** rompez! (**e**) *Am Fam (fall asleep)* s'endormir ❑

▸**fall over** *vi* (**a**) *(lose balance → person)* tomber (par terre); *(→ thing)* se renverser, être renversé (**b**) *Fam (idioms)* **she was falling over herself to make us feel welcome** elle se mettait en quatre pour nous faire bon accueil; **the men were falling over each other to help her** les hommes ne savaient pas quoi inventer pour l'aider

▸**fall through** *vi (fail)* échouer; **the deal fell through** l'affaire n'a pas abouti; **all our plans fell through at the last minute** tous nos projets sont tombés à l'eau au dernier moment

▸**fall to 1** *vt insep* (**a**) *Br (begin)* se mettre à; **we fell to work** nous nous sommes mis à l'œuvre; **we all fell to talking about the past** nous nous sommes tous mis à parler du passé

(**b**) *(devolve upon)* appartenir à, incomber à; **the task that falls to us is not an easy one** la tâche qui nous incombe *ou* revient n'est pas facile; **it fell to her to break the news to him** ce fut à elle de lui annoncer la nouvelle

2 *vi (eat)* **he brought in the food and they fell to** il a apporté à manger et ils se sont jetés dessus; **she fell to as if she hadn't eaten for a week** elle a attaqué comme si elle n'avait rien mangé depuis huit jours

►**fall upon** *vt insep* (**a**) *(attack)* attaquer, se jeter sur; *Mil* **the army fell upon the enemy** l'armée s'est abattue *ou* a fondu sur l'ennemi; **they fell upon the food** ils se sont jetés sur la nourriture (**b**) *(meet with)* tomber sur, trouver; **the family fell upon hard times** la famille a subi des revers de fortune

---

'The Fall of the House of Usher' *Poe* 'La Chute de la maison Usher'

---

fallacious [fəˈleɪʃəs] *adj (statement)* fallacieux, faux (fausse); *(hope)* faux (fausse), illusoire

fallaciousness [fəˈleɪʃəsnɪs] *n* caractère *m* fallacieux, fausseté *f*

fallacy [ˈfæləsɪ] (*pl* **fallacies**) *n (misconception)* erreur *f*, idée *f* fausse; *(false reasoning)* mauvais raisonnement *m*, sophisme *m*; *(in logic)* sophisme *m*; **it is a fallacy that...** ce serait une erreur de croire que...; **the fallacy of this argument is that...** ce qui est faux dans ce raisonnement, c'est que...

fallback [ˈfɔːlbæk] *n* (**a**) *(retreat)* retraite *f*, recul *m* (**b**) *(reserve)* réserve *f*; **what's our fallback position?** sur quoi est-ce qu'on peut se rabattre?

fallen [ˈfɔːlən] **1** *pp of* **fall**

2 *adj* (**a**) *(gen)* tombé; *(hero, soldier)* tombé, mort; *(idol)* tombé en disgrâce; *(leaf)* mort (**b**) *(immoral)* perdu; **fallen woman** fille *f* perdue

3 *npl Literary* **the fallen** ceux qui sont tombés au champ d'honneur

►► *Rel & St Exch* ***fallen angel*** ange *m* déchu; *Med* ***fallen arches*** affaissement *m* de la voûte plantaire

fallibility [ˌfæləˈbɪlətɪ] *n* faillibilité *f*

fallible [ˈfæləbəl] *adj* faillible; **everyone is fallible** tout le monde peut se tromper

falling [ˈfɔːlɪŋ] *adj (piece of masonry, tile)* qui tombe; *(population)* décroissant; *(prices, temperature, standards, value)* en baisse

►► ***falling rocks*** chute *f* de pierres; ***falling star*** étoile *f* filante

falling-away *n (of support)* affaiblissement *m*; *(of supporters)* défection *f*, désertion *f*

falling-off, fall-off *n* réduction *f*, diminution *f*; **a falling-off in production** une baisse de production; **a gradual falling-off of interest/of support** une baisse progressive d'intérêt/de soutien

Fallopian tube [fəˈləʊpɪən-] *n Anat* trompe *f* utérine *ou* de Fallope

fallout [ˈfɔːlaʊt] *n (UNCOUNT) (radioactive)* retombées *fpl* (radioactives); *Fam Fig (consequences)* retombées❑ *fpl*, répercussions❑ *fpl*

►► ***fallout shelter*** abri *m* antiatomique

fallow [ˈfæləʊ] **1** *adj* (**a**) *Agr (field, land)* en jachère, en friche; **to lie fallow** être en jachère; *Fig* **a fallow period** un passage à vide (**b**) *(colour)* fauve

2 *n* jachère *f*, friche *f*

►► *Zool* ***fallow deer*** daim *m*

fallowness [ˈfæləʊnɪs] *n Agr* jachère *f*

false [fɔːls] **1** *adj* (**a**) *(wrong)* faux (fausse); *(untrue)* erroné, inexact; **a false idea** une idée fausse *ou* erronée; **a false statement** une fausse déclaration; **to give sb a false impression of sth** donner à qn une fausse impression sur qch; **she put a false interpretation on his invitation** elle a mal interprété son invitation; **in a false position** dans une position fausse; **don't make any false moves** ne faites pas de faux pas; **false pride** vanité *f*

(**b**) *(fake)* faux (fausse); *(artificial)* artificiel; **false identity** fausse identité *f*; **false name** faux nom *m*

(**c**) *(deceptive)* faux (fausse), mensonger; **false promises** promesses *fpl* mensongères, fausses promesses *fpl*; **a false report** *or* **rumour** une fausse rumeur; *Law* **under false pretences** par des moyens frauduleux; *Fig* **you've got me here under false pretences** tu m'as bien piégé; *Law* **to bear false witness** porter un faux témoignage

(**d**) *(insincere)* perfide, fourbe; *(disloyal)* déloyal; **false modesty** fausse modestie *f*

2 *adv* faux; **her story rings false** son histoire sonne faux; **to play sb false** trahir qn

►► ***false alarm*** fausse alerte *f*; *Am* ***false arrest*** arrestation *f* illégale; *Fin* ***false bill*** fausse facture *f*; ***false bottom*** *(of box etc)* double fond *m*; **a suitcase with a false bottom** une valise à double fond; ***false dawn*** lueurs *fpl* annonciatrices de l'aube; *Fig* **it was a false dawn** ce n'était qu'un faux espoir; *Acct* ***false entry*** fausse écriture *f*; ***false eyelashes*** faux cils *mpl*; ***a false friend*** *(gen)* un ami déloyal; *Ling* un faux ami; *Psy* ***false memory syndrome*** syndrome *m* des faux souvenirs; *Mus* ***false note*** fausse note *f*; *Fig* **to strike a false note** ne pas être crédible; ***false pregnancy*** grossesse *f* nerveuse; ***false ribs*** fausses côtes *fpl*; *Sport* ***false start*** faux départ *m*; ***false teeth*** dentier *m*

false-hearted [-ˈhɑːtɪd] *adj Literary* fourbe

falsehood [ˈfɔːlshʊd] *n Formal* (**a**) *(lie)* mensonge *m*; **to tell** *or* **to utter a falsehood** mentir, dire des mensonges (**b**) *(lying)* faux *m*; **truth and falsehood** le vrai et le faux (**c**) *(falseness)* fausseté *f*

falsely [ˈfɔːlslɪ] *adv (claim, state)* faussement; *(accuse, judge)* à tort, injustement; *(interpret)* mal; *(act)* déloyalement; **she sounded falsely cheerful on the telephone** sa gaieté sonnait faux au téléphone

falseness [ˈfɔːlsnɪs] *n* (**a**) *(of belief, statement)* fausseté *f* (**b**) *(of friend, lover)* infidélité *f* (**c**) *(insincerity)* fausseté *f*, manque *m* de sincérité

falsers [ˈfɔːlsəz] *npl Br Fam Hum (teeth)* râtelier *m*, dentier❑ *m*

falsetto [fɔːlˈsetəʊ] (*pl* **falsettos**) *Mus* **1** *n* fausset *m*

2 *adj (voice)* de fausset, de tête

falsies [ˈfɔːlsɪz] *npl Fam* soutien-gorge *m* rembourré❑

falsifiable [ˌfɔːlsɪˈfaɪəbəl] *adj Phil* falsifiable

falsification [ˌfɔːlsɪfɪˈkeɪʃən] *n* falsification *f*

falsifier [ˈfɔːlsɪˌfaɪə(r)] *n* falsificateur(trice) *m,f*

falsify [ˈfɔːlsɪfaɪ] (*pt & pp* **falsified**) *vt* (**a**) *(document)* falsifier; *(evidence)* maquiller; *(accounts, figures)* truquer (**b**) *(misrepresent)* déformer, dénaturer (**c**) *(disprove)* réfuter

falsity [ˈfɔːlsətɪ] (*pl* **falsities**) *n* (**a**) *(falseness)* fausseté *f*, erreur *f* (**b**) *(lie)* mensonge *m*

falter [ˈfɔːltə(r)] **1** *vi* (**a**) *(speaker)* hésiter, parler d'une voix mal assurée; **his voice faltered** il hésita

(**b**) *(waver)* vaciller, chanceler; *(courage, memory)* faiblir; **his steps faltered as he neared the room** ses pas se firent hésitants tandis qu'il s'approchait de la pièce; **demand for luxury goods has begun to falter** la demande de produits de luxe a commencé à baisser

(**c**) *(stumble)* chanceler, tituber

2 *vt* balbutier, bredouiller; **"I'm not sure, I don't... I can't..." he faltered** "je ne suis pas sûr, je... non... non...", bredouilla-t-il *ou* balbutia-t-il

faltering [ˈfɔːltərɪŋ] *adj (attempt)* timide, hésitant; *(voice)* hésitant, mal assuré; *(steps)* chancelant, mal assuré; *(courage, memory)* défaillant

falteringly [ˈfɔːltərɪŋlɪ] *adv* avec hésitation; *(move)* d'un pas chancelant *ou* mal assuré; *(speak)* d'une voix hésitante *ou* mal assurée

Famagusta [ˌfæməˈgʊstə] *n* Famagouste

fame [feɪm] *n* célébrité *f*, renommée *f*; **the film brought her fame and fortune** le film l'a rendue riche et célèbre; **his thirst for fame and fortune** sa soif de gloire et d'argent; **to rise to fame** se faire un nom; **Mick Jagger of Rolling Stones fame** Mick Jagger, le chanteur du célèbre groupe The Rolling Stones

famed [feɪmd] *adj* célèbre, renommé; **famed for his generosity** connu *ou* célèbre pour sa générosité

familial [fəˈmɪlɪəl] *adj* familial

familiar [fəˈmɪljə(r)] **1** *adj* (**a**) *(well-known)* familier; **a familiar face** un visage familier *ou* connu; **his name is familiar** j'ai déjà entendu son nom (quelque part), son nom me dit quelque chose; **she's a familiar sight about town** tout le monde la connaît de vue en ville; **there's something familiar about the place** il me semble connaître cet endroit; **a familiar feeling** un sentiment bien connu; **an all too familiar story of drug addiction and homelessness** (c'est) toujours ce même problème de drogue et de sans-abris; *Fig* **we're on familiar territory** nous voilà en terrain de connaissance

(**b**) *(acquainted)* **to be familiar with sth** bien connaître qch; **she's familiar with the situation** elle est au courant *ou* au fait de la situation; **to become familiar with sth** se familiariser avec qch

(**c**) *(informal)* familier, intime; **to be on familiar terms with sb** entretenir des rapports amicaux avec qn; **familiar language/tone** langage *m*/ton *m* familier

(**d**) *Pej (presumptuous → socially)* familier; *(→ sexually)* trop entreprenant; **don't let him get too familiar (with you)** ne le laissez pas devenir trop entreprenant

2 *n* (**a**) *(friend)* familier *m*, ami(e) *m,f*

(**b**) *(in witchcraft → spirit)* démon *m* familier

familiarity [fəˌmɪlɪˈærətɪ] (*pl* **familiarities**) *n* (**a**) *(of face, place)* caractère *m* familier (**b**) *(with book, rules, language)* connaissance *f*; **her familiarity with his work** sa connaissance de ses œuvres; *Prov* **familiarity breeds contempt** = la familiarité engendre le mépris (**c**) *(intimacy)* familiarité *f*, intimité *f* (**d**) *(usu pl) Pej (undue intimacy)* familiarité *f*, privauté *f*

familiarization [fəˌmɪljəraɪˈzeɪʃən] *n* familiarisation *f*; **after a period of familiarization with the software** après une période de familiarisation avec le logiciel

►► ***familiarization training*** initiation *f*; *Com* ***familiarization trip*** voyage *m* d'études *ou* de familiarisation

familiarize, -ise [fəˈmɪljəraɪz] *vt* (**a**) *(inform)* familiariser; **to familiarize oneself with sth** se familiariser avec qch; **she familiarized him with the rules** elle l'a initié aux règles (**b**) *(make widely known)* répandre, vulgariser

familiarly [fəˈmɪljəlɪ] *adv* familièrement; **the Victoria theatre, familiarly known as the Old Vic** le "Victoria theatre", que l'on appelle familièrement "Old Vic"

family [ˈfæmlɪ] (*pl* **families**) **1** *n (gen) & Biol, Bot & Ling* famille *f*; **have you any family?** *(relatives)* avez-vous de la famille?; *(children)* avez-vous des enfants?; **to raise a family** élever des enfants; **a large family** une famille nombreuse; **all the children in the family are redheads** tous les enfants de la famille sont roux; **to start a family** avoir un (premier) enfant; **she's (just like) one of the family** elle fait (tout à fait) partie *ou* elle est (tout à fait) de la famille; **none of my family like him** personne ne l'aime dans ma famille; **it runs in the family** cela tient de famille; **of good family** de bonne famille; **a family audience** un public *ou* auditoire familial; **a family business** une entreprise familiale; **family butcher** boucher *m* de quartier; **family doctor** docteur *m* de famille; **a family hotel** une pension de famille; **family portraits** portraits *mpl* d'ancêtres; *Old-fashioned Fam Euph* **to be in the family way** attendre un enfant❑; **we'll keep it in the family** *(heirloom, land)* ça restera dans la famille; *(scandal)* ça ne sortira pas de la famille; **he's a family man** il aime la vie de famille, c'est un bon père de famille; **unsuitable for family viewing** non approprié aux enfants; **I wouldn't call it family viewing** ce n'est pas exactement un spectacle à conseiller aux enfants; **this film is not family viewing** ce n'est pas un film tout public

2 *comp (life)* familial, de famille; *(car, friend)* de la famille; *(dinner, likeness, quarrel)* de famille; *(programme)* pour les familles

►► *Br Formerly Admin* ***family allowance*** ≃allocations *fpl* familiales; ***family Bible*** Bible *f* familiale *ou* de famille; *Mktg* ***family brand*** marque *f* générale; ***family car*** familiale *f*; ***family circle*** cercle *m* de (la) famille; *Am Law* ***family court*** = tribunal pour toute affaire concernant des enfants; *Br Admin* ***family credit*** = prestation complémentaire pour familles à faibles revenus ayant au moins un enfant; *Br Law* ***Family Division*** = division du "High Court" s'occupant des affaires matrimoniales; *Am* ***family fare*** *(on public transport)* tarif *m* familles; *Br Formerly Admin* ***family income supplement*** ≃ complément *m* familial; *Br Formerly* ***Family Income Support*** ≃ complément *m* familial; *Fam Hum*

family jewels *(man's genitals)* bijoux *mpl* de famille; ***family law*** droit *m* de la famille; ***family leave*** congé *m* parental; ***family name*** nom *m* de famille; ***family planning*** planning *m* familial; ***Family Planning Association*** Planning *m* familial; ***family planning clinic*** centre *m* de planning familial; *Am* ***family practice*** médecine *f* générale; *Am* ***family practitioner*** médecin *m* de famille, (médecin *m*) généraliste *m*; ***Family Restaurants*** = chaîne américaine de restaurants bon marché; ***family room*** *(in hotel)* chambre *f* familiale; *Am (in house)* salle *f* de séjour; *Br (in pub)* salle *f* réservée aux familles; ***family saloon*** berline *f* familiale; ***family tree*** arbre *m* généalogique

family-run *adj (hotel, restaurant)* géré en famille, familial

family-size(d) *adj (jar, packet)* familial

famine ['fæmɪn] *n* famine *f*; *see also box on* **The Great Famine**

famished ['fæmɪʃt] *adj* affamé; *Fam* **I'm famished!** je meurs de faim!, j'ai une faim de loup!

famous ['feɪməs] **1** *adj* (**a**) *(renowned)* célèbre, renommé; **the stately home is famous for its gardens** le château est connu *ou* célèbre pour ses jardins; **a famous victory** une victoire célèbre; **so much for her famous cooking!** voilà ce que vaut *ou* on sait maintenant ce que vaut sa fameuse cuisine!; **famous last words!** c'est ce que tu crois! (**b**) *Old-fashioned (first-rate)* fameux, formidable

2 *n* **the famous** les gens célèbres, les célébrités *fpl*

►► *Literature* ***the Famous Five*** le Club des Cinq

Famous for fifteen minutes
Le peintre américain Andy Warhol déclara en 1968 qu' "à l'avenir tout le monde [aurait] droit à son quart d'heure de célébrité".
La formule est maintenant entrée dans la langue pour parler du caractère éphémère de la célébrité, et est souvent utilisée dans la structure **to have one's fifteen minutes of fame** ("connaître son quart d'heure de célébrité"), comme dans l'exemple suivant **I had my fifteen minutes of fame in 1999 when I appeared as an interviewee on Belgian television** ("j'ai connu mon quart d'heure de célébrité en 1999 lorsque j'ai été interviewé par une chaîne de télévision belge").

famously ['feɪməslɪ] *adv* (**a**) *Fam (very well)* fameusement (bien), rudement bien; **they get on famously** ils s'entendent à merveille *ou* comme larrons en foire; **the project is coming along famously** l'opération marche comme sur des roulettes

(**b**) *(with renown)* **the castle has often been the scene of important events, most famously when...** le château a souvent été la scène d'événements importants, le plus célèbre d'entre eux ayant eu lieu quand...; **as Oscar Wilde once famously said...** pour citer la formule célèbre d'Oscar Wilde...

fan [fæn] *(pt & pp* **fanned,** *cont* **fanning**) **1** *n* (**a**) *(supporter)* enthousiaste *mf*, passionné(e) *m,f*; *(of celebrity) & Sport* fan *mf*; **a football fan** un fan ou un passionné de football; [illegible] **fan** elle se passionne pour les échecs/le rap; **a crowd of football fans** une foule de supporters de football; **he's a fan of Thai cooking** c'est un amateur de cuisine thaïlandaise; **I'm not one of her fans, I'm not a great fan of hers** je suis loin d'être un de ses admirateurs; **movie fans** cinéphiles *mfpl*

(**b**) *(ventilator → mechanical)* ventilateur *m*; *(→ hand-held)* éventail *m*; **shaped like a fan** en éventail

(**c**) *Agr (machine)* tarare *m*; *(basket)* van *m*

2 *vt* (**a**) *(face, person)* éventer; **to fan oneself** s'éventer

(**b**) *(fire)* attiser, souffler sur; *(passions)* attiser, exciter; *Fig* **to fan the flames** jeter de l'huile sur le feu; **these remarks had fanned the flames of nationalist feeling** ces remarques avaient exacerbé le sentiment nationaliste; **to fan the embers of sb's passion** raviver les flammes de la passion de qn; **the terraces are fanned by cool sea breezes** les terrasses sont rafraîchies par les brises marines; *Literary* **fortune fans his sails** il a le vent en poupe

(**c**) *(spread out)* étaler (en éventail)

(**d**) *Agr (grain)* vanner

3 *vi* s'étaler (en éventail)

►► *Aut* ***fan belt*** courroie *f* de ventilateur; ***fan club*** cercle *m ou* club *m* de fans; *Fig* **her fan club is here** ses admirateurs sont là; ***fan dance*** danse *f* des éventails; ***fan heater*** radiateur *m* soufflant; ***fan jet*** *(engine)* turboréacteur *m*; *(plane)* avion *m* à turboréacteurs; ***fan letter*** lettre *f* d'un admirateur; ***fan mail*** courrier *m* des admirateurs; *Ich* ***fan mussel*** jambonneau *m (coquillage)*; ***fan oven*** four *m* à chaleur tournante; *Archit* ***fan vaulting*** *(UNCOUNT)* voûte *f ou* voûtes *fpl* en éventail

►**fan out 1** *vi (spread out)* s'étaler *ou* se déployer (en éventail); *(army, search party)* se déployer

2 *vt sep* étaler (en éventail)

fan-assisted oven *n* four *m* à chaleur tournante

fanatic [fə'nætɪk] **1** *adj* fanatique

2 *n* fanatique *mf*

fanatical [fə'nætɪkəl] *adj* fanatique

fanatically [fə'nætɪkəlɪ] *adv* fanatiquement

fanaticism [fə'nætɪˌsɪzəm] *n* fanatisme *m*

fanaticize, -ise [fə'nætɪsaɪz] *vt* fanatiser; **a fanaticized mob** une foule fanatisée

fanciable ['fænsɪəbəl] *adj Br Fam (person)* plutôt bien ❑, pas mal du tout ❑

fancied ['fænsɪd] *adj* (**a**) *(imagined)* imaginaire (**b**) *Sport (favoured)* coté, en vogue

fancier ['fænsɪə(r)] *n (of animals, birds → lover)* amateur(trice) *m,f*; *(→ breeder)* éleveur(euse) *m,f*

fanciful ['fænsɪfʊl] *adj* (**a**) *(whimsical → person)* capricieux, fantaisiste; *(→ notion)* fantasque; *(→ project)* chimérique; *(→ clothing)* extravagant; **he was being rather fanciful** *(being unrealistic)* il se faisait des idées, il rêvait; *(indulging his imagination)* il se laissait porter par son imagination (**b**) *(imaginative)* imaginatif, plein d'imagination (**c**) *(imaginary)* imaginaire

fancifully ['fænsɪfʊlɪ] *adv* (**a**) *(act)* capricieusement; *(dress)* d'une façon extravagante *ou* fantaisiste; **somewhat fancifully described as...** désigné sous le terme plutôt fantaisiste de...

(**b**) *(draw, write)* avec imagination

fancily ['fænsɪlɪ] *adv* d'une façon recherchée *ou* raffinée; **they were very fancily dressed** ils étaient habillés avec soin, ils étaient endimanchés; **fancily decorated** décoré d'une manière compliquée *ou* avec recherche

fanciness ['fænsɪnɪs] *n* caractère *m* raffiné

fan-cooled [-kuːld] *adj* refroidi par ventilateur

fancy ['fænsɪ] *(compar* **fancier,** *superl* **fanciest,** *pl* **fancies,** *pt & pp* **fancied**) **1** *adj* (**a**) *(elaborate → clothes)* recherché, raffiné, *(→ style)* recherché, travaillé; *(→ excuse)* recherché, compliqué; **fancy cakes** pâtisseries *fpl*; **a tin of fancy biscuits** un assortiment de biscuits; **a fancy dog** un chien de luxe; **just a bottle of ordinary wine, nothing fancy** juste une bouteille de vin ordinaire, rien de spécial; **to cut out the fancy stuff** arrêter les chichis

(**b**) *(upmarket → neighbourhood)* chic; *(→ shop, car)* de luxe; **fancy food** plats *mpl* compliqués

(**c**) *Pej (affected, pretentious → talk, words)* [illegible] grands airs

(**d**) *(high → price)* exorbitant

(**e**) *Zool (breed)* d'agrément

2 *n* (**a**) *(whim)* caprice *m*, fantaisie *f*; **as the fancy takes him** comme ça lui chante; **it's just a passing fancy** ce n'est qu'une lubie

(**b**) *Br (liking)* goût *m*, penchant *m*; **I've taken a fancy to avocados lately** je me suis mis depuis quelque temps à aimer les avocats; **to take a fancy to sb** *(become fond of)* se prendre d'affection pour qn; *(become sexually attracted to)* s'éprendre *ou* s'enticher de qn; **the dress took** *or* **caught her fancy** la robe lui a fait envie *ou* lui a tapé dans l'œil; *Fam* **the idea tickled my fancy** l'idée m'a séduit ❑

(**c**) *(imagination)* imagination *f*, fantaisie *f*; *Literary* **the realm of fancy** le domaine de l'imaginaire, le royaume des chimères

(**d**) *(notion)* idée *f* fantasque, fantasme *m*; **I have a fancy that...** j'ai idée que...; **one of my fancies as a child was to join the circus** enfant, je rêvais de faire partie d'un cirque; **idle fancies** chimères *fpl*

3 *vt* (**a**) *Br Fam (want)* avoir envie de ❑; *(like)* aimer ❑; **do you fancy a cup of tea?** ça te dirait une tasse de thé?; **I fancy a bit of chicken** je mangerais volontiers un morceau de poulet, j'ai envie d'un morceau de poulet; **I don't fancy travelling in this weather** cela ne me dit rien *ou* je n'ai pas envie de voyager par ce temps; **she wasn't sure if she fancied the idea** elle n'était pas sûre que l'idée la tentait; **I've never fancied science fiction** je n'ai jamais été attiré par la science-fiction; **to fancy sb** s'enticher de qn

(**b**) *Fam (imagine)* imaginer ❑, s'imaginer ❑; **fancy meeting you here!** tiens! je ne m'attendais pas à vous voir ici! ❑; **fancy anyone wanting to do that!** qu'est-ce que les gens vont chercher!; **fancy her coming!** qui aurait cru qu'elle allait venir! ❑; **fancy that!** tiens! voyez-vous cela!

(**c**) *Fam (have good opinion of)* **to fancy oneself** être infatué de sa petite personne, se gober; **she really fancies herself** elle ne se prend vraiment pas pour rien; **she fancies herself as an intellectual** elle se prend pour une intellectuelle ❑; **I don't fancy their chances of winning** je ne crois pas qu'ils aient des chances de gagner ❑, j'imagine mal qu'ils puissent gagner ❑; **they were not fancied to win** personne ne pensait qu'ils gagneraient ❑; *Sport* **which horse do you fancy?** à votre avis, quel sera le cheval gagnant? ❑, quel cheval donnez-vous gagnant? ❑

(**d**) *Literary (believe)* croire, se figurer; **he fancies he knows everything** il se figure tout savoir; **she fancied she heard the baby crying** elle a cru entendre pleurer le bébé; **I fancy we've met before** j'ai l'impression que nous nous sommes déjà rencontrés

►► *Fam* ***Fancy Dan*** *(dandy)* dandy *m*; *(show-off)* frimeur *m*; *Br* ***fancy dress*** déguisement *m*, costume *m*; **in fancy dress** déguisé; **I didn't realise it was fancy dress** je ne savais pas qu'il fallait se déguiser; ***fancy dress ball*** bal *m* masqué *ou* costumé; ***fancy dress party*** fête *f* déguisée; *Br* ***fancy goods*** articles *mpl* de fantaisie; *Fam Pej* ***fancy man*** jules *m*; **he's her new fancy man** c'est son nouveau jules *ou* mec; *Fam Pej* ***fancy woman*** maîtresse ❑ *f*, poule *f*

fancy-free *adj* sans souci

fancy-pants ['fænsɪpænts] *adj Am Fam (restaurant, hotel, neighbourhood)* classe; *(person)* frimeur

fancywork ['fænsɪwɜːk] *n (UNCOUNT)* ouvrages *mpl* d'agrément

fandangle [fæn'dæŋgəl] *n Fam* (**a**) *(ornament)* ornement *m* clinquant ❑ (**b**) *(UNCOUNT) (nonsense)* sottises ❑ *fpl*

fandango [fæn'dæŋgəʊ] *(pl* **fandangos**) *n* fandango *m*

fandom ['fændəm] *n Am* fans *mpl*, supporters *mpl*

fane [feɪn] *n Arch or Literary* temple *m*

fanfare ['fænfeə(r)] *n Mus* fanfare *f*; *Fig* **with much fanfare** *(ostentation)* avec des roulements de tambour, avec éclat

fanfaronade [ˌfænfærə'nɑːd] *n* fanfaronnade *f*, vanterie *f*

fanfold ['fænfəʊld] *adj*

►► *Comput* ***fanfold paper*** papier *m* continu plié en accordéon

fang [fæŋ] *n (of snake)* crochet *m*; *(of wolf, vampire)* croc *m*, canine *f*

fanged [fæŋd] *adj* (**a**) *(snake)* pourvu de crochets; *(wolf)* pourvu de crocs (**b**) *(tool)* muni d'une soie; *(knife)* à soie (**c**) *Med* **three-fanged molar** molaire *f* à racine avec trois prolongements

fangless ['fæŋlɪs] *adj* (**a**) *(snake)* sans crochets; *(wolf)* sans crocs (**b**) *(tool)* sans soie (**c**) *(tooth)* sans racine

fango ['fæŋgəʊ] *n Med* boue *f* des sources de Battaglia

fanlight ['fænlaɪt] *n Archit* imposte *f* (semi-circulaire)

Fannie Mae ['fænɪˌmeɪ] *n* = organisme de crédit américain

fanning ['fænɪŋ] *n* (**a**) *(of fire)* soufflement *m*; *(of quarrel)* attisage *m*, attisement *m* (**b**) *Agr (of grain)* vannage *m*

►► *Entom* ***fanning bee*** ventileuse *f*

fanny ['fænɪ] (*pl* **fannies**) *n* (**a**) *Br Vulg (female genitals)* chatte *f* (**b**) *Am Fam (buttocks)* fesses❑ *fpl*

►► *Am* ***fanny bag, fanny pack*** banane *f (sac)*

►**fanny about, fanny around** *vi Br very Fam* perdre son temps à des bricoles, glander

Fanny Adams [ˌfænɪ'ædəmz] *pr n Br Fam* **(sweet) Fanny Adams** que dalle

fan-shaped *adj* en éventail

fantabulous [fæn'tæbjʊləs] *adj Fam* chic, chouette

fantail (pigeon) ['fænteɪl-] *n Orn* pigeon *m* paon

fantailed ['fænteɪld] *adj Orn*

►► ***fantailed pigeon*** pigeon *m* paon; ***fantailed warbler*** cisticole *f* des joncs

fantasia [fæn'teɪzjə] *n Literature & Mus* fantaisie *f*

fantasist ['fæntəsɪst] *n* (**a**) *(self-deluding person)* mythomane *mf* (**b**) *Formal Art & Literature* fantaisiste *mf*

fantasize, -ise ['fæntəsaɪz] **1** *vi* fantasmer, se livrer à des fantasmes; **she fantasized about becoming rich and famous** elle rêvait de devenir riche et célèbre

2 *vt* rêver, imaginer (**that** que)

fantastic [fæn'tæstɪk] *adj* (**a**) *Fam (wonderful)* fantastique, sensationnel; **we had a fantastic time** nous nous sommes vraiment bien amusés; **what a fantastic goal!** quel but fantastique *ou* superbe! (**b**) *Fam (very great → success)* inouï❑, fabuleux❑; *(→ amount, sum, rate)* phénoménal❑, faramineux❑ (**c**) *(preposterous, strange → idea, plan, story)* fantastique, bizarre; **it sounds fantastic, but it's true** ça paraît inouï mais c'est vrai

fantastically [fæn'tæstɪklɪ] *adv* (**a**) *Fam (greatly)* fantastiquement❑, extraordinairement❑; **it's fantastically expensive** c'est incroyablement *ou* terriblement cher (**b**) *(preposterously)* **somewhat fantastically, the story ends with…** l'histoire se termine d'une manière un peu invraisemblable avec…

fantasy ['fæntəsɪ] (*pl* **fantasies**) *n* (**a**) *(dream)* fantasme *m*; *Psy* fantasme *m*; *(notion)* idée *f* fantasque; **to indulge in fantasy** se livrer à des fantasmes *ou* rêveries; **sexual fantasy** fantasme *m* (sexuel) (**b**) *(imagination)* imagination *f*, fantaisie *f*; **fantasy and reality** l'imaginaire *m* et la réalité; **to live in a fantasy world** vivre dans un monde à soi (**c**) *Literature & Mus* fantaisie *f*

►► ***fantasy football*** = jeu dans lequel les participants composent leur équipe idéale et marquent des points en fonction des performances réelles des joueurs choisis au cours de la saison

fanworm ['fænwɜːm] *n Zool* spirographe *m*

fanzine ['fænziːn] *n* revue *f* spécialisée, fanzine *m*

FAO [ˌefeɪ'əʊ] *n* (*abbr* **Food and Agriculture Organization**) FAO *f*

fao (*written abbr* **for the attention of**) à l'attention de

FAQ [ˌefeɪ'kjuː] **1** *adv Br Com* (*abbr* **free alongside quay**) FLQ

2 *n Comput* (*abbr* **frequently asked questions**) FAQ

►► *Comput* ***FAQ file*** fichier *m* FAQ

faq [ˌefeɪ'kjuː] *n Com* (*abbr* **fair average quality**) qualité *f* loyale et marchande

FAR [fɑː(r)]

loin	► **1 (a), (b)**
beaucoup	► **1 (c)**
lointain	► **2 (a)**
éloigné	► **2 (a)**
autre	► **2 (b)**
extrême	► **2 (c)**

(*compar* **farther** ['fɑːðə(r)] *or* **further** ['fɜːðə(r)], *superl* **farthest** ['fɑːðɪst] *or* **furthest** ['fɜːðɪst]) **1** *adv* (**a**) *(distant in space)* loin; **is it far?** est-ce (que c'est) loin?; **how far is it to town?** combien y a-t-il jusqu'à la ville?; **how far is he going?** jusqu'où va-t-il?; **have you come far?** êtes-vous venu de loin?; **the police are looking for them, they won't get very far** la police est à leur recherche, ils n'iront pas très loin; **he went as far north as Alaska** il est allé au nord jusqu'en Alaska; **far away** *or* **off in the distance** au loin, dans le lointain; **he doesn't live far away** *or* **off** il n'habite pas loin; **it isn't far from the station** ce n'est pas loin de la gare; **far above/below** loin au-dessus/au-dessous; **far beyond** bien au-delà; **far out at sea** en pleine mer; *Fig* **his thoughts are far away** son esprit est ailleurs; **his work is far above the others'** son travail est de loin supérieur à celui des autres; **that's far beyond me** *(physically)* c'est bien au-dessus de mes forces; *(intellectually)* ça me dépasse; **how far can you trust him?** jusqu'à quel point peut-on lui faire confiance?; **how far (on) are you in the book?** où en es-tu dans le livre?; **how far have you got with the translation?** où en es-tu de la traduction?; **far and wide** de tous côtés; **they came from far and wide** ils sont venus de partout; **he travels far and wide** il court le monde; **they searched far and wide for a suitable site** ils ont cherché partout un emplacement convenable; **far be it from me to interfere!** loin de moi l'idée d'intervenir!; **to be** *Br* **far out** *or Am* **far off** *(person)* se tromper complètement; *(report, survey)* être complètement erroné; *(guess)* être loin du compte; **he's not far off** *or* **wrong** il n'a pas tout à fait tort; **she's not far off being finished** elle n'est pas loin d'avoir fini; **to carry** *or* **to take sth too far** pousser qch trop loin; **have you got far to go?** avez-vous encore beaucoup de chemin à faire?; *Fig* êtes-vous loin du but?; **you won't get far with that attitude** vous n'irez pas loin avec ce genre de comportement; **sincerity won't get you very far** la sincérité ne vous mènera pas loin; *Literary* **far from the madding crowd** loin de la foule et du bruit

(**b**) *(distant in time)* loin; **as far back as 1800** déjà en 1800, dès 1800; **as far back as I can remember** aussi loin que je m'en souvienne; **I can't look far beyond August** je ne sais pas ce qui se passera après le mois d'août; **she worked far into the night** elle a travaillé très avant *ou* jusque tard dans la nuit; **don't look so far into the future** ne vous préoccupez pas de ce qui se passera dans un avenir aussi lointain; **the holidays aren't far off** les vacances ne sont plus loin *ou* approchent; **he's not far off sixty** il n'a pas loin de la soixantaine

(**c**) *(with comparatives) (much)* beaucoup, bien; **this is far better** c'est beaucoup *ou* bien mieux; **a far greater problem** un problème bien *ou* autrement *ou* beaucoup plus grave; **she is far more intelligent than I am** elle est bien *ou* beaucoup plus intelligente que moi

(**d**) *(idioms)* **to go far** *(person, idea)* aller loin, faire son chemin; **this has gone far enough** trop, c'est trop; **his policy doesn't go far enough** sa politique ne va pas assez loin; **I would even go so far as to say…** j'irais même jusqu'à dire…, je dirais même…; **he went so far as to claim that…** il est allé jusqu'à prétendre que…; **I wouldn't go so far as to say he's lying** je n'irais pas jusqu'à dire qu'il ment; **things went so far that…** les choses sont allées si loin que…; **to go too far** *(exaggerate)* dépasser les bornes, exagérer; **you're going too far!** vous exagérez!; **that's going too far** cela passe la mesure; **she's gone too far to back out** elle s'est trop engagée pour reculer; **this goes quite far towards solving the problem** on approche d'une solution; **£5 doesn't go far nowadays** on ne va pas loin avec 5 livres de nos jours

2 *adj* (**a**) *(distant)* lointain, éloigné; *(remote)* éloigné; **in the far distance** tout au loin; **it's a far cry from what she expected** ce n'est pas du tout *ou* c'est loin de ce qu'elle attendait

(**b**) *(more distant)* autre, plus éloigné; **on the far side** de l'autre côté; **the far end of** l'autre bout de, l'extrémité de; **at the far end of the room** au fond de la salle

(**c**) *(extreme)* extrême; **the far north** l'extrême nord *m*; *Pol* **the far left/right** l'extrême gauche *f*/droite *f*

3 as far as 1 *prep* jusqu'à; **I'll walk with you as far as the end of the lane** je vais vous accompagner jusqu'au bout du chemin **2** *conj* (**a**) *(distance)* **as far as the eye can see** à perte de vue; **that's fine as far as it goes** c'est très bien, jusqu'à un certain point

(**b**) *(to the extent that)* autant que; **as far as possible** autant que possible, dans la mesure du possible; **as far as I can** dans la mesure de mon possible; **as far as I can judge** (pour) autant que je puisse (en) juger; **as far as I know** (pour) autant que je sache; **as far as she's/I'm concerned** en ce qui la/me concerne, pour sa/ma part; **as far as money goes** *or* **is concerned** pour ce qui est de l'argent

4 by far *adv* de loin, de beaucoup; **she's by far the cleverest** *or* **the cleverest by far** c'est de loin *ou* de beaucoup la plus intelligente

5 far and away *adv* de loin

6 far from 1 *adv (not at all)* loin de; **far from clean** loin d'être propre; **the report was far from complimentary** le rapport était loin d'être flatteur; **I'm far from approving of all he does** je suis loin d'approuver tout ce qu'il fait; **he's not rich, far from it** il n'est pas riche, loin de là *ou* tant s'en faut **2** *prep (rather than)* loin de; **far from being generous, he is rather stingy** loin d'être généreux, il est plutôt radin; **far from improving, the situation got worse** loin de s'améliorer, les choses ont empiré

7 in so far as *conj* dans la mesure où

8 so far *adv* jusqu'ici, jusqu'à présent; **so far this month** depuis le début du mois; **so far so good** jusqu'ici ça va; **have you seen him? – not so far** l'avez-vous vu? – pas encore; **the story so far** ≃ résumé *m* des chapitres précédents

9 so far as = **as far as** *conj*

►► ***the Far East*** l'Extrême-Orient *m*; ***the Far North*** le Grand Nord; ***the Far South*** l'Antarctique *m*

'Far from the Madding Crowd' *Hardy, Schlesinger* 'Loin de la foule insensée'

'How far can you go?' *Lodge* 'Jeux de maux'

farad ['færəd] *n Elec* farad *m*

faraday ['færədeɪ] *n Phys* faraday *m*

farandole ['færənˌdəʊl] *n* farandole *f*

faraway ['fɑːrəweɪ] *adj (distant)* lointain, éloigné; *(isolated)* éloigné; *(sound, voice)* lointain; *(look)* absent; **her eyes had a faraway look** son regard était perdu dans le vague

farce [fɑːs] *n* (**a**) *Theat & Fig* farce *f*; **this law is a farce** cette loi est grotesque; **the trial degenerated into (a) farce** le procès a tourné à la farce (**b**) *Culin* farce *f*

farcical ['fɑːsɪkəl] *adj* risible, ridicule; **the election was completely farcical** les élections furent une véritable farce

farcically ['fɑːsɪklɪ] *adv* d'une manière ridicule *ou* grotesque

far-distant *adj (mountains, country)* lointain; **in the far-distant past** dans un passé lointain

fare [feə(r)] **1** *n* (**a**) *(charge → for bus, underground)* prix *m* du billet *ou* ticket; *(→ for boat, plane, train)* prix *m* du billet; *(→ in taxi)* prix *m* de la course; **what is the fare?** *(gen)* combien coûte le billet?; *(in taxi)* combien je vous dois?; **fares are going up** les tarifs des transports augmentent; **have you got the fare?** avez-vous de quoi payer le billet?; **fares, please!** *(in bus, train)* ≃ tickets, s'il vous plaît!

(**b**) *(taxi passenger)* client(e) *m,f*

(**c**) *(food)* nourriture *f*; **good fare** bonne chère *f*; **traditional fare** cuisine *f* traditionnelle; **hospital/prison fare** régime *m* d'hôpital/de prison

2 *vi* **how did you fare at the booking office?** comment ça s'est passé au bureau de réservation?; **she fared badly** elle ne s'en est pas bien tirée, elle ne s'est pas bien débrouillée; **she fared well** elle s'en est bien tirée, elle s'est bien débrouillée; **the company has fared better in recent months** la société s'en tire mieux depuis quelques mois; **he fared better in last year's tournament** il s'en est mieux tiré *ou* il s'est mieux débrouillé lors du tournoi de l'année dernière; **his films have fared better in Europe than in America** ses films ont eu plus de succès en Europe qu'en Amérique

►► *Fam Am* ***fare beater,*** *Br* ***fare dodger*** resquilleur(euse) *m,f*; ***fare stage*** *(of bus)* section *f*

Far Eastern *adj* extrême-oriental

fare-thee-well *n Am Fam* **to a fare-thee-well** à la perfection❑

farewell [ˌfeə'wel] **1** *n* adieu *m*; **to bid sb farewell**

dire adieu à qn; **to say** *or* **make one's farewells** faire ses adieux; **you can say farewell to your chances of winning!** tu peux dire adieu à tes chances de victoire!, tu n'as plus aucune chance de gagner!

2 *exclam* adieu!

3 *comp (dinner, party)* d'adieu

'Farewell My Lovely' *Chandler* 'Adieu ma jolie'

'A Farewell to Arms' *Hemingway* 'L'Adieu aux armes'

---

farfalle [fɑː'fælɪ] *n Culin* farfalles *fpl*

far-famed *adj Literary* dont la renommée s'est étendue au loin

far-fetched [-'fetʃt] *adj* farfelu; **a far-fetched alibi** un alibi tiré par les cheveux; **a far-fetched story** une histoire à dormir debout

far-flung *adj* (**a**) *(widespread)* étendu, vaste (**b**) *(far)* lointain; *(villages, places)* éloigné

farinaceous [ˌfærɪ'neɪʃəs] *adj* farinacé

farinose ['færɪˌnəʊs] *adj* farineux

farm [fɑːm] **1** *n* ferme *f*, exploitation *f* (agricole); **to work on a farm** travailler dans une ferme

2 *comp (equipment)* agricole

3 *vt (land)* cultiver, exploiter; *(animals)* élever

4 *vi* être fermier, être cultivateur

►► ***farm animals*** animaux *mpl* de ferme; ***farm belt*** zone *f* agricole; ***farm buildings*** bâtiments *mpl* de la ferme; *(outhouses)* dépendances *fpl*; ***farm labourer*** ouvrier(ère) *m,f* agricole; ***farm machinery*** machines *fpl* agricoles; ***farm produce*** produits *mpl* agricoles *ou* de ferme; ***farm shop*** = magasin qui vend des produits de la ferme; ***farm worker*** ouvrier(ère) *m,f* agricole

►**farm out** *vt sep* (**a**) *(shop)* mettre en gérance; *(work)* donner *ou* confier à un sous-traitant; **she farms some work out to local people** elle cède du travail à des sous-traitants locaux (**b**) *(child)* **she farms her children out to an aunt** elle confie (la garde de) ses enfants à une tante

farmable ['fɑːməbəl] *adj (land)* cultivable

farmer ['fɑːmə(r)] *n (of land)* fermier(ère) *m,f*, agriculteur(trice) *m,f*; *(of animals)* éleveur(euse) *m,f*; **sheep farmer** éleveur(euse) *m,f* de moutons; **poultry farmer** aviculteur(trice) *m,f*

farmhand ['fɑːmhænd] *n* ouvrier(ère) *m,f* agricole

farmhouse ['fɑːmhaʊs, *pl* -haʊzɪz] *n* (maison *f* de) ferme *f*; **farmhouse Cheddar** Cheddar *m* fermier

farming ['fɑːmɪŋ] **1** *n* agriculture *f*; **fish/mink farming** élevage *m* de poisson/vison; **fruit/vegetable farming** culture *f* fruitière/maraîchère

2 *comp (methods)* de culture, cultural; *(equipment, machines)* agricole; *(community, region)* rural

farmland ['fɑːmlænd] *n (UNCOUNT)* terre *f* arable, terres *fpl* arables

farmstay ['fɑːmsteɪ] *n Austr* **farmstay (accommodation)** ≃ tourisme *m* vert à la ferme

farmstead ['fɑːmsted] *n* ferme *f (et ses dépendances)*

farmyard ['fɑːmjɑːd] *n* cour *f* de ferme

►► ***farmyard animal*** animal *m* de (la) ferme; ***farmyard smells*** odeurs *fpl* de ferme

farnesol ['fɑːnɪsɒl] *n Biol & Chem* farnésol *m*

faro ['feərəʊ] *n* = jeu de cartes où l'on joue contre le donneur

Faroe, Faroese = **Faero, Faeroese**

far-off *adj (place, time)* lointain, éloigné

far-out *Fam* **1** *adj* (**a**) *(odd)* bizarre[□], farfelu; *(avant-garde)* d'avant-garde[□] (**b**) *(excellent)* génial, super

2 *exclam* super!, génial!

farrago [fə'rɑːgəʊ] *(pl* **farragoes***)* *n Pej* amas *m*; **a farrago of lies** un fatras de mensonges

far-reaching [-'riːtʃɪŋ] *adj* d'une grande portée; **to have far-reaching consequences** avoir des conséquences considérables *ou* d'une portée considérable

farrier ['færɪə(r)] *n Br* (**a**) *(blacksmith)* maréchal-ferrant *m* (**b**) *Old-fashioned (vet)* vétérinaire *mf*

farriery ['færɪərɪ] *n Br* (**a**) *(blacksmith's art)* maréchalerie *f* (**b**) *Old-fashioned (veterinary surgery)* art *m* vétérinaire

farrow ['færəʊ] **1** *n (piglets)* portée *f* (de cochons)

2 *vt (piglets)* mettre bas

3 *vi (sow)* mettre bas

far-seeing *adj (person)* prévoyant, perspicace; *(action)* prévoyant; *(decision)* pris avec clairvoyance

Farsi [ˌfɑː'siː] *n* farsi *m*

far-sighted *adj* (**a**) *(shrewd* → *person)* prévoyant, perspicace; *(*→ *action)* prévoyant; *(*→ *decision)* pris avec clairvoyance (**b**) *Am (long-sighted)* hypermétrope

far-sightedly [-'saɪtɪdlɪ] *adv* d'une manière prévoyante

far-sightedness [-'saɪtɪdnɪs] *n* (**a**) *(of person)* prévoyance *f*, perspicacité *f*; *(of action, decision)* clairvoyance *f* (**b**) *Am (long-sightedness)* hypermétropie *f*, presbytie *f*

fart [fɑːt] *Fam* **1** *n* (**a**) *(gas)* pet *m* (**b**) *(person)* birbe *m*; **he's a boring old fart** il est rasoir, c'est un raseur

2 *vi* péter

►**fart about, fart around** *vi Fam* (**a**) *(play the fool)* déconner (**b**) *(waste time)* glander; **he's been farting about with the car for days** il a passé des journées entières à trifouiller la voiture; **if you hadn't spent so much time farting about with your make-up** si tu n'avais pas autant traîné en te maquillant

farther ['fɑːðə(r)] *(compar of* **far***)* **1** *adv* (**a**) *(more distant)* plus loin; **farther north** plus (loin) au nord; **how much farther is it?** c'est encore à combien?; **have we much farther to go?** avons-nous encore beaucoup de chemin à faire?; **farther than the shop** plus loin que le magasin; **farther ahead** loin devant; **farther along the corridor** plus loin dans le couloir; **farther away, farther off** plus éloigné, plus loin; **to move farther and farther away** s'éloigner de plus en plus; **farther back** plus (loin) en arrière; **move farther back** reculez(-vous); **farther back than 1900** avant 1900; **farther down/up** plus bas/haut; **farther on** *or* **forward** plus loin; **farther west** plus à l'ouest; **farther on in the book** plus loin dans le livre

(**b**) *(in addition)* en plus, de plus

2 *adj* plus éloigné, plus lointain; **on the farther side of the room** de l'autre côté *ou* au fond de la salle; **the farther end of the tunnel** l'autre bout du tunnel

farthermost ['fɑːðəˌməʊst] *adj* plus lointain, plus éloigné; **to the farthermost ends of the earth** jusqu'aux confins de la terre

farthest ['fɑːðɪst] *(superl of* **far***)* **1** *adj* le plus lointain, le plus éloigné; **in the farthest depths of Africa** au fin fond de l'Afrique

2 *adv* le plus loin; **it's 3 km at the farthest** il y a 3 km au plus *ou* au maximum; **the farthest removed** le plus éloigné

farthing ['fɑːðɪŋ] *n Br Hist (coin)* = pièce de monnaie qui valait le quart d'un ancien penny; *Fam Fig* **we haven't a farthing** nous n'avons pas le sou

farthingale ['fɑðɪŋgeɪl] *n Hist* vertugadin *m*

fartlek ['fɑːtlek] *n Sport* fartlek *m*

fartsack ['fɑːtsæk] *n Am Fam (bed)* pieu *m*, plumard *m*; *(sleeping bag)* sac *m* à viande

FAS [ˌefeɪ'es] *adv Br Com (abbr* **free alongside ship***)* FLB, FLQ

fascia *(pl* **fasciae** [-ʃɪiː]*)* *n* (**a**) ['feɪʃə] *Archit* bandelette *f*, bande *f*; *(on shop front)* panneau *m* (**b**) ['feɪʃə] *Br Aut* tableau *m* de bord (**c**) ['fæʃɪə] *Anat* fascia *m*

fascial ['fæʃɪəl] *adj Anat* fascial, aponévrotique

fasciated ['fæʃɪeɪtɪd] *adj Bot* fascié; *(leaf)* fasciculé

►► *Bot* ***fasciated stem*** tige *f* fasciée, fascie *f*

fasciation [ˌfæʃɪ'eɪʃən] *n Bot* fasciation *f*

fascicle ['fæsɪkəl] *n* (**a**) *(gen) & Anat & Bot* faisceau *m* (**b**) *(of book)* fascicule *m*

fascicule ['fæsɪkjuːl] *n* fascicule *m*

fascinate ['fæsɪneɪt] *vt* (**a**) *(delight)* fasciner, captiver; **insects fascinate him** les insectes le fascinent; **she was fascinated by** *or* **with his story** elle était fascinée par son histoire (**b**) *(prey)* fasciner

fascinating ['fæsɪneɪtɪŋ] *adj* fascinant

fascinatingly ['fæsɪneɪtɪŋlɪ] *adv* d'une façon fascinante *ou* passionnante

fascination [ˌfæsɪ'neɪʃən] *n* fascination *f*, attrait *m*; **I don't understand the fascination of tennis** je ne comprends pas l'attrait que peut avoir le tennis; **he has always had a fascination for dinosaurs** les dinosaures ont toujours exercé une fascination sur lui, il a toujours été fasciné par les dinosaures; **she watched/listened in fascination** elle regardait/écoutait, fascinée; **her fascination with the Orient** la fascination qu'exerce sur elle l'Orient; **it holds a fascination for him** ça le fascine

fascism ['fæʃɪzəm] *n* fascisme *m*

fascist ['fæʃɪst] **1** *adj* fasciste

2 *n* fasciste *mf*

fascistic [fə'ʃɪstɪk] *adj* fasciste

fash [fæʃ] *vt Scot* **dinna fash yersel'** ne te fais pas de bile

fashion ['fæʃən] **1** *n* (**a**) *(current style)* mode *f*; **in fashion** à la mode, en vogue; **to come back into fashion** revenir à la mode; **big weddings are no longer in fashion** ça ne se fait plus, les grands mariages; **she dresses in the latest fashion** elle s'habille à la dernière mode; **the Paris fashions** les collections *fpl* (de mode) parisiennes; **hats are the fashion again** les chapeaux reviennent à la mode; **to set the fashion** donner le ton, lancer la mode; **it's the fashion to take a year out before university** il est bien vu *ou* de bon ton de prendre une année avant d'entrer à l'université; **out of fashion** démodé, passé de mode; **to go out of fashion** se démoder; *Fam* **I've been spending money/eating chocolate as if it were going out of fashion** je dépense des sommes d'argent/mange des quantités de chocolat incroyables

(**b**) *(manner)* façon *f*, manière *f*; **in an orderly fashion** d'une façon méthodique, méthodiquement; **we rubbed noses, Eskimo fashion** nous nous sommes frotté le nez à la manière des esquimaux; **after the fashion of Shakespeare** à la manière de Shakespeare; **after the French fashion** à la française; **after a fashion** tant bien que mal; **he can paint after a fashion** il peint à sa manière

2 *comp (editor, magazine, photographer)* de mode; *(industry)* de la mode

3 *vt (gen)* fabriquer, modeler; *(carving, sculpture)* façonner; *(dress)* confectionner; *Fig (character, person)* former, façonner; **to fashion sth out of clay** façonner qch en argile; **to fashion a log into a canoe** façonner un tronc d'arbre en canot

►► ***fashion designer*** modéliste *mf*; **the great fashion designers** les grands couturiers; ***fashion house*** maison *f* de (haute) couture; ***fashion model*** mannequin *m*; ***fashion plate*** gravure *f* de mode; *Fig* élégant(e) *m,f*; ***fashion show*** présentation *f* des modèles *ou* des collections, défilé *m* de mode; *Hum* ***fashion victim*** esclave *mf* de la mode

-fashion ['fæʃən] *suff* **he wore his scarf pirate-fashion** il portait son foulard comme les pirates

fashionable ['fæʃənəbəl] *adj (clothing)* à la mode; *(café, neighbourhood)* chic, à la mode; *(subject, writer)* à la mode, en vogue; **grey is fashionable this year** le gris se porte beaucoup cette année; **a café fashionable with writers** un café fréquenté par des écrivains; **it is fashionable to say that…** il est de bon ton *ou* bien vu de dire que…, **it is no longer fashionable to eat red meat** cela ne se fait plus de manger de la viande rouge; **fashionable society** les gens *mpl* à la mode

fashionably ['fæʃənəblɪ] *adv* élégamment, à la mode; **her hair is fashionably short** elle a les cheveux coupés court selon la mode

fashion-conscious *adj* qui suit la mode

fassaite ['fæseɪaɪt] *n Miner* fassaïte *f*

FAST [fɑːst]

rapide	► 1 (a)
en avance	► 1 (b); 2 (b)
solide	► 1 (c)
bon teint	► 1 (d)
libertin	► 1 (e)
vite	► 2 (a)
solidement	► 2 (c)
jeûne	► 3
jeûner	► 4

1 *adj* (**a**) *(quick)* rapide; **a fast film** une pellicule rapide; **she's a fast runner** elle court vite; **a fast time** *(in race etc)* un bon temps, un bon chrono; **at a fast pace** d'un pas vif *ou* rapide; **in fast motion** en accéléré; **a grass court is faster than a hard one** *(in tennis)* le jeu est plus rapide sur gazon que sur un court en dur; **he's a fast worker** il va vite en besogne; *Fig* il ne perd pas de temps; **he's on the fast track (to the top)** il gravit les échelons rapidement; **they see independence as the fast track to democracy** ils considèrent que l'indépendance les mènera rapidement à la démocratie; **there's no fast track to success** dans la vie, on ne réussit du jour au lendemain; *Fam* **to pull a fast one on sb** jouer un mauvais tour à qn

(**b**) *(clock)* en avance; **my watch is** *or Fam* **I'm (three minutes) fast** ma montre avance (de trois minutes)

(**c**) *(secure → knot, rope)* solide; *(→ door, window, lid)* bien fermé; *(→ grip)* ferme, solide; *(→ friend)* sûr, fidèle; **to make a boat fast** amarrer un bateau

(**d**) *(colour)* bon teint *(inv)*, grand teint *(inv)*; **the colour is not fast** la couleur déteint *ou* s'en va

(**e**) *(wild)* libertin; **fast living** vie *f* dissolue *ou* de dissipation; *Fam* **he's in with a fast set** il fréquente une bande de viveurs *ou* de fêtards

2 *adv* (**a**) *(quickly)* vite, rapidement; **how fast is the car going?** à quelle vitesse roule la voiture?; **he needs help fast** il lui faut de l'aide de toute urgence; **she ran off as fast as her legs would carry her** elle s'est sauvée à toutes jambes, elle a pris ses jambes à son cou; **the insults came fast and furious** les insultes volaient *ou* pleuvaient dru; **as fast as I ate he gave me more** il me resservait à mesure que je mangeais; **he'll do it fast enough if you pay well** il ne se fera pas prier si vous payez bien; **not so fast!** doucement!, pas si vite!; **not so fast, I haven't finished** une minute, je n'ai pas fini

(**b**) *(ahead of correct time)* en avance; **my watch is running fast** ma montre avance

(**c**) *(securely)* ferme, solidement; **shut fast** bien fermé; **to hold fast (on) to sth** tenir fermement qch; *Fig* **they held fast despite the threats** ils ont tenu bon malgré les menaces; *Fig* **to play fast and loose (with sb)** jouer double jeu (avec qn); **to play fast and loose with sb's emotions** se jouer des émotions de qn; **to play fast and loose with the statistics** truquer *ou* falsifier les statistiques

(**d**) *(soundly)* profondément; **to be fast asleep** dormir à poings fermés *ou* profondément

(**e**) *Arch (near)* tout près; **fast by the school** qui jouxte l'école, attenant à l'école

3 *n* jeûne *m*; **to break one's fast** rompre le jeûne; *Rel* **a fast day** un jour maigre *ou* de jeûne

4 *vi (gen)* jeûner, rester à jeun; *Rel* jeûner, faire maigre

►► ***fast bowler*** *(in cricket)* lanceur *m* rapide; ***fast break*** *(in basketball)* contre-attaque *f*; *Nucl* ***fast breeder reactor*** surrégénérateur *m*, surgénérateur *m*; ***fast food*** fast-food *m*, prêt-à-manger *m*; ***fast lane*** *(in UK)* voie *f* de droite; *(in Europe, US etc)* voie *f* de gauche; *Fig* **to live life in the fast lane** vivre à cent à l'heure; *Mktg* ***fast mover*** *(product)* article *m* à forte rotation; *Fam* ***fast talk*** baratin *m*; *Br* ***fast train*** rapide *m*

fastback ['fɑːstbæk] *n* voiture *f* à l'arrière profilé

fastball ['fɑːstbɔːl] *n Sport (in baseball)* balle *f* rapide *(lancée vers le batteur)*

fasten ['fɑːsən] **1** *vt* (**a**) *(attach)* attacher; *(close)* fermer; **to fasten sth with glue/nails/string to sth** coller/clouer/lier qch à qch; **fasten your seatbelt** attachez votre ceinture; **he fastened the two ends together** il a attaché les deux bouts ensemble *ou* l'un à l'autre; **to fasten one's coat** boutonner son manteau

(**b**) *(attention, eyes)* fixer; **he fastened his eyes on the door** il a fixé la porte des yeux *ou* a fixé son regard sur la porte; **to fasten one's attention on sth** fixer son attention sur qch

(**c**) *(ascribe → guilt, responsibility)* attribuer; *(→ crime)* imputer; **to fasten sth on sb** attribuer qch à qn; **they fastened the blame on him** ils ont rejeté la faute sur lui

2 *vi (bra, dress)* s'attacher; *(bag, door, window)* se fermer; **the trousers fasten at the side** le pantalon s'attache sur le côté

►**fasten down** *vt sep (flap, shutter)* fermer; *(tent, furniture)* fixer au sol; *(envelope, sticker)* coller

►**fasten on** *vt sep (belt, holster)* fixer

►**fasten onto** *vt insep* (**a**) *(seize upon)* saisir; **to fasten onto an idea** se mettre une idée en tête; **she fastened onto this kiss as evidence of his affection** elle se raccrochait à ce baiser comme à une preuve de son affection (**b**) *(grip)* se cramponner à, s'accrocher à; *Fig* **he fastened onto our group** il s'est attaché à notre groupe

►**fasten up** *vt sep* fermer, attacher

►**fasten upon** *vt insep* (**a**) *(gaze at)* fixer; **her eyes fastened upon the letter** elle fixait la lettre du regard *ou* des yeux (**b**) *(seize upon)* saisir; **to fasten upon an excuse** saisir un prétexte; **she fastened upon the idea of escaping** elle s'est mis en tête de s'échapper *ou* de s'évader

fastener ['fɑːsənə(r)], **fastening** ['fɑːsnɪŋ] *n (gen)* attache *f*; *(on box, door, window)* fermeture *f*; *(on bag, purse, necklace)* fermoir *m*; *(on clothing)* fermeture *f*; *(button)* bouton *m*; *(hook)* agrafe *f*; *(press stud)* pression *f*, bouton-pression *m*; *(zip)* fermeture *f* Éclair®; **what kind of fastener is it?** comment cela se ferme-t-il *ou* s'attache-t-il?

fast-food *adj (chain, place)* de fast-food, *Offic* de restauration rapide

►► ***fast-food restaurant*** fast-food *m*

fast-forward **1** *vi* se dérouler en avance rapide

2 *vt* **to fast-forward a tape** faire avancer *ou* défiler une cassette

►► ***fast-forward button*** touche *f* d'avance rapide

fastidious [fə'stɪdɪəs] *adj* (**a**) *(meticulous → person)* méticuleux, minutieux; *(→ work)* minutieux; **he is fastidious about the way he dresses** il est d'une coquetterie méticuleuse; **the manager is really fastidious** le patron est vraiment exigeant *ou* pointilleux; **she is fastidious about protocol** elle est pointilleuse *ou* à cheval sur le protocole (**b**) *(fussy about details)* tatillon, pointilleux; *(fussy about cleanliness)* méticuleux, maniaque

fastidiously [fə'stɪdɪəslɪ] *adv* (**a**) *(meticulously)* méticuleusement, minutieusement (**b**) *(fussily)* **he fastidiously examined the fork** il examina la fourchette avec un soin maniaque

fastidiousness [fə'stɪdɪəsnɪs] *n* (**a**) *(meticulousness)* minutie *f* (**b**) *(fussiness about detail)* caractère *m* pointilleux *ou* tatillon; *(fussiness about cleanliness)* méticulosité *f*

fastigiate [fæ'stɪdʒɪət] *adj Bot* fastigié

fasting ['fɑːstɪŋ] *n* jeûne *m*; *Med* diète *f* (absolue)

fast-moving *adj (film)* plein d'action; **fast-moving events** des évènements *mpl* rapides

►► *Mktg* ***fast-moving consumer goods*** biens *mpl* de consommation à forte rotation

fastness ['fɑːstnɪs] *n* (**a**) *(secureness)* solidité *f* (**b**) *(of colour, dye)* solidité *f*, résistance *f* (**c**) *(stronghold)* place *f* forte, repaire *m*

fast-paced [-ˌpeɪst] *adj* rapide

fast-talk *vt Fam* baratiner; **he fast-talked me into it** il m'a persuadé grâce à son baratin

fast-track *Com & Admin* **1** *adj* (**a**) *(executive, graduate, employee)* = qui gravit rapidement les échelons (**b**) *(procedure, method)* accéléré

2 *vt (application, procedure)* accélérer; **he's been fast-tracked for promotion** il a bénéficié d'une promotion accélérée

fast-tracking *n Com & Admin* (**a**) *(of applications)* traitement *m* accéléré; *(of procedure)* accélération *f* (**b**) *(of executive, graduate, employee)* avancement *m* rapide

fat [fæt] *(compar* **fatter**, *superl* **fattest**, *pt & pp* **fatted**, *cont* **fatting**) **1** *adj* (**a**) *(heavy, overweight → person)* gros (grosse), gras; *(→ cheeks, limb)* gros (grosse); *(→ face)* joufflu; **to get** *or* **to grow fat** grossir, engraisser; **she's getting fat** elle prend de l'embonpoint; **as fat as a pig** gras comme un cochon *ou* un moine; *Fig* **they had grown fat on their investments** ils s'étaient enrichis *ou* engraissés grâce à leurs investissements

(**b**) *(meat)* gras

(**c**) *(thick, hefty)* gros (grosse); **a fat book** un gros livre, un livre épais; **a fat wallet** un portefeuille bien garni

(**d**) *Fam (cheque, salary)* gros ❑; **he made a fat profit** il a fait de gros bénéfices

(**e**) *(productive → year)* gras, prospère; *(→ land, soil)* fertile, riche; *Am Fam* **to be in fat city** être plein aux as

(**f**) *Fam (idioms)* **get this into your fat head** mets-toi ça dans la tête une fois pour toutes; **I reckon you'll get it back – fat chance!** je pense qu'on te le rendra – tu parles!; **fat chance you have of winning!** comme si tu avais la moindre chance de gagner!; **a fat lot of good that'll do you!** cela vous fera une belle jambe!; **that was a fat lot of good** *or* **use!** on est bien aidé avec ça!; **a fat lot of difference that has made!** ça a bien avancé les choses!; **a fat lot of good it did him!** ça l'a bien avancé!, le voilà bien avancé!; **a fat lot he cares!** il s'en fout pas mal!; **a fat lot you know about it!** comme si tu en savais quelque chose!; **it's not over till the fat lady sings** il ne faut jamais perdre espoir ❑

2 *n* (**a**) *(gen) & Anat* graisse *f*; **rolls of fat** des bourrelets *mpl* de graisse

(**b**) *Culin (on raw meat)* graisse *f*, gras *m*; *(on cooked meat)* gras *m*; *(as cooking medium)* matière *f* grasse; *(as part of controlled diet)* lipide *m*; **we are trying to eat less fat** nous nous efforçons de manger moins de matières grasses *ou* corps gras; **this margarine is low in fat** cette margarine est pauvre en matières grasses *ou* allégée; **beef/mutton fat** graisse *f* de bœuf/de mouton; **pork fat** saindoux *m*; **fry in deep fat** faites frire; **fry in shallow fat** faites revenir; *Fam Fig* **the fat's in the fire** ça va chauffer; **to live off the fat of the land** vivre comme un coq en pâte

3 *vt* engraisser; *Fig* **to kill the fatted calf** tuer le veau gras

►► *Fam Fig* ***fat cat*** *(rich, prosperous)* richard *m*; *(in industry)* = personne touchant un salaire extrêmement élevé de façon injustifiée; ***fat content*** (teneur *f* en) matières *fpl* grasses; *Am Fam* ***fat farm*** centre *m* d'amaigrissement ❑; ***fat intake*** ration *f* de corps gras; *Agr* ***fat stock*** bétail *m* d'engraissement

fatal ['feɪtəl] *adj* (**a**) *(deadly → disease, injury, accident)* mortel; *(→ blow)* fatal, mortel; *(→ result)* fatal; **this condition can prove fatal** cela peut être mortel

(**b**) *(ruinous → action, consequences)* désastreux, catastrophique; *(→ influence)* néfaste, pernicieux; *(→ mistake)* fatal, grave; **such a decision would be fatal to our plans** une décision de ce type porterait un coup fatal *ou* le coup de grâce à nos projets

(**c**) *Literary (ordained by fate)* fatal, fatidique; **the fatal hour** l'heure *f* fatale

►► *Law* ***fatal accident enquiry*** enquête *f* à la suite d'un accident mortel; *Comput* ***fatal error*** erreur *f* fatale

fatalism ['feɪtəlɪzəm] *n* fatalisme *m*

fatalist ['feɪtəlɪst] **1** *adj* fataliste

2 *n* fataliste *mf*

fatalistic [ˌfeɪtə'lɪstɪk] *adj* fataliste

fatalistically [ˌfeɪtə'lɪstɪklɪ] *adv* avec fatalisme

fatality [fə'tælətɪ] *(pl* **fatalities**) *n* (**a**) *(accident)* accident *m* mortel; *(person killed)* mort(e) *m,f*; **bathing fatalities** noyades *fpl*; **road fatalities** morts *fpl* sur la route; **a child was one of the fatalities** il y avait un enfant parmi les victimes (**b**) *Literary (destiny)* fatalité *f*

►► ***fatality rate*** taux *m* de mortalité

fatally ['feɪtəlɪ] *adv* (**a**) *(mortally)* mortellement; **fatally ill** condamné, perdu (**b**) *(inevitably)* fatalement; **the plan was fatally flawed** le projet était fatalement *ou* forcément imparfait; **to be fatally damaging to sth, to fatally damage sth** causer un tort irréparable à qch

fat-assed [-æst] *adj Am very Fam* gros ❑

fatback ['fætbæk] *n Culin* lard *m* salé

fate [feɪt] **1** *n* (**a**) *(power)* destin *m*, sort *m*; **what does fate have in store for them?** qu'est-ce que le destin *ou* le sort leur réserve?; **stroke of fate** coup *m* du destin *ou* du sort; **fate decreed that...** le sort a voulu que...

(**b**) *(destiny of person, thing)* sort *m*; **I left her to her fate** je l'ai abandonnée à son sort; **to meet one's fate** trouver la mort; **the new project met with a similar fate** le nouveau projet a connu un destin semblable; *Fig* **a fate worse than death** un sort pire que la mort

2 Fates *npl* **the Fates** les Parques *fpl*

fated ['feɪtɪd] *adj* (**a**) *(destined)* destiné; **they seem fated to be unhappy** ils semblent destinés *ou* condamnés à être malheureux; **he was fated never to return** il devait ne plus jamais revenir (**b**) *(doomed)* voué au malheur

fateful ['feɪtfʊl] *adj* (**a**) *(decisive → day, decision)* fatal, décisif *(disastrous)* désastreux, catastrophique (**b**) *(prophetic)* fatidique

fat-free *adj* sans matières grasses, sans corps gras

fathead ['fæthed] *n Fam* andouille *f*, courge *f*

fat-headed *adj Fam* idiot ❑, imbécile ❑

father ['fɑːðə(r)] **1** *n* (**a**) *(parent)* père *m*; **he's a good father** c'est un bon père; **he's a father of three** il est père de trois enfants; **father, this is John** papa, je te présente John; **he's like a father to me** il est comme un père pour moi; **from father to son** de père en fils; **on my father's side** du côté de mon père; **yes, father** oui, père, oui, papa; **she's her father's daughter** c'est bien la fille de son père; *Prov* **like father, like son** tel père, tel fils

(**b**) *(usu pl) (ancestor)* ancêtre *m*, père *m*

(**c**) *(founder)* père *m*, fondateur *m*; **the father of cubism/modernism** le père du cubisme/du modernisme

(**d**) *(leader)* dirigeant *m*; **father of chapel** *(shop steward)* représentant *m* du personnel *(dans l'édition)*

2 *vt* (**a**) *(child)* engendrer; *Fig (idea, science)* concevoir, inventer

(**b**) *(impose)* attribuer; **to father sth on sb** attribuer qch à qn; **they fathered the blame on her** ils lui ont fait porter le blâme

3 Father *n* (**a**) *Rel (priest)* père *m*; **Father Brown** le (révérend) père Brown; **yes, Father** oui, mon père

(**b**) *Rel (God)* Père *m*; **God the Father** Dieu le Père; **the Father, the Son and the Holy Ghost** le Père, le Fils et le Saint Esprit; **Our Father who art in Heaven** Notre Père qui êtes aux cieux; **to say the Our Father** dire le Notre Père

(**c**) *Pol* **the Father of the House** = titre traditionnel donné au doyen (par l'ancienneté) des parlementaires britanniques

►► *Br* ***Father Christmas*** le Père Noël; ***father confessor*** directeur *m* de conscience, père *m* spirituel; ***Father's Day*** fête *f* des pères; ***father figure*** = personne qui joue le rôle du père; **he was a father figure for all the employees** le personnel le considérait un peu comme un père; ***(Old) Father Time*** le Temps

fatherhood ['fɑːðəhʊd] *n* paternité *f*

father-in-law *n* beau-père *m*

fatherland ['fɑːðəlænd] *n* patrie *f*, mère *f* patrie

fatherless ['fɑːðəlɪs] *adj* sans père

fatherlike ['fɑːðəˌlaɪk] *adj* paternel

fatherly ['fɑːðəlɪ] *adj* paternel

fathom ['fæðəm] (*pl* **inv** *or* **fathoms**) **1** *n Naut* brasse *f (mesure)*; **the ship lies 50 fathoms down** ≃ le navire repose par 91 mètres de fond

2 *vt* (**a**) *(measure depth of)* sonder (**b**) *(understand)* sonder, pénétrer; **I just can't fathom it** je n'y comprends rien; **I can't fathom him (out)** je ne le comprends pas

fathometer [fə'ðɒmətə(r)] *n Naut* échosondeur *m*, sondeur *m* par ultrasons

fathomless ['fæðəmlɪs] *adj* (**a**) *(unmeasurable)* insondable (**b**) *(impenetrable)* insondable, impénétrable

fatidic [feɪ'tɪdɪk], **fatidical** [feɪ'tɪdɪkəl] *adj Literary* fatidique

fatigability [ˌfætɪgə'bɪlɪtɪ] *n* fatigabilité *f*

fatigue [fə'tiːg] **1** *n* (**a**) *(exhaustion)* fatigue *f*, épuisement *m*; **to be suffering from fatigue** être épuisé

(**b**) *Tech (in material)* fatigue *f*; **metal fatigue** fatigue *f* du métal

(**c**) *Mil (chore)* corvée *f*; **I'm on fatigue(s)** je suis de corvée

2 *comp Mil (shirt, trousers)* de corvée

3 *vt* (**a**) *Formal (person)* fatiguer, épuiser; **he felt fatigued after a long day in the office** il se sentait las après une longue journée de bureau

(**b**) *Tech (material)* fatiguer

4 fatigues *npl Mil (clothing)* treillis *m*, tenue *f* de corvée

►► *Mil* ***fatigue dress*** treillis *m ou* tenue *f* de corvée; *Mil* ***fatigue duty*** corvée *f*; *Tech* ***fatigue limit*** limite *f* de fatigue; *Mil* ***a fatigue party*** une corvée; *Tech* ***fatigue test*** essai *m* de fatigue; *Mil* ***fatigue uniform*** treillis *m ou* tenue *f* de corvée

fatiguing [fə'tiːgɪŋ] *adj* fatigant, épuisant

fatless ['fætlɪs] *adj* sans matières grasses

fatling ['fætlɪŋ] *n* jeune bête *f* à l'engrais

fatness ['fætnɪs] *n* (**a**) *(of person)* embonpoint *m*, corpulence *f* (**b**) *(of meat)* teneur *f* en graisse

fat-reducing *adj* amaigrissant

fatso ['fætsəʊ] (*pl* **fatsos** *or* **fatsoes**) *n Fam Pej* gros lard *m*

fat-soluble *adj Chem* liposoluble

fatten ['fætən] **1** *vt (animal, person)* engraisser; *(ducks, geese)* gaver

2 *vi (animals)* engraisser; *(person)* engraisser, prendre de l'embonpoint

►**fatten up** *vt sep (person)* engraisser, faire grossir; *Agr (animal)* mettre à l'engrais; **we'll have to fatten you up a bit** il va falloir qu'on t'engraisse un peu

fattening ['fætənɪŋ] **1** *adj* qui fait grossir

2 *n (of animals)* engraissement *m*; *(of ducks, geese)* gavage *m*

fattish ['fætɪʃ] *adj* grassouillet, un peu gras

fatty ['fætɪ] (*pl* **fatties**, *compar* **fattier**, *superl* **fattiest**) **1** *n Fam Pej (man)* gros *m* (bonhomme *m*); *(woman)* grosse *f* (bonne femme *f*); **hey, fatty!** ohé, mon gros!/ma grosse!

2 *adj* (**a**) *(food)* gras; **avoid fatty food** évitez les matières grasses *ou* les aliments gras (**b**) *(tissue)* adipeux

►► *Chem* ***fatty acid*** acide *m* gras; *Med* ***fatty degeneration*** dégénérescence *f* graisseuse

fatuity [fə'tjuːətɪ] (*pl* **fatuities**) *n* sottise *f*, niaiserie *f*

fatuous ['fætjʊəs] *adj (person, remark)* sot (sotte), niais; *(look, smile)* niais, béat

fatuously ['fætjʊəslɪ] *adv (say)* sottement, niaisement; *(smile)* niaisement, béatement

fatuousness ['fætjʊəsnɪs] *n* sottise *f*, niaiserie *f*

fatwa ['fætwə] *n* fatwa *f*

faucet ['fɔːsɪt] *n Am* robinet *m*

faugh [fɔː] *exclam* pouah!

fault [fɔːlt] **1** *n* (**a**) *(UNCOUNT) (blame, responsibility)* faute *f*; **it's my fault** c'est (de) ma faute; **it's not my fault** ce n'est pas (de) ma faute; **whose fault is it?** à qui la faute?, qui est fautif?; **whose fault is it if you're unhappy?** et à qui la faute si vous êtes malheureux?; **it's nobody's fault but your own** vous n'avez à vous en prendre qu'à vous-même; **it's through no fault of mine** ce n'est absolument pas (de) ma faute; **to be at fault** être fautif *ou* coupable; **he's at fault this time** c'est lui le fautif *ou* il est fautif cette fois; **she's at fault for not having taken action** elle est coupable de ne pas avoir agi *ou* de ne pas être intervenue; **his memory was at fault** sa mémoire lui a fait défaut; **the judge found him to be at fault** le juge lui a donné tort

(**b**) *(mistake)* erreur *f*; **a fault in the addition** une erreur d'addition

(**c**) *(flaw → in person)* défaut *m*; *(→ in machine)* défaut *m*, anomalie *f*; **an electrical fault** un défaut électrique; **a mechanical fault** une défaillance mécanique; **a fault in the air supply** un défaut dans l'arrivée d'air; **for all her faults, in spite of her faults** malgré tous ses défauts; **honest/scrupulous to a fault** honnête/scrupuleux à l'excès; **to find fault with sth** trouver à redire à qch, critiquer qch; **to find fault with sb** critiquer qn; **she finds fault with everything** elle trouve toujours à redire

(**d**) *Geol* faille *f*

(**e**) *Sport (in tennis, badminton, squash, show jumping)* faute *f*

2 *vt* critiquer; **to fault sb/sth** trouver des défauts chez qn/à qch; **you can't fault her on her work** il n'y a rien à redire à son travail, vous ne pouvez pas prendre son travail en défaut; **you can't fault her for effort** vous ne pouvez pas critiquer ses efforts; **I can't fault her logic** je ne trouve aucune faille à sa logique

3 *vi (make mistake)* commettre une faute

►► *Geol* ***fault line*** ligne *f* de faille; *Geol* ***fault plane*** plan *m* de faille; *Com* ***fault tree*** arbre *m* de défaillances

faulted ['fɔːltɪd] *adj Geol* faillé

faultfinder ['fɔːltˌfaɪndə(r)] *n* (**a**) *Pej (person)* mécontent(e) *m,f*, chicaneur(euse) *m,f* (**b**) *(device)* détecteur *m* de défauts

faultfinding ['fɔːltˌfaɪndɪŋ] **1** *n (UNCOUNT)* (**a**) *Pej (criticism)* critiques *fpl* (**b**) *(in machinery, equipment)* localisation *f* des défauts

2 *adj Pej (critical)* chicanier, grincheux

faultiness ['fɔːltɪnɪs] *n (of machine, logic, reasoning)* défectuosité *f*; *(of work, performance)* imperfection *f*; *(of grammar)* incorrection *f*

faultless ['fɔːltlɪs] *adj (performance, work)* impeccable, irréprochable; *(behaviour, person)* irréprochable; *(logic, reasoning)* sans faille

faultlessly ['fɔːltlɪslɪ] *adv* impeccablement, parfaitement

faultlessness ['fɔːltlɪsnɪs] *n* perfection *f*, impeccabilité *f*

fault-tolerant *adj Comput* quasi insensible aux défaillances, tolérant les pannes

faulty ['fɔːltɪ] (*compar* **faultier**, *superl* **faultiest**) *adj (machine)* défectueux; *(work)* défectueux, mal fait; *(logic, reasoning)* défectueux, erroné; *(grammar)* incorrect; **the wiring is faulty** il y a un défaut dans l'installation électrique

faun [fɔːn] *n Myth* faune *m*

fauna ['fɔːnə] (*pl* **faunas** *or* **faunae** [-niː]) *n Zool* faune *f*

faunal ['fɔːnəl] *adj Zool* faunistique

Faunus ['fɔːnəs] *pr n Myth* Faune

Faustian ['faʊstɪən] *adj* faustien

Fauve [fəʊv] *n Art* fauve *m*

Fauvism ['fəʊvɪzəm] *n Art* fauvisme *m*

Fauvist ['fəʊvɪst] *Art* **1** *adj* fauve

2 *n* fauve *m*

faux pas [ˌfəʊ'pɑː] (*pl* **inv** [-'pɑːz]) *n* bévue *f*, impair *m*

fava bean ['fɑːvə-] *n Am Culin* fève *f*

fave [feɪv] *Fam* **1** *adj* préféré ❑

2 *n* préféré(e) ❑ *m,f*; **it's one of my faves** c'est un de mes préférés

favor, favorable *etc Am* = **favour, favourable** *etc*

FAVOUR, *Am* **favor** ['feɪvə(r)]

faveur	► 1 (a), (c) – (f)
service	► 1 (b)
préférer	► 2 (a)
être partisan de	► 2 (b)
favoriser	► 2 (c), (d)
ressembler à	► 2 (e)

1 *n* (**a**) *(approval)* faveur *f*, approbation *f*; **to be in favour** *(person)* être bien en cour, être bien vu; *(artist, fashion)* être à la mode *ou* en vogue; **to be out of favour** *(person)* être mal en cour, ne pas être bien vu; *(artist, book)* ne pas être à la mode *ou* en vogue; *(fashion)* être démodé *ou* dépassé; **she's in favour with the boss** elle est bien vue du patron; **he speaks in their favour** il parle en leur faveur; **to fall out of favour with sb** perdre les bonnes grâces de qn; **this method has rather fallen out of favour in recent years** cette méthode a été plus ou moins abandonnée au cours de ces dernières années; **to be restored** *or* **to return to favour** rentrer en grâce; **to find favour with sb** trouver grâce aux yeux de qn, gagner l'approbation de qn; **he is prepared to look with favour upon the suggestion** il est prêt à approuver *ou* à examiner favorablement la proposition; **he looks with favour upon us** il est bien disposé à notre égard; **to be in favour of sth** être partisan de qch, être pour qch; **to be in favour of doing sth** être d'avis de *ou* être pour faire qch

(**b**) *(act of goodwill)* service *m*; **will you do me a favour** *or* **do a favour for me?** voulez-vous me rendre (un) service?; **may I ask a favour of you** *or* **ask you a favour?** puis-je vous demander un service?; **I did it as a favour to her** je l'ai fait pour lui rendre service; **I ask you as a favour not to say anything** je vous serais très reconnaissant de ne rien dire; **do me a favour and play somewhere else** soyez gentil, allez jouer ailleurs; **she's not doing herself any favours by being so arrogant** son arrogance la dessert; **thank God for small favours** remercions le ciel pour ses petits bienfaits; *Ironic* encore heureux!; *Br Fam* **are you going to buy it? – do me a favour!** tu vas l'acheter? – je t'en prie!

(**c**) *(advantage)* **everything is in our favour** tout joue en notre faveur, nous avons tout pour nous; **the odds are in his favour** il est (donné) favori; **a point in her favour** un bon point pour

fat–fav

elle, un point en sa faveur; **the magistrates decided in his favour** les juges lui ont donné raison *ou* gain de cause; **all those in favour raise your hand** que tous ceux qui sont pour lèvent la main; **he dropped the idea in favour of our suggestion** il a laissé tomber l'idée au profit de notre suggestion; **a will in favour of the children** un testament en faveur des enfants; **a cheque in favour of Jill Adam** un chèque payable à Jill Adam; **credit in your favour** à votre crédit

(**d**) *(partiality)* faveur *f*, partialité *f*

(**e**) *Hist (badge, ribbon)* faveur *f*; *Old-fashioned (of sports fan)* rosette *f (aux couleurs d'une équipe)*

(**f**) *Literary* **a woman's favours** les faveurs *fpl* d'une femme; **she was rather too free with her favours** elle était un peu trop prodigue de ses faveurs

(**g**) *(gift)* petit cadeau *m (offert aux invités lors d'une fête)*

(**h**) *Br Arch (letter)* communication *f*

2 *vt* (**a**) *(prefer)* préférer; *(show preference for)* montrer une préférence pour

(**b**) *(support → suggestion, team)* être partisan de, être pour; *(→ candidate, project)* favoriser, appuyer; *(→ theory)* soutenir; **I favour allowing more time for the planning stage** je suis partisan d'accorder plus de temps au stade préparatoire

(**c**) *(benefit)* favoriser, faciliter; **the ground is quite firm, which favours this horse** le terrain est très ferme, ce qui est favorable à ce cheval *ou* ce qui avantage ce cheval; **circumstances that would favour a June election** des circonstances (qui seraient) favorables à une élection en juin

(**d**) *(honour)* favoriser, gratifier; **she favoured him with a smile** elle l'a gratifié d'un sourire; **he favoured us with his company** il nous a fait l'honneur de se joindre à nous; **favoured with talent** talentueux, doué; **favoured with good looks** avantagé par la nature

(**e**) *(resemble)* ressembler à; **he favours his mother** il ressemble à *ou* tient de sa mère

favourable, *Am* **favorable** ['feɪvrəbəl] *adj (answer, comparison, impression)* favorable; *(time, terms)* bon, avantageux; *(reception)* bienveillant; *(weather, wind)* propice; **in a favourable light** sous un jour favorable; **to be favourable to an idea** approuver une idée; **the election will be held at the time most favourable to the government** les élections auront lieu au moment (qui sera) le plus favorable au gouvernement

favourably, *Am* **favorably** ['feɪvrəblɪ] *adv (compare, react)* favorablement; *(consider)* d'un bon œil; **to be favourably disposed to** *or* **towards sth** voir qch d'un bon œil; **to be favourably disposed to** *or* **towards sb** être bien disposé envers qn; **she speaks very favourably of you** elle parle de vous en très bons termes; **I hope everything goes favourably for you** j'espère que tout ira bien pour toi; **to compare favourably with sth** n'avoir rien à envier à qch; **I was favourably impressed** j'ai été favorablement impressionné

favoured, *Am* **favored** ['feɪvəd] *adj* favorisé; **he is one of our most favoured clients** c'est un de nos clients privilégiés; **the favoured few** les privilégiés *mpl*

favourite, *Am* **favorite** ['feɪvrɪt] **1** *adj* favori, préféré; **he's not one of my favourite people** je ne le porte pas dans mon cœur

2 *n* (**a**) *(gen)* favori(ite) *m,f*, préféré(e) *m,f*; **chocolate cake is a firm favourite with children** c'est vraiment le gâteau au chocolat que les enfants préfèrent; **he's the teacher's favourite** c'est le chouchou du professeur; **she's everyone's favourite** tout le monde l'adore; **he's a great favourite with the old ladies** les vieilles dames l'affectionnent particulièrement; **roast duck? (that's) my favourite!** du canard rôti? c'est mon plat préféré!; **that book is one of my favourites** c'est un de mes livres préférés; **let's listen to some old favourites** écoutons de vieilles chansons à succès; *Am* **to play favourites** faire du favoritisme

(**b**) *Sport* favori *m*; **to back the favourite** jouer le favori

3 favorites *npl Comput (Web sites)* favoris *mpl*

►► ***favourite son*** *(family member)* enfant *m* chéri; *Am Pol* = candidat favorisé par les électeurs du même état que lui

favouritism, *Am* **favoritism** ['feɪvrɪtɪzəm] *n* favoritisme *m*

fawn [fɔːn] **1** *n* (**a**) *(animal)* faon *m* (**b**) *(colour)* fauve *m*

2 *adj* (de couleur) fauve

3 *vi* (**a**) **to fawn on sb** *(person)* ramper devant qn, passer de la pommade à qn; *(dog)* faire fête à qn; **he fawns on the boss** il courbe l'échine *ou* il rampe devant le patron (**b**) *(deer)* mettre bas

fawning ['fɔːnɪŋ] **1** *n* (**a**) *(adulation, flattery)* adulation *f* (**b**) *(of deer)* mise *f* bas

2 *adj (attitude, person)* servile, obséquieux; *(dog)* trop affectueux

fawningly ['fɔːnɪŋlɪ] *adv* servilement

fax [fæks] **1** *n (machine)* fax *m*, *Offic* télécopieur *m*; *(document, message)* fax *m*, *Offic* télécopie *f*; **to send sb a fax** envoyer un fax *ou Offic* une télécopie à qn; **to send sth by fax** envoyer qch par fax *ou Offic* télécopie

2 *vt (document)* faxer, *Offic* télécopier, envoyer par fax *ou Offic* télécopie; *(person)* envoyer un fax *ou Offic* une télécopie à

►► *Comput* ***fax card*** carte *f* fax; ***fax cover sheet*** feuille *f* de garde *(pour fax)*; ***fax machine*** fax *m*, *Offic* télécopieur *m*; ***fax message*** fax *m*, *Offic* télécopie *f*; *Comput* ***fax modem*** modem-fax *m*; ***fax number*** numéro *m* de fax *ou Offic* de télécopie

►**fax back** *vt sep (return by fax)* renvoyer par fax *ou Offic* par télécopie (**to** à); **I'll fax you back** je vous réponds par fax

faxable ['fæksəbəl] *adj (document)* faxable, *Offic* télécopiable; **are you faxable?** est-ce qu'on peut vous joindre par fax?

fay [feɪ] *Literary* **1** *n (fairy)* fée *f*

2 *adj* précieux

faze [feɪz] *vt Fam* démonter❑; **he wasn't remotely fazed by the fact that people were gossiping about him** le fait qu'on dise du mal de lui ne l'a pas du tout démonté

FBI [ˌefbiː'aɪ] *n Am (abbr* **Federal Bureau of Investigation***)* **the FBI** le FBI

►► ***FBI agent*** agent *m* du FBI

FC [ˌef'siː] *n (abbr* **Football Club***)* FC *m*

FCC [ˌefsiː'siː] *n Am (abbr* **Federal Communications Commission***)* = conseil fédéral de l'audiovisuel aux États-Unis, ≃ CSA *m*

FCL-FCL *Com (written abbr* **full container load-full container load***)* FCL-FCL

FCL-LCL *Com (written abbr* **full container load-less than container load***)* FCL-LCL

FCO [ˌefsiː'əʊ] *n Br (abbr* **Foreign and Commonwealth Office***)* **the FCO** le Foreign Office, le ministère britannique des Affaires étrangères

FD[1] [ˌef'diː] *n Am (abbr* **Fire Department***)* brigade *f* des pompiers

FD[2] (**a**) *Br (written abbr* **Fidei Defensor***)* = Défenseur de la foi (**b**) *Comput (written abbr* **floppy disk***)* disquette *f*

FDA [ˌefdiː'eɪ] *n (abbr* **Food and Drug Administration***)* = organisme officiel chargé de contrôler la qualité des aliments et de délivrer les autorisations de mise sur le marché pour les produits pharmaceutiques

FDD *Comput (written abbr* **floppy disk drive***)* unité *f* de disquette

FDIC [ˌefdiːˌaɪ'siː] *n Am (abbr* **Federal Deposit Insurance Corporation***)* = organisme garantissant la sécurité des dépôts dans les banques qui en sont membres

FDR [ˌefdiː'ɑː(r)] *pr n (abbr* **Franklin D Roosevelt***)* Franklin Delano Roosevelt

fealty ['fiːəltɪ] *(pl* **fealties***) n Hist* fidélité *f*, allégeance *f*

fear [fɪə(r)] **1** *n* (**a**) *(dread)* crainte *f*, peur *f*; **many people have an irrational fear of snakes** beaucoup de personnes ont une peur irrationnelle des serpents; **have no fear** ne craignez rien, soyez sans crainte; **he expressed his fears about their future** il a exprimé son inquiétude en ce qui concerne leur avenir; **my one fear is that he will hurt himself** je n'ai qu'une crainte, c'est qu'il se blesse; **there are fears that he has escaped** on craint fort qu'il ne se soit échappé; **to be** *or* **to go in fear for one's life** craindre pour sa vie; **she lives in a state of constant fear** elle vit dans la peur; **fear drove him to desperate action** sous l'effet de la peur, il a commis un acte désespéré; **for fear of what people would think** par peur du qu'en-dira-t-on; **for fear that she might find out** de peur qu'elle ne l'apprenne; **without fear or favour** impartialement; **overcome with fear** paralysé *ou* transi de peur; **(a) fear of heights** (le) vertige

(**b**) *(awe)* crainte *f*, respect *m*; **the fear of God** la crainte *ou* le respect de Dieu; *Fam* **I put the fear of God into him** *(scared)* je lui ai fait une peur bleue; *(scolded)* je lui ai passé un savon

(**c**) *(risk)* risque *m*, danger *m*; **there is no fear of her leaving** elle ne risque pas de partir, il est peu probable qu'elle parte; **there's no fear of that** ça ne risque pas d'arriver; *Fam* **will you tell him? – no fear!** lui direz-vous? – pas de danger *ou* pas question!

2 *vt* (**a**) *(be afraid of)* craindre, avoir peur de, redouter; **she fears nothing/no one** elle n'a peur de rien/de personne; **he feared asking again** il a eu peur de redemander *ou* de poser à nouveau la question; **he fears failure above all else** l'échec est ce qu'il craint *ou* redoute pardessus tout; **to fear the worst** craindre le pire; **he is a man to be feared** c'est un homme redoutable; **I fear he's in danger** je crains *ou* j'ai peur qu'il ne soit en danger; *Formal* **it is to be feared that...** il est à craindre que... + *subjunctive*

(**b**) *Formal (be sorry)* regretter; **I fear it's too late** je crois bien qu'il est trop tard

(**c**) *(revere → God)* révérer, craindre

3 *vi* **I fear for my children** je crains *ou* je tremble pour mes enfants; **I was beginning to fear for her sanity** je commençais à m'inquiéter pour son état mental; **he fears for his life** il craint pour sa vie; **they fear for the future** ils craignent *ou* sont inquiets pour l'avenir; *Formal or Old-fashioned* **never fear, fear not** ne craignez rien, soyez tranquille; **we'll be here tomorrow, never fear** nous serons là demain, n'aie pas peur

'Fear and Loathing in Las Vegas' *Thompson, Gilliam* 'Las Vegas parano'

feared [fɪəd] *adj* redouté

fearful ['fɪəfʊl] *adj* (**a**) *(very bad)* épouvantable, affreux; **he has a fearful temper** il a un caractère épouvantable (**b**) *Fam Old-fashioned (as intensifier)* affreux❑; **he's a fearful bore!** c'est un raseur de première!; **they were making a fearful din** ils faisaient un bruit épouvantable *ou* un boucan infernal (**c**) *(afraid)* peureux, craintif; **she is fearful of angering him** elle craint de le mettre en colère

fearfully ['fɪəfʊlɪ] *adv* (**a**) *(look, say)* peureusement, craintivement (**b**) *Fam Old-fashioned (as intensifier)* affreusement❑, horriblement; **he's fearfully mean** il est méchant à faire peur

fearfulness ['fɪəfʊlnɪs] *n* (**a**) *(frightening nature)* caractère *m* terrifiant; **the fearfulness of his appearance** son aspect terrifiant (**b**) *(fear)* crainte *f*; *(concern)* appréhension *f*

fearless ['fɪəlɪs] *adj* intrépide, sans peur; **they set off, fearless of the danger** ils se mirent en route sans crainte du danger *ou* bravant le danger

fearlessly ['fɪəlɪslɪ] *adv* avec intrépidité

fearlessness ['fɪəlɪsnɪs] *n* intrépidité *f*, absence *f* de peur

fearsome ['fɪəsəm] *adj* (**a**) *(frightening)* effroyable, terrifiant (**b**) *(formidable → opponent)* redoutable; *(→ performance, car, motorbike)* impressionnant (**c**) *Literary (afraid)* peureux, craintif; *(timid)* extrêmement timide

fearsomely ['fɪəsəmlɪ] *adv* (**a**) *(in frightening manner)* effroyablement (**b**) *(formidably)* redoutablement (**c**) *Literary (fearfully)* timidement

fearsomeness ['fɪəsəmnɪs] *n* (**a**) *(frightening nature)* caractère *m* terrifiant; **the fearsomeness of his appearance** son aspect terrifiant (**b**) *(formidability → of opponent)* caractère *m* redoutable; *(→ of performance, car, motorbike)* aspect *m* impressionnant (**c**) *Literary (fear)* caractère *m* craintif; *(timidity)* timidité *f*

feasibility [ˌfiːzəˈbɪlətɪ] *n* faisabilité *f*; **to show the feasibility of a plan** démontrer qu'un plan est réalisable *ou* faisable; **the feasibility of doing sth** la possibilité de faire qch
►► ***feasibility report*** rapport *m* de faisabilité; ***feasibility stage*** phase *f* de faisabilité; ***feasibility study*** étude *f* de faisabilité; ***feasibility test*** essai *m* probatoire

feasible [ˈfiːzəbəl] *adj (plan, suggestion)* faisable, réalisable

feast [fiːst] **1** *n* **(a)** *(large meal)* festin *m*; **midnight feast** festin *m* nocturne; *Fig* **a feast for the eyes** un régal *ou* une fête pour les yeux; *Fig* **a feast of entertainment** une multitude de divertissements; *Fig* **a feast of music/poetry** une véritable fête de la musique/poésie
(b) *Rel* fête *f*
2 *vi* festoyer; **to feast on** *or* **off sth** se régaler de qch
3 *vt* **(a)** *Fig* **to feast oneself on sth** se régaler de qch; **to feast one's eyes on sth** se délecter à la vue de qch
(b) *Old-fashioned (give feast to)* donner un banquet en l'honneur de
►► ***feast day*** (jour *m* de) fête *f*; *Rel* ***Feast of Tabernacles*** fête *f* des Tabernacles; *Rel* ***Feast of Weeks*** Pentecôte *f (juive)*

feasting [ˈfiːstɪŋ] *n* festin *m*

feat [fiːt] *n* exploit *m*, prouesse *f*; **it was quite a feat getting the boss to agree to the idea** ça a été un véritable exploit *ou* une véritable prouesse que de faire accepter cette idée au chef; **that was some feat!** quel exploit!, quelle prouesse!; **a feat of courage** un acte courageux; **feat of arms** fait *m* d'armes; **feat of strength/of skill** tour *m* de force/d'adresse; **a feat of engineering** une (véritable) prouesse technique, un chef-d'œuvre de la technique

feather [ˈfeðə(r)] **1** *n (of bird)* plume *f*; *(on tail, wing, of arrow)* penne *f*; **as light as a feather** léger comme une plume; **in fine feather** en pleine forme; *Fig* **to smoothe sb's ruffled feathers** rasséréner qn; *Fig* **to show the white feather** manquer de courage; **that's a feather in his cap** il peut en être fier; **that's another feather in her cap** encore une chose dont elle peut être fière *ou* se vanter; **to make the feathers fly** mettre le feu aux poudres; **you could have knocked me down with a feather** les bras m'en sont tombés
2 *comp (mattress)* de plume; *(headdress)* de plumes
3 *vt* **(a)** *(put feathers on → arrow)* empenner; *Pej* **to feather one's (own) nest** faire son beurre
(b) *Aviat (propeller)* mettre en drapeau
(c) *(in rowing)* ramener à plat; **feather your oars!** avirons à plat!
4 *vi (in rowing)* plumer
►► ***feather bed*** lit *m* de plumes; ***feather boa*** boa *m* de plumes; ***feather cut*** *(hairstyle)* coupe *f* en dégradé; ***feather duster*** plumeau *m*

featherbed [ˈfeðəbed] (*pt & pp* **featherbedded**, *cont* **featherbedding**) *vt Pej (industry, business)* protéger (excessivement)

featherbedding [ˈfeðəbedɪŋ] *n Pej (of industry, business)* protection *f* excessive

featherbrain [ˈfeðəbreɪn] *n Fam* tête *f* de linotte; **he's a real featherbrain** c'est une vraie tête de linotte

featherbrained [ˈfeðəbreɪnd] *adj Fam* étourdi, tête en l'air

feathered [ˈfeðəd] *adj (headdress)* de plumes; *Fam* **our feathered friends** nos amis les oiseaux❑

feather-edge *n Tech* biseau *m*

feather-edged *adj Tech* taillé en biseau, biseauté

feathering [ˈfeðərɪŋ] *n* **(a)** *(of birds)* plumage *m* **(b)** *(of arrow)* empennage *m* **(c)** *(in rowing)* nage *f* plate **(d)** *Aviat (of propeller)* mise *f* en drapeau

featherless [ˈfeðəlɪs] *adj (without feathers)* sans plumes; *(having lost its feathers)* déplumé

featherstitch [ˈfeðəstɪtʃ] *n Sewing* point *m* d'épines

featherweight [ˈfeðəweɪt] **1** *n* **(a)** *Boxing* poids *m* plume *inv*; **he started at featherweight** il a commencé (dans les) poids plume
(b) *Fig (person of little importance)* poids *m* plume *inv*; **he's a (political/literary) featherweight** il n'a pas beaucoup de poids (sur le plan politique/littéraire)
2 *adj Boxing (contest, championship)* poids plume *inv*; *(champion)* de la catégorie *ou* des poids plume

feathery [ˈfeðərɪ] *adj* **(a)** *(bird)* à plumes **(b)** *Fig (light and soft → snowflake)* duveteux; **feathery strokes** *(with pencil)* traits *mpl* légers

feature [ˈfiːtʃə(r)] **1** *n* **(a)** *(facial)* trait *m*; **a woman with delicate features** une femme aux traits fins
(b) *(characteristic → of style, landscape, play etc)* caractéristique *f*, particularité *f*; *(→ of personality)* trait *m*, caractéristique *f*; *(→ of car, machine, house, room)* caractéristique *f*; **safety features** dispositifs *mpl* de sécurité; **this is a feature of the novel** c'est un élément caractéristique du roman; **the most interesting feature of the exhibition** l'élément *ou* l'aspect le plus intéressant de l'exposition; **seafood is a special feature of the menu** les fruits de mer sont l'un des points forts du menu; **to make a feature of sth** mettre qch en valeur; **the novel has just one redeeming feature** le roman est sauvé par un seul élément
(c) *Rad & TV* reportage *m*; *Press (special)* article *m* de fond; *(regular)* chronique *f*
(d) *Cin* film *m*, long métrage *m*; **full-length feature** long métrage *m*; **double-feature (programme)** programme *m* proposant deux films
2 *vt* **(a)** *Cin (star → actor, actress)* avoir pour vedette; **also featuring Mark Williams** avec Mark Williams
(b) *Press (display prominently)* **the story/the picture is featured on the front page** le récit/la photo est en première page; **all the papers feature the disaster on the front page** tous les journaux présentent la catastrophe en première page
(c) *Com (promote)* promouvoir, mettre en promotion
(d) *(have as special feature → of car, appliance)* comporter, être équipé *ou* doté de; *(→ of house, room)* comporter; **all our cars feature twin airbags** toutes nos voitures sont équipées de deux airbags
3 *vi* **(a)** *Cin* figurer, jouer
(b) *(appear, figure)* figurer; **meat does not feature on the menu** la viande ne figure pas au menu; **the millionaire featured prominently in the scandal** le millionnaire était très impliqué dans le scandale; **do I feature in your plans?** est-ce que je figure dans tes projets?
►► *Press* ***feature article*** article *m* de fond; *Press* ***features editor*** = journaliste responsable d'une rubrique; *Cin* ***feature film*** long métrage *m*; *Press* ***feature story*** article *m* de fond; *Press* ***features writer*** journaliste *mf (qui écrit des articles de fond)*

feature-length *adj Cin*
►► ***feature-length cartoon*** film *m* d'animation; ***feature-length film*** long métrage *m*

featureless [ˈfiːtʃəlɪs] *adj (desert, city etc)* sans traits distinctifs *ou* marquants

Feb. (*written abbr* **February**) févr

febricity [feˈbrɪsɪtɪ] *n Med* fébrilité *f*

febrifugal [ˌfebrɪˈfjuːgəl] *adj Med* fébrifuge

febrifuge [ˈfebrɪfjuːdʒ] *Med* **1** *n* fébrifuge *m*
2 *adj* fébrifuge

febrile [ˈfiːbraɪl] *adj Med & Literary* fébrile, fiévreux

febrility [feˈbrɪlɪtɪ] *n Med & Literary* fébrilité *f*

February [ˈfebrʊərɪ] **1** *n* février *m*; **I don't like February** je n'aime pas le mois de février; **this has been the wettest February on record** cela a été le mois de février le plus pluvieux qu'on ait jamais vu; **February was a difficult month** le mois de février a été difficile; **in February** en février, au mois de février; **in the month of February** au mois de février; **the first/ninth of February, February the first/ninth,** *Am* **February first/ninth** le premier/neuf février; **during (the month of) February** pendant le mois de février; **last/next February** en février dernier/prochain; **at the beginning/end of February** au début/à la fin février; **in the middle of February** au milieu du mois de février, à la mi-février; **early/late in February, in early/late February** au début/à la fin du mois de février; **every** *or* **each February** tous les ans en février
2 *comp (evening, weather, weekend)* de février, du mois de février

fecal, feces *Am* = **faecal, faeces**

feckless [ˈfeklɪs] *adj* **(a)** *(irresponsible)* inconscient, irresponsable **(b)** *(ineffectual → person)* propre à rien, incapable; *(→ attempt)* inepte

fecklessly [ˈfeklɪslɪ] *adv* **(a)** *(irresponsibly)* de façon irresponsable **(b)** *(ineffectually)* inefficacement

fecklessness [ˈfeklɪsnɪs] *n* **(a)** *(irresponsibility)* irresponsabilité *f*, inconscience *f* **(b)** *(ineffectuality)* manque *m* d'efficacité

fecund [ˈfekənd] *adj Literary* **(a)** *(woman, female animal)* fécond **(b)** *Fig (author)* fécond; *(imagination)* fécond, fertile

fecundate [ˈfekəndeɪt] *vt Biol & Literary* féconder

fecundation [ˌfekənˈdeɪʃən] *n Biol & Literary* fécondation *f*

fecundity [fɪˈkʌndətɪ] *n* **(a)** *Biol & Literary (of woman, female animal)* fécondité *f* **(b)** *Fig Literary (of author)* fécondité *f*; *(of imagination)* fécondité *f*, fertilité *f*

Fed[1] [fed] *n Am* **(a)** *Fin* (*abbr* **Federal Reserve Board**) banque *f* centrale (des États-Unis) **(b)** *Fin* (*abbr* **Federal Reserve (System)**) (système *m* de) Réserve *f* fédérale **(c)** *Fin* (*abbr* **Federal Reserve Bank**) banque *f* membre de la Réserve fédérale **(d)** *Fam* (*abbr* **Federal Agent**) agent *m* du FBI❑

Fed[2] *Am* **(a)** (*written abbr* **federal**) fédéral **(b)** (*written abbr* **federation**) fédération *f*
►► ***Fed funds*** fonds *mpl* fédéraux

fed [fed] *pt & pp of* **feed**

federal [ˈfedərəl] **1** *adj* **(a)** *(republic, police, system)* fédéral
(b) *(responsibility, funding)* du gouvernement fédéral; *(taxes)* fédéral
2 *n Am Hist* nordiste *mf*
►► *Am* ***Federal Architecture*** = type d'architecture de la côte est des États-Unis introduit à la fin du XVIIIème siècle, inspiré du style georgien anglais; ***the Federal Aviation Administration*** = direction fédérale de l'aviation civile américaine; ***the Federal Bureau of Investigation*** le FBI; *Am* ***federal case*** = affaire du ressort d'une cour fédérale; *Am Fig* **there's no need to make a federal case out of it** il n'y a pas de quoi en faire une affaire d'État; *Am* ***Federal Communications Commission*** = conseil fédéral de l'audiovisuel aux États-Unis, ≃ Conseil *m* supérieur de l'audiovisuel; *Am* ***federal court*** cour *f* fédérale; *Am* ***Federal Debt*** dette *f* publique *ou* de l'État; *Am* ***the Federal Deposit Insurance Corporation*** = organisme garantissant la sécurité des dépôts dans les banques qui en sont membres; *Am* ***Federal funds*** fonds *mpl* fédéraux; *Am* ***Federal Housing Administration*** = organisme de gestion des logements sociaux aux États-Unis; *Am* ***Federal Insurance Contributions Act*** = loi américaine régissant les cotisations sociales; *Am* ***Federal Maritime Board*** = Conseil supérieur de la Marine marchande aux États-Unis; *Am* ***Federal Mediation and Conciliation Services*** = organisme américain de conciliation des conflits du travail; *Formerly* ***the Federal Republic of Germany*** la République fédérale d'Allemagne; *Formerly* ***the Federal Republic of Yugoslavia*** la République fédérale de Yougoslavie; *Am* ***the Federal Reserve Board*** Réserve *f* fédérale; *Am* ***the Federal Reserve Bank*** banque *f* membre de la Réserve fédérale; *Am* ***the Federal Reserve Board*** banque *f* centrale (des États-Unis); *Am* ***the Federal Reserve System*** système *m* de Réserve *f* fédérale; *Am* ***the Federal Trade Commission*** = commission fédérale chargée de veiller au respect de la concurrence sur le marché

federalese [ˌfedərəˈliːz] *n Am Fam Pej* = jargon utilisé par les bureaucrates du gouvernement fédéral

federalism [ˈfedərəlɪzəm] *n Pol* fédéralisme *m*

federalist [ˈfedərəlɪst] *Pol* **1** *adj* fédéraliste
2 *n* fédéraliste *mf*

federalization [ˌfedərəlaɪˈzeɪʃən] *n* union *f* en fédération, fédération *f*

federalize, -ise [ˈfedərəlaɪz] **1** *vt* **(a)** *(states)* fédéraliser **(b)** *(subject to federal control)* soumettre à l'autorité d'un gouvernement fédéral
2 *vi* se fédéraliser

federally ['fedərəlɪ] *adv* **to be federally funded** être financé par le gouvernement fédéral

federate 1 *vt* ['fedəreɪt] fédérer

2 *vi* ['fedəreɪt] se fédérer

3 *adj* ['fedərət] fédéré

federation [ˌfedə'reɪʃən] *n* fédération *f*

federative ['fedərətɪv] *adj* fédératif

fedex ['fedeks] *vt* envoyer par messagerie

fedora [fɪ'dɔːrə] *n (hat)* feutre *m*

fed up *adj Fam* **to be fed up** en avoir marre, en avoir ras le bol; **she's fed up with him** elle en a marre de lui; **she's fed up with it** elle en a marre; **to be fed up (to the back teeth) with sb/ with sth/with doing sth** en avoir (vraiment) marre *ou* ras le bol de qn/de qch/de faire qch; **I'm fed up with the way you don't pay any attention to me** j'en ai marre *ou* ras le bol que tu ne fasses pas attention à moi; **what are you looking so fed up about?** pourquoi as-tu l'air aussi écœuré?; **you sound fed up** tu as l'air d'en avoir marre *ou* ras le bol

fee [fiː] *n* (**a**) *(for doctor, lawyer)* honoraires *mpl*

(**b**) *(for speaker, performer)* cachet *m*; *(retainer → for company director)* jetons *mpl* de présence; *(for private tutor)* appointements *mpl*; *(for translator)* tarif *m*; *(for agency)* commission *f*; *(for private school)* frais *mpl* de scolarité; **(transfer) fee** *(of footballer)* indemnité *f* de transfert; **is there a fee for joining?** est-ce que l'inscription est payante?; **for a small fee** pour une somme modique; *Hum* **could you post that letter for me? – OK, for a small fee** tu peux poster cette lettre pour moi? – d'accord, ça sera 100 balles

(**c**) *Law* **property held in fee simple** propriété *f* inconditionnelle

> **Fee fie fo fum**
> Cette formule vient du conte de fées anglais *Jack and the Beanstalk* ("Jack et le haricot magique") dans lequel un ogre à la poursuite du jeune Jack déclare **Fee fie fo fum, I smell the blood of an Englishman, be he alive or be he dead, I'll crush his bones to make my bread** ("Fee fie fo fum, je sens le sang d'un Anglais, qu'il soit mort ou vif, je lui broierai les os pour en faire de la farine pour mon pain").
> Ces mots n'ont aucune signification particulière mais on les utilise de façon allusive lorsqu'on s'amuse à imiter un ogre, ou bien à propos d'une personne agressive ou coléreuse. On pourra dire par exemple **he can't go around fee-fie-fo-fumming and shouting at everyone. Sometimes he would do better just to stop and listen** ("il ne devrait pas s'énerver comme ça et crier sur tout le monde. Il ferait mieux de se calmer et d'écouter les autres").

feeb [fiːb] *n Am Fam* crétin(e) *m,f*

feeble ['fiːbəl] *adj* (**a**) *(lacking strength → physically, morally)* faible; **don't be so feeble!** ne sois pas une telle mauviette! (**b**) *(lacking conviction, force → attempt, excuse)* piètre; *(→ argument)* faible, peu convaincant; *(→ smile)* timide; *(→ joke)* qui manque de finesse, bête; *(→ film, book, play)* faible, médiocre; **that's a pretty feeble excuse** c'est une bien piètre excuse, c'est une excuse bien peu convaincante

feeble-minded 1 *adj* faible d'esprit

2 *npl Old-fashioned* **the feeble-minded** les débiles *mpl* mentaux

feeble-mindedness [-'maɪndɪdnɪs] *n* faiblesse *f* d'esprit

feebleness ['fiːbəlnɪs] *n (of person)* faiblesse *f*; *(of excuse, argument)* pauvreté *f*, faiblesse *f*; *(of film, book, play)* médiocrité *f*, faiblesse *f*; *(of smile)* timidité *f*; *(of joke)* manque *m* de finesse

feebly ['fiːblɪ] *adv (say, shine)* faiblement; *(smile)* timidement; *(suggest)* sans (grande) conviction

feed [fiːd] *(pt & pp* **fed** [fed]) **1** *vt* (**a**) *(provide food for → person, family)* nourrir; *(→ country)* approvisionner; *(→ army)* ravitailler; **she insisted on feeding us** elle a tenu à nous faire manger; **there are ten mouths to feed** il y a dix bouches à nourrir; *Hum* **there's enough here to feed an army** il y a de quoi nourrir toute une armée; **the country is no longer able to feed itself** le pays n'est plus capable de subvenir à ses besoins alimentaires; **he earns just enough money to feed himself** il gagne juste de quoi se nourrir; **they were well fed at the restaurant** ils ont bien mangé au restaurant

(**b**) *(give food to → person, animal)* donner à manger à; *(→ of bird)* donner la becquée à; *(→ livestock)* affourager; *(breast-feed)* allaiter; *(bottle-feed)* donner le biberon à; *(fertilize → plant, soil, lawn etc)* nourrir; **to feed sth to sb, to feed sb sth** donner qch à manger à qn; **to feed the birds** donner à manger aux oiseaux, nourrir les oiseaux; *Fam* **to feed one's face** s'en mettre plein la lampe, se goinfrer; **she's so ill she isn't even able to feed herself** elle est si malade qu'elle n'est pas capable de se nourrir *ou* de manger toute seule; **he can feed himself already** il arrive déjà à manger tout seul; **please do not feed the animals** *(sign)* prière de ne pas donner à manger aux animaux; **how much do you feed your cats?** quelle quantité de nourriture donnez-vous à vos chats?; **the chimps are fed a diet of nuts and bananas** on donne des noix et des bananes à manger aux chimpanzés; **they were fed to the lions** ils ont été jetés en pâture aux lions

(**c**) *Fig (supply → fire, furnace)* alimenter; *(→ lake, river)* se jeter dans; *(→ imagination, hope, rumour)* alimenter, nourrir; **to feed a parking meter** mettre des pièces dans un parcmètre

(**d**) *(transmit)* **the results are fed to the departments concerned** les résultats sont transmis aux services concernés; **to feed information to sb, to feed sb information** donner des informations à qn; *(in order to mislead)* donner de fausses informations à qn *(afin de le tromper)*; *Fam* **to feed sb a line** faire avaler une histoire à qn

(**e**) *Tech (introduce → liquid)* faire passer; *(→ solid)* faire avancer; *(insert → paper, wire etc)* introduire; *Comput (→ paper)* faire avancer, alimenter; **to feed data into a computer** entrer des données dans un ordinateur

(**f**) *Theat (give cue to)* donner la réplique à

(**g**) *Sport (pass)* passer la balle à, servir; **she keeps feeding her backhand** elle n'arrête pas de lui envoyer des balles qu'elle renvoie de son revers; **to feed the forwards** alimenter les avants

2 *vi (person, animal)* manger; *(baby → gen)* manger; *(→ breast-feed)* téter; **to feed on demand** *(nursing mother)* donner la tétée chaque fois que le bébé le réclame *ou* à la demande; **to put the cattle out to feed** mettre le bétail en *ou* au pâturage

3 *n* (**a**) *(foodstuff for animal)* nourriture *f*; *(hay, oats etc)* fourrage *m*

(**b**) *(meal for baby → breast milk)* tétée *f*; *(→ bottled milk)* biberon *m*; **the baby gets its last feed at midnight** le bébé boit sa dernière tétée *ou* son dernier biberon à minuit; *Fam* **the baby's off his feed** le bébé boude son biberon

(**c**) *(meal for animal)* **the dog gets two feeds a day** le chien a à manger deux fois par jour

(**d**) *Fam (meal)* repas❑ *m*; **that was the best feed I've ever had!** je n'ai jamais aussi bien bouffé!

(**e**) *Tech (introduction → of liquid)* alimentation *f*; *(→ of solid)* avancement *m*; *(device)* dispositif *m* d'alimentation/d'avancement; **petrol feed** alimentation *f* en essence

(**f**) *Fam (actor)* acteur(trice) *m,f* qui donne la réplique❑; *(comedian's partner)* faire-valoir❑ *m*; *(cue)* réplique❑ *f*

►► ***feed belt*** *(of machine gun)* bande-chargeur *f* (souple); *Tech* ***feed hopper*** trémie *f*; ***feed line*** *(of comedian)* réplique *f*; *Tech* ***feed pipe*** tuyau *m* d'alimentation; *Tech* ***feed pump*** pompe *f* d'alimentation

►**feed back** *vt sep (information, results)* renvoyer

►**feed in** *vt sep (paper, wire)* introduire; *Comput (data)* entrer

►**feed on** *vt insep* se nourrir de; *Fig* se repaître de

►**feed up** *vt sep (animal)* engraisser; *(goose)* gaver; **he needs feeding up** *(person)* il a besoin d'engraisser un peu

feedback ['fiːdbæk] *n* (**a**) *Electron* rétroaction *f*; *(in microphone)* effet *m* Larsen; *Comput* réaction *f*, rétroaction *f*, retour *m ou* remontée *f* de l'information; *Electron* **positive/negative feedback** réactions *fpl* positives/négatives

(**b**) *(UNCOUNT) (information)* réactions *fpl*, échos *mpl*; **we haven't had much feedback from them** nous n'avons pas eu beaucoup de réactions *ou* d'échos de leur part; **we welcome feedback from customers** nous sommes toujours heureux d'avoir les impressions *ou* les réactions de nos clients; **we need more feedback** nous avons besoin de plus d'information *ou* d'informations en retour; **this will provide us with much-needed feedback on public opinion** ceci nous fournira des informations dont nous avons grand besoin sur l'opinion publique

feedbag ['fiːdbæg] *n* (**a**) *(container)* sac *m* à nourriture; *(containing food)* sac *m* de nourriture (**b**) *Am (for horse)* musette *f*, mangeoire *f* portative; *Fam Fig* **to put on the (old) feedbag** bouffer

feeder ['fiːdə(r)] *n* (**a**) *(eater)* mangeur(euse) *m,f*; **to be a heavy feeder** *(person, animal)* manger beaucoup; **the plant is a heavy feeder** cette plante a besoin de beaucoup de nourriture

(**b**) *(person → of machine)* alimenteur(euse) *m,f*; *(→ of furnace)* chargeur(euse) *m,f*

(**c**) *(child's bottle)* biberon *m*; *Br (bib)* bavette *f*, bavoir *m*

(**d**) *(feeding device → for cattle)* nourrisseur *m*, mangeoire *f* automatique; *(→ for poultry)* mangeoire *f* automatique; *(→ for machine)* chargeur *m*

(**e**) *(river)* affluent *m*; *(road)* voie *f ou* bretelle *f* de raccordement; *(air route)* ligne *f* régionale de rabattement *(regroupant les passagers vers un aéroport principal)*

(**f**) *Elec (power line)* câble *m ou* ligne *f* d'alimentation

(**g**) *Comput (for printer, scanner, photocopier)* chargeur *m*

►► ***feeder airline*** compagnie *f* aérienne d'apport; ***feeder flight*** vol *m* d'apport; ***feeder network*** *(for airport)* réseau *m* d'apport; *Br Sch* ***feeder (primary) school*** = école primaire fournissant des élèves à un collège; ***feeder road*** voie *f ou* bretelle *f* de raccordement; ***feeder route*** *(in air transport)* ligne *f* régionale de rabattement *(regroupant les passagers vers un aéroport principal)*

feedhead ['fiːdhed] *n Metal* masselotte *f*

feeding ['fiːdɪŋ] *n (of person, baby, animal, machine)* alimentation *f*; *Bible* **the Feeding of the Five Thousand** la multiplication des pains; *Fam* **it'll be like the feeding of the five thousand if all those kids come to dinner** si tous ces gosses viennent dîner, comment je vais faire pour les nourrir?; **to be in a feeding frenzy** *(sharks)* être rendu fou *ou* frénétique par la présence de nourriture; *Fig* **speculators were in a feeding frenzy** les spéculateurs se sont déchaînés; *Fig* **there was a feeding frenzy on the stock market as investors rushed to buy up shares in the new company** la Bourse a connu une activité intense lors de la ruée des investisseurs sur les actions de la nouvelle société

►► ***feeding bottle*** biberon *m*; *Med* ***feeding cup*** canard *m*; *Zool* ***feeding ground, feeding grounds*** = lieux où viennent se nourrir des animaux; *Ind* ***feeding mechanism*** mécanisme *m* d'avance *ou* d'avancement; *(for liquid)* mécanisme *m* d'alimentation; ***feeding stuff*** nourriture *f ou* aliments *mpl* pour animaux; ***feeding time*** *(for child, animal)* heure *f* des repas; **it must be (his) feeding time** ce doit être l'heure de son repas; *Hum* **it's like feeding time at the zoo** c'est la ruée sur la nourriture

feedstock ['fiːdstɒk] *n Tech* matière *f* première

feedstuff ['fiːdstʌf] *n* nourriture *f ou* aliments *mpl* pour animaux

feedwater ['fiːdwɔːtə(r)] *n Tech* eau *f* d'alimentation

FEEL [fiːl]

toucher	► 1 (a); 3 (a), (b)
sentir	► 1 (b); 2 (e)
ressentir	► 1 (b), (c)
penser	► 1 (d)
avoir	► 2 (a)
être	► 2 (b)
se sentir	► 2 (b)
fouiller	► 2 (f)
avoir envie de	► 2 (g)

(*pt & pp* **felt** [felt]) **1** *vt* (**a**) *(touch)* toucher; *(explore)* tâter, palper; **feel it, it's so smooth** touche-le, c'est tellement doux; **feel the quality of this cloth** apprécie la qualité de ce tissu; **I felt the lump on my arm** j'ai tâté *ou* palpé la grosseur sur mon bras; **he felt his pockets** il tâta ses poches; **to feel one's way** avancer à tâtons; *(in new job, difficult situation etc)* avancer avec précaution; **to feel one's way into/out of/up** entrer/sortir/monter à tâtons; **I'm still feeling my way** je suis en train de m'habituer tout doucement

(**b**) *(be aware of → wind, sunshine, atmosphere, tension)* sentir; *(→ pain)* sentir, ressentir; *(be sensitive to → cold, beauty)* être sensible à; **I can't feel anything in my foot** je ne sens plus rien dans mon pied; **I felt the floor tremble** *or* **trembling** j'ai senti trembler le sol; **I could feel her foot touching mine** je sentais son pied contre le mien; **I could feel myself blushing** je me sentais rougir; **feel the weight of it!** soupèse-moi ça!; **he felt the full force of the blow** il a reçu le coup de plein fouet; **I bet he felt that!** il a dû le sentir passer!; **to make one's authority felt** affirmer son autorité, faire sentir son autorité; **I can feel a cold coming on** je sens que je suis en train de m'enrhumer; **I could feel somebody else in the room** je sentais qu'il y avait quelqu'un d'autre dans la pièce; **I can feel it in my bones** j'en ai le pressentiment

(**c**) *(experience → sadness, happiness, joy, relief)* ressentir, éprouver; *(be affected by → someone's absence, death)* être affecté par; **to feel fear/regret** avoir peur/des regrets; **he feels things very deeply** il ressent les choses très profondément; **do you feel anything for her?** est-ce que tu éprouves *ou* ressens quelque chose à son égard?; **to feel the effects of sth** ressentir les effets de qch

(**d**) *(think)* penser, estimer; **I feel it is my duty to tell you** j'estime qu'il est de mon devoir de te le dire; **I felt it necessary to intervene** j'ai jugé nécessaire d'intervenir; **she feels very strongly that...** elle est tout à fait convaincue que...; **I can't help feeling that...** je ne peux pas m'empêcher de penser que...; **what do you feel about...?** qu'est-ce que vous pensez de...?; **I feel that things have changed between us** j'ai l'impression que les choses ont changé entre nous; **you mustn't feel you have to do it** il ne faut pas que tu te sentes obligé de le faire

2 *vi (with complement)* (**a**) *(physically)* **to feel hot/cold/hungry/thirsty** avoir chaud/froid/faim/soif; **my hands/feet feel cold** j'ai froid aux mains/pieds; **my leg feels numb** j'ai la jambe engourdie, ma jambe est engourdie; **to feel good/old/full of energy** se sentir bien/vieux/plein d'énergie; **how do you feel** *or* **are you feeling today?** comment te sens-tu aujourd'hui?; *also Hum* **are you feeling all right?** *(physically)* est-ce que tu te sens bien?; **she's feeling a lot better** elle se sent beaucoup mieux; **my foot feels better** mon pied va mieux; **to feel as though** *or* **as if** *or* **like** croire que + *indicative*, avoir l'impression que + *indicative*; **I feel** *or* **it feels as if I've been hit on the head with a hammer** j'ai l'impression qu'on m'a donné un coup de marteau sur la tête; **my arm feels as if it's broken** j'ai l'impression que je me suis cassé le bras; **he's not feeling himself today** il n'est pas en forme aujourd'hui; **you'll soon be feeling (more) yourself** *or* **your old self again** tu iras bientôt mieux, tu seras bientôt remis; **you're as old as you feel** on a l'âge que l'on veut bien avoir; **I feel ten years younger** je me sens dix ans de moins

(**b**) *(emotionally)* **to feel glad/sad/undecided** être heureux/triste/indécis; **to feel (like) a fool** se sentir bête; **to feel (like) a failure** avoir l'impression d'être un raté; **to feel (like) a new woman/man** se sentir comme neuve/neuf; **I felt like a criminal** j'ai eu l'impression d'être un criminel; **I feel really stupid** je me sens vraiment stupide; **I know how you feel** je sais ce que tu ressens; **if that's how you feel...** si c'est comme ça que tu vois les choses...; **how do you think it makes ME feel?** qu'est-ce que tu crois que je ressens, moi?; **how would you feel if it happened to you?** comment te sentirais-tu *ou* qu'est-ce que ça te ferait si ça t'arrivait à toi?; **how would you feel if I were to offer you a job?** qu'est-ce que vous diriez si je vous offrais un emploi?; **how do you feel about him/the plan?** qu'est-ce que tu penses de lui/ce projet?, comment le trouves-tu/trouves-tu ce projet?; **I felt really bad about it** j'étais dans mes petits souliers; **he felt really bad about leaving her** ça l'ennuyait vraiment de la laisser; **she feels very strongly about it** elle a une position très arrêtée là-dessus; **how do you feel about him coming to stay with us for a few months?** qu'est-ce que ça te ferait s'il venait habiter chez nous pendant quelques mois?

(**c**) *(in impersonal constructions)* **it feels good to be alive/home** c'est bon d'être en vie/chez soi; **it feels strange to be back** ça fait drôle d'être de retour; **does that feel better?** est-ce que c'est mieux comme ça?; **it feels all wrong for me to be doing this** ça me gêne de faire ça; **it feels like (it's going to) rain/snow** on dirait qu'il va pleuvoir/neiger; **it feels like spring** ça sent le printemps; **what does it feel like** *or* **how does it feel to be Prime Minister?** quelle impression ça fait d'être Premier ministre?

(**d**) *(give specified sensation)* **to feel hard/soft/smooth/rough** être dur/doux/lisse/rêche (au toucher); **the room felt hot/stuffy** il faisait chaud/l'atmosphère était étouffante dans la pièce; **the room feels damp** la pièce (me) paraît humide; **the atmosphere felt tense** on sentait une certaine tension dans l'air; **your forehead feels hot** ton front est brûlant; **your neck feels swollen** on dirait que ton cou est enflé

(**e**) *(be capable of sensation)* sentir

(**f**) *(grope → in drawer, pocket)* fouiller; **I was feeling in my pocket for the keys** je fouillais dans ma poche pour trouver mes clés; **we had to feel in the dark for the light switch** il a fallu que nous cherchions l'interrupteur à tâtons dans l'obsurité

(**g**) *(idiom)* **to feel like sth** *(want)* avoir envie de qch; **I feel like a cup of coffee/something to eat** j'ai envie d'une tasse de café/de manger quelque chose; **I felt like crying** j'avais envie de pleurer; **do you feel like going out tonight?** ça te dit de sortir ce soir?; **don't do it if you don't feel like it** ne le fais pas si tu n'en as pas envie *ou* si ça ne te dit rien

3 *n* (**a**) *(tactile quality, sensation)* **I could tell by the feel of it** je m'en étais rendu compte rien qu'au toucher; **this garment has a really nice feel to it** ce vêtement est vraiment agréable au toucher; **there's a funny feel to this gearstick** le levier de vitesses fait un peu drôle; **I like the feel of cotton next to** *or* **against my skin** j'aime bien le contact du coton sur ma peau

(**b**) *(act of feeling, touching)* **to have a feel of sth** toucher qch; **can I have a feel?** je peux toucher?; *very Fam* **he's always trying to have a quick feel** *(sexually)* il a la main baladeuse

(**c**) *(knack)* **to get the feel of sth** s'habituer à qch; **to have a real feel for translation/music** avoir la traduction/la musique dans la peau

(**d**) *(atmosphere)* atmosphère *f*; **the room has a nice homely feel (to it)** on se sent vraiment bien dans cette pièce; **his music has a really Latin feel (to it)** il y a vraiment une influence latino-américaine dans sa musique

(**e**) *Sport (skill)* **he's got great feel** il est très doué *ou* habile

►**feel about, feel around** *vi (in drawer, pocket)* fouiller; **to feel about** *or* **around in one's pocket for the key** fouiller dans sa poche pour trouver sa clé; **to feel about** *or* **around in the dark for sth** chercher qch à tâtons dans le noir, tâtonner dans le noir pour trouver qch

►**feel for** *vt insep* (**a**) *(sympathize with)* **I feel for you** je compatis; *Ironic* comme je te plains!; **that poor woman, I feel for her** la pauvre, ça me fait de la peine pour elle (**b**) *(in drawer, handbag, pocket)* chercher

►**feel up** *vt sep Fam (sexually)* peloter, tripoter

►**feel up to** *vt insep* **to feel up to doing sth** *(feel like)* se sentir le courage de faire qch; *(feel physically strong enough)* se sentir la force de faire qch; *(feel qualified, competent)* se sentir capable *ou* à même de faire qch; **I don't really feel up to it** *(feel like)* je ne m'en sens pas le courage; *(feel strong enough)* je ne m'en sens pas la force; *(feel qualified, competent enough)* je ne me sens pas à la hauteur; **if you feel up to it, how about a weekend in London?** si tu t'en sens le courage, que dirais-tu d'un week-end à Londres?; **I don't feel up to a visit from your parents** je ne me sens pas le courage de recevoir tes parents

---

feeler ['fi:lə(r)] *n (of insect)* antenne *f*; *(of snail)* corne *f*; *(of mollusc)* tentacule *m*; *Fig* **to put out feelers** tâter le terrain

►► *Tech* ***feeler gauge*** jauge *f* d'épaisseur

feel-good *adj Fam* **it's a real feel-good film** c'est un film qui donne la pêche; **the feel-good factor** l'optimisme *m* ambiant, le climat *m* d'optimisme

feeling ['fi:lɪŋ] **1** *n* (**a**) *(sensation)* sensation *f*; **she gets a tingling feeling in her fingers** elle a une sensation de fourmillement dans les doigts; **I don't have any feeling in my left foot** je n'ai plus aucune sensation dans le pied gauche; **there's a feeling of spring in the air** ça sent le printemps

(**b**) *(opinion)* avis *m*, opinion *f*; **she has very strong feelings about it** elle a des opinions très arrêtées là-dessus; **I don't have any strong feelings about it** ça m'est plus ou moins égal; **what is your feeling about...?** que pensez-vous de...?; **the feeling I have is that...** à mon avis...; **the general feeling is that..., there is a general feeling that...** l'opinion générale est que...

(**c**) *(awareness → relating to the future)* pressentiment *m*; *(→ caused by external factors)* impression *f*; **I had a feeling he would write** j'avais le pressentiment qu'il allait écrire; **I had a feeling you'd say that** j'étais sûr que tu allais dire ça; **I have a nasty feeling that...** j'ai le mauvais pressentiment que...; **I have a strong feeling that...** j'ai bien l'impression que...; **it's just a feeling** c'est un pressentiment, ce n'est qu'une impression; **a feeling of unease came over her** elle a commencé à se sentir mal à l'aise; **I have a feeling that somebody's watching us** j'ai l'impression que quelqu'un nous observe; **I have the feeling you're trying to avoid me** j'ai l'impression que tu essaies de m'éviter

(**d**) *(sensitivity, understanding)* émotion *f*, sensibilité *f*; **a writer/a person of great feeling** un écrivain/une personne d'une grande sensibilité; **to play the piano/to sing with feeling** jouer du piano/chanter avec cœur *ou* sentiment; **to have a feeling for poetry/music** être sensible à *ou* apprécier la poésie/la musique; **she has a tremendous feeling for Latin-American rhythm** elle a vraiment le rythme de la musique latino-américaine dans la peau; **to show feeling for sb** faire preuve de sympathie pour qn; **you have no feeling for other people** les autres te sont indifférents; **to appeal to sb's better feelings** faire appel aux bons sentiments de qn

(**e**) *(often pl) (emotion)* sentiment *m*; **to have mixed feelings about sb/sth** avoir des sentiments mitigés à l'égard de qn/qch; **feelings are running high** les passions sont déchaînées; **feelings are running high about the new road** la nouvelle route déchaîne les passions; **to hurt sb's feelings** blesser qn; **to show one's feelings** extérioriser ses émotions; **bad** *or* **ill feeling** hostilité *f*; **it has caused a lot of bad feeling** cela a provoqué une grande hostilité; **I know the feeling** je sais ce que c'est; **the feeling is mutual** c'est réciproque; **he spoke on the subject of poverty with great feeling** il a parlé de la pauvreté avec énormément d'émotion; **to say sth with feeling** dire qch avec émotion; **no hard feelings?** sans rancune?

2 *adj (person, look)* sympathique

feelingly ['fi:lɪŋlɪ] *adv* avec émotion

fee-paying *adj (school)* privé

►► ***fee-paying pupil*** = élève qui fréquente une école privée

feet [fi:t] *pl of* **foot**

feign [feɪn] *vt (surprise, innocence)* feindre; *(madness, death)* simuler; **to feign sleep** faire semblant *ou* mine de dormir; **to feign illness/interest** faire semblant *ou* mine d'être malade/intéressé; **with feigned surprise/innocence** avec une surprise/innocence feinte

feigned [feɪnd] *adj (surprise, innocence)* feint; *(illness, madness, death)* simulé

feint [feɪnt] *Mil & Sport* **1** *n* feinte *f*
2 *vi* faire une feinte
feint-ruled *adj (paper)* à réglure légère
feistiness ['faɪstɪnɪs] *n Fam (liveliness)* entrain ❑ *m*; *(combativeness)* cran *m*
feisty ['faɪstɪ] *(compar* **feistier**, *superl* **feistiest)** *adj Fam (lively)* plein d'entrain ❑; *(combative)* qui a du cran
felafel [fə'læfəl] *n Culin* falafels *mpl*
feldspar ['feldspɑː(r)], **feldspath** ['feldspæθ] *n Miner* feldspath *m*; **glassy feldspar** sanidine *f*; **triclinic feldspar** plagioclase *f*; **white feldspar** albite *f*; **lime soda feldspar** feldspath *m* calco-sodique
feldspathic [,feld'spæθɪk] *adj Miner (rocks)* feldspathique, à feldspath
felicitate [fɪ'lɪsɪ,teɪt] *vt* (**a**) *Literary* **to felicitate sb on sth** féliciter qn de *ou* sur qch, complimenter qn sur qch (**b**) *Arch (make happy)* rendre heureux
felicitation [fɪ,lɪsɪ'teɪʃən] *n Literary* félicitation *f*, compliment *m*; **to offer sb one's felicitations** offrir ses félicitations à qn
felicitous [fɪ'lɪsɪtəs] *adj Literary* (**a**) *(happy)* heureux (**b**) *(word, term)* bien trouvé, heureux; *(choice, decision, colour combination)* heureux
felicitously [fɪ'lɪsɪtəslɪ] *adv Literary* heureusement
felicity [fɪ'lɪsətɪ] *n Literary* (**a**) *(happiness)* félicité *f* (**b**) *(aptness → of word, term)* à-propos *m*, justesse *f*; *(→ of choice, decision, colour combination)* caractère *m* heureux
felid ['fiːlɪd] *n Zool* félidé *m*
feline ['fiːlaɪn] **1** *adj* félin
2 *n* félin *m*
felinity [fɪ'lɪnɪtɪ] *n* félinité *f*
fell [fel] **1** *pt of* **fall**
2 *vt (tree)* abattre, couper; *Fig (opponent)* abattre, terrasser
3 *n* (**a**) *Br Geog* montagne *f*, colline *f*; **the fells** *(high moorland)* les landes *fpl* des plateaux
(**b**) *(hide, pelt)* fourrure *f*, peau *f*
(**c**) *(in forestry)* nombre *m* d'arbres abattus (en une fois), abattis *m*
(**d**) *Sewing (of seam)* rabattage *m*; *(seam)* couture *f* rabattue *ou* plate; **run and fell seam** couture *f* rabattue
4 *adj* (**a**) *Arch or Literary (fierce → person)* féroce, cruel; *(deadly → disease)* cruel
(**b**) *(idiom)* **in** *or* **at one fell swoop** d'un seul coup
►► ***fell runner*** coureur(euse) *m,f* en basse montagne; ***fell running*** course *f* en basse montagne; ***fell walker*** randonneur(euse) *m,f* de basse montagne; ***fell walking*** randonnée *f* en basse montagne
fella ['felə] *n Fam (man)* mec *m*, type *m*; *Br (boyfriend)* copain *m*, mec *m*
fellah ['felə] *n* (**a**) *(Arab peasant)* fellah *m* (**b**) *Fam (man)* mec *m*, type *m*; *Br (boyfriend)* copain *m*, mec *m*
fellatio [fe'leɪʃɪəʊ] *n* fellation *f*
feller ['felə(r)] *n Br Fam (man)* mec *m*, type *m*; *Br (boyfriend)* copain *m*, mec *m*
felling ['felɪŋ] *n (of tree, forest)* abattage *m*
fellow ['feləʊ] **1** *n* (**a**) *Fam Old-fashioned (man)* gars *m*, type *m*; **a good fellow** un type *ou* gars bien; **an old fellow** un vieux bonhomme; **poor old fellow** pauvre vieux; **the poor fellow's just lost his job** le pauvre vient juste de perdre son travail; **the poor little fellow** *(animal)* la pauvre bête; **hello, old fellow** salut, mon vieux; **my dear fellow** mon cher ami; **give a fellow a chance!** donne-moi une chance!
(**b**) *Literary (comrade)* ami(e) *m,f*, camarade *mf*; *(other human being)* semblable *mf*; *(person in same profession)* confrère *m*, consœur *f*; **fellows in misfortune** compagnons (compagnes) *mpl,fpl* d'infortune; **school fellow** camarade *mf* d'école
(**c**) *Univ (professor)* professeur *m (faisant également partie du conseil d'administration)*; *(postgraduate student)* étudiant(e) *m,f* de troisième cycle *(souvent chargé de cours)*
(**d**) *(of learned society)* membre *m*; **Fellow of the Craft** *(in freemasonry)* compagnon *m*; *Br* **Fellow of the Royal College of Music** = membre du "Royal College of Music"; **Fellow of the Royal College of Physicians** = membre du "Royal College of Physicians"; **Fellow of the Royal College of Surgeons** = membre du "Royal College of Surgeons"; **Fellow of the Royal College of Veterinary Surgeons** = membre du "Royal College of Veterinary Surgeons"; **Fellow of the Royal Society** = membre de la Société royale (de Londres)
(**e**) *(one of a pair)* **where is the fellow to this sock/glove?** où est la chaussette/le gant qui va avec celle-là/celui-là?
2 *adj* **fellow prisoner/student** camarade *mf* de prison/d'études; **fellow passenger/sufferer/soldier** compagnon *m* de voyage/d'infortune/d'armes; **fellow being** *or* **creature** semblable *mf*, pareil(eille) *m,f*; **one's fellow man** son semblable; **fellow worker** *(in office)* collègue *mf* (de travail); *(in factory)* camarade *mf* (de travail), compagnon *m* de travail; **fellow citizen** concitoyen(enne) *m,f*; **fellow countryman/countrywoman** compatriote *mf*; **it's rare to meet a fellow hang-glider** c'est rare de rencontrer un autre adepte du deltaplane; **an opportunity to meet your fellow translators** une occasion de rencontrer vos confrères traducteurs
►► ***fellow feeling*** sympathie *f*; ***fellow traveller*** *(companion on journey)* compagnon (compagne) *m,f* de voyage *ou* de route; *Fig* compagnon *m* de route; *Pol* communisant(e) *m,f*
fellowship ['feləʊʃɪp] *n* (**a**) *(friendship)* camaraderie *f*; *(company)* compagnie *f* (**b**) *(organization)* association *f*, société *f*; *Rel* confrérie *f* (**c**) *Univ (scholarship)* bourse *f* d'études de l'enseignement supérieur; *(position)* poste *m* de chercheur
felo-de-se [,fiːləʊdɪ'siː] *(pl* **felones-de-se** [fɪ,ləʊniːz-]) *n Law* (**a**) *(person)* suicidé(e) *m,f* (de propos délibéré) (**b**) *(act of suicide)* suicide *m*, homicide *m* de soi-même
felon[1] ['felən] *n Law* criminel(elle) *m,f*
felon[2] *n Med* panaris *m*
felonious [fɪ'ləʊnjəs] *adj Law* criminel
felony ['felənɪ] *n Law* crime *m*; **to compound a felony** pactiser avec un crime
felsite ['felsaɪt] *n Miner* felsite *f*, pétrosilex *m*
felspar ['felspɑː(r)] = **feldspar**
felt[1] [felt] *pt & pp of* **feel**
felt[2] **1** *n Tex* feutre *m*; **roofing felt** feutre *m* bitumé
2 *comp* de *ou* en feutre
3 *vt Tex (wool, hairs)* feutrer; *Constr (roof etc)* couvrir de feutre bitumé
►► ***felt hat*** (chapeau *m* de *ou* en) feutre *m*; ***felt pen*** feutre *m*
felt-tip (pen) *n* (stylo *m*) feutre *m*
fem [fem] **1** *adj (abbr* **feminine)** fém.
2 *n Fam* lesbienne *f* féminine ❑
FEMA ['fiːmə] *n (abbr* **Federal Emergency Management Agency)** = agence gouvernementale américaine pour la prévention des catastrophes et l'aide aux sinistrés
female ['fiːmeɪl] **1** *adj* (**a**) *(animal, plant, egg)* femelle; *(sex, quality, voice, employee)* féminin; *(vote)* des femmes; *(equality)* de la femme, des femmes; **a traditionally female job** un travail traditionnellement réservé aux femmes; **the young female giraffe** la jeune girafe femelle; **female slave** femme *f* esclave; **a study of the female character** une étude du caractère de la femme; **female company** la compagnie féminine *ou* des femmes; **the female sex organs** les organes sexuels féminins *ou* de la femme; **more female students than male study languages** il y a plus d'étudiantes que d'étudiants en langues; **male and female clients** des clients et des clientes; **there are not enough female politicians** il n'y a pas assez de femmes sur la scène politique; **that's typical female thinking!** c'est un raisonnement typiquement féminin!
(**b**) *Tech* femelle
2 *n* (**a**) *(animal, plant)* femelle *f*; *(person)* femme *f*; **the female of the species** la femelle
(**b**) *Pej (woman)* bonne femme *f*; **some female called for you** il y a une bonne femme qui t'a demandé au téléphone
►► ***female circumcision*** excision *f*; ***female condom*** préservatif *m* féminin; ***female impersonator*** travesti *m (dans un spectacle)*

'The Female Eunuch' *Greer* 'La Femme eunuque'

femaleness ['fiːmeɪlnɪs] *n* féminité *f*
feminine ['femɪnɪn] **1** *adj* (**a**) *(dress, woman, hands etc)* féminin; **the bedroom is very feminine** c'est une vraie chambre de femme; **this flat needs the feminine touch** cet appartement a besoin de la présence d'une femme (**b**) *Gram (ending, form)* féminin
2 *n Gram* féminin *m*; **in the feminine** au féminin
femininity [,femɪ'nɪnətɪ] *n* féminité *f*
feminism ['femɪnɪzəm] *n* féminisme *m*; **I really admire her feminism** j'admire vraiment la façon dont elle soutient la cause de la femme *ou* des femmes
feminist ['femɪnɪst] **1** *adj* féministe; **what will be the feminist reaction?** comment les féministes réagiront-elles?
2 *n* féministe *mf*
feminization [,femɪnaɪ'zeɪʃən] *n* féminisation *f*
feminize, -ise ['femɪnaɪz] **1** *vt (boy)* féminiser, rendre efféminé; *(writing)* féminiser
2 *vi* se féminiser
femoral ['femərəl] *adj Anat* fémoral
femorotibial [,femərəʊ'tɪbɪəl] *adj Anat* fémoro-tibial
femur ['fiːmə(r)] *n Anat* fémur *m*
fen [fen] **1** *n Geog* marais *m*, marécage *m*
2 Fens *npl* **the Fens** = région de plaines anciennement marécageuses dans le sud-est de l'Angleterre
fence [fens] **1** *n* (**a**) *(gen)* barrière *f*; *(completely enclosing)* barrière *f*, clôture *f*; *(high and wooden)* palissade *f*; **electric/barbed-wire fence** clôture *f* électrique/en fil barbelé
(**b**) *(in show-jumping)* obstacle *m*; **to rush one's fences** *(horse)* arriver trop vite sur l'obstacle; *Fig* aller trop vite en besogne
(**c**) *Fam Crime slang (of stolen goods)* receleur(euse) ❑ *m,f*
(**d**) *Tech (guard)* protection *f*
(**e**) *(idioms)* **to come down on the right/wrong side of the fence** choisir le bon/mauvais parti; **to be on the other side of the fence** être de l'autre côté de la barricade; **to mend one's fences** *(with fans, electorate)* se refaire une réputation; *(with friends, colleagues)* se regagner des faveurs; **to mend one's fences with sb** *(fans, electorate)* se refaire une réputation auprès *ou* regagner les faveurs de qn; *(friends, colleagues)* se réconcilier avec qn; **to sit on the fence** ne pas se prononcer, rester neutre; **stop sitting on the fence, come down off the fence** prononce-toi
2 *vt* (**a**) *(land)* clôturer
(**b**) *Fam Crime slang (stolen goods)* receler ❑
3 *vi* (**a**) *Sport* faire de l'escrime
(**b**) *(evade question)* se dérober; *(joust verbally)* s'affronter verbalement
(**c**) *Fam Crime slang (handle stolen goods)* faire du recel ❑
►► ***fence post*** piquet *m* de clôture
►**fence in** *vt sep* (**a**) *(garden)* clôturer (**b**) *Fig (restrict → person)* enfermer, étouffer; **he feels fenced in** il se sent enfermé, il étouffe; **to feel fenced in by sth** étouffer sous le poids de qch
►**fence off** *vt sep* séparer à l'aide d'une clôture
fenceless ['fenslɪs] *adj* (**a**) *(land)* ouvert, sans clôture (**b**) *Literary (person)* sans défense (**c**) *Hist (city)* nonfortifié
fence-mending *n Fig* reprise *f* des relations
fencer ['fensə(r)] *n* (**a**) *Sport* escrimeur(euse) *m,f* (**b**) *(workman)* poseur(euse) *m,f* de clôtures
fencing ['fensɪŋ] **1** *n* (**a**) *Sport* escrime *f* (**b**) *Fig (verbal)* joutes *fpl* oratoires (**c**) *(fences)* clôture *f*, barrière *f*; *(material)* matériaux *mpl* pour clôture (**d**) *(action) (of land)* action *f* de clôturer (**e**) *Fam Crime slang (handling stolen goods)* recel ❑ *m*
2 *comp Sport (lesson)* d'escrime
►► *Sport* ***fencing match*** assaut *m*
fend [fend] *vi* **to fend for oneself** se débrouiller tout seul; *(financially)* s'assumer, subvenir à ses besoins
►**fend off** *vt sep (blow)* parer; *(attack, attacker)* repousser; *(takeover bid)* se défendre contre; *Fig (question)* éluder, se dérober à; *(person at door, on telephone)* éconduire
fender ['fendə(r)] *n* (**a**) *(for fireplace)* garde-feu *m inv* (**b**) *Naut* défense *f* (**c**) *Am (on car)* aile *f*; *(on bicycle)* garde-boue *m inv*; *(on train, tram →*

shock absorber) pare-chocs *m inv*; *(→ for clearing track)* chasse-pierres *m inv*

fender-bender *n Am Fam (minor accident)* petit accrochage❑ *m*

fenestra [fə'nestrə] *(pl* **fenestrae** [-tri:]) *n*

►► *Anat* ***fenestra cochleae*** fenêtre *f* ronde; *Anat* ***fenestra ovalis*** fenêtre *f* ovale; *Anat* ***fenestra rotunda*** fenêtre *f* ronde; *Anat* ***fenestra vestibuli*** fenêtre *f* ovale

fenestrate ['fenɪstreɪt] *vt Med* fenêtrer

fenestrated ['fenɪstreɪtɪd] *adj Biol* fenestré, fenêtré

►► *Med* ***fenestrated bandage*** bandage *m* fenêtré

fenestration [,fenɪ'streɪʃən] *n* (**a**) *Archit* fenêtrage *m* (**b**) *Med* fenestration *f*

feng shui [fəŋ'ʃweɪ] *n* Feng Shui *m*

Fenian ['fi:nɪən] *n* (**a**) *Pol & Hist* Fénian *m* (**b**) *Br Fam* = terme injurieux désignant un catholique

Fenianism ['fi:nɪə,nɪzəm] *n Pol & Hist* fénianisme *m*

fenland ['fenlænd] *n Geog* pays *m* marécageux

fennec ['fenɪk] *n Zool* fennec *m*

fennel ['fenəl] *n Bot & Culin* fenouil *m*

fenugreek ['fenjʊ,gri:k] *n Bot & Culin* fenugrec *m*

feoff [fi:f, fef] *vt (property)* donner en fief

feracious [fe'reɪʃəs] *adj* fertile, fécond

feral ['fɪərəl] *adj (animal)* féral

fer-de-lance [,feədə'lɑ:ns] *(pl* **fers-de-lance**) *n Zool* fer-de-lance *m*

ferial ['fɪərɪəl] *adj Rel* (**a**) *(weekday)* férial (**b**) *(holiday)* férié

Fermat ['fɜ:mæt] *pr n*

►► *Math* ***Fermat's last theorem*** le dernier théorème de Fermat; ***Fermat's principle*** le principe de Fermat

fermata [fɜ:'mɑ:tə] *n Mus* point *m* d'orgue

ferment 1 *vt* [fə'ment] faire fermenter; *Fig* **to ferment trouble** fomenter des troubles

2 *vi* [fə'ment] fermenter

3 *n* ['fɜ:ment] (**a**) *(agent)* ferment *m*; *(fermentation)* fermentation *f* (**b**) *Fig (unrest)* agitation *f*; **to be in (a state of) ferment** être en effervescence

fermentable [fə'mentəbəl] *adj* fermentable, fermentescible

fermentation [,fɜ:mən'teɪʃən] *n* fermentation *f*

fermentative [fə'mentətɪv] *adj* fermentatif

fermented [fə'mentɪd] *adj* fermenté

fermenter [fə'mentə(r)] *n Chem* fermenteur *m*

Fermi ['fɜ:mɪ] *n Phys (measurement)* fermi *m*

►► ***Fermi age*** âge *m* de Fermi; ***Fermi constant*** constante *f* de Fermi; ***Fermi plot*** droite *f* de Fermi

Fermi-Dirac statistics [-'dɪəræk] *npl Phys* statistique *f* de Fermi-Dirac

fermion ['fɜ:mɪən] *n Phys* fermion *m*

fermium ['fɜ:mɪəm] *n Chem* fermium *m*

fern [fɜ:n] *n Bot* fougère *f*

ferocious [fə'rəʊʃəs] *adj (animal, appetite, criticism, fighting)* féroce; *(weapon)* meurtrier; *(competition)* acharné; *(heat)* terrible, intense; *(climate)* rude; **a ferocious war** une guerre sanguinaire

ferociously [fə'rəʊʃəslɪ] *adv (bark, criticize, attack)* avec férocité, férocement; *(look at someone)* d'un œil féroce; **this business is fiercely competitive** ce secteur est caractérisé par une concurrence acharnée

ferociousness [fə'rəʊʃəsnɪs], **ferocity** [fə'rɒsətɪ] *n (of person, animal, attack, criticism)* férocité *f*; *(of climate)* rudesse *f*; *(of heat)* intensité *f*, caractère *m* torride; **the ferociousness of the competition for a place at university** la concurrence acharnée pour entrer à l'université

Ferrara [fə'rɑ:rə] *n* Ferrare

ferrate ['fereɪt] *n Chem* ferrate *m*

ferreous ['ferɪəs] *adj* ferreux

ferret ['ferɪt] **1** *n Zool* furet *m*

2 *vt (hunt with ferrets)* chasser au furet

3 *vi* (**a**) *(hunt with ferrets)* chasser au furet; **to go ferreting** aller à la chasse au furet (**b**) *Fig (in pocket, drawer)* fouiller; *(in room)* fouiller, fureter

►**ferret about, ferret around** *vi (in pocket, drawer)* fouiller; *(in room)* fouiller, fureter; **to ferret about for information** fureter dans le but de trouver des renseignements; **to ferret about in sb's past** fureter dans le passé de qn; **he's been ferreting about** il a fureté un peu partout

►**ferret out** *vt sep* (**a**) *(animal)* déloger (**b**) *(information, truth)* dénicher

ferreting ['ferɪtɪŋ] *n* chasse *f* au furet

ferrety ['ferɪtɪ] *adj* de furet; *Pej (eyes, face)* de fouine

ferriage ['ferɪɪdʒ] *n* (**a**) *(transport by ferry)* passage *m* en bac, transport *m* par bac (**b**) *(fee)* droits *mpl* de passage

ferric ['ferɪk] *adj Chem* ferrique

ferriferous [fə'rɪfərəs] *adj Miner* ferrifère

ferrimagnetic [,ferɪmæg'netɪk] *adj Phys* ferrimagnétique

ferrimagnetism [,ferɪ'mægnɪtɪzəm] *n Phys* ferrimagnétisme *m*

Ferris wheel ['ferɪs-] *n (at fairground)* grande roue *f*

ferrite ['feraɪt] *n Chem* ferrite *f*

ferro- ['ferəʊ] *pref* ferro-

ferro-alloy *n* ferroalliage *m*, alliage *m* ferreux

ferro-aluminium, *Am* **ferro-aluminum** *n* ferro-aluminium *m*

ferrocerium [,ferəʊ'sɪrɪəm] *n* ferrocérium *m*

ferrochrome [,ferəʊ'krəʊm], **ferrochromium** [,ferəʊ'krəʊmɪəm] *n* ferrochrome *m*

ferroconcrete [,ferəʊ'kɒŋkri:t] *n Constr* béton *m* armé

ferrocyanide [,ferəʊ'saɪənaɪd] *n Chem & Miner* ferrocyanide *m*

ferroelectric [,ferəʊɪ'lektrɪk] *adj Phys* ferroélectrique

ferroelectricity [,ferəʊɪlek'trɪsɪtɪ] *n Phys* ferroélectricité *f*

ferromagnetic [,ferəʊmæg'netɪk] *adj Phys* ferromagnétique

ferromagnetism [,ferəʊ'mægnə,tɪzəm] *n Phys* ferromagnétisme *m*

ferromanganese [,ferəʊ'mæŋgəni:z] *n Miner* ferromanganèse *m*

ferromolybdenum [,ferəʊmɒ'lɪbdɪnəm] *n Metal* ferromolybdène *m*

ferronickel [,ferəʊ'nɪkəl] *n* ferronickel *m*

►► ***ferronickel accumulator*** accumulateur *m* au fer-nickel; ***ferronickel alloys*** alliages *mpl* ferronickel

ferrosilicon [,ferəʊ'sɪlɪkən] *n Metal* ferrosilicium *m*

ferrotitanium [,ferəʊtɪ'teɪnɪəm] *n Metal* ferrotitane *m*

ferrotungsten [,ferəʊ'tʌŋstən] *n Miner* ferrotungstène *m*

ferrous ['ferəs] *adj Chem* ferreux

ferruginous [fə'ru:dʒɪnəs] *adj Miner* ferrugineux

►► *Orn* ***ferruginous duck*** fuligule *m* nyroca, canard *m* nyroca

ferrule ['feru:l] *n (of umbrella, walking stick)* virole *f*

ferry ['ferɪ] *(pl* **ferries,** *pt & pp* **ferried**) **1** *n (large)* ferry *m*; *(small)* bac *m*; **to take the ferry** prendre le ferry *ou* le bac; **we took the ferry to France** nous sommes allés en France en ferry; **passenger ferry** ferry *m* pour passagers piétons; **car ferry** car-ferry *m*

2 *vt* (**a**) *(by large boat → of company)* transporter en ferry; *(by small boat → of company)* faire traverser en bac; *(→ of boat)* transporter; **Donald will ferry you across in his rowing boat** Donald vous fera traverser dans sa barque

(**b**) *Fig (by vehicle → goods)* transporter; *(→ people)* conduire; **he spends most of his time ferrying the kids around** il passe la majeure partie de son temps à conduire les enfants à droite et à gauche

►► ***ferry crossing*** traversée *f* en ferry *ou* bac; ***ferry service*** ligne *f* de ferry; ***ferry terminal*** gare *f* maritime

ferryboat ['ferɪbəʊt] *n (large)* ferry *m*; *(small)* bac *m*

ferrying ['ferɪɪŋ] *n (in large boat)* transport *m* en ferry; *(in small boat)* transport *m* par bac

ferryman ['ferɪmən] *(pl* **ferrymen** [-mən]) *n* passeur *m*

fertile ['fɜ:taɪl] *adj (land, soil)* fertile; *(person, couple, animal)* fécond; *Fig (imagination)* fertile, fécond; **a fertile egg** un œuf fécondé; *Fig* **to fall on fertile ground** trouver un terrain propice

►► *Geog* ***the Fertile Crescent*** le Croissant fertile

fertility [fɜ:'tɪlətɪ] **1** *n (of land, soil)* fertilité *f*; *(of person, animal)* fécondité *f*; *Fig (of imagination)* fertilité *f*, fécondité *f*

2 *comp (rate)* de fécondité; *(rite, symbol)* de fertilité

►► *Med* ***fertility clinic*** centre *m* de traitement de la stérilité; *Med* ***fertility drug*** médicament *m* pour le traitement de la stérilité; ***fertility symbol*** symbole *m* de fertilité; *Med* ***fertility treatment*** traitement *m* de la stérilité

fertilizable ['fɜ:tɪ,laɪzəbəl] *adj* (**a**) *Biol (animal, plant, egg)* fécondable (**b**) *Agr (land, soil)* fertilisable

fertilization [,fɜ:tɪlaɪ'zeɪʃən] *n* (**a**) *Biol (of animal, plant, egg)* fécondation *f* (**b**) *Agr (of land, soil)* fertilisation *f*

fertilize, -ise ['fɜ:tɪlaɪz] *vt* (**a**) *Biol (animal, plant, egg)* féconder (**b**) *Agr (land, soil)* fertiliser

fertilizer ['fɜ:tɪlaɪzə(r)] *n Agr* engrais *m*

ferula ['ferjʊlə] *(pl* **ferulae** [-li:]) *n Bot* férule *f*

ferule ['feru:l] *n* (**a**) *(of umbrella, walking stick)* virole *f* (**b**) *(cane, rod)* férule *f* (**c**) *Am (discipline)* discipline *f (à l'école)*

fervency ['fɜ:vənsɪ] *n* ferveur *f*

fervent ['fɜ:vənt] *adj (desire, supporter etc)* fervent, ardent; **he is a fervent believer in reincarnation** il croit ardemment à la réincarnation

fervently ['fɜ:vəntlɪ] *adv (beg, desire, speak)* avec ferveur; *(believe)* ardemment

fervid ['fɜ:vɪd] *Formal* = **fervent**

fervidly ['fɜ:vɪdlɪ] *Formal* = **fervently**

fervour, *Am* **fervor** ['fɜ:və(r)] *n* ferveur *f*

Fescennine ['fesənaɪn] *adj Literature* fescennin

►► ***Fescennine verses*** chants *mpl* fescennins

►**fess up** [fes-] *vi Am Fam* cracher le morceau

festal ['festəl] *adj (day, atmosphere)* de fête; *(people)* en fête

fester ['festə(r)] *vi* (**a**) *(wound)* suppurer; *Fig (situation)* s'envenimer; **resentment within the company continues to fester** le mécontentement continue de croître dans l'entreprise (**b**) *Br Fam (do nothing)* buller

festering ['festərɪŋ] *adj (wound)* suppurant; *Fig* **his festering resentment finally came to the surface** sa rancune accumulée finit par se manifester

festival ['festɪvəl] *n (of music, film etc)* festival *m*; *Rel* fête *f*; **street festival** festival *m* de rue; **the Cannes Film Festival** le Festival de Cannes

►► *Am* ***festival seating*** *(in theatre)* placement *m* libre

festive ['festɪv] *adj (atmosphere)* de fête; **their golden wedding celebration was a very festive occasion** ils ont fait une grande fête pour célébrer leurs noces d'or; **there was a really festive atmosphere** l'atmosphère était vraiment à la fête; **the festive season** la période des fêtes; **to be in festive mood** *(person)* se sentir d'une humeur de fête; **the village is in festive mood** une ambiance de fête règne dans le village; **to look festive** *(place)* être décoré comme pour une fête

festively ['festɪvlɪ] *adv* d'une manière gaie *ou* joyeuse, joyeusement

festivity [fes'tɪvətɪ] **1** *n (merriness)* fête *f*; **an air/atmosphere of festivity** un air/une atmosphère de fête

2 festivities *npl (celebrations)* festivités *fpl*; **the Christmas festivities** les fêtes *fpl* de Noël; **come and join the festivities** viens te joindre à la fête, viens faire la fête avec nous

festoon [fe'stu:n] **1** *n* feston *m*, guirlande *f*

2 *vt* orner de festons, festonner; *Fig* **to be festooned in sth** *(draped with)* être couvert de qch

►► ***festoon blind*** store *m* autrichien

feta ['fetə] *n* **feta (cheese)** feta *f*

fetal ['fi:təl] *adj Am* fœtal

►► *Med* ***fetal alcohol syndrome*** syndrome *m* d'alcoolisme fœtal

fetch [fetʃ] **1** *vt* (**a**) *(go to get)* aller chercher; **to fetch water from the river** aller puiser de l'eau dans la rivière; **to fetch sb from the airport** aller chercher qn à l'aéroport; **I'll fetch you** je viendrai te chercher; **fetch!** *(to dog)* va chercher!; **run and fetch him** va vite le chercher

(**b**) *Com (be sold for)* rapporter; *(specific price)* atteindre; **it fetched a high price** cela s'est vendu cher; **it fetched £100,000** cela a atteint les 100 000 livres; **I'd be surprised if it fetched**

fen–fet

that much cela m'étonnerait que cela rapporte autant *ou* que cela se vende aussi cher

(**c**) *Br Fam (deal)* **to fetch sb a blow** flanquer un coup à qn; **he fetched him one with his right fist** il lui a flanqué *ou* envoyé un droit; **move or I'll fetch you one!** dégage ou je t'en mets une!

(**d**) *(generate → response, laugh)* susciter; **the speech fetched a round of applause** le discours a été reçu par des applaudissements

(**e**) *Literary (utter → sigh, moan)* pousser

2 *vi* **I'm not going to fetch and carry for you!** je ne vais pas être ta bonne à tout faire!

▸**fetch back** *vt sep (bring back → person)* ramener; *(→ thing)* rapporter

▸**fetch up 1** *vi (reach)* **to fetch up at a port** parvenir *ou* arriver à un port; **the kite fetched up in the branches of a tree** le cerf-volant est resté accroché dans les branches d'un arbre; *Fam* **they finally fetched up at our house** ils ont finalement abouti chez nous❑; *Fam* **the car fetched up against a wall** la voiture s'est (finalement) arrêtée en heurtant un mur❑

2 *vt sep* (**a**) *(bring from lower place → person)* faire monter; *(→ thing)* remonter

(**b**) *Fam (vomit)* dégueuler

fet–ffa

fetching ['fetʃɪŋ] *adj (smile, person, look)* séduisant; *(hat, dress)* seyant

fetchingly ['fetʃɪŋlɪ] *adv (smile)* d'un air séduisant; **with his hat balanced fetchingly on his head** avec son chapeau élégamment posé sur la tête

fête [feɪt, fet] **1** *n* fête *f*, kermesse *f*; **village fête** fête *f* du village

2 *vt* fêter

FÊTE

En Grande-Bretagne, les "village fêtes" sont des manifestations en plein air où l'on vend des produits faits maison et où l'on organise des manifestations sportives et des jeux pour enfants; elles sont généralement destinées à réunir des fonds pour une œuvre de charité.

feticidal, feticide *Am* = **foeticidal, foeticide**

fetid ['fetɪd, 'fi:tɪd] *adj* fétide

fetidity [fe'tɪdɪtɪ, fi:'tɪdɪtɪ], **fetidness** ['fetɪdnɪs, 'fi:tɪdnɪs] *n* fétidité *f*

fetish ['fetɪʃ] *n Psy & Rel* fétiche *m*; **to have a fetish for** *or* **to make a fetish of sth** être obsédé par qch, être un(e) maniaque de qch; *Fam* **he's got a bit of a shoe fetish** il est un peu fétichiste des chaussures

fetishism ['fetɪʃɪzəm] *n Psy & Rel* fétichisme *m*; **food fetishism** obsession *f* pour la nourriture; **foot fetishism** fétichisme *m* du pied

fetishist ['fetɪʃɪst] *n Psy & Rel* fétichiste *mf*; **food fetishist** personne *f* obsédée par la nourriture; **foot fetishist** fétichiste *mf* du pied

fetishistic [,fetɪ'ʃɪstɪk] *adj Psy* fétichiste; **that borders on the fetishistic** cela confine au fétichisme

fetlock ['fetlɒk] *n Zool (of horse → part of leg)* partie *f* postérieure du pied; *(→ joint)* boulet *m*; *(→ hair)* fanon *m*

fetoscopy *Am* = **foetoscopy**

fetter ['fetə(r)] **1** *vt (slave, prisoner)* enchaîner; *(horse)* entraver; *Fig* entraver

2 fetters *npl (of prisoner)* fers *mpl*, chaînes *fpl*; *(of horse)* entraves *fpl*; *Fig (of marriage, job)* chaînes *fpl*, sujétions *fpl*; **in fetters** *(prisoner)* enchaîné; *Fig* entravé; **to put sb in fetters** mettre qn aux fers; *Fig* entraver qn

fettered ['fetəd] *adj (prisoner)* enchaîné, dans les fers; *(horse)* entravé

fetterless ['fetəlɪs] *adj (person)* sans fers; *(horse)* sans entraves; *Fig* libre, indépendant

fettle ['fetəl] *n Fam* **to be in fine** *or* **good fettle** aller bien❑

fettuccine, fettucini [fetʊ'tʃi:ni:] *n Culin* fettucines *fpl*

fetus *Am* = **foetus**

feu [fju:] *Scot Law* **1** *n* bail *m* perpétuel

2 *vt* **to feu a piece of land** concéder un terrain à perpétuité moyennant redevance; **to feu out an estate** morceler une propriété moyennant redevance

▸▸ ***feu duty*** loyer *m* (de la terre)

feud [fju:d] **1** *n (between people, families)* querelle *f*; *(more aggressive → between families)* vendetta *f*; **a bloody feud** une vendetta; **to have a feud with sb** être à couteaux tirés avec qn

2 *vi* se quereller, se disputer; **to feud with sb (over sth)** se quereller *ou* se disputer avec qn (pour qch); **they were feuding with each other over who owned the property** ils se disputaient la possession de la propriété

feudal ['fju:dəl] *adj* (**a**) *Hist (society, system)* féodal (**b**) *Pej (extremely old-fashioned)* moyenâgeux

▸▸ *Hist* ***feudal lord*** seigneur *m*

feudalism ['fju:dəlɪzəm] *n Hist* féodalisme *m*

feudalist ['fju:dəlɪst] *n* (**a**) *Hist* partisan *m* du régime féodal (**b**) *(expert in feudal law)* feudiste *mf*

feudality [fju:'dælɪtɪ] *n Hist* féodalité *f*; *(fief)* fief *m*

feudalize, -ise ['fju:dəlaɪz] *vt Hist* féodaliser

feudally ['fju:dəlɪ] *adv* féodalement

feudatory ['fju:dətərɪ] *n Hist* feudataire *m*

feuding ['fju:dɪŋ] *n (UNCOUNT)* querelle *f*, querelles *fpl*; *(more aggressive)* vendetta *f*

fever ['fi:və(r)] *n* (**a**) *Med (illness)* fièvre *f*; **a bout of fever** un accès *ou* une poussée de fièvre; **to have a fever** *(high temperature)* avoir de la température *ou* de la fièvre; **to have a high fever** avoir beaucoup de température *ou* de fièvre

(**b**) *Fig* excitation *f* fébrile; **a fever of anticipation** une attente fiévreuse *ou* fébrile; **football/election/gold fever** fièvre *f* du football/des élections/de l'or; **gambling fever** démon *m* du jeu; **the entire hall went into a fever of excitement** la salle entière s'enfiévra; **to be in a fever about sth** *(nervous, excited)* être tout excité à cause de qch; **things are at fever pitch here** l'excitation ici est à son comble; **excitement is rising to fever pitch** l'excitation est de plus en plus fébrile

'Fever Pitch' *Hornby, Evans* 'Carton jaune'

fevered ['fi:vəd] *adj (brow)* fiévreux; *Fig (imagination)* enfiévré

feverfew ['fi:vəfju:] *n Bot* grande camomille *f*, matricaire *f*

feverish ['fi:vərɪʃ] *adj Med* fiévreux; *Fig (activity, atmosphere)* fébrile, fiévreux

feverishly ['fi:vərɪʃlɪ] *adv Fig* fébrilement, fiévreusement

feverishness ['fi:vərɪʃnɪs] *n Med* état *m* fébrile, fébrilité *f*

FEW [fju:]

peu de	▸**1 (a)**
quelques	▸**1 (b); 3**
peu	▸**2**
quelques-uns	▸**3**
un assez grand nombre (de)	▸**4**

1 *adj* (**a**) *(not many)* peu de; **few people have done that** peu de gens ont fait cela; **there are very few suitable candidates for the post** très peu de candidats ont le profil requis; **so/too few books to read** si/trop peu de livres à lire; **there are four books too few** il manque quatre livres; **we are few (in number)** nous sommes peu nombreux; **with few exceptions** à peu d'exceptions près, sauf de rares exceptions; *(with def art, poss adj etc)* **on the few occasions that I have met him** les rares fois où je l'ai rencontré; **her few remaining possessions** le peu de biens qui lui restaient; **these few precious souvenirs** ces quelques précieux souvenirs; **it is one of the few surviving examples of...** c'est un des rares exemples qui restent de...; **she is one of the few women to have held the post** c'est une des rares femmes à avoir assumé ces fonctions; **visitors are few and far between** les visiteurs sont rares; **grants will be few and far between in future** les bourses se feront rares à l'avenir

(**b**) *(indicating an unspecified or approximate number)* **every few minutes** toutes les deux ou trois minutes; **the first few copies** les deux ou trois premiers exemplaires; **in the past/next few days** pendant les deux ou trois derniers/prochains jours; **he's been living in London for the past few years** ça fait quelques années qu'il habite à Londres; **these past few weeks have been wonderful** ces dernières semaines ont été merveilleuses

2 *pron (not many)* peu; **how many of them are there? – very few** combien sont-ils? – très peu nombreux; **there are very/too few of us** nous sommes très peu/trop peu nombreux; **there are so few of them** ils sont tellement peu nombreux; **I didn't realize how few there were** je ne m'étais pas rendu compte qu'ils étaient aussi peu nombreux; **few could have predicted the outcome** peu de personnes *ou* rares sont ceux qui auraient pu prévoir le résultat; **few of them could speak French** peu parmi eux parlaient français; **the few who knew her** les quelques personnes qui la connaissaient; **the chosen few** les heureux élus; *Br Hist* **the Few** = les aviateurs britanniques qui ont défendu leur pays pendant la bataille d'Angleterre; *Bible* **many are called but few are chosen** il y a beaucoup d'appelés mais peu d'élus

3 a few 1 *adj* quelques; **I have a few ideas** j'ai quelques idées; **he has a few more friends than I have** il a un peu plus d'amis que moi; **a few more days/months/years** quelques jours/mois/années de plus; **a few more days should see the job done** encore quelques jours et le travail devrait être fini

2 *pron* quelques-uns (quelques-unes) *mpl, fpl*; **do you have many friends? – I have a few** est-ce que tu as beaucoup d'amis? – (j'en ai) quelques-uns; **we need a few more/less** il nous en faut un peu plus/moins; **a few of these cakes/the survivors** quelques-uns de ces gâteaux/des survivants; **a few of you** quelques-uns d'entre vous; **there are only a few of us who attend regularly** seuls quelques-uns parmi nous y vont régulièrement; *Fam* **he's had a few (too many)** *(drinks)* il a bu un coup (de trop); **to name but a few** pour n'en citer que quelques-uns; **not a few** pas peu

4 a good few, quite a few 1 *adj* un assez grand nombre de; **there were a good few** *or* **quite a few mistakes in it** il y avait un assez grand nombre de *ou* pas mal de fautes dedans; **quite a few minutes passed** un bon moment s'est écoulé

2 *pron* un assez grand nombre; **quite a few agreed with me** ils étaient assez nombreux à être d'accord avec moi; **quite a few of us/of the books** un assez grand nombre d'entre nous/de livres; **I hadn't seen all her films, but I'd seen a good few** je n'avais pas vu tous ses films, mais j'en avais vu un assez grand nombre

fewer ['fju:ə(r)] *(compar of* **few**) **1** *adj* moins de; **more applicants are competing for fewer jobs** il y a plus de candidats et moins de postes; **there have been fewer accidents than last year** il y a eu moins d'accidents que l'an dernier; **fewer and fewer people** de moins en moins de gens; **the fewer people turn up the better** moins il y aura de monde et mieux ce sera; **no fewer than** pas moins de

2 *pron* moins; **there are fewer of you than I thought** vous êtes moins nombreux que je ne le pensais; **I've got even/far** *or* **a lot fewer than you** j'en ai encore/beaucoup moins que toi; **the fewer the better** moins il y en a mieux c'est; **how many days are you going to spend there? – the fewer the better** combien de jours vas-tu passer là-bas? – le moins possible

fewest ['fju:ɪst] *(superl of* **few**) **1** *adj* le moins de; **the fewest mistakes possible** le moins d'erreurs possible; **this is the part where the fewest people live** c'est la région la moins peuplée

2 *pron* **I had the fewest** c'est moi qui en ai eu le moins; **who's got the fewest?** qui en a le moins?

fey [feɪ] *adj* (**a**) *(whimsical → person, behaviour)* bizarre (**b**) *Scot (clairvoyant)* extralucide (**c**) *Scot (having feeling of impending death)* qui a des pressentiments de mort

Fez [fez] *n* Fès

fez [fez] *n* fez *m*

ff *(written abbr* **and the following**) et suiv., sqq.

FFA [,efef'eɪ] *n (abbr* **Future Farmers of America**) = organisation nationale d'étudiants en agriculture

FGA [ˌefdʒiːˈeɪ] *adj Ins (abbr* **free of general average**) FCA

FH *Br (written abbr* **fire hydrant**) borne *f* à incendie

FHA [ˌefeɪtʃˈeɪ] *n Am (abbr* **Federal Housing Administration**) = organisme de gestion des logements sociaux aux États-Unis

fiancé [fɪˈɒnseɪ] *n* fiancé *m*

fiancée [fɪˈɒnseɪ] *n* fiancée *f*

Fianna Fáil [ˌfiːənəˈfɔɪl] *n Ir Pol* le Fianna Fáil

fiasco [fɪˈæskəʊ] *(pl* **fiascos** *or* **fiascoes**) *n* fiasco *m*; **it was a fiasco** ça a été un véritable fiasco; **to end in fiasco** se terminer par un fiasco

fiat [ˈfaɪæt] *n (decree)* décret *m*

►► *Am Fin* **fiat money** monnaie *f* fiduciaire

fib [fɪb] *Fam* **1** *n* petit mensonge *m*; **to tell fibs** raconter des histoires; **what a fib!** c'est des histoires!; **I told them a fib about having to do some work** je leur ai raconté qu'il fallait que je travaille

2 *vi* raconter des histoires; **I'm sure he was fibbing about how much he earns** je suis sûr qu'il a menti *ou* raconté des histoires à propos de l'argent qu'il gagne; **I fibbed to them about having to do some work** je leur ai raconté qu'il fallait que je travaille

fibber [ˈfɪbə(r)] *n Fam* menteur(euse) ❑ *m,f*

Fibber McGee [ˈfɪbəməˌgiː] *pr n* = personnage d'un feuilleton radiophonique américain, surtout connu pour son placard toujours mal rangé

fiberfill [ˈfaɪbəfɪl] *n* rembourrage *m* synthétique

fibre, *Am* **fiber** [ˈfaɪbə(r)] *n* (**a**) *(of cloth, wood)* fibre *f*; **artificial/natural fibres** fibres *fpl* artificielles/naturelles; *Fig* **moral fibre** force *f* morale; *Fig* **to love sb/sth with every fibre of one's being** aimer qn/qch de tout son être

(**b**) *(UNCOUNT) (in diet)* fibres *fpl*; **to be high in fibre** *(foodstuff)* être riche en fibres; **high-fibre diet** régime *m ou* alimentation *f* riche en fibres

►► *Comput* ***fibre optics*** fibre *f* optique, fibres *fpl* optiques

fibreboard, *Am* **fiberboard** [ˈfaɪbəbɔːd] *n* panneau *m* de fibres

fibreglass, *Am* **fiberglass** [ˈfaɪbəglɑːs] **1** *n* fibre *f* de verre; **it's (made of) fibreglass** c'est en *ou* de la fibre de verre

2 *comp (boat, hull)* en fibre de verre

fibreless, *Am* **fiberless** [ˈfaɪbəlɪs] *adj* (**a**) *(diet)* sans fibres (**b**) *Fam (person)* mou (molle) ❑, sans caractère ❑

fibre-optic, *Am* **fiber-optic** *adj Comput (cable)* fibre *f* optique

fibrescope, *Am* **fiberscope** [ˈfaɪbəskəʊp] *n Med & Opt* fibroscope *m*

fibre-tip pen *n* feutre *m* pointe fibre

fibriform [ˈfaɪbrɪfɔːm] *adj* en forme de fibres, fibreux

fibril [ˈfaɪbrɪl] *(pl* **fibrils**), **fibrilla** [ˌfaɪˈbrɪlə] *(pl* **fibrillae** [-liː]) *n Biol & Bot* fibrille *f*

fibrilar [ˈfaɪbrɪlə(r)], **fibrillar** [faɪˈbrɪlə(r)] *adj Med* fibrillaire

fibrillate [ˈfaɪbrɪleɪt] *vi Med* fibriller

fibrillation [ˌfaɪbrɪˈleɪʃən] *n Med* fibrillation *f*

fibrin [ˈfaɪbrɪn] *n Biol* fibrine *f*

►► ***fibrin ferment*** fibrin-ferment *m*

fibrinogen [faɪˈbrɪnədʒən] *n Biol* fibrinogène *m*

fibrinolysis [ˌfɪbrɪˈnɒlɪsɪs] *n Med* fibrinolyse *f*

fibrinolytic [ˌfaɪbrɪnəʊˈlɪtɪk] *adj Med* fibrinolytique

fibrinous [ˈfaɪbrɪnəs] *adj Biol* fibrineux

fibroblast [ˈfaɪbrəʊˌblæst] *n Biol* fibroblaste *m*

fibrocyst [ˈfaɪbrəʊˌsɪst] *n Med* fibrokyste *m*

fibrocystic [ˌfaɪbrəʊˈsɪstɪk] *adj Med* fibrokystique

fibrocyte [ˈfaɪbrəʊˌsaɪt] *n Biol* fibrocyte *m*

fibroferrite [ˌfaɪbrəʊˈferaɪt] *n Miner* fibroferrite *f*

fibroid [ˈfaɪbrɔɪd] *Med* **1** *adj (tissue)* fibreux

2 *n (tumour)* fibrome *m*

►► ***fibroid tumour*** fibrome *m*

fibroin [ˈfaɪbrəʊɪn] *n Chem* fibroïne *f*

fibroma [faɪˈbrəʊmə] *(pl* **fibromata** [-mətə]) *n Med* fibrome *m*

fibromatous [faɪˈbrɒmətəs] *adj Med* fibromateux

fibrosis [faɪˈbrəʊsɪs] *n (UNCOUNT) Med* fibrose *f*

fibrositis [ˌfaɪbrəˈsaɪtɪs] *n (UNCOUNT) Med* fibrosite *f*

fibrous [ˈfaɪbrəs] *adj Anat & Bot* fibreux

fibrovascular bundle [ˌfaɪbrəʊˈvæskjʊlə-] *adj Bot* faisceau *m* fibrovasculaire

fibula [ˈfɪbjʊlə] *(pl* **fibulas** *or* **fibulae** [-liː]) *n Anat* péroné *m*

FICA [ˌefaɪˌsiːˈeɪ] *n Am (abbr* **Federal Insurance Contributions Act**) = loi américaine régissant les cotisations sociales

fiche [fiːʃ] *n (microfiche)* microfiche *f*

fickle [ˈfɪkəl] *adj (friend, fan)* inconstant; *(weather)* changeant, instable; *(lover)* inconstant, volage

fickleness [ˈfɪkəlnɪs] *n (of friend, fan, public, lover)* inconstance *f*; *(of weather)* instabilité *f*

fictile [ˈfɪktaɪl] *adj* céramique, plastique

►► ***fictile clay*** argile *f* figuline

fiction [ˈfɪkʃən] *n* (**a**) *(UNCOUNT) Literature* ouvrages *mpl ou* œuvres *fpl* de fiction; **first prize for fiction** premier prix *m* de fiction; **a work** *or* **piece of fiction** un ouvrage *ou* une œuvre de fiction

(**b**) *(invention)* fiction *f*; **she has difficulty separating fact from fiction** elle a du mal à distinguer la réalité de la fiction; **it's pure fiction** c'est de la pure fiction; **we'll have to keep up the fiction a little longer** il nous faudra continuer encore un peu à faire semblant

►► ***fiction list*** classement *m* des meilleures ventes de romans; ***fiction writer*** auteur *m* d'ouvrages de fiction

fictional [ˈfɪkʃənəl] *adj* fictif; **a well-known fictional character** un célèbre personnage de la littérature; **the fictional treatment of women** le thème de la femme dans les ouvrages de fiction

fictionalize, -ise [ˈfɪkʃənəlaɪz] *vt* romancer

fictitious [fɪkˈtɪʃəs] *adj (imaginary, invented)* fictif

►► *Fin* ***fictitious assets*** actif *m* fictif; *Fin* ***fictitious cost*** charge *f* fictive; *Fin* ***fictitious person*** personne *f* fictive

fictitiously [fɪkˈtɪʃəslɪ] *adv* fictivement

fictive [ˈfɪktɪv] *adj* fictif, imaginaire

►► *Elec* ***fictive layers*** *(of dielectric)* charges *fpl* de surface

ficus [ˈfaɪkəs] *n Bot* ficus *m*

fiddle [ˈfɪdəl] **1** *n* (**a**) *(musical instrument)* violon *m*; **to be as fit as a fiddle** être en pleine forme, être frais comme un gardon; **her face was as long as a fiddle** elle faisait une tête d'enterrement; *Fig* **to play second fiddle (to sb)** jouer les seconds violons *ou* rôles (auprès de qn)

(**b**) *Fam (swindle)* truc *m*, combine *f*; *Br* **to work a fiddle** combiner quelque chose; **it's a fiddle** c'est un attrape-nigaud; **to be on the fiddle** traficoter; **tax fiddle** fraude *f* fiscale

2 *vi* (**a**) *(be restless)* **stop fiddling!** tiens-toi tranquille!, arrête de remuer!; **to fiddle with sth** *(aimlessly, nervously)* jouer avec qch; *(interfere with)* jouer avec *ou* tripoter qch; **to fiddle with one's watch** jouer avec sa montre; **don't fiddle with the switch** laisse l'interrupteur tranquille, ne tripote pas l'interrupteur

(**b**) *(tinker)* bricoler; **he fiddled with the knobs on the television** il a tourné les boutons de la télé dans tous les sens

(**c**) *(play the fiddle)* jouer du violon; *Fig* **to fiddle while Rome burns** s'occuper de futilités alors qu'il est urgent d'agir

(**d**) *Fam (cheat)* trafiquer

3 *vt* (**a**) *Fam (falsify → results, financial accounts)* truquer ❑, falsifier ❑; *(→ election)* truquer ❑; **to fiddle one's income tax** falsifier sa déclaration d'impôts; **he fiddled it so that he got the results he wanted** il a trafiqué pour obtenir les résultats qu'il voulait

(**b**) *Fam (gain dishonestly → money, time off)* carotter

(**c**) *Fam (swindle → person)* **he fiddled me out of £20** il m'a refait de 20 livres; **I've been fiddled!** je me suis fait escroquer!

(**d**) *(play → tune)* jouer au violon

▸**fiddle about, fiddle around** *vi* (**a**) *(fidget)* jouer (**b**) *Fam (mess about)* bricoler; *(loaf about, waste time)* traînasser

fiddlededee [ˌfɪdəldiːˈdiː] *exclam Fam Old-fashioned (in disagreement)* balivernes!

fiddle-faddle [-fædəl] *Fam Old-fashioned* **1** *n* (**a**) *(nonsense)* balivernes *fpl*, fadaises *fpl* (**b**) *(triviality)* bagatelles *fpl*

2 *exclam* balivernes!

fiddler [ˈfɪdlə(r)] *n* (**a**) *(fiddle player)* joueur(euse) *m,f* de violon, violoniste *mf* (**b**) *Fam (swindler)* arnaqueur(euse) *m,f* (**c**) *Fam (fidget)* = personne qui gigote tout le temps

►► *Zool* ***fiddler crab*** crabe *m* appelant

fiddlesticks [ˈfɪdəlstɪks] *exclam Fam Old-fashioned (in disagreement)* balivernes!; *(in annoyance)* bon sang de bonsoir!

fiddling [ˈfɪdəlɪŋ] **1** *adj (trivial, insignificant)* futile, insignifiant

2 *n* (**a**) *(fidgeting)* **stop your fiddling!** arrête de gigoter! (**b**) *Fam (swindling)* trafic ❑ *m*, falsification ❑ *f*; **a lot of fiddling goes on around here** ça magouille *ou* ça fricote pas mal par ici; **his fiddling of the books** sa falsification des livres de comptes; **in spite of all his fiddling** malgré toutes ses combines

fiddly [ˈfɪdəlɪ] *adj Br Fam (awkward → job, task)* délicat ❑, minutieux ❑; *(→ small object)* difficile à manier ❑, difficile à tenir entre les doigts ❑; **it's a bit fiddly** ça demande de la minutie ❑

fideism [ˈfiːdɪˌɪzəm] *n Phil* fidéisme *m*

fideist [ˈfiːdɪˌɪst] *n Phil* fidéiste *mf*

fideistic [ˈfiːdɪˌɪstɪk] *adj Phil* fidéiste

fidelity [fɪˈdelətɪ] *n* (**a**) *(of people)* fidélité *f*; **they vowed fidelity to one another** ils se sont juré fidélité (**b**) *(of translation)* fidélité *f* (**c**) *Electron* fidélité *f*; **high fidelity** haute fidélité *f*

►► *Ins* ***fidelity guarantee*** assurance *f* contre les détournements

fidget [ˈfɪdʒɪt] **1** *vi (be restless)* avoir la bougeotte, gigoter; **stop fidgeting!** arrête de gigoter!; **to fidget with sth** jouer avec qch, tripoter qch

2 *n* (**a**) *(restless person)* **she's such a fidget** elle ne tient pas en place, elle gigote tout le temps; **what a fidget you are today!** tu ne tiens pas en place *ou* tu as la bougeotte aujourd'hui!; **don't be such a fidget!** arrête de gigoter!

(**b**) *(idiom)* **to have** *or* **to get the fidgets** *(be restless, nervous)* ne pas tenir en place

fidgetiness [ˈfɪdʒɪtɪnɪs] *n* agitation *f* nerveuse

fidgeting [ˈfɪdʒɪtɪŋ] *adj* (**a**) *(person)* qui ne tient pas en place (**b**) *(thing)* énervant; *(work)* minutieux

fidgety [ˈfɪdʒɪtɪ] *adj* qui ne tient pas en place; **I feel fidgety** je ne tiens plus en place

fiducial [fɪˈduːʃəl] *adj (in surveying)* fiduciel

►► ***fiducial line*** ligne *f* de foi

fiduciary [fɪˈduːʃjərɪ] *Law & Fin* **1** *adj* fiduciaire

2 *n* fiduciaire *mf*

►► *Law & Fin* ***fiduciary account*** compte *m* fiduciaire; ***fiduciary issue*** émission *f* fiduciaire

fie [faɪ] *exclam Arch or Hum* **fie (on you)!** honte à vous!

fief [fiːf] *n Hist & Fig* fief *m*

fiefdom [ˈfiːfdəm] *n Hist & Fig* fief *m*

field [fiːld] **1** *n* (**a**) *(piece of land)* champ *m*; **to work in the fields** travailler dans les *ou* aux champs; **field of wheat** champ *m* de blé; **strawberry field** plantation *f* de fraisiers

(**b**) *Sport (pitch)* terrain *m*; **the field** *(in baseball)* les défenseurs *mpl*; *(in cricket)* les chasseurs *mpl*; **Smith is way ahead of the (rest of the) field** Smith est loin devant *ou* devance largement les autres; **there's a very strong field for the 100 metres** il y a une très belle brochette de concurrents *ou* participants au départ du 100 mètres; **sports** *or* **games field** terrain *m* de sport; **to take the field** entrer sur le terrain; **to lead the field** *(in race)* mener la course, être en tête; *Fig (in sales, area of study)* être en tête; *(of theory)* faire autorité; **our company leads the field when it comes to fitted kitchens** notre entreprise est en tête du marché pour ce qui est des cuisines encastrées; *Fig* **there are three candidates in the field** trois candidatures ont été déposées; *Fam* **to play the field** *(romantically)* avoir autant de liaisons amoureuses que l'on veut

(**c**) *(of oil, minerals etc)* gisement *m*; **oil/coal/gas field** gisement *m* de pétrole/de charbon/de gaz

(**d**) *Mil* **field (of battle)** champ *m* de bataille; **bravery in the field** bravoure *f* sur le champ de bataille; **to die on the field of honour** mourir *ou* tomber au champ d'honneur; **to hold the field** ne pas lâcher de terrain, tenir; **the French now held the field** les Français étaient maintenant maîtres du champ de bataille

(**e**) *(sphere of activity, knowledge)* domaine *m*;

fga–fie

experts from every field des experts provenant de tous les domaines; **to be an expert in one's field** être expert dans son domaine; **in the political field, in the field of politics** dans le domaine politique; **to contribute to the field of human knowledge** contribuer à la connaissance humaine; **what's your field?, what field are you in?** quel est ton domaine?; **that's not my field** ce n'est pas de mon domaine *ou* dans mes compétences
(**f**) *(practice rather than theory)* terrain *m*; **to work/to study in the field** travailler/étudier sur le terrain; **to go out into the field** aller sur le terrain
(**g**) *Phys & Opt* champ *m*; **magnetic field** champ *m* magnétique *Mil*
(**h**) *Comput* champ *m*
(**i**) *Her (on coat of arms, coin)* champ *m*; *(on flag)* fond *m*
2 *vt* (**a**) *(team)* présenter; *(player)* faire jouer; *Mil (men, hardware)* réunir; *Pol (candidate)* présenter
(**b**) *(in cricket, baseball → ball)* arrêter (et renvoyer); *Fig* **to field a question** savoir répondre à une question; *Fig* **well fielded** bien répondu
3 *vi (in cricket, baseball)* être en défense
▸▸ *Mil* ***field ambulance*** ambulance *f*; *Mil* ***field artillery*** artillerie *f* de campagne; *Mil* ***field battery*** batterie *f* de campagne; *Mil* ***field colours*** *(regimental flags)* couleurs *fpl* du régiment; *Am* ***field corn*** maïs *m* de grande culture; ***field day*** *Sch* journée *f* en plein air; *Mil* jour *m* des grandes manœuvres; *Fam Fig* **to have a field day** s'en donner à cœur joie; *(do good business)* faire recette ❑; **if the press find out about this they'll have a field day!** si les journaux l'apprennent, ils vont s'en donner à cœur joie!; ***field engineer*** ingénieur *m* de chantier *ou* sur le terrain; *Sport* ***field events*** concours *mpl* de saut et de lancer; *Mil* ***field exercise*** exercice *m* en campagne, manœuvre *f*; **field of fire** champ *m* de tir; *Phys* **field of force** champ *m* de force; *Bot* ***field gentian*** gentiane *f* champêtre; ***field glasses*** jumelles *fpl*; ***field goal*** *(in American football)* but *m*; *(in basketball)* panier *m*; *Mil* ***field gun*** canon *m*; *Am* ***field hockey*** hockey *m* (sur gazon); *Mil* ***field hospital*** antenne *f* chirurgicale, hôpital *m* de campagne; ***field ice*** banquise *f*; *Mil* ***field kitchen*** cuisine *f* roulante; ***field label*** *(in dictionary)* rubrique *f*, indicateur *m* de domaine; *Bot* ***field madder*** shérardie *f* des champs; *Bot* ***field maple*** érable *m* champêtre; *Mktg* ***field marketing*** marketing *m* sur le terrain; *Mil* ***field marshal*** maréchal *m*; ***field mushroom*** agaric *m* champêtre, rosé *m* des prés; *Mil* ***field officer*** officier *m* supérieur; *Mil* ***field rations*** ration *f* de guerre; ***field sports*** = la chasse et la pêche; ***field study*** étude *f* sur le terrain; *Mil* ***field telegraph*** télégraphe *m* militaire; ***field test*** essai *m* sur le terrain; ***field trials*** *(for machine)* essais *mpl* sur le terrain; *Sch & Univ* ***field trip*** voyage *m* d'études; *(of one afternoon, one day)* sortie *f* d'études; **a geography field trip** une excursion d'études de géographie; **field of vision** champ *m* visuel *ou* de vision; ***field worker*** *(social worker)* travailleur(euse) *m,f* social(e); *(researcher)* chercheur(euse) *m,f* de terrain

fieldcraft ['fi:ldkrɑ:ft] *n (UNCOUNT)* connaissances *fpl* de la nature

field-effect transistor *n Electron* transistor *m* à effet de champ

fielder ['fi:ldə(r)] *n (in cricket, baseball)* joueur *m* de l'équipe défendante

fieldfare ['fi:ldfeə(r)] *n Orn* (grive *f*) litorne *f*

fielding ['fi:ldɪŋ] *n (in cricket, baseball)* défense *f*

fieldmouse ['fi:ldmaʊs] (*pl* **fieldmice** [-maɪs]) *n Zool* mulot *m*

fieldsman ['fi:ldzmən] (*pl* **fieldsmen** [-mən]) *n (in cricket, baseball)* joueur *m* de l'équipe défendante

field-test *vt (machine)* soumettre à des essais sur le terrain

fieldwork ['fi:ldwɜ:k] *n (UNCOUNT)* travaux *mpl* sur le terrain; *(research)* recherches *fpl* sur le terrain

fiend [fi:nd] *n* (**a**) *(demon)* démon *m*, diable *m* (**b**) *(evil person)* monstre *m* (**c**) *Fam (fanatic, freak)* mordu(e) *m,f*, fana *mf*; **tennis fiend** fana *mf ou* mordu(e) *m,f* de tennis; **a health fiend** un(e) maniaque de la santé; **dope** *or* **drug fiend** toxico *mf*; **sex fiend** satyre *m*; *(in newspaper headline)* maniaque *mf* sexuel

fiendish ['fi:ndɪʃ] *adj* (**a**) *(fierce → cruelty, look)* diabolique, démoniaque (**b**) *Fam (cunning → plan)* diabolique ❑; *(very difficult → problem)* abominable ❑, atroce ❑; **a trick of fiendish difficulty** un tour extrêmement difficile; **to take a fiendish delight** *or* **pleasure in doing sth** prendre un plaisir diabolique à faire qch

fiendishly ['fi:ndɪʃlɪ] *adv* (**a**) *(cruelly)* diaboliquement (**b**) *Fam (extremely)* **fiendishly clever** d'une intelligence diabolique; **fiendishly difficult** abominablement *ou* atrocement difficile; *Fam* **it was fiendishly cold** il faisait un froid de tous les diables

fiendishness ['fi:ndɪʃnɪs] *n (cruelty)* cruauté *f* diabolique

fiendlike ['fi:ndlaɪk] *adj* (**a**) *(fierce → cruelty, look)* diabolique, démoniaque (**b**) *Fam (cunning → plan)* diabolique ❑; *(very difficult → problem)* abominable ❑, atroce ❑; **a trick of fiendish difficulty** un tour extrêmement difficile; **to take a fiendish delight** *or* **pleasure in doing sth** prendre un plaisir diabolique à faire qch

fierce [fɪəs] *adj* (**a**) *(aggressive → animal, person, look, words)* féroce; **to give sb a fierce look** jeter un regard féroce à qn
(**b**) *(heat)* torride; *(sun)* ardent, brûlant; *(competition, fighting, loyalty, resistance)* acharné; *(battle, criticism, hatred, temper)* féroce; *(desire)* ardent; **she was fierce in her defence of him** elle le défendait avec acharnement
(**c**) *Fam (unpleasant)* désagréable ❑; **the weather has been fierce** il a fait un temps de chien

fiercely ['fɪəslɪ] *adv* (**a**) *(aggressively)* férocement; **to look fiercely at sb** regarder qn d'un air féroce
(**b**) *Fig (argue, attack, criticize, fight)* violemment; *(resist)* avec acharnement; *(independent)* farouchement; **to compete fiercely** se livrer à une concurrence acharnée; **to be fiercely opposed to sth** être ardemment opposé à qch; **it is a fiercely competitive business** c'est un secteur où la concurrence est acharnée; **to be fiercely loyal to sb** faire preuve d'une loyauté à toute épreuve *ou* farouche envers qn

fierceness ['fɪəsnɪs] *n* (**a**) *(of animal, look, person)* férocité *f* (**b**) *Fig (of desire, sun)* ardeur *f*; *(of resistance)* acharnement *m*; *(of criticism)* férocité *f*

fierily ['faɪərɪlɪ] *adv (to speak)* avec fougue

fieriness ['faɪərɪnɪs] *n* (**a**) *(of sun)* ardeur *f*; **the fieriness of the seasoning** l'assaisonnement très relevé *ou* épicé (**b**) *(of speech)* fougue *f*; *(of character)* ardeur *f*, fougue *f*, impétuosité *f*

fiery ['faɪərɪ] *adj* (**a**) *(as though on fire → heat, sun, coals)* ardent; *(→ sky, sunset)* embrasé; **a fiery red colour** une couleur rouge feu; **fiery red hair** cheveux *mpl* d'un roux flamboyant
(**b**) *(passionate, volatile → speech)* passionné, enflammé; *(→ character)* fougueux, impétueux; **fiery temper** tempérament *m* fougueux *ou* emporté
(**c**) *(with a hot taste → alcoholic drink)* extrêmement fort, brûlant; *(→ curry)* très épicé
▸▸ *Am* ***the fiery cross*** la croix en flammes *(symbole du Ku Klux Klan)*

fiesta [fɪ'estə] *n* fiesta *f*

FIFA ['fi:fə] *n (abbr* **Fédération Internationale de Football Association**) FIFA *f*

Fife [faɪf] *n* le Fife, = région du centre-est de l'Écosse; **in Fife** dans le Fife

fife [faɪf] *n Mus* fifre *m*

fifer ['faɪfə(r)] *n Mus (person)* joueur(euse) *m,f* de fifre; *(pipe)* fifre *m*

FIFO ['fi:fəʊ] *n Comput & Ind (abbr* **first in, first out**) PEPS

fifteen [fɪf'ti:n] **1** *n* (**a**) *(number, numeral)* quinze *m inv* (**b**) *(in rugby)* quinze *m*; **the opposing fifteen** l'équipe *f* rivale; **the school/Scottish fifteen** le quinze de l'école/d'Écosse
2 *pron* quinze; **about fifteen** une quinzaine
3 *adj* quinze; **about fifteen people** une quinzaine de personnes; **his fifteen minutes of fame** son quart d'heure de célébrité; *see also* **five**

fifteenth [fɪf'ti:nθ] **1** *n* (**a**) *(fraction)* quinzième *m* (**b**) *(in series)* quinzième *mf* (**c**) *(of month)* quinze *m inv*
2 *adj* quinzième
3 *adv* quinzièmement; *(in contest)* en quinzième position, à la quinzième place; *see also* **fifth**

fifth [fɪfθ] **1** *n* (**a**) *(fraction)* cinquième *m*
(**b**) *(in series)* cinquième *mf*
(**c**) *(of month)* cinq *m inv*; **the fifth** le cinq; **on the fifth** le cinq; **the fifth of July, July the fifth,** *Am* **July fifth** le cinq juillet; **today is the fifth** nous sommes le cinq aujourd'hui; **the fifth of November** = jour anniversaire de la Conspiration des poudres aussi appelé "Guy Fawkes' Day"
(**d**) *Mus* quinte *f*
(**e**) *Aut* cinquième *f*; **in fifth** en cinquième
(**f**) *Am (Fifth Amendment)* Cinquième Amendement *m (de la Constitution des États-Unis, permettant à un accusé de ne pas répondre à une question risquant de jouer en sa défaveur)*; *Hum* **I plead the Fifth** ≃ je ne parlerai qu'en présence de mon avocat
2 *adj* cinquième; **fifth finger** petit doigt *m*; *Aut* **fifth gear** cinquième vitesse *f*; *Aut* **to go** *or* **to change into fifth gear** passer en cinquième *f*; **a fifth part** un cinquième; **on the fifth day of the month** le cinq du mois; **in fifth place** en cinquième position, à la cinquième place; **fifth from the end/right** cinquième en partant de la fin/droite; **on the fifth floor** *Br* au cinquième étage; *Am* au quatrième étage; *Am* **to feel like a fifth wheel** avoir l'impression d'être la dernière roue du carrosse; **George the Fifth** Georges Cinq
3 *adv* cinquièmement; *(in contest)* en cinquième position, à la cinquième place; **she came** *or* **was fifth** *(in race, exam etc)* elle est arrivée cinquième
▸▸ ***Fifth Amendment*** Cinquième Amendement *m (de la Constitution des États-Unis, permettant à un accusé de ne pas répondre à une question risquant de jouer en sa défaveur)*; ***Fifth Avenue*** la Cinquième avenue; **she's very Fifth Avenue** elle est très Cinquième avenue *(fait référence à l'élite sociale new-yorkaise)*; *Pol* ***fifth column*** cinquième colonne *f*; *Pol* ***fifth columnist*** membre *m* de la cinquième colonne; *Br Sch* ***fifth form*** ≃ classe *f* de seconde; *Am Sch* ***fifth grade*** = classe de l'école primaire (9 à 10 ans); ***the Fifth Republic*** la Cinquième *ou* Vème République

fifth-generation *adj Comput* de cinquième génération

fifthly ['fɪfθlɪ] *adv* cinquièmement, en cinquième lieu

fifth-rate *adj Fam* médiocre ❑

fiftieth ['fɪftɪəθ] **1** *n* (**a**) *(fraction)* cinquantième *m* (**b**) *(in series)* cinquantième *mf*
2 *adj* cinquantième
3 *adv* cinquantièmement; *(in contest)* en cinquantième position, à la cinquantième place; *see also* **fifth**

fifty ['fɪftɪ] (*pl* **fifties**) **1** *n* (**a**) *(number, numeral)* cinquante *m inv*; **fifty and fifty are a hundred** cinquante et cinquante font cent; **I'm waiting for a number fifty (bus)** j'attends le (bus numéro) cinquante; *Aut* **to do fifty** ≃ faire du quatre-vingts; **to be fifty** *(in age)* avoir cinquante ans; **he must be close to** *or* **getting on for fifty** il doit approcher de la cinquantaine; **to get fifty out of a hundred** avoir cinquante sur cent; **the fifties** les années cinquante; **in the early/late fifties** au début/à la fin des années cinquante; **the temperature will be in the high fifties** la température sera environ de quinze degrés; **she is in her fifties** elle a entre cinquante et soixante ans; **to be in one's early/late fifties** avoir une petite cinquantaine/la cinquantaine bien sonnée
(**b**) *Am (money)* billet *m* de cinquante (dollars)
2 *pron* cinquante; **about fifty** une cinquantaine; **fifty is not enough** cinquante, ce n'est pas assez; **I need fifty (of them)** il m'en faut cinquante, j'en ai besoin de cinquante; **there are fifty (of them)** *(people)* ils sont cinquante; *(objects)* il y en a cinquante; **all fifty of them left** tous les cinquante sont partis, ils sont partis tous les cinquante
3 *adj* cinquante; **fifty people** cinquante personnes; **about fifty people** une cinquantaine de

personnes; **on page fifty** (à la) page cinquante; **they live at number fifty** ils habitent au numéro cinquante; **to be fifty years old** avoir cinquante ans; **he works a fifty-hour week** il travaille cinquante heures par semaine

4 *comp* **fifty-one** cinquante et un; **fifty-two** cinquante-deux; **fifty-first** cinquante et unième; **fifty-second** cinquante-deuxième

fifty-fifty **1** *adj* **on a fifty-fifty basis** moitié-moitié, fifty-fifty; **his chances of winning/surviving are fifty-fifty** il a une chance sur deux de gagner/de s'en tirer; **the animal's chances of survival are no more than fifty-fifty** les chances de survie de l'animal ne dépassent pas cinquante pour cent

2 *adv* moitié-moitié, fifty-fifty; **to split the profits fifty-fifty** partager les bénéfices à parts égales; **to go fifty-fifty (with sb on sth)** faire moitié-moitié *ou* fifty-fifty (avec qn pour qch); **I went fifty-fifty with my brother** je me suis mis de moitié avec mon frère

fig [fɪg] *n (fruit)* figue *f*; *(tree)* figuier *m*; *Fam Old-fashioned* **it's not worth a fig** ça ne vaut pas un radis; *Fam Old-fashioned* **I don't give** *or* **care a fig** je m'en moque comme de ma première chemise; **I don't give** *or* **care a fig what she thinks** je me contrefiche de ce qu'elle pense

►► ***fig leaf*** *Bot* feuille *f* de figuier; *(on statue, in painting)* feuille *f* de vigne; *Fig* camouflage *m*; ***fig tree*** figuier *m*

FIGHT [faɪt]

bagarre	► **1 (a)**
dispute	► **1 (a)**
combativité	► **1 (b)**
se battre contre	► **2**
se battre	► **3**
combattre	► **3**
se disputer	► **3**

(*pt & pp* **fought** [fɔːt]) **1** *n* (**a**) *(physical)* bagarre *f*; *(verbal)* dispute *f*; *(of army, boxer)* combat *m*, affrontement *m*; *(against disease, poverty etc)* lutte *f*, combat *m*; **the fight for life** la lutte pour la vie; **her fight against cancer** sa lutte contre le cancer; **the fight for the leadership of the party** la lutte pour la tête du parti; **do you want a fight?** tu veux te battre?; **he enjoys a good fight** *(physical)* il aime la bagarre *ou* les bagarres; *(verbal)* il aime les disputes; *(boxing match)* il aime les bons combats de boxe; **to have** *or* **to get into a fight with sb** *(physical)* se battre avec qn; *(verbal)* se disputer avec qn; **they are always having fights** ils sont toujours en train de se bagarrer *ou* se disputer; **you've been in a fight again** tu t'es encore battu *ou* bagarré; **to pick a fight (with sb)** chercher la bagarre (avec qn); **are you trying to pick a fight (with me)?** tu me provoques?, tu cherches la bagarre?; **a fight to the death** une lutte à mort; **are you going to the fight?** *(boxing match)* est-ce que tu vas voir le combat?; **to put up a (good) fight** (bien) se défendre; **the boxer put up a great fight** le boxeur s'est défendu avec acharnement; **to make a fight of it** se défendre avec acharnement; **to give in without (putting up) a fight** capituler sans (opposer de) résistance; **he realized he would have a fight on his hands** il s'est rendu compte qu'il allait devoir lutter

(**b**) *(fighting spirit)* combativité *f*; **there's not much fight left in him** il a perdu beaucoup de sa combativité; **he still has a lot of fight left in him** il n'a pas dit son dernier mot; **the news of the defeat took all the fight out of us** la nouvelle de la défaite nous a fait perdre tout cœur à nous battre *ou* nous a enlevé le courage de nous battre; **to show fight** montrer de la combativité, ne pas se laisser faire

2 *vt (person, animal)* se battre contre; *(boxer)* combattre (contre), se battre contre; *(match)* disputer; *(disease, terrorism, fire etc)* lutter contre, combattre; *(new measure, decision)* combattre; *(illness, temptation)* lutter contre; **to fight a duel** se battre en duel; **to fight a battle** livrer (une) bataille; *Fig* **I'm not going to fight your battles for you** c'est à toi de te débrouiller; **to fight a court case** *(lawyer)* défendre une cause; *(plaintiff, defendant)* être en procès; **to fight an election** *(politician)* se présenter à une élection; *Br* **to fight an election campaign** mener une campagne électorale; *Br* **John Brown is fighting Smithtown for the Tories** John Brown se présente à Smithtown pour les conservateurs; **I'll fight you for it** on réglera ça par une bagarre; **I'll fight you for custody** je me battrai contre toi pour obtenir la garde des enfants; **to fight a losing battle (against sth)** livrer une bataille perdue d'avance (contre qch); *Rel* **to fight the good fight** combattre pour la bonne cause; **she fought the urge to laugh** elle essayait de réprimer une forte envie de rire; **don't fight it** *(pain, emotion)* n'essaie pas de lutter; **you've got to fight it** il faut que tu te battes; **to fight sb/a newspaper in court** emmener qn/un journal devant les tribunaux, faire un procès à qn/à un journal; **to fight one's way through the crowd/the undergrowth** se frayer un passage à travers la foule/les broussailles; **to fight one's way to the top of one's profession** se battre pour atteindre le sommet de sa profession; **he fought his way back to power** c'est en luttant qu'il est revenu au pouvoir

3 *vi (physically → person, soldier)* se battre; *(→ boxer)* combattre; *(→ two boxers)* s'affronter; *(verbally)* se disputer; *(against disease, injustice, sleep etc)* lutter; **to fight against the enemy** combattre l'ennemi; **to fight to the death/the last** se battre à mort/jusqu'à la fin; **he fought in the war** il a fait la guerre; *Mil* **he fought in Russia** il s'est battu en Russie; **they were fighting with each other** *(physically)* ils étaient en train de se battre; *(verbally)* ils étaient en train de se disputer; **they were fighting over some islands/who would sleep where** ils se battaient pour des îles/pour décider qui allait dormir où; **they were always fighting over** *or* **about money** ils se disputaient toujours pour des problèmes d'argent; **the children were fighting over the last biscuit** les enfants se disputaient (pour avoir) le dernier biscuit; **to fight for one's country** se battre pour sa patrie; **to fight for one's rights/to clear one's name** lutter pour ses droits/pour prouver son innocence; **they fought for the leadership of the party** ils se sont disputé la direction du parti; **he fought for breath** il se débattait *ou* il luttait pour respirer; **to fight for one's life** *(ill person)* lutter contre la mort; *Fig (in race, competition)* se battre avec la dernière énergie, se démener; **to go down fighting** se battre jusqu'au bout; **to fight shy of doing sth** tout faire pour éviter de faire qch; **to fight shy of sb** éviter qn

►► ***the fight game*** la boxe

►**fight back** **1** *vi (in physical or verbal dispute)* se défendre, riposter; *(in boxing, football match)* se reprendre; *(in race)* revenir

2 *vt sep (tears)* refouler; *(despair, fear, laughter)* réprimer

►**fight down** *vt sep (passion, resistance)* vaincre; *(impulse, urge)* réprimer

►**fight off** *vt sep (attack, enemy, advances)* repousser; *(sleep)* combattre; *(disease)* résister à; **she has to fight men off** *(has a lot of admirers)* elle a des admirateurs à la pelle *ou* à ne plus savoir qu'en faire

►**fight on** *vi* continuer le combat

►**fight out** *vt sep* **just leave them to fight it out** laisse-les se bagarrer et régler cela entre eux

fightback ['faɪtbæk] *n* reprise *f*

fighter ['faɪtə(r)] **1** *n* (**a**) *(person who fights)* combattant(e) *m,f*; *(boxer)* boxeur(euse) *m,f*; *Fig* **he's a fighter** c'est un battant (**b**) *(plane)* avion *m* de chasse, chasseur *m*

2 *comp (pilot)* de chasseur, d'avion de chasse; *(squadron)* de chasseurs, d'avions de chasse; *(plane)* de chasse

►► *Mktg* ***fighter model*** modèle *m* d'attaque

fighter-bomber *n Mil* chasseur *m* bombardier

fighting ['faɪtɪŋ] **1** *n (UNCOUNT) (physical)* bagarre *f*, bagarres *fpl*; *(verbal)* dispute *f*, disputes *fpl*, bagarre *f*, bagarres *fpl*; *Mil* combat *m*, combats *mpl*; **fighting broke out between police and fans** une bagarre s'est déclenchée entre la police et les fans; **the fighting is now at its height** on est au plus fort du combat; **there has been fierce fighting in all parts of the country** des combats acharnés ont eu lieu dans l'ensemble du pays; **fighting is not allowed in the playground** il est interdit de se bagarrer dans la cour; **to be in with** *or* **to have a fighting chance** avoir de bonnes chances; **to be fighting fit** être dans une forme éblouissante, avoir la forme olympique; **fighting spirit** esprit *m* combatif; **that's fighting talk!** c'est un langage offensif!

2 *comp (forces, unit)* de combat

►► ***fighting cock*** coq *m* de combat; *Ich* ***fighting fish*** poisson *m* combattant; *Mil* ***fighting men*** combattants *mpl*; *Boxing* ***fighting weight*** poids *m* optimal *(pour un boxeur)*

figment ['fɪgmənt] *n* **a figment of the imagination** un produit *ou* une création de l'imagination

figuline ['fɪgjʊlaɪn] *Cer* **1** *n* (**a**) *(clay vessel)* figuline *f*, poterie *f* (**b**) *(clay)* argile *f* figuline, terre *f* à poterie

2 *adj* figulin

figurable ['fɪgjʊrəbəl] *adj* figurable

figurant ['fɪgjʊrənt] *n (dancer) & Theat* figurant *m*; **the figurants** la figuration

figurante [,fɪgjʊ'rɒnt] *n (dancer) & Theat* figurante *f*

figuration [,fɪgjʊ'reɪʃən] *n* (**a**) *(of idea, pronunciation)* figuration *f*; *(of object)* configuration *f*, contour *m* (**b**) *(figurative representation)* représentation *f* figurative; *(emblem)* emblème *m*; *(allegory)* allégorie *f* (**c**) *Sewing* ornementation *f* (**d**) *Mus (of melody)* embellissement *m*

figurative ['fɪgərətɪv] *adj* (**a**) *(language, meaning)* figuré; **in the figurative sense** au (sens) figuré (**b**) *Art* figuratif

figuratively ['fɪgərətɪvlɪ] *adv* (**a**) *(speak, write)* au (sens) figuré, métaphoriquement; **figuratively speaking,...** métaphoriquement parlant,... (**b**) *Art* figurativement

FIGURE [*Br* 'fɪgə(r), *Am* 'fɪgjər]

chiffre	► **1 (a)**
ligne	► **1 (b)**
silhouette	► **1 (c)**
personnage	► **1 (d), (e)**
figure	► **1 (f), (g)**
figurine	► **1 (j)**
penser	► **2 (a)**
arriver à comprendre	► **2 (b)**
figurer	► **3 (a)**
sembler logique	► **3 (b)**

1 *n* (**a**) *(number, symbol)* chiffre *m*; *(amount)* somme *f*; **six-figure number** nombre *m* de six chiffres; **figures** *(for project etc)* détails *mpl* chiffrés; *(statistics)* statistiques *fpl*; **the figures for 1995** les statistiques de 1995; **his salary is in** *or* **runs to six figures** ≃ il gagne plus d'un million de francs; **our takings have reached four figures** nous avons décroché les quatre chiffres; **in round figures** en chiffres ronds; **to be in double figures** *(inflation, unemployment)* dépasser la barre *ou* le seuil des 10 pour cent; **his score barely managed to get into double figures** son score s'élevait tout juste à un nombre à deux chiffres; **to get inflation down to single figures** réduire l'inflation à un taux inférieur à dix pour cent; **to put a figure on sth** *(give cost)* évaluer le coût de *ou* chiffrer qch; **I couldn't put a figure on the number of people there** je ne pourrais pas dire combien de personnes il y avait; **she's good at figures** elle est bonne en calcul; **he has no head for figures** il n'est pas doué en calcul; **have you done your figures?** as-tu fait tes calculs?; **name your figure** *(to purchaser, seller)* quel est votre prix?; **the boss told him to name his figure** *(for pay rise)* le patron lui a demandé combien il voulait; **to find a mistake in the figures** trouver une erreur de calcul

(**b**) *(human shape)* ligne *f*; **she is always worrying about her figure** elle s'inquiète constamment pour sa ligne; **she has a good figure** elle a une jolie silhouette, elle est bien faite; **to look after one's figure** faire attention à sa ligne; **think of your figure!** pense à ta ligne!; **to keep/to lose one's figure** garder/perdre la ligne; **a fine figure of a woman/man** une femme/un homme qui a de l'allure; **to cut a fine figure** avoir beaucoup d'allure; **to cut a sorry figure** faire piètre figure; **he was a sorry figure standing there on the doorstep** *(wet, dirty etc)* il faisait piètre figure, debout sur les marches (**c**) *(human outline)* silhouette *f*; **a figure appeared on the horizon** une silhouette est apparue à l'horizon

(**d**) *(character in novel, film, painting etc)* personnage *m*; **the group of figures on the left** le groupe de personnes à gauche; **key figure** personnage *m* central; **figure of fun** objet *m* de risée; **a hate figure, a figure of hate** un objet de haine

(**e**) *(person)* personnage *m*; **a distinguished figure** une personnalité

(**f**) *(in geometry, skating, dancing)* figure *f*

(**g**) *(illustration, diagram)* figure *f*

(**h**) *(pattern → on material)* dessin *m*

(**i**) *(rhetorical)* **figure of speech** figure *f* de rhétorique; **it was just a figure of speech** ce n'était qu'une façon de parler

(**j**) *(statuette)* figurine *f*

2 *vt* (**a**) *Fam (reckon)* penser ❑; **we figured something like that must have happened** nous pensions *ou* nous nous doutions bien que quelque chose de ce genre était arrivé ❑

(**b**) *Am Fam (understand)* arriver à comprendre ❑; **we couldn't figure it** nous n'arrivions pas à comprendre *ou* saisir ❑

(**c**) *(decorate → material, velvet etc)* façonner; *(→ silk)* brocher

(**d**) *Mus* chiffrer

3 *vi* (**a**) *(appear)* figurer, apparaître; **does he figure in your plans?** est-ce qu'il figure dans tes projets?; **where do I figure in all this?** quelle est ma place dans tout cela?; **guilt figures quite a lot in his novels** la culpabilité a *ou* tient une place relativement importante dans ses romans; **she figured prominently in the scandal** elle a été très impliquée dans le scandale

(**b**) *Fam (make sense)* sembler logique *ou* normal ❑; **that figures!** *(I'm not surprised)* tu m'étonnes!; *(that makes sense)* c'est logique ❑; **it figures that he'd do that** ça paraît logique *ou* normal qu'il ait fait ça ❑; *Am* **it just doesn't figure** ça n'a pas de sens ❑; *Am* **go figure!** qui aurait imaginé ça? ❑

►► *Br* ***figure of eight,*** *Am* ***figure eight*** huit *m*; *(knot)* (nœud *m* en) huit *m*; ***figure skater*** patineur(euse) *m,f* artistique; ***figure skating*** **1** *n* patinage *m* artistique **2** *comp (champion, championship)* de patinage artistique

►**figure in** *vt sep (in calculations)* inclure

►**figure on** *vt insep Fam* (**a**) *(plan on)* compter sur ❑; **to figure on doing sth** compter faire qch; **when are you figuring on leaving?** quand comptes-tu *ou* penses-tu partir?; **you didn't figure on that (happening), did you?** tu ne comptais *ou* pensais pas que ça arriverait, hein?, tu ne comptais pas là-dessus, hein?

(**b**) *Am (anticipate)* s'attendre à, prévoir; **with the roadworks you should figure on an hour's delay** il faut compter une heure de plus avec les travaux

►**figure out** *vt sep* (**a**) *(understand)* arriver à comprendre; **we couldn't figure it out** nous n'arrivions pas à comprendre *ou* saisir

(**b**) *(work out → sum, cost etc)* calculer; **figure it out for yourself** réfléchis donc un peu; **she still hasn't figured out how to do it** elle n'a toujours pas trouvé comment faire

►**figure up** *vt sep Am Fam* faire le total de ❑

---

figured [*Br* 'fɪgəd, *Am* fɪgjəd] *adj* (**a**) *(material, velvet etc)* façonné; *(silk)* broché (**b**) *Mus (counterpoint)* figuré; *(bass)* chiffré

figurehead [*Br* 'fɪgəhed, *Am* 'fɪgjəhed] *n Naut* figure *f* de proue; *Fig (of organization, society)* représentant(e) *m,f* nominal(e); *Pej* homme *m* de paille

figure-hugging [-,hʌgɪŋ] *adj Br (garment)* moulant

figure-skate *vi* faire des figures en patinage, faire du patinage artistique

figurine [*Br* 'fɪgəri:n, *Am* ,fɪgjə'ri:n] *n* figurine *f*

figurism ['fɪgjʊ,rɪzəm] *n Rel* figurisme *m*

figurist ['fɪgjʊrɪst] *n Rel* figuriste *mf*

figwort ['fɪgwɜ:t] *n Bot* ficaire *f*

Fiji ['fi:dʒi:] *n* Fidji; **in Fiji** à Fidji; **the Fiji Islands** les îles *fpl* Fidji; **in the Fiji Islands** aux îles Fidji

Fijian [,fi:'dʒi:ən] **1** *n* (**a**) *(person)* Fidjien(enne) *m,f* (**b**) *Ling* fidjien *m*

2 *adj* fidjien

filament ['fɪləmənt] *n* (**a**) *Elec* filament *m* (**b**) *Biol* filament *m*, filet *m*

►► ***filament lamp*** lampe *f* à incandescence

filamentary [,fɪlə'mentərɪ] *adj* filamenteux

filbert ['fɪlbət] *n (nut)* = espèce de grosse noisette

filch [fɪltʃ] *vt Fam (steal)* piquer

filcher ['fɪltʃə(r)] *n Fam* chipeur(euse) *m,f*, chapardeur(euse) *m,f*

filching ['fɪltʃɪŋ] *n Fam (theft)* fauche *f*; **there's a lot of filching from hotels** les gens piquent beaucoup dans les hôtels

---

FILE [faɪl]

chemise	►1 (a)
classeur	►1 (a)
dossier	►1 (b)
fichier	►1 (b), (c)
file	►1 (d)
lime	►1 (e)
classer	►2 (a)
intenter	►2 (b)
limer	►2 (d)
faire du classement	►3 (a)
entrer/sortir/*etc* à la file	►3 (b)

1 *n* (**a**) *(folder)* chemise *f*; *(box)* classeur *m*; **accordion file** classeur *m* accordéon

(**b**) *(dossier, documents)* dossier *m*; *(series or system of files)* fichier *m*; **the file on James Brown, the James Brown file** le dossier James Brown; **this file belongs in the customer file** ce dossier va dans le fichier clients; **to have/to keep sth on file** avoir/garder qch dans ses dossiers; **it's on file** c'est dans les dossiers, c'est classé; **we have placed your CV on file** *or* **in our files** nous avons classé votre CV dans nos dossiers; **these papers are for the file** ces papiers sont à mettre dans les dossiers *ou* sont à classer; **to have/to keep a file on** avoir/garder un dossier sur; **to open/to close a file on** ouvrir/fermer un dossier sur; **the police have closed their file on the case** la police a classé l'affaire; **he's been on our file** *or* **files for a long time** cela fait longtemps qu'il est dans nos dossiers

(**c**) *Comput* fichier *m*; **data on file** données *fpl* sur fichier; **data file** fichier *m* de données

(**d**) *(row, line)* file *f*; **in single** *or* **Indian file** en *ou* à la file indienne

(**e**) *(for metal, fingernails)* lime *f*

2 *vt* (**a**) *(documents, information)* classer; **it's filed under B** c'est classé à la lettre B; **it's filed under "invoices"** c'est classé dans le dossier "factures"

(**b**) *Law* **to file a suit against sb** intenter un procès à qn; **to file a complaint (with the police/the manager)** déposer une plainte (au commissariat/auprès du directeur); **to file a claim** déposer une demande; **to file a claim for damages** intenter un procès en dommages-intérêts; **to file a petition in bankruptcy** déposer son bilan; *Am* **to file one's tax return** remplir sa déclaration d'impôts

(**c**) *Journ* **to file a story** boucler un sujet; **to file copy** rapporter une copie

(**d**) *(metal)* limer; **to file one's fingernails** se limer les ongles; **to file through sth** limer qch

3 *vi* (**a**) *(classify documents, information)* faire du classement

(**b**) *(walk one behind the other)* **they filed up the hill** ils ont monté la colline en file (indienne) *ou* les uns derrière les autres; **the troops filed under the bridge** les soldats sont passés sous le pont en file indienne *ou* à la file; **the troops filed past the general** les troupes ont défilé devant le général; **the crowd filed slowly past the coffin** la foule a défilé lentement devant le cercueil; **to file into a room** entrer dans une pièce à la *ou* en file; **to file out of a room** sortir d'une pièce à la *ou* en file; **they all filed in/out** ils sont tous entrés/sortis à la file

►► *Am* ***file cabinet*** classeur *m*; ***file card*** fiche *f* (de classeur); *Am* ***file clerk*** documentaliste *mf*; *Comput* ***file compression*** compression *f* de fichiers; *Comput* ***file conversion*** conversion *f* de fichiers; ***file copy*** copie *f* à classer; ***file divider*** carte-guide *f*; *Comput* ***file extension*** extension *f* du nom de fichier; *Am TV* ***file footage*** images *fpl* d'archive; *Comput* ***file format*** format *m* de fichier; *Comput* ***file management*** gestion *f ou* tenue *f* des fichiers; *Comput* ***file management system*** système *m* de gestion de fichiers; *Comput* ***file manager*** gestionnaire *m* des fichiers; *Comput* ***file name*** nom *m* de fichier; *Comput* ***file name extension*** extension *f* du nom de fichier; ***file number*** *(of document in file)* cote *f*; *Comput* ***file protection*** protection *f* de fichiers; ***file separator*** carte-guide *f*; *Comput* ***file server*** serveur *m* de fichiers; *Comput* ***file sharing*** partage *m* de fichiers; *Comput* ***file structure*** structure *f* de fichiers; *Comput* ***file transfer*** transfert *m* de fichiers; *Comput* ***file transfer protocol*** protocole *m* de transfert de fichiers; ***file trolley*** bac *m* roulant; *Comput* ***file viewer*** visualiseur *m*

►**file away** *vt sep* (**a**) *(documents)* classer (**b**) *(rough edges)* polir à la lime; *(excess material)* enlever à la lime

►**file down** *vt sep* (**a**) *(remove by filing → rough edge)* enlever à la lime, limer (**b**) *(smooth by filing → metal, nails, surface)* polir à la lime, limer; *(→ horseshoe)* raboter

►**file for** *vt insep* **to file for divorce** demander le divorce

►**file off** *vt sep (remove by filing → rough edge)* enlever à la lime, limer

---

file-compatible *adj Comput* compatible du point de vue des fichiers

filer ['faɪlə(r)] *n Comput* classeur *m*, gestionnaire *m* de fichiers et de répertoires

filet ['fi:leɪ] *n (of meat)* filet *m*

►► ***filet mignon*** filet *m* mignon

filial ['fɪljəl] *adj* filial

filially ['fɪljəlɪ] *adv* filialement

filibuster ['fɪlɪ,bʌstə(r)] **1** *n* (**a**) *Am Pol* obstruction *f* (parlementaire) (**b**) *Hist (pirate)* flibustier *m*

2 *vi* faire de l'obstruction

3 *vt (legislation)* faire obstruction à

filibusterer ['fɪlɪ,bʌstərə(r)] *n Am Pol* obstructionniste *mf*

filibustering ['fɪlɪ,bʌstərɪŋ] *n Am Pol* obstructionnisme *m*

filicide ['fɪlɪsaɪd] *n* filicide *mf*

filigree ['fɪlɪgri:] **1** *n* filigrane *m*

2 *adj* en *ou* de filigrane

filigreed ['fɪlɪgri:d] *adj* filigrané, en filigrane

filing ['faɪlɪŋ] *n* (**a**) *(of documents)* classement *m*; *(for long-term storage)* archivage *m*; **I do the filing** je m'occupe du classement; **I still have a lot of filing to do** j'ai encore beaucoup de choses à classer (**b**) *Law (of complaint, claim)* dépôt *m*; *(of petition)* enregistrement *m* (**c**) *(of metal)* limage *m*

►► ***filing cabinet*** classeur *m*; ***filing clerk*** documentaliste *mf*; ***filing system*** méthode *f* de classement; ***filing tray*** corbeille *f* pour correspondance à classer

filings ['faɪlɪŋz] *npl (of metal)* limaille *f*

Filipino [,fɪlɪ'pi:nəʊ] *(pl* **Filipinos***)* **1** *n* (**a**) *(person)* Philippin(e) *m,f* (**b**) *(language)* tagalog *m*, tagal *m*

2 *adj* philippin

FILL [fɪl]

remplir	►2 (a)
boucher	►2 (b)
occuper	►2 (c), (d)
répondre à	►2 (e)
se remplir	►3

1 *n* **to eat one's fill** manger à sa faim, se rassasier; **to drink one's fill** boire tout son soûl; **when they had eaten their fill** quand ils eurent mangé tout leur content; **a fill of tobacco** *(for pipe)* une pipe de tabac; *Fam* **I've had my fill of it/her** j'en ai assez/assez d'elle ❑

2 *vt* (**a**) *(cup, glass, bottle)* remplir; *(room, streets → of people, smoke, laughter)* envahir; *(chocolates)* fourrer; *(cake, pie)* garnir; *(vegetables)* farcir; *(pipe)* bourrer; *(cart etc)* charger; **to fill a page with writing** remplir une page d'écriture; **wind filled the sails** le vent a gonflé les voiles; **she filled his head with nonsense** elle lui a bourré le crâne de bêtises; **to be filled with people** *(room, street)* être plein *ou* rempli de gens; **to be filled with horror/admiration** être rempli d'horreur/d'admiration; **she was filled with horror at the news** cette nouvelle l'a remplie d'horreur; **to be filled with hope** être plein d'espoir; **to be filled with fear/envy** être dévoré de peur/d'envie; **it filled me with sorrow** cela m'a profondément peiné; **such were the thoughts that filled his mind** telles étaient les pensées qui occupaient son esprit; **he filled the air with his cries** il a rempli l'air de ses cris

(**b**) *(plug → hole)* boucher; *(→ tooth)* plomber; **to have a tooth filled** se faire plomber une dent; **the product filled a gap in the market** le produit a comblé un vide sur le marché; *Fam* **to fill or pump sb full of lead** *(shoot)* plomber qn

(**c**) *(position, vacancy → of employee)* occuper; *(→ of employer)* pourvoir; **to fill the office of president** remplir les fonctions de président; **the post has been filled** le poste a été pris *ou* pourvu

(**d**) *(occupy → time)* occuper; **reading fills my evenings** la lecture remplit mes soirées

(**e**) *(meet → requirement)* répondre à; *Fam* **to fill the bill** faire l'affaire

(**f**) *(supply)* **to fill an order** *(in bar, restaurant)* apporter ce qui a été commandé; *(for stationery, equipment etc)* livrer une commande; **to fill a prescription** préparer une ordonnance

3 *vi (room, bath, bus)* se remplir; *(sail)* se gonfler; **her eyes filled with tears** ses yeux se sont remplis de larmes

▸**fill in** 1 *vi* faire un remplacement; **I'm often asked to fill in** on me demande souvent de faire des remplacements; **to fill in for sb** remplacer qn; **I'll fill in for you if necessary** je te remplacerai si besoin est

2 *vt sep* (**a**) *(hole, window, door)* boucher, combler; *(ditch)* remblayer; **he filled it in in green** *(outline)* il l'a colorié *ou* rempli en vert; **to fill in the gaps in one's knowledge** combler ses lacunes

(**b**) *(complete → form, questionnaire, cheque stub)* compléter, remplir; *(insert → name, missing word)* insérer; **to fill in the blanks** remplir les blancs

(**c**) *(bring up to date)* mettre au courant; **to fill sb in on sth** mettre qn au courant de qch

(**d**) *(use → time)* occuper; **he's just filling in time** il fait ça pour s'occuper *ou* pour occuper son temps; **I've got a couple of months to fill in** je dois occuper mon temps pendant environ deux mois

▸**fill out** 1 *vi* (**a**) *(cheeks)* se remplir; *(person)* s'étoffer (**b**) *(sails)* se gonfler

2 *vt sep* (**a**) *(complete → form, questionnaire, cheque stub)* compléter, remplir (**b**) *(pad out → essay, speech)* étoffer

▸**fill up** 1 *vi* se remplir; **to fill up with petrol** faire le plein d'essence; **don't fill up on biscuits, you two!** ne vous gavez pas de biscuits, vous deux!

2 *vt sep* (**a**) *(make full)* remplir; *(person with food)* rassasier; **he filled the car up** il a fait le plein (d'essence); *Aut* **fill her** *or* **it up, please** le plein, s'il vous plaît

(**b**) *(fill in → hole)* boucher; *(→ ditch)* remblayer

(**c**) *(use → day, time)* occuper

---

filled [fɪld] *adj* (**a**) *(food, soap etc)* qui contient un succédané (**b**) *Tex* chargé d'empois

►► ***filled roll*** sandwich *m (dans un petit pain rond)*

-filled [fɪld] *suff* rempli de...; **water-filled** rempli d'eau; **gas-filled** rempli de gaz

filler ['fɪlə(r)] *n* (**a**) *(for holes, cracks)* mastic *m*; *(for cavity, open space)* matière *f* de remplissage

(**b**) *(funnel)* entonnoir *m*

(**c**) *(in quilt, bean bag etc)* matière *f* de rembourrage; *(in cigar)* tripe *f*

(**d**) *Press & TV* bouche-trou *m*

(**e**) *Ling* **filler (word)** mot *m* de remplissage

(**f**) *Tech (in papermaking)* âme *f* (du carton)

►► *Aut* ***filler cap*** bouchon *m* du réservoir d'essence; *Tech* ***filler metal*** métal *m* d'apport; *Tech* ***filler rod*** baguette *f* de soudure

fillet ['fɪlɪt] 1 *n* (**a**) *(of meat, fish)* filet *m*

(**b**) *(for hair)* ruban *m*

(**c**) *Tech (strip → of metal, wood)* ruban *m*, bande *f*; *(→ raised projection)* collet *m*, bourrelet *m*

(**d**) *Tech* **fillet (weld)** soudure *f* d'angle

(**e**) *Archit* congé *m*, filet *m*

(**f**) *Aviat* carénage *m* d'emplanture d'aile

(**g**) *Typ* filet *m*

2 *vt (meat, fish → prepare)* préparer; *(cut into fillets → fish)* faire des filets dans, lever les filets de; *(→ meat)* faire des steaks dans; **filleted sole** filets *mpl* de sole

►► ***fillet steak*** filet *m* de bœuf; **two pieces of fillet steak, two fillet steaks** deux biftecks dans le filet

fill-in *n Fam (person)* remplaçant(e)❑ *m,f*

filling ['fɪlɪŋ] 1 *n* (**a**) *(in tooth)* plombage *m*; **I had to have a filling** il a fallu qu'on me fasse un plombage

(**b**) *Culin (for cake, pie, sandwich)* garniture *f*; *(for vegetables, poultry → savoury)* farce *f*; **they all have different fillings** *(chocolates)* ils sont tous fourrés différemment

(**c**) *(of hole)* comblement *m*

2 *adj (foodstuff)* bourratif; **it was very filling** cela m'a rassasié

►► ***filling in*** (**a**) *(of hole, window, door)* comblement *m*; *(of ditch)* remblayage *m* (**b**) *(of form, questionnaire)* rédaction *f*; ***filling out*** *(of sails, balloon)* gonflement *m*; ***filling station*** station-service *f*, station *f* d'essence; ***filling up*** (**a**) *(of container)* remplissage *m* (**b**) *(of hole)* bouchage *m*; *(of ditch)* remblayage *m* (**c**) *(of form)* rédaction *f*; *Mus* ***filling up parts*** parties *fpl* de remplissage

fillip ['fɪlɪp] *n* coup *m* de fouet; **to give sb/sth a fillip** donner un coup de fouet à qn/qch

fill-up *n Aut* plein *m*; **do you want a fill-up?** *(more to drink)* je te remplis ton verre?

filly ['fɪlɪ] *(pl* **fillies**) *n* (**a**) *(horse)* pouliche *f* (**b**) *Fam Old-fashioned (girl)* fille❑ *f*; **she's a fine young filly, isn't she?** c'est un beau brin de fille, non?

film [fɪlm] 1 *n* (**a**) *esp Br Cin* film *m*; **the film of the book** le film tiré du livre; **full-length/short-length film** (film *m*) long/court métrage *m*; **to shoot** *or* **to make a film (about sth)** tourner *ou* faire un film (sur qch); **the film's on at the local cinema** le film passe au cinéma du coin; **to be in films** faire du cinéma

(**b**) *Phot* pellicule *f*; **I left a film to be developed** j'ai laissé une pellicule à développer, **a roll of film** une pellicule

(**c**) *(thin layer → of oil, mist, dust)* film *m*, pellicule *f*; *Med (over eye)* taie *f*

(**d**) *(sheet)* film *m*; **plastic film** film *m* plastique

(**e**) *(UNCOUNT) Typ* films *mpl*; **a piece of film** un film

2 *comp Cin (critic, star, producer)* de cinéma; *(clip)* d'un film; *(sequence)* de film; *(archives, award, rights)* cinématographique

3 *vt (event, person)* filmer; *Cin (scene)* filmer, tourner; *(novel)* porter à l'écran

4 *vi (record)* filmer; *Cin* tourner; **we start filming next week** on commence à tourner la semaine prochaine; **to film well** *(be photogenic)* bien passer à l'écran; **her novels don't film well** ses romans ne se prêtent pas à l'adaptation cinématographique

►► ***film actor*** acteur *m* de cinéma; ***film actress*** actrice *f* de cinéma; ***film buff*** cinéphile *mf*; ***film camera*** caméra *f*; ***film club*** ciné-club *m*; ***film crew*** équipe *f* de tournage; ***film editor*** monteur(euse) *m,f*; ***film festival*** festival *m* cinématographique *ou* du cinéma; ***the film industry*** l'industrie *f* cinématographique *ou* du cinéma; ***film laboratory*** laboratoire *m* de film; [illegible]; ***film library*** cinémathèque *f*; ***film maker*** cinéaste *mf*; ***film premiere*** première *f*; ***film producer*** producteur(trice) *m,f* de cinéma; ***film script*** scénario *m*; ***film set*** plateau *m* de tournage; *Phot* ***film speed*** sensibilité *f* d'une pellicule; ***film stock*** film *m* vierge; ***film strip*** bande *f* (de film) fixe; ***film studio*** studio *m* (de cinéma); ***film test*** bout *m* d'essai

▸**film over** *vi* s'embuer, se voiler; **to film over with tears** s'embuer de larmes

filmable ['fɪlməbəl] *adj* adaptable au cinéma

filmgoer ['fɪlm,gəʊə(r)] *n* amateur *m* de cinéma, cinéphile *mf*; **she is a regular filmgoer** elle va régulièrement au cinéma

filmic ['fɪlmɪk] *adj Cin* cinématographique

filming ['fɪlmɪŋ] *n Cin* tournage *m*

filmless camera ['fɪlmlɪs-] *n Phot* caméra *f* sans film

filmography [fɪl'mɒgrəfɪ] *n* filmographie *f*

filmset ['fɪlmset] *vt Br Typ* photocomposer

filmsetter ['fɪlm,setə(r)] *n Br Typ (machine)* photocomposeuse *f*; *(person)* photocompositeur(trice) *m,f*

filmsetting ['fɪlm,setɪŋ] *n Br Typ* photocomposition *f*

filmslide ['fɪlm,slaɪd] *n Am* diapositive *f*

filmy ['fɪlmɪ] *adj (material)* léger, vaporeux, aérien

filo ['fiːləʊ] *n Br Culin* **filo (pastry)** pâte *f* (à) filo

Filofax® ['faɪləʊ,fæks] *n* agenda *m* modulaire

filter ['fɪltə(r)] 1 *n* (**a**) *Chem, Comput, Tech & Phot* filtre *m*

(**b**) *Br Aut* flèche *f* lumineuse *(autorisant le dégagement des voitures à droite ou à gauche)*

(**c**) *(on cigarette)* filtre *m*

(**d**) *Elec & Electron* filtre *m*; **frequency filter** filtre *m* de fréquences

2 *vt (coffee, oil, water, light etc)* filtrer; *(air)* épurer

3 *vi* (**a**) *(coffee, oil, water, light, air etc)* filtrer

(**b**) *Br Aut* suivre la voie de dégagement; **the cars filtered to the left** les voitures ont suivi la voie de dégagement vers la gauche

►► *Constr* ***filter bed*** couche *f* de filtration; ***filter coffee*** café *m* filtre; *Aut* ***filter element*** cartouche *f* filtrante; *Br Aut* ***filter lane*** voie *f* de dégagement; ***filter paper*** papier *m* filtre; ***filter tip*** *(tip)* (bout *m*) filtre *m*; *(cigarette)* cigarette *f* (bout) filtre

▸**filter down** *vi* filtrer; **the information finally filtered down to them** les informations ont fini par filtrer jusqu'à eux

▸**filter in** *vi (light, sound, information, news)* filtrer; *(people)* entrer petit à petit

▸**filter out** 1 *vt sep (sediment, impurities)* éliminer par filtrage *ou* filtration; *Fig (in selection procedure etc)* éliminer

2 *vi (people)* sortir petit à petit; *(news, information)* filtrer; **information is beginning to filter out that...** des informations commencent à filtrer selon lesquelles...

▸**filter through** 1 *vt insep* **the light filtered through the branches** la lumière filtrait à travers les branches

2 *vi (pass slowly)* passer lentement; **the news soon filtered through** les nouvelles n'ont pas tardé à filtrer

filterable ['fɪltərəbəl] *adj Med (virus)* filtrant

filtering ['fɪltərɪŋ] *n* filtrage *m*, filtration *f*

►► *Comput* ***filtering software*** logiciel *m* de filtrage

filter-tipped *adj (cigarette)* (bout) filtre

filth [fɪlθ] *n (UNCOUNT)* (**a**) *(on skin, clothes)* crasse *f*; *(in street)* saleté *f* (**b**) *(obscene books, films etc)* obscénités *fpl*; *(obscene words, jokes)* grossièretés *fpl*, obscénités *fpl*; **it's sheer filth** *(film, book)* c'est un ramassis d'obscénités (**c**) *Br Fam Pej* **the filth** *(police)* les flics *mpl*

filthily ['fɪlθɪlɪ] *adv* (**a**) *(dirtily)* salement (**b**) *(obscenely)* de façon obscène

filthiness ['fɪlθɪnɪs] *n* (**a**) *(dirtiness)* crasse *f*, saleté *f* (**b**) *(obscenity)* obscénité *f*

filthy ['fɪlθɪ] *(compar* **filthier,** *superl* **filthiest**) 1 *adj* (**a**) *(dirty)* dégoûtant, crasseux; **your hands are filthy!** tes mains sont dégoûtantes!

(**b**) *(obscene, smutty → language, talk, jokes)* grossier, obscène, ordurier; *(→ person)* grossier, dégoûtant; *(→ film, book, photograph)* obscène, dégoûtant; *(→ habit)* dégoûtant; **to have a filthy mind** avoir l'esprit mal tourné; **you filthy pig!** espèce de gros dégoûtant!

(**c**) *Fam (nasty → temper, day)* atroce❑, abominable❑; *(→ trick)* vicieux❑, méchant❑; **he's in a filthy mood** *or* **temper** il est de sale humeur, il est d'une humeur massacrante; **he gave me a filthy look** il m'a jeté un sale regard, il m'a regardé d'un sale œil; *Br* **it's filthy weather** il fait un temps de chien

2 *adv Fam* **filthy dirty** dégoûtant❑; **to be filthy rich** être plein aux as

filtrable ['fɪltrəbəl] *adj Med (virus)* filtrant

filtrate ['fɪltreɪt] *Chem* 1 *n* filtrat *m*

2 *vt* filtrer

3 *vi* filtrer

filtration [fɪl'treɪʃən] *n Chem* filtrage *m*, filtration *f*

►► *Tech* ***filtration plant*** station *f* d'épuration

Fimbra ['fɪmbrə] *n Br Formerly (abbr* **Financial Intermediaries, Managers and Brokers Regulatory Association**) = organisme britannique contrôlant les activités des courtiers d'assurances

fin [fɪn] **1** *n* (**a**) *(of fish, whale)* nageoire *f*; *(of shark)* aileron *m* (**b**) *(of aircraft, spacecraft)* empennage *m*; *(of boat)* dérive *f*; *(of rocket, bomb)* ailette *f* (**c**) *Tech (of cylinder, pump, radiator)* ailette *f*; **cooling fins** ailettes *fpl* de refroidissement (**d**) *Am Fam (five-dollar bill)* billet *m* de cinq dollars ❑

2 fins *npl (for swimming)* palmes *fpl*

finable [ˈfaɪnəbəl] *adj* passible d'(une) amende

finagle [fɪˈneɪgəl] *vt Am Fam (obtain → through cleverness)* se débrouiller pour avoir; *(→ through devious means)* obtenir par subterfuge ❑, carotter

final [ˈfaɪnəl] **1** *adj* (**a**) *(last)* dernier; **the final instalment** *(of hire purchase agreement)* le dernier versement, le versement libératoire; **the final irony** le comble de l'ironie; **final warning** dernier avertissement *m*

(**b**) *(definitive)* définitif; *(score)* final; **that's my final offer** c'est ma dernière offre; **I'm not moving, and that's final!** je ne bouge pas, un point c'est tout!; **the referee's decision is final** la décision de l'arbitre est sans appel; **is that your final answer?** c'est ta réponse définitive?; **nothing's final yet** il n'y a encore rien de définitif, rien n'est encore arrêté

(**c**) *Phil (cause)* final; *Gram (clause)* de but, final

2 *n* (**a**) *(of competition)* finale *f*; **to get to the final** *or* **finals** arriver en finale; **are they in the final** *or* **finals?** est-ce qu'ils sont en finale?; **how far did they get in the finals?** jusqu'où sont-ils arrivés en finale *ou* dans les épreuves de finale?

(**b**) *Press* dernière édition *f*; **late final** dernière *f* édition du soir

3 finals *npl Univ* examens *mpl* de dernière année; **to sit one's finals** passer ses examens de dernière année; **how did you do in your finals?** comment ça a marché à tes examens?

►► *Fin* ***final accounts*** compte *m* définitif; *Aviat* ***final approach*** approche *f* finale; *Cin* ***final cut*** final cut *m*; ***final date*** date *f* limite; *Com* ***final demand*** dernier rappel *m*; *St Exch* ***final dividend*** dividende *m* définitif *ou* final; ***final edition*** *(of newspaper)* dernière édition *f*; *Univ* ***final examinations*** examens *mpl* de dernière année; *Fin* ***final settlement*** solde *m* de tout compte; *Hist* ***the Final Solution*** la solution finale; *Sport* ***final whistle*** coup *m* de sifflet final

finale [fɪˈnɑːlɪ] *n Mus* finale *m*; *Fig* final *m*, finale *m*

finalism [ˈfaɪnəˌlɪzəm] *n Phil* finalisme *m*

finalist [ˈfaɪnəlɪst] *n (in competition)* finaliste *mf*

finality [faɪˈnælətɪ] *n* (**a**) *(of decision, death)* irrévocabilité *f*, caractère *m* définitif; **there was a note of finality in his voice** il y avait quelque chose d'irrévocable dans sa voix (**b**) *Phil* finalité *f*

finalization [ˌfaɪnəlaɪˈzeɪʃən] *n (of details, plans, arrangements)* mise *f* au point; *(of deal, decision, agreement)* conclusion *f*; **the work involved in the finalization of the screenplay** le travail nécessaire pour mettre la dernière main *ou* la dernière touche *ou* la touche finale au scénario

finalize, -ise [ˈfaɪnəlaɪz] *vt (details, plans, arrangements)* mettre au point; *(deal, decision, agreement)* mener à bonne fin; *(preparations)* mettre la dernière main *ou* touche à, mettre la touche finale à; *(date)* arrêter; **that hasn't been finalized yet** cela n'a pas encore été décidé *ou* arrêté; **nothing has been finalized** rien n'a encore été décidé *ou* arrêté; **details of the visit have yet to be finalized** les détails de la visite restent à préciser

finally [ˈfaɪnəlɪ] *adv* (**a**) *(eventually)* finalement, enfin; **when he finally arrived** finalement, quand il est arrivé; **she finally agreed to come** elle a fini par accepter de venir; **finally!** enfin!

(**b**) *(lastly)* enfin; **and, finally, I would like to say…** et pour finir je voudrais dire que…; **we are, finally, only human** nous ne sommes, en fin de compte, que des hommes

(**c**) *(irrevocably)* définitivement; **"no", she said finally** "non", dit-elle fermement

final-year *adj Univ (student)* en *ou* de dernière année

finance 1 *n* [ˈfaɪnæns] *(UNCOUNT) (money management)* finance *f*; *(financing)* financement *m*; **in the world of French finance** dans le monde français de la finance; **it's a problem of finance** c'est un problème de financement; **through lack of finance** à cause d'un manque de financement; **where are they going to get the finance from?** où vont-ils trouver les fonds nécessaires?; **we don't have the necessary finance** nous n'avons pas les fonds nécessaires; **high finance** la haute finance; **Minister/Ministry of Finance** ministre *m* /ministère *m* des Finances

2 *vt* [faɪˈnæns] financer; *(project, enterprise)* financer, trouver les fonds pour; *(person, company)* financer, commanditer; **to finance staff training** financer la formation du personnel

3 finances *npl* [ˈfaɪnænsəs] finances *fpl*, fonds *mpl*; **what state are your finances in?** comment vont tes finances?; **my finances are a bit low just now** je ne suis pas très en fonds en ce moment; **the company's finances are a bit low just now** les finances de l'entreprise sont un peu basses en ce moment

►► *Pol* ***Finance Act*** loi *f* de finances; *Pol* ***finance bill*** projet *m* de loi de finances; ***finance charges*** frais *mpl* financiers; ***finance company*** société *f* financière; ***finance costs*** frais *mpl* financiers *ou* de trésorerie; ***finance department*** direction *f* financière; ***finance director*** directeur(trice) *m,f* financier(ère); *Br* ***finance house*** société *f* financière, = société britannique de financement pour les achats à crédit; *Pol* ***Finance Minister*** ministre *m* de l'Économie et des Finances

financial [faɪˈnænʃəl] *adj* financier; **but does it make financial sense?** mais est-ce que c'est avantageux *ou* intéressant du point de vue financier?

►► ***financial accountant*** comptable *mf* financier(ère); ***financial accounting*** comptabilité *f* générale *ou* financière; ***financial administration*** gestion *f* financière; ***financial adviser*** conseiller(ère) *m,f* financier(ère); ***financial aid*** aide *f* financière; ***financial analyst*** analyste *mf* financier(ère); ***financial appraisal*** évaluation *f* financière; ***financial assistance*** appui *m* financier, aide *f* financière; ***financial backer*** bailleur(eresse) *m,f* de fonds; ***financial backing*** financement *m*, aide *f* financière; ***financial centre*** place *f* financière; ***financial consultant*** conseiller(ère) *m,f* financier(ère), conseil *m* financier; ***financial control*** contrôle *m* financier; ***financial controller*** contrôleur(euse) *m,f* financier(ère); *Acct* ***financial costs*** frais *mpl* financiers; ***financial deal*** opération *f* financière; ***financial director*** directeur(trice) *m,f* financier(ère); ***financial engineering*** ingénierie *f* financière; ***financial expenses*** charges *fpl* financières; *St Exch* ***financial future*** instrument *m* financier à terme; *St Exch* ***financial futures exchange*** bourse *f* d'instruments financiers à terme; ***financial gearing*** effet *m* de levier financier; ***financial healthcheck*** diagnostic *m* financier; ***financial institution*** établissement *m* financier; ***financial instrument*** instrument *m* financier; ***financial intermediary*** intermédiaire *mf* financier(ère); ***financial management*** direction *f ou* gestion *f* financière; ***financial manager*** directeur(trice) *m,f* financier(ère); ***financial market*** marché *m* financier; *Rad & TV* ***financial news*** chronique *f* financière; ***financial ombudsman*** arbitre *m* financier; ***financial pages*** pages *fpl* financières; ***financial partner*** partenaire *mf* financier(ère); ***financial period*** période *f* comptable; ***financial plan*** plan *m* de financement; ***financial planning*** planification *f* financière; ***financial position*** position *f ou* situation *f* financière; ***financial pressure*** problèmes *mpl* financiers; ***financial product*** produit *m* financier; ***financial ratio*** ratio *m* de gestion; ***financial report*** rapport *m* financier; ***financial reporting*** communication *f* de l'information financière; *Br* ***Financial Reporting Council*** = commission de contrôle de la qualité de l'information financière publiée par les entreprises; ***financial resources*** ressources *fpl*; ***financial services*** services *mpl* financiers; ***Financial Services Authority*** = organisme gouvernemental britannique chargé de contrôler les activités du secteur financier; ***financial situation*** situation *f* financière; ***financial statement*** état *m* financier, déclaration *f* de résultats; ***financial syndicate*** syndicat *m* financier; *Press* ***The Financial Times*** = quotidien britannique d'information financière; *Fin* ***Financial Times All-Share Index*** = indice boursier du *Financial Times* basé sur la valeur de 700 actions cotées à la Bourse de Londres; *Fin* ***Financial Times-(Industrial) Ordinary Share Index*** = indice boursier du *Financial Times* basé sur la valeur de 30 actions cotées à la Bourse de Londres; *Fin* ***Financial Times-Stock Exchange 100 Share Index*** = principal indice boursier du *Financial Times* basé sur la valeur de 100 actions cotées à la Bourse de Londres; ***financial transaction*** opération *f* financière; *Br* ***the financial year*** *(in business)* l'exercice *m* financier; *(in politics)* l'année *f* budgétaire

FINANCIAL TIMES 

Le *Financial Times* est un quotidien britannique de qualité, spécialisé dans l'actualité financière et économique; il est reconnaissable à la couleur rose de son papier. Il existe une édition internationale, diffusée notamment en Allemagne et en France.

FINANCIAL YEAR 

Pour les impôts sur le revenu en Grande-Bretagne, l'année fiscale commence le 5 avril.

financially [faɪˈnænʃəlɪ] *adv* financièrement; **financially sound** solvable; **are they financially sound?** est-ce qu'ils ont une bonne assise financière?; **he's financially naive** il est naïf sur les questions d'argent

financier [faɪˈnænsɪə(r)] *n* financier *m*

financing [faɪˈnænsɪŋ] *n (of project etc)* financement *m*

►► ***financing plan*** plan *m* de financement; ***financing terms*** modalités *fpl* de financement

finback [ˈfɪnbæk] *n Zool* balénoptère *m*, rorqual *m*

finch [fɪntʃ] *n Orn* fringillidé *m*; *(goldfinch)* chardonneret *m*; *(chaffinch)* pinson *m*; *(bullfinch)* bouvreuil *m*

FIND [faɪnd]

trouver	►1 (a) – (d)
retrouver	►1 (a)
chercher	►1 (b)
constater	►1 (e)
déclarer	►1 (f)
se trouver	►1 (h)
prononcer	►2
trouvaille	►3
merveille	►3

(pt & pp **found** [faʊnd]) **1** *vt* (**a**) *(by searching)* trouver; *(lost thing, person)* retrouver; **I can't find it anywhere** je ne le trouve nulle part; **did you find what you were looking for?** as-tu trouvé ce que tu cherchais?; **she couldn't find anything to say** elle ne trouvait rien à dire; **the police could find no reason** *or* **explanation for his disappearance** la police n'arrivait pas à expliquer sa disparition; **I never did find those earrings** je n'ai jamais pu trouver ces boucles d'oreilles; **the missing airmen were found alive** les aviateurs disparus ont été retrouvés sains et saufs; **I can't find my place** *(in book)* je ne sais plus où j'en suis; **my wallet/he was nowhere to be found** mon portefeuille/il était introuvable

(**b**) *(look for, fetch)* chercher; *Comput* **to find and replace** trouver et remplacer; **he went to find help/a doctor** il est allé chercher de l'aide/un médecin; **go and find me a pair of scissors** va me chercher une paire de ciseaux; **could you find me a cloth?** tu peux me trouver un chiffon?; **he said he'd try to find me a job** il a dit qu'il essaierait de me trouver un travail; **to find the time/money to do sth** trouver le temps de/l'argent nécessaire pour faire qch; **to find the courage/strength to do sth** trouver le courage/la force de faire qch; **to find one's feet** *(in new job, situation)* prendre ses repères; **I'm still finding my feet** je ne suis pas encore complètement dans le bain; **she couldn't find it in her**

heart *or* **herself to say no** elle n'a pas eu le cœur de dire non; **the bullet found its mark** la balle a atteint son but; **to find one's way** trouver son chemin; **I'll find my own way out** je trouverai la sortie tout seul; **she found her way back home** elle a réussi à rentrer chez elle; **somehow, the book had found its way into my room** sans que je sache comment, le livre s'était retrouvé dans ma chambre

(**c**) *(come across by chance)* trouver; **we left everything as we found it** nous avons tout laissé dans l'état où nous l'avions trouvé; **we found this wonderful little bistro on our last visit** nous avons découvert un adorable petit bistro lors de notre dernière visite; **you won't find a better bargain anywhere** nulle part, vous ne trouverez meilleur prix; **this bird is found all over Britain** on trouve cet oiseau dans toute la Grande-Bretagne; **the complete list is to be found on page 18** la liste complète se trouve page 18; **I found him at home** je l'ai trouvé chez lui; **I found her waiting outside** je l'ai trouvée qui attendait dehors; **they found him dead** on l'a trouvé mort; **you'll find someone else** tu trouveras quelqu'un d'autre; **to find happiness/peace** trouver le bonheur/la paix; **I take people as I find them** je prends les gens comme ils sont; **I hope this letter finds you in good health** j'espère que vous allez bien; **they found an unexpected supporter in Mr Smith** ils ont trouvé en M. Smith un partisan inattendu

(**d**) *(expressing an opinion, personal view)* trouver; **I don't find that funny at all** je ne trouve pas ça drôle du tout; **I find her very pretty** je la trouve très jolie; **she finds it very difficult/impossible to talk about it** il lui est très difficile/impossible d'en parler; **to find some difficulty in doing sth** éprouver quelque difficulté à faire qch; **he finds it very hard/impossible to make friends** il a beaucoup de mal à/il n'arrive pas à se faire des amis; **I find it hot/cold in here** je trouve qu'il fait chaud/froid ici; **how did you find your new boss/your steak?** comment avez-vous trouvé votre nouveau patron/votre steak?; **Rovers have been found wanting** *or* **lacking in defence** les Rovers ont fait preuve de faiblesse au niveau de la défense

(**e**) *(discover, learn)* constater; **I found (that) the car wouldn't start** j'ai constaté que la voiture ne voulait pas démarrer; **they came back to find the house had been burgled** à leur retour, ils ont constaté que la maison avait été cambriolée; **I find I have time on my hands now that I am no longer working** je m'aperçois que j'ai du temps à moi maintenant que je ne travaille plus; **I think you'll find I'm right** je pense que tu t'apercevras que j'ai raison

(**f**) *Law* **to find sb guilty/innocent** déclarer qn coupable/non coupable; **how do you find the accused?** déclarez-vous l'accusé coupable ou non coupable?; **the court found that the evidence was inconclusive** le tribunal a déclaré que les preuves n'étaient pas suffisantes

(**g**) *Old-fashioned or Formal (provide → one's own tools, uniform)* fournir; **£65 a week all found** 65 livres par semaine nourri et logé

(**h**) *(reflexive use)* **to find oneself** *(one's true self)* se trouver; **I woke up to find myself on a ship** je me suis réveillé sur un bateau; **he found himself out of a job** il s'est retrouvé sans emploi; **I find/found myself in an impossible situation** je me trouve/me suis retrouvé dans une situation impossible; *Formal* **I find myself unable to agree to your request** je me vois dans l'impossibilité d'accéder à votre demande; **she found herself forced to retaliate** elle s'est trouvée dans l'obligation de riposter; **he's going on a six-month backpacking trip to find himself** il va partir en voyage pendant six mois, sac au dos, à la recherche de lui-même

2 *vi Law* **to find for/against the plaintiff** prononcer en faveur de l'accusation/de la défense

3 *n (object)* trouvaille *f*; *(person)* merveille *f*

►► *Comput* ***find command*** commande *f* de recherche

►**find out 1** *vi* (**a**) *(investigate, make enquiries)* se renseigner; **to find out about sth** se renseigner sur qch

(**b**) *(learn, discover)* **his wife/his boss found out** sa femme/son chef a tout découvert; **his wife found out about his affair** sa femme a découvert qu'il avait une liaison; **what if the police find out?** et si la police l'apprend?; **I didn't find out about the party in time** on ne m'a pas mis au courant de la fête à temps; **I didn't find out about it in time** je ne l'ai pas su à temps

2 *vt sep* (**a**) *(learn, discover → truth, real identity)* découvrir; *(→ answer, phone number)* trouver; *(→ by making enquiries, reading instructions)* se renseigner sur; **we found out that she was French** nous avons découvert qu'elle était française; **what have you found out about him/it?** qu'est-ce que tu as découvert sur lui/là-dessus?; **can you find out the date of the meeting for me?** est-ce que tu peux te renseigner sur la date de la réunion?; **when I found out the date of the meeting** quand j'ai appris la date de la réunion; **to find out how to do sth/what sb is really like** découvrir comment faire qch/la véritable nature de qn; **I found out where he'd put it** j'ai trouvé où il l'avait mis

(**b**) *(catch being dishonest)* prendre; *(show to be a fraud)* prendre en défaut; **make sure you don't get found out** veille à ne pas te faire prendre; **you've been found out** tu as été découvert; **they had found her out for the liar she was** ils avaient découvert quelle menteuse elle était; **she had been found out transferring money into her own account** on avait découvert qu'elle transférait de l'argent sur son propre compte

---

finder ['faɪndə(r)] *n* (**a**) *(person)* **it becomes the property of the finder** celui/celle qui l'a trouvé en devient propriétaire; **finders keepers (, losers weepers)** celui qui le trouve le garde (**b**) *(of camera)* viseur *m*; *(of telescope)* chercheur *m*

►► ***finder's fee*** commission *f* de démarcheur

finding ['faɪndɪŋ] **1** *n Law* verdict *m*

2 findings *npl (of scientist, enquiry, investigation etc)* résultat *m*; *(of tribunal, committee, report)* conclusion *f*; **he published his findings in a scientific journal** il a fait publier les résultats de ses recherches dans un journal scientifique

---

FINE [faɪn]

excellent	► 1 (a)
beau	► 1 (a), (f)
fin	► 1 (b), (c)
bien	► 1 (d), (e); 2
subtil	► 1 (g)
amende	► 3
condamner à une amende	► 4

(*compar* **finer**, *superl* **finest**) **1** *adj* (**a**) *(of high quality → meal, speech, view)* excellent; *(beautiful and elegant → clothes, house)* beau (belle); *(→ fabric)* précieux; **this is very fine workmanship** c'est un travail d'une grande qualité; **she is a very fine athlete** c'est une excellente athlète; **this is a very fine wine** c'est un vin vraiment excellent; *Br* **a fine chap** un bon gars; **she is a fine lady** *(admirable character)* c'est une femme admirable; *(elegant)* c'est une femme élégante; **to appeal to sb's finer feelings** faire appel aux nobles sentiments de qn; **to play at being the fine lady** jouer les grandes dames; **that was a fine effort by Webb** superbe effort de la part de Webb; **a fine example** un bel exemple; **of the finest quality** de première qualité; **made from the finest barley** fabriqué à base d'orge de la meilleure qualité; **her finest hour was winning the gold** elle a eu son heure de gloire quand elle a remporté la médaille d'or

(**b**) *(very thin → hair, nib, thread)* fin; **in this case there is a fine line between fact and fiction** dans le cas présent la frontière est très mince entre la réalité et la fiction; **it's a fine line** la différence *ou* la distinction est infime *ou* très subtile

(**c**) *(not coarse → powder, grain, drizzle)* fin; *(→ features, skin)* fin, délicat; **to chop** *or* **to cut sth (up) fine** hacher qch menu; *Fig* **to cut it fine** calculer juste; **that's cutting it a bit fine** tu calcules un peu juste

(**d**) *(good, OK)* **how is everyone? – oh, they're all fine** comment va tout le monde? – tout le monde va bien; **I'm just fine, thanks** ça va très bien, merci; **how are you? – fine, thanks** comment ça va? – bien, merci; **more coffee? – no thanks, I'm fine** encore du café? – non, ça va, merci; **the tent's fine for two, but too small for three** la tente convient pour deux personnes, mais elle est trop petite pour trois; **I'll be back in about an hour or so – fine** je serai de retour d'ici environ une heure – d'accord *ou* entendu *ou* très bien; **I was a bit worried about the new job, but it turned out fine in the end** j'étais un peu inquiet à propos de mon nouveau travail mais ça s'est finalement bien passé; **(that's) fine** très bien, parfait; **that's fine by** *or* **with me** ça me va; **that's all very fine, but what about me?** tout ça c'est bien joli, mais moi qu'est-ce que je deviens dans l'affaire?; **this is fine for those who can afford it** c'est très bien pour ceux qui peuvent se le permettre

(**e**) *(well)* **that looks fine to me** cela m'a l'air d'aller; **he looks fine now** *(in health)* il a l'air de bien aller maintenant; **you look just fine, it's a very nice dress** tu es très bien, c'est une très jolie robe; **that sounds fine** *(suggestion, idea)* très bien, parfait; *(way of playing music)* cela rend très bien

(**f**) *Br (weather)* beau (belle); **a fine day** une belle journée; **there will be fine weather** *or* **it will be fine in all parts of the country** il fera beau *ou* il y aura du beau temps dans tout le pays; **it's turned out fine again** il fait encore beau; **it was a bit cloudy in the morning, but it turned out fine in the end** le temps était un peu nuageux le matin, mais finalement ça a été une belle journée; **I hope it keeps fine for the barbecue** pourvu que le beau temps continue pour le barbecue; **I hope it keeps fine for you** j'espère que tu auras du beau temps; **one of these fine days** un de ces jours; **one fine day** un beau jour

(**g**) *(subtle → distinction, language)* subtil; *(precise → calculations)* minutieux, précis; **fine detail** petit détail *m*; **to make some fine adjustments to sth** *(to text, plan)* peaufiner qch; *(to engine)* faire des petits réglages sur qch; **there are still a few fine adjustments to be made** il reste quelques petits détails à régler; **not to put too fine a point on it** pour parler carrément

(**h**) *Fam Ironic (awful, terrible)* **that's a fine thing to say!** c'est charmant de dire ça!; **she was in a fine state** elle était dans un état épouvantable; **look at you, you're in a fine state!** non mais tu t'es vu!, ah tu es dans un bel état!; **you picked a fine time to leave me/tell me!** tu as bien choisi ton moment pour me quitter/me le dire!; **this is a fine time to start that again!** c'est bien le moment de remettre ça sur le tapis!; **you're a fine one to talk!** ça te va bien de dire ça!, tu peux parler!; **here's another fine mess you've got me into!** tu m'as encore mis dans un beau pétrin!; **a fine friend you are!** eh bien, tu fais un bon copain/une bonne copine!; **this is a fine time to come in/get up!** c'est à cette heure-ci que tu rentres/te lèves?

2 *adv (well)* bien; **yes, that suits me fine** oui, cela me va très bien; **the baby is doing fine** le bébé va très bien; **we get along fine together** on s'entend très bien

3 *n (punishment)* amende *f*, contravention *f*; **to impose a fine on sb** infliger une amende à qn; **a parking fine** une contravention *ou* amende pour stationnement illégal; **she was made to pay a fine** elle a dû payer une amende; **a £25 fine** une amende de 25 livres

4 *vt (order to pay)* condamner à une amende, donner une contravention à; **she was fined heavily** elle a été condamnée à une lourde amende *ou* contravention; **she was fined for speeding** elle a reçu une contravention pour excès de vitesse; **they fined her £25 for illegal parking** ils lui ont donné *ou* elle a eu une amende *ou* contravention de 25 livres pour stationnement illégal

►► ***fine art*** *(UNCOUNT)* beaux-arts *mpl*; **to study fine art** étudier les beaux-arts; *Fig* **he's got it** down to a fine art il est expert en la matière; **she's got washing the car down to a fine art** elle est passée maître dans l'art de laver la voiture; ***fine arts*** beaux-arts *mpl*; *Fin* ***fine bill*** beau papier *m*; *Fin* ***fine trade bill*** papier *m* de haut commerce *ou* de première catégorie

▸**fine down** *vt sep (smooth → wood)* polir, poncer *Fig (hone → theory, text)* affiner

Their finest hour
Churchill utilisa cette formule dans une déclaration adressée à ses compatriotes en 1940, destinée à encourager ces derniers à résister de toutes leurs forces contre l'ennemi, en leur promettant que la postérité se souviendrait de cette époque comme de "leur heure la plus glorieuse".
Aujourd'hui on utilise cette expression de manière allusive à propos de la période la plus mémorable de la vie ou de la carrière de quelqu'un. On dira par exemple **she always felt that her time as a doctor in Africa was her finest hour** ("elle a toujours considéré que la période durant laquelle elle était médecin en Afrique fut le meilleur moment de son existence").

This is another fine mess you've gotten us into
Il s'agit d'une formule utilisée par Oliver Hardy, le plus gros des membres du célèbre duo comique américain Laurel et Hardy. Chaque fois que les deux compères se retrouvent en difficulté et quelles que soient les circonstances, Hardy s'en prend à Laurel en ces termes: **this is another fine mess you've gotten us into** ("tu nous as encore mis dans de beaux draps!"). On utilise aujourd'hui cette phrase sur le mode humoristique dans toute situation similaire.

fine-bore *vt Metal* reforer, repasser (à l'aléseuse)
fine-cut *adj (tobacco)* haché fin
fine-darn *vt Sewing* stopper
fine-draw *vt (pt* **fine-drew**, *pp* **fine-drawn**) *Sewing (a tear)* rentraire, faire une reprise perdue à
fine-drawn *adj Fig* (**a**) *(distinction)* subtil (**b**) *(features)* fin (**c**) *(wire)* finement étiré; *(thread)* délié
Fine Gael [ˌfɪnəˈgeɪl] *n Ir Pol* le Fine Gael *m*
fine-grain *adj Phot (image)* à grain fin; *(developer)* pour grain fin
fine-grained *adj (wood)* à fibres fines, à fil fin; *(leather)* à grain peu apparent
fine-looking *adj* beau (belle)
finely [ˈfaɪnlɪ] *adv* (**a**) *(grated, ground, sliced)* finement; **finely chopped** haché menu, finement haché; **finely powdered** en poudre fine (**b**) *(delicately, subtly → tuned)* avec précision; **the situation is very finely balanced** la situation est caractérisée par un équilibre précaire (**c**) *(carved, sewn etc)* délicatement
fineness [ˈfaɪnnɪs] *n* (**a**) *(of clothes, manners)* raffinement *m*; *(of work of art, features, handwriting)* finesse *f* (**b**) *(of sand, sugar, material)* finesse *f* (**c**) *(purity → of metal)* pureté *f* (**d**) *(thinness → of thread, hair, nib)* finesse *f*; *Fig (of detail, distinction)* subtilité *f*
finery [ˈfaɪnərɪ] *n (UNCOUNT)* parure *f*; **the princess in all her finery** la princesse dans *ou* parée de ses plus beaux atours; **to be dressed in all one's finery** porter sa tenue d'apparat
fine-spoken *adj (person)* au beau parler
fine-spun *adj* (**a**) *Tex (yarn, wool)* (filé) fin (**b**) *Fig (argument, logic)* subtil
finesse [fɪˈnes] **1** *n* (**a**) *(skill)* finesse *f* (**b**) *Cards* impasse *f*
2 *vi Cards* **to finesse against a card** faire l'impasse à une carte
3 *vt Cards* **to finesse a card** faire l'impasse en jouant une carte
fine-tooth(ed) comb *n* peigne *m* fin; *Fig* **to go through sth with a fine-tooth(ed) comb** passer qch au peigne fin
fine-tune *vt (machine, engine, radio)* régler avec précision; *Fig (plan)* peaufiner; *(economy)* = régler grâce à des mesures fiscales et monétaires
fine-tuning [-ˈtjuːnɪŋ] *n (of machine, engine, radio)* réglage *m* fin; *Fig (of plan)* peaufinage *m*; *(of economy)* = réglage obtenu par des mesures fiscales et monétaires
Fingal's Cave [ˈfɪŋgəlz-] *n* la grotte de Fingal
finger [ˈfɪŋgə(r)] **1** *n* (**a**) *(part of body)* doigt *m*; **to wear a ring on one's finger** porter une bague au doigt; **she ran her fingers through her hair** elle s'est passé les doigts *ou* la main dans les cheveux; **she ran her fingers through his hair** elle a passé ses doigts *ou* sa main dans ses cheveux; **to lick one's fingers** se lécher les doigts; **to eat with one's fingers** manger avec les doigts; **to hold sth between finger and thumb** tenir qch entre le pouce et l'index; **to type with two fingers** taper (à la machine) avec deux doigts; **a finger's breadth** un doigt; **to point a finger at sb/sth** montrer qn/qch du doigt; **to twist sb round one's little finger** faire ce qu'on veut de qn; **I can twist him round my little finger** j'en fais ce que je veux; **to be all fingers and thumbs** avoir des mains de beurre, avoir deux mains gauches; *Br Fam* **get** *or* **pull your finger out!** remue-toi!; **to have a finger in every pie** jouer sur tous les tableaux; **he has a finger in the pie** il a des intérêts dans l'affaire; **if you lay a finger on her** si tu touches à un seul de ses cheveux; **to keep one's fingers crossed** croiser les doigts *(pour souhaiter bonne chance)*; **I'll keep my fingers crossed for you** je croiserai les doigts pour toi; **you could count them on the fingers of one hand** on pourrait les compter sur les doigts de la main; **to point the finger (of suspicion) at sb** diriger les soupçons sur qn; **the finger of suspicion points at the accountant** les soupçons pèsent sur le comptable; **who are you to point the finger?** qui es-tu pour accuser les autres?; *Fam* **to put the finger on sb** *(inform on)* balancer qn; **to put one's finger on sth** *(identify)* mettre le doigt sur qch; **something has changed but I can't put my finger on it** il y a quelque chose de changé mais je n'arrive pas à dire ce que c'est; **to have one's finger on the pulse** *(person)* être très au fait de ce qui se passe; *(magazine, TV programme)* être à la pointe de l'actualité; *Fam* **to give sb the finger**, *Br Fam* **to stick two fingers up at sb** ≃ faire un bras d'honneur à qn; **success/happiness/the suspect slipped through his fingers** le succès/le bonheur/le suspect lui a glissé entre les doigts; **to work one's fingers to the bone** s'épuiser à la tâche; **you never lift** *or* **raise a finger to help** tu ne lèves jamais le petit doigt pour aider; **he's so lazy, I've never seen him lift a finger** il est si paresseux, je ne l'ai jamais vu faire le moindre effort
(**b**) *(of glove)* doigt *m*
(**c**) *(of alcohol)* doigt *m*; *(of land)* bande *f*; **to cut a cake into fingers** couper un gâteau en petits morceaux rectangulaires
(**d**) *Comput* = utilitaire de l'Internet permettant d'obtenir des informations sur un utilisateur du réseau
(**e**) *Tech* doigt *m*; *(of dial)* index *m*
2 *vt* (**a**) *(feel)* tâter du doigt; *Pej* tripoter; **stop fingering that food!** arrête de tripoter la nourriture!
(**b**) *Mus* doigter, indiquer le doigté de
(**c**) *Fam (inform on)* balancer, donner
▸▸ *Culin* ***finger biscuit*** biscuit *m* à la cuiller; ***finger bowl*** rince-doigts *m inv*; ***finger buffet*** = buffet où sont servis des petits sandwiches, des petits fours et des légumes crus; *Mus* ***finger exercises*** exercices *mpl* de doigté; ***finger food*** = petits fours, petits sandwiches et légumes crus, servis à un buffet et que l'on mange avec les doigts; *Mus* ***finger hole*** trou *m*; ***finger paint*** peinture *f* pour peindre avec les doigts; ***finger painting*** peinture *f* avec les doigts; **children love finger painting** les enfants adorent peindre avec leurs doigts; ***finger puppet*** marionnette *f* à doigt
fingerboard [ˈfɪŋgəbɔːd] *n Mus* touche *f*
fingered [ˈfɪŋgəd] *adj* (**a**) *(dirty, soiled)* qui a été tripoté (**b**) *Mus* doigté
fingering [ˈfɪŋgərɪŋ] *n* (**a**) *Mus (technique, numerals)* doigté *m* (**b**) *Pej (touching)* tripotage *m* (**c**) *(knitting wool)* laine *f* fine à tricoter
fingerless glove [ˈfɪŋgələs-] *n* mitaine *f*
fingermark [ˈfɪŋgəˌmɑːk] *n* trace *f ou* marque *f* de doigt
fingermarked [ˈfɪŋgəˌmɑːkt] *adj* maculé de traces de doigts
fingernail [ˈfɪŋgəneɪl] *n* ongle *m* (de la main); **to hang on by one's fingernails** se retenir du bout des doigts; *Fig* se raccrocher comme on peut
fingerplate [ˈfɪŋgəpleɪt] *n* plaque *f* de propreté *(pour protéger une porte des marques de doigts)*
fingerprint [ˈfɪŋgəprɪnt] **1** *n* empreinte *f* digitale; **five different sets of fingerprints** cinq empreintes digitales différentes; **his fingerprints are all over it** c'est couvert de ses empreintes digitales; *Fig* tout indique que c'est lui; **to take sb's fingerprints** prendre les empreintes digitales de qn
2 *vt (person)* prendre les empreintes digitales de; *(object, weapon)* relever les empreintes digitales sur; **to fingerprint sb genetically** identifier l'empreinte *ou* le code génétique de qn
▸▸ ***fingerprint expert*** spécialiste *mf* en empreintes digitales *ou* en dactyloscopie
fingerprinting [ˈfɪŋgəˌprɪntɪŋ] *n (UNCOUNT) (of person)* prise *f* d'empreintes digitales; *(of object)* relevé *m* d'empreintes digitales
fingerstall [ˈfɪŋgəstɔːl] *n* doigtier *m*
fingertip [ˈfɪŋgətɪp] *n* bout *m* du doigt; **he rolled a cigarette between his fingertips** il s'est roulé une cigarette entre les doigts; **to be Irish to one's fingertips** être irlandais jusqu'au bout des ongles; **to have information at one's fingertips** *(be conversant with)* connaître des informations sur le bout des doigts; *(readily available)* avoir des informations à portée de main
▸▸ ***fingertip controls*** commandes *fpl* à touches; ***fingertip search*** passage *m* au peigne fin, examen *m* minutieux
finial [ˈfɪnɪəl] *n Archit* fleuron *m*
finicky [ˈfɪnɪkɪ] *adj* (**a**) *(person)* pointilleux, *Pej* tatillon; *(habit)* tatillon; **to be finicky about sth** être pointilleux *or Pej* tatillon sur qch; **to be a finicky eater** être difficile sur la nourriture (**b**) *(job, task)* minutieux; *(device, recipe)* compliqué; **this is a finicky dish to make** c'est un plat très délicat à préparer

FINISH [ˈfɪnɪʃ]

fin	▸ **1 (a)**
finitions	▸ **1 (b)**
finition	▸ **1 (c)**
finish	▸ **1 (d)**
finir	▸ **2 (a), (d); 3**
terminer	▸ **2 (a)**
se terminer	▸ **3**

1 *n* (**a**) *(end, closing stage → of life, game etc)* fin *f*; *(→ of race)* arrivée *f*; **a close finish** *(in race)* une arrivée serrée *ou* dans un mouchoir; **to fight to the finish** se battre jusqu'au bout; **it was a fight to the finish** la partie fut serrée; **to be in at the finish** voir la fin; **she was exhausted by the finish** sur la fin elle était épuisée; **that was the finish of him** ce fut le coup de grâce; *St Exch* **price at the finish** prix *m* de clôture; *St Exch* **trading at the finish** opérations *fpl* de clôture; *St Exch* **shares were up at the finish** les actions étaient en hausse à la clôture
(**b**) *(created with paint, varnish, veneer)* finitions *fpl*; **paint with a gloss/matt finish** peinture *f* vernie/mate; **paper with a gloss/matt finish** papier *m* glacé/mat; **stained with a walnut finish** teinté imitation noyer; **car with a metallic/silver finish** voiture *f* métallisée/argentée
(**c**) *(quality of workmanship, presentation etc)* finition *f*; **his prose/acting lacks finish** sa prose/son jeu manque de poli
(**d**) *Sport (of athlete)* finish *m*
(**e**) *(shot at goal)* but *m*; **a superb finish** un but magnifique
2 *vt* (**a**) *(end, complete → work, meal, school)* finir, terminer, achever; *(→ race)* finir, terminer; *(consume → supplies, food, drink)* finir, terminer; **to finish doing sth** finir *ou* terminer de faire qch; **when do you finish work?** *(time)* à quelle heure est-ce que tu finis?; *(date)* quand *ou* à quelle date finis-tu?; **to finish what one was saying** finir ce qu'on avait à dire; **to be in a hurry to get sth finished** être pressé de finir *ou* terminer qch; **finish your drinks** finissez *ou* videz vos verres

(**b**) *(ruin → someone's career)* mettre un terme à; *(→ someone's chances)* détruire, anéantir; **that was the scandal that finished him** c'est le scandale qui l'a achevé

(**c**) *(exhaust)* achever, tuer

(**d**) *(put finish on → wood, garment)* finir, mettre les finitions à; *Metal (part)* usiner; *Sewing* **to finish a buttonhole** brider une boutonnière; **the wood hasn't been very well finished** le bois présente des aspérités; **the paintwork hasn't been very well finished** la peinture n'a pas été très bien faite

3 *vi (come to an end → concert, film etc)* (se) finir, se terminer, s'achever; *(complete activity → person)* finir, terminer; **to finish by doing sth** finir *ou* terminer en faisant qch; **when does the concert finish?** à quelle heure le concert (se) finit-il *ou* se termine-t-il *ou* s'achève-t-il?; **when do you finish?** *(leave work)* quand est-ce que tu finis?; **please let me finish** *(speaking)* s'il te plaît, laisse-moi finir *ou* terminer; **to finish first/third** *(in race)* arriver premier/troisième; **where did he finish?** *(in race)* en quelle position est-il arrivé *ou* a-t-il fini?; **the runner finished strongly/well** *(in race)* le coureur a fini fort/a bien fini; **the book finishes with him returning to the family house** à la fin du livre il retourne à la maison familiale

►► *Am Sport* ***finish line*** ligne *f* d'arrivée

►**finish off 1** *vi (in speech, meal)* finir, terminer; **they finished off with a coffee/by singing the national anthem** ils ont terminé par un café/en chantant l'hymne national

2 *vt sep* (**a**) *(complete → work, letter)* finir, terminer, achever; *(→ passing move in sport)* terminer, finir, conclure

(**b**) *(consume → drink)* finir, terminer

(**c**) *(kill → person, wounded animal)* achever; *Fig (exhaust → person)* achever, tuer; *Fig* **fierce competition finished the industry off** une concurrence féroce a eu raison de cette industrie

►**finish up 1** *vi (end up)* finir; **to finish up in jail/hospital** finir en prison/à l'hôpital; **they finished up arguing** ils ont fini par se disputer; **she finished up a nervous wreck** à la fin c'était une vraie boule de nerfs, elle a fini à bout de nerfs; **you might finish up dead** tu risques de te faire tuer

2 *vt sep (meal, food, drink)* finir, terminer; **finish up your drink** finissez *ou* terminez *ou* videz votre verre

►**finish with** *vt insep* (**a**) *(have no further use for)* ne plus avoir besoin de; **have you finished with the paper/milk?** tu n'as plus besoin du journal/du lait?, tu as fini avec le journal/le lait?; **I haven't finished with it yet** j'en ai encore besoin

(**b**) *(stop doing)* en finir avec; **I've finished with journalism for good** j'en ai fini à jamais avec le journalisme, moi et le journalisme, c'est fini; **I've finished with trying to help people** plus jamais je n'essaierai d'aider les gens

(**c**) *(end relationship with)* rompre avec; **she finished with her boyfriend** elle a rompu avec son petit ami

(**d**) *(stop punishing)* régler son compte à; **just wait till I finish with him** attends que je lui règle son compte, attends que j'en aie fini avec lui; **I haven't finished with you yet** je n'en ai pas encore fini avec toi

---

finished ['fɪnɪʃt] *adj* (**a**) *(completed → work, job)* fini, terminé, achevé; *(consumed → wine, cake)* fini; **the butter is finished** il n'y a plus de beurre; **the plumber was finished by 4 p.m.** le plombier avait terminé *ou* fini à 16 heures; **finished product** *or* **article** produit *m* fini

(**b**) *Fam (exhausted)* mort, crevé

(**c**) *(ruined → career)* fini, terminé; **he's finished as a politician** sa carrière d'homme politique est terminée *ou* finie, il est fini en tant qu'homme politique; **you're finished** c'est fini *ou* terminé pour vous; **you're finished in this company** tu es fini dans cette société

(**d**) *(consummate)* fini; *Fig (performance)* parfaitement exécuté; *(appearance)* raffiné; **it's beautifully finished** les finitions sont magnifiques, c'est magnifiquement fini

(**e**) *(over)* fini; **you and I are finished** toi et moi, c'est fini; **I'm finished with him/my boyfriend** lui/mon petit ami et moi, c'est fini; **I'm finished with politics/journalism** la politique/le journalisme et moi, c'est fini, j'en ai fini avec la politique/le journalisme; **the headmaster was not finished with him yet** le principal n'en avait pas encore fini avec lui

finisher ['fɪnɪʃə(r)] *n* (**a**) *Sport* finisseur(euse) *m,f*; *Ftbl* marqueur *m*; **he's a fast finisher** *(athlete)* il finit vite, il est rapide au finish (**b**) *(thorough person)* **he's not a finisher** il ne finit jamais complètement son travail (**c**) *Ind* finisseur(euse) *m,f*

finishing ['fɪnɪʃɪŋ] **1** *adj* dernier; **finishing coat** *(of paint, varnish etc)* dernière couche *f*; **the finishing stroke** le coup de grâce

2 *n* (**a**) *(completion → of task etc)* achèvement *m* (**b**) *Tech* finition *f*; *(of leather, paper)* apprêtage *m*

►► *Br Sport* ***finishing line*** ligne *f* d'arrivée; ***finishing school*** = école privée de jeunes filles surtout axée sur l'enseignement des bonnes manières; *Ind* ***finishing shop*** atelier *m* de finitions; ***finishing touches*** finitions *fpl*; **to put the finishing touches to sth** mettre la dernière main à qch

finite ['faɪnaɪt] **1** *adj* limité; *Phil & Math (number, universe)* fini; *Gram (verb)* à aspect fini

2 *n Phil* **the finite and the infinite** le fini et l'infini

finiteness ['faɪnaɪtnɪs] *n* caractère *m* fini, finitude *f*

finitude ['fɪnɪtjuːd], **finity** ['fɪnɪtɪ] *n Phil* finitude *f*

fink [fɪŋk] *Am Fam* **1** *n* (**a**) *(strikebreaker)* jaune *mf* (**b**) *(informer)* mouchard(e) *m,f*; *(to police)* indic *m*, balance *f* (**c**) *(nasty man)* salaud *m*; *(nasty woman)* salope *f*

2 *vi* **to fink on sb** *(to police)* donner *ou* balancer qn; *(to teacher, parent)* moucharder qn

►**fink out** *vi Am Fam (withdraw → from undertaking)* laisser tomber[□], se dégonfler; *(→ from promise)* ne pas tenir parole[□]; **to fink out of doing sth** laisser tomber *ou* se dégonfler et ne pas faire qch

Finland ['fɪnlənd] *n* Finlande *f*; **in Finland** en Finlande

Finlander ['fɪnləndə(r)] *n* Finlandais(e) *m,f*

Finlandization [ˌfɪnləndaɪ'zeɪʃən] *n Pol* finlandisation *f*

Finn [fɪn] *n* (**a**) *(inhabitant of Finland)* Finlandais(e) *m,f* (**b**) *Hist* Finnois(e) *m,f*

finnan haddie ['fɪnən'hædɪ] *n Scot Culin* haddock *m*

finned [fɪnd] *adj Zool* à nageoires

►► *Tech* ***finned cylinder*** cylindre *m* à ailettes

Finnish ['fɪnɪʃ] **1** *n (language)* finnois *m*

2 *adj* (**a**) *(gen)* finlandais (**b**) *Hist* finnois

3 *comp (embassy)* de Finlande; *(history)* de la Finlande; *(teacher)* de finnois

finnock ['fɪnək] *n Ich* (jeune) truite *f* saumonée

Finno-Ugrian [ˌfɪnəʊ'uːgrɪən], **Finno-Ugric** [ˌfɪnəʊ'uːgrɪk] *n* finno-ugrien *m*

finocchio [fɪ'nɒkɪəʊ] *n Bot & Culin* fenouil *m* de Florence

fiord [fjɔːd] *n Geog* fjord *m*

fioritura [ˌfjɔːrɪ'tʊərə] *(pl* **fioriture** [-riː]) *n Mus* fioriture *f*

finale [illegible] *n Mus* [illegible]

fir [fɜː(r)] *n (tree, wood)* sapin *m*

►► *Br* ***fir cone*** pomme *f* de pin; ***fir tree*** sapin *m*

FIRE ['faɪə(r)]

incendie	► **1 (a)**
feu	► **1 (a) – (d)**
appareil de chauffage	► **1 (e)**
tirer	► **2 (a); 3 (a)**
décharger	► **2 (a)**
virer	► **2 (b)**
tourner	► **3 (b)**

1 *n* (**a**) *(destructive)* incendie *m*; **fire!** au feu!; **to catch fire** prendre feu; **to set fire to sth, to set sth on fire** mettre le feu à qch; **be careful or you'll set fire to yourself** fais attention ou tu vas mettre le feu à tes vêtements; **to cause** *or* **to start a fire** *(person, faulty wiring)* provoquer un incendie; **I'm always worried about fires** j'ai toujours peur d'un incendie; **that's how fires start** c'est comme ça qu'on met le feu; **all those empty boxes are a fire hazard** toutes ces boîtes vides constituent *ou* représentent un risque d'incendie; **smoking is forbidden since it is a fire hazard** il est interdit de fumer car cela pourrait provoquer un incendie; **on fire** en feu; **the building/village was set on fire** le bâtiment/village a été incendié; *Fig* **my throat's on fire** j'ai la gorge en feu; *Fig* **his forehead is/he's on fire** *(because of fever)* son front/il est brûlant; *Fam Hum* **where's the fire?** *(what's the rush?)* il n'y a pas le feu!; *Fig* **to play with fire** jouer avec le feu; *Fig* **to fight fire with fire** combattre le mal par le mal; *Fig* **he would go through fire and water for her** il se jetterait au feu pour elle; *Fam* **this novel is not going to set the world** *or Br* **the Thames on fire** ce roman ne casse pas des briques; *Fam* **he'll never set the world** *or Br* **the Thames on fire** il n'a jamais cassé trois pattes à un canard

(**b**) *(in hearth, campsite)* feu *m*; **to lay a fire** préparer un feu; **to light** *or* **to make a fire** allumer un feu, faire du feu; **to throw sth into** *or* **onto the fire** jeter qch au feu; **open fire** feu *m* de cheminée; **wood/coal fire** feu *m* de bois/de charbon

(**c**) *(element)* feu *m*; **before man discovered fire** avant que l'homme ait découvert le feu; **to be afraid of fire** avoir peur du feu

(**d**) *Mil* feu *m*; **open fire!** ouvrez le feu!; **to open/to cease fire** ouvrir/cesser le feu; **to open fire on sb** ouvrir le feu *ou* tirer sur qn; **to draw the enemy's fire** faire diversion en attirant le feu de l'ennemi; **to return (sb's) fire** riposter (au tir de qn); **hold your fire** *(don't shoot)* ne tirez pas; *(stop shooting)* cessez le feu; **to come under fire** essuyer le feu de l'ennemi; *Fig* être vivement critiqué *ou* attaqué; **under enemy fire** sous le feu de l'ennemi; **we are under fire** on nous tire dessus; *Fig* **between two fires** entre deux feux

(**e**) *Br (heater)* appareil *m* de chauffage; **to turn the fire on/off** allumer/éteindre le chauffage

(**f**) *(passion, ardour)* flamme *f*; **the fire of youth** la fougue de la jeunesse

(**g**) *(of diamond)* lumière *f*, éclat *m*

2 *vt* (**a**) *(shot, bullet)* tirer; *(gun, cannon, torpedo)* décharger; *(arrow)* décocher; **to fire a gun at sb** tirer un coup de fusil sur qn; **only three bullets had been fired from the gun** seulement trois balles avaient été tirées avec le pistolet; **without a shot being fired** sans un seul coup de feu; **to fire a twenty-one-gun salute** tirer vingt et un coups de canon; *Fig* **to fire questions at sb** bombarder qn de questions

(**b**) *Fam (dismiss)* virer; **you're fired!** vous êtes viré!

(**c**) *(inspire → person, an audience, supporters, the imagination)* enflammer; **to fire sb with enthusiasm/desire** remplir qn d'enthousiasme/de désir

(**d**) *Cer* cuire

(**e**) *Tech (boiler, furnace)* chauffer, charger; *(fuel mix in engine)* enflammer

(**f**) *Vet* cautériser

(**g**) *Formal or Literary (set fire to)* mettre le feu à

3 *vi* (**a**) *(shoot → person)* tirer, faire feu; **the rifle failed to fire** le coup n'est pas parti; *Mil* **fire!** feu!; *Mil* **fire at will!** feu à volonté!; **to fire at** *or* **on sb** tirer sur qn; **we were fired on** nous avons reçu des coups de feu, on nous a tiré dessus

(**b**) *(engine)* tourner; *(spark plug)* s'allumer; *(pin on print head)* se déclencher; **the engine is only firing on two cylinders** le moteur ne tourne que sur deux cylindres; **to fire on all cylinders** *(engine)* tourner rond; *Fig (person)* être au mieux de sa forme; *(company)* fonctionner à plein régime

►► ***fire alarm*** alarme *f* d'incendie; *Br* ***fire appliance*** camion *m* de pompiers; ***fire blanket*** couverture *f* pare-flamme; *Br* ***fire brigade*** brigade *f* des pompiers *ou* sapeurs-pompiers, *Suisse* service *m* du feu; **have you called the fire brigade?** as-tu appelé les pompiers?; *Comput* ***fire button*** *(on joystick)* bouton *m* feu; ***fire chief*** capitaine *m* des pompiers *ou* sapeurs-pompiers; ***fire clay*** argile *f* réfractaire; *Theat* ***fire curtain*** rideau *m* de fer; ***fire damage*** dégâts *mpl* causés par le feu; *Am* ***fire department*** brigade *f* des pompiers *ou* sapeurs-pompiers, *Suisse* service *m* du feu; ***fire door*** porte *f* coupe-feu; ***fire drill*** exercice *m* de sécurité *(en cas d'incendie)*; ***fire engine*** voiture *f* de pompiers; ***fire escape*** escalier *m* de secours *ou* d'incendie; ***fire exit*** sortie *f* de secours; ***fire extinguisher*** extincteur *m*; ***fire fighter*** pompier *m*, sapeur-pompier *m* (volontaire), *Suisse* homme *m* du feu; ***fire hose*** tuyau *m* de pompe à incendie; *Br* ***fire hydrant*** bouche *f* d'incendie, *Suisse* hydrant *m*; ***fire insurance*** *(UNCOUNT)* assurance-incendie *f*; ***fire irons*** accessoires *mpl* de cheminée; *Am* ***fire marshal*** capitaine *m* des pompiers *ou* sapeurs-pompiers; ***fire notice*** *(in hotel etc)* consignes *fpl* en cas d'incendie; *Am* ***fire plug*** *(fire hydrant)* bouche *f* d'incendie, *Suisse* hydrant *m*; *Fam (person)* = personne petite et grosse; ***fire practice*** exercice *m* d'incendie; ***fire prevention*** mesures *fpl* de sécurité contre l'incendie; ***fire prevention officer*** = personne chargée des mesures de sécurité contre l'incendie; ***fire regulations*** consignes *fpl* en cas d'incendie; ***fire safety*** sécurité *f* incendie; ***fire sale*** = vente au rabais de marchandises ayant subi de légers dégâts à la suite d'un incendie; ***fire screen*** écran *m* de cheminée; ***fire service*** brigade *f* des pompiers *ou* sapeurs-pompiers; *Astrol* ***fire sign*** signe *m* de feu; ***fire station*** caserne *f* de pompiers; ***fire tender*** voiture *f* de pompiers; *Am* ***fire truck*** voiture *f* de pompiers; ***fire walker*** = personne en transe qui marche sur des braises; ***fire walking*** = rituel consistant à marcher sur des braises; ***fire warden*** *(in forest)* guetteur *m* d'incendie; ***fire worship*** culte *m* du feu

▸**fire away** *vi Fam (go ahead)* **fire away!** allez-y! ❑

▸**fire off** *vt sep (round of ammunition)* tirer; *Fig (facts, figures)* balancer; **to fire off questions at sb** bombarder qn de questions; **she fired off a letter of complaint** elle a envoyé une lettre de réclamation sur-le-champ

---

fire-and-brimstone *adj (preacher, sermon)* menaçant des feux de l'enfer

firearm ['faɪərɑːm] *n* arme *f* à feu

▸▸ ***firearms expert*** expert(e) *m,f* en armes à feu; *Law* ***firearms offence*** délit *m* lié à la détention d'armes à feu; ***firearms training*** entraînement *m* à l'utilisation des armes à feu

fireback ['faɪəbæk] *n* **(a)** *(in hearth)* plaque *f* de cheminée, contre-feu *m* **(b)** *Orn* houppifère *m* ignicolore; **fireback (pheasant)** lophophore *m*, faisan *m* pyronote

fireball ['faɪəbɔːl] *n* **(a)** *Met* éclair *m* en boule **(b)** *Astron* bolide *m* **(c)** *Fig* **she's a real fireball** elle déborde d'énergie

firebird ['faɪəbɜːd] *n Orn* loriot *m* d'Amérique

fireboat ['faɪəbəʊt] *n* bateau-pompe *m*

firebomb ['faɪəbɒm] **1** *n* bombe *f* incendiaire

2 *vt (building)* attaquer à la bombe incendiaire

firebox ['faɪəbɒks] *n Rail* foyer *m*

firebrand ['faɪəbrænd] *n* **(a)** *(burning wood)* tison *m*, brandon *m* **(b)** *Fig (agitator)* brandon *m* de discorde

firebreak ['faɪəbreɪk] *n (in forest)* coupe-feu *m inv*

firebrick ['faɪəbrɪk] *n* brique *f* réfractaire

firebug ['faɪəbʌg] *n Fam* incendiaire ❑ *mf*, pyromane ❑ *mf*

firecracker ['faɪəkrækə(r)] *n* pétard *m*

firecrest ['faɪəkrest] *n Orn* roitelet *m* à triple bandeau

-fired ['faɪəd] *suff* chauffé à; **oil-fired/gas-fired central heating** chauffage central au mazout/gaz

fire-damaged *adj* endommagé par le feu

firedamp ['faɪədæmp] *n Mining* grisou *m*

▸▸ ***firedamp explosion*** coup *m* de grisou

firedog ['faɪədɒg] *n* chenet *m*

fire-eater *n (in circus)* cracheur(euse) *m,f* de feu; *Fig* personne *f* belliqueuse, bagarreur(euse) *m,f*

fire-eating *adj* pyrophage

fire-fighting **1** *n* lutte *f* contre les incendies

2 *comp (equipment, techniques)* de lutte contre les incendies

firefly ['faɪəflaɪ] *(pl* **fireflies***) n Zool* luciole *f*

fireguard ['faɪəgɑːd] *n (for open fire)* pare-feu *m inv*, garde-feu *m*

firehouse ['faɪəhaʊs, *pl* -haʊzɪz] *n Am* poste *m* d'incendie; *(with living quarters)* caserne *f* de (sapeurs-)pompiers

firelight ['faɪəlaɪt] *n* lueur *f ou* lumière *f* du feu; **in the firelight** à la lueur *ou* lumière du feu

firelighter ['faɪəlaɪtə(r)] *n* allume-feu *m*

fireman ['faɪəmən] *(pl* **firemen** [-mən]*) n* **(a)** *(firefighter)* pompier *m*, sapeur-pompier *m*, *Suisse* homme *m* du feu; **to give sb a fireman's lift** porter qn sur son épaule, la tête en bas **(b)** *Rail (of steam engine)* chauffeur *m* de locomotive

fireplace ['faɪəpleɪs] *n* cheminée *f*

firepower ['faɪəˌpaʊə(r)] *n* puissance *f* de feu

fireproof ['faɪəpruːf] **1** *adj (door, safe)* à l'épreuve du feu; *(clothing, toys)* ininflammable; *(dish)* allant au feu

2 *vt* ignifuger, rendre ininflammable

fireproofing ['faɪəpruːfɪŋ] *adj (spray, material)* ignifuge, ignifugeant

fire-raiser *n Br* pyromane *mf*, incendiaire *mf*

fire-raising [-'reɪzɪŋ] *n* pyromanie *f*

fire-retardant *adj* ignifuge

fireside ['faɪəsaɪd] *n* coin *m* du feu; **sitting by the fireside** assis au coin du feu

▸▸ ***fireside chair*** fauteuil *m*; ***fireside chat*** *(by politician)* causerie *f* au coin du feu

firestone ['faɪəstəʊn] *n Geol* pierre *f* réfractaire

firestorm ['faɪəstɔːm] *n* tempête *f* de feu

firetrap ['faɪətræp] *n* **this building's a real firetrap** ce bâtiment est un véritable piège (en cas d'incendie)

firewall ['faɪəwɔːl] *n* **(a)** *Tech* cloison *f* pare-feu **(b)** *Comput* mur *m* coupe-feu, garde-barrière *f*

firewatch ['faɪəwɒtʃ] *vi Br* guetter les incendies

firewatcher ['faɪəˌwɒtʃə(r)] *n Br* guetteur(euse) *m,f* d'incendies

firewatching ['faɪəˌwɒtʃɪŋ] *n Br* surveillance *f* contre les incendies

firewater ['faɪəˌwɔːtə(r)] *n Fam* gnôle *f*

firewood ['faɪəwʊd] *n* bois *m* à brûler; *(for use in home)* bois *m* de chauffage; **to chop sth up for firewood** couper qch en morceaux pour en faire du bois de chauffage

firework ['faɪəwɜːk] *n* pièce *f* d'artifice; **fireworks** *(display)* feu *m* d'artifice; *Fam Fig* **there were fireworks at the meeting** il y a eu des étincelles à la réunion

▸▸ ***firework display, fireworks display*** feu *m* d'artifice

firing ['faɪərɪŋ] *n* **(a)** *(UNCOUNT) Mil* tir *m*; **firing has been heavy** de nombreux coups de feu ont été tirés; **burst of firing** fusillade *f*

(b) *Fam (dismissal)* renvoi ❑ *m*

(c) *Aut (of engine, sparkplug)* allumage *m*

(d) *(in kiln)* cuite *f*, cuisson *f*; **they'll be given a second firing** elles seront cuites une deuxième fois

(e) *Tech (of boiler furnace)* chauffage *m*, chargement *m*

(f) *Vet* cautérisation *f*

▸▸ *Mil* ***firing line*** ligne *f* de tir; *Fig* **to be in the firing line** être dans la ligne de tir; *Aut* ***firing order*** *(of engine)* ordre *m* d'allumage; ***firing pin*** percuteur *m*; ***firing position*** *(of weapon)* position *f* de tir; *(of person)* position *f* du tireur; ***firing practice*** exercice *m* de tir; ***firing range*** champ *m* de tir; **within firing range** à portée de fusil; *Aut* ***firing sequence*** *(of engine)* ordre *m* d'allumage; ***firing squad*** peloton *m* d'exécution; **to be executed by firing squad** passer devant le peloton d'exécution

firkin ['fɜːkɪn] *n* **(a)** *(barrel)* tonnelet *m*, barillet *m* **(b)** *(unit of capacity)* = mesure de capacité de 8 à 9 gallons, ≃ quartaut *m*

firm[1] [fɜːm] *n (company)* entreprise *f*; *(of solicitors)* étude *f*; *(of lawyers, barristers, consultants)* cabinet *m*; **it's a good firm to work for** cette entreprise est un bon employeur

firm[2] **1** *adj* **(a)** *(solid, hard* → *flesh, fruit, mattress etc)* ferme; **on firm ground** sur la terre ferme; *Fig* sur un terrain solide; **I'm on firmer ground when it comes to the marketing side** je suis plus à mon affaire pour ce qui touche au marketing

(b) *(stable, secure* → *basis)* solide; *(*→ *foundations)* stable; *Com & Fin (*→ *currency, market)* stable; *(*→ *offer, sale, deal)* ferme; *(*→ *contango rates)* tendu; **these shares remain firm at 370p** ces actions se maintiennent à 370 pence; **the dollar remained firm against the yen** le dollar est resté fort contre le yen

(c) *(strong* → *handshake, grip, leadership)* ferme; **to have a firm hold** *or* **grasp** *or* **grip of sth** tenir qch fermement

(d) *(unshakeable, definite* → *belief, evidence, friendship)* solide; *(*→ *view, opinion)* déterminé, arrêté; *(*→ *intention, voice, agreement, offer)* ferme; *(*→ *date)* définitif; **they are firm friends** ce sont de bons amis; **he was very firm about this** il a été très ferme à ce propos; **she gave a firm denial** elle a nié fermement; **a firm favourite for the Derby/with the crowd** un grand favori dans le Derby/auprès de la foule; **I am a firm believer in female equality** je crois fermement à l'égalité de la femme; **to be firm with a child/dog** être ferme avec un enfant/chien; **he was polite but firm** il a été poli mais ferme

2 *adv* **to stand firm on sth** ne pas céder sur qch; **he stands firm on this issue** il a une position bien arrêtée sur le sujet

3 *vt* **to firm the soil** tasser le sol

4 *vi (muscles, prices)* se raffermir

▸**firm up** **1** *vt sep (make firm* → *muscles, prices)* raffermir; **to firm up an agreement** régler les derniers détails d'un accord

2 *vi (muscles, prices)* se raffermir

firmament ['fɜːməmənt] *n Arch or Literary (sky)* firmament *m*

firmer ['fɜːmə(r)] *n*

▸▸ *Constr* ***firmer chisel*** ciseau *m* à biseau; ***firmer gouge*** ciseau *m* à gouge

firmly ['fɜːmlɪ] *adv* **(a)** *(securely* → *hold, grasp sth)* fermement; *(*→ *closed, secured)* bien; *Fig* **to keep one's feet firmly on the ground** bien garder les pieds sur terre, rester fermement ancré dans la réalité **(b)** *(say, deny, refuse, deal with)* fermement, avec fermeté; **I firmly believe that...** j'ai la ferme conviction que...

firmness ['fɜːmnɪs] *n* **(a)** *(hardness* → *of flesh, fruit, mattress)* fermeté *f* **(b)** *(stability* → *of basis)* solidité *f*; *(*→ *of foundations)* stabilité *f*; *Com & Fin (*→ *of currency, market, prices)* stabilité *f* **(c)** *(strength* → *of handshake, grip, leadership, character, belief)* fermeté *f* **(d)** *(of voice, denial, refusal)* fermeté *f*

firmware ['fɜːmweə(r)] *n Comput* firmware *m*, microprogamme *m*

FIRST [fɜːst]

premier	▸ **1 (a), (c)**
tout de suite	▸ **1 (b)**
le premier	▸ **2 (a); 3**
d'abord	▸ **2 (b)**
pour la première fois	▸ **2 (c)**
première	▸ **3 (b), (f)**

1 *adj* **(a)** *(in series)* premier; **the first few days** les deux ou trois premiers jours; **the first six months** les six premiers mois; **Louis the First** Louis Premier *ou* I; **one hundred and first** cent unième; **to be first in the queue** être le (la) premier(ère) de la queue; **I'm first** je suis *ou* c'est moi le premier; **she was first in English Literature** elle était première en littérature anglaise; **she's in first place** *(in race)* elle est en tête; **to win first prize** gagner le premier prix; **this is the first time I've been to New York** c'est la première fois que je viens à New York; **first floor** *Br* premier étage *m*; *Am* rez-de-chaussée *m*; *Aut* **first gear** première *f* (vitesse *f*); **put the car into first gear** passe la première (vitesse); *Br* **first year** *Univ* première année *f*; *Sch* sixième *f*; *Br* **a first-year university student** un étudiant de première année à l'université; **I learnt of it at first hand** je l'ai appris de la bouche de l'intéressé/l'intéressée, c'est lui-même/elle-même qui me l'a appris; **I learned of her resignation at first hand** c'est elle-même qui m'a appris sa démission; **I haven't (got) the first idea** je n'en ai pas la moindre idée; **I don't know the first thing about cars** je n'y connais absolument rien en voitures; **I'll pick you up first thing (in the morning)** je passerai te chercher demain matin à la première heure; **I'm not at my best first thing in the morning** je ne suis pas au mieux de ma forme très tôt le matin; **there's a first time for everything** il y a un début à tout; **to be the first person to do sth** être le (la) premier(ère) à faire qch

(b) *(immediately)* tout de suite; **first thing after lunch** tout de suite après le déjeuner; *Literary*

she's past her first youth elle n'est plus de la première jeunesse

(**c**) *(most important → duty, concern)* premier; **the first priority** la priorité des priorités; **to put first things first** commencer par le commencement; **first things first!** prenons les choses dans l'ordre!; **to go back to first principles** repartir sur des bases saines

2 *adv* (**a**) *(before the others → arrive, leave, speak)* le (la) premier(ère), en premier; **I saw it first!** c'est moi qui l'ai vu le (la) premier(ère) *ou* en premier!; **you go first** vas-y en premier; **ladies first** les dames d'abord; **women and children first** les femmes et les enfants d'abord; *Comput & Ind* **first in, first out** premier entré, premier sorti; *Admin* **last in, first out** dernier entré, premier sorti; **to come first** *(in race)* arriver premier; *(in exam)* avoir la première place, être premier; **her career comes first** sa carrière passe d'abord *ou* avant tout; **I've never come first with you, have I?** tu ne m'as jamais fait passer avant le reste, n'est-ce pas?; **to put one's family first** faire passer sa famille d'abord *ou* avant tout; *Prov* **first come first served** les premiers arrivés sont les premiers servis; **tickets were handed out on a first come first served basis** les billets ont été distribués par ordre d'arrivée

(**b**) *(firstly, before anything else)* d'abord; **first, I want to say thank you** tout d'abord, je voudrais vous remercier, je voudrais d'abord vous remercier; **first prepare the meat** préparez d'abord la viande; **I need to go to the lavatory first** il faut d'abord que j'aille aux toilettes; **what should I do first?** qu'est-ce que je dois faire en premier?; **first hear the arguments, then make up your mind** écoutez d'abord les arguments, ensuite vous vous déciderez; **she says first one thing then another** elle dit d'abord une chose, et puis une autre; **I'm a mother first and a wife second** je suis une mère avant d'être une épouse

(**c**) *(for the first time)* pour la première fois; *(initially)* au début; **we first met in London** nous nous sommes rencontrés à Londres; **when I first knew him** quand je l'ai connu

(**d**) *(sooner, rather)* **I'd die first** plutôt mourir; *Fam* **I'll see him damned first** *or* **in hell first** j'aimerais bien voir ça

3 *n* (**a**) *(before all others)* **the first** le (la) premier(ère); **he was among the first to realise** il a été parmi les premiers à s'en rendre compte; **we were the very first to arrive** nous sommes arrivés les tout premiers; **she was the first in our family to go to university** c'était la première de la famille à aller à l'université; **he came in an easy first** *(in race)* il est arrivé premier haut la main

(**b**) *(achievement)* première *f*; **that's a notable first for France** c'est une grande première pour la France

(**c**) *(first time)* **the first we heard/knew of it was when...** nous en avons entendu parler pour la première fois/l'avons appris quand...; **it's the first I've heard of it!** première nouvelle!

(**d**) *(in dates)* **the first of May/the month** le premier mai/du mois

(**e**) *Br Univ* **he got a first in economics** ≃ il a eu mention très bien en économie; **she got a double first in French and Russian** ≃ elle a eu mention très bien en français et en russe

(**f**) *Aut* première *f*; **in first** en première; **to put the car into first** se mettre en première, passer la première

(**g**) *Banking & Fin* **first of exchange** première *f* de change

4 at first *adv* au début

5 first and foremost *adv* d'abord et surtout

6 first and last *adv* avant tout

7 first of all *adv* tout d'abord, pour commencer

8 first off *adv Fam* pour commencer ❑

9 from first to last *adv* du début à la fin

10 from the (very) first *adv* dès le début

11 in the first instance *adv* d'abord; **apply in the first instance to the personnel department** adressez d'abord votre demande au service du personnel

12 in the first place *adv* (**a**) *(referring to a past action)* d'abord; **why did you do it in the first place?** et puis d'abord, pourquoi as-tu fait cela?; **I don't understand why he married her in the first place** d'abord, je ne comprends pas ce qui a bien pu le pousser à se marier avec elle

(**b**) *(introducing an argument)* d'abord; **in the first place... and in the second place** d'abord... et ensuite

►► ***first aid*** **1** *n (UNCOUNT) (technique)* secourisme *m*; *(attention)* premiers soins *mpl*; **does anyone know any first aid?** quelqu'un s'y connaît-il en secourisme?; **to give/to receive first aid** donner/recevoir les premiers soins **2** *comp (class, manual)* de secourisme; ***first aid box*** trousse *f* à pharmacie; ***first aid certificate*** brevet *m* de secourisme; ***first aid kit*** trousse *f* à pharmacie; *Br* ***first aid post, first aid station*** poste *m* de secours; *Am* ***the First Amendment*** le premier amendement *(de la Constitution des États-Unis garantissant les libertés individuelles du citoyen américain, notamment la liberté d'expression)*; ***first class*** *(on train, plane)* première classe *f*; *(for letter, parcel)* tarif *m* normal; ***first cousin*** cousin(e) *m,f* germain(e); *Br* ***first eleven*** *(in soccer, cricket)* = les onze meilleurs joueurs sélectionnés pour former l'équipe la plus forte dans un club; *Am* ***the First Family*** *(presidential family)* la famille présidentielle; *(in a State)* la famille du gouverneur; *Br Sch* ***first form*** sixième *f*; *also Fig* ***first fruits*** premiers fruits *mpl*; *Am Sch* ***first grade*** = classe de l'école primaire (5 à 6 ans); *Sport* ***first half*** première mi-temps *f*; ***First Lady*** *(in US)* = femme du président des États-Unis; *Fig* **the first lady of rock/of the detective novel** la grande dame du rock/du roman policier; ***first language*** langue *f* maternelle; ***first lieutenant*** *Naut* lieutenant *m* de vaisseau; *Am Mil & Aviat* lieutenant *m*; ***first love*** premier amour *m*; *Naut* ***first mate*** second *m*; *Pol* ***First Minister*** *(of Scottish Parliament)* Premier ministre *m*; ***first name*** prénom *m*; **to be on first name terms with sb** appeler qn par son prénom; *Theat* ***first night*** première *f*; *Law* ***first offender*** délinquant(e) *m,f* primaire; *Naut* ***first officer*** second *m*; *Theat* ***first performance*** première *f*; *Gram* ***first person*** première personne *f*; **in the first person** à la première personne; ***first principle*** principe *m* fondamental *ou* de base; *Fin* ***first quarter*** *(of financial year)* premier trimestre *m*; ***first refusal*** préférence *f*; **to give sb first refusal on sth** donner la préférence à qn pour qch; **I promised Nadine first refusal** j'ai promis à Nadine que je lui donnerais la préférence; *Cin* ***first showing*** première exclusivité *f*; *Am* ***the First State*** = surnom donné au Delaware; *Sport* ***first string*** les meilleurs joueurs *mpl (d'une équipe)*; *Sport* ***first team*** (équipe *f*) première *f*; *Mus* ***first violin*** *(person, instrument)* premier violon *m*; ***the First World*** les pays *mpl* industrialisés; ***the First World War*** la Première Guerre mondiale

---

first-aider [-'eɪdə(r)] *n* secouriste *mf*

first-born 1 *adj* premier-né

2 *n* premier-né (première-née) *m,f*

first-class 1 *adj* (**a**) *(seat)* en première classe; *(compartment, ticket)* de première classe

(**b**) *(letter, stamp)* au tarif normal; **to send a letter by first-class mail** envoyer une lettre au tarif normal

(**c**) *Br Univ* **she got a first-class honours degree (in French)** elle a eu mention très bien (en français); **to graduate with first-class honours** obtenir son diplôme avec mention très bien

(**d**) *(excellent → wine, meal, restaurant)* de première qualité, excellent; *(→ idea, performance, student)* excellent; *Br* **that was a first-class performance from the Scottish team** ce fut une excellente performance de l'équipe d'Écosse

2 *adv (travel)* en première classe; *(send letter)* au tarif normal

►► *Fin* ***first-class paper*** effet *m* de première catégorie

first-day cover *n (for stamp collector)* émission *f* premier jour

first-degree *adj Med (burn)* au premier degré; *Am Law* ***first-degree murder*** meurtre *m* avec préméditation

first-ever *n Fam* tout(e) premier(ère) ❑ *m,f*

first-foot *Scot* **1** *n* = premier visiteur venant souhaiter la bonne année, la nuit de la Saint-Sylvestre

2 *vt* **to first-foot sb** = être le premier à rendre visite à qn pour lui souhaiter la bonne année la nuit de la Saint-Sylvestre

first-footer *n Scot* = premier visiteur venant souhaiter la bonne année, la nuit de la Saint-Sylvestre

first-footing *n Scot* = tradition écossaise consistant à aller rendre visite à des amis ou à de la famille pour leur souhaiter la bonne année, le plus souvent immédiatement après minuit, la nuit de la Saint-Sylvestre

first-former *n Br Sch* élève *mf* de sixième

first-generation *adj* de première génération

firsthand [fɜːst'hænd] **1** *adj (knowledge, information, news)* de première main; **I know from firsthand experience what it is like to be poor** je sais d'expérience ce que c'est que d'être pauvre

2 *adv (hear of something)* de première main

first-in first-out *adj Comput & Ind* premier entré, premier sorti

firstly ['fɜːstlɪ] *adv* premièrement, en premier lieu

first-night *adj* **first-night nerves** trac *m (du soir de la première)*

first-nighter [-'naɪtə(r)] *n Theat* spectateur (trice) *m,f* assistant *ou* ayant assisté à la première

first-notice day *n St Exch* premier jour *m* de notification

first-off *n Mktg* produit *m* vedette

first-past-the-post *adj Br Pol (system)* majoritaire à un tour; **the first-past-the-post electoral system** le scrutin majoritaire à un tour

first-person *adj Gram (pronoun)* de la première personne; **a first-person narrative** un récit à la première personne

first-rate *adj (excellent → wine, meal, restaurant)* de première qualité, excellent; *(→ idea, performance, student)* excellent; **of first-rate quality** d'excellente *ou* de première qualité; **he's a first-rate badminton/chess player** il est excellent au badminton/aux échecs; *Br* **that's absolutely first-rate!** *(idea, news etc)* c'est formidable!

first-strike *adj Mil (missile)* de première frappe; **a first-strike capability** une force de frappe importante *(permettant d'attaquer en premier)*

first-string player *n Sport (regular)* joueur(euse) *m,f* régulier(ère) *(d'une équipe)*; *(best)* meilleur(e) joueur(euse) *m,f (d'une équipe)*

first-time *adj* **first-time visitors to the country** les personnes visitant le pays pour la première fois

►► ***first-time buyer*** *(of property)* = personne devenant propriétaire pour la première fois

firth [fɜːθ] *n Scot* estuaire *m*

FIS [ˌefaɪ'es] *n Br (abbr* **Family Income Supplement**) ≃ complément *m* familial

fiscal ['fɪskəl] **1** *adj* fiscal

2 *n Scot Law* **(procurator) fiscal** ≃ procureur *m* de la République

►► *Fin* ***fiscal agent*** représentant(e) *m,f* fiscal(e); *Econ* ***fiscal drag*** frein *m* fiscal, érosion *f* fiscale; *Fin* ***fiscal measure*** mesure *f* fiscale; *Am Acct* ***fiscal period*** période *f* comptable; *Fin* ***fiscal policy*** politique *f* budgétaire; *Am* ***fiscal year*** *Fin* exercice *m* (financier), année *f* fiscale *ou* d'exercice; *Admin* année *f* budgétaire

FISCAL YEAR

En Grande-Bretagne, l'année fiscale commence le 1er avril pour les entreprises et le 6 avril pour les particuliers. Aux États-Unis, l'année fiscale correspond à l'année civile pour les particuliers.

fish [fɪʃ] *(pl* **inv** *or* **fishes**) **1** *n* (**a**) *(aquatic creature)* poisson *m*; *Astrol* **the Fish** les Poissons *mpl*; **to catch a fish** pêcher un poisson; **he caught three fish** il a attrapé *ou* pris trois poissons; **I eat a lot of fish** je mange beaucoup de poisson; **fish and chips** poisson *m* frit avec des frites

(**b**) *(idioms) Fam* **he's a queer fish** c'est un drôle de type; **to feel like a fish out of water** ne pas se sentir dans son élément; *Fam* **to drink**

fir–fis

like a fish boire comme un trou; **there are plenty more fish in the sea** un de perdu, dix de retrouvés; **to have other fish to fry** avoir d'autres chats à fouetter; **to be a big fish in a small pond** être grand parmi les petits; **to be a little fish in a big pond** être perdu dans la masse; **neither fish nor fowl (nor good red herring)** ni chair ni poisson

2 *comp (course, restaurant)* de poisson

3 *vi* (**a**) *Sport* pêcher; **to fish with a line/a rod** pêcher à la ligne/avec une canne; **to go fishing** aller à la pêche; **to go trout fishing** *or* **fishing for trout** aller à la pêche à la truite, aller pêcher la truite; *Fig* **to fish in troubled waters** pêcher en eau trouble; *Am Fam Fig* **to fish or cut bait** se décider ❑

(**b**) *(search, seek)* **he fished around for his pen under the papers** il a fouillé sous ses papiers pour trouver son crayon; **to fish for information** essayer de soutirer des informations; **to fish for compliments** rechercher les compliments

4 *vt (river, lake etc)* pêcher dans

►► *Am Orn* ***fish eagle*** balbuzard *m*, *Can* aigle *m* pêcheur; ***fish farm*** établissement *m* piscicole; ***fish farmer*** pisciculteur(trice) *m,f*; ***fish farming*** pisciculture *f*; *Br* ***fish finger*** bâtonnet *m* de poisson pané; ***fish glue*** colle *f* de poisson; *Orn* ***fish hawk*** balbuzard *m*, *Can* aigle *m* pêcheur; ***fish hook*** hameçon *m*; ***fish kettle*** poissonnière *f*; ***fish knife*** couteau *m* à poisson; ***fish ladder*** échelle *f* à poissons; ***fish market*** marché *m* au poisson; ***fish meal*** farine *f* de poisson; *Orn* ***fish owl*** hibou *m* pêcheur; ***fish paste*** pâte *f* de poisson; ***fish shop*** poissonnerie *f*; ***fish slice*** pelle *f* à poisson; *Am* ***fish stick*** bâtonnet *m* de poisson pané; *Scot* ***fish supper*** poisson *m* frit avec des frites *(à emporter)*; ***fish tank*** *(in house)* aquarium *m*; *(on fish farm)* vivier *m*

►**fish out** *vt sep (from water)* repêcher; *Fig* **he fished out his wallet** il a sorti son portefeuille; *(with difficulty)* il a extrait son portefeuille; **she fished her keys out of her bag** elle a fouillé dans son sac et en a extrait ses clés

►**fish up** *vt sep (from water)* repêcher; **to fish up sth from one's memory** ressortir qch de sa mémoire; *Fam* **where did you fish that up from?** *(object)* où est-ce que tu as été dénicher ça?; *(idea)* où est-ce que tu as été pêcher ça?

fishable ['fɪʃəbəl] *adj (stream, river)* pêchable

fish-and-chip shop *n Br* = boutique où l'on vend des frites ainsi que du poisson frit, des saucisses etc

fish-bellied *adj*

►► *Tech* ***fish-bellied girder*** poutre *f* (en) ventre de poisson

fishbone ['fɪʃbəʊn] *n* arête *f* de poisson

fishbowl ['fɪʃbəʊl] *n* bocal *m* à poissons

fishcake ['fɪʃkeɪk] *n Culin* croquette *f* de poisson

fish-eating *adj* ichtyophage

fisher ['fɪʃə(r)] *n* (**a**) *Arch (fisherman)* pêcheur *m*; *Bible* **fishers of men** pêcheurs *mpl* d'hommes (**b**) *(bird, animal)* pêcheur *m*

fisherman ['fɪʃəmən] *(pl* **fishermen** [-mən]*)* *n* pêcheur *m*

►► ***fisherman's bend*** *(knot)* nœud *m* de grappin

fishery ['fɪʃərɪ] *(pl* **fisheries***)* *n (fishing ground)* pêcherie *f*; *(fishing industry)* industrie *f* de la pêche

►► ***fishery protection vessel*** vedette *f* garde-pêche

fish-eye lens *n Phot* fish-eye *m*

fishily ['fɪʃɪlɪ] *adv Fam* d'une manière louche ❑

fishiness ['fɪʃɪnɪs] *n* (**a**) *(taste)* goût *m* de poisson; *(smell)* odeur *f* de poisson (**b**) *(suspiciousness)* caractère *m* louche ❑

fishing ['fɪʃɪŋ] **1** *n* pêche *f*; **trout/salmon fishing** pêche *f* à la truite/au saumon; **there is some good fishing to be had along this river** il y a de bons coins de pêche dans cette rivière; **we can do some fishing** nous pourrons aller à la pêche; **no fishing** *(sign)* pêche interdite

2 *comp (vessel, permit, port)* de pêche; *(season)* de la pêche; *(village, party)* de pêcheurs

►► ***fishing boat*** bateau *m* de pêche; *Ich* ***fishing frog*** baudroie *f*, lotte *f* de mer; ***fishing ground*** zone *f* de pêche; ***fishing line*** ligne *f* de pêche; ***fishing net*** filet *m* de pêche; ***fishing rod*** canne *f* à pêche, gaule *f*; ***fishing tackle*** articles *mpl* de pêche

fishmonger ['fɪʃˌmʌŋgə(r)] *n Br* poissonnier(ère) *m,f*; **fishmonger's** *(shop)* poissonnerie *f*; **to go to the fishmonger's** aller à la poissonnerie *ou* chez le poissonnier

fishnet ['fɪʃnet] *n Am (for catching fish)* filet *m* (de pêche)

►► ***fishnet stockings*** bas *mpl* résille; ***fishnet tights*** collant *m* résille

fishplate ['fɪʃpleɪt] *n Rail* éclisse *f*

fishpole mike ['fɪʃpəʊl-] *n TV & Cin* micro *m* sur perche

fishpond ['fɪʃpɒnd] *n* étang *m* (à poissons)

fishskin disease ['fɪʃskɪn-] *n Med* ichtyose *f*

fishtail ['fɪʃteɪl] **1** *n* queue *f* de poisson; **fishtail gas burner** bec *m* en queue de poisson

2 *vi Aut* chasser

fishway ['fɪʃweɪ] *n Am* échelle *f* à poissons

fishwife ['fɪʃwaɪf] *(pl* **fishwives** [-waɪvz]*)* *n* poissonnière *f*, marchande *f* de poisson; *Fig* **she's a real fishwife** elle a un langage de charretier, elle parle comme un charretier

fishy ['fɪʃɪ] *(compar* **fishier**, *superl* **fishiest***)* *adj* (**a**) *(smell, taste)* de poisson (**b**) *Fam (suspicious)* louche ❑; **there's something fishy going on** il se passe quelque chose de louche; **there's something fishy about her alibi** il y a quelque chose qui ne colle pas dans son alibi

fissile ['fɪsaɪl] *adj Phys* fissible, fissile

fissilingual [ˌfɪsɪ'lɪŋgwəl] *adj Zool* fissilingue

fissility [fɪ'sɪlɪtɪ] *n Phys* fissilité *f*

fission ['fɪʃən] *n Phys* fission *f*; *Biol* scissiparité *f*; **nuclear fission** fission *f* nucléaire

►► ***fission bomb*** bombe *f* atomique; *Nucl* ***fission reactor*** pile *f* atomique

fissionable ['fɪʃənəbəl] *adj Phys* fissible

fissiped ['fɪsɪped], **fissipedal** [fɪ'sɪpɪdəl], **fissipedate** [fɪ'sɪpɪdeɪt] *adj Zool* fissipède

fissirostral [ˌfɪsɪ'rɒstrəl] *adj Zool* fissirostre

fissure ['fɪʃə(r)] *Geol* **1** *n (crevice, crack)* fissure *f*; *Fig* fissure *f*, brèche *f*

2 *vt* fissurer, fendre

3 *vi* se fissurer, se fendre

fissured ['fɪʃəd] *adj* fissuré

fist [fɪst] *n* poing *m*; **to clench one's fists** serrer les poings; **he shook his fist at me** il m'a menacé du poing; **to put one's fists up** se mettre en garde; **make a fist** serrez le poing

fistfight ['fɪstfaɪt] *n* bagarre *f* aux poings; **to have a fistfight with sb** se battre aux poings contre qn

fistful ['fɪstfʊl] *n* poignée *f*

'A Fistful of Dollars' *Leone* 'Pour une poignée de dollars'

fisticuffs ['fɪstɪkʌfs] *n (UNCOUNT) Hum* bagarre *f*

fistula ['fɪstjʊlə] *n Med* fistule *f*

FIT [fɪt]

convenable	► 1 (a)
en forme	► 1 (c)
crise	► 2 (b)
accès	► 2 (c)
aller à	► 3 (a)
correspondre à	► 3 (b)
installer	► 3 (d)
fixer	► 3 (e)
équiper	► 3 (f)
correspondre	► 4 (b)

(compar **fitter**, *superl* **fittest**, *Br pt & pp* **fitted**, *cont* **fitting**, *Am pt & pp* **fit**, *cont* **fitting***)* **1** *adj* (**a**) *(suitable)* convenable; **that dress isn't fit to wear** cette robe n'est pas mettable; **a country fit for heroes to live in** un pays digne d'accueillir ses héros; **fit to eat** *(edible)* mangeable; *(not poisonous)* comestible; **fit to drink** *(water)* potable; **this coffee is not fit to drink** ce café est imbuvable; **a meal fit for a king** un repas digne d'un roi; **she's not fit to look after children** elle ne devrait pas avoir le droit de s'occuper d'enfants; **she's not a fit mother** c'est une mère indigne; **he's not fit to polish my boots** il n'est même pas bon à cirer mes chaussures; **my grandmother is no longer fit to drive** ma grand-mère n'est plus capable de conduire; **I'm not fit to be seen** je ne suis pas présentable; **these programmes aren't fit for children** ce ne sont pas des programmes pour les enfants; **throw it in the bin, that's all it's fit for** jette-le à la poubelle, c'est tout ce que ça mérite; **that's all he's fit for** c'est tout ce qu'il mérite; **to think** *or* **to see fit to do sth** trouver *ou* juger bon de faire qch; **do as you see** *or* **think fit** fais comme tu penses *ou* juges bon

(**b**) *Fam (ready)* **to be fit to drop** être mort de fatigue; **I feel fit to burst** je me sens prêt à éclater; **to laugh fit to burst** être plié en deux de rire; *Am* **I was fit to be tied** *(extremely angry)* j'étais furax

(**c**) *(healthy)* en forme; *Br* **to get fit** retrouver la forme; *Br* **I've never felt fitter in my life** je ne me suis jamais senti en meilleure forme; **to keep** *or* **to stay fit** entretenir sa forme; **the patient is not fit enough to be discharged** le patient n'est pas en état de quitter l'hôpital; **she is not a fit woman** *(well)* elle n'est pas en bonne santé; **the fittest member of the team** la personne la plus en forme de l'équipe; **it's a case of the survival of the fittest** ce sont les plus forts qui survivent; **fit for duty** bon pour le service; *Mil* valide

(**d**) *Br Fam (good-looking)* bien foutu

2 *n* (**a**) *(size)* **it's a perfect fit** *(item of clothing)* cela me/vous/*etc* va à merveille; *(fridge, stove, piece of furniture)* cela s'adapte parfaitement; *(two interlocking pieces)* cela s'emboîte bien; **it's not a very good fit** *(too large)* c'est trop grand; *(too tight)* c'est trop juste; **tight/loose/comfortable fit** *(item of clothing)* coupe *f* ajustée/ample/confortable; **these trousers are a bit of a tight fit** ce pantalon est un peu juste; **it was a bit of a tight fit** *(in room, car)* on était un peu à l'étroit; *(parking car)* il n'y avait pas beaucoup de place

(**b**) *Med (of apoplexy, epilepsy, hysterics)* crise *f*; **fit of coughing, coughing fit** quinte *f* de toux; **fit of crying** crise *f* de larmes; *Med* **to have a fit** avoir une crise; *Fig* **she'll have a fit when she finds out** elle va faire une crise quand elle le saura; *Fam* **to throw a fit** piquer une crise; **he nearly threw a fit when he heard the news** il a failli exploser quand il a appris la nouvelle

(**c**) *(outburst → of anger)* mouvement *m*, accès *m*, moment *m*; *(→ of depression)* crise *f*; *(→ of pique, generosity)* moment *m*; *(→ of madness)* accès *m*; **he did it in a fit of rage/temper** il a fait cela dans un mouvement de rage/colère; **to be in fits (of laughter)** avoir le fou rire; **he had us all in fits** il nous a fait hurler *ou* mourir de rire; **to get a fit of the giggles** être pris d'un *ou* piquer un fou rire; **in a sudden fit of energy** dans un sursaut d'énergie; **to work by** *or* **in fits and starts** travailler par à-coups

3 *vt* (**a**) *(be of the correct size for)* **to fit sb** aller à qn; **those trousers fit you better than the other ones** ce pantalon te va mieux que l'autre; **none of the keys fitted the lock** aucune des clés n'entrait dans la serrure; **the nut doesn't fit the bolt** l'écrou n'est pas de la même taille que le boulon; **doesn't the lid fit the box/jar?** le couvercle ne va-t-il pas sur la boîte/le bocal?; **the lid doesn't fit the pot very well** ce couvercle n'est pas très bien adapté à la casserole

(**b**) *(correspond to, match → description)* correspondre à; **to make the punishment fit the crime** adapter le châtiment au crime; **the music fitted the occasion** la musique était de circonstance; **to fit the bill** faire l'affaire

(**c**) *(make suitable for)* **what do you think fits you for the job?** en quoi estimez-vous correspondre au profil de l'emploi?

(**d**) *(install → lock, door, window etc)* installer; *Br (carpet)* poser; *Br* **to have double-glazing fitted** se faire installer *ou* mettre le double vitrage; *Br* **to fit a kitchen** installer une cuisine; **to fit a key in a lock** engager *ou* mettre une clé dans une serrure; *Br* **I've got special tyres fitted** je me suis fait mettre des pneus spéciaux

(**e**) *(attach, fix on)* fixer; **to fit a nozzle on the end of a pipe** adapter un ajutage à l'extrémité d'un tuyau; **then you fit the parts together** puis vous assemblez les différentes pièces

(**f**) *(equip)* équiper; **to fit sth with sth** équiper qch de qch; **fitted with electronic security devices** équipé de dispositifs de sécurité électroniques; **she has been fitted with a hip**

replacement elle s'est fait mettre une hanche artificielle

(**g**) *(take measurements of → person)* **to be fitted for a new suit** faire un essayage pour un nouveau costume; **the next time you come back to be fitted** lors de votre prochain essayage

(**h**) *(adjust → idea, theory)* adapter; **I'll fit the dress on you** j'essaierai la robe sur vous

4 *vi* (**a**) *(be of the correct size)* **the dress doesn't fit** la robe ne lui/me/*etc* va pas; **this lid/key doesn't fit** ce couvercle/cette clé n'est pas le bon/la bonne; **the key won't fit in the lock** la clé n'entre pas dans la serrure; **do these pieces fit together?** est-ce que ces morceaux vont ensemble?; **it won't fit** cela n'ira pas; **this lid doesn't fit very well** ce couvercle n'est pas très bien adapté; **we won't all fit round one table** nous ne tiendrons pas tous autour d'une table; **the photos just fit onto the page** les photos tiennent juste sur la page; **cut the pieces to fit** couper les morceaux aux mesures adéquates

(**b**) *(correspond, match → description)* correspondre; **it all fits** tout concorde; **to fit with sth** correspondre à qch; *Fam* **my face didn't fit** je n'avais pas le profil de l'emploi ❑

►**fit in 1** *vi* (**a**) *(go in space available)* tenir; **we won't all fit in** nous ne tiendrons pas tous; **that piece fits in here** *(jigsaw)* ce morceau va là

(**b**) *(in company, group etc)* s'intégrer; **you don't fit in here** tu n'es pas à ta place ici; **I feel that I don't fit in** j'ai l'impression de ne pas être à ma place; **I've tried to fit in** j'ai essayé de m'intégrer; **to fit in with** *(statement)* correspondre à; *(colour scheme)* s'accorder avec; **your plans don't fit in with mine** vos projets ne cadrent pas avec les miens; **she doesn't fit in easily with other people** elle a du mal à s'entendre avec les autres; **I think you should fit in with what I want to do** je pense que tu devrais t'adapter à ce que je veux faire

2 *vt sep* (**a**) *(install)* installer

(**b**) *(find room for → clothes in suitcase)* faire entrer; **can you fit one more in?** *(in car)* peux-tu prendre une personne de plus?; **how on earth are you going to fit everyone in?** *(in room, car etc)* comment diable vas-tu réussir à faire tenir tout le monde?

(**c**) *(find time for → patient)* prendre; *(→ friend)* trouver du temps pour; **could you fit in this translation by the end of the week?** est-ce que vous pourriez faire cette traduction d'ici la fin de la semaine?; **could you fit in lunch this week?** *(with me)* est-ce que tu seras libre pour déjeuner avec moi cette semaine?; **I hope we've got time to fit in a visit to the Louvre** j'espère que nous aurons le temps de visiter le Louvre; **I don't know how he fits it all in** je me demande comment il trouve le temps de tout faire

►**fit into 1** *vt insep (of furniture, clothes → into room, suitcase etc)* entrer dans, tenir dans; *(of people → into room, car)* tenir dans; *(of piece → into another piece)* s'emboîter dans; **I can't fit into these jeans any more** je n'arrive plus à rentrer dans ce jean

2 *vt sep* **to fit sth into sth** faire entrer *ou* tenir qch dans qch; **to fit one part into another** emboîter une pièce dans une autre; **he fits a lot into one day** il en fait beaucoup en une journée

►**fit on 1** *vi* **this lid won't fit on** ce couvercle ne va pas; **where does this part fit on?** où va cette pièce?

2 *vt sep (attach)* mettre

►**fit out** *vt sep (ship)* armer; *(person → with equipment)* équiper; **to fit a child out with new clothes** renouveler la garde-robe d'un enfant

►**fit up** *vt sep* (**a**) *(equip → house, car)* équiper; *(→ person)* munir; **to fit sb/sth up with sth** munir qn/équiper qch de qch; **they fitted me up with an artificial leg** ils m'ont mis une jambe artificielle

(**b**) *Br Fam Crime slang* monter un coup contre; **I've been fitted up** c'est un coup monté

---

fitch [fɪtʃ] *n Zool* putois *m*

fitful ['fɪtfʊl] *adj (sleep)* intermittent; *(night)* agité; **to make fitful progress** progresser par à-coups; **attendance has been fitful** les gens ne sont pas venus régulièrement

fitfully ['fɪtfʊlɪ] *adv (work)* par à-coups; *(attend)* irrégulièrement; *(sleep)* de manière intermittente

fitment ['fɪtmənt] *n Br (in bathroom, kitchen etc)* élément *m* démontable

fitness ['fɪtnɪs] *n* (**a**) *(health)* forme *f* physique (**b**) *(suitability → of person for job)* aptitude *f*; **your fitness as a mother is not in question** vos compétences de mère ne sont pas en cause

►► *Br* ***fitness centre*** club *m* de gym; *Fam* ***fitness freak*** fana *mf* d'exercice physique; ***fitness room*** salle *f* de musculation; ***fitness training*** entraînement *m* physique

fitted ['fɪtəd] *adj* (**a**) *(garment)* ajusté

(**b**) *Br (made to measure)* **the house has fitted carpets in every room** il y a de la moquette dans toutes les pièces de la maison; **to lay a fitted carpet in a room** moquetter *ou* poser une moquette dans une pièce

(**c**) *Br (built-in → cupboard)* encastré

(**d**) *(suited)* **to be fitted for sth/doing sth** être apte à qch/à faire qch

►► ***fitted kitchen*** cuisine *f* intégrée; ***fitted sheet*** drap-housse *m*

fitter ['fɪtə(r)] *n* (**a**) *(of machine)* monteur(euse) *m,f*; *(of carpet)* poseur(euse) *m,f* (**b**) *(of clothes)* essayeur(euse) *m,f*

fitting ['fɪtɪŋ] **1** *adj (suitable → conclusion, remark)* approprié; *(socially correct)* convenable; **it was a fitting tribute to a great athlete** c'était un hommage mérité rendu à un grand athlète; **it was only fitting he should score the winning goal** ce n'était que justice qu'il marque le but gagnant; **a fitting end for a murderer** une fin appropriée pour un meurtrier

2 *n* (**a**) *(trying on → of clothes)* essayage *m*; **I'm going for a fitting tomorrow** j'ai rendez-vous pour un essayage demain (**b**) *Br (of shoe)* **have you got it in a wider/narrower fitting?** l'avez-vous en plus large/plus étroit?

3 fittings *npl Br (of office)* installations *fpl*; *(of bathroom)* accessoires *mpl*; **electrical fittings** appareillage *m* électrique

►► ***fitting out*** *(of expedition etc)* équipement *m*; *(of ship)* armement *m*; ***fitting room*** salon *m ou* salle *f* d'essayage; *(cubicle)* cabine *f* d'essayage

-fitting ['fɪtɪŋ] *suff* **close-fitting, tight-fitting** *(item of clothing)* moulant; *(screw-top lid)* qui ferme bien; *(lid of saucepan)* adapté; **loose-fitting** *(item of clothing)* ample

fittingly ['fɪtɪŋlɪ] *adv* convenablement; **fittingly, the government has agreed to ratify the treaty** comme il le fallait, le gouvernement a accepté de ratifier le traité; **fittingly, he was buried in his home town** comme il convenait, il a été enterré dans sa ville natale

fit-up *n Br Fam Crime slang* coup *m* monté

five [faɪv] **1** *n (number, numeral)* cinq *m inv*; **five times table** table *f* des cinq; **five and five are ten** cinq et cinq font dix; **I'm waiting for a number five (bus)** j'attends le (bus numéro) cinq; *Cards* **the five of hearts** le cinq de cœur; **to be five** *(in age)* avoir cinq ans; **it's five o'clock** il est cinq heures; **it's five to/past five** il est cinq heures moins cinq/cinq heures cinq; **come at five** venez à cinq heures; **to get five out of ten** avoir cinq sur dix; **a table for five** une table pour cinq (personnes)

2 *pron* cinq; **five is not enough** cinq, ce n'est pas assez; **I need five (of them)** il m'en faut cinq, j'en ai besoin de cinq; **there are five (of them)** *(people)* ils sont cinq; *(objects)* il y en a cinq; **all five of them left** tous les cinq sont partis, ils sont partis tous les cinq; *Fam* **to take five** faire un break de cinq minutes ❑; *Fam* **give me five!** tope là! *(pour conclure un marché, dire bonjour ou manifester son approbation)*

3 *adj* cinq; **five people** cinq personnes; **on page five** (à la) page cinq; **they live at number five** ils habitent au numéro cinq; **trains leave at five minutes to the hour** le train part toutes les heures à moins cinq; **to be five years old** avoir cinq ans

4 fives *n* = sorte de squash où l'on utilise ses mains ou des battes en guise de raquettes

►► *Am Hist* ***the Five Nations*** les cinq nations iroquoises; *Formerly Sport* ***the Five Nations (Championship)*** le Tournoi des Cinq Nations; *Am Fam* ***five spot*** billet *m* de cinq dollars ❑

five-and-dime, five-and-ten *n Am* bazar *m*, supérette *f*

five-a-side *n Br* football *m* à dix

►► ***five-a-side football*** football *m* à dix; ***five-a-side tournament*** tournoi *m* de football à dix

five-barred gate *adj Horseracing* barrière *f* à cinq planches *ou* à cinq barres

five-by-five *n Am Fam Hum (fat person)* petit(e) gros(grosse) *m,f*

five-day week *n Br* semaine *f* de cinq jours

five-door model *n Aut* (version *f*) cinq portes *f*

five-figure *adj* **five-figure number** nombre *m* de cinq chiffres; *Math* **five-figure logarithm tables** table *f* de logarithmes à cinq décimales

five-finger exercises *npl Mus* exercices *mpl* de doigté

fivefold ['faɪvfəʊld] **1** *adj* quintuple

2 *adv* par cinq, au quintuple; **to increase fivefold** être multiplié par cinq, augmenter au quintuple, quintupler

five-o'clock shadow *n* barbe *f* d'un jour, barbe *f* naissante; **he's always got a five-o'clock shadow** il a toujours l'air mal rasé

fiver ['faɪvə(r)] *n Fam (five-pound note)* billet *m* de cinq livres ❑; *(five-dollar bill)* billet *m* de cinq dollars ❑; *Br* **it'll cost you a fiver** ça te coûtera cinq livres ❑

five-seater *n Aut* cinq places *f*

five-speed gearbox *n Aut* boîte *f* cinq-vitesses, boîte *f* de vitesses cinq rapports

five-spice powder *n Culin* = mélange d'épices utilisé dans la cuisine chinoise

five-star *adj (hotel)* cinq étoiles

five-year *adj (plan)* quinquennal

five-yearly *adj (election)* quinquennal; *(festival, event)* qui a lieu tous les cinq ans

---

FIX [fɪks]

fixer	► **1 (a), (b)**
s'occuper	► **1 (c), (d)**
préparer	► **1 (e)**
arranger	► **1 (f)**
pétrin	► **2 (a)**
dose	► **2 (b)**

1 *vt* (**a**) *(fasten in position → mirror, sign)* fixer; *(attention, gaze)* fixer; *(something in mind)* inscrire, graver; **to fix a post in the ground** enfoncer un poteau dans le sol; *Mil* **fix bayonets!** baïonnettes aux canons!; **to fix the blame on sb** attribuer *ou* imputer la faute à qn; **to fix one's hopes on sb/sth** mettre tous ses espoirs en qn/qch

(**b**) *(set → date, price, rate, limit)* fixer; *(→ meeting place)* convenir de; **nothing has been fixed yet** rien n'a encore été fixé; **have you (got) anything fixed for Friday?** as-tu quelque chose de prévu pour vendredi?

(**c**) *(arrange, sort out)* s'occuper de; **I'll fix it** je vais m'en occuper; **try to fix it so you don't have to stay overnight** essaye de t'arranger pour que tu ne sois pas obligé de passer la nuit là-bas; **I'll fix it with your teacher** j'arrangerai cela avec ton professeur; **I've fixed it for them to come tomorrow** je me suis arrangé pour qu'ils viennent demain

(**d**) *Fam (settle a score with)* s'occuper de, (régler son compte à); **I'll fix him** je vais m'occuper de lui, je vais lui régler son compte; **that'll fix him** ça devrait lui régler son compte

(**e**) *Am Fam (prepare → meal, drink)* préparer ❑; **can I fix you a drink?** puis-je te servir un verre? ❑

(**f**) *Fam (adjust → make-up, tie)* arranger ❑; **to fix one's hair** se coiffer ❑; *(redo)* se recoiffer ❑

(**g**) *(mend, repair → car, puncture etc)* réparer; **I've been meaning to get that fixed for ages** ça fait une éternité que j'ai l'intention de faire réparer ça

(**h**) *Fam (rig → race, fight, election, result)* truquer; *(set up → interview)* arranger ❑; *(bribe → jury, official, security guard etc)* acheter

(**i**) *Am Fam (intend, plan)* prévoir de ❑; *(be determined)* être résolu à ❑; **he's fixing to go on holiday** *(planning)* il a prévu de partir en vacances; *(determined)* il est résolu à partir en vacances

(**j**) *Aviat & Naut (position)* déterminer

(**k**) *Chem (nitrogen)* fixer

(**l**) *Art & Phot (drawing, photo)* fixer

(**m**) *Fam Euph (neuter)* châtrer ❑

2 *n* (**a**) *Fam (tight spot, predicament)* pétrin *m*; **to be in a fix** être dans une mauvaise passe; **to get into/out of a fix** se mettre dans une/sortir d'une mauvaise passe; **you've put me in a bit of a fix** tu me mets dans l'embarras; **I'm in a bit of a fix financially** j'ai quelques difficultés financières ❑

(**b**) *Fam Drugs slang* dose *f*, fix *m*; **to give oneself a fix** prendre un fix, se piquer; *Hum* **to get one's fix of coffee/news** avoir sa dose de café/d'informations

(**c**) *Aviat & Naut* **to get a fix on** *(ship)* déterminer la position de; *Fig (get clear idea of)* se faire une idée de

(**d**) *Fam (unfair arrangement)* **the result was a fix** le résultat avait été truqué

▸**fix on 1** *vt sep (attach)* fixer

2 *vt insep (decide on → date, candidate)* choisir

▸**fix up 1** *vt sep* (**a**) *(install, erect)* mettre en place, installer

(**b**) *Fam (arrange → date, meeting)* fixer ❑; *(→ deal, holiday)* organiser ❑, mettre au point ❑; **it's all fixed up** c'est une affaire réglée, tout est arrangé; **fix me up with an appointment with the dentist** prends-moi un rendez-vous chez le dentiste; **he'll try to fix something up for us** il va essayer de nous arranger quelque chose; **have you got anything fixed up for this evening?** as-tu quelque chose de prévu pour ce soir?; **have you got fixed up for your holidays?** est-ce que tu t'es organisé pour tes vacances?; **I've managed to fix him up with some work** j'ai réussi à lui trouver du travail; **they fixed me up in a hotel** ils m'ont pris une chambre dans un hôtel; **you can stay here until you get fixed up (with a place to stay)** tu peux loger ici jusqu'à ce que tu trouves un endroit où habiter; **to fix sb up with a date** trouver un/une partenaire à qn

(**c**) *(room)* refaire; *(flat, house)* refaire, retaper; **we could always fix the smallest bedroom up as a study** on pourrait toujours transformer la plus petite chambre en bureau; **you should fix yourself up a bit** tu devrais t'arranger un peu

2 *vi* s'arranger pour que + *subjunctive*; **I've fixed up for us to see the flat tomorrow** je me suis arrangé pour que nous visitions l'appartement demain; **I've already fixed up to go out tonight** j'ai déjà prévu de sortir ce soir

---

fixate [fɪk'seɪt] *vt Psy* fixer les yeux *ou* le regard sur

fixated [fɪk'seɪtɪd] *adj* obsédé; **to be fixated on sth** faire une fixation sur qch, être obsédé par qch

fixation [fɪk'seɪʃən] *n* (**a**) *(obsession)* fixation *f*; **to have a fixation about sth** faire une fixation sur qch; **you've got a fixation!** c'est une idée fixe chez toi! (**b**) *Chem* fixation *f*

fixative ['fɪksətɪv] *n Phot* fixateur *m*; *Art* fixatif *m*

fixed [fɪkst] *adj* (**a**) *(immovable → glare)* fixe; *(→ idea)* arrêté; *(→ smile)* figé; **the seats are fixed to the floor** les sièges sont fixés au sol

(**b**) *(set, unchangeable → price, rate, plans)* fixe; **people on fixed incomes** des gens disposant de revenus fixes; *Law* **of no fixed abode** sans domicile fixe

(**c**) *Fam (placed)* **how are you fixed for time/money?** *(how much do you have?)* combien de temps/d'argent as-tu? ❑; *(do you have enough?)* as-tu suffisamment de temps/d'argent? ❑; **how are you fixed for accommodation/transport?** est-ce que tu as un endroit où loger/un moyen de transport? ❑

▸▸ *Fin* ***fixed assets*** immobilisations *fpl*, actif *m* immobilisé; *Fin* ***fixed capital*** capitaux *mpl* immobilisés, capital *m* fixe; *Fin* ***fixed charge*** frais *mpl* fixes; *Fin* ***fixed cost*** coût *m* fixe *ou* constant, charge *f* fixe; *Com* ***fixed deposit*** dépôt *m* à terme (fixe) *ou* à échéance fixe; *Comput* ***fixed disk*** disque *m* fixe; *Fin* ***fixed exchange rate*** taux *m* de change fixe; *Fin* ***fixed income*** revenu *m* fixe; *Fin* ***fixed interest*** intérêt *m* fixe; *Fin* ***fixed investment*** immobilisations *fpl*; *Fin* ***fixed maturity*** échéance *f* fixe; *Fin* ***fixed parity*** parité *f* fixe; *Law* ***fixed penalty*** pénalité *f* fixe; ***fixed point*** point *m* fixe, point *m* de repère; *Math* ***fixed point arithmetic*** arithmétique *f* en virgule fixe; *Fin* ***fixed property*** immeubles *mpl*; *Fin* ***fixed rate*** taux *m* fixe; *Com* ***fixed salary*** salaire *m* fixe; *Astron* ***fixed satellite*** satellite *m* géostationnaire; *Typ* ***fixed space*** espace *m* fixe; *Astron* ***fixed star*** étoile *f* fixe; *Com* ***fixed wage*** salaire *m* fixe; *Fin* ***fixed yield*** rendement *m* constant

fixed-income *adj Fin*

▸▸ ***fixed-income investment*** placement *m* à revenu fixe; ***fixed-income securities*** valeurs *fpl* à revenu fixe

fixed-interest *adj Fin* à intérêt fixe

▸▸ ***fixed-interest market*** marché *m* des obligations; ***fixed-interest securities*** valeurs *fpl* à intérêt fixe

fixedly ['fɪksɪdlɪ] *adv (stare)* fixement

fixed-price menu *n* menu *m* à prix fixe

fixed-rate *adj Fin (loan, mortgage)* à taux fixe; *(investment)* à revenu fixe

▸▸ ***fixed-rate assessment system*** régime *m* du forfait; ***fixed-rate bond*** obligation *f* à revenu fixe; ***fixed-rate borrowing*** emprunts *mpl* à taux fixe; ***fixed-rate securities*** titres *mpl* à revenu fixe

fixed-term *adj Com* à terme fixe, à date fixe

▸▸ *Fin* ***fixed-term bill*** effet *m* à date fixe; *Com* ***fixed-term contract*** contrat *m* à durée déterminée, CDD *m*; *Fin* ***fixed-term credit*** crédit *m* à durée déterminée; *Fin* ***fixed-term deposit*** dépôt *m* à terme fixe *ou* à échéance fixe

fixed-wing aircraft *n* aéronef *m* à ailes fixes

fixer ['fɪksə(r)] *n* (**a**) *Fam (person)* combinard(e) *m,f* (**b**) *Phot* fixateur *m* (**c**) *(adhesive)* adhésif *m*

fixing ['fɪksɪŋ] **1** *n* (**a**) *(repairing)* réparation *f*

(**b**) *Com (of prices etc)* établissement *m*

(**c**) *St Exch* fixage *m*

2 *Am* **fixings** *npl (trimmings)* accessoires *mpl*; *(food)* accompagnements *mpl*, garnitures *fpl*; **roast turkey with all the fixings** dinde *f* rôtie avec tout ce qui s'ensuit

▸▸ *Phot* ***fixing bath*** *(container)* cuvette *f* de fixage; *(solution)* bain *m* de fixage; *Phot* ***fixing solution*** solution *f* de fixage

fixity ['fɪksətɪ] *n (of gaze)* fixité *f*; **fixity of purpose** détermination *f*

fixture ['fɪkstʃə(r)] *n* (**a**) *(in building)* installation *f* fixe; *Fig* **she's become a fixture here** elle fait partie des meubles à présent; *Fig* **she was something of a fixture at his parties** elle apparaissait inévitablement à chacune de ses soirées; *Fig* **the Christmas party is a fixture in most offices** faire une fête à Noël est une tradition dans la plupart des bureaux; **bathroom fixtures** installations *fpl* sanitaires; **fixtures and fittings** agencements *mpl*, installations *fpl* fixes; *Acct* **fixtures and fittings £2000** *(on balance sheet)* reprise 2000 livres

(**b**) *Sport* rencontre *f*

▸▸ *Sport* ***fixture list*** calendrier *m*

fix-up *n Am Fam (repair)* réparation ❑ *f*

fizgig ['fɪzgɪg] *n Fam* (**a**) *(flighty girl)* évaporée ❑ *f* (**b**) *(toy)* toupie ❑ *f* (**c**) *(firework)* serpenteau ❑ *m* (**d**) *Fishing* foène ❑ *f*, digon ❑ *m* (**e**) *Austr (informer)* mouchard(e) *m,f*

fizz [fɪz] **1** *vi (drink)* pétiller; *(firework)* crépiter; *Fam Fig* **to be fizzing** *(extremely angry)* bouillir (de rage); **the champagne fizzed out of the bottle** le champagne est sorti de la bouteille en pétillant

2 *n* (**a**) *(of drink)* pétillement *m*; **the champagne has lost its fizz** le champagne est éventé; *Fig* **their marriage has lost its fizz** leur mariage a perdu de son piment

(**b**) *(sound)* sifflement *m*

(**c**) *Fam (soft drink)* boisson *f* à bulles ❑; *Br (champagne)* champ' *m*; *(sparkling wine)* mousseux ❑ *m*

▸**fizz up** *vi (drink)* mousser, faire de la mousse

fizziness ['fɪzɪnɪs] *n (of drink)* pétillement *m*; **the champagne has lost its fizziness** le champagne est éventé

fizzle ['fɪzəl] *vi (drink)* pétiller; *(fire, firework)* crépiter; *(gas burner)* siffler

▸**fizzle out** *vi Fig (interest, enthusiasm, desire)* tomber; *(plan, project)* tomber à l'eau; *(book, film, party, strike etc)* tourner *ou* partir en eau de boudin; *(career)* tourner court

fizzy ['fɪzɪ] (*compar* **fizzier**, *superl* **fizziest**) *adj (soft drink)* gazeux; *(wine)* pétillant, mousseux

fjord = **fiord**

FL, Fla (*written abbr* **Florida**) Floride *f*

flab [flæb] *n Fam (of person)* graisse ❑ *f*, lard *m*; *(in text)* délayage ❑ *m*, verbiage ❑ *m*; **to fight the flab** essayer de perdre sa graisse

flabbergasted ['flæbə,gɑːstɪd] *adj Fam* sidéré; **I was flabbergasted at** *or* **by the news** j'ai été sidéré par la nouvelle, la nouvelle m'a sidéré; **I was flabbergasted by how much he had improved** j'ai été sidéré *ou* époustouflé par ses progrès

flabbergasting ['flæbə,gɑːstɪŋ] *adj Fam* sidérant

flabbily ['flæbɪlɪ] *adv Fam* mollement ❑

flabbiness ['flæbɪnɪs] *n (of skin)* manque *m* de fermeté; *(of skin, arms, stomach, flesh)* manque *m* de fermeté, mollesse *f*; *(of person)* empâtement *m*; *(of person's grip)* mollesse *f*; *Fig (of prose, writing, novel)* prolixité *f*; *(of argument, idea)* faiblesse *f*

flabby ['flæbɪ] (*compar* **flabbier**, *superl* **flabbiest**) *adj (skin)* flasque; *(arms, stomach, flesh)* flasque, mou (molle); *(person)* empâté; *(grip)* mou (molle); *Fig (prose, writing, novel)* prolixe; *(argument, speech)* peu convaincant, faible

flabellate [flə'beleɪt], **flabelliform** [flə'belɪ,fɔːm] *adj Biol* flabellé, flabelliforme

flaccid ['flæsɪd] *adj* flasque

flaccidity [flæ'sɪdɪtɪ] *n* (**a**) *(flaccid condition)* flaccidité *f* (**b**) *(disease of silkworms)* flacherie *f*

flack [flæk] *n Am Fam (press agent)* agent *m* de presse ❑

flag [flæg] (*pt & pp* **flagged**, *cont* **flagging**) **1** *n* (**a**) *(emblem of country, signal)* drapeau *m*; *(for celebration)* banderole *f*, fanion *m*; *Naut* pavillon *m*; **all the flags are out in the city** la ville est pavoisée; **black flag** *(of pirate ship)* drapeau *m* noir; *Naut* **yellow flag** pavillon *m* de quarantaine; **to fly the flag** défendre les couleurs de son pays; **to go down with all flags flying** *Naut* couler pavillon haut; *Fig* échouer la tête haute; **to keep the flag flying** faire front; **to put out the flags for sb** organiser une fête en l'honneur de qn; **to show the flag** *Naut* battre pavillon; *Fig* faire acte de présence

(**b**) *(for charity)* = badge ou autocollant que l'on obtient lorsque l'on verse de l'argent à une œuvre de charité

(**c**) *(in taxi)* **the flag was down/up** le taxi était pris/libre; **the driver put the flag down** le chauffeur a éteint son signal lumineux pour indiquer qu'il n'était plus libre

(**d**) *Comput* drapeau *m*, fanion *m*

(**e**) *(on floor)* dalle *f*

(**f**) *Bot* iris *m*

(**g**) *(for file, folder)* papillon *m*

(**h**) *(in golf)* drapeau *m*

2 *vt* (**a**) *(put marker on → page of book)* marquer; *Comput (highlight)* sélectionner; *Comput* **to flag an error** indiquer *ou* signaler une erreur par un drapeau *ou* un fanion

(**b**) *(floor)* daller

3 *vi (strength)* faiblir; *(energy, enthusiasm, interest, spirits)* faiblir, tomber; *(efforts)* se relâcher; *(conversation)* tomber, s'épuiser; **I'm flagging** *(becoming physically or mentally tired)* je fatigue; *(unable to eat any more)* je commence à être rassasié, je cale

▸▸ ***flag airline*** compagnie *f* aérienne nationale; *Naut* ***flag captain*** commandant *m* du navire amiral; ***flag carrier*** *(airline)* compagnie *f* aérienne nationale; *(shipping company)* compagnie *f* maritime nationale; *Naut* ***flag of convenience*** pavillon *m* de complaisance; *Br* ***flag day*** = jour de quête d'une œuvre de charité; *Am* ***Flag Day*** le 14 juin *(fête nationale des États-Unis)*; *Naut* ***flag of distress*** pavillon *m* de détresse; *Am* ***flag football*** = sorte de football américain où le fait d'enlever le foulard qu'un joueur porte autour de la taille tient lieu de placage; *Naut* ***flag officer*** contre-amiral *m*; *Am* ***flag station*** gare *f* d'arrêt facultatif; *Naut* ***flag of truce*** pavillon *m* parlementaire

▸**flag down** *vt sep (bus, motorist etc)* faire signe de s'arrêter à; *(taxi)* héler

▸**flag out** *vt sep Sport (racetrack)* jalonner

▸**flag up** *vt sep (mark, indicate)* marquer; *(mistake)* signaler, marquer

FLAG DAY

Les "flag days" britanniques, durant lesquels on sollicite des dons auprès des passants, ont généralement lieu le samedi. Les donateurs reçoivent un papillon en papier qu'ils portent tout au long de la journée.

flagellant ['flædʒələnt] *n Rel* flagellant *m*; *(sexual)* adepte *mf* de la flagellation

flagellate ['flædʒəleɪt] **1** *vt Formal* flageller; *Fig* fustiger
2 *adj Biol & Bot* flagellé
3 *n Biol & Bot* flagellé *m*

flagellation [ˌflædʒə'leɪʃən] *n Formal* flagellation *f*

flagellator ['flædʒəˌleɪtə(r)] *n Formal* flagellateur(trice) *m,f*

flagellum [flə'dʒeləm] *n Biol & Bot* flagelle *m*

flageolet[1] ['flædʒəlet, ˌflædʒə'let] *n Mus* flageolet *m*

flageolet[2] ['flæʒəleɪ] *n Bot & Culin* (haricot *m*) flageolet *m*

flagged [flægd] *adj (floor)* dallé

flagging[1] ['flægɪŋ] *adj (enthusiasm, spirits, strength)* qui baisse; *(courage, determination, attention)* faiblissant; *(conversation)* qui tombe *ou* s'épuise

flagging[2] *n (paving)* dallage *m*

flagitious [flə'dʒɪʃəs] *adj Arch* infâme, abominable

flagon ['flægən] *n* (**a**) *(large bottle)* grosse bouteille *f* (ventrue), bonbonne *f* (**b**) *(jug)* pot *m* (à anse)

flagpole ['flægpəʊl] *n* mât *m*; *Fam Fig* **let's run it up the flagpole** soumettons-le et voyons les réactions □

flagrancy ['fleɪgrənsɪ] *n* flagrance *f*

flagrant ['fleɪgrənt] *adj (injustice, lie, abuse)* flagrant; **a flagrant disregard for the safety of others** un mépris flagrant *ou* évident pour la sécurité d'autrui

flagrante delicto [flə'græntɪdɪ'lɪktəʊ] *adv Law & Fig* **to be caught in flagrante delicto** être surpris en flagrant délit

flagrantly ['fleɪgrəntlɪ] *adv (abuse, disregard, defy etc)* d'une manière flagrante; **flagrantly unfair** d'une injustice criante; **flagrantly dishonest** d'une malhonnêteté flagrante

flagship ['flægʃɪp] *n Naut* vaisseau *m ou* bâtiment *m* amiral; *Fig Com (product)* tête *f* de gamme; **the London store is the flagship of the chain** le magasin de Londres est le plus important de la chaîne; **this latest model is the flagship of their new range** ce dernier modèle est le produit vedette de leur nouvelle gamme; **the Conservatives' flagship council** le conseil municipal qui est le fleuron du Parti conservateur
►► *Com* ***flagship branch*** succursale *f* vedette; *Com* ***flagship brand*** marque *f* étendard, marque *f* fer de lance; *Com* ***flagship product*** produit *m* fer de lance, produit *m* vedette; *Com* ***flagship store*** magasin *m* vitrine

flagstaff ['flægstɑːf] *n* mât *m*

flagstone ['flægstəʊn] *n* dalle *f*
►► ***flagstone pavement*** dallage *m* en pierre

flag-waving *n (UNCOUNT) Fam Fig* discours *mpl* cocardiers □

flail [fleɪl] **1** *n Agr* fléau *m*
2 *vt* (**a**) *Agr* battre au fléau (**b**) *(limbs)* agiter
3 *vi* (**a**) *(person, limbs)* s'agiter violemment (**b**) *(rope, cable)* se balancer violemment

►**flail about 1** *vi (person, limbs)* s'agiter dans tous les sens; **she was flailing about in the water** elle se débattait des mains et des pieds dans l'eau
2 *vt sep (arms, legs)* battre

flair [fleə(r)] *n* (**a**) *(stylishness)* style *m*; **to dress/write with flair** s'habiller/écrire avec style (**b**) *(gift)* don *m*; **to have a flair for sth** avoir un don pour qch; **to have a flair for languages/cooking** avoir le don des langues/pour cuisiner; **he had no flair for business** il n'avait pas le sens des affaires; **they have a real flair for making the right choices** ils ont vraiment le don de faire les bons choix

flak [flæk] *n* (**a**) *(gunfire)* tir *m* antiaérien *ou* de DCA (**b**) *(UNCOUNT) Fam Fig (criticism)* critiques □ *fpl*; **I took a lot of flak over it** on m'a beaucoup critiqué pour cela; **to come in for a lot of flak** se heurter à beaucoup de critiques
►► ***flak jacket*** gilet *m* pare-balles

flake [fleɪk] **1** *n* (**a**) *(of snow)* flocon *m*; *(of metal)* paillette *f*; *(of skin)* peau *f* morte; *(of paint, plaster)* écaille *f*; **flakes of dandruff** pellicules *fpl*; **a flake of skin** un bout de peau morte
(**b**) *Am Fam (person)* allumé(e) *m,f*
(**c**) *Austr Culin* = chair de requin ou de raie
2 *vi (plaster)* s'effriter, s'écailler; *(paint)* s'écailler; *(skin)* peler; *(rock)* s'effriter; *Culin (fish)* s'émietter
3 *vt Culin (fish)* émietter; **flaked almonds** amandes *fpl* effilées

►**flake off** *vi (plaster)* s'effriter, s'écailler; *(paint)* s'écailler; *(skin)* peler

►**flake out** *vi Fam (collapse)* s'écrouler □; *(fall asleep)* s'endormir □; **I just want to flake out on the sofa** j'ai envie de m'effondrer sur le canapé et de roupiller; **she was flaked out on the couch** elle roupillait sur le canapé

flakiness ['fleɪkɪnəs] *n* (**a**) *(of paint, plaster)* effritement *m*; *(of skin)* = état d'une peau sèche; *(of scalp)* = état d'un cuir chevelu sujet aux pellicules (**b**) *(UNCOUNT) Fam (of person)* bizarreries □ *fpl*

flaking ['fleɪkɪŋ] *adj (paint, plaster)* qui s'écaille; *(skin)* qui pèle; *(rock)* qui s'effrite

flaky ['fleɪkɪ] (*compar* **flakier**, *superl* **flakiest**) *adj* (**a**) *(paint, plaster)* écaillé; *(rock)* effrité; *(skin)* qui pèle; *(scalp)* sujet aux pellicules (**b**) *Fam (person)* allumé; *(idea)* loufoque
►► *Br Culin* ***flaky pastry*** pâte *f* feuilletée

flam[1] [flæm] *n Fam Old-fashioned* (**a**) *(nonsense)* histoires *fpl*, salades *fpl* (**b**) *Am (deception)* escroquerie □ *f*, filouterie □ *f*

flam[2] *vt Am Fam Old-fashioned* escroquer □, refaire

flambé ['flɑ̃beɪ] (*pt & pp* **flambéed**, *cont* **flambéing**) *Culin* **1** *vt* flamber
2 *adj* flambé

flamboyance [flæm'bɔɪəns], **flamboyancy** [flæm'bɔɪənsɪ] *n (of behaviour, lifestyle, personality)* extravagance *f*; *(of colour)* éclat *m*

flamboyant [flæm'bɔɪənt] *adj (behaviour, lifestyle, personality)* extravagant; *(colour)* éclatant; *(clothes)* aux couleurs éclatantes; *Pej* voyant; *Archit* flamboyant

flamboyantly [flæm'bɔɪəntlɪ] *adv* de manière extravagante

flame [fleɪm] **1** *n* (**a**) *(of fire, candle)* flamme *f*; **to be in flames** *(building, car)* être en flammes; **to burst into flames** prendre feu, s'enflammer; **to go up in flames** s'embraser; *Fig (hopes, chances)* s'envoler, partir en fumée; *also Fig* **to be shot down in flames** être descendu en flammes
(**b**) *Literary (of passion, desire)* flamme *f*
(**c**) *Comput* message *m* injurieux
2 *vi* (**a**) *Fig (face, cheeks)* s'empourprer; *(passion, anger)* brûler
(**b**) *Comput* rédiger un message injurieux
3 *vt* (**a**) *Culin* flamber
(**b**) *Comput* descendre en flammes
►► *Tech* ***flame cutter*** chalumeau *m* à découper; *Agr* ***flame gun*** agriflamme *m*; ***flame red*** rouge *m* feu; ***flame retardant*** retardateur *m* de flamme, ignifuge *m*; *Bot* ***flame tree*** flamboyant *m*; *Comput* ***flame war*** guerre *f* d'insultes

►**flame up** *vi (fire)* s'embraser; *Fig (person)* s'enflammer

flame-coloured *adj* ponceau *(inv)*, couleur de feu *(inv)*

flame-grilled *adj Culin* grillé au feu de bois

flameless ['fleɪmlɪs] *adj* sans flamme
►► *Mining* ***flameless explosive*** explosif *m* de sûreté

flamenco [flə'meŋkəʊ] **1** *n* flamenco *m*
2 *comp* de flamenco
►► ***flamenco dancing*** flamenco *m*; ***flamenco music*** flamenco *m*

flameout ['fleɪmˌaʊt] *n (of jet engine)* extinction *f*

flameproof ['fleɪmˌpruːf], **flame-resistant** *adj (clothing)* ininflammable, à l'épreuve des flammes; *(dish)* allant au feu

flamer ['fleɪmə(r)] *n* (**a**) *Am Fam (stupid or obnoxious person)* enflure *f* (**b**) *Comput* auteur *m* d'un message injurieux

flame-red *adj* rouge feu

flame-retardant *comp (upholstery, sofa etc)* ignifugé

flamethrower ['fleɪmˌθrəʊə(r)] *n* lance-flammes *m inv*

flaming ['fleɪmɪŋ] **1** *adj* (**a**) *(sun, sky)* embrasé; *(fire)* flamboyant
(**b**) *Br Fam (extremely angry)* **to be in a flaming temper** être d'une humeur massacrante, être furax; **we had a flaming row about it** nous avons eu une belle engueulade là-dessus
(**c**) *Fam (as intensifier)* fichu; **you flaming idiot!** espèce d'abruti!; **you're a flaming pain in the neck!** tu es un sacré enquiquineur!; **where are my flaming keys!** où sont mes fichues clés!
2 *adv Br Fam (as intensifier)* fichtrement; **don't be so flaming stupid!** ne sois donc pas aussi bête!; **you know flaming well what I mean** tu sais fichtrement bien ce que je veux dire
3 *n Comput* envoi *m* de messages injurieux

flamingo [flə'mɪŋgəʊ] *n Orn* flamant *m* rose

flammability [ˌflæmə'bɪlɪtɪ] *n* inflammabilité *f*

flammable ['flæməbəl] *adj (material, substance)* inflammable

flan [flæn] *n Culin* tarte *f*; *(savoury)* quiche *f*
►► ***flan case*** fond *m* de tarte

Flanders ['flɑːndəz] *n* Flandre *f*, Flandres *fpl*; **in Flanders** dans les Flandres, en Flandre

flange [flændʒ] *Tech* **1** *n (on pipe, tube)* bride *f*, collerette *f*; *(of piece of sheet metal)* collet *m*, rebord *m*; *(of wheel)* boudin *m*, rebord *m*; *(of beam)* aile *f*; *(on rail)* patin *m*; *Aut (on radiator)* ailette *f*
2 *vt* brider; **to flange a pipe** brider un tube, rabattre la collerette d'un tube; **to flange a piece of sheet metal** border une tôle, rabattre un collet sur une tôle; **to flange a wheel** bourreler une roue
►► ***flange coupling*** raccordement *m* à bride; ***flange girder*** poutre *f* en I

flanged [flændʒd] *adj Tech (pipe, tube)* à bride(s); *(piece of sheet metal)* à bord tombé; *(wheel)* à boudin; *(beam)* à aile; *(rail)* à patin; *Aut (radiator)* à ailettes

flank [flæŋk] **1** *n* (**a**) *(of person, animal)* flanc *m*; *Culin (of beef)* flanchet *m*
(**b**) *(of mountain etc)* côté *m*, flanc *m*
(**c**) *Mil (of army etc)* flanc *m*, **left/right flank** aile *f* gauche/droite; **to protect one's flanks** se couvrir sur les flancs; **to launch a flank attack** lancer une attaque de côté
(**d**) *Sport* aile *f*
2 *vt* (**a**) *(be on either side of)* encadrer; **flanked by two policemen** encadré de deux gendarmes; **flanked by his wife and son** entouré de sa femme et de son fils
(**b**) *Mil* flanquer
►► *Mktg* ***flank attack*** attaque *f* latérale; *Am Naut* ***flank speed*** = vitesse de pointe d'un navire

flanker ['flæŋkə(r)] *n* (**a**) *Sport (in rugby)* avant-aile *m*, flanqueur *m*; *(in American football)* = joueur qui se tient derrière la ligne de mêlée de façon à pouvoir réceptionner la balle
(**b**) *Mktg* produit *m* de protection latérale
(**c**) *Archit* ouvrage *m* flanquant
(**d**) *Mil* flanc-garde *f*
►► *Mktg* ***flanker brand*** marque *f* de protection latérale, marque *f* dérivée; *Mktg* ***flanker product*** produit *m* de protection latérale

flanking ['flæŋkɪŋ] *adj*
►► *Mil* ***flanking manoeuvre*** flanquement *m*

flannel ['flænəl] (*Br pt & pp* **flannelled**, *cont* **flannelling**, *Am pt & pp* **flanneled**, *cont* **flanneling**) **1** *n* (**a**) *Tex* flanelle *f*
(**b**) *Br (for washing)* ≃ gant *m* de toilette
(**c**) *(UNCOUNT) Br Fam (empty words)* baratin *m*, bla-bla *m*, bla-bla-bla *m*; **to talk a lot of flannel** faire beaucoup de baratin *ou* de bla-bla
2 *comp Tex (nightgown, sheet, trousers, suit)* en *ou* de flanelle
3 *vi Br Fam (use empty words)* faire du baratin *ou* du bla-bla *ou* du bla-bla-bla; **stop flannelling!** arrête ton baratin *ou* ton bla-bla
4 flannels *npl* pantalon *m* en *ou* de flanelle

flannelette [flænə'let] *Tex* **1** *n* pilou *m*
2 *comp (nightgown, sheet)* en *ou* de pilou

flannel-mouth *n Am Fam* = personne qui parle très lentement

flap [flæp] (*pt & pp* **flapped**, *cont* **flapping**) **1** *n* (**a**) *(of sails)* claquement *m*; *(of wings)* battement *m*; **the bird gave a flap of its wings** l'oiseau a battu des ailes

(**b**) *(of counter, desk, table → hinged)* abattant *m*; *(→ sliding)* rallonge *f*; *(of pocket, tent, envelope, book jacket)* rabat *m*; *(in floor, door)* trappe *f*; *(of aircraft)* volet *m* (hypersustentateur); **a flap of skin** un morceau de peau décollée

(**c**) *Fam (panic)* panique □ *f*; **to be in a flap** être dans tous ses états, être paniqué; **to get into a flap** se mettre dans tous ses états; **there's a flap on at the office** c'est la panique au bureau

(**d**) *Ling* battement *m*

2 *vi* (**a**) *(wings)* battre; *(sails, shutters, washing, curtains)* claquer; **the seagull flapped away** la mouette est partie dans un battement d'ailes

(**b**) *Fam (panic)* paniquer □, s'affoler □; **stop flapping!** du calme!, calmos!

3 *vt (wings)* battre de; *(hands, piece of paper)* agiter; **the bird flapped its wings** l'oiseau a battu des ailes; **he was flapping his arms about to keep warm** il agitait ses bras pour se tenir chaud

flapdoodle [ˌflæp'du:dəl] *n Fam* bêtises □ *fpl*, blagues *fpl*

flapjack ['flæpdʒæk] *n Culin Br* biscuit *m* à l'avoine, *Am* = petite crêpe épaisse

flapper ['flæpə(r)] *n* = jeune fille dans le vent (dans les années 20)

flapping ['flæpɪŋ] *n (of wings)* battement *m*; *(of sail)* claquement *m*

flare [fleə(r)] **1** *n* (**a**) *(bright flame → of fire, match)* flamboiement *m*; *(→ of jet engine)* flammes *fpl*

(**b**) *(signal)* signal *m* lumineux; *(rocket)* fusée *f* éclairante

(**c**) *(in clothes)* évasement *m*; **a skirt with a flare in it** une jupe à godets; **trousers with a flare** un pantalon à pattes d'éléphant

(**d**) *Chem & Petr (in chemical plant, oil refinery)* torche *f*

2 *vi* (**a**) *(flame, match)* flamboyer

(**b**) *(tempers)* s'échauffer; **tempers flared** les esprits se sont échauffés

(**c**) *(nostrils)* frémir

(**d**) *(clothes)* s'évaser

3 *vt* (**a**) *(nostrils)* dilater

(**b**) *(clothes)* évaser

4 flares *npl Br* **(a pair of) flares** un pantalon à pattes d'éléphant

►► ***flare gun*** pistolet *m* de détresse, lance-fusées *m inv*; *Br* ***flare path*** piste *f* à balises lumineuses; *Petr* ***flare stack*** torchère *f*

►**flare up** *vi (fire)* s'embraser; *Fig (dispute, quarrel, violence)* éclater; *(disease, epidemic, crisis)* apparaître, se déclarer; *(person)* s'emporter; **he flared up at me** il s'est emporté contre moi

flared [fleəd] *adj (trousers)* à pattes d'éléphant; *(dress)* évasé; *(skirt)* évasé, à godets

flare-out *n Aviat* arrondi *m*; **flare-out path** trajectoire *f* de l'arrondi

flare-up *n (of fire, light)* flamboiement *m*; *Fig (of anger, violence)* explosion *f*; *(of tension)* montée *f*; *(of disease, epidemic)* apparition *f*; *(quarrel)* dispute *f*; **renewed flare-up** *(of anger, violence)* reprise *f*, nouvelle explosion *f*; *(of tension)* remontée *f*; *(of disease, epidemic)* réapparition *f*

FLASH [flæʃ]

éclat	► 1 (a)
flash	► 1 (b), (e)
torche	► 1 (f)
clignoter	► 2 (a)
briller	► 2 (a)
filer comme l'éclair	► 2 (b)
faire clignoter	► 3 (a)
montrer rapidement	► 3 (b)
diffuser	► 3 (c)
tape-à-l'œil	► 4 (a)

1 *n* (**a**) *(of light, diamond)* éclat *m*; *(of metal)* reflet *m*, éclat *m*; **we saw a flash of light in the distance** nous avons vu l'éclat d'une lumière au loin; **give three flashes of the torch** allume la torche trois fois; **flash of wit/humour** pointe *f* d'esprit/d'humour; **flash of inspiration** éclair *m* de génie; **in a flash** *(very quickly)* en un éclair, en un clin d'œil; **it came to me in a flash** cela m'est venu d'un seul coup; **flash of lightning** éclair *m*; **a flash in the pan** un feu de paille; **(as) quick as a flash** aussi rapide que l'éclair, rapide comme l'éclair

(**b**) *(of news)* flash *m* (d'information)

(**c**) *Mil (on uniform)* écusson *m*

(**d**) *(of colour)* tache *f*

(**e**) *Phot* flash *m*; **are you going to use a flash for this one?** est-ce que tu vas la prendre au flash, celle-ci?

(**f**) *Am Fam (flashlight)* torche □ *f*

2 *vi* (**a**) *(light, torch, sign)* clignoter; *(diamond)* briller, lancer des éclats; **lightning flashed directly overhead** il y a eu des éclairs juste au-dessus; **her eyes flashed** ses yeux ont lancé des éclairs; **his eyes flashed with anger** ses yeux lançaient des éclairs de colère; *Aut* **to flash at sb** faire un appel de phares à qn

(**b**) *(move fast)* filer comme l'éclair, aller à la vitesse de l'éclair; **to flash in/out/past** *(person, car)* entrer/sortir/passer comme un éclair; **to flash past** *or* **by** *(time)* passer à toute vitesse; **the day/the days seemed to flash by** la journée a semblé passer/les jours ont semblé défiler à toute vitesse; **the thought flashed through** *or* **across her mind that...** la pensée que... lui a traversé l'esprit; **a smile flashed across his face** un sourire éclaira soudain son visage; **information flashed onto** *or* **up on the screen** des informations sont apparues sur l'écran; **my life flashed before me** ma vie a défilé devant mes yeux

(**c**) *Fam (expose oneself)* s'exhiber □; **to flash at sb** s'exhiber devant qn

3 *vt* (**a**) *(torch → turn on and off)* faire clignoter; **to flash a light in sb's face** *or* **eyes** diriger une lumière dans les yeux de qn; *Aut* **to flash (one's headlights at) sb** faire un appel de phares à qn; *Fig* **to flash a smile at sb** lancer *ou* adresser un sourire à qn; *Fig* **she flashed me a look of contempt** elle m'a décoché un regard méprisant

(**b**) *(give brief glimpse of → passport, photograph etc)* montrer rapidement; **he flashed a £50 note at them** il leur passa un billet de 50 livres sous le nez

(**c**) *(news, information)* diffuser; **to flash a message up on the screen** faire apparaître un message sur l'écran; **she flashed a report to head office** elle a envoyé un rapport-éclair au siège social

(**d**) *Am Fam (expose oneself to)* s'exhiber devant □

4 *adj Br Fam* (**a**) *(showy → car, clothes, jewellery)* tape-à-l'œil *(inv)*; *(→ person)* frimeur

(**b**) *(expensive-looking)* chic □

►► ***flash burn*** brûlure *f (causée par un éclat très violent et brûlant, comme celui d'une bombe)*; *Sch* ***flash card*** = carte portant un mot, une image etc utilisée dans l'enseignement comme aide à l'apprentissage; ***flash flood*** crue *f* subite; ***flash freezing*** surgélation *f*; ***Flash Gordon*** = héros de bandes dessinées et de films de science-fiction; *Phot* ***flash gun*** flash *m*; *Br Fam* ***flash Harry*** frimeur *m*; *Com & Mktg* ***flash pack*** *(discounted)* emballage *m* portant une réduction de prix; ***flash photography*** photographie *f* au flash; ***flash welding*** soudure *f* par étincelage

►**flash around** *vt sep Fam (show off)* montrer □, exhiber □; **he likes flashing his money around** il aime étaler sa richesse; **don't flash your money around here!** ne montre *ou* n'exhibe pas ton argent ici!

►**flash back** *vi (in novel, film etc)* **to flash back to sth** revenir en arrière sur *ou* faire un flash-back sur qch; **my mind flashed back to 1942** l'année 1942 m'est soudain revenue à l'esprit

►**flash forward** *vi (of film)* faire un saut en avant

flashback ['flæʃbæk] *n (in novel, film, etc)* flash-back *m inv*, retour *m* en arrière; *Fam Drugs slang (hallucination)* flash-back *m*; **their story is told in flashback** leur histoire est racontée par flash-back *ou* par retours en arrière; **a flashback to the war** un flash-back sur la guerre; **I had a flashback to when I was a child** mon enfance m'est revenue à l'esprit

flashbulb ['flæʃbʌlb] *n Phot* ampoule *f* de flash

flashcube ['flæʃkju:b] *n Phot* cube *m* de flash

flasher ['flæʃə(r)] *n* (**a**) *Aut (indicator)* clignotant *m* (**b**) *Fam (man)* exhibitionniste □ *m*

flash-freeze *vt* surgeler

flash-fry *vt Culin* saisir

flashily ['flæʃɪlɪ] *adv Fam Pej* d'une manière tapageuse *ou* tape-à-l'œil, tapageusement

flashiness ['flæʃɪnɪs] *n Fam Pej (of person)* côté *m* frimeur; *(of car, clothes, taste)* côté *m* tape-à-l'œil *ou* clinquant

flashing ['flæʃɪŋ] **1** *adj (indicator, light, torch)* clignotant; *(diamonds)* étincelant; **with flashing eyes, she stormed out** elle sortit brutalement, les yeux ardents (de colère); *Aut* **flashing emergency lights** feux *mpl* de détresse; **flashing light** *(on police car)* gyrophare *m*

2 *n* (**a**) *Fam (indecent exposure)* exhibitionnisme □ *m* (**b**) *(of diamond)* éclat *m* (**c**) *(UNCOUNT) Constr (on roof)* noue *f*

flashlight ['flæʃlaɪt] *n* (**a**) *Phot* ampoule *f* de flash (**b**) *esp Am (torch)* torche *f* électrique, lampe *f* électrique *ou* de poche (**c**) *(flashing signal)* fanal *m*

►► ***flashlight photography*** photographie *f* au flash

Flashman ['flæʃmən] *pr n* = personnage d'aventurier sans scrupules créé par George MacDonald Fraser, basé sur un personnage figurant dans le roman 'Tom Brown's Schooldays'

flashover ['flæʃˌəʊvə(r)] *n Elec* étincelle *f* de rupture

flashpoint ['flɒʃpɔɪnt] *n* (**a**) *Chem* point *m* d'éclair (**b**) *Fig (trouble spot)* poudrière *f*; *(situation)* situation *f* explosive *ou* critique; *Fig* **the situation has reached flashpoint** la situation est explosive *ou* sur le point d'exploser

flashy ['flæʃɪ] *adj Fam Pej (person)* frimeur; *(car, clothes, taste)* tape-à-l'œil *(inv)*, clinquant; *(colour)* voyant □, criard □

flask [flɑ:sk] *n Pharm* fiole *f*; *Chem* ballon *m*; *(for water, wine)* gourde *f*; **(vacuum** *or* **Thermos®) flask** (bouteille *f*) Thermos® *f*

FLAT [flæt]

plat	► 1 (a); 3 (b), (c)
dégonflé	► 1 (a)
crevé	► 1 (a)
à plat	► 1 (a), (d)
éventé	► 1 (b)
monotone	► 1 (c)
en dessous du ton	► 1 (e); 2 (c)
catégorique	► 1 (f)
fixe	► 1 (g)
catégoriquement	► 1 (f); 2 (a)
appartement	► 3 (a)
bémol	► 3 (e)
crevaison	► 3 (f)

1 *adj* (**a**) *(countryside, feet, stomach, chest, shoes)* plat; *(surface)* plan; *(roof)* plat, en terrasse; *(nose)* épaté, camus; *(curve)* aplati; *(tyre → deflated)* à plat, dégonflé; *(→ punctured)* crevé; *(ball, balloon)* dégonflé; *(picture)* sans relief; *(in painting → colour)* mat; *Archit (vault)* plat; *(arch)* déprimé; **to stretch out flat** *(person)* s'allonger à plat; **to stand flat against the wall** *(person)* se plaquer contre le mur; *(item of furniture)* être adossé contre le mur; **it folds up flat** c'est pliable; **he was lying flat on his back** il était allongé à plat sur le dos; *Fig* **to be flat on one's back** *(with illness)* être alité; **lay the book flat on the desk** pose le livre à plat sur le bureau; *also Fig* **to knock sb flat** faire tomber qn à la renverse; **the blow laid him flat** le coup l'a assommé; **to fall flat on one's back** tomber sur le dos; **to fall flat** *(joke)* tomber à plat; *(play etc)* faire un four; **to fall flat on one's face** tomber la tête la première; *Fig* se casser le nez; **the city had been bombed flat** les bombardements avaient rasé la ville

(**b**) *(soft drink, beer, champagne)* éventé; **to go flat** *(beer, soft drink)* s'éventer, perdre ses bulles

(**c**) *Fig (monotonous → style, voice)* monotone, terne; *(without emotion → voice)* éteint; *(stock market, business)* au point mort; *(social life)* peu animé; **to feel flat** se sentir vidé *ou* à plat; **business has been a bit flat lately** les affaires sont calmes ces derniers temps

(**d**) *(battery)* à plat

(**e**) *Mus* en dessous du ton, trop bas; **to be flat** *(singer)* chanter en dessous du ton *ou* trop bas; *(instrumentalist)* jouer en dessous du ton *ou* trop bas; **E flat** mi *m* bémol

(**f**) *(categorical → refusal, denial)* catégorique; **to give a flat refusal** refuser catégoriquement; **you're not going, and that's flat!** tu n'iras pas, un point c'est tout!
(**g**) *Com (rate, fare, fee)* fixe
2 *adv* (**a**) *(categorically)* catégoriquement; **she turned me down flat** elle m'a opposé un refus catégorique
(**b**) *(exactly)* **in thirty seconds flat** en trente secondes pile
(**c**) *Mus* en dessous du ton
(**d**) *Fam (idiom)* **flat broke** complètement fauché
3 *n* (**a**) *Br (apartment)* appartement *m*; **(block of) flats** immeuble *m* (d'habitation)
(**b**) *(of hand, blade)* plat *m*
(**c**) *Horseracing* **the flat** *(races)* le plat; *(season)* la saison des courses de plat
(**d**) **on the flat** *(horizontally)* horizontalement; *Rail (track)* en palier; *Sport* sur le plat
(**e**) *Mus* bémol *m*
(**f**) *Fam (puncture)* crevaison❑ *f*; *(punctured tyre)* pneu *m* crevé❑; *(deflated tyre)* pneu *m* à plat❑; **we got a flat** *(puncture)* nous avons crevé
(**g**) *Theat* ferme *f*
4 flats *npl* (**a**) *Geog* **salt flats** marais *mpl* salants
(**b**) *(shoes)* chaussures *fpl* plates
5 flat out 1 *adj (exhausted)* à plat, vidé; *(drunk)* fin saoul; *(knocked out)* K-O **2** *adv* **to work flat out** travailler d'arrache-pied; **to be going flat out** *(car)* être à sa vitesse maximum; *(driver, runner, horse)* être au maximum *ou* à fond; **the car does 100 mph flat out** ≃ la vitesse maximale *ou* de pointe de la voiture est de 160 km/h; **she's going flat out to win the chairmanship** elle met tout en jeu pour obtenir la présidence
►► ***flat bed*** *(of lorry)* plateau *m*; ***flat blade screwdriver*** tournevis *m* à lame plate, tournevis *m* plat; *Naut* ***flat calm*** calme *m* plat; *Br* ***flat cap*** casquette *f*; *Comput* ***flat file*** fichier *m* de données non structurées; *Comput & TV* ***flat monitor*** écran *m* plat; *Comput* ***flat panel display*** moniteur *m* à écran plat; *Horseracing* ***flat race*** course *f* de plat; *Horseracing* ***flat racing*** *(races)* plat *m*; *(season)* saison *f* des courses de plat; *Comput & TV* ***flat screen*** écran *m* plat; *Horseracing* ***flat season*** saison *f* des courses de plat; ***flat top*** *(haircut)* brosse *f*; *Am Fam (aircraft carrier)* porte-avions❑ *m inv*; *Austr* ***flat white*** *(coffee)* café *m* au lait

---

flat-bed *adj*
►► *Br* ***flat-bed lorry*** semi-remorque *f* à plateau; *Comput* ***flat-bed scanner*** scanner *m ou* scanneur *m* à plat; *Am* ***flat-bed truck*** semi-remorque *f* à plateau

flatboat ['flætbəʊt] *n Naut* bateau *m* plat, plate *f*

flat-bottomed boat [-'bɒtəmd-] *n* bateau *m* à fond plat

flatcar ['flætkɑː(r)] *n Am Rail* wagon *m* en plate-forme

flat-chested [-'tʃestɪd] *adj* **to be flat-chested** ne pas avoir de poitrine

flat-dweller *n Br* = personne vivant en appartement

flatfish ['flætfɪʃ] *n Ich* poisson *m* plat

flatfoot ['flætfʊt] *n* (**a**) *Med* pied *m* plat (**b**) *Fam Old-fashioned (policeman)* poulet *m*

flat-footed *adj* (**a**) *Med* aux pieds plats (**b**) *Fam (clumsy)* empoté; *(tactless)* maladroit❑, lourdaud (**c**) *Fam (idiom)* **to catch sb flat-footed** prendre qn par surprise❑

Flathead ['flæthed] *n* (**a**) *(member of Native American people)* Tête-plate *mf* (**b**) *Fam (fool)* nouille *f*

flat-hunt *vi Br* chercher un appartement; **I've spent the whole day flat-hunting** j'ai passé toute la journée à chercher un appartement

flat-hunting *n Br* recherche *f* d'appartement; **flat-hunting takes up all my free time** la recherche d'un appartement occupe tout mon temps libre

flatiron ['flætaɪən] *n* fer *m* à repasser *(non électrique)*
►► ***the Flatiron Building*** = immeuble à New York dont la forme rappelle celle d'un fer à repasser

flatland ['flætlænd] *n* plaine *f*

flat-leaf parsley *n Bot & Culin* persil *m* plat

flatlet ['flætlɪt] *n Br* studio *m*

flatly ['flætlɪ] *adv* (**a**) *(categorically → deny, refuse)* catégoriquement (**b**) *(without emotion → say, speak)* d'une voix éteinte; *(monotonously)* avec monotonie

flatmate ['flætmeɪt] *n Br* colocataire *mf (d'un même appartement)*; **she and I were flatmates in London** elle et moi partagions un appartement à Londres

flatness ['flætnɪs] *n* (**a**) *(of surface etc)* nature *f* plate; *(of countryside)* absence *f* de relief; *(of curve etc)* aplatissement *m* (**b**) *(of refusal)* netteté *f* (**c**) *(of existence etc)* monotonie *f*; *(of style etc)* insipidité *f*, platitude *f*; *(of beer etc)* évent *m*; *(of colour)* caractère *m* terne; *(of sound)* caractère *m* sourd; **the flatness in his voice** l'absence d'émotion dans sa voix

flat-nosed *adj* au nez épaté *ou* camus

flat-packed *adj (furniture)* en kit

flat-rate *adj*
►► *Comput* ***flat-rate connection*** *(to Internet)* connexion *f* à tarif forfaitaire; *Comput* ***flat-rate monthly charge*** *(to Internet)* forfait *m* mensuel

flat-screen *adj Comput & TV* à écran plat

flatten ['flætən] **1** *vt* (**a**) *(path, road, ground)* aplanir; *(dough, metal)* aplatir; *(animal, person → of vehicle)* écraser; *(house, village → of bulldozer, earthquake)* raser; *(crop → of wind, storm)* écraser, aplatir; *(piece of paper)* étaler; **to flatten oneself against a wall** se plaquer *ou* se coller contre un mur
(**b**) *Fam (defeat thoroughly)* écraser, battre à plate couture
(**c**) *Fam (knock to the ground)* démolir❑
(**d**) *Fam (subdue → person)* clouer le bec à; **that'll flatten her** ça lui clouera le bec, ça la remettra à sa place
(**e**) *Mus (note)* baisser d'un demi-ton, bémoliser
2 *vi (countryside)* s'aplanir
►**flatten out 1** *vi* (**a**) *(countryside, hills)* s'aplanir (**b**) *Aviat (plane)* se redresser; *(pilot)* redresser l'appareil
2 *vt sep (piece of paper, cloth)* étaler à plat; *(bump, path, road)* aplanir

flattened ['flætənd] *adj* (**a**) *(smoothed out)* aplati; *(nose)* épaté (**b**) *Mus (note)* bémolisé

flatter ['flætə(r)] **1** *vt (of person)* flatter; *(of dress, photo, colour)* avantager; **I'm flattered to have been chosen** je suis flatté d'avoir été choisi *ou* que l'on m'ait choisi; **don't flatter yourself!, you flatter yourself!** non mais tu rêves!; **we flatter ourselves on offering a more efficient service** nous nous flattons d'offrir un service plus efficace; **he flatters himself (that) he's a good singer** il a la prétention d'être un bon chanteur
2 *vi* flatter

flatterer ['flætərə(r)] *n* flatteur(euse) *m,f*

flattering ['flætərɪŋ] *adj (remark, person, offer)* flatteur; *(picture, colour)* avantageux, flatteur; *(dress)* seyant; **it is flattering to be asked to give this speech** c'est flatteur d'être sollicité pour faire ce discours; **I didn't get a very flattering impression of the city/your boss** la ville/ton patron ne m'a pas fait une impression très favorable; **how flattering!** comme c'est flatteur!

flatteringly ['flætərɪŋlɪ] *adv (speak of, describe)* en termes flatteurs, flatteusement; **the photograph had been flatteringly lit** la photo avait été prise dans une lumière flatteuse

flattery ['flætərɪ] *n (UNCOUNT)* flatterie *f*; **to use flattery** employer la flatterie *ou* des flatteries; **flattery will get you nowhere** la flatterie ne vous mènera nulle part, vous n'obtiendrez rien par la flatterie

flattie ['flætɪ] *n Fam* chaussure *f* plate❑

flatulence ['flætjʊləns] *n* flatulence *f*

flatulent ['flætjʊlənt] *adj* flatulent

flatus ['fleɪtəs] *n Med* flatuosité *f*

flatware ['flætweə(r)] *n (UNCOUNT) Am (cutlery)* couverts *mpl*; *(serving dishes)* plats *mpl*; *(plates)* assiettes *fpl*

flatways ['flætweɪz], **flatwise** ['flætwaɪz] *adv Am* à plat

flatworm ['flæt,wɜːm] *n Entom* plathelminthe *m*, ver *m* plat

flaunt [flɔːnt] *vt (wealth, beauty, knowledge)* étaler, faire étalage de; *(car, jewellery)* faire parade de, exhiber; *(bad manners, ignorance)* afficher; **to flaunt oneself** s'afficher; **if you've got it, flaunt it** si tu as ce qu'il faut, ne t'en cache pas

flaunting ['flɔːntɪŋ] *n (of wealth, beauty, knowledge)* étalage *m*; *(of car, jewellery)* fait *m* d'exhiber

flautist ['flɔːtɪst] *n Br Mus* flûtiste *mf*

flavescent [flə'vesənt] *adj* flavescent

Flavian ['fleɪvɪən] *pr n Antiq* Flavien

flavin ['fleɪvɪn] *n Chem* flavine *f*

Flavius ['fleɪvjəs] *pr n* **Flavius Josephus** Flavius Josèphe

flavone ['fleɪvəʊn] *n Chem* flavone *f*

flavour, *Am* **flavor** ['fleɪvə(r)] **1** *n (of food, drink)* goût *m*; *(of ice-cream, tea, yoghurt)* parfum *m*; **it comes in six different flavours** il existe en six parfums différents; **chocolate/coffee flavour ice-cream** glace *f* au chocolat/au café; **this coffee keeps its flavour well** ce café garde bien sa saveur; **it doesn't have much flavour** cela n'a pas beaucoup de goût; **it's got quite a spicy flavour** c'est assez épicé; *Fig* **it gives the film a South American flavour** cela donne une note sud-américaine au film; **there was a flavour of regret about his remarks** ses remarques contenaient une pointe de regret; **to be flavour of the month** *(in vogue)* être au goût du jour; *Fam* **you're not exactly flavour of the month at the moment** tu n'es pas comme qui dirait en odeur de sainteté en ce moment, tu n'as pas vraiment la cote en ce moment
2 *vt (with spices, herbs)* assaisonner; *(with fruit, alcohol)* parfumer
►► ***flavour enhancer*** agent *m* de sapidité

flavoured, *Am* **flavored** ['fleɪvəd] *adj (milk, mineral water)* aromatisé

-flavoured, *Am* **-flavored** ['fleɪvəd] *suff* **chocolate-flavoured** au chocolat; **vanilla-flavoured** à la vanille

flavouring, *Am* **flavoring** ['fleɪvərɪŋ] *n (savoury)* assaisonnement *m*; *(sweet)* parfum *m*, arôme *m*; **no artificial flavourings** *(on tin, package)* sans arômes artificiels

flavourless, *Am* **flavorless** ['fleɪvəlɪs] *adj* sans goût, insipide

flavoursome, *Am* **flavorsome** ['fleɪvəsəm] *adj (food)* savoureux

flaw [flɔː] **1** *n* (**a**) *(in material, plan, character)* défaut *m* (**b**) *Law* vice *m* de forme
2 *vt (object)* endommager; *(someone's character, beauty)* altérer

flawed [flɔːd] *adj (reasoning)* défectueux; *(novel, film)* qui a des défauts; *(sweater, scarf, fabric)* qui a un/des défaut(s); *(wood)* gercé; *(diamond)* qui a un crapaud *ou* un défaut; **the argument is, however, flawed** cette argumentation a cependant un défaut *ou* des défauts

flawless ['flɔːlɪs] *adj* parfait

flawlessly ['flɔːlɪslɪ] *adv* parfaitement

flawlessness ['flɔːlɪsnɪs] *n* perfection *f*

flax [flæks] *n* lin *m*
►► ***flax field*** linière *f*

flaxen ['flæksən] *adj (hair)* blond pâle *ou* filasse *(inv)*

flaxen-haired *adj* aux cheveux blond pâle *ou* filasse

flay [fleɪ] *vt (animal)* dépouiller, écorcher; *(person)* fouetter; *Fig (criticize)* éreinter; **to flay sb alive** faire la peau à qn

flayer ['fleɪə(r)] *n (of animals)* écorcheur *m*

flaying ['fleɪɪŋ] *n (of animals)* écorchement *m*, dépouillement *m*

flea [fliː] *n* puce *f*; **to have fleas** avoir des puces; *Fam* **to send sb off with a flea in his/her ear** *(dismiss)* envoyer balader qn; *(scold)* passer un savon à qn
►► ***flea circus*** cirque *m* de puces savantes; ***flea collar*** collier *m* antipuces; ***flea market*** marché *m* aux puces; ***flea powder*** poudre *f* antipuce

fleabag ['fliːbæg] *n Fam* (**a**) *Br (animal, person)* sac *m* à puces (**b**) *Am (cheap hotel)* hôtel *m* miteux

fleabite ['fliːbaɪt] *n* piqûre *f ou* morsure *f* de puce; *Fig (trifle)* broutille *f*

flea-bitten *adj* couvert de puces; *Fig (shabby)* miteux

fleapit ['fliːpɪt] *n Br Fam* cinéma *m* miteux; *Hum* **the local fleapit** le cinéma du coin

fleck [flek] **1** *n* (**a**) *(of colour)* moucheture *f*, tacheture *f*; *(of sunlight)* moucheture *f* (**b**) *(of dust)* particule *f*

2 *vt (with colour)* moucheter, tacheter; *(with sunlight)* moucheter; **hair flecked with grey** cheveux *mpl* grisonnants; **white flecked with brown** blanc *m* moucheté *ou* tacheté de marron

flecking ['flekɪŋ] *n* mouchetures *fpl*

fled [fled] *pt & pp of* **flee**

fledge [fledʒ] **1** *vi Orn (birds)* s'emplumer

2 *vt* (**a**) *Orn (young birds)* élever jusqu'à ce qu'ils soient en état de voler (**b**) *(arrow)* empenner

fledged [fledʒd] *adj (bird)* emplumé

fledgling, fledgeling ['fledʒlɪŋ] **1** *n* (**a**) *(young bird)* oisillon *m* (**b**) *Fig* novice *mf*, débutant(e) *m,f*

2 *comp (company, industry, political party etc)* naissant; *(doctor, lawyer)* débutant

flee [fliː] *(pt & pp* **fled** [fled]) **1** *vi* s'enfuir, fuir; **to flee from sb/sth** fuir qn/qch; **to flee from a house/country** s'enfuir d'une maison/d'un pays; **to flee from temptation** fuir la tentation

2 *vt (person, danger, temptation)* fuir; *(country, town)* s'enfuir de

fleece [fliːs] **1** *n* (**a**) *(of sheep)* toison *f* (**b**) *Tex (sheepskin)* peau *f* de mouton; *(synthetic)* laine *f* polaire, tissu *m* polaire (**c**) *(garment)* fourrure *f* polaire, polaire *f*

2 *comp Tex (made of sheepskin)* en peau de mouton; *(synthetic)* en laine polaire, en tissu polaire

3 *vt* (**a**) *Fam (cheat)* escroquer; *(overcharge)* écorcher (**b**) *(shear → sheep)* tondre

fleeced [fliːst] *adj (having a fleece → sheep)* pourvu *ou* couvert d'une toison; *Literary* **a plain fleeced with snow** une plaine couverte d'un manteau de neige

fleece-lined *adj (with sheepskin)* doublé de peau de mouton; *(with synthetic material)* doublé de laine polaire *ou* de tissu polaire

fleecing ['fliːsɪŋ] *n Fam (overcharging)* escroquerie *f (fait de faire payer trop cher)*

fleecy ['fliːsɪ] *adj (material)* laineux; *(clouds)* cotonneux

fleeing ['fliːɪŋ] *adj (army etc)* en fuite

fleet [fliːt] **1** *n* (**a**) *Naut* flotte *f*; *(smaller)* flottille *f*; **the Fleet** = la Marine nationale

(**b**) *(of buses, cars, taxis)* parc *m*; **a fleet of ambulances took the injured to hospital** plusieurs ambulances ont transporté les blessés à l'hôpital; **car fleet** parc *m* automobile

2 *adj Literary* rapide; **fleet of foot** aux pieds ailés

►► *Naut* ***fleet admiral*** ≃ amiral *m* de France; *Naut* ***the Fleet Air Arm*** = l'aéronavale britannique; *Ins* ***fleet rating*** barème *m* des flottes; ***Fleet Street*** = rue de Londres, dont le nom sert à désigner les grands journaux britanniques; **the Fleet Street papers** les journaux *mpl* nationaux; ***Fleet Street journalist*** journaliste *mf* de la presse nationale

> **FLEET STREET**
>
> Traditionnellement, cette rue de la City était celle des journaux. Aujourd'hui, beaucoup de journaux ont établi leur siège dans d'autres quartiers, notamment les Docklands. Cependant, le terme "Fleet Street" est encore employé pour désigner la presse et le monde du journalisme.

fleet-footed *adj Literary* au pied léger

fleeting ['fliːtɪŋ] *adj (memory)* fugace; *(beauty, pleasure)* passager; **for a fleeting moment** l'espace d'un instant; **to catch a fleeting glimpse of** apercevoir, entrevoir; **to give sb a fleeting glance** lancer un regard rapide à qn; **to give sth a fleeting glance** jeter un coup d'œil rapide à qch

fleetingly ['fliːtɪŋlɪ] *adv (glimpse, appear)* rapidement

fleetly ['fliːtlɪ] *adv Literary* vite, rapidement

fleetness ['fliːtnɪs] *n Literary* vitesse *f*, rapidité *f*

Fleming ['flemɪŋ] *n* Flamand(e) *m,f*

Flemish ['flemɪʃ] **1** *n Ling* flamand *m*

2 *npl* **the Flemish** les Flamands *mpl*

3 *adj* flamand

flesh [fleʃ] **1** *n* (**a**) *(of person, animal, fruit)* chair *f*; **there's not much flesh on her** elle n'est pas très grasse; **to put on flesh** *(person)* forcir; *(animal)* engraisser; *Fig* **it needs a bit more flesh** *(proposal, essay etc)* il a besoin d'être un peu étoffé; **she looks better on TV than she does in the flesh** elle est plus jolie à la télé qu'en chair et en os; **creatures of flesh and blood** êtres *mpl* de chair et de sang; **I'm only flesh and blood, you know** je suis comme tout le monde, tu sais; **it's more than flesh and blood can bear** *or* **stand** c'est plus que ce que la nature humaine peut endurer; **she's my own flesh and blood** c'est ma chair et mon sang; *Fam* **to press the flesh** *(politicians, royalty etc)* serrer des mains ❑, faire un bain de foule ❑

(**b**) *Rel* chair *f*; **to mortify the flesh** mortifier sa chair; **pleasures/sins of the flesh** plaisirs *mpl* de la/péchés *mpl* de chair; **the spirit is willing but the flesh is weak** l'esprit est prompt mais la chair est faible; **to go the way of all flesh** retourner à la *ou* redevenir poussière

(**c**) *(colour)* couleur *f* chair

2 *vt* (**a**) *Hunt (dogs)* donner le goût du sang à (**b**) *Literary (accustom to bloodshed)* donner le baptême du sang à

(**c**) *Literary (animal)* engraisser

►► ***flesh colour*** couleur *f* chair; *Theat* ***flesh tights*** collant *m* chair; *Art* ***flesh tints*** carnations *fpl*; ***flesh wound*** blessure *f* superficielle *ou* légère

►**flesh out 1** *vt sep (essay, report, character etc)* étoffer

2 *vi (person)* s'étoffer, prendre de la carrure

flesh-coloured *adj* (couleur) chair; **flesh-coloured tights** collants *mpl* chair

fleshfly ['fleʃflaɪ] *n Entom* sarcophage *m*

fleshiness ['fleʃɪnɪs] *n (of person)* rondeurs *fpl*; *(of part of the body, fruit, leaf)* état *m* charnu

fleshless ['fleʃlɪs] *adj* décharné

fleshly ['fleʃlɪ] *adj* de la chair

fleshpots ['fleʃpɒts] *npl Hum Pej* lieux *mpl* de plaisir

fleshy ['fleʃɪ] *(compar* **fleshier**, *superl* **fleshiest**) *adj (person)* bien en chair; *(part of the body, fruit, leaf)* charnu

fletch [fletʃ] *vt (arrow)* empenner

fletcher ['fletʃə(r)] *n* fabricant(e) *m,f* de flèches

fleur-de-lis, fleur-de-lys [ˌflɜːdə'liː] *n Her* fleur *f* de lis *ou* lys

fleuret [flɜː'ret] *n Archit* fleurette *f*

fleuron ['flɜːrɒn] *n Archit & Her* fleuron *m*

flew [fluː] *pt of* **fly**

flex [fleks] **1** *vt (one's arms, knees)* fléchir; **to flex one's muscles** bander *ou* faire jouer ses muscles; *Fig* faire étalage de sa force

2 *n esp Br (wire)* fil *m*; *(heavy-duty)* câble *m*

►► ***flex holder*** enrouleur *m* pour fil électrique

flexi ['fleksɪ] *n (UNCOUNT) Br Fam (flexitime)* horaires *m* à la carte *ou* flexibles ❑; **to be on** *or* **to work flexi** avoir des horaires à la carte *ou* flexibles

flexibility [ˌfleksə'bɪlətɪ] *n (of object)* flexibilité *f*, souplesse *f*; *Fig (of plan, approach)* flexibilité *f*; *(of person's character)* souplesse *f*; **he has always shown a lot of flexibility** *(in timing, arrangements)* il s'est toujours montré très disponible *ou* arrangeant; **what I like about this software is its flexibility** ce qui me plaît dans ce logiciel, c'est sa flexibilité *ou* souplesse d'emploi

flexible ['fleksəbəl] *adj* flexible, souple; *Fig (approach, plans, timetable etc)* flexible; *(person's character)* souple; *(as regards timing, arrangements)* arrangeant; **flexible working hours** horaires *mpl* (de travail) à la carte *ou* flexibles; **my working hours are very flexible** j'ai des horaires de travail très libres *ou* souples

►► *Acct* ***flexible budget*** budget *m* variable, budget *m* flexible; *Fin* ***flexible mortgage*** emprunt *m* immobilier à échéances variables; *Mil* ***flexible response*** riposte *f* graduée

flexile ['fleksaɪl] *adj Old-fashioned* souple, flexible; *(features)* mobile

flexion ['flekʃən] *n Gram* flexion *f*

flexitime ['fleksɪtaɪm] *n Br (UNCOUNT)* horaires *mpl* à la carte *ou* flexibles; **to be on** *or* **to work flexitime** avoir des horaires à la carte

flexor ['fleksə(r)] *Anat* **1** *adj (muscle)* fléchisseur

2 *n* fléchisseur *m*

flextime ['flekstaɪm] *Am* = **flexitime**

flexuose ['fleksjʊəʊs], **flexuous** ['fleksjʊəs] *adj Bot* flexueux

flexure ['flekʃə(r)] *n* (**a**) *(bending)* flexion *f*, courbure *f*; *Tech* **lateral flexure** flambement *m*, flambage *m* (**b**) *(bend)* courbe *f* (**c**) *Geom* courbure *f* (**d**) *Geol* flexure *f*, pli *m*

►► *Geol* ***flexure fault*** pli-faille *m*

flibbertigibbet [ˌflɪbətɪ'dʒɪbɪt] *n Fam* écervelé(e) *m,f*, tête *f* de linotte

flick [flɪk] **1** *n* (**a**) *(with finger)* chiquenaude *f*; *(with wrist)* petit *ou* léger mouvement *m*; *(with tail, whip, duster)* petit *ou* léger coup *m*; *Sport* petit coup *m*; **with a flick of his finger** d'une chiquenaude; **give the table a quick flick with a duster** donne un petit coup de chiffon à *ou* sur la table; **at the flick of a switch** en appuyant simplement sur un interrupteur

(**b**) *Br Fam Old-fashioned (film)* film ❑ *m*

2 *vt (switch)* appuyer sur; **he flicked the horse with his whip** il a donné un petit coup de fouet au cheval; **he had to keep flicking the hair out of his eyes** il n'arrêtait pas de chasser du doigt les cheveux qui lui tombaient dans les yeux; **don't flick your ash on the floor** ne mets pas tes cendres par terre; **she flicked the ash off the table** *(with duster)* d'un coup de chiffon, elle a enlevé la cendre de la table; *(with finger)* d'une chiquenaude, elle a enlevé la cendre de la table

3 **flicks** *npl Br Fam Old-fashioned* **the flicks** le ciné, le cinoche

►► *Br* ***flick knife*** (couteau *m* à) cran *m* d'arrêt; *Aut* ***flick wipe*** balayage *m* unique

►**flick away** *vt sep* chasser; *(with fingers)* repousser d'une chiquenaude

►**flick off** *vt sep (with finger → ash, paper etc)* envoyer promener *ou* enlever d'une chiquenaude; *(→ light, computer)* éteindre; **to flick sth off with a duster** faire envoler qch d'un coup de torchon; **he flicked the dandruff off his collar** il secoua les pellicules qui se trouvaient sur son col

►**flick on** *vt sep* (**a**) *(light, computer)* allumer (**b**) *Ftbl* **to flick the ball on** prolonger une passe

►**flick out** *vi* sortir; **the snake's tongue was flicking in and out** la langue du serpent sortait et rentrait à petits coups rapides

►**flick over** *vt sep (pages of book, newspaper etc)* tourner rapidement

►**flick through** *vt insep (book, newspaper)* feuilleter; *(photographs)* jeter un œil parmi; *TV* **to flick through the channels** passer rapidement d'une chaîne à une autre

flicker ['flɪkə(r)] **1** *vi (flame, light)* vaciller, trembler; *(eyelids, TV picture)* trembler; *(of instrument needle etc)* osciller; **the candle was flickering** la flamme de la bougie vacillait; **a smile flickered on his lips** un sourire erra sur ses lèvres

2 *n (of flame, light)* vacillement *m*, tremblement *m*; *(of eyelids)* tremblement *m*; *(of TV screen)* scintillement *m*; **a flicker of recognition** une lueur de reconnaissance; **a flicker of hope/a smile** l'ombre *f* d'un espoir/d'un sourire; **a flicker of interest/annoyance** une pointe d'intérêt/d'énervement

flicker-free *adj (screen)* anti-scintillements *(inv)*

flickering ['flɪkərɪŋ] **1** *adj (light, flame)* vacillant; *(image)* tremblotant

2 *n* (**a**) *(of light, flame)* vacillement *m* (**b**) *(of image)* scintillement *m*

flick-on *n (in soccer)* = petite passe qui en prolonge une autre

flier ['flaɪə(r)] *n* (**a**) *Aviat (pilot)* aviateur(trice) *m,f*; **she's a good/bad flier** *(passenger)* elle supporte bien/ne supporte pas l'avion; **she's a frequent flier** elle prend souvent l'avion

(**b**) *Orn* **the heron is an ungainly flier** le héron a un vol peu élégant

(**c**) *Fam (start of race)* départ *m* lancé ❑; *(false start)* faux départ ❑ *m*; **to get a flier** *(good start)* partir comme un boulet de canon

(**d**) *Fam (fall)* vol *m* plané; **to take a flier** faire un vol plané

(**e**) *Am Fam (speculative venture)* entreprise *f* à risques ❑; **to take a flier** *(financial risk)* prendre un risque financier; **it's a bit of a flier, don't you think?** c'est un peu risqué, tu ne crois pas?

(**f**) *(leaflet)* prospectus *m*

flies [flaɪz] *npl* (**a**) *(of trousers)* braguette *f*; **your flies are undone** *or* **open** ta braguette est ouverte (**b**) *Theat* dessus *mpl*, cintres *mpl*

flight [flaɪt] *n* (**a**) *(act of flying → of bird, plane)* vol *m*; *(→ of projectile, star)* course *f*; **capable of flight** capable de voler; **to be in flight** être en vol

(**b**) *(journey → of bird, spacecraft, plane, missile)* vol *m*; **manned flight** *(of spacecraft)* vol *m* habité; **a flight of 500 miles is nothing to a swallow** ≃ les hirondelles peuvent facilement effectuer des vols de 800 kilomètres

(**c**) *Aviat (journey in plane → by passenger)* voyage *m*; *(→ by pilot)* vol *m*; *(plane itself)* vol *m*; **I don't want to miss my flight** je ne veux pas rater mon avion; **my flight is at 2.15** mon avion est à 2h15; **how was your flight?** as-tu fait bon voyage?; **this is my first transatlantic flight** *(passenger)* c'est la première fois que je traverse l'Atlantique en avion; *(pilot)* c'est mon premier vol *ou* ma première traversée transatlantique; **flight BA 314 to Paris** le vol BA 314 à destination de Paris; **when is the next flight to Newcastle?** à quelle heure part le prochain vol pour *ou* à destination de Newcastle?; **all flights out of Gatwick** tous les vols en provenance de Gatwick

(**d**) *(group of birds)* vol *m*, volée *f*; *(group of aircraft)* flotte *f* aérienne; **the Queen's/King's Flight** = avions au service de la famille royale; *Fig* **to be in the first** *or* **top flight** faire partie de l'élite

(**e**) *(fleeing)* fuite *f*; **to be in full flight** être en pleine retraite; **to take flight** prendre la fuite; **in the course of her flight from justice** alors qu'elle fuyait la justice; **to put sb/the enemy to flight** mettre qn/l'ennemi en fuite; *Fig* **flight of capital** évasion *f ou* fuite *f* des capitaux; *Bible* **the Flight into Egypt** la fuite en Égypte

(**f**) *(of stairs)* **flight (of stairs** *or* **steps)** escalier *m*; **I had to walk up all ten flights** j'ai dû monter les dix étages à pied; **it's another three flights up** c'est trois étages plus haut; **I'm not carrying this wardrobe up all those flights of stairs** je refuse de monter cette penderie tout là-haut; **a short flight of steps** quelques marches *fpl*

(**g**) *Fig* **a flight of the imagination** une envolée de l'imagination; **it was just a flight of fancy** ce n'était qu'une idée folle

(**h**) *(on arrow, dart)* penne *f*, empennage *m*

►► ***flight attendant*** *(male)* steward *m*; *(female)* hôtesse *f* de l'air; **one of our flight attendants** un des membres de l'équipage; *Fin* ***flight capital*** capitaux *mpl* flottants *ou* fébriles; ***flight clearance*** autorisation *f* de vol; ***flight control*** *(action → of individual aircraft)* conduite *f*; *(→ from ground)* contrôle *m* de la navigation aérienne; *Mil* contrôle *m* des missions aériennes; *(place)* contrôle *m* aérien; *(people)* contrôleurs *mpl* aériens; ***flight crew*** équipage *m (d'un avion)*; ***flight deck*** *(of aircraft)* poste *m ou* cabine *f* de pilotage, habitacle *m*; *(of aircraft carrier)* pont *m* d'envol; ***flight engineer*** mécanicien(enne) *m,f* navigant(e) *(d'avion)*, ingénieur *m* de vol; *Orn* ***flight feather*** *(of bird)* penne *f*; ***flight formation*** formation *f* de vol; ***flight lieutenant*** = capitaine de l'armée de l'air britannique; ***flight log*** journal *m* de vol; ***flight mechanic*** mécanicien(enne) *m,f* navigant(e); ***flight number*** numéro *m* de vol; ***flight path*** trajectoire *f* de vol; ***flight pattern*** formation *f* de vol; ***flight personnel*** personnel *m* navigant; ***flight plan*** plan *m* de vol; ***flight recorder*** enregistreur *m* de vol; ***flight sergeant*** = sergent-chef de l'armée de l'air britannique; ***flight simulator*** simulateur *m* de vol; ***flight time*** *(duration)* durée *f* de vol; *(take-off time)* heure *f* du vol

flightiness ['flaɪtɪnɪs] *n* inconstance *f*

flightless ['flaɪtlɪs] *adj (bird)* coureur

flighty ['flaɪtɪ] *(compar* **flightier,** *superl* **flightiest)** *adj* inconstant; *(in romantic relationships)* volage, inconstant

flimflam ['flɪm,flæm] **1** *n (UNCOUNT)* (**a**) *(trickery)* escroquerie *f* (**b**) *(deceitful talk)* baratin *m*, bla-bla *m*, bla-bla-bla *m*

2 *vt (trick)* rouler

3 *vi (speak deceitfully)* baratiner

flimsily ['flɪmzɪlɪ] *adv (built, constructed)* d'une manière peu solide, peu solidement

flimsiness ['flɪmzɪnɪs] *n* (**a**) *(of cloth, garment, shoes)* légèreté *f*; *(of building, plane, walls, wooden beams)* manque *m* de solidité; *(of paper, toys, books)* fragilité *f* (**b**) *(of argument, case, excuse, evidence, alibi)* minceur *f*; *(of novel, plot)* faiblesse *f*

flimsy ['flɪmzɪ] *(compar* **flimsier,** *superl* **flimsiest)**

1 *adj* (**a**) *(cloth, garment)* fin, léger; *(shoes)* léger; *(building, plane, walls, wooden beams)* peu solide; *(paper)* peu résistant, fragile; *(toys, books)* fragile (**b**) *(argument, case, excuse, evidence, alibi)* mince; *(novel, plot)* faible

2 *n (paper)* papier *m* pelure; *(with typing on it)* double *m* sur pelure

flinch [flɪntʃ] *vi* (**a**) *(wince, with pain)* tressaillir; **without flinching** sans broncher (**b**) *(shy away)* **to flinch from one's duty/obligations** reculer devant son devoir/ses obligations; **she didn't flinch from doing her duty** elle n'a pas reculé devant son devoir; **she flinched at the thought** l'idée l'a fait reculer

fling [flɪŋ] *(pt & pp* **flung** [flʌŋ]) **1** *vt* lancer, jeter; **don't just fling it, aim when you throw** ne le lance pas n'importe où, vise d'abord; **to fling one's arms around sb's neck** jeter ses bras autour du cou de qn; **fling it in the dustbin** jette-le à la poubelle; **he flung himself into an armchair** il s'est jeté dans un fauteuil; **to fling oneself into a task** se lancer dans une tâche; **I flung a few things into a suitcase** j'ai fourré quelques affaires dans une valise; **you shouldn't just fling yourself into these jobs/relationships** tu ne devrais pas te lancer sans réfléchir dans ce type de travail/relation; **to fling sb into jail** jeter qn en prison; **don't just fling yourself at him** ne te jette pas dans ses bras; **he flung himself off the top of the cliff** il s'est jeté du haut de la falaise; **with his coat casually flung over his shoulders** avec son manteau négligemment jeté sur ses épaules; **she flung the windows wide open** elle ouvrit les fenêtres en grand; *Fam* **just fling in a bit of wine to give it taste** ajoute juste un peu de vin pour donner du goût ❑; **she was flinging insults left right and centre** elle lançait des insultes de toutes parts; *Fig* **to fling sth in sb's face** envoyer qch à la figure de qn

2 *n* (**a**) *Fam (attempt, try)* **to give sth a fling, to have a fling at sth** essayer qch ❑; **to have a fling at doing sth** essayer de faire qch ❑; **he had given French a fling a few years before** il avait essayé de se mettre au français quelques années auparavant; **let's give it a fling** essayons un coup

(**b**) *Fam (wild behaviour)* **youth must have its fling** il faut que jeunesse se passe; **to have a final fling** s'éclater une dernière fois

(**c**) *Fam (affair)* **to have a fling with sb** avoir une aventure avec qn; **the two of them are having a fling** ils ont une aventure; **it's nothing serious, it's just a fling** ce n'est rien de sérieux, juste une aventure

(**d**) *(dance)* = danse traditionnelle écossaise

►**fling about** *vt sep (objects)* lancer; **the luggage got flung about a bit during the flight** les bagages ont été un peu secoués pendant le vol; **he flung his arms about wildly** *(fighting)* il se démenait violemment; *(gesticulating)* il gesticulait violemment; *Fig* **to fling one's money about** mener grand train

►**fling away** *vt sep (discard)* jeter (de côté); **that's just flinging your money away** c'est jeter ton argent par les fenêtres

►**fling back** *vt sep (ball)* renvoyer; *(curtains)* ouvrir brusquement; *(sheets, blanket)* rejeter; **she flung back her head** elle a rejeté sa tête en arrière

►**fling down** *vt sep (object)* jeter par terre; **don't just fling the books down anywhere** ne jette pas les livres n'importe où; **to fling down a challenge** lancer *ou* jeter un défi; **fling down my keys, will you?** lance-moi mes clés, s'il te plaît

►**fling off** *vt sep* (**a**) *(coat, dress etc)* jeter

(**b**) *(attacker)* repousser violemment

(**c**) *(casual remarks)* dire avec désinvolture; *(poems, article)* écrire d'un trait

►**fling out** *vt sep* (**a**) *(throw out)* jeter dehors; *(get rid of → unwanted object)* jeter, balancer; *(→ bill, legislation, case)* rejeter; *Fam* **to fling sb out** flanquer qn à la porte; **she flung him out of the house** elle l'a flanqué à la porte, elle l'a viré de chez elle

(**b**) *(extend)* **to fling out one's arm** étendre le bras d'un grand geste; **he flung out a fist and knocked his assailant out** il mit son assaillant K-O d'un coup de poing; **he flung out a foot and turned the ball into the net** il tendit le pied et dévia la balle vers le filet

►**fling up** *vt sep (throw → in air)* jeter en l'air; *(→ to someone in higher position)* lancer, envoyer; **he flung up his hands in horror** horrifié, il leva les bras au ciel

flint [flɪnt] **1** *n (substance)* silex *m*; *(for cigarette lighter)* pierre *f* à briquet

2 *comp (tools, axe)* en silex

►► ***flint glass*** flint(-glass) *m*

flinthearted ['flɪnt,hɑːtɪd] *adj* au cœur de pierre

flintlock ['flɪntlɒk] *n Hist (rifle)* mousquet *m*; *(pistol)* pistolet *m* à fusil

flinty ['flɪntɪ] *(compar* **flintier,** *superl* **flintiest)** *adj (rocks, soil)* siliceux; *Fig (heart)* de pierre

flip [flɪp] *(pt & pp* **flipped,** *cont* **flipping)** **1** *n* (**a**) *(little push, flick)* petit coup *m*; **to give sth a flip** donner un petit coup à qch

(**b**) *(turning movement)* demi-tour *m (sur soi-même)*; *(somersault → in diving)* saut *m* périlleux; *(→ in gymnastics)* flip-flap *m*

(**c**) *(drink)* = boisson alcoolisée à l'œuf

(**d**) *Am (of hair)* petite boucle *f*

2 *vt* (**a**) *(move with a flick)* donner un petit coup sec à; *(switch)* basculer; **he flipped the packet shut** d'un petit coup sec il a refermé le paquet

(**b**) *(throw)* envoyer, balancer; **he casually flipped her back onto the trapeze** sans effort apparent, il l'a renvoyée sur le trapèze; **to flip a coin (for sth)** décider (qch) à pile ou face

(**c**) *Fam (idiom)* **to flip one's** *Br* **lid** *or Am* **wig** *(get angry)* exploser, piquer une crise; *(go mad)* devenir dingue, perdre la boule; *(under effects of stress)* craquer; *(become ecstatic)* être emballé, flasher

3 *vi Fam (get angry)* exploser, piquer une crise; *(go mad)* devenir dingue, perdre la boule; *(under effects of stress)* craquer; *(become ecstatic)* être emballé, flasher

4 *adj Fam (flippant)* désinvolte ❑

5 *exclam Fam* mince!, zut!

►► ***flip chart*** tableau *m* à feuilles; ***flip side*** *Fam (of record)* face *f* B ❑; *Fig* face *f* cachée; **there is, of course, a flip side to the expansion of industry** l'expansion de l'industrie a, comme toute médaille, son revers; ***flip top*** *(of packet)* couvercle *m* à rabat

►**flip off** *vt sep (flick off → dirt, dust etc)* faire tomber; **to flip sth off sth** faire tomber qch de qch

►**flip out** *vi* (**a**) *Fam (get angry)* exploser, piquer une crise; *(go mad)* devenir dingue, perdre la boule; *(under effects of stress)* craquer; *(become ecstatic)* être emballé, flasher (**b**) *(trailer of vehicle, racing car)* faire un écart

►**flip over** **1** *vt sep (turn over → stone, person, record)* retourner; *(→ page)* tourner

2 *vi (turn over → plane, boat, fish)* se retourner; *(→ page)* tourner tout seul

►**flip through** *vt insep (magazine)* feuilleter; *(photos, posters, wallpaper samples etc)* jeter un coup d'œil à

flip-flop **1** *n* (**a**) *(sandal)* tong *f* (**b**) *Electron* bascule *f* (**c**) *(somersault)* saut *m* périlleux avec appui sur les mains (**d**) *Am Fam (in attitude, policy)* volte-face ❑ *f inv*, revirement ❑ *m*; **to do a flip-flop (over sth)** faire volte-face (sur qch) ❑, retourner sa veste (sur qch)

2 *vi Am Fam* faire volte-face ❑, retourner sa veste

flippancy ['flɪpənsɪ] *n (of person, attitude)* légèreté *f*, désinvolture *f*; *(of remark)* désinvolture *f*

flippant ['flɪpənt] *adj* désinvolte; **he was just being flippant** il ne parlait pas sérieusement

flippantly ['flɪpəntlɪ] *adv* avec désinvolture

flipper ['flɪpə(r)] *n* (**a**) *(for swimming)* palme *f* (**b**) *(of seal, penguin, whale)* nageoire *f*

flipping ['flɪpɪŋ] *Br Fam* **1** *adj (as intensifier)* fichu; **you've got a flipping nerve!** tu as un fichu *ou* sacré culot!; **you flipping idiot!** espèce d'idiot!; **he's a flipping genius** c'est un super génie

2 *adv (as intensifier)* sacrément; **it's flipping hot/cold in here** il fait sacrément chaud/froid là-dedans; **he's so flipping annoying!** ce qu'il peut être embêtant!; **it's too flipping late now** il est bien trop tard maintenant; **not flipping likely!** il n'y a pas de risque!; *Ironic* **isn't it just flipping marvellous!** c'est pas formidable!; **you can flipping well do it yourself!** tu n'as qu'à le faire toi-même si c'est comme ça!; **don't flipping well talk to me like that!** t'as intérêt à me parler sur un autre ton!

flip-top *adj (carton, pack)* à rabat

flirt [flɜːt] **1** *vi* (**a**) *(sexually)* flirter; **he flirts with everybody** il flirte avec tout le monde (**b**) *Fig* **to flirt with danger/death** frayer avec le danger/la mort; **to flirt with an idea** jouer avec une idée

2 *n* (**a**) *(person)* charmeur(euse) *m,f*; **he's just a flirt** il fait du charme à tout le monde, c'est un charmeur (**b**) *(act)* badinage *m* amoureux

flirtation [flɜː'teɪʃən] *n* badinage *m* amoureux; **to have a flirtation with sb** flirter avec qn; *Fig* **his flirtation with danger/the idea ended in disaster** il a frayé avec le danger/joué avec cette idée et cela a tourné au désastre

flirtatious [flɜː'teɪʃəs] *adj* charmeur; *(look, smile)* enjôleur; **to be flirtatious with sb** faire du charme à qn

flirtatiously [flɜː'teɪʃəslɪ] *adv* d'un air charmeur; **she smiled flirtatiously at him** elle lui fit un sourire enjôleur

flirting ['flɜːtɪŋ] *n (sexual)* flirt *m*, flirtage *m*

flit [flɪt] *(pt & pp* **flitted**, *cont* **flitting**) **1** *vi* (**a**) *(bird, bat etc)* voleter; **bats were flitting about** des chauves-souris voletaient de-ci de-là; **people were constantly flitting in and out of his office** les gens n'arrêtaient pas d'entrer et de sortir de son bureau; **an idea flitted into my mind** une idée me vint soudain à l'esprit; **to flit from one subject to another** sauter d'un sujet à un autre, passer du coq à l'âne; **to flit from woman to woman/job to job** passer continuellement d'une femme à une autre/d'un emploi à un autre

(**b**) *Scot & NEng (move house)* déménager

(**c**) *Br Fam (leave stealthily)* déménager à la cloche de bois

2 *n Scot & NEng* déménagement *m*

flitch [flɪtʃ] *n (of pork)* flèche *f*

flitting ['flɪtɪŋ] *n Scot & NEng* déménagement *m*

flivver ['flɪvə(r)] *n Fam* vieux tacot *m*

float [fləʊt] **1** *n* (**a**) *(for fishing line)* bouchon *m*, flotteur *m*; *(on raft, seaplane, fishing net, in carburettor, toilet cistern)* flotteur *m*

(**b**) *(raft)* radeau *m*; *(floating logs)* train *m* (de bois); *(for swimming)* planche *f*

(**c**) *(vehicle → in parade, carnival)* char *m*; *(→ for milk delivery)* voiture *f* du livreur de lait

(**d**) *(cash advance)* avance *f*; *(business loan)* prêt *m* de lancement; *(money in cash register)* fond *m* de caisse

(**e**) *(drink)* = soda, jus de fruit ou milk-shake avec une boule de glace

(**f**) *St Exch* flottant *m*; **clean float** taux *mpl* de change libres *ou* flottants; **dirty float** taux *mpl* de change concertés

(**g**) *Theat* **the floats** *(footlights)* la rampe

2 *vi* (**a**) *(on water)* flotter; *(be afloat → boat)* flotter, être à flot; **the raft/log floated down the river** le radeau/le tronc d'arbre a descendu la rivière au fil de l'eau; **the bottle floated out to sea** la bouteille a été emportée vers le large; **the diver floated slowly up to the surface** le plongeur est remonté lentement à la surface; **we floated downstream** *(in boat)* le courant nous a portés

(**b**) *(in the air → balloon, piece of paper)* voltiger; *(→ mist, clouds)* flotter; *(→ ghost, apparition)* flotter, planer; **music/the sound of laughter floated in through the open window** de la musique est entrée/des bruits de rires sont entrés par la fenêtre ouverte; **she floated out of the room** elle est sortie de la pièce d'un pas léger; **he seems to just float through life** *(has no worries)* il semble ne jamais avoir de soucis; *(has no goals)* il semble se laisser porter par les événements

(**c**) *Fin (currency)* flotter

3 *vt* (**a**) *(put on water → ship, raft, platform)* mettre à flot; *(→ paper boat, toy)* faire flotter; **the timber is then floated downstream to the mill** le bois est ensuite flotté jusqu'à l'usine située en aval

(**b**) *(company)* lancer, créer; *St Exch (onto Stock Market)* introduire en Bourse; *Fin (bonds, share issue)* émettre; *(loan)* émettre, lancer

(**c**) *Fin (currency)* faire flotter, laisser flotter

(**d**) *Fig (idea)* lancer, proposer; *(plan)* proposer

►► *Br* **float chamber**, *Am* **float bowl** *(in carburettor)* cuve *f*; **float glass** verre *m* flotté

►**float about, float around** *vi Fam (rumours)* courir[□]; *(unoccupied person)* traîner; **there were rumours floating about that...** le bruit courait que...; **she's/it's floating about somewhere** elle/il traîne dans les parages

►**float off 1** *vt sep (free → boat)* remettre à flot

2 *vi* (**a**) *(be carried away → log, ship etc)* partir *ou* être emporté au fil de l'eau; *(in the air → balloon, piece of paper)* s'envoler (**b**) *Fig (person)* s'envoler, disparaître

floatable ['fləʊtəbəl] *adj* flottable

floatage ['fləʊtɪdʒ] *n* (**a**) *(floating → of boat etc)* flottement *m*; *(→ of timber)* flottage *m* (**b**) *(flotsam)* morceaux *mpl* d'épave (**c**) *(vessels on a river)* tonnage *m* des navires à flot (**d**) *(buoyancy)* flottabilité *f*

floatation = **flotation**

floater ['fləʊtə(r)] **1** *n* (**a**) *Am (floating voter)* électeur(trice) *m,f* indécis(e) (**b**) *Fin* effet *m* à taux flottant (**c**) *Fam (dead body)* = cadavre à la surface de l'eau (**d**) *very Fam (in toilet)* = étron qui flotte dans la cuvette des toilettes (**e**) *Austr Old-fashioned Culin* = sorte de pâté en croûte servi dans de la soupe aux pois

2 floaters *npl (in eye)* mouches *fpl* volantes, corps *mpl* flottants

floating ['fləʊtɪŋ] **1** *adj* (**a**) *(on water)* flottant

(**b**) *(not fixed)* **he has led a sort of floating existence** il a mené une vie assez vagabonde; **there's a fairly large floating vote** les indécis sont assez nombreux; **the floating vote will determine the outcome** les voix des indécis détermineront le résultat

(**c**) *Fin (currency, exchange rate)* flottant

(**d**) *Comput (accent)* flottant

(**e**) *Tech (bearing)* flottant

2 *n* (**a**) *(putting on the water)* mise *f* à flot; *(getting afloat again)* remise *f* à flot

(**b**) *(of new company)* lancement *m*, création *f*; *(onto Stock Market)* introduction *f* en Bourse; *Fin (of loan, bonds, share issue)* émission *f*, lancement *m*

(**c**) *Fin (of currency)* flottement *m*

(**d**) *(of new idea, plan)* proposition *f*

►► *Acct* ***floating assets*** actif *m* circulant; *Med* ***floating bodies*** *(in eye)* mouches *fpl* volantes, corps *mpl* flottants; ***floating bridge*** pont *m* de bateaux *ou* de radeaux; *Fin* ***floating capital*** capital *m* circulant; *Banking* ***floating charge*** nantissement *m* général; ***floating crane*** ponton-grue *m*; *Fin* ***floating debt*** dette *f* flottante *ou* non consolidée; ***floating dock*** dock *m* flottant; *Culin* ***floating islands*** île *f* flottante; *Med* ***floating kidney*** rein *m* flottant; ***floating off*** *(of wrecked ship etc)* renflouage *m*; *Comput* ***floating point*** virgule *f* flottante; ***floating population*** *(within country)* population *f* flottante; *Fin* ***floating rate*** taux *m* flottant; *Anat* ***floating rib*** côte *f* flottante; ***floating voter*** électeur(trice) *m,f* indécis(e); *Comput* ***floating window*** fenêtre *f* flottante

floating-point *adj Comput* à *ou* en virgule flottante

►► ***floating-point arithmetic*** arithmétique *f* en virgule flottante; ***floating-point notation*** notation *f* en virgule flottante; ***floating-point processor*** coprocesseur *m* arithmétique

floating-rate *adj Fin* à taux flottant

►► ***floating-rate bond*** obligation *f* à taux flottant *ou* variable; ***floating-rate certificate of deposit*** certificat *m* de dépôt à taux flottant; ***floating-rate interest*** intérêt *m* à taux flottant; ***floating-rate investment*** investissement *m* à taux flottant *ou* variable; *Banking* ***floating-rate note*** effet *m* à taux flottant; ***floating-rate securities*** titres *mpl* à taux flottant *ou* variable

float-stone *n Geol* = roche siliceuse très poreuse

floccose ['flɒkəʊs] *adj Bot* pubescent

flocculent ['flɒkjʊlənt] *adj* floconneux; *Miner* floculeux

flock[1] [flɒk] **1** *n (of sheep)* troupeau *m*; *(of birds)* vol *m*, volée *f*; *(of people)* foule *f*; *Rel* ouailles *fpl*; **they came in flocks** ils sont venus en foule *ou* en masse

2 *vi* aller *ou* venir en foule *ou* en masse, affluer; **people are flocking to see it** les gens vont le voir en foule *ou* en masse, les gens affluent pour le voir; **audiences are flocking in** les spectateurs viennent en foule *ou* en masse, les spectateurs affluent; **the people flocked around him** les gens se sont massés *ou* attroupés autour de lui; **in summer people flock to the sea** en été les gens vont en foule au bord de la mer

flock[2] *n Tex* bourre *f*

►► ***flock wallpaper*** papier *m* tontisse

►**flock together** *vi (sheep)* se regrouper, s'attrouper

Flodden [flɒdən] *n Hist* = lieu de la défaite des Écossais du roi Jacques IV contre les Anglais

floe [fləʊ] *n* **(ice) floe** glace *f* flottante

flog [flɒg] *(pt & pp* **flogged**, *cont* **flogging**) *vt* (**a**) *(beat)* fouetter; *Fam* **to flog an idea/a joke to death** accommoder une idée/blague à toutes les sauces (**b**) *Br Fam (sell)* vendre[□]; *(sell off quickly)* bazarder; *(stolen goods)* fourguer

►**flog off** *vt sep Br Fam (sell off quickly)* bazarder; **they're flogging them off cheap** ils les bazardent pour pas cher

flogging ['flɒgɪŋ] *n (beating)* flagellation *f*; *Law* supplice *m* du fouet *ou* de la flagellation

flood [flʌd] **1** *n* (**a**) *(of water)* inondation *f*; *Bible* **the Flood** le Déluge; **to be in flood** *(river)* être en crue; **you've caused a flood in the bathroom** tu as inondé la salle de bains

(**b**) *Fig (of applications, letters, offers)* déluge *m*; *(of light)* flot *m*; **floods of tears** un déluge *ou* torrent de larmes; **to be in floods of tears** pleurer à chaudes larmes

(**c**) *(tide)* marée *f* montante

(**d**) *(floodlight)* projecteur *m*

2 *vt* (**a**) *(unintentionally)* inonder; *(deliberately)* inonder, noyer; **the river flooded its banks** la rivière est sortie de son lit, la rivière a débordé; **you've flooded the bathroom** tu as inondé la salle de bains; **to be flooded** *(ship)* être envahi par l'eau; *(house)* être inondé

(**b**) *Aut (carburettor)* noyer; *(engine)* étouffer, noyer

(**c**) *(river → of rain)* faire déborder

(**d**) *(usu passive) Fig (person → with letters, replies)* inonder, submerger; **to be flooded with applications/letters** être submergé de demandes/lettres; **to be flooded in light** *(room, valley)* être inondé de lumière

(**e**) *Agr (for irrigation)* irriguer

(**f**) *Com* **to flood the market (with sth)** inonder le marché (de qch)

3 *vi* (**a**) *(river)* être en crue; *(overflow)* déborder

(**b**) *(land, area)* être inondé

(**c**) *Fig (move in large quantities)* **to flood into the streets** envahir les rues; **spectators were flooding into the stadium** les spectateurs affluaient dans le stade; **refugees are still flooding across the border** les réfugiés continuent à passer la frontière en foule *ou* en masse; **light was flooding through the window** la lumière entrait à flots par la fenêtre; **new energy was flooding through his veins** une énergie nouvelle coulait dans ses veines

(**d**) *(woman → menstruate heavily)* saigner abondamment

►► ***flood barrier*** digue *f* de retenue; ***flood control*** contrôle *m* des crues; ***flood plain*** plaine *f* d'inondation, lit *m* majeur; ***flood tide*** marée *f* montante; ***flood wall*** mur *m* de protection contre les crues; ***flood warning*** avis *m* de crue; ***flood water*** inondation *f*; **the flood waters have receded** les inondations ont diminué

►**flood back** *vi (people)* revenir en foule *ou* en masse; *(strength, memories)* revenir à flots, affluer; **suddenly it all came flooding back** soudain tout m'est revenu en mémoire

►**flood in** *vi (people)* entrer en foule *ou* en masse, affluer; *(applications, letters)* affluer; *(light, sunshine)* entrer à flots

►**flood out 1** *vt sep* inonder; **hundreds of families have been flooded out** *(from homes)* l'inondation a forcé des centaines de familles à quitter leurs maisons

2 *vi (people)* sortir en foule *ou* en masse; *(words)* sortir à flots; *(ideas)* se bousculer, affluer; **light flooded out of the open casement** des flots de lumière s'échappaient de la fenêtre ouverte; **money flooded out of the country** il y eut d'énormes fuites de capitaux

floodable ['flʌdəbəl] *adj* inondable, submersible

►► *Naut* ***floodable length*** longueur *f* envahissable

flood-damaged *adj* abîmé *ou* endommagé par les eaux

flooded ['flʌdɪd] *adj (land, house)* inondé; *Aut (carburettor, engine)* noyé

floodgate ['flʌdgeɪt] *n* vanne *f*, porte *f* d'écluse; *Fig* **the new law will open the floodgates to all kinds of fraudulent practices** cette nouvelle loi est la porte ouverte à toutes sortes de pratiques frauduleuses

flooding ['flʌdɪŋ] *n (UNCOUNT)* inondation *f*; *(of submarine's tanks)* remplissage *m*; **flooding is a major problem** les inondations sont un grand problème

floodlight ['flʌdlaɪt] *(pt & pp* **floodlit** [-lɪt] *or* **floodlighted)** 1 *n (lamp)* projecteur *m*; *(light)* lumière *f* des projecteurs; **to play under floodlights** jouer à la lumière des projecteurs

2 *vt (football pitch, stage)* éclairer (aux projecteurs); *(building)* illuminer

floodlighting ['flʌdlaɪtɪŋ] *n (UNCOUNT) (of pitch, stage)* éclairage *m* (aux projecteurs); *(of building)* illumination *f*

floodlit ['flʌdlɪt] *adj (pitch, match, stage)* éclairé (aux projecteurs); *(building)* illuminé

floodmark ['flʌdmɑːk] *n (high-tide mark)* ligne *f* de la haute marée; *(of water in flood)* niveau *m* de la crue

floodway ['flʌdweɪ] *n* canal *m* d'inondation

flooey ['fluːɪ] *adj Am Fam* bizarre ❏

floor [flɔː(r)] 1 *n* (**a**) *(ground → gen)* sol *m*; *(→ wooden)* plancher *m*, parquet *m*; *(→ tiled)* carrelage *m*; **earthen floor** sol *m* en terre battue; **to put sth/to sit on the floor** poser qch/s'asseoir par terre; **the forest floor** le sol de la forêt, la couverture; *Fig* **to wipe the floor with sb** *(in match, fight)* battre qn à plate couture, réduire qn en miettes; *(in argument)* descendre qn

(**b**) *(bottom part → of lift, cage)* plancher *m*; *(→ of sea, ocean)* fond *m*

(**c**) *(storey)* étage *m*; **we live ten floors up** nous habitons au dixième étage; **their offices are two floors down** leurs bureaux sont deux étages plus bas; **on the same floor** au même étage; **on the floor below** à l'étage en-dessous; **on the second floor** *Br* au deuxième étage; *Am* au premier étage

(**d**) *(for dancing)* piste *f* (de danse); **to take the floor** aller sur la piste (de danse); **shall we take the floor?** voulez-vous m'accorder cette danse?

(**e**) *(in parliament, assembly etc)* enceinte *f*; *Br Parl* **the floor of the House** ≃ l'hémicycle *m*; **to have/to take the floor** *(speaker)* avoir/prendre la parole; **Mr Taylor has the floor** la parole est à M. Taylor; **he had the floor for twenty minutes** il a parlé *ou* a gardé la parole pendant vingt minutes; **to give sb the floor** accorder *ou* donner la parole à qn; **questions from the floor** questions *fpl* du public; **to cross the floor** *(in parliament)* changer de parti

(**f**) *(of stock exchange)* parquet *m*; **trading on the floor was quiet today** la journée n'a pas été très animée à la Bourse

(**g**) *TV (of studio)* plateau *m*

2 *vt* (**a**) *(building, house)* faire le sol de; *(with linoleum)* poser le revêtement de sol dans; *(with parquet)* poser le parquet *ou* plancher dans, parqueter; *(with tiles)* poser le carrelage dans, carreler

(**b**) *Fam (opponent)* terrasser; **that virus really floored me** ce virus m'a complètement terrassé

(**c**) *Fam (puzzle, baffle)* dérouter; *(surprise, amaze)* abasourdir ❏

(**d**) *Fam* **to floor it** *(drive fast)* mettre le pied au plancher

►► *Mktg* ***floor ad, floor advertisement*** publicité *f* au sol; ***floor area*** *(of room, office)* surface *f*; *TV* ***floor assistant*** assistant(e) *m,f* de plateau; ***floor cleaner*** (produit *m*) nettoyant *m* pour sols; ***floor cloth*** serpillière *f*; *(old rag)* chiffon *m*; ***floor covering*** *(linoleum, fitted carpet)* revêtement *m* de sol; *(rug)* tapis *m*; *TV* ***floor crew*** personnel *m* de plateau; ***floor exercise*** *(in gymnastics)* exercice *m* au sol; *Constr* ***floor grid*** couchis *m*; *Am* ***floor lamp*** lampadaire *m*; *Pol* ***floor leader*** = chef de file d'un parti siégeant au Sénat ou à la Chambre des représentants aux États-Unis; ***floor manager*** *(in department store)* chef *m* de rayon; *TV* régisseur(euse) *m,f* de plateau; ***floor model*** modèle *m* d'exposition; ***floor plan*** plan *m*; ***floor polish*** encaustique *f*, cire *f*; ***floor polisher*** *(machine)* cireuse *f*; *Com* ***floor price*** prix *m* seuil; *Am* ***floor sample*** modèle *m* d'exposition; ***floor show*** spectacle *m* de cabaret; ***floor tile*** carreau *m*; *St Exch* ***floor trader*** commis *m*; *St Exch* ***floor trading*** cotation *f* à la corbeille; ***floor wax*** cire *f*, encaustique *f*; ***floor work*** exercices *mpl* au sol

floorboard ['flɔːbɔːd] *n* lame *f* de parquet; **to take the floorboards up** enlever les lames du parquet; **we're going to sand and varnish the floorboards** nous allons poncer et vernir le parquet

flooring ['flɔːrɪŋ] *n (UNCOUNT)* (**a**) *(act)* **the flooring has still to be done** il reste encore les sols à faire (**b**) *(material)* revêtement *m* de sol

►► ***flooring tiles*** carreaux *mpl*

floor-mounted [-'maʊntɪd] *adj (gear lever)* au plancher

floorspace ['flɔːspeɪs] *n* espace *m*

floor-through *adj Am* **a floor-through apartment** un appartement qui occupe tout un étage

floorwalker ['flɔːˌwɔːkə(r)] *n Am* ≃ chef *m* de rayon

'The Floorwalker' *Chaplin* 'Charlot chef de rayon'

floozie, floozy ['fluːzɪ] *(pl* **floozies)** *n Fam* traînée *f*

flop [flɒp] *(pt & pp* **flopped,** *cont* **flopping)** 1 *vi* (**a**) *(fall slackly → head, arm etc)* tomber; *(→ person)* s'affaler, s'effondrer

(**b**) *Fam (attempt, idea, recipe)* louper; *(fail → play, film)* faire un four *ou* un bide; *(→ actor)* faire un bide

2 *n Fam* (**a**) *(failure)* fiasco *m*, bide *m*; **this cake is a flop** ce gâteau est complètement loupé; **he was a flop as Othello** il était complètement nul dans le rôle d'Othello *ou* en Othello

(**b**) *Am Fam (hotel)* hôtel *m* borgne; *(hostel)* asile *m* de nuit ❏

3 *adv Fam* **it went flop into the water** ça a fait plouf *ou* floc en tombant dans l'eau

►**flop about, flop around** *vi* **the fish flopped about on the deck** les poissons frétillaient sur le pont; **he flopped about all day in his slippers** il traînait toute la journée en chaussons

►**flop down** *vi* se laisser tomber lourdement

►**flop over** *vi* se renverser

flophouse ['flɒphaʊs, *pl* -haʊzɪz] *n Am Fam (hotel)* hôtel *m* borgne; *(hostel)* asile *m* de nuit ❏

floppy ['flɒpɪ] *(compar* **floppier,** *superl* **floppiest)** 1 *adj (ears, tail, plant)* pendant; *(collar, brim of hat)* mou (molle); *(trousers, sweater)* flottant, large; **the jumper went all floppy when I washed it** le pull s'est complètement déformé au lavage; *Br* **this heat makes you feel all floppy** cette chaleur vous rend tout mou; **he has floppy hair** il a les cheveux qui lui tombent sur la figure

2 *n Comput* disquette *f*; **on floppy** sur disquette

►► *Comput* ***floppy disk*** disquette *f*; *Comput* ***floppy (disk) drive*** unité *f* de disquettes

floptical ['flɒptɪkəl] *adj Comput*

►► ***floptical disk*** *(hard)* disque *m* optique; *(floppy)* disquette *f* optique; ***floptical drive*** *(hard)* unité *f* de disque optique; *(floppy)* unité *f* de disquette optique

flora ['flɔːrə] 1 *npl* flore *f*; **the flora and fauna of a region** la flore et la faune d'une région

2 **Flora** *pr n Myth* Flore

floral ['flɔːrəl] *adj (arrangement, display)* floral; *(pattern, fabric, dress)* à fleurs, fleuri

►► ***floral tribute*** *(gen)* bouquet *m ou* gerbe *f* de fleurs; *(funeral wreath)* couronne *f* de fleurs

Florence ['flɒrəns] *n* Florence

►► *Bot & Culin* ***Florence fennel*** fenouil *m* de Florence

Florentine ['flɒrəntaɪn] 1 *adj* florentin

2 *n* (**a**) *(person)* Florentin(e) *m,f* (**b**) *Culin* florentin *m*

florescence [flɔː'resəns] *n Bot* fleuraison *f*, floraison *f*

floret ['flɔːrɪt] *n* fleuron *m*

floribunda [ˌflɒrɪ'bʌndə] *Hort* 1 *n* rose *f* floribunda, rosier *m* floribunda

2 *adj* floribunda *(inv)*

floriculture ['flɔːrɪˌkʌltʃə(r)] *n* floriculture *f*

floriculturist [ˌflɔːrɪ'kʌltʃərɪst] *n* horticulteur(trice) *m,f*, fleuriste *mf*

florid ['flɒrɪd] *adj* (**a**) *(complexion)* coloré (**b**) *(style, architecture)* chargé; *(speech)* fleuri; *(music)* qui comporte trop de fioritures

Florida ['flɒrɪdə] *n* la Floride; **in Florida** en Floride

►► ***the Florida Keys*** les "keys" de Floride

floridity [flɒ'rɪdɪtɪ], **floridness** ['flɒrɪdnɪs] *n* (**a**) *(of complexion)* rougeur *f*, hauteur *f* (**b**) *(of style, architecture, music)* caractère *m* chargé; *(of speech)* style *m* fleuri

floridly ['flɒrɪdlɪ] *adv* d'un style trop chargé

floriferous [flɔː'rɪfərəs] *adj Bot* florifère

floriform ['flɔːrɪfɔːm] *adj* en forme de fleur

florin ['flɒrɪn] *n (British, Dutch)* florin *m*

florist ['flɒrɪst] *n* fleuriste *mf*; **florist's (shop)** fleuriste *m*

floristry ['flɒrɪstrɪ] *n* art *m* du fleuriste

floss [flɒs] 1 *n* (**a**) *(for embroidery)* fil *m* de schappe *ou* de bourrette (**b**) *(for teeth)* fil *m ou* soie *f* dentaire

2 *vt (teeth)* nettoyer au fil *ou* à la soie dentaire

3 *vi (floss teeth)* se nettoyer les dents au fil *ou* à la soie dentaire

flossy ['flɒsɪ] *adj* (**a**) *(resembling floss)* cotonneux (**b**) *Am Fam (showy)* tape-à-l'oeil

flotation [fləʊ'teɪʃən] *n* (**a**) *(of ship → putting into water)* mise *f* à flot; *(→ off sandbank)* remise *f* à flot; *(of logs)* flottage *m*

(**b**) *(of new company)* lancement *m*, création *f*; *(onto Stock Market)* introduction *f* en Bourse; *(of loan, bonds, share issue)* émission *f*, lancement *m*

(**c**) *Fin (of currency)* flottement *m*

►► ***flotation rings*** flotteurs *mpl*; ***flotation tank*** caisson *m* à isolation sensorielle; ***flotation therapy*** thérapie *f* par isolation sensorielle; ***flotation vest*** gilet *m* de sauvetage

flotel [fləʊ'tel] *n (for oil-rig workers)* hôtel *m* flottant

flotilla [flə'tɪlə] *n* flottille *f*

flotsam ['flɒtsəm] *n (UNCOUNT)* morceaux *mpl* d'épave; **flotsam and jetsam** morceaux *mpl* d'épave et détritus; *Fig* **the flotsam and jetsam of society** les laissés-pour-compte *mpl* de la société

flounce [flaʊns] 1 *n* (**a**) *(in garment)* volant *m* (**b**) *(of indignation, impatience)* mouvement *m* vif; **with a flounce of her long skirt, she marched out of the room** elle sortit de la pièce d'un pas ferme en faisant voltiger sa longue jupe

2 *vi* **to flounce into/out of a room** entrer dans une/sortir d'une pièce de façon très théâtrale; **she's been flouncing around all morning** elle s'est agitée toute la matinée

flounced [flaʊnst] *adj (skirt)* à volants

flouncy ['flaʊnsɪ] *adj (dress, skirt)* froufroutant

flounder ['flaʊndə(r)] 1 *vi* (**a**) *(in water, mud)* patauger péniblement; **the dolphin was floundering about in a few inches of water** le dauphin se débattait dans quelques centimètres d'eau

(**b**) *(in speech, lecture etc)* perdre pied, s'empêtrer; **I knew I had put my foot in it, but floundered on regardless** je savais que j'avais gaffé mais j'ai continué à m'enfoncer lamentablement; **somehow he floundered through his speech** il est allé tant bien que mal jusqu'à la fin de son discours; **the economy is still floundering** l'économie est encore instable

2 *n Ich* flet *m*

flour ['flaʊə(r)] 1 *n* farine *f*; **to dust sth with flour** (en)fariner qch

2 *vt* saupoudrer de farine, fariner

►► ***flour bin*** boîte *f* à farine; ***flour dredger*** saupoudreuse *f* à farine; ***flour shaker*** saupoudreuse *f* à farine

flourish ['flʌrɪʃ] 1 *vi (business, economy, plant)*

prospérer; *(arts, literature etc)* fleurir, s'épanouir; *(in health)* être en pleine forme *ou* santé

2 *vt (wave, brandish → sword, diploma)* brandir

3 *n* (**a**) *(in lettering, design)* ornement *m*, fioriture *f*; *(in signature)* paraphe *m*, parafe *m*

(**b**) *(wave)* grand geste *m* de la main; **with an elaborate flourish of his hat** avec un grand mouvement de chapeau; **to carry things off with a flourish** faire les choses avec panache; **with a flourish of his sword** en faisant un moulinet avec son épée

(**c**) *(in musical or written style)* fioriture *f*; **a flourish of trumpets** une fanfare; **a little literary flourish** un petit effet de style

flourishing ['flʌrɪʃɪŋ] *adj (business, economy)* florissant, prospère; *(plant)* qui prospère; *(trader)* prospère; *(in health)* en pleine forme *ou* santé

flourmill ['flaʊə,mɪl] *n* minoterie *f*

floury ['flaʊərɪ] *adj* (**a**) *(covered in flour → hands)* enfariné; *(→ clothes)* couvert de farine; *(rolls)* saupoudré de farine (**b**) *(texture, potatoes)* farineux

flout [flaʊt] *vt (orders, instructions)* passer outre à; *(tradition, convention)* se moquer de; *(laws of physics)* défier

FLOW [fləʊ]

circulation	► **1 (a), (b)**
écoulement	► **1 (a)**
flux	► **1 (b), (e)**
mouvement	► **1 (b)**
flot	► **1 (d)**
couler	► **2 (a), (d)**
circuler	► **2 (b), (h)**

1 *n* (**a**) *(of liquid)* circulation *f*; *(volume of liquid)* volume *m*; *(of river)* écoulement *m*; *(of lava)* coulée *f*; *(of tears)* ruissellement *m*; *(of blood → in veins)* circulation *f*; *(→ from wound)* écoulement *m*; *(of air, fuel etc)* passage *m*, arrivée *f*; *Elec (of current)* passage *m*; **the decreasing flow of oil from the North Sea** la quantité décroissante de pétrole en provenance de la mer du Nord

(**b**) *(amount → of traffic, people, information, work)* flux *m*; *(→ of ideas)* flot *m*; *(movement → of work)* acheminement *m*; *(→ of information)* circulation *f*; *Fin (→ of capital)* mouvement *m*; **there is normally a very heavy flow of traffic here** il y a généralement beaucoup de circulation *ou* une circulation intense par ici; **a steady flow of immigrants** un courant ininterrompu d'immigration; *Fig* **to go with the flow** suivre le mouvement; **flow of funds** mouvement *m* de fonds; **flow of money** flux *m* monétaire

(**c**) *(of dress, cape)* drapé *m*

(**d**) *(of prose, novel, piece of music)* flot *m*; **to be in full flow** *(orator)* être en plein discours; **there's no stopping him once he's in full flow** il n'y a pas moyen de l'arrêter quand il est lancé; **to follow the flow of sb's argument** suivre le fil de l'argumentation de qn

(**e**) *(of the tide)* flux *m*

2 *vi* (**a**) *(liquid)* couler; *(electric current, air, blood in veins)* circuler; **the river flows into the sea** la rivière se jette dans la mer; **I let the waves flow over me** j'ai laissé les vagues glisser sur moi; **blood was still flowing from the wound** le sang continuait à couler *ou* s'écouler de la blessure; **a lot of blood will flow before peace is established** beaucoup de sang sera versé avant que la paix ne soit rétablie; **I could feel a new vital force flowing through my veins** je sentais un regain de force vitale m'envahir; **the tears flowed down her cheeks** les larmes coulaient sur ses joues; *Fig* **I let the sound of the music just flow over me** j'ai laissé la musique m'envahir

(**b**) *(traffic, crowd)* circuler, s'écouler; **new measures designed to enable the traffic to flow more freely** de nouvelles mesures destinées à rendre la circulation plus fluide; **the traffic isn't flowing as it should** la circulation n'est pas aussi fluide qu'elle devrait l'être

(**c**) *(hair, dress)* flotter

(**d**) *(prose, style, novel)* couler; *(work, project)* avancer, progresser; **this essay doesn't flow very well** cette dissertation n'est pas très fluide; *Mus* **play it this way, it flows better** joue-le comme ça, ça coule mieux; **in order to keep the conversation flowing** pour entretenir la conversation

(**e**) *(appear in abundance)* **the whisky flowed freely** le whisky a coulé à flots; **ideas flowed fast and furious** les idées fusaient de tous côtés

(**f**) *(tide)* monter

(**g**) *(emanate)* provenir; **decisions flowing from head office** les décisions qui proviennent *ou* émanent du siège social; **God from whom all blessings flow** Dieu, de qui découlent toutes les grâces

(**h**) *Fin (capital, money)* circuler

►► ***flow diagram*** organigramme *m*, graphique *m* d'évolution; *Comput* ordinogramme *m*; *Comput* ***flow path*** branche *f* de traitement; ***flow pipe*** conduite *f* montante; *Acct* ***flow sheet*** feuille *f* d'avancement

►**flow away** *vi (liquid)* s'écouler

►**flow back** *vi (water)* refluer; *(in pipe etc)* régorger

►**flow in** *vi (water, liquid)* entrer, s'écouler; *(contributions, messages of sympathy, people)* affluer

►**flow out** *vi (water, liquid)* sortir, s'écouler; *(people, crowds)* s'écouler; **the sewage then flows out of the pipe into the lake** les égouts se déversent ensuite du conduit dans le lac

flowage ['fləʊɪdʒ] *n* (**a**) *Geol* écoulement *m* (**b**) *Am (flooding)* inondation *f*

flowchart ['fləʊtʃɑːt] *n* organigramme *m*, graphique *m* d'évolution; *Comput* ordinogramme *m*

flower ['flaʊə(r)] **1** *n* (**a**) *Bot* fleur *f*; **to be in flower** être en fleur *ou* fleurs; **to come into flower** fleurir; **the tree is coming into flower** l'arbre commence à fleurir; **no flowers by request** *(at funeral)* ni fleurs ni couronnes; **to do the flowers** *(arrange)* s'occuper des compositions florales

(**b**) *Fig (best part)* fine fleur *f*, crème *f*; *Literary* **the flower of the youth of Athens/of the army** la fine fleur de la jeunesse athénienne/de l'armée; **in the full flower of youth** dans la fleur de la jeunesse

(**c**) *Chem* **flowers of sulphur** fleur *f* de soufre

2 *vi* (**a**) *(plant, tree)* fleurir; *(state)* être en fleur (**b**) *Literary (artistic movement, genre)* fleurir, s'épanouir

►► ***flower arrangement*** *(art)* art *m* floral; *(example)* composition *f* florale; ***flower arranging*** *(UNCOUNT)* art *m* floral; **the flower arranging took no time at all** la composition florale a été réalisée en un rien de temps; ***flower child*** hippy *mf*, hippie *mf (surtout des années soixante)*; ***flower garden*** jardin *m* d'agrément; ***flower girl*** *(selling flowers)* marchande *f* de fleurs; *(at wedding)* = petite fille qui porte des fleurs dans un mariage, ≃ demoiselle *f* d'honneur; ***flower head*** capitule *m*; ***flower market*** marché *m* aux fleurs; ***flower people*** hippies *mpl (surtout des années soixante)*; ***flower petal*** pétale *m* de fleur; ***flower power*** = pacifisme prôné par les hippies, surtout dans les années soixante; ***flower shop*** fleuriste *m*; **she owns two flower shops** elle est propriétaire de deux boutiques de fleurs; ***flower show*** exposition *f* de fleurs; *(outdoors, on a large scale)* floralies *fpl*; ***flower vase*** vase *m* à fleurs

flowerbed ['flaʊəbed] *n* parterre *m* de fleurs

flowered ['flaʊəd] *adj (dress, pattern)* fleuri, à fleurs

floweret ['flaʊəret] *n Literary* fleurette *f*, petite fleur *f*

floweriness ['flaʊərɪnɪs] *n (of language, speech, compliments)* syle *m* fleuri

flowering ['flaʊərɪŋ] **1** *n* (**a**) *(of plant, tree)* floraison *f* (**b**) *(of artistic movement, talents)* épanouissement *m*

2 *adj (plant, tree → which flowers)* à fleurs; *(→ which is in flower)* en fleurs

►► *Bot* ***flowering ash*** orne *m*; *Bot* ***flowering cherry*** cerisier *m* à fleurs

flowerpot ['flaʊəpɒt] *n* pot *m* de fleurs

flower-seller *n* vendeur(euse) *m,f* de fleurs

flowery ['flaʊərɪ] *adj* (**a**) *(fields, perfume)* fleuri; *(smell)* de fleurs; *(pattern, dress, carpet)* à fleurs (**b**) *(language, speech, compliments)* fleuri

flowing ['fləʊɪŋ] *adj (style, prose)* fluide; *(beard, hair, robes)* flottant; *(movement)* fluide, coulant

flowline ['fləʊlaɪn] *n (on organization chart)* ligne *f* de jonction de symboles

flowmeter ['fləʊ,miːtə(r)] *n (for liquid etc)* débitmètre *m*, indicateur *m* d'écoulement *ou* de débit

flown [fləʊn] *pp of* **fly**

flow-on *n Austr Ind* = hausse de salaire accordée à une catégorie de travailleurs à la suite d'une hausse consentie à une catégorie différente

flowstone ['fləʊstəʊn] *n Geol* plancher *m* stalagmitique, (dépôt *m* de) travertin *m*

flow-through method *n Am Acct* méthode *f* de l'impôt exigible

fl. oz. *(written abbr* **fluid ounce**) once *f* liquide

flu [fluː] *n* grippe *f*; **to have the flu** *or Br* **flu** avoir la grippe, être grippé

►► ***flu epidemic*** épidémie *f* de grippe; ***flu jab*** vaccin *m* contre la grippe; ***flu virus*** virus *m* de la grippe

flub [flʌb] *Am Fam* **1** *n* gaffe *f*, bourde *f*

2 *vt* rater, louper

3 *vi* faire une gaffe, gaffer

fluctuant ['flʌktjʊənt] *adj* fluctuant

fluctuate ['flʌktjʊeɪt] *vi (rate, temperature, results etc)* fluctuer; *(interest, enthusiasm, support)* être fluctuant *ou* variable; *(person → in enthusiasm, opinions etc)* être fluctuant *ou* changeant; *Fin (exchange rate, share prices)* fluctuer; **our production fluctuates from week to week** notre production est fluctuante *ou* varie d'une semaine sur l'autre

fluctuating ['flʌktjʊeɪtɪŋ] *adj (rate, figures, prices etc)* fluctuant; *(enthusiasm, support etc)* fluctuant, variable; *(needs, opinions etc)* fluctuant, changeant

fluctuation [,flʌktjʊ'eɪʃən] *n* fluctuation *f*

►► *Fin* ***fluctuation band, fluctuation margin*** marge *f* de fluctuation

flue [fluː] *n* (**a**) *(chimney)* conduit *m*; *(for stove, boiler)* tuyau *m* (**b**) *Mus (of organ)* tuyau *m*

►► ***flue brush*** hérisson *m*; *Mus* ***flue pipe*** *(of organ)* tuyau *m*

flueless ['fluːlɪs] *adj (stove)* sans tuyau

fluency ['fluːənsɪ] *n* (**a**) *(in speaking, writing)* facilité *f*, aisance *f*; **to speak with fluency** avoir la parole facile

(**b**) *(in a foreign language)* **fluency in French is desirable** la connaissance du français parlé est souhaitable; **we can identify various levels of fluency** on peut distinguer différents niveaux de maîtrise de la langue; **the course aims at fluency rather than at explicit knowledge of grammar** le cours met l'accent sur l'expression plutôt que sur une connaissance formelle de la grammaire; **I doubt whether I'll ever achieve complete fluency** je doute d'arriver un jour à parler couramment

(**c**) *Sport (of play, strokes)* facilité *f*, aisance *f*

fluent ['fluːənt] *adj* (**a**) *(prose, style)* fluide; **he's a fluent speaker** il s'exprime aisément *ou* avec facilité (**b**) *(in a foreign language)* **to be fluent in French, to speak fluent French** parler couramment (le) français; **he replied in fluent Urdu** il a répondu dans un ourdou aisé *ou* coulant; **I'll never be fluent** je ne parlerai jamais couramment (**c**) *Sport (play, strokes)* facile, aisé

fluently ['fluːəntlɪ] *adv* (**a**) *(speak, write)* avec facilité *ou* aisance (**b**) *(speak a foreign language)* couramment (**c**) *Sport (play)* avec facilité *ou* aisance

fluey ['fluːɪ] *adj Br Fam (with flu symptoms)* **I'm feeling a bit fluey** j'ai l'impression d'avoir la grippe

fluff [flʌf] **1** *n* (**a**) *(UNCOUNT) (on baby animal, baby's head)* duvet *m*; *(from pillow, material etc)* peluches *fpl*; *(collected dust)* moutons *mpl*; **a bit of fluff** une peluche; *Br Old-fashioned Fam (pretty girl)* nana *f*, gonzesse *f*

(**b**) *Br Fam (mistake)* raté *m*; **he made a complete fluff of the line** il a complètement raté sa réplique

2 *vt Br Fam (lines, entrance, interview)* rater, louper; **to fluff it** se planter; *Sport* **to fluff a shot** rater un coup

►**fluff out** *vt sep (feathers)* hérisser, ébouriffer; *(hair)* faire bouffer; *(pillows, cushions)* secouer

►**fluff up** *vt sep (feathers)* hérisser, ébouriffer; *(pillows, cushions)* secouer

fluffy ['flʌfɪ] *(compar* **fluffier,** *superl* **fluffiest)** *adj* (**a**) *(material, sweater)* pelucheux; *(chick, kitten, hair)* duveteux; *(mousse, sponge, mashed potatoes)* léger; *(clouds)* cotonneux (**b**) *(covered in fluff, dust)* couvert de moutons
►► *Br* ***fluffy toy*** (jouet *m* en) peluche *f*

flugelhorn ['flu:gəl,hɔ:n] *n Mus* bugle *m*

fluid ['flu:ɪd] **1** *adj* (**a**) *(substance)* fluide, liquide (**b**) *(flowing → style, play, match)* fluide (**c**) *(liable to change → situation)* indécis, indéterminé; *(→ plans)* indéterminé
2 *n* fluide *m*, liquide *m*; **body fluids** sécrétions *fpl* corporelles; **to be on fluids** *(patient)* ne prendre que des liquides
►► ***fluid dram*** drachme *f*; ***fluid mechanics*** *(UNCOUNT)* mécanique *f* des fluides; ***fluid ounce*** *(in UK)* = 0,028 litre; *(in US)* = 0,03 litre

fluidal ['flu:ɪdəl] *adj* fluidal
►► *Geol* ***fluidal texture*** texture *f* fluidale

fluidic [flu:'ɪdɪk] *adj* fluidique

fluidics [flu:'ɪdɪks] *n (UNCOUNT)* fluidique *f*

fluidify [flu:'ɪdɪfaɪ] *vt* fluidifier, liquéfier

fluidity [flu:'ɪdətɪ] *n* (**a**) *(of substance)* fluidité *f* (**b**) *(of style, play, match)* fluidité *f* (**c**) *(liability to change → of situation, plans)* indétermination *f*

fluidization [,flu:ɪdaɪ'zeɪʃən] *n Tech* fluidisation *f*

fluidize, -ise ['flu:ɪdaɪz] *vt Tech* fluidiser, rendre fluide
►► *Phys* ***fluidized(-fuel) reactor*** réacteur *m* à combustible fluidisé

fluke[1] [flu:k] **1** *n (piece of good luck)* coup *m* de bol *ou* pot; *(coincidence)* hasard *m*; **by (a) sheer fluke** *(coincidence)* par un pur hasard; **it was a fluke discovery** cela a été découvert par hasard
2 *comp (shot)* heureux

fluke[2] *n (on anchor)* patte *f*, bras *m*; *(on whale's tail)* lobe *m* de la nageoire caudale

fluke[3] *n Entom* douve *f*

flukiness ['flu:kɪnɪs] *n Fam* (**a**) *(luck)* **he had to admit the flukiness of their victory** il a reconnu qu'ils ont gagné grâce à un coup de bol (**b**) *Am (strangeness)* étrangeté ❑ *f*

fluky ['flu:kɪ] *adj Fam* (**a**) *(lucky → shot, guess)* heureux ❑; *(→ person)* chanceux ❑; **what a fluky goal!** quel coup de bol, ce but! (**b**) *Am (strange)* bizarre ❑

flume [flu:m] *n* (**a**) *(channel)* buse *f* (**b**) *(at swimming pool)* toboggan *m* (**c**) *Am (ravine)* ravin *m*

flummery ['flʌmərɪ] *n* (**a**) *Br (dessert)* = dessert à base de flocons d'avoine (**b**) *(UNCOUNT) Fam (flattering nonsense)* baratin *m*

flummox ['flʌməks] *vt Fam* démonter ❑

flummoxed ['flʌməkst] *adj Fam* **I was completely flummoxed** ça m'a complètement démonté ❑

flump [flʌmp] *Fam* **1** *exclam* floc!
2 *n* floc *m*
3 *vi* **to flump about** *or* **around** marcher à pas lourds ❑; **to flump down** tomber lourdement ❑
4 *vt* **to flump sth down** jeter qch à terre ❑

flung [flʌŋ] *pt & pp of* **fling**

flunk [flʌŋk] *esp Am Fam* **1** *vi (in exam, course)* se planter
2 *vt (of student → French, maths)* se planter en; *(→ exam)* se planter à; *(of teacher → student)* recaler, coller; **he flunked his test** il s'est planté à son examen; **the professor flunked her paper in geography** le prof ne lui a pas mis la moyenne à sa dissert' de géo
3 *n* raté(e) *m,f*; **he's a complete flunk** c'est un vrai raté

►**flunk out** *Am Fam vi (from college, university)* se faire virer *(à cause de la médiocrité de ses résultats)*

flunkey *(pl* **flunkeys**), **flunky** *(pl* **flunkies**) ['flʌŋkɪ] *n (manservant)* laquais *m*; *Pej (assistant)* larbin *m*

fluor ['flu:ɔ:(r)] *n Miner* spath *m* fluor, chaux *f* fluatée; **blue fluorspar** saphir *m* femelle

fluorene ['flʊəri:n] *n Chem* fluorène *m*

fluoresce [flʊə'res] *vi* entrer en fluorescence

fluorescence [flʊə'resəns] *n* fluorescence *f*

fluorescent [flʊə'resənt] *adj* fluorescent
►► ***fluorescent lighting*** éclairage *m* au néon; ***fluorescent tube*** néon *m*

fluoridate ['flʊərɪdeɪt] *vt (water)* enrichir en fluor

fluoridation [,flʊərɪ'deɪʃən] *n* fluoration *f*, fluoruration *f*

fluoride ['flʊəraɪd] **1** *n* fluorure *m*
2 *comp (toothpaste)* au fluor

fluorine ['flʊəri:n] *n* fluor *m*

fluorite ['flʊəraɪt] *n Miner* spath *m* fluor, chaux *f* fluatée

fluorocarbon [,flʊərəʊ'kɑ:bən] *n* hydrocarbone *m* fluoré, fluorocarbone *m*

fluorography [flʊə'rɒgrəfɪ] *n* fluorographie *f*

fluoroscope ['flʊərəskəʊp] *n Med* fluoroscope *m*

fluoroscopy [flʊə'rɒskəpɪ] *n Med* fluoroscopie *f*

fluorosis [flʊə'rəʊsɪs] *n Vet* fluorose *f*

fluoxetine [flʊ'ɒksəti:n] *n Pharm* fluoxétine *m*

flurried ['flʌrɪd] *adj* paniqué; **to get flurried** perdre la tête, paniquer

flurry ['flʌrɪ] *(pl* **flurries,** *pt & pp* **flurried,** *cont* **flurrying) 1** *n* (**a**) *(of snow, wind)* rafale *f* (**b**) *Fig* **a flurry of activity** un branle-bas de combat; **there has been a late flurry of activity on the Stock Market** on a assisté à une reprise soudaine de l'activité boursière en fin de journée; **to be in a flurry of excitement** être tout excité
2 *vt (usu passive)* agiter, troubler

flush [flʌʃ] **1** *n* (**a**) *(facial redness)* rougeur *f*; **to bring a flush to sb's cheeks** *(compliment, crude joke)* faire rougir qn; *(wine)* mettre le feu aux joues à qn
(**b**) *(of beauty, youth, light)* éclat *m*; *(of emotion etc)* accès *m*; *(of enthusiasm)* élan *m*; **in the full flush of youth** dans tout l'éclat de la jeunesse; **in the first flush of victory/success** dans l'ivresse de la victoire/du succès
(**c**) *(on toilet → device)* chasse *f* (d'eau); **to pull the flush** tirer la chasse (d'eau); **with a single flush** en tirant la chasse (d'eau) une seule fois; **to give sth a (good) flush (out)** *(drains, pipes etc)* nettoyer qch à grande eau
(**d**) *(in card games)* flush *m*
2 *vi* (**a**) *(face, person)* rougir; **his face flushed scarlet** il est devenu écarlate; **to flush with embarrassment** rougir d'embarras; **I can't drink punch, it makes me flush** je ne peux pas boire de punch, ça me met le feu aux joues
(**b**) *(toilet)* **it's not flushing properly** la chasse d'eau ne marche pas bien; **the toilet flushes automatically** la chasse d'eau fonctionne automatiquement; **the toilet keeps on flushing** la chasse d'eau n'arrête pas de couler
3 *vt* (**a**) *(cheeks, face)* empourprer; **the exercise had flushed their cheeks** l'exercice leur avait fait monter le sang au visage
(**b**) *(with water)* **to flush the toilet** tirer la chasse (d'eau); **you flush it by pushing this button/pulling this chain** pour actionner la chasse d'eau, appuyez sur le bouton/tirez sur la chaîne; **to flush sth down the toilet/sink** jeter qch dans les toilettes/l'évier
(**c**) *Hunt* lever, faire sortir
4 *adj* (**a**) *(level → surface)* de niveau; *(→ door, lock)* encastré; *(→ screw, nail)* noyé; *(→ rivet)* à tête noyée *ou* perdue; **flush mounted** monté à fleur; **flush with the side of the cupboard** dans l'alignement du placard; **flush with the ground** au niveau du sol, à ras de terre
(**b**) *Fam (with money)* en fonds ❑; **feeling flush today, are you?** tu es en fonds aujourd'hui? ❑
(**c**) *Typ* justifié; **flush left/right** justifié à gauche/droite
5 *adv* (**a**) *(fit, be positioned)* **this piece has to fit flush into the frame** ce morceau doit être de niveau avec la charpente
(**b**) *Typ* **out flush left/right** justifié à gauche/droite

►**flush away 1** *vt sep (in toilet)* jeter dans les toilettes; *(in sink)* jeter dans l'évier
2 *vi (down toilet)* partir; **it wouldn't flush away** ça ne voulait pas partir

►**flush out** *vt sep* (**a**) *(clean out → container, sink etc)* nettoyer à grande eau; *(→ dirt, waste)* faire partir (**b**) *Hunt (animal)* faire sortir, lever; *Fig (person)* faire sortir; *(undercover agents)* forcer à se trahir; *(truth)* faire éclater

flushed [flʌʃt] *adj* (**a**) *(person)* rouge; *(cheeks)* rouge, en feu; **he was looking rather flushed** il était plutôt rouge; **flushed with anger/joy** rouge de colère/plaisir (**b**) *Fig* **flushed with success** enivré *ou* grisé par le succès

flushing ['flʌʃɪŋ] *n* (**a**) *(of sewer)* curage *m*, chasse *f* (**b**) *Bot* pousse *f* (**c**) *(of face)* rougeur *f*; *Med* enchymose *f*, bouffée *f* de chaleur
►► ***flushing chamber*** *(of sewer)* chambre *f* de chasse; ***flushing cistern*** réservoir *m* de chasse

Flushing Meadow *n* = quartier de New York, où a lieu le tournoi de tennis du même nom

fluster ['flʌstə(r)] **1** *n* **to be in a fluster** être troublé *ou* nerveux; **to get into a fluster** se troubler, devenir nerveux
2 *vt (make agitated, nervous)* troubler, rendre nerveux; **to get flustered** se troubler, perdre contenance
3 *vi* **he doesn't fluster easily** il ne se trouble pas facilement, il ne perd pas facilement contenance

flustered ['flʌstəd] *adj* troublé; **you're looking a bit flustered** tu as l'air un peu agité; **to get flustered** se troubler, devenir nerveux

flustra ['flʌstrə] *(pl* **flustrae** [-tri:] *or* **flustras**) *n Biol* flustre *f*

flute [flu:t] *n* (**a**) *Mus* flûte *f* (**b**) *Archit (groove on column)* cannelure *f* (**c**) *(glass)* flûte *f*

fluted ['flu:tɪd] *adj* (**a**) *Archit (column)* cannelé (**b**) *(baking tin, pastry cutter, vase, dish)* à cannelures

flute-glass *n* flûte *f*

fluting ['flu:tɪŋ] *n Archit* cannelures *fpl*

flutist ['flu:tɪst] *n Am Mus* flûtiste *mf*

flutter ['flʌtə(r)] **1** *vi* (**a**) *(wings)* battre; *(flag)* flotter; *(heart)* palpiter; *(pulse)* battre irrégulièrement; **sometimes I feel my heart flutter** j'ai parfois des palpitations; *Fig* **to make sb's heart flutter** faire tressaillir le cœur de qn
(**b**) *(butterfly, bird → fly)* voleter, voltiger; *(→ flap wings)* battre des ailes; *(leaf, paper)* voltiger; **a butterfly fluttered in through the window** un papillon est entré par la fenêtre en voletant *ou* voltigeant; **to flutter away** *(bird, butterfly)* s'envoler en voletant *ou* voltigeant; **the letter fluttered to the ground** la lettre a volé par terre; **what is she fluttering about for?** pourquoi est-ce qu'elle s'agite dans tous les sens comme ça?; **her mother kept fluttering in and out of the room** sa mère entrait et sortait de la pièce sans arrêt
2 *vt (fan, piece of paper)* agiter; *(wings)* battre; **to flutter one's legs** *(swimmer)* battre des jambes; **to flutter one's eyelashes at sb** aguicher qn en battant des cils
3 *n* (**a**) *(of wings)* battement *m*; *(of heart)* battement *m* irrégulier, pulsation *f* irrégulière; *(of pulse)* battement *m* irrégulier; **with a flutter of her eyelashes** avec un battement de cils aguichant
(**b**) *Fam (nervous state)* **to be all in** *or* **of a flutter** être dans tous ses états
(**c**) *Aviat* oscillation *f*
(**d**) *Br Fam (gamble)* pari ❑ *m*; **I have a little flutter from time to time** *(on horse)* je fais un petit pari *ou* je parie de petites sommes de temps en temps; **to have a flutter on the Stock Exchange** tenter sa chance à la Bourse, boursicoter
►► ***flutter kick*** *(in swimming)* battement *m* des jambes

flutterboard ['flʌtəbɔ:d] *n Am* planche *f (de natation)*

fluttering ['flʌtərɪŋ] **1** *n (of wings)* battement *m*; *(of heart)* battement *m* irrégulier, pulsation *f* irrégulière; *(of pulse)* battement *m* irrégulier
2 *adj (bird)* voltigeant, voletant; *(flag)* flottant; *(heart)* palpitant

fluvial ['flu:vjəl] *adj Formal* fluvial

flux [flʌks] *n (UNCOUNT)* (**a**) *(constant change)* **to be in a state of (constant) flux** *(universe)* être en perpétuel devenir; *(government, private life etc)* être en proie à des changements permanents (**b**) *Med* flux *m* (**c**) *Metal* fondant *m* (**d**) *Phys* flux *m*

fluxion ['flʌkʃən] *n* (**a**) *Med* fluxion *f* (**b**) *Math* fluxion *f*, différentielle *f*; **the method of fluxions** la méthode des fluxions

fluxmeter ['flʌks,mi:tə(r)] *n Phys* fluxmètre *m*

FLY [flaɪ]

mouche	► 1 (a)
braguette	► 1 (b)
voler	► 2 (a), (c)
prendre l'avion	► 2 (a)
filer	► 2 (b)
piloter	► 3 (a)

(pl **flies,** *pt* **flew** [flu:], *pp* **flown** [fləʊn]) **1** *n* (**a**)

Entom & Fishing mouche *f*; *Fam* **they're dropping like flies** *(dying, fainting)* ils tombent comme des mouches; *Fam* **this illness is killing them off like flies** cette maladie les fait tomber comme des mouches; *Fam* **the recession is killing companies off like flies** la récession fait une véritable hécatombe parmi les entreprises; *Fig* **the fly in the ointment** *(person)* l'empêcheur(euse) *m,f* de tourner en rond; *(problem)* l'os *m*; *Fig* **there's a fly in the ointment** il y a un os; *Fam* **there are no flies on him** il n'est pas fou; *Fig* **he wouldn't hurt a fly** il ne ferait pas de mal à une mouche; *Br Fam* **I wouldn't mind being a fly on the wall** j'aimerais bien être une petite souris; *Fam* **to be catching flies** *(yawn, have mouth open)* gober les mouches; *Am Fam* **to live on the fly** vivre à cent à l'heure

(**b**) *(often pl) (on trousers)* braguette *f*; **your flies are** *or* **fly is undone** *or* **open** ta braguette est ouverte

(**c**) *(entrance to tent)* rabat *m*; *(flysheet)* auvent *m*

(**d**) *Tech (flywheel)* volant *m*

(**e**) *(in aeroplane)* **to go for a fly** faire un tour en avion

(**f**) *Br Fam (idiom)* **to do sth on the fly** *(craftily, secretively)* faire qch en douce

2 *vi* (**a**) *(bird, insect, plane, pilot)* voler; *(passenger)* prendre l'avion; *(arrow, bullet, missile)* voler, filer; **the first plane to fly faster than the speed of sound** le premier avion à dépasser la vitesse du son; **it flies well** *(plane)* il se pilote bien; **I'm flying to Berlin tomorrow** *(passenger)* je prends l'avion pour Berlin demain; *(pilot)* je vole à Berlin demain; **he flies to Paris about twice a month** *(passenger)* il va à Paris en avion environ deux fois par mois; **we fly to Berlin four days a week** *(airline)* nous avons des vols pour Berlin quatre jours par semaine; **we fly to over a dozen destinations** *(airline)* nous desservons plus d'une douzaine de destinations; **soon we'll be flying over Manchester** nous allons bientôt survoler Manchester; **to fly across the Channel** traverser la Manche en avion; **to fly via London** faire escale à Londres; **those who have flown** *Br* **in** *or Am* **with Concorde** ceux qui ont voyagé en Concorde, ceux qui ont pris le Concorde; **he flies for an American airline** il est pilote dans une compagnie aérienne américaine; **which airline did you fly with?** avec quelle compagnie aérienne as-tu voyagé?; **they don't fly from Heathrow any more** ils n'ont plus de vols au départ de Heathrow; **the trapeze artist flew through the air** le trapéziste a voltigé; *Fig* **the bird had already flown** l'oiseau s'était envolé

(**b**) *(move quickly → person)* filer; *(→ time)* passer à toute vitesse; *(flee)* s'enfuir; *(shoot into air → sparks, dust, cork, shavings)* voler; *Fam* **I really must fly!** il faut vraiment que je file *ou* que je me sauve!; **she flew out of the room** elle est sortie de la pièce comme un bolide; **he came flying round the corner** il a débouché du coin comme un bolide; **he flew to her rescue** il a volé à son secours; **the time seems to have flown!** le temps est passé à une vitesse!; **the past two years have just flown** les deux dernières années ont passé à toute vitesse *ou* se sont envolées; **time flies!, doesn't time fly!** comme le temps passe!; **the door flew open and there stood...** la porte s'est ouverte brusquement sur...; **to fly into a rage** *or* **temper** s'emporter, sortir de ses gonds; **to knock** *or* **to send sb flying** envoyer qn rouler à terre; **to knock** *or* **to send sth flying** envoyer qch voler; **his hat went flying across the room** son chapeau a volé *ou* voltigé à travers la pièce; **the insults were really flying** les insultes fusaient de toutes parts

(**c**) *(kite)* voler; *(flag)* être déployé; *(in wind → flag, coat)* flotter; *(→ hair)* voler

(**d**) *(idioms)* **to let fly** *(physically)* envoyer *ou* décocher un coup; *(verbally)* s'emporter; **he let fly with a powerful left hook** il a décoché *ou* envoyé un puissant crochet du gauche; **she then let fly with a string of accusations** elle a alors lancé un flot d'accusations; **to (let) fly at sb** *(physically)* sauter *ou* se jeter sur qn; *(verbally)* s'en prendre violemment à qn; **to fly in the face of sth** *(reason, evidence, logic)* défier qch; **this flies in the face of our agreement** cela contrecarre notre accord

3 *vt* (**a**) *(plane, helicopter → of pilot)* piloter; **to fly Concorde** *(pilot)* piloter le Concorde; *(passenger)* prendre le Concorde, voyager en Concorde

(**b**) *(passengers, people, goods)* transporter en avion; *(route → of pilot, passenger)* emprunter; *(airline)* voyager avec; *(distance → of passenger, pilot, plane)* parcourir; *(combat mission)* effectuer; **to fly the Atlantic** *(pilot, passenger)* traverser l'Atlantique en avion; *(plane)* traverser l'Atlantique; **her employers flew her to the States** ses employeurs l'ont envoyée aux États-Unis en avion; **we're flying them home on the first flight** nous les rapatrions par le premier vol

(**c**) *(flag → of ship)* arborer; *(kite)* faire voler; **a flag is flown on public buildings when...** tous les bâtiments publics arborent un drapeau quand...

(**d**) *(flee from → the country)* fuir; *Fam* **to fly the coop** se faire la malle; **to fly the nest** *(baby bird)* quitter le nid; *Fig (person)* quitter le foyer familial

4 *adj Fam* (**a**) *Br Old-fashioned (sharp)* malin (igne)[❑], rusé[❑]; **a fly guy** un malin, un rusé

(**b**) *Black Am slang (excellent)* génial, super, géant; *(stylish, attractive)* chouette

►► ***fly agaric*** amanite *f* tue-mouches; ***fly ball*** *(in baseball)* chandelle *f*; ***fly cruise*** forfait *m* avion et croisière; *Sport* ***fly half*** *(in rugby)* demi *m* d'ouverture; **to play fly half** jouer (en) demi d'ouverture; *Sport* ***fly kick*** *(in rugby)* coup *m* de pied à suivre; *Fishing* ***fly rod*** canne *f* à mouche; ***fly spray*** bombe *f* insecticide

►**fly about, fly around** *vi (bird, insect)* voleter, voltiger; *(plane, pilot)* voler dans les parages, survoler les parages; *Fig (rumours)* courir; **there are lots of figures flying about** *or* **around** on entend tellement de chiffres différents

►**fly away** *vi (bird, insect, plane)* s'envoler

►**fly back 1** *vi (bird, insect)* revenir; *(plane)* revenir; *(passenger)* rentrer en avion

2 *vt sep (person, passengers → to an area)* emmener en avion; *(→ from an area)* ramener en avion; *(→ to own country)* rapatrier en avion

►**fly by** *vi* (**a**) *(time)* passer à toute vitesse; **the time has flown by!** comme le temps a passé!; **as the days flew by** à mesure que les jours s'enfuyaient (**b**) *(plane)* passer

►**fly in 1** *vi* (**a**) *(person)* arriver en avion; *(plane)* arriver (**b**) *(bird, insect)* entrer

2 *vt sep (troops, reinforcements, food)* envoyer en avion; *(of pilot → to an area)* emmener; *(→ from an area)* amener

►**fly off 1** *vi* (**a**) *(bird, insect)* s'envoler; *(plane)* décoller; *(person)* partir en avion; **when do you fly off to Paris?** quand prenez-vous l'avion pour Paris?; **she's always flying off somewhere** elle est toujours entre deux avions

(**b**) *(hat, lid)* s'envoler; *(button)* sauter

2 *vt sep* (**a**) *(from oil rig, island)* évacuer en avion *ou* hélicoptère

(**b**) *(transport by plane → to an area)* emmener en avion; *(→ from an area)* amener en avion

►**fly out 1** *vi* (**a**) *(person)* partir (en avion), prendre l'avion; *(plane)* s'envoler; **planes fly out of the airport at a rate of 20 an hour** les avions décollent de l'aéroport au rythme de 20 par heure; **which airport did you fly out of?** de quel aéroport es-tu parti?; **a medical team flew out to the disaster area** une équipe médicale s'est rendue en avion sur la région sinistrée; **I'll fly out to join you next Monday** je prendrai l'avion pour te rejoindre lundi prochain; **we flew out but we're going back by boat** nous avons fait l'aller en avion mais nous rentrons en bateau

(**b**) *(come out suddenly → from box, pocket)* s'échapper; **the knife flew out of his hand** le couteau lui a échappé de la main

(**c**) *(bird)* sortir en volant

2 *vt sep (person, supplies → to an area)* envoyer par avion; *(→ from an area)* évacuer par avion; **they flew the President out** *(to a place)* ils ont emmené le président en avion; *(from a place)* ils ont ramené le président en avion

►**fly past** *vi* (**a**) *(plane, bird)* passer; *(plane → as part of display, ceremony)* défiler; *Fig* **he flew past on a bicycle** il est passé à toute vitesse en bicyclette (**b**) *(time, days)* passer à toute vitesse

►**fly up** *vi* (**a**) *(plane, bird)* s'envoler; **the plane flew up to 10,000 metres** l'avion est monté à 10 000 mètres; **I flew up from London on Saturday** j'ai pris l'avion depuis Londres samedi (**b**) *(end of plank, lid)* se soulever; **glass flew up into the air** des éclats de verre ont été projetés en l'air

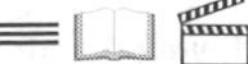

'One flew over the Cuckoo's Nest' *Kesey, Forman* 'Vol au-dessus d'un nid de coucou'

flyaway ['flaɪəweɪ] *adj* (**a**) *(hair)* indiscipliné (**b**) *(person)* frivole, étourdi; *(idea)* frivole

flyblown ['flaɪbləʊn] *adj* (**a**) *(of meat)* couvert *ou* plein d'œufs de mouches/d'asticots (**b**) *Fig (dirty, shabby)* en piteux état

flyblows ['flaɪbləʊz] *npl (eggs)* œufs *fpl* de mouches; *(maggots)* asticots *mpl*

flyboat ['flaɪbəʊt] *n* petit bateau *m* rapide

fly-boy *n Am Fam* = pilote de l'armée de l'air

flyby ['flaɪˌbaɪ] (*pl* **flybys**) *n* (**a**) *(of spacecraft)* = passage d'un avion ou d'un engin spatial à proximité d'un objectif (**b**) *Am (flypast)* défilé *m* aérien

fly-by-night *Fam* **1** *adj* (**a**) *(unreliable)* peu fiable, sur qui on ne peut pas compter; *(firm, operation)* véreux, louche (**b**) *(passing)* éphémère

2 *n* (**a**) *(person → irresponsible)* écervelé(e) *m,f*; *(→ in debt)* débiteur(trice) *m,f* qui décampe en douce (**b**) *(nightclubber)* fêtard(e) *m,f*, couche-tard *mf inv*

fly-by-wire *n* commandes *fpl* informatisées

flycatcher ['flaɪˌkætʃə(r)] *n Orn* gobe-mouches *m inv*

fly-drive *n* formule *f* avion plus voiture

►► ***fly-drive holiday, fly-drive package*** formule *f* avion plus voiture

flyer = **flier**

fly-fish *vi* pêcher à la mouche

fly-fishing *n* pêche *f* à la mouche; **to go fly-fishing** aller à la pêche à la mouche

flying ['flaɪɪŋ] **1** *n* (**a**) *(piloting plane)* pilotage *m*; *(travelling by plane)* voyage *m* en avion; **I love flying** *(as pilot)* j'adore piloter; *(as traveller)* j'adore prendre l'avion; **to be afraid of flying** avoir peur de prendre l'avion; **he goes flying at the weekends** le week-end, il fait de l'aviation

(**b**) *(of flag)* déploiement *m*

2 *adj* (**a**) *(animal, insect)* volant; **they were hurt by flying glass** ils ont été blessés par des bris de verre

(**b**) *(school)* d'aviation; *(staff)* navigant

(**c**) *(fast)* rapide; **a flying jump** *or* **leap** un saut avec élan; **she took a flying leap over the fence** elle a sauté par-dessus la barrière

(**d**) *(idiom)* **to pass with flying colours** réussir brillamment

►► ***flying ambulance*** avion-ambulance *m*; ***flying boat*** hydravion *m*; ***flying bomb*** bombe *f* volante; *Constr* ***flying buttress*** arc-boutant *m*; ***flying circus*** *(exhibition)* voltige *f* aérienne; *(group)* groupe *m* de voltige aérienne; ***flying club*** aéro-club *m*; *Mil* ***flying column*** colonne *f* mobile, groupement *m* mobile; *Am Aviat* ***flying corps*** corps *m* d'armée aérien; ***flying doctor*** médecin *m* volant; ***the Flying Dutchman*** *(legend)* le Hollandais volant; *Ich* ***flying fish*** poisson *m* volant, exocet *m*; *Aviat* ***flying fortress*** forteresse *f* volante; *Zool* ***flying fox*** roussette *f*; *Zool* ***flying lemur*** galéopithèque *m*; ***flying lessons*** leçons *fpl* de pilotage (aérien); *Zool* ***flying lizard*** dragon *m* volant; ***flying machine*** machine *f* volante; *Aviat* ***flying officer*** lieutenant *m* de l'armée de l'air; *Ind* ***flying picket*** piquet *m* de grève volant; ***flying saucer*** soucoupe *f* volante; *Zool* ***flying snake*** serpent *m* volant; ***the Flying Squad*** = brigade de détectives britanniques spécialisés dans la grande criminalité; *Zool* ***flying squirrel*** écureuil *m* volant; *Sport* ***flying start*** départ *m* lancé; **the runner got off to a flying start** le coureur est parti comme une flèche; *Fig* **she got off to a flying start in the competition** lors de la compétition, elle est partie comme une flèche *ou* elle a pris un départ foudroyant; **the campaign got off to a flying start** la campagne a démarré sur les chapeaux de roues; **his experience gives him a flying start over the others** son expérience lui donne un très net avantage sur les autres; ***flying suit*** combinaison *f* d'aviateur; *Sport* ***flying tackle*** = plongeon pour plaquer ou stopper quelqu'un; ***flying time*** heures *fpl ou* temps *m* de vol; **200 hours' flying time** 200 heures de vol; ***flying visit*** visite *f* éclair; **to pay a flying visit to London** faire une visite éclair à Londres

'The Flying Dutchman' *Wagner* 'Le Vaisseau fantôme'

flyleaf ['flaɪliːf] (*pl* **flyleaves** [-liːvz]) *n* page *f* de garde

Flymo® ['flaɪməʊ] *n* = tondeuse à gazon sur coussin d'air

fly-on-the-wall *adj* **a fly-on-the-wall documentary** un documentaire sur le vif

flyover ['flaɪ,əʊvə(r)] *n* (**a**) *Br Aut* pont *m* routier (**b**) *Am (flypast)* défilé *m* aérien

flypaper ['flaɪ,peɪpə(r)] *n* papier *m* tue-mouches, *Can* collant *m* à mouches

flypast ['flaɪpɑːst] *n Br* défilé *m* aérien

flypost ['flaɪpəʊst] *vi* coller illicitement des affiches

flyposting ['flaɪ,pəʊstɪŋ] *n* affichage *m* illégal

flyscreen ['flaɪskriːn] *n* moustiquaire *f*

flysheet ['flaɪʃiːt] *n* (**a**) *(on tent)* auvent *m* (**b**) *(leaflet)* feuille *f* volante; *(instructions)* mode *m* d'emploi

flyspeck ['flaɪspek] *n (of fly)* chiure *f* de mouche; *(gen)* tache *f*

flyspecked ['flaɪspekt] *adj* sali par les mouches

flyswat ['flaɪswɒt], **flyswatter** ['flaɪ,swɒtə(r)] *n* tapette *f (pour tuer les mouches)*

fly-tipping *n* dépôt *m* d'ordures illégal

flytrap ['flaɪtræp] *n (plant)* dionée *f*, tue-mouches *m inv*; *(device)* attrape-mouches *m inv*

flyweight ['flaɪweɪt] **1** *n Boxing* poids *m* mouche

2 *adj* de poids mouche

flywheel ['flaɪwiːl] *n Tech* volant *m*

flywhisk ['flaɪwɪsk] *n* chasse-mouches *m inv*

FM [,e'fem] *n* (**a**) (*abbr* **frequency modulation**) FM *f*; **FM radio** (radio *f*) FM *f*; **broadcast on FM only** diffusion en FM seulement (**b**) *Br Mil* (*abbr* **field marshal**) maréchal *m*

FMB [,efem'biː] *n Am* (*abbr* **Federal Maritime Board**) = conseil supérieur de la Marine marchande aux États-Unis

FMCG [,efem,siː'dʒiː] *npl Mktg* (*abbr* **fast-moving consumer goods**) biens *mpl* de consommation à forte rotation

FMCS [,efem,siː'es] *n Am* (*abbr* **Federal Mediation and Conciliation Services**) = organisme américain de conciliation des conflits du travail

f-number *n Phot* échelle *f* d'ouverture

FO [,e'fəʊ] *n* (**a**) *Mil* (*abbr* **field officer**) officier *m* supérieur (**b**) *Br Mil* (*abbr* **flying officer**) lieutenant *m* de l'armée de l'air (**c**) *Br* (*abbr* **Foreign Office**) **the FO** le Foreign Office, le ministère britannique des Affaires étrangères

foal [fəʊl] **1** *n (of horse → male)* poulain *m*; *(→ female)* pouliche *f*; *(of donkey)* ânon *m*; **the mare is in foal** la jument est pleine

2 *vi* mettre bas, pouliner

foam [fəʊm] **1** *n* (**a**) *(on beer)* mousse *f*; *(of mouth, sea)* écume *f*; **waves white with foam** vagues moutonneuses

(**b**) *(artificial substance)* mousse *f*; *(in fire-fighting)* mousse *f* (carbonique); **polystyrene foam** mousse *f* en polystyrène

2 *vi (soapy water)* mousser, faire de la mousse; *(sea)* écumer, moutonner; **to foam at the mouth** *(animal)* baver, écumer; *(person)* baver, avoir l'écume aux lèvres; *Fig (be furious)* écumer (de rage); *Fig* **she was practically foaming at the mouth** elle écumait de rage

►► ***foam bath*** bain *m* moussant; *Med* ***foam cell*** cellule *f* spumeuse; ***foam fire extinguisher*** extincteur *m* à mousse carbonique; ***foam rubber*** caoutchouc *m* Mousse®

►**foam up** *vi* mousser, faire de la mousse

foam-backed *adj* avec envers de mousse

foaming ['fəʊmɪŋ] *adj (liquid)* mousseux; *(sea)* écumeux; *(blood, saliva)* spumeux; *(beer etc)* moussant

foamy ['fəʊmɪ] (*compar* **foamier**, *superl* **foamiest**) *adj (liquid)* mousseux; *(sea)* écumeux; *(blood, saliva)* spumeux; *(beer etc)* moussant

►► *Med* ***foamy virus*** rétrovirus *m* spumeux

fob[1] [fɒb] *n (pocket)* gousset *m*; *(chain)* chaîne *f* (de gousset)

►► ***fob watch*** montre *f* de gousset

fob[2], **FOB** [,efəʊ'biː] *adv Com & Naut* (*abbr* **free on board**) FOB

►**fob off** (*pt & pp* **fobbed**, *cont* **fobbing**) *vt sep* se débarrasser de; **to fob sb off** se débarrasser de qn; **he fobbed her off with promises** il s'est débarrassé d'elle avec de belles promesses; **don't try to fob that rubbish off on me!** n'essayez pas de me refiler cette camelote!

focaccia [fə'kætʃə] *n Culin* focaccia *f (sorte de fougasse italienne)*

focal ['fəʊkəl] *adj* focal

►► *Opt* ***focal distance*** distance *f* focale, focale *f*; *Opt* ***focal length*** distance *f* focale, focale *f*; *Opt* ***focal plane*** plan *m* focal; *Phot* ***focal plane shutter*** obturateur *m* focal *ou* à rideau; ***focal point*** *Opt* foyer *m*; *Fig (of room)* point *m* de convergence; *Fig* **the focal point of the debate** le point central du débat; *Opt* ***focal ratio*** diaphragme *m*

focalization [,fəʊkəlaɪ'zeɪʃən] *n* (**a**) *(of heat, light)* convergence *f*; *(of beam, ray)* focalisation *f* (**b**) *Opt* mise *f* au point

focalize, -ise ['fəʊkəlaɪz] **1** *vt* (**a**) *(direct → heat, light)* faire converger; *(→ beam, ray)* focaliser (**b**) *Opt (eye)* mettre au point (**c**) *(illness)* localiser à son foyer

2 *vi (illness)* se localiser à son foyer

foci ['fəʊsaɪ] *pl of* **focus**

focimeter [fəʊ'sɪmɪtə(r)] *n Opt* focimètre *m*, focomètre *m*

fo'c'sle ['fəʊksəl] *n Naut* gaillard *m* d'avant; *(in merchant navy)* poste *m* d'équipage

focus ['fəʊkəs] (*pl* **focuses** *or* **foci** [-saɪ], *pt & pp* **focussed** *or* **focused**, *cont* **focussing** *or* **focusing**) **1** *n* (**a**) *Opt* foyer *m*; **the picture is in/out of focus** l'image est nette/floue, l'image est/n'est pas au point; **the binoculars are in/out of focus** les jumelles sont/ne sont pas au point; **bring the image into focus** fais la mise au point, mets l'image au point

(**b**) *(centre → of interest)* point *m* central; *(→ of trouble)* foyer *m*, siège *m*; **she was the focus of attention** elle était le centre d'attention; **taxes are currently the focus of attention** en ce moment, les impôts sont au centre des préoccupations; **the government is trying to shift the focus of the debate** le gouvernement tente de déplacer le débat; **let's try and get the problem into focus** essayons de préciser le problème; **the focus of the conference is on human rights** le point central de la conférence, ce sont les droits de l'homme; **the organization will provide some kind of a focus for opposition to the project** l'organisation fournira un point de ralliement à l'opposition au projet; **this became a focus of people's discontent** le mécontentement s'est concentré là-dessus

(**c**) *Med* siège *m*, foyer *m*

2 *vt* (**a**) *Opt (camera, microscope etc)* mettre au point; **to focus a camera (on sth)** faire la mise au point d'un appareil photo (sur qch)

(**b**) *(eyes)* fixer; **he couldn't focus his eyes** il voyait trouble; **all eyes were focussed on him** tous les regards étaient rivés sur lui

(**c**) *(direct → heat, light)* faire converger; *(→ beam, ray)* diriger; *Fig (→ attention, energies)* concentrer; *(→ interest, concern)* centrer

3 *vi* (**a**) *Opt* mettre au point

(**b**) *(eyes)* se fixer, *Spec* accommoder; **to focus on sth** *(eyes)* se fixer sur qch; *(person)* fixer le regard sur qch; **I can't focus properly** je vois trouble, je n'arrive pas à accommoder

(**c**) *(converge → light, rays)* converger; *Fig (→ attention)* se concentrer; **the debate focussed on unemployment** le débat était centré sur le problème du chômage; **his speech focussed on the role of the media** son discours a porté principalement sur le rôle des médias

►► *Mktg & Pol* ***focus group*** groupe *m* témoin

focused ['fəʊkəst] *adj* **she's very focused** elle sait où elle va

focusing ['fəʊkəsɪŋ] *n* (**a**) *(of beams, rays etc)* convergence *f*

(**b**) *(of microscope, lens etc)* mise *f* au point; **lens in focusing mount** objectif *m* à mise au point hélicoïdale

(**c**) *Opt* focalisation *f*; *Electron* focalisation *f*, concentration *f*

►► ***focusing cloth*** voile *m* noir de mise au point; ***focusing coil*** bobine *f* de concentration *ou* de focalisation; ***focusing eyepiece*** loupe *f* de mise au point; ***focusing glass*** loupe *f* de mise au point; ***focusing ring*** anneau *m* de mise au point; ***focusing scale*** échelle *f* des distances, échelle *f* de mise au point; ***focusing screen*** loupe *f* de mise au point; ***focusing screw*** vis *f* de mise au point, écrou *m* de réglage du foyer; ***focusing tube*** tube *m* de concentration *ou* de convergence, tube *m* convergent; ***focusing viewer*** viseur *m* focimétrique *ou* focométrique

focussed = **focused**

focussing = **focusing**

fodder ['fɒdə(r)] **1** *n (UNCOUNT) (feed)* fourrage *m*; *Fig Pej (material)* substance *f*, matière *f*

2 *vt (animal)* donner le fourrage à, affourager

foddering ['fɒdərɪŋ] *n* affouragement *m*

FOE [,efəʊ'iː] *n* (**a**) (*abbr* **Friends of the Earth**) AT *mpl* (**b**) *Am* (*abbr* **Fraternal Order of Eagles**) = organisation caritative américaine

foe [fəʊ] *n Literary or Formal* ennemi(e) *m,f*, adversaire *mf*

foehn = **föhn**

foeman ['fəʊmən] (*pl* **foemen** [-mən]) *n Old-fashioned Literary* ennemi *m*, adversaire *m*; **he has found a foeman worthy of his steel** il a trouvé un adversaire digne de lui

foetal, *Am* **fetal** ['fiːtəl] *adj* fœtal; **in the foetal position** en position fœtale, dans la position du fœtus

►► ***foetal distress*** souffrance *f* fœtale; ***foetal heartbeat*** rythme *m* cardiaque du fœtus

foeticidal, *Am* **feticidal** [,fiːtɪ'saɪdəl] *adj Law* fœticide

foeticide, *Am* **feticide** ['fiːtɪsaɪd] *n Law* fœticide *m*

foetid = **fetid**

foetoscopy, *Am* **fetoscopy** [fiː'tɒskəpɪ] *n Med* fœtoscopie *f*

foetus, *Am* **fetus** ['fiːtəs] *n* fœtus *m*

fog [fɒg] (*pt & pp* **fogged**, *cont* **fogging**) **1** *n* (**a**) *(mist)* brouillard *m*, brume *f*

(**b**) *Fig (mental)* brouillard *m*, confusion *f*; **my mind is in a fog today** je suis dans le brouillard *ou* je ne sais plus où j'en suis aujourd'hui; **she was in a complete fog about what she was supposed to be doing** elle ignorait complètement ce qu'elle était censée faire

(**c**) *Phot (on film, negative)* voile *m*

2 *vt* (**a**) *(glass, mirror)* embuer; *Phot (film, negative)* voiler

(**b**) *(confuse)* embrouiller; **studying for too long just fogs the mind** quand on travaille trop longtemps, ça embrouille les idées

3 *vi* **to fog (over** *or* **up)** *(glass, mirror)* s'embuer; *Phot (film, negative)* se voiler

►► ***fog bank*** banc *m* de brume; *Br* ***fog lamp,*** *Am* ***fog light*** feu *m* de brouillard; ***fog signal*** *Naut* signal *m* de brume; *Rail* pétard *m*

fogbound ['fɒgbaʊnd] *adj* pris dans le brouillard *ou* la brume

fogbow ['fɒgbəʊ] *n* = arc-en-ciel vu dans le brouillard

fogey ['fəʊgɪ] *n Fam* schnock *m*; **he's an old fogey** c'est un vieux schnock; **I'm afraid I'm turning into a bit of an old fogey** je crois que je suis en train de m'encroûter; **she's a bit of an old fogey** elle est un peu vieux jeu; *Hum* **he's a young fogey** il est jeune mais très vieux jeu

fogged [fɒgd] *adj Phot* voilé

fogger ['fɒgə(r)] *n Rail* poseur(euse) *m,f* de pétards (par temps de brouillard)

foggily ['fɒgɪlɪ] *adv* confusément, comme dans un brouillard

fogginess ['fɒgɪnɪs] *n* (**a**) *(weather)* temps *m* brumeux (**b**) *(of ideas)* confusion *f* (**c**) *Phot* voile *m*

foggy ['fɒgɪ] (*compar* **foggier**, *superl* **foggiest**) *adj* (**a**) *(misty)* brumeux; **it's foggy** il y a du brouillard *ou* de la brume; **it's getting foggy** le brouillard commence à tomber; **on a foggy day** par un jour de brouillard

(**b**) *Phot (film, negative)* voilé

(**c**) *Fam (idiom)* **I haven't the foggiest (idea** *or*

notion) je n'ai aucune idée□, je n'en ai pas la moindre idée□

►► ***Foggy Bottom*** = surnom donné au ministère américain des Affaires étrangères

foghorn ['fɒghɔːn] *n* corne *f ou* sirène *f* de brume; **a voice like a foghorn** une voix tonitruante *ou* de stentor

fogman ['fɒgmən] (*pl* **fogmen** [-mən]) *n Rail* poseur(euse) *m,f* de pétards (par temps de brouillard)

fogy (*pl* **fogies**) = **fogey**

föhn [fɜːn] *n Met* fœhn *m*, föhn *m*

FOI [ˌefəʊ'aɪ] *n* (*abbr* **freedom of information**) liberté *f* d'information

foible ['fɔɪbəl] *n (quirk)* marotte *f*, manie *f*; *(weakness)* faiblesse *f*

foie gras ['fwɑː'grɑː] *n Culin* foie *m* gras

foil [fɔɪl] **1** *n* (**a**) *(metal sheet)* feuille *f ou* lame *f* de métal; *Culin* **(silver) foil** (papier *m*) aluminium *m*, papier *m* alu; **cooked in foil** en papillote; **foil container** barquette *f* en papier aluminium

(**b**) *(complement)* repoussoir *m*; *(person)* faire-valoir *m inv*; **he's the perfect foil to his wife** il sert de faire-valoir à sa femme; **it acts as a foil to her beauty** cela met en valeur sa beauté

(**c**) *(sword)* fleuret *m*; **foils** *(fencing)* escrime *f* au fleuret

(**d**) *(in jewellery)* paillon *m*

(**e**) *Aviat & Naut (of hydrofoil)* patin *m*, aile *f*

(**f**) *Archit (of arch etc)* lobe *m*

2 *vt (thwart → attempt)* déjouer; *(→ plan, plot)* contrecarrer; **foiled again!** encore raté!; **once again they have been foiled by their own incompetence** une fois encore ils ont échoué à cause de leur propre incompétence

foiled [fɔɪld] *adj Archit* à lobes

►**foist on** [fɔɪst-] *vt sep* (**a**) *(pass on)* **you're not foisting (off) your old rubbish on** *or* **onto me** il n'est pas question que j'hérite de ta vieille camelote (**b**) *(impose on)* **she foisted her ideas on us** elle nous a imposé ses idées; **he foisted himself on us for the weekend** il s'est imposé *ou* invité pour le week-end

folacin ['fɒləsɪn, 'fəʊləsɪn], **folacine** ['fɒləsiːn, 'fəʊləsiːn] *n Biol & Chem* acide *m* folique

fold [fəʊld] **1** *vt* (**a**) *(bend)* plier; **fold the blanket in two** pliez la couverture en deux; **she sat with her legs folded under her** elle s'assit les jambes repliées sous elle; **he folded his arms** il s'est croisé les bras; **she sat with her hands folded in her lap** elle était assise, les mains jointes sur les genoux; **the bird folded its wings** l'oiseau replia ses ailes; **he folded her in his arms** il l'a serrée dans ses bras, il l'a enlacée; *Literary* **the hills were folded in mist** les collines étaient enveloppées de brume

(**b**) *Culin* incorporer

2 *vi* (**a**) *(bed, chair)* se plier, se replier

(**b**) *Fam (fail → business)* faire faillite□, fermer (ses portes)□; *(→ newspaper)* disparaître□, cesser de paraître□; *(→ play)* être retiré de l'affiche□; **the bakery folded last year** le boulanger a mis la clef sous la porte l'année dernière

3 *n* (**a**) *(crease)* pli *m*; **the soft folds of her dress** les plis soyeux de sa robe; **folds of fat** bourrelets *mpl* de graisse

(**b**) *(enclosure)* parc *m* à moutons; *(flock)* troupeau *m*

(**c**) *Fig (group)* **the fold of the Party/the Church** le sein du Parti/de l'Église; **to return to the fold** rentrer au bercail; **to welcome sb back to the fold** accueillir l'enfant prodigue

(**d**) *Geol* pli *m*

4 folds *npl Geol* plissement *m*

►**fold away 1** *vt sep* plier et ranger; **fold your clothes away neatly** plie tes affaires et range-les; **I slept on a camp bed which I folded away every morning** je dormais sur un lit de camp que je repliais tous les matins

2 *vi (chair, table)* se plier, se replier

►**fold back 1** *vt sep (sheet, sleeve)* replier, rabattre; *(door, shutter)* rabattre

2 *vi* se rabattre, se replier

►**fold down 1** *vt sep (sheet)* replier, rabattre; *(chair, table)* plier; **he folded down a corner of the page** il a corné la page

2 *vi* se rabattre, se replier

►**fold in** *vt sep Culin* incorporer; **fold in the sugar** incorporez le sucre

►**fold over 1** *vt sep (newspaper)* plier, replier; *(sheet)* replier, rabattre

2 *vi* se rabattre, se replier

►**fold under** *vt sep (edges)* replier en dessous

►**fold up 1** *vt sep* plier, replier

2 *vi (chair, table)* se plier, se replier

-fold [fəʊld] *suff* **a ten-fold increase** une multiplication par dix; **your investment should multiply six-fold** votre investissement devrait vous rapporter six fois plus

foldable ['fəʊldəbəl] *adj* pliable; **not foldable** impliable

foldaway ['fəʊldəˌweɪ] *adj* pliant

foldback ['fəʊldbæk] *n TV* ré-injection *f*, retour *m*, play-back *m inv*

folded ['fəʊldɪd] *adj* plié

►► *Geog* ***folded mountains*** montagnes *fpl* de structure plissée

folder ['fəʊldə(r)] *n* (**a**) *(cover)* chemise *f*; *(binder)* classeur *m*; *(for drawings)* carton *m*; **where's the folder on the new project?** où est le dossier sur le nouveau projet? (**b**) *(circular)* dépliant *m*, brochure *f* (**c**) *Typ (machine)* plieuse *f* (**d**) *Comput (directory)* répertoire *m*, dossier *m*

folderol ['fɒldərɒl] *n Literary* (**a**) *(UNCOUNT) (nonsense)* absurdités *fpl*, sottises *fpl* (**b**) *(trifle)* bibelot *m*, babiole *f*

folding ['fəʊldɪŋ] **1** *adj* pliant; *(joint, shutter)* brisé

2 *n* (**a**) *(of material etc)* pliage *m*

(**b**) *Typ (of pages)* pliure *f*

(**c**) *Geol (of land)* plissement *m*

►► ***folding camera*** appareil *m* à soufflet; ***folding chair*** *(without arms)* chaise *f* pliante; *(with arms)* fauteuil *m* pliant; ***folding door*** porte *f* (en) accordéon; *Fam* ***folding money*** billets *mpl* de banque□; ***folding seat*** *or* ***stool*** *(gen)* pliant *m*; *Aut & Theat* strapontin *m*; ***folding table*** table *f* pliante *ou* escamotable; *(with extending sections)* table *f* à battants; ***folding tray*** *(in plane, train)* tablette *f (qui se relève)*

foldout ['fəʊldˌaʊt] *n* encart *m*

foley ['fəʊlɪ] *n Cin* bruitage *m*

►► ***foley artist*** bruiteur(euse) *m,f*

foliaceous [ˌfəʊlɪ'eɪʃəs] *adj* (**a**) *Bot* foliacé (**b**) *Geol* foliacé, feuilleté

foliage ['fəʊlɪɪdʒ] *n* feuillage *m*

►► ***foliage plant*** plante *f* cultivée pour son feuillage

foliaged ['fəʊlɪɪdʒd] *adj* (**a**) *Bot* feuillagé, feuillé; **a light-foliaged tree** un arbre à couvert léger (**b**) *Archit* à rinceaux

foliar ['fəʊlɪə(r)] *adj Bot* foliaire

foliate ['fəʊlɪeɪt] **1** *adj Bot (plant)* feuillagé, feuillé

2 *vt* (**a**) *Typ (book)* folioter (**b**) *(metal)* battre; *(mirror)* étamer (**c**) *Archit (decorate)* orner de rinceaux

3 *vi* (**a**) *Bot* se garnir de feuilles, *Spec* feuiller (**b**) *(split)* se fendre

foliated ['fəʊlɪˌeɪtɪd] *adj Geol & Archit* folié, feuilleté

►► *Geol* ***foliated coal*** houille *f* schisteuse; *Geol* ***foliated crystalline rocks*** roches *fpl* cristallophylliennes; *Archit* ***foliated scroll*** rinceau *m*

foliation [ˌfəʊlɪ'eɪʃən] *n* (**a**) *Typ (of book)* foliotage *m* (**b**) *(of metal)* battage *m*; *(of mirror)* étamage *m* (**c**) *Bot & Geol* foliation *f* (**d**) *Archit (decoration)* rinceaux *mpl*

folic acid ['fəʊlɪk-] *n* acide *m* folique

folio ['fəʊlɪəʊ] (*pl* **folios**) *n* (**a**) *(of paper)* folio *m*, feuillet *m*; *Typ (page number)* numéro *m* (**b**) *(book)* livre *m* in-folio, in-folio *m inv* (**c**) *(paper size)* format *m* in-folio, in-folio *m inv*

►► ***folio book*** livre *m* in-folio, in-folio *m inv*

folk [fəʊk] **1** *npl* (**a**) *(people)* gens *mpl*; **they're good folk** ce sont de braves *ou* de bonnes gens; **most folk just want a quiet life** la plupart des gens veulent avoir une vie tranquille; **what will folk think?** qu'est-ce que les gens vont penser?, qu'est-ce qu'on va penser?; **the old folk** les vieux *mpl*; **the young folk** les jeunes *mpl*; **city/country folk** les gens *mpl* de la ville/de la campagne

(**b**) *(race, tribe)* race *f*, peuple *m*

2 *n (music → traditional)* musique *f* folklorique; *(→ contemporary)* musique *f* folk, folk *m*

3 *comp (concert, festival)* de folk

4 folks *npl Fam* (**a**) *(family)* famille□ *f*, parents□ *mpl*; **my folks are from Chicago** ma famille est de Chicago

(**b**) *(people)* **the old folks** les vieux□ *mpl*; **the young folks** les jeunes□ *mpl*; **hi folks!** bonjour tout le monde!□

►► ***folk art*** art *m* populaire, arts *mpl* populaires; ***folk dancing*** danse *f* folklorique; ***folk etymology*** étymologie *f* populaire; ***folk hero*** héros *m* populaire; ***folk medicine*** *(UNCOUNT)* remèdes *mpl* de bonne femme; ***folk memory*** tradition *f* populaire; ***folk music*** *(traditional)* musique *f* folklorique; *(contemporary)* musique *f* folk, folk *m*; ***folk rock*** folk-rock *m*; ***folk singer*** *(traditional)* chanteur(euse) *m,f* de chansons folkloriques; *(contemporary)* chanteur(euse) *m,f* folk; ***folk song*** *(traditional)* chanson *f ou* chant *m* folklorique; *(contemporary)* chanson *f* folk; ***folk tale*** conte *m* folklorique; ***folk wisdom*** la sagesse populaire

> **That's all folks!**
> Les dessins animés de Bugs Bunny se terminaient généralement avec ces mots qui s'inscrivaient sur l'écran. On utilise aujourd'hui cette phrase ("c'est fini, les amis!") en allusion au dessin animé, pour indiquer à un auditoire que l'on a terminé.

folklore ['fəʊklɔː(r)] *n* folklore *m*

folkloric ['fəʊkˌlɔːrɪk] *adj* folklorique

folklorist ['fəʊkˌlɔːrɪst] *n* folkloriste *mf*

folksy ['fəʊksɪ] (*compar* **folksier**, *superl* **folksiest**) *adj Fam* (**a**) *Am (friendly)* sympa (**b**) *(casual → person)* sans façon□; *(→ speech)* populaire□ (**c**) *(dress, manners)* simple□; *(tale)* populaire□

foll (*written abbr* **following**) suiv

follicle ['fɒlɪkəl] *n Anat & Bot* follicule *m*

follicle-stimulating hormone *n Physiol* hormone *f* folliculo-stimulante

follicular [fɒ'lɪkjʊlə(r)] *adj Anat & Bot* folliculeux, folliculaire

folliculated [fɒ'lɪkjʊˌleɪtɪd] *adj Bot & Zool* pourvu de follicules, folliculeux

folliculose [fɒ'lɪkjʊləʊs], **folliculous** [fɒ'lɪkjʊləs] *adj Anat & Bot* folliculeux, folliculaire

FOLLOW ['fɒləʊ] **1** *vt* (**a**) *(come after)* suivre; *(in procession)* aller *ou* venir à la suite de, suivre; **follow me** suivez-moi; **he left, followed by his brother** il est parti, suivi de son frère; **the dog follows her (about** *or* **around) everywhere** le chien la suit partout *ou* est toujours sur ses talons; **to follow sb in/out** entrer/sortir à la suite de qn; **he followed me into the house** il m'a suivi dans la maison; **his eyes followed her everywhere** il la suivait partout du regard *ou* des yeux; **she always follows the crowd** elle suit toujours la foule *ou* le mouvement; **his talk will be followed by a discussion** son exposé sera suivi d'une discussion; **she followed this remark with a rather feeble joke** elle agrémenta cette remarque d'une plaisanterie un peu facile; **in the days that followed the accident** dans les jours qui suivirent l'accident; **as sure as day follows night** aussi sûr que deux et deux font quatre; **he followed his father into politics** il est entré en politique sur les traces de son père; **George IV was followed by William IV** Guillaume IV a succédé à George IV; *Fam* **she'll be a hard act to follow** il sera difficile de lui succéder□; **to follow suit** *(in cards)* fournir; *Fig* **she sat down and I followed suit** elle s'est assise, et j'en ai fait autant *ou* j'ai fait de même; **just follow your nose** *(walk)* continuez tout droit; *(act)* suivez votre instinct

(**b**) *(pursue)* suivre, poursuivre; *(suspect)* filer; **he followed them to Rome** il les a suivis *ou* il a suivi leurs traces jusqu'à Rome; **she had her husband followed** elle a fait filer son mari; **follow that car!** suivez cette voiture!; **I'm being followed** on me suit; **we're continuing to follow this line of enquiry** nous continuons l'enquête dans la même direction

(**c**) *(go along)* suivre, longer; **follow the path** suivez le chemin; **follow the arrows** suivez les flèches; **the border follows the river** la frontière suit *ou* longe le fleuve; **the streets follow an irregular pattern** les rues suivent un schéma irrégulier (**d**) *(conform to → diet, instructions, rules)* suivre; *(→ orders)* exécuter; *(→ fashion)* suivre, se conformer à; *(→ someone's advice, example)* suivre

(**e**) *(understand)* suivre, comprendre; **do you follow me?** vous me suivez?; **I don't quite follow you** je ne vous suis pas vraiment; **I didn't follow why they killed him** je n'ai pas compris pourquoi ils l'ont tué

(**f**) *(watch)* suivre *ou* regarder attentivement; *(listen to)* suivre *ou* écouter attentivement; *Mus* **to follow a score** suivre une partition

(**g**) *(take an interest in)* suivre, se tenir au courant de; **she followed the murder case in the papers** elle a suivi l'affaire de meurtre dans les journaux; **have you been following that nature series on TV?** avez-vous suivi ces émissions sur la nature à la télé?

(**h**) *(accept → ideas)* suivre; *(→ leader)* appuyer, être partisan de; *(→ cause, party)* être partisan de, être pour; **to follow a football team** être supporter d'une équipe de foot

(**i**) *(practise → profession)* exercer, suivre; *(→ career)* poursuivre; *(→ religion)* pratiquer; *(→ method)* employer, suivre

2 *vi* (**a**) *(come after)* suivre; *(in mountaineering)* grimper en second; **my husband is following later** mon mari viendra plus tard; **in the years that followed** dans les années qui suivirent; **he answered as follows** il a répondu comme suit; **my theory is as follows** ma théorie est la suivante; **a long silence followed** un long silence s'ensuivit; **his sister followed hard on his heels** sa sœur le suivait de près *ou* était sur ses talons; **revolution followed hard on the heels of the elections** la révolution suivit de très près *ou* immédiatement les élections; *also Fig* **to follow in sb's footsteps** suivre les traces de qn; **following in her father's footsteps, she became a writer** elle a suivi les traces de son père et est devenue écrivain; **roast beef with strawberries to follow** du rosbif suivi par des fraises

(**b**) *(ensue)* s'ensuivre, résulter; **it doesn't necessarily follow that he'll die** cela ne veut pas forcément dire qu'il va mourir; **from what he says, it follows that he'll be standing for Parliament** de ce qu'il a dit, il ressort qu'il sera candidat au Parlement; **it follows from this that...** il en résulte que...; **that doesn't follow** ce n'est pas forcément *ou* nécessairement vrai; **a disturbing conclusion follows from this** une conclusion inquiétante en découle

(**c**) *(understand)* suivre, comprendre

(**d**) *(imitate)* suivre, faire de même; **Paris sets the trend and the world follows** Paris donne le ton et le reste du monde suit

►**follow on** *vi* (**a**) *(come after)* suivre; **you go ahead, we'll follow on** partez en avant, nous vous suivons; **she said she would follow on later** elle a dit qu'elle nous rejoindrait plus tard

(**b**) *(result)* **it follows on from this that...** il en résulte que...

(**c**) *(in cricket)* = reprendre la garde du guichet au début de la seconde partie faute d'avoir marqué le nombre de points requis

►**follow through 1** *vt sep (idea, plan)* poursuivre jusqu'au bout *ou* jusqu'à sa conclusion; **[illegible] didn't follow our proposal through** il n'a pas donné suite à notre proposition

2 *vi Sport* accompagner son coup *ou* sa balle; *(in billiards)* faire *ou* jouer un coulé

►**follow up 1** *vt sep* (**a**) *(pursue → advantage, success)* exploiter, tirer parti de; *(→ offer)* donner suite à; *(tip-off)* suivre; **to follow up a clue** suivre une piste

(**b**) *(maintain contact)* suivre; *(of doctor)* suivre, surveiller

(**c**) *(continue, supplement)* faire suivre, compléter; **follow up your initial phone call with a letter** confirmez votre coup de téléphone par écrit; **I followed up your suggestion for a research project** j'ai repris votre suggestion pour un projet de recherche

2 *vi* exploiter un avantage, tirer parti d'un avantage; **he followed up with a right to the jaw** il a continué avec un droit à la mâchoire

follower ['fɒləʊə(r)] *n* (**a**) *(devotee, disciple)* disciple *m*, partisan(e) *m,f*; **as followers of this programme will be aware,...** comme les personnes qui suivent cette émission le savent,...; **a follower of fashion** quelqu'un qui suit la mode

(**b**) *Sport (supporter)* partisan(e) *m,f*, fan *mf*; **a follower of tennis** quelqu'un qui s'intéresse au tennis

(**c**) *(attendant)* domestique *mf*; **the king and his followers** le roi et sa suite

(**d**) *Arch (male admirer)* amoureux *m*

(**e**) *Mktg (company, product)* suiveur *m*

following ['fɒləʊɪŋ] **1** *adj* (**a**) *(next)* suivant; **the following day** le jour suivant, le lendemain; **the following Monday** le lundi suivant; **the following names** les noms suivants, les noms que voici; **the following methods of payment are acceptable** sont acceptés les modes de paiement suivants

(**b**) *(wind)* arrière *(inv)*

2 *prep* après, suite à; **following his accident, he walked with a limp** après *ou* suite à son accident, il est resté boiteux; **following our conversation** suite à notre entretien; *Com* **following your letter** suite à *ou* en réponse à votre lettre

3 *n* (**a**) *(supporters)* partisans *mpl*, disciples *mpl*; *(entourage)* suite *f*; **she has a large following** elle a de nombreux partisans *ou* fidèles

(**b**) *(about to be mentioned)* **he said the following** il a dit ceci; **her reasons are the following** ses raisons sont les suivantes; **the following have been selected from among the candidates** les personnes suivantes ont été choisies parmi les candidats; **the following is the full list** voici la liste complète

(**c**) *(of king, prince)* suite *f*

►► *TV & Cin* ***following pan*** pano *m* de poursuite

follow-me product *n Mktg* produit *m* tactique

follow-my-leader *n Br* = jeu où tout le monde doit imiter tous les mouvements d'un joueur désigné

follow-on *n (in cricket)* = reprise de la garde du guichet par une équipe au début de la deuxième partie faute d'avoir marqué assez de points

follow-the-leader *n Am* = jeu où tout le monde doit imiter tous les mouvements d'un joueur désigné

follow-through *n* (**a**) *(to plan)* suite *f*, continuation *f* (**b**) *Sport* accompagnement *m (d'un coup)* (**c**) *(in billiards)* coulé *m*

follow-up 1 *n* (**a**) *(to event, programme)* suite *f*; *(on case, file)* suivi *m*; *Med (appointment)* visite *f ou* examen *m* de contrôle; **this meeting is a follow-up to that held in May** cette réunion est la suite de celle tenue en mai

(**b**) *(bill, letter)* rappel *m*

2 *adj (action, survey, work)* complémentaire

►► *Med* ***follow-up care*** soins *mpl* post-hospitaliers; ***follow-up interview*** *(for job, research)* deuxième entretien *m*; ***follow-up letter*** lettre *f* de rappel *ou* de relance; *Comput* ***follow-up message*** *(in newsgroups)* suivi *m* d'article; ***follow-up phone call*** coup *m* de téléphone de rappel *ou* de relance; *Mktg* ***follow-up publicity*** publicité *f* de rappel; ***follow-up visit*** visite *f* de contrôle

folly ['fɒlɪ] *(pl* **follies**) **1** *n* (**a**) *(UNCOUNT) Formal (foolishness)* folie *f*, sottise *f*; **an act of folly, a folly** une folie; **it would be folly [illegible]** serait folie de continuer; **this decision is sheer folly on the part of the government** c'est de la folie furieuse pour le gouvernement d'avoir pris cette décision (**b**) *Archit (building)* folie *f*

2 follies *npl Theat* folies *fpl*

foment [fəʊ'ment] *vt* (**a**) *(discord, discontent)* fomenter (**b**) *Med (wound)* fomenter

fomentation [,fəʊmen'teɪʃən] *n* (**a**) *(of discord, discontent)* fomentation *f* (**b**) *Med (of wound)* fomentation *f*

fomes ['fəʊmi:z] *(pl* **fomites** [-ɪ,ti:z]) *n* (**a**) *Bot* fomes *m* (**b**) *Med* matière *f* contaminée

fond [fɒnd] *adj* (**a**) **to be fond of sb** aimer beaucoup qn, avoir de l'affection pour qn; **to be fond of sth** aimer beaucoup qch, être amateur de qch; **I'm very fond of sweet things** je suis très friand de sucreries, j'aime beaucoup les sucreries; **I'm rather fond of her** je l'aime bien; **they're fond of each other** ils s'aiment bien; **he's fond of reading** il aime lire; **I'm not fond of being told I'm an idiot** je n'apprécie pas qu'on me traite d'idiot; **he is rather too fond of the sound of his own voice** il aime un peu trop s'écouter parler; **he was fond of the odd whisky** il aimait bien prendre un petit whisky de temps à autre

(**b**) *(loving → friend, wife, embrace)* affectueux, tendre; *(→ parent)* indulgent, bon; *(→ look)* tendre; **with fondest love** *(in letter)* affectueusement

(**c**) *(hope)* fervent; *(ambition, wish)* cher; *(memory)* agréable; **my fondest dream** mon rêve le plus cher

(**d**) *(foolish)* naïf; **in the fond hope of catching a glimpse of my idol** dans le fol espoir d'apercevoir mon idole; **she still retained the fond belief that he would return** elle persistait à croire qu'il reviendrait

fondant ['fɒndənt] *n Culin* fondant *m*

►► ***fondant icing*** glaçage *m* fondant

fondle ['fɒndəl] *vt* caresser; **he was fondling her leg under the table** il lui caressait la jambe sous la table

fondling ['fɒndəlɪŋ] *n* caresses *fpl*

fondly ['fɒndlɪ] *adv* (**a**) *(lovingly)* tendrement, affectueusement (**b**) *(foolishly)* naïvement; **he fondly believed she would accept** il avait la naïveté de croire *ou* il croyait naïvement qu'elle accepterait

fondness ['fɒndnɪs] *n (for person)* affection *f*, tendresse *f* (**for** pour *ou* envers); *(for things)* prédilection *f*, penchant *m* (**for** pour); **to have a fondness for drink** avoir un penchant pour la boisson

fondue ['fɒndju:] *n Culin* fondue *f*

►► ***fondue set*** service *m* à fondue

font [fɒnt] *n* (**a**) *Rel* fonts *mpl* baptismaux (**b**) *Typ & Comput* police *f*, fonte *f*

►► *Typ & Comput* ***font cartridge*** cartouche *f* de polices; *Typ & Comput* ***font cassette*** cassette *f* de polices de caractères, cassette *f* de fontes

fontanelle, *Am* **fontanel** [,fɒntə'nel] *n Anat* fontanelle *f*

food [fu:d] **1** *n* (**a**) *(UNCOUNT) (nourishment)* nourriture *f*; *(as opposed to drink)* manger *m*; *(for expedition)* vivres *mpl*; *Agr (for animals)* pâture *f*; *(for poultry)* mangeaille *f*; **is there any food?** y a-t-il de quoi manger?; **do you have enough food for everyone?** avez-vous assez à manger *ou* assez de nourriture pour tout le monde?; **they like spicy food** ils aiment la cuisine épicée; **we need to buy some food** il faut qu'on achète à manger *ou* qu'on fasse des provisions; **we gave them food** nous leur avons donné à manger; **take some food for the journey** prenez de quoi manger pendant le voyage; **the food here is especially good** dans ce restaurant la cuisine est particulièrement bonne; **he's off his food** il n'a pas d'appétit, il a perdu l'appétit; **the cost of food** le prix de la nourriture *ou* des denrées (alimentaires); **foods recommended for diabetics** aliments *mpl* conseillés aux diabétiques

(**b**) *Fig (material)* matière *f*; **the accident gave her much food for thought** l'accident l'a fait beaucoup réfléchir; **the book provides the reader with food for reflection** ce livre donne au lecteur matière à réflexion

(**c**) *Hort* engrais *m*

2 [illegible] alimentaire; *(crop)* vivrier

►► ***food additive*** additif *m* alimentaire; ***the Food and Agriculture Organization*** Organisation *f* des Nations unies pour l'alimentation et l'agriculture; ***food allergy*** allergie *f* alimentaire; *Ecol* ***food chain*** chaîne *f* alimentaire; ***food combining*** combinaisons *fpl* alimentaires; ***food court*** = partie d'un centre commercial où se trouvent les restaurants; ***food critic*** critique *mf* gastronomique; *Am* ***the Food and Drug Administration*** = organisme officiel chargé de contrôler la qualité des aliments et de délivrer les autorisations de mise sur le marché pour les produits pharmaceutiques; ***food hall*** *(in shop)* rayon *m* d'alimentation; ***food hygiene regulations*** réglementation *f* sur l'hygiène alimentaire; ***food labelling*** étiquetage *m* des produits alimentaires; ***food manufacturer*** fabricant *m* de produits comestibles; ***food mixer*** mixeur *m*; ***food packaging*** emballage *m* des produits alimentaires; ***food parcel*** colis *m* de vivres; ***food***

fol–foo

poisoning intoxication *f* alimentaire; ***food processing*** *(preparation)* traitement *m* industriel des aliments; *(industry)* industrie *f* alimentaire; ***food processor*** robot *m* ménager *ou* de cuisine; ***food products*** produits *mpl* alimentaires, comestibles *mpl*, denrées *fpl*; *Am* ***food stamp*** bon *m* alimentaire *(accordé aux personnes sans ressources)*; ***the Food Standards Agency*** = organisme britannique de contrôle de la sécurité alimentaire; ***food technology*** technologie *f* alimentaire; ***food value*** valeur *f* nutritive; *Ecol* ***food web*** réseau *m* alimentaire

foodie ['fu:dɪ] *n Fam* fin gourmet□ *m*

foodless ['fu:dlɪs] *adj* (**a**) *(person)* sans nourriture, sans vivres (**b**) *(barren → country)* stérile

foodstore ['fu:dstɔ:(r)] *n* magasin *m* d'alimentation

foodstuff ['fu:dstʌf] *n* aliment *m*

foody (*pl* **foodies**) = **foodie**

fool [fu:l] **1** *n* (**a**) *(idiot)* idiot(e) *m,f*, imbécile *mf*; **you stupid fool!** espèce d'imbécile *ou* d'abruti!; **what a fool I am!** suis-je idiot *ou* bête!; **don't be a fool!** ne fais pas l'idiot!; **she was a fool to go** elle a été idiote d'y aller; **I felt such a fool** je me suis senti bête; **he was fool enough to agree** il a été assez bête pour accepter, il a fait la bêtise d'accepter; **only a fool would pay that much for it** il faudrait être bête pour le payer aussi cher; **he's more of a fool than I thought** il est encore plus idiot que je ne pensais; **he's no fool** *or* **nobody's fool** il n'est pas bête, il n'est pas né d'hier; **some fool of a politician** un imbécile *ou* un abruti de politicien; **any fool can do it** n'importe quel imbécile peut le faire; **to make a fool of sb** *(ridicule)* ridiculiser qn, se payer la tête de qn; *(trick)* duper qn; **she doesn't want to make a fool of herself** elle ne veut pas passer pour une imbécile *ou* se ridiculiser; **more fool you!** tu n'as qu'à t'en prendre à toi-même!; **there's no fool like an old fool** il n'y a pire imbécile qu'un vieil imbécile; *Prov* **a fool and his money are soon parted** aux idiots l'argent brûle les doigts; **to go on a fool's errand** y aller pour des prunes *ou* pour le roi de Prusse; **to send sb on a fool's errand** envoyer qn décrocher la lune; **I went on a fool's errand trying to buy a turkey on Christmas Eve** j'ai essayé de trouver une dinde la veille de Noël mais il n'y a pas eu moyen; **the sales trip promised to be nothing but a fool's errand** ce voyage d'affaires avait l'air d'être une belle perte de temps en perspective

(**b**) *(jester)* bouffon *m*, fou *m*

(**c**) *Culin* = sorte de mousse aux fruits; **raspberry fool** mousse *f* aux framboises

2 *vt (deceive)* duper, berner; **(I) fooled you!** je t'ai eu!; **don't try to fool me** n'essayez pas de me faire marcher; **your excuses don't fool me** vos excuses ne prennent pas avec moi; **he fooled me into believing it** il a réussi à me le faire croire; **he had tried to fool her into providing him with an alibi** il avait essayé de l'embobiner pour qu'elle lui fournisse un alibi; **they had me completely fooled** ils m'ont bien eu; **you didn't have me fooled for a moment** je n'ai pas été dupe un seul instant; *Ironic* **her?, a socialist?, you could've fooled me!** elle?, une socialiste?, je ne l'aurais pas cru!

3 *vi* (**a**) *(joke)* faire l'imbécile *ou* le pitre; **I'm only fooling** je ne fais que plaisanter, c'est pour rire; **stop fooling!** arrête de faire l'imbécile!

(**b**) *(trifle)* traiter à la légère; **you'd better not fool with him** on ne plaisante pas avec lui

4 *adj Am* idiot, sot (sotte); **that's just the kind of fool thing he'd do** c'est tout à fait le genre de bêtise *ou* d'ânerie qu'il ferait; **that fool son of yours** ton imbécile de fils; *Fam* **what's all this (damn) fool nonsense about getting married?** se marier? qu'est-ce que c'est que ces foutaises?

▸▸ *Miner* ***fool's gold*** pyrite *f* de fer; *Bot* ***fool's parsley*** petite ciguë *f*

▸**fool about, fool around** *vi* (**a**) *(act foolishly)* faire l'imbécile *ou* le pitre; **I'm only fooling around** je ne fais que plaisanter, c'est pour rire; **she fooled around with drugs** elle a touché à la drogue

(**b**) *(waste time)* perdre du temps; **stop fooling around and get up!** arrête de traîner et lève-toi!

(**c**) *Fam (have affair)* avoir *ou* se payer des aventures□; **he's been fooling around with a married woman** il batifole avec une femme mariée

(**d**) *(fiddle)* **to fool around with sth** tripoter qch; **stop fooling around with that computer!** arrête de jouer avec cet ordinateur!; **I still enjoy fooling around with my old train set** j'aime encore bien m'amuser avec mon vieux train électrique

(**e**) *Fam (of couple)* se bécoter

▸**fool away** *vt sep Am (time, money)* gaspiller

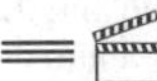

'Fools rush in' *Tennant* 'Coup de foudre et conséquences'

foolery ['fu:lərɪ] (*pl* **fooleries**) *n* *(behaviour)* bouffonnerie *f*, pitrerie *f*, pitreries *fpl*; *(act, remark)* bêtise *f*, sottise *f*; *(joke)* farce *f*, tour *m*

foolhardily ['fu:l,hɑ:dɪlɪ] *adv* témérairement, imprudemment; *(remark)* imprudemment

foolhardiness ['fu:l,hɑ:dɪnɪs] *n* *(of act, person)* témérité *f*, imprudence *f*; *(of remark)* imprudence *f*

foolhardy ['fu:l,hɑ:dɪ] *adj (act, person)* téméraire, imprudent; *(remark)* imprudent

fooling ['fu:lɪŋ] *n (UNCOUNT) (joking)* pitreries *fpl*; **fooling about, fooling around** *(foolish behaviour)* bêtises *fpl*

foolish ['fu:lɪʃ] *adj* (**a**) *(unwise)* insensé, imprudent; **it would be foolish to leave now** ce serait de la folie de partir maintenant; **that was very foolish of her** ce n'était pas très malin de sa part; **I was foolish enough to believe her** j'ai été assez bête pour la croire; **don't do anything foolish** ne faites pas de bêtises; **a foolish hope** un fol espoir

(**b**) *(ridiculous)* ridicule, bête; **I felt rather foolish** je me sentais plutôt idiot *ou* ridicule; **I feel really foolish in this costume** je me sens vraiment ridicule dans ce costume; **the question made him look foolish** la question l'a ridiculisé

foolishly ['fu:lɪʃlɪ] *adv (stupidly)* bêtement, sottement; *(unwisely)* imprudemment; **foolishly, I believed him** comme un idiot *ou* un imbécile je l'ai cru; **she looked at him rather foolishly** elle le regardait d'un air plutôt bête

foolishness ['fu:lɪʃnɪs] *n* bêtise *f*, sottise *f*; *(of plan, decision, idea etc)* stupidité *f*

foolproof ['fu:l,pru:f] **1** *adj (machine, mechanism)* indéréglable; *(plan, scheme)* infaillible, à toute épreuve

2 *vt (machine, mechanism)* rendre indéréglable, protéger contre les fausses manœuvres; *(idea, plan)* rendre infaillible

foolscap ['fu:lzkæp] **1** *n* ≃ papier *m* ministre

2 *comp (paper, size)* ministre *(inv)*

▸▸ ***foolscap envelope*** enveloppe *f* longue; ***foolscap pad*** bloc *m* de papier ministre

foosball ['fu:sbɔ:l] *n Am* baby-foot *m inv*

FOOT [fʊt] (*pl* **feet** [fi:t]) **1** *n* (**a**) *(of person, cow, horse, pig)* pied *m*; *(of bird, cat, dog)* patte *f*; **I came on foot** je suis venu à pied; **to be on one's feet** *(standing)* être *ou* se tenir debout; *(after illness)* être sur pied *ou* rétabli *ou* remis; **she's on her feet all day** elle est debout toute la journée; **on your feet!** debout!; **the speech brought the audience to its feet** l'auditoire s'est levé pour applaudir le discours; **to get** *or* **to rise to one's feet** se mettre debout, se lever; **put your feet up** reposez-vous un peu; **to put** *or* **to set sb on their feet again** *(cure)* remettre qn d'aplomb; *(in business)* remettre qn en selle; **to set foot on land** poser le pied sur la terre ferme; **I've never set foot in her house** je n'ai jamais mis les pieds dans sa maison; **never set foot in this house again!** ne remettez plus les pieds dans cette maison!; *Fig* **we got the project back on its feet** on a relancé le projet; **it's slippery under foot** c'est glissant par terre; **the children are always under my feet** les enfants sont toujours dans mes jambes; *Fig* **to sit at sb's feet** être le disciple de qn

(**b**) *(of chair, glass, lamp)* pied *m*

(**c**) *(lower end → of bed, stocking)* pied *m*; *(→ of table)* bout *m*; *(→ of cliff, mountain, hill)* pied *m*; *(→ of page, stairs)* bas *m*; *(→ of column)* base *f*; **at the foot of the page** au bas *ou* en bas de la page; **at the foot of the stairs** en bas de l'escalier; **at the foot of the ladder/mountain** au pied de l'échelle/de la montagne

(**d**) *(unit of measurement)* pied *m* (anglais); **to be five foot** *or* **feet high/thick** avoir cinq pieds de haut(eur)/d'épaisseur; **a 40-foot fall, a fall of 40 feet** une chute de 40 pieds; *Fam* **to feel ten feet tall** être aux anges *ou* au septième ciel

(**e**) *Literature* pied *m*

(**f**) *Br Mil* infanterie *f*; **the 42nd Foot** le 42ème d'infanterie

(**g**) *(idioms) Fam* **feet first** les pieds devant; *Fam* **the only way I'll leave this house is feet first** je ne quitterai cette maison que les pieds devant; **to run** *or* **to rush sb off their feet** accabler qn de travail, ne pas laisser à qn le temps de souffler; **I've been rushed off my feet all day** je n'ai pas arrêté de toute la journée; *Fam* **he claims he's divorced – divorced, my foot!** il prétend être divorcé – divorcé, mon œil!; **to fall** *or* **to land on one's feet** retomber sur ses pieds; *Fig* **to find one's feet** s'adapter; *Fig* **to get a foot in the door** poser des jalons, établir le contact; *Fig* **to have a foot in the door** être dans la place; *Fig* **well at least it's a foot in the door** au moins, c'est un premier pas *ou* contact; **to have a foot in both camps** avoir un pied dans chaque camp; *Fam* **to have one foot in the grave** *(person)* avoir un pied dans la tombe; *(business)* être moribond□; *Fig* **to have one's** *or* **both feet (firmly) on the ground** avoir les pieds sur terre; *Fam* **to have two left feet** être pataud *ou* empoté; **to have feet of clay** avoir un point faible *ou* vulnérable, avoir une faiblesse de caractère; **to put one's best foot forward** *(hurry)* se dépêcher, presser le pas; *(do one's best)* faire de son mieux; **right, best foot forward now** *(hurry)* bon, dépêchons-nous; *(do one's best)* bon, faisons de notre mieux; *Fig* **to put one's foot down** faire acte d'autorité; *Aut* accélérer; *Fam* **to put one's foot** *Br* **in it** *or Am* **in one's mouth** mettre les pieds dans le plat; *Br* **she didn't put a foot wrong** elle n'a pas commis la moindre erreur; *Br Fig* **I never seem able to put a foot right** j'ai l'impression que je ne peux jamais rien faire comme il faut; **to catch sb on the wrong foot** prendre qn au dépourvu; *Sport* prendre qn à contre-pied; **to get** *or* **to start off on the right/wrong foot** être bien/mal parti; *Scot & Ir Fam Pej* **to kick with the wrong foot** *(from a Protestant point of view)* être catholique□; *(from a Catholic point of view)* être protestant□; *Fig* **the** *Br* **boot** *or Am* **shoe is on the other foot** les rôles sont inversés

2 *vt* (**a**) *(walk) Fam* **he decided to foot it home** il a décidé de rentrer à pied□

(**b**) *(pay) Fam* **to foot the bill** payer l'addition□

▸▸ ***foot control*** commande *f* au pied; *Am* ***foot doctor*** podologue *mf*; *Tennis* ***foot fault*** faute *f* de pied; ***foot passenger*** piéton *m* *(passager sans véhicule)*; *Br Mil* ***foot patrol*** patrouille *f* à pied; ***foot powder*** poudre *f* pour pieds; ***foot pump*** pompe *f* à pied; *Bot & Vet* ***foot rot*** piétin *m*; ***foot soldier*** *Mil* fantassin *m*; *(of political party)* militant(e) *m,f* de base; ***foot spa*** bain *m* de pieds à remous

▸**foot up** *vt sep Am Fam (add up → bill)* additionner□

'Him with his Foot in his Mouth' *Bellow* 'Le Gaffeur'

footage ['fʊtɪdʒ] *n (UNCOUNT)* (**a**) *(length)* longueur *f* en pieds (**b**) *Cin (length)* métrage *m*; *(material filmed)* séquences *fpl*; **the film contains previously unseen footage on** *or* **about the war** le film contient des séquences inédites sur la guerre

foot-and-mouth disease *n Vet* fièvre *f* aphteuse

football ['fʊt,bɔ:l] *n* (**a**) *(game) Br* football *m*; *Am* football *m* américain

(**b**) *(ball)* ballon *m* (de football), balle *f*; *Fig* **the abortion issue has become a political football** les partis politiques se renvoient la balle à propos de l'avortement

▸▸ *Br* ***the Football Association*** = la Fédération britannique de football; ***football boot*** chaussure *f* de football; *Br* ***football club*** club *m* de football; *Br* ***football colours*** couleurs *fpl* d'un club de foot; *Br* ***football coupon*** ≃ grille *f* de Loto sportif; ***football fan*** *Br* fan *mf* de foot; *Am* fan *mf* de football américain; *Am* ***football field*** terrain *m* de football; *Am* ***football game*** match *m* de football américain; *Br* ***football ground*** terrain *m* de football; ***football hooligan*** hooligan *m*; ***football hooliganism*** vandalisme *m*, hooliganisme *m*; ***the Football League*** = association réunissant la majorité des clubs de football professionnels en Angleterre; *Br* ***football match*** match *m* de football; *Br* ***football pitch*** terrain *m* de football; ***football player*** *Br* joueur(euse) *m,f* de football, footballeur(euse) *m,f*; *Am* joueur(euse) *m,f* de football américain; *Br* ***football pools*** ≃ Loto *m* sportif; **to do the football pools** ≃ jouer au Loto sportif; **he won £20 on the football pools** ≃ il a gagné 20 livres au Loto sportif; *Br* ***football scarf*** = écharpe aux couleurs d'une équipe de football; ***football season*** saison *f* de football; *Br* ***football shirt*** maillot *m* de foot; *Br* ***football strip*** tenue *f* de foot; ***football supporter*** supporter *m* (de football); ***football team*** *Br* équipe *f* de football; *Am* équipe *f* de football américain

footballer ['fʊt,bɔːlə(r)] *n Br* joueur(euse) *m,f* de football, footballeur(euse) *m,f*; *Am* joueur(euse) *m,f* de football américain

footbath ['fʊtbɑːθ, *pl* -bɑːðz] *n* bain *m* de pieds

footboard ['fʊtbɔːd] *n (lever)* pédale *f*; *(on bed)* panneau *m* de pied

footboy ['fʊtbɔɪ] *n Arch* petit laquais *m*

footbrake ['fʊtbreɪk] *n* frein *m* à pied

footbridge ['fʊtbrɪdʒ] *n* passerelle *f*

-footed ['fʊtɪd] *suff* au pied...; **swift-footed** au pied léger *ou* rapide

footer ['fʊtə(r)] *n* (**a**) *Br Fam (football)* foot *m* (**b**) *Comput & Typ* bas *m* de page

-footer ['fʊtə(r)] *suff* **the boat is a 15-footer** le bateau mesure 15 pieds *ou* environ 4,50 mètres

footfall ['fʊtfɔːl] *n* (**a**) *(sound)* (bruit *m* de) pas *m*; **I heard a light footfall** j'ai entendu un pas léger (**b**) *Mktg (people entering shop, airport etc)* taux *m* de fréquentation

foot-fault *Tennis* **1** *vi* faire une faute de pied

2 *vt (of umpire)* **to foot-fault a player** pénaliser un joueur pour faute de pied

footgear ['fʊt,gɪə(r)] *n (UNCOUNT)* chaussures *fpl*

foothills ['fʊthɪlz] *npl* collines *fpl* basses *ou* avancées; *(of mountain range)* avant-monts *mpl*

foothold ['fʊthəʊld] *n* prise *f* de pied; *Fig* position *f* avantageuse; *also Fig* **to gain** *or* **to get a foothold** prendre pied; **he gained a foothold in the jazz world** il a su s'imposer dans le monde du jazz; *Com* **to get** *or* **to secure a foothold in a market** prendre pied sur un marché

footie ['fʊtɪ] *n Br Fam (football)* foot *m*

footing ['fʊtɪŋ] *n* (**a**) *(balance)* prise *f* de pied; **to get one's footing** prendre pied; **to keep/to lose one's footing** garder/perdre l'équilibre; **to miss one's footing** poser le pied à faux

(**b**) *(position → of person)* position *f*, condition *f*; *(→ of institution etc)* condition *f*, état *m*; **to be on an equal footing** être sur un pied d'égalité; **let's try to keep things on a friendly footing** essayons de rester en bons termes; **on a war footing** sur le pied de guerre; **the business is now on a firm footing** l'affaire est maintenant en bonne voie

▸**footle about, footle around** ['fuːtəl] *vi Fam* (**a**) *(potter)* bricoler, s'occuper; **to footle about** *or* **around with sth** jouer avec qch, tripoter qch (**b**) *(talk nonsense)* dire des bêtises [❑], radoter

footless ['fʊtlɪs] *adj* (**a**) *(tights)* sans pieds (**b**) *Am Fig (stupid)* idiot, stupide

footlights ['fʊtlaɪts] *npl* rampe *f*; *Fig* **the footlights** *(theatre)* le théâtre, les planches *fpl*

footling ['fuːtəlɪŋ] *adj Fam (trivial)* insignifiant [❑], futile [❑]

footloose ['fʊtluːs] *adj Fam* **footloose and fancy-free** libre comme l'air

footman ['fʊtmən] (*pl* **footmen** [-mən]) *n* valet *m* de pied

footmark ['fʊtmɑːk] *n Br* empreinte *f* (de pied)

footmen ['fʊtmən] *pl of* **footman**

footnote ['fʊtnəʊt] **1** *n (on page)* note *f* en bas de page; *(in speech)* remarque *f* supplémentaire; **as a footnote I should just mention...** en dernière remarque, je signalerai que...; *Fig* **he was doomed to become just a footnote in the history of events** il était destiné à rester en marge de l'histoire des événements *ou* à ne jouer qu'un rôle secondaire dans l'histoire des événements

2 *vt* annoter, mettre des notes de bas de page

footpad ['fʊtpæd] *n* (**a**) *Arch (thief)* voleur *m* (**b**) *Tech (of spacecraft)* semelle *f*

footpage ['fʊtpeɪdʒ] *n* petit laquais *m*

footpath ['fʊtpɑːθ, *pl* -pɑːðz] *n (path)* sentier *m*; *(paved)* trottoir *m*

footplate ['fʊtpleɪt] *n Br Rail* plate-forme *f* *(d'une locomotive)*

footplateman ['fʊtpleɪt,mən] (*pl* **footplatemen** [-mən]) *n Br Rail* agent *m* de conduite

foot-pound (*pl* **foot-pounds**) *n Phys (measurement)* pied-livre *m*

footprint ['fʊtprɪnt] *n* (**a**) *(of foot)* empreinte *f* (de pied) (**b**) *(of satellite)* empreinte *f* (**c**) *Comput* encombrement *m*

footrace ['fʊtreɪs] *n Sport* course *f* à pied

footrest ['fʊtrest] *n (gen)* repose-pieds *m inv*; *(stool)* tabouret *m*

footrope ['fʊtrəʊp] *n Naut (of sail)* ralingue *f* de fond *ou* de bordure; *(of yard)* marchepied *m*

footrule ['fʊtruːl] *n* règle *f* (d'un pied de long)

foot-second *n* (*pl* **foot-seconds**) *Phys (measurement)* pied *m* par seconde

FOOTSIE, Footsie ['fʊtsɪ] *n St Exch* (*abbr* **Financial Times-Stock Exchange 100 Index**) = principal indice boursier du 'Financial Times' basé sur la valeur de 100 actions cotées à la Bourse de Londres

footsie ['fʊtsɪ] *n Fam* **to play footsie with sb** *(rub feet)* faire du pied à qn; *Am (collaborate with)* être le (la) complice de qn [❑]

footslog ['fʊtslɒg] (*pt & pp* **footslogged**, *cont* **footslogging**) *vi Fam* marcher (d'un pas lourd) [❑]

footslogger ['fʊt,slɒgə(r)] *n Fam Mil* pousse-cailloux *m inv*, biffin *m*

footslogging ['fʊt,slɒgɪŋ] *n Fam* marche [❑] *f*; **this job involves a lot of footslogging** dans ce travail, il faut marcher beaucoup

footsore ['fʊtsɔː(r)] *adj* **I was tired and footsore** j'étais fatigué et j'avais mal aux pieds

footstalk ['fʊtstɔːk] *n* (**a**) *Bot (of leaf)* pétiole *m*, *(of flower)* pédoncule *m* (**b**) *Zool* tige *f*

footstall ['fʊtstɔːl] *n Archit* socle *m*

footstep ['fʊtstep] *n* (**a**) *(sound)* pas *m*; **I hear footsteps** j'entends des pas *ou* un bruit de pas (**b**) *(footprint)* (empreinte *f* de) pied *m* *ou* pas *m*; *Fig* **to follow** *or* **tread** *or* **walk in sb's footsteps** marcher sur les traces *ou* pas de qn; *Fig* **to follow in one's father's footsteps** suivre les traces de son père

footstool ['fʊtstuːl] *n* tabouret *m*

foot-ton (*pl* **foot-tons**) *n* pied-tonne *m*, tonne-pied *f*

foot-up *n (in rugby)* faute *f* de pied; *(in football)* pied *m* en avant

footway ['fʊtweɪ] *n Br (path)* sentier *m*; *(paved)* passerelle *f*

footwear ['fʊtweə(r)] *n (UNCOUNT)* chaussures *fpl*; **he works in the footwear department** il travaille au rayon chaussures

footwell ['fʊtwel] *n Aut* place *f* aux pieds

footwork ['fʊtwɜːk] *n* (**a**) jeu *m* de jambes; **good footwork** bon jeu *m* de jambes; *Fig* **it took some fancy footwork to avoid legal action** il a fallu manœuvrer adroitement pour éviter un procès (**b**) *(walking)* marche *f*; **the job entails a lot of footwork** le travail oblige à beaucoup marcher

footworn ['fʊtwɔːn] *adj* (**a**) *(stairs, pavement)* usé (**b**) **I was tired and footworn** j'étais fatigué et j'avais mal aux pieds

footy ['fʊtɪ] *n Fam* (**a**) *Br & Austr (soccer)* foot *m* (**b**) *Austr (rugby union)* rugby *m* à quinze; *(rugby league)* rugby *m* à treize; *(Australian Rules football)* football *m* australien

fop [fɒp] *n* dandy *m*

foppery ['fɒpərɪ] *n* dandysme *m*, élégance *f* affectée

foppish ['fɒpɪʃ] *adj (man)* dandy; *(dress, manners, elegance)* de dandy

foppishly ['fɒpɪʃlɪ] *adv* avec une élégance affectée

foppishness ['fɒpɪʃnɪs] *n* dandysme *m*, élégance *f* affectée

FOR [,efəʊ'ɑː(r)] *adv Com* (*abbr* **free on rail**) franco wagon

FOR [fɔː(r)]

pour	▸ **1A (a) – (d); B (a), (b), (d); C (b) – (e), (g), (h)**
à l'intention de	▸ **1A (c)**
dans la direction de	▸ **1A (d)**
à	▸ **1A (e)**
pendant	▸ **1B (c)**
en raison de	▸ **1C (e)**
de	▸ **1C (f)**
car	▸ **2**

1 *prep* **A.** (**a**) *(expressing purpose or function)* pour; **we were in Vienna for a holiday/for work** nous étions à Vienne en vacances/pour le travail; **what for?** pourquoi?; **I don't know what she said that for** je ne sais pas pourquoi elle a dit ça; **what's this knob for?** à quoi sert ce bouton?; **it's for adjusting the volume** ça sert à régler le volume; **what's this medicine for?** à quoi sert ce médicament?; **can you give me something for the pain?** est-ce que vous pouvez me donner quelque chose pour *ou* contre la douleur?; **an instrument for measuring temperature** un instrument pour mesurer la température; **clothes for tall men** vêtements *mpl* pour hommes grands; **not suitable for freezing** *(on packaging)* ne pas congeler

(**b**) *(in order to obtain)* pour; **write for a free catalogue** demandez votre catalogue gratuit; **for further information write to...** pour de plus amples renseignements, écrivez à...; **they play for money** ils jouent pour de l'argent

(**c**) *(indicating recipient or beneficiary)* pour, à l'intention de; **these flowers are for her** ces fleurs sont pour elle; **there's a phone call for you** il y a un appel pour vous; **I've got some news for you** j'ai une nouvelle à vous annoncer; **he left a note for them** il leur a laissé un mot, il a laissé un mot à leur intention; **opera is not for me** l'opéra, ça n'est pas pour moi; **you are the man for me/the job** vous êtes l'homme qu'il me faut/qui convient pour ce poste; **that is just the thing for you** c'est juste ce qu'il vous faut; **equal pay for women** un salaire égal pour les femmes; **parking for customers only** *(sign)* parking réservé à la clientèle; **what can I do for you?** que puis-je faire pour vous?; **he's doing everything he can for us** il fait tout son possible pour nous; **a collection for the poor** une quête pour les *ou* en faveur des pauvres; **it's for your own good** c'est pour ton bien; **he often cooks for himself** il se fait souvent la cuisine; **see for yourself!** voyez par vous-même!; **she writes for a sports magazine** elle écrit des articles pour un magazine de sport; **I work for an advertising agency** je travaille pour une agence de publicité

(**d**) *(indicating direction, destination)* pour, dans la direction de; **they left for Spain** ils sont partis pour l'Espagne; **before leaving for the office** avant de partir au bureau; **she ran for the door** elle s'est précipitée vers la porte en courant; **he made for home** il a pris la direction de la maison; **the ship made for port** le navire a mis le cap sur le port; **the train for London** le train pour *ou* à destination de *ou* en direction de Londres; **trains for the suburbs** les trains pour la banlieue; **change trains here for Beaune** changez de train ici pour Beaune; **flight 402 bound for Chicago is now boarding** les passagers du vol 402 à destination de Chicago sont invités à se présenter à l'embarquement

(**e**) *(available for)* à; **for rent** *(sign)* à louer; **for sale** *(sign)* à vendre; **these books are for reference only** ces livres sont à consulter sur place

B. (**a**) *(indicating span of time → past, future)* pour, pendant; *(→ action uncompleted)* depuis; **they're going away for the weekend** ils partent pour le week-end; **they will be gone for some time** ils seront absents (pendant *ou* pour) quelque temps; **they were in Spain for two weeks** ils étaient en Espagne pour deux semaines; **she won't be back for a month** elle ne sera pas de retour avant un mois; **I lived there for**

one month j'y ai vécu pendant un mois; **I've lived here for two years** j'habite ici depuis deux ans; **I'd only lived there for a week when the heating went wrong** je n'habitais là que depuis une semaine quand la chaudière est tombée en panne; **my mother has been here for two weeks** ma mère est ici depuis deux semaines; **you haven't been here for a long time** il y a *ou* voilà *ou* ça fait longtemps que vous n'êtes pas venu; **we've known them for years** nous les connaissons depuis des années, il y a des années que nous les connaissons; **I have not seen him for three years** il y a trois ans que je ne l'ai vu; **she won't be able to go out for another day or two** elle devra rester sans sortir pendant encore un jour ou deux; **can you stay for a while?** pouvez-vous rester un moment?; **it's the worst accident for years** c'est le pire accident qui soit arrivé depuis des années; **we have food for three days** nous avons des vivres pour trois jours

(**b**) *(indicating a specific occasion or time)* pour; **I went home for Christmas** je suis rentré chez moi pour Noël; **he took me out to dinner for my birthday** il m'a emmené dîner au restaurant pour mon anniversaire; **we made an appointment for the 6th** nous avons pris rendez-vous pour le 6; **the meeting was set for five o'clock** la réunion était fixée pour cinq heures; **it's time for bed** c'est l'heure de se coucher *ou* d'aller au lit; **there's no time for that** il n'y a pas de temps pour ça; **for the last/third time** pour la dernière/troisième fois

(**c**) *(indicating distance)* pendant; **you could see for miles around** on voyait à des kilomètres à la ronde; **we walked for several miles** nous avons marché pendant plusieurs kilomètres; **they drove for miles without seeing another car** ils ont roulé (pendant) des kilomètres sans croiser une seule voiture; **bends for one mile** *(sign)* virages sur un mil(l)e

(**d**) *(indicating amount)* **they paid him £100 for his services** ils lui ont donné 100 livres pour ses services; **you can hire a car for twenty pounds a day** on peut louer une voiture pour vingt livres par jour; **it's £2 for a ticket** c'est 2 livres le billet; **he's selling it for £200** il le vend 200 livres; **I wrote a cheque for £15** j'ai fait un chèque de 15 livres; **three for £5** trois pour 5 livres; **put me down for £5** inscrivez-moi pour 5 livres

C. (**a**) *(indicating exchange, equivalence)* **do you have change for a pound?** vous avez la monnaie d'une livre?; **he exchanged the bike for another model** il a échangé le vélo contre *ou* pour un autre modèle; **what will you give me in exchange for this book?** que me donnerez-vous en échange de ce livre?; **he gave blow for blow** il a rendu coup pour coup; **"salvia" is the Latin term for "sage"** "salvia" veut dire "sage" en latin; **what's the Spanish for "good"?** comment dit-on "good" en espagnol?; **F for François** F comme François; **what's the M for?** qu'est-ce que le M veut dire?; **red for danger** rouge veut dire danger; **he has cereal for breakfast** il prend des céréales au petit déjeuner; **to have sb for a teacher** avoir qn comme professeur; **I know it for a fact** je sais que c'est vrai; **I for one don't care** pour ma part, je m'en fiche; **do you take me for a fool?** me prenez-vous pour un imbécile?

(**b**) *(indicating ratio)* pour; **there's one woman applicant for every five men** sur six postulants il y a une femme et cinq hommes; **for every honest politician there are a hundred dishonest ones** pour un homme politique honnête, il y en a cent qui sont malhonnêtes

(**c**) *(on behalf of)* pour; **I'm speaking for all parents** je parle pour *ou* au nom de tous les parents; **the lawyer was acting for his client** l'avocat agissait au nom de *ou* pour le compte de son client; **I'll go to the meeting for you** j'irai à la réunion à votre place; **the representative for the union** le représentant du syndicat

(**d**) *(in favour of)* pour; **I'm all for it** je suis tout à fait pour; **for or against** pour ou contre; **vote for Smith!** votez (pour) Smith!; **they voted for the proposal** ils ont voté en faveur de la proposition; **he's for the ecologists** il est pour les écologistes; **I'm for shortening the hunting season** je suis pour une saison de chasse plus courte; **who's for a drink?** qui veut boire un verre?; **I'm for bed** je vais me coucher; *Law* **judgement for the plaintiff** arrêt *m* en faveur du demandeur

(**e**) *(because of)* pour, en raison de; **candidates were selected for their ability** les candidats ont été retenus en raison de leurs compétences; **she couldn't sleep for the pain** la douleur l'empêchait de dormir; **he's known for his wit** il est connu pour son esprit; **the region is famous for its wine** la région est célèbre pour son vin; **she's in prison for treason** elle est en prison pour trahison; **he couldn't speak for laughing** il ne pouvait pas parler tellement il riait; **you'll feel better for a rest** vous vous sentirez mieux quand vous vous serez reposé; **if it weren't for you, I'd leave** sans vous, je partirais; **for this reason** pour cette raison; **for fear of waking him** de crainte de le réveiller; **do it for my sake** faites-le pour moi; **for old time's sake** en souvenir du passé

(**f**) *(indicating cause, reason)* de; **the reason for his leaving** la raison de son départ; **there are no grounds for believing it's true** il n'y a pas de raison de croire que c'est vrai; **she apologized for being late** elle s'est excusée d'être en retard; **I thanked him for his kindness** je l'ai remercié de *ou* pour sa gentillesse

(**g**) *(concerning, as regards)* pour; **so much for that** voilà qui est classé; **for my part, I refuse to go** pour ma part *ou* quant à moi, je refuse d'y aller; **I'm very happy for her** je suis très heureux pour elle; **what are her feelings for him?** quels sont ses sentiments pour lui?; **for sheer impudence his remarks are hard to beat** pour ce qui est de l'effronterie, ses commentaires sont imbattables

(**h**) *(given normal expectations)* pour; **it's warm for March** il fait bon pour un mois de mars; **that's a good score for him** c'est un bon score pour lui; **she looks very young for her age** elle fait très jeune pour son âge

(**i**) *(in phrase with infinitive verbs)* **it's not for him to decide** il ne lui appartient pas *ou* ce n'est pas à lui de décider; **it's not for her to tell me what to do** ce n'est pas à elle de me dire ce que je dois faire; **it was difficult for her to apologize** il lui était difficile de s'excuser; **I have brought it for you to see** je l'ai apporté pour que vous le voyiez; **this job is too complicated for us to finish today** ce travail est trop compliqué pour que nous le finissions aujourd'hui; **there is still time for her to finish** elle a encore le temps de finir; **it took an hour for the taxi to get to the station** le taxi a mis une heure pour aller jusqu'à la gare; **for us to arrive on time we'd better leave now** si nous voulons être à l'heure, il vaut mieux partir maintenant; **the easiest thing would be for you to lead the way** le plus facile serait que vous nous montriez le chemin; **there's no need for you to worry** il n'y a pas de raison de vous inquiéter; **it is usual for the mother to accompany her daughter** il est d'usage que la mère accompagne sa fille

D. *(idioms)* **oh for a holiday!** ah, si je pouvais être en vacances!; **oh for some peace and quiet!** que ne donnerais-je pour la paix!; *Fam* **you'll be (in) for it if your mother sees you!** ça va être ta fête si ta mère te voit!; *Fam* **now we're (in) for it!** qu'est-ce qu'on va prendre!; **there's nothing for it but to pay him** il n'y a qu'à *ou* il ne nous reste qu'à le payer; **that's the postal service for you!** ça c'est bien la poste!

2 *conj Formal* car, parce que; **I was surprised when he arrived punctually, for he was usually late** je fus surpris de le voir arriver à l'heure, car il était souvent en retard

3 for all 1 *prep* (**a**) *(in spite of)* malgré; **for all their efforts** malgré tous leurs efforts; **for all his success, he's very insecure** malgré sa réussite, il manque vraiment de confiance en soi

(**b**) *(considering)* **for all the use he is he might as well go and play** pour ce qu'il fait d'utile il peut aussi bien aller jouer; **for all the sense it made** pour ce que c'était clair **2** *conj* **for all she may say** quoi qu'elle en dise; **for all the good it does** pour tout l'effet que ça fait; **it may be true for all I know** c'est peut-être vrai, je n'en sais rien

4 for all that 1 *adv* pour autant, malgré tout **2** *conj esp Literary* **for all that he wanted to believe them** pour autant qu'il veuille les croire

5 for ever *adv (last, continue)* pour toujours; *(leave)* pour toujours, sans retour; **for ever and a day** jusqu'à la fin des temps; **for ever and ever** à tout jamais, éternellement; **for ever and ever, amen** pour les siècles des siècles, amen; **to live for ever** vivre éternellement; **Scotland for ever!** vive l'Écosse!

---

fora ['fɔːrə] *pl of* **forum**

forage ['fɒrɪdʒ] **1** *n* (**a**) *(search)* fouille *f*; **to go on the forage** *(for provisions)* chercher de la nourriture; **to have a forage for sth** fouiller *ou* fourrager pour trouver qch

(**b**) *(food)* fourrage *m*

(**c**) *Mil (raid)* raid *m*, incursion *f*

2 *vi* (**a**) *(search)* fourrager, fouiller; **to forage for sth** fouiller *ou* fourrager pour trouver qch

(**b**) *Mil (raid)* faire un raid *ou* une incursion

3 *vt* (**a**) *(obtain)* trouver en fourrageant

(**b**) *(feed)* donner du fourrage à, donner à manger à

►► *Mil* ***forage cap*** calot *m*; *Agr* ***forage harvester*** fourragère *f*

►**forage about, forage around** *vi (rummage)* fourrager, fouiller (**in** dans)

forager ['fɒrɪdʒə(r)] *n* (**a**) *Mil* fourrageur *m* (**b**) *Entom* butineuse *f*

foraging ['fɒrɪdʒɪŋ] *n* **to go foraging for sth** fouiller *ou* fourrager pour trouver qch

foramen [fɒ'reɪmən] *(pl* **foramina** [-'ræmɪnə]*) n Anat* foramen *m*, trou *m*; **mental foramen** trou *m* mentonnier

►► ***foramen magnum*** trou *m* occipital; ***foramen ovale*** trou *m* de Botal

foraminate [fɒ'reɪmɪneɪt] *adj Bot & Zool* foraminé

forasmuch as [fərəz'mʌtʃ-] *conj Arch or Literary* vu que + *indicative*

foray ['fɒreɪ] **1** *n Mil (raid)* raid *m*, incursion *f*; *(excursion)* incursion *f*; **she was on one of her forays round the bookshops** elle procédait à l'une de ses excursions dans les librairies; **he made a brief foray into politics** il a fait une courte incursion dans la politique

2 *vi* faire un raid *ou* une incursion

forbad, forbade [fə'bæd] *pt of* **forbid**

forbear *(pt* **forbore** [-'bɔː(r)], *pp* **forborne** [-'bɔːn]*) Formal* **1** *vi* [fɔː'beə(r)] *(abstain)* s'abstenir; **to forbear from doing** *or* **to do sth** se garder *ou* s'abstenir de faire qch; **she forbore to make any comment** elle s'abstint de tout commentaire

2 *vt* [fɔː'beə(r)] renoncer à, se priver de

3 *n* ['fɔːˌbeə(r)] ancêtre *m*; **our forbears** nos aïeux *mpl*

forbearance [fɔː'beərəns] *n* (**a**) *(patience)* patience *f*, indulgence *f*; **to show forbearance towards sb** montrer de l'indulgence envers qn (**b**) *(restraint)* abstention *f*

forbearing [fɔː'beərɪŋ] *adj* patient, indulgent

forbearingly [fɔː'beərɪŋlɪ] *adv* avec patience, avec indulgence

forbid [fə'bɪd] *(pt* **forbad** *or* **forbade** [-'bæd], *pp* **forbidden** [-'bɪdən]*) vt* (**a**) *(not allow)* interdire, défendre; **to forbid sb alcohol** interdire l'alcool à qn; **to forbid sb to do sth** défendre *ou* interdire à qn de faire qch; **students are forbidden to talk during exams** les étudiants n'ont pas le droit de parler pendant les examens; **he was forbidden from seeing her again** on lui a interdit de la revoir; **it is strictly forbidden to smoke, smoking is strictly forbidden** il est formellement interdit de fumer

(**b**) *(prevent)* empêcher; **my condition forbids strenuous exercise** mon état ne me permet pas de me livrer à des exercices violents; **God forbid!** pourvu que non!; **if she were to die, Heaven** *or* **God forbid, I don't know what I'd do** si elle venait à mourir, Dieu (m'en) préserve, je ne sais pas ce que je ferais; **Heaven forbid (that) all her family should come too!** pourvu qu'elle ne vienne pas avec toute sa famille!

forbiddance [fə'bɪdəns] *n Arch or Literary* défense *f*, interdiction *f*

forbidden [fə'bɪdən] **1** *pp of* **forbid**

2 *adj* interdit, défendu; **to tread on forbidden ground** empiéter sur un terrain défendu; *Fig* toucher à un sujet tabou

►► **the Forbidden City** la Cité interdite; *Law* **forbidden degrees** = degrés de consanguinité au sein desquels le mariage est interdit; *Bible & Fig* **forbidden fruit** fruit *m* défendu

forbidding [fəˈbɪdɪŋ] *adj (building, look, sky)* menaçant; *(person)* sévère, menaçant; *(sky, weather)* sombre; *(face, aspect)* sinistre

forbiddingly [fəˈbɪdɪŋlɪ] *adv* **the castle towered forbiddingly over the town** le château, menaçant, dominait la ville; **forbiddingly difficult/complex** d'une difficulté/complexité rébarbative

forbore [fɔːˈbɔː(r)] *pt of* **forbear**

forborne [fɔːˈbɔːn] *pp of* **forbear**

FORCE [fɔːs]

force	► 1
puissance	► 1 (a)
violence	► 1 (b)
forcer	► 2 (a), (e) – (h)
arracher	► 2 (b)
imposer	► 2 (c)
en vigueur	► 3
en force	► 3

1 *n* (**a**) *(power)* force *f*, puissance *f*; **forces of evil/nature** forces *fpl* du mal/de la nature; **moral force** force *f* morale; **Europe is becoming a powerful economic force** l'Europe devient une grande puissance économique; **television could be a force for good** la télévision pourrait avoir une bonne influence; **to be a force for change** être le moteur du changement; **France is a force to be reckoned with** la France est une puissance *ou* force avec laquelle il faut compter; **she's a force to be reckoned with** il faudra compter avec elle; **there are several forces at work** il y a plusieurs forces en jeu

(**b**) *(strength)* force *f*; *(violence)* force *f*, violence *f*; **I'm against the use of force** je suis contre le recours à la force; **the force of the blow laid him out** la violence du coup l'a mis K-O; **they used force to control the crowd** ils ont employé la force pour contrôler la foule; **I hit it with as much force as I could muster** je l'ai frappé aussi fort que j'ai pu

(**c**) *(of argument, word)* force *f*, poids *m*; **I don't see the force of her argument** je ne perçois pas la force de son argument

(**d**) *Phys* force *f*; **centrifugal/coercive force** force *f* centrifuge/coercitive; **the force of gravity** la pesanteur; *Met* **force 10 on the Beaufort scale** force 10 sur l'échelle de Beaufort; **a force 9 gale** un vent de force 9

(**e**) *(of people)* force *f*; *Com* **our sales force** notre force de vente; *Mil* **the allied forces** les armées *fpl* alliées, les alliés *mpl*; *Mil* **the (armed) forces** les forces *fpl* armées; **the (police) force** les forces *fpl* de police; **two different police forces** deux forces de police différentes; **he was in the forces** il était dans l'armée; **forces slang** argot *m* militaire

(**f**) *(idioms)* **force of circumstances** force *f* des choses; **by** *or* **from force of habit** par la force de l'habitude; **by sheer force** de vive force; **she managed it through sheer force of will** elle y est arrivée uniquement à force de volonté; **the law comes into force this year** la loi entre en vigueur cette année

2 *vt* (**a**) *(compel)* forcer, obliger; **to force sb to do sth** contraindre *ou* forcer qn à faire qch; **I forced myself to be nice to them** je me suis forcé à être aimable avec eux; **no one's forcing you!** personne ne t'y force *ou* oblige!; *Ironic* **don't force yourself!** ne te force surtout pas!; **they were forced to admit I was right** ils ont été obligés de reconnaître que j'avais raison; **he was forced to retire** il a été mis à la retraite d'office; **to force sb's hand** forcer la main à qn

(**b**) *(wrest)* arracher, extorquer; **I forced a confession from** *or* **out of him** je lui ai arraché une confession

(**c**) *(impose)* imposer; **to force sth on** *or* **upon sb** imposer qch à qn; **to force oneself on sb** imposer sa présence à qn; **he forced himself** *or* **his attentions on her** il l'a poursuivie de ses assiduités

(**d**) *(push)* **to force one's way into a building** entrer *ou* pénétrer de force dans un immeuble; **I forced my way through the crowd** je me suis frayé un chemin *ou* passage à travers la foule; **to force sth into sth** faire entrer qch de force dans qch; **don't force it** ne force pas; **the car forced us off the road** la voiture nous a forcés à quitter la route; **to force a bill through Parliament** forcer la Chambre à voter une loi; **to force sb into a corner** pousser qn dans un coin; *Fig* mettre qn au pied du mur; **compressed air forces the liquid up the pipe** l'air comprimé fait monter le liquide dans le tuyau

(**e**) *(break open)* forcer; **to force (open) a door/lock** forcer une porte/une serrure

(**f**) *(answer, smile)* forcer; **she managed to force a smile** elle eut un sourire forcé

(**g**) *(hurry)* forcer, hâter; *Hort* **to force flowers/plants** forcer des fleurs/des plantes; **we forced the pace** nous avons forcé l'allure *ou* le pas; **I felt I had to force the issue** j'ai senti qu'il fallait que je force la décision

(**h**) *(strain → metaphor, voice)* forcer; *(→ word)* forcer le sens de

3 in force 1 *adj* en application, en vigueur; **the rules now in force** le règlement en vigueur **2** *adv* en force; **the demonstrators arrived in force** les manifestants sont arrivés en force; **the students were there in force** les étudiants étaient venus en force *ou* en grand nombre; **in full force** au grand complet

►**force back** *vt sep* (**a**) *(push back)* repousser, refouler; *Mil* faire reculer, obliger à reculer

(**b**) *(repress)* réprimer; **she forced back the urge to laugh** elle réprima une envie de rire; **I forced back my tears** j'ai refoulé mes larmes

►**force down** *vt sep* (**a**) *(push down)* faire descendre (de force); **he forced down the lid of the box** il a fermé la boîte en forçant; **to force down prices** faire baisser les prix

(**b**) *(plane)* forcer à atterrir

(**c**) *(food)* se forcer à manger *ou* à avaler; *Hum* **more cake? – I expect I could force down another slice** encore un peu de gâteau? – ma foi, je suis sûr que j'ai encore un peu de place pour un autre petit morceau

►**force out** *vt sep* (**a**) *(push out)* faire sortir (de force); **hunger eventually forced them out** la faim les a finalement obligés à sortir; **to be forced out of business** être forcé à fermer boutique; *Fig* **the opposition forced him out** l'opposition l'a poussé dehors

(**b**) *(remark)* **he forced out an apology** il s'est excusé du bout des lèvres

►**force up** *vt sep* faire monter (de force); **to force prices up** faire monter les prix

> **May the force be with you**
>
> Il s'agit d'une formule qui provient du film de science-fiction *Star Wars* (*La Guerre des étoiles*), réalisé par George Lucas en 1977. Les personnages qui luttaient pour le triomphe du bien dans l'univers se quittaient généralement sur ces mots ("que la force soit avec toi").
>
> On utilise parfois cette phrase de façon humoristique, à l'écrit ou à l'oral, pour souhaiter bonne chance à quelqu'un. On dira par exemple: **have a good business trip, and may the force be with you, you'll need it** ("j'espère que ton voyage d'affaires se passera bien, et que la force soit avec toi, tu en auras besoin").

forced [fɔːst] *adj* (**a**) *(compulsory)* forcé

(**b**) *(smile)* forcé, artificiel; **he gave a forced laugh** il a ri du bout des lèvres

(**c**) *(plant, fruit, vegetables)* forcé

►► *Fin* ***forced currency*** cours *m* forcé; ***forced feeding*** *(of person)* alimentation *f* de force; *(of livestock)* gavage *m*; ***forced labour*** travail *m* forcé; *Aviat* ***forced landing*** atterrissage *m* forcé; *Fin* ***forced loan*** emprunt *m* forcé; *Mil* ***forced march*** marche *f* forcée; ***forced sale*** vente *f* forcée; *Fin* ***forced saving*** épargne *f* forcée

forcedly [ˈfɔːsɪdlɪ] *adv* forcément

force-feed *vt (person)* nourrir de force; *(animal)* gaver

forceful [ˈfɔːsfʊl] *adj (person, personality)* énergique, fort; *(argument, style, impression)* puissant; *(language)* musclé; **he's not very forceful** il n'est pas très énergique

forcefully [ˈfɔːsfʊlɪ] *adv (speak, act)* énergiquement; *(express oneself, reason, write)* avec vigueur; *(argue)* énergiquement, avec force

forcefulness [ˈfɔːsfʊlnɪs] *n* vigueur *f*

force-land *vi Aviat* faire un atterrissage forcé

force majeure [-mæˈʒɜː] *n Law* force *f* majeure

forcemeat [ˈfɔːsmiːt] *n Culin* farce *f*

forceps [ˈfɔːseps] *npl* **(a pair of) forceps** un forceps

►► *Med* ***forceps delivery*** accouchement *m* au forceps

forcible [ˈfɔːsəbəl] *adj* (**a**) *(by force)* de *ou* par force (**b**) *(powerful → argument, style)* puissant; *(→ personality)* puissant, fort; *(→ speaker)* puissant; *(→ reminder)* brutal (**c**) *(emphatic → opinion)* catégorique; *(→ wish)* vif

►► *Law* ***forcible entry*** effraction *f*

forcibly [ˈfɔːsəblɪ] *adv* (**a**) *(by force)* de force, par la force; **they were forcibly removed from the house** on les a fait sortir de force de la maison

(**b**) *(argue, speak)* énergiquement, avec vigueur *ou* force; **she argued forcibly for their release** elle a argumenté énergiquement *ou* avec force en faveur de leur libération; **they put their case very forcibly** ils se sont défendus avec force *ou* vigueur

(**c**) *(recommend, remind)* fortement; **we were all forcibly reminded of our own mortality** nous avons été brutalement rappelés à notre condition de mortels

forcing [ˈfɔːsɪŋ] *n* (**a**) *(of lock, door)* forcement *m* (**b**) *Hort (in gardening)* forçage *m*, culture *f* forcée

►► *Culin* ***forcing bag*** poche *f* à douille; *Fin* ***forcing bid*** annonce *f* forcée *ou* de forcing; *Hort* ***forcing frame*** châssis *m*; *Hort* ***forcing house*** *(for plants)* forcerie *f*; *Fam Fig* **it's just an academic forcing house** dans cette boîte, tout ce qui compte ce sont les résultats aux examens

ford [fɔːd] **1** *n* gué *m*

2 *vt* passer *ou* traverser à gué

fordable [ˈfɔːdəbəl] *adj* guéable

fordone [fɔːˈdʌn] *adj Literary* épuisé, à bout de forces

fore [fɔː(r)] **1** *adj* (**a**) *(front)* à l'avant, antérieur; **the fore and hind legs** les pattes *fpl* de devant et de derrière

(**b**) *Naut* à l'avant

2 *n Naut* avant *m*, devant *m*; **at the fore** au mât de misaine; *Fig* **to come to the fore** *(person)* percer, commencer à être connu; *(courage)* se manifester, se révéler; **this issue came to the fore during last year's negotiations** ce problème a été mis en évidence lors des négociations de l'an dernier; **the revolt brought these issues to the fore** la révolte a mis ces problèmes en évidence, la révolte a attiré l'attention sur ces problèmes; **this question has been very much to the fore in the talks** cette question a été au tout premier plan au cours des discussions

3 *adv Naut* à l'avant; **fore and aft** de l'avant à l'arrière

4 *exclam (in golf)* attention!, gare!

►► *Typ* ***fore edge*** *(of book)* petit fond *m*, gouttière *f*; *Naut* ***fore hatch*** panneau *m* avant

fore-and-aft *adj Naut* aurique

►► *Naut* ***fore-and-aft bulkhead*** cloison *f* médiane; *Mil* ***fore-and-aft cap*** calot *m*; ***fore-and-aft movement*** *(of engine)* déplacement *m* longitudinal; *Naut* ***fore-and-aft rig*** gréement *m* aurique; *Naut* ***fore-and-aft sail*** voile *f* aurique

fore-and-after *n* (**a**) *Naut* bâtiment *m* à voiles auriques (**b**) *Hist (hat)* chapeau *m* bicorne porté en colonne

forearm 1 *n* [ˈfɔːrˌɑːm] avant-bras *m inv*

2 *vt* [ˌfɔːrˈɑːm] prémunir; **he came forearmed** il est venu prémuni *ou* préparé; **she would always ensure that she was forearmed before going** elle prenait toujours soin de se prémunir avant d'y aller

forebear [ˈfɔːbeə(r)] *n* ancêtre *m*; **our forebears** nos aïeux *mpl*

forebode [fɔːˈbəʊd] *vt Formal* augurer

foreboding [ˌfɔːˈbəʊdɪŋ] *n (feeling)* mauvais pressentiment *m*; *(omen)* présage *m* de malheur, mauvais augure *m*; **she was filled with (a sense of) foreboding** elle était envahie par un mauvais pressentiment; **she had a foreboding**

for–for

that things would go seriously wrong elle a eu le pressentiment que les choses allaient très mal tourner; **her laughter filled me with foreboding** ses rires m'ont rendu très appréhensif

forebrain ['fɔːbreɪn] *n Anat* prosencéphale *m*

forecabin ['fɔːˌkæbɪn] *n Naut* cabine *f* de l'avant, cabine *f* d'avant

forecast ['fɔːkɑːst] *(pt & pp* **forecast** *or* **forecasted**) **1** *vt* (**a**) *(gen) & Met* prévoir
(**b**) *(in betting)* pronostiquer
2 *n* (**a**) *(gen) & Met* prévision *f*; **the forecast is not good** *(gen)* les prévisions ne sont pas bonnes; *(weather)* la météo n'est pas bonne; *Com* **sales forecasts** prévisions *fpl* de ventes; **economic forecast** prévisions *fpl* économiques; **the (weather) forecast** le bulletin météorologique, la météo
(**b**) *(in betting)* pronostic *m*; **racing forecast** pronostic *m* des courses
►► *Acct* ***forecast balance sheet*** bilan *m* prévisionnel

forecaster ['fɔːˌkɑːstə(r)] *n* pronostiqueur(euse) *m,f*; **weather forecaster** météorologiste *mf*, météorologue *mf*

forecasting ['fɔːˌkɑːstɪŋ] *n (of result etc)* pronostication *f*; *(of weather, economic matters, sports)* prévision *f*
►► ***forecasting firm*** société *f* de prévisions; ***forecasting model*** modèle *m* de prévisions

forecastle ['fəʊksəl] *n Naut* gaillard *m* d'avant; *(in merchant navy)* poste *m* d'équipage

foreclose [fɔː'kləʊz] *Law* **1** *vt* **to foreclose the mortgage** saisir le bien hypothéqué
2 *vi* saisir le bien hypothéqué; **to foreclose on sb** saisir les biens de qn; **to foreclose on a mortgage** saisir un bien hypothéqué

foreclosure [fɔː'kləʊʒə(r)] *n Law* forclusion *f*, saisie *f*

forecourt ['fɔːkɔːt] *n* avant-cour *f*, cour *f* de devant; *(of petrol station)* devant *m*; **forecourt prices** prix *mpl* à la pompe

foredeck ['fɔːdek] *n Naut (of merchant ship)* pont *m* avant, gaillard *m* d'avant; *(of naval ship)* avant-pont *m*

foredoomed [fɔː'duːmd] *adj Literary* voué à l'échec

fore-end loader *n Agr* chargeur *m* frontal

forefather ['fɔːˌfɑːðə(r)] *n* ancêtre *m*; **our forefathers** nos aïeux *mpl*

forefinger ['fɔːˌfɪŋgə(r)] *n* index *m*

forefoot ['fɔːfʊt] *(pl* **forefeet** [-fiːt]) *n (of cow, horse)* pied *m* de devant *ou* antérieur; *(of cat, dog, bird)* patte *f* de devant *ou* antérieure

forefront ['fɔːfrʌnt] *n* premier rang *m*; **to be at** *or* **in the forefront of sth** *(country, firm)* être au premier rang de qch; *(person)* être une sommité dans qch

foregather [fɔː'gæðə(r)] *vi Formal* se réunir, s'assembler

forego [fɔː'gəʊ] *(pt* **forewent** [-'went], *pp* **foregone** [-'gɒn]) *vt* renoncer à, se priver de

foregoing [fɔː'gəʊɪŋ] **1** *adj* précédent, susdit; **the foregoing study** la susdite étude
2 *n* précédent(e) *m,f*; **if we are to believe the foregoing** si nous devons croire ce qui précède

foregone [fɔː'gɒn] *pp of* **forego**
►► ***foregone conclusion*** issue *f* certaine *ou* prévisible; **it was a foregone conclusion** c'était prévu d'avance

foreground ['fɔːgraʊnd] **1** *n (gen) & Art, Phot & Comput* premier plan *m*; **in the foreground** au premier plan; *Fig* **the Mayor is in the foreground** le maire est bien en évidence; **they must be hoping that this issue will fade from the foreground** ils doivent espérer que ce problème ne restera pas longtemps au premier plan
2 *vt* privilégier
►► *TV & Cin* ***foreground matte*** cache *m* d'avant-plan

forehand ['fɔːhænd] **1** *n* (**a**) *Sport* coup *m* droit; **to have a strong/weak forehand** avoir un coup droit puissant/faible; **to play a forehand** jouer un coup droit; **to serve to one's opponent's forehand** servir sur le coup droit adverse (**b**) *(of horse)* avant-main *m*
2 *adj Sport* **forehand drive** drive *m* de coup droit; **forehand stroke** coup *m* droit; **forehand volley** volée *f* de face

forehanded ['fɔːhændɪd] *adj* (**a**) *Sport* **to take a ball forehanded** jouer le coup droit (**b**) *Am (provident)* prévoyant; *(well off)* qui est à l'aise, aisé

forehandedness [fɔː'hændɪdnɪs] *n Am (providence)* prévoyance *f*, prévision *f*

forehander ['fɔːhændə(r)] *n Sport* coup *m* droit

forehead ['fɔːhed] *n* front *m*

foreign ['fɒrən] *adj* (**a**) *(country, language, person, food)* étranger; *(aid, visit → to country)* à l'étranger; *(→ from country)* de l'étranger; *(products)* de l'étranger; *(trade)* extérieur; **she looked foreign** elle paraissait étrangère; **a foreign-sounding name** un nom aux consonances étrangères; **students from foreign countries** des étudiants venant de l'étranger; **relations with foreign countries** les relations avec l'étranger; **foreign competition** concurrence *f* étrangère; **foreign investment** investissement *m* étranger; **foreign relations** relations *fpl* avec l'étranger; **foreign travel** voyages *mpl* à l'étranger
(**b**) *(alien)* étranger; **such thinking is foreign to them** un tel raisonnement leur est étranger
►► *Fin* ***foreign account*** compte *m* étranger; ***foreign affairs*** affaires *fpl* étrangères; ***foreign agent*** *(spy)* agent *m* étranger; *Com* représentant(e) *m,f* à l'étranger; *Fin* ***foreign bill*** effet *m ou* traite *f* sur l'extérieur; *Med* ***foreign body*** corps *m* étranger; ***the Foreign and Commonwealth Office*** le Foreign Office, le ministère britannique des Affaires étrangères; ***the Foreign and Commonwealth Secretary*** = le ministre britannique des Affaires étrangères; *Press* ***foreign correspondent*** correspondant(e) *m,f* à l'étranger; *Fin* ***foreign currency*** devises *fpl* étrangères; **to buy foreign currency** acheter des devises étrangères; *Fin* ***foreign currency account*** compte *m* en devises étrangères; *Fin* ***foreign currency assets*** avoirs *mpl* en devises étrangères; *Fin* ***foreign currency earnings*** apport *m* de devises étrangères; *Fin* ***foreign currency holding*** avoir *m* en devises étrangères; *Fin* ***foreign currency loan*** prêt *m* en devises étrangères; *Fin* ***foreign currency option*** option *f* de change; *Fin* ***foreign currency reserves*** réserves *fpl* de change, réserves *fpl* en devises; *Fin* ***foreign debt*** dette *f* extérieure; *Fin* ***foreign exchange*** devises *fpl* étrangères; *Fin* ***foreign exchange broker, foreign exchange dealer*** cambiste *mf*, courtier(ère) *m,f* en devises; *Fin* ***foreign exchange gain*** gain *m* de change; *Fin* ***foreign exchange loss*** perte *f* de change; *Fin* ***foreign exchange market*** marché *m* des changes; *Fin* ***foreign exchange option*** option *f* sur devises; *Fin* ***foreign exchange rate*** cours *m* des devises; *Fin* ***foreign exchange reserves*** réserves *fpl* de change, réserves *fpl* en devises; *Fin* ***foreign exchange risk*** risque *m* de change; *Fin* ***foreign exchange transfer*** transfert *m* de devises; ***the Foreign Legion*** la Légion (étrangère); ***foreign market*** marché *m* extérieur; *Med* ***foreign matter*** corps *m* étranger; *Pol* ***foreign minister*** ministre *m* des affaires étrangères; ***the Foreign Office*** le Foreign Office, le ministère britannique des Affaires étrangères; ***foreign policy*** politique *f* étrangère *ou* extérieure; ***the Foreign Secretary*** = le ministre britannique des Affaires étrangères; *Am* ***foreign service*** service *m* diplomatique

foreign-built *adj (car)* de marque étrangère; *(ship)* construit à l'étranger

foreigner ['fɒrənə(r)] *n* étranger(ère) *m,f*

foreignness ['fɒrɪnnɪs] *n* air *m* étranger; *(of place)* caractère *m* étranger; *(exotic nature)* exotisme *m*; **the foreignness of the food/their way of life** la nourriture/leur mode de vie bien à part; **given the foreignness of this concept to our culture** étant donné que ce concept est étranger à notre culture

foreign-owned company *n* firme *f* sous contrôle étranger

forejudge [ˌfɔː'dʒʌdʒ] *vt Law* **to forejudge sb** priver qn de ses droits

forejudgement, forejudgment [ˌfɔː'dʒʌdʒmənt] *n Law* privation *f* de droits

foreknow [ˌfɔː'nəʊ] *(pt* **foreknew** [-'njuː], *pp* **foreknown** [-'nəʊn]) *vt Formal* (**a**) *(have advance knowledge of)* connaître/savoir à l'avance (**b**) *(predict)* présager, prédire

foreknowledge ['fɔːˌnɒlɪdʒ] *n Formal* (**a**) *(advance knowledge)* **to have foreknowledge of sth** savoir qch à l'avance; **I had no foreknowledge of her plans** je ne savais pas à l'avance quels étaient ses projets (**b**) *(prediction)* prescience *f*

foreland ['fɔːlənd] *n* promontoire *m*, cap *m*

foreleg ['fɔːleg] *n (of horse)* jambe *f* de devant *ou* antérieure; *(of dog, cat)* patte *f* de devant *ou* antérieure

forelock ['fɔːlɒk] **1** *n* (**a**) *(of person)* mèche *f*, toupet *m*; *(of horse)* toupet *m*; **to touch** *or* **to tug one's forelock** saluer en portant la main au front; *Fig* faire des courbettes; *Literary* **to take Time by the forelock** saisir l'occasion (par les cheveux) (**b**) *Tech (of bolt)* clavette *f*, goupille *f*
2 *vt Tech (bolt)* clavetter, goupiller
►► *Tech* ***forelock bolt*** boulon *m* à clavette

foreman ['fɔːmən] *(pl* **foremen** [-mən]) *n Ind* contremaître *m*, chef *m* d'équipe; *Law* président(e) *m,f*

foremast ['fɔːmɑːst] *n Naut* mât *m* de misaine

forementioned ['fɔːˌmenʃənd] *adj Law & Admin* précité

foremost ['fɔːməʊst] **1** *adj (first → in position)* le plus en avant; *(→ in importance)* principal, le plus important; **of the foremost importance** de la plus haute importance
2 *adv* en avant

forename ['fɔːneɪm] *n Br* prénom *m*

forenamed ['fɔːneɪmd] *adj* susdit, précité

forenoon ['fɔːnuːn] *n Arch or Literary or Scot* matinée *f*

forensic [fə'rensɪk] **1** *adj* (**a**) *(chemistry)* légal; *(expert)* légiste
(**b**) *(term)* du barreau; **he showed great forensic skill at the trial** il a fait une plaidoirie remarquable
2 forensics *n (UNCOUNT)* art *m* de la discussion *ou* du débat
►► ***forensic accounting*** expertise *f* judiciaire; ***forensic department*** *(in hospital)* institut *m* médico-légal; ***forensic evidence*** expertise *f* criminalistique; ***forensic laboratory*** laboratoire *m* de criminalistique; ***forensic linguistics*** linguistique *f* appliquée à la criminalistique; ***forensic medicine*** médecine *f* légale; ***forensic pathologist*** médecin *m* légiste; ***forensic pathology*** médecine *f* légale; ***forensic science*** criminalistique *f*; ***forensic scientist*** expert *m* légiste *ou* en criminalistique; ***forensic test*** = test effectué par un expert en criminalistique; **forensic tests showed him to be the killer** les tests médico-légaux ont prouvé qu'il était l'assassin

foreordain [ˌfɔːrɔː'deɪn] *vt Formal* prédestiner

foreordination [ˌfɔːrɔːdɪ'neɪʃən] *n Formal* prédestination *f*

forepart ['fɔːpɑːt] *n Formal (gen)* devant *m*, avant *m*; *(of century, day)* début *m*

forepaw ['fɔːpɔː] *n* patte *f* de devant *ou* antérieure

forepayment ['fɔːˌpeɪmənt] *n* paiement *m* d'avance

foreperson ['fɔːˌpɜːsən] *n* (**a**) *Ind* contremaître(esse) *m,f* (**b**) *Law (of jury)* président(e) *m,f*

foreplan ['fɔːplæn] *(pt & pp* **foreplanned,** *cont* **foreplanning**) *vt* projeter

foreplay ['fɔːpleɪ] *n (UNCOUNT)* préliminaires *mpl* (amoureux)

forequarters ['fɔːˌkwɔːtəz] *npl (of animal)* avant-train *m*; *(of carcass)* quartiers *mpl* de devant

forereach ['fɔːriːtʃ] *Naut* **1** *vi* gagner au vent; **to forereach on a ship** dépasser un navire, gagner l'avant d'un navire
2 *vt (ship)* dépasser, gagner l'avant de

forerun [fɔː'rʌn] *vt (pt* **foreran** [-'ræn], *pp* **forerun,** *cont* **forerunning**) précéder, devancer; **the calm that foreruns the storm** le calme avant-coureur de la tempête

forerunner ['fɔːˌrʌnə(r)] *n* (**a**) *(precursor → person)* précurseur *m*; *(→ invention, model)* ancêtre *m* (**b**) *(omen)* présage *m*, signe *m* avant-coureur

foresaid ['fɔːsed] *adj* précité, mentionné ci-dessus

foresail ['fɔːseɪl] *n Naut* (voile *f* de) misaine *f*

foresee [fɔː'siː] *(pt* **foresaw** [-'sɔː], *pp* **foreseen** [-'siːn]) *vt* prévoir, présager

foreseeable [ˌfɔː'siːəbəl] *adj* prévisible; **in the foreseeable future** dans un avenir prévisible

foreseen [fɔː'siːn] *pp of* **foresee**

foreshadow [fɔː'ʃædəʊ] *vt* présager, annoncer; **her first novel foreshadowed this masterpiece** son premier roman a laissé prévoir ce chef-d'œuvre

foreshock ['fɔːʃɒk] *n (of earthquake)* avant-coureur *m*, choc *m* avant-coureur

foreshore ['fɔːʃɔː(r)] *n (beach)* plage *f*; *Geog* laisse *f* de mer

foreshorten [ˌfɔː'ʃɔːtən] *vt* (**a**) *Art* faire un raccourci de; *Phot (horizontally)* réduire; *(vertically)* écraser (**b**) *(reduce)* réduire; *(story)* résumer

foreshortened [ˌfɔː'ʃɔːtənd] *adj* en raccourci; **foreshortened figure** figure *f* en raccourci

foreshortening [ˌfɔː'ʃɔːtənɪŋ] *n* (**a**) *Art* raccourci *m*; *Phot (horizontal)* réduction *f*; *(vertical)* écrasement *m* (**b**) *(reduction)* réduction *f*; *(of story)* résumé *m*

foresight ['fɔːsaɪt] *n* prévoyance *f*; **lack of foresight** imprévoyance *f*; **with foresight this could all have been avoided** avec un peu de prévoyance tout ceci aurait pu être évité

foresighted ['fɔːˌsaɪtɪd] *adj (person)* prévoyant

foreskin ['fɔːskɪn] *n* prépuce *m*

forest ['fɒrɪst] **1** *n* forêt *f*; **oak/coniferous forest** forêt *f* de chênes/de conifères; **hills covered with forests, forest-covered hills** collines *fpl* boisées; *Fig* **a forest of hands** une multitude de mains; **a forest of aerials** une forêt d'antennes

2 *vt (region)* boiser (**with** de)

►► ***forest fire*** incendie *m* de forêt; ***forest floor*** sol *m* de la forêt; ***forest management*** gestion *f* des forêts; ***forest park*** parc *m* forestier; *Am* ***forest ranger*** garde *m* forestier; ***the Forest Service*** = organisme américain de gestion des forêts domaniales, ≃ les eaux et forêts *fpl*

forested ['fɒrɪstɪd] *adj* boisé (**with** de)

forestall [fɔː'stɔːl] *vt* (**a**) *(prevent)* empêcher, retenir; **she wanted to leave but he forestalled her** elle voulut partir mais il l'en empêcha (**b**) *(anticipate → desire, possibility)* anticiper, prévenir; *(→ person)* devancer, prendre les devants sur (**c**) *Com & Hist* accaparer

forestaller [ˌfɔː'stɔːlə(r)] *n* (**a**) **my forestaller** *(who anticipated me)* la personne qui m'a devancé *ou* qui m'a coupé l'herbe sous le pied (**b**) *Com & Hist* accapareur(euse) *m,f*

forestalling [ˌfɔː'stɔːlɪŋ] *n* (**a**) *(of someone's desire)* anticipation *f*; *(of competitor, rival)* devancement *m* (**b**) *Com & Hist* accaparement *m*

forestation [ˌfɒrɪ'steɪʃən] *n* boisement *m*

forestay ['fɔːsteɪ] *n Naut* étai *m* de misaine

forester ['fɒrɪstə(r)] *n* forestier(ère) *m,f*

forestland *n* ['fɒrɪstˌlənd] *n* terres *fpl* boisées

forestry ['fɒrɪstrɪ] *n* sylviculture *f*

►► ***the Forestry Commission*** = organisme britannique de gestion des forêts domaniales, ≃ les eaux et forêts *fpl*

foretaste **1** *n* ['fɔːteɪst] avant-goût *m*; **to give** *or* **offer sb a foretaste of sth** donner un avant-goût de qch à qn

2 *vt* [fɔː'teɪst] avoir un avant-goût de

foretell [fɔː'tel] (*pt & pp* **foretold** [-'təʊld]) *vt* prédire

forethought ['fɔːθɔːt] *n (premeditation)* préméditation *f*; *(foresight)* [illegible] **with a lack of forethought** manquer de prévoyance en faisant qch; **if you had given it some forethought** si tu y avais un peu réfléchi à l'avance

forethoughtful [ˌfɔː'θɔːtfʊl] *adj Literary* prudent, prévoyant

foretime ['fɔːtaɪm] *n Literary* le passé

foretold [fɔː'təʊld] *pt & pp of* **foretell**

foretooth ['fɔːtuːθ] (*pl* **foreteeth** [-tiːθ]) *n* incisive *f*, dent *f* du devant

forever [fə'revə(r)] *adv* (**a**) *(eternally)* (pour) toujours, éternellement; **it won't last forever** ça ne durera pas toujours; **I'll love you forever** je t'aimerai toujours; **United forever!** vive United!

(**b**) *(incessantly)* toujours, sans cesse; **he's forever finding fault** il trouve toujours à redire

(**c**) *(for good)* pour toujours; **dinosaurs have vanished forever** les dinosaures ont disparu pour toujours

(**d**) *Fam (a long time)* très longtemps; **it'll take forever!** ça va prendre des lustres!; **he took forever to get ready** il a mis des heures à se préparer; **we can't wait forever** nous ne pouvons pas attendre jusqu'à la saint-glinglin

forevermore [fəˌrevə'mɔː] *adv* pour toujours, à jamais

forewarn [fɔː'wɔːn] *vt* prévenir, avertir; **he forewarned them that life there would be difficult** il les a prévenus que là-bas la vie serait difficile; *Prov* **forewarned is forearmed** un homme averti en vaut deux

forewarning [ˌfɔː'wɔːnɪŋ] *n* avertissement *m*

forewent [fɔː'went] *pt of* **forego**

forewoman ['fɔːˌwʊmən] (*pl* **forewomen** [-ˌwɪmɪn]) *n* (**a**) *Ind* contremaîtresse *f* (**b**) *Law (of jury)* président *m*, présidente *f*

foreword ['fɔːwɜːd] *n* avant-propos *m inv*, préface *f*

forex ['fɔːreks] *n Fin (abbr* **foreign exchange***)* devises *fpl* étrangères

►► ***forex trading*** transactions *fpl* en devises étrangères

forfaiting ['fɔːfeɪtɪŋ] *n Banking* forfaitage *m*, forfaitisation *f*

forfeit ['fɔːfɪt] **1** *vt* (**a**) *(lose)* perdre; *(give up)* renoncer à, abandonner; **to forfeit one's rights** perdre *ou* être déchu de ses droits; **to forfeit one's life** payer de sa vie; *Fin* **to forfeit a deposit** perdre les arrhes

(**b**) *Law (lose)* perdre (par confiscation); *(confiscate)* confisquer

2 *n* (**a**) *(penalty)* prix *m*, peine *f*; *Com (sum)* amende *f*, dédit *m*

(**b**) *Law (loss)* perte *f* (par confiscation)

(**c**) *(game)* **to play forfeits** jouer aux gages; **to pay a forfeit** avoir un gage

(**d**) *St Exch* **to relinquish the forfeit** abandonner la prime

3 *adj Formal (subject to confiscation)* susceptible d'être confisqué; *(confiscated)* confisqué; *Fig* **her life could be forfeit** elle pourrait le payer de sa vie

forfeitable ['fɔːfɪtəbəl] *adj* confiscable

forfeiture ['fɔːfɪtʃə(r)] *n* (**a**) *Law (loss)* perte *f* (par confiscation); *Fig (surrender)* renonciation *f*; **forfeiture of rights** renonciation *f* aux droits (**b**) *(penalty)* prix *m*, peine *f*; *Com (sum)* amende *f*, dédit *m* (**c**) *St Exch (of shares)* déchéance *f*, forfaiture *f*

forfend [fɔː'fend] *vt Arch* détourner, empêcher; *Arch or Hum* **God** *or* **Heaven forfend!** à Dieu ne plaise!, Dieu m'en préserve!

forgather = **foregather**

forgave [fə'geɪv] *pt of* **forgive**

forge [fɔːdʒ] **1** *vt* (**a**) *(metal, sword)* forger; *Fig* **to forge an alliance/a friendship** sceller une alliance/une amitié

(**b**) *(counterfeit → money, signature)* contrefaire; *(→ picture, document)* faire un faux de, contrefaire; **a forged passport** un faux passeport; **a forged £20 note** un faux billet de 20 livres

2 *vi (go forward)* avancer; **we forged on, hoping to reach the village by nightfall** nous avons continué à toute allure dans l'espoir d'arriver au village avant la tombée de la nuit; **to forge into the lead** prendre la tête

3 *n (machine, place)* forge *f*

►**forge ahead** *vi (press forward)* faire des progrès; *(in race, election campaign)* prendre de l'avance; *(in business, undertaking)* [illegible] l'avant; **to forge ahead with one's plans** aller de l'avant dans ses projets, mener ses projets de l'avant

forgeable ['fɔːdʒəbəl] *adj* (**a**) *Metal* forgeable (**b**) *(document, signature)* qui se laisse contrefaire

forged [fɔːdʒd] *adj* (**a**) *Metal* forgé (**b**) *(document, banknote, signature)* faux (fausse), contrefait; **forged document** faux *m*; *(identity paper)* faux papier *m*

forger ['fɔːdʒə(r)] *n (gen)* faussaire *mf*; *(of money)* faux-monnayeur *m*, faussaire *mf*

forgery ['fɔːdʒərɪ] (*pl* **forgeries**) *n* (**a**) *(of money, picture, signature)* contrefaçon *f*; *(of document)* falsification *f*; **to prosecute sb for forgery** poursuivre qn pour faux (et usage de faux) (**b**) *(object)* faux *m*; **it's a forgery** *(of signature)* c'est une fausse signature (**c**) *Acct* faux *m* en écritures

forget [fə'get] (*pt* **forgot** [-'gɒt], *pp* **forgotten** [-'gɒtən]) **1** *vt* (**a**) *(be unable to recall)* oublier; **he'll never forget her** il ne l'oubliera jamais; **have you forgotten all your Latin?** avez-vous oublié tout votre latin?; **I'll never forget seeing him play Lear** je ne l'oublierai jamais *ou* je le reverrai toujours dans le rôle de Lear; **I forgot (that) you had a sister** j'avais oublié que tu avais une sœur; **he's forgotten how to type** il ne sait plus (comment) taper; **I forgot which house is his** je ne sais plus *ou* j'ai oublié quelle maison est la sienne; **I never forget a face** j'ai la mémoire des visages; **she'll never let him forget his mistake** elle n'est pas près de lui pardonner son erreur; **I forgot the time** j'ai oublié l'heure; **to forget one's manners** oublier ses manières; **have you forgotten your manners?** où sont tes bonnes manières?; *(to child)* veux-tu être poli!; **to forget oneself** s'oublier; **he was so overwhelmed by emotion that he quite forgot himself** il était tellement ému qu'il perdit toute retenue; **it's my idea and don't you forget it!** c'est moi qui ai eu cette idée, tâchez de ne pas l'oublier!; **such things are best forgotten** il vaut mieux ne pas penser à de telles choses; **that never-to-be-forgotten day** ce jour inoubliable *ou* mémorable

(**b**) *(neglect, overlook)* oublier, omettre; **she forgot to mention that she was married** elle a oublié *ou* a omis de dire qu'elle était mariée; **he seems to have forgotten his old friends** il semble avoir oublié ses anciens amis; **don't forget the poor at Christmas** n'oubliez pas les pauvres à Noël; **the forgotten man of Scottish football** le laissé-pour-compte du football écossais; **not forgetting...** sans oublier...; **let's forget our differences** oublions nos différends; *Fam* **forget it!** *(in reply to thanks)* de rien!❑; *(in reply to apology)* ce n'est pas grave!, ne t'en fais pas!; *(in irritation)* laisse tomber!; *(in reply to question)* cela n'a aucune importance!❑, peu importe!❑; **they can forget it!** *(they're being unreasonable, they've no chance)* ils peuvent faire une croix dessus!

(**c**) *(leave behind)* oublier, laisser; **don't forget your umbrella!** n'oublie pas ton parapluie!

(**d**) *(give up → idea, plan)* abandonner, renoncer à; **if we don't get financial backing, we'll just have to forget the whole thing** si nous n'obtenons pas de soutien financier il nous faudra renoncer au projet

2 *vi* oublier; **before I forget** *(can you do something?)* avant que j'oublie *ou* que je n'oublie; **to forget about sb/sth** oublier qn/qch; **sorry, I completely forgot about it** désolé, j'avais complètement oublié; **and you can forget about going to London!** et ce n'est pas la peine de songer à aller à Londres!

forgetful [fə'getfʊl] *adj (absent-minded)* distrait; *(careless)* négligent, étourdi; **she's so forgetful** elle oublie tout, elle est tellement distraite; **to be forgetful of sth** être oublieux de qch

forgetfulness [fə'getfʊlnɪs] *n (absent-mindedness)* manque *m* de mémoire; *(carelessness)* négligence *f*, étourderie *f*; **in a moment of forgetfulness** dans un moment d'étourderie

forget-me-not *n Bot* myosotis *m*

forgettable [fə'getəbəl] *adj* qui ne présente pas d'intérêt

forging ['fɔːdʒɪŋ] *n Metal (activity)* travail *m* de forge; *(forged item)* pièce *f* forgée

[illegible] ***forging press*** marteau-pilon *m*

forgivable [fə'gɪvəbəl] *adj* pardonnable

forgivably [fə'gɪvəblɪ] *adv* **she was, quite forgivably, rather annoyed with him!** elle était plutôt en colère contre lui, et on la comprend!

forgive [fə'gɪv] (*pt* **forgave** [-'geɪv], *pp* **forgiven** [-'gɪvən]) *vt* (**a**) *(pardon)* pardonner; **to forgive sb (for) sth** pardonner qch à qn; **he asked me to forgive him** il m'a demandé pardon; **forgive my ignorance, but who exactly was Galsworthy?** pardonnez mon ignorance, mais qui était Galsworthy exactement?; **can you ever forgive me?** pourras-tu jamais me pardonner?; **forgive me, but haven't we met before?** pardonnez-moi *ou* excusez-moi, mais est-ce qu'on ne s'est pas déjà rencontrés?; **one might be forgiven for thinking that...** on pourrait penser que...; **forgive and forget** pardonner et oublier

(**b**) *(debt, payment)* **to forgive (sb) a debt** faire grâce (à qn) d'une dette

forgiveable = **forgivable**

forgiveness [fə'gɪvnɪs] *n* (**a**) *(pardon)* pardon *m*; **to ask sb's forgiveness** demander pardon à qn (**b**) *(tolerance)* indulgence *f*, clémence *f*

forgiving [fə'gɪvɪŋ] *adj* indulgent, clément

forgivingly [fə'gɪvɪŋlɪ] *adv* avec indulgence *ou* clémence

forgo (*pt* **forwent** [-'went], *pp* **forgone** [-'gɒn]) = **forego**

forgot [fə'gɒt] *pt of* **forget**

forgotten [fə'gɒtən] *pp of* **forget**

forint ['fɒrɪnt] *n* forint *m*

forjudge, forjudgement = **forejudge, forejudgement**

fork [fɔːk] **1** *n* (**a**) *(for eating)* fourchette *f*
(**b**) *Agr* fourche *f*
(**c**) *(junction → in road, railway)* bifurcation *f*, embranchement *m*; **take the right fork** tournez *ou* prenez à droite à l'embranchement
(**d**) *(on bicycle, motorbike)* fourche *f*
(**e**) *(fork-shaped object → of water diviner)* baguette *f* divinatoire; *(→ to support branch etc)* poteau *m* fourchu; **fork of lightning** zigzag *m* (d'éclair)
2 *vt* (**a**) *Agr* fourcher; **they were forking hay onto the truck** ils chargeaient du foin à la fourche dans le camion
(**b**) *(food)* prendre avec une fourchette; **she was forking food into her mouth** elle enfournait la nourriture avec sa fourchette
3 *vi* (**a**) *(river, road)* bifurquer, fourcher; **the road forks at Newton** la route fait une fourche à Newton
(**b**) *(car, person)* bifurquer, tourner; **he forked left** il a pris *ou* a tourné à gauche; **fork right for the airport** prenez à droite pour l'aéroport

▶**fork in** *vt sep (compost)* enfouir en fourchant

▶**fork off** *vi (road, driver)* bifurquer

▶**fork out** *Fam* **1** *vt sep (provide, often unwillingly)* **to fork out money** allonger *ou* abouler de l'argent
2 *vi (pay out money)* **to fork out for sth** casquer pour qch; **he had to fork out (for it)** il a dû allonger la monnaie, il a dû casquer; **come on, fork out** *(what you owe me)* allez, aboule

▶**fork over** *vt sep (flower bed)* retourner légèrement à la fourche

forked [fɔːkt] *adj (tongue)* fourchu; *(river, road)* à bifurcation
▸▸ ***forked lightning*** éclair *m* en zigzags

forkful ['fɔːkfʊl] *n* (**a**) *(of food)* fourchetée *f* (**b**) *(of hay)* fourchée *f*

forking ['fɔːkɪŋ] *adj*
▸▸ *Bot* ***forking larkspur*** dauphinelle *f* consoude

forklift ['fɔːklɪft] *n* **forklift (truck)** chariot *m* élévateur

forktail ['fɔːkteɪl] *n Ich & Orn* énicure *m*

forlorn [fə'lɔːn] *adj* (**a**) *(wretched)* triste, malheureux; **a forlorn cry** un cri de désespoir
(**b**) *(lonely → person)* abandonné, délaissé; *(→ place)* désolé, désert; **the empty house had a forlorn look about it** la maison vide avait l'air abandonné
(**c**) *(desperate)* désespéré; **I went there in the forlorn hope that she'd see me** j'y suis allé dans le fol espoir qu'elle accepterait de me voir; **they made one last forlorn attempt to contact her** ils ont fait un dernier effort désespéré pour la contacter

forlornly [fə'lɔːnlɪ] *adv* (**a**) *(wretchedly)* tristement (**b**) *(desperately)* désespérément

forlornness [fə'lɔːnnɪs] *n* (**a**) *(wretchedness)* tristesse *f*, malheur *m*; **the forlornness of his appearance** son air désolé *ou* pitoyable, sa mine piteuse (**b**) *(loneliness → of person, place etc)* solitude *f*, abandon *m*; **in a state of utter forlornness** dans un abandon général (**c**) *(desperation)* désespoir *m*

FORM [fɔːm]

forme	▸ **1 (a) – (d), (f) – (m), (r), (s)**
silhouette	▸ **1 (b)**
formulaire	▸ **1 (e)**
classe	▸ **1 (n)**
former	▸ **2 (a), (b), (e), (f)**
façonner	▸ **2 (a)**
se former	▸ **2 (c); 3 (a), (b)**
créer	▸ **2 (d)**
composer	▸ **2 (e)**

1 *n* (**a**) *(shape)* forme *f*; **in the form of a heart** en forme de cœur; **her plan began to take form** son projet a commencé à prendre tournure *ou* forme
(**b**) *(body, figure)* forme *f*, silhouette *f*; **a slender form appeared at the door** une silhouette élancée apparut à la porte; **the human form** la forme humaine
(**c**) *(aspect, mode)* forme *f*; **it's written in the form of a letter** c'est écrit sous forme de lettre; **the Devil appeared in the form of a goat** le diable apparut sous la forme d'une chèvre; **the same product in a new form** le même produit présenté différemment; **what form should my questions take?** comment devrais-je formuler mes questions?; **the interview took the form of an informal chat** l'entrevue prit la forme d'une discussion informelle; **her anxiety showed itself in the form of anger** son inquiétude se manifesta par de la colère
(**d**) *(kind, type)* forme *f*, sorte *f*; **one form of cancer** une forme de cancer; **we studied three different forms of government** nous avons examiné trois systèmes de gouvernement *ou* trois régimes différents; **all forms of sugar** le sucre sous toutes ses formes; **she sent some flowers as a form of thanks** elle a envoyé des fleurs en guise de remerciements
(**e**) *(document)* formulaire *m*; *(for bank, telegram)* formule *f*; **to fill in** *or* **out a form** remplir un formulaire; **printed form** imprimé *m*
(**f**) *(condition)* forme *f*, condition *f*; **in good form** en pleine forme, en excellente condition; *Br* **on form,** *Am* **in form** en forme; **John was** *Br* **on** *or Am* **in good form at lunch** John était en forme *ou* plein d'entrain pendant le déjeuner; **I'm** *Br* **on** *or Am* **in top form** je suis en pleine forme; *Br* **on** *or Am* **in their current form they're unlikely to win** étant donné leur forme actuelle ils ont peu de chances de gagner; **he's** *Br* **off** *or Am* **out of form** il n'est pas en forme; **to study (the) form** *(in horse racing)* examiner le tableau des performances des chevaux
(**g**) *(gen) & Art, Literature & Mus* forme *f*; **form and content** la forme et le fond; **his writing lacks form** ce qu'il écrit n'est pas clair; **her ideas lack form** ses idées sont confuses
(**h**) *(standard practice)* forme *f*, règle *f*; **to do sth as a matter of form** faire qch pour la forme; **what's the usual form in these cases?** que fait-on d'habitude *ou* quelle est la marche à suivre dans ces cas-là?; *Fam* **to know the form** *(what to do)* savoir ce qu'il faut faire ❑; *Law* **in due form** en bonne et due forme
(**i**) *Old-fashioned (etiquette)* forme *f*, formalité *f*; **it's bad form** cela ne se fait pas; **it's good form** c'est de bon ton, cela se fait; **it is bad form to ask a lady her age** ce n'est pas poli de demander son âge à une dame
(**j**) *(formula)* forme *f*, formule *f*; **form of address** formule *f* de politesse; **the correct form of address for a senator** la manière correcte de s'adresser à un sénateur; **it's only a form of speech** ce n'est qu'une façon de parler; **the form of the marriage service** les rites *mpl* du mariage
(**k**) *(mould)* forme *f*, moule *m*
(**l**) *Gram & Ling* forme *f*; **the masculine form** la forme du masculin, le masculin
(**m**) *Phil (structure)* forme *f*; *(essence)* essence *f*
(**n**) *Br Sch (class)* classe *f*; **she's in the first/sixth form** ≃ elle est en sixième/première
(**o**) *Br (bench)* banc *m*
(**p**) *Br Fam (criminal record)* casier *m* judiciaire ❑; **has he got form?** est-ce qu'il a un casier judiciaire?
(**q**) *Comput (on Internet)* formulaire *m*
(**r**) *Am Typ* forme *f*
(**s**) *(of hare)* gîte *m*, forme *f*
2 *vt* (**a**) *(shape)* former, construire; *(character, mind)* former, façonner; *(sentence)* construire; *Metal* former, façonner; **he formed the model out of** *or* **from clay** il a sculpté *ou* façonné le modèle dans l'argile; **form the dough into a ball** pétrissez la pâte en forme de boule; **she has trouble forming certain words** elle a du mal à prononcer certains mots; **it was certainly a character-forming experience** c'est sans aucun doute une expérience qui forme *ou* façonne le caractère
(**b**) *(take the shape of)* former, faire; **the coastline forms a series of curves** la côte forme une série de courbes; **the children formed a circle** les enfants formèrent un cercle; **form a line please** faites la queue s'il vous plaît; **the applicants formed a queue** les candidats firent la queue
(**c**) *(develop → opinion)* se former, se faire; *(→ plan)* concevoir, élaborer; *(→ habit)* contracter; **he's wary of forming friendships** il hésite à nouer des amitiés; **to form an impression** avoir une impression
(**d**) *(organize → association, club)* créer, fonder; *(→ committee, government)* former; *Com (→ company)* fonder, créer; **they formed themselves into a committee** ils se constituèrent en comité
(**e**) *(constitute)* composer, former; **to form the basis of sth** constituer la base de *ou* servir de base à qch; **to form (a) part of sth** faire partie de qch; **the countries forming the alliance** les pays qui constituent l'alliance
(**f**) *Gram* former; **how to form the past tense** comment former le passé composé
3 *vi* (**a**) *(materialize)* se former, prendre forme; **doubts began to form in his mind** des doutes commencèrent à prendre forme dans son esprit, il commença à avoir des doutes
(**b**) *(take shape)* se former; **form into a line!** alignez-vous!; **we formed into groups** nous nous sommes mis en groupes, nous avons formé des groupes
▸▸ *Ling* ***form class*** catégorie *f* grammaticale; *Comput* ***form document*** document *m* canevas; *Comput* ***form feed*** avancement *m* du papier; ***form letter*** lettre *f* circulaire; *Br Sch* ***form master*** ≃ professeur *m* principal; *Br Sch* ***form mistress*** ≃ professeur *m* principal; *Br Sch* ***form room*** salle *f* de classe, classe *f*; *Br Sch* ***form teacher, form tutor*** ≃ professeur *m* principal; *Ling* ***form word*** mot-outil *m*, mot *m* faisant fonction de désinence

▶**form up** *vi Br* se mettre en ligne, s'aligner

FORMAL ['fɔːməl]

officiel	▸ **1 (a), (b)**
solennel	▸ **1 (a), (c)**
formel	▸ **1 (b), (g)**
formaliste	▸ **1 (d), (g)**
de forme	▸ **1 (e), (f)**

1 *adj* (**a**) *(conventional → function)* officiel, solennel; *(→ greeting)* solennel, cérémonieux; **a formal dance** un grand bal; **a formal dinner** un dîner officiel; **is it formal?** *(the party, dance etc)* est-ce que c'est habillé?; **I only wear it on formal occasions** je ne le/la porte que pour les grandes occasions
(**b**) *(official → announcement, approval)* officiel; *(→ order)* formel, explicite; **formal agreement/contract** accord *m*/contrat *m* en bonne et due forme; **a formal denial** un démenti formel *ou* catégorique; **she had no formal education** elle n'a jamais fait d'études; **no formal training is required** aucune formation spécifique n'est exigée; **we gave him a formal warning** nous l'avons averti officiellement *ou* dans les règles
(**c**) *(correct → person)* solennel; *(→ behaviour, style)* soigné, solennel; *Pej* guindé; **she's very formal** elle est très à cheval sur les conventions; **don't be so formal** ne sois pas si sérieux, sois un peu plus détendu; **in formal language** dans un style soigné *ou* soutenu; **"vous" is the formal form** "vous" est la formule de politesse
(**d**) *(ordered)* formaliste, méthodique
(**e**) *(nominal)* de forme; **formal agreement** accord *m* de forme; **she is the formal head of State** c'est elle le chef d'État officiel
(**f**) *(relating to form)* de forme; **a formal similarity** une similarité de forme
(**g**) *Gram & Ling* formaliste, formel
(**h**) *Phil* formel
2 *n Am* (**a**) *(dance)* bal *m*
(**b**) *(suit)* habit *m* de soirée
▸▸ ***formal dress*** *(for ceremony)* tenue *f* de cérémonie; *(for evening)* tenue *f* de soirée; ***formal garden*** jardin *m* à la française

formaldehyde [fɔ:'mældɪhaɪd] *n Chem* formaldéhyde *m*

formalin ['fɔ:məlɪn] *n Chem* formol *m*

formalism ['fɔ:məlɪzəm] *n Phil* formalisme *m*

formalist ['fɔ:məlɪst] *Phil* **1** *adj* formaliste

2 *n* formaliste *mf*

formalistic [,fɔ:mə'lɪstɪk] *adj* formalistique

formality [fɔ:'mælətɪ] (*pl* **formalities**) *n* (**a**) *(ceremoniousness)* cérémonie *f*; *(solemnity)* solennité *f*, gravité *f*; *(stiffness)* froideur *f*, raideur *f*; *(convention)* formalité *f*, étiquette *f*; **the formality of the dance** le caractère cérémonieux du bal (**b**) *(procedure)* formalité *f*; **it's a mere formality** c'est une simple formalité; **let's forget the formalities** dispensons-nous des formalités

formalization [,fɔ:məlaɪ'zeɪʃən] *n* officialisation *f*

formalize, -ise ['fɔ:məlaɪz] *vt* officialiser

formally ['fɔ:məlɪ] *adv* (**a**) *(with formality)* solennellement, cérémonieusement; **formally dressed** *(for ceremony)* en tenue de cérémonie; *(for evening)* en tenue de soirée

(**b**) *(officially)* officiellement, dans les règles; **the organization formally renounced violence** l'organisation a officiellement renoncé à la violence; **an agreement was formally drawn up** un accord a été rédigé en bonne et due forme

(**c**) *(speak)* de façon soignée; *(behave)* de façon solennelle; *Pej* de façon guindée

(**d**) *(study, research)* de façon méthodique; *(arrange)* de façon régulière

(**e**) *(nominally)* pour la forme; **he did consult his father before proceeding, if only formally** il a demandé conseil à son père avant d'agir, ne serait-ce que pour la forme

formant ['fɔ:mənt] *n* formant *m*

format ['fɔ:mæt] (*pt & pp* **formatted,** *cont* **formatting**) **1** *n* (**a**) *(size)* format *m* (**b**) *(layout)* présentation *f*; **the TV news now has a new format** le journal télévisé a adopté une nouvelle présentation (**c**) *Comput* format *m*

2 *vt* (**a**) *(layout)* composer la présentation de (**b**) *Comput (disk)* formater; *(page, text)* mettre en forme, formater

formate ['fɔ:meɪt] *n Chem* formiate *m*

formation [fɔ:'meɪʃən] *n* (**a**) *(establishment → of club)* création *f*, fondation *f*; *(→ of committee, company)* formation *f*, fondation *f*; *(→ of government)* formation *f*

(**b**) *(development → of character, person)* formation *f*; *(→ of idea)* développement *m*, élaboration *f*; *(→ of plan)* élaboration *f*, mise *f* en place

(**c**) *Bot, Geol & Med* formation *f*

(**d**) *(arrangement)* formation *f*, disposition *f*; *Mil (unit)* formation *f*, dispositif *m*; **battle formation** formation *f* de combat; **in close formation** en ordre serré

►► ***formation dancing*** danse *f* en formation; ***formation flying*** vol *m* en formation

formative ['fɔ:mətɪv] **1** *adj* formateur; **the formative years** les années *fpl* formatrices

2 *n Gram* formant *m*, élément *m* formateur

formatted ['fɔ:mætɪd] *adj Comput (disk)* formaté; *(page, text)* mis en forme, formaté

formatter ['fɔ:mætə(r)] *n Comput* formateur *m*

formatting ['fɔ:mætɪŋ] *n Comput (of disk)* formatage *m*; *(of page, text)* mise *f* en forme, formatage *m*

forme, *Am* **form** [fɔ:m] *n Typ* forme *f*

-formed ['fɔ:md] *suff* formé; **badly/well-formed letters** lettres *fpl* mal/bien formées

former ['fɔ:mə(r)] **1** *adj* (**a**) *(time)* passé; **in former times** *or* **days** autrefois, dans le passé

(**b**) *(earlier, previous)* ancien, précédent; **my former boss** mon ancien patron; **I'm a former student of his** je suis un de ses anciens élèves; **my former wife** mon ex-femme; **in a former life** dans une vie antérieure; **in former times** autrefois; **he's only a shadow of his former self** il n'est plus que l'ombre de lui-même; **the former Yugoslavia** l'ex-Yougoslavie *f*

(**c**) *(first)* premier; **I prefer the former idea to the latter** je préfère la première idée à la dernière

2 *n* (**a**) *(first)* premier(ère) *m,f*, celui-là *m*, celle-là *f*; **of the two methods I prefer the former** des deux méthodes je préfère la première

(**b**) *Tech* gabarit *m*

-former ['fɔ:mə(r)] *suff Br* élève *mf* de; **first-former** ≃ élève *mf* de sixième

formerly ['fɔ:məlɪ] *adv* autrefois, jadis; **Mr Martin, formerly a Liberal** M. Martin, autrefois libéral; **Mrs McBride, formerly Miss Kane** Madame McBride, auparavant Mademoiselle Kane; **formerly of London** résidant auparavant à Londres; **Burkina Faso, formerly Upper Volta** le Burkina Faso, ancienne Haute-Volta

form-filling *n* **there was a lot of form-filling** il y avait beaucoup de papier à remplir

formic ['fɔ:mɪk] *adj* formique

►► *Chem* ***formic acid*** acide *m* formique

Formica® [fɔ:'maɪkə] **1** *n* Formica® *m*, plastique *m* laminé

2 *comp (worktop, surface)* en Formica®, en plastique laminé

formicant ['fɔ:mɪkənt] *adj Med* formicant

formicary ['fɔ:mɪkərɪ] (*pl* **formicaries**) *n* fourmilière *f*

formication [,fɔ:mɪ'keɪʃən] *n Med* formication *f*, fourmillement *m*

formidable ['fɔ:mɪdəbəl] *adj* (**a**) *(inspiring fear)* redoutable, terrible; *(inspiring respect)* remarquable; **she's a formidable athlete** c'est une athlète remarquable; **a formidable intellect** un esprit brillant (**b**) *(difficult)* ardu; **a formidable problem** un problème difficile

formidably ['fɔ:mɪdəblɪ] *adv (armed, difficult)* redoutablement; *(talented, thorough)* formidablement, remarquablement

forming ['fɔ:mɪŋ] *n* (**a**) *(of company etc)* création *f*, fondation *f* (**b**) *Metal* formage *m*, façonnage *m*

formless ['fɔ:mlɪs] *adj (shape)* informe; *(idea)* vague

formlessness ['fɔ:mlɪsnɪs] *n (of shape)* absence *f* de forme; *(of idea)* caractère *m* vague

Formosa [fɔ:'məʊsə] *n Formerly* Formose *m*; **in Formosa** à Formose

Formosan [fɔ:'məʊsən] *Formerly* **1** *n* (**a**) *(person)* Formosan(e) *m,f* (**b**) *Ling* les parlers *mpl* formosans

2 *adj* formosan

formula ['fɔ:mjʊlə] (*pl sense* (**a**) **formulas** *or* **formulae** [-li:], *pl senses* (**b**), (**d**) **formulas**) *n* (**a**) *(gen) & Chem & Math* formule *f*; **a formula acceptable to both sides** une formule *ou* solution qui soit acceptable pour les deux parties; **a formula for happiness** une recette qui assure le bonheur; **these romantic novels are all done to the same formula** ces romans à l'eau de rose sont tous écrits selon la même formule

(**b**) *(expression)* formule *f*

(**c**) *Aut* formule *f*

(**d**) *Am (for baby)* ≃ bouillie *f (pour bébé)*

►► ***Formula 1/2/3 (racing)*** la formule 1/2/3; ***Formula 1/2/3 car*** voiture *f* de formule 1/2/3

formulable ['fɔ:mjʊləbəl] *adj* formulable

formulaic [,fɔ:mjʊ'leɪɪk] *adj Pej (plot)* stéréotypé; **formulaic expression** expression *f* toute faite

formulatable [,fɔ:mjʊ'leɪtəbəl] *adj* formulable

formulate ['fɔ:mjʊleɪt] *vt* (**a**) *(express)* formuler; **difficult to formulate in words** difficile à formuler (en paroles) (**b**) *(plan, policy)* élaborer

formulation [,fɔ:mjʊ'leɪʃən] *n* (**a**) *(of idea)* formulation *f*, expression *f* (**b**) *(of plan, policy)* élaboration *f*

formwork ['fɔ:mwɜ:k] *n Constr (for reinforced concrete)* coffrage *m*

fornicate ['fɔ:nɪkeɪt] *vi Formal* forniquer

fornication [,fɔ:nɪ'keɪʃən] *n Formal* fornication *f*

fornicator ['fɔ:nɪkeɪtə(r)] *n Formal (man)* fornicateur *m*, coureur *m* de jupons; *(woman)* coureuse *f*

forsake [fə'seɪk] (*pt* **forsook** [-'sʊk], *pp* **forsaken** [-'seɪkən]) *vt Formal* (**a**) *(abandon → family, spouse)* abandonner; *(→ friend)* délaisser; *(→ place)* quitter; **her customary patience forsook her** sa patience habituelle lui fit défaut (**b**) *(give up)* renoncer à; **to forsake one's religion** faire acte d'apostasie

forsaken [fə'seɪkən] **1** *pp of* **forsake**

2 *adj Literary (person)* abandonné; *(place)* abandonné, désert; **forsaken by all** abandonné de tous

forsaking [fə'seɪkɪŋ] *n* (**a**) *(of family, spouse)* abandon *m*, abandonnement *m*; *(of friend)* délaissement *m* (**b**) *(giving up)* renoncement *m* (**of** à); **forsaking of one's religion** apostasie *f*

forsook [fə'sʊk] *pt of* **forsake**

forsooth [fə'su:θ] *Arch* **1** *adv* à vrai dire, en vérité

2 *exclam* ma foi!, par exemple!

forspent [fɔ:'spent] *adj Arch* épuisé, à bout de forces

forswear [fɔ:'sweə(r)] (*pt* **forswore** [-'swɔ:(r)], *pp* **forsworn** [-'swɔ:n]) *Formal* **1** *vt* (**a**) *(renounce)* abjurer (**b**) *(deny)* désavouer; **to forswear oneself** se parjurer

2 *vi* se parjurer, commettre un parjure

forswearing [,fɔ:'sweərɪŋ] *n Formal* (**a**) *(renunciation)* abjuration *f* (**b**) *(perjury)* parjure *m*

forsworn [fɔ:'swɔ:n] *adj (person)* parjure

forsythia [fɔ:'saɪθjə] *n Bot* forsythia *m*

fort [fɔ:t] *n* fort *m*; *(smaller)* fortin *m*; *Fam Br* **to hold the fort,** *Am* **to hold down the fort** *(look after house)* garder la maison ❑; *(look after office, shop)* tenir la boutique ❑

►► ***Fort Knox*** = fort militaire dans le Kentucky contenant les réserves d'or des États-Unis; *Fig Hum* **it's like Fort Knox here** c'est une vraie forteresse ici

forte[1] ['fɔ:teɪ] *n (strong point)* fort *m*; **patience is hardly his forte** la patience n'est pas vraiment son (point) fort

forte[2] ['fɔ:tɪ] *Mus* **1** *adj* forte

2 *adv* forte

3 *n* forte *m*

fortepiano [,fɔ:tɪpɪ'ænəʊ] *n Mus* pianoforte *m*

forth [fɔ:θ] *adv* (**a**) *Literary (out, forward)* en avant; **to go** *or* **to set forth** se mettre en route; **to bring forth** produire; **to send forth** envoyer; **the ferry goes back and forth between...** le ferry fait la navette entre...; **to walk back and forth** marcher de long en large, faire les cent pas

(**b**) *Literary (forwards in time)* **from this moment forth** dorénavant, désormais; **from this day forth** à partir d'aujourd'hui *ou* de ce jour

(**c**) **and so forth** *(etcetera)* et ainsi de suite, et cetera

Forth Bridge [fɔ:θ-] *n* **the Forth (rail) Bridge** = pont ferroviaire construit au XIXème siècle sur l'estuaire du Forth, en Écosse; **the Forth (road) Bridge** = pont routier construit en 1964 sur l'estuaire du Forth, en Écosse; *Fam Fig* **it's like painting the Forth Bridge** ≃ c'est comme Sisyphe et son rocher

forthcoming [,fɔ:θ'kʌmɪŋ] *adj* (**a**) *(imminent → event)* à venir; *(→ book)* à paraître; *(→ film)* qui va sortir prochainement; **the forthcoming elections** les prochaines élections *fpl*; **forthcoming attractions** *(film, theatre advertisement)* prochainement

(**b**) *(made available)* **no answer was forthcoming** il n'y a eu aucune réponse; **no information/support was forthcoming** on ne nous a fourni aucune information/apporté aucun soutien; **the funds were not forthcoming** les fonds n'ont pas été débloqués (**c**) *(verbally)* **he wasn't very forthcoming** il n'a pas été très bavard

forthright ['fɔ:θraɪt] *adj (person, remark)* franc (franche), direct; **he's a forthright critic of the government** il critique le gouvernement ouvertement

forthrightness ['fɔ:θ,raɪtnɪs] *n* franchise *f* (**about** au sujet de)

forthwith [,fɔ:θ'wɪθ] *adv Formal* sur-le-champ

Forties ['fɔ:tɪz] *npl Geog* **the Forties** les Forties *nmpl*

fortieth ['fɔ:tɪɪθ] **1** *n* (**a**) *(fraction)* quarantième *m* (**b**) *(in series)* quarantième *mf*

2 *adj* quarantième

3 *adv* quarantièmement; *(in contest)* en quarantième position, à la quarantième place; *see also* **fifth**

fortifiable [,fɔ:tɪ'faɪəbəl] *adj* fortifiable

fortification [,fɔ:tɪfɪ'keɪʃən] *n* fortification *f*

fortified ['fɔ:tɪfaɪd] *adj* fortifié

►► *Br* ***fortified wine*** vin *m* de liqueur, vin *m* doux naturel

fortifier ['fɔ:tɪ,faɪə(r)] *n* (**a**) **the fortifier of a city** le constructeur des fortifications d'une ville, *Arch* le fortificateur d'une ville (**b**) *(drug, drink etc)* fortifiant *m*

fortify ['fɔ:tɪfaɪ] (*pt & pp* **fortified**) *vt* (**a**) *(place)* fortifier, armer; *Fig (person)* réconforter, remonter; **to fortify oneself for the coming**

struggle rassembler ses forces pour la lutte à venir; **fortified with the rites of the Church** muni des sacrements de l'Église; **have a drink to fortify yourself** prenez un verre pour vous remonter (**b**) *(wine)* augmenter la teneur en alcool, alcooliser; *(food)* renforcer en vitamines

fortifying [ˈfɔːtɪˌfaɪɪŋ] *adj* fortifiant; *(drink etc)* remontant

fortissimo [ˌfɔːˈtɪsɪməʊ] *Mus* **1** *n* fortissimo *m*
2 *adj* fortissimo
3 *adv* fortissimo

fortitude [ˈfɔːtɪtjuːd] *n* courage *m*, force *f* morale

fortnight [ˈfɔːtnaɪt] *n Br* quinzaine *f*, quinze jours *mpl*; **for a fortnight** pour quinze jours; **a fortnight ago** il y a quinze jours; **a fortnight tomorrow** demain en quinze; **a fortnight's holiday** quinze jours de vacances; **it's been postponed for a fortnight** cela a été remis à quinzaine

fortnightly [ˈfɔːtˌnaɪtlɪ] (*pl* **fortnightlies**) *Br* **1** *n* bimensuel *m*
2 *adj* bimensuel
3 *adv* tous les quinze jours

Fortnum and Mason [ˈfɔːtnəm-] *n* = grand magasin londonien réputé pour ses produits de luxe

Fortran, FORTRAN [ˈfɔːtræn] *n Comput* fortran *m*

fortress [ˈfɔːtrɪs] *n (fort)* fort *m*; *(prison)* forteresse *f*; *(castle)* château *m* fort; *(place, town)* place *f* forte
▸▸ ***fortress city*** cité *f* fortifiée; ***Fortress Europe*** forteresse *f* Europe

fortuitous [ˌfɔːˈtjuːɪtəs] *adj* fortuit, imprévu

fortuitously [ˌfɔːˈtjuːɪtəslɪ] *adv* fortuitement, par hasard

fortuitousness [ˌfɔːˈtjuːɪtəsnɪs] *n* fortuité *f*

Fortuna [ˌfɔːˈtjuːnə] *pr n Myth* Fortune

fortunate [ˈfɔːtʃənət] *adj (person)* heureux, chanceux; *(choice, meeting)* heureux, propice; **you are fortunate** vous avez de la chance; **I was fortunate enough to get the job** j'ai eu la chance d'obtenir le travail; **he is fortunate in his friends** il a de bons amis; **how fortunate!** quelle chance!; **the less fortunate among them** les plus infortunés d'entre eux; **we should help those less fortunate than ourselves** nous devons aider ceux qui n'ont pas eu notre chance

fortunately [ˈfɔːtʃənətlɪ] *adv* heureusement, par bonheur

fortune [ˈfɔːtʃuːn] *n* (**a**) *(wealth)* fortune *f*; **he came to London to make his fortune** il est venu à Londres pour faire fortune; **she makes a fortune** elle gagne beaucoup d'argent *ou* un argent fou; **he made a fortune on the house** il a gagné beaucoup d'argent en vendant la maison; **to come into a fortune** hériter d'une fortune, faire un gros héritage; **a man of fortune** un homme fortuné; **her jewels are worth a fortune** ses bijoux valent une fortune; **to cost/to pay/to spend a (small) fortune** coûter/payer/dépenser une (petite) fortune; **her face is her fortune** son visage est son grand atout
(**b**) *(future)* destin *m*; **to tell sb's fortune** dire la bonne aventure à qn; **she tells fortunes** elle dit la bonne aventure
(**c**) *(chance, fate)* sort *m*, fortune *f*; **fortune smiled upon him** *or* **has been kind to him** la chance lui a souri; **the novel traces its hero's changing fortunes** le roman retrace les tribulations de son héros; **the fortunes of war** les hasards *mpl* de la guerre
(**d**) *(luck)* fortune *f*, chance *f*; **piece of good fortune** coup *m* de chance, bonheur *m*; **ill fortune** malchance *f*, mauvais sort *m*; **he had the good fortune to win** il a eu la chance de gagner; **by good fortune** par chance, par bonheur; **to try one's fortune** tenter sa chance
▸▸ *Am* ***fortune cookie*** = biscuit chinois dans lequel est caché un horoscope; ***Fortune Five Hundred*** = les 500 plus grosses entreprises américaines (dont la liste est établie, chaque année, par le magazine 'Fortune')

fortune-hunter *n Pej (man)* coureur *m* de dot; *(woman)* aventurière *f*, femme *f* intéressée

fortune-teller *n (gen)* diseur(euse) *m,f* de bonne aventure; *(with cards)* tireur(euse) *m,f* de cartes, cartomancien(enne) *m,f*

fortune-telling *n (gen)* = fait de dire la bonne aventure; *(with cards)* cartomancie *f*

forty [ˈfɔːtɪ] (*pl* **forties**) **1** *n* quarante *m inv*
2 *pron* quarante; **about forty** une quarantaine
3 *adj* quarante; *Fam* **forty winks** petit somme ▫ *m*; **to have forty winks** faire un petit somme; *see also* **fifty**

forty-eight *n Am* **the lower forty-eight** les quarante-huit États américains *(à part l'Alaska et Hawaï)*

forty-five 1 *n* (**a**) *(record)* quarante-cinq tours *m* (**b**) *Am (pistol)* quarante-cinq *m*
2 Forty-Five *n Br Hist* **the Forty-Five** = rébellion écossaise menée en 1745 par le prince Charles Édouard pour tenter de ramener les Stuart au pouvoir

fortyish [ˈfɔːtɪɪʃ] *adj* d'une quarantaine d'années; **I'd say she was fortyish** je lui donne la quarantaine *ou* une quarantaine d'années; **he was balding, fortyish and plump** il perdait ses cheveux et avait la quarantaine rondouillarde

forty-niner [-ˈnaɪnə(r)] *n Am* **the forty-niners** = chercheurs d'or partis en Californie en 1849

forum [ˈfɔːrəm] (*pl* **forums** *or* **fora** [-rə]) *n* (**a**) *(gen) & Fig* forum *m*, tribune *f*; *Hist* forum *m*; **a forum in which workers can put forward their views** un forum permettant aux ouvriers d'exprimer leurs opinions (**b**) *Comput (on Internet)* forum *m* (de discussion)

forward [ˈfɔːwəd] **1** *adj* (**a**) *(towards front → movement)* en avant, vers l'avant; *(→ position)* avant; **the seat is too far forward** le siège est trop avancé *ou* en avant
(**b**) *(advanced)* **the project is no further forward** le projet n'a pas avancé; **forward planning** planification *f* à long terme
(**c**) *(brash)* effronté, impertinent
(**d**) *Fin & Com* à terme
2 *adv* (**a**) *(in space)* en avant; *Naut* à l'avant; **to move forward** avancer; **keep going straight forward** continuez tout droit; **he reached forward** il a tendu le bras en avant; *Fig* **three witnesses came forward** trois témoins se sont présentés; *Mil* **forward, march!** en avant, marche!; **clocks go forward one hour at midnight** il faut avancer les pendules d'une heure à minuit
(**b**) *Formal (in time)* **from this moment forward** à partir de maintenant; **from this day forward** désormais, dorénavant
(**c**) *Acct* **to carry the balance forward** reporter le solde à nouveau; **(carried) forward** report *m*
3 *vt* (**a**) *(send on)* faire suivre; *Com* expédier, envoyer; **to forward sth to sb** faire parvenir qch à qn; **we'll forward your report to the relevant department** nous transmettrons votre rapport au service correspondant; **I've arranged to have my mail forwarded** j'ai fait le nécessaire pour qu'on fasse suivre mon courrier; **please forward** *(on envelope)* faire suivre SVP, prière de faire suivre
(**b**) *(advance, promote)* avancer, favoriser
4 *n* avant *m*
▸▸ *Fin* ***forward account*** compte *m* à terme; *Fin* ***forward buying*** achat *m* à terme; *Fin* ***forward contract*** contrat *m* à terme; *Fin & Com* ***forward dealing*** opérations *fpl* à terme; *Com* ***forward delivery*** livraison *f* à terme; *Fin* ***forward exchange market*** marché *m* des changes à terme; *Fin* ***forward exchange transaction*** opération *f* de change à terme; *Aut* ***forward gears*** marches *fpl* avant; *Econ* ***forward integration*** intégration *f* en aval, intégration *f* descendante; *Sport* ***forward line*** ligne *f* des avants; *Fin & Com* ***forward market*** marché *m* à terme; *Sport* ***forward pass*** *(in rugby)* passe *f* en avant; *Fin & Com* ***forward price*** prix *m* à terme; *Fin & Com* ***forward purchase*** achat *m* à terme; *Fin* ***forward rate*** cours *m* à terme, taux *m* pour les opérations à terme; *Fin* ***Forward Rate Agreement*** accord *m* de taux à terme; *Gym* ***forward roll*** cabriole *f*, culbute *f*; *Com* ***forward sale*** vente *f* à terme; *Comput* ***forward search*** recherche *f* avant; *Br Comput* ***forward slash*** barre *f* oblique; *Fin & Com* ***forward trading*** opérations *fpl* à terme

forwardation [ˌfɔːwəˈdeɪʃən] *n Fin* report *m*

forwarder [ˈfɔːwədə(r)] *n Com* transitaire *m*; **forwarder and consolidator** transitaire-groupeur *m*

forwarding [ˈfɔːwədɪŋ] *n* (**a**) *(sending)* expédition *f*, envoi *m* (**b**) *Typ* collage *m* et endossage *m*
▸▸ ***forwarding address*** adresse *f* pour faire suivre le courrier; *Com* adresse *f* pour l'expédition; **he left no forwarding address** il est parti sans laisser d'adresse; *Com* ***forwarding agent*** transitaire *m*; *Com* ***forwarding charges*** frais *mpl* d'expédition; *Com* ***forwarding office*** bureau *m* d'expédition

forward-looking *adj (person)* tourné vers *ou* ouvert sur l'avenir; *(plans)* tourné vers l'avenir *ou* le progrès; *(company, policy)* qui va de l'avant, dynamique, entreprenant

forwardness [ˈfɔːwədnɪs] *n* (**a**) *(presumption)* effronterie *f*, impertinence *f*; *(eagerness)* empressement *m* (**b**) *Br (of child, season)* précocité *f*; *(of project)* état *m* avancé

forwards [ˈfɔːwədz] = **forward** *adv* (**a**), (**b**)

forwent [ˌfɔːˈwent] *pt of* **forgo**

Fosbury flop [ˈfɒzbərɪ-] *n Sport* fosbury-flop *m*

foss = **fosse**

fossa¹ [ˈfɒsə] (*pl* **fossae** [-siː]) *n Anat* fosse *f*

fossa² [ˈfɒsə] (*pl* **fossas**) *n Zool* fosa *m*

fosse [fɒs] *n* (**a**) *(ditch, moat)* fossé *m*; **advanced fosse** contre-fossé *m* (**b**) *Anat* fosse *f*

fossette [fɒˈset] *n Anat & Med* fossette *f*

Fosse Way [fɒs-] *n* **the Fosse Way** = voie romaine entre Lincoln et Exeter en Angleterre

fossick [ˈfɒsɪk] *Austr & NZ* **1** *vt (rummage for)* fourgonner à la recherche de
2 *vi* (**a**) *(prospect for gold, precious stones)* = chercher de l'or ou des pierres précieuses dans un site où d'autres prospecteurs ont déjà fouillé (**b**) *(rummage)* fourgonner

fossil [ˈfɒsəl] **1** *n* fossile *m*; *Fam Pej* **an old fossil** *(person)* une vieille croûte, un vieux fossile
2 *adj* fossilisé
▸▸ ***fossil fuel*** combustible *m* fossile; ***fossil man*** l'homme *m* fossile; ***fossil soil*** paléosol *m*; ***fossil water*** eau *f* fossile

fossil-fired *adj* qui brûle du combustible fossile

fossiliferous [ˌfɒsɪˈlɪfərəs] *adj* fossilifère

fossilization [ˌfɒsɪlaɪˈzeɪʃən] *n* fossilisation *f*

fossilize, -ise [ˈfɒsɪlaɪz] **1** *vt* fossiliser
2 *vi* se fossiliser

fossilized [ˈfɒsɪlaɪzd] *adj* fossilisé; *Fig* figé; *Ling* figé

fossilizing [ˈfɒsɪlaɪzɪŋ] *adj Geol (soil constituents)* fossilisateur

foster [ˈfɒstə(r)] *vt* (**a**) *Br Law (of family, person)* accueillir; *(of authorities, court)* placer; **the children were fostered (out) at an early age** les enfants ont été placés dans une famille tout jeunes
(**b**) *(idea, hope)* nourrir, entretenir
(**c**) *(promote)* favoriser, encourager
▸▸ ***foster brother*** frère *m* adoptif; ***foster child*** enfant *m* placé dans une famille d'accueil; ***foster father*** père *m* de la famille d'accueil; ***foster home*** famille *f* d'accueil; ***foster mother*** mère *f* de la famille d'accueil; ***foster parents*** famille *f* d'accueil; ***foster sister*** sœur *f* adoptive

fosterage [ˈfɒstərɪdʒ] *n* (**a**) *(of child)* prise *f* en charge par une famille d'accueil; **during his fosterage** pendant qu'il était dans une famille d'accueil (**b**) *(responsibilities of foster parent)* fonctions *fpl* d'une famille d'accueil (**c**) *(payment)* gages *mpl* payés à la famille d'accueil

fostering [ˈfɒstərɪŋ] *n* (**a**) *(of child)* prise *f* en famille d'accueil; *(fostering out)* mise *f* en famille d'accueil (**b**) *(of the arts etc)* patronage *m*, encouragement *m*

FOT [ˌefəʊˈtiː] *adj (abbr* **free on truck***)* franco camion

Foucault [ˈfuːkəʊ] *pr n* Foucault
▸▸ *Phys* ***Foucault current*** courant *m* de Foucault; *Phys* ***Foucault('s) pendulum*** pendule *m* de Foucault; *Phys* ***Foucault prism*** prisme *m* de Foucault

fought [fɔːt] *pt & pp of* **fight**

foul [faʊl] **1** *adj* (**a**) *(food, taste)* infect; *(smell)* infect, fétide; *(breath)* fétide; **to smell foul** puer; **to taste foul** avoir un goût infect
(**b**) *(filthy → linen)* sale, souillé; *(→ place)* immonde, crasseux; *(→ air)* vicié, pollué; *(→ water)* croupi
(**c**) *Fam (horrible → weather)* pourri; *(→ person)* infect, ignoble; **I've had a foul day** j'ai eu une sale journée; **she's in a foul mood** elle est d'une humeur massacrante; **he has a foul temper** il a un sale caractère *ou* un caractère de chien; **foul weather** *(gen)* sale temps *m*, temps *m* de chien; *Naut* gros temps *m*; **he's being really foul to me** il est absolument odieux *ou* ignoble avec moi

(**d**) *(language)* grossier, ordurier; **he has a foul mouth** il est très grossier

(**e**) *Literary (vile)* vil, infâme; *(unfair)* déloyal; **foul deed** infamie *f*; **murder most foul** horrible assassinat *m*

(**f**) *(clogged)* obstrué, encrassé

(**g**) *Fin (bill of lading)* avec réserves

(**h**) *(idioms)* **to fall** *or* **to run foul of sb** se brouiller avec qn; **he fell foul of the boss** il s'est mis le patron à dos; **they fell foul of the law** ils ont eu des démêlés avec la justice; **to fall foul of a reef/ship** entrer en collision avec un récif/un navire

2 *n Sport (in boxing)* coup *m* bas; *(in football, baseball etc)* faute *f*

3 *vt* (**a**) *(dirty)* salir; *(air, water)* polluer, infecter; *(of dog)* salir; *(spark plugs)* encrasser; *Br* **it is an offence to allow a dog to foul the pavement** il est contraire à la loi de laisser son chien souiller le trottoir; **to foul one's own nest** se nuire à soi-même

(**b**) *(clog)* obstruer, encrasser; *(entangle)* embrouiller, emmêler; *(nets)* se prendre dans; **to foul pipes** engorger *ou* obstruer des canalisations

(**c**) *(collide with)* entrer en collision avec

(**d**) *Sport* commettre une faute contre

(**e**) *Fig (reputation)* salir

4 *vi* (**a**) *(tangle)* s'emmêler, s'embrouiller

(**b**) *Sport* commettre une faute

►► *Sport* ***foul ball*** *(in baseball)* sortie *f*; *Sport* ***foul line*** *(in baseball)* ligne *f* de jeu; *(in basketball)* ligne *f* de lancer franc; *(in bowling)* ligne *f* de faute; *Sport* ***foul play*** jeu *m* irrégulier *ou* déloyal; *(in cards, games)* tricherie *f*; *Fig* **the police suspect foul play** la police croit qu'il y a eu meurtre *ou* croit au meurtre; **foul play is not suspected** on ne croit pas à un meurtre

►**foul out** *vi* être exclu *(pour excès de fautes)*

►**foul up 1** *vi* (**a**) *Fam (person)* merder; **don't foul up again/this time!** tâche de ne plus merder/ne pas merder cette fois!

(**b**) *(gun barrel etc)* s'encrasser; *(pump)* s'engorger

2 *vt sep* (**a**) *(contaminate)* polluer; *(clog)* obstruer, encrasser

(**b**) *Fam (bungle)* ficher en l'air, flanquer par terre

foulard ['fu:lɑ:(d)] *n Tex* foulard *m*

fouler ['faʊlə(r)] *n Sport* **he's a persistent fouler** il commet des fautes sans arrêt

foul-hook *vt (fish)* ferrer par le corps

fouling ['faʊlɪŋ] *n* (**a**) *(of pipes)* engorgement *m*; *(of spark plugs)* encrassement *m* (**b**) *Sport* **a lot of fouling** beaucoup de jeu déloyal

foully ['faʊlɪ] *adv* (**a**) *(speak)* grossièrement (**b**) *Literary (behave)* bassement, ignoblement; **he was foully murdered** il fut ignoblement assassiné

foul-mouthed *adj* grossier

foulness ['faʊlnɪs] *n* (**a**) *(dirtiness)* saleté *f*; *(of air)* fétidité *f*; **the foulness of the smell** l'odeur *f* infecte, la puanteur (**b**) *(of language etc)* grossièreté *f*, obscénité *f* (**c**) *(of act, behaviour)* infamie *f*, ignominie *f*

foul-smelling [-'smelɪŋ] *adj* puant, fétide

foul-tempered *adj* **to be foul-tempered** avoir un sale caractère

foul-up *n Fam (mix-up)* cafouillage *m*; *(mechanical difficulty)* problème *m ou* difficulté *f* mécanique; **there's been a foul-up** quelque chose a cloché *ou* cafouillé, il y a eu un cafouillage

foumart ['fu:mɑ:t] *n Zool* putois *m*

found [faʊnd] **1** *pt & pp of* **find**

2 *adj Old-fashioned* (**a**) *(furnished, equipped)* équipé; **the flat is well found** l'appartement est bien équipé

(**b**) *(idiom) Br* **all found** tout compris; **£30 a week all found** 30 livres la semaine tout compris

3 *vt* (**a**) *(establish → organization, town)* fonder, créer; *(→ business)* fonder, établir

(**b**) *(base)* fonder, baser; **to be founded on** *(principle, belief, theory, suspicions)* être fondé *ou* basé sur; **founded on fact** *(of story, novel, film)* qui est basé sur des faits véridiques; **our society is founded on the idea of equality** notre société est fondée sur la notion d'égalité

(**c**) *(cast)* fondre

►► *Art* ***found object*** objet *m* trouvé

foundation [faʊn'deɪʃən] **1** *n* (**a**) *(of business, town)* fondation *f*, création *f*

(**b**) *(institution)* fondation *f*, institution *f* dotée; *(endowment)* dotation *f*, fondation *f*; **a charitable foundation** une institution charitable

(**c**) *(basis)* base *f*, fondement *m*; **the foundation** *or* **foundations of our society** les fondements *mpl* de notre société; **his work laid the foundation** *or* **foundations of modern science** son œuvre a jeté les bases de la science moderne; **the rumour is entirely without foundation** la rumeur est dénuée de tout fondement

(**d**) *(make-up)* fond *m* de teint

(**e**) *Am (of building)* fondations *fpl*

2 foundations *npl Constr* fondations *fpl*; **to lay the foundations** poser les fondations

►► *Br* ***foundation course*** cours *m* introductif; ***foundation cream*** fond *m* de teint; *Old-fashioned* ***foundation garment*** *(girdle)* gaine *f*, combiné *m*; *(bra)* soutien-gorge *m*; ***foundation scholar*** élève *mf* boursier; *Constr* ***foundation stone*** pierre *f* commémorative; **to lay the foundation stone** poser la première pierre

foundational [faʊn'deɪʃənəl] *adj (doctrine)* fondamental

foundationer [faʊn'deɪʃənə(r)] *n Sch* boursier(-ère) *m,f*

founder ['faʊndə(r)] **1** *n* fondateur(trice) *m,f*

2 *vi* (**a**) *(ship)* sombrer; **to founder on the rocks** s'échouer sur les rochers

(**b**) *Fig (fail)* s'effondrer, s'écrouler; **the project foundered for lack of financial support** le projet s'est effondré faute de soutien financier

(**c**) *(horse → in mud)* s'embourber; *(→ go lame)* se mettre à boiter

►► *Br* ***founder member*** membre *m* fondateur; ***founder's share*** part *f* bénéficiaire *ou* de fondateur

foundering ['faʊndərɪŋ] *n (of hopes)* effondrement *m*

founding ['faʊndɪŋ] **1** *n* (**a**) *(of business, organization, town)* fondation *f*, création *f* (**b**) *Metal* fonderie *f*, moulage *m*

2 *adj* fondateur

►► ***founding father*** père *m* fondateur; **one of the founding fathers of the Society** l'un des pères fondateurs de la société; *Hist* ***the Founding Fathers*** les pères *mpl* fondateurs *(aux États-Unis)*

foundling ['faʊndlɪŋ] *n Formal* enfant *mf* trouvé(e); **foundling hospital** hospice *m* pour enfants trouvés

foundress ['faʊndres] *n* fondatrice *f*

foundry ['faʊndrɪ] *(pl* **foundries**) *n (place)* fonderie *f*; *(of articles)* fonderie *f*, fonte *f*; *(articles)* fonte *f*

fount [faʊnt] *n* (**a**) *Br Typ* fonte *f* (**b**) *Literary (spring)* source *f*; **a fount of knowledge** un puits de science; **he's the fount of all wisdom** il est plein de sagesse

fountain ['faʊntɪn] *n* (**a**) *(natural)* fontaine *f*, source *f*; *(man-made)* fontaine *f*, jet *m* d'eau (**b**) *Fig* source *f*; **the fountain of youth** la fontaine de jouvence

►► ***fountain pen*** stylo *m* à encre

fountainhead ['faʊntɪn,hed] *n* (**a**) *(spring)* source *f* (**b**) *Fig (source)* source *f*, origine *f*

four [illegible] *inv*; **on all fours** à quatre pattes; **to get** *or* **to go down on all fours** se mettre à quatre pattes

(**b**) *(in rowing)* quatre *m*

2 *pron* quatre

3 *adj* quatre; **the four corners of the earth** les quatre coins du monde; **open to the four winds** ouvert à tous les vents *ou* aux quatre vents; **the Four Freedoms** les quatre libertés *fpl (liberté d'expression et de culte, droit de ne pas vivre dans la misère et dans la peur; énoncées par Roosevelt en 1941)*; *see also* **five**

►► *Cards* ***four flush*** flush *m* de quatre cartes; *Am* ***the four hundred*** l'élite *f* sociale

'The Four Seasons' *Vivaldi* 'Les Quatre saisons'

four-ball *n* = partie de golf se jouant avec deux équipes de deux joueurs, chacun ayant sa propre balle

four-by-four *n Aut* 4 x 4 *m*, quatre-quatre *m*

four-colour, *Am* **four-color** *adj Typ* quadrichrome

►► ***four-colour (printing) process*** quadrichromie *f*; ***four-colour separation*** séparation *f* quadrichromique

four-cornered *adj* à quatre coins; *(quadrangular)* quadrangulaire

four-cycle *adj Am (engine, cylinder)* à quatre temps

four-dimensional *adj* quadridimensionnel

four-door *adj* à quatre portes

four-engined *adj* à quatre moteurs

four-eyes *n Fam* binoclard(e) *m,f*

Four-F *n* = personne inapte (physiquement) au service militaire

four-figure *adj Math (number, sum)* à quatre chiffres; *(logarithm)* à quatre décimales

four-flusher [-'flʌʃə(r)] *n Am Fam* bluffeur(euse) *m,f*

fourfold ['fɔ:,fəʊld] **1** *adj* quadruple

2 *adv* au quadruple; **to increase fourfold** quadrupler

four-footed *adj (animal)* quadrupède, à quatre pattes; *Fam* **a four-footed friend** un ami à quatre pattes

four-four *n Mus* quatre-quatre *m inv*; **in four-four (time)** à quatre-quatre

4-H (club) [fɔ:'reɪtʃ-] *n Am* = association éducative pour jeunes ruraux

four-handed *adj Cards & Mus* à quatre mains

Fourierism ['fʊrɪərɪzəm] *n* fouriérisme *m*

four-in-hand *n* (**a**) *(carriage)* attelage *m* à quatre (**b**) *(tie)* cravate *f*

four-leaf clover, four-leaved clover *n Bot* trèfle *m* à quatre feuilles

four-legged [-'legɪd] *adj* quadrupède, à quatre pattes; *Hum* **our four-legged friends** nos compagnons à quatre pattes

four-letter word *n* gros mot *m*, obscénité *f*

four-oar *n* canot *m* à quatre avirons

four-oared [-,ɔ:d] *adj* à quatre avirons

four-o'clock *n Bot* mirabilis *m*

fourpence ['fɔ:pəns] *n* (**a**) *(sum of money)* quatre pence *mpl* (**b**) *(coin)* = ancienne pièce de monnaie anglaise qui valait quatre pence

four-phase *adj Elec (system)* tétraphasé

four-ply *adj (wool)* à quatre fils; *(wood)* contreplaqué *(à quatre plis)*

four-poster (bed) *n* lit *m* à baldaquin *ou* à colonnes

fourscore [,fɔ:'skɔ:(r)] *Arch* **1** *adj* quatre-vingts; **fourscore years and ten** quatre-vingt-dix ans

2 *n* quatre-vingts *m inv*

four-seasons *adj (pizza)* quatre-saisons *(inv)*

four-seater *n Aut* voiture *f* à quatre places

foursome ['fɔ:səm] *n* (**a**) *(people)* groupe *m* de quatre personnes; *(two couples)* deux couples *mpl*; **we went as a foursome** nous y sommes allés à quatre (**b**) *(game)* partie *f* à quatre; **will you make up a foursome for bridge?** voulez-vous faire le quatrième au bridge?

four-speed *adj Aut* à quatre vitesses

foursquare [,fɔ:'skweə(r)] **1** *adj* (**a**) *(square)* carré (**b**) *(position, style)* solide; *(approach, decision)* ferme, inébranlable (**c**) *(forthright)* franc (franche)

2 *adv (solidly)* fermement

four-star *adj* à quatre étoiles

►► **four-star hotel** hôtel *m* quatre étoiles *ou* de première catégorie; *Br* ***four-star petrol*** super *m*, super-carburant *m*; *Mil* ***four-star general*** général *m* d'armée

four-stroke *Aut* **1** *adj* à quatre temps

2 *n* moteur *m* à quatre temps

fourteen [,fɔ:'ti:n] **1** *n* quatorze *m inv*

2 *pron* quatorze

3 *adj* quatorze; *see also* **five**

fourteenth [,fɔ:'ti:nθ] **1** *n* (**a**) *(fraction)* quatorzième *m*

(**b**) *(in series)* quatorzième *mf*

(**c**) *(of month)* quatorze *m inv*; **the Fourteenth of July** le quatorze juillet *(fête nationale française)*

2 *adj* quatorzième

3 *adv* quatorzièmement; *(in contest)* en quatorzième position, à la quatorzième place; *see also* **fifth**

►► ***the Fourteenth Amendment*** = amendement à la constitution américaine reconnaissant les anciens esclaves noirs comme citoyens à part entière

fourth [fɔːθ] **1** *n* (**a**) *(fraction)* quart *m*
(**b**) *(in series)* quatrième *mf*
(**c**) *(of month)* quatre *m inv*; **the Fourth of July** le quatre juillet *(fête nationale de l'Indépendance aux États-Unis)*
(**d**) *Mus* quarte *f*
(**e**) *Aut* quatrième *f*
(**f**) *Cards* **to make a fourth** faire le quatrième
2 *adj* quatrième
3 *adv* quatrièmement; *(in contest)* en quatrième position, à la quatrième place; *see also* **fifth**
►► ***the fourth dimension*** la quatrième dimension; ***the fourth estate*** le quatrième pouvoir, la presse; ***fourth finger*** annulaire *m*; *Aut* ***fourth gear*** quatrième vitesse *f*; *Am Sch* ***fourth grade*** = classe d'école primaire pour les 8 à 9 ans; ***fourth quarter*** *(of financial year)* quatrième trimestre *m*; ***the Fourth World*** le quart-monde

fourth-class mail *n Am* paquet-poste *m* ordinaire

fourth-generation language *n Comput* langage *m* de quatrième génération

fourthly [ˈfɔːθlɪ] *adv* quatrièmement, en quatrième lieu

four-toed *adj Zool* tétradactyle

four-way stop *n Am* carrefour *m* à quatre stops

four-wheel *vi Am* faire du quatre-quatre
►► *Aut* ***four-wheel drive*** propulsion *f* à quatre roues motrices; **with four-wheel drive** à quatre roues motrices; **it's a four-wheel drive** c'est un quatre-quatre; *Aut* ***four-wheel steering*** quatre roues *fpl* directrices

four-wheeled *adj* à quatre roues

four-wheeler *n* véhicule *m* à quatre roues

foussa [ˈfuːsə] *n Zool* fosa *m*, cryptoprocte *m* féroce

fousty [ˈfuːstɪ] *adj Scot* (**a**) *(mouldy)* moisi (**b**) *(smell)* de renfermé, de moisi

fowl [faʊl] *(pl* **inv** *or* **fowls**) **1** *n* (**a**) *(for eating → collectively)* volaille *f*; *(→ one bird)* volaille *f*, volatile *m* (**b**) *Arch or Literary (bird)* oiseau *m*; **all the fowls of the air** tous les oiseaux
2 *vi* chasser le gibier à plumes
►► ***fowl pest*** peste *f* aviaire

fowler [ˈfaʊlə(r)] *n* oiseleur *m*

fowling [ˈfaʊlɪŋ] *n* **to go fowling** aller à la chasse au gibier à plumes
►► ***fowling piece*** carabine *f*, fusil *m* de chasse léger

fox [fɒks] *(pl* **inv** *or* **foxes**) **1** *n* (**a**) *(animal, fur)* renard *m*; *Fig* **he's a sly old fox** c'est un vieux renard; **as sly as a fox** rusé comme un renard; **it's like setting the fox to mind the geese** c'est faire entrer le loup dans la bergerie
(**b**) *Am Fam Old-fashioned (woman)* jolie pépée *f*
2 *vt* (**a**) *(outwit)* duper, berner
(**b**) *Fam (baffle)* désarçonner; **you've got me foxed** je suis perplexe ▫
(**c**) *(paper)* marquer *ou* tacher de rousseurs
►► *Zool* ***fox bat*** *(flying fox)* roussette *f*; *(fruit bat)* chauve-souris *f* frugivore; ***fox brush*** queue *f* de renard; ***fox cub*** renardeau *m*; ***fox fur*** (peau *f* de) renard *m*; *Med* ***fox mange*** alopécie *f*; ***fox terrier*** fox *m inv*, fox-terrier *m*

foxed [fɒkst] *adj (paper)* marqué *ou* taché de rousseurs

fox-fur *adj (coat, hat)* en (peau de) renard

foxglove [ˈfɒksglʌv] *n Bot* digitale *f* (pourprée)

foxhole [ˈfɒkshəʊl] *n* (**a**) *(of fox)* terrier *m* de renard, renardière *f* (**b**) *Mil* gourbi *m*

foxhound [ˈfɒkshaʊnd] *n* fox-hound *m*, chien *m* courant

foxhunt [ˈfɒkshʌnt] *n* chasse *f* au renard

foxhunter [ˈfɒksˌhʌntə(r)] *n* chasseur(euse) *m,f* de renard

foxhunting [ˈfɒksˌhʌntɪŋ] *n* chasse *f* au renard; **to go foxhunting** aller chasser le renard *ou* à la chasse au renard

foxiness [ˈfɒksɪnɪs] *n* (**a**) *(craftiness)* ruse *f* (**b**) *Am Fam Old-fashioned (of woman)* air *m* sexy

foxing [ˈfɒksɪŋ] *n (on paper)* piqûres *fpl*, rousseurs *fpl*

foxlike [ˈfɒkslaɪk] *adj* (**a**) *(resembling a fox)* qui ressemble à un renard (**b**) *(crafty)* rusé, malin(igne)

foxtail [ˈfɒksteɪl] *n Bot (grass)* vulpin *m*; *(flower)* queue-de-renard *f*

foxtrot [ˈfɒkstrɒt] **1** *n* fox-trot *m inv*
2 *vi* danser le fox-trot

foxy [ˈfɒksɪ] *(compar* **foxier**, *superl* **foxiest**) *adj* (**a**) *(wily)* rusé, malin(igne) (**b**) *(colour)* roux (rousse) (**c**) *(paper)* marqué *ou* taché de rousseurs (**d**) *Am Fam Old-fashioned (sexy)* sexy *(inv)*; **a foxy lady** une nana sexy

foyer [ˈfɔɪeɪ] *n* (**a**) *(of cinema, hotel)* hall *m*, vestibule *m*; *(of theatre)* foyer *m* (**b**) *Am (of house)* entrée *f*, vestibule *m*

FP [ˌefˈpiː] *n* (**a**) *(abbr* **former pupil**) ancien(enne) élève *mf* (**b**) *Am (abbr* **fire-plug**) bouche *f* d'incendie

FPA [ˌefpiːˈeɪ] **1** *adj Ins (abbr* **free of particular average**) FAP
2 *n Br (abbr* **Family Planning Association**) = association pour le planning familial

FPO [ˌefpiːˈəʊ] *n Am Naut (abbr* **Fleet Post Office**) = mention figurant dans l'adresse des membres de la marine américaine

FPU [ˌefpiːˈjuː] *n Comput (abbr* **floating-point unit**) FPU *f*, coprocesseur *m* arithmétique

FQDN [ˌefkjuːˌdiːˈen] *n Comput (abbr* **Fully Qualified Domain Name**) nom *m* de domaine complet

Fr (**a**) *Rel (written abbr* **Father**) P (**b**) *(written abbr* **France**) France *f* (**c**) *Fin (written abbr* **franc**) franc *m* (**d**) *(written abbr* **friar**) F

FRA [ˌefɑːˈreɪ] *n Fin (abbr* **Future Rate Agreement, Forward Rate Agreement**) ATF *m*

fracas [*Br* ˈfrækɑː, *Am* ˈfreɪkæs] *(Br pl* **inv** [-kɑːz], *Am pl* **fracases** [-kəsɪz]) *n (brawl)* rixe *f*, bagarre *f*; *(noise)* fracas *m*

fractal [ˈfræktəl] *n Geom* fractal *m*

fraction [ˈfrækʃən] *n* (**a**) *Math* fraction *f*
(**b**) *Fig (bit)* fraction *f*, petite partie *f*; **at a fraction of the cost** pour une fraction du prix; **for a fraction of a second** pendant une fraction de seconde; **he escaped death by a fraction of a second** il a été à deux doigts de la mort; **move back just a fraction** reculez un tout petit peu
(**c**) *Fin (of share)* fraction *f*, rompu *m*
(**d**) *Chem (of distillation)* fraction *f*
(**e**) *Pol (of communist party)* fraction *f*, groupe *m* fractionnaire

fractional [ˈfrækʃənəl] *adj* (**a**) *Math* fractionnaire (**b**) *Fig (tiny)* tout petit, infime; **fractional part** fraction *f*; **a fractional difference** une différence minime
►► *Fin* ***fractional currency*** monnaie *f* divisionnaire; *Chem* ***fractional distillation*** distillation *f* fractionnée; *Fin* ***fractional money*** monnaie *f* divisionnaire *ou* d'appoint

fractionally [ˈfrækʃənəlɪ] *adv* (**a**) *(slightly)* un tout petit peu (**b**) *Chem* par fractionnement

fractionary [ˈfrækʃənərɪ] *adj* fractionnel

fractionate [ˈfrækʃəneɪt] *vt Chem & Ind (petroleum etc)* fractionner

fractionize, -ise [ˈfrækʃənaɪz] *vt Math* fractionner

fractious [ˈfrækʃəs] *adj* (**a**) *(unruly)* indiscipliné, turbulent (**b**) *(irritable → child)* grognon, pleurnicheur; *(→ adult)* irascible, revêche, irritable; **to be fractious** *or* **in a fractious mood** être de mauvaise humeur; *(baby)* pleurnicher

fractiously [ˈfrækʃəslɪ] *adv* (**a**) *(in an unruly manner)* de façon indisciplinée (**b**) *(irritably)* avec humeur

fractiousness [ˈfrækʃəsnɪs] *n* (**a**) *(unruliness)* indiscipline *f* (**b**) *(irritableness)* irritabilité *f*; *(of baby)* caractère *m* grognon

fracture [ˈfræktʃə(r)] **1** *n* fracture *f*
2 *vt (break)* fracturer; **he fractured his arm** il s'est fracturé le bras; **fractured skull** crâne *m* fracturé; **fractured ribs** côtes *fpl* enfoncées; *Fig* **their withdrawal fractured the alliance** leur retrait brisa l'alliance
3 *vi (break)* se fracturer

fraenum, *Am* **frenum** [ˈfriːnəm] *(Br pl* **fraena** [-nə], *Am pl* **frenums** *or* **frena** [-nə]) *n Anat* frein *m*, filet *m*

frag [fræg] *(pt & pp* **fragged**, *cont* **fragging**) *Am Fam Mil slang* **1** *n* grenade *f* offensive ▫
2 *vt* = tuer ou blesser intentionnellement un officier ou un compagnon d'armes avec une grenade

fragile [*Br* ˈfrædʒaɪl, *Am* ˈfrædʒəl] *adj* (**a**) *(china, glass)* fragile; *Fig (peace, happiness)* précaire, fragile; **a fragile relationship** des relations *fpl* fragiles *ou* précaires; **a fragile link with the past** un lien fragile avec le passé; **fragile: handle with care** *(on package)* fragile: manipuler avec précaution
(**b**) *(person → physically)* fragile, frêle; *(→ emotionally)* fragile; *Hum* **I'm feeling a bit fragile today** je ne suis pas dans mon assiette ce matin

fragilely [ˈfrædʒaɪllɪ] *adv* fragilement

fragility [frəˈdʒɪlətɪ] *n* fragilité *f*

fragment 1 *n* [ˈfrægmənt] *(of china, text)* fragment *m*, morceau *m*; *(of bomb)* éclat *m*; *Fig (of conversation)* bribe *f*; **the window shattered into fragments** la fenêtre a volé en éclats; **the report contains not a fragment of truth** le rapport ne contient pas un atome *ou* une once de vérité
2 *vt* [frægˈment] *(break)* fragmenter, briser; *(divide)* fragmenter, morceler
3 *vi* [frægˈment] se fragmenter

fragmental [frægˈmentəl] *adj* fragmentaire; *Geol* clastique, détritique

fragmentary [ˈfrægməntərɪ] *adj* fragmentaire

fragmentation [ˌfrægmenˈteɪʃən] *n* (*breaking*) fragmentation *f*; *(division)* fragmentation *f*, morcellement *m*; *Comput (of hard disk)* fragmentation *f*
►► ***fragmentation bomb*** bombe *f* à fragmentation; ***fragmentation grenade*** grenade *f* offensive

fragmented [frægˈmentɪd] *adj* fragmentaire, morcelé

fragrance [ˈfreɪgrəns] *n* parfum *m*; *Com* **our new fragrance** notre nouveau parfum

fragrance-free *adj* non parfumé

fragrant [ˈfreɪgrənt] *adj* parfumé; **to be** *or* **smell fragrant** sentir bon; *Literary* **a garden fragrant with flowers** un jardin où embaument les fleurs; **fragrant pine woods** des pinèdes *fpl* odorantes

fraidy cat [ˈfreɪdɪ-] *n Am Fam* poule *f* mouillée

frail [freɪl] *adj* (**a**) *(object)* fragile; *(person)* fragile, frêle; *(health)* délicat, fragile; **she's rather frail** elle a une petite santé (**b**) *(happiness, hope)* fragile, éphémère

frailness [ˈfreɪlnɪs] *n* (**a**) *(of object, person)* fragilité *f*; **the frailness of his health** sa santé délicate (**b**) *(of happiness, hope)* fragilité *f*

frailty [ˈfreɪltɪ] *(pl* **frailties**) *n (of health, hope, person)* fragilité *f*; *(of character)* faiblesse *f*; **human frailty** la faiblesse des hommes

frame [freɪm] **1** *n* (**a**) *(border → gen)* cadre *m*; *(→ of canvas, picture etc)* cadre *m*, encadrement *m*; *(→ of window)* cadre *m*, châssis *m*; *(→ of door)* encadrement *m*; *(→ for spectacles)* monture *f*; **glasses with red frames** des lunettes *fpl* avec une monture rouge
(**b**) *(support, structure → gen)* cadre *m*; *(→ of bicycle)* cadre *m*; *(→ of car)* châssis *m*; *(→ of lampshade, racket, tent)* armature *f*; *(→ of machine)* bâti *m*; *(→ of ship)* charpente *f*, carcasse *f*; *(→ in gardening)* châssis; *(→ for walking)* déambulateur *m*; *Constr* charpente *f*; *Tex* métier *m*; **the bed has a wooden frame** le lit est muni d'un cadre en bois
(**c**) *(in snooker, pool etc) (game)* partie *f*; *(wooden device)* triangle *m*
(**d**) *(body)* corps *m*; **his huge frame filled the doorway** sa large carrure s'encadrait dans la porte; **his slender frame was shaken by sobs** son corps menu *ou* fluet était secoué par des sanglots
(**e**) *(setting, background)* cadre *m*; *(area, scope)* cadre *m*; **frame of mind** état *m* d'esprit; **I'm not in the right frame of mind for celebrating** je ne suis pas d'humeur à faire la fête; **frame of reference** système *m* de référence
(**f**) *Phot* image *f*; *Cin* image *f*, photogramme *m*; *TV* trame *f*
(**g**) *(in embroidery → floor-standing)* métier *m* (à broder); *(→ hand-held)* tambour *m* (à broder)
(**h**) *Comput (of Web page)* cadre *m*
2 *vt* (**a**) *(enclose, encase)* encadrer; **she's had the photograph framed** elle a fait encadrer la photo; *Fig* **her face was framed by a white silk scarf** un foulard de soie blanc encadrait son visage
(**b**) *Formal (design, draft)* élaborer; *(formulate, express)* formuler; **to frame a plan/system** élaborer un projet/système; **the contract was**

framed in legal jargon le contrat était formulé en jargon juridique
(**c**) *Phot & TV (subject)* cadrer
(**d**) *Fam (incriminate falsely)* **to frame sb** monter un (mauvais) coup contre qn ❑; **I've been framed** j'ai été victime d'un coup monté ❑
►► *Am* ***frame backpack*** sac *m* à dos à armature; *Comput* ***frame format*** *(of network)* protocole *m*; *Am* ***frame house*** maison *f* en bois; ***frame rucksack*** sac *m* à dos à armature
framed [freɪmd] *adj (picture)* encadré; *Constr (building)* à structure discontinue, squeletté
►► *Am* ***framed house*** maison *f* en bois
framemaker ['freɪm,meɪkə(r)] *n (of umbrellas etc)* carcassier(ère) *m,f*
framer ['freɪmə(r)] *n* encadreur(euse) *m,f*
frame-up *n Fam (false incrimination)* coup *m* monté ❑
framework ['freɪmwɜːk] *n* (**a**) *(structure)* cadre *m*, structure *f*; *Constr* charpente *f*; *Tech* bâti *m* (**b**) *Fig* cadre *m*; **the bill seeks to provide a legal framework for divorce** le projet de loi vise à instaurer un cadre juridique pour les procédures de divorce; **within the framework of the UN/the EU** dans le cadre de l'ONU/l'UE
framing ['freɪmɪŋ] *n* (**a**) *(of picture, photograph)* encadrement *m* (**b**) *Cin & Phot* cadrage *m*
franc [fræŋk] *n* franc *m*
►► ***franc area*** zone *f* franc
France [frɑːns] *n* France *f*; **in France** en France
franchise ['fræntʃaɪz] **1** *n* (**a**) *Pol* suffrage *m*, droit *m* de vote (**b**) *Com & Law (granted by public body)* concession *f*; *(granted by manufacturer)* franchise *f* (**c**) *Com (shop, outlet)* boutique *f* franchisée, magasin *m* franchisé
2 *vt* accorder une franchise à
►► *Com* ***franchise agreement*** accord *m* de franchise; *Com* ***franchise outlet*** boutique *f* franchisée, magasin *m* franchisé
franchisee [,fræntʃaɪ'ziː] *n Com* franchisé(e) *m,f*
franchiser ['fræntʃaɪzə(r)] *n Com* franchiseur(euse) *m,f*
franchising ['fræntʃaɪzɪŋ] *n* franchisage *m*
franchisor ['fræntʃaɪzə(r)] *n Com* franchiseur(euse) *m,f*
Franciscan [fræn'sɪskən] *Rel* **1** *adj* franciscain
2 *n* franciscain(e) *m,f*
francium ['frænsɪəm] *n Chem* francium *m*
franco ['fræŋkəʊ] *Com* **1** *adj* franco
2 *adv* franco
►► ***franco price*** prix *m* franco
Franco- ['fræŋkəʊ-] *pref* franco-
Francoism ['fræŋkəʊɪzəm] *n* franquisme *m*
Francophile ['fræŋkə,faɪl] **1** *adj* francophile
2 *n* francophile *mf*
Francophilia [,fræŋkə'fɪlɪə] *n* francophilie *f*
Francophobe ['fræŋkə,fəʊb] **1** *adj* francophobe
2 *n* francophobe *mf*
Francophobia [,fræŋkə'fəʊbɪə] *n* francophobie *f*
Francophone ['fræŋkə,fəʊn] **1** *adj* francophone
2 *n* francophone *mf*
Franco-Prussian *adj* franco-prussien; **the Franco-Prussian War** la guerre de 70
frangibility [,frændʒɪ'bɪlɪtɪ] *n* fragilité *f*
frangible ['frændʒɪbəl] *adj* cassant, fragile
frangipane ['frændʒɪpeɪn] *n* frangipane *f*
frangipani [,frændʒɪ'pɑːnɪ] *n Bot (fruit)* frangipane *f*; *(tree)* frangipanier *m*
Franglais ['frɒŋgleɪ] *n* franglais *m*
Frank [fræŋk] *n Hist* Franc *m*, Franque *f*
frank [fræŋk] **1** *adj* franc (franche); **I'll be frank with you** je vais vous parler franchement *ou* être franc avec vous; **to be (perfectly) frank,...** franchement,..., sincèrement,...
2 *vt Br* affranchir *(à la machine)*
3 *n* (**a**) *Br (on letter)* affranchissement *m* (**b**) *Am Fam (sausage)* saucisse *f* (de Francfort) ❑; *(hot dog)* hot dog *m* ❑
Frankenstein ['fræŋkənstaɪn] *pr n* Frankenstein
►► *Fam* ***Frankenstein food*** = surnom donné aux aliments génétiquement modifiés par leurs détracteurs
Frankfurt ['fræŋkfɜt] *n* **Frankfurt (am Main)** Francfort (-sur-le-Main)
frankfurter ['fræŋk,fɜːtə(r)] *n* saucisse *f* de Francfort
frankincense ['fræŋkɪnsens] *n* encens *m*
franking ['fræŋkɪŋ] *n Br (of letter)* affranchissement *m (à la machine)*
►► ***franking machine*** machine *f* à affranchir
Frankish ['fræŋkɪʃ] **1** *adj* franc (franque)
2 *n* francique *m*
franklin ['fræŋklɪn] *n Hist* franc-tenancier *m*
franklinite ['fræŋklɪnaɪt] *n Miner* franklinite *f*
Franklin stove ['fræŋklɪn-] *n Am* poêle *m* à bois
frankly ['fræŋklɪ] *adv* franchement, sincèrement; **can I speak frankly?** puis-je parler franchement *ou* en toute franchise?

> **Frankly my dear, I don't give a damn**
> Cette phrase ("franchement ma chère, je m'en fiche complètement") provient du film *Gone With the Wind* (*Autant en emporte le vent*) (1939), où elle est prononcée par Rhett Butler, le personnage incarné par Clark Gable, et est adressée à sa femme Scarlett O'Hara, jouée par Vivien Leigh. Le film est une adaptation du roman éponyme de Margaret Mitchell (1936), où apparaît cette phrase mais sans le mot "frankly".
> Aujourd'hui on utilise cette formule pour exprimer son indifférence ou bien en n'en gardant que la première partie (**frankly, my dear**), pour exprimer une opinion sans ambages.

frankness ['fræŋknɪs] *n* franchise *f*; **I admire his frankness** j'admire sa franchise *ou* son franc-parler
frantic ['fræntɪk] *adj* (**a**) *(distraught, wild)* éperdu, affolé; **she was frantic with worry** elle était folle d'inquiétude; **frantic screams** des cris *mpl* éperdus *ou* d'affolement; **it drives him frantic** cela le met hors de lui (**b**) *(very busy)* **a scene of frantic activity** une scène d'activité frénétique; *Fam* **things are pretty frantic at the office** il y a un travail fou au bureau
frantically ['fræntɪklɪ] *adv* désespérément; **she worked frantically to finish the dress** elle travailla comme une forcenée pour terminer la robe; **the shop is frantically busy just before Christmas** il y a un monde fou au magasin juste avant Noël
frappé [*Br* 'fræpeɪ, *Am* fræ'peɪ] *n* (**a**) *(milk-shake)* milk-shake *m (épais)* (**b**) *(partly-frozen drink)* granité *m*
frat [fræt] *n Am Fam (abbr* **fraternity***)* = confrérie d'étudiants
►► ***frat rat*** = membre d'une confrérie d'étudiants
fraternal [frə'tɜːnəl] *adj* fraternel; **fraternal twins** des faux jumeaux *mpl*
►► *Am* ***Fraternal Order of Eagles*** = organisation caritative américaine
fraternally [frə'tɜːnəlɪ] *adv* fraternellement
fraternity [frə'tɜːnətɪ] *(pl* **fraternities***)* *n* (**a**) *(friendship)* fraternité *f* (**b**) *(association)* confrérie *f*; **the medical fraternity** la confrérie des médecins; *Pej* **the sailing/hunting fraternity** la clique des amateurs de voile/des chasseurs (**c**) *Am Univ* = confrérie d'étudiants
►► *Am Univ* ***fraternity house*** maison *f* communautaire (où résident des étudiants appartenant à une même confrérie); *Am Univ* ***fraternity pin*** insigne *m* de confrérie

> **FRATERNITIES AND SORORITIES**
>
> Ce type d'associations d'étudiants (les "fraternities" pour les hommes, les "sororities" pour les femmes) fut créé au XIXème siècle dans les universités de l'est des États-Unis, mais des branches furent bientôt fondées dans tout le pays. Les noms des "fraternities" et "sororities" sont composés de lettres de l'alphabet grec (Sigma Nu, Phi Delta Theta ou Phi Beta Kappa, par exemple).
> Ces associations rassemblent des étudiants de milieu culturel et d'origine sociale semblables et permettent à leurs membres d'établir facilement des réseaux de relations. Les étudiants désireux de faire partie d'une "fraternity" doivent être parrainés par des membres et doivent se soumettre à de nombreuses épreuves d'initiation. Au cours des dernières années, le système des "fraternities" et "sororities" fut sévèrement critiqué à la suite de viols, d'agressions racistes et d'incidents liés à l'abus d'alcool.

fraternization [,frætənaɪ'zeɪʃən] *n* fraternisation *f*
fraternize, -ise ['frætənaɪz] *vi* fraterniser
fratricidal [,frætrɪ'saɪdəl] *adj* fratricide
fratricide ['frætrɪsaɪd] *n* fratricide *mf*
fraud [frɔːd] *n* (**a**) *Law* fraude *f*; *Fin* escroquerie *f*; **she's been charged with fraud** elle a été inculpée de fraude; **tax fraud** fraude *f* fiscale; **credit card fraud** usage *m* frauduleux de cartes de crédit; **to obtain sth by fraud** obtenir qch frauduleusement *ou* par fraude
(**b**) *(dishonest person)* imposteur *m*; **she's a fraud** elle essaie de se faire passer pour ce qu'elle n'est pas
(**c**) *(product, work)* supercherie *f*; **the whole thing is a fraud!** c'est une vaste supercherie!
►► *Br* ***the Fraud Squad*** brigade *f* de répression des fraudes
fraudster ['frɔːdstə(r)] *n Br* fraudeur(euse) *m,f*
fraudulence ['frɔːdjʊləns], **fraudulency** ['frɔːdjʊlənsɪ] *n (of transaction)* caractère *m* frauduleux; *(of concerns, sentiments)* fausseté *f*
fraudulent ['frɔːdjʊlənt] *adj (bankrupt, trading, transaction)* frauduleux; *(sympathy, feelings)* faux (fausse), affecté; *(charge, accusation)* faux (fausse)
►► ***fraudulent balance sheet*** faux bilan *m*; ***fraudulent bankruptcy*** faillite *f* frauduleuse
fraudulently ['frɔːdjʊləntlɪ] *adv* frauduleusement
fraught [frɔːt] *adj* (**a**) *(filled)* chargé, lourd; **an atmosphere fraught with emotion/tension** une atmosphère chargée d'émotion/de tension; **fraught with danger** rempli de dangers
(**b**) *esp Br (tense)* tendu; **I'm feeling a bit fraught** je me sens un peu angoissé *ou* tendu; **things got rather fraught at work today** l'atmosphère était plutôt tendue au bureau aujourd'hui; **I've had a particularly fraught week** j'ai eu une semaine particulièrement stressante
(**c**) *(distressing)* pénible; **it's a fraught subject** c'est un thème ardu
fray [freɪ] **1** *vt (usu passive)* (**a**) *(clothing, fabric, rope)* effilocher
(**b**) *(nerves)* mettre à vif; **her nerves were frayed** elle avait les nerfs à vif
2 *vi* (**a**) *(clothing, fabric, rope)* s'effilocher; **her dress is fraying at the hem** l'ourlet de sa robe s'effiloche
(**b**) *Fig* **tempers began to fray** les gens commençaient à s'énerver *ou* perdre patience; **to fray around** *or* **at the edges** *(agreement)* battre de l'aile; **after ten months of hard work the team were starting to fray around the edges** après dix mois de dur labeur, l'équipe commençait à montrer des signes de fatigue nerveuse
3 *n* **the fray** la mêlée; **to enter** *or* **to join the fray** se jeter dans la mêlée
frayed [freɪd] *adj* (**a**) *(garment)* élimé; **her jacket was frayed at the cuffs** sa veste était élimée aux poignets (**b**) *Fig* **tempers were getting frayed** les gens étaient de plus en plus irritables; **to be frayed around** *or* **at the edges** battre de l'aile
frazil ['freɪzɪl] *n Geol* frasil *m*
frazzle ['fræzəl] *Fam* **1** *vt (exhaust)* tuer, crever
2 *n* **worn to a frazzle** crevé; **burnt to a frazzle** carbonisé, calciné; **you look burnt to a frazzle** *(by sun)* tu as l'air d'avoir pris un de ces coups de soleil
frazzled ['fræzəld] *adj Fam* (**a**) *(mentally)* à bout de nerfs; *(exhausted)* crevé; **his nerves were still frazzled** il était encore à bout de nerfs (**b**) *(burnt)* carbonisé, calciné; **I got frazzled on the beach** je me suis pris un gros coup de soleil sur la plage ❑
FRB [,efɑː'biː] *n Am Fin (abbr* **Federal Reserve Board***)* = conseil d'administration des banques centrales américaines
FRCD [,efɑː,siː'diː] *n Banking (abbr* **floating-rate certificate of deposit***)* = certificat de dépôt à taux flottant
FRCM [,efɑː,siː'em] *n Br (abbr* **Fellow of the Royal College of Music***)* = membre du "Royal College of Music"
FRCP [,efɑː,siː'piː] *n Br (abbr* **Fellow of the Royal College of Physicians***)* = membre du "Royal College of Physicians"
FRCS [,efɑː,siː'es] *n Br (abbr* **Fellow of the Royal College of Surgeons***)* = membre du "Royal College of Surgeons"

FRCVS [ˌefɑːˌsiːviːˈes] *n Br* (*abbr* **Fellow of the Royal College of Veterinary Surgeons**) = membre du "Royal College of Veterinary Surgeons"

freak [friːk] **1** *n* (**a**) *(abnormal event)* caprice *m* de la nature, aberration *f*; *(abnormal person)* phénomène *m* de foire, monstre *m*; *(eccentric person)* phénomène *m*, farfelu(e) *m,f*; **by a freak of nature** par un caprice de la nature; **by some freak (of chance)** par un hasard inouï; **just because I choose not to eat meat, that doesn't make me a freak** ce n'est pas parce que je ne mange pas de viande que je suis anormal; **freak show** exhibition *f* de monstres *(à la foire)*
(**b**) *Fam (fanatic)* fana *mf*; *(addict)* accro *mf*; **a fitness freak** un (une) fana de la forme; **a speed/cocaine freak** un (une) accro au speed/à la cocaïne
(**c**) *Fam (hippie)* hippie ❑ *mf*
(**d**) *Literary (caprice)* foucade *f*
2 *adj (storm)* anormal; *(accident)* insolite, bizarre; **freak weather conditions** des conditions *fpl* atmosphériques anormales
3 *vi Fam* (**a**) *(on drugs)* flipper
(**b**) *(lose control of one's emotions)* perdre les pédales; *(become angry)* piquer une crise, péter les plombs

▸**freak out** *Fam* **1** *vi* (**a**) *(on drugs)* flipper
(**b**) *(lose control of one's emotions)* perdre les pédales; *(become angry)* piquer une crise, péter les plombs
(**c**) *(abandon restraint)* s'éclater; **look at him freaking out on the dance floor!** regarde-le s'éclater sur la piste de danse!
2 *vt sep* (**a**) *(cause to hallucinate)* faire flipper
(**b**) *(upset emotionally)* déboussoler

freaking [ˈfriːkɪŋ] *Am very Fam* **1** *adj (for emphasis)* sacré, foutu; **where are those freaking kids?** mais où sont passés ces foutus gamins?
2 *adv (for emphasis)* vachement; **it's freaking cold out there** ça pince vachement dehors; **I don't freaking know!** j'en sais foutre rien!

freakish [ˈfriːkɪʃ] *adj* (**a**) *(strange)* étrange, bizarre; **a freakish-looking man** un homme à l'allure étrange *ou* bizarre (**b**) *(abnormal → weather)* anormal

freakishly [ˈfriːkɪʃlɪ] *adv* (**a**) *(strangely)* étrangement, bizarrement (**b**) *(abnormally)* anormalement

freakishness [ˈfriːkɪʃnɪs] *n* (**a**) *(strangeness)* étrangeté *f*, caractère *m* bizarre (**b**) *Literary (capriciousness)* caractère *m* anormal

freaky [ˈfriːkɪ] *adj Fam* bizarre ❑, insolite

freckle [ˈfrekəl] **1** *n* tache *f* de rousseur; **she's got freckles** elle a des taches de rousseur
2 *vt* marquer de taches de rousseur
3 *vi* se couvrir de taches de rousseur

freckled [ˈfrekəld], **freckly** [ˈfrekəlɪ] *adj* taché de son, marqué de taches de rousseur; **a freckled face/nose** un visage/nez couvert de taches de rousseur

Frederick [ˈfredərɪk] *pr n* **Frederick the Great** Frédéric le Grand

FREE [friː]

libre	▸ 1 (a) – (c), (e)
gratuit	▸ 1 (d)
franco	▸ 1 (i)
gratuitement	▸ 2 (a)
librement	▸ 2 (b)
libérer	▸ 3 (a), (c), (d)
dégager	▸ 3 (b)
déboucher	▸ 3 (c)

1 *adj* (**a**) *(unconfined, unrestricted → person, animal, passage, way)* libre; **as free as the air** *or* **a bird** libre comme l'air; **the hostage managed to get free** l'otage a réussi à se libérer; **to cut sb free** délivrer qn en coupant ses liens; **to let sb go free** relâcher qn, remettre qn en liberté; **to set free** *(prisoner, animal)* remettre en liberté; *(slave)* affranchir; *(hostage)* libérer; **you are free to leave** vous êtes libre de partir; **you are free to refuse** libre à vous de refuser; **they gave us free access to their files** ils nous ont donné libre accès à leurs dossiers; **to make a free choice** décider librement *ou* en toute liberté; **feel free to visit us any time** ne vous gênez pas pour nous rendre visite quand vous voulez; **feel free to speak your mind** n'hésitez pas à dire ce que vous pensez; **can I use the phone? – yes, feel free** puis-je téléphoner? – mais certainement; **free seating** *(sign)* places non numérotées
(**b**) *(unattached)* libre, sans attaches; **with his free hand** avec sa main libre; **grab the free end of the rope** attrape le bout libre de la corde
(**c**) *(democratic)* libre; **it's a free country!** on est en démocratie!; **a free press** une presse libre
(**d**) *(at no cost)* gratuit; **free admission** entrée *f* gratuite *ou* libre; **free demonstration** démonstration *f* gracieuse; *Fig* **there's no such thing as a free lunch** les gens sont tous intéressés
(**e**) *(not in use, unoccupied)* libre; **is that seat free?** est-ce que ce siège est libre?; **she doesn't have a free moment** elle n'a pas un moment de libre; **are you free for lunch today?** êtes-vous libre pour déjeuner aujourd'hui?; **could you let us know when you're free?** pourriez-vous nous faire savoir quand vous êtes libre *ou* disponible?; **what do you do in your free time?** que faites-vous pendant vos loisirs?; **she has very little free time** elle a peu de temps libre
(**f**) *(unhampered)* **the jury was not entirely free of** *or* **from prejudice** les jurés n'étaient pas entièrement sans préjugés *ou* parti pris; **to be free from care** être sans souci; **to be free from pain** ne pas souffrir; **I just want to be free of him!** je veux être débarrassé de lui!; **they're trying to keep Antarctica free from pollution** ils essaient de préserver l'Antarctique de la pollution
(**g**) *(approximate → translation, interpretation)* libre; *Pej* approximatif
(**h**) *(uninhibited)* **free and easy** désinvolte, décontracté; **she has a very free and easy attitude to life** elle prend la vie de façon très décontractée
(**i**) *Com* **free carrier** franco transporteur; **free overside** franco allège; **free in and out** bord à bord; **free alongside ship, free at quay** franco long du quai, franco long du bord; **free at frontier** franco frontière; **free of all average** franc de toute avarie; **free of general average** franc d'avarie commune; **free of particular average** franc d'avarie particulière; **free on board** franco à bord; *Customs* **free of duty** exempt de droits d'entrée; **free on rail** franco wagon; **free of tax** franc d'impôts; **free on truck** franco camion; **free on wharf** franco long du quai, franco long du bord
(**j**) *(generous)* **to be free with one's time** être généreux de son temps; **to be free with one's money** être prodigue de son argent; **he was very free with his advice** il a été très prodigue en conseils; **she's very free with her criticism** elle ne ménage pas ses critiques
(**k**) *(disrespectful)* trop familier; **he's a bit free in his manners for my liking** il est un peu trop sans gêne à mon goût
(**l**) *Chem* libre, non combiné; **free nitrogen** azote *m* à l'état libre
2 *adv* (**a**) *(at no cost)* gratuitement; **they will deliver free of charge** ils livreront gratuitement; **children travel (for) free** les enfants voyagent gratuitement; **it came free with the magazine** c'était en prime pour l'achat du magazine
(**b**) *(without restraint)* librement; **wolves roamed free through the forests** les loups rôdaient librement à travers les forêts; **to make free with sth** se servir de qch sans se gêner; **he made very free with his wife's money** il ne se gênait pas pour dépenser l'argent de sa femme
3 *vt* (**a**) *(release → gen)* libérer; *(→ prisoner)* libérer, relâcher; *(→ tied-up animal)* détacher; *(→ caged animal)* libérer; *(→ slave, colony)* affranchir; **to free sb's hands** *(untie)* détacher les mains de qn; **giving up work has freed me to get on with my painting** arrêter de travailler m'a permis de continuer à peindre
(**b**) *(disengage, disentangle)* dégager; **it took two hours to free the driver from the wreckage** il a fallu deux heures pour dégager le conducteur de sa voiture; **she tried to free herself from his grasp** elle essaya de se libérer *ou* dégager de son étreinte; *Fig* **to free sb from an obligation** libérer qn d'une obligation; **to free oneself from one's commitments** se libérer *ou* se délier de ses engagements; **he cannot free himself of guilt** il ne peut pas se débarrasser d'un sentiment de culpabilité
(**c**) *(unblock → pipe)* déboucher; *(→ passage)* libérer
(**d**) *Com (prices, trade)* libérer; *(funds)* débloquer

▸▸ ***free agent*** personne *f* libre *ou* indépendante; *(sports player)* joueur(euse) *m,f* indépendant(e); **I'm a free agent** je ne dépends de personne; *Psy* ***free association*** association *f* libre; ***Free Church*** Église *f* protestante d'Écosse; ***the Free Church of Scotland*** = secte protestante écossaise à tendance traditionnaliste; *Sport* ***free climbing*** escalade *f* libre; ***free competition*** libre concurrence *f*; *Sch* ***free composition*** composition *f* libre; ***free diver*** plongeur(euse) *m,f* autonome; ***free diving*** plongée *f* sous-marine autonome; *Golf* ***free drop*** free drop *m*, drop *m* sans pénalité; *Econ* ***free enterprise*** libre entreprise *f*; ***free fall*** chute *f* libre; ***free flight*** vol *m* ballistique; *St Exch* ***free float*** actions *fpl* disponibles (au marché); *Hist* ***Free France*** la France libre; *Hist* ***the Free French*** les Français *mpl* libres; *Com* ***free gift*** cadeau *m*; ***free hand*** liberté *f* d'action; **to give sb a free hand to do sth** donner carte blanche à qn pour faire qch; **they gave me a completely free hand** ils m'ont donné toute liberté d'action; *Br* ***free house*** = pub libre de ses approvisionnements (et non lié à une brasserie particulière); ***free indirect speech*** style *m* indirect libre; *St Exch* ***free issue*** attribution *f* d'actions gratuites; *Mus* ***free jazz*** free-jazz *m inv*; *Sport* ***free kick*** coup *m* franc; ***free love*** union *f* libre; *Econ* ***free market*** économie *f* de marché; *Law* ***free pardon*** grâce *f*; *Customs* ***free port*** port *m* franc; ***free press*** liberté *f* de la presse; *Med* ***free radical*** radical *m* libre; *Fam Ind* ***free rider*** = ouvrier non-syndiqué qui profite des avantages gagnés par les syndicats; *Com* ***free sample*** échantillon *m* gratuit; ***free skating*** figures *fpl* libres; ***free speech*** liberté *f* de parole *ou* d'expression; ***free spirit*** non-conformiste *mf*; ***Free State*** *(in South Africa)* État *m* libre; *Hist (Ireland)* État *m* libre d'Irlande; *Hist* ***Free Stater*** partisan *m* de l'État libre d'Irlande; ***free thought*** libre pensée *f*; *Sport* ***free throw*** *(in basketball)* lancer *m* franc; *Econ* ***free trade*** libre-échange *m*; *Econ* ***free trade area*** zone *f* de libre-échange; *Econ* ***free trade policy*** politique *f* antiprotectionniste, politique *f* de libre-échange; *Econ* ***free trader*** libre-échangiste *mf*; *Econ* ***free trade zone*** zone *f* de libre-échange; *Com* ***free trial*** essai *m* gratuit; *Com* ***free trial period*** période *f* d'essai gratuit; ***free verse*** vers *m* libre; ***free vote*** vote *m* libre; ***free will*** libre arbitre *m*; **to do sth of one's own free will** faire qch de son plein gré; *Pol* ***the Free World*** le monde libre

▸**free up** *vt sep (funds)* dégager; *(time, space)* libérer; **this will free up sales people to do more actual selling** cela donnera plus de temps au personnel de vente pour se consacrer à la vente même

'Free Fall' *Golding* 'Chute libre'

-free [friː] *suff* **additive-free** sans additifs; **salt-free** sans sel; **trouble-free** sans ennuis *ou* problèmes

freebase [ˈfriːbeɪs] *vi very Fam Drugs slang (purify cocaine)* purifier de la cocaïne ❑; *(smoke cocaine)* chauffer de la cocaïne et en inhaler la fumée ❑

freebie, freebee [ˈfriːbɪ] *Fam* **1** *n (for customer etc)* cadeau ❑ *m*; *(perk)* à-côté ❑ *m*; *Comput* produit *m* gratuit ❑; **it was a freebie with the magazine** c'était un cadeau offert avec le magazine
2 *adj* gratis *(inv)*

freeboard [ˈfriːbɔːd] *n Naut* franc-bord *m*

freebooter [ˈfriːˌbuːtə(r)] *n* flibustier *m*

freeborn [ˈfriːbɔːn] *adj* né libre, libre de naissance

freedman [ˈfriːdmən] (*pl* **freedmen** [-mən]) *n Hist* affranchi *m*

freedom [ˈfriːdəm] *n* liberté *f*; **the students were ready to die for freedom** les étudiants étaient prêts à mourir pour la liberté; **the journalists were given complete freedom to talk to dissidents** les journalistes ont pu parler aux dissidents en toute liberté; **freedom from hunger** le droit de manger à sa faim; **freedom from persecution** le droit de vivre sans persécution; **freedom from responsibility** l'absence *f* de responsabilités; **she had the freedom of the whole house** elle avait la maison à son entière disposition; **to be given** *or* **granted the freedom of the city** être nommé citoyen d'honneur de la ville; **freedom of the seas** liberté *f* de la haute mer

▸▸ ***freedom of association*** liberté *f* de réunion; ***freedom of conscience*** liberté *f* de conscience; ***freedom fighter*** guérillero *m*, révolutionnaire *mf*; ***freedom of information*** liberté *f* d'information; *Law* ***Freedom of Information Act*** = loi sur la communication aux citoyens des informations de source gouvernementale; ***freedom of speech*** liberté *f* d'expression; ***freedom of worship*** liberté *f* du culte

freedwoman ['fri:d,wʊmən] (*pl* **freedwomen** [-,wɪmɪn]) *n Hist* affranchie *f*

free-floating *adj* en mouvement libre

free-flowing *adj Fin (capital)* flottant

Freefone® ['fri:fəʊn] *n Br Tel* = appel gratuit, ≃ numéro *m* vert; **call Freefone® 800** appelez le numéro vert 800

free-for-all *n* mêlée *f* générale; **when the food arrived the queue quickly turned into a free-for-all** quand la nourriture est arrivée la file d'attente a tourné en mêlée générale

free-form *adj* de forme libre

▸▸ *Mus* ***free-form jazz*** free-jazz *m inv*

freehand ['fri:hænd] **1** *adj* à main levée

2 *adv* à main levée

freehanded [,fri:'hændɪd] *adj* libéral, large

freehold ['fri:həʊld] **1** *n* ≃ propriété *f* foncière inaliénable

2 *adv* **to buy/to sell sth freehold** acheter/vendre qch en propriété inaliénable

3 *adj* **freehold property** propriété *f* inaliénable

freeholder ['fri:,həʊldə(r)] *n* ≃ propriétaire *mf* foncier(ère) *(à perpétuité)*

freeing ['fri:ɪŋ] *n (of prisoner)* libération *f*, délivrance *f*; *(of slave)* affranchissement *m*; *(of funds, resources)* déblocage *m*

freelance ['fri:lɑ:ns] **1** *n* travailleur(euse) *m,f* indépendant(e), free-lance *mf*; *(journalist, writer)* pigiste *mf*

2 *adj* indépendant, free-lance *(inv)*

3 *adv* en free-lance, en indépendant

4 *vi* travailler en free-lance *ou* indépendant; *(journalist, writer)* faire de la pige, travailler comme pigiste *ou* en indépendant

freelancer ['fri:,lɑ:nsə(r)] *n* travailleur(euse) *m,f* indépendant(e), free-lance *mf*

free-liver *n* viveur(euse) *m,f*

free-living *adj* (**a**) *(person)* intempérant (**b**) *Biol* indépendant

freeload ['fri:ləʊd] *vi Fam* vivre aux crochets des autres

freeloader ['fri:ləʊdə(r)] *n Fam* pique-assiette *mf*, parasite ❑ *mf*

freeloading ['fri:ləʊdɪŋ] *adj Fam* parasite ❑

freely ['fri:lɪ] *adv* (**a**) *(without constraint)* librement; **can I speak freely?** puis-je parler librement?; **she made her confession freely** elle a avoué de son plein gré; **I freely admit that...** j'avoue sans peine que...; **traffic is moving freely again** la circulation est redevenue fluide; **the book is now freely available** on peut se procurer le livre facilement maintenant; **the wine was flowing freely** le vin coulait à flots

(**b**) *(liberally → spend)* largement; *(→ perspire, weep)* abondamment; **the plant grows freely in hot countries** cette plante pousse en abondance dans les pays chauds

freeman ['fri:mən] (*pl* **freemen** [-mən]) *n Hist* homme *m* libre; *(citizen)* citoyen *m*; **he's a freeman of the city** il est citoyen d'honneur de la ville

free-market *adj Econ*

▸▸ ***free-market economics*** libéralisme *m*; ***free-market economy*** économie *f* de marché

free-marketeer [-,mɑ:kɪ'tɪə(r)] *n Econ* libéral(e) *m,f*

freemason, Freemason ['fri:,meɪsən] *n* franc-maçon *m*

freemasonry, Freemasonry ['fri:,meɪsənrɪ] *n* franc-maçonnerie *f*

freenet ['fri:net] *n Comput* libertel *m*

Freepost® ['fri:pəʊst] *n Br* port *m* payé

free-range *adj (chicken)* fermier

▸▸ ***free-range eggs*** œufs *mpl* de poules élevées en plein air

freesheet ['fri:ʃi:t] *n* publication *f* gratuite

freesia ['fri:zjə] *n Bot* freesia *m*

free-spoken *adj* franc (franche)

freestanding [,fri:'stændɪŋ] *adj* non encastré; *Gram* indépendant

freestone ['fri:stəʊn] *n* pierre *f* de taille

freestyle ['fri:staɪl] **1** *n (in swimming)* nage *f* libre

2 *adj (skateboarding, snowboarding etc)* freestyle

▸▸ ***freestyle skiing*** ski *m* artistique

freethinker [,fri:'θɪŋkə(r)] *n* libre-penseur *m*

freethinking [,fri:'θɪŋkɪŋ] **1** *adj* de libre penseur

2 *n* libre pensée *f*

Freetown ['fri:taʊn] *n* Freetown

freeware ['fri:,weə(r)] *n Comput* logiciel *m* (du domaine) public, gratuiciel *m*

▸▸ ***freeware programs*** freewares *mpl*, logiciels *mpl* publics

freeway ['fri:weɪ] *n Am* autoroute *f*

freewheel [,fri:'wi:l] **1** *n (on bicycle)* roue *f* libre

2 *vi* (**a**) *(cyclist)* être en roue libre; **to freewheel down a slope** descendre une pente en roue libre (**b**) *(motorist)* rouler au point mort (**c**) *esp Am (travel in carefree fashion)* se laisser aller, aller sans but précis

freewheeling [,fri:'wi:lɪŋ] *adj Fam* désinvolte ❑, sans-gêne ❑ *(inv)*; **to lead a freewheeling existence** rouler sa bosse

freewoman ['fri:,wʊmən] (*pl* **freewomen** [-,wɪmɪn]) *n* (**a**) *(citizen)* citoyenne *f* (**b**) *(having the freedom of a city)* citoyenne *f* d'honneur

freeze [fri:z] (*pt* **froze** [frəʊz], *pp* **frozen** ['frəʊzən]) **1** *vi* (**a**) *(earth, pipes, water)* geler; *(food)* se congeler; **the river has frozen** la rivière est prise *ou* a gelé; **the earth had frozen hard** la terre avait gelé; **the mud/food had frozen solid** la boue/nourriture avait gelé; **to freeze to death** mourir de froid; **we'll freeze if you open the window!** nous allons geler si vous ouvrez la fenêtre!

(**b**) *Fig (stop moving)* **(everybody) freeze!** que personne ne bouge!; **she froze (in her tracks)** elle est restée figée sur place; **her blood froze** son sang se figea *ou* se glaça dans ses veines; **the smile froze on his lips** le sourire se figea sur ses lèvres

(**c**) *Comput (of screen, computer)* être bloqué

2 *vt* (**a**) *(water)* geler, congeler; *(food)* congeler; *(at very low temperatures)* surgeler; *Med (blood, human tissue)* congeler; *Fig* **she froze them with a look** d'un regard elle les glaça sur place; **to be frozen to death** mourir de froid

(**b**) *Econ & Fin (credit, wages)* geler, bloquer; *(currency, prices, assets)* geler

(**c**) *Cin* **freeze it!** arrêtez l'image!

3 *n Met* gel *m*; *Econ & Fin (of credit, wages)* gel *m*, blocage *m*; *(of currency, prices, assets)* gel *m*; **we're in for another big freeze** *Met* il va y avoir une période de très grand froid; *Econ* il va y avoir une crise économique; **they called for a freeze in the production of nuclear weapons** ils ont appelé à un gel de la production d'armes nucléaires; **pay freeze** gel *m ou* blocage *m* des salaires

▸**freeze out** [illegible] *(snub)* snober ❑

▸**freeze over** *vi* geler

▸**freeze up** *vi* (**a**) *(turn to ice)* geler (**b**) *Fam (person)* rester pétrifié

freeze-dried *adj* lyophilisé

freeze-dry *vt* lyophiliser

freeze-drying *n* lyophilisation *f*

freeze-frame *n Cin* arrêt *m* sur image

freezer ['fri:zə(r)] *n* congélateur *m*; *(in refrigerator)* freezer *m*; **in the freezer section of your supermarket** au rayon surgelés de votre supermarché

▸▸ ***freezer bag*** sac *m* congélation; ***freezer compartment*** compartiment *m* congélateur *(d'un réfrigérateur)*

freeze-up *n Fam* gel ❑ *m*

freezing ['fri:zɪŋ] **1** *adj Met* glacial; *(person)* gelé, glacé; **I'm freezing** je suis gelé; **a freezing wind was blowing** un vent glacial soufflait; **it's freezing in this room!** on gèle *ou* ça caille dans cette pièce!; **your hands are freezing** vous avez les mains gelées *ou* glacées

2 *n* (**a**) *(temperature)* **it's two degrees above/below freezing** il fait deux degrés au-dessus/au-dessous de zéro

(**b**) *Econ & Fin (of credit, wages)* blocage *m*, gel *m*; *(of currency, prices, assets)* gel *m*

3 *adv* **a freezing cold day** une journée glaciale; **it's freezing cold outside** il fait un froid glacial dehors

▸▸ ***freezing instructions*** *(for food)* consignes *fpl* pour la congélation; ***freezing point*** point *m* de congélation; *Met* ***freezing rain*** neige *f* fondue

Freiburg ['fraɪbɜ:g] *n Geog* Fribourg

freight [freɪt] **1** *n* (**a**) *(goods)* fret *m*; **to take in freight** *(load, cargo)* prendre du fret

(**b**) *(transport)* **to send goods by freight** envoyer des marchandises en régime ordinaire

2 *comp (transport)* de fret

3 *vt* (**a**) *(load → vessel)* charger

(**b**) *(hire → ship)* (af)fréter; *(→ of owner)* donner à fret

(**c**) *esp Am (transport)* transporter

▸▸ *Am* ***freight car*** wagon *m* de marchandises, fourgon *m*; ***freight charges*** fret *m*, frais *mpl* de transport; ***freight collect*** port *m* avancé; ***freight depot*** gare *f* de marchandises; *Am* ***freight elevator*** monte-charges *m inv*; ***freight forward*** port *m* avancé; ***freight forwarder*** agent *m* de fret, transitaire *m*; ***freight forwarding*** transit *m*; ***freight insurance*** assurance *f* sur fret; ***freight note*** bordereau *m* d'expédition; ***freight plane*** avion-cargo *m*, avion *m* de fret; ***freight release*** bon *m* à délivrer; ***freight shipping*** messageries *fpl* maritimes; ***freight terminal*** terminal *m* de fret; ***freight ton*** tonne *f* d'affrètement; *Am* ***freight train*** train *m* de marchandises; ***freight vehicle*** véhicule *m* de transport de marchandises; *Am* ***freight yard*** dépôt *m* de marchandises

freightage ['freɪtɪdʒ] *n* fret *m*, frais *mpl* de transport

freighter ['freɪtə(r)] *n Naut* navire *m* de charge; *Aviat* avion-cargo *m*, avion *m* de fret

Freightliner® ['freɪt,laɪnə(r)] *n* train *m* de transport de conteneurs

Fremantle doctor ['fri:,mæntəl-] *n Austr Fam (wind)* = vent du sud qui souffle sur la ville de Perth, en Australie

fremitus ['fremɪtəs] *n Med* frémissement *m*; **hydatic fremitus** frôlement *m* hydatique

French [frentʃ] **1** *npl* **the French** les Français *mpl*

2 *n (language)* français *m*; *Hum* **pardon** *or* **excuse my French!** passez-moi l'expression!

3 *adj* français; *Br Fam* **to take French leave** filer à l'anglaise

4 *comp (embassy, history)* de France; *(teacher)* de français

▸▸ ***French bean*** haricot *m* vert; ***French billiards*** billard *m* (français); ***French bread*** baguette *f*; *Geog* ***French Canada*** le Canada français; ***French Canadian*** **1** *n* Canadien(enne) *m,f* français(e) **2** *adj* canadien français; ***French chalk*** craie *f* de tailleur; ***French cricket*** = jeu pour enfants qui se joue avec une balle et une batte de cricket; *Tech* ***French curve*** pistolet *m* (de dessinateur); *Am* ***French dip*** = sandwich à la viande accompagné d'un bouillon ou d'une sauce à base de la même viande, dans lesquels on trempe le sandwich; *Am* ***French door*** porte-fenêtre *f*; *Culin* ***French dressing*** *(in UK)* vinaigrette *f*; *(in US)* = sauce de salade à base de mayonnaise et de ketchup; ***the French Foreign Legion*** la Légion étrangère; ***French franc*** franc *m* français; ***French fried potatoes*** pommes *fpl* frites; ***French fries*** frites *fpl*; ***French Guiana*** Guyane *f* française; ***French horn*** cor *m* d'harmonie; *Fam* ***French kiss*** **1** *n* patin *m* **2** *vt* rouler un patin à **3** *vi* se rouler un patin; *Br* ***French knickers*** ≃ caleçon *m (culotte pour femme)*; *Br Fam* ***French letter*** *(condom)* capote *f* anglaise; *Br* ***French loaf*** baguette *f*; ***French maid*** femme *f* de chambre française *(attachée au service particulier d'une dame)*; *Theat* soubrette *f*; ***French maid's outfit*** costume *m* de soubrette; ***French manicure*** French manucure *f*; ***French marigold*** œillet *m* d'Inde; ***French mustard*** ≃ moutarde *f* de Dijon; ***French onion soup*** gratinée *f* à l'oignon; ***French plait*** *(hairstyle)* natte *f* africaine; *Br* ***French polish*** vernis *m* (à l'alcool); ***the French Quarter*** *(in New Orleans)* le quartier

fre–fre

français, le Vieux Carré; *Hist* **the French Revolution** la Révolution (française); **the French Riviera** la Côte d'Azur; ***French roll*** *(hairstyle)* chignon *m* banane; *Sewing* **French seam** couture *f* anglaise; *Br* **French stick** baguette *f*; ***French Switzerland*** la Suisse romande; ***French toast*** pain *m* perdu; ***the French Triangle*** = région du sud des États-Unis comprise entre La Nouvelle-Orléans, Alexandria et Cameron; ***French West Africa*** l'Afrique-Occidentale *f* française; ***the French West Indies*** les Antilles *fpl* françaises; *Br* ***French window*** porte-fenêtre *f*

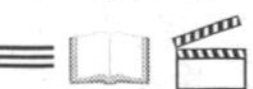

'The French Lieutenant's Woman' *Fowles, Reisz* 'Sarah et le lieutenant français' (roman), 'La Maîtresse du lieutenant français' (film)

Frenchie ['frentʃɪ] *Fam* **1** *n* (**a**) *(French person)* Français(e)□ *m,f* (**b**) *(French kiss)* patin *m* (**c**) *(French letter)* capote *f* anglaise

2 *adj* français□

Frenchified ['frentʃɪfaɪd] *adj Fam* francisé□, à la française□

Frenchify ['frentʃɪfaɪ] (*pt & pp* **Frenchified**) *vt Fam* franciser□

Frenchman ['frentʃmən] (*pl* **Frenchmen** [-mən]) *n* Français *m*

French-polish *vt Br* vernir (à l'alcool)

French-speaking *adj* francophone; **the French-speaking world** le monde francophone, la francophonie

Frenchwoman ['frentʃ,wʊmən] (*pl* **Frenchwomen** [-,wɪmɪn]) *n* Française *f*

Frenchy (*pl* **Frenchies**) = **Frenchie**

frenetic [frə'netɪk] *adj* frénétique

frenetically [frə'netɪklɪ] *adv* frénétiquement

frenum ['fri:nəm] *n Am Anat* frein *m*, filet *m*

frenzied ['frenzɪd] *adj (activity)* frénétique, forcené; *(crowd)* déchaîné; *(person)* forcené, déchaîné

frenziedly ['frenzɪdlɪ] *adv* frénétiquement

frenzy ['frenzɪ] *n* (**a**) *(fury, passion)* frénésie *f*; **to work oneself (up) into a frenzy** *(get angry)* se mettre dans une colère noire; *(get upset)* se mettre dans tous ses états; *(get very excited)* se mettre dans un état de surexcitation folle (**b**) *(fit, outburst)* accès *m*, crise *f*; **in a frenzy of anger** dans un accès *ou* une crise de colère

Freon® ['fri:ɒn] *n* Fréon® *m*

frequency ['fri:kwənsɪ] *n* fréquence *f*; **the increasing frequency of his absences** ses absences de plus en plus fréquentes

►► *Rad* ***frequency band*** bande *f* de fréquences; *Math* ***frequency distribution*** distribution *f* des fréquences; *Rad* ***frequency modulation*** modulation *f* de fréquence

frequent 1 *adj* ['fri:kwənt] *(visits etc)* fréquent; *(customer)* habituel; *(practice, custom)* très répandu; *(explanation, state of affairs etc)* commun, habituel; **it is a frequent occurrence** cela se produit souvent; **it is a frequent sight in the summer months** on en voit souvent pendant les mois d'été; **he became a frequent visitor to our house** il est devenu un habitué de la maison; **this bird is a frequent visitor to our shores** cet oiseau visite régulièrement nos rivages

2 *vt* [frɪ'kwent] *Formal* fréquenter

►► ***frequent flyer*** = personne qui prend souvent l'avion; ***frequent flyer club*** club *m* de fidélité de compagnie aérienne; ***frequent flyer programme*** programme *m* de fidélisation des passagers de compagnies aériennes; ***frequent use shampoo, frequent wash shampoo*** shampo(o)ing *m* pour lavages fréquents

frequentation [,fri:kwen'teɪʃən] *n Formal* fréquentation *f*

frequentative [frɪ'kwentətɪv] *adj Ling* fréquentatif

frequenter [frɪ'kwentə(r)] *n (of a house etc)* habitué(e) *m,f*, familier *m*; **a great frequenter of public houses** un pilier de bar

frequently ['fri:kwəntlɪ] *adv* fréquemment, souvent; **how frequently?** avec quelle fréquence?, *Fam* tous les combien?; **I can't say how frequently it happened** je ne saurais pas dire à quelle fréquence cela se produisait; *Comput* **frequently asked questions** foire *f* aux questions

fresco ['freskəʊ] (*pl* **frescoes** *or* **frescos**) *Art* **1** *n* fresque *f*; **fresco painter** fresquiste *mf*

2 *vt (wall, ceiling)* peindre à fresque

fresh [freʃ] **1** *adj* (**a**) *(recently made or produced)* frais (fraîche); **fresh bread/butter** pain *m*/beurre *m* frais; **I'll make some fresh coffee** je vais refaire du café; **fresh flowers** fleurs *fpl* fraîches; **the bread was fresh from the oven** le pain sortait du four; **the vegetables are fresh from the garden** les légumes viennent directement du jardin; **there were fresh tracks in the snow** il y avait des traces toutes fraîches dans la neige; **fresh from** *or* **out of university** (tout) frais émoulu de l'université

(**b**) *(new → idea, problem)* nouveau(elle), original; *(→ news, paint)* frais (fraîche); *(→ impression)* frais (fraîche); **a fresh approach** une approche nouvelle; **fresh capital** nouveaux capitaux *mpl*; **they have agreed to fresh talks** ils ont accepté de reprendre leurs négociations; **to make a fresh start** prendre un nouveau départ; **he put on a fresh shirt** il mit une chemise propre; **a fresh change of clothes/socks** des habits *mpl*/chaussettes *fpl* de rechange; **start on a fresh page** prenez une nouvelle page; **the incident was still fresh in his mind** le souvenir de l'incident était encore tout frais dans sa mémoire; **the memory of her loss was still fresh** le souvenir de sa mort était encore tout frais

(**c**) *(rested)* frais (fraîche); **I felt fresher after a shower** une douche m'a rafraîchi; **she looked fresh and relaxed** elle avait l'air fraîche et reposée; **as fresh as a daisy** frais comme un gardon

(**d**) *(air)* frais (fraîche), pur; *(taste)* rafraîchissant; *(cool)* frais; **I need some fresh air** j'ai besoin de prendre l'air; **in the fresh air** au grand air, en plein air; **to let fresh air into a room** aérer une pièce; **it's fresh this morning** il fait frais ce matin; **a fresh complexion** un teint frais; **the fresh scent of lemons** le parfum frais des citrons; **fresh colours** des couleurs *fpl* fraîches

(**e**) *Met (gen)* frais (fraîche); *(on Beaufort scale)* **fresh breeze** bonne brise *f*; **fresh gale** coup *m* de vent

(**f**) *(not salt → water)* doux (douce)

(**g**) *Am Fam (impudent)* insolent□; *(child)* mal élevé□; **don't you get fresh with me, young man!** pas d'insolence avec moi, jeune homme!

(**h**) *Am Fam (sexually forward)* effronté□; **he started to get fresh so she hit him** il a commencé à prendre des libertés avec elle alors elle l'a frappé

2 *adv* fraîchement; **fresh cut flowers** des fleurs *fpl* fraîchement cueillies; *Fam* **to be fresh out of sth** être en panne de qch

fresh-air fiend *n Fam* maniaque *mf* du grand air

fresh-complexioned *adj* au teint frais

freshen ['freʃən] **1** *vt* rafraîchir; *(colour)* raviver; *esp Am* **can I freshen your drink?** est-ce que je vous sers un autre verre?

2 *vi Naut (wind)* fraîchir

►**freshen up 1** *vi* faire un brin de toilette

2 *vt sep* (**a**) *(person)* faire un brin de toilette à; **to freshen oneself up** faire un brin de toilette; **to freshen up one's lipstick** se remettre du rouge à lèvres (**b**) *(house, room)* donner un petit coup de peinture à (**c**) *Am (drink)* **let me freshen up your drink** laisse-moi te resservir à boire

freshening ['freʃənɪŋ] *n (of air, atmosphere etc)* rafraîchissement *m*; *(of colour)* ravivage *m*

fresher ['freʃə(r)] *n Br Fam Univ* bizut *m*, bizuth *m*, étudiant(e) *m,f* de première année□

►► ***freshers' week*** = semaine d'accueil des étudiants de première année

freshet ['freʃɪt] *n* (**a**) *Literary (stream)* ruisseau *m*, ruisselet *m* (**b**) *(rise in water level)* crue *f*; *(flood)* inondation *f*

fresh-faced *adj (person)* au teint frais

freshly ['freʃlɪ] *adv* récemment; **freshly made coffee** du café qui vient d'être fait; **freshly squeezed orange juice** jus *m* d'oranges pressées; **the grave had been freshly dug** la fosse avait été fraîchement creusée

freshman ['freʃmən] (*pl* **freshmen** [-mən]) *Am Univ* étudiant(e) *m,f* de première année

freshness ['freʃnɪs] *n* fraîcheur *f*

fresh-run *adj Ich* nouvellement remonté de la mer

freshwater ['freʃ,wɔ:tə(r)] *adj*

►► ***freshwater fish*** poisson *m* d'eau douce; ***freshwater fishing*** pêche *f* en eau douce

fret [fret] (*pt & pp* **fretted**, *cont* **fretting**) **1** *vi (worry)* tracasser; **to fret about** *or* **over sb** se faire du souci pour qn; **don't fret, I'll be all right** ne te tracasse pas *ou* ne t'inquiète pas, tout ira bien; **the small boy was fretting for his mother** le petit garçon réclamait sa mère en pleurant; **the dog fretted for its owner** le chien s'agitait parce que son maître n'était pas là

2 *vt* (**a**) *(worry)* **to fret one's life away** passer sa vie à se tourmenter *ou* à se faire du mauvais sang

(**b**) *(erode, wear down)* ronger; **a fretted rope** une corde effilochée

(**c**) *(decorate → metal, wood)* chantourner

3 *n* (**a**) *Fam (state)* **to get in a fret about sth** se faire du mauvais sang *ou* se ronger les sangs à propos de qch

(**b**) *(on guitar)* touchette *f*, frette *f*

fretboard ['fretbɔ:d] *n (on guitar)* touche *f*

fretful ['fretfʊl] *adj* (**a**) *(anxious)* inquiet(ète); *(irritable, complaining)* grincheux, maussade; **a fretful child** un enfant grognon; **the baby's fretful crying** les pleurnichements *mpl* du bébé (**b**) *Literary (water)* agité, tourmenté; *(wind)* qui souffle par rafales

fretfully ['fretfʊlɪ] *adv* (**a**) *(anxiously → ask, say)* avec inquiétude; **the dog waited fretfully by the door** le chien attendait impatiemment à la porte (**b**) *(irritably)* d'une manière maussade; *(ask, say)* d'un ton grincheux *ou* maussade

fretfulness ['fretfʊlnɪs] *n* (**a**) *(anxiousness)* inquiétude *f* (**b**) *(irritableness)* irritabilité *f*

fretsaw ['fretsɔ:] *n Carp* scie *f* à chantourner

fretter ['fretə(r)] *n Entom* insecte *m* rongeur

fretting ['fretɪŋ] *n* (**a**) *(worrying)* inquiétude *f* (**over** à propos de); *(being upset)* agitation *f*; **I wish he'd stop his fretting!** si seulement il pouvait arrêter de se faire du mauvais sang! (**b**) *(of rope etc)* usure *f*

fretwork ['fretwɜ:k] *n Carp (technique)* découpage *m*, chantournement *m*; *(finished work)* travail *m* ajouré, bois *m* découpé *ou* chantourné

Freudian ['frɔɪdɪən] **1** *adj* freudien

2 *n* disciple *mf* de Freud

►► ***Freudian slip*** lapsus *m*

Freudianism ['frɔɪdɪənɪzəm] *n* freudisme *m*

FRG [,efɑ:'dʒi:] *n* (*abbr* **Federal Republic of Germany**) RFA *f*

Fri. (*written abbr* **Friday**) ven

friable ['fraɪəbəl] *adj* friable

friar ['fraɪə(r)] *n* frère *m*, moine *m*; **Grey Friars** Franciscains *mpl*; **Black Friars** Dominicains *mpl*; **White Friars** Carmes *mpl*

►► ***friar's balsam*** baume *m* de benjoin

friary ['fraɪərɪ] (*pl* **friaries**) *n* monastère *m*

fricassee ['frɪkəsi:] *Culin* **1** *n* fricassée *f*

2 *vt* fricasser

fricative ['frɪkətɪv] *Ling* **1** *adj* fricatif

2 *n* fricative *f*

friction ['frɪkʃən] *n* (**a**) *Phys* friction *f*; *(of two bodies)* frottement *m*; *(of scalp etc)* friction *f*

(**b**) *(discord)* friction *f*, conflit *m*; **it's an issue that often causes friction between neighbours** c'est un problème qui est souvent cause de frictions entre voisins

►► *Aut* ***friction clutch*** embrayage *m* à friction; *Aut* ***friction cylinder*** cylindre *m* de friction; *Aut* ***friction drive*** entraînement *m* par friction; *Comput* ***friction feed*** avancement *m* par friction; ***friction glove*** *(for massage)* gant *m* de crin; *Aut* ***friction lining*** garniture *f* de friction; *Aut* ***friction plate*** plateau *m* de friction; *Am* ***friction tape*** chatterton *m*

frictional ['frɪkʃənəl] *adj Tech (relating to friction)* de frottement; *(using friction)* à friction

►► ***frictional coefficient*** coefficient *m ou* indice *m* de frottement; ***frictional contact*** contact *m* par frottement; ***frictional drag*** *or* ***force*** résistance *f* de frottement; ***frictional-geared device*** appareil *m ou* dispositif *m* à embrayage à friction; ***frictional loss*** perte *f* par frottement; ***frictional resistance*** résistance *f* de frottement; ***frictional wake*** sillage *m* de frottement

frictionless ['frɪkʃənlɪs] *adj* sans friction

Friday ['fraɪdɪ] *n* vendredi *m*; **it's Friday today** nous sommes *ou* on est vendredi aujourd'hui; **I'll see you (on) Friday** je te verrai vendredi; **he leaves** *Br* **on Friday** *or Am* **Friday** il part vendredi; **the cleaning woman comes on Fridays** la femme de ménage vient le vendredi; **I work Fridays** je travaille le vendredi; **there's a market each Friday** *or* **every Friday** il y a un marché tous les vendredis *ou* chaque vendredi; **every other Friday, every second Friday** un vendredi sur deux; **the first/last Friday of every month** le premier/dernier vendredi de chaque mois; **we arrive on the Friday and leave on the Sunday** nous arrivons le vendredi et repartons le dimanche; **the programme's usually shown on a Friday** généralement cette émission passe le vendredi; **the following Friday** le vendredi suivant; **she saw the doctor last Friday** elle a vu le médecin vendredi dernier; **I have an appointment next Friday** j'ai un rendez-vous vendredi prochain; **the Friday after next** vendredi en huit; **the Friday before last** l'autre vendredi; **a week from Friday,** *Br* **a week on Friday,** *Br* **Friday week** vendredi en huit; *Br* **a fortnight on Friday, Friday fortnight** vendredi en quinze; **a week/fortnight ago Friday** il y a eu huit/quinze jours vendredi; **Friday morning** vendredi matin; **Friday afternoon** vendredi après-midi; **Friday evening** vendredi soir; **we're going out (on) Friday night** nous sortons vendredi soir; **she spent Friday night at her friend's house** elle a passé la nuit de vendredi chez son amie; **we caught the Friday morning boat** nous avons pris le bateau du vendredi matin; **Friday 26 February** vendredi 26 février; **they were married on Friday 12 June** ils se sont mariés le vendredi 12 juin; **Friday the thirteenth** vendredi treize

fridge [frɪdʒ] *n* réfrigérateur *m*

▸▸ ***fridge magnet*** aimant *m* décoratif, magnet *m*

fridge-freezer *n* réfrigérateur-congélateur *m*

fried [fraɪd] *adj* (**a**) *(cooked in frying pan)* frit; **fried egg** œuf *m* poêlé *ou* sur le plat; **fried food** friture *f*; **fried potatoes** pommes *fpl* frites; **(special) fried rice** riz *m* cantonais (**b**) *Am Fam (drunk)* bourré, pété; *(on drugs)* raide, parti

friend [frend] *n* (**a**) *(gen)* ami(e) *m,f*; **to make friends** se faire des amis; **he tried to make friends with her brother** il essaya d'être ami avec son frère; **she makes friends easily** elle se lie facilement, elle est très liante; **shall we be friends?** on est amis?; *(after a quarrel)* on fait la paix?; **his school friends** ses camarades *mfpl* d'école; **Lesley's a good friend of mine** Lesley est une grande amie à moi; **we're just good friends** nous sommes bons amis sans plus; **my best friend** mon meilleur ami, ma meilleure amie; **we're the best of friends** nous sommes les meilleurs amis du monde; **he's a friend of the family** c'est un ami de la famille; **he's always been a real friend to us** il a toujours été là quand on a eu besoin de lui; **she's someone I used to be friends with** nous avons été amies; **she's no friend of mine** elle ne fait pas partie de mes amis; **I tell you this as a friend** je vous dis ça en ami; **she doesn't realize what a good friend you are** elle n'apprécie pas votre amitié à sa juste valeur; **they wanted to part friends** ils voulaient se quitter bons amis; **you're among friends here** tu es entre amis ici; **a friend of yours is a friend of mine** tes amis sont mes amis; **she has friends in high places** elle a des amis en haut lieu *ou* bien placés; *Law* **friend of the court** = personne extérieure à un procès qui peut présenter son point de vue à la Cour; *Prov* **a friend in need is a friend indeed** = c'est dans le besoin qu'on reconnaît ses vrais amis; **friend or foe?** *(said by sentry)* qui va là?; *Ironic* **our old friend the flu virus** notre vieil ami, le virus de la grippe

(**b**) *(supporter → of law and order etc)* ami(e) *m,f*, partisan(e) *m,f*; *(→ of the arts)* mécène *m*, ami(e) *m,f*; **friend of the poor** bienfaiteur(trice) *m,f* des pauvres; **she's no friend of trade unionism** elle n'est pas favorable au syndicalisme; **the Friends of the Tate Gallery** les Amis de la Tate Gallery; *Rel* **the (Society of) Friends** la Société des Amis, les Quakers

(**c**) *(addressing someone)* **my dear friend** mon (ma) cher(ère); **listen, friend** écoute, mon vieux

(**d**) *(colleague)* collègue *mf*; **friends, we are gathered here tonight...** chers amis *ou* collègues, nous sommes réunis ici ce soir...

▸▸ ***Friends of the Earth*** les Amis de la Terre

> **How to win friends and influence people**
> Il s'agit du titre d'un ouvrage de l'auteur américain Dale Carnegie publié en 1937, que l'on pourrait traduire par "comment se faire des amis et influencer autrui".
> On utilise cette formule de manière allusive lorsque quelqu'un vient de dire une grossièreté ou vient de se comporter comme un rustre; on dira alors **he won't win friends and influence people that way** ("ce n'est pas comme ça qu'il se fera des amis et qu'il influencera autrui"); ou encore lorsque quelqu'un est mené par l'ambition: **he's got his eyes set on the top job and is desperately trying to win friends and influence people to help him get there** ("il est décidé à devenir patron et il fait tout ce qu'il peut pour se faire des amis et influencer autrui afin d'atteindre son objectif").

friendless ['frendlɪs] *adj* sans amis

friendlessness ['frendlɪsnɪs] *n* absence *f* d'amis

friendliness ['frendlɪnɪs] *n* gentillesse *f*; **an atmosphere of warmth and friendliness** une ambiance chaleureuse et sympathique

friendly ['frendlɪ] (*compar* **friendlier,** *superl* **friendliest**) **1** *adj* (**a**) *(person)* aimable, gentil; *(animal)* gentil; *(smile, advice, game)* amical; *(city, neighbours, face)* sympathique; **to be friendly to** *or* **towards sb** être gentil *ou* aimable avec qn; **a friendly welcome** *or* **reception** un accueil chaleureux; **that wasn't very friendly of him!** ce n'était pas très gentil de sa part!; **someone ought to have a friendly word with him and explain that...** quelqu'un devrait lui expliquer gentiment que...

(**b**) *(close, intimate)* ami; *(allied)* ami; **they've become very friendly lately** elles sont devenues très amies dernièrement; **she's very friendly with the boss all of a sudden** elle est très copine avec le patron tout d'un coup; **to be on friendly terms with sb** être en bons termes avec qn; **a friendly nation** un pays ami; **to get too friendly with sb** se montrer trop familier avec qn; *Fam* **don't let him get too friendly** garde tes distances avec lui; **a friendly plane** un avion allié

2 *n (game)* match *m* amical

▸▸ *Mil* ***friendly fire*** feu *m* allié; **to come under friendly fire** tomber sous le feu allié; ***the Friendly Islands*** Tonga *m*, les îles *fpl* des Amis; *Sport* ***friendly match*** match *m* amical; *Br Fin* ***friendly society*** société *f* de mutualité; *Fin* ***friendly takeover bid*** OPA *f* amicale

friendship ['frendʃɪp] *n* amitié *f*; **to form a friendship with sb** se lier d'amitié avec qn, nouer une amitié avec qn; **I would never jeopardize my friendship with him** pour rien au monde je ne compromettrais notre amitié; **he did it out of friendship for her** il l'a fait par amitié pour elle; **to live in peace and friendship** vivre en bonne intelligence; **the aim is to promote friendship between nations** le but est de promouvoir l'amitié entre les nations

frier = **fryer**

Friesian = **Frisian**

Friesland ['fri:zlənd] *n Geog* la Frise

frieze [fri:z] *n* (**a**) *Archit* frise *f* (**b**) *Tex* ratine *f*

frig [frɪg] *Vulg* (*pt & pp* **frigged,** *cont* **frigging**) **1** *vt (have sex with)* baiser avec

2 *vi (masturbate)* s'astiquer le bouton, se branler

▸**frig about, frig around** *vi very Fam (waste time)* traînailler, glandouiller; *(play the fool)* déconner

▸**frig off** *vi very Fam* **frig off!** va te faire foutre!

frigate ['frɪgət] *n* frégate *f*

▸▸ *Orn* ***frigate bird*** frégate *f*

frigging ['frɪgɪŋ] *very Fam* **1** *adj* fichu, foutu; **this frigging car** cette foutue bagnole, cette putain de bagnole; **what a frigging waste of time!** putain, quelle perte de temps!; **shut your frigging mouth!** ferme-la!, ferme ta gueule!

2 *adv* **don't frigging lie to me!** ne me mens pas, bordel!; **I'm frigging freezing!** je me les gèle!

fright [fraɪt] *n* (**a**) *(sudden fear)* frayeur *f*, peur *f*; **his face was pale with fright** il était vert de peur; **to take fright** s'effrayer (**at** de); **to give sb a fright** faire une frayeur à qn, faire peur à qn; **you gave me a terrible fright!** vous m'avez fait une de ces frayeurs *ou* peurs!; **I got the fright of my life when he said that** j'ai eu la peur de ma vie quand il a dit ça (**b**) *Fam (mess)* **you look an absolute fright** tu fais vraiment peur à voir

frighten ['fraɪtən] *vt* effrayer, faire peur à; **stop it, you're frightening me!** arrête, tu me fais peur!; **to frighten sb out of doing sth** dissuader qn de faire qch en lui faisant peur; **to frighten sb into doing sth** faire peur à qn pour qu'il fasse qch; **he is easily frightened** il s'effraie pour un rien; **these animals are easily frightened** ces animaux s'effarouchent d'un rien; **to frighten sb to death** *or* **out of their wits, to frighten the life out of sb** faire une peur bleue à qn

▸**frighten away** *vt sep* faire fuir (par la peur); *(animal)* effaroucher; **the burglars were frightened away by the police siren** effrayés par la sirène de police, les cambrioleurs ont pris la fuite

▸**frighten off** *vt sep* (**a**) *(cause to flee)* faire fuir; *(animal)* effaroucher (**b**) *(intimidate)* chasser, faire peur à, faire fuir; **rising inflation has frightened off potential investors** l'inflation croissante a fait fuir les investisseurs potentiels

frightened ['fraɪtənd] *adj* effrayé; **to be frightened of sth** avoir peur de qch; **I wasn't as frightened as you were** je n'avais pas aussi peur que vous; **I was too frightened to speak** je n'arrivais pas à parler tellement j'avais peur; **there's nothing to be frightened of** il n'y a rien à craindre; **he looked frightened** il avait l'air d'avoir peur; **frightened faces/children** des visages *mpl*/des enfants *mpl* apeurés

frightener ['fraɪtənə(r)] *n Fam* **to put the frighteners on sb** filer la trouille à qn

frightening ['fraɪtənɪŋ] *adj* effrayant; **the consequences are too frightening to think of** on n'ose pas imaginer les conséquences; **it's frightening to think what might have happened** ça fait peur de penser à ce qui aurait pu arriver

frighteningly ['fraɪtənɪŋlɪ] *adv* à faire peur; **the story was frighteningly true to life** l'histoire était d'un réalisme effrayant

frightful ['fraɪtfʊl] *adj* (**a**) *(horrible)* atroce, horrible, effroyable; **the soldier had frightful wounds** le soldat avait des blessures atroces (**b**) *Br Fam (unpleasant)* **we had a frightful time parking the car** on a eu un mal fou à garer la voiture (**c**) *Br Fam (as intensifier)* **he's a frightful bore** il est horriblement *ou* affreusement casse-pieds

frightfully ['fraɪtfʊlɪ] *adv Br* **he's a frightfully good dancer** il danse remarquablement bien; **it was frightfully generous of you to buy me lunch** c'était vraiment très généreux à vous de m'inviter à déjeuner; **I'm frightfully sorry** je suis absolument désolé; *Fam Hum* **frightfully frightfully** = maniérisme utilisé pour décrire les manières et l'accent de la haute bourgeoisie britannique

frightfulness ['fraɪtfʊlnɪs] *n* atrocité *f*

frigid ['frɪdʒɪd] *adj* (**a**) *(sexually)* frigide (**b**) *(smile, style, atmosphere)* glacial (**c**) *Geog & Met* glacial

▸▸ ***Frigid Zone*** régions *fpl* polaires

frigidity [frɪ'dʒɪdətɪ] *n* (**a**) *(coldness)* froideur *f* (**b**) *Psy* frigidité *f*

frigidly ['frɪdʒɪdlɪ] *adv (answer, reply etc)* d'un ton glacial; **frigidly polite** d'une politesse glaciale

frigidness ['frɪdʒɪdnɪs] *n (coldness)* froideur *f*

frigorific [frɪgə'rɪfɪk] *adj* frigorifique

frijoles [frɪ'həʊlɪz] *npl Culin* = purée de haricots rouges frits

frill [frɪl] **1** *n Tex* ruche *f*, volant *m*; *Culin* papillote *f*; *Zool* collerette *f*; **shirt frill** jabot *m*

2 frills *npl (ornamentation, luxuries)* **without frills** sans façon; **a cheap, basic package holiday with no frills** des vacances organisées simples et pas chères

frilled [frɪld] *adj (ribbon etc)* froncé, ruché; *(shirt)* à jabots

▸▸ *Zool* ***frilled lizard*** iguane *m* australien

frilly ['frɪlɪ] *adj* (**a**) *Tex* orné de fanfreluches (**b**) *(style)* affecté, apprêté

fringe [frɪndʒ] **1** *n* (**a**) *(decorative edge → on rug, carpet)* frange *f*; **a fringe of trees** une bordure d'arbres

(**b**) *(of hair)* frange *f*

(**c**) *(periphery)* périphérie *f*, frange *f*; **on the fringe** *or* **fringes of** en bordure de; *Fig* en marge de; **to live on the fringe of society** vivre en marge de la société; **to be on the radical fringe of a party** appartenir à la frange radicale d'un parti

(**d**) *Br Theat* **the Fringe (festival)** le festival off

(**e**) *(of golf green)* lisière *f*

2 *vt (rug, carpet)* franger; **the path was fringed with rosebushes** le sentier était bordé de rosiers; **palm-fringed beaches** des plages *fpl* bordées de palmiers

▸▸ ***fringe area*** zone *f* limitrophe; ***fringe benefits*** avantages *mpl* annexes *ou* en nature; ***fringe group*** frange *f*; ***fringe market*** marché *m* marginal; *Br* ***fringe theatre*** théâtre *m* d'avant-garde *ou* expérimental

fringed [frɪndʒd] *adj Tex* frangé, à frange; *(furniture)* garni *ou* orné d'une crépine

fringe-dweller *n Austr* = personne (généralement aborigène) vivant dans la misère à la périphérie d'une ville

fringing reef ['frɪndʒɪŋ-] *n Geog* récif *m* frangeant

frippery ['frɪpərɪ] *(pl* **fripperies***)* *n* (**a**) *(showy objects)* colifichets *mpl*, babioles *fpl*; *(on clothing)* fanfreluches *fpl* (**b**) *(ostentation)* mignardises *fpl*, chichi *m*

Frisbee® ['frɪzbɪ] *n* Frisbee® *m inv*

Frisco ['frɪskəʊ] *n Fam* = surnom donné à San Francisco

Frisian ['fri:ʒən] **1** *n* (**a**) *(person)* Frison(onne) *m,f* (**b**) *Ling* frison *m*

2 *adj* frison

▸▸ ***the Frisian Islands*** l'Archipel *m* frison

frisk [frɪsk] **1** *vi (play)* gambader; **the two kittens frisked about in the garden** les deux chatons gambadaient dans le jardin

2 *vt (search)* fouiller

3 *n (search)* fouille *f*; **to give sb a frisk** fouiller qn

friskily ['frɪskɪlɪ] *adv* (**a**) *(in a lively manner)* avec vivacité (**b**) *(sexually)* avec excitation

friskiness ['frɪskɪnɪs] *n* (**a**) *(liveliness)* vivacité *f* (**b**) *(sexual)* excitation *f* sexuelle

frisking ['frɪskɪŋ] *n (of suspect, traveller)* fouille *f*

frisky ['frɪskɪ] *(compar* **friskier**, *superl* **friskiest***)* *adj* (**a**) *(animal)* fringant, vivace (**b**) *(person → sexually)* gaillard; **to be feeling frisky** être excité

frisson ['fri:sɒn] *n* frisson *m*

fritillary [frɪ'tɪlərɪ] *n Bot & Zool* fritillaire *f*

fritter ['frɪtə(r)] **1** *n Culin* beignet *m*; **banana fritters** beignets *mpl* de banane

2 *vt (money, time)* gaspiller; *(fortune)* dissiper

▸**fritter away** *vt sep (money, time)* gaspiller; *(fortune)* dissiper; **I feel as if I've just frittered away the day** j'ai l'impression d'avoir perdu ma journée

fritz [frɪts] *n Am Fam* **to be on the fritz** *(TV, machine)* déconner, débloquer

▸**fritz out** *vi Am Fam (TV, machine)* rendre l'âme

frivolity [frɪ'vɒlətɪ] *(pl* **frivolities***)* *n* frivolité *f*

frivolous ['frɪvələs] *adj* frivole

frivolously ['frɪvələslɪ] *adv* de manière frivole

frizz [frɪz] **1** *n* **she had a frizz of blond hair** elle avait des cheveux blonds frisottés *ou* tout frisés

2 *vt* frisotter

3 *vi* frisotter

frizziness ['frɪzɪnɪs] *n* **the frizziness of my hair** mes cheveux *mpl* crépus

frizzle ['frɪzəl] **1** *vt* (**a**) *Culin (overcook)* griller; *(burn)* calciner, carboniser (**b**) *(curl)* faire friser

2 *vi* (**a**) *(cook noisily)* grésiller (**b**) *(curl)* friser

frizzy ['frɪzɪ] *adj (hair)* crêpelé, crépu

FRN [ˌefɑ:'ren] *n Banking (abbr* **floating-rate note***)* effet *m* à taux flottant

fro [frəʊ] *see* **to and fro**

frock [frɒk] *n (dress)* robe *f*; *Rel* froc *m*

▸▸ ***frock coat*** redingote *f*; *Fam Cin* ***frock flick*** film *m* en costumes ❑

Froebelian ['frø:bəljən] *adj* de Fröbel

frog [frɒg] **1** *n* (**a**) *Zool* grenouille *f*; *Fam* **to have a frog in one's throat** avoir un chat dans la gorge

(**b**) *(on uniform)* brandebourg *m*; *(on women's clothing)* soutache *f*

(**c**) *Vet (part of horse's hoof)* fourchette *f*

2 Frog *Br Fam* **1** *n (French person)* = terme xénophobe, souvent employé de manière humoristique, désignant un Français **2** *adj* français ❑; **they've got some Frog footballer playing for them** il y a un joueur français dans leur équipe; **I hate Frog food** j'ai horreur de la cuisine française

▸▸ *Culin* ***frog's legs*** cuisses *fpl* de grenouille; ***frog pond*** grenouillère *f*; *Bot* ***frog spit, frog spittle*** crachat *m* de coucou

frogfish ['frɒgfɪʃ] *(pl inv or* **frogfishes***)* *n Ich* baudroie *f*, lotte *f* de mer

frogged [frɒgd] *adj* à brandebourgs

froggery ['frɒgərɪ] *n* grenouillère *f*

Froggie = **Froggy**

frogging ['frɒgɪŋ] *n (UNCOUNT) (on clothing)* soutaches *fpl*

Froggy ['frɒgɪ] *Br Fam* **1** *n* = terme xénophobe, souvent employé de manière humoristique, désignant un Français

2 *adj* français ❑; **I hate Froggy food** j'ai horreur de la cuisine française

frogman ['frɒgmən] *(pl* **frogmen** [-mən]*)* *n* homme-grenouille *m*

frogmarch ['frɒgmɑ:tʃ] *vt Br (person)* emmener de force; **they frogmarched her out of the room** ils l'ont fait sortir de la pièce de force; **the protesters were frogmarched to a police van** les manifestants furent entraînés jusqu'au fourgon de police

frogspawn ['frɒgspɔ:n] *n Br* frai *m* de grenouilles

fro-ing ['frəʊɪŋ] *see* **to-ing and fro-ing**

frolic ['frɒlɪk] *(pt & pp* **frolicked**, *cont* **frolicking***)* **1** *vi* s'ébattre, gambader; **the children frolicked about on the grass** les enfants gambadaient sur la pelouse

2 *n (run)* gambades *fpl*, ébats *mpl*; *(game)* jeu *m*; **we let the dogs have a frolic in the park** on a laissé les chiens s'ébattre dans le parc

frolicking ['frɒlɪkɪŋ] *n (running)* gambades *fpl*, ébats *mpl*; *(games)* jeux *mpl*

frolicsome ['frɒlɪksəm] *adj* enjoué, badin

FROM [frəm, *stressed* frɒm]

de	▸ (a), (b), (d), (f), (j), (k)
à partir de	▸ (b), (c)
depuis	▸ (b)
d'après	▸ (i)

prep (**a**) *(indicating starting point → in space)* de; **Einstein came to this country from Germany** Einstein a quitté l'Allemagne pour s'établir ici; **her parents came from Russia** ses parents venaient de Russie; **where's your friend from?** d'où est *ou* vient votre ami?; **I've just come back from there** j'en reviens; **there are no direct flights from Hobart** il n'y a pas de vol direct à partir d'Hobart; **the 11:10 from Cambridge** le train de 11 heures 10 en provenance de Cambridge; **the airport is about 15 kilometres from the city centre** l'aéroport se trouve à 15 kilomètres environ du centre-ville; **it rained all the way from Calais to Paris** il a plu pendant tout le trajet de Calais à Paris; **I saw him from a long way off** je l'ai vu de loin; **it takes fifteen minutes from here to my house** il faut quinze minutes pour aller d'ici à chez moi; **from town to town** de ville en ville

(**b**) *(indicating starting point → in time)* de, à partir de, depuis; **from now on** désormais, dorénavant; **from that day** depuis ce jour, à partir de ce jour; **from morning till night** du matin au soir; **from the age of four** à partir de quatre ans; **she was unhappy from her first day at boarding school** elle a été malheureuse dès son premier jour à l'internat; **from the start** dès *ou* depuis le début; **a week from today** dans huit jours; **where will we be a year from now?** où serons-nous dans un an?; **she remembered him from her childhood** elle se souvenait de lui dans son enfance; **we've got food left over from last night** nous avons des restes d'hier soir

(**c**) *(indicating starting point → in price, quantity)* à partir de; **potatoes from 50 pence a kilo** des pommes de terre à partir de 50 pence le kilo; **knives from £2 each** des couteaux à partir de 2 livres la pièce; **the price has been increased from 50 pence to 60 pence** on a augmenté le prix de 50 pence à 60 pence; **6 from 14 is 8** 6 ôté de 14 donne 8; **we went from three employees to fifteen in a year** nous sommes passés de trois à quinze employés en un an; **the bird lays from four to six eggs** l'oiseau pond de quatre à six œufs; **every flavour of ice-cream from vanilla to pistachio** tous les parfums de glace de la vanille à la pistache

(**d**) *(indicating origin, source)* de; **who's the letter from?** de qui est la lettre?; **from...** *(on letter, parcel)* expéditeur/expéditrice...; **don't tell her that the flowers are from me** ne lui dites pas que les fleurs viennent de moi; **tell her that from me** dites-lui cela de ma part; **I got a phone call from her yesterday** j'ai reçu un coup de fil d'elle hier; **he got the idea from a book he read** il a trouvé l'idée dans un livre qu'il a lu; **where did you get the ring from?** où avez-vous eu la bague?; **you can get a money order from the post office** vous pouvez avoir un mandat à la poste; **I bought my piano from a neighbour** j'ai acheté mon piano à un voisin; **you mustn't borrow money from them** vous ne devez pas leur emprunter de l'argent; **she stole some documents from the ministry** elle a volé des documents au ministère; **who stole the key from her?** qui lui a volé la clef?; **I heard about it from the landlady** c'est la propriétaire qui m'en a parlé; **a scene from a play** une scène d'une pièce; **a quotation from Shakespeare** une citation tirée de Shakespeare; **he translates from English into French** il traduit d'anglais en français; **she still has injuries resulting from the crash** elle a encore des blessures qui datent de l'accident; **she's been away from work for a week** ça fait une semaine qu'elle n'est pas allée au travail; **they returned from their holidays yesterday** ils sont rentrés de vacances hier; **the man from the Inland Revenue** le monsieur du fisc

(**e**) *(off, out of)* **she took a book from the shelf** elle a pris un livre sur l'étagère; **he drank straight from the bottle** il a bu à même la bouteille; **she drew a gun from her pocket** elle sortit un revolver de sa poche; **he took a beer from the fridge** il a pris une bière dans le frigo; **guaranteed to remove stains from all surfaces** *(in advertisement)* enlève les taches sur toutes les surfaces

(**f**) *(indicating position, location)* de; **from the top you can see the whole city** du haut on voit toute la ville; **you get a great view from the bridge** on a une très belle vue du pont; **the rock juts out from the cliff** le rocher dépasse de la falaise

(**g**) *(indicating cause, reason)* **you can get sick from drinking the water** vous pouvez tomber malade en buvant l'eau; **his back hurt from lifting heavy boxes** il avait mal au dos après avoir soulevé des gros cartons; **I guessed she was Australian from the way she spoke** j'ai deviné qu'elle était australienne à sa façon de parler; **I know him from seeing him at the club** je le reconnais pour l'avoir vu au cercle; **he died from grief** il est mort de chagrin; **to act from conviction** agir par conviction

(**h**) *(using)* **they are made from flour** ils sont faits à base de farine; **Calvados is made from apples** le calvados est fait avec des pommes; **she played the piece from memory** elle joua le morceau de mémoire; **I speak from personal experience** je sais de quoi je parle

(**i**) *(judging by)* d'après; **from the way she talks you'd think she were the boss** à l'entendre, on croirait que c'est elle le patron; **from the way she sings you'd think she were a professional** à l'entendre chanter on dirait que c'est son métier; **from his looks you might suppose that...** à le voir on dirait que...; **from what I can see...** à ce que je vois...; **from what I gather...** d'après ce que j'ai cru comprendre...

(**j**) *(in comparisons)* de; **it's no different from riding a bike** c'est comme faire du vélo; **how do you tell one from the other?** comment les reconnais-tu l'un de l'autre?

(**k**) *(indicating prevention, protection)* de; **she**

saved me from drowning elle m'a sauvé de la noyade; **we sheltered from the rain in a cave** nous nous sommes abrités de la pluie dans une caverne; **they were hidden from view** on ne les voyait pas

frond [frɒnd] *n Bot (of fern)* fronde *f*; *(on palm tree)* feuille *f*

frondage ['frɒndɪdʒ] *n Bot* ensemble *m* des frondes

fronded ['frɒndɪd] *adj Bot* à frondes

frondose ['frɒndəʊs], **frondous** ['frɒndəs] *adj Bot* feuillu

FRONT [frʌnt]

devant	► **1 (a); 6; 7**
avant	► **1 (a)**
bord de mer	► **1 (b)**
front	► **1 (c), (d), (g)**
façade	► **1 (e), (f), (h)**
de devant	► **2 (a)**
de façade	► **2 (b)**
par devant	► **3**
diriger	► **5 (c)**
à l'avant	► **6**
en avant	► **6**

1 *n* (**a**) *(forward part)* devant *m*; *(of vehicle)* avant *m*; *(of queue)* début *m*; *(of stage)* devant *m*; *(of building)* façade *f*; *(of shop)* devanture *f*; **I'll be at the front of the train** je serai en tête de *ou* à l'avant du train; **he sat up front near the driver** il s'est assis à l'avant près du conducteur; **our seats were at the front of the theatre** nous avions des places aux premiers rangs (du théâtre); **come to the front of the class** venez devant; **she went to the front of the queue** elle alla se mettre au début de la queue; **to push one's way to the front** se frayer un chemin jusqu'au premier rang; *Fig* se pousser (en avant); **the actors stood at the front of the stage** les comédiens étaient debout sur le devant de la scène; **The Times's theatre critic is out front tonight** le critique dramatique du Times est dans la salle ce soir; **at the front of the book** au début du livre; **she wrote her name on the front of the envelope** elle écrivit son nom sur le devant de l'enveloppe; **he got wine down his front** *or* **the front of his shirt** du vin a été renversé sur le devant de sa chemise; **his portrait was in the front of every schoolbook** son portrait figurait sur la couverture de tous les livres de classe

(**b**) *(seashore)* bord *m* de mer, front *m* de mer; **the hotel is on the front** l'hôtel est au bord de la *ou* sur le front de mer; **a walk along** *or* **on the front** une promenade au bord de la mer

(**c**) *Mil* front *m*; **on the Eastern/Western front** sur le front Est/Ouest; **he fought at the front** il a combattu au front; *Fig* **the Prime Minister is being attacked on all fronts** on s'en prend au Premier ministre de tous côtés; **little had been achieved on the domestic** *or* **home front** on avait accompli peu de choses sur le plan intérieur

(**d**) [illegible] **to present a united front (on sth)** faire front commun (devant qch)

(**e**) *(appearance)* façade *f*; **his apparent optimism was only a front** son optimisme apparent n'était qu'une façade; **to put on a bold** *or* **brave front** faire preuve de courage

(**f**) *(cover)* façade *f*, couverture *f*; **the shop is just a front for a drugs ring** le magasin n'est qu'une couverture pour des trafiquants de drogue

(**g**) *Met* front *m*; **cold/warm front** front *m* froid/chaud

(**h**) *Archit* façade *f*; **the north/south front** la façade nord/sud

(**i**) *Br Fam (nerve)* **to have the front to do sth** avoir l'effronterie *ou* le front de faire qch ❑

(**j**) *Fam (idiom)* **to pay up front** payer d'avance ❑; **they want £5,000 up front** ils veulent 5000 livres d'avance; **he was very up front about it** il a été franc sur ce point ❑

2 *adj* (**a**) *(in a forward position)* de devant; *Aut* **front seat/wheel** siège *m*/roue *f* avant; **she was sitting in the front row** elle était assise au premier rang; *Press* **the front page** la première page; **his picture is on the front page** sa photo est en première page; **to be front page news** faire la une; **he came in through a front window** il est entré par une fenêtre de devant; **I'll be in the front end of the train** je serai en tête de *ou* à l'avant du train; **the front part of the brain** la partie antérieure du cerveau; **his name is on the front cover** son nom est en couverture; **a front view** une vue de face; *Archit* une élévation du devant

(**b**) *(bogus, fake)* de façade

(**c**) *Ling* **a front vowel** une voyelle avant *ou* antérieure

(**d**) *Am Fam (idiom)* **to put sth on the front burner** traiter qch en priorité ❑

3 *adv* par devant; *Mil* **eyes front!** fixe!

4 *vi* (**a**) *Br (face)* **the hotel fronts onto the beach** l'hôtel donne sur la plage; **the house fronts north** la maison est exposée *ou* orientée au nord

(**b**) *Mil* faire front; **left front!** à gauche front!, à gauche, gauche!

(**c**) *(cover)* **the newspaper fronted for a terrorist organization** le journal servait de façade à une organisation terroriste

(**d**) *Fam Black Am slang (show off)* frimer; *(tell lies)* baratiner, raconter des craques

5 *vt* (**a**) *(stand before → of building)* donner une (nouvelle) façade à; **lush gardens fronted the building** il y avait des jardins luxuriants devant le bâtiment

(**b**) *Constr* **the house was fronted with stone** la maison avait une façade en pierre

(**c**) *(lead)* être à la tête de, diriger; *TV (present)* présenter; *Mus* **to front a band** *(lead it)* diriger un orchestre

(**d**) *Am Fam (pay in advance)* avancer ❑; **the cashier can front you the money** le caissier peut vous faire une avance *ou* vous avancer l'argent

(**e**) *Am Fam (give, lend money to)* filer; **can you front me five bucks?** tu pourrais pas me filer cinq dollars?

6 in front *adv (in theatre, vehicle)* à l'avant; *(ahead, leading)* en avant; **there was a very tall man in the row in front** il y avait un très grand homme assis devant moi; **the women walked in front and the children behind** les femmes marchaient devant et les enfants derrière; **to send sb on in front** envoyer qn devant; *Sport* **to be in front** être en tête *ou* premier; **Manchester United are 5 points in front** Manchester United mène par 5 points

7 in front of *prep* devant; **she was sitting in front of the TV** elle était assise devant la télé; **he was right in front of me** il était juste devant moi; **not in front of the children!** pas devant les enfants!

►► ***front desk*** réception *f*; ***front door*** *(of house)* porte *f* d'entrée; *(of vehicle)* portière *f* avant; *Theat* ***front of house*** = partie d'un théâtre où peuvent circuler les spectateurs; *Mil* ***the front line*** la première ligne; *Fig* **she is in the front line in the fight against drug abuse** elle joue un rôle important dans la lutte contre la toxicomanie; *Am* ***front lot*** cour *f (devant un immeuble)*; ***front man*** *(representative, spokesman)* porte-parole [illegible] *(figurehead)* prête-nom *m*; *TV (presenter)* présentateur *m*; ***front matter*** = pages préliminaires (avant le texte) d'un livre; *Am Fam* ***front money*** capital *m* initial ❑ *ou* de départ ❑, mise *f* de fonds initiale ❑; *Banking* ***front office*** front-office *m*; *Cin* ***front projection*** projection *f* frontale; ***front room*** *(at front of house)* = pièce qui donne sur le devant de la maison; *(sitting room)* salon *m*; *Am* ***front yard*** jardin *m (devant une maison)*

frontage ['frʌntɪdʒ] *n* (**a**) *(of house, building)* façade *f*; *(shopfront)* devanture *f* (**b**) *(of river etc)* terrain *m* en bordure; **garden with river frontage** jardin *m* en bordure de rivière (**c**) *(land at front of building etc)* espace *m* sur le devant d'un immeuble

►► *Am* ***frontage road*** contre-allée *f*

frontager ['frʌntɪdʒə(r)] *n* riverain(e) *m,f*

frontal ['frʌntəl] **1** *adj Mil (assault, attack)* de front; *Anat & Med* frontal

2 *n Rel* parement *m* d'autel

►► *Aut* ***frontal impact*** choc *m* frontal; *Aut* ***frontal impact test*** test *m* de choc frontal; *Met* ***frontal system*** système *m* de fronts

frontbench [ˌfrʌnt'bentʃ] *n Br Pol (members of the government)* ministres *mpl*; *(members of the opposition)* ministres *mpl* du cabinet fantôme; **he's never been on the frontbench** *(government)* il n'a jamais été ministre; *(opposition)* il n'a jamais été membre du cabinet fantôme; **the frontbenches** *(in Parliament)* = à la Chambre des communes, bancs situés à droite et à gauche du président et occupés respectivement par les ministres du gouvernement en exercice et ceux du gouvernement fantôme

►► ***frontbench spokesperson*** *(of cabinet)* porte-parole *m* du gouvernement; *(of shadow cabinet)* porte-parole *m* du cabinet fantôme; ***frontbench team*** *(cabinet)* équipe *f* ministérielle; *(shadow cabinet)* cabinet *m* fantôme

frontbencher [ˌfrʌnt'bentʃə(r)] *n Br Pol (member of the government)* ministre *m*; *(member of the opposition)* membre *m* du cabinet fantôme

front-end *n Comput* interface *f*

►► *Comput* ***front-end computer*** ordinateur *m* frontal; *Fin* ***front-end fee*** frais *mpl* d'entrée; *Fin* ***front-end loading*** = système de prélèvement des frais sur les premiers versements; *Comput* ***front-end processor*** processeur *m* frontal

frontier [*Br* 'frʌnˌtɪə(r), *Am* frʌn'tɪər] **1** *n* (**a**) *also Fig (border)* frontière *f*; **the frontiers of science** les frontières *fpl ou* limites *fpl* de la science

(**b**) *Am* **the Frontier** la Frontière *(nom donné à la limite des terres habitées par les colons pendant la colonisation de l'Amérique du Nord)*

2 *comp* (**a**) *(dispute)* de frontière; *(post)* frontière

(**b**) *Am (spirit)* de pionnier

►► ***frontier town*** = ville de l'Ouest américain, à l'époque des pionniers

frontiersman [*Br* 'frʌntɪəzmən, *Am* frʌn'tɪərzmən] (*pl* **frontiersmen** [-mən]) *n* pionnier *m*

frontispiece ['frʌntɪsˌpiːs] *n* frontispice *m*

front-line *adj Mil (soldiers, troops)* en première ligne; *(ambulance)* de zone de combat

►► *Am Sport* ***front-line player*** avant *m*; *Pol* ***the front-line states*** les États *mpl* limitrophes *(d'un pays en guerre)*

front-loader *n (washing machine)* machine *f* à laver à chargement frontal

front-loading *adj (washing machine)* à chargement frontal

front-of-house *adj (staff)* en contact direct avec le public

►► ***front-of-house manager*** directeur(trice) *m,f* administratif(ive)

frontogenesis [ˌfrʌntəʊ'dʒenɪsɪs] *n Met* frontogénèse *f*

frontolysis [frʌn'tɒlɪsɪs] *n Met* frontolyse *f*

fronton ['frʌntən] *n Archit* fronton *m*

front-page *adj (article, story)* de première page; **it wasn't exactly front-page news** ça n'a pas fait la une des journaux

front-rank *adj (question, issue)* de premier ordre *ou* plan

front-row [-rəʊ] *adj Sport* **front-row forward** *(in rugby)* avant *m* de première ligne, première ligne *f*; **to have a front-row seat** *Theat* être assis [illegible] premières loges

front-runner *n* (**a**) *Sport (horse)* cheval *m* de tête; *(athlete)* coureur(euse) *m,f* de tête (**b**) *(in election etc)* favori(ite) *m,f*

front-running *n* (**a**) *St Exch* = type de délit d'initié où un opérateur vend ou achète des valeurs pour son propre compte avant d'effectuer pour un client une grosse opération susceptible d'influencer les cours (**b**) *Sport* = fait de mener la course

frontwards ['frʌntwədz] *adv* en avant, vers l'avant

front-wheel drive *n Aut* traction *f* avant

frontwise ['frʌntwaɪz] *adv* de face

frosh [frɒʃ] *n Am Fam Univ* étudiant(e) *m,f* de première année ❑

frost [frɒst] **1** *n* (**a**) *(freezing weather)* gel *m*, gelée *f*; **there was a frost last night** il a gelé hier soir; **heavy/light frost** grosse/petite gelée *f*; **a late frost** des gelées *fpl* tardives; **eight degrees of frost** huit degrés au-dessous de zéro

(**b**) *(frozen dew)* givre *m*, gelée *f* blanche; **the**

grass was covered in frost le gazon était couvert de givre
(**c**) *Am Fam (fiasco)* four *m*, fiasco *m*
2 *vt* (**a**) *(freeze)* geler; *(cover with frost)* givrer; **the rim of the glass was frosted with sugar** le bord du verre avait été givré avec du sucre
(**b**) *Am (cake)* glacer
(**c**) *Tech (glass pane)* dépolir
3 *vi (freeze)* geler; *(become covered with frost)* se givrer
►**frost over, frost up 1** *vi* se givrer
2 *vt sep* givrer
frostbite ['frɒstbaɪt] *n (UNCOUNT)* gelure *f*; **he got frostbite in his toes** il a eu les orteils gelés; **the climber died of frostbite** l'alpiniste est mort gelé
frostbitten ['frɒst,bɪtən] *adj (hands, nose)* gelé; *(plant)* gelé, grillé par le gel
frostbound ['frɒstbaʊnd] *adj (earth)* gelé
frosted ['frɒstɪd] *adj* (**a**) *(frozen)* gelé; *(covered with frost)* givré (**b**) *(pane of glass)* dépoli (**c**) *Am (cake → iced)* glacé; *(→ sugared)* recouvert de sucre (**d**) *(lipstick, nail varnish)* nacré (**e**) *(hair)* grisonnant; **his hair was frosted with white** ses cheveux grisonnaient
frost-free *adj (refrigerator, freezer)* à dégivrage automatique
frostily ['frɒstɪlɪ] *adv (greet)* de manière glaciale, froidement; *(say)* sur un ton glacial
frostiness ['frɒstɪnɪs] *n* (**a**) *(of weather, air, morning)* froid *m* glacial (**b**) *(of person)* manière *f* glaciale; **the frostiness of her smile/behaviour** son sourire *m*/comportement *m* glacial
frosting ['frɒstɪŋ] *n Am (for icing)* glaçage *m*, glace *f*
frostproof ['frɒstpruːf] *adj* résistant à la gelée
frost-shoe *vt (horse)* ferrer à glace
frostwork ['frɒstwɜːk] *n (on windows)* gelée *f*, fleurs *fpl* de givre
frosty ['frɒstɪ] (*compar* **frostier,** *superl* **frostiest**) *adj* (**a**) *(weather, air)* glacial; **we had several frosty nights** il a gelé plusieurs nuits (**b**) *(ground, window)* couvert de givre (**c**) *(answer, manner)* glacial, froid
froth [frɒθ] **1** *n (UNCOUNT)* (**a**) *(foam)* écume *f*, mousse *f*; *(on beer, coffee, chocolate)* mousse *f*; *(on lips)* écume *f*
(**b**) *(trivialities, empty talk)* futilités *fpl*
2 *vi (liquid)* écumer, mousser; *(beer, soap)* mousser; **the detergent frothed out of the washing machine** la mousse a débordé de la machine à laver; **to froth at the mouth** écumer, baver; *Fam* **he was so angry he was practically frothing at the mouth** il écumait de rage
3 *vt* faire mousser
frothiness ['frɒθɪnɪs] *n* (**a**) *(of liquid, drink)* état *m* mousseux; *(of sea)* état *m* écumeux (**b**) *(of entertainment, literature)* futilité *f*, manque *m* de substance
frothy ['frɒθɪ] (*compar* **frothier,** *superl* **frothiest**) *adj* (**a**) *(liquid)* mousseux, écumeux; *(beer, coffee, chocolate)* mousseux; *(sea)* écumeux (**b**) *(entertainment, literature)* creux, futile, sans substance (**c**) *(dress, lace)* léger, vaporeux
frottage ['frɒtɑːʒ] *n* (**a**) *Art* frottis *m* (**b**) *(sexual practice)* = pratique sexuelle qui consiste à se frotter contre une personne ou un objet
frown [fraʊn] **1** *vi* froncer les sourcils, se renfrogner; **she frowned at my remark** mon observation lui a fait froncer les sourcils; **to frown at sb** regarder qn en fronçant les sourcils
2 *n* froncement *m* de sourcils; **she looked up with a disapproving/worried frown** elle leva les yeux avec un froncement de sourcils désapprobateur/inquiet; **he gave a frown** il fronça les sourcils; *Literary* **the frowns of fortune** les rigueurs *fpl* du sort
►► ***frown lines*** rides *fpl* intersourcilières
►**frown on, frown upon** *vt insep* désapprouver; **her parents frown upon their friendship** ses parents voient leur amitié d'un mauvais œil; **such behaviour is rather frowned upon** ce type de comportement n'est pas vu d'un très bon œil *ou* n'est pas très bien vu
frowning ['fraʊnɪŋ] *adj (expression)* renfrogné
frowningly ['fraʊnɪŋlɪ] *adv* en fronçant les sourcils
frowst [fraʊst] *Br Fam* **1** *n* atmosphère *f* qui sent le renfermé ❑, odeur *f* de renfermé ❑
2 *vi* rester enfermé au coin du feu ❑
frowstiness ['fraʊstɪnɪs] *n Br Fam* manque *m* d'air ❑, odeur *f* de renfermé ❑
frowsty ['fraʊstɪ] (*compar* **frowstier,** *superl* **frowstiest**) *adj Br Fam* qui sent le renfermé ❑
frowsy, frowzy ['fraʊzɪ] (*compar* **frowsier, frowzier,** *superl* **frowsiest, frowziest**) *adj Br Fam* (**a**) *(shabby → person)* négligé ❑; *(→ clothing)* élimé ❑, râpé ❑ (**b**) *Fam (stuffy → room)* qui sent le renfermé ❑
froze [frəʊz] *pt of* **freeze**
frozen ['frəʊzən] **1** *pp of* **freeze**
2 *adj* (**a**) *(ground, lake, pipes)* gelé; *(person)* gelé, glacé; **frozen peas** petits pois *mpl* surgelés; **the lake is frozen solid** le lac est complètement gelé; **my hands are frozen** j'ai les mains gelées *ou* glacées; **I'm frozen stiff** je suis gelé jusqu'à la moelle (des os); *Fig* **frozen with terror** mort de peur
(**b**) *(credit, wages)* gelé, bloqué; *(currency, prices, assets)* gelé; *(account)* bloqué
(**c**) *Comput (screen)* bloqué
►► ***frozen food*** *(in refrigerator)* aliments *mpl* congelés; *(industrially frozen)* surgelés *mpl*; ***frozen food compartment*** congélateur *m*; *Med* ***frozen shoulder*** épaule *f* ankylosée; ***frozen yoghurt*** yaourt *m* glacé
FRS [,efɑː'res] *n* (**a**) (*abbr* **Fellow of the Royal Society**) ≃ membre *m* de l'Académie des sciences (**b**) *Am* (*abbr* **Federal Reserve System**) (système *m* de) Réserve *f* fédérale
fructiferous [frʌk'tɪfərəs] *adj Bot* frugifère, fructifère
fructification [,frʌktɪfɪ'keɪʃən] *n Formal* fructification *f*
fructiform ['frʌktɪ,fɔːm] *adj Bot* fructiforme, carpomorphe
fructify ['frʌktɪfaɪ] (*pt & pp* **fructified**) *Formal* **1** *vt* faire fructifier
2 *vi* fructifier
fructivorous [frʌk'tɪvərəs] *adj Zool* frugivore
fructose ['frʌktəʊs] *n Chem* fructose *m*
►► ***fructose syrup*** sirop *m* de fructose
fructuous ['frʌktjʊəs] *adj* fructueux; *(soil)* fertile, fécond
frugal ['fruːgəl] *adj* (**a**) *(person)* économe, frugal; *(life)* frugal, simple; **she's very frugal with her money** elle est près de ses sous (**b**) *(meal)* frugal
frugality [fruː'gælətɪ] *n* (**a**) *(of person)* parcimonie *f*, frugalité *f*; *(of life)* frugalité *f*, simplicité *f* (**b**) *(of meal)* frugalité *f*
frugally ['fruːgəlɪ] *adv (live)* simplement, frugalement; *(distribute, give)* parcimonieusement; **we dined frugally on bread and cheese** nous avons dîné simplement de pain et de fromage
frugiferous [frʊ'dʒɪfərəs] *adj Bot* frugifère, fructifère
frugivorous [frʊ'dʒɪvərəs] *adj Zool* frugivore
fruit [fruːt] (*pl sense* (**a**) **inv** *or* **fruits**) **1** *n* (**a**) *(gen)* fruit *m*; **to eat fruit** manger des fruits; **a piece of fruit** un fruit; **would you like fruit or cheese?** voulez-vous un fruit ou du fromage?; **we eat a lot of fruit** nous mangeons beaucoup de fruits; **a tree in fruit** un arbre qui porte des fruits; **the fruit** *or* **fruits of the earth** les fruits *mpl* de la terre; *Fig* **the fruit of her womb** le fruit de ses entrailles; **their plans have never borne fruit** leurs projets ne se sont jamais réalisés; **his book is the fruit of much research** son livre est le fruit de longues recherches
(**b**) *Br Fam Old-fashioned (term of address)* **old fruit** mon vieux
(**c**) *Am very Fam Pej (homosexual)* pédé *m*, tante *f*
(**d**) *Am Fam (strange person)* **he's a real fruit** il est vraiment loufoque
2 *comp (basket)* à fruits; *(diet, farm, stall)* fruitier; *(flavouring)* de *ou* aux fruits
3 *vi Bot* donner
►► *Zool* ***fruit bat*** chauve-souris *f* frugivore; *Bot* ***fruit body*** *(of mushroom)* corps *m* fructifère; ***fruit bowl*** coupe *f* à fruits, compotier *m*; ***fruit cocktail*** macédoine *f* de fruits; ***fruit cup*** *(dessert)* coupe *f* de fruits; *(drink)* boisson *f* aux fruits *(parfois alcoolisée)*; ***fruit dish*** *(individual)* coupe *f*, coupelle *f*; *(large)* coupe *f* à fruits, compotier *m*; ***fruit drop*** bonbon *m* aux fruits; ***fruit farmer*** arboriculteur(trice) *m,f* (fruitier (ère)); ***fruit farming*** arboriculture *f* (fruitière); *Entom* ***fruit fly*** mouche *f* du vinaigre, drosophile *f*; ***fruits of the forest*** fruits *mpl* des bois, *Suisse* petits fruits *mpl*; *Br* ***fruit gum*** boule *f* de gomme; ***fruit juice*** jus *m* de fruits; ***fruit knife*** couteau *m* à fruit(s); *Br* ***fruit machine*** machine *f* à sous; ***fruit salad*** salade *f* de fruits; ***fruit salts*** sels *mpl* purgatifs; ***fruit sugar*** fructose *m*; ***fruit tree*** arbre *m* fruitier
fruitarian [fruː'teərɪən] **1** *n* fruitarien(enne) *m,f*
2 *adj* fruitarien
fruit-bearing *adj (tree etc)* frugifère, fructifère
fruitcake ['fruːtkeɪk] *n* (**a**) *(cake)* cake *m* (**b**) *Fam (lunatic)* cinglé(e) *m,f*
fruit-eating *adj (animal)* frugivore
fruited ['fruːtɪd] *adj Bot* portant des fruits, chargé de fruits
fruiter ['fruːtə(r)] *n* (**a**) *Naut* navire *m* transporteur de fruits, cargo *m* fruitier (**b**) *Bot* arbre *m* fruitier; **a sure fruiter** un arbre fruitier à rendement assuré (**c**) *(person)* fructiculteur(trice) *m,f*
fruiterer ['fruːtərə(r)] *n Br* marchand(e) *m,f* de fruits, fruitier(ère) *m,f*
fruitful ['fruːtfʊl] *adj* (**a**) *(discussion, suggestion)* fructueux, utile; *(attempt, collaboration)* fructueux (**b**) *(soil)* fertile, fécond; *(plant, tree)* fécond, productif
fruitfully ['fruːtfʊlɪ] *adv* fructueusement
fruitfulness ['fruːtfʊlnɪs] *n* (**a**) *(of work, discussion etc)* caractère *m* fructueux (**b**) *(of soil)* fertilité *f*; *(of tree etc)* productivité *f*
fruiting ['fruːtɪŋ] *adj (tree etc)* frugifère, fructifère
fruition [fruː'ɪʃən] *n Formal* réalisation *f*; **to come to fruition** se réaliser; **to bring sth to fruition** réaliser qch, concrétiser qch
fruitless ['fruːtlɪs] *adj* (**a**) *(discussion, effort)* infructueux; **at least the trip won't have been entirely fruitless** au moins le voyage n'aura pas tout à fait servi à rien (**b**) *(plant, tree)* stérile, infécond; *(soil)* stérile
fruitlessly ['fruːtlɪslɪ] *adv* en vain, vainement
fruitwood ['fruːtwʊd] *n* bois *m* fruitier
fruity ['fruːtɪ] (*compar* **fruitier,** *superl* **fruitiest**) *adj* (**a**) *(flavour, sauce)* fruité, de fruit; *(perfume, wine)* fruité; **the wine has a fruity taste** le vin a un goût fruité; **it has a fruity smell** ça a une odeur fruitée (**b**) *(voice)* étoffé, timbré (**c**) *Fam (joke, story)* corsé, salé
frump [frʌmp] *n* femme *f* mal fagotée; **she looks a bit of a frump these days** elle se fagote vraiment mal ces temps-ci
frumpily ['frʌmpɪlɪ] *adv* **frumpily dressed** mal fagoté
frumpiness ['frʌmpɪnɪs] *n* manque *m* d'élégance
frumpish ['frʌmpɪʃ] *adj* mal fagoté; **she wears rather frumpish clothes** elle s'habille plutôt mal; **she was dressed in a frumpish skirt and jumper** elle portait une jupe et un pull sans aucune allure
frumpishly ['frʌmpɪʃlɪ] *adv* **frumpishly dressed** mal fagoté
frumpy ['frʌmpɪ] = **frumpish**
frustrate [frʌ'streɪt] *vt (person)* frustrer, agacer, contrarier; *(efforts, plans)* contrecarrer, faire échouer, contrarier; *(plot)* déjouer, faire échouer; **the rain frustrated our plans** la pluie a contrarié nos projets; **the prisoner was frustrated in his attempt to escape** le prisonnier a raté sa tentative d'évasion
frustrated [frʌ'streɪtɪd] *adj* (**a**) *(annoyed)* frustré, agacé; *(disappointed)* frustré, déçu; *(sexually)* frustré; **a frustrated poet** un poète manqué (**b**) *(attempt, effort)* vain; **all our efforts to contact her were frustrated** tous nos efforts pour la contacter ont été vains *ou* ont échoué
frustrating [frʌ'streɪtɪŋ] *adj* agaçant, frustrant, pénible; **it's very frustrating having to wait** c'est vraiment pénible de devoir attendre; **a frustrating person** une personne agaçante *ou* pénible
frustration [frʌ'streɪʃən] *n (gen) & Psy* frustration *f*; **it's one of the frustrations of the job** c'est un des aspects frustrants du travail
frutex ['fruːteks] (*pl* **frutices** [-ɪsiːz]) *n Bot* arbrisseau *m*
fry [fraɪ] (*pt & pp* **fried,** *pl* **fries**) **1** *vt* (**a**) *(cook in frying pan)* faire frire, frire; **he fried himself an egg** il s'est fait un œuf sur le plat; *Am Fam* **go fry an egg!** va te faire cuire un œuf!

(**b**) *Am Fam (convict)* faire passer à la chaise électrique ❑
2 *vi* (**a**) *(food)* frire; *Fig (person)* griller
(**b**) *Am Fam (convict)* passer à la chaise électrique ❑
3 *n* (**a**) *(UNCOUNT) (fish)* fretin *m*; *(frogs)* têtards *mpl*
(**b**) *Am (picnic)* = sorte de pique-nique où on mange de la friture
(**c**) *(offal)* issues *fpl*; *(of lamb, pig)* fressure *f*
4 fries *npl* frites *fpl*

▸**fry up** *vt sep* faire frire, frire

fryer ['fraɪə(r)] *n* (**a**) *(pan)* poêle *f* (à frire); *(for deep-fat frying)* friteuse *f* (**b**) *(chicken)* poulet *m* à frire

frying ['fraɪɪŋ] *n* friture *f*
▸▸ ***frying pan*** poêle *f* (à frire); **to jump out of the frying pan into the fire** tomber de Charybde en Scylla, changer un cheval borgne pour un cheval aveugle

fry-pan *n Am* poêle *f* à frire

fry-up *n Br Fam* = bacon, saucisses, tomates etc cuits à la poêle, généralement consommés au petit déjeuner

FSA [,efes'eɪ] *n* (**a**) *Fin (abbr* **Financial Services Authority**) = organisme gouvernemental britannique chargé de contrôler les activités du secteur financier (**b**) *(abbr* **Food Standards Agency**) = organisme britannique de contrôle de la sécurité alimentaire

FSH [,efes'eɪtʃ] *n Biol (abbr* **follicle-stimulating hormone**) hormone *f* folliculo-stimulante, FSH *f*

f-stop *n Phot* ouverture *f* (du diaphragme)
▸▸ ***f-stop scale*** échelle *f* des diaphragmes

FT [,ef'tiː] *n Press (abbr* **Financial Times**) Financial Times *m*
▸▸ *St Exch* ***FT Index*** (**a**) *(abbr* **Financial Times-(Industrial) Ordinary Share Index**) = indice boursier du 'Financial Times' basé sur la valeur de 30 actions cotées à la Bourse de Londres (**b**) *(abbr* **Financial Times-Stock Exchange 100 Index**) = principal indice boursier du 'Financial Times' basé sur la valeur de 100 actions cotées à la Bourse de Londres

ft (**a**) *(written abbr* **foot**) pied *m* (**b**) *(written abbr* **fort**) fort *m*

FT 100 index [,ef'tiː,wʌn'hʌndrəd-] *n St Exch* = principal indice boursier du 'Financial Times' basé sur la valeur de 100 actions cotées à la Bourse de Londres

FTC [,eftiː'siː] *n Am (abbr* **Federal Trade Commission**) = commission fédérale chargée de veiller au respect de la concurrence sur le marché

FTP [,eftiː'piː] *Comput* **1** *n (abbr* **File Transfer Protocol**) protocole *m* de transfert de fichiers
2 *vt* télécharger par FTP
▸▸ ***FTP server*** serveur *m* FTP; ***FTP site*** site *m* FTP

FT-SE index ['fʊtsɪ-] *n St Exch (abbr* **Financial Times-Stock Exchange 100 Index**) = principal indice boursier du 'Financial Times' basé sur la valeur de 100 actions cotées à la Bourse de Londres

fuchsia ['fjuːʃə] *n* (**a**) *Bot* fuchsia *m* (**b**) *(colour)* fuchsia *m*

fuchsine ['fuːksiːn] *n* fuchsine *f*

fuck [fʌk] *Vulg* **1** *vt* [illegible] *(of woman)* baiser avec; **fuck you!, go fuck yourself!** va te faire enculer!; **fuck it!** putain de merde!; **fuck me!** putain!
2 *vi* baiser; *Fig* **don't fuck with me!** essaie pas de te foutre de ma gueule!
3 *n* (**a**) *(act)* baise *f*; **to have a fuck** baiser, s'envoyer en l'air
(**b**) *(sexual partner)* **he's a good fuck** il baise bien
(**c**) *(idiot)* **you stupid fuck!** espèce de connard!
(**d**) *(as intensifier)* **what the fuck do you expect?** mais qu'est-ce que tu veux, putain de merde?; **who the fuck left the window open?** quel est le con qui a laissé la fenêtre ouverte?; **I can't really afford it, but what the fuck!** c'est un peu cher pour moi, mais je m'en fous!; **it costs a fuck of a lot of money** ça coûte la peau du cul; **it's been a fuck of a long day!** putain, la journée a été longue!; **she'd like you to apologize – like fuck I will!** elle voudrait que tu t'excuses – qu'elle aille se faire foutre!; **did you invite them? – like fuck I did!** tu les as invités? – tu déconnes ou quoi?; **shut the fuck up!** ferme ta gueule!; *Br* **get to fuck!** va te faire enculer!; **get the fuck out of here!** fous-moi le camp!, dégage!
(**e**) *(expressing surprise, disbelief)* **for fuck's sake!** merde!, putain!; *Br* **fuck knows where he is!** j'ai pas la moindre idée d'où il peut être!
(**f**) *(in comparisons)* **as stupid as fuck** con comme la lune; **as boring as fuck** chiant comme la pluie; **he ran like fuck** il a pris ses jambes à son cou
(**g**) **not to give a (flying) fuck (about)** se foutre complètement (de); **I don't give a fuck** j'en ai rien à branler; **who gives a fuck!** tout le monde s'en fout!; **are you going to apologize? – am I fuck!** est-ce que tu vas t'excuser? – des clous!
4 *exclam* putain de merde!
5 fuck all *pron (nothing)* que dalle; **it's got fuck all to do with you!** occupe-toi donc de tes fesses!; *Br* **fuck all money/time** pas un flèche/une minute; **she's done fuck all today** elle a rien foutu de la journée; **she knows fuck all about it** elle y connaît que dalle

▸**fuck about, fuck around** *Vulg* **1** *vt sep* **to fuck sb about** *or* **around** *(treat badly)* se foutre de la gueule de qn; *(waste time of)* faire perdre son temps à qn ❑
2 *vi* (**a**) *(be promiscuous)* baiser à droite à gauche
(**b**) *(act foolishly)* déconner, faire le con; *(waste time)* glander, glandouiller; **to fuck about** *or* **around with sth** tripoter qch

▸**fuck off** *Vulg* **1** *vt sep* **to fuck sb off** faire chier qn; **to be fucked off (with)** en avoir plein le cul (de)
2 *vi (leave)* se casser, calter; **fuck off!** *(go away)* casse-toi!; *(expressing contempt, disagreement)* va te faire foutre!

▸**fuck up** *Vulg* **1** *vt sep (plan, project)* foutre la merde dans; *(person)* foutre dans la merde; **he's really fucked up emotionally** il est complètement paumé; **they really fucked up their kids** ils ont complètement perturbé leurs gosses
2 *vi* merder

▸**fuck with** *vt insep* **don't fuck with me** ne me fais pas chier

fucked [fʌkt] *adj Vulg (car, stereo etc)* foutu, naze; **I'm fucked!** *(exhausted)* je suis mort *ou* crevé!; **his knee/heart/eye is fucked** son genou/cœur/œil est foutu; **his chances of winning the race were completely fucked!** il n'avait plus une chance de gagner cette putain de course!

fucker ['fʌkə(r)] *n Vulg* (**a**) *(man)* enculé *m*, enfoiré *m*; *(woman)* connasse *f*; **some fucker's stolen my bike** il y a un enculé qui m'a piqué mon vélo; **you lazy fucker!** espèce de grosse feignasse!; **you stupid fucker!** pauvre con! (**b**) *(thing)* **I can't get the fucker to start** j'arrive pas à faire démarrer cette saloperie

fuckface ['fʌkfeɪs] *n Vulg* tête *f* de con

fucking ['fʌkɪŋ] *Vulg* **1** *adj* **I'm fed up with this fucking car!** j'en ai plein le cul de cette putain de bagnole!; **you fucking idiot!** pauvre con!; **fucking hell!** putain de merde!; **where the fucking hell have you been?** où est-ce que t'étais [illegible]!; **she's here all the fucking time!** elle est toujours fourrée ici!; **fucking A!** génial!
2 *adv* **he's so fucking stupid!** tu parles d'un con!; **it was a fucking awful day!** tu parles d'une putain de journée!; **fucking stop it!** arrête, bordel de merde!; **I don't fucking know!** j'en sais foutre rien!; **it's fucking freezing!** on se les gèle!; **I'm fucking well going home!** merde! moi je rentre chez moi!

fuck-me *adj Vulg* **a fuck-me dress** une robe affriolante ❑; **fuck-me shoes** chaussures *fpl* de pute

fuck-off *Vulg* **1** *n Am (person)* glandeur(euse) *m,f*
2 *adj Br (for emphasis)* mastoc *(inv)*; **they've got a huge fuck-off house in the country** ils ont une baraque énorme à la campagne

fuck-up *n Vulg* (**a**) *(situation)* merde *f*; **to make a fuck-up of sth** foirer qch (**b**) *Am (bungler)* bousilleur(euse) *m,f*; **he's a real fuck-up** il fout sa merde partout

fuckwit ['fʌkwɪt] *n Vulg* connard (connasse) *m,f*

fucus ['fjuːkəs] *n Bot* fucus *m*

fuddle ['fʌdəl] *vt (confuse → ideas, person)* embrouiller; *(intoxicate)* griser

fuddled ['fʌdəld] *adj (ideas, mind)* embrouillé, confus; *(person → confused)* confus; *(→ tipsy)* gris, éméché

fuddy-duddy ['fʌdɪ,dʌdɪ] *(pl* **fuddy-duddies**) *Fam* **1** *n* vieux schnock *ou* schnoque *m*
2 *adj* vieux jeu *inv*

fudge [fʌdʒ] **1** *n* (**a**) *(UNCOUNT) (sweet)* caramel *m*; **a piece of fudge** un caramel; **I made some fudge** j'ai fait des caramels
(**b**) *(dodging)* faux-fuyant *m*, échappatoire *f*; **the law/agreement is a fudge** le texte de loi/de l'accord est délibérément flou
(**c**) *Typ (stop press box)* emplacement *m* de la dernière heure; *(stop press news)* (insertion *f* de) dernière heure *f*, dernières nouvelles *fpl*
(**d**) *(UNCOUNT) (nonsense)* balivernes *fpl*, âneries *fpl*
2 *vi (evade, hedge)* esquiver le problème; **the President fudged on the budget issue** le président a esquivé les questions sur le budget
3 *vt* (**a**) *(make up → excuse)* inventer; *(→ story)* monter; *(→ figures, results)* truquer
(**b**) *(avoid, dodge)* esquiver
(**c**) *Am (ruin)* rater; **I totally fudged it** je l'ai complètement raté
4 *exclam Fam Old-fashioned* balivernes!

fuel [fjʊəl] *(Br pt & pp* **fuelled,** *cont* **fuelling,** *Am pt & pp* **fueled,** *cont* **fueling**) **1** *n* (**a**) *(gen) & Aviat* combustible *m*; *(coal)* charbon *m*; *(oil)* mazout *m*, fuel *m*, fioul *m*; *(wood)* bois *m*; *Aut* carburant *m*; **what fuel do you use?** quel combustible utilisez-vous?; **coal is not a very efficient fuel** le charbon n'est pas une source d'énergie très efficace; **nuclear fuel** combustible *m* nucléaire
(**b**) *Fig* **to add fuel to the flames** jeter de l'huile sur le feu; **his words were merely fuel to her anger** ses paroles n'ont fait qu'attiser *ou* qu'aviver sa colère
2 *comp (costs)* de chauffage
3 *vt* (**a**) *(furnace)* alimenter (en combustible); *(car, plane, ship)* ravitailler en carburant
(**b**) *Fig (controversy)* aviver; *(speculation)* nourrir; **his words only fuelled their anger/their suspicions** ses paroles n'ont servi qu'à aviver leur colère/leurs soupçons
▸▸ ***fuel bill*** *(of household)* facture *f* de chauffage; *(of region)* dépenses *fpl* énergétiques; *Elec* ***fuel cell*** élément *m* de conversion; ***fuel consumption*** consommation *f* d'énergie; *(of car)* consommation *f* de carburant; ***fuel element*** élément *m* combustible; ***fuel gauge*** jauge *f* d'essence; *Tech* ***fuel injection*** alimentation *f* par injection, injection *f* (de carburant); *Tech* ***fuel injection system*** système *m* d'injection (de combustible); *Tech* ***fuel injector*** injecteur *m* de carburant; ***fuel oil*** mazout *m*, fuel *m*, fioul *m*; ***fuel pipe*** tuyau *m* d'alimentation en carburant; ***fuel pressure*** pression *f* de carburant; ***fuel pump*** pompe *f* d'alimentation; ***fuel tank*** *(in home)* cuve *f* à mazout; *(in car)* réservoir *m* de carburant *ou* d'essence; *(in ship)* soute *f* à mazout *ou* à fuel; ***fuel tax*** taxe *f* sur les carburants; ***fuel temperature gauge*** jauge *f* de température du carburant

▸**fuel up** *vi* s'approvisionner *ou* se ravitailler en carburant *ou* combustible

[illegible] *m* air/carburant

fuel-efficient *adj* économique, qui ne consomme pas beaucoup

fuel-injected *adj* à injection

fuelling, *Am* **fueling** ['fjʊəlɪŋ] *n* ravitaillement *m* en carburant
▸▸ ***fuelling stop*** escale *f* de ravitaillement (en carburant)

fug [fʌg] *n Br* **there's a terrible fug in here** *(stuffy)* ça sent vraiment le renfermé ici, on étouffe; *(smoky)* c'est complètement enfumé ici

fugacious [fjuː'geɪʃəs] *adj* (**a**) *Literary (colour, perfume)* fugace (**b**) *Biol* caduc; *Bot* fugace

fugacity [fjuː'gæsɪtɪ] *n* (**a**) *Literary (of colour, perfume)* fugacité *f* (**b**) *Biol* caducité *f*

fugal ['fjuːgəl] *adj Mus* fugué

fugato [fjʊ'gɑːtəʊ] *Mus* **1** *adv* en style fugué
2 *n* fugato *m*

fugginess ['fʌgɪnɪs] *n Br (stuffiness)* touffeur *f* de l'air; *(smokiness)* caractère *m* enfumé

fuggy ['fʌgɪ] *(compar* **fuggier,** *superl* **fuggiest**) *adj Br (stuffy)* qui sent le renfermé; *(smoky)* enfumé

fugitive ['fju:dʒətɪv] **1** *n (escapee)* fugitif(ive) *m,f*, évadé(e) *m,f*; *(refugee)* réfugié(e) *m,f*; **she's a fugitive from justice** elle fuit la justice, elle est recherchée par la justice

2 *adj* **(a)** *(debtor, slave)* fugitif

(b) *Literary (beauty, happiness)* éphémère, passager; *(impression, thought, vision)* fugitif, passager

▸▸ *Hist* ***fugitive slave law*** = loi qui obligeait tout citoyen à livrer les esclaves fugitifs à leur propriétaire, avant l'abolition de l'esclavage aux États-Unis

fugleman ['fju:gəlmən] (*pl* **fuglemen** [-mən]) *n* **(a)** *Hist & Mil* chef *m* de file **(b)** *Fam (leader)* meneur❑ *m*, chef❑ *m* **(c)** *Fam (spokesman)* porte-parole❑ *m*

fugue [fju:g] *n Mus & Psy* fugue *f*

fuguist ['fju:gɪst] *n Mus* compositeur(trice) *m,f* de fugues

Führer ['fjʊərə(r)] *n* **(a)** *Hist* Führer *m* **(b)** *Fam (dictator, boss)* tyran❑ *m*

Fula (*pl* **inv** *or* **Fulas**), **Fulah** (*pl* **inv** *or* **Fulahs**) ['fu:lə], **Fulani** [fu:'lɑ:nɪ] (*pl* **inv** *or* **Fulanis**) *n* **(a)** *(person)* Peul(e) *m,f* **(b)** *Ling* peul *m*, foulani *m*

Fulbright Scholarship ['fʊlbraɪt-] *n* = bourse américaine destinée à favoriser les échanges entre étudiants et professeurs d'universités dans différents pays

fulcrum ['fʊlkrəm] (*pl* **fulcrums** *or* **fulcra** [-krə]) *n (pivot)* pivot *m*, point *m* d'appui; *Fig (prop, support)* point *m* d'appui

fulfil, *Am* **fulfill** [fʊl'fɪl] (*pt & pp* **fulfilled,** *cont* **fulfilling**) *vt* **(a)** *(carry out → ambition, dream, plan)* réaliser; *(→ prophecy, task)* accomplir, réaliser; *(→ promise)* tenir; *(→ duty, obligation)* remplir, s'acquitter de

(b) *(satisfy → condition)* remplir; *(→ norm, regulation)* répondre à, obéir à; *(→ desire, need)* satisfaire, répondre à; *(→ prayer, wish)* exaucer; **to fulfil oneself** se réaliser, s'épanouir; **she fulfilled herself both as an artist and as a mother** elle s'est épanouie à la fois comme artiste et comme mère; **it's important to feel fulfilled** il est important de se réaliser (dans la vie)

(c) *(complete, finish → prison sentence)* achever, terminer

(d) *Com (order)* exécuter; *(contract)* remplir, respecter

fulfilled [fʊl'fɪld] *adj (life)* épanoui, heureux; *(person)* épanoui, comblé

fulfilling [fʊl'fɪlɪŋ] *adj (life, career, experience)* épanouissant

fulfilment, *Am* **fulfillment** [fʊl'fɪlmənt] *n* **(a)** *(of ambition, dream, wish)* réalisation *f*; *(of desire)* satisfaction *f*; *(of plan, condition, contract)* exécution *f*; *(of duty, prophecy, promise)* accomplissement *m*; *(of prayer)* exaucement *m*

(b) *(satisfaction)* (sentiment *m* de) contentement *m ou* satisfaction *f*; **to find** *or* **achieve fulfilment** se réaliser, s'épanouir; **to seek fulfilment** rechercher l'épanouissement; **she gets a sense** *or* **feeling of fulfilment from her work** son travail la comble

(c) *(of prison sentence)* achèvement *m*, fin *f*

(d) *Com (of order)* exécution *f*

fulgent ['fʌldʒənt] *adj Literary* fulgurant

fulgurant ['fʌlgjʊrənt] *adj* fulgurant

fulgurate ['fʌlgjʊreɪt] *vi* fulgurer; *(metals)* éclairer

fulguration [,fʌlgjʊ'reɪʃən] *n* **(a)** *(of silver, metals)* fulguration *f*, éclair *m* **(b)** *Med* fulguration *f*

fuliginous [fju:'lɪdʒɪnəs] *adj* fuligineux

FULL [fʊl]

plein	▸ **1 (a) – (c), (f), (h)**
rempli	▸ **1 (a)**
complet	▸ **1 (c), (e)**
rassasié	▸ **1 (d)**
détaillé	▸ **1 (g)**
large	▸ **1 (i)**
complètement	▸ **2 (a)**
entièrement	▸ **2 (a)**
carrément	▸ **2 (b)**
intégralement	▸ **3**
au plus haut degré	▸ **4**

1 *adj* **(a)** *(completely filled)* plein, rempli; **the cup was full to the brim** *or* **full to overflowing with coffee** la tasse était pleine à ras bord de café; **this box is only half full** cette boîte n'est remplie qu'à moitié *ou* n'est qu'à moitié pleine; **will you open the door for me, my hands are full** vous voulez bien m'ouvrir la porte, j'ai les mains occupées; **don't talk with your mouth full** ne parle pas la bouche pleine; **you shouldn't go swimming on a full stomach** tu ne devrais pas nager après avoir mangé; **I've got a full week ahead of me** j'ai une semaine chargée devant moi; **the sails are full** les voiles portent bien

(b) *Fig* **(to be) full of** *(filled with)* (être) plein de; **her arms were full of flowers** elle portait des brassées de fleurs, elle avait des fleurs plein les bras; **her eyes were full of tears** elle avait les yeux pleins de larmes; **a look full of gratitude** un regard plein *ou* chargé de reconnaissance; **his look was full of admiration** son regard était plein d'admiration; **the children were full of excitement** les enfants étaient très excités; **her parents were full of hope** ses parents étaient remplis d'espoir; **she's full of good ideas** elle est pleine de bonnes idées; **the day was full of surprises** la journée a été pleine de surprises; **her letters are full of spelling mistakes** ses lettres sont truffées de fautes d'orthographe; **full of energy** *or* **of life** plein de vie; **to be full of oneself** être plein de soi-même *ou* imbu de sa personne; **he's full of his own importance** il est pénétré de sa propre importance; **they/the papers were full of news about China** ils/les journaux ne parlaient que de la Chine; *Fam* **to be full of it** raconter n'importer quoi; *Vulg* **to be full of shit** déconner à pleins tubes

(c) *(crowded → room, theatre)* comble, plein; *(→ hotel, restaurant, train)* complet(ète); **the hotel was full (up)** l'hôtel était complet; *Theat* **house full** *(sign)* complet

(d) *(satiated)* rassasié, repu; *Br* **I'm full (up)!** je n'en peux plus!

(e) *(complete, whole)* tout, complet(ète) **she listened to him for three full hours** elle l'a écouté pendant trois heures entières; **the house is a full 10 miles from town** la maison est à 15 bons kilomètres *ou* est au moins à 15 kilomètres de la ville; **in full sunlight** en plein soleil; **the full amount** la somme totale; **she received her full share of the money** elle a reçu tout l'argent qui lui revenait; **he rose to his full height** il s'est dressé de toute sa hauteur; **to fall full length** tomber de tout son long; **he leads a very full life** il a une vie bien remplie; **the full horror of the situation** toute l'horreur de la situation; **I don't want a full meal** je ne veux pas un repas entier; **give him your full name and address** donnez-lui vos nom, prénom et adresse; **in full uniform** en grande tenue; **in full view of the cameras/of the teacher** devant les caméras/le professeur; **to get full marks** avoir vingt sur vingt; **I got full marks in my maths test** j'ai eu vingt sur vingt à mon examen de maths; *Fig* **full marks!** bravo!; **full marks for observation!** bravo, vous êtes très observateur!; *Phot* **in full colour** tout en couleur; *Naut* **full sail** toutes voiles dehors; *Fig* **in full sail** toutes voiles dehors, à toute vapeur

(f) *(maximum)* plein; **make full use of this opportunity** mettez bien cette occasion à profit, tirez bien profit de cette occasion; **they had the music on full volume** ils avaient mis la musique à fond; **on full beam** en feux de route, en pleins phares; **peonies in full bloom** des pivoines épanouies; **the trees are in full bloom** les arbres sont en fleurs; **it was going full blast** *(heating)* ça chauffait au maximum; *(radio, TV)* ça marchait à pleins tubes; *(car)* ça roulait à toute allure; **the orchestra was at full strength** l'orchestre était au grand complet; **she caught the full force of the blow** elle a reçu le coup de plein fouet

(g) *(detailed)* détaillé; **I didn't get the full story** je n'ai pas entendu tous les détails de l'histoire; **he gave us a full report** il nous a donné un rapport détaillé; **I asked for full information** j'ai demandé des renseignements complets

(h) *(plump → face)* plein, rond; *(→ figure)* rondelet, replet; *(→ lips)* charnu; **dresses designed to flatter the fuller figure** des robes qui mettent en valeur les silhouettes épanouies

(i) *(ample, wide → clothes, skirt)* large, ample; *(→ sleeve)* large, bouffant

(j) *(sound)* timbré; *(voice)* étoffé, timbré

(k) *(flavour)* parfumé; *(wine)* robuste, qui a du corps

(l) *(brother, sister)* germain

2 *adv* **(a)** *(entirely, completely)* complètement, entièrement; **I turned the heat on full** *or Br* **full on** j'ai mis le chauffage à fond; *Br* **he put the radio full on** il a mis la radio à fond; **to turn a tap on full** *or Br* **full on** ouvrir un robinet en grand

(b) *(directly, exactly)* carrément; **the blow caught her full in the face** elle a reçu le coup en pleine figure; **lying full in the sun** couché en plein (au) soleil

(c) *(idioms)* **you know full well I'm right** tu sais très bien *ou* parfaitement que j'ai raison; *Br* **full out** à toute vitesse, à pleins gaz; **to ride full out** filer à toute vitesse, foncer

3 in full *adv* intégralement; **to pay in full** payer intégralement; **we paid the bill in full** nous avons payé la facture dans son intégralité; **they refunded my money in full** ils m'ont entièrement remboursé; **write out your name in full** écrivez votre nom en toutes lettres; **they published the book in full** ils ont publié le texte intégral *ou* dans son intégralité

4 to the full *adv* au plus haut degré, au plus haut point; *Br* **enjoy life to the full** profitez de la vie au maximum

▸▸ ***full board*** pension *f* complète; *Br Mil* ***full colonel*** colonel *m*; *Fin* ***full consolidation*** intégration *f* globale; *Acct* ***full cost accounting (method)*** méthode *f* de capitalisation du coût entier; *Fin* ***full costing*** méthode *f* du coût complet; *Fin* ***full discharge*** quitus *m*; ***full dress*** *(evening clothes)* tenue *f* de soirée; *(uniform)* grande tenue *f*; *Tel* ***full duplex*** bidirectionnel *m* simultané, full duplex *m*; **to send sth full duplex** transmettre qch en full duplex; *Econ* ***full employment*** plein emploi *m*; ***full fare*** *(for adult)* plein tarif *f*; *(for child)* une place entière; ***full frontal*** = photographie montrant une personne nue de face; ***full general*** ≃ général *m* à cinq étoiles; ***full house*** *Cards* full *m*; *Theat* salle *f* comble; *Theat* **to play to a full house** jouer à guichets fermés; *Comput* ***full Internet access*** accès *m* à tout l'Internet; *Aut* ***full licence*** permis *m* tous véhicules; ***full member*** membre *m* à part entière; *Fam* ***the full monty*** *(everything)* la totale; **to do a Full Monty** *(strip)* faire un strip-tease intégral❑; ***full moon*** pleine lune *f*; **at full moon** à la pleine lune; ***full pay*** paie *f* entière; *Fin* ***full payment*** paiement *m* intégral; *Typ* ***full point*** *(in punctuation)* point *m*; ***full price*** prix *m* fort; *Am* ***full professor*** professeur *m* d'université *(titulaire d'une chaire)*; *Mus* ***full score*** partition *f*; ***full session*** *(of a committee etc)* réunion *f* plénière; *Br* ***full stop*** *(pause)* arrêt *m* complet; *Gram* point *m*; *Comput* point *m* final; **the parade came to a full stop** le défilé s'est arrêté; **the whole airport came to a full stop** toute activité a cessé dans l'aéroport; **I won't do it, full stop!** je ne le ferai pas, un point c'est tout!; *Br Univ* ***full term*** *(at Oxford and Cambridge)* = période pendant laquelle ont lieu les cours; ***full text*** texte *m* intégral; ***full time*** *(of working week)* temps *m* complet; *Sport* fin *f* de match; *Sport* ***full toss*** *(in cricket)* coup *m* plein; *Com* ***full weight*** poids *m* juste

To do a Full Monty

Cette phrase est une allusion au film britannique *The Full Monty*, qui fut un très gros succès en 1997, et qui est l'histoire d'un groupe de chômeurs de Sheffield qui décident de devenir strip-teaseurs.

L'expression **the full Monty** existait déjà avant le film dans le sens "absolument tout", mais le film a donné naissance à cette nouvelle formule (**to do a Full Monty**) qui signifie "faire un strip-tease intégral". On pourra dire par exemple: **every Saturday night drunken youths spill out of pubs and do a full Monty in the middle of the High Street** ("le samedi soir des jeunes sortent du pub complètement saouls et se mettent à poil au milieu de la rue principale").

fullback [ˈfʊlbæk] *n Sport* arrière *m*

full-blooded [-ˈblʌdɪd] *adj* (**a**) *(hearty → person)* vigoureux, robuste; *(→ effort)* vigoureux, puissant; *(→ argument)* violent; **you have our full-blooded support** vous avez notre soutien inconditionnel (**b**) *(purebred → horse)* pur sang; *(racially → person)* de race pure; *Fig* **a full-blooded Socialist** un socialiste pur et dur

full-blown *adj* (**a**) *(flower)* épanoui (**b**) *Fig (complete) Br* **a full-blown doctor** un médecin diplômé; **a full-blown crisis** une crise de la plus grande envergure; **full-blown war** la guerre totale; **the discussion developed into a full-blown argument** la discussion a dégénéré en véritable dispute (**c**) *Br Med* **full-blown AIDS** sida *m* avéré; **to have full-blown AIDS** avoir un sida avéré

full-bodied [-ˈbɒdɪd] *adj (wine)* qui a du corps, corsé

fullbred [ˌfʊlˈbred] *adj* de race pure; **fullbred horse** pur-sang *m*

full-cheeked *adj* aux grosses joues

full-chested *adj* à forte poitrine; **full-chested jacket** veston *m* à poitrine bombée

full-collision waiver *n Am Ins* assurance *f* tous risques

full-contact karate *n* boxe *f* américaine, full-contact *m*

full-cost pricing *n Mktg* fixation *f* du prix en fonction du coût

full-cream milk *n* lait *m* entier

full-dress *adj (parade)* en habit de cérémonie

►► ***full-dress debate*** débat *m* de fond; *Theat* ***full-dress rehearsal*** répétition *f* générale; ***full-dress uniform*** tenue *f* de cérémonie, grande tenue *f*

fuller's earth [ˈfʊləz-] *n* terre *f* à foulon

full-face(d) *adj* (**a**) *(person)* au visage rond (**b**) *(photograph)* de face (**c**) *Typ* gras

full-fashioned *Am* = **fully-fashioned**

full-fat *adj* entier

full-flavoured *adj* (**a**) *(tobacco)* qui a du corps; *(wine)* fruité, qui a du bouquet; **full-flavoured olive oil** huile *f* d'olive fruitée (**b**) *(story, joke etc)* épicé, corsé

full-fledged *Am* = **fully-fledged**

full-frontal *adj*

►► ***full-frontal nudity*** *(in show)* nu *m* intégral; ***full-frontal photograph*** nu *m* de face *(photographie)*

full-grown *adj* adulte

fullish [ˈfʊlɪʃ] *adj* assez plein; *(lips)* assez gros; *(sleeves)* assez ample, assez bouffant

full-length 1 *adj (portrait)* en pied; *(curtain, dress)* long (longue); **a full-length film** un long métrage

2 *adv* **he was stretched out full-length on the floor** il était étendu de tout son long par terre

►► ***full-length mirror*** glace *f* en pied; *TV & Cin* ***full-length shot*** plan *m* général

fullness [ˈfʊlnɪs] *n* (**a**) *(state)* état *m* plein, plénitude *f*; *Med (of stomach)* plénitude *f*; **in the fullness of time** avec le temps (**b**) *(of details, information)* abondance *f* (**c**) *(of face, figure)* rondeur *f*; **the fullness of his lips** ses lèvres *fpl* charnues (**d**) *(of skirt, sound, voice)* ampleur *f*

full-page *adj* pleine page

►► ***full-page advertisement*** annonce *f* pleine page; *Comput* ***full-page display*** écran *m* pleine page

full-scale *adj* (**a**) *(model, plan)* grandeur nature *(inv)* (**b**) *(all-out → strike, war)* total; *(→ attack, investigation)* de grande envergure; **the factory starts full-scale production this week** l'usine commence a tourner à plein rendement cette semaine

►► *Mil* ***full-scale fighting*** bataille *f* rangée

full-screen menu *n Comput* menu *m* plein écran

full-size(d) *adj (animal, plant)* adulte; *(drawing, model)* grandeur nature *(inv)*; *(keyboard, wheel)* aux dimensions standard; *Am* **full-size(d) car** grosse voiture *f*

full-strength *adj (solution, bleach)* non dilué; *(cigarette, aspirin)* très fort; *(team)* qui comprend les meilleurs joueurs

full-term 1 *adj (baby)* né à terme; *(pregnancy)* mené à terme

2 *adv* à terme

full-throated [-ˈθrəʊtɪd] *adj* retentissant, sonore; **to give a full-throated laugh** rire à gorge déployée; **to give a full-throated shout** crier à pleine gorge

full-time 1 *adj (job)* à plein temps; *(work, contract, employee)* à temps complet, à plein temps; **she's a full-time translator** elle est traductrice à plein temps; **it's a full-time job taking care of a baby!** s'occuper d'un bébé ne laisse pas une minute de libre!

2 *adv* à plein temps, à temps plein

►► *Sport* ***full-time score*** score *m* final

full-timer *n* = personne qui travaille à plein temps

fully [ˈfʊlɪ] *adv* (**a**) *(totally → automatic, dressed, satisfied, trained)* complètement, entièrement; *(→ furnished)* entièrement; *(→ paid)* intégralement; **I fully understand** je comprends très bien *ou* parfaitement; **I fully agree** je suis tout à fait d'accord; **I fully intend to return** j'ai la ferme intention de revenir; **I am fully aware of the implications** je suis tout à fait conscient des implications; **he is fully qualified** il a toutes les qualifications nécessaires; **fully licensed** *(hotel, restaurant etc)* autorisé à vendre de l'alcool; **fully loaded** *(van, plane etc)* en pleine charge; *Fin & St Exch* **fully diluted earnings per share** bénéfice *m* par action entièrement dilué (**b**) *(thoroughly → answer, examine, explain)* à fond, dans le détail; **this topic is dealt with more fully below** ce thème est traité plus en détail ci-après; **I'll write more fully next week** j'écrirai plus longuement la semaine prochaine (**c**) *(at least)* au moins, bien; **it was fully two hours before he arrived** au moins deux heures ont passé avant qu'il n'arrive; **fully half of the planes were faulty** la moitié des avions au moins *ou* une bonne moitié des avions étaient défectueux

fully-fashioned, *Am* **full-fashioned** [-ˈfæʃənd] *adj* moulant

fully-fitted *adj (kitchen)* intégré

fully-fledged, *Am* **full-fledged** *adj* (**a**) *(bird)* qui a toutes ses plumes (**b**) *Fig* à part entière; **a fully-fledged doctor** un médecin diplômé; **a fully-fledged member** un membre à part entière; **a fully-fledged atheist** un athée pur et dur

fully-paid capital *n Fin* capital *m* entièrement versé

fulmar [ˈfʊlmə(r)] *n Orn* fulmar *m*

fulminant [ˈfʌlmɪnənt] *adj* (**a**) *(furious)* fulminant (**b**) *Med (disease)* qui se développe subitement, foudroyant

fulminate [ˈfʌlmɪneɪt] **1** *vi* fulminer, pester; **he fulminated against** *or* **at his students** il fulminait *ou* pestait contre ses étudiants; **the preacher fulminated against the abuse of drugs** le pasteur fulminait contre l'abus de stupéfiants

2 *n Chem* fulminate *m*

►► ***fulminate of mercury*** fulminate *m* de mercure

fulmination [ˌfʌlmɪˈneɪʃən] *n* malédiction *f*, imprécation *f*

fulminatory [ˈfʌlmɪnətərɪ] *adj* fulminatoire

fulminous [ˈfʌlmɪnəs] *adj* fulminaire

fulness = **fullness**

fulsome [ˈfʊlsəm] *adj (apology, thanks)* excessif, exagéré, outré; *(welcome)* plein d'effusions; *(compliments, praise)* dithyrambique, outré; **to be fulsome in one's praise of sb/sth** porter qn/qch aux nues

fulsomely [ˈfʊlsəmlɪ] *adv (welcome)* avec effusion; **to apologize fulsomely** se répandre en excuses; **she thanked/complimented us fulsomely** elle s'est répandue en remerciements/compliments; **to praise sb/sth fulsomely** porter qn/qch aux nues; **"it's gorgeous", she said fulsomely** "c'est magnifique", dit-elle, pleine d'enthousiasme

fulsomeness [ˈfʊlsəmnɪs] *n (of apology, thanks, compliments, praise)* outrance *f*, caractère *m* excessif

fulvous [ˈfʌlvəs] *adj* fauve

fumarole [ˈfjuːmərəʊl] *n Geol* fumerolle *f*

fumatorium [ˌfjuːməˈtɔːrɪəm] *(pl* **fumatoriums** *or* **fumatoria** [-rɪə]), **fumatory** [ˈfjuːmətərɪ] *(pl* **fumatories**) *n Hort* chambre *f* pour fumigations

fumble [ˈfʌmbəl] **1** *vi* (**a**) *(grope → in the dark)* tâtonner; *(→ in pocket, purse)* fouiller; **he fumbled (about** *or* **around) in the dark for the light switch** il a cherché l'interrupteur à tâtons dans l'obscurité; **she fumbled in her bag for a pen** elle a fouillé dans son sac pour trouver un stylo; *Fig* **to fumble for words** chercher ses mots (**b**) *Sport (drop the ball)* laisser tomber la balle

2 *vt* (**a**) *(handle awkwardly)* manier gauchement *ou* maladroitement; **she fumbled her way down the dark corridor** elle chercha son chemin à tâtons le long du couloir sombre; **he fumbled his lines** il récita son texte en bafouillant

(**b**) *Sport (miss → catch)* attraper *ou* arrêter maladroitement; **to fumble the ball** laisser tomber la balle

3 *n* (**a**) *(grope)* tatônnements *mpl*

(**b**) *Sport (bad catch)* prise *f* de balle maladroite; *(dropping of the ball)* échappé *m*

fumbling [ˈfʌmblɪŋ] *adj* maladroit, gauche

fumblingly [ˈfʌmblɪŋlɪ] *adv* (**a**) *(clumsily)* maladroitement, gauchement (**b**) *(by groping)* à tâtons

fume [fjuːm] **1** *vi* (**a**) *(gas)* émettre *ou* exhaler des vapeurs; *(liquid)* fumer (**b**) *(person)* rager; **I'm fuming because I haven't been invited** je suis furieux de ne pas avoir été invité; **the boss is fuming** le patron est furieux

2 *vt* (**a**) *(treat with fumes)* fumer, fumiger (**b**) *(rage)* **"this is your fault", she fumed** "c'est de ta faute", dit-elle d'un ton rageur

3 fumes *npl (gen)* exhalaisons *fpl*, émanations *fpl*; *(of gas, liquid)* vapeurs *fpl*; **factory fumes** fumées *fpl* d'usine; **tobacco fumes** fumée *f* (de cigarette)

►► ***fume cupboard*** sorbonne *f* (de laboratoire)

fumigant [ˈfjuːmɪgənt] *n* fumigant *m*

fumigate [ˈfjuːmɪgeɪt] **1** *vt* désinfecter par fumigation

2 *vi* désinfecter par fumigation

fumigation [ˌfjuːmɪˈgeɪʃən] *n* fumigation *f*

fumigator [ˈfjuːmɪˌgeɪtə(r)] *n (device)* appareil *m* fumigatoire

fumigatorium [ˌfjuːmɪgəˈtɔːrɪəm] *(pl* **fumigatoriums** *or* **fumigatoria** [-rɪə]) *n Hort* chambre *f* étanche pour fumigations

fumigatory [ˌfjuːmɪˈgeɪtərɪ] *adj* fumigatoire

fumitory [ˈfjuːmɪtərɪ] *n (plant)* fumeterre *f*

fun [fʌn] **1** *n* (**a**) *(amusement)* amusement *m*; *(pleasure)* plaisir *m*; **to have fun** s'amuser; **we had fun at the party** nous nous sommes bien amusés à la soirée; **have fun!** amusez-vous bien!; **what fun!** ce que c'est drôle *ou* amusant!; **I don't see the fun in kicking a ball round a field** je ne trouve pas ça drôle de faire le tour d'un terrain en donnant des coups de pied dans un ballon; **skiing is good** *or* **great fun** c'est très amusant de faire du ski; **it's fun to go cycling** c'est marrant de faire du vélo; **she's tremendous fun** elle est drôlement marrante; **her brother is a lot of fun** son frère est très drôle; **the children got a lot of fun out of the bicycle** les enfants se sont bien amusés avec le vélo; **I'm learning Chinese for fun** *or* **for the fun of it** j'apprends le chinois pour mon plaisir; **he only went for the fun of it** il n'y est allé que pour s'amuser; **just for the fun of it he pretended to be the boss** histoire de rire, il a fait semblant d'être le patron; **it wasn't much fun walking home in the rain** rentrer à pied sous la pluie n'avait rien d'une partie de plaisir; **it won't be half as much fun without you** ce ne sera pas si drôle sans toi; **are you reading Marx for fun?** c'est par plaisir que tu lis Marx?; **his sister spoiled the fun** sa sœur a joué les trouble-fête *ou* les rabat-joie; **I don't want to spoil your fun, but could you keep the noise down?** je ne veux pas jouer les trouble-fête, mais est-ce que vous pourriez faire un peu moins de bruit?; **having to wear a crash helmet takes all the fun out of motorcycling** devoir porter un casque gâche tout le plaisir qu'on a à faire de la moto; *Ironic* **her boyfriend walked in and that's when the fun began** son copain est entré et c'est là qu'on a commencé à rire; **the president has become a figure of fun** le président est devenu la risée de tous; **to make fun of** *or* **to poke fun at sb** se moquer de qn; **we'll have a children's party with lots of fun and games** on va organiser une fête pour les enfants avec des tas de jeux *ou* divertissements; **I've had enough of your fun and games** *(foolish behaviour)* j'en ai assez de tes blagues *ou* farces; **there'll be some fun and games if his wife finds out** *(trouble)* ça va mal aller si sa femme l'apprend

(**b**) *(playfulness)* enjouement *m*, gaieté *f*; **to be full of fun** être plein d'entrain *ou* très gai; **he said it in fun** il l'a dit pour rire *ou* en plaisantant

2 *adj Fam* rigolo, marrant; **he's a fun guy** *or* **person** il est rigolo *ou* marrant

3 *vi Am Fam* plaisanter❑, badiner; **I was just funning!** c'était pour rire!

►► ***fun fur*** fourrure *f* synthétique

funambulist [fju:'næmbjʊlɪst] *n* funambule *mf*

funboard ['fʌnbɔ:d] *n Sport* funboard *m*

Funchal [fʊn'ʃɑ:l] *n* Funchal

function ['fʌŋkʃən] **1** *n* (**a**) *(role → of machine, organ, institution)* fonction *f*; *(→ of person)* fonction *f*, charge *f*; *Med* **vital functions** fonctions *fpl* vitales; **it is the function of a lawyer to provide sound legal advice** l'avocat a pour fonction *ou* tâche de donner de bons conseils juridiques; **he combines the functions of servant and gardener** il tient le double emploi de domestique et de jardinier; **to discharge one's functions** s'acquitter de ses fonctions; **my function in life** ma raison d'être

(**b**) *(working)* fonctionnement *m*; **they tested the heart function** ils ont examiné le fonctionnement du cœur

(**c**) *(ceremony)* cérémonie *f*; *(reception)* réception *f*; *(meeting)* réunion *f*

(**d**) *(gen) & Ling & Math* fonction *f*; **x is a function of y** x est une fonction de y

(**e**) *Comput* fonction *f*

2 *vi* fonctionner, marcher; **this room functions as a study** cette pièce sert de bureau *ou* fait fonction de bureau

►► *Comput* ***function key*** touche *f* de fonction; ***functions manager*** *(in hotel)* responsable *mf* des réceptions; ***function room*** salle *f* de réception; *Ling* ***function word*** mot *m* fonctionnel

functional ['fʌŋkʃənəl] *adj* (**a**) *(utilitarian → furniture, building, machine etc)* fonctionnel (**b**) *(in working order)* **to be functional** fonctionner; **the machine is no longer functional** la machine ne marche plus *ou* ne fonctionne plus; *Fam* **I'm barely functional before ten o'clock** je ne suis guère opérationnel avant dix heures (**c**) *Math & Med* fonctionnel

►► ***functional illiterate*** illettré(e) *m,f*

functionalism ['fʌŋkʃənəlɪzəm] *n* fonctionnalisme *m*

functionalist ['fʌŋkʃənəlɪst] **1** *adj* fonctionnaliste

2 *n* fonctionnaliste *mf*

functionality [fʌŋkʃə'nælɪtɪ] *n* fonctionnalité *f*

functionally ['fʌŋkʃənəlɪ] *adv* **to be functionally illiterate** être illettré; **to be functionally equivalent to sth** avoir la même fonction que qch; **the human appendix is functionally unnecessary** l'appendice humain est inutile du point de vue fonctionnel

functionary ['fʌŋkʃənərɪ] *(pl* **functionaries**) *n Pej (employee)* employé(e) *m,f (dans une administration)*; *(civil servant)* fonctionnaire *mf*

functioning ['fʌŋkʃənɪŋ] *n (of machine etc)* fonctionnement *m*

fund [fʌnd] **1** *n* (**a**) *(reserve of money)* fonds *m*, caisse *f*; **they've set up a fund for the earthquake victims** ils ont ouvert une souscription en faveur des victimes du séisme

(**b**) *Fig* fond *m*, réserve *f*; **she has a large fund of amusing anecdotes** elle a tout un répertoire d'anecdotes amusantes; **a fund of knowledge** un trésor de connaissances

2 *vt* (**a**) *(project)* financer; *(company)* pourvoir de fonds; *Acct* **funded from cashflow** autofinancé; **to fund money** placer de l'argent dans les fonds publics

(**b**) *Fin (debt)* consolider

3 funds *npl (cash resources)* fonds *mpl*; **public funds** fonds *mpl* publics; **secret funds** une caisse noire; **we spent all of our scarce funds on housing** nous avons dépensé le peu de capitaux dont nous disposions pour le logement; **for all other countries, remit $37 US funds** autres pays: envoyer 37 dollars US; **to be in/out of funds** être/ne pas être en fonds; **funds are low** les fonds sont bas; **I'm a bit short of funds** je n'ai pas beaucoup d'argent; *Banking* **insufficient funds** *(on returned cheque)* défaut *m* de provision; *Br* **the Funds** les bons *mpl* du Trésor; **to make a call for funds** faire un appel de capital

►► *Fin* ***funds flow statement*** tableau *m* des emplois et ressources; *Fin* ***fund of funds*** fonds *m* de fonds; *Fin* ***fund management*** gestion *f* de fonds; *Fin* ***fund manager*** gestionnaire *mf* de fonds

fundable ['fʌndəbəl] *adj Fin (debt)* consolidable

fundament ['fʌndəmənt] *n* (**a**) *(of building)* fondation *f* (**b**) *Literary (principle)* principe *m* de base, fondement *m* (**c**) *Hum (buttocks)* fondement *m*

fundamental [,fʌndə'mentəl] **1** *adj* (**a**) *(basic → concept, rule, principle)* fondamental, de base; *(→ difference, quality)* fondamental, essentiel; *(→ change, mistake)* fondamental; **a knowledge of economics is fundamental to a proper understanding of this problem** il est essentiel *ou* fondamental d'avoir des connaissances en économie pour bien comprendre ce problème; **fundamental research** recherche *f* fondamentale

(**b**) *(central)* fondamental, principal; **it's of fundamental importance** c'est d'une importance capitale

(**c**) *Mus* fondamental

2 *n* (**a**) *(usu pl)* **the fundamentals of chemistry** les principes *mpl* de base de la chimie; **when it comes to the fundamentals** quand on en vient à l'essentiel

(**b**) *Mus* fondamentale *f*

►► *Phys* ***fundamental particle*** particule *f* élémentaire; *Phys* ***fundamental unit*** unité *f* fondamentale

fundamentalism [,fʌndə'mentəlɪzəm] *n (gen) & Rel* fondamentalisme *m*; *(Muslim)* intégrisme *m*

fundamentalist [,fʌndə'mentəlɪst] **1** *adj (gen) & Rel* fondamentaliste; *(Muslim)* intégriste

2 *n (gen) & Rel* fondamentaliste *mf*; *(Muslim)* intégriste *mf*

fundamentally [,fʌndə'mentəlɪ] *adv* (**a**) *(essentially)* fondamentalement, essentiellement; **she seems hard but fundamentally she's good-hearted** elle a l'air dure, mais au fond elle a bon cœur; **fundamentally, there's nothing wrong with the idea** l'idée en soi n'est pas mauvaise; **fundamentally, it's a question of who's got more money** au fond, ce qui importe c'est qui a le plus d'argent

(**b**) *(completely)* **I disagree fundamentally with his policies** je suis radicalement *ou* fondamentalement opposé à sa politique

funded ['fʌndɪd] *adj Fin (assets)* en rentes

►► ***funded capital*** capitaux *mpl* investis; ***funded debt*** dette *f* consolidée; ***funded pension scheme*** régime *m* de retraite par capitalisation

fundholder ['fʌnd,həʊldə(r)] *n* (**a**) *(person)* rentier(ère) *m,f* (**b**) *(medical practice)* = cabinet médical ayant obtenu le droit de gérer son propre budget auprès du système de sécurité sociale britannique

funding ['fʌndɪŋ] *n (UNCOUNT) Fin* (**a**) *(for project)* financement *m*; **BP will put up half of the funding** BP financera le projet à 50 pour cent; (**b**) *(of debt)* consolidation *f*; *(of annuity, income)* assiette *f*

►► ***funding loan*** emprunt *m* de consolidation; ***funding operation*** opération *f* de financement; ***funding plan*** plan *m* de financement

fundraiser ['fʌnd,reɪzə(r)] *n (person)* collecteur(trice) *m,f* de fonds; *(event)* = projet organisé pour collecter des fonds

fundraising ['fʌnd,reɪzɪŋ] **1** *n* collecte *f* de fonds

2 *adj (dinner, project, sale)* organisé pour collecter des fonds

fundus ['fʌndəs] *n Anat* fond *m*

funeral ['fju:nərəl] **1** *n* (**a**) *(service)* enterrement *m*, obsèques *fpl*; *(more formal)* funérailles *fpl*; *(in announcement)* obsèques *fpl*; *(burial)* enterrement *m*; *Fam* **it's** *or* **that's your funeral!** débrouille-toi!, c'est ton affaire!

(**b**) *(procession → on foot)* cortège *m* funèbre; *(→ in cars)* convoi *m* mortuaire

2 *comp* funèbre

►► ***funeral ceremony*** cérémonie *f* funèbre; ***funeral director*** entrepreneur(euse) *m,f* de pompes funèbres; *Am* ***funeral home*** entreprise *f* de pompes funèbres; ***funeral march*** marche *f* funèbre; ***funeral parlour*** entreprise *f* de pompes funèbres; ***funeral procession*** cortège *m* funèbre; ***funeral pyre*** bûcher *m* (funéraire); ***funeral service*** service *m ou* office *m* funèbre

funerary ['fju:nərərɪ] *adj Formal* funéraire

funereal [fju:'nɪərɪəl] *adj (atmosphere, expression)* funèbre, lugubre; *(voice)* sépulcral, lugubre; *(pace)* lent, mesuré

funereally [fju:'nɪərɪəlɪ] *adv* funèbrement, lugubrement

funfair ['fʌnfeə(r)] *n* fête *f* foraine

funfest ['fʌn,fest] *n Am Fam* fête❑ *f (avec jeux organisés)*

fun-filled *adj* divertissant

fungal ['fʌŋgəl] *adj* fongique

►► *Med* ***fungal infection*** mycose *f*

fungi ['fʌŋgaɪ] *pl of* **fungus**

fungible ['fʌndʒɪbəl] *Law & St Exch* **1** *n* **fungibles** fongibles *mpl*

2 *adj* fongible

►► ***fungible securities*** titres *mpl* en suspens

fungicidal [,fʌndʒɪ'saɪdəl] *adj* antifongique, fongicide

fungicide ['fʌndʒɪ,saɪd] *n* fongicide *m*

fungiform ['fʌndʒɪ,fɔ:m] *adj* fongiforme

fungoid ['fʌŋgɔɪd] *adj* fongique

fungus ['fʌŋgəs] *(pl* **fungi** [-gaɪ]) *n* (**a**) *Bot* champignon *m*; *(mould)* moisissure *f* (**b**) *Med* fongus *m*

►► *Med* ***fungus infection*** mycose *f*

fungus-proof *adj* protégé contre les moisissures

funicular [fju:'nɪkjʊlə(r)] **1** *adj* funiculaire

2 *n* funiculaire *m*

►► ***funicular railway*** funiculaire *m*

funk [fʌŋk] **1** *n* (**a**) *Mus* musique *f* funk, funk *m inv*

(**b**) *Fam Old-fashioned (fear)* trouille *f*, frousse *f*; *(depression)* découragement❑ *m*; **to be in a funk** *(afraid)* avoir la trouille; *(depressed)* avoir le cafard; **to be in a blue funk** avoir une peur bleue

(**c**) *Old-fashioned (coward)* froussard(e) *m,f*

(**d**) *Am Fam (stink)* puanteur *f*, odeur *f* infecte; **what a funk!** ce que ça pue!

2 *vt* (**a**) *(be afraid of)* **to funk doing sth** ne pas avoir le courage de faire qch; **I funked telling him** je n'ai pas eu le courage de lui dire; **she had her chance and she funked it** elle a eu sa chance mais elle s'est dégonflée

(**b**) *(usu pass) (make afraid)* ficher la frousse à

3 *adj* funky *(inv)*

funkhole ['fʌŋkhəʊl] *n Fam Mil slang* abri❑ *m*, planque *f*

funky ['fʌŋkɪ] *(compar* **funkier**, *superl* **funkiest**) *adj* (**a**) *esp Am Fam (excellent)* génial, super *(inv)*; *(fashionable)* branché, cool *(inv)* (**b**) *Mus* funky *(inv)*; **funky jazz** jazz *m* funky (**c**) *Am Fam (smelly)* puant

fun-loving *adj* qui aime s'amuser *ou* rire

funnel ['fʌnəl] *(Br pt & pp* **funnelled**, *cont* **funnelling**, *Am pt & pp* **funneled**, *cont* **funneling**) **1** *n* (**a**) *(utensil)* entonnoir *m*

(**b**) *(smokestack)* cheminée *f*

(**c**) *(for ventilation)* tuyau *m ou* cheminée *f* d'aération

2 *vt* (**a**) *(liquid)* (faire) passer dans un entonnoir

(**b**) *(crowd, funds)* canaliser; **complaints are funnelled to the head office** les réclamations sont canalisées vers le bureau central

3 *vi* **the crowd funnelled out of the gates** la foule s'est écoulée par les grilles

►► *Met* ***funnel cloud*** tornade *f*

funnelled ['fʌnəld] *adj* (**a**) *(funnel-shaped)* en forme d'entonnoir (**b**) *(with numeral prefixed)* **two-funnelled steamer** bateau *m* à vapeur à deux cheminées

funnel-shaped *adj* en entonnoir; *Anat & Bot* infundibuliforme

funnel-web spider *n Entom* araignée *f* à toile en entonnoir

funnily ['fʌnɪlɪ] *adv* (**a**) *(strangely)* curieusement, bizarrement; **funnily enough, I was just thinking of you** c'est drôle *ou* chose curieuse, je pensais justement à toi (**b**) *(amusingly)* drôlement, comiquement

funniness ['fʌnɪnɪs] *n* (**a**) *(strangeness)* bizarrerie *f* (**b**) *(amusing nature)* caractère *m* amusant *ou* drôle

funny ['fʌnɪ] (*compar* **funnier,** *superl* **funniest,** *pl* **funnies**) **1** *adj* (**a**) *(amusing)* amusant, drôle, comique; **I don't think that's funny** je ne trouve pas ça drôle; **it's not funny** ce n'est pas drôle; **you looked so funny in that hat** tu étais si drôle *ou* amusant avec ce chapeau; **she didn't see the funny side of it** elle n'a pas vu le côté comique de la situation; **he's trying to be funny** il cherche à faire de l'esprit; **stop trying to be funny!** ce n'est pas le moment de plaisanter!; *Br Fam* **was it funny ha-ha or funny peculiar?** c'était drôle-rigolo ou drôle-bizarre?
(**b**) *(odd)* bizarre, curieux, drôle; **she has some funny ideas about work** elle a de drôles d'idées sur le travail; **the wine tastes funny** le vin a un drôle de goût; **it feels funny** ça fait drôle; **the engine sounds funny** le moteur fait un drôle de bruit; **I think it's funny that he should turn up now** je trouve (ça) bizarre qu'il arrive maintenant; **the funny thing (about it) is that she claimed she was away** ce qu'il y a de bizarre *ou* de curieux c'est qu'elle ait prétendu ne pas être là; **the funny thing is I just phoned you** c'est drôle, je viens juste de t'appeler; *Fam* **she's funny that way** elle est comme ça; **(that's) funny, I thought I heard the phone ring** c'est curieux *ou* drôle, j'ai cru entendre le téléphone; **(it's) funny you should say that** c'est drôle que vous disiez cela; **the whole conversation left me with a funny feeling** la conversation m'a fait un drôle d'effet; **I've got a funny feeling that's not the last we've seen of her** j'ai comme l'impression qu'on va la revoir; *Fam* **I feel a bit funny** *(odd)* je me sens tout drôle *ou* tout chose; *(ill)* je ne suis pas dans mon assiette, je suis un peu patraque; *Fam* **he went all funny when he heard the news** la nouvelle l'a rendu tout chose; *Fam* **the computer went all funny** l'ordinateur s'est détraqué; *Fam* **funny money** des sommes *fpl* mirobolantes *ou* astronomiques
(**c**) *(dubious, suspicious)* louche; *Fam* **none of your funny business!, don't try anything funny!** ne fais pas le malin!; *Fam* **there's some funny business** *or* **there's something funny going on** il se passe quelque chose de louche *ou* de pas très catholique; **there's something funny about her wanting to see him** ça me paraît louche qu'elle veuille le voir; **there's something funny about that man** cet homme n'a pas l'air très catholique
(**d**) *Br Fam (mentally)* dérangé; **he went a bit funny in his old age** il s'est mis à débloquer un peu en vieillissant
2 *n Am Fam (joke)* blague ❑ *f*; **to make a funny** raconter une blague; **to pull a funny on sb** jouer un tour à qn ❑, faire une farce à qn ❑
3 *adv Fam (walk, talk)* bizarrement ❑
4 funnies *npl Am Fam* **the funnies** les bandes *fpl* dessinées ❑ *(dans un journal)*
►► *Fam* ***funny bone*** petit juif *m*; *Fam Euph* ***funny farm*** maison *f* de fous; *Am Fam* ***funny papers*** supplément *m* bande dessinée ❑; ***fun run*** course *f* à pied pour amateurs *(pour collecter des fonds)*

'Funny Face' *Donen* 'Drôle de frimousse'

fun-packed *adj* très divertissant

fur [fɜː(r)] (*pt & pp* **furred,** *cont* **furring**) **1** *n* (**a**) *(on animal)* poil *m*, pelage *m*, fourrure *f*; *Fam* **her remark made the fur fly** *or* **set the fur flying** ça a fait du grabuge quand elle a dit ça; *Fam* **the fur really flew!** ça a bardé!
(**b**) *(coat, pelt)* fourrure *f*; **she was dressed in expensive furs** elle portait des fourrures de prix
(**c**) *(in kettle, pipe)* incrustation *f*, (dépôt *m* de) tartre *m*
(**d**) *Med (on tongue)* enduit *m*
2 *vt* (**a**) *(person)* habiller de fourrures
(**b**) *(kettle, pipe)* entartrer, incruster
(**c**) *Med (tongue)* empâter
3 *vi* **to fur (up)** *(kettle, pipe)* s'entartrer, s'incruster
►► ***fur coat*** (manteau *m* de) fourrure *f*; ***fur farm*** élevage *m* d'animaux à fourrure; *Zool* ***fur seal*** phoque *m*; ***fur skins*** peaux *fpl*; ***fur trade*** commerce *m* de fourrures, pelleterie *f*; ***fur trapper*** trappeur *m*

furbelow ['fɜːbɪləʊ] *n Arch* falbala *m*; **frills and furbelows** des falbalas *mpl*, des fanfreluches *fpl*

furbish ['fɜːbɪʃ] *vt (polish)* fourbir, astiquer; *(renovate)* remettre à neuf

furbisher ['fɜːbɪʃə(r)] *n* fourbisseur *m*; **sword furbisher** polisseur *m* d'armes blanches

furbishing ['fɜːbɪʃɪŋ] *n* fourbissage *m*, fourbissement *m*
►► ***furbishing up*** remise *f* à neuf

furcate ['fɜːkeɪt] *adj (road etc)* en bifurcation, fourché; *(hoof)* fourchu; *Biol* bifurqué

furcation [fɜː'keɪʃən] *n* bifurcation *f*

furious ['fjʊərɪəs] *adj* (**a**) *(angry)* furieux; **to be furious with sb/oneself** être furieux contre qn/soi-même; **she was furious with me for being late** elle était furieuse que je sois en retard; **he was furious when he saw the car** il s'est mis en colère quand il a vu la voiture; **a furious look** un regard furibond (**b**) *(raging, violent* → *sea, storm)* déchaîné; *(*→ *effort, struggle)* acharné; *(*→ *pace, speed)* fou (folle)

furiously ['fjʊərɪəslɪ] *adv* (**a**) *(answer, look)* furieusement (**b**) *(fight, work)* avec acharnement; *(drive, run)* à une allure folle; **the fire was blazing furiously** l'incendie faisait rage

furl [fɜːl] *vt (flag, umbrella)* rouler; *Naut (sail)* ferler, serrer

furled [fɜːld] *adj (umbrella, flag)* roulé; *Naut (sail)* serré

furlong ['fɜːlɒŋ] *n (unit of measurement)* = 201,17 m, furlong *m*

furlough ['fɜːləʊ] **1** *n* (**a**) *Mil (leave of absence)* permission *f*, congé *m*; **to be on furlough** être en permission (**b**) *Am (laying off)* mise *f* à pied provisoire
2 *vt* (**a**) *Mil (grant leave of absence)* accorder une permission à (**b**) *Am (lay off)* mettre à pied provisoirement

furnace ['fɜːnɪs] *n (for central heating)* chaudière *f*; *Ind* fourneau *m*, four *m*; *Fig* **the office was like a furnace** le bureau était une vraie fournaise

furnish ['fɜːnɪʃ] *vt* (**a**) *(supply* → *food, provisions)* fournir; *(*→ *information, reason)* fournir, donner; *(*→ *funds)* pourvoir; *(opportunity)* offrir, présenter, fournir; **they furnished us with the translation** il nous ont donné la traduction; **they furnished the ship with provisions** ils ont ravitaillé le navire
(**b**) *(house, room)* meubler; **she furnished her house with antiques** elle a meublé sa maison avec des antiquités; **a comfortably furnished house** une maison confortablement aménagée

furnished ['fɜːnɪʃt] *adj (room, apartment)* meublé

furnisher ['fɜːnɪʃə(r)] *n* (**a**) *(supplier)* fournisseur(euse) *m,f* (**of** de); *(supplier of furniture)* marchand(e) *m,f* d'ameublement; **you will find that at a (house) furnisher's** vous trouverez cela dans une maison d'ameublement (**b**) *Tex* rouleau *m* fournisseur; **brush furnisher** brosse *f* fournisseuse

furnishing fabric ['fɜːnɪʃɪŋ-] *n* tissu *m* d'ameublement

furnishings ['fɜːnɪʃɪŋz] *npl* (**a**) *(furniture)* meubles *mpl*, mobilier *m*, ameublement *m* (**b**) *Am (clothing)* habits *mpl*, vêtements *mpl*; *(accessories)* accessoires *mpl*

furniture ['fɜːnɪtʃə(r)] **1** *n (UNCOUNT)* (**a**) *(in house)* meubles *mpl*, mobilier *m*, ameublement *m*; **a piece of furniture** un meuble; **antique furniture** des meubles *mpl* anciens, du mobilier *m* ancien; **living room furniture** un salon, des meubles *mpl ou* du mobilier *m* de salon; **the room has little furniture** il n'y a pas beaucoup de meubles dans la chambre; **Louis XV furniture** du mobilier *m ou* des meubles *mpl* Louis XV; *Fam* **she feels as though she's just part of the furniture** elle a l'impression de faire partie des meubles; **he treats me as if I were part of the furniture** pour lui, je fais partie des meubles
(**b**) *Naut & Typ* garniture *f*
(**c**) *(accessories)* **street furniture** mobilier *m* urbain; **door furniture** = éléments décoratifs pour portes d'entrée
2 *comp (shop, store)* d'ameublement, de meubles
►► *Entom* ***furniture beetle*** vrillette *f*; ***furniture polish*** encaustique *f*, cire *f*; ***furniture remover*** déménageur *m*; ***furniture showroom*** magasin *m* de meubles; ***furniture van*** camion *m* de déménagement

furore [fjʊ'rɔːrɪ], *Am* **furor** ['fjʊrɔː(r)] *n* scandale *m*, tumulte *m*; **to cause** *or* **to create a furore** faire un scandale; **there's been a great furore over those scenes** ces scènes ont provoqué un énorme tumulte

furphy ['fɜːfɪ] *n Austr Fam* fausse rumeur ❑ *f*

furred [fɜːd] *adj* (**a**) *(animal)* à poils (**b**) *(kettle, pipe)* entartré; *(tongue)* pâteux, chargé

furrier ['fʌrɪə(r)] *n* fourreur *m*

furriery ['fʌrɪərɪ] *n* pelleterie *f*

furring ['fɜːrɪŋ] *n (in kettle, pipe)* tartre *m*, *(on tongue)* enduit *m*

furrow ['fʌrəʊ] **1** *n (in field)* sillon *m*; *(in garden)* rayon *m*, sillon *m*; *(on forehead, brow)* ride *f*, sillon *m*; *(on sea)* sillage *m*
2 *vt* (**a**) *(soil, surface)* sillonner (**b**) *(forehead, brow)* rider
3 *vi* se plisser; **her brow furrowed** son front se plissa

furrowed ['fʌrəʊd] *adj (forehead, brow)* ridé, sillonné de rides; **he looked up with furrowed brow** il a levé les yeux en plissant le front

furrowy ['fʌrəʊɪ] *adj* (**a**) *(field)* coupé de sillons (**b**) *(face)* ridé

furry ['fɜːrɪ] (*compar* **furrier,** *superl* **furriest**) *adj* (**a**) *(animal)* à poils; *(tail, ears)* poilu; *(fabric)* qui ressemble à de la fourrure; *(toy)* en peluche; **the husky has a furry coat** le husky a de longs poils (**b**) *(kettle, pipe)* entartré; *(tongue)* pâteux, chargé

FURTHER ['fɜːðə(r)]

plus loin	► 1 (a)
plus	► 1 (b)
de plus	► 1 (d)
plus éloigné	► 2 (a)
additionnel	► 2 (b)
avancer	► 3
suite à	► 4

1 *adv* (*compar of* **far**) (**a**) *(at a greater distance in space, time)* plus loin; **I walked further than I intended to** je suis allé plus loin que je n'en avais l'intention; **further to the south** plus au sud; **she's never been further north than Leicester** elle n'est jamais allée plus au nord que Leicester; **further along the beach** plus loin sur la plage; **how much further is it?** c'est encore loin?; **have you much further to go?** vous allez encore loin?; **he got further and further away from the shore** il a continué à s'éloigner de la rive; **to move further away** s'éloigner; **she moved further back** elle a reculé encore plus; **further back than 1960** avant 1960; **further forward, further on** plus en avant, plus loin; *Fig* **she's further on than the rest of the students** elle est en avance sur les autres étudiants; **I've got no further with finding a nanny** mes recherches pour trouver une nourrice n'ont pas beaucoup avancé; **that doesn't get us much further** cela ne nous avance pas beaucoup; **nothing could be further from the truth** rien n'est moins vrai; **nothing could be further from my mind** j'étais bien loin de penser à ça
(**b**) *(more)* plus, davantage; **I have nothing further to say** je n'ai rien à ajouter, je n'ai rien d'autre *ou* rien de plus à dire; **don't try my patience any further** ne pousse pas ma patience à bout, n'abuse pas de ma patience; **the police want to question him further** la police veut encore l'interroger; **she heard nothing further from her sister** elle n'a pas eu d'autres nouvelles de sa sœur; **I want nothing further to do with him** je ne veux plus avoir affaire à lui; **add water to the wine to make it go further** allongez le vin d'eau; **until you hear further** jusqu'à nouvel avis; **unless you hear further** sauf avis contraire
(**c**) *(to a greater degree)* **her arrival only complicated things further** son arrivée n'a fait que compliquer les choses; **play was further interrupted by rain** le jeu fut à nouveau interrompu par la pluie
(**d**) *Formal (moreover)* de plus, en outre; **and further I think it best we don't see each other again** et de plus *ou* et en outre je crois qu'il vaut mieux que nous ne nous voyions plus

fun–fur

(**e**) *(idioms)* **I would go even further and say he's a genius** j'irais même jusqu'à dire que c'est un génie; **we need to go further into the matter** il faut approfondir davantage la question; **I'll go no further** *(move)* je n'irai pas plus loin; *(say nothing more)* je vais en rester là; **this information must go no further** cette information doit rester entre nous *ou* ne doit pas être divulguée

2 *adj (compar of* **far***)* (**a**) *(more distant)* plus éloigné, plus lointain; **she walked to the further end of the room** elle est allée à l'autre bout de la pièce

(**b**) *(additional → comments, negotiations)* additionnel, autre; *(→ information, news)* supplémentaire, complémentaire; **do you have any further questions?** avez-vous d'autres questions à poser?; **I need a further £900** j'ai encore besoin de neuf cents livres; **upon further consideration** à la réflexion, après plus ample réflexion; **I have no further use for it** je ne m'en sers plus, je n'en ai plus besoin *ou* l'usage; **she needs one or two further details** elle a besoin d'un ou deux autres petits renseignements; **I would like further details of the programme** j'aimerais avoir quelques précisions *ou* indications supplémentaires sur le programme; **for further information, phone this number** pour tout renseignement complémentaire, appelez ce numéro; **please send me further information concerning the project** veuillez m'envoyer de plus amples renseignements sur *ou* concernant le projet; *esp Mil* **to await further orders** attendre les ordres; **without further delay** sans autre délai, sans plus attendre; **until further notice** jusqu'à nouvel ordre; **without further ado** sans plus de cérémonie; **without further warning** sans plus d'avertissement

3 *vt (cause, one's interests)* avancer, servir, favoriser; *(career)* servir, favoriser; *(chances)* augmenter

4 further to *prep Formal* suite à; **further to your letter of 12 July** suite à votre lettre du 12 juillet; **further to our discussion/conversation** suite à notre discussion/conversation

►► *Br* ***further education*** **1** *n* enseignement *m* postscolaire **2** *comp (class)* d'éducation permanente; ***further education college*** centre *m* de formation continue

---

furtherance ['fɜːðərəns] *n Formal* **in furtherance of their policy** pour servir leur politique

furthermore [ˌfɜːðə'mɔː(r)] *adv* en outre, par ailleurs

furthermost ['fɜːðəməʊst] *adj Literary* le plus éloigné, le plus lointain; **to the furthermost ends of the earth** jusqu'au bout du monde

furthest ['fɜːðɪst] *(superl of* **far***)* **1** *adv* le plus loin; **her house is the furthest away** sa maison est la plus éloignée; **when it's furthest from the sun** lorsqu'il se trouve le plus éloigné du soleil; **this is the furthest north I've ever been** c'est le plus au nord que j'aie jamais été

2 *adj* le plus lointain, le plus éloigné; **it's 10 miles at the furthest** il y a 16 kilomètres au plus *ou* au maximum

furtive ['fɜːtɪv] *adj (behaviour, look, smile)* furtif; *(person)* sournois

furtively ['fɜːtɪvlɪ] *adv* furtivement, en douce

furuncle ['fjʊərʌŋkəl] *n Med* furoncle *m*

furuncular [fjʊə'rʌŋkjʊlə(r)], **furunculous** [fjʊə'rʌŋkjʊləs] *adj Med* furonculeux

fury ['fjʊərɪ] *(pl* **furies***)* **1** *n* (**a**) *(anger)* fureur *f*, furie *f*; **to be in a fury** être dans une colère noire *ou* en furie; **he was beside himself with fury** il était hors de lui

(**b**) *(violence → of storm, wind)* violence *f*; *(→ of fight, struggle)* acharnement *m*; *Br* **to work like fury** travailler d'arrache-pied *ou* avec acharnement; *Br* **to run like fury** courir ventre à terre; *Br* **it's raining like fury** il pleut des cordes

(**c**) *(frenzy)* frénésie *f*; **a fury of activity** une période d'activité débordante

2 Furies *npl Myth* **the Furies** les Furies *fpl*, les Érinyes *fpl*

furze [fɜːz] *n (UNCOUNT) Bot* ajoncs *mpl*

furzy ['fɜːzɪ] *adj* couvert d'ajoncs

fusain ['fjuːzeɪn] *n* (**a**) *Art* fusain *m* (**b**) *Geol* fusain *m*, charbon *m* fossile

fuse, *Am* **fuze** [fjuːz] **1** *vi* (**a**) *(melt)* fondre; *(melt together)* fusionner; **the two metals fused (together)** les deux métaux ont fusionné

(**b**) *(join)* s'unifier, fusionner; **at some point the aims of the parties fused** à un moment donné les objectifs des partis se sont rejoints *ou* confondus

(**c**) *Br Elec* **the lights/the appliance fused** les plombs ont sauté

2 *vt* (**a**) *(melt)* fondre; *(melt together)* fondre, mettre en fusion; **to fuse two pieces together** réunir deux pièces par fusion

(**b**) *(unite)* fusionner, unifier, amalgamer; **an attempt to fuse traditional and modern methods** une tentative pour associer les méthodes modernes et traditionnelles

(**c**) *Br Elec (circuit)* faire sauter les plombs de; **to fuse the lights** faire sauter les plombs

(**d**) *(explosive)* amorcer

3 *n* (**a**) *Elec* plomb *m*, fusible *m*; **to blow a fuse** faire sauter un plomb *ou* un fusible; *Fam Fig (lose one's temper)* se mettre dans une colère noire, exploser; **the fuse keeps blowing** les plombs n'arrêtent pas de sauter; **there's a fuse blown** un des fusibles a sauté

(**b**) *(of explosive)* amorce *f*; *Mining* cordeau *m*; *Fam* **to have a short fuse** être soupe au lait, se mettre facilement en rogne; **to set a fuse** régler une fusée; *Fig* **the incident which lit the fuse of the revolution** l'incident qui a déclenché la révolution

►► ***fuse box*** boîte *f* à fusibles, coupe-circuit *m inv*; *Aut* porte-fusible *m*; ***fuse wire*** fusible *m*

fused [fjuːzd] *adj (kettle, plug)* avec fusible incorporé

fuselage ['fjuːzəlɑːʒ] *n* fuselage *m*

fusel oil [ˌfjʊːzəl-] *n* fusel *m*, huile *f* de fusel

fusible ['fjuːzəbəl] *adj* fusible

►► ***fusible alloy, fusible metal*** alliage *m* fusible

fusil ['fjuːzɪl] *n Her* fusée *f*

fusilier [ˌfjuːzə'lɪə(r)] *n Mil* fusilier *m*

fusillade [ˌfjuːzə'leɪd] *Mil* **1** *n* **a fusillade (of shots)** une fusillade; *Fig* **a fusillade of criticism/questions** une avalanche de critiques/questions

2 *vt (position)* soumettre à une fusillade; *(people)* passer par les armes, fusiller

fusinist ['fjuːzɪnɪst] *n Art* fusiniste *mf*, fusainiste *mf*

fusion ['fjuːʒən] *n* (**a**) *Metal* fonte *f*, fusion *f*; *Phys* fusion *f* (**b**) *Fig (of ideas, parties)* fusion *f*, fusionnement *m*; **their new sound is a fusion of disco and rap** leur nouveau son est un mélange de disco et de rap

►► *Nucl* ***fusion bomb*** bombe *f* thermonucléaire *ou* à hydrogène; *Culin* ***fusion food*** = cuisine qui mêle saveurs d'orient et d'occident; *Nucl* ***fusion reactor*** réacteur *m* nucléaire

fuss [fʌs] **1** *n* (**a**) *(UNCOUNT) (bother)* histoires *fpl*; **what a lot of fuss about nothing!** que d'histoires pour rien!; **all that fuss over a game of football!** tout ça pour un match de foot!; **after a great deal of fuss she accepted** après avoir fait toutes sortes de manières, elle a accepté; **can you have him ejected from the studio without too much fuss?** est-ce que vous pouvez le faire évacuer du studio discrètement?

(**b**) *(state of agitation)* panique *f*; **don't get into a fuss over it!** ne t'affole pas pour ça!; **I don't see what all the fuss is about** je ne vois pas pourquoi on fait un tel cinéma

(**c**) *(idioms)* **to kick up** *or* **to make a fuss about** *or* **over sth** faire des histoires *ou* tout un plat au sujet de qch; **he kicked up quite a fuss about the bill** il a fait toute une histoire pour la facture; **people are making a fuss about the new road** les gens protestent contre la nouvelle route; **I don't want any fuss made when I retire** je ne veux pas qu'on fasse tout un cinéma quand je prendrai ma retraite; **you should have made a fuss about it** tu n'aurais pas dû laisser passer ça; **to make a fuss of** *or* **over sb** être aux petits soins pour qn; **they made quite a fuss over her when she went to visit them** ils ont été aux petits soins pour elle quand elle est allée les voir; **he likes to be made a fuss over** il aime bien qu'on fasse grand cas de lui

2 *vi (become agitated)* s'agiter; *(worry)* s'inquiéter, se tracasser; *(rush around)* s'affairer; **she kept fussing with her hair** elle n'arrêtait pas de tripoter ses cheveux; **to fuss over sb** être aux petits soins pour qn; **he fussed over his grandchildren** il était aux petits soins pour ses petits-enfants; **stop fussing over me!** laisse-moi tranquille!; **don't fuss, we'll be on time** ne t'en fais pas, on sera à l'heure

3 *vt* (**a**) *esp Am (make nervous)* agacer, embêter

(**b**) *Br Fam (idioms)* **I'm not fussed** ça m'est égal ❑; **I don't think he's particularly fussed whether we go or not** je crois que cela lui est égal qu'on y aille ou pas ❑

►**fuss about, fuss around** *vi (rush around)* s'affairer

fussbudget ['fʌsˌbʌdʒət] *Am* = **fusspot**

fussily ['fʌsɪlɪ] *adv* (**a**) *(fastidiously)* de façon méticuleuse *ou* tatillonne; *(nervously)* avec anxiété (**b**) *(over-ornately)* de façon tarabiscotée; **fussily dressed** vêtu avec trop de recherche; **the room was rather fussily decorated** la décoration de la pièce était surchargée

fussiness ['fʌsɪnɪs] *n* (**a**) *(fastidiousness)* côté *m* tatillon; **his fussiness about food is ridiculous** il est si difficile sur la nourriture que c'en est ridicule (**b**) *(ornateness → of decoration)* tarabiscotage *m*, manque *m* de simplicité; *(→ of clothes, style)* manque *m* de simplicité

fusspot ['fʌspɒt] *n Fam* (**a**) *(worrier)* anxieux(euse) ❑ *m,f*; **don't be such a fusspot** arrête de te faire du mauvais sang (**b**) *(fastidious person)* tatillon(onne) *m,f*; **she's such a fusspot!** qu'est-ce qu'elle peut être difficile!; **don't be such a fusspot, leave the housework for one day** ne sois pas aussi tatillon, laisse tomber le ménage pour aujourd'hui

fussy ['fʌsɪ] *(compar* **fussier**, *superl* **fussiest***)* *adj* (**a**) *(fastidious)* tatillon, pointilleux; **her daughter is very fussy about what she eats** sa fille est très difficile sur la nourriture; **he's fussy about what he wears** il fait très attention à ce qu'il porte; **we can't afford to be too fussy** nous ne pouvons pas nous permettre d'être trop difficiles; **where shall we go? – I'm not fussy** où est-ce qu'on va? – ça m'est égal

(**b**) *(over-ornate → decoration)* trop chargé, tarabiscoté; *(→ style)* ampoulé, qui manque de simplicité; *(→ clothes)* trop recherché

fustian ['fʌstɪən] *n* (**a**) *(fabric)* futaine *f* (**b**) *Fig Literary (bombast)* grandiloquence *f*

fustiness ['fʌstɪnɪs] *n* (**a**) *(of room, clothes)* odeur *f* de moisi (**b**) *Fig (of theory, idea, outlook etc)* caractère *m* démodé

fusty ['fʌstɪ] *(compar* **fustier**, *superl* **fustiest***)* *adj* (**a**) *(room, clothes)* qui sent le moisi; *(smell)* de moisi (**b**) *Fig (theory, idea, outlook etc)* vieux jeu

futile [*Br* 'fjuːtaɪl, *Am* 'fuːtəl] *adj (action, effort)* vain, inutile; *(remark, question)* futile, vain; *(idea)* futile, creux; **it's futile trying to reason with him** il est inutile d'essayer de lui faire entendre raison; **all our attempts were futile** toutes nos tentatives ont été inutiles *ou* vaines

futilely [*Br* 'fjuːtaɪllɪ, *Am* 'fuːtəllɪ] *adv (act)* vainement; *(remark)* futilement

futility [fjuː'tɪlətɪ] *(pl* **futilities***)* *n (of action, effort)* inutilité *f*; *(of remark, question, idea)* futilité *f*; **an exercise in futility** une vaine entreprise

futon ['fuːtɒn] *n* futon *m*

futtock ['fʌtək] *n Naut* genou-allonge *m*, allonge *f*

►► ***futtock plate*** latte *f* de hune; ***futtock shroud*** gambe *f* (de revers), gambe *f* de hune; ***futtock staff*** bastet *m*, quenouillette *f* de trélingage

future ['fjuːtʃə(r)] **1** *n* (**a**) *(time ahead)* avenir *m*; **in (the) future** à l'avenir; **sometime in the near future** *or* **in the not so distant future** *(gen)* bientôt; *(more formal)* dans un avenir proche; **in the distant future** dans un avenir lointain; **the future is still uncertain** l'avenir est encore incertain; **I'll have to see what the future holds** *or* **has in store** on verra ce que l'avenir me réserve; **you have to think of the future** il faut songer à l'avenir

(**b**) *(prospects)* avenir *m*; **young people today don't have much of a future** les jeunes d'aujourd'hui n'ont pas beaucoup d'avenir; **he has a great future ahead of him as an actor** c'est un comédien plein d'avenir; **she wants to assure her son's future** elle veut assurer un bon avenir à son fils; **there is a future ahead for bilingual people in publishing** le monde de l'édition offre des possibilités d'avenir pour les personnes bilingues; **there's no future in farming** l'agriculture n'est pas un métier d'avenir

(**c**) *Gram* futur *m*; **the future of the verb "to be"** le futur du verbe "to be"; **in the future** au futur

2 *adj* (**a**) *(yet to happen, become)* futur; **future generations** les générations *fpl* futures *ou* à venir; **my future wife** ma future épouse *ou* femme; **current and future needs** les besoins *mpl* actuels et futurs; **at a future date** à une date ultérieure; **I kept it for future reference** je l'ai conservé comme document

(**b**) *Com (delivery, estate)* à terme; **goods for future delivery** marchandises *fpl* livrables ultérieurement

3 in future *adv* à l'avenir; **I shan't offer my advice in future!** je ne donnerai plus de conseils désormais!; **in future, please ask before taking anything** à l'avenir, je vous prie de demander la permission avant de prendre quoi que ce soit

►► *Am* ***Future Farmers of America*** = organisation nationale d'étudiants en agriculture; *Gram* ***future perfect*** futur *m* antérieur; *Fin* ***Future Rate Agreement*** accord *m* de taux à terme; *Gram* ***future tense*** futur *m*, temps *m* futur

'Future Shock' *Toffler* 'Le Choc du futur'

futureless ['fjuːtʃəlɪs] *adj* sans avenir

future-proof *esp Comput* **1** *adj* évolutif

2 *vt* rendre évolutif

futures ['fjuːtʃəz] *npl St Exch (contracts)* contrats *mpl* à terme; *(transactions)* opérations *fpl* à terme; *(securities)* titres *mpl* *ou* valeurs *fpl* à terme; **sugar futures** sucre *m* (acheté) à terme

►► ***futures contract*** contrat *m* à terme; ***futures exchange*** marché *m* à terme; ***futures market*** marché *m* à terme; ***futures option*** option *f* sur contrats à terme; ***futures and options*** contrats *mpl* à terme et options; ***futures and options fund*** fonds *m* investissant dans des contrats à terme et des options; ***futures order*** ordre *m* à terme; ***futures trading*** negociations *fpl* à terme; ***futures transaction*** opération *f* à terme; ***future value*** valeur *f* capitalisée

futurism ['fjuːtʃərɪzəm] *n Art & Literature* futurisme *m*

futurist ['fjuːtʃərɪst] *Art & Literature* **1** *adj* futuriste

2 *n* futuriste *mf*

futuristic [ˌfjuːtʃə'rɪstɪk] *adj* futuriste

futurition [ˌfjuːtʃə'rɪʃən] *n Phil* futurition *f*, futur *m*

futurity [fjuː'tjʊərətɪ] (*pl* **futurities**) *n Formal* (**a**) *(future time)* avenir *m*, futur *m* (**b**) *(event)* événement *m* futur *ou* à venir

futurologist [ˌfjuːtʃə'rɒlədʒɪst] *n* futurologue *mf*

futurology [ˌfjuːtʃə'rɒlədʒɪ] *n* futurologie *f*, prospective *f*

fuze *Am* = **fuse**

fuzz [fʌz] **1** *n (UNCOUNT)* (**a**) *(down → on peach)* duvet *m*; *(→ on body)* duvet *m*, poils *mpl* fins; *(→ on head)* duvet *m*, cheveux *mpl* fins

(**b**) *(frizzy hair)* cheveux *mpl* crépus *ou* frisottants

(**c**) *(on blanket, sweater)* peluches *fpl*

(**d**) *very Fam (police)* **the fuzz** les flics *mpl*

(**e**) *Am (lint)* peluches *fpl*

2 *vt* (**a**) *(hair)* frisotter

(**b**) *(image, sight)* rendre flou

3 *vi* (**a**) *(hair)* frisotter

(**b**) *(image, sight)* devenir flou

(**c**) *(blanket, sweater)* pelucher

fuzzball ['fʌzbɔːl] *n (on garment)* peluche *f*; *(on floor)* mouton *m*

fuzzily ['fʌzɪlɪ] *adv (describe, understand)* confusément; *(paint, print)* flou

fuzziness ['fʌzɪnɪs] *n* (**a**) *(of image, picture)* flou *m*; *(of outline, recording etc)* manque *m* de netteté (**b**) *(of ideas)* confusion *f* (**c**) *(of cloth, garment)* caractère *m* pelucheux (**d**) **the fuzziness of my hair** mes cheveux *mpl* crépus

fuzzy ['fʌzɪ] (*compar* **fuzzier**, *superl* **fuzziest**) *adj* (**a**) *(image, picture)* flou; *(outline, recording etc)* qui manque de netteté (**b**) *(confused → ideas)* confus; **my head feels a bit fuzzy today** j'ai un peu la tête qui tourne aujourd'hui (**c**) *(cloth, garment)* pelucheux (**d**) *(hair)* crépu, frisottant

►► *Comput* ***fuzzy logic*** logique *f* floue

fuzzy-wuzzy [-ˌwʌzɪ] *n Br very Fam Old-fashioned* = terme raciste désignant un Noir

fwd. (*written abbr* **forward**) vers l'avant

fwy *Am* (*written abbr* **freeway**) autoroute *f*

FX[1] [ˌef'eks] *npl Cin* effets *mpl* spéciaux *(du cinéma de science-fiction)*

FX[2] *n Fin* (*abbr* **foreign exchange**) devises *fpl* étrangères

►► ***FX broker, FX dealer*** cambiste *mf*, courtier(ère) *m,f* en devises; ***FX market*** marché *m* des changes; ***FX option*** option *f* sur devises; ***FX transfer*** transfert *m* de devises

FY *Fin* (*written abbr* **fiscal year**) année *f* fiscale *ou* d'exercice

FYI (*written abbr* **for your information**) à titre indicatif

G

G¹, g¹ [dʒiː] *n* (**a**) *(letter)* G, g *m inv*; **two g's** deux g; **G for George** ≃ G comme Gaston (**b**) *Mus (note)* sol *m inv*; **G clef** clef *f* de sol; **in G minor** en sol mineur

G² *n* (**a**) *Phys* conductance *f* (**b**) *Am Fam (abbr* **grand**) *(thousand dollars)* mille dollars *mpl*; **he earns 50G a year** il gagne cinquante mille dollars par an

G³ (**a**) *(written abbr* **good**) B (**b**) *Austr Cin (written abbr* **general (audience)**) = tous publics

g² (**a**) *(written abbr* **gramme**) g (**b**) *(written abbr* **gravity**) g

G7 [ˌdʒiːˈsevən] *n* le G7, le groupe des 7

G8 [ˌdʒiːˈeɪt] *n* le G8, le groupe des 8

GA¹ [ˌdʒiːˈeɪ] *n Ins (abbr* **general average**) avarie *f* commune

GA² *(written abbr* **Georgia**) Géorgie *f*

GAA [ˌdʒiːeɪˈeɪ] *n (abbr* **Gaelic Athletic Association**) = association qui œuvre pour le développement des sports irlandais traditionnels, notamment le football gaélique

GAAP [ˌdʒiːeɪˌeɪˈpiː] *npl Acct (abbr* **generally-accepted accounting principles**) PCGR *mpl*

gab [gæb] *(pt & pp* **gabbed,** *cont* **gabbing**) *Fam* **1** *n* (**a**) *(chatter)* parlotte *f*, parlote *f*; **we had a good gab on the phone** on a taillé une bonne bavette au téléphone (**b**) *(idiom)* **to have the gift of the gab** avoir la langue bien pendue; *(be convincing talker)* avoir du bagou(t)

2 *vi (chat)* bavarder, papoter; *(gossip)* caqueter, jaser

gabardine = **gaberdine**

gabble [ˈgæbəl] **1** *vi* (**a**) *(idly)* faire la parlote, papoter; **they gabble (away) for hours** ils papotent pendant des heures

(**b**) *(inarticulately)* bredouiller, balbutier

2 *vt* bredouiller, bafouiller; **she gabbled (out) her story** elle a raconté son histoire en bredouillant

3 *n* baragouin *m*, flot *m* de paroles; **a gabble of voices** un bruit confus de conversations; **to talk at a gabble** bredouiller, parler vite *ou* avec volubilité; **there was an incomprehensible gabble coming from the garden** on entendait une conversation inintelligible dans le jardin

gabbler [ˈgæbələ(r)] *n* bavard(e) *m,f*

gabbling [ˈgæbəlɪŋ] *n* caquetage *m*, jacasserie *f*; **stop your gabbling!** arrêtez de jacasser!

gabbro [ˈgæbrəʊ] *n Geol* gabbro *m*

gabby [ˈgæbɪ] *(compar* **gabbier,** *superl* **gabbiest**) *adj Fam* bavard

gaberdine [gæbəˈdiːn] *n* gabardine *f*

►► ***gaberdine raincoat*** gabardine *f*

gabfest [ˈgæbfest] *n Am Fam* réunion ❑ *f (où l'on parle beaucoup)*

gabion [ˈgæbjən] *n Mil & Tech* gabion *m*

gable [ˈgeɪbəl] *n (wall)* pignon *m*; *(over arch, door etc)* gâble *m*, gable *m*

►► ***gable roof*** comble *m* sur pignon(s); ***gable window*** fenêtre *f* sur pignon

gabled [ˈgeɪbəld] *adj (house)* à pignon *ou* pignons; *(wall)* en pignon; *(roof)* sur pignon *ou* pignons; *(arch)* à gâble

gable-end *n* pignon *m*

Gabon [gæˈbɒn] *n* Gabon *m*; **in Gabon** au Gabon

Gabonese [gæbɒˈniːz] **1** *npl* **the Gabonese** les Gabonais *mpl*

2 *adj* gabonais

3 *comp (embassy, history)* du Gabon

Gabriel [ˈgeɪbrɪəl] *pr n Bible* Gabriel

Gad [gæd] *exclam Arch or Hum* **(by) Gad!** sapristi!, sacrebleu!

gad [gæd] *(pt & pp* **gadded,** *cont* **gadding**) **1** *vi* **to gad about** *or* **around** se balader; **she's been out gadding about (town) all night** elle a passé toute la nuit à faire la fête (en ville); **she goes gadding all over the world** elle court le vaste monde

2 *vt Mining* casser au coin *ou* au picot

3 *n* (**a**) *Mining (chisel)* coin *m*; *(pick)* picot *m* (**b**) *(goad)* aiguillon *m* (**c**) *Am (spur)* éperon *m*

gadabout [ˈgædəbaʊt] *n Br Fam* vadrouilleur(-euse) *m,f*

Gadarene swine [gædəˈriːn-] *npl Bible* **the Gadarene swine** la guérison des deux démoniaques *(expression parfois utilisée pour décrire un mouvement de foule)*

Gaddafi [gəˈdɑːfɪ] *pr n* Kadhafi

gadfly [ˈgædflaɪ] *(pl* **gadflies**) *n* (**a**) *(insect)* taon *m* (**b**) *(annoying person)* enquiquineur(euse) *m,f*, casse-pieds *mf inv*

gadget [ˈgædʒɪt] *n* gadget *m*; **a kitchen with all the latest gadgets** une cuisine avec tous les derniers gadgets; **what's that gadget for?** à quoi sert ce truc-là?

gadgetry [ˈgædʒɪtrɪ] *n (UNCOUNT)* gadgets *mpl*

gadid [ˈgeɪdɪd] *n Ich* gadidé *m*, gade *m*

gadoid [ˈgædɔɪd] *n Ich* gade *m*, gadidé *m*

gadolinium [gædəʊˈlɪnɪəm] *n Chem* gadolinium *m*

gadwall [ˈgædwɔːl] *n Orn* canard *m* chipeau

gadzooks [gædˈzuːks] *exclam Arch or Hum* sapristi!, sacrebleu!

Gael [geɪl] *n* **the Gaels** les Gaëls *mpl*

Gaelic [*Ir* ˈgeɪlɪk, *Scot* ˈgælɪk] **1** *adj* gaélique

2 *n Ling* gaélique *m*; *Scot* **to have the Gaelic** parler gaélique

►► ***Gaelic coffee*** Irish coffee *m*; ***Gaelic football*** football *m* gaélique

> **GAELIC**
>
> Le gaélique, langue d'origine des peuples celtes d'Irlande et d'Écosse, est encore parlé aujourd'hui dans certaines régions de l'ouest de l'Irlande et de l'Écosse. En République d'Irlande, le gaélique est une matière obligatoire à l'école et la maîtrise de cette langue est exigée pour certains postes dans la fonction publique. Les régions rurales du "Gaeltacht" accueillent de nombreux séjours linguistiques pendant l'été. Plusieurs tentatives ont été faites pour renforcer le statut de la langue, telles que la création d'une chaîne de télévision gaélique en 1996.

Gaeltacht [ˈgeɪltæχt] *n* **the Gaeltacht** = les régions d'Irlande où l'on parle le gaélique

gaff [gæf] **1** *n* (**a**) *(fishhook)* gaffe *f* (**b**) *Naut (spar)* corne *f* (**c**) *Br (UNCOUNT) (nonsense)* foutaise *f*, foutaises *fpl* (**d**) *Br Fam (home)* baraque *f*; **he's staying at my gaff for the weekend** il crèche chez moi ce week-end (**e**) *Fam (idiom)* **to blow the gaff** vendre la mèche; **to blow the gaff on sb** dénoncer qn ❑, vendre qn

2 *vt (fish)* gaffer

►► *Naut* ***gaff topsail*** voile *f* de flèche

gaffe [gæf] *n (blunder)* bévue *f*; **to commit** *or* **to make a gaffe** commettre une bévue; **a social gaffe** un faux pas, un impair

gaffer [ˈgæfə(r)] *n* (**a**) *Br Fam* **the gaffer** *(boss)* le patron, le chef; *(foreman)* le contremaître ❑, le chef d'équipe ❑ (**b**) *Fam (old man)* **an old gaffer** un vieux bonhomme *m* (**c**) *Cin* chef *m* électricien, gaffer *m*

►► *TV & Cin* ***gaffer grip*** pince *f* pour projecteur; ***gaffer tape*** ruban *m* adhésif en toile

gaff-rigged *adj Naut* à gréement aurique

gaff-sail *n Naut* voile *f* aurique *ou* à corne

gag [gæg] *(pt & pp* **gagged,** *cont* **gagging**) **1** *n* (**a**) *(over mouth)* bâillon *m*; *Fig* **they want to put a gag on the press** ils veulent bâillonner la presse

(**b**) *Fam (joke)* blague ❑ *f*; *(visual)* gag ❑ *m*

(**c**) *Med* ouvre-bouche *m*

2 *vt (silence)* bâillonner; *Fig* bâillonner, museler; *Am Fam Hum* **gag me (with a spoon)!** ça me donne envie de gerber!

3 *vi* (**a**) *(retch)* avoir un haut-le-cœur; **to make sb gag** donner envie de vomir à qn; **he gagged on a fishbone** il a failli s'étrangler avec une arête de poisson; *Br Vulg* **to be gagging for it** avoir envie de se faire tirer

(**b**) *Fam (joke)* blaguer ❑, rigoler ❑

(**c**) *Theat (actor, comedian)* faire des improvisations comiques

►► *Am* ***gag law*** = toute loi limitant la liberté de la presse ou la liberté d'expression, *Can* loi du bâillon; ***gag order*** = décision de justice visant à interdire à la presse de publier tout article à propos d'une affaire, *Can* ordonnance *f* imposant le secret; **to issue a gag order** = interdire à la presse de publier tout article à propos d'une affaire; *Am* ***gag resolution, gag rule*** règle *f* du bâillon *(procédure parlementaire permettant de limiter le temps de parole et d'éviter l'obstruction systématique)*

gaga [ˈgɑːgɑː] *adj Fam (senile, crazy)* gaga; **to go gaga** devenir gaga *ou* gâteux; **he's absolutely gaga about her** il est complètement fou d'elle

Gagarin [gəˈgɑːrɪn] *pr n* **Yuri Gagarin** Iouri Gagarine

gag-bit *n* mors *m* de force

gage¹ [geɪdʒ] **1** *n* (**a**) *Arch (pledge)* gage *m* (**b**) *(challenge)* défi *m* (**c**) *Arch (glove)* gant *m*

2 *vt Arch (pledge, wager)* gager

gage² *Am* = **gauge**

gagging [ˈgægɪŋ] *n (of person, press)* bâillonnement *m*

►► ***gagging order*** = décision de justice visant à interdire à la presse de publier tout article à propos d'une affaire, *Can* ordonnance *f* imposant le secret

gaggle [ˈgægəl] **1** *n (of geese) & Fig* troupeau *m*; **a gaggle of young schoolgirls** un troupeau de jeunes élèves

2 *vi* cacarder

gagman [ˈgægmən] *(pl* **gagmen** [-men]) *n Am Cin & Theat* auteur *m* de gags, gagman *m*

Gaia [ˈgaɪə] *n Myth* Gaia

gaiety [ˈgeɪətɪ] **1** *n* gaieté *f*; **it brought a bit of gaiety into their lives** ça a apporté un peu de gaieté dans leur vie

2 gaieties *npl Literary (merry-making)* réjouissances *fpl*

gaily [ˈgeɪlɪ] *adv* (**a**) *(brightly)* gaiement; **gaily coloured clothes** des vêtements *mpl* aux couleurs vives (**b**) *(happily)* gaiement, allègrement

gain [geɪn] **1** *n* (**a**) *(profit)* gain *m*, profit *m*, bénéfice *m*; *Fig* avantage *m*; **to do sth for personal gain** faire qch par intérêt; **my gain is your loss** le profit de l'un est le dommage de l'autre

(**b**) *(acquisition)* gain *m*; **there were large Conservative gains** le Parti conservateur a gagné de nombreux sièges

(**c**) *(increase)* augmentation *f*, accroissement *m*; *(in value)* hausse *f*; **a gain in speed** une augmentation de vitesse; **a gain in weight** une prise de poids; **there has been a net gain in their income** leurs revenus ont nettement augmenté; **there has been a net gain in profits this**

year il y a eu une augmentation nette des bénéfices cette année; *St Exch* **there has been a gain of 100 points on the Dow Jones** l'indice Dow Jones a gagné 100 points; *Fin* **gain in value** plus-value *f*

(**d**) *Electron* gain *m*

2 *vt* (**a**) *(earn, win, obtain)* gagner; *(reputation)* acquérir; **you will gain nothing by it** vous n'y gagnerez rien; **what would we (have to) gain by joining?** quel intérêt avons-nous à adhérer?; **to gain friends (by doing sth)** se faire des amis (en faisant qch); **they're trying to gain our sympathy** ils essaient de gagner notre sympathie; **they managed to gain entry to the building** ils ont réussi à s'introduire dans le bâtiment; **he managed to gain a hearing** il a réussi à se faire écouter; **to gain the impression that...** avoir l'impression que... + *indicative*; **to gain an advantage** obtenir un avantage; **we've not so much lost a daughter as gained a son** nous n'avons pas perdu une fille mais gagné un fils

(**b**) *(increase)* gagner; *St Exch* **the share index has gained two points** l'indice des actions a gagné deux points

(**c**) *(obtain more)* gagner, obtenir; **to gain weight/speed** prendre du poids/de la vitesse; **to gain experience** acquérir de l'expérience; **to gain time** gagner du temps; **to gain popularity** devenir plus populaire; **he has gained prestige through this action** cette action a rehaussé son prestige; **the party has gained support** le parti a gagné des voix; **to gain ground (on)** *(of racer, pursuer)* gagner du terrain (sur); **to gain ground** *(of custom)* se répandre, se développer; **to gain a share** *(of market)* gagner des parts de marché

(**d**) *(of clock, watch)* avancer de; **my watch gains ten minutes a day** ma montre avance de dix minutes par jour

(**e**) *Literary (reach)* atteindre, gagner; **we finally gained the shore** nous avons fini par atteindre la rive

3 *vi* (**a**) *(profit)* profiter, gagner; **who stands to gain by this deal?** qui y gagne dans cette affaire?; **we have all gained by his hard work** nous avons tous bénéficié de son labeur; **we have gained by having her in the team** cela nous a aidés de l'avoir dans l'équipe

(**b**) *(increase)* **to gain in popularity** gagner en popularité; **to gain in experience** acquérir de l'expérience; **to gain in self-confidence** gagner *ou* prendre de l'assurance; **to gain in number** devenir plus nombreux

(**c**) *(clock)* avancer

►► *Electron* ***gain control*** réglage *m* du gain

►**gain on, gain upon** *vt insep (catch up)* rattraper, gagner du terrain sur

gainer ['geɪnə(r)] *n* gagnant(e) *m,f*

gainful ['geɪnfʊl] *adj* (**a**) *(profitable)* profitable, rémunérateur (**b**) *(paid)* rémunéré; **to be in gainful employment** avoir un emploi rémunéré

gainfully ['geɪnfʊlɪ] *adv* de façon profitable, avantageusement; **to be gainfully employed** avoir un emploi rémunéré

gainsay [geɪn'seɪ] *(pt & pp* **gainsaid** [-'sed]) *vt Formal (deny)* nier; *(contradict)* contredire; **you can't gainsay the facts** tu ne peux pas nier l'évidence; **there's no gainsaying her skill as an artist** on ne peut pas nier son talent artistique, son talent artistique est indéniable

gainsayer [geɪn'seɪə(r)] *n Formal (contradictor)* contradicteur *m*; *(opponent)* opposant(e) *m,f*

Gainsborough hat ['geɪnzbərə-] *n* capeline *f*

gainst [geɪnst], **'gainst** [genst] *Literary* = **against**

gait [geɪt] *n* démarche *f*, allure *f*; *(of horse)* train *m*; **to walk with an unsteady gait** marcher d'un pas chancelant

gaiters ['geɪtəz] *npl* guêtres *fpl*

Gaius ['gaɪəs] *pr n Antiq* Gaius

gal [gæl] *n* (**a**) *Fam Old-fashioned (girl)* fille ❑ *f* (**b**) *Phys (unit of acceleration)* gal *m*

gal. *(written abbr* **gallon**) gallon *m*

gala ['gɑːlə] **1** *n* (**a**) *(festivity)* gala *m* (**b**) *Br Sport* réunion *f* sportive; **swimming gala** grand concours *m* de natation

2 *comp (day, evening)* de gala

►► ***gala dress*** habit *m* de gala; **in gala dress** en habit de gala; ***a gala occasion*** une grande occasion

galactic [gə'læktɪk] *adj Astron* galactique

►► ***galactic halo*** halo *m* galactique; ***galactic plane*** plan *m* galactique; ***galactic poles*** pôles *mpl* galactiques

galactometer [gælək'tɒmɪtə(r)] *n* galactomètre *m*, pèse-lait *m inv*

galactopoiesis [gəlæktəʊpɔɪ'iːsɪs] *n* galactopoïèse *f*

galactose [gə'læktəʊs] *n* galactose *m*

galago [gə'lɑːgəʊ] *(pl* **galagos**) *n Zool* galago *m*

Galahad ['gæləhæd] *pr n Myth* **Sir Galahad** Galaad

galalith ['gæləlɪθ] *n Miner* galalithe *f*

galangal ['gæləŋgæl] = **galingale**

galantine ['gæləntiːn] *n Culin* galantine *f*

Galapagos Islands [gə'læpəgəs-] *npl* **the Galapagos Islands** les (îles *fpl*) Galapagos *fpl*; **in the Galapagos Islands** aux (îles) Galapagos

Galatian [gə'leɪʃjən] *n* **the Epistle of Paul to the Galatians** l'Épître de saint Paul aux Galates

galaxy ['gæləksɪ] *(pl* **galaxies**) *n* (**a**) *Astron* galaxie *f*; **the Galaxy** la Galaxie (**b**) *(gathering)* constellation *f*, pléiade *f*; **a galaxy of film stars** une pléiade de vedettes de cinéma

galbanum ['gælbənəm] *n Bot & Pharm* galbanum *m*

gale [geɪl] *n* (**a**) *(wind)* coup *m* de vent, grand vent *m*; *Met* **a force 9 gale** un vent de force 9; **the roof was blown off in a gale** le toit a été emporté par la tempête; **it's blowing a gale** le vent souffle en tempête (**b**) *(outburst)* éclat *m*; **gales of laughter** des éclats *mpl* de rire

►► *Met* ***gale force*** force *f* 8 à 9; *Met* ***gale warning*** avis *m* de coup de vent, avis *m* de tempête

gale-force *adj*

►► *Met* ***gale-force wind(s)*** vent *m* soufflant en tempête

galena [gə'liːnə] *n Miner* galène *f*

galenical [gə'lenɪkəl] *Pharm* **1** *adj* galénique

2 *n* médicament *m*

galenite [gə'liːnaɪt] *n Miner* galène *f*

galette [gə'let] *n Culin* galette *f*

Galicia [gə'lɪʃɪə] *n* (**a**) *(Central Europe)* Galicie *f*; **in Galicia** en Galicie (**b**) *(Spain)* Galice *f*; **in Galicia** en Galice

Galician [gə'lɪʃɪən] **1** *adj* galicien

2 *n* (**a**) *(person)* Galicien(enne) *m,f* (**b**) *Ling* galicien *m*

Galilean [gælɪ'liːən] **1** *adj* galiléen

2 *n* Galiléen(enne) *m,f*

Galilee ['gælɪliː] *n* Galilée *f*; **in Galilee** en Galilée; **the Sea of Galilee** le lac de Tibériade, la mer de Galilée

Galileo [gælɪ'leɪəʊ] *pr n* Galilée

galingale ['gælɪŋgeɪl] *n Bot* souchet *m*, galanga *m*

galiot = **galliot**

gall [gɔːl] **1** *n* (**a**) *Anat (human)* bile *f*; *(animal)* fiel *m*

(**b**) *(bitterness)* fiel *m*, amertume *f*

(**c**) *(nerve)* culot *m*, toupet *m*, effronterie *f*; **he had the gall to say it was my fault!** il a eu le culot *ou* le toupet de dire que c'était de ma faute!

(**d**) *Bot* galle *f*, cécidie *f*

(**e**) *Med & Vet* écorchure *f*, excoriation *f*; *Fig* **the criticism was a gall to his pride** la critique l'a piqué au vif

2 *vt* (**a**) *(annoy)* énerver; **it galled him to have to admit he was wrong** ça l'a forcé de devoir reconnaître qu'il avait tort

(**b**) *Med & Vet* excorier

►► *Anat* ***gall bladder*** vésicule *f* biliaire; *Anat* ***gall duct*** voie *f* biliaire; *Entom* ***gall wasp*** cynips *m*

gall. *(written abbr* **gallon**) gallon *m*

gallant **1** *adj* (**a**) ['gælənt] *(brave)* courageux, vaillant; **gallant deeds** des actions *fpl* d'éclat, des prouesses *fpl*; **the ship and her gallant crew** le navire et son valeureux équipage (**b**) [gə'lænt, 'gælənt] *(chivalrous)* galant (**c**) ['gælənt] *Literary (noble)* noble; *(splendid)* superbe, splendide

2 *n* ['gælənt] *Literary* galant *m*

gallantly ['gæləntlɪ] *adv* (**a**) *(bravely)* courageusement, vaillamment (**b**) *(chivalrously)* galamment

gallantry ['gæləntrɪ] *(pl* **gallantries**) *n* (**a**) *(bravery)* courage *m*, vaillance *f*, bravoure *f*; **a medal for gallantry** une médaille de bravoure (**b**) *(brave deed)* prouesse *f*, action *f* d'éclat (**c**) *(chivalry, amorousness)* galanterie *f*

galleon ['gælɪən] *n Naut* galion *m*

galleria [gælə'rɪə] *n* puits *m (aménagé dans un grand magasin à plusieurs étages)*

galleried ['gælərɪd] *adj Archit* à galerie *ou* galeries

gallery ['gælərɪ] *(pl* **galleries**) *n* (**a**) *(of art)* musée *m* (des beaux-arts); **private gallery** galerie *f*; **gallery owner** galeriste *mf*

(**b**) *(balcony)* galerie *f*; *(for spectators)* tribune *f*; **the press gallery** la tribune de la presse; **strangers'** *or* **public gallery** *(in Houses of Parliament)* tribune *f* du public

(**c**) *(covered passageway)* galerie *f*

(**d**) *Theat (upper balcony)* dernier balcon *m*; *(audience)* galerie *f*; *Fig* **to play to the gallery** poser pour la galerie

(**e**) *(tunnel)* galerie *f*

(**f**) *Golf (spectators)* public *m*

(**g**) *Am (veranda)* véranda *f*; *(balcony)* balcon *m*

►► ***gallery forest*** forêt-galerie *f*, galerie *f* forestière; ***gallery tray*** plateau *m* en argent *(avec rebord surélevé)*

galley ['gælɪ] *n* (**a**) *(ship)* galère *f*; **to be sent to the galleys** être condamné aux galères (**b**) *(rowing boat)* yole *f* (**c**) *(ship's kitchen)* coquerie *f*; *(aircraft kitchen)* office *m or f* (**d**) *Typ (container)* galée *f*; *(proof)* placard *m*

►► ***galley kitchen*** kitchenette *f*, cuisinette *f*; *Typ* ***galley proof*** (épreuve *f* en) placard *m*; ***galley slave*** galérien *m*

galley-west *adv Am Fam* **to knock sb galley-west** *(knock out)* mettre qn K-O; *(stupefy)* renverser qn ❑; **I was knocked galley-west!** j'en suis resté baba!; **to knock sth galley-west** *(send flying)* envoyer valser qch; *(mess up)* chambouler qch, mettre qch sens dessus dessous

gallfly ['gɔːlflaɪ] *(pl* **gallflies**) *n Entom* cynips *m*

Gallic ['gælɪk] *adj* (**a**) *(French)* français; **Gallic charm** charme *m* typiquement français; **a Gallic shrug** un haussement d'épaules (typiquement français) (**b**) *Hist (of Gaul)* gaulois

►► ***the Gallic Wars*** la guerre des Gaules

gallic ['gælɪk] *adj Chem* gallique

►► ***gallic acid*** acide *m* gallique

Gallicism ['gælɪsɪzəm] *n* gallicisme *m*

Gallicize, -ise ['gælɪsaɪz] *vt* franciser

galligaskins [,gælɪ'gæskɪnz] *npl* (**a**) *Fam (breeches)* pantalon ❑ *m*, culotte ❑ *f* (**b**) *(gaiters)* guêtres *fpl*

gallimaufry [gælɪ'mɔːfrɪ] *(pl* **gallimaufries**) *n Literary* fatras *m*, fouillis *m*

gallinaceous [gælɪ'neɪʃəs] *adj Orn* gallinacé

galling ['gɔːlɪŋ] *adj (annoying)* irritant; *(humiliating)* humiliant, vexant; **it was galling to reflect that...** ça me/la/*etc* rendait malade de penser que...

gallingly ['gɔːlɪŋlɪ] *adv* de façon irritante

gallinule ['gælɪnjuːl] *n Orn* poule *f* d'eau

galliot ['gælɪət] *n Hist & Naut* galiote *f*

gallium ['gælɪəm] *n Chem* gallium *m*

gallivant ['gælɪvænt] *vi Hum* se balader

►**gallivant about, gallivant around** *vi Hum* se balader; **he's gallivanting around the South of France** il se balade *ou* il est parti en vadrouille dans le Midi

gallnut ['gɔːlnʌt] *n* noix *f* de galle

gallon ['gælən] *n (in UK)* = 4,54 l, gallon *m*; *(in US)* = 3,78 l, gallon *m*; *Aut* **miles per gallon** ≈ consommation *f* d'essence aux cent kilomètres; *Fam* **they drink gallons of beer** ils boivent de la bière à tire-larigot

gallonage ['gælənɪdʒ] *n Tech* capacité *f* (en gallons)

galloon [gə'luːn] *n Sewing* galon *m*

gallop ['gæləp] **1** *vi (horse)* galoper; *(horse, rider)* aller au galop; **we galloped across the fields** nous avons galopé à travers les champs; **to gallop away** *or* **off** partir au galop; *Fig* **he came galloping down the stairs** il a descendu l'escalier au galop

2 *vt* faire galoper; **to gallop a horse** faire galoper un cheval

3 *n* galop *m*; **at a gallop** au galop (allongé); **(at) full gallop** au grand galop; *Fig* **to do sth at a gallop** faire qch à toute vitesse; **the pony broke into a gallop** le poney a pris le galop; **we decided to go for a gallop in the woods** nous décidâmes d'aller faire un galop dans les bois

gai–gal

►**gallop through** *vt insep Fig* faire à toute vitesse; **she galloped through her homework** elle a expédié ses devoirs; **I positively galloped through the book** j'ai vraiment lu ce livre à toute allure *or* à toute vitesse

galloping ['gæləpɪŋ] *adj (horse)* au galop; *Fig* galopant

►► ***galloping inflation*** inflation *f* galopante

Gallo-Roman [,gæləʊ-] **1** *adj (dialects)* gallo-roman; *(civilization, remains)* gallo-romain

2 *n Ling* gallo-roman *m*

gallows ['gæləʊz] *(pl* **inv**) *n* potence *f*, gibet *m*

►► *Old-fashioned* ***gallows bird*** gibier *m* de potence; *Br* ***gallows humour*** humour *m* noir; ***gallows tree*** potence *f*, gibet *m*

gallstone ['gɔːlstəʊn] *n Med* calcul *m* biliaire; **to have gallstones** avoir des calculs

Gallup Poll ['gæləp-] *n* sondage *m* (d'opinion) *(réalisé par l'institut Gallup)*

galoot [gə'luːt] *n Am & Scot Fam Pej* lourdaud *m*, empoté *m*

galore [gə'lɔː(r)] *adv* en abondance, à gogo; **we've got food galore** nous avons de la nourriture en abondance

galoshes [gə'lɒʃɪz] *npl* caoutchoucs *mpl (pour protéger les chaussures)*

galumph [gə'lʌmf] *vi Fam* courir lourdement❑ *ou* comme un pachyderme; **he came galumphing down the stairs** il a descendu l'escalier avec la légèreté d'un éléphant *ou* d'un hippopotame

galvanic [gæl'vænɪk] *adj* (**a**) *Elec* galvanique (**b**) *Med (convulsive)* convulsif (**c**) *(stimulating)* galvanisant

galvanism ['gælvə,nɪzəm] *n Med* galvanisme *m*

galvanization [,gælvənaɪ'zeɪʃən] *n Med, Metal & Fig* galvanisation *f*

galvanize, -ise ['gælvə,naɪz] *vt Med, Metal & Fig* galvaniser; **it galvanized the team into action** ça a poussé l'équipe à agir

galvanized ['gælvə,naɪzd] *adj* galvanisé

►► ***galvanized iron*** fer *m* galvanisé

galvanizing effect ['gælvə,naɪzɪŋ-] *n* effet *m* de galvanisation; *Fig* **the imminent danger had a galvanizing effect on us** la proximité du danger nous a galvanisés

galvanometer [gælvə'nɒmɪtə(r)] *n Elec* galvanomètre *m*

galvanoscope [gæl'vænəʊskəʊp] *n Elec* galvanoscope *m*

galvanotropism [gælvænəʊ'trəʊpɪzəm] *n Biol galvanotropisme m*

Galway ['gɔːlweɪ] *n* (**a**) *(town)* Galway (**b**) *(county)* le comté de Galway, = comté dans l'ouest de la République d'Irlande; **in Galway** dans le comté de Galway

Galwegian [gæl'wiːdʒən] *n* (**a**) *(inhabitant of Galway)* habitant(e) *m,f* de Galway; *(native of Galway)* originaire *mf* de Galway (**b**) *(inhabitant of Galloway)* habitant(e) *m,f* du Galloway; *(native of Galloway)* originaire *mf* du Galloway

Gambia ['gæmbɪə] *n* **(the) Gambia** (la) Gambie; **in (the) Gambia** en Gambie

Gambian ['gæmbɪən] **1** *n* Gambien(enne) *m,f*

2 *adj* gambien

gambit ['gæmbɪt] *n Chess* gambit *m*; *Fig* tactique *f*, stratagème *m*; *Chess* **king's/queen's gambit** gambit *m* du roi/de la reine; *Fig* **opening gambit** manœuvre *f* d'approche; **a gambit to get their sympathy** un stratagème pour gagner leur sympathie

gamble ['gæmbəl] **1** *vi* jouer; **I don't gamble** je ne joue pas pour de l'argent; **to gamble on a throw of the dice** miser sur un coup de dé(s); **to gamble on the Stock Exchange** jouer à la Bourse, boursicoter; *Fig* **Napoleon gambled and lost** Napoléon a joué et perdu

2 *vt* parier, miser; **to gamble one's money on horses** jouer son argent aux courses; *Fig* **the government has gambled its political future on the plan's success** le gouvernement a joué son avenir sur le succès du projet

3 *n* (**a**) *(wager)* pari *m*; **I like an occasional gamble on the horses** j'aime bien jouer aux courses de temps en temps

(**b**) *(risk)* coup *m* de poker; **I know it's a gamble but...** je sais que c'est risqué mais...; **his gamble paid off** son coup de poker a payé; **it's a gamble we have to take** c'est un risque qu'il faut prendre; **it's a bit of a gamble whether it'll work or not** nous n'avons aucun moyen de savoir si ça marchera

►**gamble away** *vt sep (fortune)* perdre au jeu

►**gamble on** *vt insep* miser *ou* tabler *ou* compter sur; **we'd gambled on having fine weather** on avait misé sur le beau temps; **I wouldn't gamble on the plan succeeding** je ne tablerais pas sur la réussite du projet; **they're gambling on there not being an inspector on the train** ils misent sur le fait qu'il n'y aura pas de contrôleur dans le train; **she's gambling on getting home by eight o'clock** elle compte rentrer avant huit heures

gambler ['gæmblə(r)] *n* joueur(euse) *m,f*

gambling ['gæmblɪŋ] **1** *n (UNCOUNT)* jeu *m*, jeux *mpl* d'argent; **no gambling** *(sign)* les jeux d'argent sont interdits; **gambling on the Stock Exchange** la spéculation en Bourse

2 *adj* joueur; **my father was a gambling man** mon père jouait; **I'm not a gambling man but I would guess that they will accept the offer** je ne suis pas homme à parier mais je crois qu'ils vont accepter la proposition

►► ***gambling debts*** dettes *fpl* de jeu; *Pej* ***gambling den*** maison *f* de jeu, tripot *m*; ***gambling fever*** démon *m* du jeu; *Br* ***gambling house,*** *Am* ***gambling parlor*** maison *f* de jeu

gamboge [gæm'buːʒ] **1** *n* gomme-gutte *f*

2 *adj (light)* jaune

gambol ['gæmbəl] *(Br pt & pp* **gambolled,** *cont* **gambolling,** *Am pt & pp* **gamboled,** *cont* **gamboling**) **1** *vi* gambader, cabrioler

2 *n* gambade *f*, cabriole *f*

gambrel roof ['gæmbrəl-] *n* toit *m* mansardé

game [geɪm] **1** *n* (**a**) *(gen)* jeu *m*; **card/party games** jeux *mpl* de cartes/de société; **a game of chance/of skill** un jeu de hasard/d'adresse; **ball games are forbidden** il est interdit de jouer au ballon; **the rules of the game** la règle du jeu; **she plays a good game of chess** c'est une bonne joueuse d'échecs, elle joue bien aux échecs; **the children were playing a game of cowboys and Indians** les enfants jouaient aux cow-boys et aux Indiens; **it's only a game!** ce n'est qu'un jeu!; **I'm off my game today** je joue mal aujourd'hui; **it put me right off my game** ça m'a complètement déconcentré; **to play sb's game** entrer dans le jeu de qn; **you're not playing the game!** tu ne joues pas le jeu!; **politics is just a game to him** pour lui, la politique n'est qu'un jeu

(**b**) *(contest)* partie *f*; *(esp professional)* match *m*; *(part of a game of cards)* manche *f*; *Chess* **opening/middle/end game** début *m*/milieu *m*/fin *f* de partie; **do you fancy a game of chess?** ça te dit de faire une partie d'échecs?; **tonight's big game** le grand match de ce soir; **he played 65 games for England** il a joué 65 fois pour l'Angleterre; **we had a good game** *(played well)* nous avons bien joué

(**c**) *(division of match – in tennis, bridge)* jeu *m*; **game, set and match** jeu, set et match; **(one) game all** un jeu partout

(**d**) *(playing equipment, set)* jeu *m*

(**e**) *Fam (scheme, trick)* ruse❑ *f*, stratagème❑ *m*; **what's your (little) game?** qu'est-ce que tu manigances?, à quel jeu joues-tu?; **I know your (little) game!** je sais bien où vous voulez en venir!; **to play a double game** jouer un double jeu; **to beat sb at his/her own game** battre qn sur son propre terrain; **the game's up!** tout est perdu!; **two can play at that game,** moi aussi je peux jouer à ce petit jeu-là; **that's not playing the game** ce n'est pas loyal; **let's stop playing games and come to the point** trêve de plaisanteries, passons aux choses sérieuses; **don't play** *or* **come that game with me!** tu ne m'auras pas à ce petit jeu-là!

(**f**) *Fam (undertaking, operation)* **at this stage in the game** à ce stade des opérations❑; **to be ahead of the game** mener le jeu

(**g**) *(activity)* travail *m*; **I'm new to this game** je suis novice en la matière; **when you've been in this game as long as I have, you'll understand** quand tu auras fait ça aussi longtemps que moi, tu comprendras

(**h**) *Culin & (in hunting)* gibier *m*; **small game** menu gibier *m*

(**i**) *(idioms)* **to give the game away** vendre la mèche; **that gave the game away** c'est comme ça qu'on a découvert le pot aux roses; *Br Fam* **to be on the game** *(prostitute)* faire le tapin *ou* le trottoir; *Br* **the game is not worth the candle** le jeu n'en vaut pas la chandelle

2 *comp* de chasse

3 *adj* (**a**) *(plucky)* courageux, brave

(**b**) *(willing)* prêt, partant; **he's game for anything** il est toujours partant; *Pej* il est prêt à tout *ou* capable de tout; **I'm game if you are!** si tu es partant, moi aussi!

(**c**) *Br (lame)* estropié; **he's got a game leg** il a une jambe estropiée

4 *vi* (**a**) *Formal (gamble)* jouer (de l'argent)

(**b**) *(play computer games)* faire des jeux électroniques

5 games *npl (international)* jeux *mpl*; *Br Sch* sport *m*; **they have games on Wednesdays** le mercredi, ils ont sport; **he's good at games** il est bon en sport, c'est un sportif

►► ***game bag*** gibecière *f*; ***game birds*** gibier *m* à plumes; **the partridge is a game bird** on chasse la perdrix; *Br Culin* ***game chips*** = frites fines servies avec le gibier; ***game fish*** poisson *m* noble *(saumon, truite, brochet)*; ***game fowl*** gibier *m* à plumes; ***game laws*** réglementation *f* de la chasse; ***game licence*** permis *m* de chasse; ***game park*** *(in Africa)* réserve *f*; *Culin* ***game pie*** tourte *f* au gibier, ≃ pâté *m* en croûte; ***game plan*** *Chess & Fig* stratégie *f*; *Mktg* stratégie *f* (de marketing); ***game point*** *(in tennis)* balle *f* de jeu; ***game reserve*** réserve *f (pour animaux sauvages)*; ***game show*** *TV* jeu *m* télévisé; *Rad* jeu *m* radiophonique; *Math* ***game theory*** théorie *f* des jeux; ***game warden*** *(gamekeeper)* garde-chasse *m*; *(in safari park)* garde *m (d'une réserve)*

gamecock ['geɪmkɒk] *n Br* coq *m* de combat

game-fishing *n* pêche *f (au saumon, à la truite, au brochet)*

gamekeeper ['geɪm,kiːpə(r)] *n* garde-chasse *m*

gamelan ['gæmɪlæn] *n Mus* gamelan *m*

gamely ['geɪmlɪ] *adv* courageusement, vaillamment

gamer ['geɪmə(r)] *n* (**a**) *(who plays computer games)* = amateur de jeux vidéo (**b**) *Am (athlete, sportsperson)* = sportif très compétitif

gamesmanship ['geɪmzmənʃɪp] *n* = art de gagner (aux jeux) en déconcertant son adversaire; **this is just gamesmanship** ce n'est qu'une astuce pour déstabiliser son adversaire

gamester ['geɪmstə(r)] *n (game-player, gambler)* joueur(euse) *m,f*

gamete ['gæmiːt] *n Biol* gamète *m*

gametic [gə'metɪk] *adj Biol* gamétique

gametocyte [gə'miːtəʊsaɪt] *n Biol* gamétocyte *m*

gametogenesis [,gæmɪtəʊ'dʒenɪsɪs] *n Biol* gamétogenèse *f*

gametophyte [gə'miːtəʊfaɪt] *n Bot* gamétophyte *m*

gameware ['geɪmweə(r)] *n Comput* ludiciel *m*

gamey *(compar* **gamier,** *superl* **gamiest**) = **gamy**

gamine ['gæmiːn] *Br* **1** *n (impish girl)* jeune fille *f* espiègle; *(tomboy)* garçon *m* manqué

2 *adj* gamin; **a gamine haircut** une coupe à la garçonne

gaming ['geɪmɪŋ] *n* (**a**) *(UNCOUNT) Old-fashioned (gambling)* jeu *m*, jeux *mpl* d'argent (**b**) *(playing of computer games)* (pratique *f* des) jeux *mpl* électroniques

►► *Old-fashioned* ***gaming house*** maison *f* de jeu; ***gaming laws*** = lois réglementant les jeux de hasard; ***gaming table*** table *f* de jeu

gamma ['gæmə] *n* gamma *m*

►► ***gamma globulin*** gammaglobuline *f*; ***gamma radiation*** *(UNCOUNT)* rayons *mpl* gamma; ***gamma ray*** rayon *m* gamma

gamma-ray therapy *n Med* gammathérapie *f*

gammon ['gæmən] **1** *n* (**a**) *Br (cut)* jambon *m*; *(meat)* jambon *m* fumé (**b**) *(in backgammon)* = victoire avant que l'adversaire ne puisse retirer aucune de ses pièces

2 *vt (in backgammon)* battre en réalisant un "gammon"

►► *Br* ***gammon steak*** = épaisse tranche de jambon fumé

gammy ['gæmɪ] *(compar* **gammier,** *superl* **gammiest**) *adj Br Fam* estropié❑; **to have a gammy leg** avoir une patte folle

gamogenesis [,gæməʊ'dʒenɪsɪs] *n* reproduction *f* sexuée

gamp [gæmp] *n Br Fam Arch* pébroque *m*, pépin *m*

gamut ['gæmət] *n Mus & Fig* gamme *f*; **to run the (whole) gamut of sth** passer par toute la gamme de qch; **this character runs the whole gamut of emotions** ce personnage passe par toute la gamme des émotions

gamy ['geɪmɪ] *(compar* **gamier**, *superl* **gamiest)** *adj (meat)* faisandé

gander ['gændə(r)] *n* (**a**) *(goose)* jars *m* (**b**) *Br Fam (simpleton)* nigaud(e) *m,f*, andouille *f* (**c**) *Fam (look)* **to have** *or* **to take a gander at sth** jeter un coup d'œil sur qch; **have a gander at this!** jette un coup d'œil là-dessus!

G&T [dʒi:ən'ti:] *n Fam* gin-tonic ❑ *m*

gang [gæŋ] **1** *n* (**a**) *(gen)* bande *f*; *(of criminals)* gang *m*; **a gang of young thugs** une bande de jeunes voyous; **she went out with a gang of friends** elle est sortie avec une bande de copains; **he's one of the gang now** il fait partie de la bande maintenant; *Fam* **the whole gang** *(of friends, colleagues)* toute la bande; *Pol & Hist* **the Gang of Four** la Bande des Quatre (**b**) *(of workmen)* équipe *f*; *(of convicts)* convoi *m*

2 *vt Tech (tools, instruments)* coupler

►► ***gang plug*** prise *f* multiple; ***gang rape*** viol *m* collectif; ***gang saw*** scie *f* multiple; ***gang show*** = spectacle de variétés organisé par les scouts; ***gang warfare*** guerre *f* des gangs

►**gang together** *vi* se réunir (en bande), se mettre à plusieurs

►**gang up** *vi* se mettre à plusieurs; **to gang up with sb** s'allier avec qn; **to gang up against** *or* **on sb** se liguer contre qn

ganga ['gændʒə] *n Fam (marijuana)* herbe *f*

gang-bang *n Vulg* (**a**) *(rape)* viol *m* collectif ❑ (**b**) *(orgy)* partouze *f*

gangbuster ['gæŋbʌstə(r)] *n Am Fam* (**a**) *(police officer)* ≃ flic *m* de la brigade antigang (**b**) *Fig (excellent thing)* **this movie is a gangbuster** ce film est vraiment super *ou* génial; *Fig* **the campaign is progressing like gangbusters** la campagne marche très fort; **to make money like gangbusters** gagner un argent fou

ganger ['gæŋə(r)] *n Br (foreman)* contremaître *m*, chef *m* d'équipe

Ganges ['gændʒi:z] *n* **the (River) Ganges** le Gange

gangland ['gæŋlænd] *n* le milieu

►► ***gangland boss*** chef *m* de gang; ***gangland killing*** règlement *m* de comptes *(dans le milieu)*; ***gangland warfare*** guerre *f* des gangs

ganglia ['gæŋglɪə] *pl of* **ganglion**

gangling ['gæŋglɪŋ] *adj* dégingandé

ganglion ['gæŋglɪən] *(pl* **ganglia** [-lɪə]) *n* (**a**) *Anat* ganglion *m* (**b**) *(centre, focus)* centre *m*, foyer *m*

gangly ['gæŋglɪ] *adj* dégingandé; **a tall, gangly young lad** un grand jeune homme dégingandé

gangplank ['gæŋplæŋk] *n* passerelle *f* (d'embarquement)

gang-rape *vt* commettre un viol collectif sur; **women who have been gang-raped** les femmes qui ont été victimes de viols collectifs; **they gang-raped her** ils l'ont violée

gangrene ['gæŋgri:n] **1** *n (UNCOUNT) Med & Fig* gangrène *f*; **to have gangrene** avoir la gangrène

2 *vi* se gangrener

gangrenous ['gæŋgrɪnəs] *adj* gangreneux; **the wound went gangrenous** la blessure s'est gangrenée

gangsta ['gæŋstə] *n* (**a**) *(music)* **gangsta (rap)** gangsta rap *m* (**b**) *(rapper)* rappeur(euse) *m,f* gangsta (**c**) *Am (gang member)* = membre d'un gang

gangster ['gæŋstə(r)] **1** *n* gangster *m*

2 *comp (film, story)* de gangsters

►► ***gangster capitalism*** = système économique débridé exclusivement basé sur la recherche du profit

gangsterism ['gæŋstərɪzəm] *n* gangstérisme *m*

gangue [gæŋ] *n Miner* gangue *f*

gangway ['gæŋweɪ] **1** *n* (**a**) *Naut* passerelle *f* (d'embarquement) (**b**) *(passage)* passage *m*; *(of bus etc)* couloir *m* central; *Br (in theatre)* allée *f*

2 *exclam* dégagez le passage!

►► ***gangway port*** sabord *m* de coupée

ganja = **ganga**

gannet ['gænɪt] *n* (**a**) *Orn* fou *m* de Bassan (**b**) *Br Fam (greedy person)* glouton(onne) ❑ *m,f*

gantry ['gæntrɪ] *(pl* **gantries**) *n* (**a**) *(for crane)* portique *m*; *Astron* **(launching) gantry** portique *m* (de lancement); *Rail* **(signal) gantry** portique *m* (à signaux) (**b**) *(for barrel)* chantier *m* (**c**) *(for drinks)* étagères *fpl* à bouteilles *(dans un bar)*

►► ***gantry crane*** grue *f* (à) portique

Ganymede ['gænɪmi:d] **1** *pr n Myth* Ganymède

2 *nm Astron* Ganymède

GAO [,dʒi:eɪ'əʊ] *n Am (abbr* **General Accounting Office**) = Cour des comptes américaine

gaol, gaolbird *etc Br* = **jail, jailbird** *etc*

gap [gæp] *n* (**a**) *(hole, opening → which needs mending)* trou *m*; *(→ in floorboards)* interstice *m*; *(→ created deliberately)* trouée *f*, ouverture *f*; *(→ in a wall)* brèche *f*; *(→ in clouds)* trou *m*; *(→ in trees)* trouée *f*; *(→ of spark plug, points)* écartement *m*; *(→ in piston ring)* jeu *m* à la coupe (des segments); **a gap in the wall** un trou dans le mur; **the sun shone through a gap in the clouds** le soleil perça à travers les nuages

(**b**) *(space between objects)* espace *m*; *(narrower)* interstice *m*, jour *m*; **a gap of 2 cm** un intervalle de 2 cm; **there was a gap of a few metres between each car** il y avait une distance de quelques mètres entre chaque voiture; **he has a gap between his front teeth** il a les dents de devant écartées; **I could see through a gap in the curtains** je voyais par la fente entre les rideaux; **there's a gap in the curtains** les rideaux bâillent; **the shelling had opened great gaps in the ranks** le bombardement avait éclairci les rangs

(**c**) *(blank)* blanc *m*; **fill in the gaps with the missing letters** remplissez les blancs avec les lettres manquantes

(**d**) *(in time)* intervalle *m*; **there's a perceptible gap between stimulus and response** il y a un intervalle sensible entre le stimulus et la réponse; **she returned to work after a gap of six years** elle s'est remise à travailler après une interruption de six ans

(**e**) *(lack)* vide *m*; *(in memory etc)* trou *m*, lacune *f*; **to bridge** *or* **to fill a gap** combler un vide; **to fill the gaps in one's education** combler les lacunes de son éducation; **his death left a gap in our lives** sa mort a laissé un vide dans notre vie; **a gap in the market** un créneau sur le marché

(**f**) *(omission)* lacune *f*; **there are several gaps in his story** il y a plusieurs trous dans son histoire

(**g**) *(silence)* pause *f*, silence *m*

(**h**) *(disparity)* écart *m*, inégalité *f*; **we need to reduce the gap between theory and practice** il nous faut réduire l'écart entre la théorie et la pratique; **there's a technology gap between our two countries** il y a un fossé technologique entre nos deux pays; **to close the gap** réduire l'écart; **age gap** différence *f* d'âge

(**i**) *Geog (opening in hills, mountains)* trouée *f*; *(mountain pass)* col *m*

(**j**) *(in recording)* blanc *m* sonore; *(in recorded tape)* plage *f* de silence

►► ***gap financing*** crédit *m* relais; ***gap site*** terrain *m* vague (entre deux bâtiments); *Br* ***gap year*** = année, souvent passée à voyager, que s'accorde un étudiant avant son entrée à l'université ou à la fin de ses études

gape [geɪp] **1** *vi* (**a**) *(stare)* regarder bouche bée; **he gaped at me** il m'a regardé bouche bée; **to gape in admiration/astonishment** être bouche bée d'admiration/d'étonnement; **what are you gaping at?** qu'est-ce que tu regardes avec cet air bête?

(**b**) *(open one's mouth wide)* ouvrir la bouche toute grande

(**c**) *(be open)* être béant, béer; **to gape (open)** *(thing)* s'ouvrir (tout grand); *(seam etc)* bâiller; *(hole)* être béant; **a chasm gaped at our feet** un gouffre béant s'ouvrait à nos pieds

2 *n (stare)* regard *m* ébahi; **with a gape of disbelief** la bouche ouverte *ou* bée en signe d'incrédulité

gaper ['geɪpə(r)] *n* (**a**) *(starer)* badaud(e) *m,f* (**b**) *Zool (clam)* mye *f*

gaping ['geɪpɪŋ] *adj* (**a**) *(staring)* bouche bée *(inv)* (**b**) *(wide open)* béant; **a gaping wound** une blessure béante

gappy ['gæpɪ] *(compar* **gappier**, *superl* **gappiest**) *adj* (**a**) *(account, knowledge)* plein de lacunes (**b**) **gappy teeth** des dents *fpl* écartées; **gappy smile** sourire *m* édenté

gap-toothed *adj (with spaces between teeth)* aux dents écartées; *(with missing teeth)* à qui il manque des dents

garage **1** *n* [*Br* 'gærɑ:ʒ, 'gærɪdʒ, *Am* gə'rɑ:ʒ] (**a**) *(for cars)* garage *m*; **there is garage space for two cars** il y a de la place pour garer deux voitures (**b**) *Mus* garage *m*

2 *vt* [*Br* 'gærɑ:ʒ, *Am* gə'rɑ:ʒ] mettre au garage

►► ***garage door*** porte *f* de garage; ***garage hand*** mécanicien(enne) *m,f*; ***garage man*** *(mechanic)* mécanicien(enne) *m,f*; *(owner)* garagiste *mf*; ***garage mechanic*** garagiste *mf*, mécanicien(enne) *m,f*; ***garage sale*** = vente d'occasion chez un particulier, ≃ vide-grenier *m*

garam masala [,gærəmmə'sɑ:lə] *n Culin* garam masala *m*

garb [gɑ:b] *Literary* **1** *n* costume *m*, mise *f*; **she was in gipsy garb** elle était en costume de gitane, elle était déguisée en gitane; **a man dressed in very strange garb** un homme bizarrement accoutré

2 *vt* vêtir; **garbed all in black** tout de noir vêtu

garbage ['gɑ:bɪdʒ] *n (UNCOUNT)* (**a**) *Am (waste matter)* ordures *fpl* (ménagères), détritus *mpl*; **throw it in the garbage** jette-le à la poubelle

(**b**) *Fam (nonsense)* bêtises ❑ *fpl*, âneries *fpl*; **you're talking garbage!** tu racontes n'importe quoi!; **this newspaper is garbage!** ce journal est nul!

(**c**) *Fam (worthless things)* **their new album is a load of garbage** leur dernier album est vraiment nul; **I've been eating too much garbage lately** je mange trop de cochonneries en ce moment

(**d**) *Comput* données *fpl* erronées; **garbage in, garbage out** la qualité des résultats est fonction de la qualité des données à l'entrée

►► *Am* ***garbage bag*** sac-poubelle *m*; *Am* ***garbage can*** poubelle *f*; *Am* ***garbage chute*** vide-ordures *m inv*; *Am* ***garbage collector*** éboueur *m*; *Am* ***garbage disposal unit*** broyeur *m* d'ordures; *Am* ***garbage dump*** décharge *f*; *Am* ***garbage heap*** tas *m* d'ordures; *Am* ***garbage man*** éboueur *m*; *Am Fam* ***garbage shoot*** vide-ordures ❑ *m inv*; *Am* ***garbage truck*** camion *m* des éboueurs

garbanzo [gɑ:'bɑ:nzəʊ] *(pl* **garbanzos**) *n Am* **garbanzo (bean)** pois *m* chiche

garble ['gɑ:bəl] *vt (involuntarily → story, message)* embrouiller; *(→ quotation)* déformer; *(deliberately → facts)* dénaturer, déformer

garbled ['gɑ:bəld] *adj (account, story, explanation → involuntarily)* embrouillé, confus; *(→ deliberately)* dénaturé, déformé

garbo ['gɑ:bəʊ] *n Austr Fam* éboueur ❑ *m*

Garda ['gɑ:də] *n* **Lake Garda** le lac de Garde

garda ['gɑ:də] *(pl* **gardai** [-di:]) *n* policier *m* *(en République d'Irlande)*

garden ['gɑ:dən] **1** *n* (**a**) *(with flowers)* jardin *m*; *(with vegetables)* (jardin *m*) potager *m*; **back/front garden** jardin *m* de derrière/de devant; **to do the garden** jardiner, faire du jardinage

(**b**) *(park)* **public garden(s)** jardin *m* public, parc *m*; **garden of remembrance** = jardin en souvenir des défunts

(**c**) *(fertile region)* jardin *m*

(**d**) *(in street names)* **Gardens** = nom donné à certaines rues en Grande-Bretagne

(**e**) *(idiom)* **everything in the garden is rosy** *or* **lovely** tout va bien

2 *comp* de jardinage, de jardin

3 *vi* jardiner, faire du jardinage

4 **gardens** *npl (park)* jardin *m* public

►► *Am* ***garden apartment*** rez-de-jardin *m inv*; *Am Culin* ***garden burger*** burger *m* végétarien; ***garden centre*** jardinerie *f*; ***garden chair*** chaise *f* de jardin; ***garden city*** cité-jardin *f*; ***the Garden of Eden*** le jardin *m* d'Éden, l'Éden *m*; ***the Garden of England*** = surnom du comté de Kent, célèbre pour ses vergers et ses champs de houblon; *Br* ***garden flat*** rez-de-jardin *m inv*; ***garden furniture*** mobilier *m* de jardin; ***garden gnome*** nain *m* de jardin; *Br* ***garden party*** garden-party *f*; ***garden path*** allée *f* *(dans un jardin)*; **he ran down the garden path** il a descendu l'allée du jardin en courant; *Fig* **she was led up the garden path** elle a été dupée, on l'a fait marcher; ***garden produce*** produits *mpl* maraîchers; ***garden seat*** banc *m* de jardin; ***garden shears*** cisaille *f ou* cisailles *fpl* de jardin; ***garden shed*** resserre *f*; ***garden snail*** petit-gris *m*; *Entom* ***garden spider*** épeire *f* diadème; ***the Garden State*** = surnom donné au New Jersey; ***garden suburb*** banlieue *f* verte; ***garden tools*** outils *mpl* de jardinage; ***garden wall*** mur *m* du jardin; *Orn* ***garden warbler*** fauvette *f* des jardins; *Am* ***garden wedding*** mariage *m* en plein air

gardener ['gɑːdnə(r)] *n* jardinier(ère) *m,f*

gardenia [gɑː'diːnjə] *n Bot* gardénia *m*

gardening ['gɑːdnɪŋ] **1** *n* jardinage *m*; **he's fond of gardening** il aime jardiner

2 *comp (book, programme)* de *ou* sur le jardinage; *(gloves)* de jardinage

garden-variety *adj Am* ordinaire

garfish ['gɑːfɪʃ] *n Ich* orphie *f*, aiguille *f* de mer

garganey ['gɑːgənɪ] *n Orn* **garganey (duck)** sarcelle *f* d'été

gargantuan [gɑː'gæntjʊən] *adj* gargantuesque

gargle ['gɑːgəl] **1** *vi* se gargariser, faire des gargarismes

2 *n* gargarisme *m*

gargoyle ['gɑːgɔɪl] *n* gargouille *f*

garibaldi [,gærɪ'bɔːldɪ] *n Br* = biscuit aux raisins secs

garish ['geərɪʃ] *adj (colour)* voyant, criard; *(clothes)* voyant, tapageur; *(light)* cru, aveuglant

garishly ['geərɪʃlɪ] *adv* **garishly dressed** vêtu de manière tapageuse; **garishly made-up** outrageusement fardé *ou* maquillé

garishness ['geərɪʃnɪs] *n (of appearance)* tape-à-l'œil *m inv*; *(of colour)* crudité *f*, violence *f*

garland ['gɑːlənd] **1** *n* **(a)** *(on head)* couronne *f* de fleurs; *(round neck)* guirlande *f ou* collier *m* de fleurs; *(hung on wall)* guirlande *f* **(b)** *Literature (of poems)* guirlande *f*, florilège *m*

2 *vt (decorate)* parer de guirlandes, enguirlander; *(crown)* couronner de fleurs; **garlanded with flowers** paré de guirlandes de fleurs

garlic ['gɑːlɪk] *n* ail *m*; **clove of garlic** gousse *f* d'ail; **head of garlic** bulbe *m* d'ail

►► ***garlic bread*** = pain chaud au beurre d'ail; ***garlic butter*** beurre *m* d'ail; ***garlic flakes*** ail *m* en flocons; ***garlic mushrooms*** champignons *mpl* à l'ail; ***garlic mustard*** alliaire *f*; ***garlic powder*** ail *m* en poudre; ***garlic press*** presse-ail *m inv*; ***garlic salt*** sel *m* d'ail; ***garlic sausage*** saucisson *m* à l'ail

garlicky ['gɑːlɪkɪ] *adj (taste)* d'ail; *(breath)* qui sent l'ail; **it smells garlicky** ça sent l'ail

garment ['gɑːmənt] *n* vêtement *m*; **the garment industry** la confection

►► ***garment bag*** housse *f* pour vêtements

garner ['gɑːnə(r)] **1** *n Literary* grenier *m* (à grain), grange *f*

2 *vt (grain)* rentrer, engranger; *Fig (information)* glaner, recueillir; *(compliments)* recueillir

►**garner in, garner up** *vt sep* engranger

garnet ['gɑːnɪt] **1** *n (stone, colour)* grenat *m*

2 *adj* **(a)** *(in colour)* grenat *(inv)* **(b)** *(jewellery)* de *ou* en grenat

garnish ['gɑːnɪʃ] **1** *vt* **(a)** *Culin* garnir; *(decorate)* embellir, orner (**with** de); **garnished with parsley** garni de persil **(b)** *Am Law* faire pratiquer une saisie-arrêt à

2 *n Culin* garniture *f*

garnishee [,gɑːnɪ'ʃiː] *n Law* tiers *m* saisi

►► ***garnishee order*** ordonnance *f* de saisie-arrêt

garnishing ['gɑːnɪʃɪŋ] *n Culin* garniture *f*; *Fig* embellissement *m*

garnishment ['gɑːnɪʃmənt] *n* **(a)** *Law* saisie-arrêt *f* **(b)** *Culin* garniture *f*

garotte = **garrote, garrotte**

garret ['gærət] *n (room)* mansarde *f*; **to live in a garret** habiter une chambre sous les combles

garrison ['gærɪsən] **1** *n* garnison *f*

2 *vt* **(a)** *(troops)* mettre en garnison; **they were garrisoned in Scotland** ils étaient en garnison en Écosse **(b)** *(town)* placer une garnison dans

►► ***garrison town*** ville *f* de garnison; ***garrison troops*** (troupes *fpl* de) garnison *f*

garrote, garrotte [gə'rɒt] **1** *n* **(a)** *(execution)* (supplice *m* du) garrot *m* **(b)** *(collar)* garrot *m*

2 *vt* garrotter

garrotting, *Am* **garroting** [gə'rɒtɪŋ] *n* **(a)** *(strangling)* strangulation *f (avec un fil ou une corde)* **(b)** *(execution)* supplice *m* du garrot

garrulity [gæ'ruːlɪtɪ] *n* loquacité *f*

garrulous ['gærələs] *adj* **(a)** *(person)* loquace, bavard **(b)** *(style)* prolixe, verbeux

garrulously ['gærələslɪ] *adv* verbeusement

garrulousness ['gærələsnɪs] *n* loquacité *f*

garryowen [,gærɪ'əʊɪn] *n Br Sport (in rugby)* (coup *m* de pied en) chandelle *f*

garter ['gɑːtə(r)] *n* **(a)** *Br (for stockings)* jarretière *f*; *(for socks)* fixe-chaussette *m*; **Knight of the (Order of the) Garter** chevalier *m* de l'ordre de la Jarretière **(b)** *Am (suspender)* jarretelle *f*

►► *Am* ***garter belt*** porte-jarretelles *m inv*; ***garter snake*** couleuvre *f (d'Amérique du Nord)*; *Knitting* ***garter stitch*** point *m* mousse

gas [gæs] (*pl* **gasses**) **1** *n* **(a)** *(domestic)* gaz *m*; **to turn on/off the gas** allumer/éteindre le gaz; **to use gas for cooking** faire la cuisine *ou* cuisiner au gaz; **a street lit by gas** une rue éclairée au gaz

(b) *Chem* gaz *m*

(c) *Mining* grisou *m*

(d) *Med* gaz *m* anesthésique *ou* anesthésiant; **to have gas** subir une anesthésie gazeuse *ou* par inhalation; **the dentist gave me gas** le dentiste m'a endormi au gaz; **gas and air** *(mask)* masque *m* à oxygène

(e) *Am Aut* essence *f*; *Fam* **step on** *or* **hit the gas!** *(in car)* appuie sur le champignon!; *Fig* grouille!, grouille-toi!

(f) *Am Fam (amusing person, thing, situation)* **the party was a real gas** on s'est bien marrés *ou* on a bien rigolé à la soirée; **to have a gas** se marrer, s'en payer une tranche; **what a gas!** quelle rigolade!; **he's a real gas!** c'est un vrai boute-en-train!

(g) *Br Fam (chatter)* bavardage ❑ *m*; **they had a good gas on the phone** ils ont taillé une bonne bavette au téléphone

(h) *(UNCOUNT) Am (in stomach)* gaz *mpl*

2 *vt* **(a)** *(poison)* asphyxier *ou* intoxiquer au gaz; **to gas oneself** *(poison)* s'asphyxier au gaz; *(suicide)* se suicider au gaz

(b) *Mil* gazer

3 *vi* **(a)** *Fam (chatter)* bavarder ❑, jacasser

(b) *Chem* dégager des gaz

4 *adj Ir Fam (fun)* marrant; **it was a gas evening** c'était une soirée super; **he's a gas man** il est marrant, on se marre bien avec lui

►► *Admin* **Gas Board** compagnie *f* du gaz; ***gas bracket*** applique *f* à gaz; ***gas burner*** brûleur *m* à gaz; ***gas central heating*** chauffage *m* central au gaz; ***gas chamber*** chambre *f* à gaz; ***gas chromatography*** chromatographie *f* en phase gazeuse; *Br* ***gas cooker*** cuisinière *f* à gaz, gazinière *f*; ***gas cylinder*** bouteille *f* de gaz; ***gas explosion*** *(in home or street)* explosion *f* due à une fuite de gaz; *(in mine)* coup *m* de grisou; ***gas field*** gisement *m* de gaz; *Br* ***gas fire*** (appareil *m* de) chauffage *m* au gaz; ***gas fitter*** installateur(trice) *m,f* d'appareils à gaz; ***gas furnace*** fourneau *m* à gaz; ***gas gangrene*** *(UNCOUNT)* gangrène *f* gazeuse; ***gas gauge*** jauge *f* d'essence; *Am Fam* ***gas guzzler*** = voiture qui consomme beaucoup; ***gas heater*** *(radiator)* radiateur *m* à gaz; *(for water)* chauffe-eau *m inv* à gaz; ***gas industry*** industrie *f* du gaz; ***gas jet*** brûleur *m*; *Br* ***gas lamp*** *(in street)* bec *m* de gaz; ***gas lighter*** *(for cooker)* allume-gaz *m inv*; *(for cigarettes)* briquet *m* à gaz; ***gas main*** conduite *f* de gaz; *(big)* gazoduc *m*; ***gas mantle*** manchon *m* à incandescence; ***gas mask*** masque *m* à gaz; ***gas meter*** compteur *m* à gaz; ***gas oil*** gas-oil *m*, gazole *m*; ***gas oven*** *(domestic)* four *m* à gaz; *(cremation chamber)* four *m* crématoire; **to put one's head in a gas oven** se suicider en mettant la tête dans un four à gaz; *Am* ***gas pedal*** accélérateur *m*; ***gas pipe*** tuyau *m* à gaz; ***gas pipeline*** gazoduc *m*; ***gas range*** fourneau *m* à gaz; *Br* ***gas ring*** *(part of cooker)* brûleur *m*; *(small cooker)* réchaud *m* à gaz; *Am* ***gas station*** poste *m* d'essence, station-service *f*; ***gas station attendant*** employé(e) *m,f* de station-service, pompiste *mf*; *Br* ***gas stove*** *(in kitchen)* cuisinière *f* à gaz, gazinière *f*; *(for camping)* réchaud *m* à gaz; ***gas tank*** *(domestic)* cuve *f* à gaz; *Am Aut (petrol tank)* réservoir *m* à essence; ***gas tap*** *(on cooker)* bouton *m* de cuisinière à gaz; *(at mains)* robinet *m* de gaz; *Ir Fam* ***gas ticket*** *(person)* marrant(e) *m,f*; ***gas turbine*** turbine *f* à gaz; ***gas turbine engine*** moteur *m* à turbine à gaz; ***gas welding*** soudage *m* au gaz

►**gas up** *Am* **1** *vt sep* **to gas the automobile up** faire le plein d'essence

2 *vi* faire le plein d'essence

gasbag ['gæsbæg] *n Br Fam Pej (chatterbox)* moulin *m* à paroles, pie *f*; *(boaster)* fanfaron (onne) ❑ *m,f*

Gascon ['gæskən] **1** *n* **(a)** *(person)* Gascon (onne) *m,f* **(b)** *Ling* gascon *m*

2 *adj* gascon

Gascony ['gæskənɪ] *n* Gascogne *f*; **in Gascony** en Gascogne

gas-cooled reactor *n* réacteur *m* à refroidissement par gaz

gaseous ['gæsjəs] *adj Phys* gazeux

gas-filled *adj (lamp)* gazeuse, à atmosphère gazeuse

►► ***gas-filled relay, gas-filled triode*** triode *f* à gaz

gas-fired *adj (boiler, heater, oven etc)* à gaz; *Br* **gas-fired central heating** chauffage *m* central au gaz

gash [gæʃ] **1** *vt* **(a)** *(knee, hand)* entailler; *(face)* balafrer, taillader; **to gash one's chin** se faire une entaille au menton; **she fell and gashed her knee** elle est tombée et s'est entaillé *ou* ouvert le genou

(b) *(material)* déchirer, lacérer

2 *n* **(a)** *(on knee, hand)* entaille *f*; *(on face)* balafre *f*, estafilade *f*; **there was a great gash in the side of the ship** il y avait une profonde entaille *ou* une large brèche dans le flanc du navire

(b) *(in material)* (grande) déchirure *f*, déchiqueture *f*

(c) *Vulg (woman's genitals)* craquette *f*, fente *f*

3 *adj Fam (surplus)* superflu ❑, en trop ❑

gasholder ['gæshəʊldə(r)] *n* gazomètre *m*

gasification [,gæsɪfɪ'keɪʃən] *n* gazéification *f*

gasify ['gæsɪfaɪ] (*pt & pp* **gasified**) **1** *vt* gazéifier

2 *vi* se gazéifier

gasket ['gæskɪt] *n* **(a)** *Tech* joint *m* (d'étanchéité); *Aut* **(cylinder) head gasket** joint *m* de culasse; **to blow a gasket** *Aut* faire sauter un joint de culasse; *Fam Fig* piquer une colère **(b)** *Naut* raban *m* de ferlage

gaslight ['gæslaɪt] *n* **(a)** *(lamp)* lampe *f* à gaz, appareil *m* d'éclairage à gaz; *(in street)* bec *m* de gaz **(b)** *(light produced)* lumière *f* produite par du gaz; **by gaslight** à la lumière d'une lampe à gaz

gaslit ['gæslɪt] *adj* éclairé au gaz

gasman ['gæsmæn] (*pl* **gasmen** [-men]) *n* employé *m* du gaz

gasohol ['gæsəhɒl] *n Am* carburol *m*

gasoline, gasolene ['gæsəliːn] *n Am Aut* essence *f*

gasometer [gæ'sɒmɪtə(r)] *n* gazomètre *m*

gasp [gɑːsp] **1** *vi* **(a)** *(be short of breath)* haleter, souffler; **to gasp for breath** *or* **for air** haleter, suffoquer

(b) *(in shock, surprise)* avoir le souffle coupé; **to gasp in** *or* **with amazement** avoir le souffle coupé par la surprise

(c) *Br Fam Fig* **I'm gasping for a cigarette** je meurs d'envie de fumer une cigarette; **I'm gasping (for a drink)** je meurs de soif

2 *vt* **"what?" he gasped** "quoi?" dit-il d'une voix pantelante; **she gasped out an explanation** elle s'est expliquée d'une voix haletante

3 *n* halètement *m*; *(of surprise)* hoquet *m*, sursaut *m*; **she gave** *or* **she let out a gasp of surprise** elle a eu un hoquet de surprise; **there were gasps of admiration from the audience** il y a eu des sursauts d'admiration dans le public; **to give a gasp of horror** avoir le souffle coupé par l'horreur; **he was at his last gasp** *(dying)* il allait rendre son dernier souffle *ou* soupir; *(exhausted)* il était à bout de souffle; **to the last gasp** jusqu'au dernier souffle

gasper ['gɑːspə(r)] *n Br Fam Old-fashioned* sèche *f*, clope *m or f*

gas-permeable *adj* **gas-permeable (contact) lenses** lentilles *fpl* semi-rigides

gas-producing *adj* **(a)** *Tech* gazogène **(b)** *(country)* producteur de gaz

gassed, *Am* **gassed up** [gæst] *adj Fam (drunk)* bourré, pété

gasser ['gæsə(r)] *n Am Fam* **to have a gasser** se marrer, s'en payer une tranche; **what a gasser!** quelle rigolade!; **the film was a real gasser!** c'était un film vachement marrant!

gassiness ['gæsɪnəs] *n* teneur *f* en gaz

gassing ['gæsɪŋ] *n* (**a**) *(of person → deliberate)* gazage *m* (**b**) *Fam (talk)* bavardage ❑ *m*

gassy ['gæsɪ] *(compar* **gassier**, *superl* **gassiest**) *adj* (**a**) *Chem* gazeux (**b**) *(drink)* gazeux (**c**) *Fam (person)* bavard ❑ (**d**) *Mining* grisouteux

gasteropod = **gastropod**

gas-tight *adj* étanche *ou* imperméable au gaz

gastrectomy [gæs'trektəmɪ] *(pl* **gastrectomies**) *n* gastrectomie *f*

gastric ['gæstrɪk] *adj* gastrique

►► ***gastric flu*** *(UNCOUNT)* grippe *f* intestinale *ou* gastro-intestinale; ***gastric juice*** suc *m* gastrique; *Med* ***gastric lavage*** lavage *m* d'estomac; ***gastric ulcer*** ulcère *m* de l'estomac, gastrite *f* ulcéreuse

gastritis [gæs'traɪtɪs] *n (UNCOUNT) Med* gastrite *f*

gastroenteritis [ˌgæstrəʊentə'raɪtɪs] *n (UNCOUNT) Med* gastro-entérite *f*; **to have gastroenteritis** avoir une gastro-entérite

gastroenterologist [ˌgæstrəʊentə'rɒlədʒɪst] *n Med* gastro-entérologue *mf*

gastroenterology [ˌgæstrəʊentə'rɒlədʒɪ] *n Med* gastro-entérologie *f*

gastrohepatitis [ˌgæstrəʊhepə'taɪtɪs] *n Med* gastro-hépatite *f*

gastrointestinal [ˌgæstrəʊɪntes'taɪnəl] *adj* gastro-intestinal

►► ***the gastrointestinal tract*** les voies *fpl* digestives

gastromycete [ˌgæstrəʊ'maɪsaɪt] *n Bot* gastromycète *m*

gastronome ['gæstrənəʊm] *n* gastronome *mf*

gastronomic [ˌgæstrə'nɒmɪk] *adj* gastronomique

gastronomist [gæs'trɒnəmɪst] *n* gastronome *mf*

gastronomy [gæs'trɒnəmɪ] *n* gastronomie *f*

gastropod ['gæstrəpɒd] **1** *n* gastéropode *m*, gastropode *m*

2 *adj* de gastéropode

gastroscope ['gæstrəskəʊp] *n Med* gastroscope *m*

gastroscopy [gæs'trɒskəpɪ] *n Med* gastroscopie *f*, fibroscopie *f* gastrique

gasworks ['gæswɜːks] *(pl* **inv**) *n* usine *f* à gaz

gat[1] [gæt] *Arch pt of* **get**

gat[2] *n Am Fam (gun)* flingue *m*, pétard *m*

gate [geɪt] **1** *n* (**a**) *(into garden)* porte *f*; *(into driveway, field)* barrière *f*; *(bigger → of mansion)* portail *m*; *(→ into courtyard)* porte *f* cochère; *(low)* portillon *m*; *(wrought iron)* grille *f*; **the main gate** la porte *ou* l'entrée *f* principale; **the gates of heaven/hell** les portes *fpl* du paradis/de l'enfer; **to pay at the gate** *(for match)* payer à l'entrée; *Am Fam* **to give sb the gate** flanquer [illegible]

(**b**) *(at airport)* porte *f*; **proceed to gate 22** embarquement porte 22

(**c**) *(on ski slope)* porte *f*

(**d**) *(on canal)* **lock gates** écluse *f*, portes *fpl* d'écluse

(**e**) *Sport (spectators)* nombre *m* de spectateurs (admis); *(money)* recette *f*, entrées *fpl*; **there was a good/poor gate** il y a eu beaucoup/peu de spectateurs; **the match needed a gate of 50,000 to break even** il fallait 50 000 spectateurs au match pour que le club rentre dans ses frais

(**f**) *Electron* gâchette *f*

(**g**) *Phot* fenêtre *f*

(**h**) *(in horse racing)* **(starting) gate** starting-gate *f*

(**i**) *Aut (for gearstick)* grille *f* *(de changement de vitesse)*

(**j**) *(of karabiner)* doigt *m*

2 *vt Br Sch* consigner, mettre en retenue; **to be gated** se faire consigner

►► ***gate lodge*** loge *f* du portier; ***gate money*** recette *f*, montant *m* des entrées

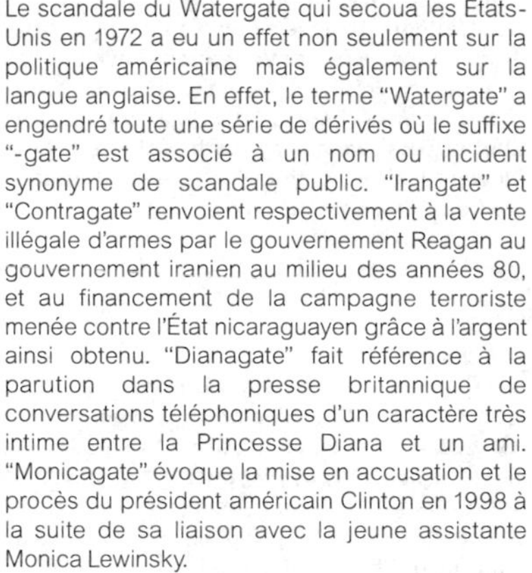

-GATE

Le scandale du Watergate qui secoua les États-Unis en 1972 a eu un effet non seulement sur la politique américaine mais également sur la langue anglaise. En effet, le terme "Watergate" a engendré toute une série de dérivés où le suffixe "-gate" est associé à un nom ou incident synonyme de scandale public. "Irangate" et "Contragate" renvoient respectivement à la vente illégale d'armes par le gouvernement Reagan au gouvernement iranien au milieu des années 80, et au financement de la campagne terroriste menée contre l'État nicaraguayen grâce à l'argent ainsi obtenu. "Dianagate" fait référence à la parution dans la presse britannique de conversations téléphoniques d'un caractère très intime entre la Princesse Diana et un ami. "Monicagate" évoque la mise en accusation et le procès du président américain Clinton en 1998 à la suite de sa liaison avec la jeune assistante Monica Lewinsky.

gateau ['gætəʊ] *(pl* **gateaux** [-təʊz]) *n* gros gâteau *m (décoré et fourré à la crème)*

gatecrash ['geɪtkræʃ] *Fam* **1** *vi (at party)* s'inviter ❑, jouer les pique-assiette; *(at paying event)* resquiller

2 *vt* **to gatecrash a party** aller à une fête sans invitation ❑; **to gatecrash a concert** aller à un concert sans payer ❑

gatecrasher ['geɪtkræʃə(r)] *n Fam (at party)* pique-assiette *mf*; *(at paying event)* resquilleur (euse) *m,f*

gatecrashing ['geɪtkræʃɪŋ] *n Fam* resquillage *m*

gated community ['geɪtɪd-] *n* = quartier de riches, sous la surveillance de vigiles, dans une ville où il y a beaucoup de ghettos pauvres

gatefold ['geɪtfəʊld] *n* encart *m* dépliant *(dans un magazine)*

gatehouse ['geɪthaʊs, *pl* -haʊzɪz] *n (of estate)* loge *f* du portier; *(of castle)* corps *m* de garde

gatekeeper ['geɪtkiːpə(r)] *n* (**a**) *(person)* gardien (enne) *m,f*; *Rail* garde-barrière *mf* (**b**) *Mktg (in purchasing department)* contrôleur *m*, relais *m*, filtre *m*

gate-leg table, gate-legged table *n* table *f* à abattant

gatepost ['geɪtpəʊst] *n* montant *m* de barrière *ou* de porte; *Br Fam* **between you, me and the gatepost** soit dit entre nous ❑

gateway ['geɪtweɪ] *n* (**a**) *(entrance)* porte *f*, entrée *f*; *Fig* porte *f*; **Istanbul, gateway to the East** Istanbul, la porte de l'Orient; **the gateway to success/happiness** la porte du succès/du bonheur (**b**) *Comput* passerelle *f* (de connexion)

►► *Am* ***gateway drug*** = drogue douce dont l'absorption peut mener à la consommation de drogues plus dures

gather ['gæðə(r)] **1** *vt* (**a**) *(pick, collect → mushrooms, wood)* ramasser; *(→ flowers, fruit)* cueillir; **to gather honey from the flowers** *(of bees)* butiner les fleurs

(**b**) *(bring together → information)* recueillir; *(→ taxes)* percevoir, recouvrer; *(→ belongings)* ramasser; **to gather a crowd** attirer une foule de gens; **we are gathered here today...** nous sommes rassemblés ici aujourd'hui [illegible]; **gather your things, we're leaving now** ramasse tes affaires, on s'en va (**c**) *(gain)* prendre; **to gather strength** prendre des forces; **to gather speed** *or* **momentum** prendre de la vitesse

(**d**) *(prepare)* **to gather one's thoughts** se concentrer; **to gather one's wits** rassembler ses esprits

(**e**) *(embrace)* serrer; **he gathered the children to him** il serra les enfants dans ses bras *ou* sur son cœur

(**f**) *(clothes)* ramasser; **she gathered her skirts about her** elle ramassa ses jupes

(**g**) *(deduce)* déduire, comprendre; **from what she told me, I gather there will be an inquiry** à l'en croire, il y aura une enquête; **I gather he isn't coming then** j'en déduis qu'il ne vient pas, donc il ne vient pas?; **as far as I can gather** d'après ce que j'ai cru comprendre; **as you may/must already have gathered** comme vous l'avez peut-être/sûrement déjà compris; **I had (already) gathered as much** *(it was not news to me)* j'avais déjà compris; **prices have gone up – so I gather** les prix ont augmenté – c'est bien ce qu'il me semble

(**h**) *Sewing* froncer; **the dress is gathered at the waist** la robe est froncée à la taille

(**i**) *Typ (signatures)* assembler

(**j**) *(idioms)* **to gather dust** ramasser la poussière; **these books are just gathering dust** ces livres ne servent qu'à ramasser *ou* prendre la poussière; *Literary* **to be gathered to one's fathers** expirer, s'éteindre

2 *vi* (**a**) *(people)* se regrouper, se rassembler; *(crowd)* se former; *(troops)* se masser; **they all gathered round the fire** ils se sont rassemblés autour du feu

(**b**) *(clouds)* s'amonceler; *(darkness)* s'épaissir; *(storm)* menacer, se préparer; **tears were gathering in her eyes** ses yeux se remplissaient de larmes

(**c**) *Med (abscess)* mûrir; *(pus)* se former

3 gathers *npl Sewing* fronces *fpl*

►**gather in** *vt sep* (**a**) *(harvest)* rentrer; *(wheat)* récolter; *(money, taxes)* recouvrer; *(books, exam papers)* ramasser

(**b**) *Sewing* **gathered in at the waist** froncé à la taille

►**gather round** *vi* se regrouper, se rassembler; **gather round and listen** approchez (-vous) et écoutez

►**gather together 1** *vi* se regrouper, se rassembler

2 *vt sep (people)* rassembler, réunir; *(books, belongings)* rassembler, ramasser

►**gather up** *vt sep* (**a**) *(objects, belongings)* ramasser; **he gathered up the toys and put them away** il ramassa les jouets et les mit de côté; **he gathered her up in his arms** il l'a prise dans ses bras

(**b**) *(skirts)* ramasser, retrousser; *(hair)* ramasser, relever; **her hair was gathered up into a bun** ses cheveux étaient ramassés *ou* relevés en chignon

gathered ['gæðəd] *adj Sewing* froncé, à fronces

►► ***gathered pages*** *(in bookbinding)* feuilles *fpl* assemblées

gatherer ['gæðərə(r)] *n* ramasseur(euse) *m,f*

gathering ['gæðərɪŋ] **1** *n* (**a**) *(group)* assemblée *f*, réunion *f*, **a gathering of top scientists** une réunion de scientifiques de haut niveau; **a social gathering** une fête; **a small gathering was listening to him** quelques personnes attroupées l'écoutaient

(**b**) *(accumulation)* accumulation *f*; *(of clouds)* amoncellement *m*

(**c**) *(bringing together → of people)* rassemblement *m*; *(→ of objects)* accumulation *f*, amoncellement *m*; **the gathering of the clans** le rassemblement des clans

(**d**) *(harvesting)* récolte *f*; *(picking)* cueillette *f*

(**e**) *(increase → in speed, force)* accroissement *m*

(**f**) *(UNCOUNT) Sewing* froncis *m*, fronces *fpl*

(**g**) *(UNCOUNT) Med (abscess)* abcès *m*

2 *adj Literary* **the gathering darkness** l'obscurité grandissante; **the gathering storm** l'orage qui se prépare *ou* qui menace

Gatling ['gætlɪŋ] *n Mil* **Gatling (gun)** mitrailleuse *f* Gatling

gator ['geɪtə(r)] *n Am Fam* alligator ❑ *m*

GATT [gæt] *n* [illegible] **Tariffs and Trade**) GATT *m*

gauche [gəʊʃ] *adj* gauche, maladroit

gauchely ['gəʊʃlɪ] *adv* gauchement, maladroitement

gaucheness ['gəʊʃnɪs] *n* gaucherie *f*, maladresse *f*

gaucherie ['gəʊʃərɪ] *n* gaucherie *f*, maladresse *f*

gaucho ['gaʊtʃəʊ] *(pl* **gauchos**) *n* gaucho *m*

gaud [gɔːd] *n Arch or Literary* babiole *f*

gaudily ['gɔːdɪlɪ] *adv (dress)* de manière voyante, tapageusement; *(decorate)* de couleurs criardes

gaudiness ['gɔːdɪnɪs] *n (of colours)* éclat *m* criard, violence *f*; *(of clothes, decor)* style *m* voyant, mauvais goût *m*

gaudy ['gɔːdɪ] *(compar* **gaudier**, *superl* **gaudiest**, *pl* **gaudies**) **1** *adj (dress)* voyant; *(colour)* voyant, criard, tape-à-l'œil *(inv)*; *(display)* tapageur

2 *n Br Univ* fête *f* annuelle *(des étudiants)*

gauge, *Am* **gage** [geɪdʒ] **1** *n* (**a**) *(instrument)* jauge *f*, indicateur *m*; **water/oil gauge** indicateur *m ou* jauge *f* de niveau d'eau/d'huile; **pressure gauge** manomètre *m*; *Aut* **(petrol** *or* **fuel) gauge** jauge *f* d'essence
(**b**) *(standard measurement)* calibre *m*, gabarit *m*; *(diameter → of wire, cylinder, gun)* calibre *m*
(**c**) *Rail (of track)* écartement *m*; *Aut (of wheels)* écartement *m*
(**d**) *Tech (of steel)* jauge *f*
(**e**) *Cin (of film)* pas *m*
(**f**) *Fig* **the survey provides a gauge of current trends** le sondage permet d'évaluer les tendances actuelles
2 *vt* (**a**) *(screw etc)* calibrer; *(oil)* jauger, mesurer; *(measure, calculate)* mesurer, jauger; **to gauge the wind** mesurer la vitesse du vent; **to gauge the temperature of the political situation** jauger la situation politique; **she tried to gauge how much it would cost her** elle a essayé d'évaluer combien ça lui coûterait; **to gauge a situation** évaluer une situation; **it was difficult to gauge how interested they were/their enthusiasm** il était difficile de juger dans quelle mesure ils étaient intéressés/de juger de leur enthousiasme
(**b**) *(predict)* prévoir; **he tried to gauge what her reaction would be** il essaya de prévoir sa réaction
(**c**) *(standardize)* normaliser

gauging rod, gauging stick ['geɪdʒɪŋ-] *n* jauge *f*

Gaul [gɔːl] *n* (**a**) *Geog* Gaule *f* (**b**) *(person)* Gaulois(e) *m,f*

gauleiter ['gaʊlaɪtə(r)] *n Hist* gauleiter *m*; *Fig Pej (petty official)* petit chef *m*

Gaulish ['gɔːlɪʃ] **1** *n Ling* gaulois *m*
2 *adj Hist* gaulois

Gaullism ['gəʊlɪzəm] *n Pol* gaullisme *m*

Gaullist ['gəʊlɪst] *Pol* **1** *adj* gaulliste
2 *n* gaulliste *mf*

gaunt [gɔːnt] *adj* (**a**) *(emaciated → face)* hâve, creux, émacié; *(→ body)* décharné, émacié (**b**) *(desolate → landscape)* morne, lugubre, désolé; *(→ building)* lugubre, désert

gauntlet ['gɔːntlɪt] *n (medieval glove)* gantelet *m*; *(for motorcyclist, fencer)* gant *m* (à crispin *ou* à manchette); **to throw down/to take up the gauntlet** jeter/relever le gant; *Mil* **to run the gauntlet** passer par les baguettes; *Fig* se faire fustiger; **to run the gauntlet of an angry mob** se forcer *ou* se frayer un passage à travers une foule hostile; **she had to run the gauntlet of their anger** elle a dû affronter leur colère

gauntness ['gɔːntnɪs] *n* (**a**) *(of face, body)* maigreur *f*, aspect *m* émacié; **the gauntness of his face** la maigreur de son visage (**b**) *(of landscape)* aspect *m* morne *ou* lugubre, désolation *f*; *(of house)* aspect *m* lugubre

gaur [gaʊə(r)] *n Zool* gaur *m*

gauss [gaʊs] *n Phys* gauss *m*

Gaussian ['gaʊsɪən] *adj Phys & Math* gaussien
►► ***Gaussian distribution*** distribution *f* de Gauss, loi *f* de Gauss

gauze [gɔːz] *n* gaze *f*

gave [geɪv] *pt of* **give**

gavel ['gævəl] *n* marteau *m (de magistrat etc)*

gavel-to-gavel *adj Am (coverage)* intégral

gavotte [gə'vɒt] *n* gavotte *f*

Gawain [gə'weɪn] *pr n Myth* Gauvain

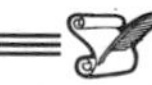

'Sir Gawain and the Green Knight' 'Sire Gauvain et le chevalier vert'

Gawd [gɔːd] *exclam Br Fam* mon Dieu!

gawk [gɔːk] *Fam* **1** *vi* être *ou* rester bouche bée ❑; **to gawk at sb** regarder qn bouche bée ❑
2 *n (person)* godiche *f*, grand dadais *m*

gawker ['gɔːkə(r)] *n Fam* badaud(e) ❑ *m,f*, curieux(euse) ❑ *m,f*

gawkily ['gɔːkɪlɪ] *adv* gauchement

gawkiness ['gɔːkɪnɪs] *n* gaucherie *f*, air *m* emprunté

gawkish ['gɔːkɪʃ] *adj* gauche, emprunté

gawky ['gɔːkɪ] (*compar* **gawkier**, *superl* **gawkiest**) *adj* gauche, emprunté

gawp [gɔːp] *vi Br Fam* être *ou* rester bouche bée ❑; **don't just stand there gawping, do something!** ne reste pas planté là, fais quelque chose!

gay [geɪ] **1** *adj* (**a**) *(cheerful, lively → appearance, party, atmosphere)* gai, joyeux; *(→ laughter)* enjoué, joyeux; *(→ music, rhythm)* gai, entraînant, allègre; **to have a gay old time** prendre du bon temps; **with gay abandon** avec insouciance, sans retenue
(**b**) *(bright → colours, lights)* gai, vif, éclatant; **the streets were gay with coloured flags/flowers** les rues étaient égayées de drapeaux/de fleurs aux couleurs vives
(**c**) *(homosexual)* gay, homosexuel
2 *n* homosexuel(elle) *m,f*, gay *mf*
3 *comp (club, disco, magazine)* pour homosexuels
►► ***the gay community*** la communauté homosexuelle *ou* gay; ***the Gay Gordons*** = quadrille écossais; ***the Gay Liberation Movement,*** *Fam* ***Gay Lib*** = mouvement de libération des homosexuels; *Fam Pej* **gay plague** sida ❑ *m*; **gay rights** les droits *mpl* des homosexuels

gay-basher [-bæʃə(r)] *n Fam* = individu qui attaque des homosexuels

gay-bashing [-bæʃɪŋ] *n Fam* = violences contre des homosexuels, violence anti-gay

gaydar ['geɪdɑː(r)] *n Fam Hum* = sixième sens que certains homosexuels sont censés posséder et qui leur permettrait de savoir qui est homosexuel et qui ne l'est pas

gayness ['geɪnɪs] *n* (**a**) *(of appearance, mood)* gaieté *f*; *(of colours)* gaieté *f*, éclat *m* (**b**) *(homosexuality)* homosexualité *f*

Gaza ['gɑːzə] *n* Gaza
►► ***the Gaza Strip*** la bande de Gaza

gaze [geɪz] **1** *vi* **to gaze at sb/sth** regarder qn/qch fixement *ou* longuement; **he was gazing at the ceiling** il regardait fixement le plafond, il fixait le plafond du regard; **she gazed at the landscape dreamily** elle regarda le paysage d'un air rêveur; **to gaze into space** avoir le regard perdu dans le vague, regarder dans le vide
2 *n* regard *m* fixe; **to meet sb's gaze** regarder qn dans les yeux; **exposed to the public gaze** exposé aux regards inquisiteurs de tous

►**gaze about, gaze around** *vi* regarder autour de soi

gazebo [gə'ziːbəʊ] (*pl* **gazebos**) *n* belvédère *m*

gazelle [gə'zel] (*pl* **inv** *or* **gazelles**) *n* gazelle *f*

gazette [gə'zet] **1** *n (newspaper)* journal *m*; *(official publication)* journal *m* officiel
2 *vt Br* publier *ou* faire paraître au journal officiel

gazetteer [gæzɪ'tɪə(r)] *n* index *m ou* nomenclature *f* géographique

gazillion [gə'zɪljən] *n Fam* **I've got a gazillion things to do** j'ai un million de choses à faire; **I've got gazillions of problems to deal with** j'ai des tas de problèmes à résoudre

gazpacho [gæz'pætʃəʊ] *n Culin* gaspacho *m*

gazump [gə'zʌmp] *Br Fam* **1** *vt* **we've been gazumped** le propriétaire de la maison est revenu sur sa promesse de vente pour accepter l'offre plus élevée d'une tierce personne ❑
2 *vi* = rompre une promesse de vente (d'une maison) à la suite d'une surenchère

gazumping [gə'zʌmpɪŋ] *n Br Fam* = fait de revenir sur une promesse de vente pour accepter une offre plus élevée

gazunder [gə'zʌndə(r)] *Br Fam* **1** *vt* = lors de l'achat d'une maison, baisser son offre juste avant la signature de l'acte de vente
2 *vi* = baisser son offre juste avant d'acheter une maison

gazundering [gə'zʌndərɪŋ] *n Br Fam* = fait de baisser son offre d'achat (d'une maison) juste avant la signature de l'acte de vente

GB[1] [ˌdʒiː'biː] *n* (*abbr* **Great Britain**) G-B *f*; **GB plate** plaque *f* GB; *Aut* **GB sticker** autocollant *m* GB

GB[2] *Comput* (*written abbr* **gigabyte**) Go

GBH [ˌdʒiːbiː'eɪtʃ] *n Law* (*abbr* **grievous bodily harm**) coups *mpl* et blessures *fpl*; *Br Fam* **to give sb GBH of the earholes** raser qn

GC [ˌdʒiː'siː] *n Br* (*abbr* **George Cross**) = distinction honorifique britannique

GCE [ˌdʒiːsiː'iː] *n Formerly Sch* (*abbr* **General Certificate of Education**) = certificat britannique de fin d'études secondaires en deux étapes (O level et A level) dont la première est aujourd'hui remplacée par le "GCSE"

GCH *Br* (*written abbr* **gas central heating**) chauffage *m* central au gaz

GCHQ [ˌdʒiːsiːˌeɪtʃ'kjuː] *n Br* (*abbr* **Government Communications Headquarters**) = centre d'interception des télécommunications étrangères en Grande-Bretagne

GCSE [ˌdʒiːsiːˌes'iː] *n Sch* (*abbr* **General Certificate of Secondary Education**) = premier examen de fin de scolarité en Grande-Bretagne

GCSE

Cet examen a remplacé les O levels, ou le GCE O level, et le CSE. On le passe après cinq ans de scolarité dans l'enseignement secondaire. Chaque élève choisit les matières dans lesquelles il veut se présenter (généralement entre cinq et dix) selon un système d'unités de valeur. Le nombre d'unités et les notes obtenues déterminent le passage dans la classe supérieure. Les élèves qui sont admis au GCSE peuvent ensuite préparer les A levels (l'équivalent du baccalauréat français). En Écosse, l'examen équivalent au GCSE s'appelle le "Standard Grade".

GD [ˌdʒiː'diː] *adj Am very Fam* (*abbr* **goddamn(ed)**) foutu, sacré; **he's a GD fool** c'est un sacré con

Gdansk [gə'dænsk] *n* Gdansk

g'day [gə'deɪ] *exclam Austr* salut!

Gdns. (*written abbr* **Gardens**) = abréviation écrite du terme "Gardens", qui est le nom donné à certaines rues en Grande-Bretagne

GDP [ˌdʒiːdiː'piː] *n Econ* (*abbr* **gross domestic product**) PIB *m*

GDR [ˌdʒiːdiː'ɑː(r)] *n* (*abbr* **German Democratic Republic**) RDA *f*

Gds (*written abbr* **Gardens**) = abréviation écrite du terme "Gardens", qui est le nom donné à certaines rues en Grande-Bretagne

gear [gɪə(r)] **1** *n* (**a**) *(UNCOUNT) (accessories, equipment → for photography, camping)* equipement *m*, matériel *m*; *(→ for manual work)* outils *mpl*, matériel *m*; *(→ for household)* ustensiles *mpl*; **he brought along all his skiing gear** il a apporté tout son équipement *ou* toutes ses affaires de ski; **he arrived with all his gear** *(his belongings)* il est arrivé avec tout son attirail; **gardening gear** matériel *m* de jardinage
(**b**) *(UNCOUNT) (personal belongings)* effets *mpl* personnels, affaires *fpl*; *(luggage)* bagages *mpl*
(**c**) *(UNCOUNT) (clothes)* vêtements *mpl*, tenue *f*; **she was in her jogging/swimming gear** elle était en (tenue de) jogging/en maillot de bain
(**d**) *(UNCOUNT) Br Fam (fashionable clothes)* fringues *fpl*; **I like the gear** j'aime bien les fringues
(**e**) *(UNCOUNT) (apparatus)* mécanisme *m*, dispositif *m*
(**f**) *(in car, on bicycle)* vitesse *f*; **to** *Br* **change** *or Am* **shift gear** changer de vitesse; **out of gear** *(car)* au point mort; **use** *or* **engage low gear** *(sign)* utiliser le frein moteur, rétrograder; **to throw** *or* **put out of gear** *(car)* débrayer; *Fig (plan, process)* perturber; **put the car in gear** passez une vitesse; **to be in first/second gear** être en première/seconde; **in gear** *(car)* embrayé, en prise; *Am Fig* **to get into gear** se magner; *Fig* **I'm back in gear again now** c'est reparti pour moi maintenant; **we're not operating in top gear** nous ne sommes pas à notre maximum *ou* au top de notre forme; *Br very Fam* **get your arse in gear!** remue-toi!
(**g**) *(cogwheel)* roue *f* dentée, pignon *m*; *(system of cogs)* engrenage *m*
(**h**) *(UNCOUNT) Br Fam (drugs)* dope *f*
2 *vt* (**a**) *(adapt)* adapter; **the army was not geared for modern warfare** l'armée n'était pas prête pour la guerre moderne; **her work schedule is geared to fit in with her holiday plans** son programme de travail concorde avec ses projets de vacances; **the government's policies were not geared to cope with an economic recession** la politique mise en place par le gouvernement n'était pas prévue pour faire face à une récession économique; **the city's hospitals were not geared to cater for such an emergency** les hôpitaux de la ville n'étaient

pas équipés pour répondre à une telle situation d'urgence

(**b**) *Aut & Tech* engrener

(**c**) *Fin (link)* indexer; **salaries are geared to the cost of living** les salaires sont indexés au coût de la vie

▸▸ ***gear change*** changement *m* de vitesse; ***gear lever*** levier *m* (de changement) de vitesse; ***gear ratio*** rapport *m* du changement de vitesse; ***gear shift*** *Am Aut* levier *m* (de changement) de vitesse; *(on bicycle)* changement *m* de vitesse; ***gear stick*** levier *m* (de changement) de vitesse; ***gear wheel*** roue *f* dentée, pignon *m*

▸**gear down** *vt sep* (**a**) *(reduce)* réduire

(**b**) *Tech* démultiplier

▸**gear up** *vt sep* (**a**) *(prepare)* **to be geared up** être paré *ou* fin prêt; **the sprinters were all geared up and ready to go** les sprinters étaient fin prêts à partir; **businesses were getting geared up for the single European market** les entreprises se préparaient en vue du marché unique européen; **she'd geared herself up to meet them** elle s'était mise en condition pour les rencontrer

(**b**) *(increase)* augmenter; **we must gear up production to meet the demand** il nous faut augmenter la production pour faire face à la demande

gearbox ['gɪəbɒks] *n* boîte *f* de vitesses

gearing ['gɪərɪŋ] *n* (**a**) *Tech* engrenage *m* (**b**) *Br Fin (leverage)* effet *m* de levier; *(as percentage)* ratio *m* d'endettement

▸▸ ***gearing adjustment*** redressement *m* financier

GEC [ˌdʒiːiː'siː] *n Br (abbr* **General Electric Company**) = société britannique fabriquant des produits électriques, électroniques et de télécommunications

gecko ['gekəʊ] *n Zool* gecko *m*

GED [ˌdʒiːiː'diː] *n Am Sch (abbr* **general equivalency diploma**) = aux États-Unis, diplôme d'études secondaires pour adultes souvent obtenu par correspondance

geddit ['gedɪt] *exclam Fam* **geddit?** tu piges?

gee [dʒiː] *exclam Am Fam* **gee (whizz)!** ça alors!; **gee, mom, can we have ice cream for dessert?** dis, maman, on peut avoir de la glace comme dessert?

▸**gee up** *Br Fam* **1** *vt sep* faire avancer ❑

2 *exclam (to horse)* hue!

gee-gee *n Br (in children's language)* dada *m*

geek [giːk] *n Am Fam Pej* (**a**) *(strange man)* mec *m* zarbi, allumé *m* (**b**) *(misfit)* ringard *m*, bouffon *m*

geeky ['giːkɪ] *adj Am Fam Pej* ringard

geese [giːs] *pl of* **goose**

geezer ['giːzə(r)] *n Fam* (**a**) *Br (man)* bonhomme *m*, coco *m*; **old geezer** vieux type *m*; **funny old geezer** drôle *m* de bonhomme (**b**) *Am (old person)* vioc (vioque) *m,f*

gefilte fish [gə'fɪltə-] *n Culin* gefilte fish *m*

Geiger counter ['gaɪgə(r)-] *n* compteur *m* Geiger

geisha (girl) ['geɪʃə-] *n* geisha *f*

gel[1] [dʒel] *(pt & pp* **gelled,** *cont* **gelling**) **1** *n* (**a**) *Chem (gen)* gel *m* (**b**) *Theat* filtre *m* coloré (**c**) *(for hair)* gel *m*

2 *vi* (**a**) *(idea, plan → take shape)* prendre forme *ou* tournure, se cristalliser; *(team)* se souder (**b**) *(jellify)* se gélifier

gel[2] [gel] *n Br Old-fashioned or Hum* fille *f*

gelatin ['dʒelətɪn], **gelatine** [dʒelə'tiːn] *n* (**a**) *(substance)* gélatine *f* (**b**) *Theat* filtre *m* coloré

▸▸ ***gelatine paper*** papier *m* gélatine

gelatinize, -ise [dʒɪ'lætɪnaɪz] **1** *vt* gélatiniser

2 *vi* se gélatiniser

gelatinized [dʒɪ'lætɪnaɪzd] *adj* gélatiné

gelatinous [dʒɪ'lætɪnəs] *adj* gélatineux

gelation [dʒɪ'leɪʃən] *n* (**a**) *(forming a gel)* gélification *f* (**b**) *(freezing)* gélation *f*

geld [geld] *vt (bull)* châtrer; *(horse)* hongrer

gelding ['geldɪŋ] *n* (cheval *m*) hongre *m*

gelid ['dʒelɪd] *adj Literary* glacial

gelignite ['dʒelɪgnaɪt] *n* gélignite *f*

gelt [gelt] *n Am Fam* fric *m*, flouze *m*, pognon *m*

gem [dʒem] **1** *n* (**a**) *(precious stone)* gemme *f*, pierre *f* précieuse; *(semiprecious stone)* gemme *f*, pierre *f* fine

(**b**) *(masterpiece)* joyau *m*, bijou *m*, merveille *f*; **the Petit Trianon is an architectural gem** le Petit Trianon est un joyau architectural; **that antique table is a real gem** cette table d'époque est une vraie merveille; **the gem of the collection** le joyau de la collection

(**c**) *(person)* **you're a gem!** tu es un ange!; **our baby-sitter is a real gem** notre baby-sitter est une perle

(**d**) *(in printing)* diamant *m*

2 *vt* orner, parer

▸▸ ***the Gem State*** = surnom donné à l'Idaho

Gemara [dʒe'mɑːrə] *n Rel & Literature* **the Gemara** la Gémara

geminate ['dʒemɪneɪt] **1** *adj* géminé

2 *vt* géminer

gemination [dʒemɪ'neɪʃən] *n* gémination *f*

Gemini ['dʒemɪnaɪ] **1** *n* (**a**) *Astron* Gémeaux *mpl* (**b**) *Astrol* Gémeaux *mpl*; **he's a Gemini** il est (du signe des) Gémeaux

2 *adj Astrol* des Gémeaux; **he's Gemini** il est (du signe des) Gémeaux

▸▸ *Astron* ***the Gemini Program*** = le programme spatial américain Gemini

Geminian [dʒemɪ'naɪən] *Astrol* **1** *n* **to be a Geminian** être (du signe des) Gémeaux

2 *adj* des Gémeaux

GEMM [ˌdʒiːiːˌem'em] *n Fin (abbr* **gilt-edged market maker**) teneur *m* de marché de premier ordre

gemma ['dʒemə] *(pl* **gemmae** [-miː]) *n Bot* gemme *f*

gemmiparous [dʒe'mɪpərəs] *adj Biol* gemmipare

▸▸ ***gemmiparous reproduction*** gemmiparité *f*

gemmologist [dʒe'mɒlədʒɪst] *n* gemmologiste *mf*

gemmology [dʒe'mɒlədʒɪ] *n* gemmologie *f*

gemmule ['dʒemjuːl] *n* gemmule *f*

Gems [dʒemz] *n Ecol (abbr* **Global Environment Monitoring System**) système *m* mondial de surveillance continue de l'environnement

gemstone ['dʒemstəʊn] *n (precious)* gemme *f*, pierre *f* précieuse; *(semiprecious)* gemme *f*, pierre *f* fine

Gen *(written abbr* **general**) G[al]

gen [dʒen] *n (UNCOUNT) Br Fam* tuyaux *mpl*, renseignements ❑ *mpl*; **she gave me the latest gen on our new assignment** elle m'a donné les derniers renseignements concernant notre nouvelle mission; **what's the gen on the new neighbours?** qu'est-ce qu'on raconte sur les nouveaux voisins?

▸**gen up** *(pt & pp* **genned,** *cont* **genning**) *Br Fam* **1** *vi* se rencarder (**on** sur)

2 *vt sep* rencarder, mettre au parfum; **she genned me up on the latest developments** elle m'a renseigné sur les *ou* elle m'a mis au parfum des derniers événements

gen. *(written abbr* **general, generally**) gen

gender ['dʒendə(r)] *n* (**a**) *Gram* genre *m*; **common gender** genre *m* commun (**b**) *(sex)* sexe *m*; **the male/female gender** le sexe masculin/féminin

▸▸ ***gender bias*** discrimination *f* sexuelle; ***the gender gap*** = les différences entre les hommes et les femmes dans la société; ***gender studies*** = à l'université, matière qui formule une critique des rôles de l'homme et de la femme tels qu'ils sont établis par la société

gender bender *n Fam* (**a**) *(cross-dresser)* travelo *m* (**b**) *Comput* commutateur ❑ *m*, changeur *m* de genre ❑

gender-changer *n* [-tʃeɪndʒə(r)] *n Comput* commutateur *m*, changeur *m* de genre

genderless ['dʒendəlɪs] *adj Gram* qui ne fait pas de distinction de genres

gender-specific *adj* propre à l'un des deux sexes

gene [dʒiːn] *n* gène *m*; **dominant/recessive gene** gène *m* dominant/récessif; *Fig* **music's in his genes** chez lui la musique, c'est héréditaire; **it's in his genes** c'est inné, il est né comme ça

▸▸ ***gene bank*** génothèque *f*, banque *f* génomique; ***gene flow*** flux *m* génétique; ***gene frequency*** fréquence *f* génétique; ***gene mapping*** cartographie *f* génétique; ***gene pool*** patrimoine *m* génétique; ***gene therapy*** thérapie *f* génique

genealogical [dʒiːnjə'lɒdʒɪkəl] *adj* généalogique

▸▸ ***genealogical tree*** arbre *m* généalogique

genealogist [dʒiːnɪ'ælədʒɪst] *n* généalogiste *mf*

genealogy [dʒiːnɪ'ælədʒɪ] *n* généalogie *f*

genera ['dʒenərə] *pl of* **genus**

general ['dʒenərəl] **1** *adj* (**a**) *(common)* général; **as a general rule** en règle générale, en général; **in general terms** en termes généraux; **in the general interest** dans l'intérêt de tous; **the general feeling was that he should have won** le sentiment général était qu'il aurait dû gagner; **there was a general movement to leave the room** la plupart des gens se sont levés pour sortir

(**b**) *(approximate)* général; **a general resemblance** une vague ressemblance; **to go in the general direction of sth** se diriger plus ou moins vers qch; **their house is over in that general direction** leur maison se trouve vers là-bas

(**c**) *(widespread)* général, répandu; **a general opinion** une opinion générale *ou* répandue; **to be in general use** être d'usage courant *ou* répandu; **to come into general use** se généraliser; **this word is no longer in general use** ce mot est tombé en désuétude; **there is general agreement on the matter** il y a consensus sur la question; **this kind of attitude is fairly general in Europe** ce genre d'attitude est assez répandu en Europe; **the rain has been pretty general** il a plu un peu partout

(**d**) *(overall → outline, plan, impression)* d'ensemble; **the general effect is quite pleasing** le résultat général est assez agréable; **I get the general idea** je vois en gros; **he gave her a general idea** *or* **outline of his work** il lui a décrit son travail dans les grandes lignes; **the general tone of her remarks was that...** ce qui ressortait de ses remarques c'est que...; **he made himself a general nuisance** il a été embêtant à tout point de vue

(**e**) *(ordinary)* **this book is for the general reader** ce livre est destiné au lecteur moyen; **the general public** le grand public

2 *n* (**a**) *(in reasoning)* **to go from the general to the particular** aller du général au particulier

(**b**) *Mil* général *m*

(**c**) *(domestic servant)* bonne *f* à tout faire

3 in general *adv* en général

▸▸ *Banking* ***general account manager*** chargé(e) *m,f* de clientèle grand public; ***general accounts*** comptabilité *f* générale; *Am* ***General Accounting Office*** = Cour des comptes américaine; *Fin & Com* ***general and administrative expenses*** frais *mpl* généraux et frais de gestion; *Com* ***general agent*** agent *m* d'affaires; ***General Agreement on Tariffs and Trade*** accord *m* général sur les tarifs douaniers et le commerce; *Med* ***general anaesthetic*** anesthésie *f* générale; ***General Assembly*** assemblée *f* générale; *Austr Cin* ***general (audience)*** = tous publics; *Ins* ***general average*** avarie *f* commune; *Com* ***general business*** *(on agenda)* questions *fpl* diverses; *Formerly Sch* ***General Certificate of Education*** = certificat de fin d'études secondaires en deux étapes (O level et A level) dont la première est aujourd'hui remplacée par le GCSE; *Sch* ***General Certificate of Secondary Education*** = premier examen de fin de scolarité en Grande-Bretagne; *see also* **GCSE**; *Am* ***general dealer*** bazar *m*; *Univ* ***general degree*** = licence comportant plusieurs matières; *Am* ***general delivery*** poste *f* restante; ***general election*** élections *fpl* législatives; *Br* ***General Electric Company*** = société britannique fabriquant des produits électriques, électroniques et de télécommunications; *Am Sch* ***general equivalency diploma*** = aux États-Unis, diplôme d'études secondaires pour adultes souvent obtenu par correspondance; *Acct & Fin* ***general expenses*** frais *mpl* généraux; ***general headquarters*** (grand) quartier *m* général; ***general hospital*** centre *m* hospitalier; ***general knowledge*** culture *f* générale; *Acct* ***general ledger*** grand-livre *m*; *Law* ***general lien*** privilège *m* général; ***general management committee*** comité *m* de direction; ***general manager*** directeur(trice) *m,f* général(e); *Br* ***General Medical Council*** ≃ conseil *m* de l'ordre des médecins; ***general meeting*** assemblée *f* générale; *Br* ***General, Municipal, Boilermakers and Allied Trades Union*** = important syndicat britannique; *Br* ***General and Municipal Workers' Union*** = syndicat britannique des employés des collectivités locales; *Br Sch* ***General National Vocational Qualification*** = formation professionnelle sur deux ans que l'on peut suivre à

gea–gen

partir de seize ans; *Fin* **general obligation bond** emprunt *m* de collectivité locale; **general officer** général *m* en chef; *Acct & Fin Br* **general overheads,** *Am* **general overhead** frais *mpl* d'administration générale; **General Post Office** *(in Britain)* = titre officiel de la Poste britannique avant 1969; *(in US)* = les services postaux américains; **general practice** médecine *f* générale; **general practitioner** médecin *m* généraliste, omnipraticien(enne) *m,f*; *Fin* **general price level** niveau *m* général des prix; **general secretary** *(of trade union, political party)* secrétaire *mf* général(e); **general staff** état-major *m*; **general store** bazar *m*; **general strike** grève *f* générale; **the General Strike** = la grève de mai 1926 en Grande-Bretagne, lancée par les syndicats par solidarité avec les mineurs; *Sch* **General Studies** ≃ cours *m* de culture générale; **General Synod** = le Synode général de l'Église anglicane; *Fin* **general wage level** niveau *m* général des salaires

general-interest station *n TV* station *f* généraliste

generalissimo [ˌdʒenərə'lɪsɪməʊ] *(pl* **generalissimos***) n* généralissime *m*

generalist ['dʒenərəlɪst] *n* non-spécialiste *mf*, généraliste *mf*

generality [dʒenə'rælətɪ] *(pl* **generalities***) n* (**a**) *(generalization)* généralité *f*; **to confine oneself to generalities** s'en tenir aux généralités; **the Minister's speech was full of generalities** lors de son discours le ministre n'a évoqué que des généralités; **a principle of great generality** un principe très général; **in the generality** en règle générale (**b**) *Formal (majority)* plupart *f*; **the generality of mankind** la plupart des hommes

generalization [ˌdʒenərəlaɪ'zeɪʃən] *n* (**a**) *(general comment)* généralisation *f*; **to make generalizations** généraliser (**b**) *(spread)* généralisation *f*

generalize, -ise ['dʒenərəlaɪz] **1** *vt* généraliser; **to become generalized** *(practice)* se généraliser

2 *vi* (**a**) *(person)* généraliser (**b**) *Med (disease)* se généraliser

generalized ['dʒenərəlaɪzd] *adj* (**a**) *(involving many)* généralisé (**b**) *(non-specific)* général

generally ['dʒenərəlɪ] *adv* (**a**) *(usually)* en général, d'habitude; **he generally comes in the afternoon** d'habitude, il vient l'après-midi

(**b**) *(in a general way)* en général, de façon générale; **generally speaking** en général, en règle générale

(**c**) *(by most)* dans l'ensemble; **it is generally agreed that it cannot be done** on s'accorde en général à penser que c'est infaisable; **this information is not generally available** le public n'a pas accès à ces informations; **it is not generally known that...** beaucoup de gens ignorent que...

general-purpose *adj (tool, adhesive)* universel; *(knife)* tous usages; *(dictionary)* général

generalship ['dʒenərəlʃɪp] *n (UNCOUNT)* (**a**) *Mil (skill, duties)* tactique *f* (**b**) *Admin* capacités *fpl* administratives

generate ['dʒenəreɪt] *vt* (**a**) *(produce → electricity, power)* produire, générer; *Fig (→ income)* créer; *(→ emotion, interest)* susciter; **tourism generated three million pounds for the region** le tourisme a rapporté trois millions de livres à la région (**b**) *Ling & Comput* générer

generating ['dʒenəreɪtɪŋ] *adj* générateur

▸▸ ***generating station*** centrale *f* électrique; ***generating unit*** groupe *m* électrogène

generation [dʒenə'reɪʃən] *n* (**a**) *(age group)* génération *f*; **the present generation is** *or* **are anxious about the future** la génération actuelle est inquiète face à l'avenir; **the 1960s saw the appearance of the hippy generation** la génération hippie est apparue au cours des années 60; **the rising generation** la jeune *ou* nouvelle génération; **a new generation of writers** une nouvelle génération d'écrivains; **from generation to generation** de génération en génération, de père en fils

(**b**) *(by birth)* **she is second generation Irish** elle est née de parents irlandais; **third generation black Britons still face racial prejudice** les noirs britanniques de la troisième génération sont encore confrontés au racisme

(**c**) *(period of time)* génération *f*; **the house has been in the family for three generations** la maison est dans la famille depuis trois générations; **traditions that have been practised for generations** des traditions en vigueur depuis des générations

(**d**) *(model → of machine)* génération *f*; **a third generation microprocessor** un microprocesseur de la troisième génération

(**e**) *(UNCOUNT) (of electricity)* génération *f*, production *f*; *(of ideas etc)* génération *f*, formation *f*; *Ling* génération *f*

▸▸ ***generation gap*** écart *m* entre les générations; *(conflict)* conflit *m* des générations; ***Generation X*** génération *f* X

generative ['dʒenərətɪv] *adj* génératif

▸▸ ***generative cell*** cellule *f* générative; *Ling* ***generative grammar*** grammaire *f* générative; *Ling* ***generative semantics*** sémantique *f* générative

generator ['dʒenəreɪtə(r)] *n* (**a**) *(electric → in power station)* générateur *m*; *(backup device → in factory, hospital etc)* groupe *m* électrogène; *(of steam)* générateur *m*, chaudière *f* (à vapeur); *(of gas)* gazogène *m* (**b**) *Comput* (programme *m*) générateur *m*; *Tech (of heat etc)* générateur *m* (**c**) *(person)* générateur(trice) *m,f*

generatrix ['dʒenəreɪtrɪks] *(pl* **generatrices** [-trɪsiːz]*) n* génératrice *f*

generic [dʒɪ'nerɪk] **1** *adj* générique

2 *n Mktg* produit *m* générique

▸▸ ***generic advertising*** publicité *f* générique; ***generic brand*** marque *f* générique; ***generic drug*** médicament *m* générique, générique *m*; ***generic market*** marché *m* générique; ***generic name*** *Biol* nom *m* du genre; *(of product, drug)* nom *m* générique; ***generic product*** produit *m* générique

generically [dʒɪ'nerɪklɪ] *adv* génériquement

generosity [dʒenə'rɒsətɪ] *n* générosité *f*

generous ['dʒenərəs] *adj* (**a**) *(with money, gifts)* généreux; **she's always generous with her time** elle n'est pas avare de son temps; **he was very generous in his praise** il ne tarissait pas d'éloges

(**b**) *(in value → gift)* généreux; *(in quantity → sum, salary)* généreux, élevé; **generous mark** *(for homework etc)* note *f* généreuse

(**c**) *(copious)* copieux, abondant; *(large)* bon, abondant; **a generous portion** une part copieuse *ou* généreuse; **food and drink were in generous supply** il y avait à boire et à manger en abondance; **she cut him a generous slice of cake** elle lui a servi une bonne tranche de gâteau; **they serve generous helpings of cream** ils ne lésinent pas sur la crème; **a generous harvest** une récolte abondante

(**d**) *Br (strong → wine)* généreux

(**e**) *(physically → size)* généreux, ample; *Euph* **to have generous curves** avoir des formes généreuses

generously ['dʒenərəslɪ] *adv* (**a**) *(unsparingly)* généreusement, avec générosité

(**b**) *(with magnanimity → agree, offer)* généreusement; *(→ forgive)* généreusement, avec magnanimité

(**c**) *(copiously)* **a plate of chips generously sprinkled with salt and vinegar** une assiette de frites généreusement salée et vinaigrée; **the soup was rather generously salted** *(oversalted)* la soupe était très généreusement salée

(**d**) *(in size)* amplement; *Euph* **to be generously built** avoir des formes généreuses

genesis ['dʒenəsɪs] *(pl* **geneses** [-siːz]*)* **1** *n* genèse *f*, origine *f*

2 Genesis *n Bible* la Genèse

genet ['dʒenɪt] *n Zool* genette *f*

genethliac [dʒə'neθlɪæk], **genethliacal** [ˌdʒeneθ'laɪəkəl] *adj Arch or Literary* généthliaque

genetic [dʒɪ'netɪk] *adj* génétique

▸▸ ***genetic code*** code *m* génétique; ***genetic counselling*** conseil *m* génétique; ***genetic engineer*** généticien(enne) *m,f*; ***genetic engineering*** génie *m* génétique; ***genetic fingerprint*** empreinte *f* génétique; ***genetic fingerprinting*** analyse *f* de l'empreinte génétique; ***genetic map*** carte *f* génétique; ***genetic marker*** marqueur *m* génétique; ***genetic parents*** parents *mpl* biologiques *ou* génétiques; ***genetic screening*** dépistage *m* des maladies génétiques

genetical [dʒɪ'netɪkəl] *adj* génétique

genetically [dʒɪ'netɪklɪ] *adv* génétiquement

genetically-modified *adj (plant, food, organism)* génétiquement modifié

geneticist [dʒɪ'netɪsɪst] *n* généticien(enne) *m,f*

genetics [dʒɪ'netɪks] *n (UNCOUNT)* génétique *f*

genetrix ['dʒenɪtrɪks] *(pl* **genetrices** [-ɪsiːz]*) n* génétrice *f*

Geneva [dʒɪ'niːvə] *n* Genève

▸▸ ***the Geneva Convention*** la Convention de Genève

Genevan [dʒɪ'niːvən], **Genevese** [dʒenɪ'viːz] *(pl* **inv***)* **1** *n* Genevois(e) *m,f*

2 *adj* genevois

Genghis Khan [ˌgeŋgɪs'kɑːn] *pr n* Gengis Khan

genial ['dʒiːnjəl] *adj* (**a**) *(friendly → person)* aimable, affable; *(→ expression, voice)* cordial, chaleureux; *(→ face)* jovial (**b**) *Literary (clement → weather)* clément

geniality ['dʒiːnɪ'ælətɪ] *n* (**a**) *(of person, expression)* cordialité *f*, amabilité *f* (**b**) *Literary (of weather)* clémence *f*

genially ['dʒiːnjəlɪ] *adv* affablement, cordialement, chaleureusement

genie ['dʒiːnɪ] *(pl* **genii** [-nɪaɪ]*) n* génie *m*, djinn *m*

genii ['dʒiːnɪaɪ] *pl of* **genie, genius**

genital ['dʒenɪtəl] **1** *adj* génital; **the genital organs** les organes *mpl* génitaux

2 genitals *npl* organes *mpl* génitaux

▸▸ ***genital herpes*** herpès *m* génital

genitalia [dʒenɪ'teɪlɪə] *npl* organes *mpl* génitaux, parties *fpl* génitales

genitival [dʒenɪ'taɪvəl] *adj* du génitif

genitive ['dʒenɪtɪv] **1** *n* génitif *m*; **in the genitive** au génitif

2 *adj* du génitif; **the genitive case** le génitif

genitor ['dʒenɪtə(r)] *n* géniteur(trice) *m,f*

genito-urinary [dʒenɪtəʊ-] *adj* génito-urinaire

▸▸ ***genito-urinary tract*** appareil *m* génito-urinaire

genius ['dʒiːnjəs] *(pl senses* (**a**)–(**c**) **geniuses,** *pl sense* (**d**) **genii** [-nɪaɪ]*) n* (**a**) *(person)* génie *m*; **she's a genius at music** c'est un génie en musique

(**b**) *(special ability)* génie *m*; **a work/writer of genius** une œuvre/un écrivain de génie; **to have a genius for sth** avoir le génie de qch; **he has a genius for public relations** il a le génie des relations publiques; **some people have great natural genius** il y a des gens très doués de naissance; **her genius lies in her power to evoke atmosphere** son génie, c'est de savoir recréer une atmosphère; **she has a genius for remembering people's faces** elle a le génie *ou* le don de se souvenir des visages; **that goal was pure genius** ce but, c'était du génie pur et simple

(**c**) *(special character → of system, idea)* génie *m* (particulier), esprit *m*

(**d**) *(spirit, demon)* génie *m*; **good/evil genius** bon/mauvais génie *m*

Genoa ['dʒenəʊə] *n* Gênes

▸▸ ***Genoa cake*** = cake recouvert d'amandes effilées

genoa ['dʒenəʊə] *n Naut* génois *m*

genocidal [ˌdʒenə'saɪdəl] *adj* génocide

genocide ['dʒenəsaɪd] *n* génocide *m*

Genoese [dʒenəʊ'iːz], **Genovese** [dʒenə'viːz] *(pl* **inv***)* **1** *n* Génois(e) *m,f*

2 *adj* génois

genome ['dʒiːnəʊm] *n Biol* génome *m*

genotype ['dʒenəʊtaɪp] *n* génotype *m*

genre ['ʒɑ̃rə] *n* genre *m*

▸▸ ***genre painting*** peinture *f* de genre

gent [dʒent] **1** *n Br Fam* (**a**) *(well-bred man)* gentleman *m*; **to behave like a (real) gent** agir en gentleman (**b**) *(man)* monsieur *m*; **gent's footwear** chaussures *fpl* pour hommes

2 gents *n (toilets)* toilettes *fpl* (pour hommes); *(sign)* messieurs; **where's the gents?** où sont les toilettes?

▸▸ ***gents' outfitters*** magasin *m* de confection *ou* d'habillement pour hommes

genteel [dʒen'tiːl] *adj* (**a**) *(refined)* comme il faut, distingué; **to live in genteel poverty** vivre dans une misère qui s'efforce de sauver les apparences (**b**) *(affected → speech)* maniéré, affecté; *(→ manner)* affecté; *(→ language)* précieux

genteelly [dʒen'tiːllɪ] *adv (affectedly → speak)*

d'un ton maniéré; *(→ behave)* d'une façon maniérée, en affectant une prétendue distinction

genteelness [dʒen'ti:lnɪs] *n* (**a**) *(good breeding)* distinction *f* (**b**) *(affected politeness)* manières *fpl* affectées

gentian ['dʒenʃən] *n* gentiane *f*
▸▸ ***gentian blue*** **1** *n* bleu *m* gentiane **2** *adj* bleu gentiane *(inv)*; ***gentian violet*** **1** *n* violet *m* gentiane **2** *adj* violet gentiane *(inv)*

Gentile ['dʒentaɪl] *Hist* **1** *n* gentil *m*
2 *adj* des gentils

gentility [dʒen'tɪlətɪ] *n* (**a**) *(good breeding)* distinction *f* (**b**) *(gentry)* petite noblesse *f* (**c**) *(UNCOUNT) (affected politeness)* manières *fpl* affectées

gentle ['dʒentəl] **1** *adj* (**a**) *(mild → person, smile, voice)* doux (douce); *(→ landscape)* agréable; **a gentle soul** une bonne âme, une âme charitable; **the gentle sex** le sexe faible; **as gentle as a lamb** doux comme un agneau
(**b**) *(light → knock, push, breeze)* léger(ère); *(→ rain)* fin, léger(ère); *(→ exercise)* modéré
(**c**) *(discreet → rebuke, reminder)* discret(ète); *Hum* **the gentle art of persuasion** l'art subtil de la persuasion; **to try gentle persuasion on sb** essayer de convaincre qn par la douceur; **we gave him a gentle hint** nous l'avons discrètement mis sur la voie
(**d**) *(gradual → slope, climb)* doux (douce); **a gentle transition** une transition progressive *ou* sans heurts; **to come to a gentle halt** s'arrêter sans à-coup
(**e**) *Arch (noble)* noble, de bonne naissance; *Literary* **gentle reader** aimable lecteur; **of gentle birth** de bonne famille
2 *vt (animal)* apaiser, calmer
3 *n (maggot)* asticot *m*

'Do not go gentle into that good night' *Thomas* 'N'entre pas sans violence dans cette bonne nuit'

Do not go gentle into that good night
Il s'agit du premier vers du poème éponyme de Dylan Thomas, publié en 1952, dans lequel le poète invite le lecteur à profiter de la vie et à ne pas accepter son destin de mortel sans se révolter **rage, rage against the dying of the light** ("insurge-toi, n'accepte pas la mort du jour").
On utilise cette phrase ("n'entre pas sans violence dans cette bonne nuit") de façon allusive à propos de la vieillesse et de la mort. On dira par exemple **the artist refused to go gentle into that good night, and was more prolific in his last years than at any other time of his life** ("le peintre refusa de s'avouer vaincu par la vieillesse et fut plus productif que jamais pendant les dernières années de sa vie").

gentlefolk ['dʒentəlfəʊk] *npl Arch* personnes *fpl* de bonne famille *ou* de la petite noblesse

gentleman ['dʒentəlmən] *(pl* **gentlemen** [-mən]) *n* (**a**) *(man)* monsieur *m*; **show the gentleman in** faites entrer monsieur; **come in, gentlemen!** entrez, messieurs!
(**b**) *(well bred man)* gentleman *m*; **he's a real gentleman** c'est un vrai gentleman; [illegible] **gentleman** agir en gentleman; **that's not how a gentleman would behave** c'est (une conduite) indigne d'un gentleman; **a born gentleman** un gentleman-né; **the word of a gentleman** la parole (d'honneur) d'un gentleman
(**c**) *(man of substance)* rentier *m*; *(at court)* gentilhomme *m*
▸▸ ***gentleman's agreement*** gentleman's agreement *m*, accord *m* reposant sur l'honneur; ***gentleman farmer*** gentleman-farmer *m*; *Br* ***gentleman's gentleman*** valet *m* de chambre

'Gentlemen Prefer Blondes' *Loos, Hawks* 'Les Hommes préfèrent les blondes'

gentleman-at-arms *n Br* gentilhomme *m* à la garde

gentleman-in-waiting *n Br* gentilhomme *m* (au service du roi)

gentlemanlike ['dʒentəlmən,laɪk] *adj (person)* bien élevé; *(appearance, behaviour)* distingué

gentlemanliness ['dʒentəlmənlɪnɪs] *n* bonnes manières *fpl*, savoir-vivre *m*

gentlemanly ['dʒentəlmənlɪ] *adj (person)* bien élevé; *(appearance, behaviour)* distingué; *(status)* noble; **to behave in a gentlemanly way** agir en gentleman

gentlemen ['dʒentəlmən] *pl of* **gentleman**
▸▸ ***gentlemen's club*** = club dont l'accès est réservé aux hommes

gentleness ['dʒentəlnɪs] *n* douceur *f*, légèreté *f*

gentlewoman ['dʒentəlwʊmən] *(pl* **gentlewomen** [-wɪmɪn]) *n* (**a**) *(of noble birth)* dame *f* (**b**) *(refined)* femme *f* du monde (**c**) *(lady-in-waiting)* dame *f* d'honneur *ou* de compagnie

gently ['dʒentlɪ] *adv* (**a**) *(mildly → speak, smile)* avec douceur
(**b**) *(discreetly → remind, reprimand, suggest)* discrètement; **he broke the news to her as gently as possible** il fit de son mieux pour lui annoncer la nouvelle avec tact *ou* ménagement
(**c**) *(lightly)* **a light breeze blew the curtains gently to and fro** une légère brise faisait onduler les rideaux; **the rain was falling gently** la pluie tombait doucement
(**d**) *(gradually)* doucement, progressivement; **the hill slopes gently down to the sea** la colline descend doucement *ou* en pente douce vers la mer; **gently rolling hills** des collines qui ondoient (doucement)
(**e**) *(slowly → move, heat)* doucement; **a gently flowing river** une rivière qui coule paisiblement; **gently does it!** doucement!

gentoo penguin [dʒentu:-] *n Orn* manchot *m* papou

gentrification [,dʒentrɪfɪ'keɪʃən] *n Br* embourgeoisement *m*

gentrified ['dʒentrɪfaɪd] *adj Br (area, street)* qui s'est embourgeoisé

gentrify ['dʒentrɪfaɪ] *(pt & pp* **gentrified**) *vt Br (suburb)* embourgeoiser, rendre chic *ou* élégant

gentry ['dʒentrɪ] *(pl* **gentries**) *n* petite noblesse *f*

genuflect ['dʒenju:flekt] *vi* faire une génuflexion

genuflection, genuflexion [,dʒenju:'flekʃən] *n* génuflexion *f*

genuine ['dʒenjʊɪn] *adj* (**a**) *(authentic → antique)* authentique; *(→ gold, mahogany)* véritable, vrai; **a genuine Van Gogh** un Van Gogh authentique; *Fig* **he's the genuine article** c'est un vrai de vrai
(**b**) *(sincere → person)* sincère, franc (franche); *(→ emotion)* sincère, vrai; *(→ smile, laugh)* vrai, franc (franche); **I think he's being genuine** je crois qu'il est sincère; **it is my genuine belief that he is innocent** je suis intimement persuadé de son innocence; **her regret seemed genuine** elle semblait sincèrement désolée
(**c**) *(real → mistake)* fait de bonne foi
(**d**) *(not impersonated → repairman, official)* vrai, véritable
(**e**) *(serious → buyer)* sérieux; **genuine enquiries only** *(in advertisement)* pas sérieux s'abstenir

genuinely ['dʒenjʊɪnlɪ] *adv (truly)* authentiquement; *(sincerely)* sincèrement, véritablement; **genuinely surprised** vraiment *ou* véritablement surpris

genuineness [illegible] *n* (**a**) *(of manuscript etc)* authenticité *f* (**b**) *(sincerity)* sincérité *f*

genus ['dʒenəs] *(pl* **genera** [-ərə]) *n Biol* genre *m*

geo- ['dʒi:əʊ] *pref* géo-

geobiology [,dʒi:əʊbaɪ'ɒlədʒɪ] *n* géobiologie *f*

geocentric [,dʒi:əʊ'sentrɪk] *adj* géocentrique

geocentricism [,dʒi:əʊ'sentrɪsɪzəm] *n* géocentrisme *m*

geochemical [,dʒi:əʊ'kemɪkəl] *adj* géochimique

geochemist [,dʒi:əʊ'kemɪst] *n* géochimiste *mf*

geochemistry [,dʒi:əʊ'kemɪstrɪ] *n* géochimie *f*

geochronological [,dʒi:əʊ,krɒnə'lɒdʒɪkəl] *adj* géochronologique

geochronology [,dʒi:əʊkrə'nɒlədʒɪ] *n* géochronologie *f*

geode ['dʒi:əʊd] *n* géode *f*

geodemographic [,dʒi:əʊdeməʊ'græfɪk] *adj Mktg* géodémographique
▸▸ ***geodemographic profile*** profil *m* géodémographique; ***geodemographic segment*** segment *m* géodémographique; ***geodemographic segmentation*** segmentation *f* géodémographique

geodemographics [,dʒi:əʊdeməʊ'græfɪks] *n (UNCOUNT) Mktg* géodémographie *f*

geodesic [,dʒi:əʊ'desɪk] *adj* géodésique
▸▸ ***geodesic dome*** dôme *m* géodésique; ***geodesic line*** (ligne *f*) géodésique *f*

geodesist [dʒi:'ɒdɪsɪst] *n* géodésien(enne) *m,f*

geodesy [dʒi:'ɒdɪsɪ] *n* géodésie *f*

geodetic [,dʒi:əʊ'detɪk] = **geodesic**

geodynamic [,dʒi:əʊdaɪ'næmɪk] *adj* géodynamique

geodynamics [,dʒi:əʊdaɪ'næmɪks] *n (UNCOUNT)* géodynamique *f*

geoglyph ['dʒɪəʊglɪf] *n Archeol* géoglyphe *m*

geographer [dʒɪ'ɒgrəfə(r)] *n* géographe *mf*

geographic [dʒɪə'græfɪk], **geographical** [dʒɪə'græfɪkəl] *adj* géographique
▸▸ ***geographical mile*** mille *m* marin

geographically [dʒɪə'græfɪkəlɪ] *adv* géographiquement

geography [dʒɪ'ɒgrəfɪ] *(pl* **geographies**) **1** *n* (**a**) *(science)* géographie *f*; **physical/social geography** géographie *f* physique/humaine (**b**) *(layout)* **I don't know the geography of the building** je ne m'oriente pas très bien dans le bâtiment
2 *comp (class, lesson)* de géographie

geoid ['dʒi:ɔɪd] *n* géoïde *m*

geological [dʒɪə'lɒdʒɪkəl] *adj* géologique
▸▸ ***geological survey*** étude *f* géologique; ***geological time*** temps *m* géologique

geologically [dʒɪə'lɒdʒɪkəlɪ] *adv* du point de vue géologique

geologist [dʒɪ'ɒlədʒɪst] *n* géologue *mf*

geology [dʒɪ'ɒlədʒɪ] *n* géologie *f*

geomagnetic [,dʒi:əʊmæg'netɪk] *adj* géomagnétique; **a geomagnetic storm** un orage magnétique

geomagnetism [,dʒi:əʊ'mægnɪtɪzəm] *n* géomagnétisme *m*, magnétisme *m* terrestre

geomancy ['dʒi:əʊ,mænsɪ] *n* géomancie *f*

geomarketing [,dʒi:əʊ'mɑ:kɪtɪŋ] *n* géomarketing *m*

geometer [dʒɪ'ɒmɪtə(r)] *n Math* géomètre *mf*
▸▸ *Entom* ***geometer moth*** géomètre *m*

geometric [dʒɪə'metrɪk] *adj* géométrique
▸▸ ***geometric distribution*** distribution *f* géométrique; ***geometric mean*** moyenne *f* géométrique; ***geometric progression*** progression *f* géométrique; ***geometric series*** série *f* géométrique

geometrical [dʒɪə'metrɪkəl] *adj* géométrique

geometrically [dʒɪə'metrɪkəlɪ] *adv* géométriquement

geometrician [,dʒɪəmə'trɪʃən] *n* géomètre *mf*

geometrization [,dʒi:ɒmɪtraɪ'zeɪʃən] *n* géométrisation *f*

geometrize, -ise [dʒi:'ɒmɪtraɪz] **1** *vt* géométriser
2 *vi* géométriser

geometry [dʒɪ'ɒmətrɪ] *n* géométrie *f*

geomorphic [,dʒi:əʊ'mɔ:fɪk] *adj* géomorphologique

geomorphologic [,dʒi:əʊmɔ:fə'lɒdʒɪk], **geomorphological** [,dʒi:əʊmɔ:fə'lɒdʒɪkəl] *adj* géomorphologique

geomorphology [,dʒi:əʊmɔ:'fɒlədʒɪ] *n* géomorphologie *f*

geophagia [,dʒi:əʊ'feɪdʒə], **geophagism** [dʒɪ'ɒfədʒɪzəm] = **geophagy**

geophagist [illegible] *mf*

geophagous [dʒɪ'ɒfəgəs] *adj* géophage

geophagy [dʒɪ'ɒfədʒɪ] *n* géophagie *f*

geophysical [dʒi:əʊ'fɪzɪkəl] *adj* géophysique

geophysicist [,dʒi:əʊ'fɪzɪsɪst] *n* géophysicien(enne) *m,f*

geophysics [,dʒi:əʊ'fɪzɪks] *n (UNCOUNT)* géophysique *f*

geopolitical [,dʒi:əʊpə'lɪtɪkəl] *adj* géopolitique

geopolitics [,dʒi:əʊ'pɒlɪtɪks] *n (UNCOUNT)* géopolitique *f*

Geordie ['dʒɔ:dɪ] *Br* **1** *n* (**a**) *(person)* = surnom des habitants du Tyneside, dans le nord-est de l'Angleterre (**b**) *(dialect)* = dialecte parlé par les habitants du Tyneside
2 *adj* = caractéristique du Tyneside

George ['dʒɔ:dʒ] *pr n* (**a**) *Fam Old-fashioned* **by George!** sapristi! (**b**) *Br Fam Aviat* = le pilote automatique
▸▸ ***George Cross*** = décoration britannique décernée aux civils pour des actes de bravoure;

George Medal = décoration britannique décernée aux civils ou aux militaires pour des actes de bravoure

georgette [dʒɔːˈdʒet] *n* crêpe *m* georgette

Georgia [ˈdʒɔːdʒjə] *n (in US, former USSR)* la Géorgie; **in Georgia** en Géorgie

Georgian [ˈdʒɔːdʒjən] **1** *n* (**a**) *(inhabitant of Georgia)* Géorgien(enne) *m,f* (**b**) *(language)* géorgien *m*

2 *adj* (**a**) *(of Georgia)* géorgien (**b**) *Hist* géorgien *(du règne des rois George I–IV 1714–1830)*; **Georgian architecture** architecture *f* de style georgien (**c**) *Literature* **Georgian poetry** poésie *f* géorgienne *(poésie britannique des années 1912–1922)*

3 *comp (embassy)* de Géorgie; *(history)* de la Géorgie; *(teacher)* de géorgien

georgic [ˈdʒɔːdʒɪk] *adj Literature* géorgique

geoscience [ˌdʒiːəʊˈsaɪəns] *n* (**a**) *(particular)* science *f* de la terre (**b**) *(UNCOUNT) (collectively)* sciences *fpl* de la terre

geoscientist [ˌdʒiːəʊˈsaɪəntɪst] *n* spécialiste *mf* des sciences de la terre

geosphere [ˈdʒiːəʊˌsfɪə(r)] *n* géosphère *f*

geostatic [ˌdʒiːəʊˈstætɪk] *adj* géostatique

geostatics [ˌdʒiːəʊˈstætɪks] *n (UNCOUNT)* géostatique *f*

geostationary [dʒiːəʊˈsteɪʃənərɪ] *adj* géostationnaire; **in geostationary orbit** en orbite géostationnaire

geostatistics [ˌdʒiːəʊˈstætɪstɪks] *n (UNCOUNT) Mining* géostatistique *f*

geostrategical [ˌdʒiːəʊstrəˈtiːdʒɪkəl] *adj* géostratégique

geostrategy [ˌdʒiːəʊˈstrætədʒɪ] *n* géostratégie *f*

geostrophic [ˌdʒiːəʊˈstrɒfɪk] *adj Met* géostrophique

geosynchronous [ˌdʒiːəʊˈsɪŋkrənəs] *adj* géosynchrone

geosyncline [ˌdʒiːəʊˈsɪŋklaɪn] *n* géosynclinal *m*

geotechnical [ˌdʒiːəʊˈteknɪkəl] *adj* géotechnique

geotechnician [ˌdʒiːəʊtekˈnɪʃən] *n* géotechnicien(enne) *m,f*

geotechnics [ˌdʒiːəʊˈteknɪks] *n (UNCOUNT)* géotechnique *f*

geotectonic [ˌdʒiːəʊtekˈtɒnɪk] *adj* géotectonique

geotextile [ˈdʒiːəʊtekstaɪl] *n* géotextile *m*

geothermal [dʒiːəʊˈθɜːməl], **geothermic** [dʒiːəʊˈθɜːmɪk] *adj* géothermique

geothermics [dʒiːəʊˈθɜːmɪks] *n (UNCOUNT)* géothermie *f*

geothermometer [ˌdʒiːəʊθəˈmɒmɪtə(r)] *n* géothermomètre *m*

geotropical [ˌdʒiːəʊˈtrɒpɪkəl] *adj* géotropique

geotropically [ˌdʒiːəʊˈtrɒpɪkəlɪ] *adv* géotropiquement

geotropism [ˌdʒiːəʊˈtrəʊpɪzəm] *n Bot* géotropisme *m*

geranium [dʒɪˈreɪnjəm] **1** *n* géranium *m*

2 *adj* rouge géranium *(inv)*, incarnat

gerbil [ˈdʒɜːbɪl] *n* gerbille *f*

geriatric [ˌdʒerɪˈætrɪk] **1** *adj Med* gériatrique

2 *n* (**a**) *(patient)* malade *mf* en gériatrie (**b**) *Pej (old person)* vieux (vieille) *m,f*

▸▸ ***geriatric hospital*** hospice *m*; ***geriatric medicine*** gériatrie *f*; ***geriatric nurse*** infirmier(ère) *m,f* (spécialisé(e)) en gériatrie; ***geriatric ward*** service *m* de gériatrie

geriatrician [dʒerɪəˈtrɪʃən] *n* gériatre *mf*

geriatrics [dʒerɪˈætrɪks] *n (UNCOUNT)* gériatrie *f*

Geritol[R] [ˈdʒerɪtɒl] *n* = tonique à forte teneur en fer, souvent pris par des personnes âgées

germ [dʒɜːm] *n* (**a**) *(microbe)* microbe *m*, germe *m* (**b**) *Biol & Agr* germe *m*, *Belg* jet *m* (**c**) *Fig* germe *m*, ferment *m*; **the germ of an idea** le germe d'une idée

▸▸ ***germ cell*** cellule *f* germinale *ou* reproductrice; ***germ killer*** germicide *m*, microbicide *m*; ***germ warfare*** guerre *f* bactériologique

German [ˈdʒɜːmən] **1** *n* (**a**) *(person)* Allemand(e) *m,f* (**b**) *(language)* allemand *m*

2 *adj* allemand

3 *comp (embassy)* d'Allemagne; *(history)* de l'Allemagne; *(teacher)* d'allemand

▸▸ *Formerly* ***the German Democratic Republic*** la République démocratique allemande, la RDA; ***German measles*** *(UNCOUNT)* rubéole *f*; *Hist* ***the German Sea*** = ancien nom de la mer du Nord; ***German shepherd*** berger *m* allemand

german [ˈdʒɜːmən] **1** *adj* (**a**) *Formal (cousin, brother)* germain (**b**) *Arch (relevant)* pertinent; **german to** en rapport avec

2 *n Am (dance)* allemande *f*

germander [dʒɜːˈmændə(r)] *n Bot* germandrée *f*

▸▸ ***germander speedwell*** véronique *f* petit-chêne

germane [dʒɜːˈmeɪn] *adj Formal* pertinent; **germane to** en rapport avec; **it is not germane to my argument** cela n'a aucun rapport avec mon argument

germaneness [dʒɜːˈmeɪnnɪs] *n* pertinence *f*

Germania [dʒɜːˈmeɪnɪə] *n Hist* Germanie *f*

Germanic [dʒɜːˈmænɪk] **1** *adj* germanique

2 *n Ling* germanique *m*

Germanism [ˈdʒɜːmənɪzəm] *n* (**a**) *Ling* germanisme *m* (**b**) *(liking for German culture etc)* germanophilie *f*

Germanist [ˈdʒɜːmənɪst] *n Ling* germaniste *mf*

germanium [dʒɜːˈmeɪnɪəm] *n Chem* germanium *m*

Germanization [ˌdʒɜːmənaɪˈzeɪʃən] *n* germanisation *f*

germanize, -ise [ˈdʒɜːmənaɪz] *vt* germaniser

Germanophile [dʒɜːˈmænəfaɪl] *n* germanophile *mf*

Germanophilia [dʒɜːˌmænəˈfɪlɪə] *n* germanophilie *f*

Germanophobe [dʒɜːˈmænəfəʊb] *n* germanophobe *mf*

Germanophobia [dʒɜːˌmænəˈfəʊbɪə] *n* germanophobie *f*

Germanophobic [dʒɜːˌmænəˈfəʊbɪk] *adj* germanophobe

Germany [ˈdʒɜːmənɪ] *n* Allemagne *f*; **in Germany** en Allemagne

germ-free *adj* stérilisé, aseptisé

germicidal [ˌdʒɜːmɪˈsaɪdəl] *adj* germicide, bactéricide

germicide [ˈdʒɜːmɪsaɪd] *n* bactéricide *m*

germinal [ˈdʒɜːmɪnəl] *adj* (**a**) *Biol* germinal (**b**) *Fig Formal* embryonnaire

germinate [ˈdʒɜːmɪneɪt] **1** *vi* (**a**) *Biol & Agr* germer, *Belg* jeter (**b**) *Fig (originate)* germer, prendre naissance

2 *vt* (**a**) *Biol* faire germer (**b**) *Fig* faire germer, donner naissance à

germination [ˌdʒɜːmɪˈneɪʃən] *n* germination *f*

germproof [ˈdʒɜːmpruːf] *adj* résistant aux microbes

Gerona [dʒəˈrəʊnə] *n* Gérone

Geronimo [dʒəˈrɒnɪməʊ] **1** *pr n* Geronimo

2 *exclam* = cri que poussent traditionnellement les parachutistes américains en sautant dans le vide

gerontocracy [ˌdʒerɒnˈtɒkrəsɪ] *(pl* **gerontocracies***)* *n* gérontocratie *f*

gerontocratic [dʒəˌrɒntəʊˈkrætɪk] *adj* gérontocratique

gerontological [ˌdʒerɒntəˈlɒdʒɪkəl] *adj* gérontologique

gerontologist [ˌdʒerɒnˈtɒlədʒɪst] *n* gérontologue *mf*

gerontology [ˌdʒerɒnˈtɒlədʒɪ] *n* gérontologie *f*

gerrymander [ˈdʒerɪˌmændə(r)] *Pej* **1** *vi* faire du charcutage électoral, redécouper des circonscriptions

2 *vt* redécouper (à des fins électorales)

3 *n* charcutage *m* électoral

gerrymandering [ˈdʒerɪˌmændərɪŋ] *n Pej* charcutage *m* électoral

gerund [ˈdʒerənd] *n Gram* gérondif *m*

gerundive [dʒɪˈrʌndɪv] *Gram* **1** *n* adjectif *m* verbal

2 *adj* du gérondif

gesso [ˈdʒesəʊ] *n (for painting)* enduit *m* (au plâtre); *(for sculpture)* plâtre *m* (de Paris)

gestalt [gəˈʃtælt] *n Psy* gestalt

▸▸ ***gestalt psychology*** gestaltisme *m*, théorie *f* de la forme

gestaltism [gəˈʃtæltɪzəm] *n Psy* gestaltisme *m*

gestaltist [gəˈʃtæltɪst] *Psy* **1** *n* gestaltiste *mf*

2 *adj* gestaltiste

Gestapo [geˈstɑːpəʊ] *n* Gestapo *f*

gestate [dʒeˈsteɪt] **1** *vi* être en gestation; *Fig* mûrir; **my ideas need time to gestate** mes idées ont besoin de mûrir

2 *vt* (**a**) *Biol (young)* porter (**b**) *Fig (idea, plan)* laisser mûrir

gestation [dʒeˈsteɪʃən] *n* gestation *f*

▸▸ ***gestation period*** période *f* de gestation

gesticulate [dʒeˈstɪkjʊleɪt] **1** *vi* gesticuler

2 *vt (answer, meaning)* mimer

gesticulation [dʒeˌstɪkjʊˈleɪʃən] *n* gesticulation *f*

gesticulatory [dʒeˈstɪkjʊlətərɪ] *adj* gesticulatoire

gestural [ˈdʒestʃərəl] *adj* gestuel

gesture [ˈdʒestʃə(r)] **1** *n* (**a**) *(expressive movement)* geste *m*; **to make a gesture** faire un geste; **a gesture of acknowledgment** un signe de reconnaissance; **he made a gesture of dismissal** il les a congédiés d'un geste

(**b**) *(sign, token)* geste *m*; **as a gesture of friendship** en signe *ou* en témoignage d'amitié; **as a gesture of protest** en signe de protestation; **it was a nice gesture** c'est une gentille attention; **they offered him a salary rise as a gesture of goodwill** ils lui ont offert une augmentation en gage de leur bonne volonté

2 *vi* **to gesture with one's hands/head** faire un signe de la main/de la tête; **he gestured to me to stand up** il m'a fait signe de me lever; **he gestured to his wife** il fit signe à sa femme; **she gestured towards the pile of books** elle désigna *ou* montra la pile de livres d'un geste

3 *vt* mimer

gesundheit [gəˈzʊnthaɪt] *exclam Am* à vos/tes souhaits!

GET [get]

recevoir	▸ **1A (a), (d), (g), (i); B (b)**
avoir	▸ **1A (a), (b)**
toucher	▸ **1A (a), (b); B (b)**
trouver	▸ **1A (b), (h)**
obtenir	▸ **1A (b), (h)**
tenir	▸ **1A (c)**
offrir	▸ **1A (e)**
acheter	▸ **1A (f)**
prendre	▸ **1A (f), (k), (l)**
gagner	▸ **1A (i)**
chercher	▸ **1A (j)**
attraper	▸ **1A (k), (l); B (a)**
réserver	▸ **1A (m)**
répondre	▸ **1A (n)**
faire faire	▸ **1C (b) – (d)**
préparer	▸ **1D (a)**
entendre	▸ **1D (b)**
comprendre	▸ **1D (d)**
atteindre	▸ **1E (a)**
devenir	▸ **2A (a), (d)**
se faire	▸ **2A (b)**
commencer à	▸ **2A (c); B (c)**
aller	▸ **2B (a)**
réussir à	▸ **2B (e)**

(Br pt & pp **got** [gɒt], *cont* **getting** [getɪŋ], *Am pt* **got** [gɒt], *pp* **gotten** [gɒtən], *cont* **getting** [getɪŋ]*)* **1** *vt* **A.** (**a**) *(receive → gift, letter, phone call)* recevoir, avoir; *(→ benefits, pension)* recevoir, toucher; *(→ medical treatment)* suivre; **I got a bike for my birthday** on m'a donné *ou* j'ai eu *ou* j'ai reçu un vélo pour mon anniversaire; **I get 'The Times' at home** je reçois le 'Times' à la maison; **this part of the country doesn't get much rain** cette région ne reçoit pas beaucoup de pluie, il ne pleut pas beaucoup dans cette région; **the living room gets a lot of sun** le salon est très ensoleillé; **I rang but I got no answer** *(at door)* j'ai sonné mais je n'ai pas obtenu *ou* eu de réponse; *(on phone)* j'ai appelé sans obtenir de réponse; **many students get grants** beaucoup d'étudiants ont une bourse; **he got five years for smuggling** il a écopé de *ou* il a pris cinq ans (de prison) pour contrebande; **he got a bullet in his shoulder** il a reçu une balle dans l'épaule; *Fam* **you're really going to get it!** qu'est-ce que tu vas prendre *ou* écoper!; *Fam* **I'll see that you get yours!** je vais te régler ton compte!

(**b**) *(obtain → gen)* avoir, trouver, obtenir; *(→ through effort)* se procurer, obtenir; *(→ licence, loan, permission)* obtenir; *(→ diploma, grades)* avoir, obtenir; **where did you get that book?** où avez-vous trouvé ce livre?; **they got him a job** ils lui ont trouvé du travail; **I got the job!** ils m'ont embauché!; **can you get them the report?**

pouvez-vous leur procurer le rapport?; **I got the idea from a book** j'ai trouvé l'idée dans un livre; **I got a glimpse of her face** j'ai pu apercevoir son visage; **you get a fine view from here** il y a une vue magnifique d'ici; **I've got six more to get** *(in collection)* il m'en manque six; **the town gets its water from the reservoir** la ville reçoit son eau du réservoir; **we get our wine directly from the vineyard** en vin *ou* pour le vin, nous nous fournissons directement chez le producteur; **they stopped in town to get some lunch** *(had lunch there)* ils se sont arrêtés en ville pour déjeuner; *(bought something to eat)* ils se sont arrêtés en ville pour acheter de quoi déjeuner; **I'm going out to get a breath of fresh air** je sors prendre l'air; **I'm going to get something to drink/eat** *(fetch)* je vais chercher quelque chose à boire/manger; *(consume)* je vais boire/manger quelque chose; **can I get a coffee?** je pourrais avoir un café, s'il vous plaît?; **get yourself a good lawyer** trouvez-vous un bon avocat; **get advice from your doctor** demandez conseil à votre médecin; **I need all the advice I can get** j'ai besoin de tous les conseils qu'on peut me donner; **to get (oneself) a wife/husband** se trouver une femme/un mari; **to get sb to oneself** avoir qn pour soi tout seul; **to get a divorce** obtenir le divorce; **get plenty of exercise** faites beaucoup d'exercice; **get plenty of sleep** dormez beaucoup; **try and get a few days off work** essayez de prendre quelques jours de congé; **I'll do it if I get the time/a moment** je le ferai si j'ai le temps/si je trouve un moment; **I got a lot from** *or* **out of my trip to China** mon voyage en Chine m'a beaucoup apporté; **she got very little from her lessons** elle a très peu appris de ses leçons; **he didn't get a chance to introduce himself** il n'a pas eu l'occasion de se présenter

(**c**) *(inherit → characteristic)* tenir; **she gets her shyness from her father** elle tient sa timidité de son père

(**d**) *(obtain in exchange)* recevoir; **they got a lot of money for their flat** la vente de leur appartement leur a rapporté beaucoup d'argent; **they got a good price for the painting** le tableau s'est vendu à un bon prix; **what did you get for your car?** combien est-ce que tu as vendu ta voiture?; **he got nothing for his trouble** il s'est donné de la peine pour rien; **you don't get something for nothing** on n'a rien pour rien

(**e**) *(offer as gift)* offrir, donner; **what did she get him for Christmas?** qu'est-ce qu'elle lui a offert *ou* donné pour Noël?; **I don't know what to get Jill for her birthday** je ne sais pas quoi acheter à Jill pour son anniversaire

(**f**) *(buy)* acheter, prendre; **get your father a magazine when you go out** achète une revue à ton père quand tu sortiras; **get the paper too** prends *ou* achète le journal aussi; **we got the house cheap** on a eu la maison (à) bon marché

(**g**) *(learn → information, news)* recevoir, apprendre; **we turned on the radio to get the news** nous avons allumé la radio pour écouter les informations; **she just got news** *or* **word of the accident** elle vient juste d'apprendre la nouvelle de l'accident; **he broke down when he got the news** en apprenant la nouvelle il a fondu en larmes

(**h**) *(reach by calculation or experimentation → answer, solution)* trouver; *(→ result)* obtenir; **multiply 5 by 2 and you get 10** multipliez 5 par 2 et vous obtenez 10

(**i**) *(earn, win → salary)* recevoir, gagner, toucher; *(→ prize)* gagner; *(→ reputation)* se faire; **plumbers get £20 an hour** un plombier gagne *ou* touche 20 livres de l'heure; **he got a good name** *or* **a reputation as an architect** il s'est fait une réputation dans le milieu de l'architecture; **someone's trying to get your attention** *(calling)* quelqu'un vous appelle; *(waving)* quelqu'un vous fait signe

(**j**) *(bring, fetch)* (aller) chercher; **he went and got a book from the library** il est allé chercher un livre à la bibliothèque; **go and get a doctor** allez chercher un médecin; **get me my coat** va me chercher *ou* apporte-moi mon manteau; **we had to get a doctor** nous avons dû faire venir un médecin; **he went to get a taxi** il est parti chercher un taxi; **what can I get you to drink?** qu'est-ce que je vous sers à boire?; **can I get you anything?** *(to somebody ill etc)* est-ce que vous avez besoin de quelque chose?; **they sent him to get help** ils l'ont envoyé chercher de l'aide

(**k**) *(catch → ball)* attraper; *(→ bus, train)* prendre, attraper; **did you get your train?** est-ce que tu as eu ton train?

(**l**) *(capture)* attraper, prendre; *(seize)* prendre, saisir; **the Mounties always get their man** la police montée attrape toujours son homme *(au Canada)*; **he got me by the arm** il m'a attrapé par le bras; **the dog got him by the leg** le chien l'a attrapé à la jambe; **(I've) got you!** je te tiens!

(**m**) *(book, reserve)* réserver, retenir; **we're trying to get a flight to Budapest** nous essayons de réserver un vol pour Budapest

(**n**) *(answer → door, telephone)* répondre; **the doorbell's ringing – I'll get it!** quelqu'un sonne à la porte – j'y vais!; **will you get the phone?** peux-tu répondre au téléphone?

B. (**a**) *(become ill with)* attraper; **he got a chill** il a pris *ou* attrapé froid; **I get a headache when I drink red wine** le vin rouge me donne mal à la tête; *Fam* **to get it bad for sb** avoir qn dans la peau

(**b**) *(experience, feel → shock)* recevoir, ressentir, avoir; *(→ fun, pain, surprise)* avoir; **I got the feeling something horrible would happen** j'ai eu l'impression *ou* le pressentiment que quelque chose d'horrible allait arriver; **I get the impression he doesn't like me** j'ai l'impression que je ne lui plais pas; **to get a thrill out of sth/doing sth** prendre plaisir à qch/faire qch; *Fam* **to get religion** devenir croyant □

(**c**) *(encounter)* **you get some odd people on these tours** il y a de drôles de gens dans ces voyages organisés; **you get a lot of people marrying young here** il y a beaucoup de gens qui se marient jeunes par ici; **we don't get many accidents here** nous n'avons pas beaucoup d'accidents par ici

C. (**a**) *(with adj or past participle) (cause to be)* **she managed to get the window closed/open** elle a réussi à fermer/ouvrir la fenêtre; **I got the car started** j'ai démarré la voiture; **don't get your feet wet!** ne te mouille pas les pieds!; **get the suitcases ready** préparez les bagages; **the children are getting themselves ready for school** les enfants se préparent pour (aller à) l'école; **I finally got her on her own** *or* **alone** j'ai fini par réussir à la voir en tête à tête; **we managed to get him in a good mood** nous avons réussi à le mettre de bonne humeur; **they've got me so I don't know whether I'm coming or going** c'en est à un tel point que je ne sais plus où j'en suis; **to get people interested (in sth)** intéresser les gens (à qch); **let me get this clear** que ce soit bien clair; **to get things under control** prendre les choses en main; **he likes his bath as hot as he can get it** il aime que son bain soit aussi chaud que possible; **the flat is as clean as I'm going to get it** j'ai nettoyé l'appartement le mieux que j'ai pu; **he got himself nominated president** il s'est fait nommer président; **don't get yourself all worked up** ne t'en fais pas

(**b**) *(with infinitive) (cause to do or carry out)* **we couldn't get her to leave** on n'a pas pu la faire partir; **get him to move the car** demande-lui de déplacer la voiture; **I got it to work, I got it working** j'ai réussi à le faire marcher; **we have to get the government to tighten up on pollution control** il faut que l'on obtienne du gouvernement qu'il renforce les lois contre la pollution; **he got the other members to agree** il a réussi à obtenir l'accord des autres membres; **I can always get someone else to do it** je peux toujours le faire faire par quelqu'un d'autre; **I got her to talk about life in China** je lui ai demandé de parler de la vie en Chine; **they can't get the landlord to fix the roof** ils n'arrivent pas à obtenir du propriétaire qu'il fasse réparer le toit; **how do you get jasmine to grow indoors?** comment peut-on faire pousser du jasmin à l'intérieur?

(**c**) *(with past participle) (cause to be done or carried out)* **to get sth done/repaired** faire faire/réparer qch; **to get one's hair cut** se faire couper les cheveux; **I didn't get anything done today** je n'ai rien fait aujourd'hui; **it's impossible to get anything done around here** *(by oneself)* il est impossible de faire quoi que ce soit ici; *(by someone else)* il est impossible d'obtenir quoi que ce soit ici

(**d**) *(cause to come, go, move)* **how are you going to get this package to them?** comment allez-vous leur faire parvenir ce paquet?; **they eventually got all the boxes downstairs/upstairs** ils ont fini par descendre/monter toutes leurs boîtes; **I managed to get the old man downstairs/upstairs** j'ai réussi à faire descendre/monter le vieil homme; **I managed to get him away from the others** j'ai réussi à l'éloigner des autres; **get him away from me** débarrassez-moi de lui; **can you get me home?** pouvez-vous me raccompagner?; **they got her to the airport on time** ils l'ont amenée à l'aéroport à l'heure; **his friends managed to get him home** ses amis ont réussi à le ramener (à la maison); **how are we going to get the bike home?** comment est-ce qu'on va ramener le vélo à la maison?; **I got a message to them** je leur ai fait parvenir un message; **he can't get the children to bed** il n'arrive pas à mettre les enfants au lit; **I can't get my boots off/on** je n'arrive pas à enlever/mettre mes bottes; **we couldn't get the bed through the door** nous n'avons pas pu faire passer le lit par la porte; *Fig* **where has all this got us?** où est-ce que tout ça nous a menés?; **this is getting us nowhere** ça ne nous mène nulle part, ça ne nous mène à rien; **that won't get you very far!** ça ne te servira pas à grand-chose!, tu ne seras pas beaucoup plus avancé!

D. (**a**) *(prepare → meal, drink)* préparer; **he's in the kitchen getting dinner** il est à la cuisine en train de préparer le dîner; **who's going to get the children breakfast?** qui va préparer le petit déjeuner pour les enfants?; **she got herself some breakfast** elle s'est préparé un petit déjeuner

(**b**) *(hear correctly)* entendre, saisir; **I didn't get his name** je n'ai pas saisi son nom

(**c**) *(establish telephone contact with)* **I got her father on the phone** j'ai parlé à son père *ou* j'ai eu son père au téléphone; **I couldn't get her at the office** je n'ai pas pu l'avoir au bureau; **did you get the number you wanted?** avez-vous obtenu le numéro que vous vouliez?; **get me extension 3500** passez-moi *ou* donnez-moi le poste 3500

(**d**) *Fam (understand)* comprendre □, saisir □; **I don't get it, I don't get the point** je ne comprends *ou* ne saisis pas, je n'y suis pas du tout; **I don't get you** *or* **your meaning** je ne comprends pas ce que vous voulez dire; **if you get my meaning** si tu vois ce que je veux dire □; **don't get me wrong** comprenez-moi bien; **I think he's got the message now** je crois qu'il a compris maintenant; **I don't get the joke** je ne vois pas ce qui est (si) drôle □; **get it?, get me?, get my drift?** tu saisis?, tu piges?; **(I've) got it!** ça y est! □, j'y suis! □; **oh, I get you!** ah! j'ai pigé!

(**e**) *(take note of)* remarquer; **did you get his address?** lui avez-vous demandé son adresse?

(**f**) *Fam (look at)* viser; **get him! who does he think he is?** vise un peu ce mec, mais pour qui il se prend?; **get (a load of) that!** vise un peu ça!

(**g**) *Fam (listen to)* écouter □; **get a load of this!** écoute un peu ça!; **get him!** écoute-le, celui-là!;

E. (**a**) *Fam (hit)* atteindre □; *(hit and kill)* tuer □; **she got him in the face with a pie** elle lui a jeté une tarte à la crème à la figure; **the bullet got him in the back** il a pris la balle *ou* la balle l'a atteint dans le dos; **a car got him** il a été tué par une voiture

(**b**) *Fam (harm, punish)* **everyone's out to get me** tout le monde est après moi

(**c**) *Fam (take vengeance on)* se venger de □; **we'll get you for this!** on te revaudra ça!; **I'll get him for that!** je lui revaudrai ça!

(**d**) *Fam (affect physically)* **the pain gets me in the back** j'ai des douleurs dans le dos □

(**e**) *Fam (affect emotionally)* émouvoir □; **that song really gets me** cette chanson me fait vraiment quelque chose

(**f**) *Fam (baffle, puzzle)* **you've got me there** alors là, aucune idée

(**g**) *Fam (irritate)* énerver □, agacer □; **it really**

gets me when you're late qu'est-ce que ça peut m'énerver quand tu es en retard!

(**h**) *Am (learn)* apprendre; **to get sth by heart** apprendre qch par cœur

(**i**) *Arch (beget)* engendrer; **to get sb with child** faire un enfant à qn

(**j**) *Rad & TV (signal, station)* capter, recevoir

(**k**) *Fam (idiom)* **he got his in Vietnam** il est mort au Viêt Nam ❑

2 *vi* **A.** (**a**) *(become)* devenir; **I'm getting hungry/thirsty** je commence à avoir faim/soif; **get dressed!** habille-toi!; **to get fat** grossir; **to get married** se marier; **to get divorced** divorcer; **don't get lost!** ne vous perdez pas!; **how did that vase get broken?** comment se fait-il que ce vase soit cassé?; **he got so he didn't want to go out any more** il en est arrivé à ne plus vouloir sortir; **to get old** vieillir; **it's getting late** il se fait tard; **this is getting boring** ça devient ennuyeux; **to get used to sth/doing sth** s'habituer à qch/à faire qch; *Fam* **will you get with it!** mais réveille-toi un peu!

(**b**) *(used to form passive)* **to get elected** se faire élire, être élu; **suppose he gets killed** et s'il se fait tuer?; **to get drowned** se noyer; **we got paid last week** on a été payés la semaine dernière; **I'm always getting invited to parties** on m'invite toujours à des soirées

(**c**) *(with present participle) (start)* commencer à, se mettre à; **let's get going** *or* **moving!** *(let's leave)* allons-y!; *(let's hurry)* dépêchons(-nous)!, grouillons-nous!; *(let's start to work)* au travail!; **I'll get going on that right away** je m'y mets tout de suite; **I can't seem to get going today** je n'arrive pas à m'activer aujourd'hui; **she got talking to the neighbours** elle s'est mise à discuter avec les voisins; **we got talking about racism** nous en sommes venus à parler de racisme; **he got to thinking about it** il s'est mis à réfléchir à la question

B. (**a**) *(go)* aller, se rendre; *(arrive)* arriver; **when did you get home?** quand es-tu rentré?; **it's nice to get home** ça fait du bien de rentrer chez soi; **how do you get to the museum?** comment est-ce qu'on fait pour aller au musée?; **how did you get in here?** comment êtes-vous entré?; **they should get here today** ils devraient arriver ici aujourd'hui; **how did you get here?** comment es-tu venu?; **how did that bicycle get here?** comment se fait-il que ce vélo se trouve ici?; **I took the train from Madrid to get there** j'ai pris le train de Madrid pour y aller; **she's successful now but it took her a while to get there** elle a une bonne situation maintenant, mais ça ne s'est pas fait du jour au lendemain; **he got as far as buying the tickets** il est allé jusqu'à acheter les billets; **I'd hoped things wouldn't get this far** j'avais espéré qu'on n'en arriverait pas là; **are you getting anywhere with that report?** il avance, ce rapport?; **now you're getting somewhere!** enfin tu avances!; **I'm not getting anywhere** *or* **I'm getting nowhere with this project** je fais du surplace avec ce projet; **we're not getting anywhere with this meeting** cette réunion est une perte de temps; **she won't get anywhere** *or* **she'll get nowhere if she's rude to people** elle n'arrivera à rien en étant grossière avec les gens; **where's your sister got to?** où est passée ta sœur?; **where did my keys get to?** où sont passées mes clés?

(**b**) *(move in specified direction)* **he got along the ledge as best he could** il a avancé le long du rebord du mieux qu'il pouvait; **she got behind a tree** elle s'est mise derrière un arbre; **to get into bed** se coucher; **get in** *or* **into the car!** monte dans la voiture!; **get over here!** viens ici!; **we couldn't get past the truck** nous ne pouvions pas passer le camion

(**c**) *(with infinitive) (start)* commencer à, se mettre à; **each city is getting to look like another** toutes les grandes villes commencent à se ressembler; **to get to know sb** apprendre à connaître qn; **we got to like her husband** nous nous sommes mis à apprécier *ou* à aimer son mari; **you'll get to like it in the end** ça finira par te plaire; **his father got to hear of the rumours** son père a fini par entendre les rumeurs; **he's getting to be known** il commence à être connu, il se fait connaître; **they got to talking about the past** ils en sont venus *ou* ils se sont mis à parler du passé

(**d**) *(become)* devenir; **it's getting to be impossible to find a flat** ça devient impossible de trouver un appartement; **she may get to be president one day** elle pourrait devenir *ou* être président un jour; **they got to be friends** ils sont devenus amis

(**e**) *(manage)* réussir à; **we never got to see that film** nous n'avons jamais réussi à *ou* nous ne sommes jamais arrivés à voir ce film; **I didn't get to speak to him in person** je n'ai pas pu lui parler en personne

(**f**) *Fam (be allowed to)* **he never gets to stay up late** on ne le laisse jamais se coucher tard ❑; **I never get to drive** on ne me laisse jamais conduire ❑

(**g**) *Fam (leave)* se tirer; **get!** fous le camp!, tire-toi!

3 *n Fam (in tennis)* beau retour ❑ *m*

►**get about** *vi* (**a**) *(be up and about, move around)* se déplacer; **how do you get about town?** comment vous déplacez-vous en ville?; **she gets about on crutches/in a wheelchair** elle se déplace avec des béquilles/en chaise roulante; **I don't get about much these days** je ne me déplace pas beaucoup ces temps-ci

(**b**) *(travel)* voyager; **I get about quite a bit in my job** je suis assez souvent en déplacement pour mon travail

(**c**) *(be socially active)* **she certainly gets about** elle connaît beaucoup de monde

(**d**) *(story, rumour)* se répandre, circuler; **the news** *or* **it got about that they were splitting up** la nouvelle de leur séparation s'est répandue

►**get across 1** *vi* (**a**) *(succeed in crossing)* traverser, passer; **the river was flooded but we managed to get across** la rivière était en crue mais nous avons réussi à traverser

(**b**) *(be communicated)* **our message is not getting across** notre message ne passe pas

2 *vt sep* (**a**) *(over water, street → person)* faire traverser; **we couldn't get the supplies across** *(across the river)* nous ne pouvions pas faire passer les vivres de l'autre côté; **it was easy to get the people across** *(across the border)* il était facile de faire passer les gens

(**b**) *(communicate)* communiquer; **I can't seem to get the idea across to them** je n'arrive pas à leur faire comprendre ça; **he managed to get his point across** il a réussi à faire passer son message

►**get after** *vt insep* poursuivre

►**get ahead** *vi (succeed)* réussir, arriver; **to get ahead in life** *or* **in the world** réussir dans la vie; **if you want to get ahead at the office, you have to work** si tu veux de l'avancement au bureau, il faut que tu travailles

►**get along** *vi* (**a**) *(fare, manage)* aller; **how are you getting along?** comment vas-tu?, comment ça va?; **she's getting along well in her new job** elle se débrouille bien dans son nouveau travail; **we can get along without him** nous pouvons nous passer de lui *ou* nous débrouiller sans lui

(**b**) *(advance, progress)* avancer, progresser; **the patient is getting along nicely** le patient est en bonne voie *ou* fait des progrès

(**c**) *(be on good terms)* s'entendre; **we get along fine** nous nous entendons très bien, nous faisons bon ménage; **she doesn't get along with my mother** elle ne s'entend pas avec ma mère; **she's easy to get along with** elle est facile à vivre

(**d**) *(move away)* s'en aller, partir; *(go)* aller, se rendre; **it's time for me to be getting along, it's time I was getting along** il est temps que je parte; **I must be getting along to the office** il faut que j'aille au bureau; *Br* **get along with you!** *(leave)* va-t'en!, fiche le camp!; *Fam (I don't believe you)* à d'autres!

►**get around 1** *vt insep (obstacle, problem)* contourner; *(law, rule)* tourner; **there's no getting around it, we'll have to tell her** il n'y a pas d'autre moyen, il va falloir que nous le lui disions; **there's no getting around the fact that he lied to us** il reste qu'il nous a menti

2 *vi* = **get about**

►**get around to** *vt insep* **she won't get around to reading it before tomorrow** elle n'arrivera pas à (trouver le temps de) le lire avant demain; **he finally got around to fixing the radiator** il a fini par *ou* il est finalement arrivé à réparer le radiateur; **it was some time before I got around to writing to her** j'ai mis pas mal de temps avant de lui écrire

►**get at** *vt insep* (**a**) *(reach → object, shelf)* atteindre; *(→ place)* parvenir à, atteindre; **I've put the pills where the children can't get at them** j'ai mis les pilules là où les enfants ne peuvent pas les prendre; *Fam* **just let me get at him!** si jamais il me tombe sous la main!

(**b**) *(discover)* trouver; **to get at the truth** découvrir la vérité

(**c**) *(mean, intend)* entendre; **I see what you're getting at** je vois où vous voulez en venir; **just what are you getting at?** qu'est-ce que vous entendez par là?, où voulez-vous en venir?; **what I'm getting at is why did she leave now?** ce que je veux dire, c'est pourquoi est-elle partie maintenant?

(**d**) *Fam (criticize)* s'en prendre à ❑, s'attaquer à ❑; **you're always getting at me** tu t'en prends toujours à moi

(**e**) *Fam (bribe, influence)* acheter, suborner ❑; **the witnesses had been got at** les témoins avaient été achetés

►**get away 1** *vi* (**a**) *(leave)* s'en aller, partir; **she has to get away from home/her parents** il faut qu'elle parte de chez elle/s'éloigne de ses parents; **I was in a meeting and couldn't get away** j'étais en réunion et je ne pouvais pas m'échapper *ou* m'en aller; **will you be able to get away at Christmas?** allez-vous pouvoir partir (en vacances) à Noël?; **to get away from the daily grind** échapper au train-train quotidien; **get away from it all, come to Florida!** quittez tout, venez en Floride!; **she's gone off for a couple of weeks to get away from it all** elle est partie quelques semaines loin de tout

(**b**) *(move away)* s'éloigner; **get away from that door!** éloignez-vous *ou* écartez-vous de cette porte!; **get away from me!** fichez-moi le camp!

(**c**) *(escape)* s'échapper, se sauver; **the murderer got away** l'assassin s'est échappé; **the thief got away with all the jewels** le voleur est parti *ou* s'est sauvé avec tous les bijoux; **there's no getting away from** *or* **you can't get away from the fact that the other solution would have been cheaper** on ne peut pas nier (le fait) que l'autre solution aurait coûté moins cher; **you can't get away from it, there's no getting away from it** c'est comme ça, on n'y peut rien

(**d**) *Br Fam (idiom)* **get away (with you)!** à d'autres!

2 *vt sep (remove → person)* emmener; **get that child away from the road!** éloignez cet enfant de la route!; **get me away from here!** fais-moi sortir d'ici!; **get your dog away from my garden!** faites sortir votre chien de mon jardin!; **they managed to get him away from the TV** ils ont fini par l'arracher de devant la télévision; **to get sth away from sb** prendre qch à qn

►**get away with** *vt insep* **he got away with cheating on his taxes** personne ne s'est aperçu qu'il avait fraudé le fisc; **I can't believe you got away with it!** je n'arrive pas à croire que personne ne t'ait rien dit!; **he got away with a small fine** il s'en est tiré avec une petite amende; **that child gets away with murder** on laisse tout faire à ce gamin; **her skirt is really tiny but she gets away with it** sa jupe est vraiment très courte mais elle peut se le permettre

►**get back 1** *vi* (**a**) *(move backwards)* reculer; **get back!** éloignez-vous!, reculez!

(**b**) *(return)* revenir, retourner; **I can't wait to get back home** je suis impatient de rentrer (à la maison); **get back in bed!** va te recoucher!, retourne au lit!; **I got back in the car/on the bus** je suis remonté dans la voiture/dans le bus; **to get back to sleep** se rendormir; **to get back to work** *(after break)* se remettre au travail; *(after holiday, illness)* reprendre le travail; **things eventually got back to normal** les choses ont peu à peu repris leur cours (normal); **getting** *or* **to get back to the point** pour en revenir au sujet qui nous préoccupe; **let's get back to your basic reasons for leaving** revenons aux raisons pour lesquelles vous voulez partir; **I'll get back to you on that** *(call back)* je vous rappelle pour vous dire ce qu'il en est; *(discuss again)* nous reparlerons de cela plus tard

(**c**) *(return to political power)* revenir; **do you think the Democrats will get back in?** croyez-vous que le parti démocrate reviendra au pouvoir?

2 *vt sep* (**a**) *(recover → something lost or lent)* récupérer; *(→ force, strength)* reprendre, récupérer; *(→ health, motivation)* retrouver; **he got his job back** il a été repris; **I got back nearly all the money I invested** j'ai récupéré presque tout l'argent que j'avais investi; **you'll have to get your money back from the shop** il faut que vous vous fassiez rembourser par le magasin

(**b**) *(return)* rendre; **we have to get this book back to her** il faut que nous lui rendions ce livre

(**c**) *(return to original place)* remettre, replacer; **I can't get it back in the box** je n'arrive pas à le remettre *ou* le faire rentrer dans le carton; **I want to get these suitcases back down to the cellar** je veux redescendre ces valises à la cave; **he managed to get the children back to bed** il a réussi à remettre les enfants au lit

(**d**) *Fam (idiom)* **to get one's own back (on sb)** se venger (de qn) ❑

►**get back at** *vt insep* se venger de; **he only said it to get back at him** il n'a dit ça que pour se venger de lui

►**get behind** 1 *vi (gen)* rester à l'arrière, se laisser distancer; *Sport* se laisser distancer; *Fig* prendre du retard; **he got behind with his work** il a pris du retard dans son travail; **we mustn't get behind with the rent** il ne faut pas qu'on soit en retard pour le loyer

2 *vt insep (support, sympathize with)* appuyer

►**get by** 1 *vi* (**a**) *(pass)* passer; **let me get by** laissez-moi passer

(**b**) *(be acceptable)* passer, être acceptable; **their work just about gets by** leur travail est tout juste passable *ou* acceptable

(**c**) *(manage, survive)* se débrouiller, s'en sortir; **how do you get by on that salary?** comment tu te débrouilles *ou* tu t'en sors avec un salaire comme ça?; **they get by as best they can** ils se débrouillent *ou* s'en sortent tant bien que mal; **we can get by without him** nous pouvons nous passer de lui *ou* nous débrouiller sans lui

2 *vt insep* (**a**) *(move past)* **can you get by the washing machine?** est-ce que vous avez assez de place pour passer à côté de la machine à laver?

(**b**) *(escape attention of → censor, editor)* échapper à; **her film got by the censors** son film a échappé à l'attention de la censure

►**get down** 1 *vi* descendre; **get down off that chair!** descends de cette chaise!; **may I get down (from the table)?** *(leave the table)* puis-je sortir de table?; **they got down on their knees** ils se sont mis à genoux; **get down!** *(hide)* couchez-vous!; *(to dog)* bas les pattes!

2 *vt sep* (**a**) *(bring, fetch down → book from shelf etc)* descendre

(**b**) *(reduce → temperature, inflation etc)* faire baisser; **to get one's weight down** perdre du poids

(**c**) *(write down)* noter; **I didn't manage to get down what she said** je n'ai pas réussi à noter ce qu'elle a dit

(**d**) *(depress)* déprimer, démoraliser; **work is really getting me down at the moment** le travail me déprime vraiment en ce moment; **this rainy weather gets him down** cette pluie lui fiche le cafard; **don't let it get you down** ne te laisse pas abattre

(**e**) *(swallow)* avaler, faire descendre

►**get down to** *vt insep* se mettre à; **I have to get down to balancing the books** il faut que je me mette à faire les comptes; **it's not so difficult once you get down to it** ce n'est pas si difficile une fois qu'on s'y met; **he got down to working on it this morning** il s'y est mis *ou* s'y est attelé ce matin; **it's hard getting down to work after the weekend** c'est difficile de reprendre le travail après le week-end; **we eventually got down to details** nous avons fini par en arriver aux détails; **when you get down to it, there's very little difference between them** en fin de compte, il y a très peu de différence entre eux

►**get in** 1 *vi* (**a**) *(into building)* entrer; **the thief got in through the window** le cambrioleur est entré par la fenêtre; **a car pulled up and she got in** une voiture s'est arrêtée et elle est montée dedans; **water had got in everywhere** l'eau avait pénétré partout

(**b**) *(return home)* rentrer; **we got in about 4 a.m.** nous sommes rentrés vers 4 heures du matin

(**c**) *(arrive)* arriver; **what time does your plane get in?** à quelle heure ton avion arrive-t-il?

(**d**) *(be admitted → to club)* se faire admettre; *(→ to school, university)* entrer, être admis *ou* reçu; **he applied to Oxford but he didn't get in** il voulait entrer à Oxford mais il n'a pas pu

(**e**) *(be elected → person)* être élu; *(→ party)* accéder au pouvoir

(**f**) *Fam (become involved)* participer ❑; **she got in at the beginning** elle est arrivée au début ❑

(**g**) *(interject)* glisser; **"what about me?" she managed to get in** "et moi?" réussit-elle à glisser

2 *vt sep* (**a**) *(fit in)* **I hope to get in a bit of reading on holiday** j'espère pouvoir lire *ou* que je trouverai le temps de lire pendant mes vacances; **she got in some last-minute revision before the exam** elle a réussi à faire des révisions de dernière minute avant l'examen

(**b**) *(insert)* faire pénétrer; **I couldn't get a word in** je n'ai pas pu placer un mot, je n'ai pas pu en placer une

(**c**) *(collect, gather → crops)* rentrer, engranger; *(→ debts)* recouvrer; *(→ taxes)* percevoir

(**d**) *(lay in)* **I must get in some more coal** je dois faire une provision de charbon; **to get in supplies** s'approvisionner

(**e**) *(call in → doctor, plumber)* faire venir; *(→ dog, cat)* faire rentrer; **shouldn't Elaine be in on this meeting? – of course, could you get her in?** on n'a pas besoin d'Elaine pour cette réunion? – si, bien sûr, tu peux lui demander de venir?

(**f**) *(hand in, submit)* rendre, remettre; **did you get your application in on time?** as-tu remis ton dossier de candidature à temps?

(**g**) *(cause to be admitted → to club, university)* faire admettre *ou* accepter; *(cause to be elected)* faire élire

(**h**) *(plant → seeds)* planter, semer; *(→ bulbs, plants)* planter

(**i**) *Br Fam (pay for, stand)* payer ❑, offrir ❑; **he got the next round in** il a payé la tournée suivante

3 *vt insep (building)* entrer dans; *(vehicle)* monter dans; **he had just got in the door when the phone rang** il venait juste d'arriver *ou* d'entrer quand le téléphone a sonné

►**get in on** 1 *vt insep* **to get in on a deal** prendre part à un marché; **to get in on the fun** se mettre de la partie

2 *vt sep* faire participer à; **he got me in on the deal** il m'a intéressé à l'affaire

►**get into** 1 *vt insep* (**a**) *(building)* entrer dans; *(vehicle)* monter dans

(**b**) *(arrive in)* arriver à; **we get into Madrid at 3 o'clock** nous arrivons à Madrid à 3 heures; **the train got into the station** le train est entré en gare

(**c**) *(put on → dress, shirt, shoes)* mettre; *(→ trousers, stockings)* enfiler, mettre; *(→ coat)* endosser; **she got into her clothes** elle a mis ses vêtements *ou* s'est habillée; **can you still get into your jeans?** est-ce que tu rentres encore dans ton jean?

(**d**) *(be admitted to → club, school, university)* entrer dans; **he'd like to get into the club** il voudrait devenir membre du club; **her daughter got into medical school** sa fille a été admise dans *ou* est entrée dans une école de médecine; **to get into office** être élu

(**e**) *(become involved in)* **he wants to get into politics** il veut se lancer dans la politique; **they got into a conversation about South Africa** ils se sont mis à parler de l'Afrique du Sud; **we got into a fight over who had to do the dishes** nous nous sommes disputés pour savoir qui devait faire la vaisselle; **this is not the moment to get into that** ce n'est pas le moment de parler de ça

(**f**) *Fam (take up)* s'intéresser à ❑; **he got into Eastern religions** il a commencé à s'intéresser aux religions orientales; **it's a hard book to get into** c'est un livre dans lequel il est difficile de rentrer ❑

(**g**) *(become accustomed to)* **he soon got into her way of doing things** il s'est vite fait *ou* s'est vite mis à sa façon de faire les choses

(**h**) *(experience a specified condition or state)* **to get into debt** s'endetter; **he got into a real mess** il s'est mis dans un vrai pétrin; **the children were always getting into mischief** les enfants passaient leur temps à faire des bêtises; **I got into a real state about the test** j'étais dans tous mes états à cause du test; **she got into trouble with the teacher** elle a eu des ennuis avec le professeur

(**i**) *(cause to act strangely)* prendre; **what's got into you?** qu'est-ce qui te prend?, quelle mouche te pique?; **I wonder what got into him to make him act like that** je me demande ce qui l'a poussé à réagir comme ça

2 *vt sep* (**a**) *(insert into)* **to get sth into sth** (faire) (r)entrer qch dans qch; **to get the key into the lock** mettre *ou* introduire la clef dans la serrure; **to get an article into a paper** faire accepter un article par un journal; **to get an idea into one's head** se mettre une idée en tête; *Fam* **when will you get it into your thick head that I don't want to go?** quand est-ce que tu vas enfin comprendre que je ne veux pas y aller? ❑

(**b**) *(cause to be admitted to → club)* faire entrer à; *(→ school, university)* faire entrer dans; **he got his friend into the club** il a permis à son ami de devenir membre du club; **the president got his son into Harvard** le président a fait entrer *ou* accepter *ou* admettre son fils à Harvard

(**c**) *(cause to be in a specified condition or state)* mettre; **she got herself into a terrible state** elle s'est mis dans tous ses états; **he got them into a lot of trouble** il leur a attiré de gros ennuis

(**d**) *(involve in)* impliquer dans, entraîner dans; **you're the one who got us into this** c'est toi qui nous as embarqués dans cette histoire

(**e**) *Fam (make interested in)* faire découvrir ❑; *(accustom to)* habituer à ❑, faire prendre l'habitude de ❑; **he got me into jazz** il m'a initié au jazz ❑

►**get in with** *vt insep* (**a**) *(ingratiate oneself with)* s'insinuer dans *ou* s'attirer les bonnes grâces de, se faire bien voir de; **they tried to get in with the new director** ils ont essayé de se faire bien voir du nouveau directeur

(**b**) *(associate with → person, group etc)* fréquenter; **he has got in with a new gang** il n'est pas plus avec la même bande; **she got in with the wrong crowd at school** elle avait de mauvaises fréquentations à l'école

►**get off** 1 *vi* (**a**) *(leave bus, train etc)* descendre; **get off at the next stop** descendez au prochain arrêt; *Fam* **I told him where to get off!** je l'ai envoyé sur les roses!, je l'ai envoyé promener!; *Fam* **where do you get off telling me what to do?** qu'est-ce qui te prend de me dicter ce que je dois faire?

(**b**) *(depart → person)* s'en aller, partir; *(→ car)* démarrer; *(→ plane)* décoller; *(→ letter, parcel)* partir; **I have to be getting off to work** il faut que j'aille au travail; *Fig* **the project got off to a bad/good start** le projet a pris un mauvais/bon départ

(**c**) *(leave work)* finir, s'en aller; *(take time off)* se libérer; **what time do you get off?** à quelle heure finissez-vous?; **can you get off early tomorrow?** peux-tu quitter le travail de bonne heure demain?

(**d**) *(escape punishment)* s'en sortir, s'en tirer, en être quitte; **she didn't think she'd get off so lightly** elle n'espérait pas s'en tirer à si bon compte; **the students got off with a fine/warning** les étudiants en ont été quittes pour une amende/un avertissement

(**e**) *(let go of something)* lâcher; **hey! get off!**

that's MY book! hé! laisse ça! c'est mon livre *ou* c'est à moi ce livre!

(**f**) *(go to sleep)* s'endormir

2 *vt insep* (**a**) *(leave → bus, train, plane etc)* descendre de

(**b**) *(descend from → bike, wall, chair etc)* descendre de; **he got off his horse** il est descendu de cheval; **if only the boss would get off my back** si seulement le patron me fichait la paix

(**c**) *(depart from)* partir de, décamper de; **get off my property** fichez le camp de chez moi; **get off the grass!** ne marche pas sur la pelouse!; **we got off the road to let the ambulance pass** nous sommes sortis de la route pour laisser passer l'ambulance

(**d**) *(let go of)* **get off me!** laisse-moi tranquille!, lâche-moi!

(**e**) *(escape from)* se libérer de; *(avoid)* échapper à; **she managed to get off work** elle a réussi à se libérer; **how did you get off doing the housework?** comment as-tu fait pour échapper au ménage?

3 *vt sep* (**a**) *(cause to leave, climb down)* faire descendre; **get the cat off the table** fais descendre le chat de (sur) la table; **the conductor got the passengers off the train** le conducteur a fait descendre les passagers du train; *Fig* **try to get her mind off her troubles** essaie de lui changer les idées

(**b**) *(send)* envoyer, faire partir; **I want to get this letter off** je veux expédier cette lettre *ou* mettre cette lettre à la poste; **she got the boys off to school** elle a expédié *ou* envoyé les garçons à l'école; **we got him off on the morning train** nous l'avons mis au train du matin

(**c**) *(remove → clothing, lid)* enlever, ôter; *(→ stains)* faire partir *ou* disparaître, enlever; **I can't get this ink off my hands** je n'arrive pas à faire partir cette encre de mes mains; **get your hands off that cake!** ne touche pas à ce gâteau!; **get your hands off me!** ne me touche pas!; **get your feet off the table!** enlève tes pieds de sur la table!; *Fig* **he'd like to get that house off his hands** il aimerait bien se débarrasser de cette maison

(**d**) *(free from punishment)* tirer d'affaire; *(in court)* faire acquitter; **he'll need a good lawyer to get him off** il lui faudra un bon avocat pour se tirer d'affaire; **to get sb off doing sth** dispenser qn de faire qch

(**e**) *(put to sleep)* endormir; **I've just managed to get the baby off (to sleep)** je viens de réussir à endormir le bébé

(**f**) *(have as holiday)* **to get a day/week off** prendre un jour/une semaine de congé; **can you get tomorrow afternoon/next week off?** est-ce que tu peux prendre un congé demain après-midi/la semaine prochaine?

(**g**) *(obtain)* **to get sth off sb** obtenir qch de qn; **I got that story off the woman next door** je tiens cette histoire de la voisine; **I got this cold off the woman next door** la voisine m'a passé son rhume

▸**get off on** *vt insep* (**a**) *Fam (sexually)* **he gets off on pornographic films** il prend son pied en regardant des films pornos; **is that what you get off on?** c'est comme ça que tu prends ton pied?; *Fig* **he gets off on teasing people** il adore taquiner les gens❑; **I really get off on hip-hop!** j'adore le hip-hop!❑

(**b**) *very Fam Drugs slang* **he gets off on heroin** il se défonce à l'héroïne

▸**get off with** *vt insep Br Fam* **to get off with sb** faire une touche avec qn

▸**get on 1** *vi* (**a**) *(on bus, plane, train)* monter; *(on ship)* monter à bord

(**b**) *(fare, manage)* **how's your husband getting on?** comment va votre mari?; **how did he get on at the interview?** comment s'est passé son entretien?, comment ça a marché pour son entretien?; **you'll get on far better if you think about it first** tout ira mieux si tu réfléchis avant

(**c**) *(make progress)* avancer, progresser; **Jennifer is getting on very well in maths** Jennifer se débrouille très bien en maths; **how's your work getting on?** ça avance, ton travail?

(**d**) *(succeed)* réussir, arriver; **to get on in life** *or* **in the world** faire son chemin *ou* réussir dans la vie; **some say that in order to get on, you often have to compromise** il y a des gens qui disent que pour réussir (dans la vie), il faut souvent faire des compromis

(**e**) *(continue)* continuer; **we must be getting on** il faut que nous partions; **do you think we can get on with the meeting now?** croyez-vous que nous puissions poursuivre notre réunion maintenant?; **get on with your work!** allez! au travail!; **they got on with the job** ils se sont remis au travail

(**f**) *(be on good terms)* s'entendre; **my mother and I get on well** je m'entends bien avec ma mère; **they don't get on** ils ne s'entendent pas; **she's never got on with him** elle ne s'est jamais entendue avec lui; **to be difficult/easy to get on with** être difficile/facile à vivre

(**g**) *(grow late → time)* **time's getting on** il se fait tard; **it was getting on in the evening, the evening was getting on** la soirée tirait à sa fin

(**h**) *(grow old → person)* se faire vieux (vieille); **she's getting on (in years)** elle commence à se faire vieille

(**i**) *(idioms)* **get on with it!** *(continue speaking)* continuez!; *(continue working)* allez! au travail!; *(hurry up)* mais dépêchez-vous enfin!; *Fam* **get on with you!** *(I don't believe you)* à d'autres!

2 *vt insep (bus, train)* monter dans; *(plane)* monter dans, monter à bord de; *(ship)* monter à bord de; *(bed, horse, table, bike)* monter sur; **he got on his bike** il est monté sur *ou* il a enfourché son vélo; **get on your feet** levez-vous, mettez-vous debout; **how did these papers get on my desk?** comment est-ce que ces papiers se sont retrouvés *ou* sont arrivés sur mon bureau?; *Fig* **it took the patient a while to get (back) on his feet** le patient a mis longtemps à se remettre

3 *vt sep* (**a**) *(help onto → bus, train)* faire monter dans; *(→ bed, bike, horse, table)* faire monter sur; **they got him on his feet** ils l'ont mis debout; *Fig* **the doctor got her on her feet** le médecin l'a remise sur pied

(**b**) *(coat, gloves, shoes)* mettre, enfiler; *(lid)* mettre; **I can't get these trousers on any more** je n'entre plus dans ce pantalon

(**c**) *Am Fam* **to get it on (with sb)** *(have sex)* s'envoyer en l'air (avec qn); *(fight)* se friter (avec qn); **to get it on** *(get started)* s'y mettre❑

▸**get on for** *vt insep* **the president is getting on for sixty** le président approche de la soixantaine *ou* a presque soixante ans; **it's getting on for midnight** il est presque minuit, il n'est pas loin de minuit; **it's getting on for three weeks since we saw her** ça va faire bientôt trois semaines que nous ne l'avons pas vue; **there were getting on for ten thousand demonstrators** il n'y avait pas loin *ou* il y avait près de dix mille manifestants

▸**get onto 1** *vt insep* (**a**) = **get on** *vt insep*

(**b**) *(turn attention to)* **to get onto a subject** *or* **onto a topic** aborder un sujet; **how did we get onto reincarnation?** comment est-ce qu'on en est venus à parler de réincarnation?; **I'll get right onto it!** je vais m'y mettre tout de suite!

(**c**) *(contact)* prendre contact avec, se mettre en rapport avec; *(speak to)* parler à; *(call)* téléphoner à, donner un coup de fil à

(**d**) *Fam (become aware of)* découvrir❑; **the plan worked well until the police got onto it** le plan marchait bien jusqu'à ce que la police tombe dessus

(**e**) *(nag, rebuke)* harceler; **his father is always getting onto him to find a job** son père est toujours à le harceler pour qu'il trouve du travail

(**f**) *(be elected to)* **he got onto the school board** il a été élu au conseil d'administration de l'école

2 *vt sep* (**a**) = **get on** *vt sep* (**a**)

(**b**) *(cause to talk about)* faire parler de, amener à parler de; **we got him onto (the subject of) his activities in the Resistance** nous l'avons amené à parler de ses activités dans la Résistance

▸**get out 1** *vi* (**a**) *(leave building, room etc)* sortir; *(leave vehicle)* descendre; *(leave organization, town)* quitter; **he got out of the car** il est sorti de la voiture; **to get out of bed** se lever, sortir de son lit; **you'd better get out of here** tu ferais bien de partir *ou* sortir; **get out!** sortez!; **get out of here!** *(leave)* sortez d'ici!; *Am Fam (I don't believe it)* mon œil!; **to get out while the going is good** partir au bon moment

(**b**) *(go out)* sortir; **they don't get out much** ils ne sortent pas beaucoup

(**c**) *(be released from prison, hospital)* sortir

(**d**) *(information, news)* se répandre, s'ébruiter; **the secret got out** le secret a été éventé

(**e**) *(escape)* s'échapper; **the prisoner got out of his cell** le prisonnier s'est échappé de sa cellule; **he was lucky to get out alive** il a eu de la chance de s'en sortir vivant

(**f**) *Am (empty)* **theaters were getting out** les gens sortaient des théâtres

2 *vt sep* (**a**) *(bring out → champagne, furniture, books, car)* sortir; *(person)* (faire) sortir; **to get a book out from the library** emprunter un livre à la bibliothèque

(**b**) *(produce, publish → book)* publier, sortir; *(→ list)* établir, dresser

(**c**) *(speak with difficulty)* prononcer, sortir; **I could barely get a word out** c'est à peine si je pouvais dire *ou* prononcer *ou* sortir un mot; *Fam* **to get out from under** s'en sortir❑, s'en tirer❑

(**d**) *(free → hostages etc)* libérer

(**e**) *(remove)* enlever; *(nail etc)* arracher; *(cork)* retirer; *(stain)* faire disparaître

(**f**) *Sport (in cricket → batsman)* renverser le guichet à

▸**get out of 1** *vt insep* (**a**) *(leave → building)* sortir de; *(car, train)* descendre de; **let's get out of here** partons d'ici; **he managed to get out of the country** *(criminal, refugee)* il a réussi à quitter le pays; **to get out of bed** se lever; **to get out of prison/the army** sortir de prison/quitter l'armée; **to get out of sb's way** s'écarter du chemin de qn, faire place à qn; *very Fam* **get the hell out of here!** fiche(-moi) le camp!

(**b**) *(avoid)* éviter, échapper à; *(obligation)* se dérober *ou* se soustraire à; **how did you get out of doing the dishes?** comment as-tu pu échapper à la vaisselle?; **he tried to get out of helping me** il a essayé de se débrouiller pour ne pas devoir m'aider; **we have to go, there's no getting out of it** il faut qu'on y aille, il n'y a rien à faire *ou* il n'y a pas moyen d'y échapper; **there's no getting out of it, you were the better candidate** il faut le reconnaître *ou* il n'y a pas à dire, vous étiez le meilleur candidat

(**c**) *(escape from)* **to get out of trouble** se tirer d'affaire; **they managed to get out of the clutches of the mafia** ils ont réussi à se tirer des griffes de la mafia; **how can I get out of this mess?** comment puis-je me tirer de ce pétrin?

(**d**) *(become unaccustomed to)* **to get out of (the habit of) doing sth** perdre l'habitude de faire qch

2 *vt sep* (**a**) *(take out of)* sortir de; **get the baby out of the house every now and then** sors le bébé de temps en temps; **she got a handkerchief out of her handbag** elle a sorti un mouchoir de son sac à main; **how many books did you get out of the library?** combien de livres as-tu emprunté à *ou* sorti de la bibliothèque?

(**b**) *(help to avoid)* **the lawyer got his client out of jail** l'avocat a fait sortir son client de prison; *Fig* **the phone call got her out of having to talk to me** le coup de fil lui a évité d'avoir à me parler; **he'll never get himself out of this one!** il ne s'en sortira jamais!; **my confession got him out of trouble** ma confession l'a tiré d'affaire

(**c**) *(extract → cork)* sortir de; *(→ nail, splinter)* enlever de; *(→ stain)* faire partir de, enlever de; **I can't get the cork out of the bottle** je n'arrive pas à déboucher la bouteille; **the police got a confession/the truth out of him** la police lui a arraché une confession/la vérité; **we got the money out of him** nous avons réussi à obtenir l'argent de lui; **I can't get anything out of him** je ne peux rien tirer de lui; **I can't get the idea out of my mind** je ne peux pas chasser cette idée de mon esprit

(**d**) *(gain from)* gagner, retirer; **to get a lot out of sth** tirer (un) grand profit de qch; **I didn't get much out of that class** ce cours ne m'a pas apporté grand-chose, je n'ai pas retiré grand-chose de ce cours; **the job was difficult but she got something out of it** la tâche était difficile, mais elle y a trouvé son compte *ou* en a tiré profit

▶**get over** 1 *vt insep* (**a**) *(cross → river, street)* traverser, franchir; *(→ fence, wall)* franchir, passer par-dessus

(**b**) *(recover from → illness)* se remettre de, guérir de; *(→ accident)* se remettre de; *(→ loss)* se remettre de, se consoler de; **I'll never get over her** je ne l'oublierai jamais; **he can't get over her death** il n'arrive pas à se remettre de sa mort *ou* disparition; **we couldn't get over our surprise** nous n'arrivions pas à nous remettre de notre surprise; **I can't get over how much he's grown!** qu'est-ce qu'il a grandi, je n'en reviens pas!; **I can't get over it!** je n'en reviens pas!; **he couldn't get over the fact that she had come back** il n'en revenait pas qu'elle soit revenue; **I can't get over your having refused** je n'en reviens pas que vous ayez refusé; **he'll get over it!** il n'en mourra pas!

(**c**) *(master, overcome → obstacle)* surmonter; *(→ difficulty)* surmonter, venir à bout de; **they soon got over their shyness** ils ont vite oublié *ou* surmonté leur timidité

2 *vt sep* (**a**) *(cause to cross)* faire traverser

(**b**) *(communicate → idea, message)* faire passer

3 *vi* (**a**) *(cross)* traverser; **to get over to France/America** aller en France/Amérique; **we'll try to get over next weekend** *(to visit)* nous essayerons de venir vous voir le week-end prochain

(**b**) *(idea, message)* passer

▶**get over with** *vt insep (finish with)* en finir avec; **let's get it over with** finissons-en; **I expect you'll be glad to get it over with** j'imagine que vous serez soulagé quand ce sera terminé

▶**get round** 1 *vt insep* (**a**) = **get around**

(**b**) *(exhibition, museum)* faire le tour de; *(corner)* passer

2 *vt sep (bring, take)* **I'll get the books round (to you) as soon as I can** je t'apporterai les livres dès que je le pourrai

3 *vi* (**a**) = **get about**

(**b**) **the doctor said she'd get round as soon as she could** le docteur a dit qu'elle viendrait *ou* passerait dès qu'elle pourrait; **I didn't manage to get round to each pupil in the class** je n'ai pas réussi à m'occuper de chaque élève de la classe

▶**get round to** *vt insep* = **get around to**

▶**get through** 1 *vi* (**a**) *(reach destination)* parvenir; **the road was blocked and no one could get through** la route était bloquée et personne ne pouvait passer; **they managed to get through to the wounded** ils ont réussi à parvenir jusqu'aux blessés; **the letter got through to her** la lettre lui est parvenue; **the message didn't get through** le message n'est pas arrivé; **despite the crowds, I managed to get through** malgré la foule, j'ai réussi à passer

(**b**) *(candidate, student → succeed)* réussir; *(→ in exam)* être reçu, réussir; **the team got through to the final** l'équipe s'est classée pour la finale

(**c**) *(bill, motion)* passer, être adopté *ou* voté

(**d**) *(make oneself understood)* se faire comprendre; **I can't seem to get through to her** elle et moi ne sommes pas sur la même longueur d'onde

(**e**) *(contact)* contacter; *Tel* obtenir la communication; **I can't get through to his office** je n'arrive pas à avoir son bureau

(**f**) *Am (finish)* finir, terminer; **call me when you get through** appelez-moi quand vous aurez *ou* avez fini

2 *vt insep* (**a**) *(come through → hole, window)* passer par; *(→ crowd)* se frayer un chemin à travers *ou* dans; *(→ military lines)* percer, franchir

(**b**) *(survive → storm, winter)* survivre à; *(→ difficulty)* se sortir de, se tirer de; **he got through it alive** il s'en est sorti (vivant)

(**c**) *(complete, finish → book)* finir, terminer; *(→ job, project)* achever, venir à bout de; **I got through an enormous amount of work** j'ai abattu beaucoup de travail; **it took us one week to get through the entire play** il nous a fallu une semaine pour venir à bout de la pièce

(**d**) *(consume, use up)* consommer, utiliser; **we get through a litre of olive oil a week** nous utilisons un litre d'huile d'olive par semaine; **they got through their monthly salary in one week** en une semaine ils avaient dépensé tout leur salaire du mois; **he gets through eight shirts a week** il salit huit chemises par semaine; **we'll never get through all this food** nous ne viendrons jamais à bout de toute cette nourriture

(**e**) *(endure, pass → time)* faire passer; **how will I get through this without you?** comment pourrai-je vivre cette épreuve sans toi?; **they got through the day without a single argument** ils ne se sont pas disputés une seule fois de toute la journée; **the Government may have difficulty getting through another six months** le gouvernement aura peut-être du mal à tenir encore six mois

(**f**) *(exam)* réussir, être reçu à

(**g**) *(of bill, motion)* passer; **the bill got through both Houses** le projet de loi a été adopté par les deux Chambres

3 *vt sep* (**a**) *(transport, send successfully)* faire parvenir; **they got the food supplies through** ils ont réussi à faire parvenir les provisions alimentaires (à destination); **to get sth through customs** (faire) passer qch à la douane; **you'll never get that desk through** tu n'arriveras jamais à faire passer ce bureau

(**b**) *(transmit → message)* faire passer, transmettre, faire parvenir; **can you get this letter through to my family?** pouvez-vous transmettre *ou* faire parvenir cette lettre à ma famille?

(**c**) *(make understood)* **I finally got it through to him that I wasn't interested** j'ai fini par lui faire comprendre que je n'étais pas intéressé; *Fam* **when will you get it through your thick head that I don't want to go?** quand est-ce que tu vas enfin comprendre que je ne veux pas y aller? ❑

(**d**) *(bill, motion)* faire adopter, faire passer; **the party got the bill through the Senate** le parti a fait voter *ou* adopter le projet de loi par le Sénat

(**e**) *(cause to succeed)* **it was your essay that got you through (the exam)** c'est grâce à ta dissertation que tu as réussi l'examen

(**f**) *(enable to endure)* **I need four cups of coffee to get me through the day** il me faut mes quatre tasses de café par jour

▶**get through with** *vt insep* terminer, finir

▶**get to** *vt insep* (**a**) *(reach)* arriver à; **where have you got to?** *(in book, work)* où en es-tu?; **it got to the point where he couldn't walk another step** il en est arrivé au point de ne plus pouvoir faire un pas

(**b**) *(deal with)* s'occuper de; **I'll get to you in a minute** je suis à toi *ou* je m'occupe de toi dans quelques secondes; **he'll get to it tomorrow** il va s'en occuper demain

(**c**) *Fam (have an effect on)* **that music really gets to me** *(moves me)* cette musique me touche vraiment ❑; *(annoys me)* cette musique me tape sur le système; **don't let it get to you!** ne t'énerve pas pour ça!

(**d**) *Am Fam* **they got to the witness** *(bribed)* ils ont acheté le témoin; *(killed)* ils ont descendu le témoin

▶**get together** 1 *vi* (**a**) *(meet)* se réunir, se rassembler; **can we get together after the meeting?** on peut se retrouver après la réunion?

(**b**) *(reach an agreement)* se mettre d'accord; **the committee got together on the date** les membres du comité se sont entendus *ou* se sont mis d'accord sur la date; **you'd better get together with him on the proposal** vous feriez bien de vous entendre avec lui au sujet de la proposition

2 *vt sep (people)* réunir, rassembler; *(things)* rassembler, ramasser; *(thoughts)* rassembler; **to get some money together** réunir une somme d'argent; **let me get my thoughts together** laissez-moi rassembler mes idées; *Fam* **to get one's act together** se secouer; *Fam* **she's really got it together** *(in life)* elle sait ce qu'elle fait ❑; *(in job etc)* elle domine son sujet ❑; *Fam* **I never thought he would get it together** je n'aurais jamais pensé qu'il y arriverait ❑

▶**get up** 1 *vi* (**a**) *(arise from bed)* se lever; **it was 6 o'clock when we got up** il était 6 heures quand nous nous sommes levés; **I like to get up late on Sundays** j'aime faire la grasse matinée le dimanche; **get up!** sors du lit!, debout!, lève-toi!

(**b**) *(rise to one's feet)* se lever, se mettre debout; **she had to get up from her chair** elle a été obligée de se lever de sa chaise; **to get up from the table** se lever *ou* sortir de table; **get up off the floor!** relève-toi!; **please don't bother getting up** restez assis, je vous prie

(**c**) *(climb up)* monter; **they got up on the roof** ils sont montés sur le toit; **she got up behind him on the motorcycle** elle est montée derrière lui sur la moto

(**d**) *(of wind)* se lever

(**e**) *(to horse)* **get up!** allez!

2 *vt insep (stairs)* monter; *(ladder, tree)* monter à; *(hill)* gravir

3 *vt sep* (**a**) *(cause to rise to feet)* faire lever; *(awaken)* réveiller

(**b**) *(move up)* monter; **how are we going to get this desk up to the fifth floor?** comment allons-nous monter ce bureau jusqu'au cinquième étage?; **to get sb up the stairs** *(help climb)* aider qn à monter l'escalier

(**c**) *(generate, work up)* **to get up speed** gagner de la vitesse; **to get one's courage up** rassembler son courage; **I can't get up any enthusiasm for the job** je n'arrive pas à éprouver d'enthousiasme pour ce travail

(**d**) *Fam (organize → entertainment, party)* organiser ❑, monter ❑; *(→ petition)* organiser ❑; *(→ play)* monter ❑; *(→ excuse, story)* fabriquer ❑, forger ❑

(**e**) *(dress up)* habiller; *(in costume)* déguiser; **their children are always so nicely got up** leurs enfants sont toujours si bien habillés; **to get oneself up** se mettre sur son trente et un

(**f**) *Fam (study → subject)* bûcher, travailler ❑; *(→ notes, speech)* préparer ❑

(**g**) *very Fam (idiom)* **to get it up** bander

▶**get up to** *vt insep* (**a**) *(do)* faire; **he gets up to all kinds of mischief** il fait des tas de bêtises; **what have you been getting up to lately?** qu'est-ce que tu deviens?

(**b**) *(reach)* **I've got up to chapter 5** j'en suis au chapitre 5; **where have you got up to?** *(in book, work)* où en êtes-vous?

---

getatable [get'ætəbəl] *adj Fam (place, shelf)* accessible ❑, d'accès facile ❑; *(person)* accessible ❑

getaway ['getəweɪ] *n* (**a**) *(escape)* fuite *f*; **to make one's getaway** s'enfuir, filer; **they made a quick getaway** ils ont vite filé (**b**) *Aut (start)* démarrage *m*; *(in racing)* départ *m*

▶▶ ***getaway car*** voiture *f* de fuyard; ***getaway vehicle*** véhicule *m* de fuyard

get-go *n Am Fam* **from the get-go** *(from the beginning)* dès le début ❑; **he's a crook from the get-go** *(completely)* c'est un escroc total, c'est un véritable escroc ❑

Gethsemane [geθ'semənɪ] *n Bible* Gethsémani

get-out *n* (**a**) *(means of escape)* échappatoire *f* (**b**) *Fam* **as nervous/boring as (all) get-out** nerveux/ennuyeux comme tout, on peut plus nerveux/ennuyeux; **as drunk as (all) get-out** ivre mort

▶▶ ***get-out clause*** clause *f* de résiliation

get-rich-quick *adj Fam* **a get-rich-quick scheme** un projet pour faire fortune rapidement ❑

get-there *n Am Fam* pêche *f*, allant *m*

get-together *n (meeting)* (petite) réunion *f*; *(party)* (petite) fête *f*; **I'm having a get-together with some friends** nous faisons une petite soirée entre amis; **you and I must have a little get-together one day** il faut qu'on se voie un de ces jours tous les deux

Gettysburg Address ['getɪzbɜːg-] *n* **the Gettysburg Address** = discours prononcé par Abraham Lincoln pendant la guerre de Sécession

THE GETTYSBURG ADDRESS 

Ce fameux discours, prononcé sur le site de la bataille du même nom par Abraham Lincoln, appelle à la volonté de construire une nation libre, dirigée "par le peuple, pour le peuple" ("a government of the people, by the people, for the people"); cette formule est souvent utilisée comme définition de la démocratie.

get-up *n Fam* (**a**) *(outfit)* accoutrement❑ *m*; *(disguise)* déguisement❑ *m*; **you're not going out in that get-up!** tu ne vas pas sortir (habillé) comme ça *ou* dans cet accoutrement! (**b**) *(of book, product)* présentation❑ *f*

get-up-and-go *n Fam* allant❑ *m*, dynamisme❑ *m*; **to have plenty of get-up-and-go** avoir beaucoup d'allant, être très dynamique; *Hum* **my get-up-and-go has got up and gone** je suis sur les rotules

get-well card *n* = carte de vœux pour un bon rétablissement

geum ['dʒiːəm] *n Bot* benoîte *f*

gewgaw ['gjuːgɔː] *n Br* bibelot *m*, babiole *f*, colifichet *m*

geyser [*Br* 'giːzə(r), *Am* 'gaɪzə(r)] *n* (**a**) *Geol* geyser *m* (**b**) *Br Old-fashioned (water heater)* chauffe-eau *m inv* (à gaz)

geyserite [*Br* 'giːzəraɪt, *Am* 'gaɪzəraɪt] *n Miner* geysérite *f*

G-force *n* pesanteur *f*

Ghana ['gɑːnə] *n* Ghana *m*; **in Ghana** au Ghana

Ghanaian [gɑː'neɪən], **Ghanian** ['gɑːnɪən] **1** *n* Ghanéen(enne) *m,f*

2 *adj* ghanéen

gharial ['gɑːrɪəl] *n Zool* garial *m*

ghastliness ['gɑːstlɪnɪs] *n* (**a**) *(of crime)* horreur *f*, atrocité *f* (**b**) *(of place, building, sight)* aspect *m* sinistre *ou* épouvantable; *(of experience, situation)* caractère *m* horrible *ou* affreux

ghastly ['gɑːstlɪ] (*compar* **ghastlier**, *superl* **ghastliest**) *adj* (**a**) *Fam (very bad)* affreux❑, épouvantable❑, atroce❑; **she wore the most ghastly outfit!** elle était accoutrée d'une façon indescriptible!; **there's been a ghastly mistake** une terrible erreur a été commise; **we went to a really ghastly party** nous sommes allés à une soirée vraiment épouvantable; **the interview was ghastly** l'interview s'est très mal passée; **you look ghastly!** vous avez l'air d'un déterré!

(**b**) *(frightening, unnatural)* horrible, effrayant; **a ghastly silence** un silence effrayant

(**c**) *(pale)* blême; *(pallor)* mortel; *(light)* blafard

ghee [giː] *n Culin* beurre *m* clarifié

Ghent [gent] *n* Gand

gherkin ['gɜːkɪn] *n* cornichon *m*

ghetto ['getəʊ] (*pl* **ghettos** *or* **ghettoes**) *n* ghetto *m*

►► *Fam* **ghetto blaster** = grand radiocassette portatif

ghettoization [,getəʊaɪ'zeɪʃən] *n* ghettoïsation *f*

ghettoize, -ise ['getəʊaɪz] *vt* ghettoïser

ghillie ['gɪlɪ] = **gillie**

ghost [gəʊst] **1** *n* (**a**) *(phantom)* fantôme *m*, revenant *m*; **to believe in ghosts** croire aux fantômes; **you look as if you've just seen a ghost!** on dirait que vous venez de voir un fantôme!

(**b**) *(shadow)* ombre *f*; **the ghost of a smile** l'ombre d'un sourire, un vague sourire; **you don't have the ghost of a chance** vous n'avez pas la moindre chance *ou* l'ombre d'une chance

(**c**) *TV* image *f* secondaire *ou* résiduelle

(**d**) *Rel* **the Holy Ghost** l'Esprit *m* saint, le Saint-Esprit

(**e**) *(writer)* nègre *m*

(**f**) *(idioms)* **to give up the ghost** rendre l'âme; *Hum* **this typewriter has given up the ghost** cette machine à écrire a rendu l'âme; **to lay any ghosts to rest about sth** dissiper le moindre doute quant à qch; *Am Fam* **to get ghost** *(leave)* se casser, s'arracher

2 *vt* **to ghost a book for an author** servir de nègre à l'auteur d'un livre

3 *adj (story, film)* de revenants, de fantômes

►► **ghost ship** vaisseau *m* fantôme; **ghost town** ville *f* fantôme; **ghost train** train *m* fantôme

ghosting ['gəʊstɪŋ] *n TV* image *f* fantôme, fantôme *m*

ghostlike ['gəʊst,laɪk] **1** *adj* spectral, de spectre

2 *adv* comme un spectre

ghostly ['gəʊstlɪ] (*compar* **ghostlier**, *superl* **ghostliest**) *adj* spectral, fantomatique; **a ghostly figure** une véritable apparition; **a ghostly silence** un silence de mort; **ghostly white** d'une pâleur mortelle

ghostwrite ['gəʊstraɪt] (*pt* **ghostwrote** [-rəʊt], *pp* **ghostwritten** [-,rɪtən]) **1** *vt* écrire *ou* rédiger (comme nègre); **I'm sure his books are ghostwritten** je suis sûr qu'il n'a écrit aucun des livres publiés sous son nom

2 *vi* **to ghostwrite for sb** servir de nègre à qn

ghostwriter ['gəʊst,raɪtə(r)] *n* nègre *m*

ghostwritten ['gəʊst,rɪtən] *pp of* **ghostwrite**

ghostwrote ['gəʊstrəʊt] *pt of* **ghostwrite**

ghoul [guːl] *n* (**a**) *(evil spirit)* goule *f* (**b**) *(macabre person)* amateur *m* de macabre; **don't be such a ghoul!** tu es vraiment morbide! (**c**) *Old-fashioned (grave robber)* déterreur *m* de cadavres

ghoulish ['guːlɪʃ] *adj* (**a**) *(ghostly)* de goule, vampirique (**b**) *(person, humour)* morbide, macabre

ghoulishly ['guːlɪʃlɪ] *adv* de façon macabre

ghoulishness ['guːlɪʃnɪs] *n (of person, humour)* caractère *m* macabre

GHQ [,dʒiːeɪtʃ'kjuː] *n* (*abbr* **general headquarters**) GQG *m*

GHz (*written abbr* **gigahertz**) GHz

GI [,dʒiː'aɪ] *n Fam* (*abbr* **Government Issue**) *(soldier)* soldat *m* américain❑, GI *m*

►► ***GI bill*** = loi adoptée aux États-Unis en 1944, accordant certains avantages aux combattants de la Seconde Guerre mondiale (notamment la possibilité de poursuivre leurs études); ***GI bride*** épouse *f* (étrangère) d'un GI; ***GI Joe*** = surnom collectif des soldats américains, notamment pendant la Seconde Guerre mondiale

giant ['dʒaɪənt] **1** *n* (**a**) *(in size)* géant(e) *m,f* (**b**) *Fig* **a literary giant** un géant de la littérature; **an industrial giant** un magnat de l'industrie; **they are one of the giants of the petrochemical industry** c'est l'un des géants de l'industrie pétrochimique

2 *adj* géant, gigantesque; **with giant strides** à pas de géant; **the company has taken giant strides towards modernizing its production techniques** la société a fait d'énormes efforts pour moderniser ses techniques de production; **the campaign has made giant strides (forward)** la campagne a progressé à pas de géant

►► ***the Giant's Causeway*** la Chaussée des Géants; *Orn* ***giant hummingbird*** oiseau-mouche *m* patagon; *Zool* ***giant panda*** panda *m* géant; *Bot* ***giant redwood*** séquoia *m* géant; *Bot* ***giant sequoia*** séquoia *m* géant; ***giant slalom*** slalom *m* géant; *Astron* ***giant star*** étoile *f* géante; *Zool* ***giant tortoise*** tortue *f* géante

giantess ['dʒaɪəntes] *n* géante *f*

giantism ['dʒaɪəntɪzəm] *n Med* gigantisme *m*

giantkiller ['dʒaɪənt,kɪlə(r)] *n Br Sport* vainqueur *m* surprise

giantkilling ['dʒaɪənt,kɪlɪŋ] *n Br Sport* = victoire surprise d'un concurrent peu coté

►► ***giantkilling act*** la victoire de David contre Goliath

giantlike ['dʒaɪənt,laɪk] *adj* gigantesque, de géant

giant-size(d) *adj (pack)* géant

giardiasis [,dʒaɪɑː'daɪəsɪs] *n Med* giardiase *f*, lambliase *f*

Gib [dʒɪb] *n Fam* Gibraltar❑

gibber ['dʒɪbə(r)] *vi* (**a**) *(person)* bredouiller, bafouiller; **to gibber with fear** bafouiller de peur; **stop gibbering and tell me exactly what happened!** arrête de bafouiller et explique-toi clairement! (**b**) *(monkey)* crier, hurler

gibbering ['dʒɪbərɪŋ] *adj* **I was a gibbering wreck!** j'étais tellement bouleversé que j'en bafouillais!; *Fam* **he's a gibbering idiot** c'est un sacré imbécile

gibberish ['dʒɪbərɪʃ] *n* baragouin *m*, charabia *m*; **it's complete gibberish to me** je ne comprends absolument rien; *Fam* **this instruction leaflet is a load of gibberish** ce mode d'emploi, c'est du charabia; **the man's talking gibberish** ce que dit cet homme est totalement incompréhensible *ou* n'a ni queue ni tête

gibbet ['dʒɪbɪt] **1** *n* potence *f*, gibet *m*

2 *vt (hang)* pendre

gibbon ['gɪbən] *n Zool* gibbon *m*

gibbous ['gɪbəs] *adj* (**a**) *Astron* gibbeux (**b**) *(humpbacked)* bossu

gibe [dʒaɪb] **1** *vt (taunt)* railler, se moquer de

2 *vi* **to gibe at sb** railler qn, se moquer de qn

3 *n (remark)* raillerie *f*, moquerie *f*

giblets ['dʒɪblɪts] *npl* abats *mpl* de volaille

Gibraltar [dʒɪ'brɔːltə(r)] *n* Gibraltar; **in Gibraltar** à Gibraltar; **the Strait of Gibraltar** le détroit de Gibraltar

Gibraltarian [,dʒɪbrɔːl'teərɪən] *n (inhabitant)* habitant(e) *m,f* de Gibraltar; *(native)* originaire *mf* de Gibraltar

giddily ['gɪdɪlɪ] *adv* (**a**) *(dizzily)* vertigineusement (**b**) *(frivolously)* étourdiment, avec insouciance

giddiness ['gɪdɪnɪs] *n (UNCOUNT)* (**a**) *(dizziness)* vertiges *mpl*, étourdissements *mpl* (**b**) *(frivolousness)* frivolité *f*, étourderie *f*

giddy ['gɪdɪ] (*compar* **giddier**, *superl* **giddiest**) *adj* (**a**) *(dizzy → person)* **to be** *or* **to feel giddy** *(afraid of height)* avoir le vertige, être pris de vertige; *(unwell)* avoir un étourdissement; **I feel giddy just watching them** j'ai la tête qui tourne *ou* le vertige rien que de les regarder

(**b**) *(lofty)* vertigineux, qui donne le vertige; **the giddy heights of success** les hautes cimes de la réussite; *Ironic* **he had reached the giddy heights of senior assistant** il avait atteint le grade prestigieux d'assistant en chef

(**c**) *(frivolous → person, behaviour)* frivole, écervelé; **she behaves just like a giddy schoolgirl** elle se comporte vraiment comme une jeune idiote *ou* écervelée; **a giddy round of parties and social events** un tourbillon de soirées et de sorties mondaines; *Br Fam Old-fashioned* **my giddy aunt!** oh là là!

►**giddy up** *exclam (to horse)* hue!

Gideon ['gɪdɪən] *pr n Bible* Gédéon

►► ***Gideon Bible*** = bible placée dans les chambres d'hôtel par l'organisation chrétienne des Gideons

GIF [gɪf] *n Comput* (*abbr* **Graphics Interchange Format**) GIF *m*

GIFT [gɪft] *n* (*abbr* **gamete intrafallopian transfer**) FIVETE *f*

gift [gɪft] **1** *n* (**a**) *(present → personal)* cadeau *m*; *(→ official)* don *m*; **to make sb a gift of sth** offrir qch à qn, faire cadeau de qch à qn; **is it a gift?** c'est pour offrir?; **I wouldn't have it as a gift!** je n'en voudrais pas même si on m'en faisait cadeau!; **her offer of help came like a gift from the gods** l'aide qu'elle nous offrait *ou* sa proposition d'aide était un cadeau tombé du ciel; *Literary* **the gift of friendship/of tears** le don de l'amitié/des larmes; *Prov* **don't** *or* **never look a gift horse in the mouth** à cheval donné on ne regarde pas la bouche

(**b**) *(talent)* don *m*; **he has a great gift for telling jokes** il n'a pas son pareil pour raconter des plaisanteries; **she has a gift for music** elle a un don *ou* elle est douée pour la musique; *Fam* **to have the gift of the gab** avoir la langue bien pendue, avoir du bagou(t)

(**c**) *Fam (bargain)* affaire❑ *f*; **at 5 pounds, it's a gift** 5 livres, c'est donné

(**d**) *Fam (easy thing)* **that exam question was a gift** ce sujet d'examen, c'était du gâteau

(**e**) *(donation)* don *m*, donation *f*; *Law* **as a gift** à titre d'avantage *ou* gracieux; **the posts abroad are in the gift of the French department** l'attribution des postes à l'étranger relève du département de français; *Law* **gift inter vivos** donation *f* inter vivos

(**f**) *Rel* **the gift of faith** la grâce de la foi; **the gift of tongues** le don des langues

2 *vt* (**a**) *Am Formal (present)* donner, faire don de; **gifted by Mr Evans** *(on plaque)* don de M. Evans

(**b**) *Fig (give away)* **their own goal gifted the game to their opponents** le but qu'ils ont marqué contre leur propre camp leur a coûté la victoire

►► *Am* ***gift certificate*** bon *m* d'achat; ***gift coupon*** bon *m* de réduction, point-cadeau *m*; ***gift shop*** boutique *f* de cadeaux; *Fin* ***gift tax*** impôt *m* sur les donations; ***gift token*** bon *m* d'achat; *Br* ***gift voucher*** *(token)* bon *m* d'achat; *(coupon)* bon *m* de réduction, point-cadeau *m*; ***gift wrapping*** papier-cadeau *m*

gifted ['gɪftɪd] *adj (person)* doué; *(performance)* talentueux; **highly gifted children** des enfants surdoués; **she's gifted with a fantastic memory** elle a une mémoire fantastique

gift-wrap *vt* **do you want it gift-wrapped?** je vous fais un paquet-cadeau?

gift-wrapped ['gɪftræp:t] *adj (article)* sous paquet-cadeau

gig [gɪg] *n* (**a**) *(carriage)* cabriolet *m* (**b**) *(boat)* yole *f*, guigue *f* (**c**) *Fam (concert)* concert ❑ *m (de rock, de jazz)*; *(show)* spectacle ❑ *m*

giga- ['gɪgə] *pref* giga-

gigabyte ['gɪgəbaɪt] *n Comput* gigaoctet *m*

gigahertz ['gɪgəhɜ:ts] *n Elec & Phys* gigahertz *m*

gigantic [dʒaɪ'gæntɪk] *adj* géant, gigantesque

gigantically [dʒaɪ'gæntɪklɪ] *adv* de façon démesurée

gigantism [dʒaɪ'gæntɪzəm] *n* gigantisme *m*

gigantomachy [,dʒaɪgæn'tɒməkɪ], **gigantomachia** [,dʒaɪgæntəʊ'meɪkɪə] *n Myth* gigantomachie *f*; *Fig* combat *m* de géants

giggle ['gɪgəl] **1** *vi (stupidly)* rire bêtement, ricaner; *(nervously)* rire nerveusement; **they couldn't stop giggling** ils ne pouvaient pas se retenir de glousser *ou* de pouffer; **what are you giggling about?** qu'est-ce qui vous fait rire?

2 *n (uncontrollable)* fou rire *m*; *(nervous)* petit rire *m* nerveux; *(stupid)* ricanement *m*; **to have a fit of the giggles** avoir le fou rire; *Br Fam* **to do sth for a giggle** faire qch pour rigoler; **the evening was a giggle from start to finish** on s'est marré toute la soirée; **she was a real giggle as usual** elle était tordante comme d'habitude

giggling ['gɪglɪŋ] **1** *adj* qui rit bêtement

2 *n (UNCOUNT) (uncontrollable)* fou rire *m*; *(nervous)* petits rires *mpl* nerveux; *(of young girl)* rires *mpl* bébêtes, gloussements *mpl*

giggly ['gɪglɪ] *adj* qui rit bêtement; **they're like giggly schoolgirls** elles n'arrêtent pas de rire comme des gamines; **to get** *or* **go all giggly** se mettre à rire bêtement; **to be in a giggly mood** être d'humeur joyeuse

giglamp ['gɪglæmp] *n (of carriage)* lanterne *f* de cabriolet

GIGO ['gaɪgəʊ, ,dʒi:aɪ,dʒi:'əʊ] *n Comput (abbr* **garbage in, garbage out**) GIGO

gigolo ['ʒɪgələʊ] *(pl* **gigolos**) *n* gigolo *m*

gigot ['dʒɪgət] *n* gigot *m*

Gila monster ['hi:lə-, 'dʒi:lə-] *n Zool* héloderme *m*

Gilbert and Sullivan ['gɪlbətən'sʌlɪvən] *pr n* **Gilbert and Sullivan opera** = opérettes satiriques dues au compositeur Sullivan et au librettiste Gilbert (fin du XIXème siècle)

gild [gɪld] *(pt* **gilded,** *pp* **gilded** *or* **gilt** [gɪlt]) **1** *n Hist (professional association)* guilde *f*, corporation *f*; **the gild of goldsmiths** la guilde des orfèvres

2 *vt* dorer; **it would be gilding the lily** ce serait du peaufinage

gilded ['gɪldɪd] *adj* doré; **to be like a bird in a gilded cage** vivre dans une prison dorée; *Fig* **gilded youth** jeunesse *f* dorée

►► ***the Gilded Age*** = l'ère du capitalisme triomphant (aux États-Unis, vers la fin du XIXème siècle)

gilding ['gɪldɪŋ] *n* dorure *f*

Gilead ['gɪlɪæd] *n Bible* Galaad; *Bot* **balm of Gilead** baume *m* de La Mecque

gilet ['ʒi:leɪ] *n* gilet *m* matelassé

gill[1] [dʒɪl] *n (liquid measure)* = 0,142l, quart *m* de pinte

gill[2] [gɪl] **1** *n* (**a**) *(of mushroom)* lamelle *f* (**b**) *Br (ravine)* ravin *m (stream)* ruisseau *m (de montagne)*

2 gills *npl (of fish)* ouïes *fpl*, branchies *fpl*; **to be green around the gills** *(from shock)* être vert (de peur); *(from illness)* avoir mauvaise mine

►► ***gill slit*** fente *f* branchiale

gillie ['gɪlɪ] *n Scot (for hunting)* guide *m*, accompagnateur *m*; *(for fishing)* accompagnateur *m*

gillion ['dʒɪljən] *n Br* milliard *m*

gillyflower ['dʒɪlɪ,flaʊə(r)] *n Bot (stock)* giroflée *f*; *(wallflower)* giroflée *f* des murailles; **(clove) gillyflower** œillet *m* giroflée

Gilsonite ['gɪlsənaɪt] *n* Gilsonite *f*

gilt [gɪlt] **1** *pp of* **gild**

2 *adj* doré

3 *n* (**a**) *(gilding)* dorure *f*; *Br* **to take the gilt off the gingerbread** gâcher le plaisir (**b**) *St Exch* fonds *m* d'État, valeur *f* de premier ordre *ou* de père de famille

►► ***gilts market*** marché *m* des valeurs de premier ordre; ***gilt switching*** rotation *f* de portefeuille-obligation

gilt-edged *adj* (**a**) *St Exch (securities, stock)* de tout repos, de père de famille (**b**) *(page)* doré sur tranche (**c**) *Fig (opportunity)* en or

►► *Am* ***gilt-edged bond*** valeur *f* du Trésor américain; ***gilt-edged market*** marché *m* des valeurs de premier ordre; ***gilt-edged market maker*** teneur *m* de marché des valeurs de premier ordre

gilthead ['gɪlthed] *n Ich* dorade *f* (méditerranéenne)

gimbal ring ['dʒɪmbəl-] *n Aviat & Naut* cardan *m*

gimbals ['dʒɪmbəlz] *npl Aviat & Naut* cardan *m*

gimcrack ['dʒɪmkræk] *adj Old-fashioned (jewellery)* en toc; *(ornament, car)* de pacotille; *(theory, idea)* bidon *(inv)*

gimlet ['gɪmlɪt] *n* (**a**) *(tool)* vrille *f*; **to have eyes like gimlets** avoir des yeux perçants; **his gimlet eyes stared at her** il la fixa de ses yeux perçants (**b**) *(drink)* = cocktail à base de vodka ou de gin et de jus de citron vert

gimlet-eyed *adj* à l'œil perçant, aux yeux perçants

gimme ['gɪmɪ] *Fam* **1** = **give me**

2 *n (in golf)* coup *m* donné

3 gimmes *npl Am* **the gimmes** la cupidité ❑

►► *Am* ***gimme cap*** = casquette donnée comme cadeau publicitaire

gimmick ['gɪmɪk] *n* (**a**) *(sales trick)* truc *m*, astuce *f*; *(in politics)* astuce *f*, gadget *m*; **advertising gimmick** trouvaille *f* publicitaire; **it's just a sales gimmick** c'est un truc pour faire vendre; **the voters aren't fooled by election gimmicks** les électeurs ne sont pas dupes des gadgets électoralistes

(**b**) *(gadget, device)* gadget *m*

(**c**) *(personal trick)* truc *m*; **he does a tap dance in the middle of the show purely as a gimmick** il fait un numéro de claquettes au milieu du spectacle simplement pour l'effet

gimmickry ['gɪmɪkrɪ] *n (UNCOUNT) Fam* truquage ❑ *m*, astuces ❑ *fpl*, gadgets ❑ *mpl*; **I'm sick of all this commercial gimmickry** j'en ai assez de tout ce tape-à-l'œil commercial

gimmicky ['gɪmɪkɪ] *adj Fam* qui relève du procédé ❑; **the show was too gimmicky** le spectacle relevait trop du procédé

gimp [gɪmp] *n Am Fam* (**a**) *Pej (person with limp)* boiteux(euse) ❑ *m,f* (**b**) *Pej (idiot)* andouille *f* (**c**) *(sado-masochist)* sadomasochiste *mf*

►► ***gimp suit*** = panoplie de sadomasochiste

gin [dʒɪn] *(pt & pp* **ginned,** *cont* **ginning**) **1** *n* (**a**) *(drink)* gin *m*; **gin and tonic** gin-tonic *m*; *Br* **gin and it** martini-gin *m* (**b**) *(trap)* piège *m* (**c**) *Ind (machine)* égreneuse *f* (de coton)

2 *vt* attraper, piéger

►► ***gin fizz*** gin-fizz *m inv*; *Am* ***gin mill,*** *Br* ***gin palace*** tripot *m*; *Cards* ***gin rummy*** gin-rummy *m*, gin-rami *m*; ***gin sling*** gin sling *m*

ginger ['dʒɪndʒə(r)] **1** *n* (**a**) *(spice)* gingembre *m*; **crystallized ginger** gingembre *m* confit; **ground ginger** gingembre *m* en poudre; **root** *or* **fresh ginger** gingembre *m* en racine *ou* frais

(**b**) *Fam Fig* entrain ❑ *m*, allant ❑ *m*, dynamisme ❑ *m*

(**c**) *(colour)* brun *m* roux

(**d**) *Fam (redhead)* roux (rousse) ❑ *m,f*; **oi ginger!** ho, poil de carotte!

(**e**) *Scot Fam (fizzy drink)* boisson *f* gazeuse ❑

2 *adj (hair)* roux (rousse), rouquin [illegible] (rousse)

3 Ginger *n Fam (nickname)* Poil de Carotte

►► ***ginger ale*** = boisson gazeuse aux extraits de gingembre pouvant servir à couper un alcool; ***ginger beer*** = limonade au gingembre; ***ginger beer plant*** = association de levure et de bactéries utilisée dans la fabrication de la "ginger beer"; ***ginger group*** = dans une organisation politique ou autre, faction dynamique cherchant à faire bouger les choses en incitant à l'action; ***ginger snap,*** *Br* ***ginger nut*** biscuit *m* au gingembre; ***ginger wine*** = boisson alcoolisée à base de gingembre

►**ginger up** *vt sep (activity, group, meeting)* animer; *(speech, story)* relever, pimenter, égayer; *(film, text, storyline etc)* donner du punch à; **we need something to ginger up the party** il nous faut quelque chose pour mettre un peu d'animation dans la soirée

gingerbread ['dʒɪndʒəbred] **1** *n* pain *m* d'épices

2 *adj (ornament, style)* tarabiscoté

►► ***gingerbread man*** = sujet en biscuit parfumé au gingembre

ginger-haired *adj* roux (rousse)

gingerly ['dʒɪndʒəlɪ] **1** *adv (cautiously)* avec circonspection, précautionneusement; *(delicately)* délicatement; **he stepped gingerly between the cowpats** il a avancé précautionneusement entre les bouses de vache

2 *adj (cautious)* circonspect, prudent; *(delicate)* délicat; **to do sth in a gingerly fashion** faire qch avec beaucoup de précaution

gingery ['dʒɪndʒərɪ] *adj* (**a**) *(taste)* de gingembre; *(colour)* roux (rousse) (**b**) *Fig (full of vigour)* animé; *(biting)* acerbe

gingham ['gɪŋəm] **1** *n* (toile *f* de) vichy *m*

2 *comp* en vichy

gingiva [dʒɪn'dʒaɪvə] *(pl* **gingivae** [-i:]) *n Anat* gencive *f*; **attached gingiva** gencive *f* adhérente; **free gingiva** gencive *f* libre

gingival [dʒɪn'dʒaɪvəl] *adj Anat* gingival

gingivitis [,dʒɪndʒɪ'vaɪtɪs] *n (UNCOUNT) Med* gingivite *f*

gingko ['gɪŋkəʊ], **gingkgo** ['gɪŋkgəʊ] *n Bot* ginkgo *m*, arbre *m* aux quarante écus

gink [gɪŋk] *n Fam* drôle d'oiseau *m*

ginormous [,dʒaɪ'nɔ:məs] *adj Fam* gigantesque

ginseng ['dʒɪnseŋ] *n* ginseng *m*

Gioconda [dʒɪɒ'kɒndə] *n Art* **la Gioconda** la Joconde; **a Gioconda smile** un sourire de Joconde

gippo ['dʒɪpəʊ] *(pl* **gippoes**) *n Br Fam* = terme injurieux désignant un gitan

gippy ['dʒɪpɪ] *adj Br Fam* **to have a gippy tummy** avoir la courante

gipsy ['dʒɪpsɪ] *(pl* **gipsies**) **1** *n* gitan(e) *m,f*, bohémien(enne) *m,f*, *Pej* romanichel(elle) *m,f*; *Fig (wanderer)* vagabond(e) *m,f*; **she's a gipsy at heart** c'est une bohème dans l'âme

2 *adj (camp)* de gitans; *(dance, music)* gitan

►► ***gipsy caravan*** roulotte *f*; ***gipsy moth*** zigzag *m*, bombyx *m* disparate

gipsyish ['dʒɪpsɪɪʃ], **gipsylike** ['dʒɪpsɪlaɪk] *adj* comme un bohémien, *Pej* comme un romanichel; *(dark-skinned)* brun de peau

gipsyweed ['dʒɪpsɪwi:d], **gipsywort** ['dʒɪpsɪwɜ:t] *n Bot* lycope *m*

giraffe [dʒɪ'rɑ:f] *n* girafe *f*; **a baby giraffe** un girafeau, un girafon

girandole ['dʒɪrəndəʊl] *n* (**a**) *(candle holder)* girandole *f* (**b**) *Tech* girandole *f*, girande *f* (**c**) *(earring, pendant)* girandole *f*

gird [gɜ:d] *(pt & pp* **girded** *or* **girt** [gɜ:t]) *vt Literary* (**a**) *(waist)* ceindre; **to gird (up) one's loins** se préparer à l'action (**b**) *(clothe)* **to gird with** revêtir de

►**gird on** *vt sep Arch or Literary* **to gird on one's sword** ceindre l'épée

girded ['gɜ:dɪd] *adj Literary* **with girded loins** les reins ceints; **with girded sword** ceint d'une épée

girder ['gɜ:də(r)] *n* poutre *f* (métallique), fer *m* profilé; *(light)* poutrelle *f*

girdle ['gɜ:dəl] **1** *n* (**a**) *(corset)* gaine *f* (**b**) *Literary (belt)* ceinture *f* (**c**) *(in tree)* incision *f* annulaire (**d**) *Scot (iron plate)* plaque *f* en fonte; *(on top of stove)* plaque *f* chauffante

2 *vt* (**a**) *Literary* **to girdle sth with sth** ceindre qch de qch (**b**) *(tree)* baguer

►► *Br* ***girdle cake, girdle scone*** = sorte de petite galette

girl [gɜ:l] *n* (**a**) *(child)* fille *f*; **a little girl** une fillette, une petite fille; **girl's name** prénom *m* féminin *ou* de fille; **a girls' school** une école de filles; **I knew her when she was a girl** je l'ai connue toute petite; **poor little girl!** pauvre petite!; **a French/an Indian girl** une jeune Française/Indienne

(**b**) *(daughter)* fille *f*; **the Murphy girl** la fille des Murphy

(**c**) *(young woman)* (jeune) fille *f*; **the other girls at the office** les autres filles du bureau; **come in, girls!** entrez, mesdemoiselles!; **she's having an evening with the girls** elle passe la soirée dehors avec les filles; **he married a French girl** il a épousé une Française; **my dear girl** ma chère

(**d**) *Fam (term of address)* **that's my girl!** je te reconnais bien là!; **my dear girl** ma chère amie; *Br* **how are you, old girl?** ça va, ma vieille?

(**e**) *Fam (girlfriend)* (petite) amie ❑ *f*, copine *f*

(**f**) *Sch (pupil)* élève *f*

(**g**) *(employee)* (jeune) employée *f*; *(maid)* bonne *f*; *(in shop)* vendeuse *f*; *(in factory)* ouvrière *f*

(**h**) *(used to address dog, horse, ship)* ma belle; **come on, girl** allez, hue cocotte!

▸▸ ***girl band*** girls band *m*; ***girl Friday*** = employée de bureau affectée à des tâches diverses; ***Girl Guide*** éclaireuse *f*; ***girl power*** = slogan associé au groupe féminin britannique The Spice Girls, revendiquant l'égalité des sexes; ***Girl Scout*** éclaireuse *f*

'The Girls of Slender Means' *Spark* 'Les Demoiselles de petite fortune'

'The Girl can't help it' *Tashlin* 'La Blonde et moi'

girlfriend ['gɜːlfrend] *n* (**a**) *(partner)* copine *f*, (petite) amie *f*; **girlfriend trouble** problèmes *mpl* de cœur (**b**) *(platonic friend)* copine *f*, amie *f*; *Am Fam* **yo, girlfriend!** salut, frangine!; *Fam* **girlfriend, you're way out of line** là, tu exagères, ma vieille

girlhood ['gɜːlhʊd] *n (as child)* enfance *f*; *(as adolescent)* adolescence *f*; **in my girlhood** dans ma jeunesse, quand j'étais jeune fille

girlie ['gɜːlɪ] *n Fam* (**a**) *(effeminate boy)* fillette *f* (**b**) *Br (young woman)* (jeune) fille ❑ *f*; **to have a girlie chat** bavarder entre filles

▸▸ ***girlie magazine*** magazine *m* de femmes à poil

girlish ['gɜːlɪʃ] *adj* (**a**) *(appearance, smile, voice)* de fillette, de petite fille (**b**) *Pej (boy)* efféminé

girlishly ['gɜːlɪʃlɪ] *adv* comme une petite fille

girlishness ['gɜːlɪʃnɪs] *n* manières *fpl ou* air *m* de petite fille

giro ['dʒaɪrəʊ] *n* (**a**) *(system)* = système de virement interbancaire introduit par la Poste britannique; **(bank) giro** virement *m* bancaire; **to pay by bank giro** payer par virement bancaire; **National Giro** ≃ Comptes *mpl* Chèques Postaux (**b**) *Fam (for unemployed)* chèque *m* d'allocation de chômage ❑; **I haven't had my giro yet** mon allocation de chômage ne m'a pas encore été payée

▸▸ ***giro account*** compte *m* chèque postal, CCP *m*; ***giro cheque*** chèque *m* postal, chèque *m* de virement; ***giro transfer*** transfert *m* par CCP

Girobank ['dʒaɪrəʊbæŋk] *n* = service bancaire de la Poste britannique, ≃ service *m* de chèques postaux

Girondist [dʒɪ'rɒndɪst] *Hist* **1** *n* Girondin(e) *m,f*

2 *adj* girondin; **the Girondist Party** le parti girondin

girt [gɜːt] *pt & pp of* **gird**

-girt [gɜːt] *suff Literary* **a sea-girt country/isle** un pays/une île encerclé(e) par la mer

girth [gɜːθ] **1** *n* (**a**) *(circumference)* circonférence *f*, tour *m* (**b**) *(stoutness)* corpulence *f*, embonpoint *m* (**c**) *(of saddle)* sangle *f*

2 *vt (horse)* sangler

gismo = **gizmo**

gist [dʒɪst] *n* essentiel *m*; **I get the gist of your argument** je comprends *ou* saisis l'essentiel de ton argument; **give me the gist of the discussion** expliquez-moi les grandes lignes du débat; **could you just give me the gist (of it) now?** pourrais-tu m'en donner l'essentiel?; **I got the gist of what she was saying** j'ai compris l'essentiel de ce qu'elle disait; **the gist of what she was saying was...** elle a dit en substance...

git [gɪt] *n Br very Fam (man)* connard *m*; *(woman)* connasse *f*; **you stupid git** espèce de connard/connasse!

GIVE [gɪv]

donner	▸ **1A (a) – (c); B (b) – (d); C (a), (d), (e); D (a), (c) – (f); 2 (a)**
offrir	▸ **1A (a), (c)**
conférer	▸ **1B (a)**
imposer	▸ **1C (b)**
reconnaître	▸ **1C (f)**
faire	▸ **1D (a) – (c), (f)**
s'affaisser	▸ **2 (b)**
élasticité	▸ **3**

(*pt* **gave** [geɪv], *pp* **given** ['gɪvən]) **1** *vt* **A.** (**a**) *(hand over)* donner; *(as gift)* donner, offrir; **I gave him the book, I gave the book to him** je lui ai donné le livre; **we gave our host a gift** nous avons offert un cadeau à notre hôte; **the family gave the paintings to the museum** la famille a fait don des tableaux au musée; **he gave his daughter in marriage** il a donné sa fille en mariage; **she gave him her hand** *(to hold)* elle lui a donné *ou* tendu la main; *(in marriage)* elle lui a accordé sa main; *Literary* **to give oneself to sb** se donner à qn; **I give you the newlyweds!** *(in toast)* je lève mon verre au bonheur des nouveaux mariés!; **I gave him my coat to hold** je lui ai confié mon manteau; **she gave them her trust** elle leur a fait confiance, elle leur a donné sa confiance; *Fam* **give it all you've got!** mets-y le paquet!; *Fam* **I'll give you something to cry about!** je vais te donner une bonne raison de pleurer, moi!; *Fam* **to give it to sb** *(beat up)* rosser qn; *(reprimand)* passer un savon à qn; **give it to them!** allez-y!; *Fam* **I gave him what for!** *(reprimanded him)* je lui ai passé un savon!; *Fam* **caviare on toast? I'll give him caviare on toast!** *(in annoyance at request)* du caviar et des toasts! je vais lui en donner, moi, du caviar et des toasts!

(**b**) *(grant → right, permission, importance)* donner; **give the matter your full attention** prêtez une attention toute particulière à cette affaire; **he gave your suggestion careful consideration** il a considéré votre suggestion avec beaucoup d'attention; *Law* **the court gave her custody of the child** la cour lui a accordé la garde de l'enfant; **she hasn't given her approval yet** elle n'a pas encore donné son consentement

(**c**) *(provide with → drink, food)* donner, offrir; (→ *lessons, classes, advice)* donner; (→ *help)* prêter; **give our guests something to eat/drink** donnez à manger/à boire à nos invités; **we gave them lunch** nous les avons invités *ou* nous leur avons fait à déjeuner; **I think I'll give them beef for lunch** je crois que je vais leur faire du bœuf au déjeuner; **let me give you some advice** laissez-moi vous donner un conseil; **I gave her the biggest bedroom** je lui ai donné la plus grande chambre; **they're giving us a pay rise** ils nous donnent une augmentation de salaire; **an investment that gives 10 percent** un placement qui rend *ou* rapporte 10 pour cent; **the children can wash up, it will give them something to do** les enfants peuvent faire la vaisselle, ça les occupera; **she gave him two lovely daughters** elle lui a donné deux adorables filles; **to give a child a name** donner un nom à un enfant; **to give sb/sth one's support** soutenir qn/qch; **do you give a discount?** faites-vous des tarifs préférentiels?; **this lamp gives a poor light** cette lampe éclaire mal; **give me time to think** donnez-moi *ou* laissez-moi le temps de réfléchir; **she didn't give him time to say no** elle ne lui a pas laissé le temps de dire non; **just give me time!** sois patient!; **we were given a choice** on nous a fait choisir; **give me a chance!** donne-moi une chance!; **such talent is not given to us all** nous n'avons pas tous un tel talent; *Fam* **give me classical music any day!** à mon avis rien ne vaut la musique classique! ❑

B. (**a**) *(confer → award)* conférer; **they gave her an honorary degree** ils lui ont conféré un diplôme honorifique

(**b**) *(dedicate)* donner, consacrer; **she gave all she had to the cause** elle s'est entièrement consacrée à cette cause; **can you give me a few minutes?** pouvez-vous m'accorder *ou* me consacrer quelques instants?; **he gave his life to save the child** il est mort *ou* il a donné sa vie pour sauver l'enfant; **I've given you six years of my life** je t'ai donné six ans de ma vie; **she gave this job the best years of her life** elle a consacré à ce travail les plus belles années de sa vie

(**c**) *(in exchange)* donner; *(pay)* payer; **I gave him my sweater in exchange for his gloves** je lui ai échangé mon pull contre ses gants; **I'll give you a good price for the table** je vous donnerai *ou* payerai un bon prix pour la table; **how much will you give me for it?** combien m'en donneras-tu?; **I would give a lot** *or* **a great deal to know...** je donnerais beaucoup pour savoir...

(**d**) *(transmit)* donner, passer; **I hope I don't give you my cold** j'espère que je ne vais pas te passer mon rhume

C. (**a**) *(cause)* donner, causer; *(headache)* donner; *(pleasure, surprise, shock)* faire; **the walk gave him an appetite** la promenade l'a mis en appétit *ou* lui a ouvert l'appétit; **the news gave me a shock** la nouvelle m'a fait un choc; **to give oneself trouble** se donner du mal

(**b**) *(impose → task)* imposer; (→ *punishment)* infliger; **the teacher gave us three tests this week** le professeur nous a donné trois interrogations cette semaine; **to give sb a black mark** infliger un blâme à qn; *Law* **he was given (a sentence of) fifteen years** il a été condamné à quinze ans de prison

(**c**) *(announce → verdict, judgment)* **the court gives its decision today** la cour prononce *ou* rend l'arrêt aujourd'hui; **the court gave the case against/for the management** la cour a décidé contre/en faveur de la direction; **given this third day of March** délivré le 3 mars; **given under my hand and seal** reçu par-devant moi et sous mon sceau; *Sport* **the umpire gave the batsman out** l'arbitre a déclaré le joueur hors jeu

(**d**) *(communicate → impression, order, signal)* donner; (→ *address, information)* donner, fournir; (→ *news, decision)* annoncer; **to give sb a message** communiquer un message à qn; **she gave her age as forty-five** elle a déclaré avoir quarante-cinq ans; **give her my love** embrassela pour moi; **he is to give his decision tomorrow** il devra faire connaître *ou* annoncer sa décision demain; **I gave a description of the suspect** j'ai donné *ou* fourni une description du suspect; **you gave me to believe he was trustworthy** vous m'avez laissé entendre qu'on pouvait lui faire confiance; **I was given to understand she was ill** on m'a donné à croire qu'elle était malade; **she gave no sign of life** elle n'a donné aucun signe de vie

(**e**) *(suggest, propose → explanation, reason)* donner, avancer; (→ *hint)* donner; **that's given me an idea** ça me donne une idée; **don't go giving him ideas!** ne va pas lui mettre des idées dans la tête!; **give us a clue** donne-nous un indice; **let me give you an example** laissez-moi vous donner un exemple; **don't give me any nonsense about missing your train!** ne me raconte pas que tu as raté ton train!; *Fam* **don't give me that (nonsense)!** ne me raconte pas d'histoires!

(**f**) *(admit, concede)* reconnaître, accorder; **she's certainly intelligent, I'll give you that** elle est très intelligente, ça, je te l'accorde; *Sport* **he gave me the game** il m'a concédé la partie

D. (**a**) *(utter → sound)* rendre, émettre; (→ *answer)* donner, faire; (→ *cry, sigh)* pousser; **he gave a laugh** il a laissé échapper un rire; **he gave a loud laugh** il a éclaté de rire; **give us a song** chantez-nous quelque chose

(**b**) *(make → action, gesture)* faire; **she gave them an odd look** elle leur a jeté *ou* lancé un regard curieux; **he gave her hand a squeeze** il lui a pressé la main; **she gave her hair a comb** elle s'est donné un coup de peigne; **he gave his face a wash** il s'est lavé le visage; **he gave the table a wipe** il a essuyé la table; **give me a kiss** *(gen)* fais-moi la bise; *(lover)* embrasse-moi; **I gave the boy a push** j'ai poussé le garçon; **the train gave a lurch** le train a cahoté; **she gave him a slap** elle lui a donné une claque; **she gave him a flirtatious smile** elle lui a adressé *ou* fait un sourire séducteur; **he gave an embarrassed smile** il a eu un sourire gêné

(**c**) *(perform in public → concert)* donner; (→ *lecture, speech)* faire; (→ *interview)* accorder; **that evening she gave the performance of a lifetime** ce soir-là elle était au sommet de son art

(**d**) *(hold → lunch, party, supper)* donner, organiser; **they gave a dinner for the professor** ils ont donné un dîner en l'honneur du professeur

(**e**) *(estimate the duration of)* donner, estimer; **I give him one week at most** je lui donne une semaine (au) maximum; **I'd give their marriage about a year if that** je donne un an maximum à leur mariage

(**f**) *Math (produce)* donner, faire; **17 minus 4**

gives 13 17 moins 4 font *ou* égalent 13; **that gives a total of 26** ça donne un total de 26

(**g**) *(idiom)* **to give way** *(ground)* s'affaisser; *(bridge, building, ceiling)* s'effondrer, s'affaisser; *(ladder, rope)* céder, (se) casser; **the ground gave way beneath** *or* **under our feet** le terrain s'est affaissé sous nos pieds; **her legs gave way (beneath her)** ses jambes se sont dérobées sous elle; **his health finally gave way** sa santé a fini par se détériorer *ou* se gâter; **their strength gave way** leurs forces leur ont manqué; **it's easier to give way to his demands than to argue** il est plus commode de céder à ses exigences que de lui résister; **don't give way if he cries** ne cède pas s'il pleure; **I gave way to tears/to anger** je me suis laissé aller à pleurer/ emporter par la colère; **he gave way to despair** il s'est abandonné au désespoir; **the fields gave way to factories** les champs ont fait place aux usines; **his joy gave way to sorrow** sa joie a fait place à la peine; **natural fibres have given way to synthetics** les fibres naturelles ont été remplacées par les synthétiques; **give way to vehicles on your right** *(sign)* priorité aux véhicules qui viennent de droite; **give way to pedestrians** *(sign)* priorité aux piétons; **give way** *(sign)* cédez le passage

2 *vi* (**a**) *(contribute)* donner; **please give generously** nous nous en remettons à votre générosité; **to give generously of one's time** donner beaucoup de son temps; *Prov* **it is better to give than to receive** donner vaut mieux que recevoir; **in any relationship you have to learn to give and take** dans toutes les relations, il faut apprendre à faire des concessions *ou* il faut que chacun y mette du sien; **to give as good as one gets** rendre coup pour coup

(**b**) *(collapse, yield → ground, wall)* s'affaisser; *(→ cloth, elastic)* se relâcher; *(→ person)* céder; **the fence gave beneath** *or* **under my weight** la barrière a cédé *ou* s'est affaissée sous mon poids; **something's got to give** quelque chose va lâcher

(**c**) *Am Fam (talk)* **now give!** accouche!, vide ton sac!

(**d**) *Am Fam* **what gives?** qu'est-ce qui se passe?❑

3 *n (of metal, wood)* élasticité *f*, souplesse *f*; **there's not enough give in this sweater** ce pull n'est pas assez ample

4 give or take *prep* à... près; **give or take a few days** à quelques jours près

►► ***give way sign*** signal *m* de priorité

►**give away** *vt sep* (**a**) *(hand over)* donner; *(as gift)* donner, faire cadeau de; *(prize)* distribuer; **it's so cheap they're practically giving it away** c'est tellement bon marché, c'est comme s'ils en faisaient cadeau; **you couldn't give them away** tu n'arriveras pas à t'en débarrasser (même si tu en faisais cadeau)

(**b**) *(bride)* conduire à l'autel

(**c**) *(throw away → chance, opportunity)* gâcher, gaspiller

(**d**) *(reveal → information)* révéler; *(→ secret)* révéler, trahir; **he didn't give anything away** il n'a rien dit

(**e**) *(betray)* trahir; **her accent gave her away** son accent l'a trahie; **no prisoner would give another prisoner away** aucun prisonnier n'en trahirait un autre; **to give oneself away** se trahir

(**f**) *Austr (renounce → habit)* renoncer à, abandonner; *(resign from → job)* quitter; *(→ position)* démissionner de

►**give back** *vt sep* (**a**) *(return)* rendre; *(property, stolen object)* restituer; **give the book back to her** rendez-lui le livre; **the store gave him his money back** le magasin l'a remboursé

(**b**) *(reflect → image, light)* refléter, renvoyer; *(→ sound)* renvoyer

►**give in 1** *vi (relent, yield)* céder; **to give in to sb/ sth** céder à qn/qch; **the country refused to give in to terrorist threats** le pays a refusé de céder aux menaces des terroristes

2 *vt sep (hand in → book, exam paper)* rendre; *(→ found object, parcel)* remettre; *(→ application, name)* donner

►**give off** *vt sep* (**a**) *(emit, produce → gas, smell)* émettre (**b**) *Bot (shoots)* former

►**give onto** *vt insep* donner sur

►**give out 1** *vt sep* (**a**) *(hand out)* distribuer

(**b**) *(emit → smell)* dégager; *(→ heat)* répandre; *(→ sound)* émettre, faire entendre

(**c**) *(make known)* annoncer, faire savoir; **the hospital gave out information on her condition to them** l'hôpital les a renseignés sur son état de santé; **it was given out that he was leaving** on a dit *ou* annoncé qu'il partait

2 *vi* (**a**) *(fail → machine)* tomber en panne; *(→ brakes)* lâcher; *(→ heart)* flancher; **the old car finally gave out** la vieille voiture a fini par rendre l'âme

(**b**) *(run out)* s'épuiser, manquer; **her strength was giving out** elle était à bout de forces, elle n'en pouvait plus; **his mother's patience gave out** sa mère a perdu patience; **my luck gave out** la chance m'a abandonné

(**c**) *Ir Fam (complain)* rouspéter; **he gave out to me because I was late** *(scolded)* il m'a enguirlandé parce que j'étais en retard

►**give out onto** *vt insep* donner sur

►**give over 1** *vt sep* (**a**) *(entrust)* donner, confier; **he gave the children over to his mother** il a confié les enfants à sa mère

(**b**) *(set aside)* donner, consacrer; *Admin* affecter; **the land was given over to agriculture** la terre a été consacrée à l'agriculture; **she gave herself over to helping the poor** elle s'est consacrée à l'aide aux pauvres

2 *vt insep Br Fam* cesser de❑, arrêter de❑; **give over crying!** cesse de pleurer!

3 *vi Br Fam* cesser❑, arrêter❑; **give over!** assez!, arrête!

►**give up 1** *vt sep* (**a**) *(renounce → habit)* renoncer à, abandonner; *(→ friend)* abandonner, délaisser; *(→ chair, place)* céder; *(→ activity)* cesser; **she'll never give him up** elle ne renoncera jamais à lui; **he's given up smoking** il a arrêté de fumer, il a renoncé au tabac; **I haven't given up the idea of going to China** je n'ai pas renoncé à l'idée d'aller en Chine; **he gave up his seat to the old woman** il a cédé sa place à la vieille dame; **don't give up hope** ne perdez pas espoir; **he was ready to give up his life for his country** il était prêt à mourir pour la patrie; **they gave up the game** *or* **the struggle** ils ont abandonné la partie; **we gave her brother up for dead** nous avons conclu que son frère était mort; **they gave the cause up for lost** ils ont considéré que c'était une cause perdue; **to give up the throne** renoncer au trône; **the doctors have given him up** les médecins disent qu'il est perdu

(**b**) *(resign from → job)* quitter; *(→ position)* démissionner de; **they gave up the restaurant business** ils se sont retirés de la restauration

(**c**) *(hand over → keys)* rendre, remettre; *(→ prisoner)* livrer; *(→ responsibility)* se démettre de; **the murderer gave himself up (to the police)** le meurtrier s'est rendu *ou* livré (à la police); **he gave his accomplices up to the police** il a dénoncé *ou* livré ses complices à la police

(**d**) *(applaud)* **give it up for...** je vous demande d'applaudir...

2 *vi* **I give up** *(in game, project)* je renonce; *(in guessing game)* je donne ma langue au chat; **we can't give up now!** on ne va pas laisser tomber maintenant!

►**give up on** *vt insep* **to give up on sb** *(stop waiting for)* renoncer à attendre qn; *(stop expecting something from)* ne plus rien attendre de qn; **I give up on him, he won't even try** j'abandonne, il ne fait pas le moindre effort

►**give up to** *vt sep* **to give oneself up to sth** se livrer à qch; **they gave themselves up to a life of pleasure** ils se sont livrés à une vie de plaisir; **he gave his life up to caring for the elderly** il a consacré sa vie à soigner les personnes âgées; **his mornings were given up to business** ses matinées étaient consacrées aux affaires

---

give-and-take *n* (**a**) *(compromise)* concessions *fpl* (mutuelles); **in a relationship there has to be some give-and-take** pour fonder une relation, il faut que chacun fasse des concessions *ou* que chacun y mette du sien

(**b**) *(in conversation)* échange *m*; **to encourage the give-and-take of ideas and opinions** favoriser l'échange d'idées

giveaway ['gɪvəˌweɪ] **1** *n* (**a**) *(free gift)* cadeau *m*; *Com* prime *f*, cadeau *m* publicitaire

(**b**) *Am Rad* jeu *m* radiophonique; *TV* jeu *m* télévisé

(**c**) *(revelation)* révélation *f* (involontaire); **her guilty expression was a dead giveaway** son air coupable l'a trahie; **the fact that he knew her name was a giveaway** le fait qu'il sache son nom était révélateur *ou* en disait long

2 *adj* (**a**) *(free)* gratuit; *(price)* dérisoire

(**b**) *Fam (revealing)* révélateur❑

►► *Am* ***giveaway program*** *Rad* jeu *m* radiophonique; *TV* jeu *m* télévisé

giveback ['gɪvbæk] *n Am Com* = restitution d'un acquis au terme d'une nouvelle négociation

given ['gɪvən] **1** *pp of* **give**

2 *adj* (**a**) *(specified)* donné; *(precise)* déterminé; **at a given moment** à un moment donné; **at any given time** à tout moment; **at a given point** à un point donné

(**b**) *(prone)* **to be given to sth** avoir une tendance à qch; **to be given to doing sth** être enclin à faire qch; **he's given to attacks of depression** il a des tendances dépressives; **I'm not given to telling lies** je n'ai pas l'habitude de mentir

(**c**) *(on official statement)* **given in Melbourne on the sixth day of March** fait à Melbourne le six mars

3 *prep* (**a**) *(considering)* étant donné; **given her age** étant donné son âge; **given the circumstances** étant donné les circonstances, les circonstances étant ce qu'elles sont

(**b**) *Math* soit; **given the rectangle ABCD** soit le rectangle ABCD

(**c**) *(idioms)* **given the chance** *or* **opportunity** si l'occasion se présentait; **she could be a good teacher, given the opportunity** elle ferait un bon professeur si l'occasion se présentait; **given the chance, I'd emigrate to Canada** si l'occasion se présentait, j'émigrerais au Canada

4 *n (sure fact)* fait *m*, acquis *m*, certitude *f*

5 given that *conj* étant donné que

►► *Am* ***given name*** prénom *m*

giver ['gɪvə(r)] *n (of blood, organ)* donneur (euse) *m,f*; *(of money)* donateur(trice) *m,f*

giving ['gɪvɪŋ] *adj (person)* généreux; **of a giving nature** d'une nature généreuse

Gîza ['giːzə] *n* Gizeh, Guizèh

gizmo ['gɪzməʊ] (*pl* **gizmos**) *n Am* gadget *m*, truc *m*

gizzard ['gɪzəd] *n* gésier *m*; *Fig* **it sticks in my gizzard** ça me reste en travers de la gorge

glabella [glə'belə] *n Anat* glabelle *f*

glacé ['glæseɪ] *adj* (**a**) *(cherries)* glacé, confit (**b**) *(leather, silk)* glacé (**c**) *Am (frozen)* glacé, gelé

►► ***glacé icing*** glaçage *m (d'un gâteau)*

glacial ['gleɪsjəl] *adj* (**a**) *(weather, wind)* glacial (**b**) *(manner, atmosphere)* glacial (**c**) *Geol (erosion, valley etc)* glaciaire (**d**) *Chem* cristallisé, en cristaux

►► ***glacial period*** période *f* glaciaire

glacially ['gleɪsjəlɪ] *adv* glacialement

glaciate ['gleɪsɪeɪt] **1** *vt (land)* couvrir de glaciers

2 *vi (of land)* se couvrir de glaciers

glaciated ['gleɪsɪeɪtɪd] *adj* glaciaire

►► ***glaciated valley*** vallée *f* glaciaire

glaciation [ˌgleɪsɪ'eɪʃən] *n* glaciation *f*

glacier ['glæsjə(r), *Am* 'gleɪʃə(r)] *n* glacier *m*

glaciofluvial [ˌgleɪsɪəʊ'fluːvɪəl] *adj* fluvioglaciaire

glaciolacustrine [ˌgleɪsɪəʊlæ'kʌstraɪn] *adj* glaciolacustre, glacio-lacustre

glaciological [ˌgleɪsɪə'lɒdʒɪkəl] *adj* glaciologique

glaciologist [ˌgleɪsɪ'ɒlədʒɪst] *n* glaciologue *mf*

glaciology [ˌgleɪsɪ'ɒlədʒɪ] *n* glaciologie *f*

glacis ['glæsɪs] (*pl* **inv** [-sɪz] *or* **glacises** ['glæsiːz]) *n* glacis *m*

glad [glæd] **1** *adj* (**a**) *(person)* heureux, content; **(I'm) glad you came** (je suis) heureux *ou* bien content que tu sois venu; **I'm glad you like him** je suis content que vous l'aimiez; **I'm feeling a lot better today – oh, I am glad!** je me sens beaucoup mieux aujourd'hui – j'en suis ravi!; **he's decided not to go – I'm glad about that** il a décidé de ne pas partir – tant mieux; **I was glad to hear the news** j'étais ravi d'apprendre la nouvelle; **he was only too glad to be asked** il n'attendait qu'une chose, c'est qu'on le lui demande; **I'd be only too glad to help** je ne demanderais pas mieux que d'aider; **could you do me a favour? – I'd be glad to** pourriez-vous me rendre service? – avec plaisir *ou* volontiers; **(I'm) glad to meet you!** enchanté!; **they were glad of the money** cet argent tombait à point nommé *ou* à pic; **we were glad of the opportunity to meet her** nous avons été heureux de pouvoir faire sa connaissance; **I was glad of your help** votre aide a été la bienvenue; **it makes my heart glad to hear him** cela me réjouit le cœur de l'entendre

(**b**) *Literary (news, occasion)* joyeux, heureux; *(laughter)* de bonheur; *(shout)* joyeux; **it's a glad day for all of us** c'est un jour de fête pour nous tous

(**c**) *Fam (idioms)* **to give sb the glad eye** faire les yeux doux à qn, faire de l'œil à qn; **to give sb the glad hand** serrer la main de qn avec de grands sourires *(souvent dans un but intéressé)*

2 *n Fam (gladiolus)* glaïeul ❑ *m*

►► *Fam* ***glad rags*** vêtements *mpl* chics ❑; **to put on one's glad rags** se mettre sur son trente et un, se saper

gladden ['glædən] *vt (person)* rendre heureux, réjouir; **it gladdens my heart to see them** cela me réjouit le cœur de les voir

glade [gleɪd] *n Literary* clairière *f*

glad-hand *vt Fam* **to glad-hand sb** serrer la main de qn avec de grands sourires ❑ *(souvent dans un but intéressé)*

gladiator ['glædɪeɪtə(r)] *n* gladiateur *m*

gladiatorial [,glædɪə'tɔːrɪəl] *adj* de gladiateurs; *Fig* **gladiatorial politics** = politique qui fait de la confrontation son moyen d'action

gladiolus [,glædɪ'əʊləs] *(pl* **gladioli** [-laɪ] *or* **gladioluses***)* *n* glaïeul *m*

gladly ['glædlɪ] *adv* avec plaisir, avec joie, de bon cœur

gladness ['glædnɪs] *n* contentement *m*, joie *f*

gladsome ['glædsəm] *adj Arch or Literary* joyeux, gai

Gladstone bag ['glædstən-] *n* = sacoche de voyage en cuir

glair [gleə(r)] *n* (**a**) *(egg white) & Med* glaire *f* (**b**) *(in bookbinding)* glairure *f*

glairy ['gleərɪ] *adj* glaireux

glam [glæm] *(pt & pp* **glammed**, *cont* **glamming***)* *adj Br Fam* glamour ❑ *(inv)*

►► ***glam rock*** glam rock *m*

►**glam up** *vt sep Fam* (**a**) *(person)* **to get glammed up** *(with clothes)* mettre ses belles fringues, se saper; *(with make-up)* se faire une beauté, se faire toute belle (**b**) *(building)* retaper; *(town)* embellir ❑

glamor *Am* = **glamour**

glamorization [,glæməraɪ'zeɪʃən] *n* idéalisation *f*

glamorize, -ise ['glæməraɪz] *vt* idéaliser, montrer *ou* présenter sous un jour séduisant; **the film glamorizes peasant life** le film idéalise la vie des paysans; **to glamorize war** présenter la guerre sous un jour attrayant; **a TV programme that glamorizes violence** une émission de télé qui rend la violence attrayante; **an advertising campaign that seeks to glamorize smoking** une campagne publicitaire qui cherche à redorer l'image des fumeurs

glamorless *Am* = **glamourless**

glamorous ['glæmərəs] *adj* (**a**) *(alluring → person)* séduisant, éblouissant; **a glamorous actress** une actrice éblouissante *ou* resplendissante; **glamorous dresses** robes *fpl* éblouissantes *ou* d'un chic inouï; **a glamorous grandmother** une grand-mère sophistiquée

(**b**) *(exciting → lifestyle)* brillant; *(→ career)* brillant, prestigieux; *(→ show)* splendide; *(→ team)* prestigieux; *(→ place)* chic; **the glamorous parts of the French Riviera** les endroits chics de la Côte d'Azur; **working in the film industry is not always glamorous** il n'y a pas que des métiers de prestige dans le cinéma

glamorously ['glæmərəslɪ] *adv* brillamment, de manière éblouissante

glamour, *Am* **glamor** ['glæmə(r)] **1** *n* (**a**) *(allure → of person)* charme *m*, fascination *f*; *(→ of appearance, dress)* élégance *f*, chic *m*

(**b**) *(excitement → of lifestyle, show)* éclat *m*, prestige *m*; **the novel captures all the glamour of London in the 1920s** le roman dépeint tout l'éclat du Londres des années vingt; **there isn't much glamour in my job** mon travail n'a rien de bien excitant *ou* passionnant

2 *comp* de charme

►► *Fam* ***glamour boy*** beau gosse *m*; *Fam* ***glamour girl*** pin-up ❑ *f inv*; *(model)* mannequin ❑ *m*; *Fam* ***glamour puss*** pin-up ❑ *f inv*; *St Exch* ***glamour stock*** valeur *f* vedette

glamourize = **glamorize**

glamourless, *Am* **glamorless** ['glæməlɪs] *adj (person)* sans charme, sans élégance, fade; *(life)* sans éclat, terne; *(job)* terne, peu intéressant

glamourous = **glamorous**

glance [glɑːns] **1** *vi* (**a**) *(look)* **to glance at sb/sth** jeter un coup d'œil (rapide) à qn/sur qch; **he glanced at his watch** il jeta un coup d'œil sur sa montre; **he glanced at her quickly** il lui jeta un rapide coup d'œil

(**b**) *(read quickly)* **she glanced through** *or* **over the letter** elle parcourut rapidement la lettre; **to glance through a book** feuilleter un livre; **to glance through a newspaper** lire un journal en diagonale, feuilleter un journal

(**c**) *(look in given direction)* **he glanced back** *or* **behind** il a jeté un coup d'œil en arrière; **she opened the door and glanced round the room** elle ouvrit la porte et jeta un coup d'œil autour de la pièce; **they glanced towards the door** leurs regards se sont tournés vers la porte

(**d**) *(gleam)* étinceler

2 *n* (**a**) *(look)* coup *m* d'œil, regard *m*; **to have** *or* **to take a glance at sb/sth** jeter un coup d'œil à qn/sur qch; **at first glance** au premier coup d'œil, à première vue; **I could tell** *or* **see at a glance** je m'en suis aperçu tout de suite; **one glance was enough** il m'a suffi d'un regard; **I didn't give it a second glance** je n'y ai guère prêté attention; **she walked away without a backward glance** elle est partie sans se retourner; **to give sb a sidelong glance** lancer un regard oblique à qn; **he cast an affectionate/anxious glance in her direction** il jeta un regard affectueux/inquiet dans sa direction

(**b**) *(gleam)* lueur *f*, éclat *m*; *(in water)* reflet *m*

►**glance away** *vi* détourner les yeux

►**glance off 1** *vi (arrow, bullet)* ricocher, faire ricochet; *(sword, spear)* être dévié, ricocher; **the arrow hit a tree and glanced off** la flèche a ricoché sur un arbre

2 *vt insep* **to glance off sth** *(of arrow, bullet)* ricocher sur qch; *(of sword, spear)* dévier sur qch

►**glance up** *vi* (**a**) *(look upwards)* regarder en l'air *ou* vers le haut

(**b**) *(from book)* lever les yeux; **he glanced up from (reading) his book** il leva les yeux de son livre

glancing ['glɑːnsɪŋ] *adj* (**a**) *(blow)* **he struck me a glancing blow** il m'asséna un coup oblique (**b**) *(gleaming → sunlight)* étincelant (**c**) *(indirect → allusion)* indirect, fortuit

gland [glænd] *n* (**a**) *Physiol* glande *f* (**b**) *Tech* presse-étoupe *m inv*

glandered ['glændəd] *adj Vet* morveux

glanders ['glændəz] *n (UNCOUNT) Vet* morve *f*

glandes ['glændiːz] *pl of* **glans**

glandiferous [glæn'dɪfərəs] *adj Bot* glandifère

glandless ['glændlɪs] *adj* (**a**) *Tech* sans garniture, sans presse-étoupe (**b**) *Biol* sans glande(s)

glandular ['glændjʊlə(r)] *adj* glandulaire, glanduleux

►► ***glandular fever*** *(UNCOUNT)* mononucléose *f* (infectieuse)

glans [glæns] *(pl* **glandes** ['glændiːz]*)* *n Anat* gland *m*

►► ***glans penis*** gland *m*

glare [gleə(r)] **1** *vi* (**a**) *(sun, light)* briller d'un éclat éblouissant; **the sun glared down from the cloudless sky** il faisait un soleil éclatant *ou* éblouissant dans un ciel sans nuages; **the sun glared down on them** un soleil de plomb les aveuglait

(**b**) *(person)* **to glare at sb** regarder qn avec colère; **they glared at each other** ils échangèrent un regard menaçant; **he glared angrily at me** il m'a lancé un regard furieux

2 *vt* **to glare hatred/defiance at sb** lancer un regard plein de haine/de défi à qn

3 *n* (**a**) *(light)* lumière *f* éblouissante *ou* aveuglante; *(of sun)* éclat *m*; **he stood in the glare of the headlights** il était pris dans la lumière (aveuglante) des phares

(**b**) *Fig* **politicians lead their lives in the (full) glare of publicity** la vie des hommes politiques est toujours sous les feux des projecteurs

(**c**) *(of anger)* regard *m* furieux; *(of contempt)* regard *m* méprisant; **she looked at him with a glare of contempt** elle lui a lancé un regard méprisant

(**d**) *Am (sheet of ice)* plaque *f* de verglas

►► *Comput* ***glare filter*** filtre *m* antireflet; *Am* ***glare ice*** verglas *m*; *Comput* ***glare screen*** écran *m* antireflet

glaring ['gleərɪŋ] *adj* (**a**) *(dazzling → light)* éblouissant, éclatant; *(→ car headlights)* éblouissant; *(→ sun)* aveuglant (**b**) *(bright → colour)* vif; *Pej* criard, voyant (**c**) *(angry)* furieux (**d**) *(obvious → error)* qui saute aux yeux, qui crève les yeux, patent; *(→ injustice, lie)* flagrant, criant; **a glaring abuse of public funds** un détournement manifeste des fonds publics; **a glaring omission** une omission flagrante

glaringly ['gleərɪŋlɪ] *adv* **it's glaringly obvious** ça crève les yeux

Glasgow ['glɑːzgəʊ] *n* Glasgow

►► *Scot Fam Hum* ***Glasgow handshake*** marron *m*, coup *m* de poing ❑; *Scot Fam Hum* ***Glasgow kiss*** coup *m* de boule

glasnost ['glæznɒst] *n* glasnost *f*

glass [glɑːs] **1** *n* (**a**) *(substance)* verre *m*; **made of glass** en verre; **a pane of glass** un carreau, une vitre; **these plants are grown under glass** ces plantes sont cultivées en serre; *Fam Boxing* **to have a glass jaw** avoir la mâchoire fragile ❑

(**b**) *(single piece → of window)* vitre *f*, carreau *m*; *(→ of car)* glace *f*, vitre *f*; *(→ of watch, lamp)* verre *m*

(**c**) *(vessel, contents)* verre *m*; **a glass of water/beer** un verre d'eau/de bière; **a glass of champagne** une coupe de champagne; **to sell wine by the glass** vendre le vin au verre; **to raise one's glass to sb** *(in toast)* lever son verre à qn

(**d**) *(in shop, museum)* vitrine *f*; **displayed under glass** exposé en vitrine

(**e**) *(glassware)* verrerie *f*

(**f**) *(telescope)* longue-vue *f*

(**g**) *(mirror)* **(looking) glass** glace *f*, miroir *m*

(**h**) *Opt (lens)* lentille *f*

(**i**) *(barometer)* baromètre *m*; **the glass is falling** le baromètre baisse

2 *comp (ornament, bottle)* en verre; *(door)* vitré; *(industry)* du verre

3 *vt (bookcase, porch)* vitrer; *(photograph)* mettre sous verre

4 **glasses** *npl* (**a**) *(spectacles)* lunettes *fpl*; **to wear glasses** porter des lunettes

(**b**) *(binoculars)* jumelles *fpl*

►► ***glass case*** *(for display)* vitrine *f*; ***glasses case*** *(for spectacles)* étui *m* à lunettes; ***glass ceiling*** = plafond de verre qui désigne métaphoriquement l'ensemble des facteurs qui empêchent les femmes de parvenir aux postes les plus élevés dans le monde professionnel; ***glass cloth*** essuie-verres *m inv*; ***glass cutting*** taille *f* du verre; ***glass eye*** œil *m* de verre; ***glass factory*** verrerie *f (usine)*; *Br* ***glass fibre***, *Am* ***glass fiber*** **1** *n* fibre *f* de verre **2** *adj* en fibre de verre; ***glass manufacturer*** verrier *m*; ***glass roof*** *(of station)* verrière *f*; ***glass slipper*** pantoufle *f* de verre; *Zool* ***glass snake*** serpent *m* de verre; ***glass wool*** laine *f* de verre

►**glass in** *vt sep (bookcase, porch)* vitrer; *(photograph)* mettre sous verre

'The Glass Menagerie' *Williams, Newman* 'La Ménagerie de verre'

glassblower ['glɑːs,bləʊə(r)] *n* souffleur *m (de verre)*

glassblowing ['glɑːs,bləʊɪŋ] *n* soufflage *m (du verre)*

glasscutter ['glɑːs,kʌtə(r)] *n* (**a**) *(person)* vitrier *m* (**b**) *(implement)* coupe-verre *m inv*, diamant *m*

glassful ['glɑːsfʊl] *n* (plein) verre *m*

glasshouse ['glɑːshaʊs, *pl* -haʊzɪz] *n* (**a**) *Br*

(greenhouse) serre *f*; *Prov* **people who live in glasshouses shouldn't throw stones** = il faut être sans défauts pour critiquer autrui (**b**) *Am (factory)* verrerie *f (usine)* (**c**) *Br Fam Mil slang (prison)* prison *f* militaire ❑, trou *m*

glassily ['glɑːsɪlɪ] *adv* d'un œil vitreux *ou* terne

glassine [glæ'siːn] *n* papier *m* cristal

glasspaper ['glɑːs,peɪpə(r)] **1** *n Br* papier *m* de verre

2 *vt* poncer au papier de verre

glassware ['glɑːsweə(r)] *n (glass objects)* verrerie *f*; *(tumblers)* verrerie *f*, gobeleterie *f*

glasswork ['glɑːswɜːk] *n (gen)* verrerie *f*; *(making windows)* vitrerie *f*

glassworks ['glɑːswɜːks] *(pl* **inv***)* *n* verrerie *f (usine)*

glasswort ['glɑːswɜːt] *n Bot (marsh samphire)* salicorne *f*; *(saltwort)* kali *m*

glassy ['glɑːsɪ] *(compar* **glassier**, *superl* **glassiest***)* *adj* (**a**) *(eye, expression)* vitreux, terne (**b**) *(smooth → surface)* uni, lisse; **a glassy sea** une mer d'huile

glassy-eyed *adj* à l'œil terne *ou* vitreux; **to be glassy-eyed** avoir le regard vitreux *ou* terne; **he looked at me glassy-eyed** il me fixa d'un œil vitreux

Glastonbury ['glæstənbərɪ] *n* Glastonbury; **the Glastonbury Festival** = festival de musique pop en plein air attirant chaque année un très grand nombre de jeunes gens

Glaswegian [glæz'wiːdʒjən] **1** *n* (**a**) *(inhabitant)* habitant(e) *m,f* de Glasgow; *(native)* originaire *mf* de Glasgow (**b**) *(dialect)* dialecte *m* de Glasgow

2 *adj* de Glasgow

glauberite ['glaʊbəraɪt] *n Miner* glaubérite *f*

glaucium ['glɔːsɪəm] *n Bot* glaucière *f*, glaucienne *f*

glaucoma [glɔː'kəʊmə] *n (UNCOUNT)* glaucome *m*; **to have glaucoma** avoir un glaucome

glauconite ['glɔːkənaɪt] *n Miner* glauconie *f*

glaucous ['glɔːkəs] *adj Literary* glauque

glaze [gleɪz] **1** *vt* (**a**) *(floor, tiles)* vitrifier; *(pottery, china)* vernisser; *(leather, silk)* glacer (**b**) *(photo, painting)* glacer (**c**) *Culin* glacer (**d**) *(window)* vitrer

2 *n* (**a**) *(on pottery)* vernis *m*; *(on floor, tiles)* vernis *m*, enduit *m* vitrifié; *(on cotton, silk)* glacé *m* (**b**) *(on painting, on paper, photo)* glacé *m*, glacis *m* (**c**) *Culin* glace *f* (**d**) *Am (ice)* verglas *m*

►► *Br* ***glaze ice*** verglas *m*

►**glaze over** *vi* **his eyes glazed over** ses yeux sont devenus vitreux

glazed [gleɪzd] *adj* (**a**) *(floor, tiles)* vitrifié; *(pottery)* vernissé, émaillé; *(leather, silk)* glacé (**b**) *(photo, painting)* glacé (**c**) *Culin* glacé (**d**) *(window)* vitré; *(picture)* sous verre (**e**) *(eyes)* vitreux, terne; **there was a glazed look in her eyes** elle avait le regard vitreux *ou* absent

glazier ['gleɪzjə(r)] *n* vitrier *m*

glazing ['gleɪzɪŋ] *n* (**a**) *(of pottery)* vernissage *m*; *(of floor, tiles)* vitrification *f*; *(of leather, silk)* glaçage *m* (**b**) *Culin (process)* glaçage *m*; *(substance)* glace *f* (**c**) *(fitting of windows)* pose *f* des vitres (**d**) *(UNCOUNT) (windows)* vitrerie *f*

GLC [,dʒiːel'siː] *n Formerly (abbr* **Greater London Council***)* = [illegible] administratif du grand Londres

gleam [gliːm] **1** *vi* (**a**) *(metal, polished surface)* luire, reluire; *(stronger)* briller; *(cat's eyes)* luire; *(water)* miroiter (**b**) *Fig* **her eyes gleamed with anticipation/mischief** ses yeux brillaient d'espoir/de malice

2 *n* (**a**) *(on surface)* lueur *f*, miroitement *m* (**b**) *Fig* lueur *f*; **a gleam of hope** une lueur d'espoir; **she had a strange gleam in her eye** il y avait une lueur étrange dans son regard; *Hum* **when you were just a gleam in your father's eye** bien avant ta naissance

gleaming ['gliːmɪŋ] *adj (metal)* luisant, brillant; *(furniture)* reluisant; *(kitchen)* étincelant

glean [gliːn] *vt* (**a**) *(collect → information, news)* glaner, grappiller; **I couldn't glean much from the brochure** je n'ai pas pu tirer grand-chose de la brochure (**b**) *Agr* glaner

gleaner ['gliːnə(r)] *n* glaneur(euse) *m,f*

gleanings ['gliːnɪŋz] *npl* (**a**) *(information)* bribes *fpl* de renseignements (glanées çà et là) (**b**) *Agr* glanure *f*, glanures *fpl*

glebe [gliːb] *n* (**a**) *Literary* glèbe *f*, terre *f* (**b**) *Br Rel* = terres faisant partie d'un bénéfice ecclésiastique

glee [gliː] *n* (**a**) *(joy)* joie *f*, allégresse *f*; *(malicious pleasure)* jubilation *f*; **to jump up and down with glee** sauter de joie; **with great glee** avec allégresse; **she announced it with some glee** elle l'a annoncé avec un malin plaisir (**b**) *Mus* chant *m* a cappella *(à plusieurs voix)*

►► *Am* ***glee club*** chorale *f*

gleeful ['gliːfʊl] *adj* joyeux, radieux; *(maliciously)* plein d'une joie malicieuse

gleefully ['gliːfʊlɪ] *adv* joyeusement, avec allégresse *ou* joie; *(maliciously)* avec une joie malicieuse

gleet [gliːt] *n* (**a**) *Med* écoulement *m* (de l'urètre), goutte *f* militaire (**b**) *Arch (pus)* pus *m*

glen [glen] *n* vallon *m*, = vallée étroite et encaissée en Écosse ou en Irlande

Glencoe [glen'kəʊ] *n* = vallée de l'ouest de l'Écosse où, en 1692, le clan des Campbell massacra, avec l'aide des Anglais, celui des MacDonald

Gleneagles [glen'iːgəlz] *n* = hôtel en Écosse possédant de célèbres terrains de golf

glengarry [glen'gærɪ] *n Scot* **glengarry (bonnet)** = béret écossais

glib [glɪb] *adj (answer, excuse)* (trop) facile, désinvolte; *(lie)* éhonté, désinvolte; **he's rather too glib** il parle trop facilement, il est trop volubile; **a glib talker** *(as salesman)* un beau parleur; **he has a glib tongue** il a la langue bien pendue

glibly ['glɪblɪ] *adv (talk, argue, reply)* avec aisance, facilement; *(lie)* avec désinvolture, sans sourciller

glibness ['glɪbnɪs] *n* (**a**) *(of person)* facilité *f* de parole (**b**) *(of argument, excuse)* facilité *f*, désinvolture *f*

glide [glaɪd] **1** *vi* (**a**) *(gen)* glisser; *(person)* **to glide in/out** *(noiselessly)* entrer/sortir sans bruit; *(gracefully)* entrer/sortir avec grâce; *(stealthily)* entrer/sortir furtivement; **the swans glided across the lake** les cygnes traversaient le lac avec grâce *ou* glissaient sur le lac; **the clouds glided across the sky** les nuages passaient dans le ciel; **the boat glided silently down the river** le bateau glissait sans bruit sur la rivière *ou* descendait la rivière sans bruit; **the actress glided majestically into the room** la comédienne entra dans la salle d'un pas majestueux; **the motorcade glided past** le cortège de voitures passa sans bruit

(**b**) *Fig (time, weeks)* **to glide by** s'écouler

(**c**) *Aviat* planer; *(in glider)* faire du vol à voile; **to go gliding** faire du vol à voile

(**d**) *(in skating, skiing)* glisser

2 *vt* (faire) glisser

3 *n* (**a**) *(gen)* glissement *m*

(**b**) *(in dance)* glissade *f*

(**c**) *Mus* port *m* de voix; *(for trombone)* piston *m*

(**d**) *(of glider)* vol *m* plané; *(of aircraft)* descente *f* en (vol) plané

(**e**) *Ling (in diphthong)* glissement *m*; *(between two vowels)* semi-voyelle *f* de transition

►► *Aviat* ***glide path, glide slope*** ligne *f* d'approche

glider ['glaɪdə(r)] *n* (**a**) *Aviat* [illegible] (**b**) *Am* *(swing)* balancelle *f*

►► ***glider pilot*** pilote *m* de planeur

gliding ['glaɪdɪŋ] *n (sport)* vol à voile

►► ***gliding club*** club *m* de vol à voile

glimmer ['glɪmə(r)] **1** *vi (moonlight, candle)* jeter une faible lueur, luire faiblement; *(water)* miroiter

2 *n* (**a**) *(of light)* (faible) lueur *f*; *(of water)* miroitement *m* (**b**) *Fig* **a glimmer of hope/interest** une (faible) lueur d'espoir/d'intérêt; **not a glimmer of interest** pas le moindre intérêt; **they haven't got the merest glimmer of a chance** ils n'ont pas l'ombre d'une chance

glimmering ['glɪmərɪŋ] **1** *adj (water)* miroitant; **a glimmering light** une faible lueur

2 *n (of light)* (faible) lueur *f*; *(of water)* miroitement *m*

glimpse [glɪmps] **1** *vt* entrevoir, entrapercevoir; *Literary* **he had glimpsed death** il avait entrevu la mort

2 *n* **to catch a glimpse of sth** entrevoir *ou* entrapercevoir qch; **she had only caught a glimpse of her assailant** elle n'avait fait qu'entrevoir son assaillant; **a glimpse of the future** un aperçu de ce que sera le futur

glint [glɪnt] **1** *vi* (**a**) *(knife)* étinceler, miroiter; *(water)* miroiter; **the blade glinted in the sunlight** la lame miroita au soleil (**b**) *Fig (eyes)* étinceler

2 *n* (**a**) *(of light → flash)* éclair *m*; *(→ continuous)* scintillement *m*; *(of knife)* reflet *m* (**b**) *Fig* **there was a strange glint in his eye** il y avait une lueur étrange dans son regard; **"perhaps not", he said, with a glint in his eye** "peut-être que non", dit-il, une lueur dans le regard; **a glint of humour/anger** une lueur d'humour/de colère

glioma [glaɪ'əʊmə] *n Med* gliome *m*

gliomatosis [,glaɪəʊmə'təʊsɪs] *n Med* gliomatose *f*

gliosis [glaɪ'əʊsɪs] *n Med* gliose *f*

glissade [glɪ'sɑːd] **1** *vi* (**a**) *(in climbing)* glisser, descendre en ramasse (**b**) *(in dance)* faire une glissade

2 *n* glissade *f*

glissando [glɪ'sændəʊ] *(pl* **glissandos** *or* **glissandi** [-diː]*)* *n* glissando *m*

glisten ['glɪsən] *vi* luire, miroiter; **his eyes glistened with tears** des larmes brillaient dans ses yeux; **dewdrops glistened in the grass** des gouttes de rosée luisaient dans l'herbe; **his forehead glistened with sweat** la sueur perlait sur son front

glistening ['glɪsənɪŋ] *adj* luisant

glister ['glɪstə(r)] *vi Arch or Literary* luire, miroiter

glitch [glɪtʃ] *n Fam (in plan)* pépin *m*; *(in machine)* = signal indiquant une baisse de tension du courant

glitter ['glɪtə(r)] **1** *vi* (**a**) *(bright object)* étinceler, scintiller, miroiter; *(jewel)* chatoyer, étinceler; *(metal)* reluire; **her fingers glittered with jewels** ses doigts brillaient de l'éclat des bijoux; *Prov* **all that glitters is not gold** tout ce qui brille n'est pas or (**b**) *(eyes)* briller

2 *n* (**a**) *(of object)* scintillement *m* (**b**) *Fig (of occasion)* éclat *m*, splendeur *f* (**c**) *(decoration, make-up)* paillettes *fpl*

glitterati [,glɪtə'rɑːtiː] *npl Fam* **the glitterati** le beau monde

glittering ['glɪtərɪŋ] *adj* (**a**) *(jewels)* scintillant, étincelant, brillant (**b**) *(glamorous)* éclatant, resplendissant; **the glittering world of show-business** le monde fascinant du showbusiness

►► *Am* ***glittering generality*** lieu *m* commun, platitude *f*

glittery ['glɪtərɪ] *adj* (**a**) *(light)* scintillant, brillant (**b**) *Pej (jewellery)* clinquant; *(make-up, decor)* voyant, tape-à-l'œil *(inv)*

glitz [glɪts] *n Fam* tape-à-l'œil *m inv*, clinquant ❑ *m*; **Hollywood glitz** le clinquant d'Hollywood

glitzy ['glɪtsɪ] *(compar* **glitzier**, *superl* **glitziest***)* *adj Fam* tape-à-l'œil *(inv)*; **the premiere was one of the year's glitziest occasions** la première fut l'un des événements les plus tape-à-l'œil de l'année

gloaming ['gləʊmɪŋ] *n Scot or Literary* crépuscule *m*; **in the gloaming** au crépuscule

gloat [gləʊt] **1** *vi* exulter, se délecter, jubiler; **don't gloat** ne te réjouis pas; **to gloat over sth** se réjouir de qch; **they gloated over their treasures** ils dévoraient leurs trésors des yeux; **he gloated over his success** son succès l'enivrait *ou* le faisait jubiler; **she gloated over the downfall of her enemy** elle se réjouissait de la chute de son ennemi

2 *n* exultation *f*, jubilation *f*; **to have a gloat** exulter

gloating ['gləʊtɪŋ] *adj (smile, look)* triomphant

gloatingly ['gləʊtɪŋlɪ] *adv* avec exultation, avec jubilation; *(over defeated enemy)* triomphalement

glob [glɒb] *n* globule *m*, (petite) boule *f*; **a glob of spittle** un crachat

global ['gləʊbəl] *adj* (**a**) *(worldwide)* mondial, planétaire (**b**) *(overall → system, view)* global

►► *Mktg* ***global audience*** audience *f* globale; *Fin* ***global banking*** banque *f* universelle; *Fin* ***global bond*** obligation *f* multimarchés; *Comput* ***global change*** changement *m* global; ***global custody*** conservation *f* globale; *Ecol* ***Global Environment Monitoring System*** système *m*

gla–glo

mondial de surveillance continue de l'environnement; *Fin* **global equities market** marché *m* mondial des actions; **global finance** la finance internationale; *Com* **global market** marché *m* global *ou* international; *Mktg* **global marketing** marketing *m* global *ou* international; *Com* **global marketplace** marché *m* global *ou* international; *Mktg* **global player** acteur *m* international; *Comput* **global search and replace** recherche *f* et remplacement *m* global; **global village** village *m* planétaire; **global warming** réchauffement *m* de la planète

globalism ['gləʊbəlɪzəm] *n* mondialisme *m*

globalist ['gləʊbəlɪst] *n* mondialiste *mf*

globalization [,gləʊbəlaɪ'zeɪʃən] *n* (**a**) *(making worldwide)* mondialisation *f* (**b**) *(generalization)* globalisation *f*

globalize, -ise ['gləʊbəlaɪz] *vt* (**a**) *(make worldwide)* rendre mondial, mondialiser; **a globalized conflict** un conflit mondial (**b**) *(generalize)* globaliser

globally ['gləʊbəlɪ] *adv* (**a**) *(worldwide)* mondialement, à l'échelle planétaire; **the problem of over-population must be dealt with globally** on doit résoudre le problème de la surpopulation à l'échelle planétaire (**b**) *(generally)* globalement

globe [gləʊb] **1** *n* (**a**) *Geog* globe *m* (terrestre), terre *f*; **all over the globe** *(surface)* sur toute la surface du globe; *(in all parts)* dans le monde entier (**b**) *(with map)* globe *m*, mappemonde *f* (**c**) *(spherical object)* globe *m*, sphère *f*; *(as lampshade)* globe *m*; *(as goldfish bowl)* bocal *m*; *(of eye)* globe *m* (**d**) *Austr & NZ (bulb)* ampoule *f (électrique)*

2 globes *npl Fam (breasts)* nichons *mpl*

▸▸ **globe artichoke** artichaut *m*; **globe lightning** éclair *m* en boule; **Globe Theatre** = théâtre de Londres où furent jouées pour la première fois les pièces de Shakespeare; détruit au XVIIème siècle, il est aujourd'hui reconstruit à l'identique

globe-fish *n* poisson-globe *m*

globe-shaped *adj* sphérique, en forme de sphère

globetrotter ['gləʊb,trɒtə(r)] *n* globe-trotter *mf*

globetrotting ['gləʊb,trɒtɪŋ] **1** *n (UNCOUNT)* voyages *mpl* aux quatre coins du monde

2 *adj* qui voyage beaucoup

globin ['gləʊbɪn] *n Biol & Chem* globine *f*

globoid ['gləʊbɔɪd] *adj* globique

▸▸ *Tech* **globoid worm** vis *f* globique

globular ['glɒbjʊlə(r)] *adj (globe-shaped)* globulaire; *(composed of globules)* globuleux

▸▸ *Astron* **globular cluster** amas *m* globulaire

globule ['glɒbju:l] *n* (**a**) *(of fat)* globule *m*; *(of wax, molten metal)* gouttelette *f* (**b**) *Astron* globule *m* (de Bok)

globulin ['glɒbjʊlɪn] *n* globuline *f*

globulous ['glɒbjʊləs] *adj (composed of globules)* globuleux

glockenspiel ['glɒkən,ʃpi:l] *n* glockenspiel *m*

glom [glɒm] *vt Am Fam (seize)* arracher ❑

▸**glom onto** *vt insep Am Fam* (**a**) *(seize)* arracher ❑ (**b**) *(catch sight of)* apercevoir ❑

glomerate ['glɒmərеɪt] *adj Bot* glomérulaire

glomerulonephritis [glɒ,merələʊnɪ'fraɪtɪs] *n Med* glomérulopathie *f*

glomerulus [glɒ'merʊləs] *(pl* **glomeruli** [-laɪ]*)* *n Anat* glomérule *m*

gloom [glu:m] **1** *n (UNCOUNT)* (**a**) *(darkness)* obscurité *f*, ténèbres *fpl*; **I could just make out a figure through the gloom** je distinguais à peine une silhouette dans l'obscurité *ou* les ténèbres

(**b**) *(despondency)* tristesse *f*, mélancolie *f*; **the news filled me with gloom** la nouvelle me plongea dans la consternation; **the announcement cast a gloom over the meeting** l'annonce jeta un froid sur la réunion; **gloom fell over the household** un voile de tristesse s'abattit sur la maison; **the news is all doom and gloom these days** les nouvelles sont des plus sombres ces temps-ci; **there is gloom in the City** la Bourse de Londres est pessimiste

2 *vi (person)* être mélancolique, broyer du noir

gloomily ['glu:mɪlɪ] *adv* sombrement, mélancoliquement, tristement; **he looked around him gloomily** il regarda autour de lui d'un air sombre *ou* morose

gloominess ['glu:mɪnɪs] *n* (**a**) *(darkness)* obscurité *f*, ténèbres *fpl*; **through the gloominess I could just see that it was him** dans l'obscurité j'arrivais tout juste à le reconnaître (**b**) *(despondency)* tristesse *f*, mélancolie *f*

gloomy ['glu:mɪ] *(compar* **gloomier,** *superl* **gloomiest**) *adj* (**a**) *(person → depressed)* triste, mélancolique; *(→ morose)* sombre, lugubre; **to feel gloomy** broyer du noir, avoir le cafard; **don't look so gloomy** ne prends pas cet air malheureux

(**b**) *(pessimistic → prediction, outlook)* sombre; *(→ news)* déprimant; **she always takes a gloomy view of things** elle voit toujours tout en noir; **gloomy thoughts** de noires pensées *fpl*; **the future looks gloomy** l'avenir se présente sous des couleurs sombres; **he paints a gloomy view of life** sa vision de la vie est assez noire

(**c**) *(sky)* obscur, sombre; *(weather)* morne, triste; *(room)* lugubre; **to become gloomy** s'assombrir

(**d**) *(place, landscape)* morne, lugubre

glop [glɒp] *n Am Fam* (**a**) *(gooey matter)* matière *f* visqueuse ❑; *(small blob)* globule ❑ *m*, (petite) boule ❑ *f* (**b**) *(sentimentality)* mièvrerie ❑ *f*

glorification [,glɔ:rɪfɪ'keɪʃən] *n* (**a**) *Rel* glorification *f* (**b**) *(of hero, writer)* exaltation *f* (**c**) *(of war, violence)* glorification *f*

glorified ['glɔ:rɪfaɪd] *adj* **he's called an engineer but he's really just a glorified mechanic** on a beau l'appeler ingénieur, il n'est que mécanicien, il n'a d'ingénieur que le nom, en réalité c'est un mécanicien; **they call it a health club but it's just a glorified swimming pool** en fait de centre de remise en forme, il ne s'agit que d'une vulgaire piscine; **it's just a glorified motor scooter** ce n'est qu'un scooter amélioré

glorify ['glɔ:rɪfaɪ] *(pt & pp* **glorified**) *vt* (**a**) *Rel* glorifier, rendre gloire à (**b**) *(praise → hero, writer)* exalter (**c**) *(war, violence)* glorifier, faire l'apologie de; **the film glorifies war** le film glorifie la guerre *ou* fait l'apologie de la guerre

gloriole ['glɔ:rɪəʊl] *n* gloire *f*, auréole *f*, nimbe *m*

glorious ['glɔ:rɪəs] *adj* (**a**) *(illustrious → reign, saint, victory)* glorieux; *(→ hero)* glorieux, illustre; *(→ deed)* glorieux, éclatant

(**b**) *(splendid, beautiful)* resplendissant, radieux; *(weather, day)* splendide, superbe, magnifique; *(colours)* superbe; **glorious in her youth and beauty** resplendissante de jeunesse et de beauté

(**c**) *(excellent)* magnifique, splendide; *(holiday, party)* merveilleux, sensationnel; **what glorious weather!** quel temps superbe!

▸▸ *Br Hist* **the Glorious Revolution** la Glorieuse Révolution; **the Glorious Twelfth** *(celebration)* = célébration par les unionistes d'Irlande du Nord de la victoire des protestants sur les catholiques à la Boyne, le 12 juillet 1690; *Hunting* = date d'ouverture de la chasse à la grouse (le 12 août)

THE GLORIOUS REVOLUTION

Face à la politique religieuse menée par le roi catholique Jacques II, ses adversaires protestants firent appel à Guillaume d'Orange pour le renverser, en 1688. Jacques II ayant fui en France, le Parlement proclama son abdication et couronna sa fille Marie conjointement à Guillaume en 1689.

gloriously ['glɔ:rɪəslɪ] *adv* glorieusement

glory ['glɔ:rɪ] *(pl* **glories,** *pt & pp* **gloried**) *n* (**a**) *(honour, fame)* gloire *f*; *(magnificence)* magnificence *f*, éclat *m*; **to be covered in glory** être couvert de gloire; **the athletes get all the glory** ce sont les athlètes qui remportent toute la gloire; **a garden at the height of its glory** un jardin au plus beau moment; **to have one's hour of glory** avoir son heure de gloire

(**b**) *(splendour)* gloire *f*, splendeur *f*; **the glory of a midsummer's day** la splendeur d'un jour au cœur de l'été; **the glories of the Irish countryside** les splendeurs de la campagne irlandaise; **in all her glory** dans toute sa splendeur *ou* gloire; **Hollywood in all its glory** Hollywood dans toute sa splendeur

(**c**) *(masterpiece)* gloire *f*, joyau *m*; **the palace is one of the greatest glories of the age** le palais est un des joyaux *ou* des chefs-d'œuvre de cette époque

(**d**) *Rel* **to give glory to God** rendre gloire à Dieu; **Christ in glory** le Christ en majesté *ou* en gloire; **to the greater glory of God** pour la plus grande gloire de Dieu; *Fam* **glory be!** mon Dieu!

(**e**) *Euph (death)* **to go to glory** passer de vie à trépas; **to send sb to glory** expédier qn ad patres

(**f**) *(halo → of saint)* gloire *f*

▸▸ **glory hole** *Naut (locker)* petit placard *m*; *(storeroom)* soute *f*; *Br Fam (cupboard)* débarras ❑ *m*; *(untidy place)* capharnaüm ❑ *m*

▸**glory in** *vt insep* **to glory in sth/doing sth** se glorifier de *ou* s'enorgueillir de qch/de faire qch; **he glories in it** il s'en glorifie, il en est très fier; **she was glorying in her new-found freedom** elle jouissait de *ou* elle savourait sa nouvelle liberté; **he glories in the title of King of Hollywood** il se donne le titre ronflant de roi d'Hollywood

Glos *(written abbr* **Gloucestershire**) Gloucestershire *m*

gloss [glɒs] **1** *n* (**a**) *(sheen)* lustre *m*, brillant *m*, éclat *m*; *(on paper, photo)* glacé *m*, brillant *m*; *(on furniture)* vernis *m*

(**b**) *(appearance)* apparence *f*, vernis *m*; **a gloss of politeness/respectability** un vernis de politesse/de respectabilité

(**c**) *(charm)* charme *m*, attrait *m*; **to take the gloss off sth** gâcher *ou* gâter qch; **the idea/victory has lost some of its gloss** l'idée/la victoire a perdu une partie de son charme *ou* attrait

(**d**) *(annotation, paraphrase)* glose *f*, commentaire *m*

(**e**) *(paint)* peinture *f* brillante

2 *vt* (**a**) *(paper)* satiner, glacer; *(metal)* faire briller, lustrer

(**b**) *(paint)* laquer

(**c**) *(explain, paraphrase)* gloser

▸▸ **gloss finish** *(painted)* brillant *m*; *Phot* glaçage *m*; **gloss paint** peinture *f* brillante

▸**gloss over** *vt insep* (**a**) *(minimize → failure, shortcomings, mistake)* glisser sur, passer sur, atténuer

(**b**) *(hide → truth, facts)* dissimuler, passer sous silence

glossary ['glɒsərɪ] *(pl* **glossaries**) *n* glossaire *m*

glossematics [,glɒsɪ'mætɪks] *n (UNCOUNT)* glossématique *f*

glosseme ['glɒsi:m] *n Ling* glossème *m*

glossina ['glɒsɪnə] *n Entom* glossine *f*, mouche *f* tsé-tsé

glossiness ['glɒsɪnɪs] *n* lustre *m*, brillant *m*, éclat *m*

glossitis [glɒ'saɪtɪs] *n Med* glossite *f*

glossodynia [,glɒsəʊ'daɪnɪə] *n Med* glossodynie *f*

glossographer [glɒ'sɒgrəfə(r)] *n* glossographe *mf*

glossography [glɒ'sɒgrəfɪ] *n* glossographie *f*

glossolalia [,glɒsə'leɪlɪə] *n* glossolalie *f*

glossology [glɒ'sɒlədʒɪ] *n* glossologie *f*

glossopharyngeal [glɒsəʊ'færɪn'dʒi:əl] *adj* glosso-pharyngien; **glossopharyngeal nerve** (nerf *m*) glosso-pharyngien *m*

glossy ['glɒsɪ] *(compar* **glossier,** *superl* **glossiest,** *pl* **glossies**) **1** *adj* (**a**) *(shiny → fur)* lustré, luisant; *(→ hair)* brillant; *(→ leather, satin)* lustré, luisant, glacé; *(→ leaves)* luisant; *(surface → polished)* brillant, poli; *(→ painted)* brillant, laqué

(**b**) *Fig (display, presentation, spectacle)* brillant, scintillant, *Pej* clinquant

(**c**) *(photo)* glacé, sur papier glacé; *(paper)* glacé

2 *n Fam Journ* magazine ❑ *m (sur papier glacé)*; *(women's magazine)* magazine *m* féminin de luxe ❑; **the glossies** la presse féminine de luxe

▸▸ *Orn* **glossy ibis** ibis *m* falcinelle; **glossy magazine** magazine *m (sur papier glacé)*

glottal ['glɒtəl] *adj* (**a**) *Anat* glottique (**b**) *Ling* glottal

▸▸ *Ling* **glottal stop** coup *m* de glotte

glottis ['glɒtɪs] *n Anat* glotte *f*

glottochronology [,glɒtəʊkrə'nɒlədʒɪ] *n Ling* glottochronologie *f*

Gloucestershire ['glɒstə,ʃɪə(r)] *n* le Gloucestershire, = comté dans le sud-ouest de l'Angleterre; **in Gloucestershire** dans le Gloucestershire

glove [glʌv] **1** *n* gant *m*; **I take size 7 in gloves** je prends du 7 pour les gants, je gante du 7; **to put on one's gloves** mettre ses gants, se ganter; **it fits like a glove** ça me/te/lui/*etc* va comme un gant; **the gloves are off** plus la peine de prendre des gants; **once the campaign started the gloves were off!** une fois la campagne partie, plus question de prendre des gants *ou* tous les coups étaient permis!

2 *vt* ganter

►► *Aut & Nucl* ***glove box*** boîte *f* à gants; *Aut* ***glove compartment*** boîte *f* à gants; ***glove counter, glove department*** *(in large store)* rayon *m* des gants, ganterie *f*; ***glove factory*** ganterie *f* *(usine)*; ***glove maker*** gantier(ère) *m,f*; *Br* ***glove puppet*** marionnette *f* *(à gaine)*; ***glove shop*** ganterie *f* *(magasin)*

gloved [glʌvd] *adj* ganté

gloveless ['glʌvlɪs] *adj* sans gants

glover ['glʌvə(r)] *n* gantier(ère) *m,f*

glow [gləʊ] **1** *vi* (**a**) *(embers, heated metal)* rougeoyer; *(sky, sunset)* s'embraser, flamboyer; *(jewel)* briller, rutiler; **the cigarette glowed red in the dark** la cigarette rougeoyait dans l'obscurité

(**b**) *(person)* rayonner; *(eyes)* briller, flamboyer; **to glow with health** éclater *ou* rayonner de santé; **her face glowed in the cold wind** elle avait le visage rougi par le vent; **to glow with pleasure** rayonner de plaisir; **to be glowing with health** être rayonnant de santé; **his cheeks were glowing** il avait les joues en feu; **his words made her glow with pride** ses mots la firent rayonner de fierté

2 *n* (**a**) *(of fire, embers)* rougeoiement *m*; *(of heated metal)* lueur *f*; *(of sky, sunset)* embrasement *m*, flamboiement *m*; *(of sun)* feux *mpl*; *(of colours, jewel)* éclat *m*; **it gives off a blue glow** cela émet une lumière bleue

(**b**) *(of complexion)* **to have a healthy glow in one's cheeks** avoir les joues bien rouges; **glow of health** bonne mine *f*; **a glow of pleasure** une rougeur de plaisir

(**c**) *Fig* *(warm feeling)* **it gave him a glow of pride** cela le faisait rayonner d'orgueil; **he felt a warm glow spread over him as the whisky went down** il sentit une sensation de chaleur dans tout le corps après avoir bu le whisky; **it gives you a warm glow** *(news, scene etc)* ça vous fait chaud au cœur

►► ***glow plug*** *(in engine)* bougie *f* de préchauffage

glower ['glaʊə(r)] *vi* avoir l'air furieux, lancer des regards furieux; **to glower at sb** *(angrily)* lancer à qn un regard noir; *(threateningly)* jeter à qn un regard menaçant; **she sat glowering in a corner** elle restait assise dans un coin, l'air furieux

glowering ['glaʊərɪŋ] *adj (expression)* mauvais, méchant, hostile; *(person)* à l'air mauvais *ou* méchant

gloweringly ['glaʊərɪŋlɪ] *adv* d'un air menaçant

glowing ['gləʊɪŋ] *adj* (**a**) *(fire, embers)* rougeoyant; *(heated metal)* incandescent; *(sky, sunset)* radieux, flamboyant; *(jewel)* brillant

(**b**) *(complexion)* éclatant; *(eyes)* brillant, flamboyant; **glowing with health** rayonnant *ou* florissant (de santé); **glowing with happiness** rayonnant de joie

(**c**) *(laudatory)* élogieux, dithyrambique; **I had read glowing reports of the play** j'avais lu des critiques dithyrambiques de la pièce; **the reviews were glowing** les critiques étaient dithyrambiques; **he spoke of you in glowing terms** il a chanté tes louanges; **to paint sth in glowing colours** présenter qch sous un jour favorable

glowingly ['gləʊɪŋlɪ] *adv* **to speak glowingly of sb/sth** parler de qn/qch en termes enthousiastes *ou* chaleureux

glow-worm *n Entom* ver *m* luisant

gloxinia [glɒk'sɪnɪə] *n Bot* gloxinia *m*

glucagon ['glu:kəgən] *n Chem* glucagon *m*

glucide ['glu:saɪd] *n Chem* glucide *m*

glucinium [glu:'sɪnɪəm], **glucinum** ['glu:sɪnəm] *n Chem* glucinium *m*, béryllium *m*

glucoprotein [ˌglu:kəʊ'prəʊti:n] *n* glycoprotéine *f*

glucose ['glu:kəʊs] *n* glucose *m*

►► ***glucose drink*** boisson *f* au glucose; ***glucose level*** glycémie *f*; ***glucose syrup*** sirop *m* de glucose

glucoside ['glu:kəsaɪd] *n* glucoside *m*

glucosuria [ˌglu:kəʊ'sjʊərɪə] *n Med* glucosurie *f*

glue [glu:] **1** *vt* (**a**) *(stick)* coller; **to glue sth to/onto sth** coller qch à/sur qch; **you'll have to glue it (back) together again** il faudra le recoller; **can't you glue it down?** vous ne pouvez pas le faire tenir avec de la colle?

(**b**) *Fig* coller; **with her face glued to the window** le visage collé à la fenêtre; **to be glued to the spot** être *ou* rester cloué sur place; **he kept his eyes glued on the ball** il garda les yeux rivés sur la balle; **they were glued to the television** ils étaient rivés à la télévision; **he's always glued to her side** il ne la quitte pas d'un pas *ou* d'une semelle

2 *n* colle *f*; *Fam* **he does a lot of glue** il est toujours en train de sniffer de la colle; *Fam* **he sticks to me like glue** il me suit partout comme un petit chien

►► *Med* ***glue ear*** otite *f* séreuse

gluepot ['glu:pɒt] *n* pot *m* de colle

glue-sniffer *n* **to be a glue-sniffer** inhaler❑ *ou* sniffer (de la colle)

glue-sniffing *n* inhalation *f* de colle

gluey ['glu:ɪ] *adj* collant, gluant

glug [glʌg] *(pt & pp* **glugged,** *cont* **glugging)** *Fam* **1** *n* **glug (glug)** glouglou *m*; **he took a long glug of lemonade** il prit une longue goulée de limonade

2 *vi* faire glouglou

gluhwein ['glu:vaɪn] *n* vin *m* chaud

glum [glʌm] *adj* triste, morose; **to be** *or* **to feel glum** avoir le cafard, broyer du noir; **to look glum** avoir l'air triste *ou* sombre; **don't look so glum!** ne fais pas cette tête-là!, ne sois pas si triste!

glumly ['glʌmlɪ] *adv* tristement, avec morosité; **he watched them glumly** il les regarda d'un œil triste *ou* morose

glumness ['glʌmnɪs] *n* tristesse *f*, morosité *f*

gluon ['glu:ɒn] *n Phys* gluon *m*

glut [glʌt] *(pt & pp* **glutted,** *cont* **glutting)** **1** *vt* (**a**) *(with food)* **to glut oneself with** *or* **on sth** se gorger *ou* se gaver de qch; *Fig* **to be glutted with television** être saturé de télévision

(**b**) *(market, economy)* encombrer, inonder; **the growers glutted the market with tomatoes** les producteurs de tomates ont saturé le marché; **the market is glutted with luxury goods** il y a surabondance d'objets de luxe sur le marché

2 *n (on market)* encombrement *m*; *(of commodity)* surabondance *f*; **there's a glut of fruit on the market** il y a surabondance de fruits sur le marché; **there's a glut of apples this year** il y a surproduction de pommes cette année; **a glut of money** une pléthore de capitaux

glutamate ['glu:təmeɪt] *n* glutamate *m*

glutamic [glu:'tæmɪk] *adj* glutamique

►► ***glutamic acid*** acide *m* glutamique

glutamine ['glu:təmi:n] *n* glutamine *f*

gluteal ['glu:tɪəl, glu:'ti:əl] *adj Anat* fessier; **gluteal muscle** muscle *m* fessier

gluten ['glu:tən] **1** *n* gluten *m*

2 *comp (bread, roll)* au gluten

gluten-free *adj* sans gluten

gluteus ['glu:tɪəs] *n Anat* (muscle) fessier *m*

►► ***gluteus maximus*** grand fessier *m*

glutinous ['glu:tɪnəs] *adj* glutineux

glutton ['glʌtən] *n* glouton(onne) *m,f*, goulu(e) *m,f*; *Fig* **to be a glutton for punishment** être un peu masochiste; **he's a glutton for work** c'est un bourreau *ou* un forcené de travail

gluttonous ['glʌtənəs] *adj* glouton, goulu

gluttonously ['glʌtənəslɪ] *adv* gloutonnement, goulûment

gluttony ['glʌtənɪ] *n* gloutonnerie *f*, goinfrerie *f*

glycaemia, *Am* **glycemia** [glaɪ'si:mɪə] *n Med* glycémie *f*

glyceric [glɪ'serɪk] *adj* glycérique

►► ***glyceric acid*** acide *m* glycérique

glyceride ['glɪsəraɪd] *n Chem* glycéride *m*

glycerin ['glɪsərɪn], **glycerine** ['glɪsəri:n] *n* glycérine *f*

glycerite ['glɪsəraɪt] *n Pharm* glycérolé *m*

glycerol ['glɪsərɒl] *n* glycérol *m*

glyceryl ['glɪsərɪl] *n Chem* glycéryle *m*

►► ***glyceryl trinitrate*** trinitrine *f*

glycine ['glaɪsi:n] *n* glycine *f*, glycocolle *m*

glycogen ['glaɪkəʊdʒən] *n* glycogène *m*

glycol ['glaɪkɒl] *n* glycol *m*

glycolic [glaɪ'kɒlɪk] *adj* glycolique

►► ***glycolic acid*** acide *m* glycolique

glycolipid [ˌglaɪkəʊ'lɪpɪd] *n Biol & Chem* glycolipide *m*

glycolysis [glaɪ'kɒlɪsɪs] *n Biol & Chem* glycolyse *f*

glycoprotein [ˌglaɪkəʊ'prəʊti:n] *n Biol & Chem* glycoprotéine *f*

glycosuria [ˌglaɪkəʊ'sjʊərɪə] *n Med* glycosurie *f*

Glyndebourne ['glaɪndˌbɔ:n] *n* = lieu d'un festival annuel d'opéra dans le Sussex

glyph [glɪf] *n* glyphe *m*

glyptic ['glɪptɪk] *adj* relatif à la glyptique

glyptography [glɪp'tɒgrəfɪ] *n* glyptique *f*

GM [ˌdʒi:'em] *adj* (**a**) *(abbr* **genetically modified)** génétiquement modifié (**b**) *(abbr* **grant maintained)** subventionné *(par l'État)*; **a GM school** une école privée subventionnée *(acceptant en échange un droit de regard de l'État sur la gestion de ses affaires)* (**c**) *(abbr* **General Motors)** General Motors *f*

►► ***GM food*** aliments *mpl* génétiquement modifiés

gm *(written abbr* **gram)** g

G-man *n* (**a**) *Am* agent *m* du FBI (**b**) *Ir* détective *m* politique *(en Irlande)*

GMAT [ˌdʒi:em,eɪ'ti:] *n Am Univ (abbr* **Graduate Management Admissions Test)** = test d'admission dans le 2ème cycle de l'enseignement supérieur aux États-Unis

GMB [ˌdʒi:em'bi:] *n Br (abbr* **General, Municipal, Boilermakers and Allied Trades Union)** = important syndicat britannique

GMC [ˌdʒi:em'si:] *n* (**a**) *(abbr* **general management committee)** comité *m* de direction (**b**) *Br (abbr* **General Medical Council)** ≃ conseil *m* de l'ordre des médecins (**c**) *(abbr* **General Motors Corporation)** General Motors *f*

GMO [ˌdʒi:em'əʊ] *n (abbr* **genetically-modified organism)** OGM *m*

GMT [ˌdʒi:em'ti:] *n (abbr* **Greenwich Mean Time)** GMT *m*

GMWU [ˌdʒi:emˌdʌbəlju:'ju:] *n Br (abbr* **General and Municipal Workers' Union)** = syndicat britannique des employés des collectivités locales

gnarl [nɑ:l] *n Bot* nœud *m*

gnarled [nɑ:ld] *adj* (**a**) *(tree, fingers)* noueux (**b**) *(character)* grincheux, hargneux

gnarly ['nɑ:lɪ] *adj Am Fam (excellent, awful)* mortel

gnash [næʃ] **1** *vt* **to gnash one's teeth** grincer des dents

2 *n* grincement *m* (de dents)

gnashers ['næʃəz] *npl Fam (teeth)* ratiches *fpl*; *(false teeth)* râtelier *m*

gnashing ['næʃɪŋ] *n* grincement *m*; *Literary or Hum* **there was much weeping and gnashing of teeth** il y eut moult pleurs et grincements de dents

gnat [næt] *n* moucheron *m*

►► *Br very Fam* ***gnat's piss*** *(drink)* eau *m* de vaisselle, pipi *m* de chat

gnaw [nɔ:] **1** *vt* ronger; **to gnaw one's fingernails** se ronger les ongles; **the rats have gnawed their way into the cupboard** les rats ont fini par percer un trou dans le placard; *Fig* **gnawed by hunger** tenaillé par la faim; **gnawed by remorse** rongé par le remords

2 *vi* **to gnaw (away) at sth** ronger qch; **to gnaw through sth** ronger qch jusqu'à le percer; *Fig* **guilt and sorrow gnawed at his heart** la culpabilité et le chagrin lui rongeaient le cœur; *Fig* **hunger gnawed at him** il était tenaillé par la faim

►**gnaw away** *vt sep* (**a**) *(animal)* ronger (**b**) *(erode)* ronger, miner

►**gnaw off** *vt sep* **to gnaw sth off** ronger qch jusqu'à le détacher

gnawing ['nɔ:ɪŋ] *adj* (**a**) *(pain)* lancinant, tenaillant; *(hunger)* tenaillant; **the gnawing pains of hunger** les affres *fpl ou* les tiraillements *mpl* de la faim (**b**) *(anxiety, doubt)* tenaillant, torturant

gneiss [naɪs] *n Geol* gneiss *m*

gnocchi ['nɒkɪ] *npl* gnocchi *mpl*, gnocchis *mpl*

gnome [nəʊm] *n* (**a**) *Myth* gnome *m*; **(garden) gnome** nain *m* de jardin (**b**) *(aphorism)* aphorisme *m*

▸▸ *Fam Banking* **the gnomes of Zurich** les grands banquiers *mpl* suisses ❑

gnomic [ˈnəʊmɪk] *adj* gnomique

gnomish [ˈnəʊmɪʃ] *adj* de gnome

gnomon [ˈnəʊmɒn] *n (on sundial)* style *m*

gnosis [ˈnəʊsɪs] *n* gnose *f*

gnostic, Gnostic [ˈnɒstɪk] **1** *adj* gnostique **2** *n* gnostique *mf*

gnosticism, Gnosticism [ˈnɒstɪsɪzəm] *n* gnosticisme *m*

GNP [ˌdʒiːenˈpiː] *n Econ (abbr* **gross national product**) PNB *m*

gnu [nuː] *n Zool* gnou *m*

GNVQ [ˌdʒiːenˌviːˈkjuː] *n Br Sch (abbr* **General National Vocational Qualification**) = formation professionnelle sur deux ans que l'on peut suivre à partir de seize ans

go¹ [gəʊ] *n (game)* jeu *m* de go

GO² [gəʊ]

aller	▸ **1A (a) – (c), (e), (f); E (a) – (c); G (a); 2 (a)**
s'en aller	▸ **1A (d)**
être	▸ **1B (a)**
devenir	▸ **1B (b)**
tomber en panne	▸ **1B (c)**
s'user	▸ **1B (d)**
se détériorer	▸ **1B (e)**
commencer	▸ **1C (a)**
aller (+ infinitif)	▸ **1C (b), (c)**
marcher	▸ **1C (d)**
disparaître	▸ **1D (a), (c)**
se passer	▸ **1E (d)**
s'écouler	▸ **1E (e)**
s'appliquer	▸ **1F (b)**
se vendre	▸ **1F (e)**
contribuer	▸ **1G (c)**
aller ensemble	▸ **1H (a)**
tenir le coup	▸ **1H (c)**
faire	▸ **2 (b), (c)**
coup	▸ **3 (a)**
essai	▸ **3 (a)**
tour	▸ **3 (b)**
dynamisme	▸ **3 (c)**

(*pl* **goes** [gəʊz], *3rd pres sing* **goes** [gəʊz], *pt* **went** [went], *pp* **gone** [gɒn]) **1** *vi* **A.** (**a**) *(move, travel → person)* aller; *(→ vehicle)* aller, rouler; **we're going to Paris/Japan/Spain** nous allons à Paris/au Japon/en Espagne; **he went to the office/a friend's house** il est allé au bureau/chez un ami; **I want to go home** je veux rentrer; **the salesman went from house to house** le vendeur est allé de maison en maison; **we went by car/on foot** nous y sommes allés en voiture/à pied; **there goes the train!** voilà le train (qui passe)!; **the bus goes by way of** *or* **through Dover** le bus passe par Douvres; **does this train go to Glasgow?** ce train va-t-il à Glasgow?; **the truck was going at 150 kilometres an hour** le camion roulait à *ou* faisait du 150 kilomètres (à l')heure; **go behind those bushes** va derrière ces arbustes; **where do we go from here?** où va-t-on maintenant?; *Fig* qu'est-ce qu'on fait maintenant?; **to go to the doctor** aller voir *ou* aller chez le médecin; **he went straight to the director** il est allé directement voir *ou* trouver le directeur; **to go to prison** aller en prison; **to go to the toilet** aller aux toilettes; **to go to sb for advice** aller demander conseil à qn; **let the children go first** laissez les enfants passer devant, laissez passer les enfants d'abord; **I'll go next** c'est à moi après; **who goes next?** *(in game)* c'est à qui (le tour)?; *Mil* **who goes there?** qui va là?, qui vive?; **here we go again!** ça y est, ça recommence!; **there he goes!** le voilà!; **there he goes again!** *(there he is again)* le revoilà!; *(he's doing it again)* ça y est, il est reparti!

(**b**) *(engage in a specified activity)* aller; **to go shopping** aller faire des courses; **to go fishing/hunting** aller à la pêche/à la chasse; **to go riding** aller faire du cheval; **let's go for a walk/bike ride/swim** allons nous promener/faire un tour à vélo/nous baigner; **they went on a trip** ils sont partis en voyage; *Br* **go and buy the paper,** *Am* **go buy the paper** va acheter le journal; **I'll go to see her** *or Am* **go see her tomorrow** j'irai la voir demain; **don't go and tell him!, don't go telling him!** ne va pas le lui dire!, ne le lui dis pas!; **don't go bothering your sister** ne va pas embêter ta sœur; **you had to go and tell him!** il a fallu que tu le lui dises!; **he's gone and locked us out!** il est parti et nous a laissé à la porte!; **you've gone and done it now!** vraiment, tu as tout gâché!

(**c**) *(proceed to specified limit)* aller; **he'll go as high as £300** il ira jusqu'à 300 livres; **the temperature went as high as 36° C** la température est montée jusqu'à 36° C; **he went so far as to say it was her fault** il est allé jusqu'à dire que c'était de sa faute à elle; **now you've gone too far!** là tu as dépassé les bornes!; **I'll go further and say he should resign** j'irai plus loin et je dirai qu'il *ou* j'irai jusqu'à dire qu'il devrait démissionner; **the temperature sometimes goes below zero** la température descend *ou* tombe parfois au-dessous de zéro; **her attitude went beyond mere impertinence** son comportement était plus qu'impertinent

(**d**) *(depart, leave)* s'en aller, partir; **I must be going** il faut que je m'en aille *ou* que je parte; **they went early** ils sont partis tôt; **you may go** vous pouvez partir; **what time does the train go?** à quelle heure part le train?; *Fam* **get going!** vas-y!, file!; *Arch* **be gone!** allez-vous-en!; **either he goes or I go** l'un de nous deux doit partir

(**e**) *(indicating regular attendance)* aller, assister; **to go to church/school** aller à l'église/l'école; **to go to a meeting** aller *ou* assister à une réunion; **to go to work** *(to one's place of work)* aller au travail

(**f**) *(indicating direction or route)* aller, mener; **that road goes to the market square** cette route va *ou* mène à la place du marché

B. (**a**) *(be or remain in specified state)* être; **to go barefoot/naked** se promener pieds nus/tout nu; **to go armed** porter une arme; **her family goes in rags** sa famille est en haillons; **the job went unfilled** le poste est resté vacant; **to go unnoticed** passer inaperçu; **such crimes must not go unpunished** de tels crimes ne doivent pas rester impunis

(**b**) *(become)* devenir; **my father is going grey** mon père grisonne; **she went white with rage** elle a blêmi de colère; **my hands went clammy** mes mains sont devenues moites; **the tea's gone cold** le thé a refroidi; **have you gone mad?** tu es devenu fou?; **to go bankrupt** faire faillite; **the country has gone Republican** le pays est maintenant républicain

(**c**) *(stop working → engine)* tomber en panne; *(→ fuse)* sauter; *(→ bulb, lamp)* sauter, griller; **the battery's going** la pile commence à être usée

(**d**) *(wear out)* s'user; *(split)* craquer; *(break)* (se) casser; **his trousers are going at the knees** son pantalon s'use aux genoux; **the jacket went at the seams** la veste a craqué aux coutures

(**e**) *(deteriorate, fail → health)* se détériorer; *(→ hearing, sight)* baisser; **all his strength went and he fell to the floor** il a perdu toutes ses forces et il est tombé par terre; **his voice is going** il devient aphone; **his voice is gone** il est aphone, il a une extinction de voix; **her mind has started to go** elle n'a plus toute sa tête *ou* toutes ses facultés

C. (**a**) *(begin an activity)* commencer; **what are we waiting for? let's go!** qu'est-ce qu'on attend? allons-y!; *Fam* **here goes!, here we go!** allez!, on y va!; **go!** partez!; **you'd better get going on** *or* **with that report!** tu ferais bien de te mettre à *ou* de t'attaquer à ce rapport!; **it won't be so hard once you get going** ça ne sera pas si difficile une fois que tu seras lancé; *Fam* **go to it!** *(get to work)* au boulot!; *(in encouragement)* allez-y!

(**b**) *(expressing intention)* **to be going to do sth** *(be about to)* aller faire qch, être sur le point de faire qch; *(intend to)* avoir l'intention de faire qch; **you were just going to tell me about it** vous étiez sur le point de *ou* vous alliez m'en parler; **I was going to visit her yesterday but her mother arrived** j'avais l'intention de *ou* j'allais lui rendre visite hier mais sa mère est arrivée

(**c**) *(expressing future)* **are you going to be at home tonight?** est-ce que vous serez chez vous ce soir?; **we're going to do exactly as we please** nous ferons ce que nous voulons; **she's going to be a doctor** elle va être médecin; **there's going to be a storm** il va y avoir un orage; **he's going to have to work really hard** il va falloir qu'il travaille très dur

(**d**) *(function → clock, machine)* marcher, fonctionner; *(start functioning)* démarrer; **is the fan going?** est-ce que le ventilateur est en marche *ou* marche?; **the car won't go** la voiture ne veut pas démarrer; **he had the television and the radio going** il avait mis la télévision et la radio en marche; **the washing machine is still going** la machine à laver tourne encore, la lessive n'est pas terminée; **to get sth going** *(car, machine)* mettre qch en marche; *(business, project)* lancer qch; **her daughter kept the business going** sa fille a continué à faire marcher l'affaire; **to keep a conversation/fire going** entretenir une conversation/un feu

(**e**) *(sound → alarm clock, bell)* sonner; *(→ alarm, siren)* retentir

(**f**) *(make movement)* **she went like this with her eyebrows** elle a fait comme ça avec ses sourcils

(**g**) *(appear)* **to go on radio/television** passer à la radio/à la télévision

D. (**a**) *(disappear)* disparaître; **the snow has gone** la neige a fondu *ou* disparu; **all the sugar's gone** il n'y a plus de sucre; **my coat has gone** mon manteau n'est plus là *ou* a disparu; **all our money has gone** *(spent)* nous avons dépensé tout notre argent; *(lost)* nous avons perdu tout notre argent; *(stolen)* on a volé tout notre argent; **I don't know where the money goes these days** l'argent disparaît à une vitesse incroyable ces temps-ci; **gone are the days when he took her dancing** elle est bien loin, l'époque où il l'emmenait danser

(**b**) *(be eliminated)* **the last paragraph must go** il faut supprimer le dernier paragraphe; **I've decided that car has to go** j'ai décidé de me débarrasser de cette voiture; **that new secretary has got to go** il va falloir se débarrasser de la nouvelle secrétaire

(**c**) *Euph (die)* disparaître, s'éteindre; **he is (dead and) gone** il nous a quittés; **his wife went first** sa femme est partie avant lui; **after I go...** quand je ne serai plus là...

E. (**a**) *(extend, reach)* aller, s'étendre; **our property goes as far as the forest** notre propriété va *ou* s'étend jusqu'au bois; **the path goes right down to the beach** le chemin descend jusqu'à la mer; *Fig* **her thinking didn't go that far** elle n'a pas poussé le raisonnement aussi loin; **my salary doesn't go very far** je ne vais pas loin avec mon salaire; **money doesn't go very far these days** l'argent part vite à notre époque; **their difference of opinion goes deeper than I thought** leur différend est plus profond que je ne pensais

(**b**) *(belong)* aller, se mettre, se ranger; **the dictionaries go on that shelf** les dictionnaires se rangent *ou* vont sur cette étagère; **where do the towels go?** où est-ce qu'on met les serviettes?; **that painting goes here** ce tableau se met *ou* va là

(**c**) *(be contained in, fit)* aller; **this last sweater won't go in the suitcase** ce dernier pull n'ira pas *ou* n'entrera pas dans la valise; **the piano barely goes through the door** le piano entre *ou* passe de justesse par la porte; **this belt just goes round my waist** cette ceinture est juste assez longue pour faire le tour de ma taille; **the lid goes on easily enough** le couvercle se met assez facilement

(**d**) *(develop, turn out)* se passer; **how did your interview go?** comment s'est passé ton entretien?; **I'll see how things go** je vais voir comment ça se passe; **we can't tell how things will go** on ne sait pas comment ça se passera; **everything went well** tout s'est bien passé; **if all goes well** si tout va bien; **the meeting went badly/well** la réunion s'est mal/bien passée; **the negotiations are going well** les négociations sont en bonne voie; **the vote went against them/in their favour** le vote leur a été défavorable/favorable; **there's no doubt as to which**

way the decision will go on sait ce qui sera décidé; **everything was going fine until she showed up** tout allait *ou* se passait très bien jusqu'à ce qu'elle arrive; **everything went wrong** ça a mal tourné; *Fam* **how's it going?, how are things going?** (comment) ça va?; **the way things are going, we might both be out of a job soon** au train où vont *ou* vu comment vont les choses, nous allons bientôt nous retrouver tous les deux au chômage

(**e**) *(time → elapse)* s'écouler, passer; *(→ last)* durer; **the journey went quickly** je n'ai pas vu le temps passer pendant le voyage; **there were only five minutes to go before...** il ne restait que cinq minutes avant...; **time goes so slowly when you're not here** le temps me paraît tellement long quand tu n'es pas là; **how's the time going?** combien de temps reste-t-il?

F. (**a**) *(be accepted)* **what your mother says goes!** fais ce que dit ta mère!; **whatever the boss says goes** c'est le patron qui fait la loi; **anything goes** on fait ce qu'on veut

(**b**) *(be valid, hold true)* s'appliquer; **that rule goes for everyone** cette règle s'applique à tout le monde; **that goes for us too** *(that applies to us)* ça s'applique à nous aussi; *(we agree with that)* nous sommes aussi de cet avis

(**c**) *(be expressed, run → report, story)* **the story** *or* **rumour goes that she left him** le bruit court qu'elle l'a quitté; **so the story goes** du moins c'est ce que l'on dit *ou* d'après les on-dit; **how does the story go?** comment c'est cette histoire?; **I forget how the poem goes now** j'ai oublié le poème maintenant; **how does the tune go?** c'est quoi *ou* c'est comment, l'air?; **her theory goes something like this** sa théorie est plus ou moins la suivante

(**d**) *(be identified as)* **to go by** *or* **under the name of** répondre au nom de; **he now goes by** *or* **under another name** il se fait appeler autrement maintenant

(**e**) *(be sold)* se vendre; **flats are going cheap at the moment** les appartements ne se vendent pas très cher en ce moment; **the necklace went for £350** le collier s'est vendu 350 livres; **going, going, gone!** *(at auction)* une fois, deux fois, adjugé!

G. (**a**) *(be given → award, prize)* aller, être donné; *(→ inheritance, property)* passer; **the contract is to go to a private firm** le contrat ira à une entreprise privée; **credit should go to the teachers** le mérite en revient aux enseignants; **every penny will go to charity** tout l'argent va *ou* est destiné à une œuvre de bienfaisance

(**b**) *(be spent)* **a small portion of the budget went on education** une petite part du budget a été consacrée *ou* est allée à l'éducation; **all his money goes on drink** tout son argent part dans la boisson

(**c**) *(contribute)* contribuer, servir; **all that just goes to prove my point** tout ça confirme bien ce que j'ai dit; **it has all the qualities that go to make a good film** ça a toutes les qualités d'un bon film

(**d**) *(have recourse)* avoir recours, recourir; **to go to arbitration** recourir à l'arbitrage

H. (**a**) *(be compatible → colours, flavours)* aller ensemble; **orange and mauve don't really go** l'orange et le mauve ne vont pas vraiment ensemble

(**b**) *(be available)* **let me know if you hear of any jobs going** faites-moi savoir si vous entendez parler d'un emploi; **are there any flats going for rent in this building?** y a-t-il des appartements à louer dans cet immeuble?; *Fam* **any whisky going?** tu as un whisky à m'offrir?

(**c**) *(endure)* tenir le coup; **we can't go much longer without water** nous ne pourrons pas tenir beaucoup plus longtemps sans eau

(**d**) *Euph (go to the toilet)* **we'll only stop if you're really desperate to go** on ne s'arrête que si tu ne tiens vraiment plus; **I went before I came** j'ai fait avant de venir

(**e**) *Math* **5 into 60 goes 12** 60 divisé par 5 égale 12; **6 into 5 won't go** 5 n'est pas divisible par 6

(**f**) *(idioms)* **she isn't bad, as teachers go** elle n'est pas mal comme enseignante; **as houses go, it's pretty cheap** ce n'est pas cher pour une maison; **as things go today** par les temps qui courent; **there goes my chance of winning a prize** je peux abandonner tout espoir de gagner un prix; **there you go again, always blaming other people** ça y est, toujours à rejeter la responsabilité sur les autres; **there you go!** *(here you are)* tiens!; *(I told you so)* voilà!; **there you go, two hamburgers and a coke** et voici, deux hamburgers et un Coca; **there you go, what did I tell you?** voilà *ou* tiens, qu'est-ce que je t'avais dit!

2 *vt* (**a**) *(follow, proceed along)* aller, suivre; **if we go this way, we'll get there much more quickly** si nous passons par là, nous arriverons bien plus vite

(**b**) *(travel)* faire, voyager; **we've only gone 5 kilometres** nous n'avons fait que 5 kilomètres; **she went the whole length of the street before coming back** elle a descendu toute la rue avant de revenir

(**c**) *(say)* faire; *(make specified noise)* faire; **ducks go "quack"** les canards font "coincoin"; **the clock goes "tick tock"** l'horloge fait "tic tac"; **the gun went bang** et pan! le coup est parti; *Fam* **then he goes "hand it over"** puis il fait "donne-le-moi"

(**d**) *(in gambling)* **to go 10** risquer 10; *Cards* **to go no/two trumps** annoncer sans/deux atout(s); *Fig* **to go one better (than sb)** surenchérir (sur qn)

(**e**) *Fam (do with)* **I could really go a beer** je me paierais bien une bière

(**f**) *(idioms) Fam Old-fashioned* **to go it** *(go fast)* filer; *(behave wildly)* se défoncer; *Fam* **how goes it?** ça marche?

3 *n* (**a**) *Br (attempt, try)* coup *m*, essai *m*; **to have a go at sth/doing sth** essayer qch/de faire qch; **he had another go** il a fait une nouvelle tentative, il a ressayé; **let's have a go!** essayons!; *Fam (let me try)* laisse-moi essayer!; **have another go!** encore un coup!; **I've never tried it but I'll give it a go** je n'ai encore jamais fait l'expérience mais je vais essayer; **she passed her exams first go** elle a eu ses examens du premier coup; **he knocked down all the skittles at one go** il a renversé toutes les quilles d'un coup; **£1 a go** *(at fair etc)* une livre la partie *ou* le tour; **to have a go on the dodgems** faire un tour d'autos tamponneuses; **he wouldn't let me have** *or* **give me a go** *(on his bicycle etc)* il ne voulait pas me laisser l'essayer

(**b**) *Br (in games → turn)* tour *m*; **it's your go** c'est ton tour *ou* c'est à toi (de jouer); **whose go is it?** à qui de jouer?, à qui le tour?

(**c**) *Fam (energy, vitality)* dynamisme *m*, entrain *m*; **to be full of go** avoir plein d'énergie, être très dynamique; **she's got plenty of go** elle est pleine d'entrain; **the new man has no go in him** le nouveau manque d'entrain

(**d**) *Fam (success)* succès *m*, réussite *f*; **he's made a go of the business** il a réussi à faire marcher l'affaire; **to make a go of a marriage** réussir un mariage; **I tried to persuade her but it was no go** j'ai essayé de la convaincre mais il n'y avait rien à faire

(**e**) *(fashion)* mode *f*; **short hair is all the go** les cheveux courts sont le dernier cri *ou* font fureur

(**f**) *Fam (idioms)* **to have a go at sb** *(physically)* rentrer dans qn; *(verbally)* passer un savon à qn; **they had a real go at one another!** qu'est-ce qu'ils se sont mis!; **she had a go at her boyfriend** elle a passé un de ces savons à son copain; *Br* **police have warned the public not to have a go, the fugitive may be armed** la police a prévenu la population de ne pas s'en prendre au fugitif car il pourrait être armé; **it's all go** ça n'arrête pas!; **all systems go!** c'est parti!; **the shuttle is go for landing** la navette est bonne *ou* est parée *ou* a le feu vert pour l'atterrissage

4 going on *adv* **he must be going on fifty** il doit approcher de la *ou* aller sur la cinquantaine; **it was going on (for) midnight by the time we finished** quand on a terminé, il était près de minuit

5 on the go *adj Fam* (**a**) *(busy)* **I've been on the go all day** je n'ai pas arrêté de toute la journée; **to be always on the go** être toujours à trotter *ou* à courir, avoir la bougeotte; **to keep sb on the go** faire trimer qn

(**b**) *(in hand)* **I have several projects on the go at present** j'ai plusieurs projets en route en ce moment

6 to go 1 *adv* à faire; **there are only three weeks/five miles to go** il ne reste plus que trois semaines/cinq miles; **five done, three to go** cinq de faits, trois à faire **2** *adj esp Am (to take out)* **two hamburgers to go** deux hamburgers à emporter!

▸**go about 1** *vi* (**a**) *(move)* circuler; *(of rumour)* courir; **policemen usually go about in pairs** en général, les policiers circulent par deux; **you can't go about saying things like that!** il ne faut pas raconter des choses pareilles!

(**b**) *Naut (change tack)* virer de bord

2 *vt insep* (**a**) *(get on with)* s'occuper de; **to go about one's business** vaquer à ses occupations

(**b**) *(set about)* se mettre à; **she showed me how to go about it** elle m'a montré comment faire *ou* comment m'y prendre; **how do you go about applying for the job?** comment doit-on s'y prendre *ou* faire pour postuler l'emploi?

(**c**) *(country)* parcourir

▸**go about with** *vt insep (frequent)* **her son goes about with an older crowd** son fils fréquente des gens plus âgés que lui; **he's going about with Rachel these days** il sort avec Rachel en ce moment

▸**go across 1** *vt insep* traverser

2 *vi* traverser; **your brother has just gone across to the shop** ton frère est allé faire un saut au magasin en face

▸**go after** *vt insep* (**a**) *(follow)* suivre

(**b**) *(pursue, seek → criminal)* poursuivre; *(→ prey)* chasser; *(→ job, prize)* essayer d'obtenir; **he goes after all the women** il court après toutes les femmes; **I'm going after that job** je vais essayer d'obtenir cet emploi

▸**go against** *vt insep* (**a**) *(disregard)* aller contre, aller à l'encontre de; **she went against my advice** elle n'a pas suivi mon conseil; **I went against my mother's wishes** je suis allé contre *ou* j'ai contrarié les désirs de ma mère

(**b**) *(conflict with)* contredire; **that goes against what he told me** c'est en contradiction avec *ou* ça contredit ce qu'il m'a dit; **the decision went against public opinion** la décision est allée à l'encontre de *ou* a heurté l'opinion publique; **it goes against my principles** c'est contre mes principes

(**c**) *(be unfavourable to → of luck, situation)* être contraire à; *(→ of opinion)* être défavorable à; *(→ of behaviour, evidence)* nuire à, être préjudiciable à; **the verdict went against the defendant** le verdict a été défavorable à l'accusé *ou* a été prononcé contre l'accusé; **if luck should go against him** si la chance lui était contraire; **her divorce may go against her winning the election** son divorce pourrait nuire à ses chances de gagner les élections

▸**go ahead** *vi* (**a**) *(precede)* passer devant; **he went ahead of us** il est parti avant nous; **I let him go ahead of me in the queue** je l'ai fait passer devant moi dans la queue

(**b**) *(proceed)* aller de l'avant; **go ahead! tell me!** vas-y! dis-le-moi!; **the mayor allowed the demonstrations to go ahead** le maire a permis aux manifestations d'avoir lieu; **the move had gone ahead as planned** le déménagement s'était déroulé comme prévu; **to go ahead with sth** démarrer qch; **they're going ahead with the project after all** ils ont finalement décidé de mener le projet à bien; **he went ahead and did it** *(without hesitating)* il l'a fait sans l'ombre d'une hésitation; *(despite warnings)* rien ne l'a arrêté

(**c**) *(advance, progress)* progresser, faire des progrès

▸**go along** *vi* (**a**) *(move from one place to another)* aller, avancer; **go along and ask your mother** va demander à ta mère; **she went along with them to the fair** elle les a accompagnés *ou* elle est allée avec eux à la foire; **we can talk it over as we go along** nous pouvons en discuter en chemin *ou* en cours de route; **I just make it up as I go along** j'invente au fur et à mesure

(**b**) *(progress)* se dérouler, se passer; **things were going along nicely** tout allait *ou* se passait bien

(**c**) *(go to meeting, party etc)* aller

▸**go along with** *vt insep (decision, order)*

accepter, s'incliner devant; *(rule)* observer, respecter; **that's what they decided and I went along with it** c'est la décision qu'ils ont prise et je l'ai acceptée; **I go along with the committee on that point** je suis d'accord avec *ou* je soutiens le comité sur ce point; **I can't go along with you on that** je ne suis pas d'accord avec vous là-dessus; **he went along with his father's wishes** il s'est conformé aux *ou* a respecté les désirs de son père

▸**go around** *vi* **(a)** *(habitually)* passer son temps à; **he goes around mumbling to himself** il passe son temps à radoter; **she just goes around annoying everyone** elle passe son temps à énerver tout le monde; **he goes around in black leather** il se promène toujours en *ou* il est toujours habillé en cuir noir

(b) *(document, illness)* circuler; *(gossip, rumour)* courir, circuler

(c) *(be long enough for)* **will that belt go around your waist?** est-ce que cette ceinture sera assez grande pour toi?

▸**go around with** = **go about with**

▸**go at** *vt insep Fam (attack → food)* attaquer, se jeter sur; *(→ job, task)* s'attaquer à; *(→ person)* attaquer; **they were still going at it the next day** ils y étaient encore le lendemain; **she went at the cleaning with a will** elle s'est attaquée au nettoyage avec ardeur

▸**go away** *vi* partir, s'en aller; **go away!** va-t'en!; **I'm going away for a few days** je pars pour quelques jours; **she's gone away to think about it** elle est partie réfléchir

▸**go back** *vi* **(a)** *(return)* revenir, retourner; **she went back to bed** elle est retournée au lit, elle s'est recouchée; **to go back to sleep** se rendormir; **they went back home** ils sont rentrés chez eux *ou* à la maison; **I went back downstairs/upstairs** je suis redescendu/remonté; **to go back to work** *(continue task)* se remettre au travail; *(return to place of work)* retourner travailler; *(return to employment)* reprendre le travail; **to go back on one's steps** rebrousser chemin, revenir sur ses pas; **let's go back to chapter two** revenons *ou* retournons au deuxième chapitre; **we went back to the beginning** nous avons recommencé; **let's go back to why you said that** revenons à la question de savoir pourquoi vous avez dit ça; **the clocks go back one hour today** on retarde les pendules d'une heure aujourd'hui

(b) *(retreat)* reculer; **go back!** recule!

(c) *(revert)* revenir; **we went back to the old system** nous sommes revenus à l'ancien système; **he went back to his old habits** il a repris ses anciennes habitudes; **the conversation kept going back to the same subject** la conversation revenait sans cesse sur le même sujet; **men are going back to wearing their hair long** les hommes reviennent aux cheveux longs *ou* se laissent à nouveau pousser les cheveux

(d) *(in time)* remonter; **our records go back to 1850** nos archives remontent à 1850; **this building goes back to the Revolution** ce bâtiment date de *ou* remonte à la Révolution; *Fam* **we go back a long way, Brad and me** ça remonte à loin, Brad et moi

(e) *(extend, reach)* s'étendre; **the garden goes back 150 metres** le jardin s'étend sur 150 mètres

▸**go back on** *vt insep (fail to keep → agreement)* rompre, violer; *(→ promise)* manquer à, revenir sur; **they went back on their decision** ils sont revenus sur leur décision; **he won't go back on his word** il ne manquera pas à sa parole

▸**go before 1** *vi (precede)* passer devant; *(happen before)* précéder; **that question has nothing to do with what went before** cette question n'a rien à voir avec ce qui précède *ou* avec ce qui a été dit avant; **the election was like nothing that had gone before** l'élection ne ressemblait en rien aux précédentes; *Euph* **those who have gone before** *(the dead)* ceux qui nous ont précédés

2 *vt insep* **(a)** *(precede)* précéder; **we are indebted to those who have gone before us** nous devons beaucoup à ceux qui nous ont précédés

(b) *(appear before)* **your suggestion will go before the committee** votre suggestion sera soumise au comité; **to go before a judge/jury** passer devant un juge/un jury; **the matter went before the court** l'affaire est allée devant les tribunaux

▸**go below** *vi Naut* descendre dans l'entrepont

▸**go by 1** *vi (pass → car, person)* passer; *(→ time)* passer, s'écouler; **as the years go by** avec les années, à mesure que les années passent; **in days** *or* **in times** *or* **in years gone by** autrefois, jadis; **to let an opportunity go by** laisser passer une occasion

2 *vt insep* **(a)** *(act in accordance with, be guided by)* suivre, se baser sur; **don't go by the map** ne vous fiez pas à la carte; **I'll go by what the boss says** je me baserai sur ce que dit le patron; **he goes by the rules** il suit le règlement

(b) *(judge by)* juger d'après; **going by her accent, I'd say she's from New York** si j'en juge d'après son accent, je dirais qu'elle vient de New York; **you can't go by appearances** on ne peut pas juger d'après *ou* sur les apparences

(c) *(be known by)* **to go by a different/false name** être connu sous un nom différent/un faux nom; **the product goes by the name of "Bango" in France** ce produit est vendu sous le nom de "Bango" en France

▸**go down 1** *vi* **(a)** *(descend, move to lower level)* descendre; **he went down on all fours** *or* **on his hands and knees** il s'est mis à quatre pattes; **going down!** *(in lift)* on descend!, pour descendre!

(b) *(proceed, travel)* aller; **we're going down to Tours/the country/the shop** nous allons à Tours/à la campagne/au magasin

(c) *(set → moon, sun)* se coucher, tomber

(d) *(sink → ship)* couler, sombrer; *(→ person)* couler, disparaître (sous l'eau)

(e) *(decrease, decline → level, price, quality)* baisser; *(→ amount, numbers)* diminuer; *(→ rate, temperature)* baisser, s'abaisser; *(→ fever)* baisser, tomber; *(→ tide)* descendre; **the dollar is going down in value** le dollar perd de sa valeur, le dollar est en baisse; **eggs are going down (in price)** le prix des œufs baisse; **my weight has gone down** j'ai perdu du poids; **he's gone down in my estimation** il a baissé dans mon estime; **the neighbourhood's really gone down since then** le quartier ne s'est vraiment pas arrangé depuis; **to have gone down in the world** avoir connu des jours meilleurs

(f) *(become less swollen → swelling)* désenfler, dégonfler; *(→ balloon, tyre)* se dégonfler

(g) *(food, medicine)* descendre; **this wine goes down very smoothly** ce vin se laisse boire (comme du petit-lait)

(h) *(produce specified reaction)* être reçu; **a cup of coffee would go down nicely** une tasse de café serait la bienvenue; **his speech went down badly/well** son discours a été mal/bien reçu; **how will the proposal go down with the students?** comment les étudiants vont-ils prendre la proposition?; **that kind of talk doesn't go down well with me** je n'apprécie pas du tout ce genre de propos

(i) *(lose)* être battu; **Mexico went down to Germany** le Mexique s'est incliné devant l'Allemagne; **Madrid went down to Milan by three points** Milan a battu Madrid de trois points; **I'm not going to go down without a fight** je me battrai jusqu'à la fin

(j) *(be relegated)* descendre; **our team has gone down to the second division** notre équipe est descendue en deuxième division

(k) *(be noted, recorded)* être noté; *(in writing)* être pris *ou* couché par écrit; **this day will go down in history** ce jour restera une date historique; **she will go down in history as a woman of great courage** elle entrera dans l'histoire grâce à son grand courage

(l) *(reach as far as)* descendre, s'étendre; **this path goes down to the beach** ce sentier va *ou* descend à la plage

(m) *(continue as far as)* aller, continuer; **go down to the end of the street** allez *ou* continuez jusqu'en bas de la rue

(n) *Br Univ* entrer dans la période des vacances

(o) *Cards (in bridge)* chuter

(p) *Comput* tomber en panne; *(of computer network)* planter; **the computer's gone down** l'ordinateur est en panne

(q) *Mus (lower pitch)* descendre

(r) *Br Fam (be sent to prison)* **how long do you think he'll go down for?** il écopera de combien, à ton avis?; **he went down for three years** il a écopé de trois ans

(s) *Am Fam (happen)* se passer ☐

2 *vt insep (hill, stairs, ladder, street)* descendre; **my food went down the wrong way** j'ai avalé de travers; *Mus* **the pianist went down an octave** le pianiste a joué une octave plus bas *ou* a descendu d'une octave; *Br Sch* **to go down a class** descendre d'une classe; *Fig* **I don't want to go down that road** je ne veux pas m'engager là-dedans

▸**go down on** *vt insep Vulg (fellate)* sucer, tailler *ou* faire une pipe à; *(perform cunnilingus on)* sucer, brouter le cresson à

▸**go down with** *vt insep* tomber malade de; **he went down with pneumonia/the flu** il a attrapé une pneumonie/la grippe

▸**go for** *vt insep* **(a)** *(fetch)* aller chercher; **he went for a doctor** il est allé *ou* parti chercher un médecin

(b) *(try to obtain)* essayer d'obtenir, viser; **she's going for his job** elle va essayer d'obtenir son poste; *Fam* **go for it!** vas-y!; **I'd go for it if I were you!** à ta place, je n'hésiterais pas!; **she was really going for it** elle donnait vraiment son maximum

(c) *(attack → physically)* tomber sur, s'élancer sur; *(→ verbally)* s'en prendre à; **dogs usually go for the throat** en général, les chiens attaquent à la gorge; **they went for each other** *(physically)* ils se sont jetés l'un sur l'autre; *(verbally)* ils s'en sont pris l'un à l'autre; **the newspapers really went for the senator** les journaux s'en sont pris au sénateur sans retenue; **go for him!** *(to dog)* attaque!

(d) *Fam (like)* aimer ☐, adorer ☐; **I don't really go for that idea** l'idée ne me dit pas grand-chose; **he really goes for her in a big way** il est vraiment fou d'elle

(e) *(choose, prefer)* choisir, préférer

(f) *(apply to, concern)* concerner, s'appliquer à; **what I said goes for both of you** ce que j'ai dit vaut pour *ou* s'applique à vous deux; **pollution is a real problem in Paris – that goes for Rome too** la pollution pose un énorme problème à Paris – c'est la même chose à Rome; **and the same goes for me** et moi aussi

(g) *(have as result)* servir à; **his twenty years of service went for nothing** ses vingt ans de service n'ont servi à rien

(h) *(be to the advantage of)* **she has a lot going for her** elle a beaucoup d'atouts; **that idea hasn't got much going for it frankly** cette idée n'est franchement pas très convaincante

▸**go forth** *vi Arch or Literary* **(a)** *(leave)* sortir; **the army went forth into battle** l'armée s'est mise en route pour la bataille; *Bible* **go forth and multiply** croissez et multipliez-vous

(b) *(be pronounced)* être prononcé; *(be published)* paraître; **the command went forth that...** il fut décrété que...

▸**go forward** *vi* (s')avancer; **the clocks go forward tomorrow** on avance les pendules demain; **if this scheme goes forward...** si ce projet est accepté...

▸**go in** *vi* **(a)** *(enter)* entrer, rentrer; **it's cold – let's go in** il fait froid – entrons; **it's too big, it won't go in** c'est trop grand, ça ne rentrera pas

(b) *(disappear → moon, sun)* se cacher

(c) *Sport (in cricket)* prendre son tour au guichet

(d) *Mil (attack)* attaquer

▸**go in for** *vt insep* **(a)** *(engage in → activity, hobby, sport)* pratiquer, faire; *(→ occupation)* se consacrer à; *(→ politics)* s'occuper de, faire; **she went in for company law** elle s'est lancée dans le droit commercial; **he thought about going in for teaching** il a pensé devenir enseignant

(b) *Fam (be interested in)* s'intéresser à ☐; *(like)* aimer ☐; **I don't go in much for opera** je n'aime pas trop l'opéra, l'opéra ne me dit rien; **he goes in for special effects in a big way** il est très branché effets spéciaux; **we don't go in for that kind of film** nous n'aimons pas ce genre de film;

this publisher doesn't really go in for fiction cet éditeur ne fait pas tellement dans le roman

(**c**) *Fam (use)* **they don't go in for injections so much nowadays** ils ne sont pas tellement pour les piqûres de nos jours; **why do scientists go in for all that jargon?** pourquoi est-ce que les scientifiques utilisent tout ce jargon?

(**d**) *(take part in → competition, race)* prendre part à; *(→ examination)* se présenter à

(**e**) *(apply for → job, position)* poser sa candidature à, postuler

►**go into** *vt insep* (**a**) *(enter → building, house)* entrer dans; *(→ activity, profession)* entrer à *ou* dans; *(→ politics, business)* se lancer dans; **she's gone into hospital** elle est (r)entrée à l'hôpital; **to go into the army** *(as profession)* devenir militaire de carrière; *(as conscript)* partir au service; **he went into medicine** il a choisi la médecine

(**b**) *(be invested → of effort, money, time)* **a lot of care had gone into making her feel at home** on s'était donné beaucoup de peine pour la mettre à l'aise; **two months of research went into our report** nous avons mis *ou* investi deux mois de recherche dans notre rapport

(**c**) *(embark on → action)* commencer à; *(→ explanation, speech)* se lancer *ou* s'embarquer dans, (se mettre à) donner; *(→ problem)* aborder; **I'll go into the problem of your taxes later** j'aborderai le problème de vos impôts plus tard; **the car went into a skid** la voiture a commencé à déraper; **to go into hysterics** avoir une crise de nerfs; **to go into fits of laughter** être pris d'un fou rire

(**d**) *(examine, investigate)* examiner, étudier; **you need to go into the question more deeply** vous devez examiner le problème de plus près; **the matter is being gone into** l'affaire est à l'étude

(**e**) *(explain in depth)* entrer dans; **the essay goes into the moral aspects of the question** l'essai aborde les aspects moraux de la question; **I won't go into details** je ne vais pas entrer dans les détails; **let's not go into that** ne parlons pas de ça

(**f**) *(begin to wear)* se mettre à porter; **to go into mourning** prendre le deuil

(**g**) *(hit, run into)* entrer dans; **a car went into him** une voiture lui est rentrée dedans

(**h**) *Comput (file, program)* aller dans; **to go into a file** aller dans un fichier

►**go off** 1 *vi* (**a**) *(leave)* partir, s'en aller; **she went off to work** elle est partie travailler; **her husband has gone off and left her** son mari l'a quittée; *Theat* **the actors went off** les acteurs ont quitté la scène

(**b**) *(stop operating → light, radio)* s'éteindre; *(→ heating)* s'éteindre, s'arrêter; *(→ pain)* partir, s'arrêter; **the electricity went off** l'électricité a été coupée

(**c**) *(become activated → bomb, firework)* exploser; *(→ gun)* partir; *(→ alarm, alarm clock)* sonner; **the grenade went off in her hand** la grenade a explosé dans sa main; **the gun didn't go off** le coup n'est pas parti; *Fig* **to go off into fits of laughter** être pris d'un fou rire

(**d**) *([illegible]ified outcome)* se passer; **the interview went off badly/well** l'entretien s'est mal/bien passé; **her speech went off well** son discours a été bien reçu

(**e**) *(fall asleep)* s'endormir

(**f**) *Br (deteriorate → food)* s'avarier, se gâter; *(→ milk)* tourner; *(→ butter)* rancir; *(→ athlete, sportsperson)* perdre sa forme; **the play goes off in the second half** la pièce se gâte pendant la seconde partie

2 *vt insep Br Fam (stop liking)* perdre le goût de❑; **he's gone off classical music/smoking** il n'aime plus la musique classique/fumer, la musique classique/fumer ne l'intéresse plus; **I've gone off the idea** cette idée ne me dit plus rien; **she's gone off her boyfriend** son copain ne l'intéresse plus; **funny how you can go off people** c'est drôle comme on se lasse des gens parfois

►**go off with** *vt insep* (**a**) *(leave with)* partir avec; **he went off with the woman next door** il est parti avec la voisine

(**b**) *(make off with)* partir avec; **someone has gone off with his keys** quelqu'un est parti avec ses clés; **he went off with the jewels** il s'est enfui avec les bijoux

►**go on** 1 *vi* (**a**) *(move, proceed)* aller; *(without stopping)* poursuivre son chemin; *(after stopping)* repartir, se remettre en route; **you go on, I'll catch up** allez-y, je vous rattraperai (en chemin); **they went on without us** ils sont partis sans nous; **after dinner they went on to Susan's house** après le dîner, ils sont allés chez Susan; **we went on home** nous sommes rentrés

(**b**) *(continue action)* continuer; **she went on (with her) reading** elle a continué à *ou* de lire; **the chairman went on speaking** le président a continué son discours; **"and that's not all", he went on** "et ce n'est pas tout", a-t-il poursuivi; **you can't go on being a student for ever!** tu ne peux pas être étudiant toute ta vie!; **go on looking!** cherchez encore!; **go on, ask her** vas-y, demande-lui; *Fam* **go on, be a devil** vas-y, laisse-toi tenter!; **go on, I'm listening** continuez, je vous écoute; **I can't go on like this!** je ne peux plus continuer comme ça!; **if he goes on like this, he'll get fired** s'il continue comme ça, il va se faire renvoyer; **their affair has been going on for years** leur liaison dure depuis des années; **the party went on into the small hours** la soirée s'est prolongée jusqu'à très tôt le matin; **life goes on** la vie continue *ou* va son train; *Br Fam* **go on (with you)!** allons, arrête de me faire marcher!; **they have enough (work) to be going on with** ils ont du pain sur la planche *ou* de quoi faire pour le moment; **here's £25 to be going on with** voilà 25 livres pour te dépanner

(**c**) *(proceed to another action)* **he went on to explain why** il a ensuite expliqué pourquoi; **to go on to another question** passer à une autre question; **she went on to become a doctor** elle est ensuite devenue médecin

(**d**) *(be placed, fit)* aller; **the lid goes on this way** le couvercle se met comme ça; **I can't get the lid to go on** je n'arrive pas à mettre le couvercle; **the cap goes on the other end** le bouchon se met *ou* va sur l'autre bout

(**e**) *(happen, take place)* se passer; **what's going on here?** qu'est-ce qui se passe ici?; **there was a fight going on** il y avait une bagarre; **a lot of cheating goes on during the exams** on triche beaucoup pendant les examens; **several conversations were going on at once** il y avait plusieurs conversations à la fois; **while the war was going on** pendant la guerre

(**f**) *(elapse)* passer, s'écouler; **as the week went on** au fur et à mesure que la semaine passait; **as time goes on** avec le temps, à mesure que le temps passe

(**g**) *Fam (chatter, talk)* parler❑, jacasser❑; **she does go on!** elle n'arrête pas de parler!, c'est un vrai moulin à paroles!; **he goes on and on about politics** il parle politique sans cesse; **don't go on about it!** ça va, on a compris!; **I don't want to go on about it, but...** je ne voudrais pas avoir l'air d'insister, mais...; **what are you going on about now?** qu'est-ce que vous racontez?

(**h**) *Fam (act, behave)* se conduire❑, se comporter❑; **what a way to go on!** en voilà des manières!

(**i**) *(start operating → light, radio, television)* s'allumer; *(→ heating, motor, power)* s'allumer, se mettre en marche

(**j**) *Sport (player)* prendre sa place, entrer en jeu

(**k**) *Theat (actor)* entrer en scène

(**l**) *(approach)* **he's going on for forty** il va sur ses quarante ans

2 *vt insep* (**a**) *(enter → boat, train)* monter dans

(**b**) *(embark on)* **to go on a journey/a holiday** partir en voyage/en vacances; **to go on a diet** se mettre au régime

(**c**) *(be guided by)* se laisser guider par, se fonder *ou* se baser sur; **the detective didn't have much to go on** le détective n'avait pas grand-chose sur quoi s'appuyer *ou* qui puisse le guider; **she goes a lot on instinct** elle se fie beaucoup à *ou* se fonde beaucoup sur son instinct

(**d**) *(approach)* **he's going on forty-five** il va sur ses quarante-cinq ans; *Hum* **she's fifteen going on forty-five** *(wise)* elle a quinze ans mais elle est déjà très mûre; *(old beyond her years)* elle a quinze ans mais elle est vieille avant l'âge

(**e**) *Br Fam (usu neg) (appreciate, like)* aimer❑; **I don't go much on abstract art** l'art abstrait ne me dit pas grand-chose

►**go on at** *vt insep Fam (criticize)* critiquer❑; *(nag)* s'en prendre à❑; **the boss went on and on at her at the meeting** le patron n'a pas cessé de s'en prendre à elle pendant la réunion; **he's always going on at his wife about money** il est toujours sur le dos de sa femme avec les questions d'argent; **I went on at my mother to go and see the doctor** j'ai embêté ma mère pour qu'elle aille voir le médecin; **don't go on at me!** laisse-moi tranquille!

►**go out** *vi* (**a**) *(leave)* sortir; **my parents made us go out of the room** mes parents nous ont fait sortir de la pièce *ou* quitter la pièce; **to go out for a meal** aller au restaurant; **to go out to dinner** sortir dîner; **to go out for a walk** aller se promener, aller faire une promenade; **she's gone out to get a paper** elle est sortie (pour) acheter un journal; **they went out to the country** ils sont allés *ou* ils ont fait une sortie à la campagne; **she goes out to work** elle travaille en dehors de la maison *ou* hors de chez elle; **he went out of her life** il est sorti de sa vie; **she was dressed to go out** *(ready to leave)* elle était prête à sortir; *(dressed up)* elle était très habillée

(**b**) *(travel)* partir; *(emigrate)* émigrer; **they went out to Africa** *(travelled)* ils sont partis en Afrique; *(emigrated)* ils sont partis vivre *ou* ils ont émigré en Afrique

(**c**) *(date)* sortir; **to go out with sb** sortir avec qn; **we've been going out together for a month** ça fait un mois que nous sortons ensemble

(**d**) *(fire, light)* s'éteindre

(**e**) *(disappear)* disparaître; **the joy went out of her eyes** la joie a disparu de son regard; **the spring went out of his step** il a perdu sa démarche légère; **all the heart went out of her** elle a perdu courage

(**f**) *(cease to be fashionable)* passer de mode, se démoder; **to go out of style/fashion** ne plus être le bon style/à la mode; *Fam* **that hairstyle went out with the ark** cette coiffure remonte au déluge

(**g**) *(tide)* descendre, se retirer; **the tide has gone out** la marée est descendue, la mer s'est retirée; **the tide goes out 6 kilometres** la mer se retire sur 6 kilomètres

(**h**) *Fig (set out)* **I went out to see for myself** j'ai décidé de voir par moi-même; **we have to go out and do something about this** il faut que nous prenions des mesures *ou* que nous fassions quelque chose

(**i**) *(be sent → letter)* être envoyé; *(be published → brochure, pamphlet)* être distribué; *(be broadcast → radio or television programme)* être diffusé

(**j**) *(feelings, sympathies)* aller; **our thoughts go out to all those who suffer** nos pensées vont vers tous ceux qui souffrent; **my heart goes out to her** je suis de tout cœur avec elle dans son chagrin

(**k**) *Sport (be eliminated)* être éliminé; **Agassi went out to Henman** Agassi s'est fait sortir par Henman

(**l**) *Cards* terminer

(**m**) [illegible] **she went all out to help us** elle a fait tout son possible pour nous aider

►**go over** 1 *vi* (**a**) *(move overhead)* passer; **I just saw a plane go over** je viens de voir passer un avion

(**b**) *(move in particular direction)* aller; *(cross)* traverser; **I went over to see her** je suis allé la voir; **they went over to talk to her** ils sont allés lui parler; **to go over to Europe** aller en Europe

(**c**) *(turn upside down)* se retourner; *(capsize → boat)* chavirer, capoter

(**d**) *(change, switch)* changer; **I've gone over to another brand of washing powder** je viens de changer de marque de lessive; **when will we go over to the metric system?** quand est-ce qu'on va passer au système métrique?

(**e**) *(change allegiance)* passer, se joindre; **he's gone over to the Socialists** il est passé dans le camp des socialistes; **she went over to the enemy** elle est passée à l'ennemi

(**f**) *(be received)* passer; **the speech went over badly/well** le discours a mal/bien passé

go–go

2 *vt insep* (**a**) *(move, travel over)* passer par-dessus; **the horse went over the fence** le cheval a sauté (par-dessus) la barrière; **we went over a bump** on a pris une bosse

(**b**) *(examine → argument, problem)* examiner, considérer; *(→ accounts, report)* examiner, vérifier; **would you go over my report?** voulez-vous regarder mon rapport?

(**c**) *(repeat)* répéter; *(review → notes, speech)* réviser, revoir; *(→ facts)* récapituler, revoir; *Sch* réviser; **she went over the interview in her mind** elle a repassé l'entretien dans son esprit; **I kept going over everything leading up to the accident** je continuais de repenser à tous les détails qui avaient conduit à l'accident; **let's go over it again** reprenons, récapitulons; **he goes over and over the same stories** il rabâche les mêmes histoires

(**d**) *(rehearse)* refaire; *(bars of music)* rejouer; *(sing)* rechanter

(**e**) *TV & Rad* **let's go over now to our Birmingham studios** passons l'antenne à notre studio de Birmingham; **we're going over live now to Paris** nous allons maintenant à Paris où nous sommes en direct

►**go past** *vt insep (move in front of)* passer devant; *(move beyond)* dépasser

►**go round** 1 *vi* (**a**) *(be enough)* **is there enough cake to go round?** est-ce qu'il y a assez de gâteau pour tout le monde?; **to make the food go round** ménager la nourriture

(**b**) *(visit)* aller; **we went round to his house** nous sommes allés chez lui; **I'm going round there later on** j'y vais plus tard

(**c**) *(circulate → rumour)* circuler, courir; *(→ bottle, cold, flu)* circuler

(**d**) *(be continuously present → idea, tune)* **that song keeps going round in my head** j'ai cette chanson dans la tête

(**e**) *(spin → wheel)* tourner; *Fig* **my head's going round** j'ai la tête qui tourne

(**f**) *(make a detour)* faire un détour; **to go round the long way** faire un long détour

2 *vt insep (tour → museum)* faire le tour de; **I hate going round the shops** j'ai horreur de faire les boutiques

►**go through** 1 *vt insep* (**a**) *(crowd, tunnel)* traverser; *Fig* **a shiver went through her** un frisson l'a parcourue *ou* traversée

(**b**) *(endure, experience)* subir, souffrir; **he's going through hell** c'est l'enfer pour lui; **we all have to go through it sometime** on doit tous y passer un jour ou l'autre; **I can't face going through all that again** je ne supporterais pas de passer par là une deuxième fois; **after everything she's gone through** après tout ce qu'elle a subi *ou* enduré; **we've gone through a lot together** nous avons vécu beaucoup de choses ensemble

(**c**) *(consume, use up → supplies)* épuiser; *(→ money)* dépenser; *(→ food)* consommer; *(wear out)* user; **she goes through a pair of tights a week** elle use une paire de collants par semaine; **I've gone through the toes of my socks** j'ai usé *ou* troué mes chaussettes au bout; *Hum* **how many assistants has he gone through now?** combien d'assistants a-t-il déjà eus?; **his novel has gone through six editions** il y a déjà eu six éditions de son roman

(**d**) *(examine → accounts, document)* examiner, vérifier; *(→ list, proposal)* éplucher; *(→ mail)* dépouiller; *(→ drawer, pockets)* fouiller (dans); *(→ files)* chercher dans; *(sort)* trier; **we went through the contract together** nous avons regardé *ou* examiné le contrat ensemble; **did customs go through your suitcase?** est-ce qu'ils ont fouillé votre valise à la douane?; **he went through her pockets** il a fouillé ses poches

(**e**) *(of bill, law)* être voté; **the bill went through Parliament last week** le projet de loi a été voté la semaine dernière au Parlement

(**f**) *(carry out, perform → movement, work)* faire; *(→ formalities)* remplir, accomplir; *Mus* **let's go through the introduction again** reprenons l'introduction; **we had to go through the whole business of applying for a visa** nous avons dû nous farcir toutes les démarches pour obtenir un visa

(**g**) *(participate in → course of study)* étudier; *(→ ceremony)* participer à

(**h**) *(practise → lesson, poem)* réciter; *(→ role, scene)* répéter; **let's go through it again from the beginning** reprenons dès le début

2 *vi* (**a**) *(travel through, penetrate)* passer, traverser

(**b**) *(offer, proposal)* être accepté; *(business deal)* être conclu, se faire; *(bill, law)* passer, être voté; *(divorce)* être prononcé; **the adoption finally went through** l'adoption s'est faite finalement

►**go through with** *vt insep* **to go through with sth** aller jusqu'au bout de qch, exécuter qch; **he'll never go through with it** il n'ira jamais jusqu'au bout; **they went through with their threat** ils ont exécuté leur menace

►**go together** *vi* (**a**) *(colours, flavours)* aller bien ensemble; *(characteristics, ideas)* aller de pair; **the two things often go together** les deux choses vont souvent de pair

(**b**) *Am (people)* sortir ensemble

►**go towards** *vt insep* (**a**) *(move towards)* aller vers

(**b**) *(effort, money)* être consacré à; **all her energy went towards fighting illiteracy** elle a dépensé toute son énergie à combattre l'analphabétisme

►**go under** 1 *vi* (**a**) *(go down → ship)* couler, sombrer; *(→ person)* couler, disparaître (sous l'eau)

(**b**) *Fig (fail → business)* couler, faire faillite; *(→ project)* couler, échouer; *(→ person)* échouer, sombrer

(**c**) *(under anaesthetic)* s'endormir

2 *vt insep* (**a**) *(move, travel underneath)* passer par-dessous

(**b**) *(be known)* **to go under a false/different name** utiliser *ou* prendre un faux nom/un nom différent; **a glue that goes under the name of Stikit** une colle qui s'appelle Stikit

►**go up** 1 *vi* (**a**) *(ascend, climb → person)* monter, aller en haut; *(→ lift)* monter; **to go up to town** aller en ville; **I'm going up to bed** je monte me coucher; **have you ever gone up in an aeroplane?** êtes-vous déjà monté en avion?; **going up!** *(in lift)* on monte!; **to go up in the world** faire son chemin

(**b**) *(increase → amount, numbers)* augmenter, croître; *(→ price)* monter, augmenter; *(→ temperature)* monter, s'élever; **rents are going up** les loyers sont en hausse; **meat is going up (in price)** (le prix de) la viande augmente; **to go up in sb's estimation** monter dans l'estime de qn

(**c**) *(sudden noise)* s'élever; **a shout went up** un cri s'éleva

(**d**) *(appear → notices, posters)* apparaître; *(be built)* être construit; **new buildings are going up all over town** de nouveaux immeubles surgissent dans toute la ville

(**e**) *(explode, be destroyed)* sauter, exploser

(**f**) *Mus (raise pitch)* monter

(**g**) *Theat (curtain)* se lever; **before the curtain goes up** avant le lever du rideau

(**h**) *Br Univ* entrer à l'université; **she went up to Oxford in 1950** elle est entrée à Oxford en 1950

(**i**) *Am Fam (be sent to prison)* **he went up for murder** il a fait de la taule pour meurtre

(**j**) *Sport (be promoted)* **they look set to go up to the First Division** ils ont l'air prêts à entrer en première division

2 *vt insep* monter; **to go up a hill/ladder** monter une colline/sur une échelle; *Mus* **the pianist went up an octave** le pianiste a monté d'une octave; *Br Sch* **to go up a class** monter d'une classe

►**go up to** *vt insep* (**a**) *(approach)* **to go up to sb/sth** se diriger vers qn/qch; **the path goes up to the front door** le chemin mène à la porte d'entrée

(**b**) *(go as far as)* **the book only goes up to the end of the war** le livre ne va que jusqu'à la fin de la guerre; **I will go up to £100** je veux bien aller jusqu'à 100 livres

►**go with** *vt insep* (**a**) *(accompany, escort)* accompagner, aller avec; *Fig* **to go with the crowd** suivre la foule *ou* le mouvement; **you have to go with the times** il faut vivre avec son temps

(**b**) *(be compatible → colours, flavours)* aller avec; **that hat doesn't go with your suit** ce chapeau ne va pas avec ton ensemble; **a white Burgundy goes well with snails** le bourgogne blanc se marie bien *ou* va bien avec les escargots

(**c**) *(be part of)* aller avec; **the flat goes with the job** l'appartement va avec le poste; **the sense of satisfaction that goes with having done a good job** le sentiment de satisfaction qu'apporte le travail bien fait; **mathematical ability usually goes with skill at chess** des capacités en mathématiques vont souvent de pair avec un don pour les échecs

(**d**) *Fam (spend time with)* sortir avec ❑; *Euph* **he's been going with other women** *(having sex)* il a été avec d'autres femmes

►**go without** 1 *vt insep* se passer de, se priver de; **he went without sleep** *or* **without sleeping for two days** il n'a pas dormi pendant deux jours

2 *vi* s'en passer; **we'll just have to go without** il faudra s'en passer, c'est tout

Do not pass go, (do not collect £200/$200)
Au Monopoly les joueurs tirent parfois une carte qui les envoie sur la case "prison". Sur cette carte sont inscrits les mots **do not pass go, do not collect £200** (ou bien **do not collect $200** s'il s'agit de la version américaine).
Cette phrase, dont la version française est "ne passez pas par la case départ, ne recevez pas 20 000 francs", est utilisée de façon allusive et sur le mode humoristique dans différents contextes: on dira par exemple **you do that again and you're going straight to jail, Bill. Do not pass go, do not collect $200** ("refais ça, Bill, et je t'assure que tu iras droit en prison).
On peut également utiliser cette expression lorsque quelqu'un essaie de mener un projet à bien mais rencontre des obstacles: **the country is trying hard to get back on its feet but because of the civil war it has not even been allowed to pass go, let alone collect £200** ("le pays fait de son mieux pour se rétablir mais la guerre civile n'arrange rien, bien au contraire").

Go ahead, make my day
C'est la formule prononcée par l'inspecteur Harry Callahan (incarné par Clint Eastwood) dans le film *Sudden Impact* (1983) lorsqu'il se trouve confronté à un gangster. Il s'agit d'une façon d'encourager le bandit à se servir de son arme afin de pouvoir l'abattre en état de légitime défense: "allez, vas-y, fais-moi plaisir".
On utilise cette formule par allusion au film et en réaction à une personne qui vient de proférer des menaces. Ainsi, le président Reagan s'en servit en s'adressant à des travailleurs qui menaçaient de se mettre en grève.

Goa ['gəʊə] *n* Goa

►► *Pharm* **Goa powder** araroba *m* pulvérisé, poudre *f* de Goa

goad [gəʊd] 1 *n* aiguillon *m*

2 *vt* (**a**) *(cattle)* aiguillonner, piquer

(**b**) *(person)* harceler, provoquer; **stop goading the poor child!** cesse de houspiller ce petit!; **to goad sb into doing sth** pousser qn à faire qch, harceler qn jusqu'à ce qu'il fasse qch; **he goaded me into losing my temper** il m'a harcelé jusqu'à ce que je me mette en colère; **the threat of redundancy goaded the men into action** la peur d'un licenciement incita les hommes à l'action

►**goad on** *vt sep* aiguillonner; **don't goad him on!** arrête de l'exciter!; **she was goaded on by the prospect of wealth and power** elle était stimulée par la perspective des richesses et du pouvoir

go-ahead 1 *n* feu *m* vert; **to give sb the go-ahead to do sth** donner le feu vert à qn pour faire qch; **to give sth the go-ahead** donner le feu vert pour qch

2 *adj (dynamic → person)* dynamique, entreprenant, qui va de l'avant; *(→ attitude, business)* dynamique

goal [gəʊl] *n* (**a**) *(aim)* but *m*, objectif *m*; **what's your goal in life?** quel est ton but *ou* quelle est ton ambition dans la vie?; **to set oneself a goal** se fixer un but *ou* objectif; **to achieve** *or* **attain**

one's goal atteindre *ou* réaliser son but; **she had achieved** *or* **attained her goal of becoming Prime Minister** elle avait atteint *ou* réalisé son but de devenir Premier ministre; **commercial and financial goals need to be clearly defined** les objectifs commerciaux et financiers doivent être clairement définis

(**b**) *Sport* but *m*; **to score a goal** marquer un but; **they won by five goals to two** ils ont gagné par cinq buts à deux; **Macleod was in goal for Rangers** Macleod était dans les buts des Rangers; **who plays in** *or* **keeps goal for Liverpool?** qui est gardien de but dans l'équipe de Liverpool?; **goal!** but!

▸▸ ***goal area*** (zone *f* des) six mètres *mpl*; ***goal average*** goal-average *m*; ***goal difference*** différence *f* de buts; ***goal kick*** coup *m* de pied au but, dégagement *m* aux six mètres; ***goal kicker*** *(in American football)* botteur *m*; ***goal line*** ligne *f* de but

goalie ['gəʊlɪ] *n Fam* goal ❑ *m*, gardien *m* (de but) ❑

goalkeeper ['gəʊl,ki:pə(r)] *n* gardien *m* (de but), goal *m*

goalkeeping ['gəʊl,ki:pɪŋ] *n* jeu *m* du gardien de but; **we saw some great goalkeeping on both sides** les deux gardiens de but ont très bien joué

▸▸ ***goalkeeping gloves*** gants *mpl* de gardien de but

goalless ['gəʊllɪs] *adj* **a goalless draw** un match sans but marqué *ou* zéro à zéro

goalminder ['gəʊl,maɪndə(r)] *n Br (in hockey, ice hockey)* gardien *m* de but

goalmouth ['gəʊl,maʊθ, *pl* -maʊðz] *n* entrée *f* de but; **in the goalmouth** directement devant le but; **a goalmouth scuffle** un cafouillage devant le but; **there was no shortage of goalmouth incidents** il y avait beaucoup d'action devant les cages

goalpost ['gəʊlpəʊst] *n* poteau *m* (de but); *Fig* **to move the goalposts** changer les règles du jeu

goalscorer ['gəʊl,skɔ:rə(r)] *n* buteur *m*; **the leading** *or* **top goalscorer** le meilleur buteur

goaltender ['gəʊl,tendə(r)] *n (in ice hockey)* gardien *m* de but

Goan ['gəʊən], **Goanese** [gəʊə'ni:z] **1** *n (inhabitant)* habitant(e) *m,f* de Goa; *(native)* originaire *mf* de Goa

2 *adj* de Goa

go-around *n* **to give sb the go-around** faire une réponse de Normand *ou* répondre en Normand à qn

goat [gəʊt] *n* (**a**) *Zool* chèvre *f* (**b**) *Fam* **old goat** *(lecherous man)* vieux *m* cochon; *Am (old woman)* vieille toupie *f*; *(old man)* vieux schnock *m* (**c**) *Fam Old-fashioned (foolish person)* andouille *f*; **you silly goat!** espèce d'andouille!; **to act** *or* **to play the (giddy) goat** faire l'andouille (**d**) *Fam (idiom)* **to get sb's goat** taper sur les nerfs *ou* le système à qn; **it gets my goat** ça me tape sur les nerfs

▸▸ ***goat's cheese*** (fromage *m* de) chèvre *m*; ***goat's milk*** lait *m* de chèvre; *Entom* ***goat moth*** gâte-bois *m*; *Bot* ***goat willow*** marceau *m*

goatee [gəʊ'ti:] *n* barbiche *f*, bouc *m*

goatherd ['gəʊthɜ:d] *n* chevrier(ère) *m,f*

goatskin ['gəʊtskɪn] *n* (**a**) *(hide)* peau *f* de chèvre (**b**) *(container)* outre *f* (en peau de chèvre)

goatsucker ['gəʊt,sʌkə(r)] *n Orn* engoulevent *m*, tète-chèvre *m*

gob [gɒb] (*pt & pp* **gobbed**, *cont* **gobbing**) *Fam* **1** *n* (**a**) *Br (mouth)* gueule *f*; **shut your gob!** fermela!, la ferme!; **he's got a bit of a gob on him** il est assez grande gueule (**b**) *(spittle)* crachat ❑ *m*, mollard *m*

2 *vi (spit)* cracher ❑, mollarder

3 gobs *npl* **gobs of** un tas de, des masses de

gobbet ['gɒbɪt] *n Fam* morceau ❑ *m*

gobble ['gɒbəl] **1** *vi (turkey)* glouglouter

2 *vt (eat greedily)* enfourner, engloutir; **don't gobble your food!** ne mange pas si vite!

3 *n (of turkey)* glouglou *m*

▸**gobble up** *vt sep (eat quickly)* engloutir, engouffrer; *Fig (money, pay rise)* engloutir; *Fig* **the empire gobbled up these territories** l'empire a absorbé ces territoires

gobbledegook, gobbledygook ['gɒbəldɪgu:k] *n Fam* charabia *m*

gobbler ['gɒblə(r)] *n Fam (male turkey)* dindon ❑ *m*

gobby [,gɒbɪ] *adj Br Fam* **to be gobby** être une grande gueule

go-between *n* intermédiaire *mf*; **to act** *or* **serve as a go-between** servir d'intermédiaire

'The Go-Between' *Hartley, Losey* 'Le Messager'

gobful ['gɒbfʊl] *n Br Fam (mouthful)* bouchée *f* pleine ❑

Gobi ['gəʊbɪ] *n* **the Gobi Desert** le désert de Gobi

goblet ['gɒblɪt] *n* coupe *f*, verre *m* à pied; *Hist* gobelet *m*

goblin ['gɒblɪn] *n* esprit *m* maléfique, lutin *m*

gobo ['geʊbəʊ] *n* (**a**) *(on camera lens, spotlight etc)* volet *m* (coupe-flux), écran *m* (de protection) (**b**) *(on microphone)* bonnette *f* de micro

gobshite ['gɒbʃaɪt] *n Br very Fam (man)* trouduc *m*; *(woman)* connasse *f*

gobsmacked ['gɒbsmækt] *adj Br Fam* estomaqué; **I was absolutely gobsmacked** j'étais complètement estomaqué

gobstopper ['gɒb,stɒpə(r)] *n Br* = gros bonbon rond qui change de couleur à mesure qu'on le suce

goby ['gəʊbɪ] (*pl* **gobies**) *n Ich* gobie *m*

go-by *n Fam* **to give sb the go-by** snober qn ❑

GOC [,dʒi:əʊ'si:] *n Mil* (*abbr* **General Officer Commanding/Commanding-in-Chief**) = général commandant en chef

go-cart *n* (**a**) = **go-kart** (**b**) *Br Old-fashioned or Am (babywalker)* trotteur *m*; *(toy wagon)* chariot *m*

go-carting = **go-karting**

god [gɒd] **1** *n* dieu *m*; **the god of War** le dieu de la Guerre; **profit is their only god** leur seul dieu, c'est le profit; *Arch or Hum* **ye gods!** grands dieux!

2 God *n* (**a**) *Rel* Dieu *m*; **God the Father, the Son and the Holy Ghost** Dieu le Père, le Fils, le Saint-Esprit; **a man of God** un homme de Dieu; **to play God** se prendre pour Dieu; **to play God with people's lives** disposer de la vie des gens; **who do you think you are – God?** tu te prends pour Dieu le père ou quoi?; **God's acre** cimetière *m*; *Fam* **he thinks he's God's gift** il ne se prend pas pour n'importe qui, il se croit sorti de la cuisse de Jupiter; *Fam* **he's not exactly God's gift to DIY** ce n'est pas vraiment un as du bricolage; *Fam* **he thinks he's God's gift to women** il croit que toutes les femmes vont tomber à ses pieds; *Fam* **he's not exactly God's gift to women** ce n'est pas vraiment l'homme dont rêvent toutes les femmes; **God's (own) country** *(beautiful place)* un endroit splendide; *(isolated place)* un trou perdu

(**b**) *(in interjections and expressions) Fam* **oh God!, my God!** mon Dieu!; **God, its warm today!** mon Dieu qu'il fait chaud aujourd'hui!; **God bless you!** Dieu vous bénisse!; *Old-fashioned (in response to sneezing)* à vos souhaits!; *Fam* **thank God!** Dieu merci!; *Fam* **thank God you didn't tell him** heureusement que tu ne lui as rien dit; **I wish to God I'd never come here** je voudrais ne jamais être venu; **I wish to God I'd never been born** j'aurais voulu ne jamais venir au monde; *Fam* **in the name of God!** nom de Dieu!; *Fam* **what in God's name are you doing?** qu'est-ce que tu fais là, nom de Dieu?; *Fam* **for God's sake!, for the love of God!** pour l'amour de Dieu!; *Fam* **for God's sake, don't tell him!** surtout ne lui dis rien!; *Fam* **God knows why/how** Dieu sait pourquoi/comment; *Fam* **she's God knows where** elle est Dieu sait où; *Fam* **God (only) knows** Dieu seul le sait; **God willing** avec de la chance

3 gods *npl Br Fam* **the gods** *(in theatre)* le poulailler

▸▸ *Fam* ***God mode*** *(in computer games)* mode *m* dieu, god mode *m*; *Fam Pej* ***the God slot*** = expression humoristique désignant les émissions religieuses à la télévision; *Fam Pej* ***the God squad*** les bigots ❑ *mpl*, les bondieusards *mpl*

godawful [gɒd'ɔ:fʊl] *adj Fam* minable, nul; **what godawful weather!** quel sale temps!; **we ended up in some godawful hotel** on a atterri dans un hôtel minable

god-botherer [-,bɒðərə(r)] *n Fam* cul-bénit *m*

godchild ['gɒdtʃaɪld] (*pl* **godchildren** [-,tʃɪldrən]) *n* filleul(e) *m,f*

goddam = **goddamn**

goddammit [,gɒd'dæmɪt] *exclam very Fam* bordel!

goddamn ['gɒdæm] *Am very Fam* **1** *exclam* nom de Dieu!, merde!

2 *n* **he doesn't care** *or* **give a goddamn** il s'en fout

3 *adj* sacré, fichu; **that goddamn dog!** ce sacré chien!; **you goddamn fool!** pauvre imbécile!

4 *adv* vachement; **it's goddamn hot** il fait vachement chaud

goddamned ['gɒdæmd] = **goddamn** *adj & adv*

goddaughter ['gɒd,dɔ:tə(r)] *n* filleule *f*

goddess ['gɒdɪs] *n* déesse *f*; *Fig* **a goddess of the screen, a screen goddess** une idole du grand écran

godet ['gəʊdeɪ] *n Sewing* godet *m*

godetia [gə'di:ʃə] *n Bot* godetia *m*

godfather ['gɒd,fɑ:ðə(r)] *n* parrain *m*

'The Godfather' *Puzo, Coppola* 'Le Parrain'

god-fearing [-fɪərɪŋ] *adj* croyant, pieux; **decent god-fearing folk** les gens croyants bien comme il faut

godforsaken ['gɒdfə,seɪkən] *adj* paumé; **what a godforsaken place!** quel bled!

godhead ['gɒdhed] *n* divinité *f*; **the godhead** Dieu

godless ['gɒdlɪs] *adj* irréligieux, impie

godlessly ['gɒdlɪslɪ] *adv (irreligiously)* de façon impie

godlessness ['gɒdlɪsnɪs] *n* impiété *f*

godlike ['gɒdlaɪk] *adj* divin, céleste

godliness ['gɒdlɪnɪs] *n* sainteté *f* (de l'âme), dévotion *f*

godly ['gɒdlɪ] *adj* (**a**) *(pious)* pieux; **to lead a godly life** vivre pieusement (**b**) *(divine)* divin

godmother ['gɒd,mʌðə(r)] *n* marraine *f*

godown ['gəʊdaʊn] *n* entrepôt *m (en Asie, surtout en Inde)*

godparent ['gɒdpeərənt] *n (woman)* marraine *f*; *(man)* parrain *m*; **my godparents** mon parrain et ma marraine

godsend ['gɒdsend] *n* aubaine *f*; **this money is a godsend to him** cet argent est un don du ciel; **the president's gaffe was a godsend to the opposition** la gaffe du président a été une aubaine pour l'opposition

godson ['gɒdsʌn] *n* filleul *m*

godspeed [,gɒd'spi:d] *exclam Arch* à-Dieu-vat!

godwit ['gɒdwɪt] *n Orn* barge *f*

goer ['gəʊə(r)] *n Br Fam* (**a**) *(fast person)* fonceur(euse) *m,f*; *(animal)* rapide ❑; *(vehicle)* bolide; **this horse is a real goer** il file *ou* il fonce, ce cheval (**b**) **to be a goer** *(idea, plan)* être réalisable ❑ (**c**) **she's a real goer** *(promiscuous)* c'est une femme facile ❑; *(good in bed)* c'est un bon coup

-goer ['gəʊə(r)] *suff* **church/cinema/theatre-goer** personne qui va souvent à l'église/au cinéma/au théâtre

GO-error [gəʊ-] *n Mktg* erreur *f* d'adoption

[illegible]

go-faster stripe *n* = bande décorative sur la carrosserie d'une voiture

gofer ['gəʊfə(r)] *n* (**a**) *esp Am Fam (menial assistant → male)* homme *m* à tout faire; *(→ female)* bonne *f* à tout faire (**b**) *Comput* (serveur *m*) gopher *m*

go-getter [-,getə(r)] *n Fam* fonceur(euse) *m,f*, battant(e) ❑ *m,f*

go-getting [-,getɪŋ] *adj Fam (person)* plein d'allant ❑, entreprenant ❑; *(approach)* dynamique ❑

goggle ['gɒgəl] **1** *vi* ouvrir de grands yeux *ou* des yeux ronds; **to goggle at sb/sth** regarder qn/qch avec des yeux ronds

2 *adj* **to have goggle eyes** avoir les yeux saillants *ou* exorbités *ou* globuleux

3 goggles *npl* (**a**) *(protective)* lunettes *fpl* (de protection); *(for motorcyclist)* lunettes *fpl* (de motocycliste); *(for diver)* lunettes *fpl* de plongée; *(for swimmer, skier)* lunettes *fpl* (**b**) *Fam (glasses)* bésicles *fpl*

▸▸ *Br Fam Hum* ***goggle box*** télé *f*

goa–gog

goggle-eyed *adj* les yeux saillants *ou* exorbités *ou* globuleux; **to stare goggle-eyed** regarder en écarquillant les yeux

goggly ['gɒglɪ] *adj* **to have goggly eyes** avoir les yeux saillants *ou* exorbités *ou* globuleux

go-go *adj*
►► ***go-go dancer*** = homme ou femme légèrement vêtu(e) qui danse sur un podium de boîte de nuit; *St Exch* ***go-go stock*** action *f* hautement spéculative

Goidel ['gɔɪdel] *n (Gael)* Gaël *m*; *(speaker of a Goidelic language)* = personne qui parle une langue goïdélique

Goidelic [gɔɪ'delɪk] **1** *n* goïdélique *m*
2 *adj* relatif au goïdélique

going ['gəʊɪŋ] **1** *n* **(a)** *(leaving)* départ *m*
(b) *(progress)* progrès *m*; **we made good going on the return journey** on est allés vite pour le retour; **that's pretty good going!** c'est plutôt rapide!; **it was slow going** *(walking, climbing)* on progressait lentement; *(working, learning)* ça avancait lentement; **it was hard going** *(walking, climbing)* on progressait difficilement; *(learning, working)* c'était dur
(c) *(condition of ground)* état *m* du terrain; *Horseracing* **good/heavy going** bon terrain *m*/terrain *m* lourd; **the going is rough** le chemin est rude; **it's rough** *or* **heavy going on these mountain roads** c'est dur de rouler sur ces routes de montagne; *Fig* **this novel is heavy going** ce roman ne se lit pas facilement; *Fig* **it's heavy going getting him to talk** on a du mal à le faire parler; *Fig* **while the going is good** tant que c'est favorable; **to get out while the going's good** partir tant que les choses vont bien; *Prov* **when the going gets tough, the tough get going** = c'est dans les moments difficiles que les vrais hommes entrent en action
2 *adj* **(a)** *(functioning)* qui marche; **to start** *or* **set sth going** mettre qch en marche
(b) *(profitable)* **the business is a going concern** c'est une affaire qui marche; **for sale as a going concern** *(sign, in property advertisement)* à vendre avec fonds
(c) *(current)* actuel; **the going price** le prix actuel, le prix sur le marché; **she's getting the going rate for the job** elle touche le tarif en vigueur *ou* normal pour ce genre de travail; **the best computer/novelist going** le meilleur ordinateur/romancier du moment

going-away *adj (party, present)* d'adieu
►► ***going-away dress*** robe *f* de voyage de noce

going-back *n (return)* retour *m*; *(retreat)* recul *m*; **going back on one's word** manque *m* de parole; **there's no going back now** il n'y a pas moyen de revenir en arrière

going-concern *adj*
►► *Acct* ***going-concern concept, going-concern convention*** principe *m* de la continuité de l'exploitation; *Com* ***going-concern status*** continuité *f* d'exploitation

going-over (*pl* **goings-over**) *n Fam* **(a)** *(check-up)* révision ❑ *f*, vérification ❑ *f*; *(clean-up)* nettoyage ❑ *m*; **the house needs a good going-over** il faudrait nettoyer la maison à fond; **the auditors gave the accounts a thorough going-over** les experts ont soigneusement examiné les comptes ❑
(b) **to give sb a going-over** *(beating)* tabasser qn; *(criticism)* sonner les cloches à qn; **the burglars had given the flat a real going-over** les cambrioleurs avaient laissé l'appartement sens dessus dessous ❑

going-rate pricing *n Mktg* alignement *m* sur les prix du marché

goings-on *npl Fam* **(a)** *Pej (behaviour)* conduite ❑ *f*, activités ❑ *fpl*; **there are some funny goings-on in that house** il s'en passe de drôles dans cette maison; **what extraordinary goings-on!** quelles histoires extraordinaires! ❑ **(b)** *(events)* événements ❑ *mpl*

goitre, *Am* **goiter** ['gɔɪtə(r)] *n* goitre *m*

go-kart *n* kart *m*
►► ***go-kart racing*** karting *m*

go-karting *n* karting *m*

Golan Heights ['gəʊ,læn-] *npl* **the Golan Heights** le plateau du Golan

gold [gəʊld] **1** *n* **(a)** *(metal, colour)* or *m*; **1,000 French francs in gold** 1000 francs français en or; **to be as good as gold** être sage comme une image; **he has a heart of gold** il a un cœur d'or; **to be worth its weight in gold** valoir son pesant d'or
(b) *(gold medal)* médaille *f* d'or; **we won two golds and a silver** nous avons remporté deux médailles d'or et une (médaille) d'argent; **to go for gold** viser la médaille d'or
(c) *(colour)* or *m*; **the reds and golds of autumn** les rouges et les ors de l'automne
2 *adj* **(a)** *(made of gold → necklace, ring)* en or
(b) *(gold-coloured)* doré; **a gold dress** une robe couleur d'or *ou* dorée; **a gold lamé dress** une robe lamée d'or; **gold paint** peinture *f* dorée
3 *adv* **to go gold** *(record)* devenir disque d'or
►► *Fin* ***gold bond*** obligation *f* or; ***gold braid*** galon *m* d'or; ***gold bullion*** or *m* en barre *ou* en lingots, encaisse *f* or; ***gold bullion standard*** étalon-or-lingot *m*; ***gold card*** carte *f* de crédit illimité; ***the Gold Coast*** *(in Australia)* = suite de stations balnéaires sur la côte est de l'Australie; *Am (expensive area)* les beaux quartiers *mpl*; *Formerly (Ghana)* le Ghana; ***gold coin*** pièce *f* d'or; ***gold content*** teneur *f* en or; *Horseracing* ***the Gold Cup*** = course de chevaux se déroulant en mars à Cheltenham; ***gold currency*** monnaie *f* d'or; ***gold disc*** disque *m* d'or; ***gold dust*** poudre *f* d'or; *Fig* **tickets for the game are like gold dust** il est pratiquement impossible de se procurer des billets pour le match; *Econ & Hist* ***gold exchange standard*** étalon *m* de change or; *Fin* ***gold export point*** point *m* de sortie de l'or; ***gold fever*** fièvre *f* de l'or; ***gold filling*** *(in tooth)* obturation *f* à l'or *ou* en or; ***gold foil*** feuille *f* d'or, or *m* en feuille; *Fin* ***gold import point*** point *m* d'entrée de l'or; ***gold ingot*** lingot *m* d'or; ***gold leaf*** feuille *f* d'or, or *m* en feuille; ***gold market*** marché *m* de l'or; ***gold medal*** médaille *f* d'or; ***gold money*** monnaie *f* d'or; ***gold plate*** *(utensils)* orfèvrerie *f*, vaisselle *f* d'or; *(plating)* plaque *f* d'or; *Fin* ***gold point*** point *m* d'or; *Mus* ***gold record*** disque *m* d'or; *Fin* ***gold reserve*** réserve *f* d'or; ***gold rush*** ruée *f* vers l'or; *Am Hist* ***the Gold Rush*** la ruée vers l'or; *St Exch* ***gold share*** valeur *f* aurifère; ***gold standard*** étalon-or *m*; ***gold star*** *(given to schoolchildren)* ≃ bon point *m*

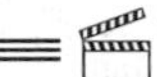

'Gold Rush' *Chaplin* 'La Ruée vers l'or'

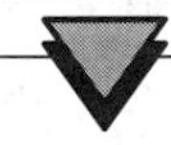

THE GOLD RUSH

Des milliers de personnes partirent pour la Californie, à la suite de la découverte de gisements d'or, en 1848. En un an, près de 80 000 pionniers atteignirent la côte ouest par terre ou par mer, après avoir échappé à la maladie et aux dangers du voyage.

goldbeater ['gəʊld,biːtə(r)] *n* batteur *m* d'or

goldbrick ['gəʊldbrɪk] *n Am Fam* **1** *n* **(a)** **to sell sb a goldbrick** rouler qn **(b)** *(malingerer)* tire-au-flanc *m inv*
2 *vt (swindle)* rouler
3 *vi (malinger)* tirer au flanc

goldbricker ['gəʊldbrɪkə(r)] *n Am Fam* tire-au-flanc *m inv*

gold-collar worker *n* col *m* doré

gold-coloured *adj* or *(inv)*, doré

goldcrest ['gəʊldkrest] *n Orn* roitelet *m* huppé

gold-digger *n* chercheur *m* d'or; *Fig (woman)* croqueuse *f* de diamants

golden ['gəʊldən] *adj* **(a)** *also Fig (made of gold)* en or, d'or; *(opinion)* favorable; **his last book won him golden opinions from the critics** son dernier livre a été encensé par la critique *ou* lui a valu l'éloge de toute la critique; **a golden opportunity** une occasion en or; **golden hours** des heures précieuses *ou* merveilleuses
(b) *(colour)* doré, (couleur) d'or; **golden brown** doré; **she has long golden hair** elle a de longs cheveux blonds; **golden yellow** jaune *m* d'or
(c) *(excellent)* **golden boy/girl** enfant *mf* chéri(e); **a golden opportunity** une occasion en or
►► ***the Golden Age*** l'âge *m* d'or; ***golden calf*** veau *m* d'or; ***Golden Delicious*** *(apple)* golden *f*; *Orn* ***golden eagle*** aigle *m* royal; *Myth* ***the Golden Fleece*** la Toison d'or; ***the Golden Gate Bridge*** le Golden Gate; *Ftbl* ***golden goal*** but *m* en or; ***Golden Gloves*** = championnat américain de boxe amateur; *Fam* ***golden handcuffs*** ❑ *fpl (versées à un cadre à intervalles réguliers pour le dissuader de partir)*; *Fam* ***golden handshake*** gratification *f* de fin de service ❑; *Fam* ***golden hello*** prime *f* d'embauche ❑; ***golden jubilee*** (fête *f* du) cinquantième anniversaire *m*; ***the golden mean*** le juste milieu; ***golden number*** nombre *m* d'or; *Fam* ***golden oldie*** vieux tube *m*; **he's a golden oldie** il a de beaux restes; *Orn* ***golden oriole*** loriot *m* (jaune); *Fam* ***golden parachute*** prime *f* de licenciement ❑ *(versé à certains cadres supérieurs en cas de rachat de l'entreprise)*; *Orn* ***golden pheasant*** faisan *m* doré; *Orn* ***golden plover*** pluvier *m* doré; *Bot* ***golden rain*** cytise *f*; ***golden retriever*** golden retriever *m*; ***golden rule*** règle *f* d'or; *Bot* ***golden samphire*** inule *f*; ***golden section*** section *f* d'or *ou* dorée; ***golden share*** participation *f* majoritaire *(souvent détenue par le gouvernement britannique dans les entreprises privatisées)*; ***the Golden State*** = surnom donné à la Californie; *Br* ***golden syrup*** mélasse *f* raffinée; ***golden triangle*** triangle *m* d'or; ***golden wedding*** noces *fpl* d'or

'The Golden Bowl' *James, Ivory* 'La Coupe d'or'

'The Golden Notebook' *Lessing* 'Le Carnet d'or'

goldeneye ['gəʊldənaɪ] *n* **(a)** *Orn* **(common** *or* **American) goldeneye** garrot *m* à œil d'or, canard *m* garrot **(b)** *Entom* chrysope *f*, œil *m* d'or

golden-eyed fly *n Entom* chrysope *f*, œil *m* d'or

golden-fleeced *adj* à la toison d'or

goldenrod ['gəʊldənrɒd] *n Bot* verge *f* d'or, solidage *m*

goldfield ['gəʊldfiːld] *n* terrain *m ou* région *f* aurifère

goldfinch ['gəʊldfɪntʃ] *n Orn* chardonneret *m*

goldfish ['gəʊldfɪʃ] *n* **(a)** *(as pet)* poisson *m* rouge **(b)** *Ich* cyprin *m* doré
►► ***goldfish bowl*** bocal *m* (à poissons rouges); *Fig* **it's like living in a goldfish bowl** c'est comme si on était tout le temps dans une vitrine

Goldilocks ['gəʊldɪlɒks] *pr n* Boucles d'or

goldmine ['gəʊldmaɪn] *n also Fig* mine *f* d'or

gold-plated *adj* plaqué or

gold-rimmed *adj (glasses)* à monture en or

goldsmith ['gəʊldsmɪθ] *n* orfèvre *m*

gold-tipped *adj* à bout doré

golem ['gəʊləm] *n* **(a)** *(in Jewish folklore)* golem *m* **(b)** *Fig (stupid or easily-controlled person)* nouille *f*

golf [gɒlf] **1** *n* golf *m*
2 *vi* jouer au golf
►► ***golf bag*** sac *m* de golf; ***golf ball*** *(for golf)* balle *f* de golf; *(for typewriter)* boule *f*; ***golf ball typewriter*** machine *f* à écrire à boule; *Br* ***golf buggy*** voiture *f* de golf; ***golf cart*** *(trolley)* chariot *m* de golf; *(car)* voiturette *f*; ***golf club*** *(stick)* club *m ou* crosse *f ou* canne *f* de golf; *(building, association)* club *m* de golf; ***golf course*** (terrain *m* de) golf *m*; ***golf glove*** gant *m* de golf; ***golf links*** links *mpl*; ***golf shoes*** chaussures *fpl* de golf; *Br* ***golf trolley*** chariot *m* de golf; ***golf umbrella*** parapluie *m* de golf; *Fam Hum* ***golf widow*** = femme délaissée par un mari qui est toujours au golf

golfer ['gɒlfə(r)] *n* joueur(euse) *m,f* de golf, golfeur(euse) *m,f*; **to be a good/bad golfer** être un bon/mauvais joueur de golf, être un bon/mauvais golfeur

golfing ['gɒlfɪŋ] *n* golf *m (activité)*; **to go golfing** faire du golf
►► ***golfing holiday*** vacances *fpl* de golf

Golgotha ['gɒlgəθə] *n* Golgotha *m*

Goliath [gə'laɪəθ] *pr n Bible* Goliath

golliwog ['gɒlɪwɒg] *n* = poupée de chiffon, au visage noir et aux cheveux hérissés

golly ['gɒlɪ] (*pl* **gollies**) *Fam* **1** *n Br* = poupée de chiffon, au visage noir et aux cheveux hérissés
2 *exclam Old-fashioned* **(good) golly!** ciel!, mince (alors)!, flûte!

gollywog = **golliwog**

goloshes = **galoshes**

GOM [,dʒiːəʊ'em] *n (abbr* **Grand Old Man)** **the GOM of English theatre/American novels** le doyen des hommes de théâtre anglais/des romanciers américains

gombeen man [gɒm'biːn-] *n Ir Pej (moneylender)* usurier *m*; *(crook)* escroc *m*

gombo ['gɒmbəʊ] *n Bot* gumbo *m*

Gomorrha, Gomorrhah [gə'mɒrə] *n Geog & Bible* Gomorrhe

gonad ['gəʊnæd] *n* gonade *f*

gonadotrophin [,gɒnədəʊ'trəʊfɪn] *n Physiol* gonadotrophine *f*

gondola ['gɒndələ] *n* (**a**) *(boat)* gondole *f* (**b**) *(on airship or balloon, for window cleaner)* nacelle *f* (**c**) *(in supermarket)* gondole *f* (**d**) *(cable car)* nacelle *f ou* cabine *f* de téléphérique (**e**) *Am Rail* **gondola (car)** wagon *m* plat
►► *Mktg* ***gondola end*** tête *f* de gondole

gondolier [,gɒndə'lɪə(r)] *n* gondolier *m*

Gondwanaland [,gɒnd'wɑːnəlænd] *n* continent *m* du Gondwana

gone [gɒn] **1** *pp of* **go**
2 *adj* (**a**) *(past)* passé, révolu; **those days are gone now** c'est bien fini tout ça; **gone is the time when…** le temps n'est plus où…
(**b**) *(away)* **be gone with you!** disparaissez de ma vue!
(**c**) *Fam (high, drunk)* parti; **to be well** *or* **far gone** être parti, planer
(**d**) *Fam (pregnant)* **she is four months gone** elle est enceinte de quatre mois ❑; **how far gone is she?** elle est enceinte de combien? ❑
(**e**) *Fam (infatuated)* **to be gone on sb/sth** être (complètement) toqué de qn/qch
(**f**) *Euph (dead)* mort; **when I'm gone** quand je ne serai plus là
(**g**) *Fam (weak)* **to be far gone** être bien faible ❑
3 *prep Br* **it's gone 11** il est 11 heures passées *ou* plus de 11 heures

'Gone with the Wind' *Mitchell, Fleming* 'Autant en emporte le vent'

goner ['gɒnə(r)] *n Fam* **I thought she was a goner** je pensais qu'elle allait mourir ❑; **if the engine fails now, we'll all be a goner** si le moteur tombe en panne, on va tous crever *ou* on est tous foutus; *Fig* **I'm a goner if she finds out where I've been** je suis fichu *ou* foutu si elle apprend où je suis allé

gong [gɒŋ] *n* (**a**) *(instrument)* gong *m* (**b**) *Br Fam Hum (medal)* médaille ❑ *f*
►► *Am TV* ***the Gong Show*** = ancienne émission mettant en scène des artistes amateurs

goniometer [,gəʊnɪ'ɒmɪtə(r)] *n* goniomètre *m*

goniometry [,gəʊnɪ'ɒmɪtrɪ] *n* goniométrie *f*

gonna ['gɒnə] *Fam* = **going to**

gonococcus [gɒnəʊ'kɒkəs] *n Med* gonocoque *m*

go-no-go *adj Am Fam (meeting)* décisif ❑; **we have to take the go-no-go decision now** il nous faut décider si l'on veut mettre notre projet à exécution maintenant ❑

gonorrhoea, *Am* **gonorrhea** [,gɒnə'rɪə] *n Med* blennorragie *f*; **to have gonorrhoea** avoir *ou* faire une blennorragie

gonorrhoeal [,gɒnə'rɪəl] *adj Med* blennorragique

Gonzaga [gɒn'zɑːgə] *pr n Hist* Gonzague

gonzo ['gɒnzəʊ] *adj Am Fam* (**a**) *(biased)* subjectif ❑, partial ❑ (**b**) *(crazy)* barjo
►► ***gonzo journalism*** = style de journalisme débridé qui laisse beaucoup de place à la subjectivité de l'auteur, popularisé par le journaliste américain Hunter S. Thompson

goo [guː] *n Fam* (**a**) *(sticky stuff)* matière *f* poisseuse ❑ (**b**) *Fig Pej* sentimentalisme ❑ *m*

goober ['guːbə(r)] *n Am Fam* crétin(e) *m,f*, andouille *f*

GOOD [gʊd]

bon	► 1A (a) – (d); B (a); C (a), (c), (d); D (a) – (e); E (a) – (d); 2 (a)
beau	► 1A (a); D (b)
gentil	► 1B (a)
sage	► 1B (b)
favorable	► 1C (b)
bien	► 2 (a), (b); 3
pour ainsi dire	► 5
pour de bon	► 6

(*compar* **better** ['betə(r)], *superl* **best** [best]) **1** *adj*
A. (**a**) *(enjoyable, pleasant → book, feeling, holiday)* bon, agréable; *(→ weather)* beau (belle); **we're good friends** nous sommes très amis; **we're just good friends** on est des amis, c'est tout; **she has a good relationship with her staff** elle a un bon contact avec ses employés; **they have a good sex life** sexuellement, tout va bien entre eux; **they had a good time** ils se sont bien amusés; **we had good weather during the holidays** il faisait beau pendant nos vacances; **good to eat/to hear** bon à manger/à entendre; **it's good to be home** ça fait du bien *ou* ça fait plaisir de rentrer chez soi; **it's good to be alive** il fait bon vivre; **wait until he's in a good mood** attendez qu'il soit de bonne humeur; **to feel good** être en forme; **he doesn't feel good about leaving her alone** *(worried)* ça l'ennuie de la laisser seule; *(ashamed)* il a honte de la laisser seule; **it's too good to be true** c'est trop beau pour être vrai *ou* pour y croire; **the good life** la belle vie; **she's never had it so good!** elle n'a jamais eu la vie si belle!; **this is as good as you can get** *or* **as it gets** c'est ce qui se fait de mieux; **have a good day!** bonne journée!; **it's good to see you** je suis/nous sommes content(s) de te voir; *Am Fam* **good to see you** content de te voir; **you can have too much of a good thing** on se lasse de tout, même du meilleur
(**b**) *(high quality → clothing, dishes)* bon, de bonne qualité; *(→ painting, film)* bon; *(→ food)* bon; **it's a good school** c'est une bonne école; **he speaks good English** il parle bien anglais; **she put her good shoes on** elle a mis ses belles chaussures; **I need a good suit** j'ai besoin d'un bon costume; **this house is good enough for me** cette maison me suffit; **if it's good enough for you, it's good enough for me** si ça vous va, alors ça me va aussi; **this isn't good enough** ça ne va pas; **this work isn't good enough** ce travail laisse beaucoup à désirer; **nothing is too good for her family** rien n'est trop beau pour sa famille; **it makes good television** ça marche bien à la télévision
(**c**) *(competent, skilful)* bon, compétent; **do you know a good lawyer?** connaissez-vous un bon avocat?; **she's a very good doctor** c'est un excellent médecin; **he's a good swimmer** c'est un bon nageur; **she's a good listener** c'est quelqu'un qui sait écouter; **to be good in bed** être bien au lit; **he's too good for that job** il mérite une meilleure situation; **to be good at sth** être doué pour *ou* bon en qch; **they're good at everything** ils sont bons en tout; **he's good with children** il sait s'y prendre avec les enfants; **to be good with one's hands** être habile *ou* adroit de ses mains; **they're not good enough to direct the others** ils ne sont pas à la hauteur pour diriger les autres; **you're as good as he is** tu le vaux bien, tu vaux autant que lui; **she's as good an artist as you are** elle vous vaut en tant qu'artiste; **to be good on French history/contract law** *(author)* être bon en histoire de France/sur le droit des contrats; **to be good on sth** *(book)* être complet sur qch; **the good gardening guide** *(title of book)* le guide du bon jardinier
(**d**) *(useful)* bon; **to be good for nothing** être bon à rien; **this product is also good for cleaning windows** ce produit est bien aussi pour nettoyer les vitres
(**e**) *(in greetings)* **good afternoon!** *(hello)* bonjour!; *(goodbye)* bon après-midi!; **good day!** *Br or Am Old-fashioned (hello)* bonjour!; *Br Old-fashioned (goodbye)* adieu!; **good evening!** bonsoir!; **good morning!** *(hello)* bonjour!; *(goodbye)* au revoir!, bonne journée!
B. (**a**) *(kind)* bon, gentil; *(loyal, true)* bon, véritable; *(moral, virtuous)* bon; **good behaviour** *or* **conduct** bonne conduite *f*; **she's a good person** c'est quelqu'un de bien; **he's a good sort** c'est un brave type; **she proved to be a good friend** elle a prouvé qu'elle était une véritable amie; **he's been a good husband to her** il a été pour elle un bon mari; **you're too good for him** tu mérites mieux que lui; **they took advantage of his good nature** ils ont profité de son bon naturel *ou* caractère; **he's a good Christian/communist** c'est un bon chrétien/communiste; **to lead a good life** *(comfortable)* avoir une belle vie; *(moral)* mener une vie vertueuse *ou* exemplaire; **they've always been good to me** ils ont toujours été gentils avec moi; **life has been good to me** j'ai eu de la chance dans la vie; **that's very good of you** c'est très aimable de votre part; **he was very good about it** il s'est montré très compréhensif; **it's good of you to come** c'est aimable *ou* gentil à vous d'être venu; **would you be good enough to ask him?** auriez-vous la bonté de lui demander?, seriez-vous assez aimable pour lui demander?; **would you be good enough to reply by return of post?** voudriez-vous avoir l'obligeance de répondre par retour du courrier?; *Old-fashioned or Hum* **and how's your good lady?** et comment va madame?; *Old-fashioned or Hum* **my good man** mon brave; *Literary* **good men and true** des hommes vaillants; *Literary* **the good ship Caledonia** le Caledonia
(**b**) *(well-behaved)* sage; **be good!** sois sage!; **be a good boy and fetch Mummy's bag** sois mignon, va chercher le sac de maman; **good dog!** *(encouraging)* oh, le beau chien!; *(congratulating)* c'est bien, le chien!
C. (**a**) *(desirable, positive)* bon, souhaitable; *(cause)* bon; **it's a good thing she's prepared to talk about it** c'est une bonne chose qu'elle soit prête à en parler; **she had the good fortune to arrive just then** elle a eu la chance d'arriver juste à ce moment-là; **it's a good job** *or* **good thing he decided not to go** c'est une chance qu'il ait décidé de *ou* heureusement qu'il a décidé de ne pas y aller; **all good wishes for the New Year** tous nos meilleurs vœux pour le nouvel an
(**b**) *(favourable → contract, deal)* avantageux, favorable; *(→ opportunity, sign)* bon, favorable; **to buy sth at a good price** acheter qch bon marché *ou* à un prix avantageux; **you've got a good chance** tu as toutes tes chances; **she's in a good position to help us** elle est bien placée pour nous aider; **there are good times ahead** l'avenir est prometteur; **he put in a good word for me with the boss** il a glissé un mot en ma faveur au patron; **it's looking good** *(is going well)* ça a l'air de bien se passer; *(is going to succeed)* ça se présente bien; **he's looking good** *(of boxer, athlete, election candidate)* il a toutes ses chances
(**c**) *(convenient, suitable → place, time)* bon, propice; *(→ choice)* bon, convenable; **it's a good holiday spot for people with children** c'est un lieu de vacances idéal pour ceux qui ont des enfants; **is this a good moment to ask him?** est-ce un bon moment pour lui demander?; **this is as good a time as any** autant le faire maintenant; **it's as good a way as any to do it** c'est une façon comme une autre de le faire
(**d**) *(beneficial)* bon, bienfaisant; **protein-rich diets are good for pregnant women** les régimes riches en protéines sont bons pour les femmes enceintes; **eat your spinach, it's good for you** mange tes épinards, c'est bon pour toi; **hard work is good for the soul!** le travail forme le caractère!; **whisky is good for a cold** le whisky est bon pour les rhumes; **to be good for business** être bon pour les affaires; **he's not good for her** il a une mauvaise influence sur elle; **this cold weather isn't good for your health** ce froid n'est pas bon pour ta santé *ou* est mauvais pour toi; **it's good for him to spend time outdoors** ça lui fait du bien *ou* c'est bon pour lui de passer du temps dehors; **he works more than is good for him** il travaille plus qu'il ne faudrait *ou* devrait; *Fig* **he doesn't know what's good for him** il ne sait pas ce qui est bon pour lui; *Fig* **if you know what's good for you, you'll listen** si tu as le moindre bon sens, tu m'écouteras
D. (**a**) *(sound, strong)* bon, valide; **I can do a lot with my good arm** je peux faire beaucoup de choses avec mon bras valide; **my eyesight/hearing is good** j'ai une bonne vue/l'ouïe fine
(**b**) *(attractive → appearance)* bon, beau (belle); *(→ features, legs)* beau (belle), joli; **you're looking good!** *(healthy)* tu as bonne mine!; *(well-dressed)* tu es très bien!; **that colour looks good on him** cette couleur lui va bien; **she has**

gom–goo

a good figure elle est bien faite; **the vase looks good there** le vase rend très bien là

(**c**) *(valid, well-founded)* bon, valable; **she had a good excuse/reason for not going** elle avait une bonne excuse pour/une bonne raison de ne pas y aller; **I wouldn't have come without good reason** je ne serais pas venu sans avoir une bonne raison; **they made out a good case against drinking tap water** ils ont bien expliqué pourquoi il ne fallait pas boire l'eau du robinet

(**d**) *(reliable, trustworthy → brand, car)* bon, sûr; *Com & Fin (→ cheque)* bon; *(→ investment, securities)* sûr; *(→ debt)* bon, certain; **my passport is good for five years** mon passeport est bon *ou* valable pour cinq ans; **this coat is good for another year** ce manteau fera encore un an; *Fam* **she's good for another ten years** elle en a bien encore pour dix ans; *Fam* **he's always good for a laugh** il sait toujours faire rire□; **how much money are you good for?** *(do you have)* de combien d'argent disposez-vous?; **he should be good for a couple of hundred pounds** on devrait pouvoir en tirer quelques centaines de livres; **they are** *or* **their credit is good for £500** on peut leur faire crédit jusqu'à 500 livres

(**e**) *(honourable, reputable)* bon, estimé; **they live at a good address** ils habitent un quartier chic; **to protect their good name** pour défendre leur réputation; **the firm has a good name** la société a (une) bonne réputation; **she's from a good family** elle est de bonne famille; **a family of good standing** une famille bien

E. (**a**) *(ample, considerable)* bon, considérable; **a good amount** *or* **deal of money** beaucoup d'argent; **a good (round) sum** une somme rondelette; **a good few people** pas mal de gens; **take good care of your mother** prends bien soin de ta mère; **to make good money** bien gagner sa vie; **I make good money** je gagne bien ma vie; **we still have a good way to go** nous avons encore un bon bout de chemin à faire; **I was a good way into the book when I realized that...** j'avais déjà bien avancé dans ma lecture quand je me suis rendu compte que...; **a good thirty years ago** il y a bien trente ans; **the trip will take you a good two hours** il vous faudra deux bonnes heures pour faire le voyage; **she's been gone a good while** ça fait un bon moment qu'elle est partie; **they came in a good second** ils ont obtenu une bonne deuxième place; **there's a good risk of it happening** il y a de grands risques que ça arrive

(**b**) *(proper, thorough)* bon, grand; **I gave the house a good cleaning** j'ai fait le ménage à fond; **have a good cry** pleure un bon coup; **we had a good laugh** on a bien ri; **I managed to get a good look at his face** j'ai pu bien regarder son visage; **take a good look at her** regardez-la bien; **he got a good spanking** il a reçu une bonne fessée; *Fam* **we were good and mad** on était carrément furax; **she'll call when she's good and ready** elle appellera quand elle le voudra bien; **I was good and sorry to have invited her** j'ai bien regretté de l'avoir invitée

(**c**) *(acceptable)* bon, convenable; **we made the trip in good time** le voyage n'a pas été trop long; **that's all very good** *or* **all well and good but**→ c'est bien joli *ou* bien beau tout ça mais...

(**d**) *(indicating approval)* bon, très bien; **I'd like a new suit – very good, sir!** j'ai besoin d'un nouveau costume – (très) bien, monsieur!; **she left him – good!** elle l'a quitté – tant mieux!; **he's feeling better – good, let him go** il va mieux – très bien, laissez-le partir; **good, that's settled** bon *ou* bien, voilà une affaire réglée; **(that) sounds good!** *(good idea)* bonne idée!; **that's a good question** c'est une bonne question; *Fam* **that's a good one!** *(joke)* elle est (bien) bonne, celle-là!; *Ironic (far-fetched story)* à d'autres!; *Fam* **good on you** *or* **for you!** bravo!, très bien!; **good old Eric, I knew he wouldn't let us down!** ce brave Eric, je savais qu'il ne nous laisserait pas tomber!; **good old London** le bon vieux Londres; **the good old days** le bon vieux temps

2 *adv* (**a**) *(as intensifier)* bien, bon; **a good hard bed** un lit bien dur; **I'd like a good hot bath** j'ai envie de prendre un bon bain chaud; **he needs a good sound spanking** il a besoin d'une bonne fessée; **the two friends had a good long chat** les deux amis ont longuement bavardé; **we took a good long walk** nous avons fait une bonne *ou* une grande promenade

(**b**) *Fam (well)* bien□; **she writes good** elle écrit bien; **the boss gave it to them good and proper** le patron leur a passé un de ces savons; **their team beat us good and proper** leur équipe nous a battus à plate couture *ou* à plates coutures; **I'll do it when I'm good and ready** je le ferai quand ça me chantera; **I like my coffee good and strong** j'aime le café bien fort; **make sure it's stuck on good and hard** vérifie que c'est vraiment bien collé; **put the paint on good and thick** appliquer la peinture en couches bien épaisses

(**c**) *(idioms)* **to make good** *(succeed)* réussir; *(reform)* changer de conduite, se refaire une vie; **a local boy made good** un garçon du pays *ou* du coin qui a fait son chemin; **the prisoner made good his escape** le prisonnier est parvenu à s'échapper *ou* a réussi son évasion; **they made good their promise** ils ont tenu parole *ou* ont respecté leur promesse; **he made good his position as leader** il a assuré sa position de leader; **to make sth good** *(mistake)* remédier à qch; *(damages, injustice)* réparer qch; *(losses)* compenser qch; *(deficit)* combler qch; *(wall, surface)* apporter des finitions à qch; **we'll make good any expenses you incur** nous vous rembourserons toute dépense; *Am* **to make good on sth** honorer qch

3 *n* (**a**) *(morality, virtue)* bien *m*; **they do good** ils font le bien; **that will do more harm than good** ça fera plus de mal que de bien; **to return good for evil** rendre le bien pour le mal; **that organization is a power for good** cet organisme exerce une influence salutaire; **she recognized the good in him** elle a vu ce qu'il y avait de bon en lui; **there is good and bad in everyone** il y a du bon et du mauvais en chacun de nous; **to be up to no good** préparer un mauvais coup; **their daughter came to no good** leur fille a mal tourné; **for good or evil, for good or ill** pour le bien et pour le mal

(**b**) *(use)* **this book isn't much good to me** ce livre ne me sert pas à grand-chose; **if it's any good to him** si ça peut lui être utile *ou* lui rendre service; **I was never any good at mathematics** je n'ai jamais été doué pour les maths, je n'ai jamais été bon *ou* fort en maths; **he's no good** il est nul; **he'd be no good as a teacher** il ne ferait pas un bon professeur; **what's the good?** à quoi bon?; **what good would it do to leave now?** à quoi bon partir maintenant?; **what good will it do you to see her?** ça te servira à quoi *ou* t'avancera à quoi de la voir?; *Fam* **a fat lot of good that did you!** te voilà bien avancé maintenant!; *Ironic* **that will do you a lot of good!** tu seras bien avancé!, ça te fera une belle jambe!; **it's no good, I give up** ça ne sert à rien, j'abandonne; **it's no good worrying about it** ça ne sert à rien de *ou* ce n'est pas la peine de *ou* inutile de vous inquiéter; **I might as well talk to the wall for all the good it does** je ferais aussi bien de parler au mur, pour tout l'effet que ça fait

(**c**) *(benefit, welfare)* bien *m*; **I did it for your own good** je l'ai fait pour ton (propre) bien; **a holiday will do her good** des vacances lui feront du bien; **she resigned for the good of her health** elle a démissionné pour des raisons de santé; **it does my heart good to see you so happy** ça me réchauffe le cœur de vous voir si heureux; **much good may it do you!** grand bien vous fasse!; **the common good** l'intérêt *m* commun

4 *npl (people)* **the good** les bons *mpl*, les gens *mpl* de bien; **the good and the bad** les bons et les méchants; **only the good die young** ce sont toujours les meilleurs qui partent les premiers

5 as good as *adv* pour ainsi dire, à peu de choses près; **I'm as good as blind without my glasses** sans lunettes je suis pour ainsi dire aveugle; **he's as good as dead** c'est comme s'il était mort; **the job is as good as finished** la tâche est pour ainsi dire *ou* est pratiquement finie; **it's as good as new** c'est comme neuf; **he as good as admitted he was wrong** il a pour ainsi dire reconnu qu'il avait tort; **they as good as called us cowards** ils n'ont pas dit qu'on était des lâches mais c'était tout comme; **are you married? – as good as** tu es marié? – non, mais c'est tout comme

6 for good *adv* pour de bon; **she left for good** elle est partie pour de bon; **they finally settled down for good** ils se sont enfin fixés définitivement; **for good and all** une (bonne) fois pour toutes, pour de bon; **I'm warning you for good and all!** c'est la dernière fois que je te le dis!

7 to the good *adv* **that's all to the good** tant mieux; **he finished up the card game £15 to the good** il a fait 15 livres de bénéfice *ou* il a gagné 15 livres aux cartes

►► ***the Good Book*** la Bible; ***Good Friday*** le vendredi saint; ***good looks*** *(attractive appearance)* beauté *f*; *Am Fam* **good old** *or* **ole** *or* **ol' boy** *(white male from Southern US)* = Blanc originaire du sud des États-Unis, aux valeurs traditionnelles; *Pej (redneck)* plouc *m*; *Bible* ***the Good Samaritan*** le bon Samaritain; *Fig* ***good Samaritan*** bon Samaritain *m*; **she's a real good Samaritan** elle a tout du bon Samaritain; *Am Law* ***the good Samaritan laws*** = lois qui protègent un sauveteur de toutes poursuites éventuelles engagées par le blessé; ***the Good Shepherd*** le Bon Pasteur

---

'A Good Enough Parent' *Bettelheim* 'Pour être des parents acceptables'

'Good as Gold' *Heller* 'Franc comme l'or'

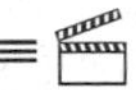

'The Good, the Bad and the Ugly' *Leone* 'Le Bon, la brute et le truand'

You've never had it so good

Ce slogan a été utilisé pour la première fois aux États-Unis en 1952 par les Démocrates. Il signifie "vous êtes aujourd'hui plus prospères que jamais". En Grande-Bretagne, ce slogan est associé au Premier ministre conservateur Harold Macmillan qui l'utilisa dans un discours en 1957. Aujourd'hui, on utilise cette formule sur le mode ironique lorsqu'une situation n'encourage pas du tout à l'optimisme.

GOOD FRIDAY

En Grande-Bretagne, il est traditionnel, le jour du vendredi saint, de manger des "hot cross buns" (petits pains ronds aux fruits secs, marqués d'une croix).

THE GOOD FRIDAY AGREEMENT

Le processus de paix en Irlande du Nord, qui a été amorcé par les cessez-le-feu des groupes paramilitaires républicains et unionistes en 1994, a abouti au "Good Friday Agreement", l'accord de paix signé à Belfast en avril 1998. Cet accord, parrainé par les Premiers ministres britannique et irlandais, et finalement approuvé par le Sinn Féin et par la plupart des partis unionistes, a mis en place la "Northern Ireland Assembly", un parlement quasi autonome avec un partage démocratique du pouvoir entre les communautés protestante et catholique. Cet accord est une étape vers la fin de trente ans de guerre civile en Ulster.

goodbye [gʊd'baɪ] **1** *exclam* au revoir!; **goodbye for now** à bientôt, à la prochaine

2 *n* adieu *m*, au revoir *m*; **I hate goodbyes** j'ai horreur des adieux; **we said our goodbyes and left** on a fait nos adieux et on est partis; **to say goodbye to sb** dire au revoir *ou* faire ses adieux à qn, prendre congé de qn; *Fig* **if you fail these exams, you can say goodbye to a career as a doctor** si tu rates ces examens, tu peux dire adieu à ta carrière de médecin; **that was goodbye to £5000** j'ai dû dire adieu à mes 5000 livres; **to give sb a goodbye kiss/hug** embrasser qn/serrer qn dans ses bras pour lui dire au revoir; **goodbye present** cadeau *m* d'adieu

'Goodbye To All That' *Graves* 'Adieu à tout cela'

'Goodbye to Berlin' *Isherwood* 'Adieu à Berlin'

good-for-nothing 1 *adj* bon *ou* propre à rien; **he's a good-for-nothing layabout!** c'est un bon à rien et un fainéant!; **that good-for-nothing husband of hers** son vaurien de mari
2 *n* vaurien(enne) *m,f*, propre-à-rien *mf*

good-hearted [-'hɑːtɪd] *adj (person)* bon, généreux; *(action)* fait avec les meilleures intentions

good-heartedness [-'hɑːtɪdnɪs] *n* bonté *f* de cœur

good-humoured, *Am* **good-humored** *adj (person → generally)* bon enfant *(inv)*; *(→ on one occasion)* de bonne humeur; *(discussion)* amical; *(joke, remark)* sans malice

good-humouredly, *Am* **good-humoredly** [-'hjuːmədlɪ] *adv* avec bonne humeur

goodie = **goody**

goodish ['gʊdɪʃ] *adj Fam* (**a**) *(quite good)* assez bon❑, passable❑ (**b**) *(number, quantity, amount)* assez grand❑; **it's a goodish step from here** c'est à un bon bout de chemin d'ici; **it's a goodish size** c'est assez grand; **add a goodish pinch of salt** ajoutez une bonne pincée de sel

good-looker *n Fam (man)* beau mec *m*; *(woman)* belle créature *f*; *(younger)* beau brin de fille *m*

good-looking *adj (person, car, shot)* beau (belle); **a good-looking woman** une belle *ou* jolie femme; **he's very good-looking** il est beau garçon; **she's quite good-looking** elle n'est pas mal; **hey, good-looking!** *(to woman)* eh, ma jolie!; *(to man)* eh, beau gosse!

goodly ['gʊdlɪ] *adj* (**a**) *Arch (amount, size)* considérable, important; **a goodly sum of money** une belle somme d'argent (**b**) *Arch or Literary (attractive)* charmant, gracieux

goodman ['gʊdmən] *(pl* **goodmen** [-mən]*)* *n Arch or Literary* maître *m* (de la maison)

good-natured *adj (person)* facile à vivre, qui a un bon naturel; *(face, smile)* bon enfant *(inv)*; *(remark)* sans malice

good-naturedly [-'neɪtʃədlɪ] *adv* avec bonne humeur, avec bonhomie

goodness ['gʊdnɪs] *n* (**a**) *(of person)* bonté *f*, bienveillance *f*, bienfaisance *f*; *(of thing)* (bonne) qualité *f*, excellence *f*, perfection *f*; **he believes in people's essential goodness** il croit en la bonté naturelle des gens; **out of the goodness of my heart** par pure bonté
(**b**) *(nourishment)* valeur *f* nutritive; **there's a lot of goodness in fresh vegetables** les légumes frais sont pleins de bonnes choses; **contains all the goodness of full-cream milk** *(in advert)* contient toutes les bonnes choses du lait entier
(**c**) *Fam (in interjections)* **(my) goodness!** mon Dieu!; **thank goodness!** Dieu merci!; **goodness gracious (me)!** Seigneur!, mon Dieu!; **for goodness' sake!** bon sang!; **goodness knows!** Dieu seul le sait!; **goodness knows why** Dieu sait pourquoi; **I wish to goodness he would shut up!** si seulement il pouvait se taire!

goodnight 1 *exclam (when leaving)* bonsoir!; *(when going to bed)* bonne nuit!
2 *n* **they said goodnight and left** ils ont dit bonsoir et sont partis; **she kissed her mother goodnight and went to bed** elle a dit bonsoir à sa mère et est allée se coucher; **give your mother a goodnight kiss** embrasse ta mère *(pour lui dire bonsoir)*

good-oh *exclam Br & Austr Fam* épatant!, chic alors!

goods [gʊdz] *npl* (**a**) *(possessions)* biens *mpl*; **he gave up all his worldly goods** il a renoncé à tous ses biens *mpl* matériels; *Br* **goods and chattels** biens *mpl* et effets *mpl*
(**b**) *Com* marchandises *fpl*, articles *mpl*; **send us the goods by rail** envoyez-nous la marchandise par chemin de fer; **these goods are not for sale** ces articles ne sont pas à vendre; **leather goods** articles *mpl* de cuir, maroquinerie *f*; *Fam* **to deliver the goods** tenir parole❑; *Fig* **a computer that can deliver the goods** un ordinateur qui tient ses promesses; *Fig* **to come up with the goods** faire le nécessaire; *Am Fam* **to have the goods on sb** avoir la preuve de la culpabilité de qn❑; *Fam* **have you got the goods?** vous avez ce qu'il faut?❑; *Fam* **he thinks she's the goods** il pense qu'elle est géniale
(**c**) *Am Fam (information)* renseignements❑ *mpl*; **can you give me the goods on him?** pouvez-vous me rencarder sur lui?
►► *Can Fin* ***goods and services tax*** taxe *f* sur les produits et services; *Br* ***goods siding*** = voie de garage pour les wagons de marchandises; *Br* ***goods train*** train *m* de marchandises; *Br* ***goods vehicle*** poids *m* lourd, véhicule *m* utilitaire; *Br* ***goods wagon*** wagon *m* de marchandises; *Br* ***goods yard*** dépôt *m* de marchandises

good-sized *adj* de bonne taille; **a good-sized room** une pièce assez *ou* suffisamment grande

good-tempered *adj (person)* qui a bon caractère, d'humeur égale; *(reply, discussion)* aimable

good-temperedly [-'tempədlɪ] *adv* aimablement, sans se fâcher

good-till-cancelled order *n St Exch* ordre *m* à révocation

good-time girl *n Fam Pej* noceuse *f*

goodwill [ˌgʊd'wɪl] **1** *n* (**a**) *(benevolence)* bienveillance *f*; **to show goodwill towards sb** faire preuve de bienveillance à l'égard de qn; **a gesture of goodwill** un geste de bonne volonté
(**b**) *(willingness)* bonne volonté *f*; **there needs to be goodwill on both sides** il faut que chacun fasse preuve de bonne volonté *ou* y mette du sien
(**c**) *Com* fonds *m* de commerce, (biens *mpl*) incorporels *mpl*
2 *comp (gesture, visit)* d'amitié, de bienveillance
3 Goodwill *n Am* = association caritative d'aide aux personnes handicapées, illettrées etc ne trouvant pas d'emploi
►► ***goodwill mission*** visite *f* d'amitié; ***Goodwill shop*** = magasin d'articles d'occasion géré par Goodwill

Goodwood ['gʊdwʊd] *n* = champ de courses en Angleterre

goody ['gʊdɪ] *(pl* **goodies***)* *Fam* **1** *exclam* génial!, chouette!, chic!
2 *n (usu pl)* (**a**) *(presents, prizes)* bonne chose❑ *f*; *(sweets, treats)* bonbon❑ *m*, friandise❑ *f*; **my mum sent me a box of goodies** ma mère m'a envoyé un colis rempli de bonnes choses (**b**) *(good person)* bon❑ *m*; *Pej* petit(e) saint(e) *m,f*; **the goodies and the baddies** les bons *mpl* et les méchants *mpl*
3 goodies *npl Am Fam (female genitals)* minou *m*; *(male genitals)* bijoux *mpl* de famille, service *m* trois pièces; *(breasts)* nichons *mpl*, nénés *mpl*

goody-goody *(pl* **goody-goodies***)* *Fam Pej* **1** *adj* de petit saint; **she's awfully goody-goody** elle prend toujours des airs de petite sainte
2 *n* petit(e) saint(e) *m,f*, *Hum* modèle *m* de vertu

goody-two-shoes *n Fam Pej* petit(e) saint(e) *m,f*, *Hum* modèle *m* de vertu

gooey ['guːɪ] *adj Fam* (**a**) *(substance)* gluant, visqueux❑, poisseux❑; *(sweets)* qui colle aux dents❑ (**b**) *(sentimental)* sentimental❑; **she goes all gooey over babies** elle devient gâteuse quand elle voit un bébé

goof [guːf] *Fam* **1** *n* (**a**) *(fool)* imbécile *mf*, andouille *f* (**b**) *(blunder)* gaffe *f*
2 *vi* (**a**) *(blunder)* faire une gaffe (**b**) *(joke)* rigoler; **to goof with sb** *(tease)* faire enrager qn (**c**) *(stare)* **to goof at sb/sth** regarder qn/qch bêtement❑

►**goof about, goof around** *vi Am Fam* (**a**) *(act foolishly)* faire le con, déconner (**b**) *(waste time)* glander, glandouiller

►**goof off** *Am Fam* **1** *vt sep* **to goof off school** sécher l'école; **to goof off work** ne pas aller bosser
2 *vi (waste time)* flemmarder; *(malinger)* tirer au flanc

►**goof on** *vt insep Am Fam* se moquer de❑

►**goof up** *Fam* **1** *vt sep* bousiller, saloper; **he goofed the job up** il a salopé le travail
2 *vi* merder

goofball ['guːfbɔːl] *Am Fam* **1** *n* (**a**) *(drug)* barbiturique❑ *m* (**b**) *(fool)* crétin(e) *m,f*, andouille *f*
2 *vi* gaffer, mettre les pieds dans le plat

goof-off *n Am Fam* tire-au-flanc *m inv*

goofy ['guːfɪ] *(compar* **goofier**, *superl* **goofiest***)* *adj Fam* (**a**) *(stupid)* dingo (**b**) *Br* **to have goofy teeth** avoir les dents qui courent après le bifteck

googly ['guːglɪ] *n (in cricket)* = balle lancée avec de l'effet qui prend le batteur à contre-pied alors qu'il pensait l'avoir bien anticipée; *Fig* **to bowl sb a googly** essayer de tromper qn

googol ['guːgɒl] *n* dix *m* puissance cent

goo-goo *adj Fam* **to go goo-goo** *(baby)* faire areu; **to make goo-goo eyes at sb** faire des yeux de velours *ou* les yeux doux à qn

gook [guːk] *n Am* (**a**) *Fam (Oriental)* bridé(e) *m,f* = terme injurieux désignant un Asiatique (**b**) *Fam (muck)* saleté❑ *f*, crasse *f*

goolies ['guːlɪz] *npl very Fam* couilles *fpl*

goombah ['guːmbə] *n Am Fam* (**a**) *(gang member)* membre *m* d'un gang❑ *(en particulier mafieux)* (**b**) *(associate)* acolyte❑ *m*

goon [guːn] *n Fam* (**a**) *(fool)* abruti(e) *m,f*; **the Goons** = groupe de comédiens loufoques très populaires dans les années 50 en Grande-Bretagne (**b**) *Am (hired thug)* casseur *m (au service de quelqu'un)*
►► ***goon squad*** *(strike-breakers)* milice *f* patronale

gooney bird ['guːnɪ-] *n Am* albatros *m*

Goonhilly [ˌguːn'hɪlɪ] *n* = station de communications par satellite en Angleterre

goosander [guː'sændə(r)] *n Orn* harle *m* bièvre

goose [guːs] *(pl* **geese** [giːs]*)* **1** *n* (**a**) *(bird)* oie *f*; **goose egg** œuf *m* d'oie; *Am Fam* zéro❑ *m*; **to kill the goose that lays the golden egg** tuer la poule aux œufs d'or; *Fig* **all his geese are swans** à l'entendre, tout ce qu'il fait tient du prodige
(**b**) *Fam Old-fashioned (fool)* **don't be such a goose!** ne sois pas si bête!; **what a little goose she is!** quelle petite dinde!
2 *vt Fam* **to goose sb** mettre la main au cul à qn
►► *esp Am* ***goose bumps*** chair *f* de poule; ***goose fat*** graisse *f* d'oie; *Bot* ***goose grass*** grateron *m*, potentille *f*, ansérine *f*; *Br* ***goose pimples*** chair *f* de poule; **to get** *or* **to come out in goose pimples** avoir la chair de poule; **horror films give me goose pimples** les films d'horreur me donnent la chair de poule

gooseberry ['gʊzbərɪ] *n* (**a**) *Bot* groseille *f* à maquereau (**b**) *(unwanted person)* **to be** *or* **to play gooseberry** tenir la chandelle
►► ***gooseberry bush*** groseillier *m*; *Hum* **we found you under a gooseberry bush** c'est la cigogne qui t'a apporté

gooseflesh ['guːsfleʃ] *n (UNCOUNT)* chair *f* de poule; **to get** *or* **to come out in gooseflesh** avoir la chair de poule; **horror films give me gooseflesh** les films d'horreur me donnent la chair de poule

goosefoot ['guːsfʊt] *n Bot* ansérine *f*, patte-d'oie *f*

goosegog ['guːzgɒg] *n Br Fam* groseille *f* à maquereau❑

gooseneck ['guːsnek] *n* (**a**) *(shape)* col *m* de cygne (**b**) *Naut (joint)* vit-de-mulet *m*
►► *Am* ***gooseneck lamp*** lampe *f* de bureau flexible

goosestep ['guːsˌstep] *(pt & pp* **goosestepped,** *cont* **goosestepping***)* **1** *n* pas *m* de l'oie
2 *vi* faire le pas de l'oie; **they goosestepped across the parade ground** ils ont traversé le terrain de manœuvres au pas de l'oie

GOP [ˌdʒiːəʊ'piː] *n Am (abbr* **Grand Old Party***)* = le parti républicain aux États-Unis

gopher[1] ['gəʊfə(r)] *n* (**a**) *(pouched rat)* gaufre *m* (**b**) *(ground squirrel)* spermophile *m* (**c**) *(tortoise)* = espèce de tortues qui s'enfouissent dans le sol

gopher[2] = **gofer**

Gorbachov ['gɔːbətʃɒf] *pr n* **Mikhail Gorbachov** Mikhaïl Gorbatchev

Gorbals ['gɔːbəlz] *npl* **the Gorbals** = quartier du sud de Glasgow autrefois connu pour ses taudis

gorblimey [gɔː'blaɪmɪ] *Br Fam* **1** *exclam* mon Dieu!, mince!
2 *n* **he's got a real gorblimey accent** il a un bon accent cockney❑

Gordian knot ['gɔ:djən-] *n* nœud *m* gordien; **to cut the Gordian knot** couper *ou* trancher le nœud gordien

Gordon Bennett ['gɔ:dən'benɪt] *exclam Br Fam* nom d'une pipe!

Gordonstoun ['gɔ:dənstən] *n* **Gordonstoun (School)** = école privée en Écosse, fréquentée notamment par la famille royale

gore [gɔ:(r)] **1** *n* (**a**) *(blood)* sang *m* (coagulé); **blood and gore** du sang et encore du sang; **there's plenty of gore in this movie** ce film est sanglant à souhait (**b**) *Sewing* godet *m*; *Naut* pointe *f* (de voile); *(land)* langue *f* de terre

2 *vt* (**a**) *(wound)* blesser à coups de cornes, encorner; **the matador was gored by the bull** le matador a été encorné par le taureau; **he was gored to death** il a été tué d'un coup de corne (**b**) *Naut (sail)* mettre une pointe à

gored [gɔ:d] *adj (skirt)* à godets

Gore-Tex® ['gɔ:teks] *n* Gore-Tex® *m*

gorge [gɔ:dʒ] **1** *n* (**a**) *Geog* défilé *m*, gorge *f* (**b**) *Arch (throat)* gorge *f*, gosier *m*; *Fig* **it made my gorge rise** cela m'a rendu malade *ou* m'a soulevé le cœur

2 *vt* **to gorge oneself (on sth)** se gaver *ou* se gorger *ou* se bourrer (de qch); **don't gorge yourself with** *or* **on sweets** ne vous bourrez *ou* gavez pas de bonbons

gorgeous ['gɔ:dʒəs] *adj* (**a**) *Fam (wonderful → person, weather)* magnifique❑, splendide❑, superbe❑; *(→ flat, clothing)* magnifique❑, très beau❑; *(→ food, meal)* délicieux❑; *Fam* **hello gorgeous!** bonjour, ma beauté! (**b**) *(magnificent → fabric, clothing)* somptueux

gorgeously ['gɔ:dʒəslɪ] *adv* (**a**) *Fam (wonderfully)* magnifiquement❑ (**b**) *(magnificently)* somptueusement

gorgeousness ['gɔ:dʒəsnɪs] *n* (**a**) *Fam (wonderfulness)* magnificence❑ *f* (**b**) *(magnificence)* somptuosité *f*

gorget ['gɔ:dʒɪt] *n Hist* (**a**) *(of wimple)* gorgerette *f* (**b**) *(of armour)* hausse-col *m*

Gorgon ['gɔ:gən] **1** *n Myth* **the Gorgons** les Gorgones *fpl*

2 gorgon *n (fierce woman)* harpie *f*, dragon *m*

Gorgonzola [,gɔ:gən'zəʊlə] *n Culin* gorgonzola *m*

gorilla [gə'rɪlə] *n* (**a**) *Zool* gorille *m* (**b**) *Fam (thug)* voyou *m*; *(bodyguard)* gorille *m*

Gorki, Gorky ['gɔ:kɪ] **1** *n* Gorki

2 *pr n* **Maxim Gorki** Maxime Gorki

gormandize, -ise ['gɔ:məndaɪz] *vi Formal* engloutir, dévorer

gormless ['gɔ:mlɪs] *adj Br Fam (person, expression)* stupide❑, abruti; **don't look so gormless!** ne prends pas cet air d'abruti!

gorp [gɔ:p] *n Am (UNCOUNT)* mélange *m* de fruits secs

gorse [gɔ:s] *n (UNCOUNT)* ajoncs *mpl*

►► ***gorse bush*** ajonc *m*

gory ['gɔ:rɪ] (*compar* **gorier**, *superl* **goriest**) *adj (battle, scene, sight, death)* sanglant; **a gory film** un film sanglant *ou* très violent; *Hum* **give me all the gory details** vas-y, raconte-moi tout; *Hum* **spare me all the gory details** épargne-moi les détails

gosh [gɒʃ] *exclam Fam* oh dis donc!, ça alors!, hé ben!

goshawk ['gɒshɔ:k] *n Orn* autour *m*

gosling ['gɒzlɪŋ] *n* oison *m*

go-slow *n Br* grève *f* du zèle, grève *f* perlée

gospel ['gɒspəl] **1** *n* (**a**) *Bible* évangile *m*; **St Mark's Gospel, the Gospel according to St Mark** l'Évangile *m* selon saint Marc; **to preach the gospel** prêcher l'évangile; *Fig* **to preach the gospel of monetarism** prêcher le monétarisme; *Fig* **to take sth as gospel** prendre qch pour parole d'évangile (**b**) *Mus* gospel *m*

2 *comp (song)* negro spiritual *m*

►► ***gospel book*** évangéliaire *m*; ***gospel music*** gospel *m*; ***gospel oath*** serment *m* prêté sur l'Évangile; ***gospel singer*** chanteur(euse) *m,f* de gospels; *Fig* ***the gospel truth*** la vérité vraie

gospeller, *Am* **gospeler** ['gɒspələ(r)] *n* évangéliste *mf*

gossamer ['gɒsəmə(r)] **1** *n (UNCOUNT) (cobweb)* fils *mpl* de la vierge, filandres *fpl*; *(gauze)* gaze *f*; *(light cloth)* étoffe *f* transparente; **like gossamer** avec une légèreté arachnéenne

2 *comp* arachnéen, très léger, très fin

gossip ['gɒsɪp] **1** *n* (**a**) *(UNCOUNT) (casual chat)* bavardage *m*, papotage *m*; *Pej (rumour)* commérage *m*, ragots *mpl*, racontars *mpl*; *(in newspaper)* potins *mpl*; **to have a good gossip** bien papoter; **have you heard the latest (bit of) gossip?** vous connaissez la dernière (nouvelle)?; **that's just (idle) gossip** ce ne sont que des bavardages (futiles); **don't listen to gossip** n'écoutez pas les racontars; **the paper gives all the local gossip** il y a tous les petits potins du coin dans le journal

(**b**) *Pej (person)* bavard(e) *m,f*, pie *f*, commère *f*; **he's such a gossip!** quelle commère!

2 *vi* bavarder, papoter; *(maliciously)* faire des commérages, dire du mal des gens; **people are always gossiping about their neighbours** les gens ont toujours des ragots à raconter sur leurs voisins

►► ***gossip column*** échos *mpl*; **in the gossip columns** dans les échos; ***gossip columnist, gossip writer*** échotier(ère) *m,f*

gossiping ['gɒsɪpɪŋ] **1** *adj* bavard; *Pej* cancanier

2 *n (UNCOUNT)* bavardage *m*, papotage *m*; *Pej* commérage *m*

gossipmonger ['gɒsɪp,mʌŋgə(r)] *n* commère *f*

gossipy ['gɒsɪpɪ] *adj Fam (person)* bavard; *Pej* cancanier; *(letter)* plein de bavardages; *(style)* de conversation mondaine

got [gɒt] *pt & pp of* **get**

gotcha ['gɒtʃə] *exclam Fam* (**a**) *(I understand)* pigé! (**b**) *(when catching someone doing something)* je t'y prends!; *(when one has an advantage over someone)* je te tiens!; *(when hitting target)* je t'ai eu!

> **Gotcha!**
> Il s'agit du titre qui fit la une du journal The *Sun* lorsque le navire argentin General Belgrano fut coulé par les Britanniques durant la guerre des Malouines. Ce mot, qui est la transcription phonétique des termes **got you!** ("je t'ai eu!"), est aujourd'hui utilisé de façon allusive: il est devenu le symbole de la frénésie nationaliste qui s'empara de la Grande-Bretagne à cette période, ainsi que du chauvinisme de la presse populaire britannique.

Goth [gɒθ] *n* (**a**) *Hist* Goth *m*; **the Goths** les Goths *mpl* (**b**) *(in 1980s, 1990s)* = amateur de musique "Gothic", aux vêtements généralement noirs et au maquillage blafard

Gotham ['gɒθəm] *n* (**a**) *(New York)* = surnom de New York (**b**) **wise man of Gotham** gribouille *m*, nigaud *m*

Gothenburg ['gɒθən,bɜ:g] *n* Göteborg

Gothic ['gɒθɪk] **1** *adj Art, Archit, Literature & Typ* gothique; *(music, style, clothes)* = relatif au mouvement "gothique"

2 *n* (**a**) *Art, Archit & Literature* gothique *m* (**b**) *Ling* gotique *m*, gothique *m*

►► ***Gothic novel*** roman *m* gothique; ***Gothic rock*** = type de musique post-punk assez sombre, des années 80–90

Gothick ['gɒθɪk] **1** *n Archit* = style architectural des XVIIIème et XIXème siècles, imitant l'architecture gothique

2 *adj* (**a**) *Archit* = qui se rapporte ou qui rappelle un style architectural des XVIIIème et XIXème siècles qui imitait l'architecture gothique (**b**) *(novel)* gothique

Gothland ['gɒθlənd], **Gotland** ['gɒtlənd] *n Geog* Gothie *f*

go-to guy *n Am Fam* **he's the go-to guy** c'est à lui qu'il faut s'adresser

gotta ['gɒtə] *Am Fam* = **have got a, have got to**

gotten ['gɒtən] *Am pp of* **get**

gouache [gʊ'ɑ:ʃ] *Art* **1** *n* (**a**) *(paint)* gouache *f* (**b**) *(painting)* gouache *f*

2 *adj* à la gouache

Gouda ['gaʊdə] *n* gouda *m*

gouge [gaʊdʒ] **1** *n* gouge *f*

2 *vt (with gouge)* gouger; **to gouge a hole** *(intentionally)* creuser un trou; *(accidentally)* faire un trou; **you've gouged a great hole in the top of the table!** vous avez fait un gros trou sur le dessus de la table!

►**gouge out** *vt sep (with gouge)* gouger, creuser (à la gouge); *(with thumb)* évider, creuser; **to gouge sb's eyes out** arracher les yeux à qn

goujon ['gu:ʒɒn] *n (of fish, meat)* = lamelles de viande ou de poisson panées et frites

goulash ['gu:læʃ] *n* goulache *m*, goulasch *m*

gourd [gʊəd] *n* (**a**) *(plant)* gourde *f*, cucurbitacée *f*; *(fruit)* gourde *f*, calebasse *f* (**b**) *(container)* gourde *f*, calebasse *f*

gourmand ['gʊəmənd] *n (glutton)* gourmand(e) *m,f*; *(gourmet)* gourmet *m*

gourmet ['gʊəmeɪ] **1** *n* gourmet *m*, gastronome *mf*

2 *comp (meal, restaurant)* gastronomique

►► ***gourmet cook*** cordon-bleu *m*

gout [gaʊt] *n* (**a**) *(UNCOUNT) Med* goutte *f* (**b**) *Arch or Literary (blob)* goutte *f*

gouty ['gaʊtɪ] *adj (leg, person)* goutteux

Gov (**a**) *(written abbr* **government**) gouvernement *m* (**b**) *(written abbr* **governor**) gouverneur *m*

.gov *Comput* = abréviation désignant les sites gouvernementaux dans les adresses électroniques

govern ['gʌvən] **1** *vt* (**a**) *(country)* gouverner, régner sur; *(city, region, bank)* gouverner; *(affairs)* administrer, gérer; *(company, organization)* diriger, gérer; **the politicians who govern Britain** les politiciens qui gouvernent la Grande-Bretagne; **when Louis XIV governed France** quand Louis XIV gouvernait la France *ou* régnait sur la France

(**b**) *(determine → behaviour, choice, events, speed)* déterminer; **laws that govern chemical reactions** lois qui régissent les réactions chimiques

(**c**) *(restrain → passions)* maîtriser, dominer

(**d**) *Gram (case, mood)* régir

(**e**) *Tech* régler

2 *vi Com & Pol* gouverner, commander, diriger

governable ['gʌvənəbəl] *adj* gouvernable

governance ['gʌvənəns] *n* (**a**) *(act, manner)* gouvernement *m*, régime *m* (**b**) *(control)* emprise *f*

governess ['gʌvənɪs] *n* gouvernante *f*

governing ['gʌvənɪŋ] **1** *adj* (**a**) *Com & Pol* gouvernant, dirigeant; **the governing party** le parti au pouvoir (**b**) *(factor)* dominant; **the governing principle** le principe directeur

2 *n* gouvernement *m*

►► ***governing body*** conseil *m* d'administration

government ['gʌvənmənt] **1** *n* (**a**) *Pol (governing authority)* gouvernement *m*; *(type of authority)* gouvernement *m*, régime *m*; *(the State)* gouvernement *m*, État *m*; **the Conservative government** le gouvernement conservateur; **to form a government** constituer *ou* former un gouvernement; **the government has fallen** le gouvernement est tombé; **the socialists have joined the coalition government** les socialistes sont entrés dans le gouvernement de coalition; **democratic government** la démocratie; **a stable government** un gouvernement stable; **the project is financed by the government** le projet est financé par l'État *ou* le gouvernement

(**b**) *(process of governing → country)* gouvernement *m*, direction *f*; *(→ company)* administration *f*, gestion *f*; *(→ affairs)* conduite *f*

2 *comp (measure, policy)* gouvernemental, du gouvernement; *(expenditure)* de l'État, public; *(minister, department)* du gouvernement

►► ***government action*** action *f* gouvernementale; ***government advertising*** publicité *f* gouvernementale; ***government auditor*** commissaire *m* aux comptes; ***government bonds*** obligations *fpl* d'État, bons *mpl* du Trésor; ***government borrowings*** emprunts *mpl* de l'État; *Br* ***government broker*** agent *m* du Trésor; *Br* ***Government Communications Headquarters*** = centre d'interception des télécommunications étrangères en Grande-Bretagne; ***government developmental grant, government developmental subsidy*** prime *f* de développement; ***government grant*** subvention *f* d'État; ***government health warning*** = avertissement officiel contre les dangers du tabac figurant sur les paquets de cigarettes et dans les publicités pour le tabac; *Fig Hum* **men like him should carry a government health warning** des bonshommes pareils, ça devrait être interdit; **this car/computer should carry a government health warning** cette voiture/cet ordinateur est une catastrophe; *Br* ***Government***

gor–gov

House palais *m* du gouverneur; ***government issue*** émission *f* d'État *ou* par le gouvernement; ***government issue uniform*** uniforme *m* fourni par l'État; ***government loan*** emprunt *m* public *ou* d'État; *Am* ***the Government Printing Office*** = maison d'édition publiant les ouvrages ou documents émanant du gouvernement, ≃ Imprimerie *f* nationale; *Fin* ***government securities, government stock*** effets *mpl* publics, fonds *mpl* publics *ou* d'État; ***government spending*** dépenses *fpl* publiques

'The Government Inspector' *Gogol* 'Le Revizor'

governmental [ˌgʌvən'mentəl] *adj* gouvernemental, du gouvernement; **governmental responsibilities** des responsabilités gouvernementales; **a governmental organization** une organisation gouvernementale

government-funded *adj* subventionné par l'État

government-sponsored *adj* parrainé par le gouvernement; **government-sponsored terrorism** terrorisme *m* d'État

governor ['gʌvənə(r)] *n* (**a**) *(of bank, country)* gouverneur *m*; *Br (of prison)* directeur(trice) *m,f*; *Br (of school)* membre *m* du conseil d'établissement; *Am* **State governor** gouverneur *m* d'État (**b**) *Br Fam (employer)* patron ❑ *m*, boss *m* (**c**) *Br Fam (form of address)* **where to, governor?** on va où, patron? (**d**) *Tech* régulateur *m*

governor-general (*pl* **governor-generals**), **Governor-General** (*pl* **Governor-Generals**) *n* gouverneur(euse) *m,f* général(e)

governor-generalship *n* poste *m* de gouverneur général

governorship ['gʌvənəʃɪp] *n* fonctions *fpl* de gouverneur

govt (*written abbr* **government**) gouv.

gown [gaʊn] *n* (**a**) *(dress)* robe *f* (**b**) *(of magistrate, teacher, academic)* robe *f*, toge *f*; *(of surgeon)* blouse *f*

goy [gɔɪ] (*pl* **goys** *or* **goyim** ['gɔɪɪm]) *n* goy *mf*, goï *mf*

GP [ˌdʒiː'piː] *n* (*abbr* **general practitioner**) (médecin *m*) généraliste *mf*, *Can* omnipracticien(enne) *m,f*

GPA [ˌdʒiːpiː'eɪ] *n Am Sch* (*abbr* **grade point average**) moyenne *f*

GPMU [ˌdʒiːpiːˌem'juː] *n Br* (*abbr* **Graphical, Paper and Media Union**) = syndicat britannique des ouvriers du livre

GPO [ˌdʒiːpiː'əʊ] *n* (**a**) *Br Formerly* (*abbr* **General Post Office**) **the GPO** = titre officiel de la Poste britannique avant 1969 (**b**) *Am* (*abbr* **Government Printing Office**) **the GPO** = maison d'édition publiant les ouvrages ou documents émanant du gouvernement, ≃ Imprimerie *f* nationale

GPS [ˌdʒiːpiː'es] *n* (*abbr* **global positioning system**) GPS *m (système de navigation par satellite)*

gr (**a**) (*written abbr* **gramme(s)**) g (**b**) (*written abbr* **gross**) brut

grab [græb] (*pt & pp* **grabbed,** *cont* **grabbing**) **1** *vt* (**a**) *(object)* saisir, empoigner; *(person)* attraper; **to grab hold of sth** saisir qch, empoigner qch; **to grab hold of sb** attraper qn; **he grabbed the book out of my hand** il m'a arraché le livre des mains; **he grabbed my purse and ran** il s'est emparé de mon porte-monnaie et est parti en courant; **she grabbed my arm** elle m'a attrapé par le bras

(**b**) *Fig (opportunity)* saisir; *(attention)* retenir; *(power)* prendre; *(land)* s'emparer de; *(quick meal)* avaler, prendre (en vitesse); *(taxi)* prendre; **I'll grab a sandwich and work through the lunch hour** je vais me prendre un sandwich en vitesse et je travaillerai pendant l'heure du déjeuner

(**c**) *Fam (idioms)* **how does that grab you?** qu'est-ce que tu en dis? ❑; **the film didn't really grab me** le film ne m'a pas vraiment emballé

2 *vi* **to grab at sb/sth** essayer d'agripper qn/qch; **don't grab!** pas touche!; *Fig* **I grabbed at the chance** j'ai sauté sur l'occasion

3 *n* (**a**) *(movement)* mouvement *m* vif; *(sudden theft)* vol *m* (à l'arraché); **to make a grab at** *or* **for sth** essayer de saisir *ou* faire un mouvement vif pour saisir qch; *Fam* **to be up for grabs** être à prendre ❑; *(be on market, for sale)* être à vendre ❑; **they're getting rid of all the furniture, so those chairs are up for grabs** ils se débarrassent de tous leurs meubles, alors ces chaises sont à qui veut les prendre; **is that last chocolate up for grabs?** est-ce que je peux prendre le chocolat qui reste?; **you can take it if you like, it's up for grabs** vous pouvez le prendre si vous voulez, il est là pour ça

(**b**) *Br Tech* benne *f* preneuse

(**c**) *Aut (of brakes)* blocage *m*

►► *Am* ***grab bag*** *(game)* = jeu consistant à chercher des cadeaux enfouis dans un grand sac; *(assortment)* fourre-tout *m inv*; *Tech* ***grab crane*** grue *f* à benne preneuse

grabber ['græbə(r)] *n* (**a**) *(greedy person)* = personne qui se précipite sur tout (**b**) *(attention-seeker)* = personne qui cherche à attirer l'attention

grabby ['græbɪ] *adj Fam* (**a**) **don't be so grabby** *(don't grab things)* ne te jette pas sur les choses ❑; *(don't grab me)* ne t'agrippe pas à moi ❑; **he's very grabby** *(of child picking things up)* il touche à tout ❑ (**b**) *(miserly)* pingre, radin

GRACE [greɪs] *n Tel* (*abbr* **group routing and charging equipment**) automatique *m*

grace [greɪs] **1** *n* (**a**) *(of movement, dancer, athlete)* grâce *f*; *(decency, politeness, tact)* tact *m*; **social graces** savoir-vivre *m*; **to do sth with good/bad grace** faire qch de bonne/mauvaise grâce; **at least he had the (good) grace to apologize** il a au moins eu la décence de s'excuser

(**b**) *Rel* grâce *f*; **by the grace of God** par la grâce de Dieu; **in a state of grace** en état de grâce; **to fall from grace** perdre la grâce; *Fig* tomber en disgrâce; **there but for the grace of God (go I)** ça aurait très bien pu m'arriver aussi; *Arch or Literary* **in the year of grace 1066** en l'an de grâce 1066

(**c**) *(amnesty)* grâce *f*; *(respite)* grâce *f*, répit *m*; *Law* **as an act of grace, the King...;** en exerçant son droit de grâce, le Roi...; **we have two days' grace** nous disposons de deux jours de répit; *Com* **days of grace** jours *mpl* de grâce

(**d**) *(prayer → before meal)* bénédicité *m*; *(→ after meal)* grâces *fpl*; **to say grace** *(before meals)* dire le bénédicité; *(after meals)* dire les grâces

(**e**) *Arch (pardon)* grâce *f*, pardon *m*

(**f**) *(idiom)* **to be in sb's good/bad graces** être bien/mal vu par qn

2 *vt* (**a**) *(honour)* honorer; *Hum* **she graced us with her presence** elle nous a honorés de sa présence

(**b**) *Formal or Literary (adorn)* orner, embellir; **some exquisite watercolours graced the walls** les murs étaient ornés de très jolies aquarelles

3 Grace *n (term of address)* **Your Grace** *(to Archbishop)* Monseigneur, (Votre) Excellence, votre Excellence l'Archevêque; *(to Duke)* Monsieur le duc; *(to Duchess)* Madame la duchesse; **His Grace the Duke** Monsieur le duc; **Her Grace the Duchess** Madame la duchesse; **His Grace the Archbishop** Monseigneur *ou* Son Excellence l'Archevêque

4 Graces *npl Myth* **the three Graces** les trois Grâces *fpl*

►► ***grace note*** note *f* d'agrément, ornement *m*; ***grace period*** délai *m* de grâce

grace-and-favour *adj Br* **grace-and-favour residence** = logement appartenant à la Couronne et prêté à une personne que le souverain souhaite honorer

graceful ['greɪsfʊl] *adj* (**a**) *(person, movement)* gracieux; **a graceful figure** une silhouette élégante; **she is a graceful dancer** elle danse avec grâce (**b**) *(speech)* gracieux, poli, bien tourné

gracefully ['greɪsfʊlɪ] *adv (dance, move)* avec grâce, gracieusement; *(apologize)* avec élégance

gracefulness ['greɪsfʊlnɪs] *n* grâce *f*, élégance *f*

graceless ['greɪslɪs] *adj (behaviour, person, movement)* gauche

gracelessly ['greɪslɪslɪ] *adv* avec maladresse, de façon peu élégante

gracious ['greɪʃəs] **1** *adj* (**a**) *(generous, kind → gesture, smile)* gracieux, bienveillant; *(→ action)* généreux; **to be gracious to** *or* **towards sb** faire preuve de bienveillance envers qn; **to be gracious in defeat** être bon perdant, accepter la défaite avec bonne grâce; **our gracious King/Queen** notre gracieux souverain; **by the gracious consent of...** par la grâce de...; **God has been gracious to us** Dieu s'est montré miséricordieux *ou* bienveillant envers nous

(**b**) *(luxurious)* **gracious living** la vie facile

2 *exclam* **(good) gracious (me)!** mon Dieu!; **good gracious no!** jamais de la vie!; *Old-fashioned* **goodness gracious!** Seigneur Dieu!, bonté divine!

graciously ['greɪʃəslɪ] *adv (smile)* gracieusement; *(accept, agree, allow)* avec bonne grâce, *Formal* gracieusement; *Rel* miséricordieusement

graciousness ['greɪʃəsnɪs] *n (of person)* bienveillance *f*, générosité *f*, gentillesse *f*; *(of action)* grâce *f*, élégance *f*; *(of lifestyle, surroundings)* élégance *f*, raffinement *m*; *Rel* miséricorde *f*, clémence *f*

grackle ['grækəl] *n Orn* (**a**) *(American songbird)* quiscale *m* (**b**) *(starling)* mainate *m*

grad [græd] *n Am Fam* (*abbr* **graduate**) diplômé(e) ❑ *m,f*

►► ***grad school*** = école où l'on poursuit ses études après la licence

gradable ['greɪdəbəl] *adj* (**a**) *(capable of being graded)* qui peut être classé (**b**) *Ling* comparatif

gradate [grə'deɪt] **1** *vt (colours)* fondre

2 *vi* se fondre (**into** en)

gradation [grə'deɪʃən] *n* (**a**) *(gen)* gradation *f*; **gradations of meaning** nuances *fpl* de sens (**b**) *(of thermometer, scale)* gradation *f*, degré *m* (**c**) *Ling* alternance *f* (vocalique), apophonie *f*

gradational [grə'deɪʃənəl] *adj* (**a**) *(gen)* graduel, progressif, échelonné (**b**) *Ling* comparatif

grade [greɪd] **1** *n* (**a**) *(level)* degré *m*, niveau *m*; *(on scale)* échelon *m*, grade *m*; *(on salary scale)* indice *m*; **the top grades of the civil service** les échelons supérieurs *ou* les plus élevés de la fonction publique

(**b**) *Mil* grade *m*, rang *m*, échelon *m*; *(in hierarchy)* échelon *m*, catégorie *f*

(**c**) *(quality → of product)* qualité *f*, catégorie *f*; *(→ of petrol)* grade *m*; *(size of products)* calibre *m*; **a high grade of coal** un charbon de haute qualité; **there are two grades of eggs** il y a des œufs de deux calibres; **grade A potatoes** pommes de terre de qualité A

(**d**) *Am Sch (mark)* note *f*; *(year)* année *f*, classe *f*; **she gets good grades at school** elle a de bonnes notes à l'école; **a grade A student** un excellent élève

(**e**) *Am (primary school)* école *f* primaire

(**f**) *Math* grade *m*

(**g**) *Am (gradient)* déclivité *f*, pente *f*; *Rail* rampe *f*

(**h**) *Agr* **grades** bétail *m* amélioré par croisement

(**i**) *(idioms)* **to make the grade** être à la hauteur; **do you think she'll make the grade?** vous pensez qu'elle est *ou* sera à la hauteur?; *Am* **up to grade** d'une qualité adéquate

2 *vt* (**a**) *(classify → by quality)* classer; *(→ by size)* calibrer; *(arrange in order)* classer; **to grade questions** classer des questions par ordre de difficulté

(**b**) *Sch (mark)* noter

(**c**) *(cross → livestock)* améliorer par sélection

(**d**) *(level)* niveler; **to grade the ground** niveler le terrain

►► *Agr* ***grade cattle*** bétail *m* amélioré par croisement; *Am Rail* ***grade crossing*** passage *m* à niveau; ***grade crossing gate*** barrière *f* de passage à niveau; *Com* ***grade label*** étiquette *f* de calibrage; *Am Sch* ***grade point average*** moyenne *f*; *Am* ***grade school*** école *f* primaire; *Am Aut* ***grade separation*** séparation *f* des niveaux de circulation; *Am* ***grade teacher*** instituteur(trice) *m,f*

►**grade down** *vt sep* mettre dans une catégorie inférieure

►**grade up** *vt sep* (**a**) *(in rank, hierarchy)* mettre dans une catégorie supérieure (**b**) *(level)* niveler

graded ['greɪdɪd] *adj (by quality, arranged in order)* classé; *(by size)* calibré; **graded exercises** exercices *mpl* gradués; **graded tax**

(upwards) impôt *m* progressif; *(downwards)* impôt *m* dégressif

grader [ˈgreɪdə(r)] *n* (**a**) *Am Sch (marker of exams)* correcteur(trice) *m,f* (**b**) *Am Sch (student)* **fourth grader** élève *mf* de 4ème année (**c**) *Tech* grader *m*, niveleuse *f*

gradient [ˈgreɪdjənt] *n* (**a**) *Br (road)* déclivité *f*, pente *f*, inclinaison *f*; *Rail* rampe *f*, pente *f*, inclinaison *f*; **a steep gradient** une ligne à forte pente; **a gradient of three in ten** *or* **30 percent** une pente de 30 pour cent (**b**) *Met & Phys* gradient *m*; **pressure gradient** gradient de pression

►► *Rail* ***gradient post*** indicateur *m* de pente

grading [ˈgreɪdɪŋ] *n* (**a**) *(classification)* classification *f*; *(by size)* calibration *f* (**b**) *Sch* notation *f* (**c**) *Am Constr & Rail (of slope)* aménagement *m*

gradiometer [ˌgreɪdɪˈɒmɪtə(r)] *n* clinomètre *m*

gradual [ˈgrædʒʊəl] **1** *adj (change, improvement)* graduel, progressif; *(slope)* doux (douce)

2 *n Rel* graduel *m*

gradualism [ˈgrædʒʊəlɪzəm] *n* gradualisme *m*; *Pol* réformisme *m*

gradually [ˈgrædʒʊəlɪ] *adv* progressivement, petit à petit, peu à peu; **it happened very gradually** ça s'est produit très progressivement; **gradually you'll be able to type without looking at the keyboard** graduellement *ou* petit à petit *ou* progressivement, tu seras capable de taper sans regarder le clavier

gradualness [ˈgrædʒʊəlnɪs] *n* progressivité *f*

graduand [ˈgrædʒʊənd] *n Br Univ* candidat(e) *m,f*, postulant(e) *m,f*, prétendant(e) *m,f*

graduate 1 *n* [ˈgrædʒʊət] (**a**) *Univ* licencié(e) *m,f*, diplômé(e) *m,f*; *Am Sch* bachelier(ère) *m,f*; **biology graduate** ≃ licencié(e) *m,f* en biologie; **she's an Oxford graduate** *or* **a graduate of Oxford** elle a fait ses études à Oxford

(**b**) *Am (container)* récipient *m* gradué

2 *adj* [ˈgrædʒʊət] *Univ* diplômé, licencié

3 *vi* [ˈgrædjʊeɪt] (**a**) *Univ* ≃ obtenir son diplôme/sa licence; *Am Sch* ≃ obtenir le *ou* être reçu au baccalauréat; **she graduated from the Sorbonne** elle a un diplôme de la Sorbonne; **he graduated in linguistics** il a une licence de linguistique; **I graduated in 1999** j'ai eu ma licence en 1999; *Am Sch* **to graduate from high school** terminer ses études secondaires

(**b**) *(gain promotion)* être promu, passer; **to graduate from sth to sth** passer de qch à qch; **he graduated from the post of foreman to that of manager** il est passé du poste de contremaître à celui de directeur; *Fam Fig* **I've graduated from cheap plonk to good wines** je suis passé du gros rouge aux bons vins

4 *vt* [ˈgrædjʊeɪt] (**a**) *(calibrate)* graduer; **the ruler is graduated in millimetres** la règle est graduée en millimètres

(**b**) *(change, improvement)* graduer; **the teacher graduated the exercises** le professeur a gradué les exercices

(**c**) *Am Sch & Univ* conférer *ou* accorder un diplôme à

►► ***graduate entry*** échelon *m* d'entrée pour les diplômés; *Am Univ* ***Graduate Management Admissions Test*** = test d'admission dans le deuxième cycle de l'enseignement supérieur aux États-Unis; *Am Univ* ***Graduate Record Exam*** = test de niveau avant l'entrée dans une "graduate school"; *Am Univ* ***graduate school*** = école où l'on poursuit ses études après la licence; *Univ* ***graduate student*** étudiant(e) *m,f* de deuxième/troisième cycle; *Am Univ* ***graduate studies*** études *fpl* de troisième cycle; ***graduate training scheme*** programme *m* de formation professionnelle pour les diplômés

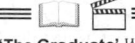

'The Graduate' *Webb, Nichols* 'Le Lauréat'

graduated [ˈgrædjʊˌeɪtɪd] *adj (tax)* progressif; *(measuring container, exercise, thermometer)* gradué; *(colours)* dégradé

►► *Br* ***graduated pension scheme*** = système de retraite complémentaire géré par l'État et alimenté par les contributions des employés et des employeurs

graduated-payment mortgage *n Am Fin* hypothèque *f* à paiements échelonnés

graduation [ˌgrædʒʊˈeɪʃən] *n* (**a**) *(gen)* graduation *f* (**b**) *Univ & Am Sch (ceremony)* (cérémonie *f* de) remise *f* des diplômes

►► ***graduation ceremony*** cérémonie *f* de remise des diplômes; ***graduation day*** jour *m* de la remise des diplômes

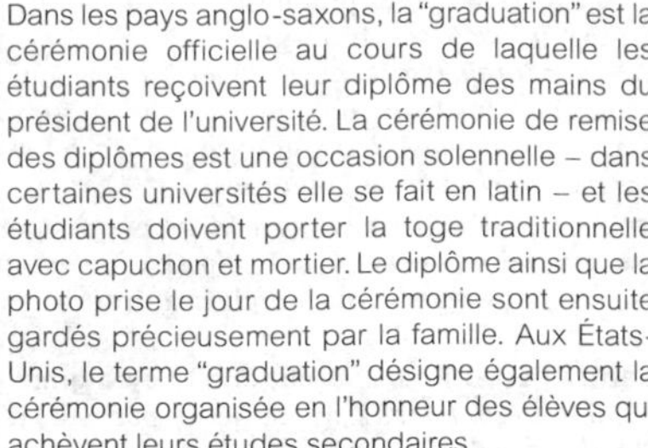

GRADUATION

Dans les pays anglo-saxons, la "graduation" est la cérémonie officielle au cours de laquelle les étudiants reçoivent leur diplôme des mains du président de l'université. La cérémonie de remise des diplômes est une occasion solennelle – dans certaines universités elle se fait en latin – et les étudiants doivent porter la toge traditionnelle avec capuchon et mortier. Le diplôme ainsi que la photo prise le jour de la cérémonie sont ensuite gardés précieusement par la famille. Aux États-Unis, le terme "graduation" désigne également la cérémonie organisée en l'honneur des élèves qui achèvent leurs études secondaires.

Graeco-, *Am* **Greco-** [ˌgriːkəʊ] *pref* gréco-; *Old-fashioned* **Graeco-Buddhist** gréco-bouddhique; **Graeco-Latin** gréco-latin; **Graeco-Roman** gréco-romain

►► *Sport* ***Graeco-Roman wrestling*** lutte *f* gréco-romaine

graffiti [grəˈfiːtɪ] *n (UNCOUNT)* graffiti *mpl*; **a piece of graffiti** un graffiti; **there's some graffiti on the wall** il y a des graffiti sur le mur

►► ***graffiti art*** tags *mpl (considérés comme un art)*; ***graffiti artist*** tagueur(euse) *m,f*

graft [grɑːft] **1** *n* (**a**) *Hort* greffe *f*, greffon *m*; *Med* greffe *f*; **they performed a cornea graft** ils ont effectué une greffe de la cornée; **bone/skin graft** greffe *f* osseuse/de peau; **I had to have a skin graft** on a dû me faire une greffe de peau

(**b**) *(UNCOUNT) (corruption)* magouilles *fpl*

(**c**) *(UNCOUNT) Br Fam (hard work)* travail *m* pénible❑; **to achieve sth by hard graft** réussir qch en bossant dur

2 *vt* (**a**) *Hort & Med* greffer; **they grafted a piece of skin onto his face** ils lui ont greffé un bout de peau sur le visage; *Fig* **this piece was grafted onto the symphony later** ce morceau a été rajouté à la symphonie plus tard; **the tower was grafted onto the original edifice** la tour a été ajoutée à l'édifice d'origine

(**b**) *(obtain by corruption)* obtenir par la corruption

3 *vi* (**a**) *(be involved in bribery)* donner *ou* recevoir des pots-de-vin

(**b**) *Hort & Med* **pears graft fairly easily** les poires se greffent assez facilement

(**c**) *Br Fam (work hard)* bosser dur

grafter [ˈgrɑːftə(r)] *n* (**a**) *Hort (instrument)* greffoir *m* (**b**) *Fam (hard worker)* bourreau *m* de travail (**c**) *Fam (corrupt person)* corrupteur❑ *m*, escroc❑ *m*; *(corrupt official)* fonctionnaire *mf* corrompu(e)❑, concussionnaire❑ *mf*

grafting [ˈgrɑːftɪŋ] *n Hort* greffe *f*, greffage *m*; *Med* greffe *f*; **skin grafting** greffe *f* de peau

graham [ˈgreɪəm] *adj*

►► *Am* ***graham cracker*** = biscuit rond légèrement sucré; *Am* ***graham flour*** farine *f* brute

Grail [greɪl] *n* Graal *m*; *Fig* **the Grail of full employment/world peace** la croisade pour parvenir au plein emploi/instaurer la paix mondiale

grain [greɪn] **1** *n* (**a**) *(UNCOUNT) (seeds of rice, wheat)* grain *m*; *(cereal)* céréales *fpl*; *Am* blé *m*; **a cargo of grain** une cargaison de céréales

(**b**) *(single)* grain *m*; **grains of rice/wheat** grains *mpl* de riz/de blé; **a grain of salt/sand** un grain de sel/de sable

(**c**) *Fig (of madness, sense, truth etc)* grain *m*, brin *m*; **a few grains of comfort** une petite consolation; *Fig* **there's not a grain of truth in what he says** il n'y a pas un grain de vérité dans ce qu'il dit; *Fig* **not a grain of common sense** pas un grain *ou* pas deux sous de bon sens, pas une once de bon sens

(**d**) *(in leather, stone, wood etc)* grain *m*; *Phot* grain *m*; **against** *or* **across the grain** contre le fil, à contre-fil; **I'll help you, but it goes against the grain** je vous aiderai, mais ce n'est pas de bon cœur; **it goes against the grain for him to accept that they are right** ce n'est pas dans sa nature d'admettre qu'ils ont raison

(**e**) *Br (unit of weight)* ≃ grain *m (poids)*

2 *vt* (**a**) *(salt)* cristalliser

(**b**) *(leather, paper)* greneler; *(paint to imitate wood)* veiner

3 *vi* se cristalliser

4 *comp (market)* céréalier

►► ***grain alcohol*** alcool *m* de grains; ***grain crop*** récolte *f* de céréales, récolte *f* céréalière; ***grain elevator*** silo *m* à céréales; ***grain mustard*** moutarde *f* à l'ancienne; ***grain store*** silo *m* à grains

grained [greɪnd] *adj* (**a**) *(salt)* cristallisé (**b**) *(leather, paper)* grenu, grené; *(painted imitation of wood)* veiné

grainy [ˈgreɪnɪ] *(compar* **grainier**, *superl* **grainiest**) *adj (surface, texture → of wood)* veineux; *(→ of stone)* grenu, granuleux; *(→ of leather, paper)* grenu, grené; *Phot* qui a du grain

gram [græm] *n* (**a**) *(metric unit)* gramme *m* (**b**) *Bot (plant)* pois *m*; *(seed)* pois *m*, graine *f* de pois

►► ***gram atom*** atome-gramme *m*; ***gram flour*** farine *f* de pois chiches; ***gram molecule*** molécule-gramme *f*

gramineous [grəˈmɪnɪəs] *adj Bot* caractéristique des graminées

graminivorous [ˌgræmɪˈnɪvərəs] *adj* = qui se nourrit d'herbe ou de céréales

grammage [ˈgræmɪdʒ] *n (of paper)* grammage *m*

grammar [ˈgræmə(r)] *n* (**a**) *Ling* grammaire *f*; **that's not very good grammar** ce n'est pas très correct du point de vue grammatical (**b**) *(book)* grammaire *f*; **a German grammar** une grammaire *ou* un livre de grammaire allemande

►► *Comput* ***grammar checker*** correcteur *m* grammatical; ***grammar school*** *(in UK)* = type d'école secondaire; *(in US)* = école primaire

GRAMMAR SCHOOL

En Grande-Bretagne, ce terme désigne une école secondaire recevant une aide de l'État mais pouvant être privée, réputée dispenser un enseignement de qualité de type traditionnel et préparant aux études supérieures. L'admission se fait sur concours ("eleven-plus") ou sur dossier. Moins de cinq pour cent des élèves britanniques fréquentent ce type d'école, qui existe en Angleterre, au pays de Galles et en Irlande du Nord.

grammarian [grəˈmeərɪən] *n* grammairien(enne) *m,f*

grammatical [grəˈmætɪkəl] *adj* (**a**) *(relating to grammar)* grammatical; **grammatical mistake** faute *f* de grammaire (**b**) *(correct)* grammaticalement correct

►► ***grammatical gender*** genre *m* grammatical

grammaticality [grəˌmætɪˈkælətɪ] *n* grammaticalité *f*

grammaticalize, -ise [grəˈmætɪkəlaɪz] *vt* grammaticaliser

grammatically [grəˈmætɪklɪ] *adv* grammaticalement, du point de vue grammatical

grammaticalness [grəˈmætɪkəlnɪs] *n* grammaticalité *f*

grammaticize, -ise [grəˈmætɪsaɪz] **1** *vt* rendre grammatical

2 *vi* discourir sur des points de grammaire

grammatologist [ˌgræməˈtɒlədʒɪst] *n* grammatologue *mf*

grammatology [ˌgræməˈtɒlədʒɪ] *n* grammatologie *f*

gramme [græm] *n (metric unit)* gramme *m*

Grammy [ˈgræmɪ] *n* **Grammy (award)** = distinction récompensant les meilleures œuvres musicales américaines de l'année (classique exclu)

gramophone [ˈgræməfəʊn] *n Br Old-fashioned* gramophone *m*, phonographe *m*

►► ***gramophone needle*** aiguille *f* de phonographe *ou* de gramophone; ***gramophone record*** disque *m*

Grampian [ˈgræmpɪən] *n* **the Grampians, the Grampian mountains** les Grampians *mpl*

►► ***Grampian Region*** les Grampians *mpl*, = région dans le nord-est de l'Écosse; **in Grampian Region** dans les Grampians

gramps [græmps] *n Fam* papy *m*, pépé *m*

grampus ['græmpəs] *n Zool* épaulard *m*, orque *f*

gran [græn] *n Br Fam (grandmother)* grand-mère *f*; *(term of address)* mamie *f*, mémé *f*

Granada [grə'nɑːdə] *n* Grenade *(en Espagne)*

granary ['grænərɪ] **1** *n* grenier *m* à blé, silo *m* (à céréales)

2 *comp (flour)* complet(ète)

►► ***granary bread, granary loaf*** pain *m* complet aux céréales

grand [grænd] **1** *adj* (**a**) *(impressive → house)* magnifique; *(→ style)* grand, noble; *(→ music, occasion)* grand; *(pretentious, self-important)* suffisant, prétentieux; *(dignified, majestic)* majestueux, digne; **to do sth in grand style** faire qch en grande pompe; **to live in grand style** mener la grande vie; **she likes to do things on a grand scale** elle aime faire les choses en grand; **to entertain on a grand scale** recevoir des gens en grande pompe; **to invest on a grand scale** faire de gros investissements; **to build on a grand scale** réaliser de grands projets de construction; **that dress is a bit too grand for me** cette robe est un peu trop chic pour moi; **it was all part of his grand design** tout cela faisait partie de son grand projet; **lexicographer is just a grand name for someone who writes dictionaries** lexicographe est simplement un mot pompeux pour désigner une personne qui écrit des dictionnaires

(**b**) *Br Old-fashioned or Ir, NEng & Scot Fam (excellent → food, accommodation)* excellent; *(→ weather)* magnifique; **I'm not feeling too grand** je ne suis pas dans mon assiette; **she sounded absolutely grand when I spoke to her on the phone** elle avait l'air en pleine forme quand je l'ai eue au téléphone; **to have a grand time** bien s'amuser; *Ironic* **we had a grand old time trying to find the house!** on s'est marré pour trouver la maison!

2 *n* (**a**) *Fam (money) Br* mille livres❑ *fpl*; *Am* mille dollars *mpl*; **two grand** *Br* deux mille livres; *Am* deux mille dollars

(**b**) *Mus* piano *m* à queue

3 *exclam Ir, NEng & Scot Fam* impec!, très bien!❑

►► ***Grand Canary (Island)*** Grande Canarie *f*; **in Grand Canary** à la Grande Canarie; ***the Grand Canyon*** le Grand Canyon; ***the Grand Canyon State*** = surnom donné à l'Arizona; ***grand duchess*** grande-duchesse *f*; ***grand duchy*** grand-duché *m*; ***grand duke*** grand-duc *m*; ***grand finale*** apothéose *f*; *Am* ***grand jury*** jury *m* d'accusation; *Am* ***grand larceny*** vol *m* qualifié; ***Grand Master*** *(in chess)* grand maître *m*; *(of masonic lodge)* Grand Maître *m*; ***the Grand National*** = la plus importante course d'obstacles de Grande-Bretagne, qui se déroule à Aintree, dans la banlieue de Liverpool; ***the Grand Old Man*** = surnom de William Gladstone; **the grand old man of trade unionism/Scottish folk music** le patriarche du syndicalisme/de la musique folklorique écossaise; *Am Pol* ***the Grand Old Party*** le parti républicain; ***grand opera*** grand opéra *m*; ***grand piano*** piano *m* à queue; *Sport & Cards* ***grand slam*** grand chelem *m*; ***Grand Slam tournament*** tournoi *m* du grand chelem; ***grand total*** total *m*; **that comes to a grand total of £536** ça fait en tout 536 livres; ***the Grand Tour*** le tour d'Europe; ***grand tour*** *(of mansion etc)* visite *f*; *Hum* **would you like a grand tour of the house?** je te fais faire le tour du propriétaire?; **she did** *or* **went on a grand tour of Italy** elle a visité toute l'Italie; *Phys* ***the Grand Unified Theory*** la théorie de grande unification; ***the Grand Union Canal*** = canal reliant Londres aux Midlands; *Hist* ***grand vizier*** grand vizir *m*; ***grand wizard*** Grand Sorcier *m*

grandad ['grændæd] *n Fam* grand-père❑ *m*; *(term of address)* pépé *m*, papy *m*; **a shirt with a grandad collar** une chemise sans col

►► ***grandad shirt*** chemise *f* sans col

grandaddy ['græn,dædɪ] *n Fam* (**a**) *(grandfather)* grand-père❑ *m*; *(term of address)* pépé *m*, papy *m* (**b**) *(most ancient)* ancêtre❑ *m*; **it's the grandaddy of them all** c'est leur ancêtre à tous

grandaunt ['grænd,ɑːnt] *n Old-fashioned* grand-tante *f*

grandchild ['grænd,tʃaɪld] *(pl* **grandchildren** [-,tʃɪldrən]*) n (boy)* petit-fils *m*; *(girl)* petite-fille *f*; **is it your first grandchild?** vous étiez déjà grand-père/grand-mère?; **she has six grandchildren** elle a six petits-enfants

granddad ['grændæd], **granddaddy** ['græn,dædɪ] *n Fam* grand-père❑ *m*; *(term of address)* pépé *m*, papy *m*

granddaughter ['græn,dɔːtə(r)] *n* petite-fille *f*

grandee [græn'diː] *n* grand *m* d'Espagne; *Fig* **Tory grandees** = personnes influentes du parti conservateur

grandeur ['grændjə(r)] *n* (**a**) *(of person)* grandeur *f*, noblesse *f*, éminence *f* (**b**) *(of building, surroundings etc)* splendeur *f*, magnificence *f*; **the grandeur of the landscape** la majesté du paysage; **an air of grandeur** quelque chose de grandiose; **faded grandeur** *(of house, furnishings etc)* splendeur *f* passée

grandfather ['grænd,fɑːðə(r)] *n* grand-père *m*

►► ***grandfather clause*** = aux États-Unis, clause de la constitution de plusieurs États du Sud qui, jusqu'en 1915, n'accordait le droit de vote qu'à ceux dont un parent votait avant 1861, excluant ainsi les Noirs – pas encore affranchis à cette date; ***grandfather clock*** horloge *f* (de parquet)

grandfatherly ['grænd,fɑːðəlɪ] *adj* de grand-père

grandiloquence [græn'dɪləkwəns] *n Formal* grandiloquence *f*

grandiloquent [græn'dɪləkwənt] *adj Formal* grandiloquent

grandiloquently [græn'dɪləkwəntlɪ] *adv Formal (speak)* d'un ton grandiloquent; *(write)* dans un style grandiloquent

grandiose ['grændɪəʊz] *adj Pej (building)* prétentieux, massif; *(style, term, theory, title)* pompeux; *(plan)* ambitieux

grandiosely ['grændɪəʊzlɪ] *adv Pej (built, designed, planned)* grandiosement; *(titled)* pompeusement

grandiosity [grændɪ'ɒsɪtɪ] *n Pej (of building)* caractère *m* prétentieux *ou* massif; *(of style, term, theory, title)* caractère *m* pompeux; *(of plan)* côté *m* ambitieux

grandly ['grændlɪ] *adv* (**a**) *(impressively)* de façon grandiose *ou* impressionnante (**b**) *Pej (pompously)* pompeusement

grandma ['grænmɑː] *n Fam* grand-mère❑ *f*; *(term of address)* mémé *f*, mamie *f*

grand mal [,grɒn'mæl] *n Med* grand mal *m*

grandmama ['grænmə,mɑː] *n Fam* grand-mère❑ *f*; *(term of address)* mémé *f*, mamie *f*

grandmother ['græn,mʌðə(r)] *n* grand-mère *f*

►► ***grandmother clock*** petite horloge *f*

grandmotherly ['græn,mʌðəlɪ] *adj* de grand-mère

grandnephew ['græn,nefjuː] *n* petit-neveu *m*

grandness ['grændnɪs] *n (of behaviour)* grandeur *f*, noblesse *f*; *(of lifestyle)* faste *m*; *(of appearance)* panache *m*

grandniece ['grænniːs] *n* petite-nièce *f*

grandpa ['grænpɑː] *n Fam* grand-père❑ *m*; *(term of address)* pépé *m*, papy *m*

grandpapa ['grænpə,pɑː] *n Fam Old-fashioned* grand-père❑ *m*; *(term of address)* pépé *m*, papy *m*

grandparent ['græn,peərənt] *n* **my grandparents** mes grands-parents *mpl*; **children are often looked after by a grandparent** les enfants sont souvent gardés par un de leurs grands-parents

grandparental [,grænpə'rentəl] *adj* des grands-parents

grand prix [,grɒn'priː] *n* grand prix *m*; **last year's grand prix winner** le vainqueur du dernier grand prix

►► ***grand prix racing*** course *f* de grand prix

grandsire ['græn,saɪə(r)] *n Arch or Literary (grandfather)* grand-père *m*, aïeul *m*; *(forefather)* aïeul *m*

grandson ['grænsʌn] *n* petit-fils *m*

grandstand ['grændstænd] **1** *n* tribune *f*; **to have a grandstand view (of sth)** être aux premières loges (pour voir qch)

2 *vi Am* faire l'intéressant

►► ***grandstand finish*** *(of race)* arrivée *f* palpitante; *(of match)* fin *f* palpitante

granduncle ['grænd,ʌŋkəl] *n Old-fashioned* grand-oncle *m*

grange [greɪndʒ] *n* (**a**) *Br (country house)* manoir *m*; *(farmhouse)* ferme *f* (**b**) *Am (farm)* ferme *f* (**c**) *Arch (granary)* grenier *m* à blé, grange *f*

granger ['greɪndʒə(r)] *n Am* fermier *m*

granite ['grænɪt] **1** *n* granit *m*, granite *m*

2 *comp* de granit *ou* granite

►► ***the Granite City*** = surnom donné à la ville d'Aberdeen, en Écosse; ***the Granite State*** = surnom donné au New Hampshire

granitic [græ'nɪtɪk] *adj* granitique, graniteux

granny, grannie ['grænɪ] *n Fam* grand-mère❑ *f*; *(term of address)* mamie *f*, mémé *f*

►► *Br Fam Fin* ***granny bond*** = type d'obligation visant le marché des retraités; *Fam* ***granny dumping*** = abandon d'une personne âgée qu'on a à charge; *Br Fam* ***granny flat*** appartement *m* indépendant *(dans une maison)*❑; ***granny knot*** nœud *m* de vache; ***Granny Smith*** *(apple)* granny-smith *f inv*

granola [grə'nəʊlə] *n Am* muesli *m*

►► ***granola bar*** barre *f* aux céréales

grant [grɑːnt] **1** *vt* (**a**) *(permission, wish)* accorder; *(request)* accorder, accéder à; *(goal, point) & Sport* accorder; *(credit, loan, pension)* accorder; *(charter, favour, privilege, right)* accorder, octroyer, concéder; *(property)* céder; **to grant sb permission to do sth** accorder à qn l'autorisation de faire qch; **the countries that have been granted autonomy** les pays qui se sont vus accorder l'autonomie; **to grant sb their request** accéder à la requête de qn; *Literary* **God grant you good fortune** que Dieu vous protège

(**b**) *(accept as true)* accorder, admettre, concéder; **will you at least grant that he is honest?** admettrez-vous au moins qu'il est honnête?; **I grant you I made an error of judgement** je vous accorde que j'ai fait une erreur de jugement; **I'll grant you that** je vous l'accorde; **granted, he's not very intelligent, but...** d'accord, il n'est pas très intelligent, mais...; **granted!** d'accord!, soit!

(**c**) *(idioms)* **to take sth for granted** considérer que qch va de soi, tenir qch pour certain *ou* établi; **you seem to take it for granted he'll agree/help you** vous semblez convaincu qu'il sera d'accord/vous aidera; **you take too much for granted** vous présumez trop; **to take sb for granted** ne plus faire cas de qn; **he takes her for granted** il la traite comme si elle n'existait pas; **you take me too much for granted** vous ne vous rendez pas compte de tout ce que je fais pour vous; **she felt that she was being taken for granted** elle avait le sentiment qu'elle ne comptait pas; **I'm tired of the way everybody just takes me for granted** j'en ai assez que personne ne fasse attention à moi

2 *n* (**a**) *(money given)* subvention *f*, allocation *f*; *(to student)* bourse *f* d'études; **I can't live on my grant** je n'arrive pas à m'en sortir avec seulement ma bourse d'études; **to give sb a grant** accorder une subvention à qn; *(student)* accorder une bourse d'études à qn; **to receive a grant** être subventionné, recevoir une subvention; *(student)* recevoir *ou* se voir accorder une bourse d'études

(**b**) *(transfer → of property)* cession *f*; *(→ of land)* concession *f*; *(permission)* octroi *m*; **grant of probate** validation *f ou* homologation *f* d'un testament

grant-aided *adj* subventionné par l'État

grant-in-aid *n* subvention *f (de l'État)*

grant-maintained *adj Br* subventionné *(par l'État)*; **grant-maintained school** école *f* privée subventionnée *(acceptant en échange un droit de regard de l'État sur la gestion de ses affaires)*

grantor [grɑːn'tɔː(r)] *n* cédant(e) *m,f*, donateur(-trice) *m,f*, concédant *m*

granular ['grænjʊlə(r)] *adj (surface)* granuleux, granulaire; *(structure)* grenu

granularity [,grænjʊ'lærɪtɪ] *n* granularité *f*

granulate ['grænjʊleɪt] *vt (lead, powder, tin)* granuler; *(salt, sugar)* grener, grainer; *(surface)* grener, greneler, rendre grenu

granulated sugar ['grænjʊleɪtɪd-] *n* sucre *m* en poudre, *Can* sucre *m* cristallisé

granulation [,grænjʊ'leɪʃən] *n (texture)* granulation *f*; *(action)* granulation *f*, grenage *m*

granuloma [,grænjʊ'ləʊmə] *n* granulome *m*

granule ['grænjuːl] *n* granule *m*; **coffee/tea granules** granules *mpl* de café/thé

grape [greɪp] *n* (**a**) *(fruit)* grain *m* de raisin; **a (variety of) grape** un raisin; **to eat grapes** manger du raisin; **to pick grapes** faire les vendanges, cueillir le raisin; **black/white grapes** du raisin noir/blanc (**b**) *(UNCOUNT) (grapeshot)* mitraille *f*

►► ***grape harvest*** vendanges *fpl*; *Bot* ***grape hyacinth*** muscari *m*; ***grape juice*** jus *m* de raisin; ***grape picking*** vendanges *fpl*; ***grape sugar*** dextrose *m*, glucose *m*

'The Grapes of Wrath' *Steinbeck, Ford* 'Les Raisins de la colère'

grapefruit ['greɪpfruːt] *n* pamplemousse *m*

►► ***grapefruit juice*** jus *m* de pamplemousse; ***grapefruit segments*** quartiers *mpl* de pamplemousse; ***grapefruit tree*** pamplemoussier *m*

grapeseed oil ['greɪpsiːd-] *n* huile *f* de pépins de raisin

grapeshot ['greɪpʃɒt] *n* mitraille *f*

grapevine ['greɪpvaɪn] *n* (**a**) *Bot* vigne *f*, treille *f* (**b**) *Fig* téléphone *m* arabe; **I heard on the grapevine that...** j'ai entendu par le téléphone arabe que...

grapey = **grapy**

graph [grɑːf] **1** *n* (**a**) *(diagram)* graphique *m*, courbe *f* (**b**) *Ling* graphie *f*

2 *vt* mettre en graphique, tracer

►► ***graph paper*** papier *m* quadrillé; *(in millimetres)* papier *m* millimétré

grapheme ['græfiːm] *n Ling* graphème *m*

graphic ['græfɪk] **1** *adj* (**a**) *Math* graphique (**b**) *(vivid)* imagé; **in graphic detail** dans tous les détails (**c**) *Art* graphique

2 graphics 1 *n (UNCOUNT) (drawing)* art *m* graphique **2** *npl Math* (utilisation *f* des) graphiques *mpl*; *(drawings)* représentations *fpl* graphiques; *Comput (images)* graphismes *mpl*, graphiques *mpl*

►► *Comput* ***graphics accelerator*** accélérateur *m* graphique; *Comput* ***graphics accelerator card*** carte *f* accélérateur graphique; ***graphic artist*** graphiste *mf*; ***graphic arts*** arts *mpl* graphiques; *Comput* ***graphics card*** carte *f* graphique; ***graphic design*** conception *f* graphique; ***graphic designer*** graphiste *mf*, maquettiste *mf*; ***graphic display*** graphisme *m*; *Comput* ***graphics display*** affichage *m* graphique; ***graphic equalizer*** égaliseur *m* graphique; *Comput* ***Graphics Interchange Format*** GIF *m*; *Comput* ***graphic interface*** interface *f* graphique; *Comput* ***graphics mode*** mode *m* graphique; ***graphic novel*** bande *f* dessinée; *Comput* ***graphics package*** grapheur *m*; *Comput* ***graphics software*** logiciel *m* graphique; ***graphic solution*** analyse *f ou* évaluation *f* graphique; *Comput* ***graphics spreadsheet*** tableur *m* de graphiques; *Comput* ***graphics tablet*** tablette *f* graphique

graphical ['græfɪkəl] *adj* graphique

►► *Br* ***Graphical, Paper and Media Union*** = syndicat britannique des ouvriers du livre; *Comput* ***graphical user interface*** interface *f* utilisateur graphique

graphically ['græfɪklɪ] *adv* (**a**) *Math* graphiquement (**b**) *(vividly)* de façon très imagée

graphite ['græfaɪt] **1** *n* graphite *m*, plombagine *f*, mine *f* de plomb

2 *adj* en graphite

graphological [ˌgræfə'lɒdʒɪkəl] *adj* graphologique

graphologist [græ'fɒlədʒɪst] *n* graphologue *mf*

graphology [græ'fɒlədʒɪ] *n* graphologie *f*

grapnel ['græpnəl] *n Naut* grappin *m*, crochet *m*; *(of balloon)* ancre *f*

grappa ['græpə] *n* grappa *f*

grapple ['græpəl] **1** *n Tech* grappin *m*

2 *vt* (**a**) *Tech* saisir avec un grappin (**b**) *Am (person)* **to grapple sb** saisir qn contre soi; **to grapple sb to the floor** mettre qn à terre

3 *vi* (**a**) *(physically)* **to grapple with sb** en venir aux mains avec qn (**b**) *Fig* **to grapple with sth** *(difficulty, problem, computer, machine)* se débattre avec qch; **to grapple with inflation** être aux prises avec l'inflation

grappling hook, grappling iron ['græplɪŋ-] *n Naut* grappin *m*, crochet *m*; *(of balloon)* ancre *f*

grapy ['greɪpɪ] *adj (wine)* fruité

grasp [grɑːsp] **1** *vt* (**a**) *(physically)* saisir; *(opportunity)* saisir; *(power)* se saisir de, s'emparer de; **to grasp (hold of) sth** saisir qch; **to grasp (hold of) sb's hand** saisir la main de qn

(**b**) *(understand)* saisir, comprendre; **I didn't quite grasp what she meant** je n'ai pas bien compris *ou* saisi ce qu'elle a voulu dire; **to grasp the importance of sth** saisir l'importance de qch

2 *n* (**a**) *(grip)* (forte) poigne *f*; *(action of holding)* prise *f*, étreinte *f*; *Fig* **to have sb in one's grasp** avoir *ou* tenir qn en son pouvoir; **to have sth in one's grasp** avoir prise sur qch; **to wrest sth from sb's grasp** arracher qch des mains de qn; **to have a strong grasp** *(handshake)* avoir de la poigne

(**b**) *Fig (reach)* portée *f*; **within/beyond sb's grasp** à la portée/hors de (la) portée de qn; **success is now within her grasp** le succès est désormais à sa portée; **to let an opportunity slip from one's grasp** rater une occasion

(**c**) *(understanding)* compréhension *f*; **she has a thorough grasp of the subject** elle a une connaissance approfondie de la question; **his grasp of the problem was poor** il dominait mal le problème

(**d**) *(handle)* poignée *f*

►**grasp at** *vt insep (attempt to seize)* chercher à saisir, essayer de saisir; *(accept eagerly)* saisir; **to grasp at an opportunity** sauter sur *ou* saisir l'occasion

grasping ['grɑːspɪŋ] *adj* avare, avide

grass [grɑːs] **1** *n* (**a**) *(gen)* herbe *f*; *(lawn)* pelouse *f*, gazon *m*; **keep off the grass** *(sign)* défense de marcher sur la pelouse, pelouse interdite; **to cut** *or* **to mow the grass** tondre la pelouse; *Tennis* **she plays well on grass** elle joue bien sur gazon; **he doesn't let the grass grow under his feet** il ne perd pas de temps; *Prov* **the grass is always greener (on the other side of the fence)** = c'est toujours mieux ailleurs

(**b**) *(pasture)* herbage *m*; **to put** *or* **turn a horse out to grass** mettre un cheval au vert; *Fig* **to put sb out to grass** mettre qn à la retraite; **to be (out) at grass** *(animal)* être au vert; **to put land under grass** enherber une terre, mettre une terre en herbe

(**c**) *Fam (marijuana)* herbe *f*

(**d**) *Br Fam (informer)* mouchard *m*, indic *m*

2 *vt* (**a**) *(field)* enherber; *(garden)* gazonner, engazonner

(**b**) *Am (animals)* mettre au vert

(**c**) *Tex* herber, blanchir au pré

3 *vi Br Fam (inform)* cafarder; **to grass on sb** balancer qn, moucharder qn

4 grasses *npl Bot* graminées *fpl*

►► ***grass court*** court *m* (en gazon); ***grass green*** vert *m* gazon; *Pol* ***the grass roots*** la base; **the feeling at the grass roots is that...** le sentiment à la base est que...; **at (the) grass roots level** au niveau de la base; ***grass roots opposition*** résistance *f* de la base; ***grass roots support*** soutien *m* de la base; ***grass seed*** *(for lawn)* graine *f* pour gazon; *(as feed)* graine *f* fourragère; ***grass skirt*** pagne *m (de feuilles)*; ***grass snake*** couleuvre *f* à collier; ***grass widow*** = femme dont le mari est toujours en déplacement; *Fig* **I'm a grass widow this weekend** je suis célibataire ce week-end; ***grass widower*** = homme dont la femme est toujours en déplacement

►**grass over** *vt sep (field)* enherber; *(garden)* gazonner, engazonner

►**grass up** *vt sep Br Fam* **to grass sb up** balancer qn, moucharder qn

grassbox ['grɑːsbɒks] *n (of lawnmower)* panier *m* à herbes

grass-cutter *n* tondeuse *f* à gazon

grass-feed *vt* mettre à pâturer

grass-green *adj (colour)* vert gazon *(inv)*

grasshopper ['grɑːsˌhɒpə(r)] *n* (**a**) *(insect)* sauterelle *f*, grillon *m*; *Fig* **he's got a grasshopper mind** il papillonne constamment (**b**) *(cocktail)* grasshopper *m (cocktail à base de crème fraîche, de crème de menthe et de crème de cacao)*

►► *Orn* ***grasshopper warbler*** locustelle *f* tachetée

grassland ['grɑːslænd] *n* prairie *f*, pré *m*

grassless ['grɑːslɪs] *adj* sans herbe

grassy ['grɑːsɪ] *adj* herbu, herbeux; *(lane)* vert; *(plain)* verdoyant

grate [greɪt] **1** *n (fireplace)* foyer *m*, âtre *m*; *(for holding coal)* grille *f* de foyer; **a fire in the grate** un feu dans la cheminée

2 *vt* (**a**) *Culin* râper

(**b**) *(chalk, metal)* faire grincer; **to grate one's teeth** grincer des dents

3 *vi* (**a**) *(machine, metal)* grincer; **to grate on the ears** écorcher les oreilles

(**b**) *Fig* **the baby's crying began to grate (on him)** les pleurs du bébé ont commencé à l'agacer; **his behaviour grates after a while** son comportement est agaçant au bout d'un moment; **to grate on the ear** *(music, particular accent)* écorcher l'oreille; *(noise)* faire mal aux oreilles

G-rated *adj Am (movie)* tous publics

grateful ['greɪtfʊl] *adj* (**a**) *(person)* reconnaissant; **to be grateful towards** *or* **to sb for sth** être reconnaissant envers qn de qch; **I am extremely grateful to you** je vous suis extrêmement reconnaissant; **I am grateful for your help** je vous suis reconnaissant de votre aide; **I would be most** *or* **very grateful if you would help me** je vous serais très reconnaissant de m'aider; **a grateful letter** une lettre de remerciements; **with grateful thanks** avec toute ma reconnaissance, avec mes sincères remerciements; **be grateful for what you've got** estime-toi heureux avec ce que tu as; **I suppose we should be grateful for that** on devrait s'en estimer heureux

(**b**) *Arch or Literary (thing)* agréable

gratefully ['greɪtfʊlɪ] *adv* avec reconnaissance *ou* gratitude; **to smile gratefully** faire un sourire reconnaissant; **all contributions gratefully accepted** toutes les contributions sont les bienvenues

gratefulness ['greɪtfʊlnɪs] *n* reconnaissance *f*, gratitude *f*

grater ['greɪtə(r)] *n* râpe *f*

graticulation [ˌgrætɪkjuː'leɪʃən] *n (of design, image)* graticulation *f*

graticule ['grætɪkjuːl] *n (on map)* quadrillage *m* cartographique; *(in microscope, telescope)* croisée *f* de fils

gratification [ˌgrætɪfɪ'keɪʃən] *n (state or action)* satisfaction *f*, plaisir *m*; *Psy* gratification *f*; **he has the gratification of knowing that...** il a la satisfaction *ou* le plaisir de savoir que...; **I noticed to my gratification that...** à ma grande satisfaction, j'ai remarqué que...; **sexual gratification** plaisir *m* sexuel, satisfaction *f* sexuelle

gratified ['grætɪfaɪd] *adj* satisfait, content (**with** de); *(smile)* de satisfaction

gratify ['grætɪfaɪ] *vt* (**a**) *(person)* faire plaisir à, être agréable à; **it gratified him** *or* **he was gratified to learn that...** ça lui a fait plaisir *ou* lui a été agréable d'apprendre que...; **I was gratified with** *or* **at the result** j'ai été très content *ou* satisfait du résultat (**b**) *(whim, wish)* satisfaire

gratifying ['grætɪfaɪɪŋ] *adj* agréable, plaisant; *Psy* gratifiant; **it's gratifying to know that...** c'est agréable *ou* ça fait plaisir de savoir que...

gratifyingly ['grætɪfaɪɪŋlɪ] *adv* agréablement

grating ['greɪtɪŋ] **1** *n (bars)* grille *f*, grillage *m*

2 *adj (irritating)* agaçant, irritant, énervant; *(sound)* grinçant, discordant; *(voice)* discordant

gratingly ['greɪtɪŋlɪ] *adv (irritatingly)* d'une façon irritante; *(laugh, talk)* d'un ton discordant

gratis ['grætɪs] **1** *adj* gratuit

2 *adv* gratuitement

gratitude ['grætɪtjuːd] *n* gratitude *f*, reconnaissance *f*; **to show/to express one's gratitude (towards sb/for sth)** témoigner/exprimer sa gratitude (envers qn/pour qch)

gratuitous [grə'tjuːɪtəs] *adj* (**a**) *(unjustified)* gratuit, sans motif, injustifié; **gratuitous violence** violence *f* gratuite (**b**) *Arch (costing nothing)* gratuit

gratuitously [grə'tjuːɪtəslɪ] *adv* (**a**) *(without good reason)* gratuitement, sans motif (**b**) *Arch (at no charge)* gracieusement, gratuitement

gratuitousness [grə'tjuːɪtəsnɪs] *n* (**a**) *(lack of justification)* gratuité *f* (**b**) *Arch (costing nothing)* gratuité *f*

gratuity [grə'tjuːɪtɪ] *n* (**a**) *Formal (tip)* gratification *f*, pourboire *m* (**b**) *Br (payment to employee)* prime *f*; *Mil* peine *f* de démobilisation

gravadlax ['grævədlæks] *n Culin* = saumon séché et mariné dans un mélange d'épices, de sel et de sucre

grave¹ [greɪv] **1** *n (hole)* fosse *f*; *(burial place)* tombe *f*; **mass grave** fosse *f* commune; *(in wartime)* charnier *m*; **to be in one's grave** être dans la tombe; **she worked herself into an early grave** elle s'est tuée au travail; **he took his secret with him to the grave** il a emporté son secret dans la tombe; **he drank himself into an early grave** l'alcool l'a prématurément tué; **he's drinking himself into an early grave** il se détruit à force de boire; *Fig* **he must have been turning in his grave** il a dû se retourner dans sa tombe; **it would make her turn in her grave** elle se retournerait dans sa tombe; **someone has just walked over my grave** j'ai eu un frisson; **to be digging one's own grave** creuser sa propre tombe; **to have one foot in the grave** avoir un pied dans la tombe; **from beyond the grave** d'outre-tombe

2 *adj (serious)* grave, sérieux; *(tone)* solennel; *(situation)* grave; *(error)* lourd; **to make a grave mistake** se tromper lourdement; **grave news** de graves nouvelles

►► *Old-fashioned* ***grave clothes*** linceul *m*; *Archeol* ***grave goods*** = objets rituels laissés dans un tombeau; ***grave robber*** *(who robs valuables from graves)* = personne qui vole les objets de valeur laissés dans les tombes; *(body snatcher)* déterreur(euse) *m,f* de cadavres

grave² [grɑːv] *Ling* **1** *n* accent *m* grave

2 *adj (accent)* grave; **it's spelled with an "a" grave** ça s'écrit avec un "a" accent grave

gravedigger ['greɪv,dɪgə(r)] *n* fossoyeur *m*

gravel ['grævəl] (*Br pt & pp* **gravelled**, *cont* **gravelling**, *Am pt & pp* **graveled**, *cont* **graveling**) **1** *n* gravier *m*; *(finer)* gravillon *m*; *Med* gravelle *f*

2 *vt* gravillonner, répandre du gravier sur

►► ***gravel path*** chemin *m* de gravier; ***gravel pit*** gravière *f*, carrière *f* de gravier

gravel-blind *adj Literary* presque aveugle

gravelled, *Am* **graveled** ['grævəld] *adj* couvert de gravier

gravelly ['grævəlɪ] *adj* (**a**) *(like or containing gravel)* graveleux; *(road)* de gravier; *(riverbed)* caillouteux (**b**) *(voice)* rauque, râpeux

gravely ['greɪvlɪ] *adv* (**a**) *(speak)* gravement, sérieusement (**b**) *(as intensifier)* **gravely ill** gravement malade; **to be gravely mistaken** se tromper lourdement; **gravely wounded** grièvement blessé

graven ['greɪvən] *adj Arch or Literary* **graven on my memory** gravé dans ma mémoire

►► *Rel* ***graven image*** idole *f*, image *f*

graveness ['greɪvnɪs] *n* gravité *f*

Graves' disease ['greɪvz-] *n Med* maladie *f* de Basedow

graveside ['greɪvsaɪd] *n* **at sb's graveside** sur la tombe de qn; **his next of kin were there at the graveside** ses proches étaient présents à l'enterrement

gravestone ['greɪvstəʊn] *n* pierre *f* tombale

graveyard ['greɪvjɑːd] *n also Fig* cimetière *m*; *Fig* **this town is a graveyard** cette ville est mortelle; **this department has been the graveyard of more than one young hopeful's ambitions** ce [illegible] fin aux ambitions de plus d'un jeune; *Fam* **to have a graveyard cough** avoir une toux qui sent le sapin

►► ***graveyard shift*** équipe *f* de nuit; **I work the graveyard shift** je suis dans l'équipe de nuit; *Rad & TV* ***graveyard slot*** tranche *f* nocturne

gravid ['grævɪd] *adj* gravide

gravimeter [grə'vɪmətə(r)] *n* gravimètre *m*

gravimetric [,grævɪ'metrɪk], **gravimetrical** [,grævɪ-'metrɪkəl] *adj* gravimétrique

gravimetry [grə'vɪmətrɪ] *n* gravimétrie *f*

graving dock ['greɪvɪŋ-] *n Naut* bassin *m* de radoub

gravitas ['grævɪtæs] *n* sérieux *m*

gravitate ['grævɪteɪt] *vi* graviter; **to gravitate towards sb/sth** graviter vers qn/qch; **many young people gravitate to the big cities** beaucoup de jeunes sont attirés par les grandes villes; **most of the guests had gravitated towards the bar/kitchen** la plupart des invités s'étaient rapprochés du bar/de la cuisine

gravitation [,grævɪ'teɪʃən] *n* gravitation *f*; *Fig* **there was a general gravitation towards the bar** tout le monde s'est dirigé vers le bar; *Phys* **law of gravitation** loi *f* de la gravitation

gravitational [,grævɪ'teɪʃənəl] *adj* gravitationnel, de gravitation

►► ***gravitational field*** champ *m* de gravitation; ***gravitational force*** force *f* de gravitation *ou* gravitationnelle; ***gravitational pull*** gravitation *f*

gravity ['grævətɪ] *n* (**a**) *(seriousness)* gravité *f*; **I don't think you appreciate the gravity of the situation** je n'ai pas l'impression que tu te rendes compte de *ou* que tu réalises la gravité de la situation (**b**) *Phys (force)* pesanteur *f*; *(phenomenon)* gravitation *f*; **the law of gravity** la loi de la pesanteur

►► ***gravity feed*** alimentation *f* par gravité; ***gravity platform*** plate-forme *f* poids

gravlax ['grævlæks] = **gravadlax**

gravure [grə'vjʊə(r)] *n (process)* gravure *f*; *(plate)* plaque *f* gravée; *(impression)* gravure *f*

gravy ['greɪvɪ] *n* (**a**) *Culin* jus *m*; *(thickened)* sauce *f* (au jus)

(**b**) *Am Fam (easy money)* bénef *m*; **it's gravy** *(easy)* c'est du gâteau

►► ***gravy boat*** saucière *f*; *Fam* ***gravy train*** assiette *f* au beurre; **to get on the gravy train** être à la recherche d'un bon filon; **she's been on the gravy train for years** elle a eu la vie facile pendant des années; **it's just a gravy train for him and his friends** c'est une véritable mine d'or pour lui et ses amis

gray, graybeard *etc Am* = **grey, greybeard** *etc*

gray-cheeked thrush *n Orn* grive *f* à joues grises

grayling ['greɪlɪŋ] *n* (**a**) *Ich* ombre *m* (**b**) *Entom* (papillon *m*) agreste *m*

Gray's Inn [greɪz-] *n* = association d'étudiants en droit et d'avocats, ainsi que les bâtiments londoniens où elle siège

graze [greɪz] **1** *vi (animals)* brouter, paître, pâturer; *(humans)* grignoter

2 *vt* (**a**) *(touch lightly)* frôler, effleurer, raser; **the boat just grazed the bottom** le bateau a effleuré le fond

(**b**) *(skin)* érafler, écorcher; **the bullet grazed his cheek** la balle lui a éraflé la joue; **she grazed her elbow on the wall** elle s'est écorché le coude sur le mur

(**c**) *(animals)* faire paître; *(grass)* brouter, paître; *(field)* pâturer

3 *n* écorchure *f*, éraflure *f*; **it's just a graze** c'est juste un peu écorché

grazier ['greɪzjə(r)] *n* herbager *m*

grazing ['greɪzɪŋ] *n (grass for animals)* pâturage *m*; *(land)* pâture *f*, pâturage *m*

GRE [,dʒiːɑː'riː] *n Am (abbr* **Graduate Record Exam**) = test de niveau avant l'entrée dans une "graduate school"

grease [griːs] **1** *n (gen)* graisse *f*; *(lubricant) & Aut* graisse *f*, lubrifiant *m*; *(used lubricant)* cambouis *m*; *(dirt)* crasse *f*; **grease stain** *(on clothing, linen)* tache *f* de gras *ou* de graisse; **to remove grease from sth** dégraisser qch; **a collar covered in grease** un col couvert de crasse

2 *vt (gen)* graisser; *Aut* graisser, lubrifier; *Culin (cake tin)* beurrer

►► ***grease gun*** (pistolet *m*) graisseur *m*, pompe *f* à graisse; *Am Fam (submachine gun)* mitraillette ☐ *f*; *Fam* **grease monkey** mécano *m*, ***grease nipple*** graisseur *m*

►**grease back** *vt sep* **to grease back one's hair** se gominer les cheveux

greased lightning [,griːst-] *n Fam* **like greased lightning** à tout berzingue, à fond la caisse

greasepaint ['griːspeɪnt] *n Theat* fard *m* (gras); **a stick of greasepaint** un crayon gras

greaseproof ['griːspruːf] *adj Br* imperméable à la graisse

►► *Culin* ***greaseproof paper*** papier *m* sulfurisé

greaser ['griːsə(r)] *n Fam* (**a**) *(mechanic)* graisseur *m*, mécano *m* (**b**) *(biker)* motard *m* (**c**) *Am (offensive use)* = terme injurieux désignant une personne d'origine latino-américaine ou italienne (**d**) *Am (hoodlum)* loubard *m*

grease-stained *adj* taché de graisse, graisseux

greasiness ['griːsɪnɪs] *n* (**a**) *(gen)* état *m* graisseux, nature *f* graisseuse; *(of cosmetics)* onctuosité *f*; *(of hair, hands)* nature *f* grasse (**b**) *(of road)* surface *f* glissante

greasy ['griːsɪ] *adj* (**a**) *(food, substance)* graisseux, gras; *(tools)* graisseux; *(cosmetics, hair, hands)* gras

(**b**) *(pavement, road)* gras, glissant

(**c**) *(clothes → dirty)* crasseux, poisseux; *(→ covered in grease marks)* taché de graisse, plein de graisse

(**d**) *(obsequious)* obséquieux; **a greasy manner** des manières obséquieuses; **a greasy smile** un sourire obséquieux

►► *Sport & Fig* ***the greasy pole*** le mât de cocagne; *Fam* ***greasy spoon*** boui-boui *m*

GREAT [greɪt] (*compar* **greater**, *superl* **greatest**) **1** *adj* (**a**) *(in size, scale)* grand; **the great fire of London** le grand incendie de Londres *(qui, en 1666, détruisit les trois quarts de la ville, et notamment la cathédrale Saint-Paul)*; **he made a great effort to be nice** il a fait un gros effort pour être agréable

(**b**) *(in degree)* grand; **a great friend** un grand ami; **they're great friends** ce sont de grands amis; **great ignorance** une grande ignorance, une ignorance complète; **there's great ignorance about the problem** les gens ne sont pas conscients du problème; **great willpower** une volonté de fer; **she's got great willpower** elle est très volontaire; **to my great satisfaction** à ma grande satisfaction; **a great surprise** une grande surprise; **with great care** avec grand soin, avec beaucoup de soin; **with great pleasure** avec grand plaisir; **it is no great matter** ce n'est pas une grosse affaire; **to be in great pain** souffrir (beaucoup); **to reach a great age** parvenir à un âge avancé; **to have a great opinion of sb/sth** avoir une haute opinion de qn/qch; **I have a great liking for that country** j'aime beaucoup ce pays

(**c**) *(in quantity)* **a great quantity of** une grande quantité de; **a great number of** un grand nombre de; **a great crowd** une grande *ou* grosse foule, une foule nombreuse; **to a great extent, in great part** en grande partie; **the great majority** la grande majorité

(**d**) *(important → person, event)* grand; **a great man** un grand homme; **Alfred the Great** Alfred le Grand; **a great poet** un grand poète; **a great lady** une grande dame; **a great moment** un grand moment; **a great occasion** une grande occasion; **a great house** une grande demeure

(**e**) *(main)* **the great hall** la grande salle, la salle principale; **France's greatest footballer** le plus grand footballeur français

(**f**) *Fam (term of approval)* génial, super; **she has a great voice** elle a une voix magnifique ☐; **he's a great guy** c'est un type super *ou* génial; **she's great!** *(nice person)* elle est super!; **to have a great time** bien s'amuser ☐; **we had a great holiday** nous avons passé des vacances merveilleuses ☐; **what's that film like? – great!** comment est ce film? – génial!; **it would be great to have lots of money** ce serait super d'avoir beaucoup d'argent; **the great thing is that...** le grand avantage *ou* ce qui est bien, c'est que... ☐; **I feel great!** je me sens super bien!; **you look great tonight!** *(in appearance)* tu es magnifique ce soir!; *Ironic* **he's coming too – oh, great!** il vient aussi – oh, génial *ou* super!

(**g**) *(keen)* **she's a great reader** elle adore lire, elle lit beaucoup; **she's a great one for television** elle adore la télévision; *Ironic* **she's a great one for borrowing things without asking people** elle est spécialiste pour emprunter les choses sans demander l'autorisation

(**h**) *Fam (good at or expert on)* **he's great at languages** il est très doué pour les langues ☐; **she's great on sculpture** elle s'y connaît vraiment en sculpture ☐; **she's great at making the past come alive** elle arrive merveilleusement bien à faire revivre le passé ☐

(**i**) *Zool* **the great apes** les grands singes *mpl*

2 *n (person)* **he's one of the greats of world cinema** c'est l'un des grands noms du cinéma mondial; **it's one of the all-time greats** c'est un des plus grands classiques; **she's one of the all-time greats** c'est une des plus grandes stars; **the great and the good** *(people)* les gens *mpl* influents

3 *adv (as intensifier)* **a great big fish** un énorme

poisson; **an enormous great house** une maison immense; *Fam* **you great fat slob!** espèce de gros lard!

4 **greats** *npl Univ* = examen final d'un diplôme de langues classiques et de philosophie à l'université d'Oxford

►► *Orn* ***great auk*** grand pingouin *m*; ***Great Australian Bight*** Grande Baie *f* Australienne; ***the Great Barrier Reef*** la Grande Barrière; ***the Great Basin*** le Grand Bassin; *Astron* ***the Great Bear*** la Grande Ourse; ***Great Bear Lake*** le Grand Lac de l'Ours; *Orn* ***great black-backed gull*** goéland *m* marin; ***Great Britain*** Grande-Bretagne *f*; **in Great Britain** en Grande-Bretagne; *Orn* ***great bustard*** outarde *f* barbue; ***great circle*** grand cercle *m*; *Orn* ***great cormorant*** grand cormoran *m*; *Orn* ***great crested glebe*** grèbe *m* huppé; ***Great Dane*** danois *m*; ***the Great Depression*** la grande dépression des années 30; ***the Great Divide*** = chaîne de montagnes dans le nord des États-Unis marquant la ligne de partage des eaux entre l'Atlantique et le Pacifique; ***the Great Exhibition*** = grande exposition sur les progrès de la technique et de l'industrie pour laquelle fut construit, en 1851, le Crystal Palace de Hyde Park; *Hist* ***the Great Famine*** la Grande Famine *(en Irlande, de 1845 à 1849)*; ***Great Glen*** Great Glen *m*, Glen *m* More *(grande ligne de faille parcourant l'Écosse du nord-est au sud-ouest)*; *Orn* ***great grey shrike*** pie-grièche *f* grise; *Hist* ***the Great Hunger*** la Grande Famine *(en Irlande, de 1845 à 1849)*; ***the Great Lakes*** les Grands Lacs *mpl*; ***the Great Lake State*** = surnom donné au Michigan; *Hist* ***the Great Leap Forward*** le Grand Bond en avant; *Orn* ***great northern diver*** plongeon *m* imbrin; ***great organ*** grand orgue *m*; *(in church)* grandes orgues *fpl*; ***the Great Plains*** les Grandes Plaines *fpl*; ***Great Power*** grande puissance *f*; ***the Great Powers*** les grandes puissances *fpl*; *Orn* ***great reed warbler*** rousserolle *f* turdoïde; *Geog* ***the Great Rift Valley*** la Rift Valley, la Great Rift Valley; *Am* ***great room*** séjour *m* cathédrale, *Can* salle *f* de séjour à toit cathédral; ***the Great Salt Lake*** le Grand Lac Salé; ***great seal*** Grand Sceau *m*; *Orn* ***great skua*** labbe *m* cataracte, grand labbe *m*; ***the Great Slave Lake*** le Grand Lac des Esclaves; ***the Great Smoky Mountains*** les Smoky Mountains *fpl*; *Orn* ***great snipe*** bécassine *f* double; *Orn* ***great spotted cuckoo*** coucou-geai *m*; *Orn* ***great spotted woodpecker*** (pic *m*) épeiche *f*; *Orn* ***great tit*** mésange *f* charbonnière, charbonnier *m*; ***the Great Wall of China*** la Grande Muraille (de Chine); ***the Great War*** la Grande Guerre, la guerre de 14 *ou* de 14–18; *Am Fam* ***the Great White Way*** Broadway[□]; *Zool* ***great white shark*** grand requin *m* blanc

'Great Expectations' *Dickens* 'Les Grandes Espérances'

'The Great Gatsby' *Fitzgerald, Clayton* 'Gatsby le Magnifique'

'The Great Escape' *Sturges* 'La Grande Évasion'

THE GREAT FAMINE

La famine qui sévit en Irlande en 1845 (époque à laquelle ce pays faisait encore partie de l'Empire britannique), fut provoquée par la maladie de la pomme de terre, aliment de base de la population paysanne. Appelée également "the Great Hunger", cette catastrophe plongea le pays dans la misère: elle fit un million de morts et contraignit plus d'un million de personnes à émigrer aux États-Unis et au Canada.

great-aunt *n* grand-tante *f*

greatcoat ['greɪtkəʊt] *n* pardessus *m*, manteau *m*; *Mil* manteau *m*, capote *f*

greater ['greɪtə(r)] *compar of* **great**

►► *Bot* ***greater knapweed*** centaurée *f* scabieuse; ***Greater London*** le Grand Londres, = zone du sud-est de l'Angleterre, comprenant Londres et son agglomération; **in Greater London** dans le Grand Londres; ***Greater Manchester*** le Grand Manchester, = zone du nord-ouest de l'Angleterre, comprenant Manchester et son agglomération; **in Greater Manchester** dans le Grand Manchester

greater-than sign *n* signe *m* "plus grand que", signe *m* "supérieur à"

greatest ['greɪtɪst] *superl of* **great**

►► ***greatest common denominator*** plus grand dénominateur *m* commun; ***greatest common divisor*** plus grand commun diviseur *m*

great-grandchild *n (boy)* arrière-petit-fils *m*; *(girl)* arrière-petite-fille *f*; **great-grandchildren** arrière-petits-enfants *mpl*

great-granddaughter *n* arrière-petite-fille *f*

great-grandfather *n* arrière-grand-père *m*, *Can* bisaïeul *m*

great-grandmother *n* arrière-grand-mère *f*, *Can* bisaïeule *f*

great-grandparents *npl* arrière-grands-parents *mpl*, *Can* bisaïeuls *mpl*, bisaïeules *fpl*

great-grandson *n* arrière-petit-fils *m*

great-great-granddaughter *n* arrière-arrière-petite-fille *f*

great-great-grandfather *n* arrière-arrière-grand -père *m*

great-great-grandmother *n* arrière-arrière-grand-mère *f*

great-great-grandparents *npl* arrière-arrière-grands-parents *mpl*

great-great-grandson *n* arrière-arrière-petit-fils *m*

great-hearted *adj Literary* au grand cœur, magnanime

greatly ['greɪtlɪ] *adv* très, beaucoup, fortement; **I was greatly impressed by her work** j'ai été très impressionné par son travail, son travail m'a beaucoup impressionné; **greatly improved** beaucoup amélioré; **you'll be greatly missed** vous nous manquerez beaucoup; **greatly irritated** très irrité; **greatly surprised** très *ou* énormément surpris; **greatly though I admired/respected him...** j'avais beau l'admirer/le respecter beaucoup...

great-nephew *n* petit-neveu *m*

greatness ['greɪtnɪs] *n* **(a)** *(size)* grandeur *f*, énormité *f*, immensité *f*; *(intensity)* intensité *f* **(b)** *(eminence)* grandeur *f*, importance *f*; **he never achieved greatness as an artist** il n'est jamais devenu un grand artiste; *Prov* **some achieve greatness, some have greatness thrust upon them** = c'est parfois dans l'adversité que se révèlent les grands hommes

great-niece *n* petite-nièce *f*

great-uncle *n* grand-oncle *m*

grebe [gri:b] *n Orn* grèbe *m*

Grecian ['gri:ʃən] **1** *adj* grec (grecque); **a Grecian profile** un profil grec

2 *n* Grec (Grecque) *m,f*

Greco ['grekəʊ] *pr n* **El Greco** le Greco; **a painting by El Greco** un tableau du Greco

Greco- *Am* = **Graeco-**

Greece [gri:s] *n* Grèce *f*; **in Greece** en Grèce

greed [gri:d] *n* **(a)** *(for material things)* avidité *f*, cupidité *f*; **greed for fame/power** la recherche avide de célébrité/pouvoir; **it's sheer greed** c'est de l'avidité pure et simple **(b)** *(gluttony)* gourmandise *f*

greedily ['gri:dɪlɪ] *adv* **(a)** *(hoard, keep for oneself etc)* avidement, cupidement **(b)** *(eat)* goulûment; *(look, say)* avec gourmandise

greediness ['gri:dɪnɪs] = **greed**

greedy ['gri:dɪ] *adj* **(a)** *(for food)* glouton, gourmand; **don't be so greedy!** ne sois pas si gourmand! **(b)** *(for fame, power, wealth)* avide (**for** de)

greedy-guts *n Fam* glouton(onne)[□] *m,f*, goinfre *mf*

Greek [gri:k] **1** *n* **(a)** *(person)* Grec *m*, Grecque *f*; *Prov* **beware of Greeks bearing gifts** = méfiez-vous des étrangers qui vous veulent du bien

(b) *(language)* grec *m*; **ancient Greek** grec *m* ancien; **modern Greek** grec *m* moderne; *Fam* **it's all Greek to me** tout ça, c'est du chinois *ou* de l'hébreu pour moi

2 *adj* grec (grecque); **the Greek islands** les îles *fpl* grecques

3 *comp (embassy)* de Grèce; *(history)* de la Grèce; *(teacher)* de grec

►► ***Greek cross*** croix *f* grecque; ***Greek gift*** cadeau *m* empoisonné; ***Greek key*** grecque *f*; *Am Univ* ***Greek letter fraternity/sorority*** = association d'étudiants ou d'étudiantes; ***Greek Orthodox*** orthodoxe grec *m*, orthodoxe grecque *f*; ***the Greek Orthodox Church*** l'Église *f* orthodoxe grecque; *Comput* ***Greek text*** texte *m* simulé

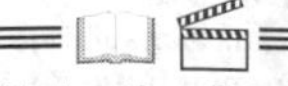

'Zorba the Greek' *Kazantzakis, Cacoyannis* 'Alexis Zorba' (roman), 'Zorba le Grec' (film)

green [gri:n] **1** *adj* **(a)** *(colour)* vert; *(field, valley)* vert, verdoyant; **the wall was painted green** le mur était peint en vert; **to go** *or* **to turn green** *(tree)* devenir vert, verdir; *(traffic light)* passer au vert; *(person)* devenir blême, blêmir; **to be** *or* **to go green with envy** être vert de jalousie; **as green as grass** vert cru; *Fig* **to have** *Br* **green fingers** *or Am* **a green thumb** avoir la main verte

(b) *(unripe fruit)* vert, pas mûr; *(undried timber)* vert; *(meat)* frais (fraîche); *(bacon)* non fumé

(c) *(naive)* naïf; *(inexperienced)* inexpérimenté; **I'm not as green as I might seem** je ne suis pas aussi naïf que j'en ai l'air; **a green reporter** un jeune reporter inexpérimenté

(d) *(ecological)* écologique, vert; **all the parties are trying to appear more green** tous les partis essaient d'adopter une image plus écolo; **to think green** penser à l'environnement; **to go green** virer écolo

(e) *Literary (alive)* vivant, vivace; **to keep sb's memory green** chérir la mémoire de qn

2 *n* **(a)** *(colour)* vert *m*; **green suits you** le vert te va bien; **the girl in green** la fille en vert; **dressed in green** habillé de *ou* en vert

(b) *(grassy patch)* pelouse *f*, gazon *m*; **village green** place *f* du village, terrain *m* communal

(c) *Golf* green *m*, *Can* vert *m*; **on the green** sur le green

(d) *Am Fam (money)* fric *m*, flouze *m*, blé *m*

3 Green *adj Br Ecol & Pol* vert

4 greens *npl* **(a)** *(vegetables)* légumes *mpl* verts; **you should eat more greens** tu devrais manger plus de légumes verts

(b) *Am (foliage)* feuillage *m (dans un bouquet)*

5 Greens *npl Br Pol* **the Greens** les Verts *mpl*, les écologistes *mpl*

►► ***green audit*** = rapport sur l'impact des activités d'une entreprise sur l'environnement; ***green bean*** haricot *m* vert; ***green belt*** ceinture *f* verte; ***the Green Berets*** les Bérets verts; ***green card*** *(for insurance)* carte *f* verte *(prouvant qu'un véhicule est assuré pour un voyage à l'étranger)*; *(work permit)* carte *f* de séjour *(temporaire, aux États-Unis)*; ***green channel*** *(at customs)* file *f* "rien à déclarer"; *Zool* ***green crab*** crabe *m* enragé *ou* vert; *Br* ***the green cross code*** le code de sécurité routière *(pour apprendre aux piétons à traverser la route avec moins de risques d'accident)*; *EU* ***green currency*** monnaie *f* verte; ***green fee*** *(in golf)* green fee *m*, droit *m* de jeu; *Br* ***green goddess*** = camion de pompiers de l'armée; *Bot* ***green hellebore*** herbe *f* à sétons; *Sport* ***green jersey*** maillot *m* vert; *also Fig* ***green light*** feu *m* vert; **to give sb/sth the green light** donner le feu vert à qn/pour qch; **to get the green light from sb** obtenir le feu vert de qn; *Zool* ***green mamba*** mamba *m* vert; ***green man*** *Br (at pedestrian crossing)* bonhomme *m* vert; *Hum (extraterrestrial)* petit homme *m* vert; **wait for the green man before crossing** attends que le bonhomme passe au vert avant de traverser; **little green men** petits hommes *mpl* verts; ***green marketing*** marketing *m* vert *ou* écologique; *Zool* ***green monkey*** vervet *m*, singe *m* vert; ***green monkey disease*** maladie *f* de Marburg; ***the Green Mountain State*** = surnom donné au Vermont; *Am* ***green onion*** ciboule *f*, cive *f*; *Br & Can Pol* ***green paper*** = document formulant des propositions destinées à orienter la politique gouvernementale; ***the Green party*** le parti écologiste, les Verts *mpl*; ***green peas*** petits pois *mpl*; ***green pepper*** poivron *m* vert; ***green peppercorn*** grain *m* de poivre vert; *Orn* ***green plover*** vanneau *m*; ***Green politics*** la politique des Verts; *Br Econ* ***green pound*** livre *f* verte; ***green rate*** taux *m* vert; ***green revolution*** révolution *f* verte; *Theat & TV* ***green room*** foyer *m* des artistes; ***green salad*** salade *f* (verte); *Orn* ***green sandpiper*** chevalier *m* cul-blanc; *Formerly* ***Green Shield stamps*** = timbres donnant droit à des cadeaux, distribués par certains magasins en fonction du montant des achats; *Fin* ***green taxation*** fiscalité *f* écologique; ***green tea*** thé *m* vert; ***green tourism*** tourisme *m* vert; *Zool* ***green turtle*** tortue *f* verte; ***green vegetables*** légumes *mpl* verts; *Br Fam* ***green wellies*** = bottes de caoutchouc vertes (le terme évoque les classes bourgeoises ou aristocratiques habitant à la campagne); *Orn* ***green woodpecker*** pivert *m*, pic-vert *m*

'How Green Was My Valley' *Llewellyn, Ford*
'Qu'elle était verte, ma vallée!'

This green and pleasant land
Il s'agit d'un vers extrait du cantique 'Jerusalem', d'après un poème de William Blake de 1804 (le poème est connu sous le même nom bien que le titre en soit différent). On chante très souvent ce cantique dans les écoles et au cours des manifestations sportives, à tel point qu'il est presque devenu un second hymne national.
On utilise la formule **this green and pleasant land** ("ce pays vert et plaisant") par allusion au cantique et à propos de l'Angleterre; elle véhicule une vision idéalisée et quelque peu désuète du pays.

greenback ['gri:nbæk] *n Am Fam* billet *m* vert
greenbottle ['gri:nbɒtəl] *n Entom* **greenbottle (fly)** mouche *f* verte *ou* dorée, lucilie *f*
greenery ['gri:nərɪ] *n* verdure *f*
green-eyed *adj* aux yeux verts; *(jealous)* jaloux
▸▸ ***the green-eyed monster*** *(jealousy)* la jalousie
greenfield site ['gri:nfi:ld-] *n* = terrain non construit à l'extérieur d'une ville
greenfinch ['gri:nfɪntʃ] *n Orn* verdier *m*
green-fingered [-'fɪŋgəd] *adj Br* qui a la main verte
greenfly ['gri:nflaɪ] *(pl* **inv** *or* **greenflies***) n Entom* puceron *m* (vert); **to have greenfly** *(plant)* avoir des pucerons
greengage ['gri:ngeɪdʒ] *n* reine-claude *f*
greengrocer ['gri:n,grəʊsə(r)] *n Br* marchand *m* de fruits et légumes; **to go to the greengrocer's** aller chez le marchand de fruits et légumes
Greenham Common ['gri:nəm-] *n* = village en Angleterre où ont eu lieu de nombreuses manifestations hostiles à l'armement nucléaire dans les années 1980
greenhorn ['gri:nhɔ:n] *n Fam* blanc-bec *m*
greenhouse ['gri:nhaʊs, *pl* -haʊzɪz] *n* serre *f*
▸▸ ***the greenhouse effect*** l'effet *m* de serre; ***greenhouse gases*** gaz *mpl* à effet de serre; ***greenhouse plants*** plantes *fpl* de serre
Greenie ['gri:nɪ] *n Austr Fam* politicien(enne) *m,f* écolo
greening ['gri:nɪŋ] *n* **the recent greening of the Labour Party** la récente conversion du Parti travailliste à l'écologie; **the greening of Great Britain** la sensibilisation des Britanniques aux problèmes écologiques
greenish ['gri:nɪʃ] *adj* tirant sur le vert
greenkeeper ['gri:n,ki:pə(r)] *n* = personne qui entretient les pelouses des terrains de golf et de jeu de boules
Greenland ['gri:nlənd] *n* Groenland *m*; **in Greenland** au Groenland
Greenlander ['gri:nləndə(r)] *n* Groenlandais(e) *m,f*
Greenlandic [,gri:n'lændɪk] **1** *n (language)* groenlandais *m*
2 *adj* groenlandais; *(history)* du Groenland
green-light *vt (approve)* donner le feu vert à
greenmail ['gri:nmeɪl] *n Am* chantage *m* au dollar *ou* au billet vert, greenmail *m*
greenness ['gri:nnɪs] *n* (**a**) *(colour)* couleur *f* verte, vert *m*; *(of field, valley)* verdure *f*; *(of fruit)* verdeur *f* (**b**) *(of person* → *inexperience)* inexpérience *f*, manque *m* d'expérience; *(*→ *naivety)* naïveté *f* (**c**) *Ecol & Pol* côté *m* écologique
greenroom ['gri:nrʊm] *n TV* salle *f* de détente; *Theat* foyer *m* des artistes
greenshank ['gri:nʃæŋk] *n Orn* chevalier *m*
greenstick fracture ['gri:nstɪk-] *n Med* fracture *f* incomplète
greenstuff ['gri:nstʌf] *n* (**a**) *(UNCOUNT) (vegetables)* légumes *mpl* verts (**b**) *Am Fam (money)* fric *m*
greensward ['gri:nswɔ:d] *n Arch or Literary* pelouse *f*, gazon *m*, tapis *m* de verdure
green-thumbed [-'θʌmd] *adj Am* qui a la main verte
greenway ['gri:nweɪ] *n Am* espace *m* vert
Greenwich ['grenɪdʒ] *n* Greenwich
▸▸ ***Greenwich Mean Time*** heure *f* (du méridien) de Greenwich; ***Greenwich meridian*** méridien *m* de Greenwich; ***Greenwich Village*** Greenwich Village *(quartier bohème de New York)*
greenwood ['gri:nwʊd] *n Arch* forêt *f* verdoyante
greeny ['gri:nɪ] *adj* tirant sur le vert
greet¹ [gri:t] *vt (meet, welcome)* saluer, accueillir; **to greet sb with a wave of the hand** saluer qn de la main; **to greet sb/sth with open arms** accueillir qn/qch les bras ouverts; **the news was greeted with a sigh of relief** les nouvelles furent accueillies avec un soupir de soulagement; **a strange sound greeted our ears** un son étrange est parvenu à nos oreilles; **the sight that greeted her (eyes) defied description** la scène qui s'offrit à ses regards défiait toute description
greet² *vi Scot (cry)* pleurer; *(complain)* se plaindre
greeter ['gri:tə(r)] *n (male)* = employé qui accueille les clients; *(female)* hôtesse *f*
greeting ['gri:tɪŋ] **1** *n* salut *m*, salutation *f*; *(welcome)* accueil *m*
2 greetings *npl (good wishes)* compliments *mpl*, salutations *fpl*; **New Year/Christmas greetings** vœux *mpl* de bonne année/Noël; **birthday greetings** vœux *mpl* d'anniversaire; **to send one's greetings to sb** envoyer son bon souvenir *ou* le bonjour à qn
▸▸ *Br* ***greetings card,*** *Am* ***greeting card*** carte *f* de vœux
gregarious [grɪ'geərɪəs] *adj (animal, bird)* grégaire; *(person)* sociable
gregariously [grɪ'geərɪəslɪ] *adv Zool (live)* en groupe; **she was not gregariously inclined** elle n'avait pas le tempérament grégaire
gregariousness [grɪ'geərɪəsnɪs] *n (of animal, bird)* grégarisme *m*; *(of person)* sociabilité *f*
Gregorian [grɪ'gɔ:rɪən] *adj* grégorien
▸▸ ***the Gregorian calendar*** le calendrier grégorien; ***Gregorian chant*** chant *m* grégorien
Gregory ['gregərɪ] *pr n* **Gregory the Great** Grégoire le Grand
gremlin ['gremlɪn] *n Fam Hum* = diablotin malfaisant que l'on dit responsable de défauts mécaniques ou d'erreurs typographiques
Grenada [grə'neɪdə] *n* Grenade *f (dans les Antilles)*; **in Grenada** à la Grenade
grenade [grə'neɪd] *n Mil* grenade *f*
▸▸ *Mil* ***grenade attack*** attaque *f* à la grenade; ***grenade launcher*** lance-grenade *m*
Grenadian [grə'neɪdɪən] **1** *n* Grenadin(e) *m,f*
2 *adj* grenadin
grenadier [,grenə'dɪə(r)] *n (soldier)* grenadier *m*
▸▸ ***the Grenadier Guards*** = régiment d'infanterie de la Garde Royale britannique
grenadine ['grenədi:n] *n* grenadine *f*
Gretna Green ['gretnə-] *n* Gretna Green

GRETNA GREEN

Le forgeron de ce village écossais fut, jusqu'en 1940, habilité à célébrer les mariages sans formalités administratives. Lorsque leurs parents s'opposaient à leur mariage, des jeunes couples choisissaient d'aller se marier à Gretna Green. Aujourd'hui, des couples choisissent de s'y marier par romantisme.

grew [gru:] *pt of* **grow**
grey, *Am* **gray** [greɪ] **1** *adj* (**a**) *(colour, weather)* gris; **to paint sth grey** peindre qch en gris; **grey skies** ciel *m* gris *ou* couvert; **a cold grey day** un jour de froid et de grisaille
(**b**) *(hair)* blanc; **to be going grey** commencer à avoir des cheveux blancs; **it's enough to make your hair go** *or* **turn grey** il y a de quoi se faire des cheveux blancs
(**c**) *(complexion)* gris, blême; **she looked grey and ill** elle avait un teint gris de malade
(**d**) *(life, situation)* morne; **Tracy leads a very grey existence** Tracy mène une vie très morne
2 *n* (**a**) *(colour)* gris *m*; *Comput* **shades of grey** niveaux *mpl* de gris
(**b**) *(horse)* (cheval *m*) gris *m*
3 *vi (hair)* **his hair is greying** il commence à avoir des cheveux blancs; **Colin is beginning to grey at the temples** Colin commence à avoir les tempes grisonnantes
▸▸ ***grey area*** zone *f* d'incertitude *ou* de flou; **the grey area between right and wrong** la frontière indistincte qui sépare le bien du mal; ***grey cell*** cellule *f* grise; *Fam* **he's a little short on grey cells** il n'a pas inventé la poudre; *Zool* ***grey fox*** urocyon *m*; ***Grey Friar*** franciscain *m*; *Orn* ***grey heron*** héron *m* cendré; ***grey import*** importation *f* grise; *St Exch* ***grey knight*** chevalier *m* gris; ***grey literature*** publications *fpl* non commerciales; *St Exch & Com* ***grey market*** marché *m* gris; *Anat* ***grey matter*** matière *f* grise; *Fam* **to exercise the grey matter** faire marcher sa matière grise; *Ich* ***grey mullet*** muge *m*; ***Grey Panthers*** = groupe de pression composé de personnes âgées; *Orn* ***grey partridge*** perdrix *f* grise; *Orn* ***grey plover*** pluvier *m* argenté *ou* varié; ***grey power*** = pouvoir économique, social etc des personnes âgées; *Zool* ***grey seal*** phoque *m* gris; *Zool* ***grey squirrel*** écureuil *m* gris, petit-gris *m*; *Orn* ***grey wagtail*** bergeronnette *f* des ruisseaux; *Zool* ***grey whale*** baleine *f* grise; *Zool* ***grey wolf*** loup *m* (gris); ***grey zone*** zone *f* grise
greybeard, *Am* **graybeard** ['greɪ,bɪəd] *n Literary* vieil homme *m*
grey-eyed, *Am* **gray-eyed** *adj* aux yeux gris
grey-haired, *Am* **gray-haired** *adj* aux cheveux gris, grisonnant
grey-headed woodpecker *n Orn* pic *m* cendré
Greyhound® ['greɪhaʊnd] *n* **Greyhound**® **buses** = réseau d'autocars couvrant tous les États-Unis
greyhound ['greɪhaʊnd] *n* lévrier *m*, levrette *f*
▸▸ ***greyhound racing*** course *f* de lévriers; ***greyhound racing track, greyhound stadium, greyhound track*** cynodrome *m*
greying, *Am* **graying** ['greɪɪŋ] *adj* grisonnant
greyish, *Am* **grayish** ['greɪɪʃ] *adj* tirant sur le gris; *(beard)* grisonnant
greylag ['greɪlæg] *n Orn* **greylag (goose)** oie *f* cendrée
greyness, *Am* **grayness** ['greɪnɪs] *n (of paint, skin)* teinte *f* grise; *(of sky, weather)* grisaille *f*; **the greyness of London** la grisaille de Londres
greyscale, *Am* **grayscale** ['greɪskeɪl] *n Comput* niveau *m* de gris
▸▸ ***greyscale monitor*** moniteur *m* de niveau de gris
gribble ['grɪbəl] *n Zool* limnoria *m*
grid [grɪd] *n* (**a**) *(grating)* grille *f*, grillage *m*
(**b**) *(electrode)* grille *f*; *Br Elec* réseau *m*
(**c**) *(on chart, map)* grille *f*; *(lines on map)* quadrillage *m*; **the earth's grid** le quadrillage terrestre; **the city was built on a grid pattern** la ville était construite en quadrillé
(**d**) *(in nuclear reactor)* grille *f*
(**e**) *Theat* gril *m*
(**f**) *Culin* gril *m*
(**g**) *(on motor racing track)* grille *f* de départ; **he was second on the grid** il était deuxième sur la grille de départ
(**h**) *Am Aut* zone *f* quadrillée; **do not enter grid unless exit is clear** *(sign)* ne pas s'arrêter dans la zone quadrillée
(**i**) *Am (game)* football *m* américain; *(pitch)* terrain *m* de football
(**j**) *Comput* grille *f*
▸▸ ***grid lines*** droites *fpl* du quadrillage; ***grid marking*** *(on charts, maps)* repères *mpl* de quadrillage; ***grid reference*** coordonnées *fpl* de la grille; ***grid system*** réseau *m* de quadrillage
gridded ['grɪdɪd] *adj* (**a**) *(grating)* grillé, grillagé (**b**) *(chart, map)* quadrillé
griddle ['grɪdəl] **1** *n (iron plate)* plaque *f* en fonte; *(on top of stove)* plaque *f* chauffante
2 *vt* cuire sur une plaque *(à galette)*
▸▸ ***griddle cake*** = sorte de galette épaisse
gridiron ['grɪd,aɪən] *n* (**a**) *Culin* gril *m* (**b**) *Theat*

gril *m* (**c**) *Am (game)* football *m* américain; *(pitch)* terrain *m* de football

gridline ['grɪdlaɪn] *n Comput* quadrillage *m*

gridlock ['grɪdlɒk] *n* (**a**) *(traffic jam)* embouteillage *m* (**b**) *Fig (situation)* impasse *f*; **to be in gridlock with sb** être dans une situation de conflit insoluble avec qn

gridlocked ['grɪdlɒkt] *adj (roads)* bloqué; *Fig (situation, negotiations)* bloqué; **the two parties are gridlocked** chaque partie campe sur ses positions

grief [gri:f] *n (UNCOUNT)* (**a**) *(sorrow)* chagrin *m*, peine *f*, (grande) tristesse *f*; **he was driven almost mad with grief** son chagrin l'a presque rendu fou; **to die of grief** mourir de chagrin

(**b**) *Fam (trouble, inconvenience)* embêtements *mpl*; **to give sb grief** embêter qn; **I'm getting a lot of grief from my parents** mes parents n'arrêtent pas de m'embêter *ou* de me prendre la tête

(**c**) *(as interjection)* **good grief!** mon Dieu!, ciel!

(**d**) *(idiom)* **to come to grief** *(person → in undertaking)* échouer; *(→ have an accident)* avoir un accident; *(project, venture)* échouer, tomber à l'eau

grief-stricken *adj* accablé de chagrin *ou* de douleur, affligé

grievance ['gri:vəns] *n* (**a**) *(cause for complaint)* grief *m*, sujet *m* de plainte; *(complaint)* réclamation *f*, revendication *f*; **my only grievance (against him) is...** le seul grief que j'aie (contre lui), c'est...; **the workers put forward a list of grievances** les travailleurs ont présenté un cahier de revendications

(**b**) *(grudge)* **to nurse a grievance** entretenir *ou* nourrir une rancune *ou* un ressentiment

(**c**) *(injustice)* injustice *f*, tort *m*; **to redress a grievance** redresser un tort *ou* une injustice

(**d**) *(discontent)* mécontentement *m*; **they voiced** *or* **aired their grievances** ils ont exprimé leur mécontentement

▸▸ ***grievance procedure*** = procédure permettant aux salariés de faire part de leurs revendications

grieve [gri:v] **1** *vt* peiner, chagriner; **it grieved me to see him so ill/unhappy** ça m'a fait de la peine de le voir si malade/si malheureux; **I was grieved to discover that...** cela m'a fait beaucoup de peine d'apprendre que...

2 *vi* (**a**) *(feel grief)* avoir de la peine *ou* du chagrin, être peiné; **to grieve at** *or* **over** *or* **about sth** avoir de la peine à cause de qch; **she is still grieving** elle a encore de la peine

(**b**) *(express grief)* pleurer; **to grieve for the dead** pleurer les morts

grieved [gri:vd] *adj* peiné, chagriné (**at** de); **to be deeply grieved (at sth)** être navré (de qch)

grieving ['gri:vɪŋ] **1** *adj (person)* en deuil; **the grieving process** le (processus de) deuil

2 *n* deuil *m*

grievous ['gri:vəs] *adj* (**a**) *Formal (causing pain)* affreux, cruel, atroce; **a grievous loss** une perte cruelle (**b**) *Literary (grave, serious)* grave, sérieux; **grievous injury** des blessures *fpl* graves; **he committed a grievous error** il a commis une grave erreur

▸▸ *Law* ***grievous bodily harm*** coups *mpl* et blessures *fpl*

grievously ['gri:vəslɪ] *adv Formal* gravement, sérieusement; **grievously mistaken** tout à fait dans l'erreur; **grievously wounded** grièvement blessé

grievousness ['gri:vəsnɪs] *n Formal* gravité *f*

griffin ['grɪfɪn] *n Myth* griffon *m*

griffon ['grɪfən] *n* (**a**) *(dog)* griffon *m* (**b**) *Myth* griffon *m* (**c**) *(bird)* **griffon (vulture)** vautour *m* griffon

grift [grɪft] *Am Fam* **1** *n (graft)* corruption □ *f*; *(cunning trickery)* escroquerie □ *f*, filouterie *f*

2 *vt* escroquer □; **to grift sth out of sb** escroquer qch à qn

3 *vi* filouter, vivre de l'arnaque □

grifter ['grɪftə(r)] *n Am Fam* arnaqueur(euse) □ *m,f*, escroc □ *m*

grill [grɪl] **1** *vt* (**a**) *Br (food)* (faire) griller (**b**) *Fam (interrogate)* cuisiner

2 *vi Br (food)* griller

3 *n* (**a**) *Br (device)* gril *m*; *(dish)* grillade *f*; **to cook sth under the grill** faire cuire qch au gril (**b**) *(room in restaurant)* grill-room *m*; *(restaurant)* grill *m* (**c**) *(grating)* grille *f*, grillage *m* (**d**) *Aut* calandre *f*

grille [grɪl] *n* (**a**) *(grating)* grille *f*, grillage *m* (**b**) *Aut* calandre *f*

grilled [grɪld] *adj Br* grillé; **grilled meat** viande *f* grillée, grillade *f*

grilling ['grɪlɪŋ] *n* (**a**) *Br (of food)* cuisson *f* sur le *ou* au gril (**b**) *Fam (interrogation)* **to give sb a grilling** cuisiner qn

grillroom ['grɪlrʊm] *n (in restaurant)* grill-room *m*; *(restaurant)* grill *m*

grilse [grɪls] *n* grilse *m*, madeleineau *m*

grim [grɪm] *adj* (**a**) *(hard, stern)* sévère; *(reality, necessity, truth)* dur; *(smile)* sardonique; *(humour)* macabre; **a grim look** un regard sévère; **to look grim** avoir l'air sévère; **with grim determination** avec une volonté inflexible

(**b**) *(gloomy)* sinistre, lugubre; *(news, report)* sombre; **grim prospects** de sombres perspectives; **a grim story** une histoire sinistre *ou* macabre; **it was a grim reminder of his years in prison** c'était un sinistre souvenir de ses années en prison; **the economic situation is looking pretty grim** la situation économique n'est pas très encourageante

(**c**) *Fam (mediocre)* nul; **his new film is pretty grim** son nouveau film n'est vraiment pas terrible; **I've had a grim day** j'ai passé une très mauvaise journée

(**d**) *Fam (unwell)* patraque; *(depressed)* déprimé □, abattu □; **I felt pretty grim this morning** *(unwell)* je ne me sentais pas bien du tout ce matin; *(depressed)* je n'avais vraiment pas le moral ce matin

grimace ['grɪmɪs] **1** *n* grimace *f*; **to make a grimace** faire une grimace

2 *vi (in disgust, pain)* grimacer, faire la grimace; *(to amuse)* faire des grimaces

grimalkin [grɪ'mɔ:lkɪn] *n Arch* (**a**) *(cat)* mistigri *m* (**b**) *(woman)* mégère *f*, vieille taupe *f*

grime [graɪm] *n (UNCOUNT)* crasse *f*, saleté *f*

griminess ['graɪmɪnɪs] *n* saleté *f*

grimly ['grɪmlɪ] *adv* (**a**) *(threateningly)* d'un air menaçant; *(unhappily)* d'un air mécontent (**b**) *(defend, struggle)* avec acharnement; *(hold on)* inflexiblement, fermement; *(with determination)* d'un air résolu, fermement

grimness ['grɪmnɪs] *n* (**a**) *(sternness)* sévérité *f*, gravité *f* (**b**) *(gloominess)* caractère *m* sinistre *ou* macabre; *(of news, report)* caractère *m* sombre; *(of situation)* difficulté *f*

grimy ['graɪmɪ] *adj* sale, crasseux

grin [grɪn] **1** *n* grand sourire *m*; **a broad grin** un large sourire

2 *vi* sourire; **to grin at sb** faire *ou* adresser un grand sourire à qn; **what are you grinning at?** qu'est-ce que tu as à sourire comme ça?; *Fig* **we'll just have to grin and bear it** il faudra le prendre avec le sourire

grind [graɪnd] *(pt & pp* **ground** [graʊnd]) **1** *n* (**a**) *Fam (monotonous work)* corvée □ *f*; **the daily grind** le train-train quotidien; **what a grind!** quelle corvée!, quelle barbe!

(**b**) *Am Fam (hard worker)* bûcheur(euse) *m,f*, bosseur(euse) *m,f*

(**c**) *Fam (when dancing)* déhanchement *m*

(**d**) *(sound)* grincement *m*, crissement *m*

(**e**) *Ir Fam Sch (private tutor)* prof *mf* particulier(ère); *(class)* cours *m* particulier □

2 *vt* (**a**) *(coffee, corn, pepper)* moudre; *(stones)* concasser; *Am (meat)* hacher; *(into powder)* pulvériser, réduire en poudre; *(crush)* broyer, écraser; **he ground his feet into the sand** il a enfoncé ses pieds dans le sable; **to grind sth under one's heel** écraser qch avec le talon; *Fig* **to grind the faces of the poor** opprimer les pauvres

(**b**) *(rub together)* écraser l'un contre l'autre; **to grind one's teeth** grincer des dents; **to grind sth between one's teeth** broyer qch entre ses dents; *Aut* **to grind the gears** faire grincer les vitesses

(**c**) *(polish → lenses)* polir; *(→ glass)* dépolir; *(→ stones)* polir, égriser; *(sharpen → knife)* aiguiser *ou* affûter (à la meule)

(**d**) *(turn handle)* tourner; **to grind a pepper mill** tourner un moulin à poivre; **to grind a barrel-organ** tourner la manivelle de *ou* jouer de l'orgue de Barbarie

(**e**) *Am Fam (irritate)* taper sur les nerfs à

3 *vi* (**a**) *(crush)* **this barley grinds well** cet orge est facile à moudre; **this pepper mill doesn't grind very well** ce moulin à poivre ne moud pas très bien

(**b**) *(noisily)* grincer; *(wheels)* grincer, crisser; *(gears)* craquer; **to grind to a halt** *or* **to a standstill** *(machine, vehicle)* s'arrêter *ou* s'immobiliser en grinçant; *Fig (company, production)* s'arrêter net; *Fig (economy)* se retrouver paralysé; *Fig* **the whole country ground to a halt** *or* **standstill during the General Strike** le pays a été complètement paralysé pendant la grève générale

(**c**) *Am Fam (work hard)* bûcher *ou* bosser (dur)

(**d**) *Vulg (copulate)* baiser

▸**grind away** *vi Fam* progresser laborieusement □; **I've been grinding away at this essay all weekend** j'ai bûché sur cette dissertation tout le week-end

▸**grind down** **1** *vt sep* (**a**) *(pulverize)* pulvériser, réduire en poudre

(**b**) *(lens)* meuler

(**c**) *Fig (oppress)* opprimer, écraser; **don't let your job grind you down** ne te laisse pas abattre par ton boulot; **the people were ground down by years of poverty** la population était écrasée par des années de misère

2 *vi (substance)* **it grinds down easily** c'est facile à moudre

▸**grind in** *vt sep* **to grind in a valve** roder une soupape

▸**grind on** *vi Fam (speaker)* parler à n'en plus finir □; *(lecture, speech, week)* traîner en longueur □; **the accordion music ground on in the background** en fond sonore on entendait l'accordéon, interminable et monotone

▸**grind out** *vt sep* (**a**) *(cigarette)* écraser

(**b**) *Fig (produce mechanically)* **he was grinding out a tune on the barrel-organ** il jouait un air sur l'orgue de Barbarie; *Fam* **she's just ground out another blockbuster** elle vient de pondre un nouveau best-seller

▸**grind up** *vt sep* pulvériser; **to grind sth up into powder** réduire qch en poudre

grinder ['graɪndə(r)] *n* (**a**) *(tooth)* molaire *f* (**b**) *(person → of minerals)* broyeur(euse) *m,f*; *(→ of knives, blades etc)* rémouleur *m* (**c**) *(machine → for crushing)* moulin *m*, broyeur *m*; *(→ for sharpening)* affûteuse *f*, machine *f* à aiguiser (**d**) *Am Fam (sandwich)* = sorte de gros sandwich

grinding ['graɪndɪŋ] **1** *n (sound)* grincement *m*

2 *adj* (**a**) *(sound)* **a grinding noise** un bruit grinçant; **to come to a grinding halt** *(vehicle)* s'immobiliser en grinçant; *(machine)* & *Fig (production)* stopper; *Fig* **to bring sth to a grinding halt** *(production)* arrêter qch d'un seul coup; *(country, rail network)* paralyser qch

(**b**) *(oppressive → boredom, monotony)* mortel; *(→ worry, insecurity)* accablant; **grinding poverty** misère *f* noire

grindingly ['graɪndɪŋlɪ] *adv* **grindingly boring/monotonous** ennuyeux/monotone à mourir; **grindingly poor** dans une misère noire

grindstone ['graɪndstəʊn] *n* meule *f*

gringo ['grɪŋgəʊ] *(pl* **gringos**) *n Fam* gringo *m*

grinning ['grɪnɪŋ] *adj (face, person)* souriant

grip [grɪp] *(pt & pp* **gripped**, *cont* **gripping**) **1** *n* (**a**) *(strong hold)* prise *f*, étreinte *f*; *(on racket, club)* tenue *f*, grip *m*; *(of tyres on road)* adhérence *f*; **to lose one's grip** lâcher prise; **he tightened his grip on the rope** il a serré la corde plus fort; **to get a grip of sb/sth** empoigner qn/qch; **your grip is wrong** *(on tennis racket, golf club etc)* tu ne tiens pas ta raquette/ton club comme il faut; *Fig* **in the grip of a disease/despair/pessimism** en proie à une maladie/au désespoir/au pessimisme; *Fig* **the country was in the grip of the worst winter for years** le pays connaissait l'hiver le plus rigoureux qu'il ait connu depuis des années

(**b**) *(handclasp)* poigne *f*; **a strong grip** une forte poigne; **she held his hand in a vice-like grip** elle lui serrait la main comme un étau *ou* tenait la main d'une poigne d'acier

(**c**) *Fam (control)* **he's losing his grip** il perd

les pédales; **Grandad is starting to lose his grip** grand-père commence à baisser; **to lose one's grip on reality** perdre le sens des réalités; **he was beginning to lose his grip on the situation** il commençait à perdre le contrôle de la situation; **get a grip (of** *or* **on yourself)!** *(control yourself)* reprends-toi!; *(behave normally, be realistic)* arrête de déconner!

(**d**) *(understanding)* **he has a good grip of the subject** il connaît *ou* domine bien son sujet

(**e**) *(handle → of oar, handlebars)* poignée *f*; *(→ of pistol)* poignée *f*, crosse *f*; *(→ of racket, club)* manche *m*, grip *m*

(**f**) **(hair) grip** pince *f* (à cheveux)

(**g**) *Cin & Theat* machiniste *mf*

(**h**) *Am Old-fashioned (bag)* sac *m* de voyage

(**i**) *Tech (device)* pince *f*

(**j**) *(idioms)* **to come** *or* **get to grips with sb** *(physically)* s'en prendre à qn; **to come** *or* **to get to grips with the enemy** être confronté à l'ennemi, être aux prises avec l'ennemi; **to come** *or* **to get to grips with a problem** s'attaquer à un problème; **I can't get to grips with Shakespeare** je n'arrive pas à comprendre Shakespeare

2 *vt* (**a**) *(grasp → rope, rail)* empoigner, saisir; **he gripped my arm** il m'a saisi le bras

(**b**) *(hold tightly)* serrer, tenir serré; **he gripped my hand** il m'a serré la main très fort; **the region has been gripped by cold weather** la région a été saisie par une vague de froid

(**c**) *(of tyres)* adhérer; **to grip the road** *(car)* coller à la route

(**d**) *(hold interest)* passionner; **the trial gripped the nation** le procès a passionné *ou* captivé le pays; **go on, I'm gripped!** continue, c'est passionnant!

3 *vi (tyres, shoes)* adhérer

gripe [graɪp] **1** *n* (**a**) *Fam (complaint)* **what's your gripe?** de quoi est-ce que tu te plains? ❑; **they've always got some gripe** ils sont toujours en train de râler (**b**) *Med* coliques *fpl*

2 *vi Fam (complain)* ronchonner, rouspéter; **he's been griping at me all day** il a ronchonné contre moi toute la journée

3 gripes *npl Med* coliques *fpl*

▸▸ ***gripe water*** calmant *m (pour coliques)*

griping ['graɪpɪŋ] **1** *n (UNCOUNT) Fam* ronchonnements *mpl*, rouspétance *f*

2 *adj* **griping pains** coliques *fpl*

gripping ['grɪpɪŋ] *adj (fascinating)* captivant, passionnant, palpitant

grippingly ['grɪpɪŋlɪ] *adv (written, told)* de manière captivante *ou* passionnante

grisette [grɪ'zet] *n Bot* coucoumelle *f*, amanite *f* vaginée

grisliness ['grɪzlɪnɪs] *n* aspect *m* sinistre *ou* macabre

grisly ['grɪzlɪ] *adj* épouvantable, macabre, sinistre

grist [grɪst] *n* blé *m* (à moudre); **it's all grist to the mill** c'est toujours ça de pris

gristle ['grɪsəl] *n (UNCOUNT) (cartilage)* cartilage *m*, tendons *mpl*; *(in meat)* nerfs *mpl*

gristly ['grɪslɪ] *adj (meat)* nerveux, tendineux

grit [grɪt] *(pt & pp* **gritted,** *cont* **gritting)** **1** *n* (**a**) *(gravel)* gravillon *m*

(**b**) *(sand)* sable *m*

(**c**) *(for fowl)* gravier *m*

(**d**) *(stone)* grès *m*

(**e**) *(dust)* poussière *f*; **I have a piece of grit in my eye** j'ai un grain de poussière dans l'œil

(**f**) *Fam (courage)* cran *m*; **she's got real grit** elle a vraiment du cran

2 *vt* (**a**) *Br (road, steps)* sabler

(**b**) *(idiom)* **to grit one's teeth** serrer les dents; *Fig* **you'll just have to grit your teeth** il va falloir que tu prennes ton mal en patience

3 grits *npl Am Culin* gruau *m* de maïs

gritstone ['grɪtstəʊn] *n* grès *m*

gritter ['grɪtə(r)] *n* camion *m* de sablage

grittiness ['grɪtɪnɪs] *n* (**a**) *(of soil)* caractère *m* cendreux; *(of coffee)* = fait de contenir du marc; *(of pear)* = fait d'être graveleux; *(of seafood)* caractère *m* sableux; *(of leek)* caractère *m* terreux (**b**) *Fam (courage)* cran *m* (**c**) *(of book, film, play)* caractère *m* réaliste et sans concessions

gritting ['grɪtɪŋ] *n (of roads)* sablage *m*

▸▸ ***gritting lorry*** camion *m* de sablage

gritty ['grɪtɪ] *(compar* **grittier,** *superl* **grittiest)** *adj* (**a**) *(soil)* cendreux; *(texture, pear)* graveleux; *(coffee)* plein de marc; *(seafood)* sableux; *(leek)* terreux; *(road)* couvert de gravier (**b**) *Fam (courageous → person)* qui a du cran; **gritty determination** détermination farouche (**c**) *(incisive → remark, comment)* incisif, mordant; **gritty realism** *(of book, film etc)* réalisme cru (**d**) *(play, film)* réaliste et sans concessions

grizzle ['grɪzəl] *vi Br Fam* (**a**) *(cry fretfully)* pleurnicher ❑, geindre (**b**) *(complain)* ronchonner

grizzled ['grɪzəld] *adj (person, hair, beard)* grisonnant

grizzling ['grɪzlɪŋ] *n Br Fam (whining)* pleurnicherie ❑ *f*, pleurnichement ❑ *m*

grizzly ['grɪzlɪ] *(compar* **grizzlier,** *superl* **grizzliest)** **1** *adj (greyish)* grisâtre; *(hair)* grisonnant

2 *n (bear)* grizzli *m*, grizzly *m*

▸▸ ***grizzly bear*** grizzli *m*, grizzly *m*

groan [grəʊn] **1** *n* (**a**) *(of pain)* gémissement *m*, plainte *f*

(**b**) *(of disapproval, dismay)* grognement *m*; **he gave a groan of annoyance** il a poussé un grognement d'exaspération

(**c**) *(of tree, timber, furniture)* grincement *m*

2 *vi* (**a**) *(in pain)* gémir

(**b**) *(in disapproval, dismay)* grogner; **everybody groaned at his corny jokes** tout le monde levait les yeux au ciel quand il sortait ses plaisanteries éculées

(**c**) *(creak)* grincer

(**d**) *(be weighed down by)* gémir; **the table groaned under the weight of the food** la table ployait sous le poids de la nourriture

(**e**) *(complain)* ronchonner

3 *vt (say)* gémir

groat [grəʊt] *n* = ancienne pièce de monnaie britannique

groats [grəʊts] *npl* gruau *m* (d'avoine)

grobag® ['grəʊbæg] *n* = sac de terreau que l'on perfore et qui sert directement de pépinière

grocer ['grəʊsə(r)] *n* épicier(ère) *m,f*; **at the grocer's (shop)** à l'épicerie, chez l'épicier

grocery ['grəʊsərɪ] *(pl* **groceries)** **1** *n (shop)* épicerie *f*; **to be in the grocery business** être dans l'épicerie

2 groceries *npl (provisions)* épicerie *f (UNCOUNT)*, provisions *fpl*; **what groceries do we need?** qu'est-ce qu'il nous faut comme épicerie *ou* provisions?

▸▸ *Am* ***grocery store*** épicerie *f*

grody ['grəʊdɪ] *adj Am Fam* dégueulasse; **grody to the max** franchement dégueulasse

grog [grɒg] *n* (**a**) *(made with rum)* grog *m* (**b**) *Austr & NZ (any alcoholic drink)* boisson *f* alcoolisée

groggily ['grɒgɪlɪ] *adv Fam* (**a**) *(weakly)* faiblement ❑ (**b**) *(unsteadily → move)* en chancelant ❑; *(→ say)* d'un air hébété ❑

grogginess ['grɒgɪnɪs] *n Fam* (**a**) *(weakness)* faiblesse ❑ *f* (**b**) *(unsteadiness)* = fait de chanceler

groggy ['grɒgɪ] *(compar* **groggier,** *superl* **groggiest)** *adj Fam* (**a**) *(weak)* faible ❑, affaibli ❑; **groggy with flu** affaibli par la grippe (**b**) *(unsteady → from exhaustion)* groggy *(inv)*; *(→ from blows)* groggy *(inv)*, sonné

grogshop ['grɒgʃɒp] *n Austr & NZ Fam* = magasin où l'on vend des boissons alcoolisées

groin [grɔɪn] *n* (**a**) *Anat* aine *f*; **groin injury** blessure *f* à l'aine (**b**) *Br Euph (testicles)* bourses *fpl*; **she kneed him in the groin** elle lui a donné un coup de genou dans l'entrejambe (**c**) *Archit* arête *f* (**d**) *Am (breakwater)* brise-lames *m inv*

groined vault [grɔɪnd-] *n Archit* voûte *f* d'arête

grommet ['grɒmɪt] *n* (**a**) *(metal eyelet)* œillet *m* (**b**) *Tech* virole *f*, rondelle *f* (**c**) *Naut* erse *f*, estrope *f*, bague *f* en corde (**d**) *Med (in ear)* diabolo *m* (**e**) *Fam (novice surfer)* surfeur(euse) *m,f* débutant(e) ❑; *(novice skateboarder)* skateboardeur(euse) *m,f* débutant(e) ❑

Groningen ['grəʊnɪŋən] *n* Groningue

groom [gru:m] **1** *n* (**a**) *(for horses)* palefrenier (ère) *m,f*, valet *m* d'écurie

(**b**) *(at wedding)* marié *m*

(**c**) *(in royal household)* gentilhomme *m*, valet *m*

2 *vt* (**a**) *(clean → horse)* panser; *(→ dog)* toiletter; **cats groom themselves** les chats font leur toilette

(**b**) *(prepare → candidate, successor)* préparer, former; **Heather is being groomed for an executive position** on prépare *ou* forme Heather pour un poste de cadre; **I'm grooming him to take over from me** c'est mon poulain, je prépare la relève

groomed [gru:md] *adj* soigné; **to be well-groomed** *(person)* être soigné (de sa personne); *(horse)* être bien entretenu

grooming ['gru:mɪŋ] *n* (**a**) *(of person)* toilette *f*; *(neat appearance)* présentation *f*; **good grooming is very important** il est important d'avoir une bonne présentation (**b**) *(of horse)* pansage *m*; *(of dog)* toilettage *m* (**c**) *Fig (of candidate)* préparation *f*

groomsman ['gru:mzmən] *(pl* **groomsmen** [-mən]) *n* = personne qui aide le marié tout au long des cérémonies

groove [gru:v] **1** *n* (**a**) *(in wood, metal, for sliding door)* rainure *f*; *(for pulley, in column)* cannelure *f*, gorge *f*; *(in folding knife)* onglet *m*

(**b**) *(in piston)* gorge *f*

(**c**) *(on record)* sillon *m*

(**d**) *(notch)* encoche *f*

(**e**) *(of sword)* gouttière *f*

(**f**) *Fam (rut)* **to get into** *or* **to be stuck in a groove** s'encroûter, être pris dans la routine ❑

(**g**) *Am Fam (idiom)* **to be in the groove** être branché, être dans le coup

2 *vt* (**a**) *Tech (make a groove in)* canneler, rainurer, rainer

(**b**) *Am Fam Old-fashioned (like)* apprécier ❑

3 *vi Fam Old-fashioned (enjoy oneself)* s'éclater; *(dance)* danser ❑; **to groove to the beat** danser en rythme ❑

grooved [gru:vd] *adj* cannelé, rainé

▸▸ ***grooved bearing*** coussinet *m* à gorges *ou* à pattes d'araignée; ***grooved block*** bossage *m* cannelé; *Carp* ***grooved board*** planche *f* bouvetée; ***grooved column*** colonne *f* cannelée *ou* striée; ***grooved panel*** panneau *m* tarabiscoté; ***grooved rail*** rail *m* à gorge *ou* à rigole *ou* à ornière; ***grooved rubber matting*** tapis *m* en caoutchouc à côtes; ***grooved shaft*** arbre *m* cannelé; *Phot* ***grooved trough*** cuve *f* à rainures; ***grooved tyre*** pneu *m* cannelé; ***grooved wheel*** roue *f* à gorge, réa *m*

groovy ['gru:vɪ] *(compar* **groovier,** *superl* **grooviest)** *Fam Old-fashioned or Hum* **1** *adj* (**a**) *(excellent)* sensationnel, sensass, super (**b**) *(trendy)* dans le vent

2 *exclam* chouette!, génial!, super!

grope [grəʊp] **1** *n Fam (sexual)* pelotage *m*; **they were having a grope** ils se pelotaient

2 *vt* (**a**) **to grope one's way in the dark** avancer à tâtons dans l'obscurité; **to grope one's way in/out** entrer/sortir à tâtons

(**b**) *Fam (sexually)* tripoter, peloter

3 *vi (seek → by touch)* tâtonner, aller à l'aveuglette; *(→ for answer)* chercher; **to grope (about** *or* **around) for sth** chercher qch à tâtons *ou* à l'aveuglette; **to grope for a word/words** chercher un mot/ses mots

groper ['grəʊpə(r)] *n Ich* mérou *m*

groping ['grəʊpɪŋ] **1** *adj* tâtonnant

2 *n* (**a**) *(in dark)* tâtonnement *m* (**b**) *Fam (sexual)* pelotage *m*

grosbeak ['grəʊsbi:k] *n Orn* gros-bec *m*, dur-bec *m*

grosgrain ['grəʊgreɪn] *n* gros-grain *m*

gros point [grəʊ'pwɛ̃, grəʊ'pɔɪnt] *n Sewing* gros point *m*

gross [grəʊs] *(pl sense* (**a**) **grosses,** *pl sense* (**b**) **inv)**

1 *n* (**a**) *(whole amount)* **the gross** la quantité totale

(**b**) *(twelve dozen)* grosse *f*, douze douzaines *fpl*

2 *adj* (**a**) *(overall, total)* brut

(**b**) *(flagrant → inefficiency, injustice, carelessness)* flagrant; *(→ error)* grossier, énorme; *(→ ignorance)* crasse

(**c**) *(vulgar, loutish → person)* grossier, fruste; *(→ joke)* cru, grossier

(**d**) *(fat)* obèse, énorme

(**e**) *Fam (disgusting)* dégueulasse

(**f**) *Naut (displacement)* global, total

3 *vt Com (of company)* faire *ou* obtenir une recette brute de; *(of sale)* produire brut; **our firm grossed $800,000 last year** notre société a fait *ou* obtenu une recette brute de 800 000 dollars l'année dernière

►► ***gross amount*** montant *m* brut; ***gross assets*** actif *m* brut; *Ins* ***gross average*** grosse(s) avarie(s) *f(pl)* commune(s); *Fin* ***gross dividend*** dividende *m* brut; ***gross domestic product*** produit *m* intérieur brut; ***gross income*** *(in accounts)* produit *m* brut; *(of individual)* revenu *m* brut; *Fin* ***gross margin*** marge *f* brute; ***gross national income*** revenu *m* national brut; ***gross national product*** produit *m* national brut; *Law* ***gross negligence*** faute *f* lourde; *Acct* ***gross operating profit*** bénéfice *m ou* résultat *m* brut d'exploitation; ***gross profit*** bénéfice *m* brut; *Acct* ***gross profit margin*** marge *f* commerciale brute; *Acct* ***gross receipts*** recettes *fpl* brutes; *Acct* ***gross redemption yield*** rendement *m* actuariel brut; *Naut* ***gross register tonnage*** (tonnage *m* de) jauge *f* brute, tonnage *m* brut; *Fin* ***gross return*** rendement *m* brut; *Naut* ***gross ton*** tonne *f* de jauge; ***gross wage*** salaire *m* brut; *Fin* ***gross yield*** rendement *m* brut

►**gross out** *vt sep Am Fam* dégoûter□, débecter; **it really grossed me out** ça m'a vraiment débecté

►**gross up** *vt sep (net figure)* convertir en chiffres bruts

grossed-up dividend ['grəʊst-] *n Fin* dividende *m* majoré

grossed-up price ['grəʊst-] *n Fin* prix *m* fort, plein tarif *m*

grossly ['grəʊslɪ] *adv* (**a**) *(coarsely)* grossièrement (**b**) *(as intensifier)* outre mesure, excessivement; **grossly unfair** extrêmement injuste; **his skills have been grossly overrated** ses capacités ont été vraiment surestimées

grossness ['grəʊsnɪs] *n* (**a**) *(obesity)* obésité *f* (**b**) *(of abuse, stupidity, error etc)* énormité *f* (**c**) *(vulgarity)* grossièreté *f*

gross-out *n Am Fam* = chose ou situation répugnante; **what a gross-out!** c'est vraiment dégueulasse!

Grosvenor Square ['grəʊvnə(r)-] *n* = grande place à Londres où se trouve notamment l'ambassade des États-Unis

grot [grɒt] *n Br Fam* crasse□ *f*, saleté□ *f*

grotesque [grəʊ'tesk] **1** *adj* grotesque

2 *n Art* grotesque *m*

grotesquely [grəʊ'tesklɪ] *adv* grotesquement, absurdement

grotesqueness [grəʊ'tesknɪs] *n* caractère *m* grotesque

grotto ['grɒtəʊ] *(pl* **grottos** *or* **grottoes***) n* grotte *f*

grotty ['grɒtɪ] *(compar* **grottier,** *superl* **grottiest***) adj Br Fam* (**a**) *(unattractive)* moche; *(unsatisfactory)* nul (**b**) *(unwell)* **to feel grotty** ne pas se sentir bien□, être mal fichu

grouch [graʊtʃ] *Fam* **1** *vi* rouspéter, ronchonner, grogner; **to grouch about sth** rouspéter *ou* ronchonner après qch, grogner contre qch

2 *n* (**a**) *(person)* rouspéteur(euse) *m,f* (**b**) *(complaint)* rouspétance *f*; **to have a grouch about sth** rouspéter contre qch

groucher ['graʊtʃə(r)] *n Fam* rouspéteur(euse) *m,f*

grouchy ['graʊtʃɪ] *(compar* **grouchier,** *superl* **grouchiest***) adj Fam* grincheux□, ronchon, grognon

GROUND [graʊnd]

terre	► 2 (a), (k)
sol	► 2 (a)
terrain	► 2 (b), (c), (e), (h)
stade	► 2 (c)
rez-de-chaussée	► 2 (f)
domaine	► 2 (g)
fond	► 2 (i), (j)
fonder	► 3 (a)
former	► 3 (b)
mettre à la terre	► 3 (e)
moulu	► 5
parc	► 6 (a)
motif	► 6 (b)
raison	► 6 (b)

1 *pt & pp of* **grind**

2 *n* (**a**) *(earth)* terre *f*; *(surface)* sol *m*; **the ground is often frozen in winter** la terre est souvent gelée en hiver; **at ground level** au niveau du sol; **the children sat on the ground** les enfants se sont assis par terre; **to pick sth up off the ground** ramasser qch par terre; **drive the stakes firmly into the ground** enfoncez solidement les pieux dans le sol; **above ground** en surface; **below ground** sous terre; **to burn sth to the ground** réduire qch en cendres; **to fall to the ground** tomber par *ou* à terre; **to go to ground** se terrer; **to run a fox to ground** traquer un renard jusqu'à son terrier; **to run sb to ground** *(criminal, suspect etc)* traquer qn; **I finally ran him to ground in the library** j'ai fini par le trouver à la bibliothèque; *Fig* **to be on firm ground** être sûr de son fait; **to change** *or* **shift one's ground** changer de tactique; **to get off the ground** *(aeroplane)* décoller; *Fig (project)* démarrer; **it suits him down to the ground** ça lui va à merveille, ça lui convient parfaitement; **to run a car into the ground** utiliser une voiture jusqu'à ce qu'elle rende l'âme; **to run a company into the ground** faire couler une entreprise; **to work oneself into the ground** se tuer au travail; *Fig* **he has built his success from the ground up** il a réussi en partant de rien; *Tennis* **to hit a ground stroke** frapper la balle au rebond

(**b**) *(UNCOUNT) (land)* terrain *m*; *(region)* région *f*, coin *m*; **there's a lot of hilly ground in Scotland** il y a beaucoup de coins vallonnés en Écosse

(**c**) *Br (piece of land)* terrain *m*; *(stadium)* stade *m*; **the crowds are leaving the ground** la foule des spectateurs sort du stade

(**d**) *(area used for specific purpose)* **fishing grounds** zones *fpl* réservées à la pêche; **training ground** terrain *m* d'entraînement *ou* d'exercice

(**e**) *Mil* terrain *m*; **to give/to lose ground** céder/perdre du terrain; **to stand** *or* **to hold one's ground** tenir bon; **to gain ground** *(in battle)* gagner du terrain; *(idea, concept)* faire son chemin, progresser; *(news)* se répandre

(**f**) *(storey)* rez-de-chaussée *m inv*

(**g**) *(UNCOUNT) (area of reference)* domaine *m*, champ *m*; **his article covers a lot of ground** dans son article, il aborde beaucoup de domaines; **this is new ground for me** pour moi, c'est un domaine nouveau

(**h**) *(subject)* terrain *m*, sujet *m*; **you're on dangerous ground** vous êtes sur un terrain glissant; **for them, politics is forbidden ground** pour eux, la politique est un sujet tabou *ou* un domaine interdit; **a middle ground** un terrain d'entente, un compromis

(**i**) *(background)* fond *m*; **on a green ground** *(painting)* sur fond vert; **the middle ground** le second plan

(**j**) *(of sea)* fond *m*

(**k**) *Am Elec* terre *f*, masse *f*; **to connect to ground** mettre à la terre *ou* à la masse

(**l**) *Mus* **ground (bass)** basse *f* contrainte

3 *vt* (**a**) *(base)* fonder, baser (**on** *or* **in** sur); **my fears proved well grounded** mes craintes se sont révélées fondées, il s'est avéré que mes craintes étaient fondées

(**b**) *(train)* former; **the students are well grounded in computer sciences** les étudiants ont une bonne formation *ou* de bonnes bases en informatique

(**c**) *(plane, pilot)* **to be grounded** être interdit de vol; **the plane was grounded for mechanical reasons** l'avion a été interdit de vol à cause d'un incident mécanique

(**d**) *(ship)* échouer

(**e**) *Am Elec* mettre à la terre *ou* à la masse

(**f**) *Fam (child)* priver de sortie□

(**g**) *(in rugby)* **to ground the ball** aplatir (le ballon)

4 *vi (ship)* échouer; **the submarine had grounded on a sandbank** le sous-marin s'était échoué *ou* avait échoué sur un banc de sable

5 *adj (wheat, coffee)* moulu; *(pepper)* concassé; *(steel)* meulé; *(meat)* haché

6 grounds *npl* (**a**) *(around house)* parc *m*, domaine *m*; *(around block of flats, hospital)* terrain *m*; *(more extensive)* parc *m*; **the house has extensive grounds** la maison est entourée d'un grand parc; **the grounds are patrolled by dogs** le terrain est gardé par des chiens

(**b**) *(reason)* motif *m*, raison *f*; *(cause)* cause *f*, raison *f*; *(basis)* base *f*, raison *f*; *(pretext)* raison *f*, prétexte *m*; **to have (good) ground** *or* **grounds for doing sth** avoir de bonnes raisons de faire qch; **you have no grounds for believing that he's lying** vous n'avez aucune raison de croire qu'il ment; **there are grounds for suspecting arson** il y a lieu de penser qu'il s'agit d'un incendie criminel; **what grounds have you for saying that?** qu'est-ce qui vous permet d'affirmer cela?; **he was excused on the grounds of poor health** il a été exempté en raison de sa mauvaise santé; **on medical/moral grounds** pour (des) raisons médicales/morales; **on what grounds?** à quel titre?; *Law* **grounds for appeal** voies *fpl* de recours; **grounds for complaint** grief *m*; **grounds for divorce** motif *m* de divorce

(**c**) *(of coffee)* marc *m*

►► *Mil* ***ground attack*** offensive *f* terrestre; *Fishing* ***ground bait*** amorce *f* de fond, appât *m* de fond; *Mus* ***ground bass*** basse *f* contrainte; *Am* ***ground beef*** steak *m* haché; *Entom* ***ground beetle*** carabidé *m*; *Bot* ***ground cherry*** physalis *m*; *Am Elec* ***ground connection*** prise *f* de terre; *Aviat* ***ground control*** contrôle *m* au sol; ***ground cover*** végétation *f* basse; ***ground cover plant*** (plante *f*) couvre-sol *m inv*; ***ground crew*** personnel *m* au sol, personnel *m* non-navigant; ***ground fire*** feu *m* de broussailles; *Br* ***ground floor*** rez-de-chaussée *m inv*; *Fig* **to get in on the ground floor** *(at beginning of project)* participer dès le début; *(buy shares)* acheter des actions dès leur émission; *Mil* ***ground forces*** armée *f* de terre; ***ground frost*** gelée *f* blanche; ***ground glass*** *(glass)* verre *m* dépoli; *(as abrasive)* verre *m* pilé; *Bot* ***ground ivy*** lierre *m* terrestre; ***ground level*** *(ground floor)* rez-de-chaussée *m inv*; *(lowest level in organization)* base *f*; **at ground level** au rez-de-chaussée; *Fishing* ***ground line*** ligne *f* de fond; *Aviat* ***ground operator*** *(who organizes services, transfers etc)* voyagiste *m ou* agence *f* de réceptif, réceptif *m*; ***ground pepper*** poivre *m* moulu; ***ground personnel*** personnel *m* au sol, personnel *m* non navigant; ***ground plan*** *(plan of ground floor)* plan *m* au sol; *(plan of action)* plan *m* préparatoire; ***ground pollution*** pollution *f* du sol; ***ground rage*** = dans un aéroport, comportement agressif de certains passagers envers le personnel au sol, dû à une attente excessive avant l'embarquement; ***ground rent*** redevance *f* foncière; ***ground rice*** farine *f* de riz; ***ground rule*** procédure *f*, règle *f*; **to lay down the ground rules** établir les règles du jeu; *Zool* ***ground squirrel*** spermophile *m*; ***ground staff*** *Sport* personnel *m* responsable de l'entretien d'un terrain de sport; *Br (at airport)* personnel *m* au sol, personnel *m* non-navigant; *Mil* ***ground war*** guerre *f* terrestre; *Geol* ***ground water*** nappe *f* phréatique; *Am Elec* ***ground wire*** fil *m* de terre; *Mil* ***ground zero*** hypocentre *m*, point *m* zéro

groundbait ['graʊndbeɪt] *n Fishing* amorce *f* de fond

ground-breaking *adj* révolutionnaire; **this is ground-breaking technology** c'est une véritable percée technologique

groundcloth ['graʊndklɒθ] *n Am* tapis *m* de sol

grounded ['graʊndɪd] *adj* (**a**) *(based → argument, belief etc)* fondé; **well/ill grounded** *(belief)* bien/mal fondé (**b**) *Am Elec* (mis) à la masse, relié à la terre

groundhog ['graʊndhɒg] *n* marmotte *f* d'Amérique

►► *Am* ***Groundhog Day*** = le 2 février, jour où les marmottes sont censées avoir fini leur hibernation et sortir de leur terrier, annonçant l'arrivée prochaine du printemps si elles restent dehors, et le prolongement de l'hiver si elles ne font qu'une brève apparition

ground-in *adj (dirt)* incrusté

grounding ['graʊndɪŋ] *n* (**a**) *(training)* formation *f*; *(knowledge)* connaissances *fpl*, bases *fpl*; **to have a good grounding in Latin** avoir de bonnes bases en latin (**b**) *(of argument)* assise *f* (**c**) *Am Elec* mise *f* à la terre *ou* à la masse (**d**) *(of ship)* échouage *m*; *(of airplane)* interdiction *f* de vol (**e**) *(of balloon)* atterrissage *m*

groundless ['graʊndlɪs] *adj* sans fondement, sans motif; **her fears proved groundless** ses craintes s'avérèrent sans fondement

groundlessly ['graʊndlɪslɪ] *adv* sans raison

groundlessness ['graʊndlɪsnɪs] *n* absence *f* de fondement *ou* motif

groundling ['graʊndlɪŋ] *n* (**a**) *(fish)* poisson *m* de fond (**b**) *(plant)* plante *f* rampante (**c**) *Theat* ≃ spectateur(trice) *m,f* du parterre; *Fig* personne *f* sans culture, philistin *m*

groundnut ['graʊndnʌt] *n Br* arachide *f*

►► ***groundnut oil*** huile *f* d'arachide

groundsel ['graʊnsəl] *n* séneçon *m*

groundsheet ['graʊndʃi:t] *n* tapis *m* de sol

groundsman ['graʊndzmən] (*pl* **groundsmen** [-mən]) *n Br* gardien *m*

groundspeed ['graʊndspi:d] *n Aviat* vitesse *f* au sol

groundswell ['graʊndswel] *n* lame *f* de fond; *Fig* **there was a groundswell of public opinion in favour of the president** l'opinion publique a basculé massivement en faveur du président; **there has been a groundswell of support for the proposal** il y a eu un raz-de-marée en faveur de la proposition

ground-to-air *adj Mil (missile)* sol-air *(inv)*

ground-to-ground *adj Mil (missile)* sol-sol *(inv)*

groundwork ['graʊndwɜ:k] *n (UNCOUNT)* travail *m* préparatoire, canevas *m*; *Fig* **to do** *or* **lay the groundwork for a project/economic reform** jeter les fondations d'un projet/de réformes économiques; **I've done the groundwork, the rest is up to you** j'ai préparé le terrain, le reste dépend de toi

group [gru:p] **1** *n* (**a**) *(of people, companies)* groupe *m*; *Pol (party)* groupement *m*; *(literary)* groupe *m*, cercle *m*

(**b**) *(of objects)* groupe *m*, ensemble *m*; *(of mountains)* massif *m*

(**c**) *(in business)* groupe *m*; **they're in** *or* **part of the Thistle group** ils font partie du groupe Thistle

(**d**) *(blood type)* groupe *m*; **what (blood) group are you? – group AB** quel est votre groupe sanguin? – le groupe AB

(**e**) *Mus* groupe *m*; **a pop/rock group** un groupe pop/rock

(**f**) *Ling* groupe *m*, syntagme *m*

(**g**) *Mil* groupe *m*

2 *comp (work)* de groupe; *(action, decision)* collectif

3 *vt* (**a**) *(bring together)* grouper, réunir; *(put in groups)* disposer en groupes; **the teacher grouped all the eight-year-olds together** l'institutrice a groupé *ou* regroupé tous les enfants de huit ans

(**b**) *(combine)* combiner

4 *vi* se grouper, se regrouper; **they all grouped round their leader** ils se groupèrent tous autour de leur chef

►► ***group booking*** réservation *f* de groupe; ***group captain*** colonel *m* de l'armée de l'air; **Group Captain Ross** le colonel Ross; *Tel* ***group dialling*** numérotation *f* groupée; ***group discount*** remise *f* pour les groupes; *Psy* ***group dynamics*** dynamique *f* de groupe; *TV & Cin* ***group fader*** potentiomètre *m* général; ***group insurance*** assurance *f* collective; ***group leader*** *(on package tour)* accompagnateur(trice) *m,f*; *(for group of children)* moniteur(trice) *m,f*; ***group manager*** chef *m* de groupe; ***group meeting*** réunion *f* de groupe; ***group photograph*** photographie *f* de groupe; *Med* ***group practice*** cabinet *m* médical; **to be in group practice** faire partie d'un cabinet médical; ***group sex*** sexe *m* de groupe; *TV & Cin* ***group shot*** plan *m* de groupe (de personnages); *Math* ***group theory*** théorie *f* des ensembles; ***group therapy*** thérapie *f* de groupe; *Fin* ***group turnover*** chiffre *m* d'affaires consolidé *ou* du groupe; ***group work*** travail *m* d'équipe *ou* en équipe

groupage ['gru:pɪdʒ] *n* groupage *m*

►► *Com* ***groupage bill*** connaissement *m* de groupage

grouped consignment [gru:pt-] *n Com* envoi *m* groupé

grouper ['gru:pə(r)] *n Ich* mérou *m*

groupie ['gru:pɪ] *n Fam* groupie *f*

grouping ['gru:pɪŋ] *n* (**a**) *(putting together → of packages, consignments)* groupage *m*; *(→ of figures)* groupement *m*; *(→ of people)* rassemblement *m* (**b**) *(group)* groupe *m*

groupware ['gru:pweə(r)] *n Comput* logiciel *m* de groupe, synergiciel *m*

grouse[1] [graʊs] *n (bird → gen)* grouse *f*, tétras *m*; *(→ red grouse)* lagopède *m* d'Écosse

►► ***grouse beating*** rabattage *m*; ***grouse moor*** chasse *f* réservée (à la chasse à la grouse); ***grouse shooting*** chasse *f* à la grouse

grouse[2] *Fam* **1** *n (grumble)* rouspétance *f*; *(complaint)* grief[❑] *m*; **to have a grouse about sth** rouspéter contre qch

2 *vi* rouspéter, râler; **what are you grousing about?** pourquoi rouspètes-tu?

grouser ['graʊsə(r)] *n Fam (complainer)* grognon *m*, rouspéteur(euse) *m,f*

grousing ['graʊsɪŋ] *n (UNCOUNT) Fam* ronchonneries *fpl*; **I've had enough of your grousing!** j'en ai assez de t'entendre ronchonner!

grout [graʊt] **1** *n* coulis *m* au ciment

2 *vt* jointoyer

grouting ['graʊtɪŋ] *n* jointoiement *m*

grove [grəʊv] *n* bosquet *m*; **beech grove** hêtraie *f*; **olive grove** oliveraie *f*; **the groves of Academe** le milieu universitaire, l'Université *f*

grovel ['grɒvəl] (*Br pt & pp* **grovelled**, *cont* **grovelling**, *Am pt & pp* **groveled**, *cont* **groveling**) *vi* (**a**) *(act humbly)* ramper, s'aplatir; **to grovel to sb (for sth)** s'aplatir devant qn (pour obtenir qch); **to grovel before sb** ramper devant qn (**b**) *(crawl on floor)* se vautrer par terre; **stop grovelling around on the floor** arrête de te traîner par terre

groveller, *Am* **groveler** ['grɒvələ(r)] *n* flagorneur(euse) *m,f*

grovelling, *Am* **groveling** ['grɒvəlɪŋ] **1** *adj* rampant, servile; **a grovelling letter** une lettre obséquieuse; **a grovelling apology** de viles excuses *fpl*

2 *n (UNCOUNT)* flagornerie *f*

grovellingly, *Am* **grovelingly** ['grɒvəlɪŋlɪ] *adv* servilement, en rampant

grow [grəʊ] (*pt* **grew** [gru:], *pp* **grown** [grəʊn]) **1** *vi* (**a**) *(plants)* croître, pousser; *(hair)* pousser; *(seeds)* germer; **orange trees grow best in a warm climate** les orangers poussent mieux en climat chaud; **she let her hair grow (long)** elle a laissé pousser ses cheveux, elle s'est laissé pousser les cheveux; **money doesn't grow on trees** l'argent ne pousse pas sur les arbres

(**b**) *(person → in age, height)* grandir; **hasn't he grown!** qu'est-ce qu'il a grandi!; **she has grown two inches** ≃ elle a grandi de 5 cm

(**c**) *(develop)* **to grow in wisdom/understanding** devenir plus sage/compréhensif

(**d**) *(originate)* **this custom grew from** *or* **out of a pagan ceremony** cette coutume est née d'une *ou* a pour origine une cérémonie païenne

(**e**) *(increase)* s'accroître, augmenter; **the crime rate in the big cities is growing** le taux de criminalité augmente dans les grandes villes; **the economy has grown by 5 percent in the last two years** la croissance de l'économie a été de 5 pour cent au cours des deux dernières années; **support for the strike is growing** la grève est de plus en plus soutenue; **our love/friendship grew over the years** notre amour/amitié a grandi au fil des ans; **he has grown in my esteem** il a grandi *ou* est monté dans mon estime; **the town grew in importance** la ville a gagné en importance

(**f**) *(become)* devenir; **to grow angry** se mettre en colère; **to grow bigger** grandir, s'agrandir; **it's beginning to grow dark** il commence à faire nuit; **to grow old** devenir vieux, vieillir

(**g**) *(with infinitive) (come gradually)* **I've grown to respect him** j'ai appris à le respecter; **to grow to like/to dislike sb/sth** finir par aimer/détester qn/qch

2 *vt* (**a**) *(crops, plants)* cultiver

(**b**) *(beard, hair)* laisser pousser; **he's trying to grow a beard** il essaie de se laisser pousser la barbe; **she's growing her hair (long)** elle se laisse pousser les cheveux

(**c**) *Fin (company)* agrandir; **to grow the business** augmenter le chiffre d'affaires

►► ***grow bag*** = sac plastique rempli d'engrais dans lequel on fait pousser une plante

►**grow apart** *vi (people)* s'éloigner; **we gradually grew apart as we got older** nous nous sommes progressivement éloignés l'un de l'autre en vieillissant

►**grow away** *vi* **they began to grow away from each other** ils ont commencé à s'éloigner l'un de l'autre

►**grow back** *vi (hair, nail, plant)* repousser

►**grow in** *vi (hair)* repousser; *(nail)* s'incarner

►**grow into** *vt insep* (**a**) *(become)* devenir (en grandissant); **both her sons grew into fine-looking men** ses deux fils sont devenus de beaux jeunes gens; **the company grew into a huge organization** l'entreprise est devenue une énorme société

(**b**) *(clothes)* **the sweater's too big for him, but he'll grow into it** le pull est trop grand pour lui, mais il pourra le mettre un jour; **he'll soon grow into those shoes** il pourra bientôt mettre ces chaussures, bientôt ces chaussures lui iront

(**c**) *(become used to)* **to grow into a job** s'habituer à *ou* s'adapter à un travail

►**grow on** *vt insep* plaire de plus en plus à; **the song began to grow on him after a while** au bout d'un certain temps, la chanson commença à lui plaire de plus en plus; **it grows on you** on y prend goût; **the idea was beginning to grow on me** l'idée commençait à me séduire

►**grow out** *vi (hairstyle)* **her hair** *or* **hairstyle has grown out** ses cheveux sont maintenant trop longs pour son genre de coiffure; **she let the dye grow out** elle a laissé pousser ses cheveux jusqu'à ce que les traces de teinture aient disparu

►**grow out of** *vt insep* (**a**) *(clothes)* **he's grown out of most of his clothes** la plupart de ses vêtements ne lui vont plus, il ne rentre plus dans la plupart de ses vêtements

(**b**) *(become too old for)* **to grow out of doing sth** passer l'âge de faire qch; **she grew out of her dolls** elle a passé l'âge de jouer à la poupée; **it's just a phase, he'll grow out of it** ce n'est qu'une tocade, ça lui passera; **to grow out of one's friends** ne plus avoir grand-chose en commun avec ses amis; **he never grew out of (the habit of) biting his nails** il n'a jamais perdu cette habitude de se ronger les ongles

►**grow up** *vi* (**a**) *(become adult)* grandir, devenir adulte; **what do you want to be when you grow up?** que veux-tu faire quand tu seras grand?; **we didn't have television when I was growing up** nous n'avions pas la télévision quand j'étais petit; **I hope he won't grow up to be a liar/thief** j'espère qu'il ne sera pas un menteur/voleur plus tard

(**b**) *(behave like adult)* **grow up!** sois un peu adulte!; **I wish you'd grow up!** j'aimerais bien que tu cesses tes gamineries!

(**c**) *(develop)* naître, se développer; **a strong feeling of hatred grew up between them** un puissant sentiment de haine est né entre eux; **a legend grew up around these events** une légende s'est développée autour de ces événements; **the town grew up around the castle** la ville s'est développée autour du château

grower ['grəʊə(r)] *n* (**a**) *(producer)* producteur(trice) *m,f*; *(professional)* cultivateur(trice) *m,f*; *(amateur gardener)* amateur *m* de jardinage; **vegetable grower** maraîcher(ère) *m,f*; **rose grower** *(professional)* rosiériste *mf*; *(amateur)* **he's a keen rose grower** il se passionne pour la culture des roses (**b**) *(plant, tree)* **a slow grower** une plante qui pousse lentement

growing ['grəʊɪŋ] **1** *adj* (**a**) *(plant)* croissant, qui pousse; *(child)* grandissant, en cours de croissance; **a growing child needs a well balanced diet** un enfant en pleine croissance a besoin d'une alimentation bien équilibrée

(**b**) *(increasing → debt)* qui augmente; *(→ amount, number)* grandissant, qui augmente; *(→ friendship, impatience)* grandissant; *(→ opinion, belief)* de plus en plus répandu; **growing numbers of people are out of work** de plus en plus de gens sont *ou* un nombre croissant de gens est au chômage; **a growing population** une population qui s'accroît; **there are growing fears of a nuclear war** on craint de plus en plus une guerre nucléaire

2 *n (of agricultural products)* culture *f*

►► ***growing pains*** *(of children)* douleurs *fpl* de croissance; *(of business, project)* difficultés *fpl* de croissance, problèmes *mpl* de départ; ***growing season*** saison *f* nouvelle

gro–gro

-growing ['grəʊɪŋ] *suff* **wine-growing region** région *f* vinicole; **wheat-/potato-growing region** région *f* qui produit du blé/de la pomme de terre, région *f* à blé/pommes de terre

growing-equity mortgage *n Am Fin* hypothèque *f* à capital croissant

growl [graʊl] **1** *vi (animal)* grogner, gronder; *(person)* grogner, grommeler; *(thunder)* tonner, gronder; *(stomach)* gargouiller; **to growl at sb** grogner contre qn

2 *vt (answer, instructions)* grommeler, grogner

3 *n* grognement *m*, grondement *m*; *(in stomach)* gargouillement *m*

growler ['graʊlə(r)] *n* **(a)** *(animal)* **the dog is a terrible growler** ce chien n'arrête pas de grogner **(b)** *(small iceberg)* petit iceberg *m* **(c)** *Br Vulg (female genitals)* chatte *f*

growling ['graʊlɪŋ] *n (of animal)* grognement *m*, grondement *m*; *(in stomach)* gargouillement *m*

grown [grəʊn] **1** *pp of* **grow**

2 *adj* **(a)** *(person)* adulte; **you don't expect grown adults to behave so stupidly** on ne s'attend pas à ce que des adultes se comportent de manière si stupide; **he's a grown man** il est adulte; **the children are fully grown now** les enfants sont grands maintenant **(b)** *(garden)* **the garden is all grown over** le jardin est tout envahi par les mauvaises herbes

-grown [grəʊn] *suff* **(a)** *(of size, development)* grand, qui a fini sa croissance, qui est arrivé à maturité; **half-grown** à mi-croissance **(b)** *(of plants)* que l'on fait pousser, que l'on cultive; **tub-grown** en bac

grown-up 1 *n* adulte *mf*, grande personne *f*

2 *adj* adulte; **our children are grown-up now** nos enfants sont grands maintenant; **he's very grown-up for his age** il est très mûr pour son âge

growth [grəʊθ] *n* **(a)** *(UNCOUNT) (development → of child, plant)* croissance *f*; *(→ of friendship)* développement *m*, croissance *f*; *(→ of organization)* développement *m*; **lack of certain vitamins can hinder growth** la carence en certaines vitamines peut entraver la croissance; **intellectual/spiritual growth** développement *m* intellectuel/spirituel

(b) *(UNCOUNT) (increase → in numbers, amount)* augmentation *f*, croissance *f*; *(→ of market, industry)* croissance *f*, expansion *f*; *(→ of influence, knowledge)* développement *m*, croissance *f*; **the experts predict a 2 percent growth in tourism/imports** les experts prédisent une croissance du tourisme/des importations de 2 pour cent; **economic growth** développement *m* *ou* croissance *f* économique; **population growth** croissance *f* de la population

(c) *(of beard, hair, weeds)* pousse *f*; **the entrance was covered by a dense growth of weeds** l'entrée était envahie par les mauvaises herbes; **growth of hair** poussée *f* de cheveux; **two days' growth (of beard)** une barbe de deux jours

(d) *Med (tumour)* excroissance *f*, tumeur *f*, grosseur *f*; **benign/malignant growth** tumeur *f* bénigne/maligne

►► ***growth area*** secteur *m* en expansion; **alternative medicine has been a growth area in recent years** les médecines parallèles ont connu un boum ces dernières années; *Mktg* ***growth developer*** stimulateur *m* de croissance; ***growth factor*** facteur *m* de croissance; ***growth hormone*** hormone *f* de croissance; ***growth industry*** industrie *f* en plein essor *ou* de pointe; *Mktg* ***growth inhibitor*** inhibiteur *m* de croissance; ***growth market*** marché *m* porteur; ***growth rate*** taux *m* de croissance; ***growth ring*** anneau *m* de croissance; ***growth sector*** secteur *m* en expansion; *St Exch* ***growth shares, growth stock*** actions *fpl* d'avenir *ou* de croissance; ***growth strategy*** stratégie *f* de croissance

growth-share matrix *n Mktg* matrice *f* croissance-part de marché

groyne, *Am* **groin** [grɔɪn] *n* brise-lames *m inv*

GRSM [ˌdʒiːɑːˌres'em] *n Br (abbr* **Graduate of the Royal Schools of Music**) = diplômé du conservatoire de musique britannique

grub [grʌb] **1** *vi* **(a)** *(animal)* fouir

(b) *(rummage)* fouiller; **I was grubbing about in the dirt looking for my key** j'étais en train de farfouiller par terre dans les saletés pour trouver ma clef; *Fig* **he grubbed around for clues** il fouinait à la recherche d'indices

2 *n* **(a)** *(larva)* larve *f*; *(maggot)* asticot *m*

(b) *Fam (food)* bouffe *f*; **grub** *or* **grub's up!** à la soupe!

►► *Tech* ***grub screw*** vis *f* noyée, vis *f* sans tête; ***Grub Street*** le monde des plumitifs

►**grub out** *vt sep (roots, stumps)* extirper

►**grub up** *vt sep (bone)* déterrer; *(roots, stumps)* extirper; *(plant)* déraciner; *(insects)* déloger

grubbily ['grʌbɪlɪ] *adv* salement, malproprement

grubbiness ['grʌbɪnɪs] *n (UNCOUNT)* saleté *f*

grubby ['grʌbɪ] *adj* sale, crasseux, malpropre; *Fig (immoral)* sordide, sale; *Fig* **I felt grubby when I found out he was married** je me suis méprisée quand j'ai appris qu'il était marié; **I don't want him getting his grubby hands on these documents** je ne veux pas que cet animal mette la main sur ces documents

grub-kick *n (in rugby)* coup *m* qui reste au sol

grubstake ['grʌbsteɪk] *n Am* = provisions données à un prospecteur contre un pourcentage de ses profits

grudge [grʌdʒ] **1** *n* rancune *f*; **to bear** *or* **to hold a grudge against sb** en vouloir à qn, avoir de la rancune contre qn; **he still bears me a grudge** il m'en veut toujours; **she's not one to bear a grudge** elle n'est pas du genre rancunier

2 *vt* **(a)** *(give unwillingly)* **to grudge sb sth** donner qch à contrecœur à qn; **she grudged them every penny she gave them** elle leur donnait chaque penny à contrecœur; **to grudge sb the food they eat** lésiner sur la nourriture de qn

(b) *(resent)* **to grudge sb their pleasures** mal supporter que qn passe du bon temps; **she grudges him his success** elle lui en veut à cause de son succès; **I don't grudge spending money but...** je ne répugne pas à dépenser mais...; **I grudge having to get up so early** je supporte très mal d'avoir à me lever si tôt

grudging ['grʌdʒɪŋ] *adj (compliment, praise)* fait *ou* donné à contrecœur; *(agreement)* réticent

grudgingly ['grʌdʒɪŋlɪ] *adv* à contrecœur, avec réticence

gruel [grʊəl] *n* bouillie *f* d'avoine, *Can* gruau *m* (d'avoine); *(thin)* brouet *m*

gruelling, *Am* **grueling** ['grʊəlɪŋ] *adj (race, interview)* éreintant, épuisant; *(punishment)* sévère; *(experience)* très difficile, très dur; **we had a gruelling time** ça a été très dur

gruellingly, *Am* **gruelingly** ['grʊəlɪŋlɪ] *adv* de manière épuisante

gruesome ['gruːsəm] *adj (sight)* horrible; *(discovery)* macabre; *Hum* **the gruesome twosome** les deux terreurs *fpl*

gruesomely ['gruːsəmlɪ] *adv* horriblement

gruesomeness ['gruːsəmnɪs] *n* caractère *m* horrible; **the gruesomeness of the situation** l'horreur *f* de la situation

gruff [grʌf] *adj* **(a)** *(manner)* brusque **(b)** *(speech, tone)* bourru; **a gruff voice** *(deep)* une grosse voix; *(brusque)* une voix bourrue

gruffly ['grʌflɪ] *adv* **(a)** *(behave)* avec brusquerie **(b)** *(speak)* d'un ton bourru

gruffness ['grʌfnɪs] *n* **(a)** *(of manner)* brusquerie *f* **(b)** *(of speech, voice, tone)* ton *m* bourru

grumble ['grʌmbəl] **1** *vi* **(a)** *(complain)* grogner, grommeler; **he's always grumbling about something** il rouspète constamment contre quelque chose; **why are you grumbling at me?** pourquoi rouspètes-tu contre moi?; **stop grumbling!** arrête de te plaindre!; **how are you? – oh, mustn't grumble!** ça va? – on fait aller!

(b) *(thunder, artillery)* gronder; **my stomach kept grumbling loudly** mon estomac n'arrêtait pas de gargouiller bruyamment

2 *vt* grommeler; **I do all the work here, he grumbled** c'est moi qui fais tout ici, a-t-il grommelé

3 *n* **(a)** *(complaint)* ronchonnement *m*, sujet *m* de plainte; **what's his latest grumble?** pourquoi se plaint-il cette fois?; **his letter contained the usual grumbles** sa lettre contenait les plaintes habituelles; **to obey without a grumble** obéir sans murmurer

(b) *(of thunder, artillery)* grondement *m*; **a distant grumble of thunder** un lointain grondement de tonnerre

grumbler ['grʌmblə(r)] *n* grincheux(euse) *m,f*, mécontent(e) *m,f*

grumbling ['grʌmblɪŋ] **1** *adj* grincheux, grognon; **grumbling noises** des ronchonnements *mpl*; **a grumbling stomach** un estomac qui gargouille

2 *n (UNCOUNT)* plaintes *fpl*, protestations *fpl*

►► *Med* ***grumbling appendix*** appendicite *f* chronique

grummet ['grʌmɪt] = **grommet**

grump [grʌmp] *n Fam* bougon(onne) *m,f*, ronchon(onne) *m,f*; **you are an old grump this morning!** t'es qu'un vieux ronchon, ce matin!; **to have the grumps** être de mauvais poil

grumpily ['grʌmpɪlɪ] *adv Fam (say, speak etc)* en ronchonnant, d'un ton ronchon; *(look at)* d'un air ronchon

grumpiness ['grʌmpɪnɪs] *n Fam* mauvaise humeur ❑ *f*, caractère *m* désagréable ❑

grumpy ['grʌmpɪ] *Fam* **1** *adj* ronchon, bougon; **a grumpy old woman** une vieille grincheuse; **don't be so grumpy!** ne sois pas si ronchon!

2 *n (term of address)* **what's wrong, grumpy?** qu'est-ce qui ne va pas, grincheux?

grundyism ['grʌndɪɪzəm] *n* pudibonderie *f*

grunge [grʌndʒ] *n* **(a)** *Am (dirt)* crasse *f* **(b)** *(fashion, music)* grunge *m*

grungy ['grʌndʒɪ] *adj* **(a)** *Am (dirty)* crasseux **(b)** *(fashion, music)* grunge

grunt [grʌnt] **1** *vi* grogner, pousser un grognement

2 *vt (reply)* grommeler, grogner; **"what?" he grunted** "quoi?", grogna-t-il

3 *n* **(a)** *(sound)* grognement *m*; **to give a grunt** pousser un grognement; **the pig gave a loud grunt** le cochon grogna bruyamment **(b)** *Am Fam Mil slang (soldier)* troufion *m*

grunting ['grʌntɪŋ] *adj* grognant, qui grogne

►► *Zool* ***grunting ox*** yack *m*, yak *m*

Gruyère ['gruːjeə(r)] *n* gruyère *m*

gryphon ['grɪfən] *n* griffon *m*

GS[1] (*written abbr* **General Staff**) EM *m*

GS[2] [ˌdʒiː'es] *n* (*abbr* **general secretary**) secrétaire *mf* général(e)

GSM [ˌdʒiːes'em] *n Tel* (*abbr* **global system for mobile communication**) GSM *m*

gsm [ˌdʒiːes'em] *n Typ* (*abbr* **grams per square metre**) grammage *m* (du papier)

g-spot *n* point *m* G

GST [ˌdʒiːes'tiː] *n Can Fin* (*abbr* **goods and services tax**) TPS *f*

G-string *n* **(a)** *Mus* (corde *f* de) sol *m* **(b)** *(item of clothing)* cache-sexe *m*, string *m*

g-suit *n* combinaison *f* anti-G

GSW [ˌdʒiːes'dʌbəljuː] *n Med* (*abbr* **gunshot wound**) blessure *f* par balle

gt (*written abbr* **great**) grand

GTi [ˌdʒiːtiː'aɪ] *n (car)* GTi *f*

GU (*written abbr* **Guam**) Guam

guacamole [ˌgwɑːkə'məʊlɪ] *n (UNCOUNT)* guacamole *m*

Guadeloupe [ˌgwɑːdə'luːp] *n* Guadeloupe *f*; **in Guadeloupe** à la *ou* en Guadeloupe

guaiac ['gwaɪæk] *n* gaïac *m*

guaiacum ['gwaɪəkəm] *n* bois *m* de gaïac

Guam [gwɑːm] *n* Guam; **in Guam** à Guam

guanine ['gwɑːniːn] *n Biol & Chem* guanine *f*

guano ['gwɑːnəʊ] *n* guano *m*

guarantee [ˌgærən'tiː] **1** *n* **(a)** *Com* garantie *f*; **a guarantee against defective workmanship** une garantie contre les malfaçons; **money-back guarantee** remboursement *m* garanti; **to be under guarantee** être sous garantie; **this cooker has a five-year guarantee** cette cuisinière est garantie cinq ans; *Comput* **on-site guarantee** garantie *f* sur site; **return-to-base guarantee** garantie *f* retour atelier

(b) *Law (pledge)* caution *f*, garantie *f*, gage *m*, cautionnement *m*; **to secure all guarantees** s'assurer toutes les garanties nécessaires; **to give sth as a guarantee** donner qch en caution *ou* en gage

(c) *(person)* garant(e) *m,f*, caution *f*; **to act as guarantee (for sb)** se porter garant (de qn)

(d) *(firm promise)* garantie *f*; **what guarantee do I have that you'll bring it back?** comment puis-je être sûr que vous le rapporterez?; **there's no guarantee it will arrive today** il n'est pas garanti *ou* dit que ça arrivera aujourd'hui

2 *vt* (**a**) *(goods)* garantir; **the watch is guaranteed waterproof** la montre est garantie étanche; **the car is guaranteed against rust for ten years** la voiture est garantie contre la rouille pendant dix ans

(**b**) *(loan, cheque)* garantir, cautionner; **to guarantee sb against loss** garantir des pertes de qn

(**c**) *(assure)* certifier, assurer; **I can't guarantee that everything will go to plan** je ne peux pas vous certifier *ou* garantir que tout se passera comme prévu; **our success is guaranteed** notre succès est garanti

►► ***guarantee agreement*** garantie *f*; ***guarantee certificate*** certificat *m* de garantie; ***guarantee commission*** commission *f* de garantie; ***guarantee company*** société *f* de sécurité; ***guarantee form*** formulaire *m ou* fiche *f* de garantie; ***guarantee fund*** fonds *m* de garantie

guaranteed [ˌgærən'tiːd] *adj (success)* garanti, assuré; **guaranteed by** *(on financial document)* pour aval, bon pour aval

►► *Fin* ***guaranteed bill*** traite *f* avalisée; *Fin* ***guaranteed bond*** obligation *f* garantie; *Fin* ***guaranteed loan*** prêt *m* garanti; *Am* ***guaranteed seat*** réservation *f* ferme

guarantor [ˌgærən'tɔː(r)] *n* garant(e) *m,f*, caution *f*; **to stand guarantor (for sb)** se porter garant (de qn)

guaranty ['gærəntɪ] *n* (**a**) *(security)* caution *f*, garantie *f* (**b**) *(guarantor)* garant(e) *m,f* (**c**) *(written guarantee)* garantie *f*

guard [gɑːd] **1** *n* (**a**) *(person)* gardien *m*, garde *m*; *(group)* garde *f*; **prison guard** gardien *m* de prison; **call out the guard!** appelez la garde!; **guard of honour** garde *f* d'honneur

(**b**) *(watch)* garde *f*; **to be on guard (duty)** être de garde; **to mount (a) guard** monter la garde; **to mount guard on** *or* **over** veiller sur; **the military kept guard over the town** les militaires gardaient la ville; **to stand guard** monter la garde; **the changing of the guard** la relève de la garde; **there was a heavy police guard for the president's visit** il y avait d'importantes forces de police pour la visite du président

(**c**) *(supervision)* garde *f*, surveillance *f*; **to keep a prisoner under guard** garder un prisonnier sous surveillance; **to put a guard on sb/sth** faire surveiller qn/qch; **the prisoners were taken under guard to the courthouse** les prisonniers furent emmenés sous escorte au palais de justice

(**d**) *(attention)* garde *f*; **on guard!** *(in fencing)* en garde!; **to be on one's guard** être sur ses gardes; **we must warn him to be on guard against robbers** nous devons lui dire de faire attention aux voleurs; **how can you put him on (his) guard?** comment le mettre en garde?; **to catch sb off guard** prendre qn au dépourvu; **his offer of help caught her off guard** elle ne s'attendait pas à ce qu'il lui propose son aide; **keep your guard up!** méfiez-vous!; **to drop** *or* **to lower one's guard** relâcher sa surveillance

(**e**) *Br Rail* chef *m* de train

(**f**) *(protective device → on machine)* dispositif *m* de sûreté ou de protection; *(→ personnel)* protection *f*

2 *vt* (**a**) *(watch over → prisoner)* garder

(**b**) *(defend → fort, town, entrance)* garder, défendre; **the house was heavily guarded** la maison était étroitement surveillée

(**c**) *(protect → life, reputation)* protéger; **to guard sb against danger** protéger qn d'un danger; **guard the letter with your life** veille bien sur cette lettre

(**d**) *(in games)* garder

3 Guards *npl Mil (regiment)* Garde *f* royale *(britannique)*; **he's in the Guards** il est dans les régiments de la Garde royale

►► ***guard dog*** chien *m* de garde; *Mil* ***Guards officer*** officier *m* de la Garde royale; *Br* ***guard's van*** fourgon *m* du chef de train

►**guard against** *vt insep* se protéger contre *ou* de, se prémunir contre; **to guard against doing sth** se garder de faire qch; **plastic sheets help guard against frost** des housses en plastique aideront à protéger du gel; **how can we guard against such accidents (happening)?** comment éviter *ou* empêcher (que) de tels accidents (arrivent)?

guarded ['gɑːdɪd] *adj* (**a**) *(cautious)* prudent, circonspect, réservé; **to give a guarded reply** répondre avec réserve (**b**) *(mechanism)* protégé (**c**) *(prisoner)* gardé à vue; *(building)* gardé, surveillé

guardedly ['gɑːdɪdlɪ] *adv (cautiously)* avec réserve, prudemment

guardhouse ['gɑːdhaʊs, *pl* -haʊzɪz] *n Mil (for guards)* corps *m* de garde; *(for prisoners)* salle *f* de garde

guardian ['gɑːdjən] *n* (**a**) *(gen)* gardien(enne) *m,f*; *(of museum)* conservateur(trice) *m,f*; *Press* **the Guardian** = quotidien britannique de qualité, plutôt de gauche (**b**) *Law (of minor)* tuteur(trice) *m,f*

►► ***guardian angel*** ange *m* gardien; ***Guardian Angels*** = vigiles bénévoles dans le métro de Londres, de New York etc; ***Guardian reader*** = lecteur du 'Guardian' (représentatif de la gauche intellectuelle)

guardianship ['gɑːdjənʃɪp] *n* (**a**) *(gen)* garde *f* (**b**) *Law* tutelle *f*; **the child was put under the guardianship of his aunt** l'enfant fut placé sous la tutelle de sa tante

guardrail ['gɑːdreɪl] *n* (**a**) *(on ship)* bastingage *m*, garde-corps *m inv* (**b**) *Rail* contre-rail *m* (**c**) *Am (on road)* barrière *f* de sécurité

guardroom ['gɑːdrʊm] = **guardhouse**

guardsman ['gɑːdzmən] (*pl* **guardsmen** [-mən]) *n Mil Br* soldat *m* de la Garde royale; *Am* soldat *m* de la garde nationale

Guatemala [ˌgwætə'mɑːlə] *n* Guatemala *m*; **in Guatemala** au Guatemala

Guatemalan [ˌgwætə'mɑːlən] **1** *n* Guatémaltèque *mf*

2 *adj* guatémaltèque

3 *comp (embassy, history)* du Guatemala

guava ['gwɑːvə] *n (tree)* goyavier *m*; *(fruit)* goyave *f*

gubbins ['gʌbɪnz] *n Fam* (**a**) *(UNCOUNT) (rubbish)* déchets❑ *mpl*, saletés❑ *fpl* (**b**) *(thing)* truc *m*, machin *m*

gubernatorial [ˌguːbənə'tɔːrɪəl] *adj Am* de *ou* du gouverneur; **gubernatorial elections** élections *fpl* des gouverneurs

guck [gʌk] *n Am Fam* substance *f* poisseuse

gudgeon[1] ['gʌdʒən] *n (socket)* tourillon *m*

►► ***gudgeon pin*** axe *m* de piston

gudgeon[2] *n Ich* goujon *m*

guelder rose [ˌgeldə(r)-] *n (shrub)* boule-de-neige *f*, obier *m*

guenon ['genɒn] *n Zool* cercopithèque *m*

gueridon ['gerɪdən] *n* guéridon *m*

guerilla = **guerrilla**

Guernica ['gɜːnɪkə] *n Art & Geog* Guernica

Guernsey ['gɜːnzɪ] **1** *n* (**a**) *(island)* Guernesey; **in Guernsey** à Guernesey (**b**) *(cow)* vache *f* de Guernesey (**c**) *(sweater)* jersey *m*, tricot *m*

2 guernsey *n Austr* **to get a guernsey** recevoir des remerciements

guerrilla [gə'rɪlə] *n* guérillero *m*

►► ***guerrilla attacks*** attaques *fpl* de guérilleros; ***guerrilla band, guerrilla group*** guérilla *f*, groupe *m* de guérilleros; ***guerrilla leader*** chef *m* de guérilla; ***guerrilla strike*** grève *f* sauvage; ***guerrilla warfare*** guérilla *f* (combat)

guess [ges] **1** *n* (**a**) *(at facts, figures)* estimation *f*; *Br* **to have** *or Am* **to take a guess at sth** (essayer de) deviner qch; **if you don't know, have a guess** si tu ne sais pas, essaie de deviner; **it was just a lucky guess** c'était un coup de chance; **at a (rough) guess, I'd say 200** à vue de nez, je dirais 200; **he made a good/a wild guess** il a deviné juste/à tout hasard; **I'll give you three guesses** devine un peu

(**b**) *(hypothesis)* supposition *f*, conjecture *f*; **it's anybody's guess** Dieu seul le sait, impossible de prévoir; **my guess is that he won't come** à mon avis il ne viendra pas, je pense qu'il ne viendra pas; **your guess is as good as mine** tu en sais autant que moi, je n'en sais pas plus que toi

2 *vt* (**a**) *(attempt to answer)* deviner; **guess what!** devine un peu!; **guess who!** devine qui c'est!; **guess who I saw in town** devine (un peu) qui j'ai vu en ville; **I guessed as much** je m'en doutais, c'est bien ce que je pensais; **you've guessed it!** tu l'as deviné!; **I guessed him to be twenty-five** je lui ai donné vingt-cinq ans

(**b**) *(imagine)* croire, penser, supposer; **I guess you're right** je suppose que vous avez raison; **I guess he isn't coming** je suppose qu'il ne viendra pas; **I guess so** je pense que oui; **I guess not** non, effectivement

3 *vi* deviner; **to guess at sth** deviner qch; **how did you guess?** comment avez-vous deviné?; **(try to) guess!** devine un peu!; **you'll never guess** tu ne devineras jamais; **the police guessed right** la police a deviné *ou* vu juste; **we guessed wrong** nous nous sommes trompés; **we could only guess at their plans** nous ne pouvions qu'essayer de deviner leurs intentions; **I couldn't begin to guess** je n'en ai pas la moindre idée; *Ironic* **I would never have guessed** je n'aurais jamais deviné; **to keep sb guessing** laisser qn dans le doute; **don't keep me guessing!** ne me laissez pas dans le doute!

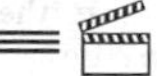

'Guess who's coming to Dinner?' *Kramer*
'Devine qui vient dîner?'

guessable ['gesəbəl] *adj* devinable

guessing ['gesɪŋ] *n* estimation *f*

►► ***guessing game*** devinette *f*

guesstimate ['gestɪmət] *Fam* **1** *n* calcul *m* au pifomètre

2 *vt* calculer au pifomètre

guesswork ['geswɜːk] *n (UNCOUNT)* conjecture *f*, hypothèse *f*; **to do sth by guesswork** faire qch au hasard; **it's pure** *or* **sheer guesswork** c'est une simple hypothèse *ou* supposition

guest [gest] **1** *n* (**a**) *(visitor → at home)* invité(e) *m,f*, hôte *mf*; *(→ at table)* invité(e) *m,f*, convive *mf*; *also Ironic* **be my guest!** fais donc!, je t'en prie!; *TV* **with a guest appearance from...** avec comme invité d'honneur...; *TV* **to make a guest appearance in a programme** être invité dans une émission

(**b**) *(in hotel)* client(e) *m,f*; *(in boarding house)* pensionnaire *mf*

(**c**) *Comput* invité(e) *m,f*

2 *vi TV & Rad* **to guest on sb's show** faire une apparition dans l'émission de qn; *Mus* **another guitarist guested on one of the tracks** un autre guitariste a participé à l'un des morceaux

►► ***guest artist*** invité-vedette (invitée-vedette) *m,f*; ***guest beer*** = bière (pression) proposée pour une durée déterminée par un pub en plus de ses bières habituelles; ***guest book*** *(in house, hotel) & Comput (of Web page)* livre *m* d'or; ***guest of honour*** invité(e) *m,f* d'honneur; ***guest list*** liste *f* des invités; ***guest night*** *(in club)* = soirée d'un club où les non-membres sont invités; ***guest speaker*** conférencier(ère) *m,f* *(invité à parler par une organisation, une association)*; ***guest star*** invité-vedette (invitée-vedette) *m,f*; **guest star Anthony Hopkins** *(in credits)* avec la participation d'Anthony Hopkins; ***guest worker*** travailleur(euse) *m,f* immigré(e)

guesthouse ['gesthaʊs, *pl* -haʊzɪz] *n* pension *f* de famille

guestroom ['gestrʊm] *n* chambre *f* d'amis

guff [gʌf] *Fam* **1** *n* (**a**) [illegible] bêtises❑ *fpl*, idioties❑ *fpl*; **don't talk guff!** ne dis pas d'âneries!; **the film was a load of guff** le film était vraiment débile (**b**) *(intestinal gas)* pet *m*

2 *vi (pass wind)* péter

guffaw [gʌ'fɔː] **1** *n* gros éclat *m* de rire

2 *vi* rire bruyamment, s'esclaffer

3 *vt* **"of course!" he guffawed** "bien sûr!", s'esclaffa-t-il

GUI ['guːiː] *n Comput (abbr* **graphical user interface)** interface *f* utilisateur graphique

Guiana [gaɪ'ɑːnə] *n* Guyane *f*; **the Guianas** les Guyanes *fpl*; **in Guiana** en Guyane; **French Guiana** Guyane *f* française; **Dutch Guiana** Guyane *f* hollandaise

Guianan [gaɪ'ɑːnən], **Guianese** [ˌgaɪə'niːz] **1** *n* Guyanais(e) *m,f*

2 *adj* guyanais

guidance ['gaɪdəns] *n* (**a**) *(advice)* conseils *mpl*; **she needs guidance concerning her education** elle a besoin de conseils pour son éducation

(**b**) *(instruction)* direction *f*, conduite *f*; *(supervision)* direction *f*, supervision *f*; **to do sth under guidance** faire qch avec les conseils *ou* sous la direction de qn; **he's writing the book under the guidance of his former professor** il écrit ce livre sous la direction de son ancien professeur
(**c**) *(information)* information *f*; **diagrams are given for your guidance** les schémas sont donnés à titre d'information *ou* à titre indicatif
(**d**) *Aviat (of missile)* guidage *m*
►► *Am* ***guidance counselor*** conseiller(ère) *m,f* d'orientation; *Aviat* ***guidance system*** système *m* de guidage

guide [gaɪd] **1** *n* (**a**) *(for tourists)* guide *mf*; **Gino was our guide during our tour of Rome** Gino nous servait de guide pendant notre visite de Rome
(**b**) *(influence, direction)* guide *m*, indication *f*; **let your conscience be your guide** laissez-vous guider par votre conscience; **to take sth as a guide** prendre qch comme règle de conduite
(**c**) *(indication)* indication *f*, idée *f*; **as a rough guide** en gros, approximativement; **are these tests a good guide to intelligence?** ces tests fournissent-ils une bonne indication de l'intelligence?; **conversions are given as a guide** les conversions sont données à titre indicatif
(**d**) *(manual)* guide *m*, manuel *m* pratique; **a guide to better French** un guide pour améliorer votre français; **a guide to France** un guide de la France
(**e**) *Br (girl scout)* **(Girl) Guide** éclaireuse *f*; **she's in the Guides** elle est éclaireuse
(**f**) *(machine part)* guide *m*
2 *vt* (**a**) *(show the way)* guider, conduire; **to guide sb in/out** conduire qn jusqu'à l'entrée/la sortie; **to guide sb upstairs** conduire qn en haut; **the children guided us through the old city** les enfants nous ont guidés à travers la vieille ville
(**b**) *(instruct)* diriger, conduire
(**c**) *(advise)* conseiller, guider, orienter; **he guided the country through some difficult times** il a su conduire le pays durant des périodes difficiles; **I'll be guided by you** je me laisserai guider par vous
(**d**) *Aviat* guider
►► ***guide dog*** chien *m* d'aveugle; ***Guide movement*** = mouvement féminin de scoutisme; ***guide rope*** *(for hoist)* corde *f* de guidage; *(for hot-air balloon)* guiderope *m*

guidebook ['gaɪdbʊk] *n* guide *m* touristique *(manuel)*

guided ['gaɪdɪd] *adj* guidé, sous la conduite d'un guide
►► ***guided missile*** missile *m* guidé *ou* téléguidé; ***guided tour*** visite *f* guidée

guideline ['gaɪdlaɪn] *n* (**a**) *(for writing)* ligne *f* (**b**) *(hint, principle)* ligne *f* directrice, directives *fpl*; **as a general** *or* **rough guideline** en règle générale

guidepost ['gaɪdpəʊst] *n* poteau *m* indicateur

guiding ['gaɪdɪŋ] **1** *adj (principle)* directeur; *Fig* **she gave me a guiding hand** elle m'a donné un coup de main
2 *n* guidage *m*, conduite *f*
3 Guiding *n* = activités des éclaireuses
►► *Fig* ***guiding light, guiding star*** guide *m*; **he's been a guiding light in my career** il m'a toujours guidé dans ma carrière

guido ['gwi:dəʊ] *n Am very Fam* Rital(e) *m,f*, Macaroni *m*, = terme injurieux désignant un Italien

guild [gɪld] *n* (**a**) *Hist (professional)* guilde *f*, corporation *f*; **the guild of goldsmiths** la guilde des orfèvres (**b**) *(association)* confrérie *f*, association *f*, club *m*; **women's/church guild** cercle *m* féminin/paroissial

guilder ['gɪldə(r)] *n* florin *m* (hollandais)

Guildford ['gɪlfəd] *n*
►► ***the Guildford Four*** = groupe de quatre Irlandais qui furent condamnés à la réclusion criminelle à perpétuité en Angleterre à la suite d'attentats à la bombe qui eurent lieu à Guildford en 1975, et qui furent libérés en 1989 lorsqu'une enquête révéla qu'ils avaient été accusés à tort par la police

guildhall ['gɪldhɔ:l] *n* palais *m* des corporations; **The Guildhall** = l'hôtel de ville de la City de Londres

guile [gaɪl] *n (UNCOUNT) Formal (trickery)* fourberie *f*, tromperie *f*; *(cunning)* ruse *f*, astuce *f*

guileful ['gaɪlfʊl] *adj Formal (deceitful)* fourbe, trompeur; *(cunning)* rusé, astucieux

guilefully ['gaɪlfʊlɪ] *adv Formal (deceitfully)* trompeusement; *(cunningly)* astucieusement

guileless ['gaɪllɪs] *adj Formal* candide, ingénu

guilelessly ['gaɪllɪslɪ] *adv Formal* candidement, ingénument

guilelessness ['gaɪllɪsnɪs] *n Formal* candeur *f*, ingénuité *f*

guillemot ['gɪlɪmɒt] (*pl* **inv** *or* **guillemots**) *n Orn* guillemot *m*

guilloche [gɪ'ləʊʃ] *Art & Archit* **1** *n* guillochis *m*; **guilloche ornamentation** ornementation *f* de *ou* en guillochis
2 *vt* guillocher

guillotine ['gɪlə,ti:n] **1** *n* (**a**) *(for executions)* guillotine *f*; **to be executed by guillotine** être guillotiné; **to go to the guillotine** aller à la guillotine, être mené à la guillotine
(**b**) *(for paper)* massicot *m*
(**c**) *Pol* = procédure parlementaire consistant à fixer des délais stricts pour l'examen de chaque partie d'un projet de loi
(**d**) *Med (for performing tonsillectomy)* amygdalotome *m*, tonsillotome *m*
2 *vt* (**a**) *(person)* guillotiner
(**b**) *(paper)* massicoter
(**c**) *Pol* **to guillotine a debate** limiter la durée d'un débat

guilt [gɪlt] *n* (**a**) *(responsibility)* culpabilité *f* (**for** pour); **the guilt does not lie with him alone** il n'est pas le seul coupable (**b**) *(feeling)* culpabilité *f*; **a sense of guilt** un sentiment de culpabilité; **guilt drove him to suicide** un sentiment de culpabilité l'a poussé au suicide; **to be on a guilt trip** culpabiliser
►► ***guilt complex*** complexe *m* de culpabilité

guiltily ['gɪltɪlɪ] *adv* d'un air coupable

guiltiness ['gɪltɪnɪs] *n* culpabilité *f*

guiltless ['gɪltlɪs] *adj* innocent

guilty ['gɪltɪ] (*compar* **guiltier**, *superl* **guiltiest**) *adj* (**a**) *Law* coupable; **guilty of murder** coupable de meurtre; **to plead guilty/not guilty** plaider coupable/non coupable; **the judge found her guilty** le juge l'a déclarée coupable
(**b**) *(responsible)* coupable; **they're guilty of a terrible lack of sensitivity** ils font preuve d'un manque terrible de sensibilité; **she's not guilty of staying out late all the time** on ne peut pas dire qu'elle rentre toujours tard le soir; **to have a guilty conscience** avoir mauvaise conscience; **I feel guilty about not telling them** je me sens coupable *ou* je culpabilise de ne pas leur avoir dit; **you're making me feel guilty** tu me culpabilises; **there's no need to feel guilty** il n'y a pas de raison de culpabiliser; **she gave me a guilty look** elle me jeta un regard coupable; **I'm sure she has some guilty secret** je suis sûr qu'elle a un secret inavouable

Guinea ['gɪnɪ] **1** *n* Guinée *f*; **in Guinea** en Guinée
2 *n Am very Fam* Rital(e) *m,f*, = terme injurieux désignant un Italien
3 guinea *n (money)* guinée *f (ancienne monnaie britannique)*
►► *Orn* ***guinea fowl*** pintade *f*; *Orn* ***guinea hen*** pintade *f (femelle)*; ***guinea pig*** cochon *m* d'Inde, cobaye *m*; *(used in experiments)* cobaye *m*; *Fig* **to use sb as a guinea pig** se servir de qn comme d'un cobaye, prendre qn comme cobaye

Guinea-Bissau [-bɪ'saʊ] *n* Guinée-Bissau *f*; **in Guinea-Bissau** en Guinée-Bissau

Guinean ['gɪnɪən] **1** *n* Guinéen(enne) *m,f*
2 *adj* guinéen

guise [gaɪz] *n* (**a**) *(appearance)* apparence *f*, aspect *m*; **the same old policies in a new guise** la même politique sous des dehors différents; **under** *or* **in the guise of** sous l'apparence de (**b**) *Arch (costume)* costume *m*

guiser ['gaɪzə(r)] *n Scot* = personne déguisée allant de porte en porte en chantant des chansons, à Halloween, en échange de friandises ou d'argent

guising ['gaɪzɪŋ] *n Scot* = activité consistant à aller de porte en porte en chantant des chansons, à Halloween, en échange de friandises ou d'argent

guitar [gɪ'tɑ:(r)] *n* guitare *f*; **to play the guitar** jouer de la guitare
►► ***guitar case*** étui *m* de guitare; ***guitar player*** guitariste *mf*; ***guitar solo*** solo *m* de guitare

guitarist [gɪ'tɑ:rɪst] *n* guitariste *mf*

Gujarat [,gʊdʒə'rɑ:t] *n Geog* le Gujerat *ou* Gujarat

Gujarati [,gʊdʒə'rɑ:tɪ] *n* gujarati *m*

gulag ['gu:læg] *n* goulag *m*

'The Gulag Archipelago' *Solzhenitsyn* 'L'Archipel du Goulag'

---

gulch [gʌltʃ] *n Am* ravin *m*

gulden ['gʊldən] *n* florin *m* (hollandais)

gulf [gʌlf] **1** *n* (**a**) *(bay)* golfe *m*
(**b**) *(chasm)* gouffre *m*, abîme *m*; *Fig* **a huge gulf has opened up between the two parties** il y a désormais un énorme fossé entre les deux partis
(**c**) *Geog* **the Gulf** le golfe Persique
2 *comp (country, oil)* du Golfe
►► ***the Gulf of Aden*** le golfe d'Aden; ***the Gulf of Bothnia*** le golfe de Botnie; ***the Gulf of California*** le golfe de Californie; ***the Gulf of Mexico*** le golfe du Mexique; ***the Gulf of Siam*** le golfe de Thaïlande; ***the Gulf States*** *(in US)* les États *mpl* du golfe du Mexique; *(round Persian Gulf)* les États *mpl* du Golfe; ***the Gulf Stream*** le Gulf Stream; ***the Gulf War*** la guerre du Golfe; ***Gulf War syndrome*** syndrome *m* de la guerre du Golfe

gulfweed ['gʌlfwi:d] *n* sargasse *f*

gull[1] [gʌl] *n (bird)* mouette *f*, goéland *m*

gull[2] *Arch* **1** *n (dupe)* dupe *f*
2 *vt* duper

gullet ['gʌlɪt] *n (oesophagus)* œsophage *m*; *(throat)* gosier *m*; *Fam Fig* **it really sticks in my gullet** ça me reste en travers du gosier

gulley (*pl* **gulleys**) = **gully**

gullibility [,gʌlə'bɪlətɪ] *n* crédulité *f*, naïveté *f*

gullible ['gʌləbəl] *adj* crédule, naïf

gullibly ['gʌləblɪ] *adv* naïvement

gull-wing door *n Aut* portière *f* en papillon

gully ['gʌlɪ] (*pl* **gullies**) *n* (**a**) *(valley)* ravin *m* (**b**) *(drain)* caniveau *m*, rigole *f*

gulp [gʌlp] **1** *vt (food)* engloutir; *(drink)* avaler à pleine gorge; *(air)* avaler
2 *vi (with emotion)* avoir un serrement de gorge; **he gulped in surprise** la surprise lui a serré la gorge
3 *n* (**a**) *(act of gulping)* **she swallowed it in one gulp** elle l'a avalé d'un seul coup
(**b**) *(with emotion)* serrement *m* de gorge; **"oh dear", he said with a gulp** "mon Dieu", dit-il, la gorge serrée
(**c**) *(mouthful)* grosse bouchée *f*; *(of drink)* goulée *f*; **he took a gulp of water** il a avalé une goulée d'eau

►**gulp back** *vt sep* avaler; **she gulped back her tears** elle a ravalé *ou* refoulé ses larmes

►**gulp down** *vt sep (food)* engloutir; *(drink)* avaler à pleine gorge; *(air)* avaler

gum [gʌm] (*pt & pp* **gummed**, *cont* **gumming**) **1** *n* (**a**) *Anat* gencive *f*
(**b**) *(chewing gum)* chewing-gum *m*; **to chew gum** mâcher du chewing-gum; **two sticks of gum** deux chewing-gums
(**c**) *(adhesive)* gomme *f*, colle *f*
(**d**) *Bot (substance)* gomme *f*
(**e**) *Br (sweet)* boule *f* de gomme
2 *vt* (**a**) *(cover with gum)* gommer; **gummed paper** papier *m* gommé
(**b**) *(stick)* coller; **gum down the flap** collez le rabat; **gum the two edges together** collez les deux bords ensemble
3 *vi Bot* exsuder de la gomme
4 *exclam Br Fam Old-fashioned* **by gum!** nom d'un chien!, mince alors!
►► ***gum arabic*** gomme *f* arabique; ***gum resin*** gomme-résine *f*; ***gum tree*** gommier *m*; *Fam* **to be up a gum tree** être dans le pétrin

►**gum up** *vt sep Fam (mechanism)* bousiller; *(plan)* ficher en l'air; *Fig* **that's gummed up the works!** ça a tout fichu en l'air!; **the kitten's eyes were all gummed up** les yeux du chaton étaient tout collés

gumball ['gʌmbɔ:l] *n Am* boule *f* de chewing-gum

gumbo ['gʌmbəʊ] (*pl* **gumbos**) *n* (**a**) *(dish)* =

soupe épaisse aux fruits de mer (**b**) *Am (okra)* gombo *m*

gumboil ['gʌmbɔɪl] *n* parulie *f*, abcès *m* gingival

gumboot ['gʌmbu:t] *n Br* botte *f* de caoutchouc

gumdrop ['gʌmdrɒp] *n* boule *f* de gomme

gummed [gʌmd] *adj (label, envelope)* gommé

gummy ['gʌmɪ] (*compar* **gummier,** *superl* **gummiest**) *adj* (**a**) *(sticky)* collant, gluant (**b**) *(gum-like)* gommeux

gumption ['gʌmpʃən] *n (UNCOUNT) Fam* (**a**) *Br (common sense)* jugeote *f*; **he didn't even have the gumption to call the police** il n'a même pas eu la présence d'esprit d'appeler la police (**b**) *(initiative)* initiative❑ *f*; **at least he had the gumption to start up business on his own** au moins il a pris l'initiative de monter sa propre affaire

gumshield ['gʌmʃi:ld] *n* protège-dents *m inv*

gumshoe ['gʌmʃu:] **1** *n* (**a**) *Am Old-fashioned Fam (detective)* privé *m* (**b**) *(rubber overshoe)* caoutchouc *m*

2 *vi* aller à pas feutrés

►► ***gumshoe movie*** film *m* de détectives

gun [gʌn] (*pt & pp* **gunned,** *cont* **gunning**) **1** *n* (**a**) *(weapon)* arme *f* à feu; *(pistol)* pistolet *m*; *(revolver)* revolver *m*; *(rifle)* fusil *m*; *(cannon)* canon *m*; **the burglar had a gun** le cambrioleur était armé; **to draw a gun on sb** braquer une arme sur qn; **a 21-gun salute** une salve de 21 coups de canon; *Mil* **the guns** l'artillerie *f*; *Fam* **to be going great guns** *(enterprise)* marcher à merveille; *Fam* **she's going great guns** ça boume pour elle; *Fam* **the big guns** les huiles *fpl*; *Fam* **to bring out one's big guns** mettre le paquet; **to jump the gun** *Sport (in race)* partir avant le signal; *Fig* brûler les étapes; *Br* **to spike sb's guns** mettre des bâtons dans les roues de qn; **to stick to one's guns** tenir bon; *Am Fam* **to give it the gun** appuyer sur le champignon; *Am Fam* **to be under the gun** être sous pression❑

(**b**) *(hunter)* fusil *m*

(**c**) *Fam (gunman)* gangster❑ *m*; **hired gun** tueur *m* à gages

(**d**) *(dispenser)* pistolet *m*; **paint gun** pistolet *m* à peinture, **(grease) gun** seringue *f ou* injecteur *m* (à graisse)

(**e**) *Electron* canon *m*

2 *vt Aut* **to gun the engine** accélérer

►► ***gun barrel*** *(of rifle)* canon *m* de fusil; *(of revolver)* canon *m* de revolver; ***gun carriage*** affût *m* de canon; *(at military funeral)* prolonge *f* d'artillerie; ***gun cotton*** fulmicoton *m*, coton-poudre *m*; ***gun crew*** servants *mpl* de pièce; ***gun law*** loi *f* réglementant le port d'armes; ***gun licence*** permis *m* de port d'armes; ***gun lobby*** lobby *m* favorable au port d'armes; ***gun mike*** micro *m* canon; ***gun room*** *(in house)* armurerie *f*; *(on warship)* poste *m* des aspirants; ***gun turret*** tourelle *f*

►**gun down** *vt sep* abattre

►**gun for** *vt insep* (**a**) *(look for)* chercher; **the boss is gunning for you** le patron te cherche *ou* est après toi (**b**) *(try hard for)* faire des pieds et des mains pour obtenir

---

'A Gun for sale' (UK), **'This Gun for Hire'** (US) *Greene* 'Tueur à gages'

GUN CONTROL

Aux États-Unis, le puissant lobby des fabricants et marchands d'armes à feu ainsi que la législation laxiste en vigueur dans de nombreux États forment un contraste très net avec la situation en Grande-Bretagne. On estime qu'outre-Atlantique 45 pour cent des ménages possèdent un fusil ou un revolver, et les crimes liés à la possession d'armes à feu y sont fréquents. Cependant, au cours des années 90, plusieurs fusillades meurtrières ont eu lieu dans des lycées américains, qui ont eu pour conséquence la mise en place d'un mouvement qui fait campagne contre les armes à feu. En dépit de cela la "National Rifle Association" continue d'invoquer "the right to bear arms" (le droit de posséder des armes à feu), inscrit dans la Constitution, et défend le tir en tant que sport légitime.

gunboat ['gʌnbəʊt] *n* canonnière *f*

►► ***gunboat diplomacy*** diplomatie *f* imposée par la force, politique *f* de la canonnière

gundeck ['gʌndek] *n Naut* batterie *f*

gundog ['gʌndɒg] *n* chien *m* de chasse

gunfight ['gʌnfaɪt] *n* fusillade *f*

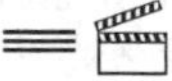

'Gunfight at the O.K. Corral' *Sturges* 'Règlement de comptes à O.K. Corral'

---

gunfighter ['gʌnfaɪtə(r)] *n (in Western film, novel)* bandit *m* armé

gunfire ['gʌnfaɪə(r)] *n (UNCOUNT)* coups *mpl* de feu, fusillade *f*; *(of cannon)* tir *m* d'artillerie

gunge [gʌndʒ] *n (UNCOUNT) Fam* substance *f* visqueuse❑; **what's this gunge on the table?** c'est quoi ce truc visqueux sur la table?

gung-ho [ˌgʌŋ'həʊ] *adj (enthusiastic)* tout feu tout flamme *(inv)*; *(ready to fight)* va-t-en-guerre *(inv)*

gungy ['gʌndʒɪ] *adj Fam* poisseux

gunk [gʌŋk] = **gunge**

gunmaker ['gʌnmeɪkə(r)] *n* armurier *m*

gunman ['gʌnmən] (*pl* **gunmen** [-mən]) *n* gangster *m* (armé); *(terrorist)* terroriste *m* (armé)

gunmetal ['gʌnˌmetəl] *n* (**a**) *(metal)* bronze *m* à canon (**b**) *(colour)* gris *m* foncé métallisé

►► ***gunmetal grey*** **1** *n* gris *m* foncé métallisé **2** *adj* gris foncé métallisé *(inv)*

gunnel = **gunwale**

gunner ['gʌnə(r)] **1** *n* artilleur *m*, canonnier *m*

2 Gunners *npl* **the Gunners** = surnom donné à l'équipe de football Arsenal

gunnery ['gʌnərɪ] *n (UNCOUNT)* artillerie *f*

►► ***gunnery officer*** officier *m* d'artillerie; ***gunnery sergeant*** sergent *m* d'artillerie

gunny ['gʌnɪ] *n* toile *f* de jute (grossière)

gunnysack ['gʌnɪsæk] *n* sac *m* de jute

►► ***gunnysack race*** course *f* en sac

gunplay ['gʌnpleɪ] *n Am* échange *m* de coups de feu

gunpoint ['gʌnpɔɪnt] *n* **to have** *or* **to hold sb at gunpoint** menacer qn d'une arme à feu; **a confession obtained at gunpoint** une confession obtenue sous la menace d'un revolver

gunport ['gʌnpɔ:t] *n Naut* sabord *m* de batterie

gunpowder ['gʌnˌpaʊdə(r)] *n* poudre *f* à canon

►► *Br Hist* ***the Gunpowder Plot*** la conspiration des poudres; ***gunpowder tea*** thé *m* gunpowder *(thé vert de Chine roulé en boulettes)*

THE GUNPOWDER PLOT

Les catholiques, menés par Guy Fawkes, organisèrent ce complot pour faire sauter le Parlement britannique et tuer le roi Jacques Ier et sa famille, le 5 novembre 1605, en réaction au refus royal d'instaurer la liberté de culte. Le complot fut déjoué. On commémore cet événement, appelé **Guy Fawkes' Night** (voir encadré), par des feux d'artifice et des feux de joie.

gunrunner ['gʌnˌrʌnə(r)] *n* trafiquant(e) *m,f* d'armes

gunrunning ['gʌnˌrʌnɪŋ] *n (UNCOUNT)* trafic *m* d'armes

gunsel ['gʌnsəl] *n Am Fam* (**a**) *(criminal)* criminel(elle) *m,f* armé(e)❑ (**b**) *(boy)* = jeune homme qui a des rapports sexuels avec un homme plus âgé

gunship ['gʌnʃɪp] *n (helicopter)* hélicoptère *m* armé

gunshot ['gʌnʃɒt] *n* (**a**) *(shot)* coup *m* de feu; **a gunshot wound** une blessure par balle (**b**) *(range)* **to be out of/within gunshot** être hors de portée de/à portée de fusil

gunshy ['gʌnʃaɪ] *adj* **to be gunshy** avoir peur des coups de feu

gunslinger ['gʌnˌslɪŋə(r)] *n Fam* bandit *m* armé❑

gunsmith ['gʌnsmɪθ] *n* armurier *m*; **gunsmith's (shop)** armurerie *f*

gunstock ['gʌnstɒk] *n* fût *m* (de fusil)

gunwale ['gʌnəl] *n Naut* plat-bord *m*; *Fig* **full to the gunwales** plein à ras bord

guppy ['gʌpɪ] (*pl* **guppies**) *n* (**a**) *Ich* guppy *m* (**b**) *Fam (gay yuppie)* homo *m* BCBG

gurgitation [ˌgɜ:dʒɪ'teɪʃən] *n Literary (of water, waves)* bouillonnement *m*

gurgle ['gɜ:gəl] **1** *n (of liquid)* glouglou *m*, gargouillis *m*; *(of stream)* murmure *m*, gazouillement *m*; *(of pleasure, delight)* gloussement *m*, roucoulement *m*; *(of baby)* gazouillis *m*

2 *vt* **she gurgled her delight** elle roucoula de plaisir

3 *vi (liquid)* glouglouter, gargouiller; *(stream)* murmurer; *(person → with pleasure, delight)* glousser, roucouler; *(baby)* gazouiller

gurgling ['gɜ:gəlɪŋ] **1** *n (of liquid)* glouglou *m*, gargouillis *m*; *(of stream)* murmure *m*, gazouillement *m*; *(of baby)* gazouillis *m*

2 *adj (liquid)* glougloutant, qui fait glouglou; *(stream)* murmurant; **a gurgling laugh** un rire perlé

Gurkha ['gɜ:kə] *n* Gurkha *m*; *Br Mil* **Gurkha regiment** régiment *m* de Gurkha

gurnard ['gɜ:nəd], **gurnet** ['gɜ:nɪt] *n Ich* grondin *m*

gurrier ['gɜ:rɪə(r)] *n Ir Fam* voyou❑ *m*, loubard *m*

guru ['gʊru:] *n Rel & Fig* gourou *m*

gush [gʌʃ] **1** *n* (**a**) *(of liquid, gas)* jet *m*, flot *m*; *(of spring, fountain)* jaillissement *m*; *Fig* **a gush of words** un flot de paroles

(**b**) *(of emotion)* vague *f*, effusion *f*; **a sudden gush of enthusiasm** une soudaine vague d'enthousiasme

2 *vt* (**a**) *(emit)* **to gush water/oil** lancer des jets d'eau/un jet de pétrole

(**b**) *Pej (say effusively)* **"how wonderful to see you!", she gushed** "qu'est-ce que ça me fait plaisir de te voir!", s'exclama-t-elle

3 *vi* (**a**) *(flow)* jaillir; **blood was gushing from his arm** le sang jaillissait de son bras; **water gushed forth** *or* **out** l'eau jaillissait

(**b**) *Pej (talk effusively)* parler avec animation; **everyone was gushing over the baby** tout le monde se répandait en compliments sur le bébé; **"darling, you were wonderful", he gushed** "chérie, tu as été formidable", lança-t-il avec exubérance

gusher ['gʌʃə(r)] *n* (**a**) *(oil well)* puits *m* jaillissant *ou* éruptif (**b**) *Fam Pej (person)* personne *f* trop exubérante❑

gushing ['gʌʃɪŋ] *adj* (**a**) *(liquid)* jaillissant, bouillonnant; **the car was swept away by a gushing torrent of water** la voiture a été emportée par un véritable torrent d'eau (**b**) *Pej (person)* trop exubérant; **gushing compliments/praise** compliments *mpl*/éloges *mpl* sans fin

gushingly ['gʌʃɪŋlɪ] *adv Pej* avec trop d'exubérance

gushy ['gʌʃɪ] (*compar* **gushier,** *superl* **gushiest**) *adj Fam Pej (person)* trop exubérant❑

gusset ['gʌsɪt] *n* (**a**) *Sewing* soufflet *m* (**b**) *Constr* gousset *m*

►**gussy up** ['gʌsɪ-] *vt sep Am* **to gussy sth up** égayer qch

gust [gʌst] **1** *n* **a gust (of wind)** un coup de vent, une rafale; **a gust of hot air** une bouffée d'air chaud; **a gust of rain** une ondée, une giboulée; *Fig* **a gust of anger** un accès de colère

2 *vi (wind)* souffler en bourrasques; *(rain)* faire des bourrasques; **winds gusting up to 50 mph were recorded** ≃ on a enregistré des pointes de vent à 80 km/h

gustatory ['gʌstətrɪ] *adj* gustatif

Gustavus Adolphus [gʊs'tɑ:vəsə'dɒlfəs] *pr n* Gustave Adolphe

gusto ['gʌstəʊ] *n* délectation *f*, enthousiasme *m*; **to do sth with (great) gusto** faire qch avec (beaucoup d')enthousiasme

gusty ['gʌstɪ] (*compar* **gustier,** *superl* **gustiest**) *adj (weather)* venteux; **it's a bit gusty out** il y a des rafales (de vent) *ou* des bourrasques dehors; **a gusty wind** un vent qui souffle en rafales, des rafales *fpl* de vent; **a gusty day** un jour de grand vent

gut [gʌt] **1** *n* (**a**) *Anat* intestin *m*

(**b**) *Fam (stomach)* bide *m*; **I've got a pain in the gut** j'ai mal au bide; **pull in your gut** rentre ton bide

(**c**) *(UNCOUNT) (thread → for violins)* corde *f* de boyau; *(→ for rackets)* boyau *m*

(**d**) *(in sea port)* goulet *m*, passage *m* étroit

2 *vt* (**a**) *(fish, poultry etc)* étriper, vider

(**b**) *(building)* ne laisser que les quatre murs de; **the house had been gutted by the fire** la maison avait été ravagée par l'incendie; **she gutted the house and completely redecorated**

it elle a cassé tout l'intérieur de la maison et a tout refait
(**c**) *(book)* résumer, extraire l'essentiel de
3 guts *npl* (**a**) *(insides)* entrailles *fpl*
(**b**) *Fam (courage)* cran *m*, courage❑ *m*; **to have guts** avoir du cran *ou* du cœur au ventre; **he has no guts** il n'a rien dans le ventre; **I didn't have the guts to tell them** je n'ai pas eu le courage de le leur dire
(**c**) *Fam (of machine)* intérieur❑ *m*
(**d**) *Fam (idioms)* **to work** *or* **to sweat one's guts out** se casser les reins, se tuer au travail; **to hate sb's guts** ne pas pouvoir blairer qn; **I'll have your guts for garters** je vais faire de toi de la chair à pâté
►► *Am Univ* ***gut course*** matière *f* facile; ***gut feeling*** pressentiment *m*; ***gut reaction*** réaction *f* instinctive *ou* viscérale
gut-churning *adj Fam* déchirant
gutless ['gʌtlɪs] *adj Fam (cowardly)* trouillard, dégonflé
gutrot ['gʌtrɒt] *n Br Fam* (**a**) *(drink)* tord-boyaux *m inv* (**b**) *(stomach upset)* mal *m* de bide
gutsy ['gʌtsɪ] *(compar* **gutsier**, *superl* **gutsiest**) *adj Fam* (**a**) *(brave → person)* qui a du cran; **she's one gutsy woman** c'est vraiment une femme qui a du cran (**b**) *(powerful → film, language, novel)* qui a du punch, musclé; *(→ performance)* plein de pêche; **she's a gutsy singer** elle chante avec ses tripes (**c**) *(greedy)* goinfre
gutta-percha [ˌgʌtə'pɜːtʃə] *n* gutta-percha *f*
gutted ['gʌtɪd] *adj Br Fam (disappointed)* dégoûté, hyper déçu
gutter ['gʌtə(r)] **1** *n* (**a**) *(on roof)* gouttière *f*; *(in street)* caniveau *m*, ruisseau *m*; *Fig* **to end up in the gutter** tomber *ou* rouler dans le ruisseau; **to rescue sb from** *or* **to drag sb out of the gutter** tirer qn du ruisseau; **to speak the language of the gutter** parler le langage des rues
(**b**) *(ditch)* rigole *f*, sillon *m (creusé par la pluie)*
(**c**) *Typ (back margin)* (blanc *m* de) petit fond *m*; *(fore-edge)* (blanc *m* de) grand fond *m*; *(space between columns)* gouttière *f*
(**d**) *(in ten-pin bowling)* rigole *f*
2 *vi (candle flame)* vaciller, trembler
►► ***gutter pipe*** tuyau *m* de descente; *Pej* ***gutter press*** presse *f* de bas étage, presse *f* à scandale
guttered ['gʌtəd] *adj Br Fam (drunk)* bourré, pété
guttering ['gʌtərɪŋ] *n (UNCOUNT) (of roof)* gouttières *fpl*
guttersnipe ['gʌtəsnaɪp] *n Pej* gosse *mf* des rues
guttural ['gʌtərəl] **1** *adj* guttural
2 *n Ling* gutturale *f*
gutturality [ˌgʌtə'rælɪtɪ] *n* ton *m* guttural; *(of a language)* accent *m* guttural
gutturally ['gʌtərəlɪ] *adv* gutturalement, d'un ton guttural
gutturalness ['gʌtərəlnɪs] *n* ton *m* guttural; *(of a language)* accent *m* guttural
gut-wrenching *adj Fam* déchirant
guv [gʌv], **guvnor** ['gʌvnə(r)] *n Br Fam* **the guv** *(boss)* le chef, le boss; *Old fashioned (father)* le pater, le paternel; **got a fag, guv?** n'auriez pas un mégot, patron?
guy [gaɪ] **1** *n* (**a**) *Fam (man)* mec *m*, type *m*, gars *m*; **a good guy** un mec *ou* un type bien; **ok guys, let's go** allez les gars *ou* les mecs, on y va; **I didn't like the look of those guys** ces types *ou* ces mecs avaient une sale tête
(**b**) *esp Am (to both men and women)* **hurry up, you guys!** allez, dépêchez-vous!; **what are you guys doing tonight?** vous faites quoi, vous, ce soir?; **ok guys, let's go** ok, les amis, on y va; **do you guys want to go out?** vous voulez sortir?; **hi guys!** salut vous!; **are you guys ready?** tout le monde est prêt?
(**c**) *Br (for bonfire)* = effigie de Guy Fawkes
(**d**) *(for tent)* corde *f* de tente
2 *vt Old-fashioned* se moquer de
►► ***guy rope*** *(for tent)* corde *f* de tente
Guyana [gaɪ'ænə] *n* Guyana *m*; **in Guyana** au Guyana
Guyanese [ˌgaɪə'niːz] **1** *n* Guyanais(e) *m,f*
2 *adj* guyanais
Guy Fawkes' Night [-'fɔːks-] *n* = fête célébrée le 5 novembre en commémoration de la conspiration des poudres

> **GUY FAWKES' NIGHT**
>
> Cette fête se déroule en plein air autour d'un grand feu de joie sur lequel on est censé brûler une effigie ("the Guy") de Guy Fawkes, l'instigateur de la conspiration des poudres. Des feux d'artifice sont également organisés.

guyot ['giːɒt] *n Geog* guyot *m*
Guy's [gaɪz] *n* = surnom donné à l'hôpital St Guy, à Londres
guzzle ['gʌzəl] *Fam* **1** *vt (food)* bouffer, bâfrer; *(drink)* siffler; **he's guzzled the whole lot!** *(food)* il a tout bouffé *ou* bâfré!; *(drink)* il a tout sifflé!; **this car really guzzles the gas** cette voiture bouffe vraiment beaucoup (d'essence)
2 *vi (eat)* s'empiffrer, se goinfrer; *(drink)* boire trop vite❑
3 *n* **I had a good guzzle** *(ate a lot)* je me suis bien empiffré; *(drank a lot)* j'ai bu comme un trou
guzzler ['gʌzlə(r)] *n Fam (person → of food)* goinfre *mf*; *(→ of drink)* soiffard(e) *m,f*
guzzling ['gʌzlɪŋ] *n Fam (of food)* = fait de s'empiffrer; *(of drink)* = fait de picoler
Gwent [gwent] *n* le Gwent, = comté du sud-est du pays de Galles; **in Gwent** dans le Gwent
Gwynedd ['gwɪneð] *n* le Gwynedd, = comté du nord-ouest du pays de Galles; **in Gwynedd** dans le Gwynedd
gym [dʒɪm] *n* (**a**) *(hall, building)* gymnase *m*; *(fitness club)* club *m* de gym (**b**) *(activity, school subject)* gymnastique *f*, gym *f*
►► ***gym shoe*** chaussure *f* de gymnastique *ou* gym
gymkhana [dʒɪm'kɑːnə] *n* concours *m* hippique
gymnasium [dʒɪm'neɪzjəm] *(pl* **gymnasiums** *or* **gymnasia** [-zɪə]) *n* gymnase *m*
gymnast ['dʒɪmnæst] *n* gymnaste *mf*; **I've never been much of a gymnast** je n'ai jamais été très fort en gymnastique
gymnastic [dʒɪm'næstɪk] *adj (exercises)* de gymnastique; *(ability)* de gymnaste
gymnastics [dʒɪm'næstɪks] *n (UNCOUNT)* gymnastique *f*; **to do gymnastics** faire de la gymnastique; *Fig* **mental gymnastics** gymnastique *f* cérébrale
►► ***gymnastics display*** exhibition *f* de gymnastique
gymnosperm ['dʒɪmnəʊˌspɜːm] *n Bot* gymnosperme *f*
gymslip ['dʒɪmˌslɪp] *n Br (part of uniform)* blouse *f* d'écolière
►► *Fam* ***gymslip mother*** très jeune mère❑ *f (encore écolière)*
gynae ['gaɪnɪ] *adj Br Fam (abbr* **gynaecological**) *(department, ward)* de gynécologie❑; **a gynae nurse** une infirmière du service de gynécologie❑
gynaeceum [gaɪ'niːsɪəm] *(pl* **gynaecea** [-sɪə]) *n Antiq* gynécée *m*
gynaecologic, *Am* **gynecologic** [ˌgaɪnɪkə'lɒdʒɪk], **gynaecological,** *Am* **gynecological** [ˌgaɪnɪkə'lɒdʒɪkəl] *adj* gynécologique
gynaecologist, *Am* **gynecologist** [ˌgaɪnɪ'kɒlədʒɪst] *n* gynécologue *mf*
gynaecology, *Am* **gynecology** [ˌgaɪnɪ'kɒlədʒɪ] *n* gynécologie *f*
gynaecomastia [ˌgaɪnəkəʊ'mæstɪə] *n Med* gynécomastie *f*
gynandrous [gaɪ'nændrəs] *adj Bot* gynandre, épistaminé
gynecology, gynecologist *etc Am* = **gynaecology, gynaecologist** *etc*
gynodioecious [ˌgaɪnəʊdaɪ'iːʃəs] *adj Bot* gynodioïque
gynoecium [gaɪ'niːsɪəm] *(pl* **gynoecia** [-sɪə]) *n Bot* gynécée *m*
gyp [dʒɪp] *(pt & pp* **gypped**, *cont* **gypping**) *Fam* **1** *n* (**a**) *Br* **to give sb gyp** *(cause pain)* dérouiller qn (**b**) *Univ (cleaning lady)* femme *f* de ménage❑ (**c**) *Am (cheat)* **what a gyp!** quelle arnaque! (**d**) *Bot (gypsophila)* gypsophile❑ *f*
2 *vt (cheat)* rouler; **you've been gypped** tu t'es fait rouler *ou* avoir
gyppo ['dʒɪpəʊ] *(pl* **gyppos**) *n Br Fam* = terme injurieux désignant un gitan
gypsophila [dʒɪp'sɒfɪlə] *n Bot* gypsophile *f*
gypsum ['dʒɪpsəm] *n* gypse *m*
gypsy *(pl* **gypsies**) = **gipsy**
gyrate [dʒaɪ'reɪt] *vi* tournoyer
gyration [dʒaɪ'reɪʃən] *n* giration *f*
gyratory ['dʒaɪrətrɪ] *adj* giratoire
gyre [dʒaɪə(r)] *Literary* **1** *n* tourbillon *m*
2 *vi* tourbillonner
gyrfalcon ['dʒɜːfɔːlkən] *n Orn* gerfaut *m*
gyro ['dʒaɪrəʊ] **1** *adj* gyroscopique
2 *n* (**a**) *(gyroscope)* gyroscope *m* (**b**) *(gyrocompass)* gyrocompas *m*
►► ***gyro control*** commande *f* gyroscopique
gyrocompass ['dʒaɪrəʊˌkʌmpəs] *n* gyrocompas *m*
gyrodyne ['dʒaɪrəʊˌdaɪn] *n Aviat* gyrodyne *m*
gyromagnetic [ˌdʒaɪrəʊmæg'netɪk] *adj* gyromagnétique
gyropilot ['dʒaɪrəʊˌpaɪlət] *n Aviat* pilote *m* automatique, gyropilote *m*; *Naut (compass)* gyropilote *m*
gyroplane ['dʒaɪrəʊˌpleɪn] *n Aviat* autogyre *m*
gyroscope ['dʒaɪrəʊˌskəʊp] *n* gyroscope *m*
gyroscopic [ˌdʒaɪrəʊ'skɒpɪk] *adj* gyroscopique
gyrostabilizer [ˌdʒaɪrəʊ'steɪbəlaɪzə(r)] *n Naut* stabilisateur *m* gyroscopique
gyrostat ['dʒaɪrəʊstæt] *n* gyrostat *m*

H, h¹ [eɪtʃ] *n (letter)* H, h *m inv*; **two h's** deux h; **H for Harry** ≃ H comme Henri; **to drop one's h's** avaler ses h *(et révéler par là ses origines populaires)*

h² *n Fam Drugs slang* (*abbr* **heroin**) héro *f*, blanche *f*

ha [hɑː] *exclam (in triumph, sudden comprehension)* ha!, ah!; *(in contempt)* peuh!; *Ironic* **ha ha, very funny!** ha ha ha, très drôle!

haar [hɑː(r)] *n Scot* brume *f* venue de la mer du Nord

habeas corpus [ˌheɪbjəs'kɔːpəs] *n Law* habeas corpus *m*; **to issue a writ of habeas corpus** délivrer un (acte d') habeas corpus

THE HABEAS CORPUS ACT

L'"Habeas Corpus Act" désigne la loi votée en Angleterre en 1679, selon laquelle toute personne arrêtée est en droit de faire examiner par un juge la légalité de son emprisonnement. Complétée par plusieurs lois postérieures (datant de 1816 et 1960), la procédure est encore applicable en Grande-Bretagne et dans tous les pays soumis à la "Common Law" (sauf l'Écosse). Elle fut également intégrée à la Constitution américaine.

habenaria [ˌhæbə'neərɪə] *n Bot* habenaria *m*

haberdasher ['hæbədæʃə(r)] *n* (**a**) *Br (draper)* mercier(ère) *m,f* (**b**) *Am (shirtmaker)* chemisier(ère) *m,f*

haberdashery [ˌhæbə'dæʃərɪ] (*pl* **haberdasheries**) *n* (**a**) *Br (draper's)* mercerie *f* (**b**) *Am (shirtmaker's)* marchand(e) *m,f* de vêtements d'hommes *(en particulier de gants et de chapeaux)*

habit ['hæbɪt] *n* (**a**) *(custom)* habitude *f*; **to be in/to get into the habit of doing sth** avoir/prendre l'habitude de faire qch; **you'd better get into the habit of being more punctual** il vaudrait mieux que tu prennes l'habitude d'être plus ponctuel; **to get sb into the habit of doing sth** faire prendre à qn *ou* donner à qn l'habitude de faire qch, habituer qn à faire qch; **to make a habit of sth/of doing sth** prendre l'habitude de qch/de faire qch; **don't worry, I'm not going to make a habit of it** ne t'en fais pas, cela ne deviendra pas une habitude; **just don't make a habit of it!** ne recommence pas!, que cela ne se reproduise pas!; **to get out of a habit** perdre une habitude; **to get sb out of the habit of doing sth** faire perdre à qn l'habitude de faire qch; **he has a very strange habit of pulling his ear when he talks** il a un tic très étrange consistant à se tirer l'oreille quand il parle

(**b**) *Fam (drug dependency)* **to have a habit** être accro; **to have a heroin habit** être accro à l'héroïne; **he steals to pay for his habit** il vole pour payer sa drogue; **to kick the habit** *(drugs, tobacco)* décrocher

(**c**) *(dress → of monk, nun)* habit *m*; *(→ for riding)* tenue *f* de cheval

habitability [hæbɪtə'bɪlɪtɪ] *n* habitabilité *f*

habitable ['hæbɪtəbəl] *adj* habitable

habitant ['hæbɪtənt] *n* (**a**) *Literary (inhabitant)* habitant(e) *m,f* (**b**) *Am (Canadian of French descent)* Canadien(enne) *m,f* français(e); *Can* habitant(e) *m,f*

habitat ['hæbɪtæt] *n Bot & Zool* habitat *m*

habitation [ˌhæbɪ'teɪʃən] *n* (**a**) *(occupation)* habitation *f*; **there were signs of recent habitation** l'endroit semblait avoir été habité dans un passé récent; **fit/unfit for habitation** habitable/inhabitable; *(from sanitary point of view)* salubre/insalubre (**b**) *Formal (place)* habitation *f*, résidence *f*, demeure *f*

habit-forming [-ˌfɔːmɪŋ] *adj (drug)* qui crée une accoutumance *ou* une dépendance; *Hum* **I'd better not have another, it could be habit-forming** il vaut mieux que je n'en prenne pas d'autre, je risquerais de ne plus pouvoir m'en passer ❑

habitual [hə'bɪtʃʊəl] *adj (customary → generosity, lateness, good humour)* habituel, accoutumé; *(→ liar, drinker)* invétéré

►► *Mktg* ***habitual buying behaviour*** comportement *m* d'achat habituel; *Law* ***habitual offender*** récidiviste *mf*

habitually [hə'bɪtʃʊəlɪ] *adv* habituellement, ordinairement

habituate [hə'bɪtʃʊeɪt] *vt Formal* **to habituate oneself/sb to sth** s'habituer/habituer qn à qch; **to become habituated to sth** s'habituer à qch

habituation [həˌbɪtʃʊ'eɪʃən] *n Formal* accoutumance *f* (**to** à)

habitus ['hæbɪtəs] *n Biol & Med* habitus *m*

haboob [hæ'buːb] *n Met* haboob *m*

Habsburg ['hæpsbɜːg] *pr n* Habsbourg

hacienda [ˌhæsɪ'endə] *n* ranch *m*, hacienda *f*

hack [hæk] **1** *n* (**a**) *(sharp blow)* coup *m* violent; *(kick)* coup *m* de pied; **to take a hack at sb** *(kick)* donner un coup de pied à qn

(**b**) *(cut)* entaille *f*

(**c**) *Pej (writer)* écrivaillon *m*; *(journalist)* journaleux(euse) *m,f*, tâcheron *m*; *(politician)* politicard *m*

(**d**) *(horse for riding)* cheval *m* de selle; *(horse for hire)* cheval *m* de louage; *(old horse, nag)* rosse *f*, carne *f*

(**e**) *(ride)* **to go for a hack** aller faire une promenade à cheval

(**f**) *(cough)* toux *f* sèche

(**g**) *Am Fam (taxi)* taxi ❑ *m*, tacot *m*; *(taxi driver)* chauffeur *m* de taxi ❑

2 *vt* (**a**) *(cut)* taillader, tailler; **to hack sb/sth to pieces** tailler qn/qch en pièces; *Fig (opponent, manuscript)* mettre *ou* tailler qn/qch en pièces; **to hack sb to death** tuer qn à coups de couteau *ou* de hache; **he hacked his way through the jungle** il s'est taillé un passage à travers la jungle à coups de machette

(**b**) *(kick → ball)* donner un coup de pied sec dans; **to hack sb on the shins** donner un coup de pied dans les tibias à qn

(**c**) *Comput* **to hack one's way into a system** entrer dans un système par effraction

(**d**) *Fam (idiom) (cope with)* **he can't hack the pace** il n'arrive pas à tenir le rythme; **I can't hack it** *(can't cope)* je n'en peux plus ❑, je craque; **the new guy can't hack it** le nouveau ne tient pas le choc

3 *vi* (**a**) *(cut)* donner des coups de couteau *(de hache etc)*; **to hack (away) at sth** taillader qch

(**b**) *(kick)* **to hack at the ball** donner un coup de pied sec dans le ballon; **to hack at sb's shins** donner des coups de pied dans les tibias à qn

(**c**) *Comput* **to hack into a system** entrer dans un système par effraction; **to hack into sth** *(system, file)* s'introduire en fraude dans qch

(**d**) *(on horseback)* aller à cheval; **to go hacking** aller faire une promenade à cheval

►► *Fam* ***hack writer*** écrivaillon *m*; *Fam* ***hack writing*** travail *m* d'écrivaillon

►**hack down** *vt sep (tree)* abattre à coups de hache; *(person)* massacrer à coups de couteau *(de hache etc)*

►**hack into** *vt sep (body, corpse)* taillader; *Fig (text, article)* massacrer

►**hack off** *vt sep* (**a**) *(chop off)* trancher (**b**) *Fam (annoy)* **to hack sb off** prendre la tête à qn; **to be hacked off (with sb/sth)** en avoir marre (de qn/qch)

►**hack out** *vt sep (centre of fruit, rotten parts)* couper; *(hole, clearing)* tailler

►**hack up** *vt sep (meat, wood)* tailler *ou* couper en menus morceaux; *(body, victim)* mettre en pièces, découper en morceaux

hacker ['hækə(r)] *n Comput* (**a**) *(illegal user)* pirate *m* informatique (**b**) *(expert user)* bidouilleur(euse) *m,f*

hackette [hæ'ket] *n Br Fam* pisse-copie *f*

hackie ['hækɪ] *n Am Fam* chauffeur *m* de taxi ❑

hacking ['hækɪŋ] **1** *n (UNCOUNT)* (**a**) *(in football, rugby etc)* coups *mpl* de pied dans les tibias (**b**) *(coughing)* toux *f* sèche (**c**) *Comput* piratage *m (informatique)* (**d**) *Br (riding)* promenade(s) *f(pl)* à cheval

►► ***hacking cough*** toux *f* sèche; ***hacking jacket*** veste *f* de cheval

hackle ['hækəl] *n (of bird)* plume *f* du cou

hackles ['hækəlz] *npl (of dog)* poils *mpl* du cou; **when a dog has its hackles up** quand un chien a le poil hérissé; *Fig* **my hackles rose** ça m'a hérissé le poil; **it gets my hackles up, it makes my hackles rise** ça me hérisse; **don't go getting your hackles up** ne t'énerve pas

hackmatack ['hækmətæk] *n Bot* mélèze *m* d'Amérique

hackney ['hæknɪ] (*pl* **hackneys**) *n* (**a**) *(taxi)* = taxi officiellement agréé (**b**) *(carriage for hire)* cabriolet *m* de louage (**c**) *(horse-drawn)* fiacre *m* (**d**) *(horse)* cheval *m* de selle; *(trotter)* trotteur *m*

►► *Br* ***hackney cab, hackney carriage*** *(horse-drawn)* fiacre *m*; *(taxi)* = taxi officiellement agréé

hackneyed ['hæknɪd] *adj (subject)* réchauffé, rebattu; *(turn of phrase)* banal, commun; **hackneyed expression** cliché *m*, lieu *m* commun

hacksaw ['hæksɔː] *n* scie *f* à métaux

hackwork ['hækwɜːk] *n* écrivaillerie *f*; **the report was a piece of shoddy hackwork** ce rapport, c'était du travail d'écrivaillon

had [həd, *stressed* hæd] *pt & pp of* **have**

haddock ['hædək] *n Ich* aiglefin *m*, églefin *m*; *(smoked)* haddock *m*

Hades ['heɪdiːz] *Myth* **1** *n (place)* Les Enfers *mpl*

2 *pr n (god)* Hadès

hadn't ['hædənt] = **had not**

Hadrian ['heɪdrɪən] *pr n* Hadrien

►► ***Hadrian's Wall*** le Mur d'Hadrien

hadrome ['hædrəʊm] *n Bot* hadrome *m*

hadron ['hædrɒn] *n Phys* hadron *m*

haem, *Am* **heme** [hiːm] *n Biol & Chem* hème *m*

haema-, *Am* **hema-** ['hiːmə] *pref Med* héma-

haemal, *Am* **hemal** ['hiːməl] *adj Physiol* hémal

haematemesis, *Am* **hematemesis** [ˌhiːmə'teməsɪs] *n Med* hématémèse *f*

haematic, *Am* **hematic** [hiː'mætɪk] *adj Physiol* hématique

haematin, *Am* **hematin** ['hiːmətɪn], **haematine,** *Am* **hematine** ['hiːmətaɪn] *n Chem & Physiol* hématine *f*

haematite, *Am* **hematite** ['hiːmətaɪt] *n Chem & Miner* hématite *f*

haemato-, *Am* **hemato-** [ˌhiːmə'tɒ, ˌhiːmə'təʊ] *pref Med* hémato-

haematoblast, *Am* **hematoblast** ['hiːmətəʊˌblæst] *n Physiol* hématoblaste *m*

haematocele, *Am* **hematocele** ['hiːmətəʊsiːl] *n Med* hématocèle *f*

haematocrit, *Am* **hematocrit** ['hiːmətəʊkrɪt] *n Med* hématocrite *m*

haematography, *Am* **hematography** [ˌhiːməˈtɒgrəfɪ] *n Med* hématographie *f*

haematological, *Am* **hematological** [ˌhiːmətəˈlɒdʒɪkəl] *adj Med* hématologique

haematologist, *Am* **hematologist** [ˌhiːməˈtɒlədʒɪst] *n Med* hématologiste *mf*, hématologue *mf*

haematology, *Am* **hematology** [ˌhiːməˈtɒlədʒɪ] *n Med* hématologie *f*

haematoma, *Am* **hematoma** [ˌhiːməˈtəʊmə] (*Br pl* **haematomas** *or* **haematomata** [-mətə], *Am pl* **hematomas** *or* **hematomata** [-mətə]) *n Med* hématome *m*

haematuria, *Am* **hematuria** [ˌhiːməˈtjʊərɪə] *n Med* hématurie *f*

haemo-, *Am* **hemo-** [ˈhiːməʊ, ˈhiːmə] *pref Med* hémo-

haemocyanin, *Am* **hemocyanin** [ˌhiːməʊˈsaɪənɪn] *n Physiol* hémocyanine *f*

haemodynamics, *Am* **hemodynamics** [ˌhiːməʊdaɪˈnæmɪks] *n Chem & Med* hémodynamique *f*

haemoglobin, *Am* **hemoglobin** [ˌhiːməˈgləʊbɪn] *n Physiol* hémoglobine *f*

haemolysin, *Am* **hemolysin** [hiːˈmɒlɪsɪn] *n Chem & Med* hémolysine *f*

haemolysis, *Am* **hemolysis** [hiːˈmɒlɪsɪs] *n Chem & Med* hémolyse *f*

haemolytic, *Am* **hemolytic** [ˌhiːməʊˈlɪtɪk] *adj Chem & Med* hémolytique

haemophilia, *Am* **hemophilia** [ˌhiːməˈfɪlɪə] *n Med* hémophilie *f*

haemophiliac, *Am* **hemophiliac** [ˌhiːməˈfɪlɪæk] *n Med* hémophile *mf*

haemophilic, *Am* **hemophilic** [ˌhiːməʊˈfɪlɪk] *adj Med* hémophile

haemoptysis, *Am* **hemoptysis** [hiːˈmɒptɪsɪs] *n Med* hémoptysie *f*, crachement *m* de sang

haemorrhage, *Am* **hemorrhage** [ˈhemərɪdʒ] **1** *n Med* hémorragie *f*

2 *vi* (**a**) *Med* faire une hémorragie (**b**) *Fig (disappear, fade → support etc)* s'évanouir, se dissiper; **party membership was haemorrhaging badly** les effectifs du parti diminuaient de façon spectaculaire

haemorrhagic, *Am* **hemorrhagic** [ˌheməˈrædʒɪk] *adj Med* hémorragique

►► *Med* ***haemorrhagic diathesis*** hémophilie *f*

haemorrhaging, *Am* **hemorrhaging** [ˈhemərɪˌdʒɪŋ] *n (UNCOUNT) Med* hémorragie *f*; **there's still some haemorrhaging** l'hémorragie n'est pas encore arrêtée

haemorrhoids, *Am* **hemorrhoids** [ˈhemərɔɪdz] *npl Med* hémorroïdes *fpl*; **to have haemorrhoids** avoir des hémorroïdes

haemostasia, *Am* **hemostasia** [ˌhiːməʊˈsteɪzɪə] *n Physiol* hémostase *f*

haemostasis, *Am* **hemostasis** [ˌhiːməʊˈsteɪsɪs] *n Physiol* hémostase *f*

haemostat, *Am* **hemostat** [ˈhiːməʊˌstæt] *n Med (instrument)* pince(s) *f(pl)* hémostatique(s)

haemostatic, *Am* **hemostatic** [ˌhiːməˈstætɪk] *adj Med* hémostatique

►► ***haemostatic forceps*** pince *f* hémostatique

haemotoxin, *Am* **hemotoxin** [ˌhiːməʊˈtɒksɪn] *n Physiol* hémotoxine *f*

hafnium [ˈhæfnɪəm] *n Chem* hafnium *m*

haft [hæft] *n (of knife)* manche *m*; *(of sword)* poignée *f*

hag [hæg] *n (witch)* sorcière *f*; *Pej (old woman)* vieille sorcière *f*, vieille chouette *f*; *(unpleasant woman)* harpie *f*; **she's a real old hag** ce n'est qu'une vieille chouette

Hagar [ˈheɪgɑː(r)] *pr n Bible* Agar

hagfish [ˈhægfɪʃ] *n Ich* myxine *f*

Haggai [ˈhægaɪ] *pr n Bible* Aggée

haggard [ˈhægəd] *adj* (**a**) *(tired, drawn)* hâve; **he looked haggard** il avait les traits tirés (**b**) *(wild → face)* égaré, hagard

haggis [ˈhægɪs] *n* = plat typique écossais fait d'une panse de brebis farcie (d'un hachis d'abats et de farine d'avoine très épicé)

haggish [ˈhægɪʃ] *adj (woman)* vieille et hideuse; *(appearance)* de vieille sorcière

haggle [ˈhægəl] **1** *vi* (**a**) *(bargain)* marchander; **to haggle over the price** marchander sur le prix (**b**) *(argue over details)* chicaner, chipoter; **to haggle over** *or* **about sth** chicaner *ou* chipoter sur qch

2 *n* **after a long haggle over the price** après un long marchandage sur le prix

haggler [ˈhæglə(r)] *n* (**a**) *(over price)* marchandeur(euse) *m,f* (**b**) *(over details, wording)* chicaneur(euse) *m,f*, chipoteur(euse) *m,f*

haggling [ˈhæglɪŋ] *n (UNCOUNT)* (**a**) *(over price)* marchandage *m* (**b**) *(about details, wording)* chicanerie *f*, chipotage *m*

hagiographer [ˌhægɪˈɒgrəfə(r)] *n* hagiographe *mf*

hagiographic [ˌhægɪəˈgræfɪk], **hagiographical** [ˌhægɪəˈgræfɪkəl] *adj* hagiographe, hagiographique

hagiography [ˌhægɪˈɒgrəfɪ] *n* hagiographie *f*

hagiolatry [ˌhægɪˈɒlətrɪ] *n* hagiolâtrie *f*

hagiologic [ˌhægɪəˈlɒdʒɪk], **hagiological** [ˌhægɪəˈlɒdʒɪkəl] *adj* hagiologique

hagiologist [ˌhægɪˈɒlədʒɪst] *n* hagiographe *mf*

hagiology [ˌhægɪˈɒlədʒɪ] *n* hagiologie *f*

hag-ridden *adj Literary (tormented)* tourmenté, ravagé; *Hum (tormented by women)* persécuté par les femmes

Hague [heɪg] *n* **The Hague** La Haye

hah = **ha**

ha-ha[1] [hɑːˈhɑː] *exclam (mock amusement)* ha ha!; *(representing laughter → in comic, novel)* ha ha ha!, hi hi hi!

ha-ha[2] [ˈhɑːˌhɑː] *n (wall, fence)* = mur ou clôture installé dans un fossé

hahnium [ˈhɑːnɪəm] *n Chem* hahnium *m*

Haifa [ˈhaɪfə] *n* Haïfa, Haiffa

haiku [ˈhaɪkuː] *n Literature* haïku *m*

hail [heɪl] **1** *n* (**a**) *Met* grêle *f*; *Fig (of stones)* grêle *f*, pluie *f*; *(of abuse)* avalanche *f*, déluge *m*; *(of blows)* grêle *f*; **he died in a hail of bullets** il est tombé sous une pluie de balles

(**b**) *Literary (call)* appel *m*; **within hail** à portée de voix

2 *vi Met* grêler; **it's hailing** il grêle

3 *vt* (**a**) *(call → taxi, ship, person)* héler; **within hailing distance** à portée de voix

(**b**) *(greet → person)* acclamer, saluer

(**c**) *(acclaim → person, new product, invention etc)* acclamer, saluer; **her book has been hailed as the most significant new novel this year** son livre a été acclamé comme le nouveau roman le plus marquant de cette année; **the plan was hailed as the solution to their problems** le projet a été salué comme la solution à tous leurs problèmes; **to hail sb emperor** proclamer qn empereur

(**d**) *(idioms)* **to hail blows on sb** faire pleuvoir les coups sur qn; **to hail insults on sb** accabler qn d'injures

4 *exclam Arch* salut à vous *ou* toi; **hail, Caesar!** Ave César!; **hail, Mary, full of grace** je te salue, Marie, pleine de grâce

►► *Rel* ***Hail Mary*** *(prayer)* Je vous salue Marie *m inv*, Ave (Maria) *m inv*; **say five Hail Marys** vous direz cinq Je vous salue Marie *ou* cinq Ave (Maria); *Am Sport* ***Hail Mary pass*** = passe au petit bonheur; *Fig* **to throw a Hail Mary pass** tenter sa chance

►**hail down 1** *vi (blows, stones etc)* pleuvoir; **blows/rocks were hailing down on us** des coups/pierres nous pleuvaient dessus; **criticism hailed down on him** il a subi une avalanche *ou* un déluge de critiques

2 *vt sep* **they hailed insults down on the President** ils ont déversé un flot d'insultes à l'intention du président; *Literary* **to hail down curses on sb** déverser un déluge de malédictions sur qn

►**hail from** *vt insep (of ship)* être en provenance de; *(of person)* venir de, être originaire de; **where does she hail from?** *(of ship)* quelle est sa provenance?; *(of person)* d'où vient-elle?

hail-fellow-well-met *adj* **he's always very hail-fellow-well-met** il fait toujours montre d'une familiarité joviale

hailstone [ˈheɪlstəʊn] *n* grêlon *m*

hailstorm [ˈheɪlstɔːm] *n* averse *f* de grêle

hair [heə(r)] **1** *n* (**a**) *(UNCOUNT) (on person's head)* cheveux *mpl*; **to have long/short hair** avoir les cheveux longs/courts; **she's got such beautiful hair** elle a vraiment de beaux cheveux; **to get** *or* **to have one's hair cut** se faire couper les cheveux; **to get one's hair done** se faire coiffer; **who does your hair?** tu te fais coiffer où?, tu vas chez quel coiffeur?; **I like the way you've done your hair** j'aime bien la façon dont tu t'es coiffé; **to wash one's hair** se laver les cheveux *ou* la tête; **to brush one's hair** se brosser (les cheveux); **to comb one's hair** se peigner (les cheveux); **she put her hair up** elle a relevé ses cheveux; **she let her hair down** elle a défait ses cheveux; **your hair looks nice** tu es bien coiffé; **my hair's a mess** je suis vraiment mal coiffé

(**b**) *(single hair → on person's head)* cheveu *m*; *(→ on person's or animal's face or body, on plant)* poil *m*; *Am Fam* **move it a hair over to the right** déplace-le un chouia vers la droite

(**c**) *(UNCOUNT) (on body, face)* poils *mpl*; *(on animal)* poils *mpl*; *(on horse)* crin *m*; *(on pig)* soie *f*; **a dog with smooth hair** un chien au pelage lisse

(**d**) *Opt (of gun sight etc)* cheveu *m*, fil *m*

(**e**) *(idioms)* **it makes your hair stand on end** *(is frightening)* c'est à vous faire dresser les cheveux sur la tête; *Fam* **it would make your hair curl** *(ride, journey)* c'est à vous faire dresser les cheveux sur la tête; *(prices, bad language)* c'est à vous faire tomber à la renverse; *(drink)* ça arrache; *Br Fam* **keep your hair on!** ne t'excite pas![❑]; **to let one's hair down** se laisser aller[❑], se défouler[❑]; *Fam* **to get in sb's hair** taper sur les nerfs de qn; *Fam* **keep him out of my hair** fais en sorte que je ne l'aie pas dans les jambes; *Fam* **I'll keep out of your hair** je ne vais pas t'embêter; *Hum* **to have a hair of the dog (that bit you)** reprendre un verre (pour faire passer sa gueule de bois); **here, a hair of the dog is what you need** bois ça, il faut guérir le mal par le mal; **to split hairs** couper les cheveux en quatre, chercher la petite bête; **not one hair of her head was harmed** elle s'en est sortie sans une égratignure; **if you harm one single hair of his head** si tu touches à un seul de ses cheveux; **she never has a hair out of place** *(is immaculate)* elle n'a jamais un cheveu de travers; **to win by a hair** gagner d'un cheveu *ou* à un quart de poil près; **to lose by a hair** perdre d'un cheveu *ou* à un quart de poil près; **she didn't turn a hair** elle n'a pas cillé; *Fam Hum* **this'll put hairs on your chest!** *(strong drink, good steak etc)* ça va te redonner du poil de la bête; **the truck missed us by a hair's breadth** le camion nous a manqués d'un cheveu *ou* de justesse; **we came within a hair's breadth of going bankrupt/of winning first prize** nous avons été à deux doigts de la faillite/de gagner le premier prix

2 *comp* (**a**) *(cream, lotion)* capillaire, pour les cheveux

(**b**) *(colour)* de cheveux

(**c**) *(mattress)* de crin

►► ***hair appointment*** rendez-vous *m* chez le coiffeur; ***hair clippers*** tondeuse *f*; **a pair of hair clippers** une tondeuse; ***hair conditioner*** après-shampooing *m*; *Br* ***hair curlers*** bigoudis *mpl*; ***hair drier, hair dryer*** *(hand-held)* sèche-cheveux *m inv*, séchoir *m*; *(over the head)* casque *m*; ***hair follicle*** follicule *m* pileux; ***hair gel*** gel *m* pour les cheveux; *Bot* ***hair grass*** canche *f*; ***hair lacquer*** laque *f* (pour les cheveux); ***hair mascara*** mascara *m* pour les cheveux; ***hair mousse*** mousse *f* coiffante; ***hair oil*** huile *f* capillaire; ***hair products*** produits *mpl* capillaires *ou* pour les cheveux; ***hair removal*** dépilation *f*; ***hair remover*** crème *f* dépilatoire; *Br* ***hair restorer*** produit *m* pour la repousse des cheveux; ***hair shirt*** haire *f*, cilice *m*; ***hair slide*** barrette *f*; ***hair straightener*** *(product)* produit *m* défrisant; ***hair straighteners*** *(appliance)* fer *m* à défriser, défriseur *m*; ***hair tonic*** lotion *f* capillaire; ***hair transplant*** implant *m* de cheveux; ***hair trigger*** *(in firearm)* détente *f* ou gâchette *f* sensible

hairball [ˈheəbɔːl] *n (of cat's fur)* boule *f* de poils

hairband [ˈheəbænd] *n* bandeau *m*

hairbreadth [ˈheəbretθ] *n* **the truck missed us by a hairbreadth** le camion nous a manqués d'un cheveu *ou* de justesse; **we came within a hairbreadth of going bankrupt/of winning first prize** nous avons été à deux doigts de la faillite/de gagner le premier prix

hairbrush [ˈheəbrʌʃ] *n* brosse *f* à cheveux

haircare [ˈheəkeə(r)] *n* soin *m* du cheveu

►► ***haircare products*** produits *mpl* de soin pour les cheveux

hairclip [ˈheəklɪp] *n* barrette *f*

haircut ['heəkʌt] *n* (**a**) *(of person)* coupe *f* (de cheveux); **I like your haircut** j'aime bien ta coupe (de cheveux); **I need a haircut** j'ai besoin de me faire couper les cheveux; **to have a haircut** se faire couper les cheveux; **to give sb a haircut** couper les cheveux à qn; **where did you get that haircut!** où est-ce que tu t'es fait couper les cheveux!; **some haircut!** quelle drôle de coupe! (**b**) *Fam St Exch* marge *f* de sécurité ❑

hairdo ['heədu:] *n Fam* coiffure ❑ *f*

hairdresser ['heə,dresə(r)] *n (person)* coiffeur(euse) *m,f*; *(shop)* salon *m* de coiffure; **to go to the hairdresser's** aller chez le coiffeur

hairdressing ['heə,dresɪŋ] *n (skill)* coiffure *f*
 ►► ***hairdressing salon*** salon *m* de coiffure; ***hairdressing school*** école *f* de coiffure

-haired [heəd] *suff* **long/short-haired** *(person)* aux cheveux longs/courts; *(animal)* à poil(s) long(s)/court(s); **wire-haired** *(dog)* à poil(s) dur(s)

hairgrip ['heəgrɪp] *n Br* pince *f* à cheveux

hairiness ['heərɪnɪs] *n* aspect *m* velu

hairless ['heəlɪs] *adj (head)* chauve, sans cheveux; *(face)* glabre; *(body)* peu poilu; *(animal)* sans poils; *(leaf)* glabre

hairline ['heəlaɪn] *n* (**a**) *(of the hair)* naissance *f* des cheveux; **to have a receding hairline** *(above forehead)* avoir le front qui se dégarnit; *(at temples)* avoir les tempes qui se dégarnissent (**b**) *(in telescope, gun sight)* fil *m* (**c**) *Typ* filet *m* ultra-fin; *(in calligraphy)* délié *m*
 ►► ***hairline crack*** fêlure *f*; *Med* ***hairline fracture*** fêlure *f*

hairnet ['heənet] *n* résille *f*, filet *m* à cheveux

hairpiece ['heəpi:s] *n (toupee)* perruque *f (pour hommes)*; *(extra hair)* postiche *m*

hairpin ['heəpɪn] *n (for hair)* épingle *f* à cheveux; *(bend)* virage *m* en épingle à cheveux
 ►► ***hairpin bend*** virage *m* en épingle à cheveux

hair-raising [-,reɪzɪŋ] *adj (adventure, experience, story, account)* à faire dresser les cheveux sur la tête, effrayant; *(prices, expenses)* affolant, exorbitant; **driving in London traffic can be a hair-raising experience** conduire à Londres peut être une expérience terrifiante; **it was pretty hair-raising** c'était à vous faire dresser les cheveux sur la tête

hairsplitting ['heə,splɪtɪŋ] **1** *adj* **that's a hairsplitting argument** *or* **distinction** c'est de la chicanerie, c'est couper les cheveux en quatre
 2 *n (UNCOUNT)* chicanerie *f*, pinaillage *m*; **that's just hairsplitting** tu es vraiment en train de couper les cheveux en quatre

hairspray ['heəspreɪ] *n* laque *f ou* spray *m* (pour les cheveux)

hairspring ['heəsprɪŋ] *n (in clock)* spiral *m (de montre)*

hairstreak ['heəstri:k] *adj*
 ►► *Entom* ***hairstreak butterfly*** thecla *m*, thècle *m*; **the hairstreak butterflies** les théclines *mpl*

hairstyle ['heəstaɪl] *n* coiffure *f*

hairstyling salon ['heə,staɪlɪŋ-] *n* salon *m* de coiffure

hairstylist ['heə,staɪlɪst] *n* styliste *mf* en coiffure

hair-trigger *adj Fig* **to have a hair-trigger temper** *(lose one's temper easily)* s'emporter facilement; **the hair-trigger tensions of a nuclear war have now eased** les tensions qui menaçaient de déclencher un conflit nucléaire sont aujourd'hui apaisées; *Fam* **to have a hair-trigger problem** *(ejaculate prematurely)* avoir des problèmes d'éjaculation précoce ❑

hairy ['heərɪ] *(compar* **hairier,** *superl* **hairiest***) adj* (**a**) *(arms, chest)* poilu, velu; *(person, animal)* poilu; *(stalk of plant, leaf)* velu
 (**b**) *Fam (frightening)* à faire dresser les cheveux sur la tête ❑; *(difficult, daunting)* qui craint; **"that was a bit hairy", he said** "j'ai eu un peu la frousse", dit-il; **there were a few hairy moments when the brakes seemed to be failing** il y a eu des moments craignos où les freins semblaient lâcher; **he gave a pretty hairy description of his two hours at the dentist** il a fait une description assez horrible *ou* atroce des deux heures qu'il a passées chez le dentiste; **he did some pretty hairy stunts** il a fait quelques cascades assez impressionnantes; **things are getting a bit hairy at the office** *(because of workload)* ça devient un peu la folie au bureau; *(because of personal or financial tension)* ça commence à craindre au bureau

Haiti ['heɪtɪ] *n* Haïti; **in Haiti** à Haïti

Haitian ['heɪʃən] **1** *adj* haïtien
 2 *n* Haïtien(enne) *m,f*

hajj [hædʒ] *n Rel* hadj *m inv*

hajji ['hædʒɪ] *n Rel* hadj *m inv*, hadji *m inv*

haka ['hɑ:kə] *n* haka *m*

hake [heɪk] *n Ich* merlu *m*, colin *m*

halal [hə'lɑ:l] **1** *n (meat)* viande *f* halal
 2 *adj* halal *(inv)*

halation [hæ'leɪʃən] *n Phot* halo *m*, irradiation *f*

halberd ['hælbɜ:d] *n Hist* hallebarde *f*

halberdier [,hælbə'di:ə(r)] *n Hist* hallebardier *m*

halcyon ['hælsɪən] **1** *n Myth (kingfisher)* halcyon *m*
 2 *adj Literary* **those halcyon days** ces temps heureux

hale [heɪl] *adj* **hale and hearty** en pleine santé

HALF [hɑ:f]

moitié	► 1 (a); 2
mi-temps	► 1 (b)
camp	► 1 (c)
demi	► 1 (d), (e)
à moitié	► 5

(pl **halves** [hɑ:vz]) **1** *n* (**a**) *(gen)* moitié *f*; *(of standard measured amount)* demi(e) *m,f*; *(of ticket, coupon)* souche *f*; **half an hour** une demi-heure; **half a dozen** une demi-douzaine; **to cut/to break sth in half** couper/casser qch en deux; **what's half of 13.72?** quelle est la moitié de 13,72?; **two and two halves, please** *(on bus, train etc)* deux billets tarif normal et deux billets demi-tarif, s'il vous plaît; *Rail* **outward/return half** *(of ticket)* coupon *m* d'aller/de retour; **you can have the smaller half** la plus petite moitié est pour toi; **she gave each of us half** elle nous en a donné la moitié à chacun; **it cuts the journey time in half** cela réduit de moitié la durée du voyage; **three and a half** trois et demi; **three and a half pieces/years** trois morceaux/ans et demi; *Br* **bigger by half** plus grand de moitié, moitié plus grand; **two halves make a whole** deux moitiés *ou* demis font un tout; **to go halves with sb** partager avec qn; **we'll go halves** on partage; **they don't do things by halves** ils ne font pas les choses à moitié; *Br* **he always was too clever by half** il a toujours été un peu trop malin; *Br* **you're too cheeky by half!** tu es bien trop effronté *ou* culotté!; *Fam* **a party/day/hangover and a half** une sacrée nouba/journée/gueule de bois; *Fam* **that was a walk and a half!** c'était une sacrée promenade!; *Fam* **I've got a headache and a half this morning!** j'ai un sacré mal de tête ce matin!; *Fam* **and that's not the half of it** et ce n'est que le début; *Fam* **you haven't heard the half of it!** tu n'en sais pas encore le quart!; **it's sort of half and half** c'est un peu de chaque; *Hum* **my better** *or* **other half** ma (chère) moitié; *Hum* **to see how the other half lives** voir comment on vit de l'autre côté de la barrière, voir comment vivent les autres
 (**b**) *(period of sports match)* mi-temps *f inv*; **France was in the lead in the first half** la France menait pendant la première mi-temps
 (**c**) *(area of football or rugby pitch)* camp *m*
 (**d**) *(rugby or football player)* demi *m*
 (**e**) *Br (half pint of beer)* demi *m* (de bière)
 2 *pron* **leave half of it for me** laisse-m'en la moitié; **half of us were students** la moitié d'entre nous étaient des étudiants
 3 *adj* **a half chicken** un demi-poulet; **oysters on the half-shell** huîtres *fpl* servies dans leurs coquilles; **at half speed** au ralenti; *Fam* **to go off at half cock** *(plan)* avorter; *Fam* **we don't want to go off at half cock on this one** cette fois-ci on ne va pas faire les choses à moitié
 4 *predet* **half the time he seems to be asleep** on a l'impression qu'il est endormi la moitié du temps; **half the time he isn't there** les trois quarts du temps, il n'est pas là; **he's half a year older than me** il a six mois de plus que moi; *Fam* **half a minute!** une (petite) minute!; *Fam* **I'll be down in half a second** je descends tout de suite ❑; **I'll be there in half an hour** j'y serai dans une demi-heure; **just half a cup for me** juste une demi-tasse pour moi; **he's not half the man he used to be** il n'est plus que l'ombre de lui-même; *Fam* **to have half a mind to do sth** avoir bien envie de faire qch ❑; **that was half the point of going there** c'était tout l'intérêt d'y aller
 5 *adv* (**a**) *(finished, asleep, dressed)* à moitié; *(full, empty, blind)* à moitié, à demi; **to be half full of sth** être à moitié rempli de qch; **you're only half right** tu n'as qu'à moitié raison; **half done** *(work)* fait à moitié; *(cooked meat etc)* à moitié cuit; **a strange colour, half green, half blue** une couleur bizarre, entre le vert et le bleu; **to be half English and half French** être moitié anglais moitié français; **I half think that...** je suis tenté de penser que...; **for a minute I half thought that...** pendant une minute, j'ai presque pensé que...; **I was half afraid you wouldn't understand** j'avais un peu peur que vous ne compreniez pas; **I was only half joking** je ne plaisantais qu'à moitié; **half laughing, half crying** moitié riant, moitié pleurant
 (**b**) *Br Fam (as intensifier)* **they're not half fit** ils sont en super-forme; **he's not half lazy** il est drôlement *ou* rudement paresseux; **it's not half cold today!** il fait rudement *ou* sacrément froid aujourd'hui!; **he didn't half yell** il a hurlé comme un fou; **she can't half run** elle court comme un lièvre; **you don't half put your foot in it sometimes!** tu mets vraiment les pieds dans le plat parfois!; **they didn't half complain** ils se sont plaints, et pas qu'un peu; **did you complain? – I didn't half!** *or* **not half!** est-ce que vous vous êtes plaint? – et comment! *ou* pas qu'un peu!; **he's/it's not half bad** il est/c'est vraiment bon
 (**c**) *(time) Br* **it's half past two, it's half two** il est deux heures et demie; *Am* **half after six** six heures et demie
 (**d**) *(idioms)* **to be half as big/fast as sb/sth** être moitié moins grand/rapide que qn/qch; **the radio was only half as loud as before** le son de la radio était moitié moins fort qu'avant; **to earn half as much as sb** gagner moitié moins que qn; **to be half as big again (as sb/sth)** être moitié plus grand (que qn/qch); **he earns half as much again as you do** il gagne moitié plus que toi
 ►► *Tech* ***half bearing*** demi-palier *m*; *Br* ***half board*** **1** *n* demi-pension *f* **2** *adv* en demi-pension; *Am Fam* ***half buck*** 50 cents *mpl*; *Comput* ***half duplex*** semi-duplex *m*; **to send sth half duplex** transmettre qch en semi-duplex; ***half fare*** demi-tarif *m*; **to travel half fare** voyager à demi-tarif; *Am Mus* ***half step*** demi-ton *m*; *Br Sch* ***half term*** = congé scolaire en milieu de trimestre; *Archit & Constr* ***half timbering*** colombage *m*; ***half year*** semestre *m*

half-a-crown = half-crown

half-and-half **1** *n Br (beer)* = mélange de deux bières; *Am (for coffee)* = mélange de crème et de lait
 2 *adv* moitié-moitié; **it's half-and-half** c'est moitié-moitié; **how shall I mix them? – half-and-half** comment faut-il les mélanger? – à doses égales

half-arsed [-'ɑ:st], *Am* **half-assed** [-'æst] *adj very Fam (incompetent)* nul à chier; **he made a half-arsed attempt at mending the fence** il a essayé de réparer la barrière mais il s'y est pris comme un manche

halfback ['hɑ:fbæk] *n* (**a**) *Old-fashioned Ftbl* demi-arrière *m* (**b**) *(in rugby)* demi *m*

half-baked [-'beɪkt] *adj Fam Fig (scheme, idea, proposal)* qui ne tient pas debout; *(person)* niais ❑

half-beam *n Naut* barrotin *m*

half-binding *n* demi-reliure *f*

half-blood *n Old-fashioned* métis(isse) *m,f*

half-boot *n* mi-botte *f*

half-bottle *n* demi-bouteille *f*

half-breed **1** *n* (**a**) *(animal)* hybride *m*; *(horse)* cheval *m* demi-sang *(inv)* (**b**) *Old-fashioned (person)* métis(isse) *m,f*
 2 *adj* (**a**) *(animal)* hybride; *(horse)* demi-sang *(inv)* (**b**) *Old-fashioned (person)* métis

half-brother *n* demi-frère *m*

half-caste *Old-fashioned* **1** *n (person)* métis(isse) *m,f*
 2 *adj* métis

half-century (*pl* **half-centuries**) *n* demi-siècle *m*
half-circle *n* demi-cercle *m*
half-cocked [-'kɒkt] *adj (gun, pistol)* à moitié armé
half-commission man *n Com* remisier *m*
half-crazy *adj* à moitié fou (folle)
half-crown *n Br Hist* demi-couronne *f*
half-cup bra *n* soutien-gorge *m* à balconnet
half-cut *adj Br Fam (drunk)* bourré, pété, fait
half-day 1 *n (at school, work)* demi-journée *f*; **tomorrow is my half-day** *(work)* demain c'est ma demi-journée de congé; **to work half-days** faire des demi-journées
2 *adj* **a half-day holiday** une demi-journée de congé
half-dead *adj Br Fam (very tired)* à moitié mort, complètement crevé
half-deck *n Naut* demi-pont *m*
half-dollar *n* pièce *f* de 50 cents
half-dozen *n* demi-douzaine *f*; **a half-dozen eggs** une demi-douzaine d'œufs
half-drowned [-'draʊnd] *adj* à moitié *ou* à demi noyé
half-eaten *adj* à moitié mangé
half-fare ticket *n* billet *m* demi-tarif
half-fill *vt (glass)* remplir à moitié *ou* à demi
half-full *adj* à moitié *ou* à demi plein
half-grown *adj* à mi-croissance
half-hardy *adj Bot* semi-rustique
half-hearted [-'hɑːtɪd] *adj (attempt, attitude)* qui manque d'enthousiasme *ou* de conviction, timide, hésitant; *(acceptance)* tiède, qui manque d'enthousiasme; **he was very half-hearted about it** il était vraiment peu enthousiaste à ce propos; **they were very half-hearted about accepting** ils ont accepté sans grand enthousiasme *ou* du bout des lèvres
half-heartedly [-'hɑːtɪdlɪ] *adv (accept, agree, say)* sans enthousiasme *ou* conviction, du bout des lèvres
half-heartedness [-'hɑːtɪdnɪs] *n* manque *m* d'enthousiasme
half-height *adj*
►► *Aut* ***half-height bulkhead*** cloison *f* basse de séparation; *Comput* ***half-height drive*** unité *f* demi-hauteur
half-hitch *n* demi-clef *f*
half-holiday *n* demi-journée *f* de congé
half-hour 1 *n (period)* demi-heure *f*; *Am* **I'll wait a half-hour** j'attendrai une demi-heure; **on the half-hour** à la demie
2 *adj* **at half-hour intervals** toutes les demi-heures
half-hourly 1 *adj* toutes les demi-heures; **there is a half-hourly train service** il y a des trains toutes les trente minutes; **he needs his half-hourly break** il lui faut faire une pause toutes les trente minutes; **at half-hourly intervals** toutes les demi-heures, toutes les trente minutes
2 *adv* toutes les demi-heures
half-inch 1 *n (unit of measurement)* = 1, 27 cm, demi-pouce *m*
2 *vt Br Fam (rhyming slang* = **pinch**) piquer, faucher; **he got his wallet half-inched** il s'est fait piquer son portefeuille
half-joking *adj* mi-figue, mi-raisin
half-jokingly *adv* d'un air mi-figue, mi-raisin
half-landing *n (on staircase)* palier *m* de repos
half-length *adj (portrait)* en buste
half-life *n* (**a**) *Phys* demi-vie *f*, période *f* (**b**) *Med* demi-vie *f*
half-light *n* demi-jour *m*
half-marathon *n* semi-marathon *m*
half-mast *n* **at half-mast** *(flag)* en berne; *Hum (trousers)* arrivant à mi-mollet; *(socks)* en accordéon
half-measure *n* demi-mesure *f*; **there's no point taking half-measures** les demi-mesures ne servent à rien
half-miler *n (runner)* coureur(euse) *m,f* de demi-mile
half-monthly *adj* semi-mensuel
half-moon *n* demi-lune *f*; *(on fingernail)* lunule *f*
half-mourning *n* demi-deuil *m*
half-naked *adj* à moitié nu
half-note *n Am Mus (minim)* blanche *f*
half-open 1 *adj (eyes, door, window)* entrouvert
2 *vt (eyes, door, window)* entrouvrir
half-pay *n* demi-salaire *m*; *(in civil service)* demi-traitement *m*; *Mil* demi-solde *f*; **to be on half-pay** toucher un demi-salaire *ou* un demi-traitement; *Mil* toucher une demi-solde
halfpenny ['heɪpnɪ] (*pl* **halfpennies**) *Br Old-fashioned* **1** *n* demi-penny *m*; **he's down to his last halfpenny** il ne lui reste que quelques sous
2 *comp* d'un demi-penny
halfpennyworth ['heɪpəθ] *n Br Old-fashioned* **a halfpennyworth of ice cream** ≃ un sou de glace
half-pint *n* (**a**) *(measurement)* ≃ quart *m* de litre; **I'll just have a half-pint** *(of beer)* je prendrai juste un demi (**b**) *Fam (small person)* demi-portion *f*
►► ***half-pint glass*** ≃ verre *m* de 25 cl
half-price 1 *n* demi-tarif *m*; **reduced to half-price** réduit de moitié; **these goods are going at half-price** ces produits sont vendus à moitié prix
2 *adj (goods)* à moitié prix; *(ticket)* (à) demi-tarif
3 *adv* **children get in half-price** les enfants payent demi-tarif; **I got it half-price** *(purchase)* je l'ai eu à moitié prix
half-rest *n Am Mus* demi-pause *f*
half-seas over *adj Fam Old-fashioned (drunk)* pompette, rond
half-shaft *n* demi-arbre *m*
half-shut *adj (eyes, door, window)* mi-clos, à moitié fermé; *Scot Fam* **to go about like a half-shut knife** être comme un zombie
half-sister *n* demi-sœur *f*
half-size 1 *adj (model)* réduit de moitié
2 *n (in shoes)* demi-pointure *f*; *(in clothing)* demi-taille *f*
half-sole *n (of shoe)* demi-semelle *f*
half-staff *n Am* **at half-staff** *(flag)* en berne
half-starved *adj* à moitié mort de faim, affamé
half-term *adj Br Sch* **half-term holiday** petites vacances *fpl*
half-tide *n Naut* mi-marée *f*
►► ***half-tide basin*** bassin *m* de *ou* accessible à mi-marée
half-timbered *adj Archit & Constr (house)* à colombages, à pans de bois
half-time 1 *n* (**a**) *Sport* mi-temps *f inv*; **at half-time** à la mi-temps; **that's the whistle for half-time** on siffle la mi-temps (**b**) *(in work)* mi-temps *m inv*; **to put sb on half-time** mettre qn à mi-temps; **to be on half-time** être *ou* travailler à mi-temps
2 *comp Sport (whistle)* de la mi-temps; *(score)* à la mi-temps
half-title *n Typ* faux-titre *m*
halftone ['hɑːftəʊn] *n* (**a**) *Phot (process)* similigravure *f* (**b**) *Art & Comput* demi-teinte *f* (**c**) *Am Mus* demi-ton *m*
half-track *n (vehicle)* half-track *m*
half-truth *n* demi-vérité *f*
half-volley *Sport* **1** *n (in tennis)* demi-volée *f*
2 *vt (in tennis)* **he half-volleyed the ball to the baseline** d'une demi-volée, il a envoyé la balle sur la ligne de fond
3 *vi (in tennis)* faire une demi-volée
halfway [hɑːf'weɪ] **1** *adv* (**a**) *(between two places)* à mi-chemin; **it's halfway between Rennes and Cherbourg** c'est à mi-chemin entre Rennes et Cherbourg; **we had got halfway to Manchester** nous étions arrivés à mi-chemin de Manchester; **they have now travelled halfway to the moon** ils sont maintenant à mi-chemin de leur voyage vers la lune; **we had climbed halfway up the mountain** nous avions escaladé la moitié de la montagne; **we had got halfway down the mountain** nous avions descendu la moitié de la montagne; **the path stops halfway up** le chemin s'arrête à mi-côte; **there's a blockage halfway up the pipe** il y a un bouchon à mi-hauteur du tuyau; **the ivy reaches halfway up the wall** le lierre monte jusqu'à la moitié du mur; **her hair hangs halfway down her back** ses cheveux lui arrivent jusqu'au milieu du dos; **he kicked the ball halfway into the French half** il a shooté dans le ballon et l'a envoyé à la moitié du camp français; **I've got halfway through chapter 6** je suis arrivé à la moitié du chapitre 6; **halfway through the programme/film** à la moitié de l'émission/du film; **to meet sb halfway** retrouver qn à mi-chemin; *Fig* couper la poire en deux, faire un compromis; *Fig* **I'm willing to meet you halfway** je veux bien couper la poire en deux, je suis prêt à t'accorder un compromis; **we're almost halfway there** *(in travelling, walking etc)* nous sommes presque à mi-chemin, nous avons fait presque la moitié du chemin; *(in work, negotiations)* nous sommes presque à mi-chemin; **this will go halfway towards covering the costs** cela couvrira la moitié des dépenses; **it's halfway between an alsatian and a collie** c'est (à mi-chemin) entre le berger allemand et le colley
(**b**) *Fam (more or less)* **a halfway decent salary** un salaire à peu près décent; **don't you have something halfway presentable to wear?** tu n'as rien d'à peu près présentable à porter?
2 *adj* **work has reached the halfway stage** le travail est à mi-chemin; **at the halfway point of his career** au milieu de sa carrière; **they're at the halfway mark** *(in race)* ils sont à mi-course
►► ***halfway house*** *(on journey)* (auberge *f*) relais *m*; *(for rehabilitation)* centre *m* de réadaptation *(pour anciens détenus, malades mentaux, drogués etc)*; *Fig (halfway stage)* (stade *m* de) transition *f*; *(compromise)* compromis *m*; *Sport* ***halfway line*** ligne *f* médiane
halfwit ['hɑːfwɪt] *n Fam* imbécile ᵒ *mf*; **some halfwit has parked right in front of the gate** il y a un imbécile qui s'est garé juste devant la grille; **only a halfwit would do something like that** il faut être débile pour faire un truc comme ça
halfwitted [ˌhɑːf'wɪtɪd] *adj Fam (person)* faible *ou* simple d'esprit; *(idea, suggestion, behaviour)* idiot; **sometimes I think he's halfwitted** parfois je le trouve débile
halfwittedly [ˌhɑːf'wɪtɪdlɪ] *adv (say)* bêtement
half-yearly 1 *adj* semestriel
2 *adv* tous les six mois
halibut ['hælɪbət] *n Ich* flétan *m*
halite ['hælaɪt] *n Miner* halite *f*, sel *m* gemme
halitosis [ˌhælɪ'təʊsɪs] *n (UNCOUNT)* mauvaise haleine *f*, *Spéc* halitose *f*
hall [hɔːl] *n* (**a**) *(of house)* entrée *f*, vestibule *m*; *(of hotel, very large house)* hall *m*; *Am (corridor)* couloir *m*; **the hall carpet** le tapis dans l'entrée; **he left the hall light on** il a laissé la lumière allumée dans l'entrée
(**b**) *(large room)* salle *f*; **dining hall** *Sch & Univ* réfectoire *m*; *(of stately home)* salle *f* à manger; *Br Univ* **to eat in hall** manger à la cantine *ou* au restaurant universitaire; **prayers were held in hall every morning** toute l'école se réunissait chaque matin dans la grande salle pour prier
(**c**) *Br Univ* **I'm living in hall** je loge à l'université
(**d**) *(mansion, large country house)* château *m*, manoir *m*; **she works up at the hall** elle travaille au château *ou* au manoir; **Fotheringham Hall** le château *ou* le manoir de Fotheringham
►► ***hall of fame*** *(group of famous people)* panthéon *m*; *(building)* musée *m*; **he's in the baseball hall of fame** il fait partie du panthéon de l'histoire du baseball; **his name will go down in the hall of fame** son nom entrera au panthéon; *Am Sport* ***hall of famer*** = personne qui fait partie du panthéon de l'histoire d'un sport; *Am Fig* ***halls of ivy*** le monde universitaire; ***hall porter*** *(in hotel)* portier *m*; *Br Univ* ***hall of residence*** résidence *f* universitaire; *Am* ***hall tree*** portemanteau *m*
halleluiah, hallelujah [ˌhælɪ'luːjə] **1** *exclam* alléluia
2 *n* alléluia *m*
►► *Mus* ***the Hallelujah Chorus*** l'Alléluia
Halley's comet ['hælɪz-] *n Astron* la comète de Halley
halliard = **halyard**
hallmark ['hɔːlmɑːk] **1** *n* (**a**) *(on precious metals)* poinçon *m* (**b**) *Fig* marque *f*; **it carries his hallmark** cela porte sa marque; **the hallmark of a creative mind** la marque *ou* le sceau d'un esprit créatif; **to have the hallmark of genius** porter la marque *ou* le sceau du génie; **the hallmark of any good author** ce qui caractérise tout bon auteur
2 *vt (precious metals)* poinçonner
hallo = **hello**
halloo [hə'luː] (*pl* **halloos**, *pt & pp* **hallooed**, *cont* **hallooing**) *Hunt* **1** *n* taïaut *m*, tayaut *m*
2 *exclam* taïaut!, tayaut!
3 *vi* crier taïaut *ou* tayaut

halloumi [hæ'lu:mɪ] *n Culin* halloumi *m*, haloumi *m*

hallow ['hæləʊ] *vt Formal* sanctifier, consacrer; **hallowed be Thy name** que Ton nom soit sanctifié

hallowed ['hæləʊd] *adj* saint, béni

►► *Rel* ***hallowed ground*** terre *f* sainte *ou* bénie; *Fig* lieu *m* de culte

Hallowe'en [ˌhæləʊ'i:n] *n* = veille de la Toussaint

HALLOWE'EN

Il s'agit d'une fête d'origine païenne célébrée dans les pays anglo-saxons la veille de la Toussaint, à l'époque de l'année où les morts étaient censés rendre visite aux vivants. Aujourd'hui la tradition demeure: on évide des citrouilles pour les transformer en lanternes en forme de crâne, et les enfants vont de maison en maison déguisés en sorcières ou en fantômes. De nos jours, la coutume britannique a adopté la tradition américaine de "trick or treat", consistant pour les enfants à demander un petit cadeau aux habitants des maisons visitées et à les menacer d'un mauvais tour s'ils refusent.

hallstand ['hɔ:lstænd] *n* portemanteau *m*

hallucinate [hə'lu:sɪneɪt] *vi* avoir des hallucinations; **it made her hallucinate** cela lui a donné des hallucinations; **I must be hallucinating!** je dois avoir des hallucinations!

hallucination [ˌhəlu:sɪ'neɪʃən] *n* hallucination *f*

hallucinatory [hə'lu:sɪnətrɪ] *adj* hallucinatoire

hallucinogen [hə'lu:sɪnəˌdʒen] *n* hallucinogène *m*

hallucinogenic [həˌlu:sɪnə'dʒenɪk] *adj* hallucinogène

hallucinosis [həˌlu:sɪ'nəʊsɪs] *n Psy* hallucinose *f*

hallway ['hɔ:lweɪ] *n (of house)* vestibule *m*, entrée *f*; *(corridor)* couloir *m*

halo ['heɪləʊ] *(pl* **halos** *or* **haloes***)* *n* (**a**) *(of saint, angel)* auréole *f*, nimbe *m*; *Hum* **her halo never slips** c'est un modèle de vertu (**b**) *Astron, Opt & Phot* halo *m*

►► *Mktg* ***halo effect*** effet *m* de halo

halocarbon [hæləʊ'kɑ:bən] *n Chem* hydrocarbure *m* halogéné

haloed ['heɪləʊd] *adj* auréolé, nimbé

halogen ['hælədʒen] *n Chem* halogène *m*

►► ***halogen headlights, halogen lamps*** phares *mpl*/lampes *fpl* à halogène; ***halogen ring*** *(on cooker)* foyer *m* halogène

halogenate ['hælədʒəneɪt] *vt Chem* halogéner

halogenation [ˌhælədʒə'neɪʃən] *n Chem* halogénation *f*

halogenous [hæ'lɒdʒənəs] *adj Chem* (composé *m*) halogène *m*

halography [hæ'lɒgrəfɪ] *n Chem* halographie *f*

haloid ['hælɔɪd] *n Chem* halogénure *m*

halology [hæ'lɒlədʒɪ] *n Chem* halochimie *f*

halometer [hæ'lɒmɪtə(r)] *n Chem* halomètre *m*

halometry [hæ'lɒmɪtrɪ] *n Chem* halométrie *f*

halon ['hælɒn] *n Chem* halon *m*

halophilous [hə'lɒfɪləs] *adj Bot* halophile

halophyte ['hæləʊˌfaɪt] *n Bot* halophyte *f*

[illegible]

halt [hɔ:lt] **1** *n* (**a**) *(stop)* halte *f*; **to bring to a halt** *(vehicle)* arrêter, immobiliser; *(horse)* arrêter; *(production, project)* interrompre; **the strike has brought production to a complete halt** la grève a complètement interrompu la production; **to call a halt to sth** mettre fin à qch; **let's call a halt for today** arrêtons-nous pour aujourd'hui; **to come to a halt** *(vehicle, horse)* s'arrêter, s'immobiliser; *(in a speech)* rester sans rien dire; **the project has come to a halt** *(temporarily)* le projet s'est interrompu; *(for good)* le projet s'est définitivement arrêté; **until the aircraft comes to a complete halt** jusqu'à l'arrêt complet de l'appareil; **this decline in education standards must come to a halt** cette baisse des niveaux scolaires doit cesser

(**b**) *Br (small railway station)* halte *f*

2 *npl Bible* **the halt and the lame** les estropiés *mpl*

3 *vi* (**a**) *(stop)* s'arrêter; *Mil* **halt!(, who goes there?)** halte! (, qui va là?)

(**b**) *Arch (limp)* boiter; *Fig (style, writing, verse)* être boiteux; **to halt between two opinions** hésiter *ou* balancer entre deux opinions

4 *vt* arrêter; *(troops)* faire faire halte à, stopper; *(production → temporarily)* interrompre, arrêter; *(→ for good)* arrêter définitivement

►► *Aut* ***halt sign*** stop *m*

halter ['hɔ:ltə(r)] *n* (**a**) *(for horse)* licou *m*, collier *m* (**b**) *(on women's clothing)* bain *m* de soleil; **a dress with a halter neck** une robe dos nu *ou* bain de soleil (**c**) *Arch (noose)* corde *f* (de pendaison)

►► ***halter top*** bain *m* de soleil

halter-neck *adj (dress, top)* dos nu, bain de soleil

halting ['hɔ:ltɪŋ] *adj (verse, style)* boiteux, heurté; *(voice, step, progress)* hésitant; *(growth)* discontinu

haltingly ['hɔ:ltɪŋlɪ] *adv (say, speak)* de façon hésitante

halva ['hælvə] *n Culin* halva *m*

halve [*Br* hɑ:v, *Am* hæv] *vt* (**a**) *(separate in two)* couper *ou* diviser en deux (**b**) *(share)* partager en deux (**c**) *(reduce by half)* réduire *ou* diminuer de moitié

halves [*Br* hɑ:vz, *Am* hævz] *pl of* **half**

halyard ['hæljəd] *n Naut* drisse *f*

Ham [hæm] *pr n Bible* Cham

ham [hæm] *(pt & pp* **hammed**, *cont* **hamming***)* **1** *n* (**a**) *(meat)* jambon *m*; **a ham** un jambon; **ham and eggs** œufs *mpl* au jambon; **ham sandwich** sandwich *m* au jambon

(**b**) *Fam (radio operator)* radioamateur □ *m*

(**c**) *Fam (actor)* cabot □ *m*, cabotin(e) □ *m,f*

(**d**) *(of leg)* cuisse *f*

2 *vt* **he hams all his parts** il charge tous ses rôles

3 *vi Fam* en faire trop

►► *Fam* ***ham acting*** cabotinage □ *m*; *Fam* ***ham actor*** cabot □ *m*, cabotin(e) □ *m,f*; *Fam* ***ham licence*** permis *m* de radioamateur □

►**ham up** *vt sep Fam* **to ham it up** en faire trop

Hamburg ['hæmbɜ:g] *n* Hambourg

hamburger ['hæmbɜ:gə(r)] *n (beefburger)* hamburger *m*; *Am (minced beef)* viande *f* hachée

►► ***hamburger relish*** condiments *mpl* pour hamburgers; ***Hamburger University*** = centre mondial de formation du personnel de la société McDonald's, situé dans la banlieue de Chicago

hames [heɪmz] *n Ir Fam* **to make a hames of sth** *(essay, speech, task)* rater qch

ham-fisted [-'fɪstɪd], **ham-handed** [-'hændɪd] *adj (person)* empoté, maladroit; *(behaviour)* maladroit

Hamitic [hæ'mɪtɪk] *adj* chamitique

hamlet ['hæmlɪt] *n (small village)* hameau *m*

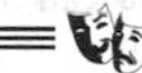

'Hamlet' *Shakespeare* 'Hamlet'

hammer ['hæmə(r)] **1** *n* (**a**) *(tool)* marteau *m*; *Sport* **the hammer** le marteau; **the hammer and sickle** *(flag)* la faucille et le marteau; **to come** *or* **to go under the hammer** *(at auction)* être mis aux enchères; **to be** *or* **to go at it hammer and tongs** *(argue)* se disputer comme des chiffonniers; *(in work, match)* mettre le paquet, ne pas y aller de main morte; *Am Fam Aut* **to let the hammer down** appuyer sur le champignon, mettre les gaz

(**b**) *(of piano)* marteau *m*; *(of firearm)* chien *m*

(**c**) *Anat (in ear)* marteau *m*

2 *vt* (**a**) *(nail, spike etc)* enfoncer au marteau; *(metal)* marteler; **to hammer a nail into sth** enfoncer un clou dans qch; **to hammer sth flat/straight** aplatir/redresser qch à coups de marteau; **to hammer home** *(nail)* enfoncer à fond au marteau; *Fig (point of view)* insister lourdement sur; **she hammered it home with the heel of her shoe** elle l'a enfoncé avec le talon de sa chaussure; **I had it hammered into me that I mustn't do that type of thing** on m'a enfoncé dans la tête que je ne devais pas faire ce genre de choses; **they're always hammering it into us that...** ils nous rabâchent sans arrêt que...; **to hammer an agreement into shape** réussir à mettre un accord au point

(**b**) *Fam Fig (beat up)* tabasser

(**c**) *Fam Fig (defeat)* battre à plate couture(s), écraser

(**d**) *Fam Fig (criticize)* descendre en flammes, massacrer

3 *vi* (**a**) *(hit with hammer)* frapper *ou* taper au marteau; *Fig (heart)* battre fort; **to hammer on the table** *(with fist)* taper du poing sur la table; **to hammer at the door** tambouriner à la porte; **the rain hammered at the window** la pluie tambourinait contre la fenêtre

(**b**) *Fam (go fast, drive fast)* foncer, aller à fond de train; **he came hammering round the final bend** il a débouché à fond de train du dernier virage; **the French champion was really hammering along the track when he tripped** le champion français était en pleine vitesse quand il a trébuché

4 Hammers *npl* **the Hammers** = surnom donné à l'équipe de football anglais West Ham

►► *Br* ***hammer drill*** perceuse *f* à percussion; ***Hammer Horror film*** = film d'horreur produit en Grande-Bretagne dans les années 50 et 60

►**hammer away** *vi (with hammer)* donner des coups de marteau; **to hammer away at sth** taper sur qch avec un marteau, donner des coups de marteau sur qch; *Fig (at agreement, contract)* travailler avec acharnement à la mise au point de qch; *(problem)* travailler avec acharnement à la solution de qch; **he hammered away at the door** *(with fists)* il a tambouriné à la porte; **to hammer away at the piano/on the typewriter** marteler le piano/la machine à écrire

►**hammer down** *vt sep (nail, spike)* enfoncer (au marteau); *(door)* défoncer

►**hammer in** *vt sep (nail, spike)* enfoncer (au marteau); *Fig* **it's no good telling him just once, you'll have to hammer it in** le lui dire une bonne fois ne suffira pas, il faudra le lui répéter sans cesse

►**hammer out** *vt sep (dent)* aplatir au marteau; *Fig (solution, agreement)* mettre au point, élaborer; *(tune, rhythm)* marteler; **unions and management hammered out an agreement** les syndicats et le patronat sont finalement parvenus à un accord

hammerbeam ['hæməˌbi:m] *n Br Archit* blochet *m* à mi-bois; **hammerbeam roof** charpente *f* à blochets

hammered ['hæməd] *adj* (**a**) *Fam (drunk)* bourré, beurré, pété (**b**) *St Exch (stockbroker)* déclaré insolvable

hammerhead ['hæməhed] *n* (**a**) *Ich* **hammerhead (shark)** requin-marteau *m* (**b**) *Orn* ombrette *f* (du Sénégal)

hammering ['hæmərɪŋ] *n* (**a**) *(noise)* martèlement *m*; *Fig (of heart)* battement *m*; *(of rain)* tambourinement *m*

(**b**) *Fam Fig (beating)* volée *f* de coups; **to give sb a hammering** tabasser qn; **to get a hammering** se faire tabasser

(**c**) *Fam Fig (defeat)* branlée *f*, pâtée *f*; **to give sb a hammering** battre qn à plates coutures; **to get a hammering** être battu à plates coutures

(**d**) *Fam Fig (criticism)* **to give sb/sth a hammering** éreinter *ou* démolir qn/qch; **to get a hammering** se faire éreinter *ou* démolir

(**e**) *St Exch (of stockbroker)* déclaration *f* d'insolvabilité

hammerlock ['hæməlɒk] *n (in wrestling)* retournement *m* de bras; **to get sb in a hammerlock** faire une clé de bras à qn

hammertoe ['hæmətəʊ] *n* orteil *m* en marteau

hammock ['hæmək] *n* hamac *m*

hammy ['hæmɪ] *(compar* **hammier**, *superl* **hammiest***)* *adj Fam (acting, performance)* de cabot □, exagéré □; **hammy actor** cabot □ *m*, cabotin(e) □ *m,f*

Hampden Park ['hæmdən-] *n* = stade de football de la fédération écossaise de football, à Glasgow, où ont lieu les rencontres les plus importantes

hamper[1] ['hæmpə(r)] *vt (impede → work, movements, person)* gêner; *(→ project)* gêner la réalisation de, entraver; **high winds hampered the rescue work** les sauveteurs ont été gênés dans leur travail par la force des vents

hamper[2] *n (for picnic)* panier *m*; *(for laundry)* panier *m* à linge sale; **a Christmas hamper** un panier de friandises de Noël

Hampshire ['hæmpˌʃɪə(r)] *n* le Hampshire, =

comté du sud de l'Angleterre; **in Hampshire** dans le Hampshire

Hampstead ['hæmpstɪd] *n* = quartier chic du nord de Londres

hamster ['hæmstə(r)] *n* hamster *m*

►► ***hamster cage*** cage *f* pour *ou* à hamster

hamstring ['hæmstrɪŋ] (*pt & pp* **hamstrung** [-strʌŋ]) **1** *n* tendon *m* du jarret; **to pull a hamstring** se claquer le tendon du jarret

2 *vt (cripple → animal, person)* couper le(s) jarret(s) à; *Fig* handicaper; **the project is hamstrung** le projet est bloqué; **we are hamstrung** nous sommes bloqués

HAND [hænd]

main	► **1 (a) – (c), (g)**
aiguille	► **1 (h)**
écriture	► **1 (i)**
paume	► **1 (j)**
ouvrier	► **1 (k)**
passer	► **2**
donner	► **2**

1 *n* (**a**) *(of person)* main *f*; **to hold sb's hand** tenir la main de qn; **I held her hand** je lui ai tenu la main; *Fig* **she's asked me to go along and hold her hand** elle m'a demandé de l'accompagner pour lui donner du courage; **to hold hands** se tenir par la main; **to take sb's hand, to take sb by the hand** prendre qn par la main, prendre la main de qn; **to lead sb by the hand** conduire qn par la main; **he writes with his left hand** il écrit de la main gauche; **to put one's hands over one's eyes** se couvrir les yeux de ses mains; **to be on one's hands and knees** être à quatre pattes; *Fig* **to go down on one's hands and knees** se mettre à genoux *ou* à plat ventre; **to be good with one's hands** être adroit de ses mains; **my hands are full** j'ai les mains occupées *ou* prises; *Fig* **to have one's hands full** avoir beaucoup à faire, avoir du pain sur la planche; **I've got my hands full trying to cope as it is** j'ai déjà assez à faire comme ça; **to lay one's hands on sth** *(find)* mettre la main sur qch; **to get** *or* **to lay one's hands on sth** *(obtain)* dénicher qch; **to lay hands on sb** faire violence à qn; *Fig* **just wait till I get** *or* **lay my hands on her!** attends un peu que je l'attrape!; **to lift** *or* **to raise a hand to sb** lever la main sur qn; *Fig* **he never lifts a hand to help** il ne lève jamais le petit doigt pour aider; **hands off!** bas les pattes!, pas touche!; **hands off the unions/education system!** pas touche aux syndicats/au système éducatif!; **he can't keep his hands to himself** il a la main baladeuse; **I only have one pair of hands!** je n'ai que deux mains!; **look – no hands!** *(cyclist)* sans les mains!; **take your hands off me!** ne me touche pas!; **(put your) hands up!** les mains en l'air!, haut les mains!; *Sch* **hands up anyone who knows the answer** que ceux qui connaissent la réponse lèvent le doigt *ou* la main; **hands up all those who agree** que ceux qui sont d'accord lèvent la main; **to tie sb's hands** attacher les mains de qn; **they tied my hands behind my back** ils m'ont lié *ou* attaché les mains dans le dos; **I could do it with one hand tied behind my back** je pourrais le faire sans aucun effort *ou* les doigts dans le nez; *Fig* **my hands are tied** j'ai les mains liées; *Fig* **to sit on one's hands** *(applaud half-heartedly)* applaudir sans enthousiasme; *(do nothing)* ne rien faire; **to ask for sb's hand in marriage** demander la main de qn, demander qn en mariage; **at hand, near** *or* **close at hand** *(about to happen)* proche; *(nearby)* à proximité; **the hour is at hand** l'heure est proche; **to suffer at the hands of sb** souffrir aux mains *ou* dans les mains de qn; **to pass sth from hand to hand** faire passer qch de mains en mains; **hand in hand** la main dans la main; *Fig* **to go hand in hand (with sth)** aller de pair (avec qch); **to be hand in glove with sb** travailler en étroite collaboration avec qn; **to make money hand over fist** gagner un argent fou; *Br Fam* **she doesn't do a hand's turn** elle n'en fiche pas une; **to live from hand to mouth** tirer le diable par la queue; *Fig* **to win hands down** gagner haut la main; **to beat sb hands down** battre qn à plates couture(s); *Prov* **many hands make light work** = à beaucoup d'ouvriers la tâche devient aisée; **on the one hand... but on the other hand...** *(used in the same sentence)* d'un côté... mais de l'autre...; **on the other hand** *(when beginning new sentence)* d'un autre côté

(**b**) *(assistance)* **to give sb a hand (with sth)** donner un coup de main à qn; **to lend a hand** mettre la main à la pâte; **do you need a hand (with that)?** as-tu besoin d'un coup de main?

(**c**) *(control, management)* **to need a firm hand** avoir besoin d'être sérieusement pris en main; **to rule with a firm hand** diriger avec de la poigne; **to take sb/sth in hand** prendre qn/qch en main; **to be out of hand** *(dog, child)* ne rien écouter; **to get out of hand** *(dog, child)* devenir indocile; *(meeting, situation)* échapper à tout contrôle; **the garden is getting out of hand** le jardin à l'air d'une vraie jungle; **to change hands** *(company, restaurant etc)* changer de propriétaire; **it's out of my hands** cela ne m'appartient plus, ce n'est plus ma responsabilité *ou* de mon ressort; **the matter is in the hands of the headmaster** la question relève maintenant *ou* est maintenant du ressort du principal; **I have put the matter in the hands of a lawyer** j'ai confié l'affaire à un avocat; **the answer lies in your own hands** la solution est entre tes mains; **to have too much time on one's hands** avoir trop de temps à soi; **to have sb/sth on one's hands** avoir qn/qch sur les bras; **now that that's off my hands** à présent que je suis débarrassé de cela; **it's out of my hands** je ne peux (plus) rien y faire; **to fall into the hands of the enemy** tomber entre les mains de l'ennemi; **to fall into the wrong hands** *(information, secret etc)* tomber en de mauvaises mains; **in the wrong hands this knowledge could be very dangerous** si elles tombaient aux mains de personnes malintentionnées, ces connaissances pourraient être très dangereuses; **in the right hands** en de bonnes mains; **to be in good** *or* **safe hands** être en de bonnes mains; **can I leave this in your hands?** puis-je te demander de t'en occuper?; **it leaves too much power in the hands of the police** cela laisse trop de pouvoir à la police; **to give sb a free hand** donner carte blanche à qn; **to take matters into one's own hands** prendre les choses en main

(**d**) *(applause)* **to give sb a (big) hand** applaudir qn (bien fort)

(**e**) *(influence, involvement)* **to have a hand in sth** avoir quelque chose à voir dans qch, être impliqué dans qch; **I had no hand in it** je n'avais rien à voir là-dedans, je n'y étais pour rien; **I see** *or* **detect your hand in this** j'y vois ta marque

(**f**) *(skill, ability)* **to have a light hand with pastry** réussir une pâte légère; **she can turn her hand to anything** elle peut tout faire; **to keep one's hand in** garder la main; **I was never much of a hand at it** je n'ai jamais été très doué pour cela; **to try one's hand at sth** s'essayer à qch

(**g**) *(in cards → cards held)* main *f*, jeu *m*; *(→ round, game)* partie *f*; *(→ player)* joueur(euse) *m,f*; **to have a good hand** avoir du jeu; **first/fourth hand** *(player)* premie(ère) *m,f*/dernier(ère) *m,f* en cartes; *Fig* **to show** *or* **to reveal one's hand** dévoiler son jeu; *Fig* **to throw in one's hand** jeter l'éponge

(**h**) *(of clock, watch)* aiguille *f*; *(of signpost, barometer)* indicateur *m*; **the little hand is pointing to three** la petite aiguille est sur le trois

(**i**) *(handwriting)* écriture *f*; **to have a good hand** avoir une belle écriture

(**j**) *(measurement of horse)* paume *f*; **a horse fifteen hands high** un cheval de quinze paumes

(**k**) *(worker)* ouvrier(ère) *m,f*; *(on ship)* homme *m*, membre *m* de l'équipage; **the ship was lost with all hands** le navire a sombré corps et biens; **old hand** expert *m*, vieux *m* de la vieille; **to be an old hand at sth** avoir une vaste expérience de qch; *also Fig* **all hands to the pump** tout le monde à la rescousse

(**l**) *(of bananas)* régime *m*; **hand of pork** jambonneau *m*

2 *vt* passer, donner; **to hand sth to sb, to hand sb sth** passer *ou* donner qch à qn; **to hand sb a letter/telegram** remettre une lettre/un télégramme à qn; *Fig* **to hand sth to sb on a plate** apporter à qn qch sur un plateau; **you've got to hand it to him** chapeau!; *Fig* **you have to hand it to her, she IS a good mother** c'est une bonne mère, il faut lui accorder cela

3 by hand *adv (written)* à la main; *(made, knitted, sewn)* (à la) main; **to wash sth by hand** laver qch à la main; **to send sth by hand** faire porter qch; **by hand** *(written on envelope)* en ville; **to rear an animal by hand** élever un animal au biberon

4 in hand *adv* (**a**) *(available → money)* disponible; *(→ time)* devant soi; *Br* **do we have any time in hand?** avons-nous du temps devant nous?

(**b**) *(being dealt with)* en cours; **the matter is in hand** on s'occupe de l'affaire; **I have the situation well in hand** j'ai la situation bien en main; **to return to the matter in hand** revenir à ses moutons; **keep your mind on the job in hand** concentre-toi sur l'affaire en cours

5 on hand *adj (person)* disponible

6 out of hand *adv (immediately)* sur-le-champ

7 to hand *adv (letter, information etc)* sous la main; **use what comes to hand** prends ce que tu as sous la main; **he took the first one that came to hand** il a pris le premier qui lui est tombé sous la main; **the first excuse to hand** le premier prétexte venu

►► ***hand baggage*** *(UNCOUNT)* bagages *mpl* à main; ***hand controls*** commandes *fpl* manuelles; ***hand cream*** crème *f* pour les mains; ***hand grenade*** grenade *f* à main; ***hand lotion*** lotion *f* pour les mains; ***hand luggage*** *(UNCOUNT)* bagages *mpl* à main; ***hand microphone*** micro *m* portatif; *Theat* ***hand puppet*** marionnette *f*; ***hand signal*** signal *m* de la main; **hand signals only** *(on vehicle)* = indique que les clignotants d'un véhicule ne fonctionnent pas; ***hand towel*** serviette *f*, essuie-mains *m inv*

►**hand around** *vt sep (distribute)* distribuer

►**hand back** *vt sep (return)* rapporter, rendre; **she handed me back the bottle** elle m'a repassé la bouteille; *Rad & TV* **I now hand you back to the studio/Jon Snow** je rends maintenant l'antenne au studio/à Jon Snow

►**hand down** *vt sep* (**a**) *(pass, give from high place)* passer, donner; **hand me down the hammer** passe-moi *ou* donne-moi le marteau (qui est là-haut)

(**b**) *(heirloom, story)* transmettre; **the necklace/property has been handed down from mother to daughter for six generations** le collier est transmis/la propriété est transmise de mère en fille depuis six générations; **all her clothes had been handed down from her older sisters** tous ses vêtements venaient de ses sœurs aînées

(**c**) *Law (decision, sentence)* annoncer; *(judgment)* rendre; *Am* **to hand down the budget** annoncer le budget

►**hand in** *vt sep (return, surrender → book)* rendre; *(→ ticket)* remettre; *(→ exam paper)* rendre, remettre; *(something found → to authorities, police etc)* déposer, remettre; **to hand in one's resignation** donner ou remettre sa démission, demissioner

►**hand off** *vt sep (in rugby)* raffûter

►**hand on** *vt sep* (**a**) *(give to someone else)* passer; **to hand sth on to sb** passer qch à qn

(**b**) = **hand down** (**b**)

►**hand out** *vt sep (distribute)* distribuer; **we hand out 200 free meals a day** nous servons 200 repas gratuits par jour; **he's very good at handing out advice** il est très fort pour ce qui est de distribuer des conseils; **he's fond of handing it out, but can't take it** *(criticism)* il se permet de critiquer les autres mais il déteste qu'on le critique; **the French boxer handed out a lot of punishment** le boxeur français a frappé à coups redoublés

►**hand over 1** *vt sep* (**a**) *(pass, give → object)* passer, donner; *Rad & TV* **we now hand you over to the weather man/Bill Smith in Moscow** nous passons maintenant l'antenne à notre météorologue/Bill Smith à Moscou; *Tel* **I'm handing him over now** je te le passe tout de suite

(**b**) *(surrender → weapons, hostage)* remettre; *(→ criminal)* livrer; *(→ power, authority)* transmettre; *Law (→ property)* céder; **he was handed over to the French police** il a été livré à la *ou* aux mains de la police française; **hand it over!** donne!

2 *vi* **to hand over to** *(government minister, chairman etc)* passer le pouvoir à; *(in meeting)* donner la parole à; *Tel* passer *ou* donner le combiné à

▸**hand round** *vt sep (distribute)* distribuer

▸**hand up** *vt sep (pass, give from low place)* passer, donner; **hand me up the hammer** passe-moi *ou* donne-moi le marteau (qui est là en bas)

---

hand- [hænd] *pref* (à la) main; **hand-stitched** cousu main; **hand-knitted** tricoté à la main

handbag ['hændbæg] **1** *n* (**a**) *(bag)* sac *m* à main (**b**) *Mus (music)* = type de house influencée par la pop commerciale

2 *vt Br Fam (attack verbally)* **she handbagged him** elle l'a violemment attaqué ❑

▸▸ ***handbag music*** = type de house influencée par la pop commerciale

handball ['hændbɔːl] *n* (**a**) *(team game)* handball *m* (**b**) *(pelota)* pelote *f* (basque) (**c**) *Ftbl (foul)* main *f*

handbasin ['hændbeɪsən] *n Br* lavabo *m*

handbell ['hændbel] *n* clochette *f*

handbill ['hændbɪl] *n Br* prospectus *m*

handbook ['hændbʊk] *n (for car, machine)* guide *m*, manuel *m*; *(for tourist's use)* guide *m*

handbrake ['hændbreɪk] *n Br Aut* frein *m* à main; **to put the handbrake on** mettre le frein à main

▸▸ ***handbrake turn*** demi-tour *m* au frein à main

h & c (*written abbr* **hot and cold**) eau *f* courante chaude et froide

handcart ['hændkɑːt] *n* charrette *f* à bras

handclap ['hændklæp] *n Br* **to get the slow handclap** *(performer)* ≃ se faire siffler; *Br* **to give sb the slow handclap** ≃ siffler qn

handclasp ['hændklɑːsp] *n Am* poignée *f* de main

hand-controlled *adj* commandé à la main

handcraft ['hændkrɑːft] *vt* fabriquer *ou* faire à la main

hand-crafted [-'krɑːftɪd] *adj* fabriqué *ou* fait à la main

handcuff ['hændkʌf] **1** *vt* passer les menottes à; **to handcuff sb to sb/sth** attacher qn à qn/qch avec des menottes; **he was handcuffed** il avait les menottes aux poignets

2 handcuffs *npl* menottes *fpl*; **to be in handcuffs** avoir les menottes (aux mains)

hand-drier *n* sèche-mains *m inv*

hand-drill *n* perceuse *f* à main

-handed ['hændɪd] *suff* **right-handed** droitier; **single-handed** tout seul; **empty-handed** les mains vides, bredouille; **two-handed sword** épée *f* (que l'on tient) à deux mains; **four-handed game of cards** jeu *m* de cartes pour quatre personnes; **one-handed catch** interception *f* à une main

Handel ['hændəl] *pr n* Haendel

-hander ['hændə(r)] *suff Theat* **two-/three-hander** *(play)* pièce *f* pour deux/trois personnes

handfeed [hænd'fiːd] (*pt & pp* **handfed** [-'fed]) **1** *n* (**a**) *Tech* alimentation *f* manuelle *ou* à la main; *(of tool)* avance *f* à la main (**b**) *Typ* marge *f* à main

2 *vt* nourrir à la main

handful ['hændfʊl] *n* (**a**) *(amount)* poignée *f*; *Fig* **a handful of** *(a few)* quelques; **a handful of people** quelques personnes; **how many people were there? – only a handful** combien de personnes y avait-il? – seulement quelques-unes

(**b**) *Fam (uncontrollable person)* **to be a handful** être difficile ❑; **that child is a real handful** cet enfant-là me donne du fil à retordre; **he's proving to be a real handful for the defence** il donne du fil à retordre à la défense adverse

'A Handful of Dust' *Waugh, Sturridge* 'Une Poignée de cendre' (book), 'A Handful of dust' (film)

---

handgrip ['hændgrɪp] *n* (**a**) *(on racket)* grip *m*; *(on bicycle)* poignée *f* (**b**) *(handshake)* poignée *f* de main (**c**) *(holdall)* fourre-tout *m inv*

handgun ['hændgʌn] *n Am* revolver *m*, pistolet *m*

hand-held 1 *adj (appliance)* à main; *(camera)* portatif

2 *n (computer)* hand-held *m*

▸▸ *Comput* ***hand-held computer*** ordinateur *m* de poche; *Comput* ***hand-held scanner*** scanner *m ou* scanneur *m* à main

handhold ['hændhəʊld] *n* prise *f* (de main)

handicap ['hændɪkæp] (*pt & pp* **handicapped**) **1** *n* (**a**) *(physical, mental)* handicap *m*; *Fig (disadvantage)* handicap *m*, désavantage *m*; **people with a (physical/mental) handicap** les gens qui souffrent d'un handicap (physique/mental); **do you find it a handicap being so small?** trouvez-vous que c'est un handicap *ou* un désavantage d'être aussi petit?

(**b**) *Sport* handicap *m*; **time/distance handicap** handicap *m* en temps/distance

2 *vt* (**a**) *Fig (disadvantage)* handicaper, désavantager; **they were always handicapped by a lack of money** ils ont toujours été handicapés par le manque d'argent

(**b**) *Sport* handicaper

handicapped ['hændɪkæpt] **1** *adj* handicapé; **to be mentally/physically handicapped** être handicapé(e) *m,f* mental(e)/physique; *Am* **handicapped parking** *(sign)* parking réservé aux handicapés

2 *npl* **the handicapped** les handicapés *mpl*

handicapper ['hændɪkæpə(r)] *n* (**a**) *(in horse racing)* handicapeur *m* (**b**) *(in golf)* **I'm a 10 handicapper** j'ai un handicap de 10

handicraft ['hændɪkrɑːft] *n* (**a**) *(items)* objets *mpl* artisanaux, artisanat *m* (**b**) *(skill)* artisanat *m*

handily ['hændɪlɪ] *adv* (**a**) *(conveniently)* de façon commode *ou* pratique; **the shop is handily situated only 100 metres from the house** le magasin n'est qu'à 100 mètres de la maison, ce qui est pratique *ou* commode; **they handily left their fingerprints** ils ont laissé leurs empreintes, ce qui était bien pratique (**b**) *Am (easily)* **to win handily** gagner haut la main

handiness ['hændɪnɪs] *n* (**a**) *(of tool etc)* commodité *f*; **the handiness of the house for the shops** l'emplacement très commode de la maison près des magasins (**b**) *(skill with hands)* adresse *f*, dextérité *f*

handing down *n (of tradition)* transmission *f*

handing over *n (of hostages, keys)* remise *f* (**to** aux mains de); *(of power)* transmission *f*; *Law (of property)* cession *f*

handiwork ['hændɪwɜːk] *n (UNCOUNT) (work)* travail *m* manuel; *(result)* œuvre *f*; **the graffiti is the handiwork of vandals** les graffiti sont l'œuvre de vandales; **this is YOUR handiwork, is it?** c'est toi qui as fait ça?

hand-job *n Vulg* **to give sb a hand-job** branler qn

handkerchief ['hæŋkətʃɪf] (*pl* **handkerchiefs** *or* **handkerchieves** [-tʃiːvz]) *n* mouchoir *m*

hand-knit 1 *n* pull *m/etc* tricoté à la main

2 *vt* tricoter à la main

hand-knitted *adj* tricoté main, tricoté à la main

HANDLE ['hændəl]

manche	▸ **1 (a)**
poignée	▸ **1 (a), (c)**
anse	▸ **1 (a)**
queue	▸ **1 (a)**
toucher à	▸ **2 (a)**
manœuvrer	▸ **2 (b)**
conduire	▸ **2 (b)**
manier	▸ **2 (b)**
traiter	▸ **2 (c), (d)**
s'occuper de	▸ **2 (d)**
répondre	▸ **3**

1 *n* (**a**) *(of broom, knife, screwdriver)* manche *m*; *(of suitcase, box, drawer, door)* poignée *f*; *(of cup)* anse *f*; *(of saucepan)* queue *f*; *(of stretcher)* bras *m*; *Br Fam* **to fly off the handle (at sb)** piquer une colère (contre qn)

(**b**) *Fam (name → of citizens' band user)* nom *m* de code ❑; *(→ which sounds impressive)* titre *m* de noblesse ❑

(**c**) *Comput* poignée *f*

(**d**) *Fam (idiom)* **to get a handle on sth** piger qch; **I'll get back to you once I've got a handle on the situation** je vous recontacterai quand j'aurai la situation en main; **the first thing to do is to get a handle on the export market** la première chose à faire est de nous familiariser avec le marché à l'exportation ❑

2 *vt* (**a**) *(touch)* toucher à, manipuler; **please do not handle the goods** *(sign)* ne pas toucher; **handle with care** *(on package)* ≃ fragile; **pesticides should be handled with caution** les pesticides doivent être manipulés avec précaution; **to handle the ball** *(in football)* faire une main

(**b**) *(operate → ship)* manœuvrer, gouverner; *(→ car)* conduire; *(→ gun)* se servir de, manier; *(→ words, numbers)* manier; **have you any experience of handling horses?** savez-vous vous y prendre avec les chevaux?

(**c**) *(cope with → crisis, problem)* traiter; *(→ situation)* faire face à; *(→ crowd, traffic, death)* supporter; **you handled that very well** tu as très bien réglé les choses; **I couldn't have handled it better myself** je n'aurais pas mieux fait; **he's good at handling people** il sait s'y prendre avec les gens; **I don't know how to handle her** je ne sais pas comment la prendre; **leave this to me, I'LL handle him** laisse-moi m'en occuper, je me charge de lui; **four babies are a lot for one person to handle** quatre bébés, cela fait beaucoup pour une seule personne; **do you think you can handle the job?** penses-tu être capable de faire le travail?; **I couldn't handle it if Dad died** si papa mourait, je ne le supporterais pas; **how is she handling it?** comment s'en sort-elle?; *Fam* **he can't handle his drink** il ne tient pas l'alcool; **it's nothing I can't handle** je me débrouille

(**d**) *(manage, process)* s'occuper de; *(address → topic, subject)* aborder, traiter; **she handles my tax for me** elle s'occupe de mes impôts; **we're too small to handle an order of that size** notre entreprise est trop petite pour traiter une commande de cette importance; **could you handle this task as well?** pourriez-vous également vous charger de ce travail?; **the airport handles two hundred planes a day** chaque jour deux cents avions passent par l'aéroport; **to handle stolen goods** receler des objets volés; **we don't handle chemical products** nous ne faisons pas de produits chimiques

3 *vi (car, ship)* répondre; **how does she handle?** *(car)* est-ce qu'elle répond bien?

---

handlebar ['hændəlbɑː(r)] *adj*

▸▸ ***handlebar moustache*** moustache *f* en guidon de vélo; ***handlebar tape*** Guidoline® *f*

handlebars ['hændəlbɑːz] *npl* guidon *m*; **she went right over the handlebars** elle est passée par-dessus le guidon

-handled ['hændəld] *suff (broom, screwdriver, knife)* à manche de; *(suitcase, box, drawer, door)* à poignée de; **a short-handled screwdriver** un tournevis à manche court; **ivory-handled knives** des couteaux *mpl* à manche d'ivoire

handler ['hændlə(r)] *n (of dogs)* maître-chien *m*; *(of baggage)* bagagiste *mf*

handless ['hændlɪs] *adj Scot (clumsy)* maladroit

handling ['hændlɪŋ] *n* (**a**) *(touching, holding)* manipulation *f*, action *f* de toucher; *(of stolen goods)* recel *m*

(**b**) *(of tool, weapon)* maniement *m*; *(of pesticides, chemicals, explosives)* manipulation *f*; *(of ship)* manœuvre *f*

(**c**) *(of car)* maniabilité *f*, comportement *m* routier; **the size of the car makes for easy handling** la taille de la voiture permet une grande maniabilité

(**d**) *(of person, situation, operation)* traitement *m*; **my handling of the problem** la façon dont j'ai traité le problème; **her handling of the interview was very professional** elle a conduit *ou* mené l'entretien en professionnelle

(**e**) *(of order, contract)* traitement *m*, exécution *f*; *(of goods, baggage)* manutention *f*

(**f**) *(of funds)* maniement *m*

(**g**) *Ftbl* (faute *f* de) main *f*; **a penalty was awarded for handling** un penalty a été accordé pour main

▸▸ ***handling capacity*** capacité *f* de traitement; ***handling charges*** frais *mpl* de traitement; *(for physically shifting goods)* frais *mpl* de manutention

handloom ['hændluːm] *n* métier *m* à tisser

handmade [ˌhænd'meɪd] *adj* fabriqué *ou* fait (à la) main

handmaid ['hændmeɪd], **handmaiden** ['hændmeɪdən] *n Arch* servante *f*, bonne *f*; *Fig* bonne *f*

'The Handmaid's Tale' *Atwood, Schlöndorff* 'La Servante écarlate'

hand-me-down *Fam* **1** *n* vêtement *m* de seconde main ❑; **this suit is a hand-me-down from my father** ce costume appartenait à mon père ❑; **why do I always have to wear his hand-me-downs?** pourquoi dois-je toujours porter ses vieux vêtements? ❑

2 *adj (clothes)* de seconde main ❑; *Fig (ideas)* reçu ❑

hand-off *n (in rugby)* raffut *m*

hand-operated *adj* à commande manuelle, commandé *ou* actionné à la main

handout ['hændaʊt] *n* (**a**) *(donation)* aide *f*, don *m*; **to live off handouts** vivre de dons; **it's not a handout** ce n'est pas de la charité; **government handouts** subventions *fpl* gouvernementales (**b**) *(printed sheet or sheets)* polycopié *m*; **press handout** communiqué *m* pour la presse (**c**) *(leaflet)* prospectus *m*; *(sample)* cadeau *m* publicitaire

handover ['hændəʊvə(r)] *n (of power)* passation *f*, transmission *f*, transfert *m*; *(of territory)* transfert *m*; *(of hostage, prisoner)* remise *f*; *(of baton)* transmission *f*, passage *m*

han–han

handpick [hænd'pɪk] *vt* (**a**) *(fruit, vegetables)* cueillir à la main (**b**) *Fig (people)* sélectionner avec soin, trier sur le volet

handpicked [ˌhænd'pɪkt] *adj (people)* trié sur le volet

handrail ['hændreɪl] *n (on bridge)* rambarde *f*, garde-fou *m*; *Naut* rambarde *f*; *(of stairway → gen)* rampe *f*; *(→ against wall)* main *f* courante

handsaw ['hændsɔː] *n* scie *f* à main; *(small)* (scie *f*) égoïne *f*

handset ['hændset] *n Tel* combiné *m*

hand-sewn *adj* cousu main, cousu à la main

hands-free [hænds-] *adj Tel* mains libres

handshake ['hændʃeɪk] *n* (**a**) *(between people)* poignée *f* de main (**b**) *Comput* dialogue *m* d'établissement de liaison

handshaking ['hændʃeɪkɪŋ] *n Comput* établissement *m* d'une liaison

hands-off [hændz-] *adj (policy)* non interventionniste, de non-intervention; *(manager)* non interventionniste; **the director has a hands-off style of management** le directeur est partisan de laisser de l'autonomie à son personnel

handsome ['hænsəm] **1** *adj* (**a**) *(good-looking → person, face, room)* beau (belle); *(→ building, furniture)* élégant; **a handsome man** un bel homme; **a handsome woman** une belle femme (**b**) *(generous → reward, compliment)* beau (belle); *(→ conduct, treatment)* généreux; *(sincere → praise, apology)* sincère; **that's very handsome of you** c'est très généreux de votre part, vous êtes bien bon; **he received very handsome treatment** on l'a traité d'une façon très généreuse

(**c**) *(substantial → profit, price)* bon; *(→ fortune)* joli; **a handsome amount** une coquette *ou* jolie somme, une somme rondelette

2 *exclam Br Fam* super!, génial!

handsomely ['hænsəmlɪ] *adv* (**a**) *(beautifully)* avec élégance, élégamment (**b**) *(generously → reward, compliment, behave, treat)* généreusement, avec générosité; *(sincerely → praise, apologize)* sincèrement (**c**) *(substantially)* **to win handsomely** gagner haut la main

handsomeness ['hænsəmnɪs] *n* (**a**) *(beauty)* beauté *f* (**b**) *(generosity)* générosité *f*; *(sincerity)* sincérité *f*

hands-on [ˌhændz-] *adj (training, experience)* pratique; *(exhibition)* = où le public peut toucher les objets exposés; **I go for a hands-on style of management** je suis le genre de patron à contribuer concrètement au fonctionnement de mon entreprise *ou* à mettre la main à la pâte

handspring ['hændsprɪŋ] *n Gym* saut *m* de mains

handstand ['hændstænd] *n Gym* appui *m* renversé, équilibre *m* sur les mains

hand-stitched *adj* cousu main

hand-to-hand **1** *adj (fighting)* corps-à-corps *(inv)*

2 *adv* **to fight hand-to-hand** se battre au corps-à-corps

hand-to-mouth **1** *adj* **to lead** *or* **to have a hand-to-mouth existence** tirer le diable par la queue

2 *adv* **to live hand-to-mouth** tirer le diable par la queue

hand-tool *vt* (**a**) *Tech (on a lathe etc)* travailler à la main (**b**) *(in bookbinding)* dorer à la main

hand-tooling *n (UNCOUNT)* (**a**) *Tech (on a lathe etc)* travail *m* à la main (**b**) *(in bookbinding)* dorure *f* à froid faite à la main

handwash ['hændwɒʃ] **1** *vt* laver à la main

2 *n* **to do a handwash** faire une lessive à la main

handwork ['hændwɜːk] *n* travail *m* à la main

handwoven [ˌhænd'wəʊvən] *adj* tissé main

handwriting ['hændˌraɪtɪŋ] *n* écriture *f*

►► ***handwriting expert*** graphologue *mf*; *Comput* ***handwriting recognition*** reconnaissance *f* de l'écriture manuscrite

handwritten ['hændˌrɪtən] *adj* manuscrit, écrit à la main

handy ['hændɪ] (*compar* **handier**, *superl* **handiest**) *adj* (**a**) *(near at hand)* proche; **I always keep my glasses handy** je range toujours mes lunettes à portée de main; **have you got a pen and paper handy?** as-tu un stylo et du papier sous la main?

(**b**) *(person → good with one's hands)* adroit de ses mains; **he's handy about the house** il est bricoleur; **he's not the handiest man in the world** ce n'est pas un très bon bricoleur; **to be handy at doing sth** être doué pour faire qch, bien savoir faire qch; **she's handy with a drill** elle sait se servir d'une perceuse; *Fam* **he's a bit handy with his fists** il sait se servir de ses poings

(**c**) *(convenient, useful)* commode, pratique; **living in the centre is handy for work** pour le travail c'est pratique d'habiter en ville; **that's handy!** c'est pratique *ou* commode!; **he's a handy guy to have around** il peut rendre des tas de services; **she's a handy person to have around in a crisis** c'est quelqu'un qu'il est bon d'avoir *ou* c'est quelqu'un d'utile en cas de crise; **a handy piece of advice** un conseil utile; **to come in handy** être utile; **don't throw it away, it might come in handy one day** ne le jette pas, ça pourrait servir un jour

handyman ['hændɪmæn] (*pl* **handymen** [-men]) *n (employee)* homme *m* à tout faire; *(DIY expert)* bricoleur *m*; *Am* **handyman's special** = maison qui a besoin de beaucoup de travaux

HANG [hæŋ]

accrocher	► 1 (a)
suspendre	► 1 (a)
fixer	► 1 (a)
coller	► 1 (a)
décorer	► 1 (b)
pendre	► 1 (c); 2 (a)
être accroché	► 2 (a)
être suspendu	► 2 (a), (c)
être étendu	► 2 (a)
tomber	► 2 (b)
flotter	► 2 (c)
être pendu	► 2 (d)

(*pt & pp vt senses* (**a**), (**b**), (**d**) *& vi senses* (**a**) – (**c**), (**e**) **hung** [hʌŋ], *pt & pp vt* (**c**) *& vi* (**d**) **hanged**) **1** *vt* (**a**) *(suspend → curtains, coat, decoration, picture)* accrocher, suspendre; *(→ door)* fixer, monter; *(→ art exhibition)* mettre en place; *(→ wallpaper)* coller, poser; *Culin (→ game, meat)* faire faisander; **to hang sth on the wall** accrocher qch au mur; **they hung banners from their windows** ils ont accroché des bannières à leurs fenêtres; **to hang a picture** suspendre un tableau; *Br* **to hang one's head (in shame)** baisser la tête (de honte); *Am Fam* **to hang one on sb** *(punch)* balancer un coup de poing à qn; **to hang fire** *(project)* être en suspens; *(decision)* traîner (en longueur); *(person)* mettre les choses en suspens

(**b**) *(usu passive) (adorn)* décorer; **a tree hung with lights** un arbre décoré *ou* orné de lumières; **to hang a room with tapestries** tendre une salle de tapisseries

(**c**) *(criminal)* pendre; **to be hanged for one's crime** être pendu pour son crime; **to hang oneself** se pendre; **hanged** *or* **hung, drawn and quartered** pendu, éviscéré et écartelé; *Fam* **hang him!** qu'il aille se faire voir!; *Br Fam* **I'll be hanged if I know** je veux bien être pendu si je le sais; *Br Fam* **I'll be hanged if I'm going out in that weather** il n'y a pas de danger que je sorte par ce temps ❑; *Br Fam* **hang it (all)!** ras le bol!; *Br* **(you) might as well be hanged for a sheep as a lamb** quitte à être puni, autant l'être pour quelque chose qui en vaille la peine

(**d**) *Am Fam (turn)* **to hang a left/right** prendre à gauche/droite ❑

2 *vi* (**a**) *(be suspended → rope, painting, light)* être accroché, être suspendu; *(→ clothes on clothes line)* être étendu, pendre; *Culin (of game)* se faisander; **to hang from sth** être accroché *ou* suspendu à qch; **to hang on sb's arm** être accroché au bras de qn; **her pictures are now hanging in several art galleries** ses tableaux sont maintenant exposés dans plusieurs galeries d'art; **the way her hair hangs down her back** la façon dont ses cheveux lui tombent le long du dos; **time hangs heavy (on) my/his hands** le temps me/lui semble long; *Fam* **how's it hanging?** ça gaze?; *Am Fam* **to hang loose** rester cool; *Am Fam* **hang loose!** détends-toi! ❑, cool!; *Am Fam* **to hang tough** s'accrocher

(**b**) *(of drapery, clothes etc)* tomber, se draper; **his suit hangs well** son costume tombe bien; **his clothes hang loosely on him** il flotte dans ses vêtements; **this door hangs badly** cette porte est mal suspendue (sur ses gonds)

(**c**) *(float → mist, smoke etc)* flotter, être suspendu; **the ball seemed to hang in the air** le ballon semblait suspendu en l'air

(**d**) *(criminal)* être pendu; **you'll hang for your crime** vous serez pendu pour votre crime; *Br Fam* **she can go hang** elle peut aller se faire voir

(**e**) *Am Fam (spend time)* traîner ❑; **he's hanging with his friends** il traîne avec ses copains

3 *n* (**a**) *Fam (knack, idea)* **to get the hang of doing sth** prendre le coup pour faire qch; **I never did get the hang of skiing** je n'ai jamais réussi à prendre le coup pour skier; **to get the hang of sth** *(understand)* piger qch; **I can't get the hang of this computer** je n'arrive pas à piger comment marche cet ordinateur; **are you getting the hang of your new job?** est-ce que tu te fais à ton nouveau travail? ❑; **you'll soon get the hang of it** tu vas bientôt t'y faire ❑

(**b**) *(of clothing)* tombé *m*; *(of material)* drapé *m*

(**c**) *(idiom) Br Fam* **he doesn't give a hang** *(couldn't care less)* il n'en a rien à taper *ou* à cirer

►**hang about, hang around** *Fam* **1** *vi* (**a**) *(wait)* poireauter; **he kept me hanging about** *or* **around for half an hour** il m'a fait poireauter pendant une demi-heure; **I've been hanging about** *or* **around waiting for her to come** je tourne en rond à l'attendre; **I hate all this hanging about** *or* **around** je déteste toute cette attente ❑, je déteste poireauter comme ça; *Br* **hang about (a bit)!** attends! ❑; **hang about, that's not what I mean!** attends *ou* doucement, ce n'est pas ce que je veux dire! ❑

(**b**) *(be idle, waste time)* traîner (à ne rien faire) ❑; **to hang about** *or* **around on street corners** traîner dans les rues; **to hang about the house doing nothing** traîner à la maison à rien faire; **we can't afford to hang about if we want that contract** nous ne pouvons pas nous permettre de traîner si nous voulons obtenir ce contrat; **she doesn't hang about** *or* **around** *(soon gets what she wants)* elle ne perd pas de temps ❑

(**c**) *(be an unwanted presence)* **Mum doesn't want me hanging around when the guests arrive** maman ne veut pas que je sois là quand les invités arriveront ❑; **that kid's been hanging around for the past hour** ça fait une heure que ce gamin traîne dans les parages

2 *vt insep* **to hang about** *or* **around a place** traîner dans un endroit ❑

►**hang about with** *vt insep Br Fam* traîner avec ❑; **I don't like the boys she hangs about with** je n'aime pas les garçons avec qui elle traîne

►**hang back** *vi (wait behind)* rester un peu plus longtemps; *(not go forward)* se tenir *ou* rester en arrière; **to hang back from doing sth** renâcler à faire qch; *Br Fig* **he hung back from saying**

what he really thought il s'est retenu de dire ce qu'il pensait vraiment

▸**hang down** *vi (light)* pendre; *(hair)* descendre, tomber

▸**hang in** *vi Fam* **hang in there!** tiens bon!, accroche-toi!

▸**hang on 1** *vi* (**a**) *(hold tight)* se tenir, s'accrocher; **hang on tight** tiens-toi *ou* accroche-toi bien

(**b**) *Fam (wait)* attendre ❑; **hang on!** *(wait)* attends! ❑; *(indicating astonishment, disagreement etc)* une minute! ❑; **hang on and I'll get him for you** *(on phone)* ne quitte pas, je te le passe ❑; **do you mind hanging on for a minute or two?** ça ne te dérange pas de patienter quelques minutes? ❑; **I've been hanging on for the past quarter of an hour!** *(on phone)* ça fait un quart d'heure que j'attends! ❑

(**c**) *(hold out, survive)* résister, tenir (bon); *Fam* **hang on in there!** *(don't give up)* tiens bon!, tiens le coup!

2 *vt insep* (**a**) *(listen to)* **she hung on his every word** elle buvait ses paroles, elle était suspendue à ses lèvres

(**b**) *(depend on)* dépendre de; **it all hangs on whether we get the loan** pour nous, tout dépend de l'obtention ou non du prêt; **this is what it all hangs on** tout dépend de cela

3 *vt sep Am Fam* **to hang one on** *(get drunk)* prendre une cuite

▸**hang onto** *vt insep* (**a**) *(cling to)* s'accrocher à (**b**) *Fam (keep)* garder ❑, conserver ❑; **I'd hang onto that table if I were you** à ta place, je garderais précieusement cette table; **he hung onto these outdated ideas** il se raccrochait à ces idées démodées ❑

▸**hang out 1** *vi* (**a**) *(protrude)* pendre; **his shirt tails were hanging out** sa chemise dépassait; **to hang out of the window** *(flags)* être déployé à la fenêtre; *(person)* se pencher par la fenêtre; *Fam* **to let it all hang out** *(person)* se relâcher complètement ❑, se laisser aller ❑; *(speak without restraint)* se défouler; *Hum (go naked)* se promener tout nu ❑

(**b**) *Fam (spend time)* traîner ❑; **he hangs out at the local bar** c'est un habitué du café du coin ❑; **where does she hang out?** quels sont les endroits qu'elle fréquente? ❑

(**c**) *(survive, not give in)* résister, tenir bon; **they won't be able to hang out for more than another two days** ils ne résisteront *ou* ne tiendront pas plus de deux jours; **the strikers are hanging out in their demands** les grévistes tiennent bon dans leurs revendications; **they're hanging out for 10 percent** ils insistent pour obtenir 10 pour cent

2 *vt sep (washing)* étendre; *(flags)* déployer

▸**hang out with** *vt insep Fam* fréquenter ❑; **she hangs out with a group of artists** elle fréquente un groupe d'artistes

▸**hang over** *vt insep* être suspendu au-dessus de, planer sur; **(a) thick fog hung over the town** un brouillard épais flottait au-dessus de la ville; **a question mark hangs over his future** un point d'interrogation plane sur son avenir; **a heavy silence hung over the meeting** un lourd silence pesait sur l'assemblée; **she has got the threat of redundancy hanging over her head** *or* **her** une menace de licenciement plane sur elle; **I can't go out with exams hanging over me** avec les examens qui approchent, je ne peux pas sortir; **we've got the threat of eviction hanging over us** nous risquons d'être expulsés d'une minute à l'autre

▸**hang together** *vi* (**a**) *(be united → people)* se serrer les coudes (**b**) *(be consistent → alibi, argument, plot etc)* (se) tenir; *(→ different alibis, statements)* concorder

▸**hang up 1** *vt sep (coat, hat etc)* accrocher; *Tel (receiver)* raccrocher; **to hang up one's boots/gloves/dancing shoes/***etc (retire)* raccrocher; *Am Fam* **to hang it up** *(stop)* laisser tomber

2 *vi* (**a**) *Tel* raccrocher; **to hang up on sb** raccrocher au nez de qn (**b**) *Comput (cease functioning)* s'arrêter

▸**hang with** *vt insep Am Fam* **to hang with sb** traîner avec qn ❑

hangar ['hæŋə(r)] *n Aviat* hangar *m*

hangdog ['hæŋdɒg] *adj* **to have a hangdog look** *or* **expression** avoir un air penaud *ou* de chien battu

hanger ['hæŋə(r)] *n (hook)* portemanteau *m*; *(coat hanger)* portemanteau *m*, cintre *m*; *(loop on garment)* cordon *m ou* ganse *f* d'accrochage *(à l'intérieur d'un vêtement)*

hanger-on *(pl* **hangers-on***) n Pej* parasite *m*

hang-glide *vi* faire du deltaplane; **to hang-glide down Mont Blanc** descendre le mont Blanc en deltaplane

hang-glider *n (aircraft)* deltaplane *m*; *(person)* libériste *mf*, adepte *mf* du deltaplane

hang-gliding *n* deltaplane *m*; **to go hang-gliding** faire du deltaplane

hanging ['hæŋɪŋ] **1** *adj (suspended)* suspendu

2 *n* (**a**) *(death penalty)* pendaison *f*; **hanging's too good for him** la pendaison, c'est encore trop bon pour lui

(**b**) *(of wallpaper)* pose *f*; *(of decorations, pictures)* accrochage *m*, mise *f* en place; *(of door)* montage *m*, accrochage *m*

(**c**) *(tapestry)* **(wall) hangings** tentures *fpl* (murales)

▸▸ ***hanging basket*** panier *m* suspendu; *Art* ***hanging committee*** = comité de réception ou jury d'admission des tableaux; ***hanging cupboard*** armoire *f* murale; ***the Hanging Gardens of Babylon*** les jardins *mpl* suspendus de Babylone; *Comput* ***hanging indent*** présentation *f* en sommaire; *Law* ***hanging judge*** juge *m* à la main lourde; ***hanging offence*** crime *m* passible de pendaison; *Fig* **it's not a hanging offence** ce n'est pas une affaire d'État; ***hanging paragraph*** paragraphe *m* en sommaire; *Geog* ***hanging valley*** vallée *f* suspendue; ***hanging wardrobe*** penderie *f*

hangman ['hæŋmən] *(pl* **hangmen** [-mən]*) n (executioner)* bourreau *m*; *(game)* le pendu; **to play hangman** jouer au pendu

hangnail ['hæŋneɪl] *n* envie *f (peau)*

hang-out *n Fam* **this is one of my favourite hang-outs** j'adore traîner dans ce coin ❑; **this is one of his hang-outs** c'est l'un des endroits où on le trouve le plus souvent ❑; **it's a real student hang-out** c'est un endroit très fréquenté par les étudiants ❑

hangover ['hæŋ,əʊvə(r)] *n* (**a**) *(from alcohol)* gueule *f* de bois; **to have a hangover** avoir la gueule de bois; **hangover cure** remède *m* contre la gueule de bois (**b**) *(relic)* reste *m*, vestige *m*, survivance *f*; **a hangover from the past** un reliquat du passé

Hang Seng index [,hæŋ'seŋ-] *n St Exch* indice *m* Hang Seng, indice *m* Hong Kong

hang-up *n* (**a**) *Fam (complex)* complexe ❑ *m*, blocage ❑ *m*; **she has a hang-up about her appearance/weight** elle est complexée par son allure/poids ❑; **you've got a lot of hang-ups** tu es très complexé ❑ (**b**) *Comput* blocage *m*, interruption *f*

▸▸ *Comput* ***hang-up loop*** boucle *f* sans fin

hank [hæŋk] *n* (**a**) *(of wool)* écheveau *m* (**b**) *Tex (measurement)* longueur *f* (**c**) *Naut* rocambeau *m*

hanker ['hæŋkə(r)] *vi* **to hanker after** *or* **for sth** rêver de qch, avoir énormément envie de qch; **to hanker after an easy life** rêver d'une vie tranquille

hankering ['hæŋkərɪŋ] *n* rêve *m*, envie *f*; **to have a hankering after** *or* **for sth** rêver de qch, avoir énormément envie de qch

hankie, hanky ['hænkɪ] *(pl* **hankies***) n Fam (abbr* **handkerchief***)* mouchoir ❑ *m*

hanky-panky [-'pæŋkɪ] *n (UNCOUNT) Fam* (**a**) *(sexual activity)* galipettes *fpl*; **to have a bit of** *or* **a little hanky-panky** faire des galipettes (**b**) *(mischief)* entourloupettes *fpl*, blagues *fpl*; **to get up to (a bit of) hanky-panky** faire des entourloupettes *ou* des blagues

Hannah ['hænə] *pr n Bible* Anne

Hannibal ['hænɪbəl] *pr n Hist* Hannibal, Annibal

Hanoi [hæ'nɔɪ] *n* Hanoi

Hanover ['hænəvə(r)] **1** *pr n Hist* Hanovre

2 *n Geog* Hanovre

Hanoverian [,hænə'veərɪən] **1** *adj* hanovrien

2 *n* Hanovrien(enne) *m,f*

Hansard ['hænsɑːd] *n Br Pol* = compte rendu quotidien des débats de la Chambre des communes

Hanseatic League [,hænsɪ'ætɪk-] *n Hist* **the Hanseatic League** la ligue hanséatique, la Hanse

hansom (cab) ['hænsəm-] *n* fiacre *m*

Hants *(written abbr* **Hampshire***)* Hampshire

Hanukkah ['hɑːnəkə] *n Rel* Hanoukka *f*

ha'penny ['heɪpnɪ] *(pl* **ha'pence** [-pəns]*) Br Fam Old-fashioned* **1** *n* demi-penny ❑ *m*; **he's down to his last ha'penny** il ne lui reste que quelques sous

2 *comp* d'un demi-penny

haphazard [,hæp'hæzəd] *adj* mal organisé; **it was done in a haphazard fashion** ça a été fait un peu n'importe comment; **the whole thing was a bit haphazard** c'était un peu n'importe quoi; **the city grew in a haphazard fashion** la ville s'est agrandie au gré des circonstances; **to choose in a haphazard fashion** choisir au petit bonheur la chance, choisir au hasard

haphazardly [,hæp'hæzədlɪ] *adv* sans organisation, n'importe comment; **there were objects lying haphazardly on the table** des choses traînaient sur la table; **to choose haphazardly** choisir au petit bonheur la chance, choisir au hasard

hapless ['hæplɪs] *adj Literary* infortuné

haplography [hæp'lɒgrəfɪ] *n Ling* haplographie *f*

haploid ['hæplɔɪd] *adj Biol* haploïde

haplology [hæp'lɒlədʒɪ] *n Ling* haplologie *f*

ha'p'orth ['heɪpəθ] *n Br Old-fashioned* **a ha'p'orth of ice cream** ≃ un sou de glace

HAPPEN ['hæpən] **1** *vi* (**a**) *(occur)* arriver, se passer, se produire; **what's happened?** qu'est-il arrivé?, que s'est-il passé?; **when did this happen?** quand cela s'est-il produit *ou* passé?, quand cela est-il arrivé?; **where did the accident happen?** où l'accident s'est-il produit *ou* est-il arrivé *ou* a-t-il eu lieu?; **it happened ten years ago** cela s'est passé il y a dix ans; **did anyone see what happened?** quelqu'un a-t-il vu ce qui s'est passé *ou* est arrivé?; **don't let it happen again** faites en sorte que cela ne se reproduise pas; **as if nothing had happened** comme si de rien n'était; **I pulled the lever, but nothing happened** j'ai tiré sur le manche, mais il ne s'est rien passé *ou* ça n'a rien fait; **whatever happens** quoi qu'il arrive *ou* advienne; **as (so) often happens** comme c'est bien souvent le cas; **it all happened so quickly** tout s'est passé si vite; **these things happen** ce sont des choses qui arrivent; **what happened next?** que s'est-il passé ensuite?; **to find out what happens next...** *(on radio, TV programme)* pour connaître la suite...; **it's all been happening this morning** ça n'a pas arrêté ce matin; **it's all happening here** ça bouge ici; **I wonder what's happened to her** *(what has befallen her)* je me demande ce qui a bien pu lui arriver; *(what she is doing now)* je me demande ce qu'elle est devenue; **whatever happened to him?** qu'est-il devenu?; **if anything happens** *or* **should happen to me** s'il m'arrivait quelque chose; **it couldn't happen to a nicer person** il/elle le mérite bien; **a funny thing happened to me last night** il m'est arrivé une drôle d'aventure hier soir; **I don't like what's happening in this country** je n'aime pas ce qui se passe dans ce pays; **what's happened to my pen?** *(where is it?)* qu'est-ce qu'on a fait de mon stylo?; *(what's wrong with it?)* qu'est-il arrivé à mon stylo?; **what's happening to us?** qu'est-ce qui nous arrive?; *Am Fam* **what's happening?** *(as greeting)* ça va? ❑

(**b**) *(chance)* **do you happen to have his address?** auriez-vous son adresse, par hasard?; **it just so happens that I do** eh bien justement, oui; **you wouldn't happen to know where I could find him, would you?** vous ne sauriez pas où je pourrais le trouver?; **as it happens** justement; **I happen to know her, it so happens that I know her, I know her, as it happens** il se trouve que je la connais; **the man you're talking about happens to be my father** il se trouve que l'homme dont vous parlez est mon père; **if you happen to see him** si jamais tu le vois

2 *adv NEng Fam (maybe)* peut-être ❑

▸**happen along, happen by** *vi Am Fam* passer par hasard ❑

han–hap

►**happen on, happen upon** *vt insep* tomber sur; **I happened on an old friend/a good pub** je suis tombé sur un vieil ami/un bon pub

'It Happened one Night' *Capra* 'New York-Miami'

happening ['hæpənɪŋ] **1** *n (occurrence)* événement *m*; *Art & Theat* happening *m*

2 *adj Fam* (**a**) *(fashionable)* branché (**b**) *(interesting)* **he's a happening kind of guy** avec lui on ne s'ennuie pas une minute❑; **this is a happening kind of place** il se passe toujours des tas de trucs ici

happenstance ['hæpənstæns] *n Am* hasard *m*; **we met by happenstance** nous nous sommes rencontrés par hasard

happily ['hæpɪlɪ] *adv* (**a**) *(contentedly → say, smile)* d'un air heureux; *(→ play, chat)* tranquillement; **I could live here very happily** je serais très heureux ici; **we were sitting there quite happily watching television** nous étions installés tout tranquillement devant la télévision; **they lived happily ever after** *(at end of fairy tale)* ≃ ils vécurent heureux et eurent beaucoup d'enfants; **I thought that when you got married you lived happily ever after** je croyais que quand on se mariait, on vivait heureux jusqu'à la fin de ses jours; **to be happily married** *(man)* être un mari comblé; *(woman)* être une épouse comblée; **I always thought you two were happily married** j'ai toujours pensé que vous étiez un couple heureux

(**b**) *(gladly)* volontiers; **she said she would happily give her consent** elle a dit qu'elle donnerait volontiers son accord *ou* qu'elle serait heureuse de donner son accord; **I could quite happily live here** je me verrais très bien vivre ici; **I could quite happily strangle him** j'ai bien envie de l'étrangler; **he'll quite happily say one thing and do the opposite** ça ne le gêne pas de dire une chose et de faire exactement le contraire

(**c**) *(luckily)* heureusement; **happily, no one was hurt** heureusement, il n'y a pas eu de blessés

(**d**) *(appropriately)* heureusement, avec bonheur; **a very happily chosen turn of phrase** une tournure de phrase très heureuse

> **And they all lived happily ever after**
> Il s'agit de la formule qui clôt tous les contes de fées en anglais ("et tous vécurent heureux pour toujours"), dont l'équivalent français est "ils vécurent heureux et eurent beaucoup d'enfants".
> Aujourd'hui on utilise cette phrase de façon allusive et parfois sur le mode sarcastique, comme dans l'exemple suivant: **Neil and Maggie were supposed to live happily ever after but actually divorced after six months** ("Neil et Maggie étaient censés vivre heureux et avoir beaucoup d'enfants mais finalement ils ont divorcé au bout de six mois").

happiness ['hæpɪnɪs] *n* bonheur *m*; *Prov* **money can't buy you happiness** l'argent ne fait pas le bonheur

happy ['hæpɪ] (*compar* **happier,** *superl* **happiest**) *adj* (**a**) *(content)* heureux; **to make sb happy** rendre qn heureux; **I want you to be happy** je veux que tu sois heureux, je veux ton bonheur; **I'm the happiest man in the world** je suis l'homme le plus heureux du monde; **I hope you'll both be very happy** je vous souhaite beaucoup de bonheur *ou* d'être très heureux; **I'm very happy for you** je suis très heureux pour toi; **if you're happy, I'm happy** si tu es satisfait, moi aussi; **would you be happy living here?** serais-tu heureux ici?; **in happier times** à une époque plus heureuse; **in happier circumstances** dans des circonstances plus heureuses; **those were happy days** c'était le bon temps; **I'm not at all happy about your decision** je ne suis pas du tout content de votre décision; **I'm still not happy about it** je n'en suis toujours pas content; **that should keep the kids happy** cela devrait occuper les enfants; **their happy smiling faces** leurs visages heureux et souriants; **it's a happy office** il y a une bonne ambiance dans ce bureau; **happy ending** *(in book, film)* fin *f* heureuse, dénouement *m* heureux; **to have a happy ending** *(book, film)* bien finir; **happy birthday!** joyeux anniversaire!; **Happy Christmas!** Joyeux Noël!; **Happy New Year!** Bonne année!; *Fam* **he's not a happy camper** *or Br* **chappy** *or* **bunny** il est pas jouasse; **to be as happy as a** *Br* **lark** *or* **sandboy** *or Am* **clam** être heureux comme tout

(**b**) *(willing)* **I'm only too happy to help** je suis ravi de rendre service; **I would be happy to do it** je le ferais volontiers; **happy to oblige** ravi de rendre service; **we'd be happy to put you up** nous serions heureux de vous loger, nous vous logerions volontiers; **I'd be happy to live here/move to Scotland** j'aimerais bien habiter ici/aller habiter en Écosse

(**c**) *(lucky, fortunate → coincidence)* heureux; **the happy few** les privilégiés *mpl*

(**d**) *(apt, appropriate → turn of phrase, choice of words)* heureux

(**e**) *Fam (drunk)* gris, pompette

►► *Br* ***happy event*** *(birth)* heureux événement *m*; ***happy families*** *(card game)* jeu *m* des sept familles; ***happy hour*** *(in pub, bar)* happy hour *f (heure, généralement en début de soirée, pendant laquelle les boissons sont moins chères)*; ***happy hunting ground*** paradis *m* des Indiens; *Fig* mine *f* d'or; **the market is a happy hunting ground for collectors** le marché est une vraie mine d'or pour les collectionneurs; ***happy medium*** équilibre *m*, juste milieu *m*; **to strike a happy medium** trouver un équilibre *ou* un juste milieu

happy-clappy [-'klæpɪ] (*pl* **happy-clappies**) *Br Fam Pej* **1** *adj (service, meeting, Christian)* agaçant de par sa joie exubérante❑ *(appliqué aux chrétiens évangéliques)*

2 *n* chrétien(enne) *m,f* évangélique❑ *(agaçant de par sa joie exubérante)*

happy-go-lucky *adj* décontracté; *Pej* insouciant

Hapsburg = **Habsburg**

hapten ['hæptən], **haptene** ['hæpti:n] *n Biol & Chem* haptène *m*, haptine *f*

haptic ['hæptɪk] *adj* haptique

haptoglobin [ˌhæptəʊ'gləʊbɪn] *n Biol & Chem* haptoglobine *f*

hara-kiri [ˌhærə'ki:rɪ] *n* hara-kiri *m*; **to commit hara-kiri** faire hara-kiri

harangue [hə'ræŋ] **1** *vt (person)* sermonner; *(crowd)* haranguer; **to harangue sb about sth** sermonner qn au sujet de qch; **to harangue sb into doing sth** sermonner qn pour qu'il fasse qch

2 *n* harangue *f*

Harare [hə'rɑ:rɪ] *n* Harare

harass ['hærəs, hə'ræs] *vt* (**a**) *Mil (enemy forces)* harceler, tenir en alerte

(**b**) *(person → pester)* tracasser, tourmenter, harceler; *(→ sexually)* harceler; **to harass sb to do sth** harceler qn pour qu'il fasse qch; **to harass sb into doing sth** harceler qn jusqu'à ce qu'il fasse qch; **he was harassing me for money** il me harcelait pour que je lui donne de l'argent; **he claimed that the police had harassed him** il a déclaré que la police l'avait harcelé; **to sexually harass sb** harceler qn sexuellement; **to be sexually harassed** être victime de harcèlement sexuel

harassed ['hærəst, hə'ræst] *adj* stressé

harassment ['hærəsmənt, hə'ræsmənt] *n (pestering)* tracasserie *f*; *(with questions, demands)* harcèlement *m*; *(stress)* stress *m*; *Mil* harcèlement *m*; **police/sexual harassment** harcèlement *m* policier/sexuel

harbinger ['hɑ:bɪndʒə(r)] *n Literary* signe *m* avant-coureur; **swallows are a harbinger of spring** les hirondelles annoncent le printemps; **a harbinger of doom** *(event, incident etc)* un mauvais présage; *(person)* un oiseau de malheur

harbour, *Am* **harbor** ['hɑ:bə(r)] **1** *n (for boats)* port *m*; *Fig* havre *m*

2 *vt* (**a**) *(person)* abriter, héberger; *(criminal)* donner asile à, receler

(**b**) *(grudge, suspicion)* nourrir, entretenir en soi; **to harbour a grudge against sb** garder rancune à qn, nourrir de la rancune envers qn

(**c**) *(conceal → dirt, germs)* renfermer, receler

►► ***harbour dues*** droits *mpl* de port; ***harbour lights*** lumières *fpl* du port; ***harbour master*** capitaine *m* de port; *Zool* ***harbour seal*** phoque *m* commun; ***harbour terminal*** gare *f* maritime

harbourless, *Am* **harborless** ['hɑ:bəlɪs] *adj* (**a**) *(coast)* sans ports (**b**) *Literary (person)* sans asile

HARD [hɑ:d]

dur	► **1 (a) – (c); 2 (a)**
difficile	► **1 (b)**
froid	► **1 (c)**
rude	► **1 (c)**
concret	► **1 (d)**
fort	► **2 (a)**
difficilement	► **2 (b)**
durement	► **2 (c)**

1 *adj* (**a**) *(not soft → substance, light, colour)* dur; **to get** *or* **to become hard** durcir; **rock hard, (as) hard as rock** dur comme la pierre; **his muscles are rock hard** *or* **(as) hard as rock** ses muscles sont durs comme le fer, il a des muscles d'acier; **she is (as) hard as nails** *(emotionally)* elle est dure, elle n'a pas de cœur; *(physically)* c'est une dure à cuire

(**b**) *(difficult → question, problem etc)* difficile, dur; **the laws make it hard to leave the country** à cause des lois, il est difficile de quitter le pays; **to have a hard fight** *or* **struggle on one's hands** avoir une lourde tâche devant soi; **it's hard to explain** c'est difficile *ou* dur à expliquer; **I find it hard to understand/believe that...** je n'arrive pas à comprendre pourquoi/croire que...; **it's hard to say** c'est difficile à dire; **he's hard to get on with** il n'est pas facile à vivre; **she is hard to please** *(never satisfied)* elle est difficile; *(difficult to buy gifts for etc)* c'est difficile de lui faire plaisir; **it's hard to beat** on trouve difficilement mieux; **it's hard to beat a good Bordeaux** il n'y a rien de meilleur qu'un bon bordeaux; **the hardest part of the job is done** le plus dur est fait; **life is hard** c'est dur, la vie; **times are hard** les temps sont durs *ou* difficiles; **these are hard times for all of us** c'est une période difficile pour tout le monde; **to fall on hard times** *(financially)* connaître des temps difficiles *ou* une période de vaches maigres; *(have difficult times)* connaître des temps difficiles, en voir de dures; **to give sb a hard time** en faire voir de dures à qn; **the boss has just been giving me a hard time** le patron vient de me faire passer un mauvais quart d'heure; **come on, don't give me a hard time!** allez, laisse-moi tranquille!; **you'll have a hard time (of it) persuading him to do that** tu vas avoir du mal à le convaincre de faire cela; **she had a hard time of it after her mother's death** elle a traversé une période difficile après la mort de sa mère; **she had a hard time of it when she was a child** la vie n'était pas drôle pour elle quand elle était enfant; **she had a hard time of it** *(in childbirth, operation)* elle a souffert; **to learn sth the hard way** *(involving personal loss, suffering etc)* apprendre qch à ses dépens; *(in a difficult way)* faire le rude apprentissage de qch; **I learnt the hard way not to be underinsured** j'ai appris à mes dépens qu'il ne faut pas être sous-assuré; **I learnt skiing the hard way** j'ai appris à skier à la dure; **I learnt my seamanship the hard way** j'ai fait le rude apprentissage du métier de marin; **to do things the hard way** *(through choice)* se compliquer la vie; *(due to circumstances)* en baver; **some people always have to do things the hard way** il y a des gens qui choisissent toujours la difficulté; **to play hard to get** *(flirt)* jouer les insaisissables; *Hum* **their financial expert is playing hard to get** leur expert financier semble jouer à cache-cache; **the hard of hearing** les malentendants *mpl*; **to be hard of hearing** être dur d'oreille; **a glass of wine, or would you prefer a drop of the hard stuff?** un verre de vin, ou bien préféreriez-vous une goutte de quelque chose de plus fort?; **keep off the hard stuff** évitez les boissons fortes

(**c**) *(severe → voice, face, eyes)* dur, froid; *(→ climate, winter)* rigoureux, rude; *(→ frost)* fort, rude; **he's hard** *(tough)* c'est un dur; **to be hard on sb** être dur avec qn; **children are hard on their shoes** les enfants font subir de mauvais traitements à leurs chaussures; **it's hard on the nerves** c'est dur pour les nerfs; **it was hard on the others** ça a été dur pour les autres; **it's hardest on the children** le plus dur, c'est pour les enfants; **to be a hard taskmaster** être dur à la tâche; **to take a long hard look at sth** examiner qch de près; **you should take a long hard look at yourself** tu devrais bien te regarder; **it's a hard blow for him** c'est un coup terrible pour lui; **no hard feelings?** tu ne m'en veux pas?; *Fam* **hard luck!**, *Br* **hard cheese!, hard lines!** pas de chance!❑, pas de veine!, pas de bol!; **it will be hard luck if he doesn't get the job** ça ne sera pas de veine *ou* de bol s'il n'obtient pas le travail; **don't give me any of your hard luck stories** ne me raconte pas tes malheurs; **he gave me some hard luck story about having lost his investments** il a essayé de m'apitoyer en me racontant qu'il avait perdu l'argent qu'il avait investi; *Fam* **a hard nut** *or* **man** un dur

(**d**) *(concrete → facts)* concret(ète), tangible; *(→ evidence)* tangible; **the hard fact is that there isn't enough money** la vérité, c'est qu'il n'y a pas assez d'argent; **the argument was not backed up by any hard fact** l'argument ne s'appuyait sur rien de concret

(**e**) *(strenuous)* **it's been a long hard day** la journée a été longue; **it's hard work** c'est dur; **it was hard work to convince him** j'ai eu fort à faire pour le convaincre; **she's hard work** *(difficult to get on with)* elle n'est pas facile à vivre; *(difficult to make conversation with)* elle n'est pas causante; **she's not afraid of hard work** le travail ne lui fait pas peur; **the climb was hard going** la montée était rude; **it's hard going making conversation with him** c'est difficile de discuter avec lui

(**f**) *(intense)* **she's a hard worker** c'est un bourreau de travail; **he's a hard drinker** c'est un gros buveur, il boit beaucoup; **he's a hard charger** c'est un fonceur; **give it a good hard shove** pousse-le un bon coup, pousse-le fort

(**g**) *Fin (stock, rates)* soutenu, ferme

(**h**) *Ling (consonant)* dur

2 *adv* (**a**) *(strenuously → pull, push, hit, breathe)* fort; *(→ work)* dur; *(→ run)* à toutes jambes; *(→ listen)* attentivement; **to work hard at sth** beaucoup travailler qch; **to work hard at improving one's service/French** beaucoup travailler pour améliorer son service/français; **to work sb hard** faire travailler qn dur; **he works hard and plays hard** il se dépense beaucoup dans son travail et dans ses loisirs; **you'll have to try harder** il faudra que tu fasses plus d'efforts; **to try hard to do sth** essayer de son mieux de faire qch; **try hard!** fais de ton mieux!; **to think hard** beaucoup réfléchir; **think hard!** réfléchis bien!; **think harder!** réfléchis un peu plus!; **we can't find it – well, look harder!** nous ne le trouvons pas – et bien cherchez mieux!; **you didn't look very hard!** tu n'as pas bien cherché; **to look hard at sb** regarder qn bien en face; **to look hard at sth** examiner qch; **as hard as possible, as hard as one can** *(work, try)* le plus qu'on peut; *(push, hit, squeeze)* de toutes ses forces; *Naut* **hard astern!** arrière, toute!; *Aut* **she hauled the wheel hard over** elle a braqué à fond; *Aut* **to turn hard to the left** braquer à gauche, faire un virage très sec vers la gauche; **to swim hard for the shore** nager de toutes ses forces vers le rivage; [illegible] **they're hard at it** *(working)* ils sont plongés dans leur travail

(**b**) *(with difficulty)* difficilement; **to be hard put** *or* **pushed** *or* **pressed to do sth** avoir du mal à faire qch; **you'll be hard put to find a shop open at this time** tu vas avoir du mal à trouver une boutique ouverte à cette heure-ci; **old habits die hard** les vieilles habitudes ont la vie dure

(**c**) *(harshly, severely → treat someone)* durement, sévèrement; *(→ rain)* à verse; *(→ freeze, snow)* fort; **he's feeling hard done by** il a l'impression d'avoir été injustement traité; **to be hard hit by sth** être durement touché par qch; **she took the news/his death pretty hard** la nouvelle/sa mort l'a beaucoup éprouvée; *Old-fashioned* **it'll go hard with him if he keeps telling lies** ça va aller mal pour lui s'il continue à raconter des mensonges

(**d**) *(solid)* **the ground was frozen hard** le gel avait complètement durci la terre; **to set hard** *(concrete, mortar)* prendre

(**e**) *(close)* **to follow hard on the heels of sb** être sur les talons de qn; **to follow** *or* **to come hard on the heels of sth** suivre qch de très près

(**f**) *Fam (idiom)* **hard up** *(short of money)* fauché, à sec; **to be hard up for ideas** manquer d'idées❑, être à court d'idées❑; **to be hard up for volunteers** manquer de volontaires❑; *Fig* **you must be hard up if you're going out with him!** il faut vraiment que tu n'aies rien à te mettre sous la dent pour sortir avec lui!

3 *n* **to try one's hardest** faire de son mieux

4 hard by *prep Old-fashioned* tout près de

►► *Typ & Comput* ***hard carriage return*** retour *m* chariot obligatoire; *Fam* ***hard case*** *(person)* dur(e) *m,f* à cuire; ***hard cash*** (argent *m*) liquide *m*; *Am* ***hard cider*** cidre *m*; ***hard coal*** anthracite *m*; *Fin* ***hard commodities*** minerais *mpl*; *Ling* ***hard consonant*** consonne *f* dure; *Comput* ***hard copy*** copie *f* sur papier, sortie *f* papier; ***hard core*** *(nucleus)* noyau *m* dur; *Constr* empierrement *m*; *Mus* hard rock *m inv*, hard *m inv*; *(pornography)* porno *m* hard; *Br* ***hard court*** *(for tennis)* court *m* en ciment; ***hard currency*** monnaie *f ou* devise *f* forte; **a hard currency shop** un magasin où on paye en devises; *Comput* ***hard disk*** disque *m* dur; *Comput* ***hard disk drive, hard drive*** unité *f* de disque dur; ***hard drug*** drogue *f* dure; *Horseriding* ***hard gallop*** galop *m* soutenu; ***hard hat*** *(of construction worker)* casque *m*; *Am Fam (construction worker)* ouvrier(ère) *m,f* du bâtiment; ***hard hat area*** = zone où le port du casque est obligatoire; **hard hat area** *(sign)* port du casque obligatoire; *Typ & Comput* ***hard hyphen*** césure *f* imposée, trait *m* d'union imposé; ***hard labour*** *(UNCOUNT)* travaux *mpl* forcés; ***hard landing*** *(by spacecraft)* atterrissage *m* avec impact; *Fig (during economic crisis)* atterrissage *m* brutal; *Metal* ***hard lead*** plomb *m* aigre; *Pol* ***the hard left*** l'extrême gauche; ***hard line*** ligne *f* de conduite dure; **to take a hard line on sb/sth** adopter une ligne de conduite dure avec qn/sur qch; ***hard liquor*** spiritueux *mpl*; *Fin* ***hard loan*** prêt *m* aux conditions du marché; *Press* ***hard news*** nouvelles *fpl* sûres *ou* vérifiées; *Vet* ***hard pad*** coussinet *m* dur; *Typ & Comput* ***hard page break*** fin *f* de page obligatoire; *Anat* ***hard palate*** voûte *f* du palais, palais *m* dur; ***hard porn*** porno *m* hard, hard *m inv*; *Comput* ***hard reset*** réinitialisation *f* totale de la machine; *Typ & Comput* ***hard return*** saut *m* de ligne manuel; *Pol* ***the hard right*** l'extrême droit; *Mus* ***hard rock*** hard rock *m inv*, hard *m inv*; *esp Am Culin* ***hard sauce*** = sauce au beurre, au sucre et au brandy ou au rhum servie avec le pudding; ***hard science*** science *f* dure; ***hard sell*** vente *f* agressive; **to give sth the hard sell** promouvoir qch de façon agressive; **the salesman gave us the hard sell** le vendeur a essayé de nous forcer la main; ***hard sell approach, hard sell tactics*** méthode *f* de vente agressive; *Aut* ***hard shoulder*** bande *f* d'arrêt d'urgence; ***hard space*** espace *m* insécable; ***hard water*** eau *f* calcaire *ou* dure

---

'Hard Times' *Dickens* 'Les Temps difficiles'

---

hard-and-fast *adj (rule)* strict, absolu; *(information)* correct, vrai; **there's no hard-and-fast rule about it** il n'existe pas de règle absolue là-dessus

hardass ['hɑːdæs] *n Am very Fam (person)* dur(e) *m,f* à cuire

hardassed ['hɑːdæst] *adj Am very Fam* vache

hardback ['hɑːdbæk] **1** *n (book)* livre *m* cartonné; **available in hardback** disponible en version cartonnée

2 *adj* cartonné

hardball ['hɑːdbɔːl] *n Am (game)* baseball *m*; *(ball)* balle *f* de baseball; *Fam Fig* **to play hardball** employer les grands moyens❑

hard-bitten [-'bɪtən] *adj Fam* endurci❑

hardboard ['hɑːdbɔːd] *n* panneau *m* de fibres; **a sheet of hardboard** un panneau dur

hard-boil *vt* **to hard-boil an egg** faire un œuf dur

hard-boiled *adj* (**a**) *(egg)* dur (**b**) *Fam (person)* dur à cuire

hardcore ['hɑːdkɔː(r)] *n (for roads, buildings)* blocaille *f*

hard-core *adj (belief in political system)* dur; *(believer)* endurci; *(support)* ferme; *(pornography, music)* hard *(inv)*

►► *Mktg* ***hard-core loyal*** fidèle *mf* absolu(e); *Mktg* ***hard-core loyalty*** fidélité *f* absolue

hardcover ['hɑːd,kʌvə(r)] **1** *n (book)* livre *m* cartonné; **available in hardcover** disponible en version cartonnée

2 *adj* cartonné

hard-drinking *adj* qui boit beaucoup

hard-earned [-'ɜːnt] *adj (money)* durement gagné; *(victory)* durement *ou* difficilement remporté; *(reputation)* durement acquis; *(holiday, reward)* bien mérité

harden ['hɑːdən] **1** *vt (person → physically, emotionally)* endurcir; *(steel)* tremper; *Ling (consonant)* durcir; *Med (arteries)* durcir, scléroser; **to harden oneself to sth** s'endurcir à qch; **to harden one's heart** endurcir son cœur; **she hardened her heart against him** elle lui a fermé son cœur

2 *vi* (**a**) *(snow, skin, steel)* durcir; *(concrete, mortar)* prendre; *Med (arteries)* durcir, se scléroser; *(person → emotionally)* s'endurcir, se durcir; *(→ physically)* s'endurcir; *(attitude)* se durcir

(**b**) *Fin (prices, market)* s'affermir

►**harden off 1** *vt sep (plant)* mettre en jauge, habituer à des conditions plus dures

2 *vi (plant)* s'habituer à des conditions plus dures

►**harden up 1** *vi Fin (shares)* se raffermir

2 *vt sep (toughen → person)* endurcir

hardened ['hɑːdənd] *adj (snow, skin, substance)* durci; *(steel)* trempé, durci; *Med (arteries)* sclérosé; **to become hardened to sth** se blinder contre qch; **a hardened criminal** un criminel endurci *ou* invétéré

hardener ['hɑːdənə(r)] *n (for glue, fingernails)* durcisseur *m*

hardening ['hɑːdənɪŋ] *n (of snow, skin, attitudes)* durcissement *m*; *(of steel)* trempe *f*; *(of person → physical)* endurcissement *m*; *(→ emotional)* durcissement *m*; *Fin (of prices)* affermissement *m*

►► *Med* ***hardening of the arteries*** durcissement *m ou* sclérose *f* des artères

hard-faced [-'feɪst] *adj* au visage dur

hard-fought [-'fɔːt] *adj (game, battle)* rudement disputé

hard-hat *adj Am* = caractéristique des attitudes conservatrices des ouvriers du bâtiment

hard-headed [-'hedɪd] *adj* (**a**) *(tough, shrewd → person)* à la tête froide; *(→ realism)* froid, brut; *(→ bargaining)* dur; *(→ decision)* froid (**b**) *Am (stubborn → person)* qui a la tête dure; *(→ attitude)* entêté

hard-hearted [-'hɑːtɪd] *adj (person)* insensible, dur, au cœur de pierre; *(attitude)* dur; **to be hard-hearted towards sb** être dur avec *ou* envers qn

hard-heartedness [-'hɑːtɪdnɪs] *n* insensibilité *f*, dureté *f* de coeur

hard-hit *adj* gravement atteint *ou* touché; **one particularly hard-hit village** un village touché de façon particulièrement dure

hard-hitting [-'hɪtɪŋ] *adj* (**a**) *(verbal attack)* rude; *(speech, report)* implacable, sans indulgence, **the speech was a hard-hitting attack on this policy** le discours était une attaque directe contre cette politique (**b**) *(boxer)* qui frappe dur

hardiness ['hɑːdɪnɪs] *n (of person)* résistance *f*, robustesse *f*; *(of plant, tree)* résistance *f*

hard-line *adj (policy, doctrine)* dur; *(politician)* intransigeant, endurci, intraitable

hardliner [,hɑːd'laɪnə(r)] *n* partisan(e) *m,f* de la manière forte

hardly ['hɑːdlɪ] *adv* (**a**) *(barely)* à peine, ne... guère; **he can hardly read** il sait à peine *ou* tout juste lire; **you can hardly move in here for furniture** c'est à peine si on peut bouger ici tellement il y a de meubles; **I have hardly started** je viens à peine *ou* tout juste de commencer; **I hardly get a minute to myself these days** c'est tout juste si j'ai une minute à moi ces jours-ci; **I can hardly believe it** j'ai du mal à le croire; *Literary* **hardly had I said these**

words when he arrived à peine avais-je prononcé ces mots qu'il arriva; **hardly anyone** presque personne; **hardly anywhere** presque nulle part; **I hardly ever see you these days** je ne te vois presque jamais ces temps-ci; **there's hardly anything in the fridge** il n'y a presque rien dans le frigo; **I paid hardly anything for it** ça m'a coûté trois fois rien; **you've hardly touched your food** tu n'as presque rien mangé; **I can hardly wait to see her** je suis très impatient de la voir; *Ironic* **I can hardly wait!** j'en frémis d'avance!; **she hardly ever goes out** elle ne sort presque jamais; **hardly a week goes by without a telephone call from her** il se passe rarement une semaine sans qu'elle téléphone; **I need hardly say that...** ai-je besoin de vous dire que...?, je n'ai pas besoin de vous dire que...

(**b**) *(expressing negative opinion)* **it's hardly MY fault!** ce n'est quand même pas de ma faute!; **it's hardly any of your business** cela ne te regarde absolument pas; **this is hardly the time to be selling your house** ce n'est vraiment pas le moment de vendre votre maison; **it's hardly surprising, is it?** ça n'a rien de surprenant, ce n'est guère surprenant; **it's hardly surprising that she left him** ce n'est pas surprenant qu'elle l'ait quitté, il n'est guère surprenant qu'elle l'ait quitté; **hardly!** *(not in the slightest)* bien au contraire!, loin de là!; **she's hardly likely to agree** elle ne risque pas d'accepter; **he'd hardly have said that** cela m'étonnerait qu'il ait dit cela

hard-mouthed [-ˈmaʊðd] *adj* (**a**) *(horse)* qui ne prend pas le mors *ou* la bride (**b**) *(person)* têtu

hardness [ˈhɑːdnɪs] *n* (**a**) *(of snow, skin, water, substance)* dureté *f*; *(of steel)* trempe *f*, dureté *f* (**b**) *(difficulty)* difficulté *f* (**c**) *(severeness → of personality)* dureté *f*; *(→ of heart)* dureté *f*, froideur *f* (**d**) *(strenuousness)* difficulté *f* (**e**) *Fin (of prices)* affermissement *m*

►► *Med* ***hardness of hearing*** surdité *f* partielle

hard-nosed [-ˈnəʊzd] *adj Fam (tough, shrewd → person)* à la tête froide❑; *(→ realism)* froid❑, brut❑; *(→ bargaining)* dur❑; *(→ decision)* froid❑

hard-on *n Vulg* **to have a hard-on** bander; **to get a hard-on** se mettre à bander; **to give sb a hard-on** faire bander qn

hard-packed [-ˈpækt] *adj (snow, soil)* tassé

hard-pressed [-ˈprest], **hard-pushed** [-ˈpʊʃt] *adj* **to be hard-pressed for money/ideas/suggestions** être à court d'argent/d'idées/de suggestions; **to be hard-pressed for time** manquer de temps; **to be hard-pressed to do sth** avoir du mal à faire qch

hard-sectored [-ˈsektəd] *adj Comput (disk)* à secteurs pré-définis

hard-shell, hard-shelled *adj* (**a**) *(animal)* à coquille dure (**b**) *Am (orthodox)* pur et dur

hardship [ˈhɑːdʃɪp] *n* épreuves *fpl*; **to go through a time of hardship** traverser de terribles épreuves; **to suffer great hardship** *or* **hardships** subir *ou* traverser de rudes épreuves; **a life of hardship** une vie pleine d'épreuves; **further hardship is in store** d'autres épreuves nous attendent

►► ***hardship allowance*** *(for student)* = aide accordée à un étudiant en cas de graves problèmes financiers

hardtack [ˈhɑːdtæk] *n Naut* biscuit *m* de marin

hardtop [ˈhɑːdtɒp] *n Aut (of car)* hard-top *m*; *(car)* voiture *f* à hard-top

hardware [ˈhɑːdweə(r)] **1** *n (UNCOUNT)* (**a**) *(ironmongery)* quincaillerie *f*

(**b**) *Comput* matériel *m*, hardware *m*; **hardware problem** problème *m* de matériel

(**c**) *Mil* matériel *m* de guerre, armement *m*

(**d**) *Fam (guns)* armes❑ *fpl*; **he wasn't carrying any hardware** il ne portait pas d'armes❑, il n'était pas armé❑

2 *comp Comput (company, manufacturer)* de matériel informatique; *(problem)* de matériel *ou* hardware

►► ***hardware dealer*** quincaillier(ère) *m,f*; ***hardware shop, hardware store*** quincaillerie *f*

hardwearing [ˌhɑːdˈweərɪŋ] *adj* robuste, résistant

hard-wired [-ˈwaɪəd] *adj Comput* câblé

hard-won [-ˈwʌn] *adj (victory, trophy, independence)* durement gagné; *(reputation)* durement acquis

hardwood [ˈhɑːdwʊd] **1** *n (wood)* bois *m* dur; *(tree)* arbre *m* à feuilles caduques

2 *comp (floor)* en bois dur

hardworking [ˌhɑːdˈwɜːkɪŋ] *adj (person)* travailleur; *(engine, machine, printer)* robuste

hardy [ˈhɑːdɪ] *(comp* **hardier**, *superl* **hardiest**) *adj* (**a**) *(strong → person, animal)* robuste, résistant; *(→ plant)* résistant (**b**) *(intrepid → explorer, pioneer)* intrépide, courageux

►► *Bot* ***hardy annual*** plante *f* annuelle; *Bot* ***hardy perennial*** plante *f* vivace; *Fig* serpent *m* de mer

Hardy Boys *npl* **the Hardy Boys** = personnages d'une série de livres d'aventures pour jeunes garçons

hardy har har [-hɑːˈhɑː(r)] *exclam Fam Ironic* ha! ha! très drôle!

hare [heə(r)] *(pl* **inv** *or* **hares**) **1** *n* (**a**) *Culin & Zool* lièvre *m*; *Br Fig* **to raise** *or* **to start a hare** mettre une question sur le tapis; *Fig* **to run with the hares and hunt with the hounds** jouer double jeu

(**b**) *Sport (at dog race)* lièvre *m*

(**c**) *Br (game)* **hare and hounds** jeu *m* de piste

2 *vi Fam* **to hare across/down/out** traverser/descendre/sortir à toutes jambes; **she came haring down the stairs** elle a dévalé les escaliers à fond de train

►► ***hare coursing*** chasse *f* à courre au lièvre; *Bot* ***hare's ear*** buplèvre *m*; *Bot* ***hare's foot clover*** pied-de-lièvre *m*

►**hare off** *vi Br Fam* prendre ses jambes à son cou, s'enfuir à toutes jambes

harebell [ˈheəbel] *n Bot* campanule *f* à feuilles rondes

harebrained [ˈheəˌbreɪnd] *adj (reckless, mad → person)* écervelé; *(→ scheme)* insensé, fou (folle)

harelip [ˌheəˈlɪp] *n Med* bec-de-lièvre *m*

harem [*Br* hɑːˈriːm, *Am* ˈhærəm] *n also Fig* harem *m*

►► ***harem pants*** pantalon *m* bouffant

haricot (bean) [ˈhærɪkəʊ-] *n* haricot *m* blanc

harissa [hæˈriːsə] *n Culin* harissa *f*

hark [hɑːk] *vi Literary* prêter l'oreille, ouïr; **hark, I hear voices!** écoutez *ou* chut, j'entends des voix!; *Br Fam* **hark at him!** écoutez-le donc!

►**hark back to** *vt insep (recall)* revenir à; **to hark back to sth** revenir (tout le temps) à qch; **the style harks back to the 1940s** le style rappelle celui des années 40

harken [ˈhɑːkən] *vi Literary* prêter l'oreille

Harlem [ˈhɑːləm] *n* Harlem

►► ***the Harlem Globetrotters*** les Harlem Globetrotters *mpl*

Harlequin [ˈhɑːlɪkwɪn] **1** *pr n* Arlequin

2 harlequin *adj (costume)* bigarré; *(dog's coat)* tacheté

►► *Orn* ***harlequin duck*** garrot *m* arlequin

harlequinade [ˌhɑːlɪkwɪˈneɪd] *n* arlequinade *f*

Harley Street [ˈhɑːlɪ-] *n* = rue du centre de Londres célèbre pour ses spécialistes en médecine

harlot [ˈhɑːlət] *n Arch or Hum* prostituée *f*

harm [hɑːm] **1** *n (UNCOUNT) (physical)* mal *m*; *(psychological)* tort *m*, mal *m*; **to do sb harm** faire du mal à qn; **I hope Ed won't come to (any) harm** j'espère qu'il n'arrivera rien à Ed; **a bath wouldn't do him any harm** un bain ne lui ferait pas de mal; **she has done you no harm** elle ne vous a fait aucun mal; **they didn't mean any harm** ils ne voulaient pas (faire) de mal; **Ted means no harm** Ted n'est pas méchant; **I know you didn't mean any harm when you said it** je sais que tu ne l'as pas dit méchamment; **the incident did a great deal of harm to his reputation** cet incident a beaucoup nui à sa réputation; **no harm done** il n'y a pas de mal; **there's no harm in trying** il n'y a pas de mal à essayer, on ne perd rien à essayer; **I see no harm in their going** je ne vois pas d'inconvénient à ce qu'ils y aillent; **what harm is there in it?** qu'est-ce qu'il y a de mal (à cela)?; **no harm will come of it** ça n'est pas grave; **too much adverse publicity will do their cause a great deal of harm** trop de mauvaise publicité nuira énormément à leur cause; **to do more harm than good** faire plus de mal que de bien; **out of harm's way** *(person)* en sûreté, en lieu sûr; *(things)* en lieu sûr

2 *vt* (**a**) *(person → physically)* faire du mal à; *(→ psychologically)* faire du tort à, nuire à; **Ray wouldn't harm a hair on her head** Ray ne lui ferait aucun mal; **he wasn't harmed by the experience** ça ne lui a pas fait de mal

(**b**) *(surface)* abîmer, endommager; *(crops)* endommager; *(environment)* nuire à

(**c**) *(cause, interests)* causer du tort à, être préjudiciable à; *(reputation)* salir

harmful [ˈhɑːmfʊl] *adj* (**a**) *(person, influence)* nuisible, malfaisant (**b**) *(chemicals)* nocif; *(effects)* nuisible; **harmful to plants** nuisible pour les plantes; **in small doses the drug is not harmful** à petites doses, ce médicament n'est pas dangereux

harmfully [ˈhɑːmfʊlɪ] *adv* de façon nuisible

harmfulness [ˈhɑːmfʊlnɪs] *n* nature *f* nuisible; *(of chemicals)* nocivité *f*

harmless [ˈhɑːmlɪs] *adj* (**a**) *(person)* inoffensif, qui n'est pas méchant; *(animal)* inoffensif (**b**) *(joke)* sans malice, anodin; *(pastime)* innocent; **it was just a bit of harmless fun** c'était pour rire; **harmless gossip** propos *mpl* inoffensifs

harmlessly [ˈhɑːmlɪslɪ] *adv* sans faire de mal, sans dommage *ou* dommages

harmlessness [ˈhɑːmlɪsnɪs] *n (of pastime)* innocence *f*

harmonic [hɑːˈmɒnɪk] **1** *n* (**a**) *Mus (of root)* harmonique *m*; *(on stringed instrument)* harmonique *m*, son *m* flûté

(**b**) *Math & Phys (of wave motion)* harmonique *m*

2 *adj* harmonique

►► *Math* ***harmonic analysis*** analyse *f* harmonique; *Math* ***harmonic mean*** moyenne *f* harmonique; *Phys* ***harmonic motion*** mouvement *m* sinusoïdal; *Math* ***harmonic progression*** progression *f* harmonique; ***harmonic series*** *Mus* échelle *f* harmonique; *Math & Phys* série *f* harmonique

harmonica [hɑːˈmɒnɪkə] *n Mus* harmonica *m*

harmonics [hɑːˈmɒnɪks] *n* (**a**) *(UNCOUNT) (science)* harmonie *f* (**b**) *Mus (sounds)* sons *mpl* harmoniques

harmonious [hɑːˈməʊnjəs] *adj* harmonieux

harmoniously [hɑːˈməʊnjəslɪ] *adv* harmonieusement; *(work, live)* en harmonie

harmonist [ˈhɑːmənɪst] *n* harmoniste *mf*

harmonium [hɑːˈməʊnjəm] *n Mus* harmonium *m*

harmonization [ˌhɑːmənaɪˈzeɪʃən] *n* harmonisation *f*

harmonize, -ise [ˈhɑːmənaɪz] **1** *vt* (**a**) *Mus (instrument, melody)* harmoniser

(**b**) *(colours)* harmoniser, assortir

(**c**) *(views, statements)* harmoniser, faire concorder; *(people)* concilier, amener à un accord

2 *vi* (**a**) *Mus (sing in harmony)* chanter en harmonie; *(be harmonious)* être harmonieux *ou* en harmonie; *(write harmony)* harmoniser, faire des harmonies

(**b**) *(colours)* aller (bien) ensemble, se marier (bien); **choose colours that harmonize with the background** choisissez des couleurs qui soient assorties au décor

(**c**) *(sounds)* s'harmoniser; *(temperaments, people, ideas etc)* se mettre en harmonie, s'accorder

harmony [ˈhɑːmənɪ] *(pl* **harmonies**) *n* (**a**) *Mus* harmonie *f*; **to study harmony** étudier l'harmonie; **to sing in harmony** chanter en harmonie; **a three-part harmony** une harmonie en trois parties; **unusual harmonies** des harmonies *fpl* inhabituelles

(**b**) *(agreement → of colours)* harmonie *f*; *(→ of temperaments, people, ideas etc)* harmonie *f*, accord *m*; **to live in harmony with sb** vivre en harmonie avec qn; **her choice is in perfect harmony with mine** ses choix sont parfaitement en harmonie *ou* en accord avec les miens; **the scene was one of perfect harmony** une harmonie parfaite se dégageait de cette scène

harness [ˈhɑːnɪs] **1** *n* (**a**) *(for horse, oxen)* harnais *m*, harnachement *m*

(**b**) *(for parachute, car seat)* harnais *m*

(**c**) *(for child)* harnais *m*

(**d**) *Tex (of loom)* harnais *m*

(**e**) *(idioms)* **to get** *or* **to be back in harness** reprendre le collier; **to die in harness** mourir à la peine *ou* au travail *ou* à la tâche; **to work in harness (with sb)** travailler de concert (avec qn)

2 *vt* (**a**) *(horse)* harnacher, mettre le harnais à; *(oxen, dogs)* atteler; **the pony was harnessed to the cart** le poney était attelé à la charrette; *Fig* **to be harnessed to sth** être étroitement lié à qch

(**b**) *(energy, resources)* exploiter, maîtriser

►► ***harness horse*** cheval *m* d'attelage; ***harness race*** course *f* attelée; ***harness racing*** *(UNCOUNT)* courses *fpl* attelées; ***harness room*** sellerie *f*

harnessing ['hɑːnɪsɪŋ] *n* (**a**) *(of horse)* harnachement *m*; *(of oxen, dogs)* attelage *m* (**b**) *(of energy, resources)* exploitation *f*

Harold ['hærəld] *pr n* Harold

harp [hɑːp] *Mus* **1** *n* harpe *f*

2 *vi* jouer de la harpe

►**harp on** *Fam* **1** *vi* chanter (toujours) le même refrain *ou* la même rengaine; **to harp on about sth** rabâcher qch, revenir sans cesse sur qch ❑; **to harp on at sb about sth** rebattre les oreilles à qn au sujet de qch; **don't keep harping on!** arrêtez de rabâcher!

2 *vt insep* **to harp on sth** revenir sans cesse sur qch ❑, rabâcher qch

harpist ['hɑːpɪst] *n* harpiste *mf*

harpoon [hɑː'puːn] **1** *n* harpon *m*

2 *vt* harponner

harpooning [hɑː'puːnɪŋ] *n* harponnage *m*, harponnement *m*

harpsichord ['hɑːpsɪkɔːd] *n Mus* clavecin *m*

harpsichordist ['hɑːpsɪˌkɔːdɪst] *n* claveciniste *mf*

harpy ['hɑːpɪ] *(pl* **harpies***)* **1** *n Fig* harpie *f*, mégère *f*

2 Harpy *n Myth* Harpye *f*, Harpie *f*; **the Harpies** les Harpyes *fpl ou* Harpies *fpl*

►► *Orn* ***harpy bat*** harpie *f*; *Orn* ***harpy eagle*** harpie *f*

harridan ['hærɪdən] *n* harpie *f*, vieille sorcière *f*

harried ['hærɪd] *adj (person)* tracassé, harcelé; **a harried husband** un mari harcelé (par sa femme); *(expression, look)* tourmenté

harrier ['hærɪə(r)] *n* (**a**) *(dog)* harrier *m* (**b**) *Sport (runner)* coureur *m* (de cross); **Plymouth Harriers** l'équipe d'athlétisme de Plymouth (**c**) *Orn* busard *m*

Harris ['hærɪs] *n (island)* Harris

►► ***Harris poll*** sondage *m* de l'institut Harris; ***Harris tweed***® tweed *m* (des Hébrides)

Harrods ['hærədz] *n* = grand magasin de luxe à Londres

Harrovian [hə'rəʊvɪən] *n Br Sch (present)* élève *m* de Harrow; *(past)* ancien élève *m* de Harrow

harrow ['hærəʊ] **1** *n Agr* herse *f*; *Fig Literary* **to be under the harrow** subir des tribulations *ou* de dures épreuves

2 *vt* (**a**) *Agr* labourer à la herse (**b**) *Fig (distress)* torturer, déchirer le cœur à (**c**) *Rel* **Christ harrowing Hell** la descente aux enfers du Christ

3 Harrow *n* = prestigieuse "public school" dans la banlieue de Londres

harrowed ['hærəʊd] *adj Fig (appearance)* meurtri

harrowing ['hærəʊɪŋ] **1** *adj (story)* terrible; *(cry)* déchirant; *(experience)* pénible, traumatisant; **the report makes harrowing reading** le rapport raconte des faits pénibles à lire

2 *n* (**a**) *Agr* hersage *m* (**b**) *Rel* **the harrowing of Hell** la descente aux enfers du Christ

harrumph [hə'rʌmf] **1** *onomat* = bruit que l'on fait en se raclant la gorge

2 *vi* se racler la gorge

Harry ['hærɪ] *n Br Fam Old-fashioned* **to play old Harry with sb** en faire voir des vertes et des pas mûres à qn; **to play old Harry with sb's health** ruiner la santé de qn ❑

harry ['hærɪ] *(pt & pp* **harried***)* *vt* (**a**) *(harass → person)* harceler, tourmenter; **he was harried by creditors** il était harcelé par ses créanciers (**b**) *(pillage → village)* dévaster, mettre à sac (**c**) *Mil (enemy, troops)* harceler

harsh [hɑːʃ] *adj* (**a**) *(cruel, severe → person)* dur, sévère, cruel; *(→ punishment, treatment)* dur, sévère; *(→ fate)* cruel; *(→ criticism, judgement, words)* dur, sévère; **to be harsh with sb** être dur envers *ou* avec qn

(**b**) *(conditions, weather, climate)* rude, rigoureux

(**c**) *(bitter → struggle)* âpre, acharné

(**d**) *(cry, voice)* criard, strident; *(tone)* dur

(**e**) *(colour, contrast)* choquant; *(light)* cru

(**f**) *(bleak → landscape, desert)* dur, austère

harshly ['hɑːʃlɪ] *adv* (**a**) *(treat, punish)* sévèrement, avec rigueur (**b**) *(answer, speak)* avec rudesse *ou* dureté; *(judge)* sévèrement, durement; **don't speak so harshly of him** ne parlez pas de lui si durement (**c**) *(cry, shout)* d'un ton strident

harshness ['hɑːʃnɪs] *n* (**a**) *(of person)* dureté *f*, sévérité *f*; *(of punishment, treatment)* sévérité *f*; *(of judgement)* dureté *f*, sévérité *f*; *(of statement, words, tone)* dureté *f* (**b**) *(of conditions, weather, climate)* rigueur *f*, rudesse *f* (**c**) *(of cry, voice)* discordance *f* (**d**) *(of light)* dureté *f*; *(of contrast)* caractère *m* choquant

hart [hɑːt] *(pl* **inv** *or* **harts***)* *n Zool* cerf *m*

hartebeest ['hɑːtəbiːst] *n Zool* bubale *m*

harum-scarum [ˌheərəm'skeərəm] *Fam* **1** *n* casse-cou *mf inv*

2 *adj (wild, reckless)* casse-cou *(inv)*

3 *adv* comme un fou (une folle) ❑

Harvard ['hɑːvəd] *n* Harvard *(prestigieuse université située à Cambridge, dans le Massachusetts)*

harvest ['hɑːvɪst] **1** *n* (**a**) *(gathering → of cereal, crops)* moisson *f*; *(→ of fruit, mushrooms)* récolte *f*, cueillette *f*; *(→ of grapes)* vendange *f*, vendanges *fpl*

(**b**) *(yield)* récolte *f*; **a good/poor harvest** une bonne/mauvaise récolte

(**c**) *(time of year)* (temps *m ou* époque *f* de la) moisson; **at harvest (time)** à l'époque de la moisson

(**d**) *Fig (from experience, research)* moisson *f*; **it yielded a rich harvest of information** on a récolté beaucoup d'informations; **a bitter harvest** une moisson amère

2 *vt* (**a**) *Agr (cereal, crops)* moissonner; *(fruit, mushrooms)* cueillir, récolter; *(grapes)* vendanger

(**b**) *Fig (benefits)* moissonner; *(consequences)* récolter

3 *vi (for cereal, crops)* moissonner, faire la moisson; *(for fruit)* faire les récoltes; *(for grapes)* vendanger

►► *Br* ***harvest festival*** = action de grâce après la rentrée des récoltes; *Br* ***harvest home*** *(festival)* fête *f* de la moisson; *(harvesting)* moisson *f*; *Entom* ***harvest mite*** aoûtat *m*; ***harvest moon*** pleine lune *f* (de l'équinoxe d'automne); *Zool* ***harvest mouse*** rat *m* des moissons; *Entom* ***harvest spider*** faucheux *m*; ***harvest supper*** = en Grande-Bretagne, dîner réunissant une communauté villageoise à la fin de la moisson; *Am & Scot* ***Harvest Thanksgiving*** = action de grâce après la rentrée des récoltes; ***harvest time*** période *f* de la moisson; **at harvest time** à la moisson

HARVEST FESTIVAL

À l'occasion de cette célébration de la moisson, les églises en Grande-Bretagne sont souvent décorées de fruits, de légumes et de blé.

harvester ['hɑːvɪstə(r)] *n* (**a**) *(machine)* moissonneuse *f* (**b**) *(person)* moissonneur(euse) *m,f*

harvesting ['hɑːvɪstɪŋ] **1** *n (UNCOUNT)* moisson *f*, moissons *fpl*

2 *adj (season)* des moissons

harvestman ['hɑːvɪstmæn] *(pl* **harvestmen** [-men]*)* *n* (**a**) *Agr* moissonneur *m* (**b**) *Entom* faucheux *m*

Harwell ['hɑːwel] *n* = centre de recherche en énergie atomique près d'Oxford

has [həz, *stressed* hæz] *3rd pers sing of* **have**

has-been ['hæzbiːn] *n Fam* has been *mf inv*

hash [hæʃ] **1** *n* (**a**) *Br Fam (muddle, mix-up)* pagaille *f*, embrouillamini *m*; *(mess, botch)* gâchis ❑ *m*; **to make a hash of sth** bousiller qch, ficher qch en l'air; **he certainly made a hash of putting that shelf up!** il a certainement fait un beau gâchis en installant cette étagère!; **I made a real hash of the interview** j'ai complètement merdé à l'entretien

(**b**) *Culin* hachis *m*

(**c**) *Fam (marijuana)* hasch *m*

(**d**) *(symbol)* dièse *m*

(**e**) *Br Fam (idiom)* **to fix** *or* **to settle sb's hash** *(in revenge, punishment)* régler son compte à qn; *(reduce to silence)* clouer le bec à qn

2 *vt Culin* hacher

►► ***hash browns*** = pommes de terre rapées et sautées (présentées parfois sous forme de galette); *Fam* ***hash head*** = personne qui fume beaucoup de cannabis; *Am Fam* ***hash house*** *(restaurant)* gargote ❑ *f*; ***hash mark, hash sign*** *(symbol)* dièse *m*; *Am Fam* ***hash slinger*** serveur(euse) *m,f* dans une gargote ❑

►**hash over** *vt sep esp Am Fam (discuss sth)* discuter ❑

►**hash up** *vt sep* (**a**) *Br Fam (mess up)* bâcler, bousiller; **I'm afraid I completely hashed up the interview** j'ai bien peur d'avoir complètement merdé à l'entretien (**b**) *Culin* hacher

hashed index [hæʃd-] *n Comput* index *m* de totalisation

hashish ['hæʃiːʃ] *n* haschisch *m*, hachisch *m*

hash-up *n Br Fam (mess)* gâchis ❑ *m*; **to make a hash-up of sth** bousiller *ou* gâcher ❑ qch

Hasid ['hæsɪd] *n Rel* hassid *m*

Hasidic [hæ'sɪdɪk] *adj Rel* hassidique

haslet ['hæzlɪt] *n (UNCOUNT) Culin* = sorte de pâté préparé avec des abats de porc

hasn't ['hæzənt] = **has not**

hasp [hɑːsp] **1** *n (for door)* loquet *m*, loqueteau *m*, moraillon *m*; *(for jewellery, lid, clothing, book)* fermoir *m*

2 *vt (door)* fermer au loquet; *(lid)* fermer; *(with padlock)* cadenasser

Hassid, Hassidic = **Hasid, Hasidic**

hassle ['hæsəl] *Fam* **1** *n* (**a**) *(trouble, inconvenience)* embêtements *mpl*, emmerdements *mpl*; **I don't want any hassle** je ne veux pas d'embêtements; **it's too much hassle** c'est trop galère; **it won't be any hassle** ça ne posera pas de problèmes ❑; **finding their house was quite a hassle** trouver leur maison n'a pas été de la tarte, on a eu un mal fou à trouver leur maison; **all the hassle of filling out the form** tous les embêtements pour remplir le formulaire

(**b**) *(quarrel)* dispute ❑ *f*, chamaillerie *f*; **there was a big hassle over who should drive** il y a eu une grosse dispute *ou* bagarre ❑ pour savoir qui allait conduire

2 *vt (annoy, nag)* embêter, harceler ❑; **don't hassle me about it** ne m'embête pas avec ça; **he keeps hassling me for money** il n'arrête pas de m'embêter pour que je lui donne de l'argent; **Yvonne's always hassling him to stop smoking** Yvonne est toujours après lui pour qu'il arrête de fumer

3 *vi (argue)* se quereller ❑, se chamailler

hassock ['hæsək] *n* (**a**) *Rel* coussin *m* d'agenouilloir (**b**) *(of grass)* touffe *f* d'herbe (**c**) *Am (pouffe)* pouf *m*

hast [həst, *stressed* hæst] *Arch or Bible 2nd pers sing of* **have**

haste [heɪst] *n (speed)* hâte *f*; *(rush)* précipitation *f*; **to do sth in haste** faire qch à la hâte, se dépêcher de faire qch; **to act in haste** agir à la hâte ou précipitamment; **to make haste** se hâter, se dépêcher; **in my haste, I forgot my hat** dans ma hâte, j'ai oublié mon chapeau; *Literary* **I am in haste to leave** j'ai hâte de partir; *Prov* **more haste less speed** hâtez-vous lentement

hasten ['heɪsən] **1** *vt* (**a**) *(speed up → event, decline)* précipiter, hâter; **the accident hastened his death** l'accident précipita *ou* accéléra sa mort; **stress can hasten the ageing process** le stress peut accélérer le vieillissement

(**b**) *(urge on → person)* presser; **we were hastened along a corridor** on nous a entraînés précipitamment dans un couloir

(**c**) *(say quickly)* **she hastened to assure us that all would be well** elle s'empressa de nous assurer que tout irait bien; **it wasn't me, I hasten to add** ce n'était pas moi, je vous assure

2 *vi Literary (verb of movement)* **to hasten away** partir à la hâte, se hâter de partir; **to hasten back** revenir à la hâte, se dépêcher de revenir

hastily ['heɪstɪlɪ] *adv* (**a**) *(hurriedly)* précipitamment, avec précipitation, à la hâte (**b**) *(impetuously, rashly)* hâtivement, sans réfléchir

hastiness ['heɪstɪnɪs] *n* (**a**) *(speed)* précipitation *f*, hâte *f* (**b**) *(rashness)* irréflexion *f*

Hastings ['heɪstɪŋz] *n* Hastings

hasty ['heɪstɪ] *adj* (**a**) *(quick, hurried)* précipité, à la hâte; **I sent him a hasty note** je lui ai envoyé un billet écrit à la hâte; **they made a hasty departure** ils sont partis à la hâte *ou* précipitamment; **she beat a hasty retreat** elle a rapidement battu en retraite

(**b**) *(rash)* irréfléchi, hâtif; **a hasty decision** une décision prise à la hâte *ou* à la légère; **let's not jump to any hasty conclusions** ne concluons pas à la légère *ou* hâtivement; **let's not be over-hasty** ne nous précipitons pas

(**c**) *(short-tempered)* vif; **to have a hasty temper** s'emporter facilement

►► *Culin* ***hasty pudding*** *Br* semoule *f* au lait; *Am* bouillie *f* de maïs *(servie avec de la mélasse)*

hat [hæt] *n* (**a**) *(for wearing)* chapeau *m*; **he always wears a hat** il porte toujours le *ou* un chapeau; *Fam* **keep this under your hat** gardez ceci pour vous❑, n'en soufflez mot à personne; *Fam* **my hat!** mon œil!; *Fam* **hats off!** chapeaux bas!; **I take my hat off to him!** chapeau!

(**b**) *Fig (role)* rôle *m*, casquette *f*; **I'm wearing three different hats at the moment** je porte trois casquettes différentes *ou* j'ai trois rôles différents en ce moment; **I'm saying that with my lawyer's hat on** je dis ça en ma qualité de juriste

(**c**) *(idioms)* **to hang up one's hat** raccrocher; **to pass the hat round** faire la quête; *Fam* **to talk through one's hat** parler à tort et à travers; *Pol* **to throw one's hat into the ring** se mettre sur les rangs; *Fam* **that's old hat** c'est dépassé

►► ***hat rack*** porte-chapeaux *m inv*; *Br* ***hat trick*** *(three goals)* hat-trick *m*; *(three wins)* trois victoires *fpl* consécutives; *(in cricket)* mise *f* hors jeu de trois batteurs avec trois balles de suite; **are you going for the hat trick?** alors, jamais deux sans trois?

hatband ['hætˌbænd] *n* ruban *m* de chapeau

hatbox ['hætˌbɒks] *n* boîte *f* à chapeau

hatch[1] [hætʃ] **1** *n* (**a**) *(hatching of egg)* éclosion *f* (**b**) *(brood)* couvée *f*

2 *vt* (**a**) *(chickens)* faire éclore; *(eggs)* incuber, (faire) couver; *(in fish farming → eggs)* incuber (**b**) *Fig (plan, plot)* tramer, manigancer

3 *vi (eggs)* éclore; *(chicks)* sortir de l'œuf

►**hatch out 1** *vt (chickens)* faire éclore; *(eggs)* incuber, (faire) couver; *(in fish farming → eggs)* incuber

2 *vi (eggs)* éclore; *(chicks)* sortir de l'œuf

►**hatch up** *vt sep (plan, plot)* tramer, manigancer

hatch[2] *n* (**a**) *Naut* écoutille *f*; **to batten down the hatches** fermer les descentes; *Fig* se préparer *(pour affronter une crise)*; *Fam* **down the hatch!** *(when drinking)* à la vôtre! (**b**) *(trapdoor)* trappe *f*; *(for inspection, access)* trappe *f*, panneau *m* (**c**) *(in aircraft, spaceship)* sas *m* (**d**) *(in dam, dike)* vanne *f (d'écluse)* (**e**) *(for serving food)* passe-plat *m*

►► *Constr* ***hatch beam*** *n* galiote *f*

hatch[3] *vt Art* hachurer

hatchback ['hætʃˌbæk] *n Aut* (**a**) *(door)* hayon *m* (**b**) *(car)* voiture *f* à hayon, cinq portes *f inv*

hatcheck ['hættʃek] *adj esp Am*

►► ***hatcheck clerk*** préposé(e) *m,f*; ***hatcheck girl*** fille *f* du vestiaire; ***hatcheck room*** vestiaire *m*

hatchery ['hætʃərɪ] (*pl* **hatcheries**) *n* (**a**) *(for chickens, turkeys)* couvoir *m* (**b**) *(for fish)* station *f* d'alevinage

hatchet ['hætʃɪt] *n* hachette *f*, hache *f* (à main)

►► *Fam* ***hatchet job*** démolissage *m*; **to do a hatchet job on sb/sth** démolir qn/qch; *Fam* ***hatchet man*** *(killer)* tueur *m* à gages❑; *Ind & Pol* = personne dont le rôle est de restructurer une entreprise ou une organisation, le plus souvent à l'aide de mesures impopulaires

hatchet-faced *adj* au visage en lame de couteau

hatching[1] ['hætʃɪŋ] *n* (**a**) *(of eggs)* éclosion *f* (**b**) *(brood)* couvée *f*

hatching[2] *n (UNCOUNT) Art* hachures *fpl*

hatchling ['hætʃlɪŋ] *n (bird)* oisillon *m*; *(chick)* poussin *m*; *(duckling)* caneton *m*

hatchway ['hætʃˌweɪ] *n Naut* écoutille *f*; *(gen)* trappe *f*

hate [heɪt] **1** *vt* (**a**) *(dislike)* détester, avoir horreur de; *(intensely)* haïr, abhorrer; **I hate Sundays** je déteste les dimanches; **I hate getting up early** j'ai horreur de me lever tôt; **she hates having to wear school uniform** elle a horreur d'avoir à porter un uniforme scolaire; **she hates having her hair washed** elle déteste qu'on lui lave les cheveux; **he hates to be contradicted** il ne peut pas souffrir qu'on le contredise; **I hate it when he's in a bad mood** je déteste quand il est de mauvaise humeur; **I hate her for what she has done** je lui en veux vraiment pour ce qu'elle a fait; **I hate myself for letting them down** je m'en veux beaucoup de les avoir laissés tomber

(**b**) *(regret)* **I would hate you to think I was avoiding you** je ne voudrais surtout pas vous donner l'impression que je cherchais à vous éviter; **I hate to mention it, but you still owe me £5** je suis désolé d'avoir à vous le faire remarquer, mais vous me devez toujours 5 livres; **I hate to bother you, but could I use your phone?** je ne voudrais surtout pas vous déranger, mais puis-je utiliser votre téléphone?; *Fam* **I hate to tell you, but I think you've missed your train** je regrette de devoir te le dire mais je pense que tu as raté ton train

2 *n* (**a**) *(emotion)* haine *f*; **I feel nothing but hate for him** je ne ressens que de la haine pour lui

(**b**) *(person hated)* personne *f* que l'on déteste; *(thing hated)* chose *f* que l'on déteste

►► *Am* ***hate crime*** = crime motivé par la haine; ***hate figure*** bête *f* noire; ***hate mail*** lettres *fpl* d'injures

hated ['heɪtɪd] *adj* détesté

hateful ['heɪtfʊl] *adj* odieux, détestable, abominable; **the very idea is hateful to him** l'idée même lui est insupportable

hatefully ['heɪtfʊlɪ] *adv* odieusement, détestablement

hater ['heɪtə(r)] *n* ennemi *m* (**of** de); **to be an animal-hater** détester les animaux

hatesheet ['heɪtˌʃiːt] *n Am Fam* torchon *m* qui incite à la haine

Hatfields and McCoys ['hætfiːldz-] *npl Am* **the Hatfields and McCoys** = noms fictifs représentant des familles rivales

hath [hæθ] *Arch or Bible 3rd pers sing of* **have**

hatless ['hætlɪs] *adj* tête nue, sans chapeau

hatmaker ['hætˌmeɪkə(r)] *n (for men)* chapelier(ère) *m,f*; *(for women)* modiste *mf*

hatpeg ['hætpeg] *n* patère *f*

hatpin ['hætˌpɪn] *n* épingle *f* à chapeau

hatred ['heɪtrɪd] *n* haine *f*; **to feel hatred for sb** avoir de la haine pour qn, haïr qn; **he had an intense hatred of the police** il avait une haine profonde de la police

hatshop ['hætʃɒp] *n (for men)* chapellerie *f*; *(for women)* boutique *f* de modiste

hatstand ['hætstænd] *n* portemanteau *m*

hatter ['hætə(r)] *n* chapelier(ère) *m,f*

haughtily ['hɔːtɪlɪ] *adv* avec arrogance, de manière hautaine

haughtiness ['hɔːtɪnɪs] *n* arrogance *f*, caractère *m* hautain

haughty ['hɔːtɪ] (*compar* **haughtier,** *superl* **haughtiest**) *adj* hautain, arrogant

haul [hɔːl] **1** *vt* (**a**) *(pull)* tirer, traîner; *(tow)* tirer, remorquer; **they hauled the boat out of the water** ils ont tiré le bateau hors de l'eau; *Fig* **she has to haul her little brother everywhere with her** elle doit traîner son petit frère partout avec elle; **they were hauled in front of** *or* **before a judge** on les traîna devant un tribunal; *Fig* **to haul sb over the coals** passer un savon à qn

(**b**) *(transport)* transporter; *(by truck)* camionner, transporter

(**c**) *(move with effort)* hisser; **he hauled himself out of bed** il s'est péniblement sorti du lit; **he hauled himself into a sitting position** il s'est hissé en position assise

(**d**) *Am very Fam (idiom)* **to haul ass** se magner

2 *vi* (**a**) *(pull)* tirer; **they hauled on the cable** ils ont tiré sur le câble

(**b**) *Naut (boat)* lofer; **to haul alongside** accoster

3 *n* (**a**) *(catch, takings → of fisherman, customs)* prise *f*, coup *m* de filet; *(→ of robbers)* butin *m*; **the thieves have made a good haul** les voleurs ont rapporté un beau butin; *Fam* **you've got a good haul!** *(of presents)* c'est un joli tas de cadeaux que tu viens de recevoir!

(**b**) *(pull)* **to give a haul on a rope/fishing net** tirer sur une corde/un filet de pêche

(**c**) *(distance)* parcours *m*, trajet *m*; **it was a long haul from Madrid to Paris** la route fut longue de Madrid à Paris; **long-/short-haul flights** vols *mpl* long courrier/moyen courrier

(**d**) *(in time)* **training to be a doctor is a long haul** les études de médecine sont très longues

►**haul down** *vt sep* (**a**) *(pull down)* descendre, faire descendre; **his parents had to haul him down from the tree** ses parents ont dû le faire descendre de l'arbre (**b**) *(lower → flag, sail)* amener

►**haul in** *vt sep (catch, net, rope)* tirer, amener; *Fam (suspects, people for questioning)* emmener; **the ship was hauled in for repairs** le bateau a été mis en cale pour réparations; *Fam* **Tom was hauled in on a drink-driving charge** Tom a été épinglé pour conduite en état d'ivresse

►**haul off 1** *vt sep (take away)* conduire, amener; **her mother hauled her off to the dentist's** sa mère l'a traînée chez le dentiste; **he was hauled off to prison** on l'a flanqué en prison

2 *vi Am Fam* lever le bras *ou* le poing❑; **she hauled off and slugged him** elle a levé le bras et lui a asséné un coup de poing

►**haul up** *vt sep* (**a**) *(hoist)* monter; *Naut (flag)* hisser; **to haul up a boat** *(on ship)* rentrer une embarcation; *(on the beach)* haler un bateau à sec

(**b**) *(call to account)* **to haul sb up (for sth)** demander des comptes à qn (de qch); **to be hauled up before the court** être traîné devant les tribunaux; **he was hauled up before the headmaster** il a dû se présenter devant le principal

haulage ['hɔːlɪdʒ] **1** *n (UNCOUNT)* (**a**) *(as business)* transports *mpl*, transport *m* (routier); **she's in the haulage business** elle travaille dans le transport routier (**b**) *(act)* transport *m* (**c**) *(cost)* (frais *mpl* de) transport *m*

2 *comp (company)* de transport routier, de transports routiers

►► ***haulage contractor*** entrepreneur *m* de transports routiers; ***haulage firm*** transporteur *m*

haulier ['hɔːlɪə(r)], *Am* **hauler** ['hɔːlə(r)] *n* (**a**) *(business)* entreprise *f* de transports routiers (**b**) *(owner)* entrepreneur *m* de transports routiers (**c**) *(driver)* routier *m*, camionneur *m*

hauling ['hɔːlɪŋ] *n Naut* halage *m*

►► ***hauling rope*** câble *m* de halage

haulm [hɔːm, hɑːm] *n* (**a**) *(of turnip, potato etc)* fane *f* (**b**) *(used for bedding)* fanes *fpl*; *(used for thatching)* chaume *m*

haunch [hɔːntʃ] **1** *n* (**a**) *Culin (of venison)* cuissot *m*; *(of beef)* quartier *m* (**b**) *(of human)* hanche *f*; **to squat down on one's haunches** s'accroupir

2 haunches *npl (of animal)* arrière-train *m*, derrière *m*

haunt [hɔːnt] **1** *vt* (**a**) *(of ghost, spirit)* hanter

(**b**) *(of problems)* hanter, tourmenter; **the memory still haunts me** le souvenir me hante encore; **she is haunted by her unhappy childhood** elle est hantée *ou* tourmentée par son enfance malheureuse; **his past continues to haunt him** son passé ne cesse de le poursuivre *ou* hanter; **these problems have returned to haunt us** ces problèmes nous minent une fois de plus

(**c**) *Fam (frequent → bar)* hanter, fréquenter❑; *(→ streets)* hanter, traîner dans❑

2 *n* (**a**) *(place)* lieu *m* que l'on fréquente beaucoup, lieu *m* de prédilection; **it's one of his favourite haunts** c'est un des endroits qu'il préfère; **we couldn't find her in any of her usual haunts** nous ne l'avons pas trouvée dans les endroits qu'elle fréquente d'habitude

(**b**) *(refuge → for animals, criminals)* repaire *m*

haunted ['hɔːntɪd] *adj* (**a**) *(house, castle)* hanté (**b**) *(look)* hagard, égaré

haunting ['hɔːntɪŋ] *adj (memory, sound)* obsédant; *(tune)* qui vous trotte dans la tête; **she has a haunting beauty** elle est d'une beauté obsédante

hauntingly ['hɔːntɪŋlɪ] *adv* **hauntingly beautiful** d'une beauté obsédante

Hausa ['haʊsə] (*pl* **inv** *or* **Hausas**) **1** *n* (**a**) *(person)* **the Hausa** les Haoussas *mpl*, les Hausas *mpl* (**b**) *Ling* haoussa *m*

2 *comp* des Haoussas

haute couture [əʊtkuː'tʊə(r)] *n* haute couture *f*

haute cuisine [əʊtkwɪ'ziːn] *n* haute cuisine *f*

Havana [hə'vænə] **1** *n (city)* la Havane

2 *n (cigar, tobacco)* havane *m*

3 *comp (cigar, tobacco)* de Havane

HAVE [hæv]

verbe auxiliaire	▸ **1**
avoir	▸ **1; 2A (a) – (c); B (b) – (e); C (a), (b); F (a), (d), (h), (i)**
être	▸ **1**
posséder	▸ **2A (a)**
disposer de	▸ **2A (b)**
prendre	▸ **2B (c)**
passer	▸ **2B (d)**
recevoir	▸ **2C (a), (b)**
vouloir	▸ **2C (c); F (f)**
tenir	▸ **2D (a)**
faire faire	▸ **2E (b), (c)**
placer	▸ **2F (b)**
devoir	▸ **2G (a), (b)**
concerner	▸ **2G (c)**

Les formes négatives, **haven't** et **hasn't**, s'écrivent **have not** and **has not** dans un style plus soutenu.

Most French verbs will conjugate with **avoir** to form the perfect tense. However, all reflexive verbs and many intransitive verbs – mainly of motion – will conjugate with **être**.

(*3rd pers sing pres* **has** [hæz], *pt & pp* **had** [hæd])

1 *v aux* (**a**) *(used to form perfect tenses)* avoir, être; **to have finished** avoir fini; **to have left** être parti; **to have sat down** s'être assis; **to have been/had** avoir été/eu; **has she slept?** a-t-elle dormi?; **have they arrived?** sont-ils arrivés?; **he has been ill** il a été malade; **when you've calmed down** quand vous vous serez calmé; **I will have forgotten by next week** j'aurai oublié d'ici la semaine prochaine; **the children will have gone to bed by the time we arrive** les enfants seront couchés quand nous arriverons; **you were silly not to have accepted** tu es bête de ne pas avoir accepté; **after** *or* **when you have finished, you may leave** quand vous aurez fini, vous pourrez partir; **she was ashamed of having lied** elle avait honte d'avoir menti; **she felt she couldn't change her mind, having already agreed to go** elle sentait qu'elle ne pouvait pas changer d'avis, étant donné qu'elle avait dit être d'accord pour y aller; **I have been thinking** j'ai réfléchi; **he has been working here for two months** il travaille ici depuis deux mois, il y a deux mois qu'il travaille ici; **I have known her for three years/since childhood** je la connais depuis trois ans/depuis mon enfance; **I had known her for years** cela faisait des années que je la connaissais, je la connaissais depuis des années; **she claimed she hadn't heard the news** elle a prétendu ne pas avoir entendu la nouvelle; **I had already gone to bed when he arrived** j'étais déjà couché quand il est arrivé; **we had gone to bed early** nous nous étions couchés de bonne heure; **when he had given his speech, I left** une fois qu'il eut terminé son discours, je partis; **had I known, I wouldn't have insisted** si j'avais su, je n'aurais pas insisté; **if I had known, I wouldn't have said anything** si j'avais su, je n'aurais rien dit; **they would have been happy if it hadn't been for the war** ils auraient vécu heureux si la guerre n'était pas survenue; **why don't you just leave him and have done with it?** pourquoi donc est-ce que vous ne le quittez pas, pour en finir?; **I'd as soon not** j'aimerais mieux pas; **he'd rather** *or* **sooner stay at home than go out dancing** il aimerait mieux rester *ou* il préférerait rester à la maison qu'aller danser; *Fam* **he's had it** *(is in trouble)* il est fichu *ou* foutu; *(is worn out)* il est à bout; *Fam* **I've had it with all your complaining!** j'en ai jusque-là de tes jérémiades!; *Fam* **I've had it up to here with him** j'en ai jusque-là de ce type-là; *Fam* **the car has just about had it** la voiture va bientôt rendre l'âme; *Fam* **this plant has had it** cette plante est fichue

(**b**) *(elliptical uses)* **have you ever had the measles? – yes, I have/no, I haven't** avez-vous eu la rougeole? – oui/non; **she hasn't finished – yes, she has!** elle n'a pas fini – (mais) si!; **you've forgotten his birthday – no, I haven't!** tu as oublié son anniversaire – mais non!; **have you ever considered going into politics? if you have.../if you haven't...** avez-vous déjà envisagé de rentrer dans la vie politique? si oui.../ si non...; **you've forgotten your gloves – so I have!** vous avez oublié vos gants – en effet! *ou* tiens, c'est vrai!

(**c**) *(in tag questions)* **you've read 'Hamlet', haven't you?** vous avez lu 'Hamlet', n'est-ce pas?; **he hasn't arrived, has he?** il n'est pas arrivé, si?; **so she's got a new job, has she?** elle a changé de travail alors?

2 *vt* **A.** (**a**) *(be in possession of, own)* avoir, posséder; **do you have** *or* **have you got a car?** avez-vous une voiture?; **they have (got) a lot of friends/money** ils ont beaucoup d'amis/d'argent; **they don't have** *or* **they haven't got any more** ils n'en ont plus; **she shares everything she has (got) with them** elle partage tout ce qu'elle a avec eux; **he has (got) £10 left** il lui reste 10 livres; **we have (got) six of them left** il nous en reste six; **do you have** *or* **have you got any children? if you have...** avez-vous des enfants? si vous en avez *ou* si oui...; **they have (got) a 50 percent interest in the business** ils ont *ou* détiennent 50 pour cent des intérêts dans l'affaire; **I have (got) a lot of work to finish** j'ai beaucoup de travail à finir; **do we have** *or* **have we got any milk in the house?** est-ce qu'on a du lait *ou* est-ce qu'il y a du lait à la maison?; **she has (got) a baker's shop/bookshop** elle tient une boulangerie/librairie; **do you have** *or* **have you got the time?** avez-vous l'heure?; **he doesn't have** *or* **hasn't got a job** il n'a pas de travail, il est sans travail; **we have (got) a deadline to meet** nous avons un délai à respecter; **I've got it!** ça y est, j'ai trouvé *ou* j'y suis!; **paper, envelopes and what have you** du papier, des enveloppes et je ne sais quoi encore; *Prov* **you can't have your cake and eat it** on ne peut pas avoir le beurre et l'argent du beurre; *Fam* **give it all you have** *or* **all you've got!** mets-y le paquet!

(**b**) *(enjoy the use of)* avoir, disposer de; **we had a couple of hours to do our errands** nous disposions de *ou* nous avions quelques heures pour faire nos courses; **I don't have time** *or* **I haven't got time to stop for lunch** je n'ai pas le temps de m'arrêter pour déjeuner; **he has (got) a month to finish** il a un mois pour finir; **he hasn't (got) long to live** il ne lui reste pas longtemps à vivre; **do you have** *or* **have you (got) a minute (to spare)?** tu as une minute?; **she had the house to herself** elle avait la maison pour elle toute seule; **such questions have an important place in our lives** ce genre de questions occupe une place importante dans notre vie; **he has (got) nothing to do/to read** il n'a rien à faire/à lire

(**c**) *(possess as quality or attribute)* avoir; **she has (got) red hair** elle a les cheveux roux, elle est rousse; **you have (got) beautiful eyes** tu as de beaux yeux; **the ticket has (got) a name on it** il y a un nom sur le billet; **to have good taste** avoir bon goût; **to have a bad temper** avoir mauvais caractère; **she has (got) a reputation for being difficult** elle a la réputation d'être difficile; **the house has (got) a beautiful view of the mountains** de la maison, on a une belle vue sur les montagnes; **she has (got) what it takes** *or* **she has it in her to succeed** elle a ce qu'il faut pour réussir; **you've never had it so good!** vous n'avez jamais eu la vie si belle!; *Fam* **he really has it bad for Emma** il a complètement craqué pour Emma

(**d**) *(possess knowledge or understanding of)* **do you have** *or* **have you got any experience of teaching?** avez-vous déjà enseigné?; **she has (got) a clear sense of what matters** elle sait très bien ce qui est important; **he has some Greek and Latin** il connaît un peu le grec et le latin; **I have a little Spanish** je parle un peu espagnol

B. (**a**) *(indicating experience of a specified situation)* **to have a dream/nightmare** faire un rêve/cauchemar; **I have no regrets** je n'ai aucun regret *ou* pas de regrets; **I didn't have any trouble in finding it** je n'ai eu aucune peine à le trouver; **we have (got) nothing** *or* **we don't have anything against dogs** on n'a rien contre les chiens; **I've had my appendix out** je me suis fait opérer de l'appendicite; **he had all his money stolen** il s'est fait voler *ou* on lui a volé tout son argent; **I love having my back rubbed** j'adore qu'on me frotte le dos; **they had some strange things happen to them** il leur est arrivé de drôles de choses

(**b**) *(be infected with, suffer from)* avoir; **to have a cold** avoir un rhume, être enrhumé; **do you have** *or* **have you got a headache?** avez-vous mal à la tête?; **he has (got) problems with his back** il a des problèmes de dos

(**c**) *(perform, take part in → bath, lesson)* prendre; *(→ meeting)* avoir; **we had our first argument last night** nous nous sommes disputés hier soir pour la première fois; **to have a stroll** se promener, faire un tour; **I want to have a think about it** je veux y réfléchir; **to have a party** *(organize)* organiser une fête; *(celebrate)* faire la fête; **I'll have no part in it** je refuse de m'en mêler

(**d**) *(pass, spend)* passer, avoir; **I had a horrible day at work** j'ai passé une journée atroce au travail; **have a nice day!** bonne journée!; **to have a good time** s'amuser; **did you have a good time?** c'était bien?, tu t'es bien amusé?; **a good time was had by all** tout le monde s'est bien amusé; **she's had a hard time of it lately** elle vient de traverser une mauvaise passe

(**e**) *(exhibit, show)* avoir, montrer; **have mercy on us!** ayez pitié de nous!; **he had the nerve to refuse** il a eu le culot de refuser; **he didn't even have the decency to apologize** il n'a même pas eu la décence de s'excuser

C. (**a**) *(obtain, receive)* avoir, recevoir; **I'd like him to have this picture** j'aimerais lui donner cette photo; **I'd like to have your advice on something** j'aimerais que vous me donniez un conseil à propos de quelque chose; **we had a phone call from the mayor** nous avons reçu *ou* eu un coup de fil du maire; **they've still had no news of the lost plane** ils n'ont toujours pas de nouvelles de l'avion (qui a) disparu; **I have it on good authority** je le tiens de bonne source; **I must have your answer by tomorrow** il me faut votre réponse pour demain; **let me have your answer by next week** donnez-moi votre réponse avant la semaine prochaine; **let me have your keys** donne-moi tes clefs; **let me have the book back when you've finished** rends-moi le livre quand tu auras fini; **she let them have the wardrobe for £300** elle leur a laissé *ou* cédé l'armoire pour 300 livres; **there are plenty of flats to be had** il y a plein d'appartements; *Fam* **I let him have it** *(attacked him)* je lui ai réglé son compte; *(told him off)* je lui ai passé un savon; *Fam* **you had it coming!** tu ne l'as pas volé!

(**b**) *(invite)* recevoir, avoir; **she's having some people (over) for** *or* **to dinner** elle reçoit *ou* elle a du monde à dîner; **let's have him round for a drink** et si on l'invitait à prendre un pot?; **did you have any visitors?** avez-vous eu de la visite?; **after the movie we had them back for coffee** après le cinéma, nous les avons invités à venir prendre le café chez nous

(**c**) *(accept, take)* vouloir; **he'd like to marry but nobody will have him!** il aimerait se marier mais personne ne veut de lui!; **do what you want, I'm having nothing more to do with your schemes** fais ce que tu veux, je ne veux plus être mêlé à tes combines

D. (**a**) *(clutch)* tenir; **to have sb in one's power** avoir qn en son pouvoir; **the teacher had (got) him by the arm/the ear** le maître le tenait par le bras/l'oreille; **he had (got) his assailant by the throat** il tenait son agresseur à la gorge

(**b**) *Fig (gain control or advantage over)* **you have me there!** là vous me tenez!; **I have (got) you right where I want you now!** je vous tiens!; *Sport* **the Bears have it!** les Bears ont gagné!

(**c**) *(bewilder, perplex)* **who won? – you've got me there** qui a gagné? – là, tu me poses une colle

E. (**a**) *(cause to be)* **the news had me worried** la nouvelle m'a inquiété; **I'll have this light fixed in a minute** j'en ai pour une minute à réparer cette lampe; **we'll have everything ready** tout sera prêt

(**b**) *(with past participle) (cause to be done)* **to have sth done** faire faire qch; **I had my hair cut** je me suis fait couper les cheveux; **we must have the curtains cleaned** nous devons faire nettoyer les rideaux *ou* donner les rideaux à nettoyer; **three houses had their windows shattered** trois maisons ont eu leurs fenêtres brisées; **she had coffee brought up to the room** elle a fait monter du café dans la chambre; **I had my watch stolen** je me suis fait voler ma montre

(**c**) *(with infinitive) (cause to do)* **to have sb do sth** faire faire qch à qn; **she had him invite all the neighbours round** elle lui a fait inviter tous les voisins; **have them come in** faites-les entrer; **the boss had him up to his office** le patron l'a convoqué dans son bureau; **he soon had them all laughing** il eut tôt fait de les faire tous rire; **I had the children go to bed early** j'ai couché les enfants de bonne heure; **as he would have us believe** comme il voudrait nous le faire croire

F. (**a**) *(consume → food, meal)* avoir, prendre; **we were having lunch** nous étions en train de déjeuner; **we're having dinner out tonight** nous sortons dîner ce soir; **to have breakfast in bed** prendre le petit déjeuner au lit; **would you like to have coffee?** voulez-vous (prendre) un café?; **do you have coffee or tea in the morning?** prenez-vous du café ou du thé le matin?; **I had tea with her** j'ai pris le thé avec elle; **we stopped and had a drink** nous nous sommes arrêtés pour boire quelque chose; **what will you have? – I'll have the lamb** *(in restaurant)* qu'est-ce que vous prenez? – je vais prendre de l'agneau; **we had fish for dinner** nous avons mangé *ou* eu du poisson au dîner; **he always has a cigarette after dinner** il fume toujours une cigarette après le dîner; **will you have a cigarette?** voulez-vous une cigarette?

(**b**) *(indicating location, position)* placer, mettre; **we'll have the wardrobe here and the table in there** nous mettrons l'armoire ici et la table par là; **she had her arm around his shoulders** elle avait mis le bras autour de ses épaules; **I had my back to the window** je tournais le dos à la fenêtre; **he had his head down** il avait la tête baissée

(**c**) *(be accompanied by)* **she had her mother with her** sa mère était avec elle; **I can't talk right now, I have someone with me** je ne peux pas parler, je ne suis pas seul *ou* je suis avec quelqu'un

(**d**) *(give birth to)* avoir; **she's had a baby** elle a eu un bébé; **she had her baby last week** elle a accouché la semaine dernière; **she's going to have a baby** elle attend *ou* elle va avoir un bébé; **he's had three children by her** il a eu trois enfants d'elle; **our dog has just had puppies** notre chien vient d'avoir des petits

(**e**) *(assert, claim)* soutenir, maintenir; **public opinion has it that he is not telling the truth** on pense généralement qu'il ne dit pas la vérité; **rumour has it that they're married** le bruit court qu'ils sont mariés; **as the government would have it** comme dirait le gouvernement; **as Plato has it** comme dit Platon, comme l'a écrit Platon

(**f**) *(with "will" or "would") (wish for)* vouloir; **what would you have me do?** que voudriez-vous que je fasse?; **I'll have you know I have a degree in French** je vous fais remarquer que j'ai une licence de français

(**g**) *(in negative) (allow, permit)* **I will not have him in my house!** il ne mettra pas les pieds chez moi!; **I won't have it!** ça ne va pas se passer comme ça!; **we can't have you sleeping on the floor** nous ne pouvons pas vous laisser dormir par terre; *Fam* **we tried to give the dog a bath but he wasn't having any of it!** nous avons essayé de donner un bain au chien, mais rien n'y a fait!; *Fam* **I'm not having any of your nonsense** pas de bêtises

(**h**) *(in passive) Fam (cheat, outwit)* avoir; **you've been had!** tu t'es fait avoir!

(**i**) *very Fam (sleep with)* avoir

G. (**a**) *(with infinitive) (indicating obligation)* **to have (got) to do sth** devoir faire qch, être obligé de faire qch; **do you have to** *or* **have you got to leave so soon?** êtes-vous obligé de partir *ou* faut-il que vous partiez si tôt?; **I have (got) to go to the meeting** il faut que j'aille *ou* je dois aller *ou* je suis obligé d'aller à la réunion; **don't you have to** *or* **haven't you got to phone the office?** est-ce que tu ne dois pas appeler le bureau?; **he'll do it if he's got to** il le fera s'il est obligé de le faire; **you don't have to** *or* **you haven't got to go** tu n'es pas obligé d'y aller; **we had to take physics at school** nous étions obligés de suivre des cours de physique à l'école; **she had to take a blood test** elle a été obligée de *ou* elle a dû faire un examen sanguin; **I hate having to get up early** j'ai horreur de devoir me lever tôt; **I won't apologize – you have to** je ne m'excuserai pas – il le faut; **you've got to be joking!** vous plaisantez!, c'est une plaisanterie!; **you didn't have to tell your father what happened!** tu n'avais pas besoin d'aller dire à ton père ce qui s'est passé!; *Ironic* **the train WOULD have to be late today of all days!** il fallait que le train soit en retard aujourd'hui!; *Fam* **that has (got) to be the stupidest idea I've ever heard!** ça doit être l'idée la plus idiote que j'aie jamais entendue!

(**b**) *(with infinitive) (indicating necessity)* devoir; **you have (got) to get some rest** il faut que vous vous reposiez, vous devez vous reposer; **I'll have to think about it** il va falloir que j'y réfléchisse; **I have (got) to know** il faut que je le sache; **we have to be careful about what we say** on doit faire attention *ou* il faut qu'on fasse attention à ce qu'on dit; **some problems still have to** *or* **have still got to be worked out** il reste encore des problèmes à résoudre; **if you finish the report this evening you won't have to come in to work tomorrow** si vous finissez le rapport ce soir, vous n'aurez pas besoin de venir travailler demain; **first the potatoes have (got) to be washed** il faut d'abord laver les pommes de terre; **I don't like housework but it has (got) to be done** je n'aime pas faire le ménage mais il faut bien que quelqu'un le fasse; **the plumbing has (got) to be redone** la plomberie a besoin d'être refaite; **you'd have to be deaf not to hear that noise** il faudrait être sourd pour ne pas entendre ce bruit; **do you have to turn the music up so loud?** vous ne pourriez pas baisser un peu la musique?

(**c**) *(with "to do") (idioms)* **the book has to do with archaeology** ce livre traite de l'archéologie; **their argument had to do with money** ils se disputaient à propos d'argent; **this has nothing to do with you** ça ne te concerne *ou* regarde pas; **I'll have nothing more to do with her** je ne veux plus avoir affaire à elle; **they had nothing to do with her being fired** ils n'avaient rien à voir avec son licenciement

3 haves *npl* **the haves** les riches *mpl*, les nantis *mpl*; **the haves and the have-nots** les riches *mpl* et les pauvres *mpl*, les nantis *mpl* et les démunis *mpl*

▸**have around** *vt sep (keep available)* garder *ou* avoir sous la main; **I have the documents around somewhere** les documents sont là quelque part, j'ai les documents quelque part; **she's a useful person to have around** il est bon de l'avoir sous la main; **I don't like having children around** je n'aime pas la compagnie des enfants

▸**have at** *vt insep Br Fencing* attaquer

▸**have away** *vt sep Br very Fam* **to have it away (with sb)** s'envoyer en l'air (avec qn)

▸**have down** *vt sep (invite from upstairs, the north)* inviter; **we're having his family down for the weekend** sa famille vient passer le week-end chez nous

▸**have in** *vt sep* (**a**) *(cause to enter)* faire entrer; **she had him in for a chat** elle l'a fait entrer pour discuter

(**b**) *(invite)* **to have friends in for a drink** inviter des amis à prendre un pot

(**c**) *(doctor, workman)* faire venir; **we had to have the doctor in** nous avons dû faire venir le médecin; **they've got workmen in at the moment** ils ont des ouvriers en ce moment

(**d**) *Fam (idiom)* **to have it in for sb** avoir une dent contre qn; **they had it in for me from the day I arrived** ils en ont eu après moi dès mon arrivée

▸**have off** *vt sep* (**a**) *(remove)* retirer; **the barber nearly had my ear off** le coiffeur a failli me couper l'oreille (**b**) *(have removed)* faire retirer; **she's having the plaster off next week** on lui retire son plâtre la semaine prochaine (**c**) *Br very Fam (have sexual intercourse)* **to have it off (with sb)** s'envoyer en l'air (avec qn)

▸**have on** *vt sep* (**a**) *(wear)* porter; **what does she have on?** qu'est-ce qu'elle porte?, comment est-elle habillée?; **she had her black dress on** elle avait *ou* portait sa robe noire; **the child had nothing on** l'enfant était tout nu

(**b**) *(radio, television)* **have you got the radio on?** avez-vous allumé la radio?, est-ce que la radio est allumée?; **he has the radio/television on all night** sa radio/sa télévision est allumée toute la nuit

(**c**) *(commitment, engagement)* **we have a lot on today** nous avons beaucoup à faire aujourd'hui; **do you have anything on for tonight?** avez-vous des projets pour *ou* êtes-vous pris ce soir?; **I have nothing on for the weekend** je n'ai rien de prévu ce week-end

(**d**) *Br Fam (tease, trick)* faire marcher; **you're having me on!** tu me fais marcher!; **I was only having you on** c'était juste pour te faire marcher

(**e**) *(idiom)* **they have nothing on me** ils n'ont aucune preuve contre moi; **the police have nothing on him** la police n'a rien sur lui

▸**have out** *vt sep* (**a**) *(tooth)* se faire arracher (**b**) *(settle)* **to have it out with sb** s'expliquer avec qn; **she had it** *or* **the matter** *or* **the whole thing out with him** elle a eu une longue explication avec lui; **let's have this out once and for all** mettons les choses au point une fois pour toutes

▸**have over** *vt sep (invite)* inviter

▸**have up** *vt sep* (**a**) *Fam (bring before the authorities)* **I'll have you up for blackmail** je vais vous poursuivre (en justice) pour chantage; **they were had up by the police for vandalism** ils ont été arrêtés pour vandalisme; **he was had up (before the court) for breaking and entering** il a comparu (devant le tribunal) pour effraction

(**b**) *(invite from downstairs, the south)* inviter; **he had them up (to his flat) for tea** il les a invités à venir prendre le thé; **we're having them up from London for the weekend** il sont venus nous voir de Londres pour le week-end

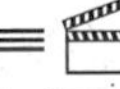

'To Have and Have Not' *Hawks* 'Le Port de l'angoisse'

have-a-go hero *n Br Fam* = membre du public, auteur d'un acte héroïque; **we don't want any have-a-go heroes** nous ne voulons pas de quelqu'un qui s'amuse à jouer les héros

haven ['heɪvən] *n* (**a**) *(refuge)* abri *m*, refuge *m*; **a safe haven** un abri sûr; *Literary* **the garden is a haven of peace and tranquillity** le jardin est un havre de paix et de tranquillité (**b**) *Arch or Literary (harbour)* havre *m*

have-nots *npl* **the have-nots** les démunis *mpl*, les défavorisés *mpl*

haven't ['hævənt] = **have not**

haver ['heɪvə(r)] *vi Fam* (**a**) *Br (dither)* tergiverser (**b**) *Scot (talk nonsense)* dire des sottises

haversack ['hævəˌsæk] *n* havresac *m*

havoc ['hævək] *n (UNCOUNT)* ravages *mpl*, chaos *m*; **to wreak havoc on sth** ravager qch; **the strike played havoc with our plans** la grève a mis nos projets par terre; **a scene of havoc** un vrai capharnaüm

haw [hɔː] **1** *n Bot (berry)* baie *f* d'aubépine, cenelle *f*; *(shrub)* aubépine *f*

2 *vi see* **hem²** *vi*, **hum** *vi*

Hawaii [hə'waɪiː] *n* Hawaii *f*, Hawaï *f*; **in Hawaii** à Hawaii, à Hawaï

Hawaiian [hə'waɪən] **1** *n* (**a**) *(person)* Hawaiien(enne) *m,f*, Hawaïen(enne) *m,f* (**b**) *Ling* hawaiien *m*; hawaïen *m*

2 *adj* hawaiien, hawaïen

▸▸ ***Hawaiian guitar*** guitare *f* hawaiienne *ou* hawaïenne; ***Hawaiian shirt*** chemise *f* hawaiienne *ou* hawaïenne; ***Hawaiian Standard Time*** heure *f* de Hawaii *ou* de Hawaï

hawfinch ['hɔːfɪntʃ] *n Orn* gros-bec *m*

haw-haw *exclam* ha, ha!

hawk [hɔːk] **1** *n* (**a**) *Orn* faucon *m*; **to watch sb/sth like a hawk** ne pas quitter qn/qch du regard; **he has eyes like a hawk** *(sharp eyesight)* il a des yeux d'aigle *ou* de lynx; *(misses nothing)* rien ne lui échappe; *Literary* **he doesn't know a hawk from a handsaw** il n'y connaît absolument rien
(**b**) *Pol* faucon *m*
(**c**) *(cough)* raclement *m* de gorge
(**d**) *Constr* taloche *f*
2 *vi* (**a**) *Hunt* chasser au faucon
(**b**) *(clear throat)* se racler la gorge; *(spit)* cracher
3 *vt* (**a**) *(sell → from door to door)* colporter; *(→ in market, street)* vendre à la criée
(**b**) *Fig (news, gossip)* colporter
(**c**) *(cough up)* cracher
►► *Bot* ***hawk's beard*** crépide *f*; *Orn* ***hawk owl*** chouette *f* épervière
►**hawk up** *vt sep* expectorer

hawkbit ['hɔːkbɪt] *n Bot* liondent *m*

hawker ['hɔːkə(r)] *n (street vendor)* marchand(e) *m,f* ambulant(e); *(door-to-door)* démarcheur (euse) *m,f*, colporteur(euse) *m,f*; **no hawkers** *(sign)* démarchage interdit

hawk-eyed *adj* (**a**) *(keen-sighted)* au regard d'aigle (**b**) *Fig (vigilant)* qui a l'œil partout

Hawkeye State ['hɔːkaɪ-] *n* **the Hawkeye State** = surnom donné à l'Iowa

hawking ['hɔːkɪŋ] *n* (**a**) *Hunt* chasse *f* au faucon (**b**) *(selling)* colportage *m*

hawkish ['hɔːkɪʃ] *adj Pol* belliciste

hawkmoth ['hɔːkmɒθ] *n Entom* sphinx *m*

hawknosed ['hɔːknəʊzd] *adj (person)* au nez aquilin

hawksbill ['hɔːksbɪl] *n Zool* tortue *f* (à écailles)

hawkweed ['hɔːkwiːd] *n Bot* épervière *f*

hawse [hɔːz] *n Naut* écubier *m*

hawser ['hɔːzə(r)] *n Naut* grelin *m*, aussière *f*; *(for mooring only)* amarre *f*

hawthorn ['hɔːθɔːn] **1** *n Bot* aubépine *f*
2 *comp (hedge, berry)* d'aubépine

hay [heɪ] *n* foin *m*; *Agr* **to make hay** faire les foins; *Prov* **to make hay while the sun shines** battre le fer pendant qu'il est chaud
►► *Med* ***hay fever*** rhume *m* des foins; **to suffer from/to have hay fever** souffrir du/avoir le rhume des foins; ***hay rake*** râteau *m*, fauchet *m*

haycart ['heɪkɑːt] *n* fourragère *f* de foin

haycock ['heɪkɒk] *n* tas *m ou* meulette *f* de foin

Haydn ['haɪdn] *pr n* Haydn

hayfork ['heɪfɔːk] *n* fourche *f* à foin

haying ['heɪɪŋ] *n Agr* fenaison *f*

hayloft ['heɪlɒft] *n* grenier *m* à foin

haymaker ['heɪˌmeɪkə(r)] *n* (**a**) *Agr (worker)* faneur(euse) *m,f*; *(machine)* faneuse *f* (**b**) *Fam (punch)* grand coup ❑ *m*

haymaking ['heɪˌmeɪkɪŋ] *n (UNCOUNT)* fenaison *f*, foins *mpl*

Haymarket ['heɪmɑːkɪt] *n* = rue de l'ouest de Londres où se trouve un théâtre du même nom

haymow ['heɪməʊ] *n (part of barn)* fenil *m*; *(hay)* tas *m* de foin *(entreposé dans un fenil)*

hayrack ['heɪræk] *n (in barn)* râtelier *m*; *(on cart)* ridelle *f*

hayrick ['heɪrɪk] *n* meule *f* de foin

hayride ['heɪraɪd] *n Am* = promenade dans un chariot rempli de paille; *Fig* **it was no hayride** ça n'a pas été une partie de plaisir

hayseed ['heɪsiːd] *n* (**a**) *Bot* graine *f* de foin (**b**) *Am, Austr & NZ Fam Pej (yokel)* péquenaud(e) *m,f*

haystack ['heɪstæk] *n* meule *f* de foin

haywain ['heɪweɪn] *n Arch* fourragère *f*

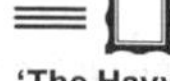

'The Haywain' *Constable* 'La Charrette à foin'

Hayward Gallery ['heɪwəd-] *n* **the Hayward Gallery** = musée d'art moderne à Londres

haywire ['heɪwaɪə(r)] *adj Fam (system, person)* détraqué; **to go haywire** *(machine)* débloquer, se détraquer; *(plans)* mal tourner

hazard ['hæzəd] **1** *n* (**a**) *(danger, risk)* risque *m*, danger *m*; *Aut (place)* point *m* dangereux; **the hazards of smoking** les dangers du tabac; **the hazards of life as a soldier** les risques *ou* dangers de la vie de militaire; **ice presents another hazard for drivers** le verglas est un danger supplémentaire pour les automobilistes; **a health/fire hazard** un risque pour la santé/d'incendie
(**b**) *(in golf)* obstacle *m*
2 *vt* (**a**) *(risk → life)* risquer, hasarder; *(→ reputation)* risquer
(**b**) *(venture → statement, advice, suggestion)* hasarder, se risquer à faire; **to hazard an opinion** risquer une opinion; **to hazard a guess** essayer de deviner; **would you care to hazard a guess as to the weight?** voulez-vous essayer de deviner combien ça pèse?
(**c**) *(stake, bet → fortune)* risquer, miser
3 hazards *npl Aut (lights)* feux *mpl* de détresse
►► *Mktg* ***hazard forecasting*** prévision *f* événementielle; *Aut* ***hazard lights*** feux *mpl* de détresse; *Am* ***hazard pay*** prime *f* de risque; *Aut* ***hazard warning*** signal *m* de danger; *Aut* ***hazard warning lights*** feux *mpl* de détresse; *Aut* ***hazard warning triangle*** triangle *m* de présignalisation; *Am* ***hazard waste*** déchets *mpl* dangereux

hazardous ['hæzədəs] *adj* (**a**) *(dangerous)* dangereux, risqué; **a hazardous stretch of road** une partie de la route qui est dangereuse (**b**) *(uncertain)* hasardeux, incertain
►► ***hazardous waste*** déchets *mpl* dangereux

hazardously ['hæzədəslɪ] *adv* (**a**) *(dangerously)* dangereusement (**b**) *(uncertainly)* hasardeusement

Hazchem *Br (written abbr* **hazardous chemicals**) *(sign)* produits dangereux

haze [heɪz] **1** *n* (**a**) *(mist)* brume *f*; **a heat haze** une brume de chaleur
(**b**) *(UNCOUNT) (steam)* vapeur *f*, vapeurs *fpl*; *(smoke)* nuage *m*
(**c**) *(confusion)* brouillard *m*; **to be in a haze** être dans le brouillard; **a haze of uncertainty surrounded the affair** une atmosphère d'incertitude entourait l'affaire
2 *vt Am* (**a**) *Univ (play tricks on, bully)* brimer, bizuter
(**b**) *Mil* faire subir des brimades à
(**c**) *(harass)* harceler
►**haze over** *vi (sky)* s'embrumer, devenir brumeux

hazel ['heɪzəl] **1** *n* (**a**) *Bot (tree)* noisetier *m* (**b**) *(colour)* (couleur *f* de) noisette *f*
2 *adj (colour)* noisette *(inv)*; **hazel eyes** yeux *mpl* (couleur) noisette
►► ***hazel grove*** coudraie *f*

hazelnut ['heɪzəlnʌt] **1** *n Bot (nut)* noisette *f*; *(tree)* noisetier *m*
2 *comp (flavour)* de noisette; *(ice cream, yoghurt)* à la noisette
►► ***hazelnut oil*** huile *f* de noisette

hazelwood ['heɪzəlwʊd] *n* (bois *m* de) noisetier *m*

hazily ['heɪzɪlɪ] *adv* vaguement

haziness ['heɪzɪnɪs] *n* (**a**) *(of sky, weather)* état *m* brumeux (**b**) *(of memory, thinking)* flou *m*, imprécision *f* (**c**) *Phot* flou *m*

hazing ['heɪzɪŋ] *n (UNCOUNT) Am* (**a**) *Univ* bizutage *m* (**b**) *Mil* brimades *fpl*
►► *Univ* ***hazing week*** (semaine *f* du) bizutage *m*

hazy ['heɪzɪ] *(compar* **hazier,** *superl* **haziest**) *adj* (**a**) *(weather, sky, air)* brumeux (**b**) *(memory, knowledge)* flou, vague; *(thinking, ideas)* flou, embrouillé; **she's rather hazy about the details of what happened** elle n'a qu'un vague souvenir de ce qui s'est passé (**c**) *Phot* flou (**d**) *(colour)* pâle

HB [ˌeɪtʃ'biː] *n Br (abbr* **hard-black**) *(on pencils)* HB

H-block *n* **the H-blocks** = les bâtiments faisant partie de la prison de Maze, près de Belfast, qui vus d'en haut, ont la forme d'un H

H-bomb *n (abbr* **hydrogen bomb**) bombe *f* H

HCF [ˌeɪtʃsiː'ef] *n Math (abbr* **highest common factor**) PGCD *m*

HD [ˌeɪtʃ'diː] *Comput* (**a**) *(abbr* **hard disk**) DD (**b**) *(abbr* **high density**) HD

HDD [ˌeɪtʃdiː'diː] *n Comput (written abbr* **hard disk drive**) unité *f* de disque dur

HDTV [ˌeɪtʃdiːˌtiː'viː] *n (abbr* **high definition television**) TVHD *f*

HE¹ (**a**) *(written abbr* **high explosive**) explosif *m* puissant (**b**) *(written abbr* **His/Her Excellency**) S Exc, SE

HE² [ˌeɪtʃ'iː] *n Br (abbr* **higher education**) enseignement *m* supérieur

he [hiː] **1** *pron* il; **he works in London** il travaille à Londres; **he and I** lui et moi; **there he is!** le voilà!; *Formal* **she is older than he is** elle est plus âgée que lui; **every politician should do what he thinks best** chaque homme politique devrait faire ce qu'il pense être le mieux; **that's what HE thinks!** c'est ce qu'il croit!
2 *n* (**a**) *Fam (male)* mâle ❑ *m*; **it's a he** *(newborn child)* c'est un garçon ❑; *(animal)* c'est un mâle ❑
(**b**) *(children's game)* (jeu *m* de) chat *m*; **you're he!** c'est toi le chat!

he- [hiː] *pref* **he-bear** ours *m* mâle; **he-goat** bouc *m*

HEAD [hed]

tête	►**1 (a), (b), (e), (i), (j), (l), (n), (p), (v)**
mal de tête	►**1 (f)**
chef	►**1 (g)**
côté face	►**1 (k)**
être à la tête de	►**2 (a)**
être en tête de	►**2 (b)**
diriger	►**2 (c)**
intituler	►**2 (d)**
aller	►**3**
principal	►**4 (a)**
premier	►**4 (b)**

(pl sense (**l**) **inv**) **1** *n* (**a**) *(of human, animal)* tête *f*; **she has a fine head of hair** elle a de très beaux cheveux *ou* une très belle chevelure; **he's already a head taller than his mother** il dépasse déjà sa mère d'une tête; *Horseracing* **to win by a head** gagner d'une tête; **from head to toe** *or* **foot** de la tête aux pieds; **he was covered in mud from head to toe** *or* **foot** il était couvert de boue de la tête aux pieds; **she was dressed in black from head to toe** *or* **foot** elle était tout en noir *ou* entièrement vêtue de noir; **to fall head over heels** tomber la tête la première; **to fall head over heels in love with sb** tomber éperdument amoureux de qn; **to have one's head in the clouds** avoir la tête dans les nuages; **he wanders around with his head in the clouds** il est toujours dans les nuages; **wine always goes to my head** le vin me monte toujours à la tête; **all this praise has gone to his head** toutes ces louanges lui ont tourné la tête; **to give a horse its head** lâcher la bride à un cheval; *Fig* **give him his head and put him in charge** lâchez-lui la bride et laissez-le prendre des responsabilités; **to stand on one's head** faire le poirier; *Fam* **I could do it standing on my head** c'est simple comme bonjour; **that's the kind of thing he could do standing on his head** c'est le genre de choses qu'il peut faire les yeux fermés; *Fam* **she's got her head screwed on (the right way)** elle a la tête sur les épaules; **the girl's got a good head on her shoulders** cette fille a la tête sur les épaules; **he's an old head on young shoulders** il est très mûr pour son âge; *Fig* **she's head and shoulders above the rest** les autres ne lui arrivent pas à la cheville; *Fam* **to laugh one's head off** rire à gorge déployée; *Fam* **to shout** *or* **to scream one's head off** crier à tue-tête; **they'll have your head (on a plate) for this** ils auront ta tête pour ça; **heads will roll** des têtes tomberont; *Am* **heads up!** attention la tête!; *Am Fam* **to give sb a heads up** tuyauter qn
(**b**) *(mind, thoughts)* tête *f*; **to do sums in one's head** calculer de tête; **to take it into one's head to do sth** se mettre en tête de faire qch; **the idea never entered my head** ça ne m'est jamais venu à l'esprit; **don't put silly ideas into his head** ne lui mettez pas des idées stupides en tête; **to get sth into one's head** se mettre qch dans la tête; **I can't get these dates into my head** je n'arrive pas à retenir ces dates; **she got it into her head that she was being persecuted** elle s'est mis en tête *ou* dans l'idée qu'on la persécutait; **I can't get that into his head** je n'arrive pas à le lui faire comprendre; **the answer has gone right out of my head** j'ai complètement oublié la réponse; **I think he made it up out of his own head** je crois

que c'est lui qui a inventé ça; *Fam* **use your head!** fais travailler tes méninges!; *Fam* **it's doing my head in!** ça me tape sur le système!, ça me prend la tête!; *Fam* **I just can't get my head round the idea that she's gone** je n'arrive vraiment pas à me faire à l'idée qu'elle est partie; *Fam* **to get one's head straight** *or* **together** se ressaisir

(**c**) *(aptitude)* **to have a good head for business** avoir le sens des affaires, s'entendre aux affaires; **she has no head for business** elle n'a pas le sens des affaires; **in my job, you need a good head for figures** pour faire mon métier, il faut savoir manier les chiffres; **to have a (good) head for heights** ne pas avoir le vertige; **I've no head for heights** j'ai le vertige

(**d**) *(clear thinking, common sense)* **keep your head!** gardez votre calme!, ne perdez pas la tête!; **to keep a cool head** garder la tête froide; **you'll need a clear head in the morning** vous aurez besoin d'avoir l'esprit clair demain matin; **to let one's head be ruled by one's heart** laisser son cœur gouverner sa raison; *Br Fam* **he's off his head** il est malade, il n'est pas net; *Fam* **he's not quite right in the head, he's a bit soft in the head** il est un peu timbré; *Fam* **to be out of one's head** *(drunk)* être bourré; *(on drugs)* être défoncé

(**e**) *(intelligence, ability)* tête *f*; **we'll have to put our heads together and find a solution** nous devrons nous y mettre ensemble pour trouver une solution; **off the top of my head, I'd say it would cost about £1,500** à vue de nez, je dirais que ça coûte dans les 1500 livres; **I don't know off the top of my head** je ne sais pas, il faudrait que je vérifie; **she made some figures up off the top of her head** elle a inventé des chiffres; **he's talking off the top of his head** il raconte n'importe quoi; **her lecture was completely over my head** sa conférence m'a complètement dépassé; **to talk over sb's head** s'exprimer de manière trop compliquée pour qn; *Prov* **two heads are better than one** deux avis valent mieux qu'un

(**f**) *Fam (headache)* mal *m* de tête❑; **I've got a bit of a head this morning** j'ai un peu mal à la tête ce matin

(**g**) *(chief, boss → of police, government, family)* chef *m*; *(→ of school, company)* directeur(trice) *m,f*; **the European heads of government** les chefs *mpl* de gouvernement européens; **the crowned heads of Europe** les têtes *fpl* couronnées de l'Europe; **head of department** *(in school)* chef *m* de département; *(in company)* chef *m* de service

(**h**) *(authority, responsibility)* **she went over my head to the president** elle est allée voir le président sans me consulter; **they were promoted over my head** ils ont été promus avant moi; **on your (own) head be it!** c'est toi qui en prends la responsabilité!, à tes risques et périls!; *Literary* **his blood will be upon your head** la responsabilité de sa mort pèsera sur vos épaules

(**i**) *(top → of racquet, pin, hammer)* tête *f*; *(→ of staircase)* haut *m*, tête *f*; *(→ of bed)* chevet *m*, tête *f*; *(→ of arrow)* pointe *f*; *(→ of page)* tête *f*; *(→ of letter)* en-tête *m*; *(→ of cane)* pommeau *m*; *(→ of valley)* tête *f*; *(→ of river)* source *f*; *(→ of mineshaft)* bouche *f*; *(→ of column, rocket, still)* chapiteau *m*; *(→ of torpedo)* cône *m*; *(→ of cask)* fond *m*; **at the head of the procession/queue** en tête de (la) procession/de (la) queue; **sitting at the head of the table** assis au bout de la *ou* en tête de table; **to be at the head of the list** venir en tête de liste

(**j**) *Bot & Culin (of corn)* épi *m*; *(of garlic)* tête *f*, gousse *f*; *(of celery)* pied *m*; *(of asparagus)* pointe *f*; *(of flower)* tête *f*; **a head of cauliflower** un chou-fleur

(**k**) *(of coin)* côté *m* face; **heads or tails?** pile ou face?; **I can't make head nor tail of this** pour moi ça n'a ni queue ni tête; *Fam Hum* **heads I win, tails you lose** pile je gagne, face tu perds; **it's a case of heads I win, tails you lose** de toutes les façons je suis gagnant

(**l**) *(of livestock)* tête *f*; **50 head of cattle** 50 têtes de bétail

(**m**) *(in prices, donations)* **tickets cost £50 a head** les billets valent 50 livres par personne

(**n**) *Electron (of tape recorder, VCR, disk drive)* tête *f*

(**o**) *(in rugby)* **to win the scrum against the head** prendre le ballon à l'adversaire sur son introduction

(**p**) *(title → of chapter)* tête *f*; **under this head** sous ce titre; **heads of agreement** *(draft)* protocole *m* d'accord

(**q**) *Typ* en-tête *m*

(**r**) *(on beer)* mousse *f*; *(on fermenting liquid)* chapeau *m*

(**s**) *Phys (of fluid, gas)* charge *f*, pression *f*; **loss of head** perte *f* de pression; **head of water** charge *f ou* pression *f* d'eau; *Fig* **to get up** *or* **to work up a head of steam** s'énerver

(**t**) *(of drum)* peau *f*

(**u**) *(of ship)* proue *f*

(**v**) *Med (of abscess, spot)* tête *f*; **to come to a head** *(abscess, spot)* mûrir; *Fig (problem)* arriver au point critique; **his resignation brought things to a head** sa démission a précipité les choses

(**w**) *Vulg (fellatio)* **to give sb head** tailler une pipe à qn

(**x**) *Am Fam or Naut (toilet)* toilettes❑ *fpl*; **I'm going to the head** je vais pisser

2 *vt* (**a**) *(command → group, organization)* être à la tête de; *(→ project, revolt)* diriger, être à la tête de; *(chair → discussion)* mener; *(→ commission)* présider; **she headed the attack on the Government's economic policy** elle menait l'attaque contre la politique économique du gouvernement

(**b**) *(be first in, on)* être *ou* venir en tête de; **Madrid heads the list of Europe's most interesting cities** Madrid vient *ou* s'inscrit en tête des villes les plus intéressantes d'Europe; *Sport* **she headed the pack from the start** elle était en tête du peloton dès le départ

(**c**) *(steer → vehicle)* diriger; *(→ person)* guider, diriger; **we headed the sheep down the hill** nous avons fait descendre les moutons de la colline; **they are heading the country into chaos** ils conduisent le pays au chaos; **just head me towards the nearest bar** dirigez-moi vers le bar le plus proche; **where are you headed?** où vas-tu?; *Naut* **to head a ship westwards** mettre le cap à l'ouest

(**d**) *(provide title for)* intituler; *(be title of)* être en tête de; **the essay is headed 'Democracy'** l'essai s'intitule *ou* est intitulé 'Démocratie'

(**e**) *Ftbl (ball)* jouer de la tête; **he headed the ball into the goal** il a marqué de la tête

(**f**) *Old-fashioned (skirt around → lake)* contourner par l'amont; *(→ river)* contourner par sa source

(**g**) *(plant)* écimer, étêter

3 *vi (car, crowd, person)* aller, se diriger; *Naut* mettre le cap sur; **where are you heading?** où vas-tu?; **you're heading in the right direction** vous allez dans la bonne direction; **I'm going to head home** je vais rentrer; **the train headed into/out of a tunnel** le train est entré dans un/sorti d'un tunnel

4 *adj* (**a**) *(main → person)* principal

(**b**) *(first in series)* premier

►► ***head barman*** chef *m* barman; *Br Sch* ***head boy*** = élève chargé d'un certain nombre de responsabilités et qui représente son école aux cérémonies publiques; ***head cashier*** chef *m* caissier; ***head chef*** chef *m* de cuisine; *Com* ***head clerk*** premier commis *m*, chef *m* de bureau; ***head cold*** rhume *m* de cerveau; ***head count*** vérification *f* du nombre de personnes présentes; **the teacher did a head count** la maîtresse a compté les élèves; ***head foreman*** chef *m* d'atelier; *Mining* ***head frame*** chevalement *m*; ***head gardener*** jardinier(ère) *m,f* en chef; *Aut* ***head gasket*** joint *m* de culasse; *Tech* ***head gate*** *(of lock)* porte *f* d'amont; *Br Sch* ***head girl*** = élève chargée d'un certain nombre de responsabilités et qui représente son école aux cérémonies publiques; ***head housekeeper*** *(in hotel)* gouvernante *f* générale; ***head louse*** pou *m*; ***head office*** siège *m* social, bureau *m* central; **it's** *Br* **head office** *or Am* **the head office on the phone** c'est le siège au téléphone; ***head porter*** *(in hotel)* chef-portier *m*; *(in university college)* appariteur *m* principal; ***head race*** (**a**) *(in rowing)* tête-de-rivière *f* (**b**) *Tech* canal *m* de prise *ou* d'amenée; *(of water mill)* bief *m* d'amont; ***head receptionist*** chef *m* de réception; *Mus* ***head register*** voix *f* de tête; *Br* ***head restraint*** appuie-tête *m*, repose-tête *m*; *TV & Cin* ***head shot*** gros plan *m* de tête; ***head start*** *(lead)* avance *f*; *(advantage)* avantage *m*; **he had a ten-minute head start over the others** il a commencé dix minutes avant les autres; **I got a head start** j'ai pris de l'avance sur les autres; **go on, I'll give you a head start** allez, vas-y, je te donne un peu d'avance; **being bilingual gives her a head start over the others** étant bilingue, elle est avantagée par rapport aux autres; ***head of state*** chef *m* d'État; *Sch* ***head teacher*** *(man)* proviseur *m*, directeur *m*, chef *m* d'établissement; *(woman)* directrice *f*, chef *m* d'établissement; ***head torch*** lampe *f* frontale; *Mus* ***head voice*** voix *f* de tête; ***head waiter*** maître *m* d'hôtel; *Br Sch* ***head of year*** conseiller(ère) *m,f* (principal(e)) d'éducation

►**head back** *vi* rentrer, retourner; **we headed back to the office** nous sommes retournés au bureau; **when are you heading back?** quand comptez-vous rentrer?

►**head for** *vt insep (of car, person)* se diriger vers; *Naut* mettre le cap sur; **where are you headed for?** où vas-tu?; **she headed for home** elle rentra (à la maison); **the country is heading for civil war** le pays va droit à la guerre civile; **he's heading for trouble** il va s'attirer des ennuis; *Fig* **to be heading for a fall** courir à l'échec; *Fam* **to head for the hills** filer

►**head off 1** *vt sep* (**a**) *(divert → animal, vehicle, person)* détourner de son chemin; *(→ enemy)* forcer à reculer; *Fig* **she headed off all questions about her private life** elle a éludé toute question sur sa vie privée (**b**) *(crisis, disaster)* prévenir, éviter; *(rebellion, revolt, unrest)* éviter

2 *vi* partir; **the children headed off to school** les enfants sont partis pour *ou* à l'école

►**head up** *vt sep (be leader of)* diriger

-head [hed] *suff Fam* **she's a bit of a whiskyhead** elle a un faible pour le whisky; **he's a real jazzhead** c'est un vrai fana de jazz

headache ['hedeɪk] *n* (**a**) *(pain)* mal *m* de tête; **to have a headache** *(gen)* avoir mal à la tête; **white wine gives me a headache** le vin blanc me donne mal à la tête; **he suffers a lot from headaches** il a souvent des maux de tête *ou* mal à la tête

(**b**) *Fig (problem)* casse-tête *m inv*; **the trip was one big headache** le voyage a été un casse-tête du début à la fin; **it can be a headache finding somewhere to park** parfois c'est la croix et la bannière pour trouver à se garer; **convincing her is your headache** pour ce qui est de la convaincre, c'est ton problème

headachy ['hedeɪkɪ] *adj Fam* **I'm feeling a bit headachy** j'ai un peu mal à la tête❑

headband ['hedbænd] *n* (**a**) bandeau *m* (**b**) *Typ* tranchefile *f*

headbang ['hedbæŋ] *vi Fam* secouer violemment la tête en rythme (sur du heavy metal)

headbanger ['hedbæŋə(r)] *n Fam* (**a**) *(heavy metal fan)* hardeux(euse) *m,f* (**b**) *Br (mad person)* cinglé(e) *m,f*, toqué(e) *m,f*

headboard ['hedbɔːd] *n* tête *f* de lit

headbutt ['hedbʌt] **1** *n* coup *m* de tête, coup *m* de boule

2 *vt* donner un coup de tête *ou* de boule à

headcase ['hedkeɪs] *n Fam* dingue *mf*

headcheese ['hed,tʃiːz] *n Am Culin* fromage *m* de tête

headdress ['hed,dres] *n (gen)* coiffure *f*; *(belonging to regional costume)* coiffe *f*

-headed ['hedɪd] *suff* à tête...; **a silver-headed cane** une canne à pommeau d'argent; **a three-headed dragon** un dragon à trois têtes

headed notepaper ['hedɪd-] *n Br* papier *m* à en-tête

header ['hedə(r)] *n* (**a**) *Fam (fall)* chute *f* (la tête la première)❑; *(dive)* plongeon *m* (la tête la première)❑; **he took a header into the ditch** il est tombé la tête la première dans le fossé

(**b**) *Ftbl* (coup *m* de) tête *f*; **he scored with a header** il a marqué de la tête

(**c**) *Comput & Typ* en-tête *m*

(**d**) *Constr* (pierre *f* en) boutisse *f*

►► *Comput* ***header block*** en-tête *m*; ***header card*** carte *f* en-tête; *Br Aut* ***header tank*** collecteur *m* de tête

headfirst [ˌhed'fɜːst] *adv* (**a**) *(dive, fall, jump)* la tête la première; **he dived headfirst into the pool** il a piqué une tête dans la piscine (**b**) *(rashly)* sans réfléchir, imprudemment; **to jump headfirst into sth** se jeter tête baissée dans qch

headgear ['hedˌgɪə(r)] *n (UNCOUNT)* couvre-chef *m*; *Hum* **they were wearing some very odd headgear** ils avaient tous un drôle de chapeau

headhunt ['hedˌhʌnt] **1** *vi* recruter des cadres (pour une entreprise)

2 *vt* **to be headhunted** être recruté par un chasseur de têtes

headhunter ['hedˌhʌntə(r)] *n also Fig* chasseur *m* de têtes

headhunting ['hedˌhʌntɪŋ] *n also Fig* chasse *f* aux têtes; *(recruiting)* chasse *f* aux têtes, recrutement *m* de cadres

headiness ['hedɪnɪs] *n* (**a**) *(of wine)* bouquet *m* capiteux; **the headiness of her perfume** son parfum capiteux; **the headiness of sudden success** la griserie *ou* l'ivresse qu'apporte un succès imprévu (**b**) *(excitement)* exaltation *f*, excitation *f*; **the headiness of the early 60s** l'euphorie du début des années 60

heading ['hedɪŋ] *n* (**a**) *(title → of article, book)* titre *m*; *(→ of chapter)* titre *m*, intitulé *m*; *Comput* titre *m*; *(in bookkeeping)* poste *m*, rubrique *f*; **page heading** tête *f* de page

(**b**) *(subject)* rubrique *f*; **this subject comes under the heading of rhetoric** cette discipline fait partie de la rhétorique

(**c**) *(letterhead)* en-tete *m*

(**d**) *Aviat & Naut (direction)* cap *m*

(**e**) *Ftbl* jeu *m* de tête

(**f**) *Mining (tunnel)* galerie *f* d'avancement; *(head of tunnel)* avancée *f*, avancement *m*

(**g**) *Constr (course)* assise *f* de boutisses

►► *Constr* ***heading course*** assise *f* de boutisses

headlamp ['hedlæmp] *n* (**a**) *Br (on car)* phare *m*; *(on train)* fanal *m*, feu *m* avant (**b**) *Mining* lampe chapeau *f*

headland ['hedlənd] *n* promontoire *m*, cap *m*

headless ['hedlɪs] *adj* (**a**) *(arrow, body, screw)* sans tête; *Hum* **he was running around like a headless chicken** il courait dans tous les sens (**b**) *(company, commission)* sans chef

headlight ['hedlaɪt] *n (on car)* phare *m*; *(on train)* fanal *m*, feu *m* avant

headline ['hedlaɪn] **1** *n* (**a**) *Press (in newspaper)* (gros) titre *m*, manchette *f*; **the hijacking made the headlines** le détournement a fait la une des journaux; **I just glanced at the headlines** j'ai juste jeté un coup d'œil sur les gros titres; **pollution has been in the headlines a lot recently** la pollution a beaucoup fait la une récemment; **it made headline news** cela a fait la une des journaux; **to hit the headlines** faire les gros titres; **news of their marriage hit the headlines** l'annonce de leur mariage a fait les gros titres *ou* a défrayé la chronique

(**b**) *Rad & TV (news summary)* grand titre *m*; **here are today's news headlines** voici les principaux titres de l'actualité

2 *vt* (**a**) *Press (place as headline → news story)* mettre en manchette

(**b**) *(provide heading for)* intituler; **the article was headlined 'The New Poor'** l'article avait pour titre 'Les Nouveaux Pauvres'

(**c**) *TV, Cin & Theat (have top billing in)* avoir le rôle principal dans; **headlining the show is Eve Arden** Eve Arden est la vedette du spectacle

3 *vi TV, Cin & Theat (have top billing)* avoir le rôle principal

headliner ['hedlaɪnə(r)] *n Am TV, Cin & Theat* vedette *f*

headlock ['hedlɒk] *n (in wrestling)* cravate *f*

headlong ['hedlɒŋ] **1** *adv* (**a**) *(dive)* la tête la première; *(fall)* de tout son long; **she dived headlong into the lake** elle a piqué une tête dans le lac

(**b**) *(rush → head down)* tête baissée; *(→ at great speed)* à toute allure *ou* vitesse; **he threw himself headlong against the door** il s'est littéralement jeté contre la porte

(**c**) *(rashly)* sans réfléchir, imprudemment; **she rushed headlong to her downfall** elle courait tout droit à sa perte; **they rushed headlong into the deal** ils se sont jetés à corps perdu dans l'affaire; **they rushed headlong into marriage** ils se sont mariés trop vite et sans réfléchir

2 *adj* (**a**) *(dive)* la tête la première

(**b**) *(impetuous → action)* imprudent, impétueux; **headlong flight** sauve-qui-peut *m inv*, débandade *f*; **the crowd made a headlong dash for the exit** la foule s'est ruée vers la sortie; **there was a headlong rush to buy the shares** tout le monde s'est précipité pour acheter les actions

headman ['hedmæn] *(pl* **headmen** [-men]*)* *n* chef *m*

headmaster [ˌhed'mɑːstə(r)] *n Sch* proviseur *m*, directeur *m*, chef *m* d'établissement

headmastership [ˌhed'mɑːstəʃɪp] *n Sch* poste *m* de proviseur *ou* de directeur

headmistress [ˌhed'mɪstrɪs] *n Sch* directrice *f*, chef *m* d'établissement

head-on **1** *adv* (**a**) *(collide, hit)* de front, de plein fouet; **he ran head-on into the tree** il a heurté l'arbre de plein fouet; **the ship ran head-on into the wharf** le navire a heurté le quai par l'avant (**b**) *(confront, meet)* de front; **to meet a problem head-on** aborder un problème de front; **management confronted the union head-on** la direction a affronté le syndicat

2 *adj* (**a**) *(collision → of car, plane)* de front, de plein fouet; *(→ of ships)* par l'avant (**b**) *(confrontation, disagreement)* violent

headphones ['hedfəʊnz] *npl* casque *m (à écouteurs)*

headpiece ['hedpiːs] *n* (**a**) *(helmet)* casque *m* (**b**) *Typ* vignette *f*, en-tete *m*

headpin ['hedpɪn] *n* quille *f* de tête

headquarter ['hedkwɔːtə(r)] *Am* **1** *vi (company)* **to headquarter in Glasgow** établir son siège à Glasgow

2 *vt* **to be headquartered in Glasgow** avoir son siège à Glasgow

headquarters [ˌhed'kwɔːtəz] *npl* (**a**) *(of bank, company, office)* siège *m* social, bureau *m* central; *(of army, police)* quartier *m* général; *(of organization, government office)* bureau *m* principal; *(of UN etc)* siège *m*; **they have their headquarters in Geneva** leur siège est à Genève; **police headquarters** le quartier général de la police (**b**) *Mil (commanding officers)* quartier *m* général

►► *Mil* ***headquarters staff*** état-major *m*

headrest ['hedrest] *n* appuie-tête *m*, repose-tête *m*

headroom ['hedrʊm] *n* hauteur *f*; **there's not much headroom in the attic** le plafond du grenier n'est pas très haut, le grenier n'est pas très haut de plafond; **there wasn't enough headroom for the bus** il n'y avait pas un dégagement suffisant au-dessus du bus; **does the car have enough headroom?** est-ce qu'il y a assez de place dans la voiture pour ne pas se cogner la tête?; **max headroom 10 metres** *(sign)* hauteur limite 10 mètres

headsail ['hedseɪl] *n Naut* foc *m*

headscarf ['hedskɑːf] *(pl* **headscarves** [-skɑːvz]*)* *n* foulard *m*

headset ['hedset] *n (with microphone)* casque *m (à écouteurs et à micro)*; *Am (headphones)* casque *m (à écouteurs)*

headship ['hedʃɪp] *n* (**a**) *(leadership)* direction *f*; **under the headship of** sous la direction de (**b**) *Sch* poste *m* de directeur *ou* de directrice

headshrinker ['hedˌʃrɪŋkə(r)] *n* (**a**) *(headhunter)* réducteur *m* de têtes (**b**) *Fam (psychiatrist)* psy *mf*

headsman ['hedzmən] *(pl* **headsmen** [-mən]*)* *n Hist (executioner)* bourreau *m*

headspring ['hedsprɪŋ] *n Literary* source *f (d'un fleuve)*

headsquare ['hedskweə(r)] *n* foulard *m*, carré *m*

headstall ['hedstɔːl] *n (for horse)* têtière *f*, licou *m*

headstand ['hedstænd] *n* **to do a headstand** faire le poirier

headstone ['hedstəʊn] *n* (**a**) *(of grave)* pierre *f* tombale (**b**) *Archit (keystone)* clef *f* de voûte

headstream ['hedstriːm] *n* source *f (d'un fleuve)*

headstrong ['hedstrɒŋ] *adj* (**a**) *(wilful)* têtu, entêté (**b**) *(rash)* impétueux, imprudent

head-up *adj*

►► ***head-up display*** *(in aeroplane, car)* affichage *m* tête-haute

headwaters ['hedˌwɔːtəz] *npl* sources *fpl (d'un fleuve)*

headway ['hedweɪ] *n* (**a**) *(progress)* **to make headway** *(gen)* avancer, faire des progrès; *Naut* faire route; **they're making some/no headway in their plans** leurs projets avancent/n'avancent pas; **I'm not making much headway with this guest list** je n'avance pas dans la préparation de cette liste d'invités, je n'ai toujours pas fini cette liste d'invités

(**b**) *(headroom)* place *f*, hauteur *f*

(**c**) *(between buses, trains)* **there is a ten-minute headway between buses** il y a dix minutes d'attente entre les bus

headwind ['hedwɪnd] *n (gen) & Aviat* vent *m* contraire; *Naut* vent *m* debout

headword ['hedwɜːd] *n* entrée *f*, adresse *f*

heady ['hedɪ] *(compar* **headier**, *superl* **headiest***)* *adj* (**a**) *(intoxicating → wine)* capiteux, qui monte à la tête; *(→ perfume)* capiteux; **the punch was a heady blend of wines and spirits** le punch était un mélange capiteux de vins et d'alcools; **she breathed in a heady draught of mountain air** elle respira l'air grisant *ou* enivrant des montagnes

(**b**) *(intoxicated)* grisé, enivré; **he felt quite heady with success** il se sentait complètement grisé par le succès

(**c**) *(exciting → experience, time)* excitant, passionnant; *(→ atmosphere)* excitant, enivrant; **she recalled her heady days as a young reporter** elle se rappelait l'époque excitante où elle était jeune reporter; **the heady heights of international finance** les sommets *mpl* de la finance internationale

heal [hiːl] **1** *vt* (**a**) *(make healthy → person)* guérir; *(→ wound)* guérir, cicatriser; **time heals all wounds** le temps guérit toutes les blessures

(**b**) *(damage, division)* remédier à, réparer; *(disagreement)* régler; **I'd do anything to heal the breach between them** je ferais n'importe quoi pour les réconcilier *ou* pour les raccommoder

2 *vi (person)* guérir; *(wound)* se cicatriser, se refermer; *(fracture)* se consolider

►**heal over** *vi* se cicatriser

►**heal up** *vi (wound)* se cicatriser, guérir; *(burn)* guérir; *(fracture)* se consolider

healer ['hiːlə(r)] *n* guérisseur(euse) *m,f*; **time is a great healer** le temps guérit toutes les blessures

healing ['hiːlɪŋ] **1** *n (of person)* guérison *f*; *(of wound)* cicatrisation *f*, guérison *f*; *(of fracture)* consolidation *f*

2 *adj* (**a**) *(remedy, treatment)* curatif; *(ointment)* cicatrisant (**b**) *(wound)* qui se cicatrise, qui guérit; *(fracture)* qui se consolide, qui guérit (**c**) *(soothing → influence)* apaisant

►► ***healing hands*** mains *fpl* de guérisseur

health [helθ] *n* (**a**) *(general condition)* santé *f*; **to be in good/poor health** être en bonne/mauvaise santé; **his health has never been good** il a toujours été fragile; **smoking is bad for your health** le tabac est mauvais pour *ou* nuisible à ta santé; *Fig* **the economic health of the nation** la (bonne) santé économique de la nation; **health problems** problèmes *mpl* de santé

(**b**) *(good condition)* (bonne) santé *f*; **has he regained his health?** s'est-il remis?, a-t-il recouvré la santé?, a-t-il guéri?; **she's the picture of health** elle respire la santé; *Hum* **I'm not doing this (just) for the good of my health!** je ne fais pas ça pour le plaisir *ou* pour m'amuser!

(**c**) *(in toast)* **(to your) good health!** à votre santé!; **we drank (to) the health of the bride and groom** nous avons porté un toast en l'honneur des mariés

►► ***health care*** soins *mpl ou* services *mpl* médicaux; ***health centre*** centre *m* médico-social; ***health certificate*** certificat *m* sanitaire; ***health club*** club *m* de remise en forme; *Br Fin* ***health cover*** assurance *f* médicale; ***health education*** sensibilisation *f* du public aux questions de santé; ***health farm*** centre *m* de remise en forme; ***health food*** aliments *mpl* diététiques *ou* biologiques; ***health food shop*** magasin *m* de produits diététiques; ***health hazard*** risque *m* pour la

hea–hea

santé; ***health inspector*** inspecteur(trice) *m,f* sanitaire; ***health insurance*** assurance *f* maladie; *Am* ***health maintenance organization*** = aux États-Unis, clinique de médecine préventive où l'on peut aller lorsqu'on a certains contrats d'assurance; ***health minister*** ministre *m* de la Santé; *Am Fin* ***health plan*** assurance *f* médicale; ***health resort*** station *f* climatique; *(by sea)* station *f* balnéaire; ***health risk*** risque *m* pour la santé; *Br* ***Health and Safety Executive*** inspection *f* du travail; *Br* ***health and safety inspector*** inspecteur(trice) *m,f* du travail; *Br* ***health and safety officer*** = membre du personnel d'une entreprise chargé de veiller à l'hygiène et à la sécurité; *Br* ***health and safety regulations*** réglementation *f* sur l'hygiène et la sécurité; ***health screening*** dépistage *m* à grande échelle; *Br* ***health service*** = système créé en 1946 en Grande-Bretagne et financé par l'État, assurant la gratuité des soins et des services médicaux, ≃ Sécurité *f* sociale; ***health services*** services *mpl* de santé; ***health tourism*** tourisme *m* de santé; *Br* ***health visitor*** = infirmière visiteuse qui s'occupe surtout des enfants en bas âge, des personnes âgées etc

healthful ['helθfʊl] *adj Old-fashioned or Literary* = **healthy** (**a**), (**d**)

health-giving *adj (effect etc)* bienfaisant, salutaire; *(air etc)* tonifiant, vivifiant

healthily ['helθɪlɪ] *adv (eat, live)* sainement

healthiness ['helθɪnɪs] *n (of climate, place)* salubrité *f*; *(of person)* bonne santé *f*; *(of diet, relationship)* caractère *m* sain

healthy ['helθɪ] (*compar* **healthier,** *superl* **healthiest**) *adj* (**a**) *(in good health → person)* sain, en bonne santé; *(→ animal, plant)* en bonne santé; **he's very healthy** il se porte très bien, il est bien portant

(**b**) *(showing good health → colour, skin, lungs)* sain; *(→ appetite)* robuste, bon

(**c**) *(beneficial → air, climate, place)* salubre; *(→ diet, food, lifestyle)* sain; *(→ exercise)* bon pour la santé, salutaire

(**d**) *(thriving → economy)* sain; *(→ business)* prospère, bien assis; *(relationship)* sain; **the new measures are designed to make the economy healthier** les nouvelles lois sont destinées à assainir l'économie

(**e**) *(substantial → profits)* considérable; *(→ sum)* considérable, important; *(→ difference)* appréciable

(**f**) *(sensible → attitude)* sain; *(→ respect)* salutaire; **he shows a healthy disrespect for opinion polls** il fait montre d'un dédain salutaire pour les sondages; **to have a healthy disregard for traditions** avoir un mépris louable des traditions

heap [hiːp] **1** *n* (**a**) *(pile)* tas *m*, amas *m*; **her things were piled in a heap** ses affaires étaient (mises) en tas; **he collapsed in a heap on the floor** il s'écroula *ou* tomba par terre comme une masse; **he started at the bottom of the heap and worked his way up** il a commencé au bas de l'échelle et a peu à peu grimpé les échelons; *Br Fam Old-fashioned* **to be struck** *or* **knocked all of a heap** être soufflé, en rester comme deux ronds de flan

(**b**) *Fam (large quantity)* tas *m*, masse *f*; **a heap** *or* **heaps of money** un paquet de fric; **I have a heap** *or* **heaps of work to do** j'ai un boulot monstre; **you've got heaps of time** tu as largement le temps *ou* tout ton temps; **he's helped us out heaps of times** il nous a rendu service mille fois *ou* des tas de fois; **they have heaps of room** ils ont de la place à ne plus savoir qu'en faire

(**c**) *Fam (old car)* vieux clou *m*

2 *vt* (**a**) *(collect into a pile)* entasser, empiler; **she heaped roast beef onto his plate** elle l'a généreusement servi en (tranches de) rosbif; **the table was heaped with food** la table était couverte de victuailles; **the lorry was heaped with food supplies** le camion regorgeait de provisions

(**b**) *Fig (lavish)* **to heap sth on sb** couvrir qn de qch; **her fiancé heaped flowers on her** son fiancé l'a couverte de fleurs; **to heap praise on** *or* **upon sb** couvrir *ou* combler qn d'éloges *ou* de compliments; **the teacher heaped homework on the students** le professeur a submergé ses élèves de devoirs

►**heap up** *vt sep (pile → books, furniture)* entasser, empiler; *(→ money, riches)* amasser; **she heaped up our plates with food** elle a rempli nos assiettes

heaped [hiːpt], *Am* **heaping** ['hiːpɪŋ] *adj* gros (grosse); *(container, bowl)* entassé, amoncelé; **a heaped teaspoonful** une cuiller à café bombée *ou* pleine

heaps [hiːps] *adv Br Fam* drôlement; **it's heaps faster to go by train** ça va drôlement plus vite en train; **I feel heaps better** je me sens drôlement *ou* rudement mieux

HEAR [hɪə(r)]

entendre	► **1 (a); 2 (a)**
écouter	► **1 (b)**
apprendre	► **1 (d)**
être au courant	► **2 (b)**

(*pt & pp* **heard** [hɜːd]) **1** *vt* (**a**) *(perceive with sense of hearing)* entendre; **can you hear me?** est-ce que vous m'entendez?; **we can't hear you** nous ne vous entendons pas, nous n'entendons pas ce que vous dites; **he could hear someone crying** il entendait (quelqu'un) pleurer; **I can hear someone at the door** j'entends sonner à la porte; **a shout was heard** un cri se fit entendre; *Formal* **he was heard to observe** *or* **remark that he was against censorship** on l'a entendu dire qu'il était opposé à la censure; **I've heard it said that...** j'ai entendu dire que...; **I've heard tell that they're engaged** j'ai entendu dire qu'ils étaient fiancés; **I've heard tell of such things** j'ai entendu parler de choses de ce genre; **I couldn't make myself heard above the noise** je n'arrivais pas à me faire entendre dans le bruit; **to hear my sister talk you'd think we were poor** à entendre ma sœur, vous pourriez croire que nous sommes pauvres; **he went on and on about it – I can just hear him!** il n'a pas arrêté d'en parler – c'est comme si j'y étais! *ou* pas la peine de me faire un dessin!; **don't believe everything you hear** n'écoutez pas tous les bruits qui courent, ne croyez pas tout ce qu'on raconte; **you're hearing things** tu t'imagines des choses; **I can hardly hear myself think** je n'arrive pas à me concentrer (tant il y a de bruit); *Ironic* **he hears what he wants to hear** il n'entend que ce qu'il veut; **let's hear it for the Johnson sisters!** un grand bravo pour les sœurs Johnson!, et on applaudit bien fort les sœurs Johnson!

(**b**) *(listen to → music, person)* écouter; *(→ concert, lecture, mass)* assister à, écouter; **be quiet, d'you hear!** taisez-vous, vous entendez!; **let's hear what you think** dites voir *ou* un peu ce que vous pensez; **so let's hear it!** allez, dis ce que tu as à dire!; **I've never heard such nonsense!** qu'est-ce qu'il ne faut pas entendre!; **I heard her rehearse her lines** je l'ai fait répéter *ou* réciter son rôle; **the Lord heard our prayers** le Seigneur a écouté *ou* exaucé nos prières

(**c**) *(of authority, official)* **the priest hears confession on Saturdays** le prêtre confesse le samedi; *Law* **the court will hear the first witness today** la cour entendra le premier témoin aujourd'hui; **the case will be heard in March** l'affaire se plaidera au mois de mars

(**d**) *(understand, be told)* entendre, apprendre; **I hear you're leaving** j'ai appris *ou* j'ai entendu (dire) que tu partais; **I hear you've lived in Thailand** il paraît que tu as vécu en Thaïlande; **have you heard the latest?** connaissez-vous la dernière?; **have you heard anything more about the accident?** avez-vous eu d'autres nouvelles de l'accident?; **for six months we heard nothing** *(received no news)* pendant six mois nous n'avons pas eu de nouvelles; **she was very famous for a while then we heard no more about her** elle a été célèbre pendant un moment puis on n'a plus entendu parler d'elle; **let me hear how you get on** donnez-moi de vos nouvelles; **from what I hear** à ce qu'on dit; **have you heard the one about the Scotsman and the Irishman?** connaissez-vous l'histoire de l'Écossais et de l'Irlandais?; **I've heard that one before!** on ne me la fait plus!; **she's heard it all before** elle connaît la musique; **I've heard good things about that school** j'ai eu des échos favorables de cette école; **you haven't heard the last of this!** *(gen)* vous n'avez pas fini d'en entendre parler!; *(threat)* vous aurez de mes nouvelles!; *Fam* **I hear you, I hear what you're saying** je comprends, j'ai compris; *Fam* **you heard!** tu m'as bien compris!

2 *vi* (**a**) *(able to perceive sound)* entendre; **she doesn't hear very well** elle n'entend pas très bien, elle est un peu dure d'oreille

(**b**) *(be aware)* être au courant; **haven't you heard? he's dead** vous n'êtes pas au courant? il est mort

(**c**) *(idiom)* **hear, hear!** bravo!, tout à fait d'accord!

►**hear about** *vt insep* (**a**) *(learn)* entendre; **have you heard about the accident?** êtes-vous au courant pour *ou* de l'accident?; **yes, I heard about that** oui, je suis au courant; **have you heard about the time she met Churchill?** connaissez-vous l'histoire de sa rencontre avec Churchill?; **I've heard so much about you** j'ai tellement entendu parler de vous

(**b**) *(have news of)* avoir *ou* recevoir des nouvelles de; **I hear about her through her sister** j'ai de ses nouvelles par sa sœur

►**hear from** *vt insep* (**a**) *(receive news of)* avoir *ou* recevoir des nouvelles de; **they'd be delighted to hear from you** ils seraient ravis d'avoir de tes nouvelles; **he never heard from her again** il n'a plus jamais eu de ses nouvelles; **you'll be hearing from me** *(gen)* je vous donnerai de mes nouvelles; *(threat)* vous allez avoir de mes nouvelles, vous allez entendre parler de moi; **you'll be hearing from my lawyer!** mon avocat vous contactera!, on en reparlera devant les tribunaux!; **(I am) looking forward to hearing from you** *(in letter)* dans l'attente de vous lire

(**b**) *(listen to)* écouter; **we hear first from one of the survivors** nous allons d'abord écouter *ou* entendre l'un des survivants

►**hear of** *vt insep* (**a**) *(know of)* entendre parler de, connaître; **I've never heard of her** je ne la connais pas

(**b**) *(receive news of)* entendre parler de; **the whole town had heard of his success** la ville entière était au courant de son succès *ou* sa réussite; **the director was never heard of again** on n'a plus jamais entendu parler du directeur; **the missing boy was never heard of again** on n'a jamais retrouvé la trace du garçon qui avait disparu; **have you ever heard of such a thing?** avez-vous déjà entendu parler d'une chose pareille?; **this is the first I have heard of it** c'est la première fois que j'en entends parler; **whoever heard of eating pizza for breakfast!** quelle (drôle d') idée de manger de la pizza au petit déjeuner!; **we hear of nothing these days but rocketing interest rates!** ces temps-ci, on nous rebat les oreilles avec la montée en flèche *ou* la croissance folle des taux d'intérêt!

(**c**) *(usu neg) (accept, allow)* **her father won't hear of it** son père ne veut pas en entendre parler *ou* ne veut rien savoir; **I won't hear of you walking home** je ne veux absolument pas que tu rentres à pied; **may I pay for dinner? – I wouldn't hear of it!** puis-je payer *ou* vous offrir le dîner? – (il n'en est) pas question!

►**hear out** *vt sep* écouter jusqu'au bout; **at least hear me out before you refuse my offer** au moins écoutez-moi jusqu'au bout avant de refuser ma proposition

heard [hɜːd] *pt & pp of* **hear**

hearer ['hɪərə(r)] *n* auditeur(trice) *m,f*

hearing ['hɪərɪŋ] *n* (**a**) *(UNCOUNT) (sense)* ouïe *f*; **to have good/bad hearing** entendre bien/mal; **a keen sense of hearing** l'oreille *f ou* l'ouïe *f* fine; **he has very little hearing left** son ouïe est défaillante, il n'entend presque plus; **his hearing gradually deteriorated** petit à petit il est devenu dur d'oreille; **cats have better hearing than humans** les chats entendent mieux *ou* ont l'ouïe plus fine que les humains

(**b**) *(UNCOUNT) (earshot)* **within hearing** à portée de voix; **you shouldn't have said that in** *or* **within hearing of his mother** tu n'aurais pas dû le dire devant *ou* en présence de sa mère

(**c**) *(act of listening)* audition *f*; **I didn't enjoy the symphony at (the) first hearing** je n'ai pas aimé la symphonie à la première audition *ou* la première fois que je l'ai écoutée

(**d**) *(chance to be heard)* audition *f*; **they were the only ones to get a hearing** ils furent les seuls à être entendus; **at least give me a hearing** laissez-moi au moins parler; **they judged the architect without a hearing** ils ont jugé l'architecte sans l'entendre *ou* sans entendre sa défense; **to give sb a fair hearing** laisser parler qn, écouter ce que qn a à dire

(**e**) *Law* audition *f* des témoins; **the hearing of witnesses** l'audition *f* des témoins; **the hearing of a trial** l'audience *f*; **the case will come up for hearing in March** l'affaire sera entendue *ou* plaidée en mars

(**f**) *(official meeting)* séance *f*

►► ***hearing aid*** appareil *m* acoustique, audiophone *m*; ***hearing dog*** *(for the deaf)* = chien entraîné à reconnaître certains bruits et aider ainsi une personne malentendante; ***the hearing impaired*** les malentendants *mpl*

hearken ['hɑːkən] *vi Arch or Literary* **to hearken to sb/sth** écouter qn/qch

hearsay ['hɪəseɪ] *n* ouï-dire *m inv*, rumeurs *fpl*; **it's only hearsay** ce ne sont que des rumeurs; **I only know it by** *or* **from hearsay** je ne le sais que par ouï-dire

►► *Law* ***hearsay evidence*** déposition *f* sur la foi d'un tiers *or* d'autrui

hearse [hɜːs] *n* corbillard *m*, fourgon *m* mortuaire

HEART [hɑːt]

cœur	► 1 (a), (b), (g), (i) – (k)
fond	► 1 (c), (h)
courage	► 1 (f)
au fond	► 2
par cœur	► 3

1 *n* (**a**) *Anat (organ)* cœur *m*; **he has a weak heart** il est cardiaque, il a le cœur malade; **to have a heart condition** souffrir du cœur, être cardiaque; *Fig* **her heart leapt** son cœur bondit; *Fig* **her heart sank** elle eut un serrement de cœur; **my heart sinks every time I think about leaving** j'ai un pincement au cœur *ou* un serrement de cœur chaque fois que je pense au départ; *Literary* **two hearts that beat as one** deux cœurs qui battent à l'unisson; *Br* **he sat there, his heart in his boots** il était là, la mort dans l'âme; **her heart was in her mouth as she watched** elle regardait en retenant son souffle

(**b**) *(seat of feelings, love)* cœur *m*; **to have a big heart** avoir très bon cœur; **he has a heart of gold/of stone** il a un cœur d'or/de pierre; **it does my heart good to see them together** cela me réchauffe le cœur de les voir ensemble; **to lose one's heart to sb** donner son cœur à qn, tomber amoureux de qn; **to win sb's heart** gagner le cœur de qn; **her words went straight to his heart** ses paroles lui sont allées droit au cœur; **the letter was written straight from the heart** la lettre était écrite du fond du cœur; **to have one's heart set on sth** s'être mis qch dans la tête; **he has his heart set on winning** il veut à tout prix gagner; **they have their heart set on that house** ils ont jeté leur dévolu sur cette maison; **they have your welfare at heart** ils ne pensent qu'à ton bien, c'est pour ton bien qu'ils font cela; **they have everything their hearts could desire** ils ont tout ce qu'ils peuvent désirer; *Literary* **my heart's desire is to see Rome again** mon plus cher désir est *ou* ce que je désire le plus au monde c'est de revoir Rome; **she hardened** *or* **steeled her heart against him** elle s'est endurcie contre lui; **affairs** *or* **matters of the heart** affaires *fpl* de cœur; *Arch or Hum* **dear heart** mon cœur, mon (ma) chéri(e); **to wear one's heart on one's sleeve** montrer *ou* laisser paraître ses sentiments

(**c**) *(innermost thoughts)* fond *m*; **in his heart of hearts** au fond de lui-même *ou* de son cœur, en son for intérieur; **in my heart I knew it was true** au fond de moi-même je savais que c'était la vérité; **there's a woman/a man after my own heart** voilà une femme/un homme selon mon cœur; **I thank you from the bottom of my heart** *or* **with all my heart** je vous remercie du fond du cœur *ou* de tout mon cœur; **do you love him? – with all my heart** vous l'aimez? – de tout mon cœur; **to take sth to heart** prendre qch à cœur; **she takes criticism too much to heart** elle prend les critiques trop à cœur; **don't take it to heart** ne le prenez pas trop à cœur; **she opened** *or* **poured out her heart to me** elle m'a dévoilé son cœur

(**d**) *(disposition, humour)* **to have a change of heart** changer d'avis

(**e**) *(interest, enthusiasm)* **I worked hard but my heart wasn't in it** j'ai beaucoup travaillé mais je n'avais pas le cœur à l'ouvrage *ou* le cœur n'y était pas; **I can tell that your heart isn't in it** je vois bien que tu n'y tiens pas tellement; **to eat/drink to one's heart's content** manger/boire tout son soûl; **she read to her heart's content** elle a lu tout son soûl; **a subject close to one's heart** un sujet qui tient à cœur; **she puts her heart** *or* **she throws herself heart and soul into her work** elle se donne à son travail corps et âme

(**f**) *(courage)* **to lose heart** perdre courage, se décourager; **take heart!** courage!; **she took heart from the fact that others shared her experience** elle était encouragée par le fait que d'autres partageaient son expérience; **the prospect of winning the prize put new heart into them** la perspective de gagner le prix leur a redonné du courage *ou* du cœur (au ventre); **to be in good heart** *(person)* avoir bon moral; *Br (land)* être fécond *ou* productif

(**g**) *(compassion)* cœur *m*; **he has no heart** il n'a pas de cœur, il manque de cœur; **she didn't have the heart to refuse, she couldn't find it in her heart to refuse** elle n'a pas eu le courage *ou* le cœur de refuser; **can you find it in your heart to forgive me?** est-ce que vous pourrez jamais me pardonner?; **her heart's in the right place** elle a bon cœur; **have a heart!** pitié!; **to be all heart** être plein de bonne volonté; *Ironic* **you're all heart** tu es charmant!

(**h**) *(core, vital part → of matter, topic)* fond *m*, vif *m*; *(→ of city, place)* centre *m*, cœur *m*; **the heart of the matter** le fond du problème; **the speaker went straight to the heart of the matter** le conférencier est allé droit au cœur du sujet *ou* du problème; **the law strikes at the heart of the democratic system** la loi porte atteinte aux fondements du régime démocratique; **in the heart of the financial district** au centre *ou* au cœur du quartier financier; **in the heart of winter** en plein hiver, au cœur de l'hiver; **in the heart of the forest** au cœur *ou* au beau milieu *ou* au fin fond de la forêt, en pleine forêt; *Am* **the Heart of Dixie** = surnom donné à l'Alabama

(**i**) *(of cabbage, celery, lettuce)* cœur *m*; *(of tree)* cœur *m*, vif *m*; *(of artichoke)* cœur *m*, fond *m*; *(of cable)* âme *f*, mèche *f*; *Br Literary* **hearts of oak** *(men)* hommes *mpl* courageux

(**j**) *Cards* cœur *m*; **to play a heart** jouer un *ou* du cœur; **hearts are trumps** atout cœur; **have you got any hearts?** avez-vous du cœur?

(**k**) *(shape)* cœur *m*; **a pattern of little red hearts** un motif de petits cœurs rouges; **she had drawn hearts all over the letter** elle avait dessiné des cœurs sur toute la lettre

(**l**) *(bosom)* poitrine *f*; **she clutched him to her heart** elle l'a serré contre sa poitrine *ou* sur son cœur

2 at heart *adv* au fond; **at heart she was a good person** elle avait un bon fond; **my sister's a gypsy at heart** ma sœur est une bohémienne dans l'âme; **to feel sad at heart** avoir le cœur triste; **to be sick at heart** avoir la mort dans l'âme

3 by heart *adv* par cœur; **to learn/to know sth by heart** apprendre/savoir qch par cœur

4 hearts *npl Cards* = jeu de cartes dont l'objet est de faire des plis ne comprenant ni des cœurs ni la dame de pique

►► *Med* ***heart attack*** crise *f* cardiaque; **to have a heart attack** avoir une crise cardiaque, faire un infarctus; *Fig* **she nearly had a heart attack when she heard about it** en apprenant la nouvelle, elle a failli avoir une attaque; *Med* ***heart disease*** maladie *f* de cœur, maladie *f* cardiaque; **heart disease is on the increase** les maladies de cœur *ou* cardiaques sont en augmentation; **smoking increases the incidence of heart disease** le tabagisme augmente le taux de maladies de cœur *ou* cardiaques; *Med* ***heart failure*** *(condition)* défaillance *f* cardiaque; *(cessation of heartbeat)* arrêt *m* du cœur; *Fig* **I nearly had heart failure when they told me I'd got the job** j'ai failli me trouver mal *ou* avoir une syncope quand ils m'ont dit que j'avais le poste; *Med* ***heart murmur*** souffle *m* au cœur; *Bot* ***heart of palm*** cœur *m* de palmier; ***heart patient*** cardiaque *mf*; *Mktg* ***heart share*** préférence *f*; ***heart surgeon*** chirurgien(enne) *m,f* cardiologue; *Med* ***heart surgery*** chirurgie *f* du cœur; *Med* ***heart trouble*** *(UNCOUNT)* maladie *f* du cœur, troubles *mpl* cardiaques; **to have** *or* **to suffer from heart trouble** souffrir du cœur, être cardiaque

---

'Heart of Darkness' *Conrad* 'Au cœur des ténèbres'

'One from the Heart' *Coppola* 'Coup de cœur'

'The Heart of the Matter' *Greene, More O'Ferrall* 'Le Fond du problème'

'The Heart is a Lonely Hunter' *McCullers* 'Le Cœur est un chasseur solitaire'

---

heartache ['hɑːteɪk] *n* chagrin *m*, peine *f*; **he caused her a lot of heartache** il lui a causé beaucoup de chagrin

heartbeat ['hɑːtbiːt] *n* battement *m* de cœur, pulsation *f*; **an irregular heartbeat** un battement arythmique *ou* irrégulier; **to be a heartbeat away from sth** être à deux doigts de qch; *Am* **in a heartbeat** sans hésiter

heartbreak ['hɑːtbreɪk] *n (grief → gen)* (immense) chagrin *m*, déchirement *m*; *(→ in love)* chagrin *m* d'amour; **I've had my share of heartbreak(s)** j'ai eu ma part de chagrins d'amour

heartbreaker ['hɑːtˌbreɪkə(r)] *n (man)* bourreau *m* des cœurs; *(woman)* femme *f* fatale

heartbreaking ['hɑːtˌbreɪkɪŋ] *adj* déchirant, navrant; **it was heartbreaking to see children starving** c'était à vous fendre le cœur de voir des enfants mourir de faim; **heartbreaking scenes** des scènes *fpl* déchirantes *ou* navrantes

heartbroken ['hɑːtˌbrəʊkən] *adj (person → gen)* qui a un immense chagrin; *(→ stronger)* qui a le cœur brisé; *(sigh, sob)* à fendre le cœur; **she's heartbroken over losing the job** elle n'arrive pas à se consoler *ou* à se remettre d'avoir perdu ce travail; **the child was heartbroken** l'enfant avait un gros chagrin

heartburn ['hɑːtbɜːn] *n (UNCOUNT) Med* brûlures *fpl* d'estomac

hearten ['hɑːtən] *vt* encourager, donner du courage à; **we were heartened to learn of the drop in interest rates** nous avons été contents d'apprendre que les taux d'intérêt avaient baissé

heartening ['hɑːtənɪŋ] *adj* encourageant, réconfortant; **I found the news heartening** la nouvelle m'a donné du courage [illegible]

heartfelt ['hɑːtfelt] *adj (apology, thanks)* sincère; **a heartfelt wish** un souhait qui vient (du fond) du cœur; **she expressed a heartfelt wish to see her country again** elle exprima le souhait sincère de revoir son pays; **with our heartfelt wishes for a speedy recovery** avec nos vœux sincères de prompt rétablissement

hearth [hɑːθ] *n* (**a**) *(of fireplace)* foyer *m*, âtre *m*; **a fire was burning in the hearth** il y avait du feu dans la cheminée (**b**) *(home)* foyer *m*; **to leave hearth and home** quitter le foyer

hearthrug ['hɑːθrʌg] *n* devant *m* de foyer

hearthstone ['hɑːθstəʊn] *n* foyer *m*, âtre *m*

heartily ['hɑːtɪlɪ] *adv* (**a**) *(enthusiastically → joke, laugh)* de tout son cœur; *(→ say, thank, welcome)* chaleureusement, de tout cœur; *(→ eat)* de bon appétit

(**b**) *(thoroughly)* **I heartily recommend it** je vous le conseille vivement; **she heartily dislikes him** elle le déteste cordialement; **to be heartily disgusted with sth** être on ne peut plus dégoûté de qch; **they were heartily sick of the work** ils en avaient par-dessus la tête *ou* ils en avaient plus qu'assez du travail

heartiness ['hɑːtɪnɪs] *n* (**a**) *(of thanks, welcome)* cordialité *f*, chaleur *f*; *(of agreement)* sincérité *f*; *(of appetite)* vigueur *f*; *(of dislike)* ardeur *f*; *(of thanks)* sincérité *f* (**b**) *(cheerfulness)* bonne humeur *f*

heartland ['hɑːtlænd] *n* cœur *m*, centre *m*; **the heartland of France** la France profonde; **the industrial heartland of Europe** le principal centre industriel de l'Europe; **the Socialist heartland** le fief des socialistes

heartless ['hɑːtlɪs] *adj (person)* sans cœur, impitoyable; *(laughter, treatment)* cruel

heartlessly ['hɑːtlɪslɪ] *adv* sans pitié

heartlessness ['hɑːtlɪsnɪs] *n (of person)* manque *m* de cœur, caractère *m* impitoyable; *(of laughter, treatment)* cruauté *f*

heart-lung *adj*

▸▸ *Med* ***heart-lung machine*** cœur-poumon *m* artificiel; *Med* ***heart-lung transplant*** greffe *f* cœur-poumon

heartrending ['hɑːtˌrendɪŋ] *adj* déchirant, qui fend le cœur; **heartrending scenes of homeless refugees** des images navrantes *ou* déchirantes de réfugiés sans abri

heart-searching *n* examen *m* de conscience; **you need to do some heart-searching before deciding** tu ferais mieux de réfléchir avant de te décider; **after much heart-searching she decided to leave** après s'être longuement interrogée *ou* tâtée, elle décida de partir

heart-shaped *adj* en forme de cœur

heartsick ['hɑːtsɪk] *adj* découragé, démoralisé; **a heartsick lover** un amoureux transi; **to be heartsick** avoir la mort dans l'âme; **heartsick and disillusioned, he gave up his search** démoralisé *ou* abattu et désenchanté, il abandonna ses recherches

heartsome ['hɑːtsəm] *adj Arch or Literary* joyeux, gai

heart-stopping *adj* terrifiant

heartstrings ['hɑːtstrɪŋz] *npl* **to play on** *or* **to pull on** *or* **to tug at sb's heartstrings** faire vibrer *ou* toucher la corde sensible de qn; **he certainly knows how to play on an audience's heartstrings** il n'y a pas de doute, il sait faire vibrer la corde sensible d'un auditoire *ou* il sait toucher la sensibilité d'un auditoire; **that song always tugs at my heartstrings** cette chanson me serre toujours le cœur

heartthrob ['hɑːtθrɒb] *n* coqueluche *f*, idole *f*; **he's her heartthrob** elle a le béguin pour lui; **he's the office heartthrob** c'est la coqueluche du bureau

heart-to-heart 1 *n* conversation *f* intime *ou* à cœur ouvert; **it's time we had a heart-to-heart** il est temps qu'on se parle (à cœur ouvert)

2 *adj* à cœur ouvert

3 *adv* à cœur ouvert

heartwarming ['hɑːtˌwɔːmɪŋ] *adj* réconfortant, qui réchauffe le cœur

heartwood ['hɑːtwʊd] *n Bot* cœur *m* du bois, bois *m* de cœur, *Spec* duramen *m*

hearty ['hɑːtɪ] *(compar* **heartier**, *superl* **heartiest**, *pl* **hearties**) **1** *adj* (**a**) *(congratulations, welcome)* cordial, chaleureux; *(thanks)* sincère; *(approval, recommendation)* sans réserves; *(laugh)* gros (grosse), franc (franche); *(knock, slap)* vigoureux; **they're hearty eaters** ils ont un bon coup de fourchette, ce sont de gros mangeurs

(**b**) *(person → robust)* vigoureux, robuste, solide; *(→ cheerful)* jovial; **they're a bit too hearty for my liking** ils sont un peu trop bruyants *ou* tapageurs à mon goût

(**c**) *(meal)* copieux, abondant

(**d**) *(thorough)* absolu; **I have a hearty dislike of hypocrisy** j'ai horreur de l'hypocrisie

2 *n* (**a**) *Arch or Hum* **my hearties!** les gars!

(**b**) *Fam (loud person)* chahuteur(euse) *m,f*

heat [hiːt] **1** *n* (**a**) *(gen) & Physiol* chaleur *f*; *(of fire, sun)* ardeur *f*, chaleur *f*; **you should avoid excessive heat and cold** il faudrait que vous évitiez les trop grosses chaleurs et les trop grands froids; **the radiator gives off a lot of heat** le radiateur chauffe bien; **you shouldn't go out in this heat** tu ne devrais pas sortir par cette chaleur; **the heat of summer** le plus fort de l'été; **in the heat of the day** au (moment le) plus chaud de la journée; **the heat of the day has passed** le plus chaud de la journée est passé; **I couldn't take the heat of the tropics** je ne pourrais pas supporter la chaleur des tropiques; *Fig* **if you can't stand the heat, get out of the kitchen** que ceux qui ne sont pas contents s'en aillent

(**b**) *(temperature)* température *f*, chaleur *f*; **heat loss** perte *f ou* déperdition *f* de chaleur; *Culin* **turn up the heat** mettre le feu plus fort; **reduce the heat** réduire le feu *ou* la chaleur; **cook at a high/low heat** faire cuire à feu vif/doux

(**c**) *(heating)* chauffage *m*; **to turn the heat on** allumer *ou* mettre le chauffage; **to turn off the heat** éteindre *ou* arrêter le chauffage; **the building was without heat all week** l'immeuble est resté toute la semaine sans chauffage

(**d**) *(intensity of feeling, fervour)* feu *m*, passion *f*; **she replied with (some) heat** elle a répondu avec feu *ou* avec passion

(**e**) *(high point of activity)* fièvre *f*, feu *m*; **in the heat of the argument** dans le feu de la discussion; **in the heat of the moment** dans l'agitation *ou* l'excitation du moment; **in the heat of battle** dans le feu du combat

(**f**) *Fam (coercion, pressure)* **the heat is on** les choses sérieuses ont commencé; **to turn up the heat** faire pression, mettre la pression; **the mafia turned the heat on the mayor** la mafia a fait pression sur le maire; **I'm lying low until the heat is off** je me tiens à carreau jusqu'à ce que les choses se calment; **the new deadline took the heat off him** le nouveau délai lui a permis de souffler un peu

(**g**) *Sport (round of contest)* manche *f*; *(preliminary round)* (épreuve *f*) éliminatoire *f*

(**h**) *Zool* chaleur *f*, rut *m*; *Br* **on heat,** *Am* **in heat** en chaleur, en rut

(**i**) *Am Fam Crime slang (police)* **the heat** les flics *mpl*

2 *vt* (**a**) *(gen) & Physiol* chauffer; *(overheat)* échauffer; **wine heats the blood** le vin échauffe le sang

(**b**) *Fig (inflame)* échauffer, enflammer

3 *vi (food, liquid)* chauffer; *(air, house, room)* se réchauffer

▸▸ *Aviat* ***heat barrier*** barrière *f* thermique; *Med* ***heat bump*** bouton *m* de chaleur; *Phys* ***heat capacity*** capacité *f* calorifique; *Phys* ***heat constant*** constante *f* calorifique; *Tech* ***heat engine*** machine *f ou* moteur *m* thermique; *Tech* ***heat exchanger*** échangeur *m* de chaleur; *Med* ***heat exhaustion*** épuisement *m* dû à la chaleur; ***heat haze*** brume *f* de chaleur; ***heat loss*** perte *f ou* déperdition *f* de chaleur; *Med* ***heat prostration*** épuisement *m* dû à la chaleur; *Tech* ***heat pump*** pompe *f* à chaleur; *Med* ***heat rash*** irritation *f ou* inflammation *f* due à la chaleur; *Aviat* ***heat shield*** bouclier *m* thermique; *Med* ***heat treatment*** traitement *m* par la chaleur, *Spec* thermothérapie *f*; *Met* ***heat wave*** vague *f* de chaleur, canicule *f*

▸**heat up 1** *vt sep* réchauffer

2 *vi (food, liquid)* chauffer; *(air, house, room)* se réchauffer; *Fig (situation)* se dégrader, s'aggraver

'In the Heat of the Night' *Jewison* 'Dans la chaleur de la nuit'

heat-conducting *adj Phys* thermoconducteur

heated ['hiːtɪd] *adj* (**a**) *(room, swimming pool)* chauffé; *(towel rail)* chauffant

(**b**) *(argument, discussion)* passionné; *(words)* vif; *(person)* échauffé; **he became quite heated about it** il s'est emporté *ou* échauffé à ce propos; **the discussion became heated** le ton de la conversation a monté; **she made a heated reply** elle a répondu avec emportement; **things got a bit heated** l'atmosphère a commencé à s'échauffer; **there were a few heated exchanges** ils échangèrent quelques propos vifs

▸▸ *Aut* ***heated rear window*** lunette *f* arrière chauffante

heatedly ['hiːtɪdlɪ] *adv (debate, talk)* avec passion; *(argue, deny, refuse)* avec passion *ou* emportement, farouchement

heater ['hiːtə(r)] *n* (**a**) *(for room)* appareil *m* de chauffage; *(for water)* chauffe-eau *m inv*; *(for car)* (appareil de) chauffage *m*; **I turned the heater on this morning** j'ai mis le chauffage ce matin (**b**) *Am Fam Crime slang (gun)* flingue *m* (**c**) *Electron* filament *m* incandescent

heath [hiːθ] *n* (**a**) *(moor)* lande *f* (**b**) *Bot* bruyère *f*

▸▸ *Bot* ***heath speedwell*** véronique *f* officinale

heathen ['hiːðən] *(pl* **inv** *or* **heathens**) **1** *n (pagan)* païen(enne) *m,f*; *(barbaric person)* barbare *mf*

2 *npl Literary* **the heathen** *(pagans)* les païens *mpl*; *(barbarians)* les barbares *mpl*

3 *adj (pagan)* païen; *(barbaric)* barbare

heathenish ['hiːðənɪʃ] *adj* (**a**) *(pagan → beliefs, rites)* païen (**b**) *(barbaric)* barbare

heathenism ['hiːðənɪzəm] *n* paganisme *m*

heather ['heðə(r)] *n Bot* bruyère *f*

heathery ['heðərɪ] *adj* de bruyère

heathland ['hiːθlænd] *n* lande *f*

Heath Robinson [ˌhiːθ'rɒbɪnsən] **1** *n* = nom évoquant une machine d'une complexité absurde (d'après le nom d'un dessinateur qui imagina de nombreux dispositifs de ce genre)

2 *adj* d'une complexité absurde

heating ['hiːtɪŋ] **1** *n* chauffage *m*; **there's no heating in the bathroom** il n'y a pas de chauffage dans la salle de bains; **to put the heating on** mettre le chauffage

2 *comp (apparatus, appliance, bill, system)* de chauffage

▸▸ ***heating element*** *(burner on stove)* plaque *f* chauffante; *(in dishwasher, kettle)* élément *m* chauffant, résistance *f*; ***heating engineer*** chauffagiste *mf*

heatproof ['hiːtpruːf] *adj (gen)* résistant à la chaleur; *(dish)* qui va au four; *(asbestos)* incombustible

heat-resistant *adj (gen)* résistant à la chaleur, *Spec* thermorésistant; *(dish)* qui va au four

heat-seeking [-ˌsiːkɪŋ] *adj (missile)* autodirecteur infrarouge

heatsink ['hiːtsɪŋk] *n Electron* dissipateur *m* thermique *ou* de chaleur

heatstroke ['hiːtstrəʊk] *n (UNCOUNT) Med* coup *m* de chaleur

heat-treat *vt* traiter par la chaleur

heave [hiːv] *(pt & pp vt & vi senses* (**a**) – (**c**) **heaved**, *pt & pp vi sense* (**d**) **hove** [həʊv], *cont* **heaving**) **1** *vt* (**a**) *(lift)* lever *ou* soulever avec effort; *(pull)* tirer fort; *(drag)* traîner avec effort; **he heaved the sacks of coal onto the truck** il a hissé les sacs de charbon dans le camion (à grand-peine); **I heaved myself out of the chair** je me suis arraché *ou* extirpé de ma chaise

(**b**) *(throw)* jeter, lancer; **he heaved a rock at the bear** il a lancé une pierre sur l'ours

(**c**) *Fig* **to heave a sigh of relief** pousser un soupir de soulagement

2 *vi* (**a**) *(rise and fall → sea, waves, chest)* se soulever; *(→ ship)* tanguer; **his shoulders heaved with suppressed laughter** il était secoué par un rire étouffé

(**b**) *(lift)* lever, soulever; *(pull)* tirer; **heave!** ho! hisse!

(**c**) *(retch)* avoir des haut-le-cœur; *(vomit)* vomir; **the sight made my stomach heave** le spectacle m'a soulevé le cœur *ou* m'a donné des nausées

(**d**) *Naut* aller, se déplacer; **the ship hove alongside the quay** le navire a accosté le quai; *Naut & Fig* **to heave into sight** *or* **into view** paraître *ou Literary* poindre à l'horizon

3 *n* (**a**) *(attempt to move)* **one more heave and we're there** encore un coup *ou* un petit effort et ça y est; **I gave the rope one more heave** j'ai tiré une fois de plus sur la corde; **with a heave he dragged the table against the door** dans un effort il traîna la table jusqu'à la porte; *Fam* **to give sb the heave** *(employee)* virer qn; *(boyfriend, girlfriend)* plaquer qn

(**b**) *(retching)* haut-le-cœur *m inv*, nausée *f*, *(vomiting)* vomissement *m*

4 heaves *npl* (**a**) *Vet* pousse *f*; **this horse has the heaves** ce cheval a la pousse *ou* est poussif

(**b**) *Fam* **to have the heaves** *(retching)* avoir des haut-le-cœur[❑]; *(vomiting)* vomir[❑]

▸**heave down** *Naut* **1** *vt sep* mettre *ou* abattre en carène, caréner

2 *vi* caréner

►**heave to** *Naut* **1** *vi* se mettre en panne
2 *vt sep* mettre en panne

heave-ho 1 *exclam Naut* oh hisse!
2 *n Fam* **to give sb the heave-ho** *(of employer)* sacquer qn, virer qn; *(of boyfriend, girlfriend)* plaquer qn

heaven ['hevən] **1** *n* **(a)** *Rel* ciel *m*, paradis *m*; **to go to heaven** aller au ciel, aller au *ou* en paradis; **in heaven** au ciel, au *ou* en paradis; **Our Father, who art in Heaven** notre Père qui es aux cieux
(b) *Fig (place or state of happiness)* **the Caribbean was like heaven on earth** les Caraïbes étaient un véritable paradis sur terre; **this is sheer heaven!** c'est divin *ou* merveilleux!, c'est le paradis!; **I wish to heaven I'd never said it** comme je regrette de l'avoir dit
(c) *(emphatic uses)* **heaven forbid!** pourvu que non!, j'espère bien que non!; **heaven forbid that I should see her** que Dieu me garde de la voir; **heaven help us if they catch us** que le ciel nous vienne en aide s'ils nous attrapent; **heaven knows I've tried!** Dieu sait si j'ai essayé!; **she bought books, magazines and heaven knows what (else)** elle a acheté des livres, des revues et je ne sais *ou* Dieu sait quoi encore; *Fam* **what in heaven's name is that?** au nom du ciel, qu'est-ce que c'est que ça?; *Fam* **who in heaven's name told you that?** qui diable vous a dit ça?, mais qui a donc pu vous dire cela?; **thank heaven (for that)!** Dieu merci!; *Fam* **good heavens!** ciel!, mon dieu!; *Fam* **(good) heavens, is that the time?** mon Dieu *ou* juste ciel, il est si tard que ça?; *Fam* **for heaven's sake!** *(in annoyance)* mince!; *(in pleading)* pour l'amour du ciel!; *Fam* **it smells** *or* **stinks to high heaven in here!** qu'est-ce que ça peut puer ici!; **she's in heaven when she's with him** elle est au septième ciel *ou* aux anges quand elle est avec lui; **to move heaven and earth to do sth** remuer ciel et terre pour faire qch
2 heavens *npl (sky) Literary* **the heavens** le ciel, le firmament; **the heavens opened** il s'est mis à pleuvoir à torrents

heavenly ['hevənlɪ] *adj* **(a)** *(from heaven, the sky)* céleste, du ciel; *(holy)* divin; **Heavenly Father** Père *m* céleste **(b)** *Fam (wonderful)* divin, merveilleux; **what heavenly peaches!** quelles pêches délicieuses!; **to have a heavenly evening** passer une soirée merveilleuse
►► ***heavenly body*** corps *m* céleste

heaven-sent *adj* providentiel; **a heaven-sent opportunity** une occasion providentielle *ou* qui tombe à pic

heavenward ['hevənwəd] **1** *adv (ascend, point)* vers le ciel; *(glance)* au ciel
2 *adj* vers le ciel; **with a heavenward glance** en levant les yeux au ciel

heavenwards ['hevənwədz] *adv Br (ascend, point)* vers le ciel; *(glance)* au ciel

heavily ['hevɪlɪ] *adv* **(a)** *(fall, land)* lourdement, pesamment; *(walk)* d'un pas lourd *ou* pesant, lourdement; **she leaned heavily on my arm** elle s'appuya de tout son poids sur mon bras; *Fig* **time hangs heavily on her** elle trouve le temps long, le temps lui pèse; **it weighed heavily on my conscience** cela me pesait sur la conscience
(b) *(laboriously → move)* avec difficulté, péniblement; *(→ breathe)* péniblement, bruyamment
(c) *(deeply → sleep)* profondément; **she left the room, sighing heavily** en poussant un énorme *ou* gros soupir, elle a quitté la pièce
(d) *(as intensifier) (drink, smoke, gamble)* beaucoup; *(fine, load, tax)* lourdement; *(stress)* fortement, lourdement; **it was raining heavily** il pleuvait des cordes; **it was snowing heavily** il neigeait très fort *ou* dru *ou* à gros flocons; **they lost heavily** *(team)* ils se sont fait écraser; *(gamblers)* ils ont perdu gros; *Fam* **they're heavily into yoga** ils donnent à fond dans le yoga; **the secret service was heavily involved in training guerillas** les services secrets étaient lourdement impliqués dans la formation des guérilleros; **they're heavily dependent on foreign trade** ils sont fortement tributaires du commerce extérieur; **heavily populated** très peuplé, à forte densité de population; **heavily wooded** très boisé

heavily-built *adj* solidement bâti; **a heavily-built man** un homme costaud *ou* bien charpenté

heavily-laden *adj* lourdement chargé; **heavily-laden with books** lourdement chargé de livres

heaviness ['hevɪnɪs] *n* **(a)** *(weight → of object)* poids *m*; *(→ of physique)* lourdeur *f*
(b) *(of burden)* poids *m*
(c) *(of movement, step)* lourdeur *f*, pesanteur *f*
(d) *(depression)* abattement *m*, découragement *m*; *(sadness)* tristesse *f*; **heaviness of heart** tristesse *f*
(e) *(of humour, irony)* manque *m* de subtilité; *(of style)* lourdeur *f*
(f) *(of food, meal)* caractère *m* indigeste; **I don't like the heaviness of their cooking** ce que je n'aime pas dans leur cuisine, c'est qu'elle est lourde
(g) *(of air, cloud, weather, silence)* lourdeur *f*

heaving ['hiːvɪŋ] *adj Br Fam (extremely busy)* hyper animé

HEAVY ['hevɪ]

lourd	► **1 (a) – (c), (e), (f), (i), (k), (m) – (o), (r), (t); 2**
chargé	► **1 (b), (k)**
important	► **1 (c), (p)**
gros	► **1 (c), (e) – (h)**
grave	► **1 (i), (r)**
pénible	► **1 (k)**
rôle tragique	► **3 (a)**
dur	► **3 (b)**

(compar **heavier**, *superl* **heaviest**, *pl* **heavies) 1** *adj* **(a)** *(in weight)* lourd; *(object)* lourd, pesant; **how heavy is he?** combien pèse-t-il?; **how heavy is it?** est-ce que c'est lourd?; **it's too heavy for me to lift** je ne peux pas le soulever, c'est *ou* ça pèse trop lourd; **heavy luggage** gros bagages *mpl*, bagages *mpl* lourds
(b) *(burdened, laden)* chargé, lourd; **the branches were heavy with fruit** les branches étaient chargées *ou* lourdes de fruits; **her eyes were heavy with sleep** elle avait les yeux lourds de sommeil; *Arch or Literary* **she was heavy with child** elle était enceinte; *Zool* **heavy with young** gravide, grosse
(c) *(in quantity → expenses, payments)* important, considérable; *(→ fine, losses)* gros (grosse), lourd; *(→ taxes)* lourd; *(→ casualties, damages)* énorme, important; *(→ crop)* abondant, gros (grosse); *(→ dew)* abondant; *(→ user)* gros (grosse); **she has a heavy cold** elle a un gros rhume, elle est fortement enrhumée; **to have heavy periods** avoir des règles abondantes; **there's a heavy demand for teachers** il y a une forte *ou* grosse demande d'enseignants; **her students make heavy demands on her** ses étudiants sont très exigeants avec elle *ou* exigent beaucoup d'elle; **heavy rain** forte pluie *f*; **heavy seas** grosse mer *f*; **heavy showers** grosses *ou* fortes averses *fpl*; **heavy sleep** sommeil *m* profond *ou* lourd; **to be a heavy sleeper** avoir le sommeil profond *ou* lourd; **heavy snow** neige *f* abondante, fortes chutes *fpl* de neige; **they expect heavy trading on the Stock Exchange** ils s'attendent à ce que le marché soit très actif; **heavy traffic** circulation *f* dense, grosse circulation *f*
(d) *(using large quantities)* **he's a heavy drinker/smoker** il boit/fume beaucoup, c'est un grand buveur/fumeur; **a heavy gambler** un(une) flambeur(euse); *Br Fam* **the car's very heavy on petrol** la voiture consomme énormément d'essence; *Fam* **you've been a bit heavy on the pepper** tu as eu la main un peu lourde avec le poivre
(e) *(laborious → movement)* lourd; *(→ step)* pesant, lourd; *(→ sigh)* gros (grosse), profond; *(→ thud)* gros (grosse); **he was dealt a heavy blow** *(hit)* il a reçu un coup violent; *(from fate)* ça a été un rude coup *ou* un gros choc pour lui; **heavy breathing** *(from effort, illness)* respiration *f* pénible; *(from excitement)* respiration *f* haletante; **heavy fighting is reported in the Gulf** on signale des combats acharnés dans le Golfe; **to rule with a heavy hand** gouverner de façon très autoritaire; **we could hear his heavy tread on the stairs** nous l'entendions monter l'escalier d'un pas lourd; **a heavy landing** un atterrissage brutal
(f) *(thick → coat, sweater, shoes)* gros (grosse); *(→ soil)* lourd, gras
(g) *(person → fat)* gros (grosse), corpulent; *(→ solid)* costaud, fortement charpenté; **a man of heavy build** un homme solidement bâti
(h) *(coarse, solid → line, lips)* gros (grosse), épais(aisse); *(thick → beard)* gros (grosse), fort; **heavy features** gros traits *mpl*, traits *mpl* épais *ou* lourds
(i) *(grave, serious → news)* grave; *(→ responsibility)* lourd; *(→ defeat)* lourd, grave; *Fam* **things got a bit heavy** les choses ont mal tourné
(j) *(depressed → mood, spirits)* abattu, déprimé; **with a heavy heart, heavy at heart** le cœur gros
(k) *(tiring → task)* lourd, pénible; *(→ work)* pénible; *(→ day, schedule, week)* chargé, difficile; **I've got a heavy day ahead of me** j'ai une journée chargée devant moi; **heavy going** *(in horseracing)* terrain *m* lourd; *Fig* **they found it heavy going** ils ont trouvé cela pénible *ou* difficile; **the rain made the trip heavy going** la pluie a rendu le voyage pénible; **it was heavy going getting them to agree** j'ai eu du mal à le leur faire accepter; **I found his last novel very heavy going** j'ai trouvé son dernier roman très indigeste
(l) *(difficult to understand → not superficial)* profond, compliqué, sérieux; *(→ tedious)* indigeste; **the report makes for heavy reading** le rapport n'est pas d'une lecture facile *ou* est ardu
(m) *(clumsy → humour, irony)* peu subtil, lourd; *(→ style)* lourd
(n) *(food, meal)* lourd, indigeste; *(wine)* corsé, lourd; **these scones are a bit on the heavy side** ces scones sont un peu lourds *ou* indigestes
(o) *(ominous, oppressive → air, cloud, weather)* lourd; *(→ sky)* couvert, chargé, lourd; *(→ silence)* lourd, pesant, profond; *(→ smell, perfume)* lourd, fort; *Fam (→ situation)* difficile ❑, menaçant ❑; **to make heavy weather of doing sth** avoir du mal à faire qch; *Fam* **to get heavy with sb** devenir agressif avec qn ❑
(p) *Fam (important)* important ❑; **to have a heavy date** avoir un rendez-vous galant
(q) *(stress)* accentué; *(rhythm)* aux accents marqués
(r) *Phys (body)* grave; *Nucl (atom)* lourd
(s) *St Exch* **the market is heavy** le marché est lourd *ou* orienté vers la baisse
(t) *Theat (part → difficult)* lourd, difficile; *(→ dramatic)* tragique
2 *adv* **(a)** *(lie, weigh)* lourd, lourdement; **the lie weighed heavy on her conscience** le mensonge pesait lourd sur sa conscience; **time hangs heavy on his hands** il trouve le temps long
(b) *(harshly)* **to come on heavy with sb** être dur avec qn
3 *n* **(a)** *Theat (serious part)* rôle *m* tragique; *(part of villain)* rôle *m* du traître; **he usually plays the heavy** d'habitude il joue des rôles de traître
(b) *Fam (tough guy)* dur *m*; **he sent round the heavies** il a envoyé les brutes *ou* les casseurs; **don't come the heavy with me** ne joue pas au dur avec moi
(c) *Fam (boxer, wrestler)* (poids *m*) lourd ❑ *m*
(d) *Mil* gros calibre *m*
(e) *Scot (beer)* = bière relativement amère, à forte teneur en houblon
(f) *Br Fam Press* **the heavies** = les quotidiens de qualité
►► *Mil* ***heavy artillery*** artillerie *f* lourde *ou* de gros calibre; *Fam* ***heavy breather*** auteur *m* de coups de téléphone obscènes ❑; *Am Culin* ***heavy cream*** ≃ crème *f* fraîche épaisse; *Mil* ***heavy fire*** feu *m* nourri, feu *m* intense; *Br Transp* ***heavy goods vehicle*** poids *m* lourd; *Am* ***heavy hitter*** *(in baseball)* = joueur qui frappe fort et marque beaucoup de points; *Fig* homme *m* influent, gros bonnet *m*; *Chem* ***heavy hydrogen*** hydrogène *m* lourd, deutérium *m*; ***heavy industry*** industrie *f* lourde; ***heavy machinery*** matériel *m* lourd; *St Exch* ***heavy market*** marché *m* lourd; ***heavy metal*** *Phys* métal *m* lourd; *Mus* heavy metal *m inv*; *Fam* ***the heavy mob*** les casseurs

hea–hea

mpl, les durs *mpl*; ***heavy oil*** huile *f* lourde; ***heavy petting*** *(UNCOUNT)* caresses *fpl* très poussées; *Typ* ***heavy type*** caractères *mpl* gras; *Phys* ***heavy water*** eau *f* lourde

heavy-duty *adj* **(a)** *(clothing, furniture)* résistant; *(boots)* solide, robuste; *(cleaning product, equipment)* à usage industriel; *(tyre)* tout-terrain *(inv)* **(b)** *Fam (meeting)* important[❑]; *(activity, discussion)* intense[❑]; **we've got to do some heavy-duty socializing** nous sommes obligés d'assister à de nombreuses réceptions

heavy-eyed *adj* aux yeux battus

heavy-footed *adj* qui marche lourdement, au pas lourd

heavy-handed *adj* **(a)** *(clumsy → person)* maladroit; *(→ style, writing)* lourd **(b)** *(harsh → person)* dur, sévère; *(→ action, policy)* arbitraire **(c)** *(tactless → remark)* qui manque de tact; *(→ joke)* lourd, qui manque de subtilité; *(→ compliment)* lourd, (trop) appuyé

heavy-handedness [-'hændɪdnɪs] *n* **(a)** *(clumsiness → of person)* maladresse *f*; *(→ of style, writing)* lourdeur *f* **(b)** *(harshness → of person)* caractère *m* dur *ou* sévère; *(→ of action, policy)* caractère *m* arbitraire **(c)** *(of remark)* manque *m* de tact; *(of joke)* manque *m* de subtilité; *(of compliment)* lourdeur *f*, maladresse *f*

heavy-hearted [-'hɑ:tɪd] *adj* abattu, découragé; **she felt sad and heavy-hearted** elle se sentait triste et avait le cœur gros

heavy-laden *adj (physically)* très chargé; *(emotionally)* accablé; **heavy-laden with worries** accablé de soucis; *Bible* **come unto me all those who are heavy-laden** venez à moi vous qui souffrez

heavy-set *adj (solidly built → woman)* fort; *(→ man)* bien charpenté, costaud; *(fat)* gros (grosse), corpulent

heavyweight ['hevɪweɪt] **1** *n* **(a)** *(large person, thing)* colosse *m*; *Fam Fig (important person)* personne *f* de poids *ou* d'envergure, ponte *m*; **a literary heavyweight** un écrivain profond *ou* sérieux, un grand écrivain

(b) *Sport* poids *m* lourd

2 *adj* **(a)** *(cloth, wool)* lourd; *(coat, sweater)* gros (grosse)

(b) *Fam Fig (important)* important[❑]; **a heavyweight industrialist** un grand *ou* gros industriel[❑]

(c) *Sport (championship, fight)* poids lourd *(inv)*; **he's a heavyweight fighter** c'est un poids lourd

▸▸ *Sport* ***heavyweight champion*** champion *m* poids lourd *ou* dans la catégorie poids lourd; ***the heavyweight title*** le titre (des) poids lourds

hebe [hi:b] *n Am Fam* youpin(e) *m,f*, = terme injurieux désignant un Juif

hebephrenia [ˌhi:bɪ'fri:nɪə] *n Psy* hébéphrénie *f*

hebephrenic [ˌhi:bɪ'frenɪk] *Psy* **1** *n* hébéphrénique *mf*

2 *adj* hébéphrénique

hebetate ['hebɪˌteɪt] *Arch or Literary* **1** *vt* hébéter, abrutir

2 *vi* s'hébéter, s'abrutir

hebetude ['hebɪˌtju:d] *n Arch or Literary* hébétement *m*, hébétude *f*

Hebraic [hi:'breɪɪk] *adj* hébraïque

Hebrew ['hi:bru:] **1** *n* **(a)** *(person → man)* Hébreu *m*, Israélite *m*, Juif *m*; *(→ woman)* Israélite *f*, Juive *f*; **the Hebrews** les Hébreux *mpl*; *Bible* **the Epistle of Paul to the Hebrews** l'Épître de saint Paul aux Hébreux **(b)** *(langue)* hébreu *m*

2 *adj (person → man)* hébreu, israélite, juif; *(→ woman)* israélite, juive; *(object, art, etc)* hébraïque

Hebridean [ˌhebrɪ'di:ən] *adj* des Hébrides

Hebrides ['hebrɪdi:z] *npl* **the Hebrides** les (îles *fpl*) Hébrides *fpl*; **in the Hebrides** aux Hébrides

Hebron ['hebrɒn] *n* Hébron

hecatomb ['hekətu:m] *n* hécatombe *f*

hechtia ['hektɪə] *n Bot* hechtia *m*

heck [hek] *Fam* **1** *n* **that's a heck of a lot of money!** c'est une sacrée somme d'argent!; **what the heck are you doing here?** qu'est-ce que tu fous là?; **where the heck did he go?** où diable est-il allé?; **who the heck said you could borrow my car?** bon sang! qui t'as dit que tu pouvais prendre ma voiture?; **why the heck didn't you tell me?** pourquoi est-ce que tu m'as pas prévenu, nom de nom!; **how the heck should I know?** mais enfin, comment veux-tu que je sache?; **he misses her a heck of a lot** elle lui manque vachement; **we saw a heck of a good film** on a vu un vachement bon film; **I went just for the heck of it** j'y suis allé, histoire de rire *ou* de rigoler; **oh, what the heck!** et puis flûte!

2 *exclam* mince alors!

heckle ['hekəl] **1** *vt (interrupt)* interrompre bruyamment; *(shout at)* interpeller, harceler

2 *vi* crier *(pour gêner un orateur)*

heckler ['heklə(r)] *n* chahuteur(euse) *m,f*

heckling ['heklɪŋ] **1** *n (UNCOUNT)* harcèlement *m*, interpellations *fpl*

2 *adj* qui fait du harcèlement, qui interpelle

hectare ['hekteə(r)] *n* hectare *m*

hectic ['hektɪk] *adj* **(a)** *(turbulent)* agité, bousculé; *(eventful)* mouvementé; **I've had a hectic day** j'ai eu une journée mouvementée, j'ai été bousculé toute la journée; **we spent three hectic weeks preparing the play** ç'a été la course folle pendant les trois semaines où on préparait la pièce; **they lead a hectic life** *(busy)* ils mènent une vie trépidante; *(eventful)* ils mènent une vie très mouvementée

(b) *(flushed)* fiévreux; *Med (fever, flush)* hectique

hectically ['hektɪklɪ] *adv* fiévreusement

hectogram, hectogramme ['hektəgræm] *n* hectogramme *m*

hectolitre, *Am* **hectoliter** ['hektəˌli:tə(r)] *n* hectolitre *m*

hectometre, *Am* **hectometer** ['hektəˌmi:tə(r)] *n* hectomètre *m*

Hector ['hektə(r)] *pr n Myth* Hector

hector ['hektə(r)] **1** *vt* harceler, tyranniser

2 *vi* être tyrannique, être une brute

3 *n* brute *f*, tyran *m*

hectoring ['hektərɪŋ] **1** *n (UNCOUNT)* harcèlement *m*, torture *f*

2 *adj (behaviour)* tyrannique; *(tone, voice)* impérieux, autoritaire

hectowatt ['hektəwɒt] *n* hectowatt *m*

he'd [hi:d] = **he had, he would**

hedge [hedʒ] **1** *n* **(a)** *(shrubs)* haie *f*; **hawthorn hedge** haie *f* d'aubépine; *Hum* **he looks like he's been dragged through a hedge backwards** il a l'air tout ébouriffé

(b) *(protection)* sauvegarde *f*; **a hedge against inflation** une sauvegarde *ou* une couverture contre l'inflation

(c) *(statement)* déclaration *f* évasive

(d) *St Exch* couverture *f*

2 *vt* **(a)** *(enclose)* entourer d'une haie, enclore; **the field was hedged with beech** le champ était entouré d'une haie de hêtres

(b) *(guard against losing)* couvrir; **to hedge one's bets** *(in betting)* répartir les risques; *Fig (cover oneself)* se couvrir

(c) *St Exch (position)* protéger, couvrir; *(shares)* arbitrer; *(transactions)* couvrir

3 *vi* **(a)** *(plant hedge)* planter une haie; *(trim hedge)* tailler une haie

(b) *(in action, discussion)* essayer de gagner du temps, atermoyer; *(in answering)* éviter de répondre, répondre à côté; *(in explaining)* expliquer avec des détours; **they are hedging slightly on the trade agreement** ils essaient de gagner du temps avant de conclure l'accord commercial; **stop hedging!** dis-le franchement!, au fait!

(c) *(protect)* se protéger; **it's a way of hedging against inflation** c'est un moyen de vous protéger *ou* vous couvrir contre l'inflation

(d) *St Exch* se couvrir; **to hedge against currency fluctuations** se couvrir contre les fluctuations monétaires

▸▸ ***hedge clippers*** cisaille *f* à haies; *St Exch* ***hedge fund*** société *f* d'investissement; *Bot* ***hedge mustard*** sisymbre *m* officinal, vélar *m*; *St Exch* ***hedge ratio*** ratio *m* de couverture; *Orn* ***hedge sparrow*** accenteur *m* mouchet, fauvette *f* d'hiver; ***hedge trimmer*** taille-haie *m*

▸**hedge about, hedge around** *vt sep* entourer; *Fig* **the offer was hedged about with conditions** l'offre était assortie de conditions

▸**hedge in** *vt sep* **(a)** *(surround with hedge)* entourer d'une haie, enclore **(b)** *(person)* **hedged in by restrictions** assorti de restrictions; **I'm feeling hedged in** je ne me sens pas libre

▸**hedge off** *vt sep (area)* entourer d'une haie; *(part of area)* séparer par une haie

hedgehog ['hedʒhɒg] *n* hérisson *m*; **to curl up like a hedgehog** se pelotonner, se recroqueviller (sur soi-même)

hedgehop ['hedʒhɒp] *(pt & pp* **hedgehopped,** *cont* **hedgehopping)** *vi Aviat* voler en rase-mottes, faire du rase-mottes

hedgehopper ['hedʒhɒpə(r)] *n Aviat (pilot)* pilote *m* qui vole en rase-mottes; *(aeroplane)* avion *m* qui fait du rase-mottes

hedgehopping ['hedʒhɒpɪŋ] *n Aviat* vol *m* en rase-mottes

hedger ['hedʒə(r)] *n St Exch* operateur(trice) *m,f* en couverture

hedgerow ['hedʒrəʊ] *n* haies *fpl*

▸▸ *Bot* ***hedgerow crane's bill*** géranium *m* des Pyrénées

hedging ['hedʒɪŋ] *n* **(a)** *(care of hedges)* entretien *m* des haies; **hedging and ditching** entretien *m* des haies et des fossés **(b)** *(hedges)* bordure *f* **(c)** *Horseracing* répartition *f* des risques **(d)** *St Exch* operations *fpl* de couverture **(e)** *(in discussion etc)* faux-fuyants *mpl*

hedonics [hi:'dɒnɪks] *n (UNCOUNT)* = branche de la psychologie ou de l'éthique qui étudie le plaisir

hedonism ['hi:dənɪzəm] *n* hédonisme *m*

hedonist ['hi:dənɪst] *n* hédoniste *mf*

hedonistic [ˌhi:də'nɪstɪk] *adj* hédoniste

heebie-jeebies [ˌhi:bɪ'dʒi:bɪz] *npl Fam* **to have the heebie-jeebies** avoir la frousse *ou* les chocottes; **the film gave me the heebie-jeebies** *(revulsion)* le film m'a donné la chair de poule; *(fright)* le film m'a donné la trouille *ou* la frousse; **he gives me the heebie-jeebies** *(revolts me)* il me hérisse; *(scares me)* il me donne la chair de poule

heed [hi:d] **1** *n* **to take heed of sth, to pay** *or* **to give heed to sth** tenir bien compte de qch; **he pays little heed to criticism** il ne se soucie guère *ou* il ne fait pas grand cas des critiques; **I took no heed of her advice** je n'ai tenu aucun compte de ses conseils; **pay no heed to him** ne faites pas attention à lui; **take heed!** prenez garde!

2 *vt* **(a)** *(warning, words)* faire bien attention à, tenir compte de, prendre garde à

(b) *(person → listen to)* bien écouter; *(→ obey)* obéir à

heedful ['hi:dfʊl] *adj Formal* attentif; **she's heedful of the importance of secrecy** elle est consciente qu'il est important de garder le secret; **they seemed heedful of what they were doing** ils semblaient attentifs à ce qu'ils faisaient

heedfully ['hi:dfʊlɪ] *adv Formal* attentivement

heedfulness ['hi:dfʊlnɪs] *n Formal* attention *f* (**of** à)

heedless ['hi:dlɪs] *adj* **heedless of the danger** sans se soucier du danger; **heedless of my warning** sans tenir compte de mon avertissement; **she seemed heedless of what was going on around her** elle ne semblait pas prêter attention à ce qui se passait autour d'elle

heedlessly ['hi:dlɪslɪ] *adv* **(a)** *(without thinking)* sans faire attention, à la légère **(b)** *(inconsiderately)* avec insouciance, négligemment

heedlessness ['hi:dlɪsnɪs] *n* **(a)** *(lack of attention)* inattention *f* (**of** à) **(b)** *(lack of consideration)* insouciance *f*

hee-haw [ˌhi:'hɔ:] **1** *n* **(a)** *(of donkey)* hi-han *m* **(b)** *(guffaw)* gros rire *m*

2 *vi* **(a)** *(donkey)* braire, faire hi-han **(b)** *(person)* rire bruyamment

3 *exclam* hi-han!

heel [hi:l] **1** *n* **(a)** *(of foot)* talon *m*; **she spun** *or* **turned on her heel and walked away** elle a tourné les talons; *Fig* **under the heel of Fascism** sous le joug *ou* la botte du fascisme; **we followed hard on her heels** *(walked)* nous lui emboîtâmes le pas; *(tracked)* nous étions sur ses talons; **famine followed hard on the heels of drought** la sécheresse fut suivie de près par la famine; **he brought the dog to heel** il a fait venir le chien à ses pieds; *Fig* **to bring sb to heel** mettre qn au pas; **to come to heel** *(dog)* venir au

pied; *Fam Fig (person, state)* se soumettre ❑; *Fam* **to take to one's heels, to show a clean pair of heels** se sauver à toutes jambes, prendre ses jambes à son cou; **he's showing the other runners a clean pair of heels** il a pris une belle avance sur les autres concurrents
(**b**) *(of boot, shoe)* talon *m*; **she was wearing heels** *(high-heeled shoes)* elle portait des talons; **to be down at heel** *(shoes)* être éculé; *Fig (person)* avoir l'air miteux
(**c**) *(of glove, golf club, hand, knife, sock, tool)* talon *m*
(**d**) *(of bread)* talon *m*, croûton *m*; *(of cheese)* talon *m*, croûte *f*
(**e**) *Fam (contemptible person)* chameau *m*
(**f**) *Naut (of keel)* talon *m*; *(of mast)* caisse *f*
(**g**) *(incline → of ship)* bande *f*; *(→ of vehicle, tower)* inclinaison *f*
2 *vt* (**a**) *(boot, shoe)* refaire le talon de; **to get one's shoes heeled** (faire) refaire le talon de ses chaussures
(**b**) *(in rugby)* talonner
3 *vi* (**a**) *(to dog)* **heel!** au pied!
(**b**) *(ship)* gîter, donner de la bande; *(vehicle, tower)* s'incliner, se pencher
►► ***heel bar*** talon-minute *m*, réparations-minute *fpl*

►**heel over** *vi (ship)* gîter, donner de la bande; *(vehicle, tower)* s'incliner, se pencher; *(cyclist)* se pencher

heel-and-toe 1 *adj* (**a**) *Sport* **heel-and-toe walking** marche *f (où le talon d'un pied est posé avant que la pointe de l'autre pied quitte le sol)* (**b**) *(driving)* **heel-and-toe driving** pointe-talon *m (façon de conduire utilisant le talon et la pointe du même pied pour appuyer sur l'accélérateur et le frein)*
2 *vi (when driving)* faire du pointe-talon

heelpiece ['hi:lpi:s] *n (of shoe)* contrefort *m* du talon

heeltap ['hi:ltæp] *n* (**a**) *(in shoe)* rondelle *f* en cuir *(pour talon)* (**b**) *(in glass)* fond *m* de verre

heft [heft] *Fam* **1** *n* (**a**) *(weight)* poids ❑ *m* (**b**) *Am (main part)* gros ❑ *m*
2 *vt* (**a**) *(lift)* soulever ❑; *(hoist)* hisser ❑ (**b**) *(test weight of)* soupeser ❑

hefty ['heftɪ] *(compar* **heftier**, *superl* **heftiest**) *adj Fam* (**a**) *(package → heavy)* lourd ❑; *(→ bulky)* encombrant ❑, volumineux ❑; *(book)* épais (aisse) ❑, gros (grosse) ❑; *(person)* costaud (**b**) *(part, profit)* gros (grosse) ❑; **a hefty sum** une jolie somme; **he paid a hefty price for them** il les a payés drôlement cher; **she earns a hefty salary** elle se fait une bonne *ou* sacrée paie (**c**) *(blow, slap)* puissant ❑

Hegelian [heɪ'gi:lɪən] *adj Phil* hégélien

Hegelianism [heɪ'gi:lɪənɪzəm] *n Phil* hégélianisme *m*

hegemony [hɪ'gemənɪ] *n* hégémonie *f*

Hegira, Hejira ['hedʒɪrə] *n Rel* hégire *f*
►► ***the Hegira calendar*** le calendrier musulman

heifer ['hefə(r)] *n* (**a**) *(animal)* génisse *f* (**b**) *Fam (fat woman)* grosse dondon *f*; *Am (attractive woman)* canon *m*

heigh-ho ['heɪ'həʊ] *exclam* (**a**) *(in weariness)* eh bien!; *(in resignation)* hélas! (**b**) *Old-fashioned or Literary (in surprise)* ça alors!, ça par exemple!; *(in happiness)* chouette alors!

height [haɪt] *n* (**a**) *(tallness → of person)* taille *f*, grandeur *f*; *(→ of building, tree)* hauteur *f*; **what height are you?** combien mesurez-vous?; **height: 1 m 80** *(on form)* taille: 1 m 80; **I'm of average height** je suis de taille moyenne; **redwoods grow to a height of 100 metres** les séquoias peuvent atteindre 100 mètres (de haut)
(**b**) *(distance above ground → of mountain, plane)* altitude *f*; *(→ of ceiling, river, stars)* hauteur *f*; **the plane was gaining/losing height** l'avion prenait/perdait de l'altitude; **to be at a height of 3 metres above the ground** être à 3 mètres au-dessus du sol; *Am Geog* **height of land** ligne *f* de partage des eaux
(**c**) *(high position)* hauteur *f*; **to fall from a great height** tomber de haut; *Geog* **the heights** les hauteurs *fpl*; **to have a good head for heights** ne pas avoir le vertige; **fear of heights** vertige *m*; **I'm afraid of heights** j'ai le vertige; *Fig* **to reach new heights** atteindre de nouveaux sommets
(**d**) *Fig (peak → of career, success)* point *m* culminant; *(→ of fortune, fame)* apogée *m*; *(→ of arrogance, stupidity)* comble *m*; **at the height of her powers** en pleine possession de ses moyens; **at its height the group had 300 members** à son apogée, le groupe comprenait 300 membres; **the tourist season is at its height** la saison touristique bat son plein; **the height of bad manners** le comble de l'impolitesse *ou* de la grossièreté; **at the height of summer** en plein été, au plus chaud de l'été; **at the height of the battle/storm** au plus fort de la bataille/de l'orage; **to dress in the height of fashion** s'habiller à la dernière mode; **it's the height of fashion** c'est le dernier cri
►► ***height restriction*** limitation *f* de hauteur

'Wuthering Heights' *Emily Brontë, Wyler* 'Les Hauts de Hurlevent'

height-adjustable *adj* réglable en hauteur

heighten ['haɪtən] **1** *vt* (**a**) *(make higher → building, ceiling, shelf)* relever, rehausser
(**b**) *(increase → effect, fear, pleasure)* augmenter, intensifier; *(→ flavour, colour)* relever; *(→ contrast)* accentuer; *(→ impression, speculation)* renforcer; *(→ fever)* faire monter, aggraver; **the incident has heightened public awareness of environmental problems** l'incident a sensibilisé encore plus le public aux problèmes de l'environnement; **the riots have heightened racial tensions in the city** les émeutes ont accentué *ou* aggravé les tensions raciales dans la ville; **the colour heightened the deathly pallor of her skin** cette couleur faisait ressortir *ou* accentuait sa pâleur cadavérique
2 *vi (fear, pleasure)* augmenter, monter; *(speculation)* s'intensifier; *(tension)* monter

heightened ['haɪtənd] *adj* (**a**) *(building, ceiling, shelf)* relevé, rehaussé (**b**) *(fear, pleasure)* intensifié; *(colour)* plus vif; **there is a heightened awareness of the dangers of pollution** il y a une prise de conscience accrue des dangers de la pollution

heightening ['haɪtənɪŋ] *n* (**a**) *(of building, ceiling, shelf)* rehaussement *m*, surélévation *f* (**b**) *(of fear, pleasure)* accroissement *m*, intensification *f*

Heimlich manoeuvre ['haɪmlɪk-] *n* méthode *f* d'Heimlich

heinie ['hi:nɪ] *n Am very Fam* cul *m*

heinous ['heɪnəs] *adj Literary or Formal* odieux, atroce; **a heinous crime** un crime abominable *ou* odieux

heinously ['heɪnəslɪ] *adv Literary or Formal* odieusement, atrocement

heinousness ['heɪnəsnɪs] *n Literary or Formal* atrocité *f*

Heinz [haɪnz] *n Fam Hum (dog)* bâtard ❑ *m*

heir [eə(r)] *n (gen)* héritier *m*; *Law* héritier *m*, légataire *mf*; **he is heir to a vast fortune** il est l'héritier d'une immense fortune; **the heir to the throne** l'héritier du trône *ou* de la couronne; *Law* **heir at law, rightful heir** héritier *m* légitime *ou* naturel; *Literary* **flesh is heir to many ills** l'humanité a hérité de bien des maux
►► ***heir apparent*** *Law* héritier *m* présomptif; *Fig (of political party, company)* dauphin *m*; *Law* ***heir presumptive*** héritier *m* présomptif *(sauf naissance d'un héritier en ligne directe)*

heirdom ['eədəm] *n* (**a**) *(right of succession)* droit *m* de succession (**b**) *Arch or Literary (inheritance)* héritage *m*

heiress ['eərɪs] *n* héritière *f*

heirless ['eəlɪs] *adj* sans héritier

heirloom ['eəlu:m] *n* (**a**) *(family property)* **(family) heirloom** objet *m* de famille (**b**) *Law (legacy)* legs *m*

heirship ['eəʃɪp] *n* (**a**) *(being an heir)* qualité *f* d'héritier (**b**) *(right of inheritance)* droit *m* d'héritier

heist [haɪst] *Am Fam* **1** *n (robbery)* vol ❑ *m*; *(in bank)* braquage *m*; *(stolen objects)* butin ❑ *m*
2 *vt (money)* voler ❑; *(bank)* braquer

held [held] *pt & pp of* **hold**

Helen ['helɪn] *pr n Myth* Hélène; **Helen of Troy** Hélène de Troie

Helena ['helɪnə] *pr n* Hélène

helenium [hɪ'li:nɪəm] *n Bot* helenium *m*

heliacal [hɪ'laɪəkəl] *adj Astron* héliaque
►► ***heliacal rising*** lever *m* héliaque; ***heliacal setting*** coucher *m* héliaque

helianthemum [ˌhi:lɪ'ænθəməm] *n Bot* hélianthème *m*

helianthus [ˌhi:lɪ'ænθəs] *n Bot* hélianthe *m*, tournesol *m*

heliborne ['helɪbɔ:n] *adj Aviat* héliporté

helical ['helɪkəl, 'hi:lɪkəl] *adj* hélicoïdal
►► *Tech* ***helical gear*** engrenage *m* hélicoïdal

helically ['helɪkəlɪ] *adv* en hélice

helices ['helɪsi:z] *pl of* **helix**

helicoid ['helɪkɔɪd], **helicoidal** ['helɪkɔɪdəl] **1** *adj (gen)* hélicoïdal; *Geom* hélicoïde
2 *n Geom* hélicoïde *m*

helicopter ['helɪkɒptə(r)] **1** *n* hélicoptère *m*; **the wounded were transported by helicopter** les blessés ont été héliportés
2 *comp (patrol, rescue)* en hélicoptère; *(pilot)* d'hélicoptère
3 *vt* transporter en hélicoptère; **they managed to helicopter in provisions** ils ont réussi à amener des provisions par hélicoptère
►► ***helicopter carrier, helicopter ship*** porte-hélicoptères *m inv*; ***helicopter gunship*** hélicoptère *m* de combat; ***helicopter transfer, helicopter transport*** héliportage *m*

helidrome ['helɪdrəʊm] *n* hélidrome *m*

heliocentric [ˌhi:lɪəʊ'sentrɪk] *adj* héliocentrique

heliograph ['hi:lɪəʊgrɑ:f] **1** *n* (**a**) *(transmitter)* héliographe *m* (**b**) *(camera)* photohéliographe *m*
2 *vt* transmettre par héliographe

heliogravure [hi:lɪəʊgrə'vjʊə(r)] *n* héliogravure *f*

heliometer [ˌhi:lɪ'ɒmɪtə(r)] *n* héliomètre *m*

Helios ['hi:lɪɒs] *pr n Myth* Hélios

helioscope ['hi:lɪəʊskəʊp] *n Astron* hélioscope *m*

heliosphere ['hi:lɪəʊsfɪə(r)] *n Astron* héliosphère *f*

heliostat ['hi:lɪəʊstæt] *n Astron* héliostat *m*

heliotherapy [ˌhi:lɪəʊ'θerəpɪ] *n Med* héliothérapie *f*

heliotrope ['helɪətrəʊp] **1** *n* (**a**) *Bot* héliotrope *m* (**b**) *(colour)* violet *m* clair
2 *adj* violet clair

heliotropic [ˌhi:lɪə'trɒpɪk] *adj Bot* héliotropique

heliotropin [ˌhi:lɪ'ɒtrəpɪn] *n Chem* héliotropine *f*

heliotropism [ˌhi:lɪ'ɒtrəpɪzəm], **heliotropy** [ˌhi:lɪ'ɒtrəpɪ] *n Bot* héliotropisme *m*

heliotype ['hi:lɪəʊˌtaɪp] *n Phot* (**a**) *(process)* héliotypie *f* (**b**) *(plate)* héliotype *m*

heliotypy ['hi:lɪəʊˌtaɪpɪ] *n Phot* héliotypie *f*

helipad ['helɪpæd] *n* héliport *m*

heliport ['helɪpɔ:t] *n* héliport *m*

helistop ['helɪstɒp] *n* héliport *m*

helium ['hi:lɪəm] *n Chem* hélium *m*
►► ***helium balloon*** ballon *m* gonflé à l'hélium

helix ['hi:lɪks] *(pl* **helices** ['helɪsi:z] *or* **helixes**) *n* (**a**) *Archit & Geom (spiral)* hélice *f* (**b**) *Anat & Zool* hélix *m*

hell [hel] **1** *n* (**a**) *Rel* enfer *m*; *Myth (underworld)* les Enfers *mpl*; **to go to hell** *(Christianity)* aller en enfer; *Myth* descendre aux Enfers; **it's (as) hot as hell in there** il fait une chaleur de tous les diables *ou* infernale là-dedans; *Fam* **go to hell!** va te faire voir!; *Fam* **to hell with him!** qu'il aille au diable!; *Fam* **to hell with society!** au diable la société!; *Fam* **to hell with what they think!** leur avis, je m'assois dessus!; *Fam* **come hell or high water** contre vents et marées, envers et contre tout; *Fam* **when hell freezes over** à la saint-glinglin, la semaine des quatre jeudis; **that won't happen until hell freezes over** ça aura lieu la semaine des quatre jeudis; *Fam* **it'll be a cold day in hell before I apologize** je m'excuserai quand les poules auront des dents; *Fam* **the boyfriend/flatmate/neighbours from hell** un petit ami/un colocataire/des voisins *mpl* de cauchemar; *Fam* **it was a journey from hell!** ce voyage, c'était l'horreur!; *Fam* **all hell broke loose** ça a bardé; *Fam* **to give sb hell** passer un savon *ou* faire sa fête à qn; *Fam* **give them hell!** rentre-leur dedans!, fais-leur en baver!; *Fam* **the damp weather plays hell with my arthritis** ce temps humide me fait rudement souffrir de mon arthrite!, par ces temps humides, qu'est-ce que je déguste avec mon arthrite!; *Fam* **there'll be hell to pay when he finds out** ça va barder *ou* chauffer quand il l'apprendra; *Fam* **they went into town to raise (a little) hell** ils sont allés faire la bringue en ville; *Fam* **the boss raised hell when he saw the report** le patron a fait une scène de tous les diables en voyant le rapport; *Fam* **I went along just for the hell of it** j'y suis allé histoire de rire *ou* de rigoler; *Fam* **he ran off hell for leather** il est parti ventre à terre; *Fam* **to ride hell for leather** aller au triple galop *ou* à bride abattue; *Am Fam* **the whole country's going to hell in a handcart** tout fout le camp dans ce pays; *Fam* **hell's bells!, hell's teeth!** mince alors!

(**b**) *Fam (torture)* enfer *m*; **it's hell in here** c'est infernal ici; **it can be hell trying to park here** quelquefois, c'est la croix et la bannière pour se garer par ici; **working there was hell on earth** *or* **on wheels** c'était l'enfer de travailler là-bas; **he made her life hell** il lui a fait mener une vie infernale

(**c**) *Fam (used as emphasis)* **it's colder/hotter than hell** il fait vachement froid/chaud; **he's as happy/tired as hell** il est vachement heureux/fatigué; **he's in a hell of a mess** il est dans un sacré pétrin; *Br* **it's a hell of a cold outside** il fait un froid de canard dehors; **a hell of a wind** un vent du diable *ou* de tous les diables; **there was a** *or* **one hell of a fight** il y a eu une bagarre terrible; **you've got a hell of a nerve!** tu as un culot du diable!; **a hell of a lot of books** tout un tas *ou* un paquet de livres; **he likes her a hell of a lot** il est dingue d'elle; **we had a hell of a good time** nous nous sommes amusés comme des fous; **it was a hell of a good film** c'était un sacrément bon film; **they had a hell of a time getting the car started** ils en ont bavé pour faire démarrer la voiture; **my arm started to hurt like hell** mon bras a commencé à me faire vachement mal; **he worked like hell** il a travaillé comme une brute *ou* une bête; **to run/to shout like hell** courir/crier comme un fou; **will you lend me $50? – like hell** *or* **the hell I will!** peux-tu me prêter 50 dollars? – tu peux toujours courir!; **I'm leaving – like hell** *or* **the hell you are!** je pars – n'y compte pas!; **I wish to hell I could remember** si seulement je pouvais me souvenir ❑; **I just hope to hell he leaves** j'espère de tout mon cœur qu'il partira; **get the hell out of here!** fous *ou* fous-moi le camp!; **what the hell** *or* **in hell's name are you doing?** qu'est-ce que tu fous?; **what the hell's going on?** qu'est-ce qui se passe, nom de Dieu?; **why the hell did you go?** qu'est-ce qui t'a pris d'y aller?; **how the hell would I know?** comment veux-tu que je le sache?; *Am* **how the hell are you doing, my friend?** comment ça va, mon pote?; **where the hell are my keys?** où diable sont mes clefs?; **who the hell do you think you are?** mais tu te prends pour qui?; **who the hell are you?** qui diable êtes-vous?; **oh well, what the hell!** oh qu'est-ce que ça peut bien faire?; **did you agree? – hell, no!** as-tu accepté? – tu plaisantes! ❑

(**d**) *Am Fam (high spirits)* **there's hell in that boy** ce garçon respire la joie de vivre ❑; **full of hell** plein d'entrain ❑ *ou* de vivacité ❑

2 *exclam* **(oh) hell!** bon Dieu!

►► ***Hell's Angels*** = nom d'un groupe de motards au comportement violent; *Am Univ* ***hell week*** = semaine au cours de laquelle les étudiants qui souhaitent devenir membres d'une "fraternity" ou d'une "sorority" sont soumis à toutes sortes d'épreuves initiatiques

'Hell's Angels' *Hughes* 'Les Anges de l'enfer'

he'll [hi:l] = **he will**

hellacious [hel'eɪʃəs] *adj Am Fam* (**a**) *(bad, unpleasant)* infernal (**b**) *(excellent)* super, génial

hellbender ['hel,bendə(r)] *n Zool* = grande salamandre aquatique des États-Unis

hell-bent *adj Fam* **to be hell-bent on doing sth** vouloir à tout prix faire qch ❑; **he's hell-bent on going** il veut à tout prix y aller, il veut y aller coûte que coûte ❑; **society seems hell-bent on self-destruction** la société semble décidée à aller tout droit à sa propre destruction ❑

hellcat ['helkæt] *n* harpie *f*, mégère *f*

hellebore ['helɪbɔ:(r)] *n Bot* hellébore *m*

helleborine [,helɪ'bɔ:ri:n] *n Bot* helléborine *f*, sérapias *m*

Hellene ['heli:n] *n* Hellène *mf*

Hellenic [he'li:nɪk] **1** *adj (people)* hellène; *(language, history)* hellénique

2 *n* langue *f* hellénique

Hellenism ['helɪnɪzəm] *n* hellénisme *m*

Hellenist ['helɪnɪst] *n* helléniste *mf*

Hellenistic [,helɪ'nɪstɪk] *adj (language, period)* hellénistique

Hellenization [,helɪnaɪ'zeɪʃən] *n* hellénisation *f*

Hellenize, -ise ['helɪnaɪz] **1** *vt* helléniser

2 *vi* s'helléniser

hellfire ['helfaɪə(r)] **1** *n* feu *m* de l'enfer; *Fig (punishment)* châtiment *m* divin

2 *exclam Fam* bon sang!, sacré nom de Dieu!

►► ***hellfire preacher*** prédicateur *m* fanatique *(qui est toujours en train de rappeler aux pécheurs qu'ils sont voués à la damnation éternelle)*

hellhole ['helhəʊl] *n Fam* trou *m* à rats

hellhound ['helhaʊnd] *n* chien *m* des Enfers; *Fig (fiend)* monstre *m*, démon *m*

hellion ['heljən] *n Am Fam (child)* galopin *m*, polisson(onne) *m,f*; *(adult)* chahuteur(euse) *m,f*, trublion *m*

hellish ['helɪʃ] **1** *adj* (**a**) *(cruel → action, person)* diabolique (**b**) *Fam (dreadful)* infernal; **she's had a pretty hellish life** elle a eu une vie absolument infernale, sa vie a été un véritable enfer; **I feel hellish** je ne me sens vraiment pas dans mon assiette

2 *adv Fam* vachement

hellishly ['helɪʃlɪ] *adv Fam* vachement

hellishness ['helɪʃnɪs] *n* **the hellishness of war** l'horreur *f* de la guerre

hello [hə'ləʊ] (*pl* **hellos**) **1** *exclam* (**a**) *(greeting)* bonjour; *(in the evening)* bonsoir; *(on answering telephone)* allô

(**b**) *(to attract attention)* hé!, ohé!; **hello there, wake up!** holà! réveille-toi!;

(**c**) *(in surprise)* tiens!; **hello, what's this?** tiens!, qu'est-ce que c'est que ça?

2 *n (greeting)* bonjour *m*, salutation *f*; **he gave me a cheery hello** il m'a salué joyeusement *ou* avec entrain; **say hello to the lady** dis bonjour à la dame; **say hello to him for me** dis-lui bonjour de ma part; **he asked me to say hello to you** il m'a demandé de vous donner le bonjour

hell-raiser *n Fam* fêtard(e) *m,f*

hell-raising *n Fam* vie *f* de patachon, vie *f* de bâton de chaise; **his hell-raising days** sa vie de patachon

helluva ['heləvə] *adj Fam* **a helluva noise** un sacré boucan; **a helluva wind** un vent du diable *ou* de tous les diables; **a helluva lot of money** un paquet de fric; **a helluva lot of kids** des tas d'enfants; **he's a helluva guy** c'est un type vachement bien; **I miss him a helluva lot** il me manque vachement; **I had a helluva time** *(awful)* je me suis emmerdé; *(wonderful)* je me suis vachement marré; **they had a helluva time convincing her** ils ont eu vachement de mal à la convaincre

helm [helm] **1** *n* (**a**) *Naut* barre *f*, gouvernail *m*; **to be at the helm** tenir la barre *ou* le gouvernail; *Fig* tenir la barre *ou* les rênes; *also Fig* **to take the helm** prendre la barre, prendre la direction des opérations; **he's at the helm of the company now** c'est lui qui dirige la société maintenant (**b**) *Arch (helmet)* casque *m*

2 *vt* (**a**) *Naut* gouverner, barrer; *Fig* diriger (**b**) *Arch (supply with helmet)* coiffer d'un casque

helmet ['helmɪt] *n (gen)* casque *m*; *(medieval)* heaume *m*

helmeted ['helmɪtɪd] *adj* casqué, portant un casque

helminth ['helmɪnθ] *n Biol & Entom* helminthe *m*, ver *m* intestinal

helminthology [,helmɪn'θɒlədʒɪ] *n Biol & Entom* helminthologie *f*

helmsman ['helmzmən] (*pl* **helmsmen** [-mən]) *n* timonier *m*, homme *m* de barre

Heloïse [heləʊ'i:z] *pr n* **Heloïse and Abelard** Héloïse et Abélard

helot ['helət] *n Hist* ilote *mf*

HELP [help]

aide	►1 (a), (b)
secours	►1 (a), (b)
personnel	►1 (c)
femme de ménage	►1 (d)
aider	►2 (a)
secourir	►2 (a)
contribuer à	►2 (b)
encourager	►2 (b)
améliorer	►2 (c)
servir	►2 (d)
être utile	►3

1 *n* (**a**) *(gen)* aide *f*, assistance *f*; *(to drowning or wounded person)* secours *m*, assistance *f*; **thank you for your help** merci de votre aide; **can I be of any help?** puis-je faire quelque chose pour vous?, puis-je vous rendre service?; **we're happy to have been of help** nous sommes contents d'avoir pu rendre service; **I had help** *(I didn't do it on my own)* on m'a aidé; **he went to get help** il est allé chercher du secours; **we yelled for help** nous avons crié au secours; **with the help of a neighbour** avec l'aide d'un voisin; **he opened the window with the help of a crowbar** il a ouvert la fenêtre à l'aide d'un levier; **she did it without any help** elle l'a fait toute seule; **the map wasn't much help** la carte n'a pas servi à grand-chose; **I could never have done it without your help** jamais je n'aurais pu le faire sans vous *ou* votre aide; **some students need help to decide which course to take** certains étudiants ont besoin qu'on les aide à choisir leur cursus; **she needs help going upstairs** il faut qu'elle se fasse aider pour *ou* elle a besoin qu'on l'aide à monter l'escalier; *Fam* **she needs help** il faut qu'elle voie un psychiatre, elle a des problèmes psychologiques; *Fam* **if you think that's funny, you need help** si tu trouves ça drôle, c'est que tu dois avoir un problème; **the situation is now beyond help** la situation est désespérée *ou* irrémédiable maintenant; **he's past help** *(is dying)* il est perdu; *(is crazy, stupid)* on ne peut rien pour lui; **there's no help for it** on n'y peut rien

(**b**) *(something that assists)* aide *f*, secours *m*; **that was a big help (to me)** ça m'a beaucoup aidé; **you've been a great help** vous m'avez été d'un grand secours, vous m'avez beaucoup aidé; *Ironic* **he's a great help!** il est d'un précieux secours!

(**c**) *(UNCOUNT) (employees)* personnel *m*, employés *mpl*; **it's hard to get good help** il est difficile de trouver des employés sérieux; **help wanted** *(sign)* cherchons employés

(**d**) *(domestic worker)* femme *f* de ménage

2 *vt* (**a**) *(assist, aid → gen)* aider; *(→ elderly, poor, wounded)* secourir, venir en aide à; **come and help me** viens m'aider; **can I help you with the dishes?** puis-je t'aider à faire la vaisselle?; **they got their neighbours to help them move** ils se sont fait aider par leurs voisins pour le déménagement; **they help one another take care of the children** ils s'entraident pour s'occuper des enfants; **we want to help poorer countries to help themselves** nous voulons aider les pays sous-développés à devenir autonomes *ou* à se prendre en main; **he helped me on/off with my coat** il m'a aidé à mettre/enlever mon manteau; *Euph* **a man is helping the police with their enquiries** la police est en train d'interroger un suspect; **she helped the old man to his feet/across the street** elle a aidé le vieux monsieur à se lever/à traverser la rue; **let me help you up/down** laissez-moi vous aider à monter/descendre; **it might help if you took more exercise** ça irait peut-être mieux si tu faisais un peu plus d'exercice; **it helped me knowing that someone was waiting for me** ça m'a aidé de savoir que quelqu'un m'attendait; **can I help you?** *(in shop)* vous désirez?; **Grant Publishing, how may I help you?** *(on telephone)* ≃ *les Éditions Grant, bonjour; Law* **do you swear to tell the truth, so help you God?** jurez-vous de dire la vérité, que Dieu vous vienne en aide?; **so help me God!** je le jure devant Dieu!; *Fam* **I'll get you for this, so help me** j'aurai ta peau, je le jure!; *Prov* **God helps those who help themselves** aide-toi, le ciel t'aidera (**b**) *(contribute to)* contribuer à; *(encourage)* encourager, favoriser; **the rain helped firefighters to bring the flames under control** la pluie a permis aux pompiers de maîtriser l'incendie; **it helped to ease my headache** cela a soulagé mon mal de tête; **it helped to give the impression that...** cela a contribué à donner l'impression que..., à cause de cela, on avait l'impression que...

(**c**) *(improve, remedy → situation)* améliorer; *(→ pain)* atténuer; **this cream should help your back pain** cette crème devrait te soulager de ton mal de dos; **that doesn't help the situation, that doesn't help much** cela ne nous avance pas (beaucoup); **crying won't help matters** cela ne sert à rien *ou* n'arrange rien de pleurer; *Ironic* **to help matters, it started to pour with rain** pour tout arranger, il s'est mis à pleuvoir des cordes

(**d**) *(serve)* servir; **she helped me to more rice** elle m'a servi du riz une deuxième fois; **I helped myself to the cheese** je me suis servi en fromage; **help yourself!** servez-vous!; **they helped themselves to more meat** ils ont repris de la viande; *Euph* **he helped himself to the petty cash** il a pioché *ou* il s'est servi dans la caisse

(**e**) *(with "can", usu negative) (avoid, refrain from)* **I can't help thinking that we could have done more** je ne peux pas m'empêcher de penser qu'on aurait pu faire plus; **we couldn't help laughing** *or* **but laugh** nous ne pouvions pas nous empêcher de rire; **I couldn't help overhearing** je n'ai pu m'empêcher de surprendre la conversation; **she never writes any more than she can help** elle ne se foule pas pour écrire, elle écrit un minimum de lettres *ou* le moins possible

(**f**) *(with "can", usu negative) (control)* **she can't help her temper** elle ne peut rien à ses colères; **I tried not to laugh but I couldn't help myself** j'essayais de ne pas rire mais c'était plus fort que moi; **they can't help being born there** ils n'ont pas demandé à naître là; **I'm not going back if I can help it** si j'ai le choix, je n'y retournerai pas; **I can't help it** je n'y peux rien, ce n'est pas de ma faute; **he can't help it if she doesn't like it** il n'y est pour rien *ou* ce n'est pas de sa faute si cela ne lui plaît pas; **can he help it if the train is late?** est-ce que c'est de sa faute si le train est en retard?; **it can't be helped** tant pis! on n'y peut rien *ou* on ne peut pas faire autrement; **are they coming? – not if I can help it!** est-ce qu'ils viennent? – pas si j'ai mon mot à dire!

3 *vi* être utile; **can I help?** est-ce que je peux faire quelque chose?; **is there anything I can do to help?** puis-je être utile?; **she helps a lot around the house** elle se rend très utile à la maison, elle rend souvent service à la maison; **he offered to help with the clearing up** il a proposé de nous/les/*etc* aider à ranger; **I was only trying to help!** je voulais seulement vous/les/*etc* aider!; **it helps if you can speak the language** c'est plus facile si on parle la langue; **losing your temper isn't going to help** ça ne sert à rien de perdre ton calme; **forgetting the map didn't help** le fait d'avoir oublié la carte n'a pas arrangé les choses; **it's near the post office if that helps** c'est près du bureau de poste si ça peut vous aider; **every little helps** les petits ruisseaux font les grandes rivières; **every penny helps** il n'y a pas de petites économies

4 *exclam (in distress)* au secours!, à l'aide!; *(in dismay)* zut!, mince!; **help!, I'm late!** mince!, je suis en retard!

►► *Comput* ***help button*** case *f* d'aide; ***help desk*** service *m* d'assistance téléphonique; *Comput (for computing queries)* service *m* d'assistance; *Comput* ***help file*** fichier *m* d'aide; *Comput* ***help key*** touche *f* d'aide; *Comput* ***help menu*** menu *m* d'aide; *Comput* ***help screen*** écran *m* d'aide

►**help along** *vt sep (person)* aider à marcher *ou* avancer; *(plan, project)* faire avancer

►**help out 1** *vt sep (gen)* aider, venir en aide à; *(with supplies, money)* dépanner; **the scholarship really helped her out** la bourse lui a été d'un grand secours; **she helps us out in the shop from time to time** elle vient nous donner un coup de main au magasin de temps en temps; **they help each other out** ils s'entraident; **she helps him out with his homework** elle l'aide à faire ses devoirs

2 *vi* aider, donner un coup de main

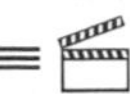

'Help!' *Lester* 'Quatre garçons dans le vent'

helper ['helpə(r)] *n* (**a**) *(gen)* aide *mf*, assistant(e) *m,f*; *(professional)* auxiliaire *mf* (**b**) *Am (home help)* femme *f* de ménage

►► *Comput* ***helper application*** = utilitaire d'un logiciel de navigation capable de reconnaître et de gérer les différents formats de fichiers; *Med* ***helper T-cell*** lymphocyte *m* T helper

helpful ['helpfʊl] *adj* (**a**) *(person)* obligeant, serviable; **he always tries to be helpful** il essaie toujours de rendre service; **his secretary was very helpful** sa secrétaire nous a été très utile *ou* nous a été d'un grand secours

(**b**) *(advice, suggestion)* utile; *(gadget, information, map)* utile; *(medication)* efficace, salutaire; **it's often helpful to talk to your doctor about it** il peut s'avérer utile d'en parler à votre médecin; **this book isn't very helpful** ce livre ne sert pas à grand-chose; **helpful hints** conseils *mpl* utiles

helpfully ['helpfʊlɪ] *adv* avec obligeance, obligeamment; **she very helpfully lent us her car** elle a eu la gentillesse *ou* l'amabilité de nous prêter sa voiture; *Ironic* **someone had very helpfully let the battery run down** quelqu'un a eu l'amabilité de décharger la pile

helpfulness ['helpfʊlnɪs] *n* (**a**) *(of person)* obligeance *f*, serviabilité *f* (**b**) *(of gadget, map etc)* utilité *f*

helping ['helpɪŋ] *n (of food)* portion *f*; **to ask for a second helping** demander à en reprendre; **who's for a second helping?** qui en reprend?; **he had four helpings** il en a repris trois fois

►► ***helping hand*** main *f* secourable; **to give** *or* **lend (sb) a helping hand** donner un coup de main *ou* prêter main-forte (à qn)

helpless ['helplɪs] *adj* (**a**) *(vulnerable)* désarmé, sans défense; **helpless children** des enfants *mfpl* sans défense

(**b**) *(physically)* faible, impotent; *(mentally)* impuissant; **he lay helpless on the ground** il était allongé par terre sans pouvoir bouger

(**c**) *(powerless → person)* impuissant, sans ressource; *(→ anger, feeling)* impuissant; *(→ situation)* sans recours, désespéré; **he gave me a helpless look** il m'a jeté un regard désespéré; **he was helpless to stop her leaving** il était incapable de l'empêcher de partir; **I feel so helpless** je ne sais vraiment pas quoi faire, je me sens vraiment désarmé; **I'm helpless in the matter** je n'y peux rien; **they were helpless with laughter** ils n'en pouvaient plus de rire, ils étaient morts de rire; **carry it yourself, you're not helpless** débrouille-toi, tu peux très bien le porter tout seul

helplessly ['helplɪslɪ] *adv* (**a**) *(without protection)* sans défense, sans ressource

(**b**) *(unable to react)* sans pouvoir réagir; *(argue, struggle, try)* en vain; **to gesture helplessly** lever les mains en signe d'impuissance; **he looked on helplessly** il a regardé sans pouvoir intervenir; **she was lying helplessly on the floor** elle était allongée par terre sans pouvoir bouger; **she smiled helplessly** elle a eu un sourire où se lisait son impuissance; **"I don't know what to say", he said helplessly** "je ne sais pas quoi vous dire", dit-il d'un ton où se sentait *ou* qui trahissait son impuissance; **they giggled helplessly** ils n'ont pas pu s'empêcher de glousser

helplessness ['helplɪsnɪs] *n* (**a**) *(defencelessness)* incapacité *f* de se défendre, vulnérabilité *f* (**b**) *(physical)* incapacité *f*, impotence *f*; *(mental)* incapacité *f* (**c**) *(powerlessness → of person)* impuissance *f*, manque *m* de moyens; *(→ of anger, feeling)* impuissance *f*; **a feeling of helplessness** un sentiment d'impuissance

helpline ['helplaɪn] *n Tel* service *m* d'assistance téléphonique; **AIDS helpline** SOS SIDA

helpmate ['helpmeɪt] *n (companion)* compagnon (compagne) *m,f*; *(helper)* aide *mf*, assistant(e) *m,f*; *(spouse)* époux (épouse) *m,f*

helpmeet ['helpmi:t] *n Arch (companion)* compagnon (compagne) *m,f*; *(helper)* aide *mf*, assistant(e) *m,f*; *(spouse)* époux (épouse) *m,f*

Helsinki [hel'sɪŋkɪ] *n* Helsinki

►► ***the Helsinki Accords, the Helsinki Agreement*** les accords *mpl* d'Helsinki

helter-skelter [ˌheltə'skeltə(r)] **1** *adv (run, rush)* en désordre, à la débandade; *(organize, throw)* pêle-mêle, en vrac

2 *adj (rush)* à la débandade; *(account, story)* désordonné

3 *n Br (at fairground)* toboggan *m*

helve [helv] *n* manche *m*

Helvellyn [hel'velɪn] *n* = sommet dans le Lake District

Helvetia [hel'vi:ʃjə] *n* Suisse *f*; *Hist* Helvétie *f*

Helvetian [hel'vi:ʃjən] **1** *n* Suisse (Suissesse) *m,f*; **the Helvetians** les Suisses *mpl*, les Helvètes *mpl*

2 *adj* suisse, helvétique; *Hist* helvète

hem[1] [hem] *(pt & pp* **hemmed**, *cont* **hemming) 1** *n* (**a**) *(of trousers, skirt)* ourlet *m*; *(of handkerchief, sheet)* bord *m*, ourlet *m*; **she let the hem down on her skirt** elle a défait l'ourlet pour rallonger sa jupe; **your hem's coming down** ton ourlet s'est défait *ou* décousu (**b**) *(hemline)* (bas *m* de l') ourlet *m* (**c**) *Metal* ourlet *m*

2 *vt* ourler, faire l'ourlet de

hem[2] [həm] **1** *exclam (to call attention)* hem!; *(to indicate hesitation, pause)* euh!

2 *vi* faire hem; **to hem and haw** *(mumble)* bafouiller; *Fig (hesitate)* tergiverser, tourner autour du pot; **he hemmed and hawed before getting to the point** il a bafouillé *ou* hésité avant d'en venir au fait

►**hem about** *vt sep* entourer, encercler; **hemmed about by trees** entouré d'arbres

►**hem in** *vt sep (house, people)* entourer, encercler; *(enemy)* cerner; **he felt hemmed in** *(in room)* il faisait de la claustrophobie, il se sentait oppressé; *(in relationship)* il se sentait prisonnier *ou* pris au piège; *Fig* **hemmed in by rules** entravé par des règles *ou* règlements

hema-, hemal *etc Am* = **haema-, haemal** *etc*

he-man *n Fam* homme *m* viril ◻; **he thinks he's a real he-man** il se croit viril

heme *Am* = **haem**

hemeralopia [hemərə'ləʊpɪə] *n Med* héméralopie *f*

hemeralopic [hemərə'ləʊpɪk] *adj Med* héméralope

hemi- ['hemɪ] *pref* hémi-

hemicycle ['hemɪˌsaɪkəl] *n* hémicycle *m*

hemidemisemiquaver ['hemɪˌdemɪ'semɪˌkweɪvə(r)] *n Br Mus* quadruple croche *f*

hemiplegia [ˌhemɪ'pli:dʒɪə] *n Med* hémiplégie *f*

hemiplegic [ˌhemɪ'pli:dʒɪk] *Med* **1** *adj* hémiplégique

2 *n* hémiplégique *mf*

hemipterous [he'mɪptərəs] *adj Zool* hémiptère

hemisphere ['hemɪˌsfɪə(r)] *n* hémisphère *m*

hemispheric [ˌhemɪ'sferɪk], **hemispherical** [ˌhemɪ'sferɪkəl] *adj* (**a**) *(in shape)* hémisphérique (**b**) *Am (pan-American)* panaméricain

hemistich ['hemɪstɪk] *n Literature* hémistiche *m*

hemline ['hemlaɪn] *n* (bas *m* de l')ourlet *m*; **hemlines are going up** les jupes vont raccourcir

hemlock ['hemlɒk] *n* (**a**) *Bot* grande ciguë *f* (**b**) *(poison)* ciguë *f* (**c**) *(tree)* sapin *m* du Canada sapin-ciguë *m*

►► ***hemlock spruce*** sapin *m* du Canada, sapin-ciguë *m*; ***the Hemlock Society*** = association américaine de défense du droit à l'euthanasie

hemo- *Am* = **haemo-**

hemocyanin *Am* = **haemocyanin**

hemodynamics *Am* = **haemodynamics**

hemoglobin *Am* = **haemoglobin**

hemolysin, hemolysis *etc Am* = **haemolysin, haemolysis** *etc*

hemophilia, hemophiliac *etc Am* = **haemophilia, haemophiliac** *etc*

hemoptysis *Am* = **haemoptysis**

hemorrhage, hemorrhagic *etc Am* = **haemorrhage, haemorrhagic** *etc*

hemorrhoids *Am* = **haemorrhoids**

hemostasia, hemostasis *Am* = **haemostasia, haemostasis**

hemostat, hemostatic *Am* = **haemostat, haemostatic**

hemotoxin *Am* = **haemotoxin**

hemp [hemp] *n* (**a**) *(fibre, plant)* chanvre *m* (**b**) *(marijuana)* marijuana *f*; *(hashish)* haschisch *m*, hachisch *m*

hempseed ['hempsiːd] *n* chènevis *m*

hemstitch ['hemstɪtʃ] *Sewing* **1** *n (stitch)* jour *m*; **a row of hemstitch** un jour

2 *vt* ourler à jour

hen [hen] *n* (**a**) *(chicken)* poule *f*

(**b**) *(female bird)* femelle *f*

(**c**) *Fam (woman)* mémère *f*; *Fam* **she's having her** *Br* **hen night** *or Am* **hen party** *(before wedding)* elle enterre sa vie de célibataire

(**d**) *Scot Fam (term of address)* **hello, hen** bonjour, ma poule *ou* ma cocotte

►► ***hen bird*** oiseau *m* femelle; ***hen coop*** mue *f*, cage *f* à poules; *Orn* ***hen harrier*** busard *m* Saint-Martin; ***hen house*** poulailler *m*; *Zool* ***hen lobster*** homard *m* femelle; *Orn* ***hen pheasant*** poule *f* faisane

henbane ['henbeɪn] *n Bot* jusquiame *f* noire

henbit ['henbɪt] *n*

►► *Bot* ***henbit dead-nettle*** lancier *m* à feuilles embrassantes

hence [hens] *adv* (**a**) *(therefore)* donc, d'où; **they are cheaper and hence more popular** ils sont moins chers et donc plus demandés; **he was born on Christmas Day, hence the name Noel** il est né le jour de Noël, d'où son nom (**b**) *Formal (from this time)* d'ici; **three days hence** dans *ou* d'ici trois jours (**c**) *Formal (from here)* d'ici; **5 kilometres hence** à 5 kilomètres d'ici; *Arch or Hum* **(get thee) hence!** hors d'ici *ou* de ma vue!

henceforth [ˌhens'fɔːθ], **henceforward** [ˌhens'fɔːwəd] *adv* dorénavant, désormais

henchman ['hentʃmən] (*pl* **henchmen** [-mən]) *n* (**a**) *(follower)* partisan *m*, *Pej* adepte *m*; *(right-hand man)* homme *m* de main, *Pej* suppôt *m* (**b**) *(squire, page)* écuyer *m*

hendecagon [hen'dekəgɒn] *n Geom* hendécagone *m*

henge [hendʒ] *n* ≃ cromlech *m*

Henley ['henlɪ] *n* = ville dans le Oxfordshire

►► ***Henley Regatta*** = importante épreuve internationale d'aviron

> **HENLEY REGATTA**
>
> Cette compétition, qui a lieu chaque année sur la Tamise à Henley, au mois de juin, est une manifestation autant mondaine que sportive.

henna ['henə] **1** *n Bot* henné *m*

2 *vt* teindre au henné; **to henna one's hair** se faire un henné

►► ***henna tattoo*** tatouage *m* au henné

hennaed ['henəd] *adj* teint au henné

henpecked ['henpekt] *adj* dominé; **a henpecked husband** un mari dominé par sa femme; **he's very henpecked** sa femme le mène par le bout du nez

Henrietta [ˌhenrɪ'etə] *pr n* **Henrietta Maria** Henriette-Marie (de France)

henroost ['henruːst] *n* (**a**) *(perch)* juchoir *m*, perchoir *m* (**b**) *(hen house)* poulailler *m*

henrun ['henrʌn] *n* poulailler *m*

Henry ['henrɪ] *pr n* Henri; **Henry the Eighth, Henry VIII** Henri VIII

henry ['henrɪ] (*pl* **henrys** *or* **henries**) *n Elec* henry *m*

hep [hep] (*compar* **hepper**, *superl* **heppest**) *adj Fam Old-fashioned* dans le coup; **he's hep to your plan** il est au courant de tes projets

heparin ['hepərɪn] *n Pharm* héparine *f*

hepatectomy [ˌhepə'tektəmɪ] (*pl* **hepatectomies**) *n Med* hépatectomie *f*

hepatic [hɪ'pætɪk] *adj Physiol* hépatique

hepatitis [ˌhepə'taɪtɪs] *n (UNCOUNT) Med* hépatite *f*; **hepatitis A/B/C** hépatite *f* A/B/C; **serum hepatitis** hépatite *f* B *ou* sérique

hepatologist [hepə'tɒlədʒɪst] *n Med* hépatologue *mf*

hepatology [hepə'tɒlədʒɪ] *n Med* hépatologie *f*

hepcat ['hepkæt] *n Fam Old-fashioned (man)* jeune homme *m* dans le vent; *(woman)* jeune femme *f* dans le vent

heptagon ['heptəgən] *n Geom* heptagone *m*

heptagonal [hep'tægənəl] *adj Geom* heptagonal

heptahedral [ˌheptə'hiːdrəl] *adj Geom* heptaédrique

heptahedron [ˌheptə'hiːdrən] *n Geom* heptaèdre *m*

heptameter [hep'tæmɪtə(r)] *n Literature* heptamètre *m*

heptane ['hepteɪn] *n Chem* heptane *m*

heptarchy ['heptɑːkɪ] *n Hist* heptarchie *f*

heptathlon [hep'tæθlɒn] *n Sport* heptathlon *m*

her [hɜː(r)] **1** *adj* (**a**) *(used of person, animal → singular)* son (sa); (→ *plural)* ses; **her book** son livre; **her secretary** sa secrétaire; **her glasses** ses lunettes; **her university** son université; **she has broken her arm** elle s'est cassé le bras; **the dog's hurt her paw** la chienne s'est fait mal à la patte

(**b**) *(used of vehicle, ship, country)* **France reassured her allies** la France rassura ses alliés; **the ship and her crew** le navire et son équipage

2 *pron* (**a**) *(direct object → unstressed)* la; (→ *stressed)* elle; **I recognize her** je la reconnais; **I heard her** je l'ai entendue; **why did you have to choose HER?** pourquoi l'as-tu choisie elle?

(**b**) *(indirect object → unstressed)* lui; (→ *stressed)* à elle; **give her the money** donne-lui l'argent; **he only told her, no-one else** il ne l'a dit qu'à elle, c'est tout; **I am thinking of her** je pense à elle; **why do they always give HER the interesting jobs?** pourquoi est-ce que c'est toujours à elle qu'on donne le travail intéressant?

(**c**) *(after preposition)* elle; **I was in front of her** j'étais devant elle; **as rich as/richer than her** aussi riche/plus riche qu'elle; **she closed the door behind her** elle a fermé la porte derrière elle

(**d**) *(with "to be")* **it's her** c'est elle; **if I were her** si j'étais elle, si j'étais à sa place

(**e**) *(used of vehicle, ship, country)* **Poland's friends deserted her** la Pologne a été abandonnée par ses amis; **the enemy sank her** il a été coulé par l'ennemi; *Fam* **I'll get her started** *(car)* je vais la faire démarrer

(**f**) *Formal (with relative pronoun)* celle; **(to) her whom we adore** (à) celle que nous adorons

3 *n Fam* **it's a her not a him** *(of baby)* c'est une fille, pas un garçon ❑; *(of animal)* c'est une femelle, pas un mâle ❑

Hera ['hɪərə] *pr n Myth* Héra

Heracles ['herəkliːz] *pr n Myth* Héraclès

Heraclitus [ˌherə'klaɪtəs] *pr n* Héraclite

Heraklion [hɪ'ræklɪən] *n* Héraklion

herald ['herəld] **1** *vt* (**a**) *(announce)* annoncer, proclamer; **his rise to power heralded a new era** son ascension au pouvoir a annoncé une nouvelle ère

(**b**) *(hail)* acclamer

2 *n* (**a**) *(medieval messenger)* héraut *m*; *Literary* **the herald of morn** le messager de l'aube

(**b**) *(forerunner)* héraut *m*, avant-coureur *m*; **a herald of spring** l'annonce *f* du printemps

(**c**) *(record keeper)* généalogiste *mf* (chargé du registre des armoiries)

3 Herald *n Press* **The Herald** = quotidien écossais publié à Glasgow

►► ***the Heralds' College*** le Collège héraldique *(à Londres)*

heraldic [he'rældɪk] *adj* héraldique

heraldry ['herəldrɪ] *n (UNCOUNT)* (**a**) *(system, study)* héraldique *f* (**b**) *(coat of arms)* blason *m* (**c**) *(pageantry)* faste *m*, pompe *f* (héraldique)

herb [*Br* hɜːb, *Am* ɜːrb] *n* (**a**) *Bot* herbe *f*; *Culin* **herbs** fines herbes *fpl*, herbes *fpl* aromatiques; **medicinal herbs** herbes *fpl* médicinales *ou* officinales, simples *mpl* (**b**) *Fam Drugs slang (marijuana)* herbe *f*

►► ***herb garden*** jardin *m* d'herbes aromatiques; *Bot* ***herb Paris*** parisette *f*; ***herb pillow*** oreiller *m* rempli d'herbes *(à effet soporifique)*; *Bot* ***herb Robert*** herbe *f* à Robert, géranium *m* robertin

herbaceous [*Br* hɜː'beɪʃəs, *Am* ɜːr'beɪʃəs] *adj (plant, stem)* herbacé

►► ***herbaceous border*** bordure *f* de plantes herbacées

herbage [*Br* 'hɜːbɪdʒ, *Am* 'ɜːrbɪdʒ] *n (UNCOUNT) (herbaceous plants)* plantes *fpl* herbacées, herbages *mpl*; *(vegetation)* herbage *m*

herbal [*Br* 'hɜːbəl, *Am* 'ɜːrbəl] **1** *adj* aux herbes

2 *n* traité *m* sur les plantes, herbier *m*

►► ***herbal cigarette*** cigarette *f* aux plantes; ***herbal infusion*** infusion *f*, tisane *f*; ***herbal medicine*** *(practice)* phytothérapie *f*; *(medication)* médicament *m* à base de plantes; ***herbal pillow*** oreiller *m* rempli d'herbes *(à effet soporifique)*; ***herbal tea*** tisane *f*

herbalism [*Br* 'hɜːbəlɪzəm, *Am* 'ɜːrbəlɪzəm] *n* médecine *f* par les herbes

herbalist [*Br* 'hɜːbəlɪst, *Am* 'ɜːrbəlɪst] *n* herboriste *mf*

herbarium [*Br* hɜː'beərɪəm, *Am* ɜːr'beərɪəm] (*pl* **herbaria** [-rɪə]) *n* herbier *m (collection)*

herbicide [*Br* 'hɜːbɪsaɪd, *Am* 'ɜːrbɪsaɪd] *n* herbicide *m*

herbivore [*Br* 'hɜːbɪvɔː(r), *Am* 'ɜːrbɪvɔː(r)] *n* herbivore *m*

herbivorous [*Br* hɜː'bɪvərəs, *Am* ɜːr'bɪvərəs] *adj* herbivore

herculean, Herculean [ˌhɜːkjʊ'liːən] *adj* herculéen; **a herculean task** un travail de Titan *ou* herculéen

Hercules ['hɜːkjʊliːz] **1** *pr n Myth* Hercule; *Fig (strong man)* hercule *m*

2 *n Astron* Hercule

►► *Comput* ***Hercules monitor*** moniteur *m* Hercules

herd [hɜːd] **1** *n* (**a**) *(of cattle, goats, sheep)* troupeau *m*; *(of wild animals)* troupe *f*; *(of horses)* troupe *f*, bande *f*; *(of deer)* harde *f*

(**b**) *Fam (of people)* troupeau *m*, foule *f*; *Pej* **the herd** le peuple, la populace

(**c**) *Arch (herdsman)* gardien *m* de troupeau, *Literary* pâtre *m*

2 *vt* (**a**) *(bring together)* rassembler (en troupeau); *(look after)* garder

(**b**) *(drive)* mener, conduire; **the cattle were herded into the barn** on a fait entrer le bétail dans la grange; **he herded the students back into the classroom** il a reconduit les élèves dans la salle de cours; **the prisoners were herded onto trucks** on a entassé les prisonniers dans des camions

3 *vi* s'assembler en troupeau, s'attrouper

►► ***herd instinct*** instinct *m* grégaire; *Pej* ***herd mentality*** panurgisme *m*

►**herd together** **1** *vi* (**a**) *(animals → live in herds)* vivre en troupeaux; (→ *form a herd)* s'assembler en troupeau (**b**) *Fam (people)* se regrouper ❑, s'assembler en troupeau ❑, s'attrouper ❑

2 *vt sep* rassembler en troupeau

►**herd up** *vt sep* rassembler en troupeau

herdboy ['hɜːdbɔɪ] *n* jeune bouvier *m*, aide-bouvier *m*

herder ['hɜːdə(r)] *n esp Am (gen)* gardien(enne) *m,f* de troupeau; *(of cattle)* vacher(ère) *m,f*, bouvier(ère) *m,f*; *(of sheep)* berger(ère) *m,f*

herdsman ['hɜːdzmən] (*pl* **herdsmen** [-mən]) *n (gen)* gardien *m* de troupeau; *(of cattle)* vacher *m*, bouvier *m*; *(of sheep)* berger *m*

HERE [hɪə(r)] **1** *adv* (**a**) *(at, in this place)* **come here!** (venez) ici!; **she left here yesterday** elle est partie d'ici hier; **I've lived here for two years** ça fait deux ans que j'habite ici, j'habite ici depuis deux ans; **is Susan here?** est-ce que Susan est là?; **he won't be here next week** il ne sera pas là la semaine prochaine; **they're here** *(I've found them)* ils sont ici; *(they've arrived)* ils sont arrivés; **winter is here** c'est l'hiver, l'hiver est arrivé; **the miniskirt is here to stay** la minijupe n'est pas près de disparaître; **where do I switch on the light? – here** où est l'interrupteur? – ici; **sign here** signez ici; **it is a question here of finances** il s'agit ici d'argent

(**b**) *(after preposition)* **around here** par ici; **it's 2 km from here** c'est à 2 km d'ici; **from here to here** d'ici jusqu'ici; **bring them in here** apportez-les (par) ici; **I'm in here** je suis là *ou* ici; **they're over here** ils sont ici; **where are you? – over here!** où êtes-vous? – (par) ici!; **the water came up to here** l'eau est montée jusqu'ici; *Fam* **I've had it up to here** j'en ai jusque là; **here today, gone tomorrow** tout passe; **any money he gets is here today and gone tomorrow** tout l'argent qu'il gagne lui file entre les doigts

(**c**) *(drawing attention to something)* voici, voilà; **here's the key!** voilà *ou* voici la clef!; **here they come!** les voilà! *ou* voici!; **here's a man who knows what he wants** voilà un homme qui sait ce qu'il veut; **here I am!** me voici!, me voilà!; **here we are!** *(I've found it)* voilà! j'ai trouvé!; *(we've arrived)* nous y sommes!, nous voilà arrivés! *ou* rendus!; **here we are in San Francisco** nous voici à San Francisco; **have you got the paper? – here you are** vous avez le journal? – le voilà *ou* voici; *Fam Br* **here goes,** *Am* **here goes nothing** allons-y!; **here we go!** *(excitedly)* c'est parti!; *(wearily)* et voilà, c'est reparti!; **here we go again!** ça y est, c'est reparti pour un tour!

(**d**) *(emphasizing specified object, person)* **ask the lady here** demandez à cette dame ici; **it's this one here that I want** c'est celui-ci que je veux; **my friend here saw it** mon ami (que voici) l'a vu; *Fam* **this here book** *(that I am pointing to)* ce livre-ci ❑; *Fam* **this here book you've all been talking about** ce bouquin dont vous n'arrêtez pas de parler tous

(**e**) *(at this point)* maintenant; *(at that point)* alors, à ce moment-là; **here I should like to remind you...** maintenant je voudrais vous rappeler...; **here I am referring to taxation** c'est aux impôts que je fais allusion; **here she paused** à ce moment-là, elle s'est arrêtée

(**f**) *(idiom)* **here's to** *(in toasts)* à; **here's to the newly-weds!** aux nouveaux mariés!; **here's to your exams!** à tes examens!; **here's to us!** à nous!, à nos amours!

2 *exclam* (**a**) *(present)* **Alex Pilard? – here!** Alex Pilard? – présent!; **Emma Lindsay? – here!** Emma Lindsay? – présente!

(**b**) *(giving, taking)* **here!** tiens!, tenez!; **here, give me that!** tiens, donne-moi ça!

(**c**) *(protesting)* **here! what do you think you're doing?** hé! qu'est-ce que tu fais?; **here, I never said that!** mais dis donc, je n'ai jamais dit ça!; **here, stop that!** écoute, tu arrêtes un peu!

3 here and now 1 *adv* sur-le-champ **2** *n* **the here and now** le présent

4 here and there *adv* ça et là; **the paintwork needs retouching here and there** la peinture a besoin d'être refaite par endroits

5 here, there and everywhere *adv Fam* un peu partout; **her things were scattered here, there and everywhere** ses affaires étaient éparpillées un peu partout

---

hereabouts ['hɪərə,baʊts], *Am* **hereabout** ['hɪərə,baʊt] *adv* par ici, près d'ici, dans les environs; **it must be somewhere hereabouts** ça doit être quelque part par ici

hereafter [,hɪər'ɑːftə(r)] **1** *n* (**a**) *(life after death)* au-delà *m inv*; **in the hereafter** dans l'autre monde (**b**) *Literary (future)* avenir *m*, futur *m*

2 *adv* (**a**) *Formal (in document)* ci-après (**b**) *Literary (after death)* dans l'au-delà (**c**) *Literary (in the future)* désormais, dorénavant

hereby [,hɪə'baɪ] *adv Formal (in statement)* par la présente (déclaration); *(in document)* par le présent (document); *(in letter)* par la présente; *(in act)* par le présent acte, par ce geste; *(in will)* par le présent testament; **I hereby declare you man and wife** en vertu des pouvoirs qui me sont conférés, je vous déclare mari et femme

hereditament [,herɪ'dɪtəmənt] *n Law* = tout bien qui peut être transmis par héritage

hereditary [hɪ'redɪtərɪ] *adj* héréditaire

▸▸ *Br Parl* ***hereditary peer*** = membre de la Chambre des lords dont le titre est héréditaire

heredity [hɪ'redɪtɪ] *n* hérédité *f*

Hereford and Worcester [,herɪfədən'wʊstə] *n* le Hereford et Worcester, = comté dans le centre de l'Angleterre; **in Hereford and Worcester** dans le Hereford et Worcester

herein [,hɪər'ɪn] *adv Formal (in this respect)* en ceci, en cela; *Law (in this document)* ci-inclus; **the letter enclosed herein** la lettre ci-incluse

hereinafter [,hɪərɪn'ɑːftə(r)] *adv Formal* ci-après; *Law* ci-après, dans la suite des présentes

hereof [,hɪər'ɒv] *adv Formal* de ceci, de cela; *Law* des présentes

hereon [,hɪər'ɒn] *adv Formal* sur ce, là-dessus

heresiarch [he'riːzɪ,ɑːk] *n* hérésiarque *mf*

heresy ['herəsɪ] *(pl* **heresies***)* *n* hérésie *f*; **an act of heresy** une hérésie

heretic ['herətɪk] *n* hérétique *mf*

heretical [hɪ'retɪkəl] *adj* hérétique

hereto [,hɪə'tuː] *adv Formal* à ceci, à cela; *Law* aux présentes

heretofore [,hɪətʊ'fɔː(r)] *adv Formal* jusqu'ici, auparavant; *Law* ci-devant

hereunder [,hɪər'ʌndə(r)] *adv Formal* (**a**) *(hereafter)* ci-après, ci-dessous (**b**) *(under the authority of this)* selon les modalités de ceci *ou* des présentes

hereupon [,hɪərə'pɒn] *adv Formal* (**a**) *(immediately following)* sur ce, là-dessus (**b**) *(on this point)* sur ce point, là-dessus

herewith [,hɪə'wɪθ] *adv Formal* (**a**) *(enclosed)* ci-joint, ci-inclus; **I enclose my curriculum vitae herewith** veuillez trouver ci-joint mon curriculum vitae (**b**) *(in statement)* par la présente (déclaration); *(in document)* par le présent (document); *(in letter)* par la présente; *(in act)* par le présent acte, par ce geste; *(in will)* par le présent testament

heritable ['herɪtəbəl] *adj Law (property)* dont on peut hériter; *(person)* qui peut hériter

heritage ['herɪtɪdʒ] *n* héritage *m*, patrimoine *m*; **the national heritage** le patrimoine national

▸▸ *Br* ***heritage centre*** = centre d'accueil et de documentation pour les visiteurs d'un site historique; ***heritage site*** site *m* patrimoine; ***heritage tourism*** tourisme *m* culturel; ***heritage trail*** = parcours touristique qui va d'un lieu historique à un autre

hermaphrodite [hɜː'mæfrə,daɪt] *Biol & Bot* **1** *adj* hermaphrodite

2 *n* hermaphrodite *m*

hermaphroditic [hɜː,mæfrə'dɪtɪk] *adj Biol & Bot* hermaphrodite

hermaphroditism [hɜː'mæfrədaɪ,tɪzəm] *n Biol & Bot* hermaphrodisme *m*

Hermaphroditus [hɜː,mæfrə'daɪtəs] *pr n Myth* Hermaphrodite

hermeneutic [,hɜːmə'njuːtɪk], **hermeneutical** [,hɜːmə'njuːtɪkəl] *adj Phil & Rel* herméneutique

hermeneutics [,hɜːmə'njuːtɪks] *n (UNCOUNT) Phil & Rel* herméneutique *f*

Hermes ['hɜːmiːz] *pr n Myth* Hermès

hermetic [hɜː'metɪk] *adj* hermétique

hermetically [hɜː'metɪkəlɪ] *adv* hermétiquement

hermeticism [hɜː'metɪ,sɪzəm] *n* hermétisme *m*

Hermione [hɜː'maɪənɪ] *pr n Myth* Hermione

hermit ['hɜːmɪt] *n (gen)* ermite *m*, solitaire *mf*; *Rel* ermite *m*; **to live like a hermit** vivre en solitaire *ou* en ermite

▸▸ *Zool* ***hermit crab*** bernard-l'ermite *m inv*, pagure *m*

hermitage ['hɜːmɪtɪdʒ] *n* ermitage *m*

hernia ['hɜːnɪə] *(pl* **hernias** *or* **herniae** [-nɪiː]*)* *n Med* hernie *f*

herniated ['hɜːnɪeɪtɪd] *adj Med* hernié

hero ['hɪərəʊ] *(pl* **heroes***)* *n* (**a**) *(person)* héros *m*; **a sporting hero** un champion sportif; **they gave him a hero's welcome** ils l'ont accueilli en héros; *Fam* **my hero!** mon héros! (**b**) *Am (sandwich)* = sorte de gros sandwich

▸▸ ***hero worship*** *(admiration)* adulation *f*, culte *m* (du héros); *Antiq* culte *m* des héros

---

'A Hero of our Time' *Lermontov* 'Un Héros de notre temps'

Herod ['herəd] *pr n Bible* Hérode

Herodias [hɪ'rəʊdɪæs] *pr n Bible* Hérodiade

Herodotus [hɪ'rɒdətəs] *pr n* Hérodote

heroic [hɪ'rəʊɪk] *adj* (**a**) *(act, behaviour, person)* héroïque (**b**) *Literary* épique, héroïque

▸▸ ***heroic age*** temps *mpl* héroïques; *Literature* ***heroic couplet*** distique *m* héroïque; *Literature* ***heroic stanza*** quatrain *m* en vers croisés; *Literature* ***heroic verse*** *(UNCOUNT)* vers *mpl* héroïques

heroically [hɪ'rəʊɪklɪ] *adv* héroïquement

heroics [hɪ'rəʊɪks] *npl* (**a**) *(language)* emphase *f*, déclamation *f*; *(behaviour)* affectation *f*, emphase *f*; **none of your heroics** inutile de chercher à nous impressionner (**b**) *Literature (heroic verse)* vers *mpl* héroïques

heroin ['herəʊɪn] *n* héroïne *f*

▸▸ ***heroin addict*** héroïnomane *mf*; ***heroin addiction*** héroïnomanie *f*; ***heroin chic*** = apparence cultivée par certains mannequins, inspirée de celle des héroïnomanes (extrême maigreur, mauvaise mine etc); ***heroin user*** héroïnomane *mf*

heroine ['herəʊɪn] *n* héroïne *f (femme)*

heroism ['herəʊɪzəm] *n* héroïsme *m*

heron ['herən] *(pl* **inv** *or* **herons***)* *n Orn* héron *m*

heronry ['herənrɪ] *n* héronnière *f*

hero-worship *vt* aduler, idolâtrer

hero-worshipper *n* = personne qui voue une admiration excessive aux idoles

herpes ['hɜːpiːz] *n (UNCOUNT) Med* herpès *m*; **to have herpes** avoir de l'herpès

▸▸ *Med* ***herpes simplex*** *(UNCOUNT)* herpès *m*; *Med* ***herpes zoster*** *(UNCOUNT)* zona *m*

herpetic [hɜː'petɪk] *adj Med* herpétique

herpetological [,hɜːpetə'lɒdʒɪkəl] *adj Zool* erpétologique

herpetologist [,hɜːpɪ'tɒlədʒɪst] *n Zool* erpétologiste *mf*

herpetology [,hɜːpɪ'tɒlədʒɪ] *n Zool* erpétologie *f*

herring ['herɪŋ] *(pl* **inv** *or* **herrings***)* *n Ich* hareng *m*

▸▸ ***herring boat*** harenguier *m*; ***herring fleet*** flotille *f* de harenguiers; *Orn* ***herring gull*** goéland *m* argenté

herringbone ['herɪŋbəʊn] **1** *n* (**a**) *(bone)* arête *f* de hareng

(**b**) *Tex (pattern)* (dessin *m* à) chevrons *mpl*; *(fabric)* tissu *m* à chevrons

(**c**) *Sewing (stitch)* point *m* croisé, point *m* de chausson

(**d**) *Constr* appareil *m* en épi

(**e**) *(in skiing)* montée *f* en ciseaux *ou* en pas de canard

2 *vt* (**a**) *Sewing & Tex* faire au point d'épine (en chevron)

(**b**) *Archit* faire un appareil en épi

3 *vi Ski* monter en ciseaux *ou* en pas de canard

▸▸ *Sewing & Tex* ***herringbone stitch*** point *m* croisé, point de *m* chausson; *Tex* ***herringbone tweed*** tweed *m* à chevrons

hers [hɜːz] *pron* (**a**) *(gen → singular)* le sien (la sienne) *m,f*; *(→ plural)* les siens (les siennes) *mpl, fpl*; **this is my book, hers is over there** ça, c'est mon livre, le sien est là-bas; **this car is hers** cette voiture lui appartient *ou* est à elle; **hers was the best photograph** sa photographie était la meilleure; **most speeches lasted ten minutes, but hers lasted half an hour** la plupart des gens ont fait un discours de dix minutes, mais le sien a duré une demi-heure; **hers is not an easy task** elle n'a pas la tâche facile

(**b**) *(after preposition)* **she took his hand in hers** elle a pris sa main dans la sienne; **he's an old friend of hers** c'est un vieil ami à elle, c'est un de ses vieux amis; **no suggestion of hers could possibly interest him** aucune suggestion venant d'elle ne risquait de l'intéresser; **when's that book of hers coming out?** quand est-ce qu'il sort, son livre?; **I blame that husband of hers** moi je dis que c'est de la faute de son sacré mari; **I can't stand that boyfriend/dog of hers** je ne supporte pas son copain/chien; **that (dreadful) voice of hers** sa voix (insupportable); **that (dreadful) habit of hers** cette habitude (insupportable) qu'elle a

(**c**) *(indicating authorship)* d'elle; **are these paintings hers?** ces tableaux sont-ils d'elle?

(**d**) *Fam (her house, flat)* chez elle ❑

herself [hɜː'self] *pron* (**a**) *(reflexive form)* se, s' *(before vowel or silent "h")*; **she introduced herself** elle s'est présentée; **she bought herself a car** elle s'est acheté une voiture; **she considers herself lucky** elle considère qu'elle a de la chance

(**b**) *(emphatic form)* elle-même; **she built the shelves herself** elle a monté les étagères elle-même; **I spoke with the teacher herself** j'ai parlé au professeur en personne

(**c**) *(with preposition)* elle; **she took it upon herself to tell us** elle a pris sur elle de nous le dire; **she has a room to herself** elle a sa propre chambre *ou* sa chambre à elle; **the old woman was talking to herself** la vieille femme parlait toute seule; **"that's odd", she thought to herself** "c'est bizarre", se dit-elle; **she did it all by herself** elle l'a fait toute seule

(**d**) *(her usual self)* **she isn't quite herself** elle n'est pas dans son état habituel; **she's feeling more herself now** elle va mieux maintenant

Hershey bar® ['hɜːʃɪ-] *n* = barre de chocolat très connue aux États-Unis

Hertfordshire ['hɑːtfəd,ʃɪə(r)] *n* le Hertfordshire,

= comté dans le sud de l'Angleterre; **in Hertfordshire** dans le Hertfordshire

Herts *(written abbr* **Hertfordshire***)* Hertfordshire *m*

hertz [hɜːts] *(pl* **inv***) n Elec & Phys* hertz *m*

hertzian, Hertzian ['hɜːtsɪən] *adj Elec & Phys* hertzien

▸▸ ***hertzian wave, Hertzian wave*** onde *f* hertzienne

he's [hiːz] = **he is, he has**

Hesiod ['hiːsɪəd] *pr n* Hésiode

hesitance ['hezɪtəns], **hesitancy** ['hezɪtənsɪ] *n* hésitation *f*, indécision *f*

hesitant ['hezɪtənt] *adj* (**a**) *(person → uncertain)* hésitant, indécis; *(→ cautious)* réticent; **I'm hesitant about sending her to a new school** j'hésite à l'envoyer dans une nouvelle école (**b**) *(attempt, speech, voice)* hésitant

hesitantly ['hezɪtəntlɪ] *adv (act, try)* avec hésitation, timidement; *(answer, speak)* d'une voix hésitante

hesitate ['hezɪˌteɪt] *vi* hésiter; **don't hesitate to call me** n'hésitez pas à m'appeler; **she wrote to them after hesitating for some time** elle leur a écrit après avoir longuement hésité; **he will hesitate at nothing** il ne recule devant rien, rien ne l'arrête; *Prov* **he who hesitates is lost** = un moment d'hésitation peut coûter cher

hesitatingly ['hezɪˌteɪtɪŋlɪ] *adv* avec hésitation, en hésitant

hesitation [ˌhezɪ'teɪʃən] *n* hésitation *f*; **after much hesitation** après bien des hésitations, après avoir longuement hésité; **she answered with some hesitation** elle a répondu d'une voix hésitante; **I would have no hesitation in recommending him** je n'hésiterais pas à le recommander; **without a moment's hesitation** sans la moindre hésitation

Hesperides [he'sperɪdiːz] *npl Myth* **the Hesperides** les Hespérides *fpl*

Hesperus ['hespərəs] *n Astron (evening star)* étoile *f* du berger; *(Venus)* Vénus *f*

Hesse [hes] *n* Hesse *f*

hessian ['hesɪən] *Tex* **1** *n* (toile *f* de) jute *m*

2 *comp (fabric, sack)* de jute

het [het] *Fam* **1** *adj* hétéro

2 *n* hétéro *mf*

hetero ['hetərəʊ] *(pl* **heteros***) Fam* **1** *adj* hétéro

2 *n* hétéro *mf*

hetero- ['hetərəʊ] *pref* hétéro-

heteroclite ['hetərəʊklaɪt] **1** *adj* hétéroclite

2 *n* mot *m* hétéroclite

heterocyclic [ˌhetərəʊ'saɪklɪk] *adj Chem* hétérocyclique

heterodox ['hetərəʊdɒks] *adj* hétérodoxe

heterodoxy ['hetərəʊdɒksɪ] *n* hétérodoxie *f*

heterodyne ['hetərəʊdaɪn] *Electron* **1** *adj* hétérodyne

2 *n* hétérodyne *f*

heterogamous [hetə'rɒgəməs] *adj Biol* hétérogame

heterogamy [hetə'rɒgəmɪ] *n Biol* hétérogamie *f*

heterogeneity [ˌhetərəʊdʒɪ'niːɪtɪ] *n* hétérogénéité *f*

heterogeneous [ˌhetərəʊ'dʒiːnɪəs] *adj* hétérogène

heterogeneousness [ˌhetərəʊ'dʒiːnɪəsnɪs] *n* hétérogénéité *f*

heterograft ['hetərəʊˌgrɑːft] *n Biol & Med* hétérogreffe *f*

heteromorphic [ˌhetərəʊ'mɔːfɪk], **heteromorphous** [ˌhetərə'mɔːfəs] *adj Biol* hétéromorphe

heteronomous [hetə'rɒnɪməs] *adj* hétéronome

heteronym ['hetərənɪm] *n Ling* homographe *m* à prononciation différente

heteroplasty ['hetərəʊˌplæstɪ] *n Med* hétéroplastie *f*

heterosexism [ˌhetərəʊ'seksɪzəm] *n* hétérosexisme *m*

heterosexual [ˌhetərə'sekʃʊəl] **1** *adj* hétérosexuel

2 *n* hétérosexuel(elle) *m,f*

heterosexuality ['hetərəʊˌsekʃʊ'ælətɪ] *n* hétérosexualité *f*

heterotrophic [ˌhetərəʊ'trəʊfɪk] *adj Biol* hétérotrophe

heterotypic [ˌhetərəʊ'tɪpɪk], **heterotypical** [ˌhetərəʊ'tɪpɪkəl] *adj Biol* hétérotypique

heterozygote [ˌhetərəʊ'zaɪgəʊt] *n Biol* hétérozygote *m*

heterozygotic [ˌhetərəʊzaɪ'gɒtɪk], **heterozygous** [ˌhetərəʊ'zaɪgəs] *adj Biol* hétérozygote

het up ['het-] *adj Fam (angry)* énervé ❑; *(excited)* excité ❑, agité ❑; **to get all het up (about sth)** se mettre dans tous ses états (pour qch)

heuristic [hjʊə'rɪstɪk] *adj Math & Phil* heuristique

▸▸ *Math & Phil* ***heuristic model*** modèle *m* heuristique

heuristics [hjʊə'rɪstɪks] *n (UNCOUNT) Math & Phil* heuristique *f*

HEW [ˌeɪtʃiː'dʌbəljuː] *n Am Formerly (abbr* **Department of Health, Education and Welfare***)* = ancien ministère américain de l'Éducation et de la Santé publique

hew [hjuː] *(pt* **hewed***, pp* **hewed** *or* **hewn** [hjuːn]*)* **1** *vt (wood)* couper; *(stone)* tailler; *(coal)* abattre; **they hewed a path through the undergrowth** ils se sont taillé *ou* frayé un chemin à travers le sous-bois (à coups de hache); **he hewed a statue out of the marble** il a taillé une statue dans le marbre

2 *vi* (**a**) *(strike with blows)* frapper (à coups de hache)

(**b**) *Am (conform)* se conformer; **they hewed to the company line** ils se sont pliés à la politique de la société

▸ **hew down** *vt sep (tree)* abattre

▸ **hew off** *vt sep (branch)* abattre

▸ **hew out** *vt sep* creuser; **the cavern had been hewn out of the rock** la caverne a été creusée dans la pierre

hewer ['hjuːə(r)] *n (of tree)* abatteur *m*; *(of stone, wood)* tailleur *m*; *(of coal)* haveur *m*

Hex [heks] *adj Comput (abbr* **hexadecimal***)* hexadécimal

hex [heks] *Am* **1** *n* (**a**) *(spell)* sort *m*, sortilège *m*; **to put a hex on sb** jeter un sort à qn (**b**) *(witch)* sorcière *f*

2 *vt* jeter un sort à

▸▸ ***hex sign*** = panneau en bois portant un emblème décoratif typique des fermes en Pennsylvanie

hexachloride [ˌheksə'klɔːraɪd] *n Chem* hexachloride *m*

hexachlorophene [ˌheksə'klɔːrəfiːn] *n Chem* hexachlorophène *m*

hexachord ['heksəkɔːd] *n Mus* hexacorde *m*

hexadecimal [ˌheksə'desɪməl] *adj Comput* hexadécimal

▸▸ ***hexadecimal notation*** codes *mpl* hexadécimaux, notation *f* hexadécimale

hexafluoride [ˌheksə'flʊəraɪd] *n Chem* hexafluorure *m*

hexagon ['heksəgən] *n Geom* hexagone *m*

hexagonal [hek'sægənəl] *adj Geom* hexagonal

hexagram ['heksəgræm] *n Geom* hexagramme *m*

hexahedron [ˌheksə'hedrən] *(pl* **hexahedrons** *or* **hexahedra** [-drə]*) n Geom* hexaèdre *m*

hexameter [hek'sæmɪtə(r)] *n Literature* hexamètre *m*

hexane ['heksem] *n Chem* hexane *m*

hexapod ['heksəpɒd] *n Entom* hexapode *m*

Hexateuch ['heksətjuːk] *n Bible* Hexateuque *m*

hexavalent [ˌheksə'veɪlənt] *adj Chem* hexavalent

hexose ['heksəʊz] *n Biol & Chem* hexose *m*

hey [heɪ] *exclam (to draw attention)* hé!, ohé!; *(to show surprise)* tiens!; **hey ho!** *(in weariness)* eh bien!; *(in resignation)* hélas!; *Old-fashioned or Literary (in surprise)* ça alors!, ça par exemple!; *(in happiness)* chouette alors!; *Br* **hey presto!** passez muscade!, et hop!; *Am* **hey (there)!** *(as greeting)* salut!; *Br Arch* **hey nonny no!** = mots que l'on trouve dans le refrain de certaines chansons médiévales, utilisés aujourd'hui en référence à cette époque

heyday ['heɪdeɪ] *n (of cinema, movement)* âge *m* d'or, beaux jours *mpl*; *(of nation, organization)* zénith *m*, apogée *m*; **in her heyday** *(youth)* quand elle était dans la force de l'âge; *(success)* à l'apogée de sa gloire, au temps de sa splendeur; **Hollywood in its heyday** l'âge d'or d'Hollywood; **the heyday of British theatre** l'âge d'or du théâtre britannique; **in its heyday it was one of the busiest ports in the world** à son heure de gloire, c'était l'un des ports les plus importants du monde

Heysel (stadium) ['haɪsəl-] *n* le stade du Heysel *(stade, à Bruxelles, où 39 supporters italiens trouvèrent la mort en 1985 à la suite d'une émeute provoquée par les supporters de Liverpool)*

Hezekiah [ˌhezɪ'kaɪə] *pr n Bible* Ézéchias

HF [ˌeɪtʃ'ef] *n Rad (abbr* **high frequency***)* HF *f*

HGH [ˌeɪtʃdʒiː'eɪtʃ] *n Biol (abbr* **human growth hormone***)* hormone *f* de croissance

HGV [ˌeɪtʃdʒiː'viː] *n Br (abbr* **heavy goods vehicle***)* PL *m*

▸▸ ***HGV licence*** permis *m* PL

HI *(written abbr* **Hawaii***)* Hawaii *f*, Hawaï *f*

hi [haɪ] *exclam Fam* (**a**) *(hello)* salut! (**b**) *(hey)* hé!, ohé!

hiatal [haɪ'eɪtəl] *adj* hiatal

hiatus [haɪ'eɪtəs] *(pl* **inv** *or* **hiatuses***) n* (**a**) *Formal (gap in series, text etc)* lacune *f* (**b**) *Formal (break in conversation)* silence *m*; *(break in negotiations)* interruption *f*; **apart from a hiatus between 1923 and 1925** mis à part une interruption entre 1923 et 1925 (**c**) *Ling* hiatus *m*

▸▸ *Med* ***hiatus hernia*** hernie *f* hiatale

Hiawatha [ˌhaɪə'wɒθə] *pr n* = chef indien qui mit fin aux guerres tribales du XVème siècle et qui devint le héros d'un poème de Longfellow

hibachi [hɪ'bɑːtʃɪ] *(pl* **inv** *or* **hibachis***) n* = petit barbecue de table

hibernal [haɪ'bɜːnəl] *adj* hibernal

hibernate ['haɪbəneɪt] *vi* hiberner

hibernation [ˌhaɪbə'neɪʃən] *n* hibernation *f*; **to go into hibernation** hiberner

Hibernia [haɪ'bɜːnjə] *n Hist* Hibernie *f (nom donné à l'Irlande par les Romains)*

Hibernian [haɪ'bɜːnjən] *Hist & Literary* **1** *adj* irlandais

2 *n* Irlandais(e) *m,f*

Hiberno-English [haɪ'bɜːnəʊ-] *n Ling* anglais *m* d'Irlande

hibiscus [hɪ'bɪskəs] *n Bot* hibiscus *m*

hiccough ['hɪkʌp], **hiccup** ['hɪkʌp] **1** *n* (**a**) *(sound)* hoquet *m*; **to have (the) hiccoughs** avoir le hoquet; **it gave me the hiccoughs** cela m'a donné le hoquet (**b**) *Fam (problem)* anicroche *f*; **there's been some sort of hiccough with the delivery** il y a eu un hic à la livraison

2 *vi* hoqueter

hick [hɪk] *Am Fam Pej* **1** *n* péquenaud(e) *m,f*, plouc *mf*

2 *adj* de péquenaud

▸▸ ***hick town*** bled *m*

hickey ['hɪkɪ] *n Am Fam* (**a**) *(gadget)* bidule *m* (**b**) *(lovebite)* suçon *m*

hickory ['hɪkərɪ] *(pl* **hickories***)* **1** *n (tree)* hickory *m*, noyer *m* blanc d'Amérique; *(wood)* (bois *m* de) hickory *m*

2 *comp (table, chair)* en (bois de) hickory

▸▸ ***hickory chips*** *(for barbecue)* copeaux *mpl* de hickory; ***hickory nut*** fruit *m* du hickory, noix *f* d'Amérique

hid [hɪd] *pt of* **hide**

hidden ['hɪdən] **1** *pp of* **hide**

2 *adj* caché; **hidden from sight** à l'abri des regards indiscrets, caché; **a village hidden away in the mountains** un village caché *ou* niché dans les montagnes; **she has hidden talents** elle a des talents cachés; **a hidden meaning** un sens caché

▸▸ ***hidden agenda*** projets *mpl* tenus secrets; *Fin* ***hidden cost*** coût *m* caché; *Com* ***hidden defects*** défauts *ou* vices *mpl* cachés; *Com* ***hidden extras*** dépenses *fpl* supplémentaires inattendues; **no hidden extras** garanti tout compris; *Comput* ***hidden file*** fichier *m* caché; *Fig* ***hidden hand*** influence *f* occulte; *Fin* ***hidden reserves*** réserve *f* latente; **I have hidden reserves** j'ai encore des réserves; *Fin* ***hidden tax*** impôt *m* indirect *ou* déguisé

hide [haɪd] *(pt* **hid** [hɪd], *pp* **hidden** ['hɪdən]*)* **1** *vt* (**a**) *(conceal → person, thing)* cacher; *(→ disappointment, dismay, fright)* dissimuler; **to hide sth from sb** *(ball, letter)* cacher qch à qn; *(emotion)* dissimuler qch à qn; **we have nothing to hide** nous n'avons rien à cacher *ou* à dissimuler; **the boy hid himself behind the door** le garçon s'est caché derrière la porte; **she hid her face** elle s'est caché le visage; **he hid it from sight** il l'a dissimulé *ou* l'a dérobé aux regards; **they hid him from the police** ils l'ont caché pour que la police ne le trouve pas; *Fig* **to hide one's light under a bushel** cacher ses talents;

she doesn't hide her light under a bushel ce n'est pas la modestie qui l'étouffe; *Am* **to hide one's head (in shame)** baisser la tête (de honte)

(**b**) *(keep secret)* taire, dissimuler; **to hide the truth (from sb)** taire *ou* dissimuler la vérité (à qn)

(**c**) *Comput (files, records)* cacher

2 *vi* se cacher; **to hide from sb** se cacher de qn; **have you been hiding from me?** tu te caches?; **he's hiding from the police** il se cache de la police; *Fig* **to hide behind an excuse/statistics** prétexter une excuse/les statistiques; *Fig* **the ambassador hid behind his diplomatic immunity** l'ambassadeur s'est réfugié derrière son immunité diplomatique

3 *n* (**a**) *Br (place)* cachette *f*; *(in hunting)* affût *m*

(**b**) *(animal skin → raw)* peau *f*; *(→ tanned)* cuir *m*

(**c**) *Fam Fig (of person)* peau[❑] *f*; **to tan sb's hide** tanner le cuir à qn; **I'll have your hide for that** tu vas me le payer cher; **I haven't seen hide nor hair of them** je n'ai eu aucune nouvelle d'eux

4 *adj* de *ou* en cuir

▸**hide away 1** *vi* se cacher; **to hide away (from sb/sth)** se cacher (de qn/ qch)

2 *vt sep* cacher

▸**hide out** *vi* se tenir caché; **he's hiding out from the police** il se cache de la police

hide-and-seek, *Am* **hide-and-go-seek** *n* cache-cache *m*; **to play hide-and-seek** jouer à cache-cache

hideaway ['haɪdəweɪ] *n* cachette *f*

hidebound ['haɪdbaʊnd] *adj (person)* obtus, borné; *(attitude, view)* borné, rigide

hideous ['hɪdɪəs] *adj* (**a**) *(physically ugly)* hideux, affreux (**b**) *(ghastly → conditions, situation)* atroce, abominable

hideously ['hɪdɪəslɪ] *adv* (**a**) *(deformed, wounded)* hideusement, atrocement, affreusement; **hideously ugly** atrocement *ou* affreusement laid (**b**) *Fam Fig (as intensifier)* terriblement, horriblement; **hideously expensive** horriblement cher

hideousness ['hɪdɪəsnɪs] *n* (**a**) *(physical ugliness)* laideur *f* (**b**) **the hideousness of his wounds/the crime** ses blessures *fpl* abominables/le crime abominable

hideout ['haɪdaʊt] *n* cachette *f*

hidey-hole ['haɪdɪ-] *n Fam* planque *f*

hiding ['haɪdɪŋ] *n* (**a**) *(concealment)* **to be in hiding** se tenir caché; **to go into hiding** *(criminal)* se cacher, se planquer; *(spy, terrorist)* entrer dans la clandestinité

(**b**) *Fam (thrashing)* rossée *f*; **to give sb a good hiding** donner une bonne raclée à qn

(**c**) *Fam (defeat)* raclée *f*, dérouillée *f*; **they got a good hiding in the election** ils ont pris une raclée aux élections

(**d**) *Br (idiom)* **to be on a hiding to nothing** être voué à l'échec

▸▸ ***hiding place*** cachette *f*

hidy-hole = **hidey-hole**

hie [haɪ] *(cont* **hieing** *or* **hying***) Arch or Hum* **1** *vi* se hâter, se presser

2 *vt* hâter, presser; **hie thee hence!** hors d'ici!

hierarch ['haɪəˌrɑːk] *n* hiérarque *m*

hierarchic [ˌhaɪə'rɑːkɪk], **hierarchical** [ˌhaɪə'rɑːkɪkəl] *adj* hiérarchique; **in hierarchic order** par ordre hiérarchique

▸▸ *Comput* ***hierarchical file system*** système *m* de fichiers hiérarchique; *Comput* ***hierarchical menu*** menu *m* hiérarchique

hierarchically [ˌhaɪə'rɑːkɪkəlɪ] *adv* hiérarchiquement

hierarchy ['haɪəˌrɑːkɪ] *(pl* **hierarchies***)* *n* (**a**) *(organization into grades)* hiérarchie *f*; *(of animals, plants)* classification *f*, classement *m* (**b**) *(upper levels of authority)* dirigeants *mpl*, autorités *fpl*

hieratic [ˌhaɪə'rætɪk] *adj* hiératique

hieroglyph ['haɪərəglɪf] *n* hiéroglyphe *m*

hieroglyphic [ˌhaɪərə'glɪfɪk] **1** *adj* hiéroglyphique

2 *n* hiéroglyphe *m*

hieroglyphics [ˌhaɪərə'glɪfɪks] *npl* écriture *f* hiéroglyphique; *Fam Fig (bad handwriting)* hiéroglyphes *mpl*

hierophant ['haɪərəˌfænt] *n Antiq* hiérophante *m*

hifalutin, hifaluting = **highfalutin, highfaluting**

hi-fi ['haɪˌfaɪ] *(abbr* **high fidelity***)* **1** *n* (**a**) *(UNCOUNT)* hi-fi *f inv* (**b**) *(stereo system)* chaîne *f* (hi-fi); *(radio)* radio *f* (hi-fi)

2 *comp (equipment, recording)* hi-fi *(inv)*

▸▸ ***hi-fi system*** chaîne *f* (hi-fi)

higgledy-piggledy [ˌhɪgəldɪ'pɪgəldɪ] *Fam* **1** *adv* pêle-mêle, en désordre[❑]

2 *adj* pêle-mêle, en désordre[❑]

HIGH [haɪ]

haut	▸ **1 (a), (b), (d), (f), (g), (m), (o), (p); 2 (a), (b); 3 (a), (b)**
élevé	▸ **1 (b) – (e), (k)**
grand	▸ **1 (c), (d)**
noble	▸ **1 (e)**
aigu	▸ **1 (g)**
excité	▸ **1 (s)**
en haut	▸ **2 (a)**

1 *adj* (**a**) *(tall)* haut; **how high is that building?** quelle est la hauteur de ce bâtiment?; **the walls are three metres high** les murs ont *ou* font trois mètres de haut, les murs sont hauts de trois mètres; **the building is eight storeys high** c'est un immeuble de *ou* à huit étages; **the highest mountain in the country** la plus haute montagne du pays; **when I was only so high** quand je n'étais pas plus grand que ça

(**b**) *(above ground level → river, tide)* haut; *(→ altitude, shelf)* haut, élevé; **built on high ground** construit sur un terrain élevé; **the sun was high in the sky** le soleil était haut

(**c**) *(above average → number)* grand, élevé; *(→ speed, value)* grand; *(→ cost, price, rate)* élevé; *(→ salary)* élevé, gros (grosse); *(→ pressure)* élevé, haut; *(→ polish)* brillant; **to the highest degree** au plus haut degré, à l'extrême; **of the highest importance** de première importance; **to pay a high price** payer le prix fort; **to fetch a high price** se vendre cher; **to make a higher bid** faire une offre supérieure, surenchérir; **highest bidder** surenchérisseur(euse) *m,f*; **she suffers from high blood pressure** elle a de la tension; *also Fig* **to play for high stakes** jouer gros (jeu); **built to withstand high temperatures** conçu pour résister à des températures élevées; **he has a high temperature** il a beaucoup de température *ou* fièvre; **areas of high unemployment** des régions à fort taux de chômage; **ore with a high mineral content** minerai *m* à haute teneur; **milk is high in calcium** le lait contient beaucoup de calcium; **high winds** des vents *mpl* violents, de grands vents *mpl*; *Math* **the highest common factor** le plus grand commun diviseur

(**d**) *(better than average → quality)* grand, haut; *(→ standard)* haut, élevé; *(→ mark, score)* élevé, bon; *(→ reputation)* bon; **our chances of success remain high** nos chances de succès restent très bonnes; **to have a high opinion of sb** avoir une bonne *ou* haute opinion de qn; **he has a high opinion of himself** il a une haute idée de lui-même; **to have a high profile** être très en vue; **she speaks of you in the highest terms** elle dit le plus grand bien de vous; **one of the highest honours in the arts** l'un des plus grands honneurs dans le monde des arts; *Com & Fin* **high value added** à haute valeur ajoutée

(**e**) *(honourable → ideal, thought)* noble, élevé; *(→ character)* noble; **a man of high principles** un homme qui a des principes (élevés); **he took a very high moral tone** il prit un ton très moralisateur; **she has very high moral standards** elle a des principes (de moralité) très élevés

(**f**) *(of great importance or rank)* haut, important; **a high official** un haut fonctionnaire; **we have it on the highest authority** nous le tenons de la source la plus sûre; **to have friends in high places** avoir des relations haut placées, avoir le bras long; **of high rank** de haut rang

(**g**) *(sound, voice)* aigu(uë); *Mus (note)* haut

(**h**) *(at peak)* **high summer** plein été *m*; **it was high summer** c'était au cœur de l'été; **it's high time we were leaving** il est grand temps qu'on parte

(**i**) *(intensely emotional)* **resentment was high** il y avait énormément de ressentiment; **moments of high drama** des moments *mpl* extrêmement dramatiques; **high adventure** grande aventure *f*; **to be high farce** tourner à la farce

(**j**) *Br (complexion)* rougeaud, rubicond; **to have a high colour** avoir le visage congestionné

(**k**) *(elaborate, formal → language, style)* élevé, soutenu

(**l**) *(prominent → cheekbones)* saillant

(**m**) *Cards* haut; **the highest card** la carte maîtresse

(**n**) *Br (meat)* avancé, faisandé; *(butter, cheese)* rance

(**o**) *(remote)* haut

(**p**) *Geog (latitude)* haut

(**q**) *(conservative)* **a high Tory** un tory ultra-conservateur; **a high Anglican** un(e) anglican(e) de tendance conservatrice

(**r**) *Ling (vowel)* fermé

(**s**) *(excited)* excité, énervé; *(cheerful)* plein d'entrain, enjoué; **to be in high spirits** être plein d'entrain; **our spirits were high** nous avions le moral; *Fam Old-fashioned* **we had a high old time** on s'est amusés comme des fous

(**t**) *Fam (person)* **to be high** *(drugged)* planer; *Fig (euphoric)* être dans un état d'euphorie[❑]; **high on cocaine** défoncé à la cocaïne; *Fig* **they were high on success** ils ne se sentaient plus après ce succès; *Fig* **he gets high on sailing** il prend son pied en faisant de la voile; **they were (as) high as kites** *(drunk)* ils étaient bien partis; *(drugged)* ils planaient; *(happy)* ils avaient la pêche

2 *adv* (**a**) *(at, to a height)* haut, en haut; *(at a great altitude)* à haute altitude, à une altitude élevée; **up high** en haut; **higher up** plus haut; **higher and higher** de plus en plus haut; **he raised both hands high** il a levé les deux mains en l'air; **the kite flew high up in the sky** le cerf-volant est monté très haut dans le ciel; **she threw the ball high into the air** elle a lancé le ballon très haut; **the geese flew high over the fields** les oies volaient très haut au-dessus des champs; **the shelf was high above her head** l'étagère était bien au-dessus de sa tête; **he rose high in the company** il a accédé aux plus hauts échelons de la société; *Fig* **we looked high and low for him** nous l'avons cherché partout; *Fig* **to set one's sights high, to aim high** viser haut; *Fig* **they're flying high** ils visent haut, ils voient grand; *also Fig* **to hold one's head high** porter la tête haute; *Fig* **to leave sb high and dry** laisser qn en plan

(**b**) *(in intensity)* haut; **they set the price/standards too high** ils ont fixé un prix/niveau trop élevé; **I turned the heating up high** j'ai mis le chauffage à fond; **he rose higher in my esteem** il est monté encore plus dans mon estime; **salaries can go as high as £50,000** les salaires peuvent monter jusqu'à *ou* atteindre 50 000 livres; **I had to go as high as £50** il a fallu que j'aille *ou* que je monte jusqu'à 50 livres; **the card players played high** les joueurs de cartes ont joué gros (jeu); **to run high** *(river)* être en crue; *(sea)* être houleuse *ou* grosse; **feelings were running high** les esprits se sont échauffés

(**c**) *(in tone)* haut; **I can't sing that high** je ne peux pas chanter aussi haut

(**d**) *Am Fam (idiom)* **to live high off** *or* **on the hog** vivre comme un roi *ou* nabab

3 *n* (**a**) *(height)* haut *m*; **on high** *(at a height)* en haut; *Fig (in heaven)* au ciel; *Hum* **the decision came from on high** la décision fut prononcée en haut lieu

(**b**) *(great degree or level)* haut *m*; **to reach a new high** atteindre un nouveau record; **prices are at an all-time high** les prix ont atteint leur maximum; **the Stock Market reached a new high** la Bourse a atteint un nouveau record *ou* maximum; **the highs and lows** *(of share prices, career, life)* les hauts *mpl* et les bas *mpl*

(**c**) *(setting → on iron, stove)* **I put the oven on high** j'ai mis le four sur très chaud

(**d**) *Aut (fourth gear)* quatrième *f*; *(fifth gear)* cinquième *f*

(**e**) *Met (anticyclone)* anticyclone *m*

(**f**) *Fam (state of excitement)* **she's been on a**

hid–hig

permanent high since he came back elle voit tout en rose depuis son retour

4 High *n Rel* **the Most High** le Très-Haut

►► *Rel* ***high altar*** maître-autel *m*; *Hist* ***High Antiquity*** Haute Antiquité *f*; *Am Aut* ***high beam*** feux *mpl* de route; *Swimming* ***high board*** plongeoir *m* le plus haut; ***high camp*** *(affectation)* affectation *f*, cabotinage *m*; *(effeminate behaviour)* manières *fpl* efféminées; *(style)* kitsch *m*; ***high chair*** chaise *f* haute (pour enfants); *Br Rel* ***High Church* 1** *n* = fraction de l'Église d'Angleterre accordant une grande importance à l'autorité du prêtre, au rituel etc **2** *adj* = de tendance conservatrice dans l'Église anglicane; *Br Rel* ***High Churchman*** = membre du mouvement conservateur à l'intérieur de l'Église anglicane; ***high comedy*** *Theat* comédie *f* au dialogue brillant; *Fig* **the debate ended in scenes of high comedy** le débat se termina par des scènes du plus haut comique; *Mil* ***high command*** haut commandement *m*; *Admin* ***high commission*** haut-commissariat *m*; *Admin* ***high commissioner*** haut-commissaire *m*; *Law* ***the High Court (of Justice)*** ≃ le tribunal de grande instance *(principal tribunal civil en Angleterre et au pays de Galles)*; *Law* ***High Court judge*** ≃ juge *m* du tribunal de grande instance; *Law* ***the High Court of Judiciary*** = la plus haute instance de justice en Écosse; ***high explosive*** explosif *m* puissant; ***high fashion*** haute couture *f*; ***high fidelity*** haute-fidélité *f*; ***high finance*** haute finance *f*; *Fam* ***high five*** = tape amicale donnée dans la paume de quelqu'un, bras levé, pour le saluer, le féliciter ou en signe de victoire; **they always give each other a high five when they meet** ils se tapent dans la main à chaque fois qu'ils se voient; *Electron* ***high frequency*** haute fréquence *f*; ***high gear*** *Aut (fourth)* quatrième *f* (vitesse *f*); *(fifth)* cinquième *f* (vitesse *f*); *Fig* **they moved into high gear** ils se sont dépêchés; ***High German*** haut allemand *m*; ***high heels*** hauts talons *mpl*; ***high jump*** *Sport* saut *m* en hauteur; *Br Fam Fig* **you're for the high jump when he finds out!** qu'est-ce que tu vas prendre quand il l'apprendra!; *Sport* ***high jumper*** sauteur(euse) *m,f (qui fait du saut en hauteur)*; ***the high life*** la grande vie; **she has a taste for the high life** elle a des goûts de luxe; **to lead** *or* **to live the high life** mener la grande vie; *Rel* ***high mass, High Mass*** grand-messe *f*; *Comput* ***high memory*** mémoire *f* haute; *Comput* ***high memory area*** zone *f* de mémoire haute; *Hist* ***the High Middle Ages*** le Haut Moyen Âge; ***high noon*** plein midi *m*; **at high noon** à midi pile; *Am* ***High Occupancy Vehicle*** = voiture particulière transportant au moins deux passagers; *Rel* ***high place*** haut lieu *m*; ***high point*** *(major event → of news)* événement *m* le plus marquant; *(→ of evening, holiday)* point *m* culminant, grand moment *m*; *(→ of film, novel)* point *m* culminant; **the high point of the party** le clou de la soirée; ***high priest*** *Rel* grand prêtre *m*; *Fig* **the high priests of fashion** les gourous *mpl* de la mode; ***high priestess*** *Rel* grande prêtresse *f*; *Fig* **the high priestess of rock** la grande prêtresse du rock; *Ling* ***high register language*** langage *m* élevé *ou* soutenu; *Art* ***high relief*** haut-relief *m*; ***high rise*** tour *f* *(immeuble)*; ***high road*** *(main road)* route *f* principale, grand-route *f*; *Fig (most direct route)* bonne voie *f*; **he's on the high road to success** il est en bonne voie de réussir; **the high road to fame** la voie de la gloire; *Am Fam* ***high roller*** *(spendthrift)* dépensier(ère)□ *m,f*; *(gambler)* flambeur(euse) *m,f*; ***high school*** *(in UK)* = établissement d'enseignement secondaire regroupant collège et lycée; *(in US)* lycée *m*; **she's still at high school** elle est toujours scolarisée *ou* va toujours au lycée; ***the high seas*** la haute mer; **on the high seas** en haute *ou* pleine mer; ***high season*** haute *ou* pleine saison *f*; **during the high season** en haute *ou* pleine saison; *Br* ***High Sheriff*** = dans les comtés anglais et gallois, représentant officiel du monarque; *Am* ***high sign*** signe *m*; **to give sb the high sign** faire signe à qn; ***high society*** haute société *f*, grand monde *m*; ***high spirits*** pétulance *f*, vitalité *f*, entrain *m*; **to be in high spirits** avoir de l'entrain, être plein d'entrain; **to put sb in high spirits** mettre qn de bonne humeur; ***high spot*** **(a)** *(major event → of news)* événement *m* le plus marquant; *(→ of evening, holiday)* point *m* culminant, grand moment *m*; *(→ of film, novel)* point *m* culminant **(b)** *Am (place)* endroit *m* intéressant; **we hit all the high spots** *(tourists)* nous avons vu toutes les attractions touristiques; *Br* ***the high street*** *(street)* la grand-rue, la rue principale; *(shops)* les commerçants *mpl*, le commerce; **the high street has been badly hit by the recession** les commerçants ont été durement touchés par la récession; *Br* ***high table*** *(for guests of honour)* table *f* d'honneur; *Sch & Univ* table *f* des professeurs; *Br* ***high tea*** = repas léger pris en début de soirée et accompagné de thé; ***high tech*** *(technology)* technologie *f* avancée *ou* de pointe; *(style)* hi-tech *m inv*; ***high tide*** *(of ocean, sea)* marée *f* haute; *Fig (of success)* point *m* culminant; **at high tide** à marée haute; *Theat* ***high tragedy*** grande tragédie *f*; ***high treason*** haute trahison *f*; *Elec* ***high voltage*** haute tension *f*; ***high water*** *(of ocean, sea)* marée *f* haute; *(of river)* crue *f*; **the river is at high water** le fleuve est en crue; ***high wire*** corde *f* raide *ou* de funambule; **to walk the high wire** marcher sur la corde raide

'High Noon' *Zinnemann* 'Le Train sifflera trois fois'

-high [haɪ] *suff* à la hauteur de...; **shoulder-high** à la hauteur de l'épaule; **waist-high** à la hauteur de la taille

high-and-mighty *adj* arrogant, impérieux; **to be high-and-mighty** se donner de grands airs; **don't act so high-and-mighty** descends de tes grands chevaux, ne prends pas tes airs de grand seigneur/grande dame

high-angle shot *n Cin* plan *m* en plongée

highball ['haɪ,bɔːl] *Am* **1** *n* = boisson à base d'un alcool avec de l'eau et des glaçons

2 *vi* aller grand train *ou* à toute vitesse, foncer

3 *vt* conduire à toute vitesse *ou* à toute allure

highbinder ['haɪ,baɪndə(r)] *n Am (politician)* politicien(enne) *m,f* corrompu(e)

highborn ['haɪbɔːn] *adj* bien né, de bonne *ou* haute naissance

highboy ['haɪbɔɪ] *n Am* commode *f* (haute)

highbrow ['haɪbraʊ] **1** *adj (literature, film)* pour intellectuels; *(taste)* intellectuel

2 *n* intellectuel(elle) *m,f*, grosse tête *f*

high-cal *adj Am Fam* calorique□

high-class *adj (person)* de la haute société, du grand monde; *(flat, neighbourhood)* de grand standing; *(job, service)* de premier ordre; *(car, hotel, restaurant)* de luxe; **a high-class prostitute** une prostituée de luxe

high-coloured *adj* rougeaud, rubicond

high-definition TV *n* télévision *f* haute définition

high-density *adj* **(a)** *(housing)* à grande densité de population **(b)** *Comput (disk, graphics, printing)* (de) haute densité

high-dependency *adj (staff, unit)* de soins semi-intensifs

high-diving *n* plongeon *m* de haut vol, haut vol *m*

high-end *adj (top-of-the-range)* haut de gamme

high-energy *adj* à haut rendement énergétique; **a high-energy diet** un régime hypercalorique *ou* riche en calories

higher ['haɪə(r)] **1** *adj* **(a)** *(at greater height)* plus haut

(b) *(advanced)* supérieur; **a sum higher than 50** une somme supérieure à 50; **people in the higher income brackets** *or* **groups** les gens appartenant aux tranches de revenus supérieurs; **institute of higher learning** institut *m* de hautes études

2 *adv* plus haut

3 Higher *n Scot Sch* = diplôme de fin d'études secondaires sanctionnant une matière déterminée

►► ***higher animals*** animaux *mpl* supérieurs; *Sch* ***the higher classes*** les grandes classes *fpl*, les classes *fpl* supérieures; *Law* ***higher court*** instance *f* supérieure; *Univ* ***higher degree*** diplôme *m* d'études supérieures; *Univ* ***higher education*** enseignement *m* supérieur; **to go on to higher education** faire des études supérieures; *Sch* ***the higher forms*** les grandes classes *fpl*, les classes *fpl* supérieures; *Scot Sch* ***Higher Grade*** = diplôme de fin d'études secondaires sanctionnant une matière déterminée; ***higher mathematics*** *(UNCOUNT)* mathématiques *fpl* supérieures; ***Higher National Certificate*** = brevet de technicien en Grande-Bretagne, ≃ BTS *m*; ***Higher National Diploma*** = brevet de technicien supérieur en Grande-Bretagne, ≃ DUT *m*

higher-up *n Fam* supérieur(e) *m,f*

highfalutin [,haɪfə'luːtɪn], **highfaluting** [,haɪfə'luːtɪŋ] *adj Fam* affecté, prétentieux; **I'm tired of her highfalutin ways** j'en ai assez de ses airs de grande dame

high-fibre *adj (food, diet)* riche en fibres

high-fidelity *adj* haute-fidélité *(inv)*

►► ***high-fidelity equipment*** matériel *m* hi-fi

high-flier *n (ambitious person)* ambitieux(euse) *m,f*, jeune loup *m*; *(talented person)* crack *m*

high-flown *adj* **(a)** *(ideas, plans)* extravagant **(b)** *(language)* ampoulé, boursouflé; *(style)* ampoulé

high-flyer = **high-flier**

high-flying *adj* **(a)** *(aircraft)* qui vole à haute altitude; *(bird)* qui vole haut **(b)** *(person)* ambitieux; *(behaviour, goal)* extravagant

high-frequency *adj* à *ou* de haute fréquence

Highgate ['haɪgeɪt] *n* = quartier du nord de Londres, connu pour son cimetière où repose entre autres Karl Marx

high-grade *adj* de haute qualité, de premier ordre; **high-grade beef/fruit** bœuf *m*/fruits *mpl* de premier choix; **high-grade minerals** minéraux *mpl* à haute teneur; *Fig* **a high-grade idiot** un(une) imbécile de premier ordre

high-handed *adj (overbearing)* autoritaire, despotique; *(arbitrary)* arbitraire; *(inconsiderate)* cavalier

high-handedly [-'hændɪdlɪ] *adv (overbearingly)* autoritairement; *(arbitrarily)* arbitrairement; *(inconsiderately)* d'une façon cavalière

high-handedness [-'hændɪdnɪs] *n (overbearing character → of person)* caractère *m* autoritaire, despotisme *m*; *(arbitrariness → of behaviour)* caractère *m* arbitraire; *(lack of consideration)* caractère *m* cavalier

high-hat *Fam* **1** *adj* snob□, hautain□

2 *vt Am* snober□, traiter de haut□

3 *n* **(a)** *Mus* cymbales□ *fpl (montées sur un pied)* **(b)** *(person)* arrogant(e)□ *m,f*, snob□ *mf* **(c)** *Cin & TV* petit pied *m* de caméra□, pied de sol□

high-heeled [-'hiːld] *adj* à talons hauts, à hauts talons

high-income *adj* à haut revenu

►► ***high-income group*** groupe *m* des gros salaires, groupe *m* des salaires élevés

high-involvement *adj Mktg (purchasing)* à forte participation des consommateurs

highjack, highjacker *etc* = **hijack, hijacker** *etc*

high-key *adj Art* comprenant peu de contraste, high-key *(inv)*

highland ['haɪlənd] **1** *n* région *f* montagneuse

2 *adj* des montagnes

3 Highland *adj (air, scenery)* des Highlands; *(holiday)* dans les Highlands

4 Highlands *npl* **the Highlands** *(of Scotland)* les Highlands *mpl*

►► ***Highland cattle*** race *f* bovine des Highlands; *Hist* ***the Highland Clearances*** = aux XVIIIème et XIXème siècles, déplacement souvent forcé des populations d'une partie des Highlands d'Écosse dans le but d'affecter les terres à l'élevage de moutons; ***Highland dress*** = costume écossais pour les hommes; ***Highland fling*** = danse des Highlands traditionnellement exécutée en solo; ***Highland games*** jeux *mpl* écossais; ***the Highland Region*** le Highland, = région dans le nord-ouest de l'Écosse; **in the Highland Region** dans le Highland

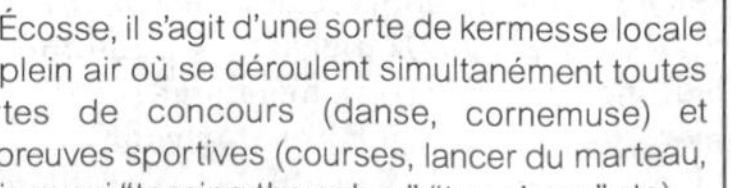

HIGHLAND GAMES

En Écosse, il s'agit d'une sorte de kermesse locale en plein air où se déroulent simultanément toutes sortes de concours (danse, cornemuse) et d'épreuves sportives (courses, lancer du marteau, mais aussi "tossing the caber", "tug o' war" etc).

highlander ['haɪləndə(r)] **1** *n (mountain dweller)* montagnard(e) *m,f*

2 Highlander *n* habitant(e) *m,f* des Highlands, Highlander *m*

high-level *adj (discussion, meeting)* à un haut niveau; *(diplomat, official)* de haut niveau, de rang élevé; *Mil* **high-level officers** officiers *mpl* supérieurs; **high-level staff** *(of company)* cadres *mpl* supérieurs
►► *Comput* ***high-level language*** langage *m* évolué *or* de haut niveau

highlight ['haɪlaɪt] **1** *vt* (**a**) *(emphasize)* souligner, mettre en relief; **the report highlights the desperate plight of the refugees** le rapport fait ressortir *ou* souligne la situation désespérée des réfugiés
(**b**) *(with pen)* surligner
(**c**) *Comput (text block)* sélectionner; **to be highlighted** *(text)* apparaître en surimpression *ou* en surbrillance
(**d**) *Art & Phot* rehausser
(**e**) *(hair)* faire des mèches dans; **to have one's hair highlighted** se faire faire des mèches
2 *n* (**a**) *(important moment → of news)* événement *m* le plus marquant; *(→ of evening, holiday)* point *m* culminant, grand moment *m*; **the news highlights** les grands titres *mpl* de l'actualité; **the highlights of today's match will be shown later** les moments forts du match d'aujourd'hui seront diffusés ultérieurement; **the highlight of the party** le clou de la soirée
(**b**) *(in hair → natural)* reflet *m*; *(→ bleached)* mèche *f*; **she has had highlights (put in her hair)** elle s'est fait faire des mèches
(**c**) *Comput* relief *m*
(**d**) *Art & Phot* rehaut *m*

highlighter (pen) ['haɪlaɪtə(r)] *n* surligneur *m*, Stabilo® *m*

highly ['haɪlɪ] *adv* (**a**) *(very)* très, extrêmement; **it's highly improbable** c'est fort peu probable; **a highly polished table** une table d'un beau poli; **the dish was highly seasoned** le plat était fortement relevé *ou* épicé
(**b**) *(very well)* très bien; **very highly paid** très bien payé
(**c**) *(favourably)* **to speak/think highly of sb** dire/penser beaucoup de bien de qn; **he praised her work highly** il a chanté (haut) les louanges de son travail; **I highly recommend it** je vous le conseille vivement *ou* chaudement
(**d**) *(at an important level)* haut; **a highly placed source** une source haut placée; **a highly placed official** *(gen)* un(une) officiel(elle) de haut rang; *Admin* un(une) haut(e) fonctionnaire

highly-geared *adj Fin* à ratio d'endettement élevé

highly-strung *adj* nerveux, tendu

high-margin product *n Com* produit *m* à forte marge

high-minded *adj (person)* de caractère noble, qui a des principes (élevés); *(action etc)* magnanime

high-mindedness [-'maɪndɪdnɪs] *n* noblesse *f* de sentiments, grandeur *f* d'âme; *(of action etc)* magnanimité *f*

high-necked [-nekt] *adj* à col haut *ou* montant

highness ['haɪnɪs] **1** *n (of building, wall)* hauteur *f*
2 Highness *n (title)* **His/Her Highness** son Altesse *f*

high octane *adj* à haut degré d'octane; *Fig* explosif
►► ***high-octane petrol*** supercarburant *m*, super *m*

high-performance *adj* performant

high-pitched *adj* (**a**) *(sound, voice)* aigu(uë); *Mus (note)* haut (**b**) *(argument, discussion)* passionné; *(style)* ampoulé; *(excitement)* intense (**c**) *(roof)* à forte pente

high-powered *adj* (**a**) *(engine, rifle)* puissant, de forte puissance; *(microscope)* à fort grossissement (**b**) *(dynamic → person)* dynamique, entreprenant; *(→ advertising, course, method)* dynamique; **she's something high-powered in the City** elle a un poste important à la Cité de Londres (**c**) *(important)* très important

high-pressure **1** *adj* (**a**) *(cylinder, gas, machine)* à haute pression (**b**) *Fig (methods, selling)* agressif; *(job, profession)* stressant; **a high-pressure salesman** un vendeur de choc
2 *vt Am Fam* forcer la main à❑; **she high-pressured me to do it** *or* **into doing it** elle m'a forcé la main pour que je le fasse
►► *Met* ***high-pressure area*** anticyclone *m*, zone *f* de hautes pressions (atmosphériques)

high-principled *adj* aux principes élevés

high-profile *adj (job, position)* qui est très en vue; *(campaign)* qui fait beaucoup de bruit

high-quality *adj* haut de gamme, de qualité supérieure

high-ranking *adj* de haut rang, de rang élevé; *Admin* **a high-ranking official** un(e) haut(e) fonctionnaire

high-rent *adj* (**a**) *(housing)* à loyer élevé (**b**) *Am (high-quality)* chic *(inv)*

high-resolution *adj Comput (screen, graphics)* à haute résolution

high-rise *adj (flat)* qui est dans une tour; *(skyline)* composé de tours

high-risk *adj* à haut risque, à hauts risques

high-school *adj Sch*
►► *Am* ***high-school diploma*** diplôme *m* de fin d'études secondaires; *Am* ***high-school teacher*** professeur *m* de lycée

high-season *adj (prices)* de haute saison

high-sounding *adj (ideas)* grandiloquent, extravagant; *(language, title)* grandiloquent, *Pej* ronflant

high-speed *adj* ultra-rapide; *Comput* à grande vitesse
►► ***high-speed train*** train *m* à grande vitesse, TGV *m*

high-spirited *adj* (**a**) *(person)* plein d'entrain *ou* de vivacité; *(activity, fun)* plein d'entrain (**b**) *(horse)* fougueux, nerveux

high-stepping *adj* (**a**) *(horse)* qui lève haut les pieds (**b**) *Fig (person)* qui aime se divertir; *(town)* qui offre beaucoup de divertissements

high-street *adj*
►► *Br* ***the high-street banks*** les grandes banques *fpl*; ***high-street fashion*** prêt-à-porter *m*; ***high-street shops*** commerces *mpl*

high-strung *adj* nerveux, tendu

hightail ['haɪteɪl] *vt esp Am Fam* **to hightail it** filer; **I hightailed it out of there** j'ai foutu le camp; **you'd better hightail it back home** tu as intérêt à rentrer le plus vite possible

high-tech [-tek] *adj* (**a**) *(industry, sector)* de pointe; *(equipment)* de haute technicité (**b**) *(furniture, style)* hi-tech *(inv)*

high-tensile steel *n Constr & Tech* acier *m* à haute résistance élastique

high-tension *adj* à haute tension
►► ***high-tension cable*** câble *m* haute tension; ***high-tension coil*** bobine *f* haute tension

high-top *n* (**a**) *(haircut)* = coupe de cheveux consistant à raser les côtés du crâne et à laisser pousser le dessus en hauteur (**b**) *(shoe)* = chaussure de sport montante

high-up *Fam* **1** *n (important person)* gros bonnet *m*, huile *f*; *(hierarchical superior)* supérieur(e)❑ *m,f*
2 *adj* haut placé❑; **she is high-up up in the government** elle est haut placée dans le gouvernement

high-viscosity *adj (oil)* à haute viscosité

high-water mark *n* (**a**) *(of ocean, river)* niveau *m* des hautes eaux (**b**) *Fig (of success)* point *m* culminant

highway ['haɪweɪ] *n (road)* route *f*; *Am (main road)* grande route *f*, route *f* nationale; *(public road)* voie *f* publique; *Am (interstate)* autoroute *f*; **all the highways and byways** tous les chemins
►► *Br* ***the Highway Code*** le code de la route; *Br* ***highway engineer*** ≃ ingénieur *m* des Ponts et Chaussées; *Am* ***highway patrol*** police *f* de la route; *Am* ***highway patrolman*** membre *m* de la police de la route; ***highway robbery*** banditisme *m* de grand chemin; *Fam Fig* **that's highway robbery!** c'est du vol!

highwayman ['haɪweɪmən] (*pl* **highwaymen** [-mən]) *n* bandit *m* de grand chemin

high-yield *adj Fin (bond, security)* à rendement élevé

hijack ['haɪdʒæk] **1** *vt* (**a**) *(plane)* détourner; *(car, train)* s'emparer de, détourner; *Fig* **the government hijacked the opposition's policy** le gouvernement s'est approprié la politique de l'opposition (**b**) *(rob)* voler
2 *n* détournement *m*

hijacker ['haɪdʒækə(r)] *n* (**a**) *(of plane)* pirate *m* (de l'air); *(of car, train)* gangster *m* (**b**) *(robber)* voleur(euse) *m,f*

hijacking ['haɪdʒækɪŋ] *n* (**a**) *(of car, plane, train)* détournement *m* (**b**) *(robbery)* vol *m*

hike [haɪk] **1** *vi* faire de la marche à pied; **to hike 5 kilometres** faire 5 kilomètres à pied; **we went hiking in the mountains** nous avons fait des excursions *ou* des randonnées à pied dans les montagnes; **he hiked through Spain** il a parcouru l'Espagne à pied; **we hiked all the way home** on a dû faire le chemin du retour à pied
2 *vt* (**a**) *(walk)* faire à pied, marcher
(**b**) *(increase → price, interest rates, rent etc)* augmenter (brusquement)
3 *n* (**a**) *(gen) & Mil* marche *f* à pied; *(long walk)* randonnée *f* à pied, marche *f* à pied; *(short walk)* promenade *f*; **they went for a four-hour hike** ils ont fait une excursion *ou* une randonnée de quatre heures à pied; *Fam* **it's a bit of a hike into town** ça fait une petite trotte pour aller en ville; *Fam* **take a hike!** dégage!
(**b**) *(increase)* hausse *f*, augmentation *f*; **price hike** hausse *f* des prix; **tax hike** augmentation *f* d'impôts

►**hike up** *vt sep* (**a**) *(hitch up → skirt)* relever; *(→ trousers)* remonter; **she hiked herself up over the wall** elle s'est hissée au-dessus du mur (**b**) *(price, interest rates, rent etc)* augmenter (brusquement)

hiker ['haɪkə(r)] *n (gen) & Mil* marcheur(euse) *m,f*; *(in mountains, woods)* randonneur(euse) *m,f*, promeneur(euse) *m,f*

hiking ['haɪkɪŋ] *n (UNCOUNT) (gen) & Mil* marche *f* à pied; *(in mountains, woods)* randonnée *f*, trekking *m*
►► ***hiking boots*** chaussures *fpl* de marche

hilarious [hɪ'leərɪəs] *adj (funny → person, joke, story)* hilarant; **his stories are hilarious** ses histoires sont à se tordre de rire; **we had a hilarious time last night** nous nous sommes amusés comme des fous hier soir

hilariously [hɪ'leərɪəslɪ] *adv* joyeusement, gaiement; **to laugh hilariously** être écroulé de rire, se tordre de rire; **it sounds hilariously unlikely** c'est complètement tiré par les cheveux; **the film's hilariously funny** le film est à se tordre de rire

hilariousness [hɪ'leərɪəsnɪs] *n (of story, joke)* caractère *m* hilarant

hilarity [hɪ'lærətɪ] *n* hilarité *f*

Hilary term ['hɪlərɪ-] *n Univ* trimestre *m* de printemps *(à Oxford et à Trinity College, Dublin)*

hill [hɪl] *n* (**a**) *(small mountain)* colline *f*, coteau *m*; **we walked up the hill** nous avons gravi la colline; **up hill and down dale, over hill and dale** par monts et par vaux; **the soldiers fought up hill and down dale** les soldats ont mené le combat avec force et persévérance; **as old as the hills** vieux comme le monde *ou* Mathusalem; *Fam* **to be over the hill** commencer à se faire vieux❑
(**b**) *(slope)* côte *f*, pente *f*; **steep hill** *(sign) (up)* montée *ou* côte raide; *(down)* descente abrupte *ou* raide
(**c**) *(mound → of earth)* levée *f* de terre, remblai *m*; *(→ of things)* tas *m*, monceau *m*; *Am Fam* **that car isn't worth a hill of beans** cette voiture ne vaut pas un clou; *Am* **on the Hill** au parlement *(par allusion à Capitol Hill, siège du Congrès)*
►► ***hill climb*** course *f* de côtes; ***hill country*** pays *m* de collines; ***hill farm*** ferme *f* à flanc de coteau; ***hill farmer*** éleveur(euse) *m,f* de moutons dans les alpages; *Aut* ***hill start*** démarrage *m* en côte; ***hill station*** *(in India)* station *f* de montagne

hillbilly ['hɪl,bɪlɪ] (*pl* **hillbillies**) *Am* **1** *n* montagnard(e) *m,f* des Appalaches; *Pej* péquenaud(e) *m,f*, plouc *mf*
2 *adj* des Appalaches
►► ***hillbilly music*** folk *m* (des Appalaches)

hill-climbing *n* randonnée *f* *(en pays de collines)*

hillfort ['hɪlfɔːt] *n* = endroit fortifié se trouvant au sommet d'une colline

hilliness ['hɪlɪnɪs] *n* vallonnement *m*, caractère *m* accidenté

hillock ['hɪlək] *n (small hill)* mamelon *m*, butte *f*; *(artificial hill)* monticule *m*, amoncellement *m*

Hillsborough ['hɪlzbrə] *n (stadium)* = stade de

football de Sheffield, Angleterre, où de nombreux supporters périrent écrasés en 1989

▸▸ *Hist* ***the Hillsborough Agreement*** = accord conclu en 1985 entre le Royaume-Uni et la république d'Irlande pour garantir la paix et la stabilité en Irlande du Nord

hillside ['hɪl,saɪd] *n* (flanc *m* de) coteau *m*; **vines grew on the hillside** des vignes poussaient à flanc de coteau

hilltop ['hɪl,tɒp] **1** *n* sommet *m* de la colline; **on the hilltop** au sommet *ou* en haut de la colline

2 *adj (village)* au sommet *ou* en haut de la colline; *(view)* d'en haut de la colline

hillwalker ['hɪl,wɔːkə(r)] *n Br* randonneur(euse) *m,f (en terrain vallonné)*

hillwalking ['hɪl,wɔːkɪŋ] *n (UNCOUNT) Br* randonnée *f (en terrain vallonné)*

hilly ['hɪlɪ] *(compar* **hillier**, *superl* **hilliest**) *adj (country, land)* vallonné; *(road)* accidenté, à fortes côtes

hilt [hɪlt] *n (of dagger, knife)* manche *m*; *(of sword)* poignée *f*, garde *f*; *(of gun)* crosse *f*; *Fig* **(up) to the hilt** au maximum; **to back sb up to the hilt** soutenir qn à fond; **mortgaged up to the hilt** *(person)* endetté jusqu'au cou, qui doit rembourser des emprunts énormes; *(property)* fortement hypothéqué

hilum ['haɪləm] *(pl* **hila** [-lə]) *n Bot & Anat* hile *m*

him [hɪm] *pron* (**a**) *(direct object → unstressed)* le, l' *(before vowel or silent 'h')*; *(→ stressed)* lui; **I recognize him** je le reconnais; **I heard him** je l'ai entendu; **why did you have to choose HIM?** pourquoi l'as-tu choisi lui?

(**b**) *(indirect object → unstressed)* lui; *(→ stressed)* à lui; **give him the money** donne-lui l'argent; **she only told him, no one else** elle ne l'a dit qu'à lui, c'est tout; **we are thinking of him** nous pensons à lui; **why do they always give HIM the interesting jobs?** pourquoi est-ce toujours à lui qu'on donne le travail intéressant?; **I object to him borrowing the car** je m'oppose à ce qu'il emprunte la voiture

(**c**) *(after preposition)* lui; **I was in front of him** j'étais devant lui; **as rich as/richer than him** aussi riche/plus riche que lui; **he closed the door behind him** il a fermé la porte derrière lui

(**d**) *(with 'to be')* **it's him** c'est lui; **if I were him** si j'étais lui, si j'étais à sa place

(**e**) *Formal (with relative pronoun)* celui; *Literary* **to him who should take offence at this I would say...** à celui qui s'en offenserait, je dirais...

Himalayan [,hɪmə'leɪən] *adj* himalayen

Himalayas [,hɪmə'leɪəz] *npl* **the Himalayas** l'Himalaya *m*; **in the Himalayas** dans l'Himalaya

himbo ['hɪmbəʊ] *n Fam* = beau mec pas très futé

himself [hɪm'self] *pron* (**a**) *(reflexive form)* se, s' *(before vowel or silent 'h')*; **he introduced himself** il s'est présenté; **he bought himself a car** il s'est acheté une voiture; **he considers himself lucky** il considère qu'il a de la chance

(**b**) *(emphatic form)* lui-même; **he built the shelves himself** il a monté les étagères lui-même; **I spoke with the teacher himself** j'ai parlé au professeur en personne

(**c**) *(with preposition)* lui; **he took it upon himself to tell us** il a pris sur lui de nous le dire; **he has a room to himself** il a sa propre chambre *ou* sa chambre à lui; **the old man was talking to himself** le vieil homme parlait tout seul; **"that's odd", he thought to himself** "c'est bizarre", se dit-il; **he did it all by himself** il l'a fait tout seul

(**d**) *(his usual self)* **he isn't quite himself** il n'est pas dans son état habituel; **he's feeling more himself now** il va mieux maintenant

hind [haɪnd] **1** *n (deer)* biche *f*; **hind calf** faon *m* femelle

2 *adj* de derrière; **hind leg** patte *f* de derrière; *Hum* **he could talk the hind legs off a donkey** il est bavard comme une pie; *Hum* **to get up on one's hind legs** se mettre debout

Hindenburg ['hɪndən,bɜːg] *n* **the Hindenburg** le Hindenburg

hinder[1] ['hɪndə(r)] *vt (person)* gêner; *(progress)* entraver, gêner; **to hinder sb in his/her work** gêner qn dans son travail; **to hinder sb from doing sth** empêcher qn de faire qch

hinder[2] ['haɪndə(r)] *adj (at the back)* de derrière, postérieur

Hindi ['hɪndɪ] **1** *n Ling* hindi *m*

2 *adj* hindi

hindmost ['haɪndməʊst] *adj* dernier, du bout

hindquarters ['haɪndkwɔːtəz] *npl* arrière-train *m*

hindrance ['hɪndrəns] *n* (**a**) *(person, thing)* obstacle *m*, entrave *f*; **you'll be more of a hindrance than a help** tu vas gêner plus qu'autre chose

(**b**) *(UNCOUNT) (action)* **without any hindrance from the authorities** *(referring to person)* sans être gêné par les autorités; *(referring to project)* sans être entravé par les autorités; **without any hindrance from the children/my husband** sans avoir les enfants/mon mari dans les jambes; **his illness has been something of a hindrance to the project** sa maladie a quelque peu retardé le projet

hindsight ['haɪndsaɪt] *n* sagesse *f* acquise après coup; **with the benefit** *or* **wisdom** *or* **gift of hindsight** avec du recul, après coup

Hindu ['hɪnduː] **1** *n* Hindou(e) *m,f*

2 *adj* hindou

Hinduism ['hɪnduːɪzəm] *n* hindouisme *m*

Hindustan [,hɪndʊ'stɑːn] *n* Hindoustan *m*; **in Hindustan** dans l'Hindoustan

Hindustani [,hɪndʊ'stɑːnɪ] **1** *n Ling* hindoustani *m*

2 *adj* hindoustani

hinge [hɪndʒ] **1** *n (of door)* gond *m*, charnière *f*; *(of box)* charnière *f*; **the door has come off its hinges** la porte est sortie de ses gonds; **(stamp) hinge** charnière *f*

2 *vt (door)* munir de gonds *ou* charnières; *(box)* munir de charnières; **the door can be hinged to open either left or right** la porte peut être montée de façon à s'ouvrir soit à gauche soit à droite

▸▸ *Anat* ***hinge joint*** diarthrose *f*

▸**hinge on, hinge upon** *vt insep (depend on)* dépendre de; **the company's future hinges on whether we get the contract** l'avenir de l'entreprise dépend de *ou* tient à *ou* repose sur ce contrat

hinged [hɪndʒd] *adj* à charnière *ou* charnières

▸▸ ***hinged flap*** *(of counter)* abattant *m*

hinny ['hɪnɪ] *(pl* **hinnies**) *n Zool* bardot *m*, bardeau *m*

hint [hɪnt] **1** *n* (**a**) *(indirect suggestion)* allusion *f*; *(clue)* indice *m*; **to drop a hint (about sth)** faire une allusion (à qch); **you could try dropping a hint that if his work doesn't improve...** tu pourrais essayer de lui faire comprendre que si son travail ne s'améliore pas...; **he can't take a hint** il ne comprend pas les allusions; **OK, I can take a hint** oh ça va, j'ai compris; **I took the hint** j'ai saisi ce qu'on essayait de me faire comprendre; **give me a hint** donne-moi un indice; **I just love plain chocolate, hint, hint** j'adore le chocolat noir, si tu vois ce que je veux dire

(**b**) *(helpful suggestion, tip)* conseil *m*, truc *m*; **the book is full of useful hints on how to save money** le livre est plein de tuyaux pour faire des économies

(**c**) *(small amount, trace → of emotion)* note *f*; *(→ of colour)* touche *f*; *(→ of flavouring)* soupçon *m*; **there's a hint of spring in the air** ça sent le printemps, il y a du printemps dans l'air

2 *vt* insinuer; **that was what he hinted** c'est ce qu'il a insinué *ou* laissé entendre

3 *vi* **to hint at sth** faire allusion à qch; **what are you hinting at?** qu'est-ce que tu insinues?; *(in neutral sense)* à quoi fais-tu allusion?; **the speech seemed to hint at the possibility of agreement being reached soon** le discours semblait laisser entendre qu'un accord pourrait être conclu prochainement; **remember, no hinting in this game** souvenez-vous que vous n'avez droit à aucun indice dans ce jeu

hinterland ['hɪntə,lænd] *n* arrière-pays *m inv*

HIP [,eɪtʃaɪ'piː] *n Am (abbr* **health insurance plan**) assurance *f* médicale

hip[1] [hɪp] *n* (**a**) *(part of body)* hanche *f*; **with one's hands on one's hips** les mains sur les hanches; **to be big/small around the hips** avoir les hanches larges/étroites; **to break one's hip** se casser le col du fémur; *Fig* **to shoot from the hip** ne pas faire dans la dentelle

(**b**) *Constr* **hip (piece** *or* **rafter)** *(of roof)* arêtier *m*, arête *f*

▸▸ *Br* ***hip bath*** bain *m* de siège; ***hip flask*** flasque *f*; *Anat* ***hip joint*** articulation *f* de la hanche; ***hip measurement*** tour *m* de hanches; *Br* ***hip pocket*** poche *f* revolver; *Med* ***hip replacement*** *(operation)* remplacement *m* de la hanche par une prothèse; *(prosthesis)* prothèse *f* de la hanche; ***hip size*** tour *m* de hanches

hip[2] *n (berry)* cynorhodon *m*, gratte-cul *m inv*

hip[3] *Fam* **1** *adj (fashionable)* branché; **to be hip to sth** être branché sur qch

2 *vt Am* **to hip sb to sth** mettre qn au courant de qch ❑; **I'll hip you to the latest** je vais te mettre au parfum

hip[4] *exclam* **hip hip, hooray!** hip hip hip, hourra!

hipbone ['hɪpbəʊn] *n Anat* os *m* iliaque

hip-hop *n (music)* hip-hop *m inv*

hiphuggers ['hɪp,hʌgəz] *npl Am* pantalon *m* à taille basse

Hipparchus [hɪ'pɑːkəs] *pr n* Hipparque

hipped [hɪpt] *adj Am Fam* **to be hipped on sb/sth** être dingue de qn/qch

-hipped [hɪpt] *suff* **broad-hipped** aux hanches larges; **narrow-hipped** aux hanches fines *ou* étroites

hippie ['hɪpɪ] **1** *n* hippie *mf*, hippy *mf*

2 *adj* hippie, hippy

▸▸ ***hippie trail*** = itinéraire menant jusqu'en Extrême-Orient, en passant par l'Inde et le Népal, suivi par de nombreux hippies au cours des années 60 et 70.

hippo ['hɪpəʊ] *(pl* **hippos**) *n Fam* hippopotame ❑ *m*

hippocampus [,hɪpəʊ'kæmpəs] *n Anat, Myth & Zool* hippocampe *m*

▸▸ *Anat* ***hippocampus major*** grand hippocampe *m*; *Anat* ***hippocampus minor*** petit hippocampe *m*

Hippocrates [hɪ'pɒkrətiːz] *pr n* Hippocrate

Hippocratic oath [,hɪpə'krætɪk-] *n* **the Hippocratic oath** le serment d'Hippocrate

hippodrome ['hɪpədrəʊm] *n* hippodrome *m*; *(not for racing)* arène *f*

hippogriff ['hɪpəgrɪf] *n Myth* hippogriffe *m*

Hippolyta [hɪ'pɒlɪtə] *pr n Myth* Hippolyté

Hippolytus [hɪ'pɒlɪtəs] *pr n Myth* Hippolyte

hippopotamus [,hɪpə'pɒtəməs] *(pl* **hippopotamuses** *or* **hippopotami** [-maɪ]) *n Zool* hippopotame *m*

hippy[1] *(pl* **hippies**) = **hippie**

hippy[2] ['hɪpɪ] *adj Fam (with large hips)* aux hanches larges ❑

hipster ['hɪpstə(r)] **1** *n esp Am Old-fashioned* beatnick *mf (des années 40 et 50)*

2 hipsters *npl Br (trousers)* pantalon *m* (à) taille basse

hiragana [hɪrə'gɑːnə] *n* hiragana *m*

hire ['haɪə(r)] **1** *n* (**a**) *Br (of car, room, suit etc)* location *f*; **for hire** *(sign)* à louer; *(taxi)* libre; **it's out on hire** il a été loué

(**b**) *(cost → of car, boat etc)* (prix *m* de) location *f*; *(→ of worker)* paye *f*

(**c**) *(of labour)* embauche *f*; *(of servant)* louage *m*

2 *vt* (**a**) *Br (car, room, suit etc)* louer; **to hire sb's services** employer les services de qn; **to hire sth from sb** louer qch à qn

(**b**) *(staff)* engager; *(labourer)* embaucher, engager; *(lawyer, private detective etc)* s'assurer les services de, engager; **hired killer** *or* **assassin** tueur *m* à gages

3 *vi* engager du personnel, embaucher (des ouvriers); **the personnel manager has the power to hire and fire** le chef du personnel a tous droits d'embauche et de renvoi

▸▸ *Br* ***hire car*** voiture *f* de location; ***hire charges*** (frais *mpl* or prix *m* de) location *f*; *Am* ***hired gun*** *(killer)* tueur *m* à gages; *(troubleshooter)* expert *m (appelé en cas de crise)*; ***hired hand*** *(on farm)* ouvrier(ère) *m,f* agricole; *(employee)* employé(e) *m,f*; ***hired help*** *(for housework)* aide *f* ménagère; *Br* ***hire purchase*** location-vente *f*, vente *f* à tempérament; **to buy** *or* **to get sth on hire purchase** acheter qch en location-vente; **I don't own it, it's on hire purchase** ce n'est pas encore à moi, je l'achète en location-vente; ***hire purchase agreement*** contrat *m* de location-vente; ***hire purchase goods*** biens *mpl* achetés en location-vente *ou* à tempérament

▸**hire on** *vi Am (take a job)* prendre un emploi

▸**hire out** *vt sep Br (car, room, suit etc)* louer, donner en location; **to hire out one's services** offrir *ou* proposer ses services; **to hire oneself out** se faire engager; *(labourer)* se faire engager *ou* embaucher

hireling [ˈhaɪəlɪŋ] *n Pej (menial)* larbin *m*; *(illegal or immoral)* mercenaire *m*

hi-res [ˈhaɪrez] *adj Fam Comput (abbr* **high-resolution**) (à) haute résolution ❑

hiring [ˈhaɪərɪŋ] *n* (**a**) *Br (of car, room, suit etc)* location *f* (**b**) *(of employee)* embauche *f*; *Fam* **he does the hiring and firing** il est chargé des embauches et des licenciements ❑

Hiroshima [hɪˈrɒʃɪmə] *n* Hiroshima

hirsute [ˈhɜːsjuːt] *adj Formal* poilu, velu

hirsuteness [ˈhɜːsjuːtnɪs] *n Formal* nature *f* poilue *ou* velue

hirudinid [hɪˈruːdɪnɪd] *n Zool* achète *m*

his [hɪz] **1** *adj (singular)* son (sa); *(plural)* ses; **his table** sa table; **his glasses** ses lunettes; **his university** son université; **it's HIS fault not mine** c'est de sa faute à lui, pas de la mienne; **he has broken his arm** il s'est cassé le bras; **with his hands in his pockets** les mains dans les poches; *Formal* **everyone must do his best** chacun doit faire de son mieux; *Formal* **I object to his borrowing the car** je m'oppose à ce qu'il emprunte la voiture; *Am* **one has his pride** on a sa fierté

2 *pron* (**a**) *(gen → singular)* le sien (la sienne) *m,f*; *(→ plural)* les siens (les siennes) *mpl, fpl*; **it's his** c'est à lui, c'est le sien; **the responsibility is his** c'est lui qui est responsable, la responsabilité lui revient; **is this coat his?** ce manteau est-il à lui?, ce manteau est-il le sien?; **no, THIS one is his** non, le sien c'est celui-ci; **whose fault is it? – his!** qui est le responsable? – lui!

(**b**) *(after preposition)* **a friend of his** un de ses amis; **that dog of his is a nuisance** son sacré chien est vraiment embêtant; **it's always been a fault of his** ça a toujours été son défaut *ou* un de ses défauts; *Formal* **everyone wants what is his** chacun veut ce qui lui revient

(**c**) *(indicating authorship)* de lui; **are these paintings his?** ces tableaux sont-ils de lui?

(**d**) *Fam (his house, flat)* chez lui ❑

3 his and hers *adj* **his and hers towels** des serviettes *fpl* brodées "lui" et "elle", *Hum* **a couple with his and hers outfits** un couple qui s'habille pareil, comme des jumeaux

Hispania [hɪˈspænɪə] *n Arch or Literary* Hispanie *f*

Hispanic [hɪˈspænɪk] **1** *n* Hispano-Américain(e) *m,f*

2 *adj* hispanique

Hispanic-American 1 *n* Hispano-Américain(e) *m,f*

2 *adj* hispano-américain

Hispanicism [hɪˈspænɪˌsɪzəm] *n Ling* hispanisme *m*

Hispanicist [hɪˈspænɪˌsɪst] *n* hispanisant(e) *m,f*

Hispanicization [hɪˌspænɪsaɪˈzeɪʃən] *n* hispanisation *f*

Hispanicize, -ise [hɪˈspænɪˌsaɪz] *vt* hispaniser

Hispaniola [ˌhɪspænɪˈəʊlə] *n* Hispaniola *f*; **in Hispaniola** en Hispaniola

Hispano-American [hɪˈspænəʊ-] **1** *n* Hispano-Américain(e) *m,f*

2 *adj* hispano-américain

hispid [ˈhɪspɪd] *adj Bot & Zool* hispide

hiss [hɪs] **1** *n (of gas, steam)* sifflement *m*, chuintement *m*; *(of person, snake)* sifflement *m*; *(of cat)* crachement *m*; **"be quiet", she said in a hiss** "tais-toi!", dit-elle nerveusement; **there was an angry hiss from the bystanders** l'assistance émit un sifflement de colère; **he was greeted with hisses** il est arrivé sous les sifflets (du public); **the cat backed away with a hiss** le chat a reculé en crachant

2 *vt (say quietly)* souffler; *(bad performer, speaker etc)* siffler; **the audience hissed its disapproval** les spectateurs ont sifflé en signe de mécontentement; **the speaker was hissed off the platform** l'orateur quitta la tribune sous les sifflets (du public)

3 *vi (gas, steam)* siffler, chuinter; *(snake)* siffler; *(cat)* cracher; *(person → speak quietly)* souffler; *(→ in disapproval, anger)* siffler; **there was a loud hissing noise** il y a eu un bruit ressemblant à un fort sifflement; **why is the radiator making all these hissing noises?** pourquoi est-ce que le radiateur siffle comme ça?

hissing [ˈhɪsɪŋ] *n (of gas, steam)* sifflement *m*, chuintement *m*; *(of person, snake)* sifflement *m*

hist [hɪst] *exclam Old-fashioned* chut!

histamine [ˈhɪstəmiːn] *n Biol & Chem* histamine *f*

histidine [ˈhɪstɪˌdiːn] *n Biol & Chem* histidine *f*

histocompatibility [ˈhɪstəʊkəmpætəˈbɪlətɪ] *n Biol* histocompatibilité *f*

histogenesis [ˌhɪstəʊˈdʒenəsɪs], **histogeny** [hɪˈstɒdʒɪnɪ] *n Biol* histogenèse *f*

histogram [ˈhɪstəgræm] *n* histogramme *m*

histologic [ˌhɪstəˈlɒdʒɪk], **histological** [ˌhɪstəˈlɒdʒɪkəl] *adj Biol* histologique

histologist [hɪsˈtɒlədʒɪst] *n Biol* histologiste *mf*

histology [hɪˈstɒlədʒɪ] *n Biol* histologie *f*

histolysis [hɪsˈtɒlɪsɪs] *n Physiol* histolyse *f*

histone [ˈhɪstəʊn] *n Biol & Chem* histon *m*, histone *f*

histopathology [ˌhɪstəʊpəˈθɒlədʒɪ] *n Biol* histopathologie *f*

historian [hɪˈstɔːrɪən] *n* historien(enne) *m,f*

historiated [hɪsˈtɔːrɪˌeɪtɪd] *adj (manuscript)* historié, enjolivé d'ornements

historic [hɪˈstɒrɪk] *adj* (**a**) *(memorable → day, occasion, meeting etc)* historique (**b**) *(of time past)* révolu, passé; *(fear)* ancestral; **in historic times** en des temps révolus

▸▸ ***historic building*** monument *m* historique

historical [hɪˈstɒrɪkəl] *adj* historique; **it's a historical fact** c'est un fait historique; **to be of historical interest** présenter un intérêt historique

▸▸ *Acct* ***historical cost*** coût *m* historique, coût *m* à l'origine; *Acct* ***historical cost accounting*** comptabilité *f* par coûts historiques; ***historical linguistics*** linguistique *f* diachronique; ***historical novel*** roman *m* historique; *Gram* ***historical present*** présent *m* historique

historically [hɪˈstɒrɪkəlɪ] *adv* historiquement; *(traditionally)* traditionnellement

historicism [hɪˈstɒrɪˌsɪzəm] *n* historicisme *m*

historicity [ˌhɪstəˈrɪsɪtɪ] *n* historicité *f*, caractère *m* historique

historicopolitical [hɪˌstɒrɪkəʊpəˈlɪtɪkəl] *adj* historicopolitique

historiographer [ˌhɪstɔːrɪˈɒgrəfə(r)] *n* historiographe *mf*

historiographic [hɪˌstɔːrɪəˈgræfɪk], **historiographical** [hɪˌstɔːrɪəˈgræfɪkəl] *adj* historiographique

historiography [ˌhɪstɔːrɪˈɒgrəfɪ] *n* historiographie *f*

history [ˈhɪstərɪ] (*pl* **histories**) **1** *n* (**a**) *(UNCOUNT) (the past)* histoire *f*; **ancient/modern history** histoire *f* ancienne/moderne; **the history of France, French history** l'histoire *f* de France; **to study history** étudier l'histoire; **I find history fascinating** l'histoire me fascine; **a character in history** un personnage historique *ou* de l'histoire; **throughout history** tout au long de l'histoire; **the history plays of Shakespeare** les pièces *fpl* historiques de Shakespeare; **tell me news, not history!** tu n'aurais pas de nouvelles un peu plus fraîches?; **to make history** entrer dans l'histoire; **a day that has gone down in history** une journée qui est entrée dans l'histoire; **that's ancient history** *(forgotten, in the past)* c'est de l'histoire ancienne; *(everyone knows that)* c'est bien connu; **the rest is history** tout le monde connaît la suite; *Fam* **there's a lot of history between them** il s'est passé beaucoup de choses entre eux ❑; *Fam* **they used to date but they're history now** ils sortaient ensemble mais maintenant c'est fini ❑; *Fam* **he's history!** *(in trouble)* il est fini!; *(no longer in my/her/etc life)* avec lui, c'est terminé

(**b**) *(UNCOUNT) (development, lifespan)* histoire *f*; **the worst disaster in aviation history** *or* **in the history of aviation** le plus grand désastre de l'histoire de l'aviation

(**c**) *(account)* histoire *f*; **Shakespeare's histories** les pièces *fpl* historiques de Shakespeare

(**d**) *(UNCOUNT) (record)* **employment history** expérience *f* professionnelle; **medical history** antécédents *mpl* médicaux; **there is a history of heart disease in my family** il y a des antécédents de maladie cardiaque dans ma famille; **there is a long history of cultural links between these cities** il existe une longue tradition de liens culturels entre ces villes; **the entire family has a history of political activity** toute la famille a fait de la politique; **he has a history of attempted rape** il a plusieurs tentatives de viol à son actif

2 *comp (book, teacher, lesson)* d'histoire

▸▸ *Comput* ***history file*** fichier *m* historique; *Comput* ***history list*** historique m

histrionic [ˌhɪstrɪˈɒnɪk] *adj* (**a**) *Pej (melodramatic)* théâtral (**b**) *Literary Theat* théâtral

histrionically [ˌhɪstrɪˈɒnɪkəlɪ] *adv* (**a**) *Pej (melodramatically)* théâtralement (**b**) *Literary Theat* théâtralement

histrionics [ˌhɪstrɪˈɒnɪks] *npl Pej* comédie *f*, simagrées *fpl*; **I've had enough of his histrionics** j'en ai assez de ses simagrées

HIT [hɪt]

coup	▸ **1 (a), (b)**
succès	▸ **1 (c)**
hit	▸ **1 (d)**
frapper	▸ **2 (a); 3 (a)**
heurter	▸ **2 (b)**
attaquer	▸ **2 (c)**
toucher	▸ **2 (d)**
arriver à	▸ **2 (e)**
buter sur	▸ **2 (f)**
marquer	▸ **2 (g)**

(*pt & pp* **hit**, *cont* **hitting**) **1** *n* (**a**) *(blow)* coup *m*; *Fig* **that was a hit at me** ça m'était destiné, c'est moi qui étais visé

(**b**) *Sport (in ball game)* coup *m*; *(in shooting)* tir *m* réussi; *(in fencing, billiards, snooker)* touche *f*; *(in baseball)* coup *m* de batte; *(in hockey)* coup *m* de crosse; **to score a hit** *(in shooting)* faire mouche, toucher la cible; *(in fencing)* faire *ou* marquer une touche; **he got three hits and one miss** il a réussi trois tirs et en a manqué un; **it only counts as a hit if the bullet goes inside the red line** le tir ne compte que si la balle se trouve à l'intérieur de la ligne rouge; **that was a hit** *(in fencing)* il y a eu touche

(**c**) *(success → record, play, book)* succès *m*; *(→ song)* succès *m*, hit *m*, tube *m*; **Frank Sinatra's greatest hits** les plus grands succès de Frank Sinatra; **to be a big hit** *(record, play, book, song)* faire *ou* être un grand succès, **a hit with the public/the critics** un succès auprès du public/des critiques; **to make a hit with sb** *(person)* conquérir qn; **she's a hit with everyone** elle a conquis tout le monde; **I think you've made a hit with him** je crois que tu l'as conquis; *(romantically)* je crois que tu as fait une touche

(**d**) *Comput (visit to website)* hit *m*, accès *m*; *(in search)* occurrence *f*; **this website counted 20,000 hits last week** ce site Web a été consulté 20 000 fois la semaine dernière

(**e**) *Fam Crime slang (murder)* liquidation *f*, **a hit by the Mafia** un meurtre perpétré par la Mafia

(**f**) *Fam Drugs slang (of hard drugs)* fix *m*; *(of joint)* taffe *f*; *(effect of drugs)* effet ❑ *m (procuré par une drogue)*; **you get a good hit off that grass** cette herbe fait rapidement de l'effet

2 *vt* (**a**) *(strike with hand, fist, stick etc → person)* frapper; *(→ ball)* frapper *ou* taper dans; *(→ nail)* taper sur; *Comput (key)* appuyer sur; **to hit sb in the face/on the head** frapper qn au visage/sur la tête; **they hit him over the head with a baseball bat** ils lui ont donné un coup de batte de baseball sur la tête; **to hit a ball over the net** envoyer un ballon par-dessus le filet; *Fig* **to hit sb where it hurts most** toucher qn là où ça fait mal; *also Fig* **to hit a man when he's down** frapper un homme quand il est à terre; *Fig* **to hit the nail on the head** mettre le doigt dessus; *Fig* **he didn't know what had hit him** il se demandait ce qui lui était arrivé

(**b**) *(come or bring forcefully into contact with → of ball, stone)* heurter; *(→ of bullet, arrow)* atteindre, toucher; **the bottle hit the wall and smashed** la bouteille a heurté le mur et s'est cassée; **the bullet hit him in the shoulder** la balle l'a atteint *ou* touché à l'épaule; **I've been hit!** j'ai été touché!; **the boat was hit by a missile** le bateau a été touché par un missile; **the windscreen was hit by a stone** une pierre a heurté le pare-brise; **he was hit by a stone** il a reçu une pierre; **the two cars didn't actually hit**

each other en fait les deux voitures ne se sont pas heurtées; **to hit the target** *(with gun, missile etc)* toucher la cible; *Fig* **his comments really hit their target** ses remarques ont vraiment fait mouche, il a mis dans le mille avec ses remarques; **the car hit a tree** la voiture a heurté *ou* est rentrée dans un arbre; **the dog was hit by a car** le chien a été heurté par une voiture; **to hit one's head/knee (against sth)** se cogner la tête/le genou (contre qch); **to hit sb's head against sth** frapper *ou* cogner la tête de qn contre qch; *Fig* **to hit the ground running** être opérationnel immédiatement; *Fig* **it suddenly hit me that...** il m'est soudain venu à l'esprit que...

(**c**) *(attack → enemy)* attaquer

(**d**) *(affect)* toucher; **the company has been hit by the recession** l'entreprise a été touchée par la récession; **how badly did the postal strike hit you?** dans quelle mesure avez-vous été touché par la grève des postes?; **the region worst hit by the earthquake** la région la plus sévèrement touchée par le tremblement de terre; **the child's death has hit them all very hard** la mort de l'enfant les a tous durement touchés *ou* frappés; **to be hard hit** être durement touché; *Fam* **it hits everyone in the pocket** tout le monde en subit financièrement les conséquences□, tout le monde le sent passer

(**e**) *(reach)* arriver à; *Fam* **the new model can hit 130 mph on the straight** le nouveau modèle peut atteindre les 210 km/h en ligne droite; *Fam* **to hit a problem** se heurter à un problème *ou* une difficulté; *Mus* **to hit a note** *(singer)* chanter une note; *(instrumentalist)* jouer une note; **to hit the wrong note** *(singer)* chanter faux; *(instrumentalist) & Fig* faire une fausse note; **I can't hit those high notes any more** je n'arrive plus à chanter ces notes aiguës; *Fam* **the circus hits town tomorrow night** le cirque arrive en ville demain soir□; *Fam* **we'll stop for dinner when we hit town** nous nous arrêterons pour dîner quand nous arriverons dans la ville; *Fam* **let's hit the beach!** allons à la plage!□; *Fam* **when it hits the shops** *(product)* quand il sera mis en vente□; **to hit an all-time high/low** *(unemployment, morale etc)* atteindre son plus haut/bas niveau□; *Fam* **to hit rock-bottom** atteindre son point le plus bas□

(**f**) *(encounter → problem, difficulty)* buter sur; **the tunnellers hit rock** les ouvriers qui creusaient le tunnel sont tombés sur de la roche; **you'll hit the rush hour traffic** tu vas te retrouver en plein dans la circulation de l'heure de pointe; **we hit a terrible snowstorm** nous nous sommes trouvés dans une tempête de neige terrible; **to hit a sticky** *or* **bad patch** rencontrer des difficultés

(**g**) *Sport (in cricket → runs)* marquer; *Fencing* toucher; **to hit three runs** *(in cricket)* marquer trois points; **to hit a home run** *(in baseball)* faire un tour complet de circuit

(**h**) *Fam Crime slang (kill)* descendre, liquider

(**i**) *Am Fam (borrow money from)* taper; **to hit sb for $10** taper qn de 10 dollars; **to hit sb for a loan** emprunter de l'argent à qn□

(**j**) *(idioms) Am Fam* **to hit the books** se mettre à étudier□; *Fam* **to hit the bottle** *(drink)* picoler; *(start to drink)* se mettre à picoler; *Fam* **to hit the ceiling** *or* **roof** sortir de ses gonds, piquer une colère folle; *Am Fam Aut* **to hit the gas** appuyer sur le champignon; *Fam* **to hit the hay** *or* **the sack** aller se mettre au pieu, aller se pieuter; *Fam* **if ever this hits the headlines we're in trouble** si jamais cela paraît dans les journaux nous aurons des problèmes□; **to hit home** *(remark, criticism)* faire mouche; **to hit the jackpot** gagner le gros lot; *Fam* **to hit the road** se mettre en route□; *Fam* **hit the road!** *(go away)* fiche le camp!; *Fam* **that really hits the spot!** *(of food, drink)* c'est juste ce dont j'avais besoin□

3 *vi* (**a**) *(person, object)* frapper, taper; **don't hit so hard, we're only playing** ne frappe *ou* tape pas si fort, ce n'est qu'un jeu; **the door was hitting against the wall** la porte cognait contre le mur; **the atoms hit against each other** les atomes se heurtent

(**b**) *(inflation, recession)* se faire sentir

►► *Fam* ***hit list*** liste *f* noire; **to be on sb's hit list** être sur la liste noire de qn; *Fam* ***hit man*** tueur *m* à gages□; *Old-fashioned* ***hit parade*** hit-parade *m*; *Mil* ***hit rate*** taux *m* de tirs réussis; *Fig* taux *m* de réussite; ***hit record*** (disque *m* à) succès *m*; ***hit single, hit song*** succès *m*, hit *m*, tube *m*; *Fam* ***hit squad*** commando *m* de tueurs□; ***hit tune*** air *m* à succès

►**hit back 1** *vi (reply forcefully, retaliate)* riposter, rendre la pareille; **he hit back with accusations that they were giving bribes** il a riposté en les accusant de verser des pots-de-vin; **to hit back at sb/sth** *(in speech)* répondre à qn/qch; **to hit back at the enemy** riposter, répondre à l'ennemi; **our army hit back with a missile attack** notre armée a riposté en envoyant des missiles

2 *vt sep* **to hit the ball back** renvoyer le ballon; **he hit me back** il m'a rendu mon coup

►**hit off** *vt sep* (**a**) *(in words)* décrire *ou* dépeindre à la perfection; *(in paint)* représenter de manière très ressemblante; *(in mimicry)* imiter à la perfection

(**b**) *Fam (idiom)* **to hit it off** *(get on well)* bien s'entendre□; **to hit it off with sb** bien s'entendre avec qn□; **we hit it off immediately** le courant est tout de suite passé entre nous

►**hit on** *vt insep* (**a**) *(find → solution, plan etc)* trouver (**b**) *Am Fam (try to pick up)* draguer

►**hit out** *vi* (**a**) *(physically → once)* envoyer un coup; *(→ repeatedly)* envoyer des coups; **he started hitting out at me** il s'est mis à envoyer des coups dans ma direction

(**b**) *(in speech, writing)* **to hit out at** *or* **against** s'en prendre à, attaquer; **he hits out in his new book** il lance l'offensive dans son nouveau livre

►**hit up** *vt sep Fam Drugs slang* **to hit it up** se piquer

►**hit upon** *vt insep (find → solution, plan etc)* trouver

---

hit-and-miss = **hit-or-miss**

hit-and-run *n* accident *m* avec délit de fuite; **a child died in a hit-and-run yesterday** un enfant est mort hier dans un accident causé par un chauffard qui a pris la fuite; **he's confessed to the hit-and-run** il s'est reconnu coupable du délit de fuite

►► ***hit-and-run accident*** accident *m* avec délit de fuite; *Mil* ***hit-and-run attack*** attaque *f* éclair; ***hit-and-run driver*** conducteur(trice) *m,f* coupable de délit de fuite; *Am Law* ***hit-and-run suit*** poursuites *fpl* pour délit de fuite *(après avoir provoqué un accident de la route)*

hitch [hɪtʃ] **1** *vt* (**a**) *Fam (hitchhike)* **to hitch a lift** *(gen)* se faire emmener en voiture□; *(hitchhiker)* se faire prendre en stop; **can I hitch a lift, Dad?** tu m'emmènes, papa?; **I hitched a lift from the woman next door** je me suis fait emmener par la voisine; **she has hitched her way round Europe** elle a fait toute l'Europe en stop *ou* auto-stop

(**b**) *(railway carriage)* attacher, atteler; *(horse → to fence)* attacher; *(→ to carriage, cart)* atteler; *(rope)* attacher, nouer

(**c**) *Fam (idiom)* **to get hitched** *(one person)* se caser; *(couple)* passer devant Monsieur le Maire

2 *vi* faire du stop *ou* de l'auto-stop; **to hitch to London** aller à Londres en stop; **I spent the summer hitching round the South of France** j'ai passé l'été à voyager dans le sud de la France en auto-stop

3 *n* (**a**) *(difficulty)* problème *m*, anicroche *f*; **there's been a hitch** il y a eu un problème; **without a hitch** *or* **any hitches** sans anicroche

(**b**) *Am Fam (length of time)* **to do a three-year hitch in prison** faire trois ans de prison□; **he's doing a five-year hitch in the navy** il s'est engagé pour cinq ans dans la marine□

(**c**) *(knot)* nœud *m*

(**d**) *(pull)* **to give sth a hitch (up)** remonter *ou* retrousser qch

(**e**) *Am (towbar)* barre *f* de remorquage

►**hitch up** *vt sep* (**a**) *(trousers, skirt etc)* remonter, retrousser (**b**) *(horse, oxen etc)* atteler

hitcher [ˈhɪtʃə(r)] *n Fam* auto-stoppeur(euse)□ *m,f*, stoppeur(euse)□ *m,f*

hitchhike [ˈhɪtʃhaɪk] **1** *vi* faire du stop *ou* de l'auto-stop; **to hitchhike to London** aller à Londres en stop; **I spent the summer hitchhiking round the South of France** j'ai passé l'été à voyager dans le sud de la France en auto-stop

2 *vt* **to hitchhike one's way round Europe** faire l'Europe en auto-stop

hitchhiker [ˈhɪtʃhaɪkə(r)] *n* auto-stoppeur(euse) *m,f*, stoppeur(euse) *m,f*; **I picked up a couple of hitchhikers on the way** j'ai pris quelques auto-stoppeurs *ou* stoppeurs en chemin

hitchhiking [ˈhɪtʃhaɪkɪŋ], **hitching** [ˈhɪtʃɪŋ] *n* auto-stop *m*, stop *m*

hi-tech [ˈhaɪˌtek] **1** *n* (**a**) *(in industry)* technologie *f* de pointe (**b**) *(style of interior design)* high-tech *m inv*

2 *adj* (**a**) *(equipment, industry)* de pointe; **they've adopted a hi-tech approach** ils ont eu recours à la technologie de pointe; **we're very hi-tech here** nous faisons un usage intensif de l'automatisation *ou* de l'informatique ici (**b**) *(design, furniture)* high-tech *(inv)*

hither [ˈhɪðə(r)] *adv Arch* ici; *Literary or Hum* **hither and thither** çà et là, de ci de là

hitherto [ˌhɪðəˈtuː] *adv Formal* jusqu'ici, jusqu'à présent; **a hitherto incurable disease** une maladie jusqu'ici *ou* jusqu'à présent incurable; **the man who had hitherto been considered guilty** l'homme qui avait jusqu'alors été tenu pour coupable

Hitlerism [ˈhɪtləˌrɪzəm] *n Hist* hitlérisme *m*

Hitlerite [ˈhɪtləraɪt] **1** *n* hitlérien(enne) *m,f*

2 *adj* hitlérien

Hitler Youth [ˈhɪtlə-] *n Hist* Jeunesses *fpl* hitlériennes

hit-or-miss *adj (method, approach)* basé sur le hasard; *(work)* fait n'importe comment *ou* à la va comme je te pousse; **the service here is a bit hit-or-miss** le service ici est fait un peu n'importe comment

Hittite [ˈhɪtaɪt] **1** *n* (**a**) *(person)* Hittite *mf* (**b**) *Ling* hittite *m*

2 *adj* hittite

HIV [ˌeɪtʃaɪˈviː] *n Med (abbr* **human immunodeficiency virus**) VIH *m*, HIV *m*; **to be HIV negative** être séronégatif; **to be HIV positive** être séropositif

►► ***HIV case*** cas *m* de séropositivité; ***HIV patients*** patients *mpl* séropositifs

hive [haɪv] **1** *n (for bees)* ruche *f*; *(group of bees)* essaim *m*; *Fig* **a hive of industry** *or* **activity** une vraie *ou* véritable ruche

2 *vt* mettre en ruche

3 *vi* entrer dans une ruche

►**hive off 1** *vt sep* (**a**) *(separate)* détacher *ou* séparer (d'un tout); **the subsidiary companies will be hived off** les filiales deviendront indépendantes

(**b**) *(department, branch of industry)* se débarrasser de; **part of the industry was hived off to private ownership** une partie de cette industrie a été privatisée

2 *vi Fam (go away, slip off)* se tirer, se casser

hives [haɪvz] *n (UNCOUNT) Med* urticaire *f*; **to have hives** avoir de l'urticaire

hiya [ˈhaɪjə] *exclam Fam* salut!

hl *(written abbr* **hectolitre**) hl

HM [ˌeɪtʃˈem] *n (abbr* **His/Her Majesty**) SM

h'm [həm] *exclam* hum, mmm

HMG [ˌeɪtʃemˈdʒiː] *n Br Admin (abbr* **His/Her Majesty's Government**) = expression utilisée sur des documents officiels en Grande-Bretagne

HMI [ˌeɪtʃemˈaɪ] *n Br Sch (abbr* **His/Her Majesty's Inspector**) = inspecteur de l'éducation nationale en Grande-Bretagne

HMMV [ˈhʌmviː] *n Am (abbr* **high-mobility multi-purpose vehicle**) = sorte de grosse jeep utilisée pour le transport de troupes

HMO [ˌeɪtʃemˈəʊ] *n Am (abbr* **Health Maintenance Organization**) = aux États-Unis, clinique de médecine préventive où l'on peut aller lorsqu'on a certains contrats d'assurance

HMP [ˌeɪtʃemˈpiː] *n Br (abbr* **His/Her Majesty's Prison**) = abréviation qui précède les noms de prison en Grande-Bretagne

HMS [ˌeɪtʃemˈes] *n Br Naut (abbr* **His/Her Majesty's Ship**) = dénomination officielle précédant le nom de tous les bâtiments de guerre de la marine britannique

HMSO [ˌeɪtʃemˌesˈəʊ] *n Br Typ (abbr* **His/Her Majesty's Stationery Office**) = maison d'édition publiant les ouvrages ou documents approuvés par le Parlement, les ministères et autres organismes officiels, ≃ l'Imprimerie *f* nationale

HNC [ˌeɪtʃen'siː] *n Br (abbr* **Higher National Certificate**) = brevet de technicien en Grande-Bretagne, ≃ BTS *m*

HND [ˌeɪtʃen'diː] *n Br (abbr* **Higher National Diploma**) = brevet de technicien supérieur en Grande-Bretagne, ≃ DUT *m*

HO [ˌeɪtʃ'əʊ] *n Br* (**a**) *(abbr* **Home Office**) ≃ ministère *m* de l'Intérieur (**b**) *Med (abbr* **House Officer**) ≃ interne *mf*

ho[1] [həʊ] *exclam* (**a**) *(attracting attention)* hé ho! (**b**) *(imitating laughter)* **ho ho!** ha ha ha! (**c**) **ho hum!** *(expressing resignation)* bon!

ho[2] *n very Fam Black Am slang* pouffiasse *f*

hoagie ['həʊgɪ] *n Am* = sorte de gros sandwich

hoar [hɔː(r)] *n* givre *m*

hoard [hɔːd] **1** *n (of goods)* réserve *f*, provisions *fpl*; *(of money)* trésor *m*, magot *m*; **he has a whole hoard of stories** il a une réserve d'histoires assez extraordinaire

2 *vt (goods)* faire provision *ou* des réserves de, stocker; *(money)* amasser, thésauriser

3 *vi* faire des réserves, stocker

hoarder ['hɔːdə] *n (gen)* = personne ou animal qui fait des réserves; *(of money)* thésauriseur(euse) *m,f*; **she's a real hoarder** elle garde absolument tout, elle ne jette absolument rien

hoarding[1] ['hɔːdɪŋ] *n (UNCOUNT) (of goods)* mise *f* en réserve *ou* en stock; *(of money)* thésaurisation *f*, accumulation *f*; **hoarding is forbidden** il est interdit de faire des réserves *ou* des stocks

hoarding[2] *n Br* (**a**) *(fence)* palissade *f* (**b**) *(billboard)* panneau *m* publicitaire *ou* d'affichage

►► *Mktg* ***hoarding site*** emplacement *m* d'affichage

hoarfrost ['hɔːˌfrɒst] *n* givre *m*

hoarse [hɔːs] *adj (person)* enroué; *(voice)* rauque, enroué; **to sound hoarse** être enroué, avoir la voix enrouée; **to shout oneself hoarse** s'enrouer à force de crier

hoarsely ['hɔːslɪ] *adv* d'une voix rauque *ou* enrouée

hoarseness ['hɔːsnɪs] *n* enrouement *m*

hoary ['hɔːrɪ] *(compar* **hoarier**, *superl* **hoariest**) *adj* (**a**) *(greyish white → hair)* blanc (blanche); *(→ person)* aux cheveux blancs, chenu (**b**) *(old → problem, story)* vieux (vieille); **a hoary old joke** une blague usée

hoatzin [həʊ'ætsɪn] *n Orn* hoazin *m*

hoax [həʊks] **1** *n* canular *m*; **to play a hoax on sb** jouer un tour à qn, monter un canular à qn; **(bomb) hoax** fausse alerte *f* à la bombe

2 *vt* jouer un tour à, monter un canular à

►► *Br* ***hoax call*** canular *m* téléphonique; *Br* ***hoax caller*** mauvais plaisant *m (qui donne de fausses informations par téléphone)*

hoaxer ['həʊksə(r)] *n* mauvais plaisant *m*

hob [hɒb] *n (on stove top)* plaque *f* (chauffante); *(by open fire)* plaque *f*

Hobbit ['hɒbɪt] *n*

'The Hobbit' *Tolkien* 'Bilbo le Hobbit'

hobble ['hɒbəl] **1** *vi* boitiller; **she hobbled across the street** elle a traversé la rue en boitillant

2 *vt (horse)* entraver

3 *n* (**a**) *(limp)* boitillement *m*; **to walk with a hobble** marcher en boitillant (**b**) *(for horse)* entrave *f*

►► ***hobble skirt*** jupe *f* entravée

hobbledehoy [ˌhɒbəldɪ'hɔɪ] *n Arch* dadais *m*, empoté *m*

hobby ['hɒbɪ] *(pl* **hobbies**) *n* (**a**) *(pastime)* passe-temps *m inv*, hobby *m* (**b**) *Orn* (faucon *m*) hobereau *m*

hobbyhorse ['hɒbɪˌhɔːs, *pl* -ˌhɔːsɪz] *n* (**a**) *(toy)* cheval *m* de bois *(composé d'une tête sur un manche)* (**b**) *(favourite topic)* sujet *m* favori, dada *m*; **she's off on her hobbyhorse again** la voilà repartie sur son sujet favori *ou* son dada; **to get sb on his/her hobbyhorse** brancher qn sur son sujet favori *ou* dada

hobbyist ['hɒbɪɪst] *n* **a computer hobbyist** un(une) fana de l'informatique

hobgoblin [ˌhɒb'gɒblɪn] *n* diablotin *m*

hobnail ['hɒbneɪl] *n* clou *m* à grosse tête, caboche *f*

►► ***hobnail boots*** chaussures *fpl* ferrées

hobnailed ['hɒbneɪld] *adj* ferré, à gros clous

►► ***hobnailed boots*** chaussures *fpl* ferrées; *Med* ***hobnailed liver*** foie *m* cirrhotique

hobnob ['hɒbnɒb] *(pt & pp* **hobnobbed**, *cont* **hobnobbing**) *vi* **to hobnob with sb** frayer avec qn, fréquenter qn

hobo ['həʊbəʊ] *(pl* **hobos** *or* **hoboes**) *n Am Fam* (**a**) *(tramp)* clochard(e)❑ *m,f*, vagabond(e)❑ *m,f* (**b**) *(itinerant labourer)* saisonnier(ère)❑ *m,f*

►► ***hobo stick*** bâton *m* de clochard

Hobson's choice ['hɒbsənz-] *n* **it's (a case of) Hobson's choice** il n'y a pas vraiment le choix *(se dit d'une situation où le choix n'est qu'apparent)*

Ho Chi Minh ['həʊˌtʃiː'mɪn] *n* Hô Chi Minh

►► ***Ho Chi Minh City*** Hô Chi Minh-Ville

hock [hɒk] **1** *n* (**a**) *(joint, piece of meat)* jarret *m*

(**b**) *(wine)* vin *m* du Rhin

(**c**) *Fam (idioms)* **in hock** *(in pawn)* au clou; *(in debt)* endetté❑; **how much are you in hock for?** de combien es-tu endetté?; **I'm in hock for $500** j'ai 500 dollars de dettes❑; **I'm in hock to him for $500** je lui dois 500 dollars❑; **to get sth out of hock** retirer qch du clou; **he was finally out of hock** enfin il n'avait plus de dettes❑

2 *vt (pawn)* mettre au clou

hockey ['hɒkɪ] **1** *n* (**a**) *Br (field hockey)* hockey *m* (sur gazon) (**b**) *Am (ice hockey)* hockey *m* sur glace

2 *comp (ball, match, pitch, team) Br* de hockey; *Am* de hockey sur glace

►► ***hockey player*** *Br* joueur(euse) *m,f* de hockey, hockeyeur(euse) *m,f*; *Am* joueur(euse) *m,f* de hockey sur glace; ***hockey stick*** *Br* crosse *f* de hockey; *Am* crosse *f* de hockey sur glace

hockshop ['hɒkʃɒp] *n Am Fam* crédit *m* municipal❑, mont-de-piété❑ *m*

hocus-pocus [ˌhəʊkəs'pəʊkəs] *n* (**a**) *(of magician → tricks)* tours *mpl* de passe-passe; *(→ chant)* abracadabra *m* (**b**) *(trickery)* tricherie *f*, supercherie *f*; *(deceptive talk)* paroles *fpl* trompeuses; *(deceptive action)* trucage *m*, supercherie *f*; **it's just hocus-pocus** ce n'est que de la supercherie

hod [hɒd] *n (for bricks)* = ustensile utilisé par les maçons pour porter les briques; *(for mortar)* auge *f*, oiseau *m*; *(for coal)* seau *m* à charbon

►► ***hod carrier*** apprenti *m ou* aide *m* maçon

ho-dad *n Am Fam* (**a**) *(poor surfer)* mauvais(e) surfeur(euse) *m,f* (**b**) *(idiot)* andouille *f*

hodgepodge ['hɒdʒpɒdʒ] *Am* = **hotchpotch**

Hodgkin's disease ['hɒdʒkɪnz-] *n Med* maladie *f* de Hodgkin

hodiernal [ˌhəʊdɪ'ɜːnəl] *adj Arch or Literary* d'aujourd'hui

hoe [həʊ] **1** *n* houe *f*, binette *f*

2 *vt* biner, sarcler

hoedown ['həʊdaʊn] *n Am* bal *m* populaire

hoeing ['həʊɪŋ] *n Agr & Hort* binage *m*, sarclage *m*; **surface hoeing** raclage *m*, raclée *f*

hog [hɒg] *(pt & pp* **hogged**, *cont* **hogging**) **1** *n* (**a**) *(castrated pig)* cochon *m ou* porc *m* châtré; *Am (pig)* cochon *m*, porc *m*

(**b**) *Fam Fig (greedy person)* goinfre *mf*; *(dirty person)* porc *m*

(**c**) *Am Fam (motorbike)* grosse cylindrée *f*, gros cube *m*

(**d**) *Fam Black Am slang (luxury car)* voiture *f* de luxe❑ *(généralement une Cadillac ou une Lincoln Continental)*

(**e**) *Fam (idioms)* **to go the whole hog** ne pas faire les choses à moitié; **why don't we go the whole hog and order champagne?** pourquoi ne pas faire les choses en grand et commander du champagne?; *Am* **to be in hog heaven** être comme un coq en pâte

2 *vt Fam* monopoliser❑; **to hog the television** monopoliser la télé; **to hog the limelight** accaparer *ou* monopoliser l'attention, se mettre en vedette; **to hog the middle of the road** prendre toute la route❑; **stop hogging all the wine for yourself** ne garde pas tout le vin pour ta poire

►► *Zool* ***hog deer*** cerf-cochon *m*

hoggish ['hɒgɪʃ] *adj Fam (habits)* de porc; *(person → dirty)* sale; *(→ greedy)* goulu; **he's very hoggish** c'est un vrai porc

Hogmanay [ˌhɒgmə'neɪ] *n Scot* la Saint-Sylvestre

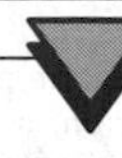

HOGMANAY

Le mot "Hogmanay" vient soit de l'ancien français, soit du gaélique. Il désigne les fêtes de la veille du nouvel an célébrées en Écosse. Traditionnellement, les Écossais préféraient célébrer la nouvelle année plutôt que Noël et jusqu'au XVIIIème siècle, la tradition était d'offrir des cadeaux le jour de l'an. Les coutumes écossaises sont aussi anciennes que diverses: à minuit, les gens chantent la chanson **Auld Lang Syne** (voir ce mot), puis vont rendre visite à leurs voisins avec un morceau de charbon en guise de cadeau, et tout le monde boit une goutte de whisky pour fêter la nouvelle année.

hogshead ['hɒgzhed] *n* tonneau *m*, barrique *f*

hogtie ['hɒgtaɪ] *vt Am (animal)* lier les quatre pattes de; *Fig* **this has hogtied us** nous voici pieds et poings liés; **to be hogtied** être pieds et poings liés

hogwash ['hɒgwɒʃ] **1** *n (UNCOUNT)* (**a**) *Fam (nonsense)* fadaises *fpl*, foutaises *fpl*; **to talk hogwash** raconter des fadaises (**b**) *(pigswill)* eaux *fpl* grasses

2 *exclam Fam* n'importe quoi!

hogweed ['hɒgwiːd] *n Bot* berce *f*

hog-wild *adj Am Fam* **she won the lottery and went hog-wild** après avoir gagné au loto elle s'est autorisé toutes les extravagances

hoick [hɔɪk] *vt Fam* soulever❑; **to hoick oneself up onto a wall** se hisser sur un mur❑; **the helicopter hoicked him out of the sea** l'hélicoptère l'a tiré de la mer avec une secousse❑; **she hoicked her skirt up and climbed the fence** elle a remonté sa jupe et a escaladé la barrière❑

hoi polloi [ˌhɔɪpə'lɔɪ] *npl Pej* **the hoi polloi** la populace

hoi sin [hɔɪ'sɪn] *n Culin* **hoi sin (sauce)** sauce *f* hoisin

hoist [hɔɪst] **1** *vt (sails, flag)* hisser; *(load, person)* lever, hisser; *Fig* **to be hoist with one's own petard** être pris à son propre piège; **she hoisted herself on to the wall** elle s'est hissée sur le mur

2 *n* (**a**) *(elevator)* monte-charge *m*; *(block and tackle)* palan *m* (**b**) *(upward push, pull)* **to give sb a hoist up** *(lift)* soulever qn; *(pull)* tirer qn

hoity-toity [ˌhɔɪtɪ'tɔɪtɪ] *adj Fam Pej* prétentieux❑, péteux; **she's very hoity-toity** c'est une vraie bêcheuse; **to go all hoity-toity** prendre ses grands airs

►**hoke up** [həʊk-] *vt sep Am* agrémenter

hokey ['həʊkɪ] *adj Am Fam (nonsensical)* absurde❑; *(sentimental)* à l'eau de rose

►► *Br* ***hokey cokey*** = danse et chanson traditionnelles londoniennes

hokum ['həʊkəm] *n (UNCOUNT) Am Fam (nonsense)* fadaises *fpl*, foutaises *fpl*; *(sentimentality)* guimauve *f*

HOLD [həʊld]

tenir	► 1A (a), (f); B (a), (b); E (b), (d); 2 (d)
avoir	► 1A (c)
retenir	► 1A (e); C (b)
contenir	► 1A (f)
exercer	► 1A (g)
[illegible]	► 1A (e), (h)
conserver	► 1A (i)
stocker	► 1A (i)
maintenir	► 1B (a)
détenir	► 1A (i); C (a)
croire	► 1D (a)
continuer	► 1D (e)
se tenir	► 2 (a)
tenir bon	► 2 (b)
durer	► 2 (c)
attendre	► 2 (f)
prise	► 3 (a) – (c)
en attente	► 4

(pt & pp **held** [held]) **1** *vt* **A.** (**a**) *(clasp, grasp)* tenir; **to hold sth in one's hand** *(book, clothing, guitar)* avoir qch à la main; *(key, money)* tenir qch dans la main; **to hold sth with both hands** tenir qch à deux mains; **will you hold my coat a second?** peux-tu prendre *ou* tenir mon manteau un instant?; **to hold the door for sb** tenir la porte à *ou* pour qn; *also Fig* **to hold sb's hand**

hnc–hol

tenir la main à qn; **to hold hands** se donner la main, se tenir (par) la main; **hold my hand while we cross the street** donne-moi la main pour traverser la rue; **to hold sb in one's arms** tenir qn dans ses bras; **to hold sb close** *or* **tight** serrer qn contre soi; **hold it tight and don't let go** tiens-le bien et ne le lâche pas; **to hold one's nose** se boucher le nez; **to hold one's sides with laughter** se tenir les côtes de rire

(**b**) *(keep, sustain)* **to hold sb's attention/interest** retenir l'attention de qn; **the film doesn't hold the attention for long** le film ne retient pas l'attention très longtemps; **to hold an audience** tenir un auditoire; **to hold one's serve** *(in tennis)* défendre son service; *Pol* **to hold a seat** *(to be an MP)* occuper un siège de député; *(to be re-elected)* être réélu; **to hold one's own** se défendre, bien se débrouiller; **the Prime Minister held her own during the debate** le Premier ministre a tenu bon *ou* ferme pendant le débat; **she is well able to hold her own** elle sait se défendre; **he can hold his own in chess** il se défend bien aux échecs; **our products hold their own against the competition** nos produits se tiennent bien par rapport à la concurrence; **to hold the floor** garder la parole; **the senator held the floor for an hour** le sénateur a gardé la parole pendant une heure

(**c**) *(have, possess → degree, permit, ticket)* avoir, posséder; *(→ job, position)* avoir, occuper; **do you hold a clean driving licence?** avez-vous déjà été sanctionné pour des infractions au code de la route?; **she holds the post of treasurer** elle occupe le poste de trésorière; **to hold office** *(chairperson, deputy)* être en fonction, remplir sa fonction; *(minister)* détenir *ou* avoir un portefeuille; *(political party, president)* être au pouvoir *ou* au gouvernement; *Rel* **to hold a living** jouir d'un bénéfice; *Fin* **to hold stock** *or* **shares** détenir *ou* avoir des actions; **to hold 5 percent of the shares in a company** détenir 5 pour cent du capital d'une société; *also Fig* **to hold a record** détenir un record; **she holds the world record for the javelin** elle détient le record mondial du javelot

(**d**) *(keep control or authority over)* *Mil* **the guerrillas held the bridge for several hours** les guérilleros ont tenu le pont plusieurs heures durant; *Mil* **to hold the enemy** contenir l'ennemi; *Fig* **to hold centre stage** occuper le centre de la scène; **hold it!, hold everything!** *(stop and wait)* attendez!; *(stay still)* arrêtez!, ne bougez plus!; *Fam Fig* **hold your horses!** pas si vite!

(**e**) *(reserve, set aside)* retenir, réserver; **we'll hold the book for you until next week** nous vous réserverons le livre *ou* nous vous mettrons le livre de côté jusqu'à la semaine prochaine; **will the restaurant hold the table for us?** est-ce que le restaurant va nous garder la table?

(**f**) *(contain)* contenir, tenir; **this bottle holds 2 litres** cette bouteille contient 2 litres; **will this suitcase hold all our clothes?** est-ce que cette valise sera assez grande pour tous nos vêtements?; **the car is too small to hold us all** la voiture est trop petite pour qu'on y tienne tous; **the hall holds a maximum of 250 people** la salle peut accueillir *ou* recevoir 250 personnes au maximum, il y a de la place pour 250 personnes au maximum dans cette salle; **to hold one's drink** bien supporter l'alcool; **the letter holds the key to the murder** la lettre contient la clé du meurtre

(**g**) *(have, exercise)* exercer; **the subject holds a huge fascination for some people** le sujet exerce une énorme fascination sur certaines personnes; **sport held no interest for them** pour eux, le sport ne présentait aucun intérêt

(**h**) *(have in store)* réserver; **who knows what the future may hold?** qui sait ce que nous réserve l'avenir?

(**i**) *(conserve, store)* conserver, détenir; *Comput* stocker; **we can't hold this data forever** nous ne pouvons pas conserver *ou* stocker ces données éternellement; **how much data will this disk hold?** quelle quantité de données cette disquette peut-elle stocker?; **the commands are held in the memory/in a temporary buffer** les instructions sont gardées en mémoire/sont enregistrées dans une mémoire intermédiaire; **my lawyer holds a copy of my will** mon avocat détient *ou* conserve un exemplaire de mon testament; **this photo holds fond memories for me** cette photo me rappelle de bons souvenirs

(**j**) *Aut* **the new car holds the road well** la nouvelle voiture tient bien la route

B. (**a**) *(maintain in position)* tenir, maintenir; **she held her arms by her sides** elle avait les bras le long du corps; **her hair was held in place with hairpins** des épingles (à cheveux) retenaient *ou* maintenaient ses cheveux; **what's holding the picture in place?** qu'est-ce qui tient *ou* maintient le tableau en place?; **hold the picture a bit higher** tenez le tableau un peu plus haut

(**b**) *(carry)* tenir; **to hold oneself upright** *or* **erect** se tenir droit; *also Fig* **to hold one's head high** garder la tête haute

C. (**a**) *(confine, detain)* détenir; **the police are holding him for questioning** la police l'a gardé à vue pour l'interroger; **they're holding him for murder** ils l'ont arrêté pour meurtre; **she was held without trial for six weeks** elle est restée en prison six semaines sans avoir été jugée

(**b**) *(keep back, retain)* retenir; *Law* **to hold sth in trust for sb** tenir qch par fidéicommis pour qn; **the post office will hold my mail for me while I'm away** la poste gardera mon courrier pendant mon absence; *Fig* **once she starts talking politics there's no holding her!** dès qu'elle commence à parler politique, rien ne peut l'arrêter!; *Am* **one burger, hold the mustard!** *(in restaurant)* un hamburger, sans moutarde!

(**c**) *(delay)* **don't hold dinner for me** ne m'attendez pas pour dîner; **they held the plane another thirty minutes** ils ont retenu l'avion au sol pendant encore trente minutes; **hold all decisions on the project until I get back** attendez mon retour pour prendre des décisions concernant le projet; **hold the front page!** ne lancez pas la une tout de suite!; **hold the lift!** ne laissez pas les portes de l'ascenseur se refermer, j'arrive!

(**d**) *(keep in check)* **we have held costs to a minimum** nous avons limité nos frais au minimum; **inflation has been held at the same level for several months** le taux d'inflation est maintenu au même niveau depuis plusieurs mois; **they held their opponents to a goalless draw** ils ont réussi à imposer le match nul

D. (**a**) *(assert, claim)* maintenir, soutenir; *(believe)* croire, considérer; *Formal* **I hold that teachers should be better paid** je considère *ou* j'estime que les enseignants devraient être mieux payés; **the Constitution holds that all men are free** la Constitution stipule que tous les hommes sont libres; **he holds strong beliefs on the subject of abortion** il a de solides convictions en ce qui concerne l'avortement; **she holds strong views on the subject** elle a une opinion bien arrêtée sur le sujet; **her statement is held to be true** sa déclaration passe pour vraie

(**b**) *(consider, regard)* tenir, considérer; **to hold sb responsible for sth** tenir qn pour responsable de qch; **I'll hold you responsible if anything goes wrong** je vous tiendrai pour responsable *ou* je vous considérerai responsable s'il y a le moindre incident; **the president is to be held accountable for his actions** le président doit répondre de ses actes; **to hold sb in contempt** mépriser *ou* avoir du mépris pour qn; **to hold sb in high esteem** avoir beaucoup d'estime pour qn, tenir qn en haute estime

(**c**) *Law (judge)* juger; **the appeal court held the evidence to be insufficient** la cour d'appel a considéré que les preuves étaient insuffisantes

(**d**) *(carry on, engage in → conversation, meeting)* tenir; *(→ party)* donner; *(organize)* organiser; **to hold an election/elections** procéder à une élection/à des élections; **the book fair is held in Frankfurt** la foire du livre se tient *ou* a lieu à Francfort; **the classes are held in the evening** les cours ont lieu le soir; **interviews will be held in early May** les entretiens auront lieu au début du mois de mai *ou* début mai; **to hold talks** être en pourparlers; **the city is holding a service for Armistice Day** la ville organise un office pour commémorer le 11 novembre; **mass is held at eleven o'clock** la messe est célébrée à onze heures

(**e**) *(continue without deviation)* continuer; *Naut* **to hold course** tenir la route; **we held our southerly course** nous avons maintenu le cap au sud, nous avons continué notre route vers le sud; *Mus* **to hold a note** tenir une note

(**f**) *Tel* **will you hold (the line)?** voulez-vous patienter?; **hold the line!** ne quittez pas!; **the line's busy just now – I'll hold** le poste est occupé pour le moment – je patiente *ou* je reste en ligne; **hold all my calls** ne me passez aucun appel

2 *vi* (**a**) *(cling → person)* se tenir, s'accrocher; **she held tight to the railing** elle s'est cramponnée *ou* accrochée à la rampe; **hold fast!, hold tight!** accrochez-vous bien!; *Fig* **their resolve held fast** *or* **firm in the face of fierce opposition** ils ont tenu bon face à une opposition acharnée

(**b**) *(remain in place → nail, fastening)* tenir bon; **the rope won't hold for long** la corde ne tiendra pas longtemps

(**c**) *(last → luck)* durer; *(→ weather)* durer, se maintenir; **prices held at the same level as last year** les prix se sont maintenus au même niveau que l'année dernière; **the pound held firm against the dollar** la livre s'est maintenue par rapport au dollar; **we might buy him a guitar if his interest in music holds** nous lui achèterons peut-être une guitare s'il continue à s'intéresser à la musique

(**d**) *(remain valid → invitation, offer)* tenir; *(→ argument, theory)* valoir, être valable; **to hold good** *(invitation, offer)* tenir; *(promises)* tenir, valoir; *(argument, theory)* rester valable; **the principle still holds good** le principe tient *ou* vaut toujours; **that theory only holds if you consider...** cette théorie n'est valable que si vous prenez en compte...; **the same holds for Spain** il en est de même pour l'Espagne

(**e**) *(stay, remain)* *Fam* **hold still!** ne bougez pas! ❑

(**f**) *(on telephone)* attendre; **the line's** *Br* **engaged** *or Am* **busy, will you hold?** la ligne est occupée, voulez-vous patienter?

3 *n* (**a**) *(grasp, grip)* prise *f*; *(in wrestling)* prise *f*; *Boxing* tenu *m*; **to catch** *or* **to grab** *or* **to seize** *or* **to take hold of sth** se saisir de *ou* saisir qch; **she caught hold of the rope** elle a saisi la corde; **grab (a) hold of that towel** tiens! prends cette serviette; **there was nothing for me to grab hold of** il n'y avait rien à quoi m'accrocher *ou* me cramponner; **get a good** *or* **take a firm hold on** *or* **of the railing** tenez-vous bien à la balustrade; **I still had hold of his hand** je le tenais toujours par la main; **to get hold of sth** *(find)* se procurer *ou* trouver qch; **it's difficult to get hold of this book** ce livre est difficile à trouver; **we got hold of the book you wanted** nous avons trouvé le livre que tu voulais; **where did you get hold of that idea?** où est-ce que tu es allé chercher cette idée?; **to get hold of sb** trouver qn; **I've been trying to get hold of you all week!** je t'ai cherché toute la semaine!; **just wait till the newspapers get hold of the story** attendez un peu que les journaux s'emparent de la nouvelle; **she kept hold of the rope** elle n'a pas lâché la corde; **you'd better keep hold of the tickets** tu ferais bien de garder les billets; **get a hold on yourself** ressaisis-toi, ne te laisse pas aller; **to take hold** *(fire)* prendre; *(idea)* se répandre; *Sport & Fig* **no holds barred** tous les coups sont permis

(**b**) *(controlling force or influence)* prise *f*, influence *f*; **the Church still exerts a strong hold on the country** l'Église a toujours une forte mainmise sur le pays; **to have a hold over sb** avoir de l'influence sur qn; **I have no hold over him** je n'ai aucune prise *ou* influence sur lui; **the Mafia obviously has some kind of hold over him** de toute évidence, la Mafia le tient d'une manière ou d'une autre

(**c**) *(in climbing)* prise *f*

(**d**) *(delay, pause)* pause *f*, arrêt *m*; **the company has put a hold on all new orders** l'entreprise a suspendu *ou* gelé toutes les nouvelles commandes

(**e**) *Am (order to reserve)* réservation *f*; **the**

association put a hold on all the hotel rooms l'association a réservé toutes les chambres de l'hôtel

(**f**) *(prison)* prison *f*; *(cell)* cellule *f*; *(fortress)* place *f* forte

(**g**) *(store → in plane)* soute *f*; *(→ in ship)* cale *f*

(**h**) *Mus* point *m* d'orgue

4 on hold *adv (gen)* & *Tel* en attente; **to put sb on hold** mettre qn en attente; **we've put the project on hold** nous avons mis le projet en attente; **the operator kept me on hold for ten minutes** le standardiste m'a mis en attente pendant dix minutes

▸**hold against** *vt sep* **to hold sth against sb** en vouloir à qn de qch; **his collaboration with the enemy will be held against him** sa collaboration avec l'ennemi lui sera préjudiciable; **he lied to her and she still holds it against him** il lui a menti et elle lui en veut toujours; **I hope you won't hold it against me if I decide not to accept** j'espère que tu ne m'en voudras pas si je décide de ne pas accepter

▸**hold back 1** *vt sep* (**a**) *(control, restrain → animal, person)* retenir, tenir; *(→ crowd, enemy forces)* contenir; *(→ anger, laughter, tears)* retenir, réprimer; *(→ inflation)* contenir; **the government has succeeded in holding back inflation** le gouvernement a réussi à contenir l'inflation

(**b**) *(keep → money, supplies)* retenir; *Fig (→ information, truth)* cacher, taire; **she's holding something back from me** elle me cache quelque chose

(**c**) *Am Sch* **they held her back a year** ils lui ont fait redoubler une classe, ils l'ont fait redoubler

(**d**) *(prevent progress of)* empêcher de progresser; **his difficulties with maths are holding him back** ses difficultés en maths l'empêchent de progresser; **lack of investment is holding industry back** l'absence d'investissements freine l'industrie

2 *vi (stay back)* rester en arrière; *Fig (restrain oneself)* se retenir; **he has held back from making a commitment** il s'est abstenu de s'engager; **the president held back before sending in the army** le président a hésité avant d'envoyer les troupes; **don't hold back, tell me everything** vas-y, dis-moi tout

▸**hold down** *vt sep* (**a**) *(keep in place → paper, carpet)* maintenir en place; *(→ person)* forcer à rester par terre, maintenir au sol; **it took four men to hold him down** il a fallu quatre hommes pour le maîtriser *ou* pour le maintenir au sol

(**b**) *(keep to limit)* restreindre, limiter; **they're holding unemployment down to 4 percent** ils maintiennent le taux de chômage à 4 pour cent; **to hold prices down** empêcher les prix de monter, empêcher la montée des prix

(**c**) *(of employee)* **to hold down a job** *(occupy)* avoir un emploi; *(keep)* garder un emploi; **he's never managed to hold down a job** il n'a jamais pu garder un emploi bien longtemps; **although she's a student, she holds down a full-time job** bien qu'elle étudie, elle occupe un poste à plein temps

(**d**) *Comput (key, mouse button)* maintenir enfoncé

▸**hold forth** *vi* pérorer, disserter; **he held forth on the evils of drink** il a fait un long discours sur les conséquences néfastes de l'alcool

▸**hold in** *vt sep* (**a**) *(stomach)* rentrer

(**b**) *(emotion)* retenir; *(anger)* contenir

▸**hold off 1** *vt sep* (**a**) *(keep at distance)* tenir à distance *ou* éloigné; **the troops held off the enemy** les troupes ont tenu l'ennemi à distance; **they managed to hold off the attack** ils ont réussi à repousser l'attaque; **I can't hold the reporters off any longer** je ne peux plus faire attendre *ou* patienter les journalistes (**b**) *(delay, put off)* remettre à plus tard; **he held off going to see the doctor until May** il a attendu le mois de mai pour aller voir le médecin; **I held off making a decision** j'ai remis la décision à plus tard

2 *vi* (**a**) *(rain)* **at least the rain held off** au moins il n'a pas plu

(**b**) *(abstain)* s'abstenir; **hold off from smoking for a few weeks** abstenez-vous de fumer *ou* ne fumez pas pendant quelques semaines

▸**hold on 1** *vi* (**a**) *(grasp, grip)* tenir bien, s'accrocher; **to hold on to sth** bien tenir qch, s'accrocher à qch, se cramponner à qch; **hold on!** accrochez-vous!; **hold on to your hat!** tenez votre chapeau (sur la tête)!

(**b**) *(keep possession of)* garder; **hold on to this contract for me** *(keep it)* garde-moi ce contrat; **all politicians try to hold on to power** tous les hommes politiques essaient de rester au pouvoir; **hold on to your dreams/ideals** accrochez-vous à vos rêves/idéaux

(**c**) *(continue, persevere)* tenir, tenir le coup; **how long can you hold on?** combien de temps pouvez-vous tenir (le coup)?; **I can't hold on much longer** je ne peux pas tenir (le coup) beaucoup plus longtemps

(**d**) *(wait)* attendre; *(stop)* arrêter; **hold on just one minute!** *(stop)* arrêtez!; *(wait)* attendez!, pas si vite!; **hold on, how do I know I can trust you?** attends un peu! qu'est-ce qui me prouve que je peux te faire confiance?; *Tel* **hold on please!** ne quittez pas!; **I had to hold on for several minutes** j'ai dû patienter plusieurs minutes

2 *vt sep (maintain in place)* tenir *ou* maintenir en place; **her hat is held on with pins** son chapeau est maintenu (en place) par des épingles

▸**hold out 1** *vi* (**a**) *(last → supplies, stocks)* durer; **will the car hold out till we get home?** la voiture tiendra-t-elle (le coup) jusqu'à ce qu'on rentre?

(**b**) *(refuse to yield)* tenir bon, tenir le coup; **the garrison held out for weeks** la garnison a tenu bon pendant des semaines; **the management held out against any suggested changes** la direction a refusé tous les changements proposés

2 *vt sep (extend)* tendre; **she held out the book to him** elle lui a tendu le livre; *also Fig* **to hold out one's hand to sb** tendre la main à qn; **I held out my hand** j'ai tendu la main; **his mother held her arms out to him** sa mère lui a ouvert *ou* tendu les bras

3 *vt insep (offer)* offrir; **I can't hold out any promise of improvement** je ne peux promettre aucune amélioration; **the doctors hold out little hope for him** les médecins ont peu d'espoir pour lui; **science holds out some hope for cancer patients** la science offre un espoir pour les malades du cancer

▸**hold out for** *vt insep* exiger; **the workers held out for a shorter working week** les ouvriers réclamaient une semaine de travail plus courte; **we're holding out for a higher offer** nous attendons qu'on nous en offre un meilleur prix

▸**hold out on** *vt insep Fam* **you're holding out on me!** tu me caches quelque chose! ❑

▸**hold over** *vt sep* (**a**) *(position)* tenir au-dessus de; **she held the glass over the sink** elle tenait le verre au-dessus de l'évier; *Fig* **they hold the threat of redundancy over their workers** ils maintiennent la menace de licenciement sur leurs ouvriers

(**b**) *(postpone)* remettre, reporter; **we'll hold these items over until the next meeting** on va remettre ces questions à la prochaine réunion; **payment was held over for six months** le paiement a été différé pendant six mois

(**c**) *(retain)* retenir, garder; **they're holding the show over for another month** ils vont laisser le spectacle à l'affiche encore un mois

(**d**) *Mus* tenir

▸**hold to 1** *vt insep (promise, tradition)* s'en tenir à, rester fidèle à; *(decision)* maintenir, s'en tenir à; **you must hold to your principles** vous devez rester fidèle à vos principes

2 *vt sep* **we held him to his promise** nous lui avons fait tenir parole; **if I win, I'll buy you lunch – I'll hold you to that!** si je gagne, je t'invite à déjeuner – je te prends au mot!

▸**hold together** *vt sep (book, car)* maintenir; *(two objects)* maintenir ensemble; *(community, family)* maintenir l'union de; **the two pieces of wood are held together by nails** les deux morceaux de bois sont cloués ensemble; **we need a leader who can hold the workers together** il nous faut un chef qui puisse rallier les ouvriers

▸**hold up 1** *vt sep* (**a**) *(lift, raise)* lever, élever; **I held up my hand** j'ai levé la main; **hold the picture up to the light** tenez la photo à contre-jour; **to hold up one's head** redresser la tête; *Fig* **she felt she would never be able to hold her head up again** elle pensait qu'elle ne pourrait plus jamais marcher la tête haute

(**b**) *(support)* soutenir; **my trousers were held up with safety pins** mon pantalon était maintenu par des épingles de sûreté

(**c**) *(present as example)* **they were held up as an example of efficient local government** on les présentaient comme un exemple de gouvernement local compétent; **to hold sb up to ridicule** tourner qn en ridicule

(**d**) *(delay)* retarder; *(stop)* arrêter; **the traffic held us up** la circulation nous a mis en retard; **the accident held up traffic for an hour** l'accident a bloqué la circulation pendant une heure; **our departure was held up by bad weather** notre départ a été retardé par le mauvais temps; **I was held up** j'ai été retenu; **the project was held up for lack of funds** *(before it started)* le projet a été mis en attente faute de financement; *(after it started)* le projet a été interrompu faute de financement; **the goods were held up at customs** les marchandises ont été immobilisées à la douane

(**e**) *(rob)* faire une attaque à main armée; **to hold up a bank** faire un hold-up dans une banque

2 *vi (clothing, equipment)* tenir; *(supplies)* tenir, durer; *(weather)* se maintenir; **the car held up well during the trip** la voiture a bien tenu le coup pendant le voyage; **she's holding up well under the pressure** elle supporte bien la pression; **my finances are holding up well** je tiens le coup financièrement

▸**hold with** *vt insep Br (agree with)* être d'accord avec; *(approve of)* approuver; **I don't hold with her ideas on socialism** je ne suis pas d'accord avec *ou* je ne partage pas ses idées concernant le socialisme; **his mother doesn't hold with private schools** sa mère est contre *ou* désapprouve les écoles privées

---

holdall ['həʊldɔːl] *n Br* (sac *m*) fourre-tout *m inv*

holder ['həʊldə(r)] *n* (**a**) *(for lamp, plastic cup etc)* support *m*

(**b**) *(person → of ticket, permit)* détenteur(trice) *m,f*; *(→ of passport, post, diploma, account)* titulaire *mf*; *(→ of lease)* locataire *mf*; *(→ of record, cup)* détenteur(trice) *m,f*; *(→ of title)* détenteur(trice) *m,f*, tenant(e) *m,f*; *(→ of opinion, belief)* tenant *m*; *Fin (→ of stock, shares, bonds, bill)* porteur(euse) *m,f*, détenteur(trice) *m,f*; *(→ of patent)* concessionnaire *mf*; *(→ of insurance policy)* assuré(e) *m,f*

holding ['həʊldɪŋ] *n* (**a**) *(of meeting)* tenue *f*

(**b**) *(in boxing)* **holding is against the rules** il est contraire au règlement de tenir son adversaire

(**c**) *(land)* propriété *f*

(**d**) *Fin* participation *f*; **holdings** *(lands)* propriétés *fpl*, terres *fpl*; *(stocks)* participation *f*, portefeuille *m*; **he has holdings in several companies** il est actionnaire de plusieurs sociétés

Fin **holding company** (société *f* en) holding *m*, société *f* à portefeuille; ***holding costs*** coûts *mpl* de détention; ***holding operation*** opération *f* de maintien; *Aviat* ***holding pattern*** circuit *m* d'attente; **we were in a holding pattern over Heathrow for two hours** nous avons eu une attente de deux heures au-dessus de Heathrow

holdover ['həʊld,əʊvə(r)] *n Am* vestige *m*; *Cin & Theat* = film ou pièce de théâtre qui reste à l'affiche plus longtemps que prévu; **a holdover from the war** un vestige de la guerre

hold-up 1 *n* (**a**) *(robbery)* hold-up *m*, vol *m* à main armée (**b**) *(delay → on road, railway track etc)* ralentissement *m*; *(→ in production, departure etc)* retard *m*; **there's been a hold-up on the line** il y a eu des perturbations sur la ligne; **there have been no hold-ups with the project** le projet n'a eu à souffrir d'aucun retard

2 hold-ups *npl (stockings)* bas *mpl* autofixants

hole [həʊl] **1** *n* (**a**) *(in the ground)* trou *m*; *(in wall, roof etc)* trou *m*; *(in clouds)* éclaircie *f*; **to dig a**

hole creuser un trou; **his socks were full of** *or* **in holes** ses chaussettes étaient pleines de trous; **his sock's got a hole in it** il a un trou à sa chaussette; **to wear a hole in sth** faire un trou à qch; *Fig* **to make a hole in one's savings/a bottle of whisky** bien entamer ses économies/une bouteille de whisky; *Fig* **money burns a hole in my pocket** l'argent me file entre les doigts; **to pick holes in an argument** trouver des failles à une argumentation; **to try to pick holes in an argument** chercher des failles à une argumentation; **his argument's full of holes** son argumentation est pleine de défauts *ou* failles; *Fam* **a hole in the wall** *(restaurant)* un restaurant minuscule □; *(cash dispenser)* un distributeur (de billets) □; *Fam* **I need that like a hole in the head** c'est vraiment la dernière chose dont j'aie besoin □; *Fam* **you're talking through a hole in your head** tu racontes n'importe quoi □; *Fam* **that's filled a hole!** ça m'a bien calé!; *Med* **hole in the heart** malformation *f* du cœur; **to have a hole in the heart** avoir une malformation du cœur, avoir la maladie bleue; **a baby born with a hole in the heart** un enfant bleu

(**b**) *Fam Pej (boring place)* trou *m*; **what a hole!** *(town)* quel trou!; **this is an awful hole!** *(house, pub, disco)* c'est mortel ici!

(**c**) *Fam (tricky situation)* pétrin *m*; **to be in a hole** être dans le pétrin; **to get sb out of a hole** sortir qn du pétrin

(**d**) *Golf* trou *m*; **to get a hole in one** faire un trou en un; **an eighteen-hole (golf) course** un parcours de dix-huit trous; **we played a few holes of golf together** nous avons fait quelques trous ensemble au golf

(**e**) *Vulg (vagina)* chagatte *f*; *Br* **to get one's hole** baiser

2 *vt* (**a**) *(make hole in)* trouer

(**b**) *Golf* **to hole a putt** faire le trou

3 *vi* (**a**) *(sock, stocking)* se trouer

(**b**) *Golf* faire le trou; **to hole in four** faire le trou en quatre (coups)

►► ***hole punch*** perforatrice *f*

►**hole out** *vi Golf* finir le trou

►**hole up 1** *vi* (**a**) *(animal)* se terrer (**b**) *Fam (hide)* se planquer

2 *vt sep (usu passive)* **they're holed up in a hotel** ils se planquent *ou* ils sont planqués dans un hôtel

hole-and-corner *adj Fam (meeting, love affair etc)* clandestin □, secret(ète) □

hole-in-the-heart *adj Med (baby)* bleu; **a hole-in-the-heart operation** une opération d'une malformation du cœur

holey ['həʊlɪ] *adj* troué, plein de trous

-holic [-ˌhɒlɪk] *suff Fam Hum* **chocaholic** accro *mf* au chocolat; **workaholic** bourreau *m* de travail; **shopaholic** maniaque *mf* du shopping; *Am* **foodaholic** goinfre *mf*

holiday ['hɒlɪdeɪ] **1** *n* (**a**) *Br (period without work)* vacances *fpl*; **Christmas holiday** vacances *fpl* de Noël; **everyone is getting ready for the Christmas holidays** tout le monde prépare les fêtes; **summer holiday** *or* **holidays** vacances *fpl* d'été; *Sch* grandes vacances *fpl*; **on holiday** en vacances; **to go on holiday** aller *ou* partir en vacances; **to go on a camping holiday** aller passer ses vacances en camping; **I'm going on holiday in a week** je pars en vacances dans une semaine; **we went to Greece for our holidays last year** nous sommes allés passer nos vacances en Grèce l'année dernière; **the holiday rush has started** la folie *ou* cohue des départs en vacances a commencé; **to take a holiday/two months' holiday** prendre des vacances/deux mois de vacances; **how much** *or* **how long a holiday do you get?** combien de vacances as-tu?; **holiday with pay, paid holidays** congés *mpl* payés; **I need** *or* **could do with a holiday** j'ai besoin de vacances; **take a holiday from the housework** oublie un peu les travaux ménagers; **I wish I could take a holiday from the children for a few days** si seulement je pouvais passer quelques jours sans les enfants; **it's no holiday!** ce n'est pas des vacances!

(**b**) *(day off)* jour *m* de congé; **tomorrow is a holiday** demain c'est férié

2 *comp (mood, feeling, destination)* de vacances; *(pay)* versé pendant les vacances

3 *vi Br* passer les vacances

►► ***holiday brochure*** catalogue *m* de vacances; *Br* ***holiday camp*** = centre de vacances familial (avec animations et activités diverses); *Br* ***holiday cottage*** gîte *m*; ***holiday entitlement*** nombre *m* de jours de vacances auquel un employé a droit, droit *m* aux vacances; *Br* ***holiday home*** maison *f* de vacances, résidence *f* secondaire; ***holiday period*** période *f* de fêtes; *Br* ***holiday resort*** lieu *m* de vacances *ou* de séjour; *Br* ***holiday season*** saison *f* des vacances; ***the holiday traffic*** la circulation des départs en vacances; ***holiday village*** village *m* des vacances

holidaymaker ['hɒlɪdeɪˌmeɪkə(r)] *n Br* vacancier(ère) *m,f*

holier-than-thou ['həʊlɪə-] *adj Pej (attitude, tone, person)* moralisateur; **to be holier-than-thou towards other people** se comporter en pharisien avec les autres

holiness ['həʊlɪnɪs] *n* sainteté *f*; **His/Your Holiness** Sa/Votre Sainteté

holism ['həʊlɪzəm] *n Med & Phil* holisme *m*

holistic [həʊ'lɪstɪk] *adj Med & Phil* holistique

►► ***holistic medicine*** médecine *f* holistique

Holland ['hɒlənd] **1** *n (country)* Hollande *f*, Pays-Bas *mpl*; **in Holland** en Hollande, aux Pays-Bas

2 Hollands *n Arch (gin)* genièvre *m* de Schiedam

holland ['hɒlənd] *n Tex* hollande *f*

hollandaise (sauce) [ˌhɒlən'deɪz-] *n Culin* sauce *f* hollandaise

holler ['hɒlə(r)] *esp Am Fam* **1** *n* braillement *m*; **to give** *or* **to let out a holler** brailler

2 *vt* brailler

3 *vi* brailler, beugler

►**holler out** *esp Am Fam* **1** *vt sep* brailler

2 *vi* brailler, beugler

hollow ['hɒləʊ] **1** *n* (**a**) *(in tree)* creux *m*, cavité *f* (**b**) *(in ground)* enfoncement *m*, dénivellation *f* (**c**) *(in hand, back)* creux *m*

2 *adj* (**a**) *(not solid → tree, container)* creux; **to have a hollow feeling in one's stomach** avoir une sensation de vide dans l'estomac; **to feel hollow** *(hungry)* avoir le ventre *ou* l'estomac creux; *Fam* **you must have hollow legs!** *(able to eat a lot)* tu dois avoir le ver solitaire!; *(able to drink a lot)* qu'est-ce que tu peux boire!, tu as une sacrée descente!

(**b**) *(sunken → eyes, cheeks)* creux, cave

(**c**) *(empty → sound)* creux, caverneux; *(→ laugh, laughter)* faux (fausse), forcé; **to feel hollow** *(emotionally)* se sentir vide *ou* vidé; **in a hollow voice** d'une voix éteinte; **she gave a hollow laugh** elle a ri d'un air un peu faux *ou* forcé, elle a ri jaune

(**d**) *(worthless → promise, words, excuse)* vain; **it was a hollow victory for her** cette victoire lui semblait dérisoire

3 *adv* (**a**) **to sound hollow** *(tree, wall)* sonner creux; *(laughter, excuse, promise)* sonner faux

(**b**) *Br Fam* **to beat sb hollow** battre qn à plate(s) couture(s)

4 *vt* creuser

►**hollow out** *vt sep* creuser

Holloway ['hɒləweɪ] *n (prison)* = grande prison pour femmes dans le nord de Londres

hollow-cheeked *adj* aux joues creuses

hollow-eyed *adj* aux yeux caves *ou* enfoncés

hollowness ['hɒləʊnɪs] *n* (**a**) *(of tree, container)* creux *m*, cavité *f* (**b**) *(of features)* **the hollowness of his eyes** ses yeux enfoncés; **the hollowness of his cheeks** ses joues creuses (**c**) *(of sound)* timbre *m* caverneux; *(of laugh, laughter)* fausseté *f*; **the hollowness of her voice** sa voix éteinte (**d**) *(of promise, words, excuse)* fausseté *f*, manque *m* de sincérité; **the hollowness of a victory** une victoire qui ne veut rien dire

holly ['hɒlɪ] *n Bot (tree, leaves)* houx *m*

►► ***holly berry*** baie *f* de houx, cenelle *f*; ***holly tree*** houx *m*

hollyhock ['hɒlɪhɒk] *n Bot* rose *f* trémière

holly-oak *n Bot* chêne *m* vert, yeuse *f*

Hollywood ['hɒlɪwʊd] **1** *n* Hollywood

2 *adj* hollywoodien

►► ***the Hollywood Bowl*** = salle de concerts semi-couverte à Hollywood

holm¹ [həʊm] *n Br (island)* petite île *f*, îlot *m (de rivière)*

holm² *n Bot* chêne *m* vert, yeuse *f*

►► ***holm oak*** chêne *m* vert, yeuse *f*

holmium ['hɒlmɪəm] *n Chem* holmium *m*

holocaust ['hɒləkɔːst] *n* holocauste *m*; **the Holocaust** l'Holocauste *m*

Holocene ['hɒləˌsiːn] *Geol* **1** *n* holocène *m*

2 *adj* holocène

Holofernes [ˌhɒlə'fɜːniːz] *pr n Bible* Holopherne

hologram ['hɒləgræm] *n* hologramme *m*

holograph ['hɒləgræf] **1** *n* document *m* olographe *ou* holographe

2 *adj* olographe, holographe

holographic [ˌhɒlə'græfɪk] *adj Phot* holographique

holography [hɒ'lɒgrəfɪ] *n* holographie *f*

holophrase ['hɒləfreɪz] *n Ling* holophrase *f*

holophrastic [hɒlə'fræstɪk] *adj Ling* holophrastique

holotype ['hɒləˌtaɪp] *n Biol* holotype *m*

hols [hɒlz] *npl Br Fam* vacances □ *fpl*

Holstein ['hɒlstaɪn] *n Am (cow)* frisonne *f*

holster ['həʊlstə(r)] *n (for gun → on waist, shoulder)* étui *m* de revolver; *(→ on saddle)* fonte *f*; *(for piece of equipment)* étui *m*

holt [hɒlt] *n* cattiche *f*

holy ['həʊlɪ] *(compar* **holier,** *superl* **holiest,** *pl* **holies) 1** *adj* (**a**) *(sacred → bread, water)* bénit; *(→ place, ground, day)* saint; **to swear by all that is holy** jurer par tous les saints

(**b**) *(devout)* saint

(**c**) *Fam (as intensifier)* **that child is a holy terror** *(mischievous)* cet enfant est un vrai démon; **the new headmaster is a holy terror** *(intimidating)* le nouveau principal est redoutable □; **to have a holy fear of sth** avoir une sainte peur de qch; *Am Pej* **he's a real holy roller** il est vraiment prêchi-prêcha; **holy smoke!, holy mackerel!, holy cow!** mince alors!, ça alors!, Seigneur!; *Am Vulg* **holy shit!** merde alors!

2 *n Rel* **the Holy of Holies** le saint des saints; *Fig Hum (inner sanctum)* sanctuaire *m*, antre *m* sacré; *(special place)* lieu *m* saint

►► ***the Holy Bible*** la Sainte Bible; ***the Holy City*** la Ville sainte; ***Holy Communion*** la Sainte Communion; **to take Holy Communion** communier, recevoir la Sainte Communion; ***the Holy Family*** la Sainte Famille; ***the Holy Father*** le Saint-Père; ***the Holy Ghost*** le Saint-Esprit, l'Esprit *m* saint; ***the Holy Grail*** le (Saint) Graal; *Rel* ***Holy Innocents' Day*** la fête des saints Innocents; ***Holy Island*** Lindisfarne; *Fam* ***Holy Joe*** *Br (religious person)* bigot *m*; *Am (parson, chaplain)* curé *m*; ***the Holy Land*** la Terre sainte; ***the Holy Loch*** = loch écossais, au nord-ouest de Glasgow, qui servit à entreposer des sous-marins nucléaires américains; ***holy matrimony*** les liens *mpl* sacrés du mariage; **to be joined in holy matrimony** être unis par les liens *mpl* sacrés du mariage; ***holy orders*** ordres *mpl*; **to take holy orders** entrer dans les ordres; *Hist* ***the Holy Roman Empire*** le Saint-Empire romain; ***the Holy Rood*** la Sainte Croix; ***Holy Scripture*** l'Écriture *f* sainte, les Saintes Écritures *fpl*; ***the Holy See*** le Saint-Siège; ***the Holy Sepulchre*** le Saint-Sépulcre; ***the Holy Spirit*** le Saint-Esprit, l'Esprit *m* saint; ***the Holy Synod*** le saint-synode; ***the Holy Trinity*** la Sainte Trinité; ***holy war*** guerre *f* sainte; ***Holy Week*** la Semaine sainte; ***Holy Writ*** l'Écriture *f* sainte, les Saintes Écritures *fpl*; *Fig* **it's not Holy Writ!** ce n'est pas parole d'évangile!

Holyrood Palace ['hɒlɪruːd-] *n* = palais à Édimbourg, propriété de la famille royale

homage ['hɒmɪdʒ] *n* hommage *m*; **to pay** *or* **to do homage to sb, to do sb homage** rendre hommage à qn; **in silent homage** en hommage silencieux

hombre ['ɒmbreɪ] *n Am Fam* mec *m*

homburg ['hɒmbɜːg] *n* chapeau *m* mou, feutre *m* souple

HOME [həʊm]

maison	►**1 (a)**
chez-soi	►**1 (a)**
foyer	►**1 (b)**
patrie	►**1 (c)**
habitat	►**1 (d)**
arrivée	►**1 (f)**
début	►**1 (g)**

chez soi	►2 (a)
au pays natal	►2 (b)
à fond	►2 (c)
familial	►3 (a)
à/pour la maison	►3 (b)
national	►3 (c), (d)

1 *n* (**a**) *(one's house)* maison *f*; *(more subjectively)* chez-soi *m inv*; **I've come straight from home** je viens (directement) de chez moi; **a home from home** un second chez-soi; **I left home at sixteen** j'ai quitté la maison à seize ans; **her home is not far from mine** sa maison n'est pas loin de chez moi; **he insulted me in my own home!** il m'a insulté sous mon propre toit!; **to have a home of one's own** avoir un foyer *ou* un chez-soi; **how long has he been missing from home?** depuis combien de temps a-t-il disparu de la maison?; **to be away from home** être parti *ou* absent *ou* en voyage; **he was found far away from home** on l'a trouvé loin de chez lui; **his home is in Nice** il habite Nice; **Glasgow is her second home** Glasgow est sa deuxième patrie; **New York will always be home for me!** c'est toujours à New York que je me sentirai chez moi!; **when did she make her home in Hollywood?** quand s'est-elle installée à Hollywood?; **emigrants came to make their homes in Canada** des émigrés sont venus s'installer au Canada; **to give sb a home** recueillir qn chez soi; **they sell lovely things for the home** ils vendent toutes sortes de très jolis accessoires pour la maison; **they have a lovely home!** c'est très agréable chez eux!; **at home** chez soi, à la maison; **to stay at home** rester à la maison; **come and see me at home** passez me voir à la maison; *Formal* **Mrs Carr is not at home on Mondays** Mme Carr ne reçoit pas le lundi; **there was nobody at home** il n'y avait personne à la maison; **make yourself at home** faites comme chez vous; **he made himself at home in the chair** il s'est mis à l'aise dans le fauteuil; **I don't feel at home here** je me sens dépaysé ici, je ne me sens pas chez moi ici; **she feels at home everywhere!** elle est à l'aise partout!; **to be** *or* **to feel at home with sth** se sentir à l'aise avec qch; **he doesn't yet feel at home with the machine** il n'est pas encore à l'aise avec la machine; **I work out of** *or* **at home** je travaille à domicile *ou* chez moi; *Fam* **what's that when it's at home?** qu'est-ce que c'est que ça?; *Ironic* **don't you have a home to go to?** tu as l'intention de passer la nuit ici?; *Prov* **there's no place like home** = on n'est vraiment bien que chez soi; *Prov* **home is where the heart is** = où le cœur aime, là est le foyer; **home sweet home** foyer, doux foyer

(**b**) *(family unit)* foyer *m*; *Admin* habitation *f*, logement *m*; **the father left home** le père a abandonné le foyer; **to start** *or* **to set up a home** fonder un foyer; **how are things at home?** comment ça va chez toi?; **are you having problems at home?** est-ce que tu as des problèmes chez toi?; **a happy home** une famille heureuse; **he comes from a good home** il vient d'une famille comme il faut; **good home wanted for three kittens** *(on notice)* je donne trois chatons

(**c**) *(native land)* patrie *f*, pays *m* natal; **it's the same at home** c'est la même chose chez nous *ou* dans notre pays; **at home and abroad** dans notre pays et à l'étranger; *Fig* **this discussion is getting a bit close to home!** on aborde un sujet dangereux!; **let's look at a situation closer to** *or* **nearer home** examinons une situation qui nous concerne plus directement; **Kentucky, the home of bourbon** Kentucky, le pays du bourbon; **the home of jazz** le berceau du jazz

(**d**) *Bot & Zool* habitat *m*

(**e**) *(mental hospital)* maison *f* de repos; *(old people's home)* maison *f* de retraite; *(children's home)* foyer *m* pour enfants

(**f**) *Sport (finishing line)* arrivée *f*; *(on board game)* case *f* départ; *(goal)* but *m*; **they play better at home** ils jouent mieux sur leur terrain; **Arsenal are playing at home on Saturday** Arsenal joue à domicile samedi; **to be at home to** recevoir; **the Rams meet the Braves at home** les Rams jouent à domicile contre les Braves

(**g**) *Comput (beginning of document)* début *m*

2 *adv* (**a**) *(to or at one's house)* chez soi, à la maison; **to go home** rentrer (chez soi *ou* à la maison); **what time did you get home?** à quelle heure est-ce que tu es rentré?; **I'd better be getting home** je crois qu'il est temps que je rentre chez moi; **it's on my way home** c'est sur mon chemin; **she'll be home tonight** elle sera à la maison ce soir; *Am* **to be home alone** être tout seul à la maison; **to see sb home** raccompagner qn jusque chez lui/elle; **to take sb home** ramener qn chez lui/elle; **Fido, home!** Fido, rentre *ou* à la maison!; *Fam* **it's nothing to write home about** ça ne casse rien; *Fam Br* **home and dry,** *Am* **home free** sauvé

(**b**) *(from abroad)* au pays natal, au pays; **when did you get** *or* **come home?** quand es-tu rentré?; **to send sb home** rapatrier qn; **the grandparents want to go** *or* **to return home** les grands-parents veulent rentrer dans leur pays

(**c**) *(all the way)* à fond; **to drive a nail home** enfoncer un clou jusqu'au bout; **the remark really went home** le commentaire a fait mouche; **to push home one's advantage** profiter au maximum d'un avantage; **it will come home to him some day** il s'en rendra compte un jour; **to bring sth home to sb** faire comprendre *ou* voir qch à qn

3 *adj* (**a**) *(concerning family, household → life)* de famille, familial; *(→ for family consumption)* familial, à usage familial

(**b**) *(to, for, at one's house)* à *ou* pour la maison

(**c**) *(national → gen)* national, du pays; *(→ market, policy, sales)* intérieur; **to be on home ground** *(near home)* être en pays de connaissance; *Fig (familiar subject)* être en terrain connu

(**d**) *Sport (team → national)* national; *(→ local)* local; ***our home ground*** notre terrain; **when they play at their home ground** quand ils jouent sur leur terrain, quand ils reçoivent

4 *vi (person, animal)* revenir *ou* rentrer chez soi; *(pigeon)* revenir au colombier

►► ***home address*** *(on form)* domicile *m* (permanent); *(not business address)* adresse *f* personnelle; ***home automation*** domotique *f*; ***home baking*** *(action)* pâtisserie *f*; *(cakes, biscuits)* gâteaux *mpl*; ***home banking*** banque *f* à domicile; *Obst* ***home birth*** accouchement *m* à la maison; ***home brew*** *(beer)* bière *f* faite maison; ***home brewing*** *(of beer)* fabrication *f* de bière chez soi; *Am (illegal distilling)* = distillation clandestine d'alcool chez soi; ***home cleaning products*** produits *mpl* ménagers; *Br* ***home comforts*** confort *m* du foyer; ***home computer*** ordinateur *m* familial; *Comput* ***home computing*** informatique *f* à domicile; ***home cooking*** cuisine *f* familiale; ***the Home Counties*** = l'ensemble des comtés limitrophes de Londres, à la population aisée et conservatrice; ***home country*** pays *m* natal; **the home country** le pays; ***home decorating*** décoration *f* intérieure; ***home delivery*** livraison *f* à domicile; ***home economics,*** *Fam* ***home ec*** *(UNCOUNT)* économie *f* domestique; ***home economist*** spécialiste *mf* d'économie domestique; *Am Fin* ***home equity loan*** prêt *m* sur valeur nette de la propriété; *Am Culin* ***home fries*** pommes de terre *fpl* sautées non pelées; ***home front*** *(during war)* arrière *m*; **on the home front** à l'arrière; **what's the news on the home front?** *(in the home country)* quelles sont les nouvelles du pays?; **how are things on the home front?** *(at home)* comment ça va à la maison?; ***home game*** match *m* à domicile; *Br Hist* ***the Home Guard*** = section de volontaires de l'armée britannique restée sur le territoire pour le défendre en cas d'invasion; *Br* ***home help*** aide *f* ménagère; ***home improvements*** travaux *mpl* de rénovation; *Fin* ***home improvement loan*** prêt *m* pour travaux de rénovation; ***home journey*** voyage *m* de retour; *Comput* ***home key*** touche *f* début; *Br* ***home leave*** congé *m* au foyer; ***home life*** vie *f* de famille; *Fin* ***home loan*** prêt *m* immobilier, prêt *m* d'épargne-logement; ***home movie*** film *m* d'amateur; ***home news*** nouvelles *fpl* nationales; ***the Home Office*** = le ministère britannique de l'Intérieur; *Am Com* ***home office*** *(of company)* siège *m* social; ***home owner*** propriétaire *mf*; ***home ownership*** = fait d'être propriétaire de son logement; **home ownership is increasing** le nombre des personnes propriétaires de leur logement augmente; *Comput* ***home page*** *(initial page)* page *f* d'accueil; *(start page in browser)* page *f* d'accueil; *(personal page)* page *f* personnelle; *Mktg* ***home party selling*** vente *f* domiciliaire; ***home plate*** *(in baseball)* bâton *m*, = plaque qui marque le début et la fin du parcours que doit effectuer le batteur pour marquer un point; *Naut* ***home port*** port *m* d'attache; *Econ* ***home products*** produits *mpl* nationaux *ou* domestiques; ***home remedy*** remède *m* de bonne femme; ***Home Rule*** *(in Ireland)* = gouvernement autonome de l'Irlande; ***home rule*** *(devolution)* décentralisation *f*; ***home run*** *(in baseball)* coup *m* de circuit *(coup de batte qui permet au batteur de marquer un point en faisant un tour complet en une seule fois)*; *Fig (last leg of trip)* dernière étape *f* du circuit; **the ship/the delivery truck is on its home run** le navire/le camion rentre à son port d'attache/au dépôt; *Sch* ***home schooling*** scolarisation *f* à domicile; ***Home Secretary*** = ministre de l'Intérieur en Grande-Bretagne; ***home shopping*** téléachat *m*; *Am* ***Home Show*** ≃ salon *m* des arts ménagers et de la décoration; *Sport & Fig Br* ***home straight,*** *Am* ***home stretch*** dernière ligne *f* droite; **they're on** *or* **in the home straight** ils sont dans la dernière ligne droite; *Sport* ***home team*** l'équipe *f* qui reçoit; ***home time*** = heure où l'on rentre à la maison; ***home town*** *(of birth)* ville *f* natale; *(of upbringing)* **his home town** la ville où il a grandi; ***home truth*** vérité *f* désagréable; **to tell sb a few home truths** dire ses (quatre) vérités à qn; **I learnt some home truths about myself** j'ai appris quelques vérités désagréables sur moi-même; ***home video*** = film vidéo réalisé par un particulier, généralement sur sa vie de famille; **to watch sb's home videos** regarder les cassettes vidéo filmées par qn; ***home visit*** *(by doctor)* visite *f* à domicile; ***home waters*** *(territorial)* eaux *fpl* territoriales; *(near home port)* eaux *fpl* voisines du port d'attache; *Sport* ***home win*** victoire *f* à domicile

►**home in on, home on to** *vt insep* (**a**) *(of missile)* se diriger (automatiquement) sur *ou* vers; *(proceed towards → goal)* se diriger vers; *Fig* mettre le cap sur

(**b**) *(direct attention to → problem, solution)* mettre l'accent sur; *(→ difficulty, question)* viser, cerner; **I made one mistake and he homed in on it** je n'ai fait qu'une seule faute mais il s'est fait un plaisir de me la faire remarquer

Don't try this at home

Il s'agit d'un conseil donné aux spectateurs dans les émissions de télévision dans lesquelles figurent des tours dangereux et des cascades. Aujourd'hui, cette formule ("n'essayez pas de faire cela chez vous") est toujours utilisée par les présentateurs de télévision avec une pointe d'ironie et d'une manière plus générale par toute personne qui est sur le point de tenter quelque chose de dangereux.

HOME RULE

On désigne ainsi le régime d'autonomie revendiqué par l'Irlande entre 1870 et 1914. Après plusieurs tentatives, une loi sur l'autonomie partielle fut votée en 1914. La mise en vigueur de cette loi, déjà compromise par l'opposition des protestants unionistes de l'Ulster, fut reportée lorsque la Première Guerre mondiale éclata en août 1914. À la suite de l'insurrection de Pâques à Dublin en 1916, les partisans du "Home Rule" revendiquèrent l'autonomie totale. La guerre pour l'indépendance (1918–21) aboutit au traité anglo-irlandais de 1921, qui établit la partition de l'île entre l'Irlande du Sud qui devenait quasiment indépendante et l'Irlande du Nord qui devait rester rattachée à la Grande-Bretagne.

home-baked *adj* (**a**) *(in home)* maison *(inv)*, fait à la maison; **home-baked bread** pain *m* fait à la maison (**b**) *(on premises)* maison *(inv)*, fait maison

homebird ['həʊmbɜːd] *n Fam (person)* casanier(ère) *m,f*

homebody ['həʊmˌbɒdɪ] *(pl* **homebodies***) n Fam* pantouflard(e) *m,f*

homebound ['həʊmbaʊnd] *adj* (**a**) *(going home)* sur le chemin du retour (**b**) *(confined to home)* obligé de rester à la maison; *(of sick people)* qui garde la chambre

homeboy ['həʊmbɔɪ] *n Fam Black Am slang* (**a**) *(man from one's home town)* compatriote ☐ *m* (**b**) *(friend)* pote *m* (**c**) *(fellow gang member)* = membre de la même bande

homebred ['həʊmbred] *adj* (**a**) *(raised at home)* élevé à la maison; *(homemade)* fait à la maison (**b**) *(manner)* naturel, rustique; *(humour, language, tastes)* peu raffiné, populaire (**c**) *(not foreign)* du pays; *Fam* **he's a homebred version of Sinatra** c'est notre Sinatra à nous

home-brewed *adj (beer)* fait maison

homecoming ['həʊm,kʌmɪŋ] **1** *n (to family)* retour *m* au foyer *ou* à la maison; *(to country)* retour *m* au pays

2 Homecoming *n Am Sch & Univ* = fête donnée en l'honneur de l'équipe de football d'une université ou d'une école et à laquelle sont invités les anciens élèves

►► *Am Sch & Univ* ***Homecoming Queen*** = élève élue "personne la plus appréciée de ses pairs", qui reçoit une couronne ainsi que le titre de reine lors du "Homecoming"

'The Homecoming' *Pinter* 'Le Retour'

homegirl ['həʊmgɜːl] *n Fam Black Am slang* (**a**) *(woman from one's home town)* compatriote ☐ *f* (**b**) *(friend)* copine *f* (**c**) *(fellow gang member)* = membre de la même bande

homegrown [,həʊm'grəʊn] **1** *adj (not foreign)* du pays; *(from own garden)* du jardin; *Br* **home-grown footballers** des footballeurs *mpl* du pays

2 *n Fam Drugs slang* = cannabis cultivé chez soi ou dans son jardin

homeland ['həʊmlænd] *n* (**a**) *(native country)* patrie *f* (**b**) *(South African political territory)* homeland *m*; **the homelands policy** la politique des homelands

homeless ['həʊmlɪs] **1** *adj* sans foyer; *(pet)* abandonné, sans foyer; **a homeless person** un(e) sans-abri; **to be homeless** être sans domicile fixe

2 *npl* **the homeless, homeless people** les sans-abri *mpl*

homelessness ['həʊmlɪsnɪs] *n* **the problem of homelessness** le problème des sans-abri; **homelessness is an increasing problem** les sans-abri représentent un problème de plus en plus grave

homeliness ['həʊmlɪnɪs] *n* (**a**) *(of food, furniture, manners)* simplicité *f* (**b**) *Am (unattractiveness → of person, features, face)* absence *f* de beauté

home-lover *n* casanier(ère) *m,f*; *(woman)* femme *f* d'intérieur

home-loving *adj* casanier

homely ['həʊmlɪ] *(compar* **homelier,** *superl* **homeliest**) *adj* (**a**) *(unpretentious)* simple, modeste; **they offer good but homely fare** on y mange bien mais sans façon; **they're homely folk** ce sont des gens sans prétention

(**b**) *(kind)* aimable, plein de bonté; *(atmosphere)* accueillant; *Fam* **my aunt was a homely old sort** ma tante était une de ces bonnes vieilles dames

(**c**) *Am (plain, unattractive → person, features, face)* peu attrayant; **what a homely woman!** elle n'est vraiment pas belle cette femme!

home-made *adj* (**a**) *(made at home)* maison *(inv)*, fait (à la) maison; **it's hard to believe your dress is home-made** c'est difficile à croire que tu as fait ta robe toi-même; **a home-made bomb** une bombe de fabrication artisanale; **the bookshelves looked rather home-made** les étagères semblaient plutôt artisanales

(**b**) *(made on premises)* maison *(inv)*, fait maison; **home-made apple pie** *(on menu)* tarte *f* aux pommes maison

homemaker ['həʊm,meɪkər] *n* femme *f* au foyer

homeo- ['həʊmɪəʊ] *pref* homéo-, homoeo-

homeopath ['həʊmɪəʊ,pæθ] *n* homéopathe *mf*

homeopathic [,həʊmɪəʊ'pæθɪk] *adj* homéopathique

►► ***homeopathic doctor*** (médecin *m*) homéopathe *mf*; ***homeopathic medecine*** homéopathie *f*; ***homeopathic remedy*** remède *m* homéopathique

homeopathy [,həʊmɪ'ɒpəθɪ] *n* homéopathie *f*

homeostasis [,həʊmɪəʊ'steɪsɪs] *n Physiol* homéostasie *f*

homeostatic [,həʊmɪəʊ'stætɪk] *adj Physiol* homéostatique

homeotherm ['həʊmɪəʊ,θɜːm] *n Physiol* homéotherme *m*

Homer ['həʊmə(r)] *pr n* Homère; *Prov* **even Homer nods, Homer sometimes nods** = même les meilleurs font des erreurs

homer ['həʊmə(r)] *n Fam* (**a**) *Am Sport (in baseball)* coup *m* de circuit ☐ (**b**) *(homing pigeon)* pigeon *m* voyageur ☐ (**c**) *Br (work)* = travail au noir exécuté par un ouvrier à l'insu de son patron

Homeric [həʊ'merɪk] *adj* homérique

homeroom ['həʊm,ruːm] *n Am Sch* (**a**) *(place)* = salle où l'on fait l'appel (**b**) *(group)* = élèves rassemblés pour l'appel

homesick ['həʊmsɪk] *adj* nostalgique; **to be homesick** avoir le mal du pays; **to be homesick for sb** s'ennuyer de qn; **to be homesick for sth** avoir la nostalgie de qch; **he's homesick for his family** sa famille lui manque

homesickness ['həʊm,sɪknɪs] *n* mal *m* du pays

homesite ['həʊmsaɪt] *n Am* terrain *m* à bâtir

homespun ['həʊmspʌn] **1** *adj* (**a**) *(wool)* filé à la maison, de fabrication domestique; *(cloth)* de homespun (**b**) *(simple)* simple, sans recherche

2 *n (cloth)* homespun *m*

homestead ['həʊmsted] **1** *n* (**a**) *Am Hist* = terre dont la propriété est attribuée à un colon sous réserve qu'il y réside et l'exploite

(**b**) *(buildings and land)* propriété *f*; *(farm)* ferme *f*; *Austr & NZ (house)* maison *f (d'un ranch)*

(**c**) *Am (birthplace)* **he's returning to the homestead** il rentre au pays

2 *vt Am (acquire)* acquérir; *(settle)* s'installer à, coloniser

3 *vi Am* = s'installer sur une terre pour en devenir propriétaire

►► ***the Homestead Act*** = décret de 1862 par lequel le Congrès américain donnait 160 acres de terre à tout nouvel arrivant qui s'engageait à s'installer dans l'ouest

homesteader ['həʊmstedə(r)] *n* (**a**) *Am Hist* = personne qui acquiert une propriété en vertu du "Homestead Act" (**b**) *(farm-owner)* propriétaire *mf* d'une ferme; *(ranch-owner)* propriétaire *mf* d'un ranch

homeward ['həʊmwəd] **1** *adj* du retour; **the homeward trip** le (voyage de) retour

2 *adv* = **homewards**

►► *Com* ***homeward freight*** fret *m* de retour

homeward-bound *adj (person)* qui rentre chez soi; *(ship)* sur le chemin du retour; **to be homeward bound** être sur le chemin du retour

homewards ['həʊmwədz] *adv* (**a**) *(to house)* vers la maison; **to head homewards** se diriger vers la maison (**b**) *(to homeland)* vers la patrie; **to be homewards bound** prendre le chemin du retour; **the plane flew homewards** l'avion faisait route vers sa base; **the ship sailed homewards** le navire faisait route vers son port d'attache

homework ['həʊmwɜːk] *n (UNCOUNT)* (**a**) *Sch* devoirs *mpl* (à la maison); *(research)* travail *m* préparatoire; **the minister hadn't done his homework** le ministre n'avait pas préparé son sujet (**b**) *(paid work)* travail *m* à domicile

►► ***homework exercise*** devoir *m* (à la maison)

homeworker ['həʊm,wɜːkə(r)] *n* travailleur (euse) *m,f* à domicile

homeworking ['həʊm,wɜːkɪŋ] *n* travail *m* à domicile

homey ['həʊmɪ] *(pl* **homies,** *compar* **homier,** *superl* **homiest**) **1** *n Fam Black Am slang* (**a**) *(from Southern US)* = Noir originaire du Sud récemment arrivé dans le Nord (**b**) *(fellow Black American → from one's home town)* compatriote ☐ *mf*; *(→ friend)* copain (copine) *m,f*; *(→ gang member)* = membre de la même bande

2 *adj* = **homy**

homicidal [,hɒmɪ'saɪdəl] *adj Law* homicide; **a homicidal maniac** un(une) maniaque à tendances homicides *ou* meurtrières

homicide ['hɒmɪsaɪd] *n Law* (**a**) *(act)* homicide *m*; **accidental homicide** homicide *m* par imprudence; **justifiable homicide** homicide *m* par légitime défense (**b**) *(person)* homicide *mf*

homie = **homey** *n*

homiletic [,hɒmɪ'letɪk] **1** *adj* homilétique

2 homiletics *n (UNCOUNT)* homilétique *f*

homily ['hɒmɪlɪ] *(pl* **homilies**) *n* (**a**) *Rel* homélie *f* (**b**) *Pej* sermon *m*, homélie *f*; **to read sb a homily** sermonner qn

homing ['həʊmɪŋ] *adj (pre-programmed)* autoguidé; *(heat-seeking)* à tête chercheuse

►► ***homing device*** mécanisme *m* d'autoguidage; ***homing guidance systems*** systèmes *mpl* d'autoguidage; ***homing instinct*** *(of animals)* instinct *m* d'orientation; *Fam Hum* **no matter how drunk I am, my homing instinct never lets me down** même quand je suis complètement soûl, j'arrive toujours à rentrer chez moi; ***homing missile*** missile *m* à tête chercheuse; ***homing pigeon*** pigeon *m* voyageur

hominid ['hɒmɪnɪd] **1** *n* hominidé *m*

2 *adj* hominidien; **the hominid family** les hominidés

hominoid ['hɒmɪnɔɪd] **1** *n* hominoïde *m*

2 *adj* hominoïde

hominy ['hɒmɪnɪ] *n Am (grits)* bouillie *f* de semoule de maïs

►► ***hominy grits*** bouillie *f* de semoule de maïs

Homo ['həʊməʊ] *n* homo *m inv*

homo ['həʊməʊ] *very Fam* **1** *n* pédé *m*, homo *mf*, = terme injurieux désignant un homosexuel

2 *adj* pédé, homo

homo- ['həʊməʊ, 'hɒmə, 'hɒməʊ] *pref* homo-

homoeo- = **homeo-**

homoeopath, homoeopathic *etc* = **homeopath, homeopathic** *etc*

homoeostasis, homoeostatic = **homeostasis, homeostatic**

homoeotherm = **homeotherm**

homoerotic [,həʊməʊɪ'rɒtɪk] *adj* homoérotique

homogamy [hə'mɒgəmɪ] *n* homogamie *f*

homogenate [həʊ'mɒdʒəneɪt] *n* résultat *m* de l'homogénéisation

homogeneity [,hɒməʊdʒə'niːɪtɪ] *n* homogénéité *f*

homogeneous [,hɒmə'dʒiːnɪəs] *adj* homogène; **a homogeneous population** une population homogène

homogeneously [,hɒmə'dʒiːnɪəslɪ] *adv* homogènement

homogenization [hə,mɒdʒənaɪ'zeɪʃən] *n* homogénéisation *f*

homogenize, -ise [hə'mɒdʒənaɪz] *vt* homogénéiser, homogénéifier

►► ***homogenized milk*** lait *m* homogénéisé

homogenous [hə'mɒdʒənɪs] *adj* homogène

homogeny [hə'mɒdʒənɪ] *n* = ressemblance due à un ancêtre génétique commun

homograft ['hɒmə,grɑːft] *n Med* allogreffe *f*, autogreffe *f*

homograph ['hɒməgrɑːf] *n Ling* homographe *m*

homographic [hɒmə'græfɪk] *adj Ling* homographe

homologate [hɒ'mɒləgeɪt] *vt* homologuer

homologous [hɒ'mɒləgəs] *adj Biol & Chem* homologue

►► *Chem* ***homologous series*** série *f* homologue

homologue ['hɒməlɒg] *n Biol & Chem* homologue *m*

homology [hə'mɒlədʒɪ] *n Biol & Chem* homologie *f*

homomorphic [,hɒmə'mɔːfɪk], **homomorphous** [,hɒmə'mɔːfəs] *adj Biol* homomorphe

homonym ['hɒmənɪm] *n Ling* homonyme *m*; **the words are homonyms (of each other)** ces mots sont homonymes (entre eux)

homonymous [hɒ'mɒnɪməs] *adj Ling* homonyme

homonymy [hɒ'mɒnɪmɪ] *n Ling* homonymie *f*

homophile ['hɒməfaɪl] *adj* homosexuel

homophobe ['həʊməʊ,fəʊb] *n* homophobe *mf*

homophobia [,həʊməʊ'fəʊbjə] *n* homophobie *f*

homophobic [,həʊməʊ'fəʊbɪk] *adj* homophobe

homophone ['hɒməfəʊn] *n Ling* homophone *m*

homophonic [,hɒmə'fɒnɪk] *adj Mus* homophonique

homophonous [hɒ'mɒfənəs] *adj Ling* homophone

homophony [hɒˈmɒfənɪ] (*pl* **homophonies**) *n Ling & Mus* homophonie *f*

Homo sapiens [ˌhəʊməʊˈsæpɪənz] *n* homo sapiens *m*

homosexual [ˌhɒməˈsekʃʊəl] **1** *n* homosexuel(elle) *m,f*

2 *adj* homosexuel

homosexuality [ˌhɒməˌsekʃʊˈælətɪ] *n* homosexualité *f*; **male/female homosexuality** homosexualité *f* masculine/féminine

homozygote [ˌhɒməʊˈzaɪgəʊt] *n Biol* homozygote *m*

homozygous [ˌhɒməʊˈzaɪgəs] *adj Biol* homozygote

homunculus [hɒˈmʌnkjʊləs] (*pl* **homunculi** [-laɪ]) *n* (**a**) *(small man)* homuncule *m*, homoncule *m* (**b**) *(in alchemy)* homuncule *m*, homunculus *m*

homy [ˈhəʊmɪ] (*compar* **homier**, *superl* **homiest**) *adj Fam* (**a**) *(comfortable)* accueillant❑, confortable❑; **you've made your place very homy** tu t'es fait un vrai chez-toi (**b**) *Br (home-loving)* casanier❑; **he's the homy type** c'est un pantouflard (**c**) *Br (private)* intime❑; **a homy little chat** une conversation intime

hon [hʌn] *n Am Fam (term of address)* chéri(e)❑ *m,f*

Hon. *Br (written abbr* **honourable**) honorable

hon. *Br (written abbr* **honorary**) honoraire

honcho [ˈhɒntʃəʊ] *n Am Fam (boss)* chef❑ *m*

Honduran [hɒnˈdjʊərən] **1** *n* Hondurien(enne) *m,f*

2 *adj* hondurien

3 *comp (embassy, history)* du Honduras

Honduras [hɒnˈdjʊərəs] *n* Honduras *m*; **in Honduras** au Honduras

hone [həʊn] **1** *vt* (**a**) *(sharpen)* aiguiser, affûter, affiler; *(re-sharpen)* repasser; **he honed the knife to a razor-sharp edge** il a affûté le couteau pour qu'il coupe comme un rasoir (**b**) *(refine → analysis, thought)* affiner; **finely honed arguments** arguments *mpl* d'une grande finesse; **practice will hone your reflexes** la pratique *ou* l'entraînement améliorera tes réflexes

2 *n* pierre *f* à aiguiser

▸**hone down** *vt sep (reduce)* tailler; *(make slim)* faire maigrir

▸**hone in on** *vt insep Am Fam (direct attention to → problem, solution)* mettre l'accent sur❑; *(→ difficulty, question)* viser❑, cerner❑

honest [ˈɒnɪst] **1** *adj* (**a**) *(not deceitful)* honnête, probe; *(trustworthy)* intègre; **an honest answer** une réponse honnête; **the honest truth** la pure vérité; **it pays to be honest** ça paie d'être honnête; **they are honest workers** ce sont des ouvriers consciencieux; **he's (as) honest as the day is long** il n'y a pas plus honnête que lui

(**b**) *(decent, upright)* droit; *(virtuous)* honnête; *Br Fam* **he's an honest bloke** c'est un brave type; *Hum* **he's decided to make an honest woman of her** il a décidé de régulariser sa situation

(**c**) *(not fraudulent)* honnête; **he charges an honest price** ses prix ne sont pas excessifs; **an honest day's work** une bonne journée de travail; **an honest day's pay for an honest day's work** toute peine mérite salaire; **they just want to make an honest profit** ils ne veulent qu'un profit légitime; **to earn an honest living** gagner honnêtement sa vie

(**d**) *(frank → face)* franc (franche), sincère; **let's be honest with each other** allons, soyons francs; **to be honest, I don't think it will work** à vrai dire, je ne crois pas que ça marchera; **give me your honest opinion** dites-moi sincèrement ce que vous en pensez

2 *adv Fam* **I didn't mean it, honest!** je plaisantais, je te le jure!; **honest to goodness** *or* **to God!** parole d'honneur!

▸▸ *Br* ***honest broker*** médiateur(trice) *m,f* neutre

honestly [ˈɒnɪstlɪ] *adv* honnêtement; **quite honestly, I don't see the problem** très franchement, je ne vois pas le problème; **it's not my fault, honestly!** ce n'est pas ma faute, je te le jure!; **honestly, the way some people behave!** franchement *ou* vraiment, il y en a qui exagèrent!; **honestly?** c'est vrai?

honest-to-goodness *adj* **a cup of honest-to-goodness English tea** une tasse de bon thé anglais

honesty [ˈɒnɪstɪ] **1** *n* (**a**) *(truthfulness → of person)* honnêteté *f*; *(→ of text, words)* véracité *f*, exactitude *f*; *Prov* **honesty is the best policy** = l'honnêteté paie toujours

(**b**) *(incorruptibility)* intégrité *f*; **we have never doubted his honesty** nous n'avons jamais douté de son intégrité

(**c**) *(upright conduct)* droiture *f*; **a man of irreproachable honesty** un homme d'une droiture irréprochable

(**d**) *(sincerity)* sincérité *f*, franchise *f*; **the honesty of his intentions is self-evident** la sincérité de ses intentions est évidente

(**e**) *Bot* monnaie-du-pape *f*, lunaire *f*

2 in all honesty *adv* en toute sincérité

▸▸ ***honesty box*** = boîte où les usagers d'un service sont invités à déposer une somme d'argent en l'absence d'un préposé à l'encaissement

honey [ˈhʌnɪ] (*pl* **honies**) **1** *n* (**a**) *(food)* miel *m*; **clear/wildflower honey** miel *m* liquide/de fleurs sauvages

(**b**) *Fig* miel *m*, douceur *f*; **he was all honey** il a été tout sucre et tout miel

(**c**) *Fam (term of endearment)* chéri(e) *m,f*; **OK, honey!** OK, chéri!

(**d**) *esp Am Fam (nice person)* amour *m*; *(good-looking person → woman)* belle nana *f*; *(→ man)* beau mec *m*; *(excellent thing)* bijou *m*; **you're such a honey!** tu es un chou!; **a honey of a dress** une super robe; **a honey of a boat** un amour de bateau

2 *adj* miellé; **honey-coloured** couleur de miel *inv*

▸▸ *Zool* ***honey badger*** ratel *m*; *Zool* ***honey bear*** *(in Europe, Asia)* ours *m* brun *(d'Europe et d'Asie)*; *(in South America)* kinkajou *m*; *Orn* ***honey buzzard*** bondrée *f* apivore; ***honey cake*** gâteau *m* d'épices au miel

honeybee [ˈhʌnɪbiː] *n Entom* abeille *f*

honeybun [ˈhʌnɪbʌn], **honeybunch** [ˈhʌnɪbʌntʃ] *n Fam (person)* chou *m* (à la crème)

honeycomb [ˈhʌnɪkəʊm] **1** *n* (**a**) *(in wax)* rayon *m ou* gâteau *m* de miel; *(for eating)* gâteau *m* de miel (**b**) *(material)* structure *f* alvéolaire (**c**) *(pattern)* nid *m* d'abeille; *Tex* nid *m* d'abeille (**d**) *Metal* soufflure *f*

2 *vt* (**a**) *(surface)* cribler (**b**) *(interior)* miner; **the hills are honeycombed with secret tunnels** les collines sont truffées de passages secrets

honeydew [ˈhʌnɪdjuː] *n (produced by insects)* miellat *m*; *(produced by plants)* miellée *f*

▸▸ ***honeydew melon*** melon *m* d'hiver *ou* d'Espagne

honey-eater [ˈhʌnɪˌiːtə(r)] *n Orn* méliphagidé *m*

honeyed [ˈhʌnɪd] *adj Fig* mielleux; **he spoke in honeyed tones** il parlait d'un ton mielleux

honeymoon [ˈhʌnɪmuːn] **1** *n* (**a**) *(period)* lune *f* de miel; *(trip)* voyage *m* de noces; **they're on (their) honeymoon** ils sont en voyage de noces

(**b**) *Fig* état *m* de grâce; **the new Prime Minister's honeymoon is over** l'état de grâce du nouveau Premier ministre est terminé

2 *comp (couple)* en voyage de noces

3 *vi* passer sa lune de miel; *(go on trip)* aller en voyage de noces; **they're honeymooning in Jamaica** ils passent leur lune de miel en Jamaïque, ils sont en voyage de noces en Jamaïque

▸▸ *Fig* ***honeymoon period*** lune *f* de miel, état *m* de grâce; ***honeymoon suite*** *(in hotel)* suite *f* nuptiale

honeymooner [ˈhʌnɪmuːnə(r)] *n* nouveau(elle) marié(e) *m,f*

honeypot [ˈhʌnɪpɒt] *n* pot *m* à miel; *Fam Fig* **to have one's fingers in the honeypot** se sucrer; *Fig* **the actress's fans clustered around her like bees around a honeypot** les admirateurs de l'actrice s'agglutinaient autour d'elle

honeysuckle [ˈhʌnɪˌsʌkəl] *n Bot* chèvrefeuille *m*

honeytrap [ˈhʌnɪˌtræp] *n* = piège tendu à une personnalité par la presse à sensation afin d'en tirer des confidences

Hong Kong [ˌhɒŋˈkɒŋ] *n* Hong Kong, Hongkong; **in Hong Kong** à Hongkong

honied = **honeyed**

honk[1] [hɒŋk] **1** *n* (**a**) *(of car horn)* coup *m* de klaxon®; **honk, honk!** tut-tut! (**b**) *(of geese)* cri *m*; *(of ganders)* jargon *m*; **honk, honk!** couin-couin!

2 *vt* **to honk one's horn** donner un coup de klaxon®; **honk your horn at him!** klaxonne-le!

3 *vi* (**a**) *(car)* klaxonner; **she honked twice on the horn** elle a donné deux coups de klaxon® (**b**) *(goose)* cacarder; *(gander)* jargonner

honk[2] *vi Br Fam* (**a**) *(smell bad)* schlinguer, chlinguer (**b**) *(vomit)* dégueuler

honker [ˈhɒŋkə(r)] *n Am Fam* (**a**) *(nose)* blaire *m*, tarin *m* (**b**) *(breast)* nichon *m* (**c**) *(device)* bécane *f*

honkie, honky [ˈhɒŋkɪ] (*pl* **honkies**) *n very Fam Black Am slang* = terme injurieux désignant un Blanc

honky-tonk [ˈhɒŋkɪˌtɒŋk] **1** *n* (**a**) *Mus* musique *f* de bastringue (**b**) *Am Fam (brothel)* maison *f* close❑; *Old-fashioned (nightclub)* beuglant *m*; *(bar)* bouge *m*; *(gambling den)* tripot *m*

2 *adj* (**a**) *Mus* de bastringue (**b**) *Am Fam (unsavoury)* louche; **a honky-tonk bar** un bar louche; **a honky-tonk district** un quartier chaud; **a honky-tonk night club** une boîte de nuit louche; **a honky-tonk woman** une putain

Honolulu [ˌhɒnəˈluːluː] *n* Honolulu

honorarium [ˌɒnəˈreərɪəm] (*pl* **honorariums** *or* **honoraria** [-rɪə]) *n* honoraires *mpl*

honorary [*Br* ˈɒnərərɪ, *Am* ɒnəˈreərɪ] *adj (titular position)* honoraire; *(in name only)* à titre honorifique, honoraire; *(unpaid position)* à titre gracieux

▸▸ *Univ* ***honorary degree*** diplôme *m* honoris causa; *Univ* ***honorary diploma*** diplôme *m* honoris causa; ***honorary member*** membre *m* honoraire; ***honorary professor*** professeur *m* honoraire; *Mil* ***honorary rank*** grade *m* honorifique; ***honorary secretary*** secrétaire *mf* honoraire

honor, honorable *etc Am* = **honour, honorable** *etc*

honorific [ˌɒnəˈrɪfɪk] **1** *n (gen)* témoignage *m* d'honneur; *(title)* titre *m* d'honneur

2 *adj* honorifique

honour, *Am* **honor** [ˈɒnə(r)] **1** *n* (**a**) *(personal integrity)* honneur *m*; **on my honour!** parole d'honneur!; **he's on his honour to behave himself** il s'est engagé sur l'honneur *ou* sur son honneur à bien se tenir; **it's a point of honour (with me) to pay my debts on time** je me fais un point d'honneur de *ou* je mets un *ou* mon point d'honneur à rembourser mes dettes; **the affair cost him his honour** l'affaire l'a déshonoré; *Prov* **(there is) honour amongst thieves** les loups ne se mangent pas entre eux; **to be honour bound (to)** être tenu par l'honneur (à)

(**b**) *(public, social regard)* honneur *m*; **they came to do her honour** ils sont venus pour lui faire *ou* rendre honneur; **peace with honour!** la paix sans le déshonneur!

(**c**) *Formal (pleasure)* **it is a great honour to introduce Mr Reed** c'est un grand honneur pour moi de vous présenter Monsieur Reed; **may I have the honour of your company/the next dance?** pouvez-vous me faire l'honneur de votre compagnie/de la prochaine danse?; **to do the honours** *(serve drinks, food)* faire le service; *(make introductions)* faire les présentations (entre invités)

(**d**) *(credit)* honneur *m*, crédit *m*; **she's an honour to her profession** elle fait honneur à sa profession; **having him on the board will do honour to the company** ça fera honneur à la société de l'avoir comme membre du conseil d'administration

(**e**) *(mark of respect)* honneur *m*; **military honours** honneurs *mpl* militaires; **to receive sb with full honours** recevoir qn avec tous les honneurs; **all honour to him!** honneur à lui!

(**f**) *Law (in title)* **Your Honour** Votre Honneur

(**g**) *(award)* distinction *f* honorifique

(**h**) *Cards (face card)* honneur *m*; **it's your honour** *(starter's right)* à vous l'honneur

2 *vt* (**a**) *(person)* honorer, faire honneur à; **she honoured him with her friendship** elle l'a honoré de son amitié; **my honoured colleague** mon (ma) cher (chère) collègue; *Formal* **I'm most honoured to be here tonight** je suis très honoré d'être parmi vous ce soir; *Ironic* **the manager honoured us with his presence today**

le directeur nous a fait l'honneur de sa présence aujourd'hui; *Ironic* **we're honoured!** quel honneur!

(**b**) *(fulfil the terms of)* honorer; *(observe → boycott, rule)* respecter; **he always honours his obligations** il honore toujours ses obligations

(**c**) *(pay → debt)* honorer; *Fin (cheque, bill of exchange)* honorer, payer

(**d**) *(dance partner)* saluer

3 honours *npl Br Univ (degree)* = diplôme universitaire obtenu avec mention; **to take honours in history** ≃ faire une licence d'histoire; *Am* **he was an honours in university/in high school** ≃ il a toujours eu mention très bien/le tableau d'honneur; **she got first-/second-class honours** elle a eu sa licence avec mention très bien/mention bien

4 in honour of *prep* en honneur de

►► *Br Univ* ***honours degree*** = diplôme universitaire obtenu avec mention; *Br* ***honours list*** = liste de distinctions honorifiques conférées par le monarque deux fois par an; *Am* ***honor roll*** tableau *m* d'honneur

honourable, *Am* **honorable** ['ɒnərəbəl] *adj* (**a**) *(worthy of honour)* honorable; **the profession is still an honourable one** la profession reste en honneur; *Old-fashioned or Hum* **are his intentions honourable?** ses intentions sont-elles honorables?; **he got an honourable discharge** il a été rendu à la vie civile; **to receive (an) honourable mention** *(in competition)* recevoir une mention spéciale

(**b**) *(title)* **the (Right) Honourable** le (très) honorable; *Parl* **my honourable friend the member for Caithness** mon collègue l'honorable député du Caithness; *Parl* **the honourable member will no doubt recall...** mon honorable collègue se rappellera sans doute...

> **HONOURABLE**
>
> Cet appellatif s'utilise avant le nom de certains membres de l'aristocratie britannique: "the Honourable James Porter" ou "the Hon. James Porter". Il est également employé à la Chambre des communes lorsqu'un député parle d'un autre député: "the honourable member for Oxford". Lorsqu'un député désigne un collègue du même parti, il emploie l'expression "my honourable friend"; lorsque son interlocuteur appartient au parti opposé, le terme consacré est "the honourable gentleman" ou "the honourable lady".

honourableness, *Am* **honorableness** ['ɒnərəbəlnɪs] *n (of person)* honorabilité *f*; *(of intentions, behaviour)* caractère *m* honorable

honourably, *Am* **honorably** ['ɒnərəblɪ] *adv* honorablement

Hons. *Br Univ* (*written abbr* **honours degree**) = diplôme universitaire obtenu avec mention

Hon. Sec. (*written abbr* **honorary secretary**) secrétaire *mf* honoraire

hooch [huːtʃ] *n Am very Fam* (**a**) *(drink)* gnôle *f* (**b**) *(marijuana)* herbe *f*

hood [hʊd] **1** *n* (**a**) *(of garment)* capuchon *m*; *(with collar)* capuche *f*; *(with eye-holes)* cagoule *f*; *Univ* épitoge *f*; **a rain hood** une capuche

(**b**) *Br Aut (soft top)* capote *f*; *Am Aut (bonnet)* capot *m*

(**c**) *(protective cover)* couvercle *m*; *(of pram)* capote *f*; *Phot (over lens)* pare-soleil *m inv*

(**d**) *(of hairdryer)* casque *m*

(**e**) *(for fumes, smoke)* hotte *f*

(**f**) *(of animals, plants)* capuchon *m*; *(for falcons)* chaperon *m*, capuchon *m*

(**g**) *Am Fam (delinquent)* voyou *m*; *(gangster)* gangster ❑ *m*, truand *m*

(**h**) *Am Fam (neighbourhood)* **the hood** le quartier ❑

2 *vt* mettre le capuchon sur; *(falcon)* chaperonner, enchaperonner

►► *Am Aut* ***hood ornament*** calicot *m*

hooded ['hʊdɪd] *adj (clothing)* à capuchon; *(person)* encapuchonné; *(executioner, thief)* au visage masqué; *Fig* **hooded eyes** yeux *mpl* aux paupières tombantes

►► *Orn* ***hooded crow*** corneille *f* mantelée; *Orn* ***hooded merganser*** harle *m* couronné

hoodlum ['huːdləm] *n Fam (delinquent)* voyou *m*; *(gangster)* gangster ❑ *m*, truand *m*

hoodmould ['hʊdməʊld], **hoodmoulding** ['hʊdməʊldɪŋ] *n Archit* larmier *m*

hoodoo ['huːduː] **1** *n* (**a**) *Am Fam (jinx)* porte-malheur ❑ *m inv*; *(bad luck)* poisse *f*, guigne *f* (**b**) *Am Geol (rock formation)* cheminée *f* de fées

2 *vt* porter la poisse *ou* la guigne à

hoodwink ['hʊdwɪŋk] *vt* tromper, avoir; **I was hoodwinked into signing** on m'a raconté des histoires pour me faire signer

hooey ['huːɪ] *n Fam* foutaises *fpl*; **that's hooey** c'est des foutaises; **to talk a load of hooey** raconter des foutaises

hoof [huːf] (*pl* **hoofs** *or* **hooves** [huːvz]) **1** *n* sabot *m (d'animal)*; **on the hoof** *(alive)* sur pied; *Fig (on ad hoc basis)* au coup par coup; **five hundred cattle on the hoof** cinq cents têtes de bétail sur pied; **I had lunch on the hoof** à midi j'ai mangé sur le pouce

2 *vt Fam (idiom)* **to hoof it** *(go on foot)* aller à pinces; *(flee)* se cavaler; *(dance)* guincher

►► *Am Vet* ***hoof and mouth disease*** fièvre *f* aphteuse

hoofbeat ['huːfbiːt] *n* bruit *m* de sabots *(d'animal)*; **the (horse's) hoofbeats came closer** on entendait s'approcher des pas (de cheval)

hoofed [huːft] *adj* à sabots; *Zool* ongulé

hoofer ['huːfə(r)] *n Fam* danseur(euse) ❑ *m,f (de métier)*

hoofprint ['huːfprɪnt] *n* empreinte *f* de sabot *(d'animal)*

hoo-ha ['huːˌhaː] *n Fam* (**a**) *(noise)* boucan *m*, potin *m*; *(chaos)* pagaille *f*, tohu-bohu *m inv*; *(fuss)* bruit *m*, histoires *fpl*; **there was a lot of hoo-ha about it** ça en a fait des histoires; **now that all the hoo-ha is over we can get down to serious business** maintenant que le calme est revenu, nous pouvons nous occuper de choses sérieuses ❑; **when all the hoo-ha about the royal wedding has died down** quand le mariage princier ne sera plus à la une de l'actualité (**b**) *Am (party)* fête *f* charivarique

hook [hʊk] **1** *n* (**a**) *(gen)* crochet *m*; *(for coats)* patère *f*; *(on clothes)* agrafe *f*; *(for meat)* croc *m*; *Naut* gaffe *f*; **hooks and eyes** *(on clothes)* agrafes *fpl* (et œillets *mpl*); **your phone was off the hook** tu avais décroché ton téléphone; *(accidentally)* tu avais mal raccroché ton téléphone; **to put the phone back on the hook** reposer le combiné (sur son support); *Fam* **to get one's hooks into sb** mettre le grappin sur qn

(**b**) *(on fishing line)* hameçon *m*; *Fam* **he swallowed the story, hook, line and sinker** il a tout avalé; *Fam* **he's fallen for her hook line and sinker** il est tombé fou amoureux d'elle ❑

(**c**) *(in advertising)* accroche *f*; *Mus (in song)* thème *m*

(**d**) *Am Fam (dismissal)* **to give sb the hook** flanquer qn à la porte, vider qn; **he'll get the hook one day** il sera flanqué à la porte *ou* vidé un jour

(**e**) *Sport (in cricket)* coup *m* tourné; *Golf* hook *m*; *Boxing* **a right/left hook** un crochet (du) droit/gauche

(**f**) *Fam (idioms)* **to get sb off the hook** tirer qn d'affaire; **to let sb off the hook** *(from obligation)* libérer qn de sa responsabilité ❑; **I'll let you off the hook this time** je laisse passer cette fois-ci; **we must do it by hook or by crook** nous devons le faire, coûte que coûte; *Am Fam* **to be on the hook** être dans le pétrin

2 *vt* (**a**) *(snag)* accrocher; *(seize → person, prey)* attraper; *(→ floating object)* gaffer, crocher; **he hooked his arm through hers** il lui a pris le bras

(**b**) *(loop)* **hook the rope around the tree** passez la corde autour de l'arbre; **she hooked one leg round the leg of the chair** elle passa *ou* enroula une jambe autour du pied de la chaise; **the two bits of wire had become hooked together** les deux fils de fer s'étaient pris l'un dans l'autre

(**c**) *Fishing (fish)* prendre; *Tech* hameçonner

(**d**) *Sport (in cricket)* renvoyer d'un coup tourné; *(in rugby)* talonner *(le ballon)*; *Golf* hooker; *Boxing* donner un crochet à

(**e**) *Fam (steal)* piquer

(**f**) *Fam Hum (marry)* passer la corde au cou à; **she'll never manage to hook him** elle n'arrivera jamais à lui mettre le grappin dessus

(**g**) *Am Fam* **to hook school** faire l'école buissonnière

(**h**) *Am Fam* **to hook it** mettre les bouts, décamper

(**i**) *Sewing (rug)* fabriquer en nouant au crochet

3 *vi* (**a**) *(fasten)* s'agrafer

(**b**) *Golf* hooker

(**c**) *Am Fam (work as prostitute)* faire le trottoir

►► ***Hook of Holland*** Hoek *m* van Holland; *Sport* ***hook shot*** *(in basketball)* bras *m* roulé; *(in cricket)* coup *m* tourné

►**hook on 1** *vt sep* accrocher

2 *vi* s'accrocher; **this strap hooks on at the back** cette bride s'accroche *ou* s'agrafe par derrière

►**hook up 1** *vt sep* (**a**) *(trailer)* accrocher; *(dress)* agrafer; *(boat)* amarrer; **they hooked up an extra coach to the train** on a accroché un wagon supplémentaire au train

(**b**) *Fam (install)* installer ❑; *(plug in)* brancher ❑

(**c**) *Rad & TV* faire un duplex entre

(**d**) *(horse, oxen etc)* atteler

2 *vi* (**a**) *(dress)* s'agrafer

(**b**) *Am Fam (meet)* se rencontrer ❑, se donner rendez-vous ❑; *(work together)* faire équipe ❑

(**c**) *Am Fam (be in relationship)* **to hook up with sb** sortir avec qn ❑

(**d**) *Rad & TV* **to hook up with** faire une émission en duplex avec

hookah ['hʊkə] *n* narguilé *m*, houka *m*

hooked [hʊkt] *adj* (**a**) *(hook-shaped)* recourbé; *(nose)* crochu (**b**) *(having hooks)* muni de crochets; *(fishing line)* muni d'un hameçon (**c**) *Fam Fig (addicted)* **he got hooked on hard drugs** il est devenu accro aux drogues dures; **she's really hooked on TV soaps** c'est une mordue des feuilletons télévisés; **to get hooked on chess** devenir fana d'échecs; **one bite and I was hooked** une bouchée et j'étais conquis

hooker ['hʊkə(r)] *n* (**a**) *Sport (in rugby)* talonneur *m* (**b**) *very Fam (prostitute)* pute *f* (**c**) *Am Fam (of drink)* **a hooker of gin/bourbon** un bon coup de gin/de bourbon

hookey ['hʊkɪ] *n Am, Austr & NZ Fam* **to play hookey** sécher les cours, faire l'école buissonnière

hook-nosed *adj* au nez recourbé *ou* crochu

hook-up *n* (**a**) *TV* relais *m* temporaire (**b**) *(for caravan, RV)* borne *f* de raccordement (**c**) *Am Fam (alliance)* alliance ❑ *f*; **a hook-up of our companies should harm the competition** une alliance de nos sociétés devrait mettre la concurrence à rude épreuve

hookworm ['hʊkwɜːm] *n Entom* ankylostome *m*

hooky = **hookey**

hooligan ['huːlɪgən] *n* hooligan *m*, vandale *m*

hooliganism ['huːlɪgənɪzəm] *n* vandalisme *m*

hoon [huːn] *n Austr Fam* loubard *m*

hoop [huːp] *n* (**a**) *(ring)* cerceau *m*; *(on barrel)* cercle *m*; *(in croquet)* arceau *m*; *Fig* **I had to jump through hoops to get the job** j'ai dû faire des pieds et des mains pour obtenir ce travail; **to put sb through the hoops** *(interrogate)* mettre qn sur la sellette; *(test)* mettre qn à l'épreuve

(**b**) *(on plumage, fur)* rayure *f*; *(around animal's neck)* collier *m*; *(on shirt)* bande *f*

(**c**) *Am Fam (basketball)* **hoop(s)** le basket; **to shoot hoops** jouer au basket

►► ***hoop earrings*** (anneaux *mpl*) créoles *fpl*

hooped [huːpt] *adj (barrel)* cerclé; *(skirt)* à cerceaux; *(earrings)* en anneau

hoopla ['huːplaː] *n* (**a**) *Br (funfair game)* jeu *m* d'anneaux *(dans les foires)* (**b**) *Am Fam* = **hoo-ha** (**a**) (**c**) *Am Fam (advertising)* publicité *f* tapageuse ❑

hoopoe ['huːpuː] *n Orn* huppe *f*

►► ***hoopoe lark*** sirli *m* du désert

hoor [hʊə(r)] *n very Fam Ir (man)* salaud *m*; *Ir & Scot (woman)* salope *f*

hooray [hʊ'reɪ] *exclam* hourra!, hurrah!

►► *Br Fam Pej* ***Hooray Henry*** = fils à papa exubérant et bruyant

hoosegow ['huːsgaʊ] *n Am Fam (prison)* taule *f*, bloc *m*; **in the hoosegow** en taule, en bloc

Hoosier ['huːsjə(r)] *n (inhabitant)* habitant(e) *m,f* de l'Indiana; *(native)* originaire *mf* de l'Indiana

▸▸ ***the Hoosier State*** = surnom donné à l'Indiana

hoot [huːt] **1** *n* (**a**) *(shout → of delight, pain)* cri *m*; *(jeer)* huée *f*; **hoots of laughter** éclats *mpl* de rire
(**b**) *(of owl)* hululement *m*
(**c**) *Aut* coup *m* de klaxon®; *(of train)* sifflement *m*; *(of siren)* mugissement *m*
(**d**) *Fam (least bit)* **I don't give** *or* **care a hoot** *or* **two hoots** je m'en fiche, mais alors complètement, je m'en contrefiche; **it doesn't matter two hoots** ça n'a strictement aucune importance ❑
(**e**) *Fam (amusing event)* **it was a hoot!** *(hilarious)* c'était tordant!; **he's a real hoot!** c'est un sacré rigolo!, il est tordant!
2 *vt (actor, speaker)* huer; *(play)* siffler
3 *vi* (**a**) *Fam (person)* **to hoot with laughter** s'esclaffer; **to hoot with anger** rugir de colère
(**b**) *(owl)* hululer
(**c**) *Aut* klaxonner; *(train)* siffler; *(siren)* mugir

▸**hoot down** *vt sep Fam (person, show)* huer ❑, conspuer ❑; **they hooted him down** ils l'ont fait taire par leurs huées ❑

hootch = **hooch**

hootenanny ['huːtənænɪ] *(pl* **hootenannies***) n* (**a**) *Am (party)* = fête populaire animée par des chanteurs de chansons folkloriques (**b**) *(thing)* machin *m*, truc *m*

hooter ['huːtə(r)] *n* (**a**) *esp Br (car horn)* klaxon® *m*; *(in factory, ship)* sirène *f* (**b**) *esp Br (party toy)* mirliton *m* (**c**) *Fam (nose)* pif *m* (**d**) *esp Am very Fam (breast)* nichon *m*

hooting ['huːtɪŋ] *n* (**a**) *(of owl)* hululement *m* (**b**) *(of person → jeering)* huées *fpl*; *(→ laughter)* hurlements *mpl* de rire (**c**) *(of cars)* coups *mpl* de klaxon®

hoover®[1] ['huːvə(r)] *n Br* aspirateur *m*

hoover[2] *Br* **1** *vt (carpet etc)* passer l'aspirateur sur; *(room)* passer l'aspirateur dans
2 *vi* passer l'aspirateur

▸**hoover up** *vt sep* (**a**) *(with vacuum cleaner)* enlever avec l'aspirateur; **I'll just hoover it up** je vais (y) donner un coup d'aspirateur (**b**) *Fam Hum (of person)* engloutir; **he hoovered up all the peanuts** il a englouti toutes les cacahuètes

hoovering ['huːvərɪŋ] *n Br* **to do the hoovering** passer l'aspirateur; **when you've finished the hoovering** quand tu auras passé l'aspirateur

hooves [huːvz] *pl of* **hoof**

hop[1] [hɒp] *(pt & pp* **hopped**, *cont* **hopping***)* **1** *n* (**a**) *(jump)* saut *m* à cloche-pied; *(in rapid series)* sautillement *m*; *Old-fashioned Sport* **the hop, skip** *or* **step and jump** le triple saut; *Br* **to catch sb on the hop** prendre qn au dépourvu; *Br* **to keep sb on the hop** ne pas laisser chômer qn
(**b**) *Aviat* étape *f*; **it's just a short hop from New York to Boston by plane** le trajet en avion de New York à Boston est très court
(**c**) *Fam Old-fashioned (dance)* sauterie ❑ *f*; *(for young people)* boum *f*, surpatte *f*
2 *vt Fam* (**a**) *Am (bus, subway etc → legally)* sauter dans ❑; *(→ illegally)* prendre en resquillant
(**b**) *(idiom)* **to hop it** décamper, décaniller; **hop it!** allez, dégage!
3 *vi* (**a**) *(jump)* sauter; *(in rapid series)* sautiller; *Fam* **to hop on/off the bus** sauter dans le/du bus; **birds hopped about in the garden** les oiseaux sautillaient dans le jardin; *Fam* **to hop into bed with sb** coucher avec qn tout de suite; *Fam* **hop in!** *(into car etc)* montez!
(**b**) *(jump on one leg)* sauter à cloche-pied; **he hopped over to the door** il est allé à cloche-pied jusqu'à la porte
(**c**) *Fam (travel by plane)* **we hopped across to Paris for the weekend** nous sommes allés à Paris en avion pour le week-end ❑

▸**hop off** *vi Fam (leave)* décamper

▸**hop up** *vt sep Am Fam* (**a**) *(excite)* exciter ❑, stimuler ❑; **all that coffee hopped him up** tout ce café l'a excité; **the crowd is really hopped up** le public est vraiment exubérant ❑ (**b**) *(make angry, nervy)* énerver ❑, exciter ❑ (**c**) *Drugs slang (drug user)* défoncer; *(athlete, racehorse)* doper ❑ (**d**) *Aut* **to hop up a car** gonfler le moteur d'une voiture

hop[2] *n* (**a**) *(plant)* houblon *m*; **to pick hops** cueillir le houblon (**b**) *Am Fam Drugs slang (drug)* came *f*

▸▸ ***hop field*** houblonnière *f*; ***hop grower*** houblonnier(ère) *m,f*; ***hop picker*** cueilleur(euse) *m,f* de houblon; ***hop picking*** cueillette *f* du houblon

hope [həʊp] **1** *n* (**a**) *(desire, expectation)* espoir *m*; *Formal* espérance *f*; **his hope is that...** ce qu'il espère *ou* son espoir c'est que...; **in the hope of a reward/of leaving early** dans l'espoir d'une récompense/de partir tôt; **I have every hope (that) he'll come** j'ai bon espoir qu'il viendra; **there's hope for him yet** il reste de l'espoir en ce qui le concerne; **don't get your hopes up** ne comptez pas là-dessus; **to give up hope (of)** perdre l'espoir (de); **the situation is past** *or* **beyond hope** la situation est sans espoir; *Euph* **she is past** *or* **beyond all hope** *(is dying)* il n'y a plus aucun espoir; **to raise sb's hopes** *(for first time)* susciter *ou* faire naître l'espoir de qn *ou* chez qn; *(anew)* faire renaître l'espoir de qn; *(increase)* renforcer l'espoir de qn; **don't raise his hopes too much** ne lui donne pas trop d'espoir; **they had high hopes for their daughter** ils avaient de grandes espérances pour leur fille; **with high hopes** avec un grand espoir; *Fam* **we live in hope!** c'est l'espoir qui fait vivre!; *Fam Ironic* **some hope!** tu parles!; **hope springs eternal (in the human breast)** l'espoir fait vivre
(**b**) *(chance)* espoir *m*, chance *f*; **he's got little hope of winning** il a peu de chances *ou* d'espoir de gagner; **one's last/only hope** le dernier/l'unique espoir de quelqu'un
(**c**) *Rel* espérance *f*
2 *vi* espérer; **to hope for sth** espérer qch; **to hope against hope** espérer contre toute attente; **we just have to hope for the best** espérons que tout finira *ou* se passera bien; **don't hope for too much** n'en attends pas trop; **you shouldn't hope for a high return** vous ne devez pas vous attendre à un rendement élevé
3 *vt* espérer; **he hopes** *or* **is hoping to go** il espère y aller; **he's hoping (that) she'll be there** il espère qu'elle sera là; **hoping** *or* **I hope to hear from you soon** *(in letter)* j'espère avoir de tes nouvelles bientôt; **I really hope so!** je l'espère bien!; **I hope not** j'espère que non; **I should hope so!** j'espère bien!; **I should hope not!** j'espère bien que non!; **I hope you don't mind me calling** j'espère que cela ne te dérange pas si je passe (te voir)

▸▸ *Am* ***hope chest*** coffre *m* à trousseau; *Fig* trousseau *m*

hopeful ['həʊpfʊl] **1** *adj* (**a**) *(full of hope)* plein d'espoir; **we're hopeful that we'll reach an agreement** nous avons bon espoir d'aboutir à un accord; **he's still hopeful that she'll come** il garde bon espoir qu'elle viendra; **he says he'll come, but I'm not that hopeful** il dit qu'il viendra mais je n'y compte pas trop; **I am hopeful about the outcome** je suis optimiste quant au résultat
(**b**) *(inspiring hope)* encourageant, prometteur; **the news is hopeful** les nouvelles sont encourageantes *ou* laissent de l'espoir; **the situation looks hopeful** la situation s'annonce meilleure
2 *n* aspirant(e) *m,f*, candidat(e) *m,f*; **a young hopeful** un jeune loup; **Davis Cup hopefuls** les prétendants à la coupe Davis

hopefully ['həʊpfəlɪ] *adv* (**a**) *(smile, speak, work)* avec espoir, avec optimisme (**b**) *(with luck)* on espère que...; **hopefully, they'll leave tomorrow** on espère qu'ils partiront demain; **will you get it finished today? – hopefully!** est-ce que tu l'auras terminé pour aujourd'hui? – je l'espère! *ou* oui, avec un peu de chance!; **hopefully not** espérons que non

hopefulness ['həʊpfʊlnɪs] *n (of person)* confiance *f*, optimisme *m*

hopeless ['həʊplɪs] *adj* (**a**) *(desperate → person)* désespéré; *(→ situation)* désespéré, sans espoir; **it's hopeless!** c'est impossible *ou* désespérant!
(**b**) *(incurable → addiction, ill person)* incurable; **a hopeless case** un cas désespéré; **to be in a hopeless condition** être dans un état désespéré
(**c**) *(inveterate → drunk, liar)* invétéré, incorrigible
(**d**) *Fam (incompetent → person)* nul; *(→ at job)* incompétent ❑; **he's a hopeless dancer** il est nul comme danseur; **she's hopeless!** c'est un cas désespéré!; **a hopeless case** un bon à rien; **I'm hopeless at this** je suis nul pour ce genre de chose; **he's hopeless at swimming** il est nul en natation
(**e**) *(pointless)* inutile; **it's hopeless trying to explain to him** il est inutile d'essayer de lui expliquer

hopelessly ['həʊplɪslɪ] *adv* (**a**) *(speak, sigh, sob)* avec désespoir (**b**) *(irremediably)* **they are hopelessly in debt/in love** ils sont complètement endettés/éperdument amoureux; **by this time we were hopelessly late/lost** nous étions maintenant vraiment en retard/complètement perdus; **hopelessly naive** d'une naïveté désespérante; **the government is hopelessly out of touch** le gouvernement a totalement perdu contact (avec le pays)

hopelessness ['həʊplɪsnɪs] *n* (**a**) *(despair)* désespoir *m* (**b**) *(of position, situation)* caractère *m* désespéré (**c**) *(pointlessness)* inutilité *f*

hophead ['hɒphed] *n Am Fam Drugs slang* défoncé(e) *m,f*

Hopi ['həʊpɪ] **1** *n* (**a**) **the Hopi** *(tribe)* les Hopi (**b**) *(member of tribe)* Hopi *mf*
2 *adj* hopi *(inv)*

hopper ['hɒpə(r)] *n* (**a**) *(jumper)* sauteur(euse) *m,f*; *Austr Fam* kangourou ❑ *m* (**b**) *Fam (grasshopper)* sauterelle ❑ *f* (**c**) *(feeder bin)* trémie *f*; *Agr (for sowing)* semoir *m*; **grain hopper** trémie *f* à blé (**d**) *(picker)* cueilleur(euse) *m,f* de houblon

▸▸ *Naut* ***hopper barge*** marie-salope *f*; *Rail* ***hopper car*** wagon-trémie *m*

hopping ['hɒpɪŋ] *adv Fam (as intensifier)* **he was hopping mad** il était fou furieux

-hopping ['hɒpɪŋ] *suff* **to go bar-hopping** aller de bar en bar, faire la tournée des bars; **to go island-hopping** aller d'île en île, faire le tour des îles

hopsack ['hɒpsæk] *n* (**a**) *(for hops)* sac *m* à houblon (**b**) *Tex* cheviote *f ou* cheviotte *f* grossière

hopscotch ['hɒpskɒtʃ] *n* marelle *f*; **to play (at) hopscotch** jouer à la marelle

Horace ['hɒrɪs] *pr n* Horace

Horatian [hə'reɪʃən] *adj Literature* d'Horace

horde [hɔːd] *n* (**a**) *(nomadic)* horde *f* (**b**) *Fig (crowd)* essaim *m*, horde *f*; *(of agitators)* horde *f*; **hordes of tourists** des hordes *fpl* de touristes; *Pej* **the horde** la horde, la foule

horehound ['hɔːhaʊnd] *n Bot* marrube *m*

horizon [hə'raɪzən] **1** *n* horizon *m*; **the sun was sinking below the horizon** le soleil descendait au-dessous de l'horizon; **we saw a boat on the horizon** nous vîmes un bateau à l'horizon; *Fig* **a new star on the political horizon** une nouvelle vedette à *ou* sur l'horizon politique
2 horizons *npl (perspectives)* horizons *mpl*; **to broaden one's horizons** élargir ses horizons; **a man of limited horizons** un homme aux vues étroites *ou* à l'esprit étroit; **China presents new horizons for investment** la Chine offre de nouveaux horizons pour les investisseurs

▸▸ *Aviat & Naut* ***horizon bar*** barre *f* d'horizon

horizontal [ˌhɒrɪ'zɒntəl] **1** *adj* (**a**) *(gen)* horizontal; **turn the lever to the horizontal position** mettez le levier à l'horizontale; *Fam* **I was horizontal for a few days with the flu** je suis resté couché *ou* au lit pendant quelques jours avec la grippe ❑ (**b**) *Admin & Com (communication, integration)* horizontal; **he asked for a horizontal move** il a demandé une mutation
2 *n* horizontale *f*

▸▸ *Sport* ***horizontal bar*** barre *f* fixe; *Fin* ***horizontal equity*** équité *f* horizontale; *Comput* ***horizontal orientation*** (format *m*) paysage *m*; *Fin* ***horizontal spread*** écart *m* horizontal

horizontality [ˌhɒrɪzɒn'tælɪtɪ] *n* horizontalité *f*

horizontally [ˌhɒrɪ'zɒntəlɪ] *adv* horizontalement; **extend your arms horizontally** tendez vos bras à l'horizontale; *Admin & Com* **to move sb horizontally (to)** muter qn (à)

Horlicks® ['hɔːlɪks] *n Br* = boisson chaude instantanée, généralement consommée le soir

hormonal [hɔː'məʊnəl] *adj* hormonal

hormone ['hɔːməʊn] *n* hormone *f*

▸▸ *Med* ***hormone deficiency*** insuffisance *f*

hormonale; *Med* ***hormone replacement therapy*** traitement *m* hormonal substitutif

Hormuz [ˌhɔːˈmuːz] *n* Hormuz, Ormuz

horn [hɔːn] **1** *n* (**a**) *(gen)* corne *f*; *(pommel)* pommeau *m*; **horns** *(of deer)* bois *mpl*; **the horn of plenty** la corne d'abondance; **the Horn of Africa** la Corne de l'Afrique, la péninsule des Somalis; *Br Fig* **to draw** *or* **to pull in one's horns** *(back off)* se calmer; *(spend less)* restreindre son train de vie; *Br* **to be on the horns of a dilemma** être pris dans un dilemme

(**b**) *Mus* cor *m*; *Fam* **he blows a mean horn** *(jazz trumpet)* il touche à la trompette; *(saxophone)* il touche au saxo; *Am Fig* **to blow one's own horn** se vanter

(**c**) *Aut* klaxon® *m*; *(manual)* corne *f*; **to sound** *or* **to blow the horn** klaxonner, corner

(**d**) *Naut* sirène *f*; **to sound** *or* **to blow the horn** donner un coup de sirène

(**e**) *Br very Fam (erection)* érection ❑ *f*; **to have the horn** avoir la trique *ou* le gourdin; **to give sb the horn** *(arouse)* exciter qn ❑

(**f**) *Am Fam (telephone)* bigophone *m*; **to get on the horn to sb** passer un coup de fil *ou* de bigophone à qn

(**g**) *Hunt* corne *f*, cor *m*, trompe *f*

(**h**) *(of loudspeaker)* pavillon *m*

(**i**) *Br Culin* cornet *m*; **cream horn** = pâtisserie en forme de cornet remplie de crème

2 *comp (handle, comb)* en corne

3 *vt (gore)* encorner, donner un coup de corne à

►► *Mus* ***horn player*** corniste *mf*; *Mus* ***horn section*** les cors *mpl*

►**horn in** *vi Fam (on conversation)* mettre son grain de sel; *(on a deal)* s'immiscer ❑

hornbeam [ˈhɔːnbiːm] *n Bot* charme *m*

hornbill [ˈhɔːnbɪl] *n Orn* calao *m*

horned [ˈhɔːnd] *adj* cornu; **a two-horned rhinoceros** un rhinocéros (d'Afrique) à deux cornes

►► *Orn* ***horned owl*** duc *m*; *Zool* ***horned toad*** crapaud *m* cornu; *Zool* ***horned viper*** vipère *f* cornue (d'Égypte)

hornet [ˈhɔːnɪt] *n Entom* frelon *m*; *Fig* **to stir up a hornet's nest** mettre le feu aux poudres

horniness [ˈhɔːnɪnɪs] *n* (**a**) *(of substance)* nature *f* cornée (**b**) *(of hands)* callosité *f* (**c**) *very Fam (state of sexual arousal)* = fait d'être excité sexuellement; *Br (sexual attractiveness)* caractère *m* sexy

hornless [ˈhɔːnlɪs] *adj* sans cornes

hornpipe [ˈhɔːnpaɪp] *n Mus* matelote *f (danse)*; **to dance a hornpipe** danser une matelote

horn-rimmed *adj* à monture d'écaille

hornswoggle [ˈhɔːnˌswɒgəl] *vt esp Am Fam (trick)* blouser, embobiner

horny [ˈhɔːnɪ] *adj* (**a**) *(substance)* corné (**b**) *(calloused* → *nail, skin)* calleux; *Vet* encorné (**c**) *very Fam (sexually excited)* excité (sexuellement); *Br (sexually attractive)* sexy *(inv)*; *Am* **he's horny as a toad** il est en rut

horologer [hɒˈrɒlədʒə(r)], **horologist** [hɒˈrɒlədʒɪst] *n* horloger(ère) *m,f*

horology [hɔːˈrɒlədʒɪ] *n* horlogerie *f*

horoscope [ˈhɒrəskəʊp] *n* horoscope *m*

horrendous [hɒˈrendəs] *adj* affreux, horrible

horrendously [hɒˈrendəslɪ] *adv* horriblement

horrible [ˈhɒrəbəl] *adj* (**a**) *(horrific)* horrible, affreux; *(morally repulsive)* abominable; **a horrible tragedy/scream** une tragédie/un cri horrible

(**b**) *(dismaying)* horrible, effroyable; **in a horrible mess** dans une effroyable *ou* horrible confusion; **I've a horrible feeling that things are going to go wrong** j'ai l'horrible pressentiment que les choses vont mal se passer

(**c**) *(very unpleasant)* horrible, atroce; *(food)* infect; **to be horrible to sb** être méchant *ou* horrible avec qn; **to say horrible things about sb** dire des horreurs *ou* des choses terribles sur qn

horribly [ˈhɒrəblɪ] *adv* (**a**) *(nastily)* horriblement, atrocement, affreusement; **he treated her horribly** il se conduisit d'une manière atroce *ou* atrocement mal envers elle; **the story of a woman who was horribly murdered** l'histoire d'une femme qui fut assassinée de manière atroce

(**b**) *(as intensifier)* affreusement; **it's horribly extravagant but...** c'est de la folie douce mais...; **things went horribly wrong** les choses ont affreusement mal tourné

horrid [ˈhɒrɪd] *adj* (**a**) *(dreadful)* horrible, affreux; *(weather)* abominable; **how horrid!** quelle horreur!; **he's such a horrid little man!** c'est un affreux petit bonhomme (**b**) *(unkind)* méchant; **he was horrid to me** il a été méchant avec moi; **to say horrid things about sb** dire des méchancetés de qn (**c**) *(ugly)* vilain, laid

horridly [ˈhɒrɪdlɪ] *adv (as intensifier)* atrocement, affreusement

horridness [ˈhɒrɪdnɪs] *n* (**a**) *(dreadfulness)* horreur *f*, caractère *m* horrible (**b**) *(unkindness)* méchanceté *f* (**c**) *(ugliness)* laideur *f*

horrific [hɒˈrɪfɪk] *adj* (**a**) *(horrendous)* horrible, terrifiant (**b**) *Fig (very unpleasant)* horrible

horrifically [hɒˈrɪfɪkəlɪ] *adv* (**a**) *(gruesomely)* atrocement (**b**) *Fig (as intensifier)* **horrifically expensive** affreusement cher

horrified [ˈhɒrɪfaɪd] *adj* horrifié; **a horrified expression** une expression d'horreur

horrify [ˈhɒrɪfaɪ] *(pt & pp* **horrified**) *vt* (**a**) *(terrify)* horrifier (**b**) *(weaker use)* horrifier, scandaliser

horrifying [ˈhɒrɪfaɪɪŋ] *adj* (**a**) *(terrifying)* horrifiant, terrifiant (**b**) *(weaker use)* scandaleux; **prices are horrifying over there** les prix sont scandaleux là-bas

horror [ˈhɒrə(r)] *n* (**a**) *(feeling)* horreur *f*; **he has a horror of snakes** il a horreur des serpents; **to my horror, I discovered...** c'est avec horreur que j'ai découvert...; *Br Fam* **he** *or* **it gives me the horrors!** il *ou* ça me donne le frisson!

(**b**) *(unpleasantness)* horreur *f*; **I began to see the horror of it all** j'ai commencé à en mesurer toute l'horreur

(**c**) *Fam (person, thing)* horreur *f*; **that child is a little horror** cet enfant est un petit monstre; **horror of horrors!** l'horreur!; *Br* **oh, horrors!** quelle horreur!

►► ***horror film, horror movie*** film *m* d'épouvante; ***horror story*** histoire *f* d'horreur; *Fam Fig* **they told some real horror stories about their holiday** ils ont raconté quelques histoires effrayantes sur leurs vacances

horror-stricken, horror-struck *adj* glacé *ou* frappé d'horreur

hors d'œuvre [ɔːˈdɜːv(r)] *(pl* **inv** *or* **hors d'œuvres**) *n* hors-d'œuvre *m inv*; *(cocktail snack)* amuse-gueule *m*

horse [hɔːs, *pl* hɔːsɪz] **1** *n* (**a**) *(animal)* cheval *m*; **to ride a horse** monter à cheval; **he fell off his horse** il a fait une chute de cheval; **to play the horses** jouer aux courses; *also Fig* **to back the wrong horse** miser sur le mauvais cheval; *Fam* **I could eat a horse!** j'ai une faim de loup!; **to eat like a horse** manger comme quatre; **(straight) from the horse's mouth** de source sûre; *Br* **that's a horse of a different colour** c'est une autre paire de manches; **to get on one's high horse** monter sur ses grands chevaux; **wild horses couldn't drag it out of me** je serai muet comme une tombe

(**b**) *(in breeding)* cheval *m* mâle, cheval *m* entier; **stud horse** étalon *m*; **to take a mare to horse** faire couvrir une jument

(**c**) *(trestle)* tréteau *m*

(**d**) *Mil & Hist (cavalry)* cavalerie *f*, troupes *fpl* montées; **regiment of horse** régiment *m* de cavalerie

(**e**) *Sport (in gymnastics)* cheval *m* d'arçons

(**f**) *Fam Drugs slang (heroin)* neige *f*, blanche *f*

2 *npl Mil* cavalière *f*

►► *Mil & Hist* ***horse artillery*** artillerie *f* montée; ***horse brass*** médaillon *m* de bronze *(fixé à une martingale)*; ***horse breeder*** éleveur(euse) *m,f* de chevaux; ***horse butcher*** boucher(ère) *m,f* hippophagique; *Bot* ***horse chestnut*** *(tree)* marronnier *m* (d'Inde); *(nut)* marron *m* (d'Inde); *Fam* ***horse doctor*** vétérinaire ❑ *mf*; *Br* ***the Horse Guards*** *(regiment)* = régiment de cavalerie attaché à la reine et remplissant certaines fonctions officielles; *(building)* = le bâtiment de Whitehall où se fait chaque jour la relève de la garde; ***Horse Guards Parade*** = grande place à Londres où ont lieu les défilés des "Horse Guards"; *Naut* ***horse latitudes*** pot *m* au noir; ***horse manure*** crottin *m* de cheval; *(as fertilizer)* fumier *m* de cheval; ***horse race*** course *f* de chevaux; ***horse racing*** *(UNCOUNT)* courses *fpl* (de chevaux); *Br* ***horse riding*** équitation *f*; *Fam* ***horse sense*** (gros) bon sens ❑ *m*; ***horse show*** concours *m* hippique; ***horse trader*** maquignon *m*; *Br Fam (hard bargainer)* négociateur(trice) *m,f* redoutable ❑; ***horse trials*** concours *m* hippique

►**horse about, horse around** *vi Fam (noisily)* chahuter

horse-and-buggy *adj Am* qui date d'avant l'automobile; *(old-fashioned)* vieillot

horseback [ˈhɔːsbæk] *n* **on horseback** à cheval

►► *Am* ***horseback riding*** équitation *f*; **do you like horseback riding?** tu aimes monter à cheval?

horsebox [ˈhɔːsbɒks] *n Br (trailer)* van *m*; *(stall)* box *m*

horsebreaker [ˈhɔːsˌbreɪkə(r)] *n Br* dresseur (euse) *m,f* de chevaux

horsecar [ˈhɔːskɑː(r)] *n Am* fourgon *m* à chevaux

horse-drawn *adj Br* tiré par des chevaux, à chevaux

horseflesh [ˈhɔːsfleʃ] *n (UNCOUNT) Fam* (**a**) *(horses)* chevaux ❑ *mpl*; **he's a good judge of horseflesh** il s'y connaît bien en chevaux (**b**) *(meat)* viande *f* de cheval ❑

horsefly [ˈhɔːsflaɪ] *(pl* **horseflies**) *n Entom* taon *m*

horsehair [ˈhɔːsheə(r)] **1** *n* crin *m* (de cheval)

2 *comp (mattress, sofa)* de crin (de cheval)

horselaugh [ˈhɔːslɑːf] *n* gros rire *m*, rire *m* tonitruant

horseman [ˈhɔːsmən] *(pl* **horsemen** [-mən]) *n* (**a**) *(rider)* cavalier *m*, écuyer *m*; **to be a good horseman** bien monter à cheval, être bon cavalier; **the four horsemen of the Apocalypse** les quatre cavaliers de l'Apocalypse (**b**) *(breeder)* éleveur(euse) *m,f* de chevaux

horsemanship [ˈhɔːsmənʃɪp] *n* (**a**) *(activity)* équitation *f* (**b**) *(skill)* talent *m* de cavalier

horsemeat [ˈhɔːsmiːt] *n* viande *f* de cheval

horseplay [ˈhɔːspleɪ] *n (UNCOUNT)* chahut *m* brutal, jeux *mpl* tapageurs *ou* brutaux; **they were having a bit of horseplay in the pool** ils faisaient les imbéciles dans la piscine; **it's just harmless horseplay** c'est une bagarre pour rire

horsepower [ˈhɔːsˌpaʊə(r)] *n (unit)* cheval-vapeur *m*, cheval *m*; **actual horsepower** puissance *f* effective en chevaux; **a 10-horsepower motor** un moteur de 10 chevaux; **it's a 4-horsepower car** c'est une 4 chevaux

horseradish [ˈhɔːsˌrædɪʃ] *n Bot* raifort *m*

►► *Culin* ***horseradish sauce*** sauce *f* au raifort

horseshit [ˈhɔːsˌʃɪt] *n (UNCOUNT) Vulg* connerie *f*, conneries *fpl*; **he's full of horseshit** il déconne complètement

horseshoe [ˈhɔːsʃuː] **1** *n* fer *m* à cheval

2 horseshoes *n (game)* jeu *m* de fer à cheval

►► *Zool* ***horseshoe bat*** fer-à-cheval *m*, rhinolophe *m*; *Zool* ***horseshoe crab*** crabe *m* des Moluques, limule *f* ; *Bot* ***horseshoe vetch*** hippocrépide *f* à toupet

horsetail [ˈhɔːsteɪl] *n Bot* prêle *f*

horse-trading *n Br Fam* négociation *f* dure ❑; *Pej* maquignonnage *m*; **after much horse-trading an agreement was reached** un accord a été obtenu à l'arraché

horsetrailer [ˈhɔːstreɪlə(r)] *n Am (trailer)* van *m*; *(stall)* box *m*

horsewhip [ˈhɔːswɪp] *(pt & pp* **horsewhipped,** *cont* **horsewhipping**) **1** *n* cravache *f*

2 *vt* cravacher; **I'll have him horsewhipped** je le ferai fouetter

horsewoman [ˈhɔːsˌwʊmən] *(pl* **horsewomen** [-ˌwɪmɪn]) *n* cavalière *f*, écuyère *f*; *(sidesaddled)* amazone *f*; **she's a good horsewoman** elle est bonne cavalière, elle monte bien

horsey, horsy [ˈhɔːsɪ] *adj Fam* (**a**) *(horse-like)* chevalin ❑ (**b**) *(fond of horses)* féru de cheval ❑; **he mixes with a very horsey crowd** il fréquente des (gens) passionnés de chevaux; **the horsey set** le monde *ou* le milieu du cheval

horsiness [ˈhɔːsɪnɪs] *n Fam* (**a**) *(of face, features)* caractère *m* chevalin (**b**) *(fondness for horses)* amour *m* des chevaux

hortative [ˈhɔːtətɪv], **hortatory** [hɔːˈteɪtərɪ] *adj Formal* exhortatif; *(words, speech)* d'exhortation

horticultural [ˌhɔːtɪˈkʌltʃərəl] *adj* horticole

►► ***horticultural show*** exposition *f* horticole *ou* d'horticulture

horticulturalist [ˌhɔːtɪˈkʌltʃərəlɪst] *n* horticulteur(trice) *m,f*

horticulturally [hɔːtɪˈkʌltjərəlɪ] *adv* **horticulturally speaking** parlant du point de vue de l'horticulture; **horticulturally superior** supérieur en fait d'horticulture

horticulture [ˈhɔːtɪkʌltʃə(r)] *n* horticulture *f*

horticulturist [ˌhɔːtɪˈkʌltʃərɪst] *n* horticulteur(-trice) *m,f*

hosanna [həʊˈzænə] **1** *n* hosanna *m*

2 *exclam* hosanna

hose [həʊz] **1** *n* (**a**) *(tube)* tuyau *m*, *Aut* Durit® *f*; **a length of rubber hose** un bout de tuyau en caoutchouc; **turn off the hose** arrêtez le jet; **garden hose** tuyau *m* d'arrosage

(**b**) *(UNCOUNT) (stockings)* bas *mpl*; *(tights)* collant *m*, collants *mpl*; *Com* articles *mpl* chaussants *(de bonneterie)*; *Hist* chausses *fpl*; *(knee breeches)* haut-de-chausse *m*, haut-de-chausses *m*, culotte *f* courte

2 *vt (lawn)* arroser au jet; *(fire)* arroser à la lance

►► ***hose reel*** dévidoir *m*

►**hose down** *vt sep* (**a**) *(wash)* laver au jet (**b**) *(with fire hose)* arroser à la lance

►**hose out** *vt sep (wash out)* laver au jet

hosepipe [ˈhəʊzpaɪp] *n* tuyau *m*; **a hosepipe ban** une interdiction d'arroser

hosier [ˈhəʊzɪə(r)] *n* bonnetier(ère) *m,f*

hosiery [ˈhəʊzɪərɪ] *n (UNCOUNT)* (**a**) *(trade)* bonneterie *f* (**b**) *(stockings)* bas *mpl*; *(socks)* chaussettes *fpl*; *Com* articles *mpl* chaussants *(de bonneterie)*; **the (women's) hosiery department** le rayon des bas; **the (men's) hosiery department** le rayon des chaussettes

hospice [ˈhɒspɪs] *n* (**a**) *(for travellers)* hospice *m* (**b**) *(for the terminally ill)* = hôpital pour grands malades en phase terminale

hospitable [hɒˈspɪtəbəl] *adj* hospitalier; *Fig* **a hospitable climate** un climat hospitalier

hospitably [hɒˈspɪtəblɪ] *adv* avec hospitalité

hospital [ˈhɒspɪtəl] **1** *n* hôpital *m*; **in hospital** à l'hôpital; *Br* **to hospital,** *Am* **to the hospital** à l'hôpital; **to go into hospital** aller à l'hôpital; **a children's hospital** un hôpital pour enfants; **to do hospital corners** *(on bed)* faire un lit au carré

2 *comp (centre, service, staff, treatment)* hospitalier; *(bed, ward)* d'hôpital

►► ***hospital care*** soins *mpl* hospitaliers; ***a hospital case*** un(une) patient(e) hospitalisé(e); ***hospital doctor*** médecin *m* hospitalier; ***hospital nurse*** infirmier(ère) *m,f (d'hôpital)*; ***hospital radio*** radio *f* diffusant dans les hôpitaux; ***hospital ship*** navire-hôpital *m*; ***hospital train*** train *m* sanitaire

hospitality [ˌhɒspɪˈtælətɪ] *n* hospitalité *f*; **thank you for your hospitality** merci pour votre hospitalité; *Old-fashioned Euph* **to enjoy His/Her Majesty's hospitality** faire de la prison

►► ***hospitality business*** hôtellerie *f*; ***hospitality industry*** industrie *f* hôtelière; ***hospitality management*** gestion *f* hôtelière; ***hospitality room, hospitality suite*** salon *m* de réception *(où sont offerts des rafraîchissements lors d'une conférence, d'un événement sportif etc)*; ***hospitality tray*** plateau *m* de courtoisie

hospitalization [ˌhɒspɪtəlaɪˈzeɪʃən] *n* hospitalisation *f*

►► *Am* ***hospitalization insurance*** assurance *f* couvrant l'hospitalisation

hospitalize, -ise [ˈhɒspɪtəlaɪz] *vt (sick person)* hospitaliser; **a couple of thugs hospitalized him** *(beat him up)* deux voyous l'ont envoyé à l'hôpital

host¹ [həʊst] **1** *n* (**a**) *(person)* hôte *m (qui reçoit)*; *(on TV show)* animateur(trice) *m,f*; *(in hotel)* hôtelier(ère) *m,f*; *(innkeeper)* aubergiste *mf*; **he acted as our host for the evening** il a été notre hôte pour la soirée; **Japan will be the next host for the conference** c'est le Japon qui accueillera la prochaine conférence

(**b**) *Biol & Zool* hôte *m*

(**c**) *Literary (denizen)* hôte *m*

(**d**) *Comput* ordinateur *m* principal; *(in network)* serveur *m*

2 *adj (cell)* hôte; *(team)* qui reçoit; **the host city for the Olympic Games** la ville organisatrice des jeux Olympiques

3 *vt* (**a**) *(TV, radio programme)* présenter; *(game show)* animer; *(event)* organiser; *(party)* donner; **she adores hosting dinner parties** elle adore recevoir à dîner

(**b**) *Comput (website)* héberger

►► *Comput* ***host computer*** ordinateur *m* principal; *(in network)* serveur *m*; ***host country*** pays *m* d'accueil; *Comput* ***host file*** fichier *m* serveur; *Comput* ***host system*** système *m* serveur *ou* hôte

host² *n* (**a**) *(large number)* foule *f*; **a host of complaints** toute une série de plaintes (**b**) *Literary* armée *f*; **the Lord God of Hosts** le Dieu des armées

host³ *n Rel (consecrated bread)* hostie *f*

hosta [ˈhɒstə] *n Bot* hosta *m*

hostage [ˈhɒstɪdʒ] *n* otage *m*; **to take/to hold sb hostage** prendre/garder qn en otage; **they released the parents but kept the child as (a) hostage** ils ont libéré les parents et gardé l'enfant en otage; *Fig* **the government doesn't want to give any hostages to fortune by promising tax cuts** le gouvernement ne veut pas prendre le risque de promettre des réductions d'impôts

►► ***hostage taker*** preneur(euse) *m,f* d'otage; ***hostage taking*** prise *f* d'otage(s)

hostel [ˈhɒstəl] *n* (**a**) *(residence)* foyer *m* (**b**) *Arch (inn)* auberge *f*

hosteller, *Am* **hosteler** [ˈhɒstələ(r)] *n* (**a**) **(youth) hosteller** ajiste *mf* (**b**) *Arch (innkeeper)* aubergiste *mf*

hostelling, *Am* **hosteling** [ˈhɒstəlɪŋ] *n Br* **hostelling is popular with students** les étudiants aiment loger dans les auberges de jeunesse au cours de leurs voyages

hostelry [ˈhɒstəlrɪ] *(pl* **hostelries***)* *n* hôtellerie *f*; *Fam Hum* **the local hostelry** le bistrot du coin

hostess [ˈhəʊstes] *n* (**a**) *(at home, on TV show)* hôtesse *f*; *(in hotel)* hôtelière *f*; *(of inn)* aubergiste *f*; *Hum* **the hostess with the mostest** la plus chouette des hôtesses (**b**) *(in nightclub)* entraîneuse *f* (**c**) **(air) hostess** hôtesse *f* de l'air

►► ***hostess agency*** agence *f* d'hôtesses; ***Hostess Trolley***® = table roulante avec chauffe-plats

hostile [*Br* ˈhɒstaɪl, *Am* ˈhɒstəl] **1** *adj* hostile; **to be hostile to sb/sth** être hostile à qn/qch; **people who are hostile to change** les gens qui n'aiment pas le changement

2 *n Am* ennemi *m*

►► *Mil* ***hostile forces*** forces *fpl* ennemies; *Com* ***hostile takeover bid*** OPA *f* hostile

hostility [hɒˈstɪlətɪ] *(pl* **hostilities***)* *n* (**a**) *(aggression)* hostilité *f*; **to show hostility to** *or* **towards sb** manifester de l'hostilité *ou* faire preuve d'hostilité envers qn (**b**) **hostilities** *(fighting)* hostilités *fpl*; **the outbreak/cessation of hostilities** l'ouverture *f*/la cessation des hostilités; **we want to avoid further hostilities** nous voulons éviter de nouvelles hostilités *ou* la poursuite des hostilités

hosting [ˈhəʊstɪŋ] *n Comput (of website)* hébergement *m*

hostler [ˈɒslə(r)] *n Br Arch* valet *m* d'écurie

HOT [hɒt]

chaud	► 1 (a), (b), (d), (k), (l), (t)
qui tient chaud	► 1 (c)
épicé	► 1 (e)
tout frais	► 1 (f)
violent	► 1 (h)
intense	► 1 (i)
enthousiaste	► 1 (j)
sévère	► 1 (m)
recherché	► 1 (o), (r)

(compar **hotter,** *superl* **hottest,** *pt & pp* **hotted,** *cont* **hotting)** **1** *adj* (**a**) *(high in temperature)* chaud; **to be hot** *(person)* avoir (très *ou* trop) chaud; *(object)* être chaud; **a hot, stuffy room** une pièce où il fait une chaleur étouffante *ou* où l'on étouffe; **the engine/glass/oven is hot** le moteur/verre/four est chaud; **I'm getting hot** je commence à avoir chaud; **the water is getting hot** l'eau devient chaude; **how hot should the oven be?** le four doit être à quelle température?; **it was hot work** le travail donnait chaud; **there's hot and cold running water** il y a l'eau courante chaude et froide; **we sat in the hot sun** nous étions assis sous un soleil brûlant; **I'd like a hot bath** j'aimerais prendre un bain bien chaud; **the doctor said not to have any hot drinks** le médecin m'a conseillé de ne pas boire chaud *ou* m'a déconseillé les boissons chaudes; **a hot meal** un repas chaud; **keep the meat hot** tenez la viande au chaud; **serve the soup while it's hot** servez la soupe bien chaude; **the bread was hot from the oven** le pain sortait tout chaud du four; **hot food always available** *(sign)* plats chauds à toute heure; *Fig* **you're getting hot!** *(in guessing game)* tu brûles!; *Fam* **to be** *or* **to get (all) hot and bothered (about sth)** être dans tous ses états *ou* se faire du mauvais sang (au sujet de qch); *Fam* **to be** *or* **to get hot under the collar (about sth)** être en colère *ou* en rogne (au sujet de qch); **the books were selling like hot cakes** les livres se vendaient comme des petits pains; *Fam* **he's full of hot air** c'est une grande gueule; **all her promises are just a lot of hot air** toutes ses promesses ne sont que des paroles en l'air; **that's nothing but hot air!** tout ça n'est que du vent!

(**b**) *(weather)* **it's hot** il fait très chaud; **it's really hot!** il fait vraiment très chaud!; **it's getting hotter** il commence à faire très chaud; **I can't sleep when it's so hot** je ne peux pas dormir par cette chaleur; **it was very hot that day** il faisait très chaud ce jour-là, c'était un jour de grande *ou* forte chaleur; **one hot afternoon in August** (par) une chaude après-midi d'août; **in (the) hot weather** pendant les chaleurs; **we had a hot spell last week** c'était la canicule la semaine dernière; **the hottest day of the year** la journée la plus chaude de l'année

(**c**) *(clothing)* qui tient chaud; **this jacket's too hot** cette veste tient trop chaud

(**d**) *(colour)* chaud, vif

(**e**) *(pungent, spicy* → *food)* épicé, piquant, relevé; *(*→ *spice)* fort; **a hot curry** un curry relevé *ou* épicé

(**f**) *(fresh, recent)* tout(e) frais (fraîche); **the news is hot off the presses** ce sont des informations de toute dernière minute; **this book is hot off the press** ce livre vient juste de paraître

(**g**) *(close, following closely)* **to be hot on the trail** être sur la bonne piste; **the police were hot on their heels** *or* **on their trail** la police les talonnait *ou* était à leurs trousses; **he fled with the police in hot pursuit** il s'est enfui avec la police à ses trousses

(**h**) *(fiery, vehement)* violent; **she has a hot temper** elle s'emporte facilement, elle est très soupe au lait

(**i**) *(intense* → *anger, shame)* intense, profond

(**j**) *(keen)* enthousiaste, passionné; *Am Fam* **he's hot on my sister** il en pince pour ma sœur; **they're very hot on formal qualifications** *(attach importance to)* ils insistent beaucoup sur les diplômes; **they're not very hot on hygiene** *(fussy about)* ils ne sont pas très portés sur l'hygiène

(**k**) *Fam (exciting)* chaud; **the reporter was onto a hot story** le journaliste était sur un coup (fumant); **to have a hot date** avoir un rendez-vous galant ❑; **this book is hot stuff** c'est un livre très audacieux ❑; **this issue is hot stuff, I wouldn't touch it** c'est un sujet brûlant, je n'y toucherais pas

(**l**) *Fam (difficult, unpleasant)* chaud, difficile ❑; **we could make it** *or* **things very hot for you if you don't cooperate** nous pourrions vous mener la vie dure *ou* vous en faire voir de toutes les couleurs si vous ne vous montrez pas coopératif; **the presence of the army made things hot for the smugglers** la présence de l'armée a rendu les choses très difficiles pour les contrebandiers ❑; **the town had got too hot for the drug dealers** l'atmosphère de la ville était devenue irrespirable pour les trafiquants de drogue; **the situation was too hot to handle** la situation était trop délicate pour qu'on s'en mêle ❑

(**m**) *Br Fam (severe, stringent)* sévère ❑, dur ❑; **the police are really hot on drunk driving** la police ne badine vraiment pas avec la conduite en état d'ivresse

(**n**) *Fam (very good)* génial, terrible; *(skilful)*

hor–hot

fort□, calé; **how is he? – not so hot** *(unwell)* comment va-t-il? – pas trop bien□; **I don't feel so hot** je ne suis pas dans mon assiette; **I'm not so hot at maths** je ne suis pas très calé en maths; **she's hot stuff at golf** c'est un as *ou* un crack au golf; **his latest book isn't so hot** son dernier livre n'est pas terrible *ou* fameux; **that isn't such a hot idea** ce n'est pas terrible *ou* fameux comme idée; **that's hot!** c'est super!; **a hot tip** un tuyau sûr *ou* increvable

(**o**) *Fam (in demand, popular)* très recherché□; **she's really hot just now** elle a vraiment beaucoup de succès en ce moment□; **to be hot property** être très demandé□; **windsurfing is hot stuff in this area** la planche à voile est très en vogue dans cette région□

(**p**) *Fam (sexually attractive)* **to be hot (stuff)** être sexy *(inv)*; **he's hot** *(sexually aroused)* il a le feu au derrière; **to be hot to trot** avoir le feu aux fesses

(**q**) *Fam (stolen)* volé□

(**r**) *Br Fam (sought by police)* recherché par la police□

(**s**) *Elec (wire)* sous tension

(**t**) *Nucl (atom)* chaud; *Fam (radioactive)* chaud, radioactif□

(**u**) *Am very Fam* **hot damn!** *(in excitement)* bon sang!, nom d'un chien!; *(in anger)* merde!

2 *adv* **to go hot and cold at the thought of sth** avoir des sueurs froides à l'idée de qch

3 hots *npl Fam* **to have the hots for sb** craquer pour qn

►► ***hot chocolate*** *(drink)* chocolat *m* chaud; ***hot desking*** = pratique qui consiste à ne pas assigner de bureaux individuels aux employés, ces derniers étant libres de s'installer à n'importe quel poste de travail inoccupé; ***hot dog*** **1** *n (sausage)* hot-dog *m*, frankfurter *m*; *Ski* ski *m* acrobatique; *(in surfing)* surf *m* acrobatique; *Am Fam (show-off)* m'as-tu-vu *mf inv* **2** *exclam Am Fam* génial!, super!; ***hot dog stand*** stand *m* de hot-dogs; **we met in front of the hot dog stand** nous nous sommes retrouvés devant le vendeur de hot-dogs; *Metal* ***hot drawing*** tirage *m* à chaud; *Br Sport* ***hot favourite*** grand(e) favori(te) *m,f*; *Am* ***hot flash,*** *Br* ***hot flush*** bouffée *f* de chaleur; ***hot gospeller*** = prêcheur évangéliste qui harangue les foules; *Br* ***hot gossip*** les tous derniers cancans *mpl*; *Fam Aut* ***hot hatch*** cinq-portes *f inv* qui pète le feu; *Fam* ***hot jazz*** (jazz *m*) hot *m inv*; *Comput* ***hot key*** touche *f* personnalisée; *Tel* ***hot line*** numéro *m* d'urgence; *Pol (between US and Kremlin)* téléphone *m* rouge; ***hot line support*** assistance *f* technique téléphonique, hot line *f*; **he has a hot line to the president** il a une ligne directe avec le président; **she's on the hot line to the director** elle téléphone au directeur; **the hot line to the Kremlin** la téléphone rouge avec le Kremlin; *Comput* ***hot link*** lien *m* hypertexte; *Fam* ***hot money*** *(UNCOUNT) (stolen)* argent *m* volé□; *Fin* capitaux *mpl* flottants *ou* fébriles□; *Br* ***hot news*** les toutes dernières nouvelles *fpl*; *Am* ***hot pad*** dessous-de-plat *m inv*; ***hot pants*** mini-short *m (très court et moulant)*; ***hot pepper*** piment *m*; *Fam Fig* ***hot potato*** sujet *m* brûlant et délicat; **a political hot potato** un sujet brûlant *ou* une question brûlante de politique; **to drop sb like a hot potato** laisser tomber qn comme une vieille chaussette *ou* savate; *Ir* ***hot press*** *(airing cupboard)* = placard chauffé où l'on fait sécher le linge; *Fam Aut* ***hot rod*** bagnole *f* trafiquée; *Metal* ***hot rolling*** laminage *m* à chaud; *Am Fam* ***hot seat*** *(electric chair)* chaise *f* électrique□; *Fig* **to be in the hot seat** *(difficult situation)* être sur la sellette; *Phot* ***hot shoe*** griffe *f* du flash, pied-sabot *m*; ***hot spot*** *(dangerous area)* point *m* chaud *ou* névralgique; *Fam (night club)* boîte *f* de nuit□; *Tech* point *m* chaud; **let's hit the town's hot spots** si on faisait la tournée des boîtes?; ***hot spring*** source *f* chaude; *Br Comput* ***hot swap*** *(of devices)* remplacement *m* à chaud; *Am Fam* ***hot ticket:*** **to be a hot ticket** faire fureur; **the play is the hottest ticket in town** c'est la pièce qui a le plus de succès actuellement□; ***hot tub*** = sorte de Jacuzzi® qu'on installe dehors; ***hot war*** guerre *f* chaude *ou* ouverte; ***hot water*** eau *f* chaude; *Fig* **their latest prank got them into** *or* **landed them in hot water** leur dernière farce leur a attiré des ennuis; **you'll be in hot water when she finds out** tu passeras un mauvais quart d'heure quand elle s'en apercevra; ***hot wire*** fil *m* sous tension

►**hot up** *Br Fam* **1** *vt sep* (**a**) *(intensify → argument, contest)* échauffer□; *(→ bombing, fighting)* intensifier□; *(→ party)* mettre de l'animation dans□; *(→ music)* faire balancer, faire chauffer; **they hotted up the pace** ils ont forcé l'allure (**b**) *Aut* **to hot up a car** gonfler le moteur d'une voiture

2 *vi (intensify → discussion, campaign)* s'échauffer□; *(→ fighting, situation)* chauffer□, s'intensifier□; **the price war has hotted up** la guerre des prix s'intensifie; **things are beginning to hot up** ça se corse

'Some like it hot' *Wilder* 'Certains l'aiment chaud'

hot-air balloon *n* montgolfière *f*

hotbed [ˈhɒtbed] *n Hort* couche *f* chaude, forcerie *f*; *Fig* pépinière *f*, foyer *m*; **a hotbed of crime/intrigue** un foyer de crime/d'intrigue

hot-blooded *adj* (**a**) *(person → passionate)* fougueux, au sang chaud (**b**) *(horse → thoroughbred)* de sang pur

hotbox [ˈhɒtbɒks] *n Rail* coussinet *m* échauffé

hotcake [ˈhɒtkeɪk] *n Am Culin* crêpe *f*

hotchpotch [ˈhɒtʃpɒtʃ] *n Br* (**a**) *(jumble)* fatras *m*, salmigondis *m*; **a hotchpotch of ideas** un fatras d'idées (**b**) *Culin* ≃ hochepot *m*, ≃ salmigondis *m*

hot-cross bun *n* = petit pain brioché aux raisins secs et marqué d'une croix que l'on vend traditionnellement à Pâques

hot-dog *vi* (**a**) *Ski* faire du ski acrobatique; *(in surfing)* faire du surf acrobatique (**b**) *Am Fam (show off)* crâner, frimer, poser (pour la galerie)

hot-dogger [-dɒɡə(r)] *n* (**a**) *Ski* skieur(euse) *m,f* acrobatique; *(in surfing)* = personne qui fait du surf acrobatique (**b**) *Am Fam (show-off)* frimeur(euse) *m,f*, crâneur(euse) *m,f*

hot-dogging [-dɒɡɪŋ] *n* (**a**) *Ski* ski *m* acrobatique; *(in surfing)* surf *m* acrobatique (**b**) *Am Fam (showing off)* frime *f*

hotel [həʊˈtel] **1** *n* (**a**) *(accommodation)* hôtel *m*; **to stay at a hotel** descendre dans un hôtel; **a two-star hotel** un hôtel deux étoiles; **a luxury hotel** un hôtel de luxe; **who paid the hotel bill?** qui a payé l'hôtel?

(**b**) *Austr (pub)* pub *m*

2 *comp (prices, reservation, room)* d'hôtel

►► ***hotel accommodation*** hébergement *m* en hôtel; **hotel accommodation not included** frais d'hôtel non inclus; **the town needs more hotel accommodation** la ville a besoin d'augmenter sa capacité hôtelière *ou* de développer ses ressources hôtelières; ***hotel administration*** gestion *f* hôtelière; ***the hotel business*** l'hôtellerie *f*; ***hotel chain*** chaîne *f* d'hôtels; ***hotel desk*** réception *f (d'un hôtel)*; **leave a message at** *or* **with the hotel desk** laissez un message à la réception; ***the hotel industry*** l'industrie *f* hôtelière, l'hôtellerie *f*; ***hotel keeping*** hôtellerie *f*; ***hotel management*** *(training)* gestion *f* hôtelière; *(people)* direction *f (de l'hôtel)*; ***hotel manager*** gérant(e) *m,f* d'hôtel, directeur(trice) *m,f* d'hôtel; ***hotel reception*** réception *f* d'hôtel; ***hotel receptionist*** réceptionniste *mf* d'hôtel; ***hotel register*** agenda *m ou* livre *m* de réservation; ***hotel staff*** personnel *m* hôtelier *ou* de l'hôtel; ***the hotel trade*** l'industrie *f* hôtelière, l'hôtellerie *f*; ***hotel transfer*** transfert *m* (de la gare/l'aéroport à l'hôtel)

hotelier [həʊˈtelɪə(r)] *n* hôtelier(ère) *m,f*

hotelkeeper [həʊˈtelˌkiːpə(r)] *n* hôtelier(ère) *m,f*

hotfoot [ˈhɒtˌfʊt] *Fam* **1** *adv* à toute vitesse□

2 *vt* **to hotfoot it** galoper à toute vitesse

hothead [ˈhɒthed] *n* tête *f* brûlée, exalté(e) *m,f*

hotheaded [ˌhɒtˈhedɪd] *adj (person)* impétueux, exalté; *(attitude)* impétueux; **she's very hotheaded** c'est une exaltée *ou* une tête brûlée

hothouse [ˈhɒthaʊs, *pl* -haʊzɪz] **1** *n* (**a**) *Hort* serre *f* (chaude) (**b**) *Fig (hotbed)* foyer *m*; **a hothouse of creativity/of decadence** un foyer de création/de décadence

2 *adj* de serre (chaude)

►► *also Fig* ***hothouse plant*** plante *f* de serre (chaude); ***hothouse tomatoes*** tomates *fpl* de serre

hot-knife *vi Fam Drugs slang* se droguer au hasch *(en coinçant un morceau de haschich entre deux lames de couteau préalablement chauffées)*

hotlist [ˈhɒtlɪst] *n Comput* liste *f* de signets

hotly [ˈhɒtlɪ] *adv (dispute)* vivement; *(deny)* vigoureusement; *(pursue)* avec acharnement; *(say)* avec flamme; **it was a hotly debated issue** c'était une question très controversée

hotplate [ˈhɒtpleɪt] *n (on stove)* plaque *f* chauffante; *(portable)* chauffe-plats *m inv*

hotpot [ˈhɒtpɒt] *n Br* = ragoût de viande et de pommes de terre

hotshot [ˈhɒtʃɒt] *Fam* **1** *n (expert)* as *m*, crack *m*; *Br (VIP)* gros bonnet *m*; *Am Pej (self-important person)* gros bonnet *m*

2 *adj* super; **they've hired some hotshot lawyer** ils ont pris un as du barreau

hotsy-totsy [ˈhɒtsɪˈtɒtsɪ] *adj Am Fam* **everything's hotsy-totsy** tout est au poil

hotted-up [ˈhɒtɪd-] *adj Fam (car)* au moteur gonflé

hot-tempered *adj* colérique, emporté; **he's very hot-tempered** il est très soupe au lait

Hottentot [ˈhɒtəntɒt] **1** *n* (**a**) *(person)* Hottentot(e) *m,f* (**b**) *Ling* hottentot *m*

2 *adj* hottentot

hotter [ˈhɒtə(r)] *n Fam* cerveau *m* brûlé

hot-water *adj*

►► ***hot-water bottle*** bouillotte *f*; ***hot-water tank*** ballon *m* d'eau chaude

hot-wire *vt Fam* **to hot-wire a car** = faire démarrer une voiture en bricolant les fils de contact

houbara bustard [ˈhʊbərə-] *n Orn* outarde *f* houbara

Houdini [ˌhuːˈdiːnɪ] *pr n* Houdini; *Fig* **a political Houdini** = un homme politique qui se tire de toutes les mauvaises passes; **to perform a Houdini act** se tirer d'une mauvaise passe avec brio

houmous, houmus = **hummus**

hound [haʊnd] **1** *n* (**a**) *(dog → gen)* chien *m*; *(→ for hunting)* chien *m* courant, chien *m* de meute; *Hunt* **the hounds, a pack of hounds** la meute; *Hunt* **to ride to** *or* **to follow the hounds** chasser à courre

(**b**) *Pej Old-fashioned (person)* canaille *f*, crapule *f*

(**c**) *Sport (in paper chase)* coureur(euse) *m,f*, poursuivant(e) *m,f*

2 *vt* (**a**) *(give chase)* traquer, pourchasser

(**b**) *(harass)* s'acharner sur, harceler; **she was hounded by reporters** elle était pourchassée *ou* harcelée par les journalistes

►► *Bot* ***hound's tongue*** cynoglosse *m* officinal, langue-de-chien *f*

►**hound down** *vt sep* prendre dans des rets, coincer; *Hunt* forcer

►**hound out** *vt sep* chasser de; **he was hounded out of town** il a été chassé de la ville

'The Hound of the Baskervilles' *Conan Doyle* 'Le Chien des Baskerville'

houndstooth, hound's-tooth [ˈhaʊndztuːθ] *Tex* **1** *n* pied-de-poule *m*

2 *comp (jacket, skirt)* en pied-de-poule

hour [ˈaʊə(r)] **1** *n* (**a**) *(unit of time)* heure *f*; **a quarter of an hour** un quart d'heure; **half an hour, a half hour** une demi-heure; **an hour and a half** une heure et demie; **an hour and three-quarters** une heure trois quarts; **at 60 km an** *or* **per hour** à 60 km à l'heure; **check it at least three times an hour** vérifie-le au moins trois fois par heure; **it's a two-hour drive/walk from here** c'est à deux heures de voiture/de marche d'ici; **the play is an hour long** la pièce dure une heure, c'est une pièce d'une heure; **he gets £10 an hour** il touche 10 livres (de) l'heure; **are you paid by the hour?** êtes-vous payé à l'heure?; **a 35-hour week** une semaine de 35 heures; **the shop is open 24 hours a day** le magasin est ouvert 24 heures sur 24; **he was an hour late** il était en retard d'une heure; **we arrived with hours to spare** nous sommes arrivés avec plusieurs heures devant nous *ou* en avance de plusieurs heures; **the situation is deteriorating by the hour** la situation s'aggrave d'heure en heure; **it will save you hours** cela te fera gagner des heures; **we waited for hours and hours** on a attendu des heures; **Miami is three hours ahead of Fresno** Miami a trois heures d'avance sur Fresno; *Tech* **output per hour** puissance *f* horaire

(**b**) *(time of day)* heure *f*; **it chimes on the hour** ça sonne à l'heure juste; **every hour on the hour** toutes les heures justes; **in the early** *or* **small hours (of the morning)** au petit matin, au petit jour; **at this late hour** vu l'heure avancée

(**c**) *Fig (specific moment)* heure *f*, moment *m*; **the hour has come** l'heure est venue, c'est l'heure *ou* le moment; **the man of the hour** l'homme de l'heure; **in one's hour of need** quand on est dans le besoin; **the burning questions of the hour** l'actualité *f* brûlante

2 hours *npl* heures *fpl*; *Ind* **flexible working hours** des horaires *mpl* mobiles *ou* souples; **opening hours** heures *fpl* d'ouverture; **you'll have to make up the hours next week** il faudra que vous rattrapiez la semaine prochaine; **what are your hours?, what hours do you work?** quels sont vos horaires de travail?; **do you work long hours?** as-tu de longues journées de travail?; **he keeps late hours** c'est un couche-tard, il veille tard; **to keep regular hours** avoir une vie réglée; **people come and go at all hours** les gens vont et viennent à toute heure; **he was out until all hours** il est rentré à une heure indue; **after hours** *(of office)* après les heures de travail; *Br (of pub)* après l'heure de la fermeture

►► ***hour hand*** petite aiguille *f*

hourglass ['aʊəglɑːs] **1** *n* sablier *m*

2 *adj* en forme d'amphore

►► ***hourglass figure*** taille *f* de guêpe; *Tech* ***hourglass worm*** vis *mf* globique

hour-long *adj* d'une heure

hourly ['aʊəlɪ] **1** *adj* (**a**) *(each hour → flights, trains)* **hourly departures** départs *mpl* toutes les heures

(**b**) *Com & Tech (per hour → earnings, rate)* horaire; **the hourly wage has been increased** le salaire horaire a été augmenté

(**c**) *(continual → anticipation)* constant, perpétuel

2 *adv* (**a**) *(each hour)* une fois par heure, chaque heure, toutes les heures; **to be paid hourly** être payé à l'heure

(**b**) *(repeatedly)* sans cesse; *(at any time)* à tout moment; **we expect them hourly** on les attend d'une minute à l'autre *ou* à tout moment

house **1** *n* [haʊs, *pl* haʊzɪz] (**a**) *(for living in)* maison *f*; **at** *or* **to his house** chez lui; **house for sale** *(sign)* propriété à vendre; **to move house** déménager; **to clean the house,** *Am* **to clean house** faire le ménage; **does he look after the house himself?** est-ce que c'est lui qui s'occupe de son ménage?; **to keep house (for sb)** tenir la maison *ou* le ménage (de qn); **to set up house** monter son ménage, s'installer; **they set up house together** ils se sont mis en ménage; **don't wake up the whole house!** ne réveille pas toute la maison!; *Fam* **we got on** *or* **along like a house on fire** nous nous entendions à merveille *ou* comme larrons en foire; *Fam* **it's coming on like a house on fire** ça marche du feu de Dieu; *Fig* **to set** *or* **to put one's house in order** mettre de l'ordre dans ses affaires; *Fig* **the government should put** *or* **set its own house in order before criticizing others** le gouvernement devrait balayer devant sa porte avant de critiquer les autres; *Br Fam* **the bus goes all round the houses** le bus fait tout le tour de la ville; *Fam Fig* **to go all round the houses** *(not get to the point)* tourner autour du pot; *Fam Fig* **he was sent all round the houses when he tried to get a work permit** on l'a renvoyé de service en service quand il a essayé d'obtenir un permis de travail

(**b**) *Com (company)* maison *f (de commerce)*, compagnie *f*; **publishing house** maison *f* d'édition; **in house** au sein de l'entreprise

(**c**) *(restaurant, bar)* **to have a drink on the house** prendre une consommation aux frais du patron *ou* de la maison; **a bottle of house red** une bouteille de (vin) rouge de la maison *ou* de l'établissement

(**d**) *Rel* maison *f* religieuse

(**e**) *(household)* maison *f*; *(dynasty)* famille *f*, maison *f*; **the House of York** la maison de York; **the whole house was down with flu** toute la maisonnée avait la grippe

(**f**) *Theat* salle *f*, auditoire *m*; **is there a good house tonight?** est-ce que la salle est pleine ce soir?; **a decent house** une salle moyenne; **they played to an empty house** ils ont joué devant les banquettes (vides); **there wasn't a soul in the house** il n'y avait personne dans la salle; **to have a full house** jouer à guichets fermés *ou* à bureaux fermés; **house full** *(sign)* complet; *Br Old-fashioned* **the first/second house** la première/deuxième séance; **to bring the house down** *(performer)* faire crouler la salle sous les applaudissements; *Fig* casser la baraque

(**g**) *Br Sch* = groupe d'élèves qui rivalise avec un autre pour les activités sportives etc

(**h**) *Mus* house *f*

(**i**) *Astrol* maison *f*

(**j**) *(of crane)* cabine *f*; *Naut (on deck)* rouf *m*; *(at helm)* kiosque *m*

(**k**) *(in debate)* **this house believes...** la motion à débattre est la suivante...

2 House *n* **the House** *Br Pol* la Chambre; *Am Pol* la Chambre des représentants; *St Exch* la Bourse (de Londres)

3 *vt* [haʊz] (**a**) *(provide with shelter → person)* héberger, loger; **we can house them temporarily in tents** nous pouvons les loger provisoirement dans des tentes; **many families are still badly housed** de nombreuses familles sont encore mal logées

(**b**) *(store → of building)* recevoir; **this wing houses a laboratory** cette aile abrite un laboratoire; **the library cannot house any more books** la bibliothèque ne peut pas abriter plus de livres; **his boat is housed in the garage during winter** son bateau est (remisé) au garage pendant l'hiver; **the archives are housed in the basement** on garde les archives dans les caves

(**c**) *(protect by covering)* **the gears are housed in a steel case** l'engrenage est contenu dans un carter d'acier; **this section houses the main engines** dans cette section se trouvent les moteurs principaux

4 *exclam* [haʊs] *(in bingo)* ≃ carton!

►► *Br* ***house agent*** agent *m* immobilier; *Am Fam* ***house ape*** *(child)* môme *mf*, chiard *m*; ***house arrest*** assignation *f* à domicile *ou* à résidence; **to put sb under house arrest** assigner qn à domicile *ou* à résidence; **he is under house arrest** il est assigné à domicile, il est en résidence surveillée; *Fin* ***house bill*** double *m* de connaissement, lettre *f* de change creuse; *also Fig* ***house of cards*** château *m* de cartes; ***the House of Commons*** la Chambre des communes; ***house detective*** responsable *m* de la sécurité, détective *m* de l'hôtel; ***house of God*** *(church)* maison *f* de Dieu; *(Protestant)* temple *m*; ***house husband*** homme *m* au foyer; ***house journal*** journal *m* interne, bulletin *m*; *Theat* ***house lights*** lumières *fpl ou* éclairage *m* de la salle; ***the House of Lords*** la Chambre des lords; ***house magazine*** journal *m* interne, bulletin *m*; *Theat* ***house manager*** directeur(trice) *m,f* de théâtre; *Orn* ***house martin*** hirondelle *f* de fenêtre; *Zool* ***house mouse*** souris *f* commune; ***house music*** house *f* (music); *Br Med* ***house officer*** ≃ interne *mf*; ***house painter*** peintre *m* en bâtiment; ***the Houses of Parliament*** le Parlement *m* (britannique); ***house party*** *(social occasion)* fête *f* de plusieurs jours *(dans une maison de campagne)*; *(guests)* invités *mpl*; *Br* ***house physician*** *(in hospital)* ≃ interne *mf* (en médecine); *(in hotel)* médecin *m (attaché à un hôtel)*; ***house of prayer*** église *f*; *(Protestant)* temple *m*; ***the House of Representatives*** la Chambre des représentants *(aux États-Unis)*; ***house rule*** règle *f* de la maison; *(in games)* règle *f* du jeu particulière; *Orn* ***house sparrow*** moineau *m* domestique; ***house special*** *(in restaurant)* spécialité *f* (de la) maison; *Br Typ & Press* ***house style*** style *m* maison; *Br* ***house surgeon*** ≃ interne *mf* (en chirurgie); *Am* ***house trailer*** caravane *f*; ***the House Un-American Activities Committee*** = organisme maccarthyste de répression anticommuniste fondé en 1938 et dissous en 1975; *Br* ***house wine*** vin *m* de la maison; *f* ***house of worship*** église *f*; *(Protestant)* temple *m*; *Orn* ***house wren*** troglodyte *m* familier

'The House of the Dead' *Dostoyevsky* 'Souvenirs de la maison des morts'

'The House of Mirth' *Wharton, Davies* 'Chez les heureux du monde'

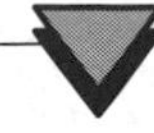

HOUSE

Dans certaines écoles en Grande-Bretagne, les élèves sont répartis en plusieurs "houses", qui regroupent des élèves de tous les âges, désignées chacune par un nom, entre lesquelles se développe un certain esprit de compétition.

HOUSE OF COMMONS

La Chambre des communes britannique est composée de 659 députés ("MPs") élus pour cinq ans et qui siègent environ 175 jours par an. Les députés du parti majoritaire s'assoient d'un côté de la Chambre (les "government benches"), tandis que les députés de l'opposition s'assoient de l'autre côté (sur les "opposition benches"). Si un projet de loi n'obtient pas l'approbation de la majorité des députés dans la Chambre des communes, il est renvoyé à la Chambre des lords, et doit par ailleurs obtenir l'assentiment du souverain avant de devenir loi.

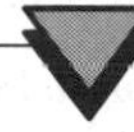

HOUSE OF LORDS

La Chambre des lords est composée de pairs et d'hommes d'Église. Il s'agit de la plus haute cour au Royaume-Uni (en excluant l'Écosse). Elle a le pouvoir d'amender certains projets de loi qui ont été votés par la Chambre des communes. Le gouvernement travailliste de Tony Blair, élu en 1997, a entrepris des réformes visant à réduire les pouvoirs de la Chambre des lords de façon radicale.

HOUSE OF REPRESENTATIVES

La Chambre des représentants constitue, avec le Sénat, l'organe législatif américain; ses membres sont élus par le peuple, en proportion de la population de chaque État.

houseboat ['haʊsbəʊt] *n* house-boat *m*, péniche *f* (aménagée)

housebound ['haʊsbaʊnd] *adj* qui ne peut quitter la maison

houseboy ['haʊsbɔɪ] *n* domestique *m*, valet *m*; *(colonial)* boy *m*

housebreaker ['haʊs,breɪkə(r)] *n* cambrioleur(euse) *m,f*

housebreaking ['haʊs,breɪkɪŋ] *n* cambriolage *m*

housebroken ['haʊs,brəʊkən] *adj Am (pet)* propre

housebuilder ['haʊsbɪldə(r)] *n* entrepreneur *m* en bâtiment

housebuilding ['haʊsbɪldɪŋ] *n* construction *f* de logements

houseclean ['haʊskliːn] *vi* faire le ménage

housecleaner ['haus,kliːnə(r)] *n* employé(e) *m,f* d'une entreprise de nettoyage

housecleaning ['haus,kliːnɪŋ] *n* nettoyage *m*, ménage *m*

housecoat ['haʊskəʊt] *n* robe *f* d'intérieur

housecraft ['haʊskrɑːft] *n* économie *f* ménagère

housefather ['haʊs,fɑːðə(r)] *n* responsable *m* (de groupe) *(dans un foyer)*

housefly ['haʊsflaɪ] (*pl* **houseflies**) *n Entom* mouche *f* (commune *ou* domestique)

houseful ['haʊsfʊl] *n* **a houseful of guests** une pleine maisonnée d'invités; **we've got a real houseful this weekend** la maison est vraiment pleine (de monde) ce week-end

houseguest ['haʊsgest] *n* invité(e) *m,f*

household ['haʊshəʊld] **1** *n (people in house)* (membres *mpl* de la) maison *f*; *(economically, statistically)* ménage *m*; **she grew up as part of a large household** elle a grandi au sein d'une

hou–hou

famille nombreuse; **the head of the household** le chef de famille; **indicate your relationship to the other members of your household** indiquez les liens de parenté existant entre vous et les autres personnes qui résident avec vous *ou* de votre foyer; **households with more than two children** ménages *mpl ou* familles *fpl* de plus de deux enfants; **95 percent of households have a television set** 95 pour cent des ménages possèdent un poste de télévision; **the Royal Household** la maison royale

2 *adj* de ménage; *Admin & Econ* des ménages; **for household use only** *(on packaging)* à usage domestique seulement

▸▸ ***household appliance*** appareil *m* ménager; ***Household Cavalry*** = division de cavalerie de la Garde royale britannique; ***household consumption*** consommation *f* des ménages; ***household expenses*** frais *mpl* de *ou* du ménage; *Hist* ***household gods*** dieux *mpl* du foyer; ***household goods*** articles *mpl* pour le ménage, produits *mpl* ménagers; ***household name*** *(brand, product)* nom *m* de marque connu; **we want to make our brand a household name** nous voulons que notre marque soit connue de tous; **she's a household name** tout le monde la connaît *ou* sait qui elle est; ***household troops*** garde *f* personnelle; *Hist* garde *f* du palais; *(in UK)* Garde *f* royale; ***household word*** = mot que tout le monde connaît

householder ['haʊsˌhəʊldə(r)] *n (occupant)* occupant(e) *m,f*; *(owner)* propriétaire *mf*; *(tenant)* locataire *mf*

househunt ['haʊsˌhʌnt] *vi* chercher un *ou* être à la recherche d'un logement

househunting ['haʊsˌhʌntɪŋ] *n* recherche *f* d'un logement; **I spent two months househunting** j'ai passé deux mois à chercher un logement *ou* à la recherche d'un logement

housekeeper ['haʊsˌkiːpə(r)] *n (institutional)* économe *f*, intendante *f*; *(in a hotel)* gouvernante *f*; *(private)* gouvernante *f*; **she's a good/bad housekeeper** c'est une bonne/mauvaise maîtresse de maison

housekeeping ['haʊsˌkiːpɪŋ] *n (UNCOUNT)* (**a**) *(of household → skill)* économie *f* domestique; *(→ work)* ménage *m* (**b**) *(of organization)* services *mpl* généraux (**c**) *Comput* gestion *f* interne

▸▸ ***housekeeping book*** carnet *m* de dépenses; ***housekeeping money*** argent *m* du ménage

houseleek ['haʊsliːk] *n Bot* joubarbe *f*

housemaid ['haʊsmeɪd] *n* bonne *f*, femme *f* de chambre

▸▸ *Med* ***housemaid's knee*** inflammation *f* du genou

houseman ['haʊsmən] *(pl* **housemen** [-mən]) *n* (**a**) *Br Med* ≃ interne *mf* (**b**) *(servant)* domestique *m*, valet *m*

housemaster ['haʊsˌmɑːstə(r)] *n Br Sch* = professeur responsable d'une "house"

housemen ['haʊsmən] *pl of* **houseman**

housemistress ['haʊsˌmɪstrɪs] *n Br Sch* = professeur responsable d'une "house"

housemother ['haʊsˌmʌðə(r)] *n* responsable *f* (de groupe) *(dans un foyer)*

house-owner *n* propriétaire *mf*

houseparent ['haʊsˌpeərənt] *n* responsable *mf* (de groupe) *(dans un foyer)*

house-parlourmaid *n* = femme de chambre qui fait aussi le service de table

houseplant ['haʊsplɑːnt] *n* plante *f* d'intérieur

house-proud *adj* **he's very house-proud** il attache beaucoup d'importance à l'aspect intérieur de sa maison, tout est toujours impeccable chez lui

houseroom ['haʊsrʊm] *n Br* place *f (pour loger quelqu'un ou quelque chose)*; **he has houseroom for two** il a de la place pour deux; **I wouldn't give that table houseroom!** je ne voudrais pas de cette table chez moi!

house-sit *vi* **to house-sit for sb** = s'occuper de la maison de quelqu'un pendant son absence

house-sitter *n* = personne qui garde une maison en l'absence de ses occupants

house-to-house *adj (enquiry)* de porte en porte; **to make a house-to-house search for sb/sth** aller de porte en porte à la recherche de qn/qch, fouiller chaque maison à la recherche de qn/qch

▸▸ *Mktg* ***house-to-house canvassing*** porte-à-porte *m inv*, démarchage *m*

housetop ['haʊstɒp] *n* toit *m*; *Fig* **to shout** *or* **to proclaim sth from the housetops** crier qch sur les toits

house-train *vt Br (pet)* dresser à la propreté; **has the dog been house-trained?** est-ce que le chien est propre?; *Fam Hum* **he used to be really untidy, but she soon got him house-trained!** avant, il était très brouillon, mais elle a eu tôt fait de le dresser!

housewares ['haʊsweəz] *npl* articles *mpl* ménagers

housewarming ['haʊsˌwɔːmɪŋ] *n* pendaison *f* de crémaillère

▸▸ ***housewarming party*** pendaison *f* de crémaillère; **to give** *or* **to have a housewarming (party)** pendre la crémaillère

housewife *n* (**a**) ['haʊswaɪf] *(pl* **housewives** [-waɪvz]) ménagère *f*; *(not career woman)* femme *f* au foyer (**b**) ['hʌzɪf] *(pl* **housewives** [-zɪvz]) *Br Old-fashioned (sewing kit)* trousse *f* de couture

housewifely ['haʊsˌwaɪflɪ] *adj* de ménagère

housewifery ['haʊswɪfərɪ] *n* économie *f* domestique

housewives ['haʊswaɪvz] *pl of* **housewife**

housework ['haʊswɜːk] *n* (travaux *mpl* de) ménage *m*; **to do the housework** faire le ménage; **we share the housework** nous nous partageons le ménage, nous faisons le ménage à tour de rôle

houseworker ['hauswɜːkə(r)] *n Am* bonne *f* (à tout faire), femme *f* de ménage

housey-housey [ˌhaʊzɪ'haʊzɪ] *n Br* ≃ loto *m (joué pour de l'argent)*

housing ['haʊzɪŋ] *n* (**a**) *(accommodation)* logement *m*; **the government has promised to provide more low-cost housing** le gouvernement a promis de fournir plus de logements à loyer modéré; **the budget allocation for housing has been cut** la part du budget réservée au logement a été réduite; **2 percent still live in substandard housing** 2 pour cent habitent encore des logements qui ne sont pas aux normes; **there's a lot of new housing going up in the area** il y a beaucoup de logements nouveaux en construction dans le quartier; **the government has no long-term housing strategy** le gouvernement n'a aucune stratégie à long terme en matière de logement; **four housing units** quatre logements *mpl ou* habitations *fpl*

(**b**) *Tech (of mechanism)* carter *m*; *Phot* boîtier *m*; **wheel housing** boîte *f* de roue; **watch housing** boîtier *m* de montre

(**c**) *Constr* encastrement *m*

▸▸ ***housing association*** = association britannique à but non lucratif qui construit ou rénove des logements pour les louer à ses membres; *Br* ***housing benefit*** = allocation de logement versée par l'État aux individus justifiant de revenus faibles; ***the local housing department*** ≃ l'antenne logement (de la commune); ***housing development*** *(estate)* lotissement *m*; *(activity)* construction *f* de logements; *Br* ***housing estate*** *(privately owned houses)* lotissement *m*; *(council owned flats)* grand ensemble *m*; *Br* ***housing list*** = liste d'attente pour bénéficier d'un logement social; ***housing market*** marché *m* de l'immobilier; *Am* ***housing project*** grand ensemble *m*; *(plan)* plan *m* d'aménagement immobilier; ***housing scheme*** *(plan)* programme *m* municipal de logement; *(privately owned houses)* lotissement *m*; *(council owned flats)* grand ensemble *m*; ***housing shortage*** crise *f* du logement; *Am* ***housing starts*** = mise en chantier de logements

Houston [*Br* 'hjuːstən, *Am* 'huːstən] *n* Houston

> **Houston, we have a problem**
> Ce sont les mots que prononça le commandant de la mission Apollo 13 (en 1970) à l'intention du centre de contrôle à Houston au Texas, lorsqu'il s'aperçut que la capsule spatiale connaissait de graves problèmes techniques.
> Aujourd'hui, on utilise cette formule ("Houston, nous avons un problème") pour indiquer à quelqu'un que quelque chose ne va pas. Il faut noter que le mot "Houston" est toujours prononcé à l'américaine, même par les Britanniques.

houting ['haʊtɪŋ] *n Ich* corégone *m*

HOV [ˌeɪtʃəʊ'viː] *n Am (abbr* **High Occupancy Vehicle**) = voiture transportant au moins deux passagers

▸▸ ***HOV lane*** = voie d'autoroute réservée aux automobiles occupées par au moins deux passagers

hove [həʊv] *pt & pp of* **heave**

hovel ['hɒvəl] *n* taudis *m*, masure *f*

hover ['hɒvə(r)] **1** *vi* (**a**) *(in air → smoke)* stagner; *(→ balloon, scent)* flotter; *(→ insects)* voltiger; *(→ helicopter, hummingbird)* faire du surplace; **bees hovered around the roses** des abeilles voltigeaient autour des roses

(**b**) *(linger → person)* rôder; *(→ smile)* flotter; *(→ danger)* planer; **a waitress was hovering near our table** une serveuse tournait autour de notre table; **I don't like him hovering over me** je n'aime pas qu'il soit sur mon dos; **it's no use hovering over the phone like that** ce n'est pas la peine de guetter la sonnerie du téléphone comme ça; **she was hovering between life and death** elle restait suspendue entre la vie et la mort; **don't just hover in the background** ne reste pas dans ton coin

(**c**) *(hesitate)* hésiter; **his finger hovered over the button** son doigt hésita à appuyer sur le bouton; **I'm hovering between the two possible options** j'hésite entre les deux options possibles; **he seemed to be hovering on the brink of saying something** il semblait hésiter à dire quelque chose

2 *n* aéroglisseur *m*

▸**hover around 1** *vt insep (move about near)* **to hover around sb** errer *ou* rôder autour de qn; **prices are hovering around the £3.50 mark** les prix oscillent autour de 3 livres 50

2 *vi (move about nearby)* tourner

hovercraft ['hɒvəkrɑːft] *n* aéroglisseur *m*

hoverfly ['hɒvəflaɪ] *(pl* **hoverflies**) *n Entom* syrphe *m*

hoverport ['hɒvəpɔːt] *n* hoverport *m*

hovertrain ['hɒvətreɪn] *n* train *m* à coussin d'air

HOW [haʊ]

comment	▸ **1 (a), (b); 2 (a), (b); 3**
comme	▸ **1 (c); 2 (c)**
que	▸ **1 (c); 2 (b)**

1 *adv* (**a**) *(in what way)* comment; **how do you spell it?** comment est-ce que ça s'écrit?; **how shall we go about it?** comment nous y prendre?; **how was she dressed?** comment est-ce qu'elle était habillée?, qu'est-ce qu'elle portait?; **how could you be so careless?** comment as-tu pu être aussi étourdi?; **how could you!** tu n'as pas honte?; **how is it that...?** comment se fait-il que...?; **how so?, how can that be?** comment cela (se fait-il)?; **how's that (again)?** comment?; **how's that for results?** alors ces résultats, qu'est-ce que vous en pensez?; **how's that for size?** ça va comme taille?; **suppose I offer you another £500, how's that?** et si je t'offre 500 livres en plus, qu'est-ce que tu en dis?; *Fam* **how the heck should I know?** mais enfin, comment veux-tu que je sache?

(**b**) *(in greetings, friendly enquiries etc)* comment; **how are you?** comment allez-vous?; **how are you doing?** comment ça va?; **how do you do?** enchanté!; **how are things?** ça marche?; **how's business?** comment vont les affaires?; *Fam* **how's life?** comment ça va?; **how did it go?** comment ça s'est passé?; **how's the dollar (doing)?** comment va le dollar?; **how's your leg?** et (comment va) ta jambe?; **how do you like this wine?** comment trouvez-vous ce vin?; **how did you like** *or* **how was the film?** comment as-tu trouvé le film?; **how was your trip?** avez-vous fait bon voyage?; **how's the water?** l'eau est bonne?

(**c**) *(in exclamations)* que, comme; **how sad she is!** qu'elle est triste!, comme elle est triste!; **how nice of you!** comme c'est aimable à vous!; **how decadent!** quelle décadence!; **how incredible!** c'est incroyable!; **how easily they forget!** comme ils oublient facilement!; **how I wish I could!** si seulement je pouvais!; *Fam* **how stupid can you get!** est-il possible d'être bête à ce point-là!

(**d**) *(with adj or adv) (to what extent)* **how wide is the room?** quelle est la largeur de la pièce?; **how tall are you?** combien mesures-tu?; **how old is she?** quel âge a-t-elle?; **how well can you see it?** est-ce que tu le vois bien?; **how angry is he?** il est vraiment fâché?; **how fast/slowly was he walking?** à quelle vitesse marchait-il?; **how far is it from here to the sea?** combien y a-t-il d'ici à la mer?; **how likely is that to happen?** quelle est la probabilité d'un tel événement?; **how keen are you on fish?** aimez-vous le poisson?; **how much does this bag cost?** combien coûte ce sac?; **how much is it/do I owe you?** combien est-ce que ça coûte/vous dois-je?; **how many are there of you?** vous êtes combien (de personnes)?; **how often did she come? – about three or four times** combien de fois est-elle venue? – trois ou quatre fois; **how often did he write?** est-ce qu'il écrivait souvent?; **how long has he been here?** depuis quand *ou* depuis combien de temps est-il ici?; **how long is the flight?** quelle est la durée du vol?; **how soon can you deliver it?** à partir de quand pouvez-vous le livrer?; **how late will you stay?** jusqu'à quelle heure resteras-tu?; **you know how useful he is to me** vous savez à quel point il m'est utile; **you don't know how right you are** vous ne savez pas combien vous dites vrai, vous ne savez pas à quel point vous avez raison

2 *conj* (**a**) *(in what way)* comment; **tell me how you do it** dites-moi comment vous faites; **he's learning how to read** il apprend à lire; **we know how to extract it** nous savons comment l'extraire; **I need more information on how the network functions** j'ai besoin de plus de renseignements sur le fonctionnement du réseau; **I don't know how he can say that!** je ne sais pas comment il peut dire une chose pareille!

(**b**) *(the fact that)* **he told us how he had seen his child born** il nous a raconté qu'il avait vu naître son enfant; **you know how he always gets his own way** tu sais bien comment il est, il finit toujours par obtenir ce qu'il veut; **we all know how smell can influence taste** tout le monde sait comment l'odorat a une influence sur le goût; **I remember how he always used to turn up late** je me souviens qui'il était toujours en retard

(**c**) *Fam (however)* comme ❑; **arrange the furniture how you like** installe les meubles comme tu veux; **did you like it? – and how!** ça t'a plu? – et comment!

3 *n* comment *m inv*; **the how and the why of it don't interest me** le pourquoi et le comment ne m'intéressent pas

4 *exclam Hum (greeting)* salut

5 how about *adv Fam* **how about a beer?** et si on prenait une bière?; **how about going out tonight?** si on sortait ce soir?; **how about Friday?** vendredi, ça va?; **how about you, what do you think?** et toi, qu'est-ce que tu en penses?; **how about that!** c'est pas vrai!

6 how come *adv Fam* **how come?** comment ça se fait?; **how come you left?** comment ça se fait que tu sois parti?

Howard ['haʊəd] *pr n*

►► ***the Howard League for Penal Reform*** – association britannique contre la torture et la peine de mort

howbeit [ˌhaʊ'biːɪt] *conj Arch* bien que + *subjunctive*

howdah ['haʊdə] *n* = siège pour monter à dos d'éléphant

howdy ['haʊdɪ] *exclam Am Fam* salut!

however [haʊ'evə(r)] **1** *adv* (**a**) *(indicating contrast or contradiction)* cependant, pourtant, toutefois; **I didn't see him, however** cependant *ou* pourtant je ne l'ai pas vu; **if, however, you have a better suggestion...** si toutefois vous avez une meilleure suggestion (à faire)...

(**b**) *(with adj or adv) (no matter how)* si... que + *subjunctive*, quelque... que + *subjunctive*; **however nice he tries to be...** si gentil qu'il essaie d'être...; **all contributions will be welcome, however small** si petites soient-elles, toutes les contributions seront les bienvenues; **he'll never do it, however much** *or* **hard he tries** quelque effort qu'il fasse, il n'y arrivera jamais; **however cold/hot the weather** même quand il fait très froid/chaud; **however late/early you arrive, call me** quelle que soit l'heure à laquelle tu arrives, appelle-moi; **however long it takes (you)** quel que soit le temps que cela (te) prend; **however much he complains** même s'il se plaint beaucoup

(**c**) *(in questions) (emphatic use)* comment; **however did he find it?** comment a-t-il bien pu le trouver?

2 *conj (in whatever way)* de quelque manière que + *subjunctive*, comme; **it'll be fine, however you do it** de quelque manière que vous le fassiez, ça ira; **we can present it however you like** *or* **want** on peut le présenter comme vous voulez

howitzer ['haʊɪtsə(r)] *n Mil* obusier *m*

howl [haʊl] **1** *n* (**a**) *(of person, animal)* hurlement *m*; *(of child)* braillement *m*, hurlement *m*; *(of wind)* mugissement *m*; **to let out a howl of pain** pousser un hurlement de douleur; **the speech was greeted with howls of derision** le discours a été accueilli par des huées

(**b**) *Electron* effet *m* Larsen

2 *vi* (**a**) *(person, animal)* hurler; *(child)* brailler; *(wind)* mugir; **to howl with laughter** hurler de rire; **to howl in** *or* **with rage** hurler de rage

(**b**) *Fam (cry)* chialer

3 *vt* crier, hurler; **they howled their defiance at the guards** ils ont hurlé leur colère aux gardes

►**howl down** *vt sep (speaker)* **they howled him down** ils l'ont réduit au silence par leurs huées

►**howl out** *vt sep* crier, hurler

howler ['haʊlə(r)] *n* (**a**) *Fam (blunder)* gaffe *f*, bourde *f* (**b**) *Zool (monkey)* (singe *m*) hurleur *m*, alouate *m*

►► *Zool* ***howler monkey*** (singe *m*) hurleur *m*, alouate *m*

howling ['haʊlɪŋ] **1** *n (of person, animal)* hurlement *m*, hurlements *mpl*; *(of child)* braillement *m*, braillements *mpl*; *(of wind)* mugissement *m*, mugissements *mpl*

2 *adj* (**a**) *(person, animal)* qui hurle; *(child)* qui braille; *(gale, wind)* furieux (**b**) *Fam (error)* énorme ❑; *(success)* fou (folle) ❑

howsoever [ˌhaʊsəʊ'evə(r)] = **however** *adv*

how's-your-father *n Br Fam Hum (sexual intercourse)* **a bit of how's-your-father** une partie de jambes en l'air

how-to *Am* **1** *n* **he gave me the how-to** il m'a expliqué comment il fallait faire

2 *adj* **he loves those how-to cookery programmes** il adore ces émissions où on explique des recettes de cuisine

howzat [haʊ'zæt] *exclam Fam (in cricket)* sortez le batteur! ❑

hoy [hɔɪ] *exclam Br (to people)* ohé!, hep!; *(to animals)* hue!

hoyden ['hɔɪdən] *n* garçon *m* manqué

hoydenish ['hɔɪdənɪʃ] *adj* garçonnier

hp[1], **HP**[1] [ˌeɪtʃ'piː] *n Br (abbr* **hire purchase**) **to buy sth on hp** acheter qch à crédit

hp[2], **HP**[2] *(written abbr* **horsepower**) CV

HP Sauce® *n* = sauce épicée vendue en bouteille

HQ [ˌeɪtʃ'kjuː] *n Mil (abbr* **headquarters**) QG *m*

HR [ˌeɪtʃ'ɑː(r)] *n (abbr* **human resources**) RH *fpl*

hr (**a**) *(written abbr* **hour**) h (**b**) *Am Sport (written abbr* **home run**) coup *m* de circuit *(coup de batte qui permet au batteur de marquer un point en faisant un tour complet en une seule fois)*

HRH *(written abbr* **His/Her Royal Highness**) SAR

HRM [ˌeɪtʃɑː'rem] *n (abbr* **human resource management**) GRH *f*

hrs *(written abbr* **hours**) h

HRT [ˌeɪtʃɑː'tiː] *n Med (abbr* **hormone replacement therapy**) traitement *m* hormonal substitutif

HS *Am (written abbr* **high school**) lycée *m*

HSC [ˌeɪtʃes'siː] *n Austr (abbr* **Higher School Certificate**) ≃ baccalauréat *m*

HSE [ˌeɪtʃes'iː] *n (abbr* **Health and Safety Executive**) inspection *f* du travail

HST [ˌeɪtʃes'tiː] *n* (**a**) *(abbr* **high speed train**) ≃ TGV *m* (**b**) *(abbr* **Hawaiian Standard Time**) heure *f* d'Hawaii

HT (**a**) *(written abbr* **high tension**) HT (**b**) *Sport (written abbr* **half-time**) mi-temps *f*

ht *(written abbr* **height**) hauteur *f*

HTML [ˌeɪtʃtiːˌem'el] *n Comput (abbr* **Hypertext Markup Language**) HTML *m*

►► ***HTML editor*** éditeur *m* HTML

HTTP [ˌeɪtʃtiːtiː'piː] *n Comput (abbr* **Hypertext Transfer Protocol**) protocole *m* HTTP

►► ***HTTP server*** serveur *m* Web

HUAC ['hjuːæk] *n Am Hist (abbr* **House Un-American Activities Committee**) = organisme maccarthyste de répression anticommuniste fondé en 1938 et dissous en 1975

hub [hʌb] *n (of wheel)* moyeu *m*; *Fig* centre *m*; *Comput* hub *m*, concentrateur *m*

►► ***hub airport*** aéroport *m* important *(qui sert de plaque tournante)*

hub-and-spoke *adj* (**a**) *Aviat* **a hub-and-spoke airline network** = un réseau aérien qui fonctionne à partir d'un aéroport principal qui sert de plaque tournante (**b**) *Am (holiday tour)* = avec excursions organisées à partir d'un lieu de séjour fixe

hubba-hubba ['hʌbə'hʌbə] *exclam Am Fam* super!

hubble-bubble ['hʌbəl-] *n Br* (**a**) *(hookah)* narguilé *m*, houka *m* (**b**) *(bubbling sound)* glouglou *m*

hubbub ['hʌbʌb] *n (of voices)* brouhaha *m*; *(uproar)* vacarme *m*, tapage *m*

hubby ['hʌbɪ] *(pl* **hubbies**) *n Fam* bonhomme *m*, petit mari *m*

hubcap ['hʌbkæp] *n Aut* enjoliveur *m* (de roue)

hubris ['hjuːbrɪs] *n* orgueil *m* démesuré, outrecuidance *f*

hubristic [hjuː'brɪstɪk] *adj* orgueilleux, outrecuidant

huckleberry ['hʌkəlbərɪ] *(pl* **huckleberries**) *n Bot* airelle *f*, myrtille *f*

huckster ['hʌkstə(r)] *n* (**a**) *(pedlar)* colporteur(euse) *m,f* (**b**) *Am Pej (in advertising)* publicitaire *mf* agressif(ive) (**c**) *(profiteer)* mercanti *m*, profiteur(euse) *m,f*; **political huckster** politicard(e) *m,f*

huckstering ['hʌkstərɪŋ] *n* (**a**) *(peddling)* colportage *m* (**b**) **political huckstering** politicailleries *fpl*, trafics *mpl*

HUD [hʌd] *n Am Formerly (abbr* **Department of Housing and Urban Development**) = ancien ministère américain de l'Urbanisme et du Logement

huddle ['hʌdəl] **1** *n* (**a**) *(of people)* petit groupe *m* (serré); *(of objects)* tas *m*, amas *m*; *(of roofs)* enchevêtrement *m*; *Fam* **to go into a huddle** se réunir en petit comité (**b**) *Sport* concentration *f (d'une équipe)*

2 *vi* (**a**) *(crowd together)* se blottir; **the sheep huddled under the trees** les moutons se blottissaient les uns contre les autres sous les arbres; **they huddled round the fire** ils se sont blottis autour du feu (**b**) *(crouch)* se recroqueviller, se blottir; **he huddled in a corner of his cell** il s'est recroquevillé dans un coin de sa cellule; **she was huddling under a blanket** elle se blottissait sous une couverture

►**huddle together** *vi* se serrer *ou* se blottir les uns contre les autres; *(for talk)* se mettre en petit groupe *ou* cercle serré; **they huddled together for warmth** ils se serraient *ou* se blottissaient les uns contre les autres pour se tenir chaud

►**huddle up** *vi* se blottir

huddled ['hʌdld] *adj* (**a**) *(for shelter)* blotti; *(curled up)* pelotonné; **I found him huddled in a ditch** je l'ai trouvé blotti dans un fossé; **huddled up in bed** couché en chien de fusil; **huddled up in a corner** blotti dans un coin; **they lay huddled under the blanket** ils étaient blottis *ou* pelotonnés les uns contre les autres sous la couverture; **the houses lay huddled in the valley** les maisons étaient blotties dans la vallée

(**b**) *(hunched)* recroquevillé; **he spends hours huddled over those maps** il passe des heures penché sur ces cartes

Hudson ['hʌdsən] *n (river)* l'Hudson *m*

►► ***Hudson Bay*** la baie d'Hudson; ***the Hudson River*** l'Hudson *m*; ***the Hudson River School*** = groupe de peintres américains du XVIIIème siècle, connus pour leurs paysages romantiques; ***the Hudson Strait*** le détroit d'Hudson

hue [hjuː] *n* (**a**) *(colour)* teinte *f*, nuance *f* (**b**) *(aspect)* nuance *f*; **that puts a different hue on the matter** cela donne à l'affaire une autre coloration, cela fait voir l'affaire sous un autre jour (**c**) *Br (idiom)* **a hue and cry** une clameur (de haro); **to raise a hue and cry against sb/sth** crier haro sur qn/qch

-hued [hju:d] *suff* **dark/light-hued** de couleur foncée/claire; **many-hued** multicolore, bigarré

huff [hʌf] **1** *vi (idiom)* **to huff and puff** *(with exertion)* haleter; *(with annoyance)* maugréer; *Br Fig* **they'll huff and puff a bit but they won't stop us** ils protesteront, mais ils nous laisseront faire

2 *vt* (**a**) *(in draughts → opponent's piece)* souffler

(**b**) *Am Fam (glue, solvents)* sniffer

3 *n Fam* **to be in a huff** faire la tête, bouder□; *Br* **to take the huff** prendre la mouche; **it's no use getting into a huff about it** ça ne sert à rien de t'énerver□; **he went off in a huff** il est parti fâché□

huffed [hʌft] *adj Fam* fâché□

huffily ['hʌfɪlɪ] *adv Fam (reply)* d'un ton vexé *ou* fâché□; *(behave)* avec (mauvaise) humeur□

huffiness ['hʌfɪnɪs] *n Fam (bad mood)* mauvaise humeur□ *f*; *(by nature)* susceptibilité□ *f*

huffy ['hʌfɪ] *adj Fam* **to be huffy** *(in bad mood)* faire la tête, bouder□; *(by nature)* être susceptible□, être chatouilleux□

hug [hʌg] *(pt & pp* **hugged,** *cont* **hugging) 1** *vt* (**a**) *(in arms)* serrer dans ses bras, étreindre; *Fig* **to hug oneself with delight (over** *or* **about sth)** se réjouir vivement (de qch)

(**b**) *Fig (idea)* tenir à, chérir; **she hugged the memory of that moment to herself** elle chérissait le souvenir de cet instant

(**c**) *(keep close to)* serrer; *(boat)* **to hug the shore** serrer la côte; *Aut* **don't hug the kerb** ne serrez pas le trottoir; **this car hugs the corners well** cette voiture prend bien les virages; **clothes that hug the figure** vêtements *mpl* qui moulent la silhouette; *Aviat* **to hug the ground** suivre le relief du terrain

2 *n* (**a**) *(gesture of affection)* étreinte *f*; **to give sb a hug** serrer qn dans ses bras, étreindre qn; **give me a hug** prends-moi dans tes bras; **they greeted each other with hugs and kisses** ils se sont accueillis avec de grandes embrassades

(**b**) *(in wrestling)* prise *f*

huge [hju:dʒ] *adj (in size, degree)* énorme, immense; *(in extent)* vaste, immense; *(in volume)* énorme, gigantesque

hugely ['hju:dʒlɪ] *adv (increase)* énormément; *(as intensifier)* énormément, extrêmement; **the project has been hugely successful/expensive** le projet a été un succès complet/a coûté extrêmement cher

hugeness ['hju:dʒnɪs] *n* immensité *f*; *(of error, demands)* énormité *f*

huggable ['hʌgəbəl] *adj* trognon

hugger-mugger ['hʌgə-] *Arch* **1** *n* (**a**) *(disorder)* fatras *m*, fouillis *m*, désordre *m* (**b**) *(secrecy)* secret *m*

2 *adj* désordonné

3 *adv* en désordre

-hugging ['hʌgɪŋ] *suff* **hip/figure/***etc***-hugging** *(of clothes)* qui moule les hanches/la silhouette/*etc*

Huguenot ['hju:gənəʊ] *Hist* **1** *n* Huguenot(e) *m,f*

2 *adj* huguenot

huh [hʌ] *exclam* **huh?** *(in surprise)* hein?; **huh!** *(in scepticism)* hum!

hula ['hu:lə], **hula-hula** *n* danse *f* polynésienne

►► ***hula skirt*** jupe *f* en paille

Hula-Hoop® ['hu:lə,hu:p] *n* Hula-Hoop® *m*

hulk [hʌlk] *n* (**a**) *(ship)* épave *f*; *Pej* vieux rafiot *m*; *Hist (used as prison, storehouse)* ponton *m*; **to be sent to the hulks** être envoyé au ponton (**b**) *(person, thing)* mastodonte *m*; **a great hulk of a man** un malabar

hulking ['hʌlkɪŋ] *adj* (**a**) *(person)* balourd, massif; *(thing)* gros (grosse), imposant (**b**) *(as intensifier)* **you hulking great oaf!** espèce de malotru!

hull [hʌl] **1** *n* (**a**) *(of ship)* coque *f*; *Mil (of tank)* caisse *f* (**b**) *(of peas, beans)* cosse *f*, gousse *f*; *(of nut)* écale *f*; *(of strawberry)* calice *m*

2 *vt* (**a**) *(peas)* écosser; *(nuts)* écaler, décortiquer; *(grains)* décortiquer; *(strawberries)* équeuter (**b**) *(ship)* percer la coque de

hullabaloo [,hʌləbə'lu:] *n Fam* raffut *m*, chambard *m*, barouf *m*; **the press made a real hullabaloo about it** la presse en a fait tout un foin

hullo = **hello**

hum [hʌm] *(pt & pp* **hummed,** *cont* **humming) 1** *vi* (**a**) *(audience, bee, wires)* bourdonner; *(person)* fredonner, chantonner; *(top, fire)* ronfler; *Electron* ronfler; *(air conditioner)* ronronner; **the motors hummed into action** les moteurs se sont mis à ronfler *ou* vrombir; *Fig* **everything was humming along nicely** tout marchait comme sur des roulettes

(**b**) *(be lively)* grouiller; **the airport/town was humming with activity** l'aéroport/la ville bourdonnait d'activité; **to make things hum** mener les choses rondement; **the party was just beginning to hum when the police arrived** la fête commençait à s'animer quand la police est arrivée

(**c**) *Br Fam (stink)* cocotter

(**d**) *(idiom)* **to hum and haw** *(mumble)* bafouiller; *Fig (hesitate)* tergiverser, tourner autour du pot; **he hummed and hawed before getting to the point** il a bafouillé *ou* hésité avant d'en venir au fait

2 *vt (tune)* fredonner, chantonner

3 *n* (**a**) *(of bees, voices)* bourdonnement *m*; *(of vehicle)* vrombissement *m*; *(of fire, top)* ronflement *m*; *Electron* ronflement *m*; *(of machine)* ronronnement *m*; **the distant hum of traffic** le ronronnement lointain de la circulation

(**b**) *Br Fam (stench)* puanteur□ *f*, mauvaise odeur□ *f*; **there's a bit of a hum in here!** ça cocotte là-dedans!

4 *exclam* hem!, hum!

human ['hju:mən] **1** *adj* humain; **the human race** le genre humain; **they were treated as less than human** ils étaient traités comme des bêtes; **he's only human** personne n'est parfait; **I can't do all that work alone, I'm only human!** je ne peux pas faire tout ce travail tout seul, je ne suis pas une bête de somme!; **the accident was caused by human error** l'accident était dû à une erreur *ou* défaillance humaine; **it's those little human touches that make all the difference** ce sont les petites touches personnelles qui font toute la différence

2 *n* (être *m*) humain *m*

►► ***human being*** être *m* humain; ***human cloning*** clonage *m* humain; *Ind* ***human engineering*** gestion *f* des relations humaines; *(ergonomics)* ergonomie *f*; ***the Human Genome Project*** le Projet génome humain; *Med* ***human growth hormone*** hormone *f* somatotrope *ou* de croissance, somatotrophine *f*; *Med* ***human immunodeficiency virus*** virus *m* d'immunodéficience humaine; *Press* ***human interest*** dimension *f* humaine; **a human interest story** un reportage à caractère social; ***human nature*** nature *f* humaine; **it's only human nature to be jealous** c'est normal *ou* humain d'être jaloux; ***the human race*** la race *ou* l'espèce *f* humaine; *Admin* ***human resources*** ressources *fpl* humaines;

human resource management gestion *f* de ressources humaines; ***human rights*** droits *mpl* de l'homme; ***a human rights organization*** une organisation pour les droits de l'homme; *Br* ***human shield*** bouclier *m* humain

---

'Of Human Bondage' *Maugham* 'Servitude humaine'

---

humane [hju:'meɪn] *adj* (**a**) *(compassionate → action, person)* humain, plein d'humanité; *(→ treatment)* humain; *(→ killing)* qui évite de faire souffrir, humain; **a humane method of killing animals** une façon humaine de tuer les animaux (**b**) *Formal Old-fashioned (education)* humaniste

►► ***humane society*** *(for animals)* société *f* protectrice des animaux; *(for good works)* société *f* *ou* association *f* humanitaire

humanely [hju:'meɪnlɪ] *adv* humainement

humaneness [hju:'meɪnnɪs] *n* humanité *f*

humanism ['hju:mənɪzəm] *n* humanisme *m*

humanist ['hju:mənɪst] **1** *n* humaniste *mf*

2 *adj* humaniste

humanistic [,hju:mə'nɪstɪk] *adj* humaniste

humanitarian [hju:,mænɪ'teərɪən] **1** *n* humanitaire *mf*

2 *adj* humanitaire

►► ***humanitarian corridor*** couloir *m* *ou* corridor *m* humanitaire

humanitarianism [hju:,mænɪ'teərɪənɪzəm] *n (philanthropy)* humanitarisme *m*; *(in theology)* monophysisme *m*

humanity [hju:'mænətɪ] **1** *n* (**a**) *(mankind)* humanité *f*; **for the good of humanity** pour le bien de l'humanité (**b**) *(compassion)* humanité *f*; **to treat sb with humanity** traiter qn avec humanité; **the prison camps stripped the inmates of their humanity** les détenus perdaient toute humanité dans les camps de prisonniers

2 humanities 1 *n (arts)* lettres *fpl*; *(classical culture)* lettres *fpl* classiques

2 *comp* en lettres

humanization [,hju:mənaɪ'zeɪʃən] *n* humanisation *f*

humanize, -ise ['hju:mənaɪz] *vt* humaniser

humankind [,hju:mən'kaɪnd] *n* l'humanité *f*, le genre humain

humanly ['hju:mənlɪ] *adv* humainement; **I'll do all that is humanly possible to help her** je ferai tout ce qui est humainement possible pour l'aider

humanoid ['hju:mənɔɪd] **1** *n* humanoïde *mf*

2 *adj* humanoïde

Humberside ['hʌmbə,saɪd] *n Formerly* le Humberside, = comté dans le nord de l'Angleterre; **in Humberside** dans le Humberside

humble ['hʌmbəl] **1** *adj* (**a**) *(meek)* humble; **please accept my humble apologies** veuillez accepter mes humbles excuses; **in my humble opinion** à mon humble avis; *Fig* **to eat humble pie** faire de plates excuses, faire amende honorable; **to force sb to eat humble pie** forcer qn à se rétracter; **your humble servant** *(in letter)* veuillez agréer, Monsieur, l'assurance de mes sentiments les plus respectueux

(**b**) *(modest)* modeste; **she has humble origins** elle a des origines modestes; **to come from a humble background** venir d'un milieu modeste; *Hum* **welcome to my humble abode** bienvenue dans mon humble *ou* ma modeste demeure; *Literary* **the humble violet** l'humble violette *f*

2 *vt* humilier, mortifier; **to humble oneself before sb** s'humilier devant qn; **a severe defeat may humble his pride** un échec sérieux servira peut-être à le rendre moins orgueilleux; **it was a humbling experience** c'était une expérience humiliante

humblebee ['hʌmbəl,bi:] *n (insect)* bourdon *m*

humbleness ['hʌmbəlnɪs] *n* humilité *f*

humbling ['hʌmbəlɪŋ] **1** *adj (experience)* humiliant

2 *n (of person)* humiliation *f*

humbly ['hʌmbəlɪ] *adv* (**a**) *(speak, ask)* humblement, avec humilité; **most humbly** en toute humilité (**b**) *(live)* modestement; **humbly born** d'origine modeste *ou* humble

humbug ['hʌmbʌg] *(pt & pp* **humbugged,** *cont* **humbugging) 1** *n* (**a**) *(person)* charlatan *m*, fumiste *mf*; *(UNCOUNT) (deception)* charlatanisme *m* (**b**) *(UNCOUNT) (nonsense)* balivernes *fpl* (**c**) *Br (sweet)* berlingot *m*

2 *vt* tromper

> **Bah humbug**
>
> Dans *A Christmas Carol* (*Un Conte de Noël*) de Charles Dickens, le personnage principal, Ebenezer Scrooge, est avare et misanthrope et rejette toute occasion de se réjouir en prononçant les mots **bah humbug!** ("sornettes que tout cela!").
>
> On utilise généralement cette expression sur le mode humoristique pour gronder quelqu'un qui fait preuve d'avarice ou qui joue les rabat-joie.

humdinger [,hʌm'dɪŋə(r)] *n Fam* (**a**) *(person)* **she's a real humdinger!** elle est vraiment extra *ou* sensass *ou* terrible! (**b**) *(thing)* **that was a humdinger of a game!** quel match extraordinaire!; **they had a real humdinger of a row!** ils se sont engueulés, quelque chose de bien!

humdrum ['hʌmdrʌm] **1** *adj (person, story)* banal; *(task, life)* monotone, banal, routinier; **I'm**

sick of this humdrum routine j'en ai marre de ce train-train

2 *n* monotonie *f*, banalité *f*

humectant [hjʊ'mektənt] *n* hydratant *m*

humeral ['hju:mərəl] *adj Anat* huméral

humerus ['hju:mərəs] (*pl* **humeri** [-raɪ]) *n Anat* humérus *m*

humid ['hju:mɪd] *adj* humide

humidifier [hju:'mɪdɪfaɪə(r)] *n* humidificateur *m*

humidify [hju:'mɪdɪfaɪ] (*pt & pp* **humidified**) *vt* humidifier

humidity [hju:'mɪdətɪ] *n* humidité *f*

humidor ['hju:mɪdɔ:(r)] *n* cave *f* à cigares

humification [ˌhju:mɪfɪ'keɪʃən] *n* humification *f*

humify ['hju:mɪfaɪ] **1** *vt* humifier

2 *vi* s'humifier

humiliate [hju:'mɪlɪeɪt] *vt* humilier; **he refused to humiliate himself by apologizing to them** il a refusé de s'humilier en leur présentant des excuses

humiliating [hju:'mɪlɪeɪtɪŋ] *adj* humiliant

humiliatingly [hju:'mɪlɪeɪtɪŋlɪ] *adv* d'une façon humiliante; **they were humiliatingly close to failure** ils étaient au bord d'un échec humiliant

humiliation [hju:ˌmɪlɪ'eɪʃən] *n* humiliation *f*

humility [hju:'mɪlətɪ] *n* humilité *f*

humming ['hʌmɪŋ] *n (of bees, voices)* bourdonnement *m*; *(of air conditioner, traffic)* ronronnement *m*; *(of tune)* fredonnement *m*

►► ***humming top*** toupie *f* ronflante

hummingbird ['hʌmɪŋbɜ:d] *n Orn* oiseau-mouche *m*, colibri *m*

hummock ['hʌmək] *n* (**a**) *(knoll)* monticule *m*, tertre *m*, mamelon *m* (**b**) *(in ice field)* hummock *m*

hummocky ['hʌməkɪ] *adj* couvert de monticules

►► ***hummocky ice*** glace *f* en hummocks

hummus ['hʊmʊs, hʌməs] *n Culin* houmous *m*

humor, -humored *etc Am* = **humour, -humoured** *etc*

humoral ['hju:mərəl] *adj Arch Med* humoral

humorist ['hju:mərɪst] *n* humoriste *mf*

humorous ['hju:mərəs] *adj (witty → remark)* plein d'humour, amusant; *(→ person)* plein d'humour, drôle; **he replied in (a) humorous vein** il a répondu sur le mode humoristique

humorously ['hju:mərəslɪ] *adv* avec humour

humour, *Am* **humor** ['hju:mə(r)] **1** *n* (**a**) *(wit, fun)* humour *m*; **the play is devoid of humour** la pièce est dénuée *ou* dépourvue d'humour; **the humour of the situation** le côté comique de la situation; **sense of humour** sens *m* de l'humour; **I like her sense of humour** j'aime son sens de l'humour; **he's got no sense of humour** il n'a aucun sens de l'humour; **he has a very dry sense of humour** il est très pince-sans-rire

(**b**) *Formal (mood)* humeur *f*, disposition *f*; **in a good/bad humour** de bonne/mauvaise humeur; **he's in no humour to talk to anybody** il n'est pas d'humeur à parler à qui que ce soit; *Literary* **to be out of humour** être de mauvaise humeur

(**c**) *Arch (bodily fluid)* humeur *f*; **the four humours** les quatre humeurs *fpl*

2 *vt (person → indulge, gratify)* faire plaisir à; *(→ treat tactfully)* ménager; *(whim, wishes)* se prêter à; **don't try to humour me** n'essaie pas de m'amadouer

-humoured, *Am* **-humored** ['hju:məd] *suff* **he's a pleasant good-humoured man** c'est un homme plaisant et d'humeur agréable; **he responded in a good-humoured enough way** il a répondu plutôt avec bonne humeur; **she seemed unpleasant and ill-humoured** elle paraissait déplaisante et de mauvaise humeur

humourless, *Am* **humorless** ['hju:məlɪs] *adj (person)* qui manque d'humour; *(book, situation, speech)* sans humour; **totally humourless** totalement dépourvu d'humour; **a humourless smile** un sourire pincé

hump [hʌmp] **1** *n* (**a**) *(on flat surface, of hunchback, camel)* bosse *f*; *(hillock)* bosse *f*, mamelon *m*; *(bump)* tas *m*; *Fig* **we're over the hump now** on a fait le plus dur *ou* gros maintenant

(**b**) *Br Fam* **to have the hump** être de mauvais poil; **to get** *or* **take the hump** se mettre à faire la gueule; **to give sb the hump** mettre qn de mauvais poil

(**c**) *Am Fam (person)* crétin(e) *m,f*, andouille *f*

2 *vt* (**a**) *(back)* arrondir, arquer

(**b**) *Fam (carry)* trimbaler, trimballer

(**c**) *very Fam (have sex with)* baiser

3 *vi very Fam (have sex)* baiser, s'envoyer en l'air

humpback ['hʌmpbæk] *n* (**a**) *(person)* bossu(e) *m,f* (**b**) *Zool (whale)* baleine *f* à bosse

►► ***humpback bridge*** pont *m* en dos d'âne; *Zool* ***humpback whale*** baleine *f* à bosse

humpbacked ['hʌmpbækt] *adj* bossu

►► ***humpbacked bridge*** pont *m* en dos d'âne

humph [mm, hʌmf] *exclam* hum!

Humpty Dumpty [ˌhʌmptɪ'dʌmptɪ] *pr n* = personnage en forme d'œuf figurant dans une comptine (désigne métaphoriquement une chose impossible à réparer)

humungous [hju:'mʌngəs] *adj Fam (huge)* énorme ❑, mastoc *(inv)*

humus ['hju:məs] *n* humus *m*

Hun [hʌn] (*pl* **inv** *or* **Huns**) *n* (**a**) *Antiq (from Asia)* Hun *m* (**b**) *Fam Old-fashioned Pej (German)* Boche *m* (**c**) *Scot Fam Pej (Protestant)* protestant(e) ❑ *m,f*

hunch [hʌntʃ] **1** *n* (**a**) *(inkling)* pressentiment *m*, intuition *f*; **I have a hunch we'll meet again** j'ai comme un pressentiment que nous nous reverrons; **to play** *or* **to follow one's hunch** suivre son intuition; **to act on a hunch** suivre son instinct; **my hunch paid off, he was there** mon intuition s'est vérifiée, il était là; **it's only a hunch** c'est une idée que j'ai

(**b**) *(hump)* bosse *f*

2 *vt* **to hunch one's back** arrondir le dos; **to hunch one's shoulders** voûter les épaules; **he was hunched against the cold** il se recroquevillait sur lui-même pour se protéger du froid; **don't hunch (up) your shoulders like that!** ne rentre pas la tête dans les épaules comme ça!

hunchback ['hʌntʃbæk] *n* (**a**) *(person)* bossu(e) *m,f* (**b**) *Anat* bosse *f*

'The Hunchback of Notre Dame' *Hugo* 'Notre-Dame de Paris'

hunchbacked ['hʌntʃbækt] *adj* bossu

hunched [hʌntʃt] *adj* voûté; **he sat hunched in a corner** il était assis recroquevillé dans un coin; **she was sitting hunched (up) over her papers** elle était assise penchée sur ses papiers

hundred ['hʌndrəd] **1** *n* cent *m*; **one hundred and one** cent un; **two hundred** deux cents; **two hundred and one** deux cent un; **about a hundred, a hundred odd** une centaine; **in nineteen hundred** en dix-neuf cents; **in nineteen hundred and ten** en dix-neuf cent dix; **to be a hundred** avoir cent ans; **I'll never forget him (even) if I live to be a hundred** même si je deviens centenaire, je ne l'oublierai jamais; **the theatre seats five hundred** la salle contient cinq cents places (assises); *Math* **in the hundred's place** dans la colonne des centaines; **give me $500 in hundreds** donnez-moi 500 dollars en billets de cent; **the temperature is in the hundreds today** il fait plus de 30 aujourd'hui; **in the seventeen hundreds** au dix-septième siècle; **hundreds of** des centaines de; **I've asked you hundreds of times!** je te l'ai demandé cent fois!; **hundreds and thousands of people** des milliers de gens; **they were dying in their hundreds** *or* **by the hundred** ils mouraient par centaines

2 *pron* cent; **about a hundred** une centaine; **I need a hundred (of them)** il m'en faut cent, j'en ai besoin de cent; **he has a hundred (of them)** il en a cent

3 *adj* cent; **a hundred guests** cent invités; **six hundred pages** six cents pages; **on page a hundred** (à la) page cent; **about a hundred metres** une centaine de mètres; **they live at number a hundred** ils habitent au numéro cent; **to be a hundred years old** avoir cent ans; **one** *or* **a hundred percent** cent pour cent; **I'm a hundred percent sure** j'en suis absolument certain; **to be a hundred percent behind sb** soutenir qn à fond; **to give a** *or* **one hundred percent** se donner à fond; **I'm not feeling a hundred percent** je ne me sens pas dans mon assiette; *Fig* **I've got a hundred and one things to do** j'ai mille choses à faire; **if I've told you once, I've told you a hundred times!** je te l'ai dit cent fois!

►► *Hist* ***the Hundred Days*** les Cent Jours *mpl*; ***hundreds and thousands*** *(confectionery)* vermicelles *mpl* en sucre, nonpareilles *fpl*; *Hist* ***the Hundred Years' War*** la guerre de Cent Ans

'One Hundred Years of Solitude' *García Márquez* 'Cent Ans de solitude'

hundredfold ['hʌndrədfəʊld] **1** *adj* centuple

2 *adv* **he has increased his initial investment (by) a hundredfold** il a multiplié par cent son investissement initial, il a centuplé son investissement initial

hundred-percenter [-pə'sentə(r)] *n Am Fam* nationaliste *mf* extrémiste ❑

hundredth ['hʌndrədθ] **1** *n* (**a**) *(fraction)* centième *m* (**b**) *(in series)* centième *mf*

2 *adj* centième

3 *adv* centièmement; *(in contest)* en centième position, à la centième place; *see also* **fifth**

hundredweight ['hʌndrədweɪt] *n Br* = 50,8 kg, (poids *m* de) 112 livres *fpl*; *Am* = 45,36 kg, (poids *m* de) 100 livres *fpl*

hundred-year-old *adj* centenaire

hung [hʌŋ] **1** *pt & pp of* **hang**

2 *adj* (**a**) *(situation)* bloqué (**b**) *Fam* **hung up** coincé; **to be hung up on sb/sth** faire une fixation sur qn/qch ❑; **to be hung up about sth** *(personal problem)* être complexé par qch ❑; *(sexual matters)* être coincé quand il s'agit de qch

►► ***hung jury*** jury *m* sans majorité; ***hung parliament*** parlement *m* sans majorité

Hungarian [hʌŋ'geərɪən] **1** *n* (**a**) *(person)* Hongrois(e) *m,f* (**b**) *(language)* hongrois *m*

2 *adj* hongrois

3 *comp (embassy)* de Hongrie; *(history)* de la Hongrie; *(teacher)* de hongrois

Hungary ['hʌŋgərɪ] *n* Hongrie *f*; **in Hungary** en Hongrie

hunger ['hʌŋgə(r)] **1** *n* faim *f*; **a conference on world hunger** une conférence sur la faim dans le monde; **to satisfy one's hunger (for sth)** satisfaire sa faim (de qch); *Fig* **he was driven by a hunger for truth/knowledge** il était poussé par une soif de vérité/de savoir

2 *vi Fig* **to hunger after** *or* **for sth** avoir faim *ou* soif de qch; **he hungered for revenge** il avait faim *ou* soif de vengeance

►► ***hunger march*** marche *f* de la faim; ***hunger pains, hunger pangs*** tiraillements *mpl* d'estomac; ***hunger strike*** grève *f* de la faim; **to go on (a) hunger strike** faire la grève de la faim; ***hunger striker*** gréviste *mf* de la faim

hungered ['hʌŋgəd] *adj Arch or Literary* affamé

hungover [hʌŋ'əʊvə(r)] *adj* **to be hungover** avoir une *ou* la gueule de bois; **he was too hungover to go to work** il avait une telle gueule de bois qu'il ne pouvait pas aller au travail

hungrily ['hʌŋgrəlɪ] *adv (eat)* voracement, avidement; *Fig (read, listen)* avidement; **she eyed his lunch hungrily** elle jeta un regard de convoitise sur son déjeuner; *Fig* **they stared hungrily at the women** ils fixaient les femmes avec avidité

hungry ['hʌŋgrɪ] (*compar* **hungrier,** *superl* **hungriest**) *adj* (**a**) *(for food)* **to be hungry** avoir faim; **we're very hungry** nous avons très faim, nous sommes affamés; **he still felt hungry** il avait encore faim; **she looked tired and hungry** elle avait l'air fatiguée et affamée; **are you getting hungry?** est-ce que tu commences à avoir faim?; **to go hungry** souffrir de la faim; **he'd rather go hungry than cook for himself** il se passerait de manger plutôt que de faire la cuisine; **that night he went hungry** cette nuit-là il est resté sur sa faim; **this is hungry work!** ce travail donne faim!

(**b**) *Fig (desirous)* avide; **hungry for affection** avide d'affection; **she was hungry for news of her family** elle attendait avec impatience des nouvelles de sa famille; *Fig* **you have to be hungry to make it to the top** ce sont les battants qui réussissent

hunk [hʌŋk] *n* (**a**) *(piece)* gros morceau *m* (**b**)

Fam (man) beau mec *m*; **he's a real hunk** il est beau mec

hunker ['hʌŋkə(r)] *vi* **to hunker (down)** *(crouch)* s'accroupir; *(squat)* s'asseoir sur ses talons, s'accroupir; *(animal)* se tapir; *Fig* **I have to hunker down and work this term** je dois donner un bon coup de collier ce trimestre

hunkers ['hʌŋkəz] *npl Fam* hanches ❑ *fpl*; **sitting on his hunkers** assis sur ses talons

hunky ['hʌŋkɪ] **1** *n Am Fam* = terme injurieux désignant un travailleur d'origine slave, balte ou hongroise

2 *adj Fam (man → with good body)* bien foutu; *(→ big and strong)* baraqué

hunky-dory [-'dɔːrɪ] *adj Fam* **to be hunky-dory** être au poil; **everything's just hunky-dory!** tout baigne (dans l'huile)!

hunt [hʌnt] **1** *vt* (**a**) *(for food, sport → of person)* chasser, faire la chasse à; *(→ of animal)* chasser; **to hunt whales** pêcher la baleine; **they were hunted to extinction** ils ont été chassés jusqu'à extinction de l'espèce

(**b**) *Br (area)* chasser dans; **to hunt the pack** diriger la meute; **he hunts his horse all winter** il monte son cheval à la chasse tout l'hiver

(**c**) *(pursue)* pourchasser, poursuivre; **he was being hunted by the police** il était pourchassé *ou* recherché par la police

(**d**) *(search)* fouiller; **I've hunted the whole office for it** j'ai retourné tout le bureau pour le retrouver

(**e**) *(drive out)* chasser; **people were hunted from their homes** des gens étaient chassés de leurs foyers

(**f**) **hunt the slipper** *or* **thimble** *(game)* ≃ cache-tampon *m*

2 *vi* (**a**) *(for food, sport)* chasser; **they hunt by night/in packs** ils chassent la nuit/en bande; **to go hunting** aller à la chasse; **do you hunt?** chassez-vous?; **to hunt for sth** *(person)* chasser *ou* faire la chasse à qch; *(animal)* chasser qch

(**b**) *(search)* chercher (partout); **she hunted (around** *or* **about) in her bag for her keys** elle a fouillé dans son sac à la recherche de ses clefs; **you'll just have to hunt until you find it** vous n'aurez qu'à chercher jusqu'à ce que vous le trouviez; *Fig* **I've hunted high and low for it** j'ai remué ciel et terre pour le retrouver; **I've hunted all over town for a linen jacket** j'ai parcouru *ou* fait toute la ville pour trouver une veste en lin

(**c**) *Tech (gauge)* osciller; *(engine)* pomper

3 *n* (**a**) *(sporting activity)* chasse *f*; *(hunters)* chasse *f*, chasseurs *mpl*; *(area)* chasse *f*; *(fox-hunt)* chasse *f* au renard; **a tiger/bear hunt** une chasse au tigre/à l'ours

(**b**) *(search)* chasse *f*, recherche *f*; **the hunt is on for the terrorists** la chasse aux terroristes est en cours; **local people joined in the hunt for the child** des gens de la région se sont joints aux recherches pour retrouver l'enfant; **the hunt for the assassin continues** la chasse à l'assassin se poursuit; **I've had a hunt for your scarf** j'ai cherché ton écharpe partout, j'ai tout retourné pour trouver ton écharpe

►► *Br* ***hunt ball*** = bal réunissant les notables locaux amateurs de chasse; *Br* ***hunt saboteur*** = personne qui tente d'arrêter une chasse

►**hunt down** *vt sep (animal)* forcer, traquer; *(person)* traquer; *(thing, facts)* dénicher; *(abuses, errors)* faire la chasse à; *(truth)* débusquer

►**hunt out** *vt sep Br* dénicher, découvrir; **I've hunted out that book you wanted to borrow** j'ai déniché le livre que vous vouliez emprunter

►**hunt up** *vt sep Br (look up)* rechercher; **I'm going to the library to hunt up that article she mentioned** je vais à la bibliothèque rechercher cet article dont elle parlait

hunted ['hʌntɪd] *adj* traqué; **he has a hunted look about him** il a un air persécuté *ou* traqué

hunter ['hʌntə(r)] *n* (**a**) *(as sport → person)* chasseur(euse) *m,f*; *(→ horse)* cheval *m* de chasse, hunter *m*; *(→ dog)* chien *m* courant *ou* de chasse (**b**) *(who searches)* chasseur(euse) *m,f*; *(pursuer)* poursuivant(e) *m,f* (**c**) *(watch)* (montre *f* à) savonnette *f*

►► ***hunter's moon*** = pleine lune qui suit celle de l'équinoxe d'automne

hunter-gatherer *n* chasseur-cueilleur *m*

hunter-killer *adj Mil* d'attaque; **a hunter-killer submarine** un sous-marin d'attaque

hunting ['hʌntɪŋ] **1** *n* (**a**) *(sporting activity)* chasse *f*; *Br (fox-hunting)* chasse *f* au renard; *Hist (mounted deer-hunt)* chasse *f* à courre; *Hist (as an art)* vénerie *f*; **huntin', shootin' and fishin'** = expression employée pour parodier l'aristocratie rurale, en insinuant que sa principale activité est la chasse et la pêche; **he's a hunting man** c'est un grand chasseur

(**b**) *(pursuit)* chasse *f*, poursuite *f*; **bargain hunting** la chasse aux soldes

2 *comp (boots, gun, knife, licence)* de chasse

►► ***hunting dog*** chien *m* de chasse; *Sport & Fig* ***hunting ground*** terrain *m* de chasse; ***hunting horn*** cor *m ou* trompe *f* de chasse; ***hunting lodge*** pavillon *m* de chasse; ***hunting pink*** **1** *n (UNCOUNT) Br* habit *m* rouge de chasse à courre **2** *adj* rouge chasseur *(inv)*; ***hunting season*** saison *f* de la chasse

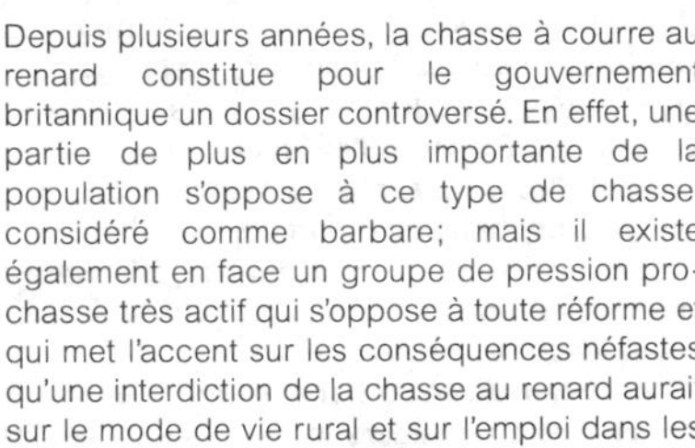

THE HUNTING DEBATE

Depuis plusieurs années, la chasse à courre au renard constitue pour le gouvernement britannique un dossier controversé. En effet, une partie de plus en plus importante de la population s'oppose à ce type de chasse, considéré comme barbare; mais il existe également en face un groupe de pression pro-chasse très actif qui s'oppose à toute réforme et qui met l'accent sur les conséquences néfastes qu'une interdiction de la chasse au renard aurait sur le mode de vie rural et sur l'emploi dans les campagnes.

En 1999, la **Countryside Alliance** (voir ce mot) organisa à Londres une grande marche contre les projets de réforme envisagés par le gouvernement. Voir aussi l'encadré sur **the Countryside Debate**.

Huntington's chorea ['hʌntɪŋtənz-] *n Med* chorée *f* de Huntington

huntress ['hʌntrɪs] *n* chasseuse *f*; *Myth* **Diana the Huntress** Diane chasseresse

huntsman ['hʌntsmən] (*pl* **huntsmen** [-mən]) *n* (**a**) *(hunter)* chasseur *m* (**b**) *(master of hounds)* veneur *m*

hurdle ['hɜːdəl] **1** *n* (**a**) *Sport* haie *f*; **the 400-metre hurdles** le 400 mètres haies; **to run a hurdle** *or* **hurdles race** faire *ou* courir une course de haies; **she's the British hurdles champion** elle est la championne britannique de course de haies; **to take** *or* **to clear a hurdle** franchir une haie

(**b**) *Fig* obstacle *m*; **she took that hurdle in her stride** elle a franchi cet obstacle sans le moindre effort; **the next hurdle will be getting funding for the project** la prochaine difficulté sera d'obtenir des fonds pour le projet

(**c**) *(for fences)* claie *f*

2 *vt* (**a**) *(jump over → obstacle)* sauter; *Sport (→ fence)* franchir

(**b**) *(surround with fences)* entourer de claies

3 *vi Sport* faire de la course de haies

hurdler ['hɜːdələ(r)] *n (person)* coureur(euse) *m,f (qui fait des courses de haies)*; *(horse)* sauteur *m*

hurdling ['hɜːdəlɪŋ] *n Sport (in athletics) & Horse-racing* course *f* de haies; *(part of competition)* courses *fpl* de haies; **the world 400-metre hurdling champion** le champion du monde du 400 mètres haies

hurdy-gurdy ['hɜːdɪ,gɜːdɪ] (*pl* **hurdy-gurdies**) *n Mus* (**a**) *(barrel organ)* orgue *m* de Barbarie; **a hurdy-gurdy man** un joueur d'orgue de Barbarie (**b**) *(medieval instrument)* vielle *f*

hurl [hɜːl] **1** *vt* (**a**) *(throw)* lancer, jeter (avec violence); **to hurl oneself at sb/sth** se ruer sur qn/qch; **he hurled a vase at him** il lui a lancé un vase à la figure; **they were hurled to the ground** ils ont été précipités *ou* jetés à terre; **she hurled herself off the top of the tower** elle s'est précipitée *ou* jetée (du haut) de la tour; **he hurled himself into the fight** il s'est jeté dans la bagarre; **the boat was hurled onto the rocks** le bateau a été projeté sur les rochers; *Fig* **they were hurled into the crisis** ils ont été précipités dans la crise

(**b**) *(yell)* lancer, jeter; **to hurl abuse at sb** lancer des injures à qn, accabler qn d'injures

2 *vi Fam (vomit)* dégobiller, gerber

hurling ['hɜːlɪŋ] *n Sport* = jeu irlandais voisin du hockey sur gazon

hurly-burly ['hɜːlɪ,bɜːlɪ] *Br* **1** *n* tohu-bohu *m inv*; **the hurly-burly of city life** le tourbillon de la vie urbaine

2 *adj* turbulent

Huron ['hjʊərən] *see* **lake**

hurrah [hʊ'rɑː], **hurray** [hʊ'reɪ] **1** *n* hourra *m*

2 *exclam* hourra!; **hurrah for the cook!** pour le chef, hip hip hip hourra!

hurricane ['hʌrɪkən] *n* ouragan *m*; *(in Caribbean)* hurricane *m*; **Hurricane Mabel** l'ouragan *m* Mabel

►► ***hurricane force*** force *f* douze (sur l'échelle Beaufort); ***hurricane lamp*** lampe-tempête *f*; ***hurricane warning*** avis *m* d'ouragan

hurricane-force *adj (winds)* de force douze

hurried ['hʌrɪd] *adj (meeting, reply, gesture, trip)* rapide; *(departure, steps)* précipité; *(judgment, decision)* hâtif; *(work)* fait à la hâte; **to have a hurried meal** manger à la hâte; **I wrote a hurried note to reassure her** j'ai écrit un mot à la hâte *ou* un mot bref pour la rassurer; **they only had time for a few hurried words** ils ont juste eu le temps d'échanger quelques mots rapides

hurriedly ['hʌrɪdlɪ] *adv (examine)* à la hâte; *(leave)* précipitamment; **she passed hurriedly over the unpleasant details** elle passa en vitesse sur les détails désagréables; **he hurriedly excused himself** il s'est empressé de s'excuser

hurry ['hʌrɪ] (*pl* **hurries**, *pt & pp* **hurried**) **1** *n* (**a**) *(rush)* hâte *f*, précipitation *f*; **to be in a hurry** être pressé; **not now, I'm in (too much of) a hurry** pas maintenant, je suis (trop) pressé; **to be in a hurry to do sth** avoir hâte de faire qch; **to do sth in a hurry** faire qch à la hâte; **to leave in a hurry** sortir à la hâte *ou* en courant; **he needs it in a hurry** il en a besoin tout de suite; **to be in a tearing** *or* **an awful hurry** être très pressé; **in his** *or* **the hurry to leave he forgot his umbrella** dans sa hâte de partir il a oublié son parapluie; **there's no big** *or* **great hurry** rien ne presse; **are you in a hurry for it?** c'est urgent?; **there's no hurry** cela ne presse pas; **what's the** *or* **your hurry?** qu'est-ce qui (vous) presse?; **it was obviously written in a hurry** de toute évidence, cela a été écrit à la hâte; **you won't see her again in a hurry** vous ne la reverrez pas de sitôt; *Br Fam* **he won't try that again in a hurry!** il ne ressayera pas de sitôt!, il n'est pas près de ressayer!

(**b**) *(eagerness)* empressement *m*; **he's in no hurry to see her again** il n'est pas pressé *ou* il n'a aucune hâte de la revoir; *Br* **a young man in a hurry** un jeune homme pressé de réussir *ou* ambitieux

2 *vi* se dépêcher, se presser, se hâter; **he's hurrying to finish some work** il se dépêche *ou* se presse *ou* se hâte de finir un travail; **I must** *or* **I'd better hurry** il faut que je me dépêche; **you don't have to hurry over that report** vous pouvez prendre votre temps pour faire ce rapport; **he hurried into/out of the room** il est entré dans/sorti de la pièce en toute hâte *ou* précipitamment; **he hurried down the stairs** il a descendu l'escalier en toute hâte *ou* précipitamment; **he hurried (over) to the bank** il s'est précipité à la banque, il s'est rendu à la banque en toute hâte; **to hurry after sb** courir après qn; **hurry! it's already started** dépêche-toi! c'est déjà commencé

3 *vt* (**a**) *(chivvy along)* faire se dépêcher, presser, bousculer; **don't hurry him** ne le bousculе pas; **he was hurried into making a choice** on l'a pressé de faire un choix; **she won't be hurried, you can't hurry her** vous ne la ferez pas se dépêcher; **they hurried him through customs** ils lui ont fait passer la douane à la hâte

(**b**) *(preparations, work)* activer, presser, hâter; **this decision can't be hurried** cette décision exige d'être prise sans hâte

(**c**) *(transport hastily)* emmener d'urgence; **aid was hurried to the stricken town** des secours ont été envoyés d'urgence à la ville sinistrée; **she was hurried to hospital** elle a été transportée à l'hôpital en (toute) hâte

►**hurry along** **1** *vi* marcher d'un pas pressé; **hurry**

along now! pressons, pressons!; **we'd better be hurrying along** on ferait mieux de se presser

2 *vt sep (person)* faire presser le pas à, faire se dépêcher *ou* s'activer; *(work)* activer, accélérer; **he wants the investigation hurried along** il veut faire accélérer *ou* faire avancer plus rapidement l'enquête

▸**hurry away 1** *vi* partir précipitamment

2 *vt sep* **he hurried the children away from the scene of the accident** il a vite éloigné les enfants du lieu de l'accident

▸**hurry back** *vi* revenir *ou* retourner à la hâte; **she'll soon come hurrying back** elle reviendra vite; **promise to hurry back afterwards** promets de revenir vite après; **don't hurry back, I'll take care of everything** ne te presse pas de revenir, je me chargerai de tout

▸**hurry off 1** *vi* partir précipitamment

2 *vt sep* **they hurried her off to hospital** ils l'ont emmenée à l'hôpital en (toute) hâte

▸**hurry on 1** *vt sep (person)* faire hâter le pas à; *(work)* activer

2 *vi* se dépêcher, continuer à la hâte *ou* en hâte; **he hurried on to the next shelter** il s'est pressé de gagner l'abri suivant; **can we hurry on to the next item on the agenda?** peut-on vite passer *ou* passer sans tarder à la prochaine question inscrite à l'ordre du jour?

▸**hurry up 1** *vi* se dépêcher, se presser; **hurry up!** dépêche-toi!; **hurry up and get dressed** dépêche-toi de t'habiller; **hurry up with that packing** dépêche-toi de faire ces bagages; **hurry up with the iron** dépêche-toi avec le fer

2 *vt sep (person)* faire se dépêcher; *(production, work)* activer, pousser; **I'll go and hurry them up** je vais leur dire de se dépêcher

hurry-up *adj Am Fam (meal)* pris sur le pouce; *(manner, procedure)* hâtif

hurt [hɜːt] *(pt & pp* **hurt***)* **1** *vt* (**a**) *(cause physical pain to)* faire mal à; **to hurt oneself** se faire mal; **mind you don't hurt yourself** faites attention de ne pas vous faire mal *ou* vous blesser; **I hurt my elbow on the door** je me suis fait mal au coude contre la porte; **is your back hurting you today?** est-ce que tu as mal au dos aujourd'hui?; **where does it hurt you?** où est-ce que vous avez mal?, où cela vous fait-il mal?; **it hardly hurts (me) at all!** ça ne me fait presque pas mal!; **the fall didn't hurt him** il ne s'est pas fait mal en tombant

(**b**) *(injure)* blesser; **two people were hurt in the crash** deux personnes ont été blessées dans la collision; **no one was hurt in the accident** personne n'a été blessé dans l'accident; *Fam* **do as I say and no one gets hurt!** faites ce que je dis et il n'y aura pas de casse!

(**c**) *(upset)* blesser, faire de la peine à; **he was very hurt by your criticism** il a été très blessé par vos critiques; **to hurt sb's feelings** blesser *ou* froisser qn; **it hurt me when they did that** ça m'a fait de la peine quand ils ont fait ça; **what hurt me most was his silence on the subject** ce qui me faisait le plus mal c'était son silence à ce propos

(**d**) *(disadvantage)* nuire à; **the new tax will hurt the middle classes most** ce sont les classes moyennes qui seront les plus touchées par le nouvel impôt; **it wouldn't hurt him to have to wait for a change** ça ne lui ferait pas de mal de devoir attendre pour changer; **a bit of fresh air won't hurt you** un peu d'air frais *ou* de grand air ne te fera pas de mal

(**e**) *(damage → crops, machine)* abîmer, endommager; *(→ eyesight)* abîmer

2 *vi* faire mal; **it hurts** ça fait mal; **my head hurts** ma tête me fait mal; **where does it hurt?** où est-ce que vous avez mal?; **I hurt all over** j'ai mal partout; **a holiday certainly wouldn't hurt** ça ne ferait certainement pas de mal de prendre des vacances; **it wouldn't hurt to make a few more photocopies** ça ne fera pas de mal de faire quelques photocopies de plus; *Am* **he's hurting** il a mal; **nothing hurts like the truth** il n'y a que la vérité qui blesse

3 *n* (**a**) *(physical pain)* mal *m*; *(wound)* blessure *f*

(**b**) *(mental pain)* peine *f*; **he wanted to make up for the hurt he had caused them** il voulait réparer la peine qu'il leur avait faite

(**c**) *(damage)* tort *m*

4 *adj* (**a**) *(physically)* blessé; **are you hurt?** êtes-vous blessé?; **he was more frightened than hurt** il a eu plus de peur que de mal; **several people were seriously/slightly hurt** plusieurs personnes ont été sérieusement/légèrement blessées

(**b**) *(offended)* froissé, blessé; **a hurt expression** un regard meurtri *ou* blessé; **I'm deeply hurt that you didn't tell me first** que vous ne me l'ayez pas dit en premier m'a profondément blessé; **don't feel hurt** ne le prends pas mal; **he's feeling a bit hurt about it all** il se sent quelque peu peiné par tout ça

▸▸ *Am* ***hurt books*** livres *mpl* endommagés

> **If it's not** (*or* **it ain't**) **hurting, it's not** (*or* **it ain't**) **working**
> Cette phrase ("si ça ne fait pas mal, c'est que ça ne marche pas") fut popularisée au début des années 90 par le Premier ministre britannique John Major, qui voulait dire par là que si l'on veut obtenir des résultats en matière d'économie, il faut être prêt à faire des sacrifices.
> On utilise aujourd'hui cette formule dans des contextes autres que politiques pour justifier des mesures d'austérité, ou bien pour encourager un patient lors d'un traitement douloureux (un régime de remise en forme éprouvant, par exemple).

hurtful ['hɜːtfʊl] *adj* (**a**) *(remark)* blessant, offensant; *(memory)* pénible; **they ended up saying hurtful things to each other** ils ont fini par se dire des méchancetés; **what a hurtful thing to say!** comme c'est méchant *ou* cruel de dire cela! (**b**) *(detrimental)* préjudiciable, nuisible

hurtfully ['hɜːtfʊlɪ] *adv* (**a**) *(remark)* d'une manière blessante *ou* offensante (**b**) *(detrimentally)* d'une manière préjudiciable *ou* nuisible

hurtfulness ['hɜːtfʊlnɪs] *n* (**a**) *(of remark)* caractère *m* blessant (**b**) *(detrimental nature)* nature *f* préjudiciable *ou* nuisible

hurtle ['hɜːtəl] **1** *vt (throw violently)* lancer

2 *vi* **to hurtle along** avancer à toute vitesse *ou* allure; **the cars hurtled round the track** les voitures tournaient autour de la piste à toute allure; **he went hurtling down the stairs** il dévala les escaliers; **the motorbike came hurtling towards him** la moto fonça sur lui; **a rock hurtled through the air** une pierre a fendu l'air

husband ['hʌzbənd] **1** *n* mari *m*, époux *m*; **are they husband and wife?** sont-ils mari et femme?; **they lived (together) as husband and wife** ils vivaient maritalement *ou* comme mari et femme

2 *vt (resources, strength)* ménager, économiser

husband-and-wife *adj* **husband-and-wife business** entreprise *f* appartenant à deux époux *ou* à un couple marié; **husband-and-wife team** équipe *f* formée par deux époux

husbandry ['hʌzbəndrɪ] *n* (**a**) *Agr* agriculture *f*; *(as science)* agronomie *f* (**b**) *Formal (thrift)* économie *f*; **good husbandry** bonne gestion *f*

hush [hʌʃ] **1** *n* silence *m*, calme *m*; **a hush fell over the room** un silence s'est installé *ou* s'est fait dans la salle; **in the hush of the early morning** dans le silence du petit matin

2 *exclam (gen)* silence!; *(stop talking)* chut!

3 *vt* (**a**) *(silence)* faire taire; **she hushed the murmurs/the crowd with a gesture** elle a fait taire les murmures/la foule d'un geste

(**b**) *(appease)* apaiser, calmer

4 *vi* se taire

▸▸ *Fam* ***hush money*** *(UNCOUNT)* pot-de-vin❑ *m (pour acheter le silence)*; **to pay sb hush money** acheter le silence de qn❑; *Am Culin* ***hush puppy*** = sorte de beignet à base de farine de maïs

▸**hush up** *vt sep* (**a**) *(affair)* étouffer; *(witness)* faire taire, empêcher de parler (**b**) *(noisy person)* faire taire

hushaby, hushabye ['hʌʃəbaɪ] *exclam* **hushaby baby!** fais dodo, mon bébé!

hushed [hʌʃt] *adj (whisper, voice)* étouffé; *(conversation)* étouffé, discret(ète); *(silence)* profond, grand; **to speak in hushed tones** parler à voix basse

hush-hush *adj Fam* archi-secret(ète); **it's all very hush-hush** tout cela c'est archi-secret *ou* top secret

husk [hʌsk] **1** *n (of wheat, oats)* balle *f*; *(of maize, rice)* enveloppe *f*; *(of nut)* écale *f*

2 *vt (oats, barley)* monder; *(maize)* éplucher; *(rice)* décortiquer; *(wheat)* vanner; *(nuts)* écaler

huskily ['hʌskɪlɪ] *adv (speak → naturally)* d'une voix rauque; *(→ because of sore throat)* d'une voix enrouée; *(sing)* d'une voix voilée

huskiness ['hʌskɪnɪs] *n* enrouement *m*

husky ['hʌskɪ] *(compar* **huskier**, *superl* **huskiest**, *pl* **huskies***)* **1** *adj* (**a**) *(voice → naturally)* rauque; *(→ because of sore throat)* enroué; **his voice was husky with emotion** il avait la voix voilée par l'émotion (**b**) *Fam (burly)* costaud

2 *n (dog)* chien *m* esquimau *ou* de traîneau, husky *m*

hussar [hʊ'zɑː(r)] *n Mil* hussard *m*

Hussite ['hʌsaɪt] *n Rel* hussite *mf*

hussy ['hʌsɪ] *(pl* **hussies***) n Arch or Hum (shameless woman)* gourgandine *f*; **you shameless** *or* **brazen hussy!** espèce de gourgandine!

hustings ['hʌstɪŋz] *npl Br* (**a**) *(campaign)* campagne *f* électorale; **to go/to be out on the hustings** partir/être en campagne électorale (**b**) *(occasion for speeches)* ≃ débat *m* public *(pendant la campagne électorale)*; **at the hustings** au cours du débat public

hustle ['hʌsəl] **1** *vt* (**a**) *(cause to move → quickly)* presser; *(→ roughly)* bousculer, pousser; **to hustle sb in/out** faire entrer/sortir qn énergiquement; **they hustled him into an alley** ils l'ont poussé dans une ruelle; **he hustled us into the president's office** il nous a pressés d'entrer chez le président; **after that, I was hustled off to boarding school** après cela, j'ai été expédié au pensionnat; **the doctor was hustled through the crowd** on a frayé un chemin au médecin dans la foule; **he was hustled away** *or* **off by two men** il a été emmené de force par deux hommes; *Am very Fam* **to hustle one's butt** se magner les fesses

(**b**) *Fam (obtain → resourcefully)* faire tout pour avoir❑; *(→ underhandedly)* magouiller pour avoir; **he's been hustling jobs since he was sixteen** il s'est décarcassé *ou* bagarré pour trouver des boulots depuis l'âge de seize ans; **they hustled that building permit** ils ont magouillé pour obtenir ce permis de construire

(**c**) *Am Fam (swindle)* rouler, arnaquer; *(pressure)* **to hustle sb into doing sth** forcer la main à qn pour qu'il fasse qch; **he hustled me out of $100** il m'a roulé *ou* arnaqué de 100 dollars; **he hustled the old lady for her savings** il a arnaqué la vieille dame de ses économies

(**d**) *Am Fam (steal)* piquer

(**e**) *Am very Fam (of prostitute)* racoler; **she hustles the bars** elle racole dans les bars

2 *vi* (**a**) *Br (shove)* bousculer; **don't hustle in the back!** ne bousculez pas derrière!

(**b**) *(hurry)* se dépêcher, se presser; **we'd better hustle!** on ferait mieux de se dépêcher *ou* presser!

(**c**) *Am Fam (work hard)* se bagarrer (pour réussir)❑; **they want that market and they're ready to hustle for it** ils veulent ce marché et ils sont prêts à tout (faire) ou à se bagarrer pour l'avoir

(**d**) *Am Fam (engage in suspect activity)* monter des coups❑, trafiquer❑; *(politically)* magouiller; **so he's hustling in Washington now?** alors il magouille à Washington maintenant?

(**e**) *Am very Fam (of prostitute)* faire le tapin, tapiner

3 *n* (**a**) *(crush)* bousculade *f*

(**b**) *(bustle)* grande activité *f*; **the hustle and bustle of the big city** le tourbillon d'activité des grandes villes

(**c**) *Am Fam (swindle)* arnaque *f*

(**d**) *(dance)* = sorte de danse disco des années 70

▸**hustle through** *vt sep Fam (deal rapidly with)* expédier❑; **they hustled the legislation through in a single day** ils ont expédié le vote de la loi en une seule journée

▸**hustle up** *Am Fam* **1** *vt sep* (**a**) *(prepare quickly)* préparer en cinq sec (**b**) *(hurry up → person)*

faire se dépêcher❑; *(→ production, work)* activer❑, pousser❑
2 *vi* se dépêcher❑, se presser❑

hustler ['hʌslə(r)] *n* (**a**) *Fam (dynamic person)* battant(e) *m,f* (**b**) *Fam (swindler)* arnaqueur (euse) *m,f* (**c**) *Am very Fam (prostitute)* putain *f*

hut [hʌt] *n (primitive dwelling)* hutte *f*; *(shed)* cabane *f*, baraque *f*; *(alpine)* refuge *m*, chalet-refuge *m*; *Mil* baraquement *m*

hutch [hʌtʃ] *n* (**a**) *(cage)* cage *f*; *(for rabbits)* clapier *m* (**b**) *(chest)* coffre *m* (**c**) *Am (Welsh dresser)* vaisselier *m* (**d**) *Tech (kneading trough)* pétrin *m*, huche *f* (**e**) *Mining (wagon)* wagonnet *m*, benne *f* (roulante)

hutment ['hʌtmənt] *n Mil* baraquements *mpl*

hyacinth ['haɪəsɪnθ] **1** *n* (**a**) *Bot* jacinthe *f*; **wood** *or* **wild hyacinth** jacinthe *f* des bois (**b**) *(gem)* hyacinthe *f* (**c**) *(colour)* bleu *m* jacinthe, bleu *m* violet
2 *adj (colour)* bleu jacinthe *(inv)*, bleu violet *(inv)*

Hyades ['haɪədi:z] *npl Myth* **the Hyades** les Hyades

hyaena = **hyena**

hyaline ['haɪəlɪn] **1** *n Literary* (**a**) *(sea)* mer *f* de cristal (**b**) *(sky)* ciel *m* pur
2 *adj Anat, Biol & Miner* hyalin, transparent
►► *Anat* ***hyaline cartilage*** cartilage *m* hyalin

hyaloid ['haɪəlɔɪd] *Anat & Biol* **1** *n* membrane *f* hyaloïde *ou* du corps vitré
2 *adj (artery, canal)* hyaloïdien
►► ***hyaloid membrane*** membrane *f* hyaloïde

hyaluronic acid [,haɪəlʊ'rɒnɪk-] *n Biol & Chem* acide *m* hyaluronique

hybrid ['haɪbrɪd] **1** *n* (**a**) *Biol & Fig* hybride *m* (**b**) *(bicycle)* vélo *m* tout chemin, VTC *m*
2 *adj* hybride
►► *Br Pol* ***hybrid bill*** = loi dont certaines dispositions sont d'application générale et d'autres d'application restreinte

hybridism ['haɪbrɪ,dɪzəm] *n Biol* hybridisme *m*

hybridization [,haɪbrɪdaɪ'zeɪʃən] *n Biol* hybridation *f*

hybridize, -ise ['haɪbrɪ,daɪz] *Biol* **1** *vt* hybrider
2 *vi* s'hybrider

hybridoma [,haɪbrɪ'dəʊmə] *n Biol* hybridome *m*

hydra ['haɪdrə] *(pl* **hydras** *or* **hydrae** [-dri:]) **1** *n Zool & Fig* hydre *f*
2 Hydra *n Myth* Hydre *f* (de Lerne)

hydra-headed *adj* à tête d'hydre

hydrangea [haɪ'dreɪndʒə] *n Bot* hortensia *m*

hydrant ['haɪdrənt] *n* prise *f* d'eau

hydrate 1 *n Chem* ['haɪdreɪt] hydrate *m*
2 *vt* [haɪ'dreɪt] hydrater
3 *vi* [haɪ'dreɪt] s'hydrater

hydration [haɪ'dreɪʃən] *n* hydratation *f*

hydraulic [haɪ'drɔ:lɪk] *adj* hydraulique
►► ***hydraulic brake*** frein *m* hydraulique; ***hydraulic cylinder*** vérin *m* hydraulique; ***hydraulic engineer*** ingénieur *m* hydraulicien, hydraulicien(enne) *m,f*; ***hydraulic engineering*** technique *f* hydraulique, hydraulique *f*; ***hydraulic jack*** *(for lifting car)* cric *m* hydraulique; ***hydraulic press*** presse *f* hydraulique; ***hydraulic ram*** vérin *m* hydraulique; ***hydraulic suspension*** suspension *f* hydraulique

hydraulically [haɪ'drɔ:lɪkəlɪ] *adv* hydrauliquement; **hydraulically controlled, hydraulically operated** à commande hydraulique, commandé *ou* fonctionnant hydrauliquement; **hydraulically driven** actionné *ou* mû hydrauliquement

hydraulics [haɪ'drɔ:lɪks] *n (UNCOUNT)* hydraulique *f*

hydric ['haɪdrɪk] *adj* hydrique
►► *Chem* ***hydric chloride*** acide *m* chlorhydrique

hydride ['haɪdraɪd] *n Chem* hydrure *m*

hydriodic [,haɪdrɪ'ɒdɪk] *adj Chem* iodhydrique

hydro ['haɪdrəʊ] **1** *n* (**a**) *Br (spa)* établissement *m* thermal *(hôtel)* (**b**) *Can (power)* énergie *f* hydroélectrique; *(plant)* centrale *f* hydroélectrique
2 *adj* hydroélectrique; *Can* **my hydro bill has gone up** ma facture d'électricité a augmenté

hydrobromic [,haɪdrə'brəʊmɪk] *adj Chem* bromhydrique

hydrocarbon [,haɪdrə'kɑ:bən] *n* hydrocarbure *m*

hydrocephalic [,haɪdrəsɪ'fælɪk] *adj Med* hydrocéphale

hydrocephalus [,haɪdrə'sefələs], **hydrocephaly** [,haɪdrə'sefəlɪ] *n Med* hydrocéphalie *f*

hydrochloric [,haɪdrə'klɒrɪk] *adj Chem* chlorhydrique
►► ***hydrochloric acid*** acide *m* chlorhydrique

hydrochloride [,haɪdrə'klɔ:raɪd] *n Chem* chlorhydrate *m*

hydrocortisone [,haɪdrə'kɔ:tɪzəʊn] *n Pharm* hydrocortisone *f*

hydrodynamic [,haɪdrəʊdaɪ'næmɪk] *adj* hydrodynamique

hydrodynamics [,haɪdrədaɪ'næmɪks] *n (UNCOUNT)* hydrodynamique *f*

hydroelectric [,haɪdrəʊɪ'lektrɪk] *adj* hydroélectrique
►► ***hydroelectric dam*** barrage *m* hydroélectrique; ***hydroelectric power*** énergie *f* hydroélectrique

hydroelectricity [,haɪdrəʊɪlek'trɪsətɪ] *n* hydroélectricité *f*

hydrofluoric acid [,haɪdrəflʊ'ɒrɪk-] *n* acide *m* fluorhydrique, fluorure *m* d'hydrogène

hydrofoil ['haɪdrəfɔɪl] *n Naut* hydrofoil *m*, hydroptère *m*

hydrogen ['haɪdrədʒən] *n* hydrogène *m*
►► ***hydrogen bomb*** bombe *f* à hydrogène; ***hydrogen bond*** liaison *f* hydrogène; ***hydrogen carbonate*** hydrogénocarbonate *m*; ***hydrogen engine*** moteur *m* hydrogène; ***hydrogen peroxide*** eau *f* oxygénée; ***hydrogen sulphide*** acide *m* sulfhydrique, hydrogène *m* sulfuré

hydrogenate [haɪ'drɒdʒɪneɪt] **1** *vt* hydrogéner
2 *vi* s'hydrogéner

hydrogenated [haɪ'drɒdʒɪneɪtɪd] *adj* hydrogéné

hydrogenation [haɪdrɒdʒɪ'neɪʃən] *n* hydrogénation *f*

hydrogenization [haɪ,drɒdʒɪnaɪ'zeɪʃən] *n* hydrogénation *f*

hydrogenize, -ise [haɪ'drɒdʒɪnaɪz] **1** *vt* hydrogéner
2 *vi* s'hydrogéner

hydrogenized [haɪ'drɒdʒɪnaɪzd] *adj* hydrogéné

hydrogenous [haɪ'drɒdʒənəs] *adj (containing hydrogen)* hydrogéné; *(relating to hydrogen)* de l'hydrogène

hydrographer [haɪ'drɒgrəfə(r)] *n* hydrographe *mf*

hydrographic [,haɪdrə'græfɪk], **hydrographical** [,haɪdrə'græfɪkəl] *adj* hydrographique

hydrography [haɪ'drɒgrəfɪ] *n* hydrographie *f*

hydroid ['haɪdrɔɪd] *Zool* **1** *n* hydroïde *m*
2 *adj* hydroïde
3 **hydroids** *npl* hydraires *mpl*

hydrokinetics [haɪdrəkɪ'netɪks] *n (UNCOUNT) Phys* cinétique *f* des fluides

hydrologist [haɪ'drɒlədʒɪst] *n* hydrologiste *mf*, hydrologue *mf*

hydrology [haɪ'drɒlədʒɪ] *n* hydrologie *f*

hydrolysis [haɪ'drɒlɪsɪs] *n Chem* hydrolyse *f*

hydrolyte ['haɪdrəlaɪt] *n Chem* corps *m* soumis à l'hydrolyse

hydrolyze, -ize ['haɪdrəlaɪz] *Chem* **1** *vt* hydrolyser
2 *vi* subir une hydrolyse

hydrometer [haɪ'drɒmɪtə(r)] *n Phys* hydromètre *m*

hydrometry [haɪ'drɒmɪtrɪ] *n Phys* hydrométrie *f*

hydronaut ['haɪdrə,nɔ:t] *n Am Naut* sous-marinier *m*

hydropathic [,haɪdrə'pæθɪk] *adj* hydrothérapique

hydropathy [haɪ'drɒpəθɪ] *n* hydropathie *f*

hydrophane ['haɪdrə,feɪn] *n Miner* hydrophane *f*, œil-du-monde *m*

hydrophilic [,haɪdrə'fɪlɪk] *adj Chem* hydrophile

hydrophobia [,haɪdrə'fəʊbjə] *n Med* hydrophobie *f*

hydrophobic [,haɪdrə'fəʊbɪk] *adj Med* hydrophobe

hydrophone ['haɪdrə,fəʊn] *n Phys* hydrophone *m*

hydrophylic = **hydrophilic**

hydroplane ['haɪdrə,pleɪn] **1** *n* (**a**) *(boat)* hydroglisseur *m* (**b**) *(seaplane)* hydravion *m* (**c**) *(pontoon)* flotteur *m (d'un hydravion)* (**d**) *(on submarine)* stabilisateur *m* d'assiette *(d'un sous-marin)*
2 *vi* se dresser comme un hydroglisseur

hydropneumatic [,haɪdrəʊnju:'mætɪk] *adj* hydropneumatique

hydroponic [,haɪdrəʊ'pɒnɪk] *adj Hort* hydroponique

hydroponics [,haɪdrəʊ'pɒnɪks] *n (UNCOUNT) Hort* culture *f* hydroponique

hydropower ['haɪdrə,paʊə(r)] *n* énergie *f* hydroélectrique

hydroquinone [,haɪdrə'kwaɪnəʊn] *n Chem & Phot* hydroquinone *f*

hydrosphere ['haɪdrə,sfɪə(r)] *n* hydrosphère *f*

hydrostat ['haɪdrəʊ,stæt] *n* hydrostat *m*

hydrostatics [,haɪdrə'stætɪks] *n (UNCOUNT)* hydrostatique *f*

hydrotherapeutic [,haɪdrəθerə'pju:tɪk] *adj* hydrothérapique

hydrotherapy [,haɪdrə'θerəpɪ] *n* hydrothérapie *f*

hydrothermal [,haɪdrə'θɜ:məl] *adj* hydrothermique, hydrothermal

hydrotropism [haɪ'drɒtrə,pɪzəm] *n Bot* hydrotropisme *m*

hydrous ['haɪdrəs] *adj (containing water)* aqueux; *Chem* hydraté

hydroxide [haɪ'drɒksaɪd] *n Chem* hydroxyde *m*

hyena [haɪ'i:nə] *n Zool* hyène *f*; *Fig* **to laugh like a hyena** rire comme un bossu

hygiene ['haɪdʒi:n] *n* hygiène *f*; **personal hygiene** hygiène *f* personnelle *ou* corporelle

hygienic [haɪ'dʒi:nɪk] *adj* hygiénique

hygienically [haɪ'dʒi:nɪkəlɪ] *adv* de façon hygiénique

hygienics [haɪ'dʒi:nɪks] *n (UNCOUNT)* hygiène *f*

hygienist [haɪ'dʒi:nɪst] *n* ≃ assistant(e) *m,f* dentaire *(qui s'occupe du détartrage etc)*

hygrograph ['haɪgrəgrɑ:f] *n* hygromètre *m* enregistreur

hygrology [haɪ'grɒlədʒɪ] *n* hygrologie *f*

hygrometer [haɪ'grɒmɪtə(r)] *n* hygromètre *m*

hygrometry [haɪ'grɒmɪtrɪ] *n* hygrométrie *f*

hygroscope ['haɪgrə,skəʊp] *n* hygroscope *m*

hygroscopic [,haɪgrə'skɒpɪk], **hygroscopical** [,haɪgrə'skɒpɪkəl] *adj* hygroscopique

hymen ['haɪmen] **1** *n Anat* hymen *m*
2 Hymen *pr n Myth* Hymen

hymn [hɪm] **1** *n* (**a**) *Rel* hymne *f*, cantique *m* (**b**) *(gen → song of praise)* hymne *m*; **a hymn to nature** un hymne à la nature
2 *vt Literary* chanter un hymne à la gloire de
►► ***hymn book*** livre *m* de cantiques; ***hymn sheet*** = feuille volante où figurent les paroles d'un cantique; *Fig* **to sing from the same hymn sheet** parler d'une seule voix; **let's meet up before the meeting to make sure we're all singing from the same hymn sheet** il faudrait qu'on se voie avant la réunion pour accorder nos violons

hymnal ['hɪmnəl] *n* livre *m* de cantiques

hymnody ['hɪmnədɪ] *n* (**a**) *(singing of hymns)* pratique *f* du chant des cantiques (**b**) *(composing of hymns)* hymnographie *f* (**c**) *(hymns collectively)* hymnologie *f*

hymnology [hɪm'nɒlədʒɪ] *n (study of hymns)* étude *f* des hymnes; *(hymns collectively)* hymnologie *f*

hyoscine ['haɪə,saɪn] *n Chem* hyoscine *f*

hypallage [haɪ'pælədʒɪ] *n Ling* hypallage *f*

hype [haɪp] *Fam* **1** *n* (**a**) *(UNCOUNT) (publicity)* battage *m* publicitaire; **the film got a lot of hype** il y a eu une publicité monstre autour de ce film; **it's all hype** ce n'est que du bla-bla; **I was put off by all the hype** toute cette pub me dégoûtait
(**b**) *Am (put-on)* baratin *m*; **don't give me any hype** ne me baratine pas, ne me fais pas d'esbroufe
(**c**) *Am Drugs slang (hypodermic)* shooteuse *f*; *(addict)* camé(e) *m,f*
2 *vt* (**a**) *(falsify)* baratiner
(**b**) *(publicize)* monter un gros coup de pub autour de; **her latest novel has been heavily hyped** son dernier roman a été lancé à grand renfort de publicité❑

►**hype up** *vt sep Fam (publicize)* **to hype sb/sth up** faire du battage autour de qn/qch; **to hype up a new film/rock group** lancer un nouveau film/groupe de rock à grand renfort de publicité❑; **it's been so hyped up in the media** on a fait un tel battage médiatique

hyped up [haɪpt-] *adj Fam* (**a**) *(heavily publicized)* lancé à grand renfort de publicité❑ (**b**) *(excited)* tout excité❑

hyper ['haɪpə(r)] *adj Fam* (**a**) *(over-excited)* tout excité ❑ (**b**) *(angry)* furax *(inv)*; **he got** *or* **went really hyper about it** ça l'a mis dans une colère noire

hyper- ['haɪpə(r)-] *pref* hyper-

hyperacidity [ˌhaɪpərə'sɪdətɪ] *n* hyperacidité *f*

hyperactive [ˌhaɪpər'æktɪv] *adj* hyperactif

hyperactivity [ˌhaɪpəræk'tɪvətɪ] *n* hyperactivité *f*

hyperaemia, *Am* **hyperemia** [ˌhaɪpər'iːmɪə] *n Med* hyperémie *f*, hyperhémie *f*

hyperaesthesia, *Am* **hyperesthesia** [ˌhaɪpərɪs'θiːzɪə] *n Med* hyperesthésie *f*

hyperalgesia [ˌhaɪpəræl'dʒiːzɪə] *n Med* hyperalgésie *f*

hyperbaric therapy [ˌhaɪpə'bærɪk-] *n Med* barothérapie *f*

hyperbaton [haɪ'pɜːbətən] *n Ling* hyperbate *f*

hyperbola [haɪ'pɜːbələ] *n Math* hyperbole *f*

hyperbole [haɪ'pɜːbəlɪ] *n Ling* hyperbole *f*

hyperbolic [ˌhaɪpə'bɒlɪk], **hyperbolical** [ˌhaɪpə'bɒlɪkəl] *adj Math & Ling* hyperbolique
▸▸ *Math* ***hyperbolic function*** fonction *f* hyperbolique

hyperbolically [ˌhaɪpə'bɒlɪkəlɪ] *adv* hyperboliquement

hyperbolize, -ise [ˌhaɪ'pɜːbəlaɪz] *vi Ling* parler par hyperboles

hyperboloid [haɪ'pɜːbəlɔɪd] *n Geom* hyperboloïde *m*

hypercharge ['haɪpəˌtʃɑːdʒ] *n* hypercharge *f*

hyperconscious [ˌhaɪpə'kɒnʃəs] *adj Am (aware)* hyperconscient; *(sensitive)* hypersensible

hypercritical [ˌhaɪpə'krɪtɪkəl] *adj* hypercritique

hyperemia *Am* = **hyperaemia**

hyperesthesia *Am* = **hyperaesthesia**

hyperfine ['haɪpəˌfaɪn] *adj Opt* hyperfin

hyperglycaemia, *Am* **hyperglycemia** [ˌhaɪpəglaɪ'siːmɪə] *n Physiol* hyperglycémie *f*

hyperglycaemic, *Am* **hyperglycemic** [ˌhaɪpəglaɪ'siːmɪk] *adj Physiol* hyperglycémiant; **to be hyperglycaemic** *(permanently)* faire de l'hyperglycémie; *(temporarily)* avoir une crise d'hyperglycémie

hypergolic [ˌhaɪpə'gɒlɪk] *adj* hypergolique

hyperinflation [ˌhaɪpərɪn'fleɪʃən] *n Econ* hyperinflation *f*

Hyperion [haɪ'pɪərɪən] *pr n Myth* Hypérion

hyperlink ['haɪpəˌlɪŋk] *n Comput* hyperlien *m*

hypermarket [ˌhaɪpə'mɑːkɪt] *n Br* hypermarché *m*

hypermedia [ˌhaɪpə'miːdɪə] *n Comput* hypermédia *m*

hypermetropia [ˌhaɪpəme'trəʊpɪə], **hypermetropy** [ˌhaɪpə'metrəpɪ] *n Opt* hypermétropie *f*

hypermnesia [ˌhaɪpəm'niːzɪə] *n Psy* hypermnésie *f*

hyperon ['haɪpərɒn] *n Phys* hypéron *m*

hyperparasite [ˌhaɪpə'pærəsaɪt] *n Biol* hyperparasite *m*

hyperpiesis [haɪpəpaɪ'iːsɪs] *n Med* hyperpiésie *f*

hyperpyrexia [haɪpəpaɪ'reksɪə] *n Med* hyperpyrexie *f*

hyperrealism [ˌhaɪpə'rɪəlɪzəm] *n* hyperréalisme *m*

hyperrealist [ˌhaɪpə'rɪəlɪst] **1** *n* hyperréaliste *mf*
2 *adj* hyperréaliste

hypersecretion [ˌhaɪpəsɪ'kriːʃən] *n Med* hypersécrétion *f*

hypersegmentation [ˌhaɪpəsegmən'teɪʃən] *n Mktg* hypersegmentation *f*

hypersensitive [ˌhaɪpə'sensɪtɪv] *adj* hypersensible

hypersensitivity ['haɪpəˌsensɪ'tɪvətɪ] *n* hypersensibilité *f*

hypersonic [ˌhaɪpə'sɒnɪk] *adj* hypersonique

hyperspace ['haɪpəspeɪs] *n* hyperespace *m*

hypertension [ˌhaɪpə'tenʃən] *n Med* hypertension *f*

hypertensive [ˌhaɪpə'tensɪv] *adj Med* hypertendu; **hypertensive patient** hypertendu(e) *m,f*

hypertext ['haɪpətekst] *n Comput & Literature* hypertexte *m*
▸▸ *Comput* ***hypertext link*** lien *m* hypertexte

hyperthermia [ˌhaɪpə'θɜːmɪə] *n Med* hyperthermie *f*

hyperthyroid [ˌhaɪpə'θaɪrɔɪd] *adj Med* hyperthyroïdien

hyperthyroidism [ˌhaɪpə'θaɪrɔɪˌdɪzəm] *n Med* hyperthyroïdie *f*

hypertonic [ˌhaɪpə'tɒnɪk] *adj Chem & Phys* hypertonique
▸▸ ***hypertonic salt solution*** solution *f* hypertonique

hypertrophic [ˌhaɪpə'trɒfɪk] *adj Med* hypertrophique

hypertrophied [haɪ'pɜːtrəfɪd] *adj Med* hypertrophié

hypertrophous [haɪ'pɜːtrəfəs] *adj Med* hypertrophique

hypertrophy [haɪ'pɜːtrəfɪ] (*pl* **hypertrophies**) *Med*
1 *n* hypertrophie *f*
2 *vt* hypertrophier
3 *vi* s'hypertrophier

hyperventilate [ˌhaɪpə'ventɪleɪt] *vi Med* faire de l'hyperventilation *ou* de l'hyperpnée

hyperventilation ['haɪpəˌventɪ'leɪʃən] *n Med* hyperventilation *f*, hyperpnée *f*

hyphen ['haɪfən] **1** *n* trait *m* d'union
2 *vt* mettre un trait d'union à

hyphenate ['haɪfəneɪt] *vt* mettre un trait d'union à; **a hyphenated word** un mot à trait d'union; **is that hyphenated?** est-ce que ça prend un trait d'union?
▸▸ *Am* ***hyphenated American*** étranger(ère) *m,f* naturalisé(e) *(Germano-Américain, Hispano-Américain etc)*

hyphenation [haɪfə'neɪʃən] *n* syllabation *f*; *(in printing)* césure *f*, coupure *f* des mots
▸▸ *Comput* ***hyphenation help*** aide *f* à la césure; *Comput* ***hyphenation logic*** logique *f* de césure; *Comput* ***hyphenation menu*** menu *m* de césure; *Comput* ***hyphenation program*** programme *m* de césure, logiciel *m* de syllabation

hypnagogic [ˌhɪpnə'gɒdʒɪk] *adj Psy* hypnagogique

hypnoid ['hɪpnɔɪd] *adj Psy* hypnoïde

hypnology [hɪp'nɒlədʒɪ] *adj Psy* hypnologie *f*

hypnopaedia, **hypnopedia** *Psy* [hɪpnəʊ'piːdɪə] *n* hypnopédie *f*

hypnosis [hɪp'nəʊsɪs] *n* hypnose *f*; **to be under hypnosis** être en état hypnotique *ou* d'hypnose; **to put sb under hypnosis** mettre qn sous hypnose

hypnotherapist [ˌhɪpnəʊ'θerəpɪst] *n* hypnothérapeute *mf*, médecin *m* hypnotiseur

hypnotherapy [ˌhɪpnəʊ'θerəpɪ] *n* hypnothérapie *f*

hypnotic [hɪp'nɒtɪk] **1** *adj* hypnotique; **hypnotic state** état *m* d'hypnose; **in a hypnotic trance** en état d'hypnose; *Fig* **to have a hypnotic effect on sb** hypnotiser qn
2 *n (drug)* hypnotique *m*; *(person)* hypnotique *mf*

hypnotism ['hɪpnətɪzəm] *n* hypnotisme *m*

hypnotist ['hɪpnətɪst] *n* hypnotiseur(euse) *m,f*

hypnotize, -ise ['hɪpnətaɪz] *vt* hypnotiser

hypo ['haɪpəʊ] *Fam* **1** *n Drugs slang (abbr* **hypodermic**) shooteuse *f*, pompe *f*
2 *adj Physiol (abbr* **hypoglycaemic**) hypoglycémiant ❑; **to be hypo** *(permanently)* faire de l'hypoglycémie ❑; *(temporarily)* avoir une crise d'hypoglycémie ❑

hypo- ['haɪpəʊ] *pref* hypo-

hypoacidity [ˌhaɪpəʊə'sɪdɪtɪ] *n Med* **gastric hypoacidity** hypochlorhydrie *f*

hypoallergenic ['haɪpəʊˌælə'dʒenɪk] *adj* hypoallergique, hypoallergénique

hypocalorific [ˌhaɪpəkælə'rɪfɪk] *adj* hypocalorique, hypoénergétique

hypocentre, *Am* **hypocenter** ['haɪpəʊˌsentə(r)] *n* (**a**) *(of earthquake)* hypocentre *m* (**b**) *Nucl* point *m* zéro

hypochondria [ˌhaɪpə'kɒndrɪə] *n* hypocondrie *f*

hypochondriac [ˌhaɪpə'kɒndrɪæk] **1** *adj* hypocondriaque
2 *n* hypocondriaque *mf*, malade *mf* imaginaire; **she's such a hypochondriac** c'est une véritable malade imaginaire

hypocorism [haɪ'pɒkəˌrɪzəm] *n Ling* hypocoristique *m*

hypocoristic [ˌhaɪpəkɔː'rɪstɪk] *adj Ling* hypocoristique

hypocrisy [hɪ'pɒkrəsɪ] (*pl* **hypocrisies**) *n* hypocrisie *f*

hypocrite ['hɪpəkrɪt] *n* hypocrite *mf*

hypocritical [ˌhɪpə'krɪtɪkəl] *adj* hypocrite; **a hypocritical remark** une remarque hypocrite; **it would be hypocritical of me to get married in church** ce serait hypocrite de ma part de me marier à l'église

hypocritically [ˌhɪpə'krɪtɪkəlɪ] *adv* hypocritement

hypocycloid [ˌhaɪpə'saɪklɔɪd] *n Math* hypocycloïde *f*, épicycloïde *f* intérieure

hypodermic [ˌhaɪpə'dɜːmɪk] *Med* **1** *adj* hypodermique
2 *n* (**a**) *(syringe)* seringue *f* hypodermique (**b**) *(injection)* injection *f* hypodermique
▸▸ ***hypodermic needle*** aiguille *f* hypodermique; ***hypodermic syringe*** seringue *f* hypodermique

hypoglycaemia, *Am* **hypoglycemia** [ˌhaɪpəʊglaɪ'siːmɪə] *n Physiol* hypoglycémie *f*

hypoglycaemic, *Am* **hypoglycemic** [ˌhaɪpəʊglaɪ'siːmɪk] *adj Physiol* hypoglycémiant; **to be hypoglycaemic** *(permanently)* faire de l'hypoglycémie; *(temporarily)* avoir une crise d'hypoglycémie

hypoid ['haɪpɔɪd] *adj Tech* hypoïde

hypomania [ˌhaɪpəʊ'meɪnɪə] *n Psy* hypomanie *f*

hyponym ['haɪpənɪm] *n* hyponyme *m*

hypostasis [haɪ'pɒstəsɪs] (*pl* **hypostases** [-siːz]) *n Med, Phil & Rel* hypostase *f*

hypostyle ['haɪpəʊˌstaɪl] *adj Archit* hypostyle

hypotension [ˌhaɪpəʊ'tenʃən] *n Med* hypotension *f*

hypotensive [ˌhaɪpəʊ'tensɪv] *adj Med* hypotendu; **hypotensive patient** hypotendu(e) *m,f*

hypotenuse [haɪ'pɒtənjuːz] *n Geom* hypoténuse *f*

hypothalamus [ˌhaɪpəʊ'θæləməs] *n Anat* hypothalamus *m*

hypothermia [ˌhaɪpəʊ'θɜːmɪə] *n Med* hypothermie *f*

hypothesis [haɪ'pɒθɪsɪs] (*pl* **hypotheses** [-siːz]) *n* hypothèse *f*; **according to your hypothesis** selon *ou* suivant votre hypothèse; **to put forward** *or* **to advance a hypothesis** émettre *ou* énoncer une hypothèse; **this confirms my hypothesis that...** cela confirme mon hypothèse selon *ou* d'après laquelle...

hypothesize, -ise [haɪ'pɒθɪsaɪz] **1** *vt* supposer; **let's hypothesize the following** faisons les hypothèses suivantes; **he hypothesized that she was not in fact the killer** il a formulé l'hypothèse selon laquelle ce ne serait pas elle l'assassin
2 *vi* faire des hypothèses *ou* des suppositions

hypothetical [ˌhaɪpə'θetɪkəl] *adj* hypothétique; **it's purely hypothetical** c'est purement hypothétique

hypothetically [ˌhaɪpə'θetɪkəlɪ] *adv* hypothétiquement

hypothyroid [ˌhaɪpəʊ'θaɪrɔɪd] *adj Med* hypothyroïdien

hypothyroidism [ˌhaɪpəʊ'θaɪrɔɪdɪzəm] *n Med* hypothyroïdie *f*

hypotonic [ˌhaɪpəʊ'tɒnɪk] *adj Physiol* hypotonique

hypoxia [haɪ'pɒksɪə] *n Med* hypoxie *f*

hypsography [hɪp'sɒgrəfɪ] (*pl* **hypsographies**) *n* (**a**) *(science of mapping)* hypsométrie *f*, hypsographie *f* (**b**) *(relief → of a region)* hypsométrie *f* (**c**) *(representation)* carte *f* hypsographique

hypsometer [hɪp'sɒmɪtə(r)] *n* hypsomètre *m*

hypsometric [ˌhɪpsə'metrɪk], **hypsometrical** [ˌhɪpsə'metrɪkəl] *adj* hypsométrique
▸▸ ***hypsometric layer, hypsometric tint*** teinte *f* hypsométrique

hypsometry [hɪp'sɒmɪtrɪ] *n* hypsométrie *f*

hyrax ['haɪræks] *n Zool* daman *m*

hyssop ['hɪsəp] *n Bot* hysope *f*; **hedge hyssop** gratiole *f* officinale, herbe *f* au pauvre homme; **false hedge hyssop** ilysanthes *m*

hysterectomy [ˌhɪstə'rektəmɪ] (*pl* **hysterectomies**) *n* hystérectomie *f*; **to have a hysterectomy** subir une hystérectomie

hysteresis [ˌhɪstə'riːsɪs] *n* hystérésis *f*

hysteria [hɪs'tɪərɪə] *n* (**a**) *Psy* hystérie *f* (**b**) *(hysterical behaviour)* crise *f* de nerfs; **his voice betrayed his mounting hysteria** sa voix trahissait la montée d'une crise de nerfs; **an atmosphere of barely controlled hysteria reigned in the office** une atmosphère de folie à peine contenue régnait dans le bureau; *Fig* **the crowd was on the edge** *or* **verge of hysteria** la foule était au bord de l'hystérie; **a country in the grip of war hysteria** un pays en proie à une hystérie guerrière

hysteric [hɪs'terɪk] *n Psy* hystérique *mf*

hysterical [hɪs'terɪkəl] *adj* (**a**) *Psy* hystérique (**b**) *(sobs, voice, reaction)* hystérique; *(laugh)* hystérique, nerveux; **hysterical passengers fought to reach the emergency exits** des passagers hystériques se battaient pour atteindre la sortie de secours; **he's the hysterical type** c'est un grand nerveux; **he was hysterical with grief** il était fou de chagrin (**c**) *(overexcited)* **it's nothing to get hysterical about!** ce n'est pas la peine de faire une crise (de nerfs)! (**d**) *Fam (very funny)* écroulant, tordant

►► *Am* ***hysterical pregnancy*** grossesse *f* nerveuse

hysterically [hɪs'terɪkəlɪ] *adv* (**a**) *(very emotionally)* sans pouvoir maîtriser ses émotions; **he was waving his arms hysterically** il agitait ses bras de façon incontrôlée; **to weep hysterically** avoir une crise de larmes; **to laugh hysterically** être pris d'un rire nerveux (**b**) *Fam* **hysterically funny** écroulant, tordant (**c**) *Fam* **to laugh hysterically** *(with great amusement)* avoir le fou rire

hysterics [hɪs'terɪks] *npl* (**a**) *(hysterical behaviour)* crise *f* de nerfs; **to go into** *or* **to have hysterics** avoir une (violente) crise de nerfs (**b**) *Fam (laughter)* crise *f* de rire; **to go into** *or* **to have hysterics** attraper un *ou* avoir le fou rire; **we were in hysterics about** *or* **over it** on était piés en deux de rire; **he had me in hysterics** il m'a fait mourir de rire

hysteroscopy [,hɪstə'rɒskəpɪ] *n Med* hystéroscopie *f*

Hz *Elec & Phys (written abbr* **hertz**) Hz

I¹, i [aɪ] *n (letter)* I, i *m inv*; **two i's** deux i; **I for Ivor** ≃ I comme Irma
►► ***I beam*** *Constr* fer *m* en I *ou* en double T; *Comput* pointeur *m* en I

I² *pron (gen)* je; *(emphatic)* moi; **I like skiing** j'aime skier; **Rosie and I have known each other for years** Rosie et moi nous connaissons depuis des années; **I found it, not you** c'est moi qui l'ai trouvé, pas vous; **I too have a twin sister** moi aussi, j'ai une jumelle; **here I am** me voici; *Formal* **it is I who should be apologizing** c'est moi qui devrais m'excuser

I. *(written abbr* **island***)* île *f*

IA *(written abbr* **Iowa***)* Iowa *m*

IAAF [ˌaɪdʌbəleɪ'ef] *n (abbr* **International Amateur Athletics Federation***)* FIAA *f*

IAEA [ˌaɪeɪˌiː'aɪ] *n (abbr* **International Atomic Energy Agency***)* AIEA *f*

Iago [ɪ'ɑːgəʊ] *pr n* Iago *(personnage dans 'Othello' de William Shakespeare dont le nom désigne métaphoriquement un individu capable de trahir jusqu'à ses plus proches amis)*

iamb ['aɪæm] *n Literature* iambe *m*

iambic [aɪ'æmbɪk] *Literature* **1** *n (line, poem)* iambe *m*
2 *adj* iambique
►► ***iambic foot*** iambe *m*; ***iambic pentameter*** pentamètre *m* iambique

iambus [aɪ'æmbəs] *n Literature* iambe *m*

IAP [ˌaɪeɪ'piː] *n Comput (abbr* **Internet Access Provider***)* fournisseur *m* d'accès à l'Internet

IASC [ˌaɪeɪˌes'siː] *n Fin (abbr* **International Accounting Standards Committee***)* comité *m* international des normes comptables

IATA [aɪ'ɑːtə, iː'ɑːtə] *n (abbr* **International Air Transport Association***)* IATA *f*

iatrogenic [aɪˌætrəʊ'dʒenɪk] *adj Med* iatrogène, iatrogénique

IBA [ˌaɪbiː'eɪ] *n Br Formerly (abbr* **Independent Broadcasting Authority***)* = organisme d'agrément et de coordination des stations de radio et chaînes de télévision du secteur privé en Grande-Bretagne

IBC [ˌaɪbiː'siː] *n Press (abbr* **inside back cover***)* troisième *f* de couverture

Iberia [aɪ'bɪərɪə] *n* Ibérie *f*; **in Iberia** en Ibérie

Iberian [aɪ'bɪərɪən] **1** *n* **(a)** *(person)* Ibère *mf* **(b)** *Ling* ibère *m*
2 *adj* ibérique
►► ***the Iberian Peninsula*** la péninsule Ibérique

Ibero-American [aɪ'bɪərəʊ-] *adj* ibéro-américain

IBEW ['aɪbiju:] *n (abbr* **International Brotherhood of Electrical Workers***)* = syndicat international d'électriciens

ibex ['aɪbeks] *(pl* **inv** *or* **ibexes***) n Zool* bouquetin *m*

ibid *(written abbr* **ibidem***)* ibid

ibis ['aɪbɪs] *(pl* **inv** *or* **ibises***) n Orn* ibis *m*

Ibiza [ɪ'biːθə] *n* Ibiza; **in Ibiza** à Ibiza

IBM-compatible [ˌaɪbiː'em-] *adj Comput* compatible IBM

Ibo ['iːbəʊ] **1** *n* **(a) the Ibo** *(people)* les Ibo *mpl* **(b)** *(member of people)* Ibo *mf* **(c)** *(language)* ibo *m*
2 *adj* ibo

IBOR ['aɪbɔː(r)] *n Fin (abbr* **interbank offered rate***)* taux *m* interbancaire offert

IBRD [ˌaɪbiːˌɑː'diː] *n (abbr* **International Bank for Reconstruction and Development***)* BIRD *f*

IBS [ˌaɪbiː'es] *n Med (abbr* **irritable bowel syndrome***)* syndrôme *m* du côlon irritable

ibuprofen [ˌaɪbjʊ'prəʊfən] *n Pharm* ibuprofène *m*

IC [ˌaɪ'siː] *n Comput (abbr* **integrated circuit***)* circuit *m* intégré
►► ***IC card*** carte *f* à circuits intégrés

i/c [ˌaɪ'siː] *(abbr* **in charge of***)* responsable de

ICA [ˌaɪsiː'eɪ] *n Br (abbr* **Institute of Contemporary Arts***)* = centre d'art moderne à Londres

ICAO [ˌaɪsiːˌeɪ'əʊ] *n (abbr* **International Civil Aviation Organization***)* OACI *f*

Icarus ['ɪkərəs] *pr n Myth* Icare

ICBM [ˌaɪsiːˌbiː'em] *n (abbr* **intercontinental ballistic missile***)* ICBM *m*

ICC [ˌaɪsiː'siː] *n* **(a)** *(abbr* **International Chamber of Commerce***)* CCI *f* **(b)** *Am (abbr* **Interstate Commerce Commission***)* = commission fédérale américaine réglementant le commerce entre les États

ice [aɪs] **1** *n* **(a)** *(UNCOUNT) (frozen water)* glace *f*; *(ice cubes)* glaçons *mpl*; **her feet were like ice** elle avait les pieds gelés; **with ice?** *(in drink)* avec des glaçons *ou* de la glace?; **the reforms have been put on ice** les réformes ont été gelées; *Fig* **to walk** *or* **to be on thin ice** avancer en terrain miné
(b) *(on road)* verglas *m*
(c) *(in ice rink)* glace *f*; **come out onto the ice** venez patiner *ou* sur la piste
(d) *Br Old-fashioned (ice-cream)* glace *f*
(e) *(UNCOUNT) Fam (diamonds)* diams *mpl*, cailloux *mpl*
(f) *Fam Drugs slang* ice *f*
2 *vt* **(a)** *(chill → drink)* rafraîchir; *(→ with ice cubes)* mettre des glaçons dans
(b) *(cake)* glacer
(c) *Fam Crime slang (kill)* liquider
3 *vi* (se) givrer
►► ***ice age*** période *f* glaciaire; *Br* ***ice axe,*** *Am* ***ice ax*** piolet *m*; ***ice bag*** sac *m* à glaçons; ***ice blue*** *n* bleu *m* très pâle; ***ice bucket*** seau *m* à glace; ***ice cap*** calotte *f* glaciaire; ***ice cube*** glaçon *m*; ***ice dancer*** danseur(euse) *m,f* sur glace; ***ice dancing*** danse *f* sur glace; ***ice floe*** glace *f* flottante; ***ice hockey*** hockey *m* sur glace; ***ice jam*** embâcle *m*; *Br* ***ice lolly*** glace *f* à l'eau; ***ice machine, ice maker*** machine *f* à glace; *Fam Pej* ***ice maiden*** glaçon *m (femme distante)*; ***ice pack*** *(pack ice)* banquise *f*; *(ice bag)* sac *m* à glaçons; *Med* poche *f* à glace; ***ice pick*** pic *m* à glace; ***ice point*** point *m* de congélation; *Fam Pej* ***ice queen*** glaçon *m (femme distante)*; ***ice rink*** patinoire *f*; ***ice scraper*** *(for car window)* raclette *f* (antigivre); ***ice screw*** *(for mountaineering)* broche *f* à glace; ***ice sculpture*** sculpture *f* de glace; ***ice sheet*** nappe *f* de glace; ***ice show*** spectacle *m* sur glace; ***ice skate*** patin *m* (à glace); ***ice storm*** chutes *fpl* de pluie verglaçante, tempête *f* de verglas; ***ice track*** piste *f* de patinage de vitesse; *Am* ***ice water*** eau *f* glacée; *Br* ***ice yacht*** char *m* à voile (sur patins)

►**ice over** **1** *vt sep* **to be iced over** *(lake, river etc)* être gelé; *(window, propellers)* être givré
2 *vi (lake, river etc)* geler; *(window, propellers)* (se) givrer

►**ice up** **1** *vt sep* **to be iced up** *(lock, windscreen, propellers)* être givré; *(road)* être verglacé
2 *vi* **(a)** *(lock, windscreen, propellers)* (se) givrer, se couvrir de givre **(b)** *(road)* se couvrir de verglas

ice-age *adj* (datant) de la période glaciaire

iceberg ['aɪsbɜːg] *n* **(a)** *(in sea)* iceberg *m* **(b)** *Fam (cold person)* glaçon *m*
►► ***iceberg lettuce*** = salade aux feuilles serrées et croquantes

iceblink ['aɪsblɪŋk] *n* reflet *m ou* clarté *f* des neiges

ice-blue *adj* bleu très pâle

iceboat ['aɪsbəʊt] *n* **(a)** *(ice yacht)* char *m* à voile (sur patins) **(b)** *(icebreaker)* brise-glace *m inv*

icebound ['aɪsbaʊnd] *adj* bloqué par les glaces

icebox ['aɪsbɒks] *n* **(a)** *Br (freezer compartment)* freezer *m* **(b)** *Am Old-fashioned (refrigerator)* réfrigérateur *m*, frigo *m* **(c)** *(coolbox)* glacière *f* **(d)** *Fig* glacière *f*; **their house is like an icebox** c'est une vraie glacière *ou* on gèle chez eux

icebreaker ['aɪsˌbreɪkə(r)] *n* **(a)** *(vessel)* brise-glace *m inv* **(b)** *(at party)* **if you're looking for an icebreaker** si tu veux briser la glace

ice-climbing *n* escalade *f* de murs de glace

ice-cold *adj (hands, drink)* glacé; *(house, manners)* glacial

ice-cream *nf* glace *f*; **chocolate/strawberry ice-cream** glace *f* au chocolat/à la fraise
►► ***ice-cream bar*** barre *f* glacée; ***ice-cream cone, ice-cream cornet*** cornet *m* de glace; *Culin* ***ice-cream maker*** sorbetière *f*; ***ice-cream man*** marchand *m* de glaces; ***ice-cream parlour*** salon *m* de dégustation de glaces; ***ice-cream soda*** soda *m* avec de la glace; ***ice-cream van*** camionnette *f* de vendeur de glaces

'An Ice-cream War' *Boyd* 'Comme neige au soleil'

iced [aɪst] *adj* **(a)** *(chilled → drink)* glacé **(b)** *(decorated → cake, biscuit)* glacé
►► ***iced water*** eau *f* avec glaçons

icefield ['aɪsfiːld] *n* champ *m* de glace, icefield *m*

icefish ['aɪsfɪʃ] *n Ich* poisson *m* des glaces

icehouse ['aɪshaʊs, *pl* -haʊzɪz] *n* glacière *f (local)*

Iceland ['aɪslənd] *n* Islande *f*; **in Iceland** en Islande

Icelander ['aɪsləndə(r)] *n* Islandais(e) *m,f*

Icelandic [aɪs'lændɪk] **1** *n (language)* islandais *m*
2 *adj* islandais
3 *comp (embassy)* d'Islande; *(history)* de l'Islande; *(teacher)* d'islandais

iceman ['aɪsmæn] *(pl* **icemen** [-men]*) n Am* livreur *m* de glace à domicile

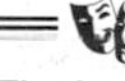

'The Iceman Cometh' *O'Neill* 'Le Marchand de glace est passé'

Iceni [ˌaɪ'siːnaɪ] *npl Hist* Icéniens *mpl*, Icènes *mpl*

iceplant ['aɪsplɑːnt] *n* **(a)** *Bot* (ficoïde *f*) cristalline *f*, (ficoïde *f*) glaciale *f* **(b)** *Ind* fabrique *f* de glace

ice-skate *vi* patiner; *(professionally)* faire du patinage (sur glace); *(for pleasure)* faire du patin (à glace)

ice-skater *n* patineur(euse) *m,f*

ice-skating *n* patinage *m* (sur glace); **to go ice-skating** faire du patin (à glace)

ice-tray *n* bac *m* à glace *ou* à glaçons

Ichabod Crane ['ɪkəbɒd-] *pr n* = personnage dans 'The Legend of Sleepy Hollow' de Washington Irving, qui se croit poursuivi par un chevalier sans tête

I Ching [ˌiː'tʃɪŋ] *n* Yijing *m*, Yi-king *m*

ichneumon [ɪk'njuːmən] *n* **(a)** *Zool* ichneumon *m*, rat *m* de Pharaon *ou* d'Égypte **(b)** *Entom* **ichneumon (fly)** ichneumon *m*

ichor ['aɪkɔː(r)] *n Myth & Med* ichor *m*

ichthyic ['ɪkθiːɪk] *adj* ichtyique

ichthyoid ['ɪkθiːɔɪd] *adj* ichtyoïde

ichthyologic [ˌɪkθɪə'lɒdʒɪk], **ichthyological** [ˌɪkθɪə'lɒdʒɪkəl] *adj* ichtyologique

ichthyologist [ˌɪkθɪ'ɒlədʒɪst] *n* ichtyologiste *mf*, ichtyologue *mf*

ichthyology [ˌɪkθɪ'ɒlədʒɪ] *n* ichtyologie *f*

ichthyophagous [ˌɪkθɪ'ɒfəgəs] *adj* ichtyophage

ichthyosaurus [ˌɪkθɪəˈsɔːrəs] *(pl* **inv** *or* **ichthyosauri** [-raɪ]) *n* ichtyosaure *m*

ichthyosis [ˌɪkθɪˈəʊsɪs] *n Med* ichtyose *f*

icicle [ˈaɪsɪkəl] *n* glaçon *m (qui pend d'une gouttière etc)*

icily [ˈaɪsɪlɪ] *adv* d'une manière glaciale; **to answer icily** répondre d'un ton *ou* sur un ton glacial; **he looked at her icily** il lui lança un regard glacial

iciness [ˈaɪsɪnɪs] *n (of wind, water)* température *f* glaciale; **because of the iciness of the steps** parce que les marches étaient verglacées; *Fig* **the iciness of her voice** son ton glacial

icing [ˈaɪsɪŋ] *n* (**a**) *esp Br Culin* glaçage *m*; *Fig* **it's the icing on the cake** c'est la cerise sur le gâteau (**b**) *(on aeroplane → process)* givrage *m*; *(→ ice)* givre *m* (**c**) *Sport (in ice hockey)* dégagement *m* interdit

►► *Br* ***icing sugar*** sucre *m* glace

ICJ [ˌaɪsiːˈdʒeɪ] *n Law (abbr* **International Court of Justice**) CIJ *f*

ick [ɪk] *Am Fam* **1** *n (UNCOUNT)* cochonneries *fpl*

2 *exclam* beurk!

icky [ˈɪkɪ] *(compar* **ickier**, *superl* **ickiest**) *adj Fam (repulsive)* dégueulasse; *(sticky)* poisseux; *(sentimental)* mièvre, à la guimauve

icon [ˈaɪkɒn] *n* (**a**) *Rel* icône *f*; *Fig* **a 60s icon** un symbole des années 60; **a gay icon** une idole gay (**b**) *Comput* icône *f*

►► *Comput* ***icon bar*** barre *f* d'icônes; *Comput* ***icon editor*** éditeur *m* d'icônes

iconic [aɪˈkɒnɪk] *adj* (**a**) *(gen) & Comput* iconique (**b**) *Fig (person)* emblématique; **to have iconic status** être une idole

iconize, -ise [ˈaɪkənaɪz] *vt Comput* représenter en icône

iconoclasm [aɪˈkɒnəklæzəm] *n* iconoclasme *m*

iconoclast [aɪˈkɒnəklæst] *n* iconoclaste *mf*

iconoclastic [aɪˌkɒnəˈklæstɪk] *adj* iconoclaste

iconographer [ˌaɪkəˈnɒɡrəfə(r)] *n* iconographe *mf*

iconographic [ˌaɪkɒnəˈɡræfɪk], **iconographical** [ˌaɪkɒnəˈɡræfɪkəl] *adj* iconographique

iconography [ˌaɪkɒˈnɒɡrəfɪ] *n* iconographie *f*

iconological [ˌaɪkɒnəˈlɒdʒɪkəl] *adj* iconologique

iconology [ˌaɪkɒˈnɒlədʒɪ] *n* iconologie *f*

iconostasis [ˌaɪkɒˈnɒstəsɪs] *n Archit & Rel* iconostase *f*

icosahedral [ˌaɪkəsəˈhiːdrəl] *adj Geom* icosaèdre

icosahedron [ˌaɪkəsəˈhiːdrən] *n Geom* icosaèdre *m*

ICR [ˌaɪsiːˈɑː(r)] *n Am (abbr* **Institute for Cancer Research**) = institut américain de recherche sur le cancer

ICT [ˌaɪsiːˈtiː] *n (abbr* **information and communication technology**) informatique *f*

icteric [ɪkˈterɪk] *Med* **1** *n* ictérique *mf*

2 *adj* ictérique

icterus [ˈɪktərəs] *n* (**a**) *Med* ictère *m*, jaunisse *f* (**b**) *Bot* ictère *m* (**c**) *Orn* ictère *m*, icterus *m*

ictus [ˈɪktəs] *n* (**a**) *Literature* ictus *m* (**b**) *Med (stroke, attack)* ictus *m*; *(beating of pulse)* battement *m* (du pouls)

ICU [ˌaɪsiːˈjuː] *n Med (abbr* **intensive care unit**) unité *f* de soins intensifs

icy [ˈaɪsɪ] *(compar* **icier**, *superl* **iciest**) *adj* (**a**) *(weather, water, wind)* glacial; *(hands)* glacé; *(ground)* gelé (**b**) *(covered in ice → road)* verglacé; *(→ window, propeller)* givré, couvert de givre; *Rail (→ points)* gelé (**c**) *Fig (reception, stare)* glacial; **his icy manner** sa froideur

ID[1] [ˌaɪˈdiː] *(pl* **ID's**, *pt & pp* **ID'd**, *cont* **ID'ing**) **1** *n (UNCOUNT) (abbr* **identification**) (**a**) *(documents)* papiers *mpl*; **do you have any ID?** vous avez une pièce d'identité? (**b**) *Comput* numéro *m* d'identification

2 *vt (abbr* **identify**) **to ID sb** identifier qn; **to be** *or* **to get ID'd** subir un contrôle d'identité

►► ***ID card*** carte *f* d'identité

ID[2] *(written abbr* **Idaho**) Idaho

I'd [aɪd] = **I had, I would**

id [ɪd] *n Psy* ça *m inv*

Idaho [ˈaɪdəhəʊ] *n* l'Idaho *m*; **in Idaho** dans l'Idaho

IDB [ˌaɪdiːˈbiː] *n Fin (abbr* **inter-dealer broker**) courtier *m* intermédiaire

IDD [ˌaɪdiːˈdiː] *n Tel (abbr* **international direct dialling**) indicatif *m* du pays

IDE [ˌaɪdiːˈiː] *n Comput (abbr* **integrated drive electronics**) IDE *m*

idea [aɪˈdɪə] *n* (**a**) *(plan, suggestion, inspiration)* idée *f*; **what a good idea!** quelle bonne idée!; **I've had an idea** j'ai une idée; **it wasn't MY idea!** l'idée n'était pas de moi!; **the idea of leaving you never entered my head** l'idée de te quitter ne m'a jamais effleuré; **where did you get the idea for your book?** d'où vous est venue l'idée de votre livre?; **I thought the idea was for them to come here** il n'était pas prévu que ce serait eux qui viendraient ici?; **that's an idea!** ça, c'est une bonne idée!; **that's the idea!** c'est ça!; **what's the idea?** *(showing disapproval)* qu'est-ce que ça veut dire *ou* signifie?; **the very idea!** en voilà une idée!

(**b**) *(notion)* idée *f*; **our ideas about the universe** notre conception de l'univers; **he has some strange ideas** il a de drôles d'idées; **I have my own ideas on the subject** j'ai mes idées personnelles sur la question; **sorry, but this is not my idea of fun** désolé, mais je ne trouve pas ça drôle *ou* ça ne m'amuse pas; **if this is your idea of a joke** si tu trouves que c'est drôle; **you've got a funny idea of loyalty** tu as une conception bizarre de la loyauté; **don't put ideas into his head** ne va pas lui fourrer *ou* lui mettre des idées dans la tête; **she hasn't an idea in her head** elle n'a pas un grain de jugeote; **it was a nice idea to phone** c'est gentil d'avoir pensé à téléphoner; **you've no idea how difficult it was** tu n'imagines pas à quel point c'était difficile; **you've no idea of the conditions in which they lived** tu ne peux pas t'imaginer les conditions dans lesquelles ils vivaient; **has anyone any idea how the accident occurred?** est-ce qu'on a une idée de la façon dont l'accident est arrivé?; **I have a rough idea of what happened** je m'imagine assez bien ce qui est arrivé; **no idea!** aucune idée!; **she had no idea what the time was** elle n'avait aucune idée de l'heure; **I haven't the slightest idea** je n'en ai pas la moindre idée; **I've no idea where it came from** je ne sais vraiment pas d'où ça vient; **what gave him the idea that it would be easy?** qu'est-ce qui lui a laissé croire que ce serait facile?

(**c**) *(estimate)* indication *f*, idée *f*; **can you give me an idea of how much it will cost?** est-ce que vous pouvez m'indiquer à peu près combien ça va coûter?

(**d**) *(suspicion)* soupçon *m*, idée *f*; **she had an idea that something was going to happen** elle se doutait que quelque chose allait arriver; **I've an idea that he'll succeed** j'ai dans l'idée qu'il finira par réussir

(**e**) *(objective, intention)* but *m*; **the idea of the game** le but du jeu; **the idea is to provide help for people in need** il s'agit d'aider ceux qui sont dans le besoin

►► ***ideas man*** concepteur *m*

ideal [aɪˈdɪəl] **1** *n* (**a**) *(perfect example)* idéal *m*; **the ideal of beauty** l'idéal *m* de la beauté

(**b**) *(principle)* idéal *m*; **a man with no ideals** un homme sans idéaux; **with such high ideals you'll never be satisfied** si tu es aussi idéaliste, tu ne seras jamais satisfait

2 *adj* idéal; **an ideal couple** un couple idéal; **that's ideal!** c'est parfait! **in an ideal world** dans l'idéal

►► *Phys* ***ideal gas*** gaz *m* parfait; ***the Ideal Home Exhibition*** ≃ le Salon de l'habitat

idealism [aɪˈdɪəlɪzəm] *n* idéalisme *m*

idealist [aɪˈdɪəlɪst] **1** *n* idéaliste *mf*

2 *adj* idéaliste

idealistic [ˌaɪdɪəˈlɪstɪk] *adj* idéaliste

idealistically [ˌaɪdɪəˈlɪstɪkəlɪ] *adv* d'une manière *ou* façon idéaliste

idealization [aɪˌdɪəlaɪˈzeɪʃən] *n* idéalisation *f*

idealize, -ise [aɪˈdɪəlaɪz] *vt* idéaliser

ideally [aɪˈdɪəlɪ] *adv* (**a**) *(perfectly)* parfaitement; **they're ideally suited** c'est un couple parfaitement assorti; **the shop is ideally situated** l'emplacement du magasin est idéal

(**b**) *(in a perfect world)* dans l'idéal; **ideally, this wine should be served at room temperature** normalement *ou* pour bien faire, ce vin doit être servi chambré; **ideally, accidents like this wouldn't happen** l'idéal serait que de tels accidents ne se produisent pas; **ideally, I would like to work in advertising** dans l'idéal, je voudrais travailler dans la publicité

idem [ˈaɪdem, ˈɪdem] *pron* idem

ident [ˈaɪdent] *n TV & Rad* indicatif *m*, identification *f*

identical [aɪˈdentɪkəl] *adj* identique; **identical to** *or* **with** identique à; **your hairstyle is identical to** *or* **with Lauren's** tu as exactement la même coiffure que Lauren; **they were wearing identical dresses** elles portaient la même robe

►► ***identical twins*** *(boys)* vrais jumeaux *mpl*; *(girls)* vraies jumelles *fpl*

identically [aɪˈdentɪkəlɪ] *adv* identiquement; **to be identically dressed** être habillé exactement de la même façon

identifiable [aɪˈdentɪˌfaɪəbəl] *adj* identifiable

identification [aɪˌdentɪfɪˈkeɪʃən] *n* (**a**) *(of body, criminal)* identification *f* (**b**) *(UNCOUNT) (identity papers)* papiers *mpl*; **the police asked me for identification** la police m'a demandé mes papiers *ou* une pièce d'identité (**c**) *(association)* identification *f*

►► ***identification card*** carte *f* d'identité; *Aviat & Naut* ***identification marks*** (lettres *fpl* et numéros *mpl* d')immatriculation *f*; ***identification papers*** papiers *mpl* d'identité; *Br* ***identification parade*** séance *f* d'identification *(au cours de laquelle on demande à un témoin de reconnaître une personne)*

identifier [aɪˈdentɪfaɪə(r)] *n Comput* identificateur *m*, identifieur *m*

identify [aɪˈdentɪfaɪ] *(pt & pp* **identified**) **1** *vt* (**a**) *(recognize, name)* identifier; **he was identified as one of the ringleaders** il fut identifié comme étant l'un des meneurs; **the winner has asked not to be identified** le gagnant a tenu à garder l'anonymat

(**b**) *(distinguish → of physical feature, badge etc)* **she wore a red rose to identify herself** elle portait une rose rouge pour se faire reconnaître *ou* pour qu'on la reconnaisse; **his accent immediately identified him to the others** les autres l'ont immédiatement reconnu à son accent

(**c**) *(acknowledge → difficulty, issue etc)* définir; **the report identifies two major problems** le rapport met en lumière deux problèmes principaux

(**d**) *(associate → people, ideas etc)* **he has long been identified with right-wing groups** il y a longtemps qu'il est assimilé *ou* identifié aux groupuscules de droite; **to identify oneself with** s'identifier avec; **she identifies herself with the activists** elle s'identifie avec les militants

2 *vi* **to identify with** s'identifier à *ou* avec; **I can't identify with the way she feels** j'ai du mal à comprendre ce qu'elle ressent; **I can't identify with his problems** j'ai du mal à comprendre ses problèmes

identifying marks [aɪˈdentɪfaɪɪŋ-] *n* signes *mpl* particuliers

Identikit® [aɪˈdentɪkɪt] *n (picture)* portrait-robot *m*

►► ***Identikit® picture*** portrait-robot *m*

identity [aɪˈdentətɪ] *(pl* **identities**) *n* (**a**) *(name, set of characteristics)* identité *f*; **only afterwards did they reveal his identity** ce n'est qu'après qu'ils ont révélé son identité; **it was a case of mistaken identity** il y a eu erreur sur la personne (**b**) *(sense of belonging)* identité *f*

►► ***identity bracelet*** bracelet *m* d'identité; ***identity card*** carte *f* d'identité; ***identity crisis*** crise *f* d'identité; *Mil* ***identity disc*** plaque *f* d'identité; ***identity papers*** papiers *mpl* d'identité; *Br* ***identity parade*** séance *f* d'identification *(au cours de laquelle on demande à un témoin de reconnaître une personne)*

ideogram [ˈɪdɪəʊɡræm], **ideograph** [ˈɪdɪəʊɡrɑːf] *n* idéogramme *m*

ideographic [ˌɪdɪəʊˈɡræfɪk] *adj* idéographique

ideography [ˌɪdɪˈɒɡrəfɪ] *n* idéographie *f*

ideological [ˌaɪdɪəˈlɒdʒɪkəl] *adj* idéologique

ideologically [ˌaɪdɪəˈlɒdʒɪkəlɪ] *adv* du point de vue idéologique, idéologiquement; **ideologically sound** *(idea)* défendable sur le plan idéologique; *(person)* dont les idées sont défendables sur le plan idéologique

ideologist [ˌaɪdɪˈɒlədʒɪst] *n* idéologue *mf*

ideologue [ˈaɪdɪəlɒɡ] *n* idéologue *mf*

ideology [ˌaɪdɪˈɒlədʒɪ] *(pl* **ideologies**) *n* idéologie *f*

ides [aɪdz] *n Antiq* ides *fpl*

►► ***the Ides of March*** les ides *fpl* de mars

idiocy ['ɪdɪəsɪ] *n* (**a**) *(stupidity)* stupidité *f*, idiotie *f* (**b**) *Arch Psy (mental retardation)* idiotie *f*

idiolect ['ɪdɪəlekt] *n Ling* idiolecte *m*

idiom ['ɪdɪəm] *n* (**a**) *(expression)* locution *f*, expression *f* idiomatique (**b**) *(language)* idiome *m* (**c**) *(style → of music, writing etc)* style *m*

idiomatic [ˌɪdɪə'mætɪk] *adj* idiomatique; **his Italian is fluent and idiomatic** il parle un italien tout à fait idiomatique

►► ***idiomatic expression*** expression *f* idiomatique

idiomatically [ˌɪdɪə'mætɪkəlɪ] *adv* de manière idiomatique

idiopathic [ˌɪdɪəʊ'pæθɪk], **idiopathical** [ˌɪdɪəʊ'pæθɪkəl] *adj Med (disease)* idiopathique, essentiel

idiosyncrasy [ˌɪdɪə'sɪŋkrəsɪ] *(pl* **idiosyncrasies***)* *n (peculiarity)* particularité *f*; *(foible)* manie *f*

idiosyncratic [ˌɪdɪəsɪŋ'krætɪk] *adj (style, behaviour)* caractéristique

idiot ['ɪdɪət] *n* (**a**) *(fool)* idiot(e) *m,f*, imbécile *mf*; **(you) stupid idiot!** espèce d'idiot!; **don't be an idiot!** ne sois pas idiot!; **to behave like an idiot** se comporter comme un imbécile *ou* un idiot; **that idiot Harry** cet imbécile de Harry (**b**) *Arch Psy* idiot(e) *m,f*

►► *Fam TV* ***idiot board*** téléprompteur[❑] *m*; *Fam Pej* ***idiot box*** télé *f*, téloche *f*; *Aut* ***idiot light*** *(on dashboard)* voyant *m* lumineux; *Psy* ***idiot savant*** autiste *mf (à la mémoire particulièrement développée)*

idiotic [ˌɪdɪ'ɒtɪk] *adj* idiot; **he looks absolutely idiotic!** il a l'air complètement idiot!

idiotically [ˌɪdɪ'ɒtɪkəlɪ] *adv* stupidement, bêtement; **he behaved idiotically** il s'est comporté comme un imbécile; **he smiled idiotically** il a souri bêtement

idiotism ['ɪdɪəˌtɪzəm] *n Am (of language)* idiotisme *m*

idiot-proof *Fam* **1** *adj* à l'épreuve de toute fausse manœuvre[❑]

2 *vt* rendre infaillible[❑]

idle ['aɪdəl] **1** *adj* (**a**) *(person → inactive)* inoccupé, désœuvré; *(→ lazy)* oisif, paresseux; **in her idle moments** à ses moments perdus; **1,500 men have been made idle** 1500 hommes ont été mis au chômage; **he's an idle good-for-nothing** c'est un fainéant et un bon à rien

(**b**) *(factory, equipment)* arrêté, à l'arrêt; *St Exch (markets)* improductif, dormant; **to stand idle** *(machine)* être arrêté *ou* au repos; **to lie idle** *(factory)* chômer; *(money)* dormir, être improductif; **to let one's money lie idle** laisser dormir son argent

(**c**) *(futile, pointless)* inutile, vain; *(empty → threat, promise etc)* vain, en l'air; *(→ rumour)* sans fondement; *(→ boast)* mal placé; **it would be idle to speculate** il ne servirait à rien de se livrer à de vaines conjectures

(**d**) *(casual)* **an idle glance** un regard distrait; **out of idle curiosity** par pure curiosité

2 *vi (engine)* tourner au ralenti

3 *vt Am (make unemployed → permanently)* mettre au chômage; *(→ temporarily)* mettre en chômage technique

►► ***idle gossip*** ragots *mpl*; ***idle pleasure*** plaisir *m* futile; ***the idle rich*** les riches *mpl* désœuvrés ou oisifs

►**idle about, idle around** *vi Br* traîner

►**idle away** *vt sep* **to idle away one's time** tuer le temps

idleness ['aɪdəlnɪs] *n* (**a**) *(laziness)* oisiveté *f*, paresse *f*; *(inactivity)* désœuvrement *m*; **to live in idleness** vivre dans l'oisiveté, mener une vie oisive (**b**) *(futility)* futilité *f*

idler ['aɪdlə(r)] *n* (**a**) *(lazy person)* paresseux (euse) *m,f*, fainéant(e) *m,f* (**b**) *Tech (pulley)* poulie *f* folle; *(wheel)* roue *f* folle

idling ['aɪdəlɪŋ] *n* (**a**) *(time-wasting)* fainéantise *f*; **that's more than enough idling for one day** assez fainéanté pour aujourd'hui (**b**) *(of engine)* (marche *f* au) ralenti *m*

►► ***idling speed*** *(of engine)* ralenti *m*

idly ['aɪdlɪ] *adv* (**a**) *(lazily)* paresseusement (**b**) *(casually)* négligemment; **"why not?" she said idly** "pourquoi pas?" dit-elle négligemment (**c**) *(unresponsively)* sans réagir; **we will not stand idly by** nous n'allons pas rester sans réagir *ou* sans rien faire

idol ['aɪdəl] *n* idole *f*; **a 1970s pop idol** une idole (pop) des années 1970

idolater [aɪ'dɒlətə(r)] *n* (**a**) *Rel* idolâtre *m* (**b**) *Fig* adorateur *m* (**of** de)

idolatress [aɪ'dɒlətrɪs] *n* (**a**) *Rel* idolâtre *f* (**b**) *Fig* adoratrice *f* (**of** de)

idolatrous [aɪ'dɒlətrəs] *adj* idolâtre

idolatrously [aɪ'dɒlətrəslɪ] *adv* d'une manière idolâtre

idolatry [aɪ'dɒlətrɪ] *n* idolâtrie *f*

idolize, -ise ['aɪdəlaɪz] *vt* idolâtrer

idolizing ['aɪdəˌlaɪzɪŋ] **1** *n* idolâtrie *f*

2 *adj* plein d'adoration

Idomeneus [aɪ'dɒmɪnjuːs] *pr n Myth* Idoménée

idyll ['ɪdɪl] *n* idylle *f*

idyllic [ɪ'dɪlɪk, aɪ'dɪlɪk] *adj* idyllique

idyllically [ɪ'dɪlɪkəlɪ, aɪ'dɪlɪkəlɪ] *adv* d'une façon idyllique

ie ['aɪ'iː] *adv (abbr* **id est***)* c'est-à-dire, à savoir

IEEE [ˌaiːˌiː'iː] *n Comput (abbr* **Institute of Electronic and Electrical Engineers***)* IEEE *m*

IF [ɪf] **1** *conj* (**a**) *(supposing that)* si; **if he comes, we'll ask him** s'il vient, on lui demandera; **if possible** si (c'est) possible; **have it done by Tuesday, if at all possible** faites-le pour mardi si possible; **if necessary** si (c'est) nécessaire, le cas échéant; **if so** si c'est le cas; **if so, when?** si oui, quand?; **if all goes well, we'll be there by midnight** si tout va bien, nous y serons pour minuit; **if anyone wants me, I'm** *or* **I'll be in my office** si quelqu'un veut me voir, je suis dans mon bureau; **if she hadn't introduced herself, I would never have recognized her** si elle ne s'était pas présentée, je ne l'aurais pas reconnue; **if I'd known you were coming, I'd have bought some wine** si j'avais su que tu venais, j'aurais acheté du vin; **if a child can do it, so can I** si un enfant peut le faire, je peux le faire aussi; **if you'd told me the truth, this would never have happened** si tu m'avais dit la vérité, ça ne serait jamais arrivé; **if I was older, I'd leave home** si j'étais plus âgé, je quitterais la maison; **if you could have anything you wanted, what would you ask for?** si tu pouvais avoir tout ce que tu désires, qu'est-ce que tu demanderais?; **if I were a millionaire, I'd buy a yacht** si j'étais millionnaire, j'achèterais un yacht; **would you mind if I invited Angie too?** ça te dérangerait si j'invitais aussi Angie?; **if he agrees and (if) we have time** s'il est d'accord et que nous avons le temps

(**b**) *(whenever)* si; **if you mix blue and yellow you get green** si on mélange du bleu et du jaune, on obtient du vert; **if you ever come** *or* **if ever you come to London, do visit us** si jamais tu passes à Londres, viens nous voir; **if you are "gratified" by something, you are pleased by it** si (on dit que) quelque chose nous "satisfait", cela veut dire que ça nous fait plaisir; **he gets angry if I so much as open my mouth** si j'ai seulement le malheur d'ouvrir la bouche, il se fâche

(**c**) *(given that)* si; **if Paul was the brains in the family, then Julia was the organizer** si Paul était le cerveau de la famille, Julia en était l'organisatrice

(**d**) *(whether)* si; **to ask/to know/to wonder if** demander/savoir/se demander si; **it doesn't matter if he comes or not** peu importe qu'il vienne ou (qu'il ne vienne) pas; **I'll see if she's up yet** je vais voir si elle est levée

(**e**) *(with verbs or adjectives expressing emotion)* si; **I'm sorry if I upset you** je suis désolé si je t'ai fait de la peine; **if I gave you that impression, I apologize** je m'excuse si c'est l'impression que je vous ai donnée; **we'd be so pleased if you could come** ça nous ferait tellement plaisir si vous pouviez venir

(**f**) *(used to qualify a statement)* **few, if any, readers will have heard of him** peu de lecteurs auront entendu parler de lui, ou même aucun; **modifications, if any, will have to be made later** les modifications éventuelles devront être apportées plus tard; **he was intelligent if a little arrogant** il était intelligent, mais quelque peu arrogant; **pleasant weather, if rather cold** temps agréable, bien qu'un peu froid; **it is well-paid, if uninteresting work** c'est un travail bien payé à défaut d'être intéressant

(**g**) *(introducing comments or opinions)* **if I could just come in here...** si je puis me permettre d'intervenir...; **it's rather good, if I say so myself** c'est assez bon, sans fausse modestie; **I'll leave it there, if I may, and go on to my next point** j'en resterai là, si vous voulez bien et passerai au point suivant; **I thought you were rather rude, if you don't mind my saying so** je vous ai trouvé assez grossier, si je peux me permettre; **well, if you want my opinion** *or* **if you ask me, I thought it was dreadful** eh bien, si vous voulez mon avis, c'était affreux; **if you think about it, it is rather odd** si vous y réfléchissez, c'est plutôt bizarre; **if I remember rightly, she was married to a politician** si j'ai bonne mémoire, elle était mariée à un homme politique; **if I know Sophie, she won't have done it!** comme *ou* telle que je connais Sophie, elle ne l'aura pas fait!

(**h**) *(in polite requests)* si; **if you could just write your name here...** si vous voulez bien inscrire votre nom ici...; **if you could all just wait in the hall, I'll be back in a second** si vous pouviez tous attendre dans l'entrée, je reviens tout de suite; **would you like me to wrap it for you? – if you would, please** vous voulez que je vous l'emballe? – oui, s'il vous plaît

(**i**) *(expressing surprise, indignation)* tiens, ça alors; **well, if it isn't my old mate Jim!** tiens *ou* ça alors, c'est ce vieux Jim!

2 *n* si *m inv*; **if you get the job – and it's a big if – you'll have to move to London** si tu obtiens cet emploi, et je dis bien si, tu devras aller t'installer à Londres; **no ifs and buts, we're going** il n'y a pas de "mais" qui tienne *ou* pas de discussions, on y va; **the agreement is full of ifs and buts** l'accord n'est qu'une suite de conditions

3 if and when *conj* au cas où; **if and when he phones, I'll simply tell him to leave me alone** au cas où il appellerait, je lui dirais tout simplement de me laisser tranquille

4 if anything *adv* plutôt; **he doesn't look any slimmer, if anything, he's put on weight** il n'a pas l'air plus mince, il a même plutôt grossi; **I am, if anything, even keener to be involved** j'ai peut-être encore plus envie d'y participer

5 if ever *conj* **there's a hopeless case if ever I saw one!** voilà un cas désespéré s'il en est!; **if ever I saw a man driven by ambition, it's him** si quelqu'un est poussé par l'ambition, c'est bien lui

6 if I were you *adv* à ta place; **if I were you I'd accept the offer** si j'étais toi *ou* à ta place, j'accepterais la proposition

7 if not *conj* sinon; **I'm happy to eat out if you want to, if not, I'll just rustle something up here** on peut aller manger quelque part si tu veux, sinon je préparerai quelque chose ici; **are you going to read this book? if not, I will** tu vas lire ce livre? sinon, je vais le lire moi; **did you finish on time? and if not, why not?** avez-vous terminé à temps? sinon, pourquoi?; **hundreds, if not thousands** des centaines, voire des milliers

8 if only *conj* (**a**) *(providing a reason)* au moins; **I think I should come along too, if only to make sure you don't get into mischief** je crois que je devrais venir aussi, ne serait-ce que pour m'assurer que vous ne faites pas de bêtises; **all right, I'll let you go to the party, if only to keep you quiet** bon d'accord, tu peux aller à la fête, comme ça au moins, j'aurai la paix

(**b**) *(expressing a wish)* si seulement; **if only!** si seulement!; **if only I could drive** si seulement je savais conduire; **if only someone would tell us what has happened** si seulement quelqu'un nous disait ce qui s'est passé; **if only we'd known** si seulement nous avions su

IFA [ˌaɪef'eɪ] *n Fin (abbr* **independent financial adviser***)* conseiller(ère) *m,f* financier(ère) indépendant(e)

IFC [ˌaɪef'siː] *n* (**a**) *Typ (abbr* **inside front cover***)* deuxième *f* de couverture (**b**) *Fin (abbr* **International Finance Corporation***)* SFI *f*

iffy ['ɪfɪ] *(compar* **iffier**, *superl* **iffiest***)* *adj Fam* (**a**) *(uncertain → situation)* aléatoire[❑]; **the picnic/project is looking very iffy** le pique-nique/

projet semble très compromis ❑; **the car's a bit iffy these days** la voiture n'est pas très fiable ces jours-ci ❑; **I'm still a bit iffy about the whole thing** *(haven't made my mind up)* j'hésite encore ❑; *Br* **my stomach's been a bit iffy lately** je me sens un peu barbouillé ces temps-ci; **that sky looks a bit iffy** le ciel est un peu menaçant ❑; **the ice looks a bit iffy** *(on pond)* la glace n'a pas l'air très sûre ❑; **it's still a bit iffy but I think I WILL be going to the conference** je ne suis pas complètement sûr mais je pense que j'irai à la conférence ❑

(**b**) *(suspect → person, appearance)* louche ❑; **it all sounded rather iffy** tout ça m'avait l'air plutôt louche; **her new man sounds really iffy** son nouveau copain a l'air vraiment louche

if-then operation *n Comput* inclusion *f*

igloo [ˈɪgluː] *n* igloo *m*, iglou *m*

Ignatius [ɪgˈneɪʃəs] *pr n* Ignace

►► ***Ignatius Loyola*** Ignace de Loyola

igneous [ˈɪgnɪəs] *adj Geol* igné

ignimbrite [ˈɪgnɪmˌbraɪt] *n Geol* ignimbrite *f*

ignite [ɪgˈnaɪt] **1** *vt (set fire to)* mettre le feu à, enflammer; *(light)* allumer; *Fig (situation, conflict)* enflammer

2 *vi (catch fire)* prendre feu, s'enflammer; *(be lit)* s'allumer; *Fig (situation, conflict)* s'enflammer

ignition [ɪgˈnɪʃən] *n* (**a**) *Aut* allumage *m*; **to turn on/off the ignition** mettre/couper le contact; **the key was still in the ignition** la clé était encore sur le contact (**b**) *Phys & Chem* ignition *f*

►► ***ignition coil*** bobine *f* d'allumage; ***ignition cycle*** cycle *m* d'allumage; ***ignition key*** clef *f* de contact; ***ignition lock*** antivol-contact *m*; ***ignition switch*** contact *m*; ***ignition system*** circuit *m* d'allumage

ignobility [ˌɪgnəˈbɪlɪtɪ] *n* ignobilité *f*

ignoble [ɪgˈnəʊbəl] *adj* infâme

ignobleness [ɪgˈnəʊbəlnɪs] *n* ignobilité *f*

ignobly [ɪgˈnəʊbəlɪ] *adv* d'une façon ignoble, ignoblement; *Arch* **to be ignobly born** être de basse naissance

ignominious [ˌɪgnəˈmɪnɪəs] *adj* ignominieux

ignominiously [ˌɪgnəˈmɪnɪəslɪ] *adv* ignominieusement

ignominy [ˈɪgnəmɪnɪ] *n* ignominie *f*

ignorable [ˌɪgˈnɔːrəbəl] *adj* qui ne présente pas d'intérêt; **it wasn't ignorable** on ne pouvait pas ne pas en tenir compte

ignoramus [ˌɪgnəˈreɪməs] (*pl* **ignoramuses**) *n* ignare *mf*

ignorance [ˈɪgnərəns] *n* (**a**) *(lack of knowledge, awareness)* ignorance *f*; **out of** *or* **through sheer ignorance** par pure ignorance; **they kept him in ignorance of his sister's existence** ils lui ont caché l'existence de sa sœur; **forgive my ignorance, but...** excuse mon ignorance, mais...; **ignorance of the law is no excuse** nul n'est censé ignorer la loi; **in a situation like this, ignorance is bliss** dans ce genre de situation, il vaut mieux ne pas savoir

(**b**) *Pej (bad manners)* grossièreté *f*

ignorant [ˈɪgnərənt] *adj* (**a**) *(uneducated)* ignorant; **I'm really ignorant about classical music/politics** je ne connais absolument rien à la musique classique/la politique

(**b**) *(lacking knowledge → person)* ignorant; *(→ question, remark)* qui trahit l'ignorance; **I was ignorant as to his whereabouts** j'ignorais où il se trouvait; **he was ignorant of the facts** il ignorait les faits

(**c**) *Pej (bad-mannered)* mal élevé, grossier; **don't be so ignorant, take your hat off!** tiens-toi bien, enlève ton chapeau!

ignorantly [ˈɪgnərəntlɪ] *adv (behave)* d'une manière grossière

ignore [ɪgˈnɔː(r)] *vt* (**a**) *(pay no attention to → person, remark)* ne pas prêter attention à, ignorer; *(→ letter, invitation)* ne pas répondre à; *(→ signal, red light)* ne pas respecter; **she completely ignored me** elle a fait semblant de ne pas me voir; **ignore him and he'll go away** fais comme s'il n'était pas là et il te laissera tranquille; **we can't continue to ignore these objections** on ne peut pas continuer à ne tenir aucun compte de ces objections; **I'll ignore that!** *(what you said)* je ferai comme si je n'avais rien entendu!

(**b**) *(take no account of → warning, request, order)* ne pas tenir compte de; **he ignored the doctor's advice and continued smoking** il n'a pas suivi les conseils de son médecin et a continué de fumer

(**c**) *(overlook)* **they can no longer ignore what is going on here** il ne leur est plus possible d'ignorer *ou* de fermer les yeux sur ce qui se passe ici; **the report ignores certain crucial facts** le rapport passe sous silence des faits cruciaux; **they seemed to ignore the fact that I was there** ils semblaient ignorer ma présence

►► *Comput* ***ignore character*** caractère *m* de suppression

Iguaçu Falls [ˌiːgwəˈsuː-] *npl* **the Iguaçu Falls** les chutes *fpl* d'Iguaçu

iguana [ɪˈgwɑːnə] *n Zool* iguane *m*

IKBS [ˌaɪkeɪˌbiːˈes] *n Comput* (*abbr* **intelligent knowledge-based system**) système *m* expert

ikebana [iːkɪˈbɑːnə] *n* ikebana *m*

ikon = **icon**

IL (*written abbr* **Illinois**) Illinois *m*

ILA [ˌaɪelˈeɪ] *n* (*abbr* **International Longshoremen's Association**) = syndicat international de dockers

ILEA [ˌaɪelˌiːˈeɪ, ˈɪlɪə] *n Br Formerly Sch* (*abbr* **Inner London Education Authority**) **the ILEA** = organisme qui, jusqu'en 1990, était chargé de gérer les services londoniens de l'enseignement

ileitis [ˌɪlɪˈaɪtɪs] *n Med* iléite *f*

ileo-colic [ˌɪlɪəʊ-] *adj Anat* iléo-colique

ileostomy [ˌɪlɪˈɒstəmɪ] *n Med* iléostomie *f*

ileum [ˈɪlɪəm] *n Anat* iléon *m*

ilex [ˈaɪleks] (*pl* **ilexes**) *n Bot* yeuse *f*, chêne *m* vert

iliac [ˈɪlɪæk] *adj Anat* iliaque

Iliad [ˈɪlɪəd] *n*

'The Iliad' *Homer* 'L'Iliade'

Ilium [ˈɪlɪəm] *pr n* Ilion *f*, Troie *f*

ilium [ˈɪlɪəm] *n Anat* ilion *m*

ilk [ɪlk] *n* (**a**) *(type)* **people of that ilk** ce genre de personnes; **books of that ilk** des livres de ce genre (**b**) *Scot* **Moray of that ilk** Moray du domaine de Moray

I'll [aɪl] = **I shall, I will**

ill [ɪl] **1** *adj* (**a**) *(sick, unwell)* malade; **to fall** *or* **to be taken ill** tomber malade; **seriously ill** gravement malade; **the smell makes me ill** l'odeur me rend malade; **I feel ill just thinking about it** rien que d'y penser, j'en suis malade

(**b**) *Br (injured)* **he is critically ill with stab wounds** il est dans un état critique après avoir reçu de nombreux coups de couteau

(**c**) *Literary (bad)* mauvais, néfaste; **ill fortune, ill luck** malheur *m*, malchance *f*; **the ill effects of alcohol** les effets *mpl* néfastes de l'alcool; **ill deeds** méfaits *mpl*; **a house of ill repute** une maison mal famée; *Prov* **it's an ill wind that blows nobody any good** à quelque chose malheur est bon

2 *n* (**a**) *Literary (evil)* mal *m*; **to think/speak ill of sb** penser/dire du mal de qn; **for good or ill** *(whatever happens)* quoi qu'il arrive

(**b**) *(difficulty, trouble)* malheur *m*; **the nation's ills** les malheurs *mpl* du pays

(**c**) *(wrong)* dommage *m*, tort *m*; **I have suffered no ill at his hands** il ne m'a fait aucun tort

3 *adv* (**a**) *(hardly)* à peine, difficilement; **we can ill afford these luxuries** ce sont des luxes que nous pouvons difficilement nous permettre; **we can ill afford to wait** nous ne pouvons vraiment pas nous permettre d'attendre

(**b**) *Formal (badly)* mal; **it ill becomes** *or* **befits you to criticize** il vous sied mal de critiquer; **to augur** *or* **to bode ill** être de mauvais augure

►► ***ill feeling*** ressentiment *m*, animosité *f*; ***ill health*** mauvaise santé *f*; **to suffer from ill health, to be in ill health** avoir des problèmes de santé; **because of ill health** pour des raisons de santé; ***ill humour*** mauvaise humeur *f*; **to be in an ill humour** être de mauvaise humeur; ***ill will*** malveillance *f*; **I bear them no ill will** je ne leur garde pas rancune, je ne leur en veux pas

ill. (*written abbr* **illustration**) ill

ill-advised *adj (remark, comment)* peu judicieux, hors de propos, déplacé; *(action)* peu judicieux, déplacé; **he was ill-advised to go away** il a eu tort *ou* il a été mal avisé de partir

ill-advisedly *adv* peu judicieusement

ill-assorted *adj* mal assorti, disparate

ill-at-ease *adj* gêné, mal à l'aise

illative [ɪˈleɪtɪv] *Ling* **1** *n* illatif *m*

2 *adj* illatif

ill-behaved *adj* qui se conduit *ou* se tient mal

ill-bred *adj* mal élevé

ill-breeding *n* manque *m* de savoir-vivre

ill-concealed *adj* mal dissimulé

ill-conceived [-kənˈsiːvd] *adj* mal pensé

ill-considered *adj (hasty)* hâtif; *(thoughtless)* irréfléchi

ill-defined [-dɪˈfaɪnd] *adj* mal défini

ill-disposed *adj* (**a**) *(unfriendly, unhelpful)* **to be ill-disposed towards sb** être mal disposé envers qn; **to be ill-disposed towards an idea/a proposal** ne pas être favorable à une idée/une proposition (**b**) *(disinclined)* **to be ill-disposed to do sth** être peu disposé à faire qch

illegal [ɪˈliːgəl] *adj* (**a**) *Law* illégal; *(parking)* interdit (**b**) *Comput (character, file name, instruction)* non autorisé

►► ***illegal entry*** violation *f* de domicile; ***illegal immigrant*** immigré(e) *m,f*, clandestin(e) *m,f*

illegality [ˌɪliːˈgælətɪ] (*pl* **illegalities**) *n* illégalité *f*

illegally [ɪˈliːgəlɪ] *adv* illégalement, d'une manière illégale; **to be illegally parked** être en stationnement interdit

illegibility [ɪˌledʒɪˈbɪlɪtɪ] *n* illisibilité *f*

illegible [ɪˈledʒɪbəl] *adj* illisible

illegibly [ɪˈledʒɪblɪ] *adv* illisiblement

illegitimacy [ˌɪlɪˈdʒɪtɪməsɪ] *n* illégitimité *f*

illegitimate [ˌɪlɪˈdʒɪtɪmət] **1** *adj* (**a**) *(child)* naturel, illégitime (**b**) *(activity)* illégitime, interdit (**c**) *(argument)* illogique

2 *n* enfant *mf* naturel(elle)

illegitimately [ˌɪlɪˈdʒɪtɪmətlɪ] *adv* (**a**) *(outside marriage)* hors du mariage (**b**) *(illegally)* illégitimement

ill-equipped *adj* (**a**) *(lacking equipment)* mal équipé, mal préparé (**b**) *(lacking qualities → for job, situation)* **to be ill-equipped (for)** ne pas être à la hauteur (de), être mal armé (pour); **he felt ill-equipped to cope with the pressures of the job** il ne se sentait pas capable d'affronter les problèmes posés par son travail

ill-fated *adj (action)* malheureux, funeste; *(person)* qui joue de malheur, malheureux; *(day)* néfaste, de malchance; *(journey)* funeste, fatal

ill-favoured, *Am* **ill-favored** *adj* (**a**) *(ugly)* laid (**b**) *(unpleasant)* désagréable

ill-fitting *adj (garment, lid, window)* mal ajusté

ill-founded [-ˈfaʊndɪd] *adj (hopes, confidence)* mal fondé; *(suspicions)* sans fondement

ill-gotten gains *npl* biens *mpl* mal acquis

ill-humoured, *Am* **ill-humored** *adj* de mauvaise humeur

illiberal [ɪˈlɪbərəl] *adj* (**a**) *(bigoted, intolerant)* intolérant; *Pol (regime)* intolérant; *(legislation)* restrictif (**b**) *(ungenerous)* avare

illiberality [ɪˌlɪbəˈrælɪtɪ] *n* (**a**) *(intolerance)* intolérance *f*, étroitesse *f* d'esprit; *Pol (of regime)* intolérance *f*; *(of legislation)* caractère *m* restrictif (**b**) *(lack of generosity)* avarice *f*

illicit [ɪˈlɪsɪt] *adj* illicite

►► ***illicit still*** alambic *m* clandestin

illicitly [ɪˈlɪsɪtlɪ] *adv* illicitement

illicitness [ɪˈlɪsɪtnɪs] *n* caractère *m* illicite

illimitable [ɪˈlɪmɪtəbəl] *adj* illimité, infini

ill-informed *adj* (**a**) *(having the wrong information → person)* mal renseigné (**b**) *(having insufficient information)* peu informé; **we continue to be ill-informed about their intentions** nous ne sommes toujours pas sûrs de savoir quelles sont leurs intentions; **he made an ill-informed attack on the government** il a attaqué le gouvernement en utilisant des arguments sans fondement

Illinois [ˌɪlɪˈnɔɪ] *n* l'Illinois *m*; **in Illinois** dans l'Illinois

ill-intentioned [-ɪnˈtenʃənd] *adj* malintentionné (**towards** envers)

illiquid [ɪˈlɪkwɪd] *adj Fin* non liquide

►► ***illiquid assets*** actif *m* non-disponible *ou* immobilisé

illiquidity [ɪlɪˈkwɪdɪtɪ] *n Fin* illiquidité *f*

►► *Fin* ***illiquidity premium*** prime *f* d'illiquidite

illiteracy [ɪ'lɪtərəsɪ] *n* analphabétisme *m*; **functional illiteracy** illettrisme *m*

illiterate [ɪ'lɪtərət] **1** *adj* (**a**) *(unable to read or write)* analphabète; **functionally illiterate** illettré

(**b**) *(uneducated)* ignorant, sans éducation; **many young people are scientifically illiterate** de nombreux jeunes gens n'ont aucune formation *ou* connaissance scientifique; *Fig* **to be emotionally illiterate** ne pas savoir exprimer ses émotions

(**c**) *(lacking culture → person)* qui n'a aucune culture; *(→ usage, style)* incorrect

2 *n* analphabète *mf*; **functional illiterate** illettré(e) *m,f*

ill-judged [-dʒʌdʒd] *adj (remark, attempt)* peu judicieux

ill-kempt [-kempt] *adj* (**a**) *(person, appearance etc)* négligé; *(hair)* hirsute, mal peigné (**b**) *(garden)* mal tenu, négligé

ill-mannered *adj (person)* mal élevé, impoli; *(behaviour)* grossier, impoli

ill-matched *adj* mal assorti

ill-natured *adj (person)* d'un mauvais caractère, désagréable; *(remark, criticism etc)* désagréable; **to be ill-natured** avoir mauvais caractère

illness ['ɪlnɪs] *n* maladie *f*

ill-nourished [-'nʌrɪʃt] *adj* mal nourri

illocution [ˌɪlə'kjuːʃən] *n* illocution *f*, acte *m* illocutoire

illocutionary [ˌɪlə'kjuːʃənrɪ] *adj* illocutoire, illocutionnaire

illogical [ɪ'lɒdʒɪkəl] *adj* illogique; **that's illogical** ce n'est pas logique; **she knew it was illogical, but she felt very bitter** elle savait que c'était absurde, mais elle éprouvait une vive amertume

illogicality [ˌɪlɒdʒɪ'kælətɪ] *(pl* **illogicalities***) n* illogisme *m*

illogically [ɪ'lɒdʒɪkəlɪ] *adv* d'une manière illogique; **he assumed, illogically, that he meant nothing to her** il supposait, sans raison, qu'il n'était rien pour elle

ill-omened [-'əʊmənd] *adj* voué à l'échec

ill-prepared *adj* mal préparé

ill-qualified *adj* incompétent; **ill-qualified to do sth** *(unqualified for)* peu qualifié pour faire qch; *(unfit for)* peu apte à faire qch

ill-starred [-stɑːd] *adj Literary (person)* né sous une mauvaise étoile; *(day)* néfaste, funeste

ill-suited *adj (couple)* mal assorti; **to be ill-suited for sth** être inapte à qch; **such clothes were ill-suited to a hot climate** ces vêtements n'étaient pas adaptés à un climat chaud; **arts graduates are ill-suited to this job** les diplômés en lettres ne sont pas aptes à ce travail

ill-tempered *adj (by nature)* grincheux, qui a mauvais caractère; *(temporarily)* de mauvaise humeur; *(remark, outburst etc)* plein de mauvaise humeur

ill-timed [-'taɪmd] *adj (arrival, visit)* inopportun, intempestif, qui tombe mal; *(remark, question)* déplacé, mal à propos *(inv)*; **the meeting was very ill-timed** cette réunion ne pouvait plus mal tomber

ill-treat *vt* maltraiter

ill-treatment *n* mauvais traitement *m*

illuminate [ɪ'luːmɪneɪt] **1** *vt* (**a**) *(light up)* illuminer, éclairer (**b**) *(make clearer)* éclairer; **this book illuminates many difficult problems** ce livre éclaire de nombreux problèmes complexes (**c**) *(manuscript)* enluminer

2 *vi* s'illuminer

illuminated [ɪ'luːmɪneɪtɪd] *adj* (**a**) *(lit up → sign, notice)* lumineux (**b**) *(decorated → manuscript)* enluminé

illuminati [ɪˌluːmɪ'nɑːtiː] *npl* illuminés *mpl*

illuminating [ɪ'luːmɪneɪtɪŋ] **1** *adj (speech, interview)* qui éclaire la situation/le sujet/*etc*; *(comparison, remark, example)* éclairant; **the programme was very illuminating** l'émission m'a appris beaucoup de choses

2 *n* (**a**) *(of building)* illumination *f* (**b**) *(of manuscript)* enluminure *f*

illuminatingly [ɪ'luːmɪneɪtɪŋlɪ] *adv (speak)* de manière à éclairer la situation/le sujet/*etc*; *(compare)* d'une manière éclairante

illumination [ɪˌluːmɪ'neɪʃən] **1** *n* (**a**) *(light)* éclairage *m*; *(of building)* illumination *f*; **a candle was the only means of illumination** il n'y avait pour tout éclairage qu'une bougie (**b**) *(of manuscript)* enluminure *f* (**c**) *Opt (of lens etc)* éclat *m*; *Phys* **(degree of) illumination** éclairement *m* (**d**) *Rel (enlightenment)* illumination *f*

2 illuminations *npl (coloured lights)* illuminations *fpl*

illuminative [ɪ'luːmɪnətɪv] *adj* (**a**) *Rel* illuminatif (**b**) *(enlightening)* qui éclaire la situation/le sujet/*etc*

►► ***illuminative art*** *(art)* enluminure *f*; *(objects)* enluminures *fpl*

illuminator [ɪ'luːmɪneɪtə(r)] *n* (**a**) *Elec* source *f* lumineuse (**b**) *(artist)* enlumineur(euse) *m,f*

illumine [ɪ'luːmɪn] *vt Literary* illuminer

ill-use *Literary* **1** *n* [ˌɪl'juːs] *(cruel treatment)* mauvais traitement *m*

2 *vt* [ˌɪl'juːz] (**a**) *(physically)* maltraiter (**b**) *(behave badly towards)* ne pas bien traiter; **he feels he's been ill-used** il a le sentiment qu'il n'a pas été bien traité

illusion [ɪ'luːʒən] *n* (**a**) *(false impression)* illusion *f*; **mirrors give an illusion of space** les miroirs donnent une illusion d'espace

(**b**) *(false belief)* illusion *f*; **to be under an illusion** se faire une illusion; **we were living under an illusion** nous étions victimes d'une illusion; **she has no illusions about her chances of success** elle ne se fait aucune illusion sur ses chances de succès *ou* de réussir; **I have no illusions** *or* **am under no illusion on that score** je ne me fais aucune illusion à ce sujet

(**c**) *(magic trick)* illusion *f*

illusionism [ɪ'luːʒənɪzəm] *n* illusionnisme *m*

illusionist [ɪ'luːʒənɪst] *n (conjurer, magician)* illusionniste *mf*

illusive, illusory [ɪ'luːsərɪ] *adj* illusoire

illustrate ['ɪləstreɪt] *vt* (**a**) *(with pictures)* illustrer; **an illustrated children's book** un livre pour enfants illustré (**b**) *(demonstrate)* illustrer; **it clearly illustrates the need for improvement** cela montre bien que des améliorations sont nécessaires; **to illustrate my point** pour illustrer ce que je veux dire; **the lecture will be illustrated by slides** la conférence sera accompagnée de diapositives

illustration [ˌɪlə'streɪʃən] *n* (**a**) *(picture)* illustration *f*; **illustrations** *(in book)* iconographie *f*

(**b**) *(publishing process)* illustration *f*; **he/she works in illustration** il est illustrateur/elle est illustratrice

(**c**) *(demonstration)* illustration *f*; **it's a clear illustration of a lack of government interest** cela illustre bien un manque d'intérêt de la part du gouvernement; **by way of illustration** à titre d'exemple

►► *Comput* ***illustration software*** logiciel *m* graphique

illustrative ['ɪləstrətɪv] *adj (picture, diagram)* qui illustre, explicatif; *(action, event, fact)* qui démontre, qui illustre; **the demonstrations are illustrative of the need for reform** les manifestations montrent que des réformes sont nécessaires

►► ***illustrative example*** exemple *m* illustratif

illustrator ['ɪləstreɪtə(r)] *n* illustrateur(trice) *m,f*

illustrious [ɪ'lʌstrɪəs] *adj* illustre

illustriously [ɪ'lʌstrɪəslɪ] *adv* de façon illustre

illustriousness [ɪ'lʌstrɪəsnɪs] *n* éclat *m*, gloire *f*

ill-wisher [-'wɪʃə(r)] *n* malveillant(e) *m,f*; **he has no ill-wishers** personne ne lui veut du mal *ou* de mal

Illyria [ɪ'lɪrɪə] *n Hist* Illyrie *f*

ilmenite ['ɪlməˌnaɪt] *n Miner* ilménite *f*

ILO [ˌaɪel'əʊ] *n Ind (abbr* **International Labour Organization***)* OIT *f*

ILWU ['ɪljuː] *n (abbr* **International Longshoremen's and Warehousemen's Union***)* = syndicat international de dockers et de magasiniers

I'm [aɪm] = **I am**

image ['ɪmɪdʒ] *n* (**a**) *(mental picture)* image *f*; **I still have an image of her as a child** je la vois encore enfant; **many people have the wrong image of her/of life in New York** beaucoup de gens se font une fausse idée d'elle/de la vie à New York

(**b**) *(public appearance)* **(public) image** image *f* de marque; **the party tried to change its image** le parti a essayé de changer son image de marque; **its image is that of a dirty industrial city** cette ville a la réputation d'être une ville industrielle sale; **she's tired of her hippy image** elle en a assez de son image baba cool; **their brief is to update the product's image** ils ont pour mission de moderniser l'image du produit; **the company is suffering from an image problem** l'entreprise a un problème d'image

(**c**) *(likeness)* image *f*; **man was made in God's image** l'homme a été créé à l'image de Dieu; **you are the (very** *or* **living) image of your mother** tu es tout le portrait *ou* le portrait craché de ta mère

(**d**) *(representation)* portrait *m*; *(sculpture)* image *f* (sculptée); *(of god etc)* représentation *f*, statue *f*; *(for worship)* idole *f*

(**e**) *(in art)* image *f*; *(in literature)* image *f*, métaphore *f*; **I tried to create an image of wartime Britain** j'ai essayé de brosser un tableau de la vie en Grande-Bretagne pendant la guerre

(**f**) *Opt, Phot & Comput* image *f*

►► *Comput* ***image bank*** banque *f* d'images; *Phys* ***image converter*** convertisseur *m* d'image(s); *Opt & Phot* ***image enhancement*** correction *f* de l'image, retouche *f* d'images; *Opt & Phot* ***image enhancer*** correcteur *m* d'images; ***image format*** format *m* graphique; *Comput* ***image file*** fichier *m* vidéo *or* image; *Opt* ***image intensifier*** intensificateur *m* d'image, amplificateur *m* de luminance; *Mktg* ***image pricing*** fixation *f* de prix en fonction de l'image; *Comput* ***image processing*** traitement *m* des images; *Comput* ***image processor*** unité *f* de traitement d'images

image-conscious *adj* conscient *ou* soucieux de son image

image-maker *n* conseiller(ère) *m,f* en image

imager ['ɪmɪdʒə(r)] *n Comput* imageur *m*

imagery ['ɪmɪdʒərɪ] *n (UNCOUNT)* (**a**) *(in literature)* images *fpl* (**b**) *(visual images)* imagerie *f*

imagesetter ['ɪmɪdʒˌsetə(r)] *n Comput* photocomposeuse *f*

imaginable [ɪ'mædʒɪnəbəl] *adj* imaginable; **the worst thing imaginable happened** ce qu'on pouvait imaginer de pire est arrivé

imaginary [ɪ'mædʒɪnərɪ] *adj* (**a**) *(in one's imagination → sickness, danger)* imaginaire (**b**) *(fictional → character)* fictif

imagination [ɪˌmædʒɪ'neɪʃən] *n* imagination *f*; **to have no imagination** n'avoir aucune imagination; **use your imagination!** fais preuve d'un peu d'imagination!; **she tends to let her imagination run away with her** elle a tendance à se laisser emporter par son imagination; **it's all in her imagination** elle se fait des idées; **it was only my imagination** c'est mon imagination qui me jouait des tours

imaginative [ɪ'mædʒɪnətɪv] *adj (person)* imaginatif; *(writing, idea, plan)* original

imaginatively [ɪ'mædʒɪnətɪvlɪ] *adv (say, think)* avec imagination; *(described, devised)* avec inventivité; **an imaginatively illustrated book** un livre illustré avec beaucoup d'imagination

imaginativeness [ɪ'mædʒɪnətɪvnɪs] *n (of person)* imagination *f*; *(of story, idea, solution)* inventivité *f*

imagine [ɪ'mædʒɪn] **1** *vt* (**a**) *(picture → scene, person)* imaginer, s'imaginer, se représenter; **I can just imagine her saying/doing that** je la vois très bien dire/faire ça; **I'd imagined him to be a much smaller man** je l'imaginais plus petit; **I can't imagine (myself) getting the job** je n'arrive pas à imaginer que je puisse être embauché; **imagine yourself in his situation** imaginez-vous dans sa situation, mettez-vous à sa place; **imagine (that) you're on a beach** imagine-toi sur une plage; **you can't imagine how awful it was** vous ne pouvez pas (vous) imaginer *ou* vous figurer combien c'était horrible; **just imagine my disgust** imaginez combien j'étais dégoûté; **(you can) imagine his delight!** vous pensez s'il était ravi!; **imagine meeting you here!** ça alors, toi ici!; **you're imagining things** tu te fais des idées; **I was beginning to imagine all sorts of things!** je commençais à m'imaginer des tas de choses (**b**) *(suppose, think)* supposer, imaginer; **I imagine you're tired** je suppose *ou* j'imagine que vous êtes fatigué; **I imagine them to be fairly rich** j'imagine qu'ils sont assez riches; **an intelligent child, I'd imagine** un enfant intelligent, j'imagine; **imagine (that) you've won** imagine que tu as gagné, suppose que tu aies gagné; **don't imagine I'll help you again** ne t'imagine pas que je t'aiderai encore

2 *vi* **he ate all of it, can you imagine?** il a tout mangé, tu t'imagines?; **I can imagine** je veux bien le croire, j'imagine; **just imagine!** tu t'imagines!

imagined [ɪ'mædʒɪnd] *adj* imaginé, imaginaire

imagines [ɪ'meɪdʒɪni:z] *pl of* **imago**

imaging device ['ɪmɪdʒɪŋ-] *n Comput* imageur *m*

imaginings [ɪ'mædʒɪnɪŋz] *npl (fears, dreams)* **never in my worst imaginings did I think it would come to this** je n'aurais jamais pensé que les choses en arriveraient là

imagism ['ɪmədʒɪzəm] *n Literature* imagisme *m*

imagist ['ɪmədʒɪst] *n Literature* imagiste *mf*

imago [ɪ'meɪgəʊ] (*pl* **imagoes** *or* **imagines** [-dʒɪni:z]) *n* (**a**) *Entom* imago *m* (**b**) *Psy* imago *f*

imam [ɪ'mɑ:m] *n* imam *m*

IMAX® ['aɪmæks] *n* (procédé *m*) Imax® *m*

▸▸ ***IMAX® cinema*** cinéma *m* Imax®

imbalance [,ɪm'bæləns] **1** *n* déséquilibre *m*

2 *vt* déséquilibrer

▸▸ *Econ* ***imbalanced growth*** croissance *f* déséquilibrée

imbecile ['ɪmbɪsi:l] **1** *n* (**a**) *(idiot)* imbécile *mf*, idiot(e) *m,f*; **to act the imbecile** faire l'imbécile; **you imbecile!** espèce d'imbécile *ou* d'idiot! (**b**) *Psy* imbécile *mf*

2 *adj* imbécile, idiot

imbecilic [,ɪmbɪ'sɪlɪk] *adj* imbécile, idiot

imbecility [,ɪmbɪ'sɪlətɪ] (*pl* **imbecilities**) *n* (**a**) *(stupidity)* idiotie *f*, imbécillité *f* (**b**) *(stupid action)* idiotie *f*, imbécillité *f* (**c**) *Psy* imbécillité *f*

imbed = **embed**

imbibe [ɪm'baɪb] **1** *vt* (**a**) *Formal or Hum (drink)* absorber (**b**) *Literary (knowledge, ideas, culture)* assimiler (**c**) *Phys* absorber

2 *vi Formal or Hum* boire

imbricate ['ɪmbrɪ,keɪt] **1** *adj* imbriqué

2 *vt* imbriquer

3 *vi* s'imbriquer

▸▸ *Bot* ***imbricate aestivation*** (préfloraison *f*) imbriquée *f*; *Bot* ***imbricate leaves*** feuilles *fpl* imbriquées; *Bot* ***imbricate petals*** pétales *fpl* imbriquées; *Geol* ***imbricate structure*** structure *f* imbriquée; ***imbricate work*** imbrication *f*

imbricated ['ɪmbrɪ,keɪtɪd] *adj Archit & Biol* imbriqué

imbrication [,ɪmbrɪ'keɪʃən] *n* imbrication *f*

imbroglio [ɪm'brəʊlɪəʊ] *n* imbroglio *m*

imbrute [ɪm'bru:t] *Arch or Literary* **1** *vt* abrutir

2 *vi* s'abrutir

imbue [ɪm'bju:] *vt* imprégner; **her parents had imbued her with high ideals** ses parents lui avaient inculqué de nobles idéaux; **his words were imbued with resentment** ses paroles étaient pleines de ressentiment

IMF [,aɪem'ef] *n Fin* (*abbr* **International Monetary Fund**) FMI *m*

imipramine [ɪ'mɪprə,mi:n] *n Pharm* imipramine *f*

imitable ['ɪmɪtəbəl] *adj* imitable

imitate ['ɪmɪteɪt] *vt* (**a**) *(copy → person)* imiter, copier; **to imitate sb's style** imiter le style de qn (**b**) *(mimic → person)* singer, mimer; *(→ call of bird etc)* imiter; **to imitate its surroundings** *(insect etc)* prendre l'aspect de son milieu

imitation [,ɪmɪ'teɪʃən] **1** *n* (**a**) *(copy)* imitation *f*; **it's a cheap imitation** c'est du toc; **a poor imitation of the real thing** une pâle imitation de l'original; **beware of imitations** *(in advertisement)* méfiez-vous des contrefaçons; **an imitation diamond necklace** un collier en faux diamants

(**b**) *(action)* imitation *f*; **to learn by imitation** apprendre par mimétisme; **he does everything in imitation of his brother** il imite *ou* copie son frère en tout; *Prov* **imitation is the sincerest form of flattery** = l'imitation est la flatterie la plus sincère qui soit

2 *comp* faux (fausse)

▸▸ ***imitation fur*** fourrure *f* synthétique; ***imitation jewellery*** bijoux *mpl* (de) fantaisie; ***imitation leather*** imitation *f* cuir, similicuir *m*; ***imitation pearls*** fausses perles *fpl*

imitative ['ɪmɪtətɪv] *adj (behaviour, sound)* imitatif; *(person, style)* imitateur; *Mktg (product)* d'imitation

imitator ['ɪmɪteɪtə(r)] *n* imitateur(trice) *m,f*

immaculate [ɪ'mækjʊlət] *adj* (**a**) *(clean → house, clothes, room)* impeccable, d'une propreté irréprochable; **he's always immaculate** il est toujours impeccable *ou* tiré à quatre épingles (**b**) *(faultless → work, behaviour, performance etc)* parfait, impeccable (**c**) *(morally pure)* irréprochable

▸▸ ***the Immaculate Conception*** l'Immaculée Conception *f*

immaculately [ɪ'mækjʊlətlɪ] *adv* (**a**) *(spotlessly → clean, tidy)* impeccablement; **immaculately dressed** tiré à quatre épingles; **immaculately clean/white** d'une propreté parfaite/blancheur éclatante (**b**) *(faultlessly → behave, perform etc)* d'une manière irréprochable, impeccablement, parfaitement; **she played immaculately throughout the match** elle a joué d'une manière remarquable pendant tout le match

immaculateness [ɪ'mækjʊlətnɪs] *n* (**a**) *(cleanness → of house, room, clothes)* caractère *m* immaculé (**b**) *(faultlessness → of work, behaviour, performance etc)* perfection *f*

immanence ['ɪmənəns], **immanency** ['ɪmənənsɪ] *n* immanence *f*

immanent ['ɪmənənt] *adj* immanent

Immanuel [ɪ'mænjʊəl] *pr n Bible* Emmanuel

immaterial [,ɪmə'tɪərɪəl] *adj* (**a**) *(unimportant)* sans importance; **whether I was there or not is immaterial** que j'aie été présent ou non est sans importance; **that point is immaterial to what we are discussing** cela n'a rien à voir avec ce dont nous sommes en train de parler; **the truth is immaterial to him** la vérité est sans importance à ses yeux (**b**) *Phil* immatériel

immaterialism [,ɪmə'tɪərɪə,lɪzəm] *n Phil* immatérialisme *m*

immaterialist [,ɪmə'tɪərɪəlɪst] *n Phil* immatérialiste *mf*

immateriality [,ɪmətɪərɪ'ælɪtɪ] *n* (**a**) *(lack of importance)* insignifiance *f*, peu *m* d'importance (**b**) *Phil* immatérialité *f*

immature [,ɪmə'tjʊə(r)] *adj* (**a**) *(childish)* immature; **she's very immature** elle manque vraiment de maturité; **stop being so immature!** arrête de te comporter comme un gamin! (**b**) *Bot & Zool* immature, jeune

immaturely [,ɪmə'tjʊəlɪ] *adv (childishly)* de façon puérile

immaturity [,ɪmə'tjʊərətɪ] *n* (**a**) *(childishness)* manque *m* de maturité, immaturité *f* (**b**) *Bot & Zool* immaturité *f*

immeasurable [ɪ'meʒərəbəl] *adj* (**a**) *(very large)* incommensurable (**b**) *Fig (as intensifier)* illimité, incommensurable; **to have an immeasurable influence on sth** avoir une influence énorme sur qch

immeasurably [ɪ'meʒərəblɪ] *adv* (**a**) *(long, high)* incommensurablement (**b**) *Fig (as intensifier)* infiniment

immediacy [ɪ'mi:djəsɪ] *n* impact *m* immédiat; **the immediacy of the famine as seen on television** l'impact immédiat des images de la famine montrées à la télévision; **the immediacy of the crisis** les effets immédiats de la crise

immediate [ɪ'mi:djət] *adj* (**a**) *(instant)* immédiat, urgent; **the problem needs immediate attention** il est urgent de régler le problème; **we need an immediate answer** il nous faut une réponse immédiate; **this pill gives immediate relief** ce cachet soulage instantanément, l'effet de ce cachet est instantané; **house for sale with immediate possession** maison à vendre avec jouissance immédiate

(**b**) *(close in time)* immédiat; **in the immediate future** dans les heures *ou* les jours qui viennent; **my immediate objective** mon objectif premier; **what are your immediate plans?** que proposez-vous de faire d'abord?; **I have no immediate plans to retire** je n'ai pas l'intention de prendre ma retraite dans un futur proche

(**c**) *(nearest)* immédiat, proche; **my immediate relatives** mes parents les plus proches; **my immediate neighbours** mes voisins immédiats

(**d**) *(direct → cause, influence)* immédiat direct

▸▸ *Comput* ***immediate access*** accès *m* direct; *Ling* ***immediate constituent*** constituant *m* immédiat

immediately [ɪ'mi:djətlɪ] **1** *adv* (**a**) *(at once)* tout de suite, immédiatement; **come immediately** viens tout de suite; **I left immediately after** je suis parti tout de suite après; **the distinction isn't immediately obvious** la distinction n'est pas évidente tout de suite

(**b**) *(directly)* directement; **it does not affect me immediately** cela ne me touche pas directement

(**c**) *(just)* juste; **immediately above the window** juste au-dessus de la fenêtre

2 *conj Br* dès que; **let me know immediately he arrives** dès qu'il sera là, prévenez-moi

immediateness [ɪ'mi:djətnɪs] = **immediacy**

immemorial [,ɪmə'mɔ:rɪəl] *adj* immémorial; **since** *or* **from time immemorial** de temps immémorial

immense [ɪ'mens] *adj* immense, considérable

immensely [ɪ'menslɪ] *adv* immensément, extrêmement; **I'm immensely grateful to you** je vous suis extrêmement reconnaissant; **she is immensely fat** elle est absolument énorme

immensity [ɪ'mensətɪ] *n* (**a**) *(of universe, fortune etc)* immensité *f* (**b**) *(of problem, task)* énormité *f*

immerse [ɪ'mɜ:s] *vt* (**a**) *(in liquid)* immerger, plonger; **I'm going to immerse myself in a hot bath** je vais me plonger dans un bain chaud (**b**) *Fig* **I immersed myself in my work** je me suis plongé dans mon travail; **they were immersed in a game of chess** ils étaient plongés dans une partie d'échecs; **she went to London to immerse herself in the English language** elle est allée à Londres en séjour linguistique (**c**) *Rel* baptiser par immersion

immerser [ɪ'mɜ:sə(r)] *n Br Fam* chauffe-eau *m inv* électrique

immersion [ɪ'mɜ:ʃən] *n* (**a**) *(in liquid)* immersion *f* (**b**) *Fig (in reading, work)* absorption *f* (**c**) *Astron & Rel* immersion *f*

▸▸ ***immersion course*** cours *m* de langue intensif *(dans lequel seule la langue apprise est utilisée)*; ***immersion heater*** chauffe-eau *m inv* électrique

immigrant ['ɪmɪgrənt] **1** *n* immigré(e) *m,f*

2 *adj* immigré

▸▸ ***immigrant children*** enfants *mpl* d'immigrés; ***immigrant worker*** travailleur(euse) *m,f* immigré(e)

immigrate ['ɪmɪgreɪt] *vi* immigrer

immigration [,ɪmɪ'greɪʃən] **1** *n* (**a**) *(act of immigrating)* immigration *f*; **the government wants to reduce immigration** le gouvernement veut restreindre l'immigration (**b**) *(control section)* services *mpl* de l'immigration; **to go through immigration** passer l'immigration

2 *comp* de l'immigration

▸▸ ***immigration authorities, immigration control*** services *mpl* de l'immigration; ***the Immigration Control Act*** = loi de 1986 permettant aux immigrés illégaux résidant aux États-Unis depuis 1982 de recevoir un visa; ***immigration figures*** chiffres *mpl* de l'immigration; ***immigration laws*** lois *fpl* sur l'immigration; ***the Immigration and Naturalization Service*** = services américains de contrôle de l'immigration; ***immigration officer*** agent *m* du service de l'immigration; ***immigration quotas*** quotas *mpl* d'immigration; ***immigration regulations*** réglementation *f* relative à l'immigration

imminence ['ɪmɪnəns] *n* imminence *f*

imminent ['ɪmɪnənt] *adj* imminent

imminently ['ɪmɪnəntlɪ] *adv* d'une manière imminente

immiscible [ɪ'mɪsəbəl] *adj* non miscible

immobile [ɪ'məʊbaɪl] *adj* immobile

immobility [,ɪmə'bɪlətɪ] *n* immobilité *f*

immobilization [ɪ,məʊbɪlaɪ'zeɪʃən] *n (gen) & Fin* immobilisation *f*

immobilize, -ise [ɪ'məʊbɪlaɪz] *vt (gen) & Fin* immobiliser

immobilizer [ɪ'məʊbɪlaɪzə(r)] *n Aut* (système *m*) antidémarrage *m*

immoderate [ɪ'mɒdərət] *adj* immodéré, excessif

immoderately [ɪ'mɒdərətlɪ] *adv* immodérément
immodest [ɪ'mɒdɪst] *adj* (**a**) *(indecent)* impudique (**b**) *(vain)* prétentieux
immodestly [ɪ'mɒdɪstlɪ] *adv* (**a**) *(indecently)* impudiquement, de façon indécente (**b**) *(vainly)* sans modestie; **he rather immodestly claims to be the best** il déclare non sans prétention qu'il est le meilleur
immodesty [ɪ'mɒdɪstɪ] *n* (**a**) *(indecency)* indécence *f*, impudeur *f* (**b**) *(vanity)* manque *m* de modestie, prétention *f*
immolate ['ɪməleɪt] *vt Literary* immoler
immolation [,ɪmə'leɪʃən] *n Literary* immolation *f*
immoral [ɪ'mɒrəl] *adj* immoral; *Law* **for immoral purposes** aux fins de débauche
immorality [,ɪmə'rælətɪ] *n* immoralité *f*
immorally [ɪ'mɒrəlɪ] *adv* immoralement
immortal [ɪ'mɔ:təl] **1** *adj* immortel
2 *n* immortel(elle) *m,f*
immortality [,ɪmɔ:'tælətɪ] *n* immortalité *f*
immortalization [ɪ,mɔ:təlaɪ'zeɪʃən] *n* immortalisation *f*
immortalize, -ise [ɪ'mɔ:tə,laɪz] *vt* immortaliser
immovable, immoveable [ɪ'mu:vəbəl] **1** *adj* (**a**) *(fixed)* fixe; *(impossible to move)* impossible à déplacer (**b**) *(determined → person, opposition)* inébranlable
2 immovables *npl Law* biens *mpl* immobiliers
►► *Rel* ***immovable feast*** fête *f* fixe; *Law* ***immovable property*** biens *mpl* immeubles *ou* immobiliers
immune [ɪ'mju:n] *adj* (**a**) *Med* immunisé; **immune to measles** immunisé contre la rougeole
(**b**) *Fig* **immune to** *(unaffected by)* à l'abri de, immunisé contre; **to be immune to temptation/flattery** être immunisé contre les tentations/la flatterie
(**c**) *(exempt)* **immune from** exempt de, exonéré de; **immune from taxation** exonéré d'impôts; **immune from prosecution** inviolable
►► *Med* ***immune deficiency*** immunodéficience *f*; *Med* ***immune response*** réaction *f* immunitaire; *Med* ***immune serum*** immun-sérum *m*, antisérum *m*; *Physiol* ***immune system*** système *m* immunitaire
immunity [ɪ'mju:nətɪ] *n* (**a**) *Med* immunité *f*, résistance *f* (**to** contre), **immunity to** *or* **against measles** immunité contre la rougeole (**b**) *(exemption)* **immunity from** exonération *f* de, exemption *f* de; **immunity from taxation** exonération *f* d'impôts (**c**) *(diplomatic, parliamentary)* immunité *f*; **immunity from prosecution** immunité *f*, inviolabilité *f*
immunization [,ɪmju:naɪ'zeɪʃən] *n* immunisation *f* (**to** contre)
immunize, -ise ['ɪmju:naɪz] *vt* immuniser, vacciner (**to** contre)
immunoassay [,ɪmju:nəʊ'æseɪ] *n Biol* immunoessai *m*, dosage *m* immunologique
immunochemistry [,ɪmju:nəʊ'kemɪstrɪ] *n* immunochimie *f*
immunodeficiency [,ɪmju:nəʊdɪ'fɪʃənsɪ] (*pl* **immunodeficiencies**) *n Med* immunodéficience *f*
immunodeficient [,ɪmju:nəʊdɪ'fɪʃənt] *adj Med* immunodéficitaire
immunodepressant [,ɪmju:nəʊdɪ'presənt] *n Med* immunodépresseur *m*
immunodepressive [,ɪmju:nəʊdɪ'presɪv] *adj Med* immunodépressif
immunogenetics [,ɪmju:nəʊdʒɪ'netɪks] *n (UNCOUNT) Med* immunogénétique *f*
immunogenic [,ɪmju:nəʊ'dʒenɪk] *adj Med* immunogène
immunoglobulin [,ɪmju:nəʊ'glɒbjʊlɪn] *n Med* immunoglobuline *f*
immunological [,ɪmju:nəʊ'lɒdʒɪkəl] *adj* immunologique
immunologist [,ɪmju:n'ɒlədʒɪst] *n* immunologiste *mf*
immunology [,ɪmju:n'ɒlədʒɪ] *n* immunologie *f*
immunopathology [,ɪmju:nəʊpə'θɒlədʒɪ] *n Med* immunopathologie *f*
immunoreaction [,ɪmju:nəʊrɪ'ækʃən] *n Med* réaction *f* immunitaire, immunoréaction *f*
immunosuppressant [,ɪmju:nəʊsə'presənt] *Med*
1 *adj* immunosuppresseur
2 *n* immunosuppresseur *m*
immunosuppression [,ɪmju:nəʊsə'preʃən] *n Med* immunosuppression *f*
immunosuppressive [,ɪmju:nəʊsə'presɪv] *adj Med* immunosuppressif
immunotherapy [,ɪmju:nəʊ'θerəpɪ] *n Med* immunothérapie *f*
immunotransfusion [,ɪmju:nəʊtræns'fju:ʒən] *n Med* immunotransfusion *f*
immure [ɪ'mjʊə(r)] *vt Arch or Literary* (**a**) *(shut away → person)* enfermer, cloîtrer; **he had immured himself in the library** il s'était enfermé dans la bibliothèque; **immured in silence** cloîtré dans le silence (**b**) *(wall up → victim)* emmurer
immutability [ɪ,mu:tə'bɪlətɪ] *n* immuabilité *f*
immutable [ɪ'mju:təbəl] *adj* immuable
immutably [ɪ'mju:təblɪ] *adv* immuablement
imp [ɪmp] *n (devil)* lutin *m*; *(child)* coquin(e) *m,f*; **she's a little imp!** c'est une petite coquine!, elle est très espiègle!
impact 1 *n* ['ɪmpækt] (**a**) *(force)* impact *m*; **on impact** au moment de l'impact
(**b**) *Fig (of speech, play, advertising campaign etc)* impact *m*, impression *f*; **the scandal had little impact on the election results** le scandale a eu peu de répercussions *ou* d'incidence sur les résultats de l'élection; **you made** *or* **had quite an impact on him** vous avez fait une forte impression sur lui; **she made quite an impact (at the meeting)** son intervention (lors de la réunion) a été très remarquée
(**c**) *Mktg* impact *m*
2 *vt* [ɪm'pækt] (**a**) *(collide with)* entrer en collision avec
(**b**) *(influence)* avoir un impact sur
3 *vi* [ɪm'pækt] (**a**) *(affect)* **to impact on** produire un effet sur
(**b**) *Comput* frapper
►► *Br* ***impact adhesive*** colle *f* instantanée; *Aut* ***impact bar*** barre *f* de renfort; *St Exch* ***impact day*** = jour où l'on annonce une nouvelle émission d'actions; *Comput* ***impact printer*** imprimante *f* à impact; *Mktg* ***impact study*** étude *f* d'impact
impacted [ɪm'pæktɪd] *adj (tooth)* inclus; *(fracture)* avec impaction
►► *Am* ***impacted area*** zone *f* affectée
impaction [ɪm'pækʃən] *n (of bone)* impaction *f*; *(of tooth)* inclusion *f*; *Obst (of head)* enclavement *m*; *Med* **impaction of the bowel** occlusion *f* intestinale
impair [ɪm'peə(r)] *vt (sight, hearing, mental faculties)* diminuer, affaiblir; *(strength)* diminuer; *(authority)* saper; *(relationship, chances, ability)* compromettre
impaired [ɪm'peəd] *adj (sight, hearing, mental faculties)* affaibli
►► *Can* ***impaired driving*** conduite *f* en état d'ivresse; ***impaired hearing*** ouïe *f* affaiblie; ***impaired vision*** vue *f* affaiblie
impairment [ɪm'peəmənt] *n (of sight, hearing, mental faculties, chances)* affaiblissement *m*, diminution *f*; *(of relationship)* détérioration *f*
impala [ɪm'pɑ:lə] *n Zool* impala *m*
impale [ɪm'peɪl] *vt* empaler; **to impale oneself on sth** s'empaler sur qch
impalement [ɪm'peɪlmənt] *n* (**a**) *(by accident)* empalement *m*; *Hist (form of torture)* empalement *m*, supplice *m* du pal; **he just avoided impalement on the railings** il a failli s'empaler sur la grille (**b**) *Her* **arms marshalled by impalement** armoiries *fpl* réunies sur un écu mi-parti
impalpable [ɪm'pælpəbəl] *adj* impalpable; *(ideas)* insaisissable
impanel [ɪm'pænəl] (*pt & pp* **impaneled,** *cont* **impaneling**) *vt Am (jury)* constituer; *(juror)* inscrire sur la liste *ou* le tableau du jury
imparidigitate [ɪm,pærɪ'dɪdʒɪteɪt] *adj Zool* imparidigité, mésaxonien
imparisyllabic [ɪm,pærɪsɪ'læbɪk] *adj Gram* imparisyllabe, imparisyllabique
impart [ɪm'pɑ:t] *vt* (**a**) *(communicate → news, truth)* apprendre (**b**) *(transmit → knowledge, wisdom)* transmettre (**c**) *(give → quality, flavour)* donner
impartial [ɪm'pɑ:ʃəl] *adj* impartial
impartiality [ɪm,pɑ:ʃɪ'ælətɪ] *n* impartialité *f*
impartially [ɪm'pɑ:ʃəlɪ] *adv* impartialement
impassability [ɪm,pɑ:sə'bɪlɪtɪ] *n (of river, frontier)* état *m* infranchissable; *(of road)* impraticabilité *f*
impassable [ɪm'pɑ:səbəl] *adj (river, frontier)* infranchissable; *(road)* impraticable
impassableness [ɪm'pɑ:səbəlnɪs] *n (of river, frontier)* état *m* infranchissable; *(of road)* impraticabilité *f*
impasse [æm'pɑ:s] *n* impasse *f*; **the talks have reached an impasse** les pourparlers sont dans une impasse; **there's no way out of this impasse** c'est une situation sans issue
impassioned [ɪm'pæʃənd] *adj* passionné; *(plea)* fervent
impassive [ɪm'pæsɪv] *adj* impassible
impassively [ɪm'pæsɪvlɪ] *adv* impassiblement; **to look at sb/sth impassively** regarder qn/qch d'un air impassible
impassiveness [ɪm'pæsɪvnɪs], **impassivity** [,ɪmpæ'sɪvɪtɪ] *n* impassibilité *f*
impasto [ɪm'pæstəʊ] *n Art* empâtement *m*
impatience [ɪm'peɪʃəns] *n* (**a**) *(lack of patience)* impatience *f*; **with impatience** avec impatience, impatiemment (**b**) *(irritation)* irritation *f*; **I fully understand your impatience at the delay** je comprends parfaitement que ce retard vous irrite (**c**) *(intolerance)* intolérance *f*; *Formal* **he was known for his impatience of sloppy work** il avait la réputation de mal supporter le travail brouillon
impatient [ɪm'peɪʃənt] *adj* (**a**) *(eager, anxious)* impatient; **I'm impatient to see her again** je suis impatient de la revoir; **they were impatient for the results** ils attendaient les résultats avec impatience; **the people were impatient for reform** le peuple réclamait des réformes
(**b**) *(irritated)* **she's impatient with her children** elle n'a aucune patience avec ses enfants; **I'm getting impatient** je commence à m'impatienter *ou* à perdre patience
(**c**) *(intolerant)* intolérant; **he's impatient with people who always ask the same questions** il ne supporte pas les gens qui lui posent toujours les mêmes questions
impatiently [ɪm'peɪʃəntlɪ] *adv* impatiemment, avec impatience
impavid [ɪm'pævɪd] *adj Literary* impavide, intrépide
impawn [ɪm'pɔ:n] *vt Literary (object)* mettre *ou* donner en gage; *Fig (one's life, honour)* engager
impeach [ɪm'pi:tʃ] *vt* (**a**) *Br Law (accuse)* accuser, inculper (**b**) *Am Law & Pol* entamer une procédure d'"impeachment" contre (**c**) *Br Formal (doubt → motives, honesty)* mettre en doute; *(→ character)* attaquer (**d**) *Law* **to impeach a witness** récuser un témoin
impeachable [ɪm'pi:tʃəbəl] *adj Am Law & Pol* = qui peut donner lieu à une procédure d'impeachment
impeachment [ɪm'pi:tʃmənt] *n* (**a**) *Br Law (accusation)* mise *f* en accusation (**b**) *Am Law & Pol* = mise en accusation d'un élu devant le Congrès
impearl [ɪm'pɜ:l] *vt Literary* emperler
impeccable [ɪm'pekəbəl] *adj (house, room)* impeccable; *(conduct, management)* irréprochable; *(manners)* impeccable, irréprochable; **he speaks impeccable English** il parle un anglais impeccable
impeccably [ɪm'pekəblɪ] *adv* impeccablement; **impeccably dressed** habillé impeccablement
impecuniosity [,ɪmpɪkju:nɪ'ɒsɪtɪ] *n Formal* impécuniosité *f*
impecunious [,ɪmpɪ'kju:nɪəs] *adj Formal* impécunieux
impedance [ɪm'pi:dəns] *n Elec* impédance *f*
impede [ɪm'pi:d] *vt* (**a**) *(obstruct → traffic, player)* gêner (**b**) *(hinder → progress)* ralentir, entraver; *(→ plan)* faire obstacle à, entraver; *(→ person)* gêner
impediment [ɪm'pedɪmənt] *n* (**a**) *(obstacle)* obstacle *m* (**b**) *(handicap)* défaut *m* (physique) (**c**) *Law* empêchement *m*
impedimenta [ɪm,pedɪ'mentə] *npl Fig* impedimenta *mpl*
impel [ɪm'pel] (*pt & pp* **impelled,** *cont* **impelling**) *vt* (**a**) *(urge, incite)* inciter; *(compel)* obliger, contraindre; **I felt impelled to intervene** je me sentais obligé d'intervenir (**b**) *(propel)* pousser
impeller [ɪm'pelə(r)] *n Tech* rotor *m*; *(of water pump)* turbine *f*; *(of converter)* roue *f* pompe
impend [ɪm'pend] *vi (be imminent)* être imminent; *(threaten → danger)* menacer

imm–imp

impending [ɪm'pendɪŋ] *adj* imminent; **the impending visit by the President** la visite imminente du Président; **the impending arrival of all my relations** l'arrivée prochaine de ma famille au grand complet; **the impending crisis** la crise imminente *ou* qui couve; **there was an atmosphere of impending doom** il planait une atmosphère de désastre imminent

impenetrability [ɪm,penɪtrə'bɪlɪtɪ] *n* (**a**) *(of wall, forest, fog, defences)* impénétrabilité *f*; *Fig (of mystery)* caractère *m* inexplicable (**b**) *(incomprehensibility → of jargon, system etc)* caractère *m* incompréhensible

impenetrable [ɪm'penɪtrəbəl] *adj* (**a**) *(wall, forest, fog, defences)* impénétrable; *Fig (mystery)* insondable, impénétrable (**b**) *(incomprehensible → jargon, system etc)* incompréhensible

impenetrably [ɪm'penɪtrəblɪ] *adv* (**a**) *(gen)* impénétrablement (**b**) *(incomprehensibly)* **an impenetrably obscure text** un texte incompréhensible

impenitence [ɪm'penɪtəns] *n* impénitence *f*

impenitent [ɪm'penɪtənt] *adj* impénitent; **he is still utterly impenitent** il n'a toujours pas le moindre remords

impenitently [ɪm'penɪtəntlɪ] *adv* avec impénitence

imperative [ɪm'perətɪv] **1** *adj* (**a**) *(essential)* (absolument) essentiel, impératif; **it's imperative that you reply immediately** il faut absolument que vous répondiez tout de suite; **it was imperative to finalize the deal** il fallait impérativement conclure l'affaire (**b**) *(categorical → orders, voice, tone)* impérieux, impératif (**c**) *Gram* impératif

2 *n Gram* impératif *m*; **in the imperative** à l'impératif

imperatively [ɪm'perətɪvlɪ] *adv* (**a**) *(absolutely)* impérativement (**b**) *(imperiously)* impérieusement, impérativement

imperceptible [,ɪmpə'septəbəl] *adj* imperceptible; **imperceptible to the human eye/ear** invisible/inaudible (pour l'homme)

imperceptibly [,ɪmpə'septəblɪ] *adv* imperceptiblement

imperceptive [,ɪmpə'septɪv] *adj* peu perspicace

imperfect [ɪm'pɜːfɪkt] **1** *adj* (**a**) *(flawed → work, argument)* imparfait (**b**) *(faulty → machine)* défectueux; *(→ goods)* de second choix; **it's slightly imperfect** *(item for sale)* il a un léger défaut (**c**) *(incomplete)* incomplet(ète), inachevé (**d**) *Gram* imparfait (**e**) *Law* inapplicable (pour vice de forme)

2 *n Gram* imparfait *m*; **in the imperfect** à l'imparfait

imperfection [,ɪmpə'fekʃən] *n* (**a**) *(imperfect state)* imperfection *f* (**b**) *(fault)* imperfection *f*, défaut *m*

imperfective [,ɪmpə'fektɪv] *Gram* **1** *n* imperfectif *m*

2 *adj* imperfectif

imperfectly [ɪm'pɜːfɪktlɪ] *adv* imparfaitement

imperial [ɪm'pɪərɪəl] **1** *adj* (**a**) *(in titles)* impérial; **His Imperial Majesty** Sa Majesté Impériale (**b**) *(majestic)* majestueux, auguste (**c**) *(imperious)* impérieux (**d**) *(paper)* grand format *(inv)* *(Br = 762 mm × 559 mm, Am= 787 mm × 584 mm)* (**e**) *Br (weights and measures)* = relatif au système de mesure anglo-saxon utilisant les miles, les pints etc

2 *n* (**a**) *(beard)* impériale *f*, barbe *f* à l'impériale (**b**) *(paper size)* grand format *m (Br = 762 mm × 559 mm, Am= 787 mm × 584 mm)*

►► ***Imperial College*** = établissement relevant de l'université de Londres et spécialisé dans la recherche scientifique, la mécanique et l'informatique; *Br* ***imperial gallon*** gallon *m* (britannique); ***imperial pint*** pinte *f* (britannique); ***the Imperial War Museum*** = musée militaire à Londres

imperialism [ɪm'pɪərɪəlɪzəm] *n* impérialisme *m*

imperialist [ɪm'pɪərɪəlɪst] **1** *n* impérialiste *mf*

2 *adj* impérialiste

imperialistic [ɪm,pɪərɪəl'ɪstɪk] *adj* impérialiste

imperially [ɪm'pɪərɪəlɪ] *adv* (**a**) *(majestically)* majestueusement (**b**) *(authoritatively)* impérieusement

imperil [ɪm'perɪl] *(Br pt & pp* **imperilled**, *cont* **imperilling**, *Am pt & pp* **imperiled**, *cont* **imperiling**) *vt* mettre en péril

imperious [ɪm'pɪərɪəs] *adj (authoritative)* impérieux, autoritaire

imperiously [ɪm'pɪərɪəslɪ] *adv (authoritatively)* impérieusement, autoritairement

imperiousness [ɪm'pɪərɪəsnɪs] *n (authoritativeness)* air *m* impérieux; *(in speech)* ton *m* impérieux

imperishable [ɪm'perɪʃəbəl] *adj (quality, truth)* impérissable; *(goods)* non perissable

imperium [ɪm'pɪərɪəm] *n Literary* pouvoir *m* absolu

impermanence [ɪm'pɜːmənəns] *n* fugacité *f*

impermanent [ɪm'pɜːmənənt] *adj* fugace

impermeability [ɪm,pɜːmɪə'bɪlɪtɪ] *n (of soil, cell, wall etc)* imperméabilité *f*; *(of container)* étanchéité *f*

impermeable [ɪm'pɜːmɪəbəl] *adj (soil, cell, wall etc)* imperméable; *(container)* étanche

impersonal [ɪm'pɜːsənəl] *adj* (**a**) *(objective)* impartial (**b**) *(cold)* froid, impersonnel (**c**) *Gram* impersonnel

►► *Fin* ***impersonal accounts*** comptes *mpl* impersonnels

impersonality [ɪm,pɜːsə'nælɪtɪ] *n* (**a**) *(objectivity)* impartialité *f* (**b**) *(coldness)* froideur *f*

impersonally [ɪm'pɜːsənəlɪ] *adv* (**a**) *(objectively)* impartialement (**b**) *(coldly)* avec froideur

impersonate [ɪm'pɜːsəneɪt] *vt* (**a**) *(imitate)* imiter (**b**) *(pretend to be)* se faire passer pour

impersonation [ɪm,pɜːsə'neɪʃən] *n* (**a**) *(imitation)* imitation *f*; **to do an impersonation of sb** imiter qn (**b**) *(pretence of being)* imposture *f*

impersonator [ɪm'pɜːsəneɪtə(r)] *n* (**a**) *(mimic)* imitateur(trice) *m,f* (**b**) *(impostor)* imposteur *m*

impertinence [ɪm'pɜːtɪnəns] *n* impertinence *f*

impertinent [ɪm'pɜːtɪnənt] *adj* (**a**) *(rude)* impertinent, insolent; **to be impertinent to sb** être impertinent envers qn (**b**) *(irrelevant)* hors de propos, non pertinent

impertinently [ɪm'pɜːtɪnəntlɪ] *adv* avec impertinence

imperturbability [ɪmpə,tɜːbə'bɪlɪtɪ] *n* imperturbabilité *f*

imperturbable [,ɪmpə'tɜːbəbəl] *adj* imperturbable

imperturbably [,ɪmpə'tɜːbəblɪ] *adv* imperturbablement

impervious [ɪm'pɜːvɪəs] *adj* (**a**) *(unreceptive, untouched → person)* imperméable, fermé; **they are impervious to new ideas** ils sont imperméables *ou* inaccessibles aux idées nouvelles; **impervious to criticism** imperméable à la critique; **he was impervious to her charm** il était insensible à son charme; **he remained impervious to our suggestions** il est resté sourd à nos propositions

(**b**) *(resistant → material)* **impervious to heat** résistant à la chaleur; **impervious to damp/water** imperméable

imperviously [ɪm'pɜːvɪəslɪ] *adv* impénétrablement

imperviousness [ɪm'pɜːvɪəsnɪs] *n* impénétrabilité *f*; **imperviousness to damp/water** imperméabilité *f*

impetigo [,ɪmpɪ'taɪgəʊ] *n (UNCOUNT) Med* impétigo *m*

impetuosity [ɪm,petjʊ'ɒsətɪ] *n* impétuosité *f*

impetuous [ɪm'petʃʊəs] *adj* impétueux; *(decision)* hâtif

impetuously [ɪm'petʃʊəslɪ] *adv* avec impétuosité

impetuousness [ɪm'petʃʊəsnɪs] *n* impétuosité *f*

impetus ['ɪmpɪtəs] *n* (**a**) *(force)* force *f* d'impulsion; *(speed)* élan *m*; *(weight)* poids *m*; **to gain impetus** prendre *ou* gagner de l'importance; **to lose impetus** perdre de son élan; **to be carried by** *or* **under one's own impetus** être entraîné par son propre élan *ou* par son propre poids (**b**) *Fig (incentive, drive)* impulsion *f*, élan *m*; **to give new impetus to sth** donner un nouvel élan à qch, relancer qch

impiety [ɪm'paɪətɪ] (*pl* **impieties**) *n* (**a**) *Rel* impiété *f* (**b**) *Formal (disrespect)* irrévérence *f*

►**impinge on, impinge upon** [ɪm'pɪndʒ] *vt insep* (**a**) *(affect)* affecter; **it impinges in a big way on all our lives** ça affecte énormément notre vie à tous; **to impinge on sb's conscious mind** venir à la conscience de qn; **it didn't even impinge on his consciousness** il ne s'en est même pas rendu compte; **in so far as it impinges on our department** dans la mesure où cela affecte *ou* a des répercussions sur notre service (**b**) *(infringe on → rights)* empiéter sur

impingement [ɪm'pɪndʒmənt] *n* empiètement *m*

impious ['ɪmpɪəs] *adj* (**a**) *Rel* impie (**b**) *Formal (disrespectful)* irrévérent

impiously ['ɪmpɪəslɪ] *adv* (**a**) *Rel* avec impiété (**b**) *Formal (disrespectfully)* avec irrévérence

impish ['ɪmpɪʃ] *adj (laughter, face)* de petit diable, d'espiègle; *(child, remark)* espiègle, malicieux

impishly ['ɪmpɪʃlɪ] *adv* de façon espiègle

impishness ['ɪmpɪʃnɪs] *n* espièglerie *f*

implacability [ɪm,plækə'bɪlɪtɪ] *n* implacabilité *f*

implacable [ɪm'plækəbəl] *adj* implacable

implacableness [ɪm'plækəbəlnɪs] *n* implacabilité *f*

implacably [ɪm'plækəblɪ] *adv* implacablement

implant 1 *n* ['ɪmplɑːnt] *(under skin)* implant *m*; *(graft)* greffe *f*

2 *vt* [ɪm'plɑːnt] (**a**) *(instil → idea, feeling)* inculquer (**in sb** à qn); **he tried to implant his own beliefs in his children's minds** il a essayé d'inculquer ses propres convictions à ses enfants (**b**) *Med (graft)* greffer; *(place under skin)* implanter

implantation [,ɪmplɑːn'teɪʃən] *n* (**a**) *(of idea)* inculcation *f* (**b**) *Med (grafting)* greffe *f*; *(placing under skin)* implantation *f* (**c**) *Biol (of egg)* nidation *f*

implausibility [ɪm,plɔːzə'bɪlɪtɪ] *n* invraisemblance *f*

implausible [ɪm'plɔːzəbəl] *adj* invraisemblable

implausibly [ɪm'plɔːzəblɪ] *adv* invraisemblablement; **to end implausibly** *(book, film etc)* se terminer de façon peu vraisemblable

impledge [ɪm'pledʒ] *vt Literary (object)* mettre en gage; *Fig (one's life, honour)* engager

implement 1 *n* ['ɪmplɪmənt] (**a**) *(tool)* outil *m*; **agricultural implements** matériel *m* agricole; **gardening implements** outils *mpl* de jardinage; **kitchen implements** ustensiles *mpl* de cuisine (**b**) *Fig (means)* instrument *m*

2 *vt* ['ɪmplɪment] *(plan, orders)* exécuter; *(ideas, policies)* appliquer, mettre en œuvre; *(product, campaign)* mettre en œuvre

implementation [,ɪmplɪmen'teɪʃən] *n (of plan, orders)* exécution *f*; *(of ideas, policies)* application *f*, mise *f* en œuvre; *(of product, campaign)* mise *f* en œuvre

implicate ['ɪmplɪkeɪt] *vt* (**a**) *(show involvement of)* impliquer; **to be implicated in sth** être impliqué dans qch (**b**) *Formal (imply)* impliquer, renfermer

implication [,ɪmplɪ'keɪʃən] *n* (**a**) *(possible repercussion)* implication *f*; **what are the implications of the survey?** quelles sont les implications de ce sondage?; **I don't think you understand the implications of what you are saying** je ne suis pas sûr que vous mesuriez la portée de vos propos; **the full implications of the report are not yet clear** il est encore trop tôt pour mesurer pleinement les implications de ce rapport

(**b**) *(suggestion)* suggestion *f*; *(insinuation)* insinuation *f*; *(hidden meaning)* sous-entendu *m*; **by implication** par voie de conséquence; **the implication was that we would be punished** tout portait à croire que nous serions punis

(**c**) *(involvement)* implication *f*

implicit [ɪm'plɪsɪt] *adj* (**a**) *(implied)* implicite; **his feelings were implicit in his words** ses paroles laissaient deviner ses sentiments (**b**) *(absolute → confidence, obedience)* total, absolu; **implicit faith** confiance *f* aveugle

implicitly [ɪm'plɪsɪtlɪ] *adv* (**a**) *(by implication)* implicitement (**b**) *(absolutely)* absolument

implicitness [ɪm'plɪsɪtnɪs] *n* (**a**) *(implied nature)* caractère *m* implicite (**b**) *(absoluteness → of confidence, obedience)* caractère *m* absolu

implied [ɪm'plaɪd] *adj* implicite, sous-entendu

►► *Law* ***implied consent*** consentement *m* tacite

implode [ɪm'pləʊd] *vi* imploser

►► *Ling* ***imploded consonant*** consonne *f* implosive

implore [ɪmˈplɔː(r)] *vt* supplier, implorer; **he implored me to give him the money** il m'a supplié *ou* imploré de lui donner l'argent; **I implore you!** je vous en supplie!

imploring [ɪmˈplɔːrɪŋ] *adj* suppliant, implorant

imploringly [ɪmˈplɔːrɪŋlɪ] *adv (say)* d'un ton suppliant *ou* implorant; *(look at)* d'un air suppliant *ou* implorant

implosion [ɪmˈpləʊʒən] *n* implosion *f*

implosive [ɪmˈpləʊsɪv] *Ling* **1** *n* implosive *f*
2 *adj* implosif

imply [ɪmˈplaɪ] *(pt & pp* **implied**) *vt* (**a**) *(insinuate)* insinuer; *(give impression)* laisser entendre *ou* supposer; **are you implying that I'm mistaken?** voulez-vous insinuer que je me trompe?; **she implied that it wouldn't take long** elle a laissé entendre que cela ne prendrait pas longtemps; **your silence implies that you are guilty** votre silence laisse à penser que vous êtes coupable
(**b**) *(presuppose)* impliquer; *(involve)* comporter; **it implies that one of them is lying** cela implique *ou* veut dire que l'un d'eux ment; **it implies a lot of hard work** cela implique beaucoup de travail

impolite [ˌɪmpəˈlaɪt] *adj* impoli; **to be impolite to sb** être *ou* se montrer impoli envers qn

impolitely [ˌɪmpəˈlaɪtlɪ] *adv* impoliment

impoliteness [ˌɪmpəˈlaɪtnɪs] *n* impolitesse *f*

impolitic [ɪmˈpɒlətɪk] *adj* peu *ou* mal avisé, maladroit

imponderability [ɪmˌpɒndərəˈbɪlɪtɪ] *n* impondérabilité *f*

imponderable [ɪmˈpɒndrəbəl] **1** *n* impondérable *m*
2 *adj* impondérable

import 1 *n* [ˈɪmpɔːt] (**a**) *Com (activity)* importation *f*; *(imported article)* importation *f*, article *m* importé; **the government has put a tax on imports** le gouvernement a instauré une taxe sur les produits d'importation *ou* les produits importés
(**b**) *Formal (meaning)* signification *f*; *(content)* teneur *f*
(**c**) *Formal (importance)* importance *f*; *(of remark)* portée *f*
2 *comp* [ˈɪmpɔːt] *(company, licence, surcharge)* d'importation; *(duty)* de douane, sur les importations; *(trade)* des importations
3 *vt* [ɪmˈpɔːt] (**a**) *Com* importer; **lamb imported from New Zealand into Britain** agneau de Nouvelle-Zélande importé en Grande-Bretagne
(**b**) *(imply)* signifier
(**c**) *Comput* importer (**from** depuis)
(**d**) *Arch or Literary (be important)* **these questions import us nearly** ces questions nous importent fort; **it imports us to know whether...,** il nous importe de savoir si..., il est important que nous sachions si...
►► ***import agent*** commissionnaire *mf* importateur(trice), agent *m* importateur; ***import ban*** interdiction *f* d'importation; **to impose an import ban on sth** interdire qch d'importation; ***import controls*** contrôles *mpl* à l'importation; ***import goods*** marchandises *fpl* à l'import; ***import list*** liste *f* des importations; *(of prices)* tarif *m* d'entrée; ***import price*** prix *m* à l'importation, prix *m* (à l')import; ***import quotas*** contingents *mpl* d'importation; ***import restrictions*** restrictions *fpl* à l'importation

importance [ɪmˈpɔːtəns] *n* importance *f*; **to be of importance** avoir de l'importance; **it is of great importance to act now** il est très important d'agir maintenant; **it's of no importance whatsoever** cela n'a aucune espèce d'importance; **to give** *or* **attach importance to sth** attacher de l'importance à qch; **a position of importance** un poste important; *Pej* **to be full of one's own importance** être imbu de sa personne

'The Importance of Being Earnest' *Wilde* 'De l'importance d'être constant'

importance-performance analysis *n Mktg* analyse *f* importance-performance

important [ɪmˈpɔːtənt] *adj* (**a**) *(gen)* important; **it's not important** ça n'a pas d'importance; **it is important that you (should) get the job** il est important que vous obteniez cet emploi; **it is important for her to know the truth** il est important pour elle de connaître *ou* il est important qu'elle connaisse la vérité; **my job is important to me** mon travail compte beaucoup pour moi; **to play an important part** jouer un rôle important *ou* capital; **stop trying to look important** cesse de te donner des airs importants
(**b**) *(influential)* **an important book/writer** un livre-clef/grand écrivain

importantly [ɪmˈpɔːtəntlɪ] *adv (look at)* d'un air important; *(say)* d'un ton important; **and, more importantly...** et, ce qui est plus important...

importation [ˌɪmpɔːˈteɪʃən] *n* (**a**) *Com (of goods)* importation *f*; *Am (imported article)* importation *f*, article *m* d'importation (**b**) *Comput* importation *f*

importer [ɪmˈpɔːtə(r)] *n Com* (**a**) *(person)* importateur(trice) *m,f* (**b**) *(country)* pays *m* importateur; **an oil importer** un pays importateur de pétrole; **this country is a big importer of luxury goods** ce pays est un gros importateur de produits de luxe; **Japan is still a net importer of technology** le Japon est toujours un importateur net de technologie

import-export *Com* **1** *n* import-export *m*
2 *comp (company)* d'import-export

importing [ɪmˈpɔːtɪŋ] **1** *n* (**a**) *Com (of goods)* importation *f* (**b**) *Comput* importation *f*
2 *adj Com (country)* importateur(trice)

importunate [ɪmˈpɔːtjʊnət] *adj Formal (visitor, beggar)* importun; *(demands, questions)* incessant

importunately [ɪmˈpɔːtjʊnətlɪ] *adv Formal* importunément

importune [ɪmˈpɔːtjuːn] *Formal* **1** *vt* (**a**) *(gen)* importuner, harceler; **to importune sb with questions** harceler *ou* presser qn de questions (**b**) *Br (of prostitute)* racoler
2 *vi Br (prostitute)* racoler

importunity [ˌɪmpɔːˈtjuːnətɪ] *n (harassment)* sollicitation *f*

impose [ɪmˈpəʊz] **1** *vt (price, tax, attitude, belief, restrictions)* imposer; *(fine, penalty)* infliger; **to impose a ban on sth** interdire qch; **the EU is in favour of imposing a ban on tobacco advertising** l'UE est en faveur d'interdire la publicité pour le tabac; **to impose a task on sb** imposer une tâche à qn; **he tried to impose his opinions on us** il a essayé de nous imposer ses opinions; **to impose oneself on sb** imposer sa présence à qn
2 *vi* s'imposer; **I'm sorry to impose** je suis désolé de vous déranger; **to impose on sb** abuser de la gentillesse de qn; **they impose upon his hospitality** ils abusent de son hospitalité

imposing [ɪmˈpəʊzɪŋ] *adj (person, building)* impressionnant; *(air, tone)* imposant; **of imposing stature** d'une taille imposante *ou* impressionnante

imposingly [ɪmˈpəʊzɪŋlɪ] *adv* d'une manière imposante

imposition [ˌɪmpəˈzɪʃən] *n* (**a**) *(of tax, sanction)* imposition *f* (**b**) *(burden)* charge *f*, fardeau *m*; *(unfair demand)* abus *m*; **I don't want to be an imposition (on you)** je ne veux pas abuser de votre gentillesse *ou* de votre bonté; **her asking me to do that was a bit of an imposition** elle abuse un peu de m'avoir demandé de faire ça (**c**) *Typ* imposition *f* (**d**) *Br Old-fashioned Sch* punition *f*

impossibility [ɪmˌpɒsəˈbɪlətɪ] *(pl* **impossibilities**) *n* impossibilité *f*; **it's a physical impossibility for us to arrive on time** nous sommes dans l'impossibilité matérielle d'arriver à l'heure; **it's a total impossibility** c'est totalement impossible

impossible [ɪmˈpɒsəbəl] **1** *adj* (**a**) *(not possible)* impossible; **it's impossible for me to leave work before 6 p.m.** il m'est impossible de quitter mon travail avant 18 heures; **you make it impossible for me to be civil to you** tu me mets dans l'impossibilité d'être poli envers toi; **I'm afraid that's quite impossible** je regrette, mais ça n'est vraiment pas possible
(**b**) *(difficult to believe)* impossible, invraisemblable; **but that's impossible!** mais ce n'est pas possible!; **it is impossible that he should be lying** il est impossible qu'il mente
(**c**) *(unbearable)* impossible, insupportable; **he's absolutely impossible** il est vraiment impossible *ou* insupportable; **he made their lives impossible** il leur a rendu la vie insupportable *ou* impossible; **you're putting me in an impossible situation** vous me mettez dans une situation impossible
2 *n* impossible *m*; **to attempt/to ask the impossible** tenter/demander l'impossible

impossibly [ɪmˈpɒsəblɪ] *adv* (**a**) *(extremely)* extrêmement; **impossibly difficult** extrêmement difficile; **the film is impossibly long** le film n'en finit pas; **the coach was travelling impossibly slowly** le car roulait incroyablement lentement (**b**) *(unbearably)* insupportablement; **they were behaving impossibly** ils sont totalement insupportables

impost[1] [ˈɪmpəʊst] *n* (**a**) *Fin* impôt *m* (**b**) *Fam Horseracing* handicap ❑ *m*, surcharge ❑ *f*

impost[2] *n Archit* imposte *f*

impostor, imposter [ɪmˈpɒstə(r)] *n* imposteur *m*

imposture [ɪmˈpɒstʃə(r)] *n Formal* imposture *f*

impotence [ˈɪmpətəns] *n* (**a**) *(sexual)* impuissance *f* (**b**) *(powerlessness)* impuissance *f*; *(weakness)* faiblesse *f*, impotence *f*

impotent [ˈɪmpətənt] *adj* (**a**) *(sexually)* impuissant (**b**) *(powerless)* impuissant; *(weak)* faible

impotently [ˈɪmpətəntlɪ] *adv (powerlessly)* de façon impuissante; *(weakly)* faiblement

impound [ɪmˈpaʊnd] *vt* (**a**) *Law (goods)* confisquer, saisir (**b**) *(put in pound → animal, car)* mettre en fourrière

impounding [ɪmˈpaʊndɪŋ] *n* (**a**) *Law (of goods)* confiscation *f*, saisie *f* (**b**) *(putting in pound → of animal, car)* mise *f* en fourrière

impoverish [ɪmˈpɒvərɪʃ] *vt* appauvrir

impoverished [ɪmˈpɒvərɪʃt] *adj* appauvri, très pauvre

impoverishment [ɪmˈpɒvərɪʃmənt] *n* appauvrissement *m*

impracticability [ɪmˌpræktɪkəˈbɪlɪtɪ] *n* impraticabilité *f*

impracticable [ɪmˈpræktɪkəbəl] *adj (not feasible)* irréalisable, impraticable

impractical [ɪmˈpræktɪkəl] *adj (plan, suggestion)* irréaliste; *(person)* qui manque d'esprit pratique; **he's completely impractical** il n'a aucun sens pratique

imprecate [ˈɪmprɪˌkeɪt] *vt Literary* maudire; **to imprecate curses upon sb** *or* **on sb's head** appeler des malédictions sur la tête de qn

imprecation [ˌɪmprɪˈkeɪʃən] *n Formal* imprécation *f*

imprecatory [ˈɪmprɪˌkeɪtərɪ] *adj Formal* imprécatoire

imprecise [ˌɪmprɪˈsaɪs] *adj* imprécis

imprecisely [ˌɪmprɪˈsaɪslɪ] *adv* sans précision

imprecision [ˌɪmprɪˈsɪʒən] *n* imprécision *f*

impregnability [ɪmˌpregnəˈbɪlɪtɪ] *n* (**a**) *(of fortress)* caractère *m* imprenable *ou* inexpugnable (**b**) *Fig (of argument)* caractère *m* irréfutable

impregnable [ɪmˈpregnəbəl] *adj* (**a**) *(fortress)* imprenable (**b**) *Fig (argument)* irréfutable; **his position is impregnable** sa position est inattaquable

impregnate [ˈɪmpregneɪt] *vt* (**a**) *(saturate)* imprégner (**with** de); **allow the oil to impregnate the wood** laissez le bois s'imprégner d'huile (**b**) *Formal (make pregnant)* féconder

impregnation [ˌɪmpregˈneɪʃən] *n* (**a**) *(saturation)* imprégnation *f* (**b**) *Formal (fertilization)* fécondation *f*

impresario [ˌɪmprɪˈsɑːrɪəʊ] *(pl* **impresarios**) *n* impresario *m*

imprescriptible [ˌɪmprəˈskrɪptəbəl] *adj Formal* imprescriptible

impress 1 *vt* [ɪmˈpres] (**a**) *(create impression on)* faire impression sur, impressionner; **I was favourably impressed by her appearance** son apparence m'a fait bonne impression; **I'm not in the least impressed** ça ne m'impressionne pas du tout; **he impressed the jury** il a fait une forte impression sur le jury; **I wasn't impressed by her friend** son ami ne m'a pas fait grande impression
(**b**) **to impress sth on sb** *(make understand)* faire comprendre qch à qn
(**c**) *(print)* imprimer, marquer; **the clay was impressed with a design, a design was impressed onto the clay** un motif était imprimé

imp–imp

dans l'argile; *Fig* **her words are impressed on my memory** ses paroles sont gravées dans ma mémoire

2 *n* ['ɪmpres] empreinte *f*

impression [ɪm'preʃən] *n* (**a**) *(impact → on person, mind, feelings)* impression *f*; **to make a good/bad impression (on)** faire bonne/mauvaise impression (sur); **he made a strong impression on them** il leur a fait une forte impression; **he always tries to make an impression** il essaie toujours d'impressionner les gens; **my words made no impression on him whatsoever** mes paroles n'ont eu absolument aucun effet sur lui; **they got a good impression of my brother** mon frère leur a fait bonne impression

(**b**) *(idea, thought)* impression *f*; **to create** *or* **give the impression that...** donner *ou* produire l'impression que...; **I don't know where she got that impression from** je ne sais pas où elle est allée chercher ça; **you should never trust first impressions** il ne faut pas se fier aux premières impressions; **it's my impression** *or* **I have the impression that she's rather annoyed with us** j'ai l'impression qu'elle est en colère contre nous; **what were your impressions of Tokyo?** quelles ont été vos impressions de Tokyo?; **I was under the impression that you were unable to come** j'étais persuadé que vous ne pouviez pas venir

(**c**) *(mark, imprint)* marque *f*, empreinte *f*; **to take an impression of sth** prendre l'empreinte *ou* l'impression de qch; **impression cylinder** cylindre *m* de rotative

(**d**) *(printing)* impression *f*; *(edition)* tirage *m*

(**e**) *(impersonation)* imitation *f*; **to do impressions** faire des imitations; **she does a very good impression of the Queen** elle imite très bien la reine

impressionability [ɪm,preʃənə'bɪlɪtɪ] *n* influençabilité *f*

impressionable [ɪm'preʃənəbəl] *adj* influençable; **he is at a very impressionable age** il est à l'âge où on se laisse facilement influencer

impressionism, Impressionism [ɪm'preʃənɪzəm] *n Art & Literature* impressionnisme *m*

impressionist [ɪm'preʃənɪst] **1** *n* (**a**) *(entertainer)* imitateur(trice) *m,f* (**b**) *Art & Literature* impressionniste *mf* **2** *adj Art & Literature* impressionniste

3 Impressionist *Art Literature* **1** *n* impressionniste *mf* **2** *adj* impressionniste

impressionistic [ɪm,preʃə'nɪstɪk] *adj (vague)* vague, imprécis

impressionistically [ɪm,preʃə'nɪstɪkəlɪ] *adv* (**a**) *(painted)* dans le genre impressionniste (**b**) *(express oneself)* selon ses impressions

impressive [ɪm'presɪv] *adj* impressionnant

impressively [ɪm'presɪvlɪ] *adv* remarquablement

impressiveness [ɪm'presɪvnɪs] *n* nature *f* impressionnante

imprest ['ɪmprest] *n Fin* avance *f*

►► ***impress account*** compte *m* d'avances (à montant fixe); ***imprest fund*** fonds *m* de caisse à montant fixe; ***imprest system*** comptabilité *f* de prévision

imprimatur [,ɪmprɪ'meɪtə(r)] *n* imprimatur *m inv*

imprint 1 *n* ['ɪmprɪnt] (**a**) *(mark)* empreinte *f*, marque *f*; **the imprint of a hand** l'empreinte *f* d'une main; *Fig* **the imprint of suffering on her face** les marques de la souffrance sur son visage; *Fig* **the war had left its imprint on all of us** la guerre nous avait tous marqués

(**b**) *Typ* adresse *f* bibliographique; **published under the Pentagon imprint** édité chez Pentagon

(**c**) *(design)* logo *m*

2 *vt* [ɪm'prɪnt] (**a**) *(print)* imprimer

(**b**) *(in sand, clay, mud)* imprimer; **to be imprinted in sth** être imprimé dans qch

(**c**) *Fig (fix)* implanter, graver; **her face was imprinted on my mind** son visage est resté gravé dans mon esprit

►► *Typ* ***imprint page*** page *f* portant l'adresse bibliographique

imprinting [ɪm'prɪntɪŋ] *n Zool* empreinte *f*

imprison [ɪm'prɪzən] *vt* (**a**) *(put in prison)* mettre en prison, incarcérer; **he has been imprisoned several times** il a fait plusieurs séjours en prison (**b**) *Fig (confine, restrain)* enfermer; **the hostages were imprisoned for five years** les otages ont été enfermés pendant cinq ans

imprisonment [ɪm'prɪzənmənt] *n* emprisonnement *m*; **to be sentenced to six months' imprisonment** être condamné à six mois de prison

improbability [ɪm,prɒbə'bɪlətɪ] (*pl* **improbabilities**) *n* (**a**) *(of event)* improbabilité *f* (**b**) *(of story)* invraisemblance *f*

improbable [ɪm'prɒbəbəl] *adj* (**a**) *(unlikely)* improbable; **I think it highly improbable that he ever came here** il me paraît fort peu probable qu'il soit jamais venu ici (**b**) *(hard to believe)* invraisemblable; **an improbable story** une histoire invraisemblable

improbably [ɪm'prɒbəblɪ] *adv* invraisemblablement; **he was wearing an improbably large hat** il portait un chapeau d'une grandeur invraisemblable

improbity [ɪm'prəʊbɪtɪ] *n Formal* improbité *f*

impromptu [ɪm'prɒmptju:] **1** *adj* impromptu, improvisé; **an impromptu speech** un discours improvisé

2 *adv* impromptu; **to speak impromptu** parler impromptu

3 *n* impromptu *m*

improper [ɪm'prɒpə(r)] *adj* (**a**) *(rude, shocking → words, action)* déplacé; **his behaviour was most improper** il a eu un comportement tout à fait déplacé; **to make improper suggestions (to sb)** faire des propositions malhonnêtes (à qn) (**b**) *(unsuitable)* peu convenable (**c**) *(dishonest)* malhonnête (**d**) *(incorrect → method, equipment)* inadapté, inadéquat

►► *Math* ***improper fraction*** expression *f* fractionnaire; ***improper practices*** pratiques *fpl* irrégulières

improperly [ɪm'prɒpəlɪ] *adv* (**a**) *(indecently)* de manière déplacée; **he behaved most improperly** il s'est comporté d'une manière tout à fait déplacée (**b**) *(unsuitably)* d'une façon convenable; **he was improperly dressed** il n'était pas habillé d'une façon convenable (**c**) *(dishonestly)* malhonnêtement (**d**) *(incorrectly)* incorrectement, de manière incorrecte

impropriety [ɪmprə'praɪətɪ] (*pl* **improprieties**) *n* (**a**) *(of behaviour)* inconvenance *f*; *(of language)* impropriété *f* (**b**) *(act, expression, gesture)* inconvenance *f*; **to commit an impropriety** commettre une inconvenance

improvable [ɪm'pru:vəbəl] *adj* perfectible

improve [ɪm'pru:v] **1** *vt* (**a**) *(make better → work, facilities, result)* améliorer; *(→ system, device)* perfectionner; *(→ wine, soil)* bonifier; **to improve one's chances** augmenter ses chances; **if you cut your hair it would improve your looks** tu serais mieux avec les cheveux plus courts; **a little basil will greatly improve the flavour** ce sera nettement meilleur avec un peu de basilic; **she's gone to Madrid to improve her Spanish** elle est allée à Madrid pour améliorer son espagnol

(**b**) *(increase → knowledge, productivity)* accroître, augmenter

(**c**) *(cultivate)* **to improve one's mind** se cultiver l'esprit; **reading improves the mind** on se cultive en lisant

2 *vi (get better)* s'améliorer; *(increase)* augmenter; *(make progress)* s'améliorer, faire des progrès; *(wine)* se bonifier; **her health is improving** son état (de santé) s'améliore; **business is improving** les affaires reprennent; **your maths has improved** vous avez fait des progrès en maths; **to improve with age/use** s'améliorer en vieillissant/à l'usage; *Formal* **he improves on acquaintance** il gagne à être connu

►**improve on, improve upon** *vt insep* (**a**) *(result, work)* améliorer; **it's difficult to see how the performance can be improved on** il semble difficile d'améliorer cette performance (**b**) *(offer)* **to improve on sb's offer** enchérir sur qn

improved [ɪm'pru:vd] *adj (gen)* amélioré; *(services)* amélioré, meilleur; *(offer, performance)* meilleur

improvement [ɪm'pru:vmənt] *n* (**a**) *(gen)* amélioration *f*; *(in person's work, performance)* progrès *m*; **what an improvement!** c'est nettement mieux!; **this is a great improvement on her previous work** c'est bien mieux que ce qu'elle faisait jusqu'à présent; **there has been some improvement** il y a un léger mieux; **there has been a slight improvement in his work** son travail s'est légèrement amélioré; **there is no improvement in the weather** le temps ne s'est pas arrangé; **her new boyfriend's a bit of an improvement** son nouveau petit ami est un peu mieux que le précédent/les précédents; **to show some improvement** *(in condition)* aller un peu mieux; *(in work)* faire quelques progrès; **there's room for improvement** ça pourrait être mieux

(**b**) *(in building, road etc)* rénovation *f*, aménagement *m*; **(home) improvements** travaux *mpl* de rénovation; **to carry out improvements** effectuer des travaux de rénovation; **motorway improvements** travaux *mpl* de réfection des autoroutes

►► *Br* ***improvement grant*** subvention *f* pour la rénovation d'une maison

improver [ɪm'pru:və(r)] *n* (**a**) *(reformer)* réformateur(trice) *m,f*; *(renovator)* rénovateur(trice) *m,f* (**b**) *(worker → in industry)* apprenti(e) *m,f*, élève *mf*; *(→ in millinery)* petite main *f*, petite *f*; *(→ in administration)* stagiaire *mf* (**d**) *Hist* **(dress) improver** *(bustle)* tournure *f*

improvidence [ɪm'prɒvɪdəns] *n Formal* (**a**) *(rashness)* imprévoyance *f* (**b**) *(carelessness with money)* prodigalité *f*

improvident [ɪm'prɒvɪdənt] *adj Formal* (**a**) *(rash → person)* imprévoyant; *(→ life)* insouciant (**b**) *(careless with money)* dépensier

improvidently [ɪm'prɒvɪdəntlɪ] *adv Formal* (**a**) *(rashly)* avec imprévoyance (**b**) *(with careless use of money)* dispendieusement

improving [ɪm'pru:vɪŋ] *adj (instructive → book)* édifiant; *(→ influence, environment)* bénéfique

improvisation [,ɪmprəvaɪ'zeɪʃən] *n* improvisation *f*

improvise ['ɪmprə,vaɪz] **1** *vt* improviser; **hastily improvised** sommairement organisé; **an improvised raft** un radeau de fortune; **an improvised speech** un discours improvisé *ou* impromptu; **they improvised bandages from bedsheets** ils ont fait des bandages de fortune avec des draps

2 *vi* improviser; **to improvise on the piano** improviser au piano; **you will have to improvise** *(make do)* il faudra que vous vous débrouilliez avec ce qu'il y a

improviser ['ɪmprə,vaɪzə(r)] *n* improvisateur(trice) *m,f*

imprudence [ɪm'pru:dəns] *n* imprudence *f*

imprudent [ɪm'pru:dənt] *adj* imprudent; **imprudent with money** imprudent dans ses dépenses; **she's rather imprudent in her choice of friends** elle choisit mal ses amis

imprudently [ɪm'pru:dəntlɪ] *adv* imprudemment

impudence ['ɪmpjʊdəns] *n* effronterie *f*, impudence *f*

impudent ['ɪmpjʊdənt] *adj* effronté, impudent; **he is impudent to his teachers** il est effronté avec ses professeurs

impudently ['ɪmpjʊdəntlɪ] *adv* effrontément, impudemment

impugn [ɪm'pju:n] *vt Formal (declaration)* contester; *(testimony)* récuser

impugnable [ɪm'pju:nəbəl] *adj Formal (declaration)* contestable; *(testimony)* récusable

impulse ['ɪmpʌls] *n* (**a**) *(desire, instinct)* impulsion *f*, besoin *m*, envie *f*; **I felt an irresistible impulse to hit him** j'ai éprouvé une irrésistible envie de le frapper; **a sudden impulse made me start running** instinctivement, j'ai commencé à courir; **to act on impulse** agir par impulsion; **I bought it on impulse** je l'ai acheté sur un coup de tête; **I'm sorry, I did it on impulse** je m'excuse, j'ai fait ça sans réfléchir; **on a sudden impulse, he kissed her** pris d'une envie irrésistible, il l'a embrassée

(**b**) *Formal (impetus)* impulsion *f*, poussée *f*; **government grants have given an impulse to trade** les subventions gouvernementales ont relancé les affaires

(**c**) *Elec & Physiol* impulsion *f*

(**d**) *Phys* impulsion *f*

►► *Mktg* ***impulse buy*** achat *m* d'impulsion; *Mktg* ***impulse buyer*** acheteur(euse) *m,f* impulsif(ive); *Mktg* ***impulse buying*** *(UNCOUNT)* achats *mpl* d'impulsion; *Mktg* ***impulse purchase*** achat *m* d'impulsion; *Mktg* ***impulse purchaser*** acheteur(euse) *m,f* impulsif(ive); *Mktg* ***impulse purchasing*** *(UNCOUNT)* achats *mpl* d'impulsion

impulsion [ɪm'pʌlʃən] *n* impulsion *f*

impulsive [ɪm'pʌlsɪv] *adj* (**a**) *(instinctive, spontaneous)* impulsif; *(thoughtless)* irréfléchi (**b**) *(force)* impulsif

impulsively [ɪm'pʌlsɪvlɪ] *adv* par *ou* sur impulsion, impulsivement; **he kissed her impulsively** pris d'une envie irrésistible, il l'embrassa; **I acted impulsively** j'ai agi par impulsion

impulsiveness [ɪm'pʌlsɪvnɪs] *n* caractère *m* impulsif

impunity [ɪm'pjuːnətɪ] *n Formal* impunité *f*; **to act with impunity** agir en toute impunité *ou* impunément

impure [ɪm'pjʊə(r)] *adj* (**a**) *(unclean → air, milk)* impur (**b**) *Literary (sinful → thought)* impur, mauvais; *(→ motive)* bas (**c**) *Archit (style)* bâtard

impurity [ɪm'pjʊərətɪ] *(pl* **impurities***)* *n* impureté *f*

imputability [ɪm,pjuːtə'bɪlɪtɪ] *n* imputabilité *f*

imputable [ɪm'pjuːtəbəl] *adj* imputable

imputation [,ɪmpjuː'teɪʃən] *n Formal* (**a**) *(attribution)* attribution *f* (**b**) *(accusation)* imputation *f*

impute [ɪm'pjuːt] *vt Formal* (**a**) *(attribute)* attribuer; **the blame must be imputed to them** la responsabilité leur en revient (**b**) *(accuse)* imputer

imputrescible [,ɪmpjuː'tresɪbəl] *adj* imputrescible

IMR [,aɪem'ɑː(r)] *n (abbr* **infant mortality rate***)* taux *m* de mortalité infantile

IMRO ['ɪmrəʊ] *n Br Formerly (abbr* **Investment Management Regulatory Organization***)* = organisme britannique contrôlant les activités de banques d'affaires et de gestionnaires de fonds de retraite

---

IN [ɪn]

dans	► **1A (a) – (e); B (c); C (d); D (a); F (a)**
à	► **1A (g); F (b)**
en	► **1A (h); B (a), (b); C (a), (b), (d); E (b); F (b)**
chez	► **1C (f)**
sur	► **1G (b)**
à l'intérieur	► **2A (a)**
à la mode	► **2E (b); 3 (a)**

1 *prep* **A.** (**a**) *(within a defined area or space)* dans; **in a box** dans une boîte; **what have you got in your pockets?** qu'est-ce que tu as dans tes poches?; **she was sitting in an armchair** elle était assise dans un fauteuil; **in the house** dans la maison; **in Catherine's house** chez Catherine; **they're playing in the garden/living room/street** ils jouent dans le jardin/le salon/la rue; **we live in a village** nous habitons un village; **he's still in bed/in the bath** il est encore au lit/dans son bain; **she shut herself up in her bedroom** elle s'est enfermée dans sa chambre; **the light's gone in the fridge** la lumière du réfrigérateur ne marche plus; *Law* **in camera** à huis clos

(**b**) [illegible] **she trailed her hand in the water** elle laissait traîner sa main dans l'eau; **there's a smell of spring in the air** ça sent le printemps; **we swam in the sea** nous nous sommes baignés dans la mer

(**c**) *(indicating movement)* dans; **put it in your pocket** mets-le dans ta poche; **throw the letter in the bin** jette la lettre à la poubelle; **we headed in the direction of the port** nous nous sommes dirigés vers le port

(**d**) *(contained by a part of the body)* dans; **he had a knife in his hand** il avait un couteau dans *ou* à la main; **she held her tight in her arms** elle la serrait dans ses bras; **with tears in his eyes** les larmes aux yeux

(**e**) *(on or behind a surface)* dans; **a hole in the wall** un trou dans le mur; **there were deep cuts in the surface** la surface était marquée de profondes entailles; **a reflection in the mirror** un reflet dans la glace; **how much is that jumper in the window?** combien coûte ce pull dans la vitrine?; **who's that man in the photo?** qui est cet homme sur la photo?

(**f**) *(in a specified institution)* **she's in hospital/in prison** elle est à l'hôpital/en prison; **he teaches in a language school** il enseigne dans une école de langues

(**g**) *(with geographical names)* **in Paris** à Paris; **in France** en France; **in Afghanistan** en Afghanistan; **in the States** aux États-Unis; **in Portugal** au Portugal; **in the Pacific** dans l'océan Pacifique; **in the Third World** dans les pays du tiers-monde

(**h**) *(wearing)* en; **he was in a suit** il était en costume; **she was still in her dressing gown** elle était encore en robe de chambre; **he always dresses in green** il s'habille toujours en vert; **who's that woman in the hat?** qui est la femme avec le *ou* au chapeau?; **in uniform/mourning** en uniforme/deuil

(**i**) *(covered by)* **sardines in tomato sauce** des sardines à la sauce tomate; **beef in a red wine sauce** bœuf mijoté dans une sauce au vin rouge; **fish in breadcrumbs** poisson pané; **we were up to our waists in mud** nous étions dans la boue jusqu'à la taille

B. (**a**) *(during a specified period of time)* en; **in 1992** en 1992; **in March** en mars, au mois de mars; **in the thirties** dans les années trente; **in (the) summer/autumn/winter** en été/automne/hiver; **in (the) spring** au printemps; **he doesn't work in the afternoon/morning** il ne travaille pas l'après-midi/le matin; **I'll come in the afternoon/morning** je viendrai l'après-midi/le matin; **at 5 o'clock in the afternoon/morning** à 5 heures de l'après-midi/du matin; **in the future** à l'avenir; **in the past** autrefois

(**b**) *(within a specified period of time)* en; **he cooked the meal in ten minutes** il prépara le repas en dix minutes

(**c**) *(after a specified period of time)* dans; **I'll be back in five minutes** je reviens dans cinq minutes, j'en ai pour cinq minutes

(**d**) *(indicating a long period of time)* **we haven't had a proper talk in ages** nous n'avons pas eu de véritable conversation depuis très longtemps; **I hadn't seen her in years** ça faisait des années que je ne l'avais pas vue

(**e**) *(during a specified temporary situation)* **in my absence** en *ou* pendant mon absence; **in the ensuing chaos** dans la confusion qui s'ensuivit

C. (**a**) *(indicating arrangement, shape)* en; **in five rows/parts** en cinq rangées/parties; **stand in a circle** mettez-vous en cercle; **line up in twos** mettez-vous par deux; **cut the cake in three/in half** coupe le gâteau en trois/en deux; **she had her hair up in a ponytail** ses cheveux étaient relevés en queue de cheval

(**b**) *(indicating form, method)* **in cash** en liquide; **in writing** par écrit; **in English/French** en anglais/français; **written in ink** écrit à l'encre; **do you have these shoes in a 5?** est-ce que vous auriez ces chaussures en 38?; **have you got this jacket in a large?** est-ce que vous auriez cette veste dans une taille plus grande?; **does it come in red?** est-ce que ça existe *ou* est-ce que ça se fait en rouge?

(**c**) *(indicating state of mind)* **she's in a bit of a state** elle est dans tous ses états; **to be in love** [illegible] **don't keep us in suspense** ne nous tiens pas en haleine plus longtemps; **he watched in wonderment** il regardait avec émerveillement

(**d**) *(indicating state, situation)* dans, en; **in the present circumstances** dans les circonstances actuelles; **in the dark** dans l'obscurité; **in this weather** par *ou* avec ce temps; **in the sun** au soleil; **in the rain/snow** sous la pluie/neige; **in danger/silence** en danger/silence; **in my presence** en ma présence; **she's got her leg in plaster** elle a une jambe plâtrée *ou* dans le plâtre

(**e**) *(referring to plants and animals)* **in blossom** en fleur *ou* fleurs; **in pup/calf/cub** plein; *Am* **in heat** en chaleur

(**f**) *(among)* chez; **a disease common in five-year-olds** une maladie très répandue chez les enfants de cinq ans; **the sense of smell is more developed in dogs** l'odorat est plus développé chez les chiens

D. (**a**) *(forming part of)* dans; **in chapter six** dans le chapitre six; **we were standing in a queue** nous faisions la queue; **she's appearing in his new play/film** elle joue dans sa nouvelle pièce/son nouveau film; **he has two Picassos in his collection** il a deux Picasso dans sa collection; **this is a common theme in Shakespeare's work** c'est un thème fréquent dans les œuvres de Shakespeare; **the best player in the team** le meilleur joueur de l'équipe; **how many feet are there in a metre?** combien de pieds y a-t-il dans un mètre?; **service is included in the price** le service est inclus dans le prix

(**b**) *(indicating a personality trait)* **she hasn't got it in her to be nasty** elle est bien incapable de méchanceté; **I didn't think she had it in her** je ne l'en croyais pas capable; **it's the Irish in me** c'est mon côté irlandais

(**c**) *(indicating feelings about a person or thing)* **she has no confidence in him** elle n'a aucune confiance en lui; **they showed no interest in my work** mon travail n'a pas eu l'air de les intéresser le moins du monde

(**d**) *(according to)* **in my opinion** *or* **view** à mon avis

E. (**a**) *(indicating purpose, cause)* **he charged the door in an effort to get free** dans un effort pour se libérer, il donna un grand coup dans la porte; **in reply** *or* **response to your letter...** en réponse à votre lettre...; **there's no point in complaining** il est inutile de *ou* ça ne sert à rien de se plaindre

(**b**) *(as a result of)* en; **in doing so, you only encourage him** en faisant cela, vous ne faites que l'encourager; **in attempting to save her son's life, she almost died** en essayant de sauver son fils, elle a failli mourir

(**c**) *(as regards)* **it's five feet in length** ça fait cinq pieds de long; **the town has grown considerably in size** la ville s'est beaucoup agrandie; **a change in direction** un changement de direction; **he's behind in maths** il ne suit pas en maths; **spinach is rich in iron** les épinards sont riches en fer; **we've found the ideal candidate in Richard** nous avons trouvé en Richard le candidat idéal

(**d**) *(indicating source of discomfort)* **I've got a pain in my arm** j'ai une douleur au *ou* dans le bras

F. (**a**) *(indicating specified field, sphere of activity)* dans; **to be in the army/navy** être dans l'armée/la marine; **she's in advertising** elle est dans la publicité; **an expert in economics** un expert en économie politique; **he's in business with his sister** il dirige une entreprise avec sa sœur; **there have been tremendous advances in the treatment of cancer** de grands progrès ont été faits dans le traitement du cancer; **a degree in Italian** une licence d'italien

(**b**) *(indicating activity engaged in)* **our days were spent in swimming and sailing** nous passions nos journées à nager et à faire de la voile; **they spent hours (engaged) in complex negotiations** ils ont passé des heures en négociations difficiles; **you took your time in getting here!** tu en as mis du temps à venir!

G. (**a**) *(indicating approximate number, amount)* **people arrived in droves/in dribs and drabs** les gens sont arrivés en foule/par petits groupes; **they came in their thousands** ils sont venus par milliers; **he's in his forties** il a la quarantaine; **the temperature was in the nineties** la température était dans les trente degrés

(**b**) *(in ratios)* sur; **one child in three** un enfant sur trois; **a one-in-five hill** une pente de 20 pour cent; **once in ten years** une fois tous les dix ans

2 *adv* **A.** (**a**) *(into an enclosed space)* à l'intérieur, dedans; **she opened the door and looked in** elle ouvrit la porte et regarda à l'intérieur; **he jumped in** il sauta dedans

(**b**) *(indicating movement from outside to inside)* **breathe in then out** inspirez puis expirez; **we can't take in any more refugees** nous ne pouvons pas accueillir plus de réfugiés; **she's been in and out of mental hospitals all her life** elle a passé presque toute sa vie dans des hôpitaux psychiatriques; **she and I were always in and out of each other's houses** nous étions tout le temps fourrées l'une chez l'autre

(**c**) *(at home or place of work)* **is your wife/the boss in?** est-ce que votre femme/le patron est là?; **it's nice to spend an evening in** c'est agréable de passer une soirée chez soi; **to eat/to stay in** manger/rester à la maison; **we've got the builders in** nous avons des ouvriers à la maison; **he usually comes in about 10 o'clock** en général, il est là vers 10 heures; *Fam* **what's he in for?** *(in prison)* pourquoi est-ce qu'il fait de la tôle?; *(in hospital)* pourquoi est-ce qu'il est à l'hôpital?

B. (**a**) *(indicating entry)* **to go in** entrer; **come in!** entrez!; **to saunter/to run in** entrer d'un pas nonchalant/en courant; **in we go!** on y va!

(**b**) *(indicating arrival)* **the bus isn't in yet** le bus n'est pas encore arrivé; **what time does your train get in?** quand est-ce que votre train arrive?

(**c**) *(towards the centre)* **the walls fell in** les murs se sont écroulés; **the edges bend in** le bord est recourbé

(**d**) *(towards the shore)* **the tide is in** la marée est haute

C. (**a**) *(indicating transmission)* **write in for further information** écrivez-nous pour plus de renseignements; **entries must be in by 1 May** les bulletins doivent nous parvenir avant le 1 mai; **offers of help poured in** les propositions d'aide sont arrivées en masse

(**b**) *(indicating participation, addition)* **to be in at the start/finish of sth** assister au début/à la fin de qch; **we asked if we could join in** nous avons demandé si nous pouvions participer; **stir in the sliced onions** ajouter les oignons en lamelles; **fill in the blanks** remplissez les espaces vides

D. (**a**) *Sport (within area of court)* **the ball was in** la balle était bonne

(**b**) *(in cricket)* à l'attaque; **the other side went in first** c'est l'autre équipe qui était d'abord à l'attaque

E. (**a**) *Pol (elected)* **he failed to get in at the last election** il n'a pas été élu aux dernières élections

(**b**) *(in fashion)* à la mode; **short skirts are coming back in** les jupes courtes reviennent à la mode

F. *(idioms)* **you're in for a bit of a disappointment** tu vas être déçu; **he's in for a surprise/shock** il va avoir une surprise/un choc; **we're in for a storm** nous aurons sûrement de l'orage; **they don't know what they're in for** ils ne savent pas ce qui les attend; **now he's really in for it** cette fois-ci, il va y avoir droit; **he's in on the secret** il est dans le secret; **he's in on it** il est dans le coup; **we were all in on the plot** on était tous au courant; **I wasn't in on that particular conversation** je n'étais pas là pendant cette conversation; *Fam* **to be in with sb** être en bons termes avec qn; **he's trying to get in with the boss** il essaie de se faire bien voir du patron

3 *adj Fam* (**a**) *(fashionable)* à la mode, branché; **that nightclub is very in** cette boîte est très à la mode; **it's the in place to go** c'est l'endroit branché du moment; **to be the in thing** être à la mode; **the in crowd** les gens dans le coup

(**b**) *(for a select few)* **it's an in joke** c'est une plaisanterie entre nous/elles/*etc*

4 *n Am Fam (influence)* **to have an in** avoir de l'influence; **he has an in with the senator** il a ses entrées chez le sénateur

5 ins *npl* **the ins and outs (of a situation)** les tenants et les aboutissants (d'une situation)

6 in all *adv* en tout; **there are 30 in all** il y en a 30 en tout

7 in between 1 *adv* (**a**) *(in intermediate position)* **a row of bushes with little clumps of flowers in between** une rangée d'arbustes séparés par des petites touffes de fleurs; **he's neither right nor left but somewhere in between** il n'est ni de droite ni de gauche mais quelque part entre les deux; **she either plays very well or very badly, never in between** elle joue très bien ou très mal, jamais entre les deux

(**b**) *(in time)* entretemps, dans l'intervalle **2** *prep* entre

8 in itself *adv* en soi; **the town is not in itself beautiful but it has style** la ville n'est pas belle en soi mais elle a de l'allure; **this was in itself an achievement** c'était déjà un exploit en soi

9 in that *conj* puisque; **I'm not badly off in that I have a job and a flat but...** je ne peux pas me plaindre puisque j'ai un emploi et un appartement mais...; **we are lucky in that there are only a few of us** nous avons de la chance d'être si peu nombreux

►► *Comput* **in box** *(for e-mail)* boîte *f* de réception, corbeille *f* d'arrivée

---

-in [ɪn] *suff* = exprime l'aspect collectif d'une activité; **love-in** célébration *f* de l'amour en commun

in. (*written abbr* **inch(es)**) inch *m*, pouce *m*

inability [ˌɪnəˈbɪlətɪ] (*pl* **inabilities**) *n* incapacité *f*; **our inability to help them** notre incapacité à les aider

in absentia [ˌɪnæbˈsentɪə] *adv* in absentia; *Law* par contumace

inaccessibility [ˌɪnəkˌsesɪˈbɪlətɪ] *n* inaccessibilité *f*

inaccessible [ˌɪnəkˈsesəbəl] *adj* (**a**) *(impossible to reach)* inaccessible; **the inaccessible parts of Antarctica** les régions inaccessibles de l'Antarctique; **the village is inaccessible by car** le village n'est pas accessible en voiture (**b**) *(unavailable → person)* inaccessible, inabordable; *(→ information)* inaccessible (**c**) *(obscure → film, book, music)* inaccessible incompréhensible

inaccuracy [ɪnˈækjʊrəsɪ] (*pl* **inaccuracies**) *n (of calculation, information, figures)* inexactitude *f*; *(of word, expression, term)* inexactitude *f*, impropriété *f*; *(of report, account)* inexactitude *f*, manque *m* de précision; *(of translation)* inexactitude *f*, infidélité *f*

inaccurate [ɪnˈækjʊrət] *adj (incorrect → translation, calculation, information, figures)* inexact; *(→ word, expression, term)* impropre; *(→ result)* erroné; *(→ description)* inexact; *(→ report, account)* erroné

inaccurately [ɪnˈækjʊrətlɪ] *adv* inexactement; **the events have been inaccurately reported** les événements ont été présentés de façon inexacte

inaction [ɪnˈækʃən] *n* inaction *f*

inactivate [ɪnˈæktɪveɪt] *vt* désactiver

inactivation [ɪnˌæktɪˈveɪʃən] *n* désactivation *f*

inactive [ɪnˈæktɪv] *adj* (**a**) *(person, animal → resting)* inactif, peu actif; *(→ not working)* inactif (**b**) *(lazy)* paresseux, oisif (**c**) *(inoperative → machine)* au repos, à l'arrêt (**d**) *(dormant → volcano)* qui n'est pas en activité; *(→ disease, virus)* inactif (**e**) *Fin (money, bank account)* inactif (**f**) *Chem & Phys* inerte

inactivity [ˌɪnækˈtɪvətɪ] *n* inactivité *f*, inaction *f*

inadaptability [ɪnəˌdæptəˈbɪlɪtɪ], **inadaptation** [ɪnˌædæpˈteɪʃən] *n* incapacité *f* de s'adapter (**to** à); **inadaptability of the soil** incapacité *f ou* impropriété *f* du sol à la culture

inadequacy [ɪnˈædɪkwəsɪ] (*pl* **inadequacies**) *n* (**a**) *(insufficiency → of resources, facilities)* insuffisance *f* (**b**) *(social)* incapacité *f*, inadaptation *f*; *(sexual)* impuissance *f*, incapacité *f*; **feelings of inadequacy** un sentiment d'impuissance (**c**) *(failing)* défaut *m*, faiblesse *f*

inadequate [ɪnˈædɪkwət] *adj* (**a**) *(insufficient)* insuffisant; **our resources are inadequate to meet our needs** nos ressources ne correspondent pas à nos besoins

(**b**) *(unsatisfactory)* médiocre; **his performance in the test was inadequate** il n'a pas bien réussi son examen; **their response to the problem was inadequate** ils n'ont pas su trouver de réponse satisfaisante au problème; **that is an inadequate explanation of his behaviour** cela ne suffit pas à justifier son comportement

(**c**) *(unsuitable → equipment)* inadéquat; **our machinery is inadequate for this type of work** notre outillage n'est pas adapté à ce genre de travail

(**d**) *(incapable)* incapable; *(sexually)* impuissant; **he's hopelessly inadequate for the job** il n'est vraiment pas fait pour ce travail; **being unemployed often makes people feel inadequate** les gens au chômage se sentent souvent inutiles; **he's socially inadequate** c'est un inadapté

inadequately [ɪnˈædɪkwətlɪ] *adv* de manière inadéquate; *(fund, invest)* insuffisamment; **they were inadequately equipped for climbing a mountain** ils n'avaient pas l'équipement adéquat pour faire une ascension; **the vehicle was felt to perform inadequately on rough terrain** la performance du véhicule sur terrain accidenté a été jugée insuffisante

inadmissibility [ˌɪnədˌmɪsɪˈbɪlɪtɪ] *n* inadmissibilité *f*, caractère *m* inacceptable; *Law* irrecevabilité *f*

inadmissible [ˌɪnədˈmɪsɪbəl] *adj* inadmissible, inacceptable

►► *Law* ***inadmissible evidence*** témoignage *m* irrecevable

inadvertence [ˌɪnədˈvɜːtəns] *n* manque *m* d'attention, étourderie *f*, inadvertance *f*; **by inadvertence** par mégarde *ou* inadvertance

inadvertent [ˌɪnədˈvɜːtənt] *adj* accidentel, involontaire

inadvertently [ˌɪnədˈvɜːtəntlɪ] *adv* par mégarde *ou* inadvertance

inadvisability [ˈɪnədˌvaɪzəˈbɪlətɪ] *n* inopportunité *f*

inadvisable [ˌɪnədˈvaɪzəbəl] *adj* déconseillé; **this plan is inadvisable** ce projet est à déconseiller; **it's inadvisable to invest all your money in one place** il est déconseillé d'investir tout son argent dans une seule entreprise

inalienability [ɪnˌeɪljənəˈbɪlɪtɪ] *n Law* inaliénabilité *f*

inalienable [ɪnˈeɪljənəbəl] *adj Law* inaliénable

►► ***inalienable right*** droit *m* inaliénable

inalienableness [ɪnˈeɪljənəbəlnɪs] *n Law* inaliénabilité *f*

inalienably [ɪnˈeɪljənəblɪ] *adv Law* inaliénablement

inalterability [ɪnˌɔːltərəˈbɪlɪtɪ] *n* immutabilité *f*; *(of colour, photo etc)* inaltérabilité *f*

inalterable [ɪnˈɔːltərəbəl] *adj* immuable; *(colour, photo etc)* inaltérable

inamorata [ɪnˌæməˈrɑːtə] *n Literary or Hum* amoureuse *f*

inamorato [ɪnˌæməˈrɑːtəʊ] *n Literary or Hum* amoureux *m*

inane [ɪˈneɪn] *adj (person)* idiot, imbécile; *(behaviour)* stupide, inepte; *(remark)* idiot, stupide, inepte

inanely [ɪˈneɪnlɪ] *adv* de façon idiote *ou* stupide *ou* inepte

inanimate [ɪnˈænɪmət] *adj* inanimé

inanition [ˌɪnəˈnɪʃən] *n* (**a**) *(debility)* = faiblesse due à une alimentation insuffisante (**b**) *(lethargy)* léthargie *f*, torpeur *f*

inanity [ɪˈnænətɪ] (*pl* **inanities**) *n* (**a**) *(stupidity)* stupidité *f* (**b**) *(stupid remark)* ineptie *f*, bêtise *f*

inappetence [ɪnˈæpɪtəns] *n Med* inappétence *f*, manque *m* d'appétit

inapplicability [ˌɪnəˌplɪkəˈbɪlɪtɪ] *n* inapplicabilité *f* (**to** à)

inapplicable [ˌɪnəˈplɪkəbəl] *adj* inapplicable (**to** à); **the rule is inapplicable to this case** dans ce cas, la règle ne s'applique pas

inapposite [ɪnˈæpəzɪt] *adj* inopportun, inapproprié

inappropriate [ˌɪnəˈprəʊprɪət] *adj (action, remark)* inopportun, mal à propos; *(behaviour, joke)* déplacé; *(time, moment)* inopportun; *(clothing, equipment)* peu approprié, inadéquat; *(name)* mal choisi; **you've come at an inappropriate time** vous arrivez au mauvais moment, vous tombez mal; **principles which are inappropriate to modern life** des principes qui ne sont pas adaptés à la vie moderne

inappropriately [ˌɪnəˈprəʊprɪətlɪ] *adv* de manière peu convenable *ou* appropriée; **she was inappropriately dressed** elle n'était pas vêtue pour la circonstance

inappropriateness [ˌɪnəˈprəʊprɪətnɪs] *n* manque *m* d'à-propos; **the inappropriateness of the way she was dressed** l'inconvenance *f* de sa tenue

inapt [ɪnˈæpt] *adj* (**a**) *(unsuitable → remark)* mal choisi; *(→ behaviour)* peu convenable (**b**) *(incapable)* inapte, incapable

inaptitude [ɪnˈæptɪtjuːd] *n* (**a**) *(unsuitability → of remark)* manque *m* d'à-propos; *(→ of behaviour)* inconvenance *f* (**b**) *(incapability)* incapacité *f*, inaptitude *f*

inaptly [ɪnˈæptlɪ] *adv* (**a**) *(unsuitably → remark)* mal à-propos; *(behave)* de façon peu convenable; **inaptly described** mal décrit (**b**) *(incapably)* avec incompétence

inarticulate [ˌɪnɑːˈtɪkjʊlət] *adj* (**a**) *(person)* qui bredouille; **an inarticulate old man** un vieil homme qui a du mal à s'exprimer; **to be inarticulate with fear/rage** bégayer de peur/de rage; **his inarticulate suffering** la souffrance qu'il ne pouvait exprimer (**b**) *(words, sounds)* indistinct; **inarticulate expressions of love** des mots d'amour bredouillés (**c**) *Anat & Biol* inarticulé

inarticulated [ˌɪnɑːˈtɪkjʊleɪtɪd] *adj* (**a**) *(words, sounds)* indistinct (**b**) *Anat & Biol* inarticulé

inarticulately [ˌɪnɑːˈtɪkjʊlətlɪ] *adv (express oneself)* de manière confuse *ou* peu claire; *(mumble)* de façon indistincte, indistinctement

inarticulateness [ˌɪnɑːˈtɪkjʊlətnɪs] *n* (**a**) *(of person)* manque *m* d'aisance dans l'expression (**b**) *(of words, sounds)* caractère *m* indistinct

inartistic [ˌɪnɑːˈtɪstɪk] *adj* (**a**) *(painting, drawing etc)* dénué de toute valeur artistique (**b**) *(person → lacking artistic taste)* sans goût artistique; *(→ unskilled)* sans talent

inasmuch as [ˌɪnəzˈmʌtʃ-] *conj Formal (given that)* étant donné que, vu que; *(insofar as)* dans la mesure où

inattention [ˌɪnəˈtenʃən] *n* manque *m* d'attention, inattention *f*; **your essay shows inattention to detail** il y a beaucoup d'erreurs de détail dans votre travail

inattentive [ˌɪnəˈtentɪv] *adj* (**a**) *(paying no attention)* inattentif (**b**) *(neglectful)* peu attentionné, négligent; **to be inattentive towards sb** être peu attentionné envers qn, négliger qn

inattentively [ˌɪnəˈtentɪvlɪ] *adv* (**a**) *(without paying attention)* sans prêter *ou* faire attention (**b**) *(neglectfully)* négligemment

inattentiveness [ˌɪnəˈtentɪvnɪs] *n* (**a**) *(lack of attention)* manque *m* d'attention, inattention *f* (**b**) *(neglectfulness)* négligence *f*

inaudibility [ɪˌnɔːdɪˈbɪlɪtɪ] *n (of sound, voice)* caractère *m* inaudible; **the inaudibility of a speaker** l'incapacité *f* d'un orateur à se faire entendre

inaudible [ɪˈnɔːdɪbəl] *adj* inaudible; **she spoke in an almost inaudible whisper** elle s'exprimait de façon presque inaudible

inaudibly [ɪˈnɔːdɪblɪ] *adv* indistinctement; **"yes", she answered inaudibly** "oui", répondit-elle d'une voix inaudible

inaugural [ɪˈnɔːgjʊrəl] **1** *adj* inaugural, d'inauguration

2 *n Am* discours *m* inaugural *(d'un président des États-Unis)*

inaugurate [ɪˈnɔːgjʊreɪt] *vt* (**a**) *(open ceremoniously → building)* inaugurer; *(→ conference, exhibition)* ouvrir (**b**) *(commence formally)* inaugurer; **to inaugurate a new policy** instaurer *ou* inaugurer une nouvelle politique (**c**) *(herald → new era)* inaugurer; *(→ new system, tradition etc)* instaurer (**d**) *(instate → official)* installer (dans ses fonctions), investir; *(→ king, bishop)* introniser

inauguration [ɪˌnɔːgjʊˈreɪʃən] *n* (**a**) *(of building)* inauguration *f*, cérémonie *f* d'ouverture (**b**) *(of policy, new era etc)* inauguration *f* (**c**) *(of official)* investiture *f*

►► ***Inauguration Day*** = jour de l'investiture du président des États-Unis (le 20 janvier)

inauspicious [ˌɪnɔːˈspɪʃəs] *adj* défavorable, peu propice; **things got off to an inauspicious start** les choses ont pris un mauvais départ; **an inauspicious event** un événement de mauvais augure *ou* de sinistre présage

inauspiciously [ˌɪnɔːˈspɪʃəslɪ] *adv* défavorablement; **to start inauspiciously** prendre un mauvais départ

inauspiciousness [ˌɪnɔːsˈpɪʃəsnɪs] *n* caractère *m* défavorable

inauthentic [ɪnɔːˈθentɪk] *adj* inauthentique

in-between **1** *n* **it's hard to find shoes to fit if you're an in-between** c'est difficile de trouver des chaussures quand on est entre deux pointures

2 *adj* intermédiaire

inboard [ˈɪnbɔːd] *adj*

►► *Naut* ***inboard motor*** en-bord *m inv*

inborn [ˌɪnˈbɔːn] *adj (characteristic, quality)* inné; *Med* congénital, héréditaire

inbound [ˈɪnbaʊnd] *adj (flight, passenger etc)* à l'arrivée

inbred [ˌɪnˈbred] *adj* (**a**) *(characteristic, quality)* inné; **their hatred of violence is inbred** leur horreur de la violence est innée (**b**) *Biol (trait)* acquis par sélection génétique; *(strain)* produit par le croisement d'individus consanguins; *(person)* de parents consanguins; *(family, group)* consanguin

inbreed [ˈɪnˈbriːd] *(pt & pp* **inbred** [-bred]) *vi* se reproduire entre eux

inbreeding [ˈɪnˈbriːdɪŋ] *n (of animals)* croisement *m*; **generations of inbreeding** *(of people)* des générations d'alliances consanguines

inbuilt [ˈɪnbɪlt] *adj* (**a**) *(device)* incorporé, intégré (**b**) *(quality, defect)* inhérent

Inc. *Am (written abbr* **incorporated**) ≃ SARL

inc. *(written abbr* **inclusive**) **12–15 April inc** du 12 au 15 avril inclus

Inca [ˈɪŋkə] *(pl* **inv** *or* **Incas**) *n* Inca *mf*

incalculability [ɪnˌkælkjʊləˈbɪlɪtɪ] *n* incalculabilité *f*

incalculable [ɪnˈkælkjʊləbəl] *adj* incalculable; *(loss, help)* inestimable

incalculably [ɪnˈkælkjʊləblɪ] *adv* de façon inestimable

incandescence [ˌɪnkænˈdesəns] *n* incandescence *f*

incandescent [ˌɪnkænˈdesənt] *adj* incandescent

►► ***incandescent lamp*** lampe *f* à incandescence

incantation [ˌɪnkænˈteɪʃən] *n* incantation *f*

incantatory [ˌɪnkænˈteɪtərɪ] *adj* incantatoire

incapability [ɪnˌkeɪpəˈbɪlətɪ] *n* incapacité *f*

incapable [ɪnˈkeɪpəbəl] *adj* (**a**) *(unable)* incapable; **to be incapable of doing sth** être incapable de faire qch; **he's incapable of showing emotion** il est incapable de montrer ce qu'il ressent; **she's incapable of such an act** elle est incapable de faire une chose pareille; **he's incapable of speech** il ne peut pas parler; *Literary* **feelings incapable of expression** des sentiments impossibles à exprimer

(**b**) *(incompetent)* incapable; *Law* **to be declared incapable** être déclaré incapable, être frappé d'incapacité juridique

incapacitant [ˌɪnkəˈpæsɪtənt] *n* incapacitant *m*

incapacitate [ˌɪnkəˈpæsɪteɪt] *vt* (**a**) *(cripple)* rendre infirme *ou* invalide; **he was temporarily incapacitated by the accident** à la suite de l'accident, il a été temporairement immobilisé (**b**) *Law* frapper d'incapacité légale

incapacitation [ˌɪnkəpæsɪˈteɪʃən] *n* (**a**) *(crippling)* **incapacitation for work** incapacité *f* de travail; **since his incapacitation** depuis qu'il est devenu infirme; **wounded soldiers who suffer permanent incapacitation** blessés *mpl* de guerre frappés d'invalidité (**b**) *Law* privation *f* de capacité légale

incapacity [ˌɪnkəˈpæsɪtɪ] *(pl* **incapacities**) *n* (**a**) *(lack of power, ability)* incapacité *f*; **his incapacity for work** son incapacité à travailler; **her incapacity to adapt** son incapacité à s'adapter (**b**) *Law* incapacité *f*

►► *Br Admin* ***incapacity benefit*** prestation *f* d'invalidité

in-car *adj*

►► *Aut* ***in-car listening*** écoute *f* de la radio en voiture; *Br* ***in-car stereo*** autoradio *f* (à cassette)

incarcerate [ɪnˈkɑːsəreɪt] *vt* incarcérer

incarcerated [ɪnˈkɑːsəreɪtɪd] *adj* (**a**) *(imprisoned)* incarcéré, en prison (**b**) *Arch Med (hernia)* incarcéré; **to become incarcerated** s'incarcérer

incarceration [ɪnˌkɑːsəˈreɪʃən] *n* incarcération *f*

incarnadine [ɪnˈkɑːnəˌdaɪn] *Literary* **1** *n* (**a**) *(flesh colour)* incarnadin *m*, incarnat *m* (**b**) *(blood-red)* rouge *m* sang

2 *adj* (**a**) *(flesh-coloured)* incarnadin, incarnat (**b**) *(blood-red)* rouge sang

incarnate [ɪnˈkɑːneɪt] *Literary* **1** *adj* (**a**) *(personified)* incarné; **the devil incarnate** le diable incarné; **he's stupidity incarnate** c'est la bêtise incarnée *ou* personnifiée (**b**) *(colour)* incarnat

2 *vt* incarner

incarnation [ˌɪnkɑːˈneɪʃən] **1** *n* incarnation *f*; **he's the very incarnation of humility** il est l'incarnation même de l'humilité, il est l'humilité incarnée; **in a previous incarnation** dans une vie antérieure; *Fam* **I must have known her in a previous incarnation** j'ai dû la connaître dans une vie antérieure

2 Incarnation *n Rel* **the Incarnation** l'Incarnation *f*

incautious [ɪnˈkɔːʃəs] *adj* imprudent

incautiously [ɪnˈkɔːʃəslɪ] *adv* imprudemment

incendiarism [ɪnˈsendjərɪzəm] *n* (**a**) *(arson)* incendie *m* volontaire *ou* criminel (**b**) *Pol* sédition *f*

incendiary [ɪnˈsendjərɪ] *(pl* **incendiaries**) **1** *n* (**a**) *(arsonist)* incendiaire *mf* (**b**) *(bomb)* bombe *f* incendiaire (**c**) *Fig (agitator)* fauteur *m* de troubles

2 *adj* (**a**) *(causing fires)* incendiaire (**b**) *(combustible)* inflammable (**c**) *Fig (speech, statement)* incendiaire, séditieux

►► ***incendiary bomb*** bombe *f* incendiaire; ***incendiary device*** dispositif *m* incendiaire

incense[1] [ˈɪnsens] **1** *n* encens *m*

2 *vt (perfume)* encenser

►► ***incense bearer*** thuriféraire *m*; ***incense burner*** encensoir *m*; ***incense stick*** bâtonnet *m* d'encens

incense[2] [ɪnˈsens] *vt (anger)* rendre furieux, excéder; **he was incensed by** *or* **at her indifference** son indifférence l'a rendu furieux; **I was absolutely incensed** j'étais hors de moi

incentive [ɪnˈsentɪv] **1** *n* (**a**) *(motivation)* motivation *f*; **they have lost their incentive** ils ne sont plus très motivés; **he has no incentive to work harder** rien ne le motive à travailler plus dur; **to give sb the incentive to do sth** motiver qn à faire qch

(**b**) *Fin & Ind* incitation *f*, encouragement *m*; *(payment)* prime *f*; *Mktg* stimulation *f*; *(reduction, free gift)* stimulant *m*; **the firm offers various incentives** la société offre diverses primes; **tax incentives** avantages *mpl* fiscaux

2 *comp* incitateur, incitatif

►► *Br* ***incentive bonus*** prime *f* de rendement *ou* d'encouragement; ***incentive marketing*** marketing *m* de stimulation; *Am* ***incentive plan,*** *Br* ***incentive scheme*** *(for buyers)* programme *m* de stimulation; *(for workers)* système *m* de primes

incentivize [ɪnˈsentɪvaɪz] *vt Am* motiver

incept [ɪnˈsept] **1** *vt* (**a**) *Biol (of cell, organism)* absorber (**b**) *Literary (undertake)* entreprendre

2 *vi Br Formerly Univ* = passer sa licence ou son doctorat à l'université de Cambridge

inception [ɪnˈsepʃən] *n* création *f*

inceptive [ɪnˈseptɪv] **1** *n Ling* inchoatif *m*

2 *adj* (**a**) *(beginning)* initial (**b**) *Ling* inchoatif

incertitude [ɪnˈsɜːtɪtjuːd] *n* incertitude *f*

incessant [ɪnˈsesənt] *adj* incessant

incessantly [ɪnˈsesəntlɪ] *adv* continuellement, sans cesse

incest [ˈɪnsest] *n* inceste *m*

incestuous [ɪnˈsestjʊəs] *adj* incestueux; *Fig* **publishing is a very incestuous business** le monde de l'édition est très fermé

incestuously [ɪnˈsestjʊəslɪ] *adv* incestueusement

incestuousness [ɪnˈsestjʊəsnɪs] *n* caractère *m* incestueux

inch [ɪntʃ] **1** *n* inch *m*, pouce *m*; **it's about 6 inches wide** ≃ cela fait à peu près 15 centimètres de large; **it's a few inches shorter** c'est plus court de quelques centimètres; **the car missed me by inches** la voiture m'a manqué de peu; **every inch of the wall was covered with posters** il n'y avait pas un centimètre carré du mur qui ne fût couvert d'affiches, le mur était entièrement couvert d'affiches; **give him an inch and he'll take a yard** *or* **a mile** on lui donne le doigt et il vous prend le bras; **inch by inch** petit à petit, peu à peu; *Fig* **we'll have to fight every inch of the way** nous ne sommes pas au bout de nos peines; **he's every inch a Frenchman** il est français jusqu'au bout des ongles; **the unions won't budge** *or* **give an inch** les syndicats ne céderont pas d'un pouce; **to beat sb to within an inch of their life** laisser qn pour mort; **to be within an inch of doing sth** être à deux doigts de faire qch

2 *vt* **to inch one's way in/out** entrer/sortir petit à petit; **he inched his way to the door** petit à petit, il s'approcha de la porte; **she inched the car forward slowly** elle fit avancer la voiture très lentement

3 *vi* **to inch in/out** entrer/sortir petit à petit; **he inched along the ledge** il avançait petit à petit le long du rebord

-inch [ɪntʃ] *suff* **a five-inch floppy disk** une disquette cinq pouces

inchoate [ɪnˈkəʊeɪt] *adj Formal (incipient)* naissant; *(unfinished)* inachevé

inchoative [ˈɪnkəʊeɪtɪv] *adj* (**a**) *Ling* inchoatif (**b**) *Formal (incipient)* naissant

inchtape [ˈɪntʃteɪp] *n Br* mètre *m* (de couturier), mètre-ruban *m*

inchworm [ˈɪntʃwɜːm] *n* arpenteuse *f*

incidence [ˈɪnsɪdəns] *n* (**a**) *(rate)* taux *m*; **there is a higher/lower incidence of crime** le taux de criminalité est plus élevé/plus faible; **the incidence of the disease in adults** la fréquence de la maladie chez les adultes (**b**) *Geom, Phys & Opt* incidence *f*; **angle/point of incidence** angle *m*/point *m* d'incidence

incident [ˈɪnsɪdənt] **1** *n* incident *m*; **the meeting went off without incident** la réunion s'est déroulée sans incident; **the match was full of incident** de nombreux incidents ont eu lieu pendant le match; **border** *or* **frontier incident** incident *m* de frontière; **diplomatic incident** incident *m* diplomatique

2 *adj* (**a**) *Formal* lié, attaché; **incident to** lié à (**b**) *Phys* incident

►► *Br* ***incident room*** *(in police station)* salle *f* des opérations

incidental [ˌɪnsɪˈdentəl] **1** *adj* (**a**) *(minor)* secondaire, accessoire; *(additional)* accessoire, supplémentaire; **the project will have other incidental benefits** ce projet aura encore d'autres avantages

(**b**) *(related)* **incidental to** en rapport avec, occasionné par; **the fatigue incidental to such work** la fatigue occasionnée par un tel travail

2 *n (chance happening)* événement *m* fortuit; *(minor detail)* détail *m* secondaire

3 incidentals *npl (expenses)* faux frais *mpl*

►► ***incidental costs, incidental expenses*** faux frais *mpl*; ***incidental music*** *(for film)* musique *f* de film; *(for play)* musique *f* de scène

incidentally [ˌɪnsɪˈdentəlɪ] *adv* (**a**) *(by chance)* incidemment, accessoirement (**b**) *(by the way)* à propos, au fait; **incidentally, I really need that money I lent you** à propos *ou* au fait, j'aurais vraiment besoin de l'argent que je t'ai prêté (**c**) *(additionally)* accessoirement

incinerate [ɪnˈsɪnəreɪt] *vt* incinérer

incineration [ɪnˌsɪnəˈreɪʃən] *n* incinération *f*

incinerator [ɪnˈsɪnəreɪtə(r)] *n* incinérateur *m*; *(in crematorium)* four *m* crématoire

incipience [ɪnˈsɪpɪəns], **incipiency** [ɪnˈsɪpɪənsɪ] *n* naissance *f*, début *m*

incipient [ɪnˈsɪpɪənt] *adj* naissant

incipit [ˈɪnsɪpɪt] *n Literature & Mus* incipit *m inv*

incise [ɪnˈsaɪz] *vt* (**a**) *Art* graver (**b**) *Med* inciser

incised [ɪnˈsaɪzd] *adj* (**a**) *Art* gravé (**b**) *Med* incisé (**c**) *Bot* découpé, incisé

incision [ɪnˈsɪʒən] *n* incision *f*; **to make an incision in sth** inciser qch, pratiquer une incision dans qch

incisive [ɪnˈsaɪsɪv] *adj (mind)* perspicace, pénétrant; *(wit, remark)* incisif

incisively [ɪnˈsaɪsɪvlɪ] *adv (think)* de façon incisive; *(ask, remark)* de manière perspicace *ou* pénétrante

incisiveness [ɪnˈsaɪsɪvnɪs] *n (of thought)* perspicacité *f*, acuité *f*; *(of remark, wit)* perspicacité *f*

incisor [ɪnˈsaɪzə(r)] *n* incisive *f*

incitation [ˌɪnsaɪˈteɪʃən] *n* (**a**) *(inciting)* incitation *f* (**to** à) (**b**) *(stimulus)* stimulant *m*, aiguillon *m*

incite [ɪnˈsaɪt] *vt* **to incite sb to do sth** inciter qn à faire qch; **to incite sb to violence** inciter qn à la violence; **they were accused of inciting racial hatred** on les accusa d'incitation à la haine raciale

incitement [ɪnˈsaɪtmənt] *n* incitation *f*; **incitement to riot/violence** incitation à la révolte/à la violence; *Law* **incitement to racial hatred** incitation *f* à la haine raciale

incivility [ˌɪnsɪˈvɪlətɪ] (*pl* **incivilities**) *n Formal* (**a**) *(rudeness)* impolitesse *f*, manque *m* de savoir-vivre, *Literary* incivilité *f* (**b**) *(act, remark)* impolitesse *f*, indélicatesse *f*

incl. (**a**) *(written abbr* **inclusive**) inclus; **from 14 to 23 November incl.** du 14 au 23 novembre inclus; **incl. of gas and electricity** gaz et électricité compris (**b**) *(written abbr* **including**) avec; **incl. VAT** TVA comprise; **350 francs incl. VAT** 350 FF TTC

in-clearing book *n Banking* livre *m* du dedans, registre *m* des chèques à rembourser

inclemency [ɪnˈklemənsɪ] *n Literary* rigueur *f*, inclémence *f*

inclement [ɪnˈklemənt] *adj Literary (weather)* inclément

inclinable [ɪnˈklaɪnəbəl] *adj* (**a**) *(person)* enclin (**to** à), porté (**to** sur); *(to somebody, a party)* favorable (**to** à) (**b**) *(table, stand etc)* inclinable

inclination [ˌɪnklɪˈneɪʃən] *n* (**a**) *(tendency)* disposition *f*, prédisposition *f*, tendance *f*; **a decided inclination towards laziness** une nette prédisposition à la paresse; **my inclination would be to say yes** je serais enclin à dire oui

(**b**) *(liking)* penchant *m*, inclination *f*; **she had no inclination to help him** elle n'avait pas du tout envie de l'aider; **to have lost all inclination for sth** n'avoir plus envie de qch; **to show little inclination to do sth** se montrer peu enclin à faire qch; **you should follow your own inclination in the matter** tu devrais suivre ta propre inclination; **I do it from necessity, not from inclination** je le fais par nécessité, pas par inclination *ou* par goût

(**c**) *(slant, lean)* inclinaison *f*; *(of body)* inclination *f*; **a slight inclination of the head** une légère inclination de la tête

(**d**) *(hill)* pente *f*, inclinaison *f*

(**e**) *Astron & Math* inclinaison *f*

incline 1 *vt* [ɪnˈklaɪn] (**a**) *(dispose)* disposer, pousser; **it's unlikely to incline them to work harder** il est peu probable que cela les pousse *ou* incite à travailler davantage; **his unhappy childhood inclined him towards cynicism** *or* **to be cynical** c'est à cause de son enfance malheureuse qu'il a tendance à être cynique

(**b**) *(lean, bend)* incliner; **to incline one's head** incliner la tête; *Literary* **to incline one's ear to sb** prêter l'oreille à qn

2 *vi* [ɪnˈklaɪn] (**a**) *(tend)* tendre, avoir tendance; **to incline to do sth** avoir tendance à faire qch; **he inclines towards exaggeration** il a tendance à exagérer, il exagère facilement

(**b**) *(lean, bend)* s'incliner

3 *n* [ˈɪnklaɪn] inclinaison *f*; *(slope)* pente *f*, déclivité *f*; *Rail* rampe *f*

inclined [ɪnˈklaɪnd] *adj* (**a**) *(tending, disposed* → *temporarily)* disposé (**to** à); *(*→ *permanently)* enclin (**to** à); **to feel** *or* **be inclined to do sth** *(tend to)* avoir tendance à faire qch; *(have desire to)* avoir envie de faire qch; **I'm inclined to agree** j'aurais tendance à être d'accord; **he's inclined to exaggeration** il a tendance à exagérer, il exagère facilement; **the drawers are inclined to stick** les tiroirs ont tendance à se coincer; **he's inclined to put on weight** il a tendance à grossir; **to be well inclined towards sb** être bien disposé envers qn; **if you are so inclined** si ça vous dit, si le cœur vous en dit; **I'm not musically inclined** *(don't like music)* je ne suis pas très porté sur la musique; *(have no talent)* je n'ai pas de talent musical; **if you're that way inclined** *(if you want to)* si cela vous dit; *Fam* **he's the other way inclined** *(in his sexual orientation)* il est de l'autre bord; *Fam* **I'm not that way inclined** je ne suis pas comme ça

(**b**) *(slanting, leaning)* incliné

►► ***inclined plane*** plan *m* incliné; *Am* ***inclined railway*** (chemin *m* de fer) funiculaire *m*

inclose = **enclose**

inclosure = **enclosure**

include [ɪnˈkluːd] *vt* comprendre, inclure; **each team includes eight forwards** chaque équipe comprend huit avants; **the price includes VAT** la TVA est comprise (dans le prix); **does that remark include me?** cette remarque vaut-elle aussi pour moi?; **don't forget to include the cheque** n'oubliez pas de joindre le chèque; **if you include Christmas Day** en comptant le jour de Noël; **to include sb among one's friends** compter qn parmi *ou* au nombre de ses amis; **my duties include sorting the mail** trier le courrier entre dans mes attributions *ou* fait partie de mon travail; **the children refused to include him in their games** les enfants ont refusé de l'inclure dans leurs jeux

►**include in** *vt sep Br Fam* **include me in!** comptez-moi aussi! ❑

►**include out** *vt sep Br Fam* **you can include me out** ne comptez pas sur moi ❑

included [ɪnˈkluːdɪd] *adj* **all his property was sold, his house included** tous ses biens furent vendus, y compris sa maison; **included in the price are two excursions** deux excursions sont comprises dans le prix; **myself included** y compris moi; **service not included** *(on bill, menu)* service non compris; **batteries not included** *(on packaging)* piles non fournies; **service charge included** *(on bill, menu)* service compris

including [ɪnˈkluːdɪŋ] *prep* (y) compris; **14 guests including the children** 14 invités y compris les enfants; **14 guests not including the children** 14 invités sans compter les enfants; **up to and including page 40** jusqu'à la page 40 incluse; **five books, including one I hadn't read** cinq livres, dont un que je n'avais pas lu

inclusion [ɪnˈkluːʒən] *n* inclusion *f*

inclusive [ɪnˈkluːsɪv] *adj* (**a**) *(including everything)* inclus, compris; *Fin* net; **inclusive of tax** taxes *fpl* comprises; **inclusive of all taxes** toutes taxes comprises; **from July to September inclusive** de juillet à septembre inclus; **inclusive prices** prix *mpl* nets; **inclusive of VAT** TVA comprise; **£200 inclusive of VAT** 200 livres TTC (**b**) *(list)* exhaustif; *(survey)* complet(ète), poussé (**c**) *Phil* inclusif; **inclusive or** ou *m* inclusif

inclusively [ɪnˈkluːsɪvlɪ] *adv* inclusivement

incognito [ˌɪnkɒgˈniːtəʊ] (*pl* **incognitos**) **1** *n* incognito *m*; **to travel under an incognito** voyager incognito

2 *adv* incognito; **to remain incognito** *(witness)* garder l'anonymat; *(star, politician)* garder l'incognito

incognizant [ɪnˈkɒgnɪzənt] *adj Formal* ignorant, inconscient; **incognizant of the danger** inconscient du danger

incoherence [ˌɪnkəʊˈhɪərəns] *n* incohérence *f*

incoherency [ˌɪnkəʊˈhɪərənsɪ] (*pl* **incoherencies**) *n* incohérence *f*

incoherent [ˌɪnkəʊˈhɪərənt] *adj (person, argument)* incohérent; *(thought)* incohérent, décousu

incoherently [ˌɪnkəʊˈhɪərəntlɪ] *adv* de manière incohérente; **to mutter incoherently** marmonner des paroles incohérentes

incohesive [ˌɪnkəʊˈhiːsɪv] *adj* incohésif, sans cohésion

incombustible [ˌɪnkəmˈbʌstəbəl] *adj* incombustible

income [ˈɪŋkʌm] *n* (**a**) *(of person)* revenu *m*; **a high/low income** un revenu élevé/faible; **to declare one's income** déclarer ses revenus; **their combined income** leurs revenus additionnés; **the income from her shares/investments** les revenus de ses actions/placements

(**b**) *(of company)* recettes *fpl*, revenus *mpl*, rentrées *fpl*; *Fin* **income and expenditure account** compte *m* de dépenses et recettes; *Acct* **income from operations** produits *mpl* de gestion courante, produits *mpl* d'exploitation

►► *Acct* ***income account*** compte *m* de produits; *Fin* ***income bond*** obligation *f* à intérêt conditionnel; ***income bracket*** tranche *f* de salaire *ou* de revenu; **most people in this area belong to the lower/higher income bracket** la plupart des habitants de ce quartier sont des économiquement faibles/ont des revenus élevés; ***income group*** tranche *f* de salaire *ou* de revenu; *Br* ***incomes policy*** politique *f* des revenus; ***income smoothing*** manipulations *fpl* de revenu; *Am Acct* ***income statement*** compte *m* de résultat; *Am St Exch* ***income stocks*** valeurs *fpl* de rendement; *Fin* ***income stream*** flux *m* de revenus; *Br* ***income support*** = prestation complémentaire en faveur des personnes justifiant de faibles revenus, ≃ revenu *m* minimum d'insertion; ***income tax*** impôt *m* sur le revenu (des personnes physiques); ***income tax allowance*** déduction *f* avant impôt, déduction *f* fiscale; **income tax is deducted at source** les impôts sont prélevés à la source; ***income tax inspector*** inspecteur *m* des contributions directes *ou* des impôts; ***income tax return*** déclaration *f* de revenus, feuille *f* d'impôt; *Fin* ***income velocity of***

capital vitesse *f* de circulation du capital en revenus; *Fin* ***income velocity of circulation*** vitesse *f* de circulation de la monnaie en revenus

incomer ['ɪnˌkʌmə(r)] *n* nouveau (nouvelle) venu(e) *m,f*

incoming ['ɪnˌkʌmɪŋ] **1** *adj* (**a**) *(in direction → flight, train, passengers)* à l'arrivée; *(→ tide)* montant

(**b**) *(telephone call)* de l'extérieur; *(fax)* en entrée; *(e-mail)* à l'arrivée; **this telephone takes incoming calls only** ce téléphone ne permet que de recevoir des appels; **please make a note of any incoming calls** veuillez noter tous les appels que vous recevez

(**c**) *(cash, interest)* qui rentre

(**d**) *(official, administration, tenant)* nouveau (nouvelle)

2 incomings *npl (revenue)* recettes *fpl*, revenus *mpl*; **incomings and outgoings** dépenses *fpl* et recettes *fpl*

►► ***incoming mail*** courrier *m* (du jour)

incommensurability [ˌɪnkəˌmenʃərə'bɪlɪtɪ] *n* incommensurabilité *f*

incommensurable [ˌɪnkə'menʃərəbəl] **1** *n Math* quantité *f* incommensurable

2 *adj (gen) & Math* incommensurable

incommensurate [ˌɪnkə'menʃərət] *adj Formal* (**a**) *(disproportionate)* disproportionné, inadéquat; **it is incommensurate with our needs** cela ne correspond pas à nos besoins (**b**) *(incommensurable)* incommensurable

incommode [ˌɪnkə'məʊd] *vt Formal* incommoder, indisposer

incommodious [ˌɪnkə'məʊdjəs] *adj Formal* (**a**) *(cramped)* exigu, étriqué (**b**) *(troublesome)* ennuyeux, fâcheux

incommunicability [ˌɪnkəˌmjuːnɪkə'bɪlɪtɪ] *n* incommunicabilité *f*

incommunicable [ˌɪnkə'mjuːnɪkəbəl] *adj* incommunicable, indicible

incommunicableness [ˌɪnkə'mjuːnɪkəbəlnɪs] *n* incommunicabilité *f*

incommunicado [ˌɪnkəmjuːnɪ'kɑːdəʊ] *adj & adv* sans communication avec le monde extérieur; **the prisoners are being kept** *or* **held incommunicado** les prisonniers sont (gardés) au secret; *Fig* **I'll be incommunicado for a month while I'm on holiday** je serai injoignable pendant un mois quand je partirai en vacances

in-company *adj Br* **in-company training** formation *f* sur le lieu de travail; **in-company training scheme** stage *m* organisé par la société; **in-company cafeteria** cantine *f* de la société

incomparable [ɪn'kɒmpərəbəl] *adj* incomparable

incomparably [ɪn'kɒmpərəblɪ] *adv* incomparablement, infiniment

incompatibility ['ɪnkəmˌpætə'bɪlətɪ] *n* incompatibilité *f*; *(grounds for divorce)* incompatibilité *f* d'humeur

incompatible [ˌɪnkəm'pætɪbəl] *adj* incompatible

incompetence [ɪn'kɒmpɪtəns], **incompetency** [ɪn'kɒmpɪtənsɪ] *n* incompétence *f*

incompetent [ɪn'kɒmpɪtənt] **1** *adj* (**a**) *(lacking skill, ability)* incompétent (**b**) *Law (judge, court)* incompétent

2 *n* incompétent(e) *m,f*, incapable *mf*

incompetently [ɪn'kɒmpɪtəntlɪ] *adv* incompétemment, sans compétence

incomplete [ˌɪnkəm'pliːt] *adj* (**a**) *(unfinished)* inachevé (**b**) *(lacking something)* incomplet(ète) (**c**) *(in logic)* incomplet(ète)

incompletely [ˌɪnkəm'pliːtlɪ] *adv* incomplètement; **her plan was incompletely thought out** son projet était incomplètement préparé

incompleteness [ˌɪnkəm'pliːtnɪs], **incompletion** [ˌɪnkəm'pliːʃən] *n* (**a**) *(unfinished nature)* inachèvement *m*; **there's a feeling of incompleteness about his paintings** ses tableaux donnent l'impression de ne pas être finis *ou* achevés (**b**) *(lacking something)* caractère *m* incomplet (**c**) *(in logic)* incomplétude *f*

incomprehensibility [ˌɪnkɒmprɪˌhensə'bɪlɪtɪ] *n* incompréhensibilité *f*

incomprehensible [ˌɪnkɒmprɪ'hensəbəl] *adj* incompréhensible

incomprehensibleness [ˌɪnkɒmprɪ'hensəbəlnɪs] *n* incompréhensibilité *f*

incomprehensibly [ˌɪnkɒmprɪ'hensəblɪ] *adv* incompréhensiblement, de manière incompréhensible; **they were incomprehensibly absent** chose incompréhensible, ils étaient absents

incomprehension [ˌɪnkɒmprɪ'henʃən] *n* incompréhension *f*

inconceivable [ˌɪnkən'siːvəbəl] *adj* inconcevable, inimaginable

inconceivably [ˌɪnkən'siːvəblɪ] *adv* incroyablement; **inconceivably rich** incroyablement riche

inconclusive [ˌɪnkən'kluːsɪv] *adj* peu concluant; **the results are inconclusive** les résultats sont peu concluants; **inconclusive data** données *fpl* peu probantes; **the talks have been inconclusive** les pourparlers n'ont pas abouti

inconclusively [ˌɪnkən'kluːsɪvlɪ] *adv* de manière peu concluante; **the meeting ended inconclusively** la réunion n'a abouti à aucune conclusion

inconclusiveness [ˌɪnkən'kluːsɪvnɪs] *n* caractère *m* peu concluant

incongruent [ɪn'kɒŋgrʊənt] *Formal* = **incongruous**

incongruity [ˌɪnkɒŋ'gruːətɪ] (*pl* **incongruities**) *n* (**a**) *(strangeness, discordancy)* incongruité *f* (**b**) *(disparity)* disparité *f*; **their statements were full of incongruities** leurs témoignages contenaient un grand nombre d'incohérences

incongruous [ɪn'kɒŋgrʊəs] *adj (strange, discordant)* incongru; *(disparate)* incohérent; **he was an incongruous figure among the factory workers** on le remarquait tout de suite au milieu des ouvriers de l'usine; **they are such an incongruous couple** ils sont tellement bizarrement assortis

incongruously [ɪn'kɒŋgrʊəslɪ] *adv* de manière incongrue, incongrûment

inconsequence [ɪn'kɒnsɪkwəns] *n* inconséquence *f*

inconsequent [ɪn'kɒnsɪkwənt], **inconsequential** [ˌɪnkɒnsɪ'kwenʃəl] *adj* (**a**) *(unimportant → matter, remarks)* sans importance; **an inconsequential detail** un détail insignifiant; **an inconsequential little man** un bonhomme sans importance (**b**) *(not following logically → reasoning, ideas)* décousu

inconsequentiality [ˌɪnkɒnsɪkwenʃɪ'ælɪtɪ] *n* (**a**) *(lack of importance)* insignifiance *f* (**b**) *(lack of logical sequence)* inconséquence *f*

inconsequentially [ˌɪnkɒnsɪ'kwenʃəlɪ], **inconsequently** [ɪn'kɒnsɪkwəntlɪ] *adv* (**a**) *(unimportantly)* de façon insignifiante (**b**) *(illogically)* de façon inconséquente

inconsiderable [ˌɪnkən'sɪdərəbəl] *adj* insignifiant, négligeable; **a not inconsiderable amount of money** une somme d'argent non négligeable

inconsiderate [ˌɪnkən'sɪdərət] *adj (person)* qui manque de prévenance; *(action, remark)* irréfléchi; **he's inconsiderate of other people's feelings** peu lui importe ce que pensent les autres; **that was very inconsiderate of you** vous avez agi sans aucun égard pour les autres; **to be inconsiderate towards sb** manquer d'égards envers qn; **don't be so inconsiderate** pense un peu aux autres

inconsiderately [ˌɪnkən'sɪdərətlɪ] *adv* sans aucune considération

inconsiderateness [ˌɪnkən'sɪdərətnɪs], **inconsideration** [ˌɪnkənˌsɪdə'reɪʃən] *n* manque *m* d'égards

inconsistency [ˌɪnkən'sɪstənsɪ] (*pl* **inconsistencies**) *n* (**a**) *(incoherence)* manque *m* de cohérence, incohérence *f* (**b**) *(contradiction)* contradiction *f*; **there are several inconsistencies in your argument** votre argumentation présente *ou* laisse apparaître plusieurs contradictions

inconsistent [ˌɪnkən'sɪstənt] *adj* (**a**) *(person)* incohérent *(dans ses comportements)*; **you're being inconsistent** *(in saying that)* tu te contredis; *(in doing that)* tu n'es pas cohérent; **they're inconsistent in what they say** leurs dires sont contradictoires

(**b**) *(performance)* inégal; *(work)* irrégulier; **his films are very inconsistent in quality** la qualité de ses films est très irrégulière

(**c**) *(reasoning, argument)* incohérent

(**d**) *(incompatible)* incompatible (**with** avec)

inconsistently [ˌɪnkən'sɪstəntlɪ] *adv (behave)* de façon incohérente; *(perform)* de façon irrégulière *ou* inégale; *(assert)* de façon contradictoire; *(argue)* de façon incohérente

inconsolable [ˌɪnkən'səʊləbəl] *adj* inconsolable

inconsolably [ˌɪnkən'səʊləblɪ] *adv* de façon inconsolable; **he cried inconsolably** il était inconsolable

inconspicuous [ˌɪnkən'spɪkjʊəs] *adj (difficult to see)* à peine visible, qui passe inaperçu; *(discreet)* peu voyant, discret(ète); **she tried to make herself as inconspicuous as possible** elle fit tout son possible pour passer inaperçue

inconspicuously [ˌɪnkən'spɪkjʊəslɪ] *adv* discrètement

inconspicuousness [ˌɪnkən'spɪkjʊəsnɪs] *n (lack of visual prominence)* caractère *m* peu frappant; *(discreetness)* discrétion *f*

inconstancy [ɪn'kɒnstənsɪ] *n* (**a**) *(of phenomenon)* variabilité *f*, instabilité *f*; *(of weather)* instabilité *f*, caractère *m* changeant (**b**) *(of person)* versatilité *f*, inconstance *f*

inconstant [ɪn'kɒnstənt] *adj* (**a**) *(weather)* variable (**b**) *(person)* inconstant, volage

incontestable [ˌɪnkən'testəbəl] *adj* incontestable

incontestably [ˌɪnkən'testəblɪ] *adv* incontestablement, sans conteste

incontinence [ɪn'kɒntɪnəns] *n* incontinence *f*

►► ***incontinence pads*** couches *fpl* pour adultes

incontinent [ɪn'kɒntɪnənt] *adj* incontinent

incontrovertible [ˌɪnkɒntrə'vɜːtəbəl] *adj (fact, proof)* irréfutable; *(truth)* indiscutable; **incontrovertible evidence** une preuve irréfutable

incontrovertibly [ˌɪnkɒntrə'vɜːtəblɪ] *adv* indiscutablement, indéniablement

inconvenience [ˌɪnkən'viːnjəns] **1** *n* (**a**) *(disadvantage)* inconvénient *m*; **the language barrier was a major inconvenience to the participants** la barrière de la langue a beaucoup gêné les participants

(**b**) *(trouble)* **to cause inconvenience** déranger, gêner; **I hope it's not putting you to too much inconvenience** j'espère que cela ne vous dérange pas trop; **we apologize for any inconvenience** nous vous prions de nous excuser pour tout désagrément éventuel

(**c**) *(disadvantages)* incommodité *f*, inconvénients *mpl*; **the inconvenience of a small flat** les désagréments d'un petit appartement; **we apologize to our customers for any inconvenience caused** nous prions notre aimable clientèle de nous excuser pour la gêne occasionnée

2 *vt* déranger, incommoder

inconvenient [ˌɪnkən'viːnjənt] *adj* (**a**) *(inopportune, awkward)* inopportun; **at an inconvenient time** au mauvais moment; **it's a bit inconvenient just now, could you call back later?** je n'ai pas vraiment le temps tout de suite, tu pourrais me rappeler plus tard?; **if it's not inconvenient** si cela ne vous dérange pas; **he has chosen to ignore any inconvenient facts** il a choisi d'ignorer tout ce qui pouvait poser problème; **Friday's a bit inconvenient** vendredi ne me convient pas tellement

(**b**) *(impractical → tool, kitchen)* peu pratique; **it's very inconvenient living so far from town** c'est très incommode d'habiter aussi loin de la ville; **the house is very inconvenient for the shops** la maison est mal située par rapport aux commerces

inconveniently [ˌɪnkən'viːnjəntlɪ] *adv* (**a**) *(happen, arrive)* au mauvais moment, inopportunément; **the announcement was inconveniently timed** le moment de l'annonce a été mal choisi (**b**) *(be situated)* de façon malcommode, mal; **the switch was inconveniently placed above the door** l'interrupteur était placé à un endroit très peu pratique au-dessus de la porte

inconvertible [ˌɪnkən'vɜːtəbəl] *adj* inconvertible, non convertible

incorporate [ɪn'kɔːpəreɪt] **1** *vt* (**a**) *(include, add)* incorporer; **she incorporated many folk tunes into her performance** son programme comprenait de nombreux airs folkloriques; **the territory was incorporated into Poland** le territoire fut incorporé *ou* annexé à la Pologne; **incorporate the butter into the flour** incorporez le beurre à la farine; **to incorporate amendments**

into a text apporter des modifications à un texte

(**b**) *Com (company)* constituer en société commerciale; *(banks)* réunir en société

(**c**) *(merge)* regrouper pour former un tout; **these organizations were incorporated into a national fire brigade** ces organismes ont été regroupés pour constituer une brigade nationale de pompiers

2 *vi Com (form a corporation)* se constituer en société commerciale; *(merge)* fusionner

incorporated [ɪn'kɔːpəreɪtɪd] *adj Am* constitué en société commerciale; **Bradley & Jones Incorporated** ≃ Bradley & Jones SARL

►► *Am* ***incorporated company*** association *f* constituée en société commerciale, société *f* par actions

incorporation [ɪnˌkɔːpə'reɪʃən] *n* (**a**) *(inclusion)* incorporation *f*, intégration *f* (**b**) *Com* constitution *f* en société commerciale

incorporeal [ˌɪnkɔː'pɔːrɪəl] *adj Literary* incorporel

incorrect [ˌɪnkə'rekt] *adj* (**a**) *(wrong → answer, result)* erroné, faux (fausse); *(→ sum, statement)* inexact, incorrect; **incorrect use of a word** usage *m* impropre d'un mot (**b**) *(improper)* incorrect; *(behaviour)* déplacé

incorrectly [ˌɪnkə'rektlɪ] *adv* (**a**) *(wrongly)* **she answered incorrectly** elle a mal répondu; **I was incorrectly quoted** j'ai été cité de façon incorrecte; **the illness was incorrectly diagnosed** il y a eu erreur de diagnostic; **you're using that tool incorrectly** vous utilisez mal cet outil (**b**) *(improperly)* incorrectement; **he behaved most incorrectly** il s'est conduit de façon déplacée, sa conduite était tout à fait déplacée

incorrectness [ˌɪnkə'rektnɪs] *n* (**a**) *(of sum, statement)* inexactitude *f*; *(of text, result)* caractère *m* fautif (**b**) *(of style, behaviour)* incorrection *f*

incorrigible [ɪn'kɒrɪdʒəbəl] *adj* incorrigible

incorrigibly [ɪn'kɒrɪdʒəblɪ] *adv* incorrigiblement

incorruptibility [ˌɪnkəˌrʌptə'bɪlɪtɪ] *n* incorruptibilité *f*

incorruptible [ˌɪnkə'rʌptəbəl] *adj* incorruptible

incorruptibleness [ˌɪnkə'rʌptəbəlnɪs] *n* incorruptibilité *f*

incoterms ['ɪnkəʊtɜːmz] *npl Com* termes *mpl* commerciaux, incoterms *mpl*

increase 1 *vi* [ɪn'kriːs] *(price, takings, salary, speed etc)* augmenter; *(noise, dissatisfaction)* augmenter, croître; *(pain, population)* s'accroître, augmenter; **to increase by 10 percent** augmenter de 10 pour cent; **production/demand/inflation has increased** la production/la demande/l'inflation a augmenté; **the growth rate is likely to increase** le taux de croissance va probablement augmenter *ou* s'accélérer; **the attacks have increased in frequency** la fréquence des attaques a augmenté; **to increase in size** grandir; **to increase in intensity** s'intensifier; **to increase in price** augmenter; **to increase in value** prendre de la valeur

2 *vt* [ɪn'kriːs] augmenter; **to increase output to 500 units a week** augmenter *ou* faire passer la production à 500 unités par semaine; **recent events have increased speculation** des événements récents ont renforcé les rumeurs

3 *n* ['ɪnkriːs] (**a**) *(in price, takings, salary, speed etc)* augmentation *f*; *(of noise, dissatisfaction)* augmentation *f*; *(in pain, population)* accroissement *m*, augmentation *f*; **the increase in productivity/in the cost of living** l'augmentation de la productivité/du coût de la vie; **a 10 percent pay increase** une augmentation de salaire de 10 pour cent; **an increase in population** un accroissement de la population; **an increase in the number of patients** une augmentation *ou* un accroissement du nombre des malades

(**b**) *Knitting* augmentation *f*

4 on the increase *adj* **crime is on the increase** la criminalité est en hausse; **shoplifting is on the increase** les vols à l'étalage sont de plus en plus nombreux

increased [ɪn'kriːst] *adj* accru; **increased investment leads to increased productivity** l'accroissement des investissements entraînera un accroissement *ou* une augmentation de la productivité

increasing [ɪn'kriːsɪŋ] *adj* croissant, grandissant; **there has been an increasing number of complaints** les réclamations sont de plus en plus nombreuses; **they make increasing use of computer technology** ils ont de plus en plus souvent recours à l'informatique

increasingly [ɪn'kriːsɪŋlɪ] *adv* de plus en plus; **increasingly, people are saying that...** de plus en plus, les gens disent que...

incredible [ɪn'kredəbəl] *adj* (**a**) *(unbelievable)* incroyable, invraisemblable; **I find it incredible that she didn't know** je n'arrive pas à croire qu'elle n'était pas au courant (**b**) *Fam (excellent)* fantastique, incroyable

incredibly [ɪn'kredəblɪ] *adv* (**a**) *(unbelievably)* **incredibly, we were on time** aussi incroyable que cela puisse paraître, nous étions à l'heure (**b**) *Fam (extremely)* incroyablement; **she was incredibly beautiful** elle était incroyablement belle

incredulity [ˌɪnkrɪ'djuːlətɪ] *n* incrédulité *f*

incredulous [ɪn'kredjʊləs] *adj* incrédule; **an incredulous look** un regard incrédule

incredulously [ɪn'kredjʊləslɪ] *adv* avec incrédulité

incredulousness [ɪn'kredjʊləsnɪs] *n* incrédulité *f*

increment ['ɪnkrɪmənt] **1** *n* (**a**) *(increase)* augmentation *f*; **a salary with yearly increments of £500** un salaire assorti d'augmentations annuelles de 500 livres; **the scale goes up in increments of 0.25** le barème augmente par paliers de 0,25 (**b**) *Comput* incrément *m* (**c**) *Math* accroissement *m*

2 *vt Comput* incrémenter

incremental [ˌɪnkrɪ'mentəl] *adj* (**a**) *(increasing)* croissant; **incremental increases** augmentations *fpl* régulières (**b**) *Comput* incrémentiel, incrémental

►► *Fin* ***incremental cash flow*** cashflow *m* marginal; *Comput* ***incremental compiler*** compilateur *m* incrémentiel; *Fin* ***incremental cost*** coût *m* marginal; *Comput* ***incremental plotter*** traceur *m* par pas

incriminate [ɪn'krɪmɪneɪt] *vt* incriminer, mettre en cause; **to incriminate oneself** se compromettre; **all the evidence seems to incriminate the maid** tous les indices semblent accuser la bonne

incriminating [ɪn'krɪmɪneɪtɪŋ] *adj* accusateur, compromettant; **incriminating evidence** pièces *fpl* à conviction

incrimination [ɪnˌkrɪmɪ'neɪʃən] *n* mise *f* en cause, incrimination *f*

incriminatory [ɪn'krɪmɪnətrɪ] *adj* accusateur, compromettant

in-crowd *n Fam* coterie *f*; **to be in with the in-crowd** être branché

incrust [ɪn'krʌst] *vt (with jewels)* incruster; *(with mud, snow, ice)* couvrir; **to be incrusted with sth** être incrusté *ou* couvert *ou* recouvert de qch

incrustation [ˌɪnkrʌs'teɪʃən] *n* incrustation *f*

incubate ['ɪnkjʊbeɪt] **1** *vt* (**a**) *Biol (eggs → of bird)* couver; *(→ of fish)* incuber; *(→ in incubator)* incuber (**b**) *Fig (plot, idea)* couver

2 *vi* (**a**) *Biol (egg)* être en incubation (**b**) *Med (virus)* incuber; **the disease incubates for several days** la maladie a une période d'incubation de plusieurs jours (**c**) *Fig (plan, idea)* couver

incubation [ˌɪnkjʊ'beɪʃən] *n Biol & Med (of egg, virus, disease)* incubation *f*

►► ***incubation period*** (période *f* d')incubation *f*

incubator ['ɪnkjʊbeɪtə(r)] *n (for premature baby)* couveuse *f*, incubateur *m*; *(for eggs, bacteria)* incubateur *m*

incubus ['ɪnkjʊbəs] *(pl* **incubuses** *or* **incubi** [-baɪ]) *n* (**a**) *(demon)* incube *m* (**b**) *Literary (nightmare)* cauchemar *m*

in-cue *n Rad & TV* signal *m* de départ

inculcate ['ɪnkʌlkeɪt] *vt* inculquer; **to inculcate sb with sth, to inculcate sth in sb** *(idea, principle, habit etc)* inculquer qch à qn

inculcation [ˌɪnkʌl'keɪʃən] *n* inculcation *f*

inculpate ['ɪnkʌlˌpeɪt] *vt* incriminer

incumbency [ɪn'kʌmbənsɪ] *(pl* **incumbencies**) *n (office)* office *m*, fonction *f*; **during my predecessor's incumbency** pendant l'exercice de mon prédécesseur

incumbent [ɪn'kʌmbənt] *Formal* **1** *adj* (**a**) *(imposed)* **it is incumbent on** *or* **upon the manager to check the takings** il incombe *ou* il appartient au directeur de vérifier la recette (**b**) *(in office)* en fonction, en exercice; **the incumbent mayor** *(current)* le maire en exercice; *(during election campaign)* le maire sortant

2 *n* (**a**) *(office holder)* titulaire *mf* (**b**) *Rel* bénéficiaire *m*, titulaire *m (d'une charge)*

incunabulum [ˌɪnkjuː'næbjʊləm] *(pl* **incunabula** [-jʊlə]) *n* incunable *m*

incur [ɪn'kɜː(r)] *(pt & pp* **incurred**, *cont* **incurring**) *vt (blame, loss, penalty)* s'exposer à, encourir; *(debt)* contracter; *(losses)* subir; *(expenses)* engager; **the expenses incurred** les dépenses encourues; **to incur sb's wrath** s'attirer les foudres de qn

►► *Acct* ***incurred expenditure, incurred expenses*** dépenses *fpl* engagées

incurable [ɪn'kjʊərəbəl] **1** *adj* (**a**) *(illness)* incurable, inguérissable (**b**) *Fig (optimist, romantic)* incorrigible

2 *n* incurable *mf*

incurably [ɪn'kjʊərəblɪ] *adv* (**a**) **to be incurably ill** avoir une maladie incurable (**b**) *Fig* **to be incurably lazy/optimistic/romantic** être un incorrigible paresseux/optimiste/romantique

incurious [ɪn'kjʊərɪəs] *adj Literary* incurieux, sans curiosité

incuriously [ɪn'kjʊərɪəslɪ] *adv Literary* sans curiosité

incursion [*Br* ɪn'kɜːʃən, *Am* ɪn'kɜːʒən] *n* incursion *f*; **an incursion into enemy territory** une incursion en territoire ennemi

incus ['ɪŋkəs] *n Anat* enclume *f*

Ind (**a**) *(written abbr* **Independent**) indépendant (**b**) *(written abbr* **Indiana**) Indiana *m*

indebted [ɪn'detɪd] *adj* (**a**) *(for help)* redevable; **I am greatly indebted to you for doing me this favour** je vous suis extrêmement reconnaissant de m'avoir rendu ce service; **I am indebted to you for your loyal support** je vous suis reconnaissant de votre soutien loyal (**b**) *(owing money)* endetté; **heavily indebted** fortement endetté

indebtedness [ɪn'detɪdnɪs] *n* (**a**) *(for help)* dette *f*, obligation *f*; **my indebtedness to her** ma dette envers elle (**b**) *(financial)* endettement *m* (**c**) *(amount owed)* dette *f*, dettes *fpl*

indecency [ɪn'diːsnsɪ] *(pl* **indecencies**) *n* indécence *f*; **he was brought in on an indecency charge** il a été mis en examen pour attentat à la pudeur; *Law* **an act of gross indecency** un grave outrage à la pudeur

indecent [ɪn'diːsənt] *adj* (**a**) *(obscene)* indécent; **an indecent proposition** une proposition indécente (**b**) *(unseemly)* indécent, inconvenant, déplacé; **an indecent display of wealth** un étalage indécent de richesse; **with indecent haste** avec une précipitation déplacée

►► *Law* ***indecent assault*** attentat *m* à la pudeur; *Law* ***indecent exposure*** outrage *m* public à la pudeur

indecently [ɪn'diːsəntlɪ] *adv* indécemment

indecipherable [ˌɪndɪ'saɪfərəbəl] *adj* indéchiffrable

indecision [ˌɪndɪ'sɪʒən] *n* indécision *f*

indecisive [ˌɪndɪ'saɪsɪv] *adj* (**a**) *(hesitating → person)* indécis, irrésolu; **she was indecisive about whether to go or stay** elle ne savait pas si elle devait partir ou rester (**b**) *(inconclusive)* peu concluant

indecisively [ˌɪndɪ'saɪsɪvlɪ] *adv* (**a**) *(hesitatingly)* de manière indécise, avec hésitation (**b**) *(inconclusively)* de manière peu convaincante *ou* concluante; **the argument ended indecisively** la discussion s'est terminée de façon peu concluante

indecisiveness [ˌɪndɪ'saɪsɪvnɪs] *n* indécision *f*

indeclinable [ˌɪndɪ'klaɪnəbəl] *adj* indéclinable

indecorous [ɪn'dekərəs] *adj* inconvenant, malséant

indecorously [ɪn'dekərəslɪ] *adv* de manière inconvenante

indecorum [ˌɪndɪ'kɔːrəm] *n* inconvenance *f*

indeed [ɪn'diːd] *adv* (**a**) *(used to confirm)* effectivement, en effet; **there was indeed a problem** il y avait effectivement *ou* bien un problème; **we are aware of the problem; indeed, we are**

already investigating it nous sommes conscients du problème; en fait, nous sommes déjà en train de l'étudier

(**b**) *(used to qualify)* **the problem, if indeed there is one, is theirs** c'est leur problème, si problème il y a; **it is difficult, indeed virtually impossible, to get in** il est difficile, pour ne pas dire *ou* voire impossible, d'entrer

(**c**) *(used as intensifier)* vraiment; **I'm very tired indeed** je suis vraiment très fatigué; **thank you very much indeed** merci beaucoup; **that's praise indeed!** ça, c'est un compliment!, voilà ce qui s'appelle un compliment!

(**d**) *(in replies)* en effet; **I believe you support their policy – I do indeed** je crois que vous soutenez leur politique – en effet; **you've been to Venice haven't you? – indeed I have!** tu es allé à Venise, n'est-ce pas? – oui, j'y suis allé; **you haven't been to Venice – indeed I have!** tu n'es jamais allé à Venise – si, j'y suis déjà allé!; **yes indeed!** mais certainement!, pour sûr!

(**e**) *(as surprised, ironic response)* **he asked us for a pay rise – indeed!** il nous a demandé une augmentation – eh bien! *ou* vraiment?; **I've bought a new car – have you indeed!** j'ai acheté une nouvelle voiture – vraiment?

indefatigability [ˌɪndɪˌfætɪgəˈbɪlɪtɪ] *n* infatigabilité *f*

indefatigable [ˌɪndɪˈfætɪgəbəl] *adj* infatigable

indefatigably [ˌɪndɪˈfætɪgəblɪ] *adv* infatigablement, sans se fatiguer, inlassablement

indefeasible [ˌɪndɪˈfiːzəbəl] *adj Law (right, possession)* irrévocable, imprescriptible

►► ***indefeasible interest*** intérêt *m* indestructible

indefensible [ˌɪndɪˈfensəbəl] *adj* (**a**) *(conduct)* injustifiable, inexcusable; *(argument, theory)* insoutenable, indéfendable (**b**) *Mil* indéfendable

indefensibly [ˌɪndɪˈfensəblɪ] *adv* de façon indéfendable

indefinable [ˌɪndɪˈfaɪnəbəl] *adj* indéfinissable

indefinably [ˌɪndɪˈfaɪnəblɪ] *adv* indescriptiblement

indefinite [ɪnˈdefɪnɪt] *adj* (**a**) *(indeterminate)* indéterminé, illimité; **for an indefinite period** pour une période indéterminée; **an indefinite strike** une grève illimitée; **of indefinite origin** d'origine incertaine (**b**) *(vague, imprecise)* flou, peu précis; **an indefinite answer** une réponse floue *ou* vague (**c**) *Gram* indéfini

►► *Gram* ***indefinite article*** article *m* indéfini; *Gram* ***indefinite pronoun*** pronom *m* indéfini

indefinitely [ɪnˈdefɪnətlɪ] *adv* (**a**) *(without limit)* indéfiniment; **we can't go on indefinitely** on ne peut pas continuer indéfiniment; **I could go on indefinitely** *(continue speaking)* je pourrais continuer à l'infini; **closed indefinitely** *(sign)* fermé jusqu'à nouvel avis *ou* ordre (**b**) *(imprecisely)* vaguement

indelible [ɪnˈdeləbəl] *adj (ink, stain)* indélébile; *(memory)* impérissable

►► *Br* ***indelible marker (pen)*** marqueur *m* indélébile

indelibly [ɪnˈdeləblɪ] *adv* de manière indélébile; *Fig* **her face remained indelibly fixed in his memory** son visage resta à jamais gravé dans [illegible]

indelicacy [ɪnˈdelɪkəsɪ] (*pl* **indelicacies**) *n* (**a**) *(of behaviour, remark)* indélicatesse *f* (**b**) *(tactless remark, action)* manque *m* de tact

indelicate [ɪnˈdelɪkət] *adj (action)* déplacé, indélicat; *(person, remark)* indélicat, qui manque de tact

indemnification [ɪnˌdemnɪfɪˈkeɪʃən] *n* (**a**) *(act of compensation)* indemnisation *f*, dédommagement *m* (**b**) *(sum reimbursed)* indemnité *f*

indemnify [ɪnˈdemnɪfaɪ] (*pt & pp* **indemnified**) *vt* (**a**) *(compensate)* indemniser, dédommager; **to be indemnified for sth** être indemnisé *ou* dédommagé de qch (**b**) *(insure)* assurer, garantir; **to be indemnified for** *or* **against sth** être assuré contre qch

indemnity [ɪnˈdemnətɪ] (*pl* **indemnities**) *n* (**a**) *(compensation)* indemnité *f*, dédommagement *m*; **war indemnities** réparations *fpl* de guerre (**b**) *(insurance)* assurance *f* (**c**) *(exemption from prosecution)* immunité *f*

indent 1 *n* [ˈɪndent] (**a**) *Br Com (order)* commande *f*; *(order form)* bordereau *m* de commande

(**b**) *(in line of text)* renfoncement *m*, alinéa *m*

(**c**) *(notch)* entaille *f*; *(in metal)* bosselure *f*

2 *vt* [ɪnˈdent] (**a**) *(line of text)* mettre en retrait

(**b**) *(edge)* denteler, découper; *(more deeply)* échancrer

(**c**) *(surface)* marquer, faire une empreinte dans

(**d**) *Br Com (goods)* commander

(**e**) *(contract)* contrat *m*; *(of apprentice)* contrat *m* d'apprentissage

3 *vi* [ɪnˈdent] (**a**) *(at start of paragraph)* faire un alinéa

(**b**) *Br Com* passer commande; **to indent on sb for sth** commander qch à qn

indentation [ˌɪndenˈteɪʃən] *n* (**a**) *(in line of text)* renfoncement *m*, alinéa *m* (**b**) *(in edge)* dentelure *f*; *(deeper)* échancrure *f*; *(in coastline)* découpure *f* (**c**) *(on surface)* empreinte *f* (**d**) *(contract)* contrat *m* synallagmatique; *(of apprentice)* contrat *m* d'apprentissage

indented [ɪnˈdentɪd] *adj (edge)* découpé, dentelé; *(coastline)* découpé; *(line, paragraph)* en retrait

indenture [ɪnˈdentʃə(r)] **1** *n (often pl)* contrat *m* synallagmatique; *(of apprentice)* contrat *m* d'apprentissage

2 *vt* (**a**) *(bind by contract)* engager par contrat (**b**) *Arch (of parent or guardian)* mettre en apprentissage (**to sb** chez qn); *(of employer)* prendre en apprentissage; **he was indentured to a carpenter** on le mit en apprentissage chez un menuisier

►► *Br* ***indentured labour*** *(workers)* main-d'œuvre *f* sous contrat; *(work)* travail *m* sous contrat; *Br* ***indentured labourer*** ouvrier *m* sous contrat

indentureship [ɪnˈdentʃə(r)ʃɪp] *n* travail *m* sous contrat

independence [ˌɪndɪˈpendəns] *n (gen) & Pol* indépendance *f*; **the country has recently gained its independence** le pays vient d'accéder à l'indépendance; **the (American) War of Independence** la guerre d'Indépendance (américaine)

►► ***Independence Day*** fête *f* nationale de l'Indépendance *(aux États-Unis)*

THE AMERICAN WAR OF INDEPENDENCE

En réaction à la dureté de l'administration britannique qui leur imposait de lourdes taxes, les treize colonies de la Nouvelle-Angleterre engagèrent cette guerre pour accéder à l'indépendance. Marqué par la Déclaration d'indépendance du 4 juillet 1776, le conflit dura cinq ans et le nouvel État fut reconnu en 1783.

independency [ˌɪndɪˈpendənsɪ] (*pl* **independencies**) *n* (**a**) *(fact of being independent)* indépendance *f* (**b**) *(country)* État *m* indépendant

independent [ˌɪndɪˈpendənt] **1** *adj* (**a**) *(person, country etc)* indépendant; **to become independent** *(country)* accéder à l'indépendance; **she is independent of her parents** elle ne dépend plus de ses parents; **two independent studies have been made** [illegible] dantes ont été menées; **he is incapable of independent thought** il est incapable de penser par lui-même; **a man of independent means** un rentier; **two independent sources have confirmed the rumour** deux sources indépendantes ont confirmé la rumeur

(**b**) *Gram, Phil & Math* indépendant

2 *n* (**a**) *(gen)* indépendant(e) *m,f*; *Press* **The Independent** = quotidien britannique de qualité sans affiliation politique particulière

(**b**) *Pol* indépendant(e) *m,f*, non-inscrit(e) *m,f*

►► *Br Formerly* ***the Independent Broadcasting Authority*** = organisme d'agrément et de coordination des stations de radio et chaînes de télévision du secteur privé en Grande-Bretagne; *Gram* ***independent clause*** proposition *f* indépendante; *Fin* ***independent financial adviser*** conseiller(ère) *m,f* financier(ère) indépendant(e); ***independent income*** revenus *mpl* indépendants, rentes *fpl*; ***independent inquiry*** enquête *f* indépendante; **an independent inquiry has been set up** une enquête indépendante a été ouverte; ***Independent Radio News*** = agence de presse radiophonique; ***independent retailer*** détaillant(e) *m,f* indépendant(e); *Br* ***independent school*** école *f* privée; *Br* ***the Independent Television Commission*** = commission de surveillance des télévisions britanniques privées

independently [ˌɪndɪˈpendəntlɪ] *adv* de manière indépendante, de manière autonome; **independently of** indépendamment de; **to be independently wealthy** vivre de sa fortune personnelle

in-depth *adj* en profondeur

indescribable [ˌɪndɪˈskraɪbəbəl] *adj* indescriptible

indescribably [ˌɪndɪˈskraɪbəblɪ] *adv* incroyablement

indestructibility [ˌɪndɪˌstrʌktəˈbɪlɪtɪ] *n* indestructibilité *f*

indestructible [ˌɪndɪˈstrʌktəbəl] *adj* indestructible

indestructibleness [ˌɪndɪsˈtrʌktəbəlnɪs] *n* indestructibilité *f*

indeterminable [ˌɪndɪˈtɜːmɪnəbəl] *adj* (**a**) *(fact, amount, distance)* indéterminable (**b**) *(controversy, problem)* insoluble

indeterminacy [ˌɪndɪˈtɜːmɪnəsɪ] *n* indétermination *f*

indeterminate [ˌɪndɪˈtɜːmɪnət] *adj* (**a**) *(undetermined, indefinite)* indéterminé; **for an indeterminate period** pour une période indéterminée; **indeterminate sentence** peine *f* (de prison) de durée indéterminée (**b**) *(vague, imprecise)* flou, vague (**c**) *Ling, Math & Phil* indéterminé

indeterminately [ˌɪndɪˈtɜːmɪnətlɪ] *adv* (**a**) *(indefinitely)* de façon indéterminée (**b**) *(vaguely)* de manière floue, imprécisément

indeterminism [ˌɪndɪˈtɜːmɪnɪzəm] *n* indéterminisme *m*

index [ˈɪndeks] (*pl senses* (**a**)–(**c**), (**h**) **indexes**, *pl senses* (**d**)–(**g**) **indices** [-dɪsiːz]) **1** *n* (**a**) *(in book, database)* index *m*; **name index** index *m* des noms propres

(**b**) *(in library)* catalogue *m*, répertoire *m*; *(on index cards)* fichier *m*

(**c**) *(finger)* index *m*

(**d**) *Econ & St Exch* indice *m*

(**e**) *Phys* indice *m*

(**f**) *(pointer on scale)* aiguille *f*, indicateur *m*; *Fig (sign)* indice *m*, indicateur *m*; **it is a good index of the current political mood** c'est un bon indicateur du climat politique actuel

(**g**) *Math (subscript)* indice *m*; *(superscript)* exposant *m*

(**h**) *Typ (pointing fist)* renvoi *m*

2 *vt* (**a**) *(word, book, database)* indexer; **all geographical names are indexed** tous les noms géographiques sont indexés; **you'll find it indexed under "science"** vous trouverez ça indexé à "science" *ou* dans l'index sous (l'entrée) "science"

(**b**) *Fin (salary, pension)* indexer; **indexed to inflation** indexé sur l'inflation

(**c**) *Tech* indexer

3 Index *Rel* Index *m*

►► *Am St Exch* ***index arbitrage*** arbitrage *m* sur indice; ***index box*** boîte *f* à fiches; ***index card*** fiche *f*; ***index finger*** index *m*; *St Exch* ***index fund*** fonds *m* à gestion indicielle, fonds *m* indiciel; ***index number*** *(in statistics)* indice *m*; *St Exch* ***index option*** option *f* sur indice; *Opt* ***index of refraction*** indice *m* de réfraction; ***index register*** registre *m* d'index

indexation [ˌɪndekˈseɪʃən] *n* indexation *f*

►► *Fin* ***indexation clause*** clause *f* d'indexation

indexing [ˈɪndeksɪŋ] *n Comput* indexation *f*

index-link *vt Fin* indexer; **this pension is index-linked to the cost of living** cette retraite est indexée sur le coût de la vie

index-linked *adj Fin* indexé

►► ***index-linked fund*** fonds *m* à gestion indicielle, fonds *m* indiciel

index-linking *n Fin* indexation *f*

India [ˈɪndɪə] *n* Inde *f*; **in India** en Inde

►► *Am* ***India ink*** encre *f* de Chine; ***India paper*** papier *m* bible; *Br* ***India rubber*** *(substance)* caoutchouc *m*; *(eraser)* gomme *f*

Indiaman [ˈɪndɪəmən] (*pl* **Indiamen** [-mən]) *n Br* =

grand voilier assurant le commerce avec les Indes

Indian ['ɪndɪən] **1** *n* (**a**) *(Asian person)* Indien(enne) *m,f*

(**b**) *(Native American)* Indien(enne) *m,f* (d'Amérique)

(**c**) *(language → in America)* langue *f* amérindienne

(**d**) *Fam (restaurant)* restau *m* indien; *(meal)* repas *m* indien ❑; **we went out for an Indian** on est allés dans un restau indien

2 *adj (American or Asian)* indien; **in Indian file** en file *f* indienne; *Pej* **to be an Indian giver** = demander la restitution de quelque chose qu'on a donné

3 *comp (embassy → of India)* d'Inde; *(history → of India)* de l'Inde

►► *Am & Can* ***Indian agent*** délégué(e) *m,f* aux affaires indiennes; ***Indian buffalo*** buffle *m* d'Asie; ***Indian club*** massue *f (pour la gymnastique)*; *Am* ***Indian corn*** maïs *m*; *Zool* ***Indian elephant*** éléphant *m* d'Asie; *Br* ***Indian hemp*** chanvre *m* indien, cannabis *m*; *Br* ***Indian ink*** encre *f* de Chine; ***the Indian Mutiny*** = grande révolte indienne contre les Britanniques en 1857; ***Indian National Trade Union Congress*** = confédération de syndicats indiens; ***the Indian Ocean*** l'océan *m* Indien; ***Indian red*** colcotar *m*, rouge *m* de Prusse; ***Indian reserve*** réserve *f* indienne; ***Indian sign*** sort *m (jeté sur quelqu'un)*; ***Indian summer*** été *m* de la Saint-Martin, été *m* indien; *Fig* vieillesse *f* heureuse; ***Indian Territory*** = région à l'ouest du Mississippi où les Indiens furent contraints d'immigrer à la fin du XIXème siècle; *Am Hist* ***Indian Wars*** = guerres entre les Indiens d'amérique et les colons aux XVIIIème et XIXème siècles; ***Indian wrestling*** bras *m* de fer

THE INDIAN MUTINY

Cette violente révolte de la population indienne contre l'Empire britannique et l'occidentalisation du pays éclata en 1857 dans une garnison et se propagea dans tout le pays. Elle dura deux ans et aboutit principalement à la fin de l'influence politique de l'East India Company.

Indiana [,ɪndɪ'ænə] *n* l'Indiana *m*; **in Indiana** dans l'Indiana

Indianapolis [,ɪndɪə'næpəlɪs] *n* Indianapolis

►► ***the Indianapolis 500*** = course automobile qui se déroule à Indianapolis, aux États-Unis

Indic ['ɪndɪk] *Ling* **1** *n* indo-aryen *m*

2 *adj* indo-aryen

indicate ['ɪndɪkeɪt] **1** *vt* (**a**) *(show, point to)* indiquer; **to indicate the way** indiquer *ou* montrer le chemin; **the footprints would seem to indicate that someone has been here** les traces de pas semblent indiquer que quelqu'un est passé par ici; **this dial indicates the temperature** ce cadran indique la température; **all the pointers indicate a rise in unemployment** tous les indicateurs font état d'une montée du chômage

(**b**) *(make clear)* signaler; **as I have already indicated** comme je l'ai déjà signalé *ou* fait remarquer; **he indicated his willingness to help** il nous a fait savoir qu'il était prêt à nous aider; **she indicated that the interview was over** elle a fait comprendre que l'entretien était terminé

(**c**) *Br Aut* **to indicate (that one is turning) left/right** mettre son clignotant à gauche/à droite (pour tourner)

(**d**) *(recommend, require)* indiquer; **surgery is indicated** l'opération semble tout indiquée; **strong measures were clearly indicated** il était évident que la situation exigeait des mesures rigoureuses

2 *vi Br Aut* mettre son clignotant

indication [,ɪndɪ'keɪʃən] *n* (**a**) *(sign)* indication *f*; **she gave no indication that she had seen me** rien ne pouvait laisser supposer qu'elle m'avait vu; **he gave early indications of his talent** son talent se révéla de bonne heure; **he gave us a clear indication of his intentions** il nous a clairement fait comprendre *ou* clairement indiqué ses intentions; **all the indications are that..., there is every indication that...** tout porte à croire que...

(**b**) *(act of indicating)* indication *f*

indicative [ɪn'dɪkətɪv] **1** *adj* (**a**) *(symptomatic)* indicatif; **his handwriting is indicative of his mental state** son écriture est révélatrice de son état mental; **it is indicative of a strong personality** cela témoigne d'une forte personnalité (**b**) *Gram* indicatif

2 *n Gram* indicatif *m*; **in the indicative** à l'indicatif

►► *Gram* ***indicative mood*** mode *m* indicatif, indicatif *m*

indicator ['ɪndɪkeɪtə(r)] *n* (**a**) *(instrument)* indicateur *m*; *(warning lamp)* voyant *m*; *(needle, pointer)* index *m*, aiguille *f*; **temperature indicator** indicateur *m* de température

(**b**) *Aut* clignotant *m*, *Belg* clignoteur *m*, *Suisse* signofil(e) *m*

(**c**) *(at station, in airport)* **arrivals/departures indicator** panneau *m* des arrivées/des départs

(**d**) *Fig* indicateur *m*; **economic indicators** indicateurs *mpl* économiques

(**e**) *Chem* indicateur *m*

(**f**) *Ling* indicateur *m*

►► ***indicator light*** signal *m* lumineux; *(on monitor)* voyant *m*

indices ['ɪndɪsi:z] *pl of* **index**

indict [ɪn'daɪt] *vt Law* inculper, *Spec* mettre en examen

indictable [ɪn'daɪtəbəl] *adj Law* (**a**) *(person)* passible de poursuites (**b**) *(crime)* passible des tribunaux

indictment [ɪn'daɪtmənt] *n* (**a**) *Law (act)* inculpation *f*, mise *f* en examen; *(document)* acte *m* d'accusation; **indictment for fraud** inculpation *f* pour fraude (**b**) *Fig* **a damning indictment of government policy** un témoignage accablant contre la politique gouvernementale

indie ['ɪndɪ] *Fam* **1** *n (music)* indie-rock *m*

2 *adj (band, charts)* indépendant ❑ *(dont les disques sont produits par des maisons indépendantes)*

►► ***indie music*** indie-rock *m*

Indies ['ɪndɪz] *npl* **the Indies** les Indes *fpl*; **in the Indies** aux Indes

indifference [ɪn'dɪfərəns] *n* (**a**) *(unconcern)* indifférence *f* (**to** *or* **towards sb/sth** à l'égard de qn/pour qch); **with total indifference** avec une indifférence totale (**b**) *(mediocrity)* médiocrité *f* (**c**) *(unimportance)* insignifiance *f*; **it is a matter of great indifference to me** c'est une question qui me laisse totalement indifférent (**d**) *Phil* indifférence *f*

indifferent [ɪn'dɪfərənt] *adj* (**a**) *(unconcerned, cold)* indifférent; **she was indifferent to the beauty of the landscape** elle était indifférente à la beauté du paysage; **he was indifferent to her pleas** il est resté sourd à ses suppliques; **indifferent to the danger** insouciant du danger

(**b**) *(unimportant)* indifférent; **it's indifferent to me whether they go or stay** qu'ils partent ou qu'ils restent, cela m'est égal *ou* indifférent

(**c**) *(mediocre)* médiocre, quelconque; **good, bad or indifferent** bon, mauvais ou ni l'un ni l'autre

(**d**) *Biol (cell, tissue)* indifférencié

indifferentism [ɪn'dɪfərən,tɪzəm] *n Rel & Pol* indifférentisme *m*

indifferently [ɪn'dɪfərəntlɪ] *adv* (**a**) *(unconcernedly)* indifféremment, avec indifférence (**b**) *(in mediocre manner)* médiocrement

indigence ['ɪndɪdʒəns] *n Formal* indigence *f*

indigenous [ɪn'dɪdʒɪnəs] *adj* (**a**) *(animal, plant, custom)* indigène; *(population)* autochtone; **rabbits are not indigenous to Australia** à l'origine, il n'y avait pas de lapins en Australie (**b**) *(innate)* inné, natif

indigent ['ɪndɪdʒənt] *Formal* **1** *n* indigent(e) *m,f*

2 *adj* indigent, nécessiteux

indigestibility [,ɪndɪ,dʒestə'bɪlɪtɪ] *n* indigestibilité *f*

indigestible [,ɪndɪ'dʒestəbəl] *adj* indigeste

indigestion [,ɪndɪ'dʒestʃən] *n (UNCOUNT)* indigestion *f*; **to have indigestion** avoir une indigestion

indign [ɪn'daɪn] *adj Literary* indigne, honteux

indignant [ɪn'dɪgnənt] *adj* indigné, outré; **he was indignant at her attitude** il était indigné par son attitude; **an indignant look** un regard outré

indignantly [ɪn'dɪgnəntlɪ] *adv* avec indignation

indignation [,ɪndɪg'neɪʃən] *n* indignation *f*; **public indignation** indignation *f* générale

indignity [ɪn'dɪgnətɪ] (*pl* **indignities**) *n* indignité *f*; **he suffered the indignity of having to ask for a loan** il a dû s'abaisser à solliciter un prêt; **the indignity of it!** quelle honte!

indigo ['ɪndɪgəʊ] (*pl* **indigos** *or* **indigoes**) **1** *n* (**a**) *(dye, colour)* indigo *m* (**b**) *(plant)* indigotier *m*

2 *adj* indigo *(inv)*

►► ***indigo blue*** indigo *m*

indirect [,ɪndɪ'rekt] *adj* indirect; **by an indirect route** par un chemin indirect *ou* détourné; **the indirect effects of radioactivity** les effets indirects *ou* secondaires de la radioactivité; **an indirect reference** une allusion voilée

►► ***indirect costs*** coûts *mpl* indirects; *Ftbl* ***indirect free kick*** coup *m* franc indirect; *Fin* ***indirect investment*** investissement *m* indirect; ***indirect lighting*** éclairage *m* indirect; *Gram* ***indirect object*** objet *m* indirect; *Mktg* ***indirect promotional costs*** coûts *mpl* de promotion indirects; ***indirect question*** question *f* indirecte; *Mktg* ***indirect selling*** vente *f* indirecte; *Gram* ***indirect speech*** discours *m* indirect; ***indirect tax*** impôt *m* indirect; *Com & Fin* ***indirect taxation*** contributions *fpl* indirectes, impôts *mpl* indirects

indirection [,ɪndɪ'rekʃən] **1** *n* (**a**) *(deceit)* tromperie *f*, déloyauté *f* (**b**) *(aimlessness)* manque *m* de but *ou* d'objectif (**c**) *Comput* adressage *m* indirect

2 by indirection *adv* indirectement, par des moyens détournés

indirectly [,ɪndɪ'rektlɪ] *adv* indirectement; **I heard about it indirectly** je l'ai appris indirectement *ou* par personnes interposées; **she felt indirectly responsible** elle se sentait indirectement responsable

indirectness [,ɪndɪ'rektnɪs] *n* caractère *m* indirect

indiscernible [,ɪndɪ'sɜ:nəbəl] *adj* indiscernable, imperceptible

indiscipline [ɪn'dɪsɪplɪn] *n* indiscipline *f*

indiscreet [,ɪndɪ'skri:t] *adj* indiscret(ète)

indiscreetly [,ɪndɪ'skri:tlɪ] *adv* indiscrètement

indiscretion [,ɪndɪ'skreʃən] *n* (**a**) *(lack of discretion)* manque *m* de discrétion, indiscrétion *f* (**b**) *(unwise act)* écart *m* de conduite; *(unwise remark)* indiscrétion *f*; **to be guilty of an indiscretion** *(blunder)* commettre une inconséquence; *(sexual)* se compromettre

indiscriminate [,ɪndɪ'skrɪmɪnət] *adj* **it was indiscriminate slaughter** ce fut un massacre aveugle; **to distribute indiscriminate punishment/praise** distribuer des punitions/des éloges à tort et à travers; **children are indiscriminate in their television viewing** les enfants regardent la télévision sans discernement; **indiscriminate admiration** admiration *f* inconditionnelle

indiscriminately [,ɪndɪ'skrɪmɪnətlɪ] *adv* **he reads indiscriminately** il lit tout ce qui lui tombe sous la main; **he fired indiscriminately into the crowd** il a tiré dans la foule sans faire de distinction; **the plague struck rich and poor indiscriminately** la peste a frappé indifféremment les riches et les pauvres; **she admired everything indiscriminately** elle admirait tout sans discernement; **I use the two terms indiscriminately** j'utilise indifféremment les deux termes

indiscrimination ['ɪndɪs,krɪmɪ'neɪʃən] *n* manque *m* de discernement

indispensability [,ɪndɪ,spensə'bɪlɪtɪ] *n* indispensabilité *f*

indispensable [,ɪndɪ'spensəbəl] *adj* indispensable (**to** à *or* pour); **to make oneself indispensable to sb** se rendre indispensable à qn

indispensableness [,ɪndɪs'pensəbəlnɪs] *n* indispensabilité *f*

indisposed [,ɪndɪ'spəʊzd] *adj Formal* (**a**) *Euph (sick)* indisposé, souffrant; **to be** *or* **feel indisposed** être indisposé *ou* souffrant (**b**) *(unwilling)* peu enclin, peu disposé; **to be indisposed to do sth** être peu enclin *ou* peu disposé à faire qch

indisposition [,ɪndɪspə'zɪʃən] *n Formal* (**a**) *Euph (illness)* indisposition *f* (**b**) *(unwillingness)* dispositions *fpl* peu favorables, manque *m* d'empressement

indisputable [,ɪndɪ'spju:təbəl] *adj* incontestable, indiscutable

indisputably [ˌɪndɪ'spjuːtəblɪ] *adv* incontestablement, indiscutablement

indissociable [ˌɪndɪ'səʊʃɪəbəl] *adj* indissociable (**from** de)

indissoluble [ˌɪndɪ'sɒljʊbəl] *adj* indissoluble

indissolubly [ˌɪndɪ'sɒljʊblɪ] *adv* indissolublement

indistinct [ˌɪndɪ'stɪŋkt] *adj* indistinct

indistinctly [ˌɪndɪ'stɪŋktlɪ] *adv* indistinctement

indistinctness [ˌɪndɪ'stɪŋktnɪs] *n* caractère *m* indistinct

indistinguishable [ˌɪndɪ'stɪŋgwɪʃəbəl] *adj* (**a**) *(alike)* impossible à distinguer; **his handwriting is indistinguishable from his brother's** son écriture est impossible à distinguer de celle de son frère; **the twins are indistinguishable** les jumeaux se ressemblent à s'y méprendre (**b**) *(imperceptible)* imperceptible

indistinguishably [ˌɪndɪ'stɪŋgwɪʃəblɪ] *adv* imperceptiblement

indium ['ɪndɪəm] *n Chem* indium *m*

individual [ˌɪndɪ'vɪdʒʊəl] **1** *adj* (**a**) *(for one person)* individuel; **his pupils get individual attention** il s'occupe de ses élèves individuellement; **individual portions** portions *fpl* individuelles *ou* pour une personne; **she has individual tuition** elle prend des cours particuliers

(**b**) *(single, separate)* particulier; **we cannot consider each individual case** nous ne pouvons pas considérer tous les cas particuliers *ou* chaque cas en particulier; **it's impossible to investigate each individual complaint** il est impossible d'étudier séparément chaque réclamation; **each individual case is different** chaque cas est différent; **everyone will have his individual copy** chacun aura son exemplaire personnel *ou* son propre exemplaire

(**c**) *(distinctive)* personnel, particulier; **she has a very individual way of working** elle a une façon très particulière *ou* personnelle de travailler

2 *n* individu *m*; **who's that strange individual?** qui est cet individu bizarre?; **as a private individual** comme simple particulier

►► *Fin* ***individual company accounts*** comptes *mpl* sociaux, comptes *mpl* d'entreprise individuelle; *Swimming* ***individual medley*** quatre nages *m inv* individuel; *Cycling* ***individual pursuit*** poursuite *f* individuelle; *Am Fin* ***individual retirement account*** plan *m* d'epargne retraite pesonnel; ***individual rights*** droits *mpl* de l'individu *ou* de la personne; *Fin* ***individual savings account*** plan *m* d'epargne en actions; *Cycling* ***individual time trial*** contre-la-montre *m inv* individuel

individualism [ˌɪndɪ'vɪdʒʊəlɪzəm] *n (gen) & Phil & Pol* individualisme *m*

individualist [ˌɪndɪ'vɪdʒʊəlɪst] *n* individualiste *mf*

individualistic [ˌɪndɪˌvɪdʒʊə'lɪstɪk] *adj* individualiste

individualistically [ˌɪndɪˌvɪdʒʊə'lɪstɪklɪ] *adv* du point de vue individualiste

individuality ['ɪndɪˌvɪdʒʊ'ælətɪ] (*pl* **individualities**) *n* individualité *f*

individualization [ˌɪndɪˌvɪdʒʊəlaɪ'zeɪʃən] *n* individualisation *f*

[illegible] liser

individually [ˌɪndɪ'vɪdʒʊəlɪ] *adv* (**a**) *(separately)* individuellement; **he spoke to us all individually** il nous a parlé à tous un par un; **individually wrapped** emballé individuellement *ou* séparément (**b**) *(distinctively)* de façon distinctive; **he dresses very individually** il s'habille de façon très originale, il a une façon très personnelle de s'habiller

individuate [ˌɪndɪ'vɪdʒʊeɪt] *vt* différencier

individuation [ˌɪndɪˌvɪdʒʊ'eɪʃən] *n Phil* individuation *f*

indivisibility [ˌɪndɪˌvɪzə'bɪlɪtɪ] *n* indivisibilité *f*

indivisible [ˌɪndɪ'vɪzəbəl] *adj* indivisible; **17 is indivisible by 3** 17 n'est pas divisible par 3

indivisibly [ˌɪndɪ'vɪzəblɪ] *adv* indivisiblement

Indo- ['ɪndəʊ] *pref* indo-; **an Indo-Pakistani agreement** un accord indo-pakistanais

Indo-Aryan 1 *n* (**a**) *(person)* Indo-Aryen(enne) *m,f* (**b**) *Ling* indo-aryen *m*

2 *adj* indo-aryen

Indochina [ˌɪndəʊ'tʃaɪnə] *n* Indochine *f*; **in Indochina** en Indochine

Indochinese [ˌɪndəʊtʃaɪ'niːz] **1** *n* Indochinois(e) *m,f*

2 *adj* indochinois

indoctrinate [ɪn'dɒktrɪneɪt] *vt* endoctriner; **they were indoctrinated with revolutionary ideas** on leur a inculqué des idées révolutionnaires

indoctrination [ɪnˌdɒktrɪ'neɪʃən] *n* endoctrinement *m*

Indo-European 1 *n* indo-européen *m*

2 *adj* indo-européen

indolence ['ɪndələns] *n* (**a**) *(laziness)* paresse *f*, indolence *f* (**b**) *Med* indolence *f*

indolent ['ɪndələnt] *adj* (**a**) *(lazy)* paresseux, indolent (**b**) *Med* indolent

indolently ['ɪndələntlɪ] *adv* paresseusement, indolemment

Indology [ɪn'dɒlədʒɪ] *n* étude *f* de la civilisation indienne

indomitable [ɪn'dɒmɪtəbəl] *adj* indomptable, irréductible

indomitably [ɪn'dɒmɪtəblɪ] *adv* de façon indomptable, irréductiblement

Indonesia [ˌɪndə'niːzjə] *n* Indonésie *f*; **in Indonesia** en Indonésie

Indonesian [ˌɪndə'niːzjən] **1** *n* (**a**) *(person)* Indonésien(enne) *m,f* (**b**) *(language)* indonésien *m*

2 *adj* indonésien

3 *comp (embassy)* d'Indonésie; *(history)* de l'Indonésie; *(teacher)* d'indonésien

indoor ['ɪndɔː(r)] *adj (toilet)* à l'intérieur; *(clothing)* d'intérieur; *(swimming pool, tennis court)* couvert; *(sport)* pratiqué en salle

►► ***indoor aerial*** antenne *f* intérieure; ***indoor athletics*** athlétisme *m* en salle; ***indoor games*** *(sports)* jeux *mpl* pratiqués en salle; *(board games, charades etc)* jeux *mpl* d'intérieur; ***indoor plants*** plantes *fpl* d'intérieur *or* d'appartement; *Cin & TV* ***indoor scene*** scène *f* tournée en intérieur

indoors [ˌɪn'dɔːz] *adv* à l'intérieur; **let's go indoors** rentrons (à l'intérieur); **it's much cooler indoors** il fait beaucoup plus frais à l'intérieur; **I don't like being indoors all day** je n'aime pas rester enfermée toute la journée

Indo-Pakistan *adj (war, relations)* indo-pakistanais

indorse, indorsee *etc* = **endorse, endorsee** *etc*

indraught, *Am* **indraft** ['ɪndrɑːft] *n (of liquid, air)* afflux *m*

indrawn [ˌɪn'drɔːn] *adj* (**a**) *(air)* aspiré; **indrawn breath** aspiration *f*, inspiration *f* (**b**) *(person)* replié sur soi-même, renfermé

indubitable [ɪn'djuːbɪtəbəl] *adj* indubitable

indubitably [ɪn'djuːbɪtəblɪ] *adv* assurément, indubitablement

induce [ɪn'djuːs] *vt* (**a**) *(cause)* entraîner, provoquer; **this drug sometimes induces sleepiness** ce médicament peut provoquer la somnolence

(**b**) *(persuade)* persuader, décider; **nothing will induce me to change my mind** rien ne me décidera à *ou* ne me fera changer d'avis

(**c**) *Med (labour)* déclencher (artificiellement); **she's had to be induced** on a dû lui faire une piqûre pour provoquer l'accouchement *ou* déclencher le travail

[illegible]

(**e**) *Elec* induire

-induced [ɪn'djuːst] *suff* **work-induced injury** accident *m* du travail; **drug-induced sleep** sommeil *m* provoqué par des médicaments

inducement [ɪn'djuːsmənt] *n* (**a**) *(encouragement)* persuasion *f*; **fears for his daughter's safety will be enough of an inducement** le fait qu'il craint pour la sécurité de sa fille sera une motivation suffisante (**b**) *(reward)* incitation *f*, récompense *f*; *(bribe)* pot-de-vin *m*; **he was offered considerable financial inducements to leave his company** on lui a offert des sommes considérables pour l'inciter à quitter son entreprise

inducer [ɪn'djuːsə(r)] *n Biol & Chem* inducteur *m*

induct [ɪn'dʌkt] *vt* (**a**) *(into office, post)* installer (**b**) *(into mystery, unknown field)* initier; **he was inducted into the Freemasons** il a été initié à la franc-maçonnerie (**c**) *Am Mil* appeler (sous les drapeaux) (**d**) *Elec* induire

►► *Aut* ***inducted gas*** gaz *m* aspiré

inductance [ɪn'dʌktəns] *n Elec* (**a**) *(property)* inductance *f* (**b**) *(component)* inducteur *m*

inductee [ˌɪndʌk'tiː] *n Am Mil* conscrit *m*, appelé *m*

induction [ɪn'dʌkʃən] *n* (**a**) *(into office, post)* installation *f*

(**b**) *(into mystery, new field)* initiation *f*

(**c**) *(causing)* provocation *f*, déclenchement *m*; **induction of sleep by drugs** sommeil *m* provoqué par des médicaments

(**d**) *Med (of labour)* déclenchement *m* (artificiel)

(**e**) *Phil* induction *f*

(**f**) *Am Mil* conscription *f*, appel *m* sous les drapeaux

(**g**) *Biol, Elec & Tech* induction *f*

►► ***induction coil*** bobine *f* d'inductance; *Br* ***induction course*** stage *m* préparatoire *ou* de formation; ***induction heating*** chauffage *m* par induction; ***induction loop*** circuit *m* d'induction; ***induction motor*** moteur *m* à induction

inductive [ɪn'dʌktɪv] *adj* (**a**) *(reasoning)* inductif, par induction (**b**) *Elec (current etc)* inducteur

inductively [ɪn'dʌktɪvlɪ] *adv* par induction

inductor [ɪn'dʌktə(r)] *n* inducteur *m*

indulge [ɪn'dʌldʒ] **1** *vt* (**a**) *(person)* gâter; **she indulges her children** elle gâte ses enfants, elle passe tout à ses enfants; **to indulge oneself** se faire plaisir; **we really indulged ourselves** on s'est vraiment fait plaisir

(**b**) *(desire, vice)* assouvir; *(hope)* nourrir; *(passion)* se livrer à, donner libre cours à; **she indulged her passion for skiing** elle a satisfait sa passion pour le ski; **he indulges her every whim** il se prête à *ou* il lui passe tous ses caprices

(**c**) *Com (debtor)* accorder un délai de paiement à

2 *vi* **to indulge in sth** se livrer à qch; **let us indulge in a little speculation** livrons-nous à quelques suppositions; **I occasionally indulge in a cigar** je me permets un cigare de temps en temps; **no thank you, I don't indulge** *(drink)* non merci, je ne bois pas; *(smoke)* non merci, je ne fume pas

indulgence [ɪn'dʌldʒəns] *n* (**a**) *(tolerance, kindness)* indulgence *f*

(**b**) *(gratification)* assouvissement *m*; **the indulgence of his every desire** l'assouvissement *m* de tous ses désirs; **indulgence in bad habits** fait *m* de se complaire dans de mauvaises habitudes

(**c**) *(privilege)* privilège *m*; *(treat)* gâterie *f*; **we allow ourselves a few small indulgences from time to time** nous nous offrons quelques petites gâteries de temps en temps; **smoking is my only indulgence** mon seul vice, c'est le tabac

(**d**) *Rel* indulgence *f*

indulgent [ɪn'dʌldʒənt] *adj (liberal, kind)* indulgent, complaisant; **you shouldn't be so indulgent with your children** vous ne devriez pas vous montrer aussi indulgent envers vos enfants

indulgently [ɪn'dʌldʒəntlɪ] *adv* avec indulgence

indulin ['ɪndjʊlɪn], **induline** ['ɪndjʊlaɪn] *n* induline *f*

indurated ['ɪndjʊəˌreɪtɪd] *adj* (**a**) *(substance)* durci; *Fig (heart)* endurci (**b**) *Geol & Med* induré (**c**) *(use)* invétéré

induration [ˌɪndjʊə'reɪʃən] *n* (**a**) *(of substance)* durcissement *m*; *Fig (of heart)* endurcissement *m* (**b**) *Geol & Med* induration *f*

Indus ['ɪndəs] *n* **the (River) Indus** l'Indus *m*

industrial [ɪn'dʌstrɪəl] **1** *adj (gen)* industriel; *(unrest)* social; **an industrial city** une ville industrielle; **in industrial quantities** en quantités *fpl* industrielles; **for industrial use only** usage *m* industriel uniquement

2 industrials *npl St Exch* valeurs *fpl* industrielles

►► ***industrial accident*** accident *m* du travail; ***industrial accident insurance*** assurance *f* contre les accidents du travail; *Br* ***industrial action*** *(UNCOUNT)* grève *f*, grèves *fpl*; **they threatened (to take) industrial action** ils ont menacé de faire grève; ***industrial archaeology*** archéologie *f* industrielle; *Am Sch* ***industrial art*** = cours technique où l'on apprend le maniement des machines propres à une industrie particulière; *Fin* ***industrial bank*** banque *f* industrielle; ***industrial centre*** centre *m* industriel; ***industrial complex*** complexe *m* industriel; ***industrial design*** dessin *m* industriel; ***industrial diamond*** diamant *m* industriel *ou* de nature; ***industrial disease*** maladie *f* professionnelle *ou* du travail; *Br* ***industrial dispute*** conflit *m* social; ***industrial espionage*** espionnage *m* industriel; *Br* ***industrial estate*** zone *f* industrielle; ***industrial injury*** accident *m* du travail; ***industrial injuries benefit*** indemnité *f* pour accidents du travail; ***industrial marketer*** mercaticien(enne) *m,f* industriel; ***industrial marketing*** marketing *m* industriel; *Med* ***industrial medicine*** médecine *f* du travail; *Fin* ***industrial monopoly*** trust *m* industriel; *Am* ***industrial park*** zone *f* industrielle; ***industrial relations*** relations *fpl* entre le patronat et les travailleurs; **industrial relations have deteriorated** le climat social s'est dégradé; ***the Industrial Revolution*** la révolution industrielle; *Am* ***industrial school*** école *f* technique; *St Exch* ***industrial shares*** valeurs *mpl* industrielles; *Br & Austr* ***industrial tribunal*** ≃ conseil *m* de prud'hommes; ***industrial unit*** atelier *m*; ***industrial workers*** travailleurs *mpl* de l'industrie; *Ind* ***Industrial Workers of the World*** = syndicat révolutionnaire américain actif au début du XXème siècle

THE INDUSTRIAL REVOLUTION

La révolution industrielle commença en Grande-Bretagne dès le XVIIIème siècle. Elle apporta de profonds changements dans la société britannique en bouleversant ses structures et son fonctionnement traditionnel. Si la richesse nationale augmenta rapidement, transformant la Grande-Bretagne en phare économique mondial, elle fut synonyme de misère pour la classe ouvrière jusqu'au XIXème siècle.

industrialism [ɪn'dʌstrɪəlɪzəm] *n* industrialisme *m*
industrialist [ɪn'dʌstrɪəlɪst] *n* industriel *m*
industrialization [ɪn,dʌstrɪəlaɪ'zeɪʃən] *n* industrialisation *f*
industrialize, -ise [ɪn'dʌstrɪəlaɪz] **1** *vt* industrialiser
2 *vi* s'industrialiser
industrialized [ɪn'dʌstrɪəlaɪzd] *adj* industrialisé
►► ***the industrialized countries*** les pays *mpl* industrialisés
industrial-strength *adj (adhesive, bleach etc)* à usage industriel; *Hum (coffee)* hyper-costaud
industrious [ɪn'dʌstrɪəs] *adj* travailleur
industriously [ɪn'dʌstrɪəslɪ] *adv* avec application
industriousness [ɪn'dʌstrɪəsnɪs] *n* application *f*, diligence *f*
industry ['ɪndʌstrɪ] (*pl* **industries**) *n* (**a**) *(business)* industrie *f*; **both sides of industry** syndicats *mpl* et patronat *m*, les partenaires *mpl* sociaux; **the oil/film industry** l'industrie *f* pétrolière/cinématographique (**b**) *(diligence)* application *f*, diligence *f*
►► ***industry expert*** expert *m* de l'industrie; ***industry forecast*** prévision *f* de l'industrie; ***industry sector*** secteur *m* industriel *ou* secondaire
industry-standard *adj* normalisé
indwell [ɪn'dwel] (*pt & pp* **indwelt** [ɪn'dwelt] *or* **indwelled**) *vi Arch or Literary* **to indwell in a place** demeurer *ou* séjourner dans un lieu
indwelling [ɪn'dwelɪŋ] *adj Arch or Literary (principle, emotion)* intérieur
Indy ['ɪndɪ] *n Fam* (*abbr* **Indianapolis**) Indianapolis ❑
►► ***Indy car*** = type de voiture de course, aux États-Unis; ***the Indy 500*** = course automobile qui se déroule à Indianapolis, aux États-Unis
inebriate *Formal* **1** *n* [ɪ'ni:brɪət] ivrogne *mf*, alcoolique *mf*
2 *adj* [ɪ'ni:brɪət] ivre
3 *vt* [ɪ'ni:brɪeɪt] enivrer, griser
inebriated [ɪ'ni:brɪeɪtɪd] *adj* ivre; *Fig* **inebriated by his success** grisé par son succès
inebriation [ɪ,ni:brɪ'eɪʃən] *n Formal* (**a**) *(act of making drunk)* enivrement *m* (**b**) *(drunkenness)* ivresse *f*, ébriété *f*

inedible [ɪn'edɪbəl] *adj* (**a**) *(unsafe to eat)* non comestible; **inedible mushrooms** des champignons non comestibles (**b**) *(unpleasant to eat)* immangeable
ineducable [ɪn'edjʊkəbəl] *adj* inéducable
ineffable [ɪn'efəbəl] *adj Literary* ineffable, indicible
ineffably [ɪn'efəblɪ] *adv Literary* ineffablement, indiciblement
ineffective [,ɪnɪ'fektɪv] *adj* (**a**) *(person)* inefficace, incapable, incompétent; **an ineffective leader** un dirigeant incompétent (**b**) *(action)* inefficace, sans effet; **the drug is ineffective against the new virus** le médicament est inefficace *ou* n'a aucun effet contre le nouveau virus
ineffectively [,ɪnɪ'fektɪvlɪ] *adv* sans résultat
ineffectiveness [,ɪnɪ'fektɪvnɪs] *n* inefficacité *f*
ineffectual [,ɪnɪ'fektʃʊəl] *adj* inefficace
ineffectuality [,ɪnɪ,fektʃʊ'ælɪtɪ] *n* inefficacité *f*
ineffectually [,ɪnɪ'fektʃʊəlɪ] *adv* inefficacement
ineffectualness [,ɪnɪ'fektʃʊəlnɪs] *n* inefficacité *f*
inefficacious [,ɪnefɪ'keɪʃəs] *adj* inefficace, sans effet
inefficacity [,ɪnefɪ'kæsətɪ], **inefficacy** [ɪn'efɪkəsɪ] *n* inefficacité *f*
inefficiency [,ɪnɪ'fɪʃənsɪ] (*pl* **inefficiencies**) *n* inefficacité *f*, manque *m* d'efficacité; **the inefficiency of the old machines** le manque de rendement *ou* le faible rendement des anciennes machines
inefficient [,ɪnɪ'fɪʃənt] *adj* inefficace; **an inefficient use of resources** une mauvaise utilisation des ressources; **these old machines are too inefficient** le rendement de ces vieilles machines est vraiment insuffisant
inefficiently [,ɪnɪ'fɪʃəntlɪ] *adv* inefficacement
inelastic [,ɪnɪ'læstɪk] *adj* (**a**) *(material)* rigide, inélastique; *(schedule)* rigide, inflexible (**b**) *Phys (collision)* inélastique
inelegance [ɪn'elɪgəns] *n (UNCOUNT)* inélégance *f*
inelegancy [ɪn'elɪgənsɪ] *n* inélégance *f*; **inelegancies of style** inélégances *fpl* de style
inelegant [ɪn'elɪgənt] *adj* inélégant
inelegantly [ɪn'elɪgəntlɪ] *adv* de façon peu élégante
ineligibility [ɪn,elɪdʒə'bɪlətɪ] *n* (**a**) *(gen)* **his ineligibility for unemployment benefit** le fait qu'il n'ait pas droit aux allocations de chômage; **the ineligibility of most of the applications** l'irrecevabilité *f* de la plupart des demandes (**b**) *(for election)* inéligibilité *f*
ineligible [ɪn'elɪdʒəbəl] *adj* (**a**) *(unqualified)* non qualifié; **he is ineligible for the post** il n'est pas qualifié pour le poste; **to be ineligible for military service** être inapte au service militaire; **they are ineligible for unemployment benefit** ils n'ont pas droit aux allocations de chômage; **they are ineligible to vote** ils n'ont pas le droit de voter (**b**) *(for election)* inéligible
ineluctability [,ɪnɪ,lʌktə'bɪlətɪ] *n Formal* inéluctabilité *f*
ineluctable [,ɪnɪ'lʌktəbəl] *adj Formal* inéluctable
ineluctably [,ɪnɪ'lʌktəblɪ] *adv Formal* inéluctablement
inept [ɪ'nept] *adj* inepte
ineptitude [ɪ'neptɪtju:d] *n* ineptie *f*
ineptly [ɪ'neptlɪ] *adv* absurdement, stupidement
ineptness [ɪ'neptnɪs] *n* ineptie *f*
inequality [,ɪnɪ'kwɒlətɪ] (*pl* **inequalities**) *n* inégalité *f*
inequitable [ɪn'ekwɪtəbəl] *adj* inéquitable
inequitably [ɪn'ekwɪtəblɪ] *adv* inéquitablement
inequity [ɪn'ekwətɪ] (*pl* **inequities**) *n Formal* injustice *f*, iniquité *f*
ineradicable [,ɪnɪ'rædɪkəbəl] *adj* indéracinable
inert [ɪ'nɜ:t] *adj* inerte
►► ***inert gas*** gaz *m* inerte
inertia [ɪ'nɜ:ʃə] *n* inertie *f*
►► *Br Mktg* ***inertia selling*** *(UNCOUNT)* vente *f* forcée
inertial [ɪ'nɜ:ʃəl] *adj* inertiel
►► *Mil* ***inertial guidance*** guidage *m* inertiel
inertia-reel seat belt *n Br* ceinture *f* de sécurité à enrouleur
inertness [ɪ'nɜ:tnɪs] *n* inertie *f*; *Chem (of body)* inactivité *f*

inescapable [,ɪnɪ'skeɪpəbəl] *adj (outcome)* inévitable, inéluctable; *(fact)* indéniable
inescapably [,ɪnɪ'skeɪpəblɪ] *adv* inévitablement, indéniablement
inessential [,ɪnɪ'senʃəl] **1** *adj* non essentiel
2 inessentials *npl* superflu *m*; **to do without inessentials** se passer du superflu
inestimable [ɪn'estɪməbəl] *adj* inestimable, incalculable
inestimably [ɪn'estɪməblɪ] *adv* **they're inestimably rich** ils ont une fortune incalculable; **he's been inestimably lucky** il a eu une chance absolument incroyable
inevitability [ɪn,evɪtə'bɪlətɪ] *n* inévitabilité *f*
inevitable [ɪn'evɪtəbəl] **1** *adj (outcome, consequence)* inévitable, inéluctable; *(end)* inévitable, fatal; **war seems inevitable** la guerre semble inévitable; **it's inevitable that someone will feel left out** il est inévitable *ou* on ne pourra empêcher que quelqu'un se sente exclu; **the inevitable cigarette in his mouth** l'éternelle *ou* l'inévitable cigarette au coin des lèvres
2 *n* inévitable *m*; **we had to resign ourselves to the inevitable** il fallut nous résoudre à accepter l'inévitable
inevitably [ɪn'evɪtəblɪ] *adv* inévitablement, fatalement
inexact [,ɪnɪg'zækt] *adj (imprecise)* imprécis; *(wrong)* inexact, erroné; **our figures are still inexact** nos chiffres sont encore imprécis; **it's an inexact science** ce n'est pas une science exacte
inexactitude [,ɪnɪg'zæktɪtju:d] *n* (**a**) *(imprecision)* imprécision *f*; *(incorrectness)* inexactitude *f* (**b**) *(mistake)* inexactitude *f*
inexactly [,ɪnɪg'zæktlɪ] *adv (imprecisely)* de façon imprécise; *(incorrectly)* inexactement, incorrectement
inexactness [,ɪnɪg'zæktnɪs] *n (imprecision)* imprécision *f*; *(incorrectness)* inexactitude *f*
inexcusable [,ɪnɪk'skju:zəbəl] *adj* inexcusable, impardonnable
inexcusably [,ɪnɪk'skju:zəblɪ] *adv* inexcusablement, impardonnablement; **inexcusably rude** d'une grossièreté impardonnable; **he behaved quite inexcusably at the party** la façon dont il s'est comporté à la soirée est inexcusable
inexhaustible [,ɪnɪg'zɔ:stəbəl] *adj* (**a**) *(source, energy, patience)* inépuisable, illimité; **she had an inexhaustible supply of jokes** elle avait un stock de blagues inépuisable (**b**) *(person)* infatigable
inexorability [ɪn,eksərə'bɪlɪtɪ] *n (of fate, event etc)* inexorabilité *f*; *(of person)* caractère *m* inexorable
inexorable [ɪn'eksərəbəl] *adj* inexorable
inexorableness [ɪn'eksərəbəlnɪs] *n (of fate, event etc)* inexorabilité *f*; *(of person)* caractère *m* inexorable
inexorably [ɪn'eksərəblɪ] *adv* inexorablement
inexpedient [,ɪnɪk'spi:djənt] *adj* peu judicieux, malavisé
inexpensive [,ɪnɪk'spensɪv] *adj* bon marché *(inv)*, peu cher
inexpensively [,ɪnɪk'spensɪvlɪ] *adv (sell)* (à) bon marché, à bas prix; *(live)* à peu de frais
inexperience [,ɪnɪk'spɪərɪəns] *n* inexpérience *f*, manque *m* d'expérience
inexperienced [,ɪnɪk'spɪərɪənst] *adj* (**a**) *(person)* inexpérimenté, sans expérience; **she is still inexperienced** elle manque encore d'expérience; **he's inexperienced in handling staff** il n'a pas l'habitude de diriger le personnel (**b**) *(eye, ear)* inexercé
inexpert [ɪn'ekspɜ:t] *adj* inexpérimenté, inexpert; **he was inexpert in such matters** il ne connaissait pas grand-chose à ces choses; **her inexpert handling of the situation** la façon maladroite dont elle a géré l'affaire
inexpertly [ɪn'ekspɜ:tlɪ] *adv* maladroitement
inexpiable [ɪn'ekspɪəbəl] *adj Formal* inexpiable
inexplicable [,ɪnɪk'splɪkəbəl] *adj* inexplicable
inexplicably [,ɪnɪk'splɪkəblɪ] *adv* inexplicablement
inexpressible [,ɪnɪk'spresəbəl] *adj* inexprimable, indicible
inexpressibly [,ɪnɪks'presəblɪ] *adv* inexprimablement, indiciblement
inexpressive [,ɪnɪk'spresɪv] *adj* inexpressif

inextinguishable [ˌɪnɪk'stɪŋgwɪʃəbəl] *adj (fire)* impossible à éteindre; *(need, desire)* insatiable; *(thirst)* inextinguible; *(passion)* irrépressible, incontrôlable

in extremis [ɪnɪk'striːmɪs] **1** *adv* à l'extrême rigueur, à la limite

2 *adj* **to be in extremis** être à l'article de la mort

inextricable [ˌɪnɪk'strɪkəbəl] *adj* inextricable

inextricably [ˌɪnɪk'strɪkəblɪ] *adv* inextricablement

INF [ˌaɪen'ef] *npl Mil (abbr* **intermediate range nuclear forces***)* FNI *fpl*

infallibility [ɪnˌfælə'bɪlətɪ] *n* infaillibilité *f*

infallible [ɪn'fæləbəl] *adj* infaillible

infallibly [ɪn'fæləblɪ] *adv* infailliblement, immanquablement

infamous ['ɪnfəməs] *adj* (**a**) *(notorious)* tristement célèbre, notoire (**b**) *(shocking → conduct)* infâme

infamously ['ɪnfəməslɪ] *adv (behave)* de manière infâme

infamy ['ɪnfəmɪ] *(pl* **infamies***)* *n* (**a**) *(notoriety)* triste notoriété *f* (**b**) *(notorious act, event)* infamie *f*

infancy ['ɪnfənsɪ] *(pl* **infancies***)* *n* (**a**) *(early childhood)* petite enfance *f*; **a child in its infancy** un enfant en bas âge (**b**) *Fig* débuts *mpl*, enfance *f*; **when electronics was still in its infancy** quand l'électronique n'en était qu'à ses balbutiements (**c**) *Law* minorité *f* (légale)

infant ['ɪnfənt] **1** *n* (**a**) *(young child)* petit(e) enfant *mf*, enfant *mf* en bas âge; *(baby)* bébé *m*; *(new-born)* nouveau-né(e) *m,f* (**b**) *Br Sch* = élève dans les premières années d'école primaire (**c**) *Law* mineur(e) *m,f*

2 *comp* (**a**) *(food)* pour bébés; *(disease)* infantile (**b**) *Br (teacher, teaching)* des premières années d'école primaire

3 *adj (organization)* naissant

►► ***the infant Church*** l'Église *f* des origines *or* des premiers jours; ***infant mortality*** mortalité *f* infantile; ***infant mortality rate*** taux *m* de mortalité infantile; *Br* ***infant school*** école *f* maternelle *(5–7 ans)*

infanta [ɪn'fæntə] *n Hist* infante *f*

infante [ɪn'fæntɪ] *n Hist* infant *m*

infanticide [ɪn'fæntɪsaɪd] *n* (**a**) *(act)* infanticide *m* (**b**) *(person)* infanticide *mf*

infantile ['ɪnfəntaɪl] *adj* (**a**) *Pej (childish)* infantile, puéril (**b**) *(of, for infants)* infantile

►► *Old-fashioned* ***infantile paralysis*** *(UNCOUNT)* paralysie *f* infantile

infantilism [ɪn'fæntɪlɪzəm] *n* infantilisme *m*

infantry ['ɪnfəntrɪ] **1** *n* infanterie *f*

2 *adj* de l'infanterie

infantryman ['ɪnfəntrɪmən] *(pl* **infantrymen** [-mən]*)* *n* soldat *m* d'infanterie, fantassin *m*

infarct [ɪn'fɑːkt] *n Med* infarctus *m (du myocarde)*

infarcted [ɪn'fɑːktɪd] *adj Med (tissue)* atteint d'un infarctus

infarction [ɪn'fɑːkʃən] *n Med* infarctus *m (du myocarde)*

infatuate [ɪn'fætjʊeɪt] *vt* **the desire for wealth that has infatuated the population** l'appât du gain qui s'est emparé de la population

infatuated [ɪn'fætjʊeɪtɪd] *adj* entiché (**with** de) **to become infatuated with sb/sth** s'enticher de qn/qch

infatuation [ɪnˌfætjʊ'eɪʃən] *n* engouement *m* (**for** *or* **with** pour)

infect [ɪn'fekt] *vt* (**a**) *Med (wound, organ, person, animal)* infecter; **is the liver infected?** est-ce que le foie est infecté *ou* atteint?; **I hope that cut won't get infected** j'espère que cette coupure ne s'infectera pas; **to infect sb with sth** transmettre qch à qn; **he infected all his friends with the flu** il a transmis *ou* donné sa grippe à tous ses amis

(**b**) *(food, water, area, clothing)* contaminer

(**c**) *Comput (file, disk)* infecter

(**d**) *Fig (of vice)* corrompre, contaminer; *(of emotion)* se communiquer à; **they infected us with their enthusiasm** ils nous ont communiqué leur enthousiasme

infected [ɪn'fektɪd] *adj* (**a**) *(wound, organ, person, animal)* infecté (**b**) *(food, water, area, clothing)* contaminé (**c**) *Comput* infecté

infection [ɪn'fekʃən] *n* (**a**) *Med* infection *f*; **a throat infection** une infection de la gorge, une angine (**b**) *Fig* contagion *f*, contamination *f*

infectious [ɪn'fekʃəs] *adj* (**a**) *Med (disease)* infectieux; *(person)* contagieux (**b**) *Fig (laughter, enthusiasm etc)* contagieux, communicatif

►► *Med* ***infectious hepatitis*** *(UNCOUNT)* hépatite *f* infectieuse, hépatite *f* virale A; *Med* ***infectious mononucleosis*** *(UNCOUNT)* mononucléose *f* infectieuse

infectiousness [ɪn'fekʃəsnɪs] *n* (**a**) *Med* caractère *m* infectieux (**b**) *Fig* caractère *m* contagieux *ou* communicatif

infectiveness [ɪn'fektɪvnɪs], **infectivity** [ˌɪnfek'tɪvɪtɪ] *n Med* infectiosité *f*

infelicitous [ˌɪnfɪ'lɪsɪtəs] *adj Literary* malheureux, malchanceux

infelicity [ˌɪnfɪ'lɪsɪtɪ] *(pl* **infelicities***)* *n Literary* (**a**) *(state of misfortune)* malchance *f*, infortune *f* (**b**) *(piece of bad luck)* malchance *f* (**c**) *(remark)* parole *f* malheureuse, maladresse *f*

infer [ɪn'fɜː(r)] *(pt & pp* **inferred**, *cont* **inferring***)* *vt* (**a**) *(deduce)* conclure, inférer, déduire; **what are we to infer from their absence?** que devons-nous conclure de leur absence?; **I inferred from his look that I had done something wrong** à son regard, j'ai compris que j'avais fait quelque chose de mal (**b**) *Fam (imply)* suggérer[❑], laisser supposer[❑]; **what are you inferring by that?** qu'insinuez-vous par là?[❑]

inference ['ɪnfərəns] *n* déduction *f*; *(in logic)* inférence *f*; **what inferences can we draw from it?** quelles conclusions pouvons-nous en tirer?, que pouvons-nous en déduire?

inferential [ˌɪnfə'renʃəl] *adj (reasoning)* déductif; **inferential proof** preuves *fpl* obtenues par déduction

inferentially [ˌɪnfə'renʃəlɪ] *adv (reason)* par déduction; **inferentially he's not to be trusted** on peut conclure de là qu'on ne peut se fier à lui

inferior [ɪn'fɪərɪə(r)] **1** *n (in social status)* inférieur(e) *m,f*; *(in rank, hierarchy)* subalterne *mf*, subordonné(e) *m,f*; **he never speaks to his inferiors** il n'adresse jamais la parole à ses subordonnés

2 *adj* (**a**) *(quality, worth, social status)* inférieur; **he always felt inferior to his brother** il a toujours éprouvé un sentiment d'infériorité par rapport à son frère; **to make sb feel inferior** donner un sentiment d'infériorité à qn; **inferior imported goods** marchandises *fpl* importées de qualité inférieure

(**b**) *(in rank)* subalterne; **she holds an inferior position in the company** elle a un poste subalterne dans la société

(**c**) *(in space, position)* inférieur

►► *Typ* ***inferior character*** (caractère *m* en) indice *m*; *Law* ***inferior court*** cour *f* de juridiction inférieure; *Anat* ***inferior maxillary*** mâchoire *f* inférieure; *Bot* ***inferior ovary*** ovaire *m* infère *or* adhérent; ***inferior planet*** planète *f* inférieure

inferiority [ɪnˌfɪərɪ'ɒrətɪ] *(pl* **inferiorities***)* *n* infériorité *f*

►► ***inferiority complex*** complexe *m* d'infériorité

infernal [ɪn'fɜːnəl] *adj* (**a**) *Fam (awful)* infernal; **stop that infernal racket** *or* **din!** arrêtez ce raffut *ou* boucan infernal!; **that infernal fuse has blown again!** ce satané fusible a encore sauté! (**b**) *(of hell)* infernal; *(diabolical)* infernal, diabolique; **the infernal regions** l'enfer *m*

infernally [ɪn'fɜːnəlɪ] *adv Fam* terriblement, épouvantablement; **it's infernally hot** il fait une chaleur d'enfer

inferno [ɪn'fɜːnəʊ] *(pl* **infernos***)* *n* (**a**) *(fire)* brasier *m*; **the hotel was a blazing inferno** l'hôtel n'était qu'un gigantesque brasier (**b**) *(hell)* enfer *m*

infertile [ɪn'fɜːtaɪl] *adj (person, animal)* stérile; *(land, soil)* stérile, infertile

infertility [ˌɪnfə'tɪlətɪ] *n (of person)* stérilité *f*; *(of soil)* stérilité, infertilité *f*

►► ***infertility clinic*** = service qui s'occupe des problèmes de stérilité dans un établissement hospitalier

infest [ɪn'fest] *vt* infester (**with** de); **shark-infested waters** eaux *fpl* infestées de requins

infestation [ˌɪnfe'steɪʃən] *n Med* infestation *f*; *Bot (of plants by parasites etc)* invasion *f*

infibulation [ɪnˌfɪbjʊ'leɪʃən] *n* infibulation *f*

infidel ['ɪnfɪdəl] **1** *n* infidèle *mf*

2 *adj* infidèle, incroyant

infidelity [ˌɪnfɪ'delətɪ] *(pl* **infidelities***)* *n* (**a**) *(betrayal)* infidélité *f* (**b**) *(lack of faith)* incroyance *f*, irréligion *f*

infield ['ɪnfiːld] *n Sport (in baseball → area)* champ *m* intérieur; *(→ players)* joueurs *mpl* positionnés dans le champ intérieur

infighting ['ɪnˌfaɪtɪŋ] *n (UNCOUNT)* (**a**) *Br (within group)* conflits *mpl* internes, luttes *fpl* intestines (**b**) *(in boxing)* corps à corps *m*

infill ['ɪnfɪl] **1** *n* matériau *m* de remplissage

2 *vt* remplir, combler

infilling ['ɪnfɪlɪŋ] *n (material)* matériau *m* de remplissage

infiltrate ['ɪnfɪltreɪt] **1** *vt* (**a**) *(organization)* infiltrer, noyauter; **the police had infiltrated the terrorist group** la police avait infiltré *ou* noyauté le groupe terroriste; **they infiltrated spies into the organization** ils ont envoyé des espions pour infiltrer l'organisation (**b**) *(of liquid → substance)* s'infiltrer dans (**c**) *(cause to enter → liquid)* faire pénétrer (**into** dans)

2 *vi* s'infiltrer

3 *n* infiltrat *m*

infiltration [ˌɪnfɪl'treɪʃən] *n* (**a**) *(of group)* infiltration *f*, noyautage *m* (**b**) *(by liquid)* infiltration *f* (**into/through** dans/à travers)

infiltrator ['ɪnfɪltreɪtə(r)] *n* agent *m* infiltré; **there are infiltrators in the party** le parti a été infiltré *ou* noyauté

infinite ['ɪnfɪnət] **1** *adj* (**a**) *(not finite)* infini (**b**) *Fig (very great)* infini, incalculable; **he showed infinite patience** il a fait preuve d'une patience infinie; *Ironic* **the government, in its infinite wisdom, has decided to close the factory** le gouvernement, dans son infinie sagesse, a décidé de fermer l'usine

2 *n* infini *m*

►► *Math* ***infinite set*** ensemble *m* infini

infinitely ['ɪnfɪnətlɪ] *adv* infiniment

infinitesimal [ˌɪnfɪnɪ'tesɪməl] *adj* (**a**) *Math* infinitésimal (**b**) *(tiny)* infinitésimal, infime

►► ***infinitesimal calculus*** calcul *m* infinitésimal

infinitesimally [ˌɪnfɪnɪ'tesɪməlɪ] *adv* infiniment

infinitival [ɪnˌfɪnɪ'taɪvəl] *adj Gram* infinitif

►► ***infinitival clause*** proposition *f* infinitive

infinitive [ɪn'fɪnɪtɪv] *Gram* **1** *n* infinitif *m*; **in the infinitive** à l'infinitif

2 *adj* infinitif

infinitude [ɪn'fɪnɪˌtjuːd] *n* infinité *f*, infinitude *f*; *Literary* **an infinitude of misfortunes** une infinité de malheurs

infinity [ɪn'fɪnətɪ] *(pl* **infinities***)* *n* (**a**) *(of space, time, quantity etc)* infinité *f*, infini *m*; *Fig* **there is an infinity of names to choose from** on peut choisir parmi une infinité de noms; **it stretches to infinity** cela s'étend jusqu'à l'infini (**b**) *Math & Phot* infini *m*; **to focus on** *or* **for infinity** mettre au point sur l'infini

infirm [ɪn'fɜːm] **1** *adj* (**a**) *(in health, body)* invalide, infirme (**b**) *Literary (in moral resolution)* indécis, irrésolu; **to be infirm of purpose** manquer de détermination (**c**) *Law* invalide

2 *npl* **the infirm** les infirmes *mpl*

infirmary [ɪn'fɜːmərɪ] *(pl* **infirmaries***)* *n (hospital)* hôpital *m*; *(sickroom)* infirmerie *f*

infirmity [ɪn'fɜːmətɪ] *(pl* **infirmities***)* *n* (**a**) *(physical)* infirmité *f* (**b**) *(moral)* défaut *m*, faiblesse *f*

infix **1** *n* ['ɪnfɪks] *Ling* infixe *m*

2 *vt* [ɪn'fɪks] (**a**) *(instil)* instiller, implanter (**b**) *Ling* insérer (comme infixe)

inflame [ɪn'fleɪm] **1** *vt* (**a**) *(rouse → person, crowd)* exciter, enflammer; *(→ anger, hatred, passion)* attiser, exacerber; **the argument became inflamed** la discussion s'est enflammée; **she was inflamed with anger/passion** elle brûlait de colère/de passion

(**b**) *Med (wound, infection)* enflammer; *(organ, tissue)* irriter, infecter

(**c**) *(set fire to)* enflammer, mettre le feu à

(**d**) *Literary (redden)* enflammer

2 *vi* (**a**) *(person, heart, passion)* s'enflammer

(**b**) *Med (wound, infection)* s'enflammer; *(organ, tissue)* s'irriter, s'infecter

(**c**) *(catch fire)* s'enflammer, s'embraser

inflamed [ɪn'fleɪmd] *adj* (**a**) *Med (eyes, throat, tendon, wound)* enflammé, irrité (**b**) *Fig (passion, hatred)* enflammé, ardent (**with** de); **inflamed with passion** brûlant d'amour

inflammability [ɪn,flæmə'bɪlɪtɪ] *n* inflammabilité *f*

inflammable [ɪn'flæməbəl] **1** *n* matière *f* inflammable

2 *adj (substance, material)* inflammable; *Fig (person, crowd)* prompt à s'échauffer; *Fig* **an inflammable situation** une situation explosive

inflammableness [ɪn'flæməbəlnɪs] *n* inflammabilité *f*

inflammation [,ɪnflə'meɪʃən] *n* inflammation *f*

inflammatory [ɪn'flæmətrɪ] *adj* (**a**) *(speech, propaganda)* incendiaire (**b**) *Med* inflammatoire

inflatable [ɪn'fleɪtəbəl] **1** *adj (toy)* gonflable; *(mattress, boat)* pneumatique

2 *n* structure *f* gonflable

inflate [ɪn'fleɪt] **1** *vt* (**a**) *(tyre, balloon, boat)* gonfler; *(lungs)* emplir d'air; *(chest)* gonfler, bomber

(**b**) *(opinion, importance)* gonfler, exagérer; **to inflate the importance of an event** exagérer *ou* grossir l'importance d'un événement

(**c**) *Econ (prices)* faire monter, augmenter; *(economy)* provoquer l'inflation de; **to inflate the currency** accroître la circulation monétaire

(**d**) *Com (account)* grossir, charger; *(expense account, figures)* gonfler

2 *vi* (**a**) *(tyre)* se gonfler; *(lungs)* s'emplir d'air; *(chest)* se gonfler, se bomber

(**b**) *Econ (prices, money)* subir une inflation; **the government decided to inflate** le gouvernement a décidé d'avoir recours à des mesures inflationnistes

inflated [ɪn'fleɪtɪd] *adj* (**a**) *(balloon, tyre)* gonflé (**b**) *(opinion, importance)* exagéré; *(style)* emphatique, pompier; **inflated with pride** bouffi d'orgueil; **he has an inflated sense of his own importance** il se fait une idée exagérée de sa propre importance (**c**) *Econ (price)* exagéré

►► ***inflated currency*** inflation *f* monétaire

inflation [ɪn'fleɪʃən] *n* (**a**) *Econ* inflation *f*; **inflation is down/up on last year** l'inflation est en baisse/en hausse par rapport à l'année dernière; **inflation now stands at 5 percent** l'inflation est maintenant à 5 pour cent (**b**) *(of tyre, balloon, boat)* gonflement *m* (**c**) *(of idea, importance)* grossissement *m*, exagération *f*

►► *Fin* ***inflation tax*** impôt *m* à la production

inflationary [ɪn'fleɪʃənrɪ] *adj* inflationniste, *Belg* inflatoire

►► ***inflationary spiral*** spirale *f* inflationniste

inflationism [ɪn'fleɪʃənɪzəm] *n* inflationnisme *m*

inflationist [ɪn'fleɪʃənɪst] **1** *n* inflationniste *mf*

2 *adj* inflationniste, *Belg* inflatoire

inflation-proof *adj* protégé contre les effets de l'inflation

inflect [ɪn'flekt] **1** *vt* (**a**) *Ling (verb)* conjuguer; *(noun, pronoun, adjective)* décliner (**b**) *(tone, voice)* moduler; *Mus (note)* altérer (**c**) *(curve, light beam)* infléchir

2 *vi Ling* se décliner; *(verb)* se conjuguer; **adjectives do not inflect in English** les adjectifs ne se déclinent pas en anglais

inflected [ɪn'flektɪd] *adj Ling (language)* à flexions, flexionnel; *(vowel)* infléchi

►► ***inflected form*** forme *f* fléchie

inflection [ɪn'flekʃən] *n* (**a**) *(of tone, voice)* inflexion *f*, modulation *f* (**b**) *Ling* désinence *f*, flexion *f* (**c**) *(curve)* flexion *f*, inflexion *f*, courbure *f* (**d**) *Math* inflexion *f*; **point of inflection** point *m* d'inflexion

inflectional [ɪn'flekʃənəl] *adj* flexionnel

inflexibility [ɪn,fleksə'bɪlətɪ] *n* inflexibilité *f*, rigidité *f*

inflexible [ɪn'fleksəbəl] *adj* inflexible, rigide

inflexibly [ɪn'fleksəblɪ] *adv* inflexiblement, rigidement

inflexion, inflexional *Br* = **inflection, inflectional**

inflict [ɪn'flɪkt] *vt* infliger; **to inflict pain/suffering on sb** faire mal à/faire souffrir qn; **to inflict a defeat on sb** infliger une défaite à qn; **I don't want to inflict myself** *or* **my company on you** je ne veux pas vous infliger ma compagnie

infliction [ɪn'flɪkʃən] *n (action)* action *f* d'infliger; **to take pleasure in the infliction of pain** prendre du plaisir à infliger de la douleur

in-flight *adj* en vol

►► ***in-flight meal*** plateau-repas *m*; ***in-flight refuelling*** ravitaillement *m* en vol; ***in-flight video*** vidéo *f* projetée en vol

inflorescence [,ɪnflə'resəns] *n Bot* (**a**) *(part of plant)* inflorescence *f* (**b**) *(blossoming)* floraison *f*

inflow ['ɪnfləʊ] *n (of water, gas)* arrivée *f*; *(of people, goods)* afflux *m*; **the inflow of capital** l'afflux *m* de capitaux

influence ['ɪnflʊəns] **1** *n* influence *f*; **to have influence** avoir de l'influence; **to bring one's influence to bear on sth** exercer son influence sur qch; **he is a man of influence** c'est un homme influent; **foreign influence in Africa** l'influence étrangère en Afrique; **I have no influence over them** je n'ai aucune influence sur eux; **he is a bad influence on them** il a une mauvaise influence sur eux; **she is a disruptive influence** c'est un élément perturbateur; **you can see the influence of Bacon in his paintings** on voit l'influence de Bacon dans ses tableaux; **his music has a strong reggae influence** sa musique est fortement influencée par le reggae; **they acted under his influence** ils ont agi sous son influence; **she was under the influence of drink/drugs** elle était sous l'emprise de l'alcool/de la drogue; **driving under the influence of alcohol** conduite *f* en état d'ivresse; *Fam* **to be under the influence** *(drunk)* être soûl ❑

2 *vt* influencer, influer sur; **influenced by cubism** influencé par le cubisme; **don't let yourself be influenced by them** ne te laisse pas influencer par eux; **to influence sb to the good** exercer une bonne influence sur qn; **he is easily influenced** il se laisse facilement influencer, il est très influençable; **how can the stars influence our lives?** comment les étoiles peuvent-elles influer sur notre vie?

influencer ['ɪnflʊənsə(r)] *n Mktg* préconisateur *m*, influenceur *m*

influential [,ɪnflʊ'enʃəl] *adj* influent, puissant; *(newspaper, TV programme)* influent, qui a de l'influence; **she's an influential woman** c'est une femme qui a de l'influence; **he was influential in getting her a job** il a fait jouer son influence pour l'aider à obtenir du travail

influentially [,ɪnflʊ'enʃəlɪ] *adv (with influential result)* **he wrote influentially on the subject** ses écrits à ce sujet ont eu une influence certaine; **she argued influentially that women should have the right to vote** ses arguments en faveur du droit de vote des femmes ont eu une grande influence

influenza [,ɪnflʊ'enzə] *n (UNCOUNT) Formal* grippe *f*; **to have influenza** avoir la grippe

influx ['ɪnflʌks] *n* (**a**) *(of water, gas)* arrivée *f*; *(of people, goods, cash)* afflux *m*; **an influx of capital** un afflux de capitaux (**b**) *(of river)* embouchure *f*

info ['ɪnfəʊ] *n (UNCOUNT) Fam* informations ❑ *fpl*, renseignements ❑ *mpl*; *(brochure, leaflet)* doc *f*, documentation ❑ *f*; **a piece of info** une information, un renseignement

infoaddict ['ɪnfəʊ,ædɪkt] *n Fam Comput* accro *mf* de l'Internet

infobahn ['ɪnfəʊbɑːn] *n Br Comput* autoroute *f* de l'information, *Can* inforoute *f*

infohighway [,ɪnfəʊ'haɪweɪ] *n Comput* autoroute *f* de l'information, *Can* inforoute *f*

infomercial [,ɪnfəʊ'mɜːʃəl] *n* infomercial *m*

inform [ɪn'fɔːm] **1** *vt* (**a**) *(tell)* informer; **will you inform him of your decision?** allez-vous l'informer de votre décision?; **I have been informed that the funds have arrived** on m'a informé que les fonds sont arrivés; **I'll keep you informed** je vous tiendrai au courant; **why was I not informed (of this)?** pourquoi est-ce que je n'en ai pas été informé?; **I regret to have to inform you that...** j'ai le regret de vous annoncer que...; **we are writing to inform you of the dispatch of...** nous vous avisons de l'envoi de...

(**b**) *Literary (pervade → literary work etc)* imprégner

2 *vi* **to inform on** *or* **against sb** dénoncer qn

informal [ɪn'fɔːməl] *adj* (**a**) *(discussion, meeting)* informel; *(dinner)* décontracté; **he's very informal for a prime minister** il est très décontracté pour un premier ministre; **British offices tend to be more informal than German ones** en Grande-Bretagne l'ambiance dans les bureaux tend à être plus décontractée qu'en Allemagne

(**b**) *(clothes)* **his dress was informal** il était habillé simplement; **informal or evening dress?** tenue de ville ou tenue de soirée?

(**c**) *(unofficial → arrangement, agreement)* officieux; *(→ visit, talks)* non officiel; **I had an informal chat with the boss** j'ai discuté un peu avec le patron; **they had informal talks with the Russians** ils ont eu des entretiens non officiels avec les Russes

(**d**) *(colloquial → speech, language, words)* familier

►► ***informal economy*** travail *m* au noir; *Austr* ***informal vote*** bulletin *m* nul

informality [,ɪnfɔː'mælətɪ] *(pl* **informalities***)* *n* (**a**) *(of gathering, meal)* simplicité *f*; *(of discussion, interview)* absence *f* de formalité; *(of manners)* naturel *m* (**b**) *(of speech, language, words)* familiarité *f*, liberté *f*

informally [ɪn'fɔːməlɪ] *adv* (**a**) *(casually → entertain, discuss)* sans cérémonie; *(→ behave)* simplement, avec naturel; *(→ dress)* simplement (**b**) *(unofficially)* officieusement (**c**) *(colloquially)* familièrement, avec familiarité

informant [ɪn'fɔːmənt] *n* informateur(trice) *m,f*; **I have it from a reliable informant** je le tiens de source sûre

informatics [,ɪnfə'mætɪks] *n (UNCOUNT)* sciences *fpl* de l'information

information [,ɪnfə'meɪʃən] *n* (**a**) *(UNCOUNT) (facts)* renseignements *mpl*, informations *fpl*; **a piece** *or* **bit of information** un renseignement, une information; **if my information is correct** si mes informations sont exactes; **do you have any information on** *or* **about the new model?** avez-vous des renseignements concernant *ou* sur le nouveau modèle?; **I'd like some information about train times** je voudrais des renseignements sur les horaires des trains; **for more information, call this number** pour plus de renseignements *ou* de précisions, appelez ce numéro; **I am sending you this brochure for your information** je vous envoie cette brochure à titre d'information; **for your information, I'm not stupid** sachez que je ne suis pas complètement idiot; **for your information, I've done the dishes for the past week!** je t'apprendrai que j'ai fait la vaisselle toute cette semaine!; **his head is full of useless information** il encombre sa mémoire de choses inutiles; **the government is operating an information blackout** le gouvernement fait de la rétention d'information

(**b**) *(communication)* information *f*; **they discussed the importance of information in our time** ils ont parlé de l'importance de l'information à notre époque; **information overload** surinformation *f*

(**c**) *(UNCOUNT) (knowledge)* connaissances *fpl*; **her information on the subject is unequalled** elle connaît ce sujet mieux que personne; *Admin* **for your information, please find enclosed...** à titre d'information, vous trouverez ci-joint...; **for your information, it happened in 1938** je vous signale que cela s'est passé en 1938

(**d**) *Comput (data)* information *f*; **the transmission of genetic information** la transmission de l'information génétique

(**e**) *(UNCOUNT) (service, department)* (service *m* des) renseignements *mpl*; **ask at the information desk** adressez-vous aux renseignements

(**f**) *Am Tel* renseignements *mpl*; **to call information** appeler les renseignements

(**g**) *Br Law* acte *m* d'accusation; **to lay an information against sb** déposer une plainte contre qn

►► *Br* ***information bureau*** bureau *m or* service *m* des renseignements; ***information carrier*** support *m* d'information; ***information copy*** *(of document)* copie *f* pour information; ***information desk*** *(in hotel etc)* bureau *m* des renseignements; ***information gathering*** collecte *f* d'informations; *Comput* ***information highway*** autoroute *f* de l'information, *Can* inforoute *f*; ***information market*** marché *m* des informations; ***information office*** bureau *m ou* service *m* des renseignements; ***information officer*** *(press officer)* responsable *mf* de la communication; *(archivist)* documentaliste *mf*; ***information pack*** dossier *m* d'information; ***information processing*** *(action)* traitement *m* de l'information; *(domain)* informatique *f*; ***information processing error*** erreur *f* dans le traitement de l'information; ***information retrieval*** recherche *f* documentaire; *Comput* recherche *f* d'information; ***information science*** science *f* de l'information; ***information scientist*** informaticien(enne) *m,f*; ***information sheet*** fiche *f* explicative; *Comput* ***information society*** société *f* de l'information; ***information storage*** mémorisation *f* des informations; ***information system*** système *m* informatique; *Comput* ***information superhighway*** autoroute *f* de l'information, *Can* inforoute *f*; ***information technology*** technologie *f* de l'information, informatique *f*; ***information theory*** théorie *f* de l'information

informational [ˌɪnfə'meɪʃənəl] *adj* (**a**) *(informative)* instructif, informant (**b**) *Comput (relating to information)* informationnel, sur le plan information

informative [ɪn'fɔːmətɪv] *adj (lecture, book, TV programme)* instructif; **he wasn't very informative about his future plans** il ne nous a pas dit grand-chose de ses projets

►► *Mktg* ***informative advertising*** publicité *f* informative

informed [ɪn'fɔːmd] *adj* (**a**) *(having information)* informé, renseigné; **informed opinion has it that...** on sait de source sûre *ou* dans les milieux renseignés que...; **she's very well informed** elle est très bien informée *ou* renseignée; **he made an informed guess** il a essayé de deviner en s'aidant de ce qu'il sait; **according to informed sources** selon des sources bien informées

(**b**) *(based on information)* **an informed choice** un choix fait en toute connaissance de cause; **it will allow us to make informed decisions** cela nous permettra de prendre des décisions en toute connaissance de cause

(**c**) *(learned, cultured)* cultivé

►► *Med* ***informed consent*** consentement *m* éclairé; ***the informed consumer*** le consommateur averti

informer [ɪn'fɔːmə(r)] *n* (**a**) *(denouncer)* informateur *m*; **police informer** indicateur *m* (de police) (**b**) *(information source)* informateur (trice) *m,f*

infotainment ['ɪnfəʊˌteɪnmənt] *n (UNCOUNT)* = documentaires télévisés à but distractif

infraction [ɪn'frækʃən] *n* infraction *f*; **infraction of the code/regulations** infraction *f* au code/règlement

infra dig [ˌɪnfrə'dɪg] *adj Br Fam* dégradant ❑

infrared [ˌɪnfrə'red] **1** *n* infrarouge *m*

2 *adj* infrarouge

►► ***infrared astronomy*** astronomie *f* infrarouge; ***infrared keyboard*** clavier *m* à infrarouge; *Med* ***infrared lamp*** lampe *f* à rayons infrarouges; *Comput* ***infrared mouse*** souris *f* à infrarouge; ***infrared photography*** photographie *f* (à l')infrarouge; ***infrared radiation, infrared rays*** radiation *f* infrarouge, infrarouge *m*; ***infrared remote control*** télécommande *f* (à) infrarouge

infrasonic [ˌɪnfrə'sɒnɪk] *adj* infrasonore

infrasound ['ɪnfrəˌsaʊnd] *n* infrason *m*

infrastructure ['ɪnfrəˌstrʌktʃə(r)] *n* infrastructure *f*

infrequency [ɪn'friːkwənsɪ] *n* rareté *f*

infrequent [ɪn'friːkwənt] *adj (event)* peu fréquent, rare; *(visitor)* épisodique

infrequently [ɪn'friːkwəntlɪ] *adv* rarement, peu souvent

infringe [ɪn'frɪndʒ] **1** *vt (agreement, rights)* violer, enfreindre; *(law)* enfreindre, contrevenir à; *(patent)* contrefaire; **to infringe copyright** enfreindre les lois de copyright

2 *vi* **to infringe on** *or* **upon** empiéter sur

infringement [ɪn'frɪndʒmənt] *n (violation)* infraction *f*, atteinte *f*; *(encroachment)* empiètement *m*; **an infringement of the treaty conditions** une violation des termes du traité; **an infringement on freedom of speech** une atteinte à la liberté d'expression; **that's an infringement of my rights** c'est une atteinte à mes droits; **infringement of copyright** non-respect *m* des droits d'auteur

infuriate [ɪn'fjʊərɪeɪt] *vt (enrage)* rendre furieux; *(exasperate)* exaspérer

infuriated [ɪn'fjʊərɪeɪtɪd] *adj* furieux

infuriating [ɪn'fjʊərɪeɪtɪŋ] *adj* agaçant, exaspérant; **it's/he's infuriating!** c'est/il est exaspérant!; **it's infuriating the way she's always right** ça me met hors de moi qu'elle ait toujours raison

infuriatingly [ɪn'fjʊərɪeɪtɪŋlɪ] *adv* **infuriatingly stubborn** d'un entêtement exaspérant; **she remained infuriatingly polite** elle restait d'une politesse exaspérante

infuse [ɪn'fjuːz] **1** *vt* (**a**) *(inspire)* inspirer, insuffler, *Literary* infuser; **to infuse sb with sth, to infuse sth into sb** inspirer *ou* insuffler qch à qn; **her speech infused them with courage** son discours leur a inspiré *ou* insufflé du courage (**b**) *Culin* (faire) infuser (**c**) *(blood)* faire une perfusion de

2 *vi Culin* infuser

infuser [ɪn'fjuːzə(r)] *n* **(tea) infuser** boule *f* à thé

infusion [ɪn'fjuːʒən] *n* (**a**) *(drink, process)* infusion *f* (**b**) *(of blood)* perfusion *f* (**c**) *(injection)* **an infusion of new blood into the company** un apport de sang neuf dans la société; **the news gave her a big infusion of energy** la nouvelle lui a redonné beaucoup d'énergie

infusoria [ˌɪnfjuː'zɔːrɪə] *npl Arch Zool* protozoaires *mpl* ciliés, infusoires *mpl*

ingenious [ɪn'dʒiːnjəs] *adj (person, idea, device)* ingénieux, astucieux

ingeniously [ɪn'dʒiːnjəslɪ] *adv* ingénieusement

ingeniousness [ɪn'dʒiːnjəsnɪs] *n* ingéniosité *f*

ingenuity [ˌɪndʒɪ'njuːətɪ] *(pl* **ingenuities***) n* ingéniosité *f*

ingenuous [ɪn'dʒenjʊəs] *adj* (**a**) *(naive)* ingénu (**b**) *(frank)* candide

ingenuously [ɪn'dʒenjʊəslɪ] *adv* (**a**) *(naively)* ingénument (**b**) *(frankly)* franchement

ingenuousness [ɪn'dʒenjʊəsnɪs] *n* (**a**) *(naivety)* ingénuité *f*, naïveté *f* (**b**) *(frankness)* franchise *f*, candeur *f*

ingest [ɪn'dʒest] *vt (food, liquid)* ingérer

ingestion [ɪn'dʒestʃən] *n* ingestion *f*

inglenook ['ɪŋgəlnʊk] *n* coin *m* du feu

►► ***inglenook fireplace*** vaste cheminée *f* à l'ancienne

inglorious [ɪn'glɔːrɪəs] *adj (shameful)* déshonorant; **an inglorious defeat** une défaite déshonorante *ou* ignominieuse

ingloriously [ɪn'glɔːrɪəslɪ] *adv* sans gloire

ingoing ['ɪnˌgəʊɪŋ] *adj (tenant, president)* nouveau (nouvelle)

►► *Com* ***ingoing inventory*** inventaire *m* d'entrée

ingot ['ɪŋgət] *n* lingot *m*; **gold/cast-iron ingot** lingot *m* d'or/de fonte

ingrained [ˌɪn'greɪnd] *adj* (**a**) **ingrained with dirt** encrassé; **ingrained dirt** crasse *f* (**b**) *(deep-seated* → *attitude, fear, prejudice)* enraciné, inébranlable; *(*→ *habit)* invétéré, tenace; *(*→ *belief)* inébranlable

ingratiate [ɪn'greɪʃɪeɪt] *vt* **to ingratiate oneself with sb** s'insinuer dans les bonnes grâces de qn; **I'll try to ingratiate myself** je vais essayer de me faire bien voir

ingratiating [ɪn'greɪʃɪeɪtɪŋ] *adj (manners, person)* insinuant; *(smile)* mielleux

ingratiatingly [ɪn'greɪʃɪeɪtɪŋlɪ] *adv* mielleusement

ingratitude [ɪn'grætɪtjuːd] *n* ingratitude *f*

ingredient [ɪn'griːdjənt] *n* (**a**) *Culin* ingrédient *m*; **ingredients: fruit juice, water** *(on packaging)* composition: jus de fruit, eau (**b**) *(element)* élément *m*, ingrédient *m*; *Literary* **what are the ingredients of her success?** qu'est-ce qui fait son succès?

ingress ['ɪngres] *n* (**a**) *Formal or Literary (entry, right to enter)* entrée *f*; **to have free ingress** avoir accès libre (**b**) *Astron* immersion *f*

ingressive [ɪn'gresɪv] *adj Ling* ingressif

in-group *n* groupe *m* d'initiés

ingrowing toenail ['ɪnˌgrəʊɪŋ-] *n Br* ongle *m* incarné

ingrown ['ɪnˌgrəʊn] *adj* (**a**) *(toenail)* incarné (**b**) *(ingrained* → *habit)* enraciné, tenace (**c**) *(introverted)* renfermé, réservé

ingurgitate [ɪn'gɜːdʒɪˌteɪt] *vt* (**a**) *(swallow greedily)* ingurgiter (**b**) *Literary (engulf)* engloutir

ingurgitation [ɪnˌgɜːdʒɪ'teɪʃən] *n* ingurgitation *f*

Ingushetia [ˌɪŋgʊ'ʃetɪə] *n* Ingouchie *f*

inhabit [ɪn'hæbɪt] *vt* habiter; **the island is no longer inhabited** l'île n'est plus habitée *ou* est maintenant inhabitée

inhabitable [ɪn'hæbɪtəbəl] *adj* habitable

inhabitant [ɪn'hæbɪtənt] *n* habitant(e) *m,f*

inhalant [ɪn'heɪlənt] *n* inhalation *f*

inhalation [ˌɪnhə'leɪʃən] *n* (**a**) *(of air)* inspiration *f* (**b**) *(of gas, glue)* inhalation *f*

inhalator ['ɪnhəleɪtə(r)] *n* inhalateur *m*

inhale [ɪn'heɪl] **1** *vt* (**a**) *(fumes, gas)* inhaler; *(fresh air, scent)* respirer; *(smoke)* avaler (**b**) *Am Fam (eat quickly)* engouffrer; *(drink quickly)* descendre

2 *vi (breathe in)* inspirer; *(smoker)* avaler la fumée

inhaler [ɪn'heɪlə(r)] *n* inhalateur *m*

inhaling [ɪn'heɪlɪŋ] *n* inhalation *f*

inharmonious [ˌɪnhɑː'məʊnjəs] *adj* inharmonieux, sans harmonie, peu harmonieux

inhere [ɪn'hɪə(r)] *vi Formal* être inhérent; **the powers that inhere in the state** les pouvoirs (qui sont) inhérents *ou* propres à l'État

inherent [ɪn'hɪərənt, ɪn'herənt] *adj* inhérent; **inherent in** *or* **to** inhérent à; **an inherent fault in the design** une anomalie inhérente à la conception

►► ***inherent stability*** *(of plane, ship etc)* stabilité *f* propre; *Com* ***inherent vice*** vice *m* inhérent

inherently [ɪn'hɪərəntlɪ, ɪn'herəntlɪ] *adv* intrinsèquement, par nature; **the system is inherently inefficient** le système est inefficace par nature

inherit [ɪn'herɪt] **1** *vt* (**a**) *(property, right)* hériter (de); *(title, peerage)* accéder à; **she inherited a million dollars** elle a hérité d'un million de dollars

(**b**) *(situation, tradition, attitude)* hériter; **the problems inherited from the previous government** les problèmes hérités du gouvernement précédent; **she inherited her father's intelligence** elle a hérité (de) l'intelligence de son père

(**c**) *Biol (characteristic, feature)* hériter (de)

2 *vi* hériter; **she stands to inherit when her aunt dies** elle doit hériter à la mort de sa tante

inheritable [ɪn'herɪtəbəl] *adj* (**a**) *(property, right, title)* dont on peut hériter; **where the crown was inheritable by females** là où les femmes pouvaient hériter de la couronne (**b**) *Biol (disease)* transmissible à ses descendants (**c**) *Law (person)* apte à hériter; **inheritable to an estate** apte à hériter d'une terre

inheritance [ɪn'herɪtəns] *n* (**a**) *(legacy)* héritage *m*; **to come into an inheritance** faire *ou* toucher un héritage

(**b**) *(succession)* succession *f*; **to claim sth by right of inheritance** revendiquer qch en faisant valoir son droit à la succession

(**c**) *Biol (of characteristic, feature)* hérédité *f*; **genetic inheritance does not explain this phenomenon** ce phénomène ne peut s'expliquer par l'héritage génétique

(**d**) *(heritage)* héritage *m*, patrimoine *m*; **our cultural inheritance** notre héritage culturel

►► *Fin* ***inheritance tax*** droits *mpl* de succession

inherited [ɪn'herɪtɪd] *adj* hérité

inheritor [ɪn'herɪtə(r)] *n* héritier(ère) *m,f*

inhibit [ɪn'hɪbɪt] *vt* (**a**) *(hinder* → *person, freedom)* gêner, entraver; **were you inhibited by him being there?** est-ce que sa présence vous a gêné?; **a law which inhibits free speech** une loi qui constitue une entrave à la liberté d'expression

(**b**) *(check* → *growth, development)* freiner, entraver; **to inhibit progress** entraver la marche du progrès

(**c**) *(suppress* → *desires, emotions)* inhiber, refouler; *Psy* inhiber

(**d**) *(forbid)* interdire

(**e**) *Chem* inhiber

►► *Comput* ***inhibit code*** code *m* inhibiteur

inhibited [ɪn'hɪbɪtɪd] *adj* inhibé; **to be sexually inhibited** souffrir d'inhibition sexuelle

inhibiter [ɪn'hɪbɪtə(r)] *n* inhibiteur *m*

inhibiting [ɪn'hɪbɪtɪŋ] *adj* inhibant

inhibition [ˌɪnhɪ'bɪʃən] *n* (**a**) *Psy* inhibition *f*; **to have no inhibitions** ne pas avoir de complexes; **he had no inhibitions about lying to her face** ça ne le gênait pas de la regarder dans les yeux et de lui raconter des mensonges (**b**) *Law* prohibition *f*

inhibitive [ɪn'hɪbɪtɪv] *adj Med* inhibiteur
inhibitor [ɪn'hɪbɪtə(r)] *n* inhibiteur *m*
inhibitory [ɪn'hɪbɪtərɪ] *adj* (**a**) *Chem & Psy* inhibiteur (**b**) *(prohibitory)* prohibitif
in-home placement testing *n Mktg* test *m* à domicile par des consommateurs-témoins
inhospitable [ˌɪnhɒ'spɪtəbəl] *adj* (**a**) *(person)* peu accueillant, inhospitalier; **I don't wish to appear inhospitable, but...** je ne voudrais pas vous mettre à la porte, mais... (**b**) *(area, climate)* inhospitalier
inhospitableness [ˌɪnhɒ'spɪtəbəlnɪs] *n (of person, area, climate)* inhospitalité *f*
inhospitably [ˌɪnhɒ'spɪtəblɪ] *adv* d'une manière peu accueillante
inhospitality [ˌɪnhɒspɪ'tælɪtɪ] *n* inhospitalité *f*
in-house **1** *adj* interne *(à une entreprise)*; *(training)* maison *(inv)*
2 *adv* sur place; **we prefer to train our staff in-house** nous préférons former notre personnel au sein de l'entreprise
►► ***in-house journal*** journal *m* interne; ***in-house staff*** personnel *m* permanent; **a very small in-house staff** un personnel permanent très peu nombreux; ***in-house training*** formation *f* interne
inhuman [ˌɪn'hjuːmən] *adj (behaviour)* inhumain, barbare; *(person, place, process)* inhumain
inhumane [ˌɪnhjuː'meɪn] *adj* cruel, inhumain
inhumanely [ˌɪnhjuː'meɪnlɪ] *adv* inhumainement, cruellement
inhumanity [ˌɪnhjuː'mænətɪ] *(pl* **inhumanities***) n* (**a**) *(quality)* inhumanité *f*, barbarie *f*, cruauté *f*; **man's inhumanity to man** la cruauté de l'homme pour l'homme (**b**) *(act)* atrocité *f*, brutalité *f*
inhumation [ˌɪnhjuː'meɪʃən] *n Formal* inhumation *f*
inhume [ɪn'hjuːm] *vt Formal* inhumer
inimical [ɪ'nɪmɪkəl] *adj* (**a**) *(unfavourable)* hostile; **inimical to** peu favorable à (**b**) *(unfriendly)* inamical
inimitable [ɪ'nɪmɪtəbəl] *adj* inimitable
inimitably [ɪ'nɪmɪtəblɪ] *adv* d'une façon inimitable
iniquitous [ɪ'nɪkwɪtəs] *adj* inique
iniquitously [ɪ'nɪkwɪtəslɪ] *adv* iniquement
iniquity [ɪ'nɪkwətɪ] *n* iniquité *f*
initial [ɪ'nɪʃəl] *(Br pt & pp* **initialled**, *cont* **initialling**, *Am pt & pp* **initialed**, *cont* **initialing***)* **1** *adj* initial; **my initial reaction** ma première réaction; **we expect a few problems in the initial stages** dans un premier temps, nous nous attendons à quelques difficultés; **the project is still in its initial stages** le projet en est encore à ses débuts; *Ling* **in initial position** en position initiale
2 *n* (**a**) *(letter)* initiale *f*; **initials** initiales *fpl*; *(to alteration of cheque etc)* paraphe *m*; *(of supervisor etc)* visa *m*; *(on garment)* monogramme *m*; **it's got his initials on it** il y a ses initiales dessus
(**b**) *Typ (of chapter)* lettrine *f*
3 *vt (memo, page, correction)* parapher, parafer, signer de ses initiales
►► *Fin* ***initial capital*** capital *m* initial *ou* d'apport; *Fin* ***initial cost*** coût *m* inital; *(of manufactured product)* prix *m* de revient; *Fin* ***initial expenditure*** frais *mpl* de premier établissement; *Fin* ***initial investment*** investissements *mpl* initiaux; ***initial letter*** initiale *f*; *St Exch* ***initial margin*** dépôt *m* initial *ou* de marge; *Am St Exch* ***initial public offering*** introduction *f* en Bourse; *Com* ***initial stock*** stock *m* de départ; *Fin* ***initial value*** valeur *f* de départ
initialism [ɪ'nɪʃəˌlɪzəm] *n* sigle *m*
initialization [ɪˌnɪʃəlaɪ'zeɪʃən] *n Comput (of computer, modem, printer)* initialisation *f*
initialize, -ise [ɪ'nɪʃəlaɪz] *vt Comput (computer, modem, printer)* initialiser
initially [ɪ'nɪʃəlɪ] *adv* au départ, à l'origine; **she was initially against the idea** au départ, elle était contre
initiate **1** *vt* [ɪ'nɪʃɪeɪt] (**a**) *(talks, debate)* amorcer, engager; *(policy)* lancer; *(measures)* instaurer; *(quarrel, reaction)* provoquer, déclencher; **the pilot has initiated landing procedures** le pilote a entamé *ou* amorcé les procédures d'atterrissage; **I find it hard to initiate conversation with him** je trouve difficile d'engager la conversation avec lui; *Law* **to initiate proceedings against sb** entamer des poursuites contre qn
(**b**) *(person)* initier; **to initiate sb into sth** initier qn à qch
2 *n* [ɪ'nɪʃɪət] initié(e) *m,f*
initiated [ɪ'nɪʃɪeɪtɪd] **1** *adj* initié
2 *npl* **the initiated** les initiés *mpl*
initiation [ɪˌnɪʃɪ'eɪʃən] *n* (**a**) *(start)* commencement *m*, début *m*; **he fought for the initiation of new policies** il s'est battu pour la mise en œuvre de politiques différentes (**b**) *(of person)* initiation *f*; **her initiation into politics** son initiation à la politique; **his initiation into the world of crime** sa première expérience de la pègre
►► ***initiation ceremony*** cérémonie *f* d'initiation
initiative [ɪ'nɪʃətɪv] **1** *n* (**a**) *(drive)* initiative *f*; **she's certainly got initiative** elle a de l'initiative, il n'y a pas de doute; **to act on one's own initiative** agir de sa propre initiative; **you'll have to use your initiative** vous devrez prendre des initiatives; *Am Pol* **citizen's initiative** initiative *f* populaire
(**b**) *(first step)* initiative *f*; **to take the initiative** prendre l'initiative; **some new initiatives have been suggested** de nouvelles initiatives ont été proposées
(**c**) *(lead)* initiative *f*; **to have the initiative** avoir l'initiative; **they lost the initiative to foreign competition** ils ont été dépassés par la concurrence étrangère
2 *adj* (**a**) *(preliminary)* préliminaire
(**b**) *(ritual)* initiatique
initiator [ɪ'nɪʃɪeɪtə(r)] *n* initiateur(trice) *m,f*, instigateur(trice) *m,f*
initiatory [ɪ'nɪʃɪətərɪ] *adj* (**a**) *(initial)* premier, introductoire; **initiatory steps** démarches *fpl* préparatoires *ou* préliminaires (**b**) *(rite, ceremony etc)* d'initiation, initiatique
inject [ɪn'dʒekt] *vt* (**a**) *Med (drug)* faire une piqûre de, injecter; **to inject sb with penicillin** faire une piqûre de pénicilline à qn; **have you been injected against tetanus?** êtes-vous vacciné contre le tétanos?; **he injected novocaine into my gum** il m'a fait une injection *ou* une piqûre de novocaïne dans la gencive; *Tech* **the resin is injected into the mould** la résine est injectée dans le moule
(**b**) *Fig (money)* injecter; **they've injected billions of dollars into the economy** ils ont injecté des milliards de dollars dans l'économie; **to inject new life into sth** donner un nouvel essor à qch; **he tried to inject some humour into the situation** il a tenté d'introduire un peu d'humour dans la situation
injectable [ɪn'dʒektəbəl] *adj (drug)* injectable
injectant [ɪn'dʒektənt] *n* substance *f* injectée
injection [ɪn'dʒekʃən] *n Med & Fig* injection *f*; *Med* **to give sb an injection** faire une injection *ou* une piqûre à qn; *Fig* **an injection of capital** une injection de capitaux
►► *Tech* ***injection moulding*** moulage *m* par injection; ***injection pump*** *Constr* pompe *f* à injection; *Aut* pompe *f* d'injection (de carburant)
injector [ɪn'dʒektə(r)] *n* injecteur *m*
injudicious [ˌɪndʒuː'dɪʃəs] *adj* peu judicieux, imprudent
injudiciously [ˌɪndʒuː'dɪʃəslɪ] *adv* peu judicieusement
Injun ['ɪndʒən] *n Am Fam* Peau-Rouge *mf*, = terme injurieux désignant un Amérindien; *Fam Old-fashioned* **honest Injun!** parole de scout!, juré, craché!
injunction [ɪn'dʒʌŋkʃən] *n* (**a**) *Law* ordonnance *f*; **to take out an injunction against sb** mettre qn en demeure (**b**) *(warning)* injonction *f*, recommandation *f* formelle; **she smokes despite her father's injunctions against it** elle fume malgré les injonctions de son père
injure ['ɪndʒə(r)] *vt* (**a**) *(physically)* blesser; **he injured his knee skiing** il s'est blessé au genou en faisant du ski; **ten people were injured in the accident** l'accident a fait dix blessés; **you could injure yourself lifting that box** vous pourriez vous faire mal en soulevant cette caisse
(**b**) *(damage → relationship, interests)* nuire à
(**c**) *(offend)* blesser, offenser; **only his pride was injured** seul son amour-propre a été blessé; **try not to injure her feelings** faites en sorte de ne pas l'offenser *ou* la blesser
(**d**) *(wrong)* faire du tort à
injured ['ɪndʒəd] **1** *adj* (**a**) *(physically)* blessé; **his injured left foot** son pied gauche blessé; **her head is badly injured** elle est grièvement blessée à la tête (**b**) *(offended → person)* offensé; **to feel injured** être offensé; **it's just his injured pride** il est blessé dans son amour-propre, c'est tout
2 *npl* **the injured** les blessés *mpl*
►► ***the injured party*** l'offensé(e) *m,f*, *Law* la partie lésée
injurious [ɪn'dʒʊərɪəs] *adj Formal* (**a**) *(detrimental)* nuisible, préjudiciable (**to** à) (**b**) *(insulting)* offensant, injurieux
injuriously [ɪn'dʒʊərɪəslɪ] *adv Formal* (**a**) *(detrimentally)* **to affect sb/sth injuriously** avoir effet nuisible *ou* préjudiciable sur qn/qch (**b**) *(insultingly)* injurieusement
injury ['ɪndʒərɪ] *(pl* **injuries***) n* (**a**) *(physical)* blessure *f*; **the explosion caused serious injuries** l'explosion a fait des blessés graves; *Sport* **the team has had very few injuries this season** il n'y a eu que très peu de blessés dans l'équipe cette saison; **he escaped without injury** il s'en est sorti indemne; *Br* **be careful, you'll do yourself an injury!** fais attention, tu vas te blesser!
(**b**) *Formal or Literary (wrong)* tort *m*, préjudice *m*; **you do him injury** vous lui faites du tort
(**c**) *(offence)* offense *f*
(**d**) *Law* préjudice *m*
►► *Sport* ***injury time*** *(UNCOUNT)* arrêts *mpl* de jeu; **to play injury time** jouer les arrêts de jeu; **they scored during injury time** ils ont marqué un but pendant les arrêts de jeu; **he scored nine minutes into injury time** il a marqué un but neuf minutes après le début des arrêts de jeu
injustice [ɪn'dʒʌstɪs] *n* (**a**) *(of law, system etc)* injustice *f* (**b**) *(unjust act, remark)* injustice *f*; **to do sb an injustice** être injuste envers qn
ink [ɪŋk] **1** *n* (**a**) *(for writing, printing)* encre *f*; **in ink** à l'encre
(**b**) *(of squid, octopus etc)* encre *f*, noir *m*
2 *vt* (**a**) *(surface)* encrer
(**b**) *Am (document, name)* signer; **the bill was inked this morning by the President** le président a signé le projet de loi ce matin; *Fig* **she inked her name in the record books** elle a établi un nouveau record
►► *Zool* ***ink bag*** poche *f* à encre; ***ink bottle*** bouteille *f* d'encre; *Bot* ***ink cap*** coprin *m*; ***ink cartridge*** cartouche *f* d'encre; *Comput* ***ink channel*** *(in printer)* canal *m* encreur; ***ink drawing*** dessin *m* à l'encre; ***ink eraser*** gomme *f* à encre; ***ink pen*** stylo *m* à encre; *Br* ***ink rubber*** gomme *f* à encre; *Zool* ***ink sac*** sac *m or* poche *f* à encre
►**ink in** *vt sep (drawing)* repasser à l'encre; *(lines)* retracer à l'encre; *(writing)* réécrire à l'encre
►**ink out** *vt sep (word)* oblitérer *ou* rayer *ou* biffer à l'encre
►**ink up** *vt sep* (**a**) *Am (stain with ink)* faire une tache d'encre à *ou* sur (**b**) *Typ* encrer
Inkatha [ɪn'kɑːtə] *n* Inkatha
inkblot ['ɪŋkblɒt] *n* tache *f* d'encre, pâté *m*; *(in Rorschach test)* tache *f* d'encre
►► ***inkblot test*** test *m* de Rorschach *ou* des taches d'encre
inking ['ɪŋkɪŋ] *n Typ (of rollers)* encrage *m*
inkjet printer ['ɪŋkdʒet-] *n Comput* imprimante *f* à jet d'encre
inkling ['ɪŋklɪŋ] *n* vague *ou* petite idée *f*; **I had some inkling of the** *or* **as to the real reason** j'avais bien une petite idée de la véritable raison; **you must have an inkling** tu dois bien avoir une petite idée; **I had no inkling** je ne m'en doutais pas du tout; **she didn't have the slightest inkling that her husband had been unfaithful** elle était à cent lieues de se douter que son mari l'avait trompée
inkpad ['ɪŋkpæd] *n* tampon *m* (encreur)
inkpot ['ɪŋkpɒt] *n* encrier *m*
inkslinger ['ɪŋkˌslɪŋə(r)] *n Pej* écrivaillon *m*
inkstain ['ɪŋksteɪn] *n* tache *f* d'encre
inkstained ['ɪŋksteɪnd] *adj* taché *ou* barbouillé d'encre
inkstand ['ɪŋkstænd] *n* encrier *m*
inkwell ['ɪŋkwel] *n* encrier *m* (encastré)

inky ['ɪŋkɪ] (*compar* **inkier,** *superl* **inkiest**) *adj* (**a**) *(inkstained)* taché d'encre (**b**) *(dark)* noir comme l'encre
►► ***inky black*** noir d'encre; ***inky blue*** bleu-noir

INLA [,aɪen,el'eɪ] *n* (*abbr* **Irish National Liberation Army**) Armée *f* de libération nationale irlandaise, INLA *f*

inlaid [,ɪn'leɪd] **1** *pt & pp of* **inlay**
2 *adj* incrusté; *(wood)* marqueté, incrusté; *(floor)* parqueté; **an inlaid table** une table en marqueterie

inland 1 *adj* ['ɪnlənd] (**a**) *(not coastal → town, sea)* intérieur
(**b**) *Br (not foreign)* intérieur
2 *adv* [ɪn'lænd] *(travelling)* vers l'intérieur; *(located)* à l'intérieur; **to go inland** pénétrer vers l'intérieur *ou* dans les terres; **the town is situated a few miles inland** la ville est située à quelques kilomètres dans les terres
►► ***inland clearance depot*** dépôt *m* de dédouanement intérieur; ***inland freight*** fret *m* intérieur; ***inland haulage*** transport *m* routier; ***inland mail*** courrier *m* intérieur; ***inland navigation*** navigation *f* fluviale; *Br* ***the Inland Revenue*** ≃ le fisc, la Direction Générale des Impôts; ***the Inland Sea*** la mer Intérieure; ***inland waterways*** voies *fpl* navigables; ***inland waterway transport*** transport *m* fluvial

in-laws *npl Fam (gen)* belle-famille❑ *f*; *(parents-in-law)* beaux-parents❑ *mpl*

inlay (*pt & pp* **inlaid**) **1** *n* [,ɪn'leɪ] (**a**) *(gen)* incrustation *f*; *(in woodwork)* marqueterie *f*; *(in metalwork)* damasquinage *m*; **the brooch has very fine inlay work** la broche a de très belles incrustations; **with ivory inlay** incrusté d'ivoire (**b**) *(in dentistry)* incrustation *f*
2 *vt* ['ɪnleɪ] incruster; **inlaid with** incrusté de; **the table was inlaid with ivory** la table avait des incrustations *ou* était incrustée d'ivoire

inlet ['ɪnlet] **1** *n* (**a**) *(in coastline)* anse *f*, crique *f*; *(between offshore islands)* bras *m* de mer (**b**) *Tech (intake)* arrivée *f*, admission *f*; *(opening)* (orifice *m* d')entrée *f*; *(for air)* prise *f* (d'air); **to regulate the inlet of steam** régler l'admission de (la) vapeur
2 *comp Tech* d'arrivée
►► ***inlet manifold*** conduits *mpl* d'admission, collecteur *m* d'admission; ***inlet pipe*** tuyau *m* d'arrivée; ***inlet valve*** soupape *f* d'admission; *(of fuel pump)* soupape *f* d'alimentation

in-line *adj*
►► *Aut* ***in-line engine*** moteur *m* en ligne; ***in-line skates*** rollers *mpl* in-line; ***in-line skating*** roller *m* in-line; **to do** *or* **go in-line skating** faire du roller in-line

inline image ['ɪnlaɪn-] *n Comput* image *f* intégrée

in loco parentis [ɪn,ləʊkəʊpə'rentɪs] *adv Law* **to act in loco parentis** agir en lieu et place des parents

inmate ['ɪnmeɪt] *n (of prison)* détenu(e) *m,f*; *(of mental institution)* interné(e) *m,f*; *(of hospital)* malade *mf*; *(of house)* occupant(e) *m,f*, résident(e) *m,f*

in memoriam [,ɪnmɪ'mɔːrɪəm] *prep* à la mémoire de; *(on gravestone)* in memoriam

inmost ['ɪnməʊst] = **innermost**

inn [ɪn] *n (pub,* [illegible]*)* [illegible] *f*
►► *Eng Law* ***the Inns of Court*** = associations auxquelles appartiennent les avocats et les juges et dont le siège se trouve dans le quartier historique du même nom à Londres

innards ['ɪnədz] *npl Fam* entrailles❑ *fpl*

innate [ɪ'neɪt] *adj (inborn)* inné, naturel; **her innate gift for music** son don inné pour la musique

innately [ɪ'neɪtlɪ] *adv* naturellement; **nobody is innately evil** aucun être n'est naturellement méchant

inner ['ɪnə(r)] **1** *adj* (**a**) *(interior → courtyard, pocket, walls, lane)* intérieur; *(→ structure, workings)* interne; **the inner wall of the stomach** la paroi interne de l'estomac; **Inner London** Londres intra-muros; **in the inner circles of power** dans les milieux proches du pouvoir; **her inner circle of advisers/friends** le cercle de ses conseillers/amis les plus proches
(**b**) *(inward → feeling, conviction)* intime; *(→ life, voice, struggle, warmth)* intérieur; **inner calm** paix *f* intérieure; **the inner meaning** le sens profond; **the inner man/woman** *(spiritual self)* l'être *m* intérieur; *Hum (stomach)* l'estomac *m*
2 *n (in archery, darts)* = zone rouge entourant le centre de la cible; **he got three inners** il a mis trois fois dans le rouge
►► *Psy* ***the inner child*** l'enfant *mf* qui est en nous; ***inner city*** = quartier défavorisé dans le centre d'une grande ville; ***inner ear*** oreille *f* interne; ***Inner Hebrides*** Hébrides *fpl* intérieures; ***Inner Mongolia*** Mongolie-Intérieure *f*; **in Inner Mongolia** en Mongolie-Intérieure; ***the Inner Temple*** = association d'étudiants en droit et d'avocats, ainsi que les bâtiments londoniens où elle siège; ***inner tube*** *(of tyre)* chambre *f* à air

inner-city *adj* **inner-city areas** = quartiers défavorisés du centre des grandes villes; **inner-city crime** = crimes se produisant dans les quartiers défavorisés du centre des grandes villes; **inner-city children** = enfants des quartiers défavorisés du centre des grandes villes

innermost ['ɪnəməʊst] *adj* (**a**) *(feeling, belief)* intime; **my innermost thoughts** mes pensées les plus secrètes; **in her innermost being** au plus profond d'elle-même (**b**) *(central → place, room)* le plus au centre; **in the innermost depths of the cave** au plus profond de la grotte

innerspring mattress ['ɪnə,sprɪŋ-] *n Am* matelas *m* à ressorts

innervate ['ɪnɜː,veɪt] *vt Physiol* innerver

innervation [,ɪnɜː'veɪʃən] *n Physiol* innervation *f*

inning ['ɪnɪŋ] *n (in baseball)* tour *m* de batte

innings ['ɪnɪŋz] (*pl* **inv**) **1** *n (in cricket)* tour *m* de batte; *Br Fig* **he's had a good innings** il a bien profité de la vie
2 *npl (reclaimed land)* polders *mpl*

innkeeper ['ɪn,kiːpə(r)] *n* aubergiste *mf*

innocence ['ɪnəsəns] *n* innocence *f*; **to take advantage of sb's innocence** abuser de l'innocence de qn; **in all innocence** en toute innocence

innocent ['ɪnəsənt] **1** *adj* (**a**) *(not guilty)* innocent; **to be innocent of a crime** être innocent d'un crime; **to be proven innocent of sth** être reconnu innocent de qch; **he was proven innocent** il a été innocenté; **an innocent person** un(e) innocent(e); **the bomb killed several innocent bystanders** la bombe a tué plusieurs innocents qui se trouvaient là; *Fam* **to act all innocent** faire l'innocent
(**b**) *(naïve)* innocent, naïf; **an innocent remark** une remarque innocente
(**c**) *Formal (devoid)* **innocent of** dépourvu de, sans
2 *n* innocent(e) *m,f*; **what an innocent you are!** quel innocent tu fais!; **don't play the innocent!** ne fais pas l'innocent!

innocently ['ɪnəsəntlɪ] *adv* innocemment

innocuous [ɪ'nɒkjʊəs] *adj* inoffensif, anodin

innocuously [ɪ'nɒkjʊəslɪ] *adv* de façon inoffensive *ou* anodine

innocuousness [ɪ'nɒkjʊəsnɪs] *n (of remark, joke etc)* caractère *m* anodin; *Med* innocuité *f*

innovate ['ɪnəveɪt] **1** *vt* innover
2 *vi* innover

innovating company ['ɪnəveɪtɪŋ-] *n Mktg* entreprise *f* innovatrice

innovation [illegible] *n* innovation *f*; **innovations in management techniques** des innovations en matière de gestion

innovative ['ɪnəvətɪv] *adj* innovateur, novateur
►► *Mktg* ***innovative product*** produit *m* novateur, produit *m* innovateur

innovator ['ɪnəveɪtə(r)] *n* innovateur(trice) *m,f*, novateur(trice) *m,f*

innovatory ['ɪnəvətərɪ] *adj* innovateur, novateur

Innsbruck ['ɪnzbrʊk] *n* Innsbruck

innuendo [,ɪnjuː'endəʊ] (*pl* **innuendos** *or* **innuendoes**) *n* (**a**) *(insinuation)* insinuation *f*; **to discredit sb by innuendo** discréditer qn par sous-entendus (**b**) *(in jokes)* allusion *f* grivoise; **the play is full of innuendos** la pièce est pleine de sous-entendus (**c**) *Law* insinuation *f*, mot *m* couvert *(destiné à atteindre quelqu'un dans son honneur)*

Innuit = **Inuit**

innumerable [ɪ'njuːmərəbəl] *adj* innombrable; **innumerable times** un nombre incalculable de fois

innumeracy [ɪ'njuːmərəsɪ] *n* incapacité *f* à compter

innumerate [ɪ'njuːmərət] **1** *n* personne *f* qui ne sait pas compter
2 *adj* qui ne sait pas compter; **he's completely innumerate** il est incapable d'additionner deux et deux

inoculate [ɪ'nɒkjʊleɪt] *vt Med (person, animal)* vacciner; **to inoculate sb against sth** vacciner qn contre qch; **they inoculated guinea pigs with the virus** ils ont inoculé le virus à des cobayes

inoculation [ɪ,nɒkjʊ'leɪʃən] *n* inoculation *f*

in-off *n (in billiards)* = boule qui entre dans un trou après en avoir touché une autre

inoffensive [,ɪnə'fensɪv] *adj* inoffensif; *(smell)* pas si désagréable

inoperable [ɪn'ɒprəbəl] *adj* (**a**) *Med* inopérable (**b**) *(unworkable)* impraticable

inoperative [ɪn'ɒprətɪv] *adj* inopérant

inopportune [ɪn'ɒpətjuːn] *adj (remark)* déplacé, mal à propos; *(time)* mal choisi, inopportun; *(behaviour)* inconvenant, déplacé

inopportunely [ɪn'ɒpətjuːnlɪ] *adv Formal* inopportunément, mal à propos

inordinate [ɪn'ɔːdɪnət] *adj (immense → size)* démesuré; *(→ pleasure, relief)* incroyable; *(→ amount of money)* exorbitant; **they spent an inordinate amount of time on it** ils y ont consacré énormément de temps

inordinately [ɪn'ɔːdɪnətlɪ] *adv* démesurément, excessivement

inorganic [,ɪnɔː'gænɪk] *adj* inorganique
►► ***inorganic chemistry*** chimie *f* inorganique *or* minérale

inotropic [,ɪnəʊ'trɒpɪk] *adj Physiol* inotrope

in-patient *n* hospitalisé(e) *m,f*, malade *mf*

in-plant agency *n Am (travel agency)* implant *m*

inpoint ['ɪnpɔɪnt] *n (on tape, film)* point *m* d'entrée

input ['ɪnpʊt] (*pt & pp* **input,** *cont* **inputting**) **1** *n* *(UNCOUNT)* (**a**) *(during meeting, discussion)* contribution *f*; **we'd like some input from marketing before committing ourselves** nous aimerions consulter le service marketing avant de nous engager plus avant
(**b**) *Comput (data)* données *fpl* (en entrée); *(action)* entrée *f*, introduction *f*; **the program requires input from the user** ce programme exige que l'utilisateur entre des données
(**c**) *Elec* énergie *f*, puissance *f*; **to reduce the voltage input to a circuit** réduire la tension d'un circuit
(**d**) *Econ* input *m*, intrant *m*
2 *comp Comput (file, program)* d'entrée
3 *vt* (**a**) *(gen)* (faire) entrer, introduire
(**b**) *Comput* entrer
►► *Comput* ***input device*** périphérique *m* d'entrée; *Fin* ***input tax*** TVA *f* récupérée; *Elec* ***input transformer*** courant *m* *ou* transformateur *m* d'entrée

input/output *n Comput* entrée/sortie *f*
►► ***input/output device*** périphérique *m* d'entrée/sortie

inquest ['ɪnkwest] *n Law* enquête *f*; *(into death)* = enquête menée pour établir les causes des morts violentes, non naturelles ou mystérieuses; *Fig (after event, match etc)* analyse *f*

inquietude [illegible] *n* [illegible] *(*[illegible]*ness)* malaise *m*, inquiétude *f*

inquire [ɪn'kwaɪə(r)] **1** *vt (ask)* demander; **to inquire sth of sb** s'enquérir de qch auprès de qn; **she inquired how to get to the park** elle a demandé qu'on lui indique le chemin du parc; **may I inquire what brings you here?** puis-je vous demander l'objet de votre visite?
2 *vi (seek information)* se renseigner, demander; **inquire within** *(sign)* s'adresser ici; **to inquire about sth** demander des renseignements *ou* se renseigner sur qch

►**inquire after** *vt insep Br* demander des nouvelles de; **she inquired after you** elle a demandé de vos nouvelles

►**inquire into** *vt insep* se renseigner sur; *(investigate)* faire des recherches sur; *Admin & Law* enquêter sur; **they should inquire into how the money was spent** ils devraient enquêter sur la façon dont l'argent a été dépensé

inquirer [ɪn'kwaɪərə(r)] *n* investigateur(trice) *m,f*

inquiring [ɪn'kwaɪərɪŋ] *adj (voice, look)* interrogateur; *(mind)* curieux

inquiringly [ɪn'kwaɪərɪŋlɪ] *adv* d'un air interrogateur; **she looked at him inquiringly** elle le regarda d'un air interrogateur, elle l'interrogea du regard

inquiry [*Br* ɪn'kwaɪərɪher, *Am* 'ɪnkwərɪ] (*pl* **inquiries**) *n* (**a**) *(request for information)* demande *f* (de renseignements); **to make inquiries** se renseigner; **to make inquiries about sb** prendre des renseignements sur qn; **to make inquiries into sth** faire des recherches sur qch; **with reference to your inquiry of 5 May,...** *(in letter)* en réponse à votre demande du 5 mai,...; **we have received hundreds of inquiries** nous avons reçu des centaines de demandes de renseignements; **could you make a few discreet inquiries?** pourriez-vous vous renseigner discrètement?
(**b**) *(investigation)* enquête *f*; **to hold** *or* **to conduct an inquiry into sth** faire une enquête sur qch; **the police are making inquiries** la police enquête, une enquête (policière) est en cours; **he is helping police with their inquiries** la police est en train de l'interroger; **upon further inquiry** après vérification; **commission of inquiry** commission *f* d'enquête
(**c**) *(questioning)* **a look/tone of inquiry** un regard/ton interrogateur
►► *Br* ***inquiry agent*** détective *m* (privé)

'Inquiry into the Nature and Causes of the Wealth of Nations' *Smith* 'Recherches sur la nature et les causes de la richesse des nations'

inquisition [,ɪnkwɪ'zɪʃən] **1** *n* (**a**) *(gen)* inquisition *f*; **the interview turned into an inquisition** l'entrevue s'est transformée en inquisition (**b**) *Law* enquête *f*
2 Inquisition *n Hist* **the Inquisition** l'Inquisition *f*

inquisitive [ɪn'kwɪzətɪv] *adj* (**a**) *(curious)* curieux; *(look)* plein de curiosité (**b**) *Pej (nosy)* indiscret(ète)

inquisitively [ɪn'kwɪzətɪvlɪ] *adv* (**a**) *(curiously)* avec curiosité (**b**) *Pej (nosily)* de manière indiscrète; **he stared inquisitively into the room** il jeta dans la pièce un regard inquisiteur

inquisitiveness [ɪn'kwɪzətɪvnɪs] *n* (**a**) *(curiosity)* curiosité *f* (**b**) *Pej (nosiness)* indiscrétion *f*

inquisitor [ɪn'kwɪzɪtə(r)] *n* (**a**) *(investigator)* enquêteur(euse) *m,f*; *(interrogator)* interrogateur(trice) *m,f* (**b**) *Hist* inquisiteur *m*

inquisitorial [ɪn,kwɪzɪ'tɔːrɪəl] *adj* inquisitorial

inquorate [ɪn'kwɔːreɪt] *adj Br* sans quorum; **the meeting is inquorate** la réunion n'a pas atteint le quorum

inroad ['ɪnrəʊd] **1** *n (raid)* incursion *f*; *(advance)* avance *f*
2 inroads *npl* (**a**) *Mil* **to make inroads into enemy territory** avancer en territoire ennemi (**b**) *Fig* **to make inroads in** *or* **into** *or* **on** *(supplies, funds)* entamer; *(spare time, someone's rights)* empiéter sur; **they have made significant inroads into our market share** ils ont considérablement mordu sur notre part du marché; **they've made great inroads on the work** ils ont bien avancé le travail

inrush ['ɪnrʌʃ] *n* afflux *m*

INS [,aɪen'es] *n Am (abbr* **Immigration and Naturalization Service**) = services américains de contrôle de l'immigration

ins (**a**) *(written abbr* **insurance**) asse. (**b**) *(written abbr* **inches**) pouces

insalubrious [,ɪnsə'luːbrɪəs] *adj Formal (district, climate)* insalubre, malsain

insane [ɪn'seɪn] **1** *adj* (**a**) *(mentally disordered)* fou (folle); **temporarily insane** en état de démence temporaire; **to go insane** perdre la raison; **to be insane with grief/jealousy** être fou de douleur/jalousie (**b**) *Fig (person)* fou (folle); *(scheme, price)* démentiel; **it's driving me insane!** ça me rend fou!
2 *npl* **the insane** les malades *mpl* mentaux
►► *Am* ***insane asylum*** hospice *m ou* asile *m* d'aliénés

insanely [ɪn'seɪnlɪ] *adv* (**a**) *(crazily → laugh, behave, talk)* comme un fou (une folle); **they clapped insanely** ils applaudissaient comme des fous (**b**) *Fig (as intensifier → funny, rich)* follement; **he was insanely jealous** il était fou de jalousie

insanitary [ɪn'sænɪtrɪ] *adj* insalubre, malsain

insanity [ɪn'sænətɪ] *n* (**a**) *(mental disorder)* folie *f*, démence *f* (**b**) *Fig (of scheme, plan etc)* folie *f*; **it's sheer insanity doing that** c'est de la folie pure et simple (que) de faire cela

insatiability [ɪn,seɪʃə'bɪlɪtɪ] *n* insatiabilité *f*

insatiable [ɪn'seɪʃəbəl] *adj* insatiable

insatiableness [ɪn'seɪʃəbəlnɪs] *n* insatiabilité *f*

insatiably [ɪn'seɪʃəblɪ] *adv* insatiablement

inscape ['ɪnskeɪp] *n* essence *f*

inscribe [ɪn'skraɪb] *vt* (**a**) *(on list)* inscrire; *(on plaque, tomb etc)* graver, inscrire; **he had the ring inscribed with her name** *or* **her name inscribed on the ring** il a fait graver son nom sur la bague; **his cigar case was inscribed with his name** son étui à cigares était gravé à son nom; *Fig* **it's inscribed on my memory** c'est inscrit *ou* gravé dans ma mémoire
(**b**) *(dedicate)* dédicacer; **an inscribed copy of the book** un exemplaire dédicacé du livre
(**c**) *Geom* inscrire
►► *Fin* ***inscribed securities*** titres *mpl* nominatifs

inscription [ɪn'skrɪpʃən] *n (on plaque, tomb)* inscription *f*; *(on coin)* inscription *f*, légende *f*; *(in book)* dédicace *f*

inscrutability [ɪn,skruːtə'bɪlɪtɪ] *n* impénétrabilité *f*

inscrutable [ɪn'skruːtəbəl] *adj (person, face)* énigmatique, impénétrable; *(remark)* énigmatique

inscrutably [ɪn'skruːtəblɪ] *adv* de façon énigmatique

insect ['ɪnsekt] *n* (**a**) *(animal)* insecte *m* (**b**) *Fam Pej (person)* vermisseau *m*
►► ***insect bite*** piqûre *f* d'insecte; ***insect repellent*** produit *m* insectifuge

insecticidal [ɪn,sektɪ'saɪdəl] *adj* insecticide

insecticide [ɪn'sektɪsaɪd] *n* insecticide *m*

insectivore [ɪn'sektɪvɔː(r)] *n* insectivore *m*

insectivorous [,ɪnsek'tɪvərəs] *adj* insectivore

insecure [,ɪnsɪ'kjʊə(r)] *adj* (**a**) *(person → temporarily)* inquiet(ète); *(→ generally)* pas sûr de soi, qui manque d'assurance; **he's so insecure** il est vraiment mal dans sa peau (**b**) *(chair, nail, scaffolding etc)* peu solide (**c**) *(place)* peu sûr (**d**) *(future, market)* incertain; *(peace, job, relationship)* précaire; **recent events have made her position/the regime insecure** les récents événements ont rendu sa position/le régime plus précaire

insecurely [,ɪnsɪ'kjʊəlɪ] *adv* (**a**) *(say)* sans aucune assurance (**b**) *(precariously)* **insecurely balanced** en équilibre instable; **insecurely closed/bolted/attached** mal fermé/verrouillé/attaché

insecurity [,ɪnsɪ'kjʊərətɪ] (*pl* **insecurities**) *n* (**a**) *(lack of confidence)* manque *m* d'assurance; *(uncertainty)* incertitude *f*; **job insecurity** précarité *f* de l'emploi (**b**) *(lack of safety)* insécurité *f*

inseminate [ɪn'semɪneɪt] *vt* inséminer

insemination [ɪn,semɪ'neɪʃən] *n* insémination *f*

insensate [ɪn'senseɪt] *adj Formal* (**a**) *(unfeeling)* insensible (**b**) *(foolish)* insensé

insensibility [ɪn,sensə'bɪlɪtɪ] (*pl* **insensibilities**) *n Formal* (**a**) *(unconsciousness)* inconscience *f* (**b**) *(indifference)* insensibilité *f*; **his insensibility to music** son manque de sensibilité pour la musique

insensible [ɪn'sensəbəl] *adj Formal* (**a**) *(unconscious)* inconscient, sans connaissance; *(numb)* insensible; **she was knocked insensible by her fall** sa chute lui a fait perdre connaissance; **her body was insensible to any pain** son corps était insensible à toute douleur
(**b**) *(cold, indifferent)* **insensible to the suffering of others** insensible *ou* indifférent à la souffrance d'autrui
(**c**) *(unaware)* inconscient; **insensible of the risks** inconscient des risques
(**d**) *(imperceptible)* insensible, imperceptible

insensibly [ɪn'sensəblɪ] *adv (imperceptibly)* insensiblement, petit à petit

insensitive [ɪn'sensətɪv] *adj* (**a**) *(cold-hearted)* insensible, dur; **they are insensitive brutes** ce sont des brutes épaisses; **the government's reaction was highly insensitive** le gouvernement a fait preuve d'une indifférence extrême (**b**) *(unaware)* insensible; **to be insensitive to sth** être insensible à qch (**c**) *(physically)* insensible; **insensitive to pain** insensible à la douleur

insensitively [ɪn'sensətɪvlɪ] *adj* avec un grand manque de tact

insensitivity [ɪn,sensə'tɪvətɪ], **insensitiveness** [ɪn'sensətɪvnɪs] *n* insensibilité *f*

insentient [ɪn'senʃənt] *adj* insensible, qui n'éprouve aucune sensation

inseparability [ɪn,sepərə'bɪlɪtɪ] *n* inséparabilité *f*

inseparable [ɪn'sepərəbəl] *adj* inséparable

inseparableness [ɪn'sepərəbəlnɪs] *n* inséparabilité *f*

inseparably [ɪn'sepərəblɪ] *adv* inséparablement

insert 1 *vt* [ɪn'sɜːt] (**a**) *(put, put in)* introduire, insérer; **insert your coin/card into the machine** introduisez votre pièce/carte dans la machine; **she inserted a small ad in the local paper** elle a mis une petite annonce dans le journal local; **before inserting your contact lenses** avant de mettre vos verres de contact; **to insert a name on a list** ajouter un nom à une liste
(**b**) *Typ (line)* intercaler
(**c**) *Comput* insérer
2 *n* ['ɪnsɜːt] (**a**) *(gen)* insertion *f*, *(in book, magazine)* encart *m*
(**b**) *Sewing* pièce *f* rapportée; *(decorative)* incrustation *f*
(**c**) *Cin* scène-raccord *f*
(**d**) *Typ (in proofs)* insertion *f*
(**e**) *Comput* insertion *f*
►► *Comput* ***insert key*** touche *f* d'insertion; *Typ* ***insert mark*** signe *m* d'insertion; *Comput* ***insert mode*** mode *m* (d')insertion; *Comput* ***insert point*** point *m* d'insertion

insertion [ɪn'sɜːʃən] *n* (**a**) *(act)* insertion *f* (**b**) *(thing inserted)* insertion *f* (**c**) *Anat & Bot* insertion *f*; **point of insertion** point *m* d'insertion
►► *Typ* ***insertion point*** point *m* d'insertion

in-service *adj*
►► *Br Sch* ***in-service training*** formation *f* permanente *ou* continue pour les enseignants

INSET ['ɪnset] *n Br Sch (abbr* **in-service training**) formation *f* permanente *ou* continue pour les enseignants

inset ['ɪnset] (*pt & pp* **inset,** *cont* **insetting**) **1** *vt* (**a**) *(detail, map, diagram)* insérer en encadré; **town plans are inset in the main map** des plans de ville figurent en encadrés sur la carte principale
(**b**) *Sewing (extra material)* rapporter
(**c**) *Typ* rentrer
(**d**) *(jewel)* incruster (**with** de)
2 *n* (**a**) *(in map, text)* encadré *m*; *(on video, TV screen)* incrustation *f*
(**b**) *(in newspaper, magazine)* encart *m*
(**c**) *Sewing* panneau *m* rapporté; **lace inset** incrustation *f* de dentelle
►► *Sewing* ***inset pocket*** poche *f* couture

inshore 1 *adj* ['ɪnʃɔː(r)] côtier
2 *adv* [ɪn'ʃɔː(r)] *(near shore)* près de la côte; *(towards shore)* vers la côte; **the boat was keeping close inshore** le bateau longeait *ou* restait près de la côte
►► ***inshore current*** courant *m* qui porte vers la côte; ***inshore fishing*** pêche *f* côtière; ***inshore waters*** eaux *fpl* près de la côte; ***inshore wind*** vent *m* de mer

INSIDE

dedans	► **1 (a)**
à l'intérieur	► **1 (a)**
au fond	► **1 (d)**
à l'intérieur de	► **2 (a)**
dans	► **2 (a)**
en moins de	► **2 (b)**
intérieur	► **3 (a); 4 (a)**

1 *adv* [ɪn'saɪd] (**a**) *(within enclosed space)* dedans, à l'intérieur; **there's nothing inside** il n'y a rien dedans *ou* à l'intérieur; **it's hollow inside** c'est creux à l'intérieur, l'intérieur est creux; **inside and out** au dedans et au dehors, à l'intérieur et à l'extérieur
(**b**) *(indoors)* à l'intérieur; **bring the chairs**

inside rentre les chaises; **she opened the door and went inside** elle ouvrit la porte et entra; **go and play inside** va jouer à l'intérieur; **come inside!** entrez!; *Br* **plenty of room inside!** *(in bus)* il y a plein de place à l'intérieur!; **move along inside there!** avancez jusqu'au fond!

(**c**) *Fam (in prison)* en taule; **he's been inside** il a fait de la taule (**d**) *(in one's heart)* au fond (de soi-même); **inside I was furious** au fond de moi-même, j'étais furieux

2 *prep* [ɪn'saɪd] (**a**) *(within)* à l'intérieur de, dans; **inside the house** à l'intérieur de la maison; *Fig* **what goes on inside his head?** qu'est-ce qui se passe dans sa tête?; *Fam* **I'll be all right once I've got a few drinks inside me** tout ira bien quand j'aurai descendu quelques verres; *Fam* **get this inside you** avale ça; **a little voice inside me kept saying "no"** une petite voix intérieure n'arrêtait pas de me dire "non"; **it's just inside the limit** c'est juste (dans) la limite; **the attack took place inside Turkey itself** l'assaut a eu lieu sur le territoire turc même; **someone inside the company must have told them** quelqu'un de l'entreprise a dû le leur dire

(**b**) *(in less than)* en moins de; **I'll have it finished inside 6 days** je l'aurai terminé en moins de 6 jours

3 *n* [ɪn'saɪd] (**a**) *(inner part)* intérieur *m*; **the inside of the box** l'intérieur de la boîte; **the door doesn't open from the inside** la porte ne s'ouvre pas de l'intérieur; **she has a scar on the inside of her wrist** elle a une cicatrice à l'intérieur du poignet

(**b**) *(of pavement, road)* **walk on the inside** marchez loin du bord; *Aut* **to overtake on the inside** *(driving on left)* doubler à gauche; *(driving on right)* doubler à droite; *Horseracing* **coming up on the inside is Golden Boy** Golden Boy remonte à la corde

(**c**) *Fig* **only someone on the inside would know that** seul quelqu'un de la maison saurait ça

4 *adj* ['ɪnsaɪd] (**a**) *(door, wall)* intérieur; *Constr (measurement, stair etc)* dans œuvre; *(diameter)* interne; *Horseracing* **to be on the inside track** tenir la corde; *Fig* être bien placé

(**b**) *Fig* **he has inside information** il a quelqu'un dans la place qui le renseigne; **it looks like an inside job** on dirait que c'est quelqu'un de la maison qui a fait le coup; **I speak with inside knowledge** ce que je dis je le sais de bonne source; **find out the inside story** essaie de découvrir les dessous de l'histoire

(**c**) *Ftbl* **inside left/right** inter *m* gauche/droit

5 insides [ɪn'saɪdz] *npl Fam (stomach)* estomac❑ *m*; *(intestines)* intestins❑ *mpl*, tripes❑ *fpl*; **to have pains in one's insides** avoir mal au ventre

6 inside of *prep Fam* (**a**) *(in less than)* en moins de❑

(**b**) *Am (within)* à l'intérieur de❑, dans❑

7 inside out *adv* (**a**) *(with inner part outwards)* **your socks are on inside out** tu as mis tes chaussettes à l'envers; **he turned his pockets inside out** il a retourné ses poches; *Fig* **they turned the room inside out** ils ont mis la pièce sens dessus dessous

(**b**) *(thoroughly)* **he knows this town inside out** il connaît cette ville comme sa poche; **she knows her job inside out** elle connaît parfaitement son travail

►► *Press* ***inside back cover*** troisième *f* de couverture; ***inside centre*** *(in rugby)* premier centre *m*; *Aut* ***inside door*** portière *f* côté trottoir; *Ftbl* ***inside forward*** inter *m*, intérieur *m*; *Press* ***inside front cover*** deuxième *f* de couverture; ***the inside lane*** *(in athletics)* la corde, le couloir intérieur; *(of road → driving on left)* la voie de gauche; *(→ driving on right)* la voie de droite; ***inside leg (measurement)*** hauteur *f* de l'entrejambe; *Typ* ***inside margin*** marge *f* de reliure, (blanc *m* de) petit fond *m*; ***the inside pages*** *(of newspaper)* les pages *fpl* intérieures; ***inside toilet*** toilettes *fpl* à l'intérieur; *Am Sport* ***inside track*** la corde, le couloir intérieur; *Fig* **to have the inside track** être en position de force; *Aut* ***inside wheel*** roue *f* côté trottoir

insider [,ɪn'saɪdə(r)] *n* initié(e) *m,f*; **according to an insider** selon une source bien informée; **I got a hot tip from an insider** quelqu'un dans la place m'a donné un bon tuyau; *St Exch* **the insiders** les initiés *mpl*

►► *St Exch* ***insider dealing, insider trading*** *(UNCOUNT)* délit *m* d'initié; **to be accused of insider dealing** être accusé de délit d'initié

insidious [ɪn'sɪdɪəs] *adj* insidieux

insidiously [ɪn'sɪdɪəslɪ] *adv* insidieusement

insidiousness [ɪn'sɪdɪəsnɪs] *n* caractère *m* insidieux

insight ['ɪnsaɪt] *n* (**a**) *(perspicacity)* perspicacité *f*; **she has great insight** elle est très fine; **his book shows remarkable insight into the problem** son livre témoigne d'une compréhension très fine du problème

(**b**) *(idea, glimpse)* aperçu *m*, idée *f*; **I managed to get** *or* **gain an insight into her real character** j'ai pu me faire une idée de sa véritable personnalité; **his book offers us new insights into human behaviour** son livre nous propose un nouveau regard sur le comportement humain

insightful ['ɪnsaɪtfʊl] *adj* pénétrant, perspicace

insignia [ɪn'sɪgnɪə] (*pl* **inv** *or* **insignias**) *n* insigne *m*, insignes *mpl*; **he wore the insignia of his office** il portait les insignes de sa fonction

insignificance [,ɪnsɪg'nɪfɪkəns] *n* insignifiance *f*; **my problems fade into insignificance beside yours** mes problèmes semblent totalement insignifiants à côté des tiens

insignificant [,ɪnsɪg'nɪfɪkənt] *adj* (**a**) *(unimportant)* insignifiant, sans importance (**b**) *(negligible)* insignifiant, négligeable

insincere [,ɪnsɪn'sɪə(r)] *adj* peu sincère; **his grief turned out to be insincere** il s'avéra que son chagrin n'était que feint; **did you think I was being insincere?** croyais-tu que je n'étais pas sincère?

insincerely [,ɪnsɪn'sɪəlɪ] *adv* sans sincérité, de manière hypocrite

insincerity [,ɪnsɪn'serətɪ] *n* manque *m* de sincérité

insinuate [ɪn'sɪnjʊeɪt] *vt* (**a**) *(imply)* insinuer, laisser entendre; **he insinuated that you were lying** il a insinué que vous mentiez (**b**) *Formal (introduce)* insinuer; **he insinuated himself into their favour** il s'est insinué dans leurs bonnes grâces

insinuating [ɪn'sɪnjʊeɪtɪŋ] *adj* (**a**) *(ingratiating)* insinuant (**b**) **an insinuating remark** une insinuation

insinuatingly [ɪn'sɪnjʊeɪtɪŋlɪ] *adv* (**a**) *(ingratiatingly)* d'une manière insinuante (**b**) *(say, reply)* d'un ton lourd de sous-entendus

insinuation [ɪn,sɪnjʊ'eɪʃən] *n* (**a**) *(hint)* insinuation *f*, allusion *f* (**b**) *(act, practice)* insinuation *f*

insipid [ɪn'sɪpɪd] *adj* insipide, fade

insipidity [,ɪnsɪ'pɪdətɪ], **insipidness** [ɪn'sɪpɪdnɪs] *n* insipidité *f*, fadeur *f*

insist [ɪn'sɪst] **1** *vi* (**a**) *(demand)* insister; **if you insist** si tu insistes; **he insisted on a new contract** il a exigé un nouveau contrat; **I insist on seeing the manager** j'exige de voir le directeur; **she insists on doing it her way** elle tient à le faire à sa façon; **he insisted on my taking the money** il a tenu à ce que je prenne l'argent

(**b**) *(maintain)* **to insist on** maintenir; **she insists on her innocence** elle maintient qu'elle est innocente

(**c**) *(stress)* **to insist on** insister sur; **I must insist on this point** je dois insister sur ce point

2 *vt* (**a**) *(demand)* insister; **I insist that you tell no one** j'insiste pour que vous ne le disiez à personne; **you should insist that you be paid** vous devriez exiger qu'on vous paye

(**b**) *(maintain)* maintenir, soutenir; **she insists that she locked the door** elle maintient qu'elle a fermé la porte à clef

insistence [ɪn'sɪstəns] *n* insistance *f*; **their insistence on secrecy has hindered negotiations** en exigeant le secret, ils ont entravé les négociations; **her insistence on her innocence** ses protestations d'innocence; **his insistence on his rights** la revendication répétée de ses droits; **because of his insistence on paying** parce qu'il tenait à payer; **at** *or* **on my insistence** sur mon insistance; **I came here at her insistence** je suis venu ici parce qu'elle a insisté

insistent [ɪn'sɪstənt] *adj (person)* insistant; *(demand)* pressant; *(denial, refusal)* obstiné; **to be insistent about sth** insister sur qch; **she was most insistent** elle a beaucoup insisté; **the child's insistent cries** les pleurs incessants de l'enfant

insistently [ɪn'sɪstəntlɪ] *adv (stare, knock)* avec insistance; *(ask, urge)* avec insistance, instamment

in situ [,ɪn'sɪtjuː] *adv* sur place, in situ

insobriety [,ɪnsə'braɪətɪ] *n Formal (drunkenness)* ébriété *f*; *(intemperance)* intempérance *f*

insofar as [,ɪnsəʊ'fɑː(r)-] *conj* dans la mesure où; **I'll help her insofar as I can** je l'aiderai dans la mesure de mes capacités; **insofar as it's possible** dans la limite *ou* mesure du possible

insolation [,ɪnsəʊ'leɪʃən] *n* insolation *f*

insole ['ɪnsəʊl] *n (inner sole)* première semelle *f*; *(separate piece → of cork, felt etc)* semelle *f* intérieure

insolence ['ɪnsələns] *n* insolence *f*

insolent ['ɪnsələnt] *adj* insolent; **he's insolent to his teachers** il est insolent *ou* il fait preuve d'insolence envers ses professeurs

insolently ['ɪnsələntlɪ] *adv* insolemment, avec insolence

insolubility [ɪn,sɒljʊ'bɪlətɪ] *n* insolubilité *f*

insoluble [ɪn'sɒljʊbəl] *adj (problem, substance)* insoluble

insolvable [ɪn'sɒlvəbəl] *adj* insoluble

insolvency [ɪn'sɒlvənsɪ] *n Fin (of person)* insolvabilité *f*; *(of company)* faillite *f*; **they're going to declare insolvency** *(people)* ils vont se déclarer insolvables; *(company)* ils vont déposer leur bilan

►► ***insolvency provision*** fonds *m* de garantie salariale

insolvent [ɪn'sɒlvənt] **1** *adj Fin (person)* insolvable; *(company)* en faillite; **he was insolvent by ten million dollars** il laissait une dette de dix millions de dollars; **to declare oneself insolvent** *(person)* se déclarer insolvable; *(company)* déposer son bilan

2 *n* insolvable *mf*

insomnia [ɪn'sɒmnɪə] *n (UNCOUNT)* insomnie *f*

insomniac [ɪn'sɒmnɪæk] **1** *adj* insomniaque

2 *n* insomniaque *mf*

insomuch as [,ɪnsəʊ'mʌtʃ-] *conj Formal (given that)* étant donné que, vu que; *(insofar as)* dans la mesure où

insouciance [ɪn'suːsɪəns] *n Literary* insouciance *f*

insouciant [ɪn'suːsɪənt] *adj Literary* insoucieux

inspect [ɪn'spekt] **1** *vt* (**a**) *(scrutinize)* examiner, inspecter; **she inspected her body for bruises** elle examina son corps à la recherche de bleus (**b**) *(check officially → school, product, prison)* inspecter; *(→ ticket)* contrôler; *(→ accounts)* contrôler; *(→ machinery, vehicle)* contrôler, vérifier; **the customs officer inspected our luggage** le douanier a inspecté nos bagages (**c**) *Mil (troops)* passer en revue

2 *vi* faire une inspection

inspecting officer [ɪn'spektɪŋ-] *n* inspecteur (trice) *m,f*

inspection [ɪn'spekʃən] *n* (**a**) *(of object)* examen *m* (minutieux); *(of place)* inspection *f*; **on closer inspection** en regardant de plus près; **to buy goods on inspection** acheter des marchandises sur examen

(**b**) *(official check)* inspection *f*; *(of ticket, passport)* contrôle *m*; *(of school, prison)* (visite *f* d')inspection *f*; *(of machinery, vehicle)* contrôle *m*, vérification *f*; **customs inspection** contrôle *m* douanier; **product quality inspection** contrôle *m* de qualité des produits

(**c**) *Mil (of troops)* revue *f*, inspection *f*

►► ***inspection chamber*** bouche *f* d'égout; ***inspection copy*** *(in publishing)* spécimen *m*; *Tech* ***inspection hole*** orifice *m ou* trou *m ou* regard *m* de visite; *Tech* ***inspection panel*** panneau *m* de visite; *Aut* ***inspection pit*** fosse *f* (de réparations); *Tech* ***inspection port*** orifice *m ou* trou *m ou* regard *m* de visite

inspector [ɪn'spektə(r)] *n* (**a**) *(gen)* inspecteur(trice) *m,f*; *(on public transport)* contrôleur(euse) *m,f* (**b**) *Br Sch* inspecteur(trice) *m,f* (**c**) *(in police force)* **(police) inspector** ≃ inspecteur *m* (de police)

►► ***inspector general*** *(gen)* inspecteur *m* général; *Mil* ≃ général *m* inspecteur; *Br* ***inspector of taxes*** ≃ inspecteur(trice) *m,f* des impôts

'An Inspector Calls' *Priestley* 'Un Inspecteur vous demande'

inspectorate [ɪn'spektərət] *n (body of inspectors)* inspection *f*; *(duties, term of office)* inspection *f*, inspectorat *m*

inspiration [ˌɪnspə'reɪʃən] *n* **(a)** *(source of ideas)* inspiration *f*; **to draw one's inspiration from** s'inspirer de; **her art draws** *or* **takes its inspiration from desert landscapes** son art s'inspire des paysages désertiques; **to be an inspiration to sb** être une source d'inspiration pour qn; **your generosity has been an inspiration to us all** votre générosité nous a tous inspirés; **the inspiration for her screenplay** l'idée de son scénario
(b) *(bright idea)* inspiration *f*; **hey, I've had an inspiration!** hé! j'ai une idée géniale!
(c) *Formal (inhalation)* inspiration *f*

inspirational [ˌɪnspə'reɪʃənəl] *adj* **(a)** *(inspiring)* inspirant **(b)** *(inspired)* inspiré

inspire [ɪn'spaɪə(r)] **1** *vt* **(a)** *(person, work of art)* inspirer; **Moore's sculptures inspired her early work** les sculptures de Moore lui ont inspiré ses œuvres de jeunesse; **to inspire sb to do sth** inciter *ou* pousser qn à faire qch; **he inspired her to become a doctor** il suscita en elle une vocation de médecin
(b) *(arouse → feeling)* inspirer; **whatever inspired you to do that?** qu'est-ce qui a bien pu te donner l'idée de faire ça?; **the decision was inspired by the urgent need for funds** la décision a dû être prise pour répondre à un besoin urgent de fonds; **to inspire confidence/respect** inspirer (la) confiance/le respect; **a man who once inspired fear** un homme qui jadis inspirait la crainte; **his success inspired me with confidence** sa réussite m'a donné confiance en moi; **to inspire courage in sb** insuffler du courage à qn
(c) *Formal (inhale)* inspirer
2 *vi Formal (inhale)* inspirer

inspired [ɪn'spaɪəd] *adj (artist, poem)* inspiré; *(moment)* d'inspiration; *(performance)* extraordinaire; *(choice, decision)* bien inspiré, heureux; **I'm not feeling very inspired today** je n'ai pas vraiment l'inspiration aujourd'hui; **an inspired idea** une inspiration; **to make an inspired guess** deviner *ou* tomber juste

inspiring [ɪn'spaɪərɪŋ] *adj (speech, book)* stimulant; *(music)* exaltant; **it wasn't a very inspiring debate** ce débat n'avait rien de bien passionnant; **the menu wasn't very inspiring** le menu n'avait rien de bien tentant

inspissate [ɪn'spɪseɪt] *vt Arch or Literary (liquid)* épaissir; *Fig* **inspissated gloom** ténèbres *fpl* épaisses

inst. *Old-fashioned Com (written abbr* **instant***)* courant; **of the 9th inst.** du 9 courant *ou* de ce mois

instability [ˌɪnstə'bɪlətɪ] *(pl* **instabilities***) n* instabilité *f*

instal *Am* = **install**

install, *Am* **instal** [ɪn'stɔːl] *vt* **(a)** *(machinery, equipment, software)* installer; **we're having central heating installed** nous faisons installer le chauffage central **(b)** *(settle → person)* installer; **she installed herself in an armchair** elle s'installa dans un fauteuil **(c)** *(appoint → manager, president)* nommer; **the Tories were installed with a huge majority** les conservateurs ont été élus avec une écrasante majorité

installation [ˌɪnstə'leɪʃən] *n* **(a)** *(of machinery, equipment, software)* installation *f* **(b)** *(thing installed)* installation *f* **(c)** *Art* installation *f* **(d)** *Mil (base)* base *f*
►► *Comput* ***installation disk*** disquette *f* d'installation; *Comput* ***installation manual*** manuel *m* d'installation; *Comput* ***installation program*** programme *m* d'installation

installer [ɪn'stɔːlə(r)] *n Comput (program)* programme *m* d'installation

instalment, *Am* **installment** [ɪn'stɔːlmənt] *n* **(a)** *(payment)* acompte *m*, versement *m* partiel; **monthly instalments** mensualités *fpl*; **to pay in** *or* **by instalments** payer par versements échelonnés; **to pay off a loan in** *or* **by instalments** rembourser un prêt en plusieurs versements *ou* tranches
(b) *(of serial, story)* épisode *m*; *(of book)* fascicule *m*; *(of TV documentary)* volet *m*, partie *f*; **the last instalment of our special report on Brazil** *(on TV)* le dernier volet de notre reportage spécial sur le Brésil; **published in instalments** publié par fascicules
(c) *(installation → of machinery, equipment, software)* installation *f*
►► *Fin* ***instalment loan*** prêt *m* à tempérament *ou* à remboursements échelonnés; *Am* ***installment plan*** système *m* de paiements échelonnés; **to buy sth on the installment plan** acheter qch à crédit *(avec remboursement par paiements échelonnés)*

instance ['ɪnstəns] **1** *n* **(a)** *(example)* exemple *m*; *(case)* occasion *f*, circonstance *f*; **as an instance of** comme exemple de; **he agrees with me in most instances** la plupart du temps *ou* dans la plupart des cas il est d'accord avec moi; **our policy, in that instance, was to raise interest rates** notre politique en la circonstance *ou* l'occurrence a consisté à augmenter les taux d'intérêt; **what would you have decided in that instance?** qu'auriez-vous décidé en pareil cas?
(b) *(stage)* **in the first/second instance** en premier/second lieu; *Law* **court of first instance** tribunal *m* de première instance
(c) *Formal (request)* demande *f*, instances *fpl*; **at the instance of** à la demande de
2 *vt* donner *ou* citer en exemple
3 for instance *adv* par exemple

instant ['ɪnstənt] **1** *adj* **(a)** *(immediate)* immédiat; **this wound needs instant attention** cette blessure doit être soignée immédiatement; **for instant weight loss** pour perdre du poids rapidement; **give yourself an instant new look** changez de look en un clin d'œil
(b) *Culin (coffee)* instantané, soluble; *(soup, sauce)* instantané, en sachet; *(milk)* en poudre; *(mashed potato)* en flocons; *(dessert)* à préparation rapide
(c) *Literary (urgent)* pressant, urgent
(d) *Old-fashioned Com (in letter → of current month)* courant
2 *n* **(a)** *(moment)* instant *m*, moment *m*; **at that instant** à ce moment-là; **the next instant he'd disappeared** l'instant d'après il avait disparu; **do it this instant** fais-le tout de suite *ou* immédiatement *ou* à l'instant; **she read it in an instant** elle l'a lu en un rien de temps; **I'll be with you in an instant** je serai à vous dans un instant; **call me the instant you arrive** appelle-moi dès que *ou* aussitôt que tu seras arrivé; **I didn't believe it for one instant** je ne l'ai pas cru un seul instant; **he left on the instant** il est parti immédiatement *ou* sur-le-champ
(b) *Fam (instant coffee)* café *m* instantané ▫; **I've only got instant, I'm afraid** je suis désolé mais je n'ai que de l'instantané
►► *TV* ***instant replay*** = répétition immédiate d'une séquence

instant-access *adj (bank account)* à accès immédiat

instantaneity [ˌɪnstəntə'niːɪtɪ] *n* instantanéité *f*

instantaneous [ˌɪnstən'teɪnjəs] *adj* instantané
►► *Mktg* ***instantaneous audience*** audience *f* instantanée

instantaneously [ˌɪnstən'teɪnjəslɪ] *adv* instantanément

instantaneousness [ˌɪnstən'teɪnjəsnɪs] *n* instantanéité *f*

instantly ['ɪnstəntlɪ] *adv (immediately)* immédiatement, instantanément; **he was killed instantly** il a été tué sur le coup; **cleans and refreshes instantly!** nettoie et rafraîchit instantanément!

Instants® ['ɪnstənts] *n (scratchcard)* = carte à gratter de la Loterie nationale britannique

instate [ɪn'steɪt] *vt Formal* installer *(dans une fonction)*

in-state *adj Am* **in-state students** étudiants *mpl* originaires de l'État; **in-state championship** championnat *m* de l'État

instead [ɪn'sted] **1** *adv* **he didn't go to the office, he went home instead** au lieu d'aller au bureau, il est rentré chez lui; **I don't like sweet things, I'll have cheese instead** je n'aime pas les sucreries, je prendrai plutôt du fromage; **since I'll be away, why not send Eva instead?** puisque je ne serai pas là, pourquoi ne pas envoyer Eva à ma place?
2 instead of *prep* au lieu de, à la place de; **instead of reading a book** au lieu de lire un livre; **her son came instead of her** son fils est venu à sa place; **I had an apple instead of lunch** j'ai pris une pomme en guise de déjeuner

instep ['ɪnstep] *n* **(a)** *Anat* cou-de-pied *m*; **to have a high instep** avoir le pied très cambré **(b)** *(of shoe)* cambrure *f*

instigate ['ɪnstɪgeɪt] *vt* **(a)** *(initiate → gen)* être à l'origine de; *(→ project)* promouvoir; *(→ strike, revolt, change)* provoquer; *(→ plot)* ourdir **(b)** *(urge)* inciter, pousser; **to instigate sb to do sth** pousser *ou* inciter qn à faire qch

instigation [ˌɪnstɪ'geɪʃən] *n (urging)* instigation *f*, incitation *f*; **at her instigation** à son instigation

instigator ['ɪnstɪgeɪtə(r)] *n* instigateur(trice) *m,f*

instil, *Am* **instill** [ɪn'stɪl] *vt (principles, ideals)* inculquer (**in** à); *(loyalty, courage, fear)* insuffler (**in** à)

instillation [ˌɪnstɪ'leɪʃən] *n (of principles, ideals)* inculcation *f*

instinct ['ɪnstɪŋkt] *n* instinct *m*; **by instinct** d'instinct; **she has an instinct for business** elle a le sens des affaires; **he has an instinct for the right word** il a le don pour trouver le mot juste; **her first instinct was to run away** sa première réaction a été de s'enfuir; **to follow one's instinct** suivre *ou* obéir à son instinct

instinctive [ɪn'stɪŋktɪv] *adj* instinctif

instinctively [ɪn'stɪŋktɪvlɪ] *adv* instinctivement; **animals are instinctively afraid of fire** les animaux ont une peur instinctive du feu

instinctual [ɪn'stɪŋktjʊəl] *adj* instinctuel

institute ['ɪnstɪtjuːt] **1** *vt* **(a)** *(establish → system, guidelines)* instituer, établir; *(→ change)* introduire, apporter; *(→ committee)* créer, constituer; *(→ award, organization)* fonder, créer
(b) *(take up → proceedings)* engager, entamer; *(→ inquiry)* ouvrir; **he threatened to institute legal action against them** il a menacé de leur intenter un procès
(c) *(induct)* installer; *Rel* instituer
2 *n* institut *m*; **institute for the blind** institut *m* pour aveugles; **research institute** institut *m* de recherche
►► ***the Institute for Cancer Research*** = institut américain de recherche sur le cancer; *Br* ***the Institute of Contemporary Arts*** = centre d'art moderne à Londres; *Br* ***institute of education*** école *f* formant des enseignants

institution [ˌɪnstɪ'tjuːʃən] *n* **(a)** *(of rules)* institution *f*, établissement *m*; *(of committee)* création *f*, constitution *f*; *(of change)* introduction *f*; *Law (of action)* début *m*; *(of official)* installation *f*
(b) *(organization)* organisme *m*, établissement *m*; *(governmental)* institution *f*; *(financial, educational, penal, religious)* établissement *m*; *(private school)* institution *f*; *(hospital)* hôpital *m*, établissement *m* hospitalier; *Euph (mental hospital)* établissement *m* psychiatrique
(c) *(custom, political or social structure)* institution *f*; **the institution of marriage** l'institution du mariage
(d) *Hum (person)* institution *f*; **she's a national institution** elle est devenue une véritable institution nationale

institutional [ˌɪnstɪ'tjuːʃənəl] *adj* **(a)** *(hospital, prison, school etc)* institutionnel; **after years of institutional life** après des années d'internement
(b) *(belief, values)* séculaire
(c) *Com* institutionnel
►► *Com* ***institutional advertising*** publicité *f* institutionnelle; *Com* ***institutional buying*** achats *mpl* institutionnels; ***institutional care*** soins *mpl* hospitaliers; **he'd be better off in institutional care** il serait mieux dans un établissement *ou* centre spécialisé; *Com* ***institutional investment*** investissement *m* institutionnel; *Com* ***institutional investors*** investisseurs *mpl* institutionnels; *Com* ***institutional savings*** épargne *f* institutionnelle

institutionalism [ˌɪnstɪ'tjuːʃənəlɪzəm] *n* institutionnalisme *m*

institutionalization [ˌɪnstɪˌtjuːʃənəlaɪ'zeɪʃən] *n* **(a)** *(establishing)* institutionnalisation *f* **(b)**

(placing in a hospital, home) = fait de placer dans un établissement médical ou médico-social

institutionalize, -ise [ˌɪnstɪ'tjuːʃənəˌlaɪz] *vt* (**a**) *(establish)* institutionnaliser (**b**) *(place in a hospital, home)* placer dans un établissement *(médical ou médico-social)*

institutionalized [ˌɪnstɪ'tjuːʃənəˌlaɪzd] *adj* (**a**) *(person)* marqué par la vie en collectivité; **after years in a psychiatric hospital, she had become completely institutionalized** après des années en hôpital psychiatrique, elle était devenue complètement dépendante; **things are less institutionalized in this establishment** cet établissement a un caractère moins institutionnel (**b**) *(practice)* établi

in-store *adj (bakery, childcare facilities etc)* dans le magasin, sur place

►► *Mktg* ***in-store advertising*** PLV *f*, publicité *f* sur le lieu de vente; *Mktg* ***in-store advertising space*** espace *m* de PLV, espace *m* de publicité sur le lieu de vente; ***in-store demonstration*** démonstration *f* sur le lieu de vente; ***in-store promotion*** promotion *f* sur le lieu de vente

instruct [ɪn'strʌkt] *vt* (**a**) *(command, direct)* charger; **we have been instructed to accompany you** nous sommes chargés de *ou* nous avons mission de vous accompagner

(**b**) *(teach)* former; **to instruct sb in sth** enseigner *ou* apprendre qch à qn

(**c**) *(inform)* informer; **I have been instructed that the meeting has been cancelled** on m'a informé *ou* avisé que la réunion a été annulée

(**d**) *Law (jury, solicitor)* donner des instructions à; **to instruct counsel** constituer avocat

instruction [ɪn'strʌkʃən] *n* (**a**) *(order)* instruction *f*; **follow my instructions carefully** suis bien mes instructions *ou* indications; **to give sb instructions to do sth** ordonner à qn de faire qch; **to carry out instructions** exécuter des ordres; **to act in accordance with/contrary to instructions** se conformer/ne pas se conformer aux instructions reçues; **our instructions were to arrest him** nous avions reçu l'ordre de l'arrêter; **she gave instructions for the papers to be destroyed** elle a donné des instructions pour qu'on détruise les documents; **they were given instructions not to let him out of their sight** ils avaient reçu l'ordre de ne pas le perdre de vue; **instructions (for use)** mode *m* d'emploi

(**b**) *(UNCOUNT) (teaching)* leçons *fpl*; *Mil* instruction *f*

(**c**) *Comput* **instructions** *(in program)* instructions *fpl*

►► ***instruction book*** livret *m* d'instruction(s); *Comput* ***instruction code*** code *m* d'instruction; ***instruction manual*** manuel *m* (d'utilisation et d'entretien); *Comput* guide *m* de l'utilisateur; *Comput* ***instruction set*** jeu *m* d'instructions

instructive [ɪn'strʌktɪv] *adj* instructif

instructively [ɪn'strʌktɪvlɪ] *adv* d'une manière instructive

instructor [ɪn'strʌktə(r)] *n* (**a**) *(gen)* professeur *m*; *Mil* instructeur *m*; **music instructor** professeur *m* de musique; **sailing instructor** moniteur(trice) *m,f* de voile (**b**) *Am Univ* ≃ assistant(e) *m,f*

instructress [ɪn'strʌktrɪs] *n* professeur *m*; *Mil* instructrice *f*; **music instructress** professeur *m* de musique; **sailing instructress** monitrice *f* de voile

instrument ['ɪnstrʊmənt] **1** *n* (**a**) *Med, Mus & Tech* instrument *m*; **to fly by** *or* **on instruments** naviguer à l'aide d'instruments

(**b**) *Fig (means)* instrument *m*, outil *m*; **to serve as the instrument of sb's vengeance** servir d'instrument à la vengeance de qn; **instrument of propaganda** outil *m* de propagande

(**c**) *Fin* effet *m*, titre *m*; *Law* instrument *m*, acte *m* juridique; **instrument of incorporation** statut *m*, acte *m* de constitution; **an instrument of payment** un moyen de paiement; **instrument to order** papier *m* à ordre

2 *comp Aviat (flying, landing)* aux instruments (de bord)

3 *vt* (**a**) *Mus* orchestrer

(**b**) *Tech* munir *ou* équiper d'instruments

4 *vi Law* instrumenter

►► *Aviat & Aut* ***instrument board*** tableau *m* de bord; *Tech* tableau *m* de contrôle; *Tech* ***instrument error*** erreur *f* due aux instruments; ***instrument panel*** *Aviat & Aut* tableau *m* de bord; *Tech* tableau *m* de contrôle

instrumental [ˌɪnstrʊ'mentəl] **1** *adj* (**a**) *(significant)* **to be instrumental in doing sth** contribuer à faire qch, jouer un rôle décisif dans qch; **her work was instrumental in bringing about the reforms** elle a largement contribué à faire passer les réformes; **an instrumental role** un rôle déterminant

(**b**) *Mus* instrumental

(**c**) *Tech* d'instruments

2 *n* (**a**) *Mus* morceau *m* instrumental; **they played a few instrumentals** ils ont joué quelques morceaux de musique instrumentale

(**b**) *Ling* instrumental *m*

►► *Ling* ***instrumental case*** (cas *m*) instrumental *m*; *Tech* ***instrumental check*** *(of devices)* vérification *f* des instruments; *(by devices)* vérification *f* par instruments; *Tech* ***instrumental error*** erreur *f* due aux instruments; *Ling* ***instrumental phrase*** complément *m* d'instrument

instrumentalism [ˌɪnstrʊ'mentəˌlɪzəm] *n Phil* instrumentalisme *m*

instrumentalist [ˌɪnstrʊ'mentəlɪst] *n Mus* instrumentiste *mf*

instrumentality [ˌɪnstrʊmen'tælɪtɪ] *n* **to obtain an appointment through the instrumentality of sb** obtenir une nomination avec le concours *ou* par l'intermédiaire *ou* à l'aide de qn

instrumentation [ˌɪnstrʊmen'teɪʃən] *n* (**a**) *(musical arrangement)* orchestration *f*, instrumentation *f*; *(musical instruments)* instruments *mpl* (**b**) *Tech* instrumentation *f*

insubordinate [ˌɪnsə'bɔːdɪnət] *adj* insubordonné

►► ***insubordinate behaviour*** conduite *f* insubordonnée *ou* rebelle

insubordination ['ɪnsəˌbɔːdɪ'neɪʃən] *n* insubordination *f*

insubstantial [ˌɪnsəb'stænʃəl] *adj* (**a**) *(structure)* peu solide; *(book)* facile, peu substantiel; *(garment, snack, mist)* léger; *(claim)* sans fondement; *(reasoning)* faible, sans substance (**b**) *(imaginary)* imaginaire, chimérique

insufferable [ɪn'sʌfərəbəl] *adj* insupportable, intolérable

insufferably [ɪn'sʌfərəblɪ] *adv* insupportablement, intolérablement; **he's insufferably arrogant** il est d'une arrogance insupportable

insufficiency [ˌɪnsə'fɪʃənsɪ] (*pl* **insufficiencies**) *n* insuffisance *f*

insufficient [ˌɪnsə'fɪʃənt] *adj* insuffisant; **there is insufficient evidence** les preuves sont insuffisantes

►► *Fin* ***insufficient capital*** insuffisance *f* de capitaux; *Fin* ***insufficient funds*** provision *f* insuffisante, insuffisance *f* de provision

insufficiently [ˌɪnsə'fɪʃəntlɪ] *adv* insuffisamment

insular ['ɪnsjʊlə(r)] *adj* (**a**) *(island → tradition, authorities)* insulaire; *(isolated)* isolé; **he leads a very insular existence** il vit comme un ermite (**b**) *Fig Pej (mentality)* limité, borné; **she's very insular** elle est très bornée *ou* a l'esprit très étroit

insularity [ˌɪnsjʊ'lærətɪ] *n* (**a**) *(of tradition, authorities)* insularité *f*; *(isolation)* isolement *m* (**b**) *Fig Pej (of mentality)* [illegible] *(of person)* étroitesse *f* d'esprit

insulate ['ɪnsjʊleɪt] *vt* (**a**) *(against cold, heat, radiation)* isoler; *(hot water pipes, tank)* calorifuger; *(soundproof)* insonoriser

(**b**) *Elec* isoler

(**c**) *Fig (protect)* protéger; **they are no longer insulated from the effects of inflation** ils ne sont plus à l'abri des effets de l'inflation; **his cynicism insulates him from any feelings of pity** son cynisme le protège contre tout sentiment de pitié

►► ***insulated screwdriver*** tournevis *m* isolant; ***insulated sleeping bag*** sac *m* de couchage isolant

insulating ['ɪnsjʊleɪtɪŋ] *adj* isolant; *(against loss of heat)* calorifuge; *(soundproofing)* insonore

►► *Elec* ***insulating material*** isolant *m*; ***insulating properties*** propriétés *fpl* isolantes; ***insulating tape*** ruban *m* isolant, chatterton *m*

insulation [ˌɪnsjʊ'leɪʃən] *n* (**a**) *(against cold)* isolation *f* (calorifuge), calorifugeage *m*; *(sound-proofing)* insonorisation *f*, isolation *f*; **loft insulation** isolation *f* thermique du toit (**b**) *Elec* isolation *f* (**c**) *(feathers, foam etc)* isolant *m* (**d**) *Fig (protection)* protection *f*

insulator ['ɪnsjʊleɪtə(r)] *n (material)* isolant *m*; *(device)* isolateur *m*

insulin ['ɪnsjʊlɪn] *n* insuline *f*

►► ***insulin reaction, insulation shock*** choc *m* insulinique

insulin-dependent *adj Med* insulinodépendant

insult **1** *vt* [ɪn'sʌlt] *(abuse)* insulter, injurier; *(offend)* faire (un) affront à, offenser; **don't be insulted if I don't tell you everything** ne le prends pas mal *ou* ne t'offense pas si je ne te dis pas tout

2 *n* ['ɪnsʌlt] insulte *f*, injure *f*, affront *m*; **they were hurling insults at each other** ils se lançaient des insultes à la figure; **his remarks were an insult to their intelligence** ses commentaires étaient une insulte à leur intelligence; **their ads are an insult to women** leurs pubs sont insultantes *ou* une insulte pour les femmes; **to add insult to injury** pour couronner le tout

insulting [ɪn'sʌltɪŋ] *adj (language)* insultant, injurieux; *(attitude)* insultant, offensant; *(behaviour)* grossier; **it is insulting to suggest that...** il est insultant de suggérer que...

insultingly [ɪn'sʌltɪŋlɪ] *adv (speak)* d'un ton insultant *ou* injurieux; *(act)* d'une manière insultante; **he behaved most insultingly towards her** son comportement a été très injurieux à son égard

insuperable [ɪn'suːprəbəl] *adj* insurmontable

insuperably [ɪn'suːprəblɪ] *adv* de façon insurmontable; **insuperably difficult** d'une difficulté insurmontable

insupportable [ˌɪnsə'pɔːtəbəl] *adj* (**a**) *(unbearable)* insupportable, intolérable (**b**) *(indefensible)* insoutenable

insurable [ɪn'ʃɔːrəbəl] *adj* assurable

►► ***insurable interest*** intérêt *m* pécuniaire

insurance [ɪn'ʃɔːrəns] **1** *n* (**a**) *(UNCOUNT) (against fire, theft, accident)* assurance *f*; *(cover)* garantie *f* (d'assurance), couverture *f*; *(premium)* prime *f* (d'assurance); **to take out insurance (against sth)** prendre *ou* contracter une assurance (contre qch), s'assurer (contre qch); **to have insurance against sth** être assuré pour *ou* contre qch; **he's in insurance** il est dans les assurances; **extend the insurance when you renew the policy** faites augmenter le montant de la garantie quand vous renouvelez le contrat d'assurance; **he bought himself a stereo out of the insurance** il s'est acheté une chaîne stéréo avec (une partie de) l'argent de l'assurance; **she got £2,000 in insurance** elle a reçu 2000 livres de l'assurance; **how much do you pay in insurance?** combien payez-vous (de prime) d'assurance?

(**b**) *Fig (means of protection)* garantie *f*, moyen *m* de protection; **take Sam with you, just as an insurance** emmenez Sam avec vous, on ne sait jamais *ou* au cas où

2 *comp (scheme)* d'assurance; *(company)* d'assurances

►► ***insurance adviser*** assureur-conseil *m*; ***insurance agent*** agent *m* d'assurance(s); ***insurance banker*** bancassureur *m*; ***insurance broker*** courtier(ère) *m,f* d'assurances; ***insurance certificate*** certificat *m* d'assurance; ***insurance claim*** demande *f* d'indemnité; *(for more serious damage)* déclaration *f* de sinistre; **to make an insurance claim** faire une demande d'indemnité; *(for more serious damage)* faire une déclaration de sinistre; ***insurance company*** société *f* d'assurances; ***insurance cover*** couverture *f* d'assurance; ***insurance group*** groupe *m* d'assurance; ***insurance inspector*** inspecteur *m* d'une société d'assurances; ***insurance policy*** police *f* d'assurance, contrat *m* d'assurance; **to take out an insurance policy** contracter une assurance; ***insurance portfolio*** portefeuille *m* d'assurances; ***insurance premium*** prime *f* d'assurance; ***insurance value*** valeur *f* d'assurance

insure [ɪn'ʃɔː(r)] **1** *vt* (**a**) *(car, building, person)* assurer; **he insured himself** *or* **his life** il a pris *ou* contracté une assurance-vie; **insured against** assuré contre (**b**) *Fig (protect)* **what strategy can insure (us) against failure?** quelle stratégie peut nous prévenir contre l'échec *ou* nous garantir que nous n'échouerons pas?; **to insure one's future** assurer son avenir

2 *vi* **to insure against sth** s'assurer *ou* se faire assurer contre qch

insured [ɪn'ʃɔːd] (*pl* **inv**) **1** *n* assuré(e) *m,f*

2 *adj* assuré

►► ***insured risk*** risque *m* couvert

insurer [ɪn'ʃɔːrə(r)] *n* assureur *m*

insurgence [ɪn'sɜːdʒənsɪ], **insurgency** [ɪn'sɜːdʒəns] *n* insurrection *f*

insurgent [ɪn'sɜːdʒənt] **1** *n* insurgé(e) *m,f*

2 *adj* insurgé

insurmountable [ˌɪnsə'maʊntəbəl] *adj* insurmontable

insurrection [ˌɪnsə'rekʃən] *n* insurrection *f*; **armed insurrection** soulèvement *m* armé, insurrection *f* armée

insurrectionary [ˌɪnsə'rekʃənərɪ] (*pl* **insurrectionaries**) **1** *n* insurgé(e) *m,f*

2 *adj* insurrectionnel

insurrectionist [ˌɪnsə'rekʃənɪst] **1** *n* insurgé(e) *m,f*

2 *adj* insurrectionnel

insusceptible [ˌɪnsə'septəbəl] *adj* insusceptible, non susceptible; *Literary* **his heart was insusceptible of pity** il était inaccessible à la pitié; **a mind insusceptible to flattery** un esprit insensible à la flatterie

intact [ɪn'tækt] *adj* intact

intaglio [ɪn'tɑːlɪəʊ] (*pl* **intaglios** *or* **intagli** [-ljiː]) *n* (*gem*) intaille *f*; (*design*) dessin *m* en intaille; (*technique*) gravure *f* en creux

intake ['ɪnteɪk] *n* (**a**) *Sch & Univ* admission *f*, inscription *f*; *Mil* recrutement *m*; **the intake of refugees** l'accueil *m* des réfugiés; **they've increased their intake of medical students** ils ont décidé d'admettre davantage d'étudiants en médecine; **this year's intake of pupils is** *or* **are of a higher standard than usual** cette année les nouveaux élèves sont d'un niveau plus élevé que d'habitude

(**b**) *Tech* (*of water*) prise *f*, arrivée *f*; (*of gas, steam*) admission *f*; **an intake rate of 10 litres per second** un débit d'admission de 10 litres par seconde; **a high energy intake** une consommation importante d'énergie; **air intake** admission *f* d'air

(**c**) (*of food, alcohol*) consommation *f*; **a daily intake of 2,000 calories** une ration quotidienne de 2000 calories; **there was a sharp intake of breath** tout le monde/il/elle/*etc* retint son souffle; **oxygen intake** absorption *f* d'oxygène

►► *Br* ***intake class*** cours *m* préparatoire; *Tech* ***intake manifold*** conduits *mpl* d'admission, collecteur *m* d'admission; *Tech* ***intake valve*** soupape *f* d'admission

intangibility [ɪnˌtændʒɪ'bɪlɪtɪ] *n* intangibilité *f*; (*of idea*) caractère *m* indéfinissable

intangible [ɪn'tændʒɪbəl] **1** *adj* (*quality, reality*) intangible, impalpable; (*idea, difficulty*) indéfinissable, difficile à cerner

2 *n* impondérable *m*

3 intangibles *npl Fin* valeurs *fpl* immatérielles, actif *m* incorporel

►► *Fin* ***intangible asset*** valeur *f* immatérielle, actif *m* incorporel; *Fin* ***intangible fixed assets*** immobilisations *fpl* incorporelles; *Law* ***intangible property*** biens *mpl* incorporels

intangibleness [ɪn'tændʒɪbəlnɪs] *n* intangibilité *f*; (*of idea*) caractère *m* indéfinissable

integer ['ɪntɪdʒə(r)] *n Math* (nombre *m*) entier *m*; (*whole unit*) entier *m*

integral ['ɪntɪgrəl] **1** *adj* (**a**) (*essential* → *part, element*) intégrant, constitutif; **it's an integral part of your job** cela fait partie intégrante de votre travail

(**b**) (*entire*) intégral, complet(ète)

(**c**) *Math* intégral

(**d**) *Tech* (*forming a part*) incorporé (**with** à); **to be integral with** faire partie intégrante de

2 *n Math* intégrale *f*

►► *Aut* ***integral body shell*** coque *f* autoporteuse; *Math* ***integral calculus*** calcul *m* intégral; *Math* ***integral number*** nombre *m* entier; ***integral power supply*** accumulateur *m* incorporé

integrality [ˌɪntɪ'grælɪtɪ] *n* intégralité *f*

integrally ['ɪntɪgrəlɪ] *adv* intégralement, en totalité

integrand ['ɪntɪgrænd] *n* expression *f* à intégrer

integrate ['ɪntɪgreɪt] **1** *vt* (**a**) (*combine*) combiner; **the two systems have been integrated** on a combiné les deux systèmes

(**b**) (*include in a larger unit*) intégrer; **to integrate sb in a group** intégrer qn dans un groupe; **his brief was to integrate the new building into the historic old quarter** il avait pour mission de concevoir un bâtiment qui soit en harmonie avec la vieille ville

(**c**) (*end segregation of*) **the law was intended to integrate racial minorities** cette loi visait à l'intégration des minorités raciales; **to integrate a school** mettre fin à la ségrégation raciale dans une école

(**d**) *Math* intégrer

2 *vi* (**a**) (*fit in*) s'intégrer (**into** dans); **at first they found it hard to integrate with the local community** au début, ils ont eu du mal à s'intégrer dans la collectivité locale

(**b**) (*desegregate*) ne plus pratiquer la ségrégation raciale

integrated ['ɪntɪgreɪtɪd] *adj* (**a**) (*gen*) intégré (**b**) (*fax, modem*) intégré; **vertically integrated company** société *f* à intégration verticale

►► ***integrated circuit*** circuit *m* intégré; ***integrated circuit card*** carte *f* à circuit intégré; *Am* ***integrated neighborhood*** quartier *m* multiracial; *Comput* ***integrated package*** logiciel *m ou* progiciel *m* intégré, intégré *m*; ***integrated port facilities*** complexe *m* portuaire intégré; *Am* ***integrated school*** = école où se pratique l'intégration (raciale); *Comput* ***Integrated Services Digital Network*** Réseau *m* Numérique à Intégration de Services; *Comput* ***integrated software*** logiciel *m* intégré; *Sch* ***integrated studies*** études *fpl* interdisciplinaires

integration [ˌɪntɪ'greɪʃən] *n* (**a**) (*process of integrating*) intégration *f*; **racial integration** déségrégation *f*; *Am* **school integration** déségrégation *f* des établissements scolaires; *Econ* **vertical/horizontal integration** intégration *f* verticale/horizontale (**b**) *Math* intégration *f*

integrationist [ˌɪntɪ'greɪʃənɪst] *n* intégrationniste *mf*

integrator ['ɪntɪgreɪtə(r)] *n* (*device*) intégrateur *m*

integrity [ɪn'tegrətɪ] *n* (**a**) (*uprightness*) intégrité *f*, probité *f*; **she's a woman of great integrity** c'est une femme d'une grande intégrité (**b**) (*wholeness*) intégrité *f*; **cultural integrity** identité *f* culturelle

integument [ɪn'tegjʊmənt] *n Biol* tégument *m*

intellect ['ɪntəlekt] *n* (**a**) (*intelligence*) intelligence *f*; **a man of intellect** un homme intelligent (**b**) (*mind, person*) esprit *m*; **he was one of the best intellects of his time** c'était un des plus grands esprits de son époque

intellectual [ˌɪntə'lektjʊəl] **1** *n* intellectuel(elle) *m,f*

2 *adj* (*mental*) intellectuel; (*attitude, image*) d'intellectuel; **an intellectual set** un petit groupe d'intellectuels

►► *Law* ***intellectual property*** propriété *f* intellectuelle

intellectualism [ˌɪntə'lektjʊəlɪzəm] *n* intellectualisme *m*

intellectuality [ˌɪntəˌlektjʊ'ælɪtɪ] *n* intellectualité *f*

intellectualization [ˌɪntəˌlektjʊəlaɪ'zeɪʃən] *n* intellectualisation *f*

intellectualize, -ise [ˌɪntə'lektjʊəˌlaɪz] **1** *vt* intellectualiser

2 *vi* tenir des discours intellectuels

intellectually [ˌɪntə'lektjʊəlɪ] *adv* intellectuellement

intelligence [ɪn'telɪdʒəns] *n* (*UNCOUNT*) (**a**) (*mental ability*) intelligence *f*; **to have the intelligence to do sth** avoir l'intelligence de faire qch; **her decision shows intelligence** elle a fait preuve d'intelligence en prenant cette décision; **use your intelligence!** réfléchis un peu!

(**b**) (*information*) renseignements *mpl*, information *f*, informations *fpl*; (*department*) services *mpl* de renseignements; **intelligence is** *or* **are working on it** les services de renseignements y travaillent; **he used to work in intelligence** il travaillait pour les services de renseignements; **army intelligence** service *m* de renseignements de l'armée

(**c**) (*intelligent being*) intelligence *f*

►► *Am Pol* ***intelligence agency*** services *mpl* de renseignements; ***intelligence knowledge-based system*** système *m* expert; ***intelligence gathering*** renseignement *m*, espionnage *m*; ***intelligence officer*** officier *m* de renseignements; ***intelligence quotient*** quotient *m* intellectuel; *Br Pol* ***intelligence service*** services *mpl* de renseignements; ***intelligence test*** test *m* d'aptitude intellectuelle

intelligent [ɪn'telɪdʒənt] *adj* intelligent

►► *Br* ***intelligent card*** carte *f* à mémoire *ou* à puce; *Comput* ***intelligent terminal*** terminal *m* intelligent

intelligently [ɪn'telɪdʒəntlɪ] *adv* intelligemment

intelligentsia [ɪnˌtelɪ'dʒentsɪə] *n* intelligentsia *f*

intelligibility [ɪnˌtelɪdʒə'bɪlətɪ] *n* intelligibilité *f*

intelligible [ɪn'telɪdʒəbəl] *adj* intelligible

intelligibly [ɪn'telɪdʒəblɪ] *adj* intelligiblement

intemperance [ɪn'tempərəns] *n Formal* (**a**) (*overindulgence*) intempérance *f*, manque *m* de modération (**b**) (*of behaviour, remark*) caractère *m* outrancier (**c**) (*harshness* → *of climate*) rigueur *f*

intemperate [ɪn'tempərət] *adj Formal* (**a**) (*overindulgent*) intempérant; **intemperate drinking** consommation *f* excessive d'alcool (**b**) (*uncontrolled* → *behaviour, remark*) excessif, outrancier; **her intemperate refusal** la violence de son refus (**c**) (*harsh* → *climate*) rigoureux, rude

intend [ɪn'tend] *vt* (**a**) (*plan, have in mind*) **to intend to do sth, to intend doing** *or Am* **on doing sth** avoir l'intention de *ou* projeter de faire qch; **how do you intend to do it?** comment avez-vous l'intention de vous y prendre?; **we arrived later than (we had) intended** nous sommes arrivés plus tard que prévu; **his statement was intended to mislead** la déclaration visait à induire en erreur; **I had intended staying** *or* **to stay longer** j'avais l'intention *ou* prévu de rester plus longtemps; **he didn't intend her to see the letter** il n'avait pas l'intention de lui laisser voir la lettre; **we intend to increase our sales** nous entendons développer nos ventes; **the board intends her to become managing director** le conseil d'administration souhaite qu'elle soit nommée P-DG; *Literary* **to intend marriage** avoir l'intention de se marier; **no harm was intended** c'était sans mauvaise intention; **I'm sorry, no criticism/insult was intended** je suis désolé, je ne voulais pas vous critiquer/offenser; **I intended it to be a joke!** je voulais plaisanter!; **no pun intended!** sans jeu de mots!

(**b**) (*destine*) destiner; **a book intended for the general public** un livre destiné *ou* qui s'adresse au grand public; **the funds were intended for disabled children** les fonds étaient destinés à l'enfance handicapée; **the device is intended to reduce pollution** ce dispositif a pour but *ou* fonction de réduire la pollution; **the reform is intended to limit the dumping of toxic waste** cette réforme vise à limiter le déversement de déchets toxiques

intended [ɪn'tendɪd] **1** *adj* (**a**) (*planned* → *event, trip*) prévu; (→ *result, reaction*) voulu; (→ *market, public*) visé (**b**) (*deliberate*) intentionnel, délibéré

2 *n Arch or Hum* **his intended** sa future, sa promise; **her intended** son futur, son promis

intense [ɪn'tens] *adj* (**a**) (*gen*) intense; (*battle, debate*) acharné; (*hatred*) violent, profond; (*pleasure*) vif; **a period of intense activity** une période d'activité intense; **to my intense satisfaction/annoyance** à ma très grande satisfaction/mon grand déplaisir (**b**) (*person*) **he's so intense** (*serious*) il prend tout très au sérieux; (*emotional*) il prend tout très à cœur (**c**) *Am Fam* (*very good*) génial

intensely [ɪn'tenslɪ] *adv* (**a**) (*with intensity* → *work, stare*) intensément, avec intensité; (→ *love*) profondément, passionnément (**b**) (*extremely* → *hot, painful, curious*) extrêmement; (→ *moving, affected, bored*) profondément

intensification [ɪnˌtensɪfɪ'keɪʃən] *n* intensification *f*

intensifier [ɪn'tensɪfaɪə(r)] *n* (**a**) *Ling* intensif *m* (**b**) *Phot* renforçateur *m*

intensify [ɪn'tensɪfaɪ] (*pt & pp* **intensified**) **1** *vt* (*feeling, impression, colour*) renforcer; (*sound*) intensifier; **the police have intensified their**

search for the child la police redouble d'efforts pour retrouver l'enfant

2 *vi* s'intensifier, devenir plus intense

intensity [ɪn'tensətɪ] (*pl* **intensities**) *n* (**a**) *(of emotion, colour etc)* intensité *f*; **the emotional intensity of his paintings** la force des sentiments exprimés dans ses tableaux; **the intensity of the debate** la véhémence du débat (**b**) *Phys (of sound, current etc)* intensité *f*; *Chem (of reaction)* énergie *f* (**c**) *Phot (of negative)* densité *f*

intensive [ɪn'tensɪv] **1** *adj* intensif; **an intensive course in English** un stage intensif d'anglais; **intensive security measures** mesures *fpl* de sécurité draconiennes

2 *n Ling* intensif *m*

►► ***intensive care*** *(UNCOUNT)* soins *mpl* intensifs; **in intensive care** en réanimation; ***intensive care unit*** unité *f* de soins intensifs; *Mktg* ***intensive distribution*** distribution *f* intensive; *Mktg* ***intensive distribution strategy*** stratégie *f* de distribution intensive; ***intensive farming*** culture *f* intensive; *Am* ***intensive security prison*** prison *f* où la surveillance est renforcée

-intensive [ɪn'tensɪv] *suff* qui utilise beaucoup de...; **labour-intensive** qui nécessitent une main-d'œuvre importante; **capital-intensive** qui mobilise beaucoup de capitaux; **energy-intensive** *(appliance, industry)* grand consommateur d'énergie

intensively [ɪn'tensɪvlɪ] *adv* intensivement

intent [ɪn'tent] **1** *n* intention *f*, but *m*; **with good/evil intent** dans une bonne/mauvaise intention; *Law* **with criminal intent** dans un but délictueux; **declaration of intent** déclaration *f* d'intention

2 *adj* (**a**) *(concentrated)* attentif, absorbé; **with intent application** avec une concentration extrême; **he was silent, intent on the meal** il était silencieux, tout à son repas

(**b**) *(determined)* résolu, déterminé; **to be intent on doing sth** être déterminé *ou* résolu à faire qch; **they left intent on murder** ils sont partis, déterminés à commettre un meurtre; **a woman intent on success** une femme déterminée à réussir

3 to all intents and purposes *adv* pratiquement, quasiment; **to all intents and purposes, it was a failure** tout bien considéré, ce fut un échec

intention [ɪn'tenʃən] *n* intention *f*; **despite my intention to say** *or* **of saying nothing** malgré mon intention de ne rien dire; **I have absolutely no intention of spending my life here** je n'ai aucune intention de passer ma vie ici; **I have every intention of calling her!** j'ai bien l'intention de l'appeler; **he went to Australia with the intention of making his fortune** il est parti en Australie dans l'intention de *ou* dans le but de faire fortune; **it was with this intention that I wrote to him** c'est dans cette intention *ou* à cette fin que je lui ai écrit; *Old-fashioned or Hum* **his intentions are honourable** *(towards her)* il a l'intention de l'épouser; *Mktg* **intention to buy** intention *f* d'achat

intentional [ɪn'tenʃənəl] *adj* intentionnel, voulu

intentionally [ɪn'tenʃənəlɪ] *adv* intentionnellement; **he didn't do it intentionally** il ne l'a pas fait exprès *ou* intentionnellement; **I intentionally didn't invite her** c'est intentionnellement que je ne l'ai pas invitée

intention-to-buy-scale *n Mktg* échelle *f* des intentions d'achat

intently [ɪn'tentlɪ] *adv (alertly → listen, watch)* attentivement; *(thoroughly → question, examine)* minutieusement

intentness [ɪn'tentnɪs] *n* contention *f* d'esprit; *(of gaze, attention etc)* attention *f* soutenue; **intentness on one's work** application *f* à son travail

inter [ɪn'tɜː(r)] (*pt & pp* **interred**, *cont* **interring**) *vt Formal* enterrer, inhumer

inter- ['ɪntə(r)] *pref* inter-

interact [ˌɪntər'ækt] *vi* (**a**) *(person)* **they interact very well together** ils ont de très bons rapports, ils s'entendent très bien; **a person who doesn't interact well with others** une personne qui a du mal dans ses rapports avec les autres; **the way the two characters in the novel interact** l'interaction entre les deux personnages dans ce roman

(**b**) *(forces)* interagir; *(substances)* avoir une action réciproque; **the cold air interacts with the warm** il se produit une réaction entre l'air chaud et l'air froid

(**c**) *Comput* dialoguer

interaction [ˌɪntər'ækʃən] *n* interaction *f*

interactive [ˌɪntər'æktɪv] *adj* interactif

►► *Comput* ***interactive CD*** CD-I *m*, disque *m* compact interactif; ***interactive learning*** apprentissage *m* interactif; ***interactive marketing*** marketing *m* interactif; *Comput* ***interactive mode*** mode *m* conversationnel *ou* interactif; ***interactive television*** télévision *f* interactive; *Comput* ***interactive terminal*** terminal *m* (informatique) interactif

interactively [ˌɪntər'æktɪvlɪ] *adv Comput* interactivement

interactiveness [ˌɪntər'æktɪvnɪs], **interactivity** [ˌɪntəræk'tɪvɪtɪ] *n* interactivité *f*

inter alia [ˌɪntər'eɪlɪə] *adv Formal* entre autres

interallied [ˌɪntər'ælaɪd] *adj* interallié

inter-American *adj* interaméricain

interbank ['ɪntəbæŋk] *adj* interbancaire

►► ***interbank deposit*** dépôt *m* interbancaire; ***interbank loan*** prêt *m* de banque à banque *ou* entre banques; ***interbank market*** marché *m* interbancaire; ***interbank money*** argent *m* de gré à gré entre banques; ***interbank offered rate*** taux *m* interbancaire offert; ***interbank transfer*** virement *m* interbancaire

interbranch [ˌɪntə'bræntʃ] *adj* entre succursales *(d'une même entreprise)*

interbreed [ˌɪntə'briːd] (*pt & pp* **interbred** [-bred])

1 *vt* (**a**) *(crossbreed → animals)* croiser; *(→ races)* métisser (**b**) *(breed from same stock)* croiser *(des animaux consanguins)*

2 *vi* (**a**) *(crossbreed → animals)* se croiser; *(→ races)* se métisser (**b**) *(within family, community)* contracter des mariages consanguins

interbreeding [ˌɪntə'briːdɪŋ] *n* (**a**) *(crossbreeding → of animals)* croisement *m*; *(→ of races)* métissage *m* (**b**) *(within breed)* croisement *m* d'animaux de même souche; *(within family, community)* union *f* consanguine, unions *fpl* consanguines

intercalary [ˌɪntə'kælərɪ] *adj* (**a**) *(day, month, year)* intercalaire (**b**) *Bot (internode)* intercalaire

►► ***intercalary contour*** *(in mapmaking)* courbe *f* intercalaire; *Geol* ***intercalary strata*** couches *fpl* intercalées

intercalate [ɪn'tɜːkəleɪt] *vt* intercaler

intercalation [ɪnˌtɜːkə'leɪʃən] *n* intercalation *f*

intercede [ˌɪntə'siːd] *vi* intercéder; **she interceded with the boss on my behalf** elle a intercédé en ma faveur auprès du patron

intercellular [ˌɪntə'seljʊlə(r)] *adj Biol* intercellulaire

intercensal [ˌɪntə'sensəl] *adj (period)* intercensitaire, entre deux recensements

intercept 1 *vt* [ˌɪntə'sept] intercepter; **to intercept a blow** parer un coup

2 *vi* [ˌɪntə'sept] *(in football)* intercepter une passe

3 *n* ['ɪntəsept] interception *f*

►► *Mktg* ***intercept interview*** entretien *m* spontané

intercepter = **interceptor**

interception [ˌɪntə'sepʃən] *n* interception *f*

interceptor [ˌɪntə'septə(r)] *n* (**a**) *(person → of message)* personne *f* qui intercepte (**b**) *Aviat & Mil (aircraft)* avion *m* d'interception, intercepteur *m*

►► *Aviat & Mil* ***interceptor aircraft*** avion *m* d'interception, intercepteur *m*

intercession [ˌɪntə'seʃən] *n* intercession *f*

interchange 1 *n* ['ɪntətʃeɪndʒ] (**a**) *(exchange)* échange *m* (**b**) *(road junction)* échangeur *m*

2 *vt* [ˌɪntə'tʃeɪndʒ] (**a**) *(exchange → opinions, information)* échanger (**b**) *(switch round)* intervertir, permuter; **these tyres can be interchanged** ces pneus sont interchangeables

interchangeability [ˌɪntəˌtʃeɪndʒə'bɪlɪtɪ] *n* interchangeabilité *f*

interchangeable [ˌɪntə'tʃeɪndʒəbəl] *adj* interchangeable

interchangeableness [ˌɪntə'tʃeɪndʒəbəlnɪs] *n* interchangeabilité *f*

interchangeably [ˌɪntə'tʃeɪndʒəblɪ] *adv* indifféremment

intercharacter spacing [ɪntə'kærəktə-] *n Typ* espacement *m* entre les caractères

intercity [ˌɪntə'sɪtɪ] (*pl* **intercities**) *Br* **1** *n (train)* (train *m*) rapide *m*, train *m* grandes lignes

2 *adj (travel)* d'une ville à l'autre, interurbain

►► ***intercity train*** (train *m*) rapide *m*, train *m* grandes lignes

intercollegiate [ˌɪntəkə'liːdʒɪət] *adj* entre collèges; *Am (between universities)* interuniversitaire

intercom ['ɪntəkɒm] *n* Interphone® *m*; **to call sb on** *or* **over the intercom** appeler qn à *ou* par l'Interphone®; **to speak over the intercom** parler dans l'Interphone®

intercommunicate [ˌɪntəkə'mjuːnɪkeɪt] *vi* communiquer

intercommunication ['ɪntəkəˌmjuːnɪ'keɪʃən] *n* intercommunication *f*

intercommunion [ˌɪntəkə'mjuːnjən] *n Rel* intercommunion *f*

intercommunity [ˌɪntəkə'mjuːnɪtɪ] (*pl* **intercommunities**) **1** *n* communauté *f*

2 *adj* entre communautés

intercompany [ˌɪntə'kʌmpənɪ] *adj* interentreprise, intersociété

interconnect [ˌɪntəkə'nekt] **1** *vt (gen)* connecter; **the buildings are interconnected by underground walkways** les immeubles sont reliés par des passages souterrains; **interconnected corridors** couloirs *mpl* communicants; *Fig* **interconnected ideas** idées *fpl* étroitement reliées

2 *vi (rooms, buildings)* communiquer; *(circuits)* être connecté

interconnecting [ˌɪntəkə'nektɪŋ] *adj (wall, room)* mitoyen; **interconnecting doors** portes *fpl* de chambres communiquantes

interconnection [ˌɪntəkə'nekʃən] *n* connexion *f*, lien *m*; *Elec* interconnexion *f*

intercontinental ['ɪntəˌkɒntɪ'nentəl] *adj* intercontinental

►► ***intercontinental ballistic missile*** missile *m* balistique intercontinental

interconvertible [ˌɪntəkən'vɜːtəbəl] *adj* interchangeable (**with** avec)

intercooled ['ɪntəˌkuːld] *adj (engine)* refroidi

intercooler ['ɪntəˌkuːlə(r)] *n Aut* intercooler *m*, refroidisseur *m* intermédiaire

intercostal [ˌɪntə'kɒstəl] *adj* intercostal

►► ***intercostal muscles*** muscles *mpl* intercostaux

intercourse ['ɪntəkɔːs] *n* (**a**) *(sexual)* rapports *mpl* (sexuels); **to have intercourse (with sb)** avoir des rapports sexuels (avec qn) (**b**) *Formal (communication)* relations *fpl*, rapports *mpl*; **commercial intercourse** relations *fpl* commerciales; **social intercourse** communication *f*

intercurrent [ˌɪntə'kʌrənt] *adj* (**a**) *Med (disease, infection)* intercurrent; *(fever)* récurrent (**b**) *(event)* intervenu, survenu (dans l'intervalle); *(time, period)* écoulé *(entre deux événements)*

intercut [ˌɪntə'kʌt] *vt TV & Cin* insérer

inter-dealer broker *n Fin* courtier(ère) *m,f* intermédiaire

interdenominational ['ɪntədɪˌnɒmɪ'neɪʃənəl] *adj* interconfessionnel

interdepartmental ['ɪntəˌdiːpɑːt'mentəl] *adj (in company, hospital)* entre services; *(in university, ministry)* interdépartemental

interdependence [ˌɪntədɪ'pendəns] *n* interdépendance *f*

interdependent [ˌɪntədɪ'pendənt] *adj* interdépendant

interdict 1 *n* ['ɪntədɪkt] (**a**) *Law* interdiction *f* (**b**) *Rel* interdit *m*

2 *vt* [ˌɪntə'dɪkt] (**a**) *Law* interdire (**b**) *Rel* jeter l'interdit sur

interdiction [ˌɪntə'dɪkʃən] *n Law & Rel* interdiction *f*

interdigital [ˌɪntə'dɪdʒɪtəl] *adj Anat* interdigital

interdisciplinary [ˌɪntəˌdɪsɪ'plɪnərɪ] *adj* interdisciplinaire

interest ['ɪntrəst] **1** *n* (**a**) *(curiosity, attention)* intérêt *m*; **centre of interest** centre *m* d'intérêt; **to take/have an interest in sb/sth** s'intéresser à qn/qch; **to show (an) interest in sth** manifester de l'intérêt pour qch; **two people have shown an interest in (buying) the house** deux personnes sont intéressées par la maison; **she takes a**

int–int

great/an active interest in politics elle s'intéresse beaucoup/activement à la politique; **he has** *or* **takes no interest whatsoever in music** il ne s'intéresse absolument pas à la musique; **he lost all interest in his work** il a perdu tout intérêt pour son travail; **pupils can often lose interest** il arrive souvent que les élèves décrochent; **to hold sb's interest** retenir l'attention de qn; **the book created** *or* **aroused a great deal of interest** le livre a suscité un intérêt considérable; **there's little interest in these old chairs nowadays** on ne s'intéresse pas beaucoup à ces vieilles chaises de nos jours

(**b**) *(appeal)* intérêt *m*; **there was little of interest on television** il n'y avait pas grand-chose d'intéressant à la télévision; **of no interest** sans intérêt; **politics has** *or* **holds no interest for me** la politique ne présente aucun intérêt pour moi; **to be of interest to sb** intéresser qn; **what he does is of no interest to me** ça ne m'intéresse pas de savoir ce qu'il fait; **this information would be of great interest to the police** cette information intéresserait sûrement la police

(**c**) *(pursuit, hobby)* centre *m* d'intérêt; **we share the same interests** nous avons les mêmes centres d'intérêt; **her interests include skiing and photography** le ski et la photographie font partie de ses centres d'intérêt; **his only interests are television and comic books** la télévision et les bandes dessinées sont les seules choses qui l'intéressent

(**d**) *(advantage, benefit)* intérêt *m*; **it's in your own interest** *or* **interests** c'est dans votre propre intérêt; **it's in my interest to do it** c'est dans mon intérêt de le faire; **it's not in their interest to offend her** ce n'est pas dans leur intérêt de l'offenser, ils n'ont pas intérêt à l'offenser; **it's in all our interests to cut costs** nous avons tout intérêt à *ou* il est dans notre intérêt de réduire les coûts; **to act in/against one's own interests** agir dans/à l'encontre de ses propres intérêts; **to act in sb's best interest(s)** agir dans l'intérêt de qn; **we look after British interests** nous défendons les intérêts britanniques; **I have your interests at heart** tes intérêts me tiennent à cœur; **a conflict of interests** un conflit d'intérêts; **of public interest** d'intérêt public; **it would not be in the public interest** ça ne serait pas dans l'intérêt public; **in the interests of justice/peace** dans l'intérêt de la justice/paix; **in the interests of hygiene** par mesure d'hygiène; **in the interests of accuracy** par souci d'exactitude

(**e**) *(group with common aim)* intérêt *m*; **the oil/steel interests in the country** l'industrie pétrolière/sidérurgique du pays; **big business interests** de gros intérêts commerciaux

(**f**) *(share, stake)* intérêts *mpl*; **he has an interest in a sawmill** il a des intérêts dans une scierie; **to have a direct interest in sth** être concerné directement par qch; **I have no financial interest in the business** je ne suis pas intéressé dans cette entreprise; **our firm's interests in Europe** les intérêts de notre société en Europe; **his interest in the company is £10,000** il a une commandite de 10 000 livres

(**g**) *Fin* intérêts *mpl*; **to pay interest on a loan** payer des intérêts sur un prêt; **to bear** *or* **yield interest** porter intérêt, rapporter; **the investment will bear 6 percent interest** le placement rapportera 6 pour cent; **interest accrued** fraction *f* d'intérêt; **interest on arrears** intérêt *m* de retard; **interest on capital** rémunération *f* de capital; **interest due** intérêts *mpl* dus *ou* exigibles; **interest due and payable** intérêts *mpl* exigibles; **interest paid** intérêts *mpl* versés; **interest payable** intérêt *m* exigible; **interest received** produits *mpl* financiers, intérêts *mpl* perçus; **to pay interest** payer des intérêts; *Fig* **he'll get it back with interest!** il va le payer cher!

2 *vt* intéresser; **can I interest you in our new model?** puis-je attirer votre attention sur notre nouveau modèle?; **we couldn't interest her in the idea** nous ne sommes pas parvenus à susciter son intérêt pour cette idée; **can I interest you in a drink?** puis-je vous proposer un verre?; **it might interest you to learn** *or* **know that...** ça t'intéressera peut-être d'apprendre *ou* de savoir que...

►► *Fin* ***interest and dividend income*** produits *mpl* financiers; *Fin* ***interest charges*** intérêts *mpl* (à payer); *(on overdraft)* agios *mpl*; *Fin* ***interest days*** jours *mpl* d'intérêt; ***interest group*** groupe *m* d'intérêt; *Fin* ***interest payment date*** date *f* d'échéance des intérêts; *Fin* ***interest rate*** taux *m* d'intérêt; **the interest rate is 4 percent** le taux d'intérêt est de 4 pour cent; *St Exch* ***interest rate differential*** differentiel *m* de taux; *St Exch* ***interest rate swap*** échange *m* de taux d'intérêt

interest-bearing *adj Fin* productif d'intérêts

►► ***interest-bearing account*** compte *m* rémunéré; ***interest-bearing capital*** capital *m* productif d'intérêts; ***interest-bearing loan*** prêt *m* à intérêt; *St Exch* ***interest-bearing securities*** titres *mpl* qui produisent des intérêts

interested ['ɪntrestɪd] *adj* (**a**) *(showing interest)* intéressé; **to be interested in sth** s'intéresser à qch; **she is interested in fashion** elle s'intéresse à la mode, la mode l'intéresse; **would you be interested in meeting him?** ça t'intéresserait de le rencontrer?; **anyone interested?** il y en a que ça intéresse?, est-ce que quelqu'un est intéressé?; **we'd be interested to know** nous aimerions *ou* voudrions savoir; **I'm interested to see how they do it** je suis curieux de voir comment c'est fait; **she seems interested in the offer** elle semble intéressée par la proposition; **a group of interested passers-by** un groupe de passants curieux

(**b**) *(involved, concerned)* intéressé; **interested party** partie *f* intéressée

interestedly ['ɪntrəstɪdlɪ] *adv* avec intérêt; **I don't speak interestedly** je ne parle pas par intérêt *ou* je parle sans calcul

interest-free *adj Fin (loan)* sans intérêt; *(credit)* gratuit

interesting ['ɪntrəstɪŋ] *adj* intéressant

interestingly ['ɪntrəstɪŋlɪ] *adv* de façon intéressante; **interestingly, a number of her supporters voted against her** il est intéressant de noter qu'un certain nombre de ses partisans ont voté contre elle; **interestingly enough, they were out** chose intéressante, ils étaient sortis

interface 1 *n* ['ɪntəfeɪs] *(gen)* & *Comput* interface *f*; **the patient-doctor interface** les relations médecin-patient

2 *vt* [,ɪntə'feɪs] (**a**) *(connect)* connecter; *(two computers)* mettre en interface, interfacer (**b**) *Sewing* entoiler

3 *vi* [,ɪntə'feɪs] avoir une interface (**with** avec); **this device interfaces with most PC's** ce dispositif permet une interface avec la plupart des ordinateurs individuels

interfacing [,ɪntə'feɪsɪŋ] *n Sewing* entoilage *m*

interfere [,ɪntə'fɪə(r)] *vi* (**a**) *(intrude)* s'immiscer, s'ingérer; **to interfere in sb's life** s'immiscer *ou* s'ingérer dans la vie de qn; **I warned him not to interfere** je l'ai prévenu de ne pas s'en mêler *ou* de rester à l'écart; **I hate the way he always interferes** je déteste sa façon de se mêler de tout; **don't interfere between them** ne vous mêlez pas de leurs affaires

(**b**) *(clash, conflict)* **to interfere with** entraver; **to interfere with the course of justice** entraver le cours de la justice; **it interferes with my work** cela me gêne dans mon travail; **he lets his pride interfere with his judgment** il laisse son orgueil troubler son jugement

(**c**) *(meddle)* **to interfere with** toucher (à); **don't interfere with those wires!** laisse ces fils tranquilles!; *Euph* **to interfere with a child** se livrer à des attouchements sur un enfant

(**d**) *Phys* interférer; *Chem* perturber

(**e**) *Rad* **local radio sometimes interferes with police transmissions** la radio locale brouille *ou* perturbe parfois les transmissions de la police

interference [,ɪntə'fɪərəns] *n* (**a**) *(gen)* ingérence *f*, intervention *f*; *Sport (from opponent)* obstruction *f*; **she won't tolerate interference in** *or* **with her plans** elle ne supportera pas qu'on s'immisce dans ses projets

(**b**) *Phys* interférence *f*; *Chem* perturbation *f*

(**c**) *(UNCOUNT) Rad* parasites *mpl*, interférence *f*

(**d**) *Ling* interférence *f*

►► *Opt* ***interference figure, interference pattern*** figure *f* d'interférence

interfering [,ɪntə'fɪərɪŋ] *adj (person)* importun

interferometer [,ɪntəfə'rɒmɪtə(r)] *n* interféromètre *m*

interferon [,ɪntə'fɪərɒn] *n* interféron *m*

intergalactic [,ɪntəgə'læktɪk] *adj* intergalactique

intergovernmental ['ɪntə,gʌvən'mentəl] *adj* intergouvernemental

►► ***the Intergovernmental Panel on Climate Change*** le Groupement Intergouvernemental de l'Étude du Climat

interim ['ɪntərɪm] **1** *n* intérim *m*

2 *adj (government, measure, report)* provisoire; *(post, function)* intérimaire; **the interim minister** le ministre par intérim *ou* intérimaire

3 in the interim *adv* entretemps

►► *Acct* ***interim accounts*** comptes *mpl* semestriels; *Fin* ***interim dividend*** dividende *m* intérimaire; *Law* ***interim order*** avant faire-droit *m*; ***interim payment*** paiement *m* provisoire; ***the interim period*** l'intérim *m*; *Acct* ***interim profit and loss statement*** compte *m* de résultat prévisionnel; ***interim report*** rapport *m* intérimaire; *Acct* ***interim statement*** bilan *m* intérimaire

interior [ɪn'tɪərɪə(r)] **1** *n* (**a**) *(gen)* intérieur *m*; **the French Minister of the Interior** le ministre français de l'Intérieur; **Secretary/Department of the Interior** = ministre/ministère chargé de l'administration des domaines et des parcs nationaux aux États-Unis (**b**) *Art* (tableau *m* d') intérieur *m*

2 *adj* intérieur

►► *Math* ***interior angle*** angle *m* interne; ***interior decoration*** décoration *f* (d'intérieurs); ***interior decorator*** décorateur (trice) *m,f* (d'intérieurs); ***interior design*** architecture *f* d'intérieurs; ***interior designer*** architecte *mf* d'intérieurs; ***interior doors*** portes *fpl* intérieures; ***interior monologue*** monologue *m* intérieur; *TV & Cin* ***interior shot*** intérieur *m*, scène *f* d'intérieur; *Aut* ***interior trim*** habillage *m* intérieur

interiority [ɪn,tɪərɪ'ɒrɪtɪ] *n* intériorité *f*

interiorization [ɪn,tɪərɪə,raɪ'zeɪʃən] *n* intériorisation *f*

interiorize, -ise [ɪn'tɪərɪə,raɪz] *vt* intérioriser

interior-sprung mattress *n Br* matelas *m* à ressorts

interject [,ɪntə'dʒekt] *vt (question, comment)* placer; **"not like that", he interjected** "pas comme ça", coupa-t-il

interjection [,ɪntə'dʒekʃən] *n* (**a**) *Ling* interjection *f* (**b**) *(interruption)* interruption *f*

interlace [,ɪntə'leɪs] **1** *vt* (**a**) *(entwine)* entrelacer (**b**) *(intersperse)* entremêler

2 *vi* s'entrelacer, s'entrecroiser

interlaced [,ɪntə'leɪst] *adj Comput (display, monitor)* entrelacé

interlanguage ['ɪntə,læŋgwɪdʒ] *n Ling* interlangue *f*

interlard [,ɪntə'lɑːd] *vt* entrelarder (**with** de)

interlay [,ɪntə'leɪ] *vt* mêler

interleaf ['ɪntəliːf] (*pl* **interleaves** [-liːvz]) *n* feuillet *m* intercalé

interleave [,ɪntə'liːv] *vt (book)* interfolier; *(sheet)* intercaler

interleukin [,ɪntə'ljuːkɪn] *vt Biol* interleukine *f*

interlibrary [,ɪntə'laɪbrərɪ] *adj* inter-bibliothèque

interline [,ɪntə'laɪn] *vt* (**a**) *(text)* interligner (**b**) *Sewing* poser une doublure intermédiaire à

►► *Typ* ***interline spacing*** interligne *m*

interlinear [,ɪntə'lɪnɪə(r)] *adj (text)* interlinéaire

interlining [,ɪntə'laɪnɪŋ] *n Sewing* doublure *f* intermédiaire

interlinked [,ɪntə'lɪŋkt] *adj* **the problems are interlinked** les problèmes sont liés

interlock 1 *n* ['ɪntəlɒk] (**a**) *Tech* enclenchement *m* (**b**) *Tex* interlock *m*

2 *vt* [,ɪntə'lɒk] (**a**) *Tech* enclencher (**b**) *(entwine)* entrelacer

3 *vi* [,ɪntə'lɒk] (**a**) *Tech (mechanism)* s'enclencher; *(cogwheels)* s'engrener (**b**) *(groups, issues)* s'imbriquer

interlocking [,ɪntə'lɒkɪŋ] *adj (parts)* emboîtable; *Tech (gears)* qui s'engrènent *ou* s'enclenchent; **interlocking chairs** chaises *fpl* empilables

interlocutor [,ɪntə'lɒkjʊtə(r)] *n* interlocuteur(trice) *m,f*

interlocutory [,ɪntə'lɒkjʊtərɪ] *adj Law* interlocutoire, préjudiciel

►► ***interlocutory decree, interlocutory judgement*** interlocutoire *m*; **to award an interlocutory decree in a case** interloquer une affaire; **to**

pronounce an interlocutory decree against sb interloquer qn

interloper ['ɪntələʊpə(r)] *n* intrus(e) *m,f*

interlude ['ɪntəlu:d] *n* (**a**) *(period of time)* intervalle *m*; **a brief interlude** un bref intervalle; **a pleasant interlude in her troubled life** un moment de répit dans sa vie mouvementée (**b**) *Theat* intermède *m*; *Mus & TV* interlude *m*

intermarriage [ˌɪntə'mærɪdʒ] *n* (**a**) *(within family)* mariage *m* consanguin; *(within tribe)* endogamie *f* (**b**) *(between different races, religions, nationalities)* mariage *m* mixte; **intermarriage between Jews and Christians** mariage mixte entre juifs et chrétiens

intermarry [ˌɪntə'mærɪ] *(pt & pp* **intermarried**) *vi* (**a**) *(within family)* se marier entre membres d'une même famille; *(within family)* pratiquer l'endogamie (**b**) *(between different groups)* **members of different religions intermarried freely** les mariages mixtes se pratiquaient librement

intermediary [ˌɪntə'mi:djərɪ] *(pl* **intermediaries**) **1** *n* intermédiaire *mf*

2 *adj* intermédiaire

intermediate [ˌɪntə'mi:djət] **1** *adj* (**a**) *(gen)* intermédiaire (**b**) *Sch (class)* moyen; **an intermediate English course** un cours d'anglais de niveau moyen *ou* intermédiaire

2 *n* (**a**) *Am (car)* voiture *f* de taille moyenne (**b**) *Chem* produit *m* intermédiaire

►► *Fin* ***intermediate broker*** intermédiaire *mf*, remisier *m* (en Bourse); *Fin* ***intermediate credit*** crédit *m* à moyen terme; *Elec* ***intermediate frequency*** fréquence *f* moyenne; ***intermediate goods*** biens *mpl* intermédiaires; *Mil* ***intermediate range ballistic missile*** IRBM *m*; *Mil* ***intermediate range missile*** missile *m* de moyenne portée *ou* de portée intermédiaire; *Mil* ***intermediate range nuclear forces*** forces *fpl* nucléaires intermédiaires; *NZ* ***intermediate school*** = école qui ne comprend que les classes de sixième et de cinquième; ***intermediate students*** étudiants *mpl* de niveau moyen *ou* intermédiaire; ***intermediate technology*** technologie *f* intermédiaire

interment [ɪn'tɜ:mənt] *n* enterrement *m*, inhumation *f*

intermezzo [ˌɪntə'metsəʊ] *(pl* **intermezzos** *or* **intermezzi** [-'metsi:]) *n Theat* intermède *m*; *Mus* intermezzo *m*

interminable [ɪn'tɜ:mɪnəbəl] *adj* interminable

interminably [ɪn'tɜ:mɪnəblɪ] *adv* interminablement; **the play seemed interminably long** la pièce semblait interminable; **the discussions dragged on interminably** les discussions s'éternisaient

intermingle [ˌɪntə'mɪŋgəl] *vi* se mêler; **the different groups intermingled freely** les différents groupes se mêlaient librement

intermingling [ˌɪntə'mɪŋglɪŋ] *n* entremêlement *m*

interministerial [ˌɪntəˌmɪnɪs'tɪərɪəl] *adj* interministériel

intermission [ˌɪntə'mɪʃən] *n* (**a**) *(break)* pause *f*, trêve *f*; *(in illness, fever)* intermission *f*; **without intermission** sans relâche (**b**) *Cin & Theat* entracte *m*

intermit [ˌɪntə'mɪt] *(pt & pp* **intermitted,** *cont* **intermitting**) **1** *vt Literary (interrupt)* interrompre, suspendre

2 *vi Med (illness, fever)* avoir des intermittences

intermittence [ˌɪntə'mɪtəns] *n* intermittence *f*

intermittent [ˌɪntə'mɪtənt] *adj* intermittent; **intermittent rain** pluies *fpl* intermittentes, averses *fpl*

►► *Aut* ***intermittent facility*** *(of wipers)* intermittence *f*

intermittently [ˌɪntə'mɪtəntlɪ] *adv* par intervalles, par intermittence; **the journal has been published only intermittently** la revue n'a connu qu'une parution irrégulière

intermixture [ˌɪntə'mɪkstʃə(r)] *n* (**a**) *(action)* mixtion *f* (**b**) *(result)* mélange *m*

intermodal [ˌɪntə'məʊdəl] *adj (container)* intermodal

►► ***intermodal points*** points *mpl* de rupture de charge; ***intermodal transport system*** réseau *m* de transport intermodal

intermolecular [ˌɪntəmə'lekjʊlə(r)] *adj* intermoléculaire

intern 1 *n* ['ɪntɜ:n] (**a**) *Med* interne *mf*; *Am Sch* (professeur *m*) stagiaire *mf*; *Am (in firm)* stagiaire *mf* (**b**) *(internee)* interné(e) *m,f* (politique)

2 *vt* [ɪn'tɜ:n] *Pol* interner

3 *vi* [ɪn'tɜ:n] *Am Med* faire son internat; *Sch* faire son stage pédagogique; *(with firm)* faire un stage en entreprise

internal [ɪn'tɜ:nəl] **1** *adj* (**a**) *(gen)* interne, intérieur; **the internal workings of the mind** les opérations *fpl* secrètes de l'esprit (**b**) *(inside country)* intérieur (**c**) *(inside organization, institution)* interne; **internal disputes are crippling the party** des luttes intestines paralysent le parti

2 *n Med* examen *m* gynécologique

►► ***internal affairs*** affaires *fpl* intérieures; ***internal audit*** audit *m* interne; ***internal auditor*** audit *m* interne, auditeur(trice) *m,f* interne; ***internal bleeding*** hémorragie *f* interne; *Tel* ***internal cable*** câble *m* d'immeuble; ***internal check*** contrôle *m* interne; *Comput* ***internal command*** commande *f* interne; ***internal company document*** document *m* interne à l'entreprise; ***internal debt*** endettement *m* intérieur; *Comput* ***internal drive*** unité *f* (de disque) interne; *Med* ***internal examination*** examen *m* interne; *Sch* ***internal examiner*** examinateur (trice) *m,f (faisant passer un examen dans son propre établissement)*; ***internal flight*** vol *m* intérieur; ***internal injuries*** lésions *fpl* internes; ***internal mail*** courrier *m* interne; ***internal marketing*** marketing *m* interne; *Am* ***internal medicine*** médecine *f* générale; ***internal memo*** note *f* à circulation interne; ***internal modem*** modem *m* interne; ***internal rate of return*** taux *m* de rentabilité interne; ***internal revenue*** recettes *fpl* fiscales; *Am Fin* ***the Internal Revenue Service*** ≃ le fisc, la Direction Générale des Impôts; ***internal rhyme*** rime *f* intérieure; ***internal telephone*** téléphone *m* intérieur; ***internal travel*** voyages *mpl* à l'intérieur d'un même pays

internal-combustion engine *n* moteur *m* à explosion *ou* à combustion interne

internalization [ɪnˌtɜ:nəlaɪ'zeɪʃən] *n (of values, behaviour)* intériorisation *f*

internalize, -ise [ɪn'tɜ:nəlaɪz] *vt* (**a**) *(values, behaviour, feeling, emotion)* intérioriser (**b**) *Ind & Fin* internaliser

internally [ɪn'tɜ:nəlɪ] *adv* intérieurement; *Pharm* **not to be taken internally** *(on packaging)* à usage externe, ne pas avaler

international [ˌɪntə'næʃənəl] **1** *adj* international; **an international singing star** une vedette internationale de la chanson

2 *n* (**a**) *Sport (match)* match *m* international; *(player)* international(e) *m,f* (**b**) *Pol* **the International** l'Internationale *f*; **the First International** la Première Internationale

►► *Acct* ***the International Accounting Standards Committee*** le comité international des normes comptables; ***the International Air Transport Association*** l'Association *f* internationale de transport aérien; ***the International Atomic Energy Agency*** l'Agence *f* internationale de l'énergie atomique; ***the International Bank for Reconstruction and Development*** la Banque internationale pour la reconstruction et le développement; ***international call*** communication *f* internationale; ***the International Chamber of Commerce*** la chambre de commerce internationale; ***the International Civil Aviation Organization*** l'Organisation *f* de l'aviation civile internationale; ***the International Court of Justice*** la cour internationale de justice; *Fin* ***international currency*** devise *f* internationale; ***the International Date Line*** la ligne de changement de date; ***international direct*** *Br* ***dialling*** *or Am* ***dial code*** indicatif *m* du pays; ***the International Finance Corporation*** la Société financière internationale; ***the International Labour Organization*** l'Organisation *f* internationale du travail; ***international law*** droit *m* international; ***the International Longshoremen's Association*** = syndicat international de dockers; ***the International Longshoremen's and Warehousemen's Union*** = syndicat international de dockers et de magasiniers; *Fin* ***the International Monetary Fund*** le Fonds monétaire international; *Fin* ***international monetary reserves*** réserves *fpl* monétaires internationales; *Fin* ***international money market*** marché *m* monétaire international; *Fin* ***international money order*** mandat *m* international; *Sport* ***the International Olympic Committee*** le comité international olympique; ***the International Phonetic Alphabet*** l'alphabet *m* phonétique international; ***the International Refugee Organization*** = organisation humanitaire pour les réfugiés; ***international relations*** relations *fpl* internationales; ***international relief agency*** organisation *f* humanitaire internationale; ***international reply coupon*** coupon-réponse *m* international; ***International Standard Book Number*** ISBN *m*; ***the International Standards Organization*** l'organisation *f* internationale de normalisation; *Com* ***international trading corporation*** société *f* de commerce international, SCI *f*; ***international waters*** eaux *fpl* internationales

Internationale [ˌɪntənæʃə'nɑ:l] *n* **the Internationale** l'Internationale *f*

internationalism [ˌɪntə'næʃənəlɪzəm] *n* internationalisme *m*

internationalist [ˌɪntə'næʃənəlɪst] **1** *n* internationaliste *mf*

2 *adj* internationaliste

internationality [ˌɪntəˌnæʃə'nælɪtɪ] *n* internationalité *f*

internationalization ['ɪntəˌnæʃənəlaɪ'zeɪʃən] *n* internationalisation *f*

internationalize, -ise [ˌɪntə'næʃənəlaɪz] *vt* internationaliser

internationally [ˌɪntə'næʃənəlɪ] *adv* internationalement; **internationally famous** de renommée internationale; **internationally (speaking), the situation is improving** sur le *ou* au plan international, la situation s'améliore

interne ['ɪntɜ:n] *n Am Med* interne *mf*

internecine [*Br* ˌɪntə'ni:saɪn, *Am* ˌɪntər'ni:sən] *adj Formal* (**a**) *(within a group)* intestin; **internecine struggles** luttes *fpl* intestines (**b**) *(mutually destructive)* **internecine warfare** guerre *f* qui ravage les deux camps

internee [ˌɪntɜ:'ni:] *n* interné(e) *m,f* (politique)

Internet ['ɪntənet] *n Comput* **the Internet** l'Internet, l'internet *m*; **to surf the Internet** naviguer sur l'Internet *ou* sur Internet

►► ***Internet access*** accès *m* (à l') Internet; ***Internet access provider*** fournisseur *m* d'accès à l'Internet; ***Internet account*** compte *m* Internet; ***Internet address*** adresse *f* Internet; *Fin* ***Internet banking*** opérations *fpl* bancaires par l'Internet; ***Internet café*** cybercafé *m*; ***Internet connection*** connexion *f* à l'Internet; ***Internet number*** numéro *m* Internet; ***Internet phone*** téléphone *m* Internet; ***Internet presence provider*** = fournisseur d'accès à l'Internet proposant l'hébergement de sites Web; ***Internet protocol*** protocole *m* Internet; ***Internet relay chat*** service *m* de bavardage Internet, canal *m* de dialogue en direct; ***Internet service provider*** fournisseur *m* d'accès à l'Internet; ***Internet Society*** = organisation non gouvernementale chargée de veiller à l'évolution de l'Internet; ***Internet surfer*** internaute *mf*; ***Internet surfing*** navigation *f* sur l'Internet; ***Internet telephone*** téléphone *m* Internet; ***Internet telephony*** téléphonie *f* sur l'Internet; ***Internet user*** internaute *mf*

internist [ɪn'tɜ:nɪst] *n Am Med* interniste *mf*, spécialiste *mf* de médecine interne

internment [ɪn'tɜ:nmənt] *n* (**a**) *(gen)* internement *m* (politique); **internment without trial** internement *m* sans jugement (**b**) *(in Ireland)* = système de détention des personnes suspectées de terrorisme en Irlande du Nord

►► ***internment camp*** camp *m* d'internement

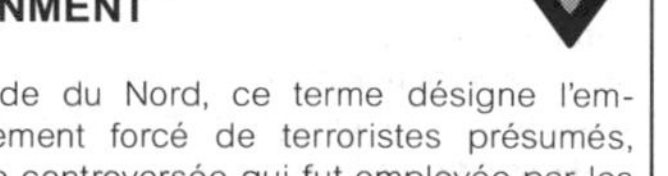

INTERNMENT

En Irlande du Nord, ce terme désigne l'emprisonnement forcé de terroristes présumés, méthode controversée qui fut employée par les autorités britanniques pour tenter de contrôler les activités de l'**IRA** (voir ce mot) au début des années 70. Cette mesure fut abandonnée en 1975.

internship ['ɪntɜ:nʃɪp] *n Am Med* internat *m*; *(with firm)* stage *m* en entreprise

interoceanic [ˌɪntərˌəʊʃɪ'ænɪk] *adj* interocéanique

interparliamentary [ˌɪntəˌpɑːləˈmentərɪ] *adj Pol* interparlementaire

interparticle [ˌɪntəˈpɑːtɪkəl] *adj Phys* interparticulaire

interparty [ˌɪntəˈpɑːtɪ] *adj (talks, negotiations)* entre différents partis politiques

interpellate [ɪnˈtɜːpeleɪt] *vt* interpeller

interpenetrate [ˌɪntəˈpenɪtreɪt] *vt (permeate)* imprégner, pénétrer

interpenetration [ˈɪntəˌpenɪˈtreɪʃən] *n (permeation)* imprégnation *f*, pénétration *f*

interpersonal [ˌɪntəˈpɜːsənəl] *adj* interpersonnel
▸▸ ***interpersonal relationships*** relations *fpl* interpersonnelles; ***interpersonal skills*** qualités *fpl* relationnelles

interplanetary [ˌɪntəˈplænɪtrɪ] *adj* interplanétaire
▸▸ ***interplanetary matter*** matière *f* interplanétaire

interplay [ˈɪntəpleɪ] *n (between forces, events, people)* interaction *f*; **the interplay of colours** le jeu des couleurs

Interpol [ˈɪntəpɒl] *n* Interpol

interpolate [ɪnˈtɜːpəleɪt] *vt* (**a**) *Formal (passage of text)* interpoler; **he interpolated several revised passages into the new edition** dans la nouvelle édition, il a interpolé plusieurs passages révisés (**b**) *Formal (interrupt)* interrompre; **"that's utter nonsense", she interpolated** "c'est complètement absurde", interrompit-elle (**c**) *Math* interpoler

interpolation [ɪnˌtɜːpəˈleɪʃən] *n* (**a**) *Formal (gen)* interpolation *f* (**b**) *Math & Comput* interpolation *f*

interpose [ˌɪntəˈpəʊz] **1** *vt* (**a**) *(between objects)* interposer, intercaler (**b**) *(interject)* lancer; **he interposed a few apt comments** il lança *ou* plaça quelques remarques pertinentes
2 *vi* intervenir, s'interposer; **"that simply isn't true!" he interposed** "c'est tout simplement faux!" lança-t-il

interpret [ɪnˈtɜːprɪt] **1** *vt* interpréter
2 *vi* servir d'interprète, faire l'interprète; **can you interpret for me?** est-ce que vous pouvez me servir d'interprète?

interpretation [ɪnˌtɜːprɪˈteɪʃən] *n* interprétation *f*; **she puts quite a different interpretation on the facts** l'interprétation qu'elle donne des faits est assez différente; **she wasn't sure what interpretation to put on the remarks** elle ne savait pas trop comment elle devait interpréter ces remarques; **to be open to interpretation** donner lieu à interprétation
▸▸ *Can* ***interpretation centre*** *(at historic site etc)* = centre d'accueil et de documentation pour les visiteurs d'un site touristique

---

'The Interpretation of Dreams' *Freud* 'L'Interprétation des rêves'

---

interpretative [ɪnˈtɜːprɪtətɪv] *adj* interprétatif

interpreter [ɪnˈtɜːprɪtə(r)] *n* (**a**) *(person)* interprète *mf* (**b**) *Comput (software)* interpréteur *m*

interpreting [ɪnˈtɜːprɪtɪŋ] *n (occupation)* interprétariat *m*, interprétation *f*

interpretive [ɪnˈtɜːprɪtɪv] *adj* interprétatif
▸▸ ***interpretive centre*** = centre d'accueil et de documentation pour les visiteurs d'un site touristique

interprofessional [ˌɪntəprəˈfeʃənəl] *adj* interprofessionnel

interprovincial [ˌɪntəprəˈvɪnʃəl] *adj (between provinces)* entre provinces; *(shared by provinces)* commun à plusieurs provinces

interracial [ˌɪntəˈreɪʃəl] *adj (relations)* interracial
▸▸ ***interracial harmony*** harmonie *f* interraciale

Inter-Rail [ˈɪntəreɪl] *Br vi* **to go Inter-Railing** voyager avec un billet Inter Rail
▸▸ ***Inter-Rail ticket*** billet *m* Inter Rail

interregnum [ˌɪntəˈregnəm] (*pl* **interregnums** *or* **interregna** [-ˈregnə]) *n* interrègne *m*; *Br Hist* **the Interregnum** l'Interrègne *m* *(intervalle (1649–1660) pendant lequel l'Angleterre, sous l'autorité de Cromwell, fut une république)*

interrelate [ˌɪntərɪˈleɪt] **1** *vt* mettre en corrélation; **interrelated questions** questions *fpl* interdépendantes *ou* intimement liées
2 *vi* être interdépendant, interagir

interrelation [ˌɪntərɪˈleɪʃən], **interrelationship** [ˌɪntərɪˈleɪʃənʃɪp] *n* corrélation *f*; **there's an interrelation between poverty levels and inflation** il y a une corrélation entre les niveaux de pauvreté et l'inflation

interrogate [ɪnˈterəgeɪt] *vt (gen) & Comput* interroger

interrogation [ɪnˌterəˈgeɪʃən] *n (gen) & Ling & Comput* interrogation *f*; *(by police)* interrogatoire *m*; **to undergo (an) interrogation** subir un interrogatoire; **she's been under interrogation** elle a subi un interrogatoire
▸▸ *Mil* ***interrogation centre*** *(for prisoners of war)* centre *m* d'interrogatoires; *Br* ***interrogation mark****, Am* ***interrogation point*** point *m* d'interrogation

interrogative [ˌɪntəˈrɒgətɪv] **1** *n Gram (word)* interrogatif *m*; *(grammatical form)* interrogative *f*; **in the interrogative** à la forme interrogative
2 *adj* (**a**) *(inquiring)* interrogateur (**b**) *Gram* interrogatif

interrogatively [ˌɪntəˈrɒgətɪvlɪ] *adv* (**a**) *(look)* interrogativement, d'un air interrogateur; *(remark)* d'un *ou* sur un ton interrogateur (**b**) *Gram* interrogativement

interrogator [ɪnˈterəgeɪtə(r)] *n* (**a**) *(questioner)* interrogateur(trice) *m,f* (**b**) *Old-fashioned Press, Rad & TV (interviewer)* interviewer *m*

interrogatory [ˌɪntəˈrɒgətrɪ] *adj* interrogateur

interrupt [ˌɪntəˈrʌpt] **1** *vt* (**a**) *(lecture, conversation)* interrompre; *(person talking)* interrompre, couper la parole à; **don't interrupt me when I'm speaking to you!** ne m'interromps pas lorsque je te parle!; **am I interrupting something?** est-ce que je vous dérange?
(**b**) *(process, activity)* interrompre; **work on the project has been interrupted** les travaux sur le projet ont été interrompus; **we interrupt this programme for a news flash** nous interrompons notre émission pour un flash d'information
(**c**) *(uniformity)* rompre; **only an occasional tree interrupted the monotony of the landscape** seul un arbre ici et là venait rompre la monotonie du paysage
2 *vi* interrompre; **he tried to explain but you kept interrupting** il a essayé de s'expliquer mais vous n'avez cessé de l'interrompre *ou* de lui couper la parole; **sorry to interrupt but...** désolé de vous interrompre mais...
3 *n Comput* interruption *f*

interrupter [ˌɪntəˈrʌptə(r)] *n Electron* interrupteur *m*

interruption [ˌɪntəˈrʌpʃən] *n* interruption *f*; **without interruption** sans interruption, sans arrêt; **he hates interruptions** il a horreur d'être interrompu

interruptor [ˌɪntəˈrʌptə(r)] = **interrupter**

interscholastic [ˌɪntəskəˈlæstɪk] *adj* interscolaire, inter-écoles

intersect [ˌɪntəˈsekt] **1** *vi* se couper, se croiser; *Math* **intersecting lines** lignes *fpl* intersectées
2 *vt* couper, croiser; **the valley is intersected by a network of small roads** la vallée est quadrillée d'innombrables petites routes; **the two lines intersect each other** les deux lignes se coupent *ou* se croisent

intersection [ˌɪntəˈsekʃən] *n* (**a**) *esp Am (road junction)* carrefour *m*, croisement *m* (**b**) *Math* intersection *f*; **point of intersection** point *m* d'intersection

interservice [ˌɪntəˈsɜːvɪs] *adj* entre les forces armées

interspace [ˌɪntəˈspeɪs] *vt Typ* espacer

intersperse [ˌɪntəˈspɜːs] *vt* parsemer, semer; **our conversation was interspersed with long silences** notre conversation était ponctuée de longs silences; **plain-clothes officers were interspersed in the crowd** des policiers en civil étaient dispersés dans la foule; **there were small blue flowers interspersed amongst the daisies** les marguerites étaient parsemées de petites fleurs bleues; **sunny weather interspersed with the odd shower** temps ensoleillé entrecoupé de quelques averses

interstate [ˈɪntəsteɪt] *Am* **1** *n* autoroute *f*
2 *adj (commerce, highway)* entre États
▸▸ ***interstate carrier*** transporteur *m* inter-État; ***Interstate Commerce Commission*** = commission régissant les relations commerciales entre les États américains

interstellar [ˌɪntəˈstelə(r)] *adj* interstellaire
▸▸ ***interstellar space*** espace *m* interstellaire

interstice [ɪnˈtɜːstɪs] *n* interstice *m*

interstitial [ˌɪntəˈstɪʃəl] **1** *n Comput* publicité *f* interstitielle
2 *adj* interstitiel
▸▸ *Comput* ***interstitial ad*** publicité *f* interstitielle

intertextual [ˌɪntəˈtekstjʊəl] *adj* intertextuel

intertextuality [ˌɪntəˈtekstjʊˈælətɪ] *n* intertextualité *f*

intertribal [ˌɪntəˈtraɪbəl] *adj* entre tribus

intertwine [ˌɪntəˈtwaɪn] **1** *vt* entrelacer; **their lives are inextricably intertwined** leurs vies sont inextricablement liées
2 *vi* s'entrelacer; **intertwining branches** branches *fpl* entrelacées

interurban [ˌɪntəˈɜːbən] *adj* interurbain

interval [ˈɪntəvəl] *n* (**a**) *(period of time)* intervalle *m*; **there was an interval of three months between applying for the job and being accepted** trois mois se sont écoulés entre la candidature et l'embauche; **I saw him again after an interval of six months** je l'ai revu après un intervalle de six mois; **at intervals** par intervalles, de temps en temps; **at regular intervals** à intervalles réguliers; **at short intervals** à intervalles rapprochés; **at weekly intervals** toutes les semaines, chaque semaine
(**b**) *(interlude)* pause *f*; *Br Theat* entracte *m*; *Sport* mi-temps *f*
(**c**) *(distance)* intervalle *m*, distance *f*; **at two-metre intervals** à deux mètres d'écart, à un intervalle de deux mètres; **trees planted at regular intervals** des arbres plantés à intervalles réguliers
(**d**) *Met* **sunny intervals** éclaircies *fpl*
(**e**) *Math & Mus* intervalle *m*
▸▸ *Am* ***interval ownership*** multipropriété *f*

inter-varsity *adj* inter-universitaire

intervene [ˌɪntəˈviːn] *vi* (**a**) *(person, government)* intervenir; **they were unwilling to intervene in the conflict** ils ne souhaitaient pas intervenir dans le conflit; **I warned him not to intervene** *(in fight)* je lui avais bien dit de ne pas intervenir *ou* s'interposer; *(in argument)* je lui avais bien dit de ne pas s'en mêler; **the government intervened to save the dollar from falling** le gouvernement est intervenu pour arrêter la chute du dollar
(**b**) *(event)* survenir; **he was about to go to college when war intervened** il allait entrer à l'université lorsque la guerre a éclaté
(**c**) *(time)* s'écouler; **three months intervened between the agreement and actually signing the contract** trois mois se sont écoulés entre l'accord et la signature du contrat
(**d**) *(interrupt)* intervenir; **if I might just intervene here...** si je peux me permettre d'intervenir sur ce point...

intervening [ˌɪntəˈviːnɪŋ] *adj (period of time)* intermédiaire; **during the intervening period** dans l'intervalle, entre-temps

intervention [ˌɪntəˈvenʃən] *n* intervention *f*; **armed intervention** intervention *f* armée
▸▸ *Econ* ***intervention price*** prix *m* d'intervention; *Fin* ***intervention rate*** taux *m* d'intervention

interventionism [ˌɪntəˈvenʃənɪzəm] *n* interventionnisme *m*

interventionist [ˌɪntəˈvenʃənɪst] **1** *n* interventionniste *mf*
2 *adj* interventionniste

intervertebral [ˌɪntəˈvɜːtəbrəl] *adj* intervertébral

interview [ˈɪntəvjuː] **1** *n* (**a**) *(for job, university place etc)* entrevue *f*, entretien *m*; **interviews will be held at our London offices** les entretiens se dérouleront dans nos bureaux de Londres; **he's already had several interviews** il a déjà eu plusieurs entretiens; **to invite** *or* **to call sb for interview** convoquer qn pour une entrevue
(**b**) *Press, Rad & TV* interview *f*; **she gave him an exclusive interview** elle lui a accordé une interview en exclusivité
(**c**) *(in survey, for research)* entretien *m*
2 *vt* (**a**) *(for job, university place etc)* avoir une entrevue *ou* un entretien avec; **shortlisted applicants will be interviewed in March** les candidats sélectionnés seront convoqués pour un entretien en mars; **we have interviewed ten**

people for the post nous avons déjà vu dix personnes pour ce poste

(**b**) *Press, Rad & TV* interviewer; **she's being interviewed by their top reporter** leur meilleur journaliste l'interviewe *ou* l'interroge en ce moment

(**c**) *(in survey, for research)* interroger, sonder; **900 voters were interviewed** 900 électeurs ont été interrogés, l'enquête a été effectuée auprès de 900 électeurs

(**d**) *(of police)* interroger, questionner; **he is being interviewed in connection with a series of thefts** on l'interroge pour une série de vols

3 *vi (job interviewer)* faire passer un entretien; **I'm interviewing all day** je fais passer des entretiens toute la journée; **he interviews well/badly** *(candidate)* il s'en sort/ne s'en sort pas bien aux entretiens; *(celebrity)* il passe/ne passe pas bien dans les interviews

▸▸ ***interview room*** salle *f* d'entretien

interviewee [ˌɪntəvjuːˈiː] *n* personne *f* interviewée

interviewer [ˈɪntəvjuːə(r)] *n* (**a**) *(for job, university place etc)* **the interviewer asked me what my present salary was** la personne qui m'a fait passer l'entretien *ou* l'entrevue m'a demandé quel était mon salaire actuel; **her skills as an interviewer** ses qualités pour faire passer les entretiens *ou* pour examiner les candidats (**b**) *Press, Rad & TV* interviewer *m*, intervieweur(euse) *m,f* (**c**) *(in survey, for research)* enquêteur(euse) *m,f*

inter vivos [ˌɪntəˈvaɪvəʊs, ˌɪntəˈviːvəʊs] *adj Law* entre vifs; **disposition inter vivos** donation *f* entre vifs

intervocalic [ˌɪntəvəˈkælɪk] *adj* intervocalique

interwar [ˌɪntəˈwɔː(r)] *adj* **the interwar period** l'entre-deux-guerres *m inv*; **interwar politics** la politique de l'entre-deux-guerres; **the interwar years** l'entre-deux-guerres *m inv*

interweave [ˌɪntəˈwiːv] (*pt* **interwove** [-ˈwəʊv] *or* **interweaved**, *pp* **interwoven** [-ˈwəʊvən] *or* **interweaved**) **1** *vt* entrelacer; **interwoven with** entrelacé de, *Fig* **our lives have become closely interwoven** nos deux vies sont devenues intimement liées

2 *vi* s'entrelacer, s'entremêler

intestacy [ɪnˈtestəsɪ] *n Law* fait *m* de mourir intestat, absence *f* de testament

intestate [ɪnˈtesteɪt] **1** *adj* intestat *(inv)*; **to die intestate** décéder intestat

2 *n* intestat *mf*

▸▸ ***intestate estate, intestate succession*** succession *f* ab intestat

intestinal [ɪnˈtestɪnəl] *adj* intestinal; *Am* **intestinal fortitude** cran *m*

intestine [ɪnˈtestɪn] *n (usu pl)* intestin *m*; **an infection of the intestine** *or* **intestines** une infection intestinale; **large intestine** gros intestin *m*; **small intestine** intestin *m* grêle

in-the-money option *n St Exch* option *f* en dedans

intimacy [ˈɪntɪməsɪ] (*pl* **intimacies**) **1** *n* (**a**) *(closeness, warmth)* intimité *f*

(**b**) *(privacy)* intimité *f*; **in the intimacy of one's own home** dans l'intimité du foyer

(**c**) *(intimate remark etc)* familiarité *f*

(**d**) *(UNCOUNT) Euph Formal (sexual relations)* relations *fpl* sexuelles, rapports *mpl*; **intimacy took place on more than one occasion** ils ont eu des rapports à plusieurs reprises

2 intimacies *npl (familiarities)* familiarités *fpl*; **they never really exchanged intimacies** ils ont toujours gardé une certaine réserve l'un envers l'autre

intimate 1 *adj* [ˈɪntɪmət] (**a**) *(friend, relationship)* intime; **we were never very intimate** nous n'avons jamais été (des amis) intimes; **we're on intimate terms with them** nous sommes très amis, ils font partie de nos amis intimes

(**b**) *(small and cosy)* intime; **an intimate little bar** un petit bar intime; **an intimate dinner for two** un dîner en amoureux; **an intimate (little) dinner party** un dîner en tête-à-tête, un petit dîner à deux

(**c**) *Euph Formal (sexually)* **they were intimate on more than one occasion** ils ont eu des rapports (intimes) à plusieurs reprises; **he admitted to having had intimate relations with her** il a reconnu avoir eu des rapports avec elle

(**d**) *(personal, private)* intime; *Hum* **spare me the intimate details!** fais-moi grâce de tous ces détails!

(**e**) *(thorough)* profond, approfondi; **she has an intimate knowledge of the field** elle connaît le sujet à fond

(**f**) *(close, direct)* étroit; **an intimate link** un lien étroit

2 *n* [ˈɪntɪmət] intime *mf*

3 *vt* [ˈɪntɪmeɪt] (**a**) *(hint, imply)* laisser entendre, insinuer; **he intimated that he had had an affair with her** il a laissé entendre qu'il avait eu une liaison avec elle; **her speech intimated strong disapproval** son discours laissait paraître son profond désaccord

(**b**) *Formal (make known → order)* intimer; *(→ one's intentions)* signifier

intimately [ˈɪntɪmətlɪ] *adv* (**a**) *(talk, behave → in a friendly way)* intimement; **to know sb intimately** connaître qn intimement (**b**) *(know → thoroughly)* à fond; *(→ closely, directly)* étroitement; **the two questions are intimately related** les deux questions sont intimement liées; **I am intimately acquainted with the details of the matter** je connais l'affaire dans ses moindres détails

intimation [ˌɪntɪˈmeɪʃən] *n Formal (suggestion)* suggestion *f*; *(sign)* indice *m*, indication *f*; *(premonition)* pressentiment *m*; **we had no intimation that disaster was imminent** rien ne laissait pressentir l'imminence d'une catastrophe; **her letter was the first intimation we had that she was in any danger** sa lettre a été pour nous le premier indice du danger qu'elle courait

intimidate [ɪnˈtɪmɪdeɪt] *vt* intimider; **to intimidate sb into doing sth** intimider qn pour qu'il fasse qch; **don't let him intimidate you** ne le laisse pas t'intimider, ne te laisse pas intimider par lui

intimidating [ɪnˈtɪmɪdeɪtɪŋ] *adj* intimidant

intimidation [ɪnˌtɪmɪˈdeɪʃən] *n (UNCOUNT)* intimidation *f*, menaces *fpl*

intimidatory [ɪnˌtɪmɪˈdeɪtərɪ] *adj* intimidateur

intimism [ˈɪntɪmɪzəm] *n Literature & Art* intimisme *m*

intimist [ˈɪntɪmɪst] *Literature & Art* **1** *n* intimiste *mf*

2 *adj* intimiste

into [ˈɪntʊ] *prep* (**a**) *(indicating direction, movement etc)* dans; **come into my office** venez dans mon bureau; **to run/stroll into a room** entrer dans une pièce en courant/d'un pas nonchalant; **they sank deeper into debt** ils se sont endettés de plus en plus; **Britain's entry into the Common Market** l'entrée *f* de la Grande-Bretagne dans le Marché commun; **to feed data into a computer** entrer des données dans un ordinateur; **planes take off into the wind** les avions décollent face au vent

(**b**) *(indicating collision)* dans; **the truck ran** *or* **crashed into the wall** le camion est rentré dans *ou* s'est écrasé contre le mur

(**c**) *(indicating transformation)* en; **the frog changed into a prince** la grenouille s'est transformée en prince; **he's grown into a man** c'est un homme maintenant; **mix the ingredients into a paste** mélangez les ingrédients jusqu'à ce qu'ils forment une pâte

(**d**) *(indicating result)* **to frighten sb into confessing** faire avouer qn en lui faisant peur; **they were shocked into silence** le choc leur a fait perdre la parole

(**e**) *(indicating division)* en; **cut it into three** coupe-le en trois; **7 into 63 goes 9** 63 divisé par 7 donne 9; **6 into 10 won't go** on ne peut pas diviser 10 par 6

(**f**) *(indicating elapsed time)* **we worked well into the night** nous avons travaillé (jusque) tard dans la nuit; **he must be well into his forties** il doit avoir la quarantaine bien passée; **a week into her holiday and she's bored already** il y a à peine une semaine qu'elle est en vacances et elle s'ennuie déjà

(**g**) *Fam (fond of)* **to be into sb/sth** *(like)* bien aimer qn/qch ☐; **I was never really into pop music** je n'ai jamais été un fana de musique pop; **is he into drugs?** est-ce qu'il se drogue? ☐; **he's into leather** il est cuir; **we're not into cheating people** *(that's not our style)* nous ne cherchons pas à rouler les gens; **if that's what you're into!** si c'est ton truc!

(**h**) *(curious about)* **the baby's into everything** le bébé est curieux de tout

(**i**) *Am (in debt to)* **he's into them for $5,000** il leur doit 5000 dollars

intolerable [ɪnˈtɒlərəbəl] *adj* intolérable, insupportable; **I find it intolerable that...** je trouve intolérable que...

intolerably [ɪnˈtɒlərəblɪ] *adv* intolérablement, insupportablement; **he had been intolerably rude** il avait été d'une grossièreté intolérable

intolerance [ɪnˈtɒlərəns] *n (gen) & Med* intolérance *f*

intolerant [ɪnˈtɒlərənt] *adj* intolérant; **she is very intolerant of noisy children** elle ne supporte absolument pas les enfants bruyants; *Med* **to be intolerant of a drug** ne pas tolérer *ou* supporter un médicament

intolerantly [ɪnˈtɒlərəntlɪ] *adv* avec intolérance

intonation [ˌɪntəˈneɪʃən] *n* intonation *f*

▸▸ *Ling* ***intonation pattern*** intonation *f*

intone [ɪnˈtəʊn] *vt* psalmodier

in toto [ˌɪn-ˈtəʊtəʊ] *adv* au total

intoxicant [ɪnˈtɒksɪkənt] *Formal* **1** *n (alcohol)* alcool *m*, boisson *f* alcoolisée; *(drug)* stupéfiant *m*

2 *adj* enivrant, grisant

intoxicate [ɪnˈtɒksɪkeɪt] *vt* (**a**) *also Fig (make drunk)* enivrer, griser (**b**) *Med (poison)* intoxiquer

intoxicated [ɪnˈtɒksɪkeɪtɪd] *adj* (**a**) *(drunk)* ivre, *Formal* en état d'ébriété (**b**) *Fig* ivre; **he was intoxicated with joy** il était ivre de joie; **she was intoxicated by success** son succès l'avait grisée *ou* lui avait fait tourner la tête

intoxicating [ɪnˈtɒksɪkeɪtɪŋ] *adj* enivrant; *Fig* grisant, enivrant, excitant; **an intoxicating perfume** un parfum enivrant *ou* capiteux

▸▸ ***intoxicating liquor*** boisson *f* alcoolisée

intoxication [ɪnˌtɒksɪˈkeɪʃən] *n* (**a**) *also Fig* ivresse *f* (**b**) *Med (poisoning)* intoxication *f*

intracardiac [ˌɪntrəˈkɑːdɪæk], **intracardial** [ˌɪntrəˈkɑːdɪəl] *adj* intracardiaque

intracellular [ˌɪntrəˈseljʊlə(r)] *adj Biol* intracellulaire

intracerebral [ˌɪntrəˈserɪbrəl] *adj Anat* intracérébral

intracervical [ˌɪntrəˈsɜːvɪkəl] *adj Med* intracervical

intra-Community [ˌɪntrəkəˈmjuːnɪtɪ] *adj EU* intracommunautaire

▸▸ ***intra-Community trade*** échange *m* intracommunautaire

intra-company [ˌɪntrəˈkʌmpənɪ] *adj* intra-entreprise

intractability [ɪnˌtræktəˈbɪlətɪ] *n* (**a**) *(of person)* intransigeance *f*, fermeté *f*, opiniâtreté *f* (**b**) *(of problem)* caractère *m* insoluble, insolubilité *f*; *(of situation)* caractère *m* inextricable

intractable [ɪnˈtræktəbəl] *adj* (**a**) *(person)* intraitable, intransigeant (**b**) *(problem)* insoluble; *(situation)* inextricable, sans issue

intradermal [ˌɪntrəˈdɜːməl], **intradermic** [ˌɪntrəˈdɜːmɪk] *adj Med* intradermique

▸▸ ***intradermal reaction*** intradermo-réaction *f*

intrados [ɪnˈtreɪdɒs] (*pl* **inv** *or* **intradoses**) *n Archit* intrados *m*

intramolecular [ˌɪntrəməˈlekjʊlə(r)] *adj Phys* intramoléculaire

intramural [illegible] *(courses, sports)* interne (à l'établissement); **intramural teams** = équipes sportives d'un même établissement jouant les unes contre les autres

intramuscular [ˌɪntrəˈmʌskjʊlə(r)] *adj* intramusculaire

Intranet [ˈɪntrənet] *n Comput* Intranet *m*

intransigence [ɪnˈtrænzɪdʒəns] *n* intransigeance *f*

intransigent [ɪnˈtrænzɪdʒənt] **1** *n* intransigeant(e) *m,f*

2 *adj* intransigeant

intransitive [ɪnˈtrænsətɪv] *Gram* **1** *n* intransitif *m*

2 *adj* intransitif

intransitively [ɪnˈtrænsətɪvlɪ] *adv Gram* intransitivement

intransitiveness [ɪnˈtrænsɪtɪvnɪs], **intransitivity** [ɪnˌtrænsɪˈtɪvɪtɪ] *n Gram* intransitivité *f*

intranuclear [ˌɪntrəˈnjuːklɪə(r)] *adj* intranucléaire

intraocular [ˌɪntrəˈɒkjʊlə(r)] *adj Anat* intraoculaire

intrapreneur [ˌɪntrəprəˈnɜː(r)] *n* = personne chargée de lancer de nouveaux projets au sein d'une entreprise

intrastate [ˌɪntrəˈsteɪt] *adj* à l'intérieur d'un même État

intrauterine [ˌɪntrəˈjuːtəraɪn] *adj* intra-utérin
►► ***intrauterine contraceptive device*** stérilet *m*

intravascular [ˌɪntrəˈvæskjʊlə(r)] *adj* intravasculaire

intravenous [ˌɪntrəˈviːnəs] *adj* intraveineux
►► ***intravenous drip*** perfusion *f* intraveineuse; ***intravenous drugs user*** toxicomane *mf* qui s'injecte sa drogue; ***intravenous injection*** (injection *f*) intraveineuse *f*

intravenously [ˌɪntrəˈviːnəslɪ] *adv* par voie intraveineuse; **he's being fed intravenously** on l'alimente par perfusion; **to take drugs intravenously** s'injecter de la drogue

in-tray *n Br* corbeille *f* de courrier à traiter *ou* "arrivée"; **put it in my in-tray** posez ça sur le courrier à traiter

intreat *Arch or Literary* = **entreat**

intrepid [ɪnˈtrepɪd] *adj* intrépide

intrepidity [ˌɪntreˈpɪdɪtɪ] *n* intrépidité *f*

intrepidly [ɪnˈtrepɪdlɪ] *adv* intrépidement

intricacy [ˈɪntrɪkəsɪ] (*pl* **intricacies**) *n* (**a**) *(complicated detail)* complexité *f*; **he knows all the legal intricacies** il connaît toutes les subtilités du droit; **I couldn't follow all the intricacies of her argument** je n'ai pas suivi toutes les subtilités de son raisonnement (**b**) *(complexity)* complexité *f*; **I admire the intricacy of her drawings** je suis en admiration devant la complexité de ses dessins

intricate [ˈɪntrɪkət] *adj (mechanism, drawing, design)* compliqué; *(question, argument, plot)* complexe

intricately [ˈɪntrɪkətlɪ] *adv* de façon complexe *ou* compliquée; **an intricately carved chair** une chaise aux sculptures complexes *ou* très travaillées

intrigue 1 *n* [ˈɪntriːg] (**a**) *(plotting)* intrigue *f*; **the boardroom was rife with intrigue** la salle du conseil d'administration sentait l'intrigue (**b**) *(plot, treason)* complot *m*; **he was involved in various intrigues against the state** il a participé à plusieurs complots contre l'État (**c**) *(love affair)* intrigue *f*
2 *vt* [ɪnˈtriːg] intriguer; **her silence intrigues me** son silence m'intrigue; **I'd be intrigued to know where they met** je serais curieux de savoir où ils se sont rencontrés
3 *vi* [ɪnˈtriːg] intriguer, comploter; **they intrigued with republicans against the throne** ils ont comploté avec des Républicains contre le roi

intriguing [ɪnˈtriːgɪŋ] *adj* curieux; **I find the whole thing most intriguing** tout cela me paraît très curieux; **it's an intriguing idea!** c'est une idée curieuse!

intriguingly [ɪnˈtriːgɪŋlɪ] *adv* bizarrement, curieusement; **did he turn up on time? – intriguingly enough, he did** est-il arrivé à l'heure? – curieusement, oui

intrinsic [ɪnˈtrɪnsɪk] *adj* intrinsèque; **the picture has little intrinsic value** ce tableau a peu de valeur en soi; **such ideas are intrinsic to my argument** de telles idées sont essentielles *ou* inhérentes à mon raisonnement
►► *St Exch* ***intrinsic value*** valeur *f* intrinsèque

intrinsically [ɪnˈtrɪnsɪklɪ] *adv* intrinsèquement

intro [ˈɪntrəʊ] (*pl* **intros**) *n Fam* introduction[❑] *f*, intro *f*

intro- [ˈɪntrəʊ] *pref* intro-

introduce [ˌɪntrəˈdjuːs] *vt* (**a**) *(present → one person to another)* présenter; **she introduced me to her sister** elle m'a présenté à sa sœur; **may I introduce you?** permettez-moi de *ou* laissez-moi vous présenter; **let me introduce myself, I'm John** je me présente? John; **has everyone been introduced?** les présentations ont été faites?; **I don't think we've been introduced, have we?** nous n'avons pas été présentés, je crois; **to introduce a speaker** présenter un conférencier; **the main character is introduced in chapter 2** le personnage principal fait son apparition au chapitre 2; *Cin* **introducing Simon McLean** et pour la première fois à l'écran, Simon McLean; **to be introduced to society** *(débutante)* faire son entrée dans le monde
(**b**) *(radio or TV programme)* présenter
(**c**) *(bring in)* introduire; **when were rabbits introduced into Australia?** quand a-t-on introduit les lapins en Australie?; **I'd like to introduce a new topic into the debate, if I may** si vous le permettez, j'aimerais introduire dans le débat un nouveau sujet; **her arrival introduced a note of sadness into the festivities** son entrée mit une note de tristesse dans la fête; *Mus* **the arpeggio introduces the final movement** l'arpège marque le début du dernier mouvement
(**d**) *(laws, legislation)* déposer, présenter; *(reform, fashion, new methods)* introduire; **the government hopes to introduce the new bill next week** le gouvernement espère déposer son nouveau projet de loi la semaine prochaine
(**e**) *(initiate)* initier; **she introduced me to the pleasures of French cooking** elle m'a initié aux *ou* révélé les délices de la cuisine française; **to introduce sb to sth** initier qn à qch, faire découvrir qch à qn; **it was my sister who introduced me to yoga** c'est ma sœur qui m'a initiée au yoga *ou* fait découvrir le yoga
(**f**) *(start)* ouvrir, donner le départ de; **a fanfare introduced the start of the ceremony** une fanfare a ouvert la cérémonie
(**g**) *Formal (insert)* introduire; **introduce the wire carefully into the cavity** introduisez doucement le fil dans le trou
(**h**) *Gram (phrase)* introduire
(**i**) *Com (product)* lancer; *St Exch (shares)* introduire

introduction [ˌɪntrəˈdʌkʃən] *n* (**a**) *(of one person to another)* présentation *f*; *Fam* **would you do** *or* **make the introductions?** peux-tu faire les présentations?; **our next guest needs no introduction** inutile de vous présenter l'invité suivant
(**b**) *(first part → of speech, piece of music)* introduction *f*; *(→ of book)* introduction *f*, avant-propos *m inv*
(**c**) *(basic textbook, course)* introduction *f*, initiation *f*; **an introduction to linguistics** une introduction à la linguistique; **an introduction to his more difficult work** une introduction aux parties difficiles de son œuvre
(**d**) *(bringing in)* introduction *f*; **the introduction of computer technology into schools** l'introduction de l'informatique à l'école
(**e**) *(of bill, law)* introduction *f*, présentation *f*; *(of reform, fashion, new methods)* introduction *f*
(**f**) *(initiation)* introduction *f*, premier contact *m*; **this was my introduction to Shakespeare** ça a été mon premier contact avec Shakespeare; **this record is a good introduction to her work** cet album constitue une bonne introduction à son œuvre
(**g**) *Formal (insertion)* introduction *f*
(**h**) *Com (of product)* lancement *m*; *St Exch (of shares)* introduction *f* au marché hors cote

introductory [ˌɪntrəˈdʌktərɪ] *adj (remarks)* préliminaire; *(chapter, course)* d'introduction; **after a few introductory words** après quelques mots d'introduction
►► *Com* ***introductory offer*** offre *f* de lancement; *Com* ***introductory price*** prix *m* de lancement

intro-ident *n TV & Rad* identification *f* d'intro

introit [ˈɪntrɔɪt] *n Mus & Rel* introït *m*

introjection [ˌɪntrəˈdʒekʃən] *n Psy* introjection *f*

intron [ˈɪntrɒn] *n Biol & Chem* intron *m*

introspection [ˌɪntrəˈspekʃən] *n* introspection *f*

introspective [ˌɪntrəˈspektɪv] *adj* introspectif

introversion [ˌɪntrəˈvɜːʃən] *n* introversion *f*

introvert [ˈɪntrəvɜːt] **1** *n* introverti(e) *m,f*
2 *vt* introvertir

introverted [ˈɪntrəvɜːtɪd] *adj* introverti; **she's become very introverted since the accident** elle est devenue très renfermée depuis l'accident

intrude [ɪnˈtruːd] **1** *vi* (**a**) *(disturb)* déranger, s'imposer; **disturbing memories kept intruding** de douloureux souvenirs continuaient à le/me/*etc* hanter; **I hope I'm not intruding** j'espère que je ne vous dérange pas
(**b**) *(interfere)* **I don't let my work intrude on my private life** je ne laisse pas mon travail empiéter sur ma vie privée; **they're intruding on our private lives** ils se mêlent de *ou* ils s'immiscent dans notre vie privée; **she didn't let the news intrude on her good mood** elle ne laissa pas cette nouvelle gâcher sa bonne humeur; **I felt I was intruding on their grief** j'ai eu l'impression de les déranger dans leur chagrin; **a supermarket would intrude on the character of the village** un supermarché gâcherait le caractère pittoresque du village
(**c**) *Geol* pénétrer par intrusion
2 *vt Formal* imposer; **a doubt intruded itself into my mind** un doute m'est venu à l'esprit

intruded [ɪnˈtruːdɪd] *adj Geol* intrusif

intruder [ɪnˈtruːdə(r)] *n (criminal)* intrus *m*; *(outsider)* intrus(e) *m,f*, importun(e) *m,f*; **they made us feel like intruders** nous avons eu l'impression de déranger *ou* d'être de trop

intrusion [ɪnˈtruːʒən] *n* (**a**) *(gen)* intrusion *f*, ingérence *f*; **it's an intrusion into our privacy** c'est une intrusion dans notre vie privée (**b**) *Geol* intrusion *f*

intrusive [ɪnˈtruːsɪv] *adj* (**a**) *(person)* importun; **he was an intrusive presence in the house** sa présence dans la maison était importune; **far away from the intrusive sounds of the city** loin de la rumeur importune de la ville (**b**) *Geol* intrusif
►► *Ling* ***intrusive consonant*** consonne *f* d'appui

intrusively [ɪnˈtruːsɪvlɪ] *adv* importunément, en importun

intrusiveness [ɪnˈtruːsɪvnɪs] *n* caractère *m* importun, importunité *f*

intubate [ˈɪntjʊbeɪt] *vt Med* intuber

intubation [ˌɪntjʊˈbeɪʃən] *n Med* intubation *f*, tubage *m*

INTUC [ˈɪntʌk] *n* (*abbr* **Indian National Trade Union Congress**) = confédération de syndicats indiens

intuit [ɪnˈtjuːɪt] *vt Formal* savoir *ou* connaître intuitivement; **I could only intuit what had happened between them** je n'ai pu que deviner ce qui s'était passé entre eux

intuition [ˌɪntjuːˈɪʃən] *n* intuition *f*; **(my) intuition tells me he won't be coming** mon intuition me dit qu'il ne viendra pas; **I had an intuition something was wrong** j'avais le sentiment que quelque chose n'allait pas

intuitionism [ˌɪntjuːˈɪʃənɪzəm] *n* intuitionnisme *m*

intuitive [ɪnˈtjuːɪtɪv] *adj* intuitif; **an intuitive understanding** une connaissance intuitive; **he's very intuitive** c'est un intuitif

intuitively [ɪnˈtjuːɪtɪvlɪ] *adv* intuitivement; **I knew intuitively that she was lying** je savais intuitivement qu'elle mentait, je sentais bien qu'elle ne disait pas la vérité

intumesce [ˌɪntjuːˈmes] *vi Med* enfler

intumescence [ˌɪntjuːˈmesəns] *n Med* enflure *f*, boursouflure *f*

intumescent [ˌɪntjuːˈmesənt] *adj Med* enflé, boursouflé

intussusception [ˌɪntəsəˈsepʃən] *n Med & Biol* intussusception *f*

Inuit [ˈɪnʊɪt] (*pl* **inv** *or* **Inuits**) **1** *n* Inuit *mf*
2 *adj* inuit

Inuktitut [ɪˈnʌktɪˌtʊt] *n Ling* inuktitut *m*

inulin [ˈɪnjʊlɪn] *n Biol & Chem* inuline *f*

inunction [ɪnˈʌŋkʃən] *n (action)* onction *f*; *(ointment)* pommade *f*

inundate [ˈɪnʌndeɪt] *vt also Fig* inonder; **the whole area was inundated** toute la région a été inondée; **we've been inundated with phone calls/letters** nous avons été submergés de coups de fil/courrier; **I'm inundated with work just now** pour l'instant, je suis débordé (de travail) *ou* je croule sous le travail

inundation [ˌɪnʌnˈdeɪʃən] *n* inondation *f*

inure [ɪˈnjʊə(r)] **1** *vt* aguerrir; **to become inured to sth** s'habituer à qch; **he became inured to the pain** il s'est habitué *ou* fait à la douleur
2 *vi (law)* entrer en vigueur

in utero [ˌɪnˈjuːtərəʊ] **1** *adj* in utero
2 *adv* in utero

invade [ɪnˈveɪd] **1** *vt* (**a**) *Mil* envahir (**b**) *Fig* envahir; **the village was invaded by reporters** les journalistes ont envahi le village; **her mind was invaded by sudden doubts** le doute

s'empara soudain de son esprit; **to invade sb's privacy** s'immiscer dans la vie privée de qn
2 *vi* envahir

invader [ɪn'veɪdə(r)] *n* envahisseur(euse) *m,f*; **to repel invaders** repousser l'envahisseur

invading [ɪn'veɪdɪŋ] *adj* (**a**) *(army)* d'invasion; **the invading barbarians** l'envahisseur barbare (**b**) *(plants, insects)* envahissant

invaginate [ɪn'vædʒɪˌneɪt] *Med & Biol* **1** *vt* invaginer
2 *vi* s'invaginer

invagination [ɪnˌvædʒɪ'neɪʃən] *n Med & Biol* invagination *f*

invalid¹ 1 *n* ['ɪnvəlɪd] *(disabled person)* infirme *mf*, invalide *mf*; *(ill person)* malade *mf*; **I'm not an invalid!** je ne suis pas infirme!
2 *adj* ['ɪnvəlɪd] *(disabled)* infirme, invalide; *(ill)* malade; **he has to look after his invalid mother** il doit s'occuper de sa mère infirme
3 *vt* ['ɪnvəliːd] (**a**) *(disable)* rendre infirme (**b**) *Br Mil* **he was invalided home** il a été rapatrié pour raisons médicales
►► *Br* ***invalid car, invalid carriage*** voiture *f* d'infirme; ***invalid chair*** fauteuil *m* roulant
►**invalid out** *vt sep Mil* **to invalid sb out of the army** réformer qn pour raisons médicales

invalid² [ɪn'vælɪd] *adj* (**a**) *(passport, ticket)* non valide, non valable; **your passport will soon be invalid** votre passeport sera bientôt périmé (**b**) *(law, marriage, election)* nul (**c**) *(argument)* non valable; **your reasoning is invalid** votre raisonnement n'est pas valable *ou* ne tient pas (**d**) *Comput* invalide
►► *Comput* ***invalid file name*** nom *m* de fichier invalide

invalidate [ɪn'vælɪdeɪt] *vt* (**a**) *(contract, agreement)* invalider, annuler; *(verdict)* casser, infirmer (**b**) *(argument)* infirmer

invalidation [ɪnˌvælɪ'deɪʃən] *n* (**a**) *(of contract, agreement)* invalidation *f*, annulation *f*; *(of verdict)* infirmation *f*, cassation *f* (**b**) *(of argument)* infirmation *f*

invalidism ['ɪnvəlɪˌdɪzəm] *n* valétudinarisme *m*, invalidité *f*

invalidity [ˌɪnvə'lɪdətɪ] *n* (**a**) *Med* invalidité *f* (**b**) *(of contract, agreement etc)* manque *m* de validité, nullité *f* (**c**) *(of argument)* manque *m* de fondement; **to demonstrate the invalidity of an argument** prouver qu'un argument n'est pas valable
►► *Br* ***invalidity benefit*** prestation *f* d'invalidité *(aujourd'hui remplacée par l'"incapacity benefit")*; *Br* ***invalidity pension*** pension *f* d'invalidité

invaluable [ɪn'væljʊəbəl] *adj* inestimable, très précieux; **your help has been invaluable (to me)** votre aide m'a été très précieuse; **she's an invaluable asset (to the company)** elle représente un atout inestimable (pour l'entreprise)

invaluably [ɪn'væljʊəblɪ] *adv* **the job that she performed so invaluably for us** l'aide précieuse qu'elle nous a apportée en faisant ce travail; **invaluably precious** d'une valeur inestimable

Invar® ['ɪnvɑː(r)] *n Metal* Invar® *m*

invariable [ɪn'veərɪəbəl] **1** *n Math* constante *f*
2 *adj* invariable

invariably [ɪn'veərɪəblɪ] *adv* (**a**) *(always)* invariablement; **almost invariably** presque toujours (**b**) *(almost always)* presque toujours; **she was invariably dressed in black** elle était presque toujours habillée en noir

invariance [ɪn'veərɪəns] *n Math* invariance *f*

invariant [ɪn'veərɪənt] **1** *adj* invariant
2 *n* invariant *m*

invasion [ɪn'veɪʒən] *n* (**a**) *Mil* invasion *f*, envahissement *m*; **the Roman invasion of England** l'invasion de l'Angleterre par les Romains (**b**) *Fig* invasion *f*, intrusion *f*; **a pitch invasion** une intrusion des supporters sur le terrain; **we expect the usual invasion of tourists this summer** nous nous attendons à l'habituelle invasion de touristes cet été; **he considered it an invasion of privacy** il l'a ressenti comme une intrusion dans sa vie privée

invasive [ɪn'veɪsɪv] *adj Mil (armies)* d'invasion; *Fig* envahissant
►► *Med* ***invasive surgery*** chirurgie *f* invasive *ou* effractoire

invective [ɪn'vektɪv] *n (UNCOUNT)* invective *f*, invectives *fpl*; **a stream of invective** un torrent d'invectives

inveigh [ɪn'veɪ] *vi Formal* **to inveigh against sb/sth** invectiver qn/qch

inveigle [ɪn'veɪgəl] *vt* entortiller; **he had been inveigled into letting them in** on l'avait adroitement manipulé pour qu'il les laisse entrer; **she inveigled him into giving her a lift** elle a réussi à l'entortiller pour qu'il la conduise en voiture

invent [ɪn'vent] *vt* (**a**) *(new machine, process)* inventer (**b**) *(lie, excuse)* inventer; **he invented a movie-star mother** il s'est inventé une mère star de cinéma

invention [ɪn'venʃən] *n* (**a**) *(discovery, creation)* invention *f*; **television is a wonderful invention** la télévision est une invention merveilleuse; **she has great powers of invention** elle a de grandes facultés d'invention; **a story of his own invention** une histoire de son cru
(**b**) *(untruth)* invention *f*, fabrication *f*; **the whole thing was an invention of the press** la presse a inventé *ou* monté cette histoire de bout en bout; **it was pure invention** ce n'était que pure invention, c'était complètement faux

inventive [ɪn'ventɪv] *adj (person, mind)* inventif; *(plan, solution)* ingénieux

inventiveness [ɪn'ventɪvnɪs] *n* esprit *m* d'invention, inventivité *f*

inventor [ɪn'ventə(r)] *n* inventeur(trice) *m,f*

inventory ['ɪnvəntərɪ] (*pl* **inventories**, *pt & pp* **inventoried**) **1** *n* (**a**) *(list)* inventaire *m*; **to draw up** *or* **to make an inventory** dresser un inventaire; **to take the inventory** faire l'inventaire (**b**) *(UNCOUNT) Am (stock)* stock *m*, stocks *mpl*; **our inventory is low** nos stocks sont bas
2 *vt* inventorier
►► *Fin* ***inventory account*** compte *m* de stock; ***inventory control*** contrôle *m* des stocks; ***inventory level*** niveau *m* des stocks; ***inventory management*** gestion *f* des stocks; ***inventory turnaround*** rotation *f* des stocks; *Fin* ***inventory turnover*** rotation *f* des stocks; ***inventory valuation*** valorisation *f* des stocks; ***inventory value*** valeur *f* d'inventaire

inverse [ɪn'vɜːs] **1** *n* inverse *m*, contraire *m*; *Math* inverse *m*
2 *adj* inverse; **to be in inverse proportion to** être inversement proportionnel à; *Comput* **in inverse video** en vidéo inverse

inversely [ɪn'vɜːslɪ] *adv* inversement; **to be inversely proportional to** être inversement proportionnel à

inversion [ɪn'vɜːʃən] *n* (**a**) *(gen)* inversion *f*; *(of roles, relations)* renversement *m* (**b**) *Mus (of chord)* renversement *m*; *(in counterpoint)* inversion *f* (**c**) *Chem* inversion *f* (**d**) *Anat* inversion *f* (**e**) *Elec & Math* inversion *f* (**f**) *Psy* **(sexual) inversion** inversion *f* sexuelle

invert 1 *vt* [ɪn'vɜːt] (**a**) *(turn upside down or inside out)* inverser, retourner; *(switch around)* intervertir; *(roles)* intervertir, renverser; **the two letters have been inverted** les deux lettres ont été interverties (**b**) *Mus (chord)* renverser; *(interval)* inverser (**c**) *Chem (sugar)* invertir
2 *n* ['ɪnvɜːt] (**a**) *Psy* inverti(e) *m,f* (**b**) *Constr* radier *m*
3 *adj* ['ɪnvɜːt] *(sugar)* inverti

invertase ['ɪnvəteɪs] *n Biol & Chem* invertase *f*

invertebrate [ɪn'vɜːtɪbrɪt] **1** *adj* invertébré
2 *n* invertébré *m*

inverted [ɪn'vɜːtɪd] *adj* (**a**) *(upside down)* renversé; *Mus (chord)* renversé (**b**) *(reversed → word order etc)* renversé; *Opt (image)* renversé (**c**) *Psy (instinct)* inverti
►► *Br* ***inverted commas*** guillemets *mpl*; **in inverted commas** entre guillemets; **her "best friend", in inverted commas, ran off with her husband** sa "meilleure amie", entre guillemets, est partie avec son mari; *Sewing* ***inverted pleat*** pli *m* inverti *ou* creux

inverter, invertor [ɪn'vɜːtə(r)] *n* (**a**) *Elec* onduleur *m* (de courant) (**b**) *Comput* inverseur *m*

invest [ɪn'vest] **1** *vi* investir, faire des placements; **to invest in shares/in the oil industry/on the Stock Market** investir en actions/dans l'industrie pétrolière/en Bourse; **to invest in property** faire des placements dans l'immobilier; **they decided to invest in an automated system** ils ont décidé d'investir dans un système automatisé; *Fam* **you ought to invest in a new coat** tu devrais t'offrir *ou* te payer un nouveau manteau
2 *vt* (**a**) *(money)* investir, placer; *(capital)* investir; **to invest money in a business** mettre de l'argent *ou* placer des fonds dans un commerce; **they invested $5 million dollars in new machinery** ils ont investi 5 millions de dollars dans de nouveaux équipements
(**b**) *(time, effort)* investir; **we've invested a lot of time and energy in this project** nous avons investi beaucoup de temps et d'énergie dans ce projet
(**c**) *Formal (confer on)* investir; **invested with the highest authority** investi de la plus haute autorité; **by the power invested in me** par les pouvoirs qui me sont conférés
(**d**) *Mil (besiege, surround)* investir
(**e**) *Arch or Literary (clothe, cover)* revêtir
(**f**) *(install → bishop, pope)* introniser; *(→ president)* installer
(**g**) *Literary (provide → person)* investir (**with** de); **to invest a subject with interest** rendre un sujet intéressant; **his novels invest criminality with too much glamour** ses romans donnent une image trop séduisante du monde du crime

investigate [ɪn'vestɪˌgeɪt] **1** *vt (allegation, crime, accident)* enquêter sur; *(problem, situation)* examiner, étudier
2 *vi* enquêter, mener une enquête; **I'll go and investigate** je vais voir ce qui se passe

investigating [ɪn'vestɪˌgeɪtɪŋ] *adj*
►► ***investigating committee*** commission *f* d'enquête; ***investigating magistrate*** juge *m* d'instruction; ***investigating officer*** officier *m* chargé de l'enquête

investigation [ɪnˌvestɪ'geɪʃən] *n (into crime, accident)* enquête *f*; *(of problem, situation)* examen *m*, étude *f*; **months of investigation turned up no clues** après des mois d'enquête, aucun indice n'a été découvert; **his activities are under investigation** une enquête a été ouverte sur ses activités; **your case is currently under investigation** nous étudions actuellement votre cas; **on further investigation** en poursuivant les recherches; **on further investigation, the ruins turned out to be...** des recherches plus approfondies ont révélé que les ruines étaient...; **to make investigations** faire des investigations; *(police)* procéder à une enquête

investigative [ɪn'vestɪgətɪv] *adj Press, Rad & TV* d'investigation
►► ***investigative journalism*** journalisme *m* d'investigation *ou* d'enquête; ***investigative reporter*** journaliste *mf ou* reporter *m* d'investigation

investigator [ɪn'vestɪˌgeɪtə(r)] *n* enquêteur(euse) *m,f*, enquêteur(trice) *mf*

investigatory [ɪn'vestɪˌgeɪtərɪ] *adj* d'investigation

investiture [ɪn'vestɪtʃə(r)] *n* investiture *f*; *(of bishop, pope)* intronisation *f*

investment [ɪn'vestmənt] *n* (**a**) *(of money, capital)* investissement *m*, placement *m*; *(money invested)* investissement *m*, mise *f* de fonds; **are these shares a good investment?** ces actions sont-elles un bon placement?; **property is no longer such a safe investment** l'immobilier n'est plus un placement aussi sûr; **the company has investments all over the world** la société a des capitaux investis dans le monde entier; **investment in industry/real estate** investissement industriel/immobilier; **I'd prefer a better return on investment** je préférerais un investissement plus rentable
(**b**) *(of time, effort)* investissement *m*
(**c**) *(investiture)* investiture *f*; *(of bishop, pope)* intronisation *f*
(**d**) *Mil (of fortress)* investissement *m*
►► ***investment account*** compte *m* d'investissement; ***investment advice*** conseil *m* en placements; ***investment adviser*** conseiller(ère) *m,f* en placements; ***investment analyst*** analyste *mf* en placements; ***investment appraisal*** appréciation *f* des investissements; *Am* ***investment bank*** banque *f* d'affaires; *Am* ***investment banker*** banquier(ère) *m,f* d'affaires; *Am* ***investment banking*** banque *f* d'affaires; ***investment boom*** boom *m* des investissements; ***investment capital*** capital-investissement *m*; ***investment certificate*** certificat *m* d'investissement; ***investment company***

inv–inv

société *f* de portefeuille *ou* d'investissement; ***investment consultancy*** société *f* de conseil en investissement; ***investment curve*** courbe *f* d'investissement; ***investment fund*** fonds *m* commun de placement, fonds *m* d'investissement; ***investment grant*** subvention *f* d'investissement; ***investment income*** revenu *m* provenant d'investissements; ***investment institution*** société *f* d'investissements; ***investment instrument*** instrument *m* de placement; ***investment management*** gestion *f* des investissements; *Br Formerly* ***Investment Management Regulatory Organization*** = organisme britannique contrôlant les activités de banques d'affaires et de gestionnaires de fonds de retraite; ***investment market*** marché *m* des capitaux; ***investment objectives*** objectifs *mpl* de placement; ***investment plan*** plan *m* d'investissement; ***investment policy*** politique *f* d'investissement; ***investment portfolio*** portefeuille *m* d'investissements; ***investment programme*** programme *m* d'investissement; ***investment return*** retour *m* sur investissements; ***investment securities*** valeurs *fpl* en portefeuille *ou* de placement; ***investment services*** services *mpl* d'investissement; ***investment stock*** valeurs *fpl* en portefeuille *ou* de placement; ***investment subsidy*** prime *f* à l'investissement; ***investment trust*** société *f* de placement, trust *m* de placement

investor [ɪn'vestə(r)] *n* investisseur *m*; *(shareholder)* actionnaire *mf*

inveterate [ɪn'vetərət] *adj* (**a**) *(habit, dislike)* invétéré; *(hatred)* tenace (**b**) *(drinker, gambler, liar, smoker)* invétéré; *(bachelor)* endurci

invidious [ɪn'vɪdɪəs] *adj* (**a**) *(unfair)* injuste; **invidious comparisons** des comparaisons injustes (**b**) *(unpleasant)* ingrat, pénible; **an invidious task** une tâche pénible; **to be in an invidious position** être dans une position peu enviable

invidiously [ɪn'vɪdɪəslɪ] *adv* (**a**) *(unfairly)* injustement (**b**) *(unpleasantly)* péniblement

invidiousness [ɪn'vɪdɪəsnɪs] *n* (**a**) *(unfairness)* injustice *f* (**b**) *(unpleasantness)* caractère *m* pénible, pénibilité *f*

invigilate [ɪn'vɪdʒɪ,leɪt] *Br Sch & Univ* **1** *vt (exam)* surveiller

2 *vi* surveiller les candidats *(à un examen)*

invigilation [ɪn,vɪdʒɪ'leɪʃən] *n Br Sch & Univ* surveillance *f (des candidats à un examen)*

invigilator [ɪn'vɪdʒɪ,leɪtə(r)] *n Br Sch & Univ* surveillant(e) *m,f (d'un examen)*

invigorate [ɪn'vɪgə,reɪt] *vt* revigorer, vivifier; **she felt invigorated by the cold wind** le vent frais la revigorait

invigorating [ɪn'vɪgə,reɪtɪŋ] *adj (air, climate)* tonique, tonifiant, vivifiant; *(walk)* revigorant; *(bath)* tonifiant; *(discussion)* enrichissant; **it's invigorating just talking to her** il suffit de lui parler pour se sentir revigoré

invincibility [ɪn,vɪnsɪ'bɪlətɪ] *n* invincibilité *f*; *(of belief, faith)* caractère *m* inébranlable

invincible [ɪn'vɪnsɪbəl] *adj (army, troops)* invincible; *(belief)* inébranlable

inviolability [ɪn,vaɪələ'bɪlətɪ] *n* inviolabilité *f*

inviolable [ɪn'vaɪələbəl] *adj* inviolable

inviolably [ɪn'vaɪələblɪ] *adv* inviolablement

inviolate [ɪn'vaɪələt] *adj Literary* inviolé; **to remain inviolate** demeurer inviolé

invisibility [ɪn,vɪzɪ'bɪlətɪ] *n* invisibilité *f*

invisible [ɪn'vɪzɪbəl] **1** *adj* invisible; **invisible to the naked eye** invisible à l'œil nu; *Fig* **I felt like the invisible man** c'était comme si j'étais invisible; **he's been the invisible man recently** il se fait rare ces temps-ci

2 invisibles *npl Fin* invisibles *mpl*

►► *Com & Fin* ***invisible assets*** biens *mpl* incorporels; *Fin* ***invisible balance*** balance *f* des invisibles; *Fin* ***invisible earnings*** gains *mpl* invisibles; *Com & Fin* ***invisible exports*** exportations *fpl* invisibles; *Com & Fin* ***invisible imports*** importations *fpl* invisibles; ***invisible ink*** encre *f* invisible *ou* sympathique; ***invisible mending*** stoppage *m*; ***invisible trade*** commerce *m* de services

invisibly [ɪn'vɪzɪblɪ] *adv* invisiblement

invitation [,ɪnvɪ'teɪʃən] *n* invitation *f*; *(card)* carte *f* d'invitation; **have you sent out the wedding invitations?** as-tu envoyé les invitations au mariage?; **she's here at my invitation** c'est moi qui l'ai invitée; **at the invitation of** sur l'invitation de; **we went to the congress at the invitation of the President himself** nous sommes allés au congrès sur l'invitation du président en personne; **by invitation only** sur invitation seulement; **your son is included in the invitation** votre fils est invité, lui aussi; **a standing invitation** une invitation permanente; *Fig* **prison conditions are an (open) invitation to violence** les conditions de détention sont une véritable incitation à la violence

►► ***invitation card*** carte *f* d'invitation

invite 1 *vt* [ɪn'vaɪt] (**a**) *(ask to come)* inviter; **to invite sb for lunch** inviter qn à déjeuner; **the Thomsons have invited us over** les Thomson nous ont invités chez eux; **I invited him up for a coffee** je l'ai invité à monter prendre un café; **the discussion took place in front of a specially invited audience** la discussion s'est déroulée devant un public spécialement invité *ou* invité pour l'occasion

(**b**) *(ask to do something)* demander, solliciter; **they invited her to become president** ils lui ont demandé de devenir présidente; **I've been invited for interview** j'ai été convoqué à un entretien

(**c**) *(solicit)* **to invite bids** *or* **tenders** faire un appel d'offres; **he invited comment on his book** il a demandé aux gens leur avis sur son livre; **applications are invited for the position** toute personne intéressée est invitée à déposer un dossier de candidature; **we invite suggestions from readers** toute suggestion de la part de nos lecteurs est la bienvenue

(**d**) *(trouble, defeat, disaster)* aller au-devant de; *(criticism)* s'exposer à; *(doubt, sympathy)* appeler, attirer; **you're just inviting failure** tu vas au-devant d'un échec; **his garbled answers simply invited disbelief** ses réponses embrouillées ne faisaient que susciter la méfiance

2 *n* ['ɪnvaɪt] *Fam* invitation ❑ *f*

►**invite out** *vt sep* inviter (à sortir); **she's invited me out tonight** elle m'a invité à sortir (avec elle) ce soir; **he's always getting invited out** il est toujours invité quelque part

inviting [ɪn'vaɪtɪŋ] *adj (gesture)* d'invitation; *(eyes, smile)* engageant; *(display)* attirant, attrayant; *(idea)* tentant, séduisant; *(place, fire)* accueillant; **not very inviting** peu attrayant; **the water looks inviting** l'eau donne envie de se baigner

invitingly [ɪn'vaɪtɪŋlɪ] *adv* d'une manière attrayante; **he gestured invitingly** il eut un geste d'invitation; **she smiled at him invitingly** elle lui adressa un sourire engageant; **she spoke invitingly of blue seas and white sand** elle parlait de mer bleue et de sable blanc, c'était plutôt tentant; **the invitingly blue sea** la mer, dont le bleu était une invitation à la baignade; **the box lay open invitingly on the desk** la boîte était ouverte sur la table, tentante

in vitro [,ɪn'viːtrəʊ] *Med* **1** *adj* in vitro

2 *adv* in vitro

►► ***in vitro fertilization*** fécondation *f* in vitro

in vivo [,ɪn'viːvəʊ] *Med* **1** *adj* in vivo

2 *adv* in vivo

invocation [,ɪnvə'keɪʃən] *n* (**a**) *Law & Pol* invocation *f* (**b**) *Rel* invocation *f*; **invocations to the gods** l'invocation des dieux

invoice ['ɪnvɔɪs] **1** *n Com* facture *f*; **to make out an invoice** établir *ou* faire une facture; **to settle an invoice** régler une facture; **invoices should be settled within 30 days** les factures doivent être réglées sous 30 jours; **as per invoice** conformément à la facture; **within 30 days of invoice** dans les 30 jours après la facturation; **payable against invoice** à payer à réception de la facture; **invoice of origin** facture *f* originale

2 *vt (goods)* facturer, porter sur une facture; *(person, company)* envoyer la facture à; **who do I invoice?** à qui dois-je adresser la facture?; **to invoice sb for sth** facturer qch à qn

►► ***invoice clerk*** facturier(ère) *m,f*; ***invoice date*** date *f* de facturation; ***invoice discounting*** escompte *m* de créances *ou* de traites; ***invoice price*** prix *m* facturé; ***invoice value*** valeur *f* de facture

invoicing ['ɪnvɔɪsɪŋ] *n (of goods etc)* facturation *f*

►► ***invoicing address*** adresse *f* de facturation; ***invoicing instructions*** instructions *fpl* de facturation; ***invoicing software*** logiciel *m* de facturation

invoke [ɪn'vəʊk] *vt* (**a**) *(cite)* invoquer; **they invoked the non-intervention treaty** ils ont invoqué le traité de non-intervention; **she invoked the principle of free speech** elle a invoqué le principe de la liberté d'expression

(**b**) *(call upon)* en appeler à, faire appel à; **to invoke sb's help** requérir l'aide de qn; **they invoked the might of the gods** ils invoquèrent la puissance des dieux

(**c**) *(summon up)* invoquer; **to invoke evil spirits** invoquer les mauvais esprits

involucre ['ɪnvəluːkə(r)] *n* (**a**) *Anat* membrane *f* externe (**b**) *Bot* involucre *m*

involuntarily [ɪn'vɒləntrəlɪ] *adv* involontairement; **she smiled involuntarily** elle ne put réprimer un sourire *ou* s'empêcher de sourire

involuntariness [ɪn'vɒləntərɪnɪs] *n* caractère *m* involontaire

involuntary [ɪn'vɒləntərɪ] *adj* involontaire

►► ***involuntary memory*** mémoire *f* involontaire; ***involuntary muscle*** muscle *m* lisse *ou* viscéral

involute ['ɪnvəluːt], **involuted** ['ɪnvəluːtɪd] *adj* (**a**) *(intricate)* compliqué (**b**) *Bot* involuté

involution [,ɪnvə'luːʃən] *n* (**a**) *(intricacy)* complexité *f* (**b**) *Bot, Math, Med & Zool* involution *f*

involve [ɪn'vɒlv] *vt* (**a**) *(entail)* impliquer, comporter; **it involves a lot of work** cela implique *ou* nécessite *ou* veut dire beaucoup de travail; **what does the job involve?** en quoi consiste le travail?; **my job involves a lot of travel** je dois beaucoup voyager dans mon travail; **a job which involves meeting people** un travail où l'on est amené à rencontrer beaucoup de gens; **it won't involve you in much expense** cela ne t'entraînera pas dans de grosses dépenses; **there's a lot of work involved in launching a new product** le lancement d'un nouveau produit implique beaucoup de travail

(**b**) *(concern, affect)* concerner, toucher; **this discussion doesn't involve you** cette discussion ne vous concerne pas; **there are too many accidents involving children** il y a trop d'accidents dont les enfants sont les victimes

(**c**) *(bring in, implicate)* impliquer; **over two hundred people were involved in planning the event** plus de deux cents personnes ont participé à la préparation de l'événement; **several vehicles were involved in the accident** plusieurs véhicules étaient impliqués dans cet accident; **it's not necessary to involve anyone else in this matter** il n'est pas nécessaire d'impliquer quelqu'un d'autre dans *ou* d'associer quelqu'un d'autre à cette affaire; **we try to involve the parents in the running of the school** nous essayons de faire participer les parents à la vie de l'école; **I'm not going to involve myself in their private affairs** je ne vais pas me mêler de leur vie privée *ou* de leurs affaires

(**d**) *(absorb, engage)* absorber; **the novel doesn't really involve the reader** le lecteur ne se sent pas impliqué dans ce roman

involved [ɪn'vɒlvd] *adj* (**a**) *(complicated)* compliqué, complexe; **I can't explain, it's all terribly involved** je ne peux pas expliquer, c'est terriblement compliqué

(**b**) *(implicated)* impliqué; **were the CIA involved?** est-ce que la CIA était impliquée?; **I don't want to get involved** je ne veux pas être impliqué, je ne veux rien avoir à faire avec cela; **they became involved in a long war** ils se sont trouvés entraînés dans une longue guerre; **the amount of work involved is enormous** la quantité de travail à fournir est énorme; **there are important principles involved** les principes en cause *ou* en jeu sont importants; **he had no idea of the problems involved** il n'avait aucune idée des problèmes en jeu *ou* en cause; **over a hundred companies are involved in the scheme** plus de cent sociétés sont associées à *ou* parties prenantes dans ce projet; **I think he's involved in advertising** je crois qu'il est dans la publicité; **to be involved in politics** prendre part à la vie politique; **he's getting involved with the school orchestra** il commence à prendre part aux activités de l'orchestre de l'école (**c**) *(absorbed)* absorbé; **she's too involved in her work to notice** elle est trop absorbée par son travail pour remarquer quoi que ce soit

(**d**) *(emotionally)* **to be involved with sb** avoir une liaison avec qn; **she's heavily involved with him** elle est très éprise de lui, elle est très accrochée; **he doesn't want to get involved** il ne veut pas s'engager

involvement [ɪn'vɒlvmənt] *n* (**a**) *(participation)* participation *f*; *(in crime)* implication *f*; **my involvement in the project is strictly limited** ma participation au projet est strictement limitée; **they were against American involvement in the war** ils étaient opposés à toute participation américaine au conflit

(**b**) *(commitment)* investissement *m*, engagement *m*; **she's looking for work that requires total involvement** elle cherche un emploi qui demanderait un investissement total

(**c**) *(relationship)* liaison *f*; **their involvement was short-lived** leur liaison fut de courte durée; **I've had no further involvement with him since** je n'ai plus jamais eu affaire à lui depuis; **he's frightened of emotional involvement** il a peur de s'engager sentimentalement, il redoute tout engagement affectif

(**d**) *(complexity)* complexité *f*, complication *f*

invulnerability [ɪn,vʌlnərə'bɪlətɪ] *n* invulnérabilité *f*

invulnerable [ɪn'vʌlnərəbəl] *adj* invulnérable; *(position)* inattaquable

-in-waiting *suff (government, leader)* prêt à prendre la relève

inward ['ɪnwəd] **1** *adj* (**a**) *(thoughts, satisfaction)* intime, secret(ète) (**b**) *(movement)* vers l'intérieur

2 *adv Am* = **inwards**

►► *Com & Fin* ***inward bill of lading*** connaissement *m* d'entrée; ***inward charges*** *(of ship)* frais *mpl* à l'entrée; *Customs* ***inward customs clearance*** entrée *f* en douane; *Fin* ***inward investment*** investissements *mpl* étrangers; *Acct* ***inward payment*** paiement *m* reçu

inward-bound *adj (flight)* à l'arrivée; *(traffic)* en direction de la ville

inward-looking *adj Br (person)* introverti, replié sur soi; *(group)* replié sur soi, fermé; *(philosophy)* introspectif, *Pej* nombriliste; **he's become very inward-looking lately** il s'est beaucoup refermé *ou* replié sur lui-même ces derniers temps

inwardly ['ɪnwədlɪ] *adv (pleased, disgusted)* secrètement; **she said nothing but was inwardly rejoicing** elle n'a rien dit mais elle se réjouissait secrètement; **he smiled inwardly** il sourit intérieurement; **inwardly I was still convinced that I was right** en mon for intérieur, j'étais toujours convaincu d'avoir raison; **we all groaned inwardly at the thought** à cette idée nous avons tous réprimé un mouvement d'humeur

inwardness ['ɪnwədnɪs] *n* (**a**) *(introspection)* introversion *f*, repli *m* sur soi (**b**) *(spirituality)* spiritualité *f*, nature *f* spirituelle

inwards ['ɪnwədz], *Am* **inward** ['inwərd] *adv* (**a**) *(turn, face)* vers l'intérieur; **the doors open inwards** les portes s'ouvrent vers l'intérieur (**b**) *(into one's own heart, soul etc)* **my thoughts turned inwards** je me suis replié sur moi-même; **he said we should look inwards to find our true selves** il a dit que c'est en nous-mêmes qu'il fallait chercher notre véritable identité

in-your-face *adj Fam* (**a**) *(uncompromising → documentary, film)* cru □ (**b**) *(aggressive → attitude, personality)* agressif □

Io ['aɪəʊ] *pr n Myth & Astron* Io

I/O *Comput (written abbr* **input/output**) E/S *f*

IOC [,aɪəʊ'si:] *n Sport (abbr* **International Olympic Committee**) CIO *m*

iodate ['aɪə,deɪt] *n Chem* iodate *m*; **potassium iodate** iodate *m* de potasse

iodide ['aɪə,daɪd] *n Chem* iodure *m*; **mercuric iodide** iodure *m* de mercure

iodinate ['aɪədɪ,neɪt] *vt Chem* iodurer

iodine [*Br* 'aɪədi:n, *Am* 'aɪədaɪn] *n* iode *m*; *Pharm* teinture *f* d'iode

iodize, -ise ['aɪədaɪz] *vt* ioder

iodoform [aɪ'ɒdəfɔ:m] *n* iodoforme *m*

IOM *(written abbr* **Isle of Man**) île *f* de Man

ion ['aɪən] *n Chem* ion *m*

►► ***ion accelerator*** accélérateur *m* d'ions; ***ion beam*** faisceau *m* ionique; ***ion engine*** moteur *m* ionique; ***ion implantation*** implantation *f* d'ions

Iona [aɪ'əʊnə] *n* Iona *f (un des premiers centres de la chrétienté en Écosse)*

Ionian [aɪ'əʊnɪən] **1** *n* (**a**) *(person)* Ionien(enne) *m,f* (**b**) *Ling* ionien *m*

2 *adj* ionien

►► ***the Ionian Islands*** les îles *fpl* Ioniennes; **in the Ionian Islands** aux îles Ioniennes; *Mus* ***Ionian mode*** mode *m* ionien; ***the Ionian Sea*** la mer Ionienne

Ionic [aɪ'ɒnɪk] *adj Archit* ionique

ionic [aɪ'ɒnɪk] *adj Chem & Phys* ionique

►► ***ionic bond*** lien *m* ionique

ionization [,aɪənaɪ'zeɪʃən] *n* (**a**) *Chem, Phys & Elec* ionisation *f* (**b**) *Med* (traitement *m* par) ionisation *f*

►► ***ionization chamber*** chambre *f* d'ionisation; ***ionization potential*** potentiel *m* d'ionisation

ionize, -ise ['aɪə,naɪz] **1** *vt* ioniser

2 *vi (of acid etc)* s'ioniser

ionized ['aɪə,naɪzd] *adj* ionisé; **ionized-gas anemometer** anémomètre *m* à ionisation

ionizer ['aɪə,naɪzə(r)] *n* ioniseur *m*

ionizing ['aɪə,naɪzɪŋ] *adj (particle, radiation)* ionisant

ionomer [aɪ'ɒnəmə(r)] *n Chem* ionomère *m*

ionosphere [aɪ'ɒnə,sfɪə(r)] *n* ionosphère *f*

ionospheric [aɪ,ɒnə'sferɪk] *adj* ionosphérique

iota [aɪ'əʊtə] *n* (**a**) *(Greek letter)* iota *m inv*

(**b**) *(tiny bit)* brin *m*, grain *m*, iota *m inv*; **she doesn't have an iota of sense** elle n'a pas un sou *ou* une once de jugeote; **there's not one iota of truth in the letter** il n'y a pas un brin *ou* un grain de vrai dans cette lettre; **I don't care one iota** cela m'est complètement égal, je m'en fiche complètement; **they haven't changed one iota** ils n'ont absolument pas changé

IOU [,aɪəʊ'ju:] *n (abbr* **I owe you**) reconnaissance *f* de dette

IOW *(written abbr* **Isle of Wight**) île *f* de Wight

Iowa ['aɪəʊə] *n* l'Iowa *m*; **in Iowa** dans l'Iowa

Iowan ['aɪəʊən] **1** *n (inhabitant)* habitant(e) *m,f* de l'Iowa; *(native)* originaire *mf* de l'Iowa

2 *adj* de l'Iowa

IP [,aɪ'pi:] *n Comput (abbr* **Internet Protocol**)

►► ***IP address*** adresse *f* IP; ***IP number*** numéro *m* IP

IPCC [,aɪpi:,si:'si:] *n (abbr* **Intergovernmental Panel on Climate Change**) GIEC *m*

ipecac ['ɪpɪkæk], **ipecacuanha** [,ɪpɪ,kækjʊ'ænə] *n Bot* ipéca *m*

Iphigenia [ɪ,fɪdʒɪ'naɪə] *pr n Myth* Iphigénie

IPO [,aɪpi:'əʊ] *n Am St Exch (abbr* **initial public offering**) introduction *f* en Bourse

ipso facto [,ɪpsəʊ'fæktəʊ] *adv* ipso facto

IQ [,aɪ'kju:] *n (abbr* **intelligence quotient**) QI *m*

IRA [,aɪɑ:'reɪ] *n* (**a**) *(abbr* **Irish Republican Army**) IRA *f* (**b**) *Am Fin (abbr* **individual retirement account**) plan *m* d'épargne retraite personnel

IRA

L'IRA est une organisation qui lutte pour la réunification de l'Irlande. En 1969, elle s'est scindée en deux factions: la "Provisional IRA", qui a recours à la violence et la "Official IRA", qui privilégiait un réglement politique du conflit en Irlande du Nord. En 1995, au début du processus de paix qui a abouti à l'accord de 1998 (le **Good Friday Agreement**, voir cet encadré) la "Provisional IRA" a déclaré un cessez-le-feu. Cependant, quelques groupes dissidents, notamment la "Continuity IRA" et la "Real IRA", ont poursuivi les actes terroristes.

Iran [ɪ'rɑ:n] *n* Iran *m*; **in Iran** en Iran

Irangate [ɪ'rɑ:ngeɪt] *n* = scandale politique sous le mandat Reagan: le Président aurait autorisé la vente d'armes à l'Iran contre la mise en liberté d'otages américains, et versé une partie des revenus de ces opérations aux contras du Nicaragua

Iranian [ɪ'reɪnjən] **1** *n* (**a**) *(person)* Iranien(enne) *m,f* (**b**) *(language)* iranien *m*

2 *adj* iranien

3 *comp (embassy)* d'Iran; *(history)* de l'Iran; *(teacher)* d'iranien

Iraq [ɪ'rɑ:k] *n* Iraq *m*, Irak *m*; **in Iraq** en Iraq

Iraqi [ɪ'rɑ:kɪ] **1** *n* Irakien(enne) *m,f*, Iraquien(enne) *m,f*

2 *adj* irakien

3 *comp (embassy)* d'Iraq; *(history)* de l'Iraq

irascibility [ɪ,ræsə'bɪlətɪ] *n* irascibilité *f*

irascible [ɪ'ræsəbəl] *adj* irascible, coléreux

irascibly [ɪ'ræsəblɪ] *adv (say etc)* sur un ton irrité

irate [aɪ'reɪt] *adj* furieux; **she got most irate about it** cela l'a rendue furieuse; **an irate letter** une lettre courroucée

irately [aɪ'reɪtlɪ] *adv* furieusement

IRBM [,aɪɑ:,bi:'em] *n (abbr* **intermediate range ballistic missile**) IRBM *m*

IRC [,aɪɑ:'si:] *n Comput (abbr* **Internet Relay Chat**) IRC *m*, service *m* de bavardage Internet, dialogue *m* en direct

►► ***IRC channel*** canal *m* IRC, canal *m* de dialogue en direct

ire ['aɪə(r)] *n Literary* courroux *m*, colère *f*

ireful ['aɪəfʊl] *adj Literary* courroucé

irefully ['aɪəfʊlɪ] *adv Literary* avec courroux, avec colère

Ireland ['aɪələnd] *n* Irlande *f*; **in Ireland** en Irlande; **Northern Ireland** l'Irlande *f* du Nord; **the Republic of Ireland** la République d'Irlande

irenic [aɪ'ri:nɪk], **irenical** [aɪ'ri:nɪkəl] *adj Literary* irénique

IRFU [,aɪɑ:r,ef'ju:] *n (abbr* **Irish Rugby Football Union**) = fédération irlandaise de rugby

iridaceous [,ɪrɪ'deɪʃəs] *adj Bot* iridacé

iridectomy [,ɪrɪ'dektəmɪ] *(pl* **iridectomies**) *n Med* iridectomie *f*

irides ['ɪrɪdi:z] *pl of* **iris** (**a**)

iridescence [,ɪrɪ'desəns] *n* irisation *f*

iridescent [,ɪrɪ'desənt] *adj* irisé, *Literary* iridescent

iridium [ɪ'rɪdɪəm] *n Chem* iridium *m*

iridologist [,ɪrɪ'dɒlədʒɪst] *n* iridologue *mf*

iridology [,ɪrɪ'dɒlədʒɪ] *n* iridologie *f*, iridodiagnostic *m*

Iris ['aɪrɪs] *pr n Myth* Iris

iris ['aɪrɪs] *(pl sense* (**a**) **irises** *or* **irides** ['ɪrɪdi:z], *pl senses* (**b**) *and* (**c**) **irises**) *n* (**a**) *Anat* iris *m* (**b**) *Bot* iris *m* (**c**) *Phot (diaphragm)* iris *m*

►► *Phot* ***iris diaphragm*** iris *m*

Irish ['aɪrɪʃ] *(pl* **Inv**) **1** *npl* **the Irish** les Irlandais *mpl*

2 *n (language)* irlandais *m*

3 *adj* (**a**) *(from or relating to Ireland)* irlandais (**b**) *Fam (illogical)* loufoque; **that's a bit Irish** c'est un peu loufoque

4 *comp (embassy)* de la République d'Irlande; *(history)* de l'Irlande; *(teacher)* d'irlandais

►► ***Irish American*** Américain(e) *m,f* d'origine irlandaise; ***Irish coffee*** irish-coffee *m*, = café noir au whiskey irlandais couronné de crème fraîche; ***Irish elk*** mégacéros *m*; ***the Irish Free State*** l'État *m* libre d'Irlande; ***the Irish Guards*** = régiment de l'armée britannique; ***Irish joke*** = histoire drôle aux dépens des Irlandais, ≃ histoire *f* belge; ***Irish pound*** livre *f* irlandaise; ***Irish pub*** pub *m* irlandais; ***the Irish Republic*** la République d'Irlande; ***the Irish Republican Army*** l'IRA *f*; *see also* **IRA**; ***the Irish Sea*** la mer d'Irlande; ***Irish setter*** setter *m* irlandais; ***Irish stew*** ≃ ragoût *m* de mouton; ***Irish wolfhound*** lévrier *m* irlandais

THE IRISH FREE STATE

En 1922, la division administrative de l'Irlande donna naissance, en même temps qu'à l'Irlande du Nord, à cet État autonome (néanmoins membre du Commonwealth) qui devint la République d'Irlande en 1949.

Irishism ['aɪrɪʃɪzəm] *n (idiom)* locution *f* irlandaise; *(custom)* coutume *f* irlandaise

Irishman ['aɪrɪʃmən] *(pl* **Irishmen** [-mən]) *n* Irlandais *m*

Irishwoman ['aɪrɪʃ,wʊmən] *(pl* **Irishwomen** [-,wɪmɪn]) *n* Irlandaise *f*

irk [ɜ:k] *vt* irriter, agacer; **it really irks me that he won't do the washing-up** cela m'agace vraiment qu'il ne fasse jamais la vaisselle

irksome ['ɜ:ksəm] *adj* irritant, agaçant

IRN [,aɪɑ:'ren] *n (abbr* **Independent Radio News**) = agence de presse radiophonique

inv–irn

IRO [ˌaɪɑː'rəʊ] *n* (*abbr* **International Refugee Organization**) = organisation humanitaire pour les réfugiés

iron ['aɪən] **1** *adj* (**a**) *(made of, containing iron)* de fer, en fer (**b**) *Fig (strong)* de fer, d'acier; **iron discipline** une discipline de fer; **an iron hand** *or* **fist in a velvet glove** une main de fer dans un gant de velours

2 *vt (laundry)* repasser

3 *vi (laundry)* se repasser

4 *n* (**a**) *(metal)* fer *m*; **made of iron** de *ou* en fer; **she has a will of iron** elle a une volonté de fer; **the iron and steel industry** la sidérurgie; **(as) hard as iron** dur comme *ou* aussi dur que le fer

(**b**) *(in diet)* fer *m*; **spinach has a high iron content** les épinards contiennent beaucoup de fer

(**c**) *(for laundry)* fer *m* (à repasser); **your shirt needs an iron** ta chemise a besoin d'un coup de fer *ou* d'être repassée

(**d**) *(tool, appliance)* fer *m*; **to have many irons in the fire** avoir plusieurs fers au feu

(**e**) *(golf club)* fer *m*; **a five iron** un fer cinq

(**f**) *SEng very Fam (rhyming slang* **iron hoof** = **poof**) pédale *f*, tantouze *f*, tapette *f*

(**g**) *Horseriding (of stirrup)* étrier *m*

5 irons *npl (chains)* fers *mpl*; **clap them in irons!** mettez-les aux fers!

►► ***the Iron Age*** l'âge *m* du fer; **an Iron Age tool** un outil de l'âge du fer; ***iron bar*** barre *f* de fer; ***iron bridge*** pont *m* en fer; ***Iron Chancellor*** chancelier *m* de fer; ***the Iron Curtain*** le rideau de fer; **the Iron Curtain countries** les pays *mpl* de l'Est; *Med* ***iron deficiency*** carence *f* en fer; *Fam Tech* ***iron fairy*** grue ᑫ *f*; ***iron filings*** limaille *f* de fer; ***iron foundry*** fonderie *f (de fonte)*; ***an iron grating*** une grille en fer; *Am Hist* ***the iron horse*** = la locomotive; *Br Pol* ***the Iron Lady*** la Dame de Fer *(surnom donné à Margaret Thatcher)*; *Med* ***iron lung*** poumon *m* d'acier; ***iron maiden*** = instrument de torture consistant en un coffre à l'intérieur parsemé de pointes, dans lequel on place la victime; ***iron ore*** minerai *m* de fer; ***iron oxide*** oxyde *m* de fer; ***iron pyrites*** pyrite *f* (de fer); ***iron shot*** coup *m* de fer; ***Iron and Steel Trades Confederation*** = syndicat britannique des ouvriers de la sidérurgie; *Med* ***iron tablet*** comprimé *m* de fer; ***an iron will*** une volonté de fer

▸**iron out** *vt sep* (**a**) *(crease)* enlever au fer (**b**) *Fig (problem, difficulty)* aplanir; **have you ironed out your differences?** est-ce que vous avez résolu vos différends?

'The Iron Man' *Hughes* 'Le Géant de fer'

ironbound ['aɪənbaʊnd] *adj* (**a**) *(cask)* cerclé de fer (**b**) *(rule, tradition)* sévère, inflexible

Ironbridge ['aɪənbrɪdʒ] *n* = ville de l'ouest de l'Angleterre considérée comme le foyer de la Révolution industrielle en Grande-Bretagne

ironclad ['aɪənklæd] **1** *adj* (**a**) *(ship)* cuirassé (**b**) *(argument)* inattaquable (**c**) *(rule)* inflexible

2 *n* cuirassé *m*

iron-grey *adj* gris acier

ironic [aɪ'rɒnɪk], **ironical** [aɪ'rɒnɪkəl] *adj* ironique

ironically [aɪ'rɒnɪkəlɪ] *adv* (**a**) *(smile, laugh)* ironiquement (**b**) *(paradoxically)* **ironically enough, he was the only one to remember** paradoxalement, il était le seul à s'en souvenir; **ironically, the box was empty** comble d'ironie, la boîte était vide

ironing ['aɪənɪŋ] *n* repassage *m*; **to do the ironing** faire le repassage, repasser; **she does the ironing on Sundays** elle fait son repassage *ou* elle repasse le dimanche; **I've got a lot of ironing to do** j'ai beaucoup de repassage à faire

►► ***ironing board*** planche *f ou* table *f* à repasser; ***ironing board cover*** housse *f* de table à repasser

ironist ['aɪrəˌnɪst] *n* ironiste *mf*

ironize, -ise ['aɪrəˌnaɪz] *vi* ironiser

ironmonger ['aɪənˌmʌŋgə(r)] *n Br* quincaillier(ère) *m,f*; **ironmonger's (shop)** quincaillerie *f*

ironmongery ['aɪənˌmʌŋgərɪ] *n Br* quincaillerie *f*

iron-on transfer *n* transfert *m (appliqué au fer à repasser)*

ironstone ['aɪənstəʊn] *n* minerai *m* de fer

ironware ['aɪənˌweə(r)] *n* ferronnerie *f*

iron-willed *adj* à la volonté de fer

ironwork ['aɪənwɜːk] *n* ferronnerie *f*

ironworker ['aɪənwɜːkə(r)] *n (in plant)* (ouvrier(ère) *m,f*) métallurgiste *mf*; *(in wrought iron)* ferronnier(ère) *m,f*

ironworks ['aɪənwɜːks] *(pl* **inv**) *n (for smelting)* fonderie *f* de fonte; *(for casting)* usine *f* sidérurgique

irony ['aɪrənɪ] *(pl* **ironies**) *n (gen) & Literature* ironie *f*; **the irony is that it might be true** ce qui est ironique *ou* ce qu'il y a d'ironique, c'est que cela pourrait être vrai; **in one of life's little ironies** par une ironie du sort; **and, irony of ironies,...** et, comble de l'ironie,...

Iroquoian [ɪrə'kwɔɪən] **1** *n* (**a**) *(person)* Iroquois(e) *m,f* (**b**) *Ling* iroquois *m*

2 *adj* iroquois

Iroquois ['ɪrəkwɔɪ] *(pl* **inv**) **1** *n* (**a**) *(person)* Iroquois(e) *m,f*; **the Iroquois** les Iroquois *mpl* (**b**) *Ling* iroquois *m*

2 *adj* iroquois

IRR [ˌaɪɑː'rɑː(r)] *n Fin* (*abbr* **internal rate of return**) taux *m* de rentabilité interne

irradiance [ɪ'reɪdɪəns] *n* (**a**) *(emission of light)* rayonnement *m*, éclat *m* (**b**) *Phys* radiance *f*, éclairement *m* énergétique

irradiancy [ɪ'reɪdɪənsɪ] = **irradiance** (**a**)

irradiate [ɪ'reɪdɪeɪt] *vt* (**a**) *Med & Phys (expose to radiation)* irradier; *(food)* irradier (**b**) *(light up)* illuminer, éclairer

irradiation [ɪˌreɪdɪ'eɪʃən] *n* (**a**) *Med & Phys (exposure to radiation)* irradiation *f*; *(X-ray therapy)* radiothérapie *f*; *(of food)* irradiation *f* (**b**) *Opt* irradiation *f* (**c**) *(by light)* illumination *f*

irrational [ɪ'ræʃənəl] **1** *adj* (**a**) *(person, behaviour, feeling)* irrationnel; *(fear)* irraisonné; *(creature, being)* incapable de raisonner; **don't be so irrational!** sois raisonnable! (**b**) *Math* irrationnel

2 *n* **the irrational** l'irrationnel *m*

►► *Math* ***irrational number*** nombre *m* irrationnel

irrationality [ɪˌræʃə'nælətɪ] *n* irrationalité *f*

irrationally [ɪ'ræʃənəlɪ] *adv* irrationnellement

irreconcilability [ɪˌrekənˌsaɪlə'bɪlɪtɪ] *n* (**a**) *(of aims, views, beliefs)* inconciliabilité *f* (**b**) *(of conflict, disagreement)* caractère *m* insoluble, insolubilité *f*; *(of enemies)* irréconciliabilité *f*

irreconcilable [ɪ'rekənˌsaɪləbəl] *adj* (**a**) *(aims, views, beliefs)* inconciliable, incompatible; **his beliefs are irreconcilable with his work** ses convictions sont incompatibles avec son travail (**b**) *(conflict, disagreement)* insoluble; **to be irreconcilable enemies** être ennemis jurés

irreconcilably [ɪˌrekən'saɪləblɪ] *adv* **they are irreconcilably different** ils sont radicalement différents; **they are irreconcilably divided** il y a entre eux des divisions irréconciliables

irrecoverable [ˌɪrɪ'kʌvərəbəl] *adj* (**a**) *(thing lost)* irrécupérable; *(debt)* irrécouvrable (**b**) *(loss, damage, wrong)* irréparable

irrecoverably [ˌɪrɪ'kʌvərəblɪ] *adv (lost)* pour toujours; *(damaged)* irrémédiablement

irrecusable [ˌɪrɪ'kjuːzəbəl] *adj* irrécusable

irrecusably [ˌɪrɪ'kjuːzəblɪ] *adv* incontestablement

irredeemable [ˌɪrɪ'diːməbəl] **1** *adj* (**a**) *Fin (share)* non remboursable; *(bond)* non amortissable; *(paper money, bill)* non convertible (**b**) *(person)* incorrigible, impénitent (**c**) *(loss, damage, wrong)* irréparable

2 irredeemables *npl Fin* obligations *fpl* non amortissables

irredeemably [ˌɪrɪ'diːməblɪ] *adv* irrémédiablement; **to be irredeemably wicked** être foncièrement méchant

irredentism [ˌɪrɪ'dentɪzəm] *n Pol* irrédentisme *m*

irredentist [ˌɪrɪ'dentɪst] *Pol* **1** *n* irrédentiste *mf*

2 *adj* irrédentiste

irreducibility [ˌɪrɪˌdjuːsɪ'bɪlɪtɪ] *n* irréductibilité *f*

irreducible [ˌɪrɪ'djuːsɪbəl] *adj* irréductible

irreducibleness [ˌɪrɪ'djuːsɪbəlnɪs] *n* irréductibilité *f*

irrefragable [ɪ'refrəgəbəl] *adj (reply, testimony)* irrécusable, irréfutable

irrefutability [ˌɪrɪˌfjuːtə'bɪlɪtɪ] *n (of argument, proof, fact)* irréfutabilité *f*; *(of testimony)* caractère *m* irrécusable, irrécusabilité *f*

irrefutable [ˌɪrɪ'fjuːtəbəl] *adj (argument, proof, fact)* irréfutable; *(testimony)* irrécusable

irrefutably [ˌɪrɪ'fjuːtəblɪ] *adv* irréfutablement; **to prove irrefutably that one is right** prouver irréfutablement *ou* sans conteste qu'on a raison

irregular [ɪ'regjʊlə(r)] **1** *adj* (**a**) *(object, shape etc)* irrégulier; *(surface)* inégal; **an irregular polygon** un polygone irrégulier

(**b**) *(intermittent, spasmodic)* irrégulier; **her visits became increasingly irregular** ses visites se firent de plus en plus irrégulières; **she works irregular hours** elle a des horaires de travail irréguliers; **irregular breathing** respiration *f* irrégulière *ou* saccadée

(**c**) *Formal (unorthodox)* irrégulier; **your request is highly irregular** votre demande n'est absolument pas régulière

(**d**) *Gram & Math* irrégulier

2 *n* (**a**) *Mil (soldier)* irrégulier *m*

(**b**) *Am Com* article *m* de second choix

►► ***irregular conduct*** conduite *f* irrégulière; *Mil* ***irregular troops*** troupes *fpl* irrégulières, irréguliers *mpl*; *Gram* ***irregular verb*** verbe *m* irrégulier

irregularity [ɪˌregjʊ'lærətɪ] *(pl* **irregularities**) **1** *n (of surface, work, breathing)* irrégularité *f*; **there was an irregularity to do with his passport** il y avait quelque chose qui n'était pas en règle dans son passeport

2 irregularities *npl Law* irrégularités *fpl*; **there were some irregularities in the paperwork** il y avait quelques irrégularités dans les écritures

irregularly [ɪ'regjʊləlɪ] *adv* (**a**) *(spasmodically)* irrégulièrement (**b**) *(unevenly)* inégalement; **irregularly shaped triangles** des triangles aux formes irrégulières

irrelevance [ɪ'reləvəns], **irrelevancy** [ɪ'reləvənsɪ] *(pl* **irrelevancies**) *n* (**a**) *(of fact, comment)* manque *m* de rapport, non-pertinence *f*; **the irrelevance of your remarks on the subject is all too obvious** il est évident que vos remarques n'ont pas de rapport avec le sujet

(**b**) *(pointless fact or matter)* inutilité *f*; **don't waste your time on irrelevances** ne perdez pas votre temps avec des choses sans importance; **the monarchy has become an irrelevance** la monarchie n'a plus de raison d'être, la monarchie a perdu sa raison d'être

irrelevant [ɪ'reləvənt] *adj* sans rapport, hors de propos; **your question is totally irrelevant to the subject in hand** votre question n'a aucun rapport *ou* n'a rien à voir avec le sujet qui nous intéresse; **that is irrelevant** cela n'a aucun rapport *ou* n'a rien à voir avec la question; **the monarchy has become irrelevant** la monarchie n'a plus de raison d'être, la monarchie a perdu sa raison d'être; **irrelevant information** information *f* non pertinente; **our personal feelings on the matter are irrelevant** nos sentiments personnels n'ont rien à voir ici; **age is irrelevant** l'âge est sans importance *ou* n'est pas un critère

irreligion [ˌɪrɪ'lɪdʒən] *n* irréligion *f*

irreligiosity [ˌɪrɪˌlɪdʒɪ'ɒsɪtɪ] *n* irréligiosité *f*

irreligious [ˌɪrɪ'lɪdʒəs] *adj* irréligieux

irreligiously [ˌɪrɪ'lɪdʒəslɪ] *adv* irréligieusement

irreligiousness [ˌɪrɪ'lɪdʒəsnɪs] *n* irréligion *f*

irremediable [ˌɪrɪ'miːdɪəbəl] *adj* irrémédiable

►► ***irremediable damage*** dégâts *mpl* irrémédiables

irremediably [ˌɪrɪ'miːdɪəblɪ] *adv* irrémédiablement

irremissible [ˌɪrɪ'mɪsɪbəl] *adj Formal* irrémissible

irremovable [ˌɪrɪ'muːvəbəl] *adj (stain)* indélébile; *(official)* inamovible

irreparable [ɪ'repərəbəl] *adj (damage)* irréparable; *(loss)* irrémédiable, irrécupérable; **he's done irreparable harm to his career** il a compromis sa carrière de façon irréparable

irreparably [ɪ'repərəblɪ] *adv (damaged)* irréparablement; *(lost)* irrémédiablement

irreplaceable [ˌɪrɪ'pleɪsəbəl] *adj* irremplaçable

irrepressible [ˌɪrɪ'presəbəl] *adj* (**a**) *(need, desire, urge)* irrépressible; *(good humour)* à toute épreuve (**b**) *(person)* que rien n'abat; **he's irrepressible** rien ne l'abat

irrepressibly [ˌɪrɪ'presɪblɪ] *adv* **irrepressibly optimistic/enthusiastic/good-humoured** d'un optimisme/d'un enthousiasme/d'une bonne humeur à toute épreuve

irreproachable [ˌɪrɪ'prəʊtʃəbəl] *adj* irréprochable; **his behaviour has always been**

irreproachable sa conduite a toujours été irréprochable
irreproachably [ˌɪrɪˈprəʊtʃəblɪ] *adv* irréprochablement, de façon irréprochable
irresistibility [ˌɪrɪˌzɪstəˈbɪlɪtɪ] *n* irrésistibilité *f*
irresistible [ˌɪrɪˈzɪstəbəl] *adj* irrésistible; **she's got an irresistible smile** elle a un sourire irrésistible; **the irresistible force of their argument** la force irrésistible de leur argument; **when they argue, it's a case of an irresistible force meeting an immovable object** quand ils se disputent, chacun campe sur ses positions
irresistibleness [ˌɪrɪˈzɪstəbəlnɪs] *n* irrésistibilité *f*
irresistibly [ˌɪrɪˈzɪstəblɪ] *adv* irrésistiblement; **he was irresistibly drawn to her** il était irrésistiblement attiré vers elle; **irresistibly delicious cakes** des gâteaux irrésistibles
irresolute [ɪˈrezəluːt] *adj* irrésolu, indécis
irresolutely [ɪˈrezəluːtlɪ] *adv* d'un air irrésolu
irresoluteness [ɪˈrezəluːtnɪs], **irresolution** [ɪˌrezəˈluːʃən] *n* indécision *f*, irrésolution *f*
irresolvable [ˌɪrɪˈzɒlvəbəl] *adj* (**a**) *(problem, question)* insoluble (**b**) *Tech (body)* indécomposable, irréductible
irrespective [ˌɪrɪˈspektɪv] **irrespective of** *prep* sans tenir compte de, indépendamment de; **irrespective of race or religion** sans discrimination de race ou de religion; **irrespective of what has been said before** indépendamment de ce qui a été dit auparavant
irresponsibility [ˌɪrɪˌspɒnsəˈbɪlətɪ] *n* irresponsabilité *f*
irresponsible [ˌɪrɪˈspɒnsəbəl] *adj (person, parent, driver)* irresponsable; *(act)* irréfléchi; **you're so irresponsible!** tu n'as aucun sens des responsabilités!
irresponsibly [ˌɪrɪˈspɒnsəblɪ] *adv* (**a**) *(act, behave, drive)* de manière irresponsable (**b**) *Law* irresponsablement
irretrievable [ˌɪrɪˈtriːvəbəl] *adj (object)* impossible à récupérer; *(loss, harm, damage)* irréparable; *Comput (file)* irrécupérable; **the damage is irretrievable** les dégâts sont irréparables; **the situation is irretrievable** la situation est irrémédiable
irretrievably [ˌɪrɪˈtriːvəblɪ] *adv (lost)* irrémédiablement, à tout jamais; **to break down irretrievably** *(of marriage)* se briser irrémédiablement
irreverence [ɪˈrevərəns] *n* irrévérence *f*
irreverent [ɪˈrevərənt] *adj* irrévérencieux; **irreverent remarks** remarques irrévérencieuses *ou* insolentes; **an irreverent sense of humour** un sens de l'humour insolent *ou* impertinent
irreverently [ɪˈrevərəntlɪ] *adv* irrévérencieusement
irreversible [ˌɪrɪˈvɜːsɪbəl] *adj* (**a**) *(decision, step)* irrévocable (**b**) *(process)* irréversible
irreversibly [ˌɪrɪˈvɜːsəblɪ] *adv* irréversiblement
irrevocable [ɪˈrevəkəbəl] *adj (gen) & Fin (letter of credit)* irrévocable
irrevocably [ɪˈrevəkəblɪ] *adv* irrévocablement
irrigable [ˈɪrɪgəbəl] *adj* irrigable
irrigate [ˈɪrɪgeɪt] *vt (gen) & Med* irriguer
irrigation [ˌɪrɪˈgeɪʃən] *n (gen) & Med* irrigation *f*
▸▸ ***irrigation canal*** canal *m* d'irrigation; ***irrigation channel*** fossé *m ou* rigole *f* d'irrigation
irritability [ˌɪrɪtəˈbɪlətɪ] *n* irritabilité *f*
irritable [ˈɪrɪtəbəl] *adj (gen) & Med* irritable
▸▸ ***irritable bowel syndrome*** syndrome *m* du côlon irritable
irritably [ˈɪrɪtəblɪ] *adv* avec irritation
irritant [ˈɪrɪtənt] **1** *n* irritant *m*; *Fig* **at least we can be an irritant** au moins nous pouvons jouer les empêcheurs de tourner en rond
2 *adj* irritant
irritate [ˈɪrɪteɪt] *vt* (**a**) *(annoy)* irriter, contrarier, énerver (**b**) *Med* irriter
irritated [ˈɪrɪteɪtɪd] *adj* (**a**) *(annoyed)* irrité, agacé; **don't get irritated!** ne t'énerve pas!
(**b**) *Med (eyes, skin)* irrité
irritating [ˈɪrɪteɪtɪŋ] *adj* (**a**) *(annoying)* irritant, contrariant, énervant (**b**) *Med* irritant, irritatif
irritatingly [ˈɪrɪteɪtɪŋlɪ] *adv* de façon agaçante *ou* irritante; **he's irritatingly slow** il est d'une lenteur irritante
irritation [ɪrɪˈteɪʃən] *n* (**a**) *(annoyance)* irritation *f*, agacement *m*; **she tried to hide her irritation** elle tenta de cacher son agacement; **it's just one of life's little irritations** ce n'est qu'une de ces petites choses énervantes de la vie (**b**) *Med* irritation *f*
irrupt [ɪˈrʌpt] *vi* faire irruption
irruption [ɪˈrʌpʃən] *n* irruption *f*
IRS [ˌaɪɑːˈres] *n Am Fin (abbr* **Internal Revenue Service***)* **the IRS** ≃ le fisc
IS [ˌaɪˈes] *n (abbr* **information system***)* système *m* informatique
is [ɪz] *see* **be**
ISA [ˈaɪsə] *n Br Fin (abbr* **individual savings account***)* ≃ PEA *m*
Isaac [ˈaɪzək] *pr n Bible* Isaac
isabel [ˈɪzəˌbel], **isabella** [ˌɪzəˈbelə] **1** *n (colour)* isabelle *m*, gris *m* jaune
2 *adj* isabelle *(inv)*, gris jaune
isagogics [aɪzəˈgɒdʒɪks] *n* isagogique *f*
Isaiah [aɪˈzaɪə] *pr n Bible* Isaïe
isallobar [aɪˈsæləˌbɑː(r)] *n Met* isallobare *f*
ISBN [ˌaɪesˌbiːˈen] *n (abbr* **International Standard Book Number***)* ISBN *m*
ischaemia, ischemia [ɪˈskiːmɪə] *n Med* ischémie *f*
ischium [ˈɪskɪəm] *(pl* **ischia** [-kɪə]*) n Anat* ischion *m*
ISDN [ˌaɪesˌdiːˈen] *(abbr* **integrated services digital network***)* **1** *n* RNIS *m*
2 *vt Fam* **to ISDN sth** envoyer qch par RNIS ❑
▸▸ ***ISDN card*** carte *f* RNIS; ***ISDN line*** ligne *f* RNIS; ***ISDN modem*** modem *m* RNIS *ou* Numéris
Iseult [ɪˈzuːlt] *pr n* Iseut
Isfahan [ˌɪsfəˈhɑːn] *n* Ispahan
-ish [ɪʃ] *suff* (**a**) *(with adjective)* **blueish** bleuâtre; **shortish** plutôt petit (**b**) *(with noun)* **girlish** de petite fille; **wolfish** de loup (**c**) *(with time, numbers etc)* **around eightish** vers huit heures, aux environs de huit heures; **he's fortyish** il a la quarantaine
Ishmael [ˈɪʃmeɪəl] **1** *pr n Bible* Ismaël
2 *n (outcast)* paria *m*, déshérité *m*
isinglass [ˈaɪzɪŋˌglɑːs] *n* (**a**) *(glue)* ichtyocolle *f* (**b**) *Miner (mica)* mica *m*
Isis [ˈaɪsɪs] *pr n Myth* Isis
Islam [ˈɪzlɑːm] *n* Islam *m*
Islamabad [ɪzˈlɑːməˌbæd] *n* Islamabad
Islamic [ɪzˈlæmɪk] *adj* islamique
Islamicist [ɪzˈlæmɪsɪst] *n* personne *f* qui étudie l'Islam
Islamicize, -ise [ɪzˈlæmɪsaɪz] *vt* islamiser
Islamism [ˈɪzləmɪzəm] *n* islamisme *m*
Islamist [ˈɪzləmɪst] *n* islamiste *mf*
Islamization [ˌɪzləmaɪˈzeɪʃən] *n* islamisation *f*
Islamize, -ise [ˈɪzləˌmaɪz] *vt* islamiser
island [ˈaɪlənd] **1** *n* (**a**) *Geog* île *f*; *Am Fam* **the Island** *(Long Island)* Long Island ❑; **they are an island race** c'est une race insulaire; **we didn't stay in one place, we went island-hopping** nous ne sommes pas toujours restés au même endroit, nous sommes allés d'île en île; **the island of Ireland** l'Irlande; *Fig* **an island of calm** une oasis de tranquillité
(**b**) *(in road)* îlot *m*; *(for pedestrians)* refuge *m*; *(of houses etc)* groupe *m*
(**c**) *(for displaying goods)* ilôt *m*
2 *vt (isolate)* isoler
▸▸ *Geol* ***island arc*** arc *m* insulaire
islander [ˈaɪləndə(r)] **1** *n* insulaire *mf*
2 Islander *n NZ* habitant(e) *m,f* des îles du Pacifique
Islay [ˈaɪlə] *n* Islay *f*
isle [aɪl] *n* île *f*
▸▸ ***the Isle of Dogs*** = quartier de l'est de Londres faisant partie des Docklands; ***the Isle of Man*** l'île *f* de Man; **in** *or* **on the Isle of Man** à l'île de Man; ***the Isle of Sheppey*** l'île *f* de Sheppey, Sheppey *f*; **in** *or* **on the Isle of Sheppey** à l'île de Sheppey; ***the Isle of Wight*** l'île *f* de Wight, = comté au sud de l'Angleterre; **in** *or* **on the Isle of Wight** à l'île de Wight
islet [ˈaɪlɪt] *n* (**a**) *(small island)* îlot *m* (**b**) *Med (cluster of cells)* îlot *m*
▸▸ ***the islets of Langerhans*** les îlots de Langerhans
ism [ˈɪzəm] *n Fam Pej* doctrine ❑ *f*, idéologie ❑ *f*
Ismaili [ˌɪzmɑːˈiːlɪ], **Ismailian** [ˌɪzmɑːˈiːlɪən] *n* ismaélien(enne) *m,f*, ismaïlien(enne) *m,f*
isn't [ˈɪzənt] = **is not**
ISO [ˌaɪesˈəʊ] *n (abbr* **International Standards Organization***)* ISO *f*
iso- [ˈaɪsəʊ] *pref* iso-
isobar [ˈaɪsəbɑː(r)] *n Met & Phys* isobare *f*
isobaric [ˌaɪsəʊˈbærɪk] *adj Met & Phys (line)* isobare; *(map)* isobarique, isobarométrique
▸▸ *Met & Phys* ***isobaric curve*** isobarique *f*; *Phys* ***isobaric spin*** spin *m* isobarique *ou* isotopique; ***isobaric surface*** surface *f* isobare
isobutane [ˌaɪsəʊˈbjuːteɪn] *n Chem* isobutane *m*
ISOC [ˌaɪesˌəʊˈsiː] *n Comput (abbr* **Internet Society***)* = organisation non gouvernementale chargée de veiller à l'évolution de l'Internet
isocaloric [ˌaɪsəʊˈkælərɪk] *adj Med* isocalorique
isochronal [aɪˈsɒkrənəl], **isochronous** [aɪˈsɒkrənəs] *adj* isochrone, isochronique
isoclinal [ˌaɪsəʊˈklaɪnəl] *adj Geol* isoclinal; *Geog* isocline
isocline [ˈaɪsəʊklaɪn] *n Geog* isocline *f*
isocracy [aɪˈsɒkrəsɪ] *n Pol* isocratie *f*
isodiametric [ˌaɪsəʊˌdaɪəˈmetrɪk] *adj Geom* isodiamétrique
isodynamic [ˌaɪsəʊdaɪˈnæmɪk] *Phys* **1** *n* ligne *f* isodynamique
2 *adj* isodynamique
isoelectric [ˌaɪsəʊɪˈlektrɪk] *adj* isoélectrique
isogamy [aɪˈsɒgəmɪ] *n Bot* isogamie *f*
isogloss [ˈaɪsəʊglɒs] *n Ling* isoglosse *f*
isoglossal [ˌaɪsəʊˈglɒsəl] *adj Ling* isoglosse
isohel [ˈaɪsəʊhel] *n Met* isohèle *f*
isohyet [ˌaɪsəʊˈhaɪət] *n Met* isohyète *f*
isolable [ˈaɪsələbəl] *adj* isolable
isolate [ˈaɪsəleɪt] *vt (gen) & Med, Biol & Elec* isoler (**from** de *ou* d'avec); **she isolated herself from other people** elle s'est isolée des autres gens
isolated [ˈaɪsəleɪtɪd] *adj* (**a**) *(alone, remote)* isolé (**b**) *(single)* unique, isolé; **an isolated incident** un incident isolé; **isolated case** cas *m* isolé; **isolated instance** cas *m* isolé
isolation [ˌaɪsəˈleɪʃən] *n (gen) & Med, Biol & Elec* isolement *m*; **a sense of complete isolation** un sentiment d'isolement total; **in isolation** en soi, isolément; **you cannot consider the problem in isolation** on ne peut pas considérer le problème isolément
▸▸ ***isolation hospital*** hôpital *m* d'isolement; ***isolation ward*** service *m* des contagieux
isolationism [ˌaɪsəˈleɪʃəˌnɪzəm] *n* isolationnisme *m*
isolationist [ˌaɪsəˈleɪʃənɪst] *adj* isolationniste
isolator [ˈaɪsəˌleɪtə(r)] *n Elec* isolant *m*, isolateur *m*
Isolde [ɪˈzɒldə] *pr n Myth* Iseult
isoleucine [ˌaɪsəʊˈluːsiːn] *n Chem* isoleucine *f*
isomer [ˈaɪsəmə(r)] *n Chem & Phys* isomère *m*
isomerase [ˌaɪˈsəʊməreɪz] *n Biol & Chem* isomérase *f*
isomeric [ˌaɪsəʊˈmerɪk] *adj Chem & Phys* isomère, isomérique
isomerism [aɪˈsɒmərɪzəm] *n Chem & Phys* isomérie *f*
isomerization [aɪˌsəʊməraɪˈzeɪʃən] *n Chem & Phys* isomérisation *f*
isomerize, -ise [aɪˈsəʊməˌraɪz] *vt Chem & Phys* isomériser
isometric [ˌaɪsəʊˈmetrɪk] *adj Geom & Physiol* isométrique
▸▸ *Gym* ***isometric exercises*** exercices *mpl* isométriques
isometrics [ˌaɪsəʊˈmetrɪks] *n (UNCOUNT) Gym* exercices *mpl* isométriques
isometry [aɪˈsɒmetrɪ] *n Geog & Math* isométrie *f*
isomorph [ˈaɪsəmɔːf] *n Biol & Chem* isomorphe *m*
isomorphic [ˌaɪsəʊˈmɔːfɪk] *adj Biol, Chem & Math* isomorphe
isomorphism [ˌaɪsəˈmɔːfɪzəm] *n Biol, Chem & Math* isomorphisme *m*
isomorphous [ˌaɪsəʊˈmɔːfəs] *adj Biol, Chem & Math* isomorphe
isonomy [aɪˈsɒnəmɪ] *n* isonomie *f*
isopentane [ˌaɪsəʊˈpenteɪn] *n Chem* isopentane *m*
isopod [ˈaɪsəʊˌpɒd] *(pl* **isopods** *or* **isopoda** [-ˈsɒpədə]*) n Zool* isopode *m*
isoprene [ˈaɪsəʊˌpriːn] *n Chem* isoprène *m*
isopropyl [ˌaɪsəʊˈprəʊpɪl] *n Chem* isopropyle *m*
▸▸ ***isopropyl alcohol*** alcool *m* isopropylique
isosceles [aɪˈsɒsɪliːz] *adj* isocèle
▸▸ ***isosceles triangle*** triangle *m* isocèle
isoseismal [ˌaɪsəʊˈsaɪzməl] *Geol* **1** *n* isoséiste *f*, isosiste *f*
2 *adj* isoséiste, isosiste

irr–iso

isoseismic [ˌaɪsəʊ'saɪzmɪk] *adj Geol* isoséiste, isosiste
isospin ['aɪsəʊspɪn] *n Phys* spin *m* isobarique *ou* isotopique
isostasy [aɪ'sɒstəsɪ] *n Geol* isostasie *f*
isostatic [ˌaɪsəʊ'stætɪk] *adj Geol* isostatique
isothere ['aɪsəʊθɪə(r)] *n Met* isothère *f*
isotherm ['aɪsəʊθɜːm] *n Met & Phys* isotherme *f*
isothermal [ˌaɪsəʊ'θɜːməl], **isothermic** [ˌaɪsəʊ'θɜːmɪk] *adj Met & Phys* isotherme, isothermique
isotonic [ˌaɪsəʊ'tɒnɪk] *adj Phys, Mus & Med* isotonique
isotope ['aɪsətəʊp] *n Chem & Phys* isotope *m*
isotopic [ˌaɪsə'tɒpɪk] *adj Chem & Phys* isotopique
isotropic [ˌaɪsə'trɒpɪk] *adj* (**a**) *Chem & Phys* isotrope, isotropique (**b**) *Biol (egg)* isotrope
isotropism [ˌaɪsə'trəʊpɪzəm], **isotropy** [aɪ'sɒtrəpɪ] *n Chem & Phys* isotropie *f*
isotype ['aɪsəʊˌtaɪp] *n Biol* isotype *m*
ISP [ˌaɪes'piː] *n Comput* (*abbr* **Internet Service Provider**) fournisseur *m* d'accès à l'Internet
I-spy *n Br* = jeu d'enfant où l'un des joueurs donne la première lettre d'un objet qu'il voit et les autres doivent deviner de quoi il s'agit; *Hum* **I-spy with my little eye a spare chocolate biscuit** mais qu'est-ce que je vois là, il reste un biscuit au chocolat?
Israel ['ɪzreɪəl] *n* Israël; **in Israel** en Israël
Israeli [ɪz'reɪlɪ] (*pl* **inv** *or* **Israelis**) **1** *n* Israélien(enne) *m,f*
2 *adj* israélien
3 *comp (embassy, history)* d'Israël
Israelite ['ɪzrəlaɪt] *n* Israélite *mf*
issuable ['ɪʃuːəbəl] *adj Fin* émissible, susceptible d'être émis
►► *Law* ***issuable matter*** matière *f* à litige
issuance ['ɪʃuːəns] *n (of official document)* délivrance *f*

ISSUE ['ɪʃuː]

question	► **1 (a)**
différend	► **1 (b)**
numéro	► **1 (c)**
distribution	► **1 (d)**
délivrance	► **1 (d)**
émission	► **1 (d)**
prêt	► **1 (d)**
issue	► **1 (e)**
publier	► **2 (a), (c)**
sortir	► **2 (a)**
délivrer	► **2 (b)**
prêter	► **2 (b)**
émettre	► **2 (d)**
distribuer	► **2 (e)**

1 *n* (**a**) *(matter, topic)* question *f*, problème *m*; **where do you stand on the abortion issue?** quel est votre point de vue sur (la question de) l'avortement?; **the issue was raised at the meeting** le problème a été soulevé à la réunion; **your personal feelings are not the issue** vos sentiments personnels n'ont rien à voir là-dedans; **that's not the issue** ce n'est pas la question; **it's become an international issue** le problème a pris une dimension internationale; **the important issues of the day** les grands problèmes du moment; **at issue** en question; **the point at issue is not the coming election** le problème n'est pas l'élection à venir; **her competence is not at issue** sa compétence n'est pas en cause; **to join issue with sb (about sth)** discuter l'opinion de qn (au sujet de qch); **to cloud** *or* **confuse the issue** brouiller les cartes; **to avoid** *or* **to duck** *or* **to evade the issue** esquiver la question; **to force the issue** forcer la décision; *Law* **issue (of fact/of law)** question *f ou* point *m* de fait/de droit
(**b**) *(cause of disagreement)* différend *m*; **the subject has now become a real issue between us** ce sujet est maintenant source de désaccord entre nous; **to be at issue with sb over sth** être en désaccord avec qn au sujet de qch; **they are at issue with the Japanese over import quotas** ils sont en désaccord avec les Japonais au sujet des quotas d'importations; **to make an issue of sth** monter qch en épingle; **don't make such an issue of it!** inutile d'en faire toute une histoire!; **to take issue with sb/sth** être en désaccord avec qn/qch; **I take issue with him on only one point** je suis en désaccord avec lui sur un point seulement; **I would take issue with that** je ne suis pas d'accord là-dessus
(**c**) *(edition → of newspaper, magazine etc)* numéro *m*; **the latest issue of the magazine** le dernier numéro du magazine
(**d**) *(distribution → of supplies, equipment)* distribution *f*; *(→ of official document, passport)* délivrance *f*; *(→ of shares, money, stamps)* émission *f*; *(→ of library book)* prêt *m*; **date of issue** date *f* de délivrance; **standard issue** modèle *m* standard; **army issue** modèle *m* de l'armée
(**e**) *Formal (result, outcome)* issue *f*, résultat *m*; **I hope your request has a favourable issue** j'espère que votre demande connaîtra une issue *ou* recevra une réponse favorable; *Law* **issue (of fact/law)** conclusion *f*
(**f**) *Arch or Law (progeny)* descendance *f*, progéniture *f*; **he died without issue** il est mort sans héritiers
(**g**) *Med (of blood, pus)* décharge *f*
2 *vt* (**a**) *(book, newspaper)* publier, sortir; *(record)* sortir; **the magazine is issued on Wednesdays** le magazine sort *ou* paraît le mercredi
(**b**) *(official document, passport)* délivrer; *Law (warrant, writ, summons)* lancer; *(library book)* prêter; **where was the passport issued?** où le passeport a-t-il été délivré?
(**c**) *(statement, proclamation)* publier; **the government has issued a denial** le gouvernement a publié un démenti
(**d**) *(shares, money, stamps)* émettre; *(letter of credit)* fournir; **the Bank of Scotland issues its own notes** la Bank of Scotland émet ses propres billets; **to issue a draft on sb** fournir une traite sur qn
(**e**) *(distribute → supplies, tickets etc)* distribuer; **the magazine is issued free to every household** le magazine est distribué gratuitement à *ou* dans tous les foyers; **we were all issued with rations** on nous a distribué à tous des rations; **each man will be issued with two uniforms** chaque homme recevra deux uniformes; **no books will be issued after eight p.m.** le service de prêt ferme à vingt heures
3 *vi Formal* (**a**) *(come or go out)* sortir (**from** de); *(blood, water)* s'écouler (**from** de); *(smoke)* s'échapper (**from** de); **delicious smells issued from the kitchen** des odeurs délicieuses provenaient de la cuisine
(**b**) *(result, originate)* **to issue from** provenir de; **all our difficulties issue from that first mistake** c'est de cette première erreur que proviennent tous nos ennuis; *Formal* **the children issuing from this marriage** les enfants issus de ce mariage
►► *Admin* ***issue card*** carte *f* (de) sortie de stock; *Fin* ***issue department*** service *m* des émissions; *Fin* ***issue premium*** prime *f* d'émission; *Fin* ***issue price*** prix *m* d'émission, valeur *f* d'émission
►**issue forth** *vi Literary* jaillir

issued ['ɪʃuːd] *adj*
►► *St Exch* ***issued capital*** capital *m* émis; ***issued securities*** titres *mpl* émis; *St Exch* ***issued share capital*** capital-action *m* émis
issueless ['ɪʃuːlɪs] *adv Formal* **to die issueless** mourir sans laisser de descendance
issuer ['ɪʃuːə(r)] *n (of shares, money, stamps)* émetteur *m*
issuing ['ɪʃʊɪŋ] *n (of loan, banknotes)* émission *f*; *(of provisions)* distribution *f*; *(of library books)* prêt *m*; *(of passport)* délivrance *f*; *(of arrest warrant)* lancement *m*
►► *Br* ***issuing bank*** banque *f* d'émission *ou* émettrice; ***issuing company*** société *f* émettrice; ***issuing house*** banque *f* émettrice, banque *f* d'émission
Istanbul [ˌɪstæn'bʊl] *n* Istanbul
ISTC [ˌaɪes,tiː'siː] *n* (*abbr* **Iron and Steel Trades Confederation**) = syndicat britannique des ouvriers de la sidérurgie
isthmus ['ɪsməs] (*pl* **isthmuses** *or* **isthmi** [-maɪ]) *n Geog & Anat* isthme *m*
Istria ['ɪstrɪə] *n* l'Istrie *f*
Istrian ['ɪstrɪən] **1** *n* Istrien(enne) *m,f*
2 *adj* istrien
IT [ˌaɪ'tiː] *n* (*abbr* **information technology**) technologie *f* de l'information; **she's our IT expert** c'est notre spécialiste en informatique; **IT has revolutionized the way we do business** l'informatique a complètement transformé le monde du commerce

IT [ɪt]

il/elle	► **1 (a)**
le/la	► **1 (a)**
lui	► **1 (a)**
en	► **1 (b)**
il	► **1 (c)**
ce	► **1 (e)**

1 *pron* (**a**) *(referring to specific thing, animal etc → as subject)* il (elle); *(→ as direct object)* le (la); *(→ as indirect object)* lui; **is it a boy or a girl?** c'est un garçon ou une fille?; **the building's dangerous, it should be pulled down** le bâtiment est dangereux, il devrait être démoli; **I'd lend you my typewriter but it's broken** je te prêterais bien ma machine à écrire mais elle est cassée; **I took my hat off and now I can't find it** j'ai enlevé mon chapeau et je ne le trouve plus; **take this plate and put it on the table** prends cette assiette et mets-la sur la table; **give it a tap with a hammer** donnez un coup de marteau dessus; **fetch the dog and give it something to eat** va chercher le chien et donne-lui à manger
(**b**) *(after preposition)* **he told me all about it** il m'a tout raconté; **as we walked away from it** tandis que nous nous en éloignions; **he's not bad, far from it** il n'est pas méchant, loin de là; **give me half of it** donnez-m'en la moitié; **there was nothing inside it** il n'y avait rien dedans *ou* à l'intérieur; **don't tread on it** ne marchez pas dessus; **I went over to it** je m'en suis approché; **did he consent to it?** est-ce qu'il y a consenti?; **I left the bag under it** j'ai laissé le sac dessous; **I cracked his head with it** je lui ai fendu la tête avec
(**c**) *(as unspecified subject)* **it's me!** c'est moi!; **it's raining/snowing** il pleut/neige; **it's cold/dark today** il fait froid/sombre aujourd'hui; **it's Friday today** nous sommes *ou* c'est vendredi aujourd'hui; **it seemed like a good idea** cela *ou* ça semblait être une bonne idée; **it's 500 miles from here to Vancouver** Vancouver est à 800 km d'ici; **it's not easy for me to say this, but...** je n'aime pas dire ce genre de chose, mais...; **it'll take us hours to get there** on va mettre des heures pour y arriver; **it'll cost (us) a fortune to have it repaired** ça va (nous) coûter une fortune pour le faire réparer; **it was agreed that we should move out** il a été convenu que nous déménagerions; **it's impossible to work in this heat** c'est impossible de travailler par cette chaleur; **it's vital to plan ahead** il est indispensable de prévoir les choses à l'avance; **it might look rude if I don't go** si je n'y vais pas, cela pourrait être considéré comme une impolitesse; **it seems** *or* **appears** *or* **would appear that there's been some trouble** il semble qu'il y ait eu des problèmes; **it says on the box/in the instructions that...** c'est écrit sur la boîte/dans les instructions que...; **it's the Johnny Carson Show!** voici le Johnny Carson Show!; **it's a goal!** but!; *Fam* **it was pouring down** il pleuvait des cordes; **it's his constant complaining I can't stand** ce que je ne supporte pas, c'est sa façon de se plaindre constamment
(**d**) *(as unspecified object)* **I like it here** je me plais beaucoup ici; **I love it when we go on a picnic** j'adore quand on va pique-niquer; **I couldn't bear it if she left** je ne supporterais pas qu'elle parte; **she found it easy to make new friends** ça lui a été facile de se faire de nouveaux amis; *Fam* **blast it!** zut!
(**e**) *(as complement)* **who is it?** qui est-ce?
2 *n Fam* (**a**) *(in games)* **you're it!** c'est toi le chat!, c'est toi qui y es!
(**b**) *(most important person)* **he thinks he's it** il s'y croit
(**c**) *Fam (Italian vermouth)* **gin and it** gin-vermouth ❑ *m*
►► *Br Fam* ***it girl*** jeune mondaine ❑ *f*

ITA [ˌaɪtiː'eɪ] *n* (*abbr* **Initial Teaching Alphabet**) **the ITA** = alphabet en partie phonétique parfois utilisé pour l'enseignement de la lecture

Italian [ɪ'tæljən] **1** *n* (**a**) *(person)* Italien(enne) *m,f* (**b**) *(language)* italien *m* (**c**) *Fam (restaurant)* restau *m* italien; *(meal)* repas *m* italien ❑; **we went out for an Italian** on est allés dans un restau italien
2 *adj* italien
3 *comp (embassy)* d'Italie; *(history)* de l'Italie; *(teacher)* d'italien
►► ***Italian dressing*** vinaigrette *f* aux fines herbes; ***Italian Switzerland*** Suisse *f* italienne; ***Italian vermouth*** vermouth *m* italien

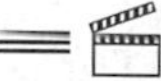

'The Italian Job' *Collinson* 'L'Or se barre'

Italianate [ɪ'tæljəneɪt] *adj Archit* italianisant
Italianism [ɪ'tæljə,nɪzəm] *n* (**a**) *Ling* italianisme *m* (**b**) *(custom)* italianisme *m*
Italianist [ɪ'tæljə,nɪst] *n* (**a**) *(specialist)* italianisant(e) *m,f* (**b**) *(devotee)* amateur(trice) *m,f* de l'Italie
Italianize, -ise [ɪ'tæljə,naɪz] *vt* italianiser
italic [ɪ'tælɪk] **1** *adj* italique; **italic(s) face** *or* **type** caractères *mpl* italiques
2 *n* italique *m*; **in italics** en italique; **the italics are mine** les italiques sont de moi
3 Italic 1 *adj (of ancient Italy)* italique **2** *n Ling* italique *m*
italicization [ɪ,tælɪsaɪ'zeɪʃən] *n* mise *f* en italique
italicize, -ise [ɪ'tælɪ,saɪz] *vt* mettre en italique; **the italicized words** les mots en italique
Italo- [ɪ'tæləʊ] *pref* italo-; **Italo-American** italo-américain
Italy ['ɪtəlɪ] *n* Italie *f*; **in Italy** en Italie
ITC [,aɪtiː'siː] *n Br (abbr* **Independent Television Commission**) = commission de surveillance des télévisions britanniques privées
itch [ɪtʃ] **1** *n* (**a**) *(physical)* démangeaison *f*; **I've got an itch** ça me démange *ou* me gratte
(**b**) *Fam Fig (desire)* envie ❑ *f*; **I've got the itch to work abroad** ça me démange d'aller travailler à l'étranger; *Fam Fig* **if you've got an itch, scratch it** si ça te dit, vas-y
2 *vi* (**a**) *(physically)* avoir des démangeaisons; **I'm itching all over** j'ai des démangeaisons partout, je suis couvert de démangeaisons; **does it itch?** est-ce que cela te démange?; **my back itches** mon dos me démange *ou* me gratte; **that sweater itches** ce pull me gratte; *Fig* **to have an itching palm** être cupide
(**b**) *Fam Fig (desire)* **I was itching to tell her** ça me démangeait de lui dire; **we're itching to go** nous ne tenons plus en place
itchiness ['ɪtʃɪnɪs] *n (itching)* démangeaison *f*
itching ['ɪtʃɪŋ] *n* démangeaison *f*
►► ***itching powder*** poil *m* à gratter
itchy ['ɪtʃɪ] *(compar* **itchier**, *superl* **itchiest**) *adj* qui gratte, qui démange; **an itchy pullover** un pull qui gratte; **I've got an itchy leg** ma jambe me démange; *Fam Fig* **to have itchy feet** avoir la bougeotte
it'd ['ɪtəd] = **it would, it had**
item ['aɪtəm] **1** *n* (**a**) *(object)* article *m*; **the items in the shop window** les articles en vitrine; **the only item he bought was a lighter** la seule chose qu'il ait achetée, c'est un briquet; **an item of clothing** un vêtement
(**b**) *(point, issue)* point *m*, question *f*; **there are two important items on the agenda** il y a deux points importants à l'ordre du jour; **I've several items of business to attend to** j'ai plusieurs affaires à régler
(**c**) *(in newspaper)* article *m*; *(very brief)* entrefilet *m*; *(on TV or radio)* point *m ou* sujet *m* d'actualité; **an item in the 'Times'** un article dans le 'Times'; **there was an item on the news about it yesterday** ils en ont parlé aux informations hier; **and here are today's main news items** et voici les principaux points de l'actualité
(**d**) *(performance in show)* numéro *m*
(**e**) *Comput (on menu)* élément *m*
(**f**) *Ling* item *m*; **lexical item** item *m* lexical
(**g**) *Acct* écriture *f*, article *m*; **item of expenditure** article *m* de dépense
(**h**) *Fam (couple)* **are they an item?** est-ce qu'ils sortent ensemble? ❑; **they're no longer an item** ils ne sortent plus ensemble ❑
2 *adv Old-fashioned (when listing)* item
itemize, -ise ['aɪtəmaɪz] *vt* détailler
►► ***itemized bill*** facture *f* détaillée; ***itemized billing, itemized invoicing*** facturation *f* détaillée; ***itemized list*** liste *f* détaillée
iterate ['ɪtəreɪt] *vt Formal (say again)* réitérer; *(do again)* refaire, répéter; *Comput & Math* itérer
iteration [,ɪtə'reɪʃən] *n Formal & Comput & Math* itération *f*
iterative ['ɪtərətɪv] *adj (gen) & Ling & Math* itératif
Ithaca ['ɪθəkə] **1** *pr n Myth* Ithaque
2 *n Geog* Ithaque
ithyphallic [,ɪθɪ'fælɪk] *adj Literature* ithyphallique
itinerant [ɪ'tɪnərənt] **1** *adj* itinérant; *(actors)* ambulant, itinérant; **itinerant preacher** prédicateur *m* itinérant; *Am* **itinerant teacher** professeur *m* remplaçant
2 *n* nomade *mf*
itinerary [aɪ'tɪnərərɪ] *(pl* **itineraries**) *n* itinéraire *m*
it'll [ɪtəl] = **it will**
ITN [,aɪtiː'en] *n Br (abbr* **Independent Television News**) = service d'actualités télévisées pour les chaînes relevant de l'"ITC"
its [ɪts] **1** *adj (singular)* son (sa); *(plural)* ses; **the committee has its first meeting on Friday** le comité se réunit pour la première fois vendredi; **the dog wagged its tail** le chien a remué la queue; **the jug's lost its handle** le pichet n'a plus de poignée
2 *pron (singular)* le sien (la sienne); *(plural)* les siens (les siennes)
it's [ɪts] = **it is, it has**
itself [ɪt'self] *pron* (**a**) *(reflexive use)* se; **the cat was licking itself clean** le chat faisait sa toilette; **the dog hurt itself** le chien s'est blessé
(**b**) *(emphatic use)* lui-même (elle-même); **the town itself is quite small** la ville elle-même est assez petite; **she's kindness itself** c'est la gentillesse même
(**c**) *(after preposition)* **it switches off by itself** ça s'éteint tout seul; **it's not dangerous in itself** ce n'est pas dangereux en soi; **working with her was in itself fascinating** le seul fait de travailler avec elle était fascinant
itsy-bitsy [,ɪtsɪ'bɪtsɪ], **itty-bitty** [,ɪtɪ'bɪtɪ] *adj Fam* tout petit ❑, minuscule ❑
ITV [,aɪtiː'viː] *n Br (abbr* **Independent Television**) = sigle désignant les programmes diffusés par les chaînes relevant de l'"ITC"
IUCD [,aɪjuː,siː'diː] *n (abbr* **intrauterine contraceptive device**) stérilet *m*
IUD [,aɪjuː'diː] *n (abbr* **intrauterine device**) stérilet *m*
IV [,aɪ'viː] *Med (abbr* **intravenous**) **1** *n* perfusion *f* intraveineuse
2 *adj* intraveineux
3 *adv* par voie intraveineuse
►► ***IV drip*** perfusion *f* intraveineuse; ***IV push*** pompe *f* de perfusion sous pression
Ivan ['aɪvən] *pr n*
►► ***Ivan the Great*** Ivan le Grand; ***Ivan the Terrible*** Ivan le Terrible
Ivanhoe ['aɪvənhəʊ] *pr n* Ivanhoé
I've [aɪv] = **I have**
IVF [,aɪviː'ef] *n (abbr* **in vitro fertilization**) FIV *f*
ivied ['aɪvɪd] *adj* couvert de lierre
Ivorian [aɪ'vɔːrɪən] **1** *n* Ivoirien(enne) *m,f*
2 *adj* ivoirien
ivory ['aɪvərɪ] *(pl* **ivories**) **1** *n* (**a**) *(substance)* ivoire *m* (**b**) *(object)* ivoire *m*
2 *adj* (**a**) *(made of ivory)* d'ivoire, en ivoire; **an ivory carving** une sculpture d'ivoire (**b**) *(ivory-coloured)* (couleur) ivoire *(inv)*
3 ivories *npl Fam* (**a**) *(piano keys)* touches ❑ *fpl*; *Hum* **to tickle the ivories** toucher du piano ❑ (**b**) *(teeth)* ratiches *fpl*
►► ***ivory tower*** tour *f* d'ivoire
Ivory Coast ['aɪvərɪ-] *n* **the Ivory Coast** la Côte d'Ivoire; **in the Ivory Coast** en Côte d'Ivoire
ivory-white *adj (teeth)* d'une blancheur d'ivoire
ivy ['aɪvɪ] *(pl* **ivies**) *n Bot* lierre *m*
►► ***the Ivy League*** = groupe des huit universités les plus prestigieuses du nord-est des États-Unis

THE IVY LEAGUE

On désigne ainsi un groupe de huit universités du nord-est des États-Unis: Brown, Columbia, Cornell, Dartmouth, Harvard, l'Université de Pennsylvanie, Princeton et Yale. Ces universités se caractérisent par une forte proportion d'étudiants de troisième cycle, des moyens financiers importants et la réputation d'excellence de leurs universitaires. Si à l'origine, "Ivy League" servait à promouvoir les rencontres sportives entre les universités qui la composaient, elle est depuis devenue synonyme d'un enseignement prestigieux très compétitif, réservé à l'élite.

ivy-leaved *adj Bot* à feuilles de lierre
►► ***ivy-leaved geranium*** géranium-lierre *m*; ***ivy-leaved speedwell*** véronique *f* à feuilles de lierre; ***ivy-leaved toadflax*** cymbalaire *f*
Ivy-League *adj* **he had an Ivy-League education** il a fait ses études dans une grande université; *Fam* **her boyfriend's very Ivy-League** son petit ami est très BCBG
IWW [,aɪdʌbəljuː'dʌbəljuː] *n (abbr* **Industrial Workers of the World**) IWW *m*, = syndicat révolutionnaire américain actif au début du XXème siècle
IYHF [,aɪwaɪ,eɪtʃ'ef] *n (abbr* **International Youth Hostel Federation**) FIAJ *f*
Izmir ['ɪzmɪə(r)] *n* Izmir
Izod test ['aɪzɒd-] *n Tech* essai *m* Izod
izzard ['ɪzəd] *n Arch* Z, z *m inv*

J

J¹, j [dʒeɪ] *n (letter)* J, j *m inv*; **two j's** deux j; **J for John** ≃ J comme Joseph

J² *n Fam Drugs slang (joint)* joint *m*

JA [ˌdʒeɪ'eɪ] *n (abbr* **judge advocate**) assesseur *m (d'un tribunal militaire)*

J/A, j/a *Banking (written abbr* **joint account**) compte *m* joint

jab [dʒæb] *(pt & pp* **jabbed**, *cont* **jabbing**) **1** *n* (**a**) *(poke)* coup *m (donné avec un objet pointu)*; **she gave him a sharp jab in the ribs (with her elbow)** elle lui a mis un coup de coude dans les côtes

(**b**) *Fam (injection)* piqûre❑ *f*; **to give sb a jab** faire une injection❑ *ou* une piqûre à qn; *(for TB, malaria etc)* vacciner qn❑; **I've got to get a tetanus jab** je dois me faire vacciner contre le tétanos❑

(**c**) *Boxing* coup *m* droit, direct *m*

2 *vt* (**a**) *(poke, prick)* **to jab sb/sth (with sth)** piquer qn/qch (avec qch *ou* du bout de qch); **to jab sb with one's elbow/a knife** donner un coup de coude/de couteau à qn; **she jabbed him in the eyes with her fingers** elle lui a planté ses doigts dans les yeux

(**b**) *(thrust)* enfoncer, planter (d'un coup sec) (**into** dans); **she jabbed a finger at him to emphasize her point** elle a pointé le doigt dans sa direction pour appuyer ses propos

3 *vi* (**a**) *(poke, prick)* **to jab at sb/sth (with sth)** piquer qn/qch (avec qch, du bout de qch); **to jab at sb with a knife/an umbrella** donner un coup de couteau/de parapluie à qn

(**b**) *Boxing* envoyer un coup droit *ou* un direct (**at** à)

jabber ['dʒæbə(r)] *Fam* **1** *vi (idly)* jacasser, *Pej* caqueter; *(inarticulately)* bredouiller, bafouiller; *(in foreign language)* baragouiner; **they jabber (away) for hours on the phone** ils passent des heures à jacasser au téléphone; **they were all jabbering away in different languages** chacun baragouinait dans sa langue

2 *vt* **to jabber (out)** bredouiller, bafouiller; **I managed to jabber a few words of thanks** j'ai réussi à bredouiller *ou* bafouiller quelques mots de remerciement

3 *n (UNCOUNT)* (**a**) *(noise)* brouhaha *m*

(**b**) *(chat)* conversation *f*, *Pej* jacasseries *fpl*; **to have a jabber** bavarder, tailler une bavette

jabbering ['dʒæbərɪŋ] *n (UNCOUNT)* (**a**) *(incomprehensible)* baragouinage *m* (**b**) *(chattering)* bavardage *m*, *Pej* jacasseries *fpl*

jabot ['ʒæbəʊ] *n* jabot *m*

jaçana [ʒɑːsə'nɑː] *n Orn* jacana *m*

jacaranda [ˌdʒækə'rændə] *n Bot* jacaranda *m*

jacinth ['dʒæsɪnθ] *n (gemstone)* hyacinthe *f*

jack [dʒæk] **1** *vt Tech* soulever avec un vérin; *Aut* mettre sur cric

2 *n* (**a**) *Tech (tool)* vérin *m*; *Aut* cric *m*

(**b**) *(playing card)* valet *m*

(**c**) *(in bowls)* cochonnet *m*

(**d**) *Tel* prise *f*; *Elec (socket)* prise *f ou* fiche *f* femelle; *(plug, connector)* prise *f ou* fiche *f* mâle; **microphone/headphone jack** prise *f* de microphone/de casque

(**e**) *Am Fam (money)* blé *m*, fric *m*

(**f**) **(roasting) jack** tournebroche *m*

(**g**) *Naut (crosstree)* barre *f* de cacatois; *(flag)* pavillon *m* beaupré

(**h**) *(medieval armour)* jaque *f*, grippon *m*, hoqueton *m*

(**i**) *(idioms) Br Fam* **every man jack (of them)** tous autant qu'ils sont; *Vulg* **I didn't understand jack shit** j'ai pigé que dalle

3 Jack *pr n Br Fam* **I'm all right, Jack** moi ça va; *Fam* **an "I'm all right, Jack" attitude** une attitude égoïste❑; *Am* **hey, Jack!** *(to stranger)* hé, vous là-bas!; *Br Fam* **before you could say Jack Robinson** avant d'avoir pu dire "ouf"

4 jacks *n (UNCOUNT) (game)* osselets *mpl*

►► *Naut* **jack crosstree** barre *f* de cacatois; ***Jack Frost*** le Bonhomme Hiver; *Tech* ***jack plug*** prise *f ou* fiche *f* mâle, jack *m*; *Zool* ***jack rabbit*** = gros lièvre d'Amérique; ***Jack Russell*** Jack Russell (terrier) *m*; *Orn* ***jack snipe*** bécassine *f* sourde; *Elec* ***jack socket*** prise *f ou* fiche *f* femelle; *Fam Old-fashioned* ***jack tar*** marin❑ *m*, matelot❑ *m*

►**jack around** *Am Fam* **1** *vt sep* **to jack sb around** *(treat badly)* se ficher de qn; *(waste time of)* faire perdre son temps à qn

2 *vi (waste time)* glander, glandouiller

►**jack in** *vt sep Br Fam* plaquer; **I've jacked my job in** j'ai plaqué mon boulot; **oh, jack it in, will you!** oh, ferme-la, tu veux!

►**jack off** *Vulg* **1** *vt sep* **to jack sb off** branler qn

2 *vi* se branler, se palucher

►**jack up 1** *vt sep* (**a**) *(car)* lever avec un cric (**b**) *Fam (price, wage)* augmenter❑, monter❑ (**c**) *Br Fam Drugs slang (inject oneself with)* s'injecter❑, se piquer à

2 *vi Br Fam Drugs slang (inject oneself)* s'injecter❑, se piquer

jackal ['dʒækəl] *n also Fig* chacal *m*

jackanapes ['dʒækəneɪps] *n Arch or Literary (arrogant person)* fat *m*, faquin *m*; *(mischievous child)* polisson(onne) *m,f*, galopin *m*

jackaroo ['dʒækəˌruː] *(pl* **jackaroos**) *n Austr Fam* bleu *m (dans une ferme)*

jackass ['dʒækæs] *n* (**a**) *(donkey)* âne *m*, baudet *m* (**b**) *Fam (imbecile)* imbécile *mf*

jackboot ['dʒækbuːt] *n* botte *f* (de militaire); *Fig* **life under the jackboot** la vie sous la botte de l'ennemi; **jackboot tactics** des tactiques dictatoriales

jackbooted ['dʒækbuːtɪd] *adj* botté

jackdaw ['dʒækdɔː] *n Orn* choucas *m*

jackeen [dʒæ'kiːn] *n Ir Fam Pej* = expression péjorative utilisée par les habitants des campagnes pour désigner les Dublinois

jacket ['dʒækɪt] **1** *n* (**a**) *(garment)* veste *f*; *(shorter)* blouson *m*; *(of man's suit)* veston *m*; *(of woman's suit)* jaquette *f*; **leather jacket** blouson *m* de cuir; *(longer)* veste *f* de cuir

(**b**) *(of book)* jaquette *f*; *Am (of record)* pochette *f*

(**c**) *(of baked potato)* peau *f*; **potato (cooked) in its jacket** pomme *f* de terre en robe des champs *ou* en robe de chambre

(**d**) *Tech (of boiler, bullet)* chemise *f*

2 *vt* (**a**) *(book)* couvrir d'une jaquette

(**b**) *Tech (boiler etc)* garnir *ou* envelopper d'une chemise, chemiser

►► ***jacket potato*** pomme *f* de terre en robe des champs *ou* en robe de chambre

jackfruit ['dʒækfruːt] *n* jaque *m*

jackhammer ['dʒækˌhæmə(r)] *n* marteau *m* piqueur

jacking point ['dʒækɪŋ-] *n* point *m* de levage, emplacement *m* prévu pour le cric

jack-in-office *n Br Pej* petit chef *m*

jack-in-the-box *(pl* **jack-in-the-boxes** *or* **jacks-in-the-box**) *n* diable *m* (à ressort); *Fam* **to jump up and down like a jack-in-the-box** ne pas tenir en place❑

jackknife ['dʒæknaɪf] *(pl* **jackknives** [-naɪvz]) **1** *n* couteau *m* de poche

2 *vi* **the truck jackknifed** le camion s'est mis en portefeuille

►► *Sport* ***jackknife dive*** saut *m* de carpe

jack-of-all-trades *(pl* **jacks-of-all-trades**) *n Pej* homme *m* à tout faire; *Prov* **jack-of-all-trades and master of none** propre à tout et bon à rien

jack-o'-lantern *n* (**a**) *(Hallowe'en lantern)* = lanterne faite dans une citrouille sur laquelle on a creusé un visage (**b**) *(will-o'-the-wisp)* feu *m* follet

jackpot ['dʒækpɒt] *n* (**a**) *Cards (in poker etc)* pot *m* (**b**) *(in competition, of lottery)* gros lot *m*; **to hit** *or* **win the jackpot** gagner le gros lot; *Fig* **to hit the jackpot** *(be successful → person)* gagner le gros lot, décrocher la timbale; **she's hit the jackpot with her latest book** elle a fait un malheur avec son dernier livre

jackshaft ['dʒækʃɑːft] *n Tech* arbre *m* de renvoi

jacksie [ˌdʒæksɪ] *n Br very Fam (buttocks)* fesses❑ *fpl*, popotin *m*

jackstones ['dʒækstəʊnz] *n (game)* osselets *mpl*

jackstraws ['dʒækstrɔːz] *n* jonchets *mpl*

jacksy = **jacksie**

Jack-the-Lad *n Fam* jeune frimeur *m*

Jacob ['dʒeɪkəb] **1** *pr n Bible* Jacob

2 *n (sheep)* mouton *m* (de) Jacob

►► ***Jacob's ladder*** *Bible* l'échelle *f* de Jacob; *Bot* valériane *f* grecque; *Naut* échelle *f* de revers, échelle *f* de pilote; *Hist* ***Jacob's staff*** *(in surveying)* mire *f*

Jacobean [ˌdʒækə'bɪən] *adj Hist & Archit* jacobéen, de l'époque de Jacques Ier (d'Angleterre)

Jacobin ['dʒækəbɪn] *Hist* **1** *n* Jacobin(e) *m,f*

2 *adj* jacobin

Jacobinism ['dʒækəbɪnɪzəm] *n Hist* jacobinisme *m*

Jacobite ['dʒækəbaɪt] *Hist* **1** *n* Jacobite *mf*

2 *adj* jacobite

►► ***the Jacobite Rising*** = nom donné aux deux tentatives conduites par les Stuarts pour s'emparer du trône d'Angleterre en 1715 et 1745

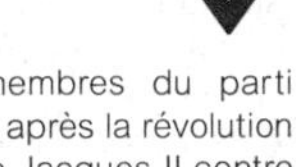

THE JACOBITES

Les "Jacobites" sont les membres du parti légitimiste anglais qui soutint, après la révolution de 1688, d'abord la cause de Jacques II contre Guillaume d'Orange, puis celle des derniers Stuarts contre la maison des Hanovre.

jaconet ['dʒækənɪt] *n Tex* jaconas *m*

jacquard ['dʒækɑːd] *n Tex (fabric)* jacquard *m*

►► ***jacquard loom*** métier *m* Jacquard, jacquard *m*

Jacuzzi® [dʒə'kuːzɪ] *(pl* **Jacuzzis**) *n* Jacuzzi® *m*, bain *m* à remous

jade [dʒeɪd] **1** *n* (**a**) *(stone)* jade *m* (**b**) *(colour)* vert jade *m inv* (**c**) *Arch (horse)* rosse *f*, haridelle *f* (**d**) *Arch (woman → shrewish)* mégère *f*; *(→ disreputable)* friponne *f*

2 *adj* (**a**) *(made of jade)* de *ou* en jade (**b**) *(colour)* vert jade *(inv)*

jaded ['dʒeɪdɪd] *adj (person → tired)* las, fatigué; *(→ unenthusiastic)* blasé; *(performance, piece of writing, cliché)* faiblard; **I'm feeling a bit jaded today** je ne suis pas très en forme aujourd'hui

►► ***jaded palate*** palais *m* blasé; *Fig* appétit *m* fatigué

jadeite ['dʒeɪdaɪt] *n* jadéite *f*

Jaffa ['dʒæfə] *n* (**a**) *(city)* Jaffa (**b**) *(orange)* orange *f* de Jaffa

JAG [ˌdʒeɪeɪ'dʒiː] *n (abbr* **judge advocate general**) assesseur *m* général

Jag [dʒæg] *n Fam (Jaguar® car)* Jaguar®❑ *f*

jag [dʒæg] *(pt & pp* **jagged,** *cont* **jagging**) **1** *n* (**a**) *(jagged projection)* pointe *f*, aspérité *f*; *(of saw)* dent *f* (**b**) *Am Fam (drinking bout)* soûlerie *f*; **to go on a (drinking) jag** se soûler, prendre une cuite; **he broke into a coughing jag** il s'est mis à tousser □; **a crying jag** une crise de larmes (**c**) *Scot Fam (injection)* piquouse *f*
2 *vt* déchiqueter; *(fabric)* taillader

jagged ['dʒægɪd] *adj (coastline, mountain top)* découpé; *(edge)* découpé, dentelé; *(line, tear)* irrégulier; *(rock)* pointu, dentelé; **the jagged outline of the coast** les dentelures *fpl ou* découpures *fpl* de la côte

jaggedness ['dʒægɪdnɪs] *n (of coastline, mountain top, edge)* état *m* découpé; *(of line, tear)* irrégularité *f*; *(of rock)* état *m* dentelé

jaggy ['dʒægɪ] *(pl* **jaggies**) **1** *n Typ* courbe *f* en escalier
2 *adj* (**a**) *(coastline, mountain top)* déchiqueté, découpé; *(edge)* déchiqueté, découpé, dentelé (**b**) *Scot (prickly)* plein de piquants

jaguar ['dʒægjʊə(r)] *n Zool* jaguar *m*

jaguarundi [,dʒægwə'rʌndɪ] *n Zool* jaguarondi *m*

jai alai [,haɪə'laɪ] *n* = jeu qui ressemble à la pelote basque, pratiqué surtout en Floride

jail [dʒeɪl] **1** *n* prison *f*; **to be in jail** être en prison; **to be sent to jail** être incarcéré *ou* emprisonné; **to go to jail** aller en prison, faire de la prison; **he was sent to jail** *or* **he went to jail for ten years** il a été condamné à dix ans de prison; **she was in jail for ten years, she went to jail for ten years** elle a fait dix ans de prison; **to break out of jail** s'évader de prison
2 *vt* emprisonner, mettre en prison, incarcérer; **to be jailed for life** être condamné à perpétuité *ou* à vie

jailbait ['dʒeɪlbeɪt] *n (UNCOUNT) Am Fam* mineur(e) *m,f*; **she's jailbait** c'est un coup à se retrouver en taule *(pour détournement de mineur)*

jailbird ['dʒeɪlbɜːd] *n Fam (actually in prison)* taulard(e) *m,f*; *(constantly going to prison)* cheval *m* de retour

jailbreak ['dʒeɪlbreɪk] *n* évasion *f*; **to carry out a jailbreak** s'évader

jailbreaker ['dʒeɪl,breɪkə(r)] *n* évadé(e) *m,f*

jailer ['dʒeɪlə(r)] *n* geôlier(ère) *m,f*

jailhouse ['dʒeɪlhaʊs, *pl* -haʊzɪz] *n Am* prison *f*

jailor = **jailer**

Jain [dʒaɪn] **1** *n* jaïn(e) *m,f*
2 *adj* jaïn

Jainism ['dʒaɪnɪzəm] *n* jaïnisme *m*

Jaipur [,dʒaɪ'pʊə(r)] *n* Jaipur

Jakarta [dʒə'kɑːtə] *n* Djakarta, Jakarta

jake [dʒeɪk] *n Br Fam Drugs slang* joint *m*

jakes [dʒeɪks] *npl Br Fam Arch* **the jakes** *(toilet)* les cabinets *mpl*

jalapeño [hɑːlə'peɪnjəʊ] *(pl* **jalapeños**) *n Am* petit piment *m* vert

jalopy, jaloppy [dʒə'lɒpɪ] *(pl* **jalopies** *or* **jaloppies**) *n Fam* (vieille) bagnole *f*, (vieux) tacot *m*

jam [dʒæm] *(pt & pp* **jammed,** *cont* **jamming**) **1** *n* (**a**) *(preserve)* confiture *f*; **strawberry jam** confiture *f* de fraises; *Br Fam* **he wants jam on it!** et avec ça, on est difficile!; *Br Fam* **it's a case of jam tomorrow** ce sont des promesses en l'air (**b**) *(traffic jam)* bouchon *m*, embouteillage *m*, encombrement *m*
(**c**) *(crowd)* **there was a great jam of people outside the theatre** il y avait une foule énorme devant le théâtre
(**d**) *Fam (predicament)* pétrin *m*; **I'm in a bit of a jam** je suis plutôt dans le pétrin
(**e**) *Fam (by musicians)* bœuf *m*, jam-session *f*
2 *comp (tart, pudding, sandwich)* à la confiture
3 *vt* (**a**) *(crowd, cram)* entasser, tasser; *(push roughly, ram)* fourrer; **we were jammed in like sardines** on était entassés *ou* serrés comme des sardines; **all my clothes are jammed into one drawer** tous mes vêtements sont entassés dans un seul tiroir; **I was jammed (up) against the wall** j'étais coincé contre le mur; **he jammed the gun into his pocket** il fourra le pistolet dans sa poche; **she jammed her hat on** elle enfonça *ou* vissa son chapeau sur sa tête; **to jam one's foot on the brake(s)** écraser le frein *ou* la pédale de frein
(**b**) *(make stick)* coincer, bloquer; *(weapon, mechanism)* enrayer, bloquer; *(pipe)* boucher; **she jammed the window shut with a wedge** elle coinça *ou* bloqua la fenêtre avec une cale; **to jam a door open with a book** maintenir une porte ouverte à l'aide d'un livre
(**c**) *(congest)* encombrer, bloquer, boucher; **a crowd of late arrivals jammed the entrance** une foule de retardataires bloquait l'entrée; **the streets were jammed with cars** les rues étaient embouteillées
(**d**) *Rad* brouiller
(**e**) *Tel (lines)* encombrer; *(switchboard)* faire sauter; **the switchboard was jammed** le standard était saturé
4 *vi* (**a**) *(crowd)* se tasser, s'entasser; **thousands of people jammed in for the concert** des milliers de personnes se sont entassées pour assister au concert
(**b**) *(drawer, window, lift etc)* se coincer, se bloquer; *(gun, machine)* s'enrayer, se bloquer; *(brakes, wheel, paper in printer)* se bloquer
(**c**) *Fam (play in a jam session)* faire un bœuf; *(play on one's own)* improviser □; **I was just jamming** c'était juste de l'impro
(**d**) *(in mountaineering)* faire un verrou, coincer
▸▸ *Br Fam Hum* ***jam sandwich*** *(police car)* voiture *f* de police □; *Fam* ***jam session*** bœuf *m*, jam-session *f*

▸**jam in 1** *vt sep* (**a**) *(wedge in)* coincer; **the crowd were jamming him in** il était coincé par la foule; **her car was being jammed in by a large truck** un gros camion était en train de la coincer
(**b**) *(pack or press tightly in → passengers etc)* (en)tasser; *(→ objects)* bourrer; **he had jammed as many quotations as he could find into the essay** il avait farci sa dissertation de toutes les citations qu'il avait trouvées
2 *vi (crowd in)* s'entasser; **they all jammed in** *(into train)* ils s'y entassèrent tous; **we won't all be able to jam in at once** nous n'allons jamais tous tenir à la fois

▸**jam on** *vt sep* (**a**) *Aut* **to jam on the brakes** écraser le frein *ou* la pédale de frein (**b**) *(lid, hat etc)* enfoncer

Jamaica [dʒə'meɪkə] *n* Jamaïque *f*; **in Jamaica** à la Jamaïque
▸▸ ***Jamaica pepper*** poivre *m* de la Jamaïque, toute-épice *m*; ***Jamaica rum*** rhum *m* jamaïquain *ou* jamaïcain *ou* de la Jamaïque

Jamaican [dʒə'meɪkən] **1** *n* Jamaïcain(e) *m,f*, Jamaïquain(e) *m,f*
2 *adj* jamaïcain, jamaïquain

jamb [dʒæm] *n* chambranle *m*, jambage *m*, montant *m*

jambalaya [,dʒæmbə'laɪə] *n* jambalaya *m*

jamboree [,dʒæmbə'riː] *n* (**a**) *(scouts' meeting)* jamboree *m* (**b**) *Fam (celebration, party)* fête □ *f*, réunion □ *f*; *(festivities)* réjouissances □ *fpl* (tapageuses); **village jamboree** fête *f* de village

James [dʒeɪmz] *pr n* Jacques; **James I/II** Jacques I/II

Jamestown ['dʒeɪmztaʊn] *n* = premier établissement anglais en Amérique du Nord en 1607, aujourd'hui lieu touristique

jam-full *adj (suitcase, bag etc)* plein à craquer, bourré (**of** de); **jam-full (of people)** *(hall, bus)* plein à craquer, bondé; *(street)* noir de monde, bondé; **this magazine is jam-full of interesting articles** ce magazine est truffé *ou* regorge d'articles intéressants

jamjar ['dʒæmdʒɑː(r)] *n* pot *m* à confiture

jammies ['dʒæmɪz] *npl (in children's language)* pyjama *m*

jamming ['dʒæmɪŋ] *n* (**a**) *(sticking)* coincement *m*; *(of brakes)* blocage *m* (**b**) *Rad* brouillage *m* (**c**) *Tel (of lines)* encombrement *m* (**d**) *(in mountaineering)* coincement *m*

jammy ['dʒæmɪ] *(compar* **jammier,** *superl* **jammiest**) *adj* (**a**) *(covered with jam)* plein de confiture (**b**) *Br Fam (lucky)* veinard, verni; **he's a jammy devil!** quel veinard, celui-là!, il est verni, celui-là! (**c**) *Br Fam (easy)* facile □; **jammy job** filon *m*, bonne planque *f*

jam-packed *adj (suitcase, bag etc)* plein à craquer, bourré (**with** de); **jam-packed (with people)** *(hall, bus)* plein à craquer, bondé; *(street)* noir de monde, bondé; **this magazine is jam-packed with interesting articles** ce magazine est truffé *ou* regorge d'articles intéressants

jampot ['dʒæmpɒt] *n* pot *m* à confiture

jams [dʒæmz] *npl Am (shorts)* bermuda *m*

Jan. *(written abbr* **January**) janv

Jane [dʒeɪn] *n Am Fam (woman)* nana *f*
▸▸ *Am* ***Jane Doe*** *(average person)* l'Américaine *f* moyenne, ≃ Madame Dupont; *(unidentified woman → under arrest)* inconnue *f*; *(→ corpse)* morte *f* non identifiée

JANET ['dʒænɪt] *n Comput (abbr* **Joint Academic Network**) = réseau Internet composé d'universités et d'organismes de recherche britanniques

jangle ['dʒæŋgəl] **1** *n (of bells)* tintamarre *m*; *(of money)* bruit *m*, cliquetis *m*; **the jangle of keys** le cliquetis des clés
2 *vt* faire retentir; *(more quietly)* faire cliqueter; *Fig* **my nerves are all jangled** j'ai les nerfs en boule *ou* en pelote
3 *vi* retentir (avec un bruit métallique *ou* avec fracas); *(more quietly)* cliqueter; **his keys jangled in his pocket** ses clés cliquetaient dans sa poche; **it jangled on my nerves** cela me mettait les nerfs en pelote

jangling ['dʒæŋglɪŋ] **1** *adj (bells)* retentissant; *(keys)* qui tintent; **a jangling noise** un bruit métallique
2 *n* bruit *m* métallique; **a jangling of keys** un bruit de clés

janitor ['dʒænɪtə(r)] *n Am & Scot (caretaker)* gardien *m*, concierge *m*; *Old-fashioned (doorkeeper)* portier *m*

jankers ['dʒæŋkəz] *n Fam Mil slang* sanction *f* disciplinaire □; **to be on jankers** être puni □

Jansenism ['dʒænsə,nɪzəm] *n* jansénisme *m*

Jansenist ['dʒænsənɪst] **1** *n* janséniste *mf*
2 *adj* janséniste

January ['dʒænjʊərɪ] *n* janvier *m*; *see also* **February**

Janus ['dʒeɪnəs] *pr n Myth* Janus

Janus-faced *adj* à deux visages, hypocrite

JAP [dʒæp] *n Am Fam Pej (abbr* **Jewish American princess**) = jeune Juive américaine issue d'une famille aisée

Jap [dʒæp] *very Fam* **1** *n* Jap *mf*, = terme injurieux désignant un Japonais
2 *adj* jap, japonais □

Japan [dʒə'pæn] *n* Japon *m*; **in Japan** au Japon

japan [dʒə'pæn] *(pt & pp* **japanned,** *cont* **japanning**) *Art* **1** *n* laque *f* du Japon
2 *vt* laquer

Japanese [,dʒæpə'niːz] *(pl* **inv**) **1** *npl* **the Japanese** les Japonais *mpl*
2 *n* (**a**) *(person)* Japonais(e) *m,f* (**b**) *(language)* japonais *m*
3 *adj* japonais
4 *comp (embassy, history)* du Japon; *(teacher)* de japonais
▸▸ ***Japanese artichoke*** crosne *m*; ***Japanese lantern*** lanterne *f* vénitienne; *Bot* ***Japanese laurel*** aucuba *m*; *Bot* ***Japanese moss*** helxine *f*

japanned [dʒə'pænd] *adj* laqué
▸▸ ***japanned leather*** cuir *m* verni; ***japanned sheet iron*** tôle *f* vernie

jape [dʒeɪp] *n Fam Old-fashioned* farce □ *f*, blague *f*

japonica [dʒə'pɒnɪkə] *n Bot* cognassier *m* du Japon

jar [dʒɑː(r)] *(pt & pp* **jarred,** *cont* **jarring**) **1** *n* (**a**) *(container → glass)* bocal *m*; *(→ for jam)* pot *m*; *(→ earthenware)* pot *m*, jarre *f*
(**b**) *Br Fam (drink)* pot *m*; **he's having a few jars with the lads** il prend un pot *ou* un verre avec les copains
(**c**) *(jolt)* secousse *f*, choc *m*
2 *vi* (**a**) *(make harsh noise)* grincer, crisser; **there's something about her voice which really jars** sa voix a quelque chose qui vous écorche les oreilles
(**b**) *(clash → note)* détonner; *(→ colour)* jurer (**with** avec); *(→ ideas, styles, remarks)* détonner, être incompatible, ne pas s'accorder (**with** avec); **it jars with your red dress** cela jure avec ta robe rouge; **his constant complaining jars on my nerves** ses lamentations continuelles me hérissent
3 *vt* (**a**) *(shake → structure)* secouer, ébranler;

the fall jarred my bones cette chute m'a secoué; **I've jarred my wrist** je me suis fait mal au poignet

(**b**) *(of news)* ébranler, secouer

4 on the jar *adj (door)* entrouvert

jardinière [ˌʒɑːdɪ'njeə(r)] *n* (**a**) *(for plants)* jardinière *f* (**b**) *Culin* jardinière *f*, macédoine *f* de légumes

jargon ['dʒɑːgən] *n* jargon *m*; **legal jargon** jargon *m* juridique, langage *m* du Palais; **to talk (in) jargon** parler en jargon, jargonner

Jarlsberg® ['jɑːlzbɜːg] *n* jarlsberg *m*

jarred [dʒɑːd] *adj Ir Fam (drunk)* bourré, beurré

jarring ['dʒɑːrɪŋ] *adj (sound)* discordant; *(colour)* criard; **a loud jarring noise** un bruit discordant

Jarrow Marches [ˌdʒærəʊ'mɑːtʃɪz] *npl* **the Jarrow Marches** = "marches de la faim", du nord-est de l'Angleterre à Londres, organisées au milieu des années trente par les chômeurs pour protester contre leur condition

jarvey ['dʒɑːvɪ] *n Br Fam Arch* cocher *m* (de fiacre)❑

Jas. *(written abbr* **James***)* James

jasmine ['dʒæzmɪn] *n Bot* jasmin *m*

▸▸ ***jasmine tea*** thé *m* au jasmin

Jason ['dʒeɪsən] *pr n Myth* Jason

jasper ['dʒæspə(r)] *n Miner* jaspe *m*

jato ['dʒeɪtəʊ] *n Aviat (abbr* **jet-assisted take-off***)* décollage *m* (avec fusées) JATO

▸▸ ***jato unit*** fusées *fpl* JATO

jaundice ['dʒɔːndɪs] *n* (**a**) *(UNCOUNT) Med* jaunisse *f* (**b**) *Fig (bitterness)* amertume *f*

jaundiced ['dʒɔːndɪst] *adj* (**a**) *Med* ictérique, bilieux (**b**) *Fig (bitter)* aigri, amer; *(jealous)* jaloux; **to look on the world** *or* **on things with a jaundiced eye** *(bitterly)* voir tout en noir; *(jealously)* tout regarder d'un œil jaloux; **to take a jaundiced view of a situation** voir une situation d'un mauvais œil

jaunt [dʒɔːnt] **1** *n* balade *f*; **to go on** *or* **for a jaunt** faire une (petite) excursion *ou* une balade

2 *vi* **she's always jaunting off to Paris** elle est toujours en balade entre ici et Paris

jauntily ['dʒɔːntɪlɪ] *adv (remark → casually)* d'une manière désinvolte, avec désinvolture; *(→ cheerfully)* gaiement, avec entrain, d'un air enjoué; *(walk)* d'un pas guilleret; *(wear one's hat)* d'une façon désinvolte

jauntiness ['dʒɔːntɪnɪs] *n (carefreeness)* désinvolture *f*, insouciance *f*; *(cheerfulness)* enjouement *m*, vivacité *f*; **the jauntiness of his step** son pas guilleret

jaunty ['dʒɔːntɪ] *adj (carefree)* désinvolte, insouciant, dégagé; *(cheerful, lively)* enjoué; **with a jaunty air** d'un air dégagé; **jaunty step** pas *m* guilleret; **he wore his cap at a jaunty angle** sa casquette était négligemment posée sur sa tête

Java¹ ['dʒɑːvə] *n Geog* (île *f* de) Java *f*

▸▸ ***Java Man*** homme *m* de Java

Java²® ['dʒɑːvə] *n Comput* Java® *m*

Java® ***script*** Javascript® *m*, (langage) Javascript® *m*

java ['dʒɑːvə] *n Am Fam (coffee)* caoua *m*, kawa *m*

Javanese [ˌdʒɑːvə'niːz] *(pl* **inv***)* **1** *npl* **the Javanese** les Javanais *mpl*

2 *n* (**a**) *(person)* Javanais(e) *m,f* (**b**) *(language)* javanais *m*

3 *adj* javanais

javelin ['dʒævəlɪn] *n (weapon)* javelot *m*, javeline *f*; *Sport* javelot *m*; *Sport* **the javelin** *(event)* l'épreuve *f* de javelot

▸▸ ***javelin thrower*** lanceur(euse) *m,f* de javelot

jaw [dʒɔː] **1** *n* (**a**) *Anat* mâchoire *f*; *(of insect)* mandibule *f*; **she has a very square jaw** elle a une mâchoire très carrée; **his jaw dropped in astonishment** il en est resté bouche bée; **upper/lower jaw** mâchoire *f* supérieure/inférieure; *Fig* **snatched from the jaws of death** arraché aux griffes de la mort; *Fig* **to set one's jaw** *(show determination)* décider de s'accrocher; *Am Fam* **to flap one's jaw** gueuler

(**b**) *(of valley, cave)* entrée *f*; *(of volcano)* bouche *f*; *Fig* **the jaws of hell** les portes *fpl* de l'enfer

(**c**) *(of tool)* mâchoire *f*

(**d**) *Fam (chat)* **to have a good old jaw** tailler une petite bavette, papoter

(**e**) *Fam (moralizing speech)* sermon❑ *m*

2 *vi Fam* (**a**) *(chat)* papoter, tailler une bavette; **she's been jawing away on the phone all morning** elle n'a pas arrêté de papoter au téléphone de toute la matinée

(**b**) *(moralize)* prêcher, moraliser❑

3 *vt Fam (remonstrate with)* sermonner❑

'Jaws' *Spielberg, Benchley* 'Les Dents de la mer'

Jaw-jaw is better than war-war
Churchill déclara lors d'un discours prononcé à la Maison Blanche en 1954 **"Talking jaw is better than going to war"** ("Mieux vaut discuter que de faire la guerre"). Cependant, c'est la formule **Jaw-jaw is better than war-war** qui est passée à la postérité.
On utilise cette expression aujourd'hui pour dire qu'il est toujours préférable de parlementer avec ses ennemis afin de résoudre un différend de façon pacifique.

jawbone ['dʒɔːbəʊn] **1** *n* maxillaire *m*

2 *vt Am Fam* exercer des pressions sur❑

jawbreaker ['dʒɔːˌbreɪkə(r)] *n Fam* (**a**) *(word)* mot *m* difficile à prononcer❑; *(name)* nom *m* à coucher dehors (**b**) *Am (sweet)* = sorte de bonbon dur

-jawed [dʒɔːd] *suff* **round/long/***etc***-jawed** à la mâchoire ronde/allongée/*etc*; *Fam Boxing* **glass-jawed** à la mâchoire fragile❑

jawline ['dʒɔːlaɪn] *n* menton *m*; **a strong jawline** un menton saillant

jay [dʒeɪ] *n Orn* geai *m*

Jaycees [ˌdʒeɪ'siːz] *npl Am* **the Jaycees** = chambre de commerce pour jeunes entrepreneurs

jaywalk ['dʒeɪwɔːk] *vi Am* = marcher en dehors des passages pour piétons

jaywalker ['dʒeɪwɔːkə(r)] *n Am* = piéton qui traverse en dehors des passages pour piétons

jaywalking ['dʒeɪwɔːkɪŋ] *n Am* = délit mineur qui consiste à traverser une rue en dehors des clous ou au feu vert

Jaz® [dʒæz] *n*

▸▸ *Comput* ***Jaz***® ***disk*** cartouche *f* Jaz®; ***Jaz***® ***drive*** lecteur *m* Jaz®

jazz [dʒæz] **1** *n* (**a**) *(music)* jazz *m*

(**b**) *Fam (rigmarole)* baratin *m*, bla-bla *m*; **don't give me that jazz!** ne me raconte pas de salades!; **what's (all) this jazz about your leaving?** qu'est-ce que c'est que cette histoire comme quoi tu t'en vas?; **and all that jazz** et tout le bataclan; **they've done a jazz version of her song** ils ont fait une version jazz de sa chanson

2 *comp (club, record, singer)* de jazz

3 *vt very Fam Black Am slang (have sex with)* baiser avec

▸▸ ***the Jazz Age*** = l'âge d'or du jazz américain; ***jazz band*** jazz-band *m*; ***jazz poetry*** = poésie récitée sur fond sonore de jazz; ***jazz rock*** jazz-rock *m*

▸**jazz up** *vt sep* (**a**) *(song)* mettre sur un rythme (de) jazz; **it's jazzed up Beethoven** c'est du Beethoven sur un rythme de jazz (**b**) *Fam (enliven)* égayer❑; **they've jazzed the hotel up** ils ont refait la déco de l'hôtel

jazzman ['dʒæzmæn] *(pl* **jazzmen** [-men]*)* *n* musicien *m* de jazz

jazzy ['dʒæzɪ] *(compar* **jazzier**, *superl* **jazziest***)* *adj* (**a**) *(music)* (de) jazz *(inv)*, sur un rythme de jazz; **a jazzy version of "Carmen"** une version jazz de "Carmen" (**b**) *Fam (gaudy)* tapageur, voyant; *(smart)* chic *(inv)*

JC [ˌdʒeɪ'siː] *n Fam (abbr* **Jesus Christ***)* J.-C.

JCB® [ˌdʒeɪsiː'biː] *n Br* tractopelle *f*

JCR [ˌdʒeɪsiː'ɑː(r)] *n Br Univ (abbr* **junior common room***)* ≃ foyer *m* des étudiants

JCS [ˌdʒeɪsiː'es] *npl Am (abbr* **Joint Chiefs of Staff***)* = organe consultatif du ministère américain de la Défense, composé des chefs d'état-major des trois armées

J-curve *n Econ* courbe *f* en J

JD [ˌdʒeɪ'diː] *n Am* (**a**) *(abbr* **Justice Department***)* ≃ le ministère de la Justice (**b**) *(abbr* **Doctor of Jurisprudence***)* ≃ docteur *m* en droit

jealous ['dʒeləs] *adj* (**a**) *(fearful of rivals)* jaloux; **a jealous lover** un amant jaloux; **he gets terribly jealous** il a des crises de jalousie terribles (**b**) *(envious)* jaloux; **to be jealous of sb** être jaloux de qn; **he became very jealous of her sudden success** sa réussite soudaine l'a rendu très jaloux (**c**) *(possessive)* jaloux, possessif; **to be jealous of one's reputation** être jaloux de *ou* veiller à sa réputation

jealously ['dʒeləslɪ] *adv* (**a**) *(enviously)* jalousement, avec jalousie (**b**) *(possessively)* avec un soin jaloux; **a jealously guarded secret** un secret jalousement gardé

jealousy ['dʒeləsɪ] *(pl* **jealousies***)* *n* jalousie *f*

jeans [dʒiːnz] *npl* jean *m*, blue-jean *m*; **a pair of jeans** un jean

▸▸ *Am* ***jeans jacket*** veste *f* en jean

Jedda ['dʒedə] *n* Djedda

Jeep® [dʒiːp] *n* Jeep® *f*

jeepers ['dʒiːpəz] *exclam Am Fam* **jeepers (creepers)!** oh là là!

jeer [dʒɪə(r)] **1** *n (scoffing)* raillerie *f*; *(boo, hiss)* huée *f*

2 *vt (scoff at)* railler; *(boo, hiss at)* huer, conspuer

3 *vi (scoff)* railler, se moquer; *(boo, hiss)* pousser des cris hostiles *ou* de dérision; **everybody jeered at me** ils se sont tous moqués de moi

jeerer ['dʒɪərə(r)] *n (scoffer)* railleur(euse) *m,f*, moqueur(euse) *m,f*

jeering ['dʒɪərɪŋ] **1** *n (UNCOUNT) (scoffing)* railleries *fpl*; *(boos, hisses)* huées *fpl*

2 *adj* railleur, moqueur

jeeringly ['dʒɪərɪŋlɪ] *adv* d'une manière railleuse *ou* moqueuse

Jeeves [dʒiːvz] *pr n* = personnage des romans de PG Wodehouse, type du valet impassible

jeez [dʒiːz] *exclam Fam* purée!

Jefferson Memorial ['dʒefəsən-] *n* **the Jefferson Memorial** = monument à la mémoire de Thomas Jefferson, à Washington

Jehovah [dʒɪ'həʊvə] *pr n* Jéhovah

▸▸ ***Jehovah's Witness*** témoin *m* de Jéhovah

jejune [dʒɪ'dʒuːn] *adj Literary* (**a**) *(puerile)* naïf, puéril (**b**) *(dull)* ennuyeux, morne; *(unrewarding)* ingrat

jejunostomy [dʒɪˌdʒuː'nɒstəmɪ] *(pl* **jejunostomies***)* *n Med* jéjunostomie *f*

jejunum [dʒɪ'dʒuːnəm] *n Anat* jéjunum *m*

Jekyll and Hyde [ˌdʒekələnd'haɪd] *n* **he's a real Jekyll and Hyde** c'est un véritable docteur Jekyll; **to have a Jekyll and Hyde personality** faire un dédoublement de la personnalité

jell [dʒel] **1** *vi* (**a**) *(idea, plan → take shape)* prendre forme *ou* tournure, se cristalliser; *(team)* se souder (**b**) *(jellify)* se gélifier

2 *n Am Fam* = **jelly**

jellied ['dʒelɪd] *adj Culin* en gelée

Jell-o® ['dʒeləʊ] *n Am Culin (dessert)* ≃ gelée *f*

jelly ['dʒelɪ] *(pl* **jellies**, *pt & pp* **jellied***)* **1** *n* (**a**) *(gen)* gelée *f*; **my legs feel like jelly** j'ai les jambes en coton *ou* comme du coton; **my legs just turned to jelly** j'en ai eu les jambes coupées, je n'avais plus de jambes (**b**) *Br Culin (dessert)* ≃ gelée *f* (**c**) *Am Culin (jam)* confiture *f* (**d**) *Fam Mil slang (gelignite)* gélignite❑ *f* (**e**) *Br Fam Drugs slang* gélule *f* de Temazepam❑

2 *vt* gélifier

▸▸ *Br* ***jelly baby*** bonbon *m* gélifié *(en forme de bébé)*; ***jelly bag*** poche *f* à gelée *(dans laquelle on presse les fruits)*; ***jelly bean*** dragée *f* à la gelée de sucre *(en forme de haricot)*; *Am* ***jelly roll*** (gâteau *m*) roulé *m*

jellyfish ['dʒelɪfɪʃ] *(pl* **inv** *or* **jellyfishes***)* *n* méduse *f*

jemmy ['dʒemɪ] *(pl* **jemmies**, *pt & pp* **jemmied***)* *Br*

1 *n* pince-monseigneur *f*

2 *vt* **to jemmy a door (open)** forcer une porte avec une pince-monseigneur

Jena glass ['jeɪnə-] *n* verre *m* d'Iéna

jennet ['dʒenɪt] *n* (**a**) *(horse)* genet *m* (**b**) *(donkey)* ânesse *f*

jenny ['dʒenɪ] *(pl* **jennies***)* *n* (**a**) *(female of bird or animal)* **jenny wren** roitelet *m* femelle; **jenny (ass)** ânesse *f* (**b**) *(machine)* jenny *f*

jeopardize, -ise ['dʒepədaɪz] *vt (health, future, life)* compromettre, mettre en danger *ou* en péril; *(chances, career)* compromettre; *(one's business)* laisser péricliter

jeopardy ['dʒepədɪ] *n* danger *m*, péril *m*; **our future is in jeopardy** notre avenir est en péril *ou* menacé *ou* compromis; **his business is in jeopardy** son affaire périclite; **to put sb in jeopardy** mettre qn en danger *ou* en péril

Jerba = **Djerba**
jerbil = **gerbil**
jerboa [dʒɜː'bəʊə] *n Zool* gerboise *f*
jeremiad [ˌdʒerɪ'maɪəd] *n Literary* jérémiade *f*, lamentation *f*
Jeremiah [ˌdʒerɪ'maɪə] **1** *pr n Bible* Jérémie
  2 *n Fig* prophète *m* de malheur
Jericho ['dʒerɪkəʊ] *n* Jéricho
jerk[1] [dʒɜːk] **1** *vt* (**a**) *(pull)* tirer d'un coup sec, tirer brusquement; **the door was jerked open** la porte s'ouvrit brusquement *ou* d'un coup sec
  (**b**) *(shake)* secouer
  2 *vi* (**a**) *(jolt)* cahoter, tressauter; **the train began to jerk violently** le train se mit à cahoter *ou* bringuebaler dans tous les sens; **to jerk to a halt** s'arrêter en cahotant
  (**b**) *(person → jump)* sursauter; **to jerk awake** se réveiller en sursaut
  (**c**) *(person, muscle → twitch)* se contracter; **her hand jerked up instinctively** instinctivement, elle leva la main
  3 *n* (**a**) *(bump)* secousse *f*, saccade *f*; **the train came to a halt with a jerk** le train s'arrêta brutalement; **she gave the rope a jerk** elle a donné une secousse à la corde, elle a tiré d'un coup sec sur la corde
  (**b**) *(wrench)* coup *m* sec; **she gave the handle a jerk** elle a tiré d'un coup sec sur la poignée
  (**c**) *(brusque movement)* mouvement *m* brusque; **with a jerk of his head he indicated that I should leave** d'un brusque signe de la tête, il me fit comprendre qu'il me fallait partir; **to wake up with a jerk** se réveiller en sursaut
  (**d**) *very Fam (person)* abruti(e) *m,f*, crétin(e) *m,f*
  (**e**) *(in weightlifting)* jeté *m*
►**jerk off** *Vulg* **1** *vt sep* **to jerk sb off** branler qn
  2 *vi* se branler, se palucher
jerk[2] *Culin* **1** *n* viande *f* séchée; **beef jerk** bœuf *m* séché
  2 *adj* **jerk chicken/pork** = poulet/porc roulé dans des épices puis cuit au four, spécialité des Caraïbes
jerkily ['dʒɜːkɪlɪ] *adv (move)* par saccades, par à-coups; *(walk)* d'un pas saccadé; *(write, speak)* d'une manière saccadée *ou* hachée
jerkin ['dʒɜːkɪn] *n* blouson *m*; *Hist* pourpoint *m*
jerkiness ['dʒɜːkɪnɪs] *n* (**a**) *(of style)* caractère *m* haché *ou* heurté (**b**) **the jerkiness of his movements was due to his illness** ses mouvements saccadés étaient dus à sa maladie
jerkoff ['dʒɜːkɒf] *n Vulg (person)* connard (connasse) *m,f*
jerkwater ['dʒɜːkwɔːtə(r)] *adj Am Fam* (**a**) *(remote)* éloigné ❑, perdu ❑ (**b**) *(inferior, unimportant)* piètre ❑, méprisable ❑; **a jerkwater show** un piètre spectacle
  ►► ***jerkwater politician*** politicien *m* méprisable ❑; ***jerkwater town*** trou *m*, bled *m*; ***jerkwater train*** train *m* de petite ligne ❑
jerky ['dʒɜːkɪ] (*compar* **jerkier**, *superl* **jerkiest**) **1** *n* viande *f* séchée; **beef jerky** bœuf *m* séché
  2 *adj* (**a**) *(movement)* saccadé; *(voice, style, speech)* saccadé, heurté, haché; **a jerky ride** un trajet cahotant; **in jerky French** dans un français heurté *ou* haché; *Fig* **we got off to a jerky start** nos débuts ont été houleux (**b**) *Am very Fam (stupid)* débile
[illegible]
jeroboam [ˌdʒerə'bəʊəm] *n* jéroboam *m*
Jerry ['dʒerɪ] (*pl* **Jerries**) *n Fam Old-fashioned Pej (German)* Fritz *m*, Boche *m*; *(the Germans)* les Boches *mpl*
jerry ['dʒerɪ] (*pl* **jerries**) *n Br Fam* pot *m* de chambre ❑
  ►► ***jerry can*** jerrican *m*, jerrycan *m*
jerry-builder *n Pej* = marchand de biens peu scrupuleux qui fait construire des maisons de mauvaise qualité
jerry-built *adj Pej (house, building)* construit en carton-pâte, peu solide
Jersey ['dʒɜːzɪ] *n* (**a**) *Geog* Jersey *f*; **in Jersey** à Jersey (**b**) *Am Fam (New Jersey)* New Jersey ❑ *m*; **in Jersey** dans le New Jersey (**c**) *(cow)* vache *f* de Jersey *ou* jersiaise
jersey ['dʒɜːzɪ] *n* (**a**) *(pullover)* pull-over *m*, tricot *m*; *Sport* maillot *m* (**b**) *(fabric)* jersey *m*
Jerusalem [dʒə'ruːsələm] *n* Jérusalem
  ►► ***Jerusalem artichoke*** topinambour *m*

jess [dʒes] *n (for falcon)* jet *m*
jessamine ['dʒesəmɪn] *n Bot* jasmin *m*
jessie ['dʒesɪ] *n Scot Fam* femmelette *f*
jest [dʒest] **1** *n* plaisanterie *f*; *(witty remark)* mot *m* d'esprit; **to say sth in jest** dire qch pour rire *ou* pour plaisanter; **(only) half in jest** en ne plaisantant qu'à moitié; **to act in jest** plaisanter; *Prov* **there's many a true word spoken in jest** = on dit souvent la vérité sous le couvert d'une plaisanterie
  2 *vi* plaisanter
jester ['dʒestə(r)] *n Hist* bouffon *m*, fou *m* (du roi); *(joker)* farceur(euse) *m,f*
jesting ['dʒestɪŋ] **1** *n (jokes)* plaisanteries *fpl*; *(witty remarks)* mots *mpl* d'esprit
  2 *adj (remark)* fait pour plaisanter *ou* pour rire
jestingly ['dʒestɪŋlɪ] *adv* en plaisantant; **jestingly known as...** désigné par le terme farceur de...
Jesuit ['dʒezjʊɪt] **1** *n* jésuite *m*
  2 *adj* jésuite; *(college, seminary)* de jésuites
  ►► ***Jesuit priest*** prêtre *m* jésuite
jesuitical [ˌdʒezjʊ'ɪtɪkəl] *adj* jésuitique
jesuitism ['dʒezjʊɪˌtɪzəm] *n* jésuitisme *m*
jesuitry ['dʒezjʊɪtrɪ] *n Pej* jésuitisme *m*
Jesus ['dʒiːzəs] **1** *pr n* Jésus; **Jesus Christ** Jésus-Christ
  2 *exclam Fam* **Jesus (Christ)!** nom de Dieu!; *Br* **Jesus wept!** bon sang!; *Am* **Jesus H. Christ!** nom de Dieu!
  ►► *Br Fam* ***Jesus creepers*** sandales ❑ *fpl*; *Fam* ***Jesus freak*** chrétien(enne) *m,f* hippie; ***the Jesus movement*** = mouvement chrétien pratiquant le prosélytisme
jet[1] [dʒet] (*pt & pp* **jetted**, *cont* **jetting**) **1** *n* (**a**) *(aircraft)* avion *m* à réaction, jet *m*; **to travel by jet** voyager en jet *ou* en avion à réaction; *Am Fam* **cool your jets!** du calme!
  (**b**) *(stream → of liquid)* jet *m*, giclée *f*; *(→ of gas, steam)* jet *m*
  (**c**) *(nozzle)* jet *m*, ajutage *m*, buse *f*; *(on printer)* buse *f*; *(of stove)* brûleur *m*; *Aut* gicleur *m*; **(water) jet** *(in whirlpool, bath etc)* gicleur *m*
  2 *comp (fighter, bomber)* à réaction; *(transport, travel)* en avion (à réaction)
  3 *vi* (**a**) *Fam (travel by jet)* voyager en avion (à réaction) ❑; **they jetted (over) to Paris for the weekend** ils ont pris l'avion pour passer le week-end à Paris ❑
  (**b**) *(liquid)* gicler, jaillir
  4 *vt* (**a**) *(transport by jet)* transporter par avion (à réaction); **supplies are being jetted into** *or* **to the disaster area** des avions apportent des vivres à la zone sinistrée
  (**b**) *(direct → liquid)* faire gicler
  ►► *Aviat* ***jet-assisted take-off*** décollage *m* (avec fusées), JATO; ***jet engine*** moteur *m* à réaction; ***jet fuel*** kérosène *m*; ***jet plane*** avion *m* à réaction; ***jet propulsion*** propulsion *f* par réaction; *Fam* ***jet set*** jet-set *m ou f*; **he's part of the jet set now** il fait partie du *ou* de la jet-set; ***jet stream*** jet-stream *m*, courant-jet *m*; ***jet trail*** traînée *f* de condensation
►**jet in** *vi* arriver par avion
►**jet off** *vi* s'envoler (**to** pour)
jet[2] **1** *n* (**a**) *Miner* jais *m* (**b**) *(colour)* noir *m* de jais
  2 *comp (necklace, earrings)* de *ou* en jais
  3 *adj (colour)* noir comme (du) jais, (noir) de jais
  ►► ***jet black*** noir *m* de jais
jet-black *adj* jais *(inv)*, noir de jais
jetfoil ['dʒetfɔɪl] *n* hydroglisseur *m*
jetlag ['dʒetlæg] *n* fatigue *f* due au décalage horaire; **I'm still suffering from jetlag** je suis encore sous le coup du décalage horaire
jetlagged ['dʒetlægd] *adj* fatigué par le décalage horaire; **I'm still a bit jetlagged** je ne suis pas complètement remis du décalage horaire
jetliner ['dʒetlaɪnə(r)] *n* avion *m* de ligne
jet-powered [-paʊəd], **jet-propelled** [-prə'peld] *adj (engine, aircraft)* à réaction
jetsam ['dʒetsəm] *n (UNCOUNT)* objets *mpl* jetés à la mer
jet-setter *n Fam* membre *m* du jet-set
jetski ['dʒetskiː] *n* scooter *m* des mers, jet-ski *m*
jet-skiing *n* scooter *m* des mers, jet-ski *m*
jettison ['dʒetɪsən] *vt* (**a**) *Naut* jeter à la mer, jeter par-dessus bord; *Aviat (bombs, cargo)* larguer (**b**) *Fig (unwanted possession)* se débarrasser de; *(theory, hope)* abandonner

jetty ['dʒetɪ] (*pl* **jetties**) *n (landing stage)* embarcadère *m*, débarcadère *m*; *(breakwater)* jetée *f*, môle *m*
Jew [dʒuː] *n* (**a**) Juif(ive) *m,f* (**b**) *Fam Old-fashioned Pej (miser)* Juif *m*; **don't be such a Jew!** ne sois pas si radin!

'The Jew of Malta' *Marlowe* 'Le Juif de Malte'

Jew-baiting [-'beɪtɪŋ] *n* persécution *f* des Juifs
jewel ['dʒuːəl] *n* (**a**) *(precious stone)* bijou *m*, joyau *m*, pierre *f* précieuse; *(in watch)* rubis *m*; **a three-jewel wristwatch** une montre trois rubis (**b**) *Fig (person, thing)* bijou *m*, perle *f*; **the new receptionist is an absolute jewel** la nouvelle réceptionniste est une vraie perle
  ►► ***jewel box*** coffret *m* à bijoux; ***jewel case*** *(for gems)* coffret *m* à bijoux; *(for compact disc)* coffret *m*
jeweled, jeweler *etc Am* = **jewelled, jeweller** *etc*
jewelled, *Am* **jeweled** ['dʒuːəld] *adj* orné de bijoux; *(watch)* monté sur rubis
jeweller, *Am* **jeweler** ['dʒuːələ(r)] *n (person)* bijoutier(ère) *m,f*, joaillier(ère) *m,f*; **jeweller's (shop)** bijouterie *f*
  ►► ***jeweller's shop*** bijouterie *f*
jewellery, *Am* **jewelry** ['dʒuːəlrɪ] *n (UNCOUNT)* bijoux *mpl*; **a piece of jewellery** un bijou
Jewess ['dʒuːɪs] *n* Juive *f*
Jewish ['dʒuːɪʃ] *adj* juif
  ►► ***the Jewish calendar*** le calendrier juif; ***Jewish New Year*** nouvel an *m* juif
Jewry ['dʒʊərɪ] *n (Jews collectively)* la communauté juive
jew's-harp *n* guimbarde *f*
Jezebel ['dʒezəˌbəl] **1** *pr n Bible* Jézabel
  2 *n Literary or Hum* dévergondée *f*
JFK [ˌdʒeɪef'keɪ] *n* (*abbr* **John Fitzgerald Kennedy**) (**a**) *(person)* John Kennedy (**b**) *(airport)* aéroport *m* JFK *(de New York)*
jib [dʒɪb] (*pt & pp* **jibbed**, *cont* **jibbing**) **1** *n* (**a**) *Naut* foc *m*; *Fig* **I don't like the cut of his jib** *(look)* je n'aime pas son allure; *(manner, behaviour)* je n'aime pas ses façons de faire (**b**) *(of crane)* flèche *f*, bras *m*
  2 *vi Br (horse)* regimber; *(person)* regimber (**at sth** devant qch), rechigner (**at sth** devant qch); **to jib at doing sth** rechigner à faire qch
  ►► *Naut* ***jib boom*** bâton *m* de foc
jibe [dʒaɪb] **1** *n (remark)* raillerie *f*, moquerie *f*
  2 *vt (taunt)* railler, se moquer de
  3 *vi* (**a**) *Am Fam (agree)* s'accorder ❑, coller ❑ (**b**) **to jibe at sb** *(taunt)* railler qn, se moquer de qn
Jibouti = **Djibouti**
jibsail ['dʒɪbseɪl] *n Naut* marabout *m*
Jidda ['dʒɪdə] = **Jedda**
jiff [dʒɪf], **jiffy** ['dʒɪfɪ] (*pl* **jiffies**) *n Fam* **to do sth in a jiff** faire qch en un rien de temps *ou* en moins de deux; **I'll be back/there in a jiff!** je reviens/j'arrive tout de suite *ou* dans un instant! ❑; **half a jiff** une petite minute
Jiffy bag® ['dʒɪfɪ-] *n Br* enveloppe *f* matelassée
jig [dʒɪg] (*pt & pp* **jigged**, *cont* **jigging**) **1** *n* (**a**) *(dance, music)* gigue *f*
  (**b**) *Tech* gabarit *m*
  (**c**) *Fishing* leurre *m*
  (**d**) *Am very Fam (black person)* nègre (négresse) *m,f*, = terme raciste désignant un Noir
  (**e**) *Mining* crible *m* (pour minerai), classeur-pulsateur *m*
  (**f**) *Am Fam (idiom)* **the jig is up** c'est cuit
  2 *vt (shake)* secouer (légèrement)
  3 *vi* (**a**) *(dance)* danser allègrement
  (**b**) *Br* **to jig (around** *or* **about)** sautiller, se trémousser
jigaboo ['dʒɪgəˌbuː] (*pl* **jigaboos**) *n Am very Fam (black person)* nègre (négresse) *m,f*, = terme raciste désignant un Noir
jigger ['dʒɪgə(r)] **1** *n* (**a**) *(spirits measure)* mesure *f (42 ml)*; **a jigger of gin/whisky** un petit verre de gin/whisky (**b**) *(golf club)* fer *m* quatre (**c**) *(in billiards)* chevalet *m*, appui-queue *m inv* (**d**) *Naut* tapecul *m* (**e**) *Am Fam (thing)* machin *m*, truc *m* (**f**) *Br (flea)* chique *f*, puce-chique *f* (**g**) *Mining* crible *m* (pour minerai), classeur-pulsateur *m*
  2 *vt Fam (break → TV, machine etc)* bousiller

jer–jig

jiggered [ˈdʒɪgəd] *adj Fam* (**a**) *Br (exhausted)* crevé, vidé (**b**) *Br (as expletive)* **well, I'll be jiggered!** mince alors!; **I'm jiggered if I'll do it!** pas question que je le fasse! (**c**) *Fam (broken → TV, machine etc)* nase, déglingué, foutu; **my ankle/back is jiggered** je me suis niqué la cheville/le dos

jiggery-pokery [ˌdʒɪgərɪˈpəʊkərɪ] *n (UNCOUNT) Br Fam* micmacs *mpl*; **there's some jiggery-pokery going on** il se passe des choses pas très catholiques

jiggle [ˈdʒɪgəl] **1** *n* secousse *f*; **give it a jiggle** secoue-le un peu

2 *vt* secouer (légèrement); **you have to jiggle the key a bit to get it in** il faut tourner et retourner un peu la clef pour la faire entrer dans la serrure

3 *vi* **to jiggle (about** *or* **around)** être légèrement secoué; *(earrings)* se balancer; **try not to let it jiggle about** fais en sorte qu'il ne soit pas trop secoué; **I can feel something jiggling about** je sens quelque chose qui remue; **her breasts jiggle when she runs** ses seins ballottent quand elle court; **stop jiggling about!** arrête de gigoter!

jigsaw [ˈdʒɪgsɔː] *n* (**a**) *(game)* puzzle *m*; *Fig* **the pieces of the jigsaw were beginning to fall into place** peu à peu tout devenait clair (**b**) *(tool)* scie *f* sauteuse

►► ***jigsaw puzzle*** puzzle *m*

jihad [dʒɪˈhɑːd] *n* djihad *m*

jillaroo [ˌdʒɪləˈruː] *(pl* **jillaroos**) *n Austr Fam* bleue *f (dans une ferme)*

jilt [dʒɪlt] *vt (lover)* laisser tomber

Jim Crow [ˌdʒɪmˈkrəʊ] *n Am Fam* (**a**) *Old-fashioned Pej (black person)* nègre (négresse) *m,f*, = terme raciste désignant un Noir (**b**) *(policy)* politique *f* raciste □ (**c**) *(tool)* presse □ *f (à cintrer les rails)*

►► ***Jim Crow laws*** lois *fpl* ségrégationnistes

jim-dandy [dʒɪm-] *adj Am Fam* chouette

jimjams [ˈdʒɪmdʒæmz] *npl Fam* (**a**) **to have the jimjams** *(fear)* avoir les chocottes; *(revulsion)* avoir la chair de poule □; *(anxiety)* avoir les nerfs en pelote (**b**) *Br (pyjamas)* pyjama □ *m*

Jimmy [ˈdʒɪmɪ] *pr n SEng Fam (rhyming slang* **Jimmy Riddle = piddle**) **to have a Jimmy** pisser; **to go for a Jimmy** aller pisser

jimmy [ˈdʒɪmɪ] *(pl* **jimmies,** *pt & pp* **jimmied**) *Am* **1** *n* pince-monseigneur *f*

2 *vt* **to jimmy a door (open)** forcer une porte avec une pince-monseigneur

jimson weed [ˈdʒɪmsən-] *n Am Bot* stramoine *f*

jingle [ˈdʒɪŋgəl] **1** *n* (**a**) *(of bells)* tintement *m*; *(of keys etc)* tintement *m*, cliquetis *m*; *(of spurs)* cliquetis *m* (**b**) *(catchy tune)* ritournelle *f*; *(for children)* comptine *f*; *Rad & TV (in advertisement)* jingle *m*, *Offic* sonal *m*

2 *vt (coins, keys etc)* faire tinter *ou* cliqueter; *(bells)* faire tinter *ou* tintinnabuler

3 *vi (bells)* tinter, tintinnabuler; *(keys, coins etc)* tinter, cliqueter

jingo [ˈdʒɪŋgəʊ] *n Fam Old-fashioned* **by jingo!** crénom de nom!

jingoism [ˈdʒɪŋgəʊˌɪzəm] *n Pej* chauvinisme *m*

jingoist [ˈdʒɪŋgəʊɪst] *Pej* **1** *n* chauvin(e) *m,f*, cocardier(ère) *m,f*

2 *adj* chauvin, cocardier

jingoistic [ˌdʒɪŋgəʊˈɪstɪk] *adj Pej* chauvin, cocardier

jink [dʒɪŋk] **1** *n (movement)* esquive *f*

2 *vi* zigzaguer, se faufiler; *Sport* **he jinked through the defence** il s'est faufilé à travers la défense adverse

jinks [dʒɪŋks] *npl Fam* **high jinks** la rigolade; **we had high jinks** on a eu une séance de rigolade, on s'est bien marrés; **stop the high jinks!** trêve de rigolade!; **that's enough high jinks for today** assez rigolé pour aujourd'hui; *Ironic* **there'll be high jinks when my parents find out** ça va barder *ou* chauffer quand mes parents l'apprendront

jinni [ˈdʒɪnɪ] *(pl* **jinn** [dʒɪn]) *n* djinn *m*

jinx [dʒɪŋks] *Fam* **1** *n (person, object)* porte-malheur □ *m inv*, porte-guigne *m inv*; *(spell, curse)* maléfice □ *m*, (mauvais) sort □ *m*; *(bad luck)* guigne *f*; **to have a jinx** avoir la guigne; **to put a jinx on sb** jeter un sort à qn; **to put a jinx on sth** porter la guigne à qch; **there's a jinx on this car** cette voiture porte malheur □ *ou* la guigne

2 *vt* porter la guigne à; **to be jinxed** avoir la guigne

jism [ˈdʒɪzəm] *n* (**a**) *Vulg (semen)* foutre *m* (**b**) *Am Fam (energy)* ressort □ *m*

JIT [ˌdʒeɪaɪˈtiː] *adj (abbr* **just-in-time**) juste à temps, JAT

►► ***JIT distribution*** distribution *f* JAT; ***JIT production*** production *f* JAT; ***JIT purchasing*** achat *m* JAT

jitterbug [ˈdʒɪtəbʌg] *(pt & pp* **jitterbugged,** *cont* **jitterbugging**) **1** *n* (**a**) *(dance)* jitterbug *m* (**b**) *Fam (nervous person)* nerveux(euse) □ *m,f*

2 *vi (dance)* danser le jitterbug

jitters [ˈdʒɪtəz] *npl Fam* frousse *f*; **to have the jitters** avoir la frousse *ou* le trac; **to give sb the jitters** flanquer la frousse à qn

jittery [ˈdʒɪtərɪ] *adj Fam (person)* nerveux □; *(situation)* tendu □, délicat □; **he's always jittery before exams** il a toujours le trac avant un examen

jiu-jitsu [dʒuːˈdʒɪtsuː] *n* jiu-jitsu *m inv*

Jivaro [ˈhiːvərəʊ] *(pl* **inv**) *n* Jivaro *mf*

jive [dʒaɪv] **1** *n* (**a**) *(dance)* swing *m*

(**b**) *(slang)* **jive (talk)** argot *m (employé par les Noirs américains, surtout les musiciens de jazz)*

(**c**) *Fam Black Am slang (lies, nonsense)* baratin *m*, bla-bla *m*; **don't give me all that jive** arrête ton char

2 *vt Fam Black Am slang (deceive, mislead)* baratiner, charrier; **stop jiving him** arrête de le charrier

3 *vi* (**a**) *(dance)* danser le swing

(**b**) *Fam Black Am slang (fool around)* déconner; **stop jiving and get to work!** assez déconné, au boulot!

4 *adj Fam Black Am slang (phoney, insincere)* bidon *(inv)*

jive-ass *adj very Fam Black Am slang* à la noix

jizz [dʒɪz] *n* = traits distinctifs d'une espèce animale ou végétale

Jnr *(written abbr* **Junior**) **Michael Roberts Jnr** Michael Roberts fils

Joan of Arc [ˌdʒəʊnəvˈɑːk] *pr n* Jeanne d'Arc

Job [dʒəʊb] *pr n Bible* Job; **to have the patience of Job** avoir la patience d'un ange; **he's a real Job's comforter** *(adds to distress)* pour remonter le moral, tu peux lui faire confiance; **as poor as Job** pauvre comme Job

►► *Bot* ***Job's tears*** larme-de-Job *f*

JOB [dʒɒb]

travail	► **1 (a) – (c), (f)**
tâche	► **1 (a)**
emploi	► **1 (c)**
mal	► **1 (d)**
faire des petits travaux	► **2 (a)**
travailler à la tâche	► **2 (b)**

(pt & pp **jobbed,** *cont* **jobbing**) **1** *n* (**a**) *(piece of work, task)* travail *m*, tâche *f*; **the job took longer than expected** le travail a pris plus longtemps qu'on ne pensait; **to do its job** *(medicine, alcohol)* faire son effet; **to do the job** faire l'affaire; *Fig* **it's not perfect, but it does the job** ce n'est pas parfait, mais ça fait l'affaire; **if that ointment doesn't do the job** si cette pommade n'a pas d'effet; **to make a good job of sth** bien réussir qch; **she made a good job of fixing the car** elle s'en est bien sortie pour réparer la voiture; **it's quite a difficult job (to do sth)** c'est tout un travail (que de faire qch); *Fig* **to lie down** *or* **fall down on the job** *(avoid working)* tirer au flanc; **on a job** en déplacement; *Fam* **to be on the job** *(be having sex)* faire une partie de jambes en l'air; **this shelf isn't strong** *or* **good enough for the job** cette étagère ne tiendra pas le coup; **to do odd jobs** faire des petits travaux, bricoler à droite et à gauche; *Ind* **it's a precision job** c'est un travail de précision; *Fam* **the car has had a paint job** la bagnole a été repeinte; **he's done a good job of work** il a fait du bon boulot

(**b**) *(responsibility, duty)* travail *m*; **they are only doing their job** ils ne font que leur travail; **I was given the job of breaking the bad news** c'est à moi que la tâche est revenue *ou* c'est moi qui ai été chargé d'annoncer la mauvaise nouvelle; **it's my job to...** je suis chargé de..., c'est mon travail de...; **it's my job to remind her** c'est à moi de le lui rappeler; **that's not your job** ce n'est pas votre travail, ce n'est pas à vous de faire ça; **I make it my job to...** je me charge de...; **I'll have the job of clearing it all up later** c'est moi qui serai obligé de ranger *ou* qui devrai ranger tout ça plus tard; **this muscle has the job of...** le rôle de ce muscle est de...; **that's not part of his job** ça n'entre pas dans ses fonctions, ça ne fait pas partie de son travail *ou* de ses attributions

(**c**) *(employment, post)* emploi *m*, travail *m*; **to find a job** trouver un emploi *ou* du travail; **to look for a job** chercher un emploi *ou* du travail; **to be out of a job** être sans emploi *ou* sans travail; **what kind of job does she do?** qu'est-ce qu'elle fait comme travail?; **to create (new) jobs** créer des emplois, créer de nouveaux emplois; **she knows her job** elle connaît son travail *ou* son affaire *ou* son métier; **to give up one's job, to resign from one's job** démissionner; *Ind* **five hundred jobs were lost** *or* **axed** il y a eu cinq cents suppressions d'emplois, cinq cents emplois *ou* postes ont été supprimés; **it's more than my job's worth** ça serait risquer de perdre mon emploi, ça ne vaut pas la peine de perdre mon emploi pour ça; *Br Fam* **to give jobs to the boys** placer ses copains; *Br Fam* **it's jobs for the boys** les boulots vont directement aux copains

(**d**) *(difficulty, trouble)* **to have (quite) a job doing** *or* **to do sth** avoir du mal à faire qch; **it was quite a job getting her to come at all** ça a déjà été difficile de la convaincre de venir; *Fam* **she had the devil of a job doing it** elle a eu tout le mal du monde *ou* un mal de tous les diables *ou* un mal fou à faire cela; *Fam* **they've got a real job on their hands with that baby** ils ont du pain sur la planche avec ce bébé; **it's a job and a half** c'est un sacré boulot

(**e**) *Fam Crime slang (robbery)* coup *m*; **to do a job** monter un coup; **they did that bank job** ils ont monté le coup de la banque

(**f**) *Comput* travail *m*; **job control** gestion *f* des travaux

(**g**) *Fam (thing)* **that TV is a really nice job** cette télé, c'est du beau travail; **his car is the red job parked on the corner** sa voiture, c'est le bel engin rouge qui est garé au coin

(**h**) *Br Fam (excrement)* caca *m*; **the baby has done a big job** le bébé a fait un gros caca

(**i**) *Fig (phrases) Br* **it's a good job (that)...** heureusement que... + *indicative*, c'est heureux que... + *subjunctive*; *Br Fam* **he got what he deserved, (and) a good job too!** il a eu ce qu'il méritait, et c'est tant mieux *ou* c'est bien fait pour lui *ou* j'en suis très heureux!; **the make-up department did a good job (on him)** les maquilleurs se sont surpassés; **you've done a really good job** tu as vraiment fait du bon travail; **that's just the job** c'est exactement ce qu'il faut; **to give sb/sth up as a bad job** laisser tomber qn/qch qui n'en vaut pas la peine; **we decided to make the best of a bad job** nous avons décidé de faire avec ce que nous avions; *Fam* **to do a job on a car** *(wreck)* bousiller une voiture; *Fam* **to do a job on sb** *(beat up)* tabasser qn; **that journalist did a real job on him** ce journaliste l'a descendu en flammes *ou* l'a vraiment soigné

2 *vi* (**a**) *(do small jobs)* faire des petits travaux, bricoler

(**b**) *(do piecework)* travailler à la tâche *ou* à la pièce

(**c**) *Br Com* **he jobs in used cars** il revend des voitures d'occasion

3 *vt* (**a**) *Br St Exch* négocier; **she jobs government securities** elle négocie des fonds d'État

(**b**) *Am Fam (swindle)* arnaquer, truander; *(betray)* vendre

►► ***job analysis*** analyse *f* des tâches *ou* du travail; ***job assignment*** assignation *f* des tâches; ***job classification*** classification *f* des emplois; *Br* ***job club*** = association *f* d'aide aux personnes sans emploi; ***job creation*** création *f* d'emplois; ***job creation scheme*** programme *m* de création d'emplois; ***job description*** description *f* de poste; **that's not in my job description** ça ne fait pas partie de mon travail; ***job design*** conception *f* des tâches; ***job enrichment*** enrichissement *m* des tâches; *Admin* ***job evaluation*** analyse *f* des postes; ***job hunting*** recherche *f* d'un emploi; **to go/to be job hunting** aller/être à la recherche d'un emploi; ***job losses*** suppressions *fpl* d'emplois; *Br Com* **job lot** lot *m*; **a job lot of books** des livres en vrac, un lot de livres; **to buy/sell sth as a job lot** acheter/vendre qch en lot *ou* en vrac; ***job offer*** offre *f* d'emploi; ***job opportunities*** perspectives *fpl* d'emploi, débouchés *mpl*; *Br Comput* **job queue** file *f* d'attente des tâches; ***job satisfaction*** satisfaction *f* professionnelle; ***job security*** sécurité *f* de l'emploi; ***job sharing*** partage *m* d'emploi; ***job specification**, Fam **job spec*** description *f* d'emploi; ***job title*** titre *m* (de fonction)

▶**job out** *vt sep* sous-traiter; **they jobbed out the work to three different firms** ils ont confié le travail à trois sous-traitants

---

jobber ['dʒɒbə(r)] *n Br* (**a**) *St Exch* courtier(ère) *m,f* (en Bourse) (**b**) *(pieceworker)* ouvrier(ère) *m,f* à la pièce; *(casual worker)* journalier(ère) *m,f* (**c**) *Com (wholesaler)* grossiste *mf*

jobbery ['dʒɒbərɪ] *n (UNCOUNT) Br* (**a**) *Fam (intrigue)* micmacs *mpl*, trafics *mpl* (**b**) *St Exch* agiotage *m*, tripotage *m*

jobbing ['dʒɒbɪŋ] *Br* **1** *adj* **jobbing gardener** jardinier(ère) *m,f* à la journée; **jobbing tailor** tailleur *m* à façon; **jobbing workman** ouvrier *m* à la tâche

2 *n* (**a**) *(piecework)* travail *m* à la tâche (**b**) *(odd jobs)* bricolage *m*

Jobcentre ['dʒɒbˌsentə(r)] *n Br* = agence locale pour l'emploi, ≃ ANPE *f*

jobholder ['dʒɒbˌhəʊldə(r)] *n* salarié(e) *m,f*

job-hop *(pt & pp* **job-hopped,** *cont* **job-hopping***) vi Am* aller d'un emploi à l'autre

jobhunter ['dʒɒbhʌntə(r)] *n Br* demandeur *m* d'emploi

jobless ['dʒɒblɪs] **1** *adj* au chômage, sans emploi

2 *npl* **the jobless** les chômeurs *mpl*, les sans-emploi *mpl*

joblessness ['dʒɒblɪsnɪs] *n* chômage *m*

jobseeker ['dʒɒbsiːkə(r)] *n Br* demandeur *m* d'emploi

▶▶ ***jobseeker's allowance*** allocation *f* (de) chômage

job-share **1** *n* partage *m* du travail; **we could do it as a job-share** nous pourrions nous partager le travail; **they applied for the post as a job-share** ils se sont présentés pour le poste en proposant de se partager le travail

2 *vi* partager le travail; **we could apply to job-share** nous pourrions nous présenter en proposant de nous partager le travail

jobsharing ['dʒɒbˌʃeərɪŋ] *n* partage *m* du travail

jobsworth ['dʒɒbzwəθ] *n Br Fam* petit employé *m (qui invoque le règlement pour éviter toute initiative)*

Joburg, Jo'burg ['dʒəʊbɜːg] *n (abbr* **Johannesburg***)* Johannesburg *m*

Jocasta [dʒə'kæstə] *pr n Myth* Jocaste

Jock [dʒɒk] *n Fam* (**a**) *(Scotsman)* = terme injurieux ou humoristique désignant un Écossais (**b**) *(Scottish soldier)* soldat *m* écossais ❑

jock [dʒɒk] *n Fam* (**a**) *Am (athlete)* sportif ❑ *m* (**b**) *Horseracing (jockey)* jockey ❑ *m* (**c**) *(disc jockey)* disc-jockey ❑ *m*, animateur(trice) ❑ *m,f*

jockey [illegible] **(woman) jockey** femme *f* jockey

(**b**) *Am Fam (driver)* conducteur(trice) ❑ *m,f*; *(operator)* opérateur(trice) ❑ *m,f*; *Hum* **desk jockey** rond-de-cuir *m*; **elevator jockey** liftier ❑ *m*; **truck jockey** routier ❑ *m*

2 *vt* (**a**) *(horse)* monter

(**b**) *(trick)* manipuler, manœuvrer; **they jockeyed him into lending them money** ils l'ont adroitement *ou* habilement amené à leur prêter de l'argent; **to jockey sb out of a job** évincer *ou* chasser qn d'un poste

3 *vi also Fig* **to jockey for position** essayer de se placer avantageusement; *Fig* **the companies were all jockeying for position** toutes les entreprises essayaient de se placer

▶▶ ***jockey cap*** casquette *f* de jockey; ***the Jockey Club*** = organisme chargé de l'organisation des courses hippiques en Grande-Bretagne

Jockey shorts® ['dʒɒkɪ-] *npl* slip *m* kangourou

jockstrap ['dʒɒkstræp] *n* suspensoir *m*

jocose [dʒə'kəʊs] *adj Literary* facétieux

jocosely [dʒə'kəʊslɪ] *adv Literary* facétieusement

jocular ['dʒɒkjʊlə(r)] *adj* (**a**) *(jovial)* gai, jovial, enjoué (**b**) *(facetious)* facétieux, badin; **a jocular remark** une remarque facétieuse

jocularity [ˌdʒɒkjʊ'lærɪtɪ] *n (humour)* humour *m*; *(jollity)* jovialité *f*

jocularly ['dʒɒkjʊləlɪ] *adv (humorously)* facétieusement; *(with jollity)* jovialement; **he was jocularly known as "the Walrus" by his pupils** ses élèves lui donnaient le surnom facétieux du "Morse"

jocund ['dʒɒkənd] *adj Literary* gai, jovial

jocundity [dʒɒ'kʌndɪtɪ] *n Literary* jovialité *f*, gaieté *f*

jocundly ['dʒɒkəndlɪ] *adv Literary* jovialement, gaiement

Jodhpur [ˌdʒɒd'pʊə(r)] *n Geog* Jodhpur

jodhpur boots ['dʒɒdpə-] *npl* bottines *fpl* d'équitation

jodhpurs ['dʒɒdpəz] *npl* jodhpurs *mpl*

Jodrell Bank ['dʒɒdrəl-] *n* = observatoire astronomique dans le Cheshire

Joe [dʒəʊ] *n Fam* (**a**) *Am (man)* type *m*, gars *m*; **he's an ordinary Joe** c'est un mec comme les autres (**b**) *Am (GI)* soldat ❑ *m*, GI ❑ *m inv*

▶▶ *Br* ***Joe Bloggs**, Am & Austr **Joe Blow*** Monsieur Tout le Monde; *Am* ***Joe College*** l'étudiant *m* type ❑; ***Joe Public, Joe Schmo**, Am **Joe Six-pack**, Br **Joe Soap*** Monsieur Tout le Monde

joey ['dʒəʊɪ] *n Austr Fam* (**a**) *(kangaroo)* jeune kangourou ❑ *m* (**b**) *(child)* môme *mf*, marmot *m*

jog [dʒɒg] *(pt & pp* **jogged,** *cont* **jogging***)* **1** *n* (**a**) *(slow run)* jogging *m*; *Horseriding* petit trot *m*; **at a jog (trot)** au petit trot; **to break into a jog** *(person, horse)* se mettre à trotter; **to go for a jog** aller faire un jogging

(**b**) *(push)* légère poussée *f*; *(nudge)* coup *m* de coude

2 *vi* (**a**) *(run)* courir à petites foulées; *(for fitness)* faire du jogging; **she jogs to work every morning** tous les matins, elle va travailler en joggant

(**b**) *(bump)* se balancer; **his rifle jogged against his back** son fusil se balançait dans son dos

3 *vt (nudge)* donner un léger coup à; **she jogged my elbow** elle m'a poussé le coude; *Fig* **to jog sb's memory** rafraîchir la mémoire de *ou* à qn; *Fig* **to jog sb into action** inciter qn à l'action; **to jog sb out of it** secouer qn; **to jog sb out of their complacency** tirer qn de sa complaisance

▶▶ ***jog pants*** pantalon *m* de jogging; ***jog top*** *(sweatshirt)* sweat *m*; ***jog trot*** petit trot *m*

▶**jog along** *vi* (**a**) *Horseriding* trottiner, aller au petit trot (**b**) *Fig (person, factory, country etc)* aller tant bien que mal; *Fig* **I'm jogging along quite happily** je vais mon petit bonhomme de chemin; **my work is jogging along pretty steadily** mon travail avance assez bien

jogger ['dʒɒgə(r)] *n* jogger *mf*, joggeur(euse) *m,f*

▶▶ *Fam* ***jogger's nipple*** = irritation des tétons due au frottement contre les vêtements

jogging ['dʒɒgɪŋ] *n* jogging *m*; **to go jogging** faire du jogging; **to like jogging** aimer faire du jogging, aimer le jogging

▶▶ ***jogging** Br **bottoms** or Am **pants*** pantalon *m* de jogging; ***jogging suit*** jogging *m*

joggle ['dʒɒgəl] **1** *n* (**a**) *(shake, jolt)* secousse *f* (**b**) *Constr* cheville *f*, goujon *m*

2 *vt* (**a**) *(shake)* secouer (légèrement) (**b**) *Constr* fixer, assembler *(au moyen d'une cheville ou d'un goujon)*

3 *vi* cahoter, ballotter; **the truck joggled along the track** le camion cahotait sur la piste; **they joggled up and down in the back** ils étaient secoués *ou* bringuebalés à l'arrière

jog-trot *(pt & pp* **jog-trotted,** *cont* **jog-trotting***) vi* trottiner, aller au petit trot

Johannesburg [dʒə'hænɪsˌbɜːg] *n* Johannesburg

John [dʒɒn] *pr n Bible* Jean *m*; **the Gospel According to (Saint) John** l'Évangile selon saint Jean; **(Saint) John the Baptist** (saint) Jean-Baptiste

▶▶ *Hum* ***John Barleycorn*** = personnage symbolisant l'alcool, notamment le whisky; ***John Birch Society*** = organisation conservatrice américaine, particulièrement hostile au communisme, influente dans les années 50-60; ***John Bull*** John Bull *(personnification de la nation anglaise, du peuple anglais)*; *Am* ***John Doe*** *(average person)* l'Américain *m* moyen, ≃ Monsieur Dupont; *Fam (unidentified man → under arrest)* inconnu ❑ *m*; *(corpse)* mort *m* non identifié ❑; *Ich* ***John Dory*** saint-pierre *m inv*; *Am Fam* ***John Hancock, John Henry*** signature ❑ *f*, gribouillis *m*; **to lay one's John Hancock** = apposer sa signature au bas d'un document; ***John Lackland*** Jean sans Terre; ***John o'Groats*** = village d'Écosse qui marque le point le plus septentrional de la Grande-Bretagne continentale; *Am Fam* ***John Q. Public*** Monsieur *m* Tout le Monde; *Fam* ***John Thomas*** *(penis)* zizi *m*, zob *m*

john [dʒɒn] *n Fam* (**a**) *Am (lavatory)* waters ❑ *mpl*, W-C ❑ *mpl* (**b**) *(prostitute's client)* micheton *m*

johnny ['dʒɒnɪ] *(pl* **johnnies***) n* (**a**) *Br Fam Old-fashioned (man)* type *m*, gars *m*; **what does that inspector johnnie want?** ce type-là, l'inspecteur, qu'est-ce qu'il veut? (**b**) *Br Fam (condom)* **(rubber) johnny** capote *f*

▶▶ *Am & Austr* ***johnny cake*** crêpe *f*

Johnny-come-lately ['dʒɒnɪ-] *(pl* **Johnny-come-latelies** *or* **Johnnies-come-lately***) n Fam (newcomer)* nouveau(elle) venu(e) *m,f*; *Pej (upstart)* parvenu(e) *m,f*

Johnny Foreigner [ˌdʒɒnɪ'fɒrɪnə(r)] *n Fam Hum* étranger(ère) ❑ *m,f*; **Johnny Foreigner is interfering too much in our affairs** les étrangers se mêlent trop de nos affaires ❑

Johnny Reb [ˌdʒɒnɪ'reb] *n Am Fam Hist* soldat *m* confédéré ❑

johnson ['dʒɒnsən] *n Am very Fam (penis)* quéquette *f*

JOIN [dʒɔɪn]

adhérer à	▶ 1 (a)
s'engager dans	▶ 1 (a)
entrer dans	▶ 1 (a)
s'inscrire à	▶ 1 (a)
rejoindre	▶ 1 (b), (e)
se joindre à	▶ 1 (b)
joindre	▶ 1 (c)
unir	▶ 1 (c), (d)
raccorder	▶ 1 (c)
relier	▶ 1 (d)
devenir membre	▶ 2 (a)
se joindre	▶ 2 (b), (c)
se raccorder	▶ 2 (b)
s'unir	▶ 2 (c)
raccord	▶ 3
couture	▶ 3
joint	▶ 3

1 *vt* (**a**) *(political party, club)* adhérer à; *(armed forces, police)* s'engager dans; *(company, group, religious order)* entrer dans; *(class, course)* s'inscrire pour *ou* à; **join the army!** engagez-vous!; *Fig* **so you've been burgled too? join the club!** alors, toi aussi tu as été cambriolé? bienvenue au club!

(**b**) *(join company with, meet)* rejoindre; *(in activity or common purpose)* se joindre à; **I'll join you later** je vous rejoindrai *ou* retrouverai plus tard; **she joined the procession** elle se joignit au cortège; **I joined the queue at the ticket office** j'ai fait la queue au guichet; **to join one's ship** rallier son navire; **to join one's regiment** rejoindre son régiment; **will you join us?** voulez-vous vous joindre à nous?; **may I join you?** puis-je me joindre à vous?; **they joined us for lunch** ils nous ont retrouvés pour déjeuner; **will you join me for** *or* **in a drink?** vous prendrez bien un verre avec moi?; **why don't you join (us at) our table?** venez donc vous asseoir à notre table!; **we are joined in the studio by Bruce Johnson** Bruce Johnson vient nous rejoindre *ou* vient se joindre à nous dans notre studio; **he didn't want to join the dancing** il n'a pas voulu se joindre *ou* se mêler aux danseurs; **my wife joins me in offering our sincere condolences** ma femme se joint à moi pour vous adresser nos sincères condoléances; *Mil* **to join one's regiment** rejoindre son régiment; *Naut* **to join one's ship** rejoindre son bâtiment

(**c**) *(attach, fasten → planks, pieces of material)* joindre, unir; *(→ pipes, electric wires)* raccorder; *(→ edges of a wound)* rapprocher, réunir; **to join**

job–joi

(up) the two ends of a rope nouer les deux bouts d'une corde; **you have to join these two electric wires** il faut raccorder ces deux fils électriques; **the workmen joined the pipes (together)** les ouvriers ont raccordé les tuyaux; **the Siamese twins are joined at the thigh** les frères siamois sont rattachés (l'un à l'autre) par la cuisse

(**d**) *(unite)* relier, unir; **to be joined in marriage** *or* **matrimony** être uni par les liens du mariage; **to join hands** *(in prayer)* joindre les mains; *(link hands)* se donner la main; **we must join forces (against the enemy)** nous devons unir nos forces (contre l'ennemi); **she joined forces with her brother** elle s'est alliée à son frère; **to join battle (with)** entrer en lutte (avec), engager le combat (avec)

(**e**) *(intersect with)* rejoindre; **does this path join the main road?** est-ce que ce chemin rejoint la grand-route?; **we camped where the stream joins the river** nous avons campé là où le ruisseau rejoint la rivière

2 *vi* (**a**) *(become a member)* devenir membre

(**b**) *(planks, pieces of material)* se joindre; *(pipes, electric wires)* se raccorder

(**c**) *(form an alliance)* s'unir, se joindre; **they joined together to fight drug trafficking** ils se sont unis pour lutter contre le trafic de drogue; **we all join with you in your sorrow** *(sympathize)* nous nous associons tous à votre douleur

3 *n (in broken china, wallpaper)* (ligne *f* de) raccord *m*; *Sewing (in fabric)* couture *f*; *Tech (junction between elements)* joint *m*

▸**join in 1** *vi* se mettre de la partie, participer, prendre part; **she started singing and the others joined in** elle a commencé à chanter et les autres se sont mis à chanter avec elle

2 *vt insep* participer à, prendre part à; **she never joins in the conversation** elle ne participe jamais à la conversation; **he joined in the protest** il s'associa aux protestations; **all join in the chorus!** reprenez tous le refrain en chœur!

▸**join on 1** *vi* s'attacher; **where does this part join on?** où cette pièce vient-elle se rattacher?; **they joined on at the end of the parade** ils se sont mis à la queue du défilé

2 *vt sep* attacher, ajouter; **we got off the train while they were joining on more coaches** nous sommes descendus du train pendant que l'on accrochait de nouveaux wagons

▸**join up 1** *vi* (**a**) *(for armed forces)* s'engager; *(for class, course)* s'inscrire (**b**) *(planks, pieces of material)* se toucher, se joindre; *(pipes, electric wires)* se raccorder (**c**) *(meet)* **to join up with sb** rejoindre qn

2 *vt sep (planks, pieces of material)* joindre, assembler; *(pipes, electric wires)* raccorder; *(two machines)* accoupler

---

joined-up [dʒɔɪnd-] *adj* **can you do joined-up writing yet?** tu sais lier les lettres?

joiner ['dʒɔɪnə(r)] *n* (**a**) *(carpenter)* menuisier *m* (**b**) *Fam (member of many clubs)* **he's a real joiner** il est de toutes les bonnes causes ❑; **he's not really a joiner** il n'est pas très sociable ❑

joinery ['dʒɔɪnərɪ] *n* menuiserie *f*; **piece of joinery** article *m ou* pièce *f* de menuiserie

joining fee ['dʒɔɪnɪŋ-] *n Comput* frais *mpl* d'accès au service

joint [dʒɔɪnt] **1** *n* (**a**) *Tech* joint *m*, jointure *f*; *Carp* assemblage *m*; **(soldered** *or* **welded) joint** soudure *f*

(**b**) *Anat* articulation *f*, jointure *f*; **out of joint** déboîté; **to put one's shoulder out of joint** se démettre *ou* se déboîter l'épaule; *Fig* **the change in schedule has put everything out of joint** le changement de programme a tout chamboulé

(**c**) *Geol* diaclase *f*

(**d**) *Br Culin* rôti *m*; **joint of beef** rôti *m* de bœuf; **joint of lamb** *(leg)* gigot *m* d'agneau; *(shoulder)* épaule *f* d'agneau

(**e**) *Fam (cannabis cigarette)* joint *m*

(**f**) *Fam (night club)* boîte *f*; *(bar)* troquet *m*, boui-boui *m*; *(gambling house)* tripot *m*; **strip joint** club *m* de strip-tease

(**g**) *Am Fam (house)* baraque *f*; **nice joint you have here!** c'est pas mal chez toi!

(**h**) *Am Fam (prison)* taule *f*, placard *m*; **in the joint** en taule, à l'ombre

(**i**) *Am very Fam (penis)* pine *f*, bite *f*

2 *adj* (**a**) *(united, combined)* conjugué, commun; **to take joint action** mener une action commune; **thanks to their joint efforts...** grâce à leurs efforts conjugués...

(**b**) *(shared, collective)* joint, commun; *(contract → between two parties)* bilatéral; *(→ between more than two parties)* collectif

3 *vt* (**a**) *Tech* assembler, emboîter

(**b**) *Br Culin* découper aux jointures

(**c**) *Constr* jointoyer

(**d**) *Carp* varloper

►► *Comput* ***the Joint Academic Network*** = réseau Internet composé d'universités et d'organismes de recherche britanniques; *Banking* ***joint account*** compte *m* joint, compte *m* conjoint; ***joint agreement*** *(gen)* accord *m* commun; *Ind* convention *f* collective; ***joint author*** coauteur *m*; *Fin* ***joint beneficiary*** bénéficiaire *mf* conjoint(e); ***the Joint Chiefs of Staff*** = organe consultatif du ministère américain de la Défense, composé des chefs d'état-major des trois armées; ***joint commission*** commission *f* mixte; ***joint committee*** *(gen)* commission *f* mixte; *Ind* comité *m* paritaire; *Fin* ***joint creditor*** cocréancier(ère) *m,f*; *Law* ***joint custody*** garde *f* conjointe; *Fin* ***joint debtor*** codébiteur(trice) *m,f*; ***joint enterprise*** entreprise *f* en participation; ***joint heir*** cohéritier *m*; ***joint holder*** *(of record, trophy etc)* codétenteur(trice) *m,f*; *Br Univ* ***joint honours*** = licence portant sur deux matières; ***joint liability*** responsabilité *f* conjointe; ***joint management*** cogestion *f*; ***joint occupancy*** colocation *f*; *Br* ***joint owner*** *(of property)* copropriétaire *mf*; **to be joint owners of sth** *(car, shares etc)* posséder *ou* détenir qch en commun; *Br* ***joint ownership*** copropriété *f*; ***joint partnership*** coassociation *f*; ***joint passport*** passeport *m* conjoint; **we have a joint passport** nous sommes sur le même passeport; *Ins* ***joint policy*** police *f* conjointe; ***joint production*** coproduction *f*; ***joint property*** biens *mpl* communs; ***joint purchase*** coacquisition *f*; ***joint report*** rapport *m* collectif; *Am Pol* ***joint resolution*** ≃ projet *m* de loi; ***joint responsibility*** responsabilité *f* conjointe; **the project is their joint responsibility** le projet relève de leur responsabilité à tous les deux; ***joint statement*** déclaration *f* commune; *Fin* ***joint stock*** capital *m* social; ***joint tenancy*** location *f* commune; ***joint tenant*** colocataire *mf*; ***joint venture*** *(undertaking)* entreprise *f* commune; *Com (agreement)* coentreprise *f*, joint-venture *m*; *(company)* société *f* commune, société *f* en participation; ***joint venture agreement*** accord *m* de partenariat; ***joint venture company*** société *f* d'exploitation en commun

joint and several *adj*

►► *Fin* ***joint and several debtor*** débiteur *m* solidaire; ***joint and several guarantor*** garant *m* solidaire; ***joint and several liability*** responsabilité *f* solidaire et indivise

jointed ['dʒɔɪntɪd] *adj* (**a**) *Tech* articulé (**b**) *Culin (poultry)* découpé

jointer ['dʒɔɪntə(r)] *n* (**a**) *Constr (tool)* mirette *f* (de maçon), tire-joint *m inv* (**b**) *Carp* varlope *f*

join-the-dots *n Br* = jeu qui consiste à relier des points numérotés pour découvrir un dessin

jointing ['dʒɔɪntɪŋ] *n* (**a**) *(joining → of boards)* assemblage *m*; *(→ of pipes)* emmanchage *m*; (**b**) *Culin* découpage *m* (**c**) *Constr (of brickwork)* jointoiement *m* (**d**) *Carp* varlopage *m*

►► *Tech* ***jointing compound*** lut *m*, mastic *m*; *Carp* ***jointing plane*** varlope *f*; *Tech* ***jointing tape*** bande *f* de collure

jointly ['dʒɔɪntlɪ] *adv* conjointement; **to own/manage jointly** coposséder/cogérer; **the house is jointly owned** la maison est en copropriété; *Law* **jointly liable** coresponsable, conjointement responsable; *Fin* **jointly and severally** conjointement et solidairement

joint-stock *adj*

►► *Br Fin* ***joint-stock bank*** banque *f* de dépôt; ***joint-stock company*** société *f* (anonyme) par actions

jointure ['dʒɔɪntʃə(r)] *n Law* douaire *m*

joist [dʒɔɪst] *n* solive *f*

jojoba [həʊ'həʊbə] *n* jojoba *m*

joke [dʒəʊk] **1** *n* (**a**) *(verbal)* plaisanterie *f*, blague *f*; **to tell a joke** raconter une histoire drôle *ou* une blague; **to make a joke** faire une plaisanterie *ou* une blague; **he's always ready with a joke** il a toujours le mot pour rire; **to make a joke of** *or* **about sth** plaisanter sur *ou* à propos de qch; **he tried to make a joke of it** il a essayé d'en rire; **we did it for a joke** nous l'avons fait pour rire *ou* pour rigoler; **he didn't see** *or* **get the joke** *(didn't appreciate something funny)* il n'a pas trouvé ça drôle; *(didn't understand somebody's joke)* il n'a pas compris la plaisanterie; **he can't take a joke** il n'a pas le sens de l'humour; **it's gone beyond a joke** la plaisanterie a assez duré; **it's a private joke** c'est une plaisanterie entre nous/eux/elles; **what a joke!** *(how ridiculous)* quelle blague!; **the joke is that...** le comique de l'histoire, c'est que...; **the test was a joke!** *(easy)* ce test, c'était de la rigolade!; **that's** *or* **it's no joke!** *(not easy)* ce n'est pas de la tarte!; *(serious)* ce n'est pas de la blague!; **it was no joke climbing that cliff!** escalader cette falaise, ce n'était pas de la tarte *ou* de la rigolade!

(**b**) *(prank)* plaisanterie *f*, farce *f*, blague *f*; **to play a joke on sb** jouer un tour à qn, faire une farce à qn; **the joke is on you** la plaisanterie s'est retournée contre toi; **the joke is on me** je suis le dindon de la farce

(**c**) *(object of derision)* risée *f*; **their so-called planning is a joke** leur soi-disant planification est risible; **his staff just regard him as a joke** il est la risée de tous ses employés; **the new legislation is just a joke** la nouvelle législation est une plaisanterie; **this is turning into a joke** *(is getting annoying)* c'est en train de tourner à la farce

2 *vi* plaisanter, blaguer (**about** sur); **I was only joking** je ne faisais que plaisanter; **I'm not joking!** je ne plaisante pas!; **you must be joking!, you have (got) to be joking!** vous plaisantez!, vous n'êtes pas sérieux!; **Nicola's passed her driving test – you're joking!** Nicola a eu son permis de conduire – sans blague! *ou* tu veux rire?; **to joke about sth** se moquer de qch

joker ['dʒəʊkə(r)] *n* (**a**) *(funny person)* farceur(euse) *m,f*, blagueur(euse) *m,f*; *Pej (frivolous person)* plaisantin *m* (**b**) *(in cards)* joker *m* (**c**) *Fam (man)* type *m*, mec *m*; *(stupid person)* abruti *m*; **some joker has stolen my umbrella** il y a un abruti qui m'a piqué mon parapluie (**d**) *(clause)* clause *f* ambiguë; **the contract contained a joker** le contrat contenait une clause piège

jokey ['dʒəʊkɪ] *(compar* **jokier,** *superl* **jokiest)** *adj (person)* blagueur; *(mood, conversation etc)* jovial; *(remark)* moqueur; *(gift, novelty)* farfelu

jokily ['dʒəʊkɪlɪ] *adv* en plaisantant

joking ['dʒəʊkɪŋ] **1** *adj (tone)* moqueur, de plaisanterie; *(comment, response)* moqueur

2 *n (UNCOUNT)* plaisanterie *f*, plaisanteries *fpl*, blagues *fpl*; **the joking must stop** assez plaisanté *ou* blagué; **joking apart** *or* **aside** plaisanterie mise à part, blague à part

jokingly ['dʒəʊkɪŋlɪ] *adv* en plaisantant, pour plaisanter

joky = **jokey**

joliotium [,dʒɒlɪ'əʊtɪəm] *n Chem* joliotium *m*

jollies ['dʒɒlɪz] *npl Am Fam* **to get one's jollies (doing sth)** prendre son pied (à faire qch)

jollification [,dʒɒlɪfɪ'keɪʃən] *n (UNCOUNT) Fam (merrymaking)* réjouissances ❑ *fpl*

jollify ['dʒɒlɪfaɪ] *(pt & pp* **jollified)** *vt* égayer

jolliness ['dʒɒlɪnɪs], **jollity** ['dʒɒlɪtɪ] *n (UNCOUNT) (cheerfulness)* jovialité *f*, gaieté *f*; *(merrymaking)* réjouissances *fpl*

jolly ['dʒɒlɪ] *(compar* **jollier,** *superl* **jolliest,** *pt & pp* **jollied,** *pl* **jollies) 1** *adj* (**a**) *(person)* gai, joyeux, jovial; **what are you so jolly about?** qu'est-ce qui te met de si bonne humeur?

(**b**) *Br (enjoyable)* agréable, plaisant; **we had a very jolly time** nous nous sommes bien amusés; **jolly hockey sticks** = expression parodique utilisée en parlant d'une femme bourgeoise, éduquée dans une "public school", caractérisée par un enthousiasme débordant et une certaine naïveté

2 *adv Br* rudement, drôlement; **it's a jolly good**

thing he came c'est rudement bien qu'il soit venu; **jolly good!** formidable!; **and a jolly good job too!** et c'est tant mieux!; **a jolly good fellow** un chic type; **you'll jolly well do what you're told!** tu feras ce qu'on te dit de faire, un point c'est tout!; **it jolly well serves them right!** c'est vraiment bien fait pour eux!

3 *vt Br (coax)* enjôler, entortiller; **she jollied me into going** avec ses paroles enjôleuses, elle a fini par me convaincre d'y aller; **he'll come if you jolly him along a bit** il viendra si tu le pousses un peu

4 *n Fam Pej* voyage *m* aux frais de la princesse

►► ***jolly boat*** chaloupe *f*, canot *m*; ***Jolly Roger*** pavillon *m* noir, drapeau *m* de pirate

►**jolly up** *vt sep Br* égayer; **we jollied up the room with some posters** nous avons égayé la pièce avec des affiches

jolt [dʒəʊlt] **1** *vt* (**a**) *(physically)* secouer; **the passengers were jolted about in the bus** les passagers étaient secoués dans le bus

(**b**) *(mentally)* secouer, choquer; **to jolt sb into action** secouer (les puces à) qn; *Fig* **the nation was jolted into action by the news** cette nouvelle a poussé le pays à entrer en action; *Fig* **to jolt sb out of a depression** faire sortir qn de son état dépressif d'un seul coup; *Fig* **that jolted him out of his smugness!** ça lui a fait perdre sa belle suffisance d'un seul coup!

2 *vi* cahoter; *(plane)* être secoué; **the Jeep® jolted along the track** la Jeep® avançait en cahotant sur la piste; **to jolt forward** *(vehicle, train)* s'ébranler avec une secousse; **his head jolted forward/back** *(on impact)* sa tête a été rejetée en avant/en arrière; **to jolt to a stop** *(vehicle, train)* s'arrêter en cahotant *ou* avec des à-coups

3 *n* (**a**) *(jar)* secousse *f*, coup *m*; *(of vehicle)* cahot *m*, secousse *f*, à-coup *m*; *(of plane)* secousse *f*; *(of engine)* à-coup *m*, secousse *f*; **the fall gave his spine a jolt** dans sa chute, il a reçu un choc à la colonne vertébrale

(**b**) *(start)* sursaut *m*, choc *m*; **to wake up with a jolt** se réveiller en sursaut; **it gave me a bit of a jolt** ça m'a fait un choc *ou* un coup

jolting ['dʒəʊltɪŋ] *n (UNCOUNT) (of vehicle)* cahots *mpl*; *(of plane)* secousses *fpl*

Jonah ['dʒəʊnə] *n Bible* Jonas; *Fig (jinx)* porte-malheur *m inv*

Jonathan ['dʒɒnəθən] *pr n Bible* Jonathan

Joneses ['dʒəʊnzɪz] *npl Fam* **to keep up with the Joneses** vouloir faire aussi bien que le voisin, ne pas vouloir être en reste

jonquil ['dʒɒŋkwɪl] *n Bot* (petite) jonquille *f*

Jordan ['dʒɔːdən] *n* Jordanie *f*; **in Jordan** en Jordanie; **the (River) Jordan** le Jourdain

Jordanian [ˌdʒɔː'deɪnɪən] **1** *n* Jordanien(enne) *m,f*

2 *adj* jordanien

3 *comp (embassy)* de Jordanie; *(history)* de la Jordanie

Joseph ['dʒəʊzɪf] *pr n Bible* Joseph; **Joseph of Arimathea** Joseph d'Arimathie

Josephine ['dʒəʊzəfiːn] *pr n* **the Empress Josephine** l'impératrice *f* Joséphine

josh [dʒɒʃ] *Fam* **1** *vi* blaguer; **I'm only joshing** je plaisante

2 [illegible] (**about** sur), mettre en boîte (**about** à cause de)

3 *n* quolibet *m*, moquerie *f*

Joshua ['dʒɒʃʊə] *pr n Bible* Josué

Josiah [dʒəʊ'saɪə] *pr n Bible* Josias

joss stick [dʒɒs-] *n* bâtonnet *m* d'encens

jostle ['dʒɒsəl] **1** *vi* se bousculer; **they were jostling for seats** ils se bousculaient pour avoir des places; *Fig* **to jostle for position** essayer de bien se placer

2 *vt* bousculer, heurter; **she was jostled by the demonstrators** elle a été bousculée par les manifestants; **to jostle sb out of the way** écarter qn à coups de coudes *ou* en jouant des coudes; **to jostle one's way (through)** se frayer un chemin à coups de coude

3 *n* bousculade *f*

jostling ['dʒɒsəlɪŋ] *n (UNCOUNT) (of crowd)* bousculade(s) *f(pl)*

jot [dʒɒt] *(pt & pp* **jotted**, *cont* **jotting**) *n* **it won't change his mind one jot** ça ne le fera absolument pas changer d'avis; **there isn't a jot of truth in what he says** il n'y a pas un brin de vérité dans ce qu'il raconte; **it doesn't matter a jot** cela n'a pas la moindre importance; **not one jot or tittle** pas un iota

►**jot down** *vt sep* noter, prendre note de; **she jotted a few ideas down before the meeting** elle a rapidement noté quelques idées avant la réunion

jotter ['dʒɒtə(r)] *n Br (exercise book)* cahier *m*, carnet *m*; *(pad)* bloc-notes *m*

jottings ['dʒɒtɪŋz] *npl* notes *fpl*; **her private jottings** ses notes personnelles

joual [ʒwɑːl] *n Ling* joual *m*

joule [dʒuːl] *n Phys* joule *m*

►► ***Joule effect*** effet *m* Joule; ***Joule's law*** loi *f* de Joule

journal ['dʒɜːnəl] *n* (**a**) *(publication)* revue *f* (**b**) *(diary)* journal *m* intime (**c**) *Naut (logbook)* journal *m* de bord (**d**) *Acct (for transactions)* livre *m* de comptes, (livre) journal *m* (**e**) *Law* procès-verbal *m* (**f**) *Tech* tourillon *m*

►► *Tech* ***journal bearing*** palier *m* (de tourillon); ***journal entry*** écriture *f* comptable, contre-passation *f*

'A Journal of the Plague Year' *Defoe* 'Journal de l'année de la peste'

journalese [ˌdʒɜːnə'liːz] *n Pej* jargon *m* journalistique

journalism ['dʒɜːnəlɪzəm] *n* journalisme *m*

►► ***journalism college*** école *f* de journalisme; ***journalism diploma*** diplôme *m* de journalisme

journalist ['dʒɜːnəlɪst] *n* journaliste *mf*

journalistic [dʒɜːnə'lɪstɪk] *adj* journalistique

journey ['dʒɜːnɪ] **1** *n* (**a**) *(gen)* voyage *m*; **have a good journey!** bon voyage!; **it was quite a journey to get here** ça a été toute une épopée pour arriver jusqu'ici; **it is a two-day journey by car** c'est à deux journées de route en voiture; **to set out on a journey** partir en voyage; **to go (away) on a journey** partir en voyage; **she went on a journey to Europe** elle a fait un voyage en Europe; **to go on a train journey** prendre le train, voyager par le train; **the journey back** *or* **home** le (voyage du) retour; **to break one's journey** *(in plane, bus)* faire escale; *(in car)* faire une halte, s'arrêter; **to reach (one's) journey's end** *(arrive)* arriver à destination; *Fig (die)* arriver au bout du voyage; *Fig* **the journey into adulthood** le passage à l'âge adulte

(**b**) *(shorter distance)* trajet *m*; **a short tube journey** un court trajet en métro; **the journey to work takes me ten minutes** je mets dix minutes pour aller à mon travail

2 *vi Formal* voyager

►► ***journey time*** *(gen)* durée *f* du voyage; *(shorter distance)* durée *f* du trajet

journeyman ['dʒɜːnɪmən] *(pl* **journeymen** [-mən]) *n* (**a**) *(qualified apprentice)* compagnon *m*; **journeyman carpenter** compagnon *m* charpentier (**b**) *Arch (day-worker)* journalier *m*

journo ['dʒɜːnəʊ] *(pl* **journos**) *n Fam* journaleux(euse) *m,f*

joust [dʒaʊst] **1** *n Hist* joute *f*

2 *vi Hist* jouter (**with** contre); *Fig* batailler

jousting ['dʒaʊstɪŋ] *n (UNCOUNT) Hist* joutes *fpl*; *Fig (verbal)* joutes *fpl* oratoires

►► *Fig* ***jousting match*** joutes *fpl* oratoires

Jove [dʒəʊv] *pr n* Jupiter; *Br Fam Old-fashioned* **by Jove!** par Jupiter!

jovial ['dʒəʊvɪəl] *adj* jovial, enjoué; **she's in a jovial mood** elle est d'humeur joviale; **to feel jovial** être enjoué

joviality [ˌdʒəʊvɪ'ælətɪ] *n* jovialité *f*, entrain *m*

jovially ['dʒəʊvɪəlɪ] *adv* jovialement

Jovian ['dʒəʊvɪən] *adj* (**a**) *Myth* jupitérien (**b**) *Astron* jovien

jowl [dʒaʊl] *n* (**a**) *(jaw)* mâchoire *f* (**b**) *(hanging flesh on cheek)* bajoue *f*; **he had heavy jowls** il avait de grosses bajoues

-jowled [dʒaʊld] *suff* **a heavy-jowled man** un homme aux joues flasques

joy [dʒɔɪ] *n* (**a**) *(pleasure)* joie *f*, plaisir *m*; **to shout with** *or* **for joy** crier de joie; **she moved out, to the great joy of her neighbours** elle a déménagé, à la grande joie de ses voisins; **her grandchildren are a great joy to her** ses petits-enfants sont la joie de sa vie; **it was a joy to see him laughing again** c'était un plaisir de le voir rire à nouveau; **the joys of gardening** les plaisirs *ou* les charmes du jardinage; **full of the joys of spring** au comble du bonheur; **the joys of having children** les joies qu'apportent les enfants; **the joys of having a car** les joies d'avoir une voiture; **her style is a joy to watch** son style est un plaisir pour les yeux; **he's a joy to work for** c'est un plaisir de travailler pour lui; **our new car is a joy to drive** avec notre nouveau modèle, la conduite est un plaisir; **she's a joy to be with, it's a joy to be with her** c'est un plaisir que d'être à ses côtés; *Ironic* **oh joy!** ô joie!

(**b**) *Br Fam (success)* **they had no joy at the casino** ils n'ont pas eu de chance au casino; **any joy at the job centre?** tu as trouvé quelque chose à l'agence pour l'emploi?; **(did you have** *or* **get) any joy?** ça a marché?, tu as réussi?; **no joy!** ça n'a rien donné!, ça n'a pas marché!; **you won't get any joy from him** tu n'arriveras à rien avec lui

joybells ['dʒɔɪbelz] *npl Arch or Literary* carillon *m* (de fête); **the joybells were ringing** les cloches carillonnaient

Joycean ['dʒɔɪsɪən] *adj* de (James) Joyce

joyful ['dʒɔɪfʊl] *adj* joyeux, enjoué

joyfully ['dʒɔɪfʊlɪ] *adv* joyeusement

joyfulness ['dʒɔɪfʊlnɪs] *n* joie *f*, allégresse *f*

joyless ['dʒɔɪlɪs] *adj (unhappy)* triste, sans joie; *(dull)* morne, maussade

joylessly ['dʒɔɪlɪslɪ] *adv (unhappily)* tristement, sans joie; *(dully)* de façon morne

joyous ['dʒɔɪəs] *adj Literary* joyeux; *(news)* heureux

joyously ['dʒɔɪəslɪ] *adv Literary* joyeusement

joyousness ['dʒɔɪəsnɪs] *n Literary* joie *f*, allégresse *f*

joypad ['dʒɔɪpæd] *n Comput* joypad *m*

joypop ['dʒɔɪˌpɒp] *(pt & pp* **joypopped**, *cont* **joypopping**) *vi Fam Drugs slang* = prendre de la drogue sans devenir dépendant

joyride ['dʒɔɪraɪd] *(pt* **joyrode** [-rəʊd], *pp* **joyridden** [-rɪdən]) **1** *n* virée *f* (dans une voiture volée); **to go for a** *or* **on a joyride** faire une virée (dans une voiture volée); *Fig* **it's no joyride working with him** travailler avec lui, ce n'est pas une partie de plaisir

2 *vi* **to go joyriding** faire une virée dans une voiture volée; **they were had up for joyriding** ils ont été convoqués devant les tribunaux pour vol de voiture

joyrider ['dʒɔɪraɪdə(r)] *n* = personne qui vole une voiture pour faire un tour

joyrode ['dʒɔɪrəʊd] *pt of* **joyride**

joystick ['dʒɔɪstɪk] *n* (**a**) *Aviat* manche *m* à balai (**b**) *Comput* manette *f* de jeu, manche *m* à balai

JP [ˌdʒeɪ'piː] *n Br Law* (*abbr* **Justice of the Peace**) ≃ juge *m* d'instance

JPEG ['dʒeɪpeg] *n Comput* (*abbr* **Joint Photographic Experts Group**) (format *m*) JPEG *m*

Jr. (*written abbr* **Junior**) junior, fils

jubate ['dʒuːbeɪt] *adj Zool* à crinière

jubilance ['dʒuːbɪləns] *n Literary* réjouissance *f*, jubilation *f*

jubilant ['dʒuːbɪlənt] *adj (shouts)* de joie; *(expression)* épanoui, radieux; *(crowd)* exultant; *(party, celebration)* joyeux; **the Prime Minister was jubilant at the election results** le Premier ministre fut transporté de joie à la vue des résultats du scrutin; **the jubilant champion** le champion radieux

jubilantly ['dʒuːbɪləntlɪ] *adv* avec jubilation

jubilation [ˌdʒuːbɪ'leɪʃən] *n (UNCOUNT) (rejoicing)* joie *f*, jubilation *f*; *(celebration)* réjouissances *fpl*; **to be a cause for (great) jubilation** être l'occasion de (grandes) réjouissances; **scenes of jubilation** scènes de réjouissance

jubilee ['dʒuːbɪliː] *n* jubilé *m*; **silver/diamond jubilee** (fête *f* du) vingt-cinquième/soixantième anniversaire *m*

Judaea [dʒuː'dɪə] *n* Judée *f*; **in Judaea** en Judée

Judaeo-Christian [dʒuː'diːəʊ-] *adj* judéo-chrétien

Judaeo-Christianity [dʒuː'diːəʊ-] *n* judéo-christianisme *m*

Judaeo-Spanish [dʒuː'diːəʊ-] *n Ling* judéo-espagnol *m*

jol-jud

Judah ['dʒu:də] *pr n Bible* Juda

Judaic [dʒu:'deɪɪk] *adj* judaïque

Judaica [dʒu:'deɪɪkə] *npl (literature)* littérature *f* judaïque; *(objects)* objets *mpl* ayant trait à la culture judaïque

Judaism ['dʒu:deɪˌɪzəm] *n* judaïsme *m*

Judaize, -ise ['dʒu:deɪˌaɪz] *vt* judaïser; *(convert to Judaism)* convertir au judaïsme

Judas ['dʒu:dəs] **1** *pr n Bible* Judas; **Judas Iscariot** Judas Iscariote

2 *n (traitor)* judas *m*

▸▸ ***Judas kiss*** baiser *m* de Judas; ***Judas tree*** arbre *m* de Judée, gainier *m*

judas ['dʒu:dəs] *n (peephole)* judas *m*

judder ['dʒʌdə(r)] **1** *n* trépidation *f*; *(of vehicle, machine)* broutement *m*

2 *vi Br* vibrer; *(brakes, clutch)* brouter; **the bus juddered to a halt** le bus s'est arrêté en cahotant

Jude [dʒu:d] *pr n* Jude

Judea = **Judaea**

Judeo-Christian, Judeo-Christianity *etc* = **Judaeo-Christian, Judaeo-Christianity** *etc*

judge [dʒʌdʒ] **1** *n* **(a)** *Law* juge *m*; **Judge Jeffries** le juge Jeffries; **presiding judge** président *m* du tribunal; *Fig* **you can't just appoint yourself judge and jury** tu n'as pas le droit de décider sans consulter personne

(b) *(in a competition)* membre *m* du jury; *Sport* juge *m*; **the judges were divided** le jury était partagé

(c) *Fig* juge *m*; **a good judge (of)** *(of cars, horses, wine)* un/une spécialiste (en); **she fancies herself as a good judge of men** elle croit savoir juger les hommes; **I'm not sure he's the best judge of such things** je ne suis pas sûr qu'il soit très bon juge en la matière; **to be a good** *or* **keen judge of character** être bon *ou* fin psychologue; **I'll let you be the judge of that** je vous en fais juge, je vous laisse juge; **I will be the judge of that** c'est moi qui jugerai de cela

2 *vt* **(a)** *(pass judgment on, adjudicate)* juger; **the case will be judged tomorrow** l'affaire sera jugée demain; **a panel of critics judged the competition** le concours a été jugé par un panel de critiques; **the assistant referee judged him offside** le juge de touche a estimé qu'il était hors jeu; **don't judge him too harshly** ne le juge pas trop sévèrement

(b) *(consider)* juger, considérer; **she judged it her duty to protest** elle a considéré qu'il était de son devoir de protester; **her latest novel has been judged a failure by the critics** les critiques ont estimé que son dernier roman était mauvais

(c) *(estimate)* juger de, estimer; **can you judge the distance?** peux-tu évaluer la distance?; **I'd judge him to be about thirty** je lui donnerais la trentaine

3 *vi* juger; **who will be judging?** *(in competition)* qui va faire fonction de juge?; **if you don't believe me, judge for yourself** si vous ne me croyez pas, jugez-en par vous-même; **it isn't for me to judge** ce n'est pas à moi d'en juger; **you're in no position to judge** vous n'êtes pas en mesure d'en juger; **as far as I can judge** pour autant que je puisse en juger; **judging from** *or* **by what he said** si j'en juge par ce qu'il a dit; **to judge from** *or* **by her accent** à en juger par son accent, d'après son accent

4 Judges *n Bible* **(the) book of Judges** (le livre des) Juges

▸▸ *Mil* ***judge advocate*** assesseur *m (d'un tribunal militaire)*; *Mil* ***judge advocate general*** assesseur *m* général

judgment, judgement ['dʒʌdʒmənt] *n* **(a)** *Law & Rel* jugement *m*; **to pass judgment on sb** prononcer *ou* rendre un jugement sur qn; *Fig* **to pass judgment on sb/sth** porter un jugement sur qn/qch; **to sit in judgment on** juger; **to sit in judgment** *(court)* siéger; *Fig* **they have no right to sit in judgment over us!** ils n'ont pas le droit de nous juger!

(b) *(opinion)* jugement *m*, opinion *f*, avis *m*; **to give one's judgment on** donner *ou* exprimer son avis sur; **to form a judgment** se faire une opinion; **in my judgment** à mon sens, à mon avis; **to reserve judgment on sth** réserver son jugement *ou* opinion sur qch; *Fig* **we will have to reserve judgment on the new arrangements** nous devrons attendre avant de nous prononcer sur les nouvelles dispositions; **against my better judgment we decided to go** je pensais que c'était une erreur, mais nous avons quand même décidé d'y aller

(c) *(discernment)* jugement *m*; **he is a man of judgment** c'est un homme perspicace; **political/financial judgment** discernement *m* en matière de politique/finances; **to have/lack (good** *or* **sound) judgment** avoir du/manquer de jugement; **to have very sound judgment** avoir une grande sûreté de jugement, avoir un jugement très sûr; **this decision shows good judgment** cette décision montre du discernement; **to trust sb's judgment** s'en remettre au jugement de qn

▸▸ ***Judgment Day*** (jour *m* du) Jugement *m* dernier; *Mktg* ***judgment sample*** échantillon *m* discrétionnaire; *Mktg* ***judgment sampling*** échantillonnage *m* discrétionnaire

judgmental, judgemental [dʒʌdʒ'mentəl] *adj (person, book etc)* critique; **I don't want to seem judgmental, but...** je ne veux pas avoir l'air de critiquer, mais...

▸▸ *Mktg* ***judgmental forecasting*** prévision *f* par estimation; *Mktg* ***judgmental method*** méthode *f* estimative

judicature ['dʒu:dɪkətʃə(r)] *n Law* **(a)** *(judge's authority)* justice *f* **(b)** *(court's jurisdiction)* juridiction *f*; **court of judicature** cour *f* de justice **(c)** *(judges collectively)* magistrature *f*

judicial [dʒu:'dɪʃəl] *adj* **(a)** *Law* judiciaire; **to take** *or* **to bring judicial proceedings against sb** attaquer qn en justice **(b)** *(impartial)* impartial, critique; **a judicial mind** un esprit critique

▸▸ ***judicial inquiry*** enquête *f* judiciaire; *Am* ***judicial review*** *(of ruling)* examen *m* d'une décision de justice *(par une juridiction supérieure)*; *(of law)* examen *m* de la constitutionnalité d'une loi; ***judicial separation*** séparation *f* de corps

judicially [dʒu:'dɪʃəlɪ] *adv* judiciairement

judiciary [dʒu:'dɪʃərɪ] **1** *n* **(a)** *(judicial authority)* pouvoir *m* judiciaire **(b)** *(judges collectively)* magistrature *f*

2 *adj* judiciaire

judicious [dʒu:'dɪʃəs] *adj* judicieux

judiciously [dʒu:'dɪʃəslɪ] *adv* judicieusement

judiciousness [dʒu:'dɪʃəsnɪs] *n (of person, mind)* discernement *m*, bon sens *m*; *(of thought, remark)* caractère *m* judicieux

Judith ['dʒu:dɪθ] *pr n Bible* Judith

judo ['dʒu:dəʊ] *n* judo *m*

judogi ['dʒu:dəʊgɪ] *n* judogi *m*

judoist ['dʒu:dəʊɪst], **judoka** ['dʒu:dəʊkə] *n* judoka *mf*

Judy ['dʒu:dɪ] *(pl* **Judies***) n Br Fam Old-fashioned* pépée *f*

jug [dʒʌg] *(pt & pp* **jugged**, *cont* **jugging***)* **1** *n* **(a)** *Br (small → for milk)* pot *m*; *(→ for water)* carafe *f*; *(→ for wine)* pichet *m*, carafe *f*; *(large → earthenware)* cruche *f*; *(→ metal, plastic)* broc *m*; **a jug of wine** une carafe de vin; **wine jug** carafe *f* à vin; *Fam* **his ears are like jug handles** il a les oreilles en contrevent *ou* comme des esgourdes

(b) *Br (beer glass)* chope *f (contenant une pinte)*

(c) *Fam (jail)* tôle *f*, cabane *f*; **five years in (the) jug** cinq ans en tôle

(d) *Am (narrow-necked)* bonbonne *f*

(e) *very Fam* **jugs** *(breasts)* nichons *mpl*, roberts *mpl*

2 *vt* **(a)** *Culin* cuire à l'étouffée *ou* à l'étuvée

(b) *Fam (imprison)* mettre en tôle *ou* en cabane

▸▸ *Am* ***jug band*** orchestre *m* de folk/jazz *(jouant avec des instruments de fortune)*; ***jug kettle*** = bouilloire électrique haute; *Am* ***jug wine*** vin *m* ordinaire

jugate ['dʒu:geɪt] *adj Bot* conjugué

jug-eared *adj Fam* aux oreilles protubérantes ❑

jugful ['dʒʌgfʊl] *n* (contenu *m* d'un) pot *m*, (contenu *m* d'une) carafe *f*; **he drank a whole jugful of water** il a bu toute une carafe d'eau

jugged hare [dʒʌgd-] *n* civet *m* de lièvre

juggernaut ['dʒʌgənɔ:t] *n* **(a)** *Br (large lorry)* gros poids *m* lourd **(b)** *(force)* force *f* fatale; **the juggernaut of history** la force aveugle de l'histoire; **the juggernaut of war** le pouvoir destructeur de la guerre

juggins ['dʒʌgɪnz] *n Br Fam Old-fashioned (simpleton)* nigaud(e) *m,f*, cruche *f*

juggle ['dʒʌgəl] **1** *vi (as entertainment)* jongler; *Fig* **to juggle with sth** *(figures, dates)* jongler avec qch

2 *vt also Fig* jongler avec; *Fig* **he juggled all the different possibilities** il envisagea toutes les possibilités

3 *n* jonglerie *f*

juggler ['dʒʌglə(r)] *n* **(a)** *(entertainer)* jongleur(euse) *m,f* **(b)** *(deceitful person)* tricheur(euse) *m,f*

juggling ['dʒʌglɪŋ], **jugglery** ['dʒʌglərɪ] *n also Fig* jonglerie *f*

Jugoslav, Jugoslavia *etc* = **Yugoslav, Yugoslavia** *etc*

jugular ['dʒʌgjʊlə(r)] **1** *n* jugulaire *f*; *Fam* **to go for the jugular** attaquer qn sur ses points faibles ❑

2 *adj* jugulaire

▸▸ ***jugular vein*** jugulaire *f*

juice [dʒu:s] **1** *n* **(a)** *(of fruit, vegetables, meat)* jus *m*; **grapefruit juice** jus *m* de pamplemousse; **meat juice** jus *m* de viande

(b) *Biol* suc *m*

(c) *Fam (electricity)* jus *m*; *(petrol)* essence ❑ *f*; *Br (gas)* gaz ❑ *m*

(d) *Am Fam (spirits)* tord-boyaux *m*; *(wine)* pinard *m*

(e) *Am Fam (popularity, recognition)* succès ❑ *m*; **to have a lot of juice** faire un tabac

2 *vt (fruit)* presser

▸▸ ***juice bar*** = bar où l'on sert des jus de fruit; *Br* ***juice extractor*** centrifugeuse *f (pour faire des jus de fruit)*

▸**juice up** *vt sep Am Fam* **(a)** *(battery)* recharger ❑ **(b)** *(enliven)* égayer ❑, animer ❑ **(c)** *(intoxicate)* soûler; **he got juiced up on whisky** il s'est soûlé au whisky

juiced [dʒu:st] *adj Am Fam (drunk)* pété, bourré, beurré

juicehead ['dʒu:shed] *n Am Fam (alcoholic)* alcolo *mf*, poivrot(e) *m,f*

juicer ['dʒu:sə(r)] *n* **(a)** *(machine)* presse-fruits *m inv* **(b)** *Am Fam (alcoholic)* alcolo *mf*, poivrot(e) *m,f*

juiciness ['dʒu:sɪnɪs] *n* **(a)** *(of fruit)* **I chose these oranges for their juiciness** j'ai choisi ces oranges parce qu'elles sont juteuses **(b)** *Fam (of story)* piquant *m*

juicy ['dʒu:sɪ] *(compar* **juicier**, *superl* **juiciest***) adj* **(a)** *(fruit)* juteux; *(meat)* plein de jus, qui rend du jus; **a big juicy steak** un bon steak bien tendre **(b)** *Fam (profitable)* juteux; **a juicy deal** une affaire juteuse **(c)** *Fam (racy)* savoureux; **a juicy story** une histoire osée *ou* piquante; **let's hear all the juicy details** raconte-nous les détails croustillants

ju-jitsu = **jiu-jitsu**

juju ['dʒu:dʒu:] *n (charm)* amulette *f*

jujube ['dʒu:dʒu:b] *n (fruit)* jujube *m*; *(tree)* jujubier *m*

jukebox ['dʒu:kbɒks] *n* juke-box *m*

Jul. *(written abbr* **July***)* juill

julep ['dʒu:lɪp] *n* **(a)** *(soft drink)* boisson *f* sucrée **(b)** *(alcoholic drink)* **(mint) julep** = cocktail au bourbon et à la menthe **(c)** *Pharm* julep *m*

Julian ['dʒu:lɪən] **1** *pr n* **Julian the Apostate** Julien l'Apostat

2 *adj (relating to Julius Caesar)* julien, de Jules César

▸▸ *Geog* ***Julian Alps*** Alpes *fpl* Juliennes; ***Julian calendar*** calendrier *m* julien; ***Julian year*** année *f* julienne

julienne [ˌdʒu:lɪ'en] **1** *n (soup)* (potage *m* à la) julienne *f*

2 *adj* **julienne carrots/courgettes** julienne *f* de carottes/courgettes

Juliet ['dʒu:lɪet] *pr n* Juliette

Julius Caesar [ˌdʒu:lɪəs'si:zə(r)] *pr n* Jules César

'Julius Caesar' *Shakespeare* 'Jules César'

July [dʒu:'laɪ] *n* juillet *m*; *see also* **February**

jumbal ['dʒʌmbəl] *n Am Culin* = petit gâteau en forme d'anneau

jumble [ˈdʒʌmbəl] **1** *n* (**a**) *(confusion, disorder)* fouillis *m*, désordre *m*; **my things are all in a jumble** mes affaires sont tout en désordre; **a jumble of colours** un kaléidoscope de couleurs

(**b**) *(of thoughts, ideas)* méli-mélo *m*, fouillis *m*, fatras *m*; *(of words)* fatras *m*

(**c**) *Br (articles for jumble sale)* bric-à-brac *m*

(**d**) *Am Culin* = petit gâteau en forme d'anneau

2 *vt* (**a**) *(objects, belongings)* mélanger; **the pages got all jumbled** les pages se sont complètement mélangées; **her clothes were all jumbled (up** *or* **together) in a suitcase** ses vêtements étaient fourrés pêle-mêle dans une valise

(**b**) *(thoughts, ideas)* embrouiller; **his essay was just a collection of jumbled ideas** sa dissertation n'était qu'un fourre-tout d'idées confuses

►► *Br* ***jumble sale*** = vente de charité où sont vendus des articles d'occasion et des produits faits maison

jumbo [ˈdʒʌmbəʊ] *(pl* **jumbos***)* *Fam* **1** *n* (**a**) *(elephant)* éléphant ◻ *m*, pachyderme ◻ *m* (**b**) *(aircraft)* avion *m* gros porteur ◻, gros-porteur ◻ *m*

2 *adj* (**a**) *(giant-sized)* énorme ◻, géant ◻ (**b**) *Am Fin (loan)* géant ◻

►► *Fin* ***jumbo certificate of deposit*** certificat *m* de très grand dépôt ◻; ***jumbo jet*** avion *m* gros porteur ◻, gros-porteur ◻ *m*; *St Exch* ***jumbo trade*** opération *f* jumbo

jumbo-size, jumbo-sized *adj Fam* énorme, géant; **a jumbo-size packet of washing powder** un paquet de lessive familial

JUMP [dʒʌmp]

saut	► **1 (a), (d)**
bond	► **1 (a), (b)**
hausse	► **1 (b)**
obstacle	► **1 (c)**
prise	► **1 (e)**
sauter	► **2 (a), (c); 3 (a), (d)**
faire sauter	► **2 (b)**
bondir	► **3 (a)**
sursauter	► **3 (b)**
monter en flèche	► **3 (c)**

1 *n* (**a**) *(leap, bound)* saut *m*, bond *m*; **she got up with a jump** elle se leva d'un bond; *Fig* **we need to keep one jump ahead of the competition** nous devons garder une longueur d'avance sur nos concurrents; *Fam* **to have the jump on sb** avoir pris une longueur d'avance sur qn dès le départ; *Fam* **to get the jump on sb** devancer qn ◻; *Am Fam* **to be on the jump** être pressé *ou* débordé; *Fam* **go take a jump!** va te faire voir (ailleurs)!, va te faire cuire un œuf!

(**b**) *(sharp rise)* bond *m*, hausse *f*; **there has been a sudden jump in house prices** il y a eu une flambée des prix de l'immobilier; **inflation took a sudden jump last month** l'inflation a subitement augmenté le mois dernier

(**c**) *Horseriding (fence, obstacle)* obstacle *m*

(**d**) *Comput* saut *m*

(**e**) *(in board games)* prise *f* (de pion)

2 *vt* (**a**) *(leap over)* sauter; **to jump a fence** sauter *ou* franchir un obstacle; *Am* **to jump rope** sauter à la corde; **to jump a piece** *(in draughts)* prendre un pion; *Fig* **he jumped all the others in his field** il a dépassé tout le monde dans sa spécialité

(**b**) *(horse)* faire sauter; **she jumped her horse over the stream** elle a fait sauter *ou* franchir le ruisseau à son cheval

(**c**) *(omit, skip)* sauter; **to jump a line** sauter une ligne

(**d**) *Fam (attack)* sauter sur ◻, agresser ◻; **two men jumped him in the park** deux hommes lui ont sauté dessus dans le parc

(**e**) *Fam (leave, abscond from)* **to jump bail** ne pas comparaître au tribunal ◻ *(après avoir été libéré sous caution)*; *also Fig* **to jump ship** quitter le navire ◻; *Am* **the fugitive jumped town** le fugitif a réussi à quitter la ville ◻

(**f**) *(not wait one's turn at)* **to jump the queue** ne pas attendre son tour, resquiller; **she jumped the lights** elle a grillé *ou* brûlé le feu (rouge)

(**g**) *esp Am Fam* **to jump a train** *(not buy ticket for)* voyager sans billet ◻

(**h**) *Am Fam* **he jumped a (mining) claim** *(took illegally)* il s'est approprié une concession (minière) ◻

3 *vi* (**a**) *(leap)* sauter, bondir; **they jumped across the crevasse** ils ont traversé la crevasse d'un bond; **to jump back** faire un bond en arrière; **can you jump over the hedge?** peux-tu sauter par-dessus la haie?; **he jumped up, he jumped to his feet** il se leva d'un bond; **to jump to the ground** sauter à terre; **the frog jumped from stone to stone** la grenouille bondissait de pierre en pierre; **to jump for joy** sauter de joie; **she was jumping up and down with rage** elle trépignait de rage; *Fam* **jump to it!** grouille!; *Fam* **to jump down sb's throat** *(reply sharply to)* rabrouer qn, rembarrer qn; *(criticize)* engueuler qn; *Am Fam* **to jump all over sb** passer un savon à qn, engueuler qn; **let's wait and see which way she jumps** attendons de voir sa réaction, attendons de voir comment elle va réagir

(**b**) *(make a sudden movement → person)* sursauter, tressauter; *(→ record player, needle, chisel, drill)* sauter; **the noise made her jump** le bruit l'a fait sursauter; **when the phone rang his heart jumped** il tressaillit en entendant la sonnerie du téléphone; **this record jumps** ce disque saute; **we nearly jumped out of our skins** *(from surprise)* nous avons failli sauter au plafond; *(from fear, shock)* ça nous a fait un de ces coups

(**c**) *(rise sharply)* monter *ou* grimper en flèche; **prices jumped dramatically in 1974** les prix ont grimpé de façon spectaculaire en 1974

(**d**) *(go directly)* sauter; **he jumped from one topic to another** il passait rapidement d'un sujet à un autre; **to jump to conclusions** tirer des conclusions hâtives; **she immediately jumped to the conclusion that he was being unfaithful** elle en a immédiatement conclu qu'il la trompait; **I jumped to the third chapter** je suis passé directement au troisième chapitre; **the film then jumps to the present** puis le film fait un saut jusqu'au présent; *Comput* **to jump from one Web page to another** passer d'une page Web à une autre

(**e**) *Fam (be lively)* être très animé ◻; **by nightfall the joint was jumping** à la tombée de la nuit, ça chauffait dans la boîte

►► *Sport* ***jump ball*** *(in basketball)* entre-deux *m inv*; *Cin* ***jump cut*** faux *m* raccord, saut *m* de montage; *Br* ***jump jet*** avion *m* à décollage vertical; *Br* ***jump leads*** câbles *mpl* de démarrage; *Am* ***jump rope*** corde *f* à sauter; *Br* ***jump seat*** strapontin *m*; ***jump shot*** *(in basketball)* tir *m* en suspension

►**jump aboard** **1** *vt insep* (**a**) *(boat)* monter à bord de (**b**) *(campaign, bandwagon)* se joindre à

2 *vi* (**a**) *(get on boat)* embarquer

(**b**) *(join campaign, bandwagon)* **they've been campaigning for years but few people have jumped aboard** ça fait des années qu'ils font campagne, mais ils ont fait peu d'adeptes; **the anti-gun lobby received a boost when the State Governor jumped aboard** le lobby qui fait campagne contre les armes à feu a été très aidé par l'adhésion du gouverneur

►**jump about, jump around** *vi* sautiller; *Fig (story, film)* partir dans toutes les directions

►**jump at** *vt insep (offer, chance, suggestion)* sauter sur, saisir; **he jumped at the chance to go abroad** il sauta sur l'occasion de partir à l'étranger

►**jump in** *vi* (**a**) *(into vehicle)* monter; *(into water, hole, ditch)* sauter; **go on, jump in!** vas-y, monte!; **if you want a lift, jump in!** si tu veux que je te dépose, monte!; *Fig* **to jump in at the deep end** se jeter tête baissée dans les problèmes

(**b**) *Fam Fig (intervene)* intervenir ◻; **he jumped in to defend her** il est intervenu pour la défendre, il est venu à sa rescousse ◻

►**jump into** *vt insep* sauter dans; **she jumped into her car** elle a sauté dans sa voiture; **to jump into bed with sb** coucher avec qn tout de suite

►**jump off** **1** *vi* (**a**) *(leap → from wall)* sauter (**from** de); *(get off → from bicycle, bus, train, horse)* descendre

(**b**) *Horseriding* faire un barrage

2 *vt insep (leap from → wall)* sauter de; *(get off from → bicycle, bus, train, horse)* descendre de; **he jumped off the train** *(leapt from)* il a sauté du train; *(got off from)* il est descendu du train; **he jumped off the bridge** il s'est jeté du haut du pont

►**jump on** **1** *vt insep* (**a**) *(bicycle, horse)* sauter sur; *(bus, train)* monter dans; *(person)* sauter sur

(**b**) *Fig (mistake)* repérer; **the boss jumps on every little mistake** aucune faute n'échappe au patron; *Fam* **to jump on sb** *(reprimand)* passer un savon à qn

2 *vi (on to bicycle, horse)* sauter dessus; *(on to bus, train)* monter

►**jump out** *vi (from hiding place)* sortir d'un bond (**from** de); *(from high place)* sauter; *(from vehicle)* descendre (**of** *or* **from** de); **I'll jump out at the traffic lights** je vais descendre au feu rouge; **to jump out of bed** sauter (à bas) du lit; **to jump out of the window** sauter par la fenêtre; **to jump out of the bushes/one's hiding place** bondir d'entre les buissons/de sa cachette; **why did he jump out of the window?** pourquoi a-t-il sauté par la fenêtre?; *Fig* **the answer suddenly jumped out at me** la réponse m'a subitement sauté aux yeux

jumped-up [dʒʌmpt-] *adj Br Fam Pej* parvenu; **she's just a jumped-up shop assistant** ce n'est qu'une petite vendeuse qui se donne de grands airs *ou* qui se prend au sérieux

jumper [ˈdʒʌmpə(r)] *n* (**a**) *Br (sweater)* pull(-over) *m* (**b**) *Am (dress)* robe-chasuble *f* (**c**) *(person)* sauteur(euse) *m,f* (**d**) *Comput (pin)* cavalier *m*

►► *Am* ***jumper cables*** câbles *mpl* de démarrage

jumpily [ˈdʒʌmpɪlɪ] *adv (nervously)* nerveusement

jumpiness [ˈdʒʌmpɪnɪs] *n (of person)* nervosité *f*; *St Exch (of markets)* instabilité *f*

jumping [ˈdʒʌmpɪŋ] **1** *n Horseriding* jumping *m*

2 *adj Fam (party, nightclub)* hyper animé

►► ***jumping bean*** pois *m* sauteur; ***jumping jack*** *(firework)* pétard *m* mitraillette; *(puppet)* pantin *m*; *Am* ***jumping rope*** corde *f* à sauter

jumping-off point, jumping-off place *n* point *m* de départ, tremplin *m*; *Fig* **his success could be a jumping-off point for a new career** sa réussite pourrait être le point de départ d'une nouvelle carrière

jump-jockey *n* jockey *m* d'obstacles

jumpmaster [ˈdʒʌmpˌmæstə(r)] *n Am Mil* moniteur(trice) *m,f* de parachutisme

jump-off *n Horseriding* barrage *m*

jump-start **1** *n* **to give sb a jump-start** *(by pushing or rolling car)* faire démarrer la voiture de qn en la poussant/en la mettant dans une pente; *(with jump leads)* faire démarrer la voiture de qn avec des câbles *(branchés sur la batterie d'une autre voiture)*; *Fig* **to give a jump-start to the economy** relancer l'économie

2 *vt* **to jump-start a car** *(by pushing or rolling)* faire démarrer une voiture en la poussant/en la mettant dans une pente; *(with jump leads)* faire démarrer une voiture avec des câbles *(branchés sur la batterie d'une autre voiture)*; *Fig* **to jump-start the economy** relancer l'économie

jumpsuit [ˈdʒʌmpsuːt] *n* combinaison-pantalon *f*

jumpy [ˈdʒʌmpɪ] *(compar* **jumpier**, *superl* **jumpiest***)* *adj* (**a**) *Fam (edgy)* nerveux ◻ (**b**) *St Exch* instable, fluctuant (**c**) *(fitful, jerky → style, gestures etc)* saccadé

Jun. (**a**) *(written abbr* **June***)* juin (**b**) *(written abbr* **Junior***)* junior, fils

junction [ˈdʒʌŋkʃən] *n* (**a**) *(of roads)* carrefour *m*, croisement *m*; *(of railway lines, traffic lanes)* embranchement *m*; *(of rivers, canals)* confluent *m*; *(in pipes)* embranchement *m*, jonction *f*, raccordement *m*; *Br* **junction 5** *(on motorway → exit)* la sortie 5; *(→ entrance)* l'entrée *f* 5

(**b**) *Elec (of wires)* raccordement *m*; *(between semiconductors)* jonction *f*

(**c**) *Formal (joining)* jonction *f*

►► *Br* ***junction box*** boîte *f* de dérivation

juncture [ˈdʒʌŋktʃə(r)] *n* (**a**) *Formal (moment)* conjoncture *f*; **at this juncture** dans la conjoncture actuelle, dans les circonstances actuelles; **at a crucial juncture** à un moment critique (**b**)

Ling joncture *f*, jointure *f*, frontière *f* (**c**) *Tech* jointure *f*

June [dʒuːn] *n* juin *m*; *see also* **February**

►► *Entom* ***June beetle, June bug*** hanneton *m*

Jungian ['jʊŋɪən] **1** *n* jungien(enne) *m,f*

2 *adj* jungien

jungle ['dʒʌŋgəl] **1** *n* (**a**) *(tropical forest)* jungle *f*

(**b**) *Fig* jungle *f*; **the world of business is a real jungle** le monde des affaires est une véritable jungle; **it's a jungle out there** c'est la jungle là-bas; **the jungle of tax laws** le labyrinthe du droit fiscal

2 *comp (animal)* de la jungle

►► *very Fam* ***jungle bunny*** nègre (négresse) *m,f*, = terme injurieux désignant un Noir; ***jungle fever*** *(UNCOUNT)* paludisme *m*; ***jungle fowl*** coq *m* sauvage; *Am* ***jungle gym*** cage *f* à poules *(jeu)*; *Br Fam* ***jungle juice*** gnôle *f*; ***jungle warfare*** combat *m* de jungle

'The Jungle Book' *Kipling, Reithermann* 'Le Livre de la jungle'

junior ['dʒuːnjə(r)] **1** *n* (**a**) *(younger person)* cadet(ette) *m,f*; **he is five years her junior** il est de cinq ans son cadet, il a cinq ans de moins qu'elle

(**b**) *(subordinate)* subordonné(e) *m,f*, subalterne *mf*

(**c**) *Br (pupil)* écolier(ère) *m,f (entre 7 et 11 ans)*; **she teaches juniors** elle est institutrice

(**d**) *Am Sch* élève *mf* de troisième année; *Am Univ* étudiant(e) *m,f* de troisième année

2 *comp Br (teaching, teacher)* dans le primaire; *Sport (event, team)* junior

3 *adj* (**a**) *(younger)* cadet, plus jeune; **to be junior to sb** être plus jeune que qn

(**b**) *(lower in rank)* subordonné, subalterne; **a junior member of staff** un employé subalterne; **he's junior to her in the department** il est son subalterne dans le service

(**c**) *(juvenile)* jeune

(**d**) *(small)* petit

4 Junior *n* (**a**) **Hudson Junior** *(the son)* Hudson fils *ou* junior; *(one of two or more brothers)* Hudson junior

(**b**) *Am Fam (term of address)* fiston *m*; **bring Junior with you next time** amène ton fiston la prochaine fois

►► ***Junior Chamber of Commerce*** *(in US)* = chambre de commerce pour jeunes entrepreneurs; ***Junior College*** *(in US)* = établissement d'enseignement supérieur où l'on obtient un diplôme en deux ans; *Br Univ* ***junior common room*** salle *f* des étudiants; ***junior doctor*** interne *mf*; ***junior executive*** cadre *m* débutant, jeune cadre *m*; *Am Univ* ***the junior faculty*** les enseignants *mpl* non titulaires; *Am* ***junior high school*** ≃ collège *m* d'enseignement secondaire; *Br* ***junior hospital doctor*** ≃ interne *mf*; ***Junior League*** = association américaine de jeunes femmes de droite; ***junior minister*** sous-secrétaire *m* d'État; ***junior miss*** *(clothes size)* fillette *f*; ***junior partner*** associé(e) *m,f* adjoint(e); ***junior portion*** *(in restaurant)* portion *f* enfants; *Br* ***junior school*** école *f* élémentaire *(pour les enfants de 7 à 11 ans)*; *Com* ***junior sizes*** petites tailles *fpl*; *Am Sch & Univ* ***junior year*** avant-dernière année *f*

juniper ['dʒuːnɪpə(r)] *n Bot* genévrier *m*

►► ***juniper berry*** baie *f* de genièvre; ***juniper oil*** essence *f* de genièvre

junk [dʒʌŋk] **1** *n* (**a**) *(UNCOUNT) Fam (poor-quality, worthless things)* pacotille *f*, camelote *f*; **this watch is a real piece of junk** cette montre, c'est vraiment de la camelote *ou* c'est de la vraie camelote; **all his so-called antiques were just a pile of junk** ses prétendues antiquités n'étaient en fait qu'un ramassis de vieilleries; **his latest film is utter junk** son dernier film est absolument nul *ou* un vrai navet; **she eats nothing but junk** elle mange que des saloperies

(**b**) *(UNCOUNT) (second-hand or unwanted goods)* bric-à-brac *m*

(**c**) *(UNCOUNT) Fam (stuff)* trucs *mpl*, machins *mpl*; **can you get your junk off the table?** tu peux enlever tes trucs *ou* ton bazar de la table?; **what's all that junk in the hall?** qu'est-ce que c'est que ce bric-à-brac *ou* ce bazar dans l'entrée?

(**d**) *(boat)* jonque *f*

(**e**) *(UNCOUNT) Fam Drugs slang* came *f*

2 *vt Fam* jeter (à la poubelle)[□], balancer

►► *St Exch* ***junk bond*** junk bond *m (obligation à haut rendement mais à haut risque)*; *Biol* ***junk DNA*** ADN *m* non génique; *Comput* ***junk e-mail*** messages *mpl* publicitaires; *Fam* ***junk food*** nourriture *f* de mauvaise qualité[□]; **their kids eat nothing but junk food** leurs gosses ne mangent que des cochonneries; ***junk heap*** dépotoir *m*; ***junk jewellery*** *(UNCOUNT)* bijoux *mpl* fantaisie; ***junk mail*** *(UNCOUNT)* courrier *m* publicitaire; ***junk room*** pièce *f* de débarras; ***junk shop*** magasin *m* de brocante; **at the junk shop** chez le brocanteur

junker ['dʒʌŋkə(r)] *n Am Fam (old car)* vieille bagnole *f*

junket ['dʒʌŋkɪt] **1** *n* (**a**) *Fam Pej (trip)* voyage *m* aux frais de la princesse (**b**) *Fam (festive occasion)* banquet[□] *m*, festin[□] *m* (**c**) *Culin* ≃ lait *m* caillé (sucré et parfumé)

2 *vi* (**a**) *Fam (feast)* banqueter[□], festoyer[□] (**b**) *Fam Pej (go on trip)* voyager aux frais de la princesse

junketing ['dʒʌŋkɪtɪŋ] *n (UNCOUNT) Fam Pej* voyages *mpl* aux frais de la princesse

junkie ['dʒʌŋkɪ] *n Fam* (**a**) *(drug addict)* drogué(e)[□] *m,f*, junkie *mf* (**b**) *Fig* dingue *mf*, accro *mf*; **a television/football junkie** un dingue de la télé/du football

junkman ['dʒʌŋkmæn] *(pl* **junkmen** [-men]*) n Am (dealer in old furniture)* brocanteur *m*; *(ragman)* chiffonnier *m*; *(scrap metal dealer)* ferrailleur *m*, marchand *m* de ferraille

junky = **junkie**

junkyard ['dʒʌŋk,jɑːd] *n* (**a**) *(for scrap metal)* entrepôt *m* de ferraille; **at the junkyard** chez le ferrailleur (**b**) *(for discarded objects)* dépotoir *m*; *Fig* **their garden is a real junkyard** leur jardin est un véritable dépotoir

Juno ['dʒuːnəʊ] *pr n Myth* Junon

Junoesque [,dʒuːnəʊ'esk] *adj (woman)* imposant

Junr *(written abbr* **Junior***)* junior, fils

junta [*Br* 'dʒʌntə, *Am* 'hʊntə] *n* junte *f*

Jupiter ['dʒuːpɪtə(r)] **1** *pr n Myth* Jupiter

2 *n Astron* Jupiter *f*

Jurassic [dʒʊ'ræsɪk] **1** *adj* jurassique

2 *n* jurassique *m*

juridical [dʒʊ'rɪdɪkəl] *adj* juridique

juridically [dʒʊ'rɪdɪkəlɪ] *adv* juridiquement

jurisconsult [,dʒʊərɪs'kɒnsʌlt] *n (lawyer)* jurisconsulte *m*; *(legal expert)* juriste *mf*

jurisdiction [,dʒʊərɪs'dɪkʃən] *n* (**a**) *Law & Admin* juridiction *f*; **the federal government has no jurisdiction over such cases** de tels cas ne relèvent pas de la compétence *ou* des attributions du gouvernement fédéral; **to come** *or* **to fall within the jurisdiction of** relever de la juridiction de; **this territory is within the jurisdiction of the United States** ce territoire est soumis à l'autorité judiciaire des États-Unis

(**b**) *(general authority)* autorité *f*; **to have jurisdiction over sb** avoir autorité sur qn; **he has no jurisdiction over his brother's activities** il n'a aucune emprise *ou* aucun pouvoir sur ce que fait son frère

(**c**) *Fig (field of activity)* compétence *f*, ressort *m*; **this matter does not come within** *or* **is not in** *or* **falls outside our jurisdiction** cette affaire ne relève pas de notre compétence, cette affaire n'est pas de notre compétence *ou* de notre ressort

jurisdictional [,dʒʊərɪs'dɪkʃənəl] *adj* juridictionnel; *Am* **jurisdictional dispute** querelle *f* d'attributions

jurisprudence [,dʒʊərɪs'pruːdəns] *n* jurisprudence *f*

jurisprudential [,dʒʊərɪspruː'denʃəl] *adj* jurisprudentiel

jurist ['dʒʊərɪst] *n Formal (expert)* juriste *mf*, légiste *m*; *(writer)* juriste *mf*; *Am (lawyer)* avocat(e) *m,f*; *(student)* étudiant(e) *m,f* en droit

juror ['dʒʊərə(r)] *n* juré *m*

jury ['dʒʊərɪ] *(pl* **juries***)* **1** *n* (**a**) *Law* jury *m*; **to serve on a jury** faire partie d'un jury; **ladies and gentlemen of the jury, members of the jury** *(term of address)* Mesdames et Messieurs les jurés; **the jury is out** le jury est en délibération; *Fig* **the jury is still out on that one** ça reste à voir

(**b**) *(in contest)* jury *m*

2 *adj Naut* de fortune, improvisé

►► ***jury box*** sièges *mpl* des jurés; **she was in the jury box** elle faisait partie des jurés; ***jury duty, jury service*** participation *f* à un jury; **to do (one's) jury service** s'acquitter de son devoir de participation au jury; **to be called (up) for jury service** être convoqué comme juré; *Am* ***jury shopping*** choix *m* vétilleux des jurés *(par les avocats de la défense)*

juryman ['dʒʊərɪmən] *(pl* **jurymen** [-mən]*) n* juré *m*

jury-rig *(pt & pp* **jury-rigged**, *cont* **jury-rigging***) vt* (**a**) *Am (improvise)* bricoler (**b**) *Naut (boat)* gréer tant bien que mal

jury-rigged *adj* (**a**) *Am (improvised)* bricolé, de fortune (**b**) *Naut* avec un gréement de fortune

jury-rigging *n Law* truquage *m* d'un jury

jurywoman ['dʒʊərɪ,wʊmən] *(pl* **jurywomen** [-,wɪmɪn]*) n* jurée *f*

JUST[1] [dʒʌst]

juste	► **1 (a) – (f)**
seulement	► **1 (c)**
exactement	► **1 (d)**
à peine	► **1 (e)**
absolument	► **1 (i)**
presque	► **2 (a)**

1 *adv* (**a**) *(indicating immediate past)* juste; **just the other day** pas plus tard que l'autre jour; **just last week** pas plus tard que la semaine dernière; **she has just gone out** elle vient juste de sortir; **they had (only) just arrived** ils venaient (tout) juste d'arriver; **I've (only) just seen him going downstairs** je viens de le voir à l'instant qui descendait; **I've just been speaking to him on the phone** je viens juste de lui parler au téléphone, je lui parlais au téléphone à l'instant; **she's just this moment** *or* **minute left the office** elle vient de sortir du bureau à l'instant; **he's just been to Mexico** il revient *ou* rentre du Mexique; **I saw him just yesterday, I just saw him yesterday** je l'ai vu pas plus tard qu'hier; **he has just left school** il sort du lycée; *Scot & Ir Fam* **I'm just after seeing him** je viens de le voir[□]

(**b**) *(indicating present or immediate future)* juste; **I was just going to phone you** j'allais juste *ou* justement te téléphoner, j'étais sur le point de te téléphoner; **my hair is just turning grey** *or* **is just beginning to turn grey** mes cheveux commencent juste à grisonner; *Fam* **I'm just off** je m'en vais[□]; *Fam* **just coming!** j'arrive tout de suite![□]; **to be just about to do sth** être sur le point de faire qch; **I was just about to tell you** j'allais justement te le dire; **I'm just making tea, do you want some?** je suis en train de faire du thé, tu en veux?

(**c**) *(only, merely)* juste, seulement; **just a few** quelques-uns/quelques-unes seulement; **just a little** juste un peu; **just a minute** *or* **a moment** *or* **a second, please** une (petite) minute *ou* un (petit) instant, s'il vous plaît; **just a minute, aren't you supposed to be somewhere else?** une seconde, tu n'es pas censé être ailleurs?; **tell him just to wait** dites-lui qu'il n'a qu'à attendre; *Fam* **I'll just pop in** je ne ferai qu'entrer et sortir; **just ask if you need money** vous n'avez qu'à demander si vous avez besoin d'argent; **do you want some whisky? – just a drop** est-ce que tu veux du whisky? – juste une goutte; **it costs just $10** ça ne coûte que 10 dollars, ça coûte 10 dollars seulement; **we have just a few copies left** il nous (en) reste quelques exemplaires seulement *ou* juste quelques exemplaires; **it was just a dream** ce n'était qu'un rêve; **he's just a clerk** ce n'est qu'un simple employé; **she's just a baby** ce n'est qu'un bébé; **we're just friends** nous sommes amis, c'est tout; **I have come just to see you** je viens seulement *ou* juste *ou* uniquement pour vous voir; **he was just trying to help** il voulait juste *ou* simplement rendre service; **if he could**

just work a little harder! si seulement il pouvait travailler un peu plus!; **if the job is so unpleasant you should just leave** si le travail est désagréable à ce point, tu n'as qu'à démissionner; **don't argue, just do it!** ne discute pas, fais-le, c'est tout!; **if you can just sign here please** juste une petite signature ici, s'il vous plaît; **you can't ask just anybody to present the prizes** tu ne peux pas demander au premier venu de présenter les prix; **this is not just any horse race, this is the Derby!** ça n'est pas n'importe quelle course de chevaux, c'est le Derby!

(**d**) *(exactly, precisely)* exactement, juste; **just here/there** juste ici/là; **just at that moment** juste à ce moment-là; **that's just what I needed** c'est exactement *ou* juste ce qu'il me fallait; *Ironic* il ne me manquait plus que ça; **just what are you getting at?** où veux-tu en venir exactement?; **just why does she do it?** pour quelles raisons exactement le fait-elle?, pourquoi exactement le fait-elle?; **he's just like his father** c'est son père tout craché; **she's just the person for the job** elle a exactement le profil requis pour ce poste; **that dress is just the same as yours** cette robe est exactement la même que la tienne; **oh, I can just picture it!** oh, je vois tout à fait!; **that hat is just you** ce chapeau te va à merveille; **you speak French just as well as I do** ton français est tout aussi bon que le mien; **I'd just as soon go tomorrow** j'aimerais autant y aller demain; **it's just ten o'clock** il est dix heures juste(s) *ou* pile, il est tout juste dix heures; *Ironic* **(it's) just my luck!** c'est bien ma chance!; **don't come in just yet** n'entre pas tout de suite; **that's just it** *or* **just the point!** précisément!, justement!, voilà!

(**e**) *(barely)* (tout) juste, à peine; **I could just make out what they were saying** je parvenais tout juste à entendre ce qu'ils disaient; **you came just in time!** tu es arrivé juste à temps!; **she's just in time for a drink** elle arrive pile pour *ou* elle arrive juste à temps pour prendre un verre; **he (only) just managed to catch the train** il a eu le train de justesse, c'est tout juste s'il a eu le train; **she caught the train but (only) just** elle a eu le train mais c'était juste *ou* c'était de justesse; **they (only) just missed the train** ils ont manqué le train de peu; **I just missed a lorry** j'ai failli heurter un camion; **the trousers just fit me** je rentre tout juste dans le pantalon

(**f**) *(a little)* **it costs just over/under £50** ça coûte un tout petit peu plus de/moins de 50 livres; **it's just after/before two o'clock** il est un peu plus/moins de deux heures; **just after my birthday** juste après *ou* peu après mon anniversaire; **just afterwards** juste après; **just in front/behind/above/below** juste devant/derrière/au-dessus/au-dessous; **it's just to the right of the painting** c'est juste à droite du tableau

(**g**) *(possibly)* **I may** *or* **might just be able to do it** il n'est pas impossible que je puisse le faire; **his story might** *or* **could just be true** son histoire pourrait être vraie, il est possible que son histoire soit vraie

(**h**) *(emphatic use)* **just think what might have happened!** imagine un peu ce qui aurait pu arriver!; **we just can't understand it** nous n'arrivons vraiment pas à comprendre!; **just wait till I find the culprit!** attends un peu que je trouve le coupable!; **just be quiet, will you!** veux-tu bien te taire!; **now just you wait a minute, Kate!** hé, une petite minute, Kate!; **just (you) try!** essaie donc un peu!; **I just won't do it** il n'est pas question que je le fasse; **it just isn't good enough** c'est loin d'être satisfaisant, c'est tout; *Br* **he looks terrible in that suit – doesn't he just!** ce costume ne lui va pas du tout – je ne te le fais pas dire!; *Br* **do you remember? – don't I just!** tu t'en souviens? – et comment (que je m'en souviens)!; **why don't you want to go? – I just don't** pourquoi est-ce que tu ne veux pas y aller? – je ne veux pas, c'est tout!

(**i**) *(utterly, completely)* absolument; **the meal was just delicious** le repas était tout simplement *ou* vraiment délicieux; **everything is just fine** tout est parfait; **this is just ridiculous!** c'est vraiment ridicule!; **don't you just love that hat?** adorable, ce chapeau, non?; **I just loved Barcelona** j'ai vraiment adoré Barcelone

(**j**) *(on signs)* **just picked** cueilli du jour; **just cooked** cuit du jour; **just arrived** fraîchement arrivé

2 just about *adv* (**a**) *(very nearly)* presque, quasiment; **it's just about ten o'clock** il est plus ou moins *ou* à peu près dix heures; **dinner is just about ready** le dîner est presque prêt; **she's just about as tall as you** elle est presque aussi grande que toi; *Fam* **that just about does it!** ça suffit comme ça!; **I've just about had enough of your sarcasm!** j'en ai franchement assez de tes sarcasmes!; **have you finished? – just about** est-ce que vous avez terminé? – presque

(**b**) *(barely)* (tout) juste; **can you reach the shelf? – just about!** est-ce que tu peux atteindre l'étagère? – (tout) juste!; **his handwriting is just about legible** son écriture est tout juste *ou* à peine lisible

(**c**) *(approximately)* **their plane should be taking off just about now** leur avion devrait être sur le point de décoller

3 just as *conj* (**a**) *(at the same time as)* juste au moment où; **they arrived just as we were leaving** ils sont arrivés juste au moment où nous partions; **just as the door was opening** au moment même où la porte s'ouvrait

(**b**) *(exactly as)* **just as I thought/predicted** comme je le pensais/prévoyais; **just as you like** *or* **wish** comme vous voulez *ou* voudrez; **why not come just as you are?** pourquoi ne viens-tu pas comme tu es?

4 just in case 1 *conj* juste au cas où; **just in case we don't see each other** juste au cas où nous ne nous verrions pas **2** *adv* au cas où; **take a coat, just in case** prends un manteau, on ne sait jamais *ou* au cas où

5 just like that *adv Fam* comme ça; **he told me to clear off, just like that!** il m'a dit de me tirer, carrément!; **I can't do it just like that, I need some notice** je ne peux pas le faire comme ça, sans être prévenu à l'avance

6 just now *adv* (**a**) *(at this moment)* **I'm busy just now** je suis occupé pour le moment; **not just now** pas en ce moment; **she's not leaving just now** elle ne part pas encore, elle ne part pas tout de suite

(**b**) *(a short time ago)* **I heard a noise just now** je viens juste d'entendre un bruit; **I've just now come from there** j'en viens à l'instant; **when did this happen? – just now** quand cela s'est-il passé? – à l'instant

7 just on *adv Br* exactement; **they've been married just on thirty years** ça fait exactement trente ans qu'ils sont mariés; **the fish weighed just on 3 kilos** le poisson pesait exactement 3 kilos; **it's just on ten o'clock** il est dix heures juste(s) *ou* pile, il est tout juste dix heures

8 just so 1 *adv Formal (expressing agreement)* c'est exact; **are you a magistrate? – just so** vous êtes magistrat? – c'est exact **2** *adj Br (properly arranged)* parfait; **she likes everything (to be) just so** elle aime que tout soit parfait; **he set the vase down just so** *(carefully)* il a posé le vase avec soin

9 just then *adv* à ce moment-là; **I was just then getting ready to go out** je me préparais justement à sortir; **just then, a strange figure appeared** à ce moment-là, une silhouette étrange apparut

10 just the same *adv (nonetheless)* quand même; **just the same, it's as well to check** il vaut quand même mieux vérifier

---

'Just So Stories' *Kipling* 'Histoires comme ça'

---

just² **1** *adj* (**a**) *(fair, impartial)* juste, équitable; **a just law** une loi juste *ou* équitable; **a ruler who was just to** *or* **towards all men** un souverain qui a su faire preuve d'équité (envers tous)

(**b**) *(reasonable, moral)* juste, légitime; **a just cause** une juste cause; **he has just cause for complaint** il a de bonnes raisons pour se plaindre; **to show just cause for concern, to have just cause to be concerned** avoir de bonnes raisons de s'inquiéter

(**c**) *(deserved)* juste, mérité; **a just reward** une juste récompense, une récompense bien méritée; **he got his just deserts** il n'a eu que ce qu'il méritait, ce n'est que justice

(**d**) *(accurate)* juste, exact; **a just account of the facts** un compte rendu exact des faits

(**e**) *Rel (righteous)* juste

2 *npl* **the just** les justes *mpl*; **to sleep the sleep of the just** dormir du sommeil du juste

justice ['dʒʌstɪs] *n* (**a**) *Law (power of law)* justice *f*; **a court of justice** une cour de justice; **to dispense justice** rendre la justice; **to bring sb to justice** traduire qn en justice; *Am* **the Department of Justice** ≃ le ministère de la Justice

(**b**) *(fairness)* justice *f*, équité *f*; **where's your sense of justice?** qu'est-il advenu de ton sens de la justice?; **they believe in the justice of their cause** ils croient à la justesse de leur cause; **there's no justice in their claim** leur demande est dénuée de fondement; **to do sb/sth justice** *(represent fairly)* rendre justice à qn/qch; **the portrait didn't do her justice** son portrait ne lui rendait pas justice; **to do oneself justice** se mettre en valeur, se montrer sous son meilleur; **to do him justice, he wasn't informed of the decision** il faut lui rendre cette justice que *ou* il faut reconnaître que l'on ne l'avait pas mis au courant de la décision; **to do justice to a meal** faire honneur à un repas

(**c**) *(punishment, vengeance)* justice *f*; **the whole town called for justice** la ville entière réclamait vengeance

(**d**) *(judge)* juge *mf*; **Mr Justice Long** *(title)* Monsieur le juge Long; **Mrs Justice Long** Madame le *ou* la juge Long

►► *Am* ***the Justice Department*** ≃ le ministère de la Justice; ***Justice of the Peace*** ≃ juge *m* d'instance

JUSTICE OF THE PEACE

Les "JPs" sont nommés par le Lord Chancellor. Ce sont en général des notables locaux (médecins, propriétaires terriens) jouissant d'une bonne réputation.

justiceship ['dʒʌstɪsʃɪp] *n (office of justice, judge)* fonction *f* de juge

justiciary [dʒʌ'stɪʃərɪ] *(pl* **justiciaries***) n (judge)* juge *m*

justifiability [ˌdʒʌstɪˌfaɪə'bɪlɪtɪ] *n* caractère *m* justifiable

justifiable ['dʒʌstɪˌfaɪəbəl] *adj* justifiable; *Law* légitime

►► ***justifiable homicide*** *(killing in self-defence)* homicide *m* justifiable; *(state execution)* application *f* de la peine de mort

justifiableness ['dʒʌstɪˌfaɪəbəlnɪs] *n* caractère *m* justifiable

justifiably ['dʒʌstɪˌfaɪəblɪ] *adv* légitimement, à juste titre; **she was justifiably angry** elle était fâchée, et à juste titre

justification [ˌdʒʌstɪfɪ'keɪʃən] *n* (**a**) *(gen)* justification *f*; **what justification do you have for such a statement?** comment justifiez-vous une telle affirmation?; **poverty is no justification for theft** la pauvreté ne saurait justifier le vol; **he was accused of cheating, with some justification** il fut accusé d'avoir triché, non sans raison; **he spoke out in justification of his actions** il a parlé pour justifier ses actes; **that's no justification!** ce n'est pas une raison!

(**b**) *Comput & Typ* justification *f*; **left/right justification** justification *f* à gauche/à droite; **vertical justification** justification *f* verticale

justificative ['dʒʌstɪfɪˌkeɪtɪv], **justificatory** ['dʒʌstɪfɪˌkeɪtərɪ] *adj* justificatif, justificateur

justified ['dʒʌstɪfaɪd] *adj* (**a**) *(right, fair → action)* justifié, légitime; **to be justified in doing sth** avoir raison de faire qch (**b**) *Comput & Typ (aligned)* justifié; **left/right justified** justifié à gauche/droite; **vertically justified** justifié verticalement

justify ['dʒʌstɪfaɪ] *(pt & pp* **justified***) vt* (**a**) *(gen)* justifier; **nothing can justify such cruelty** rien ne saurait excuser *ou* justifier une telle cruauté; **she tried to justify her behaviour to her parents** elle a essayé de justifier son comportement aux yeux de ses parents (**b**) *Comput & Typ (text)* justifier (**c**) *Law* **to justify a lawsuit** justifier une action en justice

Justinian [dʒʌ'stɪnɪən] *pr n* Justinien

►► ***the Justinian Code*** le Code Justinien

jus–jus

just-in-time *adj Com & Mktg* juste à temps
►► ***just-in-time distribution*** distribution *f* juste à temps; ***just-in-time production*** production *f* juste à temps; ***just-in-time purchasing*** achat *m* juste à temps

justly ['dʒʌstlɪ] *adv* (**a**) *(fairly)* justement, avec justice (**b**) *(accurately, deservedly)* à juste titre; **a justly unpopular decision** une décision impopulaire à juste titre

justness ['dʒʌstnɪs] *n (of claim, demand)* bien-fondé *m*, légitimité *f*; *(of idea, reasoning)* justesse *f*

jut [dʒʌt] *(pt & pp* **jutted,** *cont* **jutting)** *vi* **to jut out** dépasser, faire saillie; **a rocky peninsula juts (out) into the sea** une péninsule rocheuse avance dans la mer; **a large rock jutted out over the path** un gros rocher surplombait le sentier; **his chin juts out** il a un menton en galoche

Jute [dʒu:t] *n* Jute *mf*

jute [dʒu:t] *n (textile)* jute *m*

Jutland ['dʒʌtlənd] *n* Jütland *m*, Jylland *m*; **in Jutland** dans le Jütland

Juvenal ['dʒu:vənəl] *pr n* Juvénal

juvenescence [ˌdʒu:vɪ'nesəns] *n Literary* passage *m* de la jeunesse à l'adolescence

juvenescent [dʒu:vɪ'nesənt] *adj Literary* en train de passer de la jeunesse à l'adolescence

juvenile ['dʒu:vənaɪl, *Am* 'dʒu:vənəl] **1** *adj* (**a**) *(young, for young people)* jeune, *Formal* juvénile (**b**) *(immature)* puéril, enfantin; **don't be so juvenile!** ne sois pas si puéril!
2 *n* (**a**) *Formal* mineur(e) *m,f*
(**b**) *Theat* jeune acteur(trice) *m,f*
►► ***juvenile court*** tribunal *m* pour enfants *(10-16 ans)*; ***juvenile delinquency*** délinquance *f* juvénile; ***juvenile delinquent*** jeune délinquant(e) *m,f*, mineur(e) *m,f* délinquant(e); ***juvenile lead*** jeune premier *m*; ***juvenile literature*** *(UNCOUNT)* livres *mpl* pour enfants *ou* pour la jeunesse; ***juvenile offender*** accusé(e) *m,f* mineur(e)

juvenilia [ˌdʒu:və'nɪlɪə] *npl* œuvres *fpl* de jeunesse

juxtapose [ˌdʒʌkstə'pəʊz] *vt* juxtaposer

juxtaposition [ˌdʒʌkstəpə'zɪʃən] *n* juxtaposition *f*; **to be in juxtaposition** se juxtaposer

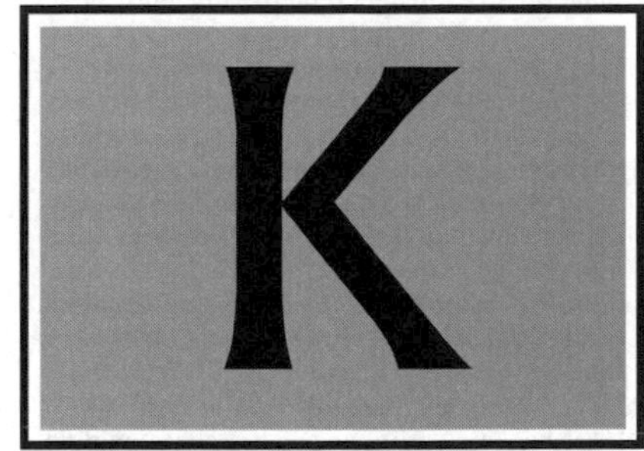

K¹, k [keɪ] *n* (**a**) *(letter)* K, k *m inv*; **two k's** deux k; **K for Kevin** ≃ K comme Kléber
(**b**) *Comput* (*abbr* **kilobyte**) K, Ko; **how many K are left?** combien de Ko reste-t-il?; **720K diskette** disquette *f* de 720 Ko
(**c**) (*abbr* **thousand**) K
(**d**) *Fam* (*abbr* **thousand pounds**) **he earns 30K** il gagne 30 000 livres ❏
(**e**) *Fam* (*abbr* **kilometre(s)**) kilomètre(s) ❏ *m(pl)*; **a 10K race** une course de 10 kilomètres
►► *Am Mil* ***K ration*** ration *f* (alimentaire)
K² (*written abbr* **Knight**) chevalier *m*
K-12 [ˌkeɪ'twelv] *n Am Sch* = terme désignant l'ensemble de l'enseignement public du jardin d'enfant au terme du secondaire
K2 [ˌkeɪ'tuː] *n* K2 *m*; **they climbed K2** ils ont escaladé le (pic) K2
kabala, kabalism *etc* = **cabala, cabalism** *etc*
kabbala, kabbalism *etc* = **cabala, cabalism** *etc*
kabob [kə'bɒb] = **kebab**
kabuki [kə'buːkɪ] *n* kabuki *m*
Kabul ['kɑːbəl] *n* Kaboul, Kabul
Kabyle [kə'baɪl] (*pl* **inv** *or* **Kabyles**) *n* (**a**) *(person)* Kabyle *mf* (**b**) *Ling* kabyle *m*
Kabylia [kə'bɪlɪə] *n* Kabylie *f*
Kabylian [kə'bɪlɪən] *adj* kabyle
kaccha ['kʌtʃə] *n* kaccha *m*
kaddish ['kædɪʃ] *n Rel* kaddish *m*
kaffeeklatsch ['kæfeɪˌklætʃ] *n Am* = réunion de femmes qui bavardent en prenant le café
Kaffir, Kafir ['kæfə(r)] **1** *n* (**a**) *SAfr very Fam* nègre (négresse) *m,f*, = terme raciste désignant un Noir (**b**) *(member of ethnic group)* Cafre *mf*
2 kaffir *n Fam St Exch* valeur-or *f* sud-africaine ❏
kaffiyeh [kɑː'fiːje] *n* keffieh *m*
Kafkaesque [ˌkæfkə'esk] *adj* kafkaïen
kaftan ['kæftæn] *n* caftan *m*, cafetan *m*
kagu ['kæguː] *n Orn* cagou *m*
kail = **kale**
kainite ['kaɪnaɪt] *n Miner* kaïnite *f*
Kaiser ['kaɪzə(r)] *n* Kaiser *m*
kaka ['kɑːkə] *n Orn* = perroquet vert de Nouvelle-Zélande
kakapo ['kɑːkəpəʊ] (*pl* **kakapos**) *n Orn* kakapo *m*, perroquet-hibou *m*
Kalahari Desert [ˌkælə'hɑːrɪ-] *n* **the Kalahari Desert** le (désert du) Kalahari
kalanchoe [kælən'kəʊɪ] *n Bot* kalanchoe *m*
kalashnikov [kə'læʃnɪkɒv] *n* kalachnikov *m ou f*
kale [keɪl] *n* chou *m* frisé
kaleidoscope [kə'laɪdəskəʊp] *n also Fig* kaléidoscope *m*
kaleidoscopic [kəˌlaɪdə'skɒpɪk] *adj* kaléidoscopique
kalends = **calends**
kali ['kælɪ] *n Bot* kali *m*
Kalinin [kə'lɪnɪn] *n Formerly* Kalinine
kalmia ['kælmɪə] *n Bot* kalmia *m*
Kama Sutra [ˌkɑːmə'suːtrə] *n* **the Kama Sutra** le Kama-sutra
kameez [kə'miːz] *n* = tunique à manches étroites portée par les femmes d'Asie du sud
kamikaze [ˌkæmɪ'kɑːzɪ] **1** *n* kamikaze *m*
2 *adj Fig* suicidaire
►► ***kamikaze pilot*** kamikaze *m*; ***kamikaze plane*** kamikaze *m*, avion-suicide *m*
Kampala [kæm'pɑːlə] *n* Kampala
Kampuchea [ˌkæmpʊ'tʃɪə] *n Formerly* Kampuchéa *m*; **in Kampuchea** au Kampuchéa
Kampuchean [ˌkæmpʊ'tʃɪən] **1** *n* Cambodgien(enne) *m,f*
2 *adj* cambodgien

Kanak [kə'næk] *n* (**a**) *(Melanesian)* Mélanésien(enne) *m,f* (**b**) *(from New Caledonia)* Kanak(e) *m,f*, Canaque *mf*
Kandinsky [kæn'dɪnskɪ] *pr n* Kandinsky
kanga [kæŋgə] *n* boubou *m*
kangaroo [ˌkæŋgə'ruː] (*pl* **kangaroos**, *pt & pp* **kangarooed**) **1** *n* (**a**) *(animal)* kangourou *m* (**b**) *Fam St Exch* valeur *f* australienne ❏
2 *vi Fam (car)* avoir des à-coups
►► *Aut* ***kangaroo bars*** pare-buffles *m inv*; ***kangaroo court*** tribunal *m* illégal; *(held by strikers, prisoners etc)* ≃ tribunal *m* populaire; *Zool* ***kangaroo rat*** rat-kangourou *m*
kangha ['kʌŋhə] *n* kangha *m*
kanji ['kændʒɪ] *n* kanji *m inv*
Kansan ['kænzən] **1** *n* (**a**) *Geol* kansanien *m* (**b**) *(inhabitant)* habitant(e) *m,f* du Kansas; *(native)* originaire *mf* du Kansas
2 *adj* (**a**) *Geol* kansanien (**b**) *(of or from Kansas)* du Kansas
Kansas ['kænzəs] *n* le Kansas; **in Kansas** au Kansas
Kantian ['kæntɪən] **1** *adj* kantien
2 *n* kantien(enne) *m,f*
kaolin ['keɪəlɪn] *n* kaolin *m*
kaolinite ['keɪəlɪnaɪt] *n Miner* kaolinite *f*
kaon ['keɪɒn] *n Phys* kaon *m*
kapok ['keɪpɒk] **1** *n* kapok *m*
2 *comp* de kapok
►► ***kapok tree*** kapokier *m*
Kaposi's sarcoma [kæ'pəʊsɪz-] *n Med* sarcome *m* de Kaposi
kaput, kaputt [kə'pʊt] *adj Fam* fichu, foutu
kara ['kʌrə] *n* kara *m*
karabiner [ˌkærə'biːnə(r)] *n Sport* mousqueton *m*
Karachi [kə'rɑːtʃɪ] *n* Karachi
karakul ['kærəkʊl] *n (sheep, fur)* karakul *m*, caracul *m*
karaoke [ˌkærɪ'əʊkɪ] *n* karaoké *m*
►► ***karaoke machine*** karaoké *m*
karat *Am* = **carat**
karate [kə'rɑːtɪ] *n* karaté *m*
►► ***karate chop*** coup *m* de karaté *(donné avec le tranchant de la main)*
karateka [ˌkərɑː'teɪkə] *n* karatéka *mf*
Karelia [kə'riːlɪə] *n Geog* Carélie *f*
Kariba Dam [kə'riːbə-] *n* **the Kariba Dam** le barrage de Kariba
karma ['kɑːmə] *n* karma *m*, karman *m*
Karnak ['kɑːnæk] *n Geog* Carnac, Karnac
karri ['kærɪ] *n Bot* karri *m*
[illegible]
2 *adj* karstique
►► ***karst country*** pays *m*/région *f* karstique
kart [kɑːt] *n* kart *m*
karting ['kɑːtɪŋ] *n* karting *m*; **to go karting** faire du karting
karyokinesis [ˌkærɪəʊkɪ'niːsɪs] *n Biol* caryocinèse *f*
karyology [ˌkærɪ'ɒlədʒɪ] *n Biol* caryologie *f*
karyotype ['kærɪəˌtaɪp] *n Biol* caryotype *m*
karyotyping ['kærɪəˌtaɪpɪŋ] *n Biol* analyse *f* des chromosomes
kasbah ['kæzbɑː] *n* casbah *f*
Kashmir [kæʃ'mɪə(r)] *n Geog* Cachemire *m*, Kashmir *m*
Kashmiri [kæʃ'mɪərɪ] **1** *n* (**a**) *(person)* Cachemirien(enne) *m,f* (**b**) *Ling* kashmiri *m*
2 *adj* cachemirien
Kashrut, Kashruth [kæʃ'ruːt] *n* kashrout *f*
kat [kæt] *n (shrub, drug)* qat *m*, khat *m*
kata ['kɑːtə] *n* kata *m*

katakana [ˌkætə'kɑːnə] *n* katakana *m*
Katanga [kə'tæŋgə] *n Geog* Katanga *m*
Katar ['kætɑː(r)] *n* Qatar *m*, Katar *m*,; **in Katar** au Qatar
Katari [kæ'tɑːrɪ] **1** *n (inhabitant)* habitant(e) *m,f* du Qatar; *(native)* originaire *mf* du Qatar
2 *adj* du Qatar
katharometer [ˌkæθə'rɒmətə(r)] *n Chem* catharomètre *m*
Katmandu [ˌkætmæn'duː] *n* Katmandou
katydid ['keɪtɪdɪd] *n Entom* sauterelle *f* (d'Amérique du Nord)
kauri ['kaʊrɪ] *n Bot* kauri *m*, kaori *m*
kava ['kɑːvə] *n (plant, drink)* kawa *m*, kava *m*
kayak ['kaɪæk] *n* kayak *m*
kayaker ['kaɪækə(r)] *n* kayakiste *mf*
kayaking ['kaɪækɪŋ] *n* kayak *m*, kayakisme *m*; **to go kayaking** faire du kayak
kayo [ˌkeɪ'əʊ] (*pl* **kayos**, *pt & pp* **kayoed**) *Fam* **1** *n Sport* K-O *m*
2 *vt* mettre K-O
Kazakh ['kæzæk] **1** *n* (**a**) *(person)* Kazakh(e) *m,f* (**b**) *(language)* kazakh *m*
2 *adj* kazakh
3 *comp (embassy, history)* du Kazakhstan; *(teacher)* de kazakh
Kazakhstan [ˌkæzæk'stɑːn] *n* Kazakhstan *m*; **in Kazakhstan** au Kazakhstan
kazoo [kə'zuː] (*pl* **kazoos**) *n* (**a**) *(instrument)* mirliton *m* (**b**) *Am Fam (buttocks)* derrière *m*, arrière-train *m*; **to have problems/debts up the kazoo** avoir des problèmes/des dettes jusqu'au cou
KB [ˌkeɪ'biː] *n Comput* (*abbr* **kilobyte**) Ko *m*
Kb [ˌkeɪ'biː] *n Comput* (*abbr* **kilobit**) Kb *m*
KBE [ˌkeɪbiː'iː] *n Br* (*abbr* **Knight (Commander of the Order) of the British Empire**) Chevalier *m* de l'Ordre de l'Empire britannique
Kbps [ˌkeɪbiːˌpiː'es] *n Comput* (*abbr* **kilobits per second**) Kb/s
KC [ˌkeɪ'siː] *n Br Law* (*abbr* **King's Counsel**) = avocat de la Couronne
kcal (*written abbr* **kilocalorie**) Kcal
KCB [ˌkeɪsiː'biː] *n Br* (*abbr* **Knight Commander (of the Order) of the Bath**) Chevalier *m* Commandeur de l'Ordre du Bain
kd [ˌkeɪ'diː] *adj* (*abbr* **knocked down**) = livré en kit à monter soi-même
kea ['kɪə] *n Orn* kéa *m*
Keatsian ['kiːtsɪən] *adj (of Keats)* de Keats; *(characteristic of Keats)* à la manière de Keats
kebab [kɪ'bæb] *n* brochette *f*; **shish kebab** chi- [illegible]
►► ***kebab house*** = restaurant grec ou turc
keck [kek] *vi Am Fam* avoir des haut-le-cœur ❏, avoir mal au cœur ❏
kecks [keks] *npl Br Fam (trousers)* fute *m*, falzar *m*
kedge [kedʒ] **1** *n* ancre *f* à jet
2 *vt* haler, touer
3 *vi* se haler, se touer
kedgeree ['kedʒəriː] *n Br* = riz pilaf au poisson fumé et aux œufs durs
keek [kiːk] *Scot* **1** *n* coup *m* d'œil furtif; **to have a keek at sb/sth** jeter un coup d'œil furtif à qn/qch
2 *vi* **to keek at sb/sth** jeter un coup d'œil furtif à qn/qch
keel [kiːl] **1** *n* (**a**) *Naut* quille *f*; **on an even keel** à tirant d'eau égal; *Fig* en équilibre; **to be back on an even keel** *(situation)* être de nouveau stable, s'être stabilisé; *(person)* avoir retrouvé son équilibre; **to put a company/the economy**

back on an even keel remettre une entreprise/ l'économie d'aplomb

(**b**) *Literary (ship)* navire *m*

2 *vt* faire chavirer, cabaner

3 *vi* chavirer

▸**keel over 1** *vt sep Naut* faire chavirer, cabaner

2 *vi* (**a**) *Naut* chavirer (**b**) *(fall)* s'effondrer; *(faint)* s'évanouir; *(drop dead)* tomber raide mort

keelhaul ['ki:lhɔ:l] *vt* (**a**) *Naut* faire passer sous la quille (**b**) *Fam Fig (rebuke)* houspiller, enguirlander

keelson ['ki:lsən, 'kelsən] *n Naut* carlingue *f*; **bilge keelson** carlingue *f* de bouchain; **middle-line keelson** carlingue *f* centrale

keen [ki:n] **1** *adj* (**a**) *(eager, enthusiastic)* passionné, enthousiaste; **she's a keen gardener** c'est une passionnée de jardinage; **he was keen to talk to her** il tenait à *ou* voulait absolument lui parler; **I'm keen that they should get a second chance** je tiens à ce qu'ils aient une deuxième chance; **I'm not so keen on the idea** l'idée ne m'enchante *ou* ne m'emballe pas vraiment; **they aren't so keen on going out tonight** ils n'ont pas (très) envie *ou* ça ne leur dit pas grand-chose de sortir ce soir; **Suzanne is really keen on Stuart** Suzanne a vraiment le béguin pour Stuart; *Fam* **to be as keen as mustard** *(enthusiastic)* être très enthousiaste; *(clever)* avoir l'esprit vif

(**b**) *(senses, mind, wit)* fin, vif; **to have a keen sense of smell** avoir un odorat subtil; **to have a keen eye** avoir le coup d'œil

(**c**) *(fierce → competition, rivalry)* acharné

(**d**) *Br (cold → wind)* glacial

(**e**) *Br (sharp → blade, knife)* affilé

(**f**) *(intense)* intense, profond; **she felt a keen desire to break free** elle ressentit une profonde envie de partir; **keen appetite** rude appétit *m*; **to have a keen appetite for success** avoir un appétit de succès dévorant

(**g**) *Br (competitive → price)* imbattable

(**h**) *Am Fam (very good)* génial

2 *vt (mourn)* pleurer

3 *vi (mourn)* pleurer

4 *n (dirge)* mélopée *f* funèbre

keen-eyed *adj (observant)* observateur

keenly ['ki:nlɪ] *adv* (**a**) *(deeply, intensely)* vivement, profondément; **she's keenly interested in the project** elle s'intéresse vivement *ou* elle porte un vif intérêt au projet; **he felt her death keenly** sa mort l'a profondément affecté (**b**) *(fiercely)* âprement; **a keenly contested game** un match âprement disputé (**c**) *(eagerly)* ardemment, avec enthousiasme; *(attentively)* attentivement

keenness ['ki:nnɪs] *n* (**a**) *(enthusiasm)* enthousiasme *m*, empressement *m*, ardeur *f*; **there's no doubting her keenness to help** son empressement à rendre service ne fait aucun doute (**b**) *(of senses)* acuité *f*, finesse *f*; **keenness of eye** acuité *f* visuelle; **keenness of mind** perspicacité *f*, finesse *f* (**c**) *(intensity, fierceness)* intensité *f*, âpreté *f* (**d**) *(of blade, knife)* tranchant *m*

keen-sighted *adj* à la vue perçante

KEEP [ki:p]

garder	▸ **1A (a) – (c); B (e); D (d)**
mettre	▸ **1A (c)**
retenir	▸ **1B (d)**
avoir	▸ **1C (b)**
tenir	▸ **1C (c)**
vendre	▸ **1C (d)**
élever	▸ **1C (e)**
observer	▸ **1D (b)**
maintenir	▸ **1D (c)**
continuer	▸ **2 (a)**
rester	▸ **2 (b)**
se tenir	▸ **2 (b)**
se conserver	▸ **2 (c)**
aller	▸ **2 (d)**

(*pt & pp* **kept** [kept]) **1** *vt* **A.** (**a**) *(retain → receipt, change)* garder; **you can keep the book I lent you** vous pouvez garder le livre que je vous ai prêté; **she's kept her English accent** elle a gardé son accent anglais; **please keep your seats** veuillez rester assis; **he's never kept a job for more than a year** il n'a jamais gardé *ou* conservé le même emploi plus d'un an; **to keep a secret** garder un secret; **to keep one's temper/ composure** garder son calme/son sang-froid; **to keep one's figure** garder la ligne; **to keep its shape/colour** *(garment)* conserver sa forme/ couleur; **to keep sth to oneself** garder qch pour soi; **they kept the discovery to themselves** ils ont gardé la découverte pour eux; **keep it to yourself!** garde ça pour toi!; **you can keep your snide remarks to yourself!** tu peux garder tes remarques déplaisantes pour toi!; **keep your hands to yourself!** bas les mains!; **to keep oneself to oneself** rester dans son coin; **they keep themselves very much to themselves** ils ne se mêlent pas du tout aux autres; *Fam* **if that's your idea of a holiday, you can keep it!** si c'est ça ton idée des vacances, tu peux te la garder!; *Fam* **tell him he can keep his rotten job!** dis-lui qu'il peut se le garder, son sale boulot!

(**b**) *(save)* garder; **to keep sth for sb** garder qch pour qn; **we've kept some cake for you** on t'a gardé du gâteau; **can you keep my seat?** pouvez-vous (me) garder ma place?; **we'll keep the tickets for you until Wednesday** nous vous garderons les tickets jusqu'à mercredi; **I'm keeping this cigar for later** je garde ce cigare pour plus tard

(**c**) *(store, put)* mettre, garder; **she keeps her money in the bank** elle met son argent à la banque; **I keep my comb in my pocket** je mets toujours mon peigne dans ma poche; **how long can you keep fish in the freezer?** combien de temps peut-on garder *ou* conserver du poisson au congélateur?; **where do you keep the playing cards?** où est-ce que vous rangez les cartes à jouer?; **I've got nowhere to keep my books** je n'ai nulle part où mettre mes livres; **keep out of the reach of children** *(on medicine, harmful products)* ne pas laisser à la portée des enfants

B. (**a**) *(with adj complement) (maintain in the specified state)* **to keep sth clean/secret** tenir qch propre/secret; **to keep sb quiet** faire tenir qn tranquille; **to keep oneself warm** *(by staying in the warmth)* se tenir au chaud; *(by dressing warmly)* s'habiller chaudement; **to keep sth warm** garder qch au chaud; **the noise kept me awake** le bruit m'a empêché de dormir, le bruit m'a tenu éveillé; **to keep the door open/shut** garder *ou* laisser la porte ouverte/fermée; **the doors are kept locked** les portes sont toujours fermées à clef; **to keep sth up to date** tenir qch à jour

(**b**) *(with adv complement) (maintain in the specified manner or place)* **a well-kept/badly kept office** un bureau bien/mal tenu; **the weather kept us indoors** le temps nous a empêchés de sortir; **troops were kept on the alert** les soldats ont été maintenus en état d'alerte; **he kept his hands in his pockets** il a gardé les mains dans les poches; **keep your eyes on the red dot** ne quittez pas le point rouge des yeux; **keep the noise to a minimum** essayez de ne pas faire trop de bruit

(**c**) *(with present participle)* **to keep sb waiting** faire attendre qn; **keep the engine running** n'arrêtez pas le moteur; **we kept the fire burning all night** nous avons laissé le feu allumé toute la nuit; **to keep sth going** *(organization, business)* faire marcher qch; *(music, conversation)* ne pas laisser qch s'arrêter; **alcohol is the only thing that keeps me going** l'alcool est la seule chose qui me permette de tenir *(le coup)*

(**d**) *(delay)* retenir; **I hope I've not kept you** j'espère que je ne vous ai pas retenu; **what kept you?** qu'est-ce qui t'a retenu?

(**e**) *(detain)* garder; **to keep sb in hospital/ prison** garder qn à l'hôpital/en prison; **the doctor kept him in bed** le médecin l'a obligé à garder le lit; **I don't want to keep you from your work** je ne veux pas vous empêcher de travailler; **there was nothing to keep me in England/ with that company** rien ne me retenait en Angleterre/dans cette entreprise

C. (**a**) *(support)* **he hardly earns enough to keep himself** il gagne à peine de quoi vivre; **she has a husband and six children to keep** elle a un mari et six enfants à nourrir; **it keeps me in cigarettes** ça paie mes cigarettes; **the grant barely keeps me in food** ma bourse me permet tout juste de me payer de quoi manger

(**b**) *(have as dependant or employee)* avoir; **he keeps a mistress** il a une maîtresse; **they keep a maid and a gardener** ils ont une bonne et un jardinier

(**c**) *(run → shop, business)* tenir

(**d**) *Com (have in stock)* vendre; **I'm afraid we don't keep that article** je regrette, nous ne vendons pas *ou* nous ne faisons pas cet article

(**e**) *(farm animals)* élever; **they keep pigs/bees** ils élèvent des porcs/des abeilles

(**f**) *(diary, list etc)* tenir; **my secretary keeps my accounts** ma secrétaire tient *ou* s'occupe de ma comptabilité; **to keep a record of events** prendre les événements en note; **to keep a note of sth** noter qch

D. (**a**) *(fulfil → a promise)* tenir; **to keep one's word** tenir sa parole

(**b**) *(observe → silence)* observer; *(→ the Sabbath)* respecter; *(→ law)* respecter, observer; *(→ vow)* rester fidèle à; *(→ treaty)* tenir, respecter, observer; *(→ date, appointment)* ne pas manquer; *Rel* **to keep the commandments** observer les commandements

(**c**) *(uphold)* maintenir; **to keep order/the peace** maintenir l'ordre/la paix; **to keep a lookout** faire le guet

(**d**) *(guard)* garder; **to keep goal** être gardien de but; **to keep wicket** *(in cricket)* garder le guichet; *Arch* **God keep you!** Dieu vous garde!

E. (**a**) *(prevent)* **to keep sb from doing sth** empêcher qn de faire qch; **nothing will keep me from going** rien ne m'empêchera d'y aller

(**b**) *(withhold)* **to keep sth from sb** cacher qch à qn; **to keep information from sb** dissimuler des informations à qn; **I can't keep anything from her** je ne peux rien lui cacher; **they deliberately kept the news from his family** ils ont fait exprès de cacher les nouvelles à sa famille

2 *vi* (**a**) *(with present participle) (continue)* continuer; **letters keep pouring in** les lettres continuent d'affluer; **don't keep apologizing** arrête de t'excuser; **they keep teasing him** ils n'arrêtent pas de le taquiner; **to keep smiling** garder le sourire; **don't keep asking questions** ne posez pas tout le temps des questions; **I wish you wouldn't keep saying that** j'aimerais bien que tu arrêtes de répéter cela; **she had several failures but kept trying** elle a essuyé plusieurs échecs mais elle a persévéré; **to keep going** *(not give up)* continuer; **keep going till you get to the crossroads** allez jusqu'au croisement; **she kept going when everyone else had given up** elle a continué alors que tous les autres avaient abandonné; **with so few customers, it's a wonder the shop keeps going** avec si peu de clients, c'est un miracle que le magasin ne ferme pas

(**b**) *(stay, remain)* rester, se tenir; **to keep quiet** se tenir *ou* rester tranquille; **keep calm!** restez calmes!, du calme!; **she kept warm by jumping up and down** elle se tenait chaud en sautillant sur place; **keep to the path** ne vous écartez pas du chemin; **to keep in touch with sb** rester en contact avec qn; **to keep to oneself** se tenir à l'écart

(**c**) *(last, stay fresh)* se conserver, se garder; **it will keep for a week in the refrigerator** vous pouvez le garder *ou* conserver au réfrigérateur pendant une semaine; **what I've got to tell you won't keep till tomorrow** ce que j'ai à te dire n'attendra pas jusqu'à demain; **will it keep till later?** *(news)* est-ce que ça peut attendre?

(**d**) *(in health)* aller; **how are you keeping?** comment allez-vous?, comment ça va?; **I'm keeping well** je vais bien, ça va (bien); **she doesn't keep well** elle ne jouit pas d'une bonne santé

3 *n* (**a**) *(board and lodging)* **the grant is supposed to be enough to pay your keep** la bourse est censée vous permettre de payer la nourriture et le logement; **he gives his mother £50 a week for his keep** il donne 50 livres par semaine à sa mère pour sa pension; **to earn one's keep** = payer ou travailler pour être nourri et logé; **our cat certainly earns his keep** notre chat vaut bien ce qu'il nous coûte

(**b**) *(in castle)* donjon *m*

(**c**) *(idiom) Fam* **for keeps** pour de bon ❑

►**keep at 1** *vt sep* **the sergeant kept us hard at it all morning** le sergent nous a fait travailler toute la matinée
2 *vt insep* (**a**) *(pester)* harceler; **she kept at him until he agreed** elle l'a harcelé jusqu'à ce qu'il accepte
(**b**) *(idiom)* **to keep at it** persévérer; **he kept at it until he found a solution** il a persévéré jusqu'à trouver une solution
►**keep away 1** *vt sep* tenir éloigné, empêcher d'approcher; **keep the baby away from the fire** empêche le bébé d'approcher du feu; **the rain kept a lot of spectators away** la pluie a dissuadé bien des spectateurs de venir; **keep that dog away (from me)!** tenez ce chien loin de moi!; **the wind will keep the rain away** le vent empêchera la pluie
2 *vi* ne pas s'approcher; **keep away (from me)!** n'approchez pas!; **keep away from the cooker** ne t'approche pas de la cuisinière; **keep away from those people** évitez ces gens-là; **I felt my visits were unwelcome and so I kept away** je n'avais pas l'impression que mes visites étaient bienvenues, alors je n'y suis plus allé; **I can't keep away from chocolates** je ne peux pas résister quand je vois des chocolats
►**keep back 1** *vt sep* (**a**) *(keep at a distance* → *crowd, spectators)* tenir éloigné, empêcher de s'approcher
(**b**) *(not reveal* → *names, facts)* cacher; **I'm sure he's keeping something back (from us)** je suis sûr qu'il (nous) cache quelque chose
(**c**) *(retain)* retenir; **part of our salary is kept back every month** une partie de notre salaire est retenue tous les mois
(**d**) *(detain)* retenir; **to be kept back after school** être en retenue; *Sch* **to be kept back a year** redoubler
(**e**) *(restrain)* retenir; **he struggled to keep back the tears** il s'est efforcé de retenir ses larmes
2 *vi* rester en arrière, ne pas s'approcher; **keep back!** restez où vous êtes!, n'approchez pas!
►**keep behind** *vt sep (after meeting, class)* retenir
►**keep down 1** *vt sep* (**a**) *(not raise)* ne pas lever; **keep your head down!** ne lève pas la tête!, garde la tête baissée!; **keep your voices down!** parlez moins fort *ou* plus bas
(**b**) *(prevent from increasing)* limiter; **we must keep our expenses down** il faut que nous limitions nos dépenses; **our aim is to keep prices down** notre but est d'empêcher les prix d'augmenter; **to keep one's weight down** garder la ligne
(**c**) *(repress)* réprimer; *(control* → *vermin, weeds)* empêcher de proliférer; **the army kept the population/the revolt down** l'armée a tenu la population en respect/a maté la révolte; **you can't keep a good man down** rien n'arrête un homme de mérite
(**d**) *(food)* garder; **she can't keep solid foods down** son estomac ne garde aucun aliment solide
(**e**) *Sch* faire redoubler; **to be kept down a year** redoubler une année
2 *vi* ne pas se relever; **keep down!** ne vous relevez pas!
►**keep from** *vt insep* s'empêcher de, se retenir de; **I couldn't keep from laughing** je n'ai pas pu m'empêcher de rire
►**keep in 1** *vt sep* (**a**) *(not allow out)* empêcher de sortir; *Sch* donner une consigne à, garder en retenue; **the bad weather kept us in** le mauvais temps nous a empêchés de sortir; **they're keeping him in overnight** *(in hospital)* ils le gardent pour la nuit
(**b**) *(fire)* entretenir
(**c**) *(stomach)* rentrer
(**d**) *(idiom)* **to keep one's hand in** garder la main
2 *vi (not go out)* ne pas sortir, rester chez soi
►**keep in with** *vt insep* **to keep in with sb** ne pas se mettre mal avec qn
►**keep off 1** *vt sep* (**a**) *(dogs, birds, trespassers)* éloigner; *(rain, sun)* protéger de; **this cream will keep the mosquitoes off** cette crème vous/le/te/*etc* protégera contre les moustiques; **keep your hands off!** pas touche!, bas les pattes!
(**b**) *(coat, hat)* ne pas remettre
2 *vt insep* (**a**) *(avoid)* éviter; **keep off drink and tobacco** évitez l'alcool et le tabac; **we tried to keep off the topic** on a essayé d'éviter le sujet
(**b**) *(keep at a distance from)* ne pas s'approcher de; **keep off the grass** *(sign)* pelouse interdite
3 *vi* (**a**) *(keep at a distance)* ne pas s'approcher; **that's mine, keep off!** c'est à moi, n'y touchez pas!
(**b**) *(weather)* **the rain/snow kept off** il n'a pas plu/neigé; **if the storm keeps off** si l'orage n'éclate pas
►**keep on 1** *vt sep* (**a**) *(coat, hat)* garder
(**b**) *(employee)* garder
(**c**) *(not turn off)* **to keep the central heating on** laisser le chauffage central en marche; **don't keep the lights on all day** ne laissez pas la lumière allumée toute la journée
2 *vi* (**a**) *(continue)* continuer; **keep on until you come to a crossroads** continuez jusqu'à ce que vous arriviez à un carrefour; **they kept on talking** ils ont continué à parler; **don't keep on asking questions** ne posez pas tout le temps des questions; **I keep on making the same mistakes** je fais toujours les mêmes erreurs
(**b**) *Fam (talk continually)* parler sans cesse; **he keeps on about his kids** il n'arrête pas de parler de ses gosses; **don't keep on about it!** ça suffit, j'ai compris!; **he just keeps on and on about it** il n'arrête pas d'en parler
►**keep on at** *vt insep Fam (pester)* **to keep on at sb (to do sth)** harceler qn (pour qu'il fasse qch)[❑]
►**keep out 1** *vt sep* empêcher d'entrer; **a guard dog to keep intruders out** un chien de garde pour décourager les intrus; **a scarf to keep the cold out** une écharpe pour vous protéger du froid
2 *vi* ne pas entrer; **keep out** *(sign)* défense d'entrer, entrée interdite; **to keep out of an argument** ne pas intervenir dans une discussion; **to keep out of danger** rester à l'abri du danger; **try to keep out of trouble** essaie de ne pas t'attirer d'ennuis
►**keep to** *vt insep* (**a**) *(observe, respect)* respecter; **you must keep to the deadlines** vous devez respecter les délais
(**b**) *(not deviate from)* ne pas s'écarter de; **to keep to the script** *(actors)* s'en tenir au script; **keep to the point** *or* **the subject!** ne vous écartez pas du sujet!; **keep to the main roads when it's icy** restez sur les grandes routes quand il y a du verglas
(**c**) *(stay in)* garder; **to keep to one's room/bed** garder la chambre/le lit
►**keep together 1** *vt sep* ne pas séparer; **I'd like them to be kept together** j'aimerais qu'ils ne soient pas séparés
2 *vi* rester ensemble
►**keep under** *vt sep* (**a**) *(repress)* réprimer
(**b**) *(with drug)* **he's being kept under with Pentothal**® on le garde sous Pentothal®
►**keep up 1** *vt sep* (**a**) *(prevent from falling* → *shelf, roof)* maintenir; **I need a belt to keep my trousers up** j'ai besoin d'une ceinture pour empêcher mon pantalon de tomber; *Fig* **it will keep prices up** ça empêchera les prix de baisser; **it's to keep the troops' morale up** c'est pour maintenir le moral des troupes; **keep your spirits up!** ne te laisse pas abattre!
(**b**) *(maintain* → *attack, bombardment)* poursuivre; *(*→ *correspondence, contacts, conversation)* entretenir; **you have to keep up the payments** on ne peut pas interrompre les versements; **she kept up a constant flow of questions** elle ne cessait de poser des questions; **it's a tradition which hasn't been kept up** c'est une tradition qui s'est perdue; **keep up the good work!** c'est du bon travail, continuez!; **you're doing well, keep it up!** c'est bien, continuez!; **once they start talking politics, they can keep it up all night** une fois lancés sur la politique, ils sont capables d'y passer la nuit
(**c**) *(prevent from going to bed)* empêcher de dormir; **the baby kept us up all night** nous n'avons pas pu fermer l'œil de la nuit à cause du bébé
(**d**) *(not allow to deteriorate* → *house, garden)* entretenir; **the lawns haven't been kept up** les pelouses n'ont pas été entretenues; **she goes to evening classes to keep up her French** elle suit des cours du soir pour entretenir son français
2 *vi* (**a**) *(continue)* continuer; **if this noise keeps up much longer, I'm going to scream!** si ce bruit continue, je crois que je vais hurler!
(**b**) *(not fall)* se maintenir; **if prices keep up** si les prix se maintiennent; **how are their spirits keeping up?** est-ce qu'ils gardent le moral?
(**c**) *(not fall behind)* suivre; **he's finding it hard to keep up in his new class** il a du mal à suivre dans sa nouvelle classe; **things change so quickly I can't keep up** les choses bougent si vite que j'ai du mal à suivre
►**keep up with** *vt insep* (**a**) *(stay abreast of)* **to keep up with the news** se tenir au courant de l'actualité; **I can barely keep up with her** *(she changes so much)* ça change tellement vite avec elle que j'ai du mal à suivre; **to keep up with the times** être à la page
(**b**) *(keep in touch with)* rester en contact avec; **have you kept up with your cousin in Australia?** est-ce que tu es resté en contact avec ton cousin d'Australie?
(**c**) *(remain level with)* **to keep up with sb** aller à la même allure que qn; **I can't keep up with you** vous marchez/parlez/*etc* trop vite pour moi; **he couldn't keep up with the rest of the children in his class** il n'arrivait pas à suivre dans sa classe

'Keep the Aspidistra Flying' *Orwell, Biermann*
'Et vive l'aspidistra!'

keeper ['ki:pə(r)] *n* (**a**) *(gen)* gardien(enne) *m,f*; *(in museum)* conservateur(trice) *m,f*; *Bible* **am I my brother's keeper?** suis-je le gardien de mon frère?; *Fig* **I'm not his keeper!** je ne suis pas responsable de ses actions (**b**) *Fam (goalkeeper)* goal *m*, gardien *m* de but[❑] (**c**) *Tech (safety catch)* cran *m* de sûreté
keep-fit *n* culture *f* physique, gymnastique *f* (d'entretien); **she goes to keep-fit (classes) every week** toutes les semaines elle va à son cours de gymnastique
keeping ['ki:pɪŋ] **1** *n* (**a**) *(care, charge)* garde *f*; **he left the manuscript in his wife's keeping** il a confié le manuscrit à son épouse; **in safe keeping** en sécurité, sous bonne garde
(**b**) *(observing* → *of rule, custom etc)* observation *f*
2 in keeping *adj* conforme
3 in keeping with *prep* conformément à; **in keeping with government policy** conformément à la politique du gouvernement; **it's in keeping with everything I have been told about her** cela concorde avec tout ce qu'on m'a dit sur elle; **their dress was not at all in keeping with the seriousness of the occasion** leur tenue ne convenait pas du tout à la gravité de la circonstance
4 out of keeping with *prep* **to be out of keeping with** être en désaccord avec; **it was rather out of keeping with the spirit of the occasion** cela détonnait avec l'esprit de l'occasion
keepsake ['ki:pseɪk] *n* souvenir *m (objet)*; **he gave it to her as a keepsake** il le lui a donné en souvenir
kef [kef] *n Fam* kif *m*
kefir ['kefə(r)] *n* kéfir *m*, képhir *m*
keg [keg] *n* (**a**) *(barrel)* tonnelet *m*, baril *m*; *(of fish)* baril *m*; *(of beer)* tonnelet *m*; *(of herring)* caque *f* (**b**) *(beer)* bière *f* (à la) pression
►► ***keg beer*** bière *f* pression
kegger ['kegə(r)] *n Am Fam (party)* = soirée, le plus souvent en plein air, où l'on boit de la bière pression
keister ['ki:stə(r)] *n Am Fam (buttocks)* derrière *m*, derche *m*
keks = **kecks**
kelim = **kilim**
kelly-green ['kelɪ-] *adj inv Am* vert pomme
keloid ['ki:lɔɪd] *n Med* chéloïde *f*
►► ***keloid acne*** acné *f* chéloïdienne
kelp [kelp] *n* varech *m*
Kelper ['kelpə(r)] **1** *n* Kelper *mf*, habitant(e) *m,f* des îles Falkland
2 *adj* des îles Falkland
kelpie ['kelpɪ] *n Scot* = dans le folklore écossais,

kee–kel

esprit des eaux généralement représenté sous forme de cheval

kelson ['kelsən] *n Naut* carlingue *f*; **bilge kelson** carlingue *f* de bouchain; **middle-line kelson** carlingue *f* centrale

kelt [kelt] *n (salmon)* kelt *m*

kelvin ['kelvɪn] *n Phys* kelvin *m*

Kempton Park ['kemptən-] *n* = champ de courses dans le Surrey

ken [ken] *(pt & pp* **kenned,** *cont* **kenning) 1** *n Old-fashioned or Hum* **it is beyond my ken** cela dépasse mon entendement

2 *vt Scot* savoir; *(person, place)* connaître

3 *vi Scot* savoir

kendo ['kendəʊ] *n* kendo *m*

Kennedy ['kenɪdɪ] *pr n* Kennedy

►► ***the Kennedy assassination*** l'assassinat *m* de Kennedy; ***the Kennedy Space Center*** le Kennedy Space Center, le centre spatial Kennedy

THE KENNEDY ASSASSINATION

Le 22 novembre 1963, le jeune président américain J F Kennedy fut assassiné à Dallas, au Texas. Le meurtrier présumé, Lee Harvey Oswald, fut arrêté mais il fut assassiné à son tour deux jours plus tard. Bien qu'officiellement close, cette affaire suscite encore aujourd'hui une controverse, en particulier de la part de ceux qui y voient un complot mettant en cause la CIA.

kennel ['kenəl] *(Br pt & pp* **kennelled,** *cont* **kennelling** *Am pt & pp* **kenneled,** *cont* **kenneling) 1** *n* **(a)** *Br (doghouse)* niche *f* **(b)** *Am (for boarding or breeding)* chenil *m* **(c)** *Hunt* **the kennel** *(hounds)* la meute

2 *vt* mettre dans un chenil

3 kennels *n pl Br (for boarding or breeding)* chenil *m*

►► ***the Kennel Club*** ≃ la société centrale canine

kennelmaid ['kenəl,meɪd] *n* employée *f* d'éleveur de chiens *ou* de chenil

kennelman ['kenəl,mən] *(pl* **kennelmen** [-mən]*) n* valet *m* de chenil, employé *m* d'éleveur de chiens

Kensington ['kenzɪŋtən] *n* Kensington

►► ***Kensington Gardens*** Kensington Gardens, les jardins de Kensington; ***Kensington Palace*** Kensington Palace, le palais de Kensington

Kent [kent] *n* le Kent, = comté dans le sud-est de l'Angleterre; **in Kent** dans le Kent; **Man of Kent** = natif de la partie est du Kent

THE KENT STATE INCIDENT

Il s'agit de l'incident qui eut lieu le 4 mai 1970 sur le campus de Kent State University (dans l'Ohio) entre des étudiants manifestant contre la guerre du Viêt-Nam et la Garde nationale américaine. Quand les manifestants se sont mis à lancer des pierres, la Garde nationale a riposté en tirant sur la foule, tuant quatre personnes et en blessant une dizaine.

Kentish ['kentɪʃ] *adj* du Kent

►► *Entom* ***Kentish glory*** endromis *m*; ***Kentish Man*** = natif de la partie ouest du Kent

Kentuckian [ken'tʌkɪən] **1** *n (inhabitant)* habitant(e) *m,f* du Kentucky; *(native)* originaire *mf* du Kentucky

2 *adj* du Kentucky

Kentucky [ken'tʌkɪ] *n* le Kentucky; **in Kentucky** dans le Kentucky

►► ***the Kentucky Derby*** = course pour chevaux de trois ans, qui a lieu chaque année à Louisville

Kenya ['kenjə] *n* Kenya *m*; **in Kenya** au Kenya

Kenyan ['kenjən] **1** *n* Kenyan(e) *m,f*

2 *adj* kenyan

3 *comp (embassy, history)* du Kenya

kepi ['keɪpi:] *n* képi *m*

Keplerian [kep'lɪərɪən] *adj Astron* képlérien

Kepler's laws ['kepləz-] *npl Astron* lois *fpl* de Kepler

kept [kept] **1** *pt & pp of* **keep**

2 *adj Hum or Pej* **a kept man** un homme entretenu; **a kept woman** une femme entretenue

keratectomy [,kerə'tektəmɪ] *(pl* **keratectomies***) n Med* kératectomie *f*

keratin ['kerətɪn] *n Biol* kératine *f*

keratinization [,kerətɪnaɪ'zeɪʃən] *n Biol* kératinisation *f*

keratinized ['kerətɪ,naɪzd] *adj Biol* kératinisé

keratitis [,kerə'taɪtɪs] *n Med* kératite *f*

keratogenous [,kerə'tɒdʒɪnɪs] *adj Physiol* kératogène

keratosis [,kerə'təʊsɪs] *n Med & Physiol* kératose *f*

keratotomy [,kerə'tɒtəmɪ] *(pl* **keratotomies***) n Med* kératotomie *f*

kerb, *Am* **curb** [kɜ:b] *n* **(a)** *(on road)* bord *m* du trottoir; **he stepped off the kerb** il est descendu du trottoir; **the bus pulled into the kerb** l'autobus s'est arrêté le long du trottoir

(b) *Fam St Exch* **to buy/sell on the kerb** acheter/vendre après la clôture officielle de la Bourse❑; **business done on the kerb** opérations *fpl* effectuées en coulisse *ou* après clôture de Bourse❑

►► *Fam St Exch* ***kerb broker*** coulissier❑ *m*, courtier(ère) *m,f* hors Bourse❑; ***kerb crawler*** = personne qui longe le trottoir en voiture à la recherche d'une prostituée; ***kerb crawling*** = recherche d'une prostituée en voiture; ***kerb drill*** précautions *fpl* pour traverser la rue; *Fam St Exch* ***kerb market*** marché *m* hors cote❑, coulisse❑ *f*; ***kerb weight*** poids *m* à vide

kerbstone, *Am* **curbstone** ['kɜ:bstəʊn] *n* pierre *f* de bordure *(d'un trottoir)*

►► *Fam St Exch* ***kerbstone market*** marché *m* hors cote❑, coulisse❑ *f*

kerchief ['kɜ:tʃɪf] *n Old-fashioned* foulard *m*, fichu *m*

kerfuffle [kə'fʌfəl] *n Br Fam (disorder)* désordre❑ *m*, chahut *m*; *(fight)* bagarre❑ *f*; **there was a kerfuffle at the exit** il y a eu des remous à la sortie

kermes ['kɜ:mi:z] *n* **(a)** *(dye)* kermès *m* **(b)** *(tree)* kermès *m*, chêne *m* kermès

kern [kɜ:n] *Typ & Comput* **1** *n* approche *f*

2 *vt* créner, rapprocher

kernel ['kɜ:nəl] *n* **(a)** *(fruit stone)* amande *f*; *(of nut)* intérieur *m*; *(of cereal)* graine *f* **(b)** *Fig (heart, core)* cœur *m*, noyau *m*; **the kernel of the problem** le fond du problème; **a kernel of truth** un fond de vérité

kerning ['kɜ:nɪŋ] *n Typ & Comput* crénage *m*, rapprochement *m* de caractères

kerogen ['kerədʒən] *n Geol* kérogène *m*

kerosene, kerosine ['kerəsi:n] **1** *n Am (for aircraft)* kérosène *m*; *(for lamps, stoves)* pétrole *m*

2 *comp (lamp, stove)* à pétrole

Kerry ['kerɪ] *n* le Kerry, = comté dans le sud-ouest de la République d'Irlande; **in Kerry** dans le Kerry

►► ***Kerry blue terrier*** terrier *m* Kerry blue; ***Kerry cow*** vache *f* du Kerry

kesh [keʃ] *n* kesh *m*

kestrel ['kestrəl] *n Orn* crécerelle *f*

ketch [ketʃ] *n Naut* ketch *m*

ketchup ['ketʃəp] *n* ketchup *m*

ketone ['ki:təʊn] *n Chem* cétone *f*

ketose ['ki:təʊs] *n Biol & Chem* cétose *m*

ketosis [kɪ'təʊsɪs] *n Med* cétose *f*

ketoxime [ki:'tɒksi:m] *n Biol & Chem* cétoxime *f*

kettle ['ketəl] *n* **(a)** *(for water)* bouilloire *f*; **to put the kettle on** mettre de l'eau à chauffer; **the kettle's boiling** l'eau bout **(b)** *(for fish)* poissonnière *f*; *Fam* **that's another** *or* **a different kettle of fish** c'est une autre paire de manches; *Br Fam* **this is a fine** *or* **pretty kettle of fish!** quelle salade!, quel sac de nœuds!

kettledrum ['ketəldrʌm] *n* timbale *f*

Kevin ['kevɪn] *n Br Fam Pej* jeune beauf *m*

Kew Gardens [kju:-] *n* = parc et jardin botanique dans l'ouest de Londres

key [ki:] **1** *n* **(a)** *(for lock)* clé *f*, clef *f*; *(for clock, mechanism etc)* clé *f*, remontoir *m*; **the key to the drawer** la clé du tiroir; **where are the car keys?** où sont les clés de la voiture?; **he was given the keys to the city** on lui a remis les clés de la ville; *Br Old-fashioned* **to get the key of the door** atteindre sa majorité; *esp Am Hum* **to get the key to the executive washroom** obtenir une promotion importante; **the (House of) Keys** = une des deux chambres du parlement de l'île de Man

(b) *Fig (means)* clé *f*, clef *f*; **the key to happiness** la clé du bonheur; **communication is the key to a good partnership** la communication est la clé d'une bonne association

(c) *(on typewriter, computer, piano, organ)* touche *f*; *(on wind instrument)* clé *f*, clef *f*

(d) *Mus* ton *m*; **in the key of B minor** en si mineur; **to play in/off key** jouer dans le ton/dans le mauvais ton; **to sing in/off key** chanter juste/faux

(e) *(on map, diagram)* légende *f*

(f) *(answers)* corrigé *m*, réponses *fpl*; *Comput (of sort, identification etc)* indicatif *m*, critère *m*; **the key to the exercises is on page 155** le corrigé des exercices se trouve page 155

(g) *Tech* clé *f ou* clef *f* (de serrage)

(h) *(island)* îlot *m*; *(reef)* (petit) récif *m (qui s'étend au sud de la Floride)*

(i) *Constr (roughness of surface)* rappointis *m*

(j) *Fam Drugs slang* kilo❑ *m (de marijuana)*

2 *adj* clé, clef; **the key conspirator** la cheville ouvrière du complot; **a key factor** un élément décisif; **one of the key issues in the election** un des enjeux fondamentaux de ces élections; **she was appointed to a key post** elle a été nommée à un poste clé

3 *vt* **(a)** *(data, text)* taper, saisir

(b) *(adjust, adapt)* adapter; **his remarks were keyed to the occasion** ses commentaires étaient adaptés aux circonstances

►► *Com & Mktg* ***key account*** compte-clé *m*; ***key bar*** *(in shop)* stand *m* de clef-minute; *Mktg* ***key brand*** marque *f* clé; ***key case*** porte-clés *m inv*; *Mus* ***key change*** changement *m* de ton; *Am* ***key club*** = club privé dont les membres possèdent chacun une clef; *Comput* ***key combination*** combinaison *f* de touches; *Cin* ***key grip*** technicien(enne) *m,f* en chef *(chargé(e) de l'installation des décors et des rails de caméra au cinéma)*; ***key industries*** industries *fpl* clés, industries-clés *fpl*; ***Key Lime pie*** tarte *f* au citron vert; ***key man*** homme *m* clé; ***key money*** pas *m* de porte; ***key numbers*** *(on squared map)* numéros *mpl* de repérage; ***key position*** position *f* clé; ***key rack*** *(in hotel etc)* tableau *m* (des clés); ***key ring*** porte-clés *m inv*; *Mus* ***key signature*** armature *f*, armure *f*; *Br Sch* ***key stage*** étape *f* clé de la scolarité; ***key word*** mot clé *m*

►**key in, key up** *vt sep Comput (word, number)* entrer; *(data, text)* taper, saisir

key-account *adj Com & Mktg*

►► ***key-account management*** gestion *f* de comptes-clés; ***key-account sales*** ventes *fpl* aux comptes-clés

keyboard ['ki:bɔ:d] **1** *n (of instrument, typewriter, computer)* clavier *m*; **who's on keyboards?** qui est aux claviers?

2 *vt* taper, saisir

3 *vi* introduire des données par clavier

►► ***keyboard instrument*** instrument *m* à clavier; ***keyboard layout*** disposition *f* de clavier; ***keyboard map*** schéma *m* de clavier; ***keyboard operator*** claviste *mf*; ***keyboard shortcut*** raccourci *m* clavier; ***keyboard skills*** compétences *fpl* de claviste

keyboarder ['ki:bɔ:də(r)] *n Comput* claviste *mf*, opérateur(trice) *m,f* de saisie

keyboarding ['ki:bɔ:dɪŋ] *n Comput (of data)* frappe *f*, saisie *f*

►► ***keyboarding accuracy*** précision *f* de frappe; ***keyboarding error*** faute *f* de frappe; ***keyboarding problems*** problèmes *mpl* au niveau de la frappe; ***keyboarding skills*** compétences *fpl* de claviste; ***keyboarding speed*** vitesse *f* de frappe

keyboardist ['ki:bɔ:dɪst] *n (pianist)* pianiste *mf*; *(on synthesizer)* joueur(euse) *m,f* de synthétiseur

keyboardless computer ['ki:bɔ:dlɪs-] *n* ordinateur *m* sans clavier

keycard ['ki:kɑ:d] *n* carte *f* magnétique *(servant à ouvrir la porte d'une chambre d'hôtel)*

key-driven *adj* commandé par clavier *ou* par touche

►► ***key-driven computer*** ordinateur *m* comptable (à clavier)

keyed up [ki:d-] *adj* excité; **the fans were all keyed up for the match** les supporters attendaient le match, très excités

key-escrow *n Fin & Comput* système *m* du tiers de

confiance *(permettant de confier sa clé privée de cryptage à un tiers de confiance agréé)*

keyhole ['ki:həʊl] *n* trou *m* de serrure; **he looked through the keyhole** il regarda par le trou de la serrure

►► ***keyhole surgery*** chirurgie *f* endoscopique

keying ['ki:ɪŋ] *n Comput (of data, text)* frappe *f*, saisie *f*

►► ***keying error*** faute *f* de frappe; ***keying speed*** vitesse *f* de frappe

Keynesian ['keɪnzɪən] *adj Econ* keynésien

keynote ['ki:nəʊt] **1** *n* (**a**) *(main point)* point *m* capital; **industrial recovery is the keynote of government policy** le redressement industriel constitue l'axe central de la politique gouvernementale (**b**) *Mus* tonique *f*

2 *adj (address)* introductif; *(speaker)* principal

3 *vt* insister sur, mettre en relief; **she keynoted the need for party unity** elle a insisté sur la nécessité de cohésion au sein du parti

►► ***keynote speech*** discours *m* introductif *ou* liminaire

keynoter ['ki:nəʊtə(r)] *n Am* = orateur qui prononce le discours d'ouverture

keypad ['ki:pæd] *n Comput* pavé *m*

keyphone ['ki:fəʊn] *n* téléphone *m* à touches

keypunch ['ki:pʌntʃ] *n* perforatrice *f* à clavier

keystone ['ki:stəʊn] *n Constr & Fig* clé *f ou* clef *f* de voûte

►► ***the Keystone State*** = surnom donné à la Pennsylvanie

keystroke ['ki:strəʊk] *n* frappe *f* (de touche); **codes are entered with a single keystroke** une seule touche suffit pour entrer les codes; **keystrokes per minute/hour** vitesse *f* de frappe à la minute/à l'heure

KG [,keɪ'dʒi:] *n Br* (*abbr* **Knight of the (Order of the) Garter**) Chevalier *m* de l'Ordre de la Jarretière

kg (*written abbr* **kilogram(me)**) kg

KGB [,keɪdʒi:'bi:] *n Formerly* (*abbr* **Komitet Gosudarstvennoi Bezopasnosti**) KGB *m*

►► ***KGB agent*** agent *m* du KGB; ***KGB officer*** officier *m* du KGB

Khachaturian [,kætʃə'tjʊrɪən] *pr n* Khatchatourian

khaki ['kɑ:kɪ] **1** *n (colour)* kaki *m*; *(material)* treillis *m*

2 *adj* kaki *(inv)*

3 khakis *npl Am (khaki trousers)* pantalon *m* de treillis

►► *Br* ***khaki election*** = élection dont la date est fixée dans la foulée d'une victoire militaire, assurant le succès du gouvernement au pouvoir

khalif = **calif**

Khalsa ['kælsə] *n* Khalsa *m*

khan [kɑ:n] *n Hist* khan *m*

khanate ['kɑ:neɪt] *n Hist* khanat *m*

Khaniá [χɑ:'njə] *n* Khaniá, La Canée

Khartoum [kɑ:'tu:m] *n* Khartoum

khat [kæt] = **kat**

khedive [kə'di:v] *n Hist* khédive *m*

Khmer [k'meə(r)] **1** *n* (**a**) *(person)* Khmer(ère) *m,f*; **Khmer Rouge** Khmer rouge (**b**) *Ling* khmer *m*

2 *adj* khmer

Khyber Pass ['kaɪbə-] *n* **the Khyber Pass** la passe de Khaybar *ou* de Khaïbar *ou* de Khyber

kHz (*written abbr* **kilohertz**) kHz

KIA [,keɪaɪ'eɪ] *adj Am Mil* (*abbr* **killed in action**) tué au combat

kibble[1] ['kɪbəl] *n Mining* benne *f*, cuffat *m*

kibble[2] *vt Agr (grain)* égruger

kibbutz [kɪ'bʊts] (*pl* **kibbutzes** *or* **kibbutzim** [-bʊt'sim]) *n* kibboutz *m*

kibbutznik [kɪ'bʊtsnɪk] *n* kibboutznik *mf*

kibitz ['kɪbɪts] *vi Am Fam (gen)* mettre son grain de sel; *(during card game)* = commenter une partie sans y avoir été invité

kibitzer ['kɪbɪtsə(r)] *n Am Fam (meddler)* mouche *f* du coche; *(at card game)* donneur(euse) *m,f* de conseils ❑; *(joker)* plaisantin *m*; **he's a real kibitzer** il fourre son nez partout

kiblah ['kɪblɑ:] *n Rel* qibla *f*

kibosh ['kaɪbɒʃ] *n Fam* **to put the kibosh on sth** ficher qch en l'air

KICK [kɪk]

coup de pied	► 1 (a)
plaisir	► 1 (b)
entrain	► 1 (d)
engouement	► 1 (e)
recul	► 1 (f)
retour en arrière	► 1 (g)
donner un/des coup(s) de pied (à)	► 2 (a); 3 (a)
lancer les jambes en l'air	► 3 (b)
reculer	► 3 (c)

1 *n* (**a**) *(with foot)* coup *m* de pied; **to give sb/sth a kick** donner un coup de pied à qn/qch; **to aim a kick at sb/sth** lancer *ou* donner un coup de pied en direction de qn/qch; **a long kick upfield** un long coup de pied en avant; **to have a powerful kick** *(footballer, horse)* avoir un coup de pied puissant; *(swimmer)* avoir un battement de pied puissant; *Fam* **it was a real kick in the teeth for him** ça lui a fait un sacré coup; *Fam* **she needs a kick up the backside** *or* **in the pants** elle a besoin d'un coup de pied aux fesses

(**b**) *Fam (thrill)* plaisir ❑ *m*; **to get a kick from** *or* **out of doing sth** prendre son pied à faire qch; **to do sth for kicks** faire qch pour rigoler *ou* pour s'amuser

(**c**) *Fam (strength → of drink)* **his cocktail had quite a kick** son cocktail était costaud; **this beer's got no kick in it** cette bière est un peu plate *ou* manque de vigueur ❑

(**d**) *Fam (vitality, force)* entrain ❑ *m*, allant ❑ *m*; **she's still got plenty of kick in her** elle a encore du ressort

(**e**) *Fam (fad)* engouement ❑ *m*; **she's on a yoga kick at the moment** elle est emballée *ou* elle ne jure que par le yoga en ce moment

(**f**) *(recoil → of gun)* recul *m*; *(of mechanism)* cahot *m*, secousse *f*

(**g**) *(of engine)* retour *m* en arrière

2 *vt* (**a**) *(once)* donner un coup de pied à; *(several times)* donner des coups de pied à; **she kicked the ball over the wall** elle a envoyé la balle par-dessus le mur (d'un coup de pied); **I kicked the door open** j'ai ouvert la porte d'un coup de pied; *Fam* **to kick sb's behind** flanquer à qn un coup de pied au derrière; **he had been kicked to death** il avait été tué à coups de pied; **the dancers kicked their legs in the air** les danseurs lançaient les jambes en l'air; **to kick a penalty** *(in rugby)* marquer *ou* réussir une pénalité; *(in football)* tirer un penalty; **to kick the ball into touch** mettre la balle en touche, botter (la balle) en touche; *Fam* **to kick the bucket** *(die)* passer l'arme à gauche, casser sa pipe; *Fam Fig* **to get kicked in the teeth** recevoir un coup en vache; *Fig* **you shouldn't kick a man when he's down** il ne faut pas s'acharner sur quelqu'un qui a déjà été fortement éprouvé; **I could have kicked myself!** je me serais donné des gifles!; **I could kick myself!** quel imbécile je fais!; **they must be kicking themselves** ils doivent s'en mordre les doigts; *Br Fam* **he was kicked upstairs** *(promoted)* on l'a promu pour se débarrasser de lui ❑; *Pol* on s'est débarrassé de lui en l'envoyant siéger à la chambre des Lords ❑; *Fam* **to kick one's heels** faire le pied de grue, poireauter; *Fam* **to kick a habit** se défaire d'une mauvaise habitude ❑

(**b**) *Fam* **I used to smoke but I've managed to kick the habit** je fumais, mais j'ai réussi à m'arrêter ❑

3 *vi* (**a**) *(once)* donner un coup de pied; *(several times)* donner des coups de pied; **I told you not to kick!** je t'ai dit de ne pas donner de coups de pied!; **they dragged him away kicking and screaming** il se débattait comme un beau diable quand ils l'ont emmené; **the baby lay on its back kicking** le bébé gigotait, allongé sur le dos; *Sport* **to kick for touch** *(in rugby)* chercher une touche; *Br* **to kick over the traces** ruer dans les brancards

(**b**) *(in dance)* lancer les jambes en l'air

(**c**) *(gun)* reculer

(**d**) *Am Fam (die)* calancher, passer l'arme à gauche

►► ***kick boxer*** tireur(euse) *m,f*, personne *f* pratiquant la boxe française; ***kick boxing*** boxe *f* française; ***kick turn*** *(in skiing, skateboarding)* conversion *f*

►**kick about, kick around 1** *vt sep* (**a**) **to kick a ball about** jouer au ballon; **they were kicking a tin can about** ils jouaient au foot avec une boîte de conserves (**b**) *Fam Fig (idea)* débattre; **we kicked a few ideas about** on a discuté à bâtons rompus (**c**) *Fam Fig (mistreat)* malmener, maltraiter; **I'm not going to let her kick me about any more** je ne vais plus me laisser faire par elle

2 *vt insep Fam (spend time in)* **to kick about the world/Africa** rouler sa bosse *ou* traîner ses guêtres autour du monde/en Afrique; *Br* **is my purse kicking about the kitchen somewhere?** est-ce que mon porte-monnaie traîne quelque part dans la cuisine?

3 *vi Fam* traîner; **I know my old overalls are kicking about here somewhere** je suis sûr que mon vieux bleu de travail traîne quelque part par là

►**kick about with, kick around with** *vt insep Fam* traîner avec; **who are you kicking about with these days?** avec qui tu traînes en ce moment?

►**kick against** *vt insep Fam* regimber contre; **he was always trying to kick against the system** il n'arrêtait pas de regimber contre le système; *Br* **to kick against the pricks** se rebeller en pure perte

►**kick at** *vt insep Fam* regimber contre

►**kick back 1** *vt sep* (**a**) *(ball)* renvoyer du pied (**b**) *(person)* rendre un coup de pied à; **I immediately kicked him back** je lui ai tout de suite rendu son coup de pied (**c**) *Am (money)* verser; **he got 10 percent kicked back on the contract** il a touché 10 pour cent du contrat en dessous-de-table

2 *vi Am Fam (relax)* se détendre ❑; **they kicked back after the midterm exams** ils se sont détendus après les partiels

►**kick down** *vt sep (person)* abattre *ou* faire tomber à coups de pied; *(door)* défoncer à coups de pied

►**kick in 1** *vt sep* défoncer à coups de pied; *Fam* **I'll kick his teeth in!** je vais lui casser la figure!

2 *vi Fam* entrer en action ❑; **the painkillers haven't kicked in yet** les analgésiques n'ont pas encore fait effet ❑

►**kick off 1** *vt sep* (**a**) *(shoes)* enlever d'un coup de pied (**b**) *Fam Fig (start)* démarrer ❑ (**c**) *Sport* donner le coup d'envoi à

2 *vi* (**a**) *Sport* donner le coup d'envoi; **they kicked off an hour late** le match a commencé avec une heure de retard (**b**) *Fam Fig (start)* démarrer ❑, commencer ❑ (**c**) *Am Fam (die)* calancher, passer l'arme à gauche (**d**) *Br Fam (become violent)* **it's going to kick off** ça va bastonner

►**kick out 1** *vt sep Fam (person)* chasser à coups de pied ❑; *Fig* foutre dehors

2 *vi* (**a**) *(person)* lancer des coups de pied; *(horse, donkey)* ruer; **she would kick out at anyone who came near** elle donnait des coups de pied à tous ceux qui s'approchaient (**b**) *Fam (complain)* râler, rouspéter; *(revolt)* se révolter ❑

►**kick over** *vt sep* renverser du pied *ou* d'un coup de pied

►**kick up** *vt sep* (**a**) *(dust, sand)* faire voler (du pied) (**b**) *Fam Fig* **to kick up a fuss** *or* **a row (about sth)** faire toute une histoire *ou* tout un plat (au sujet de qch); **to kick up a din** *or* **a racket** faire un boucan d'enfer

kickabout ['kɪkəbaʊt] *n Br Fam (soccer game)* partie *f* de foot; **to have a kickabout** jouer au foot

kickback ['kɪkbæk] *n* (**a**) *Fam (bribe)* dessous-de-table ❑ *m inv*, pot-de-vin ❑ *m* (**b**) *Tech* recul *m* (**c**) *(backlash)* contrecoup *m*

kickdown switch ['kɪkdaʊn-] *n Aut* rétro-contact *m*

kicker ['kɪkə(r)] *n* (**a**) *Sport (in rugby)* buteur *m*; *(in American football)* botteur *m*

(**b**) *(horse)* cheval *m* qui rue; *(mule)* mulet *m* qui rue

(**c**) *TV (light)* projecteur *m* de décrochement, contre-jour *m*

(**d**) *Am Fam (hidden drawback)* os *m*, hic *m*

(**e**) *Am Fam (worst part of situation)* **the work's tough and the kicker is the pay's lousy** le travail est dur, et en plus de ça, c'est payé avec un lance-pierres

▸▸ *TV* ***kicker light*** projecteur *m* de décrochement, contre-jour *m*

kicking ['kɪkɪŋ] *Fam* **1** *n Br* **to give sb a kicking** tabasser qn à coups de latte; **to get a kicking** se faire tabasser à coups de latte

2 *adj (party, nightclub)* hyper animé

kickoff ['kɪkɒf] *n* (**a**) *Sport* coup *m* d'envoi; **the kickoff is at three o'clock** le coup d'envoi sera donné à trois heures (**b**) *Br Fam Fig* **for a kickoff** pour commencer❑

kickpleat ['kɪkpliːt] *n (in skirt)* pli *m* d'aisance

kickshaw ['kɪkʃɔː] *n Arch* (**a**) *Culin* friandise *f* (**b**) *(trinket)* bagatelle *f*, colifichet *m*

kickstand ['kɪkstænd] *n* béquille *f (de moto)*

kick-start 1 *n* kick *m*

2 *vt* démarrer (au kick); *Fig* **measures to kick-start the economy** des mesures pour faire repartir l'économie

kick-starter *n* kick *m*

kicky ['kɪkɪ] *(compar* **kickier**, *superl* **kickiest**) *adj Am Fam (excellent)* super *(inv)*, génial

kid [kɪd] *(pt & pp* **kidded**, *cont* **kidding**) **1** *n* (**a**) *Fam (child, young person)* gosse *mf*, môme *mf*, gamin(e) *m,f*; **she's just a kid** ce n'est qu'une gamine *ou* une enfant; **listen to me, kid!** écoute-moi bien, petit!; **that's kids' stuff** c'est pour les bébés; *Am* **college kids** étudiants *mpl*; *NEng Fam* **our kid** *(brother)* le petit frère, le frérot; *(sister)* la petite sœur, la sœurette

(**b**) *(young goat)* chevreau(ette) *m,f*

(**c**) *(hide)* chevreau *m*

2 *adj* (**a**) *Fam (young)* **kid brother** petit frère *m*, frérot *m*; **kid sister** petite sœur *f*, sœurette *f*

(**b**) *(coat, jacket)* en chevreau

3 *vi Fam (joke)* blaguer; **I won it in a raffle – no kidding!** *or* **you're kidding!** je l'ai gagné dans une tombola – sans blague! *ou* tu rigoles!; **don't get upset, I was just kidding** ne te fâche pas, je plaisantais *ou* c'était une blague

4 *vt Fam* (**a**) *(tease)* taquiner❑, se moquer de❑; **they kidded him about his accent** ils se moquaient de lui à cause de son accent

(**b**) *(deceive, mislead)* charrier, faire marcher; **don't kid yourself!** il ne faut pas te leurrer *ou* te faire d'illusions!; **who do you think you're kidding?** tu te fous de moi?; **you're not kidding!** je ne te le fais pas dire!; **I kid you not** sans blague, sans rigoler

▸▸ ***kid gloves*** gants *mpl* de chevreau; **to handle** *or* **to treat sb with kid gloves** prendre des gants avec qn

▸**kid around** *vi Fam* raconter des blagues, rigoler

▸**kid on** *Br Fam* **1** *vt sep* charrier, faire marcher

2 *vi* faire semblant; **they were kidding on that I'd won** ils voulaient me faire croire que j'avais gagné

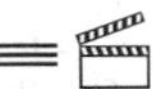

'Butch Cassidy and the Sundance Kid' *Hill* 'Butch Cassidy et le kid'

kiddie = **kiddy**

kidding ['kɪdɪŋ] *n (UNCOUNT) Fam* plaisanteries❑ *fpl*, blagues *fpl*; **kidding aside** blague à part, sans rigoler

kiddo ['kɪdəʊ] *(pl* **kiddos**) *n Fam (addressing boy or young man)* mon grand; *(addressing girl or young woman)* ma grande

kiddush ['kɪdəʃ] *n Rel* kiddush *m*

kiddy ['kɪdɪ] *(pl* **kiddies**) *n Fam* gosse *mf*, gamin(e) *m,f*

kid-glove *adj* **to give sb the kid-glove treatment** prendre des gants avec qn

kidnap ['kɪdnæp] *(Br pt & pp* **kidnapped**, *cont* **kidnapping**, *Am pt & pp* **kidnaped**, *cont* **kidnaping**) **1** *n* enlèvement *m*, rapt *m*, kidnapping *m*

2 *vt* enlever, kidnapper

'Kidnapped' *Stevenson, Mann* 'Enlevé'

kidnapper, *Am* **kidnaper** ['kɪdnæpə(r)] *n* ravisseur(euse) *m,f*, kidnappeur(euse) *m,f*

kidnapping, *Am* **kidnaping** ['kɪdnæpɪŋ] *n* enlèvement *m*, rapt *m*, kidnapping *m*

kidney ['kɪdnɪ] **1** *n* (**a**) *Anat* rein *m* (**b**) *Culin* rognon *m*; **pork kidneys** rognons *mpl* de porc (**c**) *Br Literary (temperament)* nature *f*, caractère *m*; **a man of (quite) a different kidney** un homme d'un (tout) autre caractère

2 *comp Anat (ailment, trouble)* des reins, rénal

▸▸ ***kidney bean*** *(red)* haricot *m* rouge; *(white)* haricot *m* de Soissons; ***kidney donor*** donneur(euse) *m,f* de rein; ***kidney failure*** insuffisance *f* rénale; ***kidney machine*** rein *m* artificiel; **he's on a kidney machine** il est sous rein artificiel *ou* en dialyse *ou* en hémodialyse; ***kidney specialist*** néphrologue *mf*; ***kidney stone*** calcul *m* rénal; *Med* ***kidney tray*** cuvette *f* à pansements réniforme; *Bot* ***kidney vetch*** (anthyllide *f*) vulnéraire *f*

kidney-shaped *adj* en forme de haricot, réniforme

kidology [kɪ'dɒlədʒɪ] *n Br Fam* esbroufe *f*, bluff *m*

kidskin ['kɪdskɪn] *n* (peau *f* de) chevreau *m*

kidvid ['kɪdvɪd] *n Am Fam* émission *f* pour enfants❑

Kiev ['kiːev] *n* Kiev

kif [kɪf, kiːf] *n Fam* kif *m*

kike [kaɪk] *n Am very Fam* youpin(e) *m,f*, = terme antisémite désignant un Juif

Kildare [kɪl'deə(r)] *n* le comté de Kildare, = comté dans l'est de la République d'Irlande; **in Kildare** dans le comté de Kildare

kilim [kɪ'liːm] *n* kilim *m*

Kilimanjaro [ˌkɪlɪmən'dʒɑːrəʊ] *n* **(Mount) Kilimanjaro** le Kilimandjaro

Kilkenny [kɪl'kenɪ] *n* (**a**) *(town)* Kilkenny (**b**) *(county)* le comté de Kilkenny, = comté du sud-est de la République d'Irlande; **in Kilkenny** dans le comté de Kilkenny

kill [kɪl] **1** *vt* (**a**) *(person, animal)* tuer; **to kill oneself** se tuer, *Formal* se donner la mort; **the frost killed the flowers** le gel a tué les fleurs; **I'll finish it even if it kills me** j'en viendrai à bout même si je dois me tuer à la tâche; **don't kill yourself working** ne te tue pas au travail; **this'll kill you or cure you!** si ça ne te fait pas de mal, ça te fera peut-être du bien!; *Hum* **he didn't exactly kill himself to find a job** il ne s'est pas trop fatigué pour trouver du travail; *Hum* **don't kill yourself!** ne te fatigue pas trop!, ne te tue pas à la tâche!; **if you tell them, I'll kill you!** si tu leur dis, je te tue!; **this joke will kill you** cette plaisanterie va te faire mourir de rire; **they were killing themselves (laughing** *or* **with laughter)** ils étaient morts de rire; *Prov* **to kill two birds with one stone** faire d'une pierre deux coups; **to kill time** tuer le temps

(**b**) *Fam Fig (cause pain to)* faire très mal à❑; **these shoes are killing me** ces chaussures me font souffrir le martyre; **my back's killing me** j'ai très *ou* horriblement mal au dos❑; **the heat will kill you** tu vas crever de chaleur

(**c**) *(put an end to)* tuer, mettre fin à; **the accident killed all his hopes of becoming a dancer** avec son accident ses espoirs de devenir danseur se sont évanouis *ou* envolés

(**d**) *(alleviate, deaden)* atténuer, soulager; *(smell)* neutraliser; **this injection should kill the pain** cette piqûre devrait atténuer la douleur; **to kill the sound** étouffer *ou* amortir le son

(**e**) *Fam (defeat)* rejeter❑, faire échouer❑; **the Senate killed the appropriations bill** le Sénat a fait échouer le projet de loi de finances

(**f**) *Fam (cancel, remove)* supprimer❑, enlever❑; *(computer file)* effacer❑; *Press* **the editor had to kill the story** le rédacteur en chef a dû supprimer l'article

(**g**) *Fam (switch off)* arrêter❑, couper❑; **to kill the engine** arrêter le moteur; **to kill the lights** éteindre les lumières❑

2 *vi* tuer; **to shoot to kill** tirer dans l'intention de tuer; *Bible* **thou shalt not kill** tu ne tueras point; **it's a case of kill or cure** c'est un remède de cheval; *Fam* **I'd kill for a beer** je me damnerais pour une bière

3 *n* (**a**) *(act of killing → animal)* mise *f* à mort; **the tiger had made three kills that week** le tigre avait tué à trois reprises *ou* avait fait trois victimes cette semaine-là; **to be in at the kill** assister au coup de grâce; **to move in for the kill** donner *ou* porter le coup de grâce

(**b**) *(prey → killed by animal)* proie *f*; *(→ killed by hunter)* chasse *f*; **the kill was plentiful** la chasse a été bonne

(**c**) *Mil (destruction → of enemy aircraft)* descente *f*; *(→ of enemy warship)* coulée *f*

▸**kill off** *vt sep* (**a**) *(gen)* exterminer; *Fig* **high prices could kill off the tourist trade** des prix élevés pourraient porter un coup fatal au tourisme

(**b**) *(fictional character)* faire mourir

killdeer ['kɪldɪə(r)] *n Orn* pluvier *m* kildir

killer ['kɪlə(r)] **1** *n* (**a**) *(murderer)* tueur(euse) *m,f*; **a convicted killer** une personne reconnue coupable d'homicide; **tuberculosis was once a major killer** jadis, la tuberculose faisait de nombreuses victimes *ou* des ravages

(**b**) *Fam (thing)* **the exam was a real killer** l'examen était vraiment coton; **their new album's a killer** *(excellent)* leur dernier album est vraiment génial *ou* mortel; **that walk was a killer!** cette promenade était vraiment crevante!; **this one's a killer** *(joke)* celle-là est à mourir de rire

2 *comp (disease)* meurtrier

3 *adj Am very Fam (excellent)* d'enfer

▸▸ *Fig* ***killer instinct*** agressivité *f*; **he's got the killer instinct** c'est un battant; **he lacks the killer instinct** il manque d'agressivité *ou* de combativité, il a trop de scrupules; *Zool* ***killer shark*** requin *m* tueur; ***killer T-cell*** lymphocyte *m* cytotoxique; *Zool* ***killer whale*** épaulard *m*, orque *f*

killing ['kɪlɪŋ] **1** *n* (**a**) *(of person)* assassinat *m*, meurtre *m*; **a wave of killings** une vague d'assassinats; **the killing of endangered species is forbidden** il est interdit de tuer un animal appartenant à une espèce en voie de disparition

(**b**) *Fam (profit)* **to make a killing** se remplir les poches, s'en mettre plein les poches

2 *adj Br Fam* (**a**) *(tiring)* crevant, tuant

(**b**) *Old-fashioned (hilarious)* tordant, bidonnant; **it was absolutely killing** c'était à se tordre *ou* à mourir de rire

'The Killing' *Kubrick* 'L'Ultime Razzia'

killingly ['kɪlɪŋlɪ] *adv Br Fam* **it was killingly funny** c'était à se tordre *ou* à mourir de rire

killjoy ['kɪldʒɔɪ] *n* trouble-fête *mf inv*; **don't be such a killjoy!** ne sois pas rabat-joie!

kiln [kɪln] *n* four *m (à céramique, à briques etc)*

▸▸ ***kiln drying*** séchage *m* au four

kiln-dried *adj* séché au four

Kilner jar® ['kɪlnə-] *n Br* bocal *m* (à conserves)

kilo ['kiːləʊ] *(pl* **kilos**) *n (abbr* **kilogram(me)**) kilo *m*

kilobar ['kɪləbɑː(r)] *n* kilobar *m*

kilobaud ['kɪləbɔːd] *n* kilobaud *m*

kilobit ['kɪləbɪt] *n Comput* kilobit *m*

kilobyte ['kɪləbaɪt] *n Comput* kilo-octet *m*

kilocalorie ['kɪləˌkælərɪ] *n* kilocalorie *f*, grande calorie *f*

kilocycle ['kɪləˌsaɪkəl] *n* kilocycle *m*, kilohertz *m*

kilogram, kilogramme ['kɪləˌgræm] *n* kilogramme *m*

kilogray ['kɪləgreɪ] *n Phys* kilogray *m*

kilohertz ['kɪləˌhɜːts] *n* kilohertz *m*

kilojoule ['kɪləˌdʒuːl] *n* kilojoule *m*

kilolitre, *Am* **kiloliter** ['kɪləˌliːtə(r)] *n* kilolitre *m*

kilometre, *Am* **kilometer** ['kɪləˌmiːtə(r), kɪ'lɒmɪtə(r)] *n* kilomètre *m*

kilometric [ˌkɪlə'metrɪk] *adj* kilométrique

kiloton ['kɪləˌtʌn] *n* kilotonne *f*

kilovolt ['kɪləˌvəʊlt] *n* kilovolt *m*

kilowatt ['kɪləˌwɒt] *n* kilowatt *m*

kilowatt-hour *n* kilowattheure *m*

kilt [kɪlt] *n* kilt *m*

kilted ['kɪltɪd] *adj* (**a**) *(person)* en kilt (**b**) *(pleated)* **kilted skirt** kilt *m*

kilter ['kɪltə(r)] **out of kilter** *adj* en dérangement, en panne

kimchi ['kɪmtʃɪ] *n Culin* kimchi *m*

kimono [kɪ'məʊnəʊ] *(pl* **kimonos**) *n* kimono *m*

kin [kɪn] *npl* parents *mpl*, famille *f*

kinaesthesia, *Am* **kinesthesia** [ˌkɪnɪs'θiːzɪə] *n Med* kinesthésie *f*

kinaesthesis, *Am* **kinesthesis** [ˌkɪnɪs'θiːsɪs] *n Med* kinesthésie *f*

kinaesthetic, *Am* **kinesthetic** [ˌkɪnɪs'θetɪk] *adj Med* kinesthésique

kinase ['kɪneɪz, 'kaɪneɪz] *n Biol & Chem* kinase *f*

KIND¹ [kaɪnd] **1** *n* (**a**) *(sort, type)* sorte *f*, type *m*, genre *m*; **hundreds of different kinds of books** des centaines de livres de toutes sortes; **they have every kind of bird imaginable** ils ont tous les oiseaux possibles et imaginables; **it's a kind of fish** c'est une espèce de poisson; **what kind of fish is this?** quel type *ou* quelle sorte de poisson est-ce?; **what kind of computer have you got?** qu'est-ce que vous avez comme (marque d')ordinateur?; **have you got any other kind?** en avez-vous d'autres?; **they did have some flour, but it wasn't the right kind** ils avaient bien de la farine, mais ce n'était pas la bonne; **all kinds of people** toutes sortes de gens; **what kind of people go there? – oh, all kinds** quel type de gens y va? – oh, des gens très différents; **the worst kind of people** des gens de la pire espèce; **the place was packed with paintings of all kinds** il y avait là toutes sortes de tableaux; **it's a different kind of problem** c'est un tout autre problème, c'est un problème d'un autre ordre; **I think he's some kind of specialist** *or* **a specialist of some kind** je crois que c'est un genre de spécialiste; **he's that kind of person** il est comme ça; *Fam* **are you some kind of nut?** tu es malade ou quoi?; **what kind of person do you think I am?** pour qui me prenez-vous?; **it's all right, if you like that kind of thing** c'est bien si vous aimez ce genre de choses; **is this the kind of thing you're looking for?** est-ce que c'est quelque chose de ce genre que vous cherchez?; **this is not the kind of thing you can do overnight** ce n'est pas le genre de chose qu'on fait du jour au lendemain; **his books are not the kind to become best-sellers** ses livres ne sont pas du genre à devenir des best-sellers; **he's not the kind that would betray his friends** il n'est pas du genre à trahir ses amis; **they're not our kind of people** *(not the sort we mix with)* nous ne sommes pas du même monde; **Las Vegas is my kind of town** Las Vegas est le genre de ville que j'aime; **you're my kind of girl** tu es mon type de femme, tu es le type de femme que j'aime; **I'm not that kind of girl** ce n'est pas mon genre; **he's not the understanding kind** il n'est pas du genre compréhensif; **she's not the marrying kind** elle n'est pas du genre à se marier; **she's more the stay-at-home kind** elle est plus du genre à rester à la maison; **I know your kind!** je connais les gens de ton espèce!; **I said nothing of the kind!** je n'ai rien dit de pareil *ou* de tel!; **you were drunk last night – I was nothing of the kind!** tu étais ivre hier soir – absolument pas *ou* mais pas du tout!

(**b**) *(class of person, thing)* **he's a traitor to his kind** il a trahi les siens; **it's one of the finest of its kind** *(animal)* c'est l'un des plus beaux spécimens de son espèce; *(object)* c'est l'un des plus beaux dans son genre

(**c**) *(idioms)* **a kind of** une sorte de, une espèce de; **a hat with a kind of (a) veil** un chapeau avec une espèce de voilette; **it was a kind of saucer-shaped thing** c'était une espèce de truc en forme de soucoupe; **she had a kind of fit** elle a eu une sorte d'attaque; **I had a kind of (a) feeling you'd come** j'avais comme l'impression que tu viendrais; **I heard a kind of thump** j'ai entendu une espèce de cognement *ou* comme un cognement; *Fam* **kind of** plutôt; **it's kind of big and round** c'est plutôt *ou* dans le genre grand et rond; **I'm kind of sad about it** ça me rend un peu triste; **did you hit him? – well, kind of** tu l'as frappé? – oui, si on veut; **do you agree? kind of** tu es d'accord? plus ou moins; **we just kind of wandered about** on s'est un peu baladés; **they're two of a kind** ils sont de la même espèce; **one of a kind** unique (en son genre); **did he give you any tips? – of a kind** vous a-t-il donné des conseils? – si on peut appeler ça des conseils; **well, it's beer of a kind, I suppose** oui, on peut appeler ça de la bière, je suppose; **he speaks French – of a kind** il parle français – plus ou moins; **it's work of a kind, but only as a stopgap** c'est un emploi, d'accord, mais pas pour très longtemps

2 in kind *adv* (**a**) *(with goods, services)* en nature; **to pay sb in kind** payer qn en nature

(**b**) *(in similar fashion)* de même; **he insulted me, and I replied in kind** il m'a insulté, et je lui ai rendu la monnaie de sa pièce

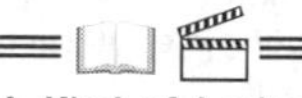

'A Kind of Loving' *Barstow, Schlesinger* 'Un Amour pas comme les autres'

kind² *adj* (**a**) *(good-natured, considerate)* gentil, aimable; **she's a very kind woman** c'est une femme très gentille *ou* une femme d'une grande bonté; **to be kind to sb** être gentil avec qn; **it's very kind of you to take an interest** c'est très gentil à vous de vous y intéresser; **how kind!** comme c'est gentil!; **you are really too kind** vous êtes vraiment trop aimable; **she was kind enough to say nothing** elle a eu la gentillesse de ne rien dire; **would you be so kind as to post this for me?** auriez-vous l'amabilité de mettre ceci à la poste pour moi?; **by kind permission of...** avec l'aimable autorisation de...; **give him my kind regards** faites-lui mes amitiés

(**b**) *(favourable)* favorable; **most of the reviews were kind to the actors** la plupart des critiques étaient favorables aux acteurs

(**c**) *(delicate, not harmful)* doux (douce); **a detergent that is kind to your hands** une lessive qui n'abîme pas les mains

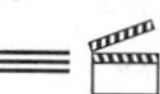

'Kind Hearts and Coronets' *Hamer* 'Noblesse oblige'

kinda ['kaɪndə] *Am Fam* = **kind of**

kindergarten ['kɪndəˌgɑːtən] *n* jardin *m* d'enfants, (école *f*) maternelle *f*, *Suisse* école *f* enfantine, *Belg* gardienne *f*

kindergartener ['kɪndəˌgɑːtənə(r)] *n (child)* petit(e) enfant *mf*; **kindergarteners** les tout-petits *mpl*

kind-hearted *adj* bon, généreux; **she's very kind-hearted** elle a bon cœur, elle est d'une grande générosité

kind-heartedly [-'hɑːtɪdlɪ] *adv* avec bonté, généreusement

kind-heartedness [-'hɑːtɪdnɪs] *n* bonté *f*, générosité *f*

kindle ['kɪndəl] **1** *vt* (**a**) *(wood)* allumer, faire brûler; *(flame, fire)* allumer (**b**) *Fig (interest)* susciter; *(passion, desire)* embraser, enflammer; *(hatred, jealousy)* attiser, susciter

2 *vi* (**a**) *(wood)* s'enflammer, brûler (**b**) *Fig (interest)* s'éveiller; *(passion, desire)* s'embraser, s'enflammer; *(hatred, jealousy)* s'éveiller

kindliness ['kaɪndlɪnɪs] *n* gentillesse *f*, amabilité *f*, bonté *f*

kindling ['kɪndlɪŋ] *n* petit bois *m*, bois *m* d'allumage

kindly ['kaɪndlɪ] *(compar* **kindlier**, *superl* **kindliest**) **1** *adv* (**a**) *(affably, warmly)* chaleureusement, affablement; **he has always treated me kindly** il a toujours été gentil avec moi

(**b**) *(obligingly)* gentiment, obligeamment; **she kindly offered to help us** elle a gentiment offert de nous aider

(**c**) *(favourably)* **to look kindly on sth** voir qch d'un bon œil; **they don't take kindly to people arriving late** ils n'apprécient pas beaucoup *ou* tellement qu'on arrive en retard; **I have always thought kindly of him** j'ai toujours eu une bonne opinion de lui; **she spoke very kindly of you** elle a dit des choses très aimables *ou* gentilles à votre égard; **to be kindly disposed towards sb/sth** être bien disposé envers qn/qch

(**d**) *(in polite requests)* **would** *or* **will you kindly pass the salt?** auriez-vous la gentillesse *ou* l'amabilité de me passer le sel?; **kindly reply by return of post** prière de répondre par retour du courrier; **kindly refrain from smoking** prière de ne pas fumer

(**e**) *(in anger or annoyance)* **will you kindly sit down!** asseyez-vous, je vous prie!

2 *adj (person, attitude)* gentil; *(smile)* bienveillant

kindness ['kaɪndnɪs] *n* (**a**) *(thoughtfulness)* bonté *f*, gentillesse *f*; **an act of kindness** un acte de bonté; **she did it out of the kindness of her heart** elle l'a fait par bonté d'âme; *Ironic* **and I suppose it was out of the kindness of your heart that you did that?** et je suppose que c'est ton bon cœur qui t'a poussé à faire ça?

(**b**) *Br (considerate act)* service *m*; **to do sb a kindness** rendre service à qn; *Formal* **please do me the kindness of replying** pourriez-vous être assez gentil pour *ou* pourriez-vous avoir l'amabilité de me donner une réponse?

kindred ['kɪndrɪd] **1** *n Arch or Literary (relationship)* parenté *f*; *(family)* famille *f*, parents *mpl*

2 *adj (related)* apparenté; *(similar)* similaire, analogue

►► ***kindred spirits*** âmes *fpl* sœurs

kinematic [ˌkɪnə'mætɪk, ˌkaɪnə'mætɪk] *adj Phys* cinématique

►► ***kinematic chain*** chaîne *f* cinématique; ***kinematic viscosity*** viscosité *f* cinématique

kinematics [ˌkɪnɪ'mætɪks] *n (UNCOUNT)* cinématique *f*

kinesics [kɪ'niːsɪks] *n (UNCOUNT)* kinésique *f*

kinesiologist [kɪˌniːsɪ'ɒlədʒɪst] *n* kinésiologue *mf*

kinesiology [kɪˌniːsɪ'ɒlədʒɪ] *n* kinésiologie *f*

kinesthesia, kinesthesis *etc* = **kinaesthesia, kinaesthesis** *etc*

kinetic [kɪ'netɪk, kaɪ'netɪk] *adj* cinétique

►► ***kinetic art*** art *m* cinétique; ***kinetic energy*** énergie *f* cinétique

kinetically [kɪ'netɪkəlɪ, kaɪ'netɪkəlɪ] *adv* cinétiquement

kinetics [kɪ'netɪks] *n (UNCOUNT)* cinétique *f*

kinfolk ['kɪnfəʊk] *npl Am* parents *mpl*, famille *f*

king [kɪŋ] **1** *n* (**a**) *(person)* roi *m*; **King Henry the Eighth** le roi Henri VIII; **the King of Spain/Belgium** le roi d'Espagne/des Belges; **the Three Kings** les trois Mages, les Rois mages; *Fig* **the king of (the) beasts** le roi des animaux; *Fig* **the fast-food king** le roi *ou* le magnat de la restauration rapide; **to live like a king** vivre en grand seigneur; *Fam* **I'm the king of the castle!** *(in children's games)* c'est moi le plus fort!; *Br Law* **to turn King's evidence** témoigner contre ses complices; **to pay a king's ransom (for sth)** payer une fortune *ou* un prix fou (pour qch)

(**b**) *(in cards, chess)* roi *m*; *(in draughts)* dame *f*; **the king of hearts** le roi de cœur

2 Kings *n Bible* **(the book of) Kings** (le livre des) Rois

►► *Law* ***King's Bench*** = en Angleterre et au Pays de Galles, l'une des trois divisions de la High Court, ≃ tribunal *m* de grande instance; ***King's Bench Division*** ≃ cour *f* d'assises *(en Grande-Bretagne et au Canada)*; ***King Charles spaniel*** king-charles *m inv*, épagneul *m* du roi Charles; *Zool* ***king cobra*** cobra *m* royal, hamadryade *f*; ***King's Counsel*** avocat(e) *m,f* de la Couronne *(en Grande-Bretagne)*, *Can* conseil *m* du roi; *Zool* ***king crab*** limule *f*, crabe *m* des Moluques; ***King Edward*** *(potato)* (pomme *f* de terre) King Edward *f*; *Br* **the King's English** le bon anglais; *Old-fashioned Med* ***King's evil*** *(scrofula)* écrouelles *fpl*; *Br* ***the King's highway*** la voie publique; ***King James Bible, King James Version*** = version anglaise de la Bible publiée en 1611, "autorisée" par le roi Jacques Ier d'Angleterre; *Orn* ***king penguin*** manchot *m* royal; *Br* ***king prawn*** (grosse) crevette *f*; ***the King's Road*** = rue chic de Londres, très à la mode dans les années 60; ***king scallop*** grosse coquille *f* Saint-Jacques; *Zool* ***king snake*** serpent-roi *m*; *Orn* ***king vulture*** condor *m* papa

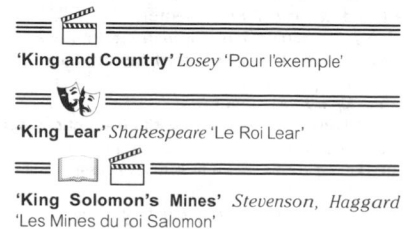

'King and Country' *Losey* 'Pour l'exemple'

'King Lear' *Shakespeare* 'Le Roi Lear'

'King Solomon's Mines' *Stevenson, Haggard* 'Les Mines du roi Salomon'

kingbird ['kɪŋbɜːd] *n Orn* tyran *m*

kingbolt ['kɪŋbəʊlt] *n Tech* pivot *m*, cheville *f* ouvrière

kingcup ['kɪŋkʌp] *n Br Bot* populage *m*, souci *m* d'eau

kingdom ['kɪŋdəm] *n* (**a**) *(realm)* royaume *m*; *Bible* **the kingdom of God/Heaven** le royaume de Dieu/des cieux; **Thy kingdom come** que Ton règne vienne; **till kingdom come** jusqu'à la fin des temps; **they were blown to kingdom come** ils ont été expédiés dans l'autre monde *ou* dans l'au-delà (**b**) *(division)* règne *m*; **the animal/vegetable/mineral kingdom** le règne animal/végétal/minéral

kingfisher ['kɪŋˌfɪʃə(r)] *n Orn* martin-pêcheur *m*

kinglet ['kɪŋlɪt] *n* (**a**) *(petty king)* roitelet *m* (**b**) *Orn* roitelet *m*

kingly ['kɪŋlɪ] *(compar* **kinglier,** *superl* **kingliest)** *adj* royal, majestueux; **to behave in a kingly manner** *(be like a king)* se conduire en roi; *(be generous)* se conduire comme un prince

kingmaker ['kɪŋˌmeɪkə(r)] *n Hist* faiseur *m* de rois; *Fig* = personne qui fait ou défait les candidats politiques

king-of-the-herrings *n Ich* régalec *m* roi *m* des harengs

kingpin ['kɪŋˌpɪn] *n* (**a**) *Tech* pivot *m* (**b**) *Fig (of organization, company)* pivot *m*, cheville *f* ouvrière (**c**) *(in tenpin bowling)* quille *f* du milieu

kingship ['kɪŋʃɪp] *n* royauté *f*

king-size, king-sized *adj (bed, mattress)* (très) grand format *(de 2 mètres sur 1,95 mètre)*; *(cigarette)* long (longue); *(packet, container)* géant; *Fam Fig* **I've got a king-size hangover** j'ai une gueule de bois carabinée

Kingston ['kɪŋstən] *n* Kingston

kinin ['kaɪnɪn] *n Biol & Bot* kinine *f*

kink [kɪŋk] **1** *n* (**a**) *(in hair)* ondulation *f*; **the rope has got a kink in it** la corde fait une boucle; **the hose has got a kink in it** le tuyau est tordu (**b**) *Fam Fig (sexual deviation)* perversion❑ *f*, aberration❑ *f*; *(quirk)* bizarrerie❑ *f*, excentricité❑ *f* (**c**) *Am Fam (flaw)* problème❑ *m*

2 *vt (cable, hose)* tordre

3 *vi (rope)* faire une boucle; *(cable, hose)* être tordu

kinkajou ['kɪŋkədʒuː] *n Zool* kinkajou *m*

kinkiness ['kɪŋkɪnɪs] *n Fam (of sexual tastes)* bizarrerie❑ *f*

kinky ['kɪŋkɪ] *(compar* **kinkier,** *superl* **kinkiest)** *adj* (**a**) *Fam (behaviour)* farfelu, loufoque; *(sexually → person)* qui a des goûts spéciaux❑; *(→ tastes)* bizarre❑, spécial❑; **he likes kinky sex** il a des goûts sexuels un peu spéciaux; **she wears kinky clothes** elle a une façon très spéciale de s'habiller (**b**) *(rope)* qui fait des boucles; *(cable, hose)* tordu; *(hair)* ondulé

kinsfolk ['kɪnzfəʊk] *npl* parents *mpl*, famille *f*

Kinshasa [kɪn'ʃɑːsə] *n* Kinshasa

kinship ['kɪnʃɪp] *n (relationship)* parenté *f*; *Fig (closeness)* intimité *f*; **I feel no real kinship with my colleagues** je ne me sens pas du tout proche de mes collègues

kinsman ['kɪnzmən] *(pl* **kinsmen** [-mən]) *n* parent *m*

kinswoman ['kɪnzˌwʊmən] *(pl* **kinswomen** [-ˌwɪmɪn]) *n* parente *f*

kiosk ['kiːɒsk] *n (for newspapers, magazines)* kiosque *m*; *Am (for advertisements)* ≃ colonne *f* Morris; *Comput* borne *f* interactive

kip [kɪp] *(pt & pp* **kipped,** *cont* **kipping)** *Br Fam* **1** *n* (**a**) *(sleep)* roupillon *m*; **to have a** *or* **to get some kip** faire *ou* piquer un roupillon; **I got no kip last night** je n'ai pas fermé l'œil de la nuit (**b**) *(bed)* pieu *m*, plumard *m*; **to be still in one's kip** être encore au plumard

2 *vi* roupiller

►**kip down** *vi Br Fam* se pieuter

kipper ['kɪpə(r)] **1** *n* hareng *m* fumé, kipper *m*

2 *vt (fish)* fumer; **kippered herring** hareng *m* fumé, kipper *m*

►► ***kipper tie*** large cravate *f*

KIPS [kɪps] *n Comput* (*abbr* **kilo instructions per second**) = millier d'instructions par seconde

kir [kɪə(r)] *n (drink)* kir *m*, blanc *m* cassis

►► ***kir royale*** kir *m* royal

kirby-grip ['kɜːbɪ-] *n Br* pince *f* à cheveux

Kirgizia, Kirghizia [kɜː'gɪzɪə] *n* Kirghizie *f*, Kirghizstan *m*, Kirghizistan *m*; **in Kirgizia** en Kirghizie *ou* Kirghizstan *ou* Kirghizistan

kirk [kɜːk] *n Scot* église *f*; **the Kirk** l'Église *f* (presbytérienne) d'Écosse

kirkyard ['kɜːkjɑːd] *n Scot (grounds)* terrain *m* autour de l'église; *(graveyard)* cimetière *m (autour d'une église)*

kirpan [kɪə'pɑːn] *n* kirpan *m*

kirsch [kɪəʃ] *n* kirsch *m*

kiskadee ['kɪskədiː] *n Orn* pitanga *m*, pitagua *m*

kismet ['kɪzmet] *n* sort *m*, destin *m*

KISS [kɪs] *adj Am Fam* (*abbr* **keep it simple, stupid**) = sobre et simple

kiss [kɪs] **1** *n* (**a**) *(with lips)* baiser *m*; **they gave her a kiss** ils l'ont embrassée; *Fam* **give us a kiss!** fais-moi un (gros) bisou!; **she gave him a goodnight kiss** elle lui a souhaité une bonne nuit en l'embrassant, elle l'a embrassé pour lui souhaiter (une) bonne nuit; **to give sb the kiss of life** faire du bouche-à-bouche à qn; *Fig* **it could be the kiss of life for the building trade** cela pourrait permettre à l'industrie du bâtiment de retrouver un *ou* son second souffle; **kiss of death** coup *m* fatal; **the new supermarket was the kiss of death for local shopkeepers** l'ouverture du supermarché a entraîné la ruine des petits commerçants

(**b**) *(sweet)* **chocolate kiss** (petit) bonbon *m* au chocolat

(**c**) *(in snooker, pool)* touche *f*, contre *m*

2 *vt* (**a**) *(with lips)* embrasser; **he kissed her on the lips/forehead** il l'embrassa sur la bouche/le front; **he kissed her hand** il lui a baisé la main, il lui a fait le baisemain; **to kiss hands** = baiser la main du souverain pour signifier officiellement que l'on accepte une fonction; **I kissed her goodnight** je l'ai embrassée *ou* je lui ai fait une bise pour lui souhaiter (une) bonne nuit; **kiss your dad goodnight!** embrasse ton père *ou* fais une bise à ton père avant d'aller te coucher!; **mummy will kiss it better** maman va te faire un bisou et tu n'auras plus mal; *Fam* **you can kiss your money goodbye!** tu peux faire ton deuil de *ou* tu peux faire une croix sur ton fric!

(**b**) *Literary (touch lightly)* caresser; **the sunlight kissed her hair** le soleil lui caressait les cheveux

(**c**) *(in snooker, pool)* toucher

3 *vi* (**a**) *(people)* s'embrasser; **they kissed goodbye** ils se sont dit au revoir en s'embrassant; **to kiss and make up** s'embrasser et faire la paix; **to kiss and tell** = dévoiler les détails de sa liaison avec une personne connue

(**b**) *(in snooker, pool)* se toucher

►► *Br* ***kiss curl*** accroche-cœur *m*

►**kiss away** *vt sep* **she kissed away my tears** ses baisers ont séché mes larmes

►**kiss off** *Am Fam* **1** *vt sep* (**a**) *(dismiss)* envoyer promener (**b**) *(kill)* descendre, buter (**c**) *(give up hope of)* faire une croix sur, dire adieu à; **you can kiss off your promotion!** tu peux faire une croix sur *ou* dire adieu à ta promotion!

2 *vi* aller se faire voir; **kiss off!** va te faire voir!

'The Kiss' *Rodin* 'Le Baiser'

kissable ['kɪsəbəl] *adj Fam* qu'on voudrait embrasser❑

kissagram = **kissogram**

kiss-and-tell *adj Press* = se dit d'un article où une personne dévoile les détails de sa liaison avec une personne connue

kisser ['kɪsə(r)] *n* (**a**) *(person)* **to be a great kisser** bien embrasser (**b**) *Fam (face, mouth)* tronche *f*

kissing ['kɪsɪŋ] *n (UNCOUNT)* baisers *mpl*, embrassades *fpl*; **kissing of hands** baisemain *m*; **I know her quite well but we're not on kissing terms** je la connais assez bien mais on ne s'embrasse pas; **the kissing of the stone is supposed to bring good luck** on dit que ça porte bonheur d'embrasser la pierre

►► *Am Fam* ***kissing cousin*** = parent que l'on connaît assez pour l'embrasser lorsqu'on le rencontre; *Fam* ***kissing disease*** maladie *f* du baiser; ***kissing gate*** portillon *m (avec battant entre chicanes)*

kiss-me-quick hat *n Br* = chapeau portant les mots "kiss me quick", traditionnellement vendu dans les stations balnéaires

kiss-off *n Am Fam* **to give sb the kiss-off** envoyer promener qn

kissogram ['kɪsəgræm] *n Br* = message délivré par une personne déguisée et accompagné d'un baiser

►► ***kissogram girl*** = fille qui délivre des messages et est chargée d'embrasser le destinataire

kit [kɪt] *(pt & pp* **kitted,** *cont* **kitting)** *n* (**a**) *(set)* trousse *f*; **tool/sewing kit** trousse *f* à outils/à couture

(**b**) *(equipment, clothing)* affaires *fpl*, matériel *m*; **have you got your squash kit?** as-tu tes affaires de squash?; *Fam* **to get one's kit off** se désaper, se mettre à poil; *Fam* **get your kit off!** à poil!; *Fam* **the whole kit and caboodle** tout le bazar *ou* bataclan

(**c**) *(soldier's gear)* fourniment *m*; **in full battle kit** en tenue de combat

(**d**) *(parts to be assembled)* kit *m*; **it's sold in kit form** c'est vendu en kit; **model aircraft kit** maquette *f* d'avion

►► *Br* ***kit bag*** musette *f*, sac *m* de toile; ***kit inspection*** revue *f* de détail

►**kit out, kit up** *vt sep Br Fam* équiper❑; **we kitted ourselves out for a long trip** nous nous sommes équipés pour un long voyage; **he was kitted out for golf** il était en tenue de golf

kitchen ['kɪtʃɪn] **1** *n* cuisine *f*

2 *comp (salt, scissors, table, utensil)* de cuisine

►► ***kitchen cabinet*** *(furniture)* buffet *m* (de cuisine); *Br Pol* = conseillers proches du chef du gouvernement; ***kitchen floor*** sol *m* de la cuisine; ***kitchen foil*** aluminium *m* ménager, papier *m* d'aluminium *ou* d'alu; *Br* ***kitchen garden*** (jardin *m*) potager *m*; ***kitchen hand*** aide *mf* de cuisine; *Br* ***kitchen paper, kitchen roll*** essuie-tout *m*, Sopalin® *m*; ***kitchen shop*** magasin *m* d'articles de cuisine; ***kitchen sink*** évier *m*; *Fam Fig* **to take everything but the kitchen sink** *(on holiday)* emporter toute la maison; *(thief, person moving out etc)* ne laisser que les murs; ***kitchen sink drama*** = théâtre et cinéma réalistes des années 50–60 dépeignant l'ennui et la misère des gens ordinaires; ***kitchen stove*** cuisinière *f*; ***kitchen unit*** élément *m* (de cuisine)

kitchenette [ˌkɪtʃɪ'net] *n* kitchenette *f*, *Offic* cuisinette *f*

kitchenmaid ['kɪtʃɪnˌmeɪd] *n* fille *f* de cuisine

kitchenware ['kɪtʃɪnˌweə(r)] *n (UNCOUNT)* vaisselle *f* et ustensiles *mpl* de cuisine

kite [kaɪt] **1** *n* (**a**) *(toy)* cerf-volant *m*; **to fly a kite** faire voler un cerf-volant; *Fig* lancer un ballon d'essai; **go fly a kite!** va voir là-bas si j'y suis!

(**b**) *Orn* milan *m*

(**c**) *Fam Fin* traite *f* en l'air❑, billet *m* de complaisance❑; **to fly** *or* **to send up a kite** tirer en l'air *ou* à découvert

(**d**) *Br Fam Old-fashioned (aeroplane)* zinc *m*

2 *vt Fam Fin* **to kite a cheque** faire un chèque en bois

3 *vi* s'envoler

►► ***kite balloon*** ballon *m* observateur; ***kite flyer*** cerf-voliste *mf*, lucanophile *mf*; *Fam Fin* tireur *m* en l'air *ou* à découvert; ***kite flying*** le cerf-volant; *Fam Fin* tirage *m* en l'air *ou* à découvert; **he enjoys kite flying** il aime faire du cerf-volant; ***Kite mark*** = label représentant un petit cerf-volant, apposé sur les produits conformes aux normes officielles britanniques; ***kite surfing*** surf *m* tracté par cerf-volant

kith [kɪθ] *npl* **kith and kin** amis *mpl* et parents *mpl*; **he's one of our own kith and kin** il est l'un des nôtres

kiting ['kaɪtɪŋ] *n Fam Fin* tirage *m* en l'air❑, tirage *m* à découvert❑

kitsch [kɪtʃ] **1** *adj* kitsch *(inv)*

2 *n* kitsch *m inv*

kitschy ['kɪtʃɪ] *adj (compar* **kitschier,** *superl* **kitschiest)** kitsch *(inv)*

kitten ['kɪtən] *n* (**a**) *(animal)* chaton *m*; **our cat has had kittens** notre chatte a eu des petits; *Br Fam* **he was having kittens** il était dans tous ses états *ou* aux cent coups (**b**) *(term of endearment)* ma petite, ma mignonne

►► ***kitten heels*** talons *mpl* bobine

kittenish ['kɪtənɪʃ] *adj (playful)* joueur, espiègle; *(flirtatious)* coquet

kittiwake ['kɪtɪweɪk] *n Orn* mouette *f* tridactyle

kitty ['kɪtɪ] *(pl* **kitties)** *n* (**a**) *Fam (kitten)* chaton❑ *m*; **here, kitty kitty** viens, mon minou *ou* minet (**b**) *(funds held in common)* cagnotte *f*, caisse *f* (commune); *(in gambling)* cagnotte *f* (**c**) *(in bowls)* cochonnet *m*

kitty-cornered *Am Fam* **1** *adj* diagonal ❑
 2 *adv* diagonalement ❑

kiwi ['ki:wi:] **1** *n* (**a**) *Orn* kiwi *m*, aptéryx *m* (**b**) *(fruit)* kiwi *m*
 2 Kiwi *n Fam (New Zealander)* Néo-Zélandais(e) ❑ *m,f*; **the Kiwis** *(rugby team)* les Kiwis
 ►► ***kiwi fruit*** kiwi *m*

KIWI

Le kiwi est l'emblème national de la Nouvelle-Zélande. Cet oiseau coureur, qui n'existe que dans ce pays, figure non seulement sur les pièces de monnaie et les billets de Nouvelle-Zélande, mais aussi sur le drapeau de la fameuse équipe de rugby des All Blacks. "Kiwi" est également devenu le surnom donné aux Néo-Zélandais.

KKK [,keɪkeɪ'keɪ] *n Am (abbr* **Ku Klux Klan**) Ku Klux Klan *m*

Klan [klæn] *n* **the Klan** le Ku Klux Klan

Klansman ['klænzmən] *(pl* **Klansmen** [-mən]) *n* membre *m* du Ku Klux Klan

Klaxon® ['klæksən] *n Br Aut* Klaxon® *m*

Kleenex® ['kli:neks] *n* Kleenex® *m inv*, mouchoir *m* en papier

klepto ['kleptəʊ] *(pl* **kleptos**) *n Fam* kleptomane ❑ *mf*, cleptomane ❑ *mf*

kleptomania [,kleptə'meɪnɪə] *n* kleptomanie *f*, cleptomanie *f*

kleptomaniac [,kleptə'meɪnɪæk] **1** *adj* kleptomane, cleptomane
 2 *n* kleptomane *mf*, cleptomane *mf*

klieg light [kli:g-] *n Am* lampe *f* à arc

klipspringer ['klɪp,sprɪŋə(r)] *n Zool* oréotrague *m*

Klondike ['klɒndaɪk] *n* (**a**) *(river)* **the Klondike** le Klondike (**b**) *Fig (source of wealth)* mine *f* d'or
 ►► ***the Klondike gold rush*** = la ruée vers l'or (1897–99), au Canada; ***the Klondike River*** le Klondike

Klondiker, Klondyker ['klɒndaɪkə(r)] *n* navire-usine *m*

kloof [klu:f] *n SAfr* ravin *m*, gorge *f*

klutz [klʌts] *n Am Fam* balourd(e) *m,f*, godiche *f*

klystron ['klaɪstrɒn] *n* klystron *m*

km *(written abbr* **kilometre**) km

km/h *(written abbr* **kilometres per hour**) km/h

knack [næk] *n* tour *m* de main, truc *m*; **there's a knack to it** il y a un truc; **it's easy once you get the knack (of it)** c'est facile une fois qu'on a compris le truc; **she's got a knack of finding the right word** elle sait toujours trouver le mot juste; *Hum* **he's got a knack of turning up at meal-times** il a le chic pour arriver à l'heure du repas

knacker ['nækə(r)] *Br* **1** *vt very Fam* (**a**) *(exhaust)* crever; **that run completely knackered me** cette course m'a mis sur les genoux (**b**) *(break, wear out)* bousiller; **I've knackered my hi-fi** j'ai bousillé ma chaîne stéréo
 2 *n* (**a**) *(slaughterer)* équarrisseur *m* (**b**) *(of buildings, ships)* démolisseur *m*
 3 knackers *npl Br Vulg (testicles)* couilles *fpl*
 ►► ***knacker's yard*** équarrissoir *m*, abattoir *m*

knackered ['nækəd] *adj Br very Fam* (**a**) *(exhausted)* crevé, lessivé, naze (**b**) *(broken, worn out)* bousillé

knapsack ['næpsæk] *n* havresac *m*, sac *m* à dos

knapweed ['næpwi:d] *n Bot* **(common) knapweed** centaurée *f* (noire)

knave [neɪv] *n* (**a**) *Arch (rogue)* fripon *m*, canaille *f* (**b**) *Cards* valet *m*; **knave of clubs** valet *m* de trèfle

knavery ['neɪvərɪ] *(pl* **knaveries**) *n Arch* friponnerie *f*, canaillerie *f*

knavish ['neɪvɪʃ] *adj Arch (person)* fripon; *(trick, deed)* de fripon, de canaille

knead [ni:d] *vt (dough, clay, muscles)* pétrir, malaxer

knee [ni:] **1** *n* (**a**) *(part of body)* genou *m*; **the snow was up to our knees, we were up to our knees in snow** on avait de la neige jusqu'aux genoux; **at knee level** à hauteur du genou; **to go down on one's knees, to fall to one's knees** se mettre à genoux; *also Fig* **to be on one's knees** être à genoux; *Literary* **to bend** *or* **to bow the knee to** *or* **before sb** fléchir le genou devant qn, s'incliner devant qn; **to bring sb to his/her knees** faire capituler qn; **the war nearly brought the country to its knees** la guerre a failli entraîner la ruine du pays
 (**b**) *(of trousers)* genou *m*; **worn at the knees** usé aux genoux
 (**c**) *(lap)* genoux *mpl*; **come and sit on my knee** viens t'asseoir sur mes genoux; **to put sb over one's knee** donner la fessée à *ou* corriger qn; **I learnt it at my mother's knee** j'ai appris cela dès ma plus tendre enfance; **on bended knee** à genoux; **to go down on bended knee** se mettre à genoux
 (**d**) *Tech (in pipe)* genou *m*, coude *m*; *(device)* rotule *f*
 2 *vt* donner un coup de genou à; **he kneed me in the groin** il m'a donné un coup de genou dans l'aine; **she kneed the door open** elle poussa la porte du genou
 ►► *Tech* ***knee bracket*** console-équerre *f*; *Br* ***knee breeches*** knickers *mpl*; ***knee drop*** *(in wrestling)* projection *f* sur le genou; ***knee jerk*** réflexe *m* rotulien; ***knee joint*** articulation *f* du genou; ***knee pad*** genouillère *f*; ***knee plate*** gousset *m* (de charpente); ***knee reflex*** réflexe *m* rotulien; *Carp* ***knee timber*** bois *m* courbant *ou* coudé

kneecap ['ni:kæp] *(pt & pp* **kneecapped**, *cont* **kneecapping**) **1** *n Anat* rotule *f*
 2 *vt* **to kneecap sb** punir qn en lui brisant les rotules *(pratique terroriste)*

kneecapping ['ni:kæpɪŋ] *n* mutilation *f* des rotules

knee-deep *adj* **the snow was knee-deep** on avait de la neige jusqu'aux genoux; **the water was only knee-deep** l'eau ne nous arrivait qu'aux genoux; **we were knee-deep in water** l'eau nous arrivait *ou* nous étions dans l'eau jusqu'aux genoux; *Fig* **he was knee-deep in trouble** il était dans les ennuis jusqu'au cou

knee-high *adj (grass)* à hauteur de genou; **the grass was knee-high** l'herbe nous arrivait (jusqu')aux genoux; *Fam Hum* **knee-high to a grasshopper** haut comme trois pommes
 ►► ***knee-high socks*** chaussettes *fpl* montantes

kneehole ['ni:həʊl] *n (in desk)* trou *m* pour l'entrée des genoux
 ►► ***kneehole desk*** bureau *m* ministre

knee-jerk *adj (reflex)* automatique
 ►► *Fig Pej* ***knee-jerk reaction*** réflexe *m*, automatisme *m*; *Pol* ***knee-jerk support*** soutien *m* systématique *ou* inconditionnel

kneel [ni:l] *(pt & pp* **knelt** [nelt] *or* **kneeled**) *vi* s'agenouiller, se mettre à genoux; **she was kneeling on the floor** elle était agenouillée *ou* à genoux par terre; **to kneel in prayer** s'agenouiller pour prier; **to kneel before sb** se mettre à genoux devant qn

►**kneel down** *vi* se mettre à genoux, s'agenouiller

knee-length *adj (dress)* qui descend jusqu'aux genoux; *(boot, socks)* qui monte jusqu'aux genoux

kneeler ['ni:lə(r)] *n (cushion in church)* agenouilloir *m*

kneeling ['ni:lɪŋ] *adj* agenouillé, à genoux; **in a kneeling position** à genoux

kneepan ['ni:pæn] *n Anat* patelle *f*, rotule *f*

kneeroom ['ni:rʊm] *n* **have you got enough kneeroom?** avez-vous assez de place pour vos genoux *ou* vos jambes?

knees-up [ni:z-] *n Br Fam* java *f*; **to have a knees-up** faire la java; **there was a bit of a knees-up in the pub** on a un peu fait la java au pub

knee-trembler [-tremblə(r)] *n Br Fam Hum* **to have a knee-trembler** faire l'amour debout ❑

knell [nel] *n Literary* glas *m*; **to toll the knell** sonner le glas

knelt [nelt] *pt & pp of* **kneel**

knew [nju:] *pt of* **know**

knickerbocker glory ['nɪkə,bɒkə-] *n* = coupe de glace avec fruits et crème Chantilly

knickerbockers ['nɪkə,bɒkəz] *npl* knickers *mpl*; *(for golf)* culotte *f* de golf

knickers ['nɪkəz] **1** *npl* (**a**) *Br (underwear)* **(pair of) knickers** culotte *f*, slip *m (de femme)*; *Fam* **don't get your knickers in a twist!** *(don't panic)* ne t'affole pas! ❑; *(don't get angry)* du calme!, calme-toi!; *Vulg* **to get into sb's knickers** s'envoyer qn, culbuter qn (**b**) *Am (knickerbockers)* knickers *mpl*; *(for golf)* culotte *f* de golf
 2 *exclam Br Fam Old-fashioned* mon œil!

knick-knack ['nɪknæk] *n (trinket)* bibelot *m*; *(brooch)* colifichet *m*

knife [naɪf] *(pl* **knives** [naɪvz]) **1** *n* (**a**) *(for eating)* couteau *m*; **a knife and fork** une fourchette et un couteau; **her words cut me like a knife** ses paroles m'ont piqué au vif *ou* m'ont profondément blessé; **fish knife** couteau *m* à poisson; **like a knife through butter** comme dans du beurre; **this knife wouldn't cut butter** ce couteau ne coupe que ce qu'il voit *ou* ne coupe rien; *Fam* **to be** *or* **to go under the knife** passer sur le billard; *Fam Old-fashioned* **before you could say knife** en un rien de temps, en moins de rien
 (**b**) *(as a weapon)* couteau *m*; **to carry a knife** porter un couteau sur soi; *Fig* **she really got her knife into them** elle en avait drôlement après eux, elle leur en voulait drôlement; *Fig* **the knives are out** ils sont à couteaux tirés *ou* en guerre ouverte; *Fam* **you really stuck the knife in!** tu ne l'as pas loupé!; *Fig* **to turn** *or* **to twist the knife (in the wound)** retourner le couteau dans la plaie
 2 *vt* donner un coup de couteau à; **to knife sb to death** tuer qn à coups de couteau; **he's been knifed** il a reçu un coup de couteau; **he was knifed in the back** il a reçu un coup de couteau *ou* on lui a planté un couteau dans le dos; *Fig* on lui a tiré dans le dos *ou* dans les pattes
 ►► ***knife attack*** attaque *f* à coups de couteau; ***knife pleat*** pli *m* plat; *Elec* ***knife switch*** interrupteur *m* à lame; ***knife wound*** blessure *f* à coups de couteau

knife-edge *n* (**a**) *(blade)* fil *m* du couteau; *Fig* **we were on a knife-edge** on était sur des charbons ardents; **his decision was (balanced) on a knife-edge** sa décision ne tenait qu'à un fil (**b**) *(of scales)* couteau *m*

knife-edged *adj*
 ►► ***knife-edged file*** lime *f* à couteau; ***knife-edged pleat*** pli *m* plat; ***knife-edged wit*** esprit *m* mordant

knife-grinder *n (person)* rémouleur *m*; *(instrument)* meule *f* à aiguiser

knife-point *n* **at knife-point** sous la menace du couteau

knife-rest *n* porte-couteau *m*

knife-sharpener *n (automatic)* aiguisoir *m*; *(manual)* fusil *m* (à aiguiser)

knifing ['naɪfɪŋ] *n* agression *f* à coups de couteau

knight [naɪt] **1** *n* (**a**) *Hist* chevalier *m*; **a knight in shining armour** *(romantic hero)* un prince charmant; *(saviour)* un sauveur, un redresseur de torts
 (**b**) *Br (honorary title)* chevalier *m*; **Laurence Olivier was made a knight** Laurence Olivier a été anobli *ou* fait chevalier
 (**c**) *(chess piece)* cavalier *m*
 2 *vt* faire chevalier
 ►► *Br* ***knight bachelor*** chevalier *m (n'appartenant à aucun ordre)*; ***the Knights of Columbus*** les Chevaliers de Colomb, = organisation catholique fondée aux États-Unis en 1882, présente dans de nombreux pays; *Br* ***Knight Commander (of the Order) of the Bath*** Chevalier *m* Commandeur de l'Ordre du Bain; ***Knight of (the Order of) the Garter*** Chevalier de l'Ordre de la Jarretière; ***the Knights of the Round Table*** les Chevaliers de la Table ronde; ***Knight Templar*** Templier *m*

knight-errant *(pl* **knights-errant**) *n Hist* chevalier *m* errant

knighthood ['naɪthʊd] *n* (**a**) *Br (title)* titre *m* de chevalier; **to receive a knighthood** être fait chevalier, être anobli (**b**) *Hist* chevalerie *f*

knightly ['naɪtlɪ] *adj* chevaleresque

Knightsbridge ['naɪtsbrɪdʒ] *n* = quartier chic de Londres, connu pour ses magasins de luxe

kniphofia [nɪ'fəʊfɪə] *n Bot* tritoma *m*

knit [nɪt] *(pt & pp* **knit** *or* **knitted**, *cont* **knitting**) **1** *vt* (**a**) *(garment)* tricoter; **he knitted himself a scarf** il s'est tricoté une écharpe
 (**b**) *(in instructions)* **knit 2 purl 2** (tricoter) 2 mailles à l'endroit, 2 mailles à l'envers; **knit 2 together** tricoter 2 mailles ensemble
 (**c**) *(unite)* unir

kit–kni

(**d**) *(idiom)* **to knit one's brows** froncer les sourcils

2 *vi* (**a**) *(make garment)* tricoter; **I like to knit in the evenings** j'aime bien tricoter *ou* faire du tricot le soir

(**b**) *(as opposed to purl)* tricoter à l'endroit

(**c**) *(bones)* se souder

►**knit together 1** *vt sep (unite)* unir; *Med (bones)* souder

2 *vi (heal → bones)* se souder

►**knit up 1** *vt sep (garment)* tricoter; **she knitted up a scarf from the spare wool** elle a fait une écharpe avec la laine qui restait

2 *vi (yarn)* **this wool knits up easily** cette laine se tricote facilement

-knit [nɪt] *suff* (**a**) *(of woollen garment)* **a chunky-knit sweater** un gros pull, un pull en grosse laine (**b**) *(united)* **a close-knit family** une famille très unie

knitted ['nɪtɪd] *adj* tricoté, en tricot

►► ***knitted fabric*** tricot *m*; ***knitted goods*** tricots *mpl*, articles *mpl* en tricot

knitter ['nɪtə(r)] *n* tricoteur(euse) *m,f*; **she's a good/a quick knitter** elle tricote bien/vite

knitting ['nɪtɪŋ] **1** *n* (**a**) *(garment)* tricot *m*; **have you seen my knitting?** avez-vous vu mon tricot?

(**b**) *(activity)* tricot *m*; *(on industrial scale)* tricotage *m*; **to do some knitting** faire du tricot; **knitting helps me relax** le tricot m'aide à me détendre; **machine knitting** tricots *mpl* faits à la machine; *Am & Scot Fam* **to stick to one's knitting** s'occuper de ses oignons

(**c**) *(of bones)* soudure *f*

2 *comp (wool)* à tricoter; *(pattern)* de tricot; *(factory)* de tricotage

►► ***knitting machine*** machine *f* à tricoter; ***knitting needle, knitting pin*** aiguille *f* à tricoter

knitwear ['nɪtweə(r)] *n (UNCOUNT) (garments)* lainages *mpl*; *(in department store)* rayon *m* lainages

►► ***knitwear manufacturer*** fabricant *m* de lainages

knives [naɪvz] *pl of* **knife**

knob [nɒb] *n* (**a**) *(handle → of door, drawer)* poignée *f*, bouton *m*; *Br Fam* **the same to you with knobs on!** toi-même!

(**b**) *(control → on appliance)* bouton *m*

(**c**) *(ball-shaped end → of walking stick)* pommeau *m*; *(→ on furniture)* bouton *m*

(**d**) *(of butter)* noix *f*

(**e**) *(hillock)* monticule *m*

(**f**) *Br Vulg (penis)* queue *f*, bite *f*

(**g**) *Br Vulg (man)* trou *m* du cul

knobbed [nɒbd] *adj (stick)* à pommeau

knobbly ['nɒblɪ] (*compar* **knobblier,** *superl* **knobbliest**) *adj Br* noueux; **knobbly knees** genoux *mpl* couverts de bosses

knobby ['nɒbɪ] (*compar* **knobbier,** *superl* **knobbiest**) *adj Am* noueux; **knobby knees** genoux *mpl* couverts de bosses

KNOCK [nɒk]

coup	►1 (a) – (c)
critique	►1 (d)
cognement	►1 (e)
heurter	►2 (b); 3 (b)
cogner	►2 (b); 3 (b), (c)
éreinter	►2 (c)
frapper	►3 (a)

1 *n* (**a**) *(blow)* coup *m*; **give it a knock with a hammer** donne un coup de marteau dessus; **there was a knock at the door/window** on a frappé à la porte/fenêtre; **she gave three knocks on the door** elle a frappé trois fois *ou* coups à la porte; **to hear a knock** entendre frapper; **no one answered my knock** personne n'a répondu quand j'ai frappé; **knock! knock!** toc! toc!; **can you give me a knock tomorrow morning?** est-ce que vous pouvez (venir) frapper à ma porte demain matin pour me réveiller?

(**b**) *(bump)* coup *m*; **to give sb a knock on the head** porter à qn un coup à la tête; **I got a nasty knock on the elbow** *(in fight, accident)* j'ai reçu un sacré coup au coude; *(by one's own clumsiness)* je me suis bien cogné le coude; **the car's had a few knocks, but nothing serious** la voiture est un peu cabossée mais rien de grave

(**c**) *(setback)* coup *m*; **his reputation has taken a hard knock** sa réputation en a pris un sérieux coup; **I've taken a few knocks in my time** j'ai encaissé des coups moi aussi

(**d**) *Fam (criticism)* critique❑ *f*; **she's taken a few knocks from the press** la presse n'a pas toujours été très tendre avec elle

(**e**) *Aut (in engine)* cognement *m*

2 *vt* (**a**) *(hit)* **to knock a nail in** enfoncer un clou; **she knocked a nail into the wall** elle a planté un clou dans le mur; **she knocked a hole in the wall** elle a fait un trou dans le mur; **he was knocked into the ditch** il a été projeté dans le fossé; **the boy was knocking the ball against the wall** le garçon lançait *ou* envoyait la balle contre le mur; **the force of the explosion knocked us to the floor** la force de l'explosion nous a projetés à terre; *Fam* **to knock sb unconscious** *or* **cold** assommer qn; **the boom knocked him off balance** la bôme, en le heurtant, l'a déséquilibré *ou* lui a fait perdre l'équilibre; *Fig* **the news knocked me off balance** la nouvelle m'a sidéré *ou* coupé le souffle

(**b**) *(bump)* heurter, cogner; **I knocked my head on** *or* **against the low ceiling** je me suis cogné la tête contre le *ou* au plafond

(**c**) *Fam (criticize → author, film)* éreinter; *(→ driving, cooking)* critiquer❑; **knocking your colleagues isn't going to help** ce n'est pas en débinant vos collègues *ou* en cassant du sucre sur le dos de vos collègues que vous changerez quoi que ce soit; **they're always knocking the trade unions** ils n'arrêtent pas de taper sur les syndicats; **don't knock it till you've tried it!** n'en dis pas de mal avant d'avoir essayé❑

(**d**) *Br very Fam (have sex with)* se faire, se taper

(**e**) *(idioms)* **to knock holes in a plan/an argument** démolir un projet/un argument; **maybe it will knock some sense into him** cela lui mettra peut-être du plomb dans la cervelle, cela le ramènera peut-être à la raison; **the army soon knocked his enthusiasm out of him** l'armée a eu tôt fait de tuer en lui toute trace d'enthousiasme; **to knock sb into shape** mettre qn au pas; *Br Fam* **to knock sth on the head** *(put a stop to)* faire cesser qch❑; *Br Fam* **our plans have been knocked on the head** nos projets sont tombés à l'eau; *Br Fam* **knock it on the head, will you!** c'est pas bientôt fini?; *Br Fam* **he can knock spots off me at chess/tennis** il me bat à plate couture aux échecs/au tennis; *Am Fam* **it really knocked me for a loop** ça m'a vraiment scié; **to knock sb dead** *(impress)* en mettre plein la vue à qn; **Texas knocked them dead last night** hier soir, Texas a fait un tabac

3 *vi* (**a**) *(hit)* frapper; **to knock on** *or* **at the door** frapper (à la porte); **she came in without knocking** elle est entrée sans frapper; **they knock on the wall when we're too noisy** ils tapent *ou* cognent contre le mur quand on fait trop de bruit; **it was a branch knocking against the window** c'était une branche qui cognait contre la fenêtre

(**b**) *(bump)* **to knock against** *or* **into** heurter, cogner; **she knocked into the desk** elle s'est heurtée *ou* cognée contre le bureau; **my elbow knocked against the door frame** je me suis cogné *ou* heurté le coude contre le chambranle de la porte

(**c**) *(make sound)* cogner; **my heart was knocking** je sentais mon cœur cogner dans ma poitrine, j'avais le cœur qui cognait; **the car engine is knocking** le moteur cogne; *Hum* **his knees were knocking** ses genoux jouaient des castagnettes; **the pipes knock when you run the taps** les tuyaux cognent quand on ouvre les robinets

►**knock about, knock around 1** *vi Fam (loiter)* traîner; **Vicky must be knocking about here somewhere** Vicky doit traîner quelque part dans le coin; **I knocked about in Australia for a while** j'ai bourlingué *ou* roulé ma bosse en Australie pendant quelque temps; *Br* **are my fags knocking about?** est-ce que mes clopes sont dans le coin?; **that's what I wear to knock about in** ce sont mes vêtements d'intérieur❑

2 *vt insep Fam* traîner dans; **I knocked about town all day** j'ai traîné en ville toute la journée; **she spent a year knocking about Europe** elle a passé une année à se balader en Europe; **these clothes are OK for knocking about the house in** ces vêtements, ça va pour traîner à la maison; **your keys are knocking about the kitchen somewhere** tes clés traînent dans un coin de la cuisine

3 *vt sep* (**a**) *(beat)* battre; *(ill-treat)* malmener; **he used to knock his wife about a lot** il tapait sur *ou* il battait sa femme; **the old car's been knocked about a bit** la vieille voiture a pris quelques coups ici et là; **the furniture has been badly knocked about** les meubles ont été fort maltraités

(**b**) *(jolt, shake)* ballotter; **we were really knocked about in the back of the truck** nous étions ballottés à l'arrière du camion

(**c**) *Fam (discuss)* débattre❑; **we knocked the idea about for a while** nous en avons vaguement discuté pendant un certain temps

►**knock about with, knock around with** *vt insep Fam* fréquenter❑; **they knocked about together at school** ils se fréquentaient à l'école

►**knock back** *vt sep Fam* (**a**) *(drink)* descendre; **she could knock back ten vodkas in an hour** elle pouvait s'envoyer dix vodkas en une heure; **he certainly knocks it back!** qu'est-ce qu'il descend!

(**b**) *(cost)* coûter à❑; **that car must have knocked him back a few thousand pounds** cette voiture a bien dû lui coûter quelques milliers de livres

(**c**) *(surprise, shock)* secouer, bouleverser; **the news really knocked me back** la nouvelle m'a vraiment abasourdi *ou* m'a laissé pantois

(**d**) *Br (reject)* **to knock sb back** rejeter qn❑; **to knock sth back** *(offer, invitation)* refuser qch❑; **she knocked him back** il s'est pris une veste

►**knock down** *vt sep* (**a**) *(person)* renverser; *(in fight)* envoyer par terre, étendre; **she was knocked down by a bus** elle a été renversée par un bus; **he knocked the champion down in the first round** il a envoyé le champion au tapis *ou* il a mis le champion knock-down dans la première reprise

(**b**) *(hurdle, vase, pile of books)* faire tomber, renverser

(**c**) *(demolish → building)* démolir; *(→ wall)* démolir, abattre; *(→ argument)* démolir

(**d**) *(price)* baisser; *(salesman)* faire baisser; **I managed to knock him down to $500** j'ai réussi à le faire baisser jusqu'à 500 dollars

(**e**) *Br (at auction)* adjuger; **it was knocked down to her for £300** on le lui a adjugé pour 300 livres

►**knock off 1** *vt sep* (**a**) *(from shelf, wall etc)* faire tomber; **the statue's arm had been knocked off** la statue avait perdu un bras; **he knocked the earth off the spade** il fit tomber la terre qui était restée collée à la bêche; **he was knocked off his bicycle by a car** il s'est fait renverser à vélo par une voiture; *Fig* **to knock sb off their pedestal** *or* **perch** faire tomber qn de son piédestal; *Fam* **to knock sb's block off** casser la figure à qn

(**b**) *(reduce by)* faire une réduction de; **the salesman knocked 10 percent off (for us)** le vendeur nous a fait un rabais *ou* une remise de 10 pour cent; **I managed to get something knocked off the price** j'ai réussi à faire baisser un peu le prix

(**c**) *Fam (write rapidly)* torcher; **she can knock off an article in half an hour** elle peut pondre un article en une demi-heure

(**d**) *very Fam (kill)* descendre, buter

(**e**) *Br very Fam (steal)* piquer, faucher; *(rob)* braquer; **they knocked off a bank** ils ont braqué une banque

(**f**) *Br Vulg (have sex with)* baiser

(**g**) *Fam (idiom)* **knock it off!** *(stop it)* arrête ton char!

2 *vi Fam (stop work)* cesser le travail❑; **we knock off at five o'clock** on finit à cinq heures

►**knock on 1** *vt sep (in rugby)* **to knock the ball on** faire un en-avant

2 *vt insep Br Fam* **he's knocking on sixty** il va sur la soixantaine; **there were knocking on fifty people in the hall** il n'y avait pas loin de cinquante personnes dans la salle

3 *vi* (**a**) *(in rugby)* faire un en-avant

(**b**) *Br Fam (age)* **my dad's knocking on a bit**

now mon père commence à prendre de la bouteille

▸**knock out** *vt sep* (**a**) *(nail)* faire sortir; *(wall)* abattre; **one of his teeth was knocked out** il a perdu une dent

(**b**) *(make unconscious)* assommer; *(in boxing)* mettre K-O; *Fam (of drug, pill)* assommer❑, mettre K-O; *Fam* **the sleeping pill knocked her out for ten hours** le somnifère l'a assommée *ou* mise K-O pendant dix heures

(**c**) *Fam (astound)* épater; **her performance really knocked me out!** son interprétation m'a vraiment épaté!

(**d**) *(eliminate)* éliminer; **our team was knocked out in the first round** notre équipe a été éliminée au premier tour

(**e**) *(put out of action)* mettre hors service; **it can knock out a tank at 2,000 metres** cela peut mettre un tank hors de combat à 2000 mètres

(**f**) *Fam (exhaust)* crever; **I'm not going to knock myself out working for him** je ne vais pas m'esquinter à travailler pour lui

(**g**) *Am Fam* **to knock oneself out** *(indulge oneself)* se faire plaisir❑; **there's plenty of food left, knock yourself out!** il reste plein de nourriture, sers-toi autant que tu veux!❑

(**h**) *(pipe)* débourrer

▸**knock over** *vt sep* (**a**) *(capsize)* renverser, faire tomber; **I knocked a pile of plates over** j'ai renversé *ou* fait tomber une pile d'assiettes; **she was knocked over by a bus** elle a été renversée par un bus

(**b**) *Am Fam (rob)* braquer

▸**knock together 1** *vt sep* (**a**) *(hit together)* cogner l'un contre l'autre; **they make music by knocking bamboo sticks together** ils font de la musique en frappant des bambous l'un contre l'autre; *Fam* **they need their heads knocking together, those two** ces deux-là auraient bien besoin qu'on leur secoue les puces

(**b**) *Fam (make quickly)* faire à la hâte❑; **we knocked together a rough shelter** on s'est fabriqué une espèce d'abri❑

2 *vi* s'entrechoquer

▸**knock up 1** *vt sep* (**a**) *Fam (make quickly)* faire à la hâte❑; **these buildings were knocked up after the war** ces bâtiments ont été construits à la hâte après la guerre; **he knocked up a delicious meal in no time** en un rien de temps, il a réussi à nous préparer quelque chose de délicieux❑

(**b**) *Br (waken)* réveiller (en frappant à la porte)

(**c**) *Br Fam (exhaust)* crever; *(make ill)* rendre malade❑; **that walk yesterday really knocked me up** la promenade d'hier m'a complètement crevé; **he's knocked up with the flu** il a chopé la grippe

(**d**) *Am Fam (damage)* esquinter; **the furniture is pretty knocked up** les meubles sont plutôt esquintés *ou* amochés

(**e**) *very Fam (make pregnant)* mettre en cloque; **she got knocked up** elle s'est fait mettre en cloque

(**f**) *(in cricket)* marquer; **he knocked up 50 runs before rain stopped play** il a marqué 50 points avant que la pluie n'interrompe la partie

2 *vi Br (in ball games)* faire des balles

---

knockabout ['nɒkəbaʊt] **1** *n* (**a**) *(game)* partie *f* pour rire (**b**) *Naut* dériveur *m*

2 *adj (game)* pour rire; **a knockabout comedy** *or* **farce** une grosse farce; **a knockabout comedian** un clown

knockback ['nɒkbæk] *n Br Fam (rejection)* veste *f*; **to get a knockback** prendre une veste

knockdown ['nɒk,daʊn] **1** *adj* (**a**) *(forceful)* **a knockdown blow** un coup à assommer un bœuf; **a knockdown argument** un argument massue

(**b**) *(easy to dismantle)* démontable; **sold in knockdown form** vendu en kit

(**c**) *Br (reduced)* **for sale at knockdown prices** en vente à des prix imbattables *ou* défiant toute concurrence; **I got it for a knockdown price** je l'ai eu pour trois fois rien

2 *n* (**a**) *(in boxing)* knock-down *m inv*

(**b**) *Am Fam Old-fashioned (introduction)* présentation❑ *f*; **I'll give you a knockdown to him** je te le présenterai❑

knocker ['nɒkə(r)] **1** *n* (**a**) *(on door)* heurtoir *m*, marteau *m* (de porte) (**b**) *Fam (critic)* débineur(euse) *m,f*

2 knockers *npl very Fam (breasts)* nichons *mpl*

knocker-up *(pl* **knockers-up**) *n Br Old-fashioned* = autrefois, personne qui réveillait les gens en frappant à leur porte

knock-for-knock agreement *n Br Ins* = accord à l'amiable selon lequel, lors d'un accident, chaque compagnie d'assurance paie les dégâts de son propre assuré

knocking ['nɒkɪŋ] *n* (**a**) *(noise)* bruit *m* de coups, cognement *m* (**b**) *(in engine)* cognement *m*, cliquetis *m* (**c**) *Br Fam (injury, defeat)* **to take a knocking** *(in fight)* se faire rouer de coups; *(in match)* se faire battre à plate(s) couture(s); **their prestige took a knocking** leur prestige en a pris un coup

▸▸ ***knocking copy*** *(UNCOUNT)* publicité *f* comparative; ***knocking sheet*** = feuille sur laquelle sont inscrits les points faibles de ses principaux concurrents commerciaux; *Br Fam* ***knocking shop*** bordel *m*

knocking-off time *n Br Fam* **it's knocking-off time** c'est l'heure de se tirer

knock-kneed [-'ni:d] *adj* cagneux

knock-knock joke *n* = blague fondée sur un jeu de mots, qui débute toujours par "knock-knock – who's there?"

knock-on *n (in rugby)* en-avant *m inv*

▸▸ ***knock-on effect*** répercussion *f*; **to have a knock-on effect** déclencher une réaction en chaîne; **businesses are feeling the knock-on effect of a strong pound** les entreprises subissent le contrecoup d'une livre forte

knockout ['nɒkaʊt] *n* (**a**) *Boxing* knock-out *m inv*, K-O *m*; **to win by a knockout** gagner par K-O

(**b**) *Fam (sensation)* **to be a knockout** être sensationnel *ou* génial; **she's a knockout!** *(beautiful)* elle est canon!

(**c**) *Sport* tournoi *m* (par élimination directe)

(**d**) *(at auction)* entente *f (entre concurrents pour baisser les prix)*

▸▸ *Boxing* ***knockout blow*** coup *m* qui met K-O; *Fig* coup *m* de grâce; **to deliver the knockout blow** *Boxing* mettre K-O; *Fig* donner le coup de grâce; *Sport* ***knockout competition*** tournoi *m* par élimination; *Fam* ***knockout drops*** soporifique❑ *m*, somnifère❑ *m*; ***knockout stages*** *(of competition)* (épreuves *fpl*) éliminatoires *mpl*

knockover ['nɒkəʊvə(r)] *n Am Fam (robbery)* casse *m*

knock-up *n Br Sport (in ball games)* échauffement *m*; **to have a knock-up** faire des balles

knoll [nəʊl] *n* monticule *m*, tertre *m*

Knossian ['knɒsɪən] *adj* de Cnossos, de Knossos

Knossos ['knɒsɒs] *n* Cnossos, Knossos

knot [nɒt] *(pt & pp* **knotted**, *cont* **knotting**) **1** *n* (**a**) *(fastening)* nœud *m*; *Fig (bond)* lien *m*; **to tie sth in a knot, to tie a knot in sth** nouer qch, faire un nœud à qch; **to tie/to untie a knot** faire/défaire un nœud; *Fam Fig* **to tie the knot** se maquer; *Br Fam* **tie a knot in it!** ferme-la!

(**b**) *(tangle)* nœud *m*; **the wool is full of knots** la laine est toute emmêlée; *Fig* **my stomach was in knots** j'avais l'estomac noué; *Fam* **to get tied up in knots, to tie oneself (up) in knots** s'emmêler les pinceaux

(**c**) *(in wood)* nœud *m*

(**d**) *Anat & Med* nœud *m*, nodule *m*; *(in muscle)* raideur *f*

(**e**) *(cluster of people)* petit groupe *m*

(**f**) *Naut* nœud *m*; **we are doing 15 knots** nous filons 15 nœuds; *Fig* **at a rate of knots** à toute allure, à un train d'enfer; *Fam* **she was spending her money at a rate of knots** elle jetait l'argent par les fenêtres

(**g**) *Orn* bécasseau *m* maubèche, canut *m*

2 *vt (string)* nouer, faire un nœud dans; *(tie)* nouer; **he knotted the rope around his waist** il s'est attaché *ou* noué la corde autour de la taille

3 *vi (stomach)* se nouer; *(muscles)* se contracter, se raidir; **my stomach knotted up with fear** j'avais l'estomac noué par la peur

knotgrass ['nɒtgrɑ:s] *n Bot* renouée *f* des oiseaux

knothole ['nɒthəʊl] *n* trou *m (laissé par un nœud dans du bois)*

knotted ['nɒtɪd] *adj* noué; *Br very Fam* **get knotted!** va te faire voir!

knotty ['nɒtɪ] *(compar* **knottier**, *superl* **knottiest**) *adj* (**a**) *(wood, hands)* noueux (**b**) *(wool, hair, rope)* plein de nœuds (**c**) *(question, problem)* épineux

knout [naʊt] *n* knout *m*

KNOW [nəʊ]

connaître	▸ **1 (a) – (c), (g)**
savoir	▸ **1 (c); 2**
reconnaître	▸ **1 (e)**
distinguer	▸ **1 (f)**
discerner	▸ **1 (f)**
considérer	▸ **1 (i)**

(pt **knew** [nju:], *pp* **known** [nəʊn]) **1** *vt* (**a**) *(person)* connaître; **to know sb by sight/by reputation** connaître qn de vue/de réputation; **we've known each other for years** ça fait des années que nous nous connaissons; **I don't know him to speak to** je ne le connais pas assez pour lui parler; **I know him to say hello to** nous nous saluons; **when I first knew her** quand j'ai fait sa connaissance; **knowing him, he'll still be in bed** tel que je le connais, il sera encore au lit; **you'll like her once you get to know her better** elle vous plaira une fois que vous la connaîtrez mieux; **I'd like to get to know him better** j'aimerais bien le connaître mieux

(**b**) *(place)* connaître; **I know Budapest well** je connais bien Budapest

(**c**) *(fact, information)* **do you know her phone number?** vous connaissez son numéro de téléphone?; **it'll be easier once you get to know the system** ce sera plus facile une fois que tu te seras familiarisé avec le système; **civilization as we know it** la civilisation telle que nous la connaissons; **how was I to know she wouldn't come?** comment aurais-je pu savoir *ou* deviner qu'elle ne viendrait pas?; **I know for a fact that he's lying** je sais pertinemment qu'il ment; **she is known to be a keen photographer** on sait qu'elle aime beaucoup la photographie; **he let it be known that he was available** il a fait savoir qu'il était disponible; **I don't know that it's the best solution** je ne suis pas certain *ou* sûr que ce soit la meilleure solution; **you don't know** *or* **you'll never know how glad I am that it's over** tu ne peux pas savoir combien *ou* à quel point je suis content que ce soit terminé; **she thinks she knows all the answers** elle croit tout savoir; **she didn't quite know what to say** elle ne savait trop que dire; **I know what I'm talking about** je sais de quoi je parle; **I'll let you know how it turns out** je te dirai comment ça s'est passé; **any problems, let me know** au moindre problème, n'hésitez pas; **do you know anything about him that could help us?** est-ce que vous savez quelque chose à son sujet qui pourrait nous aider?; **do you know anything about physics?** est-ce que tu connais quelque chose en physique?; **she knows a lot about politics** elle s'y connaît en politique; **she doesn't know what fear is** elle ne sait pas ce que c'est que d'avoir peur; **there's no knowing how he'll react** on ne peut pas savoir comment il réagira; *Fam* **she knows a thing or two about business** elle s'y connaît en affaires❑; **she knows her own mind** elle sait ce qu'elle veut; *Fam* **it's not an easy job – don't I know it!** ce n'est pas un travail facile – à qui le dis-tu!; *Fam* **wouldn't you know it!** comme par hasard!; **you know what I mean** tu vois ce que je veux dire; *Fam* **he was just sort of lying there, know what I mean?** il était allongé là, tu vois; *Fam* **well, what do you know!** ça alors!, ça par exemple!; **what do YOU know?** qu'est-ce que tu en sais?; *very Fam* **you know what you can do with it!** tu sais où tu peux te le mettre!; *Fam* **God** *or* **Heaven knows why!** Dieu sait pourquoi!

(**d**) *(language, skill)* **he knows French** il comprend le français; **I know a few words of Welsh** je connais quelques mots de gallois; **she really knows her job/subject** elle connaît son boulot/sujet; **to know how to do sth** savoir faire qch; **does he know how to cook?** sait-il cuisiner?; **they knew how to make cars in those days!** en ce temps-là, les voitures, c'était du solide!

(**e**) *(recognize)* reconnaître; **I knew her the**

kno–kno

moment I saw her je l'ai reconnue dès que je l'ai vue; **I'd know him anywhere** je le reconnaîtrais n'importe où; **I knew her by her walk** je l'ai reconnue à son allure *ou* à sa démarche; **the town centre has changed so much you wouldn't know it** le centre-ville a tellement changé que vous auriez du mal à le reconnaître; **she knows a bargain when she sees one** elle sait reconnaître une bonne affaire; **he wouldn't know a good novel if it hit him** il est tout à fait incapable de reconnaître un bon roman

(**f**) *(distinguish)* distinguer, discerner; **she doesn't know right from wrong** elle ne sait pas discerner le bien du mal *ou* faire la différence entre le bien et le mal; *Fam* **he doesn't know one end of a car from another** il n'y connaît absolument rien en voitures❑

(**g**) *(experience)* connaître; **I've known poverty/failure** j'ai connu la pauvreté/l'échec; **I've never known anything like it** je n'ai jamais rien vu de semblable; **I have never known him tell a lie** à ce que je sache, il n'a jamais menti; **I've never known him (to) be this late** je ne l'ai jamais vu être aussi en retard; **it has been known (to happen)** c'est une chose qu'on a vue se produire, ça s'est vu; **such coincidences have been known** de telles coïncidences se sont déjà vues

(**h**) *(nickname, call)* **Ian White, known as "Chalky"** Ian White, connu sous le nom de "Chalky"; **they're known as June bugs in America** on les appelle des "June bugs" en Amérique

(**i**) *(regard)* considérer; **she's known as one of our finest singers** elle est considérée comme l'une de nos meilleures chanteuses

(**j**) *Arch or Bible (have sex with)* connaître

2 *vi* savoir; **who knows?** qui sait?; *Fam* **I wouldn't know** je ne saurais dire❑; **I don't want to know** je ne veux pas le savoir; **when I mentioned that he just didn't want to know** quand j'ai mentionné ça, il n'a rien voulu savoir; **you never know** on ne sait jamais; **he might** *or* **should have known better** ce n'était pas très sage de sa part; **he's old enough to know better** à son âge, il devrait être plus raisonnable; **you can't blame him, he doesn't know any better** on ne peut pas lui en vouloir, il ne se rend pas compte; **he always thinks he knows best** il croit toujours avoir raison; **Mother knows best** maman sait de quoi elle parle; **to know about sth** être au courant de qch; **I've known about it for a week** je le sais *ou* je suis au courant depuis une semaine; **do you know about the new arrangements?** est-ce que vous êtes au courant *ou* avez-vous entendu parler des nouvelles dispositions?; **he knows about cars** il s'y connaît en voitures; **I don't know about that** *(I'm not certain)* je n'en suis pas sûr; **I don't know about you, but I'm exhausted** toi, je ne sais pas, mais moi, je suis épuisé; **to know of sb/sth** avoir entendu parler de qn/qch; **do you know her? – well, I know of her** est-ce que tu la connais? – non, mais j'ai entendu parler d'elle; **do you know of a good bookshop?** vous connaissez une bonne librairie?; **not that I know (of)** pas que je sache; **have they got much money? – not that I know of** ont-ils beaucoup d'argent? – pas que je sache; **it's just so difficult – oh, I know** c'est tellement difficile – oh, je sais; **it's difficult, I know, but not impossible** c'est difficile, je sais, mais pas impossible; **what's his name? – I don't know** comment s'appelle-t-il? – je ne sais pas; **are you going to accept? – I don't know** tu vas accepter? – je ne sais pas

3 *n (idiom) Fam* **to be in the know** être au courant❑

4 as far as I know *adv* (pour) autant que je sache; **not as far as I know** pas que je sache; **as far as I know, he lives in London** autant que je sache, il vit à Londres

5 you know *adv* (**a**) *(for emphasis)* **I was right, you know** j'avais raison, tu sais

(**b**) *(indicating hesitancy)* **he was just, you know, a bit boring** il était juste un peu ennuyeux, si tu vois ce que je veux dire

(**c**) *(to add information)* **it was that blonde woman, you know, the one with the dog** c'était la femme blonde, tu sais, celle avec le chien

(**d**) *(to introduce a statement)* **you know, sometimes I wonder why I do this** tu sais, parfois je me demande pourquoi je fais ça

'What Maisie knew' *James* 'Ce que savait Maisie'

knowable ['nəʊəbəl] *adj* connaissable

know-all, *Am* **know-it-all** *n Fam Pej* je-sais-tout *mf*, monsieur *m*/madame *f*/mademoiselle *f* je-sais-tout; **she's a real know-all** c'est une vraie (madame) je-sais-tout

know-how *n* savoir-faire *m inv*, know-how *m inv*; *(technical)* connaissances *fpl* techniques

knowing ['nəʊɪŋ] *adj* (**a**) *(look, laugh)* entendu, complice; **she gave him a knowing look** elle l'a regardé d'un air entendu (**b**) *(intelligent, educated)* intelligent, instruit (**c**) *(cunning)* fin, malin(igne), rusé

knowingly ['nəʊɪŋlɪ] *adv* (**a**) *(act)* sciemment, consciemment (**b**) *(look, laugh)* d'un air entendu

know-it-all *Am* = **know-all**

knowledgable = **knowledgeable**

knowledge ['nɒlɪdʒ] *n* (**a**) *(learning)* connaissance *f*, savoir *m*; *(total learning)* connaissances *fpl*; **she has a good knowledge of English** elle a une bonne connaissance de l'anglais; **he has a basic knowledge of computing** il a un minimum de connaissances en informatique; **to have a thorough knowledge of sth** connaître qch à fond; *Prov* **knowledge is power** savoir c'est pouvoir

(**b**) *(awareness)* connaissance *f*; **I have no knowledge of what happened** je ne sais absolument rien de *ou* j'ignore totalement ce qui s'est passé; **it has come to my knowledge that...** j'ai appris que...; **he brought the theft to my knowledge** il a porté le vol à ma connaissance, il m'a fait part du vol; **to (the best of) my knowledge** (pour) autant que je sache, à ma connaissance; **not to my knowledge** pas que je sache; **without my knowledge** à mon insu, sans que je le sache; **it's (a matter of) common knowledge** c'est de notoriété publique, personne ne l'ignore

►► *Comput* ***knowledge base*** base *f* de connaissances; *Comput* ***knowledge engineer*** cogniticien(enne) *m,f*

knowledgeable ['nɒlɪdʒəbəl] *adj* (**a**) *(well researched)* bien documenté (**b**) *(expert)* bien informé; **he's very knowledgeable about computing** il connaît bien l'informatique, il s'y connaît en informatique

knowledgeably ['nɒlɪdʒəblɪ] *adv* en connaisseur; **he speaks very knowledgeably about art** il parle d'art en connaisseur

knowledge-based system *n Comput* système *m* basé sur les connaissances

known [nəʊn] **1** *pp of* **know**

2 *adj* (**a**) *(notorious)* connu, notoire; **he's a known drugs dealer** c'est un revendeur de drogue notoire (**b**) *(recognized)* reconnu; **she's a known expert in the field** c'est un expert reconnu *ou* qui fait autorité dans ce domaine; **it's a known fact** c'est un fait établi; **to make oneself known** se faire connaître; **to let it be known** faire savoir

►► ***known reserves*** *(of oil)* réserves *fpl* prouvées

knuckle ['nʌkəl] **1** *n* (**a**) *(of human)* articulation *f ou* jointure *f* (du doigt); *(of animal)* première phalange *f*; **I grazed my knuckles on the wall** je me suis écorché les doigts contre le mur; **near the knuckle** *(joke, remark)* limite (**b**) *(joint of meat)* jarret *m*

2 knuckles *npl Am* coup-de-poing *m* américain

►► *Fam* ***knuckle sandwich*** coup *m* de poing❑; **I gave him a knuckle sandwich** je lui ai mis mon poing sur la gueule

►**knuckle down** *vi Br* s'y mettre; **we'd better knuckle down to some work** il vaudrait mieux se mettre *ou* s'atteler au travail

►**knuckle under** *vi* céder, se soumettre; **don't knuckle under to the pressure/management** ne cédez pas à la pression/la direction

knucklebone ['nʌkəlbəʊn] *n* articulation *f* du doigt

knuckle-duster *n* coup-de-poing *m* américain

knucklehead ['nʌkəlhed] *n Fam* andouille *f*

knurl [nɜːl] **1** *n* (**a**) *(in wood)* nœud *m* (**b**) *(on screw)* moletage *m*

2 *vt Tech* moleter

►► *Tech* ***knurled ring*** bague *f* moletée

KO [ˌkeɪ'əʊ] *(pl* **KO's,** *pt & pp* **KO'd,** *cont* **KO'ing)** *Fam (abbr* **knockout)** **1** *n* K-O *m*

2 *vt* mettre K-O; *(in boxing)* battre par K-O

koa ['kəʊə] *n* = espèce d'acacia originaire de Hawaii

koala [kəʊ'ɑːlə] *n Zool* koala *m*

►► ***koala bear*** koala *m*

kob [kɒb] *n Zool* cobe *m*

Koch's bacillus [kɒχs-] *n Med* bacille *m* de Koch

Kodiak ['kəʊdɪæk] *n (bear)* kodiak *m*

►► ***Kodiak bear*** kodiak *m*

kohl [kəʊl] *n* kohol *m*, khôl *m*

kohlrabi [kəʊl'rɑːbɪ] *n* chou-rave *m*

koi [kɔɪ] *n Ich* carpe *f* koi

►► ***koi carp*** carpe *f* koi

koine ['kɔɪneɪ] *n Ling* koinè *f*

kola = **cola**

kolinsky [kə'lɪnskɪ] *(pl* **kolinskies)** *n (animal)* loutre *f* de Sibérie; *(fur)* kolinski *m*

kolkhoz [kɒl'χɒz] *n* kolkhoz(e) *m*

kombi = **combi**

Komodo dragon, Komodo lizard [kə'məʊdəʊ-] *n Zool* dragon *m* de Komodo

kook [kuːk] *n Am Fam* dingo *m*, cinglé(e) *m,f*

kookaburra ['kʊkəˌbʌrə] *n Orn* martin-chasseur *m* (australien), kookaburra *m*

kookie, kooky ['kuːkɪ] *(compar* **kookier,** *superl* **kookiest)** *adj Am Fam* loufoque, loufedingue

koori ['kuːrɪ] *n Austr* Aborigène *mf*

Kop [kɒp] *n* **the Kop** = partie du stade d'Anfield à Liverpool où se tiennent les supporters de l'équipe de la ville

kopeck, kopek ['kəʊpek] *n* kopeck *m*

kora ['kɔːrə] *n* kora *f*

Koran [kə'rɑːn] *n* **the Koran** le Coran

Koranic [kə'rænɪk] *adj* coranique

Korea [kə'rɪə] *n* Corée *f*; **in Korea** en Corée; **the Democratic People's Republic of Korea** la République populaire démocratique de Corée

Korean [kə'rɪən] **1** *n* (**a**) *(person)* Coréen(enne) *m,f* (**b**) *(language)* coréen *m*

2 *adj* coréen

3 *comp (embassy)* de Corée; *(history)* de la Corée; *(teacher)* de coréen

►► ***the Korean War*** la guerre de Corée

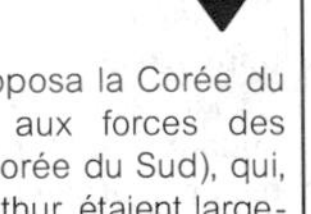

THE KOREAN WAR

De 1950 à 1953, ce conflit opposa la Corée du Nord (régime communiste) aux forces des Nations unies (soutenant la Corée du Sud), qui, dirigées par le général MacArthur, étaient largement composées d'Américains. Un traité mit fin à cette guerre en établissant la frontière entre les deux pays sur la ligne de front.

korfball ['kɔːfbɔːl] *n* korfbal *m*

korma ['kɔːmə] *n Culin* **chicken/prawn korma** poulet *m*/crevettes *fpl* korma

koruna [kɒ'ruːnə] *n* couronne *f* tchèque

kosher ['kəʊʃə(r)] **1** *adj* (**a**) *Rel* kasher *(inv)*, cacher *(inv)* (**b**) *Fam (honest)* honnête❑, régulier; **it's not kosher** c'est louche, c'est pas catholique

2 *n* nourriture *f* kasher

Kosovan ['kɒsəvən] **1** *n* Kosovar *mf*

2 *adj* kosovar

Kosovo ['kɒsəvəʊ] *n* Kosovo *m*; **in Kosovo** au Kosovo

Koweit [kə'weɪt] = **Kuwait**

kowhai ['kəʊhaɪ] *n Bot* sophora *m*

kowtow [ˌkaʊ'taʊ] *vi* **to kowtow to sb** faire des courbettes à qn

KP [ˌkeɪ'piː] *n Am Fam Mil slang (abbr* **kitchen police)** **looks like we're on KP tonight** on dirait qu'on est de corvée de cuisine ce soir

kph *(written abbr* **kilometres per hour)** km/h

kraal [krɑːl] *n* kraal *m*

kraft [krɑːft] *n* papier *m* kraft

krait [kraɪt] *n* = serpent venimeux d'Asie du Sud

kraken ['krɑːkən] *n Myth* kraken *m*

Krakow = **Cracow**

Kraut [kraʊt] *Fam Pej* **1** *n* Boche *mf*

2 *adj* boche

Krebs cycle [krebz-] *n Biol & Chem* cycle *m* de Krebs
Kremlin ['kremlɪn] *n* **the Kremlin** le Kremlin
Kremlinologist [ˌkremlɪ'nɒlədʒɪst] *n* kremlinologiste *mf*
Kremlinology [ˌkremlɪ'nɒlədʒɪ] *n* kremlinologie *f*
krill [krɪl] *n* krill *m*
kris [krɪs] *n* kriss *m*, criss *m*
Krishna ['krɪʃnə] *n* Krishna
Krishnaism ['krɪʃnəɪzəm] *n* krishnaïsme *m*
kriss = **kris**
Kriss Kringle [-'krɪŋgəl] *n Am* le Père Noël
krona ['krəʊnə] *n (in Sweden)* couronne *f* suédoise; *(in Iceland)* couronne *f* islandaise
krone ['krəʊnə] *n (in Norway)* couronne *f* norvégienne; *(in Denmark)* couronne *f* danoise
Krugerrand ['kru:gərænd] *n* Krugerrand *m*
krummhorn ['krʌmhɔ:n] *n Mus* cromorne *m*
Krushchev ['krʊstʃɒf] *pr n* **Nikita Krushchev** Nikita Khrouchtchev
krypton ['krɪptɒn] *n Chem* krypton *m*
KS[1] [ˌkeɪ'es] *n Med (abbr* **Kaposi's sarcoma**) sarcome *m* de Kaposi
KS[2] *(written abbr* **Kansas**) Kansas *m*
KT *(written abbr* **Knight**) chevalier *m*
Kuala Lumpur [ˌkwɑ:lə'lʊmˌpʊə(r)] *n* Kuala Lumpur
kudos ['kju:dɒs] *n* gloire *f*, prestige *m*
kudu ['ku:du:] *n Zool* coudou *m*
kudzu vine ['kʊdzu:-] *n* = plante fourragère très envahissante qui pousse dans le sud des États-Unis
Ku Klux Klan [ˌku:klʌks'klæn] *n* Ku Klux Klan *m*
kukri ['kʊkrɪ] *n* kukri *m*
kümmel ['kʊməl] *n* kummel *m*
kumquat ['kʌmkwɒt] *n* kumquat *m*
kung fu [ˌkʌŋ'fu:] *n* kung-fu *m inv*
Kurd [kɜ:d] *n* Kurde *mf*
Kurdish ['kɜ:dɪʃ] **1** *n Ling* kurde *m*
2 *adj* kurde
Kurdistan [ˌkɜ:dɪ'stɑ:n] *n* Kurdistan *m*; **in Kurdistan** au Kurdistan
Kuril Islands, Kurile Islands [kʊ'ri:l-] *npl* **the Kuril Islands** les îles *fpl* Kouriles; **in the Kuril Islands** aux îles Kouriles
kurtosis [kɜ:'təʊsɪs] *n* kurtosis *m*
Kuwait [kʊ'weɪt] *n* (**a**) *(country)* Koweït *m*; **in Kuwait** au Koweït (**b**) *(city)* Koweït
Kuwaiti [kʊ'weɪtɪ] **1** *n* Koweïtien(enne) *m,f*
2 *adj* koweïtien
3 *comp (embassy, history)* du Koweït
kV *(written abbr* **kilovolt**) kV
kvell [kvel] *vi Am Fam* jubiler; **he must be kvelling at the news** la nouvelle doit le faire jubiler
kvetch [kvetʃ] *vi Fam* rouspéter
kW *(written abbr* **kilowatt**) kW
kwacha ['kwætʃə] *n* kwacha *m*
kwanza, kwanzaa ['kwænzə] *n* kwanza *m*
kwashiorkor [ˌkwɒʃɪ'ɔ:kɔ:(r)] *n Med* kwashiorkor *m*
kWh *(written abbr* **kilowatt-hour**) kWh
KY *(written abbr* **Kentucky**) Kentucky *m*
kyanite ['kaɪənaɪt] *n* cyanite *f*
KY jelly® ['keɪwaɪ-] *n* gel *m* intime
kyle [kaɪl] *n Scot* détroit *m*
►► ***the Kyles of Bute*** les détroits *mpl* de Bute
kylie ['kaɪlɪ] *n Austr* = sorte de boomerang
kymograph ['kaɪməgrɑ:f] *n Ling & Med* kymographe *m*; *Aviat* indicateur *m* de virage
Kyoto ['kjəʊtəʊ] *n* Kyoto
kyphosis [kaɪ'fəʊsɪs] *n* cyphose *f*
Kyrgyz ['kɪəgɪz] **1** *n* (**a**) *(person)* Kirghiz(e) *m,f* (**b**) *(language)* kirghiz *m*
2 *adj* kirghiz
3 *comp (embassy, history)* du Kirghizistan; *(teacher)* de kirghiz
Kyrgyzstan [ˌkɜ:gɪ'stɑ:n] *n* Kirghizstan *m*, Kirghizistan *m*; **in Kyrgyzstan** au Kirghizstan *ou* Kirghizistan
Kyrie ['kɪrɪeɪ] *n Rel* **Kyrie (eleison)** Kyrie (eleison) *m inv*

L

L[1], **l**[1] [el] *n (letter)* L, l *m inv*; **two l's** deux l; **L for Larry** ≃ L comme Louis

L[2] (**a**) *(written abbr* **lake**) lac *m* (**b**) *(written abbr* **large**) L (**c**) *(written abbr* **left**) g (**d**) *(written abbr* **learner**) = lettre apposée sur une voiture et signalant un apprenti conducteur (en Grande-Bretagne)

l[2] *(written abbr* **litre**) l

LA[1] [ˌel'eɪ] *n (abbr* **Los Angeles**) Los Angeles *m*

LA[2] *(written abbr* **Louisiana**) Louisiane *f*

la [lɑː] *n Mus* la *m*

laager ['lɑːgə(r)] *n Mil* camp *m*

Lab *(written abbr* **Labour, Labour Party**) parti *m* travailliste

lab [læb] **1** *n* (**a**) *(abbr* **laboratory**) labo *m* (**b**) *Fam (abbr* **labrador**) labrador ❑ *m*

2 *comp (book)* de laboratoire

►► ***lab assistant*** laborantin(e) *m,f*, assistant(e) *m,f* de laboratoire; ***lab coat*** blouse *f*

label ['leɪbəl] *(Br pt & pp* **labelled**, *cont* **labelling**, *Am pt & pp* **labeled**, *cont* **labeling**) **1** *n* (**a**) *also Fig* étiquette *f*; **they brought out the record on the Mega label** ils ont sorti le disque chez Mega; **it's a good label** c'est une bonne marque; **designer label** marque *f*, griffe *f*

(**b**) *Comput (of tape, file)* label *m*

(**c**) *Chem* marque *f*

2 *vt* (**a**) *(suitcase, jar)* étiqueter; **you must label your clothes clearly** tous vos vêtements doivent être clairement marqués à votre nom; **the bottle was labelled "shake before use"** la bouteille portait l'étiquette "agiter avant emploi"

(**b**) *Fig (person)* étiqueter, cataloguer; **he's been labelled (as) a troublemaker** on l'a étiqueté *ou* catalogué comme fauteur de troubles

(**c**) *Chem* marquer

labelling, *Am* **labeling** ['leɪbəlɪŋ] *n* étiquetage *m*

labellum [lə'beləm] *(pl* **labella** [-lə]) *n Bot* labelle *m*

labia ['leɪbɪə] *npl Anat* lèvres *fpl*; **labia minora/majora** petites/grandes lèvres *fpl*

labial ['leɪbɪəl] *Ling* **1** *n* labiale *f*

2 *adj* labial

►► ***labial consonant*** consonne *f* labiale

labialization [ˌleɪbɪəlaɪ'zeɪʃən] *n Ling* labialisation *f*

labialize, -ise ['leɪbɪəlaɪz] *vt Ling* labialiser

labiate ['leɪbɪeɪt] *Bot* **1** *n* labiée *f*

2 *adj* labié

labile ['leɪbaɪl] *adj* labile

lability [lə'bɪlɪtɪ] *n* labilité *f*

labiodental [ˌleɪbɪəʊ'dentəl] *Ling* **1** *n* labiodentale *f*

2 *adj* labiodental

labionasal [ˌleɪbɪəʊ'neɪzəl] *n Ling* nasale *f* bilabiale

►► *Ling* ***labionasal consonant*** consonne *f* nasale bilabiale

labiovelar [ˌleɪbɪəʊ'viːlə(r)] *Ling* **1** *n* labiovélaire *f*

2 *adj* labiovélaire

labor *Am* = **labour**

laboratory [*Br* lə'bɒrətrɪ, *Am* 'læbrəˌtɔːrɪ] *(pl* **laboratories**) **1** *n* laboratoire *m*; **tested under laboratory conditions** testé en laboratoire

2 *comp (assistant, equipment, experiment)* de laboratoire

laboratory-tested *adj* testé en laboratoire

labored, laborer *etc Am* = **laboured, labourer** *etc*

laborious [lə'bɔːrɪəs] *adj* laborieux

laboriously [lə'bɔːrɪəslɪ] *adv* laborieusement

laboriousness [lə'bɔːrɪəsnɪs] *n* caractère *m* laborieux

labour, *Am* **labor** ['leɪbə(r)] **1** *n* (**a**) *(work, task)* travail *m*; *(hard effort)* labeur *m*; **a labour of love** un travail fait pour le plaisir; **her book was the result of five years' hard labour** son livre était le fruit de cinq ans de dur labeur *ou* de travail acharné; **the twelve labours of Hercules** les douze travaux *mpl* d'Hercule

(**b**) *Ind (manpower)* main-d'œuvre *f*; *(workers)* ouvriers *mpl*, travailleurs *mpl*; **cost of labour** prix *m* de la main-d'œuvre; **capital and labour** le capital et la main-d'œuvre

(**c**) *Obst* travail *m*; **to be in labour** être en travail; **to go into labour** commencer le travail; **it was a difficult labour** ça a été un accouchement difficile

2 *comp (movement)* social; *(shortage)* de main-d'œuvre

3 *vi* (**a**) *(work)* travailler dur

(**b**) *(struggle → person)* **he laboured up the stairs** il monta péniblement l'escalier; *Fig* **to labour under a misapprehension** *or* **a delusion** se méprendre, être dans l'erreur

(**c**) *(move with difficulty → vehicle)* peiner; **the car laboured up the slope** la voiture peinait dans la montée; **the ship was labouring through heavy seas** le bateau avançait péniblement dans la mer démontée

4 *vt (stress)* insister sur; **there's no need to labour the point** ce n'est pas la peine de t'étendre *ou* d'insister là-dessus

5 Labour *Pol* **1** *n* = le parti travailliste britannique; **to vote Labour** voter travailliste **2** *adj (policy, government, MP)* travailliste

►► ***labour camp*** camp *m* de travail; ***Labor Code*** code *m* du travail *(aux États-Unis et au Canada)*; *Am* ***labor contract*** contrat *m* de travail; *Ind* ***labour costs*** coûts *mpl* de la main-d'œuvre; *Am* ***Labor Day*** fête *f* du travail *(aux États-Unis et au Canada, célébrée le premier lundi de septembre)*; ***labour dispute*** conflit *m* du travail; *Br & Can Formerly* ***labour exchange*** agence *f* pour l'emploi; ***labour force*** *(in country)* population *f* active; *(in company)* main-d'œuvre *f*; ***labour laws*** législation *f* du travail; *Pol* ***Labour leader*** dirigeant(e) *m,f* (du parti) travailliste; ***labour market*** marché *m* du travail; *Pol* ***Labour Member (of Parliament)*** député *m* travailliste; *Pol* ***the Labour Party*** le parti travailliste; *Obst* ***labour pains*** douleurs *fpl* de l'accouchement; *Ind* ***labour relations*** relations *fpl* sociales; *Am* ***labor union*** syndicat *m*; *Obst* ***labour ward*** salle *f* d'accouchement

laboured, *Am* **labored** ['leɪbəd] *adj* (**a**) *(breathing)* pénible, difficile (**b**) *(style, joke)* lourd, laborieux

labourer, *Am* **laborer** ['leɪbərə(r)] *n (gen)* ouvrier(ère) *m,f*; *(on building site)* manœuvre *m*; *Prov* **the labourer is worthy of his hire** toute peine *ou* tout travail mérite salaire

labouring, *Am* **laboring** ['leɪbərɪŋ] *adj* **the labouring class** la classe ouvrière; **a labouring job** un travail manuel

labour-intensive, *Am* **labor-intensive** *adj* **craftwork is very labour-intensive** le travail artisanal nécessite un travail considérable; **a labour-intensive industry** une industrie à forte main-d'œuvre

Labourite ['leɪbəraɪt] *Pol* **1** *n* travailliste *mf*

2 *adj* travailliste

labour-saving device, *Am* **labor-saving device** *n (in home)* appareil *m* ménager; *(at work)* = appareil permettant un gain de temps

Labrador ['læbrədɔː(r)] **1** *n Geog* Labrador *m*; **in Labrador** au Labrador

2 labrador *n (dog)* labrador *m*

labradorite [ˌlæbrə'dɔːraɪt] *n Miner* laboradorite *f*, labrador *m*

laburnum [lə'bɜːnəm] *n Bot* cytise *m*, faux ébénier *m*

►► ***laburnum tree*** cytise *m*, faux ébénier *m*

labyrinth ['læbərɪnθ] *n* labyrinthe *m*, dédale *m*

labyrinthine [ˌlæbə'rɪnθaɪn] *adj* labyrinthique

labyrinthodont [ˌlæbə'rɪnθəˌdɒnt] *n Archeol & Zool* labyrinthodonte *m*

lac [læk] *n* gomme *f* laque, laque *f*

Lacanian [læ'keɪnɪən] *adj* lacanien

laccase ['lækeɪz] *n Biol & Chem* laccase *f*

laccolite ['lækəlaɪt], **laccolith** ['lækəlɪθ] *n Geol* laccolite *f*, laccolithe *f*

lace [leɪs] **1** *n* (**a**) *Tex* dentelle *f*

(**b**) *(in shoe, boot, corset)* lacet *m*

2 *comp (handkerchief, tablecloth etc)* en dentelle

3 *vt* (**a**) *(tie)* lacer; *(put laces in)* mettre des lacets à; **he's already learned to lace his own shoes** il a déjà appris à lacer ses souliers

(**b**) *(add alcohol to)* ajouter de l'alcool à; **he laced my orange juice with gin** il a mis du gin dans mon jus d'orange; *Fig* **he laced his story with salacious details** il ajoutait des détails salaces à son histoire

4 *vi (shoes, boots)* se lacer

►**lace into** *vt insep Br Fam (physically)* rosser; *(in criticism)* attaquer violemment ❑

►**lace up** *Br* **1** *vt sep (shoes, boots)* lacer

2 *vi (shoes, boots)* se lacer; **they lace up at the sides** elles se lacent *ou* s'attachent sur le côté

lacemaker ['leɪsˌmeɪkə(r)] *n* dentellier(ère) *m,f*

lacemaking ['leɪsˌmeɪkɪŋ] *n* industrie *f* dentellière

lacerate ['læsəreɪt] *vt* lacérer; **his hands were lacerated by the broken glass** il avait les mains lacérées par le verre brisé; *Fig* **the encounter left her emotions lacerated** la rencontre lui avait déchiré le cœur *ou* l'avait meurtrie

►► *Bot* ***lacerate leaves*** feuilles *fpl* dentées *or* dentelées

laceration [ˌlæsə'reɪʃən] *n* (**a**) *(action)* lacération *f* (**b**) *(gash)* entaille *f*; **he had deep lacerations on his back** il avait le dos profondément lacéré *ou* entaillé

lace-up 1 *adj (shoe, boot)* à lacets

2 lace-ups *npl Br* chaussures *fpl* à lacets

lacewing ['leɪswɪŋ] *n Entom* hémérobe *m*

lacework ['leɪswɜːk] *n (art)* dentellerie *f*

►► ***lacework objects*** objets *mpl* en dentelle

laches ['lætʃɪz] *n Law* = délai immotivé pour s'acquitter d'une obligation légale ou pour faire valoir un droit

lachrymal ['lækrɪməl] *adj* lacrymal

►► ***lachrymal duct*** conduit *m* lacrymal; ***lachrymal gland*** glande *f* lacrymale

lachrymose ['lækrɪməʊs] *adj Literary* larmoyant

lacing ['leɪsɪŋ] *n* (**a**) *(on shoe, garment)* laçage *m* (**b**) *(of food, drink)* adjonction *f* d'alcool

laciniate [læ'sɪnɪeɪt], **laciniated** [læ'sɪnɪeɪtɪd] *adj Bot* lacinié

laciniate-leaved *adj Bot* lacinifolié

lack [læk] **1** *n* manque *m*; **through** *or* **for lack of** par manque de, faute de; **there's no lack of volunteers** ce ne sont pas les volontaires qui manquent

2 *vt* manquer de; **they certainly don't lack confidence** ils ne manquent certes pas de confiance en eux; **we lack the necessary resources** nous n'avons pas les ressources nécessaires; **what the country lacks in modern tourist amenities, it more than makes up for in natural beauty** la beauté naturelle du paysage compense largement le manque d'infrastructures touristiques

▸**lack for** *vt insep* manquer de; **he lacks for nothing** il ne manque de rien, il a tout ce qu'il lui faut

lackadaisical [ˌlækə'deɪzɪkəl] *adj (person → apathetic)* apathique; *(→ lazy)* indolent

lackaday ['lækədeɪ] *exclam Arch* hélas!

lackey ['lækɪ] **1** *n* laquais *m*; *Pej* larbin *m*
 2 *vi* **I refuse to lackey for him** je refuse d'être son larbin

lacking ['lækɪŋ] *adj* (**a**) *(wanting)* **to be lacking** *(not present)* faire défaut; **to be lacking in sth** manquer de qch; **to be lacking in confidence/experience** manquer de confiance/d'expérience; **originality is sadly lacking in his new novel** son nouveau roman manque malheureusement d'originalité (**b**) *Fam Euph (stupid)* demeuré, simple d'esprit ❑

lacklustre, *Am* **lackluster** ['lækˌlʌstə(r)] *adj* terne

laconic [lə'kɒnɪk] *adj* laconique

laconically [lə'kɒnɪkəlɪ] *adv* laconiquement

lacquer ['lækə(r)] **1** *n* (**a**) *(varnish, hairspray)* laque *f* (**b**) *(varnished object)* laque *m*
 2 *vt (wood)* laquer; *(hair)* mettre de la laque sur; **to lacquer one's hair** se mettre de la laque (sur les cheveux)

lacquered ['lækəd] *adj* laqué; **a lacquered box** une boîte laquée

lacquerware ['lækəweə(r)] *n (UNCOUNT)* laques *mpl*

lacquerwork ['lækəwɜːk] *n (objects)* laques *mpl*

lacrimal = **lachrymal**

lacrosse [lə'krɒs] **1** *n* lacrosse *f*, crosse *f*
 2 *comp (player)* de crosse
 ▸▸ ***lacrosse stick*** crosse *f*

lacrymal = **lachrymal**

lactalbumen [læk'tælbjʊmɪn] *n Chem* lactalbumine *f*

lactarian [læk'teərɪən] **1** *n* lacto-végétarien(enne) *m,f*
 2 *adj* lacto-végétarien

lactase ['lækteɪz] *n Physiol* lactase *f*

lactate 1 *n* ['lækteɪt] *Chem* lactate *m*
 2 *vi* [læk'teɪt] sécréter du lait

lactation [ˌlæk'teɪʃən] *n* lactation *f*

lacteal ['læktɪəl] *Anat & Med* **1** *n* veine *f* lactée
 2 *adj* lacté

lactic ['læktɪk] *adj Chem* lactique
 ▸▸ ***lactic acid*** acide *m* lactique

lactobacillus [ˌlæktəʊbə'sɪləs] *(pl* **lactobacilli** [-laɪ]) *n* lactobacille *m*, lactobacillus *m*

lactogenic [ˌlæktə'dʒenɪk] *adj* lactogène

lactoglobulin [ˌlæktəʊ'glɒbjʊlɪn] *n* lactoglobuline *f*

lactose ['læktəʊs] *n* lactose *m*

lactovegetarian [ˌlæktəʊvedʒə'teərɪən] **1** *n* lacto-végétarien(enne) *m,f*
 2 *adj* lacto-végétarien

lacuna [lə'kjuːnə] *(pl* **lacunas** *or* **lacunae** [-niː]) *n* lacune *f*

lacustrine [lə'kʌstraɪn] *adj* lacustre

lacy ['leɪsɪ] *(compar* **lacier,** *superl* **laciest**) *adj (lace-like)* fin comme de la dentelle; *(made of lace)* en dentelle

lad [læd] *n* (**a**) *(young boy)* garçon *m*; *(son)* fils *m*; **he's only a lad** c'est seulement un gamin; **when I was a lad** quand j'étais jeune; **come here, lad** viens ici, mon petit gars
 (**b**) *Br Fam (friend)* copain *m*; *(colleague)* collègue ❑ *m*, gars *m*; **he went out for a drink with the lads** il est allé boire un coup avec des copains; **the lads from work** les copains de travail; **morning lads!** salut les gars!; **to be one of the lads** aimer sortir en bande
 (**c**) *Br Fam (rake)* noceur *m*; **he was a bit of a lad when he was young** il a eu une jeunesse assez tumultueuse
 (**d**) *Br Horseracing* **(stable) lad** lad *m*

ladder ['lædə(r)] **1** *n* (**a**) *also Fig* échelle *f*; *also Fig* **to be at the top of the ladder** être arrivé au sommet *ou* en haut de l'échelle; *Fig* **to get one's foot on the ladder** mettre un pied dans le circuit; **fish** *or* **salmon ladder** échelle *f* à saumons (**b**) *Br (in stocking, tights)* maille *f* filée; **you've got a ladder in your stocking** ton bas a filé, tu as filé ton bas
 2 *vt Br* filer
 3 *vi Br* filer
 ▸▸ ***ladder back*** chaise *f* à barrettes

laddered portfolio [lædəd-] *n Am Fin* portefeuille *m* d'obligations à rendement échelonné

ladderproof ['lædəpruːf] *adj Br (stockings, tights)* indémaillable

laddie ['lædɪ] *n Scot Fam* gars *m*; **come here, laddie** viens là, mon petit gars

laddish ['lædɪʃ] *adj Br Fam* = typique d'un style de vie caractérisé par de fréquentes sorties entre copains, généralement copieusement arrosées, un comportement arrogant et macho, et un goût prononcé pour le sport et les activités de groupe

lade [leɪd] *(pt* **laded,** *pp* **laden** ['leɪdən] *or* **laded**) *vt Formal (ship)* charger

laden ['leɪdən] **1** *pp of* **lade**
 2 *adj* chargé (**with** de); **I was laden with shopping** j'avais les bras chargés de commissions; **apple-laden trees** arbres *mpl* couverts de pommes; **a heavily laden ship** un navire à forte charge; *Literary* **laden with grief** accablé de douleur

ladette [læ'det] *n Br Fam* = jeune femme se revendiquant l'égale des hommes pour ce qui est des sorties, de la vulgarité etc

la-di-da [ˌlɑːdɪ'dɑː] *Fam Pej* **1** *adj (manner)* snob ❑, prétentieux ❑; *(voice)* maniéré ❑; **she speaks in a very la-di-da way** elle est assez pimbêche
 2 *adv* d'une façon prétentieuse ❑

ladies ['leɪdɪz] *n Br* toilettes *fpl* pour dames; *(sign)* dames; **can you tell me where the ladies is?** pouvez-vous m'indiquer où sont les toilettes?
 ▸▸ *Culin* ***ladies fingers*** gombo *m*; ***ladies' man*** don Juan *m*, homme *m* à femmes; ***ladies' night*** *(in bar)* = soirée où les femmes ont droit à des réductions; *(in gym)* = soir réservé aux femmes; *Am* ***ladies room*** toilettes *fpl* pour dames

lading ['leɪdɪŋ] *n* (**a**) *(action → of ship)* chargement *m*; *(of merchandise)* mise *f* à bord (**b**) *(cargo)* cargaison *f*, chargement *m*

ladle ['leɪdəl] **1** *n* (**a**) *(for soup)* louche *f* (**b**) *Ind* puisoir *m*; *Metal* **foundry ladle** poche *f* de fonderie
 2 *vt* servir (à la louche)

▸**ladle out** *vt sep Br* (**a**) *(soup)* servir (à la louche) (**b**) *Fam Fig (money, advice)* distribuer à droite et à gauche

ladleful ['leɪdəlfʊl] *n* pleine louche *f* (**of** de)

lady ['leɪdɪ] *(pl* **ladies**) **1** *n* (**a**) *(woman)* dame *f*; **Ladies and Gentlemen** Mesdames et Messieurs; **the lady of the house** la maîtresse de maison; *Old-fashioned* **a lady doctor** une femme médecin; **young lady** *(girl)* jeune fille *f*; *(young woman)* jeune femme *f*; **ask the young lady over there** *(in shop)* demandez à la demoiselle que vous voyez là-bas; **well, young lady, what have you got to say for yourself?** eh bien, ma fille, qu'avez-vous à répondre?; **the Old Lady of Threadneedle Street** = surnom donné à la Banque d'Angleterre
 (**b**) *(refined woman)* dame *f*; **she's a real lady** c'est une vraie dame; **she's no lady** elle n'a aucune classe
 (**c**) *(term of address)* **my Lady** Madame
 (**d**) *(as title)* **Lady Browne** Lady Browne *(titre de noblesse féminin)*; **to act like Lady Muck** jouer à la grande dame
 (**e**) *Am Fam (term of address)* madame ❑ *f*; **hey lady!** eh, ma petite dame!
 (**f**) *Old-fashioned (wife)* femme *f*, épouse *f*; **how's your good lady?** comment va votre dame?; **this is my lady wife** voici mon épouse; **my young lady** *(fiancée)* ma fiancée, ma future
 (**g**) *Rel* **Our Lady** Notre-Dame *f*
 2 *comp* **lady doctor** femme *f* médecin; **lady novelist** romancière *f*; **lady teacher** institutrice *f*
 ▸▸ *Pej or Hum* ***lady bountiful*** généreuse bienfaitrice *f*; ***Lady Chapel*** chapelle *f* de la Sainte Vierge; ***Lady Day*** (fête *f* de) l'Annonciation *f*; *Culin Br* ***lady's finger,*** *Am* ***lady finger*** *(biscuit)* boudoir *m*; ***Lady Godiva*** = au XIème siècle, dame de haut rang qui aurait parcouru la ville de Coventry nue et à cheval pour forcer son mari à réduire les impôts locaux; ***the Lady of the Lake*** la Dame du lac; ***the Lady with the Lamp*** la Dame à la Lampe *(Florence Nightingale, célèbre infirmière anglaise)*; ***Lady Luck*** la chance; ***lady's maid*** femme *f* de chambre; ***lady's man*** don Juan *m*, homme *m* à femmes; *Br* ***Lady Mayoress*** femme *f* du maire; *Bot* ***lady's slipper*** sabot-de-Vénus *m*; *Bot* ***lady's smock*** cardamine *f* des prés; *Bot* ***(autumn) lady's tresses*** spiranthe *f* spiralée, spiranthe *f* d'automne

'The Lady in the Lake' *Chandler* 'La Dame du lac'

'The Lady and the Tramp' *Disney* 'La Belle et le clochard'

'The Lady's Not for Burning' *Fry* 'La Dame ne brûlera pas'

'The Lady Vanishes' *Hitchcock* 'Une Femme disparaît'

'Lady Chatterley's Lover' *Lawrence* 'L'Amant de Lady Chatterley'

ladybird ['leɪdɪbɜːd] *n Br* coccinelle *f*

ladyboy ['leɪdɪbɔɪ] *n Br Fam (transsexual)* = jeune transsexuel asiatique

ladybug ['leɪdɪbʌg] *n Am* coccinelle *f*

ladyfriend ['leɪdɪfrend] *n Old-fashioned or Hum* petite amie *f*

lady-in-waiting *n* dame *f* d'honneur

ladykiller ['leɪdɪˌkɪlə(r)] *n Fam* bourreau *m* des cœurs

'The Ladykillers' *Mackendrick* 'Les Tueurs de dames'

ladylike ['leɪdɪlaɪk] *adj (person)* distingué, bien élevé; *(manners)* raffiné, élégant; **it's not very ladylike to smoke in the street!** une fille comme il faut ne fume pas dans la rue!

ladylove ['leɪdɪlʌv] *n Literary* **his ladylove** sa bien-aimée

ladyship ['leɪdɪʃɪp] *n* **Your/Her Ladyship** Madame (la baronne/la vicomtesse/la comtesse); *Fig or Hum* Madame; **you'd better get some nice wine for her ladyship** tu ferais bien d'acheter du bon vin pour Madame

lag [læg] *(pt & pp* **lagged,** *cont* **lagging**) **1** *n* (**a**) *(gap)* décalage *m*; **there was a lag between completion and publication** il y a eu un décalage entre l'achèvement de l'œuvre et sa publication
 (**b**) *Br very Fam (convict)* **an old lag** un cheval de retour
 2 *vt (pipe)* calorifuger
 3 *vi* rester en arrière, traîner

▸**lag behind 1** *vt insep (competitor)* traîner derrière, avoir du retard sur
 2 *vi* (**a**) *(dawdle)* traîner, lambiner; *(be at the back)* rester derrière; **the youngest children were lagging behind** les enfants les plus jeunes restaient en arrière
 (**b**) *(be outdistanced)* se laisser distancer; **our country is lagging behind in medical research** notre pays a du retard en matière de recherche médicale; **salaries are still lagging behind** les salaires sont restés à un niveau inférieur

lager ['lɑːgə(r)] *n* (**a**) *Br (beer)* bière *f* blonde (**b**) *Mil* camp *m*
 ▸▸ *Br Fam* ***lager lout*** = jeune qui, sous l'influence de l'alcool, cherche la bagarre ou commet des actes de vandalisme

laggard ['lægəd] *n* (**a**) *(person)* traînard(e) *m,f* (**b**) *Mktg (product)* innovateur(trice) *m,f* tardif(ive)

lagging ['lægɪŋ] *n* (**a**) *(action)* calorifugeage *m* (**b**) *(material)* isolant *m*, calorifuge *m*

lagniappe ['lænjæp] *n Am Com* prime *f*

lagomorph ['lægəʊmɔːf] *n Zool* lagomorphe *m*

lagoon [lə'guːn] *n (gen)* lagune *f*; *(in coral reef)* lagon *m*

Lagos ['leɪgɒs] *n* Lagos

lah = **la**

lahar ['lɑːhɑː(r)] *n* coulée *f* de boue, avalanche *f* boueuse

lah-di-dah = **la-di-da**
laic ['leɪɪk], **laical** ['leɪɪkəl] *adj* laïque
laicism ['leɪɪsɪzəm] *n* laïcisme *m*
laicization [ˌleɪɪsaɪ'zeɪʃən] *n* laïcisation *f*
laicize, -ise ['leɪɪˌsaɪz] *vt* laïciser
laid [leɪd] *pt & pp of* **lay**
laid-back *adj Fam* décontracté ❑, cool
lain [leɪn] *pp of* **lie**
lair [leə(r)] *n (for animals)* tanière *f*; *Fig* repaire *m*, tanière *f*
laird [leəd] *n* laird *m*, propriétaire *m* foncier *(en Écosse)*
laisser-faire, laissez-faire [ˌleseɪ'feə] *n* non-interventionnisme *m*
►► ***laisser-faire economy*** économie *f* basée sur le non-interventionnisme; ***laisser-faire policy*** politique *f* du laisser-faire
laity ['leɪətɪ] *n (UNCOUNT)* (**a**) *Rel* laïcs *mpl* (**b**) *(non-specialists)* profanes *mpl*
lake [leɪk] **1** *n* (**a**) *Geog* lac *m*; *Fig* **a wine lake** des excédents *mpl* de vin; *Fam* **go jump in a lake!** va te faire cuire un œuf!
(**b**) *(pigment)* laque *f*
2 Lakes *npl Br* **the Lakes** la région des lacs
►► ***Lake Baikal*** le lac Baïkal; ***Lake Balaton*** le lac Balaton; ***Lake Como*** le lac de Côme; ***Lake Constance*** le lac de Constance; ***the Lake District*** le Lake District, la région des lacs *(dans le nord-ouest de l'Angleterre)*; ***lake dwelling*** habitation *f* lacustre; ***Lake Erie*** le lac Érié; ***Lake Garda*** le lac de Garde; ***Lake Geneva*** le lac Léman, le lac de Genève; ***Lake Huron*** le lac Huron; ***Lake Kariba*** le lac Kariba; ***Lake Ladoga*** le lac Ladoga; ***Lake Maggiore*** le lac Majeur; ***Lake Malawi*** le lac Malawi; ***Lake Michigan*** le lac Michigan; ***Lake Nasser*** le lac Nasser; ***Lake Ontario*** le lac Ontario; ***the Lake Poets*** les lakistes *mpl (poètes anglais du début du XIXème siècle, dont Wordsworth et Coleridge)*; ***Lake Superior*** le lac Supérieur; ***Lake Tanganyika*** le lac Tanganyika; ***Lake Tiberias*** le lac de Tibériade; ***Lake Titicaca*** le lac Titicaca; ***Lake Victoria*** le lac Victoria; ***Lake Winnipeg*** le lac Winnipeg
Lakeland ['leɪklənd] *adj (of or in Lake District)* de la région des lacs
lakeshore ['leɪkʃɔː(r)], **lakeside** ['leɪksaɪd] **1** *n* rive *f* d'un lac
2 *adj* au bord du lac
la-la land *n Fam* = surnom donné à la ville de Los Angeles; *Fig* **to be in la-la land** planer
Lallans ['lælənz] *n* lallans *m (dialecte du sud de l'Écosse)*
lallation [læ'leɪʃən] *n Ling* lallation *f*, lambdacisme *m*
lallygag ['lælɪgæg] *(pt & pp* **lallygagged**, *cont* **lallygagging**) *vi Am Fam* traîner
lam [læm] *(pt & pp* **lammed**, *cont* **lamming**) *Fam* **1** *vt (beat)* rosser
2 *n Am (escape)* cavale *f*; **on the lam** en cavale; **to take it on the lam** faire la belle
►**lam into** *vt insep Br Fam* (**a**) *(physically)* rentrer dans ❑; **he lammed into me** il m'est rentré dedans (**b**) *(verbally)* enguirlander, sonner les cloches à
lama ['lɑːmə] *n Rel* lama *m*
Lamaism ['lɑːməɪzəm] *n Rel* lamaïsme *m*
La Mancha [lɑː'mæntʃə] *n* la Manche *(province d'Espagne)*
Lamarckism [lə'mɑːkɪzəm] *n* lamarckisme *m*
lamasery ['lɑːməsərɪ] *(pl* **lamaseries**) *n* couvent *m* de lamas, lamaserie *f*
Lamaze method [lə'mɑːz-] *n Obst* = méthode d'accouchement sans douleur
lamb [læm] **1** *n* (**a**) *(animal)* agneau *m*; **like lambs to the slaughter** comme des veaux que l'on mène à l'abattoir
(**b**) *(meat)* agneau *m*
(**c**) *Fig (innocent person)* agneau *m*; *(lovable person)* **she's a lamb** c'est un ange, elle est adorable; **be a lamb and fetch my glasses** sois un ange *ou* sois gentil, va me chercher mes lunettes; **you poor lamb!** mon pauvre chou!
2 *comp (chop, cutlet)* d'agneau
3 *vi* agneler, mettre bas
►► *Rel* ***the Lamb of God*** l'Agneau *m* de Dieu; ***lamb's lettuce*** mâche *f*; *Fam* ***lamb's tails*** *(of hazel tree)* chatons *mpl*
lambada [ˌlæm'bɑːdə] *n* lambada *f*
lambast [læm'bæst], **lambaste** [læm'beɪst] *vt* *(scold)* réprimander; *(thrash)* battre, rosser
lambda ['læmdə] *n* lambda *m*
lambency ['læmbənsɪ] *n Literary* (**a**) *(of star)* lueur *f* blafarde (**b**) *(of wit, humour)* éclat *m*
lambent ['læmbənt] *adj Literary* (**a**) *(glowing)* chatoyant, brillant; *(sparkling)* étincelant (**b**) *(wit, humour)* brillant
lambert ['læmbət] *n Phys* lambert *m*
Lambeth ['læmbəθ] *n* Lambeth
►► ***Lambeth Conference*** conférence *f* de Lambeth; ***Lambeth Palace*** = résidence londonienne de l'archevêque de Cantorbéry; ***the Lambeth walk*** = célèbre chanson et danse à la mode dans les années 40, où tout le monde avance en ligne
lambing ['læmɪŋ] *n* agnelage *m*; **at lambing time** au moment de l'agnelage
lambkin ['læmkɪn] *n* agnelet *m*; **my little lambkin** *(term of affection)* mon petit chou
lambrequin ['læmbrəkɪn] *n* lambrequin *m*
lambskin ['læmskɪn] **1** *n* (peau *f* d')agneau *m*
2 *comp (coat, gloves)* en agneau
lambswool ['læmzwʊl] *comp (scarf, sweater etc)* en laine d'agneau, en lambswool
LAMDA ['læmdə] *n (abbr* **London Academy of Music and Dramatic Art**) = conservatoire de musique et d'art dramatique, à Londres
lame [leɪm] **1** *adj* (**a**) *(person, horse)* boiteux; **to be lame** boiter; **to go lame** se mettre à boiter; **his left leg is lame, he's lame in his left leg** il boite de la jambe gauche
(**b**) *(weak → excuse)* piètre, bancal; *(→ argument, reasoning)* boiteux; *(→ plot)* boiteux, bancal; **what a lame joke!** quelle blague idiote!, quelle astuce vaseuse!
(**c**) *Am Fam (conventional)* vieux jeu ❑ *(inv)*; *(stupid)* cloche, nouille
2 *vt* estropier
3 *n Am Fam (stupid person)* andouille *f*, cruche *f*
4 *npl* **the lame** les boiteux *mpl*
►► *Fig* ***lame duck*** *(gen) & Ind* canard *m* boiteux; *Am Pol* = candidat sortant non réélu qui attend l'arrivée de son successeur
lamé ['lɑːmeɪ] *n* lamé *m*; **a gold lamé dress** une robe en lamé d'or
lamebrain ['leɪmbreɪn] *n Fam* crétin(e) *m,f*, andouille *f*
lame-duck *adj Am Pol* **lame-duck president** = président sortant non réélu
lamella [lə'melə] *(pl* **lamellas** *or* **lamellae** [-liː]) *n Anat & Bot* lame *f*
lamellibranch [lə'melɪbræŋk] *n Zool* lamellibranche *m*
lamellicorn [lə'melɪkɔːn] *n Entom* lamellicorne *m*
lamely ['leɪmlɪ] *adv* de façon peu convaincante, maladroitement
lameness ['leɪmnɪs] *n* (**a**) *(limping)* boiterie *f*, *Spec* claudication *f*; **his lameness is the result of a childhood accident** il boite à la suite d'un accident qu'il a eu dans son enfance (**b**) *(weakness → of excuse, argument etc)* faiblesse *f*
lament [lə'ment] **1** *vt (feel sorrow for)* regretter, pleurer; *(complain about)* se lamenter sur, se plaindre de; **she lamented the passing of her youth** elle pleurait sa jeunesse perdue; **"I'll never finish in time!" she lamented** "je n'aurai jamais fini à temps!", gémit-elle
2 *vi* se lamenter; **she was lamenting loudly over the loss of her jewels** elle se lamentait bruyamment *ou* à grands cris d'avoir perdu ses bijoux
3 *n* (**a**) *(lamentation, complaint)* lamentation *f* (**b**) *(poem)* élégie *f*; *(song)* complainte *f*
lamentable ['læməntəbəl] *adj (regrettable)* regrettable; *(poor)* lamentable; **the lamentable state of the economy** l'état lamentable *ou* déplorable de l'économie
lamentably ['læməntəblɪ] *adv* lamentablement
lamentation [ˌlæmen'teɪʃən] **1** *n* lamentation *f*
2 Lamentations *npl Bible* **the Lamentations (of Jeremiah)** les Lamentations (de Jérémie)
lamented [lə'mentɪd] *adj* **the late lamented Mr Jones** le regretté M. Jones
lamina ['læmɪnə] *(pl* **laminas** *or* **laminae** [-niː]) *n Anat & Bot* lame *f*
laminal ['læmɪnəl] *adj Ling* laminal
laminar ['læmɪnə(r)] *adj* laminaire
►► ***laminar boundary layer*** couche *f* limite laminaire; *Phys* ***laminar flow*** écoulement *m* laminaire; *Miner* ***laminar fracture*** cassure *f* laminaire
laminar-flow airfoil *n Aviat* profil *m* (d'aile) laminaire
laminate ['læmɪneɪt] *Tech* **1** *vt* (**a**) *(bond in layers)* laminer; *(glass)* feuilleter; *(plastic)* stratifier; *(wood)* contreplaquer (**b**) *(split)* diviser en lamelles (**c**) *(veneer)* plaquer (**d**) *(document, card)* plastifier
2 *vi* (**a**) *(bond)* se laminer (**b**) *(split)* se diviser en lamelles
3 *n* stratifié *m*; **a table covered in white laminate** une table recouverte de stratifié blanc
laminated ['læmɪneɪtɪd] *adj* (**a**) *(glass)* feuilleté; *(plastic)* stratifié; *(wood)* contreplaqué (**b**) *(document, card)* plastifié
►► ***laminated spring*** ressort *m* à lames (superposées); ***laminated windscreen*** pare-brise *m inv* (en verre) feuilleté
laminectomy [ˌlæmɪ'nektəmɪ] *(pl* **laminectomies**) *n Med* laminectomie *f*
lamington ['læmɪŋtən] *n Austr* = gâteau au chocolat, recouvert de noix de coco
Lammas ['læməs] *n* **Lammas (Day)** le premier août
lammergeier ['læməˌgaɪə(r)] *n Orn* gypaète *m* barbu
lamp [læmp] *n* (**a**) *(gen)* lampe *f*; *(street lamp)* réverbère *m*; *(on car, train)* lumière *f*, feu *m* (**b**) *Med* lampe *f*; **infrared lamp** lampe *f* à infrarouges
►► ***lamp bracket*** applique *f*; ***lamp standard*** lampadaire *m*
lampblack ['læmpblæk] *n* noir *m* de carbone *ou* de fumée
lampern ['læmpən] *n Ich* lamproie *f* d'alose, lamproie *f* fluviatile
lamplight ['læmplaɪt] *n* **her hair shone in the lamplight** la lumière de la lampe faisait briller ses cheveux; **to read by lamplight** lire à la lumière d'une lampe; **to work by lamplight** travailler à la lumière d'une lampe
lamplighter ['læmplaɪtə(r)] *n* (**a**) *(person)* allumeur *m* de réverbères (**b**) *Am (device)* programmeur *m* d'éclairage
lamplit ['læmplɪt] *adj* éclairé par une lampe
lampoon [læm'puːn] **1** *n (satire)* satire *f*; *(written)* pamphlet *m*
2 *vt* ridiculiser, tourner en dérision
lampoonist [læm'puːnɪst] *n (satirist)* satiriste *mf*; *(in writings)* pamphlétaire *mf*
lamppost ['læmppəʊst] *n* réverbère *m*
lamprey ['læmprɪ] *n Ich* lamproie *f*
lampshade ['læmpʃeɪd] *n* abat-jour *m inv*
lampshell ['læmpʃel] *n Zool* brachiopode *m*
lampstand ['læmpstænd] *n* pied *m* de lampe
LAN [læn] *n Comput (abbr* **local area network**) réseau *m* local
Lancashire ['læŋkəˌʃɪə(r)] *n* le Lancashire, = comté du nord-ouest de l'Angleterre; **in Lancashire** dans le Lancashire
►► ***Lancashire heeler*** *(dog)* Lancashire-heeler *m*
Lancaster ['læŋkəstə(r)] (**a**) *(town)* Lancaster (**b**) *(royal house) Hist* Lancastre
Lancastrian [læŋ'kæstrɪən] *n* (**a**) *(from Lancaster)* habitant(e) *m,f* de Lancaster; *(from Lancashire)* habitant(e) *m,f* du Lancashire (**b**) *Hist* lancastrien(enne) *m,f*
lance [lɑːns] **1** *n* (**a**) *(weapon)* lance *f*; *Br Fig* **to break a lance with sb** se disputer avec qn (**b**) *Med* lancette *f*, bistouri *m*
2 *vt Med* percer, inciser
►► *Br* ***lance corporal*** ≃ caporal *m*, *Suisse* ≃ appointé *m*
lancelet ['lɑːnslɪt] *n Zool* amphioxus *m*
Lancelot ['lɑːnsəlɒt] *pr n* Lancelot
lanceolate ['lɑːnsɪəˌleɪt], **lanceolated** ['lɑːnsɪəˌleɪtɪd] *adj* lancéolé
lancer ['lɑːnsə(r)] **1** *n Hist & Mil* lancier *m*
2 lancers *npl (dance)* (quadrille *m* des) lanciers *mpl*
lancet ['lɑːnsɪt] *n Med* lancette *f*, bistouri *m*; *Br Press* **the Lancet** = revue médicale britannique
►► *Archit* ***lancet arch*** arc *m* lancéolé *ou* en lancette; *Archit* ***lancet window*** fenêtre *f* en ogive
lanceted ['lɑːnsɪtɪd] *adj Archit (window)* à lancette; *(church)* aux fenêtres à lancette

lancewood ['lɑːnswʊd] *n* (**a**) *Bot (Cuban)* duguétie *f*; *(Jamaican)* oxandre *m* (**b**) *Com* = bois souple pour brancards ou cannes à pêche

Lancs (*written abbr* **Lancashire**) Lancashire *m*

LAND [lænd]

terre(s)	▸ 1 (a), (b), (d)
région	▸ 1 (c)
pays	▸ 1 (e), (f)
royaume	▸ 1 (f)
poser	▸ 2 (a)
débarquer	▸ 2 (a)
hisser	▸ 2 (b)
décrocher	▸ 2 (c)
atterrir	▸ 3 (a)
arriver à quai	▸ 3 (b)
tomber	▸ 3 (c)
finir	▸ 3 (d)

1 *n* (**a**) *(for farming, building etc)* terre *f*; **he works on the land** il travaille la terre; **this is good farming land** c'est de la bonne terre; **building land** terrain constructible; **land for sale** *(sign)* terrain à vendre; **a piece of land** *(for farming)* un lopin de terre; *(for building)* un terrain (à bâtir); **to live off the land** vivre des ressources naturelles de la terre; *Fig* **to see how the land lies, to find out the lie** *or* **lay of the land** tâter le terrain

(**b**) *(property)* terre *f*, terres *fpl*; **their lands were confiscated** leurs terres ont été confisquées; **get off my land!** sortez de mes terres!

(**c**) *(area, region)* région *f*; **the desert lands of Northern Australia** les régions désertiques du nord de l'Australie

(**d**) *(not sea)* terre *f*; *Naut* **to make land** reconnaître la terre; *Naut* **they sighted land** ils aperçurent la terre; **we travelled by land to Cairo** nous sommes allés au Caire par la route; **over land and sea** sur terre et sur mer

(**e**) *Literary or Formal (nation, country)* pays *m*; **to travel in distant lands** voyager dans des pays lointains; **the victory was celebrated throughout the land** le pays tout entier a fêté la victoire; **a land of opportunity** un pays où tout est possible

(**f**) *Fig (realm)* royaume *m*, pays *m*; **he is no longer in the land of the living** il n'est plus de ce monde; **she lives in a land of make-believe** elle vit dans un monde de chimères

2 *vt* (**a**) *(plane)* poser; *(cargo, passengers)* débarquer; **they landed him on the deck of the ferry** ils l'ont fait atterrir sur le pont du ferry; **they have succeeded in landing men on the moon** ils ont réussi à envoyer des hommes sur la Lune

(**b**) *(fish → onto bank)* hisser sur la rive; *(→ onto boat)* hisser dans le bateau

(**c**) *Fam (job, contract)* décrocher; **he's just landed a good job** il vient juste de décrocher *ou* dégoter un bon boulot

(**d**) *Fam (put, place)* ficher; **he caught me a blow that nearly landed me in the water** il m'a flanqué un tel coup que j'ai bien failli me retrouver dans l'eau; **this could land us in real trouble** ça pourrait nous attirer de gros ennuis *ou* nous mettre dans le pétrin; **you've landed us in a nice mess!** tu nous as mis dans de beaux draps!; **it'll land you in prison!** tu finiras en prison!

(**e**) *(blow)* flanquer; **I landed him a blow** *or* **landed him one on the nose** je lui ai flanqué *ou* collé mon poing dans la figure

(**f**) *Fam (encumber)* **I got landed with the job of organizing the party** c'est moi qui me suis retrouvé avec la fête à organiser ❑, c'est moi qui me suis tapé l'organisation de la fête; **I've been landed with the job of telling him** c'est à moi qu'il est revenu de le lui dire; **we got landed with their children for the weekend** ils nous ont refilé leurs gosses *ou* il a fallu se farcir leurs gosses tout le week-end; **as usual, I got landed with all the work** comme d'habitude, c'est moi qui me suis tapé tout le travail; **they landed me with the bill** c'est moi qui ai écopé de l'addition

3 *vi* (**a**) *Aviat & Astron* atterrir; **they land at 7 p.m.** ils atterrissent *ou* leur avion arrive à 19 heures; **to land on the moon** atterrir sur la Lune, alunir; **to land in the sea** amerrir; **to land on an aircraft carrier** apponter (sur un porte-avions)

(**b**) *Naut (boat)* arriver à quai; *(passengers)* débarquer

(**c**) *(ball)* tomber, retomber; *(gymnast, ski-jumper, horse, high jumper)* se réceptionner; *(falling object, bomb, parachutist)* tomber; *(bird)* se poser; **an apple/the ball landed on her head** elle a reçu une pomme/le ballon sur la tête; **to land on one's feet** retomber sur ses pieds; *(of cat)* retomber sur ses pattes; *Fam Fig* **he always manages to land on his feet** il arrive toujours à retomber sur ses pattes

(**d**) *Fam (finish up)* finir ❑, atterrir; **he slipped and landed in a puddle** il a glissé et a atterri dans une flaque d'eau; **I hope that problem doesn't land on my desk** j'espère que ce problème ne va pas atterrir sur mon bureau; **the car landed in the ditch** la voiture a terminé sa course dans le fossé ❑; **he landed in jail** il s'est retrouvé en prison ❑

4 *comp (prices → in town)* du terrain; *(→ in country)* de la terre; *(ownership)* foncier; *Br Hist (army)* de terre; *(worker)* agricole

▸▸ *Law* ***land act*** loi *f* agraire; ***land agent*** *(administrator)* régisseur *m*, intendant(e) *m,f*; *Br (estate agent)* agent *m* immobilier; ***land bank*** crédit *m* foncier; ***land breeze*** brise *f* de terre; ***land bridge*** isthme *m*; *Acct* ***land charge*** dette *f* foncière; ***land crab*** crabe *m* terrestre; ***the Land of Enchantment*** = surnom donné au Nouveau-Mexique; ***Land's End*** = pointe de la Cornouailles; ***Land of Lincoln*** = surnom donné à l'Illinois; ***the Land of the Midnight Sun*** la terre du soleil de minuit; ***land reform*** réforme *f* agraire; ***land register*** cadastre *m*; ***land registration*** inscription *f* au cadastre; ***land registry*** cadastre *m*; ***land registry office*** bureau *m* du cadastre; ***land route*** voie *f* de terre; ***land tax*** impôt *m* foncier, contribution *f* foncière

▸**land up** *vi Fam (finish up)* finir ❑, atterrir; **the letter landed up in Finland** la lettre a atterri en Finlande; **you'll land up in jail!** tu finiras en prison!; **I landed up at a friend's house** j'ai atterri *ou* échoué chez un ami; **I landed up having to dance with him** il a fallu que je danse avec lui ❑; **I always landed up with the worst jobs** je me tapais toujours les tâches les plus ingrates à faire

---

A land fit for heroes

Cette expression ("un pays digne de ses héros") trouve son origine dans un discours que le Premier ministre britannique Lloyd George prononça en 1918. Il y expliquait la façon dont il envisageait l'avenir de son pays au sortir de la Première Guerre mondiale, et déclarait qu'il incombait au gouvernement de faire de la Grande-Bretagne **a fit country for heroes to live in** ("un pays qui ferait honneur à ses héros").

On utilise aujourd'hui cette formule dans sa version modifiée et souvent sur le mode ironique en parlant de la façon dont un pays traite ses soldats. On dira par exemple **if the returning veterans hoped for a land fit for heroes, they were to be sadly disappointed** ("si, une fois de retour au pays, les anciens combattants s'étaient imaginé trouver un pays digne de héros, ils allaient être amèrement déçus").

---

landau ['lændɔː] *n* landau *m*

land-based *adj Econ* basé sur la propriété terrienne

▸▸ *Mil* ***land-based forces*** forces *fpl* terrestres, armée *f* de terre; ***land-based missile*** missile *m* terrestre

landed ['lændɪd] *adj Br* foncier

▸▸ *Com* ***landed cost*** *(of goods)* prix *m* à quai; *Fin* ***landed costs*** coûts *mpl* fonciers; ***the landed gentry*** la noblesse terrienne; ***landed immigrant*** résident(e) *m,f* permanent(e); ***landed property*** propriété *f* foncière *ou* territoriale; ***landed proprietor*** propriétaire *mf* terrien(enne)

lander ['lændə(r)] *n Mining* receveur *m*, ouvrier *m* de la recette

landfall ['lændfɔːl] *n Naut (arrival)* atterrissage *m*; *(sight of land)* arrivée *f* en vue de terre; **to make landfall** apercevoir la terre, arriver en vue d'une côte

landfill ['lændfɪl] *n* ensevelissement *m* de déchets; **to use sth as landfill** utiliser qch pour remblayer *ou* comme remblai

▸▸ ***landfill site*** décharge *f* publique

landgirl ['lændgɜːl] *n Br Hist* = membre du "Women's Land Army", corps féminin qui assurait des travaux agricoles pendant la Seconde Guerre mondiale

land-grant college *n Am* = université construite sur un terrain offert par le gouvernement fédéral

landgrave ['lændgreɪv] *n Hist* landgrave *m*

landholder ['lænd,həʊldə(r)] *n* propriétaire *mf* terrien(enne)

landholding ['lænd,həʊldɪŋ] **1** *n* propriété *f*

2 *adj* foncier

landing ['lændɪŋ] *n* (**a**) *(of plane, spacecraft)* atterrissage *m*; *(on moon)* alunissage *m*; *(on sea)* amerrissage *m*; *(on deck of ship)* appontage *m*; *(of passengers, foods)* débarquement *m*; *Hist* **the Normandy landings** le débarquement (en Normandie)

(**b**) *Sport (of skier, high jumper, gymnast)* réception *f*; **he made a bad landing** il s'est mal reçu

(**c**) *(in staircase)* palier *m*; *(floor)* étage *m*

(**d**) *(jetty)* débarcadère *m*, embarcadère *m*

▸▸ *Aviat* ***landing beacon*** balise *f* d'atterrissage; ***landing card*** carte *f* de débarquement; ***landing certificate*** certificat *m* de déchargement; ***landing charges*** frais *mpl* de déchargement; ***landing craft*** navire *m* de débarquement; ***landing field*** terrain *m* d'atterrissage; ***landing flap*** volet *m* d'atterrissage; *Mil & Naut* ***landing force*** troupes *fpl* de débarquement; *Aviat* ***landing gear*** train *m* d'atterrissage; ***landing lights*** *(on plane)* phares *mpl* d'atterrissage; *(at airport)* balises *fpl* (d'atterrissage); ***landing net*** épuisette *f (filet)*; ***landing operation*** opération *f* de débarquement; ***landing order*** permis *m* de débarquement; *Mil & Naut* ***landing party*** compagnie *f* de débarquement; *Com* ***landing and port charges*** frais *mpl* de débarquement et de port; ***landing stage*** débarcadère *m*; ***landing strip*** piste *f* d'atterrissage; ***landing wheels*** train *m* d'atterrissage; *Mil & Aviat* ***landing zone*** zone *f* d'atterrissage *(des troupes aéroportées)*

landlady ['lænd,leɪdɪ] (*pl* **landladies**) *n* (**a**) *(from whom one rents accommodation → owner)* propriétaire *f*; *(→ living on premises)* logeuse *f* (**b**) *Br (of pub → owner)* propriétaire *f*; *(→ manager)* gérante *f* (**c**) *(of small hotel)* aubergiste *f*, hôtelière *f*; *(of guesthouse)* patronne *f*

landlegs ['lændlegz] *npl Fam* **to get one's landlegs** *(sailor)* se familiariser de nouveau avec la terre ❑

landless ['lændlɪs] *adj* sans terre

land-line *n Tel* ligne *f* terrestre

landlocked ['lændlɒkt] *adj (country)* enclavé, sans accès à la mer; *(sea)* intérieur

landlord ['lændlɔːd] *n* (**a**) *(of property)* bailleur *m*; *(from whom one rents accommodation → owner)* propriétaire *m*; *(→ living on premises)* logeur *m* (**b**) *Br (of pub → owner)* propriétaire *m*; *(→ manager)* gérant *m*; *(form of address)* patron *m* (**c**) *(landowner)* propriétaire *m* (foncier)

landlubber ['lænd,lʌbə(r)] *n Fam Hum* terrien ❑ *m*, éléphant *m*

landmark ['lændmɑːk] **1** *n* (**a**) *(building, statue etc)* point *m* de repère; **the major Paris landmarks** les principaux monuments de Paris (**b**) *Fig* étape *f* décisive, jalon *m*; *Fig* **the trial was a landmark in legal history** le procès a fait date dans les annales juridiques

2 *comp (decision)* qui fait date

landmass ['lændmæs] *n* étendue *f* de terre; **the American landmass** le continent américain

landmine ['lændmaɪn] *n* mine *f* (terrestre)

land-office *adj Am (booming → business)* qui monte en flèche

landowner ['lænd,əʊnə(r)] *n* propriétaire *mf* foncier(ère)

landowning ['lænd,əʊnɪŋ] *adj*

▸▸ ***the landowning classes*** la classe des propriétaires fonciers

Land Rover® ['lænd,rəʊvə(r)] *n* Land-Rover® *f*

landscape ['lændskeɪp] **1** *n* (**a**) *(gen)* paysage *m*; *Fig* **the political landscape** le paysage politique (**b**) *Comput & Typ (paper format)* (format *m*) paysage *m*; **to print sth in landscape** *Comput* imprimer qch en (mode) paysage; *Typ* imprimer qch à l'italienne

2 *adj Comput* paysage; *Typ* à l'italienne

3 *vt (garden)* dessiner; *(waste land)* aménager; **they had their garden landscaped** ils ont fait dessiner leur jardin par un paysagiste

►► ***landscape architect*** architecte *mf* paysagiste; ***landscape architecture*** architecture *f* de paysage; ***landscape design*** architecture *f* de paysage; ***landscape designer*** paysagiste *mf*; *Hort* ***landscape gardener*** jardinier(ère) *m,f* paysagiste; *Hort* ***landscape gardening*** paysagisme *m*; *Comput* ***landscape mode*** mode *m* paysage; *Art* ***landscape painter*** (peintre *m*) paysagiste *mf*; ***landscape painting*** le paysage

landscaping ['lænd,skeɪpɪŋ] *n* aménagement *m* paysager

landscapist ['lænd,skeɪpɪst] *n Art* (peintre *m*) paysagiste *mf*

landslide ['lændslaɪd] **1** *n* **(a)** *(of earth, rocks)* glissement *m* de terrain **(b)** *(victory)* victoire *f* écrasante; **to win the elections by a landslide** gagner les élections avec une majorité écrasante

2 *comp (majority, victory)* écrasant

landslip ['lændslɪp] *n Br* éboulement *m*

landward ['lændwəd] *Naut* **1** *adj* du côté de la terre; **landward breeze** vent *m* marin *ou* qui souffle de la mer; **on the landward side** du côté terre

2 *adv* en direction de la terre; *(on land)* vers l'intérieur (des terres)

landwards ['lændwədz] *adv Naut* en direction de la terre; *(on land)* vers l'intérieur (des terres)

lane [leɪn] *n* **(a)** *(road → in country)* chemin *m*; *(→ in street names)* rue *f*, allée *f*

(b) *(for traffic)* voie *f*; *(line of vehicles)* file *f*; *(for shipping, aircraft)* couloir *m*; **get into the right-hand lane** mettez-vous dans la file *ou* sur la voie de droite; **keep in lane** *(sign)* ne changez pas de file; **get in lane** *(sign)* mettez-vous sur la bonne file; **lane ends** *(sign)* chaussée rétrécie (à droite/à gauche); **a 4-lane road** une route à 4 voies; **to be in the wrong lane** être dans la mauvaise file; **traffic is reduced to two lanes** la circulation ne se fait plus que sur deux voies

(c) *(in athletics, swimming)* couloir *m*

►► ***lane closure*** fermeture *f* de voies; **the traffic was held up by lane closures** la circulation a été ralentie par des rétrécissements (dus à des travaux); ***lane markings*** *(on road)* signalisation *f* au sol *ou* horizontale des voies; *Sport (on track)* lignes *fpl* de marquage des couloirs; *(in swimming pool)* lignes *fpl* d'eau

lang *Sch & Univ* (*written abbr* **language**) langue *f*

langlauf ['læŋlaʊf] *n* ski *m* de fond

►► ***langlauf skier*** skieur(euse) *m,f* de fond

langouste ['lɒŋgʊst] *n* langouste *f*

langoustine ['lɒŋgʊsti:n] *n* langoustine *f*

language ['læŋgwɪdʒ] **1** *n* **(a)** *(concept, vocabulary)* langage *m*; **I prefer language to literature** je préfère l'étude des langues à celle de la littérature; **the child's acquisition of language** l'acquisition du langage par l'enfant

(b) *(specific tongue)* langue *f*; *Sch & Univ (area of study)* langue *f*; **the French language** la langue française; **to study languages** faire des études de langue; **she speaks three languages fluently** elle parle trois langues couramment; **to speak the same language** parler le même langage; *Fig* **you speak my language** nous parlons le même langage; *Fig* **we don't talk the same language** nous ne parlons pas le même langage

(c) *(code)* langage *m*; **a computer language** un langage machine; **the language of love/flowers** le langage de l'amour/des fleurs

(d) *(terminology)* langue *f*, langage *m*; **medical/legal language** langage *m* médical/juridique; **the language of diplomacy** *(jargon)* le langage diplomatique

(e) *(manner of expression)* expression *f*, langue *f*; **I find his language very pompous** je trouve qu'il s'exprime avec emphase *ou* de façon très pompeuse

(f) *(rude words)* gros mots *mpl*, grossièretés *fpl*; **(mind your) language!** surveille ton langage!

2 *comp (acquisition)* du langage; *(teaching, learning, course)* de langues; *(barrier)* linguistique; *(student)* en langues

►► ***language laboratory,*** *Fam* ***language lab*** labo *m* de langues; ***language studies*** études *fpl* de langues

languid ['læŋgwɪd] *adj* langoureux, alangui

languidly ['læŋgwɪdlɪ] *adv* langoureusement

languidness ['læŋgwɪdnɪs] *n* langueur *f*

languish ['læŋgwɪʃ] *vi* **(a)** *(suffer)* languir; **to languish in prison** croupir en prison **(b)** *(become weak)* dépérir; **to languish in the heat** *(plant)* dépérir à la chaleur; *(person)* souffrir de la chaleur; **the project was languishing for lack of funds** le projet traînait, faute d'argent **(c)** *Literary (pine)* languir; **he languished for love of his lady** il languissait d'amour pour sa bien-aimée

languishing ['læŋgwɪʃɪŋ] *adj* langoureux, alangui

languor ['læŋgə(r)] *n* langueur *f*

languorous ['læŋgərəs] *adj* langoureux

languorously ['læŋgərəslɪ] *adv* langoureusement

langur [lʌŋ'gʊə(r)] *n Zool* langur *m*, entelle *m*

laniard = **lanyard**

lank [læŋk] *adj (hair)* terne; *(plant)* étiolé, grêle

lankiness ['læŋkɪnɪs] *n* aspect *m* efflanqué

lankness ['læŋknɪs] *n (of hair)* aspect *m* terne

lanky ['læŋkɪ] (*compar* **lankier**, *superl* **lankiest**) *adj* grand et maigre, efflanqué

lanner ['lænə(r)] *n Orn* faucon *m* lanier

lanneret ['lænəret] *n Orn* laneret *m*

lanolin, lanoline ['lænəlɪn] *n* lanoline *f*

lantern ['læntən] *n (lamp)* lanterne *f*; *Naut (of lighthouse)* fanal *m*

►► ***lantern fish*** poisson-lanterne *m*; ***lantern slide*** plaque *f* de lanterne magique

lantern-jawed [-dʒɔ:d] *adj* aux joues creuses

lanthanide ['lænθə,naɪd] *n Chem* lanthanide *m*

►► ***lanthanide series*** lanthanides *mpl*

lanthanum ['lænθənəm] *n Chem* lanthane *m*

lanugo [lə'nju:gəʊ] *n* lanugo *m*

lanyard ['lænjəd] *n* corde *f*, cordon *m*; *Naut* ride *f*

Lanzarote [,lænzə'rɒtɪ] *n* Lanzarote; **in Lanzarote** à Lanzarote

Lao [laʊ] **1** *n* **(a)** *(person)* Laotien(enne) *m,f* **(b)** *(language)* laotien *m*

2 *adj* laotien

3 *comp (embassy, history)* du Laos; *(teacher)* de laotien

Laodicean [,leɪəʊdɪ'sɪən] **1** *n* **(a)** *Antiq* Laodicéen(enne) *m,f* **(b)** *Literary* = personne peu intéressée par la religion ou la politique

2 *adj* **(a)** *Antiq* laodicéen **(b)** *Literary (person)* peu intéressé par la religion ou la politique

Laoighis, Laois ['leɪʃ] *n* le comté de Leix, = comté dans le centre de la République d'Irlande; **in Laoighis** *or* **Laois** dans le comté de Leix

Laos [laʊs] *n* Laos *m*; **in Laos** au Laos

Laotian ['laʊʃən] **1** *n* **(a)** *(person)* Laotien(enne) *m,f* **(b)** *(language)* laotien *m*

2 *adj* laotien

3 *comp (embassy, history)* du Laos; *(teacher)* de laotien

lap [læp] (*pt & pp* **lapped**, *cont* **lapping**) **1** *n* **(a)** *(knees)* genoux *mpl*; **come and sit on my lap** viens t'asseoir sur mes genoux; *Fam* **don't think it's just going to fall into your lap!** ne t'imagine pas que ça va te tomber tout cuit dans le bec!; *Fig* **to drop sth in sb's lap** coller qch à qn; **it's in the lap of the gods** c'est entre les mains des dieux; **the lap of luxury** le grand luxe; **to live in the lap of luxury** vivre dans le plus grand luxe

(b) *Sport* tour *m* de piste; **we ran two laps** nous avons fait deux tours de piste; **a 30-lap race** une course sur 30 tours; **the last lap** le tour de l'arrivée, le dernier tour (avant l'arrivée); *Fig* **we're on the last lap** on arrive au bout de nos peines; **lap of honour** tour *m* d'honneur

(c) *(of journey)* étape *f*

(d) *Tech (overlap)* recouvrement *m*; *Constr (of tiles, slates)* chevauchement *m*, recouvrement *m*

(e) *(of wire around cylinder etc)* tour *m*

2 *vt* **(a)** *Sport (competitor, car)* dépasser, prendre un tour d'avance sur; **the slower drivers were soon lapped by the leaders** les pilotes les plus rapides n'ont pas tardé à prendre un tour d'avance sur les autres concurrents

(b) *(time)* chronométrer; **Kelly was lapped at over 200 mph** Kelly a été chronométré sur un tour à plus de 300 km/h

(c) *(milk)* laper

(d) *(of waves)* clapoter contre; **the waves lapped the hull** les vagues clapotaient contre la coque

(e) *(wrap)* **to lap sth round sth** enrouler qch autour de qch

(f) *Constr (planks)* enchevaucher, poser à recouvrement; *(tiles)* donner du recouvrement à; **to lap a joint with sheet metal** chaperonner un assemblage

3 *vi* **(a)** *Sport* tourner, faire un tour de circuit; **Kelly was lapping at over 200 mph** Kelly tournait à plus de 300 km/h de moyenne

(b) *(waves)* clapoter; **the waves lapped against the boat** les vagues clapotaient contre le bateau

►► *Aut* ***lap belt*** ceinture *f* ventrale; ***lap dancer*** = entraîneuse qui danse nue pour un client; ***lap dancing*** = type de danse exécutée par une entraîneuse nue pour un client; *Tech* ***lap joint*** enchevauchure *f*, assemblage *m* par recouvrement; *Am* ***lap robe*** plaid *m*; *Aut* ***lap and shoulder belt*** ceinture *f* trois points; *Metal* ***lap weld*** soudure *f* à recouvrement; *Metal* ***lap welding*** soudage *m* à recouvrement

►**lap over 1** *vt insep (tiles)* chevaucher sur

2 *vi* se chevaucher

►**lap up** *vt sep* **(a)** *(milk)* laper

(b) *Fam Fig (praise)* boire; *(information)* avaler, gober; **he laps up every word she says** il gobe tout ce qu'elle dit; **they were all paying her compliments and she was just lapping it up** tous lui faisaient des compliments et elle s'en délectait

laparoscope ['læpərəskəʊp] *n* laparoscope *m*

laparoscopy [,læpə'rɒskəpɪ] *n* laparoscopie *f*

laparotomy [,læpə'rɒtəmɪ] (*pl* **laparotomies**) *n Med* laparotomie *f*

La Paz [læ'pæz] *n* La Paz

lapdog ['læpdɒg] *n* petit chien *m* d'appartement; *Fig Pej (person)* toutou *m*, caniche *m*

lapel [lə'pel] *n* revers *m*; **he grabbed me by the lapels** il m'a saisi par le revers de ma veste

lap-held *adj (typewriter, computer)* portatif *(que l'on peut poser sur ses genoux)*

lapidary ['læpɪdərɪ] (*pl* **lapidaries**) **1** *n* lapidaire *m*

2 *adj (cut in stone)* lapidaire

lapidate ['læpɪdeɪt] *vt Literary* lapider

lapidation [,læpɪ'deɪʃən] *n Literary* lapidation *f*

lapidification [lə,pɪdɪfɪ'keɪʃən] *n Literary* lapidification *f*

lapidify [lə'pɪdɪfaɪ] *vt Literary* lapidifier

lapis lazuli [,læpɪs'læzjʊlaɪ] *n* lapis *m*, lapis-lazuli *m inv*

Lapland ['læplænd] *n* Laponie *f*; **in Lapland** en Laponie

Laplander ['læplændə(r)] *n* Lapon(one) *m,f*

Lapp [læp] **1** *n* **(a)** *(person)* Lapon(one) *m,f* **(b)** *(language)* lapon *m*

2 *adj* lapon

lapping ['læpɪŋ] *n (of waves)* clapotis *m*

Lappish ['læpɪʃ] **1** *n (language)* lapon *m*

2 *adj* lapon

lapsang souchong ['læpsæŋ'su:ʃɒŋ] *n* lapsang souchong *m*

lapse [læps] **1** *n* **(a)** *(failure)* **lapse of memory** trou *m* de mémoire; **lapse in concentration** moment *m* d'inattention

(b) *(in behaviour)* écart *m* (de conduite); *(in standards)* baisse *f*; **she has occasional lapses** elle fait des bêtises de temps en temps; **the slightest lapse was punished harshly** la moindre faute était sévèrement punie; **a lapse from virtue** un manquement à la vertu

(c) *(interval)* laps *m* de temps, intervalle *m*; **after a lapse of six months** au bout de six mois

(d) *(of contract)* expiration *f*; *(of custom)* disparition *f*; *(of legal right)* déchéance *f*

2 *vi* **(a)** *(decline)* baisser, chuter; *Rel* **to lapse from grace** pécher; **he only lapsed once** il n'a fait qu'une seule erreur; **his concentration lapsed for a split second** il a relâché sa concentration pendant une fraction de seconde; **if standards of education are allowed to lapse** si on laisse baisser les niveaux scolaires

(b) *(drift)* tomber; **she lapsed into a coma** elle

est tombée dans le coma; **to lapse into bad habits** prendre de mauvaises habitudes; **to lapse into silence** garder le silence, s'enfermer dans le silence; **she kept lapsing into Russian** elle repassait sans cesse au russe

(**c**) *(pass → time)* passer; **weeks lapsed before I saw her again** il se passa plusieurs semaines avant que je ne la revoie

(**d**) *(law, custom)* tomber en désuétude; *(licence, passport)* se périmer; *(subscription)* prendre fin, expirer; *(estate)* devenir disponible; *(legacy)* devenir caduc; **he let his insurance lapse** il a laissé périmer son assurance

(**e**) *Rel (cease practising one's faith)* cesser de pratiquer

lapsed [læpst] *adj (law)* caduc; *(passport)* périmé; *Fin (fund)* périmé

►► ***lapsed Catholic*** catholique *mf* qui ne pratique plus; *St Exch* ***lapsed option*** option *f* expirée

laptop ['læptɒp] *n* ordinateur *m* portable, *Can* ordinateur *m* portatif

►► ***laptop computer*** ordinateur *m* portable, *Can* ordinateur *m* portatif

lapwing ['læpwɪŋ] *n Orn* vanneau *m*

larboard ['lɑːbəd] *n Arch* bâbord *m*

larceny ['lɑːsənɪ] (*pl* **larcenies**) *n Law* vol *m* simple

larch [lɑːtʃ] *n Bot* mélèze *m*

lard [lɑːd] **1** *n* saindoux *m*; *Fam* **he's a tub of lard** c'est un sac de graisse

2 *vt* larder; *Fig* **an essay larded with quotations** une rédaction truffée de citations

lardarse ['lɑːdɑːs], *Am* **lardass** ['lɑːdæs] *n very Fam (man)* gros *m* plein de soupe; *(woman)* grosse vache *f*

larder ['lɑːdə(r)] *n (room)* cellier *m*; *(cupboard)* garde-manger *m inv*; *Fam* **to raid the larder** faire une razzia dans le garde-manger

lares and penates ['lɑːreɪzənpə'nɑːteɪz] *npl Myth* lares *mpl* et pénates *mpl*

large [lɑːdʒ] **1** *adj* (**a**) *(in size)* grand; *(family)* grand, nombreux; *(person, organization)* gros (grosse), grand; **large size** *(clothes)* grande taille *f*; *(of product)* grand modèle *m*; **a large coat** un grand manteau; **on a large scale** à grande échelle; **to a large extent** dans une large mesure; **he lives in a large house** il habite une grande maison; **she's a large woman** c'est une femme plutôt grosse *ou* forte

(**b**) *(in number, amount)* grand, important; **a large proportion** une grande proportion, une part importante; **she wrote him a large cheque** elle lui a fait un chèque pour une somme importante *ou* une grosse somme; **a large helping of potatoes/apple pie** une grosse portion de pommes de terre/part de tarte aux pommes; **a large number of** beaucoup de; **there are a large number of entrants this year** il y a beaucoup de participants *ou* candidats cette année, les participants *ou* candidats sont nombreux cette année; **to grow** *or* **get larger** *(town, deficit)* s'agrandir; *(person, amount)* grossir; **he was standing there as large as life** il était là, en chair et en os; **larger than life** exagéré, outrancier

(**c**) *(extensive, significant → changes)* considérable, important; **a large part of my time/job/day** une grande partie de mon temps/mon travail/ma journée

(**d**) *(liberal → views, ideas)* libéral, large *(generous → heart)* grand, généreux

2 *adv* (**a**) **to loom large** menacer, sembler imminent; **to be writ large** être évident

(**b**) *Br Fam (to a large extent)* **Arsenal got thrashed large** Arsenal s'est fait ratatiner *ou* s'est fait battre à plates coutures; **we got ratted large last night** on s'est pris une cuite maison hier soir

3 *n (size)* **I take a large** je prends une grande taille; **this T-shirt's a large** ce tee-shirt est une grande taille

4 at large 1 *adj (at liberty)* en liberté; *(prisoner)* en fuite; **the rapist is at large somewhere in the city** le violeur se promène en (toute) liberté quelque part dans cette ville; **he was acting as the UN's ambassador at large** il a été ambassadeur itinérant des Nations unies **2** *adv* (**a**) *(as a whole)* dans son ensemble; **the country at large** le pays dans son ensemble; **people at large** le grand public, la grande masse du public; **teachers at large** la masse des professeurs (**b**) *(in detail)* tout au long, en détail; **to talk at large** parler au hasard

5 by and large *adv* de manière générale, dans l'ensemble; **by and large they vote Conservative** ils votent conservateur pour la plupart

6 in large *adv Am* en profondeur

►► *Fin* ***large denominations*** grosses coupures *fpl*; *Anat* ***the large intestine*** le gros intestin; *Entom* ***large white*** piéride *f* (du chou)

large-hearted *adj* au grand cœur

largely ['lɑːdʒlɪ] *adv (mainly)* en grande partie, pour la plupart; *(in general)* en général, en gros

large-minded *adj* large d'esprit, ouvert

largeness ['lɑːdʒnɪs] *n (in size)* grandeur *f*, (grande) taille *f*; *(of sum)* importance *f*; *(of number)* grandeur *f*, importance *f*

large-print *adj* en gros caractères

large-scale *adj* à grande échelle; **large-scale disaster** grande catastrophe *f*

►► *Comput* ***large-scale integration*** intégration *f* à grande échelle

large-size, large-sized *adj (clothes)* grande taille *(inv)*; *(product)* grand modèle *(inv)*; *(envelope)* grand format *(inv)*

largesse [lɑː'dʒes] *n (UNCOUNT)* largesse *f*, largesses *fpl*

larghetto [lɑː'getəʊ] *Mus* **1** *n* larghetto *m*

2 *adv* larghetto

largish ['lɑːdʒɪʃ] *adj (in size)* assez grand; *(in amount)* assez grand, assez gros; *(in number)* assez nombreux

largo ['lɑːgəʊ] **1** *n* largo *m*

2 *adj* largo

3 *adv* largo

lariat ['lærɪət] **1** *n* (**a**) *Am (lasso)* lasso *m* (**b**) *(for tethering animals)* corde *f* à piquet

2 *vt* prendre au lasso

larid ['lærɪd] (*pl* **laridae** [-diː]) *n Orn* lariforme *m*

lark [lɑːk] *n* (**a**) *Orn* alouette *f*; **to rise** *or* **to be up with the lark** se lever avec les poules *ou* au chant du coq; *Br* **as happy as a lark** gai comme un pinson

(**b**) *Fam (joke)* rigolade *f*; *(prank)* blague *f*, farce *f*; **for a lark** pour blaguer, pour rigoler; **what a lark!** quelle rigolade!, quelle bonne blague!

(**c**) *Fam (rigmarole, business)* histoire *f*; **I don't like the sound of this fancy dress lark** je n'aime pas beaucoup cette histoire de déguisement, cette idée de déguisement ne me dit rien qui vaille; **are you still at the teaching lark?** tu fais toujours ce sacré métier de prof?

►**lark about, lark around** *vi Br Fam* faire le fou (la folle); **stop larking about!** arrêtez de faire les fous *ou* les imbéciles!; **some children were larking around with an old tyre** des enfants s'amusaient avec un vieux pneu

larkspur ['lɑːkspɜː(r)] *n Bot* pied-d'alouette *m*

larrikin ['lærɪkɪn] *n Austr & NZ Fam* vaurien *m*

larva ['lɑːvə] (*pl* **larvae** [-viː]) *n* larve *f*

larvacide ['lɑːvəsaɪd] *n Agr* larvicide *m*

larval ['lɑːvəl] *adj* larvaire

larvicide ['lɑːvɪsaɪd] *n Agr* larvicide *m*

laryngal [lə'rɪŋgəl], **laryngeal** [ˌlærɪn'dʒiːəl] *adj* (**a**) *Med* laryngé, laryngien (**b**) *Ling* laryngal, glottal

laryngectomy [ˌlærɪn'dʒektəmɪ] (*pl* **laryngectomies**) *n* laryngectomie *f*

laryngitis [ˌlærɪn'dʒaɪtɪs] *n (UNCOUNT)* laryngite *f*; **to have laryngitis** avoir une laryngite

laryngoscope [lə'rɪŋgəskəʊp] *n* laryngoscope *m*

laryngoscopy [ˌlærɪŋ'gɒskəpɪ] *n Med* laryngoscopie *f*

laryngotomy [ˌlærɪŋ'gɒtəmɪ] (*pl* **laryngotomies**) *n Med* laryngotomie *f*

larynx ['lærɪŋks] *n* larynx *m*

lasagne, lasagna [lə'zænjə] *n (UNCOUNT)* lasagnes *fpl*

lascar ['læskə(r)] *n* matelot *m* indien

lascivious [lə'sɪvɪəs] *adj* lascif, lubrique

lasciviously [lə'sɪvɪəslɪ] *adv* lascivement

lasciviousness [lə'sɪvɪəsnɪs] *n* lasciveté *f*

laser ['leɪzə(r)] *n* laser *m*

►► ***laser beam*** rayon *m ou* faisceau *m* laser; ***laser card*** carte *f* à puce; ***laser checkout*** *(in supermarket)* caisse *f* munie de lecteurs laser; ***laser disc*** disque *m* laser; ***laser engraving*** gravure *f* au laser; ***laser mass spectrometer*** spectromètre *m* de masse à laser; ***laser pen*** pointeur *m* laser; ***laser printer*** imprimante *f* (à) laser; *Comput* ***laser quality*** qualité *f* laser; ***laser show*** spectacle *m* laser; ***laser surgery*** chirurgie *f* (au) laser

laser-guided *adj* guidé au laser

lash [læʃ] **1** *n* (**a**) *(whip)* lanière *f*; *(blow from whip)* coup *m* de fouet; **he was given sixty lashes** on lui a donné *ou* il a reçu soixante coups de fouet; **the lash** *(punishment)* le (supplice du) fouet

(**b**) *Fig (of scorn, criticism)* **he'd often felt the lash of her tongue** il avait souvent été la cible de ses propos virulents

(**c**) *(of rain, sea)* **the lash of the rain on the windows** le bruit de la pluie qui fouette les vitres; **the lash of the waves against the shore** le déferlement des vagues sur la grève

(**d**) *(eyelash)* cil *m*

2 *vt* (**a**) *(with whip)* fouetter

(**b**) *(of rain, waves)* battre, fouetter; **the waves lashed the shore** les vagues venaient se fracasser sur la grève; **the cold rain lashed my face** la pluie froide me cinglait *ou* me fouettait le visage; **the hail lashed the window** la grêle s'abattait sur la vitre; *Fig* **he lashed them with his tongue** il leur adressa quelques remarques cinglantes

(**c**) *(move)* **the tiger lashed its tail** le tigre fouettait l'air de sa queue

(**d**) *(tie)* attacher; **they lashed him to the chair** ils l'ont attaché solidement à la chaise; **they lashed the cargo to the deck** ils arrimèrent la cargaison sur le pont

3 *vi* **its tail lashed wildly** il fouettait l'air furieusement de sa queue; **the hail lashed against the window** la grêle cinglait la vitre

►**lash down 1** *vt sep (cargo)* arrimer, fixer; **the crates were lashed down** les caisses étaient solidement arrimées

2 *vi (rain, hail)* s'abattre, tomber avec violence

►**lash into** *vt insep (criticize)* se déchaîner contre; **she really lashed into them** elle était véritablement déchaînée contre eux

►**lash out 1** *vt sep Br Fam (spend)* **I lashed out £10 on a bottle of wine** j'ai claqué 10 livres sur une bouteille de vin

2 *vi* (**a**) *(struggle → with fists)* donner des coups de poing; *(→ with feet)* donner des coups de pied; **she lashed out in all directions** elle se débattit de toutes ses forces

(**b**) *Fig (verbally)* **he lashed out at his critics** il a fustigé ses détracteurs

(**c**) *Br Fam (spend)* **to lash out (on sth)** dépenser un fric monstre (pour qch); **he lashed out and bought himself a new suit** il a claqué son fric pour s'acheter un nouveau costume

lashing ['læʃɪŋ] **1** *n* (**a**) *(with whip)* flagellation *f*, fouet *m*; **to give sb a lashing** donner des coups de fouet à qn (**b**) *Fig (scolding)* réprimandes *fpl*, correction *f* (**c**) *(rope)* corde *f*; *Naut* amarre *f*

2 *adj (rain)* cinglant

3 lashings *npl Br (in amount)* des montagnes; **with lashings of chocolate sauce** [illegible] sauce au chocolat

Las Palmas [ˌlæs'pælməs] *n* Las Palmas

lass [læs] *n Scot & NEng (girl)* fille *f*

Lassa ['lɑːsə] *n* Lhassa

►► ***Lassa fever*** fièvre *f* de Lhassa

lassie ['læsɪ] *n Scot & Ir* fillette *f*, gamine *f*

lassitude ['læsɪtjuːd] *n* lassitude *f*

lasso [læ'suː] (*pl* **lassos** *or* **lassoes**, *pp & pt* **lassoed**, *cont* **lassoing**) **1** *n* lasso *m*

2 *vt* prendre au lasso

LAST[1] [lɑːst] **1** *adj* (**a**) *(with dates, times of day)* dernier; **last Monday** lundi dernier; **last week/year** la semaine/l'année dernière; **last July** en juillet dernier, l'année dernière au mois de juillet; **last night** *(at night)* cette nuit, la nuit dernière; *(in the evening)* hier soir

(**b**) *(final)* dernier; **the last train** le dernier train; **the last guest to arrive** le dernier des invités à arriver; **the last syllable but one** l'avant-dernière syllabe; **that was the last time**

I saw him c'était la dernière fois que je le voyais; **that's the last time I do HIM a favour** c'est la dernière fois que je lui rends service; **it's your last chance** c'est votre dernière chance; **at the last minute** *or* **moment** à la dernière minute, au dernier moment; **it's our last day here** c'est notre dernière journée ici; **I'm down to my last cigarette** il ne me reste plus qu'une seule cigarette; **they were down to their last few bullets** il ne leur restait pratiquement plus de munitions; **one of the last few survivors** un des tout derniers survivants; **the last two pages** les deux dernières pages; **I'll sack every last one of them!** je vais tous les virer!; **every last scrap of bread had been eaten** on avait mangé jusqu'à la dernière miette; **she used up every last ounce of energy** elle a utilisé tout ce qui lui restait d'énergie; **to the last detail** dans les moindres détails; *Am* **the movie was her last hurrah** c'est avec ce film qu'elle a fait ses adieux au cinéma; **the concert was her last hurrah** c'est avec ce concert qu'elle a fait ses adieux au public; **they were prepared to fight to the last man** ils étaient prêts à se battre jusqu'au dernier; **she was on her last legs** elle était au bout du rouleau; **your car is on its last legs** votre voiture ne va pas tarder à vous lâcher; **the regime is on its last legs** le régime vit ses derniers jours *ou* est au bord de l'effondrement; **I'll get my money back if it's the last thing I do** je récupérerai mon argent coûte que coûte; **I always clean my teeth last thing at night** je me brosse toujours les dents juste avant de me coucher; **we finished the work last thing on Tuesday afternoon** on a terminé le travail juste avant de partir mardi après-midi

(**c**) *(most recent)* dernier; **you said that last time** c'est ce que tu as dit la dernière fois; **this time last year we were in New York** l'année dernière à cette époque nous étions à New York; **I've been here for the last five years** je suis ici depuis cinq ans, cela fait cinq ans que je suis ici; **I haven't been to church for the last few weeks** je ne suis pas allé à l'église ces dernières semaines; **I didn't like her last film** je n'ai pas aimé son dernier film

(**d**) *(least likely)* **he's the last person I expected to see** c'est bien la dernière personne que je m'attendais à voir; **he's the last person I'd ask to help me** c'est (bien) la dernière personne à qui je demanderais de l'aide; **that's the last thing that's worrying me** ça c'est le cadet de mes soucis; **that's the last place I'd have looked** c'est bien le dernier endroit où j'aurais cherché; **that's the last thing I wanted** je n'avais vraiment pas besoin de ça; **you're the last one to criticize** tu es vraiment mal placé pour critiquer

2 *adv* (**a**) *(finally)* **she arrived last** elle est arrivée la dernière *ou* en dernier; **she came** *or* **finished last** *(in race)* elle est arrivée dernière; **and last but not least...** et en dernier, mais non par ordre d'importance,...; **last but not least on the list we have M. Livingstone** et enfin sur la liste, je ne voudrais pas oublier M. Livingstone

(**b**) *(most recently)* **when did you last see him?** quand l'avez-vous vu la dernière fois?; **they last came to see us in 1989** leur dernière visite remonte à 1989; **I can't remember when I last ate** je ne sais plus quand j'ai pris mon dernier repas; *Com & Fin* **last in, first out** dernier entré, premier sorti

(**c**) *(lastly)* enfin, en dernier lieu; **last, I would like to say...** et pour finir, je voudrais dire...

3 *n* (**a**) *(final one)* dernier(ère) *m,f*; **am I the last?** *(to arrive)* suis-je le dernier?; **the last in the class** le dernier de la classe; **she was the last to arrive** elle est arrivée la dernière; **the last of the Romanovs** le dernier des Romanov; **the next to last, the last but one** l'avant-dernier; *Bible* **the last shall be first** les derniers seront les premiers

(**b**) *(previous one)* **each more handsome than the last** tous plus beaux les uns que les autres; **the day before last** avant-hier; **the night before last** *(at night)* la nuit d'avant-hier; *(in the evening)* avant-hier soir; **the winter before last** l'hiver d'il y a deux ans; **the Prime Minister before last** l'avant-dernier Premier ministre

(**c**) *(end)* **that was the last I saw of her** c'est la dernière fois que je l'ai vue, je ne l'ai pas revue depuis; **I hope that's the last we see of them** j'espère qu'on ne les reverra plus; **I'll never see the last of this!** je n'en verrai jamais la fin!, je n'en viendrai jamais à bout!; **I think we've heard the last of him** je pense qu'on n'en entendra plus parler; **we'll never hear the last of it** on n'a pas fini d'en entendre parler; **you haven't heard the last of this!** *(as threat)* vous aurez de mes nouvelles!; **leave the pans till last** gardez les casseroles pour la fin, lavez les casseroles en dernier; *Literary* **to look one's last on sth** voir qch pour la dernière fois; *Literary* **to breathe one's last** rendre le dernier soupir; *Literary* **to be near one's last** *(death)* être proche de sa fin

(**d**) *(remainder)* reste *m*; **we drank the last of the wine** on a bu ce qui restait de vin

4 at last *adv* enfin; **free at last** enfin libre; **at long last** enfin; **now at last I understand** enfin, je comprends; **at long last she's found a job she enjoys** elle a enfin trouvé un emploi qui lui plaît; **at last! where on earth have you been?** (te voilà) enfin! mais où étais-tu donc?; **at last he said: "do you forgive me?"** enfin il demanda: "tu me pardonnes?"

5 at the last *adv Formal* **at the last the judges came out in her favour** à la dernière minute, les juges ont décidé en sa faveur; **she was there at the last** elle est restée jusqu'au bout

6 to the last *adv* jusqu'au bout; **faithful to the last** fidèle jusqu'au bout; **she insisted to the last that she was not guilty** elle a dit jusqu'au bout qu'elle n'était pas coupable

►► *Am* ***last call*** = dans un bar, moment où le barman annonce que l'heure de la fermeture approche et qu'il s'apprête à servir les dernières consommations; ***the Last Frontier*** = surnom donné à l'Alaska; ***the Last Judgment*** le Jugement dernier; ***last name*** nom *m* de famille; *Tel* ***last number redial*** touche *f* bis; *Br* ***last orders*** = dans un pub, moment où le barman annonce que l'heure de la fermeture approche et qu'il s'apprête à servir les dernières consommations; *Br Mil* ***last post*** *(at night)* extinction *f* des feux; *(at funeral)* sonnerie *f* aux morts; **to sound the last post (over the grave)** jouer la sonnerie aux morts; ***last rites*** derniers sacrements *mpl*; ***the Last Supper*** la (sainte) Cène; *St Exch* ***last trading day*** dernier jour *m* de cotation; ***last word*** *(final decision)* dernier mot *m*; *(latest style)* dernier cri *m*; **the Treasury has the last word on defence spending** le ministère des Finances a le dernier mot en matière de dépenses militaires; **she was wearing the very last word in hats** elle portait un chapeau du dernier cri

'Last Exit to Brooklyn' *Selby, Edel* 'Dernière sortie pour Brooklyn'

LAST[2] [lɑːst] **1** *vi* (**a**) *(continue to exist or function)* durer; **it's too good to last** c'est trop beau pour durer; **if the good weather lasts** si le beau temps se maintient; **it lasted (for) ten days** cela a duré dix jours; **how long did the film last?** combien de temps le film a-t-il duré?, quelle était la durée du film?; **how long can we last without water?** combien de temps tiendrons-nous sans eau?; **the supplies will not last two months** les vivres ne feront pas deux mois; **he didn't last more than a year as a singer** il n'a pas tenu plus d'un an dans la chanson; **their romance didn't last (for) long** leur idylle n'a pas duré longtemps; **he won't last long** *(in job)* il ne tiendra pas longtemps; *(will soon die)* il n'en a plus pour longtemps; **the batteries didn't last (for) long** les piles n'ont pas duré longtemps; *Fam* **cakes never last long in this house** *(they get eaten quickly)* les gâteaux ne durent jamais très longtemps dans cette maison; **built/made to last** construit/fait pour durer

(**b**) *(be enough)* **we've got enough food to last another week** nous avons assez à manger pour une semaine encore

(**c**) *(keep fresh → food)* se conserver; **these flowers don't last (long)** ces fleurs ne tiennent *ou* ne durent pas (longtemps)

2 *vt* **his money didn't last him to the end of the holiday** il n'a pas eu assez d'argent pour tenir jusqu'à la fin des vacances; **have we got enough to last us until tomorrow?** en avons-nous assez pour tenir *ou* aller jusqu'à demain?; **my camera's lasted me ten years** mon appareil photo a duré dix ans; **that fountain pen will last you a lifetime** vous pourrez garder ce stylo à plume toute votre vie; **it has lasted him well** ça lui a fait de l'usage; **she couldn't last the pace** elle n'a pas pu tenir le rythme

►**last out 1** *vi* (**a**) *(survive)* tenir; **I'm not sure I'll last out at this job** je ne sais pas si je pourrai faire ce travail longtemps; **how long will he last out?** combien de temps peut-il tenir?

(**b**) *(be enough)* suffire; **will our supplies last out till the end of the month?** les provisions suffiront-elles jusqu'à la fin du mois?

2 *vt sep* **he didn't last the night out** il n'a pas passé la nuit, il est mort pendant la nuit; **will the play last out the month?** est-ce que la pièce tiendra le mois?; **to last the year out** *(person)* survivre jusqu'à la fin de l'année; *(supplies)* suffire pour l'année; **my overcoat will last the winter out** mon pardessus fera encore l'hiver; **I don't know if I'll be able to last out the afternoon without any coffee** je ne sais pas si j'arriverai à tenir tout l'après-midi sans café

last[3] *n (for shoes)* forme *f*

last-chance saloon *n Fam Hum* **you're drinking in the last-chance saloon** c'est ta dernière chance

last-ditch *adj (ultimate)* ultime; *(desperate)* désespéré; **a last-ditch attempt** *or* **effort** un ultime effort

lasting ['lɑːstɪŋ] *adj* durable; **to their lasting regret/shame** à leur plus grand regret/plus grande honte

lastingly ['lɑːstɪŋlɪ] *adv* d'une manière durable

lastly ['lɑːstlɪ] *adv* enfin, en dernier lieu

last-minute *adj* de dernière minute

Las Vegas [ˌlæs'veɪgəs] *n* Las Vegas

lat *(written abbr* **latitude**) lat.

latch [lætʃ] **1** *n* loquet *m*; **leave the door on the latch** ne fermez pas la porte à clé; **the door was on the latch** la porte n'était pas fermée à clé

2 *vt* fermer au loquet

3 *vi* se fermer

►**latch on** *vi Fam* piger

►**latch onto** *vt insep Fam* (**a**) *(attach oneself to)* s'accrocher à; **to latch onto an idea** s'accrocher à une idée; **she always latches onto older children** elle s'accroche toujours à des enfants plus âgés

(**b**) *Br (understand)* piger; **I suddenly latched onto the fact that they were following me** d'un seul coup j'ai pigé qu'ils me suivaient

(**c**) *Am (obtain)* se procurer, obtenir

latchkey ['lætʃkiː] *n* clef *f ou* clé *f (de la porte d'entrée)*

►► ***latchkey child*** = enfant dont les parents travaillent et ne sont pas là quand il rentre de l'école

LATE [leɪt]

en retard	►1 (a)
tardif	►1 (b)
tard	►1 (b), (c); 2 (a)
défunt	►1 (d)
feu	►1 (d)
récent	►1 (e)
récemment	►2 (b); 3
autrefois	►2 (c)

1 *adj* (**a**) *(behind schedule)* en retard; **to be late (for sth)** être en retard (pour qch); **the train is late** le train a du retard; **to be ten minutes late** avoir dix minutes de retard; **she's often late** elle est *ou* elle arrive souvent en retard; **to make sb late** retarder qn, mettre qn en retard; **we apologize for the late arrival of flight 906** nous vous prions d'excuser le retard du vol 906; **it was too late to do anything about it** il était trop tard pour faire quoi que ce soit; **her baby was five days late** son bébé est né avec cinq jours de retard

(**b**) *(in time)* tardif; *(news, edition)* dernier; **at a late hour** à une heure tardive; **to keep late**

las–lat

hours veiller, se coucher tard; **in the late afternoon** tard dans l'après-midi, en fin d'après-midi; **she's in her late fifties** elle approche de la soixantaine; **in the late seventies** à la fin des années soixante-dix; **in late 1970** fin 1970; **at this late date** à cette date avancée; **at this late stage** à ce stade avancé; **to have a late lunch** déjeuner tard; **there have been some late developments in the talks** il y a du nouveau dans les discussions; **he was a late developer** *(physically)* il a eu une croissance tardive; *(intellectually)* son développement intellectuel fut un peu tardif

(**c**) *(far on in the day)* tard; **it's late** il est tard; **it's getting late** il se fait tard; **it is too late** il est trop tard; **I was late going to bed** je me suis couché tard

(**d**) *(deceased)* **the late lamented president** le regretté président; **the late Mr Fox** le défunt M. Fox, *Formal* feu M. Fox; **her late husband** son défunt mari, *Formal* feu son mari; **his late wife** sa défunte femme, *Formal* feu sa femme

(**e**) *(recent)* récent, dernier

(**f**) **to be late** *(with one's period)* avoir un retard de règles; **I'm two days late** je suis en retard de deux jours

2 *adv* (**a**) *(in time)* tard; **to arrive/to go to bed late** arriver/se coucher tard; **to arrive ten minutes late** arriver avec dix minutes de retard; **late in the afternoon** tard dans l'après-midi; **she came to poetry late in life** elle est venue à la poésie sur le tard; **they came too late** ils sont arrivés trop tard; **late in the day** vers la fin de la journée; *Fig* **it's rather late in the day to be thinking about that** c'est un peu tard pour penser à ça

(**b**) *(recently)* récemment; **even as late as last year he was still painting** pas plus tard que l'année dernière, il peignait encore

(**c**) *Formal (formerly)* autrefois, anciennement; **Mr Fox, late of Delhi** M. Fox, anciennement domicilié à Delhi

3 of late *adv* récemment; **I haven't seen him of late** je ne l'ai pas vu récemment *ou* ces derniers temps; **as events of late have shown...** comme les récents événements l'ont montré...

►► *Mktg* ***late adopter*** utilisateur *m* tardif; ***late arrival*** *(at hotel)* arrivée *f* tardive; **he will be a late arrival** il arrivera tard; ***late booking*** réservation *f* de dernière minute; *Mktg* ***late entrant*** concurrent(e) *m,f* tardif(ive); *Mktg* ***late entry*** lancement *m* tardif; *Mktg* ***late majority*** majorité *f* conservatrice; *Fin* ***late payment*** retard *m* de paiement; *Fin* ***late payment penalty*** pénalité *f* de retard; ***late tackle*** *(in rugby)* plaquage *m* à retardement; *(in football)* tacle *m* à retardement; *St Exch* ***late trading*** opérations *fpl* de clôture

---

late-blooming *adj Bot* tardiflore

latecomer ['leɪtˌkʌmə(r)] *n* retardataire *mf*; **latecomers must wait in the foyer** les retardataires doivent attendre dans le foyer; **latecomers will not be admitted** *(sign)* ≃ les retardataires ne sont pas admis après la fermeture des portes; **he was a latecomer to football** il est venu au football sur le tard

lateen [lə'tiːn] *n* **lateen (sail)** voile *f* latine

lateen-rigged *adj* gréé avec une voile latine

►► ***lateen-rigged boat*** bâtiment *m* latin

late-flowering *adj Bot* tardiflore

lately ['leɪtlɪ] *adv* récemment, ces derniers temps, dernièrement; **I haven't been feeling well lately** je ne me sens pas bien ces temps-ci; **until lately** jusqu'à ces derniers temps, jusqu'à récemment

laten ['leɪtən] *Literary* **1** *vt* retarder

2 *vi (hour, season)* avancer

latency ['leɪtənsɪ] *n* latence *f*

lateness ['leɪtnɪs] *n* (**a**) *(of bus, train, person)* retard *m*; **I find persistent lateness infuriating** les gens qui sont toujours en retard m'exaspèrent (**b**) *(late time)* heure *f* tardive; **given the lateness of the hour** étant donné *ou* vu l'heure tardive

late-night *adj (play, show, film)* ≃ de minuit; **what's tonight's late-night movie?** *(on TV)* qu'est-ce qu'il y a au ciné-club ce soir?; **a late-night film** *(in cinema)* une séance de minuit; **a late-night bus service** un bus de nuit; *Com* **late-night opening on Thursdays** *(sign)* nocturne le jeudi; **late-night opening is on Thursdays** le magasin reste ouvert tard le jeudi

►► ***late-night shopping*** courses *fpl* en nocturne

latent ['leɪtənt] *adj* latent

►► ***latent defect*** vice *m* caché; ***latent heat*** chaleur *f* latente; ***latent image*** image *f* latente; ***latent period*** *Med* incubation *f*; *Psy* latence *f*, état *m* latent, temps *m* de latence; *Psy* ***latent time*** latence *f*, état *m* latent, temps *m* de latence

latently ['leɪtəntlɪ] *adv* d'une manière latente

later ['leɪtə(r)] *(compar of* **late***)* **1** *adj* ultérieur; **we can always catch a later train** on peut toujours prendre un autre train, plus tard; **a collection of her later poems** un recueil de ses derniers poèmes; **later events proved that...** la suite des événements a démontré que...; **at a later date** à une date ultérieure; **at a later stage** à un stade plus avancé; **in later life** plus tard dans la vie

2 *adv* plus tard; **later that day** plus tard dans la journée; **later on** plus tard; **see you later!** à plus tard!; **no later than tomorrow** demain dernier délai, demain au plus tard

3 *exclam Fam* ciao!, à plus!, à toute!

lateral ['lætərəl] **1** *n Ling* (consonne *f*) latérale *f*

2 *adj* latéral

►► *Ich* ***lateral line*** ligne *f* latérale; ***lateral thinking*** approche *f* originale; **we need a bit of lateral thinking on this problem** il nous faut adopter une approche du problème plus originale

laterality [ˌlætə'rælɪtɪ] *n Psy* latéralité *f*

laterally ['lætərəlɪ] *adv* latéralement

laterite ['lætəraɪt] *n Geol* latérite *f*

latest ['leɪtɪst] *(superl of* **late***)* **1** *adj* dernier; **the latest date/time** la date/l'heure *f* limite; **the latest news** les dernières nouvelles *fpl*; **the latest fashions** la dernière mode; **the latest model** le dernier modèle; **let's hope her latest novel won't be her last** espérons que le roman qu'elle vient de publier ne sera pas le dernier

2 *n* (**a**) *(most recent → news)* **have you heard the latest?** vous connaissez la dernière?; **what's the latest on the trial?** qu'y a-t-il de nouveau sur le procès?; **tune in at 7 p.m. for the latest on the elections** soyez à l'écoute à 19 heures pour les dernières informations sur les élections; *Fam* **have you met his/her latest?** *(boyfriend, girlfriend)* avez-vous fait la connaissance de sa dernière conquête?

(**b**) *(in time)* **at the latest** au plus tard; **when is the latest you can come?** jusqu'à quelle heure pouvez-vous venir?

latex ['leɪteks] *n* latex *m*

lath [lɑːθ] *n (wooden)* latte *f*; *(in venetian blind)* lame *f*

lathe [leɪð] **1** *n* tour *m (à bois ou à métal)*; **precision lathe** tour *m* de précision; **capstan** *or* **turret lathe** tour *m* (à) revolver; **polishing lathe** touret *m* à polir *ou* de polisseur

2 *vt* tourner

►► ***lathe bed*** banc *m ou* bâti *m* de tour; ***lathe operator*** tourneur(euse) *m,f*

lather ['lɑːðə(r)] **1** *n* (**a**) *(from soap)* mousse *f*

(**b**) *(foam → on horse, seawater)* écume *f*; *Br* **to get into a lather (about** *or* **over sth)** s'énerver *ou* se mettre dans tous ses états (à propos de qch); **he got into a real lather over the unpaid bills** les factures impayées l'ont mis dans tous ses états

2 *vt* (**a**) *(clean)* savonner; **to lather one's face** se savonner le visage

(**b**) *Fam Old-fashioned (defeat)* rosser

3 *vi* (**a**) *(soap)* mousser

(**b**) *(horse)* écumer

lathe-turned *adj* fait au tour, tourné

lathi ['lɑːtiː] *n (in India)* bâton *m* ferré (de policier), bambou *m* ferré

Latin ['lætɪn] **1** *n* (**a**) *(person)* Latin(e) *m,f*; **the Latins** *(in Europe)* les Latins *mpl*; *(in US)* les Latino-Américains *mpl* (**b**) *Ling* latin *m*

2 *adj* latin

►► ***Latin America*** Amérique *f* latine; **in Latin America** en Amérique latine; ***Latin American*** **1** *n* Latino-Américain(e) *m,f* **2** *adj* latino-américain; ***Latin cross*** croix *f* latine; *Fam* ***Latin lover*** latin lover *m*; ***the Latin Quarter*** le Quartier latin

Latinate ['lætɪneɪt] *adj (vocabulary)* d'origine latine; *(style)* empreint de latinismes

Latinism ['lætɪˌnɪzəm] *n* (**a**) *Ling* latinisme *m*, tournure *f* latine (**b**) *Rel* influence *f* de l'Église latine

Latinist ['lætɪnɪst] *n* latiniste *mf*

Latinization [ˌlætɪnaɪ'zeɪʃən] *n* latinisation *f*

Latinize, -ise ['lætɪnaɪz] *vt* latiniser

Latino [læ'tiːnəʊ] *(pl* **Latinos***)* *n* latino *mf*

latish ['leɪtɪʃ] *adj* (**a**) *(after the appointed time)* un peu en retard (**b**) *(far on in the day)* un peu tardif; **at a latish hour** à une heure assez avancée; **it was getting latish** il commençait à se faire tard

latitude ['lætɪtjuːd] *n* (**a**) *Astron & Geog* latitude *f*, **at a latitude of 50° south** à 50° de latitude sud; **in northern/southern latitudes** dans les latitudes boréales/australes; **few animals live in these latitudes** rares sont les animaux qui vivent sous ces latitudes; *Literary* **in other latitudes** sous d'autres cieux (**b**) *(freedom)* latitude *f*; **they don't allow** *or* **give the children much latitude for creativity** ils n'encouragent guère les enfants à être créatifs

latitudinal [ˌlætɪ'tjuːdɪnəl] *adj* latitudinal

latitudinarian [ˌlætɪtjuːdɪ'neərɪən] **1** *n* latitudinaire *mf*

2 *adj* latitudinaire

Latium ['leɪʃjəm] *n* Latium *m*

latrine [lə'triːn] *n* latrines *fpl*

latte ['læteɪ] *n* café *m* au lait

latter ['lætə(r)] **1** *adj* (**a**) *(in relation to former)* dernier, second; **the latter proposal is unrealistic** la seconde *ou* cette dernière proposition est irréaliste; **the latter half of the book was better** la seconde moitié du livre était meilleure

(**b**) *(later)* dernier, second; **in the latter years of her life** au cours des dernières années de sa vie; **the latter part of the holiday** la seconde partie des vacances

2 *n* **the former... the latter** le premier... le second, celui-là... celui-ci; **the latter is definitely the better book** le second livre est sans aucun doute le meilleur; **of tigers and cheetahs, the latter are by far the faster runners** des tigres et des guépards, ces derniers sont de loin les plus rapides

latter-day *adj* d'aujourd'hui; **a latter-day St Francis** un saint François moderne; **Church of the Latter-day Saints** Église *f* de Jésus-Christ des saints des derniers jours

latterly ['lætəlɪ] *adv* (**a**) *(recently)* récemment, dernièrement (**b**) *(towards the end)* vers la fin

lattermost ['lætəməʊst] *adj* dernier

lattice ['lætɪs] *n (fence, frame)* treillage *m*; *(design)* treillis *m*; *(pastry)* en croisillons

►► ***lattice beam, lattice girder*** poutre *f* en treillis *ou* à croisillons; ***lattice window*** fenêtre *f* à croisillons

latticed ['lætɪst] *adj (fence)* à claire-voie; *(ceramics)* treillissé; *(pastry)* en croisillons; *(dress)* ajouré

latticework ['lætɪswɜːk] *n (UNCOUNT)* treillis *m*

Latvia ['lætvɪə] *n* Lettonie *f*; **in Latvia** en Lettonie

Latvian ['lætvɪən] **1** *n* (**a**) *(person)* Letton(onne) *m,f* (**b**) *(language)* letton *m*

2 *adj* letton

3 *comp (embassy)* de Lettonie; *(history)* de la Lettonie; *(teacher)* de letton

laud [lɔːd] *vt Formal or Literary* louer, chanter les louanges de, glorifier

laudability [ˌlɔːdə'bɪlɪtɪ] *n* caractère *m* louable

laudable ['lɔːdəbəl] *adj* louable, digne de louanges

laudably ['lɔːdəblɪ] *adv* de manière louable; **you behaved laudably** votre comportement a été admirable

laudanum ['lɔːdənəm] *n Pharm* laudanum *m*

laudation [lɔː'deɪʃən] *n Formal* louanges *fpl*

laudatory ['lɔːdətrɪ] *adj Formal* laudatif, élogieux

lauds [lɔːdz] *npl Rel* laudes *fpl*

laugh [lɑːf] **1** *vi* (**a**) *(in amusement)* rire; **we all laughed at the joke/the film** la blague/le film nous a tous fait rire; **she was laughing about his gaffe all day** sa gaffe l'a fait rire toute la journée; **you have to laugh** mieux vaut en rire; **to burst out laughing** éclater de rire; **we laughed until we cried** on a ri aux larmes, on a pleuré de rire; **we laughed about it afterwards** après coup, cela nous a fait bien rire, on en a ri après coup; **it's easy for you to laugh!** vous pouvez rire!; **to**

lat–lau

laugh aloud *or* **out loud** rire aux éclats; **he was laughing to himself** il riait dans sa barbe; **they didn't know whether to laugh or cry** ils ne savaient pas s'ils devaient en rire ou en pleurer; *Br* **to laugh up one's sleeve** rire dans sa barbe; *Br* **I'll make him laugh on the other side of his face** je lui ferai passer l'envie de rire, moi; *Br* **you'll laugh on the other side of your face one of these days** un de ces jours tu vas rire jaune; *Prov* **he who laughs last laughs** *Br* **longest** *or Am* **best** rira bien qui rira le dernier

(**b**) *(in contempt, ridicule)* rire; **to laugh at sb/sth** se moquer de qn/qch, rire de qn/qch; **to laugh at someone else's misfortunes** se moquer des malheurs des autres; **they laughed at the dangers** ils (se) riaient des dangers; **they laughed in my face** ils m'ont ri au nez; **he laughed about his mistakes** il a ri de ses erreurs; *Fam Ironic* **don't make me laugh!** laisse-moi rire!

(**c**) *Br Fam Fig (be in comfortable situation)* **once we get the contract, we're laughing** une fois qu'on aura empoché le contrat, on sera tranquilles; **you've already got your visa, you're laughing** toi, tu as déjà ton visa, tu n'as pas de problèmes *ou* tu es tranquille ❑; **if you've already done this before, you're laughing** si tu as déjà fait ça, c'est un jeu d'enfant ❑; **if we win this match, we'll be laughing** si on gagne ce match, on n'a plus de souci à se faire ❑; **if your offer's accepted, you'll be laughing** s'ils acceptent ta proposition, ce sera super pour toi; **she's laughing all the way to the bank** elle s'en met plein les poches

2 *vt* (**a**) *(in amusement)* **to laugh oneself silly** se tordre de rire, être plié en deux de rire

(**b**) *(in contempt, ridicule)* **he was laughed off the stage/out of the room** il a quitté la scène/la pièce sous les rires moqueurs; *Br* **they laughed him to scorn** ils se sont moqués de lui; *Fig* **to laugh sth out of court** tourner qch en dérision

(**c**) *Br (express)* **she laughed her scorn** elle eut un petit rire méprisant

3 *n* (**a**) *(of amusement)* rire *m*; *(burst of laughter)* éclat *m* de rire; **to give a laugh** rire; **we had a good laugh about it** ça nous a bien fait rire; **she left the room with a laugh** elle sortit en riant *ou* dans un éclat de rire; **look outside if you want a laugh** regarde dehors si tu veux rigoler

(**b**) *(of contempt, ridicule)* rire *m*; **we all had a good laugh at his expense** nous nous sommes bien moqués de lui; **to have the last laugh** avoir le dernier mot

(**c**) *Br Fam (fun)* rigolade *f*; **to have a laugh** rigoler *ou* se marrer un peu; **he's always good for a laugh** avec lui, on se marre bien; **these old horror films are usually good for a laugh** ces vieux films d'horreur sont souvent marrants; **he's a laugh a minute** il est très marrant

(**d**) *Fam (joke)* **we did it for a laugh** *or* **just for laughs** on l'a fait pour rigoler; **what a laugh!** qu'est-ce qu'on s'est marré!; *Ironic* **home-made cakes? that's a laugh!** gâteaux faits maison? c'est une blague *ou* ils plaisantent!

▸**laugh away** *vt sep* **she laughed away her tears/cares** ça l'a amusée et elle a séché ses larmes/oublié ses soucis

▸**laugh down** *vt sep (objection, proposal)* ridiculiser

▸**laugh off** *vt sep (difficulty)* rire de, se moquer de; *(difficult situation)* désamorcer; **I managed to laugh off an awkward situation** j'ai réussi à éviter une situation fâcheuse en plaisantant; **how can they just laugh it off like that?** comment osent-ils prendre ça à la légère?; **he tried to laugh off the defeat** il s'efforça de ne pas prendre sa défaite trop au sérieux

laughable ['lɑːfəbəl] *adj* ridicule, risible; **the whole situation is just laughable** tout ça est parfaitement ridicule; **he made a laughable attempt at reconciliation** il fit une tentative de réconciliation pitoyable

laughably ['lɑːfəblɪ] *adv* ridiculement

laughing ['lɑːfɪŋ] **1** *n* rires *mpl*; **we could hear the sound of laughing** nous entendions des rires

2 *adj* riant; **I'm in no laughing mood** je n'ai pas envie de rire; **this is no laughing matter** il n'y a pas de quoi rire

▸▸ ***laughing gas*** gaz *m* hilarant; *Br Fam* ***laughing gear*** bouche ❑ *f*, clapet *m*; ***laughing hyena*** hyène *f* tachetée; ***laughing jackass*** martin-chasseur *m (d'Australie)*, kookaburra *m*; ***laughing stock*** risée *f*; **they were the laughing stock of the whole neighbourhood** ils étaient la risée de tout le quartier; **they made laughing stocks of themselves** ils se sont couverts de ridicule

'The Laughing Cavalier' *Hals* 'Le Chevalier souriant'

laughingly ['lɑːfɪŋlɪ] *adv* (**a**) *(cheerfully)* en riant (**b**) *(inappropriately)* **this noise is laughingly called folk music** c'est ce bruit qu'on appelle le plus sérieusement du monde de la musique folk

laughter ['lɑːftə(r)] *n (UNCOUNT)* rire *m*, rires *mpl*; **a burst of laughter** un éclat de rire; **to cause laughter** provoquer les rires *ou* l'hilarité; **there was much laughter over the misunderstanding** le malentendu provoqua des éclats de rire; **she continued to speak amid loud laughter** elle a continué à parler au milieu des éclats de rire

'Laughter in the Dark' *Nabokov, Richardson* 'Chambre obscure'

launch [lɔːntʃ] **1** *n* (**a**) *(boat)* vedette *f*; *(long boat)* chaloupe *f*; **(pleasure) launch** bateau *m* de plaisance

(**b**) *(of ship, spacecraft, new product)* lancement *m*; **a book launch** le lancement d'un livre; **the launch of a new job creation scheme** le lancement d'un nouveau programme de création d'emplois

2 *vt* (**a**) *(boat → from ship)* mettre à la mer; *(→ from harbour)* faire sortir; *(→ for first time)* lancer

(**b**) *Com* lancer; **our firm has launched a new perfume on** *or* **onto the market** notre société a lancé un nouveau parfum; **to launch a £3 million cash bid** lancer une offre au comptant de 3 millions de livres

(**c**) *St Exch (company)* introduire en Bourse; *(shares)* émettre

(**d**) *(start)* **that was the audition that launched me on my career** cette audition a donné le coup d'envoi de ma carrière; **to launch a military offensive** déclencher *ou* lancer une attaque

(**e**) *Comput* lancer

▸▸ *Astron* ***launch complex*** base *f ou* station *f* de lancement; *Astron* ***launch pad*** rampe *f ou* plate-forme *f* de lancement; ***launch party*** réception *f (pour le lancement d'un produit)*; *Astron* ***launch site*** base *f* de lancement; *Astron* ***launch vehicle*** fusée *f* de lancement

▸**launch forth** *vi* (**a**) *(set off)* **to launch forth on a new career** se lancer dans une nouvelle carrière

(**b**) *(start speaking)* **he launched forth into a long explanation** il s'est lancé dans une longue explication

▸**launch into** *vt insep (start)* se lancer dans; **she launched into her work with vigour** elle s'est lancée dans son travail avec énergie

▸**launch out** *vi* se lancer; **Blakes have launched out into distilling** Blakes s'est lancé dans la distillation; **she's just launched out on her own** elle vient de se mettre à son compte

launcher ['lɔːntʃə(r)] *n (vehicle)* lanceur *m*; *(launching pad)* rampe *f ou* plate-forme *f* de lancement; *(for planes)* catapulte *f* de lancement

launching ['lɔːntʃɪŋ] *n* (**a**) *(of ship, spacecraft)* lancement *m*; *(of lifeboat → from ship)* mise *f* à la mer; *(→ from shore)* sortie *f* (**b**) *(of new product)* lancement *m*

▸▸ *Aviat* ***launching catapult*** catapulte *f* de lancement; ***launching ceremony*** cérémonie *f* de lancement; ***launching pad, launching platform*** rampe *m ou* plate-forme *f* de lancement; ***launching ramp*** rampe *f* de lancement; ***launching site*** aire *f* de lancement; ***launching vehicle*** fusée *f* de lancement

launder ['lɔːndə(r)] *vt* (**a**) *(clothes)* laver; *(at laundry)* blanchir; **the sheets have been freshly laundered** *(at home)* les draps viennent d'être lavés; *(at laundry)* les draps reviennent de chez le blanchisseur *ou* le teinturier (**b**) *Fig (money)* blanchir

launderette [,lɔːndə'ret] *n Br* laverie *f* automatique

laundering ['lɔːndrɪŋ] *n* (**a**) *(of clothes)* blanchissage *m* (**b**) *Fig (of money)* blanchiment *m*

laundress ['lɔːndrɪs] *n* blanchisseuse *f*

laundrette [lɔːn'dret] *n Br* laverie *f* automatique

Laundromat® ['lɔːndrəmæt] *n Am* laverie *f* automatique

laundry ['lɔːndrɪ] (*pl* **laundries**) *n* (**a**) *(shop)* blanchisserie *f*; *(in house)* buanderie *f*; **to send sth to the laundry** envoyer qch à la blanchisserie (**b**) *(washing)* linge *m*; **to do the laundry** faire la lessive

▸▸ ***laundry bag*** sac *m* de blanchisserie; ***laundry basket*** panier *m* à linge; ***laundry list*** liste *f* de blanchissage; ***laundry mark*** étiquette *f* de la blanchisserie; ***laundry room*** buanderie *f*; ***laundry service*** service *m* de blanchissage; ***laundry van*** camionnette *f* du blanchisseur

laundryman ['lɔːndrɪmən] (*pl* **laundrymen** [-mən]) *n* (**a**) *(van-driver)* livreur *m* de blanchisserie (**b**) *(worker in laundry)* blanchisseur *m*

laundrywoman ['lɔːndrɪ,wʊmən] (*pl* **laundrywomen** [-,wɪmɪn]) *n* blanchisseuse *f*

Laurasia [lɔː'reɪʒə] *n Geol* Laurasie *f*

laureate ['lɔːrɪət] *n* (**a**) *(prize winner)* lauréat *m*; **a Nobel laureate** un prix Nobel (**b**) *(poet)* poète *m* lauréat

laurel ['lɒrəl] **1** *n Bot* laurier *m*

2 *comp (crown, wreath)* de lauriers

3 laurels *npl (honours)* lauriers *mpl*; **to look to one's laurels** ne pas s'endormir sur ses lauriers; **to rest on one's laurels** se reposer sur ses lauriers

LAUTRO ['laʊtrəʊ] *n Br* (*abbr* **Life Assurance and Unit Trust Regulatory Organization**) = organisme britannique contrôlant les activités de compagnies d'assurance-vie et de SICAV

LAV [,eleɪ'viː] *n Med* (*abbr* **lymphadenopathy associated virus**) LAV *m*

lav [læv] *n Br Fam* cabinets ❑ *mpl*, W-C ❑ *mpl*

lava ['lɑːvə] *n* lave *f*

▸▸ ***lava bed*** champ *m* de lave; ***lava flow*** coulée *f* de lave; ***lava lamp*** = objet décoratif apparu dans les années 70, composé d'un cylindre transparent contenant un liquide dans lequel des bulles colorées montent et descendent lentement; ***lava stream*** coulée *f* de lave

lavabo [lə'veɪbəʊ] (*pl* **lavabos**) *n Rel* lavabo *m*

lavage [læ'vɑːʒ] *n Med* lavement *m*

lavalier, lavaliere [læ,vælɪ'eə(r)] *n Am* pendentif *m*

lavatorial [,lævə'tɔːrɪəl] *adj (style, humour)* scatologique

lavatory ['lævətrɪ] (*pl* **lavatories**) **1** *n Br* toilettes *fpl*, cabinets *mpl*; *(bowl)* cuvette *f*; **to go to the lavatory** aller aux toilettes

2 *adj* des W-C; *(humour)* scatologique

▸▸ *Br* ***lavatory bowl, lavatory pan*** cuvette *f* (de W-C); *Br* ***lavatory paper*** papier *m* hygiénique

lave [leɪv] *vt Arch or Literary* (**a**) *(clean)* laver (**b**) *(of current, river, waves → move over)* baigner; *(→ carry away)* emporter, entraîner

lavender ['lævəndə(r)] **1** *n* lavande *f*

2 *adj (colour)* lavande

▸▸ ***lavender bag*** sachet *m* de lavande; ***lavender blue*** bleu *m* lavande; ***lavender water*** eau *f* de lavande

lavender-blue *adj* bleu lavande

laver ['leɪvə(r)] *n* porphyra *f*

▸▸ ***laver bread*** galette *f* d'algues

laverock ['lævərək] *n Literary* alouette *f*

lavish ['lævɪʃ] **1** *adj* (**a**) *(abundant)* copieux, abondant; *(luxurious)* somptueux, luxueux (**b**) *(generous)* généreux; **he can afford to be lavish** il peut se permettre d'être généreux; **to be lavish with one's money** dépenser sans compter; **he was lavish in his praise** il ne tarissait pas d'éloges

2 *vt* prodiguer; **to lavish money on sb** dépenser des fortunes pour qn; **they lavish all their attention on their son** ils sont aux petits soins pour leur fils; **he lavished praise on the book** il ne tarissait pas d'éloges sur le livre

lavishly ['lævɪʃlɪ] *adv* (**a**) *(generously, extravagantly)* généreusement, sans compter; **she spends lavishly** elle dépense sans compter, elle ne regarde pas à la dépense; **he praised us lavishly** il n'a pas tari d'éloges à notre égard (**b**) *(luxuriously)* luxueusement, somptueusement; **lavishly decorated/furnished** somptueusement décoré/meublé

lavishness ['lævɪʃnɪs] *n* (**a**) *(generosity)* générosité *f*; *(extravagance)* extravagance *f* (**b**) *(luxuriousness)* luxe *m*, somptuosité *f*

law [lɔː] **1** *n* (**a**) *(legal provision)* loi *f*; **a law against gambling** une loi qui interdit les jeux d'argent; **there's no law against it!** il n'y a pas de mal à cela!; *Hum* **there ought to be a law against it** ça devrait être interdit par la loi; **to be a law unto oneself** ne connaître ni foi ni loi

(**b**) *(legislation)* loi *f*; **it's against the law to sell alcohol** la vente d'alcool est illégale; **by law** selon la loi; **in** *or* **under British law** selon la loi britannique; **to break/to uphold the law** enfreindre/respecter la loi; **the bill became law** le projet de loi a été voté *ou* adopté; **the law of the land** la loi, les lois *fpl*; **the law of the jungle** la loi de la jungle; *Fig* **to lay down the law** imposer sa loi, faire la loi; *Fig* **her word is law** ses décisions sont sans appel

(**c**) *(legal system)* droit *m*; **a student of law** un(e) étudiant(e) en droit

(**d**) *(justice)* justice *f*, système *m* juridique; *Br* **to go to law** aller en justice; *Br* **to take a case to law** porter une affaire en justice *ou* devant les tribunaux; **to take the law into one's own hands** (se) faire justice soi-même; **law and order** l'ordre *m* public

(**e**) *Fam* **the law** *(police)* les flics *mpl*; **the law soon arrived** les flics n'ont pas tardé à rappliquer; **I'll have the law on you!** je vais appeler les flics!

(**f**) *(rule → of club, sport)* règle *f*; **the laws of rugby** les règles *fpl* du rugby

(**g**) *(principle)* loi *f*; *Phys* **the laws of gravity** les lois *fpl* de la pesanteur; *Econ* **the law of supply and demand** la loi de l'offre et de la demande

2 *comp (faculty, school)* de droit

►► ***law centre*** bureau *m* d'aide judiciaire; ***law court*** tribunal *m*, cour *f* de justice; ***law enforcement*** application *f* de la loi; ***law enforcement agency*** organisme *m* chargé de faire respecter la loi; ***law enforcement officer*** agent *m* de police; ***law firm*** cabinet *m* d'avocats, cabinet *m* juridique; *Br* ***Law Lords*** = membres de la Chambre des lords siégeant en tant que cour d'appel de dernière instance; ***law officer*** conseiller(ère) *m,f* juridique; ***law school*** faculté *f* de droit; *Br* ***the Law Society*** = conseil de l'ordre des avocats chargé de faire respecter la déontologie; ***law student*** étudiant(e) *m,f* en droit

law-abiding *adj* respectueux de la loi; **a law-abiding citizen** un honnête citoyen

law-and-order *adj* **law-and-order issues** questions *fpl* d'ordre public; **he presents himself as the law-and-order candidate** il se présente comme le candidat de l'ordre (public)

law-breaker *n* personne *f* qui transgresse la loi

law-breaking *n* infraction *f* à la loi

lawful ['lɔːfʊl] *adj (legal)* légal; *(legitimate)* légitime; *(valid)* valide; **to go about one's lawful business** vaquer à ses occupations; **by all lawful means** par tous les moyens légaux; **my lawful wedded wife** mon épouse légitime

lawfully ['lɔːfəlɪ] *adv* légalement, de manière légale; **did you come by that money lawfully?** est-ce que vous avez gagné cet argent par des moyens légaux?

lawfulness ['lɔːfʊlnɪs] *n* légalité *f*

lawgiver ['lɔːˌgɪvə(r)] *n* législateur(trice) *m,f*

lawk [lɔːk], **lawks** [lɔːks] *exclam Fam* mon Dieu!, Seigneur!

lawless ['lɔːlɪs] *adj (person)* sans foi ni loi; *(activity)* illégal; *(country)* livré à l'anarchie; **a lawless frontier territory** un territoire sauvage situé aux confins du monde civilisé

lawlessness ['lɔːlɪsnɪs] *n* non-respect *m* de la loi; *(anarchy)* anarchie *f*; *(illegality)* illégalité *f*; **the town was in a state of utter lawlessness** la ville était plongée dans l'anarchie la plus totale

lawmaker ['lɔːˌmeɪkə(r)] *n* législateur(trice) *m,f*

lawman ['lɔːmæn] (*pl* **lawmen** [-men]) *n Am (policeman)* policier *m*; *(sheriff)* shérif *m*

lawn [lɔːn] *n* (**a**) *(grass)* pelouse *f*, gazon *m*; **to mow** *or* **cut the lawn** tondre le gazon (**b**) *Tex* linon *m*

►► *Am* ***lawn bowling*** boules *fpl*; *Am* ***lawn chair*** chaise *f* de jardin; ***lawn fertilizer, lawn food*** engrais *m* à gazon; *Am* ***lawn party*** garden-party *f*; ***lawn sprinkler*** arrosoir *m* de pelouse; *(spinning)* tourniquet *m* arroseur; ***lawn tennis*** tennis *m* sur gazon; *Br* ***Lawn Tennis Association*** = la Fédération britannique de tennis; ***lawn tennis club*** club *m* de tennis

lawnmower ['lɔːnˌməʊə(r)] *n* tondeuse *f* à gazon

Lawrence ['lɒrəns] *pr n* **Lawrence of Arabia** Lawrence d'Arabie

lawrencium [lə'rensɪəm] *n Chem* lawrencium *m*

Lawrentian [lə'renʃɪən] *adj Literature* lawrencien

lawsuit ['lɔːsuːt] *n* action *f* en justice; **to bring a lawsuit against sb** intenter une action (en justice) contre qn

lawyer ['lɔːjə(r)] *n* (**a**) *(barrister)* avocat(e) *m,f* (**b**) *(solicitor → for wills, conveyancing etc)* notaire *m* (**c**) *(legal expert)* juriste *mf*; *(adviser)* conseil *m* juridique

LAX *(written abbr* **Los Angeles Airport**) = sigle désignant l'aéroport international de Los Angeles

lax [læks] *adj* (**a**) *(person)* négligent; *(behaviour, discipline)* relâché; *(justice)* laxiste; **to be lax about sth** négliger qch (**b**) *(not tense → string)* lâche, relâché; *Ling (phoneme)* lâche, relâché; *Med (bowels)* relâché (**c**) *(imprecise → definition, usage)* imprécis, vague

laxative ['læksətɪv] **1** *n* laxatif *m*

2 *adj* laxatif

laxity ['læksətɪ] *n* (**a**) *(negligence)* négligence *f*; **moral laxity** relâchement *m* moral (**b**) *(lack of tension)* relâchement *m* (**c**) *(imprecision)* imprécision *f*

laxly ['lækslɪ] *adv* (**a**) *(negligently)* négligemment (**b**) *(not tensely)* mollement (**c**) *(imprecisely)* vaguement

laxness ['læksnɪs] = **laxity**

LAY [leɪ]

poser	► **2 (a)**
mettre	► **2 (a), (c)**
étendre	► **2 (a)**
préparer	► **2 (d)**
pondre	► **2 (e); 3 (a)**
imposer	► **2 (f)**
porter	► **2 (g)**
soumettre	► **2 (h)**
dissiper	► **2 (i)**
laïque	► **4 (a)**
profane	► **4 (b)**

(*pt & pp* **laid** [leɪd]) **1** *pt of* **lie**

2 *vt* (**a**) *(in specified position)* poser, mettre; *(spread out)* étendre; **to lay sb/sth flat** coucher *ou* étendre qn/qch (par terre); **lay the cards face upwards** posez les cartes face en l'air; **lay the photos on the shelf to dry** mettez les photos à plat sur l'étagère pour qu'elles sèchent; **he laid the baby on the bed** il a couché l'enfant sur le lit; **she laid her head on my shoulder** elle a posé sa tête sur mon épaule; *Euph* **to lay sb to rest** enterrer qn; **she laid the blanket on the ground** elle a étendu la couverture par terre; *Fam* **to lay eyes on sb/sth** voir qn/qch □; **to lay it on the line** ne pas y aller par quatre chemins

(**b**) *(tiles, bricks, pipes, cable, carpet, foundations)* poser; *(wreath)* déposer; *(mine)* poser, mouiller; *(concrete)* couler; **to lay lino on the floor, to lay the floor with lino** poser du linoléum; **a roof laid with zinc** un toit recouvert de zinc; *Fig* **the plan lays the basis** *or* **the foundation for economic development** le projet jette les bases du développement économique

(**c**) *(set → table)* mettre; **lay the table for six** mettez la table pour six (personnes), mettez six couverts; **they hadn't laid enough places** ils n'avaient pas mis assez de couverts, il manquait des couverts

(**d**) *(prepare, arrange → fire)* préparer; **to lay a trail** tracer un chemin; **they laid a trap for him** ils lui ont tendu un piège

(**e**) *(egg)* pondre; *Am Fam Fig* **to lay an egg** faire une gaffe; *Fam Fig* **he nearly laid an egg** *(in surprise)* il a failli en faire une jaunisse

(**f**) *(impose → burden, duty, penalty)* imposer; *(→ fine)* infliger; **to lay emphasis** *or* **stress on sth** mettre l'accent sur qch; **to lay the blame (for sth) on sb** faire porter la responsabilité (de qch) à qn; **to lay a curse on sb/sth** jeter un sort à qn/qch

(**g**) *Law (lodge)* porter; **to lay a complaint** déposer une plainte, porter plainte; **to lay a matter before the court** saisir le tribunal d'une affaire; **to lay an accusation against sb** porter une accusation contre qn; **charges have been laid against five men** cinq hommes ont été inculpés

(**h**) *(present, put forward → question, request)* soumettre (**before sb** devant qn); **he laid all the facts before me** il me présenta tous les faits; **she laid the scheme before him** elle lui soumit le projet

(**i**) *(allay → fears)* dissiper; *(exorcize → ghost)* exorciser; *(refute → rumour)* démentir

(**j**) *(bet)* faire; **I'll lay you ten to one that she won't come** je te parie à dix contre un qu'elle ne viendra pas

(**k**) *very Fam (have sex with)* s'envoyer; **to get laid** s'envoyer en l'air

(**l**) *Literary (strike)* **to lay a whip across sb's back** fouetter qn

(**m**) *Literary (cause to settle)* faire retomber; **the rain helped to lay the dust** la pluie a fait retomber la poussière

(**n**) *(with adjective complements)* **to lay oneself open to criticism** s'exposer à la critique

3 *vi* (**a**) *(bird, fish)* pondre

(**b**) = **lie** *vi* (**b**)

4 *adj* (**a**) *(non-clerical)* laïque; **in lay dress** en habit laïque

(**b**) *(not professional)* profane, non spécialiste; **the book is intended for a lay audience** le livre est destiné à un public de profanes

5 *n* (**a**) *very Fam (person)* **he's/she's a good lay** c'est un bon coup

(**b**) *(poem, song)* lai *m*

►► *Rel* ***lay brother*** frère *m* lai; ***lay days*** starie *f*, jours *mpl* de planche; *Art* ***lay figure*** mannequin *m*; ***lay person*** profane *mf*, non-initié(e) *m,f*; ***lay preacher*** prédicateur(trice) *m,f* laïque; ***lay reader*** prédicateur(trice) *m,f* laïque; ***lay sister*** sœur *f* converse

►**lay about** *vt insep Fam (attack)* attaquer □, taper sur □; **she laid about him with her umbrella** elle l'a attaqué à coups de parapluie, elle lui a tapé dessus avec son parapluie; **to lay about one** *(hit out)* frapper de tous côtés

►**lay aside** *vt sep* (**a**) *(put down)* mettre de côté; **she laid her knitting aside to watch the news** elle posa son tricot pour regarder les informations; *Fig* **you should lay aside any personal opinions you might have** vous devez faire abstraction de toute opinion personnelle

(**b**) *(save)* mettre de côté; **we have some money laid aside** nous avons de l'argent de côté

►**lay back** *vt sep (of horse → ears)* rabattre, coucher

►**lay by** *vt sep Br (provisions)* mettre de côté

►**lay down** *vt sep* (**a**) *(put down)* poser; **she laid her knife and fork down** elle posa son couvert; **to lay down one's arms** déposer *ou* rendre les armes

(**b**) *(renounce, relinquish)* [illegible] à; **to lay down one's life** se sacrifier

(**c**) *(formulate, set out → plan, rule)* formuler, établir; *(→ condition)* imposer; *(→ duties)* spécifier; **as laid down in the contract, the buyer keeps exclusive rights** il est stipulé *ou* il est bien précisé dans le contrat que l'acheteur garde l'exclusivité

(**d**) *Naut (ship)* mettre en chantier *ou* sur cale

(**e**) *(store → wine)* mettre en cave

(**f**) *Mus (record → song, track)* enregistrer

(**g**) *Agr (field, land)* **he has laid down five acres of barley** il a semé deux hectares et demi d'orge

►**lay in** *vt sep (stores)* faire provision de; **to lay in provisions** faire des provisions; **we've laid in plenty of food for the weekend** nous avons prévu beaucoup de nourriture pour le week-end; *Com* **to lay in goods** *or* **stock** faire provision de marchandises

►**lay into** *vt insep* (**a**) *(attack → physically)* tomber (à bras raccourcis) sur; *(→ verbally)* prendre à partie, passer un savon à; **he really laid into his opponent** il est tombé à bras raccourcis sur son adversaire; **she laid into the government for their hard-line attitude** elle a pris le gouvernement à partie pour son attitude intransigeante

(**b**) *(eat greedily)* se jeter sur

▸**lay off 1** *vt sep* (**a**) *(employees)* licencier; *(temporarily)* mettre en chômage technique

(**b**) *(in gambling → bet)* couvrir

(**c**) *Ins* **to lay off a risk** effectuer une réassurance

(**d**) *Ftbl* **to lay the ball off for sb** placer le ballon en bonne position pour qn

2 *vt insep Fam* (**a**) **to lay off sb** *(stop annoying, nagging)* ficher la paix à qn; **just lay off me!** fiche-moi la paix!; **I told her to lay off my husband** je lui ai dit de laisser mon mari tranquille❑

(**b**) *(abstain from)* **to lay off the chocolate** ne plus manger de chocolat❑; **to lay off the cigarettes** s'arrêter de fumer❑; **you'd better lay off the booze for a while** tu devrais t'arrêter de boire pendant quelque temps❑; *Fam* **lay off it, will you!** laisse tomber, tu veux!

3 *vi Fam (drop the subject)* laisser tomber; **lay off!** *(leave me alone)* fiche-moi la paix!

▸**lay on** *vt sep* (**a**) *(provide)* fournir; **drinks will be laid on** les boissons seront fournies; **the meal was laid on by our hosts** le repas nous fut offert par nos hôtes; **they had transport laid on for us** ils s'étaient occupés de nous procurer un moyen de transport; **I'll lay on a car for you at the station** j'enverrai une voiture vous chercher à la gare

(**b**) *Br (install)* installer, mettre; **the caravan has electricity laid on** la caravane a l'électricité

(**c**) *(spread → paint, plaster)* étaler; *Fam Fig* **to lay it on thick** *or* **with a trowel** en rajouter

(**d**) *Am Fam* **to lay sth on sb** *(give)* filer qch à qn; *(tell)* raconter qch à qn❑; **let me lay some advice on you** je vais te filer un bon conseil; **did she lay a heavy one on me!** elle n'a pas mâché ses mots!

(**e**) *Fam (idiom)* **if you're not careful, I'll lay one on you!** *(hit)* fais gaffe ou je t'en mets une!

▸**lay out** *vt sep* (**a**) *(arrange, spread out)* étaler; **he laid his wares out on the ground** il a étalé *ou* déballé sa marchandise sur le sol

(**b**) *(present, put forward)* exposer, présenter; **her ideas are clearly laid out in her book** ses idées sont clairement exposées dans son livre

(**c**) *(design)* concevoir; **the house is badly laid out** la maison est mal agencée

(**d**) *(corpse)* faire la toilette de

(**e**) *(spend)* mettre; **we've already laid out a fortune on the project** nous avons déjà mis une fortune dans ce projet

(**f**) *(knock out)* assommer, mettre K-O; **he was laid out cold** il a été mis K-O

(**g**) *Typ* faire la maquette de, monter

▸**lay over** *vi Am (stop off)* faire une halte, faire escale

▸**lay to** *Naut* **1** *vi* se mettre en panne

2 *vt sep* mettre en panne

▸**lay up** *vt sep Br* (**a**) *(store, save)* mettre de côté; *Fig* **you're just laying up trouble for yourself** tu te prépares des ennuis

(**b**) *(confine to bed)* aliter; **she's laid up with mumps** elle est au lit avec les oreillons

(**c**) *(ship)* désarmer; *(car)* mettre au garage; **my car is laid up** ma voiture est au garage

---

layabout ['leɪəbaʊt] *n Br Fam* paresseux(euse)❑ *m,f*, fainéant(e) *m,f*

lay-away plan *n Am Com* vente *f* réservée *ou* à terme

lay-by (*pl* **lay-bys**) *n* (**a**) *Br Aut* aire *f* de stationnement (**b**) *Rail* voie *f* de garage (**c**) *Austr & NZ (deposit)* arrhes *fpl*; **to buy sth on lay-by** retenir qch en versant des arrhes

layer ['leɪə(r)] **1** *n* (**a**) *(of skin, paint, wood)* couche *f*; *(of fabric, clothes)* épaisseur *f*; *Fig* **the poem has many layers of meaning** le poème peut être lu de différentes façons

(**b**) *Geol* strate *f*, couche *f*

(**c**) *Hort* marcotte *f*

(**d**) *(hen)* pondeuse *f*

(**e**) *Comput* couche *f*

2 *vt* (**a**) *(arrange in layers)* poser *ou* disposer en couches

(**b**) *(hair)* couper en dégradé; **I'd like my hair layered** j'aimerais un dégradé; **a layered cut** une coupe en dégradé

(**c**) *Hort* marcotter

▸▸ ***layer cake*** génoise *f*; **chocolate layer cake** génoise *f* au chocolat

layered ['leɪəd] *adj Sewing (skirt)* à volants

layette [leɪ'et] *n* layette *f*

laying ['leɪɪŋ] *n* (**a**) *(of egg)* ponte *f* (**b**) *(of cables, carpets, rails, pipes)* pose *f*; *(of mine)* pose *f*, mouillage *m*; *(of wreath)* dépôt *m*; **a wreath-laying ceremony** un dépôt de gerbe; *Rel* **laying on of hands** imposition *f* des mains

▸▸ ***laying down*** *(of principle, rule etc)* établissement *m*; *(of sewage system, cable)* pose *f*; *(of ship)* mise *f* en chantier *ou* sur cale; *(of arms)* dépôt *m*; ***laying hen*** poule *f* pondeuse; ***laying out*** *(of dead body)* toilette *f*

layman ['leɪmən] (*pl* **laymen** [-mən]) *n* (**a**) *(non-specialist)* non-initié(e) *m,f*, profane *mf*; **the book is incomprehensible to the layman** le livre est incompréhensible pour le profane; **a layman's guide to the stock market** un manuel d'initiation au système boursier (**b**) *(non-clerical)* laïc (laïque) *m,f*

lay-off *n* (**a**) *(sacking)* licenciement *m* (**b**) *(inactivity)* chômage *m* technique

▸▸ *Am* ***lay-off pay*** indemnité *f* de licenciement

layout ['leɪaʊt] *n* (**a**) *(gen)* disposition *f*; *(of building, park)* agencement *m*; *(of essay)* plan *m*; **the layout of the controls is very straightforward** la disposition des commandes est très simple (**b**) *Typ* maquette *f*, mise *f* en page (**c**) *(diagram)* schéma *m*

▸▸ *Typ* ***layout artist*** maquettiste *mf*; *Typ* ***layout card*** *(for pages)* plan *m* de maquette; *Typ* ***layout compositor*** maquettiste *mf*; *Typ* ***layout sheet*** *(for pages)* maquette *f*, trame *f* de maquette

layover ['leɪəʊvə(r)] *n Am* escale *f*, halte *f*; **we had a three-hour layover in Miami** nous avons eu *ou* fait une escale de trois heures à Miami

layshaft ['leɪʃɑːft] *n Tech* arbre *m* secondaire *ou* intermédiaire

laywoman ['leɪˌwʊmən] (*pl* **laywomen** [-ˌwɪmɪn]) *n* (**a**) *(non-specialist)* *f* non-initiée *f*, profane *f* (**b**) *(non-clerical)* laïque *f*

Lazarus ['læzərəs] *pr n Bible* Lazare; *Fig* **the company has risen like Lazarus from the dead** tel le Phénix, la société renaquit de ses cendres

laze [leɪz] **1** *vi (relax)* se reposer; *(idle)* paresser; **to laze in bed** traîner au lit; **we spent the holidays lazing on the beach** nous avons passé nos vacances à paresser sur la plage

2 *n* farniente *m*; **to have a laze in bed** traîner au lit

▸**laze about, laze around** *vi* paresser, fainéanter; **we just lazed about** on a traîné

▸**laze away** *vt sep* **to laze one's time away** passer son temps à ne rien faire

lazily ['leɪzɪlɪ] *adv* paresseusement, avec paresse

laziness ['leɪzɪnɪs] *n* paresse *f*, fainéantise *f*

lazulite ['læzjʊˌlaɪt] *n Miner* lazulite *f*, pierre *f* d'azur

lazurite ['læzjʊˌraɪt] *n Miner* outremer *m*

lazy ['leɪzɪ] (*compar* **lazier**, *superl* **laziest**) *adj* (**a**) *(idle)* paresseux, fainéant; *(relaxed)* indolent, nonchalant; **he's always been lazy about getting up** il a toujours eu du mal à se lever; **we spent a lazy afternoon on the beach** on a passé l'après-midi à paresser sur la plage; **I feel too lazy to do it** je n'ai pas l'énergie de le faire; **these lazy summer days** ces journées d'été où l'on ne fait rien

(**b**) *(movement)* paresseux, lent

▸▸ ***lazy eye*** amblyopie *f*; **to have a lazy eye** être amblyope; ***lazy Susan*** *(on table)* plateau *m* tournant

lazybones ['leɪzɪbəʊnz] *n Fam* fainéant(e)❑ *m,f*; **come on, lazybones!** allez, secoue-toi *ou* remue-toi un peu!

LB *(written abbr* **Labrador***)* Labrador *m*

lb *(written abbr* **pound***)* **3 lb** *or* **lbs** 3 livres

LBJ [ˌelbiː'dʒeɪ] *n (abbr* **Lyndon Baines Johnson***)* Lyndon Johnson

LBO [ˌelbiː'əʊ] *n Fin (abbr* **leveraged buy-out***)* rachat *m* d'entreprise financé par l'endettement

lbw [ˌelbiː'dʌbəljuː] *n Br Sport (abbr* **leg before wicket***)* = au cricket, faute d'un joueur qui intercepte avec sa jambe une balle qui allait frapper le guichet

LC [ˌel'siː] *n Am (abbr* **Library of Congress***)* bibliothèque *f* du Congrès *(équivalent américain de la Bibliothèque nationale)*

lc *Typ (written abbr* **lower case***)* bdc

L/C *Com (written abbr* **letter of credit***)* lettre *f* de crédit

LCD [ˌelsiː'diː] *n Comput (abbr* **liquid crystal display***)* affichage *m* à cristaux liquides, LCD *m*

▸▸ ***LCD screen*** écran *m* LCD

LCL *Com (written abbr* **less than container load***)* conteneur *m* chargé en partie

LCM [ˌelsiː'em] *n Math (abbr* **lowest common multiple***)* PPCM *m*

LD [ˌel'diː] *n Pharm (abbr* **lethal dose***)* dose *f* létale *ou* mortelle

Ld *(written abbr* **lord***)* Lord

L-dopa [ˌel'dəʊpə] *n* L-dopa *f*, lévodopa *f*

LDR [ˌeldiː'ɑː(r)] *n Electron (abbr* **light dependent resistor***)* LDR *m*

L-driver *n Br (abbr* **learner-driver***)* = personne qui apprend à conduire

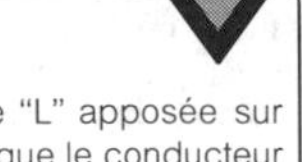

L-DRIVER

En Grande-Bretagne, la lettre "L" apposée sur l'arrière d'un véhicule indique que le conducteur n'a pas encore son permis mais qu'il est en conduite accompagnée.

LDS [ˌeldiː'es] *n (abbr* **Licentiate in Dental Surgery***)* *(person)* = titulaire d'un diplôme en chirurgie dentaire; *(qualification)* diplôme *m* en chirurgie dentaire

LEA [ˌeliː'eɪ] *n Br Admin & Sch (abbr* **local education authority***)* = organisme chargé de l'enseignement au niveau régional

lea [liː] *n Literary* pré *m*

leach [liːtʃ] **1** *vt* (**a**) *Tech* lessiver, extraire par lessivage (**b**) *Chem & Pharm* lixivier

2 *vi (liquid)* filtrer (**through** à travers); **fertilizers have been leaching into the water supply** des engrais ont infiltré la réserve d'eau

leaching ['liːtʃɪŋ] *n* (**a**) *Tech* lessivage *m* (**b**) *Chem & Pharm* lixiviation *f*

lead[1] [led] **1** *n* (**a**) *(metal)* plomb *m*; **it's made of lead** c'est en plomb

(**b**) *Fam (bullets)* plomb *m*; **they pumped him full of lead** ils l'ont plombé

(**c**) *(in pencil)* mine *f*

(**d**) *(piece of lead → for sounding)* plomb *m* (de sonde); *(→ on car wheel, fishing line)* plomb *m*; *Typ* interligne *m*

(**e**) *(idioms) Am Fam* **to get the lead out (of one's pants)** se magner (le train); *very Fam* **that'll put some lead in your pencil!** *(invigorate)* ça te requinquera!; *very Fam* **to have lead in one's pencil** *(be sexually potent)* ne pas avoir de problèmes pour bander

2 *vt* (**a**) *(seal)* plomber

(**b**) *Typ* interligner

3 *adj (made of lead)* de *ou* en plomb; *(containing lead)* plombifère; *Fam* **to go down like a lead balloon** tomber à plat❑

4 leads *npl Br Constr (on roof)* plombs *mpl* (de couverture); *(on window)* plombures *fpl*, plombs *mpl*

▸▸ ***lead crystal*** verre *m* de *ou* au plomb; ***lead glass*** verre *m* de *ou* au plomb; ***lead ore*** minerai *m* de plomb; ***lead oxide*** oxyde *m* de plomb; ***lead paint*** peinture *f* à base de plomb; ***lead pencil*** crayon *m* noir *ou* à papier *ou* à mine de plomb; ***lead poisoning*** *Med* intoxication *f* par le plomb, saturnisme *m*; *Am Fam (death)* mort *f* par balle(s); *(injury)* blessure *f* par balle(s); *Am Fam* **to get lead poisoning** être tué/blessé par balle(s); ***lead pipe*** tuyau *m* de plomb; ***lead shot*** grenaille *f* de plomb

▸**lead out** *vt sep Typ (lines of text)* augmenter l'interlignage de

LEAD[2] [liːd]

tête	▸ **1 (a)**
initiative	▸ **1 (b)**
indice	▸ **1 (c)**
gros titre	▸ **1 (d)**
rôle principal	▸ **1 (e)**

laisse	► 1 (g)
fil	► 1 (h)
mener	► 2 (a), (c), (e)
être à la tête de	► 2 (b)
diriger	► 2 (b)
amener	► 2 (d)
aller devant	► 3 (d)
principal	► 4

(*pt & pp* **led** [led]) **1** *n* (**a**) *Sport* tête *f*; **to be in the lead** être en tête, mener; **to go into** *or* **to take the lead** *(in race)* prendre la tête; *(in match)* mener; **to have a 10-point/10-length lead** avoir 10 points/10 longueurs d'avance; **to have a good lead over the rest of the field** avoir une bonne avance sur les autres concurrents; **he's opened up a tremendous lead** il a pris une avance considérable; **France are hanging on to the lead** *(in race)* la France reste en tête de la course; *(in points table)* la France reste en tête du classement

(**b**) *(initiative)* initiative *f*; **he took the lead in asking questions** il fut le premier à poser des questions; **take your lead from me** prenez exemple sur moi; **to follow sb's lead** suivre l'exemple de qn; **it's up to the government to give a lead on housing policy** c'est au gouvernement (qu'il revient) de donner l'exemple en matière de politique du logement

(**c**) *(indication, clue)* indice *m*, piste *f*; **to give sb a lead** mettre qn sur la voie; **the police have several leads** la police tient plusieurs pistes; **we're currently following up an important lead** nous sommes actuellement sur une piste prometteuse

(**d**) *Br Press* gros titre *m*; **the news made the lead in all the papers** la nouvelle était à la une de tous les journaux; **the 'Telegraph' opens with a lead on the Middle East crisis** le 'Telegraph' consacre sa une à la crise au Proche-Orient

(**e**) *Cin & Theat (role)* rôle *m* principal; *(actor)* premier rôle *m* masculin; *(actress)* premier rôle *m* féminin; **Jude Law plays the male lead** Jude Law tient le premier rôle masculin

(**f**) *Cards* **to have the lead** jouer le premier; **your lead!** à vous de jouer!; **whose lead is it?** c'est à qui de jouer?; **you must follow the lead** il faut fournir à la couleur demandée; **a heart lead** une ouverture à cœur

(**g**) *(for dog)* laisse *f*; **dogs must be kept on a lead** *(sign)* les chiens doivent être tenus en laisse

(**h**) *Elec* fil *m*

(**i**) *(in ice)* chenal *m*

2 *vt* (**a**) *(take, guide)* mener, emmener, conduire; **to lead sb somewhere** mener *ou* conduire qn quelque part; **I was led into the garden** on m'a emmené *ou* conduit dans le jardin, **he led them across the lawn** il leur fit traverser la pelouse; **she led him down the stairs** elle lui fit descendre l'escalier; **she led them to safety** elle les a conduits en lieu sûr; **to lead an army into battle** mener une armée au combat; **to lead a team to victory** mener une équipe à la victoire; **the captain led the team onto the field** le capitaine a conduit son équipe sur le terrain; **she led them through the garden** *(to get out)* elle les fit passer par le jardin; *(to visit)* elle leur fit visiter le jardin; *Literary* **he led her to the altar** il la prit pour épouse; **to lead the way** montrer le chemin; **police motorcyclists led the way** des motards de la police ouvraient la route; **they led the cable along the edge of the floor** ils ont fait passé le câble par terre, le long du mur; *Bible* **lead us not into temptation** ne nous soumets pas à la tentation; *Prov* **you can lead a horse to water but you cannot make him drink** on ne saurait faire boire un âne qui n'a pas soif; *Fig* **to lead sb up the garden path** mener qn en bateau

(**b**) *(be leader of)* être à la tête de, diriger; *(orchestra)* diriger; **to lead the prayers/singing** diriger la prière/les chants

(**c**) *Sport (be in front of)* mener; **Stardust is leading Black Beauty by 10 lengths** Stardust a pris 10 longueurs d'avance sur Black Beauty; **to lead the field** mener; **to lead sb by 8 points** avoir une avance sur qn de 8 points; *Fig* **Great Britain leads the field in heart transplant technology** la Grande-Bretagne est le pays le plus avancé dans le domaine des greffes cardiaques

(**d**) *(induce)* amener; **to lead sb to do sth** amener qn à faire qch; **despair led him to commit suicide** le désespoir l'a poussé au suicide; **he led me to believe (that) he was innocent** il m'a amené à croire qu'il était innocent; **everything leads us to believe (that) she is still alive** tout porte à croire *ou* nous avons toutes les raisons de croire qu'elle est encore en vie; **I was led to the conclusion that he had been lying all along** je suis arrivé à la conclusion qu'il mentait depuis le début; **what led you to apply for this job?** qu'est-ce qui vous a conduit *ou* amené à postuler?; **he is easily led** il se laisse facilement influencer; *Fig* **subsequent events led the country into war** des événements ultérieurs ont entraîné le pays dans la guerre; **this leads me to my second point** ceci m'amène à ma seconde remarque; **he led the conversation round to money again** il a ramené la conversation sur la question de l'argent

(**e**) *(life)* mener; **he has lead a life of debauchery** il a mené une vie de débauche; **she has led a full and happy life** elle a eu une vie heureuse et bien remplie

(**f**) *Cards* demander, jouer; **to lead trumps** demander *ou* jouer atout; **what was led?** qu'est-ce qui a été demandé?

(**g**) *Law* **to lead a witness** poser des questions tendancieuses à un témoin

3 *vi* (**a**) *(go)* mener; **this path leads to the village** ce chemin mène au village; **where does this door lead to?** sur quoi ouvre cette porte?; **the stairs lead to the cellar** l'escalier mène *ou* conduit à la cave; **take the street that leads away from the station** prenez la rue qui part de la gare; **that road leads nowhere** cette route ne mène nulle part; *Fig* **this is leading nowhere!** cela ne rime à rien!

(**b**) *Sport* mener, être en tête; **to lead by 2 metres** avoir 2 mètres d'avance; **to lead by 3 points to 1** mener par 3 points à 1; **Black Beauty is leading** Black Beauty est en tête

(**c**) *Cards* **hearts led** cœur (a été) demandé; **Joanne to lead** c'est à Joanne de jouer

(**d**) *(go in front)* aller devant; *(in mountaineering)* grimper en tête; **if you lead, I'll follow** allez-y, je vous suis

(**e**) *Br Press* **to lead with sth** mettre qch à la une; **the 'Times' led with news of the plane hijack** le détournement d'avion faisait la une *ou* était en première page du 'Times'

(**f**) *Boxing* **he leads with his right** il attaque toujours du droit *ou* de la droite

(**g**) *(in dancing)* conduire

(**h**) *Law* être l'avocat principal; **he led for the prosecution** il dirigea l'accusation en tant qu'avocat principal

4 *adj (actor, singer)* principal, premier; *Press (article)* de tête

►► *Com* ***leads and lags*** termaillage *m*; *Banking & St Exch* ***lead manager*** (banque *f*) chef *m* de file; ***lead time*** *Ind* délai *m* de préparation; *Com* délai *m* de livraison; *Mktg* ***lead user*** utilisateur(trice) *m,f* pilote

►**lead away** *vt sep* emmener; **the guards led him away** les gardes l'ont emmené; **he led her away from the scene of the accident** il l'éloigna du lieu de l'accident

►**lead back 1** *vt sep* ramener, reconduire; **they led him back to his room** ils l'ont ramené *ou* reconduit à sa chambre; **she led the conversation back to the question of money** elle a ramené la conversation sur la question de l'argent

2 *vi* **this path leads back to the beach** ce chemin ramène à la plage

►**lead off 1** *vi (in conversation)* commencer, débuter; *(in debate)* entamer les débats; *(in game)* jouer le(la) premier(ère); *(at dance)* ouvrir le bal; *(in relay race)* être le premier relayeur

2 *vt insep* (**a**) *(begin)* commencer, entamer

(**b**) *(go from)* partir de; **several avenues lead off the square** plusieurs avenues partent de la place

3 *vt sep (person)* conduire; **they were led off to jail** ils ont été conduits *ou* emmenés en prison

►**lead on 1** *vi* aller *ou* marcher devant; **lead on!** allez-y!

2 *vt sep* (**a**) *(trick)* **to lead sb on** faire marcher qn; **you shouldn't lead him on like that** vous ne devriez pas le faire marcher comme ça

(**b**) *(bring on)* faire entrer; **lead on the horses!** faites entrer les chevaux!

(**c**) *(in progression)* amener; **this leads me on to my second point** ceci m'amène à mon deuxième point

►**lead to** *vt insep (result in, have as consequence)* mener *ou* aboutir à; **what's all this leading to?** sur quoi tout ceci va-t-il déboucher?; **the decision led to panic on Wall Street** la décision a semé la panique à Wall Street; **one thing led to another** une chose en amenait une autre; **a course leading to a degree** un cursus qui débouche sur un diplôme; **several factors led to his decision to leave** plusieurs facteurs le poussèrent *ou* l'amenèrent à décider de partir; **this led to several of them losing their jobs** à cause de cela, plusieurs d'entre eux ont perdu leur emploi; **drinking too much can lead to violence** l'excès d'alcool peut conduire à la violence; **his statement led to a misunderstanding** sa déclaration est à l'origine d'un malentendu; **this could lead to some confusion** ça pourrait provoquer une certaine confusion; **her research led to nothing** ses recherches n'ont abouti à rien *ou* n'ont rien donné

►**lead up to** *vt insep* (**a**) *(path, road)* conduire à, mener à; **a narrow path led up to the house** un étroit sentier menait jusqu'à la maison; **those stairs lead up to the attic** cet escalier mène au grenier

(**b**) *(in reasoning)* **she's leading up to something** je me demande où elle veut en venir; **what are you leading up to?** où voulez-vous en venir?; **I was just leading up to that** j'allais justement y venir

(**c**) *(precede, cause)* **the events leading up to the war** les événements qui devaient déclencher la guerre; **in the months leading up to her death** pendant les mois qui précédèrent sa mort; *Mus* **the chords that lead up to the final movement** les accords qui introduisent le dernier mouvement

Lead on, MacDuff

Cette phrase ("après toi, MacDuff") est une déformation d'un vers de *Macbeth* de Shakespeare, dans un passage où Macbeth défie à l'épée son ennemi MacDuff en prononçant les mots **lay on, MacDuff** ("frappe, MacDuff").

On utilise la version modifiée de cette phrase de façon humoristique lorsque l'on demande à quelqu'un d'ouvrir la marche.

lead-bearing [led-] *adj* plombifère

leaded ['ledɪd] *adj* (**a**) *(door, box, billiard cue)* plombé (**b**) *(petrol)* au plomb (**c**) *Typ* interligné

►► ***leaded window*** fenêtre *f* avec verre cathédrale

leaden ['ledən] *adj* (**a**) *(made of lead)* de *ou* en plomb (**b**) *(dull → sky)* de plomb, plombé; *(heavy → sleep)* de plomb; *(→ heart)* lourd; **he walked with leaden steps** il marchait d'un pas lourd (**c**) *(oppressive → atmosphere)* lourd, pesant; *(→ silence)* de mort

leaden-eyed *adj* aux yeux ternes *ou* morts

leader ['liːdə(r)] *n* (**a**) *(head)* chef *m*; *Pol* chef *m*, leader *m*, dirigeant(e) *m,f*; *(of association)* dirigeant(e) *m,f*; *(of strike, protest, riot)* meneur(euse) *m,f*; **to be a born leader** être fait pour donner des ordres *ou* commander; **the leaders of the march were arrested** les organisateurs de la manifestation ont été arrêtés

(**b**) *Sport (horse)* cheval *m* de tête; *(athlete)* coureur *m* de tête; *(in championship)* leader *m*; **she was up with the leaders** elle était parmi les premiers *ou* dans le peloton de tête

(**c**) *(main body or driving force)* **the institute is a world leader in cancer research** l'institut occupe une des premières places mondiales en matière de recherche contre le cancer; **the leaders of fashion** ceux qui font la mode

(**d**) *Mus (of orchestra) Br* premier violon *m*; *Am* chef *m* d'orchestre

(**e**) *(in newspapers → editorial)* éditorial *m*

(**f**) *Br Law* avocat(e) *m,f* principal(e)

(**g**) *Mktg (product)* leader *m*; *(company)* chef *m* de file, leader *m*; *Am (loss leader)* produit *m* d'appel
(**h**) *(for film, tape)* amorce *f*
(**i**) *(in mountaineering)* premier *m* de cordée
(**j**) *St Exch* valeur *f* vedette
▸▸ *Pol* ***the Leader of the House*** *(in the Commons)* = parlementaire de la majorité chargé de certaines fonctions dans la mise en place du programme gouvernemental; *(in the Lords)* = porte-parole du gouvernement; ***the Leader of the Opposition*** le chef de l'opposition; *Br Journ* ***leader writer*** éditorialiste *mf*

leaderboard ['li:dəbɔ:d] *n (in golf)* leaderboard *m*; *Fig* **to be top of the leaderboard** être en tête du classement

leaderless ['li:dəlɪs] *adj* sans chef, dépourvu de chef

leadership ['li:dəʃɪp] *n* (**a**) *(direction)* direction *f*; **during** *or* **under her leadership** sous sa direction; **he was offered the party leadership** on lui a offert la direction du parti; **she is clearly cut out for leadership** elle est manifestement née pour diriger; **no one showed any leadership** personne n'a montré des qualités de chef; **he has great leadership qualities** c'est un excellent meneur d'hommes; **they looked to us for leadership** ils comptaient sur nous pour leur montrer le chemin
(**b**) *(leaders)* direction *f*, dirigeants *mpl*; **the leadership of the movement is divided on this issue** les chefs *ou* les dirigeants du mouvement sont divisés sur cette question
▸▸ ***leadership battle, leadership contest*** bataille *f* pour la direction; ***leadership potential*** qualités *fpl* de chef

lead-foot [led-] *vt Am Fam* **to lead-foot it** *(drive quickly)* conduire pied au plancher

lead-footed [led-] *adj Fam* (**a**) *(clumsy)* maladroit ◻, gauche ◻ (**b**) *Am* **a lead-footed driver** un fou du volant

lead-free [led-] *adj (paint, petrol)* sans plomb; *(toy)* (garanti) sans plomb

lead-in [li:d-] *n Br* (**a**) *(introductory remarks)* introduction *f*, remarques *fpl* préliminaires; *(introductory music)* introduction *f* (**b**) *Elec & Tel (of cable)* entrée *f*; *(to aerial)* descente *f* d'antenne
▸▸ ***lead-in groove*** *(on record)* sillon *m* initial

leading¹ ['li:dɪŋ] **1** *adj* (**a**) *(prominent)* premier, de premier plan; *(major)* majeur, principal, dominant; **leading figure** figure *f* de premier plan; **they played a leading part in the discussions** ils ont joué un rôle prépondérant dans le débat; **he is the leading actor in the company** c'est le meilleur acteur de la troupe; **to play the leading role in a film** être la vedette d'un film; *Econ* **leading indicators** principaux indicateurs *mpl* économiques
(**b**) *Sport (in race)* de tête; *(in championship)* premier; **to be in the leading position** être en tête; **the leading runners/riders** les coureurs/cavaliers de tête; **the leading cyclists, the leading motorcyclists** le peloton de tête
(**c**) *(in front → car)* de tête
(**d**) *Math (coefficient)* premier
2 *n (of horses)* conduite *f*, manège *m*
▸▸ ***leading article*** *Br* éditorial *m*; *Am* article *m* leader *ou* de tête; ***leading axle*** *(of vehicle)* essieu *m* porteur d'avant; *Cards* ***leading card*** première carte *f*; *Elec* ***leading current*** courant *m* déphasé en avant; *Aviat* ***leading edge*** *(of wing)* bord *m* d'attaque; *Fig* **to be at the leading edge of technology** être à la pointe de la technologie; ***leading edge technology*** technologie *f* de pointe; *Cin & Theat* ***leading lady*** premier rôle *m* (féminin); **Vivien Leigh was the leading lady** Vivien Leigh tenait le premier rôle féminin; ***leading light*** personnage *m* (de marque); **she's a leading light in the environmental lobby** c'est une personnalité très influente du mouvement écologiste; *Cin & Theat* ***leading man*** premier rôle *m* (masculin); **he was the leading man** il tenait le premier rôle masculin; *Mus* ***leading note*** sensible *f*; *Cin & Theat* ***leading part*** premier rôle *m*; *Mil* ***leading patrol*** patrouille *f* de tête; *Am* ***leading price indicator*** indice *m* composite des principaux indicateurs; ***leading question*** question *f* orientée; *Law* = question posée au témoin de manière à suggérer la réponse; ***leading rein*** *(for horse)* longe *f*; *Br* ***leading reins*** *(for child)* harnais *m*; *Cin & Theat* ***leading role*** premier rôle *m*; *St Exch* ***leading shares*** valeurs *fpl* vedettes; *St Exch* ***a leading shareholder*** un des principaux actionnaires; ***leading shoot*** *(of plant)* pousse *f* principale; *Am* ***leading strings*** harnais *m (pour enfant)*; ***leading technology*** technologie *f* de pointe; ***leading wheels*** *(of vehicle)* essieu *m* porteur d'avant

leading² ['ledɪŋ] *n Typ & Comput (process)* interlignage *m*; *(space)* interligne *m*

leading-edge ['li:dɪŋ-] *comp* de pointe

lead-off [li:d-] *adj*
▸▸ ***lead-off runner*** *(in relay race)* premier(ère) relayeur(euse) *m,f*

lead-out [li:d-] *n Elec & Tel (of wire etc)* sortie *f*
▸▸ ***lead-out groove*** *(of record)* sillon *m* de sortie

lead-up [li:d-] *n* veille *f*; **in the lead-up to independence** dans la période qui a précédé l'indépendance

leadwork ['ledwɜ:k] *n Archit (of window)* plombs *mpl*

leaf [li:f] *(pl* **leaves** [li:vz]) **1** *n* (**a**) *(on plant, tree)* feuille *f*; **to come into leaf** se couvrir de feuilles; **the tree has lost its leaves** l'arbre a perdu son feuillage *ou* ses feuilles; **the trees are in leaf** les arbres sont en feuilles
(**b**) *(page)* feuillet *m*, page *f*; **to take a leaf out of sb's book** prendre exemple *ou* modèle sur qn
(**c**) *(on table → hinged)* abattant *m*; *(→ inserted board)* allonge *f*, rallonge *f*
(**d**) *(of door)* battant *m*, vantail *m*; *(of shutter)* battant *m*; *(of spring)* lame *f*
(**e**) *(of metal)* feuille *f*
(**f**) *Fam Drugs slang (marijuana)* marie-jeanne *f inv*, herbe *f*
2 *vi (tree)* se feuiller
▸▸ ***leaf beet*** bette *f*; *Entom* ***leaf beetle*** chrysomèle *f*; ***leaf bud*** bourgeon *m* à feuille; ***leaf curl*** frisolée *f*; ***leaf green*** vert prairie *m inv*; *Entom* ***leaf insect*** phyllie *f*; ***leaf mould*** terreau *m* de feuilles; ***leaf spot*** *(UNCOUNT)* (maladie *f* des) taches *fpl* noires; *Tech* ***leaf spring*** ressort *m* à lames; *Aut* ***leaf spring suspension*** suspension *f* à lames; ***leaf tobacco*** tabac *m* en feuilles

▸**leaf through** *vt insep (book, magazine)* feuilleter, parcourir

---

'Leaves of Grass' *Whitman* 'Feuilles d'herbe'

---

leafage ['li:fɪdʒ] *n* feuillage *m*

leafcutter bee ['li:fkʌtə-] *n Entom* abeille *f* coupeuse de feuilles

leaf-green *adj* vert prairie *(inv)*

leafhopper ['li:fhɒpə(r)] *n* cicadelle *f*, cicadellide *m*

leafiness ['li:fɪnɪs] *n (of tree)* abondance *f* de feuillage

leafless ['li:flɪs] *adj* sans feuilles; **the leafless trees** les arbres dénudés

leaflet ['li:flɪt] **1** *n* (**a**) *(brochure)* prospectus *m*, dépliant *m*; *(political)* tract *m* (**b**) *(instruction sheet)* notice *f* (explicative), mode *m* d'emploi (**c**) *Bot* foliole *f*
2 *vt* distribuer des prospectus *ou* des tracts à; **has the area been leafleted?** est-ce qu'on a distribué des tracts dans le quartier?
▸▸ ***leaflet drop*** distribution *f* de prospectus

leafstalk ['li:fstɔ:k] *n Bot* pétiole *f*

leafy ['li:fɪ] *(compar* **leafier**, *superl* **leafiest**) *adj (tree)* feuillu; *(woodland)* boisé, vert; **a leafy avenue** une avenue bordée d'arbres; **a leafy canopy** un dais de feuillage *ou* de verdure; **a leafy suburb** une banlieue verte
▸▸ *Bot* ***leafy lousewort*** pédiculaire *f* feuillée

league [li:g] **1** *n* (**a**) *(alliance)* ligue *f*; **to be in league (with sb)** être de mèche *ou* de connivence (avec qn); **they are in league together** ils sont complices *ou* de mèche; **they're all in league against me** ils se sont tous ligués contre moi
(**b**) *Sport (competition)* championnat *m*; *(division)* division *f*; **United are league leaders at the moment** United est en tête du championnat en ce moment
(**c**) *Fig (class)* **I'm not in your league, I'm not in the same league as you** je ne suis pas de votre niveau; **they're not in the same league** ils ne sont pas du même niveau; **I thought I was good but he's in another league** je pensais que j'étais bon mais il est bien meilleur que moi; **to be in the big league** être parmi les meilleurs; **that's way out of our league** ce n'est pas du tout dans nos possibilités
(**d**) *Arch (distance)* lieue *f*
2 *vt* **to be leagued with sb** être allié à *ou* avec qn
3 *vi* se liguer
▸▸ *Ftbl* ***league champions*** champion *m*; **to become league champions** remporter le championnat; *Ftbl* ***league championship*** championnat *m*; ***league championship match*** match *m* de championnat *ou* comptant pour le championnat; *Ftbl* ***league match*** match *m* de championnat; *Hist* ***the League of Nations*** la Société des Nations; *Br Ftbl* ***league table*** (classement *m* du) championnat *m*; *Fig* **a league table of statistics** un classement statistique

Leah ['lɪə] *pr n Bible* Lia

leak [li:k] **1** *n* (**a**) *(in pipe, tank, roof)* fuite *f*; *(in boat)* voie *f* d'eau
(**b**) *(disclosure → of information, secret)* fuite *f*
(**c**) *very Fam (idioms)* **to go for** *or* **to take a leak** *(urinate)* pisser un coup
2 *vi* (**a**) *(pen, roof, bucket, pipe)* fuir; *(boat, shoe)* prendre l'eau; **the roof leaks** il y a une fuite dans le toit; **his pen leaked in his pocket** son stylo a fui *ou* coulé dans sa poche
(**b**) *(gas, liquid)* fuir, s'échapper; **the rain leaks through the ceiling** la pluie s'infiltre par le plafond
3 *vt* (**a**) *(liquid)* répandre, faire couler; **the can leaked oil onto my trousers** de l'huile du bidon s'est répandue sur mon pantalon; **the radiator had been leaking water everywhere** le radiateur avait fui et il y avait de l'eau partout
(**b**) *(information)* divulguer; **to leak sth to the press** divulguer qch à la presse; **the budget details were leaked** il y a eu des fuites sur le budget; **the documents had been leaked to a local councillor** quelqu'un avait communiqué *ou* avait fait parvenir les documents à un conseiller municipal

▸**leak in** *vi* s'infiltrer; **the rain had leaked in through a crack in the wall** la pluie s'était infiltrée par une lézarde dans le mur

▸**leak out** *vi* (**a**) *(liquid, gas)* fuir, s'échapper
(**b**) *(news, secret)* filtrer, transpirer; **the truth finally leaked out** la vérité a fini par se savoir

leakage ['li:kɪdʒ] *n (UNCOUNT)* fuite *f*; **damage caused by leakage** des dégâts dus à des fuites

leakiness ['li:kɪnɪs] *n (of pen, roof, bucket, pipe)* = fait de fuir; *(of boat, shoes)* = fait de prendre l'eau

leakproof ['li:kpru:f] *adj* étanche

leaky ['li:kɪ] *(compar* **leakier**, *superl* **leakiest**) *adj* (**a**) *(pen, roof, bucket, pipe)* qui fuit; *(boat, shoes)* qui prend l'eau (**b**) *Fam Fig* **this department is very leaky** il y a plein de fuites dans ce service

leal [lɪəl] *adj Literary or Scot* loyal

lean¹ [li:n] *(Br pt & pp* **leaned** *or* **leant** [lent], *Am pt & pp* **leaned**) **1** *vt* (**a**) *(prop → ladder, bicycle)* appuyer; **he leant the ladder/bike (up) against the tree** il appuya l'échelle/le vélo contre un arbre
(**b**) *(rest → head, elbows)* appuyer; **to lean one's elbows on sth** s'accouder à qch; **she leant her head on his shoulder** elle posa sa tête sur son épaule
(**c**) *(incline)* pencher; **to lean one's head to one side** pencher *ou* incliner la tête
2 *vi (be on incline)* pencher, s'incliner; **she/a ladder was leaning (up) against the wall** elle/une échelle était appuyée contre le mur; **he was leaning with his back to** *or* **against the wall** il était adossé au mur; **she leant down to speak to me** elle s'est penchée pour me parler; **to lean in through the window** pencher la tête par la fenêtre; **lean on my arm** appuyez-vous *ou* prenez appui sur mon bras; **she was leaning with her elbows on the window sill** elle était accoudée à la fenêtre

lean² [li:n] **1** *n* (**a**) *(slope)* inclinaison *f*
(**b**) *(meat)* maigre *m*
2 *adj* (**a**) *(animal, meat)* maigre; *(person → thin)*

maigre; *(→ slim)* mince; *Fig* **the company is now fitter and leaner than it was before** l'entreprise se porte mieux depuis que sa structure a été allégée

(**b**) *(poor → harvest)* maigre, pauvre; *(→ period of time)* difficile; **we had a lean time** nous avons eu une période de vaches maigres

(**c**) *(deficient → ore, mixture)* pauvre

▸**lean back** 1 *vt sep* pencher en arrière; **to lean one's head back** pencher *ou* renverser la tête en arrière; **to lean one's chair back** pencher sa chaise en arrière

2 *vi* (**a**) *(person)* se pencher en arrière; **he leaned back against the wall** il s'est adossé au mur; **don't lean back on your chair!** ne te balance pas sur ta chaise!; **he leaned back in his armchair** il s'est renversé dans son fauteuil

(**b**) *(chair)* basculer; **this chair leans back if you pull that lever** on peut incliner *ou* faire basculer le siège en poussant ce levier

▸**lean forward** 1 *vt sep* pencher en avant

2 *vi* se pencher en avant

▸**lean on, lean upon** *vt insep* (**a**) *(depend)* s'appuyer sur; **to lean on sb's advice** compter sur les conseils de qn; **she leans heavily on her family for financial support** financièrement, elle dépend beaucoup de sa famille

(**b**) *Br Fam (pressurize)* faire pression sur❑; **they leaned on him for more information** ils ont fait pression sur lui pour qu'il parle; **they kept leaning on him until they got him to agree** ils ne l'ont pas lâché avant qu'il ait dit oui

▸**lean out** 1 *vt sep* pencher au dehors; **he leaned his head out of the window** il a passé la tête par la fenêtre

2 *vi* se pencher au dehors; **don't lean out of the window!** ne te penche pas par la fenêtre!; **do not lean out of the window** *(sign)* interdiction de se pencher au dehors

▸**lean over** *vi (person)* se pencher en avant; *(tree, wall)* pencher, être penché; **he leaned over to speak to me** il s'est penché vers moi pour me parler; **to lean over backwards** se pencher en arrière; *Fig* remuer ciel et terre, se mettre en quatre

▸**lean towards** *vt insep (tend)* pencher pour; **I rather lean towards the view that we should sell** je pencherais plutôt pour la vente, j'ai tendance à penser que nous devrions vendre; **I think I'm leaning towards the opinion that you were right after all** je commence à penser qu'en fin de compte tu avais raison; **politically she leans towards the right** politiquement, elle se situe plutôt à droite

lean-burn *adj (engine)* à mélange pauvre

Leander [lɪ'ændə(r)] *pr n Myth* Léandre

leaning ['li:nɪŋ] 1 *n (tendency)* inclination *f* (**towards** pour), penchant *m* (**towards** pour *ou* vers), tendance *f* (**towards** à); **she has communist leanings** elle a des penchants communistes; **she has literary leanings** elle aimerait être écrivain

2 *adj (tree, wall)* penché

▸▸ ***the Leaning Tower of Pisa*** la tour de Pise

leanness ['li:nnɪs] *n* maigreur *f*

leant [lent] *Br pt & pp of* **lean**

lean-to *n Br* appentis *m*

▸▸ ***lean-to garage*** = garage attenant à la maison, avec un toit incliné; ***lean-to roof*** comble *m* en appentis

leap [li:p] (*Br pt & pp* **leaped** *or* **leapt** [lept], *Am pt & pp* **leaped**) 1 *n* (**a**) *(jump)* saut *m*, bond *m*; **with one leap she cleared the ditch** d'un saut *ou* d'un bond elle franchit le fossé; *also Fig* **to take a leap forward** faire un bond en avant, sauter en avant; **it's a great leap forward in medical research** c'est un grand bond en avant pour la recherche médicale; **his heart gave a leap** son cœur bondit, son cœur fit un bond; **by leaps and bounds** à pas de géant; **his French had improved by leaps and bounds** il avait fait des progrès phénoménaux en français; *Fig* **a leap in the dark** un saut dans l'inconnu; **to take a leap in the dark** faire un saut dans l'inconnu

(**b**) *(in prices)* bond *m*

2 *vt* (**a**) *(fence, stream)* sauter (par-dessus), franchir d'un bond

(**b**) *(horse)* faire sauter

3 *vi* (**a**) *(person, animal)* bondir, sauter; *(flame)* jaillir; **she leapt a good four feet** ≃ elle a sauté un bon mètre vingt; **to leap to one's feet** se lever d'un bond; **to leap for joy** *(person)* sauter de joie; *(heart)* faire un bond; **we leapt back in fright** de frayeur, nous fîmes un bond en arrière; **she nearly leapt out of her skin** elle a sauté au plafond; **to leap into the air** sauter en l'air; **the cat leapt off the chair onto the table** le chat sauta de la chaise sur la table; **we had to leap over the stream** nous avons dû sauter par-dessus le ruisseau

(**b**) *Fig* faire un bond; **the price of petrol leapt by 10 percent** le prix du pétrole a fait un bond de 10 pour cent; **the answer almost leapt off the page at me** la réponse m'a pour ainsi dire sauté aux yeux; **the idea suddenly leapt into my mind** l'idée m'est soudain venue à l'esprit; **she leapt to the wrong conclusion** elle a conclu trop hâtivement

▸▸ ***leap day*** jour *m* intercalaire; ***leap year*** année *f* bissextile

▸**leap about, leap around** 1 *vt insep* gambader dans; **he kept leaping about the room** il n'a cessé de gambader dans la pièce

2 *vi* gambader

▸**leap at** *vt insep* (**a**) *(in attack)* sauter sur; **the dog leapt at me** le chien m'a sauté dessus

(**b**) *Fig* **to leap at an opportunity** sauter sur l'occasion; **she leapt at the chance** elle a sauté sur l'occasion

▸**leap out** *vi (from hiding place)* sortir d'un bond; **to leap out at sb** bondir sur qn; **they leapt out from behind the bushes** ils sont sortis d'un bond de derrière les buissons; *Fig* **a familiar face leapt out at me from the newspaper** soudain, je remarquai dans le journal un visage que je connaissais; **he almost leapt out of his skin** il a failli tomber à la renverse

▸**leap up** *vi (into the air)* sauter (en l'air); *(to one's feet)* se lever d'un bond; **to leap up in surprise** sauter au plafond, sursauter; **to leap up in indignation** bondir d'indignation; **the dog leapt up at him** le chien lui a sauté dessus

One small step for a man, one giant leap forward for mankind

Il s'agit des mots que prononça Neil Armstrong lorsqu'il devint le premier homme à marcher sur la Lune le 20 juillet 1969 : "un petit pas pour l'homme, un pas de géant pour l'humanité".

On utilise aujourd'hui cette formule en référence aux mots d'Armstrong pour mettre en contraste le caractère apparemment anodin d'un phénomène et l'ampleur de son effet, comme **it's a small step for nanotechnology but a giant leap forward for computers** ("c'est un petit pas pour la nanotechnologie mais un pas de géant pour les ordinateurs").

leapfrog ['li:pfrɒg] (*pt & pp* **leapfrogged**, *cont* **leapfrogging**) 1 *n* saute-mouton *m*; **to play leapfrog** jouer à saute-mouton

2 *vt* **to leapfrog sb/sth** sauter par-dessus qn/qch à saute-mouton; *Br Fig* dépasser qn/qch; **he leapfrogged several of his more senior colleagues to get the post** il a obtenu le poste en passant devant plusieurs de ses collègues d'un échelon supérieur

3 *vi Br* **to leapfrog over sb** sauter par-dessus qn; *Fig* **to leapfrog into the computer age** se trouver propulsé à l'ère de l'informatique

leapt [lept] *Br pt & pp of* **leap**

learn [lɜ:n] (*Br pt & pp* **learned** *or* **learnt** [lɜ:nt], *Am pt & pp* **learned**) 1 *vt* (**a**) *(by instruction)* apprendre; **to learn (how) to do sth** apprendre à faire qch; **she's learning the violin** elle apprend à jouer du violon, elle étudie le violon; **to learn sth by heart** apprendre qch par cœur; *Fig* **he's learnt his lesson now** cela lui a servi de leçon; **when will she learn her lesson?** quand est-ce qu'elle comprendra?

(**b**) *(discover, hear)* apprendre; **I subsequently learnt that he wouldn't be coming** j'ai appris par la suite qu'il ne viendrait pas

(**c**) *Fam (teach)* apprendre❑; **that'll learn you!** ça t'apprendra!

2 *vi* (**a**) *(by instruction, experience)* apprendre; **to learn about sth** apprendre qch; **to learn by** *or* **from one's mistakes** tirer la leçon de ses erreurs; **they learnt the hard way** ils ont été à dure école; **it's never too late to learn** il n'est jamais trop tard pour apprendre

(**b**) *(be informed)* **to learn of sth** apprendre qch; **we only learnt of her death today** ce n'est qu'aujourd'hui que nous avons appris sa mort

▸**learn off** *vt sep Br* apprendre par cœur

▸**learn up** *vt sep Br Fam* bûcher, potasser; **I've been learning up all about the town's history** j'ai potassé tout ce qui a trait à l'histoire de la ville

learnable ['lɜ:nəbəl] *adj* qui peut être appris, qui peut s'apprendre

learned [*senses* (**a**), (**b**) 'lɜ:nɪd, *sense* (**c**) lɜ:nd] *adj* (**a**) *(erudite → person)* savant, érudit; *(→ subject, book, society)* savant (**b**) *Law (lawyer)* **my learned friend** mon éminent confrère (**c**) *Psy (behaviour)* acquis

▸▸ ***learned profession*** profession *f* intellectuelle

learnedly ['lɜ:nɪdlɪ] *adv* savamment, avec érudition

learnedness ['lɜ:nɪdnɪs] *n* érudition *f*, savoir *m*

learner ['lɜ:nə(r)] *n* apprenant(e) *m,f*; *Br (driver)* = personne qui apprend à conduire; **to be a quick learner** apprendre vite; **learners of English** les apprenants d'anglais, les gens qui apprennent l'anglais

▸▸ *Br* ***learner driver*** = personne qui apprend à conduire; *Am* ***learner's permit*** permis *m* de conduire provisoire *(autorisation que l'on doit obtenir avant de prendre des leçons)*

learning ['lɜ:nɪŋ] *n* (**a**) *(erudition)* érudition *f*, savoir *m*; **a man of great learning** *(in sciences)* un grand savant; *(in arts)* un homme d'une grande érudition *ou* culture

(**b**) *(acquisition of knowledge)* étude *f*; *Mktg* apprentissage *m*; **language learning** l'étude *f ou* l'apprentissage *m* des langues; **adults/children with learning difficulties** adultes *mpl*/enfants *mpl* qui ont des difficultés d'apprentissage

▸▸ ***learning capacity*** capacités *fpl* d'apprentissage; ***learning curve*** courbe *f* d'assimilation; **it was a steep learning curve** l'apprentissage a été difficile; *Am* ***learning disability*** difficultés *fpl* d'apprentissage; ***learning support*** = soutien scolaire pour les enfants ayant des difficultés d'apprentissage

'A Little Learning' *Waugh* 'Un peu de savoir'

learning-disabled *adj Am* **to be learning-disabled** avoir des difficultés d'apprentissage

learnt [lɜ:nt] *Br* 1 *pt & pp of* **learn**

2 *adj Psy* acquis

lease [li:s] 1 *n* (**a**) *Law* bail *m*; *(of equipment)* location *f*; *(of house to let)* bail *m* (à loyer); *(of farming land)* bail *m* à ferme; *(document)* (contrat *m* de) bail *m*; **a 99-year lease** un bail de 99 ans; **to take (out) a lease on a house, to take a house on lease** prendre une maison à bail; **to sign a lease** signer un bail; **the lease runs out in May** le bail expire en mai

(**b**) *(idioms)* **to take on a new lease of life** *(person)* renaître à la vie; *(industry, town, football club)* retrouver un nouveau souffle; **the trip has given her a new lease** *Br* **of** *or Am* **on life** le voyage l'a remise en forme *ou* lui a redonné du tonus; **cleaning the engine will give the car a new lease of life** ça va retaper la voiture de nettoyer le moteur

2 *vt* (**a**) *(of owner → house)* louer *ou* céder à bail; *(→ equipment, vehicle)* louer; *(→ land)* affermer;

(**b**) *(of tenant → house)* louer, prendre à bail; *(of person → equipment, vehicle)* louer; *(→ land)* prendre en fermage

▸▸ *Acct* ***lease charges*** charges *fpl* locatives; ***lease contract*** *(for property)* contrat *m* de bail; *(for equipment)* contrat *m* en location; *Fin* ***lease financing*** leasing *m*, location *f* avec option d'achat; *Comput* ***leased line*** ligne *f* louée; *Acct* ***lease revenue*** loyers *mpl*

▸**lease back** *vt sep Fin* = louer dans le cadre d'une cession-bail

▸**lease out** *vt sep (of owner → house)* louer *ou* céder à bail; *(→ equipment, vehicle)* louer; *(→ land)* affermer

leaseback ['li:sbæk] *n* cession-bail *f*

leasehold ['li:shəʊld] **1** *n (lease)* bail *m*; *(property)* location *f* à bail
2 *adj* loué à bail

leaseholder ['li:sˌhəʊldə(r)] *n (tenant)* locataire *mf*

lease-purchase *n* crédit-bail *m*
▸▸ ***lease-purchase contract*** contrat *m* de crédit-bail

leash [li:ʃ] *n (for dog)* laisse *f*; **to put a dog on the leash** mettre une laisse à un chien; **dogs must be kept on a leash** *(sign)* les chiens doivent être tenus en laisse; *Fig* **to keep sb on a tight leash** tenir la bride haute à qn; **to keep one's emotions on a tight leash** avoir étroitement en mains les rênes de ses émotions

leasing ['li:sɪŋ] *n (of house)* location *f* à bail; *(of equipment, vehicle)* location *f*; *(of land)* affermage *m*; *(on lease-purchase)* location-bail *f*; *(system)* location *f* avec option d'achat, crédit-bail *m*, leasing *m*

LEAST [li:st]

le moins	▸ **1 (a); 3**
le/la moindre	▸ **1 (b); 2 (b)**
le moins de	▸ **2 (a)**
au moins	▸ **4 (a) – (c)**
du moins	▸ **4 (c), (d)**

1 *pron* (**a**) *(in quantity, size)* **he's the one who drank the least** c'est lui qui a bu le moins; **he's got the least** c'est lui qui en a le moins

(**b**) *(slightest)* **it was the least we could do** c'était la moindre des choses; **that's the least of our worries** c'est le moindre *ou* c'est le cadet de nos soucis; *Prov* **least said, soonest mended** moins on en dit, mieux on se porte

2 *adj (superl of* **little**) (**a**) *(in quantity, size)* **I ate the least chocolate** c'est moi qui ai mangé le moins de chocolat; **she has the least money out of all of us** c'est elle qui a le moins d'argent d'entre nous tous

(**b**) *(slightest)* **I haven't the least idea** je n'en ai pas la moindre idée; **the least thing upsets her** un rien la contrarie; **the government clamps down on the least sign of opposition** le gouvernement serre la vis au moindre signe d'opposition; **I'm not the least bit musical** je ne suis pas musicien pour un sou; **I'm not the least bit interested** cela ne m'intéresse pas le moins du monde

3 *adv* (le) moins; **which do you find (the) least useful?** à votre avis, lequel est le moins utile?; **the least interesting film I've ever seen** le film le moins intéressant que j'aie jamais vu; **it's what we least expected** c'est ce à quoi nous nous attendions le moins; **it always happens when you are least expecting it** ça arrive toujours au moment où tu t'y attends le moins

4 at least *adv* (**a**) *(not less than)* au moins; **at least $500** au moins 500 dollars; **she's at least seventy** elle a au moins soixante-dix ans; **he smokes at least forty cigarettes a day** il fume au moins quarante cigarettes par jour; **she's at least as tall as you** elle est au moins aussi grande que toi

(**b**) *(as a minimum)* au moins; **I can at least try** je peux toujours essayer; **you could at least have phoned** vous auriez pu au moins téléphoner; **at the very least he might have warned us** la moindre des choses aurait été de nous avertir

(**c**) *(indicating an advantage)* au moins, du moins; **at least we've got an umbrella** au moins *ou* du moins on a un parapluie

(**d**) *(used to qualify)* du moins; **I didn't like him, at least not at first** il ne m'a pas plu, en tout cas *ou* du moins pas au début; **I understand now, at least I think I do** ça y est, je comprends, du moins je crois

5 in the least *adv (with negative)* **not in the least** pas du tout, pas le moins du monde; **am I boring you? – not in the least** je t'ennuie? – pas du tout; **she's not in the least angry** elle n'est pas du tout fâchée; **she didn't seem to mind in the least** ça ne semblait pas la déranger le moins du monde

6 least of all *adv* surtout pas, encore moins; **nobody could understand it, Liz least of all** *or* **least of all Liz** personne ne comprenait, surtout pas Liz *ou* Liz encore moins que les autres; **we didn't expect to win any prizes, least of all this one** nous ne nous attendions pas à gagner un prix, et en tout cas, certainement pas celui-là

7 not least *adv* **many politicians, not least the Foreign Secretary, are in favour** de nombreux hommes politiques y sont favorables, notamment le ministre des Affaires étrangères

▸▸ *Br* ***the least common denominator*** le plus petit dénominateur commun; *Orn* ***least sandpiper*** bécasseau *m* minuscule

leastways ['li:stweɪz], *Am* **leastwise** *adv Fam* du moins❑

leather ['leðə(r)] **1** *n* (**a**) *(material)* cuir *m*; **real leather** cuir *m* véritable; **made of leather** de *ou* en cuir; *Br Fam* **leathers** *(clothes)* cuir *m* (**b**) *(for polishing)* **(wash** *or* **window) leather** peau *f* de chamois (**c**) *(of pump, valve etc)* cuir *m*; **stirrup leather** étrivière *f*

2 *comp* (**a**) *(jacket, shoes, sofa, bag)* de *ou* en cuir (**b**) *(bar, club)* cuir *(inv)*

3 *vt (punish)* tanner le cuir à

▸▸ ***leather goods*** *(ordinary)* articles *mpl* en cuir; *(finer)* maroquinerie *f*

leatherback ['leðəbæk] *n Zool* tortue *f* luth, fausse tortue *f*

leatherbound ['leðəbaʊnd] *adj* relié (en) cuir

leatherboy ['leðəbɔɪ] *n Fam* cuir *m*, pédé *m* cuir

leathercloth ['leðəklɒθ] *n* toile *f* cuir

leatherette [ˌleðə'ret] **1** *n* similicuir *m*
2 *comp (purse, bag, clothing)* en similicuir

leathering ['leðərɪŋ] *n Br Fam* raclée *f*; **to give sb a leathering** tanner le cuir à qn

leatherjacket ['leðəˌdʒækɪt] *n Entom* larve *f* de la tipule

leather-look *adj* en similicuir

leathern ['leðən] *adj Fam Old-fashioned* de cuir❑, en cuir❑

leatherneck ['leðənek] *n Am Fam* marine❑ *m*, ≃ marsouin *m*

leatherwork ['leðəwɜ:k] *n (activity, products)* maroquinerie *f*

leatherworker ['leðəwɜ:kə(r)] *n* maroquinier(ère) *m,f*

leathery ['leðərɪ] *adj (meat)* coriace; *(skin)* parcheminé, tanné
▸▸ *Zool* ***leathery turtle*** tortue *f* luth, fausse tortue *f*

LEAVE¹ [li:v]

partir	▸ **1 (a), (b)**
quitter	▸ **2 (a), (b), (d)**
laisser	▸ **2 (c), (d) – (h), (j), (l)**
oublier	▸ **1 (g)**
léguer	▸ **1 (n)**
congé	▸ **3 (a), (c)**
permission	▸ **3 (a), (b)**

(pt & pp **left** [left]) **1** *vi* (**a**) *(depart)* partir; **my flight leaves at ten** mon avion part à dix heures; **when did you leave?** quand est-ce que vous êtes partis?; **we're leaving for Mexico tomorrow** nous partons pour le Mexique demain; **which station do you leave from?** vous partez de quelle gare?; **he's just left for lunch** il vient de partir déjeuner; **if you'd rather I left...** si vous voulez que je vous laisse...

(**b**) *(quit)* partir; **half of the staff have left** la moitié du personnel est partie; **fewer schoolchildren are now leaving at sixteen** les élèves sont aujourd'hui moins nombreux à quitter l'école à seize ans

(**c**) *(end relationship)* **Charles, I'm leaving!** Charles, je te quitte!

2 *vt* (**a**) *(depart from → place)* quitter; **she left London yesterday** elle est partie de *ou* elle a quitté Londres hier; **he left the room** il est sorti de *ou* il a quitté la pièce; **I leave home at 8 o'clock every morning** je pars *ou* je sors de chez moi tous les matins à 8 heures; **she never leaves the house** elle ne sort jamais de la maison; **to leave the table** se lever de table; **may I leave the table?** est-ce que je peux sortir de table?; **the boat finally left port at 6 o'clock** le bateau quitta finalement le port à 6 heures; **his brakes failed and the car left the road** ses freins ont lâché et la voiture a quitté la route; **the train left the rails** le train a déraillé; **his eyes never left her** il ne la quittait pas des yeux

(**b**) *(quit → job, institution)* quitter; **she left the firm last year** elle a quitté l'entreprise l'année dernière; **I left home at eighteen** je suis parti de chez moi *ou* de chez mes parents à dix-huit ans; **to leave school** quitter l'école; **he left Oxford without finishing his studies** il a quitté Oxford sans avoir terminé ses études; *Mil* **to leave the service** quitter le service

(**c**) *(in specified place or state)* laisser; **you can't leave them alone for a minute** on ne peut pas les laisser seuls une minute; **he left her asleep on the sofa** elle était endormie sur le canapé lorsqu'il la quitta; **I left him to his reading** je l'ai laissé à sa lecture; **I left him to himself** je l'ai laissé seul; **left to himself, who knows what he'd do?** qui sait ce qu'il ferait s'il était livré à lui-même?; **just leave me alone!** laissez-moi tranquille!; **let's leave it at that, we'll leave it at that** *(not do any more work)* arrêtons-nous là; *(not argue any more)* n'en parlons plus

(**d**) *(abandon → person)* quitter; *(take leave of → person)* laisser; **she left him for another man** elle l'a quitté pour un autre; **the prisoners were left to die** les prisonniers furent abandonnés à une mort certaine; **it's getting late, I must leave you now** il se fait tard, je dois vous laisser; **you may leave us now** vous pouvez disposer maintenant

(**e**) *(deposit, set down)* laisser; **it's no trouble to leave you at the station** ça ne me dérange pas de vous laisser *ou* déposer à la gare

(**f**) *(for someone's use, information etc)* laisser; **I've left your dinner in the oven for you** je t'ai laissé de quoi dîner dans le four; **leave your name with the receptionist** laissez votre nom à la réception; **he's out, do you want to leave (him) a message?** il n'est pas là, voulez-vous (lui) laisser un message?; **she left word for you to call her back** elle a demandé que vous la rappeliez

(**g**) *(forget)* laisser, oublier; **I must have left my gloves at the café** j'ai dû oublier mes gants au café

(**h**) *(allow or cause to remain)* laisser; **leave some cake for your brother** laisse du gâteau pour ton frère; **if you don't like your dinner, then leave it** si tu n'aimes pas ton dîner, laisse-le; **leave enough space for the address** laissez assez de place pour l'adresse; **leave the stew to cook for two hours** laissez mijoter le ragoût pendant deux heures; **leave yourself an hour to get to the airport** prévoyez une heure pour aller à l'aéroport; **I only left myself £20 a week to live on** je n'avais plus que 20 livres par semaine pour me nourrir; **don't leave things to the last minute** n'attendez pas la dernière minute (pour faire ce que vous avez à faire); **he left his work unfinished** il n'a pas terminé son travail; **he left his dinner untouched** il ne toucha pas à son dîner; **please leave the windows closed** veuillez laisser les fenêtres fermées; **to leave sth unsaid** passer qch sous silence; **their behaviour leaves a lot to be desired** leur conduite laisse beaucoup à désirer; **her words left me curious to know more** le peu qu'elle a dit m'a donné l'envie d'en savoir plus; **the decision leaves me in a bit of a quandary** cette décision me place devant un dilemme; **I want to be left on/off the list** je veux que mon nom reste/je ne veux pas que mon nom figure sur la liste; **I was left with the bill** c'est moi qui ai dû payer l'addition; **she had been left a widow at thirty** elle s'était retrouvée veuve à l'âge de trente ans; **the flood has left thousands homeless** les inondations ont fait des milliers de sans-abri

(**i**) *(passive use)* **to be left** *(remain)* rester; **we finished what was left of the cake** on a fini ce qui restait du gâteau; **there's nothing left** il ne reste (plus) rien; **there wasn't enough left to go round** il n'en restait pas assez pour tout le monde; **I've got £10/10 minutes left** il me reste 10 livres/10 minutes; **there's no doubt left in my mind** il n'y a plus le moindre doute dans mon esprit; **he had nothing left to do but lock up the house** il ne lui restait (plus) qu'à fermer la maison

(**j**) *(mark, trace)* laisser; **the wine left a stain** le vin a fait une tache

(**k**) *(allow)* **can I leave you to deal with it, then?** vous vous en chargez, alors?; **she leaves**

me to get on with things elle me laisse faire; **to leave sb in charge of sth** confier la responsabilité de qch à qn; **right then, I'll leave you to it** bon, eh bien, je te laisse

(**l**) *(entrust)* laisser, confier; **can I leave my suitcase with you for a few minutes?** puis-je vous confier ma valise quelques instants?; **she left the detailed arrangements to her secretary** elle a laissé à sa secrétaire le soin de régler les détails; **you should leave such tasks to a specialist** vous devriez laisser *ou* confier ce genre de travail à un spécialiste; **nothing was left to chance** on avait paré à toutes les éventualités; **I'll leave it to you to finish it off** je vous laisse (le soin de) finir; **leave it to me!** je m'en occupe!, je m'en charge!; **leave it with me** laissez-moi faire, je m'en charge

(**m**) *Br Math* **9 from 16 leaves 7** 16 moins 9 égale 7; **what does 29 from 88 leave?** 29 ôté de 88 égale combien?

(**n**) *(bequeath)* léguer; **she left all her money to charity** elle légua toute sa fortune à des œuvres de charité

(**o**) *(be survived by)* **he leaves a wife and two children** il laisse une femme et deux enfants

3 *n* (**a**) *(from work)* congé *m*; *Mil* permission *f*; **to be/to go on leave** *(gen)* être/partir en congé; *Mil* être/partir en permission

(**b**) *(permission)* permission *f*, autorisation *f*; **he asked leave to address the meeting** il a demandé la permission de prendre la parole devant l'assemblée; **by** *or* **with your leave** avec votre permission; **without so much as a by your leave** sans même en demander la permission

(**c**) *(farewell)* congé *m*; **to take one's leave (of sb)** prendre congé (de qn); **to take leave of sb** prendre congé de qn; *Fig* **to take leave of one's senses** perdre la tête *ou* la raison

►► ***leave of absence*** congé *m* (exceptionnel); *(without pay)* congé *m* sans solde; *Mil* permission *f* exceptionnelle

►**leave about, leave around** *vt sep* laisser traîner; **he leaves his stuff around everywhere** il laisse traîner ses affaires partout

►**leave aside** *vt sep* laisser de côté; **leaving aside the question of cost for the moment** si on laisse de côté pour le moment la question du coût

►**leave behind** *vt sep* (**a**) *(not take)* laisser; **it's hard to leave all your friends and relations behind** c'est dur de laisser tous ses amis et sa famille derrière soi; **they left me behind** ils sont partis sans moi

(**b**) *(forget)* laisser, oublier; **somebody left their watch behind** quelqu'un a laissé *ou* oublié sa montre

(**c**) *(leave as trace)* laisser; **the cyclone left behind a trail of destruction** le cyclone a tout détruit sur son passage

(**d**) *(outstrip)* distancer, devancer; **she soon left the other runners behind** elle a vite distancé tous les autres coureurs; **if you don't work harder you'll soon get left behind** si tu ne travailles pas plus, tu vas vite te retrouver loin derrière les autres

►**leave in** *vt sep (word, paragraph)* garder, laisser

►**leave off 1** *vi (stop)* s'arrêter; **we'll carry on from where we left off** nous allons reprendre là où nous nous étions arrêtés; *Br Fam* **leave off, will you!** arrête, tu veux!

2 *vt insep Br Fam (stop)* **to leave off doing sth** arrêter de faire qch□; **if it leaves off raining, we'll go for a walk** s'il s'arrête de pleuvoir *ou* si la pluie cesse, nous irons nous promener

3 *vt sep* (**a**) *(not put on)* ne pas remettre; **who left the top of the toothpaste off?** qui a laissé le tube de dentifrice débouché?; **you can leave your jacket off** ce n'est pas la peine de remettre ta veste

(**b**) *(not switch or turn on → tap, gas)* laisser fermé; *(→ light)* laisser éteint; *(not plug in → appliance)* laisser débranché; **we left the heating off while we were away** nous avons arrêté *ou* coupé le chauffage pendant notre absence

►**leave on** *vt sep* (**a**) *(not take off → garment)* garder; *(→ top, cover)* laisser; **don't leave the price tag on** enlève l'étiquette

(**b**) *(not switch or turn off → tap, gas)* laisser ouvert; *(→ light)* laisser allumé; *(not unplug → appliance)* laisser branché; **I hope I didn't leave the gas on** j'espère que j'ai éteint le gaz

►**leave out** *vt sep* (**a**) *(omit)* omettre; **several names have been left out** plusieurs noms ont été omis; **leave out any reference to her husband in your article** dans votre article, évitez toute allusion à son mari

(**b**) *(exclude)* exclure; **I felt completely left out at the party** j'ai eu le sentiment d'être totalement tenu à l'écart *ou* exclu de leur petite fête; **leave her out of this!** laissez-la en dehors de ça!, ne la mêlez pas à ça!

(**c**) *(not put away → by accident)* ne pas ranger; *(→ on purpose)* laisser sorti, ne pas ranger; **he left a meal out for the children** il a laissé un repas tout prêt pour les enfants; **leave the disks out where I can see them** laisse les disquettes en évidence; **who left the milk out overnight?** qui a oublié de mettre le lait au frigo hier soir?

(**d**) *(leave outdoors)* laisser dehors; **to leave the washing out to dry** mettre le linge à sécher (dehors)

(**e**) *Br Fam (idiom)* **leave it out!** arrête!

►**leave over** *vt sep (allow or cause to remain)* laisser; **to be left over** rester; **there are still one or two left over** il en reste encore un ou deux

leave² [li:v] (*pt & pp* **leaved,** *cont* **leaving**) *vi Bot (produce leaves)* feuiller

-leaved [li:vd] *suff* **three-leaved** *(screen)* à trois panneaux; **broad-leaved** feuillu; **ivy-leaved** à feuilles de lierre

leaven ['levən] **1** *n (yeast)* levain *m*; *Fig* **he brought a leaven of humour to the dullest occasion** il apportait une touche *ou* pointe d'humour dans les occasions les plus sinistres

2 *vt* (**a**) *Culin* faire lever (**b**) *Fig (occasion, atmosphere)* égayer

►► ***leavened bread*** pain *m* au levain

leavening ['levənɪŋ] *n also Fig* levain *m*

Leavenworth ['levənwɜ:θ] *n* = ville du Kansas connue pour sa prison

leaves [li:vz] *pl of* **leaf**

leave-taking *n (UNCOUNT)* adieux *mpl*

leaving ['li:vɪŋ] *n* départ *m*

►► *Ir Sch* ***Leaving Certificate*** ≃ baccalauréat *m*

leavings ['li:vɪŋz] *npl (from meal)* restes *mpl*

Lebanese [,lebə'ni:z] (*pl* **inv**) **1** *n* Libanais(e) *m,f*

2 *adj* libanais

3 *comp (embassy, history)* du Liban

Lebanon ['lebənən] *n* Liban *m*; **in (the) Lebanon** au Liban

lebensraum ['leɪbənz,raʊm] *n* espace *m* vital

lech [letʃ] *Fam* **1** *n* obsédé□ *m*

2 *vi* **stop leching!** ne prends pas ce regard lubrique!□; **he's always leching after my secretary** il n'arrête pas de reluquer ma secrétaire

lecher ['letʃə(r)] *n* débauché *m*, obsédé *m* (sexuel)

lecherous ['letʃərəs] *adj* lubrique

lecherously ['letʃərəslɪ] *adv* lubriquement, avec lubricité; **to look at sb lecherously** regarder qn d'un œil lubrique

lechery ['letʃərɪ] *n* lubricité *f*

lecithin ['lesɪθɪn] *n Chem* lécithine *f*

lectern ['lektən] *n* lutrin *m*; *(in library)* pupitre *m*, lutrin *m*

lectionary ['lekʃənərɪ] (*pl* **lectionaries**) *n Rel* lectionnaire *m*

lector ['lektə(r)] *n Rel & Univ* lecteur(trice) *m,f*

lecture ['lektʃə(r)] **1** *n* (**a**) *(talk)* conférence *f*, exposé *m*; *Univ (as part of course)* cours *m* (magistral); **she gave a very good lecture on Yeats** elle a fait un très bon cours sur Yeats; **have you been to his linguistics lectures?** avez-vous suivi ses cours de linguistique?

(**b**) *Fig (sermon)* sermon *m*, discours *m*; **I'm tired of his lectures about the virtues of healthy living** j'en ai assez de ses discours *ou* de ses sermons sur les vertus d'une vie saine; **to give sb a lecture** sermonner qn, faire des remontrances à qn; **she gave the children a lecture on how to behave** elle a donné aux enfants une leçon de bonne conduite

2 *comp (notes)* de cours

3 *vi (talk)* faire *ou* donner une conférence; *(teach)* faire (un) cours; **he lectures twice a week** il fait cours deux fois par semaine; **she lectures in linguistics** elle enseigne la *ou* donne des cours de linguistique; **she lectures on Dante** elle donne des cours sur Dante; **he lectures at Stirling** il enseigne à l'université de Stirling

4 *vt (reprimand)* réprimander, sermonner; **he's always lecturing his children about their manners** il est toujours à sermonner *ou* réprimander ses enfants sur leurs manières

►► ***lecture hall*** salle *f* de cours, amphithéâtre *m*; ***lecture room*** salle *f* de cours *ou* de conférences; ***lecture theatre*** salle *f* de cours, amphithéâtre *m*

lecturer ['lektʃərə(r)] *n (speaker)* conférencier(ère) *m,f*; *Univ (teacher)* enseignant(e) *m,f* du supérieur; **she's a lecturer in English at the University of Dublin** elle enseigne l'anglais à l'université de Dublin; **assistant lecturer** ≃ assistant(e) *m,f*; **is she a good lecturer?** est-ce que c'est un bon professeur?; **senior lecturer** ≃ maître *m* de conférences

lectureship ['lektʃəʃɪp] *n Univ* poste *m* d'enseignant dans le supérieur; **he got a lectureship at the University of Oxford** il a obtenu un poste à l'université d'Oxford; **senior lectureship** ≃ poste *m* de maître de conférences

lecturing ['lektʃərɪŋ] *n* cours *mpl*, conférences *fpl*

LED [,eli:'di:] *n Comput (abbr* **light-emitting diode**) DEL *f*, LED *f*

►► ***LED display*** affichage *m* (par) LED

led [led] *pt & pp of* **lead²**

Leda ['li:də] *pr n Myth* Léda

lederhosen ['leɪdə,həʊzən] *npl* culotte *f* de peau tyrolienne

ledge [ledʒ] *n* (**a**) *(shelf)* rebord *m* (**b**) *Geog (on mountain)* saillie *f*; *(on rock or cliff face)* corniche *f*; *(on seabed)* haut-fond *m* (**c**) *Geol (vein)* filon *m*

ledger ['ledʒə(r)] *n* (**a**) *Com & Fin* grand-livre *m*, livre *m* de comptabilité *ou* de comptes (**b**) *Tech* longrine *f*

►► *Mus* ***ledger line*** ligne *f* supplémentaire

ledger-bait *n Fishing* appât *m* de fond

ledger-line *n Fishing* ligne *f* dormante *ou* de fond

ledger-tackle *n Fishing* appareil *m* de fond

lee [li:] **1** *n* (**a**) *Naut* bord *m* sous le vent (**b**) *(shelter)* abri *m*; **in the lee of a rock** à l'abri d'un rocher

2 *adj* sous le vent

►► ***lee shore*** terre *f* sous le vent

leeboard ['li:bɔ:d] *n Naut* aile *f ou* semelle *f* de dérive

leech [li:tʃ] **1** *n also Fig* sangsue *f*; **to cling to sb like a leech** s'accrocher *ou* coller à qn comme une sangsue

2 *vt Med* saigner (avec des sangsues)

3 *vi Fam* **to leech onto sb** s'accrocher *ou* coller à qn comme une sangsue

Lee-Enfield [li:'enfi:ld] *n* = fusil utilisé par l'armée britannique pendant les deux guerres

leek [li:k] **1** *n* poireau *m*

2 *comp (soup, tart)* aux poireaux

LEEK

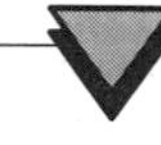

Le poireau est l'emblème national du pays de Galles. D'après la légende, saint David, patron du pays de Galles, ordonna à ses soldats d'accrocher des poireaux à leur casque lors d'une bataille contre les Saxons qui avait lieu dans un champ de poireaux. Le 1er mars, jour de la Saint-David et fête nationale du pays de Galles, certains accrochent à leur chapeau un poireau ou une jonquille, autre emblème du pays de Galles.

leer [lɪə(r)] **1** *n (malevolent)* regard *m* méchant; *(lecherous)* regard *m* concupiscent *ou* lubrique

2 *vi* **to leer at sb** *(malevolently)* regarder qn méchamment; *(lecherously)* lorgner qn

leering ['lɪərɪŋ] *adj (malevolent)* méchant; *(lecherous)* concupiscent, lubrique

leeringly ['lɪərɪŋlɪ] *adv* (**a**) *(malevolently)* avec un regard méchant (**b**) *(lecherously)* avec un regard concupiscent *ou* lubrique

leery ['lɪərɪ] (*compar* **leerier,** *superl* **leeriest**) *adj Fam* méfiant□; **to be leery of sth** se méfier de qch

lees [li:z] *npl (sediment)* lie *f*; *Fig* **to drink** *or* **to drain sth to the lees** boire qch jusqu'à la lie

leeward ['li:wəd] **1** *n* bord *m* sous le vent; *Naut* **to leeward** sous le vent

2 *adj* sous le vent

lea–lee

Leeward Islands ['liːwəd-] *npl* **the Leeward Islands** les îles *fpl* Sous-le-Vent; **in the Leeward Islands** aux îles Sous-le-Vent

leeway ['liːweɪ] *n (UNCOUNT)* (**a**) *(margin)* marge *f* (de manœuvre); **it doesn't give us much leeway** cela ne nous laisse pas une grande marge de manœuvre; **a quarter of an hour should be enough leeway** une marge de sécurité d'un quart d'heure devrait suffire (**b**) *(lost time)* retard *m*; **he has a lot of leeway to make up** il a un fort retard à rattraper (**c**) *Aviat & Naut (drift)* dérive *f*; **to make leeway** dériver (à la voile)

left¹ [left] *pt & pp of* **leave**

left² [left] **1** *n* (**a**) *(gen)* gauche *f*; **on the left** sur la gauche, à gauche; **to drive on the left** rouler à gauche; **the building on the left** le bâtiment de gauche; **on your left** à *ou* sur votre gauche; **it's to the left of the fireplace** c'est à gauche de la cheminée; **it's to** *or* **on the left of the picture** *(in the picture)* c'est sur la gauche du tableau; *(next to the picture)* c'est à gauche du tableau; **move a bit to the left** déplacez-vous un peu vers la gauche; **to keep to the left** tenir sa gauche; **the second figure from the left** le deuxième chiffre en partant de la gauche; **he doesn't know his left from his right** il ne reconnaît pas sa droite de sa gauche

(**b**) *Pol* gauche *f*; **the far** *or* **extreme left** l'extrême gauche; **the parties of the left** les partis de (la) gauche; **she is further to the left than her husband** elle est (politiquement) plus à gauche que son mari

(**c**) *(in boxing)* gauche *m*; **he knocked him out with a left to the chin** il l'a étendu d'un gauche au menton

2 *adj (foot, eye)* gauche; **on the left side** sur la gauche, du côté gauche; **I always sleep on my left side** je dors toujours sur le côté gauche; **with her left hand** de la main gauche; *Aut* **left hand down a bit!** braquez un peu à gauche!; **to make a left turn** tourner à gauche; **take the left fork** prenez à gauche à l'embranchement; *Fam* **to be way out in left field** être complètement excentrique ❑; *Fam* **it came out of left field** *(of comment, question)* c'est tombé comme un cheveu sur la soupe

3 *adv* (**a**) *(gen)* à gauche; **turn left at the junction** tournez *ou* prenez à gauche au croisement; *Mil* **eyes left!** tête à gauche!; *Mil* **left turn!** à gauche! gauche!; **left, right and centre** *(in, from all directions)* de tous les côtés; *Typ* **left justified** justifié à gauche

(**b**) *Pol* à gauche; **to vote left** voter à gauche

►► *Comput* ***left arrow*** flèche *f* vers la gauche; *Comput* ***left arrow key*** touche *f* de déplacement vers la gauche; ***the Left Bank*** *(in Paris)* la rive gauche; *Sport* ***left back*** arrière *m* gauche; *Sport* ***left half*** demi *m* gauche; *Br* ***left luggage*** *(UNCOUNT) (cases)* bagages *mpl* en consigne; *(office)* consigne *f*; ***left margin*** marge *f* de gauche; *TV & Cin* ***left pan*** panoramique *m* horizontal DG; ***left wing*** *Pol* gauche *f*; *Sport (position)* aile *f* gauche; *(player)* ailier *m* gauche; **the left wing of the party** l'aile *f* gauche du parti

left-click *Comput* **1** *vt* cliquer avec le bouton gauche de la souris sur

2 *vi* cliquer avec le bouton gauche de la souris (**on** sur)

left-footed [-'fʊtɪd] *adj* qui se sert de son pied gauche

left-footer *n* (**a**) *Sport* joueur(euse) *m,f* qui joue du pied gauche (**b**) *Br Fam Pej (Catholic)* catholique ❑ *mf*, catho *mf*

left-hand *adj* (**a**) *(gen)* gauche; **a left-hand bend** un virage à gauche; **on the left-hand side** à gauche, sur la gauche; **on my left-hand side, the Grand Palace** à *ou* sur ma gauche, le Grand Palais (**b**) *Tech (lock, screw, drill)* à gauche

►► ***left-hand drive*** conduite *f* à gauche; **my car is a left-hand drive** ma voiture a le volant à gauche; *Tech* ***left-hand thread*** filetage *m* à gauche

left-handed **1** *adj* (**a**) *(person)* gaucher; **she's left-handed** elle est gauchère (**b**) *(scissors, instrument, golf club)* pour gauchers (**c**) *(blow, punch, shot)* de la main gauche

2 *adv* de la main gauche

►► *Am* ***a left-handed compliment*** un faux compliment

left-handedness [-'hændɪdnɪs] *n* gaucherie *f*, latéralité *f* de gauche; **do you find left-handedness a problem?** est-ce qu'être gaucher vous pose des problèmes?

left-hander *n (person)* gaucher(ère) *m,f*; *(blow)* coup *m* (donné de la main gauche)

leftie = **lefty**

leftism ['leftɪzəm] *n (gen)* idées *fpl* de gauche; *(extreme left)* gauchisme *m*

leftist ['leftɪst] **1** *n (gen → man)* homme *m* de gauche; *(→ woman)* femme *f* de gauche; *(extreme left-winger)* gauchiste *mf*

2 *adj (gen)* de gauche; *(extremely left-wing)* gauchiste

left-luggage *adj*

►► *Br* ***the left-luggage lockers*** la consigne automatique; *Br* ***left-luggage office*** consigne *f*

left-of-centre *adj Pol* de centre gauche; **his views are slightly left-of-centre** ses opinions sont plutôt de centre gauche

leftover ['leftəʊvə(r)] **1** *adj (food, material)* qui reste; *(stock)* en surplus; **she used the leftover wool to knit a scarf** elle a tricoté une écharpe avec la laine qui restait; **there was some leftover chicken** il restait du poulet

2 *n (throwback, vestige)* vestige *m*; **the gun is a leftover from the war** le fusil est un souvenir de la guerre

leftovers ['leftəʊvəz] *npl (food)* restes *mpl*

leftward ['leftwəd] **1** *adj* de gauche

2 *adv Am* à gauche

leftwards ['leftwədz] *adv* à gauche

left-wing *adj Pol* de gauche; **a left-wing publication** une publication de gauche; **she's very left-wing** elle est très à gauche; **he has slightly left-wing ideas** il a des idées gauchisantes

left-winger *n* (**a**) *Pol (man)* homme *m* de gauche; *(woman)* femme *f* de gauche (**b**) *Sport* ailier *m* gauche

lefty ['leftɪ] (*pl* **lefties**) *n Fam* (**a**) *Pej Pol (man)* homme *m* de gauche ❑; *(woman)* femme *f* de gauche ❑ (**b**) *Am (left-handed person)* gaucher(ère) ❑ *m,f*

leg [leg] (*pt & pp* **legged**, *cont* **legging**) **1** *n* (**a**) *Anat (of human, horse)* jambe *f*; *(of smaller animals and birds)* patte *f*; **his legs went from under him** ses jambes se sont dérobées sous lui; *Fig* **you don't have a leg to stand on** vos arguments ne tiennent pas debout; **you won't have a leg to stand on if they find this letter** s'ils trouvent cette lettre, vous êtes fichu; *very Fam* **to get one's leg over** s'envoyer en l'air; *Fam* **to pull sb's leg** faire marcher qn

(**b**) *Culin (of lamb)* gigot *m*; *(of pork)* jambon *m*; *(of chicken)* cuisse *f*; **frog's legs** cuisses *fpl* de grenouille

(**c**) *(of chair, table)* pied *m*; *(of compasses)* branche *f*; *(of tripod)* jambe *f*; *(of trestle)* montant *m*

(**d**) *(of trousers, pyjamas, stockings)* jambe *f*; **these trousers are a bit short in the leg** ce pantalon est un peu court au niveau des jambes

(**e**) *(stage → of journey)* étape *f*; *(→ of competition)* manche *f*; *(→ in relay race)* relais *m*; *Sport* **they won the first/second leg** ils ont gagné le match aller/retour

(**f**) *Sport* **leg (side)** *(when the batsman is right-handed)* côté *m* gauche du terrain; *(when the batsman is left-handed)* côté *m* droit du terrain; **leg before wicket** = au cricket, faute d'un joueur qui intercepte avec sa jambe une balle qui allait frapper le guichet

2 *vt Fam* **to leg it** *(run)* courir; *(walk)* aller à pied; *(flee)* se sauver, se tirer

►► *Med* ***leg iron*** appareil *m* orthopédique; ***leg rest*** appui-jambes *m inv*; *Med* étrier *m*; *Fam* ***leg show*** revue *f* légère ❑

legacy ['legəsɪ] (*pl* **legacies**) *n* (**a**) *Law* legs *m*; **to leave sb a legacy** faire un legs *ou* laisser un héritage à qn; **to come into a legacy** faire un héritage; **the money is a legacy from my aunt** j'ai hérité cet argent de ma tante, ma tante m'a légué cet argent

(**b**) *Fig* héritage *m*; **this desk is a legacy from my predecessor** j'ai hérité ce bureau de mon prédécesseur; **the legacy of the war was a divided Europe** l'héritage de la guerre fut une Europe divisée; **the crisis left a legacy of bitterness** la crise a créé un climat d'amertume

legal ['liːgəl] **1** *adj* (**a**) *(lawful)* légal; *(legitimate)* légal, légitime; **to make sth legal** légaliser qch; **to have a legal claim to sth** avoir légalement droit à qch; **they're below the legal age** ils n'ont pas atteint l'âge légal; **to be above the legal limit** *(for drinking)* dépasser le taux légal (d'alcoolémie); **legal, decent, honest, truthful** = devise de la "Advertising Standards Authority"

(**b**) *(judicial → mind, matter, question)* juridique; *(→ power, investigation, error)* judiciaire; **to take legal action** engager des poursuites judiciaires, intenter un procès; **to take legal advice** consulter un juriste *ou* un avocat; **this is the legal procedure** c'est la procédure à suivre; **by legal process** par voies légales, par voies de droit; **he's a member of the legal profession** c'est un homme de loi

(**c**) *Comput (character, symbol)* autorisé

(**d**) *Am (paper format)* légal *(216 mm × 356 mm)*

2 *n Am (paper size)* légal *m (216 mm × 356 mm)*

►► ***legal action*** action *f* en justice; **to take legal action (against sb)** intenter une action (en justice) (contre qn); ***legal adviser*** conseil *m* juridique; ***legal aid*** aide *f* juridique; *Fin* ***legal currency*** monnaie *f* courante; ***legal department*** *(in bank, company)* (service *m* du) contentieux *m*; ***legal dispute*** litige *m*; ***legal document*** acte *m* authentique; *Fam Hum* ***legal eagle*** jeune avocat(e) *m,f* dynamique ❑; ***legal entity*** personne *f* morale; ***legal executive*** assistant(e) *m,f (d'un avocat)*; *Am* ***legal holiday*** jour *m* férié, fête *f* légale; ***legal manager*** responsable *mf* juridique; ***legal medicine*** médecine *f* légale; ***legal owner*** propriétaire *mf* légitime; *Am* ***legal pad*** bloc-notes *m*; ***legal proceedings*** poursuites *fpl* judiciaires; **to initiate legal proceedings against sb** engager des poursuites judiciaires contre qn; ***legal secretary*** secrétaire *mf* juridique; *Law* ***legal separation*** séparation *f* de corps; ***legal status*** statut *m* légal, statut *m* juridique; ***legal system*** système *m* juridique; ***legal technicality*** vice *m* de forme; ***legal tender*** cours *m* légal; **to be legal tender** avoir cours (légal); **these coins are no longer legal tender** ces pièces n'ont plus cours *ou* ont été démonétisées

legalese [,liːgə'liːz] *n Pej* jargon *m* juridique

legalism ['liːgə,lɪzəm] *n* (**a**) *(strict respect of law)* légalisme *m* (**b**) *(technicality)* argutie *f* juridique

legalist ['liːgəlɪst] *n* légaliste *mf*

legalistic [,liːgə'lɪstɪk] *adj* légaliste, formaliste

legalistically [,liːgə'lɪstɪklɪ] *adv* avec légalisme, de façon légaliste

legality [liː'gælətɪ] *n* légalité *f*

legalization [,liːgəlaɪ'zeɪʃən] *n* légalisation *f*

legalize, -ise ['liːgəlaɪz] *vt* légaliser, rendre légal

legally ['liːgəlɪ] *adv* légalement; **to act legally** agir légalement *ou* dans la légalité; **to be legally binding** avoir force de loi, être juridiquement contraignant; **to be held legally responsible for sth** être tenu légalement *ou* juridiquement responsable de qch; **legally you're not responsible** légalement *ou* du point de vue légal, vous n'êtes pas responsable; **they were not legally married** ils vivaient maritalement

legal-tender value *n Fin* valeur *f* numéraire

legate ['legɪt] *n Rel* légat *m*; *(gen)* messager(ère) *m,f*

legatee [,legə'tiː] *n* légataire *mf*

legation [lɪ'geɪʃən] *n* légation *f*

legato [lɪ'gɑːtəʊ] *Mus* **1** *n* legato *m*

2 *adv* legato

legator [lɪ'geɪtə(r)] *n* testateur(trice) *m,f*

legend ['ledʒənd] *n* (**a**) *(myth)* légende *f*; **she became a legend in her own lifetime** elle est entrée dans la légende de son vivant (**b**) *(inscription)* légende *f*

legendary ['ledʒəndrɪ] *adj* légendaire

legerdemain [,ledʒədə'meɪn] *n (UNCOUNT) (conjuring)* (tours *mpl* de) prestidigitation *f*; *(cunning)* tours *mpl* de passe-passe

-legged ['legɪd, legd] *suff* **short-/bare-legged** aux jambes courtes/nues

leggings ['legɪŋz] *npl* caleçon *m* long

leggo [le'gəʊ] *exclam Fam* = **let go**

leggy ['legɪ] (*compar* **leggier**, *superl* **leggiest**) *adj (person)* tout en jambes; *(colt, young animal)* haut sur pattes

Leghorn [,leg'hɔːn] *n* Livourne

legibility [ˌledʒɪˈbɪlətɪ] *n* lisibilité *f*

legible [ˈledʒəbəl] *adj* lisible

legibly [ˈledʒəblɪ] *adv* lisiblement

legion [ˈliːdʒən] **1** *n Mil & Fig* légion *f*

2 *adj Formal* légion *(inv)*; **their name is legion** ils sont légion; **the difficulties were legion** les difficultés étaient innombrables

legionary [ˈliːdʒənərɪ] (*pl* **legionaries**) **1** *n* légionnaire *m*

2 *adj* de la légion

legionella pneumophilia [ˌliːdʒəˈneləˌnjuːməʊˈfɪlɪə] *n Biol* légionelle *f*

legionnaire [ˌliːdʒəˈneə(r)] *n* légionnaire *m*

▸▸ ***legionnaire's disease*** maladie *f* du légionnaire

legislate [ˈledʒɪsleɪt] *vi* légiférer; **to legislate in favour of/against sth** légiférer en faveur de/contre qch; **we can't legislate for all possible situations** nous ne pouvons pas prévoir des lois pour tous les cas de figure possibles; **child labour had been legislated out of existence by 1900** grâce à la législation, le travail des enfants fut interdit à partir de 1900

legislation [ˌledʒɪsˈleɪʃən] *n* législation *f*; **the legislation on immigration** la législation sur l'immigration; **a piece of legislation** une loi; **to bring in legislation in favour of/against sth** légiférer en faveur de/contre qch

legislative [ˈledʒɪslətɪv] *adj* législatif

▸▸ ***legislative assembly*** assemblée *f* législative; ***the Legislative Assembly*** *(in Ireland, Australia, India, Canada)* l'Assemblée *f* législative; ***legislative council*** conseil *m* législatif; ***the Legislative Council*** *(in Australia, India)* le Conseil législatif; ***legislative power*** pouvoir *m* législatif

legislator [ˈledʒɪsˌleɪtə(r)] *n* législateur(trice) *m,f*

legislature [ˈledʒɪsˌleɪtʃə(r)] *n* (corps *m*) législatif *m*

legit [ləˈdʒɪt] *adj Fam* réglo

legitimacy [lɪˈdʒɪtɪməsɪ] *n* légitimité *f*

legitimate 1 *adj* [lɪˈdʒɪtɪmət] (**a**) *(legal, lawful)* légitime; **legitimate child** enfant *mf* légitime (**b**) *(valid)* légitime, valable; **his criticisms are perfectly legitimate** ses critiques sont parfaitement légitimes *ou* fondées; **it would be perfectly legitimate to ask them to pay** on serait tout à fait en droit d'exiger qu'ils paient (**c**) *(theatre)* sérieux

2 *vt* [lɪˈdʒɪtɪmeɪt] légitimer

legitimately [lɪˈdʒɪtɪmətlɪ] *adv* (**a**) *(legally, lawfully)* légitimement; **both legitimately and effectively** de droit comme de fait (**b**) *(justifiably)* légitimement, avec raison; **it could legitimately be argued that...** on peut soutenir, non sans raison, que...

legitimatize, -ise [lɪˈdʒɪtɪməˌtaɪz] *vt* légitimer

legitimism [lɪˈdʒɪtɪmɪzəm] *n* légitimisme *m*

legitimize, -ise [lɪˈdʒɪtɪˌmaɪz] *vt* légitimer

legless [ˈleglɪs] *adj* (**a**) *(without legs)* cul-de-jatte (**b**) *Br Fam (drunk)* bourré, pété

legman [ˈlegmæn] (*pl* **legmen** [-mən]) *n Am* (**a**) *Journ* = reporter qui fait la chronique des chiens écrasés (**b**) *(errand boy etc)* factotum *m*

leg-of-mutton *adj*

▸▸ ***leg-of-mutton sleeves*** manches *fpl* gigot

leg-pull *n Fam* canular ❑ *m*, farce ❑ *f*; **it was only a leg-pull!** on te faisait marcher!

leg-puller [-ˌpʊlə(r)] *n Fam* blagueur(euse) ❑ *m,f*, farceur(euse) ❑ *m,f*

leg-pulling *n (UNCOUNT) Fam* blagues ❑ *fpl*, mise *f* en boîte; **he got a lot of leg-pulling about his marriage** on l'a beaucoup charrié sur son mariage

legroom [ˈlegrʊm] *n* place *f* pour les jambes; **these little cars don't give you any legroom** dans ces petites voitures, on n'a aucune place pour les jambes

legume [leˈgjuːm] *n* légumineuse *f*

leguminous [leˈgjuːmɪnəs] *adj* légumineux

leg-up *n* **to give sb a leg-up** faire la courte échelle à qn; *Fig* donner un coup de main *ou* de pouce à qn

legwarmers [ˈlegˌwɔːməz] *npl* jambières *fpl*

legwork [ˈlegwɜːk] *n Fam* **who's going to do the legwork?** qui va se taper la marche?; **there's a lot of legwork in this job** c'est un travail où l'on marche beaucoup

lei [leɪ] *n* collier *m* de fleurs

Leibnitzian, Leibnizian [laɪbˈnɪtsɪən] *Phil* **1** *n* leibnizien(enne) *m,f*

2 *adj* leibnizien

Leicester [ˈlestə(r)] *n* (**a**) *(city)* Leicester (**b**) *(cheese)* leicester *m* (**c**) *(sheep)* dishley *m*

▸▸ ***Leicester Square*** = place populaire de Londres connue pour ses grands cinémas

Leicestershire [ˈlestəˌʃɪə(r)] *n* le Leicestershire, = comté dans le centre de l'Angleterre; **in Leicestershire** dans le Leicestershire

Leics *(written abbr* **Leicestershire***)* Leicestershire *m*

Leipzig [ˈlaɪpzɪg] *n* Leipzig

leishmania [liːʃˈmeɪnɪə] *n Zool* leishmanie *f*

leishmaniasis [ˌliːʃməˈnaɪəsɪs] *n Med* leishmaniose *f*; **visceral leishmaniasis** kala-azar *m*; **post-kala-azar dermal leishmaniasis** leishmanide *f*

leisure [*Br* ˈleʒə(r), *Am* ˈliːʒər] **1** *n (UNCOUNT)* (**a**) *(spare time)* loisir *m*, loisirs *mpl*, temps *m* libre; **during my leisure (time)** pendant mes loisirs, à mes heures perdues; **to be at leisure to do sth** avoir (tout) le loisir de faire qch; **to do sth at one's leisure** faire qch à loisir *ou* dans ses moments de loisir; **I'll read it at (my) leisure** je le lirai à tête reposée

(**b**) *(relaxation)* loisir *m*; **to lead a life of leisure** mener une vie oisive; **he's a man of leisure** il mène une vie de rentier

2 *comp (activity, clothes)* de loisir *ou* loisirs

▸▸ ***leisure break*** court séjour *m* de détente; ***leisure centre*** centre *m* de loisirs; ***leisure club*** club *m* de loisirs; ***leisure hours*** heures *fpl* de loisir; ***leisure industry*** industrie *f* des loisirs; ***leisure market*** marché *m* des loisirs; ***leisure time*** temps *m* libre; ***leisure tourism*** tourisme *m* de loisir, tourisme *m* ludique

leisured [*Br* ˈleʒəd, *Am* ˈliːʒərd] *adj* oisif, qui mène une vie oisive

leisureliness [*Br* ˈleʒəlɪnɪs, *Am* ˈliːʒərlɪnɪs] *n (of pace)* caractère *m* mesuré; *(of weekend)* caractère *m* détendu; **the leisureliness of sea travel** la détente apportée par une croisière

leisurely [*Br* ˈleʒəlɪ, *Am* ˈliːʒərlɪ] **1** *adj (gesture)* mesuré, nonchalant; *(lifestyle)* paisible, indolent; **to do sth in a leisurely fashion** faire qch sans se presser; **we went for a leisurely stroll through the park** nous sommes allés faire une petite balade dans le parc; **they moved with a leisurely grace** ils se déplaçaient avec grâce et lenteur; **at a leisurely pace** sans se presser; **he spoke in a leisurely way** il parlait en prenant son temps

2 *adv (calmly)* paisiblement, tranquillement; *(unhurriedly)* sans se presser

leisurewear [*Br* ˈleʒəweə(r), *Am* ˈliːʒəweər] *n* vêtements *mpl* décontractés

leitmotiv, leitmotif [ˈlaɪtməʊˌtiːf] *n (gen) & Mus* leitmotiv *m*

Leitrim [ˈliːtrɪm] *n* le comté de Leitrim, = comté dans le nord de la République d'Irlande; **in Leitrim** dans le comté de Leitrim

Leix [liːʃ] *n* le comté de Leix, = comté dans le centre de la République d'Irlande; **in Leix** dans le comté de Leix

lek[1] [lek] *n Orn* arène *f*, lek *m*

lek[2] *n (unit of currency)* lek *m*

LEM [lem] *n Astron (abbr* **lunar excursion module***)* module *m* lunaire

lemma [ˈlemə] (*pl* **lemmas** *or* **lemmata** [-mətə]) *n Ling* lemme *m*

lemmatize, -ise [ˈlemətaɪz] *vt Ling* lemmatiser

lemme [ˈlemɪ] *exclam Fam* = **let me**

lemming [ˈlemɪŋ] *n Zool* lemming *m*; *Fig* mouton *m*

lemon [ˈlemən] **1** *n* (**a**) *(fruit)* citron *m*; *(tree)* citronnier *m*

(**b**) *(colour)* jaune citron *m inv*

(**c**) *Br Fam (awkward person)* idiot(e) *m,f*; **I'm going to look a right lemon** je vais avoir l'air plutôt débile

(**d**) *Fam (useless object)* **it's a lemon** c'est de la camelote; **she got sold a lemon** elle s'est fait rouler

(**e**) *Am Fam (useless car)* = voiture de mauvaise qualité

2 *adj (colour)* (jaune) citron *(inv)*; *(flavour)* citron *(inv)*

3 *comp (ice-cream, tart)* au citron

▸▸ *Bot* ***lemon balm*** mélisse *f*, citronnelle *f*; ***lemon cheese, lemon curd*** lemon curd *m*, crème *f* au citron; ***lemon drop*** bonbon *m* au citron; ***lemon grass*** citronnelle *f*, lemon-grass *m*; ***lemon juice*** jus *m* de citron; *(lemon squash)* citronnade *f*; *(freshly squeezed)* citron *m* pressé; *Am* ***lemon juicer*** presse-citron *m*; *Am Fam* ***lemon law*** = loi qui oblige les constructeurs automobiles à rembourser ou à remplacer les pièces défectueuses; ***lemon meringue pie*** tarte *f* au citron meringuée; ***lemon sole*** limande-sole *f*; ***lemon squash*** citronnade *f*, sirop *m* de citron; *Br* ***lemon squeezer*** presse-citron *m*; ***lemon tea*** thé *m* au citron; ***lemon thyme*** thym *m* citronné; ***lemon verbena*** verveine *f* citronnelle; ***lemon zest*** zeste *m* de citron; ***lemon zester*** zesteur *m*

lemonade [ˌleməˈneɪd] *n (freshly squeezed)* citron *m* pressé; *Br (carbonated)* limonade *f*

lemony [ˈlemənɪ] *adj (smell, taste)* citronné

lemur [ˈliːmə(r)] *n Zool* lémur *m*; *(ring-tailed)* maki *m*

lend [lend] (*pt & pp* **lent** [lent]) **1** *vt* (**a**) *(money, object)* prêter; **to lend sth to sb, to lend sb sth** prêter qch à qn; **to lend money at interest** prêter de l'argent à intérêt; **to lend money against security** prêter de l'argent sur titres

(**b**) *(contribute)* apporter, conférer; **to lend credibility/drama to a story** rendre une histoire crédible/dramatique; **her presence lent glamour to the occasion** sa présence a conféré un certain éclat à l'événement; **the bright uniforms lent colour to the ceremony** les uniformes éclatants apportaient une touche de couleur à la cérémonie; **distance lends enchantment to the view** tout paraît beau (vu) de loin

(**c**) *(give → support)* apporter; *(→ name)* prêter; **to lend sb a hand** donner un coup de main à qn; **you can't expect me to lend my name to such an enterprise** ne comptez pas sur moi pour prêter mon nom à *ou* cautionner cette affaire; *Fig* **to lend an ear** prêter l'oreille

(**d**) *(adapt → to circumstances, interpretation)* **the novel doesn't lend itself to being filmed** le roman ne se prête pas à une adaptation cinématographique; **his voice really lends itself to reading aloud** sa voix se prête très bien à la lecture à voix haute

2 *n Br Fam* **can I have a lend of your book?** tu peux me prêter ton livre? ❑

3 *vi Fin* prêter; **to lend at 12 percent** prêter à 12 pour cent

lender [ˈlendə(r)] *n* prêteur(euse) *m,f*; *Fin (institution)* organisme *m* de crédit; **lender of last resort** prêteur *m* en dernier ressort

lending [ˈlendɪŋ] *n* prêt *m*; **bank lending has increased** le volume des prêts bancaires a augmenté

▸▸ *Fin* ***lending bank*** banque *f* de crédit; *Fin* ***lending banker*** banquier *m* prêteur; ***lending country*** pays *m* créancier; ***lending library*** bibliothèque *f* de prêt; *Fin* ***lending limit*** plafond *m* de crédit; ***lending policy*** *(of bank, country)* politique *f* de prêt; *Fin* ***lending rate*** taux *m* de prêt

lend-lease *n (UNCOUNT) Econ & Hist* prêt-bail *m*

length [leŋθ] **1** *n* (**a**) *(measurement, distance)* longueur *f*; **what length is the room?** quelle est la longueur de la pièce?; **the room is 20 metres in length** la pièce fait 20 mètres de long *ou* de longueur; **a river 200 kilometres in length** un fleuve long de 200 kilomètres; **we walked the length of the garden** nous sommes allés jusqu'au bout du jardin; **flower beds ran the length of the street** il y avait des massifs de fleurs tout le long de la rue; *Br* **the ship can turn in its own length** le navire peut virer sur place; **throughout the length and breadth of the continent** partout sur le continent; **what length skirts are in this year?** *(in fashion)* quelle est la longueur des jupes cette année?

(**b**) *(effort)* **to go to considerable** *or* **great lengths to do sth** se donner beaucoup de mal pour faire qch; **he would go to any lengths to meet her** il ferait n'importe quoi pour la rencontrer; **I never dreamed that they would go to such lengths** je n'aurais jamais imaginé qu'ils iraient si loin

(**c**) *(duration)* durée *f*, longueur *f*; **the length of time required to do sth** le temps qu'il faut pour faire qch; **the wine is kept in casks for a great**

length of time le vin séjourne très longtemps dans des fûts; **bonuses are given for length of service** les primes sont accordées selon l'ancienneté
(**d**) *(of text)* longueur *f*; **articles must be less than 5,000 words in length** les articles doivent faire moins de 5 000 mots; **his essay was a bit over/under length** sa dissertation était un peu trop longue/courte
(**e**) *Sport (in racing, rowing)* longueur *f*; *(in swimming)* longueur *f* (de bassin); **to win by a length/by half a length** gagner d'une longueur/d'une demi-longueur; **to have a three-length lead** avoir trois longueurs d'avance; **I swam ten lengths** j'ai fait dix longueurs
(**f**) *(piece → of string, tubing)* morceau *m*, bout *m*; *(→ of wood)* morceau *m*; *(→ of wallpaper)* lé *m*; *(→ of fabric)* pièce *f*; **a length of curtain material** une pièce de tissu pour faire des rideaux; **what length of material do I need to make these curtains?** quel métrage faut-il pour faire ces rideaux?
(**g**) *Ling (of syllable, vowel)* longueur *f*
(**h**) *Sport* longueur *f* de balle
(**i**) *Br Vulg* **to slip sb a length** *(have sex with)* glisser un bout à qn, tringler qn
2 at length *adv (finally)* finalement, enfin; *(in detail, for a long time)* longuement; **she went on** *or* **spoke at some length about her experience** elle a parlé assez longuement de son expérience

-length [leŋθ] *suff* à hauteur de; **knee-length socks** chaussettes *fpl* (montantes), mi-bas *mpl*

lengthen ['leŋθən] **1** *vt (garment)* allonger, rallonger; *(holiday, visit)* prolonger; *Ling (vowel)* allonger
2 *vi (shadow)* s'allonger; *(day)* rallonger; *(holiday, visit)* se prolonger

lengthening ['leŋθənɪŋ] *n (of garment, vowel)* allongement *m*; *(of holiday, visit)* prolongement *m*

lengthily ['leŋθɪlɪ] *adv* longuement

lengthiness ['leŋθɪnɪs] *n* longueur *f*

lengthways ['leŋθweɪz], **lengthwise** ['leŋθwaɪz] **1** *adj* en longueur, longitudinal
2 *adv* dans le sens de la longueur, longitudinalement

lengthy ['leŋθɪ] (*compar* **lengthier**, *superl* **lengthiest**) *adj* (très) long (longue); **after a lengthy wait** après avoir attendu très longtemps, après une attente interminable; **his speech was a bit lengthy** son discours n'en finissait plus

leniency ['li:njənsɪ] *n* clémence *f*, indulgence *f*

lenient ['li:njənt] *adj (jury, sentence)* clément; *(attitude, parent)* indulgent; **his parents are too lenient with him** ses parents sont trop indulgents avec lui; **you shouldn't be so lenient with them** vous devriez être plus strict avec eux

leniently ['li:njəntlɪ] *adv* avec clémence *ou* indulgence; **the magistrate had treated him leniently** le magistrat s'était montré indulgent *ou* avait fait preuve d'indulgence à son égard

Lenin ['lenɪn] *pr n* Lénine

Leningrad ['lenɪngræd] *n* Leningrad

Leninism ['lenɪnɪzəm] *n* léninisme *m*

Leninist ['lenɪnɪst] **1** *n* léniniste *mf*
2 *adj* léniniste

lenis ['li:nɪs] (*pl* **lenes** [-ni:z]) *Ling* **1** *n* consonne *f* douce
2 *adj* doux (douce)

lenitive ['lenɪtɪv] **1** *n* lénitif *m*
2 *adj* lénitif

lenity ['lenətɪ] (*pl* **lenities**) *n Literary* clémence *f*

leno ['li:nəʊ] *n Tex* toile *f* à patron

lens [lenz] *n* (**a**) *Opt (in microscope, telescope)* lentille *f*; *(in spectacles)* verre *m*; *(in camera)* objectif *m*; *(contact lens)* lentille *f ou* verre *m* (de contact) (**b**) *Anat (in eye)* cristallin *m*
►► ***lens attachment*** accessoire *m* d'objectif; ***lens cap*** bouchon *m* d'objectif; ***lens cleaning fluid*** produit *m* de nettoyage pour lentilles; ***lens holder*** étui *m* à objectif; ***lens hood*** pare-soleil *m inv*; ***lens paper*** papier *m* pour surfaces optiques

lensman ['lenzmən] (*pl* **lensmen** [-mən]) *n Fam (photographer)* photographe ❑ *m*; *(cameraman)* cameraman ❑ *m*, cadreur ❑ *m*

Lent [lent] *n Rel* le carême; **to keep Lent** faire carême, observer le carême; **I've given up sugar for Lent** j'ai renoncé au sucre pour le carême
►► *Br Univ* ***Lent term*** deuxième trimestre *m (de janvier à Pâques)*

lent [lent] *pt & pp of* **lend**

Lenten ['lentən] *adj* de carême

lentic ['lentɪk] *adj* lénitique, lentique

lenticel ['lentɪsəl] *n Bot* lenticelle *f*

lenticle ['lentɪkəl] *n Geol* amas *m* lenticulaire, lentille *f*

lenticular [len'tɪkjʊlə(r)] *adj* lenticulaire, lenticulé

lentigo [len'taɪgəʊ] *n Med* lentigine *f*, lentigo *m*

lentil ['lentɪl] **1** *Bot & Culin n* lentille *f*
2 *comp (soup)* aux lentilles

lentisk ['lentɪsk] *n Bot* lentisque *m*

lentivirus ['lentɪvaɪrəs] *n* lentivirus *m*

lento ['lentəʊ] *Mus* **1** *n* lento *m*
2 *adj* lento
3 *adv* lento

Leo ['li:əʊ] **1** *n* (**a**) *Astron* Lion *m* (**b**) *Astrol* Lion *m*; **he's a Leo** il est (du signe du) Lion
2 *adj Astrol* du Lion; **he's Leo** il est (du signe du) Lion

Leon [leɪ'ɒn] *n Geog* Léon *m*

Leonardo da Vinci [ˌli:ə'nɑ:dəʊdə'vɪntʃɪ] *pr n* Léonard de Vinci

leone [lɪ'əʊn] *n (unit of currency)* leone *m*

leonine ['li:ənaɪn] *adj Literary* de lion, léonin

leopard ['lepəd] *n* léopard *m*; *Prov* **a leopard can't change its spots** chassez le naturel, il revient au galop
►► *Bot* ***leopard's bane*** doronic *m*; *Entom* ***leopard moth*** zeuzère *f*; *Zool* ***leopard seal*** léopard *m* de mer; ***leopard skin*** **1** *n* peau *f* de léopard **2** *comp (coat, rug)* en (peau de) léopard

leopardess ['lepədɪs] *n* léopard *m* femelle

Leopold ['lɪəpəʊld] *pr n (emperor)* Léopold

leotard ['li:ətɑ:d] *n* body *m (pour le sport)*

LEP [ˌeli:'pi:] *n* (**a**) *Am* (*abbr* **Limited English Proficiency**) = niveau d'expression moyen en anglais (**b**) (*abbr* **Large Electon-Positron Collider**) LEP *m*

Lepanto [lɪ'pæntəʊ] *n Hist* Lépante

leper ['lepə(r)] *n* lépreux(euse) *m,f*; *Fig* pestiféré(e) *m,f*
►► ***leper colony*** léproserie *f*

Lepidoptera [ˌlepɪ'dɒptərə] *npl* lépidoptères *mpl*

lepidopteran [ˌlepɪ'dɒptərən] (*pl* **lepidopterans** *or* **lepidoptera** [-rə]) **1** *n* lépidoptère *m*
2 *adj* lépidoptère

lepidopterist [ˌlepɪ'dɒptərɪst] *n* lépidoptériste *mf*

lepidopterous [ˌlepɪ'dɒptərəs] *adj* lépidoptère

leporine ['lepəˌreɪn] *adj* du lièvre

leprechaun ['leprəkɔ:n] *n* lutin *m*

leprosarium [ˌleprə'seərɪəm] (*pl* **leprosaria** [-rɪə]) *n* léproserie *f*

leprosy ['leprəsɪ] *n* lèpre *f*; **to have leprosy** avoir la lèpre

leprous ['leprəs] *adj* lépreux

leptin ['leptɪn] *n Biol* leptine *f*

leptokurtic [ˌleptəʊ'kɜ:tɪk] *adj* leptocurtique

lepton ['leptɒn] *n Phys* lepton *m*

leptosome ['leptəʊˌsəʊm] **1** *n* leptosome *mf*
2 *adj* leptosome

leptospirosis [ˌleptəʊspaɪ'rəʊsɪs] *n Med* leptospirose *f*

leptotene ['leptəʊˌti:n] *n Biol* leptotène *m*

Lermontov ['leəmɒntɒf] *pr n* Lermontov

Lerwick ['lɜ:wɪk] *n* Lerwick

lesbian ['lezbɪən] **1** *n* lesbienne *f*
2 *adj* lesbien

lesbianism ['lezbɪənɪzəm] *n* lesbianisme *m*

lesbo ['lezbəʊ] *n very Fam* gouine *f*, = terme injurieux désignant une lesbienne

lese-majesty [ˌli:z-] *n* (crime *m* de) lèse-majesté *f inv*

lesion ['li:ʒən] *n* lésion *f*

Lesotho [lə'su:tu:] *n* Lesotho *m*; **in Lesotho** au Lesotho

LESS [les]

moins de	►1; 7 1
moins	►2; 3 (a)
de moins en moins	►5
encore moins	►6
moins que	►7 2
rien de moins	►8 (b)
pas moins de	►9

1 *adj (compar of* **little***)* moins de; **less money/time/bread** moins d'argent/de temps/de pain; **we have less time than we thought** nous avons moins de temps que nous ne pensions; **of less importance/value** de moindre importance/valeur
2 *pron (compar of* **little***)* moins; **a bit less** un peu moins; **the evening was less of a success than she had hoped** la soirée était moins réussie qu'elle ne l'avait espéré; **let's hope we see less of them in future** espérons que nous les verrons moins souvent à l'avenir; **less of your noise!** faites moins de bruit!; *Fam* **less of that!, less of it!** ça suffit!
3 *adv* (**a**) *(forming comparatives)* moins; **they couldn't be less friendly if they tried** il leur serait difficile d'être plus désagréables; **she is less musical than her sister** elle est moins musicienne que sa sœur; **he was less amusing than I remembered** il était moins drôle que dans mes souvenirs
(**b**) *(to a lesser extent or degree)* **the blue dress costs less** la robe bleue coûte moins cher; **not a penny less** pas un sou de moins; **we saw his books less as literature than as propaganda** nous considérions ses livres moins comme de la littérature que comme de la propagande; **I don't think any (the) less of her** *or* **I think no less of her because of what happened** ce qui s'est passé ne l'a pas fait baisser dans mon estime; **we don't like her any the less for all her faults** nous ne l'aimons pas moins à cause de ses défauts; **the more I see of her the less I like her** plus je la vois moins elle me plaît; **the less you know the better** moins tu en sais, mieux c'est; **there's nothing I want less than to hurt him** je ne veux surtout pas le blesser
4 *prep* **that's £300 less ten percent for store card holders** ça fait 300 livres moins dix pour cent avec la carte du magasin; **8 less 3 is 5** 8 moins 3 *ou* 3 ôté de 8 égale 5
5 less and less 1 *adj* de moins en moins; **I seem to have less and less energy** on dirait que j'ai de moins en moins d'énergie **2** *adv* de moins en moins; **less and less interesting** de moins en moins intéressant; **we found we had less and less to say to each other** nous nous sommes rendu compte que nous avions de moins en moins de choses à nous dire; **I see him less and less these days** je le vois de moins en moins ces temps-ci
6 much less, still less *conj* encore moins; **they don't own a fridge, much less a freezer** ils n'ont pas de réfrigérateur, et encore moins de congélateur; **he wouldn't even phone her, much less visit her** il ne voulait même pas l'appeler, encore moins aller la voir; **I hadn't really thought about it, much less talked to anyone else** je n'y avais pas vraiment réfléchi, et j'en avais encore moins parlé à qui que ce soit
7 less than 1 *prep (with numbers, measurements etc)* moins de; **it took me less than five minutes** ça m'a pris moins de cinq minutes; **you won't get another one like it for less than $1,000** vous n'en retrouverez pas un comme ça à moins de 1000 dollars; **nothing less than a four-star hotel is good enough for them** il leur faut au moins un quatre étoiles; **in less than no time** en un rien de temps, en moins de deux **2** *adv* moins que; **there was less than I expected** il y en avait moins que je m'y attendais; **he eats less than he used to** il mange moins qu'avant; **the weather was rather less than ideal** le temps était vraiment loin d'être idéal; **it would have been less than fair to have kept it from her** ça aurait été vraiment injuste de le lui cacher
8 no less *adv* (**a**) *(in size, amount, degree)* **I expected no less from you** je n'en attendais pas moins de vous; **the news of his death came as no less of a shock for being expected** on avait beau s'y attendre, la nouvelle de sa mort n'en fut pas moins un choc
(**b**) *(for emphasis)* **he won the Booker prize, no less!** il a gagné le prix Booker, rien que ça!; **she married a duke, no less!** elle a épousé un duc, s'il vous plaît!; **she had invited no less a person than the President himself** elle avait invité rien moins que le président lui-même; **the letter was signed by Vincent, no less!** la lettre était signée de Vincent, s'il vous plaît!

9 no less than *adv* pas moins de; **this wall is no less than a metre thick** ce mur n'a pas moins d'un mètre d'épaisseur; **taxes rose by no less than 15 percent** les impôts ont augmenté de 15 pour cent, ni plus ni moins

lessee [le'si:] *n* preneur(euse) *m,f* (à bail)

lessen ['lesən] **1** *vt (cost, importance)* diminuer, réduire; *(impact, effect)* atténuer, amoindrir; *(shock)* amortir; *(noise)* atténuer; *(activity)* ralentir; *(fervour, enthusiasm)* calmer
2 *vi* s'atténuer, s'amoindrir

lessening ['lesənɪŋ] *n (UNCOUNT) (of cost, importance)* diminution *f*; *(of value, rate)* réduction *f*, diminution *f*, baisse *f*; *(of powers)* réduction *f*, baisse *f*; *(of impact, effect)* amoindrissement *m*; *(of shock)* amortissement *m*

lesser ['lesə(r)] *adj* **(a)** *(gen)* moindre; **to be of lesser intelligence** être moins intelligent; **Wordsworth, Coleridge and their lesser contemporaries** Wordsworth, Coleridge et leurs contemporains de moindre envergure; **to a lesser extent** dans une moindre mesure; **she treats them as though they were lesser mortals** elle les traite de haut; **it's the lesser evil** *or* **of two evils** c'est le moindre mal; *Hum* **lesser mortals like me** les simples mortels comme moi
(b) *Bot, Geog, Orn & Zool* petit
►► *Orn* ***lesser black-backed gull*** goéland *m* brun; *Orn* ***lesser kestrel*** faucon *m* crécerellette; *Bot* ***lesser meadow-rue*** petit pigamon *m*; *Zool* ***the lesser panda*** le petit panda; *Entom* ***lesser purple emperor*** petit mars *m* (changeant); *Orn* ***lesser redpoll*** sizerin *m* cabaret; *Orn* ***lesser short-toed lark*** alouette *f* pispolette; *Orn* ***lesser spotted woodpecker*** (pic *m*) épeichette *f*; *Orn* ***lesser whitethroat*** fauvette *f* babillarde

lesser-known *adj* moins connu

lesson ['lesən] *n* **(a)** *(gen)* leçon *f*; *Sch* leçon *f*, cours *m*; **an English lesson** une leçon *ou* un cours d'anglais; **a dancing/driving lesson** une leçon de danse/de conduite; **to give a lesson** donner un cours *ou* une leçon; **lessons start at half past eight** les cours commencent à huit heures et demie; **private lessons** cours *mpl* particuliers
(b) *(example)* leçon *f*; **her downfall was a lesson to us all** sa chute nous a servi de leçon à tous; **to teach sb a lesson** donner une (bonne) leçon à qn; **that'll teach him a lesson!** cela lui servira de leçon!; **the experience has taught me a lesson I won't forget!** cette expérience m'a servi de leçon, croyez-moi!; **let that be a lesson to you!** que cela vous serve de leçon!
(c) *Rel* leçon *f*, lecture *f*
►► ***lesson plan*** plan *m* de cours

lessor [le'sɔ:(r)] *n* bailleur(eresse) *m,f*

less-than sign *n* signe *m* inférieur à

lest [lest] *conj* **(a)** *Literary (in case)* de peur que + *subjunctive*, de crainte que + *subjunctive*; **they whispered lest the children should hear** ils parlèrent à voix basse de peur *ou* de crainte que les enfants ne les entendent; **she wrote it down, lest she forget** *or* **lest she might forget** elle l'a noté, de peur d'oublier; **lest we forget** *(on memorial)* in memoriam **(b)** *Arch (after verbs of fearing)* **I feared lest he should fall** je craignais qu'il (ne) tombât

let¹ [let] *(pt & pp* **let**, *cont* **letting) 1** *n* **(a)** *(rental)* location *f*; **she took a six-month let on a house** elle a loué une maison pour six mois; **a short/long let** une location de courte/longue durée
(b) *Sport (in tennis, squash)* balle *f* let; **let!** let!; **the ball was a let** la balle était let; **to play a let** jouer une balle let
(c) *Law (hindrance)* **without let or hindrance** librement, sans entrave
2 *vt* **(a)** *(rent)* louer; **to let** *(sign)* à louer
(b) *Arch or Literary* **to let (sb's) blood** faire une saignée (à qn)
►► *Sport* ***let ball*** balle *f* let

LET² [let] *(pt & pp* **let**, *cont* **letting) 1** *vt* **(a)** *(permit)* laisser, permettre; *(allow)* laisser; **to let sb do sth** laisser qn faire qch, permettre à qn de faire qch; **she let them watch the programme** elle les a laissés regarder l'émission; **I couldn't come because my parents wouldn't let me** je ne suis pas venu parce que mes parents ne me l'ont pas permis; **I let the cakes burn** j'ai laissé brûler les gâteaux; **let me buy you all a drink** laissez-moi vous offrir un verre; **don't let me stop you going** je ne veux pas t'empêcher d'y aller; **let me see the newspaper** fais-moi voir le journal; **to let sb past** laisser passer qn; **they don't let anyone near the reactor** ils ne laissent personne approcher du réacteur; **let me tell you that...** permettez-moi de vous dire que...; **it wasn't easy, let me tell you!** ça n'a pas été facile, crois-moi!; *Fam* **don't let it get you down!** ne te laisse pas abattre pour ça!; **don't let him get to you** ne te soucie pas de lui; **to let sb have sth** donner qch à qn; **don't be selfish, let him have a cake!** ne sois pas égoïste, donne-lui un gâteau!; **I'll let you have a copy of the report** je vous ferai parvenir une copie du rapport; **she let him know what she thought of him** elle lui a fait savoir ce qu'elle pensait de lui; **let me know when he wakes up** prévenez-moi quand il se réveillera; **I'll let him know you're here** je vais le prévenir que vous êtes arrivé; **please let me know if there's any change** veuillez me prévenir s'il y a du changement; **please God don't let anything happen to her!** faites qu'il ne lui arrive rien!; **to let sth pass** laisser passer qch; *Fam* **to let sb have it** *(physically)* casser la figure à qn; *(verbally)* dire ses quatre vérités à qn
(b) *(followed by "go")* **to let sb go** *(allow to leave)* laisser partir qn; *(release)* relâcher qn; *(allow to escape)* laisser échapper qn; *Euph (dismiss, fire)* licencier qn; **to let sb go, to let go of sb** *(stop holding)* lâcher qn; **they let the hostages go** ils ont relâché les otages; **she let her assistant go** elle a licencié son assistant; **let me go!, let go of me!** lâchez-moi!; **to let sth go** *(allow to escape)* laisser échapper qch; **to let sth go, to let go of sth** *(stop holding)* lâcher qch; **hold the rope and don't let go (of it)!** tiens la corde et ne la lâche pas!; **to let oneself go** *(neglect oneself, relax)* se laisser aller; **he's really let the garden go** il a vraiment négligé le jardin; **that remark was uncalled-for but I'll let it go** cette réflexion était déplacée mais restons-en là; **give me £5 and we'll let it go at that** donne-moi 5 livres et on n'en parle plus
(c) *(in making suggestions)* **let's hurry!** dépêchons-nous!; **let's go to bed** allons nous coucher; **let's go!** allons-y!; **don't let's go out** *or* **let's not go out tonight** ne sortons pas ce soir; **let's not have an argument about it!** on ne va pas se disputer pour ça!; **now, let's not have any nonsense!** allons, pas de bêtises!; **shall we have a picnic? – yes, let's!** si on faisait un pique-nique? – d'accord!; *Formal* **let us pray** prions ensemble
(d) *(to focus attention)* **let me start by saying how pleased I am to be here** laissez-moi d'abord vous dire combien je suis ravi d'être ici; **let me put it another way** je vais tâcher d'être plus clair; **let me try and explain** je vais essayer de vous expliquer
(e) *(in hesitation)* **let me think** attends, voyons voir; **let me see, let's see** voyons
(f) *(to express criticism or defiance)* **if she doesn't want my help, let her do it herself!** si elle ne veut pas de mon aide, qu'elle le fasse toute seule!; **let them talk!** laisse-les dire!
(g) *(in threats)* **don't let me catch you at it again!** que je ne t'y reprenne plus!; *Fam* **let me catch you doing that again and you're for it!** si je te reprends à faire ça, ça va être ta fête!
(h) *(in commands) Bible* **let there be light** que la lumière soit; **let the festivities begin!** que la fête commence!; **let them be!** laisse-les tranquilles!, fiche-leur la paix!
(i) *(in making assumptions)* **let us suppose that...** supposons que...; *Math* **let x equal 17** soit x égal à 17; *Math* **let ABC be a right-angled triangle** soit un triangle rectangle ABC
2 let alone *conj* **I wouldn't go out with him, let alone marry him** je ne sortirais même pas avec lui, alors pour ce qui est de l'épouser...; **he's never even used a computer, let alone surfed the Internet** il ne s'est jamais servi d'un ordinateur et encore moins de l'Internet

►**let by** *vt sep* **to let sb by** laisser passer qn

►**let down** *vt sep* **(a)** *(disappoint)* décevoir; **to let sb down gently** ménager qn; **I felt really let down** j'étais vraiment déçu; **our old car has never let us down** notre vieille voiture ne nous a jamais lâchés; **he has been badly let down** il a été gravement déçu
(b) *(lower, let fall → object)* baisser, (faire) descendre; *(→ hair)* dénouer; *Fig* **to let sb down gently** traiter qn avec ménagement
(c) *(garment)* rallonger; **to let the hem of a dress down** rallonger une robe
(d) *(deflate)* dégonfler

►**let in** *vt sep* **(a)** *(person, animal)* laisser entrer; **to let sb in** ouvrir (la porte) à qn, faire entrer qn; **his mother let me in** sa mère m'a fait entrer *ou* m'a ouvert (la porte); **here's the key to let yourself in** voici la clé pour entrer; **she let herself in with a pass key** elle est entrée avec un passe
(b) *(air, water)* laisser passer; **the roof lets the rain in** le toit laisse entrer *ou* passer la pluie; **my shoes let in water** mes chaussures prennent l'eau
(c) *Aut* **to let in the clutch** embrayer

►**let in for** *vt sep* **he didn't realize what he was letting himself in for** il ne savait pas à quoi il s'engageait; **we're letting ourselves in for a lot of work** nous allons avoir beaucoup de travail

►**let in on** *vt sep* **to let sb in on sth** mettre qn au courant de qch; **have you let him in on the secret?** lui avez-vous confié le secret?

►**let into** *vt sep* **(a)** *(allow to enter)* laisser entrer; **my mother let her into the flat** ma mère l'a laissée entrer dans l'appartement
(b) *(allow to know)* **I'll let you into a secret** je vais te confier un secret
(c) *(insert)* encastrer; **the pipes are let into the wall** les tuyaux sont encastrés dans le mur; **to let a door/window into a wall** percer une porte/fenêtre dans un mur

►**let off 1** *vt sep* **(a)** *(excuse)* dispenser; **to let sb off doing sth** dispenser qn de faire qch; **I've been let off work** je suis dispensé de travailler
(b) *(allow to leave)* laisser partir; *(allow to disembark)* laisser descendre; **we were let off an hour early** on nous a laissés partir une heure plus tôt; **they let us off the bus** on nous a laissés descendre du bus
(c) *(criminal, pupil, child)* ne pas punir; **the judge let him off lightly** le juge a fait preuve d'indulgence à son égard; **she was let off with a fine** elle s'en est tirée avec une amende; **I'll let you off this time** pour cette fois, je passe; **you let him off too easily** vous n'avez pas été assez sévère avec lui
(d) *(bomb, explosive)* faire exploser; *(firework)* faire partir; *(gun)* laisser partir
(e) *(release → steam, liquid)* laisser échapper; *Fig* **to let off steam** se défouler
(f) *(rent)* louer; **the whole building is let off as offices** tout l'immeuble est loué en bureaux
2 *vi Fam (break wind)* péter

►**let on 1** *vt sep (allow to embark)* laisser monter; **they let us on the train** on nous a laissés monter dans le train
2 *vi Fam* parler[❑]; **she never let on** elle ne l'a jamais dit; **somebody let on about the wedding to the press** quelqu'un a parlé du mariage à *ou* a révélé le mariage à la presse; **he didn't let on that he saw her** *(didn't tell anyone)* il n'a pas dit qu'il l'avait vue; *(didn't acknowledge her)* il a fait semblant de ne pas la voir; **don't let on!** pas un mot!

►**let out 1** *vt sep* **(a)** *(allow to leave)* laisser sortir; *(bird)* laisser échapper; *(prisoner)* libérer; **the teacher let us out early** le professeur nous a laissés sortir plus tôt; **my secretary will let you out** ma secrétaire va vous reconduire; **don't get up, I'll let myself out** ne vous levez pas, je connais le chemin
(b) *(water, air)* laisser échapper; **someone's let the air out of the tyres** quelqu'un a dégonflé les pneus
(c) *(shout, oath, whistle)* laisser échapper
(d) *(secret)* révéler; **who let it out that they're getting married?** qui est allé raconter qu'ils allaient se marier?
(e) *(garment)* élargir
(f) *Aut* **to let out the clutch** débrayer

(**g**) *Br (rent)* louer; **they let out boats by the hour** ils louent des bateaux à l'heure

2 *vi Am (end)* finir

►**let up** *vi* (**a**) *(stop)* arrêter; *(diminish)* diminuer; **the rain didn't let up all day** il n'a pas cessé *ou* arrêté de pleuvoir de toute la journée; **once he's started he never lets up** une fois lancé, il ne s'arrête plus

(**b**) *(relax)* **he never lets up** il ne s'accorde aucun répit; **don't let up now, you're in the lead** ce n'est pas le moment de faiblir, tu es en tête

►**let up on** *vt insep Fam* **to let up on sb** lâcher la bride à qn

letch = **lech**

letdown ['letdaʊn] *n Fam* déception ☐ *f*; **the party was a bit of a letdown** la fête a été plutôt décevante

lethal ['li:θəl] *adj* fatal, mortel; *Med* létal; **in the hands of a child, a plastic bag can be lethal** dans les mains d'un enfant, un sac en plastique peut être dangereux; **this substance is lethal to rats** c'est une substance mortelle pour les rats; *Fam Fig* **this vodka's lethal!** cette vodka est mortelle!

►► ***lethal dose*** dose *f* mortelle *ou* létale; ***lethal gene*** gène *m* létal; ***lethal weapon*** arme *f* meurtrière

lethality [li:'θælɪtɪ] *n* mortalité *f*; *Med* létalité *f*

lethally ['li:θəlɪ] *adv* mortellement

lethargic [lə'θɑ:dʒɪk] *adj (person, sleep)* léthargique; *(atmosphere)* soporifique; **I feel really lethargic today** je me sens complètement à plat aujourd'hui

lethargically [lɪ'θɑ:dʒɪklɪ] *adv* d'une manière léthargique; **to move lethargically** se déplacer mollement

lethargy ['leθədʒɪ] *n* léthargie *f*; **to fall into a state of lethargy** tomber en léthargie

Lethe ['li:θɪ] *n Myth* le Léthé

let-out *n Br (excuse)* prétexte *m*; *(way out)* échappatoire *f*; **I've been invited but I'm looking for a let-out** j'ai été invité, mais je cherche un prétexte pour ne pas y aller

►► ***let-out clause*** échappatoire *f*

Letraset® ['letrəset] *n* Letraset®

LETS [lets] *n Com (abbr* **Local Exchange Trading System***)* = système d'échange de services dans une communauté donnée, basé sur une monnaie nominale

let's [lets] = **let us**

Lett [let] *n* Letton(onne) *m,f*

lettable ['letəbəl] *adj* qui peut se louer; *(building)* en état d'être loué

letter ['letə(r)] **1** *n* (**a**) *(of alphabet)* lettre *f*; **the letter B** la lettre B; **a six-letter word** un mot de six lettres; **to have letters after one's name** *(have academic qualifications)* être diplômé; *(have official title)* avoir un titre

(**b**) *(communication)* lettre *f*; *(mail)* courrier *m*; **I've had a letter from him** j'ai reçu une lettre de lui; **by letter** par lettre *ou* courrier; **he's a good letter writer** il écrit régulièrement; **I'm a bad letter writer** je n'écris pas souvent; *Br* **to post letters** poster des lettres *ou* du courrier; **letters to the editor** *(in newspapers, magazines)* courrier *m* des lecteurs; **the letters of DH Lawrence** la correspondance de DH Lawrence

(**c**) *Fig (exact meaning)* lettre *f*; **the letter of the law** la lettre de la loi; **to keep** *or* **to stick to the letter of the law** respecter la loi au pied de la lettre *ou* à la lettre; **she obeyed the instructions to the letter** elle a suivi les instructions à la lettre *ou* au pied de la lettre

(**d**) *Am (paper size)* lettre *f (216 mm × 279 mm)*

2 *adj Am (paper)* lettre *(216 mm × 279 mm)*

3 *vt (write)* inscrire des lettres sur; *(engrave)* graver (des lettres sur); *(manuscript)* enluminer; **the title was lettered in gilt** le titre était inscrit en lettres dorées; **the rooms are lettered from A to K** les salles portent des lettres de A à K

4 letters *npl Formal (learning)* belles-lettres *fpl*; **a man of letters** *(scholar)* un lettré; *(writer)* un homme de lettres; *Br* **English letters** littérature *f* anglaise

►► ***letter of acknowledgement*** accusé *m* de réception; ***letter of advice*** lettre *f* d'avis; *St Exch* ***letter of allotment*** avis *m* d'attribution *ou* de répartition, lettre *f* d'allocation; ***letter of apology*** lettre *f* d'excuse; ***letter of application*** *(for job)* lettre *f* de demande d'emploi; *St Exch (for shares)* lettre *f* de souscription; ***letter of appointment*** lettre *f* de nomination *ou* d'affectation; ***letter bomb*** lettre *f* piégée; ***letter card*** carte-lettre *f*; ***letter of complaint*** lettre *f* de réclamation; ***letter of confirmation*** lettre *f* de confirmation; *Com* ***letter of credit*** lettre *f* de crédit *ou* de créance; *Admin* ***letters of credence*** lettres *fpl* de créance; ***letter of dismissal*** lettre *f* de licenciement; *Com* ***letter of exchange*** lettre *f* de change; ***letter of guarantee*** lettre *f* de garantie; *Fin* ***letter of guaranty*** lettre *f* d'aval; *Fin* ***letter of indemnity*** cautionnement *m*, lettre *f* de garantie (d'indemnité); *Fin* ***letter of intent*** lettre *f* d'intention; ***a letter of introduction*** une lettre de recommandation; ***letter opener*** coupe-papier *m inv*; ***the letters page*** le courrier des lecteurs; ***letters patent*** lettres *fpl* patentes; *Comput* ***letter quality*** qualité *f* courrier; ***near letter quality*** qualité *f* quasi-courrier *(pour une imprimante)*; ***letter rack*** porte-lettres *m inv*; ***letter rate*** tarif *m* lettres; ***letter of reference*** lettre *f* de recommandation; ***letter scales*** pèse-lettre *m*; ***letter tray*** corbeille *f ou* panier *m* à courrier

letterbox ['letəbɒks] **1** *n Br (for mail)* boîte *f* à *ou* aux lettres

2 *adj Cin (film)* recadré pour la télévision

letterboxing ['letəbɒksɪŋ] *n Cin* = recadrage d'un film en Cinémascope pour la télévision

lettered ['letəd] *adj* (**a**) *Formal (person)* lettré (**b**) *(inscribed)* **lettered in gold** inscrit en lettres d'or; **a briefcase lettered with my initials** une mallette gravée à mes initiales

letterhead ['letəhed] *n* en-tête *m (de lettre)*; *(paper)* papier *m* à en-tête

lettering ['letərɪŋ] *n (UNCOUNT)* (**a**) *(action)* lettrage *m* (**b**) *(inscription)* inscription *f* (**c**) *(characters)* caractères *mpl*; **gold lettering** lettres *fpl* en or

letter-perfect *adj Am (person)* qui connaît son texte parfaitement; *(text)* parfait

letterpress ['letəpres] *n (technique)* typographie *f*; *(text)* texte *m* (imprimé)

letter-quality *adj* qualité courrier *(inv)*

letterset ['letəset] *n* offset *m* sec

letters-of-marque *npl* lettres *fpl* de marque

Lettic ['letɪk] **1** *n Ling* lette *m*, lettique *m*, letton *m*

2 *adj* letton

letting ['letɪŋ] *n (of house, property)* location *f*

►► ***letting agency*** agence *f* de location

Lettish ['letɪʃ] **1** *n Ling* lette *m*, lettique *m*, letton *m*

2 *adj* letton

lettuce ['letɪs] *n* (**a**) *(gen) & Culin* salade *f*; *Bot* laitue *f* (**b**) *Am Fam (money)* blé *m*, oseille *f*

►► ***lettuce leaf*** feuille *f* de salade *ou* de laitue

let-up *n (stop)* arrêt *m*, pause *f*; *(abatement)* répit *m*; **it's been raining for days without let-up** ça fait des jours qu'il n'arrête pas de pleuvoir *ou* qu'il pleut sans arrêt

leu ['leɪu:] *n (unit of currency)* leu *m*

leucin ['lu:sɪn], **leucine** ['lu:si:n] *n Biol & Chem* leucine *f*

leucite ['lu:saɪt] *n Miner* leucite *f*, amphigène *m*

leuco- ['lu:kəʊ] *pref* leuco-; *Biol & Chem* **leucobase** leucobase *f*, leucodérivé *m*

leucoblast ['lu:kəʊˌblæst] *n Biol* leucoblaste *m*

leucocratic [ˌlu:kəʊ'krætɪk] *adj Geol* leucocrate

leucocyte ['lu:kəˌsaɪt] *n Anat* leucocyte *m*

leucocytic [ˌlu:kə'sɪtɪk] *adj Anat* leucocytaire

leucocytosis [ˌlu:kəsaɪ'təʊsɪs] *n Med* leucocytose *f*

leucoma ['lu:kəʊmə] *n Med* leucome *m*

leucopenia [ˌlu:kəʊ'pi:nɪə] *n Med* leucopénie *f*

leucopoiesis [ˌlu:kəʊpɔɪ'i:sɪs] *n Med* leucopoïèse *f*

leucotomy [lu:'kɒtəmɪ] *(pl* **leucotomies***) n Med* leucotomie *f*

leukaemia, *Am* **leukemia** [lu:'ki:mɪə] *n (UNCOUNT)* leucémie *f*; **he has leukaemia** il a une leucémie, il est atteint de leucémie

leukaemic, *Am* **leukemic** [lu:'ki:mɪk] *adj Med* leucémique

leuko- = **leuco-**

lev [lef] *n (unit of currency)* lev *m*

Levant [lɪ'vænt] *n* **the Levant** le Levant

Levantine ['levəntaɪn] **1** *n* Levantin(e) *m,f*

2 *adj* levantin

levator [lɪ'veɪtə(r)] *n Anat* élévateur *m*, (muscle *m*) releveur *m*

levee[1] ['levɪ] *n Am* (**a**) *(embankment)* levée *f*; *(surrounding field)* digue *f* (**b**) *(landing place)* quai *m*

levee[2] ['levɪ] *n Hist (in royal chamber)* lever *m* (du roi); *Br (at court)* réception *f* à la cour

LEVEL ['levəl]

niveau	► 1 (a) – (d), (f)
hauteur	► 1 (a)
taux	► 1 (b)
échelon	► 1 (c)
étage	► 1 (f)
plat	► 1 (g); 2 (a)
au même niveau	► 2 (b)
à la même hauteur	► 2 (b)
horizontal	► 2 (c)
de/à niveau	► 2 (c)
à égalité	► 2 (d)
calme	► 2 (e)
à l'horizontale	► 3
aplanir	► 4 (a)
niveler	► 4 (a)

(Br pt & pp **levelled,** *cont* **levelling,** *Am pt & pp* **leveled,** *cont* **leveling***)* **1** *n* (**a**) *(height → in a horizontal plane)* niveau *m*; *(→ in a vertical plane)* hauteur *f*; **at ground level** au niveau du sol; **water seeks its own level** c'est le principe des vases communicants; *Fig* on se heurte toujours à ses propres limites; **the level of the river has risen overnight** le niveau de la rivière a monté pendant la nuit; **the flood waters have reached the level of the bridge** la crue a atteint le niveau du pont; **the sink is on a level with the work surface** l'évier est au niveau du *ou* de niveau avec le plan de travail; **on the same level** au même niveau

(**b**) *(amount)* niveau *m*; *(percentage)* taux *m*; **noise levels are far too high** le niveau sonore est bien trop élevé; **a low level of sugar in the bloodstream** un faible taux de sucre dans le sang; **inflation has reached new levels** l'inflation a atteint de nouveaux sommets; **check the oil level** *(in car)* vérifiez le niveau d'huile; **her ambition is on a level with mine** son ambition est du même ordre que la mienne; *Comput* **levels of grey** échelle *f* des gris

(**c**) *(rank)* niveau *m*, échelon *m*; **at cabinet/national level** à l'échelon ministériel/national; **at a regional level** au niveau régional; **talks are being held at the highest level** on négocie au plus haut niveau

(**d**) *(standard)* niveau *m*; **her level of English is poor** elle n'a pas un très bon niveau en anglais; **students at beginners' level** étudiants *mpl* au niveau débutant; **a high level of competence/intelligence** un haut niveau de compétence/d'intelligence; **they're not on the same level at all** ils ne sont pas du tout du même niveau, ils n'ont absolument pas le même niveau; **she's on a different level from the others** elle n'est pas au même niveau que les autres; **to come down to sb's level** se mettre au niveau de qn; **don't descend** *or* **sink to their level** ne t'abaisse pas à leur niveau

(**e**) *(point of view)* **on a personal level, I really like him** sur le plan personnel, je l'aime beaucoup; **on a practical level** du point de vue pratique

(**f**) *(storey)* niveau *m*, étage *m*; **the library is on level three** la bibliothèque est au niveau trois *ou* au troisième étage

(**g**) *(flat land)* plat *m*; **100 km/h on the level** 100 km/h sur le plat

(**h**) *(for woodwork, building etc)* **(spirit) level** niveau *m* (à bulle)

(**i**) *Fam (idiom)* **on the level** *(honest)* honnête ☐, réglo; **do you think he's on the level?** tu crois qu'il est réglo *ou* que c'est un type réglo?; **I'm giving it to you on the level** je te dis ça franchement *ou* sans détour; **this deal is definitely on the level** cette affaire est tout ce qu'il y a de plus réglo

2 *adj* (**a**) *(flat)* plat; **a level spoonful** une cuillerée rase; **to make sth level** aplanir qch

(**b**) *(at the same height)* au même niveau, à la même hauteur; *(at the same standard)* au même niveau; **the terrace is level with the pool** la terrasse est au même niveau que *ou* de plain-pied avec la piscine; **his head is just level with my shoulder** sa tête m'arrive exactement à l'épaule

(**c**) *(horizontal)* horizontal; *(ground)* de niveau, à niveau

(**d**) *(equal)* à égalité; **the leading cars are almost level** les voitures de tête sont presque à la même hauteur; **to draw level** se trouver à égalité; **the other runners drew level with me** les autres coureurs m'ont rattrapé

(**e**) *(calm, steady)* calme, mesuré; **to speak in a level voice** parler d'une voix calme *ou* posée; **she gave me a level look** elle me regarda posément; **to keep a level head** garder la tête froide

(**f**) *Fam (honest)* honnête ❑, réglo; **you're not being level with me** tu ne joues pas franc jeu avec moi

(**g**) *(idioms)* **to do one's level best** faire de son mieux; **she did her level best to irritate me** elle a tout fait pour me mettre en colère; *Br* **it's level pegging** *(between the two)* il y a égalité; **they're level pegging** ils sont à égalité

3 *adv* à l'horizontale; **hold the tray level** tenez le plateau à l'horizontale *ou* bien à plat; *Aviat* **to fly level** voler en palier

4 *vt* (**a**) *(flatten)* aplanir, niveler; **to level a town (to the ground)** raser une ville

(**b**) *(aim)* **to level a gun at sb** braquer une arme sur qn; **to level accusations at sb** lancer des accusations contre qn; **a lot of criticism has been levelled at me** on m'a beaucoup critiqué

(**c**) *(in surveying)* effectuer des opérations de nivellement dans, niveler

5 *vi Fam* **to level with sb** être franc avec qn ❑, jouer franc jeu avec qn ❑

►► *Br & Can* ***level crossing*** passage *m* à niveau; *Aviat* ***level flight*** vol *m* horizontal

►**level down** *vt sep (surface)* aplanir, niveler; *(standard)* niveler par le bas

►**level off 1** *vi* (**a**) *(production, rise, development)* s'équilibrer, se stabiliser; **the curve on the graph levels off at this point** la courbe du graphique se stabilise à partir d'ici; **the team's performance has levelled off this season** les résultats de l'équipe se sont stabilisés cette saison

(**b**) *Aviat* amorcer un palier

2 *vt sep (flatten)* aplatir, niveler

►**level out 1** *vi* (**a**) *(road, surface)* s'aplanir

(**b**) *(stabilize)* se stabiliser

2 *vt sep* niveler

►**level up** *vt sep* niveler (par le haut)

---

leveler *Am* = **leveller**

level-headed *adj* équilibré, pondéré, réfléchi; **he's a level-headed boy** c'est un garçon qui a la tête sur les épaules

level-headedness [-'hedɪdnɪs] *n* esprit *m* bien équilibré, pondération *f*

leveling *Am* = **levelling**

leveller, *Am* **leveler** ['levələ(r)] **1** *n Pol* égalitariste *mf*, niveleur(euse) *m,f*; **death is a great leveller** nous sommes tous égaux devant la mort

2 Levellers *npl Hist* **the Levellers** les niveleurs *mpl*

THE LEVELLERS

Ce mouvement de républicains [illegible] pendant la guerre civile en Angleterre. Les "niveleurs" réclamaient un renforcement des pouvoirs du Parlement ainsi qu'une plus large représentation populaire, mais furent durement réprimés par Cromwell.

levelling, *Am* **leveling** ['levəlɪŋ] **1** *n* nivellement *m*, aplanissement *m*; **earth levelling** nivellement *m* du terrain; **a levelling up/down of salaries is desirable** un nivellement des salaires par le haut/par le bas est souhaitable; **a levelling off of prices** une stabilisation des prix

2 *adj* de nivellement

►► ***levelling screw*** vis *f* d'ajustement (de niveau); ***levelling staff*** mire *f* (parlante)

levelness ['levəlnɪs] *n* (**a**) *(flatness)* nature *f* plate

(**b**) *(being at same height)* = fait d'être au même niveau

lever [*Br* 'li:və(r), *Am* 'levər] **1** *n also Fig* levier *m*; *(smaller)* manette *f*

2 *vt* manœuvrer à l'aide d'un levier; **he levered the box open with a piece of wood** il a forcé la caisse à l'aide d'un morceau de bois; **they levered the engine into position** ils installèrent le moteur à l'aide d'un levier; *Fig* **he has levered himself into a very strong position** il s'est hissé à un poste très important

►► *Tech* ***lever arm*** bras *m* de levier; *Tech & Fig* ***lever effect*** effet *m* de levier

►**lever off** *vt sep (lid, top, tyre)* enlever (avec un levier); *(padlock)* faire sauter

►**lever out** *vt sep* extraire *ou* extirper (à l'aide d'un levier); *Fig* **he levered himself out of bed** il s'extirpa du lit; **they levered the president out of office** ils ont délogé le président de son poste

►**lever up** *vt sep* soulever (au moyen d'un levier); *Fig* **she levered herself up onto the rock** elle se hissa sur le rocher

leverage [*Br* 'li:vərɪdʒ, *Am* 'levərɪdʒ] *n* (**a**) *Tech* force *f* (de levier); **I can't get enough leverage** je n'ai pas assez de prise

(**b**) *(influence)* influence *f*; **to exert some leverage on sb** exercer de l'influence sur qn; **he has no leverage with the management** il n'a aucun moyen de pression sur la direction; **the committee's findings give us considerable (political) leverage** les conclusions de la commission constituent pour nous des moyens de pression considérables (sur le plan politique)

(**c**) *Am Econ (gearing)* effet *m* de levier; *(as percentage)* ratio *m* d'endettement, ratio *m* de levier

leveraged [*Br* 'li:vərɪdʒd, *Am* 'levərɪdʒd] *adj Fin* **the company is highly leveraged** la société est fortement endettée

►► *Fin* ***leveraged buyout*** rachat *m* d'entreprise financé par l'endettement; *Fin* ***leveraged management buyout*** rachat *m* d'entreprise par les salariés

lever-arch file *n* classeur *m* à levier

leveret ['levərɪt] *n* levraut *m*

Levi ['li:vaɪ] *pr n Bible* Lévi

leviathan [lɪ'vaɪəθən] **1** *n (ship)* navire *m* géant; *(institution, organization)* institution *f ou* organisation *f* géante

2 Leviathan *pr n Bible* Léviathan

levigate ['levɪ,geɪt] *vt Tech* (**a**) *(crush, pulverize)* léviger (**b**) *(smooth)* lisser

Levis® ['li:vaɪz] *npl* jean *m ou* jeans *mpl* (Levi's®)

levitate ['levɪteɪt] **1** *vt* faire léviter, soulever par lévitation

2 *vi* léviter

levitation [,levɪ'teɪʃən] *n* lévitation *f*

Levite ['li:vaɪt] *n* lévite *m*

Levitical [lɪ'vɪtɪkəl] *adj Bible* lévitique, des lévites

►► ***Levitical degrees*** = degrés de parenté qui n'autorisent pas le mariage; **marriage within the Levitical degrees** = mariage *m* prohibé entre parents

Leviticus [lɪ'vɪtɪkəs] *n Bible* le Lévitique

levity ['levətɪ] (*pl* **levities**) *n* légèreté *f*, manque *m* de sérieux

levodopa [,li:vəʊ'dəʊpə] *n Pharm* lévodopa *f*

levy ['levɪ] (*pl* **levies,** *pt & pp* **levied**) **1** *n* (**a**) *(action)* prélèvement *m*; **tax levy** prélèvement *m* fiscal; **a capital levy of 10 percent** un prélèvement de 10 pour cent sur le capital

(**b**) *(tax, duty)* impôt *m*, taxe *f*, droit *m*; **to impose a levy on sugar imports** taxer les importations de sucre; **special levy** taxe *f* exceptionelle

(**c**) *Mil* levée *f*

2 *vt* (**a**) *(impose → tax)* prélever; *(→ fine)* imposer, infliger; **to levy a duty on imports** prélever une taxe sur les importations

(**b**) *(collect → taxes, fine)* lever, percevoir

(**c**) *Mil (troops)* lever

(**d**) *(wage)* **to levy war on small states** faire la guerre à de petits États

►**levy on** *vt insep Formal or Law* **to levy on sb's property** saisir les biens de qn

lewd [lju:d] *adj (behaviour)* lubrique; *(speech)* obscène

lewdly ['lju:dlɪ] *adv (behave)* lubriquement; *(speak)* de façon obscène

lewdness ['lju:dnɪs] *n (of behaviour)* lubricité *f*; *(of speech)* obscénité *f*

lewis ['lu:ɪs] *n (lifting device)* louve *f*

Lewis ['lu:ɪs] *n Geog* Lewis

►► ***Lewis gun*** mitrailleuse *f (utilisée pendant la Première et Seconde Guerre mondiale)*

lewisite ['lu:ɪsaɪt] *n Chem* lewisite *f*

lexeme ['leksi:m] *n Ling* lexème *m*

lexical ['leksɪkəl] *adj* lexical

lexicalize, -ise ['leksɪkəlaɪz] *vt* lexicaliser

lexicographer [,leksɪ'kɒgrəfə(r)] *n* lexicographe *mf*

lexicographical [,leksɪkə'græfɪkəl] *adj* lexicographique

lexicography [,leksɪ'kɒgrəfɪ] *n* lexicographie *f*

lexicological [,leksɪkə'lɒdʒɪkəl] *adj* lexicologique

lexicologist [,leksɪ'kɒlədʒɪst] *n* lexicologue *mf*

lexicology [,leksɪ'kɒlədʒɪ] *n* lexicologie *f*

lexicon ['leksɪkən] *n* lexique *m*

lexigram ['leksɪgræm] *n* logogramme *m*

lexigraphy [lek'sɪgrəfɪ] *n* lexigraphie *f*

lexis ['leksɪs] *n* lexique *m*

ley [leɪ] *n* pâturage *m*

►► ***ley line*** = ensemble de repères indiquant le tracé probable d'un chemin préhistorique

Leyden ['laɪdən] *n Geog* Leyde

►► *Elec* ***Leyden jar*** bouteille *f* de Leyde

lez [lez], **lezzy** ['lezɪ] *n very Fam* gouine *f*, = terme injurieux désignant une lesbienne

lh [,el'eɪtʃ] *Mus* (*abbr* **left hand**) main *f* gauche

Lhasa ['lɑ:sə] *n* Lhassa

lhasa apso ['lɑ:sə'ɑ:psəʊ] *n* Lhassa apso *m*

LI (*written abbr* **Long Island**) Long Island

liability [,laɪə'bɪlətɪ] (*pl* **liabilities**) **1** *n* (**a**) *(UNCOUNT) Law (responsibility)* responsabilité *f* (légale); **he refused to admit liability for the damage** il refusa d'endosser la responsabilité des dégâts

(**b**) *(UNCOUNT) (eligibility)* assujettissement *m*; **liability for tax** assujettissement *m* à l'impôt; **liability for military service** obligations *fpl* militaires

(**c**) *(hindrance)* gêne *f*, handicap *m*; **some qualifications are more of a liability than an asset** certains diplômes sont un handicap plus qu'un atout; **the house he had inherited was a real liability** la maison dont il avait hérité lui coûtait une petite fortune *ou* lui revenait cher; **that man is a (total) liability** ce type est un vrai poids mort *ou* un véritable boulet

(**d**) *Acct & Fin* dette *f*

(**e**) *Com (on bills of exchange)* encours *m*

2 liabilities *npl Acct & Fin (debts)* passif *m*, dettes *fpl*; **to meet one's liabilities** rembourser ses dettes; **liabilities on an estate** passif *m* d'une succession; **assets and liabilities** actif *m* et passif *m*

►► *Am Law* ***liability suit*** procès *m* en responsabilité civile

liable ['laɪəbəl] *adj* (**a**) *Law (responsible)* responsable; **to be held liable for sth** être tenu (pour) responsable de qch; **employers are liable for their staff's mistakes** les employeurs sont (civilement) responsables des erreurs de leur personnel; **to be liable for sb's debts** répondre des dettes de qn; **you'll be liable for damages** on sera en droit de vous demander *ou* réclamer des dommages et intérêts

(**b**) *(likely)* **to be liable to do sth** *(person, thing)* risquer de faire qch; **the programme is liable to change** le programme est susceptible d'être modifié, il se peut que le programme subisse des modifications; **he's liable to arrive at any moment** il peut arriver d'une minute à l'autre; **the bomb is liable to explode at any moment** la bombe risque d'exploser à tout instant; **we are all liable to make mistakes** tout le monde peut se tromper; **if you don't remind him, he's liable to forget** si on ne lui rappelle pas, il risque d'oublier; **to be liable to headaches** être sujet aux maux de tête

(**c**) *Admin* **to be liable for tax** *(person)* être assujetti à *ou* redevable de l'impôt; *(goods)* être assujetti à une taxe; **offenders are liable to a fine** les contrevenants sont passibles d'une amende; **he is liable to be prosecuted** il s'expose à des poursuites judiciaires; *Mil* **to be liable for military service** être astreint au service militaire

liaise [lɪ'eɪz] *vi* **to liaise with sb** *(be in contact*

lev–lia

with) être en contact avec qn; *(work together with)* collaborer avec qn; **the two parties have agreed to liaise** les deux parties ont accepté de collaborer; **the successful applicant will be required to liaise with head office** le candidat retenu sera en contact direct avec le siège; **her role is to liaise with the accounts department** son rôle est d'assurer la liaison avec le service de la comptabilité

liaison [lɪ'eɪzɒn] *n* liaison *f*

►► ***liaison officer*** *(between services, companies)* agent *m* de liaison; *Mil* officier *m* de liaison

liana [lɪ'ɑːnə] *n* liane *f*

liar ['laɪə(r)] *n* menteur(euse) *m,f*; **you liar!** espèce de menteur!

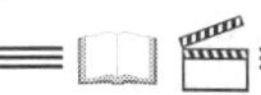

'Billy Liar' *Waterhouse, Schlesinger* 'Billy le menteur'

lias ['laɪəs] *n Geol (rock, stratum)* lias *m*

liassic [laɪ'æsɪk] *adj Geol* liasique

Lib [lɪb] *n (abbr* **Liberal**) libéral(e) *m,f*

►► ***Lib Dem*** **1** *n* = membre du parti libéral démocrate **2** *adj* libéral démocrate

lib [lɪb] *n Fam (abbr* **liberation**) libération ❑ *f*

libation [laɪ'beɪʃən] *n Literary (offering)* libation *f*; *Hum* **can I offer you a small libation?** puis-je vous offrir un petit quelque chose?

libber ['lɪbə(r)] *n Fam* **women's libber** féministe ❑ *f*, ≃ adhérente *f* du MLF ❑

libel ['laɪbəl] *(Br pt & pp* **libelled**, *cont* **libelling**, *Am pt & pp* **libeled**, *cont* **libeling**) **1** *n Law (act of publishing)* diffamation *f*; *(publication)* écrit *m* diffamatoire; *Fig (calumny)* calomnie *f*, mensonge *m*; **to sue sb for libel** poursuivre qn en justice pour diffamation; **that's libel!** c'est une calomnie *ou* de la diffamation!

2 *vt Law* diffamer; *Fig* calomnier

►► ***libel case*** procès *m* en diffamation; ***libel laws*** législation *f* en matière de diffamation; ***libel suit*** procès *m* en diffamation

libellee, *Am* **libelee** [,laɪbə'liː] *n* personne *f* poursuivie pour diffamation

libellous, *Am* **libelous** ['laɪbələs] *adj* diffamatoire

libellously, *Am* **libelously** ['laɪbələslɪ] *adv* de façon diffamatoire, calomnieusement

liberal ['lɪbərəl] **1** *adj* **(a)** *(tolerant → person)* libéral, large d'esprit; *(→ ideas, mind)* libéral, large; *(→ education)* libéral

(b) *(generous)* libéral, généreux; **the cook was a bit too liberal with the salt** le cuisinier a eu la main un peu lourde avec le sel; **he was always very liberal with his praise** il n'était jamais avare de compliments

(c) *(copious → helping, portion)* abondant, copieux

2 *n (moderate)* **she's a liberal** elle est de centre gauche

3 Liberal *Pol* **1** *adj (19th century)* libéral; *(today)* centriste **2** *n (party member)* libéral(e) *m,f*

►► ***the liberal arts*** les sciences *fpl* humaines; ***Liberal Democrat*** **1** *n* = membre du parti libéral démocrate **2** *adj* libéral démocrate; ***the Liberal Democrats*** parti *m* libéral démocrate *(parti politique britannique de tendance centriste)*; ***the Liberal Party*** le parti libéral; ***liberal studies*** ≃ programme *m* de culture générale

liberalism ['lɪbərəlɪzəm] *n* libéralisme *m*

liberality [,lɪbə'rælətɪ] *(pl* **liberalities**) *n* **(a)** *(tolerance)* libéralisme *m* **(b)** *(generosity)* libéralité *f*, largesse *f*

liberalization [,lɪbərəlaɪ'zeɪʃən] *n* libéralisation *f*

liberalize, -ise ['lɪbərəlaɪz] *vt* libéraliser

liberally ['lɪbərəlɪ] *adv* libéralement; **a liberally spiced dish** un plat généreusement épicé

liberal-minded *adj* large d'esprit

liberate ['lɪbəreɪt] *vt* **(a)** *(gen)* libérer; *Fin* **to liberate capital** libérer des capitaux **(b)** *Chem & Phys (gas, heat)* libérer, dégager **(c)** *Hum (steal)* piquer

liberated ['lɪbəreɪtɪd] *adj (person)* libéré; *(ideas, views)* progressiste; **a liberated woman** une femme libérée; **these are liberated times** on vit une époque libérée; **her ideas aren't liberated** elle n'est pas libérée

liberating ['lɪbəreɪtɪŋ] *adj* libérateur

liberation [,lɪbə'reɪʃən] *n* **(a)** *(gen)* libération *f*; **she doesn't believe in women's liberation** elle ne croit pas à la libération de la femme **(b)** *Chem & Phys (of gas, heat)* dégagement *m*

►► ***liberation movement*** mouvement *m* de libération; ***liberation theology*** théologie *f* de la libération

liberationist [,lɪbə'reɪʃənɪst] *n* = défenseur des droits des franges défavorisées de la société ou des minorités

liberator ['lɪbəreɪtə(r)] *n* libérateur(trice) *m,f*

Liberia [laɪ'bɪərɪə] *n* Liberia *m*; **in Liberia** au Liberia

Liberian [laɪ'bɪərɪən] **1** *n* Libérien(enne) *m,f*

2 *adj* libérien

3 *comp (embassy, history)* du Liberia

libertarian [,lɪbə'teərɪən] **1** *adj* libertaire

2 *n* libertaire *mf*

libertarianism [,lɪbə'teərɪənɪzəm] *n (doctrine)* doctrine *f* libertaire; *(political ideas)* convictions *fpl* libertaires

liberticide [lɪ'bɜːtɪ,saɪd] **1** *n* **(a)** *(person)* liberticide *mf* **(b)** *(crime)* liberticide *m*

2 *adj* liberticide

libertinage ['lɪbətɪnɪdʒ] *n* **(a)** *(licentiousness)* libertinage *m*, mœurs *fpl* dissipées, débauche *f* **(b)** *(freethinking)* libertinisme *m*, libre-pensée *f*

libertine ['lɪbətiːn] **1** *n* libertin(e) *m,f*

2 *adj* libertin

libertinism ['lɪbətɪnɪzəm] *n* **(a)** *(licentiousness)* libertinage *m*, mœurs *fpl* dissipées, débauche *f* **(b)** *(freethinking)* libertinisme *m*, libre-pensée *f*

liberty ['lɪbətɪ] *(pl* **liberties**) **1** *n (in behaviour)* liberté *f*; **to take liberties with sb** prendre *ou* se permettre des libertés avec qn; **the government is taking liberties** le gouvernement se fiche du monde; **to take liberties with the truth** prendre des libertés avec la vérité; **I took the liberty of inviting them** j'ai pris la liberté *ou* je me suis permis de les inviter; **what a liberty!** *(cheek)* quel toupet!; *Fam Pej* **it's liberty hall in this house** chacun fait ce qui lui plaît ❑ *ou* c'est la pétaudière dans cette maison

2 at liberty *adj* **the criminals are still at liberty** les criminels sont toujours en liberté *ou* courent toujours; **you are at liberty to leave** vous êtes libre de partir; **I'm not at liberty to say** il ne m'est pas possible *ou* permis de le dire; **I'm not at liberty to comment** je n'ai pas le droit de *ou* il ne m'est pas permis de faire de commentaires

►► ***the Liberty Bell*** = cloche qui retentit pour annoncer l'indépendance des États-Unis en 1776, actuellement conservée à Philadelphie; ***liberty bodice*** chemise *f* américaine; ***liberty cap*** bonnet *m* phrygien *ou* d'affranchi; ***Liberty Island*** île *f* de la Liberté; ***liberty ship*** = navire de marchandises préfabriqué construit par les États-Unis pendant la Seconde Guerre mondiale; *Naut* ***liberty ticket*** permission *f* de terre *ou* d'aller à terre

'On Liberty' *Mill* 'La Liberté'

libidinal [lɪ'bɪdɪnəl] *adj* libidinal

libidinous [lɪ'bɪdɪnəs] *adj* libidineux

libidinously [lɪ'bɪdɪnəslɪ] *adv* de façon libidineuse

libidinousness [lɪ'bɪdɪnəsnɪs] *n* caractère *m* libidineux, libidinosité *f*

libido [lɪ'biːdəʊ] *(pl* **libidos**) *n* libido *f*

Lib-Lab *adj Br Fam (abbr* **Liberal-Labour**) *(agreement, talks)* entre libéraux et travaillistes; **a Lib-Lab pact** un accord entre libéraux et travaillistes

LIBOR ['laɪbɔː(r)] *n Br Fin (abbr* **London Inter-Bank Offer Rate**) ≃ TIOP *m*

Libra ['liːbrə] **1** *n* **(a)** *Astron* Balance *f* **(b)** *Astrol* Balance *f*; **he's a Libra** il est (du signe de la) Balance

2 *adj Astrol* de la Balance; **he's Libra** il est (du signe de la) Balance

Libran ['liːbrən] *Astrol* **1** *n* **to be a Libran** être (du signe de la) Balance

2 *adj* de la Balance

librarian [laɪ'breərɪən] *n* bibliothécaire *mf*

librarianship [laɪ'breərɪənʃɪp] *n (science)* bibliothéconomie *f*; **to study librarianship** faire des études de bibliothécaire *ou* de bibliothéconomie

library ['laɪbrərɪ] *(pl* **libraries**) **1** *n* **(a)** *(gen)* bibliothèque *f* **(b)** *(series → of books)* bibliothèque *f*, collection *f*; *(→ of records, tapes, CDs)* discothèque *f*; *(→ of films, videos)* collection *f* **(c)** *Comput (of programs)* bibliothèque *f*

2 *comp (book, card)* de bibliothèque

►► ***the Library of Congress*** la bibliothèque du Congrès *(équivalent américain de la Bibliothèque nationale)*; ***library edition*** édition *f* de luxe; ***library film*** film *m* d'archives; *Br* ***library footage, library pictures*** images *fpl* d'archives; ***library science*** bibliothéconomie *f*; **she's studying library science** elle fait des études de bibliothécaire; ***library steps*** escabeau *m* de bibliothèque

libration [laɪ'breɪʃən] *n* **(a)** *(oscillating)* oscillation *f*, balancement *m* **(b)** *(equilibrium)* équilibre *m* **(c)** *Astron (of moon)* libration *f*

librettist [lɪ'bretɪst] *n* librettiste *mf*

libretto [lɪ'bretəʊ] *(pl* **librettos** *or* **libretti** [-tɪ]) *n Mus* livret *m*, libretto *m*

Libreville ['liːbrəvɪl] *n* Libreville

Librium® ['lɪbrɪəm] *n* Librium® *m*

Libya ['lɪbɪə] *n* Libye *f*; **in Libya** en Libye

Libyan ['lɪbɪən] **1** *n* Libyen(enne) *m,f*

2 *adj* libyen

3 *comp (embassy)* de Libye; *(history)* de la Libye

►► ***the Libyan Desert*** le désert de Libye

lice [laɪs] *pl of* **louse**

licence, *Am* **license¹** ['laɪsəns] *n* **(a)** *(permit)* permis *m*; *(for marriage)* certificat *m* de publication des bans; *(for trade, bar)* licence *f*; *(for TV, radio)* redevance *f*; *(for pilot)* brevet *m*; *(for driver)* permis *m* (de conduire); **do you have a TV licence?** avez-vous payé la redevance (télé)?; **a licence to sell alcoholic drinks** une licence de débit de boissons

(b) *Admin & Com (permission)* licence *f*, autorisation *f*; **to manufacture sth under licence** fabriquer qch sous licence; **to marry by special licence** ≃ se marier sans publication de bans; *Fig* **that job's a licence to print money!** ce travail est une sinécure!

(c) *(liberty)* licence *f*, liberté *f*; **the biographer has allowed himself a certain licence in his interpretation** le biographe s'est permis certaines libertés d'interprétation; **artistic licence** licence *f* artistique

(d) *(immoral behaviour)* licence *f*, débordements *mpl*; **sexual licence** débordements *mpl* sexuels

►► *Comput* ***licence agreement*** licence *f*; *Br* ***licence fee*** redevance *f* télévisuelle; ***licence number*** *(on vehicle)* numéro *m* d'immatriculation; *(on driving licence)* numéro *m* de permis de conduire; ***licence plate*** plaque *f* minéralogique *ou* d'immatriculation

license² *vt* **(a)** *Admin & Com (premises, trader)* accorder une licence *ou* une autorisation à; **licensed to practise medicine** habilité à exercer la médecine; **to license a car** immatriculer une voiture; *Br* **is this vehicle licensed?** ce véhicule est-il immatriculé? **(b)** *(allow)* **to license sb to do sth** autoriser qn à faire qch, permettre à qn de faire qch

licensed ['laɪsənst] *adj* **(a)** *Com (product)* fabriqué sous licence; **these premises are licensed to sell alcoholic drinks** cet établissement est autorisé à vendre des boissons alcoolisées **(b)** *(pilot)* breveté; *(driver)* qui a son permis (de conduire)

►► ***licensed brand name*** nom *m* de marque sous licence; *Am* ***licensed practical nurse*** infirmier(ère) *m,f*; ***licensed premises*** *(bar, pub)* débit *m* de boissons; *(restaurant, cafeteria)* établissement *m* autorisé à vendre des boissons alcoolisées; ***licensed product*** produit *m* sous licence; *Formal* ***licensed victualler*** débitant *m* de boissons

licensee [,laɪsən'siː] *n (gen)* titulaire *mf* d'une licence *ou* d'un permis; *(pub-owner, landlord)* débitant *m* de boissons

licensing ['laɪsənsɪŋ] *n (of car)* immatriculation *f*; *(of activity)* autorisation *f*

►► ***licensing agreement*** accord *m* de licence; ***licensing authority*** = organisme chargé de la délivrance des licences; ***licensing hours*** *(in UK)* = heures d'ouverture des pubs; ***licensing***

laws** (in UK)* = lois réglementant la vente d'alcools; ***licensing requirements conditions *fpl* d'autorisation

LICENSING HOURS

Traditionnellement, les heures d'ouverture des pubs répondent à une réglementation très stricte (liée à la législation sur la vente des boissons alcoolisées), mais celle-ci a été assouplie en 1988. Au lieu d'ouvrir uniquement de 11h30 à 14h30 et de 18h à 22h30, les pubs en Angleterre peuvent désormais rester ouverts de 11h à 23h. En Écosse, en revanche, la réglementation est moins stricte et les pubs qui en font la demande peuvent ouvrir plus tard certains soirs. Dans l'avenir, la réglementation en vigueur en Angleterre et au pays de Galles, qui fait actuellement l'objet de débats au Parlement, va probablement être assouplie sur le modèle écossais.

licensor ['laɪsənsə(r)] *n* concédant *m*

licentiate [laɪ'senʃɪət] *n* diplômé(e) *m,f*

►► *Mus* ***Licentiate of the Royal Academy of Music*** = membre de la "Royal Academy of Music"

licentious [laɪ'senʃəs] *adj* licencieux

licentiously [laɪ'senʃəslɪ] *adv* licencieusement

licentiousness [laɪ'senʃəsnɪs] *n* licence *f*

lichee = **lychee**

lichen ['laɪkən, 'lɪtʃən] *n* lichen *m*

lich-gate = **lych-gate**

licit ['lɪsɪt] *adj* licite

lick [lɪk] **1** *n* (**a**) *(with tongue)* coup *m* de langue; **to give sth a lick** lécher qch; **can I have a lick of your ice-cream?** je peux goûter ta glace?; **a lick of paint** un (petit) coup de peinture; *Fam Old-fashioned* **to give oneself a lick and a promise** faire un brin de toilette

(**b**) *Br Fam (speed)* **at a tremendous lick** à fond la caisse, à fond de train

(**c**) **lick (of hair)** mèche *f*

(**d**) *Agr* pierre *f* à lécher

(**e**) *Am Fam* **we got our last licks on the beach before the weather changed** on est allé à la plage une dernière fois avant que le temps ne se gâte; **he started the debate so you get last licks** c'est lui qui a entamé le débat, ce sera donc à toi de le clore

2 *vt* (**a**) *(gen)* lécher; *(stamp)* humecter; **the dog licked its bowl clean** le chien a nettoyé sa gamelle à coups de langue; **the dog licked her hand** le chien lui a léché la main; **the cat licked (up) the milk from the plate** le chat a lapé le lait qui était dans l'assiette; **he licked the jam off the bread** il lécha la confiture de la tartine; **the dog licked the crumbs off the floor** le chien léchait les miettes par terre; *Fam* **to lick one's chops** se lécher les babines; *Fig* **the flames licked the walls of the house** les flammes léchaient les murs de la maison; *Fam* **to lick sb's boots** lécher les bottes à qn; *Br Vulg* **to lick sb's arse** lécher le cul de qn; **to lick one's lips** se lécher les lèvres; *Fig (with satisfaction, lust)* se frotter les mains; *(with eager anticipation)* se lécher les babines; **to lick one's wounds** *(of animal)* lécher ses plaies; *Fig* panser ses blessures; *Br* **how long did it take to lick the garden into shape?** combien de temps vous a-t-il fallu pour que le jardin prenne forme?; **a spell in the army will soon lick him into shape** un séjour à l'armée lui fera le plus grand bien

(**b**) *Fam (defeat)* battre à plate couture; *(in fight)* donner une raclée à; **this crossword has got me licked** ces mots croisés sont trop forts pour moi; **we've finally got the problem licked** nous sommes enfin venus à bout du problème; **when it comes to marketing, they've got us licked** pour ce qui est du marketing, on ne leur arrive pas à la cheville

►**lick out** *vt sep Br Vulg* **to lick sb out** brouter le cresson à qn

lickety-split [,lɪkətɪ'splɪt] *adv Am Fam* à toute(s) pompe(s)

licking ['lɪkɪŋ] *n Fam (thrashing)* raclée *f*, dégelée *f*; *(defeat)* raclée *f*, déculottée *f*; **to get a good licking** prendre une raclée

lickspittle ['lɪk,spɪtəl] *n Fam* lèche-bottes *mf inv*

licorice *Am* = **liquorice**

lid [lɪd] *n* (**a**) *(gen)* couvercle *m*

(**b**) *Anat (eyelid)* paupière *f*

(**c**) *Fam (hat)* galure *m*, galurin *m*; *(helmet)* casque ❑ *m*

(**d**) *Fam (idioms)* **the scandal put the lid on the Chicago operation** le scandale mit fin à l'opération de Chicago; **the firm is keeping a lid on expenses** l'entreprise met un frein aux dépenses; *Br* **that puts the (tin) lid on it!** ça, c'est le bouquet!; **to take** *or* **to lift the lid off sth** percer *ou* mettre qch à jour; *Am Fam* **keep a lid on it!** la ferme!

lidded ['lɪdɪd] *adj* (**a**) *(container)* à couvercle (**b**) **heavy lidded eyes** des yeux aux paupières lourdes

lidless ['lɪdlɪs] *adj* (**a**) *(container)* sans couvercle (**b**) *(eyes)* sans paupières

lido ['liːdəʊ] *(pl* **lidos**) *n (pool)* piscine *f* découverte; *(resort)* station *f* balnéaire

Lidocaine® ['laɪdəʊkeɪn] *n Pharm* lidocaïne *f*

LIE [laɪ]

mentir	► 1 (a)
se coucher	► 1 (b)
reposer	► 1 (c)
être classé	► 1 (d)
se trouver	► 1 (e), (g)
rester	► 1 (f)
mensonge	► 3 (a)
configuration	► 3 (b)
position	► 3 (c)

(*cont* **lying**, *pt & pp sense* (**a**) **lied**, *pt senses* (**b**) – (**j**) **lay** [leɪ], *pp senses* (**b**) – (**j**) **lain** [leɪn])

1 *vi* (**a**) *(tell untruth)* mentir; **he lied about his age** il a menti sur son âge; **"it wasn't me", she lied** "ce n'était pas moi", dit-elle en mentant; **to lie through one's teeth** mentir effrontément; *Fig* **the camera never lies** une photo ne ment pas

(**b**) *(person, animal → recline)* se coucher, s'allonger, s'étendre; *(→ be in lying position)* être couché (à plat); **to lie on one's back/side** être couché sur le dos/côté; **to be lying ill in bed** être (malade et) alité; **she lay on the beach all day** elle est restée allongée sur la plage toute la journée; **she was lying on the couch** elle était couchée *ou* allongée sur le divan; **we found him lying dead** nous l'avons trouvé mort; **he lay helpless on the floor** il gisait là sans pouvoir bouger; **lie still!** ne bouge pas!; **I like lying in bed on Sunday mornings** j'aime rester au lit *ou* faire la grasse matinée le dimanche matin; **they lay sound asleep** ils dormaient profondément, ils étaient profondément endormis; **she lay awake for hours** elle resta plusieurs heures sans pouvoir s'endormir; **to lie in wait for sb** guetter l'arrivée de qn

(**c**) *(corpse)* reposer; **he** *or* **his body lies in the village graveyard** il *ou* son corps repose au cimetière du village; **he will lie in state at Westminster Abbey** son corps sera exposé solennellement à l'abbaye de Westminster; **here lies John Smith** *(on gravestone)* ci-gît John Smith

(**d**) *(team, competitor → rank)* être classé, se classer; **France lies second, after Italy** la France est classée deuxième, après l'Italie; **she was lying fourth** *(in race)* elle était en quatrième position

(**e**) *(thing → be, be placed)* être, se trouver; **the papers lay on the table** les papiers étaient sur la table; **a folder lay open on the desk before her** un dossier était ouvert devant elle sur le bureau; **a pile of ammunition lay ready** des munitions étaient là, prêtes à servir; **I found your watch lying on the floor** j'ai trouvé ta montre qui traînait par terre; **several boats lay in the harbour** plusieurs bateaux étaient mouillés dans le port; **thick fog lay over the plain** un brouillard épais recouvrait la plaine; **snow lay (thick) on the ground** il y avait une (épaisse) couche de neige; **the castle now lies in ruins** le château est aujourd'hui en ruines; *Fig* **all her hopes and dreams lay in ruins** tous ses espoirs et ses rêves étaient anéantis *ou* réduits à néant; **the obstacles that lie in our way** les obstacles qui bloquent notre chemin

(**f**) *(thing → remain, stay)* rester; **the jewel lay hidden for many years** le bijou est resté caché pendant de nombreuses années; **our machines are lying idle** nos machines sont arrêtées *ou* ne tournent pas; **the money is just lying in the bank doing nothing** l'argent dort à la banque; **the snow didn't lie** la neige n'a pas tenu

(**g**) *(place → be situated)* se trouver, être; *(land → stretch, extend)* s'étendre; **Texas lies to the south of Oklahoma** le Texas se trouve *ou* s'étend au sud de l'Oklahoma; **these hills lie between us and the sea** ces collines sont entre nous et la mer; **the valley lay at our feet** la vallée s'étendait à nos pieds; **a vast desert lay before us** un immense désert s'étendait devant nous

(**h**) *(future event)* **they didn't know what lay ahead of them** ils ne savaient pas ce qui les attendait; **who knows what may lie in store for us** qui sait ce qui nous attend *ou* ce que l'avenir nous réserve

(**i**) *(answer, explanation, duty etc)* **the problem lies in getting them motivated** le problème, c'est de réussir à les motiver; **where do our real interests lie?** qu'est-ce qui compte vraiment pour nous?; **the fault lies with you** c'est de votre faute; **responsibility for the strike lies with the management** la responsabilité de la grève incombe à la direction; **the onus of proof lies with them** c'est à eux qu'il incombe de fournir la preuve; **my talents do not lie in that direction** je n'ai pas de dispositions *ou* de talent pour cela

(**j**) *Law (appeal, claim)* être recevable

2 *vt* **she lied her way into the building** elle a pénétré dans l'immeuble grâce à quelques mensonges; **he always lies his way out of difficulties** il se sort toujours des difficultés en mentant

3 *n* (**a**) *(untruth)* mensonge *m*; **to tell lies** dire des mensonges, mentir; **a pack of lies** un tissu de mensonges; *Literary* **to give the lie to sth** démentir qch; **it was in June, no, I tell a lie, in July** c'était en juin, non, je me trompe, en juillet; **there are lies, damned lies and statistics** on fait dire ce que l'on veut aux chiffres

(**b**) *(of land)* configuration *f*, disposition *f*

(**c**) *Golf (of golf ball)* position *f*; **he's got a bad lie** c'est une balle difficile

►► ***lie detector*** détecteur *m* de mensonges; **to take a lie detector test** passer au détecteur de mensonges

►**lie about, lie around** *vi* (**a**) *(person)* traîner; **I lay about all weekend doing nothing** j'ai traîné tout le week-end à ne rien faire

(**b**) *(thing)* traîner; **don't leave your things lying about** ne laisse pas traîner tes affaires

►**lie back** *vi* **he lay back in his armchair** il s'est renversé dans son fauteuil; *Fig* **just lie back and take it easy!** repose-toi un peu!; **when you've finished you'll be able to lie back and take things easy** quand tu auras fini tu pourras te reposer

►**lie behind** *vt insep* se cacher derrière; **what can lie behind this unexpected decision?** qu'est-ce qui peut bien se cacher derrière cette décision soudaine?; **deep insecurity lay behind his apparently successful life** sa vie, en apparence réussie, cachait une profonde insécurité

►**lie down** *vi* se coucher, s'allonger, s'étendre; **go and lie down for an hour** va t'allonger une heure; **to lie down on the ground** se coucher *ou* s'allonger par terre; **to take sth lying down** accepter qch sans réagir *ou* sans broncher; **I won't take this lying down!** je ne vais pas me laisser faire comme ça!

►**lie in** *vi* (**a**) *(stay in bed)* faire la grasse matinée

(**b**) *Arch Med* être en couches

►**lie off** *vi Naut* rester au large

►**lie to** *vi Naut* se tenir *ou* (se) mettre à la cape

►**lie up** *vi (person)* rester au lit, garder le lit; *(machine)* ne pas tourner, être arrêté; *(car)* rester au garage

'As I Lay Dying' *Faulkner* 'Tandis que j'agonise'

> **Lie back and think of England**
> Peu de gens savent que la phrase à l'origine de cette formule ("allonge-toi et pense à l'Angleterre") fut prononcée par Lady Hillingdon en 1912, mais elle n'en évoque pas moins dans l'esprit de tous l'époque victorienne et son idéologie. En fait la phrase exacte était **I lie down on my bed, close my eyes, open my legs, and think of England** ("je m'allonge sur mon lit, je ferme les yeux, j'écarte les jambes, et je pense à l'Angleterre").
> Aujourd'hui on utilise cette phrase dans son contexte d'origine à propos d'une femme qui accepte à contrecœur d'avoir des rapports sexuels, et de manière générale pour parler d'une attitude caractérisée par un certain stoïcisme, comme dans l'exemple **I know life's tough for you at the moment working out there in the Antarctic but you'll just have to lie back and think of England** ("je sais que la vie n'est pas facile pour toi qui travailles là-bas dans l'Antarctique, mais il faut que tu prennes ton mal en patience").

lie-abed *n Arch* paresseux(euse) *m,f*

Liechtenstein ['lɪktənstaɪn] *n* Liechtenstein *m*; **in Liechtenstein** au Liechtenstein

lied [li:d] (*pl* **lieder** ['li:də(r)]) *n Mus* lied *m*

lie-down *n Br Fam* **to have a lie-down** se coucher❑, s'allonger❑; **I think I'll go for a little lie-down** je crois que je vais aller m'allonger un peu; **that lie-down has done me good** ça m'a fait du bien de m'allonger un peu

lief [li:f] *adv Arch or Literary* **I'd as lief die as marry him** plutôt mourir que de l'épouser

liege [li:dʒ] *Arch* **1** *n* seigneur *m*, suzerain *m*
2 *adj (vassal, homage)* lige
▸▸ ***liege lord*** seigneur *m*, suzerain *m*; ***liege man*** homme *m* lige

lie-in *n Br Fam* **to have a lie-in** faire la grasse matinée

lien ['lɪən] *n Law (on property)* privilège *m*, droit *m* de rétention; **to have a lien on a cargo** avoir un recours sur un chargement; *Fin* **lien on shares** nantissement *m* d'actions

lieu [lju:, lu:] **1 in lieu** *adv* **take Monday off in lieu** prends ton lundi pour compenser
2 in lieu of *prep* au lieu de, à la place de; **two weeks salary in lieu of notice** deux semaines de salaire en guise de préavis

Lieut *Mil (written abbr* **lieutenant**) Lieut.

Lieut-Col *Mil (written abbr* **Lieutenant-Colonel**) Lieut.-Col.

lieutenancy [*Br* lef'tenənsɪ, *Am* lu:'tenənsɪ] *n* (**a**) *Mil (in army)* grade *m* de lieutenant; *(in navy)* grade *m* de lieutenant de vaisseau (**b**) *Hist* lieutenance *f*

lieutenant [*Br* lef'tenənt, *Am* lu:'tenənt] *n* (**a**) *Mil (in army)* lieutenant *m*; *(in navy)* lieutenant *m* de vaisseau
(**b**) *(in US and Canadian police)* inspecteur *m* (de police)
(**c**) *Fig* lieutenant *m*, second *m*; **the marketing director and his lieutenants** le directeur du marketing et ses lieutenants
(**d**) *Hist* lieutenant *m*
▸▸ ***lieutenant colonel*** lieutenant-colonel *m*; ***lieutenant commander*** capitaine *m* de corvette; ***lieutenant general*** *(in army)* général *m* de corps d'armée; *(in US airforce)* général *m* de corps aérien; ***lieutenant governor*** *(in Canada)* lieutenant(e) *m,f* gouverneur(e); *(in US)* gouverneur(e) *m,f* adjoint(e)

LIFE [laɪf]

vie	▸ 1 (a) – (d), (f) – (i), (k)
sensation	▸ 1 (e)
nature	▸ 1 (j)
réalité	▸ 1 (j)
prison à vie	▸ 1 (l)
durée	▸ 1 (m)
à vie	▸ 2

(*pl* **lives** [laɪvz]) **1** *n* (**a**) *(existence)* vie *f*; **to give life to sb** donner la vie à qn; **they believe in life after death** ils croient à la vie après la mort; **it's a matter of life and death** c'est une question de vie ou de mort; **life is hard** la vie est dure; **life has been good to us** la vie nous a gâtés; **he hasn't seen much of life** il ne connaît pas grand-chose de la vie; **you really see life as a cop** quand on est flic, on en voit de toutes les couleurs; **there have been several attempts on her life** elle a été victime de plusieurs attentats; **he's in hospital fighting for his life** il lutte contre la mort à l'hôpital; *Fam* **how's life?** comment ça va?; **what a life!** quelle vie!; **just relax and enjoy life!** profite donc un peu de la vie!; **I want to live my own life** je veux vivre ma vie; **is life worth living?** la vie vaut-elle la peine d'être vécue?; **life is worth living when I'm with her** avec elle, la vie vaut la peine d'être vécue; **meeting him has made my life worth living** le rencontrer *ou* notre rencontre a donné un sens à ma vie; **he makes her life a misery** il lui rend la vie impossible; **to live life to the** *Br* **full** *or Am* **fullest** croquer la vie à belles dents; **hundreds lost their lives** des centaines de personnes ont trouvé la mort; **he emigrated in order to make a new life for himself** il a émigré pour commencer une nouvelle vie *ou* pour repartir à zéro; **to depart this life** quitter ce monde; **to save sb's life** sauver la vie à qn; **to risk one's life (to do sth)** risquer sa vie (à faire qch); **to risk life and limb** risquer sa peau; **a cat has nine lives** *(person)* avoir l'âme chevillée au corps; **to take sb's life** tuer qn; **she took her own life** elle s'est donné la mort; **she's the only woman in his life** c'est la seule femme dans sa vie; **to run for one's life** *or* **for dear life** s'enfuir à toutes jambes; **run for your lives!** sauve qui peut!; **she was hanging on for dear life** elle s'accrochait de toutes ses forces; **for the life of me I can't remember where we met** rien à faire, je n'arrive pas à me rappeler où nous nous sommes rencontrés; *Fam* **get a life!** t'as rien de mieux à faire de ton temps?; *Br Fam* **my life!** c'est pas vrai!; *Fam* **he can't sing to save his life** il chante comme un pied; **not on your life!** jamais de la vie!; **you take your life in your hands when cycling in London** on risque sa vie quand on fait du vélo à Londres; **that's life!, such is life!** c'est la vie!; **this is the life!** (ça, c'est) la belle vie!; **I had the time of my life** je ne me suis jamais autant amusé; *Arch* **upon my life** seigneur!, mon Dieu!
(**b**) *(period of existence)* vie *f*; **I've worked hard all my life** j'ai travaillé dur toute ma vie; **in his early life** quand il était jeune; **I began life as a labourer** j'ai débuté dans la vie comme ouvrier; **it began life as a car chassis** à l'origine c'était un châssis de voiture; **we don't want to spend the rest of our lives here** on ne veut pas finir nos jours ici; **I've never eaten snails in my life** je n'ai jamais mangé d'escargots de ma vie; **I ran the race of my life!** j'ai fait la course de ma vie!; **it gave me the fright of my life** je n'ai jamais eu aussi peur de ma vie; **my/her/***etc* **life's work** l'œuvre *f* de toute ma/sa/*etc* vie; **the fire destroyed her life's work** l'incendie a détruit l'œuvre de toute sa vie; **to mate for life** *(animal, bird)* s'unir pour la vie
(**c**) *(mode of existence)* vie *f*; **they lead a strange life** ils mènent une drôle de vie; **school life** la vie scolaire; **she's not used to city life** elle n'a pas l'habitude de vivre en ville; **married life** la vie conjugale; *Fam* **to live the life of Riley** mener une vie de pacha; **life at the top!** la grande vie!
(**d**) *(living things collectively)* vie *f*; **is there life on Mars?** y a-t-il de la vie sur Mars?
(**e**) *(UNCOUNT) (physical feeling)* sensation *f*; **life began to return to her frozen fingers** le sang se remit peu à peu à circuler dans ses doigts gelés
(**f**) *(liveliness)* vie *f*; **she's still young and full of life** elle est encore jeune et pleine de vie; **there's no life in this place** ça manque d'entrain ici; **there's a lot more life in Sydney than in Wellington** Sydney est nettement plus animé que Wellington; **to come to life** s'animer; **to bring sb to life** *(play, book etc)* faire vivre qn; **his arrival put new life into the firm** son arrivée a donné un coup de fouet à l'entreprise; **there's life in the old dog yet!** il est encore vert, le bonhomme!; **she was the life and soul of the party** c'est elle qui a mis de l'ambiance dans la soirée, elle fut le boute-en-train de la soirée
(**g**) *(living person)* vie *f*; **a phone call can save a life** un coup de fil peut sauver une vie; **200 lives were lost in the disaster** 200 personnes ont perdu la vie dans la catastrophe, la catastrophe a fait 200 morts; **no lives were lost** il n'y a eu aucune victime, on ne déplore aucune victime
(**h**) *(durability)* (durée *f* de) vie *f*; **double the life of your batteries** multipliez par deux la durée de vos piles; **the average life of an isotope** la durée de vie moyenne d'un isotope; **during the life of the previous government** sous le gouvernement précédent
(**i**) *(biography)* vie *f*; **she's writing a life of James Joyce** elle écrit une biographie de James Joyce
(**j**) *Art* nature *f*; *Literature* réalité *f*; **to draw from life** dessiner d'après nature; **his novels are very true to life** ses romans sont très réalistes; **that's her to the life** c'est elle tout craché
(**k**) *(in games)* vie *f*; **when you lose three lives you're out** quand on perd trois vies, on est éliminé
(**l**) *Fam (imprisonment)* prison *f* à vie❑; **the kidnappers got life** les ravisseurs ont été condamnés à perpétuité *ou* à la prison à vie; **he's doing life** il purge une peine à perpétuité
(**m**) *Fin (of loan)* durée *f*
2 *comp (post, member, president)* à vie
3 for life *adv* **he was crippled for life** il a été estropié à vie; **sent to prison for life** condamné à perpétuité; **if you help me, I'll be your friend for life** si tu m'aides, je serai ton ami pour la vie; **a job for life** un emploi à vie
▸▸ *Fin* ***life annuity*** rente *f* viagère; *Br* ***life assurance*** assurance-vie *f*; ***Life Assurance and Unit Trust Regulatory Organization*** = organisme britannique contrôlant les activités de compagnies d'assurance-vie et de SICAV; ***life belt*** bouée *f* de sauvetage; ***life buoy*** bouée *f* de sauvetage; *Fin* ***life capitalization*** capitalisation *f* viagère; ***life class*** cours *m* de dessin avec modèle nu; ***life cycle*** cycle *m* de vie; *Mktg* ***life cycle chart, life cycle curve*** *(of product)* courbe *f* du cycle de vie; ***life drawing*** dessin *m* d'après modèle; ***life expectancy*** *(of human, animal)* espérance *f* de vie; *(of machine, product)* durée *f* (utile) de vie; ***the Life Guards*** = régiment de cavalerie de la garde royale britannique; ***life history*** vie *f*; **the organism takes on many different forms during its life history** l'organisme prend de nombreuses formes au cours de sa vie *ou* de son existence; **she told me her whole life history** elle m'a raconté l'histoire de sa vie; ***life imprisonment*** prison *f* à vie; ***life insurance*** assurance-vie *f*; **to take out life insurance** contracter une assurance-vie; ***life jacket*** gilet *m* de sauvetage; ***life member*** membre *m* à vie; ***life membership*** adhésion *f* à vie; *Br* ***life peer*** pair *m* à vie; *Br* ***life peerage*** pairie *f* à vie; *Fin* ***life pension*** pension *f* à vie; *Am* ***life preserver*** *(life belt)* bouée *f* de sauvetage; *(life jacket)* gilet *m* de sauvetage; ***life raft*** radeau *m* de sauvetage; *Am* ***Life Saver®*** = bonbon acidulé en forme de bouée de sauvetage; ***the life sciences*** les sciences *fpl* de la vie; **anthropology is a life science** l'anthropologie fait partie des sciences de la vie; ***life sentence*** condamnation *f* à vie *ou* à perpétuité; ***life skills*** = aptitude à fonctionner efficacement en société; ***life span*** *(of human, animal)* espérance *f* de vie; *(of machine, product)* durée *f* de vie; ***life story*** biographie *f*; **she told me her whole life story** elle m'a raconté l'histoire de sa vie; *Fam* **just give us the facts, we don't need your life story!** tenez-vous-en aux faits, inutile de nous raconter votre vie!; ***life subscription*** abonnement *m* à vie; ***life tenant*** usufruitier(ère) *m,f*; ***life vest*** gilet *m* de sauvetage

life-and-death *adj* **a life-and-death matter** une question de vie ou de mort; **this is a life-and-death decision** c'est une décision vitale; **a life-and-death struggle** un combat à mort, une lutte désespérée

lifeblood ['laɪfblʌd] *n (of company etc)* âme *f*; *Literary (of person)* sang *m*; **the government are draining the lifeblood from small businesses** le gouvernement est en train de saigner les petites entreprises; **the lifeblood of the economy** le pivot de l'économie

lifeboat ['laɪfbəʊt] *n* (**a**) *(launched from coast)* canot *m* de sauvetage (**b**) **(ship's) lifeboat** chaloupe *f* de sauvetage
▸▸ *lifeboat station* poste *m* de sauvetage

lifeboatman ['laɪfbəʊtmən] *(pl* **lifeboatmen** [-mən]) *n* sauveteur *m* (en mer)

life-force *n* force *f* vitale

life-form *n* forme *f* de vie

life-giving *adj* qui insuffle la vie, vivifiant

lifeguard ['laɪfgɑːd] *n (at seaside)* surveillant *m* de baignade; *(at swimming pool)* maître *m* nageur; **to be on lifeguard duty** surveiller la baignade

lifeless ['laɪflɪs] *adj* (**a**) *(dead body)* sans vie; **his lifeless form** son corps sans vie; **she fell lifeless to the floor** elle est tombée raide sur le sol (**b**) *(where no life exists)* sans vie; **a lifeless desert** un désert sans vie (**c**) *(dull → eyes)* éteint; *(→ hair)* terne; *(→ town)* mort; *(→ style, performance)* plat

lifelessly ['laɪflɪslɪ] *adv* (**a**) *(inanimately)* sans vie (**b**) *(dully → perform, write, speak)* platement

lifelessness ['laɪflɪsnɪs] *n* (**a**) *(of body)* absence *f* de vie (**b**) *(dullness → of town)* manque *m* d'animation; *(→ of style, performance)* platitude *f*

lifelike ['laɪflaɪk] *adj* (**a**) *(portrait)* ressemblant (**b**) *(seeming alive)* **the new robots are extremely lifelike** ces nouveaux robots ont l'air *ou* paraissent vraiment vivants

lifeline ['laɪflaɪn] *n* (**a**) *Naut (thrown to boat)* remorque *f*; *(stretched across deck)* sauvegarde *f*, filière *f* de mauvais temps *ou* de sécurité; **they threw the drowning man a lifeline** ils ont lancé un filin à l'homme qui se noyait
(**b**) *(for diver)* corde *f* de sécurité
(**c**) *Fig* **it's his lifeline to the outside world** c'est son lien avec le monde extérieur; **to cut off sb's lifeline** couper les vivres à qn; **to throw sb a lifeline** venir à l'aide de qn; *Fig* **for us it was a financial lifeline** cet argent a permis notre survie
(**d**) *(in palmistry)* ligne *f* de vie

lifelong ['laɪflɒŋ] *adj* de toute une vie; **a lifelong friend** un ami de toujours; **it's been my lifelong ambition to meet her** toute ma vie, j'ai espéré la rencontrer
▸▸ *lifelong learning* éducation *f* permanente

life-or-death = **life-and-death**

lifer ['laɪfə(r)] *n Fam* condamné(e) *m,f* à perpète

life-renter *n Scot Law* usufruitier(ère) *m,f* à vie

lifesaver ['laɪf,seɪvə(r)] *n* (**a**) *(lifeguard)* maître *m* nageur (**b**) *Fam Fig* **thank you, you're a lifesaver!** merci, tu m'as sauvé la vie!; **that money was a lifesaver** cet argent m'a sauvé la vie; **that cup of tea was a lifesaver!** cette tasse de thé m'a redonné vie

life-saving *adj* **life-saving apparatus** appareils *mpl ou* engins *mpl* de sauvetage; **life-saving vaccine** vaccin *m* qui sauve la vie

life-size(d) *adj* grandeur nature *(inv)*

lifestyle ['laɪfstaɪl] *n* style *m ou* mode *m* de vie
▸▸ *Mktg* ***lifestyle analysis*** analyse *f* du style de vie; *Mktg* ***lifestyle data*** données *fpl* de style de vie; *Mktg* ***lifestyle group*** sociostyle *m*; *Mktg* ***lifestyle segmentation*** segmentation *f* par styles de vie

life-support system *n Med* respirateur *m* artificiel; *Aviat & Astron* équipement *m* de vie; **he's on a life-support system** il est sous assistance respiratoire

life-threatening *adj (illness)* qui peut être mortel; **it's not life-threatening** ce n'est pas mortel

lifetime ['laɪftaɪm] *n (of person)* vie *f*; *(of lamp, machine) & Fin (of option)* durée *f*, vie *f*; *Nucl (of atom, isotope)* durée *f* de vie, longévité *f*; *St Exch (of an option)* durée *f* de vie; **in** *or* **during one's lifetime** de son vivant; **such a bill is unlikely within the lifetime of this parliament** un tel projet de loi est peu probable tant que ce parlement est en place; **a lifetime of happiness** toute une vie de bonheur; **it's the chance** *or* **opportunity of a lifetime** cette chance n'arrive qu'une fois dans la vie; **the holiday of a lifetime** des vacances sensationnelles; **a lifetime supply** une réserve pour la vie; **he's bought enough envelopes to last him a lifetime** il a acheté suffisamment d'enveloppes pour tenir jusqu'à la fin de ses jours

LIFFE [laɪf, 'lɪfɪ] *n Fin (abbr* **London International Financial Futures Exchange**) = marché à terme britannique d'instruments financiers, ≃ MATIF *m*

LIFO ['laɪfəʊ] *n Com & Fin (abbr* **last in, first out**) DEPS

lift [lɪft] **1** *vt* (**a**) *(object)* soulever, lever; *(one's head, eyes, arm)* lever; **help me lift the wardrobe** aide-moi à soulever l'armoire; **she lifted the washing basket off** *or* **from the table** elle a soulevé le panier à linge de la table; **I lifted the books out of the crate** j'ai sorti les livres de la caisse; **she lifted her eyes from her magazine** elle leva les yeux de sa revue; **she lifted the suitcase down from the top of the wardrobe** elle a descendu la valise de dessus l'armoire; **to lift weights** *(as exercise)* faire des haltères; **I feel as if a burden has been lifted from my shoulders** j'ai l'impression qu'on m'a enlevé un poids des épaules; **the forward lifted the ball over the goalkeeper** l'avant a lobé le gardien de but; *Literary* **the church lifts its spire to the skies** l'église dresse sa flèche vers le ciel
(**b**) *Formal (voice)* élever
(**c**) *(spirits, heart)* remonter; **his music never fails to lift my spirits** sa musique me remonte toujours le moral
(**d**) *(end → blockade, embargo etc)* lever; *(→ control, restriction)* supprimer; *(→ mortgage)* déshypothéquer
(**e**) *Fam (steal)* piquer, faucher; *(plagiarize)* plagier❑, piquer; **he had his wallet lifted** il s'est fait piquer son portefeuille; **to lift a passage from an author/a book** piquer un passage chez un auteur/dans un livre
(**f**) *Br Fam (arrest)* agrafer, alpaguer; **he got lifted for stealing cars** il s'est fait agrafer *ou* alpaguer pour vol de voitures
(**g**) *(bulbs, potatoes, turnips)* arracher
(**h**) *Am (debt)* rembourser
(**i**) *(face)* **she's had her face lifted** elle s'est fait faire un lifting
2 *vi* (**a**) *(rise)* se lever, se soulever; **our spirits lifted at the news** la nouvelle nous a remonté le moral
(**b**) *(fog, mist)* se lever, se dissiper; *(cloud)* se dissiper; **his bad mood didn't lift all day** sa mauvaise humeur ne s'est pas dissipée de la journée
(**c**) *Sport (in walking race)* marcher sur la pointe des pieds
3 *n* (**a**) *(act of lifting)* **to give sth a lift** soulever qch
(**b**) *(in morale, energy)* **to give sb a lift** remonter le moral à qn; **glucose tablets are good if you need a quick lift** les comprimés de glucose sont bons si vous avez besoin d'un coup de fouet
(**c**) *Br (elevator)* ascenseur *m*; **goods lift** monte-charge *m inv*
(**d**) *(car ride)* **to give sb a lift** prendre *ou* emmener qn en voiture; **could you give me a lift to the station?** *(it's on your way)* est-ce que tu peux me déposer à la gare?; *(make special trip)* est-ce que tu peux m'emmener à la gare?; **can I give you a lift?** est-ce que je peux vous conduire *ou* déposer quelque part?; **I'll try to arrange a lift for anyone who hasn't got a car** je ferai en sorte que tout le monde ait une place dans une voiture; **we've been waiting over two hours for a lift** cela fait deux heures que nous attendons que quelqu'un veuille bien nous prendre; **we got a great lift yesterday, all the way to Lyons** on a eu de la chance hier, il y a quelqu'un qui nous a emmenés jusqu'à Lyon
(**e**) *(extent of rise → of crane etc)* hauteur *f* de levage; *(→ of pump)* hauteur *f* d'élévation; *Tech (→ of valve, cam)* levée *f*; *(→ of millrace)* (hauteur *f* de) chute *f*; *(between bearings)* différence *f* de niveau
(**f**) *(raising power → of balloon, gas)* force *f* ascensionnelle; *Aviat* portance *f*, poussée *f* (aérodynamique), sustentation *f*
(**g**) *(shoe)* talonnette *f*
▸▸ *Br* ***lift attendant*** liftier(ère) *m,f*; *Br* ***lift engineer*** ascensoriste *mf*; *Br* ***lift operator*** liftier(ère) *m,f*; *Br* ***lift shaft*** cage *f* d'ascenseur

▸**lift down** *vt sep (object from shelf)* descendre

▸**lift off 1** *vt sep (hat, lid)* enlever, ôter
2 *vi (plane, rocket)* décoller

▸**lift out** *vt sep (from box etc)* sortir (**from** de); *Mil (troops)* évacuer (par avion *ou* hélicoptère)

▸**lift up** *vt sep* (**a**) *(object)* soulever, lever; *(part of body)* lever; **to lift sb up** *(who has fallen)* aider qn à se relever; **lift me up so I can see the parade** soulève-moi pour que je puisse voir le défilé; **she lifted up the mat and found a key** elle souleva le paillasson et trouva une clé; **to lift up one's head** lever la tête
(**b**) *Formal (voice, heart)* élever; **the choir lifted up their voices in song** le chœur s'est mis à chanter; **lift up your hearts in prayer** élevez vos âmes *ou* cœurs dans la prière

liftboy ['lɪftbɔɪ] *n Br* liftier *m*

liftgate ['lɪftgeɪt] *n Am Aut* hayon *m*

lifting ['lɪftɪŋ] *n* (**a**) *(of weight)* levage *m* (**b**) *(of blockade, embargo etc)* levée *f*; *(of control, restriction)* suppression *f* (**c**) *(of bulbs, potatoes, turnips)* arrachage *m*, récolte *f*
▸▸ *lifting gear* appareil *m* de levage; ***lifting jack*** cric *m* (de levage)

liftman ['lɪftmæn] *(pl* **liftmen** [-men]) *n Br* liftier *m*

lift-off *n* décollage *m*; **we have lift-off!** lancement réussi!

lig [lɪg] *vi Br Fam* (**a**) *(spend time idly)* paresser❑ (**b**) *(freeload)* vivre en parasite❑

ligament ['lɪgəmənt] *n Anat* ligament *m*; **to tear a ligament** se déchirer un ligament

ligand ['lɪgənd] *n Chem* ligand *m*

ligase ['laɪgeɪz] *n Biol & Chem* ligase *f*

ligate ['laɪgeɪt] *vt Med* ligaturer, faire une ligature à

ligation [laɪ'geɪʃən] *n Med* ligature *f*

ligature ['lɪgətjə(r)] **1** *n* (**a**) *Med* ligature *f* (**b**) *Typ* ligature *f* (**c**) *Mus* liaison *f*
2 *vt* (**a**) *Med (vein)* ligaturer, barrer (**b**) *Typ (two vowels)* ligaturer; **o e ligatured** e dans l'o

liger ['laɪgə(r)] *n Zool* ligre *m*

ligger ['lɪgə(r)] *n* (**a**) *(idler)* paresseux(euse) *m,f* (**b**) *(freeloader)* parasite *m*

LIGHT [laɪt]

lumière	▸ 1 (a), (b)
lampe	▸ 1 (b)
lueur	▸ 1 (c)
feu	▸ 1 (d), (e), (g)
phare	▸ 1 (d), (j)
jour	▸ 1 (f)
fenêtre	▸ 1 (h)
solution	▸ 1 (i)
clair	▸ 2 (a), (b)
atone	▸ 2 (c)
léger	▸ 2 (d) – (f); 3
éclairer	▸ 4 (a)
allumer	▸ 4 (b)
s'allumer	▸ 5 (a)

(pt & pp **lit** [lɪt] *or* **lighted**) **1** *n* (**a**) *(luminosity, brightness)* lumière *f*; **there's not enough light to read by** il n'y a pas assez de lumière pour lire; **it looks brown in this light** on dirait que c'est marron avec cette lumière; **by the light of our flashlamps** à la lumière de nos lampes de poche; **by the light of the moon** au clair *ou* à la clarté de la lune; **the light was beginning to fail** le jour commençait à baisser; **she took the picture against the light** elle a pris la photo à contre-jour; *Literary* **at first light** au point *ou* au lever du jour; **you're (standing) in my light** tu me fais de l'ombre; **in the cold light of the morning** dans la lueur pâle du matin; *Fig* **to bring sth to light** révéler qch; **to be brought** *or* **to come to light** être découvert *ou* révélé; **the trial will throw** *or* **cast light on their real motives** le procès permettra d'en savoir plus sur *ou* de percer à jour leurs véritables mobiles; **can you throw any light on this problem?** peux-tu apporter tes lumières sur ce problème?, peux-tu éclaircir cette question?; **the light at the end of the tunnel** le bout du tunnel; **at last we can see (some** *or* **the) light at the end of the tunnel** enfin on voit le bout du tunnel; **to see the light** *(understand)* comprendre; *(be converted)* trouver le chemin de la vérité; **to see the light of day** voir le jour
(**b**) *(light source)* lumière *f*; *(lamp)* lampe *f*; **the lights of the city** les lumières de la ville; **a light went on in the window** une lumière s'est allumée à la fenêtre; **turn the light on/off** allume/

lif–lig

éteins (la lumière); **put the lights out before you go to bed** éteins les lumières avant de te coucher; **during the storm the lights went out** il y a eu une panne d'électricité *ou* de lumière pendant l'orage; **to go out like a light** *(fall asleep)* s'endormir tout de suite; *(faint)* tomber dans les pommes; *Fam Hum* **the lights are on but there's nobody home** c'est pas une lumière

(**c**) *Fig (in someone's eyes)* lueur *f*

(**d**) *Aut (gen)* feu *m*; *(headlamp)* phare *m*; **we were dazzled by the lights of the oncoming cars** les phares des véhicules qui venaient en face nous éblouissaient; **dip your lights** roulez en code

(**e**) *(traffic light)* feu *m* (rouge); **turn left at the lights** tournez à gauche au feu rouge; **she jumped the lights** elle a brûlé le feu rouge; **the lights were (on) amber** le feu était à l'orange

(**f**) *(aspect, viewpoint)* jour *m*; **I see the problem in a different light** je vois le problème sous un autre jour; **in a good/bad/new light** sous un jour favorable/défavorable/nouveau; *Literary* **to act according to one's lights** agir selon ses principes

(**g**) *(flame)* feu *m*; **could you give me a light?** pouvez-vous me donner du feu?; **have you got a light?** vous avez du feu?; **to set light to sth** mettre le feu à qch

(**h**) *(window)* fenêtre *f*; *(small round)* lucarne *f*; *(of mullioned window)* jour *m*; *(of greenhouse)* carreau *m*

(**i**) *(in crossword)* solution *f*

(**j**) *(lighthouse)* phare *m*

2 *adj* (**a**) *(bright, well-lit)* clair; **a large, light room** une grande pièce claire; **it isn't light enough to read** il n'y a pas assez de lumière pour lire; **it's getting light already** il commence déjà à faire jour; **it stays light until 10** il fait jour jusqu'à 10 heures du soir

(**b**) *(pale)* clair; **she has light hair** elle a des cheveux clairs; **light yellow/brown** jaune/marron clair *(inv)*

(**c**) *Ling (in phonetics)* atone

(**d**) *(in weight)* léger; **as light as a feather** léger comme une plume; **light clothes** vêtements *mpl* légers; **to be light on one's feet** être leste; **light touch** *(of painter, author, film director)* finesse *f*; **she's got a very light touch with pastry** les pâtisseries qu'elle fait sont très légères

(**e**) *(comedy, music etc)* léger, facile; **light conversation** conversation *f* peu sérieuse, propos *mpl* anodins

(**f**) *(not intense, strong etc)* léger; **there was a light tap at the door** on frappa tout doucement à la porte; **the traffic was light** la circulation était fluide; **I had a light lunch** j'ai mangé légèrement à midi, j'ai déjeuné léger; **a light rain was falling** il tombait une pluie fine; **take some light reading** prends quelque chose de facile à lire; **I'm a light sleeper** j'ai le sommeil léger; **a light wine** un vin léger; **he can only do light work** il ne peut faire que des travaux peu fatigants; **to make light of sth** prendre qch à la légère

3 *adv* **to travel light** voyager léger

4 *vt* (**a**) *(illuminate)* éclairer; **the room was lit by a single bare bulb** la pièce n'était éclairée que par une ampoule nue; **I'll light the way for you** je vais t'éclairer le chemin

(**b**) *(lamp, candle, cigarette)* allumer; *(match)* craquer; **to light a fire** allumer un feu, faire du feu

5 *vi* (**a**) *(lamp)* s'allumer; *(match)* s'enflammer; *(fire, coal)* prendre

(**b**) *Literary (alight)* se poser; **to light from a horse** descendre d'un cheval

6 lights *npl (lungs)* mou *m*

7 in (the) light of *prep* **in (the) light of these new facts** à la lumière de ces faits nouveaux

►► ***light air*** *(on Beaufort scale)* très légère brise *f*; ***light aircraft*** avion *m* de tourisme; *Br* ***light ale*** = bière brune légère; *Mil* ***light artillery*** artillerie *f* légère *ou* de petit calibre; ***light beam*** faisceau *m* lumineux; ***light box*** table *f* lumineuse; ***light breeze*** *(gen)* petite brise *f*, brise *f* légère; *(on Beaufort scale)* légère brise *f*; ***light bulb*** ampoule *f* (électrique); *Metal* ***light castings*** petites pièces *fpl* de fonderie; *Am* ***light cream*** crème *f* liquide; *TV* ***light cue*** signal *m* lumineux; ***light entertainment*** variétés *fpl*; *Fam* **it's not exactly light entertainment** *(job)* ce n'est pas ce qu'on fait de plus divertissant; *(music, play, film)* ce n'est pas ce qu'il y a de plus léger; ***light fitting*** applique *f* (électrique); ***light flare*** fusée *f* éclairante; ***light industry*** industrie *f* légère; ***light infantry*** infanterie *f* légère; ***light meter*** posemètre *m*; ***light opera*** opéra *m* comique, opérette *f*; *Comput* ***light pen*** crayon *m* optique; ***light pollution*** excès *m* de lumière artificielle; ***light ray*** rayon *m* lumineux; ***light show*** spectacle *m* de lumière; **a laser light show** un spectacle laser; ***light soil*** terre *f* légère; ***light switch*** interrupteur *m*; ***light table*** *(for viewing negatives, film)* table *f* lumineuse; *Mktg* ***light user*** faible utilisateur(-trice) *m,f*; ***light vehicle*** véhicule *m* léger; ***light wave*** onde *f* lumineuse; ***light weapons*** armes *fpl* légères

►**light into** *vt insep Fam* **to light into sb** *(attack)* rentrer dans le lard à qn

►**light on** *vt insep* tomber (par hasard) sur, trouver par hasard

►**light out** *vi Am Fam* se tirer

►**light up 1** *vt sep* éclairer; **the house was all lit up** la maison était tout *ou* toute éclairée; **joy lit up her face** son visage rayonnait de bonheur

2 *vi* (**a**) *(lamp)* s'allumer; **the whole sky lit up** le ciel entier s'illumina

(**b**) *(face, eyes)* s'éclairer, s'illuminer

(**c**) *Fam (light cigarette)* allumer une cigarette ❑

►**light upon** = **light on**

light-coloured *adj* clair, de couleur claire

light-duty *adj*

►► ***light-duty machine*** machine *f* de faible puissance, machine *f* auxiliaire; ***light-duty vehicle*** véhicule *m* de poids léger

lighted ['laɪtɪd] *adj (room)* éclairé; *(candle)* allumé

light-emitting diode [-ɪ'mɪtɪŋ-] *n* diode *f* électroluminescente

lighten ['laɪtən] **1** *vt* (**a**) *(make brighter)* éclairer, illuminer; **a single candle lightened the darkness** seule une bougie trouait l'obscurité

(**b**) *(make paler)* éclaircir; **lighten the blue with a little white** éclaircissez le bleu avec un peu de blanc; **to have one's hair lightened** se faire éclaircir les cheveux

(**c**) *(make less heavy)* alléger; **having an assistant will lighten my workload** avec un assistant ma charge de travail sera moins lourde

2 *vi* (**a**) *(become light)* s'éclairer, s'éclaircir; **the sky has lightened a little** le ciel s'est légèrement éclairci; **her mood lightened** sa mauvaise humeur se dissipa

(**b**) *(load, burden)* s'alléger; **my heart lightened** j'ai été soulagé

►**lighten up** *vi Fam* se remettre ❑; **oh come on, lighten up!** allez, remets-toi *ou* ne fais pas cette tête!

lighter ['laɪtə(r)] **1** *n* (**a**) *(for cigarettes)* briquet *m*; *(in car)* allume-cigare *m*; *(for gas)* allume-gaz *m inv* (**b**) *Naut* allège *f*, chaland *m*, gabare *f*

2 *comp (flint, fluid, fuel)* à briquet

lighterage ['laɪtərɪdʒ] *n Naut (unloading)* déchargement *m* par allèges *ou* par gabares, gabarage *m*; *(fee)* droits *mpl ou* frais *mpl* d'allège *ou* de gabarage

lighterman ['laɪtəmən] *(pl* **lightermen** [-mən]) *n Naut* gabarier *m*, batelier *m*

lighter-than-air 1 *n* appareil *m* plus léger que l'air

2 *adj (aircraft)* plus léger que l'air

lightface ['laɪtfeɪs] *n Typ* (caractère *m*) maigre *m*

light-fingered *adj* chapardeur

light-flyweight *Boxing* **1** *n* poids *m* mi-mouche

2 *adj* mi-mouche *(inv)*

light-footed [-'fʊtɪd] *adj* au pied léger, à la démarche légère

light-haired *adj* aux cheveux clairs, blond

light-headed *adj (dizzy)* étourdi; *(tipsy)* ivre, enivré; **to feel light-headed** avoir des vertiges *ou* la tête qui tourne; **the wine had made me light-headed** le vin m'était monté à la tête; **the realization that she had won made her feel quite light-headed** elle était tout excitée de réaliser qu'elle avait gagné

light-headedness [-'hedɪdnɪs] *n (dizziness)* étourdissement *m*, vertige *m*; *(tipsiness)* ivresse *f*

light-hearted *adj (person, atmosphere)* enjoué, gai; *(poem, irony)* léger; **a light-hearted remark** une remarque bon enfant; **this programme takes a light-hearted look at politics** cette émission pose un regard amusé sur la politique

light-heartedly [-'hɑːtɪdlɪ] *adv* joyeusement, gaiement

light-heartedness [-'hɑːtɪdnɪs] *n (of person, atmosphere)* gaieté *f*; *(of poem, irony)* légèreté *f*

light-heavyweight *Boxing* **1** *n* (poids *m*) mi-lourd *m*

2 *adj* mi-lourd

lighthouse ['laɪthaʊs, *pl* -haʊzɪz] *n* phare *m*

►► ***lighthouse keeper*** gardien *m* de phare

'To the Lighthouse' *Woolf* 'La Promenade au phare'

---

lighting ['laɪtɪŋ] *n* (**a**) *(gen)* éclairage *m*; **artificial/neon lighting** éclairage *m* artificiel/au néon (**b**) *(UNCOUNT) Theat & Cin* éclairages *mpl*

►► *Theat & Cin* ***lighting cameraman*** directeur *m* de la photographie, chef opérateur *m* cadreur; ***lighting effects*** effets *mpl* d'éclairage *ou* de lumière; ***lighting engineer*** éclairagiste *mf*

lighting-up time *n Br* = heure où les automobilistes doivent obligatoirement allumer leurs phares

lightly ['laɪtlɪ] *adv* (**a**) *(not heavily)* légèrement; **lightly dressed** légèrement vêtu; **it was raining lightly** il tombait une pluie fine; **she stepped lightly onto the dance floor** elle entra sur la piste de danse d'un pas léger; **lightly fry the onions** faites légèrement dorer les oignons; **to sleep lightly** *(generally)* avoir le sommeil léger; *(on one occasion)* dormir d'un sommeil léger

(**b**) *(casually)* légèrement, à la légère; **to take sth lightly** prendre qch à la légère; **"I'm getting married tomorrow", he said lightly** "je me marie demain", annonça-t-il d'un air détaché; **this is not a decision that we took lightly** ce n'est pas une décision que nous avons prise à la légère

(**c**) *(idiom)* **to get off lightly** s'en tirer à bon compte

light-middleweight *Boxing* **1** *n* (poids *m*) mi-moyen *m*

2 *adj* mi-moyen

light-negative *adj Phys* photorésistant

lightness ['laɪtnɪs] *n* (**a**) *(brightness, light)* clarté *f* (**b**) *(of object, tone, step)* légèreté *f*; **lightness of heart** gaieté *f* de cœur; **lightness of touch** *(of pianist, tennis player)* légèreté *f*; *(of artist)* légèreté *f* de pinceau; *(of writer)* légèreté *f* de style

lightning ['laɪtnɪŋ] **1** *n (UNCOUNT)* éclairs *mpl*, foudre *f*; **lightning frightens me** les éclairs me font peur; **a flash of lightning** un éclair; **to be struck by lightning** être frappé par la foudre *ou* foudroyé; *Fam* **as quick as lightning, with lightning speed, like greased lightning** rapide comme l'éclair ❑; *Prov* **lightning never strikes twice in the same place** la foudre ne frappe jamais deux fois au même endroit

2 *adj (raid, visit)* éclair *(inv)*

►► ***lightning arrester*** parafoudre *m* (de surtension); *Am* ***lightning bug*** luciole *f*; *Br* ***lightning chess*** échecs *mpl* rapides; ***lightning conductor, lightning rod*** paratonnerre *m*; ***lightning strike*** grève *f* surprise *(inv)*

light-positive *adj Phys* photoconducteur

lightproof ['laɪtpruːf] *adj* opaque

light-sensitive *adj Phys* photosensible

lightship ['laɪtʃɪp] *n Naut* bateau-feu *m*, bateau-phare *m*

lightsome ['laɪtsəm] *adj Arch or Literary* (**a**) *(light-hearted)* au cœur léger, gai (**b**) *(nimble)* agile, preste

lights-out *n* extinction *f* des feux

lightweight ['laɪtweɪt] **1** *n* (**a**) *Boxing* poids *m* léger; **the world lightweight championship** le championnat du monde des poids légers (**b**) *(insignificant person)* personne *f* sans envergure; **he's a literary lightweight** c'est un écrivain sans envergure

2 *adj* (**a**) *(clothes, equipment)* léger (**b**) *Boxing* léger

light-year *n* année-lumière *f*; **it seems light-years away** ça paraît si loin

ligneous ['lɪgnɪəs] *adj* ligneux

lignification ['lɪgnɪfɪ,keɪʃən] *n Bot* lignification *f*

lignify ['lɪgnɪfaɪ] (*pt & pp* **lignified**) *vi Bot* se lignifier

lignin ['lɪgnɪn] *n Bot* lignine *f*

lignite ['lɪgnaɪt] *n Geol* lignite *m*

lignum vitae [,lɪgnəm'viːtaɪ] *n Bot (tree)* gaïac *m*; *(wood)* bois *m* de gaïac

Liguria [lɪ'gjʊərɪə] *n Geog* Ligurie *f*

Ligurian [lɪ'gjʊərɪən] **1** *n* Ligurien(enne) *m,f*
 2 *adj* ligurien

likable = **likeable**

LIKE[1] [laɪk] **1** *vt* (**a**) *(find pleasant)* aimer (bien); **I like him** je l'aime bien, il me plaît bien; **I like her, but I don't love her** je l'aime bien, mais je ne suis pas amoureux d'elle; **I don't like him** je ne l'aime pas beaucoup, il ne me plaît pas; **I like Elaine better than Simon** j'aime mieux Elaine que Simon; **I like Sally best** c'est Sally que je préfère; **what do you like about him?** qu'est-ce qui te plaît chez lui?; **do you like coffee?** est-ce que tu aimes le café?; **these plants don't like direct sunlight** ces plantes ne supportent pas l'exposition directe à la lumière du soleil; *Hum* **I like curry but it doesn't like me!** j'aime le curry mais ça ne me réussit pas tellement!
 (**b**) *(enjoy)* aimer; **he likes school** il aime l'école; **to like doing** *or* **to do sth** aimer faire qch; **I like dancing** *or* **to dance** j'aime danser; **I like spending** *or* **to spend my weekends at home** j'aime passer mes week-ends à la maison; **I don't like being shouted at** je n'aime pas qu'on me crie dessus; **he doesn't like people talking about it** il n'aime pas qu'on en parle; **how would HE like being kept waiting in the rain?** ça lui plairait, à lui, qu'on le fasse attendre sous la pluie?
 (**c**) *(approve of)* aimer; **I like people to be frank with me** j'aime qu'on soit franc avec moi; **if he doesn't like it he can go elsewhere** si ça ne lui plaît pas il peut aller ailleurs; **I don't like you swearing, I don't like it when you swear** je n'aime pas que tu dises des gros mots; **they're not going to like it!** ça ne va pas leur plaire!; **whether you like it or not!** que ça te plaise ou non!; *Ironic* **well, I like that!** ça, c'est le bouquet!; *Ironic* **I like the way you say "don't worry"** "ne t'inquiète pas", c'est facile à dire
 (**d**) *(want, wish)* aimer, vouloir; **I'd like some tea** je prendrais bien une tasse de thé; **take any dress you like** prends la robe que tu veux *ou* qui te plaît; **as much as you like** tant que vous voudrez; **do what you like** fais ce que tu veux *ou* ce qui te plaît; **he thinks he can do anything he likes** il se croit tout permis; **she is free to do as she likes** elle est libre d'agir à sa guise *ou* de faire comme il lui plaira; **as you like** comme vous voudrez; **what I'd like to know is where he got the money from** ce que je voudrais savoir, c'est où il a obtenu cet argent; **come whenever you like** venez quand vous voulez; **I didn't like to say anything, but...** je ne voulais rien dire mais...; **I'd like nothing better than a hot bath** il n'y a rien qui me ferait autant plaisir qu'un bon bain chaud; **I'd like your opinion on this wine** j'aimerais savoir ce que tu penses de ce vin; **I would** *or* **I'd like to go out tonight** j'aimerais (bien) sortir ce soir
 (**e**) *(in polite offers, requests)* **would you like to go out tonight?** ça te dirait de *ou* tu as envie de sortir ce soir?; **would you like tea or coffee?** voulez-vous du thé ou du café?; **would you like to leave a message?** voulez-vous laisser un message?; **would you like me to do it for you?** veux-tu que je le fasse à ta place?; **I'd like to speak to Mr Smith, please** je voudrais parler à M. Smith, s'il vous plaît; **I'd like the soup followed by a salad** je prendrai la soupe puis une salade; **I'd like my steak rare, please** je voudrais mon steak saignant, s'il vous plaît
 (**f**) *(asking opinion)* **how do you like my jacket?** comment trouves-tu ma veste?; **how would you like a trip to Paris?** ça te dirait d'aller à Paris?
 (**g**) *(asking preference)* **how do you like your coffee, black or white?** vous prenez votre café noir ou avec du lait?
 (**h**) *(in generalizations)* **I like to be in bed by 10 p.m.** j'aime être couché pour 10 heures; **one doesn't like to interrupt** c'est toujours délicat d'interrompre quelqu'un
 2 likes *npl (preferences)* goûts *mpl*; **try to discover their likes and dislikes** essayez de découvrir ce qu'ils aiment et ce qu'ils n'aiment pas
 3 if you like *adv* (**a**) *(expressing willingness)* si tu veux; **I can do it, if you like** je peux le faire, si tu veux; **I'll get lunch, shall I? – if you like** je vais chercher de quoi manger, d'accord? – si tu veux
 (**b**) *(as it were)* si tu veux; **it was a surprise, a shock, if you like** ça m'a surpris, choqué si tu veux
 4 like it or not *adv* **like it or not, we're heading for a confrontation** qu'on le veuille ou non, nous ne pouvons éviter une confrontation

LIKE[2] [laɪk] **1** *prep* (**a**) *(similar to)* comme; **to be like sb/sth** être semblable à qn/à qch, ressembler à qn/à qch; **there's a car like ours** voilà une voiture comme la nôtre; **their house is a bit like ours** leur maison est un peu comme la nôtre; **there's no place like home** rien ne vaut son chez-soi; **we're like sisters** nous sommes comme des sœurs; **she's nothing like her sister** elle ne ressemble pas du tout à sa sœur; **he was like a father to me** il a été comme un père pour moi; **he talks like his father** il parle comme son père; **it's shaped like an egg** ça a la forme d'un œuf; **it tastes a bit like celery** ça a un peu le goût de céleri; **do you have any more like this?** en avez-vous d'autres?; **I want to find one just like it** je veux trouver le/la même; **there's nothing like it** il n'y a rien de mieux; **it seemed like hours** c'était comme si des heures entières s'étaient écoulées; **it looks like rain** on dirait qu'il va pleuvoir
 (**b**) *(asking for opinion or description)* **what's your new boss like?** comment est ton nouveau patron?; **what's the weather like?** quel temps fait-il?; **what does it taste like?** quel goût ça a?; **what was it like?** c'était comment?
 (**c**) *(such as)* comme; **in a family like ours** dans une famille comme la nôtre; **I've had enough of people like him!** j'en ai assez des gens comme lui!; **it makes me angry to hear things like that** ça me met en colère d'entendre des choses pareilles; **cities like Toronto and Ottawa** des villes comme Toronto et Ottawa; **I'm useless at things like sewing** je ne suis bon à rien quand il s'agit de couture et de choses comme ça
 (**d**) *(indicating typical behaviour)* **you know what she's like** vous savez comme elle est; **kids are like that, what do you expect?** les gosses sont comme ça, qu'est-ce que tu veux!; **it's not like him to be rude** ça ne lui ressemble pas *ou* ce n'est pas son genre d'être impoli; **it's just like him not to show up!** c'est bien son style *ou* c'est bien de lui de ne pas venir!; *Fam* **be like that then!** tant pis pour toi!; *Fam* **don't be like that, he didn't mean what he said** ne le prends pas mal, ce n'est pas ce qu'il voulait dire □; **that's just like a man!** c'est typiquement masculin!; **like father like son** tel père, tel fils
 (**e**) *(in the same manner as)* comme; **I think like you** je pense comme vous; **you're acting like a fool** tu te comportes comme un imbécile; **they chattered like monkeys** ils ont bavardé comme de vraies pipelettes; **to speak French like a native** parler français comme un natif; **we, like everyone else, were forced to queue all night** nous avons dû faire la queue toute la nuit, comme tout le monde; **do it like this/that** voici/voilà comment il faut faire; **like so** comme ça; **sorry to interrupt you like this** désolé de t'interrompre comme ça; **don't talk to me like that!** ne me parle pas sur ce ton!
 (**f**) *(in approximations)* **it cost something like £200** ça a coûté dans les 200 livres; **we don't have anything like as many people as we need** on est loin d'avoir tout le monde qu'il nous faut; **it will cost more like £20** ça coûtera plutôt dans les 20 livres; **it was more like midnight when we got home** il était plus près de minuit quand nous sommes arrivés à la maison; **that's more like it!** voilà qui est mieux!; **she is nothing like as intelligent as you** elle est loin d'être aussi intelligente que vous; *Fam* **he ran like anything** *or* **like hell** *or* **like blazes** il a couru comme un dératé *ou* comme s'il avait le feu aux fesses
 2 *adj* **we were treated in like manner** on nous a traités de la même façon; **they are of like temperament** ils ont le même tempérament; *Math* **like terms/quantities** termes *mpl*/quantités *fpl* semblables
 3 *conj Fam* (**a**) *(as)* comme □; **like I was saying** comme je disais; **they don't make them like they used to!** ils/elles ne sont plus ce qu'ils/elles étaient!; **I wish I could dance like you!** j'aimerais bien pouvoir danser comme toi!; **it was just like in the films** c'était exactement comme au cinéma; **tell it like it is** dis les choses comme elles sont
 (**b**) *(as if)* comme si □; **he acted like he was in charge** il se comportait comme si c'était lui le chef; **she felt like she wanted to cry** elle avait l'impression qu'elle allait pleurer; **he looked like he'd seen a ghost** on aurait dit qu'il avait vu un fantôme
 4 *adv Fam (in conversation, reported speech)* **I was hungry, like, so I went into this café** j'avais faim, tu vois, alors je suis entré dans un café; **there were like three thousand people there** il devait y avoir environ trois mille personnes □; **I was busy, like, that's why I didn't call you** j'étais occupé, c'est pour ça que je t'ai pas appelé, tu comprends?; **he just came up behind me, like** il s'est approché de moi par derrière □; **I was like "no way"** alors je lui ai fait "pas question"; **so he was like "in your dreams, pal!"** alors il a dit "c'est ça, compte là-dessus mon vieux!"
 5 *n* **he and his like** lui et ses semblables; **like attracts like** qui se ressemble s'assemble; **you can only compare like with like** on ne peut comparer que ce qui est comparable; **to give** *or* **to return like for like** rendre la pareille; **she goes in for shiatzu, yoga and the like** elle fait du shiatsu, du yoga et d'autres choses comme ça; **I've never seen the like of it!** je n'ai jamais rien vu de pareil!; **he was a president the like** *or* **likes of which we will probably never see again** c'était un président comme on n'en verra probablement plus jamais
 6 likes *npl* **the likes of us/them/***etc* les gens comme nous/eux/*etc*; **it's not for the likes of us** ça n'est pas pour les gens comme nous
 7 like enough, like as not *adv Br Fam* probablement □; **he's still at the office, like enough** il y a des chances qu'il soit encore au bureau; **like enough, she hasn't even read it yet** elle ne l'a probablement même pas encore lu

-like [laɪk] *suff* **dream-like** onirique, de rêve; **ghost-like** fantomatique

likeable ['laɪkəbəl] *adj* sympathique, agréable; **he's a likeable person** c'est un type sympathique

likeableness ['laɪkəbəlnɪs] *n* caractère *m* sympathique *ou* agréable

likelihood ['laɪklɪhʊd] **1** *n* probabilité *f*; **there's not much likelihood of us moving** il est peu probable que nous déménagions; **there is little likelihood of us still being here** *or* **that we'll still be here in August** il y a peu de chances (pour) que nous soyons encore là en août; **there is every likelihood of an agreement** tout porte à croire qu'un accord sera conclu
 2 in all likelihood *adv* vraisemblablement, selon toute vraisemblance

likely ['laɪklɪ] (*compar* **likelier**, *superl* **likeliest**) **1** *adj* (**a**) *(probable)* vraisemblable, probable; **it's not a very likely scenario** ce scénario n'est pas très vraisemblable; **the pub is a likely place to find him** le pub est probablement l'endroit où le trouver; *Fam Ironic* **that's a likely story!** la belle histoire!, en voilà une bonne!; **it's more than likely** c'est plus que probable; **it's not very likely** c'est peu probable; **it's not** *or* **hardly likely to happen** il est peu probable *ou* il y a peu de chances que cela se produise; **it's likely to rain** il y a des chances pour qu'il pleuve; **she is quite likely to do it** il y a des chances qu'elle le fasse; **books likely to interest young people** ouvrages susceptibles d'intéresser les jeunes; **this plan is most likely to succeed** ce projet a beaucoup de chances de réussir; **are the neighbours likely to object?** y a-t-il des chances que les voisins s'y opposent?; **rain is likely in the east** il risque de pleuvoir dans l'Est

(**b**) *(promising)* prometteur; **we found a likely** *or* **likely-looking spot for a picnic** on a trouvé un endroit qui a l'air idéal pour pique-niquer; *NEng Fam* **a likely lad** un gars qui promet

2 *adv* probablement, sans doute; **they'll very likely** *or* **most likely forget** ils vont très probablement oublier; **as likely as not she's already home** elle est sûrement déjà rentrée; *Fam* **would you do it again? – not likely!** tu recommencerais? – ça risque pas *ou* y a pas de risque!

like-minded *adj* du même avis; *(having same tastes)* qui ont les mêmes goûts

liken ['laɪkən] *vt* comparer; **his style has been likened to that of Peter Wolfe** on a comparé son style à celui de Peter Wolfe

likeness ['laɪknɪs] *n* (**a**) *(resemblance)* ressemblance *f*; **a family likeness** un air de famille; **she bears a strong likeness to her mother** elle ressemble beaucoup à sa mère; **God created man in his own likeness** Dieu a créé l'homme à son image

(**b**) *(portrait)* portrait *m*; **to paint sb's likeness** faire le portrait de qn; **it's a very good likeness of him** c'est tout à fait lui; **it isn't a very good likeness of him** ça ne lui ressemble pas beaucoup

likewise ['laɪkwaɪz] *adv* (**a**) *(similarly)* de même; **likewise in Israel, talks are in progress** en Israël aussi, des pourparlers ont été entamés; **he worked hard and expected his daughters to do likewise** il travaillait beaucoup et attendait de ses filles qu'elles fassent de même; **and I suggest you do likewise** et je suggère que tu en fasses autant; **pleased to meet you – likewise** ravi de vous rencontrer – moi de même

(**b**) *(by the same token)* de même, de plus, en outre

liking ['laɪkɪŋ] *n* (**a**) *(affection)* sympathie *f*, affection *f*; **I have a great liking for Alan** j'ai beaucoup de sympathie pour Alan; **to take a liking to sb** se prendre d'amitié pour qn; **I took an instant liking to Rome** j'ai tout de suite aimé Rome

(**b**) *(taste)* goût *m*, penchant *m*; **to have a liking for sth** avoir du goût pour qch, aimer qch; **she has a liking for expensive jewellery** elle a un faible pour les bijoux de prix; **the decor is not really to my liking** le décor n'est pas tout à fait à mon goût; **is everything to your liking?** est-ce que tout est à votre convenance?; **it's too small for my liking** c'est trop petit à mon goût

lilac ['laɪlək] **1** *n (colour, flower)* lilas *m*

2 *adj (colour)* lilas *(inv)*

Lilith ['lɪlɪθ] *pr n Myth* Lilith

Lilliputian [ˌlɪlɪ'pjuːʃən] **1** *n* lilliputien(enne) *m,f*

2 *adj* lilliputien

Lilo® ['laɪləʊ] (*pl* **Lilos**) *n Br* matelas *m* pneumatique

Lilongwe [lɪ'lɒŋweɪ] *n* Lilongwe

lilt [lɪlt] *n* (**a**) *(in voice)* modulation *f*; **her voice has a lilt to it** sa voix a des inflexions mélodieuses; **to speak with a Welsh lilt** parler avec des intonations galloises (**b**) *(in music)* rythme *m*, cadence *f* (**c**) *(in movement)* balancement *m* harmonieux (**d**) *Scot (tune)* chant *m*, air *m*

lilting ['lɪltɪŋ] *adj* (**a**) *(voice, accent)* mélodieux (**b**) *(music, tune)* chantant, mélodieux (**c**) *(movement)* souple, harmonieux

lily ['lɪlɪ] (*pl* **lilies**) *n Bot* lis *m*, lys *m*; **lily of the valley** muguet *m*

►► ***lily pad*** feuille *f* de nénuphar

lily-livered [-'lɪvəd] *adj* froussard

lily-white *adj* d'une blancheur de lis, d'un blanc immaculé; *Fam (character)* blanc comme neige

Lima ['liːmə] *n* Lima

lima bean ['laɪmə-] *n* haricot *m* de Lima *ou* du Cap, pois *m* de sept ans

limb [lɪm] *n* (**a**) *(of body)* membre *m*; *Hum* **let's rest our weary limbs!** si on soufflait un peu!; **I'll tear him limb from limb!** je le taillerai en pièces!; *Fam Fig* **limb of Satan** petit diable *m*

(**b**) *(of tree)* (grosse) branche *f*; *Fam* **to be out on a limb** *(be alone)* être en plan❑; *(be in dangerous position)* être dans une situation délicate❑; *Fam* **his refusal to compromise left him out on a limb** son refus d'accepter un compromis l'a mis dans une situation délicate; *Fam* **to go out on a limb** prendre des risques❑

(**c**) *Astron, Bot & Math* limbe *m*

-limbed [lɪmd] *suff* **to be long-limbed** avoir les membres longs, être élancé; **to be loose-limbed** être délié *ou* souple

limber ['lɪmbə(r)] **1** *n Mil (of gun carriage)* avant-train *m*

2 *adj* souple, agile

3 *vt Mil* **to limber a gun** attacher une pièce de canon à l'avant-train

►**limber up 1** *vt sep (muscles)* se chauffer

2 *vi* s'échauffer, faire des assouplissements; **do some limbering-up exercises first** commencez par des exercices d'assouplissement; *Fig* **they're limbering up for a fight with the unions** ils se préparent à une bataille *ou* ils fourbissent leurs armes en vue d'une bataille avec les syndicats

limbic system ['lɪmbɪk-] *n Anat* système *m* limbique

limbless ['lɪmlɪs] *adj (person)* = à qui il manque un ou plusieurs membres; *(with no arms or legs)* sans membres; **limbless ex-servicemen** grands mutilés *mpl* de guerre

limbo ['lɪmbəʊ] (*pl sense* (**c**) **limbos**) *n* (**a**) *(UNCOUNT) Rel* limbes *mpl* (**b**) *(dance)* limbo *m* (**c**) *Fig* **to be in (a state of) limbo** être dans l'incertitude; **they kept us in limbo for weeks** ils nous ont laissés dans l'incertitude pendant des semaines

►► ***limbo dancer*** danseur(euse) *m,f* de limbo

limbus ['lɪmbəs] *n Bot* limbe *m*

lime [laɪm] **1** *n* (**a**) *(substance)* chaux *f*; **caustic/slaked lime** chaux *f* vive/éteinte; **burnt lime** chaux *f* vive

(**b**) *(fruit)* citron *m* vert, lime *f*; **lager and lime** bière *f* blonde au sirop de citron vert

(**c**) *(citrus tree)* limettier *m*

(**d**) *(linden)* tilleul *m*

(**e**) *(for catching birds)* glu *f*

2 *vt* (**a**) *Agr (soil)* chauler

(**b**) *(with birdlime → branch, bird)* engluer

►► ***lime cordial*** sirop *m* de citron vert; ***lime green*** vert *m* jaune; ***lime juice*** jus *m* de citron vert; ***lime kiln*** four *m* à chaux; ***lime pit*** *(quarry)* fosse *f* à chaux; *(in tanning)* pelain *m*; ***lime tree*** tilleul *m*; ***lime twig*** gluau *m*

limeade [laɪ'meɪd] *n* boisson *f* au citron vert

limed [laɪmd] *adj (wood, furniture)* cérusé

lime-green *adj* vert jaune *(inv)*

limelight ['laɪmlaɪt] *n* **in the limelight** sous les feux de la rampe, très en vue; **she doesn't like the limelight** elle n'aime pas sentir les projecteurs braqués sur elle; **an actor who's never out of the limelight** un acteur très en vue; **to seek the limelight** rechercher la vedette; **to steal the limelight** voler la vedette

Limerick ['lɪmərɪk] *n* (**a**) *(town)* Limerick (**b**) *(county)* le comté de Limerick, = comté dans le sud-ouest de la République d'Irlande; **in Limerick** dans le comté de Limerick

limerick ['lɪmərɪk] *n* limerick *m (poème absurde ou indécent en cinq vers, dont les rimes doivent suivre un ordre précis)*

limestone ['laɪmstəʊn] *Geol* **1** *n* calcaire *m*, roche *f* calcaire

2 *comp (cave, rock formation)* calcaire; *(quarry)* de calcaire

►► ***limestone landscape*** relief *m* calcaire; ***limestone pavement*** lapiaz *m*

limewash ['laɪmwɒʃ] **1** *n* blanc *m* de chaux, badigeon *m*

2 *vt (wall)* blanchir à la chaux, chauler

limewater ['laɪmˌwɔːtə(r)] *n* eau *f* de chaux

limey ['laɪmɪ] *Am Fam Pej* **1** *n* (**a**) *(English person)* ≃ Angliche *mf* (**b**) *(English sailor)* matelot *m* anglais❑

2 *adj* ≃ angliche

liminal ['lɪmɪnəl] *adj* liminal

limit ['lɪmɪt] **1** *n* (**a**) *(boundary, greatest extent, maximum)* limite *f*; **the eastern limits of the empire** les limites orientales de l'empire; **I know my limits** je connais mes limites, je sais ce dont je suis capable; **his arrogance knows no limits** son arrogance ne connaît pas de limites; **there is no limit to his powers** ses pouvoirs sont illimités; **our resources are stretched to the limit** nous sommes au bout de nos ressources; **there's a limit to my patience** ma patience a des limites; **within limits** dans une certaine mesure; **within the limits of the present regulations** dans le cadre délimité par le présent règlement; **I'd like to help but there are limits** je veux bien aider mais il y a des limites; **I agree with you, within limits** je suis d'accord avec toi, jusqu'à un certain point; **off limits** interdit d'accès; **the bar's off limits to servicemen** le bar est interdit aux militaires; **that's the (absolute) limit!** c'est le comble!; **she really is the limit!** elle dépasse vraiment les bornes!; **what is the limit on this road?** *(speed)* quelle est la limitation *ou Can* limite de vitesse sur cette route?; **to fix a limit** *(in insurance)* fixer les pleins

(**b**) *(restriction)* limitation *f*; **the limit on Japanese imports** la limitation des importations japonaises; **to put** *or* **to set a limit on sth** limiter qch; **weight limit** limitation *f* de poids; *Br* **to be over the limit** *(driver)* dépasser le taux d'alcoolémie autorisé

2 *vt* limiter; **we're trying to limit costs** nous essayons de limiter les coûts; **they are limiting their research to one kind of virus** ils limitent leurs recherches à un seul type de virus; **to limit oneself to two whiskies** se limiter à deux whiskies; **she limits herself to one visit a week** elle se contente d'une visite par semaine; **I will limit myself to observing that...** je me bornerai à observer que...

►► *St Exch* ***limit order*** ordre *m* limite

limitation [ˌlɪmɪ'teɪʃən] *n* (**a**) *(restriction, control)* limitation *f*, restriction *f*; **we will accept no limitation on our freedom** nous n'accepterons aucune entrave à notre liberté; **arms limitation talks** négociations *fpl* sur la limitation des armements (**b**) *(shortcoming)* limite *f*; **we all have our limitations** nous avons tous nos limites; **to know one's limitations** connaître ses limites (**c**) *Law* prescription *f*

limited ['lɪmɪtɪd] *adj* (**a**) *(restricted)* limité, restreint; **the choice was rather limited** le choix était plutôt limité; **only a limited number of players will be successful** seul un nombre limité *ou* un petit nombre de participants gagneront; **the play met with only limited success** la pièce n'a connu qu'un succès relatif; **to a limited extent** jusqu'à un certain point; **they are of limited intelligence** ils ont une intelligence limitée

(**b**) *Am (train, bus)* semi-direct

►► ***limited circulation*** circulation *f* restreinte; ***limited company*** ≃ société *f* à responsabilité limitée, SARL *f*; ***limited edition*** édition *f* à tirage limité; ***limited liability*** responsabilité *f* limitée; ***limited liability company*** ≃ société *f* à responsabilité limitée, SARL *f*; *Fin* ***limited partner*** commanditaire *m*; *Fin* ***limited partnership*** société *f* en commandite (simple); ***limited stop bus*** bus *m* à nombre d'arrêts limité; ***limited stop train*** train *m* à nombre d'arrêts limité

limiter ['lɪmɪtə(r)] *n Electron* limiteur *m*

limiting ['lɪmɪtɪŋ] *adj* contraignant

limitless ['lɪmɪtlɪs] *adj* illimité; **limitless resources** des ressources illimitées *ou* inépuisables; *Literary* **the limitless sea** la mer infinie

limn [lɪm] *vt Arch or Literary* (**a**) *(describe)* décrire (**b**) *(draw)* dessiner; *(paint)* peindre

limnology [lɪm'nɒlədʒɪ] *n* limnologie *f*

limo ['lɪməʊ] (*pl* **limos**) *n Fam* limousine❑ *f*

limonite ['laɪməˌnaɪt] *n Miner* limonite *f*; **nodular limonite** œtite *f*

limonium [lɪ'məʊnɪəm] *n Bot* limonium *m*

limousine ['lɪməziːn] *n* limousine *f*

limp [lɪmp] **1** *n* **to walk with a limp, to have a limp** boiter; **the accident left him with a limp** depuis son accident il boite; **a man with a limp** un boiteux

2 *adj* (**a**) *(cloth, lettuce, handshake)* mou (molle); *(skin)* flasque; **the plants had gone limp through lack of water** les plantes s'étaient étiolées faute d'être arrosées; **his body went completely limp** il s'affaissa; **to feel limp** *(person)* se sentir mou *ou* sans énergie; **to be limp**

with exhaustion tomber d'épuisement (**b**) *(book → cover, binding)* souple

3 *vi* boiter; *(slightly)* clopiner; **he limped into the room** il entra dans la pièce en boitant; **she limped along the corridor** elle remonta le couloir en boitant; **she was limping badly** elle boitait beaucoup; *Fig* **the ship limped into harbour** le navire gagna le port tant bien que mal

limpet ['lɪmpɪt] *n Zool* patelle *f*, bernique *f*, chapeau *m* chinois; *Fig (person)* sangsue *f*; **to cling to sth like a limpet** se cramponner à qch de toutes ses forces

►► ***limpet mine*** mine-ventouse *f*

limpid ['lɪmpɪd] *adj* limpide, clair

limpidity [lɪm'pɪdɪtɪ] *n* limpidité *f*, clarté *f*

limpidly ['lɪmpɪdlɪ] *adv* avec limpidité, clairement

limpidness ['lɪmpɪdnɪs] *n* limpidité *f*, clarté *f*

limpkin ['lɪmpkɪn] *n Orn* courlan *m*

limply ['lɪmplɪ] *adv* mollement, flasquement; *(without energy)* mollement, sans énergie

limpness ['lɪmpnɪs] *n (of handshake, bearing)* mollesse *f*; *(of temperament)* manque *m* de vigueur; *(of attitude)* manque *m* de fermeté

limp-wristed [-'rɪstɪd] *adj Fam Pej* efféminé ❑

limy ['laɪmɪ] (*compar* **limier**, *superl* **limiest**) *adj* (**a**) *(containing lime)* calcaire (**b**) *(smeared with lime)* englué, gluant

linage = **lineage²**

linchpin ['lɪntʃpɪn] *n* (**a**) *Tech* esse *f* (d'essieu), cheville *f* d'essieu (**b**) *Fig (person)* pivot *m*, cheville *f* ouvrière; **it's the linchpin of government policy** c'est l'axe central de la politique du gouvernement

Lincoln ['lɪŋkən-] *pr n*

►► ***Lincoln's birthday*** = le 12 février, jour férié dans certains États américains; ***the Lincoln Center*** = complexe culturel à New York; ***Lincoln green*** vert *m* vif *(couleur associée à Robin des Bois, souvent représenté dans un habit de cette teinte)*; ***Lincoln's Inn*** = association d'étudiants en droit et d'avocats, ainsi que les bâtiments londoniens où elle siège; ***the Lincoln Memorial*** = monument à la mémoire d'Abraham Lincoln, à Washington

Lincolnshire ['lɪŋkən,ʃɪə(r)] *n* le Lincolnshire, = comté dans l'est de l'Angleterre; **in Lincolnshire** dans le Lincolnshire

Lincs *(written abbr* **Lincolnshire***)* Lincolnshire *m*

linctus ['lɪŋktəs] *n* sirop *m* (pour la toux)

lindane ['lɪndeɪn] *n Chem* lindane *m*

Lindbergh ['lɪndbɜːg] *pr n* Lindbergh

►► ***the Lindbergh kidnapping*** = l'enlèvement et le meurtre en 1932 du fils, âgé de deux ans, du célèbre aviateur américain Charles Lindbergh, à la suite duquel le kidnapping devint un crime fédéral puni de mort aux États-Unis

linden ['lɪndən] *n (tree)* tilleul *m*

►► ***linden tree*** tilleul *m*

Lindisfarne ['lɪndɪsfɑːn] *n* Lindisfarne

LINE [laɪn]

ligne	► **1 (a) – (c), (e), (j) – (o), (r), (v)**
trait	► **1 (a)**
ride	► **1 (a)**
rang	► **1 (c)**
queue	► **1 (c)**
mot	► **1 (f)**
corde	► **1 (g)**
tuyau	► **1 (h)**
voie	► **1 (i)**
frontière	► **1 (p)**
branche	► **1 (q)**
chaîne	► **1 (s)**
lignée	► **1 (t)**
border	► **2 (a)**
régler	► **2 (b)**
doubler	► **2 (c)**
garnir	► **2 (c), (d)**

1 *n* (**a**) *(mark, stroke)* ligne *f*, trait *m*; *(wrinkle)* ride *f*; *Math, Sport & TV* ligne *f*; **to draw a line** tracer *ou* tirer une ligne; *Sport* **to beat sb on the line** *(at the finishing line)* coiffer qn au poteau; **to score 50 points above/below the line** *(in bridge)* marquer 50 points d'honneur/de marche; **straight line** *(gen)* ligne *f* droite; *Math* droite *f*; **there are five lines to a stave** une portée est constituée de cinq lignes; **his face was covered with lines** son visage était plein de rides

(**b**) *(path)* ligne *f*; **light travels in a straight line** la lumière se propage en ligne droite; **it's on a line between Houston and Dallas** c'est sur la ligne qui va de Houston à Dallas; **the two grooves must be exactly in line** les deux rainures doivent être parfaitement alignées; **I don't follow your line of thinking** je ne suis pas ton raisonnement; **to be in the line of fire** être dans la ligne de tir; **line of sight** *or* **of vision** ligne *f* de visée; **let's try a different line of attack** essayons une approche différente; **it's all in the line of duty** cela fait partie de mes fonctions; **the problems I meet in the line of duty** les problèmes auxquels je suis confronté dans l'exercice de mes fonctions; **to be killed in the line of duty** *(policeman)* mourir dans l'exercice de ses fonctions; *(soldier)* mourir au champ d'honneur; *Br* **to take the line of least resistance** choisir la solution de facilité; **there's been a terrible mistake somewhere along the line** il s'est produit une erreur grave quelque part; **I'll support them all along** *or* **right down the line** je les soutiendrai jusqu'au bout *ou* sur toute la ligne; **the population is split along religious lines** la population est divisée selon des critères religieux; **he reorganized the company along more rational lines** il a réorganisé l'entreprise sur une base plus rationnelle; **we shall take action along the lines suggested** nous agirons dans le sens de ce qui a été proposé; **another idea along the same lines** une autre idée dans le même genre; **we seem to be thinking along the same lines** il semble que nous voyions les choses de la même façon; **to be on the right lines** être sur la bonne voie

(**c**) *(row → side by side)* ligne *f*, rang *m*, rangée *f*; *(→ one behind another)* rang *m*, file *f*; *Am (queue)* file *f* (d'attente), queue *f*; **a line of traffic** une colonne de véhicules; **to fall** *or* **get into line, to form a line** *(people)* se mettre en ligne; *(children)* se mettre en rang; *(soldiers)* former les rangs; **stand in line, children** mettez-vous en rang, les enfants; **to step into line** se mettre en rang; **a line of trees** une rangée d'arbres; **we joined the line at the bus stop** nous avons fait la queue à l'arrêt de bus; **they wanted to be first in line** ils voulaient être les premiers dans la file d'attente; *Fig* **he's in line for promotion** il est sur les rangs pour une promotion; **he's next in line for promotion** la prochaine promotion sera pour lui; **he's first in line for the throne** c'est l'héritier du trône; **to be on the line** *(job, reputation)* être en jeu; **to put one's job/reputation on the line** mettre son travail/sa réputation en jeu; **to lay one's reputation/life on the line (for sb/sth)** mettre sa réputation/vie en jeu (pour qn/qch)

(**d**) *Fig (conformity)* **it's in/out of line with company policy** c'est conforme/ce n'est pas conforme à la politique de la société; **it's more or less in line with what we'd expected** cela correspond plus ou moins à nos prévisions; **to bring wages into line with inflation** actualiser les salaires en fonction de l'inflation; **the rebels have been brought into line** les rebelles ont été mis au pas; **to fall into line with government policy** accepter la politique gouvernementale; **to step out of line** s'écarter du droit chemin

(**e**) *(of writing, text)* ligne *f*; *(of poem, song)* vers *m*; *(of play)* réplique *f*; **new line** *(in dictation)* à la ligne; *Comput* **a 20-line program** un programme de 20 lignes; *Sch* **she gave me 100 lines** elle m'a donné 100 lignes (à faire); **she quoted a line from Wordsworth** elle a cité un vers de Wordsworth; **I only have two lines in the whole play!** je n'ai que deux répliques dans toute la pièce!; **he forgot his lines** il a oublié son texte; **he gave me the usual line about his wife not understanding him** il m'a fait son numéro habituel comme quoi sa femme ne le comprend pas; *Fam* **to shoot a line** *(boast)* frimer; *(smooth talk)* baratiner; *Am Fam* **to hand** *or* **give** *or* **pass sb a line** *(chat up)* draguer qn

(**f**) *Fam (letter)* mot *m*; **to drop sb a line** envoyer un mot à qn

(**g**) *(rope)* corde *f*; *Naut* bout *m*; *Fishing* ligne *f*; *(in surveying) & Constr* cordeau *m*; **to hang the washing on the line** mettre le linge à sécher, étendre le linge; **your clothes are out on the line** tes vêtements sont sur la corde à linge

(**h**) *(pipe)* tuyau *m*; *(pipeline)* pipeline *m*

(**i**) *Br Rail (track)* voie *f*; *(single rail)* rail *m*; **the train left the line** le train a déraillé

(**j**) *(travel route)* ligne *f*; **underground line** ligne *f* de métro; **there's a new coach line to London** il y a un nouveau service d'autocars pour Londres; **to keep the lines of communication open** maintenir ouvertes les lignes de communication; **shipping line** compagnie *f* de navigation

(**k**) *Elec* ligne *f*; **the power lines have been cut** les lignes électriques ont été coupées; **the lines are still down after the gale** les lignes n'ont pas été rétablies depuis la tempête; **the power station comes on line in June** la centrale entre en service en juin

(**l**) *Tel* ligne *f*; **the line went dead** la communication a été coupée; **I was on the line to Paris** je téléphonais à Paris; **all the lines to London are busy** toutes les lignes pour Londres sont occupées; **then a voice came on the other end of the line** alors une voix a répondu à l'autre bout du fil; **I have Laura on the line** j'ai Laura en ligne; **a direct line to Washington** une ligne directe avec Washington; **hold the line** ne quittez pas; **the line is** *Br* **engaged** *or Am* **busy** la ligne est occupée; **there's someone on the line** il y a quelqu'un sur la ligne; **the line's very bad** la communication est mauvaise; **she's on the other line** elle est sur l'autre ligne; *Comput* **on line** en ligne

(**m**) *(outline)* ligne *f*; **the graceful line** *or* **lines of the new model** la ligne harmonieuse du nouveau modèle; **can you explain the main** *or* **broad lines of the project to me?** pouvez-vous m'expliquer les grandes lignes du projet?

(**n**) *(policy)* ligne *f*; **they took a hard** *or* **tough line on terrorism** ils ont adopté une politique de fermeté envers le terrorisme; **the opposition takes a harder line on this issue** l'opposition a une politique plus dure sur cette question; **to follow** *or* **to toe the party line** suivre la ligne du parti; **what line are you going to take?** quel parti allez-vous prendre?; **we must take a firm line with such people** il nous faut être ferme avec des gens comme ça

(**o**) *Mil* ligne *f*; **they struggled vainly to hold the line** ils ont vainement tenté de maintenir leur position; **battle lines** lignes *fpl* de bataille; **to infiltrate enemy lines** infiltrer les lignes ennemies; **regiment/ship of the line** régiment *m*/navire *m* de ligne

(**p**) *(boundary)* frontière *f*, limite *f*; **the distant line of the horizon** la ligne lointaine de l'horizon; **the (dividing) line between frankness and rudeness** la limite entre la franchise et l'impolitesse; **to overstep the line** dépasser la mesure; **the poverty line** le seuil de pauvreté; **they crossed the state line into Nevada** ils ont franchi la frontière du Nevada; **to cross the Line** *(equator)* traverser l'équateur

(**q**) *(field of activity)* branche *f*; *(job)* métier *m*; *(field of interest)* domaine *m*; **she's in the same line (of work) as you** elle travaille dans la même branche que toi; **what line (of business) are you in?, what's your line (of business)?** qu'est-ce que vous faites dans la vie?; **if you need anything doing in the plumbing line** si vous avez besoin de faire faire des travaux de plomberie; **that's not my line** ce n'est pas mon rayon; **that's more in Katy's line** c'est plus du domaine de Katy; **opera isn't really my line** l'opéra n'est pas vraiment mon genre

(**r**) *(range → of products)* ligne *f*; **a new line of office furniture** une nouvelle ligne de meubles de bureau; **they produce** *or* **do an interesting line in chairs** ils produisent une gamme intéressante de chaises; *Fam* **a rice pudding or something in that line** un gâteau de riz ou quelque chose dans ce genre(-là)

(**s**) *(production line)* chaîne *f*; **the new model will be coming off the line in May** le nouveau modèle sortira de l'usine en mai

(**t**) *(lineage, ancestry)* lignée *f*; **line of descent** filiation *f*; **to be descended in (a) direct line from sb** descendre en droite ligne de qn; **the**

Windsor line la lignée des Windsor; **the title is transmitted by the male line** le titre se transmet par les hommes; **he comes from a long line of doctors** il est issu d'une longue lignée de médecins

(**u**) *Fam (information)* **I'll try and get a line on what actually happened** j'essaierai d'avoir des tuyaux sur ce qui s'est réellement passé; **the police have got a line on him** la police sait des choses sur lui

(**v**) *Fam Drugs slang (of powdered drugs)* ligne *f*

2 *vt* (**a**) *(road, river)* border; **the avenue is lined with trees** l'avenue est bordée d'arbres; **crowds lined the streets** la foule était *ou* s'était massée sur les trottoirs

(**b**) *(paper)* régler, ligner

(**c**) *(clothes, curtains)* doubler; *(container, drawer, cupboard)* tapisser, garnir; **lined with silk** doublé de soie; **the tissue that lines the digestive tract** la paroi interne de l'appareil digestif; **you need something to line your stomach** il faut que tu avales quelque chose avant; *Culin* **line the baking tin with pastry** disposez la pâte dans le moule; **walls lined with books** des murs tapissés de livres; *Fam* **to line one's (own) pockets** s'en mettre plein les poches

(**d**) *Tech (bearing)* garnir, recouvrir; *(brakes)* garnir; *(wall, furnace)* revêtir, incruster; *(well)* cuveler; **to line a shaft with metal** blinder un puits; **the tubes are lined with plastic** l'intérieur des tubes est revêtu d'une couche de plastique

►► *Mktg* ***line addition*** ajout *m* à la ligne; *Typ* ***line block*** cliché *m* au trait; *Comput* ***line break*** saut *m* de ligne; ***line call*** *(in tennis)* décision *f* du juge de ligne; *Comput* ***line command*** ligne *f* de commande; *Fin* ***line of credit*** ligne *f* de crédit, ligne *f* de découvert; ***line dancing*** = danse de style country effectuée en rangs; *Mktg* ***line differentiation*** différenciation *f* de ligne; ***line drawing*** dessin *m* au trait; *Sport* ***line drive*** *(in baseball)* flèche *f*; *Typ & Comput* ***line end*** fin *f* de ligne; *Typ & Comput* ***line end hyphen*** tiret *m* de fin de ligne; ***line engraving*** gravure *f* au trait; *Mktg* ***line extension*** extension *f* de ligne; *Comput* ***line feed*** changement *m* de ligne; *Am* ***line fence*** clôture *f*; *Mktg* ***line filling*** consolidation *f* de ligne; ***line fishing*** pêche *f* à la ligne; *Typ* ***line gauge*** typomètre *m*; *Sport* ***line judge*** juge *m* de ligne; *Com* ***line management*** organisation *f* hiérarchique; *Com* ***line manager*** chef *m* hiérarchique; ***line noise*** parasites *mpl*; ***line organization*** organisation *f* hiérarchique; *Comput* ***line printer*** imprimante *f* ligne à ligne; *Comput* ***line printout*** imprimé *m* ligne à ligne; *Theat* ***line rehearsal*** lecture *f* collective; *Tel* ***line rental*** abonnement *m*; *Typ & Comput* ***line space*** interligne *m*; **three line spaces** un triple interligne; *Typ & Comput* ***line spacing*** interlignage *m*, espacement *m* de lignes; *Mktg* ***line stretching*** extension *f* de ligne; *Typ & Comput* ***line width*** longueur *f* de ligne

►**line up 1** *vt sep* (**a**) *(put in line → objects)* aligner, mettre en ligne; *(→ people)* faire aligner; **he lined up the troops for inspection** il fit aligner les hommes pour passer l'inspection

(**b**) *(bring into alignment)* aligner; **the two grooves must be lined up exactly** les deux rainures doivent être parfaitement alignées; **he had the pheasant lined up in his sights** il avait le faisan dans sa ligne de mire

(**c**) *Fam (plan)* préparer ❑, prévoir ❑; **I've got a treat lined up for the kids** j'ai préparé une surprise pour les gosses; **he's lined up an all-star cast for his new film** la distribution de son nouveau film ne comprend que des stars; **have you got anyone lined up for the job?** avez-vous quelqu'un en vue pour le poste?; **what have you got lined up for us?** qu'est-ce que vous nous préparez?

2 *vi (stand in line)* s'aligner, se mettre en ligne; *Am (queue up)* faire la queue; *Fig* **the Liberals lined up behind the government** les libéraux ont apporté leur soutien au gouvernement

---

lineage¹ ['lɪnɪɪdʒ] *n (ancestry)* ascendance *f*, famille *f*; *(descendants)* lignée *f*, descendance *f*; **of noble lineage** de famille *ou* d'ascendance noble; **to boast an ancient lineage** se vanter d'une longue généalogie; **to trace one's lineage** retracer sa généalogie

lineage² ['laɪnɪdʒ] *n (for newspaper advertisement)* lignage *m*

lineal ['lɪnɪəl] *adj* en ligne directe

lineament ['lɪnɪəmənt] *n Literary* linéament *m*

linear ['lɪnɪə(r)] *adj* linéaire

►► *Phys* ***linear accelerator*** accélérateur *m* linéaire; ***linear equation*** équation *f* linéaire; *Phys* ***linear expansion*** dilatation *f* linéaire; ***linear measure*** mesure *f* linéaire, mesure *f* de longueur; *Mktg* ***linear metre*** mètre *m* linéaire; *Phys* ***linear momentum*** moment *m* linéaire; ***linear motor*** moteur *m* linéaire; ***linear perspective*** perspective *f* linéaire; *Comput* ***linear programming*** programmation *f* linéaire

linearity [,lɪnɪ'ærɪtɪ] *n* linéarité *f*

linearization [,lɪnɪəraɪ'zeɪʃən] *n* linéarisation *f*

linearize, -ise ['lɪnɪəraɪz] *vt* linéariser

linearly ['lɪnɪəlɪ] *adv* linéairement

lineation [,lɪnɪ'eɪʃən] *n* (**a**) *Literary (marking with lines)* traçage *m* de lignes; *(lines)* lignes *fpl* (**b**) *Geol* linéation *f*

linebacker ['laɪn,bækə(r)] *n Sport* secondeur(euse) *m,f*

lined [laɪnd] *adj* (**a**) *(paper)* réglé (**b**) *(face, skin)* ridé (**c**) *(jacket)* doublé; *(box)* tapissé (**d**) *Aut (brake)* garni

lineman ['laɪnmən] (*pl* **linemen** [-mən]) *n Am Elec & Tel* monteur *m ou* ouvrier *m* de ligne

linen ['lɪnɪn] **1** *n* (**a**) *(fabric)* (toile *f* de) lin *m*

(**b**) *(sheets, tablecloths, towels etc)* linge *m* (de maison); *Old-fashioned (underclothes)* linge *m* (de corps); **dirty linen** linge *m* sale; *Br Fig* **to wash one's dirty linen in public** laver son linge sale en public; **table linen** linge *m* de table

2 *comp (garment, sheet)* en lin; *(thread)* de lin

►► ***linen basket*** corbeille *f* à linge; ***linen cupboard,*** *Am* ***linen closet*** armoire *f ou* placard *m* à linge; *Typ* ***linen counter*** compte-fils *m*; ***linen paper*** papier *m* toilé; ***linen room*** *(in hospital, hotel)* lingerie *f*; *Typ* ***linen tester*** compte-fils *m*

linenfold panel ['lɪnɪn,fəʊld-] *n Archit* panneau *m* à étoffe(s) pliée(s)

line-out *n Sport* touche *f*, remise *f* en jeu

liner ['laɪnə(r)] *n* (**a**) *(ship)* paquebot *m* (de grande ligne) (**b**) *(eyeliner)* eye-liner *m* (**c**) *(for clothing)* doublure *f* (**d**) *Tech* chemise *f*

linesman ['laɪnzmən] (*pl* **linesmen** [-mən]) *n* (**a**) *Sport (in rugby, football)* juge *m ou* arbitre *m* de touche; *(in tennis)* juge *m* de ligne (**b**) *Br Elec & Tel* monteur *m ou* ouvrier *m* de ligne

line-up *n* (**a**) *(queue)* queue *f* (de personnes); *(identity parade)* séance *f* d'identification; *(line of suspects)* rangée *f* de suspects

(**b**) *(composition)* **a jazz band with a traditional line-up** une formation de jazz traditionnelle; **the England line-up for tonight's match** la composition de l'équipe anglaise pour le match de ce soir; **we have an all-star line-up for tonight's programme** nous avons un plateau de vedettes pour l'émission de ce soir

linework ['laɪnwɜːk] *n Art* dessin *m* au trait

ling [lɪŋ] *n* (**a**) *(sea fish)* lingue *f*, julienne *f*; *(freshwater fish)* lotte *f* (**b**) *(heather)* bruyère *f*

linger ['lɪŋgə(r)] *vi* (**a**) *(memory, custom)* persister, subsister; *(smell, taste, sound)* persister; **a doubt lingered (on) in my mind** il subsistait un doute dans mon esprit

(**b**) *(person)* s'attarder, traîner; **we lingered over lunch** nous nous sommes attardés à table; **a few students lingered outside the classroom** quelques étudiants s'attardaient devant la salle de cours; **the camera lingered on the scene** la caméra s'est attardée sur cette scène; **her gaze lingered on the painting** son regard s'attardait sur le tableau

(**c**) *(stay alive)* **she might linger on for years yet** il se pourrait qu'elle tienne encore des années; **those attitudes still linger on today** ces attitudes survivent *ou* perdurent encore aujourd'hui

lingerie ['lænʒərɪ] *n* lingerie *f*

lingering ['lɪŋgrɪŋ] *adj* (**a**) *(long)* long (longue); **he gave her a long lingering look** il lui lança un long regard langoureux; **they had no time for lingering goodbyes** ils n'avaient pas le temps d'échanger des adieux prolongés

(**b**) *(persistent)* persistant; **a lingering feeling of dissatisfaction** un irréductible sentiment d'insatisfaction; **a lingering doubt** un doute persistant

(**c**) *(illness)* qui traîne, chronique; *(death)* lent; **she died a lingering death** la mort l'a emportée lentement

lingo ['lɪŋgəʊ] (*pl* **lingoes**) *n Fam* **I don't speak the lingo** je ne parle pas la langue du pays ❑; **technical/scientific lingo** jargon *m* technique/scientifique ❑

lingua franca [,lɪŋgwə'fræŋkə] (*pl* **lingua francas** *or* **linguae francae** [,lɪŋgwiː'fræŋkiː]) *n* lingua franca *f inv*, langue *f* véhiculaire

lingual ['lɪŋgwəl] *adj Anat & Ling* lingual

linguini [lɪŋ'gwiːnɪ] *n (UNCOUNT) Culin* linguinis *mpl*

linguist ['lɪŋgwɪst] *n* (**a**) *Br (in foreign languages → student)* étudiant(e) *m,f* en langues étrangères; *(→ specialist)* spécialiste *mf* en langues étrangères; **to be a good linguist** être doué pour les langues (**b**) *(in linguistics)* linguiste *mf*

linguistic [lɪŋ'gwɪstɪk] *adj* linguistique; **he had no linguistic ability** il n'avait aucune aptitude pour les langues

►► ***linguistic atlas*** atlas *m* linguistique

linguistically [lɪŋ'gwɪstɪklɪ] *adv* linguistiquement

linguistician [,lɪŋgwɪs'tɪʃən] *n* linguiste *mf*

linguistics [lɪŋ'gwɪstɪks] **1** *n (UNCOUNT)* linguistique *f*

2 *comp (textbook, professor, degree)* de linguistique

liniment ['lɪnɪmənt] *n* pommade *f*

lining ['laɪnɪŋ] *n* (**a**) *(of clothes, curtains)* doublure *f*; *(of hat)* coiffe *f* (**b**) *Tech (of container, bearing)* revêtement *m*; *(of brake, clutch)* garniture *f* (**c**) *Anat* paroi *f* interne; **the stomach lining** la paroi de l'estomac

►► ***lining paper*** *(for drawer)* papier *m* pour tiroirs; *(for shelves)* papier *m* pour recouvrir les étagères

Link® [lɪŋk] *n* = système reliant différents établissements bancaires britanniques et permettant à leurs clients d'utiliser indifféremment les guichets automatiques des uns et des autres

link [lɪŋk] **1** *n* (**a**) *(of chain)* chaînon *m*, maillon *m*; *Fig* **the weak link** le maillon faible

(**b**) *(bond, relationship)* lien *m*; **she's severed all links with her family** elle a coupé les ponts avec sa famille; **Britain's trade links with Spain** les relations commerciales entre la Grande-Bretagne et l'Espagne; **he is a link between the old world and the new** il sert de trait d'union entre le vieux monde et le nouveau; **the link between inflation and unemployment** le lien *ou* rapport entre l'inflation et le chômage

(**c**) *(physical connection)* liaison *f*; **a road/rail/radio link** une liaison routière/ferroviaire/radio

(**d**) *Comput (hyperlink)* lien *m* (**to** avec)

(**e**) *Tech* pièce *f* de liaison, tige *f* d'assemblage

(**f**) *(unit of measurement)* = 7,92 pouces, centième partie *f* de la chaîne (d'arpenteur)

2 *vt* (**a**) *(relate)* lier; **the two crimes are linked** les deux crimes sont liés; **the two companies are in no way linked** il n'y a aucun lien entre les deux sociétés; **his name has been linked with several well-known actresses** son nom a été associé à plusieurs actrices bien connues; **it's all linked together** tout cela se tient; **wages linked to the cost of living** salaires indexés sur le coût de la vie

(**b**) *(connect physically)* relier; *Comput* lier, relier (**to** à); **it can be linked (up) to a computer** on peut le relier *ou* connecter à un ordinateur; **to link hands/arms** se donner la main/le bras; **a tunnel linking Britain and France** un tunnel reliant la Grande-Bretagne à la France

3 *vi Comput* **to link to** être relié à

►► ***link road*** route *f* de jonction; ***link sausage*** saucisse *f (vendue en chapelet)*

►**link up 1** *vi* (**a**) *(meet → people, roads, paths)* se rejoindre; *(→ troops)* effectuer une jonction; *(→ spacecraft)* s'arrimer; **the space rocket will link up with the orbiting satellite** la navette spatiale rencontrera le satellite en orbite

(**b**) *(form a partnership)* s'associer; **we'll be linking up with a French company for this project** nous serons associés à une entreprise française pour ce projet (**c**) *(be connected)* se relier; **it can link up to a computer** on peut le relier *ou* connecter à un ordinateur

2 *vt sep* relier (**to** à); **the computers are all linked up** les ordinateurs sont tous reliés les uns aux autres; **they haven't been linked up to the network yet** ils n'ont pas encore été reliés au réseau

linkage ['lɪŋkɪdʒ] *n* (**a**) *(connection)* lien *m*, rapport *m*; **they deny any linkage between the two issues** ils nient l'existence d'un lien *ou* rapport quelconque entre les deux problèmes (**b**) *Tech* transmission *f* par tringles, tringlerie *f*; *Aut* timonerie *f*

linking verb ['lɪŋkɪŋ-] *n Gram* copule *f* verbale

linkman ['lɪŋkmən] *(pl* **linkmen** [-mən]) *n Rad & TV* journaliste *m (qui annonce les reportages des envoyés spéciaux)*

links [lɪŋks] *npl (golf course → any)* terrain *m* de golf; *(→ beside the sea)* links *mpl*

link-up *n* (**a**) *(physical connection)* liaison *f*; **a telephone/satellite link-up** une liaison téléphonique/par satellite (**b**) *(of spacecraft, troops)* jonction *f*

linkwoman ['lɪŋk,wʊmən] *(pl* **linkwomen** [-,wɪmɪn]) *n Rad & TV* journaliste *f (qui annonce les reportages des envoyés spéciaux)*

linkword ['lɪŋkwɜːd] *n Ling* mot-outil *m*

Linnaean, Linnean [lɪ'niːən] *adj Bot* linnéen

Linnaeus, Lineus [lɪ'neɪəs] *pr n* Linné

linnet ['lɪnɪt] *n Orn* linotte *f*

lino ['laɪnəʊ] *n Br* lino *m*

►► ***lino tile*** dalle *f* de linoléum

linocut ['laɪnəʊkʌt] *n* linogravure *f*, gravure *f* sur linoléum

linoleum [lɪ'nəʊljəm] *n* linoléum *m*

Linotype® ['laɪnəʊtaɪp] *n* Linotype® *f*

linseed ['lɪnsiːd] *n* graine *f* de lin

►► ***linseed oil*** huile *f* de lin

lint [lɪnt] *n (UNCOUNT)* (**a**) *Med* pansement *m* ouatiné (**b**) *(fluff)* peluches *fpl*

lintel ['lɪntəl] *n* linteau *m*

lint-free *adj (cloth)* sans peluches

lion ['laɪən] **1** *n* (**a**) *(animal)* lion *m*; **to fight like a lion** se battre comme un lion; **to put one's head in the lion's mouth** se jeter dans la gueule du loup; **born under the sign of the lion** né sous le signe du Lion; **the lion's share** la part du lion (**b**) *Fig (courageous person)* lion(onne) *m,f*; *(celebrity)* célébrité *f*; **a literary lion** un grand nom de la littérature

2 Lions *npl Sport* **the Lions** = équipe de rugby à quinze constituée des joueurs sélectionnés dans les quatre équipes nationales (Angleterre, pays de Galles, Écosse et Irlande)

►► ***Lions Club*** = association caritative internationale regroupant des entreprises et des membres des professions libérales; ***lion cub*** lionceau *m*; ***the lion's den*** l'antre *m* du lion; ***lion house*** *(at zoo)* fauverie *f*; ***lion hunter*** chasseur *m* de lions; ***lion tamer*** dompteur(euse) *m,f* (de lions)

lioness ['laɪənes] *n* lionne *f*

lionheart ['laɪən,hɑːt] *n Hist* **(Richard) the Lionheart** Richard Cœur de Lion

lionhearted ['laɪən,hɑːtɪd] *adj* courageux comme un lion

lionize, -ise ['laɪənaɪz] *vt Br (make a celebrity)* célébrer; *(treat like a celebrity)* porter aux nues

lip [lɪp] *n* (**a**) *(of* [illegible]*)* [illegible], *(of animal)* lèvre *f*, babine *f*; **her lip trembled** ses lèvres tremblaient; **my lips are sealed** je ne dirai rien; **her name is on everyone's lips** son nom est sur toutes les lèvres; **to read sb's lips** lire sur les lèvres de qn; *Fam* **read my lips** *(believe what I say)* écoutez-moi bien ❑; **to do** *or* **pay lip service to sth** faire semblant de s'intéresser à qch; **the company is paying lip service to the need for a crèche** l'entreprise prétend s'intéresser à la nécessité d'une crèche

(**b**) *(of jug)* bec *m*; *(of cup, bowl)* rebord *m*; *(of wound)* lèvre *f*, bord *m*; *(of well)* margelle *f*; *(of crater, golf hole)* bord *m*

(**c**) *Fam (impertinence)* culot *m*; **enough of your lip!** ne sois pas insolent!; **don't give me any of your lip!** ne te fiche pas de moi!

►► ***lip balm*** baume *m* pour les lèvres; ***lip gloss*** brillant *m* à lèvres; ***lip microphone*** microphone *m* labial; ***lip pencil*** crayon *m* à lèvres; ***lip salve*** pommade *f ou* baume *m* pour les lèvres

►**lip off** *vi Am Fam* se montrer insolent ❑

lipaemia, *Am* **lipemia** [lɪ'piːmɪə] *n Med* lipémie *f*

Lipari ['lɪpərɪ] *n*

►► *Geog* ***the Lipari Islands*** les îles *f* Lipari

lipase ['lɪpeɪs] *n Biol & Chem* lipase *f*

lipemia *Am* = **lipaemia**

lip-flap *n (in dubbing)* lèvres *fpl* non synchro

lipid ['lɪpɪd] *n Biol & Chem* lipide *m*

lipidic [lɪ'pɪdɪk] *adj Biol & Chem* lipidique

Lipizzaner [,lɪpɪ'zɑːnə(r)] *n* lipizzan *m*

lipochrome ['lɪpəʊ,krəʊm] *n Biol & Chem* lipochrome *m*

lipogenesis [,lɪpəʊ'dʒenɪsɪs] *n Biol* lipogenèse *f*

lipogram ['lɪpəgræm] *n Literature* lipogramme *m*

lipography [lɪ'pɒgrəfɪ] *n Ling* haplographie *f*

lipoid ['lɪpɔɪd] *Biol* **1** *n* lipoïde *m*

2 *adj* lipoïde, lipoïdique

lipolysis [lɪ'pɒlɪsɪs] *n Physiol* lipolyse *f*, adipolyse *f*

lipolytic [lɪpə'lɪtɪk] *adj Physiol* lipolytique

lipoma [lɪ'pəʊmə] *n Med* lipome *m*

lipophilic [,lɪpəʊ'fɪlɪk] *adj Biol* lipophile

lipophobic [,lɪpəʊ'fəʊbɪk] *adj Biol* lipophobe

lipoprotein [,lɪpəʊ'prəʊtiːn] *n Biol* lipoprotéine *f*

liposoluble [,lɪpəʊ'sɒljʊbəl] *adj Biol* liposoluble

liposome ['lɪpəʊsəʊm] *n Biol* liposome *m*

liposuction ['lɪpəʊ,sʌkʃən] *n* liposuccion *f*

lipothymia [,lɪpəʊ'θaɪmɪə] *n Med* lipothymie *f*

lipotropic [,lɪpəʊ'trɒpɪk] *adj Biol* lipotrope

lipoxygenase [lɪ'pɒksɪgə,neɪs] *n* lipoxygénase *f*

-lipped [lɪpt] *suff* **thin-lipped** aux lèvres minces

lippy ['lɪpɪ] (*compar* **lippier**, *superl* **lippiest**) *Fam* **1** *n Br (lipstick)* rouge *m* à lèvres ❑

2 *adj* insolent ❑, culotté

lip-read (*pt & pp* **lip-read** [-red]) **1** *vt* lire sur les lèvres de; **she can lip-read what you're saying** elle peut lire sur vos lèvres

2 *vi* lire sur les lèvres

lip-reader *n* **to be a good lip-reader** bien savoir lire sur les lèvres

lip-reading *n* lecture *f* sur les lèvres

lip-smacking *adj Fam* appétissant ❑, qui met l'eau à la bouche ❑

lipstick ['lɪpstɪk] *n* (**a**) *(substance)* rouge *m* à lèvres (**b**) *(stick)* (tube *m* de) rouge *m* à lèvres

►► *Fam* ***lipstick lesbian*** lesbienne *f* glamoureuse ❑

lip-synch 1 *vt (song)* chanter en play-back

2 *vi* chanter en play-back

liquefaction [,lɪkwɪ'fækʃən] *n* liquéfaction *f*

liquefied ['lɪkwɪ,faɪd] *adj* **liquefied natural/petroleum gas** gaz *m* naturel/de pétrole liquéfié

liquefy ['lɪkwɪ,faɪ] (*pt & pp* **liquefied**) **1** *vt* liquéfier

2 *vi* se liquéfier

liqueur [lɪ'kjʊə(r)] *n* (**a**) *(drink)* liqueur *f*; **cherry liqueur** liqueur *f* aux cerises (**b**) *(sweet)* chocolat *m* à la liqueur

►► ***liqueur chocolate*** chocolat *m* à la liqueur; ***liqueur glass*** verre *m* à liqueur

liquid ['lɪkwɪd] **1** *adj* (**a**) *(fluid)* liquide; *Hum* **to have a liquid lunch** boire de l'alcool en guise de déjeuner; *Hum* **how about some liquid refreshment?** et si nous prenions un petit quelque chose?

(**b**) *Fin* liquide

(**c**) *(clear → eyes, sound)* limpide

(**d**) *Ling (consonant)* liquide

2 *n* (**a**) *(fluid)* liquide *m*

(**b**) *Ling (consonant)* liquide *f*

►► ***liquid air*** air *m* liquide; ***liquid assets, liquid capital*** actif *m* liquide, liquidités *fpl*; ***liquid crystal*** cristal *m* liquide; ***liquid crystal display*** affichage *m* à cristaux liquides; ***liquid debt*** dette *f* liquide; ***liquid diet*** régime *m* ne comprenant que des liquides, *Spec* diète *f* hydrique; ***liquid fuel*** combustible *m* liquide; *Fig* ***liquid gold*** *(oil)* or *m* noir; ***liquid measure*** mesure *f* de capacité pour les liquides; ***liquid nitrogen*** azote *m* liquide; ***liquid oxygen*** oxygène *m* liquide; ***Liquid paper***® correcteur *m* liquide; ***liquid paraffin*** huile *f* de paraffine; ***liquid securities*** valeurs *fpl* liquides

liquidable ['lɪkwɪdəbəl] *adj Fin* liquidable

liquidambar [,lɪkwɪd'æmbə(r)] *n Bot* liquidambar *m*, copalme *m*

liquidate ['lɪkwɪdeɪt] **1** *vt* (**a**) *Fam Crime slang (kill, eliminate)* liquider, éliminer (**b**) *Fin & Law (debt, company, estate)* liquider; *(capital)* mobiliser; *St Exch* **to liquidate a position** liquider une position

2 *vi Fin & Law* entrer en liquidation, déposer son bilan

liquidation [,lɪkwɪ'deɪʃən] *n* (**a**) *Fam Crime slang (killing, elimination)* liquidation *f* (**b**) *Fin & Law (of debt, company, estate)* liquidation *f*; *(of capital)* mobilisation *f*; **to go into liquidation** entrer en liquidation, déposer son bilan

liquidator ['lɪkwɪdeɪtə(r)] *n Fin & Law* liquidateur(trice) *m,f*

liquidity [lɪ'kwɪdɪtɪ] *n* (**a**) *(of substance)* liquidité *f* (**b**) *Fin* liquidité *f*

►► *Fin* ***liquidity ratio*** ratio *m* de liquidité, coefficient *m* de liquidité

liquidize, -ise ['lɪkwɪdaɪz] *vt* (**a**) *Culin* passer au mixeur (**b**) *Phys* liquéfier

liquidizer ['lɪkwɪdaɪzə(r)] *n* mixer *m*, mixeur *m*

liquor ['lɪkə(r)] *n* (**a**) *Am (alcohol)* alcool *m*, boissons *fpl* alcoolisées; **he can't hold** *or* **take his liquor** il ne supporte pas l'alcool; **to be the worse for liquor** être ivre

(**b**) *Culin* jus *m*, bouillon *m*

(**c**) *Pharm* solution *f* aqueuse

(**d**) *(in brewing)* = eau chaude que l'on mélange au malt pour obtenir le moût

►► ***liquor cabinet, liquor case*** bar *m (meuble)*; *Am* ***liquor store*** magasin *m* de vins et spiritueux; *Am* ***state liquor store*** = magasin de vins et spiritueux agréé par l'État

►**liquor up** *Am Fam* **1** *vt sep* saouler ❑; **to get liquored up** se pinter *ou* se beurrer (la gueule)

2 *vi* se pinter *ou* se beurrer (la gueule)

liquorice, *Am* **licorice** ['lɪkərɪs] *n (plant, root, sweet)* réglisse *f*

►► ***liquorice allsorts*** = bonbons à la réglisse de différentes couleurs; ***liquorice root*** racine *f* de réglisse; ***liquorice stick*** bâton *m* de réglisse

lira ['lɪərə] (*pl* **lire** [-rɪ] *or* **liras**) *n* lire *f*

LISA [,elaɪ,es'eɪ] *n Br Fin* (*abbr* **long-term individual savings account**) plan *m* de retraite en actions

Lisbon ['lɪzbən] *n* Lisbonne

lisle [laɪl] *n (thread)* fil *m* d'Écosse

►► ***lisle thread*** fil *m* d'Écosse

lisp [lɪsp] **1** *n* zézaiement *m*; **to speak with** *or* **to have a lisp** avoir un cheveu sur la langue, zézayer

2 *vt* dire en zézayant

3 *vi* parler avec un cheveu sur la langue, zézayer

lispingly ['lɪspɪŋlɪ] *adv* en zézayant

lissom, lissome ['lɪsəm] *adj Literary* souple, agile

list [lɪst] **1** *n* (**a**) *(record)* liste *f*, *Admin* bordereau *m*; **list of names** liste *f* nominative; *Fig* **it's (at the) top of my list** *(I'll do it first)* c'est la première chose que je doive faire; **a fridge is top of my list** *(to buy)* la première chose que je doive acheter, c'est un réfrigérateur; **a diamond necklace is top of my list** *(as gift)* le cadeau que je préférerais avoir est un collier de diamants; **top of the list for the government is the appointment of...** ce qui figure en tête des priorités du gouvernement c'est de nommer...; *Fig* **it's (at the) bottom of the list** *(least important)* ce n'est pas à faire en priorité; **you're/your name's not on the list** [illegible] sur la liste; **to make out** *or* **draw up a list** établir *ou* dresser une liste; **to enter sth on a list** porter qch sur une liste; *St Exch* **list of applicants** *or* **applications** *(for loan, shares)* liste *f* des souscripteurs; *Fin* **list of bills for collection/for discount** bordereau *m* d'effets à l'encaissement/à l'escompte

(**b**) *(lean)* inclinaison *f*; *Naut* gîte *f*, bande *f*; **to have a list** donner de la bande, prendre de la gîte

2 *vt* (**a**) *(make list of)* dresser la liste de; *(enumerate)* énumérer; *(enter in a list)* inscrire (sur une liste); **I've listed the things to be done** j'ai dressé une liste de choses à faire; **she listed the reasons for her decision** elle a énuméré les raisons pour lesquelles elle avait pris cette décision; **my name isn't listed** mon nom ne figure pas sur la liste; **his phone number isn't listed (in the directory)** son numéro de téléphone ne figure pas dans l'annuaire

(**b**) *(classify)* classer; **they are listed by family**

lin–lis

name ils sont classés par nom de famille; **it was officially listed as suicide** ce fut officiellement classé comme un suicide

(**c**) *(price)* **what are the new laptops listed at?** les nouveaux portables sont vendus combien?

(**d**) *Comput* lister

(**e**) *St Exch (shares)* coter

3 *vi* (**a**) *(lean)* pencher, être incliné; *Naut* gîter, donner de la bande

(**b**) *Am* **this car lists (at** *or* **for) $10,000** cette voiture se vend *ou* s'est vendue 10 000 dollars

►► *Fin* ***list of investments*** (bordereau *m* de) portefeuille *m*; ***list price*** prix *m* du catalogue; **I can get 20 percent off (the) list price** je peux avoir un rabais de 20 pour cent sur le prix de vente; *St Exch* ***list of quotations*** bulletin *m* des cours

'Schindler's List' *Spielberg* 'La Liste de Schindler'

listed ['lɪstɪd] *adj Fin* **to be listed on the Stock Exchange** être coté en Bourse

►► *Br* ***listed building*** bâtiment *m* classé; *Br St Exch* ***listed company*** société *f* cotée en Bourse; *St Exch* ***listed securities, listed stock*** valeurs *fpl* admises *ou* inscrites à la cote officielle

listen ['lɪsən] **1** *vi* (**a**) *(gen)* écouter; **to listen to sb/sth** écouter qn/qch; **to listen with half an ear** n'écouter que d'une oreille; **you're not listening to a word I'm saying!** tu n'écoutes pas un traître mot de ce que je dis!; **we listened to their daughter singing** nous avons écouté chanter leur fille; **I listened to her singing** je l'ai écoutée chanter

(**b**) *(pay attention)* faire attention, écouter; **he wouldn't listen** il n'a rien voulu savoir; **to listen to reason** écouter la voix de la raison; **don't listen to him, make up your own mind** n'écoute pas ce qu'il te dit, prends la décision toi-même; **listen! I've got an idea** écoutez, j'ai une idée; **if only I'd listened to my mother!** si seulement j'avais écouté ma mère *ou* suivi les conseils de ma mère!

2 *n Fam* **have a listen to their latest record** écoute un peu leur dernier disque; **give it another listen** écoute-le encore une fois ❑

►**listen for** *vt insep* **will you listen for the phone?** peux-tu surveiller le téléphone?; **to listen for the postman/doctor** tendre l'oreille pour entendre l'arrivée du facteur/docteur; **will you listen for the baby?** si le bébé pleure, est-ce que tu peux aller voir?; **he listened for the sound of the car driving off** il tendit l'oreille pour être sûr d'entendre la voiture quand elle partirait; **she tapped on the wall, listening for a hollow sound** elle cherchait à quel endroit le mur était creux en tapant avec ses doigts

►**listen in** *vi* (**a**) *(to radio)* écouter, être à l'écoute; **listen in tomorrow at the same time** soyez à l'écoute demain à la même heure

(**b**) *(eavesdrop)* écouter; **it's rude to listen in on other people's conversations** c'est impoli d'écouter les conversations; **I'd like to listen in on the discussion** j'aimerais assister à cette discussion

►**listen out for** = **listen for**

►**listen up** *vi Am Fam* **hey you guys, listen up!** hé, écoutez un peu!

listener ['lɪsənə(r)] *n* (**a**) *(gen)* personne *f* qui écoute; **he's a good/bad listener** il sait/il ne sait pas écouter (les autres) (**b**) *Rad* auditeur(trice) *m,f*

listening ['lɪsənɪŋ] *n* écoute *f*; *(in language learning)* compréhension *f* orale

►► ***listening device*** écoute *f*; ***listening post*** poste *m* d'écoute

listeria [lɪ'stɪərɪə] *n Biol* listeria *f inv*

listeriosis [lɪˌstɪərɪ'əʊsɪs] *n Med* listériose *f*

listing ['lɪstɪŋ] **1** *n* (**a**) *(gen → list)* liste *f*; *(→ entry)* entrée *f*; **I found no listing for the company in the directory** je n'ai pas trouvé la société dans l'annuaire; **do you have a listing for Jacqui Dunn?** est-ce que vous avez une Jacqui Dunn dans vos fichiers?

(**b**) *Comput* listing *m*, listage *m*

(**c**) *St Exch* admission *f* à la cote officielle; **to have a listing** être coté en Bourse

2 listings *npl* **cinéma/TV listings** programme *m* des films/émissions de la semaine

►► *St Exch* ***listing agreement*** dossier *m* de demande d'introduction en Bourse; ***listings magazine*** magazine *m* de spectacles; ***listing paper*** papier *m* continu, papier *m* listing; ***listing particulars*** prospectus *m* d'admission à la cote

listless ['lɪstlɪs] *adj (torpid, unenergetic)* apathique, endormi, avachi; *(weak)* mou (molle), inerte; *(bored)* indolent, alangui; *(indifferent)* indifférent, insensible

listlessly ['lɪstlɪslɪ] *adv (without energy)* sans énergie *ou* vigueur, avec apathie; *(weakly)* mollement; *(without interest)* d'un air absent

listlessness ['lɪstlɪsnɪs] *n (lack of energy)* manque *m* d'énergie *ou* de vigueur, apathie *f*; *(weakness)* mollesse *f*; *(boredom)* langueur *f*, indolence *f*; *(indifference)* indifférence *f*

lists [lɪsts] *npl Hist* lice *f*; *also Fig* **to enter the lists** entrer en lice

lit[1] [lɪt] **1** *pt & pp of* **light**

2 *adj* (**a**) *(illuminated)* éclairé; **the room is well/badly lit** la pièce est bien/mal éclairée (**b**) *Am Fam (drunk)* allumé

lit[2] *n Fam (abbr* **literature***)* **she teaches English lit** elle enseigne la littérature anglaise ❑

►► ***lit crit*** critique *f* littéraire ❑

litany ['lɪtənɪ] *(pl* **litanies***) n Rel* litanies *fpl*; *Fig* **a litany of complaints** des jérémiades *fpl*

litchi = **lychee**

liter *Am* = **litre**

literacy ['lɪtərəsɪ] *n (of individual)* capacité *f* de lire et d'écrire; *(of population)* alphabétisation *f*; **a literacy campaign** une campagne d'alphabétisation *ou* contre l'illettrisme; **the work requires a high degree of literacy** le poste exige une solide culture générale; **literacy level** degré *m* d'instruction *ou* d'alphabétisation; **adult literacy** l'alphabétisation *f* des adultes

►► ***literacy test*** test *m* pour mesurer le niveau d'alphabétisation

literal ['lɪtərəl] **1** *adj* (**a**) *(translation)* littéral, mot à mot; **in the literal sense of the word** au sens propre du mot; **to take sth in a literal sense** prendre qch au pied de la lettre; **it meant literal starvation for thousands of farmers** cela signifiait que des milliers de fermiers allaient littéralement mourir de faim (**b**) *Math (coefficient)* littéral

2 *n Typ* coquille *f*

►► *Typ* ***literal error*** coquille *f*

literalism ['lɪtərəˌlɪzəm] *n* littéralisme *m*

literalist ['lɪtərəlɪst] *n* littéraliste *mf*

literalistic [ˌlɪtərə'lɪstɪk] *adj* littéraliste

literally ['lɪtərəlɪ] *adv* (**a**) *(not figuratively)* littéralement, au sens propre; *(word for word)* littéralement; **to take sth literally** prendre qch au pied de la lettre *ou* à la lettre; **to translate literally** faire une traduction littérale; **literally speaking** à proprement parler; **he was literally bleeding to death** il se vidait de son sang

(**b**) *(in exaggeration)* littéralement; **we've had literally hundreds of letters** nous avons reçu littéralement des centaines de lettres

literal-minded *adj* sans imagination, terre à terre *(inv)*

literalness ['lɪtərəlnɪs] *n* littéralité *f*

literary ['lɪtərərɪ] *adj* (**a**) *(style, work etc)* littéraire; **a literary man** un homme de lettres (**b**) *(formal, written → language)* littéraire

►► ***literary agent*** agent *m* littéraire; ***literary criticism*** critique *f* littéraire

literate ['lɪtərət] **1** *n (literate person)* personne *f* sachant lire et écrire

2 *adj* (**a**) *(able to read and write)* qui sait lire et écrire; **only 20 percent of the population is literate** 20 pour cent seulement de la population sait lire et écrire (**b**) *(educated)* instruit, cultivé

-literate ['lɪtərət] *suff* **to be computer-literate** avoir des connaissances en informatique

literati [ˌlɪtə'rɑːtɪ] *npl Formal* gens *mpl* de lettres, lettrés *mpl*

literature ['lɪtrətʃə(r)] *n (UNCOUNT)* (**a**) *(written works)* littérature *f*; **French literature** la littérature française (**b**) *(printed material)* documentation *f*; **scientific/medical literature** la documentation scientifique/médicale; **can you give me some literature?** pouvez-vous me donner de la documentation?; **sales literature** documentation *f*, brochures *fpl* de vente

litharge ['lɪθɑːdʒ] *n Chem* litharge *f*

lithe [laɪð] *adj (movement, person)* agile; *(body)* souple

litheness ['laɪðnɪs] *n (of movement, person)* agilité *f*; *(of body)* souplesse *f*

lithesome ['laɪðsəm] *adj Literary* souple, agile

lithia ['lɪθɪə] *n Chem* lithine *f*

lithium ['lɪθɪəm] *n Chem* lithium *m*

litho ['lɪθəʊ, 'laɪðəʊ] **1** *adj (abbr* **lithographic***)* lithographique

2 *n* (**a**) *(abbr* **lithograph***)* lithographie *f* (**b**) *(abbr* **lithography***)* lithographie *f*

litho- ['lɪθəʊ, 'lɪθə] *pref* litho-

lithograph ['lɪθəgrɑːf] **1** *n* lithographie *f (estampe)*

2 *vt* lithographier

lithographer [lɪ'θɒgrəfə(r)] *n* lithographe *mf*

lithographic [ˌlɪθə'græfɪk] *adj* lithographique

lithography [lɪ'θɒgrəfɪ] *n* lithographie *f (procédé)*

lithological [ˌlɪθə'lɒdʒɪkəl] *adj Geol* lithologique

lithology [lɪ'θɒlədʒɪ] *n Geol* lithologie *f*

lithophyte ['lɪθəˌfaɪt] *n* (**a**) *Bot* lithophyte *m* (**b**) *Zool* lithophyte *m*

lithosphere ['lɪθəˌsfɪə(r)] *n Geol* lithosphère *f*

lithospheric [ˌlɪθə'sferɪk] *adj Geol* lithosphérique

lithotomy [lɪ'θɒtəmɪ] *(pl* **lithotomies***) n Med* lithotomie *f*

lithotripsy ['lɪθəʊtrɪpsɪ] *n Med* lithotritie *f*

lithotriptor ['lɪθəˌtrɪptə(r)], **lithotrite** ['lɪθəˌtraɪt] *n Med* lithotriteur *m*

lithotrity [lɪ'θɒtrɪtɪ] *(pl* **lithotrities***) n Med* lithotritie *f*

Lithuania [ˌlɪθjʊ'eɪnjə] *n* Lituanie *f*; **in Lithuania** en Lituanie

Lithuanian [ˌlɪθjʊ'eɪnjən] **1** *n* (**a**) *(person)* Lituanien(enne) *m,f* (**b**) *(language)* lituanien *m*

2 *adj* lituanien

3 *comp (embassy)* de Lituanie; *(history)* de la Lituanie; *(teacher)* de lituanien

litigant ['lɪtɪgənt] *Law* **1** *n* plaideur(euse) *m,f*, partie *f*

2 *adj* en litige; **the litigant parties** les parties *fpl* plaidantes *ou* en litige

litigate ['lɪtɪgeɪt] *Law* **1** *vt* contester (en justice)

2 *vi* plaider, intenter une action en justice

litigation [ˌlɪtɪ'geɪʃən] *n Law* litige *m*; **the case went to litigation** le cas est passé en justice; **they are in litigation** ils sont en procès; **the issue is still in litigation** l'affaire est toujours devant *ou* entre les mains de la justice

litigator ['lɪtɪgeɪtə(r)] *n Law (lawyer)* avocat-conseil (avocate-conseil) *m,f*

litigious [lɪ'tɪdʒəs] *adj* (**a**) *Formal Pej (fond of lawsuits)* procédurier (**b**) *Formal Pej (argumentative)* chicaneur, chicanier (**c**) *Law* litigieux, contentieux

litigiousness [lɪ'tɪdʒəsnɪs] *n* (**a**) *Formal Pej (fondness of lawsuits)* amour *m* de la procédure (**b**) *Formal Pej (argumentativeness)* esprit *m* chicaneur *ou* chicanier (**c**) *Law* nature *f* litigieuse *ou* contentieuse

litmus ['lɪtməs] *n Chem* tournesol *m*

►► ***litmus paper*** papier *m* de tournesol; ***litmus test*** réaction *f* au tournesol; *Fig* test *m* décisif; **this will be a litmus test of the government's will** ce sera un test décisif pour juger de la détermination du gouvernement

litotes ['laɪtəʊtiːz] *(pl* **inv***) n Ling* litote *f*

litre, *Am* **liter** ['liːtə(r)] *n* litre *m*

litter ['lɪtə(r)] **1** *n* (**a**) *(UNCOUNT) (rubbish)* détritus *mpl*, ordures *fpl*; *(dropped in street)* papiers *mpl* (gras); **no litter** *(sign)* respectez la propreté des lieux

(**b**) *(clutter)* fouillis *m*; **his desk was covered in a litter of papers** son bureau était envahi par les papiers

(**c**) *(of animal)* portée *f*; **five young at a litter** *or* **in one litter** cinq petits d'une portée; *Fig* **the pick of the litter** le gratin, le dessus du panier

(**d**) *(for carrying wounded)* civière *f*; *Hist (conveyance)* litière *f*

(**e**) *Agr (of straw, hay → to bed animals)* litière *f*; *(→ to protect plants)* paille *f*, paillis *m*

(**f**) *(for cat)* litière *f*

2 *vt* (**a**) *(make untidy → public place)* laisser des détritus dans; *(→ house, room)* mettre du désordre dans; *(→ desk)* encombrer; **don't litter**

the table (up) with your tools n'encombre pas la table avec tes outils

(**b**) *(usu passive) (cover, strew)* joncher, couvrir; *Fig* parsemer; **beer cans littered the dance floor** la piste de danse était jonchée de cannettes de bière; **his life is littered with failed love affairs** sa vie est jalonnée d'échecs amoureux; **her works are littered with allusions to the classics** ses écrits sont encombrés d'allusions aux auteurs classiques; **the pages of the book are littered with obscenities** le livre est un tissu d'obscénités; *Fig* **beaches littered with tourists** des plages jonchées de touristes

(**c**) *(horse)* faire la litière à; *(plants)* empailler; **to litter (down) a stable** étendre de la paille dans une écurie

3 *vi* (**a**) *Zool* mettre bas

(**b**) *Am* **no littering** *(sign)* respectez la propreté des lieux

▸▸ ***litter basket*** *(in street)* poubelle *f*, boîte *f* à ordures; *Br* ***litter bin*** poubelle *f*, boîte *f* à ordures; *Br Fam* ***litter lout*** = personne qui jette des papiers ou des détritus par terre; ***litter tray*** caisse *f* (pour litière)

litterbug ['lɪtəbʌg] *n Fam* = personne qui jette des papiers ou des détritus par terre

littermates ['lɪtəˌmeɪts] *npl* petits *m* d'une même portée

LITTLE¹ ['lɪtəl] *adj* (**a**) *(in size, quantity)* petit; **a little group of children** un petit groupe d'enfants; **would you like a little drop of gin?** tu veux un peu de gin?; **he has a little antiques shop** il a une petite boutique d'antiquités; **a little smile/sob/cry** un petit sourire/sanglot/cri; **here's a little something for your new house** voilà un petit quelque chose pour ta nouvelle maison; **would you like a little something to eat?** voudriez-vous manger un petit quelque chose?; **the little hand** *(of clock)* la petite aiguille; *Hist* **the battle of the Little Bighorn** la bataille de Little Bighorn

(**b**) *(young, younger → child, animal)* petit; **a little boy** un petit garçon; **a little girl** une petite fille, une fillette; **when I was little** quand j'étais petit; **my little sister** ma petite sœur

(**c**) *(short → time, distance)* **we spent a little time in France** nous avons passé quelque temps en France; **a little while ago** *(moments ago)* il y a quelques instants; *(days, months ago)* il y a quelque temps; **she only stayed (for) a little while** elle n'est pas restée très longtemps; **the shop is a little way along the street** le magasin se trouve un peu plus loin dans la rue

(**d**) *(unimportant)* petit; **we had a little difference of opinion** nous avons eu un petit différend; **they had a little argument** ils se sont un peu disputés

(**e**) *(expressing affection, pleasure, irritation)* petit; **what a nice little garden!** quel joli petit jardin!; **I've got my own little house in Oxford now** j'ai ma petite maison à moi à Oxford maintenant; **a little old lady** une petite vieille; **poor little thing!** pauvre petit!; **she's a little horror!** c'est une petite peste!; *Fam* **you're a filthy little pig!** espèce de petit cochon!; **I'm used to his little ways** je connais ses petites habitudes; *Fam* **I've worked out his little game!** j'ai compris son petit jeu!

▸▸ *Astron* ***the Little Bear*** la Petite Ourse; *Orn* ***little bittern*** butor *m* blongois; ***little black dress*** petite robe *f* noire; *Orn* ***little bustard*** outarde *f* canepetière; *Orn* ***little crake*** marouette *f* poussin, râle *m* poussin; *Am Astron* ***the Little Dipper*** la Petite Ourse; *Orn* ***little egret*** aigrette *f* garzette, petite aigrette *f*; *Br Aut* ***little end*** pied *m* de bielle; ***little Englander*** *Hist* isolationniste *mf (hostile à l'expansion de l'empire britannique)*; *(chauvinistic)* = anglais chauvin et xénophobe; ***little finger*** auriculaire *m*, petit doigt *m*; **to twist sb round one's little finger** faire ce qu'on veut de qn; *Orn* ***little grebe*** petit grèbe *m*; *Fam Hum* ***little green men*** petits hommes verts *mpl*, extraterrestres❑ *mpl*; *Orn* ***little gull*** mouette *f* pygmée; *Am Sport* ***Little League*** = championnat de baseball pour les jeunes de 8 à 12 ans; ***Little Orphan Annie*** = personnage de bande dessinée américaine, petite orpheline protégée par un riche homme d'affaires, Daddy Warbucks; *Orn* ***little owl*** chevêche *f*; *Ir* ***the little people*** les lutins *mpl*; *Orn* ***little ringed plover*** petit gravelot *m*; *Cards* ***little slam*** *(in bridge)* petit chelem *m*; *Orn* ***little stint*** bécasseau *m* minute; *Orn* ***little tern*** sterne *f* naine; ***little toe*** petit orteil *m*; *Old-fashioned* ***the little woman*** *(wife)* ma/ta/sa tendre moitié *f*; *Pej* **she plays the little woman** *(helpless)* elle joue les faibles femmes

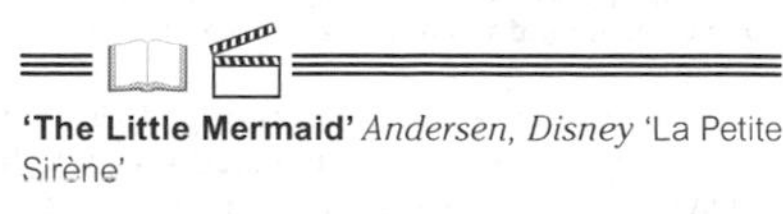

'The Little Mermaid' *Andersen, Disney* 'La Petite Sirène'

'Little Red Riding Hood' *Perrault* 'Le Petit Chaperon rouge'

'Little Women' *Alcott, Armstrong* 'Les Quatre Filles du Docteur March'

THE BATTLE OF THE LITTLE BIGHORN

Il s'agit de l'ultime bataille menée par le général américain Custer, qui lança sa cavalerie aux trousses des Indiens sioux de Sitting Bull et Crazy Horse dans l'État du Montana, en 1876. Custer ayant sous-estimé les forces indiennes, celles-ci firent face et massacrèrent la troupe entière. Cet épisode est également connu sous le nom de "Custer's last stand".

LITTLE²

peu de	▸ 1
pas grand-chose	▸ 2 (a)
peu	▸ 3 (b)
un peu de	▸ 4 (1)
un peu	▸ 4 (2); 4 (3) (a), (b)
peu à peu	▸ 6

(compar **less** [les], *superl* **least** [liːst]) **1** *adj (opposite of "much")* peu de; **very little time/money** très peu de temps/d'argent; **I had little time to relax** je n'ai guère eu le temps de me détendre; **I watch very little television** je regarde très peu la télévision; **I'm afraid there's little hope left** je crains qu'il n'y ait plus beaucoup d'espoir; **to have little chance of doing sth** avoir peu de chances de faire qch; **there is little point in complaining** ça ne vaut pas vraiment la peine de porter plainte; **it makes little sense** ça n'a pas beaucoup de sens; **they have so little freedom** ils ont si peu de liberté; **there was too little money** il y avait trop peu d'argent; **if you think how little money they actually have** quand on pense au peu d'argent dont ils disposent; **with what little French I knew** avec le peu de français que je connaissais; *Formal* **with no little difficulty** non sans peine

2 *pron* (**a**) *(small amount)* pas grand-chose; **there's little one can say** il n'y a pas grand-chose à dire; **I see very little of him now** je ne le vois plus que très rarement; **he has done little for us** il n'a pas fait grand-chose pour nous; **very little is known about his childhood** on ne sait pas grand-chose *ou* on ne sait que très peu de choses sur son enfance; **given the little that I know about this subject** étant donné le peu de connaissances que j'ai dans ce domaine; **I gave her as little as possible** je lui ai donné le minimum; **you may be paid as little as £3 an hour** tu ne seras peut-être payé que 3 livres de l'heure; **so little** si peu; **you know so little about me** tu ne sais presque rien de moi; **too little** trop peu; **to make little of sth** *(fail to understand)* ne pas comprendre grand-chose à qch; *(not emphasize)* minimiser qch; *(scorn)* faire peu de cas de qch

(**b**) *(certain amount)* **a little of everything** un peu de tout; **the little I saw looked excellent** le peu que j'en ai vu paraissait excellent; *Prov* **a little of what you fancy does you good** il n'y a pas de mal à se faire du bien

3 *adv* (**a**) *(to a limited extent)* **it's little short of madness** ça frise la folie; **he's little more than a waiter** il n'est rien de plus qu'un simple serveur; **he's little known outside Birmingham** il n'est pas très connu en dehors de Birmingham; **I realized how little I knew him** je me suis rendu compte à quel point je le connaissais peu; **little more than an hour ago** il y a à peine une heure

(**b**) *(rarely)* peu; **we go there as little as possible** nous y allons le moins possible; **we talk very little now** nous ne nous parlons presque plus

(**c**) *Formal (never)* **I little thought** *or* **little did I think we would be friends one day** jamais je n'aurais cru que nous serions amis un jour; **little did he suspect that his wife was the culprit** il ne se doutait pas que c'était sa femme qui était coupable

4 a little 1 *adj* un peu de; **there's still a little time/bread left** il reste encore un peu de temps/pain; **I speak a little French** je parle quelques mots de français; *Prov* **a little knowledge** *or* **learning is a dangerous thing** = il est moins dangereux de ne rien savoir que d'en savoir trop peu **2** *pron* un peu **3** *adv* (**a**) *(slightly)* un peu; **he laughed a little** il a ri un peu; **I'm a little tired** je suis un peu fatigué; **a little too late** un peu trop tard; **a little less/more sugar** un (petit) peu moins/plus de sucre; **not even a little interested** pas le moins du monde intéressé; **I was not a little afraid** j'avais très peur (**b**) *(for a short time or distance)* un peu; **I walked on a little** j'ai marché encore un peu; **I paused there (for) a little and then said...** j'ai marqué un petit temps d'arrêt, puis j'ai dit...

5 a little bit *adv Fam* = **a little**

6 little by little *adv* peu à peu, petit à petit; **he pieced the story together little by little** il reconstitua l'histoire peu à peu

little- [lɪtəl] *pref* **a little-understood phenomenon** un phénomène (encore) mal compris; **a little-explored area** une zone presque inexplorée *ou* (encore) peu explorée

little-boy *adj* de petit garçon, de garçonnet; *(haircut)* à la garçonne

little-girl *adj* de petite fille, de fillette

little-known *adj* peu connu

little-league *adj Am Fam (unimportant)* de rien du tout; **a little-league politician** un politicard de rien du tout

littleness ['lɪtəlnɪs] *n (in size)* petitesse *f*, petite taille *f*

littoral ['lɪtərəl] **1** *n* littoral *m*

2 *adj* littoral

liturgical [lɪ'tɜːdʒɪkəl] *adj* liturgique

liturgist ['lɪtədʒɪst] *n* liturgiste *mf*

liturgy ['lɪtədʒɪ] *(pl* **liturgies**) *n* liturgie *f*

livable ['lɪvəbəl] *adj Fam* (**a**) *(inhabitable)* habitable❑; **we're trying to make the house livable (in)** nous essayons de rendre la maison habitable (**b**) *(bearable)* supportable❑; **his visits made her life livable** ses visites lui ont rendu la vie supportable; **she's not livable with** elle est invivable

LIVE¹ [lɪv]

vivre	▸ 1 (a), (b), (d), (f); 2
habiter	▸ 1 ([illegible])
se nourrir	▸ 1 (e)

1 *vi* (**a**) *(be or stay alive)* vivre; **plants need oxygen to live** les plantes ont besoin d'oxygène pour vivre; **as long as I live** tant que je vivrai, de mon vivant; **was she still living when her grandson was born?** est-ce qu'elle était encore en vie quand son petit-fils est né?; **he hasn't long to live** il ne lui reste pas beaucoup de temps à vivre; **she didn't live long after her son died** elle n'a pas survécu longtemps à son fils; **the doctors think she'll live** les médecins pensent qu'elle vivra; *Ironic* **you'll live!** tu n'en mourras pas!; **I won't live to see them grow up** je ne vivrai pas assez vieux pour les voir grandir; **she'll live to be 100** elle vivra jusqu'à 100 ans, elle sera centenaire; **we live in interesting times** nous vivons une époque intéressante; **to live on borrowed time** être en sursis; **to live to a ripe old age** vivre vieux *ou* jusqu'à un âge avancé; *Fig* **the dialogue is what makes the**

lit–liv

characters live ce sont les dialogues qui donnent de la vie aux personnages; **your words will live in our hearts/memories** vos paroles resteront à jamais dans nos cœurs/notre mémoire

(**b**) *(have a specified way of life)* vivre; **to live dangerously** vivre dangereusement; *Fam* **go on, live dangerously!** allez, vas-y, on n'a qu'une vie!; **to live well** vivre bien; **they lived happily ever after** ils vécurent heureux jusqu'à la fin de leurs jours; **he lives by the rules** il mène une vie bien rangée; **the rules we all live by** les règles auxquelles nous nous plions tous; **she lives for her children/for skiing** elle ne vit que pour ses enfants/que pour le ski; **he lived for music** il ne vivait que pour la musique; **we're living for the day we emigrate** nous vivons dans l'attente du jour où nous émigrerons; **she was living for the chance of revenge** la perspective de vengeance était sa raison de vivre; **to live in poverty/luxury** vivre dans la pauvreté/le luxe; **to live in fear** vivre dans la peur; **he lives in the past** il vit dans le passé; **we live in uncertain times** nous vivons une époque incertaine; *Hum* **he lives in that shirt!** il a cette chemise sur le dos en permanence!; *Prov* **live and let live!** = il faut savoir faire preuve de tolérance!; **well, you live and learn!** on en apprend tous les jours!

(**c**) *(reside)* habiter; **where does she live?** où habite-t-elle?; **they have nowhere to live** ils sont à la rue; **the giant tortoise lives mainly in the Galapagos** la tortue géante vit surtout aux Galapagos; **they live in Rome** ils habitent (à) Rome, ils vivent à Rome; **I lived in France for a year** j'ai vécu en France pendant un an; **to live in a flat/a castle** habiter (dans) un appartement/un château; **she lives in a fifth-floor flat** elle vit dans un appartement au cinquième étage; **to live at Number 10** habiter au numéro 10; **to live in the town/country** habiter *ou* vivre en ville/à la campagne; **I live in** *or* **on Bank Street** j'habite Bank Street; **they live in** *or* **on my street** ils habitent (dans) ma rue; **to live on the street** être à la rue; **she lives on the ground floor** elle habite au rez-de-chaussée; **he practically lives in** *or* **at the library** il passe sa vie à la bibliothèque; **do you live with your parents?** habitez-vous chez vos parents?; *Old-fashioned or Hum* **to live in sin (with sb)** vivre dans le péché (avec qn)

(**d**) *(support oneself)* vivre; **they don't earn enough to live** ils ne gagnent pas de quoi vivre; **he lives by teaching** il gagne sa vie en enseignant; **the tribe lives by hunting** la tribu vit de la chasse

(**e**) *(obtain food)* se nourrir; **we've been living out of cans** *or* **tins lately** on se nourrit de conserves depuis quelque temps; **he was reduced to living out of rubbish bins** il en était réduit à fouiller les poubelles pour se nourrir

(**f**) *(exist fully, intensely)* vivre; **she really knows how to live** elle sait vraiment profiter de la vie; **let's live for the moment** *or* **for today!** vivons l'instant présent!; **I want to live a little** je veux profiter de la vie; **if you haven't been to New York, you haven't lived!** si tu n'es jamais allé à New York, tu n'as rien vu!

2 *vt* vivre; **to live a life of poverty** vivre dans la pauvreté; **to live a life of luxury** mener la grande vie; **to live a solitary life** mener une vie solitaire; **to live a lie** être dans une situation fausse; **she lived the life of a film star for six years** elle a vécu comme une star de cinéma pendant six ans; *Fam* **to live it up** faire la fête; **my father lives and breathes golf** mon père ne vit que pour le golf

▶**live down** *vt sep (recover from → error, disgrace, ridicule)* **they'll never let him live that down** ils ne lui passeront *ou* pardonneront jamais cela; **if I forget her birthday, I'll never live it down!** si j'oublie son anniversaire, elle ne me le pardonnera jamais!; **you'll never live this down!** tu n'as pas fini d'en entendre parler!

▶**live in** *vi* (**a**) *(servant)* être logé et nourri; *(worker, nurse)* être logé *ou* habiter sur place; **all their farm hands live in** tous leurs ouvriers agricoles sont logés sur place

(**b**) *(pupil)* être interne

▶**live off** *vt insep* (**a**) *(sponge off)* vivre aux crochets de; **he lives off his parents** il vit aux crochets de ses parents

(**b**) *(savings)* vivre de; *(nuts, berries)* se nourrir de; **they live off the fruit of other people's labours** ils vivent du produit du travail d'autrui; **to live off the land** vivre de la terre

▶**live on 1** *vi (person)* continuer à vivre; *(custom, ideal)* persister; **she lived on to the end in the same house** elle a vécu dans la même maison jusqu'à sa mort; **his memory lives on** son souvenir est encore vivant

2 *vt insep* (**a**) *(food)* vivre de, se nourrir de; **to live on fruit and vegetables** vivre de fruits et de légumes

(**b**) *(salary)* vivre de; **it's not enough to live on** ce n'est pas suffisant pour vivre; **to earn enough to live on** gagner de quoi vivre; **how does she live on that salary?** comment s'en sort-elle avec ce salaire?; **his pension is all they have to live on** ils n'ont que sa retraite pour vivre; **to live on $800 a month** vivre avec 800 dollars par mois

(**c**) *Fig* **to live on one's wits** vivre d'expédients; **to live on one's name** vivre sur sa réputation

▶**live out 1** *vt sep* (**a**) *(spend)* passer; **she lived out the rest of her life in Spain** elle a passé le reste de sa vie en Espagne

(**b**) *(fulfil)* vivre; **he lived out his destiny** sa destinée s'est accomplie, il a suivi son destin; **to live out one's fantasies** réaliser ses rêves

2 *vi* **the maid lives out** la bonne ne loge pas sur place; **he studies here but lives out** il est étudiant ici mais il n'habite pas sur le campus

▶**live out of** *vt insep* **they live out of tins** ils ne mangent que des conserves

▶**live through** *vt insep (experience → war, hard times etc)* vivre, connaître; *(survive → war, drought)* survivre à; **they've lived through war and famine** ils ont connu la guerre et la famine; **he's unlikely to live through the winter** il est peu vraisemblable qu'il passe l'hiver

▶**live together** *vi (as a couple)* vivre ensemble, cohabiter

▶**live up to** *vt insep (name, reputation)* se montrer à la hauteur de; *(expectation)* être *ou* se montrer à la hauteur de, répondre à; **we have a reputation to live up to!** nous avons une réputation à défendre!; **it's too much for me to live up to** on m'en demande trop; **the holiday didn't live up to our expectations** les vacances n'étaient pas à la hauteur de nos espérances

▶**live with** *vt insep* (**a**) *(cohabit with)* vivre avec; **she lived with him for a couple of years before they got married** elle a vécu avec lui pendant quelques années avant qu'ils se marient

(**b**) *(put up with)* **she's not easy to live with** elle n'est pas facile à vivre; **I don't like the situation, but I have to live with it** cette situation ne me plaît pas, mais je n'ai pas le choix; **I couldn't live with myself if I didn't tell him the truth** je ne supporterais pas de ne pas lui dire la vérité; **you'll always live with the guilt** la culpabilité vous poursuivra toute la vie; **it's not ideal but I can live with it** ce n'est pas l'idéal mais je m'y ferai

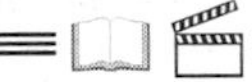

'You only live twice' *Fleming, Gilbert* 'On ne vit que deux fois'

To live fast, die young and leave a beautiful corpse

À l'origine, cette phrase provient du titre d'un film de 1949 mis en scène par Nicholas Ray intitulé *Knock on Any Door* ("Les Ruelles du malheur"), dont le personnage principal, un marginal joué par John Derek, voulait "vivre vite, mourir jeune et laisser un beau cadavre". Aujourd'hui cette formule est davantage associée aux personnages de rebelles qu'incarnaient James Dean et d'autres jeunes acteurs des années 50 et 60, et à la vie trépidante qu'ils menaient dans la réalité.

Cette formule est généralement utilisée dans sa version tronquée (**live fast and die young**) pour faire référence à un style de vie débridé. On dira par exemple **I don't like these modern pop stars and their live fast, die young attitude** ("je n'aime pas les vedettes de la musique pop d'aujourd'hui qui ne pensent qu'à s'amuser sans jamais penser aux conséquences").

live² [laɪv] **1** *adj* (**a**) *(alive → animal, person)* vivant; **the live weight of the animal** le poids de l'animal sur pied; **they feed the snakes on live mice** ils nourrissent les serpents de souris vivantes; *Fam* **a real live cowboy** un cow-boy, un vrai de vrai

(**b**) *Mus, Rad & TV (programme, interview, concert)* en direct; **live pictures from Mars** des images en direct de Mars; **Sinatra live at the Palladium** Sinatra en concert au Palladium; **recorded before a live audience** enregistré en public

(**c**) *Elec (connected)* sous tension

(**d**) *Tech (load)* roulant, mobile

(**e**) *(unexploded)* non explosé

(**f**) *(still burning → coals, embers)* ardent

(**g**) *(not extinct → volcano)* actif

(**h**) *(controversial)* controversé; **a live issue** un sujet controversé

2 *adv* en direct; **to perform live** *(singer, group)* chanter en direct; **they've never performed live** ils n'ont jamais fait de scène; **the match can be seen/is going out live at 3.30 p.m.** on peut suivre le match/le match est diffusé en direct à 15 heures 30; **the show comes live from New York City** le spectacle nous arrive en direct de New York

▶▶ ***live ammunition*** balles *fpl* réelles; *Tech* ***live axle*** essieu *m* moteur, pont *m*; ***live births*** naissances *fpl* viables; *Comput* ***live cam*** caméra *f* Internet; *Elec* ***live circuit*** circuit *m* alimenté *ou* sous tension; ***live entertainment*** spectacle *m*; *(broadcast)* spectacles *mpl* en direct; **nobody goes to see live entertainment any more** plus personne ne va au spectacle de nos jours; **the theatre and other forms of live entertainment** le théâtre et autres formes de divertissement; ***live music*** musique *f* live; ***live oak*** chêne *m* vert; *Am Fam* ***live one*** *(dupe)* poire *f*, pigeon *m*; ***live recording*** enregistrement *m* live *ou* public; *Elec* ***live wire*** fil *m* sous tension; *Fam Fig* **she's a real live wire** elle déborde d'énergie ❑; ***live yoghurt*** yaourt *m* actif

liveable = **livable**

livebait ['laɪvbeɪt] *n (in fishing)* vif *m*, appât *m* vivant

lived-in ['lɪvd-] *adj (house, flat)* accueillant; *Fig (face)* marqué; **the cottage has a lived-in feel (to it)** la maison est accueillante et confortable

live-in ['lɪv-] *adj (maid)* logé et nourri; *(nurse, governess)* à demeure; **his live-in girlfriend** sa compagne, la femme avec qui il vit

▶▶ ***live-in accommodation*** *(for staff)* logement *m* à demeure; *Hum* ***live-in lover*** compagnon (compagne) *m,f* (avec qui l'on vit)

livelihood ['laɪvlɪhʊd] *n (UNCOUNT)* moyens *mpl* d'existence, gagne-pain *m inv*; **to earn** *or* **gain one's livelihood** gagner sa vie *ou* son pain; **tourism is our livelihood** le tourisme est notre gagne-pain; **to lose one's livelihood** perdre son gagne-pain; **writing isn't a hobby, it's my livelihood** écrire n'est pas un passe-temps, c'est mon gagne-pain *ou* mon métier

liveliness ['laɪvlɪnɪs] *n (of person)* vivacité *f*; *(of conversation, party)* animation *f*; *(of debate, style)* vigueur *f*; *(of music, dance)* gaieté *f*, allégresse *f*; *(of colours)* éclat *m*, gaieté *f*

livelong ['lɪvlɒŋ] **1** *n Br Bot* grand orpin *m*

2 *adj Literary* **all the livelong day** toute la journée, tout au long du jour; **the livelong night** toute la nuit

lively ['laɪvlɪ] *(compar* **livelier**, *superl* **liveliest**) *adj* (**a**) *(full of life → person)* vif, plein d'entrain; *(→ kitten, puppy)* plein de vie, espiègle; *(→ horse)* fringant; *(→ car, engine)* nerveux; *(→ music)* gai, entraînant; **she's lively company** on ne s'ennuie pas avec elle

(**b**) *(keen → mind, curiosity)* vif; *(→ imagination)* fertile; **to take a lively interest in sth** s'intéresser vivement à qch

(**c**) *(exciting → place, description, party, conversation)* animé; **a very lively debate** un débat très animé; **the town gets a bit livelier in summer** la ville s'anime un peu en été; **a lively performance** une interprétation très enlevée

(**d**) *(eventful → day, time)* mouvementé, agité; **things got lively when the police arrived** il y a eu de l'animation quand la police est arrivée; *Fam* **to make it** *or* **things lively for sb** rendre la vie dure à qn; *Br Fam* **look lively!** grouille-toi!

(**e**) *(brisk → pace)* vif

(**f**) *(vivid → colour)* vif, éclatant

liven ['laɪvən] *vi Am (respond)* **I didn't liven to his plan** son projet n'a pas éveillé mon intérêt

►**liven up 1** *vt sep (person, meeting, party)* animer, égayer; *(proceedings)* activer; **to liven up the conversation** ranimer la conversation; **you need to liven up your style** vous devriez mettre plus de mouvement dans votre style; **some pictures would liven up the text a bit** quelques photos égaieraient un peu le texte

2 *vi* s'animer, s'activer

liver[1] ['lɪvə(r)] *n* (**a**) *Anat* foie *m* (**b**) *Culin* foie *m* (**c**) *(colour)* rouge brun *m inv*, brun roux *m inv*

►► *Anat* **liver complaint** maladie *f* du foie; *Vet* **liver fluke** grande douve *f*; *Culin* **liver pâté** pâté *m* de foie; *Br* **liver salts** lithiné *m*; **liver sausage** pâté *m* de foie; **liver spot** tache *f* de vieillesse

liver[2] *n (person) Fam* **fast** *or* **high liver** fêtard(e) *m,f*, noceur(euse) *m,f*

Liver Building ['laɪvə-] *n* **the Liver Building** = édifice de Liverpool orné de deux statues d'oiseaux imaginaires, les "Liver Birds"

liveried ['lɪvərɪd] *adj* en livrée

liverish ['lɪvərɪʃ] *adj Fam* (**a**) *(ill)* **to be** *or* **to feel liverish** avoir mal au foie ❑ (**b**) *(peevish)* irritable ❑, bilieux ❑

Liverpool ['lɪvəpu:l] *n* Liverpool

Liverpudlian [ˌlɪvə'pʌdlɪən] **1** *n (inhabitant)* habitant(e) *m,f* de Liverpool; *(native)* originaire *mf* de Liverpool

2 *adj* de Liverpool

liverwort ['lɪvəwɜ:t] *n Bot* hépatique *f*

liverwurst ['lɪvəwɜ:st] *n Am* pâté *m* de foie

livery ['lɪvərɪ] (*pl* **liveries**) *n* (**a**) *(uniform)* livrée *f*; **full livery** grande livrée *f*; **in livery** en livrée; *Fig Literary* **the livery of spring** la livrée du printemps (**b**) *(of company)* couleurs *fpl*; **the cars have been painted in the new company livery** les voitures ont été peintes aux nouvelles couleurs de la maison

►► *Br* **livery company** confrérie *f (de la cité de Londres)*; **livery horse** cheval *m* de louage; **livery stable** *(for boarding)* écurie *f* prenant des chevaux en pension; *(for hiring)* écurie *f* de chevaux de louage

liveryman ['lɪvərɪmən] (*pl* **liverymen** [-mən]) *n Br (member of livery company)* membre *m* d'une confrérie londonienne

lives [laɪvz] *pl of* **life**

livestock ['laɪvstɒk] *n* bétail *m*, cheptel *m*

liveware ['laɪvweə(r)] *n Fam Comput* personnel *m* informaticien ❑

livid ['lɪvɪd] *adj* (**a**) *(blue-grey)* livide; **he went livid with rage** il a blêmi de rage; **a livid sky** un ciel de plomb (**b**) *Fam (angry)* furax; *Fam* **to be livid with anger, to be absolutely livid** être fou de rage; **it makes me livid!** ça me met en rage!

lividity [lɪ'vɪdɪtɪ], **lividness** ['lɪvɪdnɪs] *n* lividité *f*

living ['lɪvɪŋ] **1** *n* (**a**) *(livelihood)* vie *f*; **I have to work for a living** je suis obligé de travailler pour vivre; **what do you do for a living?** qu'est-ce que vous faites dans la vie?; **to write for a living** vivre de sa plume; **she made a (good) living as a pianist** elle gagnait (bien) sa vie comme pianiste; **to make a living** gagner sa vie; **you can't make a decent living in this business** on gagne mal sa vie *ou* on a du mal à gagner sa vie dans ce métier

(**b**) *(life, lifestyle)* vie *f*; **come to California where the living is easy** venez en Californie, la vie y est facile; **plain living** la vie simple

(**c**) *Br Rel* bénéfice *m*

2 *adj (alive)* vivant; **the study of living organisms** l'étude des organismes vivants; **he has no living relatives** il n'a plus de famille; **who's the greatest living boxer?** quel est le plus grand boxeur vivant?; **while she was living** de son vivant; **it was the worst storm in living memory** de mémoire d'homme on n'avait jamais vu une tempête aussi violente; **I didn't see a living soul** je n'ai pas vu âme qui vive; **she's living proof that the treatment works** elle est la preuve vivante que le traitement est efficace; **they made her life a living hell** ils lui ont rendu la vie infernale; **the living dead** les morts *mpl* vivants; **living death** vie *f* de souffrances; **his life became a living death** sa vie ne fut plus qu'une longue souffrance

3 *npl* **the living** les vivants *mpl*

4 *comp (conditions)* de vie

►► **living allowance** indemnité *f* de séjour; **living area** aire *f* de séjour; **the living area is separated from the bedrooms** la partie séjour est séparée des chambres; *Fin* **living expenses** indemnité *f* de séjour; **living quarters** *(for servants)* logements *mpl*; *(on ship)* partie *f* habitée; **these are the crew's living quarters** ce sont les quartiers de l'équipage; *Geol* **the living rock** la roche non exploitée; **sculpted from the living rock** taillé à même le roc; **living room 1** *n* (salle *f* de) séjour *m* **2** *comp* du salon; **living space** espace *m* vital; **living standards** niveau *m* de vie; **living thing** être *m* vivant; **a living wage** le minimum vital; **£400 a month isn't a living wage** on ne peut pas vivre avec 400 livres par mois; **living will** = testament dans lequel le testataire exprime sa volonté de ne pas être maintenu en vie artificiellement s'il sombre dans un état végétatif irréversible à la suite d'une maladie ou d'un accident

living-flame *adj* **living-flame gas fire** = chauffage au gaz à flammes réelles, imitant un feu de charbon

living-in *adj Br (maid, cook)* logé sur place

Livingstone daisy ['lɪvɪŋstən-] *n Bot* mésembryanthème *m*

Livy ['lɪvɪ] *pr n* Tite-Live

lizard ['lɪzəd] **1** *n* (**a**) *(reptile)* lézard *m* (**b**) *Geog* **the Lizard** le cap Lizard

2 *comp (belt, shoes)* en lézard

►► *Geog* **Lizard Point** le cap Lizard

lizardskin ['lɪzədskɪn] **1** *n* lézard *m*

2 *comp (belt, shoes)* en lézard

llama ['lɑ:mə] *n Zool* lama *m*

LLB [ˌelel'bi:] *n (abbr* **Bachelor of Laws**) *(person)* = titulaire d'une licence de droit; *(qualification)* licence *f* de droit

LLD [ˌelel'di:] *n (abbr* **Doctor of Laws**) *(person)* docteur *m* en droit; *(qualification)* doctorat *m* en droit

LLM [ˌelel'em] *n (abbr* **Master of Laws**) *(person)* = titulaire d'une maîtrise de droit; *(qualification)* maîtrise *f* de droit

Lloyd's [lɔɪdz] *n* = compagnie d'assurances britannique

►► **Lloyd's name** = titre réservé aux membres investissant leur fortune personnelle dans la compagnie d'assurances Lloyd's et s'engageant à avoir une responsabilité illimitée en cas de sinistre; **Lloyd's register** = registre de tous les bâtiments non militaires tenu par la compagnie d'assurances Lloyd's

LMBO [ˌelem,bi:'əʊ] *n Fin (abbr* **leveraged management buy-out**) = rachat d'entreprise par les salariés

LMS [ˌelem'es] *n Admin (abbr* **local management of schools**) = système où l'administration des écoles publiques est confiée à l'échelon local

LMT [ˌelem'ti:] *n (abbr* **Local Mean Time**) = heure locale

LNG [ˌelen'dʒi:] *n (abbr* **liquefied natural gas**) GNL *m*

lo [ləʊ] *exclam* (**a**) *Arch or Literary* regardez!, voyez! (**b**) *(idiom)* **and lo and behold there he was!** et voilà, il était là!

loach [ləʊtʃ] *n Ich* loche *f*

load [ləʊd] **1** *n* (**a**) *(of lorry, ship etc)* charge *f*, chargement *m*; *(carrying capacity)* charge *f*; **maximum load 5 tonnes** *(sign)* charge maximum 5 tonnes; **she was carrying a load of books/washing** elle portait des livres/du linge; **to be carrying a heavy load** être lourdement chargé; **a load of gravel** un chargement de gravier; **one horse can't pull such a heavy load** un seul cheval ne peut pas tirer une charge aussi lourde; **we moved all the stuff in ten loads** nous avons tout transporté en dix voyages

(**b**) *Fig (burden)* fardeau *m*, charge *f*; **the reforms should lighten the load of classroom teachers** les réformes devraient faciliter la tâche des enseignants; **hire somebody to share the load** embauchez quelqu'un pour vous faciliter la tâche **that's a load off my mind!** me voilà soulagé d'un poids!; **take a load off!** détends-toi!

(**c**) *(batch of laundry)* machine *f*; **I've two more loads to do** j'ai encore deux machines à faire

(**d**) *Elec, Constr & Tech* charge *f*; **safe load** charge *f* de sécurité; **the machine is working at full load** la machine fonctionne *ou* travaille à pleine charge; **under load** en charge; *Elec* **to shed the load** délester

(**e**) *St Exch* frais *mpl* d'achat *ou* d'acquisition

(**f**) *(idioms) Fam* **get a load of this** *(look)* vise un peu ça; *(listen)* écoute-moi ça; *Am Fam* **he has a load on, he's carrying a load** il est complètement bourré; *Vulg* **to shoot one's load** *(ejaculate)* décharger

2 *vt* (**a**) *(person, animal, vehicle)* charger; **to load sth with sth** charger qch sur qch; **load the bags into the car** chargez *ou* mettez les sacs dans la voiture; **the ship is loading grain** on est en train de charger le navire de céréales; **he was loaded with shopping** il avait les bras chargés de courses; **loaded with cares** accablé de soucis; **I'm going to load some more work onto you** je vais vous confier encore un peu de travail; **I don't think it's fair to load all the work onto one person** je trouve que ce n'est pas juste de donner tout le travail à une seule personne

(**b**) *(camera, gun, machine)* charger; **load! take aim! fire!** chargez! en joue! feu!; **to load a film/tape** mettre une pellicule/une cassette; **load the cassette into the recorder** introduisez la cassette dans le magnétophone

(**c**) *Comput* charger; **to load a program into the memory** charger un programme en mémoire

(**d**) *(insurance premium)* majorer, augmenter

(**e**) *Tech (spring)* serrer, bander

(**f**) *(idioms)* **to load the dice** piper les dés; *Fig* **to load the dice against sb** défavoriser qn; **the dice are loaded against us** nous n'aurons pas la partie facile

3 *vi* (**a**) *(receive freight)* faire le chargement; **the ship is loading** le navire est en cours de chargement; **the tankers load off shore** les pétroliers font le chargement en mer; *Aut* **no loading or unloading between 9 a.m. and 4 p.m.** *(sign)* chargement ou déchargement interdits entre 9 h et 16 h

(**b**) *(camera, gun)* se recharger

(**c**) *Comput (computer program)* se charger

4 *comp Comput (program)* de chargement; *(module)* chargeable

5 a load of *adj Br Fam* **what a load of rubbish!** c'est vraiment n'importe quoi!

►► **load bed** *(of truck)* plateau *m* de chargement; **load box** *(on vehicle)* soute *f*; **load carrying capacity** charge *f* utile; **load factor** *(of plane)* coefficient *m* de remplissage; *Elec* facteur *m ou* coefficient *m* de charge; *Tech* facteur *m* de charge; *Naut* **load line** ligne *f* de charge; *Comput* **load mode** mode *m* chargement; *Elec* **load shedding** délestage *m*

►**load down** *vt sep* charger (lourdement); **he was loaded down with packages** il avait des paquets plein les bras; **I'm loaded down with work** je suis surchargé de travail; **to be loaded down with worry** être accablé de soucis

►**load up 1** *vt sep* (**a**) *(truck, ship etc)* charger; **load the wheelbarrow up with bricks** remplissez la brouette de briques

(**b**) *Comput (disk, program)* charger

2 *vi* charger

loadable ['ləʊdəbəl] *adj Comput (software)* qui peut se charger, chargeable

load-bearing *adj (wall)* porteur

loaded ['ləʊdɪd] *adj* (**a**) *(vehicle)* chargé; **is the lorry fully loaded?** le camion est-il vraiment plein?

(**b**) *Fig* **to be loaded with** être chargé de *ou* plein de; **his writing is loaded with metaphors** ses textes sont pleins de métaphores; **she's loaded with talent** elle est bourrée de talent; **the word is loaded with meaning** c'est un mot lourd de sens

(**c**) *(gun, camera)* chargé

(**d**) *(dice)* pipé

(**e**) *(statement, comment, question)* insidieux

(**f**) *Fam (rich)* plein aux as

(**g**) *Fam (drunk)* plein, bourré; *(on drugs)* défoncé

►► *Ins* **loaded premium** prime *f* majorée, surprime *f*; **loaded question** question *f* insidieuse

loader ['ləʊdə(r)] *n* (**a**) *(person)* chargeur(euse) *m,f* (**b**) *Elec, Mil & Phot (device)* chargeur *m* (**c**)

Constr (machine) chargeuse *f*, loader *m* (**d**) *Comput* (programme *m*) chargeur *m* (**e**) *(with shooting party)* chargeur *m* des fusils

loading [ˈləʊdɪŋ] *n* (**a**) *(of vehicle, machine, gun, computer program)* chargement *m* (**b**) *Austr (payment)* indemnité *f*, allocation *f*

▸▸ ***loading bay*** aire *f* de chargement; ***loading dock*** embarcadère *m*; ***loading gauge*** gabarit *m* de chargement; ***loading point*** point *m* de chargement; ***loading ramp*** rampe *f* de chargement; ***loading time*** délai *m* de chargement; *(on ship)* délai *m* d'embarquement

loadmaster [ˈləʊdmɑːstə(r)] *n* responsable *mf* de la cargaison

loads [ləʊdz] *Fam* **1** *npl* **loads of** des tas de, des masses de; **it'll be loads of fun** ça va être super marrant; **it'll be loads of work** on va bosser comme des malades; **she's got loads of money** elle est bourrée de fric, elle a un fric monstre; **we've done it loads of times** on l'a fait plein de fois; **we've got loads of time** nous avons largement le temps ❑

2 *adv* vachement; **it's loads easier than I thought** c'est vachement plus facile que je croyais; **it'll cost loads** ça va coûter un max *ou* vachement cher

loadstar = **lodestar**

loadstone = **lodestone**

loaf [ləʊf] (*pl* **loaves** [ləʊvz]) **1** *n* (**a**) *(of bread)* pain *m*; *(large, round)* miche *f*; **two loaves (of bread) please** deux pains, s'il vous plaît; *Prov* **half a loaf is better than none** faute de grives, on mange des merles

(**b**) *Br Fam (rhyming slang* **loaf of bread = head***)* **to use one's loaf** faire marcher son ciboulot; **use your loaf!** fais un peu marcher ton ciboulot!

2 *vi Fam* fainéanter ❑, traîner; **I spent the day loafing about** *or* **around the house** j'ai passé la journée à traîner chez moi

▸▸ ***loaf sugar*** sucre *m* en pains; ***loaf tin*** *(for bread)* moule *m* à pain; *(for cake)* moule *m* à cake

loafer [ˈləʊfə(r)] *n* (**a**) *Fam (person)* fainéant(e) ❑ *m,f* (**b**) *(shoe)* mocassin *m*

loam [ləʊm] *n* (**a**) *Agr & Hort* terreau *m* (**b**) *Constr* pisé *m*

loamy [ˈləʊmɪ] (*compar* **loamier**, *superl* **loamiest**) *adj (soil)* riche en terreau

loan [ləʊn] **1** *n* (**a**) *(money → from borrower's point of view)* emprunt *m*; *(→ from lender's point of view)* prêt *m*; **a £500 loan** un prêt de 500 livres; **to take out a loan** faire un emprunt; **to apply for a loan** demander un prêt; **to repay a loan** rembourser un emprunt; **he asked me for a loan** il m'a demandé de lui prêter de l'argent; **it's a loan, you can have it as a loan** je vous le prête; **long/short-term loan** prêt *m*/emprunt *m* à long/court terme; **secured loan** prêt *m*/emprunt *m* gagé *ou* garanti; **unsecured loan, loan without security** prêt *m*/emprunt *m* à découvert; **loan on** *or* **against securities** emprunt *m* sur titre; **loan against security** prêt *m* sur gage; **loan without security** prêt *m* à fonds perdus; **loan at interest** prêt *m* à intérêts; **loan at reduced rate of interest** prêt *m* bonifié; **loan to value** = rapport entre le capital restant dû et la valeur du bien financé; *Acct* **loans and advances to customers** créances *fpl* clients; *Acct* **loans outstanding** encours *m*; *Fin* **loan at call, loan repayable on demand** prêt *m* remboursable sur demande; *Fin* **loan at notice** prêt *m* à terme; *Fin* **loan on collateral** prêt *m* sur gage *ou* sur nantissement; *Fin* **loan on mortgage** prêt *m* hypothécaire *ou* sur hypothèque; *Fin* **loan on overdraft** prêt *m* à découvert; *Fin* **loan on trust** prêt *m* d'honneur

(**b**) *(act of lending)* **to give sb a loan of sth** prêter qch à qn; *Br* **may I have the loan of your typewriter?** peux-tu me prêter ta machine à écrire?; *Br Fam* **give me a loan of your scissors** prête-moi tes ciseaux ❑; **I have three books on loan from the library** j'ai emprunté trois livres à la bibliothèque; **the book you want is out on loan** le livre que vous voulez est sorti; **the picture is on loan to an American museum** le tableau a été prêté à un musée américain; **she's on loan from head office** le siège l'a envoyée chez nous pour un temps

(**c**) *Ling* (mot *m* d')emprunt *m*

2 *vt* prêter; **to loan sb sth, to loan sth to sb** prêter qch à qn; **he asked me to loan him £20/my car** il m'a demandé de lui prêter 20 livres/ma voiture

▸▸ *Banking* ***loan account*** compte *m* de prêt; ***loan agreement*** contrat *m* de prêt; *Fin* ***loan capital*** capital *m* sur prêt *ou* d'emprunt; *Fin* ***loan certificate*** titre *m* de prêt; *Fin* ***loan charges*** frais *mpl* financiers; ***loan collection*** collection *f* en prêt; *Fin* ***loan company*** société *f* de crédit, maison *f* de prêt; *Fin* ***loan department*** service *m* des crédits; *Fin* ***loan guarantee scheme*** prêts *mpl* bonifiés d'aide au développement des entreprises; ***loan insurance*** assurance *f* crédit; *Fin* ***loan market*** marché *m* des prêts; *Fin* ***loan note*** titre *m* d'obligation, titre *m* de créance; *Fin* ***loan office*** organisme *m* de crédit, maison *f* de prêt; *Fin* ***loan origination fee*** commission *f* de montage; ***loan repayment insurance*** assurance *f* crédit; ***loan maturity*** échéance *f* emprunt; ***loan risk cover*** couverture *f* du risque de crédit; *Fam Pej* ***loan shark*** usurier(ère) ❑ *m,f*; ***loan stock*** emprunt *m* obligataire; ***loan transaction*** opération *f* de prêt; *Ling* ***loan translation*** calque *m*

loan-back, loanback [ˈləʊnbæk] *n Fin* cession-bail *f*

▸▸ ***loan-back facility*** *(in insurance)* = possibilité d'emprunt sur le montant de son assurance-vie; ***loan-back pension*** retraite *f* par capitalisation

loaner [ˈləʊnə(r)] *n* prêteur(euse) *m,f*

loanword [ˈləʊnwɜːd] *n Ling* (mot *m* d')emprunt *m*

loath [ləʊθ] *adj* **to be loath to do sth** n'avoir pas du tout envie de faire qch, répugner à faire qch; **I'm very loath to admit it** j'ai beaucoup de mal à l'admettre; **they were loath to leave** ils étaient peu disposés à partir; **I am somewhat loath to contradict you, but...** je n'aime pas vous contredire, mais...; **nothing loath** avec plaisir, très volontiers

loathe [ləʊð] *vt* détester; **I loathe having to get up in the mornings** j'ai horreur d'être obligé de me lever le matin; **I loathe milk** j'ai horreur du lait, je déteste le lait; **I loathe being mistaken for a tourist** je déteste *ou* j'ai horreur qu'on me prenne pour un touriste; **you know how much I loathe him** tu sais à quel point je le déteste

loathing [ˈləʊðɪŋ] *n* aversion *f*, répugnance *f*; **I have an absolute loathing for people like them** j'ai horreur des gens comme eux; **it fills me with loathing** ça me révolte

loathsome [ˈləʊðsəm] *adj (person)* répugnant; *(habit)* détestable; *(smell)* nauséabond; **that was a loathsome thing to do/say!** c'était vraiment dégoûtant de faire/dire ça!

loathsomely [ˈləʊðsəmlɪ] *adv* d'une manière répugnante; **loathsomely ugly** dégoûtant par sa laideur

loathsomeness [ˈləʊðsəmnɪs] *n* nature *f* répugnante *ou* dégoûtante

loaves [ləʊvz] *pl of* **loaf**

lob [lɒb] (*pt & pp* **lobbed**, *cont* **lobbing**) **1** *n Sport* lob *m*

2 *vt* (**a**) *(throw)* lancer; **he lobbed the stone into the air** il envoya la pierre en l'air; *Fam* **lob me those cigarettes** balance-moi ces cigarettes (**b**) *Sport (ball)* envoyer haut; *(opponent)* lober; **she lobbed the ball over my head** elle m'a lobé; **to lob a goalkeeper** lober un gardien de but

3 *vi Sport (player)* faire un lob

lobar [ˈləʊbə(r)] *adj Zool & Med* lobaire

▸▸ ***lobar pneumonia*** pneumonie *f* lobaire

lobate [ˈləʊbeɪt] *adj Zool* lobé, lobaire

lobby [ˈlɒbɪ] (*pl* **lobbies**, *pt & pp* **lobbied**) **1** *n* (**a**) *(in hotel)* hall *m*; *Theat* foyer *m*; *(in large house, apartment block)* entrée *f*

(**b**) *Pol (pressure group)* groupe *m* de pression, lobby *m*; *(action)* pression *f*; **the ecology lobby** le lobby écologiste; **yesterday's lobby of parliament** la pression exercée hier sur le parlement; **the nurses' lobby for increased pay** la pression exercée par les infirmières pour obtenir une augmentation de salaire

(**c**) *Br Pol (hall)* salle *f* des pas perdus; **division lobbies** = vestibules où passent les députés lorsqu'ils se divisent pour voter

2 *vi* faire campagne; **he has been lobbying hard in recent weeks** il a mené une campagne intensive ces dernières semaines; **ecologists are lobbying for the closure of the plant** les écologistes font pression pour obtenir la fermeture de la centrale; **he's being paid to lobby on behalf of the dairy farmers** il est payé par les producteurs laitiers pour défendre leurs intérêts

3 *vt (person, parliament)* faire pression sur; **a group of teachers came to lobby the minister** un groupe d'enseignants est venu faire pression sur le ministre

▸▸ *Br Pol* ***lobby correspondent*** journaliste *mf* parlementaire

lobbying [ˈlɒbɪɪŋ] *n (UNCOUNT) Pol* pressions *fpl*; **there has been intense lobbying against the bill** il y a eu de fortes pressions pour que le projet de loi soit retiré

lobbyist [ˈlɒbɪɪst] *n* lobbyiste *mf*, membre *m* d'un groupe de pression

lobe [ləʊb] *n Anat, Bot & Rad* lobe *m*

lobectomy [ləʊˈbektəmɪ] (*pl* **lobectomies**) *n Med* lobectomie *f*

lobed [ləʊbd] *adj Bot* lobé

lobelia [ləˈbiːljə] *n Bot* lobélie *f*

lobo [ˈləʊbəʊ] (*pl* **lobos**) *n* loup *m* gris

lobotomize, -ise [ləˈbɒtəmaɪz] *vt* lobotomiser

lobotomized [ləˈbɒtəmaɪzd] *adj Am Fam* apathique ❑, éteint ❑; **he acts like he's lobotomized** on dirait qu'il est tombé sur la tête

lobotomy [ləˈbɒtəmɪ] (*pl* **lobotomies**) *n* lobotomie *f*, leucotomie *f*

lobster [ˈlɒbstə(r)] (*pl* **inv** *or* **lobsters**) *n* homard *m*; *(spiny lobster)* langouste *f*

▸▸ ***lobster boat*** homardier *m*; *(for spiny lobster)* langoustier *m*; ***lobster thermidor*** homard *m* thermidor

lobsterpot [ˈlɒbstəpɒt] *n* casier *m* à homards; *(for spiny lobster)* casier *m* à langoustes

lobular [ˈlɒbjʊlə(r)] *adj* lobulaire, lobulé

lobule [ˈlɒbjuːl] *n* lobule *m*

lobworm [ˈlɒbwɜːm] *n Zool* arénicole *f* des pêcheurs

local [ˈləʊkəl] **1** *adj* (**a**) *(gen)* local; *(hospital, shop)* de quartier; *(inhabitants)* du quartier, du coin; **a local woman** une femme du quartier *ou* du coin; **the local doctor** le médecin du quartier; **they voted for the local man** ils ont voté pour le candidat local; **local traders** les commerces *mpl* de proximité

(**b**) *Admin & Pol (services, council)* local, communal, municipal

(**c**) *Med (infection, pain)* localisé

2 *n* (**a**) *(person)* habitant(e) *m,f* (du lieu); **the locals** les gens *mpl* du pays *ou* du coin; **ask one of the locals** demande à quelqu'un du coin

(**b**) *Br Fam (pub)* troquet *m* du coin; **it used to be our local** c'est là qu'on allait boire un pot

(**c**) *Am (train)* omnibus *m*; *(bus)* bus *m* local

(**d**) *Am (union branch)* section *f* syndicale

(**e**) *Fam (anaesthetic)* anesthésie *f* locale ❑

(**f**) *Can Tel* poste *m*; **local 476 please** le poste 476, s'il vous plaît

(**g**) *Am Press (item)* nouvelle *f* locale

▸▸ *Med* ***local anaesthetic*** anesthésie *f* locale; **to give sb a local anaesthetic** faire une anesthésie locale à qn; *Comput* ***local area network*** réseau *m* local; *Pol* ***local authorities*** autorités *fpl* locales *ou* régionales; ***local authority*** administration *f* locale; *(in town)* municipalité *f*; *Comput* ***local bus*** bus *m* local; ***local bus card*** carte *f* de bus local; *Tel* ***local call*** communication *f* locale; ***local colour*** couleur *f* locale; ***local currency*** monnaie *f* locale; ***local edition*** édition *f* locale; ***local education authority*** direction *f* régionale de l'enseignement *(en Angleterre et au pays de Galles)*; *Com* ***Local Exchange Trading System*** = système d'échange de services dans une communauté donnée, basé sur une monnaie nominale; ***local government*** administration *f* municipale; ***local government elections*** élections *fpl* municipales; ***local government official*** fonctionnaire *mf* de l'administration municipale; ***local health authority*** services *mpl* municipaux de la santé; ***local housing department*** ≃ antenne *f* logement (de la commune); *Admin* ***local management of schools*** = système où l'administration des écoles publiques est confiée à l'échelon local; ***Local Mean Time*** =

heure locale; ***local news*** informations *fpl* régionales; ***local paper*** journal *m* local; ***local radio*** radio *f* locale; ***local radio station*** station *f* de radio locale; *Br* ***local rate number*** numéro *m* à tarification locale; ***local showers*** averses *fpl* éparses; *Am Fin* ***local taxes*** impôts *mpl* locaux; ***local television*** télévision *f* locale; ***local time*** heure *f* locale; **6 a.m. local time** 6 heures du matin heure locale; ***local train*** (train *m*) omnibus *m*

locale [ləʊ'kɑːl] *n (place)* endroit *m*, lieu *m*; *(scene, setting)* cadre *m*; **a rural locale** un cadre champêtre

localism ['ləʊkə,lɪzəm] *n* (**a**) *(attachment to one's locality)* amour *m* de sa ville/de sa région; *Pej* esprit *m* de clocher (**b**) *(local idiom)* locution *f* régionale (**c**) *(local custom)* coutume *f ou* habitude *f* du pays

locality [lə'kælətɪ] (*pl* **localities**) *n* (**a**) *(neighbourhood)* voisinage *m*, environs *mpl*; *(general area)* région *f*; **a man was seen in the locality at around 8 o'clock** un homme a été vu dans les environs vers 8 heures; **he was seen in the (general) locality of the station** on l'a vu dans le quartier de la gare (**b**) *(location → of building, place)* lieu *m*, site *m*; *(→ of species)* localité *f*

localization [,ləʊkəlaɪ'zeɪʃən] *n* localisation *f*

localize, -ise ['ləʊkəlaɪz] *vt* (**a**) *(locate)* localiser, situer; **the source of the problem has been localized** on a réussi à localiser l'origine du problème (**b**) *(confine)* localiser, limiter; **they have tried to localize the effect of the strike** ils ont essayé de limiter l'effet de la grève; **to become localized** *(disease, pain)* se localiser (**c**) *(concentrate → power, money)* concentrer (**d**) *(acclimatize → species, plant)* acclimater (**e**) *(adapt → software, product)* localiser

localized ['ləʊkəlaɪzd] *adj* localisé; **localized flooding** des inondations par endroits

localizer ['ləʊkəlaɪzə(r)] *n* (**a**) *Aviat* radiophare *m* d'alignment de piste (**b**) *Med* localisateur *m*

locally ['ləʊkəlɪ] *adv* localement; **she is well known locally** *(in region)* elle est très connue dans la région; *(in neighbourhood)* elle est très connue dans le quartier; **there have been no disturbances locally** *(in region)* il n'y a pas eu de troubles dans la région; *(in neighbourhood)* il n'y a pas eu de troubles dans le quartier; **he lives locally** il vit par ici; **we shop locally** nous faisons nos courses dans le quartier; **many issues have to be decided locally, not nationally** de nombreux problèmes doivent être résolus au niveau local, et non au niveau national; **locally grown potatoes/carrots** *(sign)* pommes de terre/carottes du pays; **locally manufactured goods** articles *mpl* de fabrication locale

locate [*Br* ləʊ'keɪt, *Am* 'ləʊkeɪt] **1** *vt* (**a**) *(find → lost object, person)* retrouver; *(→ fault, technical problem)* localiser; *(on a map → place)* repérer; **they have located the cause of the trouble** ils ont localisé la cause du problème; **the police are trying to locate possible witnesses** la police recherche des témoins éventuels; **we are trying to locate his sister** nous essayons de savoir où se trouve sa sœur; **to locate a ship** déterminer la position d'un navire (en mer); **he had hoped to locate precisely the site of Troy** il avait espéré trouver l'emplacement exact de Troie

(**b**) [illegible] *(situate)* situer; **to be located** se situer, être situé; **the house is conveniently located for shops and public transport** la maison est située à proximité des magasins et des transports en commun

2 *vi* (**a**) *Com (company, factory)* s'établir, s'implanter

(**b**) *Am (settle)* s'installer, s'établir

locater = **locator**

location [ləʊ'keɪʃən] *n* (**a**) *(place, site)* emplacement *m*, site *m*; **what a beautiful location for a campus!** quel site magnifique pour un campus universitaire!; **the firm has moved to a new location** la société a déménagé; **what is your present location?** *(whereabouts)* où te trouves-tu en ce moment?; **show me the exact location of the tower** montrez-moi l'emplacement exact de la tour

(**b**) *Cin* **to be on location** tourner en extérieur; **filmed on location** filmé en extérieur

(**c**) *(finding → on map)* repérage *m*; *(→ of fault, technical problem)* localisation *f*; **location of the wreckage is proving difficult** l'endroit exact du naufrage s'avère difficile à localiser

(**d**) *Comput* position *f*; **memory location** position *f* (en) mémoire

(**e**) *Comput* adresse *f* URL

(**f**) *SAfr (township)* township *m*; *(reservation)* réserve *f* (noire)

►► *Cin* **location marks** *(in studio)* points *mpl* de repère au sol; *Mktg* ***location pricing*** fixation *f* des prix selon l'endroit; ***location shot*** plan *m* en extérieur

locative ['lɒkətɪv] *Gram* **1** *n* locatif *m*

2 *adj* locatif

locator [lə'keɪtə(r)] *n* (**a**) *(person)* trouveur(euse) *m,f* (**b**) *Comput* localisateur *m* (**c**) *Tech* pièce *f* de repérage, repère *m* (**d**) *Electron* phare *m* (pour radiocompas); *Petr* **electronic pipe locator** localisateur *m* de canalisation en place

loc. cit. (*written abbr* **loco citato**) loc. cit.

loch [lɒχ] *n Scot* loch *m*, lac *m*; **sea loch** bras *m* de mer, fjord *m*

►► ***Loch Lomond*** le loch Lomond; ***Loch Ness*** le loch Ness; ***the Loch Ness monster*** le monstre du loch Ness

lochia ['lɒkɪə] *n (UNCOUNT) Med* lochies *fpl*

loci ['ləʊsaɪ, 'ləʊkaɪ] *pl of* **locus**

LOCK [lɒk]

serrure	► **1 (a)**
écluse	► **1 (b)**
prise	► **1 (c)**
braquage	► **1 (d)**
verrou	► **1 (e)**
verrouillage	► **1 (f)**
boucle	► **1 (h)**
fermer à clef	► **2 (a); 3 (a)**
enfermer	► **2 (b)**
serrer	► **2 (c)**
bloquer	► **2 (d)**
verrouiller	► **2 (e)**
se joindre	► **3 (b)**
se bloquer	► **3 (c)**

1 *n* (**a**) *(on door, drawer etc)* serrure *f*; **under lock and key** *(object)* sous clef; *(person)* sous les verrous; **the whole gang is now safely under lock and key** toute la bande est désormais sous les verrous

(**b**) *(on canal)* écluse *f*

(**c**) *(grip → gen)* prise *f*; *(→ in wrestling)* clef *f*, prise *f*

(**d**) *Br Aut* (rayon *m* de) braquage *m*; **on full lock** braqué à fond; **the car has a good/poor lock** la voiture a un bon/médiocre rayon de braquage

(**e**) *Tech (device → gen)* verrou *m*; *(→ on gun)* percuteur *m*

(**f**) *Comput* verrouillage *m*; **shift** *or* **caps lock** touche *f* de verrouillage majuscule

(**g**) *Sport (in rugby)* **lock (forward)** deuxième ligne *m*

(**h**) *(curl)* boucle *f*; *(stray strand)* mèche *f*

(**i**) *(idioms)* **lock, stock and barrel** en entier; **she bought the company lock, stock and barrel** elle a acheté la société en bloc; **his essay was lifted lock, stock and barrel from a textbook** il a copié sa rédaction telle quelle [illegible] dans un manuel scolaire; **he swallowed the story lock, stock and barrel** il a tout avalé; **the family has moved lock, stock and barrel to Canada** la famille est partie avec armes et bagages s'installer au Canada

2 *vt* (**a**) *(door, drawer, room etc → with key)* fermer à clef; *(→ with bolt)* verrouiller; **check that all the doors and windows are locked** vérifiez que toutes les portes et les fenêtres sont bien fermées

(**b**) *(valuables, person)* enfermer; **lock all these papers in the safe** enfermez tous ces papiers dans le coffre-fort; *Fig* **they were locked into the agreement** ils étaient tenus par l'accord

(**c**) *(hold tightly)* serrer; **they were locked in a passionate embrace** ils étaient unis *ou* enlacés dans une étreinte passionnée; **to lock arms** *(police cordon)* former un barrage; **the armies were locked in battle** les armées étaient engagées à fond dans la bataille; **the unions were locked in a dispute with the management** les syndicats étaient aux prises avec la direction; **to be locked in combat** être engagé dans un combat; *Fig* être aux prises; **to lock horns** *(stags)* s'entremêler les bois; *Fig* être aux prises; *Fig* **to lock horns with the enemy** livrer bataille avec l'ennemi

(**d**) *(device, wheels, brakes)* bloquer

(**e**) *Comput (file, disk, keyboard)* verrouiller

3 *vi* (**a**) *(door, drawer, car etc)* (se) fermer à clef; **the door locks on the inside** la porte se ferme de l'intérieur; **the safe locks automatically** le coffre-fort se verrouille automatiquement

(**b**) *(engage)* se joindre; **push the lever back until it locks into place** pousse le levier jusqu'à ce qu'il s'enclenche

(**c**) *(wheels, brakes, nut)* se bloquer

4 locks *npl Literary* chevelure *f*

►► ***lock chamber*** *(on canal)* sas *m* (d'écluse); ***lock gate*** porte *f* d'écluse; ***lock keeper*** éclusier(ère) *m,f*; *Br Aut* ***lock ring*** jonc *m* d'arrêt; ***lock turns*** tours *mpl* de volant

►**lock away** *vt sep (valuables)* mettre sous clef; *(criminal)* incarcérer, mettre sous les verrous; **we keep the alcohol locked away** nous gardons l'alcool sous clef

►**lock in** *vt sep* (**a**) *(in building, room)* enfermer; **he locked himself in** il s'est enfermé (à l'intérieur)

(**b**) **to be locked in** *(to pension scheme)* ne pas avoir la possibilité de changer; *(to contract)* être lié; *St Exch* **to lock in a hedge** immobiliser une couverture

►**lock onto** *vt insep (of radar)* capter; *(of homing device)* se caler sur; *(of missile)* se fixer *ou* se verrouiller sur; **to lock onto a signal** capter un signal

►**lock out** *vt sep* (**a**) *(accidentally)* enfermer dehors; *(deliberately)* laisser dehors; **her father threatened to lock her out if she was late home** son père a menacé de la laisser à la porte *ou* dehors si elle rentrait en retard; **I've locked myself out** j'ai fermé la porte en laissant les clés à l'intérieur, je me suis enfermé dehors

(**b**) *Ind (workers)* lock-outer

►**lock up 1** *vt sep* (**a**) *(house, shop)* fermer à clef

(**b**) *(valuables)* mettre sous clef; *(criminal)* incarcérer, mettre sous les verrous; **he should be locked up!** il faudrait l'enfermer!

(**c**) *Fin (capital)* immobiliser

(**d**) *Typ (type)* caler; *(forme)* serrer

2 *vi* fermer à clef; **it's time to lock up** c'est l'heure de fermer; **the last to leave locks up** le dernier à partir ferme la porte à clef

lockable ['lɒkəbəl] *adj* qu'on peut fermer à clef

lockage ['lɒkɪdʒ] *n* (**a**) *(system of locks)* écluses *fpl* (**b**) *(toll)* péage *m* d'écluse (**c**) *(difference in level)* différence *f* de niveau *(entre biefs)*

locked [lɒkt] *adj (door, room → with key)* fermé à clé; *(→ with bolt)* verrouillé

►► *Am Fam* ***locked bowels*** constipation ❑ *f*; **to have locked bowels** être constipé ❑

locked-in syndrome *n Med* locked-in syndrome *m*, syndrome *m* d'enfermement

locker ['lɒkə(r)] *n* (**a**) *(for luggage, in school)* casier *m*; *Naut* coffre *m*; *Aviat* **overhead locker** coffre *m* à bagages (**b**) *Am (freezer)* congélateur *m*

►► *Am* ***locker room*** vestiaire *m (avec casiers)*

locker-room *adj (humour, joke)* corsé, salé

locket ['lɒkɪt] *n* médaillon *m*

locking ['lɒkɪŋ] *adj (door, briefcase)* à serrure, qui ferme à clef

►► ***locking mechanism*** mécanisme *m* de verrouillage; ***locking up*** mise *f* sous clef; *(of house, room)* fermeture *f*; *Fin (of capital)* immobilisation *f*

lockjaw ['lɒkdʒɔː] *n* tétanos *m*; **to have lockjaw** avoir le tétanos

locknut ['lɒknʌt] *n (supplementary nut)* contre-écrou *m*; *(self-locking)* écrou *m* autobloquant

lockout ['lɒkaʊt] *n (of workers)* lock-out *m inv*

locksmith ['lɒksmɪθ] *n* serrurier *m*

lockstitch ['lɒkstɪtʃ] *n Sewing* point *m* de piqûre

lock-to-lock *adv Aut* de butée à butée

lockup ['lɒkʌp] *n* (**a**) *Am (jail)* prison *f*; *(cell)* cellule *f* (**b**) *Br (for storage)* remise *f*; *(garage)* garage *m* (**c**) *(act of locking up)* fermeture *f*

lock-up *adj*
►► *Br* ***lock-up garage*** garage *m*; *Br & NZ* ***lock-up shop*** (petite) boutique *f (sans logement attenant)*

loco ['ləʊkəʊ] *(pl* **locos**) **1** *n (train)* loco *f*
2 *adj* (**a**) *Am Fam (crazy)* dingue, cinglé (**b**) *Com* loco *(inv)*
3 *adv Com* loco; **the prices are loco Hull** les prix incluent le transport jusqu'à Hull
►► *Am Vet* ***loco disease*** vertigo *m*; *Com* ***loco price*** prix *m* loco

locoism ['ləʊkəʊɪzəm] *n Vet* vertigo *m*

locomotion [,ləʊkə'məʊʃən] *n* locomotion *f*

locomotive [,ləʊkə'məʊtɪv] **1** *n* locomotive *f*
2 *adj* locomotif; *Anat* locomoteur
►► *Rail* ***locomotive roundhouse*** rotonde *f*; ***locomotive works*** usine *f* de construction de machines

locomotor [,ləʊkə'məʊtə(r)] *adj* locomoteur
►► *Med* ***locomotor ataxia*** ataxie *f* locomotrice

locomotory [,ləʊkə'məʊtərɪ] *adj* locomotif; *Anat* locomoteur

locoregional [,ləʊkə'ri:dʒənəl] *adj Med* locorégional

locoweed ['ləʊkəʊwi:d] *n* (**a**) *Bot* astragale *m* toxique (**b**) *Fam (marijuana)* herbe *f*

loculus ['lɒkjələs] *(pl* **loculi** [-laɪ]) *n Biol* loge *f*

locum ['ləʊkəm] *n Br* remplaçant(e) *m,f (de prêtre, de médecin)*; **to take a locum job** faire un remplacement, prendre un emploi de remplaçant; **she's working as a locum in a hospital in London** elle fait un remplacement dans un hôpital de Londres
►► *Br Formal* ***locum tenens*** remplaçant(e) *m,f (de prêtre, de médecin)*

locus ['ləʊkəs] *(pl* **loci** [-saɪ, -kaɪ]) *n* (**a**) *Formal (place)* lieu *m*; *Law* lieux *mpl* (**b**) *Math* lieu *m* (géométrique) (**c**) *Biol (of gene)* locus *m*

locust ['ləʊkəst] *n* (**a**) *(insect)* locuste *f*, criquet *m* migrateur (**b**) *Bot (false acacia)* robinier *m*; *(carob tree)* caroubier *m*
►► ***locust bean*** caroube *f*; *Orn* ***locust bird*** glaréole *f* à ailes noires; *Bot* ***locust tree*** *(false acacia)* robinier *m*; *(carob tree)* caroubier *m*

locution [lə'kju:ʃən] *n Formal Ling* (**a**) *(phrase)* locution *f* (**b**) *(style)* style *m*, phraséologie *f*; *(manner of speech)* élocution *f*

locutionary act [ləʊ'kju:ʃənərɪ-] *n Ling* acte *m* de parole

lode [ləʊd] *n (vein → of metallic ore)* veine *f*; *(→ of gold, copper, silver)* filon *m*

loden ['ləʊdən] *adj (coat, jacket)* en loden

lodestar ['ləʊdstɑ:(r)] *n* (étoile *f*) Polaire *f*; *Fig* guide *m*, point *m* de repère

lodestone ['ləʊdstəʊn] *n Miner* pierre *f* à aimant, magnétite *f*; *Fig* aimant *m*

lodge [lɒdʒ] **1** *n* (**a**) *(cabin → for hunters)* pavillon *m*; *(→ for skiers)* chalet *m*
(**b**) *Br (on country estate)* maison *f* du gardien; *(of porter)* loge *f*; **shooting lodge** pavillon *m* de chasse
(**c**) *Am (in park, resort)* bâtiment *m* central
(**d**) *(Masonic)* loge *f*
(**e**) *(hotel)* hôtel *m*, relais *m*
(**f**) *(of beavers)* hutte *f*
(**g**) *(of Native Americans)* hutte *f*, wigwam *m*
2 *vt* (**a**) *(house)* héberger, loger; **the rescued passengers were lodged overnight in schools** les rescapés ont été hébergés pour la nuit dans des écoles; **the hotel can lodge 65 people** l'hôtel peut accueillir 65 personnes
(**b**) *(stick, embed)* mettre, placer; **a fish bone had lodged itself in his throat** il s'était coincé une arête dans le gosier; **his words were lodged in my memory** ses paroles étaient gravées dans ma mémoire
(**c**) *(make, file → claim)* déposer; **to lodge a complaint** porter plainte; **she lodged a formal complaint with the authorities** elle a déposé une plainte officielle auprès de l'administration; *Law* **to lodge an accusation against sb** porter plainte contre qn; **to lodge an appeal** interjeter appel, faire appel
(**d**) *(deposit for safekeeping)* consigner, déposer, mettre en sûreté; **to lodge securities with a bank** déposer des titres dans une banque
(**e**) *(invest → power, authority etc)* investir
3 *vi* (**a**) *(stay)* loger, être logé; **he is lodging at Mrs Smith's** *or* **with Mrs Smith** il loge chez Mme Smith; *(with board)* il est en pension chez Mme Smith
(**b**) *(stick, become embedded)* se loger; **a fishbone lodged in his throat** il s'est coincé une arête dans le gosier; **a bullet lodged close to his spine** il a reçu une balle qui est allée se loger près de sa colonne vertébrale
►► ***lodge keeper*** portier *m*; ***lodge meeting*** *(Masonic)* tenue *f*

lodgement = **lodgment**

lodger ['lɒdʒə(r)] *n* locataire *mf*; *(with board)* pensionnaire *mf*; **to take (in) lodgers** louer des chambres; *(provide meals too)* prendre des pensionnaires

lodging ['lɒdʒɪŋ] **1** *n* logement *m*; **they offered the family free lodging** ils ont offert d'héberger gratuitement la famille; **to find a night's lodging** trouver où coucher pour la nuit; **full board and lodging** pension *f* complète
2 lodgings *npl Br* chambre *f* meublée *(chez un particulier)*; **most of the students live in lodgings** la plupart des étudiants habitent dans des chambres meublées
►► ***lodging house*** garni *m*

lodgment ['lɒdʒmənt] *n Formal* (**a**) *(placing)* emplacement *m* (**b**) *(accumulation)* accumulation *f*; *(obstruction)* bouchon *m*

loess ['ləʊɪs] *n* lœss *m*

loft [lɒft] **1** *n* (**a**) *(attic)* grenier *m*
(**b**) *(elevated space → in church)* tribune *f*, galerie *f*
(**c**) *(warehouse apartment)* loft *m*
(**d**) *(for pigeons)* pigeonnier *m*
(**e**) *(of golf club)* angle *m* de la face
2 *vt Sport (hit)* envoyer très haut
►► ***loft conversion*** combles *mpl* aménagés, loft *m*; **they spent a lot of money on the loft conversion** ils ont dépensé beaucoup d'argent pour aménager les combles; ***loft ladder*** échelle *f* escamotable *(permettant d'accéder au grenier)*

loftily ['lɒftɪlɪ] *adv* avec mépris, dédaigneusement

loftiness ['lɒftɪnɪs] *n* (**a**) *(of mountain, tree, building)* hauteur *f* (**b**) *Pej (of person, manner)* arrogance *f*, hauteur *f*

lofty ['lɒftɪ] *(compar* **loftier**, *superl* **loftiest**) *adj* (**a**) *(mountain, tree, building)* haut, élevé; **the lofty peaks of the Alps** les hauts sommets des Alpes; **a lofty interior** des pièces hautes (de plafond)
(**b**) *Pej (person, manner)* hautain, arrogant
(**c**) *(exalted → in spirit)* noble, élevé; *(→ in rank, position)* éminent
(**d**) *(elevated → style, prose)* relevé, soutenu; **the lofty words in which the argument is expressed** le style relevé de l'argumentation

log¹ [lɒg] *(pt & pp* **logged**, *cont* **logging**) **1** *n* (**a**) *(for firewood)* bûche *f*; *(for building)* rondin *m*
(**b**) *(record)* journal *m*, registre *m*; *Comput (file)* fichier *m* compte-rendu; *Naut* journal *m*, livre *m* de bord; *Aviat* carnet *m* de vol; *(lorry driver's)* carnet *m* de route; **keep a log of all phone calls** notez tous les appels téléphoniques; **to write up the log** noter les détails du voyage
(**c**) *Naut (apparatus)* loch *m*
(**d**) *(cake)* **Yuletide** *or* **Christmas log** bûche *f* de Noël
(**e**) *Br Vulg (excrement)* étron *m*
2 *vt* (**a**) *(information → on paper)* consigner, inscrire; *(→ in computer memory)* entrer
(**b**) *(speed, distance, time)* **he has logged 2,000 hours' flying time** il a 2000 heures de vol à son actif, il totalise 2000 heures de vol; **the ship logged 15 knots** le navire filait 15 nœuds
(**c**) *(tree)* tronçonner; *(forest)* mettre en coupe
3 *vi Am (company)* exploiter une forêt; *(person)* travailler comme bûcheron
►► ***log cabin*** cabane *f* en rondins; *Comput* ***log file*** fichier *m* compte-rendu; ***log fire*** feu *m* de bois; ***log running*** flottage *m* du bois; *Math* ***log tables*** tables *fpl* de logarithmes; ***log transporter*** fardier *m*

►**log in** *Comput* **1** *vt sep (user name, password)* entrer, introduire
2 *vi* entrer, ouvrir une session

►**log off** *Comput* **1** *vt sep* faire sortir
2 *vi (user)* sortir, terminer *ou* clore une session

►**log on** *Comput* **1** *vt sep* faire entrer
2 *vi (user)* entrer, ouvrir une session; *(to remote system)* entrer en communication; **to log on to a system** se connecter à un système; **to log on to a data base** entrer dans une base de données

►**log out** *vi Comput (user)* sortir, se déconnecter

►**log up** *vt sep Br* (**a**) *(do, achieve)* avoir à son actif; **I've logged up three extra days' work** j'ai fait trois journées de travail supplémentaires; **they managed to log up 80 miles a day** ils ont réussi à faire 130 km par jour; **he has logged up yet another victory** il a remporté une nouvelle victoire
(**b**) *(write up)* consigner, inscrire

LOG CABIN

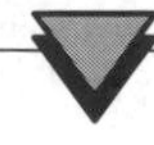

Certains hommes politiques américains prétendent être nés dans une "log cabin", comme ce fut réellement le cas d'Abraham Lincoln, exprimant ainsi leur aptitude à comprendre les problèmes des gens ordinaires.

log² [lɒg] *n Math (abbr* **logarithm**) log *m*

loganberry ['ləʊgənbərɪ] *(pl* **loganberries**) *n (plant)* framboisier *m* (hybride); *(fruit)* ronce-framboise *f*, mûre-framboise *f*

logarithm ['lɒgərɪðəm] *n* logarithme *m*

logarithmic [,lɒgə'rɪðmɪk] *adj* logarithmique
►► ***logarithmic function*** fonction *f* logarithme; ***logarithmic table*** table *f* des logarithmes

logarithmically [,lɒgə'rɪðmɪkəlɪ] *adv* au moyen de(s) logarithmes

logbook ['lɒgbʊk] *n* (**a**) *(record)* journal *m*, registre *m*; *Naut* journal *m ou* livre *m* de bord; *Aviat* carnet *m* de vol; *(of machine)* journal *m* de travail (**b**) *Br Aut* ≃ carte *f* grise

loge [ləʊʒ] *n Theat (box)* loge *f*; *(gallery)* galerie *f*, balcon *m*

logger ['lɒgə(r)] *n* (**a**) *Am (lumberjack)* bûcheron *m* (**b**) *Br (tractor)* tracteur *m* forestier

loggerhead ['lɒgəhed] *n Zool* caouanne *f*
►► *Orn* ***loggerhead shrike*** pie-grièche *f* migratrice; *Zool* ***loggerhead turtle*** caouanne *f*

loggerheads ['lɒgəhedz] *npl* **to be at loggerheads with sb (about sth)** avoir un différend avec qn (au sujet de qch); **they were constantly at loggerheads** ils se disputaient tout le temps; **his views were at loggerheads with...** ses opinions étaient en contradiction avec...

loggia ['ləʊdʒə] *(pl* **loggias** *or* **loggie** [-dʒe]) *n* loggia *f*; *Theat* galerie *f*

logging ['lɒgɪŋ] *n* (**a**) *(of details, events)* inscription *f* dans un journal; *(of order) & Comput* enregistrement *m* (**b**) *(felling timber etc)* exploitation *f* forestière; **the logging of mahogany** l'abattage *m* de l'acajou
►► ***logging camp*** camp *m* forestier; ***logging company*** société *f* d'exploitation forestière; ***logging road*** route *f* d'accès aux zones d'abattage

logic ['lɒdʒɪk] *n (gen) & Comput* logique *f*; *(reasoning)* raisonnement *m*; **I don't see the logic of it** je ne vois pas la logique (dans tout cela); **if you follow my logic** si tu suis mon raisonnement; **that's typical male logic!** c'est un raisonnement typiquement masculin!
►► *Comput* ***logic bomb*** bombe *f* logique *ou* à retardement; *Comput* ***logic card*** carte *f* logique; *Comput* ***logic chip*** puce *f* logique; *Comput* ***logic circuit*** circuit *m* logique; ***logic gate*** porte *f* logique; *Comput* ***logic operator*** opérateur *m* logique

logical ['lɒdʒɪkəl] *adj* logique; **it's a logical impossibility** c'est logiquement impossible; **he is incapable of logical argument** il est incapable d'avoir un raisonnement logique; **a logical conclusion** une conclusion logique
►► *Comput* ***logical file*** fichier *m* logique; *Ling* ***logical form*** forme *f* logique; *Comput* ***logical operator*** opérateur *m* logique; *Phil* ***logical positivism*** positivisme *m* logique, néopositivisme *m*; ***logical positivist*** logicopositiviste *mf*

logicality [,lɒdʒɪ'kælɪtɪ] *n* logique *f*

logically ['lɒdʒɪkəlɪ] *adv* logiquement; **if you think about it logically** si on y réfléchit bien; **logically, he should win** logiquement *ou* normalement, il devrait gagner

logic-chopper *n* ergoteur(euse) *m,f*

logic-chopping *n* ergotage *m*

logician [lə'dʒɪʃən] *n* logicien(enne) *m,f*

logicism ['lɒdʒɪˌsɪzəm] *n Phil* logicisme *m*

login ['lɒgɪn] *n Comput* ouverture *f* de session

►► ***login name*** nom *m* d'utilisateur, nom *m* de login

logistic [lɒ'dʒɪstɪk], **logistical** [lɒ'dʒɪstɪkəl] *adj* logistique; **a logistic problem** un problème de logistique; **it's a logistic nightmare** c'est un casse-tête du point de vue de la logistique

►► ***logistic support*** soutien *m* logistique

logistically [lə'dʒɪstɪkəlɪ] *adv* d'un point de vue logistique

logistics [lə'dʒɪstɪks] *npl* logistique *f*; **the logistics of the situation** les données logistiques de la situation

logjam ['lɒgdʒæm] *n* (**a**) *(in river)* bouchon *m* de bois flottés, *Can* digue *f* (**b**) *Fig (deadlock)* impasse *f*

logo ['ləʊgəʊ] *(pl* **logos***)* *n* logo *m*

logocentrism [ˌlɒgəʊ'sentrɪzəm] *n* logocentrisme *m*

logodaedalus [ˌlɒgəʊ'diːdələs] *n* personne *f* habile à manier le langage

logoff ['lɒgɒf] *n Comput* fin *f* de session

logogram ['lɒgəgræm], **logograph** ['lɒgəgrɑːf] *n* logogramme *m*

logographer [lɒ'gɒgrəfə(r)] *n* logographe *mf*

logography [lɒ'gɒgrəfɪ] *n* logographie *f*

logomachic [lɒ'gɒməkɪk] *adj* logomachique

logomachy [lɒ'gɒməkɪ] *n* logomachie *f*

logon ['lɒgɒn] *n Comput* ouverture *f* de session

logorrhoea, *Am* **logorrhea** [ˌlɒgə'rɪə] *n* logorrhée *f*

logos ['lɒgɒs] **1** *n Phil* logos *m*

2 Logos *n Rel* Logos *m*

logotype ['lɒgətaɪp] *n Typ* logotype *m*

logout ['lɒgaʊt] *n Comput* fin *f* de session

logrolling ['lɒgrəʊlɪŋ] *n* (**a**) *(sport)* = sport pratiqué par les bûcherons, qui consiste à se maintenir debout sur un tronc d'arbre flottant que l'on fait tourner sous ses pieds, *Can* concours *m* de draveurs (**b**) *Am Pej* échange *m* de faveurs *(accord entre hommes politiques selon lequel on se rend mutuellement des services)*

logwood ['lɒgwʊd] *n (wood)* campêche *m*, bois *m* de campêche; *(tree)* campêche *m*

logy ['ləʊgɪ] *(compar* **logier**, *superl* **logiest***)* *adj Am Fam* patraque; **you look a bit logy** tu n'as pas l'air en forme

loin [lɔɪn] **1** *n Culin (of pork)* longe *f*, échine *f*, filet *m*; *(of beef)* aloyau *m*; *(of veal)* longe *f*; *(of lamb)* carré *m*

2 loins *npl Anat* reins *mpl*; *Euph (genitals)* parties *fpl*; *Literary* **sprung from the loins of...** sorti des reins de...

►► ***loin chop*** côtes *fpl* premières

loincloth ['lɔɪnklɒθ] *n* pagne *m*

loiter ['lɔɪtə(r)] *vi* (**a**) *(hang about)* traîner; *(lurk)* rôder; **there was someone loitering in the car-park** il y avait quelqu'un qui rôdait dans le parking; **no loitering** *(sign)* zone sous surveillance *(où il est interdit de s'attarder)*; **to loiter with intent** *Law* rôder d'une manière suspecte; *Fig Hum* rôder (**b**) *(dawdle)* traîner; *(lag behind)* traîner (en route)

loitering ['lɔɪtərɪŋ] *n Law* **loitering with intent** = délit qui consiste à rôder dans le but de commettre un méfait

loll [lɒl] *vi* (**a**) *(lounge)* se prélasser; **he was lolling against the wall** il était nonchalamment appuyé contre le mur (**b**) *(head)* tomber en avant; *(tongue)* pendre

►**loll about, loll around** *vi (in grass, armchair etc)* se prélasser; **I just lolled about** *or* **around all day** j'ai paressé toute la journée

►**loll out** *vi (tongue)* pendre (mollement)

lollapalooza [ˌlɒləpə'luːzə] *n Am Fam* merveille ❑ *f*, phénomène ❑ *m*; **her last film's a lollapalooza** son dernier film est vraiment prodigieux ❑

Lollard ['lɒləd] *n Hist* lollard *m*

lollipop ['lɒlɪpɒp] *n* (**a**) *(sweet)* sucette *f* (**b**) *Br (ice lolly)* Esquimau® *m*, sucette *f* glacée

►► *Br Fam* ***lollipop lady*** = femme chargée d'aider les enfants à traverser la rue; *Br Fam* ***lollipop man*** = homme chargé d'aider les enfants à traverser la rue

lollop ['lɒləp] *vi (person)* marcher lourdement; *(animal)* galoper; **the rabbit lolloped off** le lapin s'éloigna en bondissant

lollo rosso [ˌlɒləʊ'rɒsəʊ] *n Bot & Culin* lollo rosso *m*

lolly ['lɒlɪ] *(pl* **lollies***)* *n* (**a**) *Br Fam (on stick)* sucette ❑ *f* (**b**) *Br Fam (money)* fric *m*, pognon *m* (**c**) *Austr & NZ Fam (sweet)* bonbon ❑ *m*

lollypop = **lollipop**

Lombard ['lɒmbəd] **1** *n* Lombard(e) *m,f*

2 *adj* Lombard

►► *Banking* ***Lombard rate*** taux *m* Lombard; ***Lombard Street*** *(in London)* = rue de Londres, cœur de l'activité financière; *(in San Francisco)* = rue de San Francisco que l'on prétend la plus sinueuse du monde

Lombardy ['lɒmbədɪ] *n* Lombardie *f*; **in Lombardy** en Lombardie

►► *Bot* ***Lombardy poplar*** peuplier *m* d'Italie

Lomé ['ləʊmeɪ] *n* Lomé

London ['lʌndən] **1** *n* Londres

2 *comp (museums, bus, taxi)* londonien; *(life)* à Londres; *(street)* de Londres

►► ***the London Academy of Music and Dramatic Art*** = conservatoire de musique et d'art dramatique, à Londres; ***London Bridge*** = pont construit sur la Tamise en 1968 pour remplacer l'ancien pont, qui fut vendu et remonté dans l'Arizona; ***the London Coliseum*** = théâtre londonien, siège du "English National Opera"; ***the London Eye*** = la grande roue construite à Londres pour le nouveau millénaire; *Fin* ***London Inter-Bank Offer Rate*** ≃ taux interbancaire offert à Paris; *Fin* ***the London International Financial Futures Exchange*** = marché à terme britannique d'instruments financiers, ≃ MATIF *m*; ***the London Palladium*** = théâtre londonien connu pour ses spectacles de variétés; *Bot* ***London pride*** saxifrage *f* à feuilles en coin, mignonnette *f*; ***London (Regional) Transport*** = régie des transports publics londoniens; *Univ* ***London School of Economics*** = grande école de sciences économiques et politiques à Londres; ***the London Season*** = série de manifestations mondaines, courses hippiques etc organisées chaque année à Londres et dans les alentours; *St Exch* ***the London Stock Exchange*** = la Bourse de Londres; ***the London Symphony Orchestra*** = orchestre symphonique de Londres; *Br* ***London weighting*** = indemnité de vie chère venant compléter certains salaires londoniens

Londonderry [ˌlʌndən'derɪ] *n* Londonderry

Londoner ['lʌndənə(r)] *n* Londonien(enne) *m,f*; **a Londoner born and bred** un Londonien pure souche

lone [ləʊn] *adj (gunman, rider, stag)* solitaire; *(isolated → house)* isolé; *(single, unique)* unique, seul; **a lone fishing boat on the horizon** un seul bateau de pêche à l'horizon; *Fig* **to play a lone hand** agir tout seul, être seul contre tous

►► ***lone parent*** parent *m* unique; ***the Lone Ranger*** = cow-boy masqué dans un feuilleton télévisé américain; ***the Lone Star State*** = surnom donné au Texas; *Fig* ***lone wolf*** solitaire *mf*; **to be a bit of a lone wolf** être un peu solitaire

loneliness ['ləʊnlɪnɪs] *n (of person)* solitude *f*, isolement *m*; *(of place)* isolement *m*; **with only the loneliness of old age to look forward to** avec la seule perspective de vieillir dans la solitude

'The Loneliness of the Long Distance Runner' *Sillitoe, Richardson* 'La Solitude du coureur de fond'

lonely ['ləʊnlɪ] *(compar* **lonelier**, *superl* **loneliest***)* *adj* (**a**) *(sad → person)* seul; *(→ life)* solitaire; **to be** *or* **to feel lonely** se sentir seul; **a lonely figure** une silhouette; *Fig (politician etc)* une figure isolée; *Fig* **to travel a lonely road** avoir un parcours solitaire; **the house seems lonely without you** la maison paraît vide sans toi; **life is very lonely since the children left home** la vie est bien morne depuis que les enfants ont quitté la maison; **he went home to his lonely room** il regagna la solitude de sa chambre; **the loneliest hour of the day** l'heure de la journée où l'on se sent le plus seul

(**b**) *(unfrequented → spot, farmhouse)* isolé; *(→ street)* peu fréquenté, vide; **I find the village too lonely** je trouve le village trop isolé

►► ***lonely hearts club*** club *m* de rencontres; ***lonely hearts column*** rubrique *f* rencontres *(des petites annonces)*

loner ['ləʊnə(r)] *n Fam (person)* solitaire ❑ *mf*; **he's a bit of a loner** il est un peu sauvage *ou* farouche ❑

lonesome ['ləʊnsəm] **1** *adj Am* solitaire, seul; **to feel lonesome** se sentir seul

2 *n* **on one's lonesome** tout seul

LONG [lɒŋ] *(compar* **longer** ['lɒŋgə(r)], *superl* **longest** ['lɒŋgɪst]) **1** *adj* (**a**) *(in size)* long (longue); **how long is the pool?** quelle est la longueur de la piscine?, la piscine fait combien de long?; **the pool's 33 metres long** la piscine fait 33 mètres de long; **the article is 80 pages long** l'article fait 80 pages; **is it a long way (away)?** est-ce loin (d'ici)?; **it's a long way to the beach** la plage est loin; **she can throw a long way** elle lance loin; **to take the long way round** prendre le chemin le plus long; **the best by a long way** de loin le meilleur; **to get** *or* **grow longer** *(shadows)* s'allonger; *(hair, beard)* pousser; **long in the leg** aux longues jambes; **a long face** un visage allongé; *Fig* **to have** *or* **pull a long face** faire la tête, faire une tête de six pieds de long; **why the long face?** pourquoi est-ce que tu fais cette tête de six pieds de long?

(**b**) *(in time → pause, speech, separation)* long (longue); **how long will the flight be/was the meeting?** combien de temps durera le vol/a duré la réunion?; **the film is three hours long** le film dure trois heures; **her five-year-long battle with the authorities** sa lutte de cinq années contre les autorités; **to have a long memory** avoir une bonne mémoire; **to have a long talk with sb** parler longuement avec qn; **to get longer** *(days, intervals)* devenir plus long; **they want longer holidays** ils veulent des vacances plus longues; **she took a long swig of beer** elle a bu une grande gorgée de bière; **they took a long look at the view** ils restèrent longtemps à regarder la vue qui s'offrait à eux; **it was a long two months** ces deux mois ont été longs; **I've had a long day** j'ai eu une journée bien remplie; **in the long term** à long terme; **it will take a long time** cela prendra longtemps, ce sera long; **a long time ago** il y a (bien) longtemps; **it's a long time since I was (last) in Paris** ça fait longtemps que je ne suis pas allé à Paris; **I've been wanting to go for a long time** ça fait longtemps que j'ai envie d'y aller; **I've known her (for) a long time** *or* **while** je la connais depuis longtemps, cela fait longtemps que je la connais; **it was a long haul** *(journey)* le voyage a été long; *(task, recovery)* c'était un travail de longue haleine; **at long last!** enfin!

(**c**) *Gram (vowel, syllable)* long (longue)

(**d**) *St Exch* **they're long on copper, they've taken a long position on copper** ils ont investi dans le cuivre

(**e**) *Fam (in tennis)* **that serve was long** ce service était trop long

(**f**) *(idioms)* **she's long on good ideas** elle n'est pas à court de bonnes idées, ce ne sont pas les bonnes idées qui lui manquent; **his speeches are long on rhetoric but short on substance** ce n'est pas la rhétorique qui manque dans ses discours, c'est la substance

2 *n* (**a**) *Gram (vowel, syllable)* longue *f*

(**b**) *Fin (bill)* effet *m* à longue échéance

(**c**) *(idioms) Fam* **the long and the short of it is that I got fired** enfin bref, j'ai été viré; **that's the long and the short of it!** un point c'est tout!

3 *adv* (**a**) *(a long time)* longtemps; **they live longer than humans** ils vivent plus longtemps que les êtres humains; **he won't keep you long/much longer** il ne vous gardera pas longtemps/beaucoup plus longtemps; **I haven't been here long** ça ne fait pas longtemps que je suis là; **they haven't been married long** ça ne fait pas longtemps qu'ils sont mariés, ils ne sont pas mariés depuis longtemps; **how long will he be/was he in jail?** (pendant) combien de temps restera-t-il/est-il resté en prison?; **how long has he been in jail?** ça fait combien de temps qu'il est en prison?, depuis combien de temps est-il en prison?; **how long is it since we last visited them?** quand sommes-nous allés les voir pour la dernière fois?; **it happened long ago/not long ago** cela s'est passé il y a longtemps/il n'y a pas longtemps; **as long ago as 1937** déjà en 1937; **long before you were born** bien avant que tu sois né; **not long before/after their divorce** peu avant/après leur divorce; **the decision had been taken long before** la décision avait été prise depuis longtemps; **long after** *or* **afterwards, when these events were mostly forgotten...** bien après, alors que ces évènements étaient presque complètement oubliés...; **colleagues long since promoted** des collègues promus depuis longtemps; **a law which had come into force not long since** une loi qui était entrée en vigueur depuis peu; **to look at sb/sth long and hard** fixer qn/qch longuement; *Fig* **to look at sth long and hard** se pencher longuement sur qch; **I've thought long and hard about this** j'y ai longuement réfléchi; **we talked long into the night** nous avons parlé jusque tard dans la nuit

(**b**) *(with "be", "take")* **will you be long?** tu en as pour longtemps?; **I won't be long** je n'en ai pas pour longtemps; **please wait, she won't be long** attendez, s'il vous plaît, elle ne va pas tarder; **are you going to be much longer?** tu en as encore pour longtemps?; **how much longer will he be?** *(when will he be ready?)* il en a encore pour longtemps?; *(when will he arrive?)* dans combien de temps sera-t-il là?; **don't be** *or* **take too long** fais vite; **it wasn't long before he realized, it didn't take long for him to realize** il n'a pas mis longtemps à s'en rendre compte, il s'en est vite rendu compte; **he wasn't long in coming** il n'a pas tardé à venir; **he took** *or* **it took him so long to make up his mind...** il a mis si longtemps à se décider..., il lui a fallu tellement de temps pour se décider...; **how long does it take to get there?** combien de temps faut-il pour y aller?; **this won't take long** ça va être vite fait; **this won't take longer than five minutes** ça sera fait en moins de cinq minutes

(**c**) *(in wishes, toasts)* **long may our partnership continue!** à notre collaboration!; **long live the Queen!** vive la reine!

(**d**) *(for a long time)* depuis longtemps; **it has long been known that...** on sait depuis longtemps que...; **I have long suspected that he was involved in it** cela fait longtemps que je le soupçonne *ou* je le soupçonne depuis longtemps d'être impliqué là-dedans; **the longest-running TV series** le feuilleton télévisé qui existe depuis le plus longtemps

(**e**) *(throughout)* **all day/week long** toute la journée/la semaine; **all my life long** toute ma vie

(**f**) *St Exch* **to go long** acheter à la hausse, prendre une position longue; **to buy long** acheter à long terme

(**g**) *Fam (idiom)* **so long!** salut!, à bientôt! □

4 *vi* **I long for him** il me manque énormément; **she was longing for a letter from you** elle attendait impatiemment que vous lui écriviez; **we were longing for a cup of tea** nous avions très envie d'une tasse de thé; **to long** *or* **to be longing to do sth** être impatient *ou* avoir hâte de faire qch; **he's longing to go back to Italy** il meurt d'envie de retourner en Italie; **I was longing to tell her the truth** je mourais d'envie de lui dire la vérité; **I've been longing to meet you for years** cela fait des années que je souhaite faire votre connaissance

5 longs *npl St Exch* titres *mpl* longs, obligations *fpl* longues

6 as long as, so long as *conj* (**a**) *(during the time that)* aussi longtemps que, tant que; **as long as he's in power, there will be no hope** tant qu'il sera au pouvoir, il n'y aura aucun espoir; **I'll never forget that day for as long as I live** jamais de ma vie je n'oublierai ce jour

(**b**) *(providing)* à condition que, pourvu que; **you can have it as long as you give me it back** vous pouvez le prendre à condition que *ou* pourvu que vous me le rendiez; **I'll do it as long as I get paid for it** je le ferai à condition d'être payé; **you can go out as long as you're back before midnight** tu peux sortir à condition de rentrer avant minuit; **as long as you're happy** du moment que tu es heureux

(**c**) *Am Fam (seeing that)* puisque □; **as long as you're going to the post office get me some stamps** puisque tu vas à la poste, achète-moi des timbres

7 before long *adv (soon)* dans peu de temps, sous peu; *(soon afterwards)* peu (de temps) après; **she'll be back before long** elle sera de retour dans peu de temps *ou* sous peu; **before long, everything had returned to normal** tout était rapidement rentré dans l'ordre

8 for long *adv* longtemps; **he's still in charge here, but not for long** c'est encore lui qui s'en occupe, mais plus pour longtemps

9 no longer *adv* ne...plus; **not any longer** plus maintenant; **she no longer loves him** elle ne l'aime plus; **I can't wait any longer** je ne peux pas attendre plus longtemps, je ne peux plus attendre; **they used to live there, but not any longer** ils habitaient là autrefois, mais plus maintenant

►► ***long black*** grand café *m* noir; *Fin* ***long credit*** crédit *m* à long terme; ***long dress*** *(for evening wear)* robe *f* longue; ***long drink*** long drink *m*; *(non-alcoholic)* = grand verre de jus de fruits, de limonade etc; *Fin* ***long hedge*** couverture *f* longue, achat *m* par couverture; ***Long Island*** Long Island; **on Long Island** à Long Island; ***Long Island iced tea*** = cocktail composé de cinq alcools, de bitter et de Coca-Cola; *Fam* ***long johns*** caleçon *m* long □, caleçons *mpl* longs □; *Sport* ***long jump*** saut *m* en longueur; *Sport* ***long jumper*** sauteur(euse) *m,f* en longueur; *Hist* ***the Long March*** la Longue Marche; *Am* ***long pants*** pantalon *m* long; ***the Long Parliament*** le Long Parlement, = Parlement convoqué par Charles Ier en 1640, renvoyé par Cromwell en 1653 et dissous en 1660; ***long pig*** chair *f* humaine; *St Exch* ***long position*** position *f* acheteur *ou* longue; **to take a long position** acheter à la hausse, prendre une position longue; ***long shot*** *(competitor, racehorse etc)* outsider *m*; *(bet)* pari *m* risqué; *Cin* plan *m* éloigné; *Fig* entreprise *f* hasardeuse; **it's a bit of a long shot** il y a peu de chances pour que cela réussisse; **it's a bit of a long shot, but we may be successful** c'est une entreprise hasardeuse mais nous réussirons peut-être; **I haven't finished, not by a long shot** je n'ai pas fini, loin de là; *Tech* ***long ton*** tonne *f* anglaise; ***long trousers*** pantalon *m* long; *Univ* ***long vacation*** grandes vacances *fpl*, vacances *fpl* d'été; ***long view*** prévisions *fpl* à long terme; **to take the long view** envisager les choses à long terme; ***long vodka*** = cocktail à base de vodka, de bitter, de sirop de citron vert et de soda ou limonade; *Rad* ***long wave*** grandes ondes *fpl*; **on long wave** sur les grandes ondes; ***long weekend*** week-end *m* prolongé; **to take a long weekend** prendre un week-end prolongé

'Long Day's Journey into Night' *O'Neill* 'Long Voyage vers la nuit'

long. *(written abbr* **longitude***)* long.

longan [ˈlɒŋgən] *n Bot (tree)* longanier *m*; *(fruit)* longane *m*

longanimity [ˌlɒŋgəˈnɪmɪtɪ] *n Literary* longanimité *f*

long-awaited [-əˈweɪtɪd] *adj* très attendu

longbed [ˈlɒŋbed] *adj Am*

►► ***longbed truck*** gros camion *m*

longboat [ˈlɒŋbəʊt] *n Naut* chaloupe *f*; *(of Vikings)* drakkar *m*

longbow [ˈlɒŋbəʊ] *n* arc *m*

longcase clock [ˈlɒŋkeɪs-] *n* horloge *f* (de parquet)

long-chain *adj Chem (molecule)* à longue chaîne

long-dated *adj St Exch* à longue échéance

►► ***long-dated bill*** effet *m ou* traite *f* à longue échéance; ***long-dated securities*** titres *mpl* longs, obligations *fpl* longues

long-distance 1 *adj Tel* longue distance; **is it long-distance?** est-ce que c'est un appel longue distance?

2 *adv* **to telephone long-distance** faire un appel longue distance; **I'm phoning long-distance from Aberdeen** c'est un appel interurbain, j'appelle d'Aberdeen

►► ***long-distance call*** communication *f* hors circonscription; *Math* ***long division*** division *f* posée; **to do long division/a long division** faire des divisions/une division *(à la main)*; ***long-distance footpath*** sentier *m* de grande randonnée; *Br* ***long-distance lorry driver*** conducteur(trice) *m,f* de poids lourd, *Fam* routier *m*; *Sport* ***long-distance race*** course *f* de fond; *Sport* ***long-distance runner*** coureur(euse) *m,f* de fond

long-drawn-out *adj (sigh)* prolongé; *(story, explanation)* interminable; **long-drawn-out account** récit *m* prolongé *ou* à n'en plus finir

long-eared *adj* aux grandes oreilles

►► *Zool* ***long-eared bat*** oreillard *m*; *Orn* ***long-eared owl*** hibou *m* moyen-duc

longed-for [ˈlɒŋd-] *adj* très attendu

longeron [ˈlɒndʒərən] *n Aviat* longeron *m*

long-established *adj (tradition)* qui existe depuis longtemps

longevity [lɒnˈdʒevətɪ] *n* longévité *f*

Longford [ˈlɒŋfəd] *n* (**a**) *(town)* Longford (**b**) *(county)* le comté de Longford, = comté dans le nord de la République d'Irlande; **in Longford** dans le comté de Longford

long-forgotten *adj* oublié depuis longtemps; **a long-forgotten tradition** une tradition tombée en désuétude

long-grain rice *n* riz *m* long

longhair [ˈlɒŋheə(r)] *Am* **1** *n Fam* (**a**) *Old-fashioned (intellectual)* intello *mf* (**b**) *(hippie)* chevelu *m*

2 *adj* (**a**) *(cat, dog)* à poil(s) long(s) (**b**) *Fam Old-fashioned (for intellectuals)* pour les intellos

►► ***longhair music*** musique *f* classique

longhaired [ˈlɒŋheəd] *adj* (**a**) *(cat, dog)* à poil(s) long(s); *(person)* aux cheveux longs (**b**) *Am Fam Old-fashioned (for intellectuals)* pour les intellos

longhand [ˈlɒŋhænd] *n* écriture *f* courante; **in longhand** *(not on a typewriter)* à la main; *(not in shorthand)* en entier

long-haul *adj (aircraft)* long-courrier

►► ***long-haul carrier*** long-courrier *m*

longheaded [ˌlɒŋˈhedɪd] *adj (shrewd)* astucieux, malin(igne)

longhorn [ˈlɒŋhɔːn] *n Agr* longhorn *m*

longhouse [ˈlɒŋhaʊs, *pl* -haʊzɪz] *n* long house *f*

longicorn [ˈlɒŋgɪkɔːn] *adj Entom* longicorne

►► ***longicorn beetle*** longicorne *m*

longing [ˈlɒŋɪŋ] **1** *n* envie *f*, désir *m*; **I had a longing to see the sea** j'avais très envie de voir la mer; **the sight of her filled him with longing** en la voyant le désir s'empara de lui

2 *adj* d'envie, de désir; **a longing look** un regard plein d'envie

longingly [ˈlɒŋɪŋlɪ] *adv (with desire)* avec désir *ou* envie; *(with regret)* avec regret; **to look longingly at sth** couver qch des yeux; **to think longingly of the past** penser au passé avec nostalgie

longish [ˈlɒŋɪʃ] *adj* assez long (longue)

longitude [ˈlɒndʒɪtjuːd] *n* longitude *f*; **at a longitude of 60° east** par 60° de longitude est

longitudinal [ˌlɒndʒɪˈtjuːdɪnəl] *adj* longitudinal

►► ***longitudinal section*** coupe *f* longitudinale; *Phys* ***longitudinal wave*** onde *f* longitudinale

longitudinally [ˌlɒndʒɪˈtjuːdɪnəlɪ] *adv* longitudinalement

long-lasting *adj* durable, qui dure longtemps

Longleat [ˈlɒŋliːt] *n* = château dans le sud-ouest de l'Angleterre connu pour son "safari park"

long-legged *adj (person)* aux jambes longues; *(animal)* aux pattes longues

long-life *adj (milk, juice)* longue conservation *(inv)*; *(lightbulb, battery)* longue durée *(inv)*

long-limbed *adj* aux longs membres

long-line *adj*

►► ***long-line bra*** soutien-gorge *m* à basque; *(strapless)* bustier *m*

longlist [ˈlɒŋlɪst] *n* première liste *f*

long-lived [-lɪvd] *adj (person, animal, plant)* qui vit longtemps; *(family, species)* d'une grande longévité; *(friendship, theory)* durable; *(prejudice)* tenace, qui a la vie dure

►► *Acct* ***long-lived assets*** actifs *mpl* à long terme, actifs *mpl* à longue durée de vie

long-lost *adj (manuscript, painting etc)* perdu depuis longtemps; **she has been reunited with her long-lost brother** elle a retrouvé son frère dont elle avait été séparée depuis très longtemps; **I'm seeking some long-lost cousins** je suis à la recherche de cousins que j'ai perdus de vue depuis longtemps; **he welcomed me like a long-lost friend** il m'a accueilli comme si on était des amis qui ne s'étaient pas vus depuis des années

long-nosed *adj* au nez long

long-playing record *n* 33 tours *m inv*, microsillon *m*

long-range *adj* (**a**) *(weapon)* à longue portée; *(vehicle, aircraft)* à long rayon d'action (**b**) *(plan)* à long terme
▸▸ *Met* ***long-range forecast*** prévisions *fpl* météorologiques à long terme

long-running *adj (film, play)* qui tient l'affiche; *(TV or radio programme)* qui est diffusé depuis longtemps

longship ['lɒŋʃɪp] *n* drakkar *m*

longshore ['lɒŋʃɔ:(r)] *adj* qui vit sur la côte

longshoreman ['lɒŋʃɔ:mən] *(pl* **longshoremen** [-mən]) *n Am* docker *m*

longsighted [,lɒŋ'saɪtɪd] *adj* (**a**) *Med* hypermétrope; *(in old age)* presbyte (**b**) *Fig (policy, decision)* prévoyant

longsightedness [,lɒŋ'saɪtɪdnɪs] *n* (**a**) *Med* hypermétropie *f*; *(in old age)* presbytie *f* (**b**) *Fig (of policy, decision)* prévoyance *f*, discernement *m*

long-sleeved *adj* à manches longues

long-stalked [-stɔ:kt] *adj Bot* à longue tige
▸▸ ***long-stalked crane's bill*** géranium *m* colombin

long-standing *adj* de longue date
▸▸ *Fin* ***long-standing accounts*** vieux comptes *mpl*

long-stay *adj*
▸▸ *Med* ***long-stay bed*** lit *m* (de) long séjour; ***long-stay car park*** parking *m* longue durée; ***long-stay hospital*** unité *f ou* centre *m* de soins de longue durée

long-stemmed *adj Bot* à longue tige

long-suffering *adj* (extrêmement) patient, d'une patience à toute épreuve; *(resigned)* résigné; **she gave a long-suffering sigh** elle poussa un soupir résigné *ou* de résignation

long-tailed *adj* à longue queue
▸▸ *Orn* ***long-tailed bird of paradise*** épimaque *m*; *Orn* ***long-tailed cormorant*** cormoran *m* africain; *Orn* ***long-tailed duck*** canard *m* de Miquelon, *Can* cacaoui *m*; *Orn* ***long-tailed skua*** labbe *f* longicaude

long-term *adj* (**a**) *(detainee, prisoner)* qui subit un emprisonnement de longue durée; **the long-term unemployed** les chômeurs de longue durée
(**b**) *Fin (loan, policy etc)* à long terme
▸▸ *Fin* ***long-term bond*** obligation *f* à long terme; *Fin* ***long-term bond rate*** taux *m* long obligataire; *Acct* ***long-term borrowings*** emprunts *mpl* à long terme; *Acct* ***long-term capital*** capitaux *mpl* permanents; *Fin* ***long-term credit*** crédit *m* (à) long terme; *Fin* ***long-term debt*** dette *f* à long terme; *Br Fin* ***long-term individual savings account*** plan *m* de retraite en actions; *Fin* ***long-term financing*** financement *m* à long terme; *Fin* ***long-term interest rate*** taux *m* d'intérêt à long terme; *Fin* ***long-term investments*** placements *mpl* à long terme; [illegible] immobilisations *fpl* financières; *Fin* ***long-term liabilities*** dettes *fpl ou* passif *m* à long terme; *Fin* ***long-term loan*** prêt *m* à long terme; *Fin* ***long-term maturity*** échéance *f* à long terme; ***long-term memory*** mémoire *f* à long terme; ***long-term planning*** planification *f* à long terme; ***long-term unemployment*** chômage *m* de longue durée

long-time *adj (friend, acquaintance)* de longue date; *(interest, affiliation)* ancien, qui dure depuis longtemps

long-waisted *adj (garment)* à taille basse; *(person)* au buste long

long-wave *adj* sur grandes ondes

longways ['lɒŋweɪz] *adv* longitudinalement, dans le sens de la longueur

longwearing [,lɒŋ'weərɪŋ] *adj Am* solide, résistant

long-winded [-'wɪndɪd] *adj (person)* prolixe, bavard; *(article, essay, lecture)* interminable; *(style)* verbeux, diffus

longwise ['lɒŋwaɪz] *adv* longitudinalement, dans le sens de la longueur

long-woolled [-wʊld] *adj (sheep)* à grosse laine

Lonsdale Belt ['lɒnzdeɪl-] *n* = la plus haute distinction pour les boxeurs professionnels en Grande-Bretagne

loo [lu:] *n* (**a**) *Br Fam* cabinets *mpl*, petit coin *m*; **to go to the loo** aller aux toilettes ❑; **in the loo** aux toilettes ❑, aux cabinets (**b**) *(card game)* = ancien jeu de cartes où l'on joue de l'argent
▸▸ *Br Fam* ***loo paper*** papier *m* hygiénique ❑; *Br Fam* ***loo roll*** rouleau *m* de papier hygiénique ❑; *(paper)* papier *m* hygiénique ❑; *Br Fam* ***loo seat*** siège *m* des toilettes *ou* des WC ❑

loofa, loofah ['lu:fə] *n* luffa *m*, loofa *m*

LOOK [lʊk]

coup d'œil	▸ **1 (a)**
regard	▸ **1 (c)**
air	▸ **1 (d)**
mode	▸ **1 (e)**
regarder	▸ **2 (a); 3 (a)**
chercher	▸ **3 (b)**
écouter	▸ **3 (c)**
avoir l'air	▸ **3 (d)**
chercher à	▸ **3 (f)**
beauté	▸ **4**

1 *n* (**a**) *(gen)* coup *m* d'œil; **to have** *or* **to take a look (at sth)** jeter un coup d'œil (sur *ou* à qch), regarder (qch); *Fam* **let's have a look** *(show me)* fais voir; **would you like a look through my binoculars?** voulez-vous regarder avec mes jumelles?; **one look at him is enough to know he's a crook** on voit au premier coup d'œil que c'est un escroc; **it's worth a quick look** ça vaut le coup d'œil; **we need to take a long hard look at our image abroad** il est temps que nous examinions de près notre image de marque à l'étranger; **did you get a good look at him?** vous l'avez vu clairement?; **did the mechanic have a proper look at the car?** est-ce que le mécanicien a bien regardé la voiture?; **and now a look ahead to next week's programmes** et maintenant, un aperçu des programmes de la semaine prochaine; **do you mind if I take a look around?** ça vous gêne si je jette un coup d'œil?; **we'll just have a quick look round the garden** nous allons jeter un coup d'œil dans le jardin; **we had a look round the town** nous avons fait un tour dans la ville; **I took a quick look through the drawers** j'ai jeté un rapide coup d'œil dans les tiroirs
(**b**) *(search)* **to have a look for sth** chercher qch; **have you had a good look for it?** est-ce que tu as bien cherché?; **have another look** cherche encore
(**c**) *(glance)* regard *m*; **a suspicious/nasty/angry look** un regard soupçonneux/mauvais/méchant; **she gave me a dirty look** elle m'a jeté un regard mauvais; **you should have seen the looks we got from passers-by!** si tu avais vu la façon dont les passants nous regardaient!; **we were getting some very odd looks** on nous regardait d'un drôle d'air; **he didn't say anything, but if looks could kill!** il n'a pas dit un mot, mais il y a des regards qui tuent!
(**d**) *(appearance, air)* air *m*; **he had a strange look in his eyes** *(expression)* il avait un drôle de regard; **the old house has a neglected look** la vieille maison a l'air négligé; **she has the look of a troublemaker** elle a une tête à faire des histoires; **she has the look of someone who's going places** elle a l'air de quelqu'un qui réussira dans la vie; **by the look** *or* **looks of her, I'd say she failed the exam** à la voir *ou* rien qu'en la voyant, je dirais qu'elle a raté son examen; **it has the look of a successful marriage** cela a l'air d'un mariage heureux; **there's trouble brewing by the look of it** *or* **things** on dirait que quelque chose se trame; **I quite like the look of the next candidate** j'aime assez le profil du prochain candidat; **I don't like the look of it** ça ne me dit rien de bon *ou* rien qui vaille; **I didn't like the look of her at all** son allure ne m'a pas du tout plu; **I don't like the look of the weather** le temps a l'air inquiétant
(**e**) *(fashion)* mode *f*, look *m*; **the sporty/punk look** le look sportif/punk

2 *vt* (**a**) *(in imperative)* **look who's coming!** regarde qui arrive!; **look who's talking!** tu peux parler, toi!; **look what you've done/where you're going!** regarde un peu ce que tu as fait/où tu vas!
(**b**) *(idioms)* **to look one's last on sth** jeter un dernier regard à qch; **to look sb up and down** regarder qn de haut en bas, toiser qn du regard; **to look sb (full** *or* **straight) in the face** regarder qn (bien) en face *ou* dans les yeux; **I can never look her in the face again** je ne pourrai plus jamais la regarder en face

3 *vi* (**a**) *(gen)* regarder; **look, there's Brian!** regarde, voilà Brian!; **what's happening outside? let me look** qu'est-ce qui se passe dehors? laissez-moi voir; **have you cut yourself? let me look** tu t'es coupé? montre-moi *ou* laisse-moi voir; **go on, nobody's looking** vas-y, personne ne regarde; **they crept up on me while I wasn't looking** ils se sont approchés de moi pendant que j'avais le dos tourné; **I'm just looking** *(in shop)* je regarde; **look and see if there's anyone there** regarde voir s'il y a quelqu'un; **if you look very carefully you can see a tiny crack in it** si tu regardes bien, tu verras une toute petite fissure; **look this way** regardez par ici; **to look into sb's eyes** regarder qn dans les yeux; **she looked along the row/down the list** elle a parcouru la rangée/la liste du regard; **he was looking out of the window/over the wall/up the chimney** il regardait par la fenêtre/par-dessus le mur/dans la cheminée; **to look on the bright side** voir les choses du bon côté; **to look over sb's shoulder** regarder par-dessus l'épaule de qn; *Fig* surveiller ce que fait qn; **to look the other way** détourner les yeux; *Fig* fermer les yeux; *Prov* **look before you leap** = il faut réfléchir deux fois avant d'agir
(**b**) *(search)* chercher; **you can't have looked hard enough** tu n'as pas dû beaucoup chercher
(**c**) *(in imperative → listen, pay attention)* écouter; **look, I can't pay you back just yet** écoute, je ne peux pas te rembourser tout de suite; **now look, Paul, I've had enough of this!** bon écoute, Paul, ça suffit maintenant!; **look here!** dites donc!
(**d**) *(seem, appear)* avoir l'air; **to look old** avoir l'air *ou* faire vieux; **to look ill** avoir l'air malade, avoir mauvaise mine; **to look well** *(person)* avoir bonne mine; **that looks delicious!** ça a l'air délicieux!; **you look** *or* **are looking better today** tu as l'air (d'aller) mieux aujourd'hui; **how do I look?** comment tu me trouves?; **you look absolutely stunning in that dress** tu es vraiment ravissante dans cette robe; **it makes him look ten years older/younger** ça le vieillit/rajeunit de dix ans; **he's 70, but he doesn't look it** il a 70 ans mais il n'en a pas l'air *ou* mais il ne les fait pas; **I can't hang the picture there, it just doesn't look right** je ne peux pas mettre le tableau là, ça ne va pas; **it looks all right to me** moi, je trouve ça bien; **how does the situation look to you?** que pensez-vous de la situation?; **that's not how it looks to the man in the street** ce n'est pas comme ça que l'homme de la rue voit les choses; **things will look very different when you leave school** les choses te sembleront très différentes quand tu quitteras l'école; **it'll look bad if I don't contribute** ça fera mauvaise impression si je ne contribue pas; **things are looking black for the economy** les perspectives économiques sont assez sombres; **the crops look promising** la récolte s'annonce bien; **she's not as stupid as she looks** elle est moins bête qu'elle n'en a l'air; **I must have looked a fool** j'ai dû passer pour un imbécile; **to make sb look a fool** *or* **an idiot** tourner qn en ridicule; **he makes the rest of the cast look very ordinary** à côté de lui, les autres acteurs ont l'air vraiment quelconques; **to look like sb/sth** *(resemble)* ressembler à qn/qch; **she looks like her mother** elle ressemble à sa mère; **what does she look like?** *(describe her)* comment est-elle?; *(she looks a mess)* non mais, à quoi elle ressemble!; **it looks like an oil refinery** ça ressemble à une raffinerie de pétrole, on dirait une raffinerie de pétrole; **I don't know what it is, but it looks like blood** je ne sais pas ce que c'est, mais on dirait *ou* ça ressemble à du sang; **it looks like rain** on dirait qu'il va pleuvoir; **it**

looks (to me) like he was lying j'ai l'impression qu'il mentait; **is this our room? – it looks like it** c'est notre chambre? – ça m'en a tout l'air; **the meeting looked like going on all day** la réunion avait l'air d'être partie pour durer toute la journée; **you look as if you've seen a ghost** on dirait que tu as vu un revenant; **it looks as if Natalie's going to resign** Natalie a l'air de vouloir démissionner; **it looks as if he didn't want to go** il semble qu'il ne veuille pas y aller; **it doesn't look as if they're coming** on dirait qu'ils ne vont pas venir; **you're looking good** tu as l'air en forme; **he looks good in jeans** les jeans lui vont bien; **that hat looks very good on you** ce chapeau te va très bien; **it'll look good on your CV** ça fera bien sur ton curriculum *ou* CV; **things are looking pretty good here** les choses ont l'air de se présenter plutôt bien ici

(**e**) *(face → house, window)* **to look (out) onto a park** donner sur un parc; **to look north/west** être exposé au nord/à l'ouest

(**f**) *(intend)* **to be looking to do sth** chercher à faire qch; **she'll be looking to improve on her previous best time** elle cherchera à améliorer son meilleur temps; **we're looking to expand our export business** nous cherchons à développer nos exportations; **I'm not looking to cause any trouble** je ne veux pas causer de problèmes

4 **looks** *npl (beauty)* **she's got everything – looks, intelligence, youth...** elle a tout pour elle, elle est belle, intelligente, jeune...; **he's kept his looks** il est resté beau; **looks don't matter** l'apparence ne compte pas; **she's got her mother's looks** elle a la beauté de sa mère; **he's lost his looks** il n'est plus aussi beau qu'avant

►**look after** *vt insep* (**a**) *(take care of)* s'occuper de; **my mother's looking after the kids/the cat this weekend** ma mère va s'occuper des enfants/du chat ce week-end; **she has a sick mother to look after** elle a une mère malade à charge; **you should look after your clothes more carefully** tu devrais prendre plus grand soin de tes vêtements; **he helps me to look after the garden** il m'aide à m'occuper du jardin; *Fig* **look after yourself!** fais bien attention à toi!; **you're well looked after** on s'occupe bien de vous; **the car has been well looked after** la voiture est bien entretenue; **don't worry, he can look after himself** ne t'inquiète pas, il est capable de se débrouiller tout seul

(**b**) *(be responsible for)* s'occuper de; **they look after our interests in Europe** ils s'occupent de nos affaires en Europe

(**c**) *(watch over)* surveiller; **can you look after my bag for a couple of minutes?** tu peux surveiller mon sac deux minutes?

►**look ahead** *vi* regarder vers l'avenir; **looking ahead three or four years** dans trois ou quatre ans; **let's look ahead to the next century/to next month's meeting** pensons au siècle prochain/à la réunion du mois prochain

►**look around** = **look round**

►**look at** *vt insep* (**a**) *(gen)* regarder; **she looked at herself in the mirror** elle se regarda dans la glace; **they looked at each other** ils ont échangé un regard; **oh dear, look at the time!** oh là là, regardez l'heure!; **just look at you!** *(you look awful)* mais regarde-toi donc!; **it's not much to look at** ça ne paie pas de mine; **she's not much to look at** ce n'est pas une beauté; **he's not much to look at** il n'est pas très beau; **you wouldn't think, to look at him, that he's a multi-millionaire** à le voir on ne croirait pas avoir affaire à un multi-millionnaire; **I haven't looked at another woman in the last forty years** en quarante ans, je n'ai pas regardé une autre femme; **just look at the mess we're in!** regarde les ennuis qu'on a!

(**b**) *(consider)* considérer; **look at the problem from my point of view** considérez le problème de mon point de vue; **that's not the way I look at it** ce n'est pas comme ça que je vois les choses; **they won't even look at the idea** ils refusent même de prendre cette idée en considération; **if you don't have money, he won't even look at you** si vous n'avez pas d'argent, il ne vous regardera même pas; *Fam* **my brother can't even look at an egg** mon frère ne supporte pas *ou* déteste les œufs

(**c**) *(check)* vérifier, regarder; **could you look at the tyres?** pouvez-vous regarder les pneus?; **to have one's teeth looked at** se faire examiner les dents; *Fam* **you need your head looking at!** ça va pas, la tête?

►**look away** *vi* détourner les yeux

►**look back** *vi* (**a**) *(in space)* regarder derrière soi; **she walked away without looking back** elle est partie sans se retourner

(**b**) *(in time)* regarder en arrière; **there's no point in looking back** ça ne sert à rien de regarder en arrière; **the author looks back on the war years** l'auteur revient sur les années de guerre; **it seems funny now we look back on it** ça semble drôle quand on y pense aujourd'hui; **we can look back on some happy times** nous avons connu de bons moments; *Fig* **after she got her first job she never looked back** à partir du moment où elle a trouvé son premier emploi, tout lui a réussi

►**look down** *vi* regarder en bas; *(in embarrassment)* baisser les yeux; **we looked down on** *or* **at the valley** nous regardions la vallée en dessous

►**look down on** *vt insep (despise)* mépriser

►**look for** *vt insep* (**a**) *(seek)* chercher; **go and look for him** allez le chercher; **she's still looking for a job** elle est toujours à la recherche d'un emploi; **are you looking for a fight?** tu cherches la bagarre?

(**b**) *(expect)* attendre; **it's not the result we were looking for** ce n'est pas le résultat que nous attendions

►**look forward** *vi (to the future)* regarder vers l'avenir

►**look forward to** *vt insep* attendre avec impatience; **we're looking forward to the end of term** nous attendons la fin du trimestre avec impatience; **I'm looking forward to the weekend** vivement le week-end!; **to look forward to doing sth** être impatient de faire qch; **I'm looking forward to seeing her again** *(eager)* il me tarde de la revoir; *(polite formula)* je serai heureux de la revoir; **I look forward to meeting you** je serai heureux de faire votre connaissance; **see you on Saturday – right, I'll look forward to it** à samedi alors – oui, c'est entendu; **I'm not exactly looking forward to going** je n'ai pas vraiment envie d'y aller; **they had been looking forward to this moment for months** cela faisait des mois qu'ils attendaient cet instant; **I look forward to hearing from you soon** *(in letter)* dans l'attente de votre réponse; **I'm not looking forward to the operation** la perspective de cette opération ne m'enchante guère

►**look in** *vi* (**a**) *(inside)* regarder à l'intérieur

(**b**) *(pay a visit)* passer; **to look in on sb** rendre visite à *ou* passer voir qn; **I'll look in again tomorrow** je repasserai demain; **he looked in at the pub on the way home** il s'est arrêté au pub en rentrant chez lui

(**c**) *(watch TV)* regarder la télévision

►**look into** *vt insep* examiner, étudier; **it's a problem that needs looking into** c'est un problème qu'il faut examiner *ou* sur lequel il faut se pencher

►**look on** 1 *vt insep* considérer; **I look on him as my brother** je le considère comme mon frère; **to look on sb/sth with favour/disfavour** voir qn/qch d'un œil favorable/défavorable

2 *vi* regarder; **the passers-by just looked on** les passants se sont contentés de regarder

►**look out** 1 *vt sep Br* **I'll look that book out for you** je te chercherai ce livre; **have you looked out those photos to give me?** est-ce que tu as trouvé les photos que tu devais me donner?

2 *vi* (**a**) *(person)* regarder dehors

(**b**) *(room, window)* **the bedroom looks out on** *or* **over the garden** la chambre donne sur le jardin

(**c**) *(be careful)* faire attention; **look out, it's hot!** attention, c'est chaud!; **you'll be in trouble if you don't look out** tu vas t'attirer des ennuis si tu ne fais pas attention

►**look out after** *vt insep Am (take care of)* prendre soin de

►**look out for** *vt insep* (**a**) *(be on watch for)* guetter; **I'll look out for you at the station** je te guetterai à la gare; **look out for the sign to Dover** guettez le panneau pour Douvres; **she's always looking out for bargains** elle est toujours à la recherche *ou* à l'affût d'une bonne affaire; **you have to look out for snakes** il faut faire attention *ou* se méfier, il y a des serpents

(**b**) *Fam (idioms)* **to look out for oneself** penser à soi; **you've got to look out for number one!** chacun pour soi!

►**look over** *vt insep (glance over)* jeter un coup d'œil sur; *(examine)* examiner, étudier

►**look round** 1 *vt insep (museum, cathedral, factory)* visiter; *(shop, room)* jeter un coup d'œil dans

2 *vi* (**a**) *(look at surroundings)* regarder (autour de soi); **I'm just looking round** *(in shop)* je regarde; **I'd rather look round on my own than take the guided tour** je préférerais faire le tour moi-même plutôt que de suivre la visite guidée; **I looked round for an exit** j'ai cherché une sortie

(**b**) *(look back)* regarder derrière soi, se retourner

►**look through** *vt insep* (**a**) *(window, screen)* regarder à travers

(**b**) *(book, report)* jeter un coup d'œil sur *ou* à, regarder

(**c**) *Fig (person)* **he looked straight through me** il m'a regardé comme si je n'étais pas là

►**look to** *vt insep* (**a**) *(turn to)* se tourner vers; **it's best to look to an expert** il est préférable de consulter un expert *ou* de demander l'avis d'un expert; **don't look to her for help** ne compte pas sur elle pour t'aider; **they are looking to us to find a solution to this problem** ils comptent sur nous pour trouver une solution à ce problème

(**b**) *Formal (attend to)* veiller à; **he should look to his reputation** il devrait veiller à sa réputation; **look to it that discipline is properly maintained** veillez à ce que la discipline soit bien maintenue

►**look up** 1 *vt sep* (**a**) *(in reference work, directory etc)* chercher; **look the word up in the dictionary** cherche le mot dans le dictionnaire

(**b**) *(visit)* passer voir, rendre visite à; **look us up when you're in New York** passe nous voir quand tu seras à New York

2 *vi* (**a**) *(raise one's eyes)* lever les yeux

(**b**) *(improve)* s'améliorer; **things are looking up for the economy** les perspectives économiques semblent meilleures

►**look upon** *vt insep* considérer

►**look up to** *vt insep* respecter, avoir du respect pour

'Don't look now' *Du Maurier, Roeg* 'Ne vous retournez pas'

'Look back in Anger' *Osborne, Richardson* 'La Paix du dimanche' (pièce), 'Les Corps sauvages' (film)

> **Here's looking at you kid**
> Ce sont les mots que prononce Rick Blaine, le personnage incarné par Humphrey Bogart dans le film *Casablanca* (1942), lorsqu'il dit adieu à la femme qu'il aime, jouée par Ingrid Bergman.
> Aujourd'hui on utilise souvent cette phrase en référence au film lorsque l'on porte un toast à quelqu'un.

look-ahead *adj Am* tourné vers l'avenir

lookalike ['lʊkəˌlaɪk] *n (double)* sosie *m*; **a Brad Pitt lookalike** un sosie de Brad Pitt; **it's just another Renault lookalike** c'est la copie conforme de la Renault

looked-for ['lʊkd-] *adj* recherché, attendu

looker ['lʊkə(r)] *n Fam* **she's a real looker** elle est vraiment canon; **she's not much of a looker** ce n'est pas une beauté

looker-on (*pl* **lookers-on**) *n (spectator)* spectateur(trice) *m,f*, *Pej* badaud(e) *m,f*

look-in *n Br Fam* (**a**) *(chance)* **she talked so much that I didn't get a look-in** elle ne m'a pas laissé le temps de placer un mot *ou* d'en placer une;

the other people applying for the job don't have a look-in les autres candidats n'ont aucune chance ▫ (**b**) *(visit)* **to give sb a look-in** passer voir qn ▫, faire un saut chez qn

-looking ['lʊkɪŋ] *suff* **kind-looking** qui a l'air gentil; **filthy-looking** (d'aspect) très sale *ou* répugnant

looking-glass *n Old-fashioned* miroir *m*, glace *f*
▸▸ *Fig* ***a looking-glass world*** un monde à l'envers

lookout ['lʊkaʊt] *n* (**a**) *(post)* poste *m* d'observation *ou* de vigie
(**b**) *(person) & Mil* guetteur *m*; *Naut* homme *m* de veille *ou* de vigie
(**c**) *(action)* surveillance *f*, observation *f*; *Naut* veille *f*; **to keep a lookout** être aux aguets; *Naut* veiller, être en *ou* de vigie; **to be on the lookout for** *(person)* guetter; *(thing)* être à la recherche de; **to be on lookout duty** être de guet
(**d**) *Fam* **it's a poor lookout when even doctors are on the dole** il y a de quoi s'inquiéter quand même les médecins sont au chômage; **that's your lookout!** ça c'est tes oignons!
▸▸ ***lookout post*** poste *m* d'observation *ou* de vigie

look-over *n Fam* coup *m* d'œil ▫; **I've given the report a look-over** j'ai jeté un coup d'œil sur le rapport

look-see *n Fam* **to have** *or* **to take a look-see** jeter un petit coup d'œil

look-up *n Comput* recherche *f*, consultation *f*
▸▸ ***look-up table*** table *f* de recherche *ou* de référence

LOOM [lu:m] *n Am (abbr* **Loyal Order of the Moose**) = association caritative américaine

loom [lu:m] **1** *vi* (**a**) *(appear)* surgir; **an iceberg loomed out of** *or* **through the fog** un iceberg a soudain surgi du brouillard; **a figure loomed in the doorway** une silhouette est apparue dans l'encadrement de la porte; **above us loomed a high cliff** une falaise se dressait au-dessus de nos têtes
(**b**) *(approach)* être imminent; **the deadline was looming nearer and nearer** la date fatidique approchait; **he's getting worried with the elections looming ahead** l'approche des élections l'inquiète
(**c**) **to loom large** *(threaten)* menacer; **the idea of eviction loomed large in their minds** l'idée d'être expulsés ne les quittait pas
2 *n* (**a**) *Tex* métier *m* à tisser; **hand/power loom** métier *m* manuel/mécanique
(**b**) *(of oar)* manche *f*

▸**loom up** *vi* apparaître indistinctement, surgir

looming ['lu:mɪŋ] *adj* (**a**) *(cliffs, mountains etc)* imposant (**b**) *(deadline)* qui s'approche dangereusement

loon [lu:n] **1** *n* (**a**) *Fam (lunatic)* dingue *mf*; *(fool)* imbécile *mf*
(**b**) *Arch (commoner)* roturier(ère) *m,f*; **lord and loon** seigneur et vilain
(**c**) *Am Orn* plongeon *m*, *Can* huart *m*
(**d**) *(in N Scotland) (boy)* garçon *m*
2 *vi Br Fam* **to loon (about)** faire le fou *ou* l'imbécile
3 loons *npl* = pantalon taille basse à pattes d'éléphant
▸▸ ***loon pants*** = pantalon taille basse à pattes d'éléphant

looney, loony ['lu:nɪ] (*pl* **loonies,** *compar* **loonier,** *superl* **looniest**) *Fam* **1** *n* dingue *mf*, malade *mf*
2 *adj* dingue, loufoque; *Am Fam* **loony tunes** *(crazy)* barjo, foldingue
▸▸ *Fam Hum* ***loony bin*** maison *f* de fous; **he's ready for the loony bin** il est bon pour l'asile; *Pej* ***the loony left*** = l'aile gauche extrémiste du parti travailliste

loop [lu:p] **1** *n* (**a**) *(of ribbon, film etc)* boucle *f*; *(of fingerprint)* anse *f*; *(of river)* méandre *m*, boucle *f*; *(in skating)* croisé *m*; *(of spiral, spool)* tour *m*; **a loop of string served as a handle** une ficelle servait de poignée; **the film/the tape runs in a loop** le film/la bande défile en continu; **the Loop** = quartier des affaires de Chicago (délimité par une ligne de métro faisant une boucle); *Am Fam* **to be out of the loop** ne pas être dans le coup; *Am Fam* **to cut sb out of the loop** mettre qn aux oubliettes
(**b**) *Comput* boucle *f*
(**c**) *Elec* boucle *f*, bouclage *m*; *Nucl (of reactor)* boucle *f*, circuit *m*
(**d**) *(contraceptive device)* stérilet *m*
(**e**) *Aviat* boucle *f*, looping *m*
(**f**) *Rail (line)* voie *f* d'évitement, voie *f* de raccordement; *(at terminus)* boucle *f* d'évitement
2 *vt* (**a**) *(in string, rope etc)* faire une boucle à; **loop the rope around your waist/through the ring** passez la corde autour de votre taille/dans l'anneau; **streamers were looped across the room** la pièce était tendue de guirlandes
(**b**) *Aviat* **to loop the loop** faire un looping, boucler la boucle
3 *vi (road)* faire des lacets; *(river)* faire des méandres *ou* des boucles; **the path looped round the side of the mountain** le sentier montait en lacet à flanc de montagne
▸▸ *Rad* ***loop aerial*** cadre *m*; *Elec* ***loop circuit*** circuit *m* bouclé; *Rail* ***loop line*** voie *f* d'évitement, voie *f* de raccordement; *(at terminus)* boucle *f* d'évitement; ***loop stitch*** point *m* de bouclette

▸**loop back 1** *vt sep (curtain)* retenir avec une embrasse
2 *vi (river etc)* faire une boucle; *Comput (program)* faire une boucle pour retourner (**to** à)

looper ['lu:pə(r)] *n Entom* chenille *f* arpenteuse

loopey = **loopy**

loophole ['lu:phəʊl] *n* (**a**) *(in law, regulations etc)* point *m* faible; **to find a loophole** trouver une échappatoire; **a legal loophole** un vide juridique (**b**) *(gap)* trou *m*, ouverture *f*; *(in fortified wall)* meurtrière *f*

loopy ['lu:pɪ] (*compar* **loopier,** *superl* **loopiest**) *adj* (**a**) *(curly)* bouclé; *(knotted)* plein de nœuds (**b**) *Fam (crazy)* dingue, cinglé

LOOSE [lu:s] **1** *adj* (**a**) *(not tightly fixed → nail)* mal enfoncé; *(→ screw, bolt)* desserré; *(→ button)* qui pend, mal cousu; *(→ knot)* qui se défait; *(→ floor tile)* décollé; *(→ shelf)* mal fixé; *(→ handle, brick)* branlant; *(→ floorboard)* disjoint; *(→ slate)* mal fixé; *(→ tooth)* qui bouge; **your button's loose** ton bouton est décousu; **he prised a brick loose** il a réussi à faire bouger une brique; **remove all the loose plaster** enlève tout le plâtre qui se détache; **the steering seems loose** il y a du jeu dans la direction; **to work loose** *(nail)* sortir; *(screw, bolt)* se desserrer; *(knot)* se défaire; *(tooth, slate)* bouger; *(button)* se détacher; **the wind blew some slates loose** le vent a déplacé quelques ardoises; *Br* **to have a loose cough** avoir une toux grasse
(**b**) *(free, unattached)* libre; **tie the loose end of the rope to the post** attache le bout libre de la corde au poteau; **she picked up all the loose newspapers** elle a ramassé tous les journaux qui traînaient; **a loose sheet of paper** une feuille volante; **the cutlery was loose in the drawer** les couverts étaient en vrac dans le tiroir; **her hair hung loose about her shoulders** ses cheveux flottaient librement sur ses épaules; **several pages have come loose** plusieurs pages se sont détachées; **I got one hand loose** j'ai réussi à dégager une de mes mains; **if I manage to tear myself loose** si je réussis à me libérer *ou* à me dégager; **he decided to cut loose from his family** il a décidé de couper les ponts avec sa famille; **all the cows were loose in the village** toutes les vaches se promenaient *ou* étaient en liberté dans les rues du village; **a lion got loose from the zoo** un lion s'est échappé du zoo; **he set** *or* **let** *or* **turned a mouse loose in the kitchen** il a lâché une souris dans la cuisine; *Fig* **he let loose a torrent of abuse** il a lâché un torrent d'injures
(**c**) *Com (not packaged)* en vrac; **loose coal** charbon *m* en vrac; **loose cheese** fromage *m* à la coupe; **I always buy vegetables loose** j'achète mes légumes au poids
(**d**) *(slack → grip, hold)* mou (molle); *(→ skin, flesh)* flasque; *(→ bowstring, rope, knot)* lâche; *Fig (→ discipline)* relâché; **she tied the ribbon in a loose bow** elle noua le ruban sans le serrer; **his arms hung loose at his sides** il avait les bras ballants; **to have a loose tongue** ne pas savoir tenir sa langue
(**e**) *(not tight-fitting → dress, jacket)* ample, flottant; **this skirt is much too loose at the waist** cette jupe est bien trop large à la taille
(**f**) *(weak → connection, link)* vague; **they have loose ties with other political groups** ils sont vaguement liés à d'autres groupes politiques
(**g**) *(informal → organization)* peu structuré; *(→ agreement)* officieux; **a loose political grouping** un regroupement politique peu organisé
(**h**) *(imprecise, broad → thinking, application)* peu rigoureux; *(→ translation, terminology)* approximatif; **we can make a loose distinction between the two phenomena** nous pouvons faire une vague distinction entre les deux phénomènes
(**i**) *Pej (woman)* facile; *(morals)* léger
(**j**) *(not dense or compact → earth)* meuble; *(→ knit, weave)* lâche
(**k**) *(relaxed → muscles)* détendu, relâché, au repos; *(→ athlete, sportsman)* échauffé; **to have loose bowels** avoir la diarrhée
(**l**) *Fin* disponible
(**m**) *Am Fam* **to keep** *or* **to stay loose** rester cool; *Fam* **hang** *or* **stay loose!** relax!, du calme!
(**n**) *(idiom)* **I have a few loose ends to tie up** j'ai encore quelques petits détails à régler; **to be** *Br* **at a loose end** *or Am* **at loose ends** être dans un moment creux
2 *n (in rugby)* **in the loose** dans la mêlée ouverte
3 *vt Literary* (**a**) *(unleash → dogs)* lâcher; *(→ panic, chaos)* semer; **she loosed her tongue** *or* **fury upon me** elle s'est déchaînée contre moi
(**b**) *(let fly → bullet)* tirer; *(→ arrow)* décocher; *Fig* **he loosed a volley of threats/abuse at her** il s'est répandu en menaces/invectives contre elle
(**c**) *(undo → knot)* défaire; *(→ hair)* détacher; *(unfasten → boat, raft)* démarrer, détacher; *(→ sail)* déferler
4 on the loose *adj* **to be on the loose** *(gen)* être en liberté; *(on the run)* être en fuite; **a gang of hooligans on the loose** une bande de jeunes voyous qui rôdent; **there was a gunman on the loose in the neighbourhood** il y avait un homme armé qui rôdait dans le quartier; *Hum* **her husband's on the loose tonight** son mari est en vadrouille ce soir
▸▸ ***loose change*** petite monnaie *f*; *Elec* ***loose connection*** mauvais contact *m*; *Br* ***loose cover*** *(for armchair, sofa)* housse *f*; ***loose insert*** *(in newspaper, magazine)* encart *m* libre; ***loose living*** débauche *f*, vie *f* dissolue; *Fin* ***loose money*** argent *m* disponible, liquidités *fpl*; ***loose talk*** des propos *mpl* lestes

▸**loose off 1** *vt sep (bullet)* tirer; *(arrow)* décocher; *(gun)* décharger; *(curses)* lâcher
2 *vi (with gun)* tirer; **he loosed off into the crowd** il tira au hasard dans la foule; *Am Fig* **to loose off at sb** *(with insults, criticism etc)* se déchaîner contre qn, s'en prendre violemment à qn

---

loosebox ['lu:sbɒks] *n Br Horseriding* box *m*

loose-fitting *adj (garment)* ample, large, flottant

loose-head prop *n Sport (in rugby)* pilier *m* gauche

loose-jointed *adj (supple)* souple; *(gangling)* dégingandé

loose-leaf(ed) *adj* à feuilles mobiles *ou* volantes
▸▸ ***loose-leaf binder*** classeur *m* (à feuilles mobiles); ***loose-leaf paper*** feuillets *mpl* mobiles

loose-limbed *adj* souple, agile

loosely ['lu:slɪ] *adv* (**a**) *(not firmly → pack, fit, hold, wrap)* sans serrer; *(not closely → knit, weave)* lâchement; **the dress was loosely gathered at the waist** la robe était peu ajustée à la taille; **the rope hung loosely** *(unattached)* la corde pendait; *(slackly)* la corde était lâche
(**b**) *(apply, interpret)* mollement; **loosely translated** *(freely)* traduit librement; *(inaccurately)* mal traduit; **loosely speaking, I'd say...** en gros, je dirais...; **the word is often used loosely** le mot est souvent employé de façon imprécise
(**c**) *(vaguely → connect, relate)* vaguement; **the book is only loosely based on my research** le livre n'a qu'un rapport lointain avec mes

recherches; **the exhibition is loosely organized around four themes** l'exposition tourne autour de quatre grands thèmes

loosen ['lu:sən] **1** *vt* (**a**) *(knot, screw, lid)* desserrer; *(rope, cable)* détendre; *(grip, reins)* relâcher; *Agr (soil)* ameublir; **this mixture helps loosen the cough** ce sirop aide à dégager les bronches; **he loosened his grip** il relâcha *ou* desserra son étreinte; **I loosened my belt a notch** j'ai desserré ma ceinture d'un cran; **he loosened his tie** il a desserré son nœud de cravate; **the accident loosened the front wheels** depuis l'accident, il y a du jeu dans le train avant; **the punch has loosened several of his teeth** le coup lui a déchaussé plusieurs dents; **loosen the cake from the sides of the tin** détachez le gâteau des bords du moule; **it loosens the bowels** c'est un laxatif; **loosen the soil with a hoe** ameublissez le sol avec une binette; **the wine soon loosened his tongue** le vin eut vite fait de lui délier la langue; **they have loosened their ties with Moscow** leurs liens avec Moscou se sont relâchés

(**b**) *(rules, restrictions)* assouplir

2 *vi (knot, screw, lid)* se desserrer; *(rope, cable)* se détendre; *(grip)* se relâcher; **one of the bolts had loosened during the flight** un des boulons s'était desserré pendant le vol

▸**loosen up** **1** *vt sep (muscles)* assouplir

2 *vi* (**a**) *(become less severe)* se montrer moins sévère; **to loosen up on discipline** relâcher la discipline; **will they loosen up on immigration?** vont-ils adopter une position plus souple vis-à-vis de l'immigration?

(**b**) *(relax socially)* se détendre; **loosen up a bit!** détends-toi un peu!; **he began to loosen up once the meal was served** il commença à se détendre quand le repas fut servi

(**c**) *(athlete, musician)* s'échauffer

looseness ['lu:snɪs] *n* (**a**) *(of screw, nail, lever)* jeu *m*; *(of rope)* relâchement *m*, mou *m*

(**b**) *(of clothing)* ampleur *f*

(**c**) *(of thinking, interpretation)* manque *m* de rigueur; *(of translation, terminology)* manque *m* de précision; **he shows a certain looseness in his interpretation of the rules** il interprète le règlement de façon assez fantaisiste

(**d**) *Pej (of way of life)* débauche *f*, licence *f*; **a growing looseness of morals** un relâchement croissant des mœurs

loosening ['lu:sənɪŋ] *n* (**a**) *(of knot, screw, lid)* desserrage *m*; *(of rope, cable)* relâchement *m*; *Agr (of soil)* ameublissement *m* (**b**) *(of rules, restrictions)* assouplissement *m*

loosestrife ['lu:sstraɪf] *n Bot* **(yellow) loosestrife** lysimachie *f*, lysimaque *f*; **(purple) loosestrife** salicaire *f* commune

loose-tongued [-tʌŋd] *adj* bavard

loose-weave *adj (fabric)* lâche, à mailles lâches

loot [lu:t] **1** *n* (**a**) *(stolen goods)* butin *m* (**b**) *Fam (money)* pognon *m*, fric *m*; **where's the loot stashed?** où est planqué le fric?; **he's got plenty of loot** il est plein aux as

2 *vt (town, goods, tomb)* piller; *Fig* **state coffers were looted to finance the war** les coffres de l'État ont été pillés pour financer la guerre

3 *vi* piller, se livrer au pillage

looter ['lu:tə(r)] *n (in war, riot)* pillard(e) *m,f*, pilleur(euse) *m,f*; *(of tombs, churches)* pilleur(euse) *m,f*

looting ['lu:tɪŋ] *n* pillage *m*

lop [lɒp] *(pt & pp* **lopped**, *cont* **lopping**) *vt* (**a**) *(tree)* élaguer, tailler; *(branch)* couper; **farmers have to lop and top all trees and hedges** les agriculteurs doivent tailler tous les arbres et toutes les haies (**b**) *Fig (budget)* élaguer, faire des coupes sombres dans; *(sum of money, item of expenditure)* retrancher, supprimer

▸**lop off** *vt sep* (**a**) *(branch)* couper, tailler (**b**) *Fig (price, time)* réduire; **they could easily lop another 10 percent off fares** ils pourraient facilement baisser le prix des billets de 10 pour cent; **the new motorway will lop 30 minutes off travelling time** la nouvelle autoroute va raccourcir le trajet de 30 minutes

lope [ləʊp] **1** *n (of runner)* pas *m* de course *(rapide et souple)*; *(of animal)* course *f (avec des bonds)*

2 *vi (runner)* courir à grandes foulées; *(animal)* courir en bondissant

▸**lope along** *vi (person)* avancer à grandes enjambées; *(leopard)* courir tout en puissance; *(hare)* avancer en bondissant

▸**lope off** *vi (person)* partir d'une démarche élastique; **the tiger loped off into the jungle** le tigre pénétra dans la jungle de sa démarche souple

lop-eared *adj Br* aux oreilles tombantes *ou* pendantes

lophophore ['ləʊfəˌfɔ:(r)] *n Orn & Zool* lophophore *m*

lopsided [ˌlɒp'saɪdɪd] *adj* qui manque de symétrie, asymétrique; *(picture, roof)* de guingois, de travers; **a lopsided grin** un sourire en coin; **a lopsided group with twice as many women as men** un groupe déséquilibré comptant deux fois plus de femmes que d'hommes; **her handwriting is all lopsided** son écriture part dans tous les sens; **the article presents a rather lopsided picture of events** l'article présente les événements de façon plutôt partiale

lopsidedness [lɒp'saɪdɪdnɪs] *n* manque *m* de symétrie

loquacious [lə'kweɪʃəs] *adj Formal* loquace, volubile

loquaciously [lə'kweɪʃəslɪ] *adv Formal* avec loquacité

loquacity [lə'kwæsətɪ] *n Formal* volubilité *f*, loquacité *f*

loquat ['lɒkwæt] *n Bot (fruit)* nèfle *f* du Japon; *(tree)* néflier *m* du Japon

lor [lɔ:(r)] *exclam Br Fam Old-fashioned* crénom!, nom d'une pipe!

loran ['lɔ:rən] *n* loran *m*

lord [lɔ:d] **1** *n* (**a**) *(master)* seigneur *m*; *(nobleman)* noble *m*; **lord of the manor** châtelain *m*; **to live like a lord** mener grand train, vivre en grand seigneur; **she mixes with lords and ladies** elle fréquente la haute société; *Hum* **her lord and master** son seigneur et maître

(**b**) *Astrol* maître *m*

2 Lord **1** *n Br* (**a**) *(title)* lord *m*; **Lord (Peter) Snow** lord (Peter) Snow (**b**) *(term of address)* **my Lord** *(to noble)* monsieur le marquis, monsieur le baron; *(to judge)* monsieur le juge; *(to bishop)* monseigneur, Excellence **2** *pr n* (**a**) *Rel* **the Lord** le Seigneur; **in the year of our Lord 1897** en l'an de grâce 1897 (**b**) *Fam (in interjections and expressions)* **Good Lord!** Seigneur!; **oh Lord!** mon Dieu!; **Lord (only) knows!** Dieu seul le sait!; **Lord knows where he's put it** Dieu sait où il l'a mis; *Br Old-fashioned* **Lord love a duck!** crénom de nom!

3 *vt* **to lord it** mener la grande vie; *Br* **to lord it over sb** prendre des airs supérieurs avec qn

▸▸ *Law* ***Lord Advocate*** ≃ procureur *m* de la République, ≃ procureur *m* général *(en Écosse)*; ***Lord Chamberlain*** grand chambellan *m (en Grande-Bretagne)*; ***Lord Chancellor*** lord *m* Chancelier, ≃ ministre *m* de la Justice *(en Grande-Bretagne)*; ***Lord Chief Justice*** ≃ président *m* de la Haute Cour *(en Grande-Bretagne)*; *Rel* ***the Lord's day*** le jour du Seigneur; ***Lord God Almighty*** Seigneur Dieu Tout-puissant; ***Lord High Chancellor*** lord *m* Chancelier, ≃ ministre *m* de la Justice *(en Grande-Bretagne)*; ***Our Lord Jesus Christ*** Notre Seigneur Jésus-Christ; ***Lord Justice of Appeal*** ≃ président *m* de la cour d'appel; ***Lord Justice General*** = président de la juridiction pénale suprême *(en Écosse)*; *Bot* ***lords and ladies*** arum *m* maculé, pied-de-veau *m*; ***Lord Lieutenant*** lord-lieutenant *m (en Grande-Bretagne)*; ***Lord Mayor*** lord-maire *m*; ***the Lord Mayor's Banquet*** = dîner officiel donné à l'occasion de l'élection du maire de Londres, et où le Premier ministre fait traditionnellement un discours; ***the Lord Mayor's Show*** = défilé officiel où le nouveau maire de Londres se déplace en carrosse doré; *Br Fig* **after their brilliant victory their next match was a case of after the Lord Mayor's Show** après leur magnifique victoire, le match qui suivit ne pouvait être que décevant; ***the Lord's Prayer*** le Notre Père; ***Lord President*** = président de la juridiction civile suprême *(en Écosse)*; ***the Lord Privy Seal*** = titre du doyen du gouvernement britannique; ***Lord Protector*** lord-protecteur *m*; ***Lord Provost*** maire *m (dans les villes d'Aberdeen, Dundee, Édimbourg, Glasgow et Perth)*; ***Lords Spiritual*** = membres ecclésiastiques de la Chambre des lords; ***the Lord's Supper*** l'eucharistie *f*; ***Lords Temporal*** = membres laïques de la Chambre des lords

'Lord of the Flies' *Golding, Brook* 'Sa Majesté des Mouches'

'The Lord of the Rings' *Tolkien* 'Le Seigneur des anneaux'

lordliness ['lɔ:dlɪnɪs] *n* (**a**) *(arrogance)* hauteur *f*, arrogance *f* (**b**) *(splendour)* somptuosité *f*

lordling ['lɔ:dlɪŋ] *n* petit seigneur *m*

lordly ['lɔ:dlɪ] *adj* (**a**) *(arrogant)* arrogant, hautain; **with lordly indifference** avec une indifférence souveraine (**b**) *(noble → gesture)* noble, auguste; *(splendid → feast, occasion, lifestyle)* somptueux; **he lives in a lordly mansion** il vit dans une maison princière

lordosis [lɔ:'dəʊsɪs] *n Med* lordose *f*

lordotic [lɔ:'dɒtɪk] *adj Med* lordosique

Lord's [lɔ:dz] *n* = célèbre terrain de cricket londonien et siège de la fédération anglaise de cricket

lordship ['lɔ:dʃɪp] *n* (**a**) *(form of address)* **Your/His Lordship** *(to noble)* monsieur le marquis, monsieur le baron; *(to judge)* monsieur le juge; *(to bishop)* Excellence/Son Excellence; *Hum* **if His Lordship would care to sit down** si Votre Altesse daigne s'asseoir (**b**) *(lands, rights)* seigneurie *f*; *(power)* autorité *f*

lordy ['lɔ:dɪ] *exclam esp Am Fam* Seigneur!

lore [lɔ:(r)] *n* (**a**) *(folk legend)* tradition *f*, traditions *fpl*, coutume *f*, coutumes *fpl*; **according to Celtic lore, it was built by fairies** la tradition celtique veut qu'il ait été construit par des fées (**b**) *(traditional knowledge)* science *f*, savoir *m*; **she knows all the countryside lore** elle connaît tous les us et coutumes du pays

Lorenzo [lə'renzəʊ] *pr n* **Lorenzo the Magnificent** Laurent le Magnifique

lorgnette [lɔ:'njet] *n* (**a**) *(spectacles)* lorgnon *m*, face-à-main *m* (**b**) *(opera glasses)* jumelles *fpl* de théâtre, lorgnette *f*

lorikeet [lɒrɪ'ki:t] *n Orn* loriquet *m*

loris ['lɒrɪs] *n Zool* loris *m*

lorn [lɔ:n] *adj Literary* délaissé, solitaire

Lorraine [lɒ'reɪn] *n* Lorraine *f*; **in Lorraine** en Lorraine

lorry ['lɒrɪ] *(pl* **lorries**) *n Br* camion *m*, poids *m* lourd; *Fam Euph* **it fell off the back of a lorry** c'est de la marchandise volée

▸▸ ***lorry driver*** chauffeur *m* de camion, routier(ère) *m,f*; ***lorry park*** aire *f* de stationnement pour poids lourds

lorry-load *n Br* chargement *m*; **he had a lorry-load of bricks to deliver** il avait un chargement de briques à livrer

lory ['lɔ:ri:] *(pl* **lories**) *n Orn* lori *m*

Los Angeles [lɒs'ændʒɪli:z] *n* Los Angeles

LOSE [lu:z]

perdre	▸ 1 (a) – (c)
semer	▸ 1 (d)
coûter	▸ 1 (e)
retarder	▸ 2 (b)

(pt & pp **lost** [lɒst]) **1** *vt* (**a**) *(gen → limb, job, money, patience etc)* perdre; **I've lost my umbrella again** j'ai encore perdu mon parapluie; **to lose one's way** se perdre, s'égarer; **what have you got to lose?** qu'est-ce que tu as à perdre?; **you've got nothing to lose** tu n'as rien à perdre; **we haven't got a moment to lose** il n'y a pas une seconde à perdre; **he lost no time in telling her she was wrong** il ne s'est pas gêné pour lui dire qu'elle avait tort; **his shop is losing money** son magasin perd de l'argent; **they are losing their markets to the Koreans** ils sont en train de perdre leurs marchés au profit des Coréens; **we lost 80 days in strikes last year** l'année dernière, nous avons perdu 80 journées de travail à cause des grèves; **don't talk so fast, you've lost me** ne parle pas si vite, je n'arrive pas à te suivre; **you lost me when you**

started using technical terms j'ai perdu le fil quand tu as commencé à employer des termes techniques; **at what age did he lose his mother?** à quel âge a-t-il perdu sa mère?; **they lost their homes in the flood** ils ont perdu leur maison dans l'inondation; **thirty lives were lost in the fire** trente personnes ont péri dans l'incendie, l'incendie a fait trente morts; **she lost a leg/her eyesight in an accident** elle a perdu une jambe/la vue dans un accident; **to lose one's voice** avoir une extinction de voix; **his work loses a lot in translation** son œuvre se prête très mal à la traduction; **the play didn't lose much in the television version** la pièce n'a pas perdu beaucoup en étant adaptée pour la télévision; **to lose one's appetite** perdre l'appétit; **it made me lose my appetite** ça m'a coupé l'appétit; **the plane is losing altitude** *or* **height** l'avion perd de l'altitude; **to lose one's balance** perdre l'équilibre; **to lose consciousness** perdre connaissance; **to lose face** perdre la face; **to lose ground** perdre du terrain; **I've lost interest in it** ça ne m'intéresse plus; **he lost his nerve at the last minute** le courage lui a manqué au dernier moment; *Fam* **to lose one's head** perdre la tête; *Fam* **to lose it** *(go mad)* perdre la boule; *(lose one's temper)* piquer une crise, péter les plombs; *Br Fam* **to lose the plot** perdre la boule; *Br Fam* **to lose the place** devenir gaga

(**b**) *(not win)* perdre; **he lost four games to Karpov** il a perdu quatre parties contre Karpov

(**c**) *(shed, get rid of)* perdre; **to lose weight** perdre du poids; **I've lost several pounds** j'ai perdu plusieurs kilos; **the trees lose their leaves in winter** les arbres perdent leurs feuilles en hiver

(**d**) *(elude, shake off)* semer; **she managed to lose the detective** elle a réussi à semer le détective

(**e**) *(cause to lose)* coûter à, faire perdre à; **it lost him his job** ça lui a fait perdre son emploi; **it lost us the contract** cela nous a fait perdre le contrat; **his attitude lost him our respect** à cause de son attitude, il a perdu notre estime; **that mistake lost him the match** cette faute lui coûta la partie

(**f**) *(of clock, watch)* **my watch loses five minutes a day** ma montre prend cinq minutes de retard par jour

2 *vi* (**a**) *(gen)* perdre; **they lost by one goal** ils ont perdu d'un but; **either way, I can't lose** je suis gagnant à tous les coups; **the dollar is losing in value (against the deutschmark)** le dollar baisse (par rapport au deutsche Mark); **if you sell the house now you'll lose on it** si tu vends la maison maintenant tu vas perdre de l'argent; **I lost on the deal** j'ai été perdant dans l'affaire

(**b**) *(clock, watch)* retarder

▸**lose out** *vi* perdre, être perdant; **to lose out on a deal** être perdant dans une affaire; **will the Americans lose out to the Japanese in computers?** les Américains vont-ils perdre le marché de l'informatique au profit des Japonais?

---

loser ['lu:zə(r)] **1** *n* (**a**) *(gen)* & *Sport* perdant(e) *m f*; **to be a good/bad loser** être bon/mauvais joueur; **you'll be the loser** c'est toi qui y perdras; *Br Fig* **they're the losers by it** ce sont eux les perdants dans cette affaire (**b**) *Fam (failure → man)* raté *m*, loser *m*; *(→ woman)* ratée *f*; **he's a born loser** c'est un vrai raté (**c**) *St Exch* valeur *f* en baisse

2 *adj Am Fam* **a real loser guy** un vrai raté

losing ['lu:zɪŋ] **1** *adj* (**a**) *(gen)* & *Sport* perdant; **to fight a losing battle** engager une bataille perdue d'avance (**b**) *(unprofitable)* **the business was a losing concern** cette entreprise n'était pas viable; **it's a losing proposition** ce n'est pas rentable

2 losings *npl (losses)* pertes *fpl*

▸▸ ***the losing side*** les vaincus *mpl*; *Sport* l'équipe *f* perdante

losingest ['lu:zɪŋəst] *adj Am* **the losingest** le/la pire

loss [lɒs] *n* (**a**) *(gen)* perte *f*; **have you reported the loss to the police?** avez-vous signalé cette perte à la police?; **it's your gain and their loss** c'est vous qui y gagnez et eux qui y perdent; **it's your loss!** tant pis pour vous!; **her retirement will be a great loss to us all** son départ à la retraite sera une grande perte pour nous tous; **it's no great loss to me** ce n'est pas une grosse perte pour moi; **he would be no great loss to the firm** ce ne serait pas une grande perte pour l'entreprise; **it can cause temporary loss of vision** cela peut provoquer *ou* entraîner une perte momentanée de la vue; **the loss of a close relative** la perte *ou* la mort d'un parent proche; **the party suffered heavy losses in the last elections** le parti a subi de lourdes pertes *ou* a perdu de nombreux sièges lors des dernières élections; **the closure will cause the loss of hundreds of jobs** la fermeture provoquera la disparition de centaines d'emplois; **fortunately there was little loss of life** heureusement, il n'y eut que peu de victimes; **there was terrible loss of life in the last war** la dernière guerre a coûté beaucoup de vies humaines; **they inflicted heavy losses on the enemy** ils infligèrent de lourdes pertes à l'ennemi; **to sustain** *or* **suffer heavy losses** subir de grosses pertes; **to cut one's losses** faire la part du feu

(**b**) *(financial)* déficit *m*; **to make a loss** perdre de l'argent; **the company announced losses of** *or* **a loss of a million pounds** la société a annoncé un déficit d'un million de livres; **we made a loss of 10 percent on the deal** nous avons perdu 10 pour cent dans l'affaire; **to sell at a loss** vendre à perte; **to run at a loss** *(business)* tourner à perte; *Fin* **loss attributable** perte *f* supportée; *Fin* **loss carry back** report *m* déficitaire sur les exercices précédents; *Fin* **loss carry forward** déficit *m* reportable, report *m* déficitaire sur les exercices ultérieurs; *Fin* **loss transferred** perte *f* transférée

(**c**) *(feeling of pain, unhappiness)* malheur *m*, chagrin *m*; **his family rallied round him in his loss** sa famille l'a beaucoup entouré dans son chagrin; **she tried to hide her sense of loss from her friends** elle essayait de cacher son chagrin à ses amis; **to feel a sense of loss** ressentir un vide

(**d**) *Ins* sinistre *m*; **the following losses are not covered by the policy** les sinistres suivants ne sont pas couverts par cette police

(**e**) *Com (of product being manufactured or transported)* freinte *f*; **loss in transit** freinte *f* de route

(**f**) *(idioms)* **to be at a loss** ne savoir que faire; *(not know what to say)* ne savoir que dire; *(not know what to answer)* ne savoir que répondre; **to be at a (total) loss to explain...** être (totalement) incapable d'expliquer...; **to be at a loss (to know) what to do/say** ne savoir que faire/dire; **she's never at a loss for an answer** elle a *ou* trouve toujours réponse à tout; **he's never at a loss for something to say** il n'est jamais à court (de mots)

▸▸ *Br* ***loss adjuster*** *Ins* expert *m*; *Naut* dispatcheur *m*; ***loss assessment*** fixation *f* des dommages; ***loss of earnings*** manque *m* à gagner; **to sue for loss of earnings** intenter une action en justice pour recouvrement d'un manque à gagner; *Rel* ***loss of grace*** amission *f* de la grâce; *Mktg* ***loss leader*** produit *m* d'appel; ***loss leader price*** prix *m* d'appel; ***loss pricing*** fixation *f* d'un prix d'appel

loss-maker *n* gouffre *m* financier

loss-making *adj Br Com* qui tourne à perte, déficitaire

lost [lɒst] **1** *pt & pp of* **lose**

2 *adj* (**a**) *(mislaid, not found)* perdu; **all is not yet lost** tout n'est pas perdu; **they have discovered a lost masterpiece** ils ont découvert un chef-d'œuvre disparu; **to give sth up for lost** abandonner tout espoir de retrouver qch; **the lost city of Atlantis** Atlantide, la ville engloutie

(**b**) *(person → in direction)* perdu, égaré; **can you help me, I'm lost** pouvez-vous m'aider, je me suis perdu *ou* égaré; **to get lost** se perdre; **they got lost on the way back** ils se sont perdus sur le chemin du retour; *Mil* **lost in action** mort au combat; **30 people were reported lost at sea** 30 personnes auraient péri en mer; *also Fig* **a lost sheep** une brebis égarée; **he looks like a lost sheep without his wife** sans sa femme, il a l'air complètement perdu; **a lost soul** une âme en peine; *Old-fashioned* **a lost woman** une femme perdue; *Fam* **get lost!** va te faire voir!

(**c**) *Fig (engrossed)* perdu, plongé, absorbé; **she was lost in her book** elle était plongée dans son livre; **to be lost in thought** être perdu dans ses pensées

(**d**) *(wasted → time)* perdu; *(→ opportunity)* perdu, manqué; *(→ youth)* gâché; **the allusion was lost on me** je n'ai pas compris *ou* saisi l'allusion; **your advice would be lost on them** leur donner un conseil serait peine perdue; **the hint/the suggestion was not lost on him** l'allusion/la suggestion ne lui a pas échappé; **your compliment was lost on her** elle ne s'est pas rendu compte que tu lui faisais un compliment; **French humour is lost on us** nous ne comprenons rien à l'humour français

(**e**) *(confused, bewildered)* perdu; **I'm lost, start again!** je suis perdu *ou* je ne vous suis plus, recommencez!; **I felt quite lost in the new job** je me sentais complètement perdu dans mon nouveau travail; **I'm lost for words** je ne sais pas quoi dire

(**f**) *(oblivious)* insensible; **he was lost to the world** il avait l'esprit ailleurs

▸▸ ***lost cause*** cause *f* perdue; ***the Lost Generation*** la génération perdue; ***lost property*** objets *mpl* trouvés; *Br* ***lost property office*** bureau *m* des objets trouvés; *Am* ***lost river*** rivière *f* souterraine

'The Lost Weekend' *Wilder* 'Le Poison'

---

lost-and-found *n Am* **lost-and-found (office)** bureau *m* des objets trouvés; **I put an advert in the lost-and-found column** j'ai mis une annonce dans la rubrique des objets trouvés

---

LOT [lɒt]

groupe	▸ **1 (a), (b)**
lot	▸ **1 (c)**
sort	▸ **1 (d)**
tirage au sort	▸ **1 (e)**
terrain	▸ **1 (f)**
studio	▸ **1 (g)**
paquet	▸ **1 (h)**
beaucoup	▸ **2; 3**
plein de	▸ **4**
le tout	▸ **5**

1 *n* (**a**) *(group of people)* **this lot are leaving today and another lot are arriving tomorrow** ce groupe part aujourd'hui et un autre (groupe) arrive demain; **the new recruits are quite an interesting lot** les nouveaux sont tous assez intéressants; **I don't want you getting mixed up with that lot** je ne veux pas que tu traînes avec cette bande; *Pej* **that lot next door** la bande d'à côté; **I'm taking my lot to the cinema** j'emmène les miens au cinéma; **come here, you lot!** venez ici, vous autres!; **you rotten lot!** bande de vauriens!; **he's a bad lot** c'est un sale type

(**b**) *(group of things)* **most of the last lot of fans we had in were defective** presque tous les ventilateurs du dernier lot étaient défectueux; **take all this lot and dump it in my office** prends tout ça et mets-le dans mon bureau; **I've just been given another lot of letters to sign** il me vient de me donner un autre paquet de lettres à signer

(**c**) *(item in auction, in lottery)* lot *m*; **lot 49 is a set of five paintings** le lot 49 est un ensemble de cinq tableaux; **the winner of lot 20** le gagnant du lot 20

(**d**) *(destiny, fortune)* sort *m*, destin *m*; **to be content with one's lot** être content de son sort; **it was his lot in life to be the underdog** il était destiné à rester un sous-fifre; **it fell to my lot to be the first to try** le sort a voulu que je sois le premier à essayer; **to throw in one's lot with sb** se mettre du côté de qn

(**e**) *(random choice)* **the winners are chosen by lot** les gagnants sont choisis par tirage au sort; **to draw** *or* **cast lots** tirer au sort

(**f**) *Am (plot of land)* terrain *m*; **a vacant lot** un terrain vague; **a used car lot** un parking de voitures d'occasion

(**g**) *Am Cin* studio *m* (de cinéma)

(**h**) *Fin & St Exch (of bonds, shares)* paquet *m*; **in**

lots par lots; **to buy/sell in one lot** acheter/vendre en bloc

2 lots *Fam* **1** *pron* beaucoup □; **do you need any paper/envelopes? I've got lots** est-ce que tu as besoin de papier/d'enveloppes? j'en ai plein; **there are lots to choose from** il y a du choix **2** *adv* beaucoup □; **are you feeling better now? – oh, lots, thank you** vous vous sentez mieux maintenant? – oh, beaucoup mieux, merci; **this is lots easier than the last exam** c'est vachement plus facile que le dernier exam

3 a lot 1 *pron* beaucoup; **there's a lot still to be done** il y a encore beaucoup à faire; **there's an awful lot wrong with the plan** il y a beaucoup de choses qui ne vont pas dans ce projet; **there's not a lot you can do about it** tu n'y peux pas grand-chose; **what did you think of his speech? – not a lot!** qu'as-tu pensé de son discours? – pas grand-chose!; **I'd give a lot to know** je donnerais beaucoup *ou* cher pour savoir; **it did me a lot of good** ça m'a fait beaucoup de bien; **a lot of people think it's true** beaucoup de gens pensent que c'est vrai; **what a lot of people!** quelle foule!, que de monde!; **there's an awful lot of work still to be done** il reste encore beaucoup de travail à faire; **I've got a lot to do before bedtime** j'ai beaucoup à faire avant d'aller me coucher; **you have a lot of explaining to do** tu me dois des explications; **I've had such a lot of cards from well-wishers** j'ai vraiment reçu beaucoup de cartes de sympathie; **she takes a lot of care over her appearance** elle fait très attention à son apparence; **the party was a lot of fun** la soirée était vraiment bien; **we see a lot of them** nous les voyons beaucoup *ou* souvent; *Ironic* **a (fat) lot of help you were!, you were a (fat) lot of help!** ça, pour être utile, tu as été utile! **2** *adv* beaucoup; **a lot better/more** beaucoup mieux/plus; **their house is a lot bigger** leur maison est beaucoup plus grande; **he's changed a lot since I last saw him** il a beaucoup changé depuis la dernière fois que je l'ai vu; **she travels a lot on business** elle voyage beaucoup pour ses affaires; **thanks a lot!** merci beaucoup!; *Ironic* **a (fat) lot she cares!** elle s'en fiche pas mal!

4 lots of *adj Fam* plein de □; **we had lots of fun** on s'est bien marrés; **I've been there lots of times** j'y suis allé plein de fois; **lots and lots of lovely money** tout plein de sous; **lots of love** *(at end of letter)* je t'embrasse, grosses bises; **they've got money and lots of it!** ils ont de l'argent, et pas qu'un peu!

5 the lot *pron* le tout; **there isn't much, take the lot** il n'y en a pas beaucoup, prenez tout; **there aren't many, take the lot** il n'y en a pas beaucoup, prenez-les tous; **she ate the (whole) lot** elle a tout mangé; **the (whole) lot of them came** ils sont tous venus; **clear off, the lot of you** débarrassez-moi tous le plancher; **it only cost me a pound for the lot** le tout ne m'a coûté qu'une livre; **that's the lot** tout est là; *Fam* **that's the** *or* **your lot for tonight** c'est tout pour ce soir

►► *Fin & St Exch* ***lot number*** numéro *m* de lot; *Fin & St Exch* ***lot size*** unité *f* de transaction

Lot [lɒt] *pr n Bible* Lot, Loth

loth = **loath**

Lothario [lə'θɑːrɪəʊ] (*pl* **Lotharios**) *n* don Juan *m*, libertin *m*

Lothian ['ləʊðɪən] *n* les Lothians *mpl*, = région dans l'est de l'Écosse; **in Lothian** dans les Lothians

lotion ['ləʊʃən] *n* lotion *f*

lottery ['lɒtərɪ] (*pl* **lotteries**) *n* loterie *f*; *Fig* **it's a bit of a lottery** c'est une loterie

►► *St Exch* ***lottery bonds*** valeurs *fpl* à lot; *Br* ***lottery funding*** = fonds provenant de la loterie nationale; *Fin* ***lottery loan*** emprunt *m* à lots; *Fin* ***lottery loan bond*** titre *m* à lots; ***lottery ticket*** billet *m* de loterie

lotto ['lɒtəʊ] *n* loto *m (jeu de société)*

lotus ['ləʊtəs] *n* lotus *m*

►► ***lotus position*** position *f* du lotus

lotus-eater *n Myth* lotophage *m*; *Fig* doux rêveur *m*

loud [laʊd] **1** *adj* **(a)** *(noise, shout)* grand, puissant; *(voice, music)* fort; *(explosion)* fort, violent; *(protest, applause)* vif; **the television is too loud** la télévision est trop forte, le son de la télévision est trop fort; **in a loud voice** à haute voix; **the door slammed with a loud bang** la porte a claqué très fort; **a loud argument was going on in the next room** on se disputait bruyamment dans la pièce voisine; **there were loud protests among politicians** de vives protestations se sont élevées dans la classe politique, la classe politique a vivement protesté; **they were loud in their support/condemnation of the project** ils ont vigoureusement soutenu/condamné le projet

(b) *Pej (loudmouthed, brash)* bruyant, tapageur; **he's a bit loud, isn't he?** ce n'est pas le genre discret!

(c) *(garish → colour)* criard, voyant; *(→ pattern, clothes)* voyant; **he wore a suit with a loud check** il portait un costume à carreaux très voyant

2 *adv* fort; **can you speak a little louder?** pouvez-vous parler un peu plus fort?; **the music was turned up loud** on avait mis la musique à fond; **to read out loud** lire à haute voix; **I was thinking out loud** je pensais tout haut; **I hear you loud and clear** je te reçois cinq sur cinq; *Fam (I understand)* j'ai compris □

►► *Mus* ***loud pedal*** pédale *f* forte

loudhailer [ˌlaʊd'heɪlə(r)] *n Br* porte-voix *m inv*, mégaphone *m*; **they spoke to him by loudhailer** ils lui ont parlé à l'aide d'un porte-voix

loudly ['laʊdlɪ] *adv* **(a)** *(noisily → speak)* d'une voix forte; *(→ laugh)* bruyamment; *(vigorously)* avec force *ou* vigueur; **our neighbour banged loudly on the wall** notre voisin a donné de grands coups contre le mur; **the supporters cheered loudly** les supporters ont applaudi bruyamment; **we protested loudly** nous avons protesté vigoureusement **(b)** *(garishly)* de façon tapageuse *ou* voyante

loudmouth ['laʊdmaʊθ, pl -maʊðz] *n Fam Pej* **to be a loudmouth** *(noisy)* être *ou* avoir une grande gueule; *(indiscreet)* avoir une grande langue

loudmouthed ['laʊdmaʊðd] *adj Fam Pej (noisy)* fort en gueule, gueulard; *(indiscreet)* bavard, frimeur

loudness ['laʊdnɪs] *n* **(a)** *(of sound)* intensité *f*, force *f*; *(of voice)* intensité *f*; *(of cheers)* vigueur *f*; **the loudness of the music makes conversation impossible** la musique est tellement forte qu'on ne s'entend pas **(b)** *(of colours)* éclat *m*; **the loudness of his ties** ses cravates voyantes

►► ***loudness control*** *(on hi-fi system)* bouton *m* de compensation physiologique

loudspeaker [ˌlaʊd'spiːkə(r)] *n* haut-parleur *m*; *(on stereo)* enceinte *f*, baffle *m*

lough [lɒk] *n Ir (lake)* lac *m*; *(inlet)* lagune *f*

louis ['luːɪ] (*pl* **inv** [-iːz]) *n (coin)* louis *m* (d'or)

Louisiana [luːˌiːzɪ'ænə] *n* la Louisiane; **in Louisiana** en Louisiane

►► ***the Louisiana Purchase*** l'achat *m* de la Louisiane

> **THE LOUISIANA PURCHASE**
>
> On désigne ainsi la cession par la France aux États-Unis du territoire de la Louisiane, en 1803. Craignant l'expansion de l'empire napoléonien, Thomas Jefferson négocia avec la France, qui céda facilement l'immense territoire contre de l'argent liquide. La surface du pays s'en trouva doublée.

lounge [laʊndʒ] **1** *n* **(a)** *(in house, on ship, in hotel)* salon *m*; *(at airport)* salle *f* d'attente

(b) *(bar)* (salle *f* de) bar *m*

(c) *(rest)* **to have a lounge in the sun** paresser *ou* se prélasser au soleil

(d) *(seat)* méridienne *f*

2 *vi* **(a)** *(recline)* s'allonger, se prélasser; *(sprawl)* être allongé; **he spent the afternoon lounging on the sofa reading** il a passé l'après-midi à lire allongé sur le canapé; **he lounged against the counter** il était appuyé nonchalamment contre le comptoir

(b) *(laze)* paresser; *(hang about)* traîner; **gangs of kids were lounging on street corners** des bandes de gosses traînaient au coin des rues

►► *Br* ***lounge bar*** = salon dans un pub (plus confortable et plus cher que le "public bar"); ***lounge chair*** fauteuil *m*; *Fam Old-fashioned* ***lounge lizard*** salonnard *m*; *Br* ***lounge suit*** costume *m* de ville; *(on invitation)* tenue *f* de ville

►**lounge about, lounge around** *vi (laze)* paresser; *(hang about)* traîner

lounger ['laʊndʒə(r)] *n* **(a)** *(sunbed)* lit *m* bain de soleil **(b)** *(person)* paresseux(euse) *m,f*

loupe [luːp] *n* loupe *f* d'horloger

lour ['laʊə(r)] *vi* **(a)** *(sky, weather)* être menaçant **(b)** *(person)* prendre un air menaçant; **to lour at sb** regarder qn d'un air menaçant

louse [laʊs] (*pl sense* **(a) lice** [laɪs], *pl sense* **(b) louses**) **1** *n* **(a)** *Entom* pou *m* **(b)** *Fam (person)* peau *f* de vache

2 *vt (remove lice from)* épouiller

►**louse up** *vt sep Fam (spoil)* foutre en l'air

lousewort ['laʊswɜːt] *n Bot* pédiculaire *f* des forêts

lousily ['laʊzɪlɪ] *adv* très mal

lousiness ['laʊzɪnɪs] *n* **(a)** *Fam (poor quality → of performance, weather, service, salary)* nullité *f* **(b)** *(louse infestation)* = fait d'être infesté de poux

lousy ['laʊzɪ] (*compar* **lousier**, *superl* **lousiest**) *adj* **(a)** *Fam (appalling → film, singer)* nul; *(→ weather)* pourri; **we had a lousy holiday** on a passé des vacances nulles; **they made a lousy job of it** ils ont fait ça n'importe comment; **he's in a lousy mood** il est d'une humeur de chien; **I've got a lousy hangover!** j'ai une de ces gueules de bois!; **I feel lousy this morning** je suis mal fichu ce matin; **I'm lousy at tennis, I'm a lousy tennis player** je suis nul au tennis, je joue au tennis comme un pied; **it's in lousy condition** il est en très mauvais état □; **you're a lousy liar** *(lie badly)* tu ne sais pas mentir □; *(as intensifier)* tu n'es qu'un sale menteur

(b) *Fam (annoying)* fichu, sacré; **I've got these lousy letters to write!** j'ai ces fichues lettres à écrire!; **all for a lousy £5** tout ça à cause de 5 malheureuses livres

(c) *Fam (mean)* vache; **that's a lousy thing to do/say** c'est dégueulasse *ou* moche de faire/dire une chose pareille; **he's lousy to his wife** il est dégueulasse avec sa femme; **a lousy trick** un sale tour

(d) *Fam (guilty)* **I feel lousy about what happened** je culpabilise à cause de ce qui est arrivé

(e) *Fam (full)* **the town was lousy with police** la ville grouillait de flics; **they're lousy with money** ils sont bourrés de fric *ou* pleins aux as

(f) *(lice-infested)* pouilleux

lout [laʊt] *n (bumpkin)* rustre *m*; *(hooligan)* voyou *m*; **you ignorant lout!** espèce de brute épaisse!

Louth [laʊθ] *n* le comté de Louth, = comté dans le nord-est de la République d'Irlande; **in Louth** dans le comté de Louth

loutish ['laʊtɪʃ] *adj (behaviour)* grossier; *(manners)* de rustre, mal dégrossi

loutishness ['laʊtɪʃnɪs] *n* grossièreté *f*; **there's too much loutishness at football matches these days** de nos jours il y a trop de voyous aux matchs de football

louvre, *Am* **louver** ['luːvə(r)] *n* **(a)** *Archit (board)* abat-vent *m inv*, abat-son *m* **(b)** *(in door, window)* persienne *f*; *Naut* louvre *m*; *Aut & Aviat (of ventilation inlet, car bonnet)* persienne *f*, volet *m*; *Tech (of air intake)* ouïe *f*

►► *Archit* ***louvre board*** abat-vent *m inv*, abat-son *m*; ***louvre door*** porte *f* à persiennes

louvred, *Am* **louvered** ['luːvəd] *adj* à claire-voie

lovable ['lʌvəbəl] *adj* charmant, attachant; **lovable rogue** petit coquin *m*

lovage ['lʌvɪdʒ] *n Bot* livèche *f*

lovat ['lʌvət] *n* = couleur bleu-vert ou jaune-vert qu'on trouve en particulier dans les lainages et dans les tweeds

LOVE [lʌv]

amour	►**1 (a) – (c)**
passion	►**1 (d)**
zéro	►**1 (f)**
aimer	►**2 (a) – (c)**

1 *n* **(a)** *(for person)* amour *m*; **motherly love** amour *m* maternel; **we didn't marry for love** nous n'avons pas fait un mariage d'amour; **he did it out of love for her** il l'a fait par amour pour elle; **it was love at first sight** ce fut le coup de foudre; **to be in love (with sb)** être amoureux (de qn), *Can* être en amour (avec qn); **they were deeply in love** ils s'aimaient profondément; **to fall in love (with sb)** tomber amoureux (de qn), *Can* tomber en amour (avec qn); **to make love** *(have sex)* faire l'amour; *Literary (flirt)* se faire la cour; **to make love to sb** *(have sex with)* faire l'amour à qn; *Literary (court)* faire la cour à qn; *Literary* **to make violent love to sb** faire une cour ardente à qn; **make love not war!** faites l'amour, pas la guerre!; *Fam* **for the love of God** *or Br* **Mike!** pour l'amour du ciel!; **Mark sends** *or* **gives you his love** Mark t'embrasse; **give my love to Gordon** embrasse Gordon de ma part *ou* pour moi; **(lots of) love from Jayne, all my love, Jayne** *(in letter)* affectueusement, Jayne; *Fam* **I wouldn't do it for love nor money** je ne le ferais pas pour tout l'or du monde, je ne le ferais pour rien au monde ❑; *Fam* **you can't get a taxi for love nor money round here** pas moyen de trouver un taxi par ici; **there's no love lost between them** ils se détestent cordialement

(**b**) *(for object, hobby, one's country etc)* amour *m*; **his love of good food** sa passion pour la bonne chère; **he has a great love of Scotland** il a beaucoup d'amour pour l'Écosse; **she fell in love with the house immediately** elle a eu le coup de foudre pour la maison; **I don't do this job for the love of it** je ne fais pas ce travail pour le *ou* par plaisir

(**c**) *(beloved person)* amour *m*; **he's one of her many loves** c'est un des nombreux hommes qu'elle a aimés; **she's the love of his life** c'est la femme de sa vie; *Br Fam* **isn't he a love!** ce qu'il est mignon *ou* chou!

(**d**) *(favourite activity)* passion *f*; **music is his great love** la musique est sa grande passion

(**e**) *(term of endearment)* **(my) love** mon amour; *Br Fam* **more coffee, love?** tu prends encore du café, mon petit/ma petite?; *Br Fam* **there you are, love!** *(speaking to customer)* voilà madame/mademoiselle/monsieur!

(**f**) *Sport (in tennis)* zéro *m*; **40 love** 40 zéro; **two sets to love** deux sets à rien *ou* à zéro

2 *vt* (**a**) *(partner, spouse)* aimer; *(friends, relatives)* aimer beaucoup *ou* bien; **I like you but I don't love you** je t'aime bien mais je ne suis pas amoureux de toi; *Fam* **I love my brother but he drives me round the bend** j'aime beaucoup mon frère, mais il me rend chèvre; *Fam* **I'll have to love you and leave you** ce n'est pas le tout mais il faut que j'y aille

(**b**) *(enjoy)* aimer, adorer; **don't you just love that little dress?** cette petite robe est vraiment adorable, tu ne trouves pas?; **I love lying** *or* **to lie in bed on Sunday mornings** j'adore faire la grasse matinée le dimanche; **she loves to hear you sing** elle adore vous entendre chanter; **I'd love to come** j'aimerais beaucoup venir; **I'd love you to come** j'aimerais beaucoup que *ou* cela me ferait très plaisir que tu viennes; **she'd love to see you again** elle serait enchantée *ou* ravie de vous revoir; **would you like to come too? – I'd love to** voudriez-vous venir aussi? – avec grand plaisir

(**c**) *(prize → one's country, freedom etc)* aimer

►► **love affair** liaison *f* (amoureuse); *Fig* passion *f*; **his love affair with Paris** sa passion pour Paris; ***love aid*** *(sex toy)* gadget *m* érotique; ***love child*** enfant *mf* de l'amour; *Fam Hum* ***love handles*** poignées *fpl* d'amour; ***love knot*** lacs *m* d'amour; ***love letter*** lettre *f* d'amour, billet *m* doux; ***love life*** vie *f* sentimentale; *Fam* **how's your love life?** comment vont tes amours?; ***love match*** mariage *m* d'amour; ***love nest*** nid *m* d'amour; ***love potion*** philtre *m*; ***love scene*** scène *f* d'amour; ***love song*** chanson *f* d'amour; ***love story*** histoire *f* d'amour; ***love token*** gage *m* d'amour; ***love triangle*** ménage *m* à trois

'Love in a Cold Climate' *Mitford* 'L'Amour dans un pays froid'

'Love's Labour's Lost' *Shakespeare* 'Peines d'amour perdues'

loveable = **lovable**

lovebird ['lʌvbɜːd] *n* (**a**) *Orn* perruche *f*; **lovebirds** inséparables *mpl* (**b**) *Hum (lover)* amoureux(euse) *m,f*; **the lovebirds are in the other room** les amoureux *ou* les tourtereaux sont dans l'autre pièce

lovebite ['lʌvbaɪt] *n Br* suçon *m*

loved up [lʌvd-] *adj Br Fam Drugs slang* tout gentil *(sous l'effet de l'ecstasy)*

love-hate *adj*

►► ***a love-hate relationship*** une relation d'amour-haine

love-in *n* (**a**) *Old-fashioned (hippie gathering)* rassemblement *m* de hipppies (**b**) *Fig* = situation dans laquelle des gens passent leur temps à se faire des compliments les uns aux autres

love-in-a-mist *n (UNCOUNT) Bot* cheveux *mpl* de Vénus, nigelle *f* de Damas

loveless ['lʌvlɪs] *adj (marriage)* sans amour; *(person → unloved)* mal aimé; *(→ unloving)* sans cœur, incapable d'aimer

lovelessness ['lʌvlɪsnɪs] *n* (**a**) *(incapacity for love)* insensibilité *f* à l'amour (**b**) *(absence of love)* privation *f* d'amour

love-lies-bleeding *n (UNCOUNT) Bot* queue-de-renard *f*, amarante *f*

loveliness ['lʌvlɪnɪs] *n* beauté *f*

lovelorn ['lʌvlɔːn] *adj* qui a des peines d'amour; **to be lovelorn** avoir le mal d'amour

lovely ['lʌvlɪ] (*compar* **lovelier**, *superl* **loveliest**) **1** *adj* (**a**) *(in appearance → person)* beau (belle), joli; *(→ child)* joli, mignon; *(→ home, scenery, dress)* joli

(**b**) *(view, evening, weather)* beau (belle); *(holiday)* (très) agréable; *(meal)* excellent; **what a lovely day!** quelle belle journée!; **we had a lovely day at the beach** nous avons passé une très agréable journée à la plage; **have a lovely time!** amusez-vous bien!; **it's a lovely idea** c'est une très bonne idée; **it's lovely to see you** je suis enchanté *ou* ravi de vous voir; *Br* **this wool is lovely and soft** cette laine est très douce au toucher; *Br* **it's lovely and warm by the fire** il fait bon près de la cheminée; **it sounds lovely** cela a l'air très bien; **would you like to come to dinner next week? – that'd be lovely** tu veux venir dîner la semaine prochaine? – ça serait vraiment bien *ou* avec plaisir

(**c**) *(in character)* charmant, très aimable; **what a lovely woman!** quelle femme charmante!; **her parents are lovely people** ses parents sont des gens charmants

2 *n Fam (girl)* mignonne *f*; **come on, my lovely** *(said to a horse)* allez, hue cocotte

'Oh! What a Lovely War' *Chilton, Attenborough* 'Ah Dieu! que la guerre est jolie!'

lovemaking ['lʌvˌmeɪkɪŋ] *n* (**a**) *(sexual intercourse)* ébats *mpl* (amoureux); **during their lovemaking** pendant qu'ils faisaient l'amour (**b**) *Arch (courtship)* cour *f*

lover ['lʌvə(r)] *n* (**a**) *(sexual partner)* amant(e) *m,f*; **he fancies himself as a great lover** il se considère comme un merveilleux amant

(**b**) *Old-fashioned (suitor)* amoureux *m*, soupirant *m*; **the young lovers** les jeunes amoureux *mpl*

(**c**) *(enthusiast)* amateur(trice) *m,f*; **he's a real music lover** c'est un mélomane; **I'm not a dog lover myself** moi-même je n'aime pas beaucoup les chiens; **for all lovers of good food** pour tous les amateurs de bonne cuisine; **she's a great lover of the cinema** elle adore le cinéma, c'est une grande cinéphile

lover-boy *n Fam Ironic (womanizer)* don Juan ❑ *m*, tombeur *m*, séducteur ❑ *m*; **morning, lover-boy!** bonjour, chéri!; **she's gone out with lover-boy** elle est sortie avec son jules; **when's lover-boy coming round to see you?** quand est-ce qu'il vient te voir, ton jules?

loveseat ['lʌvsiːt] *n* causeuse *f*

lovesick ['lʌvsɪk] *adj* **to be lovesick** se languir d'amour

lovesickness ['lʌvsɪknɪs] *n* mal *m* d'amour

lovey-dovey ['lʌvɪˌdʌvɪ] *adj Fam Pej* doucereux

loving ['lʌvɪŋ] *adj (affectionate)* affectueux; *(tender)* tendre; **loving kindness** bonté *f*; **your loving mother** *(at end of letter)* ta mère qui t'aime

►► ***loving cup*** coupe *f* de l'amitié

-loving ['lʌvɪŋ] *suff* **wine-loving** qui aime le vin, amateur de vin; **music-loving** amateur de musique, mélomane; **home-loving** casanier

lovingly ['lʌvɪŋlɪ] *adv (affectionately)* affectueusement; *(tenderly)* tendrement; *(passionately)* avec amour, amoureusement; *(with great care)* soigneusement, avec soin

LOW [ləʊ]

bas	► 1 (a) – (d), (f), (i), (j); 2 (a) – (d); 3 (a)
faible	► 1 (b) – (e), (i)
mauvais	► 1 (e)
grossier	► 1 (g)
niveau bas	► 3 (b)
dépression	► 3 (c)

1 *adj* (**a**) *(in height)* bas; **this room has a low ceiling** cette pièce est basse de plafond; **low hills** collines peu élevées; **a low neckline** un décolleté; **the sun was already low in the sky** le soleil était déjà bas dans le ciel; **the houses are built on low ground** les maisons sont bâties dans une cuvette; **the river is low today** la rivière est basse aujourd'hui; **low bridge** *(sign)* hauteur limitée

(**b**) *(in scale → temperature)* bas; *(→ level)* faible; **the temperature is in the low twenties** il fait un peu plus de vingt degrés; **old people are given very low priority** les personnes âgées ne sont absolument pas considérées comme prioritaires; **I've reached a low point in my career** j'ai atteint un creux dans ma carrière; **their relationship is at a low ebb** leurs relations sont au plus bas; **a low blood count** une numération globulaire basse

(**c**) *(in degree, intensity → probability, visibility)* faible; *(→ fire)* bas; *(→ lighting)* faible, tamisé; **cook on a low heat** faire cuire à feu doux; **to keep a low profile** garder un profil bas

(**d**) *(below average → number, cost, price, rate)* bas, faible; *(→ profit)* faible, maigre; *(→ salary)* peu élevé; **low economic growth** faible croissance économique; **attendance was low** il y avait peu de monde; **we're only playing for low stakes** nous ne jouons que de petites mises, nous ne jouons pas de grosses sommes; **we're rather low on whisky** on n'a plus beaucoup de whisky; **we're getting low on kerosene** nous allons bientôt être à court de kérosène; **our water supply is getting low** notre réserve d'eau baisse; **the ammunition is getting low** nous aurons bientôt épuisé les munitions; **low in calories** pauvre en calories; **the soil is very low in nitrogen** la terre est très pauvre en azote

(**e**) *(poor → intelligence, standard)* faible; *(→ opinion)* faible, piètre; *(→ in health)* mauvais, médiocre; *(→ in quality)* mauvais; **he's very low at the moment** il est bien bas *ou* bien affaibli en ce moment; **I'm in rather low spirits, I feel rather low** je n'ai pas le moral, je suis assez déprimé; **the pupils in this school have a low standard of reading** les élèves de cette école ont un niveau faible en lecture; **a low quality carpet** une moquette de mauvaise qualité

(**f**) *(in rank)* bas, inférieur; **to be of low birth** être de basse extraction *ou* d'origine modeste; **low ranking officials** petits fonctionnaires *mpl*, fonctionnaires *mpl* subalternes

(**g**) *(vulgar → behaviour)* grossier; *(→ tastes)* vulgaire; **to keep low company** fréquenter des gens peu recommandables; **that was a low trick** c'était un sale tour; **that was rather a low thing to do** ce n'était pas très joli de faire une chose pareille; **a man of low cunning** un homme d'une ruse ignoble

(**h**) *(primitive)* **low forms of life** des formes de vie inférieures *ou* peu évoluées

(**i**) *(soft → voice, music)* bas, faible; *(→ light)* faible; **keep your voice low** ne parlez pas trop fort; **in a low voice** à voix basse, à mi-voix; **turn the radio down low** mettez la radio moins fort; **turn the lights down low** baissez les lumières; **she gave a low groan** elle poussa un faible gémissement; **we heard a low moan** nous avons entendu une plainte étouffée

(**j**) *(deep → note, voice)* bas

lov–low

(**k**) *Cards* **to play a low trump** jouer un petit atout

2 *adv* (**a**) *(in height)* bas; **lower down** plus bas; **aim low** visez bas; **I can't bend down that low** je ne peux pas me pencher si bas; **a helicopter flew low over the town** un hélicoptère a survolé la ville à basse altitude; **the sun sank low on the horizon** le soleil est descendu très bas sur l'horizon; **she was sitting very low in her chair** elle était avachie sur sa chaise; **he bowed low** il s'inclina profondément; **to lie low** *(hide)* se cacher; *(keep low profile)* adopter un profil bas; **to be laid low** *(ill)* être immobilisé

(**b**) *(in intensity)* bas; **the fire had burnt low** le feu avait baissé; **stocks are running low** les réserves baissent; **the batteries are running low** les piles sont usées; **turn the music down low** baisse la musique

(**c**) *(in tone)* bas; **I can't sing that low** je ne peux pas chanter aussi bas

(**d**) *(in price)* **to buy low** acheter à bas prix; *St Exch* acheter quand les cours sont bas

(**e**) *(morally)* **I wouldn't stoop** *or* **sink so low as to tell lies** je ne m'abaisserais pas à mentir

3 *n* (**a**) *(in height)* bas *m*

(**b**) *(degree, level)* niveau *m* bas, point *m* bas; **the dollar has reached a record low** le dollar a atteint son niveau le plus bas; **the share price has reached a new low** l'indice des actions est descendu à son plus bas niveau; **inflation is at an all-time low** l'inflation est à son niveau le plus bas; **relations between them are at an all-time low** leurs relations n'ont jamais été si mauvaises; *St Exch* **the highs and lows** les hauts *mpl* et les bas *mpl*

(**c**) *(setting)* minimum *m*; **the heating is on low** le chauffage est au minimum

(**d**) *Met* dépression *f*

(**e**) *Am Aut* **in low** en première/seconde

(**f**) *Literary (of cattle)* meuglement *m*, beuglement *m*

4 *vi* meugler, beugler

▸▸ ***the low cards*** les basses cartes *fpl*; ***Low Church*** **1** *n* = section de l'Église anglicane qui se distingue par la simplicité du rituel **2** *adj* = de tendance conservatrice, dans l'Église anglicane; *Theat* ***low comedy*** farce *f*; ***the Low Countries*** les Pays-Bas *mpl*; **in the Low Countries** aux Pays-Bas; *Fam* ***low five*** = tape amicale donnée dans la paume de quelqu'un pour le saluer, le féliciter ou en signe de victoire; *Am* ***low gear*** première (vitesse) *f*; *Aut* **engage low gear** *(sign)* utilisez le frein moteur; ***Low German*** bas allemand *m*; ***Low Latin*** bas latin *m*; ***low life*** pègre *f*; *(individual → disreputable)* voyou *m*, crapule *f*; *(→ criminal)* membre *m* du milieu *ou* de la pègre; *Rel* ***Low Mass*** messe *f* basse; ***low pressure*** basse pression *f*; *Met* **a low pressure area, an area of low pressure** une zone de basse pression; ***the low season*** la basse saison; ***low season holidays*** vacances *fpl* hors saison; ***low technology*** technologie *f* de base; ***low tide*** marée *f* basse; **at low tide** à marée basse; ***low water*** *(UNCOUNT)* basses eaux *fpl*

---

low-alcohol *adj* à faible teneur en alcool

low-angle shot *n TV & Cin* contre-plongée *f*

low-born *adj* d'origine modeste, de basse extraction

lowboy ['ləʊbɔɪ] *n* commode *f* (basse)

lowbrow ['ləʊbraʊ] *Pej* **1** *n* personne *f* sans prétentions intellectuelles *ou* terre à terre

2 *adj (person)* peu intellectuel, terre à terre *(inv)*; *(book, film)* sans prétentions intellectuelles; *(literature)* de hall de gare

low-browed [-braʊd] *adj* (**a**) *(person)* au front bas (**b**) *(building)* à entrée basse; *(rock)* surplombant

low-budget *adj* économique

low-calorie, low-cal [-kæl] *adj* (à) basses calories

low-class *adj (lower-class)* populaire

low-cost *adj* à bas prix; *(housing, accommodation)* à loyer modéré

▸▸ *Mktg* ***low-cost purchase*** achat *m* à petit prix; *Mktg* ***low-cost purchasing*** achats *mpl* à petits prix

low-cut *adj* décolleté

low-density housing *n* zones *fpl* d'habitation peu peuplées

lowdown ['ləʊdaʊn] *n (UNCOUNT) Fam* renseignements❑ *mpl*; **can you give me the lowdown on what happened?** tu peux me mettre au courant de ce qui s'est passé?❑

low-down *adj* (**a**) *(shameful)* honteux, bas; *(mean)* mesquin; **that was a dirty low-down trick** c'était un sale tour (**b**) *Am (depressed)* cafardeux; **I'm feeling low-down** j'ai le cafard

low-end *adj Mktg* bas de gamme

lower[1] ['ləʊə(r)] **1** *adj (compar of* **low**) inférieur, plus bas; **people in the lower income brackets** *or* **groups** les gens appartenant aux tranches de revenus inférieures

2 *adv (compar of* **low**) **the lower paid** la tranche inférieure du salariat

3 *vt* (**a**) *(eyes, blind, head, window)* baisser; *(sails)* abaisser, amener; *(lifeboat)* mettre à la mer; **lower your aim a bit** visez un peu plus bas; **supplies were lowered down to us on a rope** on nous a descendu des provisions au bout d'une corde; *Theat* **to lower the curtain** baisser le rideau; **she lowered herself into the water** elle se laissa glisser dans l'eau; *Am* **lowered control button** = dans un ascenseur, bouton accessible aux personnes en fauteuil roulant; **to lower one's guard** *Boxing* baisser sa garde; *Fig* prêter le flanc

(**b**) *(reduce → price, interest rate, pressure, standard)* baisser, diminuer; *(→ temperature)* abaisser; **lower your voice** parlez moins fort, baissez la voix

(**c**) *(morally)* **she wouldn't lower herself to talk to them** elle ne s'abaisserait pas au point de leur adresser la parole

4 *vi (diminish → pressure)* diminuer; *(→ price)* baisser

▸▸ ***lower back*** reins *mpl*; **to have lower back pain** avoir mal aux reins; ***Lower California*** la Basse-Californie *f*; **in Lower California** en Basse-Californie; ***the lower classes*** les classes *fpl* inférieures; ***the lower deck*** *(of ship)* le pont inférieur; *Am Fam* ***the lower forty-eight*** = les États continentaux américains à l'exception de l'Alaska; *Br Pol* ***the lower Chamber, the Lower House*** la Chambre basse *ou* des communes; *Anat* ***lower jaw*** mâchoire *f* inférieure; ***the lower middle class*** la petite bourgeoisie; ***the lower ranks*** *(in army)* les rangs *mpl* inférieurs; ***the lower school*** les petites classes *fpl*; ***lower vertebrates*** vertébrés *mpl* inférieurs

▸ **lower away** *vi* **lower away!** laissez descendre!

'The Lower Depths' *Gorky* 'Les Bas-Fonds'

---

lower[2] ['laʊə(r)] *vi* (**a**) *(sky, weather)* se couvrir; **a lowering sky** un ciel menaçant *ou* couvert (**b**) *(person)* regarder d'un air menaçant; **he sat in the corner and lowered at me** il s'assit dans un coin et il me regarda d'un œil *ou* d'un air menaçant

lower-case ['ləʊə-] *Typ* **1** *n* bas *m* de casse, minuscule *f*

2 *adj* en bas de casse, minuscule

lower-class ['ləʊə-] *adj* populaire

lowering[1] ['ləʊərɪŋ] **1** *n* (**a**) *(of flag)* abaissement *m*; *(of boat)* mise *f* à la mer; **the lowering of the coffin into the grave** la descente du cercueil dans la tombe (**b**) *(reduction → of temperature, standards, prices)* baisse *f*

2 *adj* humiliant

lowering[2] ['laʊərɪŋ] *adj (sky)* sombre, couvert; *(clouds, look)* menaçant

loweringly ['laʊərɪŋlɪ] *adv (look)* d'un air menaçant; **the clouds gathered loweringly** les nuages menaçants s'amoncelaient

lowermost ['ləʊəməʊst] *adj Formal* le plus bas

lowest ['ləʊɪst] *adj (superl of* **low**) le plus bas; **the sun was at its lowest** le soleil était très bas sur l'horizon; **the lowest of the low** le dernier des derniers; *Fig* **the newspaper panders to the views of the lowest in society** ce journal flatte les instincts les plus bas de la société

▸▸ ***lowest bidder*** moins-disant *m*; *Math* ***the lowest common multiple*** le plus petit commun multiple; *Math & Fig* ***the lowest common denominator*** le plus petit dénominateur commun; *Fig Pej* **TV is dumbing down to appeal to the lowest common denominator** la télévision vise le niveau le plus bas pour plaire au plus grand nombre; **why do you always have to reduce things to the lowest common denominator?** pourquoi est-ce que tu ramènes tout à ce qu'il y a de plus vulgaire?

low-fat *adj (yoghurt, crisps)* allégé; *(milk)* demi-écrémé

low-flying *adj* volant à basse altitude

low-frequency *adj* (à) basse fréquence

low-grade *adj (in quality)* de qualité inférieure; *(in rank)* (de rang) inférieur, subalterne

low-heeled [-hi:ld] *adj* à talons plats

lowing ['ləʊɪŋ] *n (UNCOUNT) Literary* meuglement *m*, beuglement *m*, mugissement *m*

low-interest *adj Fin (credit, loan)* à taux réduit

low-involvement *adj Mktg (purchasing)* à faible participation des consommateurs

low-key *adj (style)* discret(ète); *(person)* réservé; **the meeting was a very low-key affair** la réunion s'est tenue dans la plus grande discrétion; **a low-key approach** une approche discrète

lowland ['ləʊlənd] **1** *n* plaine *f*, basse terre *f*

2 Lowlands *npl* **the Lowlands** *(in Scotland)* les Lowlands *fpl*

▸▸ ***Lowland Scots*** écossais *m (parlé dans les Lowlands)*

lowlander ['ləʊləndə(r)] **1** *n* habitant(e) *m,f* de la plaine

2 Lowlander *n (in Scotland → inhabitant)* habitant(e) *m,f* des Lowlands; *(→ native)* originaire *mf* des Lowlands

low-lather *adj* peu moussant

low-level *adj (talks)* à bas niveau; *(operation)* de faible envergure

▸▸ *Aviat* ***low-level flying*** vol *m* à basse altitude; *Med* ***low-level infection*** infection *f* bénigne; *Comput* ***low-level language*** langage *m* non évolué *ou* de bas niveau; *Nucl* ***low-level radiation*** irradiation *f* de faible intensité

low-life *adj (criminal)* du milieu; *(disreputable)* louche

lowlights ['ləʊlaɪts] *npl* (**a**) *(in hair)* mèches *fpl* (**b**) *Fam (worst points)* points *mpl* noirs❑

lowliness ['ləʊlɪnɪs] *n* humilité *f*

low-loader *n Rail* wagon *m* à plate-forme surbaissée; *Aut* camion *m* à plate-forme surbaissée

lowly ['ləʊlɪ] *(compar* **lowlier**, *superl* **lowliest**) *adj (modest)* modeste; *(meek)* humble; *(simple)* sans prétention *ou* prétentions; **of lowly birth** issu d'un milieu humble

low-lying *adj (land → gen)* bas; *(→ below sea level)* au-dessous du niveau de la mer; *(cloud)* bas

low-maintenance *adj (pet)* qui ne demande pas beaucoup de soins; *(garden, hairstyle)* qui ne demande pas beaucoup d'entretien; *Hum (girlfriend)* peu exigeant

low-minded *adj* vulgaire, grossier

low-necked *adj* décolleté

lowness ['ləʊnɪs] *n* (**a**) *(of wall, building)* faible hauteur *f*; *(of land)* faible élévation *f* (**b**) *(of wages, prices)* modicité *f* (**c**) *(of temperature)* faible élévation *f* (**d**) *(of voice → softness)* douceur *f*; *(→ in pitch)* profondeur *f*

low-octane fuel *n* carburant *m* à faible indice d'octane

low-paid 1 *adj* mal payé

2 *npl* **the low-paid** les petits salaires *mpl*

low-pitched *adj* (**a**) *(voice, note)* bas, grave (**b**) *(roof)* à faible pente

low-powered *adj* de faible puissance

low-pressure *adj* (**a**) *(gas)* sous faible pression, de basse pression; *(tyre)* à basse pression (**b**) *(job)* peu stressant

low-price(d) *adj* bon marché, peu cher

low-profile *adj (talks, visit)* discret(ète)

▸▸ *Aut* ***low-profile tyre*** pneu *m* à profil bas

low-radiation monitor *n* moniteur *m* basse radiation

low-rent *adj* (**a**) *(housing)* à loyer modéré (**b**) *Pej (low-quality)* bas de gamme

low-resolution *adj* à basse résolution

lowrider ['ləʊraɪdə(r)] *n* voiture *f* surbaissée

low-rise 1 *n* immeuble *m* bas

2 *adj (building)* de faible hauteur, bas

low-slung *adj (furniture)* bas; *Aut (chassis)* surbaissé

low-sodium *adj* à faible teneur en sodium

low-speed *adj (engine)* à petite vitesse, à vitesse réduite

low-spirited *adj* déprimé, démoralisé

low-tar *adj*
▸▸ ***low-tar cigarettes*** cigarettes *fpl* à faible teneur en goudron

low-tech *adj* rudimentaire

low-tension *adj Elec* (de) basse tension

low-voltage *adj* à faible voltage, à faible tension

low-water mark *n* niveau *m* des basses eaux

lox¹ [lɒks] *n Culin* saumon *m* fumé

lox² *n* (*abbr* **liquid oxygen**) oxygène *m* liquide

loxodromic [ˌlɒksəˈdrɒmɪk] *adj Naut* loxodromique
▸▸ ***loxodromic tables*** tables *fpl* loxodromiques

loxodromics [ˌlɒksəˈdrɒmɪks] *n* (*UNCOUNT*) *Naut* navigation *f* loxodromique

loxodromy [lɒkˈsɒdrəmɪ] *n Naut* loxodromie *f*

loyal [ˈlɔɪəl] *adj* loyal, fidèle; *Mktg* (*customer*) fidèle; **to be loyal to sb** être loyal envers qn, faire preuve de loyauté envers qn; **a loyal friend** un ami fidèle; **loyal supporters** partisans *mpl* fidèles
▸▸ *Am* ***Loyal Order of the Moose*** = association caritative américaine; ***the loyal toast*** = toast porté à la reine d'Angleterre à la fin d'un dîner

loyal-customer discount *n Mktg* remise *f* de fidélité

loyalism [ˈlɔɪəlɪzəm] *n* loyalisme *m*

loyalist [ˈlɔɪəlɪst] **1** *n* loyaliste *mf*
2 *adj* loyaliste
3 Loyalist *n* loyaliste *mf*

LOYALIST

Dans le contexte britannique, le mot "Loyalist" désigne un protestant d'Irlande du Nord souhaitant rester au sein du Royaume-Uni.

loyally [ˈlɔɪəlɪ] *adv* loyalement, fidèlement

loyalty [ˈlɔɪəltɪ] (*pl* **loyalties**) *n* (**a**) (*faithfulness*) loyauté *f*, fidélité *f*; **she's always shown great loyalty** elle a toujours fait preuve d'une grande loyauté; **the party demands loyalty to the principles of democracy** le parti exige le respect des principes de la démocratie; **her loyalty to the cause is not in doubt** son dévouement à la cause n'est pas mis en doute
(**b**) (*tie*) **tribal loyalties** liens *mpl* tribaux; **my loyalties are divided** je suis déchiré (entre les deux), entre les deux mon cœur balance
▸▸ *Mktg* ***loyalty card*** carte *f* de fidélité; *Mktg* ***loyalty discount*** remise *f* de fidélité; *Mktg* ***loyalty magazine*** = magazine publié par une chaîne de magasins, une banque etc, pour ses clients; *Mktg* ***loyalty programme, loyalty scheme*** programme *m* de fidélisation

Loyola [lɔɪˈəʊlə] *pr n* **Saint Ignatius Loyola** saint Ignace de Loyola

lozenge [ˈlɒzɪndʒ] *n* (**a**) (*sweet*) pastille *f*; **throat lozenge** pastille *f* pour la gorge (**b**) (*rhombus*) losange *m*

LP [ˌelˈpiː] *n* (*abbr* **long-player**) **an LP** un 33 tours

LPG [ˌelpiːˈdʒiː] *n* (*abbr* **liquefied petroleum gas**) GPL *m*, *Belg* LPG *m*

L-plate *n Br* = plaque apposée sur une voiture et signalant un apprenti conducteur (en Grande-Bretagne)

LPN [ˌelpiːˈen] *n* (*abbr* **licensed practical nurse**) = [illegible]

LQ [ˌelˈkjuː] *Comput* (*abbr* **letter quality**) qualité *f* courrier
▸▸ ***LQ printer*** imprimante *f* de qualité courrier

LRAM [ˌelɑːˌreɪˈem] *n* (*abbr* **Licentiate of the Royal Academy of Music**) = membre de la "Royal Academy of Music"

LSAT [ˌelesˌeɪˈtiː] *n* (*abbr* **Law School Admissions Test**) = aux États-Unis, test d'admission aux études de droit

LSD¹ [ˌelesˈdiː] *n* (*abbr* **lysergic acid diethylamide**) LSD *m*

LSD², lsd *n Formerly* (*abbr* **librae, solidi, denarii**) = symboles représentant les "pounds", les "shillings" et les "pence" de l'ancienne monnaie britannique avant l'adoption du système décimal en 1971

LSE [ˌelesˈiː] *n* (**a**) *Univ* (*abbr* **London School of Economics**) = grande école de sciences économiques et politiques à Londres (**b**) *St Exch* (*abbr* **London Stock Exchange**) = la Bourse de Londres

L-shaped *adj* en (forme de) L

LSI [ˌelesˈaɪ] *n Comput* (*abbr* **large scale integration**) intégration *f* à grande échelle

LSO [ˌelesˈəʊ] *n* (*abbr* **London Symphony Orchestra**) = orchestre symphonique de Londres

LT¹ [ˌelˈtiː] *n* (*abbr* **London Transport**) = régie des transports londoniens

LT² (*written abbr* **low tension**) BT

Lt. *Mil* (*written abbr* **lieutenant**) Lieut.

LTA [ˌeltiːˈeɪ] *n* (*abbr* **Lawn Tennis Association**) = la Fédération britannique de tennis

Ltd, ltd (*written abbr* **limited**) ≃ SARL, *Can* limité; **Smith and Sons Ltd** ≃ Smith & Fils, SARL

Luanda [luːˈændə] *n* Luanda

luau [ˈluːaʊ] *n Am* fête *f* hawaïenne

lube [luːb] *Fam* **1** *n* (*lubricant*) lubrifiant❑ *m*; (*lubrication*) lubrification❑ *f*
2 *vt* lubrifier❑
▸▸ ***lube bay*** poste *m* de graissage; ***lube job*** graissage *m*; ***lube oil*** huile *f* de graissage

lubricant [ˈluːbrɪkənt] **1** *n* lubrifiant *m*
2 *adj* lubrifiant

lubricate [ˈluːbrɪkeɪt] *vt* (*gen*) lubrifier; (*mechanism*) lubrifier, graisser, huiler

lubricated [ˈluːbrɪkeɪtɪd] *adj Fam Hum* (*drunk*) bourré

lubricating [ˈluːbrɪkeɪtɪŋ] *n* lubrification *f*
▸▸ ***lubricating oil*** huile *f* de graissage

lubrication [ˌluːbrɪˈkeɪʃən] *n* (*gen*) lubrification *f*; (*of mechanism*) lubrification *f*, graissage *m*, huilage *m*; *Fam Hum* (*alcohol*) gnôle *f*
▸▸ ***lubrication nipple*** graisseur *m*; ***lubrication oil*** huile *f* de lubrification; ***lubrication system*** circuit *m* de lubrification

lubricator [ˈluːbrɪkeɪtə(r)] *n* graisseur *m*

lubricious [luːˈbrɪʃəs] *adj Literary* lubrique

lubricity [luːˈbrɪsətɪ] *n* (**a**) *Literary* (*lewdness*) lubricité *f* (**b**) *Tech* onctuosité *f*

Lucca [ˈlʌkə] *n Geog* Lucques

lucency [ˈluːsənsɪ] *n* brillance *f*, luminosité *f*

lucent [ˈluːsənt] *adj* (**a**) (*bright*) brillant, lumineux (**b**) (*clear*) clair, transparent

Lucerne [luːˈsɜːn] *n* Lucerne

lucerne [luːˈsɜːn] *n Br Bot* luzerne *f*

lucid [ˈluːsɪd] *adj* (**a**) (*clear-headed*) lucide; **he has his lucid moments** il a des moments de lucidité (**b**) (*clear*) clair, limpide; **a lucid narrative style** un style d'une grande clarté; **she gave a lucid account of events** elle donna un compte rendu net et précis des événements (**c**) *Literary* (*shining*) brillant, lumineux

lucidity [luːˈsɪdətɪ] *n* (**a**) (*of mind*) lucidité *f* (**b**) (*of style, account*) clarté *f*, limpidité *f*

lucidly [ˈluːsɪdlɪ] *adv* lucidement, avec lucidité

Lucifer [ˈluːsɪfə(r)] *pr n* Lucifer

luciferin [luːˈsɪfərɪn] *n Biol & Chem* luciférine *f*

luck [lʌk] *n* (**a**) (*fortune*) chance *f*; **to have good luck** avoir de la chance; **good luck!** bonne chance!; *Ironic* **good luck to you!** je vous souhaite bien du plaisir!; **good luck in your new job!** bonne chance pour ton nouveau travail!; **we had a bit of bad luck with the car** on a eu un pépin avec la voiture; **you've brought me nothing but bad luck** tu ne m'as causé que des malheurs; **it's bad luck to spill salt** renverser du sel porte malheur; **bad** *or* **hard** *or* **tough luck!** pas de chance!; **we thought the exam** [illegible] que l'examen était annulé – ç'aurait été trop beau; **to be down on one's luck** avoir la poisse *ou* la guigne; **to push one's luck** jouer avec le feu; **with (any) luck** avec un peu de chance; **worse luck** tant pis; **no, he hasn't asked me out, worse luck!** non, il ne m'a pas invitée à sortir, tant pis!
(**b**) (*good fortune*) **that's a bit of luck!** c'est de la chance!; **luck was with us** *or* **on our side** la chance était avec nous; **you're in luck, your luck's in** vous avez de la chance; **we're out of luck** on n'a pas de chance; **one more for luck** et un pour le pot; **better luck next time** vous aurez plus de chance la prochaine fois; **any luck?** alors, ça a marché?; **some people have all the luck!** il y en a qui ont vraiment de la chance!; *Ironic* **it would be just my luck to bump into my boss** ce serait bien ma veine de tomber sur mon patron
(**c**) (*chance, opportunity*) hasard *m*; **it's the luck of the draw** c'est une question de chance; **to try one's luck** tenter sa chance; **as luck would have it** (*by chance*) par hasard; (*by good luck*) par bonheur; (*by bad luck*) par malheur; **as luck would have it I'd forgotten my keys** et comme par hasard, j'avais oublié mes clés
▸**luck into** *vt insep Fam* **to luck into sth** dégoter qch
▸**luck out** *vi Fam* (*succeed*) avoir de la veine

luckily [ˈlʌkɪlɪ] *adv* heureusement, par chance; **luckily for him, he escaped** heureusement pour lui, il s'est échappé

luckless [ˈlʌklɪs] *adj* (*person*) malchanceux; (*escapade, attempt*) malheureux

lucklessness [ˈlʌklɪsnɪs] *n* malchance *f*

lucky [ˈlʌkɪ] (*compar* **luckier**, *superl* **luckiest**) *adj* (**a**) (*fortunate* → *person*) chanceux; (→ *encounter, winner*) heureux; **to be lucky** (*person*) avoir de la chance; (*thing*) porter bonheur; *Fam* **to get lucky** avoir un coup de bol; (*sexually*) faire une touche; **you're lucky to have escaped with your life** vous avez eu de la chance de vous en tirer vivant; **what a lucky escape!** on l'a échappé belle!; **it was lucky for them that we were there** heureusement pour eux que nous étions là; **it's my lucky day** c'est mon jour de chance; **to be born lucky** être né coiffé; **who's the lucky man?** (*she's going to marry*) qui est l'heureux élu?; *Fam* **you lucky devil** *or* **thing!** sacré veinard!; **I'd like a pay rise – you'll be lucky** *or* **you should be so lucky!** j'aimerais une augmentation – tu peux toujours courir!; **lucky you!** vous en avez de la chance!
(**b**) (*token, number*) porte-bonheur (*inv*)
(**c**) (*guess*) heureux
▸▸ *Fam* ***lucky break*** coup *m* de pot *ou* de bol; ***lucky charm*** porte-bonheur *m inv*; *Br* ***lucky dip*** = jeu consistant à chercher des cadeaux enfouis dans une caisse remplie de sciure ou dans un sac; *Fig* **the job market is a real lucky dip at the moment** de nos jours, trouver un emploi, c'est vraiment une question de chance; *Sport* ***lucky loser*** = perdant que l'on repêche, le plus souvent pour avoir un nombre pair de participants

'Lucky Jim' *Amis* 'Jim-la-Chance'

Lucozade® [ˈluːkəzeɪd] *n* = boisson gazeuse à base de glucose

lucrative [ˈluːkrətɪv] *adj* (*job*) bien rémunéré, lucratif; (*activity, deal*) lucratif, rentable

lucratively [ˈluːkrətɪvlɪ] *adv* d'une manière lucrative, lucrativement

lucrativeness [ˈluːkrətɪvnɪs] *n* bon rapport *m*

lucre [ˈluːkə(r)] *n Hum Pej* **(filthy) lucre** lucre *m*

Lucretia Borgia [ˌluːˈkriːʃəˈbɔːdʒə] *pr n* Lucrèce Borgia

Lucretius [luːˈkriːʃəs] *pr n* Lucrèce

lucubration [ˌluːkjuːˈbreɪʃən] *n Literary* (*studying*) travail *m* laborieux, élucubration *f*; (*literary work*) élucubration *f*

Luddism [ˈlʌdɪzəm] *n Hist* luddisme *m*

Luddite [ˈlʌdaɪt] **1** *n* luddite *m*; *Fig* personne *f* opposée au progrès
2 *adj* luddite
▸▸ ***the Luddite Riots*** les émeutes *fpl* luddites

THE LUDDITE RIOTS

Au cours de ces émeutes ouvrières, qui eurent lieu en Grande-Bretagne pendant la dépression de 1811 à 1813, des chômeurs parcoururent le nord du pays en détruisant les nouvelles machines textiles, jugées responsables de leur sort. Ces émeutes furent durement réprimées par le gouvernement.

ludic [ˈluːdɪk] *adj* ludique

ludicrous [ˈluːdɪkrəs] *adj* ridicule, absurde

ludicrously [ˈluːdɪkrəslɪ] *adv* ridiculement

ludicrousness [ˈluːdɪkrəsnɪs] *n* absurdité *f*, ridicule *m*

ludism [ˈluːdɪzəm] *n* ludisme *m*

ludo [ˈluːdəʊ] *n Br* ≃ (jeu *m* des) petits chevaux *mpl*

Ludwig [ˈlʊdvɪg] *pr n* **Ludwig of Bavaria** Louis de Bavière

luff [lʌf] *Naut* **1** *n* guindant *m*
2 *vi* lofer, aller au lof

luffa ['lʌfə] = **loofa**

lug [lʌg] *(pt & pp* **lugged**, *cont* **lugging**) **1** *n* (**a**) *(for fixing)* ergot *m*, (petite) patte *f*; *(handle)* anse *f*, poignée *f* (**b**) *Br Fam (ear)* esgourde *f* (**c**) *Am (fool)* niais *m*; **of course I love you, you big lug!** bien sûr que je t'aime, gros bêta!

2 *vt Fam (carry, pull)* trimbaler; **I had to lug my bags all the way from the station** j'ai dû trimbaler mes bagages de la gare jusqu'ici; **he lugged his bicycle up the stairs** il s'est trimbalé sa bicyclette jusqu'en haut des escaliers

►► ***lug screw*** vis *f* sans tête

►**lug about, lug around** *vt sep Fam* trimbaler; **he always has to lug his little sister about with him** il doit toujours trimbaler *ou* traîner sa petite sœur à droite et à gauche

luge [lu:ʒ] *n Sport* luge *f*

luger ['lu:ʒə(r)] *n Sport* lugeur(euse) *m,f*

luggable ['lʌgəbəl] *n Comput* portable *m* (lourd)

luggage ['lʌgɪdʒ] *n (UNCOUNT)* bagages *mpl*; **a piece of luggage** un bagage

►► ***luggage carrier*** porte-bagages *m inv*; ***luggage compartment*** compartiment *m* à bagages; *Br* ***luggage handler*** bagagiste *m*; *Naut* ***luggage hold*** soute *f* à bagages; ***luggage label*** étiquette *f* à bagages; ***luggage locker*** consigne *f* automatique; *Br* ***luggage rack*** *Rail (shelf)* porte-bagages *m inv*; *(net)* filet *m* (à bagages); *Aut* galerie *f* (de toit); *Naut* ***luggage room*** soute *f* à bagages; ***luggage trolley*** chariot *m* à bagages; *Br Rail* ***luggage van*** fourgon *m* (à bagages)

lugger ['lʌgə(r)] *n* lougre *m*

lughole ['lʌghəʊl] *n Br Fam (ear)* esgourde *f*

lugsail ['lʌgseɪl] *n Naut* voile *f* à bourcet

lugubrious [lʊ'gu:brɪəs] *adj* lugubre

lugubriously [lʊ'gu:brɪəslɪ] *adv* lugubrement, de façon lugubre

lugubriousness [lʊ'gu:brɪəsnɪs] *n* caractère *m* lugubre

lugworm ['lʌgwɜ:m] *n Zool* arénicole *f*

Luke [lu:k] *pr n Bible* Luc; **the Gospel According to (Saint) Luke** l'Évangile selon saint Luc

lukewarm ['lu:kwɔ:m] *adj (water, soup)* tiède; *Fig* **a lukewarm reception** *(of person)* un accueil peu chaleureux; *(of book, film)* un accueil mitigé

LULAC ['lu:læk] *n (abbr* **League of United Latin-American Citizens**) = ligue américaine pour la défense des droits de la population d'origine latino-américaine

lull [lʌl] **1** *n (in weather)* accalmie *f*; *(in fighting)* accalmie *f*, pause *f*; *(in conversation)* pause *f*; **the lull before the storm** le calme avant la tempête

2 *vt (calm → anxiety, person)* calmer, apaiser; **she lulled the child to sleep** elle berça l'enfant jusqu'à ce qu'il s'endorme; **the sound of the engine lulled me to sleep** le ronronnement du moteur m'a endormi; **they were lulled into a false sense of security** ils ont fait l'erreur de se laisser rassurer par des propos lénifiants

lullaby ['lʌləbaɪ] *(pl* **lullabies**) *n* berceuse *f*

lulu ['lu:lu:] *n Am Fam* **it's a lulu!** c'est du tonnerre!; **her latest film's a real lulu** son dernier film est génial

lumbago [lʌm'beɪgəʊ] *n Med (UNCOUNT)* lumbago *m*, lombalgie *f*

lumbar ['lʌmbə(r)] *adj Anat* lombaire

►► ***lumbar adjustable seat*** siège *m* à réglage lombaire; *Med* ***lumbar puncture*** ponction *f* lombaire, rachicentèse *f*; ***lumbar vertebra*** lombaire *f*

lumber ['lʌmbə(r)] **1** *n* (**a**) *Am (cut wood)* bois *m* (d'œuvre); *(ready for use)* bois *m* de construction *ou* de charpente

(**b**) *Br (junk)* bric-à-brac *m inv* (**c**) *Scot Fam* **to get a lumber** faire une touche

2 *vt Am (logs)* débiter; *(tree)* abattre, couper

3 *vi* (**a**) *(large person, animal)* marcher pesamment; **I could hear him lumbering down the stairs** je l'entendais descendre l'escalier d'un pas pesant; **she lumbered into the room** elle entra dans la pièce d'un pas lourd; **the tanks lumbered into the centre of the town** la lourde colonne de chars avançait vers le centre de la ville

(**b**) *Am (fell trees)* abattre des arbres *(pour le bois)*

►► ***lumber jacket*** grosse veste *f* de bûcheron; *Br* ***lumber room*** débarras *m*

►**lumber with** *vt sep Fam (usu passive) (encumber)* **to lumber sb with sth** refiler qch à qn; **I'll get lumbered with it** ça va me retomber dessus; **they've lumbered me with the cooking** c'est moi qui me suis tapé tous les repas; **I was lumbered with him for the whole evening** je l'ai eu sur le dos pendant toute la soirée

lumbering ['lʌmbərɪŋ] **1** *n Am* exploitation *f* forestière

2 *adj (heavy → step)* pesant, lourd; *(→ person)* lourd, maladroit

lumberjack ['lʌmbədʒæk] *n* bûcheron(onne) *m,f*

►► ***lumberjack shirt*** chemise *f* de bûcheron *(chemise épaisse à grands carreaux)*

lumberman ['lʌmbəmən] *(pl* **lumbermen** [-mən]) *n Am* bûcheron *m*

lumbermill ['lʌmbə,mɪl] *n Am* scierie *f*

lumberyard ['lʌmbəjɑ:d] *n Am* dépôt *m* de bois

lumen ['lu:mɪn] *n Phys* lumen *m*; *Anat* lumière *f*

luminance ['lu:mɪnəns] *n* luminance *f*

luminary ['lu:mɪnərɪ] *(pl* **luminaries**) *n* (**a**) *(celebrity)* lumière *f*, sommité *f* (**b**) *Literary (heavenly body)* astre *m*, luminaire *m*

luminescence [,lu:mɪ'nesəns] *n* luminescence *f*

luminescent [,lu:mɪ'nesənt] *adj* luminescent

luminosity [,lu:mɪ'nɒsətɪ] *n* luminosité *f*

luminous ['lu:mɪnəs] *adj (paint, colour, sky, watch face)* lumineux; *Fig (explanation, argument)* lumineux, limpide; *(clothing)* fluorescent

►► *Phys* ***luminous flux*** flux *m* lumineux; *Phys* ***luminous intensity*** intensité *f* lumineuse

lumme ['lʌmɪ] *exclam Br Fam Old-fashioned* ben mon vieux!

lummox ['lʌməks] *n Fam* empoté(e) *m,f*

lummy = **lumme**

lump [lʌmp] **1** *n* (**a**) *(of sugar)* morceau *m*; **one lump or two?** un ou deux sucres?

(**b**) *(of solid matter → small)* morceau *m*; *(→ large)* masse *f*; *(in food)* grumeau *m*; *(of stone, marble)* bloc *m*; *(of earth, clay)* motte *f*; **a shapeless lump of melted plastic** une masse informe de plastique fondu; **to have a lump in one's throat** avoir une boule dans la gorge, avoir la gorge serrée; *Am Fam* **you've got to take your lumps** tout n'est pas toujours rose

(**c**) *(bump)* bosse *f*; **I've got a lump on my forehead** j'ai une bosse au front; **there are lots of lumps in this mattress** ce matelas est plein de bosses

(**d**) *Med (swelling)* grosseur *f*, protubérance *f*; **she has a lump in her breast** elle a une grosseur au sein

(**e**) *(of money)* **you don't have to pay it all in one lump** vous n'êtes pas obligé de tout payer en une seule fois

(**f**) *Fam Pej (clumsy person)* empoté(e) *m,f*

(**g**) *Br Constr* **the lump** *(casual workers)* ouvriers *mpl* indépendants (non déclarés); *Fam* **to work on the lump** travailler au noir❑ *(avec rémunération au forfait)*

2 *vt Fam (put up with)* **if that's her final decision, we'll just have to lump it!** puisque c'est sa décision définitive, on n'a plus qu'à s'écraser!; **if you don't like it you can lump it!** si ça ne te plaît pas, tant pis pour toi!

►► ***lump labour*** main-d'œuvre *f* non déclarée; ***lump sugar*** sucre *m* en morceaux; ***lump sum*** somme *f* forfaitaire, montant *m* forfaitaire; **they pay me a lump sum** je touche une somme forfaitaire; **to work for a lump sum** travailler à forfait; **to be paid in a lump sum** être payé en une seule fois

►**lump together** *vt sep* (**a**) *(gather together)* réunir, rassembler; **couldn't you lump all these paragraphs together under one heading?** ne pourrais-tu pas réunir *ou* regrouper tous ces paragraphes sous un même titre?

(**b**) *(consider the same)* mettre dans la même catégorie

lumpectomy [,lʌm'pektəmɪ] *(pl* **lumpectomies**) *n Med* ablation *f* d'une tumeur au sein

lumpen ['lʌmpən] *adj* grossier

lumpenproletariat ['lʌmpən,prəʊlɪ'teərɪət] *n* lumpenprolétariat *m*

lumpfish ['lʌmpfɪʃ] *(pl* **inv** *or* **lumpfishes**) *n Ich* lump *m*, lompe *m*

►► ***lumpfish roe*** œufs *mpl* de lump

lumpish ['lʌmpɪʃ] *adj (clumsy)* maladroit; *(dull-witted)* idiot, abruti

lumpishness ['lʌmpɪʃnɪs] *n (clumsiness)* maladresse *f*; *(dull-wittedness)* bêtise *f*

lumpsucker ['lʌmp,sʌkə(r)] *n Ich* lump *m*, lompe *m*

lumpy ['lʌmpɪ] *(compar* **lumpier**, *superl* **lumpiest**) *adj (sauce)* plein de grumeaux; *(mattress)* plein de bosses, défoncé

lunacy ['lu:nəsɪ] *(pl* **lunacies**) *n* (**a**) *(madness)* démence *f*, folie *f* (**b**) *(folly)* folie *f*; **it would be lunacy to accept such a proposal** ce serait de la folie d'accepter pareille proposition; **it's sheer lunacy!** c'est de la folie pure et simple!

lunar ['lu:nə(r)] *adj (rock, month, cycle)* lunaire; *(eclipse)* de Lune

►► *Astron* ***lunar landing*** alunissage *m*; *Astron* ***lunar excursion module*** module *m* lunaire; ***lunar month*** lunaison *f*

lunaria [lu:'neərɪə] *n Bot* lunaire *f*

lunate ['lu:neɪt] *adj Anat & Bot* en forme de croissant

lunatic ['lu:nətɪk] **1** *n* (**a**) *(madman)* aliéné(e) *m,f*, dément(e) *m,f* (**b**) *Fam (fool)* cinglé(e) *m,f*; **he's a complete lunatic!** il est fou à lier!, il est complètement cinglé!

2 *adj* (**a**) *(insane)* fou (folle), dément (**b**) *Fam (crazy → person)* cinglé, dingue; *(→ idea)* dément, démentiel

►► ***lunatic asylum*** asile *m* d'aliénés; *Pej* ***lunatic fringe*** extrémistes *mpl* fanatiques

lunch [lʌntʃ] **1** *n* déjeuner *m*, *Can & Belg* dîner *m*; **to have lunch** déjeuner; **after lunch** après le déjeuner; **she's gone out for lunch** elle est partie déjeuner; **what's for lunch?** qu'y a-t-il pour le déjeuner?; **we're having trout for lunch** il y a de la truite au déjeuner; **I've invited him for lunch on Tuesday** je l'ai invité à déjeuner mardi prochain; **I have a lunch date** je déjeune avec quelqu'un, je suis pris pour le déjeuner; *(for business)* j'ai un déjeuner d'affaires; **what did you have for lunch?** qu'est-ce que tu as mangé à midi?; **they're giving a lunch at the Savoy** ils donnent un déjeuner au Savoy; *Fam* **to lose** *or Am* **shoot one's lunch** *(vomit)* gerber, dégobiller; **he's out to lunch** il est parti déjeuner; *Fam Fig* il débloque

2 *vi Formal* déjeuner, *Can & Belg* dîner; **we lunched on sandwiches** nous avons déjeuné de sandwichs

►► ***lunch break*** *(in course of working day)* pause *f* du déjeuner; *Am* ***lunch counter*** *(in store)* bar *m* de restauration rapide; ***lunch hour*** heure *f* du déjeuner; **she's not here, it's her lunch hour** elle n'est pas là, c'est l'heure à laquelle elle déjeune; ***lunch menu*** menu *m* déjeuner

lunchbox ['lʌntʃbɒks] *n* (**a**) *(for carrying lunch → gen)* = boîte dans laquelle on transporte son déjeuner; *(→ for workmen)* gamelle *f* (**b**) *Br Fam Hum (man's genitals)* service *m* trois pièces, bijoux *mpl* de famille

lunchbucket ['lʌntʃbʌkɪt] *n Am (for carrying lunch → gen)* = boîte dans laquelle on transporte son déjeuner; *(→ for workmen)* gamelle *f*

luncheon ['lʌntʃən] *n Formal* déjeuner *m*; **a literary luncheon** un déjeuner littéraire

►► ***luncheon meat*** = bloc de viande de porc en conserve; *Br* ***luncheon voucher*** Ticket-Restaurant® *m inv*

luncheonette [,lʌntʃə'net] *n Am* snack *m*, snack-bar *m*

luncher ['lʌntʃə(r)] *n* déjeuneur(euse) *m,f*

lunchpail ['lʌntʃpeɪl] *n Am (for carrying lunch → gen)* = boîte dans laquelle on transporte son déjeuner; *(→ for workmen)* gamelle *f*

lunchroom ['lʌntʃrʊm] *n Am* = pièce où l'on peut manger ses sandwichs etc à l'heure du déjeuner

lunchtime ['lʌntʃtaɪm] *n* heure *f* du déjeuner; **I saw him at lunchtime** je l'ai vu à midi *ou* à l'heure du déjeuner; **it's lunchtime** c'est l'heure de déjeuner

lunette [lu:'net] *n Archit* lunette *f*

lung [lʌŋ] **1** *n* poumon *m*; **to shout at the top of one's lungs** crier à tue-tête; **he filled his lungs with air** il inspira profondément

2 *comp (artery, congestion, disease)* pulmonaire; *(transplant)* du poumon

►► ***lung cancer*** cancer *m* du poumon; ***lung specialist*** pneumologue *mf*

lunge [lʌndʒ] **1** *n* (**a**) *(sudden movement)* **to make a lunge for sth** se précipiter vers qch (**b**) *Fencing* fente *f* (avant) (**c**) *Horseriding* longe *f*

2 *vi (move suddenly)* faire un mouvement brusque en avant; **she lunged at him with a knife** elle se précipita sur lui avec un couteau; *Fencing* **he lunged at his opponent** il allongea une botte à son adversaire

3 *vt (horse)* mener à la longe

►**lunge forward** *vi* se jeter en avant; *Fencing* se fendre

lungfish ['lʌŋfɪʃ] (*pl* **inv** *or* **lungfishes**) *n Ich* dipneuste *m*

lungful ['lʌŋfʊl] *n* **she breathed in a lungful of cold air** elle aspira l'air froid à pleins poumons, elle aspira une grande bouffée d'air froid; **take a lungful of air** inspirez à fond

lungwort ['lʌŋwɜːt] *n Bot* pulmonaire *f*

lunisolar [ˌluːnɪ'səʊlə(r)] *adj* luni-solaire

lunkhead ['lʌŋkhed] *n Am Fam* cruche *f*, andouille *f*

lunula ['luːnjʊlə], **lunule** ['luːnjuːl] *n Anat* lunule *f*

Lupercalia [ˌluːpə'keɪlɪə] *npl Antiq* lupercales *fpl*

lupin ['luːpɪn] *n Bot* lupin *m*

lupine ['luːpaɪn] **1** *n Am* lupin *m*

2 *adj* de loup

lupus ['luːpəs] *n Med* lupus *m*; **lupus vulgaris** lupus *m* vulgaire

lurch [lɜːtʃ] **1** *vi (person)* tituber, chanceler; *(car → swerve)* faire une embardée; *(→ jerk forwards)* avancer par à-coups; *(ship)* tanguer; **he lurched into the room** il entra dans la pièce en titubant; **the car lurched out of control** la voiture livrée à elle-même fit une embardée; *Fig* **his opinions lurch from one extreme to another** dans ses opinions, il passe d'un extrême à l'autre

2 *n (of ship)* embardée *f*, coup *m* de roulis; *(of car)* embardée *f*; **the car gave a sudden lurch and left the road** la voiture fit une embardée et quitta la route; **with a lurch, the train was off again** le train est reparti avec un à-coup; **to leave sb in the lurch** laisser qn en plan

lurcher ['lɜːtʃə(r)] *n* = chien bâtard, croisement de lévrier et de colley

lure [ljʊə(r)] **1** *n* (**a**) *(attraction)* attrait *m*; *(charm)* charme *m*; *(temptation)* tentation *f* (**b**) *Fishing & Hunt* leurre *m*

2 *vt* (**a**) *(person)* attirer (sous un faux prétexte); **he lured them into a trap** il les a attirés dans un piège (**b**) *Fishing & Hunt* leurrer

►**lure away** *vt sep* **he lured me away from my friends** il a fait en sorte que je ne voie plus mes amis, il m'a éloigné de mes amis; **she invited me over in order to lure me away from the office** elle m'a invité chez elle pour m'éloigner du bureau

Lurex® ['lʊəreks] *n (thread)* Lurex® *m*, *(cloth)* tissu *m* en Lurex®

lurgy ['lɜːgɪ] *n Br Fam Hum* **I've got the dreaded lurgy** j'ai attrapé quelque chose ❑

lurid ['ljʊərɪd] *adj* (**a**) *(sensational → account, story)* macabre, atroce, horrible; *(salacious)* salace, malsain; **many newspapers go in for lurid sensationalism** de nombreux journaux exploitent le goût du public pour le sensationnel; **he gave me a lurid account of the plane crash** il m'a décrit l'accident d'avion sans m'épargner le moindre détail; **their affair was described in lurid details** leur liaison était décrite avec force détails scabreux; **the book gives a lurid description of life at the castle** le livre donne une description haute en couleur de la vie au château

(**b**) *(glaring → sky, sunset)* sanglant, rougeoyant; *(→ wallpaper, shirt)* criard, voyant; **a lurid green dress** une robe d'un vert criard; **harsh neon lights** la lumière crue des néons

luridly ['ljʊərɪdlɪ] *adv (garishly)* violemment, tapageusement

luridness ['ljʊərɪdnɪs] *n* (**a**) *(of account, story)* horreur *f* (**b**) *(of sky)* lueurs *fpl* rougeoyantes; *(of wallpaper, shirt, colour)* aspect *m* criard

lurk [lɜːk] *vi* (**a**) *(person, animal)* se tapir; *(danger)* se cacher, menacer; *(doubt, worry)* persister; **the burglar was lurking behind the trees** le cambrioleur était tapi derrière les arbres (**b**) *Comput* rôder

lurker ['lɜːkə(r)] *n Comput* rôdeur(euse) *m,f*, badaud(e) *m,f*

lurking ['lɜːkɪŋ] *adj (suspicion)* vague; *(danger)* menaçant

Lusaka [luː'sɑːkə] *n* Lusaka

luscious ['lʌʃəs] *adj* (**a**) *(fruit)* succulent; *(colour)* riche (**b**) *(woman)* séduisant; *(lips)* pulpeux

lusciousness ['lʌʃəsnɪs] *n* (**a**) *(of fruit)* succulence *f*; *(of colour)* richesse *f* (**b**) *(of lips)* sensualité *f*

lush [lʌʃ] **1** *adj* (**a**) *(vegetation)* riche, luxuriant; *(fruit)* succulent; *Fig (description)* riche (**b**) *(luxurious)* luxueux

2 *n Fam* poivrot(e) *m,f*

lushed [lʌʃt] *adj Am Fam (drunk)* pété, bourré

lushness ['lʌʃnɪs] *n* (**a**) *(of vegetation)* richesse *f*, luxuriance *f*; *(of fruit)* succulence *f*; *Fig (of description)* richesse *f* (**b**) *(luxuriousness)* luxe *m*

Lusitania [ˌluːsɪ'teɪnjə] *n* (la) Lusitanie *f*; **in Lusitania** en Lusitanie

Lusitanian [ˌluːsɪ'teɪnjən] **1** *n* Lusitanien(enne) *m,f*

2 *adj* lusitanien

lust [lʌst] *n* (**a**) *(sexual desire)* désir *m* sexuel, concupiscence *f*; *(as sin)* luxure *f* (**b**) *(greed)* soif *f*, convoitise *f*; **lust for power** soif *f* de pouvoir

►**lust after** *vt insep (person)* désirer, avoir envie de, convoiter; *(money, property)* convoiter

►**lust for** *vt insep (money)* convoiter; *(revenge, power)* avoir soif de

luster *Am* = **lustre**

lusterware *Am* = **lustreware**

lustful ['lʌstfʊl] *adj* (**a**) *(lecherous)* lascif, sensuel (**b**) *(greedy)* avide

lustfully ['lʌstfʊlɪ] *adv* (**a**) *(lecherously)* lascivement (**b**) *(greedily)* avidement

lustily ['lʌstɪlɪ] *adv (sing, shout)* à pleine gorge, à pleins poumons

lustiness ['lʌstɪnɪs] *n* vigueur *f*

lustral ['lʌstrəl] *adj* (**a**) *(purificatory)* lustral (**b**) *(occurring every five years)* quinquennal

►► *Antiq* **lustral games** jeux *mpl* lustraux; *Rel* ***lustral water*** eau *f* lustrale

lustre, *Am* **luster** ['lʌstə(r)] *n* (**a**) *(sheen)* lustre *m*, brillant *m* (**b**) *Fig (glory)* éclat *m*; *Literary* **to shed lustre on a name** donner du lustre à un nom (**c**) *Cer (glaze)* lustre *m*

lustreless, *Am* **lusterless** ['lʌstəlɪs] *adj* terne, sans éclat

lustreware, *Am* **lusterware** ['lʌstəweə(r)] *n Cer* poterie *f* à reflets métalliques, poterie *f* lustrée

lustrous ['lʌstrəs] *adj* (**a**) *(shiny → pearls, stones)* lustré, chatoyant; *(→ eyes)* brillant; *(→ cloth)* lustré; **lustrous black hair** cheveux *mpl* d'un noir de jais (**b**) *Literary (illustrious → career)* illustre; *(→ name)* glorieux

lustrousness ['lʌstrəsnɪs] *n (of pearls, stones)* brillant *m*; *(of eyes, hair)* éclat *m*; *(of cloth)* lustre *m*

lustrum ['lʌstrəm] (*pl* **lustra** [-trə] *or* **lustrums**) *n Antiq* lustre *m (espace de cinq ans)*

lusty ['lʌstɪ] (*compar* **lustier,** *superl* **lustiest**) *adj (strong → person, baby)* vigoureux, robuste; *(→ voice, manner)* vigoureux

lute [luːt] **1** *n* (**a**) *Mus* luth *m* (**b**) *Tech* lut *m*

2 *vt Tech* luter

►► *Mus* ***lute stop*** jeu *m* de luth

luteal ['luːtɪəl] *adj Biol* lutéal

lutecium = **lutetium**

lutein ['luːtɪɪn] *n Biol & Chem* lutéine *f*

luteinizing hormone ['luːtɪɪnaɪzɪŋ-] *n Biol* hormone *f* lutéinisante

lutenist ['luːtənɪst] *n Mus* joueur(euse) *m,f* de luth, luthiste *mf*

Lutetia [luː'tiːʃə] *n* Lutèce

lutetium [luː'tiːʃəm] *n Chem* lutécium *m*

Luther ['luːθə(r)] *pr n* **Martin Luther** Martin Luther

Lutheran ['luːθərən] **1** *n* Luthérien(enne) *m,f*

2 *adj* luthérien

Lutheranism ['luːθərənɪzəm] *n* luthéranisme *m*

lutz [lʊts] *n (in ice skating)* lutz *m*

luv *Br Fam* = **love**

luvvie ['lʌvɪ] *n Fam Hum* acteur(trice) *m,f* prétentieux(euse) ❑

lux [lʌks] *n Phys* lux *m*

luxate [lʌk'seɪt] *vt Med* luxer

luxation [lʌk'seɪʃən] *n Med* luxation *f*

Luxembourg ['lʌksəmbɜːg] *n* (**a**) *(country)* Luxembourg *m*; **in Luxembourg** au Luxembourg (**b**) *(town)* Luxembourg

►► ***Luxembourg franc*** franc *m* luxembourgeois

Luxembourger ['lʌksəmbɜːgə(r)] *n* Luxembourgeois(e) *m,f*

Luxor ['lʌksɔː(r)] *n* Louqsor, Louxor

luxuriance [lʌg'ʒʊərɪəns] *n* (**a**) *(luxury)* luxe *m*, somptuosité *f* (**b**) *(of vegetation)* luxuriance *f*, richesse *f*; *(of plants)* exubérance *f*, abondance *f*; *(of hair)* abondance *f*

luxuriant [lʌg'ʒʊərɪənt] *adj* (**a**) *(luxurious → surroundings)* luxueux, somptueux (**b**) *(vegetation)* luxuriant; *(crops, undergrowth)* abondant, riche; *(countryside)* couvert de végétation, luxuriant; *Fig (style)* luxuriant, riche (**c**) *(flowing → hair, beard)* abondant

luxuriantly [lʌg'ʒʊərɪəntlɪ] *adv (grow)* en abondance, de façon luxuriante

luxuriate [lʌg'ʒʊərɪeɪt] *vi* (**a**) *(take pleasure)* **to luxuriate in sth** se délecter de qch; **to luxuriate in the sun/in a hot bath** se prélasser au soleil/dans un bain chaud (**b**) *Literary (proliferate, flourish)* proliférer

luxurious [lʌg'ʒʊərɪəs] *adj* (**a**) *(opulent → house, decor, clothes)* luxueux, somptueux; *(→ car)* luxueux; **to have luxurious tastes** avoir des goûts de luxe (**b**) *(voluptuous)* voluptueux

luxuriously [lʌg'ʒʊərɪəslɪ] *adv* (**a**) *(with, in luxury)* luxueusement; **luxuriously furnished** luxueusement *ou* richement meublé; **to live luxuriously** vivre dans le luxe *ou* dans l'opulence (**b**) *(voluptuously)* voluptueusement; **she stretched out luxuriously on the grass** elle s'allongea voluptueusement sur l'herbe

luxuriousness [lʌg'ʒʊərɪəsnɪs] *n* luxe *m*

luxury ['lʌkʃərɪ] (*pl* **luxuries**) **1** *n* (**a**) *(comfort)* luxe *m*; **to live in luxury, to lead a life of luxury** vivre dans le luxe

(**b**) *(treat)* luxe *m*; **whisky is the one luxury I still allow myself** le whisky est le seul luxe que je me permette encore; **one of life's little luxuries** un des petits plaisirs de la vie; **it's a luxury for them to eat meat** manger de la viande est, pour eux, un luxe

2 *comp (car, restaurant, kitchen)* de luxe; *(apartment)* de luxe, de standing

►► ***luxury brand*** marque *f* de luxe; ***luxury goods*** articles *mpl* de luxe; *Fin* ***luxury tax*** taxe *f* (sur les produits) de luxe

LV (*written abbr* **luncheon voucher**) Ticket-Restaurant® *m inv*

LW *Rad* (*written abbr* **long wave**) GO

LWOP ['elwɒp] *n Am* (**a**) (*abbr* **leave without pay**) congé *m* sans solde (**b**) (*abbr* **life without parole**) = réclusion criminelle à perpétuité sans possibilité de remise en liberté conditionnelle

LWT [ˌeldʌbəljuː'tiː] *n* (*abbr* **London Weekend Television**) = chaîne de télévision relevant de l'ITC

lycanthrope ['laɪkənˌθrəʊp] *n* (**a**) *Psy* lycanthrope *mf* (**b**) *(werewolf)* loup-garou *m*

lycanthropy [laɪ'kænθrəpɪ] *n Psy* lycanthropie *f*

lyceum [laɪ'sɪəm] *n* (**a**) *(in names of public buildings)* théâtre *m* (**b**) *Am (hall)* salle *f* publique; *(organization)* association *f* culturelle

lychee [ˌlaɪ'tʃiː] *n* litchi *m*, lychee *m*

lych-gate ['lɪtʃ-] *n* porche *m* de cimetière

Lycia ['lɪsɪə] *n Antiq* Lycie *f*

Lycian ['lɪsɪən] *Antiq* **1** *n* Lycien(enne) *m,f*

2 *adj* lycien

Lycra® ['laɪkrə] *n* Lycra® *m*

lyddite ['lɪdaɪt] *n* lyddite *f*

Lydia ['lɪdɪə] *n Antiq* Lydie *f*

Lydian ['lɪdɪən] *Antiq* **1** *n* Lydien(enne) *m,f*

2 *adj* lydien

►► *Mus* ***Lydian mode*** mode *m* lydien

lye [laɪ] *n Chem* lessive *f*

lying ['laɪɪŋ] **1** *adj* (**a**) *(reclining)* couché, étendu, allongé (**b**) *(dishonest → person)* menteur; *(→ story)* mensonger, faux (fausse); *very Fam* **you lying bastard!** sale menteur!

2 *n* (**a**) *(corpse)* **lying in state** exposition *f* du corps (**b**) *(UNCOUNT) (dishonesty)* mensonges *mpl*

lying-in *n Med* couches *fpl*

Lyme disease [laɪm-] *n* maladie *f* de Lyme

lyme grass [laɪm-] *n* elymus *m*

lymph [lɪmf] *n* lymphe *f*
►► ***lymph gland, lymph node*** ganglion *m Med* lymphatique

lymphadenectomy [lɪmˌfædɪ'nektəmɪ] (*pl* **lymphadenectomies**) *n Med* lymphadénectomie *f*

lymphadenitis [lɪmˌfædɪ'naɪtɪs] *n Med* lymphadénite *f*; *Vet* **caseous lymphadenitis** pseudotuberculose *f*

lymphadenopathy [lɪmˌfædɪ'nɒpəθɪ] *n Méd* lymphadénopathie *f*
►► ***lymphadenopathy associated virus*** virus *m* associé à la lymphadénopathie

lymphangitis [ˌlɪmfæn'dʒaɪtɪs] *n Med* lymphangite *f*

lymphatic [lɪm'fætɪk] *adj* lymphatique
►► ***lymphatic drainage*** drainage *m* lymphatique; ***lymphatic system*** système *m* lymphatique; ***lymphatic tissue*** tissu *m* lymphatique; ***lymphatic vessels*** vaisseaux *mpl* lymphatiques

lymphoblast ['lɪmfəʊˌblæst] *n Biol* lymphoblaste *m*

lymphocyte ['lɪmfəʊsaɪt] *n* lymphocyte *m*

lymphocytosis [ˌlɪmfəʊsaɪ'təʊsɪs] *n Med* lymphocytose *f*

lymphoma [lɪm'fəʊmə] *n Med* lymphome *m*

lymphosarcoma [ˌlɪmfəʊsɑː'kəʊmə] *n Med* lymphosarcome *m*

lynch [lɪntʃ] *vt* lyncher
►► ***lynch law*** loi *f* de Lynch; ***lynch mob*** lyncheurs *mpl*

lynching ['lɪntʃɪŋ] *n* lynchage *m*

lynchpin = **linchpin**

lynx [lɪnks] (*pl* **inv** *or* **lynxes**) *n Zool* lynx *m inv*; *(European)* loup-cervier *m*

lynx-eyed *adj* aux yeux de lynx

Lyon, Lyons [liːɔ̃] *n* Lyon

lyophilic [ˌlaɪəʊ'fɪlɪk] *adj* lyophile

lyophilization [laɪˌɒfɪlaɪ'zeɪʃən] *n* lyophilisation *f*

lyophilize, -ise [laɪ'ɒfɪlaɪz] *vt* lyophiliser

lyophobic [ˌlaɪəʊ'fəʊbɪk] *adj* lyophobe

lyre ['laɪə(r)] *n* lyre *f*

lyrebird ['laɪəbɜːd] *n Orn* oiseau-lyre *m*

lyric ['lɪrɪk] **1** *adj* lyrique
2 *n (poem)* poème *m* lyrique
3 lyrics *npl (of song)* paroles *fpl*
►► ***lyrics writer*** parolier(ère) *m,f*

lyrical ['lɪrɪkəl] *adj* (**a**) *(poetic)* lyrique (**b**) *Fig (enthusiastic)* passionné; **he was positively lyrical about his visit to China** son séjour en Chine l'a véritablement enthousiasmé

'Lyrical Ballads' *Coleridge & Wordsworth* 'Ballades lyriques'

lyrically ['lɪrɪkəlɪ] *adv* (**a**) *(poetically)* avec lyrisme (**b**) *(enthusiastically)* avec enthousiasme; **she spoke/wrote lyrically of her voyage to Africa** elle a évoqué son voyage en Afrique avec beaucoup d'enthousiasme

lyricism ['lɪrɪsɪzəm] *n* lyrisme *m*

lyricist ['lɪrɪsɪst] *n (of poems)* poète *m* lyrique; *(of song, opera)* parolier(ère) *m,f*

Lysander [laɪ'sændə(r)] *pr n* Lysandre

lysergic [laɪ'sɜːdʒɪk] *adj* lysergique
►► ***lysergic acid*** acide *m* lysergique

lysine ['laɪsiːn] *n* lysine *f*

lysis ['laɪsɪs] (*pl* **lyses** [-siːz]) *n Biol* lyse *f*; *Med* lysis *f*

Lysol® ['laɪsɒl] *n Pharm* lysol® *m*

lysosome ['laɪsəsəʊm] *n* lysosome *m*

lytic ['lɪtɪk] *adj Biol* lytique

M[1], m[1] [em] *n (letter)* M, m *m inv*; **two m's** deux m; **M for mother** ≃ M comme Marcel; *Br* **the M5** *(road)* l'autoroute *f* M5

'M' *Lang, Losey* 'M le Maudit'

M[2] *(written abbr* **medium**) M

m[2] (**a**) *(written abbr* **metre**) m (**b**) *(written abbr* **million**) M (**c**) *(written abbr* **mile**) mile *m*

MA[1] [ˌem'eɪ] *n* (**a**) *Univ* (*abbr* **Master of Arts**) *(in England, Wales and US → person)* = titulaire d'une maîtrise de lettres; *(→ qualification)* maîtrise *f* de lettres; *(in Scotland → person)* = titulaire du premier examen universitaire, équivalent de la licence; *(→ qualification)* = premier examen universitaire, équivalent de la licence, **to have an MA in Russian** avoir une maîtrise/licence de russe; **Susan Long, MA** Susan Long, Maîtrise de lettres/licenciée ès lettres (**b**) *(abbr* **military academy**) école *f* militaire

MA[2] *(written abbr* **Massachusetts**) Massachusetts *m*

ma [mɑː] *n Fam* maman *f*; *Hum* **Ma Baker** la mère Baker

ma'am [mæm] *n* madame *f*

Maastricht ['mɑːstrɪkt] *n* Maastricht

Mac [mæk] *n Comput* Mac *m*; **available for the Mac** disponible en version Mac
▸▸ ***Mac disk*** disquette *f* pour Mac; ***Mac OS*** Mac-OS *m*

mac[1] [mæk] *n Am Fam (term of address)* chef *m*

mac[2] *n Br Fam (abbr* **mackintosh**) imper *m*

macabre [mə'kɑːbrə] *adj* macabre

macaco [mə'keɪkəʊ] *n Zool* maki *m*, mococo *m*

macadam [mə'kædəm] **1** *n* macadam *m*
2 *comp (road)* macadamisé, en macadam

macadamia nut [ˌmækə'deɪmɪə-] *n* noix *f* de macadamia

macadamize, -ise [mə'kædəmaɪz] *vt* macadamiser

Macao [mə'kaʊ] *n* Macao; **in Macao** à Macao

macaque [mə'kɑːk] *n Zool* macaque *m*

macaroni [ˌmækə'rəʊnɪ] *n (UNCOUNT)* macaronis *mpl*; **a piece of macaroni** un macaroni
▸▸ *Br* ***macaroni cheese,*** *Am* ***macaroni and cheese*** gratin *m* de macaronis

macaronic [ˌmækə'rɒnɪk] *Literature* **1** *n* vers *m* macaronique, poésie *f* macaronique
2 *adj* macaronique

macaronicism [ˌmækə'rəʊnɪsɪzəm] *n Literature* macaronisme *m*

macaroon [ˌmækə'ruːn] *n Culin* macaron *m*

macassar [mæ'kæsə(r)] *n* macassar *m*
▸▸ ***macassar oil*** huile *f* de macassar; ***macassar wood*** (bois *m* de) macassar *m*

macaw [mə'kɔː] *n Orn* ara *m*

Maccabean [ˌmækə'biːən] *adj Hist* Macchabéen, des Macchabées

Maccabees ['mækəbiːz] *npl Hist* **the Maccabees** les Macchabées

Mac-compatible *adj Comput* compatible Mac

Mace® [meɪs] **1** *n (spray)* gaz *m* lacrymogène
2 *vt Am Fam* bombarder au gaz lacrymogène

mace [meɪs] *n* (**a**) *(spice)* macis *m* (**b**) *(club)* massue *f*, masse *f* d'armes; *(ceremonial)* masse *f*
▸▸ ***mace bearer*** massier *m*

macédoine [ˌmæseɪ'dwɑːn] *n Culin* macédoine *f*

Macedonia [ˌmæsɪ'dəʊnɪə] *n* Macédoine *f*; **in Macedonia** en Macédoine

Macedonian [ˌmæsɪ'dəʊnɪən] **1** *n* (**a**) *(person)* Macédonien(enne) *m,f* (**b**) *(language)* macédonien *m*
2 *adj* macédonien
3 *comp (embassy)* de Macédoine; *(history)* de la Macédoine; *(teacher)* de macédonien

macerate ['mæsəreɪt] **1** *vt* macérer
2 *vi* macérer

maceration [ˌmæsə'reɪʃən] *n* macération *f*

Mach [mæk] *n* Mach; **to fly at Mach 3** voler à Mach 3
▸▸ ***Mach number*** nombre *m* de Mach

machete [mə'ʃetɪ] *n* machette *f*

Machiavelli [ˌmækɪə'velɪ] *pr n* Machiavel

Machiavellian [ˌmækɪə'velɪən] *adj* machiavélique

Machiavellianism [ˌmækɪə'velɪənɪzəm] *n* machiavélisme *m*

machinable [mə'ʃiːnəbəl] *adj* usinable

machinate ['mækɪneɪt] *vt* machiner

machinations [ˌmæʃkɪ'neɪʃənz] *npl* machinations *fpl*

machine [mə'ʃiːn] **1** *n* (**a**) *(mechanical device)* machine *f*; **to do sth by machine** *or* **on a machine** faire qch à la machine
(**b**) *Fig Pej (person)* machine *f*, automate *m*; **he thinks she's just a machine for doing housework** il la considère comme une machine à faire le ménage; **a thinking machine** une machine à penser
(**c**) *Fig (organization)* machine *f*, appareil *m*; **the party machine** l'appareil *m* du parti
(**d**) *(car, motorbike)* machine *f*; *(plane)* appareil *m*
(**e**) *(computer)* ordinateur *m*
2 *vt Sewing* coudre à la machine; *Ind (manufacture)* fabriquer à la machine; *(work on machine)* usiner
▸▸ ***the machine age*** l'ère *f* de la machine; *Comput* ***machine code*** code *m* machine; ***machine gun*** mitrailleuse *f*; ***machine intelligence*** intelligence *f* artificielle; *Comput* ***machine language*** langage *m* machine; ***machine operator*** opérateur(trice) *m,f* (sur machine); ***machine pistol*** mitraillette *f*, pistolet *m* mitrailleur; ***machine room*** salle *f* des machines; ***machine shop*** atelier *m* d'usinage; ***machine time*** temps-machine *m*; ***machine tool*** machine-outil *f*; ***machine tool operator*** machiniste *mf*; *Comput* ***machine translation*** traduction *f* assistée par ordinateur

▸**machine down** *vt sep Ind (metal)* amincir

machine-cut *vt* tailler à la machine

machined [mə'ʃiːnd] *adj Sewing* cousu à la machine; *Ind* usiné

machine-down time *n* = durée d'immobilisation d'une machine

machine finish *vt (paper)* apprêter (à la machine), calandrer; *(clothes)* finir à la machine

machine-finished *adj (paper)* apprêté, calandré; *(clothes)* fini à la machine

machine-gun *vt* mitrailler

machine-gunner *n* mitrailleur *m*

machine-gunning [-'gʌnɪŋ] *n* mitraillage *m*

machine-hour *n* heure-machine *f*

machine-made *adj* fait à la machine

machine-produced *adj* fait à la machine *ou* en série

machine-readable *adj Comput* lisible par ordinateur

machinery [mə'ʃiːnərɪ] *(pl* **machineries**) *n* (**a**) *(UNCOUNT) (machines)* machines *fpl*, machinerie *f*; *(mechanism)* mécanisme *m* (**b**) *Fig* rouages *mpl*; **the machinery of state/of government** les rouages de l'État/du gouvernement

machine-stitch **1** *n* point *m* (de piqûre) à la machine
2 *vt* piquer (à la machine)

machine-time intensive *adj* qui nécessite beaucoup de temps-machine

machine-washable *adj* lavable à la *ou* en machine

machining [mə'ʃiːnɪŋ] *n Ind* usinage *m*

machinist [mə'ʃiːnɪst] *n* (**a**) *Ind* opérateur(trice) *m,f* (sur machine) (**b**) *Sewing* mécanicien(enne) *m,f*

machismo [mə'tʃɪzməʊ, mə'kɪzməʊ] *n* machisme *m*

machmeter ['mækˌmiːtə(r)] *n* machmètre *m*

macho ['mætʃəʊ] **1** *n* macho *m*
2 *adj* macho

Machu Picchu [ˌmætʃuː'pɪtʃuː] *n* Machu Picchu

macintosh = **mackintosh**

mack [mæk] *n Am Fam* (**a**) *(pimp)* maquereau *m*, mac *m* (**b**) *(seducer)* tombeur *m*

▸**mack on** *vt insep Am Fam* **to mack on sb** draguer qn

mackerel ['mækərəl] *(pl* **inv** *or* **mackerels**) *n Ich* maquereau *m*
▸▸ *Ich* ***mackerel shark*** touille *f*; ***mackerel sky*** ciel *m* pommelé

Mackinaw coat ['mækɪnɔː-] *n Am* = grosse veste de laine croisée à carreaux

mackintosh ['mækɪntɒʃ] *n Br* imperméable *m*

mackle ['mækəl] *Typ* **1** *n* maculage *m*
2 *vt* mâchurer

mackled ['mækəld] *adj Typ* bavocheux

mackling ['mækəlɪŋ] *n Typ* maculage *m*

Mack truck® [mæk-] *n Am* = semi-remorque à seize roues

macle ['mækəl] *n* macle *f*

macramé [mə'krɑːmɪ] **1** *n* macramé *m*
2 *comp* en macramé

macro ['mækrəʊ] *(pl* **macros**) *n Comput* macro-instruction *f*, macro *f*, macrocommande *f*
▸▸ ***macro instruction*** macroinstruction *f*; ***macro language*** macrolangage *m*; ***macro virus*** virus *m* de macro

macro- ['mækrəʊ] *pref* macro-

macrobiotic [ˌmækrəʊbaɪ'ɒtɪk] **1** *adj* macrobiotique
2 macrobiotics *n (UNCOUNT)* macrobiotique *f*

macrocephalic [ˌmækrəʊse'fælɪk], **macrocephalous** [ˌmækrəʊ'sefələs] *adj Anat* macrocéphale

macrocephaly [ˌmækrəʊ'sefəlɪ] *n Anat* macrocéphalie *f*

macrochemical [ˌmækrəʊ'kemɪkəl] *adj* macrochimique

macrochemistry [ˌmækrəʊ'kemɪstrɪ] *n* macrochimie *f*

macroclimate ['mækrəʊˌklaɪmət] *n* macroclimat *m*

macroclimatic [ˌmækrəʊklaɪ'mætɪk] *adj* macroclimatique

macrocomputing [ˌmækrəʊkəm'pjuːtɪŋ] *n Comput* macroinformatique *f*

macrocosm ['mækrəʊˌkɒzəm] *n* macrocosme *m*

macrocosmic [ˌmækrəʊ'kɒzmɪk] *adj* macrocosmique

macrocyte ['mækrəʊsaɪt] *n Med* macrocyte *m*

macrocytic [ˌmækrəʊ'sɪtɪk] *adj Med* macrocytaire

macrocytosis [ˌmækrəʊsaɪ'təʊsɪs] *n Med* macrocytose *f*

macrodecision [ˌmækrəʊdɪ'sɪʒən] *n* macrodécision *f*

macroeconomic ['mækrəʊˌiːkə'nɒmɪk] **1** *adj* macroéconomique
2 macroeconomics *n (UNCOUNT)* macroéconomie *f*

macroenvironment [ˌmækrəʊɪnˈvaɪərənmənt] *n Mktg* macroenvironnement *m*

macrofauna [ˌmækrəʊˈfɔːnə] *npl Ecol* macrofaune *f*; **soil macrofauna** macrofaune *f* du sol

macroglobulin [ˌmækrəʊˈglɒbjʊlɪn] *n* macroglobuline *f*

macroglobulinaemia [ˈmækrəʊˌglɒbjʊlɪˈniːmɪə] *n Med* macroglobulinémie *f*

macrograph [ˈmækrəʊˌgrɑːf] *n* épreuve *f* macrographique, macrographie *f*

macrographic [ˌmækrəʊˈgræfɪk] *adj* macrographique

macroinstruction [ˌmækrəʊɪnˈstrʌkʃən] *n Comput* macroinstruction *f*

macromarketing [ˌmækrəʊˈmɑːkɪtɪŋ] *n* macromarketing *m*

macromolecular [ˌmækrəʊməˈlekjʊlə(r)] *adj Chem* macromoléculaire

macromolecule [ˌmækrəʊˈmɒlɪkjuːl] *n Chem* macromolécule *f*

macromutation [ˌmækrəʊmjuːˈteɪʃən] *n Biol* macromutation *f*

macron [ˈmækrɒn] *n Typ* macron *m*

macronutrient [ˌmækrəʊˈnjuːtrɪənt] *nm Physiol* macronutriment *m*, macronutrient *m*

macrophage [ˈmækrəʊfeɪdʒ] *n Physiol* macrophage *m*

macrophagic [ˌmækrəʊˈfeɪdʒɪk] *adj Physiol* macrophage

macrophotographic [ˌmækrəʊfəʊtəˈgræfɪk] *adj* macrophotographique, photomacrographique

macrophotography [ˌmækrəʊfəˈtɒgrəfɪ] *n* macrophotographie *f*, photomacrographie *f*

macrophysics [ˌmækrəʊˈfɪzɪks] *n (UNCOUNT)* macrophysique *f*

macropod [ˈmækrəʊpɒd] *n Zool* macropodidé *m*

macropterous [məˈkrɒptərəs] *adj Zool* macropode

macroscopic [ˌmækrəʊˈskɒpɪk] *adj* macroscopique

macrosegment [ˈmækrəʊˌsegmənt] *n Mktg* macrosegment *m*

macrosegmentation [ˈmækrəʊˌsegmənˈteɪʃən] *n Mktg* macrosegmentation *f*

macrosociology [ˈmækrəʊˌsəʊsɪˈɒlədʒɪ] *n* macrosociologie *f*

macrosporangium [ˈmækrəʊˌspəˈrændʒɪəm] *n Bot* macrosporange *m*

macrostructure [ˈmækrəʊˌstrʌktʃə(r)] *n* macrostructure *f*

MACRS [ˌemeɪˌsiːɑːˈres] *n Am Acct* (*abbr* **modified accelerated cost recovery system**) = méthode d'amortissement accéléré

macruran [məˈkrʊərən] *n Zool* macroure *m*

macula [ˈmækjʊlə] (*pl* **maculae** [-liː]) *n* (**a**) *Med* macule *f* (**b**) *Anat (on retina)* tache *f* jaune, macula *f*

▸▸ ***macula acustica*** tache *f* auditive; ***macula lutea*** macula *f* (lutea)

macular [ˈmækjʊlə(r)] *adj Med* pigmentaire, maculeux

maculation [ˌmækjʊˈleɪʃən] *n* maculation *f*, maculage *m*

MAD [mæd] *n* (**a**) *Am Nucl* (*abbr* **mutual assured destruction**) = équilibre de la terreur (**b**) *Acct* (*abbr* **mean absolute deviation**) écart *m* moyen absolu

mad [mæd] **1** *adj* (**a**) *esp Br (crazy)* fou (folle); **to go mad** devenir fou; **you must have been mad to do it** il fallait être fou pour faire ça; **that's a mad idea** c'est une idée folle *ou* insensée; **to be mad with joy/grief** être fou de joie/douleur; **it's a case of patriotism gone mad** c'est du patriotisme poussé à l'extrême *ou* qui frise la folie; **to drive sb mad** rendre qn fou; **it's enough to drive you mad** il y a de quoi devenir fou, c'est à vous rendre fou; **you're driving me mad with all your questions** tu me rends fou avec toutes tes questions; **to be as mad as a hatter** *or* **a March hare** être fou à lier; *Am Press* **MAD (magazine)** = magazine satirique très populaire

(**b**) *(absurd → ambition, plan)* fou (folle), insensé; **he's always full of mad schemes for making money** il a toujours des plans insensés pour se faire de l'argent

(**c**) *(angry)* en colère, furieux; **he went mad when he saw them** il s'est mis dans une colère noire en les voyant; **to be mad at** *or* **with sb** être en colère *ou* fâché contre qn; **she makes me mad** elle m'énerve; **don't get mad** ne vous fâchez pas

(**d**) *(frantic)* **there was a mad rush for the door** tous les gens se sont rués vers la porte comme des fous; *Fam* **I'm in a mad rush** je suis très pressé ❑, je suis à la bourre; **there was a mad panic to sell** les gens n'avaient plus qu'une idée en tête, vendre; *Fig* **don't go mad and try to do it all yourself** tu ne vas pas te tuer à essayer de tout faire toi-même?; *Fam* **to run like mad** courir comme un fou *ou* un dératé; *Fam* **they were arguing like mad** ils discutaient comme des perdus; *Fam* **the kettle was boiling away like mad** la bouilloire s'emballait

(**e**) *Fam (enthusiastic, keen)* **to be mad about** *or* **on sth** être fou (folle) *ou* dingue de qch; **she's mad about cats** elle adore les chats ❑; **he's mad about her** il est fou d'elle; **I can't say I'm mad about going** je ne peux pas dire que ça m'emballe *ou* que je meure d'envie d'y aller; *Br* **to be mad for it** *(raring to go)* être prêt à s'éclater

(**f**) *(dog)* enragé; *(bull)* furieux

2 *n Am Fam* accès *m* de colère ❑; **to have a mad on** être en pétard

3 *adv Br Fam* **to be mad keen on** *or* **about sth** être dingue *ou* un(une) mordu(e) de qch

▸▸ *Vet* ***mad cow disease*** maladie *f* de la vache folle; *Fam Fin* ***mad dog*** *(company)* société *f* en pleine expansion ❑; **there are several rising mad dogs in the IT sector** il existe plusieurs sociétés en pleine expansion dans le secteur de l'informatique ❑

Madagascan [ˌmædəˈgæskən] **1** *n* Malgache *mf*

2 *adj* malgache

Madagascar [ˌmædəˈgæskə(r)] *n* Madagascar *f*; **in Madagascar** à Madagascar

madam [ˈmædəm] *n* (**a**) *Formal (form of address)* madame *f*; **Dear Madam** (Chère) Madame; **madam Chairman** Madame la Présidente; *Br Fam* **that's enough of your cheek, madam!** ça suffit comme ça, petite insolente! (**b**) *Br Fam Pej (arrogant girl)* **she's a little madam** c'est une petite pimbêche (**c**) *Fam (of brothel)* (mère *f*) maquerelle *f*

madcap [ˈmædˌkæp] **1** *n* fou (folle) *m,f*, hurluberlu(e) *m,f*

2 *adj* fou (folle), insensé; **a madcap scheme** un projet insensé

MADD [mæd] *n Am* (*abbr* **Mothers Against Drunk Driving**) = association américaine de lutte contre l'alcool au volant, fondée par la mère d'une enfant tuée par un conducteur en état d'ébriété

madden [ˈmædən] *vt (drive insane)* rendre fou (folle); *(exasperate)* exaspérer, rendre fou (folle); **her silence maddened him** son silence l'exaspérait

maddening [ˈmædənɪŋ] *adj* exaspérant; **a maddening noise** un bruit à vous rendre fou; **the really maddening thing is that we could so easily have won** ce qui est rageant c'est qu'on aurait facilement pu gagner

maddeningly [ˈmædənɪŋlɪ] *adv* de façon exaspérante; **a maddeningly long wait** une attente interminable; **maddeningly slow** d'une lenteur exaspérante

madder [ˈmædə(r)] *n Bot & Tex* garance *f*

▸▸ *Bot* ***madder root*** alizari *m*

madding [ˈmædɪŋ] *adj Arch or Literary* effréné, frénétique

made [meɪd] *pt & pp of* **make**

-made [meɪd] *suff* **factory-made** industriel; **British-made** fabriqué au Royaume-Uni; **man-made** *(gen)* artificiel; *(fabric, fibre)* synthétique

Madeira [məˈdɪərə] *n* (**a**) *(island)* Madère; **in Madeira** à Madère (**b**) *(wine)* vin *m* de Madère, madère *m*

▸▸ ***Madeira cake*** ≃ quatre-quarts *m inv*

made-to-measure *adj* (fait) sur mesure

made-to-order *adj* (fait) sur commande

made-up *adj* (**a**) *(wearing make-up)* maquillé; **a heavily made-up face** un visage très maquillé (**b**) *(invented → story)* fabriqué; *(→ evidence)* faux (fausse) (**c**) *NEng Fam (very pleased)* vachement content

madhouse [ˈmædhaʊs, *pl* -haʊzɪz] *n Fam also Fig* maison *f* de fous; **the place was a complete madhouse when we arrived** lorsque nous sommes arrivés, on se serait crus dans une maison de fous

Madison Avenue [ˈmædɪsən-] *n* = rue de New York dont le nom évoque le milieu de la publicité

Madison Square Garden *n* = grande salle à New York où ont lieu concerts et événements sportifs

madly [ˈmædlɪ] *adv* (**a**) *(passionately)* follement; **madly excited** surexcité; **madly in love** éperdument *ou* follement amoureux; **madly jealous** fou (folle) de jalousie; **I can't say I'm madly interested in it** je ne peux pas dire que ça m'intéresse follement

(**b**) *(frantically)* comme un fou (une folle), frénétiquement; *(wildly)* comme un fou (une folle), follement; **to run/to shout madly** courir/crier comme un fou (une folle); **the dog was barking madly** le chien aboyait frénétiquement

(**c**) *(desperately)* désespérément; **she was madly trying to contact her parents** elle essayait désespérément de contacter ses parents

madman [ˈmædmən] (*pl* **madmen** [-mən]) *n* fou *m*, aliéné *m*; **he's a complete madman!** il est complètement fou!

madness [ˈmædnɪs] *n* (**a**) *(insanity)* folie *f*, démence *f*; **in a fit of madness** dans un accès *ou* dans un moment de folie (**b**) *(folly)* folie *f*; **it's madness even to think of going away now** il faut être fou pour songer à partir maintenant

Madonna [məˈdɒnə] *pr n Rel* Madone *f*; *(image)* madone *f*

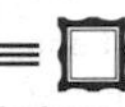

'Madonna and Child' 'Vierge à l'enfant'

Madras [məˈdrɑːs] *n* Madras

madras [məˈdrɑːs] *n* madras *m*

▸▸ ***madras curry*** curry *m* de Madras

madrepore [ˈmædrɪpɔː(r)] *n Zool* madrépore *m*

madreporite [ˌmædrɪˈpɔːraɪt] *n Zool* madréporite *f*, plaque *f* madréporique

Madrid [məˈdrɪd] *n* Madrid

madrigal [ˈmædrɪgəl] *n Mus* madrigal *m*

madrigalist [ˈmædrɪgəlɪst] *n* madrigaliste *mf*

madwoman [ˈmædˌwʊmən] (*pl* **madwomen** [-ˌwɪmɪn]) *n* folle *f*, aliénée *f*

Maecenas [miːˈsiːnæs] *pr n Antiq* Mécène

maelstrom [ˈmeɪlˌstrɒm] *n* maelström *m*, malstrom *m*; *Fig* **a maelstrom of violence** un ouragan de violence; *Fig* **the maelstrom of modern life** le tourbillon de la vie moderne

maenad [ˈmiːnæd] *n Myth* ménade *f*

maestro [ˈmaɪstrəʊ] (*pl* **maestros**) *n* maestro *m*; **he's a real maestro on the violin** c'est un vrai virtuose du violon

Mae West [ˌmeɪˈwest] *n Am Fam Old-fashioned* gilet *m* de sauvetage (gonflable) ❑

MAFF [mæf] *n Br* (*abbr* **Ministry of Agriculture, Fisheries and Food**) ≃ ministère *m* de l'Agriculture

mafia [ˈmæfɪə] **1** *n Fig* mafia *f*, maffia *f*

2 Mafia *n* **the Mafia** la Mafia, la Maffia

mafioso [ˌmæfɪˈəʊsəʊ] (*pl* **mafiosi** [-siː]) *n* mafioso *m*, maffioso *m*

mag[1] [mæg] *n Fam (magazine)* revue ❑ *f*, magazine ❑ *m*

mag[2] *adj* (*abbr* **magnetic**)

▸▸ ***mag tape*** bande *f* magnétique; ***mag tape cassette*** cassette *f* à bande magnétique; ***mag tape reader*** lecteur *m* de bandes magnétiques

magazine [ˌmægəˈziːn] *n* (**a**) *(publication)* magazine *m*, revue *f*; *Rad & TV (programme)* magazine *m* (télévisé), émission *f* magazine

(**b**) *(in gun)* magasin *m*; *(cartridges)* chargeur *m*

(**c**) *Mil (store)* magasin *m*; *(for weapons)* dépôt *m* d'armes; *(munitions)* munitions *fpl*

(**d**) *Phot* magasin *m*; *(for slides)* panier *m*, magasin *m*

▸▸ *Rad & TV* ***magazine programme*** magazine *m* (télévisé), émission *f* magazine; ***magazine rack*** porte-revues *m*; ***magazine rifle*** fusil *m* à répétition *ou* à chargeur

Magdalene [ˈmægdəlɪn] *pr n Bible* **Mary Magdalene** Marie Madeleine

Magellan [məˈgelən] *pr n* Magellan; **the Strait of Magellan** le détroit de Magellan

Magellanic [ˌmægɪ'lænɪk] *adj* magellanique
▸▸ *Astron* ***Magellanic clouds*** Nuages *fpl* de Magellan

magenta [mə'dʒentə] **1** *n* magenta *m*
2 *adj* magenta *(inv)*

Maggiore [ˌmædʒɪ'ɔːrɪ] *n* **Lake Maggiore** le lac Majeur

maggot ['mægət] *n* asticot *m*

maggoty ['mægətɪ] *adj (food)* véreux

Maghreb ['mɑːgrəb] *n* **the Maghreb** le Maghreb; **in the Maghreb** au Maghreb

Magi ['meɪdʒaɪ] *npl Bible* **the Magi** les Rois *mpl* mages

magic ['mædʒɪk] **1** *n* (**a**) *(enchantment)* magie *f*; *Fig* **like** *or* **as if by magic** comme par enchantement *ou* magie; **the medicine worked like magic** le remède a fait merveille
(**b**) *(conjuring)* magie *f*, prestidigitation *f*
(**c**) *(special quality)* magie *f*; **the magic of Greta Garbo** la magie *ou* le charisme de Greta Garbo; **discover the magic of Greece** découvrez les merveilles de la Grèce; **the magic had gone out of their marriage** leur vie conjugale n'avait plus rien de magique
2 *adj* (**a**) *(supernatural)* magique; **just say the magic words** il suffit de dire la formule magique; *Fam* **say the magic word!** *(say please!)* qu'est-ce qu'on dit?
(**b**) *(special → formula, moment)* magique
(**c**) *Br Fam (excellent)* super, génial
▸▸ ***magic carpet*** tapis *m* volant; ***the Magic Circle*** = association britannique de magiciens; ***magic eye*** œil *m* cathodique *ou* magique; ***the Magic Kingdom*** = surnom de Disneyland; ***magic lantern*** lanterne *f* magique; *Fam* ***magic mushroom*** champignons *mpl* (hallucinogènes); ***magic number*** nombre *m* magique; *Literature* ***Magic Realism*** réalisme *m* magique; ***magic spell*** sortilège *m*; ***magic square*** carré *m* magique; ***magic wand*** baguette *f* magique
▸**magic away** *vt sep* faire disparaître comme par enchantement

'The Magic Flute' *Mozart* 'La Flûte enchantée'

'The Magic Roundabout' 'Le Manège enchanté'

magical ['mædʒɪkəl] *adj* magique; **her songs had a magical quality** ses chansons avaient quelque chose de magique
▸▸ *Literature* ***Magical Realism*** réalisme *m* magique

> **A magical mystery tour**
> Il s'agit du titre d'un album des Beatles de 1967, que l'on pourrait traduire par "voyage mystère". Aujourd'hui on utilise cette expression à propos d'un long trajet dont la destination est incertaine; on dira par exemple **the guide led us on a magical mystery tour around the Kent countryside in search of the country pub that he remembered from his youth** ("le guide nous a fait parcourir la campagne du Kent dans tous les sens à la recherche d'un pub qu'il connaissait dans sa jeunesse")

magically ['mædʒɪkəlɪ] *adv* magiquement; **don't think it will just happen magically** ne t'imagine pas que cela va se produire comme par enchantement

magician [mə'dʒɪʃən] *n* magicien(enne) *m,f*

magilp [mə'gɪlp] *n Art* = mélange d'huile de lin et de vernis au mastic utilisé en peinture

Maginot Line ['mæʒɪˌnəʊ-] *n Hist* ligne *f* Maginot

magisterial [ˌmædʒɪ'stɪərɪəl] *adj* (**a**) *Law* de magistrat (**b**) *Fig* magistral

magisterially [ˌmædʒɪ'stɪərɪəlɪ] *adv* magistralement

magistracy ['mædʒɪstrəsɪ] (*pl* **magistracies**) *n* magistrature *f*

magistral [mə'dʒɪstrəl] *adj* magistral

magistrate ['mædʒɪstreɪt] *n* magistrat *m*
▸▸ *Eng Law* ***magistrates' court*** = tribunal de première instance compétent en matière civile et pénale

maglev ['mæglev] *n Transp* (*abbr* **magnetic levitation**) lévitation *f* magnétique
▸▸ ***maglev train*** train *m* à lévitation magnétique

magma ['mægmə] *n Geol* magma *m*

magmatic [ˌmæg'mætɪk] *adj Geol* magmatique
▸▸ ***magmatic water*** eau *f* magmatique *ou* juvénile

Magna Carta, Magna Charta [ˌmægnə'kɑːtə] *n Br Hist* la Grande Charte

> **MAGNA CARTA** 
> Souvent prise pour le symbole de la lutte contre l'oppression, cette charte, imposée en 1215 au roi Jean sans Terre par les barons anglais, énonce les droits et privilèges des nobles, de l'Église et des hommes libres ("freemen") face à l'arbitraire royal.

magna cum laude [ˌmægnəkʊm'laʊdeɪ] *adv Univ* avec mention très bien

magnaflux test ['mægnəflʌks-] *n Electron* essai *m* magnétique à la limaille

magnanimity [ˌmægnə'nɪmətɪ] *n* magnanimité *f*

magnanimous [ˌmæg'nænɪməs] *adj* magnanime

magnanimously [ˌmæg'nænɪməslɪ] *adv* avec magnanimité, magnanimement

magnate ['mægneɪt] *n* magnat *m*; **a press magnate** un magnat de la presse

magnesia [mæg'niːʃə] *n Chem* magnésie *f*

magnesium [mæg'niːzɪəm] *n Chem* magnésium *m*
▸▸ ***magnesium hydroxide*** hydroxyde *m* de magnésium; ***magnesium oxide*** magnésie *f*, oxyde *m* de magnésium

magnet ['mægnɪt] *n* (**a**) *Phys* aimant *m* (**b**) *Fig (for tourists etc)* pôle *m* d'attraction; *Fam* **his new car's a babe** *or* **chick magnet** sa nouvelle voiture est super pour emballer les gonzesses
▸▸ *Am* ***magnet school*** = lycée spécialisé dans une matière donnée en plus des disciplines habituelles

magnetic [mæg'netɪk] *adj* magnétique; *Fig* **a magnetic personality** une personnalité magnétique *ou* charismatique
▸▸ *Comput* ***magnetic bubble*** mémoire *f* à bulles; *Comput* ***magnetic card*** carte *f* magnétique; *Comput* ***magnetic character reader*** lecteur *m* de cartes; *Comput* ***magnetic disk*** disque *m* magnétique; *(floppy)* disquette *f* magnétique; *Comput* ***magnetic drive*** dérouleur *m* de bande magnétique, unité *f* de bande magnétique; *Comput* ***magnetic drum*** tambour *m* magnétique; ***magnetic equator*** équateur *m* magnétique; ***magnetic field*** champ *m* magnétique; *Phys* ***magnetic flux*** flux *m* (d'induction) magnétique; *Phys* ***magnetic induction*** induction *f* magnétique; *Comput* ***magnetic ink character recognition*** reconnaissance *f* magnétique de caractères; *Phys* ***magnetic levitation*** lévitation *f* magnétique; ***magnetic lock*** serrure *f* magnétique; ***magnetic media*** supports *mpl* magnétiques; *Phys* ***magnetic moment*** moment *m* magnétique; ***magnetic mine*** mine *f* magnétique; ***magnetic needle*** aiguille *f* aimantée; ***magnetic north*** nord *m* magnétique; ***magnetic pole*** pôle *m* magnétique; *Med* ***magnetic resonance imaging*** imagerie *f* par résonance magnétique; ***magnetic storm*** orage *m* magnétique; ***magnetic strip, magnetic stripe*** piste *f* magnétique; ***magnetic stripe card*** carte *f* à piste magnétique; ***magnetic stripe reader*** lecteur *m* de pistes magnétiques; ***magnetic tape*** bande *f* magnétique; *Comput* ***magnetic tape unit*** dérouleur *m* de bande magnétique, unité *f* de bande magnétique

magnetically [mæg'netɪkəlɪ] *adv* magnétiquement

magnetism ['mægnɪtɪzəm] *n* magnétisme *m*

magnetite ['mægnɪtaɪt] *n Geol* magnétite *f*

magnetization [ˌmægnɪtaɪ'zeɪʃən] *n Phys* aimantation *f*, magnétisation *f*
▸▸ ***magnetization coefficient*** coefficient *m* d'aimantation; ***magnetization curve*** courbe *f* de magnétisation

magnetize, -ise ['mægnɪtaɪz] *vt* (**a**) *Phys* aimanter, magnétiser (**b**) *Fig (charm)* magnétiser; **he was magnetized by her good looks** il était fasciné par sa beauté

magnetizing ['mægnɪtaɪzɪŋ] *adj (current, field etc)* magnétisant
▸▸ *Phys* ***magnetizing coil*** bobine *f* d'aimantation

magneto [mæg'niːtəʊ] *n Elec* magnéto *f*
▸▸ ***magneto bell*** sonnerie *f* magnétique, sonnette *f* à magnéto; ***magneto booster*** magnéto *f* de départ; ***magneto (telephone) system*** système *m* téléphonique à magnéto

magnetochemical [mægˌniːtəʊ'kemɪkəl] *adj* magnétochimique

magneto-electric *adj Phys* magnétoélectrique

magnetometer [ˌmægnɪ'tɒmɪtə(r)] *n Phys* magnétomètre *m*

magneton ['mægnɪtɒn] *n Phys* magnéton *m*

magneto-optical *adj Comput* magnéto-optique

magnetosphere [mæg'niːtəʊˌsfɪə(r)] *n* magnétosphère *f*

magnetostatics [mægˌniːtəʊ'stætɪks] *n (UNCOUNT) Phys* magnétostatique *f*

magnetron ['mægnɪtrɒn] *n Phys* magnétron *m*

magnific [mæg'nɪfɪk] *adj Arch or Literary* magnifique

magnificat [mæg'nɪfɪkæt] *n Rel* magnificat *m inv*; **the Magnificat** le Magnificat

magnification [ˌmægnɪfɪ'keɪʃən] *n* (**a**) *Opt* grossissement *m*; *(acoustics)* amplification *f* (**b**) *Rel* glorification *f*

magnificence [mæg'nɪfɪsəns] *n* magnificence *f*, splendeur *f*

magnificent [mæg'nɪfɪsənt] *adj* magnifique, splendide; **Lorenzo the Magnificent** Laurent le Magnifique

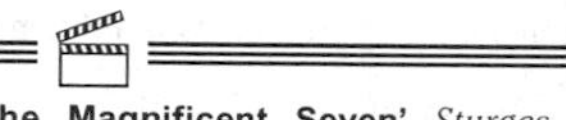
'The Magnificent Seven' *Sturges* 'Les Sept Mercenaires'

'The Magnificent Ambersons' *Welles* 'La Splendeur des Amberson'

magnificently [mæg'nɪfɪsəntlɪ] *adv* magnifiquement

magnifico [mæg'nɪfɪkəʊ] (*pl* **magnificos** *or* **magnificoes**) *n* grand seigneur *m*

magnifier ['mægnɪfaɪə(r)] *n Opt* verre *m* grossissant

magnify ['mægnɪfaɪ] (*pt & pp* **magnified**) *vt* (**a**) *Opt* grossir; *(acoustics)* amplifier; *Comput* agrandir (**b**) *(exaggerate)* exagérer, grossir; **the incident was magnified out of all proportion** on a terriblement exagéré l'importance de cet incident (**c**) *Literary (exalt)* exalter, magnifier; *Rel* glorifier

magnifying ['mægnɪfaɪɪŋ] *adj*
▸▸ ***magnifying glass*** loupe *f*; *Opt* ***magnifying power*** *(of lens, microscope)* grossissement *m*

magniloquence [mæg'nɪləkwəns] *n Formal* grandiloquence *f*, emphase *f*

magniloquent [mæg'nɪləkwənt] *adj Formal* grandiloquent, emphatique

magnitude ['mægnɪtjuːd] *n* (**a**) *(scale)* ampleur *f*, étendue *f*; *Astron & Geol* magnitude *f*; *Math* grandeur *f*, valeur *f*; *Astron* **star of the first magnitude** étoile *f* de première magnitude; **magnitude 7 on the Richter scale** magnitude 7 sur l'échelle (de) Richter (**b**) *(of problem → importance)* importance *f*; *(→ size)* ampleur *f*; *Fig* **of the first magnitude** de premier ordre

magnolia [mæg'nəʊlɪə] **1** *n Bot* magnolia *m*
2 *adj* couleur magnolia *(inv)*, blanc rosé *(inv)*
▸▸ ***the Magnolia State*** = surnom donné au Mississippi

magnox® ['mægnɒks] *n* Magnox® *m*

magnum ['mægnəm] *n (wine bottle, gun)* magnum *m*

magnum opus *n* œuvre *f* maîtresse, chef-d'œuvre *m*

magpie ['mægpaɪ] *n* (**a**) *Orn* pie *f* (**b**) *Fam Fig (chatterbox)* pie *f*, moulin *m* à paroles; *Br (hoarder)* chiffonnier(ère) *m,f*

magus ['meɪgəs] (*pl* **magi** [-dʒaɪ]) *n* mage *m*

MAG welding [mæg-] *n Tech* (*abbr* **metallic active-gas**) soudage *m* MAG

Magyar ['mægjɑː(r)] **1** *n* (**a**) *(person)* Magyar(e) *m,f* (**b**) *Ling* magyar *m*
2 *adj* magyar

Magyarization [ˌmægjəraɪ'zeɪʃən] *n* magyarisation *f*

Magyarize, -ise ['mægjəraɪz] *vt* magyariser

maharaja, maharajah [ˌmɑːhə'rɑːdʒə] *n* maharaja *m*, maharadjah *m*

mag–mah

maharani [ˌmɑːhəˈrɑːniː] *n* maharani *f*

maharishi [ˌmɑːhəˈriːʃɪ] *n* maharishi *m*

mahatma [məˈhɑːtmə] *n Rel* mahatma *m*

Mahayana [ˌmɑːhəˈjɑːnə] *Rel* **1** *n* Mahayana *m*

2 *adj* du Mahayana

▸▸ ***Mahayana Buddhism*** Mahayana *m*

Mahdi [ˈmɑːdɪ] *n Rel* mahdi *m*

Mahdism [ˈmɑːdɪzəm] *n Rel* mahdisme *m*

Mahdist [ˈmɑːdɪst] *Rel* **1** *n* mahdiste *mf*

2 *adj* mahdiste

mah-jong, mah-jongg [mɑːˈdʒɒŋ] *n* mah-jong *m*

mahogany [məˈhɒɡənɪ] (*pl* **mahoganies**) **1** *n (wood, colour)* acajou *m*

2 *adj* (**a**) *(colour)* acajou *(inv)* (**b**) *(furniture)* en acajou

▸▸ ***mahogany brown*** brun acajou *(inv)*; ***mahogany tree*** acajou *m*

Mahomet [məˈhɒmɪt] *pr n Old-fashioned Rel* Mahomet

Mahometan [məˈhɒmɪtən] *Old-fashioned Rel* **1** *n* Mahométan(e) *m,f*

2 *adj* mahométan

Mahometanism [məˈhɒmɪtənɪzəm] *n Old-fashioned Rel* islamisme *m*

mahout [məˈhaʊt] *n* cornac *m*

MAI [ˌemeɪˈaɪ] *n Fin (abbr* **multilateral agreement on investment**) AMI *m*

maid [meɪd] *n* (**a**) *(servant)* bonne *f*, domestique *f*; *(in hotel)* femme *f* de chambre; **maid of all work** bonne *f* à tout faire; **lady's maid** femme *f* de chambre

(**b**) *Literary* jeune fille *f*, demoiselle *f*

(**c**) *Pej* **old maid** vieille fille *f*

▸▸ ***maid of honour*** *(to queen)* demoiselle *f* d'honneur; *Am (at wedding)* première demoiselle *f* d'honneur; *Br Culin (cake)* petit gâteau *m* aux amandes; ***Maid Marian*** Marianne *(dans les histoires de Robin des Bois)*; ***the Maid of Orléans*** la Pucelle d'Orléans; ***maid service*** *(at self-catering apartment)* service *m* de femme de ménage

maiden [ˈmeɪdən] *n* (**a**) *Literary (young girl)* jeune fille *f*; *(virgin)* vierge *f* (**b**) *Sport* **maiden (over)** *(in cricket)* = série de six balles pendant laquelle aucun point n'est marqué

▸▸ ***maiden aunt*** tante *f* célibataire; ***maiden flight*** premier vol *m*, vol *m* inaugural; ***maiden name*** nom *m* de jeune fille; *Br* ***maiden speech*** = premier discours prononcé par un parlementaire nouvellement élu; ***maiden voyage*** voyage *m* inaugural

maidenhair [ˈmeɪdənheə(r)] *n Bot (fern)* capillaire *m*, cheveu-de-Vénus *m*

▸▸ ***maidenhair fern*** capillaire *m*, cheveu-de-Vénus *m*

maidenhead [ˈmeɪdənhed] *n Literary (hymen)* hymen *m*; *(virginity)* virginité *f*

maidenhood [ˈmeɪdənhʊd] *n* virginité *f*

maidenly [ˈmeɪdənlɪ] *adj* virginal

maid-in-waiting (*pl* **maids-in-waiting**) *n* dame *f* d'honneur

maidservant [ˈmeɪdˌsɜːvənt] *n* servante *f*

maieutics [meɪˈjuːtɪks] *n (UNCOUNT) Phil* maïeutique *f*

mail [meɪl] **1** *n* (**a**) *(postal service)* poste *f*; **to send a letter by mail** envoyer une lettre par la poste; **the parcel got lost in the mail** le colis a été égaré par la poste; **your cheque is in the mail** votre chèque a été posté

(**b**) *(letters, parcels)* courrier *m*; **has the mail arrived?** est-ce que le courrier est arrivé?; **it came in the mail** c'est arrivé au courrier; **was there anything in the mail for me?** est-ce qu'il y avait du courrier pour moi?; **the mail is only collected twice a week** il n'y a que deux levées par semaine

(**c**) *Comput* courrier *m* électronique, *Offic* mél *m*, *Can* courriel *m*

(**d**) *Arch (coach)* malle *f*, malle-poste *f*

(**e**) *(UNCOUNT) (armour)* mailles *fpl*

2 *vt (parcel, goods, cheque)* envoyer *ou* expédier par la poste; *(letter)* poster; **I've just mailed some money home** je viens d'expédier *ou* d'envoyer de l'argent à ma famille

3 Mail *n Press* **the Mail** = nom abrégé du 'Daily Mail'; *Press* **the Mail on Sunday** = édition dominicale du 'Daily Mail'

▸▸ *Comput* ***mail address*** adresse *f* électronique; ***mail bomb*** (**a**) *Am (letter)* lettre *f* piégée; *(parcel)* colis *m* piégé (**b**) *Comput* = messages envoyés en masse pour bloquer une boîte aux lettres, *Can* message *m* piégé, bombard *m*; *Am* ***mail carrier*** facteur(trice) *m,f*; *Am* ***mail clerk*** employé(e) *m,f* responsable du courrier; *Am* ***mail drop*** boîte *f* à *ou* aux lettres; *Comput* ***mail forwarding*** réexpédition *f* du courrier électronique; *Comput* ***mail gateway*** passerelle *f* (de courrier électronique); ***mail order*** vente *f* par correspondance; **to buy sth by mail order** acheter qch par correspondance *ou* sur catalogue; *Comput* ***mail path*** chemin *m* du courrier électronique; *Comput* ***mail reader*** logiciel *m* de courrier électronique, client *m* de messagerie électronique; *Comput* ***mail server*** serveur *m* de courrier; *Mktg* ***mail survey*** enquête *f* postale; ***mail train*** train *m* postal; ***mail transfer*** virement *m* par courrier; *Am* ***mail truck,*** *Br* ***mail van*** camionnette *f* ou fourgonnette *f* des postes; *Rail* voiture-poste *f*

mailable [ˈmeɪləbəl] *adj Am* conforme aux règlements postaux

mailbag [ˈmeɪlbæɡ] *n* sac *m* postal

mailboat [ˈmeɪlbəʊt] *n* navire *m* postal

mailbox [ˈmeɪlbɒks] *n* (**a**) *esp Am (postbox)* boîte *f* à lettres (**b**) *Am (letterbox)* boîte *f* aux lettres (**c**) *Comput* boîte *f* à *ou* aux lettres

mailcoach [ˈmeɪlkəʊtʃ] *n Rail* voiture-poste *f*; *Arch (horse-drawn)* malle-poste *f*

mailed [meɪld] *adj (armour)* maillé

mailer [ˈmeɪlə(r)] *n Com & Mktg* mailing *m*, publipostage *m*

mailing [ˈmeɪlɪŋ] *n* (**a**) *(posting)* expédition *f*, envoi *m* par la poste; **our prices are correct up to the time of mailing** nos prix sont valables au moment où nous vous les adressons

(**b**) *Com, Mktg & Comput* mailing *m*, publipostage *m*; **to do** *or* **send a mailing** faire un mailing

▸▸ ***mailing address*** adresse *f* postale; *Mktg* ***mailing card*** carte *f* de publicité; ***mailing list*** *Mktg* liste *f* de publipostage; *Comput* liste *f* de diffusion; **are you on our mailing list?** est-ce que vous êtes sur notre fichier?; *Mktg* ***mailing shot*** mailing *m*, publipostage *m*; **to do** *or* **send a mailing shot** faire un mailing

mailman [ˈmeɪlmən] (*pl* **mailmen** [-mən]) *n Am* facteur *m*

mailmerge [ˈmeɪlmɜːdʒ] *n Comput* publipostage *m*

▸▸ ***mailmerge letter*** lettre *f* envoyée par publipostage; ***mailmerge program*** programme *m* de publipostage

mail-order *adj*

▸▸ ***mail-order bride*** = nom donné aux jeunes femmes originaires de pays pauvres cherchant à épouser des occidentaux par le biais d'agences matrimoniales spécialisées; ***mail-order catalogue*** catalogue *m* de vente par correspondance; ***mail-order company*** maison *f* de vente par correspondance; ***mail-order firm*** maison *f* de vente par correspondance; ***mail-order goods*** marchandises *fpl* vendues *ou* achetées par correspondance; ***mail-order organization*** vépéciste *m*; ***mail-order retailing*** vente *f* par correspondance

mailroom [ˈmeɪlruːm] *n* service *m* du courrier

mailshot [ˈmeɪlʃɒt] **1** *n* mailing *m*, publipostage *m*; **to do** *or* **send a mailshot** faire un mailing

2 *vt* envoyer un mailing *ou* un publipostage à

maim [meɪm] *vt* (**a**) *(disable)* mutiler, estropier; *(injure)* blesser; **people were badly maimed in the attack** des gens ont été grièvement blessés au cours de l'attaque (**b**) *(psychologically)* marquer, perturber; **the experience maimed her for life** l'expérience l'a marquée pour la vie

main [meɪn] **1** *adj* (**a**) *(principal)* principal; *(largest)* principal, plus important; *(essential → idea, theme, reason)* principal, essentiel; **the main body of public opinion** le gros de l'opinion publique; **the main points** les points *mpl* principaux; **the main thing we have to consider is his age** la première chose à prendre en compte, c'est son âge; **you're safe, that's the main thing** tu es sain et sauf, c'est le principal; **that's the main thing to remember** c'est ce dont il faut se souvenir avant tout; *Fam* **he always has an eye to the main chance** il ne perd jamais de vue ses propres intérêts[❑]; *Fam* **main man** *(friend)* pote *m*; *Fam* **yo, my main man, how ya doin'?** salut mon pote, comment ça va?; *Br Fam* **when it comes to scoring goals, Michael Owen's the main man** pour ce qui est de marquer des buts, Michael Owen est champion

(**b**) *Literary (sheer)* **to do sth by main force** employer la force pour faire qch

2 *n* (**a**) *(for gas, water → public)* canalisation *f* principale; *(for electricity)* conducteur *m* principal

(**b**) *Arch* **the main** *(ocean)* le grand large, l'océan *m*; **the Spanish Main** la mer des Antilles

(**c**) *Naut* grand mât *m*

3 in the main *adv* en gros, dans l'ensemble

▸▸ ***main beam*** *Aut* feux *mpl* de route; *Constr* poutre *f* maîtresse; *Aut* **to be on main beam** rouler pleins phares; ***main bearing*** palier *m (dans un moteur)*; ***main branch*** *(of bank)* établissement *m* principal; *Gram* ***main clause*** proposition *f* principale; *St Exch* ***main cost centre*** centre *m* d'analyse principal; ***main course*** plat *m* principal; *(on menu)* plat *m*; *Agr* ***main crop*** culture *f* principale; *Naut* ***main deck*** pont *m* principal; *Am Fam* ***main drag*** rue *f* principale[❑], grande rue[❑] *f*; ***main entrance*** entrée *f* principale; ***main line*** (**a**) *Rail* grande ligne *f*; *Am (road)* grande route *f* (**b**) *Fam Drugs slang (vein)* veine *f* apparente *(choisie pour s'injecter de la drogue)*; *St Exch* ***main market*** = marché principal de la Bourse de Londres; *Naut* ***main mast*** grand mât *m*; ***main office*** *(gen)* bureau *m* principal; *(headquarters)* siège *m* (social); *Br* ***main road*** grande route *f*, route *f* à grande circulation, ≃ nationale *f*; ***main sewer*** égout *m* collecteur; *Fam* ***main squeeze*** *(boyfriend)* mec *m*, jules *m*; *(girlfriend)* nana *f*, gonzesse *f*; ***main street*** rue *f* principale, grand-rue *f*; *Am Fig* ***Main Street*** *(shops)* les commerçants *mpl*, le commerce; **Main Street has been badly hit by the recession** les commerçants ont été durement touchés par la recé ssion

'Main Street' *Lewis* 'Grand-rue'

mainbrace [ˈmeɪnbreɪs] *n Naut* grand bras *m* de vergue

Maine [meɪn] *n* le Maine; **in Maine** dans le Maine

mainframe [ˈmeɪnfreɪm] *n (computer)* ordinateur *m* central

▸▸ ***mainframe computer*** ordinateur *m* central

mainland [ˈmeɪnlənd] **1** *n* continent *m*; **she sailed back to the mainland** elle regagna le continent en bateau; **you can see the Scottish mainland** on voit la côte écossaise; **the Danish mainland** le Danemark continental; **the British mainland** la Grande-Bretagne *(le Royaume-Uni sans l'Irlande du Nord)*

2 *adj* continental; **in mainland Europe** en Europe continentale; **in mainland Britain** en Grande-Bretagne proprement dite *(par opposition aux îles qui l'entourent)*

mainlander [ˈmeɪnˌləndə(r)] *n* habitant(e) *m,f* du continent, continental(e) *m,f*

mainline [ˈmeɪnlaɪn] *Fam Drugs slang* **1** *vt* se faire un shoot de; *(habitually)* se shooter à

2 *vi* se piquer, se shooter

main-line *adj (train, station)* de grande ligne

mainliner [ˈmeɪnˌlaɪnə(r)] *n Fam Drugs slang* junkie *mf*, shooté(e) *m,f*

mainly [ˈmeɪnlɪ] *adv (chiefly)* principalement, surtout; *(in the majority)* pour la plupart, dans l'ensemble; **the passengers were mainly old men** la plupart des passagers étaient des vieux messieurs; **a mainly Spanish-speaking population** une population à majorité *ou* principalement *ou* surtout hispanophone; **their diet consists mainly of insects** ils se nourrissent essentiellement *ou* principalement *ou* surtout d'insectes; **she was mainly to blame** c'est elle la principale responsable, c'est surtout de sa faute

mains [meɪnz] *n* (**a**) *(main supply)* réseau *m*; **where's the mains?** où est la conduite principale?; **did you turn the electricity/gas off at the mains?** as-tu fermé l'arrivée de gaz/d'électricité?; **the village doesn't have mains electricity** le village n'est pas raccordé au réseau électrique

(**b**) *Elec* secteur *m*; **my shaver works on battery or mains** mon rasoir marche sur piles ou sur (le) secteur

▸▸ ***mains adaptor*** adaptateur *m* secteur; ***mains gas*** gaz *m* de ville; ***mains razor*** rasoir *m* fonctionnant sur secteur; ***mains set*** poste *m* secteur; ***mains supply*** réseau *m* de distribution de gaz/d'eau/d'électricité; ***mains water*** eau *f* courante

mainsail ['meɪnseɪl, 'meɪnsəl] *n Naut* grand-voile *f*

mainsheet ['meɪnshi:t] *n Naut* écoute *f* de (la) grand-voile

mains-operated [-ˌɒpəreɪtɪd], **mains-powered** *adj* fonctionnant sur secteur

mainspring ['meɪnsprɪŋ] *n* (**a**) *Tech* ressort *m* moteur (**b**) *Fig* moteur *m*; **his courage was the mainspring of his success** son courage était la raison profonde de son succès

mainstay ['meɪnsteɪ] *n* (**a**) *Naut* étai *m* (de grand mât) (**b**) *Fig* soutien *m*, point *m* d'appui; **maize is the mainstay of their diet** le maïs constitue la base de leur alimentation

mainstream ['meɪnstri:m] **1** *n* courant *m*; **the mainstream of modern European literature** la tendance qui prédomine dans la littérature européenne moderne; **he is in the mainstream of politics** en politique, il suit la plus forte pente *ou* la tendance générale; **to live outside the mainstream of society** vivre en marge de la société

2 *adj* **mainstream French politics** le courant dominant de la politique française; **mainstream Hollywood movies** films *mpl* dans la grande tradition hollywoodienne; **mainstream America** l'Américain *m* moyen; **their music is hardly what you'd call mainstream!** leur musique se démarque nettement de ce qu'on entend habituellement!; **mainstream jazz** = style de jazz qui se situe entre le traditionnel et le moderne

mainstreet ['meɪnstri:t] *vi Can Pol* prendre un bain de foule

mainstreeting ['meɪnˌstri:tɪŋ] *n (UNCOUNT) Can Pol* bains *mpl* de foule; **to go mainstreeting** prendre un bain de foule

maintain [meɪn'teɪn] **1** *vt* (**a**) *(retain → institution, tradition)* conserver, préserver; **the old rules have been maintained** les anciennes règles ont été conservées

(**b**) *(preserve → peace, standard)* maintenir; **to maintain law and order** maintenir l'ordre; **we must maintain our output** nous devons maintenir notre niveau de production; *Mil & Fig* **to maintain a position** tenir une position

(**c**) *(look after → roads, machinery)* entretenir; **the grounds are well maintained** les jardins sont bien entretenus *ou* tenus

(**d**) *(uphold, keep → correspondence, friendship)* entretenir; *(→ silence, advantage, composure)* garder; *(→ reputation)* défendre

(**e**) *(financially → dependants)* entretenir; **they have two children at university to maintain** ils ont deux enfants à charge à l'université; **he has a wife and seven children to maintain** il a une femme et sept enfants à nourrir

(**f**) *(assert → opinion)* soutenir, défendre; *(→ innocence)* affirmer; **I still maintain she's innocent** je soutiens *ou* je maintiens toujours qu'elle est innocente

2 *vi Am Fam* **I'm maintaining!** *(I'm fine)* ça va!

maintainable [meɪn'teɪnəbəl] *adj (attitude, opinion, position)* soutenable, défendable

maintained school [meɪn'teɪnd-] *adj Br* ≃ école *f* publique

maintainer [meɪn'teɪnə(r)] *n (of opinion, cause)* défenseur *m*

maintenance ['meɪntənəns] **1** *n* (**a**) *(of roads, building)* entretien *m*; *(of machinery, computer)* maintenance *f*

(**b**) *(financial support)* entretien *m*; **he has very little money left for his own maintenance** il lui reste très peu d'argent pour vivre

(**c**) *Law (alimony)* pension *f* alimentaire

(**d**) *(of order)* maintien *m*; *(of regulations)* application *f*; *(of situation)* maintien *m*; **maintenance of a reasonable standard of living** le maintien d'un niveau de vie correct

2 *comp (costs, crew)* d'entretien

▸▸ ***maintenance allowance*** *(to student)* bourse *f* d'études; *(to businessman)* indemnité *f* pour frais de déplacement; ***maintenance contract*** contract *m* de maintenance *ou* d'entretien; ***maintenance costs*** frais *mpl* d'entretien; ***maintenance department*** service *m* de maintenance *ou* d'entretien; ***maintenance engineer*** technicien(enne) *m,f* de maintenance; ***maintenance equipment*** matériel *m* d'entretien; ***maintenance grant*** *(to student)* bourse *f* d'études; ***maintenance handbook*** manuel *m* d'entretien; ***maintenance kit*** trousse *f* d'entretien; ***maintenance man*** ouvrier *m* chargé de l'entretien *ou* de la maintenance; ***maintenance manual*** manuel *m* d'entretien; *Law* ***maintenance order*** obligation *f* alimentaire; **she got a maintenance order against him** elle a obtenu du tribunal qu'il lui verse une pension alimentaire; ***maintenance staff*** personnel *m* d'entretien; ***maintenance vehicle*** camion-atelier *m*

maintenance-free *adj* sans entretien, sans maintenance

maintop ['meɪntɒp] *n Naut* grande hune *f*

Mainz [maɪnts] *n* Mayence

maisonette [ˌmeɪzə'net] *n Br (small house)* maisonnette *f*; *(flat)* duplex *m*

maître d' [ˌmetrə'di:], **maître d'hôtel** [ˌmetrədəʊ'-tel] *n* maître *m* d'hôtel

maize [meɪz] *n* maïs *m*

Maj. *Mil (written abbr* **Major**) ≃ Cdt; *Can & Belg* Maj.

majestic [mə'dʒestɪk] *adj* majestueux

majestically [mə'dʒestɪkəlɪ] *adv* majestueusement

majesty ['mædʒəstɪ] *(pl* **majesties**) *n* (**a**) *(impressiveness)* majesté *f*; **God in all His majesty** Dieu dans toute sa majesté

(**b**) *(sovereign)* majesté *f*; **yes, your majesty** oui, Votre Majesté; *Hum* à vos ordres!; **His Majesty the King** Sa Majesté le Roi; **Her Majesty the Queen** Sa Majesté la Reine; *Br* **on His/Her Majesty's Service** (pour le) service de Sa Majesté (≃ service de l'État); *(on envelope)* ≃ en franchise

▸▸ *Br Admin* ***His/Her Majesty's Government*** = expression utilisée sur des documents officiels en Grande-Bretagne; *Br Sch* ***His/Her Majesty's Inspector*** = inspecteur de l'Éducation nationale en Grande-Bretagne; *Br* ***Her Majesty's Prison Service*** = système pénitentiaire britannique; *Br* ***His/Her Majesty's Ship*** = dénomination officielle précédant le nom de tous les bâtiments de guerre de la marine britannique; *Br* ***Her Majesty's Stationery Office*** = maison d'édition publiant les ouvrages ou documents approuvés par le Parlement, les ministères et autres organismes officiels, ≃ l'Imprimerie nationale

Maj. Gen. *Mil (written abbr* **Major General**) ≃ général *m* de division; *Belg* ≃ général-major *m*, *Suisse* ≃ divisionnaire *m*, *Can* ≃ major-général *m*

majolica [mə'jɒlɪkə] *n* majolique *f*

major ['meɪdʒə(r)] **1** *adj* (**a**) *(main)* **the major part of our research** l'essentiel de nos recherches; **the major portion of my time is devoted to politics** la majeure partie *ou* la plus grande partie de mon temps est consacrée à la politique

(**b**) *(significant → decision, change, factor, event)* majeur; **we shouldn't have any major problems** nous ne devrions pas rencontrer de problèmes majeurs; **don't worry, it's not a major problem** ne t'inquiète pas, ce n'est pas très grave; **any problems? – nothing major** des problèmes? – rien d'important; **of major importance** d'une grande importance, d'une importance capitale; **a major role** *(in play, film)* un grand rôle; *(in negotiations, reform)* un rôle capital *ou* essentiel; **we invested in a major way** nous avons investi de manière considérable; **he's taken up Spanish in a major way** il s'est mis à fond à l'espagnol; **he's fallen for Fiona in a major way** il est tombé follement amoureux de Fiona

(**c**) *(serious → obstacle, difficulty)* majeur; **the roof is in need of major repair work** la toiture a grand besoin d'être remise en état; **she underwent major surgery** elle a subi une grosse opération

(**d**) *Mus* majeur; **a sonata in E major** une sonate en mi majeur; **in a major key** en (mode) majeur; **a major third** une tierce majeure

(**e**) *Br Old-fashioned Sch (elder)* **Smith major** Smith aîné

(**f**) *Cards* majeur; **major suit** majeure *f*

2 *n* (**a**) *Mil (in airforce)* ≃ commandant *m*; *Can & Belg* ≃ major *m*; *(in infantry)* ≃ chef *m* de bataillon, *Belg, Can & Suisse* ≃ major *m*; *(in cavalry)* ≃ commandant *m*, *Belg, Can & Suisse* ≃ major *m*

(**b**) *Formal (person over 18)* personne *f* majeure

(**c**) *Am Univ (subject)* matière *f* principale; **Tina is a physics major** Tina fait des études de physique

(**d**) *Mus* (mode *m*) majeur *m*

(**e**) *Am (big company)* **the oil majors** les grandes compagnies *fpl* pétrolières; **the Majors** *(film companies)* = les cinq compagnies de production les plus importantes à Hollywood

(**f**) *Golf* tournoi *m* du grand chelem

3 *vi Am Univ* (**a**) *(specialize)* se spécialiser; **Joe majors in chemistry** Joe se spécialise en chimie

(**b**) *(be a student)* **she majored in sociology** elle a fait des études de sociologie

▸▸ *Mil* ***major general*** ≃ général *m* de division, *Belg* ≃ général-major *m*, *Suisse* ≃ divisionnaire *m*, *Can* ≃ major-général *m*; *Am Sport* ***major league*** *(in baseball)* = une des deux principales divisions de baseball professionnel aux États-Unis et au Canada; *(gen)* première division *f*; *Mil* ***major offensive*** vaste offensive *f*; **to launch a major offensive** lancer une vaste offensive; *Phil* ***major premise*** majeure *f*; ***major road*** route *f* principale *ou* à grande circulation, ≃ nationale *f*; *Fin* ***major shareholder*** actionnaire *mf* de référence; *Univ* ***major subject*** matière *f* principale

'Major Barbara' *Shaw* 'La Commandante Barbara'

Majorca [mə'jɔ:kə] *n* Majorque; **in Majorca** à Majorque

Majorcan [mə'jɔ:kən] **1** *n* Majorquin(e) *m,f*

2 *adj* majorquin

majordomo [ˌmeɪdʒə'dəʊməʊ] *(pl* **majordomos**) *n* majordome *m*

majorette [ˌmeɪdʒə'ret] *n* majorette *f*

majorite ['meɪdʒəreɪt] *Pol* **1** *n* partisan *m* de John Major

2 *adj* partisan de John Major

majority [mə'dʒɒrətɪ] *(pl* **majorities**) **1** *n* (**a**) *(of a group)* majorité *f*, plupart *f*; **the majority of people** la plupart des gens; **in the majority of cases** dans la plupart des cas; **the majority was** *or* **were in favour** la majorité *ou* la plupart d'entre eux était pour; **the vast majority of the tourists were Japanese** les touristes, dans leur très grande majorité, étaient des Japonais

(**b**) *(in voting, opinions)* majorité *f*; **to be in a majority** être majoritaire; **a two-thirds majority** une majorité des deux tiers; **the proposition had an overwhelming majority** la proposition a recueilli une écrasante majorité; **she was elected by a majority of 6** elle a été élue avec une majorité de 6 voix *ou* par 6 voix de majorité

(**c**) *Law (voting age)* majorité *f*; **to attain** *or* **reach one's majority** atteindre sa majorité, devenir majeur

2 *comp* majoritaire

▸▸ ***majority decision*** décision *f* prise à la majorité; ***majority government*** gouvernement *m* majoritaire; ***majority holding, majority interest*** participation *f* majoritaire; *Am Pol* ***majority leader*** leader *m* de la majorité *(à la Chambre des représentants et au Sénat américains)*; ***majority party*** parti *m* majoritaire; ***majority rule*** gouvernement *m* à la majorité absolue, système *m* majoritaire; *Br* ***majority shareholder***, *Am* ***majority stockholder*** actionnaire *mf* majoritaire; ***majority verdict*** verdict *m* majoritaire; ***majority world*** tiers-monde *m*

major-league *adj Am* (**a**) *Sport* **major-league team** grande équipe *f (sportive)* (**b**) *Fam (significant)* balèze; **she's a major-league researcher in the field** dans son domaine de recherche, c'est une pointure; **he's a major-league jerk** c'est un imbécile de première

mai–maj

MAKE [meɪk]

faire	► 1A (a) – (c), (e) – (g); B (b) – (d); C (d); D (a) – (c)
fabriquer	► 1 (a)
établir	► 1 (c)
former	► 1 (d)
rendre	► 1B (a)
atteindre	► 1C (a), (b)
gagner	► 1C (d)
marquer	► 1D (d)
faire le succès de	► 1E (a)
marque	► 3 (a)

(*pt & pp* **made** [meɪd]) **1** *vt* **A.** (**a**) *(construct, create, manufacture)* faire, fabriquer; **to make one's own clothes** faire ses vêtements soi-même; **to make a meal** préparer un repas; **I'll make some tea** je vais préparer du thé; **they make computers** ils fabriquent des ordinateurs; **made in Japan** *(on packaging)* fabriqué au Japon; **a vase made of** *or* **from clay** un vase en *ou* de terre cuite; **what's it made of?** en quoi est-ce que c'est fait?; **what do you make aluminium from?** à partir de quoi est-ce qu'on fabrique l'aluminium?; **he makes models out of matchsticks** il fait des maquettes avec des allumettes; *Knitting* **to make one/two** faire un jeté simple/double; **they're made for each other** ils sont faits l'un pour l'autre; *Fam* **we're not made of money!** on n'a pas d'argent à jeter par les fenêtres!; *Fam* **I'll show them what I'm made of!** je leur montrerai de quel bois je me chauffe *ou* qui je suis!

(**b**) *(cause to appear or happen → hole, tear, mess, mistake, noise)* faire; **it made a dent in the bumper** ça a cabossé le pare-chocs; **he's always making trouble** il faut toujours qu'il fasse des histoires

(**c**) *(establish → law, rule)* établir, faire; **I don't make the rules** ce n'est pas moi qui fais les règlements

(**d**) *(form → circle, line)* former

(**e**) *Cin & TV (direct, act in)* faire; **she's making a documentary** elle fait un documentaire; **he's made several films with Ridley Scott** il a fait plusieurs films avec Ridley Scott

(**f**) *(indicating action performed)* **to make an offer** faire une offre; **to make a request** faire une demande; **to make a note of sth** prendre note de qch; **to make a speech** faire un discours; **to make a phone call** passer un coup de fil; **the Queen will make an official visit to Japan** la reine va se rendre en visite officielle au Japon; **we've made a few changes** nous avons fait *ou* apporté quelques modifications; **the police are making inquiries** la police procède à une enquête; **I have no further comments to make** je n'ai rien à ajouter

(**g**) *(tidy)* **to make one's bed** faire son lit

B. (**a**) *(with adj or pp complement) (cause to be)* rendre; **to make sb happy/mad** rendre qn heureux/fou(folle); **to make oneself useful** se rendre utile; **this will make things easier** cela facilitera les choses; **it makes her tired** ça la fatigue; **what makes the sky blue?** qu'est-ce qui fait que le ciel est bleu?; **I'd like to make it clear that it wasn't my fault** je voudrais qu'on comprenne bien que je n'y suis pour rien; **make yourselves comfortable** mettez-vous à l'aise; **it was hard to make myself heard/understood** j'ai eu du mal à me faire entendre/comprendre; **a child would make our happiness complete** il ne nous manque qu'un enfant pour que notre bonheur soit parfait

(**b**) *(with noun complement or with "into") (change into)* faire; **the film made her (into) a star** le film a fait d'elle une vedette; **to make a success of sth** réussir qch; **he was made president for life** il a été nommé président à vie; **they made Bonn the capital** ils ont choisi Bonn pour capitale; **they made Strasbourg the capital of Europe** ils ont fait de Strasbourg la capitale de l'Europe; **he makes a joke of everything** il tourne tout en plaisanterie; **the building has been made into offices** l'immeuble a été réaménagé *ou* converti en bureaux; **I'll make you a present of it** je t'en ferai cadeau; **the latest cheque makes the total £10,000** le dernier chèque porte la somme totale à 10 000 livres; **I can't come in the morning, shall we make it 2 p.m.?** je ne peux pas venir le matin, est-ce que 14 heures vous conviendrait?; **if we made it a Wednesday...** si on faisait ça un mercredi...; **can we make it your place?** est-ce qu'on peut faire ça chez toi?; **better make it** *or* **that TWO whiskies** mettez-moi un deuxième whisky

(**c**) *(with verb complement) (cause)* faire; **what makes you think they're wrong?** qu'est-ce qui te fait penser qu'ils ont tort?; **peeling onions makes my eyes water** les oignons me font pleurer; **I can't make the coffee machine work** je n'arrive pas à faire marcher la machine à café; **you make it look easy** à vous voir, on croirait que c'est facile; **the hat/photo makes you look ridiculous** tu as l'air ridicule avec ce chapeau/sur cette photo; **don't make me laugh!** ne me fais pas rire!

(**d**) *(force, oblige)* **to make sb do sth** faire faire qch à qn; *(stronger)* forcer *ou* obliger *ou* contraindre qn à faire qch; **they made me wait** ils m'ont fait attendre; **if he doesn't want to do it you can't make him** s'il ne veut pas le faire, tu ne peux pas l'y obliger *ou* forcer; **she made herself keep running** elle s'est forcée à continuer à courir

C. (**a**) *(attain, achieve → goal)* atteindre; **we made all our production targets** nous avons atteint tous nos objectifs de production; **their first record made the top ten** leur premier disque est rentré au top ten; **you won't make the team if you don't train** tu n'entreras jamais dans l'équipe si tu ne t'entraînes pas; **the story made the front page** l'histoire a fait la une des journaux

(**b**) *(arrive at, get to → place)* atteindre; **we should make Houston/port by evening** nous devrions arriver à Houston/atteindre le port d'ici ce soir; **did you make your train?** as-tu réussi à avoir ton train?

(**c**) *(be available for)* **I won't be able to make lunch** je ne pourrai pas déjeuner avec toi/elle/vous/*etc*; **can you make Friday afternoon?** vendredi après-midi, ça vous convient?; **I can make two o'clock** je peux être là à deux heures

(**d**) *(earn, win)* faire, gagner; **how much do you make a month?** combien gagnes-tu par mois?; **she made her first million selling beauty products** elle a gagné son premier million en vendant des produits de beauté; **what do they make out of the deal?** qu'est-ce qu'ils gagnent dans l'affaire?, qu'est-ce que l'affaire leur rapporte?

D. (**a**) *(amount to, add up to)* faire; **17 and 19 make** *or* **makes 36** 17 plus 19 font *ou* égalent 36; **if Kay comes, that will make eight** si Kay vient, ça fera huit; **that makes £4, Madam** ça fait *ou* fera 4 livres, Madame; **that makes the third time you've been late this week** c'est la troisième fois que vous êtes en retard cette semaine; **how old does that make him?** quel âge ça lui fait?

(**b**) *(reckon to be)* **I make the answer 257** d'après moi, ça fait 257; **I make it $14 each** si je compte bien, ça fait 14 dollars par personne; **what time do you make it?** quelle heure as-tu?

(**c**) *(with noun complement) (fulfil specified role, function etc)* faire; **these shoes will make an excellent Christmas present** ces chaussures feront un très beau cadeau de Noël; **he'll make somebody a good husband** ce sera un excellent mari; **he'd make a good teacher** il ferait un bon enseignant; **they make a handsome couple** ils forment un beau couple; **her reminiscences make interesting reading** ses souvenirs sont intéressants à lire

(**d**) *(score)* marquer; **Smith made his second century** Smith a marqué deux cents points

E. (**a**) *(make successful)* faire le succès de; **it's her performance that makes the film** tout le film repose sur son interprétation; **if this deal comes off we're made!** si ça marche, on touche le gros lot!; **you've got it made!** tu n'as plus de souci à te faire!; **what happens today will make us or break us** notre avenir dépend entièrement de ce qui va se passer aujourd'hui

(**b**) *Am (in directions)* **make a right/left** tournez à droite/à gauche

(**c**) *(idioms)* **to make it** *(arrive)* arriver; *(be successful)* réussir; *(be able to attend)* être là; **I'll never make it for ten o'clock** je ne pourrai jamais y être pour dix heures; **we made it to the airport with an hour to spare** nous sommes arrivés à l'aéroport avec une heure d'avance; **if he doesn't make it back in ten minutes, start without him** s'il n'est pas revenu dans dix minutes, commencez sans lui; **I hope she makes it through the winter** j'espère qu'elle passera l'hiver; **he'll never make it as a businessman** il ne réussira jamais dans les affaires; **I can't make it for supper tomorrow** je ne peux pas dîner avec eux/toi/*etc* demain; *Am Fam* **to make sb, to make it with sb** *(have sex with)* coucher avec qn

2 *vi (act)* **to make (as if) to** faire mine de; **she made (as if) to stand up** elle fit mine de se lever; *Fam* **I walked in trying to make like a businessman** je suis entré en essayant d'avoir l'air d'un homme d'affaires ☐; *Fam* **he's always making like a tough guy** il essaie toujours de jouer les durs; *Fam* **make like you don't know anything** fais comme si tu ne savais pas; *Fam* **make like you're asleep!** fais semblant de dormir! ☐; *Fam* **I didn't know what it was all about but I made like I did** je ne savais pas de quoi il était question, mais j'ai fait comme si; **to make believe** imaginer; **make believe you're a bird** imagine que tu es un oiseau; **to make do (with)** *(manage)* se débrouiller (avec); *(be satisfied)* se contenter (de); **it's broken but we'll just have to make do** c'est cassé mais il faudra faire avec *ou* nous débrouiller avec; **we could make do with ten** nous pourrions nous débrouiller avec dix

3 *n* (**a**) *(brand)* marque *f*; **what make of washing machine have you got?** quelle est la marque de votre machine à laver?, qu'est-ce que vous avez comme machine à laver?

(**b**) *(in bridge)* contrat *m*

(**c**) *Fam (idiom)* **to be on the make** *(financially)* chercher à se faire du fric, chercher à s'en mettre plein les poches; *(looking for sexual partner)* chasser, draguer

►**make away with** *vt insep* partir avec; **he made away with the cash** il est parti avec l'argent

►**make for** *vt insep* (**a**) *(head towards)* se diriger vers; *(hastily)* se précipiter vers; **the plane is making for Berlin** l'avion se dirige sur Berlin; **he made straight for the fridge** il se dirigea tout droit vers le frigo; **when it started to rain everyone made for the trees** quand il s'est mis à pleuvoir, tout le monde s'est précipité vers les arbres; **the truck was making right for him** le camion fonçait droit sur lui; **he made for his gun** il fit un geste pour saisir son pistolet

(**b**) *(contribute to)* mener à; **the treaty should make for a more lasting peace** le traité devrait mener *ou* aboutir à une paix plus durable; **this typeface makes for easier reading** cette police permet une lecture plus facile; **a good diet makes for healthier babies** un bon régime alimentaire donne des bébés en meilleure santé

►**make of 1** *vt sep* (**a**) *(understand)* comprendre à; **I don't know what to make of that remark** je ne sais pas comment interpréter cette remarque; **can you make anything of these instructions?** est-ce que tu comprends quelque chose à ce mode d'emploi?

(**b**) *(attach importance to)* **I think you're making too much of a very minor problem** je pense que tu exagères l'importance de ce petit problème; **you're making too much of this** tu y attaches trop d'importance; **the press has made a lot of this visit** la presse a fait beaucoup de bruit autour de cette visite; **the prosecution made much of this fact** l'accusation a fait grand cas de ce fait; *Fam* **do you want to make something of it, then?** *(threat)* tu cherches des histoires ou quoi?

2 *vt insep (think of)* penser de; **what do you make of the Caines?** qu'est-ce que tu penses des Caine?

►**make off** *vi* partir

►**make off with** *vt insep* partir avec; **he made off with the cash** il est parti avec l'argent

►**make out 1** *vt sep* (**a**) *(see)* distinguer; *(hear)* entendre, comprendre; *(read)* déchiffrer; **I could just make out the outline of the castle** je distinguais juste la silhouette du château; **I**

couldn't make out what he said je ne comprenais pas ce qu'il disait; **I can't make out the address** je n'arrive pas à déchiffrer l'adresse

(**b**) *(understand)* comprendre; **I couldn't make out how to fit it together** je ne comprenais pas comment l'assembler; **I can't make her out at all** je ne la comprends pas du tout

(**c**) *(claim)* prétendre; **she made out that she was busy** elle a fait semblant d'être occupée; **don't make yourself out to be something you're not** ne prétends pas être ce que tu n'es pas; **it's not as bad as everyone makes out** ce n'est pas aussi mauvais qu'on le prétend

(**d**) *(fill out → form)* remplir; **to make out a cheque (to sb)** faire un chèque (à l'ordre de qn); **who shall I make the cheque out to?** je fais le chèque à quel ordre?

(**e**) *(draw up → list)* dresser, faire; *(→ will, contract)* faire, rédiger, établir; *(→ receipt)* faire

2 *vi* (**a**) *Fam (manage)* se débrouiller❑; **I'm sure she'll make out whatever happens** je suis sûr qu'elle se débrouillera quoi qu'il arrive; **how did you make out at work today?** comment ça s'est passé au boulot aujourd'hui?

(**b**) *very Fam (sexually)* se peloter; **to make out with sb** peloter qn

▸**make over** *vt sep* (**a**) *(transfer)* transférer, céder; **she has made the estate over to her granddaughter** elle a cédé la propriété à sa petite-fille

(**b**) *Am (convert → room, house)* réaménager; **the garage had been made over into a workshop** le garage a été transformé en atelier

(**c**) *(change the appearance of)* transformer

▸**make up 1** *vt sep* (**a**) *(put make-up on)* maquiller; **to make oneself up** se maquiller; **he was heavily made up** il était très maquillé *ou* fardé

(**b**) *(prepare)* faire, préparer; **we can make up a bed for you in the living room** nous pouvons vous faire un lit dans le salon; **the chemist made up the prescription** le pharmacien a préparé l'ordonnance; **the fire needs making up** il faut remettre du charbon/du bois sur le feu

(**c**) *(invent)* inventer; **I'm sure he made the story up** je suis sûr qu'il a inventé cette histoire (de toutes pièces); **I'm making it up as I go along** j'improvise au fur et à mesure

(**d**) *Typ* mettre en pages

(**e**) *(idiom)* **to make up with sb**, *Br* **to make it up with sb** se réconcilier avec qn; **have you made up** *or Br* **made it up with him?** est-ce que vous vous êtes réconciliés?

2 *vt insep* (**a**) *(constitute)* composer, constituer; **the different ethnic groups that make up our organization** les différents groupes ethniques qui constituent notre organisation; **the cabinet is made up of eleven ministers** le cabinet est composé de onze ministres; **it's made up of a mixture of different types of tobacco** c'est un mélange de plusieurs tabacs différents

(**b**) *(compensate for → losses)* compenser; **to make up lost ground** regagner le terrain perdu; **he's making up time** il rattrape son retard

(**c**) *(complete)* **this cheque will help you make up the required sum** ce chèque vous aidera à atteindre le montant requis; **we need two more players to make up the team** nous avons besoin de deux joueurs de plus pour que l'équipe soit au complet; **I'll make up the difference** je mettrai la différence

3 *vi* (**a**) *(put on make-up)* se maquiller

(**b**) *(become reconciled)* se réconcilier

▸**make up for** *vt insep* compenser; **the pay doesn't make up for the poor conditions** le salaire ne compense pas les piètres conditions de travail; **how can I make up for all the trouble I've caused you?** que puis-je faire pour me faire pardonner tous les ennuis que je vous ai causés?; *also Fig* **she's making up for lost time now!** elle est en train de rattraper le temps perdu!

▸**make up to 1** *vt sep (idiom)* **I promise I'll make it up to you someday** tu peux être sûr que je te revaudrai ça (un jour)

2 *vt insep* **to make up to sb** *(try to win favour)* essayer de se faire bien voir par qn; *(make advances)* faire du plat à qn

▸**make with** *vt insep Am Fam* **make with the drinks!** à boire!; **make with the music!** musique!

---

make-believe 1 *n* **it's only make-believe** ce n'est qu'illusion; **a world of make-believe** un monde d'illusions; **to play at make-believe** jouer à faire semblant

2 *adj* imaginaire; **a make-believe friend** un ami imaginaire; **they turned the bed into a make-believe raft** ils imaginèrent que le lit était un radeau

make-or-break *adj* **it's make-or-break time!** maintenant, ça passe ou ça casse!; **it was one of those make-or-break moments** c'était un moment décisif

makeover ['meɪkˌəʊvə(r)] *n* (**a**) *(of building, room)* transformation *f* (**b**) *(of person)* changement *m* de look; *(at cosmetics counter)* séance *f* de maquillage

maker ['meɪkə(r)] **1** *n* (**a**) *(craftsman)* fabricant(e) *m,f* (**b**) *(manufacturer)* fabricant(e) *m,f*

2 Maker *n Rel* Créateur *m*; *Euph or Hum* **to go to meet one's Maker** passer de vie à trépas; **that's between you and your Maker** c'est entre toi et le Seigneur

▸▸ ***maker's price*** prix *m* de fabrique; ***maker's trademark*** cachet *m* de fabrique

-maker ['meɪkə(r)] *suff* (**a**) *(manufacturer)* fabricant *m* (**b**) *(machine)* **electric coffee-maker** cafetière *f* électrique

make-ready *n Typ* mise *f* en train

makeshift ['meɪkʃɪft] **1** *n (solution)* pis-aller *m inv*, expédient *m*; *(object)* moyen *m* de fortune

2 *adj* de fortune; **a makeshift shelter** un abri de fortune; **the accommodation was very makeshift** le logement était plutôt improvisé

make-up *n* (**a**) *(cosmetics)* maquillage *m*; **to put (one's) make-up on** se maquiller; **she had a lot of make-up on** elle était très maquillée; **eye make-up** fard *m* pour les yeux

(**b**) *(constitution)* constitution *f*; **she changed the make-up of the cabinet** elle a procédé à un remaniement ministériel

(**c**) *(nature, character)* nature *f*, caractère *m*; **spontaneous generosity is not really in her make-up** elle n'est pas généreuse de nature

(**d**) *Typ* mise *f* en pages

(**e**) *Am (test, exam)* examen *m* de rattrapage

▸▸ ***make-up artist*** maquilleur(euse) *m,f*; ***make-up bag*** trousse *f* de maquillage; ***make-up box*** boîte *f* à maquillage; *Am Sch* ***make-up classes*** cours *mpl* de rattrapage; ***make-up remover*** démaquillant *m*; *TV* ***make-up room*** salle *f* de maquillage; *Am Sch* ***make-up test*** examen *m* de rattrapage

makeweight ['meɪkweɪt] *n (on scales)* complément *m* de poids; *Fig* **I'm only here as a makeweight** je ne suis là que pour faire nombre

making ['meɪkɪŋ] **1** *n* (**a**) *(manufacture, creation)* fabrication *f*; **the situation is entirely of his own making** il est entièrement responsable de la situation dans laquelle il se trouve; **the incident was to be the making of his career as a politician** c'est cet incident qui a lancé sa carrière politique; **the two years she spent abroad were the making of her success** les deux années qu'elle a passées à l'étranger ont été la clé de sa réussite; *Elec* **making and breaking** *(of circuit)* fermeture *f* et ouverture *f*

(**b**) *(preparation → of cake)* confection *f*, préparation *f*; *(→ of film)* tournage *m*

2 in the making *adj (idea)* en gestation; *(plan)* à l'étude; *(building)* en construction; **it's history in the making** c'est une page d'histoire qui s'écrit sous nos yeux; **the film was three years in the making** le tournage du film a duré trois ans

3 makings *npl* (**a**) *(essential elements)* ingrédients *mpl*; **his war stories have the makings of a good film** il y a de quoi faire un bon film avec ses récits de guerre; **the affair has all the makings of a national scandal** il y a dans cette affaire largement de quoi déclencher un scandale national

(**b**) *(potential)* **that child has the makings of a genius** cet enfant présente toutes les caractéristiques du génie

-making ['meɪkɪŋ] *suff* **cake-making** fabrication *f* de gâteaux; **decision-making** prise *f* de décisions; **film-making** tournage *m* d'un film; *Br Fam* **it's absolutely sick-making** c'est à vous donner la nausée

making-up *n*

▸▸ *St Exch* ***making-up day*** jour *m* de liquidation; ***making-up price*** cours *m* de compensation

Malabar Coast ['mæləbɑː-] *n* **the Malabar Coast** la côte de Malabar

malabsorption [ˌmæləb'sɔːpʃən] *n Med* malabsorption *f*

Malacca [mə'lækə] *n* (**a**) *Geog* Malacca; **the Malacca Straits** le détroit de Malacca (**b**) *(cane)* (canne *f* de) jonc *m*

▸▸ ***Malacca cane*** canne *f* de jonc *m*

Malachi ['mæləkaɪ] *pr n Bible* Malachie

malachite ['mæləkaɪt] *n Miner* malachite *f*

malacologist [ˌmælə'kɒlədʒɪst] *n* malacologiste *mf*

malacology [ˌmælə'kɒlədʒɪ] *n* malacologie *f*

maladaptation [ˌmælædæp'teɪʃən] *n* défaut *m* d'adaptation

maladapted [ˌmælə'dæptɪd] *adj* inadapté

maladjusted [ˌmælə'dʒʌstɪd] *adj* (**a**) *Psy (person)* inadapté; **maladjusted children** l'enfance *f* inadaptée; **to be socially maladjusted** être socialement inadapté (**b**) *(engine, TV picture)* mal réglé; *(mechanism)* mal ajusté

maladjustment [ˌmælə'dʒʌstmənt] *n* (**a**) *(psychological or social)* inadaptation *f*; *(emotional)* déséquilibre *m* (**b**) *(of engine, TV)* mauvais réglage *m*; *(of mechanism)* mauvais réglage *m*, mauvais ajustement *m*

maladminister [ˌmæləd'mɪnɪstə(r)] *vt* mal administrer, mal gérer

maladministration ['mælədˌmɪnɪs'treɪʃən] *n (of country, economy)* mauvaise administration *f*; *(of business)* mauvaise gestion *f*

maladroit [ˌmælə'drɔɪt] *adj* maladroit, gauche, malhabile

maladroitly [ˌmælə'drɔɪtlɪ] *adv* maladroitement, gauchement

maladroitness [ˌmælə'drɔɪtnɪs] *n* maladresse *f*

malady ['mælədɪ] (*pl* **maladies**) *n Literary* maladie *f*, affection *f*, mal *m*

Malaga ['mæləgə] *n* Malaga

Malagasy [ˌmælə'gæsɪ] **1** *n* (**a**) *(person)* Malgache *mf* (**b**) *(language)* malgache *m*

2 *adj* malgache

3 *comp (embassy, history)* de Madagascar; *(teacher)* de malgache

malaise [mæ'leɪz] *n* malaise *m*

malanders ['mæləndəz] *npl Vet* malandre *f*, malandres *fpl*

malapert ['mæləpɜːt] *Arch* **1** *n* insolent(e) *m,f*

2 *adj* insolent, impertinent

malapropism ['mæləprɒpɪzəm] *n* lapsus *m*

malaria [mə'leərɪə] *n Med* malaria *f*, paludisme *m*; **to have malaria** avoir la malaria *ou* le paludisme

malarial [mə'leərɪəl] *adj (disease, fever)* paludéen

malarkey [mə'lɑːkɪ] *n (UNCOUNT) Fam* bêtises❑ *fpl*, sottises *fpl*; **I don't believe in ghosts or any of that malarkey** je ne crois pas aux fantômes et à toutes ces sottises; **he can't be bothered with that fancy-dress malarkey** il n'aime pas du tout les soirées où les gens doivent se déguiser❑

Malawi [mə'lɑːwɪ] *n* Malawi *m*; **in Malawi** au Malawi

Malawian [mə'lɑːwɪən] **1** *n* Malawite *mf*

2 *adj* malawite

Malay [mə'leɪ] **1** *n* (**a**) *(person)* Malais(e) *m,f* (**b**) *(language)* malais *m*

2 *adj* malais

3 *comp (embassy)* de Malaisie; *(history)* de la Malaisie; *(teacher)* de malais

▸▸ ***the Malay Peninsula*** (la presqu'île de) Malacca, la presqu'île Malaise

Malaya [mə'leɪə] *n* Malaisie *f*, Malaysia *f* occidentale; **in Malaya** en Malaisie

Malayan [mə'leɪən] **1** *n* Malais(e) *m,f*

2 *adj* malais

Malayo-Polynesian [məˌleɪəʊ-] **1** *n Ling* malayo-polynésien *m*

2 *adj* malayo-polynésien

Malaysia [mə'leɪzɪə] *n* Malaysia *f*; **in Malaysia** en Malaysia

Malaysian [mə'leɪzɪən] **1** *n* Malais(e) *m,f*

2 *adj* malais

malcontent [ˈmælkənˌtent] *n Formal* mécontent(e) *m,f*

Maldives [ˈmɔːldiːvz] *npl* **the Maldives** les (îles *fpl*) Maldives *fpl*; **in the Maldives** aux Maldives

Maldivian [mɔːlˈdɪvɪən] **1** *n (inhabitant)* habitant(e) *m,f* des Maldives; *(native)* natif(ive) *m,f* des Maldives

2 *adj* des Maldives

Malé [ˈmɑːleɪ] *n* Malé

male [meɪl] **1** *adj* **(a)** *Zool & Bot* mâle; **male attitudes** l'attitude *f* des hommes; **a male friend** un ami; **when I phoned her, a male voice answered** quand je l'ai appelée, c'est une voix d'homme qui a répondu

(b) *(virile)* mâle, viril

(c) *Tech (plug)* mâle; **male to female adaptor** adaptateur *m* mâle/femelle

2 *n Zool & Bot* mâle *m*; *(man)* homme *m*; **the average French male** le Français moyen

▸▸ ***male bonding*** amitié *f* virile; *Fam Hum* **they're doing some male bonding in the pub** ils sont au pub, entre hommes; ***male chauvinism*** phallocratie *f*; ***male chauvinist*** phallocrate *m*; ***male chauvinist pig*** sale phallocrate *m*; ***male child*** enfant *m* mâle; *Bot* ***male fern*** fougère *f* mâle; *Anat* ***male member*** membre *m* viril; ***male menopause*** andropause *f*; ***male nurse*** infirmier *m*; ***male pattern baldness*** alopécie *f* séborrhéique masculine, alopécie *f* androgénogénétique; ***the male sex*** le sexe masculin; ***male voice choir*** chœur *m* d'hommes

malediction [ˌmælɪˈdɪkʃən] *n Literary* malédiction *f*

malefaction [ˌmælɪˈfækʃən] *n Literary* méfait *m*

malefactor [ˈmælɪˌfæktə(r)] *n Literary* malfaiteur *m*

malefic [məˈlefɪk] *adj Literary* maléfique

maleficent [məˈlefɪsənt] *adj Literary* maléfique

maleic [məˈleɪɪk] *adj Chem* maléique

▸▸ ***maleic acid*** acide *m* maléique

maleness [ˈmeɪlnɪs] *n* masculinité *f*

malevolence [məˈlevələns] *n* malveillance *f*

malevolent [məˈlevələnt] *adj* malveillant

malevolently [məˈlevələntlɪ] *adv* avec malveillance

malfeasance [mælˈfiːzəns] *n Law* méfait *m*, malversation *f*

malformation [ˌmælfɔːˈmeɪʃən] *n* malformation *f*

malformed [ˌmælˈfɔːmd] *adj* difforme

malfunction [ˌmælˈfʌŋkʃən] **1** *n (fault)* fonctionnement *m* défectueux; *(breakdown)* panne *f*, défaillance *f*

2 *vi (go wrong)* mal fonctionner; *(break down)* tomber en panne

▸▸ *Comput* ***malfunction routine*** programme *m* de diagnostic

Mali [ˈmɑːlɪ] *n* Mali *m*; **in Mali** au Mali

Malian [ˈmɑːlɪən] **1** *n* Malien(enne) *m,f*

2 *adj* malien

3 *comp (embassy, history)* du Mali

malic [ˈmælɪk] *adj Chem* malique

▸▸ ***malic acid*** acide *m* malique

malice [ˈmælɪs] *n* méchanceté *f*, malveillance *f*; **I don't bear any malice towards them, I don't bear them any malice** je ne leur en veux pas, je ne leur veux aucun mal; **out of** *or* **through malice** par méchanceté, par malveillance; *Law* **with malice aforethought** avec préméditation

malicious [məˈlɪʃəs] *adj* **(a)** *(gen)* méchant, malveillant; **malicious gossip** médisances *fpl* **(b)** *Law* criminel

▸▸ *Br Law* ***malicious damage*** ≃ dommage *m* causé avec intention de nuire; *Am Law* ***malicious mischief*** ≃ dommage *m* causé avec intention de nuire

maliciously [məˈlɪʃəslɪ] *adv* **(a)** *(gen)* méchamment, avec malveillance **(b)** *Law* avec préméditation, avec intention de nuire

maliciousness [məˈlɪʃəsnɪs] *n* méchanceté *f*, malveillance *f*

malign [məˈlaɪn] **1** *vt (slander)* calomnier; *(criticize)* critiquer, dire du mal de; **the much-maligned government** le gouvernement, dont on dit beaucoup de mal *ou* que l'on a souvent critiqué

2 *adj* **(a)** *(evil)* pernicieux, nocif **(b)** *Med* malin(igne)

malignancy [məˈlɪgnənsɪ] (*pl* **malignancies**) *n* **(a)** *(ill will)* malignité *f*, malveillance *f*, méchanceté *f* **(b)** *Med* malignité *f*

malignant [məˈlɪgnənt] *adj* **(a)** *(person, behaviour, intentions)* malveillant, malfaisant, méchant **(b)** *Med* malin(igne)

▸▸ *Med* ***malignant tumour*** tumeur *f* maligne

malignantly [məˈlɪgnəntlɪ] *adv* avec malveillance, méchamment

malignity [məˈlɪgnətɪ] *n* **(a)** *(ill will)* malignité *f*, malveillance *f*, méchanceté *f* **(b)** *Med* malignité *f*

malinger [məˈlɪŋgə(r)] *vi* simuler la maladie, faire semblant d'être malade

malingerer [məˈlɪŋgərə(r)] *n* faux(fausse) malade *m,f*, personne *f* qui fait semblant d'être malade

malingering [məˈlɪŋgərɪŋ] *n* simulation *f* (de maladie)

mall [mɔːl] **1** *n* **(a)** *(avenue)* mail *m*, avenue *f*

(b) **(shopping) mall** galerie *f* marchande, centre *m* commercial

(c) *Austr (pedestrian precinct)* zone *f* piétonnière

2 **Mall** *n* **the Mall** **(a)** *(in London)* = large avenue reliant Buckingham Palace à Trafalgar Square **(b)** *(in Washington)* = jardin public sur lequel donnent les principaux musées de la ville

▸▸ *Am Fam Pej* ***mall rat*** = jeune qui traîne dans les galeries marchandes

mallard [ˈmælɑːd] *n Orn* colvert *m*

▸▸ ***mallard duck*** colvert *m*

malleability [ˌmælɪəˈbɪlətɪ] *n* malléabilité *f*

malleable [ˈmælɪəbəl] *adj (substance)* malléable; *(person)* influençable, malléable

mallenders [ˈmæləndəz] *npl Vet* malandre *f*, malandres *fpl*

malleolus [məˈliːələs] (*pl* **malleoli** [-laɪ]) *n Anat* malléole *f*

mallet [ˈmælɪt] *n* maillet *m*

mallow [ˈmæləʊ] *n Bot* mauve *f*; **common mallow** grande mauve *f*

malnourished [ˌmælˈnʌrɪʃt] *adj* sous-alimenté

malnutrition [ˌmælnjuːˈtrɪʃən] *n* malnutrition *f*

malocclusion [ˌmæləˈkluːʒən] *n Med* inocclusion *f*

malodorous [ˌmælˈəʊdərəs] *adj* malodorant, nauséabond

malposition [ˌmælpəˈzɪʃən] *n Obst* malposition *f*, position *f* anormale

malpractice [ˌmælˈpræktɪs] *n (UNCOUNT) (professional)* faute *f* professionnelle; *(financial)* malversation *f*, malversations *fpl*; *(political)* fraude *f*

▸▸ *Law* ***malpractice insurance*** = assurance souscrite pour parer à des poursuites judiciaires pour négligence; *Am Law* ***malpractice suit*** = procès pour faute ou négligence professionnelle

malt [mɔːlt] **1** *n* **(a)** *(substance)* malt *m* **(b)** *(whisky)* whisky *m* de malt **(c)** *Am (milk shake)* milk-shake *m* au malt, *Can* lait *m* frappé au malt

2 *comp (extract, sugar, vinegar)* de malt

3 *vt* malter

▸▸ *Am* ***malt liquor*** = boisson alcoolisée tirée du malt; ***malt whisky*** whisky *m* au malt

Malta [ˈmɔːltə] *n* Malte *f*; **in Malta** à Malte

maltase [ˈmɔːlteɪz] *n Chem* maltase *f*

malted [ˈmɔːltɪd] *n* **(a)** *(milk)* lait *m* malté **(b)** *Am (milk shake)* = milk-shake à base de lait malté

▸▸ ***malted milk*** lait *m* malté

Maltese [ˌmɔːlˈtiːz] (*pl* **inv**) **1** *n* **(a)** *(person)* Maltais(e) *m,f* **(b)** *(language)* maltais *m* **(c)** *(dog)* maltais *m*

2 *adj* maltais

3 *comp (embassy, history)* de Malte; *(teacher)* de maltais

▸▸ ***Maltese cat*** chat *m* maltais; ***the Maltese Cross*** la croix de Malte; ***Maltese dog*** chien *m* maltais; ***Maltese terrier*** bichon *m* maltais

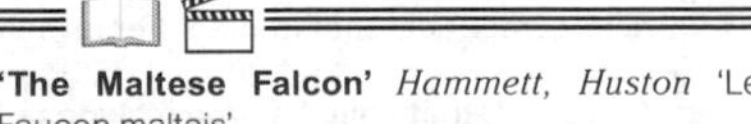

'The Maltese Falcon' *Hammett, Huston* 'Le Faucon maltais'

malthouse [ˈmɔːlthaʊs, *pl* -haʊzɪz] *n* malterie *f*

Malthusian [ˌmælˈθjuːzɪən] *adj* malthusien

Malthusianism [ˌmælˈθjuːzɪənɪzəm] *n* malthusianisme *m*

maltings [ˈmɔːltɪŋs] (*pl* **inv**) *n* malterie *f*

maltose [ˈmɔːltəʊz] *n Chem* maltose *m*

maltreat [ˌmælˈtriːt] *vt* maltraiter

maltreatment [ˌmælˈtriːtmənt] *n (UNCOUNT)* mauvais traitement *m ou* traitements *mpl*, sévices *mpl*

malty [ˈmɔːltɪ] (*compar* **maltier**, *superl* **maltiest**) *adj (in smell)* qui sent le malt; *(in taste)* qui a un goût de malt; **a malty taste** un goût de malt

malversation [ˌmælvəˈseɪʃən] *n Formal* malversation *f*

mam [mæm] *n NEng Fam* maman ◻ *f*

mama [*Br* məˈmɑː, *Am* ˈmɑːmə] *n Br Old-fashioned or Hum or Am* maman ◻ *f*; *Am Fam* ***mama's boy*** fils *m* à sa maman

mamba [ˈmæmbə] *n Zool* mamba *m*

mambo [ˈmæmbəʊ] (*pl* **mambos**) *n* mambo *m*

mamelon [ˈmæmələn] *n* mamelon *m*, butte *f*

Mameluke [ˈmæmɪluːk] *n Hist* mamelouk *m*

mamilla [məˈmɪlə] (*pl* **mamillae** [-liː]) *n Anat & Zool* mamelon *m*

mamillary [məˈmɪlərɪ] *adj Anat & Zool* **(a)** *(relating to the breast)* mamillaire **(b)** *(nipple-shaped)* mammiforme

mamma [ˈmæmə] *n esp Am Fam* **(a)** *(mother)* maman ◻ *f* **(b)** *(woman)* môme *f*, nana *f* **(c)** **big mamma** *(object)* mastodonte *m*

mammal [ˈmæməl] *n* mammifère *m*

mammalian [məˈmeɪlɪən] *adj* mammalien

mammalogical [ˌmæməˈlɒdʒɪkəl] *adj* mammalogique

mammalogy [mæˈmælədʒɪ] *n Zool* mammalogie *f*

mammary [ˈmæmərɪ] *adj Anat* mammaire

▸▸ ***mammary gland*** glande *f* mammaire

mammiferous [mæˈmɪfərəs] *adj Zool* mammifère

mammogram [ˈmæməgræm], **mammograph** [ˈmæməgrɑːf] *n Med* mammographie *f*

mammography [mæˈmɒgrəfɪ] *n Med* mammographie *f*

Mammon [ˈmæmən] *pr n* Mammon *m*

mammoth [ˈmæməθ] **1** *n* mammouth *m*

2 *adj* immense, colossal, gigantesque; **a mammoth task** un travail de Titan

mammy [ˈmæmɪ] (*pl* **mammies**) *n Fam* **(a)** *(mother)* maman ◻ *f* **(b)** *Pej Old-fashioned (black nanny)* = bonne d'enfants noire

Man (*written abbr* **Manitoba**) Manitoba *m*

MAN [mæn]

homme	▸ **1 (a) – (i), (o)**
valet	▸ **1 (k)**
ouvrier	▸ **1 (l)**
soldat	▸ **1 (m)**
matelot	▸ **1 (m)**
joueur	▸ **1 (n)**
pièce	▸ **1 (q)**
armer	▸ **2 (a)**
s'occuper de	▸ **2 (b)**
assurer le service de	▸ **2 (b)**

(*pl* **men** [men], *pt & pp* **manned**, *cont* **manning**) **1** *n* **(a)** *(adult male)* homme *m*; **a young man** un jeune homme; **an old man** un vieillard; **a blind man** un aveugle; **he seems a nice man** il a l'air gentil; **he's lived here, man and boy, for forty years** c'est ici qu'il a grandi et vécu pendant quarante ans; **there's a new man in her life** il y a un nouvel homme dans sa vie; **I'm just a man** je ne suis qu'un homme comme les autres; **one move and you're a dead man!** un (seul) geste et tu es un homme mort!; **he's a man's man** il aime bien être avec ses copains; **he's a man of the world** c'est un homme d'expérience; **the man in the moon** le visage de la lune; **men's clothes/trousers** vêtements *mpl*/pantalon *m* pour homme; **men's department** *(in shop)* rayon *m* hommes

(b) *(type)* homme *m*; **he's not a betting/drinking man** ce n'est pas un homme qui parie/boit; **he was never a man for taking risks** il n'a jamais été homme à *ou* ce n'est pas le genre d'homme à prendre des risques; **he's not a man to make a mistake like that** il ne ferait pas une telle erreur

(c) *(appropriate person)* homme *m*; **he's the man for the job** c'est l'homme qu'il faut pour

mal–man

faire ce travail; **I'm your man** je suis votre homme; **he's not the man for that kind of work** il n'est pas fait pour ce genre de travail

(**d**) *(professional)* **a medical man** un médecin; **a man of God** un homme d'église; **a man of learning** un savant; **a man of letters** un homme de lettres

(**e**) *(with manly qualities)* homme *m*; **to act like a man** se comporter en homme; **he took the news like a man** il a pris la nouvelle avec courage; **he's not man enough to own up** il n'aura pas le courage d'avouer; **the army will make a man of him!** l'armée en fera un homme!; **a holiday will make a new man of me** des vacances me feront le plus grand bien; *Fig* **this will separate** *or* **sort the men from the boys** c'est là qu'on verra les vrais hommes

(**f**) *(person, individual)* homme *m*, individu *m*; **what more can a man do?** qu'est-ce qu'on peut faire de plus?; **any man would have reacted in the same way** n'importe qui aurait réagi de la même façon; **all men are born equal** tous les hommes naissent égaux; **the man must be mad!** il doit être fou!; **I've never met the man** je n'ai jamais rencontré l'individu en question; **to be one's own man** être indépendant *ou* son propre maître; **to the last man** *(without exception)* sans exception; *(until defeat)* jusqu'au dernier; **it's every man for himself** c'est chacun pour soi; **the man in the street** l'homme *m* de la rue; *Prov* **one man's meat is another man's poison** le malheur des uns fait le bonheur des autres; *Br Fam* **every man jack of them** chacun d'eux sans exception ▫

(**g**) *(as husband, father)* homme *m*; **man and wife** mari *m* et femme *f*; **to live as man and wife** vivre maritalement *ou* en concubinage; **he's a real family man** c'est un vrai père de famille; **the man of the house** l'homme *m* de la maison; *Hum* le pater familias; *Fam* **my old man** *(husband)* mon homme; *(father)* mon vieux

(**h**) *Br Fam (boyfriend, lover)* homme *m*, mec *m*; **she's got a new man** elle a un nouveau mec; **have you met her young man?** *(boyfriend)* avez-vous rencontré son petit ami?; *(fiancé)* avez-vous rencontré son fiancé?

(**i**) *(inhabitant, native)* **I'm a Dublin man** je suis de Dublin; **he's a local man** c'est un homme du pays

(**j**) *(student)* **he's a Harvard man** *(at present)* il fait ses études à Harvard; *(in the past)* il a fait ses études à Harvard

(**k**) *(servant)* valet *m*, domestique *m*

(**l**) *(employee → in industry, on farm)* ouvrier *m*; *(→ in business, shop)* employé *m*; **the men have gone on strike** les hommes se sont mis en grève; **a TV repair man** un réparateur télé; **I'll need to get a man in to fix it** il faut que je fasse venir un réparateur; **we'll send a man round to look at it** nous vous envoyons quelqu'un pour voir; **our man in Paris** *(representative)* notre représentant *m* à Paris; *(journalist)* notre correspondant *m* à Paris; *(diplomat)* notre envoyé *m* diplomatique à Paris; *(spy)* notre agent *m* à Paris

(**m**) *(in armed forces → soldier)* soldat *m*, homme *m* (de troupe); *(→ sailor)* matelot *m*, homme *m* (d'équipage); **officers and men** *(in army)* officiers *mpl* et hommes *mpl* de troupe; *(in navy)* officiers *mpl* et matelots *mpl*

(**n**) *(player)* joueur *m*, équipier *m*; **a three-man team** une équipe de trois joueurs; **the man of the match** le héros du match

(**o**) *(mankind)* homme *m*; **primitive/modern man** l'homme *m* primitif/moderne; **one of the most deadly poisons known to man** un des plus dangereux poisons connus de l'homme; *Prov* **man cannot live by bread alone** l'homme ne vit pas que de pain

(**p**) *Fam (as term of address)* **come on, man!** allez, viens!; **hey, man!** *(as greeting)* salut vieux!; **what can I do for you, young man?** que puis-je faire pour vous, jeune homme?; *Old-fashioned* **my good man** mon cher monsieur *m*; **good man!** c'est bien!; *Old-fashioned* **how are you, old man?** comment tu vas, mon vieux?

(**q**) *(in chess)* pièce *f*; *(in draughts)* pion *m*

(**r**) *Fam Black Am slang (drug dealer)* dealer *m*; **the Man** *(whites)* les Blancs *mpl*; *(police)* les flics *mpl*

2 *vt* (**a**) *Mil (ship)* armer, équiper; *(pumps)* armer; *(cannon)* servir; **to man the barricades** défendre les barricades; **the tanker was manned by Greek seamen** le pétrolier avait un équipage grec; **man the pumps!** armez les pompes!; **man the lifeboats!** mettez les canots à la mer!; **manned space flight** vol *m* spatial habité; **the sentries manned the battlements** il y avait des sentinelles sur les remparts; **the plane is manned by a pilot and a navigator** l'équipage de l'avion consiste en un pilote et un navigateur; **the fort was manned by twenty soldiers** le fort était tenu par une garnison de vingt soldats

(**b**) *(staff → machine)* faire tourner, s'occuper de; *(→ switchboard)* assurer le service *ou* la permanence de; **who's manning the telephone?** qui assure la permanence téléphonique?; **reception wasn't manned at the time** personne n'assurait *ou* n'était à la réception à ce moment-là; **someone has to be there to man the phone** quelqu'un doit être là pour répondre au téléphone; **the campaign office was manned by volunteers** la permanence de la campagne était assurée par des volontaires; **the office is manned by a skeleton staff** le bureau tourne à effectif réduit; **to man a night-shift** composer une équipe de nuit

3 *exclam Fam* la vache!; **man, was it big!** bon sang, qu'est-ce que c'était grand!; **you should have seen it, man!** bon sang, tu aurais dû voir ça!

4 as one man *adv* comme un seul homme; **they replied as one man** ils répondirent d'une seule voix

5 to a man *adv* sans exception; **they agreed to a man** ils ont accepté à l'unanimité; **they were patriots/communists to a man** ils étaient tous patriotes/communistes

▸▸ *Literature* **Man Friday** Vendredi; ***man Friday*** *(servant)* fidèle serviteur *m*; *(office worker)* = employé de bureau affecté à des tâches diverses; *Br* ***man management*** gestion *f* des ressources humaines

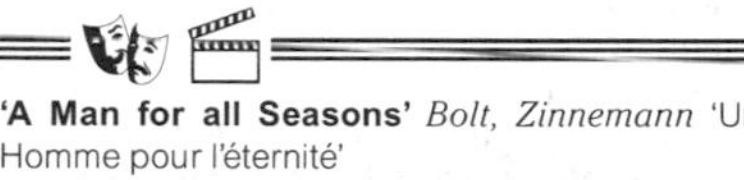

'A Man for all Seasons' *Bolt, Zinnemann* 'Un Homme pour l'éternité'

'The Man who knew too much' *Hitchcock* 'L'Homme qui en savait trop'

'The Man who would be King' *Kipling, Huston* 'L'Homme qui voulut être roi'

'The Man in the White Suit' *MacKendrick* 'L'Homme au complet blanc'

'Man and Superman' *Shaw* 'L'Homme et le surhomme'

'A Man in Full' *Wolfe* 'Un homme, un vrai'

A man's gotta do what a man's gotta do

Il s'agit d'une phrase que l'on associe généralement aux vieux westerns dans lesquels les héros expriment leur détermination à agir en hommes, en dépit du danger. Cette formule ("un homme, un vrai, ne recule pas devant l'obstacle") s'utilise aujourd'hui de façon allusive et sur le mode ironique lorsque quelqu'un doit exécuter une tâche simple (l'équivalent français est "quand il faut y aller, il faut y aller").

man-about-town (*pl* **men-about-town**) *n Br* homme *m* du monde, mondain *m*

manacle ['mænəkəl] **1** *vt (shackle)* enchaîner; *(handcuff)* mettre *ou* passer les menottes à; **his wrists were manacled** il portait des menottes

2 manacles *npl (shackles)* fers *mpl*, chaînes *fpl*; *(handcuffs)* menottes *fpl*

manage ['mænɪdʒ] **1** *vt* (**a**) *(business, hotel, shop)* gérer, diriger; *(property, estate, economy, money, resources)* gérer; *(finances, resources)* s'occuper de; *(crisis, illness)* gérer; *(team)* être le manager de, diriger; **she manages a shoe shop** elle est gérante d'une boutique de chaussures; **he manages his father's company** il dirige la société de son père; **he manages Melchester United** c'est le manager de *ou* il manage Melchester United; **to manage sb's affairs** gérer les affaires de qn; **I'm very bad at managing money** je suis incapable de gérer un budget

(**b**) *(accomplish)* réussir; **you'll manage it** ça ira; **she managed a smile** elle trouva la force de sourire; **to manage to do sth** réussir *ou* parvenir *ou* arriver à faire qch; **he managed to keep a straight face** il est parvenu à garder son sérieux; **did you manage to get anything to eat?** as-tu finalement trouvé quelque chose à manger?; **he always manages to arrive at meal times** il se débrouille toujours pour arriver *ou* il trouve toujours le moyen d'arriver à l'heure des repas

(**c**) *(handle → person, animal)* savoir s'y prendre avec; *(manipulate → machine, tool)* manier, se servir de; **she's a difficult child to manage** c'est une enfant difficile, c'est une enfant dont on ne fait pas ce qu'on veut; **he doesn't know how to manage people** il ne sait pas s'y prendre avec les gens; **I can't manage these new typewriters** je ne sais pas bien me servir de ces nouvelles machines à écrire

(**d**) *(be available for)* **can you manage nine o'clock/next Saturday?** pouvez-vous venir à neuf heures/samedi prochain?; **can you manage lunch tomorrow?** pouvez-vous déjeuner avec moi demain?

(**e**) *(cope with)* **I can't manage all this extra work** je ne peux pas faire face à ce surcroît de travail; **can you manage that rucksack?** pouvez-vous porter ce sac à dos?; **he can't manage the stairs any more** il n'arrive plus à monter l'escalier; **we can't manage any more guests** nous ne pouvons pas accueillir plus de gens; **I think I could manage another slice** j'en reprendrais volontiers une tranche; **I couldn't manage another thing** je ne peux plus rien avaler; **can you manage £10?** pouvez-vous aller jusqu'à 10 livres?

2 *vi (cope)* se débrouiller, y arriver; *(financially)* se débrouiller, s'en sortir; **we'll have to manage on our own** nous devrons nous débrouiller tout seuls; **can you manage?** ça ira?; **give me a fork, I can't manage with chopsticks** donne-moi une fourchette, je ne m'en sors pas avec des baguettes; **we had to manage without heating** nous avons dû nous passer de chauffage; **they just about manage on the dole** ils arrivent tout juste à s'en sortir avec les allocations de chômage; **how am I going to manage without a job?** comment vais-je faire *ou* m'en sortir sans travail?

manageable ['mænɪdʒəbəl] *adj (size, amount)* raisonnable; *(tool, car, boat)* maniable; *(hair)* facile à coiffer; **this new shampoo leaves your hair shiny and manageable** ce nouveau shampooing rendra vos cheveux brillants et faciles à coiffer; **cut the wood into manageable pieces** coupez le bois en morceaux faciles à manipuler; **the smaller suitcase is a more manageable size** la plus petite valise est plus maniable

managed ['mænɪdʒd] *adj (farmland, woodland, estate)* exploité

▸▸ *Fin* ***managed costs*** coûts *mpl* maîtrisables; *Fin* ***managed currency*** devise *f* contrôlée, monnaie *f* dirigée; *Fin* ***managed fund*** *(in insurance)* fonds *m* géré; *Fin* ***managed unit trust*** fonds *m* commun de placement géré

management ['mænɪdʒmənt] *n* (**a**) *(control → of firm, finances, property)* gestion *f*, direction *f*; *(of economy, money, resources)* gestion; **the management of the country's economy** la gestion de l'économie du pays; **all their problems are due to bad management** tous leurs problèmes sont dus à une mauvaise gestion; **under Gordon's management sales have increased significantly** depuis que c'est Gordon qui s'en occupe, les ventes ont considérablement augmenté; **who looks after the management of the**

farm? qui s'occupe de l'exploitation de la ferme?; **management by exception** direction *f* par exceptions; **management by objectives** gestion *f* par objectifs

(**b**) *(handling → of crisis, illness etc)* gestion *f*; **she was praised for her management of the situation** on a applaudi la façon dont elle s'est comportée dans cette situation

(**c**) *(of shop, hotel etc)* direction *f*; **the management cannot accept responsibility for any loss or damage** *(sign)* la direction décline toute responsabilité en cas de perte ou de dommage; **under new management** *(sign)* changement de direction *ou* de propriétaire; **they're on the management** ils font partie de la direction

(**d**) *Ind (managers, employers)* administration *f*, direction *f*; **negotiations between management and unions have broken down** les négociations entre le patronat et les syndicats ont échoué

►► ***management accountant*** contrôleur(euse) *m,f* de gestion; ***management accounting*** comptabilité *f* de gestion; ***management accounts*** comptes *mpl* de gestion; ***management audit*** contrôle *m* de gestion; *Fin* ***management buy-in*** apport *m* de gestion; *Br* ***management buy-out*** rachat *m* d'une société par la direction; ***management committee*** comité *m* de direction; ***management consultancy*** *(activity)* conseil *m* en gestion (d'entreprise); *(firm)* cabinet *m* (de) conseil; ***management consultant*** conseiller(ère) *m,f* en *ou* de gestion (d'entreprise); ***management contract*** contrat *m* de gestion; ***management expenses*** frais *mpl* de gestion; ***management fee*** honoraires *mpl* d'un consultant; ***management function*** fonction *f* d'encadrement; ***management information system*** système *m* intégré de gestion; ***management operating system*** système *m* intégré de gestion; ***management report*** rapport *m* de gestion; *(accounts statistics)* tableau *m* de bord; ***management skills*** qualités *fpl* de gestionnaire; ***management studies*** *(UNCOUNT)* études *fpl* de gestion; ***management style*** mode *m* de gestion; ***management summary*** résumé *m* managérial; ***management team*** équipe *f* dirigeante; ***management technique*** méthode *f* de gestion; ***management theory*** théorie *f* de la gestion de l'entreprise; ***management tool*** outil *m* de gestion; ***management training*** formation *f* des cadres

manager [ˈmænɪdʒə(r)] *n* (**a**) *(of company, bank)* directeur(trice) *m,f*; *(of shop)* directeur(trice) *m,f*, gérant(e) *m,f*; *(of bar, restaurant)* gérant(e) *m,f*; *(of pop star, celebrity)* manager *m*; *(of sports team)* manager *m*, entraîneur(euse) *m,f*; *Fin (of funds, money)* gestionnaire *mf*; *(of assets)* administrateur(trice) *m,f*; *(of estate)* régisseur *m*; **he's been made manager** il est passé cadre

(**b**) *(organizer)* **she's a good home manager** elle sait tenir une maison

(**c**) *Comput (of disk etc)* gestionnaire *m*

manageress [ˌmænɪdʒəˈres] *n (of company, bank)* directrice *f*, *(of shop)* directrice *f*, gérante *f*; *(of bar, restaurant)* gérante *f*

managerial [ˌmænɪˈdʒɪərɪəl] *adj* gestionnaire, directorial; *(position)* de commande; **at managerial level** au niveau de la direction; **managerial experience** expérience *f* de la direction

►► ***managerial skills*** qualités *fpl* de gestionnaire; ***managerial staff*** cadres *mpl*, encadrement *m*

managership [ˈmænɪdʒəʃɪp] *n* direction *f*

managing [ˈmænɪdʒɪŋ] **1** *adj* **a managing woman** une maîtresse femme

2 *n (handling)* gestion *f*; **she was praised for her managing of the situation** on a applaudi la façon dont elle s'est comportée dans cette situation

►► ***managing director*** directeur(trice) *m,f* général(e), P-DG *m*; ***managing editor*** rédacteur(trice) *m,f* en chef

Managua [məˈnægwə] *n* Managua

manakin [ˈmænəkɪn] *n Orn* manakin *m*

man-at-arms *(pl* **men-at-arms***) n Hist* homme *m* d'armes

manatee [ˌmænəˈtiː] *n Zool* lamantin *m*

man-bites-dog story *n Journ* = article paru dans la rubrique des chiens écrasés

Manc [mæŋk] *n Br Fam (abbr* **Mancunian***) (inhabitant)* habitant(e) *m,f* de Manchester; *(native)* originaire *mf* de Manchester

Manchester [ˈmænˌtʃestə(r)] **1** *n* Manchester

2 manchester *n Austr (household linen)* draps *mpl* et serviettes *fpl*

man-child *(pl* **man-children***) n Literary* enfant *m* mâle

Manchu [mænˈtʃuː] **1** *n* Mandchou(e) *m,f*

2 *adj* mandchou

Manchukuo [mænˈtʃuːkwəʊ] *n Hist* Mandchoukouo *m*

Manchuria [mænˈtʃʊərɪə] *n* Mandchourie *f*; **in Manchuria** en Mandchourie

Manchurian [mænˈtʃʊərɪən] **1** *n* (**a**) *(person)* Mandchou(e) *m,f* (**b**) *(langue)* mandchou *m*

2 *adj* mandchou

manciple [ˈmænsɪpəl] *n* intendant *m*

Mancunian [mæŋˈkjuːnjən] **1** *n (inhabitant)* habitant(e) *m,f* de Manchester; *(native)* originaire *mf* de Manchester

2 *adj* de Manchester

M&A [ˌemənˈeɪ] *n Fin (abbr* **mergers and acquisitions***)* fusions et acquisitions *fpl*

mandala [mænˈdɑːlə] *n Rel & Art* mandala *m*

Mandalay [ˌmændəˈleɪ] *n* Mandalay

mandamus [mænˈdeɪməs] *n Law* ordonnance *f* d'exécution

mandarin [ˈmændərɪn] **1** *n* (**a**) *Hist & Fig* mandarin *m* (**b**) *Bot (tree)* mandarinier *m* (**c**) *(fruit)* mandarine *f* (**d**) *(colour)* mandarine *f*

2 Mandarin *n Ling* mandarin *m*

►► *Ling* ***Mandarin Chinese*** mandarin *m*; ***mandarin collar*** col *m* Mao; *Orn* ***mandarin duck*** (canard *m*) mandarin *m*; ***mandarin orange*** mandarine *f*

mandate 1 *n* [ˈmændeɪt] (**a**) *Pol* mandat *m*; **the government receives its mandate from the electorate** c'est l'électorat qui mandate les membres du gouvernement; **the government has no mandate to introduce the new tax** le gouvernement n'a pas été mandaté pour mettre en place ce nouvel impôt

(**b**) *(country)* (territoire *m* sous) mandat *m*; **under British mandate** sous mandat britannique

(**c**) *(task)* tâche *f*, mission *f*

2 *vt* [ˌmænˈdeɪt] (**a**) *(give authority)* mandater; **to mandate sb to do sth** donner mandat à qn de faire qch

(**b**) *(country)* mettre sous mandat, administrer par mandat

►► *Fin* ***mandate form*** lettre *f* de signatures autorisées

mandatory [ˈmændətərɪ] *(pl* **mandatories***)* **1** *adj* (**a**) *(obligatory)* obligatoire; **participation is mandatory** la participation est obligatoire (**b**) *(of a mandate)* découlant d'un mandat

2 *n* mandataire *mf*

►► *Fin* ***mandatory liquid assets*** liquidités *fpl* obligatoires; ***mandatory powers*** pouvoirs *mpl* donnés par mandat; *St Exch* ***mandatory quote period*** période *f* de cotation obligatoire

man-day *n Br* jour-homme *m*; **thirty man-days** trente journées *fpl* de travail

mandible [ˈmændɪbəl] *n* (**a**) *(of insect)* mandibule *f* (**b**) *(of vertebrate)* mâchoire *f* inférieure

mandibular [mænˈdɪbjʊlə(r)] *adj Zool* mandibulaire

mandolin(e) [ˈmændəlɪn] *n* mandoline *f*

mandolinist [ˌmændəˈlɪnɪst] *n* mandoliniste *mf*

mandragora [mænˈdrægərə] *n Bot* mandragore *f*

mandrake [ˈmændreɪk] *n Bot* mandragore *f*

mandrel, mandril [ˈmændrəl] *n Tech* mandrin *m*, arbre *m* (de tour)

mandrill [ˈmændrɪl] *n Zool* mandrill *m*

►► ***mandrill ape*** mandrill *m*

mane [meɪn] *n (of horse, lion)* crinière *f*; *Fig* **a mane of golden hair** une crinière blonde

man-eater *n* (**a**) *(animal)* mangeur *m* d'hommes; *(cannibal)* cannibale *m*, anthropophage *m* (**b**) *Fam Hum (woman)* dévoreuse *f* d'hommes, mangeuse *f* d'hommes

man-eating *adj (animal)* mangeur d'hommes, anthropophage; *(people)* cannibale, anthropophage

►► ***man-eating shark*** requin *m* mangeur d'hommes

manege, manège [mæˈneɪʒ] *n (training)* manège *m*; *(school)* école *f* d'équitation, centre *m* hippique

maneuver, maneuverable *etc Am* = **manoeuvre, manoeuvrable** *etc*

man-for-man *adj Br Sport* **man-for-man marking** marquage *m* individuel

manful [ˈmænfʊl] *adj (courageous)* vaillant, ardent

manfully [ˈmænfʊlɪ] *adv (courageously)* vaillamment, courageusement; **he was struggling manfully with the suitcases/his second steak** il se démenait vaillamment avec les valises/son deuxième steak

manganese [ˈmæŋgəniːz] *n Chem* manganèse *m*

►► ***manganese steel*** acier *m* au manganèse

manganic [mæŋˈgænɪk] *adj Chem* manganique

►► ***manganic oxide*** oxyde *m* manganique

Manganin® [ˈmæŋgənɪn] *n Metal* manganin®

manganous [ˈmæŋgənəs] *adj Chem* manganeux

►► ***manganous oxide*** oxyde *m* manganeux

mange [meɪndʒ] *n Vet* gale *f*

mangel-wurzel [ˈmæŋgəlˌwɜːzəl] *n* betterave *f* fourragère

manger [ˈmeɪndʒə(r)] *n* (**a**) *(trough)* mangeoire *f* (**b**) *Bible* crèche *f*

mangetout [ˌmɑ̃ʒˈtuː] *n Br* mange-tout *m inv*

mangey = **mangy**

manginess [ˈmeɪndʒɪnɪs] *n (of animal)* état *m* galeux

mangle [ˈmæŋgəl] **1** *n (for clothes)* essoreuse *f* (à rouleaux)

2 *vt* (**a**) *(body)* mutiler, déchiqueter; *(vehicle)* rendre méconnaissable; **their bodies were horribly mangled** leurs corps ont été atrocement mutilés; **the mangled wreckage of the two cars** les carcasses en accordéon des deux voitures

(**b**) *(quotation, text)* estropier, mutiler

(**c**) *(laundry, linen)* essorer *(dans une essoreuse à rouleaux)*

mango [ˈmæŋgəʊ] *(pl* **mangos** *or* **mangoes***) n* (**a**) *(fruit)* mangue *f* (**b**) *(tree)* manguier *m*

►► ***mango chutney*** = condiment *m* à la mangue

mangold(-wurzel) [ˈmæŋgəld(ˌwɜːzəl)] = **mangel-wurzel**

mangonel [ˈmæŋgənel] *n Hist* mangonneau *m*

mangosteen [ˈmæŋgəstiːn] *n* mangoustan *m*; *(tree)* mangoustanier *m*

►► ***mangosteen tree*** mangoustanier *m*

mangrove [ˈmæŋgrəʊv] *n* manglier *m*, palétuvier *m*

►► ***mangrove swamp*** mangrove *f*

mangy [ˈmeɪndʒɪ] *(compar* **mangier**, *superl* **mangiest***) adj* (**a**) *(having mange → animal)* galeux (**b**) *Fam (shabby → coat, carpet)* miteux, pelé

manhandle [ˈmænˌhændəl] *vt* (**a**) *(treat roughly)* maltraiter, malmener (**b**) *(move)* porter *ou* transporter (à bras d'homme); **they manhandled the piano into position** ils ont poussé le piano pour le mettre à sa place

Manhattan [mænˈhætən] *n* (**a**) *Geog* Manhattan (**b**) *(cocktail)* manhattan *m*

►► ***the Manhattan Project*** = projet secret de construction d'une bombe nucléaire en 1942

manhole [ˈmænhəʊl] *n* bouche *f* d'égout, regard *m*

►► ***manhole cover*** plaque *f* d'égout

manhood [ˈmænhʊd] *n* (**a**) *(age)* âge *m* d'homme; **he has reached manhood** c'est un homme maintenant

(**b**) *(virility)* virilité *f*

(**c**) *(men collectively)* hommes *mpl*, population *f* masculine; **British manhood** les hommes *mpl* britanniques

(**d**) *Fam Hum (genitals)* bijoux *mpl* de famille

man-hour *n Br* heure-homme *f*; **300 man-hours** 300 heures *fpl* de travail

manhunt [ˈmænˌhʌnt] *n* chasse *f* à l'homme

mania [ˈmeɪnjə] *n* (**a**) *Psy* manie *f*; *(obsession)* obsession *f* (**b**) *(zeal)* passion *f*, *Pej* manie *f*; **he has a mania for collecting old photographs** il a la manie de collectionner les vieilles photos; **he's got football mania** c'est un passionné de football

maniac [ˈmeɪnɪæk] **1** *n* (**a**) *(dangerous person)* fou (folle) *m,f*; *(sexual)* obsédé(e) *m,f*; **I've been working like a maniac for the past two months** ça fait deux mois que je travaille comme un fou; **to drive like a maniac** conduire comme un fou

(**b**) *(fan)* fou (folle) *m,f*; **he's a football maniac** c'est un fan *ou* un mordu de football
(**c**) *Psy* maniaque *mf*
2 *adj* (**a**) *(gen)* fou (folle)
(**b**) *Psy* maniaque

maniacal [mə'naɪəkəl] *adj* (**a**) *(crazy)* fou (folle); **maniacal laughter** rire *m* hystérique (**b**) *Psy* maniaque

maniacally [mə'naɪəklɪ] *adv* de manière hystérique

manic ['mænɪk] **1** *n* maniaque *mf*
2 *adj* (**a**) *(crazy)* fou (folle) (**b**) *Psy* maniaque
►► ***manic depression*** psychose *f* maniaco-dépressive

manic-depressive **1** *n* maniaco-dépressif(ive) *m,f*
2 *adj* maniaco-dépressif

Manichean [ˌmænɪ'kiːən] *Rel* **1** *n* manichéen(enne) *m,f*
2 *adj* manichéen

Manicheism [ˌmænɪ'kiːɪzəm] *n Rel* manichéisme *m*

manicure ['mænɪˌkjʊə(r)] **1** *n* manucure *f*; **to give sb a manicure** faire les mains à qn, manucurer qn
2 *comp (case, scissors)* de manucure, à ongles
3 *vt* faire les mains à, manucurer; **she was manicuring her nails** elle était en train de se faire les ongles; **a manicured lawn** une pelouse impeccable
►► ***manicure set*** trousse *f* de manucure

manicurist ['mænɪˌkjʊərɪst] *n* manucure *mf*

manifest ['mænɪfest] **1** *n (of ship, plane)* manifeste *m*
2 *adj Formal* manifeste, évident
3 *vt* manifester; **to manifest open hostility** manifester une franche hostilité; **how did this mania manifest itself?** comment cette obsession s'est-elle manifestée?
4 *vi (ghost, spirit)* se manifester
►► *Am Hist* ***Manifest Destiny*** = au XIXème siècle, idée selon laquelle l'établissement des colons en Amérique du Nord relevait de la volonté divine

manifestation [ˌmænɪfes'teɪʃən] *n* manifestation *f*

manifestly ['mænɪfestlɪ] *adv* manifestement, à l'évidence

manifesto [ˌmænɪ'festəʊ] *(pl* **manifestos** *or* **manifestoes**) *n* manifeste *m*

manifold ['mænɪfəʊld] **1** *n Tech* **(exhaust) manifold** collecteur *m* d'échappement; **(inlet** *or* **intake) manifold** conduits *mpl* d'admission, collecteur *m* d'admission
2 *adj Formal (numerous)* multiple, nombreux; *(varied)* varié, divers

manikin = **mannikin**

Manila [mə'nɪlə] *n* Manille

manila, manilla [mə'nɪlə] *adj* en chanvre de Manille
►► ***manila envelope*** enveloppe *f* en papier kraft; ***manila hemp*** chanvre *m* de Manille; ***manila paper*** papier *m* kraft; ***manila rope*** (cordage *m* en) manille *f*

manioc ['mænɪɒk] *n* manioc *m*

manipulate [mə'nɪpjʊleɪt] *vt* (**a**) *(equipment)* manœuvrer, manipuler; *(tool)* manier; *(vehicle)* manœuvrer
(**b**) *Pej (person)* manipuler, manœuvrer; *(facts, figures)* manipuler; **he skilfully manipulates situations to his own end** il a l'art de tirer profit de toutes les situations; *Fin* **to manipulate the accounts** trafiquer les comptes; *St Exch* **to manipulate the market** agir sur le marché
(**c**) *Med* **to manipulate bones** pratiquer des manipulations

manipulation [məˌnɪpjʊ'leɪʃən] *n* (**a**) *(of equipment)* manœuvre *f*, manipulation *f* (**b**) *Pej (of people, facts, situation)* manipulation *f* (**c**) *Med* manipulation *f*

manipulative [mə'nɪpjʊlətɪv] *adj Pej* manipulateur; **he can be very manipulative** il n'hésite pas à manipuler les gens; **that's so manipulative** *(remark, action)* c'est de la manipulation

manipulator [mə'nɪpjʊleɪtə(r)] *n* manipulateur(trice) *m,f*

Manitoba [ˌmænɪ'təʊbə] *n* le Manitoba; **in Manitoba** au Manitoba

manitou ['mænɪtuː] *n* manitou *m*

mankind [mæn'kaɪnd] *n* (**a**) *(species)* humanité *f*, espèce *f* humaine; **for the good of mankind** pour le bien de l'humanité (**b**) *(men in general)* hommes *mpl*

manky ['mæŋkɪ] *(compar* **mankier,** *superl* **mankiest**) *adj Br Fam (worthless)* nul; *(dirty)* miteux, pourri

manlike ['mænlaɪk] *adj* (**a**) *(virile)* viril, masculin (**b**) *(woman)* masculin

manliness ['mænlɪnɪs] *n* virilité *f*

manly ['mænlɪ] *(compar* **manlier,** *superl* **manliest**) *adj (sport, activity)* d'homme, masculin; *(behaviour, character, voice)* mâle, viril

man-mad *adj* obsédé par les hommes, nymphomane

man-made *adj (fibre, fabric, product)* synthétique; *(construction, lake, beach)* artificiel; *(landscape)* modelé *ou* façonné par l'homme

manna ['mænə] *n* (**a**) *Bible & Fig* manne *f*; *Fig* **manna from heaven** manne *f* céleste (**b**) *Bot* manne *f*

manned [mænd] *adj (ship, machine)* ayant un équipage
►► ***manned spacecraft*** vaisseau *m* spatial habité

mannequin ['mænɪkɪn] *n* mannequin *m*

manner ['mænə(r)] **1** *n* (**a**) *(way)* manière *f*, façon *f*; **in the same manner** de la même manière *ou* façon; **it's just a manner of speaking** c'est juste une façon de parler; **in a manner of speaking** en quelque sorte, dans un certain sens; **it was the manner in which he did it that upset me** c'est la manière *ou* la façon dont il s'y est pris qui m'a blessé; **she dealt with them in a very gentle manner** elle a été d'une grande douceur avec eux; **to keep sb in the manner to which he/she is accustomed** permettre à qn de maintenir son train de vie; **he does it (as if** *or* **as) to the manner born** il le fait comme s'il avait fait ça toute sa vie; *Gram* **adverb of manner** adverbe *m* de manière
(**b**) *(attitude)* attitude *f*, manière *f*; *(behaviour)* comportement *m*, manière *f* de se conduire; **to have a pleasant manner** avoir des manières agréables; **I don't like his manner** je n'aime pas ses façons; **he has a good telephone manner** il fait bonne impression au téléphone; **there was something in his manner that made me suspicious** quelque chose dans son comportement a éveillé mes soupçons; **in a manner of speaking** pour ainsi dire, dans un certain sens; **by all manner of means** *(of course)* bien entendu; **not by any manner of means** en aucune manière, aucunement
(**c**) *(style)* manière *f*, **in the manner of Rembrandt** dans le style *ou* à la manière de Rembrandt; **painted in the Italian manner** peint à la manière italienne; *Literary* **it sounds rather like Verdi in his early manner** cela ressemble à du Verdi de la première manière
(**d**) *(kind)* sorte *f*, genre *m*; **all manner of rare books** toutes sortes de livres rares; *Arch* **what manner of man is he?** quel genre d'homme est-ce?
2 manners *npl* (**a**) *(social etiquette)* manières *fpl*; **(good) manners** bonnes manières; **bad manners** mauvaises manières; **to have good/bad table manners** savoir/ne pas savoir se tenir à table; **it's bad manners to talk with your mouth full** c'est mal élevé *ou* ce n'est pas poli de parler la bouche pleine; **she has no manners** elle n'a aucune éducation, elle est mal élevée; **where are your manners?** *(say thank you)* qu'est-ce qu'on dit quand on est bien élevé?; *(behave properly)* est-ce que c'est une façon de se tenir?; **I'm forgetting my manners, would you like some tea?** je manque à tous mes devoirs, je ne vous ai pas proposé de thé; *Prov* **manners maketh the man** = un homme n'est rien sans les manières
(**b**) *Literary (social customs)* mœurs *fpl*, usages *mpl*

mannered ['mænəd] *adj* maniéré, affecté, précieux

-mannered ['mænəd] *suff* **mild-mannered** aux manières douces; **well/bad-mannered** bien/mal élevé

mannerism ['mænərɪzəm] **1** *n* tic *m*, manie *f*
2 Mannerism *n Art* maniérisme *m*

Mannerist ['mænərɪst] *Art* **1** *n* maniériste *mf*
2 *adj* maniériste

mannerliness ['mænəlɪnɪs] *n* bonnes manières *fpl*, courtoisie *f*

mannerly ['mænəlɪ] *adj* bien élevé, courtois

mannikin ['mænɪkɪn] *n* (**a**) *(dwarf)* nain(e) *m,f* (**b**) *(model)* mannequin *m* (**c**) *Orn* spermète *m*, capucin *m*

mannish ['mænɪʃ] *adj (woman)* masculin; **she has a mannish voice** elle a une voix d'homme

mannishly ['mænɪʃlɪ] *adv* comme un homme

mannishness ['mænɪʃnɪs] *n* caractère *m* masculin

mannitol ['mænɪtɒl] *n Chem* mannitol *m*

manoeuvrability, *Am* **maneuverability** [məˌnuːvrə'bɪlətɪ] *n* manœuvrabilité *f*, maniabilité *f*

manoeuvrable, *Am* **maneuverable** [mə'nuːvrəbəl] *adj* manœuvrable, maniable

manoeuvre, *Am* **maneuver** [mə'nuːvə(r)] **1** *n* (**a**) *Mil & Naut (action)* manœuvre *f*; **to be on manoeuvres** être en manœuvres
(**b**) *(action, remark)* manœuvre *f*; **it was only a manoeuvre to get him to resign** ce n'était qu'une manœuvre pour l'amener à démissionner; **there wasn't much room for manoeuvre** *(physically)* il n'y avait pas beaucoup de place pour manœuvrer; *Fig* il y avait peu de marge de manœuvre
2 *vt* (**a**) *(physically)* manœuvrer; **he manoeuvred the ladder through the window** il a manœuvré pour faire passer l'échelle par la fenêtre; **they manoeuvred the animal into the pen** ils ont fait entrer l'animal dans l'enclos
(**b**) *(by influence, strategy)* manœuvrer; **she manoeuvred her way to the top** elle a réussi à se hisser jusqu'au sommet; **they manoeuvred him into resigning** ils l'ont poussé à démissionner
3 *vi* manœuvrer; *Naut (ship)* évoluer; **to manoeuvre for position** manœuvrer pour se placer avantageusement

manoeuvring, *Am* **maneuvering** [mə'nuːvərɪŋ] *n* (**a**) *Mil & Naut* manœuvres *fpl* (**b**) *Pej (plotting)* menées *fpl*, intrigues *fpl*

man-of-war [ˌmænəˈwɔː(r)] *(pl* **men-of-war** [ˌmen-]) *n Naut* bâtiment *f* de guerre

manometer [mə'nɒmɪtə(r)] *n* manomètre *m*

manometric [ˌmænəʊ'metrɪk], **manometrical** [ˌmænəʊ'metrɪkəl] *adj* manométrique

manometry [mæ'nɒmɪtrɪ] *n Phys* manométrie *f*

manor ['mænə(r)] *n* (**a**) *(house)* manoir *m*, château *m* (**b**) *Hist* seigneurie *f*, domaine *m* seigneurial; **lord of the manor** châtelain *m*; **lady of the manor** châtelaine *f* (**c**) *Br Fam Crime slang (police district)* îlot□ *m*
►► ***manor house*** manoir *m*, château *m*

manorial [mə'nɔːrɪəl] *adj Hist* seigneurial

man-o'-war [ˌmænə'wɔː(r)] *n* = **man-of-war**

manpower ['mænˌpaʊə(r)] *n (UNCOUNT) (personnel)* main-d'œuvre *f*; *Mil* effectifs *mpl*; **we don't have the necessary manpower** nous ne disposons pas des effectifs nécessaires
►► ***manpower forecasting*** prévision *f* de l'emploi; ***manpower management*** gestion *f* de l'emploi; ***manpower planning*** planification *f* de la main-d'œuvre; ***Manpower Services Commission*** = agence britannique pour l'emploi, aujourd'hui remplacée par la "Training Agency" ≃ ANPE *f*; ***manpower shortage*** manque *m* de main-d'œuvre

manqué ['mɒŋkeɪ] *adj* manqué

mansard ['mænsɑːd] *n (roof)* toit *m* mansardé; *(attic)* mansarde *f*

manse [mæns] *n* presbytère *m*

manservant ['mænˌsɜːvənt] *n (gen)* domestique *m*; *(valet)* valet *m* (de chambre)

mansion ['mænʃən] *n (in town)* hôtel *m* particulier; *(in country)* château *m*, manoir *m*; **their house is more like a mansion** leur maison est un vrai château
►► ***mansion block*** résidence *f* de standing; ***the Mansion House*** = la résidence officielle du maire de Londres

man-size, man-sized *adj (job, task)* ardu, difficile; *(meal)* copieux
►► ***man-sized tissues*** grands mouchoirs *mpl* (en papier)

manslaughter ['mænˌslɔːtə(r)] *n Law* homicide *m* involontaire

mansuetude ['mænswɪtju:d] *n Arch* mansuétude *f*

manta ray ['mæntə-] *n Ich* mante *f*

mantel ['mæntəl] *n (shelf)* (tablette *f* de) cheminée *f*; *(frame)* manteau *m*

mantelpiece ['mæntəl,pi:s] *n* (**a**) *(surround)* (manteau *m* de) cheminée *f* (**b**) *(shelf)* (tablette *f* de) cheminée *f*

mantelshelf ['mæntəl,ʃelf] (*pl* **mantelshelves** [-ʃelvz]) *n* (tablette *f* de) cheminée *f*

mantic ['mæntɪk] *adj* divinatoire, prophétique

mantilla [mæn'tɪlə] *n* mantille *f*

mantis ['mæntɪs] *n Entom* mante *f*
▸▸ *Ich* ***mantis shrimp*** squille *f* mante

mantissa [mæn'tɪsə] *n Math* mantisse *f*

mantle ['mæntəl] **1** *n* (**a**) *(cloak)* cape *f*; *Fig (covering)* manteau *m*; **a mantle of fog** un manteau de brume; *Fig* **to take on** *or* **to assume the mantle of** assumer le rôle de
(**b**) *Zool & Geol* manteau *m*
(**c**) *(of gas lamp)* manchon *m*; *Br* **turn up the mantle** montez le gaz
(**d**) *(shelf)* (tablette *f* de) cheminée *f*; *(frame)* manteau *m*
2 *vt Arch or Literary* (**a**) *(cover with cloak)* envelopper d'une cape
(**b**) *(obscure)* cacher, voiler
(**c**) *(cover)* couvrir, envelopper (**with** de); **the wall is mantled with ivy** le mur est tapissé de lierre
3 *vi Arch or Literary* (**a**) *(liquid → froth)* écumer, mousser
(**b**) *(blood, blush)* se répandre; *(face, cheeks)* rougir; **the blood mantled over her cheeks** elle s'empourpra; *Fig* **the dawn mantled in the sky** l'aurore envahit le ciel

man-to-man **1** *adj* entre hommes, d'homme à homme
2 *adv* entre hommes, d'homme à homme

mantra ['mæntrə] *n* mantra *m*

mantrap ['mæntræp] *n* piège *m* à hommes

Mantua ['mæntjʊə] *n* Mantoue

Mantuan ['mæntjʊən] **1** *n* Mantouan(e) *m,f*
2 *adj* mantouan

manual ['mænjʊəl] **1** *n* (**a**) *(handbook)* manuel *m*
(**b**) *(of organ)* clavier *m*
(**c**) *(car)* voiture *f* à embrayage manuel
(**d**) *(mode of operation)* **to be on manual** être sur commande manuelle
2 *adj* manuel
▸▸ ***manual dexterity*** dextérité *f*, habileté *f* manuelle; *Aut* ***manual gears, manual gearbox*** boîte *f* de vitesses mécanique, boîte *f* manuelle *ou* mécanique; ***manual labour*** travail *m* manuel; ***manual operation*** fonctionnement *m* manuel; *Aut* ***manual transmission*** transmission *f* mécanique; ***manual typewriter*** machine *f* à écrire mécanique; ***manual worker*** travailleur(euse) *m,f* manuel(le)

manually ['mænjʊəlɪ] *adv* manuellement, à la main

manufactory [,mænjʊ'fæktərɪ] *n Arch* fabrique *f*, usine *f*

manufacture [,mænjʊ'fæktʃə(r)] **1** *n* (**a**) *(making)* fabrication *f*; *(of clothes)* confection *f*; *(of cars, aircraft, computers)* construction *f*
(**b**) *Tech (product)* produit *m* manufacturé
2 *vt* (**a**) *(produce)* fabriquer, produire; *(car, aircraft, computer)* construire; *(clothes)* confectionner; **manufactured goods** produits *mpl* manufacturés
(**b**) *(invent → news, story)* inventer; *(→ evidence)* fabriquer; **to manufacture an opportunity to do sth** inventer une occasion de faire qch

manufacturer [,mænjʊ'fæktʃərə(r)] *n* fabricant(e) *m,f*; *(of cars, aircraft, computers)* constructeur(trice) *m,f*; **send it back to the manufacturers** renvoyez-le au fabricant
▸▸ ***manufacturer's agent*** agent *m* exclusif; ***manufacturer's brand*** marque *f* de fabricant; ***manufacturer's instructions*** notice *f* du constructeur; ***manufacturer's liability*** responsabilité *f* du fabricant; ***manufacturer's price*** prix *m* de fabrique; ***manufacturer's recommended price*** prix *m* conseillé par le fabricant

manufacturing [,mænjʊ'fæktʃərɪŋ] **1** *n* fabrication *f*; **the decline of manufacturing** le déclin de l'industrie manufacturière
2 *adj (city, area)* industriel
▸▸ *Acct* ***manufacturing account*** compte *m* de production; ***manufacturing capacity*** capacité *f* de production; ***manufacturing company*** entreprise *f* industrielle; ***manufacturing costs*** frais *mpl* de fabrication; ***manufacturing defect*** vice *m* *ou* défaut *m* de fabrication; ***manufacturing industry*** les industries *fpl* manufacturières *ou* de transformation; ***manufacturing licence*** licence *f* de fabrication; ***manufacturing overheads*** = **manufacturing costs;** ***manufacturing plant*** usine *f* de fabrication; ***manufacturing process*** procédé *m* de fabrication; ***manufacturing rights*** droits *mpl* de fabrication

manumission [,mænjʊ'mɪʃən] *n Hist* manumission *f*

manumit [,mænjʊ'mɪt] (*pt & pp* **manumitted,** *cont* **manumitting**) *vt Hist* affranchir, émanciper

manure [mə'njʊə(r)] **1** *n (farmyard)* fumier *m*; *(fertilizer)* engrais *m*; **liquid manure** purin *m*, lisier *m*; **manure heap** tas *m* de fumier
2 *vt (with dung)* fumer; *(with fertilizer)* répandre de l'engrais sur

manuscript ['mænjʊskrɪpt] **1** *n* manuscrit *m*; *(for music)* papier *m* à musique; **I read the book in manuscript** j'ai lu le manuscrit du livre
2 *adj* manuscrit, (écrit) à la main
▸▸ ***manuscript paper*** *(for music)* papier *m* à musique

Manx [mæŋks] **1** *npl* **the Manx** les habitants *mpl* de l'île de Man
2 *n Ling* mannois *m*
3 *adj* de l'île de Man
▸▸ ***Manx cat*** chat *m* (sans queue) de l'île de Man; *Orn* ***Manx shearwater*** puffin *m* des Anglais

Manxman ['mæŋksmən] (*pl* **Manxmen** [-mən]) *n* habitant *m* de l'île de Man

Manxwoman ['mæŋks,wʊmən] (*pl* **Manxwomen** [-,wɪmɪn]) *n* habitante *f* de l'île de Man

many ['menɪ] (*compar* **more** [mɔ:], *superl* **most** [məʊst]) **1** *adj* beaucoup de, de nombreux; **many people** beaucoup de *ou* bien des gens; **many years** bien des années, de nombreuses années; **many times** souvent, bien des fois; **she had cards from all her many admirers** elle a reçu des cartes de ses nombreux admirateurs; **take as many books as you like** prenez autant de livres *ou* tous les livres que vous voudrez; **they admitted as many people as they could** ils ont laissé entrer autant de gens que possible; **we visited six cities in as many days** nous avons visité six villes en autant de jours; **how many...?** combien de...?; **how many students came?** combien d'étudiants sont venus?; **so many people** tant de gens; **there are only so many ways you can cook chicken** il n'y a pas une infinité de façons de préparer le poulet; **too many people** trop de gens; **we met a good many times** on s'est vus bien des fois; **I've received a great many applications** j'ai reçu de très nombreuses *ou* un grand nombre de candidatures
2 *pron* beaucoup; **many of the audience were children** il y avait de nombreux enfants *ou* beaucoup d'enfants dans l'assistance; **many of them** beaucoup d'entre eux; **many's the time** bien des fois; **many's the holiday I spent there** j'y ai passé bien des vacances; **they admitted as many as they could** ils ont laissé entrer autant de gens que possible; **as many again** encore autant; **twice/three times as many** deux/trois fois plus; **as many as 8,000 students enrolled** jusqu'à *ou* près de 8000 étudiants se sont inscrits; **how many?** combien?; **how many were there?** combien étaient-ils?; **we can only fit in so many** nous n'avons de place que pour un certain nombre de personnes; **don't give me too many** ne m'en donne pas trop; **a good many** un bon nombre; **a great many** un grand nombre
3 *predet* **many a time** bien des fois; *Literary* **many a time and oft** maintes et maintes fois; **many a child would be glad of it** bien des enfants s'en contenteraient
4 *npl (masses)* **the many** la majorité; **the many who loved her** tous ceux qui l'aimaient; **the sacrifices made by the few for the many** les sacrifices faits par la minorité pour la masse

many-coloured *adj Br* multicolore

man-year *n Br* année-personne *f*

many-headed *adj (monster)* à plusieurs têtes

many-sided *adj* (**a**) *(figure, shape)* qui a de nombreux côtés (**b**) *(problem)* aux aspects multiples, multiforme (**c**) *(personality)* qui a de nombreuses facettes; *(individual)* aux talents multiples

Maoism ['maʊɪzəm] *n* maoïsme *m*

Maoist ['maʊɪst] **1** *n* maoïste *mf*
2 *adj* maoïste

Maori ['maʊrɪ] (*pl* **inv** *or* **Maoris**) **1** *n* (**a**) *(person)* Maori(e) *m,f* (**b**) *Ling* maori *m*
2 *adj* maori

Mao Tse-tung, Mao Zedong [,maʊtse'tʊŋ] *pr n* Mao Tsé-toung, Mao Zedong

MAP [mæp] *n Am* (*abbr* **Modified American Plan**) = dans un hôtel américain, séjour en demi-pension

map [mæp] (*pt & pp* **mapped,** *cont* **mapping**) **1** *n* (**a**) *(of country)* carte *f*; *(of town, network)* plan *m*; **to read a map** lire une carte; **a map of India** une carte de l'Inde; **it doesn't look far on the map** ça n'a pas l'air loin sur la carte; *Fig* **the city was wiped off the map** la ville a été rayée de la carte; *Fig* **to put sth on the map** faire connaître qch; **the election results put them firmly on the political map** le résultat des élections leur assure une place sur l'échiquier politique; **the legend of the monster put Loch Ness on the map** la légende du monstre a rendu le loch Ness célèbre
(**b**) *Math* fonction *f*, application *f*
(**c**) *Am Fam (face)* tronche *f*, trombine *f*
2 *vt* (**a**) *(country, region)* faire *ou* dresser la carte de; *(town)* faire *ou* dresser le plan de
(**b**) *Math* faire un graphique de; **to map sth onto sth** représenter qch sur qch
(**c**) *Fig (plot → progress etc)* consigner
▸▸ *Aut* ***map pocket*** vide-poche *m*, bac *m* à cartes; ***map reading*** lecture *f* de carte; ***map reading lamp*** lecteur *m* de carte, spot *m* de lecture; ***map reference*** référence *f* topographique, coordonnées *fpl*

▸**map out** *vt sep (itinerary)* tracer; *(essay)* faire le plan de; *(plan)* établir les grandes lignes de; *(career, future)* organiser, prévoir; **they have Laura's future all mapped out for her** ils ont déjà planifié l'avenir de Laura; **to map out one's time** organiser son emploi du temps

maple ['meɪpəl] *n* érable *m*
▸▸ ***maple bush*** érablière *f*; ***maple leaf*** feuille *f* d'érable; ***maple sugar*** sucre *m* d'érable; ***maple syrup*** sirop *m* d'érable

> **MAPLE LEAF**
>
> La feuille d'érable est l'emblème national du Canada. Il fut un temps où elle apparaissait sur toutes les pièces de monnaie canadiennes. Elle figure sur les insignes militaires canadiens, et depuis 1965 elle orne le drapeau national.

mapmaker ['mæp,meɪkə(r)] *n* cartographe *mf*

mapmaking ['mæp,meɪkɪŋ] *n* cartographie *f*

mapping ['mæpɪŋ] *n* (**a**) *(of region)* établissement *m* d'une carte (**b**) *Math* application *f*, fonction *f* (**c**) *Comput (in network)* unité *f* logique (**d**) *Mktg* mapping *m*
▸▸ ***mapping pen*** plume *f* à dessin

Maputo [mə'pu:təʊ] *n* Maputo

Mar. (*written abbr* **March**) mars *m*

mar [mɑ:(r)] (*pt & pp* **marred,** *cont* **marring**) *vt* gâter, gâcher; **to make or mar sb** faire la fortune ou la ruine de qn; **today will make or mar their future** c'est aujourd'hui que se décide *ou* se joue leur avenir

marabou ['mærəbu:] *n Orn* marabout *m*

marabout ['mærəbu:t] *n Rel* marabout *m*

maraca [mə'rækə] *n Mus* maraca *f*

maraschino [,mærə'ski:nəʊ] (*pl* **maraschinos**) *n* marasquin *m*
▸▸ ***maraschino cherry*** cerise *f* au marasquin

marathon ['mærəθən] **1** *n Sport* marathon *m*; *Fig* **dance marathon** marathon *m* de danse
2 *adj* marathon *(inv)*; **a marathon exam** un examen-marathon
▸▸ ***marathon race*** marathon *m*; ***marathon runner*** coureur(euse) *m,f* de marathon, marathonien(enne) *m,f*

maraud [mə'rɔ:d] *vi* marauder, être en maraude; **to go marauding** partir en maraude

marauder [mə'rɔːdə(r)] *n (person)* maraudeur(-euse) *m,f*; *(animal, bird)* maraudeur *m*, prédateur *m*

marauding [mə'rɔːdɪŋ] **1** *n* maraude *f*; *Law* maraudage *m*

2 *adj* maraudeur, en maraude; **marauding soldiers** des soldats en maraude

marble ['mɑːbəl] **1** *n* (**a**) *(stone, sculpture)* marbre *m*

(**b**) *(for game)* bille *f*; **to play marbles** jouer aux billes; *Fam Fig* **to lose one's marbles** perdre la boule; *Fam Fig* **she's still got all her marbles** elle a encore toute sa tête

2 *comp (fireplace, staircase, statue)* de *ou* en marbre; *(industry)* marbrier

3 *vt* marbrer

▸▸ ***Marble Arch*** = grande arche monumentale dans le centre de Londres; ***marble cake*** gâteau *m* marbré; ***marble cutter*** *(person)* marbrier *m*; ***marble quarry*** marbrière *f*, carrière *f* de marbre

marbled ['mɑːbəld] *adj* marbré; *(meat)* persillé

▸▸ *Orn* ***marbled teal*** sarcelle *f* marbrée

marbleize ['mɑːbəlaɪz] *vt Am* marbrer

marbler ['mɑːbələ(r)] *n (person)* marbreur(euse) *m,f*

marbling ['mɑːbəlɪŋ] *n (gen)* marbrure *f*; *(in meat)* marbré *m*

marc [mɑːk] *n* marc *m*

marcasite ['mɑːkəsaɪt] *n Miner* marcassite *f*

marcato [mɑː'kɑːtəʊ] *Mus* **1** *adj* marcato

2 *adv* marcato

marcel wave [mɑː'sel-] *n* = coiffure ondulée prisée par les femmes des années 20 et 30

marcescent [mɑː'sesənt] *adj Bot* marcescent

March [mɑːtʃ] *n* mars *m*; *see also* **February**

▸▸ ***March hare*** lièvre *m* en rut; ***the March Hare*** *(in stories)* le Lièvre

march [mɑːtʃ] **1** *n* (**a**) *Mil* marche *f*; **troops on the march** des troupes en marche; *Fig* **the middle classes are on the march** la classe moyenne s'est mobilisée; **the march on Versailles** la marche sur Versailles; **a march of 20 km** une marche de 20 km; **their camp was a day's march away** leur camp était à une journée de marche; *Fig* **the march of time/events** la marche du temps/des événements; **quick march!** en avant, marche!; *Am Hist* **Sherman's march to the sea** la marche vers l'océan du général Sherman

(**b**) *(demonstration)* manifestation *f*, marche *f*; **to go on a march** manifester, descendre dans la rue; **peace march** marche *f* pour la paix

(**c**) *(music)* marche *f*; **slow/quick march** marche *f* lente/rapide

(**d**) *(usu pl) (frontier)* frontière *f*; **the Welsh Marches** les marches *fpl* galloises

2 *vt* (**a**) *Mil* faire marcher au pas; **the troops were marched out of the citadel** on fit sortir les troupes de la citadelle

(**b**) *(lead forcibly)* **the prisoner was marched away/back to his cell** on conduisit/ramena le prisonnier dans sa cellule; **the shoplifter was marched into the manager's office** on conduisit le voleur dans le bureau du directeur; **the children were marched off to bed** les enfants ont été expédiés au lit (au pas de gymnastique)

3 *vi* (**a**) *Mil* marcher (au pas); *(at a ceremony, on parade)* défiler; **the regiment marched past the President** le régiment défila devant le Président; **the soldiers marched for three days and nights** les soldats ont marché pendant trois jours et trois nuits; **to march against the enemy** marcher contre l'ennemi; **to march off to war/into battle** partir à la guerre/au combat; **to march on a city** marcher sur une ville

(**b**) *(walk briskly)* avancer d'un pas ferme *ou* résolu; **to march down the street/into a room** descendre la rue/entrer dans une pièce d'un pas résolu; **they marched off in a huff** ils partirent furieux; **she marched up to him and slapped him across the face** elle se dirigea droit sur lui et le gifla; **he marched impatiently up and down the station platform** il arpentait le quai impatiemment; **he marched upstairs** il monta l'escalier d'un air décidé

(**c**) *(in demonstration)* manifester; **the students marched alongside the workers** les étudiants manifestèrent aux côtés des ouvriers

(**d**) *Fig (time, seasons)* avancer, s'écouler; **time marches on** le temps s'écoule inexorablement

▸▸ ***March of Dimes*** = association caritative américaine d'aide aux enfants handicapés

SHERMAN'S MARCH TO THE SEA

Il s'agit d'une opération menée en 1864 par le général nordiste Sherman en Géorgie pendant la guerre de Sécession. À la tête de 60 000 hommes et après avoir incendié la ville d'Atlanta, Sherman rejoignit la côte en détruisant sur son passage toute l'infrastructure sudiste: voies de chemin de fer, cultures, bétail, bâtiments etc.

marcher ['mɑːtʃə(r)] *n (in demonstration)* manifestant(e) *m,f*

marching ['mɑːtʃɪŋ] **1** *n (gen) & Mil* marche *f*

2 *adj* cadencé; **the sound of marching feet** le bruit de pas cadencés

▸▸ ***marching band*** fanfare *f*; *Mil* ***marching orders*** feuille *f* de route; *Br Fam Fig* **to give sb his/her marching orders** flanquer qn à la porte; *Br Fam Fig* **she got her marching orders** elle a été virée; ***Marching Season*** = période où se déroulent en Irlande du nord divers défilés orangistes, les principaux ayant lieu le 12 juillet et commémorant la bataille de la Boyne

marchioness [ˌmɑːʃə'nes] *n (aristocrat)* marquise *f*

marchpane ['mɑːtʃpeɪn] *n Arch Culin* massepain *m*

march-past *n* défilé *m* (militaire)

Marcus Aurelius [ˌmɑːkəsɔː'riːljəs] *pr n Antiq* Marc Aurèle

Mardi Gras [ˌmɑːdɪ'grɑː] *n* mardi *m* gras, carnaval *m*

mare[1] [meə(r)] *n* (**a**) *(animal)* jument *f* (**b**) *Br Fam Pej (woman)* grognasse *f*; **you silly mare!** espèce d'andouille!

▸▸ ***mare's nest*** *(illusion)* illusion *f*; *(disappointment)* déception *f*; *Bot* ***mare's tail*** pesse *f* d'eau

mare[2] *n Br Fam (nightmare)* cauchemar ❑ *m*; **it was a total mare!** c'était un vrai cauchemar!

Margaret ['mɑːgrɪt] *pr n* **Margaret of Anjou** Marguerite d'Anjou; **Margaret of Navarre** Marguerite de Navarre

margarine [ˌmɑːdʒə'riːn, ˌmɑːgə'riːn] *n* margarine *f*

margarita [ˌmɑːgə'riːtə] *n* margarita *f*

margay ['mɑːgeɪ] *n Zool* margay *m*, chat-tigre *m*

marge [mɑːdʒ] *n Br Fam* margarine ❑ *f*

margin ['mɑːdʒɪn] *n* (**a**) *(on page)* marge *f*; **written in the margin** écrit dans la *ou* en marge

(**b**) *(leeway)* marge *f*; **a margin of error/of safety** une marge d'erreur/de sécurité

(**c**) *(distance, gap)* marge *f*; **the opposition candidate won by a 10 percent margin** le candidat de l'opposition a gagné avec une marge de 10 pour cent; **to beat sb by a margin of twenty seconds** battre qn de vingt secondes; **they won by a narrow/wide margin** ils ont gagné de justesse/avec une marge confortable

(**d**) *Com, Fin & Mktg (profit)* marge *f*; *St Exch* acompte *m (versé à un courtier)*, marge *f* de garantie; **to have a low/high margin** avoir une faible/forte marge; **we make a 10 percent margin** nous faisons 10 pour cent de marge; **they want more margin** ils veulent augmenter leur marge bénéficiaire; **the margins are very tight** les marges sont très réduites

(**e**) *Austr (bonus payment)* prime *f*

(**f**) *(periphery → of field, lake)* bord *m*; *(→ of wood)* lisière *f*, orée *f*; *(→ of society)* marge *f*

▸▸ *St Exch* ***margin call*** appel *m* de couverture *ou* de marge *ou* de garantie; *St Exch* ***margin dealing*** *(method of dealing commodities or financial futures)* cotation *f* par appel de marge; *(high-gear dealing)* arbitrage *m* à la marge *ou* marginal; *(transactions on margin of loan)* arbitrage *m* sur dépôt de titres de garantie; *St Exch* ***margin default*** défaut *m* de couverture; *Fin* ***margin of fluctuation*** *(of a currency)* marge *f* de fluctation; *Fin* ***margin of interest*** marge *f* d'intérêt; *Typ* ***margin release*** déclenche-marge *m inv*; *St Exch* ***margin requirement*** niveau *m* de dépôt requis, couverture *f* (boursière) obligatoire; *Typ* ***margin setting*** marge *f*; *(action)* pose *f* de marges; *Typ* ***margin stop*** margeur *m*

marginal ['mɑːdʒɪnəl] **1** *adj* (**a**) *(slight → improvement)* léger; *(→ effect)* minime, insignifiant; *(→ importance)* mineur, secondaire; *(→ case)* limite; *(→ problem)* d'ordre secondaire

(**b**) *Com (business, profit)* marginal

(**c**) *(in margin → notes)* marginal, en marge

2 *n Pol* = en Grande-Bretagne, circonscription dont le député ne dispose que d'une majorité très faible

▸▸ *Com* ***marginal cost*** coût *m* marginal; *Com* ***marginal costing*** méthode *f* des coûts marginaux; *Com* ***marginal cost pricing*** méthode *f* des coûts marginaux; *Com* ***marginal disinvestment*** désinvestissement *m* marginal; *Agr* ***marginal land*** terre *f* de faible rendement; *Com* ***marginal profit*** bénéfice *m* marginal; *Com* ***marginal relief*** dégrèvement *m* marginal; *Fin* ***marginal return on capital*** rendement *m* marginal du capital; *Fin* ***marginal revenue*** revenu *m* marginal; *Pol* ***marginal seat*** = en Grande-Bretagne, circonscription dont le député ne dispose que d'une majorité très faible; *Fin* ***marginal value*** valeur *f* marginale

marginalia [ˌmɑːdʒɪ'neɪljə] *npl* annotations *fpl ou* notes *fpl* en marge

marginalism ['mɑːdʒɪnəlɪzəm] *n Econ* marginalisme *m*

marginality [ˌmɑːdʒɪ'nælɪtɪ] *n* caractère *m* marginal

marginalization [ˌmɑːdʒɪnəlaɪ'zeɪʃən] *n* marginalisation *f*

marginalize, -ise ['mɑːdʒɪnəlaɪz] *vt* marginaliser

marginally ['mɑːdʒɪnəlɪ] *adv* à peine, légèrement; **his health has improved only marginally** son état ne s'est guère amelioré

margrave ['mɑːgreɪv] *n Hist* margrave *m*

margravine ['mɑːgrəviːn] *n Hist* margrave *f*, margravine *f*

marguerite [ˌmɑːgə'riːt] *n Bot* marguerite *f*

Maria [mə'raɪə] *see* **black**

Maria de Medici [məˌrɪəde'medɪtʃiː] *pr n* Marie de Médicis

Mariana Islands [ˌmærɪ'ɑːnə-] *npl* **the Mariana Islands** les îles *fpl* Mariannes; **in the Mariana Islands** aux îles Mariannes

Marie-Antoinette ['mærɪˌæntwə'net] *pr n* Marie-Antoinette

marigold ['mærɪgəʊld] *n Bot (African)* rose *f* d'Inde; *(French)* œillet *m* d'Inde; **(pot) marigold** souci *m* (des jardins)

marihuana, marijuana [ˌmærɪ'wɑːnə] *n* marihuana *f*, marijuana *f*

marimba [mə'rɪmbə] *n* marimba *m*

marina [mə'riːnə] *n* port *m* de plaisance, marina *f*

marinade [ˌmærɪ'neɪd] *Culin* **1** *n* marinade *f*

2 *vt* mariner

marinate ['mærɪneɪt] *Culin* **1** *vt* mariner

2 *vi* mariner

marine [mə'riːn] **1** *n* (**a**) *(ships collectively)* marine *f*

(**b**) *(soldier)* fusilier *m* marin; *(British or American)* marine *m*; *Fam* **go tell it to the marines!** mon œil!, à d'autres!

2 *adj* (**a**) *(underwater)* marin

(**b**) *(naval)* maritime

▸▸ ***marine architect*** ingénieur *m* des constructions navales; ***marine artist*** peintre *m* de marines; ***marine bill of lading*** connaissement *m* maritime; ***marine biologist*** biologiste *mf* marin; ***marine biology*** biologie *f* marine; *Am Mil* **Marine Corps** Marines *mpl*; ***marine engineer*** mécanicien *m* de bord; ***marine engineering*** génie *m* maritime; ***marine insurance*** assurance *f* maritime; ***marine insurance policy*** police *f* d'assurance maritime; ***marine life*** vie *f* marine; ***marine risk*** risque *m* maritime; ***marine surveyor*** visiteur *m ou* inspecteur *m* de navires

mariner ['mærɪnə(r)] *n Formal or Literary* marin *m*

Mariolatry [ˌmeərɪ'ɒlətrɪ] *n Rel* culte *m* excessif de la Vierge

Mariology [ˌmeərɪ'ɒlədʒɪ] *n Rel* mariologie *f*

marionette [ˌmærɪə'net] *n* marionnette *f*

Marist ['meərɪst] *n Rel* mariste *mf*

marital ['mærɪtəl] *adj (vows, relations, duty)* conjugal; *(problem)* conjugal, matrimonial

▸▸ ***marital aid*** gadget *m* érotique; ***marital bliss*** bonheur *m* conjugal; ***marital home*** foyer *m* conjugal; ***marital rape*** viol *m* conjugal; ***marital rights*** droits *mpl* conjugaux; ***marital status*** situation *f* de famille; ***marital vows*** serment *m* du mariage

maritally ['mærɪtəlɪ] *adv* maritalement

maritime ['mærɪtaɪm] **1** *adj* maritime

2 Maritimes *npl* **the Maritimes** les (provinces *fpl*) Maritimes *fpl*

►► ***maritime climate*** climat *m* maritime; ***maritime law*** droit *m* maritime; *Bot* ***maritime pine*** pin *m* maritime; ***the Maritime Provinces*** les Provinces *fpl* Maritimes

marjoram ['mɑːdʒərəm] *n Bot* marjolaine *f*

Mark [mɑːk] *pr n Bible* Marc; **Mark Antony** Marc Antoine; **the Gospel According to (Saint) Mark** l'Évangile selon saint Marc

MARK [mɑːk]

marque	► **1 (a), (b), (d) – (f), (h)**
niveau	► **1 (b)**
modèle	► **1 (c)**
trace	► **1 (f)**
note	► **1 (g)**
empreinte	► **1 (h)**
but	► **1 (j)**
cible	► **1 (j)**
mark	► **1 (m)**
marquer	► **2 (a) – (c), (e) – (g), (j)**
tacher	► **2 (b)**
tacheter	► **2 (d)**
célébrer	► **2 (f)**
corriger	► **2 (h)**

1 *n* **(a)** *(symbol, sign)* marque *f*, signe *m*; **to make a mark on sth** faire une marque sur qch, marquer qch

(b) *(on scale, in number, level)* marque *f*, niveau *m*; **sales topped the 5 million mark** les ventes ont dépassé la barre des 5 millions; **to reach the half-way mark** arriver à mi-course; **don't go beyond the 50-metre mark** ne dépassez pas les 50 mètres; *Br Culin* **gas mark 6** thermostat 6

(c) *Com (model)* **mark 3** modèle *m ou* série *f* 3

(d) *(feature)* marque *f*; **the town bears the mark of Greek classicism** la ville porte la marque du classicisme grec

(e) *(token)* marque *f*, signe *m*; **a mark of affection** une marque d'affection; **as a mark of my esteem/friendship** en témoignage de mon estime/de mon amitié; **as a mark of respect** en signe de respect

(f) *(trace, stain, blemish)* trace *f*, marque *f*; *(wound)* trace *f* de coups; **to leave marks in the snow** *(of car)* laisser des traces dans la neige; **there are finger marks on the mirror** il y a des traces *ou* des marques de doigts sur la glace; **there are muddy marks on the carpet** il y a des traces de boue sur la moquette; **the years she spent in prison have left their mark (on her)** ses années en prison l'ont marquée; **the cup has left a mark on the table** la tasse a laissé une marque sur la table; **there wasn't a mark on the body** le corps ne portait aucune trace de coups

(g) *Sch (grade)* note *f*; *(point)* point *m*; **to give sb/sth marks out of ten/twenty** noter qn/qch sur dix/vingt; **the mark is out of 100** la note est sur 100; **to get good marks** avoir de bonnes notes; **to get full marks** obtenir la meilleure note (possible); **you need ten more marks** il vous faut encore dix points; *Fig* **it will be a black mark against his name** ça va jouer contre lui, ça ne va pas jouer en sa faveur; **she deserves full marks for imagination** il faut saluer son imagination; **no marks for guessing the answer!** il ne faut pas être sorcier pour deviner la réponse!

(h) *(impact)* empreinte *f*, impression *f*; *(distinction)* marque *f*; **to make one's mark** s'imposer, se faire un nom; **she made her mark as a singer** elle s'est imposée *ou* elle s'est fait un nom dans la chanson; **they left their mark on 20th-century history** ils ont profondément marqué l'histoire du XXème siècle; *Br* **to be of little mark** avoir peu d'importance

(i) *Br (standard)* **to be up to the mark** *(be capable)* être à la hauteur; *(meet expectations)* être satisfaisant; **I'm afraid the work just isn't up to the mark** malheureusement le travail laisse à désirer; **I still don't feel quite up to the mark** je ne suis pas encore en pleine forme

(j) *Br (target)* but *m*, cible *f*; **to hit the mark** atteindre la cible; *Fig* faire mouche; **to miss the mark** rater la cible; *Fig* mettre à côté de la plaque; **your answer was nearest the mark** c'est vous qui avez donné la meilleure réponse

(k) *Sport* **on your marks, (get) set, go!** à vos marques, prêts, partez!; *Br Fig* **she's quick/slow off the mark** *(clever)* elle est/n'est pas très maligne, elle a/n'a pas l'esprit très vif; *(in reactions)* elle est/n'est pas très rapide; **you have to be quick off the mark** il faut réagir tout de suite *ou* immédiatement; **he's sometimes a bit too quick off the mark in his criticism** il lui arrive d'avoir la critique un peu trop facile; **you were too slow off the mark** tu as mis trop de temps

(l) *Sport (in rugby)* arrêt *m* de volée; **to call for the mark** crier "marque" (en faisant un arrêt de volée)

(m) *(currency)* mark *m*, Deutschmark *m*

2 *vt* **(a)** *(label)* marquer; **the towels were marked with his name** les serviettes étaient à son nom, son nom était marqué sur les serviettes; **mark the text with your initials** inscrivez vos initiales sur le texte; **shall I mark her absent?** est-ce que je la marque absente?; **the table was marked "sold"** la table portait l'étiquette "vendue"

(b) *(stain)* tacher, marquer; **the red wine marked the carpet** le vin rouge a taché la moquette

(c) *(face, hands)* marquer; **his face was marked by suffering** son visage était marqué par la souffrance; **the scandal marked him for life** *(mentally)* le scandale l'a marqué pour la vie

(d) *Zool* tacheter; **brown wings marked with blue** des ailes *fpl* brunes tachetées de bleu

(e) *(indicate)* indiquer, marquer; **the stream marks the boundary of the estate** le ruisseau marque la limite de la propriété; **X marks the spot** l'endroit est marqué d'un X; **this decision marks a change in policy** cette décision marque un changement de politique; **today marks a turning point in our lives** aujourd'hui marque un tournant dans notre vie

(f) *(celebrate → anniversary, event)* célébrer, marquer; **let's have some champagne to mark the occasion** ouvrons une bouteille de champagne pour fêter l'événement

(g) *(distinguish)* marquer; **he has all the qualities that mark a good golfer** il possède toutes les qualités d'un bon golfeur; **the period was marked by religious persecution** cette époque fut marquée par des persécutions religieuses

(h) *Sch (essay, homework)* corriger; *(student)* noter; **the exam was marked out of 100** l'examen a été noté sur 100; **to mark sth wrong/right** marquer qch comme étant faux/juste

(i) *(pay attention to)* **(you) mark my words!** souvenez-vous de ce que je vous dis!; *Br* **mark how he does it** observez bien la façon dont il s'y prend; *Br* **mark you, I didn't believe him** remarquez, je ne l'ai pas cru

(j) *Sport (opponent)* marquer; **he marked him out of the game** il l'a si bien marqué qu'il n'a rien pu faire

(k) *(idiom)* **to mark time** *Mil* marquer le pas; *Fig* attendre son heure *ou* le moment propice; **the government is just marking time until the elections** le gouvernement fait traîner les choses en attendant les élections

3 *vi (garment)* être salissant, se tacher facilement; **this material marks easily** ce tissu est salissant

►**mark down** *vt sep* **(a)** *(write)* noter, prendre note de, inscrire; **mark the address down in your diary** notez l'adresse dans votre agenda

(b) *(reduce → price)* baisser; *(→ article)* baisser le prix de, démarquer; **everything has been marked down to half price** tout a été réduit à moitié prix; *St Exch* **prices were marked down in early trading** les valeurs étaient en baisse *ou* ont reculé en début de séance

(c) *Sch (essay, student)* baisser la note de; **he was marked down for bad grammar** il a perdu des points à cause de la grammaire

(d) *(single out)* désigner; **my brother was marked down for the managership** mon frère a été désigné pour le poste de directeur; **I marked him down as a troublemaker** j'avais remarqué qu'il n'était bon qu'à créer des ennuis

►**mark off** *vt sep* **(a)** *(divide, isolate → area, period of time)* délimiter; **one corner of the field had been marked off by a fence** un coin du champ avait été isolé par une barrière

(b) *(measure → distance)* mesurer; **the route was marked off in 1 km sections** le trajet était divisé en tronçons d'un kilomètre

(c) *Br (distinguish)* distinguer; **his intelligence marked him off from his school friends** il se distinguait de ses camarades d'école par son intelligence

(d) *(on list)* cocher

►**mark out** *vt sep* **(a)** *(with chalk, paint → court, pitch)* tracer les lignes de; *(with stakes)* jalonner; *(with lights, flags)* baliser; *Fig* **his path in life is clearly marked out** son avenir est tout tracé

(b) *(designate)* désigner; **Steven was marked out for promotion** Steven était désigné pour obtenir une promotion; **they were marked out for special treatment** ils ont bénéficié d'un régime particulier

(c) *Br (distinguish)* distinguer; **her ambition marks her out from her colleagues** son ambition la distingue de ses collègues

►**mark up** *vt sep* **(a)** *(on notice)* marquer; **the menu is marked up on the blackboard** le menu est sur le tableau

(b) *(increase → price)* augmenter, majorer; *(→ goods)* augmenter le prix de, majorer; *St Exch* **prices at last began to be marked up** les cours sont enfin à la hausse

(c) *(proofs, manuscript → correct)* corriger; *(→ annotate)* annoter

'The Mark of Zorro' *Niblo* 'Le Signe de Zorro'

markdown ['mɑːkdaʊn] *n (article)* article *m* démarqué; *(action)* démarque *f*

marked [mɑːkt] *adj* **(a)** *(noticeable)* marqué, sensible; *(accent)* prononcé **(b)** *(bearing a mark → gen)* marqué; *(→ path)* balisé; *Fig* **he's a marked man** c'est l'homme à abattre **(c)** *Ling* marqué

►► *Mktg* ***marked price*** prix *m* marqué

marked-down *adj Com* démarqué; **marked down shirts** chemises démarquées *ou* soldées

markedly ['mɑːkɪdlɪ] *adv* nettement, sensiblement; **markedly better** nettement meilleur; **markedly different** nettement *ou* sensiblement différent

marked-up *adj Com* majoré

marker ['mɑːkə(r)] *n* **(a)** *(pen)* feutre *m*, marqueur *m*

(b) *(indicator, landmark)* jalon *m*, balise *f*; *(flag)* fanion *m*; *(stick)* piquet *m* d'alignement *ou* de jalonnement

(c) *(scorekeeper)* marqueur(euse) *m,f*

(d) *Sch* correcteur(trice) *m,f*; **to be a hard marker** noter sévèrement

(e) *(page marker)* marque-page *m*, signet *m*

(f) *Sport* marqueur(euse) *m,f*; **to lose one's marker** se démarquer (d'un adversaire)

(g) *Ling* marque *f*

(h) *Am Fam (gambling debt)* dette *f* de jeu ❑; *(note)* reconnaissance *f* de dette de jeu ❑; *Fig* **he called in his marker** il a demandé à ce qu'on lui renvoie l'ascenseur

►► *Econ* ***marker barrel*** prix *m* du baril de pétrole; *Aviat* ***marker beacon*** radiobalise *f*; *Naut* ***marker buoy*** bouée *f* de balisage; ***marker pen*** feutre *m*, marqueur *m*

market ['mɑːkɪt] **1** *n* **(a)** *(gen)* marché *m*; **to go to (the) market** aller au marché, aller faire son marché

(b) *Econ* marché *m*; *(demand)* demande *f*, marché *m*; *(outlet)* débouché *m*, marché *m*; **to be on the market** être en vente; **to come onto the market** arriver sur le marché; **home and foreign market** marché *m* intérieur et extérieur; **the job market** le marché de l'emploi; **the property market** le marché immobilier; **to put sth on the market** mettre qch en vente *ou* sur le marché; **they've just put their house on the market** ils viennent de mettre leur maison en vente; **the most economical car on the market** la voiture la plus économique du marché; **new products are always coming onto the market** de nouveaux produits apparaissent constamment sur le marché; **a new electric car has been brought onto the market** une nouvelle voiture électrique a été mise sur le marché; **to be on the open market** être sur le marché libre; **to take sth off the market** retirer qch du marché; **she's in the market for Persian rugs** elle cherche à acheter des tapis persans, elle est acheteuse de tapis persans; **there's always a (ready) market for computer software** il y a toujours une forte demande pour les logiciels; **he's unable to find a market for his products** il ne trouve pas de débouchés pour ses produits; **we hope to conquer the Australian market** nous espérons conquérir le marché australien; **this ad should appeal to the teenage market** cette pub devrait séduire les jeunes; **to find a market for sth** trouver un débouché *ou* des acheteurs pour qch; **to find a ready market** trouver à vendre facilement; **to price oneself out of the market** perdre sa clientèle en demandant trop cher; **the bottom has fallen out of the market** le marché s'est effondré

(**c**) *St Exch* marché *m*; *(index)* indice *m*; *(prices)* cours *mpl*; **the market has risen 10 points** l'indice est en hausse de 10 points; **to play the market** jouer en bourse, spéculer

2 *vt (sell)* vendre, commercialiser; *(launch)* lancer *ou* mettre sur le marché

3 *vi Am (go shopping)* faire le marché; **to go marketing** aller faire ses courses

►► ***market analysis*** analyse *f* de marché; ***market analyst*** analyste *mf* du marché; ***market appeal*** attrait *m* commercial; ***market appraisal*** évaluation *f* du marché; *St Exch* ***market capitalization*** capitalisation *f* boursière; ***market challenger*** challengeur *m*; ***market choice*** choix *m* sur le marché; *(product preferred by market)* choix *m* du marché; *St Exch* ***market commentator*** chroniqueur *m* boursier; ***market competition*** concurrence *f* du marché; ***market conditions*** conditions *fpl* du marché; *St Exch* ***market crisis*** choc *m* boursier; ***market day*** jour *m* de marché; ***market demand*** demande *f* du marché; ***market development*** développement *m* du marché; ***market economy*** économie *f* de marché *ou* libérale; ***market entry*** lancement *m* sur le marché; ***market expansion*** extension *f* de marché; ***market exploration*** prospection *f* du marché; ***market exposure*** exposition *f* sur le marché; ***market fluctuation*** mouvement *m* du marché; ***market follower*** suiveur *m* (sur le marché); ***market forces*** les forces *fpl* du marché; ***market forecast*** prévisions *fpl* du marché, pronostic *m* du marché; ***market gap*** manque *m* sur le marché; *Br* ***market garden*** jardin *m* maraîcher; *Br* ***market gardener*** maraîcher(ère) *m,f*; *Br* ***market gardening*** culture *f* maraîchère; ***market growth*** croissance *f* du marché; ***market indicator*** indicateur *m* de marché; ***market intelligence*** intelligence *f* marketing, information *f* commerciale; ***market leader*** *(product)* premier produit *m* sur le marché; *(firm)* leader *m* du marché; *St Exch* ***market maker*** mainteneur *m* *ou* teneur *m* du marché, intermédiaire *mf*; ***market mechanism*** mécanisme *m* du marché; ***market minimum*** *(base sales)* ventes *fpl* de base; *St Exch* ***market order*** ordre *m* au mieux; ***market orientation*** orientation *f* marché; ***market participant*** intervenant(e) *m,f* *ou* acteur *m* sur le marché; ***market penetration*** pénétration *f* du marché; ***market penetration pricing*** tarification *f* de pénétration du marché; ***market pioneer*** pionnier *m*; ***market player*** acteur *m* de marché; ***market positioning*** positionnement *m* sur le marché; ***market potential*** *(of product)* potentiel *m* sur le marché; *(of market)* potentiel *m* du marché; ***market price*** *Com* prix *m* courant; *St Exch* cours *m* de (la) Bourse; *St Exch* ***market price list*** mercuriale *f*; ***market profile*** profil *m* du marché; ***market prospects*** perspectives *fpl* commerciales; *St Exch* ***market quotation*** cotation *f* au cours du marché; ***market rate*** taux *m* du marché; ***market rate of discount*** taux *m* d'escompte hors banque; *St Exch* ***market rating*** cours *m* en Bourse; ***market report*** étude *f* de marché, rapport *m* ou bilan *m* commercial; ***market research*** recherche *f* commerciale; étude *f* ou études *fpl* de marché; **market research has shown that the idea is viable** des études de marché ont montré que l'idée a des chances de réussir; **he works in market research** il travaille dans le marketing; ***market research company*** société *f* d'études de marché; ***market researcher*** chargé(e) *m,f* d'étude de marché; *Br* ***Market Research Society*** = société d'étude de marché britannique; ***market risk*** risque *m* du marché; ***market rollout*** élargissement *m* du marché; ***market segment*** segment *m* de marché; ***market segmentation*** segmentation *f* du marché; ***market share*** part *f* de marché; ***market size*** *(of product)* part *f* de marché; *(of market)* taille *f* du marché; *St Exch* taille *f* boursière; *Br* ***market square*** place *f* du marché; ***market study*** étude *f* de marché; ***market survey*** enquête *f* de marché; ***market test*** marché-test *m*, test *m* de marché, test *m* de vente; ***market thrust*** percée *f* commerciale; ***market town*** bourg *m*; *Br* ***market trader*** vendeur(euse) *m,f* qui fait les marchés; *St Exch* ***market trend*** conjoncture *f* boursière; ***market value*** *Com (of object, product)* valeur *f* marchande; *St Exch (of share)* valeur *f* boursière *ou* en bourse

marketability [ˌmɑːkɪtə'bɪlətɪ] *n* possibilité *f* de commercialisation; **we are doubtful about the marketability of these machines** nous doutons que ces machines soient commercialisables

marketable ['mɑːkɪtəbəl] *adj* vendable, commercialisable; *St Exch (shares, securities)* négociable

market-driven *adj* déterminé par les contraintes du marché

►► ***market-driven economy*** économie *f* de marché

marketeer [ˌmɑːkə'tɪə(r)] *n* (**a**) **black marketeer** trafiquant(e) *m,f* (au marché noir) (**b**) *Br Pol* **pro-marketeer** partisan(e) *m,f* du Marché commun; **anti-marketeer** adversaire *mf* du Marché commun

marketer ['mɑːkɪtə(r)] *n Mktg* mercaticien(enne) *m,f*, spécialiste *mf* en marketing

marketing ['mɑːkɪtɪŋ] *n (selling)* commercialisation *f*, distribution *f*; *(promotion, study, theory, field)* marketing *m*, mercatique *f*, commercialisation *f*; **to work in marketing** travailler dans le marketing

►► ***marketing analyst*** analyste *mf* mercaticien(enne); ***marketing approach*** démarche *f* marketing; ***marketing audit*** audit *m* marketing; ***marketing auditor*** audit *m* marketing, auditeur(trice) *m,f* marketing; ***marketing budget*** budget *m* marketing; ***marketing campaign*** campagne *f* de marketing; ***marketing channel*** circuit *m* de commercialisation *ou* distribution; ***marketing communications channel*** canal *m* de communication commerciale; ***marketing company*** entreprise *f* de marketing; ***marketing concept*** concept *f* de marketing; ***marketing consultancy*** *(service, activity)* conseil *m* en marketing; ***marketing consultancy firm*** société *f* de conseil en marketing; ***marketing consultant*** conseiller(ère) *m,f* commercial(e), mercaticien(enne) *m,f*; ***marketing costs*** frais *mpl* de commercialisation; ***marketing department*** service *m* du marketing; ***marketing director*** directeur(trice) *m,f* du marketing, dirco *m*, directeur(trice) *m,f* commercial(e); ***marketing engineering*** marketing *m* informatisé; ***marketing environment*** environnement *m* commercial, environnement *m* marketing; ***marketing executive*** responsable *mf* du marketing, cadre *m* en marketing; ***marketing expert*** mercaticien(enne) *m,f*; ***marketing fit*** ajustement *m* stratégique; ***marketing information system*** système *m* d'information marketing; ***marketing intelligence*** intelligence *f* marketing; ***marketing intelligence system*** système *m* d'intelligence marketing; ***marketing management*** gestion *f* du marketing; ***marketing manager*** directeur(trice) *m,f* du marketing, responsable *mf* du marketing; ***marketing mix*** marchéage *m*, marketing mix *m*, logistique *f* commerciale; ***marketing myopia*** myopie *f* marketing; ***marketing network*** réseau *m* *ou* circuit *m* de commercialisation; ***marketing orientation*** optique *f* marketing; ***marketing plan*** plan *m* marketing; ***marketing policy*** politique *f* de commercialisation; ***marketing research*** recherche *f* commerciale; ***marketing spectrum*** marchéage *m*; ***marketing spend*** dépenses *fpl* de marketing; ***marketing strategy*** stratégie *f* marketing; ***marketing study*** étude *f* commerciale, étude *f* marketing; ***marketing subsidiary*** filiale *f* de distribution; ***marketing team*** équipe *f* commerciale; ***marketing technique*** technique *f* commerciale; ***marketing tool*** outil *m* de marketing

marketization [ˌmɑːkɪtaɪ'zeɪʃən] *n* marchéisation *f*

marketplace ['mɑːkɪtpleɪs] *n* (**a**) *(in town)* place *f* du marché (**b**) *Com* marché *m*; **the ethics of the marketplace** l'éthique *f* du marché; **the international/European marketplace** le marché international/européen; **the products in the marketplace** les produits sur le marché

markhor ['mɑːkɔː(r)] *n Zool* markhor *m*

marking ['mɑːkɪŋ] **1** *n* (**a**) *(gen)* marquage *m*

(**b**) *Sch (of homework)* correction *f*; *(work to be marked)* copies *fpl* (à corriger)

(**c**) *Sport* marquage *m*

(**d**) *St Exch (of shares)* cotation *f*; **marking to market** comptabilisation *f* au prix de marché

2 markings *npl (distinctive marks)* marques *fpl*; *(on animal → spots)* taches *fpl*; *(→ stripes)* rayures *fpl*; *Aviat* insignes *mpl*

►► ***marking ink*** encre *f* à marquer; ***marking scheme*** barème *m*

markka ['mɑːkə] *n* mark *m* finlandais

marksman ['mɑːksmən] (*pl* **marksmen** [-mən]) *n* tireur *m* d'élite; **police marksmen** des tireurs *mpl* d'élite de la police

marksmanship ['mɑːksmənʃɪp] *n* habileté *f* au tir

markswoman ['mɑːksˌwʊmən] (*pl* **markswomen** [-ˌwɪmɪn]) *n* tireuse *f* d'élite

mark-up *n Com* majoration *f*; **we operate a 2.5 times mark-up** nous appliquons une marge de 2,5

►► ***mark-up pricing*** fixation *f* du prix au coût moyen majoré; ***mark-up ratio*** taux *m* de marge

marl [mɑːl] *Agr* **1** *n* marne *f*

2 *vt* marner

Marlborough ['mɑːlbrə] *n* = ville du Wiltshire où se trouve Marlborough College, prestigieuse école privée

marled [mɑːld] *adj Scot* bigarré

marlin¹ ['mɑːlɪn] *n Ich* makaire *m*

marlin², marline ['mɑːlɪn] *n Naut* merlin *m*

►► *Naut* ***marlin spike*** épissoir *m*

marlinespike ['mɑːlɪnspaɪk] *n Naut* épissoir *m*

marling ['mɑːlɪŋ] *n Agr* marnage *m*

marlinspike = **marlinespike**

marly ['mɑːlɪ] *adj* marneux

marmalade ['mɑːməleɪd] **1** *n (gen)* confiture *f* d'agrumes; *(orange)* marmelade *f* d'orange

2 *adj (cat)* roux (rousse)

►► ***marmalade orange*** orange *f* amère, bigarade *f*

Marmara ['mɑːmərə] = **Marmora**

Marmite® ['mɑːmaɪt] *n* = pâte à tartiner végétale à base d'extrait de levure

marmite ['mɑːmaɪt] *n (cooking pot)* marmite *f*

Marmora, Marmara ['mɑːmərə] *n* **the Sea of Marmora** la mer de Marmara

marmoreal [mɑː'mɔːrɪəl] *adj Literary* marmoréen

marmoset ['mɑːməzet] *n Zool* ouistiti *m*

marmot ['mɑːmət] *n Zool & (fur)* marmotte *f*

marocain ['mærəkeɪn] *n Tex* crêpe *m* marocain

Maronite ['mærənaɪt] **1** *n* Maronite *mf*

2 *adj* maronite

maroon [mə'ruːn] **1** *n* (**a**) *(colour)* bordeaux *m* (**b**) *Br (rocket)* fusée *f* de détresse

2 *adj (colour)* bordeaux *(inv)*

3 *vt (abandon)* abandonner *(sur une île ou une côte déserte)*; **to be marooned** *(shipwrecked)* faire naufrage; *Fig* **he felt marooned in his suburban flat** il se sentait abandonné dans son appartement de banlieue

Marplan ['mɑːplæn] *n* = nom d'un institut de sondage

marque [mɑːk] *n (brand)* marque *f*

marquee [mɑː'kiː] *n* (**a**) *Br (tent)* grande tente *f*; *(for circus)* chapiteau *m* (**b**) *Am (canopy at hotel, theatre)* marquise *f* (**c**) *Am Fam (successful film, play etc)* succès □ *m*

Marquesas Islands [mɑː'keɪsæs-] *npl* **the Marquesas Islands** les îles *fpl* Marquises; **in the Marquesas Islands** aux îles Marquises

marquess ['mɑːkwɪs] *n* marquis *m*

marquetry ['mɑːkɪtrɪ] **1** *n* marqueterie *f*

2 *adj (table)* en marqueterie

marquis = **marquess**

marquisate ['mɑːkwɪzɪt] *n* marquisat *m*

marquise [mɑː'kiːz] *n* (**a**) *(noblewoman)* marquise *f* (**b**) *(ring)* marquise *f*; *(gem)* pierre *f* taillée marquise

Marrakech, Marrakesh [,mærə'keʃ] *n* Marrakech

marram ['mærəm] *n Bot* gourbet *m*

►► ***marram grass*** gourbet *m*

marriage ['mærɪdʒ] **1** *n* (**a**) *(state, relationship)* mariage *m*; *(ceremony)* mariage *m*, noces *fpl*; **to make an offer of marriage** faire une proposition de mariage; **to give sb in marriage** donner qn en mariage; **to take sb in marriage** prendre qn pour époux(épouse), épouser qn; **he's my uncle by marriage** c'est mon oncle par alliance; **a marriage made in heaven** un mariage idéal

(**b**) *Fig (union)* mariage *m*, alliance *f*; **a marriage of minds** une union des esprits; **a marriage made in heaven** un mélange exquis

2 *comp* conjugal, matrimonial

►► ***marriage bed*** lit *m* conjugal; ***marriage broker*** agent *m* matrimonial; *Br* ***marriage bureau*** agence *f* matrimoniale; ***marriage ceremony*** cérémonie *f* de mariage; ***marriage certificate*** extrait *m* d'acte de mariage; ***marriage contract*** contrat *m* de mariage; ***marriage of convenience*** mariage *m* de raison; ***marriage guidance*** conseil *m* conjugal; ***marriage guidance counsellor*** conseiller(ère) *m,f* conjugal(e); ***marriage licence*** ≃ certificat *m* de non-opposition au mariage; *Br Fam Old-fashioned* ***marriage lines*** extrait *m* d'acte de mariage[□]; ***marriage settlement*** *(dowry)* dot *f*; *(between couple)* ≃ contrat *m* de mariage, ≃ régime *m* matrimonial; ***marriage vows*** vœux *mpl* de mariage

'The Marriage of Figaro' *Beaumarchais, Mozart* 'Le Mariage de Figaro' (pièce), 'Les Noces de Figaro' (opéra)

'The Marriage of Heaven and Hell' *Blake* 'Le Mariage du ciel et de l'enfer'

marriageable ['mærɪdʒəbəl] *adj* mariable; **to be of marriageable age** être en âge de se marier

married ['mærɪd] **1** *adj (man, woman)* marié; *(life)* conjugal; **just married** *(on car)* jeunes mariés; *Fig* **he's married to his job** il ne vit que pour son travail

2 *npl* **marrieds** *(married couples)* couples *mpl* mariés

►► ***married couple*** couple *m* marié; ***married name*** nom *m* de femme mariée; *Br* ***married quarters*** logements *mpl* pour familles

marrow ['mærəʊ] *n* (**a**) *Biol & Fig* moelle *f*; **frozen** *or* **chilled to the marrow** gelé jusqu'à la moelle des os (**b**) *(vegetable)* courge *f*

marrowbone ['mærəʊbəʊn] *n* os *m* à moelle

marrowfat ['mærəʊfæt] *n* pois *m* carré

►► ***marrowfat pea*** pois *m* carré

marry ['mærɪ] *(pt & pp* **married**) **1** *vt* (**a**) *(of fiancé)* épouser, se marier avec; **to get married** se marier; **to be married (to sb)** être marié (avec qn); **they're happily married** ils forment un ménage heureux; **will you marry me?** veux-tu m'épouser?; **to marry money** faire un mariage d'argent

(**b**) *(of priest, minister, official)* marier; **they were married by the archbishop** ils ont été mariés par l'archevêque

(**c**) *Fig (combine)* marier, allier

2 *vi* (**a**) *(person, couple)* se marier; **she never married** elle ne s'est jamais mariée; **he's not the marrying type** ce n'est pas le genre à se marier; **she married beneath herself/above herself** elle s'est mésalliée/a fait un beau mariage; **to marry for money** faire un mariage d'argent; **to marry into money** épouser quelqu'un issu d'une famille riche; **she married into a farming family** elle a épousé un agriculteur; *Prov* **marry in haste, repent at leisure** tel se marie à la hâte qui s'en repent à loisir

(**b**) *Fig (combine)* se marier, s'allier; **the flavours marry well** les saveurs se marient bien

►**marry off** *vt sep* marier; **she married off her daughter to an aristocrat** elle a marié sa fille à un aristocrate

►**marry up 1** *vt sep (bring together → two parts)* joindre; *(→ colours)* marier

2 *vi (line up, fit)* coïncider, concorder; *(colours)* aller bien ensemble, se marier; **check that the two parts marry up** vérifier que les deux parties coïncident

Mars [mɑːz] **1** *pr n Myth* Mars

2 *n Astron* Mars *f*

Marsala [mɑː'sɑːlə] *n* marsala *m*

Marseille, Marseilles [mɑː'seɪ] *n* Marseille

marsh [mɑːʃ] *n* marais *m*, marécage *m*

►► ***marsh fever*** fièvre *f* des marais, paludisme *m*; ***marsh gas*** gaz *m* des marais, méthane *m*; *Bot* ***marsh gentian*** gentiane *f* pneumonanthe; *Orn* ***marsh harrier*** busard *m* des roseaux; *Orn* ***marsh hawk*** busard *m* St Martin; *Orn* ***marsh hen*** poule *f* d'eau, râle *m* d'eau; *Bot* ***marsh lousewort*** pédiculaire *f* des marais; *Bot* ***marsh marigold*** souci *m* d'eau, populage *m*; *Bot* ***marsh pennywort*** écuelle *f* d'eau; *Bot* ***marsh samphire*** salicorne *f*; *Orn* ***marsh tit*** nonnette *f* (cendrée); *Orn* ***marsh warbler*** rousserolle *f* verderolle

marshal ['mɑːʃəl] *(Br pt & pp* **marshalled,** *cont* **marshalling,** *Am pt & pp* **marshaled,** *cont* **marshaling**) **1** *n* (**a**) *Mil* maréchal *m*

(**b**) *(at public event)* membre *m* du service d'ordre; *(in law court)* huissier *m*; *(at race-track)* commissaire *m*

(**c**) *Am (police chief)* commissaire *m* de police; *(fire chief)* capitaine *m* des pompiers; *(district police officer)* commissaire *m*

2 *vt* (**a**) *Mil (troops)* masser, rassembler; *(people, group)* canaliser, diriger; **the troops were marshalled into the square** on rassembla les troupes sur la place; **she marshalled the children out of the room** elle dirigea les enfants vers la porte

(**b**) *(organize → arguments, thoughts)* rassembler; **he's trying to marshal support for his project** il essaie d'obtenir du soutien pour son projet

(**c**) *Rail (trucks, wagons)* trier, manœuvrer

►► *Br Mil* ***marshal of the Royal Air Force*** ≃ chef *m* d'état-major de l'armée de l'air, *Can* ≃ maréchal *m* de l'ARC

Marshall ['mɑːʃəl] *pr n*

►► ***the Marshall Islands*** les îles *fpl* Marshall; **in the Marshall Islands** aux îles Marshall; ***the Marshall Plan*** le Plan Marshall

MARSHALL PLAN

Le Plan Marshall, du nom du général et secrétaire d'État américain l'ayant élaboré, est le programme américain d'aide à la reconstruction économique de l'Europe d'après-guerre.

Marshallese [,mɑːʃə'liːz] *n (language)* marshallais

marshalling yard ['mɑːʃəlɪŋ-] *n Br Rail* centre *m ou* gare *f* de triage

marshiness ['mɑːʃɪnɪs] *n* état *m* marécageux

marshland ['mɑːʃlænd] *n* marais *m*, terrain *m* marécageux

marshmallow [*Br* ,mɑːʃ'mæləʊ, *Am* 'marʃ,meləʊ] *n* (**a**) *Bot* guimauve *f* (**b**) *Culin (sweet)* guimauve *f*

marshy ['mɑːʃɪ] *(compar* **marshier,** *superl* **marshiest**) *adj* marécageux

Marston Moor ['mɑːstən'mɔː(r)] *n Hist* = première grande victoire, en 1644, des armées alliées du Parlement anglais et de l'Écosse contre les royalistes, pendant la guerre civile en Angleterre

marsupial [mɑː'suːpjəl] **1** *adj* marsupial

2 *n* marsupial *m*

►► *Zool* ***marsupial frog*** nototrème *m*; *Zool* ***marsupial mole*** notorycte *m*

mart [mɑːt] *n* (**a**) *(market)* marché *m*; **second-hand car mart** magasin *m* de voitures d'occasion (**b**) *(auction room)* salle *f* des ventes

martagon ['mɑːtəgən] *n Bot* martagon *m*

►► ***martagon lily*** martagon *m*

Martello tower [mɑː'teləʊ-] *n* = tour anciennement utilisée pour la défense des côtes anglaises

marten ['mɑːtɪn] *n Zool* marte *f*, martre *f*

martensite ['mɑːtɪnsaɪt] *n Metal* martensite *f*

martensitic [,mɑːtɪn'sɪtɪk] *adj Metal* martensitique

Martha ['mɑːθə] *pr n Bible* Marthe

►► *Geog* ***Martha's Vineyard*** Martha's Vineyard

martial ['mɑːʃəl] *adj (military)* martial; *(warlike)* martial, guerrier

►► ***martial art*** art *m* martial; ***martial law*** loi *f* martiale; **to declare martial law** proclamer l'état de siège; ***martial music*** musique *f* militaire

martially ['mɑːʃəlɪ] *adv (militarily)* martialement; *(in a warlike manner)* en guerrier

Martian ['mɑːʃən] **1** *n* Martien(enne) *m,f*

2 *adj* martien

martin ['mɑːtɪn] *n Orn* hirondelle *f*

martinet [,mɑːtɪ'net] *n* tyran *m*

martingale ['mɑːtɪngeɪl] *n* (**a**) *(of horse)* martingale *f* (**b**) *Naut* martingale *f* du beaupré

►► *Naut* ***martingale guy, martingale stay*** martingale *f* du beaupré

Martini® [mɑː'tiːnɪ] *n* Martini® *m*

martini [mɑː'tiːnɪ] *n (cocktail)* martini *m*

Martinican [,mɑːtɪ'niːkən] **1** *n* Martiniquais(e) *m,f*

2 *adj* martiniquais

Martinique [,mɑːtɪ'niːk] *n* Martinique *f*; **in Martinique** à la *ou* en Martinique

Martinmas ['mɑːtɪnməs] *n* la Saint-Martin *f*; **at Martinmas** à la Saint-Martin

martlet ['mɑːtlɪt] *n* (**a**) *Orn* hirondelle *f* de fenêtre (**b**) *Her* merlette *f*

martyr ['mɑːtə(r)] **1** *n* martyr(e) *m,f*; **to die a martyr** mourir en martyr; *Fig* **she's always making a martyr of herself** elle joue toujours les martyres; **he's a martyr to rheumatism** ses rhumatismes lui font souffrir le martyre

2 *vt* martyriser

martyrdom ['mɑːtədəm] *n Rel* martyre *m*; *Fig* martyre *m*, calvaire *m*

martyred ['mɑːtəd] *adj* de martyr; **to put on a martyred look** prendre des airs de martyr

martyrization [,mɑːtəraɪ'zeɪʃən] *n* martyre *m*

martyrize, -ise ['mɑːtəraɪz] *vt* martyriser

martyrological [,mɑːtərə'lɒdʒɪkəl] *adj* martyrologique

martyrologist [,mɑːtə'rɒlədʒɪst] *n* martyrologiste *mf*

martyrology [,mɑːtə'rɒlədʒɪ] *n* (**a**) *(list of martyrs)* martyrologe *m*; *(in the Greek Church)* ménologe *m* (**b**) *(history of martyrs)* martyrologie *f*

MARV [mɑːv] *n Mil (abbr* **manoeuvrable re-entry vehicle**) MARV *m*

marvel ['mɑːvəl] *(Br pt & pp* **marvelled,** *cont* **marvelling,** *Am pt & pp* **marveled,** *cont* **marveling**) **1** *n* (**a**) *(miracle)* merveille *f*, miracle *m*, prodige *m*; **the marvels of science/the world** les merveilles *fpl* de la science/du monde; **to do** *or* **to work marvels** faire des merveilles; **it's a marvel to me that she managed to survive** pour moi, c'est un miracle qu'elle ait survécu

(**b**) *(marvellous person)* **you're a marvel!** tu es une vraie petite merveille!

2 *vt* **he marvelled that she had kept so calm** il n'en revenait pas qu'elle ait pu rester si calme

3 *vi* **to marvel at sth** s'émerveiller de qch; **I marvel at the speed they get things done** je suis émerveillé par la vitesse à laquelle ils font les choses

marvellous, *Am* **marvelous** ['mɑːvələs] *adj (amazing)* merveilleux, extraordinaire; *(miraculous)* miraculeux

marvellously, *Am* **marvelously** ['mɑːvələslɪ] *adv* merveilleusement, à merveille

Marxian ['mɑːksɪən] *adj* marxien

Marxism ['mɑːksɪzəm] *n* marxisme *m*

Marxism-Leninism *n* marxisme-léninisme *m*

Marxist ['mɑːksɪst] **1** *n* marxiste *mf*

2 *adj* marxiste

Marxist-Leninist 1 *n* marxiste-léniniste *mf*

2 *adj* marxiste-léniniste

Mary ['meərɪ] *pr n Bible* Marie; **Mary Magdalene** Marie Madeleine; **the Virgin Mary** la Vierge Marie; **Mary, Queen of Scots** Marie Stuart

Maryland ['meərɪlənd] *n* le Maryland; **in Maryland** dans le Maryland

marzipan ['mɑːzɪpæn] **1** *n* pâte *f* d'amandes

2 *comp (cake, sweet etc)* à la pâte d'amandes

►► *Fam Com* ***marzipan layer*** cadres *mpl* moyens

Masai ['mɑːsaɪ] **1** *n* (**a**) *(person)* Masaï *mf inv*
(**b**) *(language)* maa *m*
2 *adj* masaï *(inv)*

masala [mə'sɑːlə] *n Culin* masala *m*

mascara [mæs'kɑːrə] *n* mascara *m*
▸▸ ***mascara brush, mascara wand*** brosse *f* à mascara

mascaraed [mæs'kɑːrəd] *adj* **she had heavily mascaraed eyelashes** elle portait beaucoup de mascara

mascarpone [mæskə'pəʊnɪ] *n* mascarpone *m*

mascon ['mæskɒn] *n Astron* mascon *m*, réplétion *f*

mascot ['mæskət] *n* mascotte *f*

masculine ['mæskjʊlɪn] **1** *n Gram* masculin *m*; **in the masculine** au masculin
2 *adj* masculin

masculinity [ˌmæskjʊ'lɪnətɪ] *n* masculinité *f*

masculinization [ˌmæskjʊlɪnaɪ'zeɪʃən] *n* masculinisation *f*

masculinize, -ise ['mæskjʊlɪnaɪz] *vt* masculiniser

maser ['meɪzə(r)] *n Phys* maser *m*

MASH [mæʃ] *n Am (abbr* **mobile army surgical hospital**) = hôpital militaire de campagne

mash [mæʃ] **1** *n* (**a**) *Br Fam (mashed potatoes)* purée *f* (de pommes de terre) ❑
(**b**) *(for horses)* mash *m*; *(for pigs, poultry)* pâtée *f*
(**c**) *(in brewing)* empâtage *m*
(**d**) *Fam (pulp)* pulpe ❑ *f*, bouillie ❑ *f*
2 *vt* (**a**) *(crush)* écraser, broyer; **mash it all together** écraser le tout; **mash it (up) well** bien écraser
(**b**) *Culin* faire une purée de; **mashed potato** *or* **potatoes** purée *f* (de pommes de terre); **instant mashed potatoes** purée *f* instantanée, purée *f* Mousseline®
(**c**) *(in brewing)* empâter
▸▸ ***mash tun*** cuve *f* d'empâtage

masher ['mæʃə(r)] *n* broyeur *m*; *(for potatoes)* presse-purée *m inv*

mashie ['mæʃɪ] *n Golf* mashie *m*

mask [mɑːsk] **1** *n* (**a**) *also Fig* masque *m*; *Fig* **a mask of happiness/confidence** une apparence de bonheur/confiance trompeuse; *Fig* **the mask had slipped** le masque était tombé; *Fig* **to throw off** *or* **drop the mask** lever le masque, se démasquer
(**b**) *(in photography)* cache *m*
(**c**) *Comput* masque *m*
2 *vt* (**a**) *(face)* masquer
(**b**) *(truth, feelings)* masquer, cacher, dissimuler; **an apparent cheerfulness masked her deep pessimism** une gaieté apparente masquait son profond pessimisme
(**c**) *(house)* masquer, cacher; *(view)* boucher, masquer; *(flavour, smell)* masquer, recouvrir
(**d**) *(in painting, photography)* masquer, cacher

▸**mask out** *vt sep Phot* masquer, cacher

▸**mask up** *vi (surgeon)* se masquer, se mettre un masque

masked [mɑːskt] *adj (face, man)* masqué
▸▸ ***masked ball*** bal *m* masqué; *Mil* ***masked battery*** batterie *f* masquée; *Comput* ***masked ROM*** mémoire *f* morte masquée

> **Who was that masked man?**
> Il s'agit d'une formule extraite de la série télévisée américaine des années 50 *Zorro*, dans laquelle le héros éponyme porte un masque.
> On utilise aujourd'hui cette formule ("qui est cet homme masqué?") sur le mode humoristique lorsque l'on demande à connaître l'identité de quelqu'un que l'on ne connaît pas ou que l'on n'a fait qu'apercevoir.

masking ['mɑːskɪŋ] *n* masquage *m*
▸▸ ***masking tape*** ruban *m* adhésif *(utilisé pour masquer une surface que l'on ne veut pas peindre)*

maslin ['mæzlɪn] *n Agr* méteil *m*, dragée *f*

masochism ['mæsəkɪzəm] *n* masochisme *m*

masochist ['mæsəkɪst] **1** *n* masochiste *mf*
2 *adj* masochiste

masochistic [ˌmæsə'kɪstɪk] *adj* masochiste

mason ['meɪsən] **1** *n (stoneworker)* maçon(-onne) *m,f*
2 Mason *n (Freemason)* Maçon *m*, franc-maçon *m*
▸▸ ***Mason jar*** bocal *m* à conserves

Mason-Dixon Line [ˌmeɪsən'dɪksən-] *n Hist* = frontière sud de la Pennsylvanie qui marquait aussi la limite entre les États esclavagistes et les États anti-esclavagistes

Masonic [mə'sɒnɪk] *adj* maçonnique, franc-maçonnique
▸▸ ***Masonic lodge*** loge *f* maçonnique

masonite ['meɪsənaɪt] *n Miner* masonite *f*

masonry ['meɪsənrɪ] **1** *n (stonework, skill)* maçonnerie *f*; **a large piece of masonry** un gros bloc de pierre; **beware of falling masonry** *(sign)* attention, chute de matériaux
2 Masonry *n (Freemasonry)* Maçonnerie *f*, franc-maçonnerie *f*
▸▸ ***masonry bit*** foret *m* de maçonnerie; ***masonry drill*** foret *m* de maçonnerie

Masora, Masorah [mə'sɔːrə] *n Rel* massore *f*, massorah *f*

Masorete ['mæsəriːt], **Masorite** ['mæsəraɪt] *n Rel* massorète *m*

masque [mɑːsk] *n Theat* masque *m*

masquerade [ˌmæskə'reɪd] **1** *n also Fig* mascarade *f*
2 *vi* **to masquerade as** *(pretend to be)* se faire passer pour; *(disguise oneself as)* se déguiser en

Mass [mæs] *n Rel* (**a**) *(music)* messe *f*; **Mass in B Minor** messe *f* en si mineur (**b**) *(ceremony)* messe *f*; **to go to Mass** aller à la messe; **to say Mass** dire la messe

Mass. *(written abbr* **Massachusetts**) Massachusetts *m*

mass [mæs] **1** *n* (**a**) *Phys* masse *f*; *Tex* **dyed in the mass** teinté dans la masse
(**b**) *(large quantity or amount)* masse *f*, quantité *f*; **a mass of documents** une masse de documents; **a mass of work** une quantité de travail; **the streets were a solid mass of people/traffic** les rues regorgeaient de monde/de voitures
(**c**) *(bulk)* masse *f*; **the dark mass of the mountains** la masse sombre des montagnes
(**d**) *(majority)* majorité *f*, plupart *f*; **the mass of the people are in favour of this policy** la majorité des gens est favorable à cette politique; **in the mass** dans l'ensemble
(**e**) *Geog* **land mass** masse *f* continentale
2 *adj (for all → communication, education)* de masse; *(large-scale → starvation, unemployment)* à *ou* sur une grande échelle; *(involving many → resignation)* massif, en masse; *(collective → funeral)* collectif; **this product will appeal to a mass audience** ce produit plaira à un large public
3 *vi (people)* se masser; *(clouds)* s'amonceler; **the crowds were massing in the square** des milliers de personnes se massaient sur la place
4 *vt (troops)* masser
5 masses *npl* (**a**) **the masses** les masses *fpl*; **culture for the masses** la culture à la portée de tous
(**b**) *Fam (large amount)* **we've got masses** on en a plein; **masses of** des masses de, plein de; **we ate masses of sweets** on a mangé plein de bonbons
▸▸ ***mass circulation*** grande diffusion *f*, diffusion *f* de masse; ***mass communication*** communication *f* de masse; ***mass consumption*** consommation *f* de masse; ***mass culture*** culture *f* de masse; ***mass demonstration*** grande manifestation *f*; *Mktg* ***mass display*** présentation *f* en masse; ***mass distribution*** distribution *f* de masse, grande distribution *f*; ***mass distribution sector*** secteur *m* de la grande distribution; ***mass execution*** exécution *f* en masse; ***mass extinction*** extinction *f* de masse *ou* massive; ***mass grave*** charnier *m*; ***mass hypnosis*** hypnose *f* collective; ***mass hysteria*** hystérie *f* collective; ***mass mailing*** envoi *m* en nombre; ***mass market*** marché *m* de masse; ***mass marketing*** marketing *m* de grande consommation, marketing *m* de masse; ***mass media*** mass media *mpl*; ***mass meeting*** grand rassemblement *m*; ***mass murder*** tuerie *f*; ***mass murderer*** *(serial killer)* tueur(euse) *m,f* en série; *(tyrant, dictator)* boucher *m*; *Gram* ***mass noun*** nom *m* non comptable; *Chem* ***mass number*** nombre *m* de masse; ***mass production*** fabrication *f ou* production *f* en série; **it goes into mass production next week** la production en série commence la semaine prochaine; ***mass protest*** protestation *f* en masse; *Chem & Phys* ***mass spectrograph*** spectrographe *m* de masse; *Chem & Phys* ***mass spectrography*** spectrographie *f* de masse; *Chem & Phys* ***mass spectrometer*** spectromètre *m* de masse; *Comput* ***mass storage*** mémoire *f* de masse; ***mass suicide*** suicide *m* collectif; ***mass tourism*** tourisme *m* de masse; ***mass unemployment*** chômage *m* sur une grande échelle

Massachusetts [ˌmæsə'tʃuːsɪts] *n* le Massachusetts; **in Massachusetts** dans le Massachusetts

massacre ['mæsəkə(r)] **1** *n* massacre *m*; *Bible* **the Massacre of the Innocents** le massacre des Innocents
2 *vt* (**a**) *(kill)* massacrer (**b**) *Sport* écraser

massacrer ['mæsəkrə(r)] *n* massacreur(euse) *m,f*

massage [*Br* 'mæsɑːʒ, *Am* mə'sɑːʒ] **1** *n* massage *m*; *(of scalp)* friction *f*
2 *vt* masser; *Fig (statistics, facts)* manipuler
▸▸ ***massage parlour*** salon *m* de massage

masse [mæs] *see* **en masse**

massed [mæst] *adj* (**a**) *(crowds, soldiers)* massé, regroupé (**b**) *(collective)* de masse; **the massed weight of public opinion** le poids de l'opinion publique
▸▸ *Br* ***massed bands*** ensemble *m* de fanfares

mass-energy *comp* masse-énergie
▸▸ ***mass-energy equation, mass-energy relation*** relation *f* masse-énergie

masseur [*Br* mæ'sɜː(r), *Am* mæ'sʊər] *n* masseur *m*

masseuse [*Br* mæ'sɜːz, *Am* mæ'suːz] *n* masseuse *f*

massif ['mæsiːf] *n* massif *m* (montagneux)

massive ['mæsɪv] *adj (in size)* massif, énorme; *(dose, increase)* massif; *(majority)* écrasant; *(change, explosion)* énorme; *(sound)* retentissant; *(heart attack, stroke)* foudroyant; **the general was a massive man** le général était un homme massif

massively ['mæsɪvlɪ] *adv (increase, reduce)* considérablement; *(invest, fund)* massivement; *(popular, successful)* extrêmement; **he's massively built** il est solidement bâti

massiveness ['mæsɪvnɪs] *n* caractère *m* massif

massotherapy [ˌmæsəʊ'θerəpɪ] *n* massothérapie *f*

mass-produce *vt* fabriquer en série

mass-produced *adj* fabriqué en série

mast [mɑːst] *n* (**a**) *(on ship, for flag)* mât *m*; *(for radio or TV aerial)* pylône *m*; **the masts** les mâts *mpl*, la mâture; **to sail before the mast** servir comme simple matelot (**b**) *(animal food)* faine *f (destinée à l'alimentation animale)*

mastaba ['mæstəbə] *n Archeol* mastaba *m*

mastectomy [mæs'tektəmɪ] *(pl* **mastectomies**) *n Med* mastectomie *f*, mammectomie *f*

-masted ['mɑːstɪd] *suff Naut* **three/four/***etc***-masted** à trois/quatre/*etc* mâts

master ['mɑːstə(r)] **1** *n* (**a**) *(of household, dog, servant, situation)* maître *m*; **the master of the house** le maître de maison; **to be master in one's own house** être maître chez soi; **to be one's own master** être son propre maître; **to be (the) master of one's fate** être maître de son destin; **he's master of the situation** il est maître de la situation; *Prov* **like master like man** tel maître, tel valet
(**b**) *(expert)* maître *m*; **chess master** maître *m*; **he's a master at the art of ducking questions** il est maître dans l'art d'éluder les questions
(**c**) *Sch (in primary school)* instituteur *m*, maître *m* d'école; *(in secondary school)* professeur *m*; *(private tutor)* maître *m*; **history master** professeur *m* d'histoire
(**d**) *Univ* **Master of Arts/Science** *(person)* titulaire *mf* d'une maîtrise de lettres/de sciences; *(qualification)* maîtrise *f* ès lettres/ès sciences; **she's doing a master's (degree) in philosophy** elle prépare une maîtrise de philosophie
(**e**) *Old-fashioned Formal (boy's title)* **Master David Thomas** Monsieur David Thomas; **Master David** *(said by servant)* Monsieur David
(**f**) *Art* maître *m*
(**g**) *Naut (of ship)* capitaine *m*; *(of fishing boat)* patron *m*; *Naut* **master's certificate** brevet *m* de capitaine
(**h**) *Univ (head of college)* principal *m*

mas–mas

(**i**) *(original copy)* original *m*; *(standard)* étalon *m*; *Comput* **master (disk)** disque *m* maître

2 *adj* (**a**) *(overall)* directeur, maître

(**b**) *(in trade)* maître; **master chef/craftsman** maître chef *m* /artisan *m*; **a master thief** un(une) voleur(euse) de génie

(**c**) *(controlling)* principal; **master switch** interrupteur *m* général

(**d**) *(original)* original

3 *vt* (**a**) *(person, animal)* maîtriser, dompter; *(problem, difficulty)* surmonter, venir à bout de; *(emotions)* maîtriser, surmonter; *(situation)* maîtriser, se rendre maître de; **to master oneself** se maîtriser, se dominer

(**b**) *(subject, technique)* maîtriser; **she mastered Portuguese in only six months** six mois lui ont suffi pour maîtriser le portugais; **I never really mastered the language** je n'ai jamais eu une bonne maîtrise de la langue

►► *Constr* ***master beam*** poutre *f* maîtresse; ***master bedroom*** chambre *f* principale; *Fin* ***master budget*** budget *m* global; ***master builder*** maître *m* bâtisseur; ***master card*** carte *f* maîtresse; ***master of ceremonies*** *(at reception)* maître *m* des cérémonies; *(on TV show)* présentateur *m*; ***master class*** cours *m* de maître; *Mus* master class *m*; *Fig* **the press conference was a master class in how to handle the media** pour ceux qui veulent savoir comment se comporter face aux médias, cette conférence de presse pourrait servir de leçon; ***master copy*** original *m*; *Can Mil* ***master corporal*** ≃ caporal-chef *m*; *Aut* ***master cylinder*** maître-cylindre *m*; *Comput* ***master disk*** disque *m* maître; *Comput* ***master file*** fichier *m* principal *ou* maître; *Hunt* ***master of hounds, master of foxhounds*** maître *m* d'équipage; ***master key*** passe-partout *m inv*; *Naut* ***master mariner*** capitaine *m*; *TV* ***master monitor*** récepteur *m* de contrôle final; ***master plan*** stratégie *f* globale; ***master race*** race *f* supérieure; *Mus* ***master record*** disque *m* original; *Br Law* ***Master of the Rolls*** ≃ président *m* de la cour d'appel *(en Grande-Bretagne)*; *Am Mil* ***master sergeant*** ≃ sergent-chef *m*; ***master soundtrack*** mixage *m* magnétique final; ***master tape*** bande *f* originale; *Com* ***master of works*** maître *m* d'œuvre

master-at-arms *(pl* **masters-at-arms***)* *n Naut* capitaine *m* d'armes

masterbrand [ˈmɑːstəˌbrænd] *n Mktg* marque *f* vedette

Mastercard® [ˈmɑːstəkɑːd] *n* carte *f* Mastercard®

masterful [ˈmɑːstəfʊl] *adj* (**a**) *(dominant → person)* qui sait se faire obéir; **she was wrapped in his masterful arms** il l'enveloppait de ses bras puissants

(**b**) *(tone, voice, performance)* magistral; **the race was another masterful display of formula 1 driving by the world champion** le Grand Prix de formule 1 fut une nouvelle démonstration magistrale du champion du monde

masterfully [ˈmɑːstəfʊlɪ] *adv* (**a**) *(dominatingly)* fermement, autoritairement; **to speak masterfully** parler sur un ton autoritaire (**b**) *(skilfully)* magistralement

masterly [ˈmɑːstəlɪ] *adj* magistral; **a masterly performance** une performance magistrale; **in a masterly fashion** magistralement, avec maestria

mastermind [ˈmɑːstəmaɪnd] **1** *n (genius)* cerveau *m*, génie *m*; *(of crime, operation)* cerveau *m*

2 *vt* diriger, organiser; **she masterminded the whole operation** c'est elle qui a dirigé toute l'opération, c'est elle le cerveau de toute l'opération

masterpiece [ˈmɑːstəpiːs] *n also Fig* chef-d'œuvre *m*

mastership [ˈmɑːstəʃɪp] *n* (**a**) *(rule, domination)* autorité *f* (**over** sur), maîtrise *f* (**over** de) (**b**) *Sch* poste *m* de principal *(de certains collèges universitaires ou d'une école secondaire)*; **(assistant) mastership** poste *m* de professeur (**c**) *(of subject)* connaissance *f* approfondie

mastersinger [ˈmɑːstəˌsɪŋə(r)] *n* maître *m* chanteur

master-slave *adj (relationship)* maître-esclave *(inv)*

►► *Tech* ***master-slave system*** système *m* maître-esclave

masterstroke [ˈmɑːstəstrəʊk] *n* coup *m* de maître

masterwork [ˈmɑːstəwɜːk] *n* chef-d'œuvre *m*

mastery [ˈmɑːstərɪ] *(pl* **masteries***)* *n* (**a**) *(domination, control → gen)* maîtrise *f*, domination *f*; *(→ of situation)* maîtrise *f* (**of** *or* **over** sur); *(→ of opponent)* supériorité *f* (**of** *or* **over** sur); **to gain mastery over sth** se rendre maître de qch; **to gain mastery over sb** soumettre qn

(**b**) *(of art, subject, language)* maîtrise *f*, connaissance *f*

(**c**) *(masterly skill)* maestria *f*, brio *m*

masthead [ˈmɑːsthed] *n* (**a**) *Naut* tête *f* de mât (**b**) *Press* cartouche *f* de titre

mastic [ˈmæstɪk] *n* mastic *m*

►► ***mastic tree*** lentisque *m*, arbre *m* à mastic

masticate [ˈmæstɪkeɪt] **1** *vt* (**a**) *(food)* mâcher, mastiquer (**b**) *Ind (rubber etc)* triturer, malaxer

2 *vi* mastiquer, mâcher

mastication [ˌmæstɪˈkeɪʃən] *n* mastication *f*

masticatory [ˈmæstɪkətrɪ] **1** *n Med* masticatoire *m*

2 *adj (muscle)* masticateur; *(function)* masticatoire

mastiff [ˈmæstɪf] *n* mastiff *m*

mastitis [mæsˈtaɪtɪs] *n Med & Vet* mastite *f*

mastodon [ˈmæstədɒn] *n Zool* mastodonte *m*

mastoid [ˈmæstɔɪd] **1** *n* (**a**) *Anat (bone)* mastoïde *f* (**b**) *Fam Med (mastoiditis)* mastoïdite ☐ *f*

2 *adj Anat* mastoïdien, mastoïde

mastoiditis [ˌmæstɔɪˈdaɪtɪs] *n (UNCOUNT) Med* mastoïdite *f*

masturbate [ˈmæstəbeɪt] **1** *vt* masturber

2 *vi* se masturber

masturbation [ˌmæstəˈbeɪʃən] *n* masturbation *f*; *Fig Pej* **mental masturbation** masturbation *f* intellectuelle

masturbatory [ˌmæstəˈbeɪtərɪ] *adj* masturbatoire

mat [mæt] *(pt & pp* **matted**, *cont* **matting***)* **1** *n* (**a**) *(floor covering → of wool etc)* (petit) tapis *m*, carpette *f*; *(→ of straw, rushes)* natte *f*; *(→ doormat)* paillasson *m*; *(→ in gym)* tapis *m*; *Fam* **to be on the mat** être sur la sellette; *Fam* **to have sb on the mat** faire passer un mauvais quart d'heure à qn; *Am Fam* **to go to the mat** se démener

(**b**) *(on table)* set *m* de table; *(for hot dishes)* dessous-de-plat *m inv*; *(for vase, ornament)* napperon *m*

2 *adj* mat

3 *vt (hair etc)* emmêler

4 *vi* (**a**) *(hair)* s'emmêler

(**b**) *(material)* (se) feutrer

Matabele [ˌmætəˈbiːlɪ] *n* Matabélé(e) *m,f*

Matabeleland [ˌmætəˈbiːlɪlænd] *n* Matabélé *m*, Matabeleland *m*

matador [ˈmætədɔː(r)] *n* matador *m*

MATCH [mætʃ]

match	► 1 (a)
égal	► 1 (b)
couple	► 1 (c)
allumette	► 1 (e)
mèche	► 1 (f)
égaler	► 2 (a), (e)
s'assortir à	► 2 (b)
opposer	► 2 (d)
aller (bien) ensemble	► 3
correspondre	► 3

1 *n* (**a**) *Sport (of football, rugby, baseball, cricket)* match *m*; *(of tennis)* match *m*, partie *f*; *(of golf)* partie *f*; *(swimming)* compétition *f*; **a rugby/boxing match** un match de rugby/de boxe; **game, set and match** *(in tennis)* jeu, set et match; **to play a match** jouer un match; *Br* **I haven't reached full match fitness yet** je n'ai pas encore retrouvé ma forme (pour jouer)

(**b**) *(equal)* égal(e) *m,f*; **he's found** *or* **met his match (in Heather)** il a trouvé à qui parler (avec Heather); **he's a match for her any day** il est de taille à lui faire face; **David is no match for Andrew** David ne fait pas le poids contre Andrew; **they were more than a match for us** nous ne faisions pas le poids contre eux

(**c**) *(couple)* couple *m*; *(marriage)* mariage *m*; **to make a good match** faire un bon mariage; **they are** *or* **make a good match** ils vont bien ensemble; **he's a good match** c'est un bon *ou* un excellent parti

(**d**) *(combination)* **these colours are a good match** ces couleurs se marient bien *ou* vont bien ensemble; **the new paint's not quite a perfect match** la nouvelle peinture n'est pas exactement de la même couleur que la précédente; **to find a match for a wallpaper** *(find curtains etc in suitable colour)* assortir un papier peint; *(find the same)* réassortir un papier peint

(**e**) *(for lighting)* allumette *f*; **to light** *or* **to strike a match** frotter *ou* craquer une allumette; **to put** *or* **to set a match to sth** mettre le feu à qch; **a box/book of matches** une boîte/une pochette d'allumettes

(**f**) *(fuse)* mèche *f*

2 *vt* (**a**) *(be equal to)* être l'égal de, égaler; **his arrogance is matched only by that of his father** son arrogance n'a d'égale que celle de son père; **will their deeds match their words?** est-ce que leurs actes seront à la hauteur de leurs paroles?; **there's nobody to match him** il n'a pas son pareil

(**b**) *(go with → of clothes, colour)* s'assortir à, aller (bien) avec, se marier (harmonieusement) avec; **the gloves match the scarf** les gants sont assortis à l'écharpe; **his jacket doesn't match his trousers** sa veste ne va pas avec son pantalon; **the music didn't match her mood** la musique ne correspondait pas à son humeur

(**c**) *(coordinate)* **I'm trying to match this paint** je cherche une peinture identique à celle-ci; **can you match the names with the photographs?** pouvez-vous attribuer à chaque photo le nom qui lui correspond?; **I tried to match my gestures to theirs** j'ai essayé d'imiter leurs gestes; **he and his wife are well matched** lui et sa femme vont bien ensemble

(**d**) *(oppose)* **to match sb against sb** opposer qn à qn; **he matched his skill against the champion's** il mesura son habileté à celle du champion; **the two teams are well matched** les deux équipes sont de force égale

(**e**) *(find equal to)* égaler; **to match an offer** égaler une offre; **we can't match their prices** nous ne pouvons pas rivaliser avec leurs prix; **this restaurant can't be matched for quality** ce restaurant n'a pas son pareil pour ce qui est de la qualité

3 *vi (colours etc)* aller (bien) ensemble, être bien assorti; *(fingerprints, descriptions etc)* correspondre; **these colours don't match** ces couleurs ne vont pas très bien ensemble; **a red hat with a scarf to match** un chapeau rouge avec un foulard assorti; **I can't find two socks that match** je ne parviens pas à trouver deux chaussettes identiques; **none of the glasses matched** les verres étaient tous dépareillés

►► *Golf* ***match play*** match-play *m*, partie *f* par trous; *Sport* ***match point*** *(in tennis)* balle *f* de match

►**match up 1** *vt sep* faire correspondre; **to match up the names with the faces** faire correspondre les noms et les visages; **to match up two colours** harmoniser *ou* assortir deux couleurs; **I want to match up this colour** *(find exact match)* j'aimerais trouver exactement la même couleur

2 *vi (dates, figures)* correspondre; *(clothes, colours)* aller (bien) ensemble, être bien assorti; **the descriptions didn't match up** les descriptions ne correspondaient pas; **the suit jacket and trousers don't match up** la veste et le pantalon ne vont pas ensemble

►**match up to** *vt insep* valoir; **his jokes don't match up to Mark's** ses plaisanteries ne valent pas celles de Mark; **the hotel didn't match up to our expectations** l'hôtel nous a déçus *ou* ne répondait pas à notre attente

matchboard [ˈmætʃbɔːd], **matchboarding** [ˈmætʃˌbɔːdɪŋ] *n (UNCOUNT) (for floor)* lames *fpl* de parquet; *(for walls, ceiling)* lambris *mpl*

matchbook [ˈmætʃbʊk] *n* pochette *f* d'allumettes

matchbox [ˈmætʃbɒks] *n* boîte *f* d'allumettes

matched [mætʃt] *adj*

►► *St Exch* ***matched bargain*** mariage *m*; *Am* ***matched orders*** ordres *mpl* couplés d'achat et de vente *(pour stimuler le marché)*

match-fit *adj Br* **they only have ten match-fit**

players ils n'ont que dix joueurs en état de jouer

match-fixing *n Br* **they were accused of match-fixing** on les a accusés d'avoir truqué le match

matching ['mætʃɪŋ] **1** *n* (**a**) *Acct* rapprochement *m*, rattachement *m* (**b**) *Am St Exch* application *f*

2 *adj* assorti; **a blue suit with a matching tie** un costume bleu avec une cravate assortie

►► ***matching pair*** paire *f* assortie; *Am St Exch* ***matching principle*** principe *m* du rapprochement *ou* rattachement des produits et des charges

matchless ['mætʃlɪs] *adj Literary* sans égal, sans pareil

matchlock ['mætʃlɒk] *n* fusil *m* à mèche

matchmaker ['mætʃ,meɪkə(r)] *n* (**a**) *(gen)* entremetteur(euse) *m,f*; *(for marriage)* marieur(-euse) *m,f* (**b**) *(manufacturer)* fabricant *m* d'allumettes

matchmaking ['mætʃ,meɪkɪŋ] *n* **he loves matchmaking** *(gen)* il adore jouer les entremetteurs; *(for marriage)* il adore jouer les marieurs

match-play *adj Golf*

►► ***match-play tournament*** match-play *m*

matchstick ['mætʃstɪk] *n Br* allumette *f*; **to have matchstick legs** avoir des jambes comme des allumettes

►► ***matchstick men*** personnages *mpl* stylisés *(dessinés de simples traits)*

match-winner *n* atout *m* pour gagner, joker *m*; **he is the possible match-winner in the team** il est sans doute le meilleur atout de l'équipe (pour gagner)

matchwood ['mætʃwʊd] *n* bois *m* d'allumettes; *Br* **smashed** *or* **reduced to matchwood** réduit en miettes

mate[1] [meɪt] **1** *n* (**a**) *Br & Austr Fam (friend)* pote *m*; **listen, mate!** écoute, mon vieux!; **thanks, mate** *(to friend)* merci vieux; *(to stranger)* merci chef; **watch where you're going, mate!** hé, regarde devant toi!

(**b**) *(colleague)* camarade *mf* (de travail)

(**c**) *(workman's helper)* aide *mf*; **plumber's mate** aide-plombier *m*

(**d**) *Naut (in navy)* second maître *m*; *(on merchant vessel)* **(first) mate** second *m*; **second mate** lieutenant *m*

(**e**) *(sexual partner → animal)* mâle *m*, femelle *f*; *Hum (→ husband)* époux *m*; *(→ wife)* épouse *f*; *(→ lover)* partenaire *mf*; **some animals pine when separated from their mate** certains animaux dépérissent quand on les sépare de leur compagnon

(**f**) *(in chess)* mat *m*

2 *vt* (**a**) *Zool* accoupler; **to mate a cow with a bull** accoupler une vache à un taureau

(**b**) *(in chess)* mettre échec et mat, mater

3 *vi* s'accoupler

mate[2], **maté** ['mæteɪ] *n* (**a**) *(tree)* (variété *f* de) houx *m* (**b**) *(drink)* maté *m*

mater ['meɪtə(r)] *n Br Old-fashioned or Hum* **(the) mater** ma mère, maman *f*

material [mə'tɪərɪəl] **1** *n* (**a**) *(wood, plastic, stone etc)* matière *f*, substance *f*; *Constr & Ind* matériau *m*; **building materials** matériaux *mpl* de construction

(**b**) *(cloth)* tissu *m*, étoffe *f*; **curtain material** tissu *m* pour faire des rideaux

(**c**) *(UNCOUNT) (ideas, data)* matériaux *mpl*, documentation *f*; **I'm collecting material for a novel** je rassemble des matériaux pour un roman; **background material** documentation *f* de base

(**d**) *(finished work)* **written material** des textes *mpl*; **published material** des publications *fpl*; **a comic who writes his own material** un comique qui écrit ses propres textes *ou* sketches; **a singer who writes his own material** un auteur-compositeur; **publicity material** publicité *f*; **reading material** lecture *f*

(**e**) *(necessary equipment)* matériel *m*; **writing material** matériel *m* pour écrire; *Sch* **teaching materials** supports *mpl* pédagogiques; **reference materials** documents *mpl* de référence

(**f**) *(suitable person or persons)* **is he officer material?** a-t-il l'étoffe d'un officier?; **he's not university material** il n'est pas au niveau pour aller en fac; **they're not first division material** ils ne sont pas de taille à jouer en première division

2 *adj* (**a**) *(concrete)* matériel; **the material world** le monde matériel; **of material benefit** d'un apport capital

(**b**) *Formal (relevant)* pertinent; **that is not material to the present discussion** cela n'a aucun rapport *ou* n'a rien à voir avec ce dont nous discutons; **the facts material to the investigation** les faits qui présentent un intérêt pour l'enquête

►► ***material comforts*** confort *m* matériel; *Law* ***material evidence*** preuve *f* matérielle *ou* tangible; ***material possessions*** biens *mpl* matériels; ***material requirements planning*** prévision *f* des besoins matériels; *Law* ***material witness*** témoin *m* de fait

materialism [mə'tɪərɪəlɪzəm] *n* matérialisme *m*

materialist [mə'tɪərɪəlɪst] **1** *n* matérialiste *mf*

2 *adj* matérialiste

materialistic [mə,tɪərɪə'lɪstɪk] *adj* matérialiste

materialistically [mə,tɪərɪə'lɪstɪkəlɪ] *adv* matériellement

materiality [mə,tɪərɪ'ælɪtɪ] *n* (**a**) *(concreteness)* matérialité *f* (**b**) *Law (of fact etc)* importance *f*

materialization [mə,tɪərɪəlaɪ'zeɪʃən] *n* matérialisation *f*

materialize, -ise [mə'tɪərɪəlaɪz] **1** *vi* (**a**) *(become fact)* se matérialiser, se réaliser; *(take shape)* prendre forme; **the promised pay rise never materialized** l'augmentation promise ne s'est jamais matérialisée *ou* concrétisée; **she promised to lend me £1000 but the money never materialized** elle avait promis de me prêter 1000 livres mais je n'en ai jamais vu la couleur

(**b**) *Fam (arrive)* se pointer; **he eventually materialized around ten** il a fini par se pointer vers dix heures

(**c**) *(ghost, apparition)* se matérialiser

2 *vt* matérialiser

materially [mə'tɪərɪəlɪ] *adv* (**a**) *Phil, Phys & Rel* matériellement (**b**) *(appreciably → affect, alter)* sensiblement

materiel, matériel [mə,tɪərɪ'el] *n Mil* matériel *m*

maternal [mə'tɜːnəl] *adj* (**a**) *(motherly → love, instinct)* maternel (**b**) *(related through mother)* maternel; **maternal grandfather** grand-père *m* maternel

►► *Psy* ***maternal deprivation*** séparation *f* d'avec la mère; ***maternal smoking*** consommation *f* de tabac pendant la grossesse

maternally [mə'tɜːnəlɪ] *adv* maternellement

maternity [mə'tɜːnətɪ] **1** *n* maternité *f*

2 *comp (clothes)* de grossesse

►► ***maternity allowance*** = allocation de maternité versée par l'État à une femme n'ayant pas droit à la "maternity pay"; ***maternity benefit*** ≃ allocations *fpl* de maternité; ***maternity dress*** robe *f* de grossesse; ***maternity home, maternity hospital*** maternité *f*; ***maternity leave*** congé *m* (de) maternité; ***maternity pay*** = allocation de maternité versée par l'employeur; ***maternity ward*** maternité *f*

mateship ['meɪtʃɪp] *n Austr Fam* camaraderie *f*

matey ['meɪtɪ] *Br Fam* **1** *n (term of address)* **all right, matey?** ça va, mon vieux?; **just watch it, matey!** fais gaffe!

2 *adj (pally)* copain, copain-copain; **they're very matey all of a sudden** ils sont très copains tout d'un coup

mateyness = **matiness**

math [mæθ] *n (UNCOUNT) Am* maths *fpl*

mathematical [,mæθə'mætɪkəl] *adj* mathématique; **a mathematical genius** un génie en mathématiques; **I haven't got a mathematical mind, I'm not very mathematical** je ne suis pas matheux; **victory for the party is now a mathematical impossibility** mathématiquement, le parti ne peut pas gagner

►► ***mathematical linguistics*** linguistique *f* mathématique; ***mathematical logic*** logique *f* mathématique

mathematically [,mæθə'mætɪkəlɪ] *adv* mathématiquement; **I'm not very mathematically minded** je ne suis pas très matheux

mathematician [,mæθəmə'tɪʃən] *n* mathématicien(enne) *m,f*

mathematics [,mæθə'mætɪks] **1** *n (UNCOUNT) (science, subject)* mathématiques *fpl*

2 *npl (calculations involved)* **can you explain the mathematics of it to me?** pouvez-vous m'expliquer comment on parvient à ce résultat *ou* ce chiffre?

maths [mæθs] *n (UNCOUNT) Br* maths *fpl*

►► *Comput* ***maths coprocessor*** coprocesseur *m* mathématique

Matilda [mə'tɪldə] *n Austr* baluchon *m*, balluchon *m*; **to waltz Matilda** vagabonder

matinee, matinée ['mætɪneɪ] *n Cin & Theat* matinée *f*

►► *Br* ***matinee coat*** veste *f* de bébé; *Old-fashioned or Hum* ***matinee idol*** = acteur idolâtré par les femmes surtout dans les années 30 ou 40; *Br* ***matinee jacket*** veste *f* de bébé; *Cin & Theat* ***matinee performance*** matinée *f*

matiness ['meɪtɪnɪs] *n Br Fam* camaraderie ❑ *f*

mating ['meɪtɪŋ] *n* accouplement *m*

►► ***mating call*** appel *m* du mâle *ou* de la femelle; ***mating instinct*** instinct *m* sexuel ; ***mating ritual*** parade *f* nuptiale; ***mating season*** saison *f* des amours

matins ['mætɪnz] *n Rel (in Roman Catholic church)* matines *fpl*; *(in Church of England)* office *m* du matin

matriarch ['meɪtrɪɑːk] *n (ruler, head of family)* femme *f* chef de famille; *(old woman)* matrone *f*

matriarchal [,meɪtrɪ'ɑːkəl] *adj* matriarcal

matriarchy ['meɪtrɪɑːkɪ] *(pl* **matriarchies***) n* matriarcat *m*

matric [mə'trɪk] *n Br Fam Univ (abbr* **matriculation***)* inscription ❑ *f*

►► ***matric card*** carte *f* d'étudiant ❑

matrices ['meɪtrɪsiːz] *pl of* **matrix**

matricidal [,mætrɪ'saɪdəl] *adj* matricide

matricide ['mætrɪsaɪd] *n* (**a**) *(act)* matricide *m* (**b**) *(person)* matricide *mf*

matriculant [mə'trɪkjʊlənt] *n Sch* = étudiant qui s'inscrit à l'université

matriculate [mə'trɪkjʊleɪt] *vi* (**a**) *(register)* s'inscrire, se faire immatriculer; *(at university)* s'inscrire (**b**) *Br Formerly Sch* ≃ obtenir son baccalauréat

matriculation [mə,trɪkjʊ'leɪʃən] **1** *n* (**a**) *(registration)* inscription *f*, immatriculation *f*; *(at university)* inscription *f* (**b**) *Br Formerly Sch* = ancien examen équivalent au baccalauréat

2 *comp (exam)* d'inscription; *(card)* d'étudiant

►► ***matriculation fees*** droits *mpl* d'inscription

matrilineal [,mætrɪ'lɪnɪəl] *adj* matrilinéaire

matrimonial [,mætrɪ'məʊnjəl] *adj* matrimonial, conjugal

matrimony ['mætrɪmənɪ, *Am* 'mætrɪməʊnɪ] *(pl* **matrimonies***) n Formal* mariage *m*; *Rel* **joined in holy matrimony** unis par les liens sacrés du mariage

matrix ['meɪtrɪks] *(pl* **matrixes** *or* **matrices** [-trɪsiːz]*) n* matrice *f*; *Miner* gangue *f*

►► ***matrix management*** organisation *f* matricielle; *Fin* ***matrix organization*** organisation *f* matricielle; *Comput* ***matrix printer*** imprimante *f* matricielle

matron ['meɪtrən] *n* (**a**) *Br (in hospital)* infirmière *f* en chef; *(in school)* = personne assumant le rôle d'infirmière ainsi que certaines tâches matérielles

(**b**) *(in retirement home, orphanage)* directrice *f*

(**c**) *Literary (married woman)* matrone *f*, mère *f* de famille

(**d**) *Am (in prison)* gardienne *f*, surveillante *f*

►► ***matron of honour*** *(at wedding)* dame *f* d'honneur

matronly ['meɪtrənlɪ] *adj (figure, stature, appearance)* de matrone; **she looks very matronly** elle fait très matrone

matronymic [,mætrə'nɪmɪk] *n* matronyme *m*

matt [mæt] *adj* mat

►► ***matt paint*** peinture *f* mate

matte [mæt] **1** *n Metal* matte *f*, maton *m*

2 *adj* mat

►► *Cin* ***matte shot*** cache contre-cache *m*

matted ['mætɪd] *adj (material)* feutré; *(hair)* emmêlé; *(vegetation, roots)* enchevêtré; **to become matted** *(hair, wool)* s'emmêler; **his hair was matted with blood** il avait du sang séché dans les cheveux

MATTER ['mætə(r)]

affaire	▸ **1 (a)**
sujet	▸ **1 (a)**
question	▸ **1 (b)**
matière	▸ **1 (c), (d)**
importer	▸ **1 (f); 2**

1 *n* (**a**) *(affair)* affaire *f*; *(subject)* sujet *m*; **I reported the matter to the police** j'ai rapporté les faits à la police; **business matters** affaires *fpl*; **money matters** questions *fpl* d'argent; **the matter in hand** les faits *mpl* qui nous préoccupent; **I consider the matter closed** pour moi, c'est une affaire classée; **it is a matter for regret** c'est regrettable; **this is no laughing matter** il n'y a pas de quoi rire; **it's no easy matter** c'est une question difficile *ou* un sujet délicat; **that is a matter for the courts to decide** sur ce point, c'est à la justice de trancher; **I will give the matter my immediate attention** j'accorderai toute mon attention à ce problème; **I think we should let the matter drop** je pense que nous devrions laisser tomber le sujet; **you're not going out, and that's the end of** *or* **there's an end to the matter!** tu ne sortiras pas, un point c'est tout!

(**b**) *(question)* question *f*; **there's the small matter of the £100 you owe me** il y a ce petit problème des 100 livres que tu me dois; **a matter of life and death** une question de vie ou de mort; **that's quite another matter, that's a different matter altogether** ça c'est une (tout) autre affaire; **a matter of taste** une question de goût; **that's a matter of opinion** ça c'est une question d'opinion; **as a matter of course** automatiquement; **as a matter of principle** par principe; **as a matter of urgency** d'urgence; **she'll do it in a matter of minutes** cela ne lui prendra que quelques minutes; **it'll be a matter of days rather than weeks before we get a result** obtenir le résultat sera une question de jours plutôt que de semaines; **it's only** *or* **just a matter of time** ce n'est qu'une question de temps; **it's just a matter of replacing a few worn-out parts** il suffit de remplacer quelques pièces usées; **it's only** *or* **just a matter of filling in a few forms** il ne s'agit que de remplir quelques formulaires

(**c**) *(physical substance)* matière *f*; **organic/inorganic matter** matière *f* organique/inorganique

(**d**) *(written material)* matière *f*, copie *f*; *(sent by post)* imprimés *mpl*; **advertising matter** matériel *m* publicitaire; **printed matter** texte *m* imprimé

(**e**) *Med (pus)* pus *m*

(**f**) *(idioms)* **what's the matter?** qu'est-ce qu'il y a?, qu'est-ce qui ne va pas?; **what's the matter with you?** qu'est-ce que tu as?, qu'est-ce qui ne va pas?; **what's the matter with Susan?** qu'est-ce qu'elle a, Susan?; **what's the matter with your eyes?** qu'est-ce que vous avez aux yeux?; **what's the matter with the television?** qu'est-ce qu'elle a, la télévision?; **what's the matter with the way I dress?** qu'est-ce que vous reprochez à ma façon de m'habiller?; **what's the matter with telling him the truth?** quel mal y a-t-il à lui dire la vérité?; **I don't know what's the matter with me** je ne sais pas ce que j'ai; **there's something the matter** il y a quelque chose (qui ne va pas), il se passe quelque chose; **there's something the matter with my leg** j'ai quelque chose à la jambe; **there's something the matter with the aerial** il y a un problème avec l'antenne; **is there something** *or* **is anything the matter?** il y a quelque chose qui ne va pas?, il y a un problème?; **something must be the matter** il doit y avoir quelque chose; **nothing's the** *or* **there's nothing the matter** il n'y a rien, tout va bien; **nothing's the matter with me** je vais parfaitement bien; **there's nothing the matter with the engine** le moteur est en parfait état de marche; **no matter!** peu importe!; **no matter what I do** quoi que je fasse; **no matter what the boss thinks** peu importe ce qu'en pense le patron; **don't go back, no matter how much he begs you** même s'il te le demande à genoux, n'y retourne pas; **no matter what** quoi qu'il arrive; **I'll be there tomorrow no matter what** j'y serai demain quoi qu'il arrive; **we've got to win, no matter what** il faut que nous gagnions à tout prix; **no matter how** par n'importe quel moyen; **no matter how hard I try** quels que soient les efforts que je fais; **I must speak to her, no matter how ill she is** je dois lui parler, quel que soit son état de santé; **no matter when** à n'importe quel moment; **no matter when it happens** peu importe quand ça arrivera; **no matter who** qui que ce soit; **no matter who gave it to you** peu importe qui te l'a donné; **no matter where** où que ce soit; **no matter where I am** où que je sois

2 *vi* importer, avoir de l'importance; **nothing matters much to him any more since his wife died** plus rien n'a d'importance pour lui depuis la mort de sa femme; **nothing else matters** tout le reste est sans importance; **these things matter** ces choses-là comptent; **what does it matter?** quelle importance est-ce que ça a?, qu'importe?; **it matters a lot** cela a beaucoup d'importance, c'est très important; **it doesn't matter** cela n'a pas d'importance, ça ne fait rien; **it doesn't matter how much it costs** peu importe le prix; **it doesn't matter to me what you do with your money** ce que tu fais de ton argent m'est égal; **it doesn't matter to her what people think** elle se moque de ce que pensent les gens; **money is all that matters to him** il n'y a que l'argent qui l'intéresse; **I forgot to tell him, not that it matters, he'll find out soon enough** j'ai oublié de le lui dire mais c'est sans importance, il s'en rendra vite compte; **she matters a lot to him** il tient beaucoup à elle, elle compte beaucoup pour lui; **that's what matters most** c'est le plus important; **she knows all the people who matter** elle connaît tous les gens qui comptent

3 matters *npl* **as matters stand** les choses étant ce qu'elles sont; **getting angry won't help matters at all** se mettre en colère n'arrangera pas les choses; **matters have taken a turn for the worse** les choses ont pris un tour plus alarmant; **her remarks made matters worse** ses remarques n'ont fait qu'aggraver les choses; **to make matters worse, it had started to rain** pour tout arranger, il s'était mis à pleuvoir

4 as a matter of fact *adv* en fait, à vrai dire, en réalité

5 for that matter *adv* d'ailleurs; **and so am I for that matter** moi aussi d'ailleurs; **he isn't very well known in London or anywhere else for that matter** il n'est pas très connu à Londres, et nulle part ailleurs en fait

---

Matterhorn ['mætəhɔːn] *n* **the Matterhorn** le mont Cervin

matter-of-fact *adj (down-to-earth)* terre-à-terre *(inv)*; *(prosaic)* prosaïque; *(unemotional)* neutre; **Frank has a very matter-of-fact approach** Frank a une façon très pratique d'approcher les choses; **he has a very matter-of-fact way of speaking** il dit les choses comme elles sont; **in a matter-of-fact voice** d'une voix neutre; **she took the news in a very matter-of-fact way** elle a pris les nouvelles avec beaucoup de sang-froid

matter-of-factly [-'fæktlɪ] *adv (in a down-to-earth manner)* de façon pragmatique; *(prosaically)* prosaïquement; *(unemotionally)* d'un air détaché; **she announced that he was dead quite matter-of-factly** elle annonça qu'il était mort d'un air détaché

matter-of-factness [-'fæktnɪs] *n (down-to-earth character)* caractère *m* pragmatique; *(prosaicness)* prosaïsme *m*; *(lack of emotion)* détachement *m*

Matthew ['mæθjuː] *pr n Bible* Matthieu; **the Gospel According to (Saint) Matthew** l'Évangile selon saint Matthieu

Matthias [mə'θaɪəs] *pr n Bible* Matthias, Mathias

matting ['mætɪŋ] *n (UNCOUNT) (used as mat)* natte *f*, tapis *m*

mattins = **matins**

mattock ['mætək] *n Agr* pioche *f*

mattress ['mætrɪs] *n* matelas *m*; **inflatable** *or* **air mattress** matelas *m* pneumatique

maturate ['mætjʊreɪt] **1** *vt (fruit)* faire mûrir; *(wine, whisky)* faire vieillir

2 *vi (fruit, abscess)* mûrir; *(wine, whisky)* vieillir

maturation [,mætjʊ'reɪʃən] *n (of fruit, abscess)* maturation *f*; *(of wine, whisky)* vieillissement *m*; *(of cheese)* maturation *f*, affinage *m*

mature [mə'tjʊə(r)] **1** *adj* (**a**) *(person → physically)* mûr; *(→ mentally)* mûr, mature; *(animal)* adulte; **to be mature for one's age** *or* **years** être mûr pour son âge; **a man of mature years** un homme d'âge mûr; *Br Euph* **would suit a mature person** *(in job advertisement)* conviendrait à une personne d'âge mûr; **her style is not yet mature** son style n'est pas encore arrivé à maturité

(**b**) *(fruit)* mûr; *(plante)* adulte; **the more mature trees are slower to come into leaf** les arbres les plus vieux ont des feuilles plus tard que les autres

(**c**) *(cheese)* fait; *(wine, spirits)* arrivé à maturité

(**d**) *Fin (bill, bond, insurance policy)* échu

2 *vi* (**a**) *(person, attitude) & Fig (plan)* mûrir; **she had matured into a sophisticated young woman** elle était devenue une jeune femme sophistiquée

(**b**) *(wine)* vieillir; *(cheese)* se faire

(**c**) *Fin* arriver à échéance, échoir

3 *vt (cheese)* faire mûrir, affiner; *(wine, spirits)* faire vieillir

▸▸ *Fin* ***mature economy*** économie *f* en pleine maturité; ***mature garden*** jardin *m* planté depuis plusieurs années; *Br Univ* ***mature student*** = étudiant plus âgé que la moyenne ou qui entreprend des études sur le tard, *Can* étudiant(e) *m,f* adulte

maturely [mə'tjʊəlɪ] *adv (decide)* de façon raisonnable; **to behave maturely** se comporter en adulte

maturity [mə'tjʊərətɪ] *n* (**a**) *(of person, fruit, wine, cheese etc)* maturité *f*; **to reach maturity** *(person)* devenir majeur; **she lacks maturity** elle n'est pas très mûre; **the novels/poetry of his maturity** les romans/la poésie de sa maturité

(**b**) *Fin* **(date of) maturity** échéance *f*

(**c**) *Mktg (of market)* maturité *f*

▸▸ *Fin* ***maturity date*** date *f* d'échéance; *Fin* ***maturity value*** valeur *f* à l'échéance

matutinal [mə'tjuːtɪnəl] *adj Literary* matutinal, matinal

MATV [,emeɪ,tiː'viː] *n Br* (*abbr* **Master Antenna Television**) télévision *f* à antenne maîtresse

matzo ['mætsəʊ] (*pl* **matzos**) *n* pain *m* azyme

▸▸ ***matzo balls*** boulettes *fpl* à la chapelure de pain azyme; ***matzo meal*** farine *f* de pain azyme

Maud [mɔːd] *pr n Hist* **the Empress Maud** Mathilde *ou* Mahaut d'Angleterre

maudlin ['mɔːdlɪn] *adj* larmoyant; **he gets maudlin when he drinks** il a le vin triste

maul [mɔːl] **1** *vt* (**a**) *(attack → of animal)* déchiqueter; *(→ of person, crowd)* malmener; **he was mauled to death by a lion** il a été déchiqueté par un lion

(**b**) *Fam (sexually → grope)* tripoter

(**c**) *(criticize)* démolir, mettre en pièces, éreinter

2 *vi* (**a**) *(fight)* se battre

(**b**) *(in rugby)* faire un maul

3 *n Sport (in rugby)* maul *m*

maulers ['mɔːləz] *npl Br very Fam (hands)* pattes *fpl*

mauling ['mɔːlɪŋ] *n* (**a**) *(attack)* **to get a mauling** *(from animal)* être blessé; *(more seriously)* être mutilé; *(from person, crowd)* être malmené (**b**) *Fam* **to get a mauling** *(get defeated)* être battu à plates coutures, recevoir une raclée; *(get criticized)* se faire éreinter *ou* démolir

maulstick ['mɔːlstɪk] *n Art* appuie-main *m*

maunder ['mɔːndə(r)] *vi Br* (**a**) *(talk)* divaguer, parler à tort et à travers; **what's he maundering on about?** qu'est-ce qu'il raconte? (**b**) *(walk)* errer

Maundy ['mɔːndɪ] *n*

▸▸ *Br* ***Maundy money*** *(UNCOUNT)* = pièces de monnaie spéciales offertes par le souverain britannique à certaines personnes âgées le jour du jeudi saint; *Rel* ***Maundy Thursday*** jeudi *m* saint

Mauritania [,mɒrɪ'teɪnjə] *n* Mauritanie *f*; **in Mauritania** en Mauritanie

Mauritanian [,mɒrɪ'teɪnjən] **1** *n* Mauritanien(enne) *m,f*

2 *adj* mauritanien

Mauritian [mə'rɪʃən] **1** *n* Mauricien(enne) *m,f*
2 *adj* mauricien

Mauritius [mə'rɪʃəs] *n* l'île *f* Maurice; **in Mauritius** à l'île Maurice

Mauser ['maʊzə(r)] *n* Mauser *m*
►► ***Mauser rifle*** Mauser *m*

mausoleum [,mɔːzə'lɪəm] *n* mausolée *m*

mauve [məʊv] **1** *n* mauve *m*
2 *adj* mauve

MAV [,emeɪ'viː] *n* (*abbr* **micro air vehicle**) microdrone *m (avion espion téléguidé en modèle réduit)*

maven ['meɪvən] *n Am Fam* expert ☐ *m*

maverick ['mævərɪk] **1** *n* (**a**) *(person)* franc-tireur *m*, indépendant(e) *m,f* (**b**) *(calf)* veau *m* non marqué
2 *adj* non conformiste, indépendant; **a maverick Marxist** un franc-tireur du marxisme; **a maverick MP** un député non conformiste

mavis ['meɪvɪs] *n Orn* grive *f* musicienne

maw [mɔː] *n Zool* (**a**) *(stomach → of cow)* caillette *f*; *(of bird)* jabot *m* (**b**) *(mouth)* gueule *f*; *Fig* gouffre *m*

mawkish ['mɔːkɪʃ] *adj (sentimental)* mièvre; *(nauseating)* écœurant; **a mawkish smile** un sourire niais

mawkishly ['mɔːkɪʃlɪ] *adv (sentimentally)* mièvrement

mawkishness ['mɔːkɪʃnɪs] *n (sentimentality)* mièvrerie *f*

mawworm ['mɔːwɜːm] *n* (**a**) *Arch (worm)* ver *m* intestinal (**b**) *Arch or Literary (hypocrite)* hypocrite *mf*

max [mæks] (*abbr* **maximum**) **1** *n* max *m*; *Am Fam* **to the max** *(totally)* un max; **did you have a good time? – to the max!** tu t'es bien amusé? – vachement bien!, un max!
2 *adv Fam (at the most)* maxi; **it'll take three days max** ça prendra trois jours maxi
3 *vt Am Fam* **to max an exam** = obtenir le maximum de points à un examen

►**max out** *Am Fam* **1** *vt sep* **to max out one's credit card** = dépenser le maximum autorisé avec sa carte de crédit
2 *vi* **to max out on chocolate** se gaver de chocolat; **to max out on booze** picoler un max

maxed [mækst] *adj Am Fam* (**a**) *(extremely drunk)* bourré comme un coing, pété à mort (**b**) **to be maxed out on one's credit card** = avoir dépensé le maximum autorisé avec sa carte de crédit; **to be maxed out on chocolate/sci-fi movies** avoir fait une overdose de chocolat/de films de science-fiction

maxi ['mæksɪ] **1** *n (skirt)* jupe *f* maxi
2 *adj (skirt, dress etc)* maxi *(inv)*

maxilla [mæk'sɪlə] (*pl* **maxillae** [-liː]) *n Anat* maxillaire *m*

maxillary [mæk'sɪlərɪ] *adj Anat* maxillaire

maxim ['mæksɪm] *n* maxime *f*

maxima ['mæksɪmə] *pl of* **maximum**

maximal ['mæksɪməl] *adj* maximal

maximalism ['mæksɪməlɪzəm] *n* maximalisme *m*

maximalist ['mæksɪməlɪst] **1** *n* maximaliste *mf*
2 *adj* maximaliste

Maximilian [,mæksɪlmɪ'ɪən] *pr n* Maximilien

maximin ['mæksɪmɪn] *n Math* maximin *m*

maximization [,mæksɪmaɪ'zeɪʃən] *n* maximalisation *f*, maximisation *f*

maximize, -ise ['mæksɪmaɪz] *vt* maximiser, maximaliser; *Comput (window)* agrandir

maximum ['mæksɪməm] (*pl* **maximums** *or* **maxima** [-mə]) **1** *n* (**a**) *(gen)* maximum *m*; **a maximum of forty people** un maximum de quarante personnes, quarante personnes au maximum; **at the maximum** au (grand) maximum; **to the maximum** au maximum
(**b**) *(in snooker, darts)* maximum *m*
2 *adj* maximum, maximal; **maximum temperatures** températures *fpl* maximales
3 *adv* au maximum; **it happens twice a year maximum** ça se produit deux fois par an au maximum; **you can stay for two hours maximum** vous ne pouvez pas rester plus de deux heures
►► ***maximum efficiency*** rendement *m* maximum; ***maximum load*** charge *f* maximale *ou* limite; ***maximum security prison*** prison *f* de haute sécurité; ***maximum speed*** *(highest possible)* vitesse *f* maximale *ou* maximum; *(highest permitted)* vitesse *f* limite

maxwell ['mækswel] *n Phys* maxwell *m*

May [meɪ] *n* mai *m*; *Literary* **in the May of life** au printemps de la vie; **a May to December relationship/marriage** = une relation/un mariage entre une jeune femme et un homme plus âgé; *see also* **February**
►► *Br Univ* ***May ball*** = bal qui se tient au mois de juin à l'université de Cambridge; *Entom* ***May beetle*** hanneton *m*; *Entom* ***May bug*** hanneton *m*; ***May Day*** le Premier mai; ***May Day parade*** défilé *m* du Premier mai; ***May queen*** = reine des festivités du Premier mai; ***May week*** = semaine du mois de juin pendant laquelle se tiennent les "May balls"

MAY¹ [meɪ]

> **May** et **might** peuvent s'utiliser indifféremment ou presque dans les expressions de la catégorie (**a**).

v aux (**a**) *(expressing possibility)* **this may take some time** ça prendra peut-être *ou* il se peut que ça prenne du temps; **symptoms may disappear after a few days** les symptômes peuvent disparaître après quelques jours; **you may be right** vous avez peut-être raison, il se peut que vous ayez raison; **you may well be right** il est fort possible *ou* il se peut bien que vous ayez raison; **what he says may be true** ce qu'il dit est peut-être vrai; **it may well be that he misunderstood** il est fort possible *ou* il se peut bien qu'il ait mal compris; **I may live to regret this!** il se peut que je le regrette un jour!; **she may have missed the plane** elle a peut-être manqué l'avion, il se peut qu'elle ait manqué l'avion; **she may not have arrived yet** il se peut *ou* il se pourrait qu'elle ne soit pas encore arrivée; **he may have been right** il avait peut-être raison; **you may be wondering why I'm doing that** vous vous demandez peut-être pourquoi je fais cela
(**b**) *(expressing permission)* **you may go** vous pouvez partir; **you may sit down** vous pouvez vous asseoir; **only close relatives may attend** seuls les parents proches sont invités à assister à la cérémonie; **passengers may take only one item of hand luggage** les passagers ne peuvent prendre *ou* ne sont autorisés à prendre qu'un bagage à main; **candidates may consult a dictionary** l'utilisation d'un dictionnaire est autorisée pendant l'examen; **I will go home now, if I may** je vais rentrer chez moi, si vous me le permettez; **if I may be allowed to express an opinion** si je puis me permettre; **if I may say so** si je peux *ou* puis me permettre cette remarque; **you may well ask!** bonne question!
(**c**) *(in polite questions, suggestions)* **may I interrupt?** puis-je vous interrompre?, vous permettez que je vous interrompe?; **may I?** vous permettez?; **may I make a suggestion?** puis-je me permettre de faire une suggestion?; **may I help you?** puis-je vous aider?; **may I buy you ladies a drink?** puis-je vous offrir un verre, mesdames?; **may I come too? – yes, you may** puis-je venir aussi? – oui, je vous en prie; **and how, may I ask, did you find out?** et comment vous en êtes-vous rendu compte, s'il vous plaît?; **may I say how pleased we are that you could come** permettez-moi de vous dire à quel point nous sommes ravis que vous ayez pu venir; **we may remind ourselves at this point that…** il n'est pas inutile de rappeler ici que…
(**d**) *(contradicting a point of view)* **you may think I'm imagining things, but I think I'm being followed** tu vas croire que je divague mais je crois que je suis suivi; **such facts may seem insignificant, but they could prove vital** de telles choses peuvent paraître insignifiantes mais elles pourraient se révéler vitales; **whatever faults he may have he's never dull** quels que soient ses défauts, il n'est jamais ennuyeux; **he may not be very bright, but he's got a heart of gold** il n'est peut-être pas très brillant mais il a un cœur d'or; **be that as it may** quoi qu'il en soit; **brilliant she may be, but is she reliable?** elle est peut-être brillante, mais peut-on compter sur elle?; **that's as may be** c'est possible; **that's as may be, but we can't afford it** peut-être, mais nous ne pouvons pas nous le permettre; **that's as may be, but I still don't think you're right** c'est possible mais je ne suis toujours pas convaincu que tu aies raison
(**e**) *(giving additional information)* **this, it may be said, is yet another example of government interference** c'est là, on peut le dire, un autre exemple de l'interventionnisme de l'État
(**f**) *Formal (expressing purpose)* **they work hard so that their children may have a better life** ils travaillent dur pour que leurs enfants aient une vie meilleure; **so that others may sleep in peace** pour que les autres puissent dormir en paix
(**g**) *(expressing wishes, hopes)* **long may he reign** vive le roi; **may she rest in peace** qu'elle repose en paix; **may he rot in hell!** qu'il aille au diable!; **may the best man win!** que le meilleur gagne!; **much good may it do you!** grand bien vous fasse!; **I pray that you may be mistaken** j'espère que tu te trompes
(**h**) *(idioms)* **can I go home now? – you may as well** est-ce que je peux rentrer chez moi maintenant? – tu ferais aussi bien; **you may as well apply for the job anyway** tu n'as qu'à poser quand même ta candidature pour le poste; **we may as well have another drink** tant qu'à faire, autant prendre un autre verre

may² *n Br Bot (hawthorn)* aubépine *f*, épine *f* de mai
►► ***may blossom*** *(UNCOUNT)* fleurs *fpl* d'aubépine; ***may tree*** aubépine *f*

Maya ['maɪə] (*pl sense* (**a**) **inv** *or* **Mayas**) *n* (**a**) *(person)* Indien(enne) *m,f* maya; **the Maya(s)** les Mayas *mpl* (**b**) *Ling* maya *m*

Mayan ['maɪən] **1** *n* (**a**) *(person)* Indien(enne) *m,f* maya (**b**) *Ling* maya *m*
2 *adj* maya

mayapple ['meɪ,æpəl] *n Bot* podophylle *m* en bouclier

maybe ['meɪbiː] **1** *adv* peut-être; **maybe she won't accept** peut-être qu'elle n'acceptera pas, elle n'acceptera peut-être pas; **maybe so** peut-être bien que oui; **maybe not** peut-être bien que non; **maybe so, but…** peut-être bien, mais…
2 *n Fam* **I don't want any maybes** c'est oui ou non! ☐

Mayday ['meɪdeɪ] *n (emergency call)* SOS *m*; **to send out a Mayday (signal)** envoyer un signal de détresse *ou* un SOS

Mayfair ['meɪfeə(r)] *n* = quartier chic de Londres

mayflower ['meɪ,flaʊə(r)] **1** *n Bot (gen)* fleur *f* printanière; *Br (marsh marigold)* souci *m* d'eau; *Br (hawthorn)* aubépine *f*
2 Mayflower *n Am Hist* **the Mayflower** le Mayflower; **the Mayflower Compact** le covenant du Mayflower

> **THE MAYFLOWER COMPACT**
>
> On désigne ainsi le pacte conclu par les pèlerins puritains à bord du "Mayflower" en novembre 1620, avant de débarquer sur le site de Plymouth, par lequel ils s'engageaient à fonder une société civile régie par leurs propres lois. Cette convention est considérée comme la première Constitution de l'Amérique du Nord.

mayfly ['meɪflaɪ] (*pl* **mayflies**) *n Entom* éphémère *m*

mayhap ['meɪhæp] *adv Arch or Literary* peut-être

mayhem ['meɪhem] *n* (**a**) *(disorder)* désordre *m*; **it was absolute mayhem in that office** c'était le désordre le plus complet dans ce bureau; **to create** *or* **to cause mayhem** semer la panique (**b**) *Law* mutilation *f* du corps humain

mayn't [meɪnt] *Br* = **may not**

Mayo ['meɪəʊ] *n* le comté de Mayo, = comté dans le nord-ouest de la république d'Irlande; **in Mayo** dans le comté de Mayo

mayo ['meɪəʊ] *n Fam* mayonnaise ☐ *f*

mayonnaise [,meɪə'neɪz] *n* mayonnaise *f*

mayor [meə(r)] *n (man)* maire *m*; *(woman)* maire *m ou f*, mairesse *f*

mayoral ['meərəl] *adj (robes, car, responsibilities)* du maire

mayoralty ['meərəltɪ] (*pl* **mayoralties**) *n* mandat *m* de maire

mayoress ['meərɪs] *n* (**a**) *(woman mayor)* maire

m ou f, mairesse *f* (**b**) *(wife of mayor)* femme *f* du maire, mairesse *f*

maypole ['meɪpəʊl] *n* ≃ arbre *m* de mai *(mât autour duquel on danse le Premier mai)*

may've ['meɪəv] *Fam* = **may have**

mayweed ['meɪwiːd] *n Bot (scentless)* camomille *f* inodore; *(scented)* camomille *f* allemande

mazard ['mæzəd] *n Bot* cerise *f* noire, guigne *f*

maze [meɪz] **1** *n also Fig* labyrinthe *m*, dédale *m*; **the hospital is a maze of corridors** cet hôpital est un vrai labyrinthe; **a maze of streets/lanes** un dédale de rues/ruelles

2 Maze *n* **the Maze (Prison)** = prison à haute sécurité d'Irlande du Nord

mazuma [mə'zuːmə] *n Am Fam* fric *m*, oseille *f*

mazurka [mə'zɜːkə] *n Mus* mazurka *f*

mazzard = **mazard**

MB (**a**) *Comput (written abbr* **megabyte**) Mo (**b**) *(written abbr* **Manitoba**) Manitoba *m*

Mb *n Comput (written abbr* **megabit**) Mb

MBA [,embiː'eɪ] *n Univ (abbr* **Master of Business Administration**) *(person)* = titulaire d'une maîtrise de gestion; *(qualification)* maîtrise *f* de gestion, MBA *m*

MBBS [,embiː,biː'es] *n Univ (abbr* **Bachelor of Medicine and Surgery**) *(person)* = titulaire d'une licence de médecine et de chirurgie; *(qualification)* licence *f* de médecine et de chirurgie

MBE [,embiː'iː] *n (abbr* **Member of the Order of the British Empire**) *(award)* ordre *m* de l'Empire britannique; *(person)* = membre de l'ordre de l'Empire britannique

MBI [,embiː'aɪ] *n Fin (abbr* **management buy-in**) apport *m* de gestion

MBO [,embiː'əʊ] *n Br Fin* (**a**) *(abbr* **management buy-out**) rachat *m* d'une société par la direction (**b**) *(abbr* **management by objectives**) gestion *f ou* direction *f* par objectifs

Mbps *Comput (written abbr* **megabits per second**) mbps

MBS [,embiː'es] *n Fin (abbr* **mortgage-backed security**) titre *m* garanti par des créances hypothécaires

MC [,em'siː] *n* (**a**) *(abbr* **master of ceremonies**) *(at reception)* maître *m* de cérémonie; *(on TV show)* présentateur *m* (**b**) *Br Mil (abbr* **Military Cross**) = distinction militaire britannique (**c**) *Am (abbr* **Member of Congress**) membre *m* du Congrès (**d**) *Am Mil (abbr* **Marine Corps**) Marines *mpl*

MCAT [,emsiː,eɪ'tiː] *n Am (abbr* **Medical College Admissions Test**) = test d'admission aux études de médecine aux États-Unis

MCC [,emsiː'siː] *n (abbr* **Marylebone Cricket Club**) = célèbre club de cricket de Londres

McCarthyism [mə'kɑːθɪɪzəm] *n Pol* maccartisme *m*, maccarthysme *m*

MCCARTHYISM

Il s'agit du mouvement anti-communiste américain né dans les années 40–50, qui a donné lieu à une chasse aux sorcières dans les milieux artistique, professionnel et politique de l'époque.

McCarthyist [mə'kɑːθɪɪst], **McCarthyite** [mə'kɑːθɪaɪt] **1** *n* partisan(e) *m,f* du maccartisme

2 *adj* maccartiste

McCoy [mə'kɔɪ] *n Fam (idiom)* **it's the real McCoy** c'est du vrai de vrai, c'est de l'authentique

MCG [,emsiː'dʒiː] *n (abbr* **Melbourne Cricket Ground**) = principal terrain de cricket de Melbourne

Mcjob [mək'dʒɒb] *n Am Fam* boulot *m* à la con *(ennuyeux et mal payé)*

McNaughten Rules [mək'nɔːtən-] *npl* = article de la loi anglaise autorisant l'accusé à plaider la démence temporaire

m-commerce *n* commerce *m* mobile

MCP [,emsiː'piː] *n Fam (abbr* **male chauvinist pig**) phallo *m*, macho *m*

MD[1] [,em'diː] *n* (**a**) *(abbr* **Doctor of Medicine**) docteur *m* en médecine (**b**) *(abbr* **managing director**) P-DG *m*

MD[2] *(written abbr* **Maryland**) Maryland *m*

MDF [,emdiː'ef] *n (abbr* **medium-density fibreboard**) MDF *m*, panneaux *mpl* de fibres de moyenne densité

MDMA [,emdiː,em'eɪ] *n (abbr* **methylenedioxymethamphetamine**) MDMA *f*

MDS [,emdiː'es] *n (abbr* **Master of Dental Surgery**) *(person)* = titulaire d'une maîtrise de médecine dentaire; *(qualification)* maîtrise *f* de médecine dentaire

MDT [,emdiː'tiː] *n Am (abbr* **Mountain Daylight Time**) heure *f* d'été des montagnes Rocheuses

ME [,em'iː] *n* (**a**) *(UNCOUNT) Med (abbr* **myalgic encephalomyelitis**) encéphalomyélite *f* myalgique (**b**) *Am (abbr* **medical examiner**) médecin *m* légiste

Me *(written abbr* **Maine**) Maine *m*

me[1] [miː] **1** *pron* (**a**) *(direct or indirect object → unstressed)* me; *(→ stressed)* moi; **do you love me?** tu m'aimes?; **give me a light** donne-moi du feu; **lend it (to) me** prêtez-le-moi; **what, me, tell a lie?** moi, mentir?

(**b**) *(after preposition)* moi; **they're talking about me** ils parlent de moi; **come with me** viens avec moi

(**c**) *(as complement of verb "to be")* moi; **it's me** c'est moi; **it's always me who pays** c'est toujours moi qui paie; **is it just me or is it cold in here?** c'est moi, ou bien il fait froid ici?; **she's bigger than me** elle est plus grande que moi; *Fig* **this hairstyle isn't really me** cette coiffure, ce n'est pas vraiment mon style

(**d**) *(in interjections)* **poor me!** pauvre de moi!; **silly me!** que je suis bête!

2 *n* moi *m*; **now I'm going to show you the real me** maintenant je vais te montrer qui je suis; **the me generation** = la génération des années 80, considérées comme celles de l'individualisme

3 *adj Br Fam (my → singular)* mon (ma); *(→ plural)* mes; **where's me specs?** où sont mes binocles?

me[2] = **mi**

mead [miːd] *n* (**a**) *Literary (meadow)* pré *m*, prairie *f* (**b**) *(drink)* hydromel *m*

meadow ['medəʊ] *n* pré *m*, prairie *f*

►► *Bot* ***meadow clary*** sauge *f* des prés; *Bot* ***meadow crane's-bill*** géranium *m* des prés; *Bot* ***meadow grass*** pâturin *m*; *Orn* ***meadow pipit*** pipit *m* des prés, farlouse *f*; *Br Bot* ***meadow saffron*** safran *m* des prés, colchique *m* d'automne; *Bot* ***meadow saxifrage*** saxifrage *f* granulée, casse-pierre *m*

meadowland ['medəʊlænd] *n* prairie *f*, pâturages *mpl*

meadowlark ['medəʊlɑːk] *n Orn* **(eastern) meadowlark** grande sturnelle *f*; **(western) meadowlark** sturnelle *f* de l'ouest

meadow-rue *n Bot* pigamon *m*

meadowsweet ['medəʊswiːt] *n Bot* (**a**) *(Filipendula ulmaria)* reine-des-prés *f* (**b**) *(Spiraea)* spirée *f*

meagre, *Am* **meager** ['miːgə(r)] *adj* maigre; **I can't live on such a meagre salary** je ne peux pas vivre avec un salaire aussi maigre

meagrely, *Am* **meagerly** ['miːgəlɪ] *adv* maigrement, piètrement

meagreness, *Am* **meagerness** ['miːgənɪs] *n* maigreur *f*

meal [miːl] *n* (**a**) *(breakfast, lunch etc)* repas *m*; **to have a meal** prendre un repas; **I've had a huge meal** j'ai mangé comme quatre; **go to bed as soon as you've finished your meal** va te coucher dès que tu as fini de manger; **children need three meals a day** les enfants ont besoin de trois repas par jour; **have a nice meal!, enjoy your meal!** bon appétit!; **they've invited us round for a meal** ils nous ont invités à manger; **evening meal** dîner *m*; **we have our evening meal early** nous dînons tôt; *Fam Fig* **to make a meal of sth** faire tout un plat de qch

(**b**) *(flour)* farine *f*

(**c**) *(UNCOUNT) Scot (oatmeal)* flocons *mpl* d'avoine

►► ***meal ticket*** *Am* ticket *m* restaurant; *Fam Fig (source of income)* gagne-pain *m inv*; **I can't leave Harry, he's my meal ticket** je ne peux pas quitter Harry, c'est lui qui fait bouillir la marmite; *Br* ***meals on wheels*** = service de repas à domicile à l'intention des invalides et des personnes âgées; **she gets meals on wheels** on lui livre ses repas à domicile

mealies ['miːlɪz] *npl SAfr* maïs *m*

mealtime ['miːltaɪm] *n (lunch)* heure *f* du déjeuner; *(dinner)* heure *f* du dîner; **at mealtimes** aux heures des repas

mealworm ['miːlwɜːm] *n Zool* ver *m* de farine

mealy ['miːlɪ] *(compar* **mealier**, *superl* **mealiest**) *adj* (**a**) *(floury)* farineux; **mealy potatoes** des pommes *f* de terre farineuses (**b**) *(pale)* pâle

►► *Entom* ***mealy bug*** cochenille *f* farineuse

mealy-mouthed [-'maʊðd] *adj Pej* doucereux, patelin; **don't be so mealy-mouthed!** arrête de tourner autour du pot!

MEAN [miːn]

avare	► **1 (a)**
méchant	► **1 (b)**
moyen	► **1 (d)**
miteux	► **1 (f)**
milieu	► **2 (a)**
moyenne	► **2 (b)**
vouloir dire	► **3 (a), (b), (e)**
signifier	► **3 (c)**
compter	► **3 (d)**
avoir l'intention	► **3 (f)**
être censé	► **3 (g), (h)**

(pt & pp **meant** [ment]) **1** *adj* (**a**) *(miserly)* avare, mesquin; **he's mean with his money** il est près de ses sous; **they're very mean about pay rises** ils accordent les augmentations de salaire au compte-gouttes; **to be mean with one's praise** être avare de compliments

(**b**) *(nasty, unkind)* méchant; **don't be mean to your sister!** ne sois pas méchant avec ta sœur!; **go on, don't be mean!** allez, ne sois pas vache!; **he has a mean streak** il peut être méchant quand il veut; **to play a mean trick on sb** jouer un sale tour à qn; **I feel mean about not inviting her** j'ai un peu honte de ne pas l'avoir invitée; **that's mean of her** ce n'est pas chic de sa part; *Am Fam* **he gets mean after a few drinks** il devient mauvais *ou* méchant après quelques verres ❑; *Am Fam* **the sky was a mean shade of gray** le ciel était d'une méchante couleur grise ❑; *Am Fam* **mean weather** sale temps *m*

(**c**) *(inferior)* **the meanest intelligence** l'esprit *m* le plus borné; **he's no mean architect/guitarist** c'est un architecte/guitariste de talent; **it was no mean feat** ce n'était pas un mince exploit

(**d**) *(average)* moyen

(**e**) *Fam (excellent)* super, génial; **she's a mean chess player** elle joue super bien aux échecs, elle touche sa bille aux échecs; **he makes a mean curry** il fait super bien le curry; **she plays a mean guitar** elle joue super bien de la guitare, elle touche sa bille à la guitare

(**f**) *(shabby)* miteux, misérable; **mean slums** taudis *mpl* misérables

(**g**) *Literary (of lower rank or class)* **of mean birth** de basse extraction

(**h**) *Am (unwell)* **to feel mean** ne pas se sentir dans son assiette

2 *n* (**a**) *(middle point)* milieu *m*, moyen terme *m*; **the golden** *or* **happy mean** le juste milieu

(**b**) *Math* moyenne *f*

3 *vt* (**a**) *(signify → of word, gesture)* vouloir dire, signifier; *(→ of person)* vouloir dire; **what is meant by...?** que veut dire...?; **what does this term mean?** que signifie *ou* que veut dire ce terme?; **what do you mean?** qu'est-ce que tu veux dire?; **how do you mean?** qu'entendez-vous par là?; **what do you mean by that?** qu'entendez-vous par là?; **what do you mean by "wrong"?** qu'entendez-vous par "faux"?; **what do you mean you don't like the cinema?** comment ça, vous n'aimez pas le cinéma?; **do you mean** *or* **you mean it's over already?** tu veux dire que c'est déjà fini?; **what, take them to court, you mean?** tu veux dire les traîner en justice?; **what, me?, I don't know what you mean!** qui moi?, je ne vois pas ce que vous voulez dire!; **the name means nothing to me** ce nom ne me dit rien; **does the name Heathcliff mean anything to you?** est-ce que le nom de Heathcliff vous dit quelque chose?; **that was when the word "friendship" still meant something** c'était à l'époque où le mot "amitié" avait encore un sens; **that doesn't mean a thing!** ça ne veut (strictement) rien dire!

may–mea

(**b**) *(giving clarification, speaking sincerely)* **when he says early afternoon he really means around four** quand il dit en début d'après-midi, il veut dire vers quatre heures; **do you mean it?** tu es sérieux?; **do you mean him?** c'est de lui que tu parles?; **I didn't mean that** ce n'est pas ce que je voulais dire; **you don't mean it!** vous voulez rire!, vous plaisantez!; **I mean it** je parle sérieusement; **she always says what she means** elle dit toujours ce qu'elle pense; **I'll never speak to you again, I mean it** *or* **I mean what I say** je ne t'adresserai plus jamais la parole, je suis sérieux; **I want to see him now, and I mean now!** je veux le voir tout de suite, et quand je dis tout de suite, c'est tout de suite!; **I mean** *(that is to say)* je veux dire; **I was with Barry, I mean Harry** j'étais avec Barry, je veux dire Harry; **why diet? I mean, you're not exactly fat** pourquoi te mettre au régime? on ne peut pas dire que tu sois grosse; **I know what you mean!** *(I quite agree)* et comment!; **I mean to say...** ce que je veux dire c'est...; **do you mean to tell me...?** est-ce que tu es en train de me dire que...?

(**c**) *(imply, entail → of event, change)* signifier; **this means war/the end of our relationship** c'est la guerre/la fin de notre amitié; **this will mean more unemployment** ça veut dire *ou* signifie qu'il y aura une augmentation du chômage; **going to see a film means driving into town** pour voir un film, nous sommes obligés de prendre la voiture et d'aller en ville; **it would mean the children having to change school again** cela signifierait que les enfants devraient changer d'école une fois de plus; **does that mean we shouldn't wait for him?** est-ce que cela veut dire *ou* signifie que nous ne devrions pas l'attendre?; **just because you've been to university doesn't mean you know everything** ce n'est pas parce que tu es allé à l'université que tu sais tout; **it doesn't mean we have to stop seeing each other** ça ne veut pas dire que nous devons cesser de nous voir; **she's never known what it means to be loved** elle n'a jamais su ce que c'est que d'être aimée

(**d**) *(matter, be of value)* compter; **this watch means a lot to me** je suis très attaché à cette montre; **your friendship means a lot to her** votre amitié compte beaucoup pour elle; **doesn't your daughter's education mean anything to you?** est-ce que l'éducation de ta fille ne t'intéresse pas?; **you mean everything to me** tu es tout pour moi; **he means nothing to me** il n'est rien pour moi; **I can't tell you what this means to me** je ne peux pas te dire ce que ça représente pour moi; **$20 means a lot to me** 20 dollars, c'est une grosse somme *ou* c'est beaucoup d'argent pour moi; **my Sundays mean a lot to me** le dimanche est sacré pour moi; **my independence means a lot to me** mon indépendance est sacrée pour moi

(**e**) *(refer to)* **do you mean us?** tu veux dire nous?; **it was you she meant when she said that** c'était à vous qu'elle pensait *ou* qu'elle faisait allusion quand elle a dit ça

(**f**) *(intend)* **to mean to do sth** avoir (bien) l'intention de faire qch, (bien) compter faire qch, vouloir faire qch; **what do you mean to do?** que comptez-vous faire?, qu'est-ce que vous avez l'intention de faire?; **we mean to win** nous avons (bien) l'intention de gagner, nous comptons (bien) gagner; *Formal* **I mean to be obeyed** j'entends qu'on m'obéisse; *Formal* **I mean to see justice done** je veux que justice soit faite; **I meant to tell you about it** j'avais l'intention de t'en parler; **I meant to phone you last night** je voulais *ou* j'avais l'intention de vous téléphoner hier soir; **I never meant to go** je n'ai jamais eu l'intention d'y aller; **I didn't mean to hurt you** je ne voulais pas te faire de mal; **I only meant to help** je voulais seulement me rendre utile; **I mean to see him now – and I mean now!** j'ai l'intention de le voir tout de suite, et quand je dis tout de suite, c'est tout de suite!; **I didn't mean it!** *(action)* je ne l'ai pas fait exprès!; *(words)* je n'étais pas sérieux!; **you annoyed him when you said that – I meant to!** il n'a pas apprécié que tu dises ça – c'était bien mon intention!; **without meaning to** involontairement; **I mean him no harm** je ne lui veux pas de mal; **I meant it as a joke** c'était une plaisanterie; **it was meant as a compliment/an insult** c'était censé être un compliment/une insulte; **that remark was meant for you** cette remarque s'adressait à vous; **that remark wasn't meant to be overheard** cette remarque n'était pas censée être entendue; **the present was meant for your brother** le cadeau était destiné à ton frère; **they're meant for each other** ils sont faits l'un pour l'autre; **what's this switch meant to be for?** à quoi est censé servir cet interrupteur?; **it's meant to be a horse** c'est censé représenter un cheval; **perhaps I was meant to be a doctor** peut-être que j'étais fait pour être médecin; **it was meant to be** c'était écrit; **he means well** il a de bonnes intentions; **he meant well** il croyait bien faire

(**g**) *(consider, believe)* **it's meant to be good for arthritis** il paraît que c'est bon pour l'arthrite; **this painting is meant to be by Rembrandt** ce tableau est censé être un Rembrandt

(**h**) *(suppose)* **that box isn't meant to be in here** cette boîte n'est pas censée être ici; **this portrait is meant to be of the duke** ce portrait est censé représenter le duc; **you're meant to bow when she comes in** tu dois faire la révérence quand elle entre; **you weren't meant to open the presents until tomorrow** tu n'étais pas censé ouvrir les cadeaux avant demain

►► *Math* ***mean absolute deviation*** écart *m* moyen absolu; *Math* ***mean deviation*** écart *m* moyen; ***mean distance*** distance *f* moyenne; ***mean duration*** durée *f* moyenne; ***mean price*** prix *m* moyen; *Comput* ***mean time between failures*** moyenne *f* de temps entre deux pannes

---

meander [mɪ'ændə(r)] **1** *n* méandre *m*

2 *vi* (**a**) *(river)* serpenter, faire des méandres (**b**) *(person)* errer (sans but), se promener au hasard; *(in speaking)* divaguer; **we meandered off into the night** nous sommes partis sans but dans la nuit

meandering [mɪ'ændərɪŋ] *adj* (**a**) *(river)* qui serpente *ou* fait des méandres (**b**) *(speech)* sans plan, sans suite

meanie ['mi:nɪ] *n Fam* (**a**) *Br (miser)* radin(e) *m,f*, pingre *mf* méchant(e); **you old meanie!** vieux radin! (**b**) *(unpleasant person)* méchant(e) *m,f*

meaning ['mi:nɪŋ] **1** *n* sens *m*, signification *f*; **what is the meaning of this word?** que signifie *ou* que veut dire ce mot?; **I don't know the meaning of this word** je ne connais pas le sens de ce mot, je ne sais pas ce que veut dire ce mot; **loyalty? you don't know the meaning of the word!** tu ne sais pas ce que c'est que la loyauté!; **he doesn't know the meaning of hard work** il ne sait pas ce que c'est que de travailler dur; **...if you get my meaning** ...si vous voyez ce que je veux dire; **what's the meaning of this?** *(in anger)* qu'est-ce que ça veut dire?; **the meaning of life** le sens de la vie; **our success gives meaning to what we're doing** notre réussite donne un sens à ce que nous faisons; **a building that has given new meaning to the term skyscraper** un bâtiment qui redéfinit le concept de gratte-ciel; **a look full of meaning** un regard lourd de sens

2 *adj (look, smile)* significatif, éloquent

meaningful ['mi:nɪŋfʊl] *adj* (**a**) *(expressive → gesture)* significatif, éloquent; **she gave him a meaningful look** elle lui adressa un regard qui en disait long

(**b**) *(significant)* significatif; **the experiment produced no meaningful results** l'expérience n'a donné aucun résultat significatif; **meaningful talks** conversations *fpl* constructives

(**c**) *(comprehensible → explanation)* compréhensible; **nobody had ever explained it to me in such a meaningful way** personne ne me l'avait jamais expliqué de façon aussi claire *ou* compréhensible

(**d**) *(profound → experience, relationship)* profond; **I wouldn't say we had a very meaningful relationship** je ne qualifierais pas notre relation de profonde

meaningfully ['mi:nɪŋfʊlɪ] *adv* de façon significative; **he smiled meaningfully at her** le sourire qu'il lui fit en disait long; **"they left together", she said meaningfully** "ils sont partis ensemble", dit-elle d'un ton lourd de sous-entendus

meaningless ['mi:nɪŋlɪs] *adj* (**a**) *(devoid of sense → act, word, question, world)* dénué de sens; **the lyrics of this song are completely meaningless** les paroles de cette chanson n'ont absolument aucun sens; **meaningless poems** des poèmes *mpl* dénués de sens *ou* qui ne veulent rien dire

(**b**) *(futile → life)* futile, vain; *(→ violence)* gratuit; **they lead very meaningless lives** ils mènent une vie très futile; **a meaningless task** une tâche inutile

meanly ['mi:nlɪ] *adv* (**a**) *esp Br (in miserly fashion)* en lésinant, chichement (**b**) *(ignobly → to act, behave)* méchamment (**c**) *(wretchedly)* misérablement, pauvrement

meanness ['mi:nnɪs] *n* (**a**) *esp Br (with money)* avarice *f* (**b**) *(nastiness, unkindness)* méchanceté *f*, mesquinerie *f* (**c**) *Literary (wretchedness)* pauvreté *f*

means [mi:nz] *(pl* **inv**) **1** *n* (**a**) *(way, method)* moyen *m*; **a means of doing sth** un moyen de faire qch; **is there no means of doing it any faster?** n'y a-t-il pas moyen de le faire plus vite?; **he has no means of support** il est sans ressources; **there is no means of escape** il n'y a pas d'issue; **it's just a means to an end** ce n'est qu'un moyen d'arriver au but; *Prov* **the end justifies the means** la fin justifie les moyens; **by what means may I send it to him?** par quel moyen *ou* quels moyens puis-je le lui faire parvenir?; **by some means or other** *or* **another** d'une façon ou d'une autre; **means of payment** moyens *mpl* de paiement; **means of transport** moyen *m* de transport; **means of production** moyens *mpl* de production

(**b**) *(idiom)* **she's not his friend by any (manner of) means** elle est loin d'être son amie

2 *npl (money, resources)* moyens *mpl*, ressources *fpl*; **to have the means to do sth** avoir les moyens de faire qch; **to live within one's means** vivre selon ses moyens; **to live beyond one's means** vivre au-dessus de ses moyens; **the means at our disposal** les moyens *mpl* dont nous disposons; **her family obviously has means** il est évident qu'elle vient d'une famille aisée; **a man of means** un homme riche

3 by means of *prep* au moyen de; **by means of a screwdriver** à l'aide d'un tournevis; **they communicate by means of signs** ils communiquent par signes

4 by all means *adv (of course)* bien sûr; **may I leave? – by all means!** puis-je partir? – je vous en prie *ou* mais bien sûr!; **by all means go if you really want to** surtout, si tu veux y aller, vas-y

5 by no means *adv* pas du tout; **it's by no means easy** c'est loin d'être facile; **he's by no means the worst in the class** il est loin d'être le plus mauvais de la classe

►► ***means test*** enquête *f* sur les revenus *(d'une personne désirant bénéficier d'une allocation d'État)*; **to undergo a means test** faire l'objet d'une enquête sur les revenus; **the grant is subject to a means test** cette allocation est assujettie à des conditions de ressources

mean-spirited *adj* mesquin

means-test *vt* **is unemployment benefit means-tested?** les allocations de chômage sont-elles attribuées en fonction des ressources *ou* des revenus du bénéficiaire?; **all applicants are means-tested** tous les candidats font l'objet d'une enquête sur leurs revenus

meant [ment] *pt & pp of* **mean**

meantime ['mi:n,taɪm] **1** *adv* pendant ce temps; **meantime things were changing** pendant ce temps, les choses étaient en train de changer

2 in the meantime *adv* entre-temps; **in the meantime I had got married** entre-temps, je m'étais marié

3 for the meantime *adv* pour l'instant; **for the meantime, at least, the situation is resolved** le problème est résolu, au moins pour l'instant

meanwhile ['mi:n,waɪl] *adv* entre-temps, pendant ce temps; **I, meanwhile, was stuck in the lift** pendant ce temps, moi, j'étais coincé dans l'ascenseur; **meanwhile, another 2,000 people have lost their jobs** entre-temps *ou* en attendant, 2000 personnes de plus ont perdu leur emploi

Meanwhile, back at the ranch
Il s'agit d'une phrase qui évoque les séries télévisées américaines réalisées dans les années 60 et 70 dont l'action se déroulait au Far-West, telles que *The High Chaparral* (*Chaparral* en français). La continuité du récit était assurée par un récitant qui prononçait ces mots ("pendant ce temps, au ranch") pour introduire une séquence qui avait lieu au ranch où la famille des héros habitait. Aujourd'hui, on utilise souvent cette phrase sur le mode humoristique à la place de **meanwhile** ("pendant ce temps").

meany (*pl* **meanies**) = meanie

measles ['mi:zəlz] *n Med* rougeole *f*; **to have (the) measles** avoir la rougeole

measly ['mi:zəlɪ] (*compar* **measlier**, *superl* **measliest**) *adj Fam* minable, misérable❑; **all I got was one measly bar of chocolate!** je n'ai eu qu'une misérable tablette de chocolat!; **all that for a measly £5!** tout ça pour cinq malheureuses livres!

measurability [ˌmeʒərə'bɪlɪtɪ] *n* mesurabilité *f*

measurable ['meʒərəbəl] *adj* (**a**) *(rate, change, amount)* mesurable (**b**) *(noticeable, significant)* sensible, perceptible; **we've made measurable progress** nous avons sensiblement progressé

measurably ['meʒərəblɪ] *adv (noticeably, significantly)* sensiblement, notablement

measure ['meʒə(r)] **1** *n* (**a**) *(measurement)* mesure *f*; **the metre is a measure of length** le mètre est une mesure de longueur; **weights and measures** les poids *mpl* et mesures; **linear/square/cubic measure** mesure *f* de longueur/de superficie/de volume; **to give good** *or* **full measure** *(in length, quantity)* faire bonne mesure; *(in weight)* faire bon poids; **to give short measure** *(in quantity)* tricher sur la quantité; *(in weight)* tricher sur le poids; *Fig* **for good measure** pendant qu'il/elle y est; **then he painted the door, just for good measure** et puis, pendant qu'il y était, il a peint la porte; **then she insulted the other man for good measure** elle a aussi insulté l'autre pour ne pas faire de jaloux; **he gave him a couple of kicks for good measure** il lui a donné quelques coups de pied en prime; *Fig* **to take** *or* **to get the measure of sb** jauger qn, se faire une opinion de qn; **by now the authorities had taken the full measure of the gravity of the situation** les autorités mesuraient désormais pleinement la gravité de la situation; **this award is a measure of their success** ce prix ne fait que refléter leur succès; **her joy was beyond measure** sa joie était incommensurable; **irritated/shocked beyond measure** extrêmement irrité/choqué

(**b**) *(degree)* mesure *f*; **a measure of success** un certain succès; **the country has gained a measure of independence** le pays a acquis une certaine indépendance; **in some measure** dans une certaine mesure, jusqu'à un certain point; **in large measure** dans une large mesure, en grande partie; **she inspired fear and respect in equal measure** elle inspirait autant de crainte que de respect

(**c**) *(instrument → ruler)* mètre *m*, règle *f*; *(→ container)* mesure *f*; **a pint measure** une mesure d'une pinte

(**d**) *(portion)* portion *f*, dose *f*; **she poured me a generous measure of gin** elle m'a servi une bonne dose de gin

(**e**) *(step, legislation)* mesure *f*; **to take measures** prendre des mesures; **we have taken measures to correct the fault** nous avons pris des mesures pour rectifier l'erreur; **as a precautionary measure** par mesure de précaution; **parliament must draft measures to halt this trade** le parlement doit élaborer des mesures pour mettre fin à ce trafic

(**f**) *Mus & Literature* mesure *f*

2 *vt* (**a**) *(take measurement of)* mesurer; **he measured me for a suit** il a pris mes mesures pour me faire un costume; **a thermometer measures temperature** un thermomètre sert à mesurer la température; *Fam Fig* **to measure one's length** s'étaler de tout son long

(**b**) *(judge)* jauger, mesurer, évaluer; **to measure oneself** *or* **one's strength against sb** se mesurer à qn; *Fig* **to measure one's words** mesurer *ou* peser ses paroles

3 *vi* mesurer; **the room measures 18 feet by 12** la pièce mesure 18 pieds sur 12; **an earthquake measuring 6.2 on the Richter scale** un tremblement de terre d'une magnitude de 6,2 sur l'échelle de Richter

►**measure off** *vt sep* mesurer; **he measured off a metre of ribbon** il mesura un mètre de ruban

►**measure out** *vt sep* mesurer; **measure out a pound of flour** mesurez une livre de farine; **he measured out a double gin** il versa un double gin

►**measure up 1** *vt sep (wood)* mesurer; **to measure sb up for a suit** prendre les mesures de qn pour un costume; **to get measured up for a new suit** se faire prendre ses mesures pour un nouveau costume; *Fig* **to measure sb up** jauger qn, prendre la mesure de qn

2 *vi* être *ou* se montrer à la hauteur; **to measure up to sb's expectations** être à la mesure des espérances de qn; **the hotel didn't measure up** l'hôtel nous a déçus

'Measure for Measure' *Shakespeare* 'Mesure pour mesure'

measured ['meʒəd] *adj* (**a**) *(distance, length etc)* mesuré; *Sport* **the record over a measured mile** le record officiel sur un mile (**b**) *(careful, deliberate)* mesuré; **a measured speech** un discours mesuré *ou* modéré; **with measured steps** à pas mesurés *ou* comptés

measureless ['meʒəlɪs] *adj* infini, incommensurable; **a measureless expanse** un paysage fuyant à perte de vue; **measureless insolence** une insolence sans bornes

measurement ['meʒəmənt] *n* (**a**) *(dimension)* mesure *f*; **to take (down) the measurements of a piece of furniture** prendre les dimensions d'un meuble; **he took my measurements** il a pris mes mesures; **waist/hip measurement** tour *m* de taille/de hanches; **what are her measurements?** quelles sont ses mensurations?

(**b**) *(of freight)* cubage *m*, encombrement *m*

(**c**) *(action)* mesurage *m*

►► ***measurement ton*** tonne *f* d'encombrement; ***measurement tonnage*** jaugeage *m*

measuring ['meʒərɪŋ] *n* mesurage *m*

►► ***measuring chain*** *(in surveying)* chaîne *f* d'arpenteur *ou* d'arpentage; ***measuring cup*** gobelet *m* doseur, *Can* tasse *f* à mesurer; ***measuring glass*** verre *m* gradué *ou* doseur; ***measuring jug*** verre *m* gradué *ou* doseur; ***measuring spoon*** cuillère *f* à doser; ***measuring tape*** mètre *m* (à) ruban; *Entom* ***measuring worm*** (chenille *f*) arpenteuse *f*

meat [mi:t] *n* (**a**) *(from animal)* viande *f*; *(from crab, lobster etc)* chair *f*; **red/white meat** viande *f* rouge/blanche; **cooked** *or* **cold meats** viande *f* froide; *Am Fig* **the meat and potatoes of computing/gardening** le BAba de l'informatique/du jardinage; *Br* **meat and two veg** *Fam (stereotypical British meal)* plat *m* comportant de la viande et deux légumes *(typique de la gastronomie britannique traditionnelle)*; *very Fam Hum (male genitals)* service *m* trois pièces; *Fam* **there isn't much meat on him** il n'est pas très gras❑; *Fam* **you're dead meat!** t'es mort!

(**b**) *Literary (food)* nourriture *f*; **meat and drink** de quoi manger et boire; *Fig* **such incidents are meat and drink to novelists** les romanciers se repaissent de ce genre d'incidents

(**c**) *(substance, core)* substance *f*; **there's not much meat in his report** il n'y a pas grand-chose dans son rapport

(**d**) *Vulg (penis)* bite *f*, queue *f*

►► ***meat cleaver*** hachoir *m*, couperet *m*; ***meat diet*** régime *m* carné; ***meat hook*** crochet *m* de boucherie; ***meat loaf*** pain *m* de viande; *Br Fam Pej* ***meat market*** *(nightclub)* = boîte réputée pour être un lieu de drague; ***meat pie*** pâté *m* de viande en croûte; ***meat products*** produits *mpl* à base de viande; *Fam* ***meat rack*** lieu *m* de drague *(en particulier chez les homosexuels)*; ***meat safe*** garde-manger *m inv*; *Am Fam* ***meat wagon*** *(ambulance)* ambulance❑ *f*; ***meat-and-potatoes*** *adj Am Fam (no-nonsense)* **I'm a meat-and-potatoes kind of guy** je ne suis pas un mec compliqué

meatball ['mi:tbɔ:l] *n* (**a**) *Culin* boulette *f* (de viande) (**b**) *Am Fam (person)* crétin(e) *mf*, andouille *f*

meat-eater *n* carnivore *mf*; **we aren't big meat-eaters** nous ne mangeons pas beaucoup de viande, nous ne sommes pas de gros mangeurs de viande

meat-eating *adj* carnivore

Meath [mi:ð] *n* le comté de Meath, = comté dans l'est de la république d'Irlande; **in Meath** dans le comté de Meath

meathead ['mi:tˌhed] *n Am Fam* crétin(e) *mf*, andouille *f*

meatheaded ['mi:tˌhedɪd] *adj Am Fam* débile

meatless ['mi:tlɪs] *adj (not containing meat)* sans viande; *Arch (without food)* maigre

meatpacking ['mi:tˌpækɪŋ] *n Am* abattage *m* et boucherie *f*

meatus [mɪ'eɪtəs] *n Anat* conduit *m*, méat *m*

meaty ['mi:tɪ] (*compar* **meatier**, *superl* **meatiest**) *adj* (**a**) *(taste, smell)* de viande; *(food)* riche en viande; **a good, meaty meal** *(full of meat)* un bon repas riche en viande (**b**) *(fleshy → hands, limbs)* épais (**c**) *(substantial → role)* substantiel; *(→ topic, story)* riche; *(→ wine)* qui a du corps; **a meaty novel** un roman riche

mebbe, mebby ['mebɪ] *adv Fam* peut-être❑

Mecca ['mekə] *n* la Mecque; *Fig* **it's a Mecca for book lovers** c'est la Mecque des bibliophiles; **the Mecca of country music** le haut lieu de la country

mechanic [mɪ'kænɪk] **1** *n* mécanicien(enne) *m,f*

2 mechanics 1 *n (UNCOUNT) (study)* mécanique *f* **2** *npl (functioning)* mécanisme *m*; **the mechanics of government** les mécanismes *mpl* gouvernementaux, les rouages *mpl* du gouvernement; **I haven't got to grips yet with the mechanics of the system** je n'ai pas encore compris comment fonctionne le système

mechanical [mɪ'kænɪkəl] *adj* (**a**) *(device, process)* mécanique; **I'm not very mechanical** je ne suis pas très doué pour tout ce qui est mécanique

(**b**) *(machine-like)* machinal, mécanique; **a mechanical gesture** un geste machinal; **her playing is very mechanical** *(of musician)* elle joue d'une façon très mécanique

►► *Tech* ***mechanical advantage*** effet *m* mécanique; ***mechanical digger*** pelleteuse *f* mécanique; ***mechanical drawing*** dessin *m* aux instruments; ***mechanical engineer*** ingénieur *m* mécanicien; ***mechanical engineering*** génie *m* mécanique; ***the mechanical engineering industries*** les industries *fpl* mécaniques; ***mechanical failure*** défaillance *f* mécanique, panne *f* mécanique; ***mechanical fault*** défaut *m* mécanique; ***mechanical shovel*** pelle *f* mécanique, pelleteuse *f*

mechanically [mɪ'kænɪkəlɪ] *adv* (**a**) *(operated)* mécaniquement; **I'm not mechanically minded** je ne suis pas très doué pour tout ce qui est mécanique; **mechanically recovered meat** viande *f* séparée mécaniquement (**b**) *Fig (like a machine)* machinalement, mécaniquement; **he answered mechanically** il a répondu machinalement

mechanician [mekə'nɪʃən] *n* mécanicien(enne) *m,f*

mechanism ['mekənɪzəm] *n also Fig* mécanisme *m*

mechanistic [ˌmekə'nɪstɪk] *adj* mécaniste

mechanization [ˌmekənaɪ'zeɪʃən] *n* mécanisation *f*

mechanize, -ise ['mekənaɪz] *vt* (**a**) *(equip with machinery)* mécaniser; **a highly mechanized industry** une industrie fortement mécanisée (**b**) *Mil (motorize)* motoriser

mechanotherapy [ˌmekənəʊ'θerəpɪ] *n* mécanothérapie *f*

Mecklenburg ['meklənbɜ:g] *n* Mecklembourg *m*

meconium [mɪ'kəʊnɪəm] *n Biol* méconium *m*

MEd [ˌem'ed] *n Univ* (*abbr* **Master of Education**) *(person)* = titulaire d'une maîtrise en sciences de l'éducation; *(qualification)* maîtrise *f* en sciences de l'éducation

Med [med] *n Br Fam* **the Med** la Méditerranée❑

medal ['medəl] *n* médaille *f*; **gold medal** médaille *f* d'or; **to be awarded a medal for bravery** être décoré pour sa bravoure; *Fam* **you deserve a medal!** tu mérites une médaille!

►► ***medal holder*** médaillé(e) *m,f*; *Am Mil* ***Medal of Honor*** = la plus haute distinction américaine donnée en récompense à un soldat

medalist *Am* = **medallist**

medallion [mɪ'dæljən] *n* médaillon *m*

►► *Br Fam Hum* ***medallion man*** = individu entre deux âges à l'allure machiste et vulgaire, qui essaie de passer pour plus jeune qu'il n'est

medallist, *Am* **medalist** ['medəlɪst] *n (winner of medal)* médaillé(e) *m,f*; **the bronze medallist** le(la) détenteur(trice) de la médaille de bronze

medalplay ['medəlpleɪ] *n Golf* partie *f* par coups

meddle ['medəl] *vi* (**a**) *(interfere)* **to meddle in sth** se mêler de qch; **stop meddling in my affairs!** cessez de vous mêler de mes affaires!; **he can't resist the temptation to meddle** il ne peut pas s'empêcher de se mêler de tout *ou* de ce qui ne le regarde pas; **I do try not to meddle** j'essaie vraiment de ne pas m'occuper des affaires des autres

(**b**) *(tamper)* **to meddle with sth** toucher à qch, tripoter qch; **someone's been meddling with the carburettor** quelqu'un a touché au carburateur

meddler ['medələ(r)] *n* (**a**) *(busybody)* **she's such a meddler** il faut toujours qu'elle fourre son nez partout (**b**) *(tamperer)* touche-à-tout *mf inv*

meddlesome ['medəlsəm] *adj* indiscret(ète), qui se mêle de tout

meddlesomeness ['medəlsəmnɪs] *n* manie *f* de se mêler des affaires d'autrui

meddling ['medəlɪŋ] **1** *n (action)* ingérence *f* (**in** dans)

2 *adj* indiscret(ète), qui se mêle de tout

Medea [mɪ'dɪə] *pr n Myth* Médée

medevac ['medɪvæk] *n Mil* hélicoptère *m* sanitaire *(qui évacue les blessés)*

media ['mi:dɪə] **1** *pl of* **medium**

2 *npl* (**a**) *(often sg)* **the media** les médias *mpl*; **he works in the media** il travaille dans les médias; **the power of the media** la puissance des médias; **the news media** la presse; **he knows how to handle the media** il sait s'y prendre avec les journalistes; **the media follow** *or* **follows her everywhere** les journalistes la suivent partout; *Fam Pej* **he's a bit of a media whore** il ferait n'importe quoi pour faire parler de lui dans les médias

(**b**) *Comput (hardware)* support *m*

3 *comp* des médias; *(interest, coverage)* médiatique

►► ***media advertising*** publicité *f* média; ***media analysis*** analyse *f* des médias; ***media analyst*** analyste *mf* des médias; ***media buyer*** acheteur(euse) *m,f* d'espaces (publicitaires); ***media buying*** achat *m* d'espace; ***media circus*** cirque *m* médiatique; ***media consultant*** conseil *m* en communication; ***media coverage*** couverture *f* médiatique, médiatisation *f*; **to get too much media coverage** être surmédiatisé; ***media event*** événement *m* médiatique; ***media exposure*** couverture *f* médiatique, médiatisation *f*; ***media hype*** battage *m* médiatique; ***media mix*** mix *m* média; ***media mogul*** magnat *m* des médias; ***media person*** homme *m* de communication, femme *f* de communication; ***media plan*** plan *m* média; ***media planner*** médiaplaneur *m*, média planner *m*; ***media planning*** média planning *m*; ***media research*** médialogie *f*; ***media schedule*** calendrier *m* de campagne; ***media scrum*** ruée *f* de journalistes; ***media studies*** = études en communication et journalisme; ***media vehicle*** support *m* publicitaire

media-conscious *adj (politician etc)* médiatique

mediaeval, mediaevalism *etc* = **medieval, medievalism** *etc*

media-friendly *adj* médiatique

mediagenic ['mi:dɪə,dʒenɪk] *adj (person)* médiatique

medial ['mi:dɪəl] **1** *n Ling* médiale *f*

2 *adj* (**a**) *(average)* moyen (**b**) *(middle)* médian (**c**) *Ling* médial, médian

medially ['mi:dɪəlɪ] *adv Ling* médialement

median ['mi:djən] **1** *n* (**a**) *Math* médiane *f*

(**b**) *Am Aut* terre-plein *m* central, *Belg & Suisse* berme *f* centrale

2 *adj* médian

►► ***median lethal dose*** dose *f* létale 50 pour cent; ***median line*** ligne *f* médiane; *Am* ***median strip*** terre-plein *m* central, *Belg & Suisse* berme *f* centrale

mediant ['mi:dɪənt] *n Mus* médiante *f*

media-shy *adj* qui fuit les médias

mediastinitis [,mi:dɪəstaɪ'naɪtɪs] *n Med* médiastinite *f*

mediastinum [,mi:dɪə'staɪnəm] *n Anat* médiastin *m*

mediate ['mi:dɪeɪt] **1** *vt* (**a**) *(agreement, peace)* obtenir par médiation; *(dispute)* servir de médiateur dans, se faire le médiateur de; **to mediate a dispute** servir de médiateur dans un conflit; **the United States mediated an agreement between the two countries** les États-Unis ont servi de médiateur pour qu'un accord soit conclu entre les deux pays; **to mediate an industrial dispute** servir de médiateur dans un conflit social

(**b**) *(moderate)* modérer

2 *vi (act as a peacemaker)* servir de médiateur; **to mediate in a dispute** servir de médiateur dans un conflit; **to mediate between** servir d'intermédiaire entre

mediating ['mi:dɪeɪtɪŋ] *adj* médiateur

mediation [,mi:dɪ'eɪʃən] *n* médiation *f*; **to go to mediation** recourir à une médiation

mediatization [,mi:dɪətaɪ'zeɪʃən] *n Hist* médiatisation *f*

mediatize, -ise ['mi:dɪətaɪz] *vt Hist* médiatiser

mediator ['mi:dɪeɪtə(r)] *n* médiateur(trice) *m,f*

mediatory ['mi:dɪətərɪ] *adj* médiateur

medic ['medɪk] *n Fam* (**a**) *(doctor)* toubib *m* (**b**) *Br (medical student)* étudiant(e) *m,f* en médecine ❑

medicable ['medɪkəbəl] *adj* guérissable, curable

Medicaid ['medɪkeɪd] *n* = aux États-Unis, programme fédéral d'assistance médicale pour les personnes défavorisées de moins de 65 ans

medical ['medɪkəl] **1** *adj* médical

2 *n* visite *f* médicale; **to have a medical** passer une visite médicale; **to pass/fail a medical** être déclaré apte/inapte à un travail après un bilan de santé

►► ***medical board*** commission *f* médicale; *Mil* conseil *m* de révision; ***medical care*** soins *mpl* médicaux; ***medical certificate*** certificat *m* médical; ***medical examination*** visite *f* médicale; *Am* ***medical examiner*** médecin *m* légiste; ***medical history*** *(of patient → file)* dossier *m* médical; *(→ previous problems)* antécédents *mpl* médicaux; ***medical insurance*** assurance *f* maladie; *Br* ***medical officer*** *Ind* médecin *m* du travail; *Mil* médecin *m* militaire; ***Medical Officer of Health*** directeur(trice) *m,f* de la santé publique; ***medical practitioner*** (médecin *m*) généraliste *mf*; ***the medical profession*** *(people)* le corps médical; *(activity)* la profession médicale; ***medical record*** dossier *m* médical; ***Medical Research Council*** = organisme public de financement des centres de recherche médicale et des hôpitaux en Grande-Bretagne; ***medical school*** faculté *f* de médecine; ***medical student*** étudiant(e) *m,f* en médecine; ***medical supervision*** surveillance *f* médicale; ***medical technician*** infirmier(ère) *m,f*; ***medical ward*** = salle commune dans un service de médecine générale

medicalization [,medɪkəlaɪ'zeɪʃən] *n* médicalisation *f*

medicalize, -ise ['medɪkəlaɪz] *vt* médicaliser

medically ['medɪkəlɪ] *adv* médicalement; **medically speaking** d'un point de vue médical; **medically approved** approuvé par les autorités médicales; **to be medically examined** passer une visite médicale

medicament [mɪ'dɪkəmənt] *n* médicament *m*

Medicare ['medɪkeə(r)] *n* = aux États-Unis, programme fédéral d'assistance médicale pour les personnes âgées qui a largement contribué à réhabiliter socialement le troisième âge

medicate ['medɪkeɪt] *vt (patient)* faire suivre un traitement à; **he's heavily medicated** il prend beaucoup de médicaments

medicated ['medɪkeɪtɪd] *adj (shampoo, soap)* traitant

►► ***medicated shampoo*** shampooing *m* traitant; ***medicated soap*** savon *m* traitant

medication [,medɪ'keɪʃən] *n* médication *f*; **to be on medication** être sous traitement

Medici ['medɪtʃɪ] *pr npl Hist* **the Medici** les Médicis; **Lorenzo de' Medici** Laurent de Médicis

medicinal [mə'dɪsɪnəl] *adj* médicinal; *Hum* **it's just for medicinal purposes** *(when having a drink)* c'est mon médicament

►► ***medicinal plants*** plantes *fpl* médicinales; ***medicinal properties*** vertus *fpl* curatives

medicinally [mə'dɪsɪnəlɪ] *adv (use a herb, substance)* médicalement, comme médicament; *(treat)* médicalement

medicine ['medsɪn] *n* (**a**) *(practice, science)* médecine *f*; **preventive medicine** médecine *f* préventive; **to practise medicine** exercer la médecine; **he studies medicine** il est étudiant en médecine; **she studied medicine** elle a fait des études de médecine

(**b**) *(substance)* médicament *m*, remède *m*; **don't forget to take your medicine** n'oublie pas de prendre tes médicaments; *Br Fig* **to take one's medicine** avaler la pilule; **to give sb a dose** *or* **taste of his/her own medicine** rendre à qn la monnaie de sa pièce

►► ***medicine ball*** medicine-ball *m*, médecine-ball *m*; ***medicine bottle*** flacon *m* de pharmacie; *Br* ***medicine cabinet, medicine chest*** (armoire *f* à) pharmacie *f*; ***medicine man*** sorcier *m*, medicine-man *m*

medick ['medɪk] *n Bot* lupuline *f*

medico ['medɪkəʊ] *(pl* **medicos**) *Br Fam* (**a**) *(doctor)* toubib *m* (**b**) *(medical student)* étudiant(e) *m,f* en médecine ❑

medico-legal *adj* médico-légal

►► *Am* ***Medico-Legal Institute*** institut *m* médico-légal

medieval [,medɪ'i:vəl] *adj* (**a**) *Hist (art, literature, city)* médiéval; *(castle, church)* médiéval, du Moyen Âge; *(poet, lord)* du Moyen Âge; **in medieval times** au Moyen Âge (**b**) *Fig Pej (primitive → attitudes, facilities, person)* moyenâgeux

►► ***Medieval Latin*** latin *m* médiéval

medievalism [,medɪ'i:vəlɪzəm] *n* médiévisme *m*

medievalist [,medɪ'i:vəlɪst] *n* médiéviste *mf*

medina [me'di:nə] *n* médina *f*

mediocarpal [,mi:dɪəʊ'kɑ:pəl] *adj Anat* médiocarpien

mediocre [,mi:dɪ'əʊkə(r)] *adj* médiocre

mediocrity [,mi:dɪ'ɒkrətɪ] *(pl* **mediocrities**) *n* (**a**) *(gen)* médiocrité *f* (**b**) *(mediocre person)* médiocre *mf*, incapable *mf*

mediodorsal [,mi:dɪəʊ'dɔ:səl] *adj Anat* médiodorsal

mediopalatal [,mi:dɪəʊ'pælətəl] *adj Anat* médiopalatal

mediotarsal [,mi:dɪəʊ'tɑ:səl] *adj Anat* médiotarsien

meditate ['medɪteɪt] **1** *vi* (**a**) *(practise meditation)* méditer (**b**) *(reflect, ponder)* réfléchir, songer; **to meditate on** *or* **upon sth** réfléchir *ou* songer à qch

2 *vt* songer à

meditation [,medɪ'teɪʃən] *n* méditation *f*, réflexion *f*; **to spend one's days in prayer and meditation** passer ses journées en prière et en méditation

meditative ['medɪtətɪv] *adj* méditatif; **meditative atmosphere** atmosphère *f* de recueillement; **meditative exercise** exercice *m* de méditation

meditatively ['medɪtətɪvlɪ] *adv* d'un air méditatif *ou* songeur

Mediterranean [,medɪtə'reɪnɪən] **1** *n* (**a**) **the Mediterranean (Sea)** la (mer) Méditerranée (**b**) *(person)* Méditerranéen(enne) *m,f*

2 *adj* méditerranéen

►► *Orn* ***Mediterranean gull*** mouette *f* mélanocéphale

medium ['mi:dɪəm] *(pl sense* (**a**) **media** [-dɪə], *pl senses* (**b**) *and* (**c**) **media** [-dɪə] *or* **mediums,** *pl senses* (**d**), (**e**) *and* (**f**) **mediums**) **1** *n* (**a**) *(means of communication)* moyen *m* (de communication), médium *m*, support *m*; *Art (for working in)* matériau *m*; **the decision was made public through the medium of the press** la décision fut rendue publique par voie de presse *ou* par l'intermédiaire des journaux; **television is a powerful medium in education** la télévision est un très bon instrument éducatif; **his favourite medium is watercolour** son moyen d'expression favori est l'aquarelle

(**b**) *Phys (means of transmission)* véhicule *m*,

milieu *m*; **sound travels through the medium of air** les sons sont propagés *ou* véhiculés par l'air; **a refractive medium** un milieu réfringent

(**c**) *Biol (environment)* milieu *m*; **in its natural medium** dans son milieu naturel

(**d**) *(spiritualist)* médium *m*

(**e**) *(middle course)* milieu *m*; **the happy medium** le juste milieu

(**f**) *(size)* taille *f* moyenne; **this T-shirt's a medium** ce tee-shirt est une taille moyenne *ou* un deux; **available in small, medium and large** disponible en petit, moyen et grand

2 *adj* (**a**) *(gen)* moyen; **in the medium term** à moyen terme; **she's of medium height** elle est de taille moyenne

(**b**) *Culin (meat)* à point

►► ***medium brown*** châtain *m*; *Cin* ***medium close-up*** plan *m* rapproché; *Econ* ***medium of exchange*** moyen *m* d'échange; *Rad Am* ***medium frequency,*** *Br* ***medium wave*** *(UNCOUNT)* ondes *fpl* moyennes; **on medium wave** sur (les) ondes moyennes

medium-dated *adj Fin (gilts, securities)* à échéance moyenne

medium-dry *adj (wine)* demi-sec

medium-fine *adj (pen)* à pointe moyenne

medium-haul *adj (flight, route)* moyen-courrier

mediumism ['mi:djəmɪzəm] *n* médiumnité *f*

medium-range *adj*

►► ***medium-range missile*** missile *m* à moyenne portée

medium-rare *adj Culin (meat)* entre saignant et à point

mediumship ['mi:djəmʃɪp] *n* médiumnité *f*, profession *f* de médium

medium-sized *adj* moyen, de taille moyenne

medium-term *adj* à moyen terme

►► ***medium-term credit*** crédit *m* (à) moyen terme; ***medium-term liabilities*** dettes *fpl* à moyen terme; ***medium-term maturity*** échéance *f* à moyen terme; ***medium-term note*** billet *m* à moyen terme (négociable)

medium-wave *adj (broadcast)* sur ondes moyennes; *(station, transmitter)* émettant sur ondes moyennes

medlar ['medlə(r)] *n Bot (fruit)* nèfle *f*; *(tree)* néflier *m*

medley ['medlɪ] *n* (**a**) *(mixture)* mélange *m* (**b**) *Mus* pot-pourri *m* (**c**) *(in swimming)* quatre nages *m inv*

medulla [mɪ'dʌlə] *n* (**a**) *Anat (part of organ, structure)* moelle *f* (**b**) *Bot* moelle *f*

►► *Anat* ***medulla oblongata*** *(of brain)* bulbe *m* rachidien

medullary [mɪ'dʌlərɪ] *adj* (**a**) *Anat* médullaire (**b**) *Bot* médullaire, médulleux

►► *Anat* ***medullary canal*** canal *m* médullaire; *Anat* ***medullary cavity*** cavité *f* médullaire; *Bot* ***medullary ray*** rayon *m ou* prolongement *m* médullaire; ***medullary sheath*** *Bot* étui *m* médullaire; *Anat* myéline *f*

Medusa [mɪ'dju:zə] *pr n Myth* Méduse

meed [mi:d] *n Literary* récompense *f*; **to offer one's meed of praise** apporter sa part d'éloges

meek [mi:k] *adj* doux (douce), docile; **meek and mild** doux comme un agneau

meekly ['mi:klɪ] *adv* doucement, docilement

meekness ['mi:knɪs] *n* douceur *f*, docilité *f*

meerkat ['mɪəkæt] *n* suricate *m*

meerschaum ['mɪəʃəm] *n* (**a**) *(pipe)* pipe *f* en écume (**b**) *(mineral)* écume *f* de mer, magnésite *f*

MEET [mi:t]

rencontrer	► **1 (a), (h), (i)**
retrouver	► **1 (b)**
rejoindre	► **1 (b)**
attendre	► **1 (c)**
aller/venir chercher	► **1 (c)**
faire la connaissance de	► **1 (e)**
satisfaire	► **1 (f)**
régler	► **1 (g)**
accueillir	► **1 (j)**
se rencontrer	► **2 (a), (c), (e) – (g)**
se retrouver	► **2 (b)**
se rejoindre	► **2 (b)**
faire connaissance	► **2 (c)**
se réunir	► **2 (d)**

(pt & pp **met** [met]*)* **1** *vt* (**a**) *(by chance)* rencontrer; **guess who I met this morning** devine qui j'ai rencontré ce matin; **to meet sb on the stairs** croiser qn dans l'escalier; *Fam* **fancy meeting you here!** je ne m'attendais pas à te trouver ici! ☐

(**b**) *(by arrangement)* retrouver, rejoindre; **I'll meet you on the platform in twenty minutes** je te retrouve sur le quai dans vingt minutes; **I'll meet you after work** je te retrouverai après le travail; **I'm meeting Gregory this afternoon** j'ai rendez-vous avec Gregory cet après-midi; **the train meets the ferry at Dover** le train assure la correspondance avec le ferry à Douvres

(**c**) *(wait for, collect)* attendre, aller *ou* venir chercher; **nobody was at the station to meet me** personne ne m'attendait à la gare; **I'll be there to meet the bus** je serai là à l'arrivée du car; **he'll meet us at the station** il viendra nous chercher à la gare; **I'll send a car to meet you** j'enverrai une voiture vous chercher *ou* vous prendre

(**d**) *(greet)* **she came to meet us** elle est venue à notre rencontre

(**e**) *(make acquaintance of)* rencontrer, faire la connaissance de; **I met him last year** je l'ai rencontré *ou* j'ai fait sa connaissance l'année dernière; **have you met my husband?** vous connaissez mon mari?; **I'd like you to meet Mr Jones** j'aimerais vous présenter M. Jones; **meet Mrs Dickens** je vous présente Mme Dickens; **(I'm very) glad** *or* **pleased to meet you** enchanté (de faire votre connaissance); **nice meeting you** *or* **to have met you** enchanté d'avoir fait votre connaissance; **she's the nicest person I've ever met** c'est la personne la plus gentille que j'ai jamais rencontrée; **I get to meet a lot of people in my job** mon travail m'amène à rencontrer beaucoup de gens; **I like meeting people** j'aime rencontrer des gens

(**f**) *(satisfy)* satisfaire, répondre à; **to meet sb's requirements** satisfaire aux besoins de qn; **we couldn't meet their needs** nous n'avons pu répondre à leurs besoins; **supply isn't meeting demand** l'offre est inférieure à la demande; **it didn't meet my expectations** ce n'était pas aussi bien que je l'espérais; *Fig* **to meet sb halfway** trouver un compromis avec qn; **they decided to meet each other halfway** ils décidèrent de couper la poire en deux

(**g**) *(settle)* régler; **I couldn't meet the payments** je n'ai pas pu régler *ou* payer les échéances; **to meet sb's expenses** subvenir aux frais de qn; **the cost will be met by the company** les frais seront pris en charge par la compagnie

(**h**) *(face)* rencontrer, affronter; **he meets the champion on Saturday** il rencontre le champion samedi; **to meet an obstacle** se heurter à *ou* rencontrer un obstacle; **to meet the enemy** affronter l'ennemi; **how are we going to meet the challenge?** comment allons-nous relever le défi?; **to meet one's death** trouver la mort

(**i**) *(come in contact with)* rencontrer; **it's the first case of this sort I've met** c'est la première fois que je vois un cas semblable; **his hand/mouth met hers** leurs mains/bouches se rencontrèrent; **my eyes met his** nos regards se croisèrent *ou* se rencontrèrent; **he couldn't meet her eye** il ne pouvait pas la regarder dans les yeux

(**j**) *(treat)* accueillir; **his suggestion was met with howls of laughter** sa proposition a été accueillie par des éclats de rire; **we shall meet violence with violence** à la violence, nous répondrons par la violence

(**k**) *(join)* **the stream meets the river** le ruisseau se jette dans la rivière; **where East meets West** où l'est et l'ouest se rencontrent; **here the road meets the railway** c'est ici que la route rejoint *ou* croise le chemin de fer

2 *vi* (**a**) *(by chance)* se rencontrer; **we met on the stairs** nous nous sommes croisés dans l'escalier

(**b**) *(by arrangement)* se retrouver, se rejoindre, se donner rendez-vous; **let's meet for lunch** on déjeune ensemble?; **shall we meet at the station?** on se retrouve *ou* on se donne rendez-vous à la gare?; **we arranged to meet at the station** nous nous sommes donné rendez-vous à la gare; **we should meet more often** on devrait se voir plus souvent; **they weren't to meet again for a long time** ils ne devaient pas se revoir avant longtemps; **I think they meet every day** je crois qu'ils se voient tous les jours

(**c**) *(become acquainted)* se rencontrer, faire connaissance; **we first met in 1989** nous nous sommes rencontrés pour la première fois en 1989; **have you two met?** est-ce que vous vous connaissez déjà?, vous vous êtes déjà rencontrés?

(**d**) *(assemble)* se réunir; **the delegates will meet in the conference room** les délégués se réuniront dans la salle de conférence; **the committee meets once a month** le comité se réunit une fois par mois; **the classes have begun to meet** les cours ont commencé

(**e**) *(join → lines, wires)* se rencontrer, se joindre; **the cross stands where four roads meet** la croix se trouve à la jonction de quatre routes; **their eyes met** leurs regards se rencontrèrent *ou* se croisèrent; **his eyebrows meet in the middle** ses sourcils se touchent

(**f**) *(teams, opponents)* se rencontrer, s'affronter; *(armies)* s'affronter, se heurter

(**g**) *(come into contact)* se rencontrer; **the two cars met head on** les deux voitures se sont heurtées de plein fouet

3 *n* (**a**) *Br (in hunting)* rendez-vous *m* (de chasse)

(**b**) *esp Am Sport* rencontre *f*; **athletics meet** rencontre *f ou* meeting *m* d'athlétisme

4 *adj Arch or Formal (suitable)* séant, convenable; *(right)* juste; **it is only meet that they should be the ones to leave** ce n'est que justice que ce soient eux qui partent; **as was meet** comme il convenait

►**meet up** *vi (by chance)* se rencontrer; *(by arrangement)* se retrouver, se donner rendez-vous; **to meet up with sb** retrouver qn; **we met up with them in Paris** nous les avons retrouvés à Paris

►**meet with** *vt insep* (**a**) *(encounter → difficulty)* rencontrer; **they met with considerable difficulties** ils ont rencontré d'énormes difficultés; **the agreement met with general approval** l'accord a reçu l'approbation générale; **to meet with a refusal** se heurter à *ou* essuyer un refus; **the proposal has met with fierce opposition** la proposition s'est heurtée à une opposition très vive; **the expedition met with disaster** l'expédition a tourné au désastre; **the play met with great success** la pièce a eu beaucoup de succès; **I'm afraid your dog has met with an accident** j'ai bien peur que votre chien n'ait eu un (petit) accident

(**b**) *esp Am (person → by chance)* rencontrer; *(→ by arrangement)* rejoindre, retrouver; **I'm meeting with him tomorrow to discuss the budget** je le vois demain pour discuter du budget; **I'll meet with you after work** je te retrouverai après le travail

meeting ['mi:tɪŋ] *n* (**a**) *(assembly)* réunion *f*; *Pol* assemblée *f*, meeting *m*; *Br Sport* rencontre *f*, meeting *m*; **to hold a meeting** tenir une réunion; **he's in a meeting** il est en réunion; **to call a meeting of the committee/the workforce** convoquer les membres du comité/le personnel; **to open the meeting** déclarer la séance ouverte; **to address the meeting** prendre la parole; **the meeting voted in favour of the measure** l'assemblée a voté la proposition; **the (general) meeting of shareholders** l'assemblée (générale) des actionnaires; **athletics meeting** rencontre *f ou* meeting *m* d'athlétisme; **committee meeting** réunion *f* du comité

(**b**) *(encounter)* rencontre *f*; **during my first meeting with him** lors de notre première rencontre; **a chance meeting in the street** une rencontre fortuite dans la rue; *Fig* **meeting of minds** accord *m* possible

(**c**) *(arranged)* rendez-vous *m*; **I have a meeting with the boss this morning** j'ai rendez-vous avec le patron ce matin; **the Governor had a meeting with Church dignitaries** le Gouverneur s'est entretenu avec *ou* a rencontré les dignitaires de l'Église

(**d**) *(junction → of roads)* jonction *f*, rencontre *f*; *(→ of rivers)* confluent *m*

(**e**) *Rel (for Quakers)* culte *m*; **to go to meeting** aller au culte

►► **meeting place** *(for gatherings)* lieu *m* de réunion; *(for rendez-vous)* (lieu *m* de) rendez-vous *m*

meetinghouse ['mi:tɪŋhaʊs, *pl* -haʊzɪz] *n Rel* temple *m*

meg [meg] *n Fam Comput* méga *m*

mega ['megə] *Fam* **1** *adj (excellent)* génial, super *(inv), géant; (enormous)* énorme □; **all their records have been mega hits** tous leurs disques ont eu un succès énorme

2 *adv (very)* hyper, méga

mega- ['megə] *pref Fam* hyper; **mega-rich** hyper riche; **mega-famous** hyper célèbre; **mega-angry** hyper en colère

megabit ['megəbɪt] *n Comput* mégabit *m*

megabucks ['megəbʌks] *n Fam* un fric fou, une fortune; **her job pays megabucks** elle gagne une fortune dans son travail

megabyte ['megəbaɪt] *n Comput* méga-octet *m*; **20 megabyte memory** mémoire *f* de 20 méga-octets

megacephalic [,megəse'fælɪk], **megacephalous** [,megə'sefələs] *adj Anat* mégacéphale, mégalocéphale

megacephaly [,megə'sefəlɪ] *n Anat* macrocéphalie *f*

megacycle ['megə,saɪkəl] *n* mégacycle *m*

megadeath ['megədeθ] *n* million *m* de morts; **weapons capable of causing 100 megadeaths** des armes capables de faire des centaines de millions de morts

megadose ['megədəʊs] *n Fam* superdose *f*

Megaera [mə'gɪərə] *pr n Myth* Mégère

megaflop ['megəflɒp] *n Fam* flop *m* retentisssant

megahertz ['megəhɜ:ts] *(pl* **inv***) n Comput* méga-hertz *m*

megalith ['megəlɪθ] *n* mégalithe *m*

megalithic [,megə'lɪθɪk] *adj* mégalithique

megaloblast ['megələʊ,blæst] *n Physiol* mégaloblaste *m*

megaloblastic [,megələʊ'blæstɪk] *adj Physiol* mégaloblastique

megalocephalic [,megələʊse'fælɪk], **megalocephalous** [,megələʊ'sefələs] *adj Anat* macrocéphale, mégacéphale

megalocephaly [,megələʊ'sefəlɪ] *n Anat* macrocéphalie *f*, mégacéphalie *f*

megalomania [,megələ'meɪnjə] *n* mégalomanie *f*

megalomaniac [,megələ'meɪnɪæk] **1** *n* mégalomane *mf*

2 *adj* mégalomane

megalopolis [,megə'lɒpəlɪs] *n* mégapole *f*, mégalopole *f*

megalopolitan [,megələ'pɒlɪtən] **1** *n* mégalopolitain(e) *m,f*

2 *adj* mégalopolitain

megalosaur ['megələʊ,sɔ:(r)], **megalosaurus** [,megələʊ'sɔ:rəs] *n* mégalosaure *m*

megamerger ['megə,mɜ:dʒə(r)] *n Fin* méga-fusion *f*

megaphone ['megəfəʊn] *n* porte-voix *m inv*, mégaphone *m*

megaphyll ['megəfɪl] *n Bot* mégaphylle *f*

megaplex ['megəpleks] *n Am Cin* complexe *m* multisalles, cinéma *m* multisalle

megascopic [,megə'skɒpɪk] *adj* macroscopique

megaspore ['megəspɔ:(r)] *n Bot* macrospore *f*, mégaspore *f*

megastar ['megəstɑ:(r)] *n Fam* superstar *f*

megastore ['megəstɔ:(r)] *n* très grand magasin *m*

megaton ['megətʌn] *n* mégatonne *f*; **a 5 megaton bomb** une bombe de 5 mégatonnes

megavolt ['megəvɒlt] *n* mégavolt *m*

megawatt ['megəwɒt] *n* mégawatt *m*

megilla [mə'gɪlə] *n Am Fam* **the whole megilla** tout le tremblement; **I don't need the whole megilla, just give me the main points** t'as pas besoin de tout me raconter en détail *ou* par le menu, dis-moi le principal

megilp [mə'gɪlp] *n Art* = mélange d'huile de lin et de vernis au mastic utilisé en peinture

megrim ['mi:grɪm] *n Arch* (**a**) *Med* migraine *f*; **to have the megrims** avoir le spleen *ou* les vapeurs; *Vet* avoir le vertigo (**b**) *(whim)* fantaisie *f*, lubie *f*

meiosis [maɪ'əʊsɪs] *(pl* **meioses** [-si:z]*) n* (**a**) *Biol* méiose *f* (**b**) *(in rhetoric)* litote *f*

meiotic [maɪ'ɒtɪk] *adj Biol* méiotique

meitnerium [maɪt'neərɪəm] *n Chem* meitnérium *m*

Mekong ['mi:kɒŋ] *n* **the Mekong** le Mékong

melaena [me'li:nə] *n Med* melæna *m*, méléna *m*

melamine ['meləmi:n] *n* mélamine *f*

melancholia [,melən'kəʊlɪə] *n Old-fashioned Psy* mélancolie *f*

melancholic [,melən'kɒlɪk] **1** *n* mélancolique *mf*

2 *adj* mélancolique

melancholically [,melən'kɒlɪkəlɪ] *adv* mélancoliquement

melancholy ['melənkəlɪ] **1** *n Literary* mélancolie *f*

2 *adj (person, mood)* mélancolique; *(news, sight, thought)* sombre, triste

Melanesia [,melə'ni:zjə] *n* Mélanésie *f*; **in Melanesia** en Mélanésie

Melanesian [,melə'ni:zjən] **1** *n* (**a**) *(person)* Mélanésien(enne) *m,f* (**b**) *Ling* mélanésien *m*

2 *adj* mélanésien

melanic [mə'lænɪk] *adj Med (pigment, tumour)* mélanique; *(person)* atteint de mélanose

melanin ['melənɪn] *n* mélanine *f*

melanism ['melənɪzəm] *n* mélanisme *m*

melanocyte ['melənəʊsaɪt] *n* mélanocyte *m*

melanoderma [,melənəʊ'dɜ:mə], **melanodermia** [,melənəʊ'dɜ:mɪə] *n Med* mélanodermie *f*

melanodermic [,melənəʊ'dɜ:mɪk] *adj Med* mélanoderme

melanoma [,melə'nəʊmə] *n Med* mélanome *m*

melatonin [,melə'təʊnɪn] *n Physiol* mélatonine *f*

Melba ['melbə] *adj Culin* Melba *(inv)*

►► **Melba toast** = tartine de pain grillé très fine

Melbourne ['melbən] *n* Melbourne

►► **the Melbourne Cup** = course hippique prestigieuse qui a lieu à Melbourne au mois de novembre

Melchior ['melkɪ,ɔ:(r)] *pr n Bible* Melchior

Melchite ['melkaɪt] *n Rel* Melchite *mf*

meld [meld] **1** *n Cards* pose *f*

2 *vt Am (merge)* fusionner, amalgamer

3 *vi* poser ses cartes

melee, mêlée ['meleɪ] *n* mêlée *f*

melilot ['melɪlɒt] *n Bot* mélilot *m*

melinite ['melɪnaɪt] *n Miner* mélinite *f*

meliorate ['mi:lɪəreɪt] *Formal* **1** *vt* améliorer

2 *vi* s'améliorer

melioration [,mi:lɪə'reɪʃən] *n Formal* amélioration *f*

meliorative ['mi:lɪərətɪv] *adj Formal* dont l'effet est positif

melliferous [me'lɪfərəs] *adj* mellifère

mellific [me'lɪfɪk] *adj* mellifique

mellifluous [me'lɪflʊəs], **mellifluent** [me'lɪflʊənt] *adj Literary* mélodieux, doux (douce); **mellifluous prose** un style fluide

mellophone ['meləʊfəʊn] *n* cor *m* d'harmonie

mellow ['meləʊ] **1** *adj* (**a**) *(fruit)* mûr; *(wine)* velouté

(**b**) *(bricks)* patiné; *(light)* doux (douce), tamisé; *(colour)* doux (douce); *(voice, music)* doux (douce), mélodieux

(**c**) *(person, mood)* serein, tranquille; **to become** *or* **to grow mellow** s'adoucir; *(with age)* mûrir; **mellow thoughts** des pensées langoureuses

(**d**) *Fam (tipsy)* éméché, gai

(**e**) *Fam (on drugs)* **to be mellow** être parti, planer

(**f**) *Fam Black Am slang (attractive)* sexy *(inv)*, craquant

(**g**) *Fam Black Am slang (fine, acceptable)* cool *(inv)*; **see you at six? – yeah, that's mellow** on se voit à six heures? – ouais, ça marche!

2 *vt (of age, experience)* adoucir, faire mûrir; *(of food, alcohol)* détendre, décontracter

3 *vi* (**a**) *(fruit)* mûrir; *(wine)* devenir moelleux, se velouter

(**b**) *(light, colour)* s'adoucir; *(stone, brick, building)* se patiner; *(sound, music)* s'adoucir, devenir plus mélodieux; **her voice has mellowed** sa voix s'est adoucie

(**c**) *(person → with age)* s'adoucir; *(→ with food, alcohol)* se décontracter; **he's mellowed a lot since those days** il s'est beaucoup adouci depuis cette époque; **after the second whisky he began to mellow** après le deuxième whisky, il a commencé à se décontracter

4 *n Fam Black Am slang (friend)* pote *m*

►**mellow out** *vi Fam (relax)* se calmer, se détendre

mellowing ['meləʊɪŋ] **1** *n* (**a**) *(of fruit, wine)* maturation *f* (**b**) *(of person, mood, light)* adoucissement *m*

2 *adj* adoucissant; **the alcohol had a mellowing effect on them** l'alcool les a détendus

mellowness ['meləʊnɪs] *n* (**a**) *(of fruit)* douceur *f*; *(of wine)* moelleux *m*, velouté *m* (**b**) *(of light, colour)* douceur *f*; *(of voice, music)* douceur *f*, mélodie *f* (**c**) *(of person, mood)* douceur *f*, sérénité *f*

melodic [mɪ'lɒdɪk] *adj* mélodique

melodically [mɪ'lɒdɪkəlɪ] *adv* mélodiquement

melodious [mɪ'ləʊdjəs] *adj* mélodieux

►► *Orn* ***melodious warbler*** hypolaïs *f* polyglotte

melodiously [mɪ'ləʊdjəslɪ] *adv* mélodieusement

melodiousness [mɪ'ləʊdjəsnɪs] *n* caractère *m* mélodieux, mélodie *f*

melodist ['melədɪst] *n* mélodiste *mf*

melodrama ['melə,drɑ:mə] *n* mélodrame *m*

melodramatic [,melədrə'mætɪk] **1** *adj* mélodramatique; **don't be so melodramatic!** n'en fais pas tout un drame!

2 **melodramatics** *npl* goût *m* du mélodrame; **I'm fed up with his melodramatics** j'en ai assez de son cinéma

melodramatically [,melədrə'mætɪkəlɪ] *adv* de façon mélodramatique; **he spoke melodramatically of leaving her** d'un air mélodramatique, il parla de la quitter

melodramatist [,melə'dræmətɪst] *n* auteur *m* de mélodrames, mélodramatiste *mf*

melodramatize, -ise [,melə'dræmətaɪz] *vt* mélodramatiser

melody ['melədɪ] *(pl* **melodies***) n* mélodie *f*

►► *Press* ***Melody Maker*** = ancien hebdomadaire britannique consacré à la musique pop

melon ['melən] *n* (**a**) *(fruit)* melon *m* (**b**) *Am Fam (profits, money)* gros bénéfices *mpl* (à distribuer) □; **to carve** *or* **cut up the melon** distribuer les bénéfices (**c**) *Fam* **melons** *(breasts)* nichons *mpl*, roberts *mpl*

►► *Culin* ***melon baller*** cuillère *f* parisienne

meloplasty ['meləʊ,plæstɪ] *n Med* méloplastie *f*

Melpomene [mel'pɒmɪnɪ] *pr n Myth* Melpomène

melt [melt] **1** *vi* (**a**) *(become liquid)* fondre; **that chocolate melts in your mouth** ce chocolat fond dans la bouche; **his heart melted** ça l'a attendri

(**b**) *(disappear)* **to melt (away), to melt into thin air** disparaître, s'évaporer

(**c**) *(blend)* se fondre; **he tried to melt into the crowd** il a essayé de se fondre *ou* de disparaître dans la foule; **the green melts into the blue** le vert se fond dans le bleu *ou* se confond avec le bleu; **the images melted into one another** les images se fondaient les unes dans les autres

2 *vt (gen)* (faire) fondre; *(metal)* fondre; **the sun will melt the ice** le soleil fera fondre la glace; **melt the butter in a pan** faire fondre le beurre dans une poêle; **to melt sb's heart** attendrir (le cœur de) qn

3 *n (sandwich)* **bacon/tuna melt** sandwich *m* au bacon/au thon recouvert de fromage fondu

►**melt away** *vi* (**a**) *(snow)* fondre complètement (**b**) *(clouds, vapour)* se dissiper; *(crowd)* se disperser; *(anger, objections, resistance etc)* se dissiper, s'évanouir

►**melt down** **1** *vt sep* (faire) fondre

2 *vi* (faire) fondre

meltdown ['meltdaʊn] *n* (**a**) *Nucl* fusion *f* (du cœur) (**b**) *Fig* désintégration *f*; *(of Stock Exchange)* dégringolade *f*

melted cheese ['meltɪd-] *n* fromage *m* fondu; **a melted cheese sandwich** un toast au fromage

melting ['meltɪŋ] **1** *adj* (**a**) *(becoming liquid)* fondant; **melting ice/snow** de la glace/neige qui fond

(**b**) *Fig* attendrissant; **she gave him a melting look** elle lui a lancé un regard attendrissant

2 *n (of ice, snow)* fonte *f*; *(of metal)* fusion *f*, fonte *f*

►► ***melting point*** point *m* de fusion; ***melting pot*** creuset *m*; *Fig* melting-pot *m*; *Fig* **a melting pot of several cultures** un mélange de plusieurs cultures; *Fig* **the American melting pot** le melting-pot *ou* le creuset américain

meltwater ['melt,wɔ:tə(r)] *n* eaux *fpl* de fonte

member ['membə(r)] **1** *n* (**a**) *(of club, union, political party etc)* membre *m*, adhérent(e) *m,f*; **to become a member of a club/society** devenir membre d'un club/d'une association; **he became a member of the party in 1995** il a adhéré au parti en 1995

(**b**) *(of group, family, class)* membre *m*; **to be a member of the family** faire partie de la famille; **it's a member of the cat family** il fait partie de *ou* il appartient à la famille des félins; **a member of the opposite sex** une personne du sexe opposé; **a member of the audience** un spectateur; **a member of the public** un membre du public

(**c**) *Archit* membre *m*

(**d**) *Math* membre *m*

(**e**) *Anat* membre *m*; **(male) member** membre *m* (viril)

2 Member *n (of legislative body)* **the Member (of Parliament) for Oxford** le député d'Oxford

►► *Am Fin* ***member bank*** banque *f* membre de la Réserve fédérale; ***Member of Congress*** membre *m* du Congrès; ***member country*** pays *m* membre; *St Exch* ***member firm*** société *f* membre; ***Member of the House of Representatives*** membre *m* de la Chambre des représentants; ***Member of Parliament*** membre *m* de la Chambre des communes, ≃ député(e) *m,f*; ***Member of the Scottish Parliament*** député(e) *m,f* du parlement écossais; ***member state*** État *m* membre

membership ['membəʃɪp] *n* (**a**) *(condition)* adhésion *f*; **membership of the union will entitle you to vote in meetings** l'adhésion au syndicat vous donne le droit de voter lors des réunions; **his country's membership of UNESCO is in question** l'adhésion de son pays à l'UNESCO est remise en question; **to apply for membership** faire une demande d'adhésion; **they have applied for membership to the EC** ils ont demandé à entrer dans *ou* à faire partie de la CEE; **to take up party membership** prendre sa carte du *ou* adhérer au parti; **she resigned her membership of the party** elle a rendu sa carte du parti; **it's hard to get membership of the golf club** il est difficile de devenir membre du club de golf

(**b**) *(body of members)* **our club has a large membership** notre club compte de nombreux adhérents *ou* membres; **membership increased last year** le nombre d'adhérents a augmenté l'année dernière; **the rank and file membership of the party** la base militante du parti; **we have a membership of about 20** nous avons environ 20 adhérents

►► ***membership card*** carte *f* d'adhérent *ou* de membre; ***membership fee*** cotisation *f*; ***membership list*** liste *f* des membres

membrane ['membreɪn] *n* membrane *f*

membranous ['membrənəs] *adj* membraneux

memento [mɪ'mentəʊ] *(pl* **mementos** *or* **mementoes**) *n* souvenir *m*; **a memento of our visit** un souvenir de notre visite

►► ***memento mori*** memento *m* mori

memo ['meməʊ] *(pl* **memos**) *n* note *f* de service

►► *Fin* ***memo account*** poste *m* de mémoire; ***memo pad*** bloc-notes *m*

memoir ['memwɑː(r)] **1** *n* (**a**) *(biography)* biographie *f* (**b**) *(essay, monograph)* mémoire *m*

2 memoirs *npl (autobiography)* mémoires *mpl*

memoirist ['memwɑːrɪst] *n* mémorialiste *mf*

memorabilia [ˌmemərə'bɪlɪə] *npl* souvenirs *mpl*

memorable ['memərəbəl] *adj* mémorable, inoubliable; **one of the more memorable scenes in the film** l'une des scènes les plus mémorables du film

memorably ['memərəblɪ] *adv* **a memorably hot summer** un été torride dont on se souvient encore; **as Racine so memorably puts it...** comme l'a si bien dit Racine...

memorandum [ˌmemə'rændəm] *(pl* **memoranda** [-də]) *n* (**a**) *Com* note *f*; **I've received a memorandum from head office** j'ai reçu une note (de service) du siège

(**b**) *Law* sommaire *m*; **memorandum and articles of association** statuts *mpl* de société

(**c**) *(diplomatic communication)* mémorandum *m*

(**d**) *(of contract, sale)* mémoire *m*

►► ***memorandum of association*** charte *f* constitutive d'une société à responsabilité limitée, acte *m* de société; ***memorandum book*** carnet *m*, calepin *m*, agenda *m*; *Banking* ***memorandum of satisfaction*** = document certifiant le paiement d'une hypothèque

memorial [mɪ'mɔːrɪəl] **1** *n* (**a**) *(monument)* monument *m* (commémoratif), mémorial *m*

(**b**) *(diplomatic memorandum)* mémorandum *m*; *(petition)* pétition *f*; *(official request)* requête *f*, mémoire *m*

2 *adj* (**a**) *(commemorative → statue, festival, tablet, plaque etc)* commémoratif; **the Marcel Proust memorial prize** le prix Marcel Proust

(**b**) *(of memory)* mémoriel

►► *Am* ***Memorial Day*** = dernier lundi du mois de mai (férié aux États-Unis en l'honneur des soldats américains morts pour la patrie); *Am* ***memorial park*** cimetière *m*; ***memorial service*** commémoration *f*

memorialist [mɪ'mɔːrɪəlɪst] *n* (**a**) *(petitioner)* pétitionnaire *mf* (**b**) *(writer of memoirs)* mémorialiste *mf*, auteur *m* de mémoires

memorialization [mɪˌmɔːrɪəlaɪ'zeɪʃən] *n Am (commemoration → of event, dead person)* commémoration *f*

memorialize [mɪ'mɔːrɪəlaɪz] *vt Am (commemorate → event, dead person)* commémorer

memorization [ˌmeməraɪ'zeɪʃən] *n* mémorisation *f*

memorize, -ise ['meməraɪz] *vt* mémoriser

memory ['memərɪ] *(pl* **memories**) **1** *n* (**a**) *(faculty)* mémoire *f*; **to have a good/bad memory** avoir (une) bonne/mauvaise mémoire; **to have a short memory** avoir la mémoire courte; **I've got a very good/bad memory for names** j'ai/je n'ai pas une très bonne mémoire des noms; **to quote a figure from memory** citer un chiffre de mémoire *ou* de tête; **to commit sth to memory** apprendre qch par cœur; **to lose one's memory** perdre la mémoire; **memory loss, loss of memory** perte *f* de mémoire; **it will long remain in our memories** nous nous en souviendrons longtemps; **if (my) memory serves me well** *or* **right, to the best of my memory** si j'ai bonne mémoire, autant que je m'en souvienne; **within living memory** de mémoire d'homme

(**b**) *(recollection)* souvenir *m*; **childhood memories** des souvenirs *mpl* d'enfance; **to have good/bad memories of sth** garder un bon/mauvais souvenir de qch; **I have very bad memories of that evening** j'ai de très mauvais souvenirs *ou* j'ai (gardé) un très mauvais souvenir de cette soirée; **to have no memory of sb/sth** n'avoir aucun souvenir de qn/qch; **her earliest memories are of music** ses plus anciens souvenirs sont des airs de musique; **to the memory of** à la mémoire de; **to keep the memory of sb/sth alive** *or* **green** garder vivant *ou* entretenir le souvenir de qn/qch; **I cherish his memory** je chéris sa mémoire *ou* son souvenir; **to take a trip down memory lane** *(visit place)* aller sur les lieux de son passé; **it's a real trip down memory lane hearing that song** cette chanson me rappelle ma jeunesse; **this television programme will take viewers on a trip down memory lane** cette émission rappellera de vieux souvenirs aux téléspectateurs

(**c**) *Comput* mémoire *f*; **how much memory does this computer have?** cet ordinateur a combien de mémoire?; **data is stored in the memory** les données sont (entrées) en mémoire

2 in memory of *prep* en souvenir de

►► *Comput* ***memory bank*** bloc *m* de mémoire; *Comput* ***memory capacity*** capacité *f* de mémoire; *Comput* ***memory card*** carte *f* mémoire; *Comput* ***memory cell*** cellule *f* mémoire; *Comput* ***memory chip*** puce *f* mémoire; *Comput* ***memory dump*** vidage *m* de mémoire; *Comput* ***memory expansion card*** carte *f* d'extension de mémoire; *Comput* ***memory management*** gestion *f* de mémoire; *Comput* ***memory mapping*** adresses *fpl* mémoire; ***memory span*** capacité *f* de mémorisation (de courte durée), *Spec* empan *m* mnémonique; *Psy* ***memory trace*** trace *f* mnésique; *Comput* ***memory upgrade*** ajout *m* de mémoire

memory-intensive *adj Comput (application)* qui prend beaucoup de place en mémoire

memory-loadable *adj Comput* chargeable en résident

memory-resident *adj Comput* résident en mémoire

Memphis ['memfɪs] *n* Memphis

memsahib ['memˌsɑːhɪb] *n Old-fashioned (in colonial India)* Européenne *f*; *(form of address)* Madame *f*

men [men] *pl of* **man**

►► *Am* ***men's room*** toilettes *fpl (pour hommes)*

menace ['menəs] **1** *n* (**a**) *(source of danger)* danger *m*; **these steps are a real menace at night** ces escaliers sont vraiment dangereux la nuit; **some drivers are a public menace** certains conducteurs constituent un véritable danger public *ou* sont de véritables dangers publics

(**b**) *(threat)* menace *f*; **the new weapon is a menace to world peace** cette nouvelle arme constitue une menace pour la paix mondiale; *Br Law* **to demand money with menaces** = exiger de l'argent sous la menace

(**c**) *Fam (annoying person or thing)* plaie *f*; **that kid's a menace** cet enfant est une véritable plaie

2 *vt* menacer

menacing ['menəsɪŋ] *adj* menaçant

menacingly ['menəsɪŋlɪ] *adv (act)* de manière menaçante; *(speak, look)* d'un air menaçant; *(say)* d'un ton menaçant

menagerie [mɪ'nædʒərɪ] *n* ménagerie *f*

menarche [me'nɑːkɪ] *n Physiol* ménarche *m*

Mencap ['menkæp] *n* = association britannique pour les enfants et les adultes handicapés mentaux

mend [mend] **1** *n* (**a**) *(darn)* reprise *f*; *(patch)* pièce *f*

(**b**) *Fam (idiom)* **to be on the mend** *(economy, situation)* s'améliorer ❑; *(ill person)* se remettre ❑, être en voie de guérison ❑

2 *vt* (**a**) *(repair → machine, television, broken vase)* réparer; *(→ clothes)* raccommoder; *(→ hem)* recoudre; *(darn → socks)* repriser, ravauder; **to get** *or* **to have sth mended** faire réparer qch

(**b**) *(rectify)* rectifier, réparer; **to mend matters** arranger les choses; **to mend one's ways** s'amender

3 *vi (improve → patient)* se remettre, être en voie de guérison; *(→ weather)* s'améliorer; *(→ fracture, broken bones)* se ressouder; *Fam* **you'll soon mend** tu t'en remettras ❑

mendacious [men'deɪʃəs] *adj Formal (statement, remark)* mensonger, fallacieux; *(person)* menteur

mendaciously [men'deɪʃəslɪ] *adv Formal* mensongèrement

mendacity [men'dæsətɪ] *(pl* **mendacities**) *n (UNCOUNT) Formal* (**a**) *(characteristic)* propension *f* au mensonge (**b**) *(of account, report)* caractère *m* mensonger (**c**) *(lie)* mensonge *m*, mensonges *mpl*

mendelevium [ˌmendɪ'liːvɪəm] *n Chem* mendélévium *m*

Mendelian [ˌmen'diːljən] *adj* mendélien

Mendelianism [ˌmen'diːljənɪzəm], **Mendelism** ['mendəlɪzəm] *n* mendélisme *m*

mendicant ['mendɪkənt] **1** *n* mendiant(e) *m,f*

2 *adj* mendiant

►► *Rel* ***mendicant order*** ordre *m* mendiant

mendicity [men'dɪsətɪ] *n* mendicité *f*

mending ['mendɪŋ] *n* raccommodage *m*; **I've got a whole pile of mending to do** j'ai toute une pile de raccommodage à faire

Menelaus [ˌmenɪ'leɪəs] *pr n Myth* Ménélas

menfolk ['menfəʊk] *npl* hommes *mpl*; **all the menfolk of the village** tous les hommes du village

MEng [ˌem'eŋ] *n Univ (abbr* **Master of Engineering**) *(person)* = titulaire d'une maîtrise d'ingénierie; *(qualification)* maîtrise *f* d'ingénierie

menhaden ['menˌheɪdən] *n Ich* menhaden *m*

menhir ['menˌhɪə(r)] *n* menhir *m*

menial ['miːnjəl] **1** *adj* **I find the work a bit menial** je trouve le travail un peu ingrat; **menial tasks** tâches *fpl* ingrates *ou* sans intérêt

2 *n (subordinate)* subalterne *mf*; *(servant)* domestique *mf*, *Pej* laquais *m*

meningeal [me'nɪndʒɪəl], **meningic** [me'nɪndʒɪk] *adj Anat* méningé

►► *Anat* ***meningeal artery*** artère *f* méningée;

Med ***meningeal involvement*** complication *f* méningée

meninges [me'nɪndʒiːz] *pl of* **meninx**

meningitis [ˌmenɪn'dʒaɪtɪs] *n Med* méningite *f*; **to have meningitis** avoir la méningite

meningococcus [meˌnɪŋgəʊ'kɒkəs] (*pl* **meningococci** [-'kɒksaɪ]) *n Med* méningocoque *m*

meningoencephalitis [meˌnɪŋgəʊensefə'laɪtɪs] *n Med* méningo-encéphalite *f*

meninx [me'nɪŋks] (*pl* **meninges** [me'nɪndʒiːz]) *n Anat* méninge *f*

meniscus [mə'nɪskəs] (*pl* **meniscuses** *or* **menisci** [-'nɪsaɪ]) *n* ménisque *m*

Mennonite ['menənaɪt] *n Rel* Mennonite *mf*

menology [mɪ'nɒlədʒɪ] (*pl* **menologies**) *n* ménologe *m*

menopausal [ˌmenə'pɔːzəl] *adj* ménopausique; *(woman)* à la ménopause

menopause ['menəpɔːz] *n* ménopause *f*; **the male menopause** l'andropause *f*

menorah [mə'nɔːrə] *n* menora *f*, chandelier *m* à sept branches

menorrhagia [ˌmenə'reɪdʒɪə] *n Med* ménorragie *f*

menorrhagic [ˌmenə'reɪdʒɪk] *adj Med* ménorragique

menorrhoea [ˌmenə'rɪə] *n Med* ménorrhée *f*

Mensa ['mensə] *n* = association de personnes ayant un QI particulièrement élevé

mensch [menʃ] *n Am Fam (man)* chic type *m*; *(woman)* brave femme *f*

menservants ['menˌsɜːvənts] *pl of* **manservant**

menses ['mensiːz] *npl Physiol* menstruations *fpl*, règles *fpl*

Menshevik ['menʃəvɪk] **1** *n* menchevik *mf*

2 *adj* menchevik

Menshevism ['menʃəvɪzəm] *n* menchévisme *m*

Menshevist ['menʃəvɪst] **1** *n* menchéviste *mf*

2 *adj* menchéviste

mens rea [menz'rɪə] *n Law* intention *f* délictueuse

menstrual ['menstrʊəl] *adj* menstruel

►► ***menstrual cycle*** cycle *m* menstruel

menstruate ['menstrʊeɪt] *vi* avoir ses règles

menstruation [ˌmenstrʊ'eɪʃən] *n* menstruation *f*, règles *fpl*

mensurable ['menʃərəbəl] *adj* mesurable

mensuration [ˌmenʃə'reɪʃən] *n* mesurage *m*, mensuration *f*

menswear ['menzˌweə(r)] *n (UNCOUNT)* vêtements *mpl* pour hommes

►► ***menswear department*** rayon *m* hommes

mental ['mentəl] *adj* (**a**) *(intellectual)* mental

(**b**) *(in the mind)* mental; **golf is fundamentally a mental game** le golf est un jeu qui se joue avant tout avec la tête; **to make a mental note of sth** prendre note de qch; **she made a mental note to speak to him about the matter** elle se promit de lui en parler

(**c**) *(psychiatric)* mental; **it can cause great mental strain** cela peut provoquer une grande tension nerveuse; **he had a mental breakdown** il a fait une dépression nerveuse

(**d**) *Fam (mad)* dingue, cinglé; **to go mental** *(go mad)* devenir dingue *ou* cinglé, perdre la boule; *(lose one's temper)* péter les plombs, péter une durite, piquer une crise; *Br* **it was a mental party!** c'était une fête vraiment démente *ou* dingue!; *Br* **you should have seen the way they were shouting at each other, it was mental!** t'aurais vu comme ils se criaient dessus, c'était dingue!

►► ***mental age*** âge *m* mental; ***mental arithmetic*** calcul *m* mental; ***mental block*** blocage *m* psychologique; **to have a mental block about sth** faire un blocage à propos de qch; ***mental cruelty*** cruauté *f* mentale; ***mental defective*** handicapé(e) *m,f* mental(e); ***mental deficiency*** déficience *f* ou débilité *f* mentale; ***mental faculties*** facultés *fpl* mentales *ou* intellectuelles; ***mental handicap*** handicap *m* mental; **to suffer from mental handicap** être handicapé(e) mental(e); ***mental health*** santé *f* mentale; ***mental home, mental hospital*** hôpital *m* psychiatrique; ***mental illness*** maladie *f* mentale; ***mental image*** image *f*; ***mental nurse*** infirmier(ère) *m,f* psychiatrique; ***mental patient*** malade *mf* mental(e); ***mental reservation*** doute *m*; ***mental ward*** service *m* psychiatrique

mentalism ['mentəlɪzəm] *n Phil* mentalisme *m*

mentality [men'tælətɪ] (*pl* **mentalities**) *n* mentalité *f*; **a civil servant mentality** une mentalité de fonctionnaire

mentally ['mentəlɪ] *adv* mentalement; **she's mentally and physically exhausted** elle est épuisée mentalement et physiquement; **mentally handicapped** handicapé mental; **to be mentally handicapped** être un (une) handicapé(e) mental(e); **the mentally handicapped** les handicapés mentaux; **mentally ill** malade *(mentalement)*; **the mentally ill** les malades *mpl* mentaux; **mentally defective** mentalement déficient; **mentally disturbed** déséquilibré (mental); **mentally retarded** (mentalement) arriéré

menthol ['menθɒl] *n* menthol *m*

►► ***menthol cigarette*** cigarette *f* au menthol *ou* mentholée

mentholated ['menθəleɪtɪd] *adj* au menthol, mentholé

mention ['menʃən] **1** *vt* (**a**) *(talk about)* mentionner, faire mention de, parler de; **he didn't mention his divorce** il n'a pas parlé de son divorce; **the newspapers didn't mention it** les journaux n'en ont pas fait mention *ou* n'en ont pas parlé; **she never mentions her past** elle ne parle jamais de son passé; **how dare you mention such a thing!** comment osez-vous parler d'une chose pareille!; **I shall never mention it again** je n'en parlerai jamais plus; **I'll mention it to him sometime** je lui en parlerai *ou* toucherai un mot à l'occasion; **thank you very much – don't mention it!** merci beaucoup – il n'y a pas de quoi! *ou* je vous en prie!; **it's not worth mentioning** ça ne vaut pas la peine d'en parler

(**b**) *(remark, point out)* signaler; **I should mention that it was dark at the time** il faut signaler *ou* je tiens à faire remarquer qu'il faisait nuit; **she did mention a couple of good restaurants to me** elle m'a bien donné l'adresse de *ou* elle m'a bien signalé quelques bons restaurants

(**c**) *(name, cite)* mentionner, citer, nommer; **don't mention any names** ne citez aucun nom; **someone, without mentioning any names, has broken my hairdryer** je ne citerai personne, mais quelqu'un a cassé mon séchoir à cheveux; **just mention my name to her** dites-lui que c'est de ma part; **to mention sb in one's will** coucher qn sur son testament; **a range of subjects too numerous to mention** des sujets trop nombreux pour être tous cités

2 *n* mention *f*; **there's no mention of it in the papers** les journaux n'en parlent pas; **to make no mention of sth** passer qch sous silence, ne pas faire mention de qch; **there is no mention of this extra charge in the brochure** la brochure ne mentionne pas ce supplément; **it got a mention in the local paper** le journal local en a parlé *ou* y a fait allusion; **special mention should be made of all the people behind the scenes** n'oublions pas tous ceux qui ont travaillé dans l'ombre *ou* en coulisse; **honourable mention** mention *f*

3 not to mention *prep* sans parler de; **not to mention the children** sans parler des enfants

> **Don't mention the war**
> Cette phrase vient de la série comique britannique des années 70 *Fawlty Towers*, dans laquelle John Cleese joue le rôle de Basil Fawlty, le patron d'un hôtel situé quelque part sur la côte sud de l'Angleterre. Dans un épisode intitulé *The Germans*, des clients allemands séjournent dans l'hôtel; Basil Fawlty a reçu un coup sur la tête et n'arrête pas de répéter à ses employés **whatever you do, don't mention the war** ("surtout, ne parlez pas de la guerre") mais lui-même ne cesse de faire référence à la Seconde Guerre mondiale en parlant aux clients allemands.
> Le sketch est tellement connu qu'aujourd'hui cette phrase est souvent utilisée par les Britanniques de façon humoristique lorsqu'ils parlent des Allemands.

mentor ['mentɔː(r)] **1** *n* mentor *m*

2 Mentor *pr n Myth* Mentor

menu ['menjuː] *n* (**a**) *(in restaurant)* menu *m*; *(written)* menu *m*, carte *f*; **on the menu** au menu; **they have a very varied menu** ils ont une carte très variée *ou* des menus très variés

(**b**) *Comput* menu *m*

►► *Comput* ***menu bar*** barre *f* de menu; *Comput* ***menu item*** élément *m* de menu; *Comput* ***menu option*** option *f* de menu

menu-controlled *adj Comput* contrôlé par menu

menu-driven *adj Comput* commandé par menu

meow = **miaow**

MEP [ˌemiː'piː] *n EU* (*abbr* **Member of the European Parliament**) député *m* à l'Assemblée européenne, membre *m* du Parlement européen

Mephistophelean, Mephistophelian [ˌmefɪstə'fiːljən] *adj* méphistophélique

Mephistopheles [ˌmefɪ'stɒfɪliːz] *pr n* Méphistophélès

mephitic [mɪ'fɪtɪk] *adj* méphitique

►► ***mephitic air*** air *m* méphitique, mofette *f*

meprobamate [mə'prəʊbəmeɪt] *n Pharm* méprobamate *m*

Merc [mɜːk] *n Fam* (*abbr* **Mercedes**) Mercedes® *f*

mercantile ['mɜːkəntaɪl] *adj* (**a**) *Com & Fin* commercial

(**b**) *Econ (concerning mercantilism)* mercantiliste

►► ***mercantile agency*** agence *f* commerciale; ***mercantile agent*** agent *m* commercial; ***mercantile agreement*** accord *m* commercial; ***mercantile bank*** banque *f* de commerce; ***mercantile broker*** agent *m* de change; ***mercantile company*** société *f* commerciale; ***mercantile law*** droit *m* commercial; ***mercantile nation*** nation *f* commerçante; ***mercantile operations*** opérations *fpl* mercantiles; ***mercantile paper*** papier *m* commercial *ou* de commerce; ***the mercantile system*** le système marchand

mercantilism ['mɜːkəntɪlɪzəm] *n* mercantilisme *m*

mercantilist ['mɜːkəntɪlɪst] **1** *n* mercantiliste *mf*

2 *adj* mercantiliste

mercaptan [mɜː'kæptæn] *n Chem* mercaptan *m*

mercaptide [mɜː'kæptaɪd] *n Chem* mercaptide *m*

Mercator's projection [mɜː'keɪtɔːz-] *n* projection *f* de Mercator

mercenarily ['mɜːsɪnərɪlɪ] *adv* de manière intéressée

mercenariness ['mɜːsɪnərɪnɪs] *n* caractère *m* intéressé; **they were surprised at his mercenariness** ils étaient étonnés qu'il agisse par intérêt

mercenary ['mɜːsɪnərɪ] (*pl* **mercenaries**) **1** *n* mercenaire *m*

2 *adj* (**a**) *Pej* intéressé; **for purely mercenary reasons** uniquement pour l'argent; **must you be so mercenary?** tu ne penses qu'à l'argent!

(**b**) *Mil* mercenaire

mercer ['mɜːsə(r)] *n Br Old-fashioned* négociant(e) *m,f* en tissus

mercerize, -ise ['mɜːsəraɪz] *vt* merceriser

mercerized ['mɜːsəraɪzd] *adj (cotton)* mercerisé

merchandise ['mɜːtʃəndaɪz] **1** *n (UNCOUNT)* marchandises *fpl*

2 *vt* commercialiser, marchandiser

merchandiser ['mɜːtʃəndaɪzə(r)] *n (object)* présentoir *m*; *(person)* marchandiseur *m*

merchandising ['mɜːtʃəndaɪzɪŋ] *n* merchandising *m*, marchandisage *m*, commercialisation *f*; **merchandising techniques** techniques *fpl* marchandes

merchant ['mɜːtʃənt] **1** *n* (**a**) *(trader)* négociant(e) *m,f*; *(shopkeeper)* marchand(e) *m,f*; **wool merchant** lainier(ère) *m,f*, négociant(e) *m,f* en laines; **wine merchant** marchand(e) *m,f* de vin

(**b**) *Fig* **a merchant of death** un marchand de mort; **a doom merchant** un prophète de malheur; *Fam* **speed merchant** *Br (fast driver)* chauffard *m*; *Am (athlete)* = coureur à pied très rapide; *Br Fam* **gossip merchant** commère *f*; *Br Fam* **rip-off** *or* **con merchant** arnaqueur(euse) *m,f*

2 *adj* marchand

►► ***merchant bank*** banque *f* d'affaires, banque *f* d'investissement; ***merchant banker*** banquier(-ère) *m,f* d'affaires; *Am* ***merchant marine*** marine *f* marchande; *Br* ***merchant navy*** marine *f* marchande; ***merchant seaman*** marin *m* de la marine marchande; ***merchant ship*** navire *m* de commerce; ***merchant wholesaler*** grossiste *mf*

'The Merchant of Venice' *Shakespeare* 'Le Marchand de Venise'

merchantable quality ['mɜːtʃəntəbəl-] *n Mktg* qualité *f* marchande; **all goods must be of merchantable quality** tous les articles doivent être vendables

merchantman ['mɜːtʃəntmən] (*pl* **merchantmen** [-mən]) *n Naut* navire *m* de commerce

Mercia ['mɜːsɪə] *n Hist* Mercie *f*

Mercian ['mɜːsɪən] *Hist* **1** *n* Mercien(enne) *m,f*
2 *adj* mercien

merciful ['mɜːsɪfʊl] *adj* clément, miséricordieux; **to be merciful to** *or* **towards sb** faire preuve de clémence *ou* de miséricorde envers qn; **a merciful act** un geste charitable; **her death was a merciful release** sa mort a été une délivrance

mercifully ['mɜːsɪfʊlɪ] *adv* (**a**) *(luckily)* heureusement, par bonheur; **mercifully, nobody was hurt** par bonheur il n'y a pas eu de blessés (**b**) *(with clemency)* avec clémence; **he acted mercifully** il a fait preuve de clémence *ou* de miséricorde

mercifulness ['mɜːsɪfʊlnɪs] *n* miséricorde *f*, clémence *f*

merciless ['mɜːsɪlɪs] *adj* impitoyable, implacable

mercilessly ['mɜːsɪlɪslɪ] *adv* sans merci, impitoyablement, implacablement; **the rain beat down mercilessly** la pluie tombait sans répit

mercilessness ['mɜːsɪlɪsnɪs] *n* caractère *m* impitoyable, manque *m* de pitié

mercurial [mɜː'kjʊərɪəl] *adj* (**a**) *(changeable → temperament, character, person)* versatile, changeant (**b**) *(lively)* vif, plein de vie, gai (**c**) *Chem* mercuriel

mercuriality [mɜːˌkjʊərɪ'ælɪtɪ] *n* (**a**) *(changeableness)* versatilité *f* (**b**) *(liveliness)* vivacité *f*

mercuric [mɜː'kjʊərɪk] *adj Chem* mercurique

mercurous ['mɜːkjʊrəs] *adj Chem* mercureux

mercury ['mɜːkjʊrɪ] **1** *n* (**a**) *Chem* mercure *m* (**b**) *Bot* mercuriale *f*
2 Mercury 1 *pr n Myth* Mercure
2 *n Astron* Mercure *f*
►► ***mercury poisoning*** empoisonnement *m* au mercure; ***the Mercury program*** = le programme spatial américain Mercury (1961-1963)

mercy ['mɜːsɪ] (*pl* **mercies**) **1** *n* (**a**) *(clemency)* clémence *f*, pitié *f*, indulgence *f*; *Rel* miséricorde *f*; **without mercy** sans pitié, sans merci; **she had** *or* **showed no mercy** elle n'a eu aucune pitié, elle a été sans pitié; **to have mercy on sb** avoir pitié de qn; **(have) mercy!** (ayez) pitié!; *Fig* **I'll have him begging** *or* **crying for mercy!** il va le regretter!; **may God in his mercy forgive you** que Dieu vous pardonne en sa miséricorde; **to throw oneself on sb's mercy** s'abandonner à la merci de qn
(**b**) *(blessing)* chance *f*, bonheur *m*; **it's a mercy that he doesn't know** heureusement qu'il ne sait pas, c'est une chance qu'il ne sache pas; **we must be thankful** *or* **grateful for small mercies** il faut savoir apprécier les moindres bienfaits; **it was really a mercy that she left** son départ fut un véritable soulagement *ou* une véritable délivrance
(**c**) *(power)* merci *f*; **to be at sb's/sth's mercy** être à la merci de qn/qch; **the ship was at the mercy of the storm** le navire était à la merci de la tempête; *Formal* **I throw myself on your mercy** je mets mon sort entre vos mains; *Ironic* **to leave sb to the tender mercies of sb** abandonner qn aux bons soins de qn
2 *comp (flight)* de secours, humanitaire
3 *exclam Old-fashioned* grâce!
►► ***mercy dash*** course *f* contre la mort; ***mercy killing*** *(euthanasia)* euthanasie *f*; *(individual death)* acte *m* d'euthanasie; ***mercy mission*** mission *f* humanitaire; **on a mercy mission** en mission humanitaire

mere[1] [mɪə(r)] *adj* seul, simple, pur; **I'm a mere beginner** je ne suis qu'un débutant; **it's a mere formality** ce n'est qu'une simple formalité; **the mere thought of it disgusts her** rien que d'y penser ça lui répugne; **the mere sight of fish makes me queasy** la seule vue du poisson me donne la nausée; **a mere 5 percent of the population** 5 pour cent seulement de la population; **she earns a mere £100 a week** elle ne gagne que 100 livres par semaine; **it's a mere memory now** ce n'est qu'un souvenir lointain maintenant; **his eyes light up at the merest mention of money** son regard s'allume dès qu'on commence à parler d'argent; **a mere assistant like me** un simple assistant comme moi; *Hum* **us mere mortals** nous autres, simples mortels

mere[2] *n Arch or Literary (lake)* (petit) lac *m*, étang *m*

merely ['mɪəlɪ] *adv* seulement, (tout) simplement; **I'm merely a beginner** je ne suis qu'un débutant; **I was merely wondering if this is the best solution** je me demandais seulement *ou* simplement si c'était la meilleure solution; **she merely glanced at it** elle n'a fait qu'y jeter *ou* elle s'est contentée d'y jeter un coup d'œil; **I mention this merely to draw attention to...** je n'ai dit cela que pour attirer l'attention sur...

meretrices [ˌmerɪ'traɪsiːz] *pl of* **meretrix**

meretricious [ˌmerɪ'trɪʃəs] *adj Formal (glamour, excitement)* factice; *(impression)* faux (fausse); *(ornamentation, design)* clinquant, tape-à-l'œil *(inv)*; *(style)* ampoulé, pompier

meretriciously [ˌmerɪ'trɪʃəslɪ] *adv Formal (designed)* dans un style clinquant *ou* tape-à-l'œil; *(written)* dans un style ampoulé

meretriciousness [ˌmerɪ'trɪʃəsnɪs] *n Formal (of ornamentation, design, style)* clinquant *m*

meretrix ['merɪtrɪks] (*pl* **meretrices** [ˌmerɪ'traɪsiːz]) *n* (**a**) *Arch or Literary* courtisane *f*, prostituée *f* (**b**) *Zool (mollusc)* mérétrice *f*, mérétrix *f*

merganser [mɜː'gænsə(r)] *n Orn* harle *m*

merge [mɜːdʒ] **1** *vi* (**a**) *(join → rivers)* se rejoindre, confluer; *(→ roads)* se rejoindre; *(→ colours, voices)* se confondre; *(→ cultures)* se mélanger; *Pol* s'unir; **the sea and sky merged** le ciel et la mer se confondaient
(**b**) *(vanish)* **the thief merged into the crowd** le voleur s'est fondu dans la foule
(**c**) *Fin (banks, companies)* s'amalgamer, fusionner; **they have merged with their former competitor** ils ont fusionné avec leur ancien concurrent
2 *vt* joindre, fusionner; *(banks, companies)* amalgamer, fusionner; *Comput* fusionner; *Pol* unifier; **the two regiments were merged (into one)** les deux régiments ont été regroupés

merger ['mɜːdʒə(r)] *n Fin (of banks, companies)* fusion *f*; *(takeover)* absorption *f*; **mergers and acquisitions** fusions *fpl* et acquisitions *fpl*
►► ***merger accounting*** = bases de préparation des comptes consolidés où deux sociétés se sont unifiées; ***merger premium*** prime *f* de fusion; ***merger talks*** discussions *fpl* en vue d'une fusion

meridian [mə'rɪdɪən] **1** *n* (**a**) *Astron, Geog & Med* méridien *m*; **the Greenwich meridian** le méridien de Greenwich
(**b**) *Math* méridienne *f*
(**c**) *Fig (zenith)* zénith *m*, sommet *m*, apogée *m*
2 *adj* (**a**) *(gen)* méridien
(**b**) *Literary* culminant; **he was at his meridian splendour** il était au zénith *ou* à l'apogée de sa gloire
►► ***meridian angle*** angle *m* méridien; ***meridian latitude*** latitude *f* méridienne; ***meridian line*** (ligne *f*) méridienne *f*

meridional [mə'rɪdɪənəl] **1** *n* méridional(e) *m,f*
2 *adj* (**a**) *(relating to a meridian)* méridien (**b**) *(southern)* méridional

meringue [mə'ræŋ] *n* meringue *f*

merino [mə'riːnəʊ] (*pl* **merinos**) **1** *n (sheep, wool)* mérinos *m*
2 *adj* en mérinos

meristem ['merɪstem] *n Bot* méristème *m*

merit ['merɪt] **1** *n* mérite *m*; **in order of merit** par ordre de mérite; **its great merit is its simplicity** ça a le grand mérite d'être simple; **promotion is on merit alone** l'avancement se fait uniquement au mérite; **I don't see much merit in the idea** cette idée ne me paraît pas particulièrement intéressante; **a work of great merit** une œuvre remarquable; **to judge a proposal on its merits** juger une proposition pour ce qu'elle vaut; **the relative merits of theatre and cinema** les avantages *mpl* respectifs du théâtre et du cinéma; **the project has the further merit of being cheap** le projet a de plus l'avantage d'être bon marché
2 *vt* mériter; **the case merits closer examination** le cas mérite d'être examiné de plus près
►► ***merit bonus*** prime *f* de rendement; ***merit increase*** augmentation *f* au mérite; ***merit rating*** notation *f* du personnel; *Am Admin* ***merit system*** système *m* d'avancement fondé sur le mérite

meritocracy [ˌmerɪ'tɒkrəsɪ] (*pl* **meritocracies**) *n* méritocratie *f*

meritorious [ˌmerɪ'tɔːrɪəs] *adj (person)* méritant; *(act)* méritoire, louable

meritoriously [ˌmerɪ'tɔːrɪəslɪ] *adv* méritoirement, d'une façon méritoire

meritoriousness [ˌmerɪ'tɔːrɪəsnɪs] *n* mérite *m*

Merlin ['mɜːlɪn] *pr n* Merlin; **Merlin the Wizard** Merlin l'Enchanteur

merlin ['mɜːlɪn] *n Orn* émerillon *m*

merlon ['mɜːlən] *n* merlon *m*

mermaid ['mɜːmeɪd] *n Myth* sirène *f*

merman ['mɜːmæn] (*pl* **mermen** [-men]) *n Myth* triton *m*

Merovingian [ˌmerə'vɪndʒɪən] **1** *n* Mérovingien(enne) *m,f*
2 *adj* mérovingien

merrie ['merɪ] *adj Arch or Literary* **merrie England** l'Angleterre du bon vieux temps

merrily ['merɪlɪ] *adv (happily)* joyeusement, gaiement; *(blithely)* allègrement

merriment ['merɪmənt] *n (joy)* joie *f*, gaieté *f*; *(laughter)* rire *m*, rires *mpl*, hilarité *f*; **there was much merriment at the thought of this** l'idée fit beaucoup rire; **sounds of merriment came from the garden** on entendait des éclats de rire venant du jardin

merry ['merɪ] (*compar* **merrier**, *superl* **merriest**) *adj* (**a**) *(happy)* joyeux, gai; **Merry Christmas!** Joyeux Noël!; **to make merry** s'amuser; *Prov* **the more the merrier** plus on est de fous, plus on rit
(**b**) *Fam (tipsy)* éméché, pompette
(**c**) *(good)* **the merry month of May** le joli mois de mai; *Literature* **the merry men** Robin des Bois et ses joyeux compères; *Hum* **the Minister and his merry men** le ministre et son état-major; **Merry England** l'Angleterre du bon vieux temps
(**d**) *Fam* **the weather is playing merry hell with the rail timetables** le mauvais temps a complètement chamboulé l'horaire des trains; *Fam* **my back is giving me merry hell** mon dos me fait souffrir le martyre; *Br* **to lead sb a merry dance** *(exasperate)* donner du fil à retordre à qn; *(deceive)* faire marcher qn; *(in romantic context)* mener qn en bateau
►► ***the Merry Monarch*** = surnom du roi Charles II

'The Merry Widow' *Lehar* 'La Veuve joyeuse'

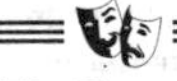

'The Merry Wives of Windsor' *Shakespeare* 'Les Joyeuses commères de Windsor'

merry-go-round *n* manège *m*, *Can, Belg & Suisse* carrousel *m*; *Fig (whirl)* tourbillon *m*

merrymaker ['merɪˌmeɪkə(r)] *n* fêtard(e) *m,f*

merrymaking ['merɪˌmeɪkɪŋ] *n (UNCOUNT)* réjouissances *fpl*, festivités *fpl*

Mersey ['mɜːzɪ] *n* **the (river) Mersey** la Mersey

Merseyside ['mɜːzɪˌsaɪd] *n* le Merseyside, = comté dans le nord-ouest de l'Angleterre; **in Merseyside** dans le Merseyside

mesa ['meɪsə] *n* mesa *f*

mescal ['meskæl] *n* (**a**) *Bot* peyotl *m* (**b**) *(alcohol)* mescal *m*, mezcal *m*

mescaline ['meskəliːn], **mescalin** ['meskəlɪn] *n* mescaline *f*

meseems [miː'siːmz] *vt Arch or Literary* ce me semble

mesembryanthemum [ˌmezəmbraɪ'ænθɪməm] *n Bot* mésembryanthème *m*

mesencephalic [ˌmesense'fælɪk] *adj Anat* mésencéphalique

mesencephalon [ˌmesen'sefəlɒn] *n Anat* mésencéphale *m*

mesenteric [ˌmesen'terɪk] *adj Anat* mésentérique

mesentery ['mesəntərɪ] *n Anat* mésentère *m*; *Zool* fraise *f*

mesh [meʃ] **1** *n* (**a**) *(of net)* mailles *fpl*; *(of sieve)* grille *f*; **the mesh is too fine** les mailles sont trop serrées; **fine-mesh stockings** des bas *mpl* à

mailles fines; **3 cm mesh netting** du filet *m* à mailles de 3 cm; **a mesh shopping bag** un filet à provisions
(**b**) *(fabric)* tissu *m* à mailles; **nylon mesh** tulle *m* de nylon
(**c**) *Fig (trap)* rets *mpl*, piège *m*; **caught in a mesh of lies** enfermé dans *ou* prisonnier de ses propres mensonges
(**d**) *Fig (network)* réseau *m*; **a mesh of intrigue** un réseau d'intrigues
(**e**) *Tech (of gears)* engrenage *m*; **in mesh** en prise
2 *vi* (**a**) *(be in harmony)* s'harmoniser, s'accorder; **our temperaments just don't mesh** nos caractères ne s'accordent pas
(**b**) *(tally, coincide)* cadrer, concorder; **to mesh with** cadrer *ou* concorder avec
(**c**) *Tech (gears)* s'engrener

meshing ['meʃɪŋ] *n (UNCOUNT)* rets *mpl*, mailles *fpl*

meshuga, meshugga [mə'ʃʊgə] *adj Am Fam* dingue, taré, cinglé

mesial ['mi:zɪəl] *adj Anat* médian

mesmeric [mez'merɪk] *adj Formal* magnétique, hypnotique

mesmerism ['mezmərɪzəm] *n* (**a**) *(hypnotism)* hypnotisme *m* (**b**) *(Mesmer's doctrine)* mesmérisme *m*

mesmerist ['mezmərɪst] *n* hypnotiseur(euse) *m,f*

mesmerize, -ise ['mezməraɪz] *vt* (**a**) *(hypnotise)* hypnotiser (**b**) *(entrance)* ensorceler, envoûter

mesmerizing ['mezməraɪzɪŋ] *adj* fascinant

mesoblast ['mesəʊblæst] *n Biol* mésoblaste *m*

mesocarp ['mesəʊkɑ:p] *n Bot* mésocarpe *m*

mesocephalic [,mesəʊse'fælɪk] *adj Anat* mésocéphalique

mesoderm ['mesəʊdɜ:m] *n Biol* mésoderme *m*

mesodermal [,mesəʊ'dɜ:məl], **mesodermic** [,mesəʊ'dɜ:mɪk] *adj Biol* mésodermique

Mesolithic [,mesə'lɪθɪk] *Geol* **1** *n* mésolithique *m*
2 *adj* mésolithique

mesomorph ['mesəʊmɔ:f] *n* mésomorphe *m*

mesomorphic [,mesəʊ'mɔ:fɪk], **mesomorphous** [,mesəʊ'mɔ:fəs] *adj* mésomorphe

meson ['mi:zɒn] *n Phys* méson *m*

mesophyll ['mesəʊfɪl], **mesophyllum** [,mesəʊ'fɪləm] *n Bot* mésophylle *m*

mesophyte ['mesəʊfaɪt] *n Bot* mésophyte *f*

Mesopotamia [,mesəpə'teɪmjə] *n* Mésopotamie *f*; **in Mesopotamia** en Mésopotamie

Mesopotamian [,mesəpə'teɪmjən] **1** *n* Mésopotamien(enne) *m,f*
2 *adj* mésopotamien

mesosphere ['mesəʊsfɪə] *n* mésosphère *f*

mesothermal [,mesəʊ'θɜ:məl] *adj* (**a**) *Phys & Geol* mésothermal (**b**) *Bot* mésotherme

mesothorax [,mesəʊ'θɔ:ræks] *n Anat & Zool* mésothorax *m*

Mesozoic [,mesə'zəʊɪk] *adj Geol* mésozoïque

MESS [mes]

désordre	▸ **1 (a)**
saleté	▸ **1 (b)**
gâchis	▸ **1 (c)**
pétrin	▸ **1 (d)**
mess	▸ **1 (e)**
salir	▸ **2**
embêter	▸ **3 (a)**

1 *n* (**a**) *(untidiness)* désordre *m*, fouillis *m*; **what a mess!** quel désordre!, quelle pagaille!; **Fiona's room is (in) a real mess!** il y a une de ces pagailles *ou* un de ces fouillis dans la chambre de Fiona!; **my papers are in a mess** mes papiers sont en désordre; **clear up this mess!** mets un peu d'ordre là-dedans!, range un peu tout ce fouillis!; *Fam* **your essay is a real mess!** ta rédaction est un vrai torchon!; *Fam* **his face was a complete mess after the fight** après la bagarre il avait le visage tout amoché; **my hair's a mess!** je suis coiffé n'importe comment!; **I feel a mess** je suis dans un état lamentable; **you're a mess, go and clean up** tu n'es pas présentable, va t'arranger
(**b**) *(dirtiness)* saleté *f*, saletés *fpl*; **clean up that mess!** nettoie un peu ces saletés *ou* cette crasse!; **the cooker is (in) a horrible mess** la cuisinière est vraiment sale *ou* dégoûtante; **the dog has made a mess on the carpet** le chien a fait des saletés sur le tapis
(**c**) *(muddle)* gâchis *m*; **to make a mess of sth** gâcher qch; **she's made a real mess of her life** elle a vraiment gâché sa vie; **to make a mess of things** tout gâcher; **I'm afraid I've made a mess of the travel arrangements** je suis désolé, je me suis trompé dans les préparatifs de voyage; **this country is in a mess!** la situation dans ce pays n'est pas vraiment réjouissante!
(**d**) *Fam (predicament)* pétrin *m*; **he's got himself into a bit of a mess** il s'est fourré dans de beaux draps *ou* dans le pétrin; **thanks for getting me out of that mess** merci de m'avoir tiré de ce pétrin
(**e**) *Mil (canteen)* mess *m*; **the whole mess got food poisoning** tous ceux qui ont pris leur repas au mess ont été victimes d'une intoxication alimentaire
(**f**) *Mil (food)* ordinaire *m*, gamelle *f*
(**g**) *Arch (dish)* plat *m*; *Bible* **a mess of pottage** un plat de lentilles
2 *vt (dirty)* salir, souiller
3 *vi* (**a**) *Fam (meddle)* **to mess with sb** embêter qn; **don't mess with me!** ne me cherche pas!; **you shouldn't mess with people like that** *(get involved with)* tu ne devrais pas fréquenter des gens comme ça; *(get on wrong side of)* tu ne devrais pas mécontenter ces gens-là; **that's what happens when you mess with drugs!** voilà ce qui arrive quand on touche à la drogue!
(**b**) *Br Fam (joke)* **it's true, no messing!** c'est vrai, sans blagues!
(**c**) *Mil* manger *ou* prendre ses repas au mess; **they don't mess with the other officers** ils ne mangent pas avec les autres officiers
▸▸ *Naut* ***mess deck*** poste *m* d'équipage; *Mil* ***mess hall*** cantine *f*; *Mil* ***mess jacket*** veston *m* de tenue de soirée; *(civilian)* veste *f* courte; ***mess kit*** *Mil (eating equipment)* gamelle *f*; *Br Fam (clothes)* tenue *f* de soirée; *Br* ***mess tin*** gamelle *f*

▸**mess about, mess around** *Fam* **1** *vt sep (person)* **to mess sb about** se moquer de qn, faire tourner qn en bourrique; **I'm fed up with being messed about by men** j'en ai marre des hommes qui me font tourner en bourrique
2 *vt insep (potter about)* bricoler, *(lounge about)* traîner; **I'm just going to mess about the house this weekend** je vais rester à la maison et me la couler douce ce week-end
3 *vi Br* (**a**) *(waste time)* glander, glandouiller; *(dawdle, hang around)* traîner; **get on with the job and stop messing about!** mettez-vous au travail et que ça saute!
(**b**) *(potter)* bricoler; **I spent the weekend messing about in the house** j'ai passé le week-end à faire des bricoles dans la maison; **he likes messing about in the garden** il aime s'occuper dans le jardin
(**c**) *(play the fool)* faire l'imbécile; **stop messing about and listen to me!** arrête de faire l'imbécile et écoute-moi!
(**d**) *(meddle, fiddle)* tripoter, tripatouiller; **don't mess about with my computer** ne tripote pas mon ordinateur; *Fig* **to mess about with sb** *(annoy)* embêter qn; *(have an affair)* coucher avec qn; **if I catch her messing about with my husband I'll kill her!** si je l'attrape à faire du gringue à mon mari, je la tue!

▸**mess up** **1** *vt sep* (**a**) *(make disorderly → room, papers)* mettre en désordre; **stop it, you'll mess up my hair!** arrête, tu vas me décoiffer!
(**b**) *Fam (spoil)* ficher en l'air; **that's really messed up our plans!** ça a vraiment fichu nos projets en l'air!
(**c**) *(dirty)* salir, souiller
2 *vi esp Am Fam (make a mistake)* tout rater; **to mess up on an exam** merdouiller dans *ou* à un examen

message ['mesɪdʒ] **1** *n* (**a**) *(communication)* message *m*, commission *f*; *(written)* message *m*, mot *m*; *Comput (e-mail)* message *m*; **to take/to leave a message** prendre/laisser un message; **can you give her a message?** pouvez-vous lui transmettre un message?; **would you like to leave a message for him?** voulez-vous (lui) laisser un message?
(**b**) *(theme → of book, advert)* message *m*; *(teaching → of prophet)* message *m*, enseignement *m*; **a book/film with a message** un livre/film qui fait passer un message; **the film's message is clear** le message qui ressort du film est clair; **to get one's message across** se faire comprendre; *Fam* **(do you) get the message?** tu piges?; *Fam* **people seem to be getting the message, the message seems to be getting across** les gens ont l'air de commencer à comprendre ❑
(**c**) *Scot* commission *f*, course *f*; **to go a message for sb** faire une commission pour qn
(**d**) *Ling* message *m*
2 messages *npl Ir & Scot (shopping)* courses *fpl*; **he's out doing the messages** il est sorti faire les courses
▸▸ *Br Comput* ***message body*** corps *m* du message; *Comput* ***message box*** boîte *f* de dialogue; *Comput* ***message handling*** messagerie *f* (électronique); *Comput* ***message header*** en-tête *m* de message; *Comput* ***message switching*** commutation *f* de messages

messaging ['mesɪdʒɪŋ] *n Comput* messagerie *f* électronique

messenger ['mesɪndʒə(r)] *n (gen)* messager(ère) *m,f*; *(errand boy → in office)* coursier *m*; *(in hotel)* chasseur *m*, coursier *m*; *(in post office)* télégraphiste *mf*; *Br* **King's/Queen's messenger** ≃ courrier *m* d'État; **by special messenger** par porteur spécial; **bicycle messenger** coursier(ère) *m,f* à bicyclette
▸▸ ***messenger boy*** coursier *m*, garçon *m* de courses; *Biol* ***messenger RNA*** ARN *m* messager; ***messenger service*** messagerie *f*

Messenia [me'si:nɪə] *n Geog* la Messénie

messiah [mɪ'saɪə] **1** *n* messie *m*
2 Messiah *n Rel* Messie *m*

♫

'Messiah' *Handel* 'Le Messie'

messianic [,mesɪ'ænɪk] *adj* messianique

messianism [me'saɪənɪzəm] *n* messianisme *m*

messily ['mesɪlɪ] *adv* (**a**) *(untidily)* mal, de façon peu soignée; *(in a disorganized way)* n'importe comment; **she did it really messily** elle l'a vraiment fait n'importe comment; *Fig* **the affair ended messily** l'affaire s'est mal terminée (**b**) *(dirtily)* comme un cochon

Messina [me'si:nə] *n* Messine

messiness ['mesɪnɪs] *n* (**a**) *(disorder)* désordre *m*, pagaille *f* (**b**) *(dirt)* saleté *f* (**c**) *(unpleasant situation)* difficultés *fpl*, confusion *f*

messmate ['mes,meɪt] *n* = personne qui mange à la même table

mess-room *n Naut* carré *m*

Messrs, Messrs. ['mesəz] *npl (abbr* **Messieurs**) MM *mpl*

messuage ['meswɪdʒ] *n Law* propriété *f*, maison *f* avec ses dépendances

mess-up *n Fam* confusion ❑ *f*; **there was a mess-up over the dates** on s'est embrouillé dans les dates

messy ['mesɪ] *(compar* **messier**, *superl* **messiest**) *adj* (**a**) *(dirty → hands, clothes)* sale, malpropre; *(→ job)* salissant; **he's a messy eater** il mange salement; **don't get all messy** ne te salis pas; **he did some painting and got all messy** il a fait de la peinture et il s'en est mis partout
(**b**) *(untidy → place)* en désordre, désordonné, mal tenu; *(→ person)* peu soigné, négligé, débraillé; *(→ hair)* ébouriffé, en désordre, en bataille
(**c**) *(badly done)* bâclé; **a messy piece of homework** un devoir bâclé
(**d**) *Fig (complicated)* compliqué, embrouillé, délicat; **a messy situation** une situation délicate *ou* difficile; **a very messy business** une affaire très embrouillée; **a messy divorce** un divorce difficile *ou* compliqué

mestiza [me'sti:zə] *n* = métisse d'Hispano-Américain et d'Indien d'Amérique

mestizo [me'sti:zəʊ] *(pl* **mestizos**) *n* = métis d'Hispano-Américain et d'Indien d'Amérique

Met [met] *n Fam* (**a**) *Am (abbr* **Metropolitan Opera**) **the Met** le Metropolitan Opera ❑ *(opéra de New York)* (**b**) *Am (abbr* **Metropolitan Museum of Art**) = un des principaux musées américains, à New York (**c**) *Br (abbr* **Metropolitan Police**) police *f* londonienne ❑

►► *Br Met* ***Met Office*** = services météorologiques britanniques

met [met] *pt & pp of* **meet**

meta- ['metə] *pref* méta-

metabolic [ˌmetə'bɒlɪk] *adj* métabolique; **metabolic rate** taux *m* métabolique

metabolism [mɪ'tæbəlɪzəm] *n* métabolisme *m*; **to have a fast metabolism** avoir un métabolisme rapide

metabolite [mɪ'tæbəlaɪt] *n* métabolite *m*

metabolize, -ise [mɪ'tæbəlaɪz] *vt* métaboliser

metacarpal [ˌmetə'kɑːpəl] *Anat* **1** *n* métacarpien *m*

2 *adj* métacarpien

metacarpus [ˌmetə'kɑːpəs] (*pl* **metacarpi** [-paɪ]) *n Anat* métacarpe *m*

metacentre, *Am* **metacenter** ['metəsentə(r)] *n Phys* métacentre *m*; **height of the metacentre** hauteur *f* métacentrique

metacentric [ˌmetə'sentrɪk] *adj Phys* métacentrique

metadyne ['metədaɪn] *n Elec* métadyne *f*

metagenesis [ˌmetə'dʒenɪsɪs] *n Biol* métagénèse *f*

metal ['metəl] (*Br pt & pp* **metalled,** *cont* **metalling,** *Am pt & pp* **metaled,** *cont* **metaling**) **1** *n* (**a**) *(gen) & Chem* métal *m*; **made of metal** en métal

(**b**) *Typ* plomb *m*

(**c**) *(for road-building)* cailloutis *m*, empierrement *m*

(**d**) *(in glassmaking)* pâte *f* de verre

2 *comp* en métal

3 *vt* (**a**) *(cover with metal)* couvrir de métal

(**b**) *(road)* empierrer

4 metals *npl Br Rail* voie *f* ferrée, rails *mpl*

►► ***metal detector*** détecteur *m* de métaux; ***metal engraver*** graveur(euse) *m,f* sur métaux; ***metal fatigue*** fatigue *f* du métal; ***metal polish*** produit *m* pour faire briller les métaux; ***metal wood*** *(golf club)* bois-métal *m*

metalanguage ['metəˌlæŋgwɪdʒ] *n* métalangue *f*, métalangage *m*

metaldehyde [me'tældɪhaɪd] *n Chem* métaldéhyde *m*

metaled *Am* = **metalled**

metalhead ['metəlˌhed] *n Fam* fan *mf* de heavy metal ❑, hardeux(euse) *m,f*

metaling *Am* = **metalling**

metalinguistic [ˌmetəlɪŋ'gwɪstɪk] *adj* métalinguistique

metalinguistics [ˌmetəlɪŋ'gwɪstɪks] *n (UNCOUNT)* métalinguistique *f*

metalled, *Am* **metaled** ['metəld] *adj (road)* revêtu *(de macadam, de pierres etc)*

metallic [mɪ'tælɪk] *adj* (**a**) *Chem* métallique (**b**) *(voice)* métallique; *(sound)* métallique, grinçant; *(taste)* de métal; **metallic blue** bleu *m* métallisé; **metallic grey** gris *m* métallisé

►► *Chem* ***metallic bond*** liaison *f* métallique; *Chem* ***metallic oxide*** oxyde *m* métallique; ***metallic paint*** peinture *f* métallisée

metalliferous [ˌmetə'lɪfərəs] *adj* métallifère

metalling, *Am* **metaling** ['metəlɪŋ] *n (of road)* revêtement *m (en macadam, en pierre etc)*

metallize, -ise ['metəlaɪz] *vt* métalliser

metalloid ['metəlɔɪd] *n Chem* métalloïde *m*

metallurgic [ˌmetə'lɜːdʒɪk], **metallurgical** [ˌmetə'lɜːdʒɪkəl] *adj* métallurgique

metallurgist [me'tælədʒɪst] *n* métallurgiste *mf*, ingénieur *m* en métallurgie

metallurgy [me'tælədʒɪ] *n* métallurgie *f*

metalware ['metəlweə(r)] *n* ustensiles *mpl* (domestiques) en métal

metalwork ['metəlwɜːk] *n* (**a**) *(objects)* ferronnerie *f* (**b**) *(activity)* travail *m* des métaux (**c**) *(metal framework)* tôle *f*, métal *m*; *(of crashed car, plane)* carcasse *f*

metalworker ['metəlˌwɜːkə(r)] *n* (**a**) *(in factory)* métallurgiste *mf* (**b**) *(craftsman)* ferronnier(ère) *m,f*

metalworking ['metəlˌwɜːkɪŋ] *n* travail *m* des métaux

metamathematics [ˌmetəmæθə'mætɪks] *n (UNCOUNT)* métamathématique *f*

metamere ['metəmɪə(r)] *n Zool* métamère *m*

metameric [ˌmetə'merɪk] *adj Chem* métamère

metamerism [me'tæmərɪzəm], **metamery** [me'tæmərɪ] *n Zool & Chem* métamérie *f*

metamorphic [ˌmetə'mɔːfɪk] *adj* métamorphique

metamorphism [ˌmetə'mɔːfɪzəm] *n* métamorphisme *m*

metamorphose [ˌmetə'mɔːfəʊz] **1** *vt* métamorphoser

2 *vi* se métamorphoser; **to metamorphose into sth** se métamorphoser en qch

metamorphosis [ˌmetə'mɔːfəsɪs,ˌmetəmɔː'fəʊsɪs] (*pl* **metamorphoses** [-siːz]) *n* métamorphose *f*

'Metamorphosis' *Kafka* 'La Métamorphose'

metamorphous [ˌmetə'mɔːfəs] *adj* métamorphique

metaphase ['metəfeɪz] *n Biol* métaphase *f*

metaphor ['metəfə(r)] *n* métaphore *f*; **it's a metaphor for loneliness** c'est une métaphore de la solitude

metaphoric [ˌmetə'fɒrɪk], **metaphorical** [ˌmetə'fɒrɪkəl] *adj* métaphorique

metaphorically [ˌmetə'fɒrɪkəlɪ] *adv* métaphoriquement; **metaphorically speaking** métaphoriquement

metaphrase ['metəfreɪz] **1** *n* traduction *f* littérale *ou* mot à mot

2 *vt* traduire littéralement *ou* mot à mot

metaphysic [ˌmetə'fɪzɪk] *n* métaphysique *f*

metaphysical [ˌmetə'fɪzɪkəl] *adj* métaphysique; *Fig (abstract)* métaphysique, abstrait

metaphysically [ˌmetə'fɪzɪkəlɪ] *adv* métaphysiquement

metaphysician [ˌmetəfɪ'zɪʃən] *n* métaphysicien(enne) *m,f*

metaphysics [ˌmetə'fɪzɪks] *n (UNCOUNT)* métaphysique *f*

metaplasia [ˌmetə'pleɪzɪə] *n Physiol* métaplasie *f*

metaplasm ['metəˌplæzəm] *n Ling* métaplasme *m*

metapsychology [ˌmetəsaɪ'kɒlədʒɪ] *n* métapsychologie *f*

metastable ['metəˌsteɪbəl] *adj Phys* métastable

metastasis [me'tæstəsɪs] (*pl* **metastases** [-siːz]) *n* métastase *f*

metastasize, -ise [me'tæstəsaɪz] *vi* métastaser

metastatic [ˌmetə'stætɪk] *adj* métastatique

metatarsal [ˌmetə'tɑːsəl] *Anat* **1** *n* métatarsien *m*

2 *adj* métatarsien

metatarsus [ˌmetə'tɑːsəs] (*pl* **metatarsi** [-saɪ]) *n Anat* métatarse *m*

metatheory [ˌmetə'θɪərɪ] (*pl* **metatheories**) *n Phil* métathéorie *f*

metathesis [mɪ'tæθəsɪs] (*pl* **metatheses** [-siːz]) *n Ling & Chem* métathèse *f*

metazoan [ˌmetə'zəʊən] *n Zool* métazoaire *m*

►**mete out** [miːt-] *vt sep (punishment)* infliger; *(judgment, justice)* rendre; *(reward)* décerner

metempsychosis [ˌmetəmsaɪ'kəʊsɪs] *n* métempsychose *f*

meteor ['miːtɪə(r)] *n Astron* météore *m*

►► ***meteor shower*** pluie *f* d'étoiles filantes, averse *f* météorique

meteoric [ˌmiːtɪ'ɒrɪk] *adj* (**a**) *Astron* météorique (**b**) *Fig* fulgurant, très rapide; **Hitler's meteoric rise to power** l'ascension fulgurante d'Hitler au pouvoir

meteorically [ˌmiːtɪ'ɒrɪkəlɪ] *adv* comme un météore

meteorite ['miːtjəraɪt] *n Astron* météorite *f*

meteoritic [ˌmiːtɪə'rɪtɪk] *adj Astron* météoritique

meteorograph ['miːtjərəˌgrɑːf] *n Met* météorographe *m*

meteoroid ['miːtjərɔɪd] *n Astron* météoroïde *m*

meteorological [ˌmiːtjərə'lɒdʒɪkəl] *adj* météorologique

►► *Met* ***meteorological office*** office *m* météorologique

meteorologist [ˌmiːtjə'rɒlədʒɪst] *n* météorologue *mf*, météorologiste *mf*

meteorology [ˌmiːtjə'rɒlədʒɪ] *n* météorologie *f*

meter ['miːtə(r)] **1** *n* (**a**) *(for water, gas, electricity)* compteur *m*; **to read the meter** relever le compteur; **to feed the meter** mettre des pièces dans le compteur

(**b**) **(parking) meter** parcmètre *m*, parcomètre *m*; **(taxi) meter** taximètre *m*, compteur *m*; *Fam* **I'm on a meter** je suis garé à un parcmètre ❑

(**c**) *Am* = **metre**

2 *vt* (**a**) *(electricity, water, gas)* mesurer à l'aide d'un compteur

(**b**) *(mail)* affranchir *(avec une machine)*

►► *Am Fam* ***meter maid*** contractuelle ❑ *f*, pervenche *f*, *Can* préposée *f* au stationnement

meterage ['miːtərɪdʒ] *n* mesurage *m* à l'aide d'un compteur

metering ['miːtərɪŋ] *n* mesurage *m* à l'aide d'un compteur

►► ***metering device*** dispositif *m* de mesure; ***metering head*** sonde *f* de mesure; ***metering pin*** pointeau *m* calibreur; ***metering screw*** vis *f* de réglage

methadone ['meθəˌdəʊn] *n Pharm* méthadone *f*

►► ***methadone programme*** traitement *m* d'entretien à la méthadone; **to be on the methadone programme** suivre un traitement d'entretien à la méthadone

methaemoglobin, *Am* **methemoglobin** [meˌθiːmə'gləʊbɪn] *n Chem* méthémoglobine *f*

methaemoglobinaemia, *Am* **methemoglobinemia** [meˌθiːməgləʊbɪ'niːmɪə] *n Med* méthémoglobinémie *f*

methamphetamine [ˌmeθæm'fetəmiːn] *n Pharm* méthamphétamine *f*

methane ['miːθeɪn] *n Chem* méthane *m*

►► ***methane series*** alcanes *mpl*

methanoic acid [meθə'nəʊɪk-] *n Chem* acide *m* formique

methanol ['meθənɒl] *n Chem* méthanol *m*

methemoglobin, methemoglobinemia *Am* = **methaemoglobin, methaemoglobinaemia**

methinks [mɪ'θɪŋks] (*pt* **methought** [-'θɔːt]) *vt Arch or Hum* ce me semble

methionine [me'θaɪəniːn] *n Biol & Chem* méthionine *f*

method ['meθəd] **1** *n* (**a**) *(means)* méthode *f*, moyen *m*; *(manner)* manière *f*; *(instruction)* méthode *f*, mode *m* d'emploi; **method of doing sth** manière *f* de faire qch, méthode *f* (employée) pour faire qch; *Fin* **method of payment** mode *m ou* modalité *f* de paiement, mode *m ou* modalité *f* de règlement

(**b**) *(procedure)* méthode *f*, procédé *m*; *(theory)* théorie *f*, méthode *f*; **experimental methods** des méthodes *fpl* expérimentales; **their methods of investigation have come under fire** la façon dont ils mènent leurs enquêtes a été critiquée, on a critiqué leur façon d'enquêter; *Sch* **the Montessori method** la méthode Montessori

(**c**) *(organization)* méthode *f*, organisation *f*; **his work lacks method** son travail manque de méthode; **there's method in her madness** elle n'est pas aussi folle qu'elle en a l'air

2 Method *n Cin & Theat* **the Method** la méthode Stanislavski

►► *Cin & Theat* ***Method acting*** la méthode Stanislavski; *Cin & Theat* ***Method actor*** acteur *m* adepte de la méthode de Stanislavski; *Cin & Theat* ***Method actress*** actrice *f* adepte de la méthode de Stanislavski; ***methods engineer*** ingénieur *m* des méthodes; ***methods engineering*** étude *f* des méthodes; ***method study*** étude *f* des méthodes

methodical [mə'θɒdɪkəl] *adj* méthodique

methodically [mə'θɒdɪkəlɪ] *adv* méthodiquement, de façon méthodique, avec méthode

Methodism ['meθədɪzəm] *n* méthodisme *m*

Methodist ['meθədɪst] **1** *n* méthodiste *mf*

2 *adj* méthodiste

methodize, -ise ['meθədaɪz] *vt* systématiser

methodological [ˌmeθədə'lɒdʒɪkəl] *adj* méthodologique

►► ***methodological uniformitarianism*** actualisme *m*

methodologically [ˌmeθədə'lɒdʒɪkəlɪ] *adv* d'un point de vue méthodologique

methodology [ˌmeθə'dɒlədʒɪ] (*pl* **methodologies**) *n* méthodologie *f*

meths [meθs] *n Br Fam* (*abbr* **methylated spirits**) alcool *m* à brûler ❑

►► ***meths drinker*** = alcoolique qui boit de l'alcool à brûler

Methuselah [mɪ'θjuːzələ] **1** *pr n Bible* Mathusalem; **as old as Methuselah** vieux comme Mathusalem *ou* Hérode

2 *n (bottle)* mathusalem *m*

methyl ['meθɪl] *n Chem* méthyle *m*

▸▸ ***methyl acetate*** acétate *m* de méthyle; ***methyl alcohol*** méthanol *m*, alcool *m* méthylique; ***methyl group*** groupe *m* méthyle; ***methyl orange*** méthylorange *m*

methylal ['meθəlæl] *n Chem* méthylal *m*

methylate ['meθɪˌleɪt] *Chem* **1** *n* méthyle *m*

2 *vt* méthyler

methylated spirits ['meθɪˌleɪtɪd-] *n Chem* alcool *m* à brûler

methylation [ˌmeθɪ'leɪʃən] *n Chem* méthylation *f*

methylene ['meθəli:n] *n Chem* méthylène *m*

▸▸ ***methylene blue*** bleu *m* de méthylène

metic ['metɪk] *n Antiq* métèque *m*

meticulous [mɪ'tɪkjʊləs] *adj* méticuleux, minutieux; **with meticulous attention to detail** avec une attention méticuleuse *ou* minutieuse pour les détails

meticulously [mɪ'tɪkjʊləslɪ] *adv* méticuleusement; **meticulously honest** d'une honnêteté scrupuleuse

meticulousness [mɪ'tɪkjʊləsnɪs] *n* minutie *f*, *Literary* méticulosité *f*; **with great meticulousness** avec un soin tout particulier

metol ['mi:tɒl] *n* métol *m*

metonym ['metənɪm] *n Ling* = mot employé par métonymie

metonymic [ˌmetə'nɪmɪk] *adj Ling* métonymique

metonymically [ˌmetə'nɪmɪkəlɪ] *adv Ling* par métonymie

metonymy [mɪ'tɒnɪmɪ] *n Ling* métonymie *f*

me-too *adj*

▸▸ *Mktg* ***me-too product*** produit *m* tactique; *Mktg* ***me-too strategy*** stratégie *f* d'imitation

metope ['metəpɪ] *n Archit* métope *f*

metre, *Am* **meter** ['mi:tə(r)] *n* (**a**) *(measurement)* mètre *m* (**b**) *Literature* mètre *m*; **in iambic metre** en vers *mpl* iambiques (**c**) *Mus* mesure *f*

metric ['metrɪk] *adj Math* métrique; **to go metric** adopter le système métrique

▸▸ ***metric hundredweight*** 50 kilogrammes *mpl*; ***the metric system*** le système métrique; ***metric ton*** tonne *f*

metrical ['metrɪkəl] *adj Literature* métrique

metrically ['metrɪkəlɪ] *adv* (**a**) *Literature* en vers (**b**) *Math* selon le système métrique

metricate ['metrɪkeɪt] *vt* convertir au système métrique

metrication [ˌmetrɪ'keɪʃən] *n* conversion *f* au système métrique, métrisation *f*

metricize, -ise ['metrɪsaɪz] **1** *vt* convertir au système métrique

2 *vi* se convertir au système métrique

metrics ['metrɪks] *n (UNCOUNT) (in poetry)* métrique *f*

metrify ['metrɪfaɪ] *(pt & pp* **metrified***) vt Literature* versifier

metro ['metrəʊ] *(pl* **metros***) n* métro *m*

Metroland ['metrəʊˌlænd] *n* = terme légèrement péjoratif désignant la banlieue de Londres, notamment dans l'entre-deux-guerres

Metroliner® ['metrəʊˌlaɪnə(r)] *n* = ligne de chemin de fer entre Boston et New York

metrological [ˌmetrə'lɒdʒɪkəl] *adj* métrologique

metrology [me'trɒlədʒɪ] *n* métrologie *f*

metronome ['metrənəʊm] *n* métronome *m*

metronomic [ˌmetrə'nɒmɪk] *adj* métronomique

metronymic [ˌmetrə'nɪmɪk] **1** *n* matronyme *m*

2 *adj* matronymique

metroplex ['metrəʊˌpleks] *n Am* mégapole *f*, mégalopole *f*

metropolis [mɪ'trɒpəlɪs] *(pl* **metropolises** [-i:z]) *n* métropole *f*, grande ville *f*, grand centre *m* urbain

metropolitan [ˌmetrə'pɒlɪtən] **1** *n Rel* métropolitain *m*; *(in orthodox church)* métropolite *m*

2 *adj* (**a**) *Geog* métropolitain; **metropolitan France/Spain** la France/l'Espagne *f* métropolitaine; **metropolitan Milan/Glasgow** l'agglomération *f* de Milan/Glasgow

(**b**) *Rel* métropolitain

▸▸ ***metropolitan bishop*** métropolitain *m*; ***metropolitan district*** *(in UK)* circonscription *f* administrative; ***Metropolitan Museum of Art*** = un des principaux musées américains, à New York; *Am* ***the Metropolitan Opera*** le Metropolitan Opera *(opéra de New York)*; ***Metropolitan Police*** *Br* police *f* londonienne; *Am* police *f* urbaine

metrorrhagia [ˌmetrəʊ'reɪdʒɪə] *n Med* métrorragie *f*

Mets [mets] *npl* **the (New York) Mets** = l'une des équipes de base-ball de New York

mettle ['metəl] *n* courage *m*; **to show** *or* **to prove one's mettle** montrer ce dont on est capable; **to be on one's mettle** faire de son mieux; **this new challenge has really put him on his mettle** ce nouveau défi l'a vraiment forcé à donner le meilleur de lui-même

mettlesome ['metəlsəm] *adj Literary* courageux; *(horse)* fougueux

mew [mju:] **1** *n* (**a**) *(of cat)* miaulement *m*; *(of gull)* cri *m* (**b**) *(gull)* mouette *f*

2 *vi (cat)* miauler; *(gull)* crier

mewing ['mju:ɪŋ] *n (of cat)* miaulement *m*; *(of gull)* cris *mpl*

mewl [mju:l] *vi* vagir, geindre

mewling ['mju:lɪŋ] **1** *n* vagissement *m*

2 *adj (child)* vagissant

mews [mju:z] **1** *n Br* (**a**) *(flat)* = appartement chic aménagé dans une écurie rénovée (**b**) *(street)* ruelle *f (sur laquelle donnaient des écuries)*

2 *npl Arch* écurie *f*, écuries *fpl*

▸▸ *Br* ***mews flat*** = appartement chic aménagé dans une écurie rénovée

Mex [meks] *Am Fam (abbr* **Mexican**) **1** *n* = terme injurieux désignant un Mexicain

2 *adj* mexicain

Mexican ['meksɪkən] **1** *n* Mexicain(e) *m,f*

2 *adj* mexicain

3 *comp (embassy, history)* du Mexique

▸▸ ***Mexican American*** **1** *n* Américain(e) *m,f* d'origine mexicaine **2** *adj (history, culture)* de la population américaine d'origine mexicaine; *(population)* américaine d'origine mexicaine; ***Mexican jumping bean*** pois *m* sauteur; *esp Am* ***Mexican standoff*** impasse *f*; ***the Mexican War*** la guerre du Mexique; ***Mexican wave*** ola *f*

THE MEXICAN WAR

On désigne ainsi le conflit qui opposa, de 1846 à 1848, les États-Unis au Mexique. Vaincu, ce dernier renonça à ses prétentions sur le Texas et céda un vaste territoire comprenant plusieurs États américains actuels (y compris le Nouveau Mexique et la Californie).

Mexico ['meksɪkəʊ] *n* Mexique *m*; **in Mexico** au Mexique; **the Gulf of Mexico** le golfe du Mexique

▸▸ ***Mexico City*** Mexico

mezzanine ['metsəni:n] *n* (**a**) *(floor)* mezzanine *f* (**b**) *Am Theat (first balcony)* corbeille *f*

(**c**) *Br Theat (beneath stage)* premier dessous *m (de la scène)*

▸▸ ***mezzanine bed*** lit *m* en mezzanine; *Fin* ***mezzanine debt*** dette *f* subordonnée *ou* mezzanine; ***mezzanine finance*** = méthode de financement d'une partie du capital nécessaire pour acheter une entreprise *(utilisée principalement par ses employés)*

mezzo ['metsəʊ] *Mus* **1** *n Fam* (**a**) *(singer)* mezzo-soprano ❑ *f* (**b**) *(voice)* mezzo-soprano ❑ *m*

2 *adv* mezzo

mezzo-forte *adv Mus* mezzo forte

mezzo-piano *adv Mus* mezzo piano

mezzo-soprano *(pl* **mezzo-sopranos**) *n Mus* (**a**) *(singer)* mezzo-soprano *f* (**b**) *(voice)* mezzo-soprano *m*

mezzotint ['medzəʊˌtɪnt] *n* mezzotinto *m inv*

MFA [ˌemef'eɪ] *n Univ (abbr* **Master of Fine Arts**) *(person)* = titulaire d'une maîtrise en beaux-arts; *(qualification)* maîtrise *f* en beaux-arts

mfd *Com (written abbr* **manufactured**) fabriqué

mfr *(written abbr* **manufacturer**) fabricant *m*

mg *(written abbr* **milligram**) mg

Mgr (**a**) *Rel (written abbr* **Monseigneur, Monsignor**) Mgr (**b**) *(written abbr* **manager**) directeur(trice) *m,f*

MHC [ˌemeɪtʃ'si:] *n Med (abbr* **major histocompatibility complex**) CMH *m*

mho [məʊ] *n Old-fashioned Elec* MHO *m*

MHR [ˌemeɪtʃ'ɑ:(r)] *n Am Pol (abbr* **Member of the House of Representatives**) membre *m* de la Chambre des représentants

MHz *Elec (written abbr* **megahertz**) MHz

MI[1] [ˌem'aɪ] (**a**) *(written abbr* **Michigan**) Michigan *m* (**b**) *Comput (written abbr* **machine intelligence**) IA *f*

MI[2] *n Med (abbr* **myocardial infarction**) infarctus *m* du myocarde

mi [mi:] *n Mus* mi *m inv*

MI5 [ˌemaɪ'faɪv] *n Br (abbr* **Military Intelligence 5**) = service de contre-espionnage britannique

MI6 [ˌemaɪ'sɪks] *n Br (abbr* **Military Intelligence 6**) = service de renseignements britannique

MIA [ˌemaɪ'eɪ] *Mil (abbr* **missing in action**) **1** *n* soldat *m* porté disparu

2 *adj* porté disparu au combat

Miami [maɪ'æmɪ] *n* Miami

miaow [mi:'aʊ] *Br* **1** *n* miaulement *m*

2 *exclam* miaou!

3 *vi* miauler

miasma [mɪ'æzmə] *n Literary* (**a**) *(vapour)* miasme *m*; *(of smoke)* bouffée *f* (**b**) *(evil influence)* emprise *f*, empire *m*; **the miasma of despair/of poverty** l'emprise *f* du désespoir/de la misère

miasmal [mɪ'æzməl], **miasmatic** [ˌmɪæz'mætɪk], **miasmic** [mɪ'æzmɪk] *adj* miasmatique

mic [maɪk] *n TV & Rad* micro *m*

mica ['maɪkə] *n Miner* mica *m*

Micah ['maɪkə] *pr n Bible* Michée

Micawber [mɪ'kɔ:bə(r)] *pr n* **Mr Micawber** = personnage du roman de Charles Dickens 'David Copperfield', qui fait preuve d'un optimisme à toute épreuve malgré des difficultés financières

mice [maɪs] *pl of* **mouse**

micella [maɪ'selə] *(pl* **micellae** [-li:]) *n Chem* micelle *f*

micellar [maɪ'selə(r)] *adj Chem* micellaire

micelle [maɪ'sel] *n Chem* micelle *f*

Mich. *(written abbr* **Michigan**) Michigan *m*

Michael ['maɪkəl] *pr n Br Fam Hum* **are you taking the Michael?** tu me fais marcher ou quoi?

Michaelmas ['mɪkəlməs] *n* (**a**) *Rel* Saint-Michel *f*; **at Michaelmas** à la Saint-Michel (**b**) *Br Univ* premier trimestre *m (de l'année scolaire dans certaines universités)*

▸▸ *Bot* ***Michaelmas daisy*** aster *m* (d'automne); *Br Univ* ***Michaelmas term*** premier trimestre *m*

Michelangelo [ˌmaɪkəl'ændʒɪləʊ] *pr n* Michel-Ange

Michelin ['mɪtʃəlɪn] *n*

▸▸ ***Michelin Guide*** Guide *m* Michelin; ***the Michelin man*** le bonhomme Michelin, Bibendum *m*; *Fam Hum* **he looked like a Michelin man** on aurait dit le bonhomme Michelin *ou* Bibendum

Michigan ['mɪʃɪgən] *n* le Michigan; **in Michigan** dans le Michigan, au Michigan

Mick [mɪk] *n Fam (Irishman)* = terme injurieux désignant un Irlandais

mick [mɪk], **mickey** ['mɪkɪ] *n Br Fam* **to take the mickey out of sb/sth** se ficher de qn/qch; **are you taking the mickey?** tu te fiches de moi?

Mickey (Finn) [ˌmɪkɪ(ˌfɪn)] *n Fam* = boisson alcoolisée dans laquelle on a versé un sédatif

Mickey Mouse **1** *pr n* Mickey

2 *adj Fam Pej* à la gomme, à la noix; *(car)* à la noix; *(job, course, firm)* bidon *(inv)*, pas sérieux; *(degree)* bidon *(inv)*, sans aucune valeur ❑; *(watch etc)* de pacotille

mickle ['mɪkəl] *n Scot & NEng Prov* **many a mickle makes a muckle** les petits ruisseaux font les grandes rivières

MICR [ˌemaɪˌsi:'ɑ:(r)] *n Comput (abbr* **magnetic ink character recognition**) RMC *f*

micro ['maɪkrəʊ] *(pl* **micros**) **1** *n (microcomputer)* micro-ordinateur *m*, micro *m*

2 *adj* très petit, microscopique

▸▸ ***micro air vehicle*** microdrone *m (avion espion téléguidé en modèle réduit)*

micro- ['maɪkrəʊ] *pref* micro-

microampere ['maɪkrəʊˌæmpeə(r)] *n Phys* microampère *m*

microanalysis [ˌmaɪkrəʊə'næləsɪs] *(pl* **microanalyses** [-si:z]) *n* microanalyse *f*

microanalytic [ˌmaɪkrəʊænə'lɪtɪk], **microanalytical** [ˌmaɪkrəʊænə'lɪtɪkəl] *adj* microanalytique

microbe ['maɪkrəʊb] *n Biol* microbe *m*

microbial [maɪ'krəʊbɪəl], **microbic** [maɪ'krəʊbɪk] *adj Biol* microbien

microbiological ['maɪkrəʊˌbaɪə'lɒdʒɪkəl] *adj* microbiologique

microbiologist [ˌmaɪkrəʊbaɪˈɒlədʒɪst] *n* microbiologiste *mf*

microbiology [ˌmaɪkrəʊbaɪˈɒlədʒɪ] *n* microbiologie *f*

microbrewery [ˈmaɪkrəʊˌbrʊərɪ] *n* microbrasserie *f*

microcalorimeter [ˌmaɪkrəʊkəˈlɒrɪmɪtə(r)] *n* microcalorimètre *m*

microcalorimetry [ˌmaɪkrəʊkəˈlɒrɪmɪtrɪ] *n* microcalorimétrie *f*

microcamera [ˌmaɪkrəʊˈkæmərə] *n* appareil *m* de microphotographie

microcapsule [ˌmaɪkrəʊˈkæpsjuːl] *n* microcapsule *f*

microcassette [ˌmaɪkrəʊkəˈset] *n* microcassette *f*

microcephalic [ˌmaɪkrəʊseˈfælɪk] *Anat* **1** *n* microcéphale *mf*
2 *adj* microcéphale

microcephaly [ˌmaɪkrəʊˈsefəlɪ] *n Anat* microcéphalie *f*

microchannel architecture [ˌmaɪkrəʊˈtʃænəl-] *n Comput* architecture *f* à micro-canaux

microchemistry [ˌmaɪkrəʊˈkemɪstrɪ] *n* microchimie *f*

microchip [ˈmaɪkrəʊtʃɪp] *n* puce *f*

microcircuit [ˈmaɪkrəʊˌsɜːkɪt] *n* microcircuit *m*

microcircuitry [ˌmaɪkrəʊˈsɜːkɪtrɪ] *n (UNCOUNT)* microcircuits *mpl*

microclimate [ˈmaɪkrəʊˌklaɪmət] *n* microclimat *m*

microclimatic [ˌmaɪkrəʊklaɪˈmætɪk] *adj* microclimatique

microclimatologic [ˌmaɪkrəʊklaɪmətəˈlɒdʒɪk], **microclimatological** [ˌmaɪkrəʊklaɪmətəˈlɒdʒɪkəl] *adj* microclimatologique

microclimatology [ˌmaɪkrəʊklaɪməˈtɒlədʒɪ] *n* microclimatologie *f*

micrococcus [ˌmaɪkrəʊˈkɒkəs] (*pl* **micrococci** [-kaɪ]) *n Biol* microcoque *m*, micrococcus *m*

microcode [ˈmaɪkrəʊkəʊd] *n* microcode *m*

microcoding [ˈmaɪkrəʊˌkəʊdɪŋ] *n* microprogrammation *f*

microcomputer [ˌmaɪkrəʊkəmˈpjuːtə(r)] *n* micro-ordinateur *m*

microcomputing [ˌmaɪkrəʊkəmˈpjuːtɪŋ] *n* micro-informatique *f*

microcopy [ˈmaɪkrəʊˌkɒpɪ] (*pl* **microcopies**) *n* microcopie *f*

microcosm [ˈmaɪkrəʊˌkɒzəm] *n* microcosme *m*

microcosmic [ˌmaɪkrəʊˈkɒzmɪk] *adj* microcosmique

microcredit [ˈmaɪkrəʊˌkredɪt] *n* micro-crédit *m*

microcrystal [ˈmaɪkrəʊˌkrɪstəl] *n Miner* microcristal *m*

microcrystalline [ˌmaɪkrəʊˈkrɪstəlaɪn] *adj Miner* microcristallin

microcyte [ˈmaɪkrəʊˌsaɪt] *n Biol* microcyte *m*

microcytosis [ˌmaɪkrəʊsaɪˈtəʊsɪs] *n Med* microcytose *f*

microdissection [ˌmaɪkrəʊdɪˈsekʃən] *n Biol* microdissection *f*

microdot [ˈmaɪkrəʊdɒt] *n* micropoint *m*, micro-image *f*

microeconomic [ˈmaɪkrəʊˌiːkəˈnɒmɪk] *adj* microéconomique

microeconomics [ˈmaɪkrəʊˌiːkəˈnɒmɪks] *n (UNCOUNT)* microéconomie *f*

microelectronic [ˈmaɪkrəʊɪˌlekˈtrɒnɪk] *adj* microélectronique

microelectronics [ˈmaɪkrəʊɪˌlekˈtrɒnɪks] *n* microélectronique *f*

microfibre, *Am* **microfiber** [ˈmaɪkrəʊˌfaɪbə(r)] *n Tex* microfibre *m*

microfiche [ˈmaɪkrəʊfiːʃ] *n* microfiche *f*

microfilament [ˌmaɪkrəʊˈfɪləmənt] *n Biol* microfilament *m*

microfilm [ˈmaɪkrəʊfɪlm] **1** *n* microfilm *m*
2 *vt* microfilmer, mettre sur microfilm
►► ***microfilm reader*** micro-lecteur *m*, lecteur *m* de microfilms

microfilming [ˈmaɪkrəʊˌfɪlmɪŋ] *n* microfilmage *m*

microfloppy [ˈmaɪkrəʊˌflɒpɪ] *n Comput* microdisquette *f*

microflora [ˌmaɪkrəʊˈflɔːrə] *n* microflore *f*

microform [ˈmaɪkrəʊfɔːm] *n* microforme *f*

microfossil [ˈmaɪkrəʊˌfɒsəl] *n Geol* microfossile *m*

microglobulin [ˌmaɪkrəʊˈglɒbjʊlɪn] *n Biol* microglobuline *f*

microgram¹ [ˈmaɪkrəʊgræm] *n* = **micrograph**

microgram², microgramme [ˈmaɪkrəʊgræm] *n (metric unit)* microgramme *m*

micrograph [ˈmaɪkrəʊgrɑːf] **1** *n* micrographie *f*
2 *vt* micrographier

micrographic [ˌmaɪkrəˈgræfɪk] *adj* micrographique

micrography [maɪˈkrɒgrəfɪ] *n* micrographie *f*

microgravity [ˈmaɪkrəʊˌgrævɪtɪ] *n* microgravité *f*

microgroove [ˈmaɪkrəˌgruːv] *n* microsillon *m*

microhabitat [ˌmaɪkrəʊˈhæbɪtæt] *n Ecol* microécosystème *m*, synasie *f*

microinstruction [ˌmaɪkrəʊɪnˈstrʌkʃən] *n Comput* micro-instruction *f*

microlight [ˈmaɪkrəʊlaɪt] *n Aviat* ultraléger *m* motorisé, ULM *m*

microlinguistics [ˌmaɪkrəʊlɪŋˈgwɪstɪks] *n (UNCOUNT)* microlinguistique *f*

microlith [ˈmaɪkrəʊlɪθ] *n Archeol* microlithe *m*

micromanipulation [ˌmaɪkrəʊməˌnɪpjʊˈleɪʃən] *n Tech* micromanipulation *f*

micromarketing [ˌmaɪkrəʊˈmɑːkɪtɪŋ] *n* micromarketing *m*

micromechanics [ˌmaɪkrəʊməˈkænɪks] *n* micromécanique *f*

micromesh [ˈmaɪkrəʊmeʃ] **1** *n* micromesh *m*
2 *adj (tights)* surfin

micrometeorite [ˌmaɪkrəʊˈmiːtɪəraɪt] *n Astron* micrométéorite *f*

micrometeorology [ˌmaɪkrəʊˌmiːtɪəˈrɒlədʒɪ] *n* micrométéorologie *f*

micrometer [maɪˈkrɒmɪtə(r)] *n* (**a**) *Tech (device)* micromètre *m (instrument)* (**b**) *Am* = **micrometre**
►► ***micrometer screw*** vis *f* micrométrique; ***micrometer screw gauge*** palmer *m*

micrometre, *Am* **micrometer** [ˈmaɪkrəʊˌmiːtə(r)] *n* micromètre *m (mesure)*

micrometric [ˌmaɪkrəʊˈmetrɪk], **micrometrical** [ˌmaɪkrəʊˈmetrɪkəl] *adj* micrométrique

micrometry [maɪˈkrɒmətrɪ] *n* micrométrie *f*

microminiaturization [ˈmaɪkrəʊˌmɪnətʃəraɪˈzeɪʃən] *n* microminiaturisation *f*

microminiaturize, -ise [ˌmaɪkrəʊˈmɪnətʃəraɪz] *vt* microminiaturiser

micromodule [ˈmaɪkrəʊˌmɒdjuːl] *n Electron* micromodule *m*

micron [ˈmaɪkrɒn] (*pl* **microns** *or* **micra** [-krə]) *n* micron *m*

Micronesia [ˌmaɪkrəˈniːzjə] *n* Micronésie *f*; **in Micronesia** en Micronésie

Micronesian [ˌmaɪkrəˈniːzjən] **1** *n* (**a**) *(person)* Micronésien(enne) *m,f* (**b**) *Ling* micronésien *m*
2 *adj* micronésien

micronutrient [ˌmaɪkrəʊˈnjuːtrɪənt] *n Biol* micronutriment *m*, substance *f* micronutritive

microorganism [ˌmaɪkrəʊˈɔːgənɪzəm] *n Biol* micro-organisme *m*

microparticle [ˌmaɪkrəʊˈpɑːtɪkəl] *n Phys* microparticule *f*

microphone [ˈmaɪkrəfəʊn] *n* microphone *m*; **to talk into a microphone** parler dans un micro

microphotograph [ˌmaɪkrəʊˈfəʊtəgrɑːf] *n* microphotographie *f*

microphotography [ˌmaɪkrəʊfəˈtɒgrəfɪ] *n* microphotographie *f*

microphysical [ˌmaɪkrəʊˈfɪzɪkəl] *adj* microphysique

microphysics [ˌmaɪkrəʊˈfɪzɪks] *n (UNCOUNT)* microphysique *f*

microprint [ˈmaɪkrəʊprɪnt] *n Phot* microcarte *f*

microprobe [ˈmaɪkrəʊprəʊb] *n Electron* microsonde *f*

microprocessing [ˌmaɪkrəʊˈprəʊsesɪŋ] *n Comput* micro-informatique *f*

microprocessor [ˈmaɪkrəʊˌprəʊsesə(r)] *n Comput* microprocesseur *m*

microprogram [ˈmaɪkrəʊˌprəʊgræm] *n Comput* microprogramme *m*

microprogramming [ˌmaɪkrəʊˈprəʊgræmɪŋ] *n Comput* microprogrammation *f*

micropyle [ˈmaɪkrəʊpaɪl] *n Biol & Bot* micropyle *m*

microreader [ˈmaɪkrəʊˌriːdə(r)] *n* micro-lecteur *m*, lecteur *m* de microformes

microscope [ˈmaɪkrəskəʊp] *n* microscope *m*; **to look at sth under the microscope** observer *ou* examiner qch au microscope; *Fig* examiner qch à la loupe

microscopic [ˌmaɪkrəˈskɒpɪk] *adj* (**a**) *(tiny)* microscopique (**b**) *(using a microscope)* au microscope, microscopique

microscopically [ˌmaɪkrəˈskɒpɪkəlɪ] *adv (examine)* au microscope; **microscopically small** invisible à l'œil nu

microscopist [maɪˈkrɒskəpɪst] *n* microscopiste *mf*

microscopy [maɪˈkrɒskəpɪ] *n* microscopie *f*

micro-scooter *n* trottinette *f*

microsecond [ˈmaɪkrəʊˌsekənd] *n* microseconde *f*

microsegment [ˈmaɪkrəʊˌsegmənt] *n Mktg* microsegment *m*

microsegmentation [ˌmaɪkrəʊsegmənˈteɪʃən] *n Mktg* microsegmentation *f*

microsome [ˈmaɪkrəʊsəʊm] *n Biol* microsome *m*

microspacing [ˈmaɪkrəʊˌspeɪsɪŋ] *n Comput* micro-espacement *m*

microstructural [ˌmaɪkrəʊˈstrʌktʃərəl] *adj* microstructural

microstructure [ˈmaɪkrəʊˌstrʌktʃə(r)] *n* microstructure *f*

microsurgery [ˌmaɪkrəʊˈsɜːdʒərɪ] *n* microchirurgie *f*

microsurgical [ˌmaɪkrəʊˈsɜːdʒɪkəl] *adj* microchirurgical

microtechnology [ˌmaɪkrəʊtekˈnɒlədʒɪ] *n* microtechnologie *f*, microtechnique *f*

microtext [ˈmaɪkrəʊtekst] *n* texte *m* microfilmé *ou* sur microfilm

microtome [ˈmaɪkrəʊtəʊm] *n Biol* microtome *m*
►► ***microtome section*** tranche *f* coupée au microtome, tranche *f* microtomique

microtraumatism [ˌmaɪkrəʊˈtrɔːmətɪzəm] *n Med* microtraumatisme *m*

microtubule [ˌmaɪkrəʊˈtjuːbjʊl] *n Biol* microtubule *m*

microvillus [ˌmaɪkrəʊˈvɪləs] *n Anat* microvillosité *f*

microvolt [ˈmaɪkrəvəʊlt] *n* microvolt *m*

microwatt [ˈmaɪkrəwɒt] *n* microwatt *m*

microwave [ˈmaɪkrəweɪv] **1** *n* (**a**) *Phys* micro-onde *f* (**b**) *(oven)* (four *m* à) micro-ondes *m inv*
2 *vt* faire cuire au micro-ondes
►► ***microwave oven*** (four *m* à) micro-ondes *m inv*

microwaveable [ˈmaɪkrəˌweɪvəbəl] *adj* micro-ondable

microwriter [ˈmaɪkrəʊˌraɪtə(r)] *n Comput* micro-ordinateur *m* de traitement de texte

micturate [ˈmɪktjʊəreɪt] *vi Formal* uriner

micturition [ˌmɪktjʊəˈrɪʃən] *n Formal* miction *f*

mid [mɪd] *adj* (**a**) *(middle)* **in mid October** à la mi-octobre, au milieu du mois d'octobre; **in mid ocean** en plein océan, en pleine mer; **mid season** demi-saison *f*; **he's in his mid fifties** il a environ cinquante-cinq ans; **she stopped in mid sentence** elle s'est arrêtée au milieu de sa phrase, sa phrase est restée en suspens
(**b**) *(half)* **mid green** vert *m* ni clair ni foncé
(**c**) *(central)* central, du milieu; **mid Wales** le centre *ou* la région centrale du pays de Galles
►► *Ling* ***mid vowel*** voyelle *f* centrale

'mid [mɪd] *prep Literary* au milieu de, parmi

mid-afternoon *n* milieu *m* de l'après-midi; **we had a mid-afternoon break** on a fait une pause en milieu d'après-midi

midair [ˌmɪdˈeə(r)] **1** *n* **in midair** en plein ciel
2 *adj (collision)* en plein ciel

Midas [ˈmaɪdəs] *pr n Myth* Midas; **to have the Midas touch** transformer tout ce que l'on touche en or

mid-Atlantic **1** *n* **in (the) mid-Atlantic** au milieu de l'Atlantique
2 *adj (accent)* mi-américain mi-britannique

midbrain [ˈmɪdbreɪn] *n Anat* mésencéphale *m*

MidCap [ˈmɪdkæp] *n Am St Exch* = indice boursier américain composé d'actions de sociétés à moyenne capitalisation, ≃ MidCAC *m*

midcourse [ˈmɪdkɔːs] *n* **in midcourse** à mi-course
►► *Astron* ***midcourse corrections*** corrections *fpl* de trajectoire

midday [ˈmɪddeɪ] *n* midi *m*; **at midday** à midi; **the midday heat** la chaleur de midi
►► ***midday meal*** repas *m* de midi

midden ['mɪdən] *n* (**a**) *Fam (dung heap)* (tas *m* de) fumier *m* (**b**) *Archeol* ordures *fpl* ménagères, rejets *mpl* domestiques (**c**) *Fam (dustbin)* poubelle *m*; *Scot* **this room is like a midden!** cette pièce est une vraie porcherie!

middle ['mɪdəl] **1** *n* (**a**) *(in space)* milieu *m*, centre *m*; **in the middle (of)** au milieu (de), au centre (de); **a square with a dot in the middle** un carré avec un point au milieu; **two seats in the middle of the row** deux places en milieu de rangée; **in the middle of the crowd** au milieu de la foule; **in the middle of London** en plein Londres; **right in the middle of the target** en plein dans le mille; **in the middle of the road** au milieu de la route; **in the middle of the Atlantic** au milieu de l'Atlantique, en plein Atlantique; **they live in the middle of nowhere** ils habitent dans un coin perdu *ou* loin de tout, *Pej* ils habitent dans un trou perdu; **we broke down in the middle of nowhere** on est tombés en panne dans un endroit perdu; *Fam* **they split the money down the middle** ils ont partagé l'argent en deux parties égales

(**b**) *(in time)* milieu *m*; **in the middle of the week** au milieu de la semaine; **in the middle of October** à la mi-octobre, au milieu (du mois) d'octobre; **in the middle of the night** en pleine nuit, en plein milieu de la nuit; **in the middle of winter** en plein hiver

(**c**) *(in activity)* **to be in the middle of doing sth** être en train de faire qch; **I'm in the middle of something, can you call back?** là je suis occupé mais est-ce que tu peux me rappeler plus tard?; **I was in the middle of the ironing** j'étais en plein repassage

(**d**) *(stomach)* ventre *m*; *(waist)* taille *f*; **he's got rather fat around the middle** il a pris du ventre

2 *adj* (**a**) *(in the centre)* du milieu; **the middle book/shelf** le livre/l'étagère *f* du milieu; **she was the middle child of three** elle était la deuxième de trois enfants; *Fig* **the middle course** *or* **way** *(happy medium)* le juste milieu; *(compromise)* la solution intermédiaire; *Fig* **to steer a middle course** adopter une position intermédiaire; **in the middle distance** à mi-distance; *(in picture)* au second plan; **to gaze into the middle distance** regarder dans le vague; **the middle path** le chemin du milieu; *Fig* la voie de la modération

(**b**) *(average)* moyen; *(intermediate)* moyen, intermédiaire; *Br* **of middle height** de taille moyenne; **this car is in the middle price range** cette voiture se situe dans un ordre de prix moyen; **the middle ranks of the civil service/party** les échelons *mpl* intermédiaires de la fonction publique/du parti

3 *vt* (**a**) *Naut (sail)* plier en deux

(**b**) *(ball)* frapper franchement

4 Middle *adj Ling* **Middle Irish/French** le moyen gaélique/français

▸▸ ***middle age*** la cinquantaine; **a man in middle age** un homme d'un certain âge; **to reach middle age** atteindre la cinquantaine; **in early middle age he...** quand il avait la quarantaine, il...; **she's well into middle age** elle a plus de cinquante ans; ***the Middle Ages*** le Moyen Âge *m*; **in the Middle Ages** au Moyen Âge; **the early/late Middle Ages** le haut/bas Moyen Âge; ***Middle America*** *Geog* Amérique *f* centrale; *Fig (American middle class)* l'Amérique *f* moyenne; *Pej* l'Amérique *f* bien pensante; ***Middle American*** **1** *n* Américain(e) *m,f* du Middle-West; *Fig* Américain(e) *m,f* moyen(enne) **2** *adj Geog* du Middle-West; *Fig* de l'américain moyen; *Mus* ***middle C*** do *m inv* du milieu du clavier; ***the middle class, the middle classes*** les classes *fpl* moyennes; *Pej* la bourgeoisie *f*; *Anat* ***middle ear*** oreille *f* moyenne; ***the Middle East*** le Moyen-Orient; **in the Middle East** au Moyen-Orient; ***Middle Eastern*** moyen-oriental; ***Middle England*** l'Angleterre *f* moyenne *(aux tendances conservatrices)*; *Pej* ***Middle Englander*** Anglais(e) *m,f* moyen(enne); *Ling* ***Middle English*** le moyen anglais; ***middle finger*** majeur *m*, médius *m*; *Br Fam* ***middle finger salute*** doigt *m* d'honneur; **to give sb the middle finger salute** faire un doigt d'honneur à qn; *Chess* ***middle game*** milieu *m* de partie; ***middle ground*** *(in picture)* second plan *m*; *Fig* terrain *m* neutre; *Fig* **to occupy the middle ground** adopter une position de compromis; *Ling* ***Middle High German*** le moyen haut-allemand; *Hist* ***the Middle Kingdom*** *(in Egyptian history)* le Moyen Empire; *(China)* l'Empire *m* du Milieu; *Bot* ***middle lamella*** lamelle *f* moyenne; ***middle management*** *(UNCOUNT)* cadres *mpl* moyens; ***middle manager*** cadre *m* moyen; ***middle name*** deuxième prénom *m*; **honesty is her middle name** c'est l'honnêteté même; **laziness is his middle name** c'est un incorrigible paresseux; **generosity isn't exactly his middle name!** on ne peut pas dire qu'il soit particulièrement généreux; *St Exch* ***middle price*** cours *m* moyen; ***middle school*** *Br* = école pour enfants de 8 ou 9 à 13 ans; *Am* = école pour enfants de 10 à 13 ans, ≃ collège *m*; *Br Law* ***Middle Temple*** = association d'étudiants en droit et d'avocats, ainsi que les bâtiments londoniens où elle siège; *Phil* ***middle term*** moyen terme *m (d'un syllogisme)*; *Am Geog* ***the Middle West*** le Midwest

middle-age spread *n Fam* **he's got middle-age spread** il prend du ventre

middle-aged *adj* d'une cinquantaine d'années; **she was already middle-aged when she changed career** elle avait déjà un certain âge quand elle a changé de carrière

middlebrow ['mɪdəlbraʊ] *Pej* **1** *n* personne *f* aux activités intellectuelles limitées; *(reader)* lecteur(trice) *m,f* moyen(enne); *(audience)* spectateur(trice) *m,f* moyen(enne)

2 *adj (reader, audience)* moyen; **their music's very middlebrow** leur musique s'adresse à un public moyen; **middlebrow books** livres *mpl* sans prétentions intellectuelles; **middlebrow programmes** émissions *fpl* s'adressant à un public moyen

middle-class *adj* des classes moyennes; *Pej* bourgeois

middle-distance *adj*

▸▸ *Sport* ***middle-distance race*** course *f* de demi-fond; *Sport* ***middle-distance runner*** coureur(-euse) *m,f* de demi-fond

middle-income group *n Mktg* groupe *m* de contribuables à revenus moyens

middle-level *adj Am*

▸▸ ***middle-level management*** *(UNCOUNT)* cadres *mpl* moyens; ***middle-level manager*** cadre *m* moyen

middleman ['mɪdəlmæn] *(pl* **middlemen** [-men]) *n* intermédiaire *mf*

▸▸ ***middleman's business*** commerce *m* intermédiaire; ***middleman's market*** marché *m* intermédiaire

middlemost ['mɪdəlməʊst] *adj* le plus proche du centre

middle-of-the-road *adj (opinions, policies)* modéré; *Pej* timide, circonspect; **middle-of-the-road music** musique *f* grand public; *Pej* musique *f* passe-partout

middle-roader [-'rəʊdə(r)] *n Am Pol* modéré(e) *m,f*

middle-sized *adj* de taille moyenne

middle-spotted woodpecker *n Orn* pic *m* mar

middleweight ['mɪdəlweɪt] **1** *n* poids *m* moyen

2 *adj (championship)* de poids moyen; **he's the world middleweight champion** c'est le champion du monde des poids moyens

middling ['mɪdlɪŋ] *adj Fam (average)* moyen □; *(mediocre)* médiocre □; **how are you? – (fair to) middling** ça va? – on fait aller *ou* comme ci comme ça

Middx *(written abbr* **Middlesex**) Middlesex *m*

middy ['mɪdɪ] *n Fam* (**a**) *Naut* midship □ *m* (**b**) *Austr (glass of beer)* ≃ demi *m* de bière

Mideast [,mɪd'iːst] *n Am* **the Mideast** le Moyen-Orient

midfield [,mɪd'fiːld] *n Sport* milieu *m* du terrain; **in midfield** au milieu du terrain

▸▸ ***midfield player*** (joueur *m* du) milieu *m* de terrain

midfielder [,mɪd'fiːldə(r)] *n Ftbl* milieu *m* de terrain

midge [mɪdʒ] *n Entom* moucheron *m*

midget ['mɪdʒɪt] **1** *n (dwarf)* nain(e) *m,f*

2 *adj (gen)* minuscule; *(by design)* miniature

▸▸ ***midget submarine*** sous-marin *m* de poche

Mid Glamorgan [-glə'mɔːgən] *n* le Mid Glamorgan, = comté du sud du pays de Galles; **in Mid Glamorgan** dans le Mid Glamorgan

MIDI ['mɪdɪ] *n Comput (abbr* **musical instrument digital interface**) MIDI *m*

midi ['mɪdɪ] *n (coat)* manteau *m* à mi-mollet; *(skirt)* jupe *f* à mi-mollet

▸▸ ***midi system*** *(stereo)* chaîne *f* midi

mid-iron *n (in golf)* fer *m* moyen

midland ['mɪdlənd] *adj* au centre du pays

Midlands ['mɪdləndz] *npl* **the Midlands** les Midlands *mpl*, = comtés du centre de l'Angleterre; **a Midlands accent** un accent des Midlands

midlife ['mɪdlaɪf] *n* la cinquantaine; **in midlife, it's hard to find a new job** la cinquantaine passée, il est difficile de retrouver un emploi; **he's having** *or* **going through a midlife crisis** il a du mal à passer le cap de la cinquantaine

mid-month account *n St Exch* liquidation *f* de quinzaine

mid-morning [,mɪd'mɔːnɪŋ] *n* milieu *m* de la matinée; **we had a mid-morning snack** nous avons mangé quelque chose vers onze heures

midmost ['mɪdməʊst] *adj* le plus proche du centre

midnight ['mɪdnaɪt] **1** *n* minuit *m*; **at midnight** à minuit

2 *adj (swim)* de minuit; **to burn the midnight oil** travailler tard dans la nuit

▸▸ ***midnight blue*** bleu nuit *m inv*; ***midnight feast*** = petit repas pris en cachette la nuit par des enfants, à l'insu de leurs parents; ***midnight Mass*** messe *f* de minuit; *Am Hist* ***the midnight ride*** = épisode héroïque de la guerre d'Indépendance américaine; ***midnight sun*** soleil *m* de minuit

'Midnight's Children' *Rushdie* 'Les Enfants de minuit'

'Midnight Cowboy' *Schlesinger* 'Macadam cowboy'

THE MIDNIGHT RIDE

C'est le nom donné à l'acte héroïque de Paul Revere, qui, en 1775, pendant la guerre d'Indépendance, parcourut au galop la distance de Boston à Lexington et Concord et parvint à alerter les patriotes américains du débarquement des troupes anglaises.

mid-off *n* = au cricket, position d'un joueur, à droite du batteur si celui-ci est droitier, à sa gauche s'il est gaucher

mid-on *n* = au cricket, position d'un joueur, à gauche du batteur si celui-ci est droitier, à sa droite s'il est gaucher

midpoint ['mɪdpɔɪnt] *n (in space, time)* milieu *m*

mid-range *adj Com (computer, car)* de milieu de gamme

midrib ['mɪdrɪb] *n Bot* nervure *f* centrale

midriff ['mɪdrɪf] *n* (**a**) *(stomach)* ventre *m* (**b**) *Anat* diaphragme *m*

midrise ['mɪdraɪz] *adj*

▸▸ *Am* ***midrise apartment block*** immeuble *m* de hauteur moyenne *(dix étages au maximum)*

midsection ['mɪd,sekʃən] *n* section *f ou* partie *f* médiane

midshipman ['mɪd,ʃɪpmən] *(pl* **midshipmen** [-mən]) *n Naut* ≃ aspirant *m*, *Can* ≃ cadet *m*

midships ['mɪdʃɪps] *adv Naut* au milieu du navire, par le travers

midst [mɪdst] *n* **in the midst of sth** au milieu de qch; **in the midst of winter** au milieu *ou* au cœur de l'hiver, en plein hiver; **in the midst of all this** *(these events)* sur ces entrefaites; **in the midst of the celebration** en plein milieu de la fête; **in our/your/their midst** parmi nous/vous/eux; **there are traitors in our midst** il y a des traîtres parmi nous

midstream [,mɪd'striːm] *n* **in midstream** au milieu du courant; *Fig* **he stopped talking in midstream** il s'arrêta au beau milieu d'une phrase; *Fig* **to change horses in midstream** se raviser en cours de route

midsummer ['mɪd,sʌmə(r)] *n (middle of summer)* milieu *m* de l'été, cœur *m* de l'été; *(solstice)* solstice *m* d'été; **in midsummer** au milieu de

l'été, en été; **a midsummer night** une nuit d'été
▸▸ ***Midsummer Day, Midsummer's Day*** la Saint-Jean; ***midsummer madness*** folie *f* estivale

'A Midsummer Night's Dream' *Shakespeare* 'Le Songe d'une nuit d'été'

midterm [ˌmɪd'tɜːm] **1** *n* (**a**) *Sch & Univ* milieu *m* du trimestre; **at** *or* **in midterm** au milieu du trimestre
(**b**) *Med (of pregnancy)* milieu *m*
2 midterms *npl Am Sch & Univ* examens *mpl* du milieu du trimestre
▸▸ *Sch & Univ* ***midterm break*** vacances *fpl* de milieu de trimestre; *Pol* ***midterm elections*** = aux États-Unis, élections législatives qui ont lieu au milieu du mandat présidentiel; *Sch & Univ* ***midterm exams*** examens *mpl* du milieu du trimestre

midtown ['mɪdtaʊn] *n Am* = partie d'une ville située à mi-chemin entre le centre et les quartiers périphériques; **a midtown apartment** un appartement pas très loin du centre

Midway ['mɪdweɪ] *n* archipel *m* des Midway; **the Battle of Midway** la bataille de Midway

midway 1 *adv* [ˌmɪd'weɪ] à mi-chemin; **we broke our journey midway** nous avons interrompu notre voyage à mi-chemin; **she was midway through writing the first chapter** elle avait déjà écrit la moitié du premier chapitre; **midway between... and...** à mi-distance *ou* à mi-chemin entre... et...; **a style midway between Craig's and Andrew's** un style intermédiaire entre celui de Craig et celui d'Andrew
2 *n* ['mɪdweɪ] *Am (in fairground)* allée *f* centrale
▸▸ ***midway point*** *(in time, space)* milieu *m*; **we've reached a midway point in the negotiations** nous avons parcouru la moitié du chemin dans les négociations

midweek 1 *adj* ['mɪdwiːk] *(travel, prices, performance)* au milieu de la semaine; *Rail* ≃ (en) période bleue
2 *adv* [ˌmɪd'wiːk] *(travel, arrive, meet)* au milieu de la semaine; *Rail* ≃ en période bleue

Midwest [ˌmɪd'west] *n* **the Midwest** le Midwest; **in the Midwest** dans le Midwest

Midwestern [ˌmɪd'westən] *adj* du Midwest

mid-wicket *n Sport* = au cricket, position d'un joueur du côté "leg" du batteur

midwife ['mɪdwaɪf] (*pl* **midwives** [-waɪvz]) *n* sage-femme *f*
▸▸ *Zool* ***midwife toad*** crapaud *m* accoucheur, alyte *m*

midwifery ['mɪdˌwɪfərɪ] *n* (**a**) *(profession)* profession *f* de sage-femme (**b**) *(obstetrics)* obstétrique *f*

midwinter [ˌmɪd'wɪntə(r)] *n (middle of winter)* milieu *m* de l'hiver, cœur *m* de l'hiver; *(solstice)* solstice *m* d'hiver; **in midwinter** au milieu de l'hiver; **a midwinter** *or* **midwinter's day** un jour d'hiver

midyear [ˌmɪd'jɪə(r)] **1** *n* milieu *m* de l'année
2 *adj* du milieu de l'année
3 midyears *npl Am Univ* ≃ partiels *mpl* du deuxième trimestre

mien [miːn] *n Literary* mine *f*, air *m*

miffed [mɪft] *adj Fam (person, expression)* froissé □; **to be miffed at sb** être fâché contre qn □

miffy ['mɪfɪ] (*compar* **miffier**, *superl* **miffiest**) *adj Fam* en rogne

MIG welding [mɪg-] *n Tech* (*abbr* **metallic-electrode inert gas**) soudage *m* MIG

MIGHT¹ [maɪt]

La forme négative **mightn't** s'écrit **might not** dans un style plus soutenu. **Might** et **may** peuvent s'utiliser indifféremment ou presque dans les expressions de la catégorie (**a**).

v aux (**a**) *(expressing possibility)* **you might well be right** il se pourrait bien que vous ayez raison; **I might be home late tonight** je rentrerai peut-être tard ce soir; **why not come with us? – I might** pourquoi ne viens-tu pas avec nous? – peut-être; **don't eat it, it might be poisonous** n'en mange pas, tu pourrais t'empoisonner; **hundreds of lives might have been lost unnecessarily** des centaines de gens sont peut-être morts inutilement; **she might well have decided to turn back** il se pourrait *ou* il se peut bien qu'elle ait décidé de rentrer; **they might have reached the summit by now** ils ont peut-être déjà atteint le sommet; **she might have decided not to go** il se peut qu'elle ait décidé de ne pas y aller
(**b**) *(past form of may)* **I never considered that she might want to come** je n'avais jamais pensé qu'elle pouvait avoir envie de venir; **we feared you might be dead** nous avons eu peur que vous ne soyez mort
(**c**) *(in polite questions, suggestions)* **might I interrupt?** puis-je me permettre de vous interrompre?; **and what, might I ask, was the reason?** et puis-je savoir quelle en était la raison?; **might I** *or* **if I might make a suggestion?** puis-je me permettre de suggérer quelque chose?; **you might try using a different approach altogether** vous pourriez adopter une approche entièrement différente; **I thought we might have tea together somewhere** je m'étais dit que nous pourrions aller prendre un thé ensemble quelque part; **you might want to ask the managing director first** ce serait une bonne idée de demander au directeur avant
(**d**) *(commenting on a statement made)* **that, I might add, was not my idea** cela n'était pas mon idée, soit dit en passant; **this, as one might expect, did not go down well with the government** le gouvernement, est-il nécessaire de le préciser, n'a guère apprécié
(**e**) *(ought to)* **you might at least tidy up your room!** tu pourrais au moins ranger ta chambre!; **I might have known he'd be the last (to arrive)** j'aurais dû savoir qu'il serait le dernier (à arriver); **you might have warned me!** tu aurais pu me prévenir!
(**f**) *(used to contradict or challenge)* **they might say they support women, but they do nothing practical to help them** ils ont beau dire qu'ils soutiennent les femmes, concrètement ils ne font rien pour les aider; **whatever problems she might have, at least she keeps them to herself** elle a peut-être des problèmes, mais au moins elle n'embête pas les autres avec; **he might not be the best-looking man in the world but he's very kind** ce n'est peut-être pas un apollon mais il est très gentil
(**g**) *Formal or Hum (in questions)* **and who might you be?** et qui êtes-vous donc?; **and what might you be up to?** et que faites-vous donc?
(**h**) *(idioms)* **we might as well go home (as stay here)** nous ferions aussi bien de rentrer chez nous (plutôt que de rester ici); **I might as well have stayed in bed** j'aurais aussi bien fait de rester au lit; **he's regretting it now, as well he might!** il le regrette maintenant, et pour cause!

might² *n* (**a**) *(power → of nation)* pouvoir *m*, puissance *f*; *(→ of army)* puissance *f*
(**b**) *(physical strength)* force *f*; **with all one's might** de toutes ses forces; **he started yelling with all his might** il se mit à crier à tue-tête; *Literary* **with might and main** de toutes ses forces; **she strove with might and main to prevent it** elle a fait tout ce qu'elle a pu pour empêcher cela; *Prov* **might is right** la raison du plus fort est toujours la meilleure

might-have-been *n* (**a**) *(opportunity)* occasion *f* manquée; *(hope)* espoir *m* déçu (**b**) *Fam (person)* raté(e) *m,f*

mightily ['maɪtɪlɪ] *adv* (**a**) *(with vigour)* avec vigueur, vigoureusement (**b**) *(extremely)* extrêmement; **to be mightily relieved** être vraiment soulagé

mightiness ['maɪtɪnɪs] *n (power)* puissance *f*

mightn't ['maɪtənt] = **might not**

might've ['maɪtəv] = **might have**

mighty ['maɪtɪ] (*compar* **mightier**, *superl* **mightiest**) **1** *adj* (**a**) *(powerful)* puissant
(**b**) *(impressive)* imposant; *(enormous)* énorme
(**c**) *Am Fam (considerable)* grand □; **you're in a mighty hurry** vous êtes diablement pressé
2 *adv Am Fam* rudement, vachement; **that's mighty kind of you** c'est rudement gentil de votre part; **you're making a mighty big mistake** vous commettez là une erreur colossale □; **she looked mighty pleased with herself** elle avait l'air très contente d'elle □

migmatite ['mɪgmətaɪt] *n Geol* migmatite *f*

mignonette [ˌmɪnjə'net] *n Bot* réséda *m*, mignonnette *f*

migraine ['miːgreɪn, 'maɪgreɪn] *n* migraine *f*; **to suffer from migraines** avoir des migraines; **I've got a migraine** j'ai la migraine

migrainous ['miːgreɪnəs, 'maɪgreɪnəs] *adj Med* migraineux

migrant ['maɪgrənt] **1** *n* (**a**) *(bird, animal)* migrateur *m*
(**b**) *(worker → in agriculture)* saisonnier(ère) *m,f*, travailleur(euse) *m,f* saisonnier(ère); *(→ foreign)* travailleur(euse) *m,f* immigré(e)
(**c**) *Austr* immigré(e) *m,f*
2 *adj* (**a**) *(bird, animal)* migrateur
(**b**) *Austr (immigrant)* immigrant
▸▸ ***migrant accommodation*** logement *m* pour les immigrés; ***migrant worker*** *(seasonal)* (travailleur(euse) *m,f*) saisonnier(ère) *m,f*; *(foreign)* travailleur(euse) *m,f* immigré(e)

migrate [*Br* maɪ'greɪt, *Am* 'maɪgreɪt] *vi* (**a**) *(bird, animal)* migrer; **to migrate south** migrer vers le sud (**b**) *(person, family → from region)* migrer, se déplacer; *(→ from country)* émigrer; **the people migrated to the cities** les gens ont migré vers les villes

migration [maɪ'greɪʃən] *n (of birds, animals)* migration *f*; *(of people)* émigration *f*

migrator [maɪ'greɪtə(r)] *n (bird, animal)* migrateur *m*

migratory ['maɪgrətərɪ] *adj* (**a**) *(bird, fish)* migrateur (**b**) *(habit, movement)* migratoire

mikado [mɪ'kɑːdəʊ] (*pl* **mikados**) *n* mikado *m* *(empereur)*

Mike [maɪk] *pr n Fam* **for the love of Mike!** pour l'amour du ciel, c'est pas vrai!

mike [maɪk] *n Fam* (*abbr* **microphone**) micro *m*

mil [mɪl] *n* (**a**) *(unit of length)* millième *m* de pouce (**b**) *(thousand)* mille *m inv* (**c**) *Fam (millimetre)* millimètre □ *m* (**d**) *Fam (millilitre)* millilitre □ *m*

milady [mɪ'leɪdɪ] (*pl* **miladies**) *n Arch* madame *f*

Milan [mɪ'læn] *n* Milan

Milanese [ˌmɪlə'niːz] **1** *n* Milanais(e) *m,f*
2 *adj* milanais

milch [mɪltʃ] *adj* laitier
▸▸ ***milch cow*** vache *f* laitière; *Fig* vache *f* à lait

mild [maɪld] **1** *adj* (**a**) *(person, remark)* doux (douce); *(answer)* conciliant; *(criticism)* léger, anodin
(**b**) *(punishment)* peu sévère, léger
(**c**) *(climate)* doux (douce), tempéré; *(winter)* doux (douce), clément; **the weather is getting milder** le temps s'adoucit
(**d**) *(dish)* peu épicé; *(cigar, tobacco, soap)* doux (douce); *(sedative, medicine)* léger; **a mild curry** un curry peu épicé
(**e**) *Med (illness, infection)* bénin(igne); **a mild form of measles** une forme bénigne de rougeole
(**f**) *(slight → astonishment)* léger; **the joke caused some mild amusement** la plaisanterie a fait sourire; **the play caused a mild sensation** la pièce a fait un peu de bruit; **the play was a mild success** la pièce a obtenu un succès modéré
2 *n Br* = bière moins riche en houblon et plus foncée que la "bitter"
▸▸ ***mild cheddar*** cheddar *m* doux; ***mild steel*** acier *m* doux

mildew ['mɪldjuː] **1** *n* (**a**) *(on cereals, flowers)* rouille *f*; *(on vines, potatoes, tomatoes)* mildiou *m* (**b**) *(on paper, leather, food)* moisissure *f*
2 *vi* (**a**) *(cereals, flowers)* se rouiller; *(vines, potatoes, tomatoes)* être atteint par le mildiou (**b**) *(paper, leather, food)* moisir

mildewed ['mɪldjuːd] *adj (cereals, flowers)* rouillé; *(vines, potatoes, tomatoes)* mildiousé; *(paper, leather, food)* moisi

mildewy ['mɪldjuːɪ] *adj (food, wallpaper, leather)* moisi; **a mildewy smell** une odeur de moisi; **to go mildewy** *(plant)* se rouiller; *(bread, paper)* moisir; *(vine)* être atteint par le mildiou

mildly ['maɪldlɪ] *adv* (**a**) *(say, act)* doucement, avec douceur
(**b**) *(slightly)* modérément, légèrement; **it has**

a mildly laxative effect ça a un léger effet laxatif; **to be mildly successful** *(play)* obtenir un succès modéré; **that's putting it mildly!** c'est le moins qu'on puisse dire!; **it was rather silly, to put it mildly** c'était plutôt idiot, c'est le moins qu'on puisse dire; **he's a bastard, and that's putting it mildly!** c'est un salaud, et c'est peu dire!

mild-mannered *adj* doux (douce)

mildness ['maɪldnɪs] *n* (**a**) *(of person, weather)* douceur *f*; *(of criticism)* caractère *m* anodin; *(of punishment)* légèreté *f* (**b**) *(of disease)* bénignité *f*

mile [maɪl] **1** *n* (**a**) *(measurement)* = 1609 m, mile *m*; **it's 10 miles away** ≃ c'est à une quinzaine de kilomètres d'ici; **she lives 30 miles from Birmingham** ≃ elle habite à une cinquantaine de kilomètres de Birmingham; **the two towns are 50 miles apart** ≃ les deux villes sont (situées) à 80 kilomètres l'une de l'autre; **it's 10 miles back** ≃ c'est à une quinzaine de kilomètres derrière nous; **miles per hour** milles par heure; **smaller cars do more miles to the** *or* **per gallon** les petites voitures consomment moins; **we passed a restaurant a few miles back** nous sommes passés devant un restaurant quelques kilomètres plus haut; **a 100-mile journey** ≃ un voyage de 160 kilomètres; **a 10-mile tailback (of traffic)** ≃ un bouchon d'une quinzaine de kilomètres; **mile after mile of sandy beaches** ≃ des plages de sable sur des kilomètres et des kilomètres

(**b**) *(long distance)* **you can see it a mile off** ça se voit de loin; **they live miles apart** ils habitent à des kilomètres l'un de l'autre; **the best doctor for miles around** le meilleur médecin à des kilomètres à la ronde; **we're miles from the nearest town** on est à des kilomètres de la ville la plus proche; **it's miles from anywhere** c'est un endroit complètement isolé; **you can see for miles and miles** on voit à des kilomètres à la ronde; **we walked (for) miles and miles** on a fait des kilomètres (à pied); *Fig* **I've had to use miles of string** il m'a fallu des kilomètres de ficelle; *Fam* **it sticks out a mile** ça vous crève les yeux, ça se voit comme le nez au milieu de la figure

(**c**) *Fig* **they're miles ahead of their competitors** ils ont une avance considérable sur leurs concurrents; **the two judges are miles apart on capital punishment** les deux juges ont des points de vue *ou* des avis radicalement opposés sur la peine de mort; **he was miles away** *(daydreaming)* il était dans la lune; **you could see what was going to happen a mile off** on voyait d'ici ce qui allait arriver; **you can tell she's Italian a mile off** elle a vraiment le type italien; **your calculations are miles out** vous vous êtes complètement trompé dans vos calculs; **someone not a million miles from us** une certaine personne qui ne se trouve pas très loin de nous; **it's not a million miles from what we tried to do** cela ressemble assez à ce que nous avons essayé de faire; **to go the extra mile** faire un petit effort supplémentaire

2 *adv Fam (very much)* **I feel miles better** je me sens vachement mieux; **it's miles more interesting** c'est vachement plus intéressant; **you're miles too slow** t'es vachement trop lent, t'es mille fois trop lent; **she's miles better than me at languages** elle est vachement plus forte que moi en langues

▶▶ *Am* ***mile marker*** ≃ borne *f* kilométrique

mileage ['maɪlɪdʒ] *n* (**a**) *Aut (distance)* distance *f* en milles, ≃ kilométrage *m*; **the car's got a very high mileage** la voiture a beaucoup roulé *ou* a un kilométrage élevé; *Fig* **the papers got tremendous mileage out of the scandal** les journaux ont exploité le scandale au maximum; *Fam Fig* **there's no mileage in it** *(in idea etc)* ça ne nous mènera nulle part ❑, on ne peut rien en tirer ❑

(**b**) *(consumption)* consommation *f* (d'essence); **you get better mileage with a small car** on consomme moins avec une petite voiture; **how much mileage do you get?** combien est-ce que la voiture consomme aux cent?

▶▶ ***mileage allowance*** ≃ indemnité *f* kilométrique

Mile-High City *n* = surnom de la ville de Denver

mile-high club *n Fam* **we're members of the mile-high club** nous faisons partie de ceux qui se sont envoyés en l'air dans un avion

mileometer [maɪ'lɒmɪtə(r)] *n* compteur *m* (kilométrique)

milepost ['maɪlpəʊst] *n* ≃ borne *f* (kilométrique)

miler ['maɪlə(r)] *n* coureur(euse) *m,f* du mile

Milesian [maɪ'li:zɪən] *Hist* **1** *n* Milésien(enne) *m,f*, Milésiaque *mf*

2 *adj* milésien, milésiaque

milestone ['maɪlstəʊn] *n* (**a**) *(on road)* ≃ borne *f* (kilométrique) (**b**) *Fig (important event)* jalon *m*, étape *f* importante; **a milestone in the history of aviation** une étape importante dans l'histoire de l'aviation

milfoil ['mɪlfɔɪl] *n Bot* mille-feuille *f*

miliaria [,mɪlɪ'eərɪə] *n Med* fièvre *f* miliaire, miliaire *f*, suette *f* miliaire

milieu [*Br* 'mi:ljɜ:, *Am* mi:l'ju:] *n* environnement *m*, milieu *m*

militancy ['mɪlɪtənsɪ] *n* militantisme *m*

militant ['mɪlɪtənt] **1** *n* militant(e) *m,f*

2 *adj* militant; **she's a militant feminist** c'est une féministe militante

3 Militant (Tendency) *n Br Pol* = groupe d'extrême gauche à l'intérieur du Parti travailliste britannique

militaria [mɪlɪ'teərɪə] *n* objets *mpl* militaires

militarily [*Br* 'mɪlɪtərɪlɪ, *Am* ,mɪlə'terəlɪ] *adv* militairement

militarism ['mɪlɪtərɪzəm] *n* militarisme *m*

militarist ['mɪlɪtərɪst] *n* militariste *mf*

militaristic [,mɪlɪtə'rɪstɪk] *adj* militariste

militarization [,mɪlɪtəraɪ'zeɪʃən] *n* militarisation *f*

militarize, -ise ['mɪlɪtəraɪz] *vt* militariser

▶▶ ***militarized zone*** zone *f* militarisée

military ['mɪlɪtərɪ] **1** *adj (aircraft, base etc)* militaire; **a strong military presence** une forte présence militaire

2 *npl* **the military** les militaires *mpl*, l'armée *f*; **the military were called in** on a fait venir l'armée

▶▶ ***military academy*** école *f* militaire; ***military attaché*** attaché(e) *m,f* militaire; *Law* ***military court*** tribunal *m* militaire; ***Military Cross*** = distinction militaire britannique; ***military honours*** honneurs *mpl* militaires; *Br* ***military man*** militaire *m*; ***military police*** police *f* militaire; ***military policeman*** = membre de la police militaire; ***military science*** science *f* militaire; ***military service*** service *m* militaire; *Law* ***military tribunal*** tribunal *m* militaire

military-industrial *adj* militaro-industriel

▶▶ ***military industrial complex*** complexe *m* militaro-industriel

▶**militate against** ['mɪlɪteɪt-] *vt insep (facts, actions)* militer contre; **her temperament militates against her** son tempérament joue contre elle

militia [mɪ'lɪʃə] *n* (**a**) *(body of citizens)* milice *f* (**b**) *Am (reserve army)* réserve *f*

militiaman [mɪ'lɪʃəmən] *(pl* **militiamen** [-mən]*)* *n* milicien *m*

milk [mɪlk] **1** *n* lait *m*; **mother's milk** lait *m* maternel; **cow's milk** lait *m* de vache; **goat's milk** lait *m* de chèvre; **Milk of Magnesia**® lait *m* de magnésie; **a land flowing with milk and honey** un pays de cocagne; *Fig* **the milk of human kindness** le lait de la tendresse humaine

2 *comp (bottle, churn, jug etc* → *empty)* à lait; *(*→ *full)* de lait

3 *vt* (**a**) *(cow, goat)* traire

(**b**) *(snake)* extraire le venin de

(**c**) *Fig* **to milk a country of its resources** dépouiller un pays de ses ressources; **he really milks his clients** il plume ses clients; **she milked the subject dry** elle a épuisé le sujet; **the newspapers milked the story for all it was worth** les journaux ont tiré tout ce qu'ils ont pu de l'histoire; **they just milked all his ideas** ils se sont approprié toutes ses idées

4 *vi* **the cow milks well** la vache donne beaucoup de lait

▶▶ ***milk bank*** lactarium *m*; ***milk bar*** milk-bar *m*; *Am* ***milk can*** bidon *m* de lait; *Bot* ***milk cap*** *(fungus)* lactaire *m*; ***milk chocolate*** chocolat *m* au lait; ***milk duct*** canal *m* galactophore; *Vet* ***milk fever*** fièvre *f* lactée; *Br* ***milk float*** camionnette *f* du laitier; ***milk gland*** glande *f* lactéale *ou* galactophore; ***milk loaf*** pain *m* brioché; ***milk powder*** lait *m* en poudre; *Br* ***milk pudding*** entremets *m* au lait; *Formerly* ***the Milk Race*** = course cycliste en Grande-Bretagne *(ainsi nommée parce qu'elle était parrainée par l'industrie laitière)*; *Br* ***milk round*** *(for milk delivery)* tournée *f* du laitier; *Univ* = tournée des universités par les employeurs pour recruter des étudiants en fin d'études; *Fam* ***milk run*** *Aviat* vol *m* sans histoire, partie *f* de rigolade; *(regular journey)* trajet *m* habituel ❑, tournée *f* habituelle ❑; ***milk shake*** milk-shake *m*, *Can* lait *m* frappé; *Br* ***milk stout*** bière *f* brune; ***milk tooth*** dent *f* de lait; ***milk train*** premier train *m* (du matin); *Am* ***milk truck*** camionnette *f* du laitier; *Bot* ***milk vetch*** astragale *m*, tragacanthe *f*; *Bot* ***milk willowherb*** salicaire *f*

milk-and-water *adj Br Old-fashioned* insipide

milker ['mɪlkə(r)] *n* (**a**) *(cow)* **a good milker** une bonne laitière (**b**) *(dairy hand)* trayeur(euse) *m,f* (**c**) *(machine)* trayeuse *f*

milkiness ['mɪlkɪnɪs] *n (of liquid etc)* couleur *f* laiteuse, aspect *m* laiteux

milking ['mɪlkɪŋ] *n* traite *f*; **to do the milking** traire les vaches

▶▶ ***milking machine*** machine *f* à traire, trayeuse *f*; ***milking pail*** seau *m* à traire; ***milking parlour*** salle *f* de traite; ***milking stool*** tabouret *m* à traire; ***milking time*** l'heure *f* de la traite

milkmaid ['mɪlkmeɪd] *n* vachère *f*, trayeuse *f*

milkman ['mɪlkmən] *(pl* **milkmen** [-mən]*)* *n (who delivers milk)* laitier *m*; *Br (who milks)* vacher *m*, trayeur *m*

milkpail ['mɪlkpeɪl] *n Am* seau *m*

milksop ['mɪlksɒp] *n* chiffe *f* molle; **he's such a milksop!** c'est une vraie chiffe molle!

milkweed ['mɪlkwi:d] *n Bot (gen)* plante *f* à suc laiteux; *(sow thistle)* laiteron *m*, lait *m* d'âne; *(silkweed)* asclépiade *f* de Syrie

▶▶ *Entom* ***milkweed butterfly*** danaïde *f*

milk-white *adj* d'un blanc laiteux

milkwort ['mɪlkwɜ:t] *n Bot* polygale *m*

milky ['mɪlkɪ] *(compar* **milkier**, *superl* **milkiest***)* *adj* (**a**) *(taste)* laiteux, de lait; *(dessert)* lacté, à base de lait; *(tea, coffee)* avec du lait; **do you have your tea milky?** est-ce que vous prenez beaucoup de lait dans votre thé? (**b**) *(colour)* laiteux; *(skin)* d'un blanc laiteux (**c**) *(cloudy* → *liquid)* laiteux, lactescent

▶▶ *Astron* ***the Milky Way*** la Voie lactée

mill [mɪl] **1** *n* (**a**) *(for flour)* moulin *m*; *(on industrial scale)* meunerie *f*, minoterie *f*; *Fig* **she's been through the mill** elle a souffert; *Fig* **she put him through the mill** elle lui en a fait voir

(**b**) *(factory)* usine *f*; **steel mill** aciérie *f*

(**c**) *(domestic* → *for coffee, pepper)* moulin *m*

(**d**) *Tech (for coins)* machine *f* à créneler; *(for metal)* fraiseuse *f*; *(for rolling)* laminoir *m*

2 *vt* (**a**) *(grain)* moudre; *(ore)* broyer

(**b**) *(mark* → *coin)* créneler; *(*→ *screw)* moleter; *(*→ *surface)* strier, rainer; **a coin with a milled edge** une pièce crénelée

▶▶ *Old-fashioned* ***mill hand*** ouvrier(ère) *m,f*

▶**mill about, mill around** *vi (crowd, people)* grouiller

'The Mill on the Floss' *George Eliot* 'Le Moulin sur la Floss'

---

millboard ['mɪlbɔ:d] *n* carton *m* gris

milled [mɪld] *adj (grain etc)* moulu

▶▶ ***milled edge*** *(on coin)* crénelage *m*, grènetis *m*

millefiori [,mɪlɪ'fjɔ:rɪ] *n* sulfure *m*, millefiori *m inv*

millenarian [,mɪlɪ'neərɪən] **1** *n* millénariste *mf*

2 *adj* millénariste

millenarianism [,mɪlɪ'neərɪənɪzəm] *n* millénarisme *m*, chiliasme *m*

millenary [mɪ'lenərɪ] *(pl* **millenaries***)* **1** *n* millénaire *m*

2 *adj* millénaire

millennial [mɪ'lenɪəl] *adj* du millénaire; **the millennial celebrations** les festivités *fpl* organisées pour le passage à l'an 2000

millennium [mɪ'lenɪəm] *(pl* **millenniums** *or* **millennia** [-nɪə]*)* *n* (**a**) *(thousand years)* millénaire *m*; **what did you do for the millennium?** *(New*

Year's Eve, 1999) qu'est-ce que vous avez fait pour le millénaire *ou* pour le passage à l'an 2000?

(**b**) *Rel & Fig* **the millennium** le millénium

▸▸ ***Millennium Bridge*** = pont piétonnier au-dessus de la Tamise, à Londres, construit à l'occasion du nouveau millénaire; *Comput* ***the millennium bug*** le bogue de l'an 2000; ***the Millennium Commission*** = commission britannique chargée d'allouer des fonds provenant de la Loterie nationale à des projets liés aux festivités organisées pour le passage à l'an 2000; ***the Millennium Dome*** = centre d'expositions en forme de dôme construit à Londres à l'occasion de l'an 2000; ***the Millennium Stadium*** = stade de rugby construit à Cardiff pour accueillir les championnats du monde de rugby en 1999

THE MILLENNIUM DOME

Le projet du "Millennium Dome" (Dôme du Millénaire) fut mis en route par le gouvernement conservateur de John Major et se poursuivit sous le gouvernement Blair. À l'origine, le Dôme devait servir de vitrine pour présenter ce que la Grande-Bretagne avait de mieux à offrir en ce début de millénaire. Construit à Greenwich dans l'est de Londres et inauguré le 31 décembre 1999, le Dôme accueillit pendant toute l'année 2000 une exposition sur les enjeux importants de notre époque tels que la mondialisation, la génétique et l'environnement. Mais il s'avéra être un véritable gouffre financier. Son énorme déficit d'exploitation était payé en grande partie par des fonds de la Loterie nationale, et à défaut d'attirer suffisamment de visiteurs, l'édifice s'attira les foudres du public et devint un sujet de grande controverse.

millepede = **millipede**

miller ['mɪlə(r)] *n* (**a**) *(mill worker)* meunier(ère) *m,f* (**b**) *Tech (operator)* fraiseur *m*; *(machine)* fraiseuse *f* (**c**) *Entom* hanneton *m*

▸▸ *Ich* ***miller's thumb*** meunier *m*

millerandage ['mɪlərændɪdʒ] *n* millerandage *m*

millesimal [mɪ'lesɪməl] **1** *n* millième *m*

2 *adj* millième

millet ['mɪlɪt] *n* millet *m*

milli- ['mɪlɪ] *pref* milli-

milliard ['mɪljɑːd] *n Br* milliard *m*

millibar ['mɪlɪbɑː(r)] *n Met* millibar *m*

milligram, milligramme ['mɪlɪɡræm] *n* milligramme *m*

millilitre, *Am* **milliliter** ['mɪlɪˌliːtə(r)] *n* millilitre *m*

millimetre, *Am* **millimeter** ['mɪlɪˌmiːtə(r)] *n* millimètre *m*

milliner ['mɪlɪnə(r)] *n* modiste *mf*

millinery ['mɪlɪnrɪ] *n (manufacture)* fabrication *f* de chapeaux de femmes; *(sale)* vente *f* de chapeaux de femmes

milling ['mɪlɪŋ] *n* (**a**) *(of grain)* mouture *f*, moulage *m* (**b**) *Metal* fraisage *m*; *(of screw etc)* moletage *m*; *(of coin)* cordonnage *m* (**c**) *(on coin)* cordon *m*, grènetis *m*, tranche *f* cannelée

▸▸ ***milling cutter*** fraise *f*, fraiseuse *f*; ***milling machine*** fraiseuse *f*

million ['mɪljən] *n* (**a**) *(a thousand thousand)* million *m*; **two million dollars** deux millions *mpl* de dollars; **half a million** un demi-million; **millions of pounds** des millions *mpl* de livres; **the population of Scotland is five million** l'Écosse a cinq millions d'habitants; **the chance of that happening is one in a million** il y a une chance sur un million que ça arrive; **her secretary is one in a million** sa secrétaire est une perle rare; **he's worth millions** il est plusieurs fois milliardaire

(**b**) *(enormous number)* **an actor who gave pleasure to millions** un acteur qui a diverti des millions de gens; **there were millions of people at the concert!** il y avait un monde fou au concert!; **I've told you a million times not to do that** je t'ai dit cent fois de ne pas faire ça; **there are a million and one ways of cooking vegetables** il y a mille et une façons de préparer les légumes

millionaire [ˌmɪljə'neə(r)] *n* millionnaire *mf*; *(multi-millionaire)* milliardaire *mf*; **he's a dollar millionaire** il possède des millions de dollars; **to be a millionaire twice/three times over** être deux/trois fois millionnaire; **I've got a millionaire uncle** j'ai un oncle millionnaire/milliardaire

millionairess [ˌmɪljə'neərɪs] *n* millionnaire *f*; *(multi-millionairess)* milliardaire *f*

million-selling *adj* **a million-selling record** un disque qui s'est vendu à plus d'un million d'exemplaires

millionth ['mɪljənθ] **1** *n* (**a**) *(ordinal)* millionième *mf* (**b**) *(fraction)* millionième *m*

2 *adj* millionième

millipede ['mɪlɪpiːd] *n Entom* mille-pattes *m inv*

millisecond ['mɪlɪˌsekənd] *n* milliseconde *f*, millième *m* de seconde

millivolt ['mɪlɪvɒlt] *n* millivolt *m*

milliwatt ['mɪlɪwɒt] *n* milliwatt *m*

millowner ['mɪlˌəʊnə(r)] *n (factory owner)* propriétaire *mf* d'usine

millpond ['mɪlpɒnd] *n* retenue *f* de moulin; *Fig* **the sea was like a millpond** la mer était d'huile

millrace ['mɪlreɪs] *n (channel)* bief *m* (de moulin); *(water)* courant *m* du bief

Mills and Boon® ['mɪlzənˌbuːn] *n* = maison d'édition publiant des romans sentimentaux

Mills bomb ['mɪlz-] *n* = grenade à main utilisée par les Alliés pendant la Seconde Guerre mondiale

millstone ['mɪlstəʊn] *n* (**a**) *(stone)* meule *f* (**b**) *Fig* fardeau *m*; **another millstone round the taxpayer's neck** une charge supplémentaire pour le contribuable; **a millstone round my neck** un boulet que je traîne

millstream ['mɪlstriːm] *n* courant *m* du bief

millwheel ['mɪlwiːl] *n* roue *f* (de moulin)

millwright ['mɪlraɪt] *n* constructeur *m* de moulins

milometer = **mileometer**

milord [mɪ'lɔːd] *n Arch* milord *m*

milquetoast ['mɪlktəʊst] *n Am* chiffe *f* molle

milt [mɪlt] *n (of fish → fluid)* laitance *f*; *(→ organ)* testicule *m*

Miltonian [mɪl'təʊnɪən], **Miltonic** [mɪl'tɒnɪk] *adj Literature* miltonien

mim [mɪm] *adj Br Fam* bégueule

MIME [maɪm] *n Comput (abbr* **Multipurpose Internet Mail Extensions**) (protocole *m*) MIME *m*

mime [maɪm] **1** *n (performance)* mime *m*; *(actor)* mime *mf*; **to explain something in mime** expliquer quelque chose par gestes; **to study mime** étudier l'art du mime

2 *vt* mimer; *(derisively)* singer

3 *vi* (**a**) *Theat* faire du mime

(**b**) *(pop singer)* chanter en play-back; **to mime to a song** chanter en play-back

▸▸ ***mime artist*** mime *mf*

mimeograph ['mɪmɪəˌɡrɑːf] **1** *n* (**a**) *(machine)* Ronéo® *f*, duplicateur *m* (à stencil) (**b**) *(text)* polycopié *m*, texte *m* ronéotypé

2 *vt* ronéotyper, ronéoter

mimesis [mɪ'miːsɪs] *n* (**a**) *Biol* mimétisme *m* (**b**) *Art & Literature* mimésis *f*

mimetic [mɪ'metɪk] *adj Biol, Art & Literature* mimétique

mimetically [mɪ'metɪkəlɪ] *adv* (**a**) *Biol* par mimétisme (**b**) *Art & Literature* de façon réaliste

mimetism ['mɪmətɪzəm] *n Biol* mimétisme *m*

mimic ['mɪmɪk] *(pt & pp* **mimicked**, *cont* **mimicking**) **1** *vt* (**a**) *(person)* mimer; *(satirically)* parodier, singer; *(voice, walk, behaviour, nature etc)* imiter

(**b**) *Biol* imiter (par mimétisme)

2 *n* imitateur(trice) *m,f*; **she's an excellent mimic** c'est une excellente imitatrice

3 *adj* (**a**) *(mock → battle, warfare)* simulé

(**b**) *Theat* mimique

▸▸ *Biol* ***mimic colouring*** mimétisme *m* des couleurs

mimicry ['mɪmɪkrɪ] *n* (**a**) *(imitation)* imitation *f* (**b**) *Biol* mimétisme *m*

mimosa [mɪ'məʊzə] *n Bot* mimosa *m*

Min. *(written abbr* **ministry**) ministère *m*

min. (**a**) *(written abbr* **minute**) min (**b**) *(written abbr* **minimum**) min

mina = **myna**

minacious [mɪ'neɪʃəs] *adj Literary* menaçant

minaciously [mɪ'neɪʃəslɪ] *adv Literary* d'un air menaçant; *(speak)* d'un ton menaçant

minaret [mɪnə'ret] *n* minaret *m*

minatory ['mɪnətərɪ] *adj Formal* comminatoire

mince [mɪns] **1** *vt* (**a**) *Culin* hacher

(**b**) *(idiom)* **he doesn't mince his words** il ne mâche pas ses mots

2 *vi* (**a**) *(speak)* parler avec affectation

(**b**) *(move)* marcher en se trémoussant; **he minced into the room** il est entré dans la salle en se trémoussant

3 *n* (**a**) *Br (meat)* viande *f* hachée

(**b**) *Am (sweet filling)* = mélange de fruits secs et d'épices qui sert de garniture à des tartelettes

▸▸ ***mince pie*** = tartelette fourrée avec un mélange de fruits secs et d'épices que l'on sert à Noël en Grande-Bretagne

mincemeat ['mɪnsmiːt] *n* (**a**) *(meat)* viande *f* hachée

(**b**) *(sweet filling)* = mélange de fruits secs et d'épices qui sert de garniture à des tartelettes

(**c**) *Fam (idiom)* **to make mincemeat of sb** *(in fight, boxing match)* réduire qn en bouillie, démolir qn; *(in football, tennis match)* écraser qn; *(in debate, argument)* démolir qn; **the lawyer made mincemeat of his testimony** l'avocat a démoli son témoignage

mincer ['mɪnsə(r)] *n* hachoir *m*, hache-viande *m inv*

mincing ['mɪnsɪŋ] *adj* affecté, maniéré; **he came in with mincing steps** il est entré en se trémoussant

▸▸ ***mincing machine*** hachoir *m*, hache-viande *m inv*

mincingly ['mɪnsɪŋlɪ] *adv* en minaudant

MIND [maɪnd] *n* = organisme d'aide aux handicapés mentaux

MIND [maɪnd]

esprit	▸ **1 (a), (b), (e) – (g)**
attention	▸ **1 (c)**
avis	▸ **1 (h)**
faire attention à	▸ **2 (a) – (c)**
déranger	▸ **1 (d)**
garder	▸ **2 (e)**
faire attention	▸ **3 (c)**

1 *n* (**a**) *(reason)* esprit *m*; **the power of mind over matter** le pouvoir de l'esprit sur la matière; **to be strong in mind and body** être physiquement et mentalement solide; **to be of sound mind** être sain d'esprit; **to be/to go out of one's mind** être/devenir fou(folle); **are you out of your mind?, you must be out of your mind!** est-ce que tu as perdu la tête?; **he was out of his mind with worry** il était fou d'inquiétude; **he isn't in his right mind** il n'a pas tous ses esprits; **no one in their right mind would do such a thing** aucune personne sensée n'agirait ainsi; **to be bored out of one's mind** mourir d'ennui

(**b**) *(thoughts)* **such a thought had never entered his mind** une telle pensée ne lui était jamais venue à l'esprit; **there's something on her mind** il y a quelque chose qui la tracasse; **I have a lot on my mind** j'ai beaucoup de soucis; **what's going on in her mind?** qu'est-ce qui se passe dans son esprit *ou* sa tête?; **at the back of one's mind** au fond de soi-même; **at the back of my mind was the fear that we would arrive too late** au fond de moi-même, je craignais que nous n'arrivions trop tard; **to put sth to the back of one's mind** chasser qch de son esprit; **I just can't get him out of my mind** je n'arrive absolument pas à l'oublier; **to have sb/sth in mind** penser à qn/qch de précis; **the person I have in mind** la personne à laquelle je pense; **who do you have in mind for the role?** à qui songez-vous pour le rôle?, qui avez-vous en vue pour le rôle?; **what kind of holiday did you have in mind?** qu'est-ce que tu voulais *ou* voudrais faire pour les vacances?; **I had something smaller in mind** je pensais à quelque chose de plus petit; **you must put the idea out of your mind** tu dois te sortir cette idée de la tête; **put it out of your mind** n'y pensez plus; **to set one's mind on doing sth** se mettre en tête de faire qch; **to have one's mind set on sth** vouloir qch à tout prix; **a drink will take your mind off the accident** bois un verre, ça te fera oublier l'accident; **to put** *or* **set sb's mind at rest** rassurer qn; **to see things in one's mind's eye** bien se représenter qch; **it's**

all in your mind! tu te fais des idées!; **it's all in the mind** tout ça, c'est dans la tête

(**c**) *(attention)* **to give one's whole mind to sth** accorder toute son attention à qch; **I can't seem to apply my mind to the problem** je n'arrive pas à me concentrer sur le problème; **I'm sure if you put your mind to it you could do it** je suis sûr que si tu essayais vraiment, tu pourrais le faire; **keep your mind on the job** ne vous laissez pas distraire; **your mind is not on the job** tu n'as pas la tête à ce que tu fais; **she does crosswords to keep her mind occupied** elle fait des mots croisés pour s'occuper l'esprit; *Am* **don't pay him any mind** ne fais pas attention à lui

(**d**) *(memory)* **my mind has gone blank** j'ai un trou de mémoire; **it brings to mind the time we were in Spain** cela me rappelle l'époque où nous étions en Espagne; **Churchill's words come to mind** on pense aux paroles de Churchill; **it went clean** *or* **right out of my mind** cela m'est complètement sorti de l'esprit *ou* de la tête; **to put sb in mind of sb/sth** rappeler qn/qch à qn; **it puts me in mind of Japan** cela me fait penser au Japon, cela me rappelle le Japon; **to bear** *or* **keep sth in mind** *(think about)* songer à qch; *(take into account)* tenir compte de qch; *(not forget)* ne pas oublier qch, garder qch à l'esprit; **we must bear in mind that she is only a child** il ne faut pas oublier que ce n'est qu'une enfant; **I'll bear it in mind** *(what you suggested)* je prends note; **it must have slipped my mind** j'ai dû oublier; *Fam* **to have a mind like a sieve** avoir (une) très mauvaise mémoire ❑; *Br* **time out of mind I've warned him not to go there** cela fait une éternité que je lui dis de ne pas y aller

(**e**) *(intellect)* esprit *m*; **she has an outstanding mind** elle est d'une très grande intelligence; **he has the mind of a child** il a l'esprit d'un enfant

(**f**) *(intelligent person, thinker)* esprit *m*, cerveau *m*; **the great minds of our century** les grands esprits *ou* cerveaux de notre siècle; *Prov* **great minds think alike(, fools seldom differ)** les grands esprits se rencontrent; *Hum* **how about a drink? – great minds think alike!** si on prenait une verre? – les grands esprits se rencontrent!

(**g**) *(way of thinking)* **the Western mind** la pensée occidentale; **I haven't got a scientific mind** je n'ai pas l'esprit scientifique; **you've got a dirty mind!** tu as l'esprit mal placé!; **she has a nasty mind** elle voit le mal partout; **he has a suspicious mind** il est soupçonneux de nature; **it's probably just my suspicious mind but I don't trust him** c'est probablement que je suis trop suspicieux *ou* soupçonneux, mais je n'ai pas confiance en lui

(**h**) *(opinion)* **to be of the same** *or* **of like** *or* **of one mind** être du même avis; **they're all of one** *or* **the same mind** ils sont tous d'accord *ou* du même avis; **to know one's own mind** savoir ce qu'on veut; **you've got a mind of your own** tu peux décider toi-même; **the car seemed to have a mind of its own** la voiture semblait faire ce que bon lui semblait; **to my mind,...** à mon avis,..., selon moi,...; **I'm in two minds about where to go for my holidays** je ne sais pas très bien où aller passer mes vacances; **I'm in two minds about going** je ne sais pas si je vais y aller; **to make up one's mind** se décider, prendre une décision; **make up your mind!** décidez-vous!; **I can't make up your mind for you** je ne peux pas décider à ta place; **my mind is made up** ma décision est prise; **to make up one's mind about sth** décider qch; **to make up one's mind to do sth** se décider à faire qch; **she's made up her mind to move house** elle s'est résolue à déménager

(**i**) *(desire)* **I've half a mind to give up** j'ai presque envie de renoncer; **I've a good mind to tell him what I think** j'ai bien envie de lui dire ce que je pense

(**j**) *(intention)* **nothing was further from my mind** je n'en avais nullement l'intention; **I've had it in mind for some time now** j'y songe depuis un moment

2 *vt* (**a**) *(pay attention to)* faire attention à; **he didn't mind my advice** il n'a pas fait attention à *ou* n'a pas écouté mes conseils; **mind your own business!** occupe-toi de ce qui te regarde!, mêle-toi de tes oignons!; **mind your language!** surveille ton langage!; **to mind one's manners** se surveiller; **mind the step** *(sign)* attention à la marche; **mind the cat!** attention au chat!; **mind what you say** *(pay attention)* réfléchissez à *ou* faites attention à ce que vous dites; *(don't be rude)* mesurez vos paroles; **mind what you're doing!** regarde ce que tu fais!; **would you mind where you're putting your feet, please?** est-ce que tu peux faire attention où tu mets les pieds, s'il te plaît?; *Br Fam* **mind how you go!** fais attention à toi!

(**b**) *(be sure that)* faire attention à; **mind you write to him!** n'oubliez pas de lui écrire!; **mind you don't fall!** faites attention de ne pas tomber!; **mind you don't forget** n'oubliez surtout pas; **mind you don't break it** fais bien attention de ne pas le casser; **mind you're not late!** faites en sorte de ne pas être en retard!; **mind you post my letter** n'oubliez surtout pas de poster ma lettre

(**c**) *(concern oneself with)* faire attention à, s'inquiéter de *ou* pour; **don't mind me, I'll just sit here quietly** ne vous inquiétez pas de moi, je vais m'asseoir ici et je ne dérangerai personne; **don't mind him, he's always like that** ne fais pas attention à lui, il est toujours comme ça; *Ironic* **don't mind me, I only live here!** je t'en prie, fais comme chez toi!; **I really don't mind what he says/thinks** je me fiche de ce qu'il peut dire/penser

(**d**) *(object to)* **I don't mind him** il ne me dérange pas; **I don't mind the cold** le froid ne me gêne pas; **I don't mind trying** je veux bien essayer; **you don't mind me using the car, do you? – I mind very much** cela ne te dérange pas que je prenne la voiture? – cela me dérange beaucoup; **do you mind going out when the weather's cold?** est-ce que cela vous ennuie de sortir quand il fait froid?; **do you mind me smoking?** cela ne vous ennuie *ou* dérange pas que je fume?; **did you mind me inviting her?** tu aurais peut-être préféré que je ne l'invite pas?, ça t'ennuie que je l'aie invitée?; **would you mind turning out the light, please?** est-ce que tu peux éteindre la lumière, s'il te plaît?; **how much do you earn, if you don't mind my** *or* **me asking?** combien est-ce que vous gagnez, sans indiscrétion?; **I wouldn't mind having his salary** ça ne me dérangerait pas de gagner autant que lui; **I wouldn't mind a cup of tea** je prendrais bien *ou* volontiers une tasse de thé

(**e**) *(look after → children)* garder; *(→ bags, possessions)* garder, surveiller; *(→ shop, business)* garder, tenir; *(→ plants, garden)* s'occuper de, prendre soin de; **can you mind the house for us while we're away?** *(watch)* pouvez-vous surveiller la maison pendant notre absence?; *(look after)* pouvez-vous vous occuper de la maison pendant notre absence?

(**f**) *Scot (remember)* se rappeler, se souvenir de

(**g**) *(idioms)* **mind (you), I'm not surprised** remarque *ou* tu sais, cela ne m'étonne pas; **mind you, he's a bit young** ceci dit, il est un peu jeune; **mind you, I've always thought he was a bit strange** remarquez, j'ai toujours trouvé qu'il était un peu bizarre; **but, mind you, it was late** mais, voyez-vous, il était tard; **never mind that now** *(leave it)* ne vous occupez pas de cela tout de suite; *(forget it)* ce n'est plus la peine de s'en occuper; **never mind the consequences** ne vous préoccupez pas des conséquences, peu importent les conséquences; **never mind what people say/think** peu importe ce que disent/pensent les gens; **never mind his feelings, I've got a business to run!** je me moque de ses états d'âme, j'ai une entreprise à diriger!; **never mind him, just run for it!** ne t'occupe pas de lui, fonce!

3 *vi* (**a**) *(object → in requests)* **do you mind if I open the window?** cela vous dérange si j'ouvre la fenêtre?; **would you mind if I opened the window?** est-ce que cela vous dérangerait si j'ouvrais la fenêtre?; **do you mind if I smoke?** est-ce que cela vous gêne *ou* dérange que je fume?; **I don't mind in the least** cela ne me dérange pas le moins du monde; **if you don't mind** si vous voulez bien, si vous n'y voyez pas d'inconvénient; **I can't say I really mind** je ne peux pas dire que cela m'ennuie *ou* me dérange vraiment; **do you mind if I take the car? – of course I don't mind** est-ce que cela vous ennuie que je prenne la voiture? – bien sûr que non; *Fam* **I don't mind if I do** *(in reply to offer)* je ne dis pas non, ce n'est pas de refus

(**b**) *(care, worry)* **I don't mind if people laugh at me – but you should mind!** je ne me soucie guère que les gens se moquent de moi – mais vous devriez!; **if you don't mind, I haven't finished** si cela ne vous fait rien, je n'ai pas terminé; **do you mind?** *(politely)* vous permettez?; *Ironic* **do you mind!** *(indignantly)* non mais!; **never mind** *(it doesn't matter)* cela ne fait rien, tant pis; *(don't worry)* ne vous en faites pas; **never you mind!** *(don't worry)* ne vous en faites pas!; *(mind your own business)* ce n'est pas votre affaire!; **never mind about the money now** ne t'en fais pas pour l'argent, on verra plus tard

(**c**) *Br (be careful)* faire attention; **mind when you cross the road** fais attention en traversant la route; **mind!** attention!

▸▸ ***mind reader*** voyant(e) *m,f*; **he must be a mind reader** il lit dans les pensées comme dans un livre; **I'm not a mind reader** je ne suis pas devin; *Mktg* ***mind share*** part *f* de notoriété

▸**mind out** *vi Br* faire attention; **mind out!** attention!; **mind out for the rocks!** attention aux rochers!

---

mind-altering *adj (drug)* hallucinogène, psychédélique

mind-bender *n Fam (drug)* hallucinogène ❑ *m*

mind-bending [-bendɪŋ] *adj Fam* (**a**) *(complicated)* compliqué ❑ (**b**) *(drug)* hallucinogène ❑, psychédélique ❑

mind-blowing *adj Fam (amazing)* époustouflant; **it was a mind-blowing experience** ce fut une expérience époustouflante

mind-boggling *adj Fam* extraordinaire ❑, stupéfiant ❑; **he earns a mind-boggling £72,000 a month** il gagne la somme astronomique de 72 000 livres par mois; **his adventures make mind-boggling reading** le récit de ses aventures constitue une lecture fascinante ❑

minded ['maɪndɪd] *adj Formal* disposé; **she could easily lend us the money, if she were minded to do so** elle pourrait facilement nous prêter l'argent, si elle y était disposée *ou* le voulait

-minded ['maɪndɪd] *suff* (**a**) *(with adjective)* **simple-minded** simple d'esprit; **they're so narrow-minded** ils sont tellement étroits d'esprit

(**b**) *(with adverb)* **to be politically-minded** s'intéresser beaucoup à la politique; **many young people are scientifically-minded** beaucoup de jeunes ont l'esprit scientifique

(**c**) *(with noun)* **she isn't very money-minded** *(money isn't important to her)* elle n'est pas très préoccupée par les questions d'argent; **he's very sports-minded** c'est un passionné de sports

minder ['maɪndə(r)] *n* (**a**) *Fam (bodyguard)* garde *m* du corps ❑, gorille *m* (**b**) *(gen)* gardien(enne) *m,f*, surveillant(e) *m,f* (**c**) **(child** *or* **baby) minder** nourrice *f*

mind-expanding *adj (drug)* hallucinogène, psychédélique

mindful ['maɪndfʊl] *adj Formal* **to be mindful of sth** *(remember)* se souvenir de qch, ne pas oublier qch; **mindful of her feelings on the subject, he fell silent** attentif à ce qu'elle ressentait à ce sujet, il se tut; **he was always mindful of his children's future** il a toujours été soucieux *ou* il s'est toujours préoccupé de l'avenir de ses enfants; **he is always mindful of others** il pense toujours aux autres

mindless ['maɪndlɪs] *adj* (**a**) *(stupid → film, book)* idiot, stupide; *(senseless → cruelty, violence)* gratuit (**b**) *(boring)* bête, ennuyeux; **a mindless job** un travail ingrat *ou* stupide (**c**) *Formal (heedless)* **mindless of the danger, he dived into the river** insouciant du danger, il plongea dans la rivière

mind-numbing *adj* abêtissant

mindset ['maɪndset] *n* façon *f* de voir les choses

mine[1] [maɪn] **1** *pron* (**a**) *(gen → singular)* le mien (la mienne) *m,f*; *(→ plural)* les miens (les miennes) *mpl, fpl*; **is this pen mine? – no, it's mine!** il est à moi ce stylo? – non, c'est le mien!; **this bag**

is mine ce sac m'appartient *ou* est à moi; **the furniture is his but the house is mine** les meubles lui appartiennent mais la maison est à moi; **he's an old friend of mine** c'est un vieil ami à moi; **where did that brother of mine get to?** mais où est-ce que mon frère est encore passé?; **I took her hands in mine** j'ai pris ses mains dans les miennes; **mine is an exceptional situation** je me trouve dans une situation exceptionnelle; **what's mine is yours** ce qui est à moi est à toi; *Br Fam* **mine's a beer** *(in pub)* pour moi, ce sera une bière ❑
(**b**) *Fam (my house, flat)* chez moi ❑
2 *adj Arch (singular)* mon(ma); *(plural)* mes; **mine only hope** mon seul espoir; *Hum* **mine host** l'aubergiste *m*

mine² **1** *n* (**a**) *(for coal, gold, salt etc)* mine *f*; **he went down the mine** *or* **mines at sixteen** il est descendu à la mine à seize ans
(**b**) *Fig (valuable source)* mine *f*; **she's a mine of information** c'est une véritable mine de renseignements
(**c**) *(explosive)* mine *f*; **to clear a road of mines** déminer une route; **to lay a mine** *(on land)* poser une mine; *(at sea)* mouiller une mine
2 *vt* (**a**) *Geol (coal, gold etc)* extraire; *(coal seam)* exploiter; **they mine coal in the area** il y a des mines de charbon dans la région
(**b**) *Mil (road, sea)* miner; **the path was mined** le chemin était miné; **their jeep was mined** leur jeep a sauté sur une mine
(**c**) *(undermine → fortification)* saper
3 *vi* exploiter une mine; **to mine for uranium** *(prospect)* chercher de l'uranium, prospecter pour trouver de l'uranium; *(extract)* exploiter une mine d'uranium
▸▸ ***mine detector*** détecteur *m* de mines; ***mine workings*** chantiers *mpl* d'exploitation minière

minefield ['maɪnfiːld] *n* (**a**) *(containing mines)* champ *m* de mines (**b**) *Fig* **the minefield of high-level diplomacy** les chausse-trappes de la haute diplomatie; **a political minefield** une situation épineuse du point de vue politique

minehunter ['maɪn,hʌntə(r)] *n Naut* chasseur *m* de mines

minelayer ['maɪn,leɪə(r)] *n Naut* mouilleur *m* de mines

minelaying ['maɪn,leɪɪŋ] *n Mil* pose *f* de mines; *Naut* mouillage *m* de mines

mineowner ['maɪn,əʊnə(r)] *n* propriétaire *mf* de mine(s)

miner ['maɪnə(r)] *n Mining* mineur *m*
▸▸ ***miner's lamp*** lampe *f* de mineur; *Med* ***miner's lung*** anthracose *f*; ***miners' strike*** grève *f* des mineurs

mineral ['mɪnərəl] **1** *n* (**a**) *Geol* minéral *m*; **the mineral resources of a country** les ressources *fpl* minières d'un pays
(**b**) *Br (soft drink)* boisson *f* gazeuse (non alcoolique), soda *m*
2 *adj* minéral
▸▸ *Br* ***mineral jelly*** vaseline *f*; ***the mineral kingdom*** le monde minéral; ***mineral oil*** *Br* huile *f* minérale; *Am* huile *f* de paraffine; ***mineral ore*** minerai *m*; ***mineral spring*** source *f* d'eau minérale; ***mineral water*** eau *f* minérale; ***mineral wool*** laine *f* minérale, laine *f* de roche

mineralization [,mɪnərəlaɪ'zeɪʃən] *n* (**a**) *(of water, metal etc)* minéralisation *f* (**b**) *(of bones)* calcification *f*, minéralisation *f*; *(of teeth)* calcification *f*

mineralize, -ise ['mɪnərəlaɪz] *vt* minéraliser

mineralized ['mɪnərəlaɪzd] *adj (water, metal etc)* minéralisé
▸▸ *Com* ***mineralized methylated spirits*** alcool *m* dénaturé additionné de naphte

mineralocorticoid [,mɪnerælәʊ'kɔːtɪkɔɪd] *n Med* minéralocorticoïde *m*

mineralogical [,mɪnərə'lɒdʒɪkəl] *adj* minéralogique

mineralogist [,mɪnə'rælədʒɪst] *n* minéralogiste *mf*

mineralogy [,mɪnə'rælədʒɪ] *n* minéralogie *f*

Minerva [mɪ'nɜːvə] *pr n Myth* Minerve

mineshaft ['maɪnʃɑːft] *n* puits *m* de mine

minestrone (soup) [,mɪnɪ'strəʊnɪ-] *n* minestrone *m*

minesweeper ['maɪn,swiːpə(r)] *n* dragueur *m* de mines

minesweeping ['maɪn,swiːpɪŋ] *n* dragage *m* des mines

mineworker ['maɪn,wɜːkə(r)] *n* ouvrier(ère) *m,f* de la mine, mineur *m*

Ming [mɪŋ] *adj* Ming *(inv)*; **a Ming vase** un vase Ming; **the Ming dynasty** la dynastie des Ming

ming [mɪŋ] *n Scot Fam* puanteur ❑ *f*

minge [mɪndʒ] *n Br Vulg (vagina)* chatte *f*

minging ['mɪŋɪŋ] *adj Scot Fam* (**a**) *(having a bad smell)* qui pue ❑ (**b**) *(disgusting)* dégueulasse

mingle ['mɪŋgəl] **1** *vt* mélanger, mêler; **he mingled truth with lies** il mélangeait le vrai et le faux; **joy mingled with sadness** joie *f* mêlée de tristesse; *Literary* **to mingle one's tears with sb's** mêler ses larmes à celles de qn
2 *vi* se mêler aux gens; **to mingle with the crowd** se mêler à la foule; **excuse me, I must mingle** excusez-moi, il faut que je salue d'autres invités

mingy ['mɪndʒɪ] *(compar* **mingier**, *superl* **mingiest**) *adj Br Fam (mean → person)* radin, pingre; *(→ salary, gift, amount of money)* minable; **a mingy helping** une portion minuscule; **a mingy five pounds** cinq malheureuses livres

mini ['mɪnɪ] **1** *n Fam* (**a**) *(skirt)* minijupe ❑ *f* (**b**) *Comput* mini-ordinateur ❑ *m*, mini *m*
2 *adj* mini *(inv)*
3 **Mini**® *n (car)* mini *f* (Austin®)
▸▸ *Comput* ***mini tower*** mini-tour *f*

mini- ['mɪnɪ] *pref* mini(-); **minibiography** minibiographie *f*; **minirecording studio** mini-studio *m* d'enregistrement

miniature ['mɪnətʃə(r)] **1** *n (gen) & Art* miniature *f*; **in miniature** en miniature
2 *adj (in miniature)* en miniature; *(model)* miniature; *(tiny)* minuscule; **a miniature Eiffel Tower** une tour Eiffel miniature
▸▸ ***miniature golf*** golf *m* miniature, minigolf *m*; ***miniature poodle*** caniche *m* nain; ***miniature railway*** chemin *m* de fer miniature

miniaturist ['mɪnətʃərɪst] *n Art* miniaturiste *mf*

miniaturization [,mɪnətʃəraɪ'zeɪʃən] *n* miniaturisation *f*

miniaturize, -ise ['mɪnətʃəraɪz] *vt* miniaturiser

miniaturized ['mɪnətʃəraɪzd] *adj* miniaturisé

minibar ['mɪnɪbɑː(r)] *n* minibar *m*

mini-break *n (holiday)* mini-séjour *m*

minibudget ['mɪnɪ,bʌdʒɪt] *n Br Pol* budget *m* auxiliaire

minibus ['mɪnɪbʌs] *(pl* **minibuses**) *n* minibus *m*

minicab ['mɪnɪkæb] *n Br* = voiture de série convertie en taxi, radio-taxi *m*

minicam ['mɪnɪkæm] *n* caméra *f* de télévision miniature

minicomputer [,mɪnɪkəm'pjuːtə(r)] *n* mini-ordinateur *m*

minicourse ['mɪnɪkɔːs] *n Am Sch* stage *m* (intensif), *Can* mini-cours *m*

mini-cruise *n* mini-croisière *f*

MiniDisc® ['mɪnɪdɪsk] *n* MiniDisc® *m*

minidisk ['mɪnɪdɪsk] *n* mini-disquette *f*

minidress ['mɪnɪdres] *n* mini-robe *f*

mini-flyweight *n Boxing* poids *m* mouche

minigolf ['mɪnɪgɒlf] *n* minigolf *m*

minim ['mɪnɪm] *n* (**a**) *Br Mus* blanche *f* (**b**) *(measure)* 0,5 ml, ≃ goutte *f*
▸▸ *Br Mus* ***minim rest*** demi-pause *f*

minima ['mɪnɪmə] *pl of* **minimum**

minimal ['mɪnɪməl] *adj* (**a**) *(very small)* minime; **there has been only a minimal improvement** il n'y a eu qu'une infime amélioration; **there was minimal interest** cela n'a suscité qu'un intérêt minime *ou* que peu d'intérêt
(**b**) *(minimum)* minimal, minimum
▸▸ ***minimal art*** art *m* minimal, minimalisme *m*; *Med* ***minimal invasive therapy*** chirurgie *f* à invasion minimale; *Ling* ***minimal pair*** paire *f* minimale; ***minimal value*** valeur *f* minimale

minimalism ['mɪnɪməlɪzəm] *n* minimalisme *m*

minimalist ['mɪnɪməlɪst] **1** *n* minimaliste *mf*
2 *adj* minimaliste

minimalize, -ise ['mɪnɪməlaɪz] *vt* minimaliser

minimally ['mɪnɪməlɪ] *adv* à peine; **the new system is only minimally more efficient** le nouveau système n'est guère plus efficace; *Med* **minimally invasive surgery** chirurgie *f* à invasion minimale

minimarket ['mɪnɪ,mɑːkɪt], **minimart** ['mɪnɪmɑːt] *n* supérette *f*, petit supermarché *m*

minimax ['mɪnɪmæks] *n Math* minimax *m*

minimization [,mɪnɪmaɪ'zeɪʃən] *n* minimisation *f*

minimize, -ise ['mɪnɪmaɪz] *vt* (**a**) *(reduce → size, amount, impact)* réduire au minimum, diminuer le plus possible; **they are trying to minimize the levels of CO_2 in the atmosphere** on essaie de réduire les niveaux de CO_2 dans l'atmosphère
(**b**) *(diminish → importance, achievement)* minimiser; **he tried to minimize her success as a novelist** il essayait de minimiser son succès en tant que romancière
(**c**) *Comput (window)* réduire

minimum ['mɪnɪməm] *(pl* **minimums** *or* **minima** [-mə]) **1** *n* minimum *m*; **a minimum of two years' experience** un minimum de deux ans d'expérience; **as a minimum** au minimum; **to reduce sth to a minimum** réduire qch au minimum; **keep the questions to a minimum** essayez de poser le moins de questions possible; **in order to keep mistakes to a minimum** de façon à avoir le minimum d'erreurs; **in order to reduce delays to a minimum** de façon à réduire l'attente au maximum; **at the (very) minimum it will cost £2,000** (en mettant les choses) au mieux, cela coûtera 2000 livres; **we will need £50 each minimum** *or* **a minimum of £50 each** il nous faudra 50 livres chacun (au) minimum
2 *adj* minimum, minimal
▸▸ ***minimum charge*** charge *f ou* tarif *m* minimum; *Fin* ***minimum deposit*** acompte *m* minimum; *Br Formerly Fin* ***minimum lending rate*** taux *m* de base, taux *m* officiel d'escompte; *Fin* ***minimum payment*** paiement *m* minimum; ***minimum rate*** taux *m* minimum; *Br* ***minimum safeguard price*** prix *m* minimum de sauvegarde *(du pétrole)*; ***minimum speed*** vitesse *f* minimum *ou* minimale; *Com* ***minimum stock level*** stock *m* d'alerte; ***minimum wage*** salaire *m* minimum *(légal)*, ≃ SMIC *m*

mining ['maɪnɪŋ] **1** *n* (**a**) *Mining* exploitation *f* minière, extraction *f*; **the mining industry** l'industrie *f* minière (**b**) *Mil (on land)* pose *f* de mines; *(at sea)* mouillage *m* de mines
2 *adj (town, area, company)* minier; *(family)* de mineurs
▸▸ ***mining engineer*** ingénieur *m* des mines; ***mining engineering*** ingénierie *f* des mines

minion ['mɪnjən] *n Pej* laquais *m*; *Fam Ironic (subordinate)* sous-fifre *m*

minipill ['mɪnɪpɪl] *n* minipilule *f*

mini-roundabout *n Br* mini rond-point *m*

miniscule ['mɪnɪskjuːl] *adj* minuscule

mini-series *n TV* mini-feuilleton *m*

miniskirt ['mɪnɪskɜːt] *n* minijupe *f*

minister ['mɪnɪstə(r)] **1** *n* (**a**) *Pol* ministre *m*; **the Minister of Education/Defence** le ministre de l'Éducation/de la Défense; **Minister of State** secrétaire *mf* d'État; **Minister without Portfolio** ministre *m* sans portefeuille
(**b**) *(diplomat)* ministre *m*
(**c**) *Rel* pasteur *m*, ministre *m*; **minister of God** ministre *m* du culte
2 *vi* (**a**) *(provide care)* **to minister to sb** prodiguer des soins à qn; **to minister to sb's needs** pourvoir aux besoins de qn; **he ministered to the sick** il secourait les malades
(**b**) *Rel* **he ministered to St Luke's for twenty years** il a été le pasteur de l'église St-Luc pendant vingt ans

ministerial [,mɪnɪ'stɪərɪəl] *adj* (**a**) *Pol (project, crisis)* ministériel; *(post)* de ministre; **to hold ministerial office** être ministre; **ministerial functions** fonctions *fpl* exécutives; **ministerial responsibility** responsabilité *f* ministérielle (**b**) *Rel* pastoral, sacerdotal (**c**) *Law* exécutif
▸▸ *Br Parl* ***ministerial benches*** banc *m* des ministres

ministering angel ['mɪnɪstərɪŋ-] *n Fig* ange *m* de bonté

ministration [,mɪnɪ'streɪʃən] **1** *n Rel* ministère *m*, sacerdoce *m*
2 ministrations *npl Formal* soins *mpl*; **despite her ministrations the animal died** malgré les soins qu'elle lui a prodigués, l'animal est mort

ministry ['mɪnɪstrɪ] *(pl* **ministries**) *n* (**a**) *Pol (department)* ministère *m*; *(government)* gouvernement *m*; *Br* **Ministry of Agriculture, Fisheries and Food** ≃ ministère *m* de l'Agriculture; *Br* **the**

Ministry of Defence le ministère de la Défense (**b**) *Rel (collective body)* sacerdoce *m*, saint ministère *m*; *(period of office)* ministère *m*; **to join the ministry** *(Roman Catholic)* se faire ordonner prêtre; *(Protestant)* devenir pasteur; **at the end of his ministry in London he moved away** il quitta Londres au terme de son ministère dans cette ville

minium ['mɪnɪəm] *n Miner* minium *m*

minivan ['mɪnɪvæn] *n* fourgonnette *f*

miniver ['mɪnɪvə(r)] *n Zool* petit-gris *m*

mink [mɪŋk] *n* (**a**) *Zool* **(American) mink** vison *m*, martre *f* du Canada (**b**) *(fur)* vison *m*; **a mink (coat)** un manteau de vison, un vison

►► ***mink farm*** visonnière *f*; ***mink oil*** huile *f* de vison; ***mink ranch*** visonnière *f*

minke (whale) ['mɪŋkɪ-] *n Zool* petit rorqual *m*

Minn *(written abbr* **Minnesota***)* Minnesota *m*

Minnehaha [,mɪnɪ'hɑːhɑː] *pr n* = femme de Hiawatha

Minnesota [,mɪnɪ'səʊtə] *n* le Minnesota; **in Minnesota** dans le Minnesota

minnow ['mɪnəʊ] *(pl* **inv** *or* **minnows***)* *n* (**a**) *Ich (specific fish)* vairon *m*; *(any small fish)* fretin *m* (**b**) *Br Fig (insignificant person)* (menu) fretin *m*

Minoan [mɪ'nəʊən] **1** *n* minoen(enne) *m,f*

2 *adj* minoen

minor ['maɪnə(r)] **1** *adj* (**a**) *(secondary → road, position)* secondaire; *(→ writer)* mineur; *(→ importance, interest)* secondaire, mineur; *(→ share)* petit, mineur; **to play a minor part** *or* **role** *Cin & Theat* avoir un petit rôle; *Fig* jouer un rôle mineur *ou* accessoire

(**b**) *(unimportant → problem, worry)* mineur, peu important

(**c**) *(small → alteration, disagreement)* mineur, petit; *(→ detail, expense)* mineur, petit, menu

(**d**) *(not serious → accident)* mineur, petit; *(→ illness, injury)* bénin(igne); *Med* **to have a minor operation** subir une petite intervention chirurgicale *ou* une intervention chirurgicale bénigne

(**e**) *(for emphasis)* **the film is a minor classic** le film est un petit chef-d'œuvre; **it was a minor miracle that we got there on time** ça tient presque du miracle que nous soyons arrivés à l'heure

(**f**) *Mus* mineur; **in A minor** en la mineur; **in a minor key** en mode mineur

(**g**) *Br Old-fashioned Sch* **Jones minor** Jones junior

(**h**) *Am Univ (subject)* facultatif

2 *n* (**a**) *(in age)* mineur(e) *m,f*

(**b**) *Am Univ* matière *f* secondaire

(**c**) *Am* **the Minors** *(film companies)* = les trois compagnies de production secondaires (par rapport aux "Majors") à Hollywood: Universal, United Artists, Columbia

3 *vi Am Univ* **she minored in French** elle a pris le français comme matière secondaire

►► ***minor league*** **1** *n Am Sport* ≃ division *f* d'honneur, *Can* ligue *f* mineure **2** *adj Fig* secondaire, de peu d'importance; **they're minor league compared with some American corporations** ils sont loin d'avoir l'envergure de certaines grandes sociétés américaines; *Law* ***minor offence*** délit *m* mineur; *Rel* ***minor orders*** ordres *mpl* mineurs; *Astron* ***minor planet*** astéroïde *m*; ***minor premise*** *(in logic)* (proposition *f*) mineure *f*; *Mus* ***minor seventh*** septième *f* mineure; *Fin* ***minor shareholder*** actionnaire *mf* minoritaire; *Cards* ***minor suit*** couleur *f* mineure; *Mus* ***minor third*** tierce *f* mineure

Minorca [mɪ'nɔːkə] *n* Minorque; **in Minorca** à Minorque

Minorcan [mɪ'nɔːkən] **1** *n* Minorquin(e) *m,f*

2 *adj* minorquin

Minorite ['maɪnəraɪt] *n Rel* Frère *m* mineur, Franciscain *m*; **the Minorite order** l'ordre *m* des Frères mineurs, l'ordre *m* de saint François d'Assise

minority [maɪ'nɒrɪtɪ] *(pl* **minorities***)* **1** *n* (**a**) *(small group)* minorité *f*; **to be in a** *or* **the minority** être en minorité; **only a minority (of people) watch late-night TV** seule une minorité (de gens) regarde la télé tard le soir; *Hum* **I'm afraid you're in a minority of one** j'ai bien peur que vous ne soyez le seul de cet avis; **the vocal minority** la minorité qui se fait entendre; **a minority TV programme** = une émission de télévision destinée à un public restreint

(**b**) *Law (age)* minorité *f*

2 *comp (government, party, tastes)* minoritaire

►► ***minority group*** minorité *f*; *Fin* ***minority holding, minority interest*** participation *f* minoritaire; *Fin* ***minority investor*** investisseur(euse) *m,f* minoritaire; *Am Pol* ***minority leader*** = chef d'un parti minoritaire au Congrès; ***minority opinion*** opinion *f* d'une minorité; **minority opinion must be respected** on doit respecter l'opinion de la minorité; ***minority report*** contre-rapport *m (soumis par une minorité)*; *Fin Br* ***minority shareholder,*** *Am* ***minority stockholder*** actionnaire *mf* minoritaire; *Law* ***minority verdict*** verdict *m* de la minorité

Minos ['maɪnɒs] *pr n Myth* Minos

Minotaur ['maɪnətɔː(r)] *n* **the Minotaur** le Minotaure

Minsk [mɪnsk] *n* Minsk

minster ['mɪnstə(r)] *n (abbey church)* (église *f*) abbatiale *f*; *(cathedral)* cathédrale *f*

minstrel ['mɪnstrəl] *n* (**a**) *(in Middle Ages)* ménestrel *m* (**b**) *Literary (poet)* poète *m*; *(musician)* musicien *m*; *(singer)* chanteur *m* (**c**) *(actor, singer with blackened face)* = acteur/musicien blanc maquillé en noir

►► ***minstrel gallery*** tribune *f* des musiciens; *Theat* ***minstrel show*** = spectacle de music-hall avec des acteurs blancs déguisés en Noirs

minstrelsy ['mɪnstrəlsɪ] *n* art *m* du ménestrel

mint[1] [mɪnt] **1** *n* (**a**) *(plant)* menthe *f*

(**b**) *(sweet)* bonbon *m* à la menthe

2 *comp (chocolate, sauce, tea)* à la menthe

►► ***mint julep*** cocktail *m* au bourbon et à la menthe

mint[2] **1** *n* (**a**) *(for coins)* **the (Royal) Mint** l'Hôtel *m* de la Monnaie, la Monnaie

(**b**) *Fam (fortune)* fortune❑ *f*; **to make a mint** faire fortune; **it's worth a mint** cela vaut une fortune

2 *adj (stamps, coins)* (tout) neuf; *Fig* **in mint condition** en parfait état, à l'état neuf

3 *vt* (**a**) *(coins)* frapper; *Fam Fig* **he must be minting it** il doit rouler sur l'or

(**b**) *(invent → word)* inventer, créer; *(→ expression)* forger

►► *Fin* ***mint par*** pair *m* intrinsèque

mintage ['mɪntɪdʒ] *n (process of minting)* monnayage *m*, frappe *f* (de monnaie)

minted ['mɪntɪd] *adj Br Fam* plein aux as, bourré de fric

Minton ['mɪntən] *n (china)* = porcelaine tendre fabriquée à Stoke-on-Trent en Angleterre

minuend ['mɪnjʊend] *n Math* nombre *m* à diminuer

minuet [,mɪnjʊ'et] *n Mus* menuet *m*

minus ['maɪnəs] *(pl* **minuses** *or* **minusses***)* **1** *prep* (**a**) *Math* moins; **seven minus two leaves** *or* **equals five** sept moins deux font cinq; **minus twelve** moins douze

(**b**) *(in temperature)* **it's minus 5° outside** il fait moins 5° dehors

(**c**) *Fam (without)* sans❑; **he came home minus his shopping** il est rentré sans ses achats; **that chair is minus a leg** cette chaise a un pied en moins

2 *n* (**a**) *(sign)* moins *m*; **put a minus in front of the twelve** mettez un moins devant le douze

(**b**) *(drawback)* inconvénient *m*; **one of the minuses is that we risk losing money** un des inconvénients est que nous risquons de perdre de l'argent

3 *adj* (**a**) *(number)* négatif; *Sch* **B minus** B moins

(**b**) *Fig* négatif; **but, on the minus side, the pay is low** mais le revers de la médaille, c'est que c'est mal payé

►► ***minus sign*** signe *m* moins, moins *m*

minuscule ['mɪnəskjuːl] **1** *n* minuscule *f*

2 *adj* (**a**) *(tiny)* minuscule (**b**) *(lower-case)* en (lettres) minuscules

minute[1] ['mɪnɪt] **1** *n* (**a**) *(period of sixty seconds)* minute *f*; **for ten minutes** pendant dix minutes; **I'll be ready in ten minutes** je serai prêt dans dix minutes; **it's only a few minutes' walk (from here)** c'est seulement à quelques minutes (d'ici) à pied; **he got there with only a minute to spare** il y est arrivé avec une seule minute d'avance; **to observe a minute's silence** observer une minute de silence; **two minutes past/to ten** dix heures deux/moins deux

(**b**) *(moment)* instant *m*, minute *f*; **I'll be back in a minute** je reviens dans une minute *ou* dans un instant *ou* tout de suite; **it only took him a minute** il en a eu pour une minute; **a minute's rest** un moment de repos; **wait a minute, please** attendez un instant, s'il vous plaît; **just a minute!** un instant!, une minute!; *(aggressively)* une minute!; **come here this minute!** viens ici tout de suite!; **I think of you every minute of the day** je pense à vous à chaque instant de la journée; **I'll talk to him the minute he arrives** je lui parlerai dès qu'il arrivera; **the minute my back was turned she...** j'avais à peine le dos tourné qu'elle...; **the weather here changes from one minute to the next** ici, le temps change d'une minute à l'autre; **any minute now** d'un instant à l'autre; **at the minute** en ce moment; **right up till the last minute** jusqu'à la toute dernière minute; **at the last minute** à la dernière minute; **she left the house within minutes of his arrival** elle a quitté la maison dans les minutes qui ont suivi son arrivée; **the flight took two hours to the minute** le vol a duré deux heures à la minute près *ou* exactement; *Br* **she arrived at six o'clock to the minute** elle est arrivée à six heures précises *ou* à six heures pile

(**c**) *Geom (of degree)* minute *f*

(**d**) *(note)* note *f* (de service)

2 *vt* (**a**) *(facts, comments)* prendre note de; *(meeting)* dresser le procès-verbal *ou* le compte rendu de

(**b**) *(time)* minuter, chronométrer

3 **minutes** *npl* (**a**) *(of meeting)* procès-verbal *m*, compte rendu *m*; **to take the minutes of a meeting** faire le compte rendu d'une réunion

(**b**) *(report)* note *f*

►► ***minute bell*** glas *m (qui sonne toutes les minutes)*; ***minute book*** registre *m* des délibérations *ou* des procès-verbaux; ***minute gun*** = canon dont les coups sont tirés à intervalles d'une minute, pour des funérailles par exemple; ***minute hand*** grande aiguille *f*, aiguille *f* des minutes; ***minute steak*** entrecôte *f* minute; ***minute timer*** minuterie *f*

minute[2] [maɪ'njuːt] *adj* (**a**) *(tiny)* minuscule, infime; *(very slight → difference, improvement)* infime, minime (**b**) *(precise)* minutieux, détaillé; **with minute care** avec un soin minutieux; **in minute detail** par le menu; **in the minutest detail** dans les moindres détails

minutely [maɪ'njuːtlɪ] *adv* (**a**) *(carefully)* minutieusement, avec un soin minutieux; *(in detail)* en détail, par le menu (**b**) *(fold)* tout petit; *(move)* imperceptiblement, très légèrement

Minuteman ['mɪnɪt,mæn] *(pl* **Minutemen** [-men]*)* *n* (**a**) *Am Hist (soldier)* homme-minute *m (soldat volontaire de la guerre d'Indépendance américaine)* (**b**) *(missile)* Minuteman *m (missile balistique)*

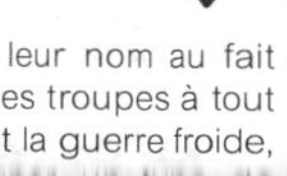

MINUTEMEN

Les "hommes-minute" doivent leur nom au fait qu'ils étaient prêts à rejoindre les troupes à tout moment pour se battre. Pendant la guerre froide, ce nom fut repris pour désigner un type de missile américain.

minuteness [maɪ'njuːtnɪs] *n* (**a**) *(tininess)* caractère *m* minuscule; *(slightness → of difference, improvement)* caractère *m* infime (**b**) *(preciseness)* minutie *f*

minutiae [maɪ'njuːʃɪaɪ] *npl* menus détails *mpl*, petits détails *mpl*; *Pej (trivialities)* vétilles *fpl*, riens *mpl*

minx [mɪŋks] *n Fam* coquine *f*, friponne *f*; **you little minx!** petite espiègle!, petite polissonne!

Miocene ['maɪəsiːn] *Geol* **1** *n* miocène *m*

2 *adj* miocène

miosis [maɪ'əʊsɪs] *n Med* myosis *m*

mips [mɪps] *n Comput (abbr* **million instructions per second***)* MIPS *m*

miracle ['mɪrəkəl] *n* (**a**) *Rel & Fig* miracle *m*; **to work miracles** faire *ou* accomplir des miracles; **she's worked miracles with those kids** elle a fait des miracles avec ces enfants; **by a miracle, disaster was averted** la catastrophe a été évitée par miracle; **it was a miracle (that) she survived** c'est un miracle qu'elle ait survécu; **economic miracle** miracle *m* économique; **a miracle of modern science** un prodige *ou* miracle de la science moderne

(**b**) *(play)* miracle *m (drame)*

►► *Fig* ***miracle cure*** remède *m* miracle; *Pharm* ***miracle drug*** remède *m* miracle; ***miracle play*** miracle *m (drame)*; ***miracle worker*** faiseur(-euse) *m,f* de miracles; *Fig* **I'm not a miracle worker you know!** je ne peux pas faire de miracles

miraculous [mɪ'rækjʊləs] *adj* miraculeux; **they had a miraculous escape** c'est un miracle qu'ils s'en soient tirés (vivants); *Ironic* **she made a miraculous recovery as soon as the weekend arrived** comme par miracle, son état de santé s'est amélioré juste avant le week-end

miraculously [mɪ'rækjʊləslɪ] *adv* (**a**) *(by a miracle)* miraculeusement, par miracle; **miraculously, no one was hurt** tout le monde s'en est sorti miraculeusement indemne (**b**) *(extremely)* merveilleusement, prodigieusement; **miraculously low prices** des prix *mpl* incroyablement bas

miraculousness [mɪ'rækjʊləsnɪs] *n* caractère *m* miraculeux

mirador [mɪrə'dɔː(r)] *n Archit* mirador *m*, belvédère *m*

mirage [mɪ'rɑːʒ] *n* mirage *m*

Miranda [mə'rændə] *n*

►► *Am* ***Miranda decision*** = décision rendue par la Cour suprême en 1966 obligeant la police à informer toute personne arrêtée de ses droits; *Am* ***Miranda rights*** = droit accordé à tout prévenu d'être défendu par un avocat et de garder le silence

Mirandize [mə'rændaɪz] *vt Am* **to Mirandize sb** lire ses droits à qn

MIRAS ['maɪræs] *n Br Formerly Fin (abbr* **Mortgage Interest Relief at Source**) = système par lequel les intérêts dus à une société de crédit immobilier sont déductibles des impôts

mire [maɪə(r)] *Literary* **1** *n* boue *f*, bourbe *f*, fange *f*; *(deep)* bourbier *m*; *Fig* **to drag sb's name through the mire** traîner le nom de qn dans la boue

2 *vt (usu passive)* (**a**) *(in debt, difficulty)* empêtrer; **the project was mired in controversy from the start** dès le début, le projet a été freiné par toutes sortes de controverses (**b**) *(in mud)* embourber

mirin ['mɪrɪn] *n Culin* mirin *m*, vin *m* de riz doux

mirror ['mɪrə(r)] **1** *n* (**a**) *(looking glass)* miroir *m*, glace *f*; *Aut (rearview mirror, side mirror)* rétroviseur *m*; **when I look at my face in the mirror** quand je me regarde dans le miroir *ou* la glace; *Aut* **check your mirrors before moving off** regardez dans les rétroviseurs avant de démarrer; *Aut* **mirror, signal, manoeuvre** = phrase utilisée par les moniteurs d'auto-école pour rappeler qu'il faut regarder dans le rétroviseur puis mettre son clignotant avant d'entreprendre une manœuvre quelconque; *Fig* **it's all done with mirrors** c'est de la magie; *Fig* **to hold up a mirror to sth** refléter qch; **the tabloid press is not necessarily a mirror of national opinion** la presse à sensation ne reflète pas nécessairement l'opinion du pays; *Literary* **the eyes are the mirrors of the soul** les yeux sont les miroirs de l'âme

(**b**) *Press* **the Mirror** = nom abrégé du 'Daily Mirror'

2 *vt* (**a**) *(reflect)* réfléchir, refléter; **the water mirrored her face** l'eau réfléchissait son visage; **the steeple is mirrored in the lake** le clocher se reflète *ou* se mire dans le lac

(**b**) *(imitate)* imiter; **his experience exactly mirrors my own** nous avons eu des expériences identiques

►► *Ich* ***mirror carp*** carpe *f* miroir; ***mirror finish*** fini *m* spéculaire; *Press* **the Mirror Group, Mirror Group Newspapers** = grand groupe de presse britannique; ***mirror image*** image *f* en miroir, image *f* spéculaire; *Fig* copie *f* conforme; ***mirror polish*** polissage *m* spéculaire; *Comput* ***mirror site*** *(on Internet)* site *m* miroir; *Psy* ***the mirror stage*** le stade du miroir; ***mirror writing*** écriture *f* spéculaire *ou* en miroir

mirrorball ['mɪrəbɔːl] *n* sphère *f* à facettes de verre

mirrored ['mɪrəd] *adj (ceiling)* couvert de miroirs; **mirrored sunglasses** lunettes *fpl* métallisées

mirrorlike ['mɪrəlaɪk] *adj (sea, lake)* lisse comme un miroir

mirth [mɜːθ] *n (UNCOUNT)* (**a**) *(laughter)* rires *mpl*, hilarité *f*; **he could barely control his mirth** il avait du mal à se retenir de rire (**b**) *(gaiety)* allégresse *f*, joie *f*

mirthful ['mɜːθfʊl] *adj Literary (laughing)* rieur; *(merry)* joyeux

mirthfully ['mɜːθfʊlɪ] *adv Literary* joyeusement

mirthfulness ['mɜːθfʊlnɪs] *n Literary (laughter)* rires *mpl*; *(gaiety)* gaieté *f*

mirthless ['mɜːθlɪs] *adj Literary* triste, sombre, morne; *(laugh)* faux (fausse), forcé

mirthlessly ['mɜːθlɪslɪ] *adv Literary* sans joie; **she laughed mirthlessly** elle eut un rire forcé

mirthlessness ['mɜːθlɪsnɪs] *n Literary* tristesse *f*

MIRV [mɜːv] *n Mil (abbr* **multiple independently targeted re-entry vehicle**) MIRV *m*

miry ['maɪərɪ] *(compar* **mirier**, *superl* **miriest**) *adj Literary* boueux, fangeux

MIS [,emaɪ'es] *n* (**a**) *Comput (abbr* **management information system**) système *m* intégré de gestion (**b**) *Mktg (abbr* **marketing information system**) système *m* d'information marketing

misaddress [,mɪsə'dres] *vt* mal adresser

misadventure [,mɪsəd'ventʃə(r)] *n (accident)* mésaventure *f*; *(misfortune)* malheur *m*; *Law* **a verdict of death by misadventure** un verdict de mort accidentelle

misalign [,mɪsə'laɪn] *adj* mal aligner

misaligned [,mɪsə'laɪnd] *adj* mal aligné

misalliance [,mɪsə'laɪəns] *n* mésalliance *f*

misanthrope ['mɪsənθrəʊp] *n* misanthrope *mf*

misanthropic [,mɪsən'θrɒpɪk] *adj (person)* misanthrope; *(thoughts, mood)* misanthropique

misanthropist [mɪ'sænθrəpɪst] *n* misanthrope *mf*

misanthropy [mɪ'sænθrəpɪ] *n* misanthropie *f*

misapplication ['mɪs,æplɪ'keɪʃən] *n* mauvaise utilisation *f*, mauvaise application *f*; *(of law)* mauvaise application *f*; *(of money)* détournement *m*

misapply [,mɪsə'plaɪ] *(pt & pp* **misapplied**) *vt* mal utiliser, mal exploiter; *(law)* mal appliquer, appliquer à tort; *(money)* détourner

misapprehend ['mɪs,æprɪ'hend] *vt Formal* mal comprendre; *(person's words)* mal comprendre, se méprendre sur

misapprehension ['mɪs,æprɪ'henʃən] *n Formal* malentendu *m*, méprise *f*; **to be** *or* **to labour under a misapprehension** se méprendre, se tromper; **the Government appears to be (labouring) under the misapprehension that...** le gouvernement semble s'imaginer que...

misappropriate [,mɪsə'prəʊprɪeɪt] *vt Formal (money, funds)* détourner; *(property)* voler

misappropriation ['mɪsə,prəʊprɪ'eɪʃən] *n Formal* détournement *m*

►► *Fin* ***misappropriation of funds*** détournement *m* de fonds, abus *m* de biens sociaux

misbegotten [,mɪsbɪ'gɒtən] *adj Formal* (**a**) *(plan)* mal conçu, bâtard (**b**) *(child)* bâtard, illégitime (**c**) *(illegally obtained)* d'origine douteuse

misbehave [,mɪsbɪ'heɪv] *vi* **to misbehave (oneself)** se conduire mal; *(child)* se tenir mal; **he has been misbehaving at school** il n'a pas été sage à l'école; **stop misbehaving!** sois sage!; *Fig* **the VCR has been misbehaving again** le magnétoscope fait encore des siennes

misbehaviour, *Am* **misbehavior** [,mɪsbɪ'heɪvjə(r)] *n (bad behaviour)* mauvaise conduite *f*; *(more serious)* inconduite *f*

misc *(written abbr* **miscellaneous**) divers

miscalculate [,mɪs'kælkjʊleɪt] **1** *vt (amount, distance)* mal calculer; *Fig* mal évaluer

2 *vi Math* se tromper dans ses calculs; *Fig (judge wrongly)* se tromper

miscalculation [,mɪskælkjʊ'leɪʃən] *n Math* erreur *f* de calcul; *Fig* mauvais calcul *m*

miscall [,mɪs'kɔːl] *vt Formal* appeler à tort

miscarriage [,mɪs'kærɪdʒ] *n* (**a**) *Med* fausse couche *f*, *Spec* avortement *m* spontané; **to have a miscarriage** faire une fausse couche (**b**) *(failure)* échec *m* (**c**) *Br (in post → of letter, package)* égarement *m*, perte *f*

►► *Law* ***miscarriage of justice*** erreur *f* judiciaire

miscarry [,mɪs'kærɪ] *(pt & pp* **miscarried**) *vi* (**a**) *Med* faire une fausse couche (**b**) *(fail → plan, hopes)* échouer, avorter, mal tourner (**c**) *Br (letter, parcel)* s'égarer, se perdre; *(reach wrong address)* parvenir à une fausse adresse

miscast [,mɪs'kɑːst] *(pt & pp* **miscast**) *vt Cin & Theat (play)* se tromper dans la distribution de; *(actor)* mal choisir le rôle de; **Ralph was hopelessly miscast as Romeo** Ralph n'était vraiment pas fait pour jouer le rôle de Roméo; **he was miscast in the part** ce n'était pas un rôle qui lui convenait

miscegenation [,mɪsɪdʒɪ'neɪʃən] *n Biol* métissage *m (de races humaines)*

miscellanea [,mɪsə'leɪnɪə] *npl* miscellanées *fpl*

miscellaneous [,mɪsə'leɪnɪəs] *adj (assorted)* divers, varié; *(jumbled)* hétérogène, hétéroclite, disparate; **the file marked miscellaneous** le dossier divers

►► ***miscellaneous expenses*** frais *mpl* divers; *Journ* ***miscellaneous news*** faits *mpl* divers; *St Exch* ***miscellaneous shares*** valeurs *fpl* diverses

miscellanist [*Br* mɪ'selənɪst, *Am* 'mɪsə,leɪnɪst] *n* anthologiste *mf*

miscellany [*Br* mɪ'selənɪ, *Am* 'mɪsəleɪnɪ] *(pl* **miscellanies**) *n* (**a**) *(mixture, assortment)* amalgame *m*, mélange *m* (**b**) *(anthology)* recueil *m*, anthologie *f*

mischance [,mɪs'tʃɑːns] *n Formal (bad luck)* malheur *m*, malchance *f*; *(stroke of bad luck)* mésaventure *f*; **by mischance** par malchance; *(stronger)* par malheur

mischief ['mɪstʃɪf] *n* (**a**) *(UNCOUNT) (naughtiness)* espièglerie *f*, malice *f*; **to get up to mischief** faire des bêtises *ou* sottises; **to keep sb out of mischief** *(prevent from being naughty)* empêcher qn de faire des sottises *ou* des bêtises; *(keep busy)* occuper qn; **to do sth out of sheer mischief** faire qch par pure espièglerie *ou* par pure malice; **he's full of mischief** il est très espiègle; **they're always up to (some) mischief** ils trouvent toujours des bêtises à faire; **a smile full of mischief** un sourire espiègle; **she looked at me with mischief in her eyes** elle me regardait d'un air taquin *ou* malicieux

(**b**) *(UNCOUNT) (trouble)* **to make mischief** semer la zizanie

(**c**) *(UNCOUNT) Formal (damage)* dommages *mpl*, dégâts *mpl*

(**d**) *Br (injury)* **to do oneself a mischief** se blesser, se faire mal; **he did himself a mischief carrying the suitcases** il s'est fait mal en portant les valises

(**e**) *Fam Hum (child)* polisson(onne) *m,f*, (petite) canaille *f*; **little mischief** petit(e) espiègle *mf*, petit(e) coquin(e) *m,f*

mischief-maker *n* faiseur(euse) *m,f* d'histoires *ou* d'embarras; **she's a terrible mischief-maker** *(naughty)* elle est très espiègle; *(nasty)* elle est toujours en train d'intriguer *ou* de semer la zizanie

mischief-making *n* (**a**) *(naughtiness)* espièglerie *f* (**b**) *(trouble-making)* intrigues *fpl*

mischievous ['mɪstʃɪvəs] *adj* (**a**) *(child)* espiègle, malicieux; *(look)* taquin, narquois; *(thought)* malicieux; **mischievous trick** *or* **prank** espièglerie *f*; **to play a mischievous trick on sb** jouer un tour *ou* faire une farce à qn (**b**) *(harmful)* méchant, malveillant; **mischievous gossip** médisances *fpl*

mischievously ['mɪstʃɪvəslɪ] *adv* (**a**) *(naughtily, teasingly)* malicieusement (**b**) *(nastily)* méchamment, avec malveillance

mischievousness ['mɪstʃɪvəsnɪs] *n* (**a**) *(naughtiness)* espièglerie *f*, malice *f* (**b**) *(nastiness)* malveillance *f*, méchanceté *f*

miscibility [,mɪsɪ'bɪlɪtɪ] *n* miscibilité *f*

miscible ['mɪsɪbəl] *adj* miscible (**with** avec)

misconceive [,mɪskən'siːv] *vt (misunderstand)* mal comprendre, mal interpréter; *(have wrong idea of)* se faire une idée fausse de

misconceived [,mɪskən'siːvd] *adj (plan)* mal conçu; *(idea)* faux (fausse), erroné

misconception [,mɪskən'sepʃən] *n (poor understanding)* mauvaise compréhension *f*; *(complete misunderstanding)* idée *f* fausse, méprise *f*; **the whole scheme is based on a basic**

misconception tout le projet repose sur une idée fausse; **a popular misconception** une idée fausse couramment répandue

misconduct **1** *n* [ˌmɪs'kɒndʌkt] (**a**) *(bad behaviour)* mauvaise conduite *f*; *(immoral behaviour)* inconduite *f*; *(adultery)* adultère *m*; **(professional) misconduct** faute *f* professionnelle

(**b**) *(bad management)* mauvaise gestion *f*; **they accused her of misconduct of the company's affairs** ils l'ont accusée d'avoir mal géré la société

2 *vt* [ˌmɪskən'dʌkt] *(mismanage → business)* mal gérer; *(→ affair)* mal conduire

misconstruction [ˌmɪskən'strʌkʃən] *n* (**a**) *(gen)* fausse interprétation *f*; **the law is open to misconstruction** la loi peut prêter à des interprétations erronées (**b**) *Gram* mauvaise construction *f*

misconstrue [ˌmɪskən'struː] *vt* mal interpréter

miscount **1** *n* ['mɪskaʊnt] *(miscalculation)* erreur *f* de calcul; *(mistake in addition)* erreur *f* d'addition; *Pol (of votes)* erreur *f* dans le dépouillement du scrutin

2 *vt* [ˌmɪs'kaʊnt] mal compter, faire une erreur en comptant

3 *vi* [ˌmɪs'kaʊnt] se tromper dans le compte

miscreant ['mɪskrɪənt] *n* (**a**) *Literary (villain)* scélérat(e) *m,f*, vaurien(enne) *m,f* (**b**) *Arch (unbeliever)* mécréant(e) *m,f*

miscue **1** *n* ['mɪsˌkjuː] (**a**) *(in billiards, snooker)* fausse queue *f* (**b**) *Fig (mistake)* erreur *f*

2 *vi* [ˌmɪs'kjuː] (**a**) *(in billiards, snooker)* faire fausse-queue, toucher la bille à faux (**b**) *Theat* manquer sa réplique

misdate [ˌmɪs'deɪt] *vt* mal dater; **the letter was misdated** la lettre ne portait pas la bonne date

misdeal [ˌmɪs'diːl] *(pt & pp* **misdealt** [-'delt]*)* *Cards* **1** *n* maldonne *f*

2 *vt* **to misdeal the cards** faire (une) maldonne

3 *vi* faire (une) maldonne

misdeed [ˌmɪs'diːd] *n Formal* méfait *m*; *Law* délit *m*

misdemean [ˌmɪsdɪ'miːn] *vt Arch or Literary* **to misdemean oneself** mal se comporter, mal se conduire

misdemeanour, *Am* **misdemeanor** [ˌmɪsdɪ'miːnə(r)] *n* (**a**) *Law* délit *m* (**b**) *(minor act of misbehaviour)* écart *m* de conduite; *(more serious)* méfait *m*

misdiagnose [ˌmɪs'daɪəgnəʊz] *vt Med* **to misdiagnose the symptoms/illness/***etc* faire une erreur de diagnostic; **she was misdiagnosed as having cancer** les médecins ont diagnostiqué un cancer mais ils se sont trompés; *Fig* **to misdiagnose the situation** faire une mauvaise analyse de la situation

misdiagnosis [ˌmɪsdaɪəg'nəʊsɪs] *(pl* **misdiagnoses** [-siːz]*)* *n Med & Fig* erreur *f* de diagnostic, mauvais diagnostic *m*

misdirect [ˌmɪsdɪ'rekt] *vt* (**a**) *(to destination → traveller)* mal orienter, mal renseigner; *(→ letter, parcel)* mal adresser (**b**) *(misuse → efforts, talents)* mal employer, mal orienter; **misdirected energy** énergie *f* mal utilisée (**c**) *(blow)* mal diriger (**d**) *Law (jury)* mal renseigner

misdirected [ˌmɪsdɪ'rektɪd] *adj* (**a**) *(letter, parcel)* envoyé à la mauvaise adresse (**b**) *(efforts, talents)* mal employé (**c**) *(blow)* frappé à faux, mal dirigé

misdirection [ˌmɪsdɪ'rekʃən] *n* (**a**) *(of traveller)* mauvaise orientation *f* (**b**) *(of efforts, talents)* mauvais emploi *m*, mauvais usage *m*

misdoing [ˌmɪs'duːɪŋ] *n* méfait *m*

misentry [ˌmɪs'entrɪ] *n Acct* contre-position *f*

miser ['maɪzə(r)] *n* (**a**) *(person)* avare *mf*; **he's a real miser** c'est un vrai grippe-sou (**b**) *(tool)* tarière *f* à gravier

'The Miser' *Molière* 'L'Avare'

miserable ['mɪzərəbəl] *adj* (**a**) *(unhappy)* malheureux, triste; **to look miserable** avoir l'air déprimé *ou* malheureux; **I feel really miserable today** je n'ai vraiment pas le moral aujourd'hui; **to make sb miserable** rendre qn malheureux, faire de la peine à qn; **don't be so miserable!** allez! ne fais pas cette tête!; **they make her life miserable** ils lui rendent *ou* mènent la vie dure

(**b**) *(unpleasant → evening, sight)* pénible; *(→ weather, summer)* épouvantable, pourri; *(→ conditions, holiday)* déplorable, lamentable; **if only I didn't have this miserable cold!** si je n'avais pas cet affreux rhume!; **what a miserable day** quelle journée épouvantable; **what miserable weather!** quel temps épouvantable!; **he had a miserable time of it at the dentist's** il a passé un sale quart d'heure chez le dentiste; **to have a miserable time** passer un mauvais moment; **we had a miserable time on holiday** nous avons passé des vacances atroces *ou* détestables

(**c**) *(poor → hotel)* miteux; *(→ tenement)* misérable; *(→ meal)* maigre; **a miserable performance** une piètre performance; **a miserable failure** *(plan etc)* un ratage complet *ou* lamentable; *(person)* un(une) raté(e)

(**d**) *(mean → reward)* minable, misérable; *(→ salary)* de misère, minable; *(→ donation, amount)* dérisoire; **I've only got a miserable £70** je n'ai que 70 malheureuses livres

(**e**) *Pej* méchant; **you miserable brat!** sale gosse!

(**f**) *Scot & Austr (stingy)* avare

miserably ['mɪzərəblɪ] *adv* (**a**) *(unhappily)* malheureusement, d'un air malheureux; *(say)* d'un ton malheureux; **she sat miserably at the back of the class** elle était assise, l'air malheureux *ou* pitoyable, au fond de la classe

(**b**) *(unpleasantly → unhappy, cold)* extrêmement

(**c**) *(poorly → perform, play)* de façon lamentable *ou* déplorable; *(→ fail)* lamentablement; **to be miserably paid** avoir un salaire de misère

(**d**) *(in poverty)* misérablement, dans la misère; **he died miserably in a garret** il est mort pauvre dans une mansarde

misère [mɪ'zeə(r)] *n (in cards)* misère *f*

Miserere [mɪzə'rɪərɪ] *n Rel* (**a**) *(psalm)* miséréré *m*, miserere *m inv* (**b**) *(seat)* miséricorde *f*, patience *f* (de stalle)

►► ***miserere seat*** miséricorde *f*, patience *f* de stalle

misericord [mɪ'zerɪkɔːd] *n Rel* (**a**) *(in monastery)* miséricorde *f* (**b**) *(seat)* miséricorde *f*, patience *f* (de stalle)

miserliness ['maɪzəlɪnɪs] *n* avarice *f*

miserly ['maɪzəlɪ] *adj* avare

misery ['mɪzərɪ] *(pl* **miseries***)* *n* (**a**) *(unhappiness)* malheur *m*, tristesse *f*; **to make sb's life a misery** rendre la vie insupportable à qn

(**b**) *(suffering) Hum* **to put sb out of their misery** mettre fin aux souffrances *ou* au supplice de qn; **go on, put me out of my misery and tell me the worst** continue, mets fin à mon supplice, dis-moi tout; *Euph* **to put an animal out of its misery** achever un animal

(**c**) *(misfortune)* malheur *m*, misère *f*

(**d**) *(poverty)* misère *f*

(**e**) *Br Fam (gloomy person)* rabat-joie *m inv*, grincheux(euse) *m,f*; **don't be such an old misery!** cesse de jouer les rabat-joie!

misery-guts *n Fam* rabat-joie *m inv*, grincheux(euse) *m,f*

misfeasance [ˌmɪs'fiːzəns] *n Law (breach of law)* infraction *f* à la loi; *(misuse of authority)* abus *m* d'autorité

misfile **1** *n* ['mɪsfaɪl] *Comput* erreur *f* de classement

2 *vt* [ˌmɪs'faɪl] *(papers, information)* mal classer

misfire **1** *n* ['mɪsfaɪə(r)] *Mil & Aut* raté *m*

2 *vi* [ˌmɪs'faɪə(r)] (**a**) *(gun)* faire long feu; *(joke)* manquer son effet; *(plan)* rater (**b**) *(engine)* avoir des problèmes d'allumage *ou* des ratés

misfit ['mɪsfɪt] *n* inadapté(e) *m,f*, marginal(e) *m,f*; **she was always a misfit at school** à l'école, elle n'a jamais été acceptée par les autres; **a social misfit** un(une) inadapté(e) social(e)

'The Misfits' *Huston* 'Les Désaxés' *ou* 'Les Misfits'

misfortune [ˌmɪs'fɔːtʃuːn] *n* (**a**) *(bad luck)* malchance *f*, infortune *f*; **allies** *or* **companions in misfortune** compagnons *mpl* d'infortune; **I had the misfortune to meet him in Paris** j'ai eu la malchance de le rencontrer à Paris (**b**) *(unfortunate event)* malheur *m*; **to be plagued by misfortunes** jouer de malchance

misgive [ˌmɪs'gɪv] *(pt* **misgave** [ˌmɪs'geɪv], *pp* **misgiven** [ˌmɪs'gɪvən]*)* *vt Arch or Literary* **my mind misgives me** j'ai de mauvais pressentiments; **my heart misgives me that…** j'ai le pressentiment que…

misgiving [ˌmɪs'gɪvɪŋ] *n* doute *m*, appréhension *f*; **not without misgiving(s)** non sans hésitation; **to have misgivings about sth** avoir des doutes quant à qch, douter de qch; **she had misgivings about allowing them to go** elle hésitait à les laisser y aller; **the whole idea fills me with misgiving** l'idée même me remplit d'appréhension

misgovern [ˌmɪs'gʌvən] **1** *vt* mal gouverner

2 *vi* mal gouverner

misgovernment [ˌmɪs'gʌvənmənt] *n (of country)* mauvais gouvernement *m*; *(of affairs)* mauvaise gestion *f*

misguidance [ˌmɪs'gaɪdəns] *n* mauvaise influence *f*

misguided [ˌmɪs'gaɪdɪd] *adj (person)* malavisé, mal inspiré; *(attempt)* malencontreux; *(decision)* peu judicieux *ou* pertinent; *(attack)* malavisé, maladroit; *(idealist)* égaré; *(nationalism)* dévoyé; **a misguided genius** un génie dévoyé; **it was very misguided of him to try to intervene** il a commis une grosse bévue en essayant d'intervenir; **in the misguided belief that…** croyant à tort que…

misguidedly [ˌmɪs'gaɪdɪdlɪ] *adv* malencontreusement

misguidedness [ˌmɪs'gaɪdɪdnɪs] *n (of person)* manque *m* de jugement; *(of attempt)* caractère *m* malencontreux; *(of decision)* manque *m* de pertinence; *(of attack)* maladresse *f*

mishandle [ˌmɪs'hændəl] *vt* (**a**) *(equipment)* mal utiliser, mal se servir de; *(substance, product)* manipuler sans prendre les précautions nécessaires (**b**) *(affair, situation)* mal gérer; **the case was mishandled from the outset** l'affaire a été mal menée depuis le début (**c**) *(treat insensitively → customer)* malmener, traiter avec rudesse

mishandling [mɪs'hændəlɪŋ] *n (of situation, staff etc)* mauvaise gestion *f*

mishap ['mɪshæp] *n (misadventure)* mésaventure *f*, accident *m*; **he arrived without mishap** il est arrivé sans encombre; **she had a slight mishap on the way here** il lui est arrivé une petite mésaventure en venant ici

mishear [ˌmɪs'hɪə(r)] *(pt & pp* **misheard** [-'hɜːd]*)* *vt* mal entendre, mal comprendre

mishit *(pt & pp* **mishit***)* *Sport* **1** *n* ['mɪshɪt] mauvais coup *m*, coup *m* manqué

2 *vt* [ˌmɪs'hɪt] *(ball)* mal frapper

3 *vi* [ˌmɪs'hɪt] mal frapper la balle

mishmash ['mɪʃmæʃ] *n Fam* méli-mélo *m*, micmac *m*

misinform [ˌmɪsɪn'fɔːm] *vt (unintentionally)* mal renseigner; *(intentionally)* donner de faux renseignements à, tromper; **I think you have been misinformed** je pense qu'on vous a mal renseigné

misinformation [ˌmɪsɪnfə'meɪʃən] *n (UNCOUNT)* fausse information *f*

misinterpret [ˌmɪsɪn'tɜːprɪt] *vt* mal comprendre, mal interpréter; **this decision should not be misinterpreted as…** cette décision ne doit pas être interprétée comme…; **she misinterpreted his silence as contempt** elle a pris à tort son silence pour du mépris

misinterpretation ['mɪsɪnˌtɜːprɪ'teɪʃən] *n* mauvaise interprétation; **the rules are open to misinterpretation** l'interprétation du règlement prête à confusion

misjudge [ˌmɪs'dʒʌdʒ] *vt (distance, reaction)* mal juger, mal évaluer; *(person)* mal juger; **it appears I misjudged you** il semblerait que je vous ai mal jugé

misjudgement, misjudgment [ˌmɪs'dʒʌdʒmənt] *n* erreur *f* de jugement; *(of distance)* mauvaise évaluation *f* *ou* estimation *f*

miskey **1** *n* [ˌmɪs'kiː] faute *f* de frappe

2 *vt* ['mɪskiː] ne pas taper correctement

mis–mis

miskick *Sport* **1** *n* ['mɪskɪk] coup *m* de pied raté
2 *vt* [,mɪs'kɪk] **he miskicked the ball** il a raté son coup de pied
3 *vi* [,mɪs'kɪk] rater le ballon

Miskito [,mɪs'kiːtəʊ] **1** *npl* **the Miskito** les Miskito *mpl*, les Mosquito *mpl*
2 *n* (**a**) *(person)* Miskito *mf*, Mosquito *mf* (**b**) *(language)* miskito *m*
3 *adj* miskito *(inv)*, mosquito *(inv)*

mislay [,mɪs'leɪ] *(pt & pp* **mislaid** [-'leɪd]) *vt* égarer

mislead [,mɪs'liːd] *(pt & pp* **misled** [-'led]) *vt* tromper, induire en erreur; **we were misled into believing he was dead** on nous a fait croire qu'il était mort; **her behaviour misled him into thinking her feelings were stronger** sa conduite lui a laissé croire que ses sentiments étaient plus profonds, mais il n'en était rien

misleading [,mɪs'liːdɪŋ] *adj (false)* trompeur, fallacieux; *(confusing)* équivoque; **the map is very misleading** cette carte n'est pas claire du tout; **the description she gave was deliberately misleading** elle a fait exprès de donner une fausse description
►► ***misleading advertising*** publicité *f* mensongère

misleadingly [,mɪs'liːdɪŋlɪ] *adj (falsely)* trompeusement

misled [,mɪs'led] *pt & pp of* **mislead**

mismanage [,mɪs'mænɪdʒ] *vt* mal gérer, mal diriger; **the whole operation was mismanaged** l'opération tout entière a été mal gérée

mismanagement [,mɪs'mænɪdʒmənt] *n* mauvaise gestion *f*, mauvaise administration *f*

mismatch **1** *n* ['mɪsmætʃ] (**a**) *(clash)* **the colours are a mismatch** ces couleurs ne vont vraiment pas ensemble *ou* sont vraiment mal assorties
(**b**) *(in marriage)* mésalliance *f*
(**c**) *Sport* match *m* inégal
(**d**) *Comput* incohérence *f*
2 *vt* [,mɪs'mætʃ] (**a**) *(colours, clothes)* mal assortir
(**b**) *(in marriage)* **they were totally mismatched** *(socially)* ils étaient vraiment mal assortis; *(by temperament)* ils n'étaient absolument pas faits pour s'entendre

misname [,mɪs'neɪm] *vt* mal nommer

misnomer [,mɪs'nəʊmə(r)] *n* nom *m* inapproprié; **to call it a democratic country is a complete misnomer** ce pays ne mérite vraiment pas le nom de démocratie

miso ['miːsəʊ] *n Culin* miso *m*

misogamy [mɪ'sɒgəmɪ] *n* misogamie *f*

misogynist [mɪ'sɒdʒɪnɪst] *n* misogyne *mf*

misogynistic [mɪ,sɒdʒɪ'nɪstɪk], **misogynous** [mɪ'sɒdʒɪnəs] *adj* misogyne

misogyny [mɪ'sɒdʒɪnɪ] *n* misogynie *f*

misoneism [,mɪsəʊ'niːɪzəm] *n* misonéisme *m*

misplace [,mɪs'pleɪs] *vt* (**a**) *(put in wrong place)* **to misplace sth** ne pas mettre qch à sa place *ou* au bon endroit; *Fig* **she's utterly misplaced in social work** elle n'est vraiment pas à sa place dans le secteur social (**b**) *(mislay)* égarer (**c**) *(trust, confidence)* mal placer

misplaced [,mɪs'pleɪst] *adj (trust, confidence)* mal placé; **misplaced remark** remarque *f* déplacée *ou* hors de propos

misplacement [,mɪs'pleɪsmənt] *n* **the misplacement of luggage** le fait d'égarer des bagages; **due to the misplacement of this title on the shelves** du fait que le livre n'a pas été rangé dans le bon rayonnage

misplay **1** *n* ['mɪspleɪ] faute *f*
2 *vt* [,mɪs'pleɪ] **to misplay the ball** faire une faute

misprint **1** *n* ['mɪsprɪnt] faute *f* d'impression, coquille *f*
2 *vt* [,mɪs'prɪnt] imprimer incorrectement; **my name was misprinted in the newspaper** il y a eu une coquille dans mon nom sur le journal

misprision [,mɪs'prɪʒən] *n Law* non-dénonciation *f* de crime

mispronounce [,mɪsprə'naʊns] *vt (word)* mal prononcer, prononcer incorrectement; *(name)* estropier, écorcher

mispronunciation ['mɪsprə,nʌnsɪ'eɪʃən] *n (act)* prononciation *f* incorrecte; *(instance)* faute *f* de prononciation

misquotation [,mɪskwəʊ'teɪʃən] *n* citation *f* inexacte

misquote **1** *n* ['mɪskwəʊt] *Fam* citation *f* inexacte❑
2 *vt* [,mɪs'kwəʊt] *(author, text)* citer inexactement; *(speaker)* déformer les propos de; **I've been misquoted** *(by the press etc)* on a déformé mes propos

misread *(pt & pp* **misread** [-'red]) **1** *n* ['mɪsriːd] *Comput* erreur *f* de lecture
2 *vt* [,mɪs'riːd] *(word, text)* mal lire; *Fig (actions, motives, situation)* mal interpréter, mal comprendre

misreport [,mɪsrɪ'pɔːt] **1** *n* rapport *m* inexact
2 *vt* rapporter inexactement

misrepresent ['mɪs,reprɪ'zent] *vt (facts, events)* déformer, dénaturer; *(person)* donner une image fausse de; **I have been grossly misrepresented by my opponents** mes adversaires donnent de moi une image entièrement fausse

misrepresentation ['mɪs,reprɪzen'teɪʃən] *n (of truth)* déformation *f*; **what they say is a complete misrepresentation of the facts** ils déforment complètement la réalité

misroute [,mɪs'ruːt] *vt (message, telephone call etc)* mal acheminer, mal diriger

misrule [,mɪs'ruːl] **1** *n* (**a**) *(misgovernment)* mauvais gouvernement *m* (**b**) *(anarchy)* désordre *m*, anarchie *f*
2 *vt* mal gouverner

Miss[1] *(written abbr* **Mississippi**) Mississippi *m*

Miss[2] [mɪs] *n* (**a**) *(term of address)* mademoiselle *f*; **Dear Miss Brett** Chère Mademoiselle Brett, Chère Mlle Brett; *Formal* **the Misses Brett** Mesdemoiselles Brett; **the Miss Bretts** les demoiselles Brett; **Miss West Indies** Miss Antilles (**b**) *Br Sch* la maîtresse; *(in secondary school)* la prof; **yes Miss** oui, madame; *Br Sch* **please Miss!** Madame!

MISS[1] [mɪs]

manquer	► **1 (a), (b), (d); 2 (c)**
rater	► **1 (a)**
faillir	► **1 (c)**
manquer de	► **1 (e)**
se passer de	► **3 (b)**

1 *vt* (**a**) *(bus, film, target)* manquer, rater; *(opportunity, turn)* manquer, laisser passer; **a life of missed opportunities** une vie d'occasions manquées; **we missed the train by five minutes** on a manqué le train de cinq minutes; **he missed breakfast** *(was too late)* il a manqué le petit déjeuner; *(didn't go)* il a sauté le petit déjeuner; **this film is not to be missed** c'est un film à ne pas manquer *ou* à ne manquer sous aucun prétexte; **I missed the first five minutes of the programme** j'ai raté les cinq premières minutes de l'émission; **at that price, it's a bargain not to be missed** à ce prix, c'est une affaire à ne pas manquer; **you didn't miss much** vous n'avez pas raté grand-chose; **it's too good an opportunity to miss** c'est une occasion trop belle pour qu'on la manque; *Fam* **you don't know what you're missing** tu ne sais pas ce que tu rates; *Fig* **to miss the boat** rater une occasion, manquer le coche; **you're going to miss the boat if you delay your application** vous allez manquer le coche si vous tardez à poser votre candidature; **to miss one's cue** *Theat* manquer sa réplique; *Fig* rater l'occasion
(**b**) *(fail to do, find, see, attend etc)* manquer; **to miss school** manquer l'école; **it's at the end of the street, you can't miss it** c'est au bout de la rue, vous ne pouvez pas le manquer; **to miss one's stop** *(of passenger)* rater son arrêt; **to miss a turning** rater un tournant; **I'm sorry, I missed you in the crowd** désolé, je ne vous ai pas vu *ou* remarqué *ou* aperçu dans la foule; **I missed seeing them in Australia** *(for lack of time)* je n'ai pas eu le temps de les voir en Australie; *(for lack of opportunity)* je n'ai pas eu l'occasion *ou* la possibilité de les voir en Australie; **I missed the beginning of your question** je n'ai pas entendu le début de votre question; **they've missed my name off the list** ils ont oublié mon nom sur la liste; **you miss a lot if you read this novel in translation** on perd beaucoup à ne pas lire ce roman dans le texte; **you've missed** *or* **you're missing the point!** vous n'avez rien compris!; **he missed the point of the exercise** il n'a pas compris *ou* saisi le but de l'exercice; *Br* **she missed her footing** *or* **step** elle a glissé *ou* trébuché; **you don't miss much!** rien ne t'échappe!; **the boss doesn't miss a thing** rien n'échappe au patron; **he never misses a chance to put other people down** il ne manque jamais une occasion de rabaisser les autres; *Br* **they never** *or* **don't miss a trick** rien ne leur échappe
(**c**) *(escape, manage to avoid)* **I narrowly** *or* **just missed being killed** j'ai bien failli me faire tuer
(**d**) *(regret the absence of)* **I miss her** elle me manque; **don't you miss your family?** est-ce que ta famille ne te manque pas?; **you'll be missed when you retire** on vous regrettera *ou* vous nous manquerez quand vous serez à la retraite; **I miss the warm weather/the sea** la chaleur/la mer me manque; **I miss being able to do what I like** ça me manque de ne pas pouvoir faire ce que je veux; **I missed my umbrella** mon parapluie m'aurait été bien utile; **you can't miss what you've never had** ce que l'on n'a jamais eu ne nous manque pas
(**e**) *(be short of, lack)* manquer de; **I'm missing two books from my collection** il me manque deux livres dans ma collection, deux livres de ma collection ont disparu; **the table's missing one of its legs** il manque un pied à la table
(**f**) *(notice disappearance of)* **when did you first miss your passport?** quand est-ce que vous vous êtes aperçu pour la première fois de la perte de *ou* que vous aviez perdu votre passeport?; **he disappeared for a week and no one ever missed him** il a disparu pendant une semaine et personne ne s'en est aperçu; **we're sure to be missed** on va sûrement remarquer notre absence; **he's got so many records he won't miss one** il a tellement de disques qu'il ne s'apercevra pas qu'il lui en manque un
2 *vi* (**a**) *(fail to hit target)* manquer *ou* rater son coup; **missed!** raté!
(**b**) *(engine)* avoir des ratés
(**c**) **to be missing** manquer; **there's a piece missing** il manque une pièce; **there's one missing, one is missing** il en manque un; **two of the children are still missing** il manque encore deux enfants, deux enfants manquent encore
3 *n* (**a**) *(gen) & Sport* coup *m* raté *ou* manqué; *Br Prov* **a miss is as good as a mile** = rater de peu ou de beaucoup, c'est toujours rater
(**b**) *(idiom) Br* **to give sth a miss** *(do without)* se passer de qch; *(avoid)* éviter qch; **I gave work a miss yesterday** je ne suis pas allé travailler hier; **I gave lessons a miss last week** je n'ai pas assisté aux cours la semaine dernière; **I'll give the soup a miss** je ne prendrai pas de soupe; **why don't you give the TV a miss tonight?** pourquoi ne pas te passer de (la) télé ce soir?

►**miss out** **1** *vt sep (omit)* omettre, sauter; *(forget)* oublier; *(in distribution)* oublier, sauter; **they missed out my first name** on a oublié mon prénom; **you've missed out one important fact** vous avez omis *ou* oublié un fait important
2 *vi* **he missed out because he couldn't afford to go to college** il a été désavantagé parce qu'il n'avait pas les moyens de poursuivre ses études

►**miss out on** *vt insep (advantage, opportunity)* manquer, rater; **you're missing out on all the fun** tu rates une occasion de bien t'amuser; **he missed out on a proper education** il n'a pas eu la possibilité de faire de vraies études; **we missed out on the deal** l'affaire nous est passée sous le nez *ou* nous a échappé; **a lot of people are missing out on state benefits they are entitled to** bien des gens ne profitent pas des allocations auxquelles ils ont droit

miss[2] *n* (**a**) *Fam (girl)* **(young) miss** jeune demoiselle❑ *f*; **everything for the modern miss** tout ce qu'il faut pour la jeune fille moderne❑; **impudent little miss!** petite effrontée! (**b**) *(size)* = taille de vêtements pour les pré-adolescentes

missal ['mɪsəl] *n Rel* missel *m*

misshape ['mɪsʃeɪp] *n* = chocolat, bonbon ou biscuit mal moulé et vendu moins cher

misshapen [,mɪs'ʃeɪpən] *adj* difforme, tordu, déformé

missile [*Br* 'mɪsaɪl, *Am* 'mɪsəl] *n* (**a**) *Mil* missile *m* (**b**) *(object thrown)* projectile *m*

►► ***missile base*** base *f* de missiles; ***missile carrier*** porte-missiles *m inv*; ***missile launcher*** lance-missiles *m inv*

missilery, missilry ['mɪsəlrɪ] *n* (**a**) *(stocks)* (ensemble *m* des) missiles *mpl* (**b**) *(science)* étude *f* des missiles

missing ['mɪsɪŋ] *adj* (**a**) *(lacking)* manquant; **there are two cups missing** il manque deux tasses, il y a deux tasses qui manquent; **the table had one leg missing** il manquait un pied à la table; **fill in the missing words** complétez avec les mots manquants

(**b**) *(lost → person)* disparu; *(→ object)* manquant, égaré, perdu; **to go missing** disparaître; *(in war)* être porté disparu; **the missing diamonds were found in her suitcase** les diamants qui avaient disparu ont été retrouvés dans sa valise; **the missing climbers are safe** les alpinistes dont on était sans nouvelles sont sains et saufs; **the expedition was reported missing** l'expédition a été portée disparue; *Mil* **missing in action** porté disparu au combat; *Mil* **missing presumed dead** porté disparu, présumé mort

►► *also Fig Hum* ***missing link*** chaînon *m* manquant; ***missing person*** personne *f* disparue; *Mil* disparu(e) *m,f*; ***missing persons*** *(department)* service *m* des personnes disparues

mission ['mɪʃən] *n* (**a**) *(task)* mission *f*; **mission of inquiry** mission *f* d'enquête; **he was sent on a rescue mission** il fut envoyé en mission de sauvetage; **she's found her mission in life** elle a trouvé sa vraie vocation; **his mission in life is to raise awareness of the environment** il tient absolument à sensibiliser l'opinion publique aux problèmes d'environnement

(**b**) *(delegation)* mission *f*; *Am (permanent)* représentation *f* diplomatique; **a Chinese trade mission** une mission commerciale chinoise

(**c**) *(organization, charity)* mission *f*; **Mission to Seamen** Mission *f* aux Marins

(**d**) *Rel (campaign, building)* mission *f*

(**e**) *Mil, Com & Astron* mission *f*; **he had flown twenty missions** il avait effectué vingt missions; **mission accomplished** mission accomplie

►► ***mission control*** centre *m* de contrôle; ***mission controller*** chef *m* du centre de contrôle; ***mission creep*** = opération militaire dont les objectifs ne sont pas clairement définis et qui risque de s'éterniser; ***mission statement*** ordre *m* de mission; ***mission station*** mission *f*

missionary ['mɪʃənrɪ] (*pl* **missionaries**) **1** *n* missionnaire *mf*

2 *adj (work)* missionnaire

►► ***missionary position*** position *f* du missionnaire; *Mktg* ***missionary selling*** ventes *fpl* de prospection; ***missionary society*** société *f* de missionnaires; *also Fig* ***missionary zeal*** fanatisme *m*

missioner ['mɪʃənə(r)] *n* missionnaire *mf (préposé aux œuvres d'une paroisse)*

missis = **missus**

Mississippi [ˌmɪsɪ'sɪpɪ] *n* (**a**) *(river)* **the Mississippi (River)** le Mississippi (**b**) *(state)* le Mississippi; **in Mississippi** dans le Mississippi

►► ***Mississippi mud pie*** = sorte de gâteau au chocolat

Mississippian [ˌmɪsɪ'sɪpɪən] **1** *n* habitant(e) *m,f* du Mississippi

2 *adj* du Mississippi

missive ['mɪsɪv] *n Formal* missive *f*

Missouri [mɪ'zʊərɪ] *n* (**a**) *(river)* **the Missouri (river)** le Missouri (**b**) *(state)* le Missouri; **in Missouri** dans le Missouri, au Missouri

►► ***the Missouri Compromise*** le compromis du Missouri

> **THE MISSOURI COMPROMISE**
>
> Il s'agit de l'admission simultanée dans l'Union (des États américains), en 1820, de l'État libre du Maine et de l'État du Missouri. Ce dernier, bien qu'esclavagiste, se trouvait au nord de la ligne de séparation entre les États esclavagistes et les États non esclavagistes. Cette admission fit basculer l'équilibre numérique entre le Nord et le Sud au Congrès et souleva une violente opposition malgré le réajustement de la ligne de démarcation.

Missourian [mɪ'zʊərɪən] **1** *n (inhabitant)* habitant(e) *m,f* du Missouri; *(native)* natif(ive) *m,f* du Missouri

2 *adj* du Missouri

misspeak [ˌmɪs'spiːk] (*pt* **misspoke** [-spəʊk], *pp* **misspoken** [-'spəʊkən]) *vi Am* se tromper *(en disant quelque chose)*

misspell [ˌmɪs'spel] (*pt & pp* **misspelt** [-'spelt] *or* **misspelled**) *vt (in writing)* mal écrire, mal orthographier; *(in speaking)* mal épeler

misspelling [ˌmɪs'spelɪŋ] *n* faute *f* d'orthographe

misspelt [ˌmɪs'spelt] *pt & pp of* **misspell**

misspend [ˌmɪs'spend] (*pt & pp* **misspent** [-'spent]) *vt (money, talents)* gaspiller, gâcher; **my misspent youth** ma folle jeunesse; *Hum* **his skill at snooker is the sign of a misspent youth** il est adroit au billard parce qu'il a passé le plus clair de son temps à y jouer quand il était plus jeune

misspoke [ˌmɪs'spəʊk] *pt of* **misspeak**

misspoken [ˌmɪs'spəʊkən] *pp of* **misspeak**

misstate [ˌmɪs'steɪt] *vt (case, argument)* rapporter *ou* exposer incorrectement; *(truth)* déformer

misstatement [ˌmɪs'steɪtmənt] *n (report)* rapport *m* inexact; *(mistake)* inexactitude *f*

mis-suit [ˌmɪs'sjuːt] *vt Literary* convenir mal à, messeoir à

missus ['mɪsɪz] *n Br Fam* (**a**) *(wife)* **the missis** la patronne, ma bourgeoise; **I'll have to ask the missus** je dois demander à la patronne (**b**) *(woman)* **eh, missus!** dites, m'dame *ou* ma p'tite dame!

missy ['mɪsɪ] (*pl* **missies**) *n Fam Old-fashioned* mademoiselle❑ *f*

mist [mɪst] **1** *n* (**a**) *(fog)* brume *f*; **the morning mist will clear by noon** les brumes matinales se dissiperont avant midi; *Fig* **the mists of time** la nuit des temps

(**b**) *(on window, glasses)* buée *f*; *(from spray)* brouillard *m*, nuage *m*

2 *vt* **to mist (over** *or* **up)** embuer; **tears misted his eyes** ses yeux étaient brouillés par les larmes

3 *vi* **to mist (over** *or* **up)** *(landscape)* disparaître dans la brume; *(mirror)* se couvrir de buée, s'embuer; *(eyes)* se voiler, s'embuer

mistakable [mɪ'steɪkəbəl] *adj* **easily mistakable (for)** facile à confondre (avec)

mistake [mɪ'steɪk] (*pt* **mistook** [-'stʊk], *pp* **mistaken** [-'steɪkən]) **1** *n* (**a**) *(error)* erreur *f*; *(in grammar, spelling)* faute *f*; **to make a mistake** *(gen)* se tromper; *(in grammar, spelling)* faire une faute; *(in sums, calculations)* faire une faute *ou* une erreur; **to make the mistake of doing sth** faire *ou* commettre l'erreur de faire qch; **I made the mistake of losing my temper** j'ai commis l'erreur de *ou* j'ai eu le tort de me fâcher; **anybody can make a mistake** tout le monde peut se tromper; **you're making a big mistake** vous faites une grave erreur; **it would be a mistake to make promises that we can't keep** ce serait une erreur de faire des promesses que nous ne pouvons pas tenir; **she made a mistake about the date** elle s'est trompée de date; **make no mistake (about it)** ne vous y trompez pas; **there must be some mistake** il doit y avoir erreur *ou* un malentendu; **it's an easy mistake to make** c'est une erreur qu'il est facile de faire; **she knew it was a mistake ever to have married him** elle savait bien qu'elle n'aurait pas dû commettre l'erreur de l'épouser; **sorry, my mistake** *(my fault)* excusez-moi, c'est (de) ma faute; *(I got it wrong)* excusez-moi, c'est moi qui me trompe

(**b**) *(inadvertence)* **by** *or Br* **in mistake** par mégarde *ou* erreur; **I took her scarf in mistake for mine** en croyant prendre mon écharpe, j'ai pris la sienne; **I went into the wrong room by mistake** je suis entré par erreur dans la mauvaise pièce

(**c**) *Br (idiom)* **he's a big man and no mistake!** pour être costaud, il est costaud!

2 *vt* (**a**) *(misunderstand → meaning, intention)* se méprendre sur; **there's no mistaking what she said** on ne peut pas se méprendre sur le sens de ses propos

(**b**) *(fail to distinguish)* se tromper sur; **you can't mistake our house, it's got green shutters** vous ne pouvez pas vous tromper *ou* il n'y a pas de confusion possible, notre maison a des volets verts; **there's no mistaking the influence of Brahms on his music** l'influence de Brahms sur sa musique est indéniable

(**c**) *(confuse)* se tromper de; **I'm often mistaken for my sister** on me prend souvent pour ma sœur; **I mistook him for someone else** je l'ai pris pour quelqu'un d'autre, je l'ai confondu avec quelqu'un d'autre; **I mistook his shyness for arrogance** j'ai pris sa timidité pour de l'arrogance

mistaken [mɪ'steɪkən] **1** *pp of* **mistake**

2 *adj (opinion)* erroné; *(idea)* faux (fausse); **to be mistaken** se tromper, être dans l'erreur; **I was mistaken about the date** je faisais erreur en ce qui concerne la date; **if I'm not mistaken** si je ne me trompe, si je ne m'abuse; **it was a case of mistaken identity** il y avait erreur sur la personne; **unless I'm very much mistaken,...** si je ne m'abuse,... **he proposed to her in the mistaken belief that she loved him** il la demanda en mariage, croyant à tort qu'elle l'aimait

mistakenly [mɪ'steɪkənlɪ] *adv (in error)* par erreur; *(wrongly)* à tort; **they quite mistakenly believed that it would be easy** ils croyaient, tout à fait à tort, que ce serait facile

mister ['mɪstə(r)] *n Fam* monsieur❑ *m*; **hey mister!** dites, m'sieur!; *Br* **mister know-all**, *Am* **mister know-it-all** monsieur je-sais-tout

mistime [ˌmɪs'taɪm] *vt (announcement)* faire au mauvais moment; *(entrance on stage)* rater; *(counterattack, shot, tackle)* mal calculer; **the launch of the new product had been badly mistimed** le nouveau produit n'avait pas été lancé au moment propice; **she mistimed her volley** elle a mal calculé sa volée, le timing de sa volée était mauvais; **he badly mistimed it** il a vraiment choisi le mauvais moment

mistiness ['mɪstɪnɪs] *n* (**a**) *(mist)* brume *f*; *(drizzle)* bruine *f*; **there may be some mistiness early on** on peut s'attendre à des brumes matinales (**b**) *(condensation)* condensation *f*, buée *f*

mistle thrush ['mɪsəl-] *n Orn* (grive *f*) draine *f*

mistletoe ['mɪsəltəʊ] *n Bot* gui *m*

mistook [mɪ'stʊk] *pt of* **mistake**

Mistra ['mɪstrə] *n* Mistra

mistranslate [ˌmɪstræns'leɪt] **1** *vt* mal traduire

2 *vi* faire des contresens

mistranslation [ˌmɪstræns'leɪʃən] *n* (**a**) *(mistake)* contresens *m*, faute *f ou* erreur *f* de traduction (**b**) *(faulty text)* traduction *f* inexacte, mauvaise traduction *f*

mistreat [ˌmɪs'triːt] *vt* maltraiter

mistreatment [ˌmɪs'triːtmənt] *n* mauvais traitement *m*

mistress ['mɪstrɪs] *n* (**a**) *(woman in control)* maîtresse *f*; **she's her own mistress** elle est sa propre maîtresse; **she was mistress of the situation** elle était maîtresse de la situation, elle maîtrisait la situation; **to be mistress of oneself** *or* **of one's emotions** être maîtresse de soi(-même); **the mistress of the house** la maîtresse de maison

(**b**) *(lover)* maîtresse *f*; **he kept a mistress for years** il a eu une maîtresse pendant des années

(**c**) *Br Sch (in primary school)* maîtresse *f*; *(in secondary school)* professeur *m (femme)*; **the PE mistress** le professeur de gymnastique

(**d**) *Br (of servants)* maîtresse *f*; **the mistress wouldn't like it** cela déplairait à Madame

(**e**) *Arch (title)* **Mistress Bacon** Madame *ou* Mme Bacon

(**f**) *(of pet)* maîtresse *f*

mistrial ['mɪstraɪəl] *n Law* jugement *m* entaché d'un vice de procédure; *Am (because jury cannot agree)* procès *m* ajourné *(l'unanimité n'ayant pas été atteinte parmi le jury)*

mistrust [ˌmɪs'trʌst] **1** *n* méfiance *f*, défiance *f*; **she has an instinctive mistrust of doctors** elle éprouve une méfiance instinctive à l'égard des médecins

2 *vt (be suspicious, wary of)* se méfier de; *(doubt)* douter de, ne pas avoir confiance en; **he mistrusts his own abilities** il doute de ses propres capacités

mistrustful [ˌmɪs'trʌstfʊl] *adj* méfiant, défiant; **to be mistrustful of sb** se méfier de qn

mistrustfully [ˌmɪs'trʌstfʊlɪ] *adv* avec méfiance, avec défiance

mistrustfulness [ˌmɪs'trʌstfʊlnɪs] *n* méfiance *f*, défiance *f*

misty ['mɪstɪ] *(compar* **mistier**, *superl* **mistiest**) *adj* (**a**) *(weather, morning)* brumeux; **it's misty** le temps est brumeux (**b**) *(window, eyes)* embué; *(horizon, mountain)* embrumé; **her eyes were misty with tears** ses yeux étaient embués *ou* voilés de larmes (**c**) *(vague → idea, memory)* flou, nébuleux (**d**) *(like mist)* vaporeux; **a misty veil of cloud** un léger voile de nuages; **misty blue** bleu *m* pâle

mistype ['mɪstaɪp] **1** *n* faute *f* de frappe

2 *vt* [,mɪs'taɪp] faire une faute de frappe dans; **the address has been mistyped** il y a une faute de frappe dans l'adresse

misunderstand [,mɪsʌndə'stænd] *(pt & pp* **misunderstood** [-'stʊd]) **1** *vt* (**a**) *(misinterpret)* mal comprendre, comprendre de travers; **I misunderstood the message** j'ai mal compris le message; **we misunderstood each other** il y a eu un malentendu entre nous; **don't misunderstand me** comprenez-moi bien; **your irony could be misunderstood** votre ironie pourrait être mal interprétée

(**b**) *(usu passive) (misjudge)* méconnaître; **a misunderstood artist** un(une) artiste méconnu(e); **he feels misunderstood** il se sent incompris

2 *vi* mal comprendre; **if I have not misunderstood** si j'ai bien compris

misunderstanding [,mɪsʌndə'stændɪŋ] *n* (**a**) *(misapprehension)* méprise *f*, quiproquo *m*, malentendu *m*; **there seems to have been some misunderstanding** il semble qu'il y ait eu méprise *ou* une erreur; **his statement is open to misunderstanding** sa déclaration prête à confusion; **the whole dispute hinges on a misunderstanding** cette discussion repose toute entière sur un malentendu; **to clear up a misunderstanding** dissiper un malentendu; **through a misunderstanding** à cause d'un malentendu

(**b**) *(disagreement)* malentendu *m*, désaccord *m*, différend *m*; **we've had a misunderstanding with the neighbours** nous nous sommes brouillés avec les voisins

misunderstood [,mɪsʌndə'stʊd] *pt & pp of* **misunderstand**

misusage [,mɪs'ju:sɪdʒ] = **misuse** *n*

misuse 1 *vt* [,mɪs'ju:z] (**a**) *(privilege, position etc)* abuser de; *(word, phrase)* employer abusivement; *(equipment, gun)* mal employer, mal utiliser; *(money, time)* mal employer; **the government is misusing our natural resources** le gouvernement fait un mauvais usage de nos ressources naturelles

(**b**) *(funds)* détourner

(**c**) *(ill-treat)* maltraiter, malmener

2 *n* [,mɪs'ju:s] (**a**) *(of privilege, one's position)* abus *m*; *(of word, phrase)* emploi *m* abusif; *(of equipment, gun)* mauvais usage *m*, mauvaise utilisation *f*; *(of money, time)* mauvais emploi *m*

(**b**) *(of funds)* détournement *m*

MIT [,emaɪ'ti:] *n Am (abbr* **Massachusetts Institute of Technology**) l'Institut *m* de Technologie du Massachusetts

mite [maɪt] *n* (**a**) *Entom* acarien *m* (**b**) *(little bit)* grain *m*, brin *m*, tantinet *m*; **I am a mite tired after my journey** je me sens un tantinet fatigué après mon voyage; **it's a mite expensive** c'est un peu cher (**c**) *Fam (child)* mioche *mf*; *(animal)* petite bête[□] *f*; **poor little mite!** pauvre petit! (**d**) *Arch or Literary (coin)* denier *m*; *(donation)* obole *f*; **the widow's mite** le denier de la veuve

miter *Am* = **mitre**

Mithraic [mɪ'θreɪɪk] *adj Rel* mithriaque

Mithraism ['mɪθreɪɪzəm] *n Rel* mithriacisme *m*, mithraïsme *m*

Mithras ['mɪθræs] *pr n Rel* Mithra

Mithridates [,mɪθrɪ'deɪti:z] *pr n* Mithridate

Mithridatic [,mɪθrɪ'deɪtɪk] *adj Hist* mithridatique

mithridatism [,mɪθrɪ'deɪtɪzəm] *n Med* mithridatisation *f*, mithridatisme *m*

mitigate ['mɪtɪgeɪt] *vt (anger, grief, pain)* adoucir, apaiser, alléger; *(conditions, consequences, harm)* atténuer

mitigating ['mɪtɪgeɪtɪŋ] *adj*

▸▸ *Law* ***mitigating circumstances*** circonstances *fpl* atténuantes

mitigation [,mɪtɪ'geɪʃən] *n Formal (of anger, grief, pain)* adoucissement *m*, allègement *m*; *(of conditions, consequences, harm)* atténuation *f*, mitigation *f*; **in mitigation, it is obvious that she was provoked** il est évident qu'elle a été provoquée, ce qui constitue une circonstance atténuante

mitochondrion [,maɪtəʊ'kɒndrɪən] *(pl* **mitochondria** [-rɪə]) *n Biol* mitochondrie *f*

mitosis [maɪ'təʊsɪs] *(pl* **mitoses** [-si:z]) *n Biol* mitose *f*

mitotic [maɪ'tɒtɪk] *adj Biol* mitotique

mitral valve ['maɪtrəl-] *n Anat* valvule *f* mitrale

mitre, *Am* **miter** ['maɪtə(r)] **1** *n* (**a**) *Rel* mitre *f*; **bishop's mitre** mitre *f* d'évêque (**b**) *(in carpentry)* onglet *m*

2 *vt (in carpentry → cut)* tailler en onglet; *(join)* assembler en onglet

▸▸ ***mitre block, mitre box*** boîte *f* à onglet; ***mitre joint*** (assemblage *m* à *ou* en) onglet *m*; ***mitre square*** équerre *f* à onglet

mitred ['maɪtəd] *adj (in carpentry)* en onglet, à onglet

mitt [mɪt] *n* (**a**) *(with fingers joined)* moufle *f*; *(fingerless)* mitaine *f*; *(glove)* gant *m*; *(boxing glove)* gant *m* (de boxe), mitaine *f*; **oven/baseball mitt** gant *m* isolant/de baseball (**b**) *Fam (hand)* patte *f*, pogne *f*; **keep your mitts off my lunch!** touche pas à mon déjeuner!; **get your mitts off me!** bas les pattes!

mitten ['mɪtən] *n (with fingers joined)* moufle *f*; *(fingerless)* mitaine *f*; *(boxing glove)* gant *m* (de boxe), mitaine *f*

MIX [mɪks]

mélange	▸ 1 (a)
préparation	▸ 1 (c)
mixage	▸ 1 (d)
mélanger	▸ 2 (a)
préparer	▸ 2 (b)
tourner	▸ 2 (c)
mixer	▸ 2 (d)
se mélanger	▸ 3 (a)
aller ensemble	▸ 3 (b)

1 *n* (**a**) *(combination, blend)* mélange *m*; **it's a mix of gothic and baroque** c'est un mélange de gothique et de baroque; **a fascinating mix of cultures** un mélange de cultures fascinant; **there's not enough cement in the mix** le mélange ne contient pas assez de ciment; **there was a good mix of people at the party** il y avait un mélange intéressant de personnes à la soirée; **he's put together the right mix of talent for the show** il est parvenu à réunir pour ce spectacle un superbe choix de talents

(**b**) *Br (act of mixing)* **give the paint a (good) mix** mélangez (bien) la peinture

(**c**) *Culin (in package)* préparation *f*; *(batter)* pâte *f*; **a packet of cake mix** un paquet de préparation pour gâteau

(**d**) *Cin, Electron & Mus* mixage *m*; **the record has been released as a dance mix** ils ont sorti une version dance du disque

2 *vt* (**a**) *(combine, blend)* mélanger; **mix the sugar and** *or* **with the flour** mélangez le sucre et *ou* avec la farine; **mix the sugar into the batter** incorporez le sucre à la pâte; **the screws and nails were all mixed together** les vis et les clous étaient tous mélangés; **I never mix business and pleasure** je ne mélange jamais les affaires et le plaisir; **never mix your drinks** ne faites jamais de mélanges de boissons; **to mix metaphors** faire des amalgames de métaphores; *Br Fam* **to mix it** *(fight)* chercher la bagarre, être bagarreur; *Br Fam* **do you want to mix it?** tu veux te battre?[□]

(**b**) *(prepare → cocktail, medicine)* préparer; *(→ cement, plaster)* malaxer; **sit down and I'll mix you a drink** assieds-toi, je te sers un verre

(**c**) *(stir → salad)* tourner, retourner, fatiguer

(**d**) *Cin, Electron & Mus* mixer

3 *vi* (**a**) *(combine, blend)* se mélanger; **oil and water don't mix** l'huile et l'eau ne se mélangent pas; **the fuel mixes with air in the carburettor** le mélange air carburant s'effectue dans le carburateur

(**b**) *(go together)* aller ensemble, faire bon ménage; **drinking and driving don't mix** l'alcool et le volant ne font pas bon ménage

(**c**) *(socialize)* **she mixes well** elle est très sociable; **he mixes with a strange crowd** il fréquente de drôles de gens; **I don't mix much** je ne fréquente pas beaucoup de gens; **my friends and his just don't mix** mes amis et les siens ne sympathisent pas

▸**mix in 1** *vt sep* mélanger; **add the sugar and mix it in well** ajoutez le sucre et mélangez bien (la préparation)

2 *vi* **she makes no effort to mix in** elle ne fait aucun effort pour se montrer sociable

▸**mix up** *vt sep* (**a**) *(mistake)* confondre; **I always mix her up with her sister** je la confonds toujours avec sa sœur

(**b**) *(baffle, confuse)* embrouiller; **I'm mixed up about how I feel about him** mes sentiments pour lui sont très confus; **I was getting all mixed up** je ne savais plus où j'en étais

(**c**) *(scramble)* **you've got the story completely mixed up** tu t'es complètement embrouillé dans cette histoire

(**d**) *(usu passive) (involve)* impliquer; **he was mixed up in a burglary** il a été impliqué *ou* mêlé à une affaire de cambriolage; **she got mixed up with some awful people** elle s'est mise à fréquenter des gens épouvantables; **I got mixed up in their quarrel** je me suis trouvé mêlé à leur querelle

(**e**) *(disorder)* mélanger; **you've mixed all my papers up** tu as mélangé tous mes papiers

(**f**) *(combine, blend)* mélanger; **mix up all the ingredients** mélangez tous les ingrédients

(**g**) *Am Fam* **to mix it up** *(fight)* se castagner, se bastonner

mix-and-match *adj (clothes)* que l'on peut coordonner à volonté

mix-down *n TV* mixage *m* avec réduction de pistes

mixed [mɪkst] *adj* (**a**) *(assorted)* mélangé; **there was a very mixed crowd at the party** il y avait toutes sortes de gens à la fête; **a bag of mixed sweets** un sachet de bonbons assortis; **we had rather mixed weather** nous avons eu un temps assez variable

(**b**) *(not wholly positive)* mitigé; **to meet with a mixed reception** recevoir un accueil mitigé; **I have mixed feelings about it** je ne sais pas très bien ce que j'en pense, je suis partagé à ce sujet; **it was with mixed feelings that I took up the position** c'est sans grand enthousiasme que j'ai accepté le poste; *Fam* **it's a bit of a mixed bag** il y a un peu de tout; **her resignation was a mixed blessing** sa démission avait du bon et du mauvais

(**c**) *(sexually, racially)* mixte; **it's not a proper topic for mixed company** ce n'est pas un sujet à aborder devant les dames; **man of mixed race** métis *m*; **woman of mixed race** métisse *f*

▸▸ *Hort* ***mixed border*** = plate-bande composée de fleurs de variétés différentes; *Sport* ***mixed doubles*** double *m* mixte; ***mixed economy*** économie *f* mixte; *Tex* ***mixed fabric*** tissu *m* mélangé; *Agr* ***mixed farming*** agriculture *f* mixte; *Culin* ***mixed grill*** assortiment *m* de grillades, mixed grill *m*; *Culin* ***mixed herbs*** herbes *fpl* de Provence; ***mixed marriage*** mariage *m* mixte; ***mixed metaphor*** mélange *m* de métaphores; *Math* ***mixed number*** nombre *m* mixte (fractionnaire); *Ins* ***mixed policy*** police *f* d'assurance mixte; *Br* ***mixed school*** école *f* mixte; ***mixed vegetables*** jardinière *f* de légumes

mixed-ability *adj (class, teaching)* sans niveaux

mixed-media *adj* multimédia

mixed-up *adj (confused)* désorienté, déboussolé; *Fam* **she's a crazy mixed-up kid** elle est un peu paumée, cette gamine

mixer ['mɪksə(r)] *n* (**a**) *(device → gen)* mélangeur *m*; *Culin (→ mechanical)* batteur *m*; *(→ electric)* mixeur *m*, mixer *m*

(**b**) *Cin, Electron & Mus* mixeur *m*, mélangeur *m* de signaux

(**c**) *(sociable person)* **to be a good/poor mixer** être sociable/peu sociable

(**d**) *Fam (troublemaker)* provocateur(trice)[□] *m,f*

(**e**) *(soft drink)* boisson *f* gazeuse *(que l'on ajoute à une boisson alcoolisée)*

(**f**) *Am Fam Univ (party)* = soirée pour permettre aux étudiants de faire connaissance

►► ***mixer tap*** (robinet *m*) mélangeur *m*; *(with single control)* mitigeur *m*

mixing ['mɪksɪŋ] *n* (**a**) *(gen)* mélange *m* (**b**) *Cin, Electron & Mus* mixage *m*

►► ***mixing bowl*** *(big)* saladier *m*; *(smaller)* bol *m*; ***mixing chamber*** *(in engine)* chambre *f* de mélange *ou* de carburation; ***mixing desk*** table *f* de mixage; ***mixing drum*** mélangeur *m* (à tambour); *TV* ***the mixing room*** la régie

mixture ['mɪkstʃə(r)] *n* (**a**) *(gen)* mélange *m*; **they speak a mixture of French and English** ils parlent un mélange de français et d'anglais; **(cake) mixture** préparation *f* pour gâteaux (**b**) *Med* mixture *f*

mix-up *n (confusion)* confusion *f*; *(misunderstanding)* malentendu *m*; *Fam (mess)* pagaïe *f*, pagaille *f*; **there's been a mix-up with the reservations** ils se sont embrouillés dans les réservations

mizzen ['mɪzən] *n Naut* artimon *m*

mizzenmast ['mɪzənmɑːst] *n Naut* artimon *m*, mât *m* d'artimon

mizzle ['mɪzəl] *n Br* bruine *f*

mk, MK *(written abbr* **mark**) version *f*

mkt *(written abbr* **market**) marché *m*

ml *(written abbr* **millilitre**) ml

MLA [,eme'leɪ] *n (abbr* **Member of the Legislative Assembly**) membre *m* de l'Assemblée législative *(en Irlande du Nord, en Australie, en Inde et au Canada)*

MLC [,emel'siː] *n (abbr* **Member of the Legislative Council**) membre *m* du Conseil législatif *(en Australie, en Inde)*

MLitt [,em'lɪt] *n Univ (abbr* **Master of Literature, Master of Letters**) *(person)* = titulaire d'une maîtrise de lettres; *(qualification)* maîtrise *f* de lettres

MLM [,eme'lem] *n Mktg (abbr* **multi-level marketing**) VRC *f*

MLR [,emel'ɑː(r)] *n Br Formerly Fin (abbr* **minimum lending rate**) taux *m* de base

M'lud [mə'lʌd] *n* = manière conventionnelle de représenter la prononciation de "My Lord", terme utilisé lorsqu'on s'adresse à un juge

mm *(written abbr* **millimetre**) mm

MMC [,emem'siː] *n Com (abbr* **Monopolies and Mergers Commission**) = commission britannique veillant au respect de la législation antitrust

MMF [,emem'ef] *n St Exch (abbr* **money market fund**) ≃ SICAV *f* monétaire

MMR [,emem'ɑː(r)] *n Med (abbr* **measles, mumps and rubella**) vaccin *m* contre la rougeole, les oreillons et la rubéole

MMX [,emem'eks] *n Comput (abbr* **multimedia extensions**) MMX *m*

MN[1] [,em'en] *n Br (abbr* **Merchant Navy**) marine *f* marchande

MN[2] *(written abbr* **Minnesota**) Minnesota *m*

MNA [,emen'eɪ] *n Can (abbr* **Member of the National Assembly**) *(in Quebec)* MAN *m*

mnemonic [nɪ'mɒnɪk] **1** *n* formule *f* mnémotechnique, aide *f* à la mémoire; *Comput* mnémonique *m*

2 *adj* (**a**) *(aiding memory)* mnémonique, mnémotechnique (**b**) *(relating to memory)* mnémonique

►► [illegible]

mnemonics [nɪ'mɒnɪks] *n (UNCOUNT)* mnémotechnique *f*

mnemonist ['niːmənɪst] *n* mnémotechnicien(enne) *m,f*

MO[1] [,em'əʊ] *n* (**a**) *(abbr* **medical officer**) *Ind* médecin *m* du travail; *Mil* médecin *m* militaire (**b**) *(abbr* **modus operandi**) *(of criminal)* façon *f* d'agir (**c**) *(abbr* **money order**) mandat-poste *m*

MO[2] *(written abbr* **Missouri**) Missouri *m*

mo, mo' [məʊ] *n Br Fam* moment ❑ *m*, instant ❑ *m*; **half a mo!, wait a mo!** une seconde!, une minute!; **(I) won't be a mo** j'en ai pour une seconde *ou* minute

moa ['məʊə] *n Orn* dinornis *m*, moa *m*

Moabite ['məʊəbaɪt] *Bible* **1** *n* Moabite *mf*

2 *adj* moabite

moan [məʊn] **1** *n* (**a**) *(sound)* gémissement *m*, plainte *f* (**b**) *Fam (complaint)* plainte ❑ *f*, jérémiades ❑ *fpl*; **to have a (good) moan** râler un bon coup

2 *vt Arch or Literary* se lamenter sur, gémir sur

3 *vi* (**a**) *(make sound)* gémir, pousser des gémissements; *(wind)* mugir, gémir (**b**) *Fam (complain)* râler, ronchonner; **to moan about sth** râler contre qch; **he's always moaning (and groaning)** il est toujours à râler; **what are they moaning about now?** de quoi se plaignent-ils maintenant?

moaner ['məʊnə(r)] *n Fam* râleur(euse) *m,f*, ronchonneur(euse) *m,f*

moaning ['məʊnɪŋ] **1** *n (UNCOUNT)* (**a**) *(sound)* gémissement *m*, gémissements *mpl*; *(of wind)* mugissement *m*, gémissement *m* (**b**) *Fam (complaining)* plaintes *fpl*, jérémiades *fpl*; **stop your moaning!** arrête de ronchonner!

2 *adj* (**a**) *(groaning)* gémissant; **a moaning sound** un gémissement (**b**) *(complaining)* grognon, râleur

►► *Mil* ***moaning Minnie*** sirène *f* d'alerte aérienne; *Br Fam* **she's a real moaning Minnie** quelle râleuse, celle-là!; *Br Fam* **don't be such a moaning Minnie!** arrête de râler!

moat [məʊt] *n* douves *fpl*, fossé *m*, fossés *mpl*

moated ['məʊtɪd] *adj* entouré d'un fossé *ou* de fossés

mob [mɒb] *(pt & pp* **mobbed,** *cont* **mobbing**) **1** *n* (**a**) *(crowd)* foule *f*, cohue *f*; **we were surrounded by an angry mob** nous étions cernés par une foule en colère; **mobs of drunken hooligans** des hordes *fpl* de hooligans ivres

(**b**) *Pej (common people)* **the mob** la populace

(**c**) *Fam (of criminals)* gang ❑ *m*

(**d**) *Fam (bunch, clique)* bande ❑ *f*, *Pej* clique ❑ *f*; **he was surrounded by the usual mob of hangers-on** il était entouré par sa bande habituelle de parasites; **which mob were you in?** *(in armed forces)* dans quel régiment étais-tu?

2 *vt (person)* assiéger, assaillir; *(place)* assiéger; **the crowds mobbing the entrance** la foule qui se pressait à l'entrée

3 Mob *n Fam* **the Mob** la Mafia ❑

►► ***mob cap*** charlotte *f (bonnet)*; ***mob hysteria*** hystérie *f* collective; ***mob rule*** règne *m* de la populace

mobbed [mɒbd] *adj Fam (crowded)* bondé

mob-handed [-'hændɪd] *adj Fam (with many people)* avec plein de gens; **they arrived mob-handed** ils sont arrivés avec plein d'autres gens

mobile ['məʊbaɪl] **1** *adj* (**a**) *(capable of moving, being moved)* mobile; **she's no longer mobile** elle ne peut plus se déplacer seule

(**b**) *(features, face)* mobile, expressif

(**c**) *(socially)* **the middle classes tend to be particularly mobile** les classes moyennes se déplacent plus facilement que les autres

(**d**) *Fam (having transport)* **are you mobile?** tu es motorisé?

2 *n* (**a**) *(hanging decoration)* mobile *m*

(**b**) *Fam (phone)* (téléphone *m*) portable *m*, *Belg* GSM ❑ *m*, G *m*, *Suisse* Natel® ❑ *m inv*, *Can* cellulaire ❑ *m*

►► *Am Mil* ***mobile army surgical hospital*** = hôpital militaire de campagne; ***mobile home*** *(caravan)* camping-car *m*; *(house)* = maison sans fondations qui peut être déplacée; *Mil* ***mobile kitchen*** cuisine *f* roulante; ***mobile library*** bibliobus *m*; ***mobile phone*** (téléphone *m*) portable *m*, *Belg* GSM *m*, *Suisse* Natel® *m inv*, *Can* cellulaire *m*; ***mobile shop*** commerce *m* ambulant; *Mil* ***mobile troops*** troupes *fpl* mobiles; *Mil* ***mobile warfare*** guerre *f* de mouvement

mobility [mə'bɪlətɪ] *n* mobilité *f*; **she has very little mobility in her right arm** elle peut à peine bouger son bras droit

►► ***mobility allowance*** indemnité *f* de déplacement *(versée aux personnes handicapées)*

mobilization [,məʊbɪlaɪ'zeɪʃən] *n* mobilisation *f*; *Fin* **mobilization of capital** mobilisation *f* des capitaux *ou* des fonds

mobilize, -ise ['məʊbɪlaɪz] **1** *vt* mobiliser

2 *vi* mobiliser

Möbius strip [,mɜːbɪəs-] *n* ruban *m* de Möbius

mobocracy [mɒb'ɒkrəsɪ] *(pl* **mobocracies**) *n Br* voyoucratie *f*

mobster ['mɒbstə(r)] *n Fam* gangster ❑ *m (particulièrement de la Mafia)*

moccasin ['mɒkəsɪn] *n* (**a**) *(shoe)* mocassin *m* (**b**) *Zool* mocassin *m*

mocha ['mɒkə] **1** *n* (**a**) *(coffee)* (café *m*) moka *m* (**b**) *(coffee and chocolate flavour)* parfum *m* café-chocolat (**c**) *(colour)* couleur *f* chocolat

2 *adj (colour)* (couleur) chocolat *(inv)*

3 *comp (ice cream, icing)* café-chocolat *(inv)*

mochaccino [mɒkə'tʃiːnəʊ] *n* mokaccino *m*

mock [mɒk] **1** *n* (**a**) *Br Fam Sch & Univ (examination)* examen *m* blanc ❑

(**b**) *(idiom) Literary* **to make a mock of sb/sth** tourner qn/qch en dérision

2 *adj* (**a**) *(imitation)* faux (fausse), factice; **mock tortoiseshell** *(rims, frame)* en imitation écaille

(**b**) *(feigned)* feint; **mock horror/surprise** horreur *f*/surprise *f* feinte; **mock trial/elections** simulacre *m* de procès/d'élections

3 *vt* (**a**) *(deride)* se moquer de, tourner en dérision; **don't mock the afflicted!** ne te moque pas des malheureux!

(**b**) *(imitate)* singer, parodier

(**c**) *Literary (thwart)* déjouer

4 *vi* se moquer; **you shouldn't mock** tu ne devrais pas te moquer

►► ***mock battle*** exercice *m* de combat; *Sch & Univ* ***mock examination*** examen *m* blanc; *Bot* ***mock orange*** seringa *m*; ***mock trial*** simulacre *m* de procès; *Am* ***mock turtleneck*** pull *m* à col cheminée; ***mock turtle soup*** consommé *m* à la tête de veau

►**mock up** *vt sep Br* faire une maquette de

mock-epic *adj* burlesque

mocker ['mɒkə(r)] *n* moqueur(euse) *m,f*

mockers ['mɒkəz] *npl Br Fam* **to put the mockers on sth** ficher qch en l'air, bousiller qch

mockery ['mɒkərɪ] *(pl* **mockeries**) *n* (**a**) *(derision)* moquerie *f*, raillerie *f*; **to hold sth up to mockery** tourner qch en ridicule *ou* en dérision; **he soldiered on despite the mockery of his colleagues** il persévéra en dépit des railleries de ses collègues

(**b**) *(person, thing)* **to make a mockery of sb** ridiculiser qn; **to make a mockery of oneself** se ridiculiser; **to make a mockery of sth** faire perdre toute crédibilité à qch

(**c**) *(pretence)* parodie *f*, simulacre *m* (**of** de); **the trial was a mockery** le procès n'a été qu'un simulacre

mock-heroic *adj* burlesque

mocking ['mɒkɪŋ] **1** *n* moquerie *f*, raillerie *f*

2 *adj* moqueur, railleur

mockingbird ['mɒkɪŋbɜːd] *n Orn* moqueur *m* (polyglotte)

mockingly ['mɒkɪŋlɪ] *adv* de façon moqueuse

mock-up *n* maquette *f*

MOD [,eməʊ'diː] *n Br (abbr* **Ministry of Defence**) ministère *m* de la Défense

mod [mɒd] **1** *adj Fam Old-fashioned (fashionable)* à la mode ❑

2 *n* (**a**) *(person)* = en Grande-Bretagne, dans les années 60–70, membre d'un groupe de jeunes au code vestimentaire particulier (parkas, pantalons étroits, socquettes blanches) qui s'opposait aux rockers (**b**) *(festival)* = festival de littérature et de musique gaélique en Écosse

modal ['məʊdəl] **1** *n Gram* verbe *m* modal

2 *adj Gram, Phil & Math* modal

►► *Gram* ***modal verb*** verbe *m* modal

modality [mə'dælətɪ] *(pl* **modalities**) *n* modalité *f*

modally ['məʊdəlɪ] *adv* de manière modale

mod cons [-kɒnz] *npl Br Fam (abbr* **modern conveniences**) **all mod cons** tout confort ❑, tt. conf

mode [məʊd] *n* (**a**) *(manner)* mode *m*, manière *f*; **mode of life** mode *m* de vie; **modes of transport** moyens *mpl* de transport (**b**) *Gram, Phil & Math* mode *m* (**c**) *Comput* mode *m*; **access/control mode** mode *m* d'accès/de contrôle (**d**) *(fashion)* mode *f*; **the current mode is for sixties fashion** le dernier cri, c'est la mode des années soixante

model ['mɒdəl] *(Br pt & pp* **modelled,** *cont* **modelling,** *Am pt & pp* **modeled,** *cont* **modeling**) **1** *n* (**a**) *(copy, representation)* modèle *m*, maquette *f*; *(built as hobby)* modèle *m* réduit; *(theoretical pattern)* modèle *m*

(**b**) *(perfect example)* modèle *m*; **your essay is a model of concision** votre rédaction est un modèle de concision; **to take sb as one's model** prendre modèle sur qn; **they always**

hold my brother up as a model of intelligence ils citent toujours mon frère comme un modèle d'intelligence
(**c**) *Art & Phot (sitter)* modèle *m*
(**d**) *(in fashion show)* mannequin *m*; **male model** mannequin *m* (homme)
(**e**) *Com* modèle *m*; **it's the latest model** c'est le dernier modèle; **demonstration model** modèle *m* de démonstration; **we plan to bring out a new model for the millennium** nous projetons de sortir un nouveau modèle pour le nouveau millénaire
(**f**) *Am (showhouse)* résidence *f* témoin
2 *vt* (**a**) *(shape)* modeler; **to model clay** modeler l'argile; **to model figures out of clay** modeler des figures en argile; **to model oneself on sb** prendre modèle sur qn; **he had modelled them into a well-disciplined team** il en avait fait une équipe très disciplinée
(**b**) *(in fashion show)* **she models clothes** elle est mannequin; **Jacqueline is modelling a grey chinchilla coat** Jacqueline porte un manteau de chinchilla gris
3 *vi (for artist, photographer)* poser; *(in fashion show)* être mannequin; **she has modelled for Dior** elle a été mannequin chez Dior
4 *adj* (**a**) *(miniature)* (en) miniature
(**b**) *(exemplary)* modèle; **he's a model pupil/husband** c'est un élève/mari modèle
▸▸ ***model aeroplane*** maquette *f* d'avion; ***model car*** *(toy)* petite voiture *f*; *(for collectors)* modèle *m* réduit; ***model factory*** usine *f* modèle, usine-pilote *f*; ***model maker*** *(as hobby)* modéliste *mf*; ***model making*** *(as hobby)* modélisme *m*; ***Model T (Ford)*** Ford T *f*

modeller, *Am* **modeler** ['mɒdələ(r)] *n (of clay etc)* modeleur(euse) *m,f*

modelling, *Am* **modeling** ['mɒdəlɪŋ] *n* (**a**) *(building models)* modelage *m*; *(as a hobby)* construction *f* de maquettes
(**b**) *(in fashion shows)* **modelling is extremely well-paid** le travail de mannequin est très bien payé, les mannequins sont très bien payés; **to make a career in modelling** faire une carrière de mannequin
(**c**) *Math* modélisation *f*
▸▸ ***modelling clay*** pâte *f* à modeler

modem ['məʊdem] **1** *n* modem *m*; **to send sth to sb by modem** envoyer qch à qn par modem
2 *vt* envoyer par modem; **to modem sth to sb** envoyer qch à qn par modem
▸▸ ***modem card*** carte *f* modem

Modena ['mɒdɪnə] *n* Modène

moderate 1 *adj* ['mɒdərət] (**a**) *(restrained, modest)* modéré; *(language)* mesuré; **a moderate wage increase** une augmentation raisonnable des salaires; **the candidate holds moderate views** le candidat défend des idées modérées; **he's a moderate drinker** il boit avec modération
(**b**) *(average)* moyen; **pupils of moderate ability** élèves *mfpl* moyens(ennes); **a moderate performance** une prestation moyenne
(**c**) *Met* modéré
2 *n* ['mɒdərət] *Pol* modéré(e) *m,f*
3 *vt* ['mɒdəreɪt] (**a**) *(make less extreme)* modérer; **they have since moderated their demands** depuis, ils ont modéré leurs exigences
(**b**) *(meeting, debate)* présider
(**c**) *Nucl (neutrons)* modérer, ralentir
4 *vi* ['mɒdəreɪt] (**a**) *(storm)* s'apaiser, se calmer
(**b**) *(at meeting)* présider
▸▸ ***moderate breeze*** *(on Beaufort scale)* jolie brise *f*; ***moderate gale*** *(on Beaufort scale)* grand frais *m*; *Comput* ***moderated list*** liste *f* de diffusion modérée, liste *f* de diffusion gérée par un modérateur

moderately ['mɒdərətlɪ] *adv* (**a**) *(with moderation)* modérément, avec modération; **moderately priced** d'un prix raisonnable *ou* abordable (**b**) *(slightly)* moyennement; **she was only moderately pleased with her new job** elle n'était que moyennement satisfaite de son nouvel emploi

moderation [mɒdə'reɪʃən] *n* (**a**) *(restraint)* modération *f*, mesure *f*; *(of language)* sobriété *f*; **in moderation** avec modération, modérément; **taken in moderation alcohol is not harmful** consommé avec modération, l'alcool n'est pas nocif (**b**) *Br Univ (at Oxford University)* **(Honour) Moderations** = premier examen pour le grade de "Bachelor of Arts"

moderato [ˌmɒdə'rɑːtəʊ] *Mus* **1** *adj* moderato
2 *adv* moderato

moderator ['mɒdəreɪtə(r)] *n* (**a**) *(at meeting)* président(e) *m,f*; *(mediator)* médiateur(trice) *m,f*; *Mktg (of group meeting)* animateur(trice) *m,f*; *Rel* modérateur *m* (**b**) *Nucl* modérateur *m*, ralentisseur *m* (**c**) *Comput & Phys* modérateur *m*

modern ['mɒdən] **1** *n* (**a**) *(person)* moderne *mf* (**b**) *Typ* didot *m*
2 *adj* moderne; **in modern times** à l'époque moderne; **modern English/French/Greek** anglais *m*/français *m*/grec *m* moderne
▸▸ ***modern art*** art *m* moderne; ***modern dance*** modern dance *f*; *Theat* ***modern dress*** costumes *mpl* modernes; *Typ* ***modern face*** didot *m*; ***modern jazz*** jazz *m* moderne; ***modern languages*** langues *fpl* vivantes; ***modern maths*** mathématiques *fpl* modernes; *Sport* ***modern pentathlon*** pentathlon *m* moderne

modern-day *adj* d'aujourd'hui; **a modern-day Joan of Arc** la Jeanne d'Arc des temps modernes

modernism ['mɒdənɪzəm] *n* (**a**) *(in art, literature etc)* modernisme *m* (**b**) *(expression, word)* néologisme *m*

modernist ['mɒdənɪst] **1** *n* moderniste *mf*
2 *adj* moderniste

modernistic [ˌmɒdə'nɪstɪk] *adj* moderniste

modernity [mɒ'dɜːnətɪ] *n* modernité *f*

modernization [ˌmɒdənaɪ'zeɪʃən] *n* modernisation *f*

modernize, -ise ['mɒdənaɪz] **1** *vt* moderniser
2 *vi* se moderniser

modest ['mɒdɪst] *adj* (**a**) *(unassuming)* modeste; **she's very modest about her success** son succès ne lui est pas monté à la tête (**b**) *(moderate, simple)* modeste; *(meagre)* modique; **a modest salary** un salaire modique; **a modest house** une maison sans prétentions *ou* à l'aspect modeste; **we are very modest in our needs** nous avons besoin de très peu (**c**) *(decent)* pudique

'A Modest Proposal' *Jonathan Swift* 'Modeste proposition'

modestly ['mɒdɪstlɪ] *adv* (**a**) *(unassumingly)* modestement, avec modestie (**b**) *(simply)* modestement, simplement; **they live very modestly** ils vivent très simplement, ils mènent une vie très simple (**c**) *(in sexual sense)* avec pudeur, pudiquement; **to dress modestly** s'habiller avec pudeur

modesty ['mɒdɪstɪ] *n* (**a**) *(lack of conceit)* modestie *f*; **in all modesty** en toute modestie; **false modesty** fausse modestie *f* (**b**) *(moderation)* modestie *f*; *(meagreness)* modicité *f* (**c**) *(decency)* pudeur *f*; **she lowered her gaze out of modesty** la pudeur lui a fait baisser les yeux (**d**) *Old-fashioned (item of dress)* modestie *f*

modicum ['mɒdɪkəm] *n* **a modicum of...** un petit peu de..., un brin de...; **a modicum of truth** une petite part de vérité; **she doesn't have even a modicum of taste** elle n'a aucun goût

modifiable ['mɒdɪfaɪəbəl] *adj* modifiable

modification [ˌmɒdɪfɪ'keɪʃən] *n* modification *f*; **he made several modifications in** *or* **to the text** il apporta plusieurs modifications au texte; **the rules need some modification** il faut modifier les règles

modified ['mɒdɪfaɪd] *adj*
▸▸ ***Modified American Plan*** = dans un hôtel américain, séjour en demi-pension; *Mktg* ***modified rebuy*** rachat *m* modifié

modifier ['mɒdɪfaɪə(r)] *n Gram* modificateur *m*
▸▸ *Comput* ***modifier key*** touche *f* de modification

modify ['mɒdɪfaɪ] *(pt & pp* **modified***)* *vt* (**a**) *(alter)* modifier; **once they had modified the engine it worked perfectly** après quelques modifications, le moteur était en parfait état de marche (**b**) *(reduce – punishment, demands)* modérer (**c**) *Gram* modifier; **the adjective agrees with the noun it modifies** l'adjectif s'accorde avec le nom auquel il se rapporte

modish ['məʊdɪʃ] *adj* à la mode

modishly ['məʊdɪʃlɪ] *adv* selon la mode

modishness ['məʊdɪʃnɪs] *n* conformité *f* à la mode

modiste [məʊ'diːst] *n* modiste *mf*

Mods [mɒdz] *npl Br Univ (abbr* **(Honour) Moderations***)* *(at Oxford University)* = premier examen pour le grade de "Bachelor of Arts"

modular ['mɒdjʊlə(r)] *adj* modulaire
▸▸ *Electron* ***modular construction*** construction *f* modulaire; *Br Univ* ***modular degree*** ≃ licence *f* à UV; ***modular furniture*** mobilier *m* modulaire *ou* à éléments

modularity [ˌmɒdjʊ'lærətɪ] *n* modularité *f*

modulate ['mɒdjʊleɪt] *vt* (**a**) *(voice)* moduler (**b**) *Electron & Mus* moduler (**c**) *(moderate)* adapter, ajuster; **they modulate their prices to the US market** ils adaptent leurs prix au marché américain

modulated ['mɒdjʊleɪtɪd] *adj* modulé

modulating ['mɒdjʊleɪtɪŋ] *adj Elec & Electron* modulateur
▸▸ ***modulating choke*** self *f* modulatrice *ou* de modulation; ***modulating electrode*** électrode *f* modulatrice *ou* de modulation; ***modulating frequency*** fréquence *f* de modulation; ***modulating tube*** tube *m* (à vide) modulateur; ***modulating valve*** lampe *f* (à vide) modulatrice; ***modulating voltage*** tension *f* de modulation

modulation [ˌmɒdjʊ'leɪʃən] *n* (**a**) *(of voice)* modulation *f*, inflexion *f* (**b**) *Mus, Elec & Electron* modulation *f*

modulator ['mɒdjʊleɪtə(r)] *n Elec & Electron* modulateur *m*

module ['mɒdjuːl] *n* (**a**) *(gen)* module *m* (**b**) *Br Univ* ≃ unité *f* de valeur, UV *f*

modulus ['mɒdjʊləs] *n Phys & Math* module *m*
▸▸ *Phys* ***modulus of elasticity*** module *m ou* coefficient *m* d'élasticité; *Phys* ***modulus of rupture*** module *m ou* coefficient *m* de rupture

modus operandi ['məʊdəsˌɒpə'rændiː] *n Formal or Literary* méthode *f* (de travail), procédé *m*

modus vivendi ['məʊdəsvɪ'vendiː] *n Formal or Literary* modus vivendi *m*

mofo ['məʊˌfəʊ] *n Vulg Black Am slang* enfoiré(e) *m,f*

mog [mɒg] *n Br Fam* minou *m*

Mogadiscio, Mogadishu [ˌmɒgə'dɪʃuː] *n* Mogadiscio, Mogadishu, Mudisho

moggie, moggy ['mɒgɪ] *(pl* **moggies***)* *n Br Fam* minou *m*

mogul ['məʊgəl] **1** *n* (**a**) *(magnate)* magnat *m*; **movie mogul** grand manitou *m* du cinéma (**b**) *(on ski slope)* bosse *f*; **moguls** *(event)* bosses *fpl*
2 Mogul 1 *n* Moghol(e) *m,f*
2 *adj* moghol

MOH [ˌeməʊ'eɪtʃ] *n Br (abbr* **Medical Officer of Health***)* directeur(trice) *m,f* de la santé publique

mohair ['məʊheə(r)] **1** *n* mohair *m*
2 *comp (sweater, blanket)* en *ou* de mohair

Mohammed [mə'hæmɪd] *pr n Rel* Mahomet

Mohammedan [mə'hæmɪdən] *Rel* **1** *n* mahométan(e) *m,f*
2 *adj* mahométan

Mohammedanism [mə'hæmɪdəˌnɪzəm] *n Rel* mahométisme *m*

Mohawk ['məʊhɔːk] *(pl* **inv** *or* **Mohawks***)* **1** *n* Mohawk *mf*
2 mohawk *n* (**a**) *(in ice-skating)* mohawk *m* (**b**) *Am (hairstyle)* iroquoise *f*

Mohican [məʊ'hiːkən, 'məʊɪkən] *(pl* **inv** *or* **Mohicans***)* **1** *n* (**a**) *(person)* Mohican(e) *m,f* (**b**) *Ling* mohican *m*
2 *adj* mohican
3 mohican *n Br (hairstyle)* iroquoise *f*

moiety ['mɔɪətɪ] *n Law* moitié *f*

Moirai ['mɔɪəraɪ] *npl Myth* **the Moirai** les Moires *fpl*

moire [mwɑː(r)] *n Tex* moire *f*

moiré ['mwɑːreɪ] **1** *Tex n* moiré *m*
2 *adj* moiré
▸▸ ***moiré silk*** moire *f* de soie

moist [mɔɪst] *adj (climate, soil, surface)* humide; *(skin, air, heat)* moite; *(cake)* moelleux; **her eyes were moist with tears** ses yeux étaient mouillés de larmes, ses yeux étaient embués; **to grow moist** se mouiller, s'humecter

moisten ['mɔɪsən] **1** *vt* humecter, mouiller; **she moistened her lips** elle s'humecta les lèvres

2 *vi (eyes)* se mouiller; *(palms)* devenir moite

moistness ['mɔɪstnɪs] *n (of climate, soil, surface)* humidité *f*; *(of skin, air, heat)* moiteur *f*; *(of cake)* moelleux *m*

moisture ['mɔɪstʃə(r)] *n* humidité *f*; *(on mirror, window etc)* buée *f*; **he wiped the moisture from the window** il essuya la buée de la fenêtre
▸▸ ***moisture content*** teneur *f* en humidité *ou* en eau

moistureproof ['mɔɪstʃə,pruːf] *adj (clothing, shoes)* imperméable; *(watch, container)* étanche; *(finish, sealant)* hydrofuge

moisturize, -ise ['mɔɪstʃəraɪz] **1** *vt (skin)* hydrater; *(air)* humidifier
2 *vi* appliquer une crème hydratante; **it is important to moisturize twice daily** il est important d'utiliser une crème hydratante deux fois par jour

moisturizer ['mɔɪstʃəraɪzə(r)] *n (cream)* crème *f* hydratante; *(lotion)* lait *m* hydratant

Mojave Desert [,məʊ'hɑːvɪ-] *n* **the Mojave Desert** le désert Mohave *ou* Mojave

moke [məʊk] *n Br Fam (donkey)* bourricot❑ *m*; *Austr (horse)* canasson *m*

mol [məʊl] *n Chem* mole *f*

molal ['məʊləl] *adj Chem* molaire

molar ['məʊlə(r)] **1** *n (tooth)* molaire *f*
2 *adj Chem (quantity, solution)* molaire

molarity [məʊ'lærɪtɪ] *n Chem* molarité *f*

molasses [mə'læsɪz] *n (UNCOUNT)* mélasse *f*; *Am Fam* **to be as slow as molasses (in winter)** être d'une lenteur de limace *ou* d'escargot *ou* de tortue

mold, molder *etc Am* = **mould, moulder** *etc*

Moldavia [mɒl'deɪvɪə] *n* Moldavie *f*; **in Moldavia** en Moldavie

Moldavian [mɒl'deɪvɪən] **1** *n* (**a**) *(person)* Moldave *mf* (**b**) *(language)* moldave *m*
2 *adj* moldave
3 *comp (embassy)* de Moldavie; *(history)* de la Moldavie; *(teacher)* de moldave

Moldova [mɒl'dəʊvə] *n* **the Republic of Moldova** la république de Moldova

Moldovan [mɒl'dəʊvən] = **Moldavian**

mole [məʊl] *n* (**a**) *(on skin)* grain *m* de beauté
(**b**) *(animal)* taupe *f*
(**c**) *Fig (spy)* taupe *f*
(**d**) *(breakwater)* môle *m*, digue *f*
(**e**) *Chem* mole *f*
(**f**) *Med* môle *m*
▸▸ *Entom* ***mole cricket*** courtilière *f*; *Zool* ***mole rat*** rat-taupe *m*, spalax *m*

molecular [mə'lekjʊlə(r)] *adj Phys* moléculaire
▸▸ ***molecular biology*** biologie *f* moléculaire; ***molecular formula*** formule *f* moléculaire; ***molecular genetics*** génétique *f* moléculaire; ***molecular structure*** structure *f* moléculaire; ***molecular volume*** volume *m* moléculaire; ***molecular weight*** poids *m* moléculaire

molecule ['mɒlɪkjuːl] *n* molécule *f*

molehill ['məʊlhɪl] *n* taupinière *f*

moleskin ['məʊlskɪn] **1** *n* (**a**) *(fur)* (peau *f* de) taupe *f* (**b**) *(cotton)* coton *m* sergé
2 *comp* (**a**) *(fur)* en (peau *f* de) taupe *f* (**b**) *(cotton)* en coton sergé

molest [mə'lest] *vt (bother)* importuner, tracasser; *(more violently)* molester, malmener; *(sexually)* agresser (sexuellement)

molestation [,məʊle'steɪʃən] *n (UNCOUNT)* brutalité *f*, violences *fpl*; *(sexual)* attentat *m* à la pudeur

molester [mə'lestə(r)] *n* agresseur *m*; **child molester** pédophile *mf*

moll [mɒl] *n Fam* **(gangster's) moll** poule *f*, môme *f (d'un gangster)*

Moll Flanders [,mɒl'flɑːndəz] *pr n* = héroïne haute en couleurs du roman éponyme de Daniel Defoe

mollification [,mɒlɪfɪ'keɪʃən] *n* apaisement *m*

mollify ['mɒlɪfaɪ] *vt (pt & pp* **mollified**) apaiser, amadouer

mollifying ['mɒlɪfaɪɪŋ] *adj (words)* apaisant; **in a mollifying tone** d'un ton doux

mollusc, *Am* **mollusk** ['mɒləsk] *n Zool* mollusque *m*

molluscum [mə'lʌskəm] *n Med* molluscum *m*

mollycoddle ['mɒlɪ,kɒdəl] *vt Fam* dorloter, materner

Molly Maguires [,mɒlɪmə'gwaɪəz] *npl Am Hist* = organisation clandestine luttant pour de meilleures conditions de travail dans les mines de Pennsylvanie au XIXème siècle

Moloch ['məʊlɒk] *pr n Bible* Moloch

moloch ['məʊlɒk] *n Zool* moloch *m* (épineux)

Molotov cocktail ['mɒlətɒf-] *n* cocktail *m* Molotov

molt, molting *Am* = **moult, moulting**

molten ['məʊltən] *adj (metal, lava)* en fusion

molto ['mɒltəʊ] *Mus* **1** *adj* molto
2 *adv* molto

Molucca [məʊ'lʌkə] *npl* **the Molucca Islands, the Moluccas** les îles *fpl* Moluques

molybdate [mə'lɪbdeɪt] *n Chem* molybdate *m*

molybdenite [mə'lɪbdənaɪt] *n Miner* molybdénite *f*

molybdenum [mə'lɪbdənəm] *n Chem* molybdène *m*

mom [mɒm] *n Am Fam* maman❑ *f*
▸▸ ***mom and pop store*** = petit magasin familial

MOMA ['məʊmə] *n Am (abbr* **Museum of Modern Art**) = musée d'art moderne à New York

moment ['məʊmənt] *n* (**a**) *(period of time)* moment *m*, instant *m*; **at the moment** en ce moment; **at that moment** à ce moment-là; **at this moment** *(now)* en ce moment; **at this moment in time** à l'heure qu'il est; **from that moment on** désormais; **the man of the moment** l'homme *m* du jour *ou* du moment; **for the moment** pour le moment; **let me think (for) a moment** laissez-moi réfléchir un moment *ou* une seconde; **for a long moment he remained silent** pendant un long moment il est resté sans parler; **I'll do it in a moment** je le ferai dans un instant; **I didn't believe them for a** *or* **for one moment** je ne les ai pas crus un seul instant; **wait a moment!, just a moment!, one moment!** une seconde!, une minute!, un instant!; **one moment, please** *(on telephone)* ne quittez pas; **just a moment, you haven't paid yet** un instant, vous n'avez pas encore payé; **she's just this moment gone out** elle vient de sortir; **I have just** *or* **only this moment heard about it** je viens de l'apprendre, je l'apprends à l'instant; **at the last moment** à la dernière minute, au dernier moment; **the next moment the phone rang** l'instant d'après le téléphone a sonné; **he may return at any moment** il peut revenir d'un instant à l'autre; **I saw her a moment ago** je l'ai vue il y a un instant *ou* une seconde; **a moment's hesitation** un instant d'hésitation; **without a moment's hesitation** sans la moindre hésitation; **the moment he arrives** dès qu'il arrivera, dès son arrivée; **the moment she saw him** dès l'instant où elle le vit; **it was her darkest moment** ce fut l'époque la plus sombre de sa vie; **it was one of the worst moments of my life** ce fut un des pires moments de ma vie; **her moment of glory** son heure de gloire; **to live for the moment** profiter du moment présent; **the moment of truth** l'heure de vérité; **in the heat of the moment** dans le feu de l'action; **the film has its moments** le film est parfois intéressant *ou* a de bons passages; **I have my moments, you know** ça m'arrive, des fois!
(**b**) *Formal (importance)* **of great moment** d'une importance considérable, de grande *ou* haute importance; **of little moment** de peu d'importance; **to be of no moment** n'avoir aucune importance
(**c**) *Phys* moment *m*
▸▸ *Phys* ***moment of inertia*** moment *m* d'inertie

momentarily [*Br* 'məʊməntərɪlɪ, *Am* ,məʊmən'terɪlɪ] *adv* (**a**) *(briefly, temporarily)* momentanément (**b**) *Am (immediately)* immédiatement, tout de suite; **I'll be with you momentarily** je suis à vous dans une seconde

momentary ['məʊməntərɪ] *adj* (**a**) *(brief, temporary)* momentané; **there will be a momentary delay** il y aura un retard de quelques minutes (**b**) *Literary (continual)* constant, continuel

momentous [mə'mentəs] *adj* capital, d'une importance capitale; **on this momentous occasion** en cette occasion mémorable; **a momentous decision** une décision d'une importance capitale

momentousness [mə'mentəsnɪs] *n* importance *f* capitale

momentum [mə'mentəm] *n* (**a**) *(impetus)* vitesse *f*, élan *m*; **to gain** *or* **gather momentum** *(of moving object)* prendre de la vitesse; *(of political movement etc)* prendre de l'ampleur, s'amplifier; **to lose momentum** *(vehicle)* perdre de la vitesse, être en perte de vitesse; *(campaign)* s'essouffler; *Fig* **we'll never get that momentum back again** on ne retrouvera jamais ce rythme
(**b**) *Tech & Phys* moment *m*

MOMI ['məʊmɪ] *n (abbr* **Museum of the Moving Image**) = musée de l'image à Londres

momma ['mɒmə] *n Am Fam* maman❑ *f*; **he's a momma's boy** il est toujours fourré dans les jupons de sa mère

mommy ['mɒmɪ] *n Am Fam* maman❑ *f*; **to be on the mommy track** = pour une femme, devoir renoncer à faire carrière lorsqu'on travaille à temps partiel pour pouvoir s'occuper de ses enfants; **she's headed for the mommy track** elle est enceinte❑

MON [,eməʊ'en] *n Aut (abbr* **motor octane numbers**) IOM *m*

Mon. *(written abbr* **Monday**) Lu

Monacan ['mɒnəkən] **1** *n* Monégasque *mf*
2 *adj* monégasque

Monaco ['mɒnəkəʊ] *n* **(principality of) Monaco** (principauté *f* de) Monaco

monad ['məʊnæd] *(pl* **monads** *or* **monades** [-diːz]) *n* (**a**) *Phil* monade *f* (**b**) *Biol* organisme *m* unicellulaire

monadic [mɒ'nædɪk] *adj* (**a**) *Phil* monadiste, monadaire (**b**) *Biol* unicellulaire (**c**) *Chem* univalent, monoatomique
▸▸ *Mktg* ***monadic test*** test *m* monadique; ***monadic testing*** tests *mpl* monadiques

Monaghan ['mɒnəhən] *n* le comté de Monaghan, = comté dans le nord-est de la République d'Irlande; **in Monaghan** dans le comté de Monaghan

Mona Lisa [,məʊnə'liːzə] *n* **she had a Mona Lisa smile** elle avait un sourire énigmatique

'The Mona Lisa' *da Vinci* 'La Joconde'

monandrous [mɒ'nændrəs] *adj* (**a**) *Bot* monandre (**b**) *(person, society)* monogame

monandry [mɒ'nændrɪ] *n* (**a**) *Bot* monandrie *f* (**b**) *(of person, society)* monogamie *f*

monarch ['mɒnək] *n (ruler)* monarque *m*
▸▸ *Entom* ***monarch butterfly*** danaïde *f*

monarchical [mə'nɑːkɪkəl] *adj* monarchique

monarchism ['mɒnəkɪzəm] *n* monarchisme *m*

monarchist ['mɒnəkɪst] **1** *n* monarchiste *mf*
2 *adj* monarchiste

monarchy ['mɒnəkɪ] *(pl* **monarchies**) *n* monarchie *f*

MONARCHY

Malgré la disparition de l'Empire britannique, la monarchie subsiste en Grande-Bretagne. Cependant au cours des dernières années une série d'événements a terni sa réputation. Le divorce de trois des quatre enfants de la reine, le désir exprimé par cette dernière que les contribuables britanniques payent les réparations des dégâts causés par l'incendie du château de Windsor en 1991, et la froideur apparente de la famille royale lors du décès de la princesse Diana en 1997, ont fait le plus mauvais effet. D'autre part le statut du prince Charles en tant qu'héritier de la couronne est sujet à controverse en raison de son divorce et de sa liaison avec une femme divorcée – le monarque britannique étant également le chef de l'Église anglicane.

monastery ['mɒnəstərɪ] *(pl* **monasteries**) *n* monastère *m*

monastic [mə'næstɪk] *adj* monastique

monasticism [mə'næstɪsɪzəm] *n* (**a**) *(way of life)* vie *f* monastique (**b**) *(system)* système *m* monastique, monachisme *m*

monatomic [,mɒnə'tɒmɪk] *adj Chem* monoatomique

monaural [mɒ'nɔːrəl] *adj* monaural

Monday ['mʌndɪ] *n* lundi *m*; **I've got that Monday morning feeling** je me sens comme on peut se sentir un lundi matin; *see also* **Friday**

►► *Br Pol* **the Monday Club** = club conservateur britannique; *Am Fam* **Monday morning quarterback** stratège *m* en chambre *(qui commente notamment les résultats sportifs)*

mondo ['mɒndəʊ] *adv Am Fam* vachement; **mondo bizarro** vachement bizarre

Monegasque [,mɒnɪ'gæsk] **1** *n* Monégasque *mf*
2 *adj* monégasque

moneme ['məʊni:m] *n Ling* monème *m*

MONEP ['məʊnep] *n St Exch* MONEP *m*

monetarism ['mʌnɪtərɪzəm] *n* monétarisme *m*

monetarist ['mʌnɪtərɪst] **1** *n* monétariste *mf*
2 *adj* monétariste

monetary ['mʌnɪtərɪ] *adj Econ & Fin* monétaire
►► ***monetary adjustment, monetary alignment*** alignement *m* monétaire; ***monetary area*** zone *f* monétaire; ***monetary assets*** liquidités *fpl*; ***monetary bloc*** bloc *m* monétaire; ***monetary compensatory amounts*** montants *mpl* compensatoires monétaires; ***monetary control*** contrôle *m* monétaire; ***monetary convention*** convention *f* monétaire; ***monetary parity*** parité *f* des monnaies; ***monetary policy*** politique *f* monétaire; *Br* ***monetary policy committee*** = comité formé de quatre membres de la Banque d'Angleterre et de quatre économistes nommés par le gouvernement, dont l'un des rôles est de fixer les taux d'intérêt; ***monetary reform*** réforme *f* monétaire; ***monetary reserves*** réserves *fpl* de change; ***monetary standard*** étalon *m* monétaire; ***monetary surplus*** surplus *m* monétaire; ***monetary system*** système *m* monétaire; ***monetary unit*** unité *f* monétaire

monetization [,mʌnɪtaɪ'zeɪʃən] *n* monétisation *f*

monetize, -ise ['mʌnɪtaɪz] *vt* monétiser

money ['mʌnɪ] *(pl* **moneys** *or* **monies**) **1** *n* **(a)** *(gen)* argent *m*; **have you got any money on you?** est-ce que tu as de l'argent *ou* du liquide sur toi?; **they don't accept foreign money** ils n'acceptent pas l'argent étranger *ou* les devises étrangères; **your money or your life!** la bourse ou la vie!; **to get one's money's worth** en avoir pour son argent; **to put money into sth** investir dans qch; **to put up the money for sth** fournir les fonds pour qch, financer qch; **it's money well spent** c'est une bonne affaire; **the best dictionary that money can buy** le meilleur dictionnaire qui existe *ou* qui soit; **to make money** *(person)* gagner de l'argent; *(business, investment)* rapporter de l'argent; **the shop isn't making any money** la boutique ne rapporte pas; **how did she make her money?** comment a-t-elle gagné son argent?; **to be worth a lot of money** *(thing)* valoir cher, avoir beaucoup de valeur; *(person)* être riche; **the deal is worth a lot of money** c'est un contrat qui porte sur de très grosses sommes; **to get one's money back** *(get reimbursed)* se faire rembourser; *(recover one's expenses)* rentrer dans ses fonds; **money is no object** peu importe le prix, l'argent n'entre pas en ligne de compte; **I'm no good with money** je n'ai pas la notion de l'argent; **there's no money in translating** la traduction ne rapporte pas *ou* ne paie pas; **toys cost money, you know** les jouets, ce n'est pas gratuit, tu sais; **the job's boring but the money's good** le travail est ennuyeux mais ça paye bien *ou* c'est bien payé; **we paid good money for it** cela nous a coûté cher; **you can earn big money selling carpets** on peut gagner beaucoup d'argent en vendant des tapis; **I'm not made of money, you know** tu as l'air de croire que je roule sur l'or; **to put money on a horse** miser sur un cheval; *Fam* **to be in the money** être plein aux as; *Sport* **to finish out of/in the money** remporter/ne pas remporter un prix en argent; *Fig* **put your money where your mouth is** il est temps de joindre le geste à la parole; *Fig* **to have money to burn** avoir de l'argent à jeter par les fenêtres; *Fig* **to throw good money after bad** s'enfoncer davantage dans une mauvaise affaire; *Fig* **it's throwing money away, it's money down the drain** c'est de l'argent gaspillé *ou* jeté par la fenêtre; *Br Fam Fig* **it's money for old rope** *or* **for jam** c'est de l'argent vite gagné *ou* du fric vite fait; **for my money, he's the best candidate** à mon avis, c'est le meilleur candidat; **money talks** l'argent peut tout; **money doesn't grow on trees** l'argent ne tombe pas du ciel; *Prov* **money is the root of all evil** l'argent est la source de tous les maux; *Fam* **on the money** *(correct → guess, answer)* correct, exact; *(on time)* à l'heure
(b) *Fin (currency)* monnaie *f*; **to coin** *or* **to mint money** battre *ou* frapper de la monnaie; **counterfeit money** fausse monnaie *f*; *Banking* **money at call** argent *m* au jour le jour, argent *m* à vue; **money at short notice** argent *m* à court terme
(c) *St Exch* **to be in the money** être dans les cours; **at the money** à parité; **out of the money** hors des cours
2 *comp (problems, matters)* d'argent, financier
3 moneys, monies *npl Law (sums)* sommes *fpl* (d'argent); **public moneys** deniers *mpl* publics
►► ***money belt*** ceinture *f* portefeuille; *Fin* ***money broker*** prêteur(euse) *m,f* sur titre; ***money laundering*** blanchiment *m* d'argent; *Am* ***money machine*** distributeur *m* de billets; *Fam* ***money man*** financier ❑ *m*; *Am Fin* ***money manager*** gestionnaire *mf* de portefeuille; *Fin* ***money market*** marché *m* monétaire *ou* financier; *Am Fin* ***money market certificate*** instrument *m* de marché monétaire; *Fin* ***money market fund*** fonds *m* commun de placement, ≃ SICAV *f* monétaire; *Fin* ***money measurement*** estimation *f* monétaire; *Fin* ***money order*** mandat *m* (postal); *Fin* ***money rate*** taux *m* de l'argent; *Br* ***money spider*** = petite araignée censée apporter bonheur et richesse à ceux qu'elle touche; *Fin* ***money supply*** masse *f* monétaire; *Fin* ***money trader*** cambiste *mf*

> **Show me the money**
> Cette phrase ("fais-moi voir l'argent") vient du film américain *Jerry Maguire* (1996), dans lequel Tom Cruise joue le rôle d'un manager sportif. L'un de ses clients, incarné par Cuba Gooding, prononce ces mots à maintes reprises lors de négociations.
> On utilise cette phrase de façon allusive en anglais américain dans des contextes similaires, comme dans l'exemple suivant: **forget about the free CDs and baseball caps, just show me the money** ("les casquettes de base-ball et les CDs gratuits ne m'intéressent pas, parlons argent"), ou bien lorsqu'on réclame une somme due: **I won the bet, so show me the money** ("j'ai gagné le pari, alors donne-moi mon argent").

money-back *n*
►► ***money-back guarantee*** garantie *f* de remboursement; *(sign)* satisfait ou remboursé; ***money-back offer*** offre *f* de remboursement

moneybag ['mʌnɪbæg] **1** *n (bag)* sac *m* à argent; *(of bus conductor etc)* sacoche *f*
2 moneybags *npl Fam (person)* richard(e) *m,f*, rupin(e) *m,f*; **lend us a fiver, moneybags!** passe-moi cinq livres, toi qui es plein aux as!

moneybox ['mʌnɪbɒks] *n Br* tirelire *f*

moneychanger ['mʌnɪ,tʃeɪndʒə(r)] *n* **(a)** *(person)* cambiste *mf*, courtier(ère) *m,f* de change **(b)** *Am (machine)* changeur *m ou* distributeur *m* de monnaie

moneyed ['mʌnɪd] *adj* riche, nanti; **the moneyed classes** les classes *fpl* possédantes

money-grubber [-,grʌbə(r)] *n Fam* rapace *m*, requin *m*

money-grubbing [-,grʌbɪŋ] *Fam* **1** *n* radinerie *f*
2 *adj* radin

moneylender ['mʌnɪ,lendə(r)] *n Fin* prêteur(-euse) *m,f*; *(usurer)* usurier(ère) *m,f*; *(pawnbroker)* prêteur(euse) *m,f* sur gages

moneyless ['mʌnɪlɪs] *adj* sans argent

moneymaker ['mʌnɪ,meɪkə(r)] *n* affaire *f* qui rapporte, mine *f* d'or; **to be a moneymaker** *(shop, business, product)* rapporter

moneymaking ['mʌnɪ,meɪkɪŋ] *adj* lucratif; **it's another of her moneymaking schemes** c'est encore une de ses idées pour faire fortune

money-off *n*
►► ***money-off deal*** *(discount)* réduction *f* de prix; *(reimbursement)* offre *f* de remboursement; ***money-off voucher*** bon *m* de remboursement

money-spinner *adj Br Fam* affaire *f* qui rapporte ❑, mine *f* d'or

money-spinning *adj Br Fam* lucratif ❑

mong [mɒŋ] *n Br very Fam* mongol(e) *m,f*, gol *m*

Mongol ['mɒŋgəl] *Hist* **1** *n* **(a)** *(person)* Mongol(e) *m,f* **(b)** *(language)* mongol *m*
2 *adj* mongol

mongol ['mɒŋgəl] *Old-fashioned* **1** *n* mongolien(enne) *m,f*, = terme injurieux désignant un trisomique
2 *adj* mongolien, = terme injurieux désignant un trisomique

Mongolia [mɒŋ'gəʊlɪə] *n* Mongolie *f*; **in Mongolia** en Mongolie; **Inner Mongolia** Mongolie-Intérieure *f*; *Formerly* **Outer Mongolia** Mongolie-Extérieure *f*

Mongolian [mɒŋ'gəʊlɪən] **1** *n* **(a)** *(person)* Mongol(e) *m,f* **(b)** *(language)* mongol *m*
2 *adj* mongol; **the Mongol hordes** les hordes *fpl* mongoles
3 *comp (embassy)* de Mongolie; *(history)* de la Mongolie; *(teacher)* de mongol

Mongolic [mɒŋ'gɒlɪk] *adj* **(a)** *Ling* mongol **(b)** *(people, customs etc)* mongoloïde

mongolism ['mɒŋgəlɪzəm] *n Old-fashioned* mongolisme *m*, trisomie *f*, = terme injurieux désignant la trisomie 21

Mongoloid ['mɒŋgəlɔɪd] **1** *n* mongol(e) *m,f*, mongolique *mf*
2 *adj* mongol, mongolique

mongoloid ['mɒŋgəlɔɪd] *Old-fashioned* **1** *n* mongolien(enne) *m,f*, = terme injurieux désignant un trisomique
2 *adj* mongolien, = terme injurieux se rapportant à la trisomie 21

mongoose ['mɒŋgu:s] *n Zool* mangouste *f*

mongrel ['mʌŋgrəl] **1** *n (dog)* bâtard(e) *m,f*; *(other animal)* hybride *m*
2 *adj (dog)* bâtard; *(other animal)* hybride

mongrelize, -ise ['mʌŋgrəlaɪz] *vt* métisser

mongst, 'mongst [mʌŋst] *Literary* = **among(st)**

monicker = **moniker**

monied = **moneyed**

monies ['mʌnɪz] *pl of* **money**

moniker ['mɒnɪkə(r)] *n Fam (name)* blase *m*; *(nickname)* surnom ❑ *m*

monism ['mɒnɪzəm] *n Phil* monisme *m*

monist ['mɒnɪst] *n Phil* moniste *mf*

monistic [mɒ'nɪstɪk] *adj Phil* monistique, moniste

monition [mɒ'nɪʃən] *n Formal (warning)* avertissement *m*; *(reproach)* admonition *f*

monitor ['mɒnɪtə(r)] **1** *n* **(a)** *Med & Tech (checking device)* moniteur *m*
(b) *Comput & TV (screen)* moniteur *m*
(c) *Sch* ≃ chef *m* de classe; **dinner monitor** = élève chargé de veiller au bon déroulement des repas à la cantine
(d) *Rad* employé(e) *m,f* d'un service d'écoute
2 *vt* **(a)** *(check)* suivre, surveiller; *Mktg (market)* surveiller, contrôler; **their progress is carefully monitored** leurs progrès sont suivis de près; **the FBI is monitoring his movements** le FBI surveille ses déplacements; **this instrument monitors the pulse rate** cet instrument surveille le pouls du patient
(b) *(broadcasts, telephone conversation)* écouter
►► *Zool* ***monitor lizard*** varan *m*

monitoring ['mɒnɪtərɪŋ] *n* **(a)** *(of progress)* suivi *m*; *(of patient)* surveillance *f* continue, monitorage *m*; *Mktg (of market)* surveillance *f*, contrôle *m* continu **(b)** *(of broadcasts, phone calls)* écoute *f*; *(of conversation)* surveillance *f*
►► *Rad* ***monitoring service*** = service d'écoute des émissions de radio étrangères; *Rad* ***monitoring station*** station *f ou* centre *m* d'écoute

monitory ['mɒnɪtərɪ] *adj Formal (warning)* d'avertissement; *(reproving)* d'admonition

monk [mʌŋk] *n* moine *m*, religieux *m*; **he's been living like a monk** *(not having sex)* il mène une vie de moine
►► *Orn* ***monk parakeet*** perruche *f* souris

monkey ['mʌŋkɪ] *n* **(a)** *(animal)* singe *m*; **female monkey** guenon *f*; *Fam* **to make a monkey out of sb** se payer la tête de qn; *Br Fam* **I don't give a monkey's** je m'en fiche pas mal, j'en ai rien à battre; *Am Fam Drugs slang* **to have a monkey on one's back** *(be addicted to drugs)* être accro
(b) *Fam (scamp)* polisson(onne) *m,f*, galopin *m*; **you little monkey!** petit polisson!, petit espiègle!
(c) *Constr (of pile-driver)* mouton *m*
(d) *Br Fam (£500)* 500 livres ❑

mon–mon

►► *Am* **monkey bars** cage *f* d'écureuil; *Fam* **monkey business** *(UNCOUNT) (suspect activity)* combines *fpl*; *(mischief)* bêtises ☐ *fpl*; **they're up to some monkey business** ils sont en train de combiner quelque chose; **monkey jacket** spencer *m (de garçon de café etc)*; *Br* **monkey nut** cacahouète *f*, cacahuète *f*; *Bot* **monkey puzzle tree** désespoir *m* des singes, *Spec* araucaria *m*; *Am* **monkey shine** farce *f*; *Fam* **monkey suit** *(formal suit)* costard *m* chic *m*; *Am (uniform)* uniforme ☐ *m*; **monkey wrench** clef *f* anglaise *ou* à molette; *Am Fam Fig* **to throw a monkey wrench into sth** faire foirer qch

►**monkey about, monkey around** *vi Fam* (**a**) *(play the fool)* faire l'imbécile

(**b**) *(tamper)* **to monkey about** *or* **around with sth** tripoter qch; **somebody's been monkeying about with the lock** quelqu'un a essayé de forcer la serrure ☐; **they've been monkeying about with the brakes on my car** ils ont saboté les freins de ma voiture

monkeyflower ['mʌŋkɪ,flaʊə(r)] *n Bot* mimule *m* tacheté

monkeywrench ['mʌŋkɪrentʃ] *vt Am* (**a**) *(open with monkey wrench)* ouvrir avec une clef à molette (**b**) *Fam Fig (scupper)* faire foirer, foutre en l'air; **the rain monkeywrenched our barbecue** la pluie a foutu notre barbecue en l'air

monkfish ['mʌŋkfɪʃ] *(pl* **inv** *or* **monkfishes**) *n Ich (angler fish)* baudroie *f*, lotte *f*; *(angel shark)* ange *m* de mer

monkhood ['mʌŋkhʊd] *n* (**a**) *(institution)* monachisme *m*; *(way of life)* vie *f* monastique; **to enter the monkhood** entrer dans les ordres (monastiques) (**b**) *(monks collectively)* **the monkhood** les moines *mpl*

monkish ['mʌŋkɪʃ] *adj* monacal, de moine

monkshood ['mʌŋkshʊd] *n Bot* aconit *m* (normal)

mono ['mɒnəʊ] *(pl* **monos**) **1** *n* (**a**) *(abbr* **monophony**) monophonie *f*; **in mono** en mono (**b**) *Am Fam (abbr* **mononucleosis**) mononucléose *f* (infectieuse) ☐

2 *adj (abbr* **monophonic**) mono *(inv)*, monophonique; **mono record player** électrophone *m* mono

mono- ['mɒnəʊ] *pref* mono-

monoacid [,mɒnəʊ'æsɪd] *n Chem* monoacide *m*

monoamine [,mɒnəʊ'eɪmi:n] *n Chem* monoamine *f*

►► ***monoamine oxidase*** monoamine-oxydase *f*

monobasal [,mɒnəʊ'beɪsəl] *adj Miner* monobase

monobase [,mɒnəʊ'beɪs] *n Chem* monobase *f*

monobasic [,mɒnəʊ'beɪsɪk] *adj* (**a**) *Chem* monobasique (**b**) *Bot* monobase

monobox ['mɒnəʊbɒks] *n Aut* monocorps *m*

monocarp ['mɒnəʊkɑ:p] *n Bot* plante *f* monocarpe

monocarpian [,mɒnəʊ'kɑ:pɪən], **monocarpic** [,mɒnəʊ'kɑ:pɪk] *adj Bot* monocarpien, monocarpique

monochromatic [,mɒnəkrə'mætɪk] *adj Phys* monochromatique

monochromator [,mɒnəʊ'krəʊmətə(r)] *n Phys* monochromateur *m*

monochromaticity [,mɒnəʊ,krəʊmə'tɪsɪtɪ] *n Phys* monochromie *f*

monochrome ['mɒnəkrəʊm] **1** *n* (**a**) *(technique)* monochromie *f*; *Phot & TV* noir et blanc *m*; *Art* camaïeu *m*

(**b**) *(photograph)* photographie *f* en noir et blanc; *(painting)* camaïeu *m*; *(in modern art)* monochrome *m*

2 *adj (photograph, television set)* en noir et blanc *(inv)*; *(computer screen)* monochrome; *(painting)* en camaïeu; *Fig* **he leads a very monochrome existence** il mène une existence très terne

monocle ['mɒnəkəl] *n* monocle *m*

monocled ['mɒnəkəld] *adj* qui porte un monocle

monoclinal [,mɒnəʊ'klaɪnəl] *adj Geol* monoclinal

monocline ['mɒnəʊklaɪn] *n Geol* monoclinal *m*

monoclinic [,mɒnə'klɪnɪk] *adj Geol* monoclinique

monoclonal [,mɒnə'kləʊnəl] *adj Biol* monoclonal

monocoque ['mɒnəkɒk] *n Aviat* construction *f* monocoque; *Aut* monocoque *f*

monocotyledon [,mɒnəʊkɒtɪ'li:dən] *n Bot* monocotylédone *f*

monocotyledonous [,mɒnəʊkɒtɪ'li:dənəs] *adj Bot* monocotylédone, monocotylé

monocracy [mɒ'nɒkrəsɪ] *(pl* **monocracies**) *n* monocratie *f*

monocratic [,mɒnəʊ'krætɪk] *adj* monocratique

monocrystal [,mɒnəʊ'krɪstəl] *n Miner* monocristal *m*

monocrystalline [,mɒnəʊ'krɪstəlaɪn] *adj Miner* monocristallin

monocular [mɒ'nɒkjʊlə(r)] *adj* monoculaire

monoculture ['mɒnə,kʌltʃə(r)] *n* monoculture *f*

monocyclic [,mɒnə'saɪklɪk] *adj Chem & Zool* monocyclique

monocyte ['mɒnəsaɪt] *n Biol* monocyte *m*, mononucléaire *m*

monodactylous [,mɒnəʊ'dæktɪləs] *adj Zool* monodactyle

monodic [mɒ'nɒdɪk] *adj Mus* monodique

monody ['mɒnədɪ] *(pl* **monodies**) *n Mus* monodie *f*

monoecious [mɒ'ni:ʃəs] *adj* (**a**) *Bot* monœcique, monoïque (**b**) *Zool* hermaphrodite

monoecism [mɒ'ni:sɪzəm] *n* (**a**) *Bot* monœcie *f* (**b**) *Zool* hermaphrodisme *m*

monoethylene glycol [,mɒnəʊ,i:θɪli:n'glaɪkɒl] *n Chem* monoéthylèneglycol *m*

monofilament ['mɒnə,fɪləmənt] *n* monofilament *m*

monogamist [mɒ'nɒgəmɪst] *n* monogame *mf*

monogamous [mɒ'nɒgəməs] *adj (person, animal)* monogame; *(relationship)* monogamique

monogamy [mɒ'nɒgəmɪ] *n* monogamie *f*

monogenesis [,mɒnəʊ'dʒenəsɪs] *n* (**a**) *(of human race)* monogénisme *m* (**b**) *Biol (asexual reproduction)* multiplication *f* asexuée

monogenetic [,mɒnəʊdʒə'netɪk] *adj Biol & Geol* monogénique

monogenic [,mɒnəʊ'dʒenɪk] *adj Biol* monogénique

monoglot ['mɒnəʊglɒt] *adj Ling* monolingue, monoglotte

monogram ['mɒnəgræm] *(pt & pp* **monogrammed**, *cont* **monogramming**) **1** *n* monogramme *m*

2 *vt* marquer d'un monogramme

monogrammatic [,mɒnəgrə'mætɪk] *adj* monogrammatique

monogrammed, *Am* **monogramed** ['mɒnəgræmd] *adj* qui porte un monogramme; **monogrammed handkerchiefs** mouchoirs *mpl* avec un monogramme brodé

monograph ['mɒnəgrɑ:f] *n* monographie *f*

monographic [,mɒnəʊ'græfɪk], **monographical** [,mɒnəʊ'græfɪkəl] *adj* monographique

monogynous [mɒ'nɒdʒɪnəs] *adj Bot* monogyne

monogyny [mɒ'nɒdʒɪnɪ] *n Bot* monogynie *f*

monohull ['mɒnə,hʌl] *n Naut* monocoque *m*

monohybrid [,mɒnəʊ'haɪbrɪd] *n Biol* monohybride *m*

monohydrate [,mɒnəʊ'haɪdreɪt] *n Chem* monohydrate *m*

monokinetic [,mɒnəʊkɪ'netɪk] *adj* monocinétique

monokini ['mɒnəki:nɪ] *n* monokini *m*

monolingual [,mɒnə'lɪŋgwəl] *adj* monolingue

monolith ['mɒnəlɪθ] *n Geol & Fig* monolithe *m*

monolithic [,mɒnə'lɪθɪk] *adj Geol* monolithe, monolithique; *Fig (government, state)* monolithique

monologue, *Am* **monolog** ['mɒnəlɒg] *n Theat & Fig* monologue *m*

monomania [,mɒnə'meɪnjə] *n Psy* monomanie *f*

monomaniac [,mɒnə'meɪnɪæk] *Psy* **1** *n* monomaniaque *mf*, monomane *mf*

2 *adj* monomaniaque, monomane

monomer ['mɒnəmə(r)] *n Chem* monomère *m*

monomeric [,mɒnəʊ'merɪk] *adj Chem* monomère

monometallic [,mɒnəʊmə'tælɪk] *adj Fin* monométalliste

monometallism [,mɒnəʊ'metəlɪzəm] *n Fin* monométallisme *m*

monometer [mɒ'nɒmɪtə(r)] *n (in prosody)* monomètre *m*

monometric [,mɒnəʊ'metrɪk], **monometrical** [,mɒnəʊ'metrɪkəl] *adj* monométrique

monomial [mɒ'nəʊmɪəl] *Math* **1** *n* monôme *m*

2 *adj* de *ou* en monôme

►► ***monomial function*** fonction *f* monôme

monomorphic [,mɒnəʊ'mɔ:fɪk] *adj Biol* monomorphe

monomorphism [,mɒnəʊ'mɔ:fɪzəm] *n Biol* monomorphisme *m*

mononuclear [,mɒnəʊ'nju:klɪə(r)] *adj Biol* mononucléé; *(white blood cell)* mononucléaire

mononucleosis ['mɒnəʊ,nju:klɪ'əʊsɪs] *n (UNCOUNT) Med* mononucléose *f* (infectieuse)

monophonic [,mɒnə'fɒnɪk] *adj* monophonique, monaural

monophony [mɒ'nɒfənɪ] *n* monophonie *f*

monophthong ['mɒnəfθɒŋ] *n Ling* monophtongue *f*

monophyletic [,mɒnəʊfaɪ'letɪk] *adj Biol* monophylétique

monophysite [mɒ'nɒfɪsaɪt] *Rel* **1** *n* monophysite *mf*

2 *adj* monophysite

monophysitism [mɒ'nɒfɪsaɪ,tɪzəm] *n Rel* monophysisme *m*

monoplane ['mɒnəpleɪn] *n* monoplan *m*

monoplegia [,mɒnə'pli:dʒə] *n Med* monoplégie *f*

monopolist [mə'nɒpəlɪst] *n* monopoleur(euse) *m,f*

monopolistic [mə,nɒpə'lɪstɪk] *adj* monopoliste, monopolistique

monopolization [mə,nɒpəlaɪ'zeɪʃən] *n* monopolisation *f*

monopolize, -ise [mə'nɒpəlaɪz] *vt* (**a**) *(power, access, use)* monopoliser; **he always monopolizes the conversation** il monopolise systématiquement la conversation; **she monopolized him the whole evening** elle l'a monopolisé toute la soirée; **I don't want to monopolize your time** je ne veux pas vous accaparer (**b**) *Com & Mktg (market, trade)* monopoliser

monopoly [mə'nɒpəlɪ] *(pl* **monopolies**) **1** *n also Fig* monopole *m*; **to have a monopoly of sth** *or* **on sth** avoir *ou* détenir le monopole de qch, monopoliser qch; **to form a monopoly** constituer un monopole; *Fig* **no political party has a monopoly on morality** aucun parti politique ne détient le monopole de la moralité; **state monopoly** monopole *m* d'État; **the Monopolies and Mergers Commission** = commission veillant au respect de la législation antitrust en Grande-Bretagne

2 Monopoly® *n (game)* Monopoly® *m*

►► ***monopoly control*** contrôle *m* monopolistique; ***monopoly market*** marché *m* monopolistique; *Fig* ***Monopoly money*** des sommes *fpl* astronomiques

monopsony [mə'nɒpsənɪ] *(pl* **monopsonies**) *n Econ* monopsone *m*

monorail ['mɒnəreɪl] *n* monorail *m*

monosaccharide [,mɒnəʊ'sækəraɪd] *n Chem* monosaccharide *m*, ose *m*

monosemic [,mɒnəʊ'si:mɪk] *adj Ling* monosémique

monosemy ['mɒnəʊ,si:mɪ] *n Ling* monosémie *f*

monosepalous [,mɒnəʊ'sepələs] *adj Bot* monosépale

monoski ['mɒnəʊskɪ] **1** *n* monoski *m*

2 *vi* faire du monoski

monosodium glutamate [,mɒnə'səʊdjəm'glu:təmeɪt] *n Culin* glutamate *m* de sodium

monospaced [,mɒnəʊ'speɪsd] *adj Comput & Typ* non proportionnel

monostable [,mɒnəʊ'steɪbəl] *adj Electron* monostable

monostylous [,mɒnəʊ'staɪləs] *adj Bot* monostyle

monosyllabic [,mɒnəsɪ'læbɪk] *adj* (**a**) *Ling* monosyllabe, monosyllabique (**b**) *(person)* qui s'exprime par monosyllabes; **he's very monosyllabic** il ne parle que par monosyllabes

monosyllable ['mɒnə,sɪləbəl] *n* monosyllabe *m*; **to speak in monosyllables** parler par monosyllabes

monotheism ['mɒnəθi:,ɪzəm] *n Rel* monothéisme *m*

monotheist ['mɒnəθi:,ɪst] *Rel* **1** *n* monothéiste *mf*

2 *adj* monothéiste

monotheistic [,mɒnəθi:'ɪstɪk] *adj Rel* monothéiste

monotint ['mɒnəʊtɪnt] *n Art* monochrome *m*

monotone [ˈmɒnətəʊn] **1** *n* ton *m* monocorde *ou* monotone; **to speak in a monotone** parler d'un ton monocorde *ou* monotone
2 *adj* monocorde

monotonic [ˌmɒnəˈtɒnɪk] *adj Math* monotone
▸▸ *Math* ***monotonic function*** fonction *f* monotone; *Phys & Math* ***monotonic quantity*** invariant *m*

monotonous [məˈnɒtənəs] *adj (gen)* monotone; *(voice)* monotone, monocorde

monotonously [məˈnɒtənəslɪ] *adv* de façon monotone; **he droned monotonously on** il ânonnait d'un ton monotone

monotony [məˈnɒtənɪ] *(pl* **monotonies***) n* monotonie *f*; **her visits broke the monotony of his life** les visites qu'elle lui rendait rompaient la monotonie de son existence; **the monotony of the landscape** l'uniformité *f ou* la monotonie du paysage

monotreme [ˈmɒnəʊtriːm] *n Zool* monotrème *m*

monotype [ˈmɒnətaɪp] **1** *n* **(a)** *Art* monotype *m* **(b)** *Biol* monotype *m*
2 Monotype® *n Typ (machine)* Monotype® *f*

monotypic [ˌmɒnəʊˈtɪpɪk] *adj Bot & Zool* monotype

monounsaturated [ˌmɒnəʊʌnˈsætʃəreɪtɪd] *adj (fat)* mono-insaturé

monovalence [ˌmɒnəʊˈveɪləns], **monovalency** [ˌmɒnəʊˈveɪlənsɪ] *n Chem* monovalence *f*

monovalent [ˌmɒnəʊˈveɪlənt] *adj Chem* monovalent, univalent

monoxide [mɒˈnɒksaɪd] *n Chem* monoxyde *m*; **carbon monoxide** monoxyde *m* de carbone; **nitrogen monoxide** protoxyde *m* d'azote

monozygotic [ˌmɒnəʊzaɪˈgɒtɪk], **monozygous** [ˌmɒnəʊˈzaɪgəs] *adj Biol* monozygote, univitellin

Monroe Doctrine [mənˈrəʊ-] *n* **the Monroe Doctrine** la doctrine Monroe

> **MONROE DOCTRINE**
>
> La doctrine Monroe, énoncée en 1823, inaugura une période isolationniste aux États-Unis, en interdisant le continent américain à l'Europe colonialiste, et en se détournant délibérément des affaires européennes.

Monrovia [mənˈrəʊvɪə] *n* Monrovia

Monsignor [mɒnˈsiːnjə(r)] *(pl* **Monsignors** *or* **Monsignori** [-siːˈnjɔːrɪ]*) n Rel* monseigneur *m*

monsoon [mɒnˈsuːn] *n* mousson *f*; **the monsoon season** la mousson

monsoonal [mɒnˈsuːnəl] *adj* de la mousson

monster [ˈmɒnstə(r)] **1** *n* **(a)** *(beast, cruel person)* monstre *m*
(b) *Fam (large person, thing)* colosse □ *m*, géant(e) □ *m,f*; **his last novel was a monster** son dernier roman est un pavé; **it's a monster of a machine** c'est un vrai monstre, cette machine
2 *adj Fam* colossal □, monstre
▸▸ *Br Pol* ***the Monster Raving Loony Party*** = parti politique parodique qui attire souvent les votes des déçus de la politique

monstrance [ˈmɒnstrəns] *n Rel* ostensoir *m*

monstrosity [mɒnˈstrɒsətɪ] *(pl* **monstrosities***) n* **(a)** *(monstrous nature)* monstruosité *f* **(b)** *(ugly person, thing)* horreur *f*; **the town hall is a huge Victorian monstrosity** la mairie est une horreur de l'époque victorienne

monstrous [ˈmɒnstrəs] *adj* **(a)** *(appalling)* monstrueux, atroce **(b)** *(enormous)* colossal, énorme **(c)** *(abnormal)* monstrueux

monstrously [ˈmɒnstrəslɪ] *adv* affreusement

monstrousness [ˈmɒnstrəsnɪs] *n (of crime etc)* monstruosité *f*, atrocité *f*

mons veneris [mɒnzˈvenərɪs] *n Anat* mont *m* de Vénus

Mont *(written abbr* **Montana***)* Montana *m*

montage [ˈmɒntɑːʒ] *n Art, Cin & Phot* montage *m*

Montagu's harrier [ˈmɒntəgjuːz-] *n Orn* busard *m* de Montagu

Montana [mɒnˈtænə] *n* le Montana; **in Montana** dans le Montana

Mont Blanc [ˌmɔ̃ˈblɑ̃] *n* mont Blanc *m*

montbretia [mɒnˈbriːʃə] *n Bot* montbrétie *f*, montbrétia *f*

Monte Carlo [ˌmɒntɪˈkɑːləʊ] *n* Monte-Carlo

Montenegrin [ˌmɒntɪˈniːgrɪn] **1** *n* Monténégrin(e) *m,f*
2 *adj* monténégrin

Montenegro [ˌmɒntɪˈniːgrəʊ] *n* Monténégro *m*

Montevideo [ˌmɒntɪvɪˈdeɪəʊ] *n* Montevideo

Montezuma [mɒntɪˈzuːmə] *pr n* Moctezuma, Montezuma
▸▸ *Fam Hum* ***Montezuma's revenge*** la turista *f*

month [mʌnθ] *n* mois *m*; **how much does she earn a month?** combien gagne-t-elle par mois?; **in the month of August** au mois d'août; **in the summer/winter months** pendant les mois d'été/d'hiver; **he's six months old** il a six mois; *Fam* **he got six months** il a été condamné à six mois de prison □; **every month** tous les mois; **in a month's time** dans un mois; **by the month** au mois; **two months' holiday** *or* **vacation** deux mois de vacances; **I can't keep it up month after month** je ne pourrai pas tenir ce rythme éternellement; **month by month you can see an improvement** on constate une amélioration de mois en mois; *Fam* **she hasn't heard from him in a month of Sundays** ça fait des siècles *ou* un bail qu'elle n'a pas de nouvelles de lui; *Fam* **never in a month of Sundays** jamais de la vie; *Euph* **is it that** *or* **your time of the month?** *(are you menstruating?)* tu es indisposée?

monthly [ˈmʌnθlɪ] *(pl* **monthlies***)* **1** *n (periodical)* mensuel *m*
2 *adj* mensuel
3 *adv* tous les mois, mensuellement
4 monthlies *npl Fam Old-fashioned (menstrual period)* règles □ *fpl*
▸▸ ***monthly instalment*** mensualité *f*; *Fin* ***monthly investment plan*** plan *m* d'investissement mensuel; ***monthly payment*** mensualité *f*; *Med* ***monthly period*** règles *fpl*; ***monthly statement*** relevé *m* mensuel, relevé *m* de fin de mois

montmorillonite [mɒntməˈrɪlənaɪt] *n Geol* montmorillonite *f*

Montreal [ˌmɒntrɪˈɔːl] *n* Montréal

Montserrat [ˈmɒntsəˌræt] *n* Montserrat

monument [ˈmɒnjʊmənt] *n* **(a)** *(memorial)* monument *m*; **a monument to the war dead** un monument aux morts; **it is a monument to man's stupidity** c'est un monument à la bêtise humaine **(b)** *(historic building)* monument *m* historique; **a national monument** un monument national

monumental [ˌmɒnjʊˈmentəl] *adj (statue, literary work, error, stupidity)* monumental; *(ignorance)* prodigieux; **the film is a monumental failure** le film est un échec monumental *ou* complet; **he's a monumental bore** il est prodigieusement ennuyeux
▸▸ ***monumental mason*** marbrier *m*

monumentally [ˌmɒnjʊˈmentəlɪ] *adv* **(a)** *(build)* de façon monumentale **(b)** *(extremely)* extrêmement; **it was monumentally boring** c'était extrêmement ennuyeux

moo [muː] **1** *n* **(a)** *(sound)* meuglement *m*, beuglement *m*, mugissement *m* **(b)** *Br Fam (woman)* vieille bique *f*, vieille toupie *f*; **you silly moo!** espèce d'andouille!; **shut up you old moo!** la ferme, espèce de vieille toupie!
2 *vi* meugler, beugler, mugir
3 *onomat* meuh

mooch [muːtʃ] *Fam* **1** *vi* **(a)** *Br (wander aimlessly)* traîner; **he mooched down the street** il descendit la rue en flânant
(b) *(cadge)* taxer; **he's always mooching off** *or* **on people** il passe son temps à quémander, il est toujours en train de taper quelqu'un
2 *vt* **(a)** *(cadge)* taper; **to mooch $10 off** *or* **from sb** taper qn de 10 dollars; **can I mooch a cigarette off you?** est-ce que je peux te piquer une cigarette?
(b) *(steal)* chiper, piquer
3 *n Am* tapeur(euse) *m,f*

▸**mooch about, mooch around** *Fam* **1** *vt insep* **to mooch about the house** traîner dans la maison
2 *vi (loaf)* glander, glandouiller; **I was just mooching about at home** je traînais *ou* flemmardais à la maison

moocher [ˈmuːtʃə(r)] *n Am Fam* tapeur(euse) *m,f*

moocow [ˈmuːˌkaʊ] *n Fam (in children's language)* vache □ *f*, meu-meu *f*

mood [muːd] *n* **(a)** *(humour)* humeur *f*, disposition *f*; **to be in a good/bad mood** être de bonne/mauvaise humeur; **to be in a generous mood** être en veine de générosité; **it's hard to predict the mood of the electorate** il est difficile de prédire l'état d'esprit *ou* l'humeur des électeurs; **she can be quite funny when the mood takes her** elle peut être plutôt drôle quand l'envie lui en prend; **to be in the mood for reading/dancing** avoir envie de lire/danser; **are you in the mood for a hamburger?** un hamburger, ça te dit?; **he's in no mood for jokes** il n'est pas d'humeur à rire; **I'm not in the mood** ça ne me dit rien; **I wasn't in the mood (for it)** je n'étais pas d'humeur à ça
(b) *(bad temper, sulk)* mauvaise humeur *f*, bouderie *f*; **to be in a mood** être de mauvaise humeur; **she's in one of her moods** elle est de mauvaise humeur, elle fait la tête
(c) *(atmosphere)* ambiance *f*, atmosphère *f*; **the mood is one of cautious optimism** l'ambiance est à l'optimisme prudent
(d) *Gram* mode *m*; **imperative mood** impératif *m*
▸▸ ***mood elevator*** *(drug)* stimulant *m*; ***mood music*** musique *f* d'ambiance; ***mood swing*** saute *f* d'humeur

moodily [ˈmuːdɪlɪ] *adv (behave)* maussadement, d'un air morose; *(talk, reply)* d'un ton maussade; **"oh, do what you like", he said moodily** "oh! faites ce que vous voulez", dit-il d'un ton maussade *ou* boudeur

moodiness [ˈmuːdɪnɪs] *n* **(a)** *(sullenness)* humeur *f* maussade, maussaderie *f* **(b)** *(volatility)* humeur *f* changeante; **it's his moodiness I can't stand** ce sont ses sautes d'humeur que je ne supporte pas

moody [ˈmuːdɪ] *(compar* **moodier**, *superl* **moodiest***) adj* **(a)** *(sullen)* de mauvaise humeur, maussade, grincheux **(b)** *(temperamental)* versatile, d'humeur changeante; **he's very moody** il est d'humeur très changeante, il est très lunatique **(c)** *Br Fam (goods)* volé □; *(passport, document)* faux (fausse) □

moola, moolah [ˈmuːlə] *n Fam* flouze *m*, fric *m*

mooli [ˈmuːlɪ] *n* daikon *m (d'Afrique)*

moon [muːn] **1** *n* **(a)** *(of planet)* lune *f*; **Saturn has several moons** Saturne a plusieurs lunes; **there's a moon tonight** on voit la lune ce soir; **by the light of the moon** au clair de (la) lune; **many moons ago** il y a bien des lunes; *Fam* **to be over the moon** être aux anges; *Fig* **he promised her the moon (and the stars)** il lui promit la lune *ou* monts et merveilles; *Fam* **once in a blue moon** tous les trente-six du mois
(b) *Am Fam (bare buttocks)* lune *f*
2 *comp (base, flight, rocket)* lunaire
3 *vt Fam (show one's buttocks to)* montrer ses fesses à □
4 *vi Fam (bare one's buttocks)* montrer ses fesses □
▸▸ ***moon boots*** après-skis *mpl*; ***moon buggy*** Jeep® *f* lunaire; *Ich* ***moon jellyfish*** méduse *f* bleue; ***moon landing*** atterrissage *m* sur la lune, alunissage *m*; *Astron* ***moon shot*** lancement *m* d'un vaisseau lunaire; *Astron* ***moon walk*** marche *f* sur la lune

▸**moon about, moon around** *vi Fam (idly)* paresser, traîner, flemmarder; *(dreamily)* rêvasser; *(gloomily)* se morfondre □

▸**moon over** *vt insep Fam* soupirer après □; **she's still mooning over her old boyfriend** elle soupire toujours après son ancien petit ami

moonbeam [ˈmuːnbiːm] *n* rayon *m* de lune

mooncalf [ˈmuːnkɑːf] *n Arch* **(a)** *(stillborn freak)* monstre *m ou* avorton *m* non viable **(b)** *(fool)* idiot(e) *m,f*, crétin(e) *m,f*

moon-faced *adj* joufflu, aux joues rebondies

moonfish [ˈmuːnfɪʃ] *n Ich* poisson-lune *m*

moonflower [ˈmuːnflaʊə(r)] *n Bot* **(a)** *(oxeye daisy)* marguerite *f* des champs **(b)** *(tropical climber)* ipomée *f* bonne-nuit

Moonie [ˈmuːnɪ] *n Fam* adepte *mf* de la secte Moon □, mooniste □ *mf*

moonless [ˈmuːnlɪs] *adj* sans lune

moonlight [ˈmuːnlaɪt] **1** *n* clair *m* de lune; **they took a walk by moonlight** ils se sont promenés au clair de (la) lune; *Br Fam* **to do a moonlight flit** déménager à la cloche de bois
2 *adj (walk)* au clair de (la) lune

mon–moo

3 *vi Fam (have second job)* avoir un deuxième emploi ❑; *(illegally)* travailler au noir

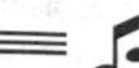

'The Moonlight Sonata' *Beethoven* 'La Sonate au clair de lune'

moonlighter ['mu:n,laɪtə(r)] *n* travailleur(euse) *m,f* non déclaré(e)
moonlighting ['mu:n,laɪtɪŋ] *n (illegal work)* travail *m* au noir
moonlit ['mu:nlɪt] *adj* éclairé par la lune; **a moonlit night** une nuit de lune; **a bright moonlit night** une nuit très claire; **we walked through the moonlit fields** nous avons marché à travers champs, au clair de lune
moonquake ['mu:nkweɪk] *n* tremblement *m* de lune
moonrise ['mu:nraɪz] *n* lever *m* de la lune
moonscape ['mu:nskeɪp] *n* paysage *m* lunaire
moonshine ['mu:nʃaɪn] *n (UNCOUNT)* (**a**) *(moonlight)* clair *m* de lune (**b**) *Fam (foolishness)* sornettes *fpl*, sottises *fpl*; **that's a bag** *or* **a load of moonshine** c'est des contes bleus, c'est des conneries (**c**) *Am Fam (illegally made spirits)* alcool *m* de contrebande ❑
moonshiner ['mu:nʃaɪnə(r)] *n Am Fam (maker)* bouilleur *m* non patenté ❑; *(seller)* trafiquant(e) *m,f* d'alcool de contrebande ❑
moonshining ['mu:nʃaɪnɪŋ] *n Am Fam* = fabrication clandestine d'alcool
moonstone ['mu:nstəʊn] *n* pierre *f* de lune, adulaire *f*

'The Moonstone' *Collins* 'La Pierre de lune'

moonstruck ['mu:nstrʌk] *adj Fam (dreamy)* dans la lune; *(mad)* détraqué, toqué
moony ['mu:nɪ] *(compar* **moonier**, *superl* **mooniest**) *adj Fam* (**a**) *(dreamy)* dans la lune (**b**) *Br (crazy)* dingue, timbré
Moor [mɔ:(r)] *n* Maure *m*, Mauresque *f*
moor [mɔ:(r)] **1** *n* lande *f*
2 *vt (boat)* amarrer; *(buoy)* mouiller
3 *vi* mouiller
moorage ['mɔ:rɪdʒ] *n* (**a**) *(place)* mouillage *m* (**b**) *(fee)* droit *m* d'ancrage
moorcock ['mɒ:kɒk] *n Br Orn* lagopède *m* d'Écosse mâle
moorfowl ['mɔ:faʊl] *n Orn* lagopède *m* d'Écosse
moorgrass ['mɔ:grɑ:s] *n Bot* (**a**) *(Drosera rotundifolia)* drosère *f* à feuilles rondes (**b**) *(Potentilla anserina)* potentille *f* ansérine, argentine *f* (**c**) *(cotton grass)* linaigrette *f* commune, lin *m* des marais
moorhen ['mɔ:hen] *n Orn* (**a**) *(waterfowl)* poule *f* d'eau (**b**) *(female grouse)* lagopède *m* d'Écosse femelle
mooring ['mɔ:rɪŋ] **1** *n* (**a**) *(act)* amarrage *m*, mouillage *m*
(**b**) *(place)* mouillage *m*
2 moorings *npl (cables, ropes etc)* amarres *fpl*; **the boat was (riding) at her moorings** le bateau tirait sur ses amarres; **the boat broke its moorings** le bateau a rompu ses amarres; *Fig* **he's lost his moorings** il est à la dérive
▸▸ ***mooring buoy*** corps-mort *m*; ***mooring line*** câble *m* d'amarrage; ***mooring ring*** organeau *m*
Moorish ['mɔ:rɪʃ] *adj* maure; *(art, architecture)* mauresque
moorland ['mɔ:lənd] *n* lande *f*
moose [mu:s] *(pl* **inv**) *n Zool* (**a**) *(in North America)* orignal *m*, élan *m* du Canada (**b**) *(in Europe)* élan *m*, orignal *m*
moot [mu:t] **1** *vt (question, topic)* soulever; **a change in the rules has been mooted** il a été question de modifier le règlement
2 *n* (**a**) *Hist* assemblée *f* (**b**) *Univ (in law faculties)* tribunal *m* fictif
3 *adj* **that's a moot point** c'est discutable, ce n'est pas sûr
mop [mɒp] *(pt & pp* **mopped**, *cont* **mopping**) **1** *n* (**a**) *(for floor → string, cloth)* balai *m* (à franges), balai *m* espagnol; *(→ sponge)* balai-éponge *m*; *Naut* vadrouille *f*; *(for dishes)* lavette *f* (à vaisselle)
(**b**) *(of hair)* tignasse *f*; **a mop of blond hair** une tignasse blonde
2 *vt (floor)* laver; *(table, face, spilt liquid)* essuyer, éponger; **he mopped the sweat from his brow** il s'épongea le front
▸**mop up** *vt sep* (**a**) *(floor, table, spilt liquid)* essuyer, éponger; **have some bread to mop up the sauce** prenez un morceau de pain pour saucer votre assiette
(**b**) *Fam (win, make off with)* rafler; **they mopped up all the gold medals** ils ont raflé toutes les médailles d'or
(**c**) *Mil (resistance)* liquider
mopboard ['mɒpbɔ:rd] *n Am* plinthe *f*
mope [məʊp] *vi* broyer du noir; **he's been moping around** *or* **about all week** il a passé la semaine à broyer du noir; **there's no use moping about** *or* **over it** ça ne sert à rien de passer ton temps à ressasser ce qui s'est passé
moped ['məʊped] *n* vélomoteur *m*
mophead ['mɒphed] *n (scruffy person)* épouvantail *m*
moppet ['mɒpɪt] *n Fam (term of affection)* chou *m*
mopping-up operation ['mɒpɪŋ-] *n* opération *f* de nettoyage
moquette [mɒ'ket] *n Tex* moquette *f (étoffe)*
MOR [,eməʊ'ɑ:(r)] *adj (abbr* **middle-of-the-road**) *(music)* grand public *(inv)*; *Pej* passe-partout *(inv)*
morainal [mɒ'reɪnəl] *adj Geol* morainique
moraine [mɒ'reɪn] *n Geol* moraine *f*
morainic [mɒ'reɪnɪk] *adj Geol* morainique
moral ['mɒrəl] **1** *adj* moral; **it's a very moral story** c'est une histoire très morale; **he complains about the decline in moral standards** il se plaint du déclin des valeurs morales *ou* du relâchement des mœurs; **we have a moral duty to help them** nous sommes moralement obligés de les aider; **young people today have no moral fibre** les jeunes d'aujourd'hui n'ont ni caractère ni moralité; **to give sb moral support** soutenir qn moralement
2 *n (lesson)* morale *f*; **what's the moral of the story?** quelle est la morale de l'histoire?
3 morals *npl (standards)* sens *m* moral, moralité *f*; **he has no morals** il n'a aucun sens moral
▸▸ ***the moral majority*** les néo-conservateurs *mpl (surtout aux États-Unis)*; ***moral philosophy*** morale *f*, éthique *f*; ***Moral Rearmament*** = mouvement international pour un renouveau moral et spirituel fondé en 1938; ***moral victory*** victoire *f* morale
morale [mə'rɑ:l] *n* moral *m*; **morale is high/low among the troops** les troupes ont bon/mauvais moral, les troupes ont/n'ont pas le moral; **she tried to raise their morale** elle a essayé de leur remonter le moral *ou* de leur redonner (du) courage; **news of the defeat sapped the troops' morale** la nouvelle de la défaite a sapé le moral des troupes
morale-booster *n* **it was a morale-booster** ça nous/leur/*etc* a remonté le moral
moralism ['mɒrəlɪzəm] *n* moralisme *m*
moralist ['mɒrəlɪst] *n* moraliste *mf*
moralistic [,mɒrə'lɪstɪk] *adj* moraliste
morality [mə'rælətɪ] *(pl* **moralities**) *n (of person, decision, principles)* moralité *f*
▸▸ *Theat* ***morality play*** moralité *f*
moralization [,mɒrəlaɪ'zeɪʃən] *n* moralisation *f*
moralize, -ise ['mɒrəlaɪz] **1** *vi* moraliser, **to moralize about sth** moraliser sur qch; **he's forever moralizing about things** il passe son temps à faire la morale
2 *vt* moraliser
moralizing ['mɒrəlaɪzɪŋ] **1** *adj* moralisateur, moralisant
2 *n (UNCOUNT)* leçons *fpl* de morale, *Pej* prêches *mpl*
morally ['mɒrəlɪ] *adv* moralement; **to be morally bound to do sth** être obligé moralement de faire qch; **the parents are morally responsible** les parents sont moralement responsables; **morally wrong** contraire à la morale
morass [mə'ræs] *n* (**a**) *(disordered situation)* bourbier *m*; *(of paperwork, information)* fouillis *m*, fatras *m*; **bogged down in a morass of rules and regulations** empêtré dans un fatras de règles et de règlements (**b**) *(marsh)* marais *m*, bourbier *m*
moratorium [,mɒrə'tɔ:rɪəm] *(pl* **moratoriums** *or* **moratoria** [-rɪə]) *n* (**a**) *(suspension of activity)* moratoire *m*; **they are calling for a moratorium on arms sales** ils appellent à un moratoire sur les ventes d'armes (**b**) *Econ, Law & Fin* moratoire *m*; *(of debt)* moratoire *m*, suspension *f*; **to declare a moratorium** décréter un moratoire
Moravia [mə'reɪvjə] *n* Moravie *f*; **in Moravia** en Moravie
Moravian [mə'reɪvjən] **1** *n* Morave *mf*
2 *adj* morave
moray ['mɒreɪ] *n Ich* murène *f*
▸▸ ***moray eel*** murène *f*
morbid ['mɔ:bɪd] *adj* (**a**) *(gen)* morbide; *(curiosity)* malsain; **he has a morbid outlook on life** il voit les choses en noir; **morbid thoughts** pensées *fpl* morbides; **don't be so morbid!** ne sois pas si morbide! (**b**) *Med (state, growth, symptom)* morbide
▸▸ *Med* ***morbid anatomy*** anatomie *f* pathologique
morbidity [mɔ:'bɪdətɪ] *n* (**a**) *(gen)* morbidité *f* (**b**) *Med* morbidité *f* (relative)
▸▸ *Med* ***morbidity rate*** morbidité *f* (relative)
morbidly ['mɔ:bɪdlɪ] *adv* maladivement
morbidness ['mɔ:bɪdnɪs] *n* morbidité *f*
mordacity [mɔ:'dæsɪtɪ], **mordancy** ['mɔ:dənsɪ] *n* mordacité *f*, causticité *f*
mordant ['mɔ:dənt] *adj* mordant, caustique
mordent ['mɔ:dənt] *n Mus* mordant *m*

MORE [mɔ:(r)]

plus de	▸ **1 (a); 6 1**
davantage de	▸ **1 (a)**
plus	▸ **2 (a), (b); 3 (a), (b)**
davantage	▸ **2 (a); 3 (b)**
encore	▸ **2 (b)**
plutôt	▸ **3 (c)**
de plus en plus	▸ **4**
plus que	▸ **6 2**

1 *adj* (**a**) *(compar of* **many, much**) *(larger quantity or number of)* plus de, davantage de; **there were more boys than girls** il y avait plus de garçons que de filles; **there's much** *or* **a lot** *or* **far more room in the other building** il y a beaucoup plus de place dans l'autre bâtiment
(**b**) *(additional quantity or number of)* **you should eat more fish** tu devrais manger davantage de *ou* plus de poisson; **I need more time** j'ai besoin de plus de temps; **three more people arrived** trois autres personnes sont arrivées; **there's only one more problem to solve** il n'y a plus qu'un problème à résoudre; **do you have any more questions?** avez-vous d'autres questions?; **do you have any more stamps?** est-ce qu'il vous reste des timbres?; **I have no more money** je n'ai plus d'argent; **is there any more butter?** est-ce qu'il reste du beurre?; **just wait a few more minutes** patiente encore quelques instants; **a little more sugar?** encore un peu de sucre?; **have some more wine** reprends du vin; **there are no more** *or* **there aren't any more green lampshades** il n'y a plus d'abat-jour verts; **no more talking** maintenant, taisez-vous *ou* silence!; **there'll be no more skiing this winter** le ski est fini pour cet hiver; **there have been several more incidents in the same area** plusieurs autres incidents se sont produits dans le même quartier; **bring me some more potatoes, please** apporte-moi encore des pommes de terre, s'il te plaît; **there's some more paper in that drawer** il y a encore du papier dans ce tiroir; **would you like some more soup?** voulez-vous un peu plus de soupe?
2 *pron* (**a**) *(compar of* **many, much**) *(larger amount)* plus, davantage; *(greater number)* plus; **he earns more than I do** *or* **than me** il gagne plus que moi; **I wish I could do more for her** j'aimerais pouvoir l'aider plus *ou* davantage; **it'll take a lot more than that to persuade them** il en faudra bien plus (que ça) *ou* bien davantage pour les convaincre; **some opted for A, but many more chose B** certains ont choisi A, mais ceux qui ont choisi B étaient bien plus nombreux; **there are more of them than there are of us** ils sont plus nombreux que nous; **he's even more of a coward than I thought** il est encore plus lâche que je ne pensais; **it's more of a problem now than it used to be** ça pose plus de problèmes maintenant qu'avant; **she's**

moo–mor

more of a singer than a dancer c'est une chanteuse plus qu'une danseuse

(**b**) *(additional amount)* plus, encore; **there's more if you want it** il y en a encore si tu veux; **he asked for more** il en redemanda; **I couldn't eat any more, thanks** je ne pourrais plus rien avaler, merci; **she just can't take any more** elle n'en peut vraiment plus; **please can I have some more?** *(food)* puis-je en reprendre, s'il vous plaît?; **there are some more here that you haven't washed** il en reste ici que tu n'as pas lavés; **I could say more, but...** je pouvais en dire plus mais...; **something/nothing more** quelque chose/rien de plus; **I have something/nothing more to say** j'ai encore quelque chose/je n'ai plus rien à dire; **he's just a good friend, nothing more** c'est un bon ami, rien de plus; **what more can I say?** que puis-je dire de plus?; **what more do you want?** que voulez-vous de plus?; *Fam* **what more could you ask for!** que demande le peuple!; **but more of that later...** mais nous reparlerons de ça plus tard...; **I want no more of this defeatist talk** je ne veux plus de ces discours défaitistes; **that's more like it!** voilà, c'est mieux!; **no more no less** ni plus ni moins; **more of the same** la même chose; **the government simply promises more of the same** le gouvernement se contente de refaire les mêmes promesses; **there's plenty more where that came from** si vous en revoulez, il n'y a qu'à demander; **need I say more?** si tu vois ce que je veux dire; *Fam* **say no more!** cela suffit!, n'en dis pas plus!

(**c**) *Fam (additional people)* **any more for the ferry?** qui d'autre prend le ferry?❑; *Hum* **any more for any more?** *(food)* est-ce que quelqu'un veut du rab?

3 *adv* (**a**) *(forming comparatives)* plus; **more intelligent** plus intelligent; **more comfortably** plus confortablement

(**b**) *(to a greater extent or degree)* plus, davantage; **you should read more** tu devrais lire plus *ou* davantage; **it worries me more than it used to** ça m'inquiète plus qu'avant; **this more than makes up for it** ça fait plus que compenser; **I like wine more than beer** je préfère le vin à la bière, j'aime mieux le vin que la bière; **I would think more of her if she owned up** j'aurais une plus haute opinion d'elle si elle avouait; **he's intelligent but his sister is more so** il est intelligent mais sa sœur l'est davantage; **I'll give you £20, not a penny more** je te donnerai 20 livres, pas un sou de plus

(**c**) *(rather)* plutôt; **she was more disappointed than angry** elle était plus déçue que fâchée; **do it more like this** fais-le plutôt comme ceci; **it's more a question of who foots the bill** il s'agit plutôt de savoir qui paiera la facture

(**d**) *(again)* **once/twice more** encore une/deux fois

4 more and more 1 *adj* de plus en plus; **more and more people are using it** de plus en plus de gens l'utilisent **2** *adv* de plus en plus; **more and more interesting** de plus en plus intéressant; **I was growing more and more tired** j'étais de plus en plus fatigué; **I like him more and more each time I see him** à chaque fois que je le vois je l'apprécie davantage

5 more or less *adv* (**a**) *(roughly)* plus ou moins; **that's more or less what I expected** c'est plus ou moins ce à quoi je m'attendais; **is that correct? – well, more or less** est-ce que c'est vrai? – plus ou moins, oui

(**b**) *(almost)* presque; **we've more or less finished** nous avons presque terminé

6 more than 1 *prep (with numbers, measurements etc)* plus de; **more than 500 people** plus de 500 personnes; **it costs much** *or* **a lot more than $50** ça coûte bien plus de 50 dollars; **for little more than £500** pour à peine plus de 500 livres; **I won't be more than two hours** je n'en ai pas pour plus de deux heures, j'en ai pour deux heures au maximum **2** *adv* plus que; **I'd be more than happy to do it** je serais ravi de le faire; **you've been more than generous** vous avez été plus que généreux; **that's more than enough** c'est plus qu'il n'en faut; **this more than makes up for his previous mistakes** voilà qui rachète largement ses anciennes erreurs

7 more than a little *adv* vraiment; **we were more than a little shocked** nous étions vraiment choqués

8 no more *adv* (**a**) *(neither)* non plus; **he doesn't believe the rumours and no more do I** il ne croit pas les rumeurs and moi non plus

(**b**) *(as little)* pas plus; **she's no more a spy than I am!** elle n'est pas plus espionne que moi!; **I would no more have suspected him than I would my own mother** je ne l'aurais pas soupçonné davantage que ma propre mère; **it's no more dangerous than crossing the street** ce n'est pas plus dangereux que de traverser la rue; *Fam* **they can no more act than fly in the air** ils jouent comme des pieds

(**c**) *Literary (no longer)* **no more will she grace our company** plus jamais elle ne nous tiendra compagnie; **the Empire is no more** l'Empire n'est plus

9 not...any more *adv* **we don't go there any more** nous n'y allons plus; **he still works here, doesn't he? – not any more (he doesn't)** il travaille encore ici, n'est-ce pas? – non, plus maintenant

10 the more *adv Formal* d'autant plus; **I was the more disappointed** j'étais d'autant plus déçu; **they went the more willingly on that account** ils y sont allés d'autant plus volontiers; **the more so because...** d'autant plus que...

11 the more...the more *conj* plus...plus; **the more they have, the more they want** plus ils en ont, plus ils en veulent; **the more I see him, the more I like him** plus je le vois, plus il me plaît

12 what is more, what's more *adv* qui plus est

---

moreish ['mɔːrɪʃ] *adj Br Fam* appétissant❑; **these peanuts are very moreish** on en mangerait de ces cacahuètes, ces cacahuètes ont un petit goût de revenez-y

morel [mə'rel] *n* morille *f*

morello [mə'reləʊ] *(pl* **morellos***)* *n* griotte *f*

▸▸ ***morello cherry*** griotte *f*

morendo [mə'rendəʊ] *Mus* **1** *adj* morendo

2 *adv* morendo

moreover [mɔː'rəʊvə(r)] *adv* de plus

mores ['mɔːreɪz] *npl Formal* mœurs *fpl*

Moresque [mɔː'resk] *adj* mauresque

morganatic [ˌmɔːgə'nætɪk] *adj* morganatique

morgue [mɔːg] *n* (**a**) *(mortuary)* morgue *f*; *Fam* **it's like a morgue here** c'est complètement mort ici (**b**) *Fam Journ* archives❑ *fpl*

MORI ['mɒrɪ] *n Br (abbr* **Market & Opinion Research Institute***)* = institut britannique de sondage

moribund ['mɒrɪbʌnd] *adj* moribond

morish = **moreish**

Mormon ['mɔːmən] *Rel* **1** *n* mormon(e) *m,f*

2 *adj* mormon

Mormonism ['mɔːmənɪzəm] *n Rel* mormonisme *m*

morn [mɔːn] *n* (**a**) *Literary (morning)* matin *m* (**b**) *Scot* **the morn** *(tomorrow)* demain; **the morn's morn** après-demain

morning ['mɔːnɪŋ] **1** *n* (**a**) *(gen)* matin *m*; *(referring to duration)* matinée *f*; **at three/ten o'clock in the morning** à trois/dix heures du matin; **I worked all morning** j'ai travaillé toute la matinée; **one summer morning** un matin d'été; **when I awoke it was morning** quand je me suis réveillé il faisait jour; **every Saturday/Sunday morning** tous les samedis/dimanches matin; **from morning till night** du matin jusqu'au soir; **there's a flight in the morning** *(before noon)* il y a un vol le matin; *(sometime during)* il y a un vol dans la matinée; *(tomorrow)* il y a un vol demain matin; **he's leaving in the morning** il s'en va dans la matinée; **it's open in the morning** *or* **mornings** c'est ouvert le matin; **see you in the morning!** à demain matin!; **in the early/late morning** en début/fin de matinée; **I'll be back on Monday morning** je serai de retour lundi matin; **the cleaning lady comes on Monday mornings** la femme de ménage vient le lundi matin; **on the morning of the twelfth** le matin du douze, le douze au matin; **do you work mornings?** est-ce que vous travaillez le matin?; **I'm on mornings this week** je travaille le matin cette semaine; **could I have the morning off?** puis-je avoir la matinée de libre?; **(good) morning!** *(hello)* bonjour!; *(goodbye)* au revoir!; **this morning** ce matin; **that morning** ce matin-là; **the previous morning, the morning before** la veille au matin; **the next morning, the morning after** le lendemain matin; *Fam* **the morning after the night before** un lendemain de cuite; **the morning rush hour** les heures *fpl* de pointe du matin; **cancel the Monday morning meeting** annulez le rendez-vous de lundi matin; **we have morning coffee around eleven** nous faisons une pause-café vers onze heures du matin

(**b**) *Literary (beginning)* matin *m*, aube *f*; **in the morning of one's life** à l'aube de sa vie

2 *comp (dew, sun, bath)* matinal, du matin; *(newspaper, broadcast)* du matin

3 mornings *adv esp Am* le matin

▸▸ ***morning coat*** queue-de-pie *f*; ***morning dress*** (**a**) *(UNCOUNT) Br (suit)* = habit porté lors des occasions importantes et comportant queue-de-pie, pantalon gris et haut-de-forme gris (**b**) *Am (dress)* robe *f* d'intérieur; *Bot* ***morning glory*** ipomée *f*, volubilis *m*; *Rel* ***Morning Prayer*** office *m* du matin *(Église anglicane)*; ***morning room*** petit salon *m*; ***morning sickness*** nausées *fpl* matinales *ou* du matin; *Press* ***the Morning Star*** = ancien quotidien britannique d'obédience communiste; ***morning star*** étoile *f* du matin

morning-after pill *n* pilule *f* du lendemain

Moroccan [mə'rɒkən] **1** *n* Marocain(e) *m,f*

2 *adj* marocain

3 *comp (embassy, history)* du Maroc

Morocco [mə'rɒkəʊ] **1** *n* Maroc *m*; **in Morocco** au Maroc

2 morocco *n* maroquin *m*

▸▸ ***morocco leather*** maroquin *m*

moron ['mɔːrɒn] *n* (**a**) *Fam (stupid person)* imbécile *mf*, crétin(e) *m,f*; **you moron!** pauvre imbécile! (**b**) *Old-fashioned (mentally retarded person)* débile *mf* léger(ère)

Moroni [mə'rəʊnɪ] *n* Moroni

moronic [mə'rɒnɪk] *adj* imbécile, débile

moronically [mə'rɒnɪkəlɪ] *adv* comme un imbécile

morose [mə'rəʊs] *adj* morose

morosely [mə'rəʊslɪ] *adv* avec morosité

moroseness [mə'rəʊsnɪs] *n* morosité *f*, humeur *f* morose

morph [mɔːf] **1** *n Ling* morphe *f*

2 *vt Comput (image)* transformer par morphing

3 *vi Comput* **to morph into sth** se transformer en qch

morpheme ['mɔːfiːm] *n Ling* morphème *m*

morphemic [mɔː'fiːmɪk] *adj Ling* morphématique

morphemics [mɔː'fiːmɪks] *n (UNCOUNT) Ling* morphématique *f*

Morpheus ['mɔːfjuːs] *pr n Myth* Morphée; **in the arms of Morpheus** dans les bras de Morphée

morphine ['mɔːfiːn], **morphia** ['mɔːfjə] *n* morphine *f*

▸▸ ***morphine addict*** morphinomane *mf*; ***morphine addiction*** morphinomanie *f*

morphing ['mɔːfɪŋ] *n Comput* morphing *m*

morphinism ['mɔːfɪnɪzəm] *n Med* morphinisme *m*

morphogenesis [ˌmɔːfəʊ'dʒenɪsɪs] *n Biol* morphogenèse *f*

morphogenetic [ˌmɔːfəʊdʒə'netɪk] *adj Biol* morphogénétique, morphogène

morphological [ˌmɔːfə'lɒdʒɪkəl] *adj Biol & Ling* morphologique

morphologically [ˌmɔːfə'lɒdʒɪkəlɪ] *adv Biol & Ling* morphologiquement

morphologist [ˌmɔː'fɒlədʒɪst] *n Biol & Ling* morphologue *mf*

morphology [ˌmɔː'fɒlədʒɪ] *n Biol & Ling* morphologie *f*

morphometry [ˌmɔː'fɒmɪtrɪ] *n Biol* morphométrie *f*

morphophoneme [ˌmɔːfəʊ'fəʊniːm] *n Ling* morphophonème *m*

morphophonemics [ˌmɔːfəʊfə'niːmɪks] *n (UNCOUNT) Ling* morphophonémique *f*

morphosis [ˌmɔː'fəʊsɪs] *(pl* **morphoses** [-siːz]*)* *n Biol* morphose *f*

morris ['mɒrɪs] *n*

▸▸ ***morris dance*** = danse folklorique anglaise; ***morris dancer*** = danseur folklorique anglais; ***morris dancing*** = danses folkloriques anglaises; ***morris man*** = danseur folklorique anglais

morrow ['mɒrəʊ] *n* (**a**) *Literary (next day)* lendemain *m*; **on the morrow** le lendemain; **what has**

the morrow in store for us? qu'est-ce que demain nous réserve? (**b**) *Arch or Literary (morning)* matin *m*

Morse [mɔːs] *n (code)* morse *m*

►► ***Morse alphabet*** alphabet *m* morse; ***Morse code*** morse *m*; ***Morse signals*** signaux *mpl* en morse

morsel ['mɔːsəl] *n (gen)* morceau *m*; *(mouthful)* bouchée *f*; **a choice morsel** un morceau de choix

mortadella [,mɔːtə'delə] *n* mortadelle *f*

mortal ['mɔːtəl] **1** *adj* (**a**) *(not immortal)* mortel; **all men are mortal** tous les hommes sont mortels; *Euph* **mortal remains** dépouille *f* mortelle

(**b**) *(fatal → blow, disease, injury)* mortel, fatal; *(deadly → enemy, danger)* mortel; **they were locked in mortal combat** ils étaient engagés dans un combat mortel

(**c**) *Fam Old-fashioned (as intensifier)* sacré, satané; **I've tried every mortal thing!** j'ai absolument tout essayé!

(**d**) *(very great)* **he lived in mortal fear of being found out** il vivait dans une peur mortelle d'être découvert

2 *n* mortel(elle) *m,f*; **a mere mortal** un simple mortel

►► ***mortal sin*** péché *m* mortel

mortality [mɔː'tælətɪ] *(pl* **mortalities***) n* (**a**) *(loss of life)* mortalité *f*; **no mortalities have been reported** on ne fait état d'aucun mort, aucun décès n'a été enregistré; **infant mortality** la mortalité infantile (**b**) *(of mortal)* mortalité *f*

►► ***mortality rate*** taux *m* de mortalité; ***mortality tables*** tables *fpl* de mortalité *ou* de létalité

mortally ['mɔːtəlɪ] *adv* mortellement; **mortally offended** mortellement offensé; **mortally wounded** blessé à mort; **to be mortally afraid (of sb)** être mort de peur (devant qn)

mortar ['mɔːtə(r)] **1** *n* (**a**) *Constr* mortier *m* (**b**) *Pharm & Culin* mortier *m*; **mortar and pestle** pilon *m* et mortier *m* (**c**) *Mil* mortier *m*

2 *vt Constr* cimenter

►► ***mortar attack*** attaque *f* au mortier; ***mortar shell*** obus *m* de mortier

mortarboard ['mɔːtəbɔːd] *n* (**a**) *Sch & Univ* ≃ mortier *m (couvre-chef de professeur, d'universitaire)* (**b**) *Constr* taloche *f*

mortgage ['mɔːgɪdʒ] **1** *n* (**a**) *(to buy house)* prêt *m* (immobilier), crédit *m* immobilier; **a 25-year mortgage at 13 percent** un emprunt sur 25 ans à 13 pour cent; **to take out a mortgage** prendre un crédit *ou* un prêt immobilier; **to pay off** *or* **clear one's mortgage** rembourser l'emprunt sur sa maison; **we can't meet our mortgage repayments** nous ne pouvons pas payer les mensualités de notre emprunt; **second mortgage** hypothèque *f*

(**b**) *(raised on property)* hypothèque *f*; **to take out** *or* **raise a mortgage** lever une hypothèque; **to secure a debt by mortgage** hypothéquer une créance; **to pay off a mortgage** purger une hypothèque

2 *vt (land, house)* hypothéquer, prendre une hypothèque sur; *(title deeds)* engager, mettre en gage; **to be mortgaged to the hilt** *(person)* crouler sous les remboursements; **to mortgage one's happiness** engager son bonheur

►► ***mortgage bank*** banque *f* hypothécaire; ***mortgage bond*** obligation *f* hypothécaire; ***mortgage broker*** courtier(ère) *m,f* en prêts hypothécaires; ***mortgage charge*** affectation *f* hypothécaire; ***mortgage debenture*** obligation *f* hypothécaire; ***mortgage deed*** acte *m* hypothécaire; ***mortgage lender*** prêteur(euse) *m,f* hypothécaire; ***mortgage loan*** emprunt *m ou* prêt *m* hypothécaire, prêt *m* sur hypothèque; ***mortgage market*** marché *m* hypothécaire; ***mortgage rate*** taux *m* de crédit immobilier; ***mortgage registrar*** conservateur(trice) *m,f* des hypothèques; ***mortgage repayment*** remboursement *m* d'emprunt; ***mortgage repossession*** mainlevée *f* d'une hypothèque; ***mortgage security*** garantie *f* hypothécaire

mortgageable ['mɔːgɪdʒəbəl] *adj* hypothécable

mortgage-backed security *n Fin* titre *m* garanti par des créances hypothécaires

mortgagee [,mɔːgɪ'dʒiː] *n* créancier(ère) *m,f* hypothécaire, prêteur(euse) *m,f (sur une hypothèque)*

mortgagor [,mɔːgɪ'dʒɔː(r)] *n* débiteur(trice) *m,f* hypothécaire, emprunteur(euse) *m,f (sur une hypothèque)*

mortice = **mortise**

mortician [mɔː'tɪʃən] *n Am* entrepreneur(euse) *m,f* de pompes funèbres

mortification [,mɔːtɪfɪ'keɪʃən] *n* (**a**) *(humiliation)* humiliation *f*; **to my (eternal) mortification** à ma (grande) honte (**b**) *Rel (of the flesh)* mortification *f* (**c**) *Med* nécrose *f*

mortified ['mɔːtɪfaɪd] *adj* mortifié, gêné; **I was absolutely mortified** j'étais mortifié *ou* profondément gêné

mortify ['mɔːtɪfaɪ] *(pt & pp* **mortified***)* **1** *vt* mortifier

2 *vi Med (become gangrenous)* se gangrener; *(undergo tissue death)* se nécroser, se mortifier

mortifying ['mɔːtɪfaɪɪŋ] *adj (experience etc)* humiliant

mortise ['mɔːtɪs] **1** *n* mortaise *f*

2 *vt* mortaiser; **to mortise two beams together** emmortaiser *ou* emboîter deux poutres

►► ***mortise lock*** serrure *f* encastrée

mortmain ['mɔːt,meɪn] *n Law* mainmorte *f*; **goods in mortmain** biens *mpl* de mainmorte; **to hold sth in mortmain** conserver qch posthumement sous son empire

mortuary ['mɔːtʃʊərɪ] *(pl* **mortuaries***)* **1** *n* morgue *f*

2 *adj* mortuaire

morula ['mɔːrjʊlə] *(pl* **morulae** [-liː]*) n Biol* morula *f*

MOS [,eməʊ'es] *n Electron (abbr* **metal oxide semiconductor***)* MOS *m*

Mosaic [məʊ'zeɪɪk] *adj Bible* mosaïque, de Moïse

mosaic [məʊ'zeɪɪk] **1** *n* (**a**) *(decorative work)* mosaïque *f* (**b**) *Bot* mosaïque *f*

2 *adj* en mosaïque

►► *Bot* ***mosaic disease*** mosaïque *f*

mosaicist [mə'zeɪɪsɪst] *n Art* mosaïste *mf*

moschatel [,mɒskə'tel] *n Bot* **(tuberous) moschatel** moscatelle *f*

Moscow ['mɒskəʊ] *n* Moscou

Moselle [məʊ'zel] *n* (**a**) *(region)* Moselle *f*; **in Moselle** en Moselle (**b**) *(wine)* (vin *m* de) Moselle *m*

Moses ['məʊzɪz] *pr n Bible* Moïse; *Fam* **Holy Moses!** Seigneur!

►► ***Moses basket*** couffin *m*

mosey ['məʊzɪ] *vi Am Fam (amble)* marcher d'un pas tranquille ▫; **I'll just mosey along to the bar** je vais faire un tour au bar; **to mosey along** aller *ou* se promener sans se presser ▫; **I'll be moseying along now** *(leaving)* je vais y aller ▫

mosh [mɒʃ] *vi Fam* = danser de façon agressive

►► ***mosh pit*** = groupe de personnes qui dansent de façon agressive

Moslem ['mɒzləm] *Rel* **1** *n* musulman(e) *m,f*

2 *adj* musulman

mosque [mɒsk] *n Rel* mosquée *f*

mosquito [mə'skiːtəʊ] *(pl* **mosquitos** *or* **mosquitoes***) n Entom* moustique *m*

►► ***mosquito bite*** piqûre *f* de moustique; ***mosquito net*** moustiquaire *f*; ***mosquito repellent*** produit *m* antimoustique

moss [mɒs] *n Bot* mousse *f*

►► *Mining* ***moss agate*** agate *f* mousseuse; ***moss green*** vert *m* mousse; *Bot* ***moss rose*** rose *f* moussue *ou* mousseuse; *Sewing* ***moss stitch*** point *m* de riz; *Sewing* ***double moss stitch*** point *m* de blé

mossback ['mɒsbæk] *n Am Pol* ultraconservateur(trice) *m,f*, réactionnaire *mf*

Moss Bros® ['mɒsbrɒs] *n* = célèbre entreprise britannique de location de vêtements de soirée qui vend aussi désormais des costumes pour hommes

moss-green *adj* vert mousse *(inv)*

moss-grown *adj* couvert de mousse, moussu

mossy ['mɒsɪ] *(compar* **mossier,** *superl* **mossiest***) adj* moussu, couvert de mousse

MOST [məʊst]

le plus de	► 1 (a)
la plupart de	► 1 (b)
le plus	► 2 (a); 3 (a), (b)
la plus grande partie	► 2 (b)
la plupart	► 2 (b)
bien	► 3 (c)
au plus	► 4

1 *adj (superl of* **many, much***)* (**a**) *(largest quantity or number of)* **(the) most** le plus de; **the candidate who gets (the) most votes** le candidat qui obtient le plus de voix *ou* le plus grand nombre de voix; **which of your inventions gave you (the) most satisfaction?** laquelle de vos inventions vous a procuré la plus grande satisfaction?; **for the most part** *(in largest number of cases)* pour la plupart; *(most often)* le plus souvent *ou* la plupart du temps

(**b**) *(the majority of)* la plupart de, la majorité de; **most Europeans** la plupart *ou* la majorité des Européens; **I like most kinds of fruit** j'aime presque tous les fruits; **I go out most evenings** je sors presque tous les soirs; **I don't like most modern art** en général, je n'aime pas l'art moderne; **most French wine is excellent** presque tous les vins français sont excellents

2 *pron (superl of* **many, much***)* (**a**) *(the largest amount)* **(the) most** le plus; **he is more reliable than most** on peut compter sur lui plus que sur bien des gens; **we all earn a lot but Diana earns (the) most** nous gagnons tous beaucoup d'argent mais c'est Diana qui en gagne le plus; **which of the three applicants has (the) most to offer?** lequel des trois candidats a le plus à offrir?; **that is the most one can say in his defence** c'est tout ce qu'on peut dire en sa faveur; *Am Fam Old-fashioned* **her latest album is the most!** son dernier album est vraiment génial!; **to make the most of sth** *(advantage, chance, good weather)* profiter de qch; *(bad situation, ill-luck)* tirer le meilleur parti de qch; *(resources, skills)* employer *ou* utiliser qch au mieux; **let's try and make the most of our last day** essayons de profiter au maximum de notre dernière journée; **she made the most of her time in Mexico** elle a profité au maximum du temps qu'elle a passé au Mexique; **the opposition made the most of the scandal** l'opposition a tiré tout ce qu'elle pouvait du scandale; **he knows how to make the most of himself** il sait se mettre en valeur

(**b**) *(the larger part)* la plus grande *ou* la majeure partie; *(the larger number)* la plupart *ou* majorité; **most of my salary** la majeure partie de mon salaire; **most of the snow has melted** presque toute la neige a fondu; **most of the time** la plupart du temps; **most of my friends are on holiday** presque tous *ou* la plupart de mes amis sont en vacances; **most of us/them** la plupart d'entre nous/eux

3 *adv* (**a**) *(forming superlatives)* **the most populated region in the world** la région la plus peuplée du monde; **it's the most beautiful house I've ever seen** c'est la plus belle maison que j'aie jamais vue; **she was the one who explained things most clearly** c'est elle qui expliquait les choses le plus clairement

(**b**) *(to the greatest extent or degree)* **(the) most** le plus; **the people who complain (the) most** les gens qui se plaignent le plus; **what worries you (the) most?, what most worries you?** qu'est-ce qui vous inquiète le plus?; **it's the one I like most of all** de tous, c'est celui que je préfère

(**c**) *(as intensifier)* bien, fort; **a most interesting theory** une théorie fort intéressante; **we had the most awful weather** nous avons eu un temps détestable; **it's most kind of you to say so** c'est extrêmement *ou* bien gentil à vous de dire ça; **she sang most delightfully** elle a chanté de façon exquise; **most certainly you may!** mais bien entendu!

(**d**) *Am Fam (almost)* presque ▫; **most everybody had heard of it** presque *ou* pratiquement tout le monde était au courant

4 at (the) most *adv* au plus, au maximum; **there's at most a 30 percent chance of success** les chances de succès sont de 30 pour cent tout au plus; **at the very most** tout au plus, au grand maximum

►► *Am Sport* ***most valuable player*** = titre décerné au meilleur joueur d'une équipe; *Am* ***most wanted list*** = liste des criminels les plus recherchés; **he's on the most wanted list** il fait partie des criminels les plus recherchés

most-favoured nation *n* nation *f* la plus favorisée; **this country has most-favoured nation**

status ce pays bénéficie de la clause de la nation la plus favorisée

mostly ['məʊstlɪ] *adv* (**a**) *(mainly)* principalement, surtout; **it's mostly sugar** c'est surtout du sucre; **the soldiers were mostly young men** il s'agissait pour la plupart *ou* surtout *ou* principalement de jeunes soldats; **I've travelled a lot, mostly in Europe** j'ai beaucoup voyagé, en Europe surtout
(**b**) *(usually)* le plus souvent, la plupart du temps; **mostly I get home quite early** la plupart du temps, je rentre assez tôt

MOT [,eməʊ'ti:] *(pt & pp* **MOT'd** [-'ti:d], *cont* **MOT'ing** [-'ti:ɪŋ]) *Br (abbr* **Ministry of Transport**)
1 *n* (**a**) *Formerly (ministry)* ministère *m* des Transports
(**b**) *(certificate)* = contrôle technique annuel obligatoire pour les véhicules de plus de trois ans; **that old car of yours will never pass its MOT** ta vieille voiture n'obtiendra jamais son certificat de contrôle technique
2 *vt* **to have one's car MOT'd** soumettre sa voiture au contrôle technique
▸▸ ***MOT certificate*** = contrôle technique annuel obligatoire pour les véhicules de plus de trois ans

mote [məʊt] *n Literary* atome *m*, grain *m*, particule *f*; *Bible* **the mote in thy brother's eye** la paille dans l'œil de ton frère

motel [məʊ'tel] *n* motel *m*

motet [məʊ'tet] *n Mus* motet *m*

moth [mɒθ] *n* (**a**) *Zool* papillon *m* (nocturne) (**b**) *(in clothes)* mite *f*

mothball ['mɒθbɔ:l] **1** *n* boule *f* de naphtaline; **it smells of mothballs in here** ça sent la naphtaline ici; *Fig* **to put sth in mothballs** mettre qch au placard *ou* en sommeil
2 *vt (project)* mettre en suspens

moth-eaten *adj* (**a**) *(clothing)* mité (**b**) *Fam Fig (shabby)* miteux

mother ['mʌðə(r)] **1** *n* (**a**) *(parent)* mère *f*; **she's a good mother** c'est une bonne mère; **she's a mother of three** elle est mère de trois enfants; **mother, this is Douglas** maman, je te présente Douglas; **she's like a mother to me** elle est comme une mère pour moi; **from mother to daughter** de mère en fille; **on my mother's side** du côté de ma mère; **yes, Mother** oui, mère, oui, maman; **she's her mother's daughter** c'est bien la fille de sa mère; **mother's milk** lait *m* maternel; *Br* **shall I be mother?** c'est moi qui fais le service?; **every mother's son** tous sans exception; **mother's little helper** *(helpful child)* = enfant qui aide sa mère dans les tâches ménagères; *Fig Hum* = alcool ou médicament consommé pour oublier ses soucis; **mother and toddler group** réunion *f* de mamans
(**b**) *(original cause, source)* mère *f*; **the Mother of parliaments** le Parlement britannique *(qui a servi de modèle à d'autres parlements)*
(**c**) *Am very Fam (character)* type *m*; **he was a big mother** c'était une véritable armoire à glace; **some mother's stolen my drink** il y a un enfoiré qui m'a pris mon verre; **the mother's broken down again** cette saloperie est encore tombée en panne
(**d**) *Fam (large person, thing)* mastodonte *m*; **I've got a mother of a hangover** j'ai une vache de gueule de bois; **her boyfriend's a big mother** son copain est un balaise; **we had the mother and father of a row** nous avons eu une de ces empoignades!
2 *adj* (**a**) *(motherly)* maternel
(**b**) *(as parent)* **the mother bird feeds her young** l'oiseau (femelle) nourrit ses petits
3 *vt* (**a**) *(give birth to)* donner naissance à
(**b**) *(take care of)* servir de mère à; *(coddle)* dorloter, materner; **she mothers him too much** elle le dorlote trop
4 Mother *n Rel* mère *f*; **Mother superior** Mère *f* supérieure; **Mother Anna** la Mère Anna; **yes, Mother** oui, Mère; **Mother of God** *(Virgin Mary)* Mère *f* de Dieu
▸▸ ***mother's boy*** fils *m* à sa maman, poule *f* mouillée; ***mother church*** église *f* mère; ***mother company*** maison *f* mère; ***mother country*** (mère) patrie *f*; ***Mother's Day*** la fête des Mères; ***Mother Earth*** la Terre; ***mother figure*** figure *f* maternelle; *Am* ***Mother Goose rhyme*** comptine *f*; ***mother hen*** mère *f* poule; ***mother lode*** *Mining* filon *m* nourricier *ou* principal; *Fig* mine *f*; ***mother love*** amour *m* maternel; ***Mother Nature*** la Nature; *Geol* ***mother rock*** roche *f* mère; *Br Hum* ***mother's ruin*** gin *m*; *Mil* ***mother ship*** ravitailleur *m*; ***mother tongue*** langue *f* maternelle; *Chem* ***mother of vinegar*** mère *f* de vinaigre; ***mother wit*** bon sens *m*

motherboard ['mʌðəbɔ:d] *n Comput* carte *f* mère

Mothercare® ['mʌðəkeə(r)] *n* = magasins britanniques spécialisés dans les articles pour nouveaux-nés, jeunes enfants et femmes enceintes

mothercraft ['mʌðəkrɑ:ft] *n* puériculture *f*

motherfucker ['mʌðə,fʌkə(r)] *n Am Vulg* (**a**) *(person)* enculé(e) *m,f*; **he's a stupid motherfucker** c'est un pauvre con (**b**) *(thing)* saloperie *f*; **the motherfucker won't start** cette saloperie ne veut pas démarrer; **I've a motherfucker of a hangover** j'ai une gueule de bois pas possible

motherfucking ['mʌðə,fʌkɪŋ] *adj Am Vulg* foutu; **open up or I'll kick the motherfucking door in!** ouvre ou j'enfonce cette putain de porte!

motherhood ['mʌðəhʊd] *n* maternité *f*; *esp Am* **it's motherhood and apple pie** c'est quelque chose qui va de soi

mothering ['mʌðərɪŋ] *n* soins *mpl* maternels
▸▸ ***mothering skills*** capacité *f* à s'occuper d'un petit; *Br* ***Mothering Sunday*** la fête des Mères

mother-in-law *(pl* **mothers-in-law**) *n* belle-mère *f*
▸▸ *Bot* ***mother-in-law's tongue*** sansevière *f*

motherland ['mʌðəlænd] *n* (mère) patrie *f*, pays *m* natal

motherless ['mʌðəlɪs] *adj* sans mère

motherliness ['mʌðəlɪnɪs] *n* affection *f* maternelle

motherly ['mʌðəlɪ] *adj* maternel

mother-of-pearl **1** *n* nacre *f*
2 *comp* en *ou* de nacre

mother-to-be *(pl* **mothers-to-be**) *n* future mère *f*

motherwort ['mʌðəwɜ:t] *n Bot* agripaume *f*

mothproof ['mɒθpru:f] **1** *adj* traité à l'antimite
2 *vt* traiter à l'antimite

motif [məʊ'ti:f] *n Art, Literature & Mus* motif *m*

motile [*Br* 'məʊtaɪl, *Am* 'məʊtəl] *adj* mobile

motility [məʊ'tɪlətɪ] *n* motilité *f*

motion ['məʊʃən] **1** *n* (**a**) *(movement)* mouvement *m*; **the gentle motion of the boat** le mouvement léger du bateau
(**b**) *(gesture)* geste *m*, mouvement *m*; **he made a motion as if to step back** il esquissa un geste de recul; **with a swaying motion of the hips** en ondulant des hanches; **to go through the motions of doing sth** faire qch machinalement; **they just went through the motions of applauding** ils ont applaudi machinalement; **he's just going through the motions** il fait juste semblant
(**c**) *(proposal)* motion *f*, résolution *f*; **to carry a motion** faire adopter une motion; **to propose** *or* **to bring a motion** présenter une motion, soumettre une proposition; **to table a motion of no confidence** déposer une motion de censure
(**d**) *Law (application)* requête *f*
(**e**) *Med (faeces)* selles *fpl*; **to have** *or* **to pass a motion** aller à la selle
(**f**) *Mus* mouvement *m*; **contrary motion** mouvement *m* contraire
2 *vi* **to motion to sb (to do sth)** faire signe à qn (de faire qch)
3 *vt* **to motion sb to do sth** faire signe à qn de faire qch; **to motion sb in/away/out** faire signe à qn d'entrer/de s'éloigner/de sortir
4 in motion 1 *adj (moving)* en mouvement; *(working)* en marche; **do not alight while the train is in motion** il est interdit de descendre du train avant l'arrêt complet **2** *adv* **he set the machine in motion** il mit la machine en marche; **we'll be setting the new system in motion next year** nous mettrons le nouveau système en place l'année prochaine; **to set the wheels in motion** démarrer
▸▸ *Am Cin* ***motion picture*** film *m*; *Am* ***motion sickness*** mal *m* des transports

motionless ['məʊʃənlɪs] *adj* immobile

motivate ['məʊtɪveɪt] *vt* motiver; **how can I motivate my pupils?** comment puis-je motiver mes élèves?; **what motivated your choice?** qu'est-ce qui a motivé votre choix?; **what motivated you to change your mind?** qu'est-ce qui vous a poussé à changer d'avis?

motivated ['məʊtɪveɪtɪd] *adj* motivé; **a highly motivated young woman** une jeune femme extrêmement motivée *ou* débordant d'ardeur

motivating ['məʊtɪveɪtɪŋ] *adj* motivant

motivation [,məʊtɪ'veɪʃən] *n* motivation *f*; **the pupils lack motivation** les élèves sont peu motivés
▸▸ *Mktg* ***motivation research*** recherche *f* de motivation; *Mktg* ***motivation study*** étude *f* de motivation

motivational [,məʊtɪ'veɪʃənəl] *adj* motivationnel
▸▸ *Mktg* ***motivational research*** recherche *f* de motivation; *Mktg* ***motivational study*** étude *f* de motivation

motivator ['məʊtɪveɪtə(r)] *n* **he's a good motivator** il sait motiver les gens

motive ['məʊtɪv] **1** *n* (**a**) *(reason)* motif *m*, raison *f*; **the motives for her behaviour** ce qui explique sa conduite, les raisons *fpl* de sa conduite; **my motive for asking is simple** la raison pour laquelle je pose cette question est simple
(**b**) *Law* mobile *m*; **what could have been his motive for committing the crime?** quelles sont les raisons qui ont pu le pousser à commettre ce crime?
(**c**) *Art (of painting)* motif *m*
2 *adj* moteur
▸▸ ***motive energy*** énergie *f* motrice; ***motive power*** force *f* motrice

motiveless ['məʊtɪvlɪs] *adj* immotivé, injustifié; **an apparently motiveless murder** un meurtre sans mobile apparent

mot juste [,məʊ'ʒu:st] *n* mot *m* juste

motley ['mɒtlɪ] **1** *adj* (**a**) *(diverse, assorted)* hétéroclite, composite, disparate; **a motley crew** une foule bigarrée (**b**) *(multicoloured)* multicolore, bariolé
2 *n* (**a**) *(mixture)* mélange *m* hétéroclite (**b**) *Arch (jester's dress)* livrée *f* de bouffon

motocross ['məʊtəkrɒs] *n* motocross *m*

motor ['məʊtə(r)] **1** *n* (**a**) *(engine)* moteur *m*; **electric motor** moteur *m* électrique
(**b**) *Br Fam (car)* bagnole *f*
2 *adj* (**a**) *(equipped with motor)* à moteur
(**b**) *Br (concerning cars)* automobile; **the motor industry** l'industrie *f* automobile; **she had a motor accident** elle a eu un accident de voiture; **the motor show** le salon de l'automobile
(**c**) *Anat (nerve, muscle)* moteur
3 *vi Br* (**a**) *Old-fashioned (go by car)* aller en voiture; **we motored up to London/across Europe** nous sommes allés à Londres/nous avons traversé l'Europe en voiture
(**b**) *Fam* **to be motoring** *(going fast)* foncer; *Fig* **now we're motoring!** cette fois on y vient!
▸▸ ***motor barge*** chaland *m* automoteur, péniche *f* automotrice; *Formal* ***motor car*** automobile *f*, voiture *f*; ***motor caravan*** camping-car *m*; ***motor coach*** autocar *m*; *Am* ***motor court*** motel *m*; ***motor engineer*** ingénieur *m* en automobile, motoriste *mf*; ***motor fuel*** carburant *m*; *Am* ***motor home*** camping-car *m*; *Am* ***motor inn*** motel *m*; ***motor insurance*** assurance *f* automobile; ***motor launch*** vedette *f*; *Am* ***motor lodge*** motel *m*; ***motor mechanic*** mécanicien(enne) *m,f*; ***motor mower*** tondeuse *f* à moteur; *Med* ***motor neurone disease*** maladie *f* de Charcot; *Aut* ***motor octane numbers*** indice *m* d'octane moteur; ***motor race*** course *f* automobile; ***motor racing*** courses *fpl* automobiles; ***motor rally*** rallye *m* automobile; *Anat* ***motor response*** réponse *f* motrice; ***motor scooter*** scooter *m*; ***motor sport*** sport *m* automobile; ***motor vehicle*** véhicule *m* automobile; *Naut* ***motor vessel*** bateau *m* à moteur

Motorail ['məʊtəreɪl] *n Br* train *m* autocouchette *ou* autos-couchettes

motor-assisted *adj*
▸▸ ***motor-assisted bicycle*** cyclomoteur *m*

motorbike ['məʊtəbaɪk] *n* moto *f*

motorboat ['məʊtəbəʊt] *n* canot *m* automobile *ou* à moteur

motorbus ['məʊtəbʌs] *n* autobus *m*

motorcade ['məʊtəkeɪd] *n* cortège *m* (de voitures)

motorcraft ['məʊtə,kræft] *n Am (boat)* vedette *f*

motorcycle ['məʊtə,saɪkəl] **1** *n* motocyclette *f*, moto *f*
2 *vi* aller en moto

▸▸ *Am Fam* ***motorcycle cop*** motard *m (de la police)*; ***motorcycle courier*** coursier(ère) *m,f*, porteur(euse) *m,f*; ***motorcycle racing*** motocyclisme *m*

motorcycling ['məʊtəˌsaɪkəlɪŋ] *n* motocyclisme *m*

motorcyclist ['məʊtəˌsaɪkəlɪst] *n* motocycliste *mf*

motor-driven *adj* à moteur; *(device)* actionné *ou* commandé par un moteur

motoring ['məʊtərɪŋ] *n (UNCOUNT)* l'automobile *f*

▸▸ ***motoring correspondent*** chroniqueur(euse) *m,f* automobile; ***motoring offence*** infraction *f* au code de la route; ***motoring organization*** association *f* d'automobilistes; ***motoring trip*** voyage *m* en voiture

motorist ['məʊtərɪst] *n* automobiliste *mf*

motorization [ˌməʊtəraɪ'zeɪʃən] *n* motorisation *f*

motorize, -ise ['məʊtəraɪz] *vt* motoriser; **a motorized wheelchair** un fauteuil roulant à moteur

▸▸ ***motorized troops*** troupes *fpl* motorisées

motorman ['məʊtəmən] *(pl* **motormen** [-mən]) *n* mécanicien *m*, conducteur *m*

motormouth ['məʊtəˌmaʊθ, *pl* -maʊðz] *n Fam Pej* **he's a bit of a motormouth** c'est un véritable moulin à paroles

motorway ['məʊtəˌweɪ] *n Br* autoroute *f*

▸▸ ***motorway café*** restauroute *m*, restoroute *m*; ***motorway driving*** conduite *f* sur autoroute; ***motorway exit*** sortie *f* d'autoroute; ***motorway madness*** la folie de l'autoroute; ***motorway network*** réseau *m* autoroutier; ***motorway police*** police *f* de l'autoroute; ***motorway restaurant*** restauroute *m*, restoroute *m*; ***motorway services*** services *mpl* autoroutiers

Motown ['məʊtaʊn] *n* (**a**) *Am Fam* = surnom de la ville de Détroit (**b**) *Mus* style *m* Motown

motte and bailey [mɒt-] *n Hist* = type de fortifications normandes constituées d'une colline artificielle entourée d'un fossé et flanquée d'une cour

mottle ['mɒtəl] *vt* tacheter, moucheter

mottled ['mɒtəld] *adj* tacheté, moucheté; *(skin)* marbré

motto ['mɒtəʊ] *(pl* **mottos** *or* **mottoes**) *n* (**a**) *(maxim)* devise *f*; **the college motto** la devise du collège (**b**) *(in Christmas cracker → joke)* blague *f*; *(→ riddle)* devinette *f* (**c**) *Typ (in book)* épigraphe *f*

mouflon, moufflon ['mu:flɒn] *n Zool* mouflon *m*

mould, *Am* **mold** [məʊld] **1** *vt* (**a**) *(fashion → statue, vase)* façonner, modeler; **to mould sth in** *or* **from** *or* **out of clay** sculpter qch dans de l'argile; **the waves have moulded the cliff** les vagues ont modelé la falaise; *Fig* **to mould sb's character** façonner *ou* former le caractère de qn; **an easily moulded character** un caractère docile *ou* malléable *ou* influençable; *Fig* **they're trying to mould public opinion** ils essaient de façonner l'opinion publique

(**b**) *Art & Metal (make in a mould)* mouler; **moulded metal** métal *m* moulé; **moulded plastic chairs** chaises *fpl* en plastique moulé

(**c**) *(cling to → body, figure)* mouler

2 *vi (become mouldy)* moisir

3 *n* (**a**) *Art & Metal (hollow form)* moule *m*; *(prototype)* modèle *m*, gabarit *m*

(**b**) *(moulded article)* pièce *f* moulée; **rice mould** gâteau *m* de riz

(**c**) *Fig (pattern)* moule *m*; **they're all cast in the same mould** ils sortent tous du *ou* ils ont tous été coulés dans le même moule; **cast in a heroic mould** fait de l'étoffe des héros; **a star in the John Wayne mould** une star du style John Wayne; **to break the mould** sortir des sentiers battus; **when they made him they broke the mould** il n'y en a pas deux comme lui

(**d**) *Archit* moulure *f*

(**e**) *(mildew)* moisissure *f*

(**f**) *(soil)* humus *m*, terreau *m*

moulder, *Am* **molder** ['məʊldə(r)] *vi* (**a**) *(decay → corpse, compost)* se décomposer; *(→ house, beams)* se délabrer; *(→ bread)* moisir (**b**) *(languish → person, article)* moisir; *(→ economy, institution)* dépérir; **he's mouldering away in prison** il moisit *ou* croupit en prison

mouldering, *Am* **moldering** ['məʊldərɪŋ] *adj (corpse)* en décomposition; *(house, beams)* dans un état de délabrement avancé

mouldiness, *Am* **moldiness** ['məʊldɪnɪs] *n* (**a**) *(mouldy condition)* état *m* moisi (**b**) *(mould)* moisissure *f*, moisi *m*

moulding, *Am* **molding** ['məʊldɪŋ] *n* (**a**) *Archit (decorative)* moulure *f*; *(at join of wall and floor)* baguette *f*, plinthe *f* (**b**) *(moulded article)* objet *m* moulé, pièce *f* moulée (**c**) *(act of shaping)* moulage *m*; *Fig (of character, public opinion)* formation *f*, façonnement *m*

mouldy, *Am* **moldy** ['məʊldɪ] *(Br compar* **mouldier**, *superl* **mouldiest**, *Am compar* **moldier**, *superl* **moldiest**) *adj* (**a**) *(covered with mould)* moisi; **it smells mouldy** ça sent le moisi (**b**) *Fam (measly)* minable; *(nasty)* vache, rosse

Mouli® ['mu:lɪ] *Br* **1** *n* moulin *m* à légumes

2 *vt* passer à la Moulinette®

moult, *Am* **molt** [məʊlt] *Zool* **1** *vi* muer; *(cat, dog)* perdre ses poils

2 *vt (hair, feathers)* perdre

3 *n* mue *f*

moulting, *Am* **molting** ['məʊltɪŋ] **1** *n* mue *f*

2 *adj* en mue

mound [maʊnd] *n* (**a**) *(of earth, stones)* butte *f*, monticule *m*, tertre *m*; **burial mound** tertre *m* funéraire, tumulus *m* (**b**) *(heap)* tas *m*; **a huge mound of junk mail** une gigantesque pile de prospectus; *Fam* **he ate mounds of rice** il a mangé une montagne de riz (**c**) *(in palmistry)* mont *m*

moundsman [maʊndzmən] *(pl* **moundsmen** [-mən] *n Am Fam (in baseball)* lanceur ☐ *m*

mount [maʊnt] **1** *n* (**a**) *(mountain)* mont *m*, montagne *f*

(**b**) *(horse)* monture *f*; *Horseracing (ride)* monte *f*

(**c**) *(support → of photo)* carton *m*, support *m*; *(→ of gem, lens, tool)* monture *f*; *(→ of machine)* support *m*; *(→ for stamp in collection)* charnière *f*; *(→ for object under microscope)* lame *f*

2 *vt* (**a**) *(climb → slope, steps)* monter

(**b**) *(climb onto → horse, bicycle)* monter sur, enfourcher; *(→ stage, throne etc)* monter sur; **a truck mounted the pavement** un camion monta sur le trottoir

(**c**) *(organize, put on → exhibition, campaign etc)* monter, organiser; *Mil* **to mount an offensive** lancer une offensive; *Mil* **to mount guard** monter la garde; **they mounted an attack on the party leadership** ils montèrent une attaque contre la direction du parti

(**d**) *(fix, support)* monter; **to mount a gem** monter une pierre; **to mount photographs/stamps** coller des photos/timbres (dans un album); **they mounted machine guns on the roofs** ils installèrent des mitrailleuses sur les toits; **an old sword mounted in a glass case** une épée de collection exposée dans une vitrine

(**e**) *(mate with)* monter, saillir, couvrir

3 *vi* (**a**) *(onto horse)* monter (à cheval), se mettre en selle

(**b**) *(rise, increase)* monter, augmenter, croître; **her anger mounted** sa colère montait; **the cost was mounting** le coût augmentait

▸▸ ***Mount Ararat*** le mont Ararat; ***Mount Athos*** le mont Athos; ***Mount Etna*** le mont Etna, l'Etna *m*; ***Mount Everest*** le mont Everest, l'Everest *m*; ***Mount Fuji*** le (mont) Fuji-Yama; ***Mount Kilimanjaro*** le Kilimandjaro; ***the Mount of Olives*** le mont des Oliviers; ***Mount Olympus*** le mont Olympe, l'Olympe *m*; ***Mount Palomar*** le mont Palomar; ***Mount Parnassus*** le mont Parnasse; ***Mount Rushmore*** le mont Rushmore *(dans lequel sont sculptés les visages des Présidents Washington, Jefferson, Lincoln et Th. Roosevelt)*; ***Mount Rushmore State*** = surnom donné au Dakota du Sud; ***Mount Sinaï*** le (mont) Sinaï; ***Mount Vernon*** = propriété où vécut George Washington et où il est enterré; ***Mount Vesuvius*** le (mont) Vésuve; ***Mount Whitney*** le mont Whitney

▸**mount up** *vi* (**a**) *(increase)* monter, augmenter, s'accroître; **the bill was mounting up** la facture augmentait (**b**) *(accumulate)* s'accumuler, s'amonceler; **you'll be amazed how quickly the money mounts up** vous serez stupéfait de voir la somme qu'on peut atteindre en si peu de temps

mountain ['maʊntɪn] **1** *n* (**a**) *(geographical feature)* montagne *f*; **we spent a week in the mountains** on a passé une semaine à la montagne; **to make a mountain out of a molehill** se faire une montagne d'un rien; **to move mountains** déplacer des montagnes, faire l'impossible; **you can't expect him to move mountains just to please you!** il ne peut pas faire l'impossible uniquement pour te faire plaisir!; **if the mountain won't go to Mohammed, Mohammed will have to go to the mountain** si la montagne ne vient pas à Mahomet, Mahomet ira à la montagne; *Fig* **they've got a (huge) mountain to climb** ils ont du pain sur la planche

(**b**) *(heap, accumulation)* montagne *f*, tas *m*; **a mountain of papers** une énorme pile de papiers; **a mountain of evidence** des quantités *fpl* de preuves; **he had bought mountains of rice** il avait acheté des montagnes de riz; **I've got mountains of work to get through** j'ai un travail fou *ou* monstre à terminer; *Econ* **the butter/beef mountain** la montagne de beurre/bœuf

2 *comp (people)* montagnard; *(resort, stream, guide)* de montagne; *(air)* de la montagne; *(life)* en montagne; *(flora, fauna)* de montagne, des montagnes

▸▸ *Bot* ***mountain ash*** *(rowan)* sorbier *m* des oiseleurs *ou* des oiseaux; *(eucalyptus)* eucalyptus *m*; *Zool* ***mountain beaver*** = rongeur d'Amérique du Nord, semblable à l'écureuil; ***mountain bike*** VTT *m*, vélo *m* tout-terrain; ***mountain biking*** VTT *m*, vélo *m* tout-terrain; **to go mountain biking** faire du VTT; *Zool* ***mountain cat*** *(lynx)* lynx *m*; *(puma)* puma *m*, cougouar *m*; ***mountain climber*** alpiniste *mf*; ***mountain climbing*** alpinisme *m*; **to go mountain climbing** faire de l'alpinisme; ***Mountain Daylight Time*** heure *f* d'été des montagnes Rocheuses; *Br* ***mountain dew*** whisky *m* (produit illégalement); *Zool* ***mountain goat*** chamois *m*; ***mountain hut*** *(for walkers)* refuge *m*; *Zool* ***mountain lion*** puma *m*, cougouar *m*; ***mountain pass*** col *m*, défilé *m*; *Bot* ***mountain pine*** pin *m* de montagne; ***mountain range*** chaîne *f* de montagnes; ***mountain rescue*** secours *m* en montagne; ***mountain rescue service*** service *m* de secours en montagne; *Zool* ***mountain sheep*** bighorn *m*; ***mountain sickness*** mal *m* des montagnes; ***Mountain (Standard) Time*** heure *f* d'hiver des montagnes Rocheuses; ***the Mountain State*** = surnom donné à la Virginie-Occidentale; ***mountain top*** sommet *m*, cime *f*; ***mountain troops*** chasseurs *mpl* alpins

mountaineer [ˌmaʊntɪ'nɪə(r)] *n* alpiniste *mf*

mountaineering [ˌmaʊntɪ'nɪərɪŋ] *n* alpinisme *m*; **to go mountaineering** faire de l'alpinisme

▸▸ ***mountaineering club*** club *m* d'alpinisme

mountainous ['maʊntɪnəs] *adj* (**a**) *(region)* montagneux (**b**) *Fig (huge)* énorme, colossal; **mountainous seas** vagues *f* énormes

mountainside ['maʊntɪnsaɪd] *n* flanc *m ou* versant *m* d'une montagne; **a village perched on the mountainside** un village juché à flanc de montagne

mountainy ['maʊntɪnɪ] *adj* (**a**) *Am (terrain)* montagneux (**b**) *Am & Ir (people)* montagnard

mountebank ['maʊntɪbæŋk] *n* charlatan *m*

mounted ['maʊntɪd] *adj (troops)* monté, à cheval

▸▸ ***the mounted police*** la police montée; ***mounted policeman*** policier *m* à cheval

Mountie ['maʊntɪ] *(pl* **Mounties**) *n Fam* membre *m* de la police montée *(au Canada)*; **the Mounties** la police montée *(au Canada)*

mounting ['maʊntɪŋ] **1** *n* (**a**) *(act of fixing)* installation *f*

(**b**) *(support → of photo)* carton *m*, support *m*; *(→ of gem, lens, tool)* monture *f*; *(→ of machine)* support *m*; *(→ for stamp in collection)* charnière *f*; *(→ for object under microscope)* lame *f*

2 *adj (pressure, anxiety)* croissant; **there is mounting evidence against her** il y a de plus en plus de preuves contre elle; **there is mounting dissatisfaction with the government** le gouvernement fait de plus en plus de mécontents; **he felt a mounting sense of panic** il sentait la panique le gagner

mounting-block *n Horseriding* montoir *m*

Mounty = **Mountie**

mourn [mɔ:n] **1** *vt (person)* pleurer, porter le deuil de; *(death, loss)* pleurer; **the whole town mourns the tragedy** cette tragédie a plongé la ville entière dans le malheur; **there's no point**

mourning what might have been cela ne sert à rien de se lamenter sur ce qui aurait pu se passer
2 *vi (feel grief)* pleurer; *(be in mourning)* être en deuil, porter le deuil; **to mourn over the loss of sb** pleurer qn, être en deuil de qn; **we mourn with you** nous partageons votre douleur; **he mourns for** *or* **over his lost youth** il se lamente sur *ou* il pleure sa jeunesse perdue

mourner ['mɔːnə(r)] *n (friend, relative)* proche *mf* du défunt; **the mourners followed the hearse** le cortège funèbre suivait le corbillard; **the streets were lined with mourners** la foule en deuil s'était massée sur les trottoirs

mournful ['mɔːnfʊl] *adj (person, eyes, mood)* triste, mélancolique; *(tone, voice)* lugubre; *(place)* lugubre, sinistre; **a mournful occasion** tristes *ou* douloureuses circonstances *fpl*

mournfully ['mɔːnfʊlɪ] *adv* mélancoliquement, tristement

mournfulness ['mɔːnfʊlnɪs] *n* tristesse *f*, mélancolie *f*

mourning ['mɔːnɪŋ] **1** *n (UNCOUNT)* **(a)** *(period)* deuil *m*; *(clothes)* (vêtements *mpl* de) deuil *m*; **to be in mourning** être en deuil, porter le deuil; **to be in mourning for sb** porter le deuil de qn; **in deep mourning** en grand deuil; **to go into/come out of mourning** prendre/quitter le deuil; **a day of mourning was declared** une journée de deuil a été décrétée
(b) *(cries)* lamentations *fpl*
2 *comp (dress, suit)* de deuil
▸▸ *Orn* ***mourning dove*** tourterelle *f* triste

'Mourning Becomes Electra' *O'Neill* 'Le Deuil sied à Électre'

mouse [maʊs] *(pl* **mice** [maɪs]) **1** *n* **(a)** *(animal)* souris *f* **(b)** *(shy person)* timide *mf*, timoré(e) *m,f* **(c)** *Comput* souris *f*
2 *vi (cat)* chasser les souris
▸▸ *Comput* ***mouse button*** bouton *m* de souris; *Comput* ***mouse driver*** programme *m* de commande de la souris; *Comput* ***mouse mat, mouse pad*** tapis *m* de souris

▸**mouse out** *vt sep Am Fam* dénicher

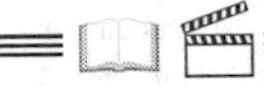

'Of Mice and Men' *Steinbeck, Milestone, Sinise* 'Des souris et des hommes'

mousebird ['maʊsbɜːd] *n Orn* coliou *m*, oiseau-souris *m*

mousehole ['maʊshəʊl] *n* trou *m* de souris

mouser ['maʊsə(r)] *n (cat)* chasseur(euse) *m,f* de souris; **she's a good mouser** elle attrape bien les souris

mousetrap ['maʊstræp] **1** *n* souricière *f*; *Am Fig Com* **to build a better mousetrap** élaborer un meilleur produit
2 *vt Am* piéger
▸▸ *Br* ***mousetrap cheese*** = fromage de qualité inférieure

'The Mousetrap' *Christie* 'La Souricière'

mousey = **mousy**

moussaka [muː'sɑːkə] *n* moussaka *f*

mousse [muːs] *n* mousse *f*; **chocolate mousse** mousse *f* au chocolat

mousseline ['muːsəliːn] *n* **(a)** *(fabric)* mousseline *f* **(b)** *(glass)* verre *m* mousseline **(c)** *Culin* plat *m* à base de sauce mousseline
▸▸ ***mousseline sauce*** sauce *f* mousseline

moustache [mə'stɑːʃ], *Am* **mustache** ['mʌstæʃ] *n* moustache *f*, moustaches *fpl*; **he's growing a moustache** il se fait pousser la moustache

moustached [məs'tɑːʃt], *Am* **mustached** ['mʌstæʃt] *adj* moustachu
▸▸ *Orn* ***moustached warbler*** lusciniole *f* à moustaches

Mousterian [muːs'tɪərɪən] *Archeol* **1** *adj* moustérien
2 *n* moustérien *m*

mousy ['maʊsɪ] *(compar* **mousier**, *superl* **mousiest**) *adj* **(a)** *Pej (shy)* timide, effacé **(b)** *Pej (hair)* châtain terne **(c)** *(colour)* gris sale

mouth 1 *n* [maʊθ, *pl* maʊðz] **(a)** *(of person, horse)* bouche *f*; *(of other animal)* gueule *f*; **don't talk with your mouth full!** ne parle pas la bouche pleine!; **breathe through your mouth** respirez par la bouche; **I have five mouths to feed** j'ai cinq bouches à nourrir; *Pharm* **to be taken by mouth** *(on packaging)* à prendre par voie orale; **he didn't open his mouth once during the meeting** il n'a pas ouvert la bouche *ou* il n'a pas dit un mot pendant toute la réunion; **keep your mouth shut** n'en parlez à personne, gardez-le pour vous; **he's incapable of keeping his mouth shut** il ne sait pas tenir sa langue; *Fam* **he's all mouth** c'est une grande gueule *ou* un fort en gueule; *Br Fam* **he's all mouth and trousers** il essaie de passer pour un Don Juan; *Fam* **he's got a big mouth** il ne peut pas s'empêcher de l'ouvrir; **you had to open your big mouth, didn't you!** il a fallu que tu ouvres ta grande gueule!; *Fam* **to be down in the mouth** avoir le cafard; **me and my big mouth!** j'ai encore perdu une occasion de me taire!; **to put words into sb's mouth** *(misquote)* faire dire à qn ce qu'il ne dit pas; *Prov* **out of the mouths of babes (and sucklings)** de la bouche des enfants *ou* des innocents
(b) *(of river)* embouchure *f*, bouche *f*, bouches *fpl*
(c) *(opening → gen)* ouverture *f*, orifice *m*, bouche *f*; *(→ of bottle)* goulot *m*; *(→ of cave)* entrée *f*
2 *vt* [maʊð] **(a)** *(silently → insults, obscenities)* dire à voix basse, marmonner; **don't talk/sing, just mouth the words** ne parle/chante pas, fais seulement semblant
(b) *(pompously)* déclamer; *(mechanically)* débiter; *(insincerely → excuses)* dire qch du bout des lèvres; *(→ regrets)* formuler sans conviction; **to mouth platitudes** débiter des lieux communs
3 *vi* [maʊð] *esp Am (grimace)* grimacer, faire des grimaces
▸▸ ***mouth organ*** harmonica *m*; ***mouth ulcer*** aphte *m*

▸**mouth off** *vi Fam* **(a)** *(brag)* se vanter[❑], crâner **(b)** *(be insolent)* se montrer insolent[❑]; *(talk indiscreetly)* parler à tort et à travers

-mouthed [maʊðd] *suff* **open-mouthed** bouche bée; **wide-mouthed** *(bottle)* à large goulot

mouthful ['maʊθfʊl] *n* **(a)** *(of food)* bouchée *f*; *(of liquid)* gorgée *f*; **I couldn't eat another mouthful!** je ne pourrais rien avaler de plus!
(b) *Fam (word → hard to pronounce)* mot *m* difficile à prononcer[❑]; *(→ complicated)* mot *m* compliqué[❑]; **his name's a bit of a mouthful** il a un nom à coucher dehors; **"myalgic encephalomyelitis" is quite a mouthful** "myalgic encephalomyelitis", voilà un terme bien compliqué[❑]
(c) *Am Fam (important remark)* **you said a mouthful!** ça, tu peux le dire!, tu l'as dit, bouffi!
(d) *Br Fam (abusive language)* **to give sb a mouthful** traiter qn de tous les noms

mouthparts ['maʊθpɑːts] *npl Zool* pièces *fpl* buccales

mouthpiece ['maʊθpiːs] *n* **(a)** *(of clarinet, oboe)* bec *m*, embouchure *f*; *(of flute, recorder)* bec *m*; *(of trumpet, trombone)* embouchure *f*; *(of pipe)* tuyau *m*; *(of telephone)* microphone *m* **(b)** *(spokesperson)* porte-parole *m inv*; *(newspaper, magazine)* organe *m*, porte-parole *m inv* **(c)** *Am Fam (lawyer)* avocat(e) *m,f* (au criminel)[❑]

mouth-to-mouth *n* bouche-à-bouche *m inv*
▸▸ ***mouth-to-mouth resuscitation*** bouche-à-bouche *m inv*; **to give sb mouth-to-mouth resuscitation** faire du bouche-à-bouche à qn

mouthwash ['maʊθwɒʃ] *n (for cleansing)* bain *m* de bouche; *(for gargling)* gargarisme *m*

mouthwatering ['maʊθ,wɔːtərɪŋ] *adj* appétissant, alléchant; **a mouthwatering display of pastries** un appétissant étalage de pâtisseries, un étalage de pâtisseries qui vous mettent l'eau à la bouche

mouthy ['maʊðɪ] *(compar* **mouthier**, *superl* **mouthiest**) *adj Fam* grande gueule

movable ['muːvəbəl] **1** *adj* mobile
2 *n Law* **movables** effets *mpl* mobiliers, biens *mpl* meubles
▸▸ *Law* ***movable assets*** valeurs *fpl* mobilieres; *Law* ***movable effects*** effets *mpl* mobiliers; *Rel* ***movable feast*** fête *f* mobile; *Law* ***movable property*** biens *mpl* meubles

'A Movable Feast' *Hemingway* 'Paris est une fête'

MOVE [muːv]

mouvement	▸ 1 (a)
déménagement	▸ 1 (b)
changement d'emploi	▸ 1 (c)
pas	▸ 1 (d)
tour	▸ 1 (e)
déplacer	▸ 2 (a), (c)
bouger	▸ 2 (a); 3 (a)
transférer	▸ 2 (b)
déménager	▸ 2 (d); 3 (f)
émouvoir	▸ 2 (e)
pousser	▸ 2 (f)
céder	▸ 2 (g)
partir	▸ 3 (d)
jouer	▸ 3 (e)
se déplacer	▸ 3 (e)
avancer	▸ 3 (h)

1 *n* **(a)** *(movement)* mouvement *m*; **with one move she was by his side** en un éclair, elle fut à ses côtés; **one move out of you and you're dead!** un seul geste et tu es mort!; **he made a move to take out his wallet** il s'apprêta à sortir son portefeuille; **the police were watching her every move** la police surveillait ses moindres gestes; **to make a move** *(leave)* y aller, bouger; **it's late, I ought to be making a move** il se fait tard, il faut que j'y aille *ou* que je parte; **she made a move to leave** elle se leva pour partir; *Fam* **to get a move on** se grouiller; *Fam* **get a move on!** grouille-toi!, active!
(b) *(change of home, premises)* déménagement *m*; **how did the move go?** comment s'est passé le déménagement?; **we're considering a move to bigger premises** nous envisageons d'emménager dans des locaux plus spacieux
(c) *(change of job)* changement *m* d'emploi; **after ten years in the same firm she felt it was time for a move** après dix ans dans la même société elle avait le sentiment qu'il était temps de changer d'air *ou* d'horizon
(d) *(step, measure)* pas *m*, démarche *f*; **she made the first move** elle a fait le premier pas; **she wondered when he would make his move** elle se demandait quand il allait se décider; **don't make a move without contacting me** ne fais rien sans me contacter; *Fam* **to make a move on sb** faire des avances à qn; **the new management's first move was to increase all salaries** la première mesure de la nouvelle direction a été de relever tous les salaires; **at one time there was a move to expand** à un moment, on avait envisagé de s'agrandir; **what do you think their next move will be?** selon vous, que vont-ils faire maintenant?; **they made an unsuccessful move to stop the war** ils firent une tentative infructueuse pour arrêter la guerre; **the government has made moves towards resolving the problem** le gouvernement a pris des mesures pour résoudre le problème
(e) *(in games → turn to move)* tour *m*; *(→ act of moving)* coup *m*; *(→ way piece moves)* marche *f*; **it's my move** c'est à moi (de jouer); *Chess* **white mates in two moves** les blancs font mat en deux coups; **white always has first move** c'est toujours les blancs qui commencent; **in chess the first thing to learn is the moves** la première chose à apprendre aux échecs, c'est la façon dont les pièces se déplacent sur l'échiquier *ou* le déplacement des pièces sur l'échiquier
2 *vt* **(a)** *(put elsewhere → object)* déplacer; *(→ part of body)* bouger, remuer; *(in games → piece)* jouer; **this key moves the cursor towards the right** cette touche déplace le curseur vers la droite; **move the lever to the left** poussez le levier vers la gauche; **we moved all the chairs indoors/outdoors** nous avons rentré/sorti toutes les chaises; **move your chair closer to the table** rapproche ta chaise de la table; **we've moved the couch into the spare room** nous

avons mis le canapé dans la chambre d'amis; **move all those papers off the table!** enlève tous ces papiers de la table!, débarrasse la table de tous ces papiers!; **don't move anything on my desk** ne touche à rien sur mon bureau; **I can't move my leg** je n'arrive pas à bouger la jambe; **can you move your leg (out of the way), please** est-ce que tu peux pousser ta jambe, s'il te plaît?; **move your head to the left** inclinez la tête vers la gauche; **he moves his lips when he reads** il remue les lèvres en lisant; *Chess* **she moved a pawn** elle a joué un pion; *Fam* **move it!** grouille-toi!

(**b**) *(send elsewhere → prisoner, troops etc)* transférer; **move all these people out of the courtyard** faites sortir tous ces gens de la cour; **she's been moved to the New York office/to accounts** elle a été mutée au bureau de New York/affectée à la comptabilité; **he asked to be moved to a room with a sea view** il a demandé qu'on lui donne une chambre avec vue sur la mer; **troops are being moved into the area** des troupes sont envoyées dans la région; **he's decided to move his family to England** *(he is in England)* il a décidé de faire venir sa famille en Angleterre; *(he is elsewhere)* il a décidé d'envoyer sa famille en Angleterre

(**c**) *(change time or date of)* déplacer; **the meeting has been moved to Friday** *(postponed)* la réunion a été remise à vendredi; *(brought forward)* la réunion a été avancée à vendredi

(**d**) *(to new premises, location)* **the company that moved us** la firme qui s'est chargée de *ou* qui a effectué notre déménagement; **to move house** déménager

(**e**) *(affect, touch)* émouvoir; **I was deeply moved** j'ai été profondément ému *ou* touché; **to move sb to anger** provoquer la colère de qn; **to move sb to tears** émouvoir qn (jusqu')aux larmes; **to move sb to pity** exciter la pitié de qn

(**f**) *(motivate, prompt)* pousser, inciter; **to move sb to do sth** pousser *ou* inciter qn à faire qch; **what moved you to change your mind?** qu'est-ce qui vous a fait changer d'avis?

(**g**) *(usu negative) (cause to yield)* **you won't move me** tu ne me feras pas changer d'avis; **nothing will move him** il est inflexible; **the Prime Minister will not be moved** le Premier ministre ne cédera pas d'un pouce; **we shall not be moved!** nous ne céderons pas!

(**h**) *(propose)* proposer; **to move an amendment** proposer un amendement; **I move that we vote on it** je propose que nous procédions au vote

(**i**) *Com (sell)* écouler, vendre; **we must move these goods quickly** nous devons vendre ces marchandises rapidement

(**j**) *Med* **to move one's bowels** aller à la selle

3 *vi* (**a**) *(shift, change position)* bouger; **don't move!** ne bougez pas!; **I'm sure the curtains moved** je suis sûr d'avoir vu les rideaux bouger; **something moved in the bushes** quelque chose a bougé dans les buissons; **I was so scared I couldn't move** j'étais pétrifié (de terreur); **the train was so crowded, I could barely move** le train était tellement bondé que je pouvais à peine bouger *ou* faire un mouvement; **you can't move for furniture in their flat** il y a tellement de meubles dans leur appartement qu'il n'y a pas la place de se retourner; **the handle won't move** la poignée ne bouge pas; **she wouldn't move out of my way** elle ne voulait pas s'écarter de mon chemin; **could you move so that we can get in?** pourriez-vous vous pousser que nous puissions entrer?; **the dancers move so elegantly** les danseurs évoluent avec beaucoup de grâce

(**b**) *(be in motion → vehicle)* **the line of cars was moving slowly down the road** la file de voitures avançait lentement le long de la route; **wait till the car stops moving** attends que la voiture soit arrêtée; **I jumped off while the train was still moving** j'ai sauté avant l'arrêt du train; **the truck started moving backwards** le camion a commencé à reculer

(**c**) *(travel in specified direction)* **the guests moved into/out of the dining room** les invités passèrent dans/sortirent de la salle à manger; **the depression is moving westwards** la dépression se déplace vers l'ouest; **the demonstrators were moving towards the embassy** les manifestants se dirigeaient vers l'ambassade; **the hands of the clock moved inexorably towards midnight** les aiguilles de l'horloge s'approchaient inexorablement de minuit; **small clouds moved across the sky** de petits nuages traversaient le ciel; **the earth moves round the sun** la Terre tourne autour du Soleil; *Fig* **public opinion is moving to the left/right** l'opinion publique évolue vers la gauche/droite; **to move in high circles** fréquenter la haute société

(**d**) *(leave)* partir; **it's getting late, I ought to be** *or* **get moving** il se fait tard, il faut que j'y aille *ou* que je parte

(**e**) *(in games → player)* jouer; *(→ piece)* se déplacer; **you can't move until you've thrown a six** on ne peut pas jouer avant d'avoir fait sortir *ou* d'avoir amené un six; *Chess* **white to move and mate in three** les blancs jouent et font mat en trois coups; *Chess* **pawns can't move backwards** les pions ne peuvent pas reculer

(**f**) *(to new premises, location)* déménager; **when are you moving?** quand est-ce que vous déménagez?; **when are you moving to your new apartment?** quand est-ce que vous emménagez dans votre nouvel appartement?; **she's moving to San Francisco** elle va habiter (à) San Francisco; **the company has moved to more modern premises** la société s'est installée dans des locaux plus modernes

(**g**) *(change job, profession)* **he's moved to a job in publishing** il travaille maintenant dans l'édition

(**h**) *(develop, progress)* avancer, progresser; **things have started moving now** les choses ont commencé à avancer; **to get things moving** faire avancer les choses

(**i**) *Fam (travel fast)* filer, foncer; **that car can really move!** cette voiture a quelque chose dans le ventre!; **she's really moving now** maintenant elle fonce vraiment

(**j**) *(take action)* agir; **if you want to succeed now is the time to move** si vous voulez réussir, il vous faut agir maintenant *ou* dès à présent; **the town council moved to have the school closed down** la municipalité a pris des mesures pour faire fermer l'école; **I'll get moving on it first thing tomorrow** je m'en occuperai demain à la première heure

(**k**) *(yield)* céder; **they won't move on the question of compensation** ils ne céderont *ou* ne fléchiront pas sur la question des compensations

(**l**) *Com (sell)* se vendre, s'écouler; **the new model isn't moving very quickly** le nouveau modèle ne se vend pas très vite

(**m**) *Med* **have your bowels moved today?** êtes-vous allé à la selle aujourd'hui?

4 on the move *adj* **to be on the move** être en déplacement; **he's a travelling salesman, so he's always on the move** c'est un représentant de commerce, voilà pourquoi il est toujours en déplacement *ou* il est toujours par monts et par vaux; **the enemy forces on the move** les colonnes ennemies en marche *ou* en mouvement; **I've been on the move all day** je n'ai pas arrêté de la journée; **we're a firm on the move** nous sommes une entreprise dynamique

►**move about** *Br* **1** *vi* se déplacer, bouger; **I can hear somebody moving about upstairs** j'entends des bruits de pas là-haut; **it's hard to move about on crutches** c'est dur de se déplacer avec des béquilles

2 *vt sep* déplacer; **they keep moving her around from one department to another** ils n'arrêtent pas de la faire passer d'un service à l'autre

►**move along** **1** *vi* (**a**) *(to make room)* se déplacer, se pousser; **move along and let the old lady sit down** poussez-vous un peu pour laisser la vieille dame s'asseoir

(**b**) *(leave)* partir, s'en aller; **I ought to be moving along** il faut que je m'en aille; **the policeman told us to move along** le policier nous a dit de circuler; **move along please!** circulez, s'il vous plaît!

(**c**) *(continue)* **moving along to my next question** pour passer à ma question suivante; **the procession moved along painfully slowly** le cortège avançait *ou* progressait terriblement lentement

2 *vt sep (bystanders, busker)* faire circuler

►**move around** = **move about**

►**move away** **1** *vi* (**a**) *(go in opposite direction)* s'éloigner, partir; **he held out his arms to her but she moved away** il lui tendit les bras mais elle s'éloigna; **the train moved slowly away** le train partit lentement

(**b**) *(change address)* déménager; **her best friend moved away** sa meilleure amie a déménagé

2 *vt sep* éloigner

►**move back** **1** *vi* (**a**) *(back away)* reculer

(**b**) *(return to original position)* retourner; **they've moved back to the States** ils sont retournés habiter *ou* ils sont rentrés aux États-Unis

2 *vt sep* (**a**) *(push back → person, crowd)* repousser; *(→ chair)* reculer

(**b**) *(return to original position)* remettre; **you can change the furniture around as long as you move it back afterwards** vous pouvez déplacer les meubles à condition de les remettre ensuite à leur place *ou* là où ils étaient

►**move down** **1** *vi* (**a**) *(from higher level, floor, position)* descendre; *Sch* **he moved down a class** on l'a fait descendre d'une classe; **the team moved down to the fourth division** l'équipe est descendue en quatrième division

(**b**) *(make room)* se pousser; **move down, there's plenty of room inside** poussez-vous, il y a de la place à l'intérieur

2 *vt insep* **move down the bus, please** avancez jusqu'au fond de l'autobus, s'il vous plaît

3 *vt sep (from higher level, floor, position)* descendre; *Sch* **he was moved down a class** on l'a fait passer dans la classe inférieure; **move this section down** mettez cette section plus bas

►**move forward** **1** *vi* avancer

2 *vt sep* avancer; **she moved the clock forward one hour** elle a avancé l'horloge d'une heure

►**move in** **1** *vi* (**a**) *(into new home, premises)* emménager; **his mother-in-law has moved in with them** sa belle-mère s'est installée *ou* est venue habiter chez eux

(**b**) *(close in, approach)* avancer, s'approcher; **the police began to move in on the demonstrators** la police a commencé à avancer *ou* à se diriger vers les manifestants; **the camera then moves in on the bed** la caméra s'approche ensuite du lit

(**c**) *(take control)* **another gang is trying to move in** un autre gang essaie de mettre la main sur l'affaire; **the unions moved in and stopped the strike** les syndicats prirent les choses en main et mirent un terme à la grève; **the market changed when the multinationals moved in** le marché a changé quand les multinationales ont fait leur apparition

2 *vt sep* (**a**) *(install → furniture)* installer; **the landlord moved another family in** le propriétaire a loué à une autre famille

(**b**) *(send → troops)* envoyer; **troops were moved in by helicopter** les troupes ont été transportées par hélicoptère

►**move off** *vi* s'éloigner, partir; **the train finally moved off** le train partit *ou* s'ébranla enfin

►**move on** **1** *vi* (**a**) *(proceed on one's way)* poursuivre son chemin; **we spent a week in Athens, then we moved on to Crete** on a passé une semaine à Athènes avant de partir pour la Crète; **a policeman told me to move on** un policier m'a dit de circuler

(**b**) *(progress → to new job, new subject etc)* **she's moved on to better things** elle a trouvé une meilleure situation; **after five years in the same job I feel like moving on** après avoir occupé le même emploi pendant cinq ans, j'ai envie de changer d'air; **technology has moved on since then** la technologie a évolué depuis; **can we move on to the second point?** pouvons-nous passer au deuxième point?

2 *vt sep (bystanders, busker)* faire circuler

►**move out** **1** *vi* (**a**) *(of home, premises)* déménager; **when are you moving out of your room?** quand est-ce que tu déménages de *ou* tu quittes ta chambre?; **his girlfriend has moved out** sa petite amie ne vit plus avec lui

(**b**) *Mil (troops)* se retirer

2 *vt sep Mil (troops)* retirer; **the troops will be moved out** les troupes se retireront; **people were moved out of their homes to make way for the new road** les gens ont dû quitter leur maison pour permettre la construction de la nouvelle route

►**move over** *vi* (**a**) *(make room)* se pousser; **move over and let me sit down** pousse-toi pour que je puisse m'asseoir

(**b**) *(stand down → politician)* se désister; **it's time he moved over to make way for a younger man** il serait temps qu'il laisse la place à un homme plus jeune

(**c**) *(change over)* **we're moving over to mass production** nous passons à la fabrication en série

►**move up 1** *vi* (**a**) *(to make room)* se pousser; **move up and let me sit down** pousse-toi pour que je puisse m'asseoir

(**b**) *(to higher level, floor, position)* monter; *(in company)* avoir de l'avancement; *Sch* **to move up a class** passer dans la classe supérieure; **you've moved up in the world!** tu en as fait du chemin!

(**c**) *Mil (troops)* avancer; **our battalion's moving up to the front** notre bataillon monte au front

(**d**) *St Exch (shares)* se relever, reprendre; **shares moved up three points today** les actions ont gagné trois points aujourd'hui

2 *vt sep* (**a**) *(to make room)* pousser, écarter

(**b**) *(to higher level, floor, position)* faire monter; *Sch* **he's been moved up a class** on l'a fait passer dans la classe supérieure; **move this section up** mettez cette section plus haut

(**c**) *Mil (troops)* faire avancer; **another division has been moved up** une autre division a été envoyée sur place

---

moveable = **movable**

movement ['muːvmənt] *n* (**a**) *(change of position)* mouvement *m*; **population/troop movements** mouvements *mpl* de populations/de troupes; **the movement of goods** le transport des marchandises; **there was a general movement towards the bar** tout le monde se dirigea vers le bar; **she heard movement in the next room** elle a entendu des bruits dans la pièce voisine; **his movements are being watched** ses faits et gestes sont surveillés; **I'm not sure what my movements are going to be over the next few weeks** je ne sais pas exactement ce que je vais faire *ou* quel sera mon emploi du temps dans les quelques semaines à venir; **freedom of movement** la liberté de circulation

(**b**) *(gesture)* mouvement *m*, geste *m*; **all her movements were rapid and precise** tous ses gestes étaient rapides et précis

(**c**) *(change, tendency)* mouvement *m*, tendance *f*; **there's a growing movement towards privatization** la tendance à la privatisation s'accentue; **his speeches over the last year show a movement towards the right** les discours qu'il a prononcés depuis un an font apparaître un glissement vers la droite; **the upward/downward movement of interest rates** la hausse/baisse des taux d'intérêts

(**d**) *Fin (of capital)* circulation *f*; *(of share prices)* mouvement *m*; *(of market)* activité *f*

(**e**) *(group)* mouvement *m*; **liberation movement** mouvement *m* de libération

(**f**) *Tech (mechanism → of clock etc)* mouvement *m*

(**g**) *Mus (of symphony, sonata etc)* mouvement *m*

(**h**) *Med (faeces)* selles *fpl*; **to have a (bowel) movement** aller à la selle

mover ['muːvə(r)] *n* (**a**) *(physical)* **sloths are extraordinarily slow movers** les paresseux sont des animaux à mouvements extrêmement lents; *Fam* **she's a lovely mover** elle bouge bien; *Fam* **he's a fast mover** c'est un tombeur; **the movers and the shakers** *(key people)* les acteurs *mpl*

(**b**) *(of a proposal, motion)* motionnaire *mf*; **who was the mover of this amendment?** qui a proposé cet amendement?

(**c**) *Am (removal company)* déménageur *m*

movie ['muːvɪ] **1** *n* film *m*; **the movie of the book** le film tiré du livre; **full-length/short-length movie** (film *m*) long/court métrage *m*; **to shoot** *or* **to make a movie (about sth)** tourner *ou* faire un film (sur qch)

2 *comp (clip)* d'un film; *(sequence)* de film; *(archives, award, rights)* cinématographique

3 movies *npl* **to go to the movies** aller au cinéma; **she's in the movies** elle travaille dans le cinéma

►► ***movie actor*** acteur *m* de cinéma; ***movie actress*** actrice *f* de cinéma; ***movie camera*** caméra *f*; ***movie channel*** chaîne *f* de cinéma; ***movie critic*** critique *mf* de cinéma; ***movie director*** metteur *m* en scène; *Am* ***movie house*** (salle *f* de) cinéma *m*; ***the movie industry*** l'industrie *f* cinématographique *ou* du cinéma; ***movie maker*** cinéaste *mf*; ***movie premiere*** première *f*; ***movie producer*** producteur(trice) *m,f* de cinéma; ***movie reviewer*** critique *mf* de cinéma; ***movie script*** scénario *m*; ***movie star*** vedette *f* de cinéma; *Am* ***movie theater*** cinéma *m*

moviegoer ['muːvɪˌgəʊə(r)] *n* cinéphile *mf*; **she is a regular moviegoer** elle va régulièrement au cinéma

moving ['muːvɪŋ] **1** *n* mouvement *m*; *(being moved)* déplacement *m*; *(leaving house, premises)* déménagement *m*

2 *adj* (**a**) *(in motion)* en mouvement; *(vehicle)* en marche; *(target)* mouvant; **slow-/fast-moving** qui se déplace lentement/rapidement

(**b**) *(not fixed)* mobile

(**c**) *(touching)* émouvant, touchant

(**d**) *(motivating)* **she's the moving force** *or* **spirit behind the project** c'est elle l'instigatrice *ou* le moteur du projet

(**e**) *(for moving house)* de déménagement; **on moving day** le jour du déménagement

►► *Fin* ***moving averages*** moyennes *fpl* mobiles; ***moving in*** *(into house, premises)* emménagement *m*; ***moving out*** *(from house, premises)* déménagement *m*; *Tech* ***moving parts*** pièces *fpl* mobiles; *Br* ***moving pavement*** trottoir *m* roulant; *Old-fashioned* ***moving picture*** film *m*; ***moving staircase*** escalier *m* roulant, escalator *m*; *Am* ***moving van*** camion *m* de déménagement; *Am Law* ***moving violation*** infraction *f* aux règles de la circulation; ***moving walkway*** tapis *m* ou trottoir *m* roulant

movingly ['muːvɪŋlɪ] *adv* de façon émouvante *ou* touchante

mow¹ [məʊ] (*pt* **mowed**, *pp* **mowed** *or* **mown** [məʊn]) *vt (lawn)* tondre; *(hay, corn, field)* faucher

►**mow down** *vt sep* faucher, abattre

mow² [maʊ] *Arch or Literary* **1** *n* grimace *f*

2 *vi* grimacer

mower ['məʊə(r)] *n* (**a**) *(person)* faucheur(euse) *m,f* (**b**) *(machine → for lawn)* tondeuse *f*; *(→ for hay)* faucheuse *f*

mowing ['məʊɪŋ] *n Agr* fauchage *m*

►► ***mowing machine*** faucheuse *f*

mown [məʊn] *pp of* **mow**

moxa ['mɒksə] *n Bot & Med* moxa *m*

moxie ['mɒksɪ] *n Am Fam* (**a**) *(courage)* cran *m* (**b**) *(energy)* punch *m*, pêche *f*

Mozambican [ˌməʊzæm'biːkən] **1** *n* Mozambicain(e) *m,f*

2 *adj* mozambicain

Mozambique [ˌməʊzæm'biːk] *n* Mozambique *m*; **in Mozambique** au Mozambique

►► ***the Mozambique Channel*** le canal de Mozambique

Mozarab [məʊ'zærəb] *n Hist* Mozarabe *mf*

Mozarabic [məʊ'zærəbɪk] *adj Hist* mozarabique, mozarabe

Mozart ['məʊtsɑːt] *pr n* Mozart

Mozartian [məʊt'sɑːtɪən] *adj* mozartien

mozzarella [ˌmɒtsə'relə] *n* mozzarelle *f*

mozzie ['mɒzɪ] *n Fam (mosquito)* moustique ☐ *m*

MP [ˌem'piː] *n* (**a**) (*abbr* **Military Police**) PM *f* (**b**) *Br & Can* (*abbr* **Member of Parliament**) ≃ député *m*; **the MP for Finchley** le député de Finchley (**c**) *Can* (*abbr* **Mounted Policeman**) policier *m*

MP3 [ˌempiː'θriː] *n Comput* (*abbr* **MPEG1 Audio Layer**) (format *m*) MPEG *m*

MPC [ˌempiː'siː] *n Fin* (*abbr* **monetary policy committee**) = comité formé de quatre membres de la Banque d'Angleterre et de quatre économistes nommés par le gouvernement, dont l'un des rôles est de fixer les taux d'intérêt

MPEG ['emˌpeg] *n Comput* (*abbr* **Moving Pictures Expert Group**) (format *m*) MPEG *m*

mpg [ˌempiː'dʒiː] *n* (*abbr* **miles per gallon**) consommation *f* d'essence; **my old car did 20 mpg** mon ancienne voiture faisait *ou* consommait 3,5 litres au cent

mph [ˌempiː'eɪtʃ] *n* (*abbr* **miles per hour**) miles *mpl* à l'heure; **100 mph** ≃ 160 km/h

MPhil [ˌem'fɪl] *n Univ* (*abbr* **Master of Philosophy**) *(person)* = titulaire d'une maîtrise de lettres; *(qualification)* maîtrise *f* de lettres

mps [ˌempiː'es] *n* (*abbr* **master production schedule**) plan *m* de production principal

MPV [ˌempiː'viː] *n Aut* (*abbr* **multi-purpose vehicle**) monospace *m*

Mr ['mɪstə(r)] *n* (*abbr* **mister**) M., Monsieur; **Mr Brown** M. Brown; **Mr President** Monsieur le Président; *Fam* **no more Mr Nice Guy!** j'en ai assez d'être la bonne pâte!; *Fam Fig* **he's a regular Mr Fixit** on peut toujours compter sur lui pour trouver une solution

►► *Fam* ***Mr Big*** le chef, le patron ☐; *Fam* ***Mr Right*** l'homme idéal ☐, le prince charmant; **she's waiting for Mr Right** elle attend le prince charmant *ou* l'homme de ses rêves

MRC [ˌemɑː'siː] *n Br* (*abbr* **Medical Research Council**) = institut de recherche médicale situé à Londres

MRCP [ˌemɑːˌsiː'piː] *n Br* (*abbr* **Member of the Royal College of Physicians**) = membre du "Royal College of Physicians"

MRCS [ˌemɑːˌsiː'es] *n Br* (*abbr* **Member of the Royal College of Surgeons**) = membre du "Royal College of Surgeons"

MRCVS [ˌemɑːsiːˌviː'es] *n Br* (*abbr* **Member of the Royal College of Veterinary Surgeons**) = membre du "Royal College of Veterinary Surgeons"

MRI [ˌemɑː'raɪ] *n* (*abbr* **magnetic resonance imaging**) IRM *f*

MRM [ˌemɑː'rem] *n* (*abbr* **mechanically-recovered meat**) viande *f* séparée mécaniquement

mrp [ˌemɑː'piː] *n Mktg* (*abbr* **manufacturer's recommended price**) prix *m* conseillé par le fabricant

MRS [ˌemɑː'res] *n Mktg* (*abbr* **Market Research Society**) = société d'étude de marché britannique

Mrs ['mɪsɪz] *n* (*abbr* **mistress**) Mme, Madame; **Mrs Brown** Mme Brown

►► ***Mrs Beeton*** = célèbre auteur anglais de livres de cuisine au dix-neuvième siècle; *Br Fam* ***Mrs Mop*** *(cleaner)* femme *f* de ménage ☐; **I'm not your Mrs Mop, you know!** hé, je ne suis pas ta bonne!

MS¹ [ˌem'es] *n* (**a**) *Med* (*abbr* **multiple sclerosis**) SEP *f* (**b**) *Am Univ* (*abbr* **Master of Science**) *(person)* = titulaire d'une maîtrise de sciences; *(qualification)* maîtrise *f* de sciences

MS² (**a**) (*written abbr* **Mississippi**) Mississippi *m* (**b**) (*written abbr* **manuscript**) ms

Ms [mɪz, məz] *n* = titre que les femmes peuvent utiliser au lieu de "Mrs" ou "Miss" pour éviter la distinction entre les femmes mariées et les célibataires

ms. (*pl* **mss**) (*written abbr* **manuscript**) ms

MSA [ˌemes'eɪ] *n Univ* (*abbr* **Master of Science in Agriculture**) *(person)* = titulaire d'une maîtrise en sciences agricoles; *(qualification)* maîtrise *f* en sciences agricoles

MSB [ˌemes'biː] *n Comput* (*abbr* **most significant bit/byte**) = bit de poids fort

MSC [ˌemes'siː] *n Formerly* (*abbr* **Manpower Services Commission**) = agence britannique pour l'emploi, aujourd'hui remplacée par la "Training Agency", ≃ ANPE *f*

MSc [ˌemes'siː] *n Br Univ* (*abbr* **Master of Science**) *(person)* = titulaire d'une maîtrise de sciences; *(qualification)* maîtrise *f* de sciences

MS-DOS [ˌemes'dɒs] *n Comput* (*abbr* **Microsoft Disk Operating System**) MS-DOS *m*

MSF [ˌemes'ef] *n Br* (*abbr* **Manufacturing, Science, Finance**) = confédération syndicale britannique

MSG [ˌemes'dʒiː] *n* (*abbr* **monosodium glutamate**) glutamate *m* de sodium

Msgr *Rel* (*written abbr* **Monsignor**) Mgr

MSP [ˌemes'piː] *n* (*abbr* **Member of the Scottish Parliament**) député *m* du parlement écossais

mss (*written abbr* **manuscripts**) manuscrits *mpl*

MST [ˌemes'tiː] *n* (*abbr* **Mountain Standard Time**) heure *f* d'hiver des montagnes Rocheuses

MSW [ˌemes'dʌbəljuː] *n Univ* (*abbr* **Master of Social Work**) *(person)* = titulaire d'une maîtrise en travail social; *(qualification)* maîtrise *f* en travail social

MT¹ [ˌem'tiː] *n Comput* (*abbr* **machine translation**) TA *f*

MT² (*written abbr* **Montana**) Montana *m*

Mt (*written abbr* **mount**) Mt

MTBF [ˌemtiːˌbiː'ef] *n Comput* (*abbr* **mean time between failures**) moyenne *f* de temps entre deux pannes

MTFA [ˌemtiːˌef'eɪ] *n Fin & EU* (*abbr* **medium-term financial assistance**) aide *f* financière à moyen terme

MTN [ˌemtiː'en] *n Fin* (*abbr* **medium-term note**) bon *m* à moyen terme (négociable)

MUCH [mʌtʃ]

beaucoup de	▶ **1**
beaucoup	▶ **2 (a); 3**
autant de	▶ **5 1**
autant que	▶ **5 2; 6 2**
combien (de)	▶ **8**
tant de	▶ **10**
tellement (de)	▶ **3**

1 *adj*

Hormis dans la langue soutenue et dans certaines expressions, ne s'utilise que dans des structures négatives ou interrogatives.

beaucoup de; **we don't have much time** on n'a pas beaucoup de temps; **there isn't much cake/money left** il ne reste pas beaucoup de gâteau/d'argent; **the tablets didn't do much good** les comprimés n'ont pas servi à grand-chose *ou* n'ont pas fait beaucoup d'effet; *Ironic* **much good may it do you!** grand bien vous fasse!

2 *pron* (**a**) *(gen)* beaucoup; **is there much left?** est-ce qu'il en reste beaucoup?; **is there any left? – not much** est-ce qu'il en reste? – pas beaucoup; **there's still much to be decided** il reste encore beaucoup de choses à décider; **he hadn't much to say on the subject** il n'avait pas grand-chose à dire à ce sujet; **there's not much anyone can do about it** personne n'y peut grand-chose; **we have much to be thankful for** nous avons beaucoup de raisons d'être reconnaissants; **much of the time** *(long period)* la majeure partie du temps; *(very often)* la plupart du temps; **much of the coffee had to be thrown away** on a dû jeter une grande partie du café; **there is not much of it** il n'y en a pas beaucoup; **I agreed with much of what she said** j'étais d'accord avec presque tout ce qu'elle a dit

(**b**) *(as intensifier)* **I'm not much of a hiker** je ne suis pas un très bon marcheur; **it hasn't been much of a holiday** ce n'était pas vraiment des vacances; **it wasn't much of a surprise** ce n'était pas une grande surprise; **it wasn't much of a joke** ce n'était pas terrible comme plaisanterie; **what he said didn't amount to much** il n'avait pas grand-chose d'important à dire; **his plans didn't come to much** ses projets n'ont pas abouti à grand-chose; **the defence made much of the witness's criminal record** la défense a beaucoup insisté sur le casier judiciaire du témoin; **I couldn't make much of the figures** je n'ai pas compris grand-chose aux chiffres; **I don't think much of him/of his technique** je n'ai pas une très haute opinion de lui/de sa technique; **there's much to be said for the old-fashioned method** la vieille méthode a beaucoup d'avantages; **there's much to be said for his suggestions** il y a des choses fort intéressantes dans ce qu'il propose; **it's not up to much** ça ne vaut pas grand-chose; **he's not up to much** ce n'est pas une lumière; **there's not much to choose between them** ils se valent; **there's not much in it** il n'y a pas une grande différence; *Fam Ironic* **he doesn't want** *or* **ask** *or* **expect much, does he?** il n'est pas difficile, lui, au moins!

3 *adv* beaucoup; **I don't drink much** je ne bois pas beaucoup; **I don't like them much, I don't much like them** je ne les aime pas beaucoup; **much admired/appreciated** très admiré/apprécié; **much happier/more slowly** beaucoup plus heureux/plus lentement; **much worse** bien pire; **I feel very much better** je me sens beaucoup mieux; **thank you very much (for)** merci beaucoup (de *ou* pour); *Formal* **it is much to be regretted that...** il est fort regrettable que...; **it doesn't matter much** cela n'a pas beaucoup d'importance; **much to my surprise** à mon grand étonnement; **we are much obliged to you for...** nous vous sommes très obligés de *ou* pour...; **I'm not much good at making speeches** je ne suis pas très doué pour faire des discours; **it's much the best/the fastest way to travel** c'est de beaucoup le meilleur moyen/le moyen le plus rapide de voyager; **it's much the best/the fastest** c'est le meilleur/le plus rapide de beaucoup; **much the same** presque pareil; **it's (pretty** *or* **very) much the same thing** c'est à peu près la même chose; **she's still much the same as yesterday** son état n'a pas changé depuis hier; **I feel much the same as you** je pense plutôt comme vous; *Fam Ironic* **he doesn't like beer, does he? – not much he doesn't!** il n'aime pas la bière, non? – et comment, il aime ça!

4 as much 1 *pron (that, the same)* **I thought/suspected as much** c'est bien ce que je pensais/soupçonnais; **I expected as much** je m'y attendais; **I said as much to him yesterday** c'est ce que je lui ai dit hier; **would you do as much for me?** en ferais-tu autant pour moi? **2** *adv (with multiples, fractions)* **twice/three times as much** deux/trois fois plus; **half as much** la moitié (de ça); **a quarter as much** un quart (de ça); **as much again** encore autant

5 as much...as 1 *adj (the same amount as)* **as much...as** autant de...que; **I've got as much money as you** j'ai autant d'argent que vous; **take as much sugar as you like** prenez autant de *ou* tout le sucre que vous voulez **2** *conj* autant...que; **he's as much to blame as her** elle n'est pas plus responsable que lui, il est responsable autant qu'elle; **it is as much your fault as (it is) mine** c'est autant de votre faute que de la mienne

6 as much as 1 *pron* (**a**) *(the same as)* **it costs as much as the Japanese model** ça coûte le même prix que le modèle japonais; **he looked at me as much as to say...** il me regarda avec l'air de (vouloir) dire...; **that's as much as to say that I'm a liar** ça revient à me traiter de menteur (**b**) *(all)* **it was as much as I could do to keep a straight face** j'ai failli éclater de rire; **it was as much as we could do to stand upright** nous avions le plus grand mal à nous tenir debout **2** *conj* autant que; **I hate it as much as you do** ça me déplaît autant qu'à vous; **as much as ever** toujours autant; **as much as before** autant qu'avant; **not quite as much as...** pas tout à fait autant que...; **I don't dislike them as much as all that** ils ne me déplaisent pas autant que ça

7 however much 1 *adj* **however much money you give him, it won't be enough** vous pouvez lui donner autant d'argent que vous voulez, ça ne suffira pas **2** *pron* **however much they offer, take it** quelle que soit la somme qu'ils proposent, acceptez-la **3** *adv* **however much you dislike the idea...** quelle que soit votre aversion pour cette idée...; **however much I try, it doesn't work** j'ai beau essayer, ça ne marche pas

8 how much 1 *adj* combien de; **how much flour have we got left?** combien de farine nous reste-t-il? **2** *pron* combien; **how much do you want?** *(gen)* combien en voulez-vous?; *(money)* combien voulez-vous?; **how much is the record** *or* **does the record cost?** combien coûte ce disque?

9 much as *conj* **much as I admire him, I have to admit that...** malgré toute mon admiration pour lui, je dois admettre que...; **much as I would like to, I can't come** à mon grand regret, il m'est véritablement impossible de venir; **much as I try, I can't succeed** j'ai beau essayer, je n'y arrive pas; **the result was much as I expected** le résultat correspondait bien à ce que j'attendais

10 so much 1 *adj* tant de, tellement de; **it takes up so much time** ça prend tellement de temps; **it's just so much nonsense** c'est tellement bête

2 *pron* (**a**) *(such a lot)* tant; **I've learnt so much on this course** j'ai vraiment appris beaucoup (de choses) en suivant ces cours; **there's still so much to do** il y a encore tant à faire; **he has drunk so much that...** il a tellement bu que... (**b**) *(this amount)* **there's only so much one can do** il y a une limite à ce qu'on peut faire; **how much water will I put in? – about so much** combien d'eau est-ce que je dois mettre? – à peu près ça; **so much a kilo** tant le kilo **3** *adv* tellement; **I miss you so much** tu me manques tellement; **I wouldn't mind so much, only he promised to do it** ça ne me gêne pas tellement, mais il avait promis de le faire; **it's not so much his unpunctuality, it's his rudeness I can't stand** ce n'est pas tellement ses retards, c'est sa grossièreté que je ne supporte pas; **thank you ever so much** merci infiniment *ou* mille fois; **so much the better** tant mieux; **so much so that...** au point que..., à tel point que...; **not so much a..., more a...** pas vraiment un..., mais plutôt un...

11 so much as *adv* même; **if you so much as breathe a word of this...** si seulement tu répètes un mot de tout ça...; **without so much as asking permission** sans même demander la permission; **I would not so much as raise a finger to help him** je ne lèverais pas même le petit doigt pour l'aider

12 so much for *prep* **so much for the agenda; now let us consider...** voilà pour ce qui est de l'ordre du jour; maintenant, je voudrais que nous nous penchions sur la question de...; **so much for that idea!** on peut oublier cette idée!; **so much for his friendship!** et voilà ce qu'il appelle l'amitié!

13 that much 1 *adj* **there was that much food, we thought we'd never finish it** il y avait tellement à manger qu'on pensait ne jamais arriver à finir **2** *pron* **was there much damage? – not that much** y a-t-il eu beaucoup de dégâts? – pas tant que ça; **did it cost that much?** ça a coûté autant que ça?; **how much do you want? – about that much** combien en veux-tu? – à peu près ça **3** *adv (with comparative)* (**a**) *(a lot)* beaucoup plus; **it'll be that much easier to organize** ce sera d'autant plus facile à organiser; **not that much better** pas beaucoup mieux (**b**) *(this amount)* **she's that much taller than me** elle est plus grande que moi de ça

14 this much 1 *adj* **there was this much coffee left** il restait ça de café **2** *pron* (**a**) *(this amount)* **I had to cut this much off the hem of my skirt** j'ai dû raccourcir ma jupe de ça (**b**) *(one thing)* une chose; **this much is true...** une chose au moins est vraie...; **I'll say this much for her, she's got guts** il faut reconnaître une chose, c'est qu'elle a du cran

15 too much 1 *adj* trop de **2** *pron* trop; **there's too much to do** il y a trop à faire; **don't expect too much** *(be too demanding)* ne soyez pas trop exigeant, n'en demandez pas trop; *(be too hopeful)* ne vous faites pas trop d'illusions; **to cost too much** coûter trop cher; **£10 too much** 10 livres de trop; *Fam* **she's too much!** elle est trop!; *Fam* **that's too much!** ça, c'est trop!; *Fam* **that's a bit much!** c'est un peu fort!; **you can't have too much of a good thing** abondance de biens ne nuit pas **3** *adv (work, speak)* trop

much-loved *adj* bien-aimé

muchly ['mʌtʃlɪ] *adv esp Am Fam Hum* **thanks muchly!** merci beaucoup!

muchness ['mʌtʃnɪs] *n Br Fam (idiom)* **they're all much of a muchness** *(objects)* c'est du pareil au même ❑; *(people)* ils se valent ❑

mucilage ['mjuːsɪlɪdʒ] *n* (**a**) *Bot* mucilage *m* (**b**) *Am (glue)* colle *f*

muck [mʌk] *(UNCOUNT) Fam* **1** *n* (**a**) *(mud)* boue ❑ *f*, gadoue ❑ *f*; *(dirt)* saletés ❑ *fpl*; *(manure)* fumier ❑ *m*; *(dung – of horse)* crottin ❑ *m*; *(– of dog)* crotte ❑ *f*; *Br Hum* **they think they're Lord and Lady Muck** ils ne se prennent pas pour n'importe qui, ils se croient sortis de la cuisse de Jupiter; *Br Prov* **where there's muck, there's brass** = c'est peut-être sale, mais ça rapporte! *(fait référence aux travaux salissants mais rentables)*

(**b**) *Fig (inferior literature, films etc)* idioties *fpl*; *(bad food)* cochonneries *fpl*; *(worthless objects)*

mst–muc

camelote *f*; **his book's a load of muck** son livre ne vaut pas un clou; **he eats nothing but muck** il ne mange que des cochonneries
(**c**) *Br Fam* **to make a muck of sth** *(bungle)* bousiller qch
2 *vt Agr* fumer
▸▸ *Ir Pej* ***muck savage*** plouc *m*, péquenot *m*

▸**muck about, muck around** *Fam* **1** *vi* (**a**) *(waste time)* traîner, perdre son temps ❑
(**b**) *(act foolishly)* faire l'imbécile; **stop mucking about!** arrête de faire l'imbécile!
(**c**) *(interfere)* **to muck about with sth** *(equipment)* toucher à qch, tripoter qch; *(belongings)* déranger qch, mettre la pagaille dans qch
2 *vt sep* (**a**) *(person → waste time of)* faire perdre son temps à; *(→ be inconsiderate to)* malmener
(**b**) *(belongings, papers)* déranger, toucher à

▸**muck in** *vi Br Fam (share task)* mettre la main à la pâte, donner un coup de main ❑; *(share costs)* participer aux frais ❑

▸**muck out** *Br* **1** *vt sep (horse, stable)* nettoyer, curer
2 *vi* nettoyer l'écurie/les écuries

▸**muck up** *vt sep Fam* (**a**) *(dirty)* cochonner (**b**) *(ruin)* bousiller, foutre en l'air (**c**) *Austr (lark around)* faire des bêtises ❑

muck-a-muck *n Am Fam (important person)* huile *f*; **her dad's a muck-a-muck in the police department** son père a un poste haut placé dans la police ❑

mucker [ˌmʌkə(r)] *n Br Fam* (**a**) *(friend)* pote *m* (**b**) *(term of address)* vieux *m*; **alright, me old mucker!** salut vieux!, salut mon pote!

muckheap [ˈmʌkhiːp] *n Br Fam* tas *m* de fumier ❑

muckiness [ˈmʌkɪnɪs] *n* (**a**) *(of hands, shoes etc)* saleté *f* (**b**) *(obscenity)* obscénité *f*

muckle [ˈmʌkəl] *Scot* **1** *adj* très; **a muckle big house** une très grande maison
2 *adv (with verb)* beaucoup; *(with adjective)* très

mucklucks [ˈmʌklʌks] *npl Am* = bottes de neige portées sur de grosses chaussettes ou des chaussures

muckraker [ˈmʌkˌreɪkə(r)] *n Pej (journalist)* fouineur(euse) *m,f*

muckraking [ˈmʌkˌreɪkɪŋ] *n Pej* **it's the kind of paper that specializes in muckraking** c'est le type de journal spécialisé dans les scandales

muckspreader [ˈmʌkˌspredə(r)] *n Agr* épandeur *m* (d'engrais)

muckspreading [ˈmʌkˌspredɪŋ] *n Agr* épandage *m*

muck-up *n Br Fam* pagaille *f*, bordel *m*; **to make a muck-up of sth** foutre qch en l'air, bousiller qch
▸▸ *Austr* ***muck-up day*** = dernier jour de l'année scolaire dans les lycées australiens, au cours duquel les élèves font du chahut

mucky [ˈmʌkɪ] (*compar* **muckier**, *superl* **muckiest**) *adj Fam* (**a**) *(dirty, muddy → hands)* sale ❑, crasseux; *(→ shoes)* sale ❑, crotté ❑; *(→ water, road)* sale ❑, boueux ❑; *Br* **the weather was mucky** il faisait un sale temps (**b**) *Br (obscene → book, film)* obscène

mucoid [ˈmjuːkɔɪd] *n Chem* mucoïde *m*

mucopolysaccharide [ˌmjuːkəʊˌpɒlɪˈsækəraɪd] *n Biol & Chem* mucopolysaccharide *m*

mucoprotein [ˌmjuːkəʊˈprəʊtiːn] *n Biol & Chem* mucoprotéine *f*

mucopurulent [ˌmjuːkəʊˈpjʊərʊlənt] *adj Med* muco-purulent

mucosa [mjuːˈkəʊsə] *n Anat* muqueuse *f*

mucosity [mjuːˈkɒsɪtɪ] *n* mucosité *f*

mucous [ˈmjuːkəs] *adj* muqueux
▸▸ *Anat* ***mucous membrane*** muqueuse *f*

mucus [ˈmjuːkəs] *n* mucus *m*, mucosité *f*; *(from nose)* morve *f*

MUD [ˌemjuːˈdiː] *n Comput* (*abbr* **multi-user dungeon**) environnement *m* MUD

mud [mʌd] (*pt & pp* **mudded**, *cont* **mudding**) **1** *n* *(gen)* boue *f*; *(in river, lake)* vase *f*; *(in swamp)* bourbe *f*; **my car got stuck in the mud** ma voiture s'est embourbée; *Fam Old-fashioned* **here's mud in your eye!** à la tienne!; **to drag sb** *or* **sb's name through the mud** traîner qn dans la boue; *Fam* **my name is mud in certain circles** je suis en disgrâce *ou* persona non grata dans certains milieux; **to throw** *or* **to sling mud at sb** couvrir qn de boue; *Fam* **as clear as mud** clair comme du jus de boudin
2 *vt* couvrir de boue, crotter
▸▸ ***mud hut*** case *f* en pisé *ou* en terre; ***mud pie*** *(made of mud)* pâté *m* (de sable); *(cake)* = sorte de gâteau au chocolat; ***mud wrestler*** = personne qui pratique le catch dans la boue; ***mud wrestling*** catch *m* dans la boue

mudbank [ˈmʌdbæŋk] *n* banc *m* de vase

mudbath [ˈmʌdbɑːθ, *pl* -bɑːðz] *n* bain *m* de boue

muddiness [ˈmʌdɪnɪs] *n* (**a**) *(of shoes etc)* état *m* crotté; *(of road, stream)* état *m* boueux (**b**) *Fig (of complexion)* aspect *m* terreux; *(of liquid)* turbidité *f*, état *m* trouble

muddle [ˈmʌdəl] **1** *n* *(confusion)* confusion *f*; *(mess)* désordre *m*, fouillis *m*; **all her belongings were in a muddle** toutes ses affaires étaient en désordre *ou* sens dessus dessous; **my finances are in an awful muddle** ma situation financière n'est pas claire du tout *ou* est complètement embrouillée; **Holly was in a real muddle over the holiday plans** Holly ne savait plus où elle en était dans ses projets de vacances; *Fig* **let's try to sort out this muddle** essayons de démêler cet écheveau; **there must have been a muddle over the train times** quelqu'un a dû se tromper dans les horaires de train
2 *vt* (**a**) *(mix up → dates)* confondre, mélanger; *(→ facts)* embrouiller, mélanger; **the dates got muddled** il y a eu une confusion dans les dates
(**b**) *(confuse → person)* embrouiller (l'esprit *ou* les idées de); **now you've got me muddled** maintenant, je ne sais plus où j'en suis; **she'll get muddled if you all talk at once** vous allez lui embrouiller l'esprit si vous parlez tous à la fois
(**c**) *(stir → cocktail)* remuer

▸**muddle along** *vi* se débrouiller

▸**muddle through** **1** *vt insep* se tirer de
2 *vi* se tirer d'affaire

▸**muddle up** *vt sep* (**a**) *(mix up → dates)* confondre, mélanger; *(→ facts)* embrouiller (**b**) *(confuse → person)* embrouiller

muddled [ˈmʌdəld] *adj* (**a**) *(objects)* en désordre (**b**) *(person, ideas)* confus, embrouillé

muddleheaded [ˌmʌdəlˈhedɪd] *adj (person)* désordonné, brouillon, écervelé; *(idea, speech, essay)* confus

muddler [ˈmʌdələ(r)] *n* (**a**) *(person)* personne *f* désordonnée; **he's such a muddler!** il est tellement brouillon! (**b**) *(for stirring)* bâtonnet *m* à cocktail

muddle-up *n* (**a**) *(misunderstanding)* quiproquo *m*, malentendu *m*; **there was a muddle-up over the dates** il y a eu une confusion dans les dates (**b**) *(situation)* embrouillement *m*, imbroglio *m*

muddy [ˈmʌdɪ] (*compar* **muddier**, *superl* **muddiest**) **1** *adj* (**a**) *(hand, car)* plein *ou* couvert de boue; *(shoes)* plein de boue, crotté; *(road, path, stream)* boueux
(**b**) *Fig (complexion)* terreux; *(colour)* terne, sale; *(flavour, drink)* boueux; *(liquid)* boueux, trouble; **muddy brown** couleur (de) terre
(**c**) *(indistinct → thinking, ideas)* confus, embrouillé, peu clair; *(out of focus → image)* brouillé, trouble, flou
2 *vt* (**a**) *(hands, shoes)* salir, couvrir de boue; *(road, stream)* rendre boueux; *Fig* **to muddy the waters** semer la confusion
(**b**) *(situation)* compliquer, embrouiller

Mudejar [muːˈdeɪhɑː(r)] *Hist* **1** *n* Mudéjar(e) *m,f*
2 *adj* mudéjar

mudflap [ˈmʌdflæp] *n (on car)* bavette *f*; *(on truck)* pare-boue *m inv*

mudflat [ˈmʌdflæt] *n* laisse *f ou* banc *m* de boue

mudguard [ˈmʌdgɑːd] *n* garde-boue *m inv*

mudhopper [ˈmʌdˌhɒpə(r)] *n Br Ich* gobie *m* marcheur *ou* des marais

mudlark [ˈmʌdlɑːk] *n* (**a**) *Literary (person)* gamin(e) *m,f* des rues, gavroche *m* (**b**) *(horse)* = cheval qui court bien sur terrain lourd

mudpack [ˈmʌdpæk] *n* masque *m* à l'argile

mudpuppy [ˈmʌdpʌpɪ] *n Zool (salamander)* = salamandre aquatique d'Amérique du Nord; *(Necturus maculosus)* necture *m* tacheté

mudskipper [ˈmʌdˌskɪpə(r)] *n Ich* gobie *m* marcheur *ou* des marais

mudslinger [ˈmʌdˌslɪŋə(r)] *n* fauteur(trice) *m,f* de scandales; **the mudslingers will be disappointed** les amateurs de scandales en seront pour leurs frais

mudslinging [ˈmʌdˌslɪŋɪŋ] *n* calomnie *f*; **a lot of mudslinging went on during the elections** ils ont passé leur temps à se traîner les uns les autres dans la boue pendant les élections

mud-spattered *adj* couvert *ou* maculé de boue

mud-stained *adj* taché de boue

muesli [ˈmjuːzlɪ] *n* muesli *m*, *Suisse* bircher *m*
▸▸ *Br Pej* ***the muesli belt*** = quartiers où vit une certaine bourgeoisie de gauche, soucieuse de diététique et sensible aux problèmes de l'environnement

muezzin [muːˈezɪn] *n* muezzin *m*

muff [mʌf] **1** *n* (**a**) *(for hands)* manchon *m*; *(for ears)* oreillette *f* (**b**) *Vulg (woman's genitals)* chatte *f*, con *m* (**c**) *Zool* aigrette *f* (**d**) *(bungled attempt)* coup *m* manqué
2 *vt (bungle)* rater, manquer; **to muff a catch** rater une prise

muffin [ˈmʌfɪn] *n* (**a**) *(sponge cake)* muffin *m*, = petit gâteau (**b**) *Br (served warm)* muffin *m*, = petit pain rond servi chaud et beurré

muffle [ˈmʌfəl] *vt (quieten → sound)* étouffer, assourdir; *(→ engine)* étouffer le bruit de; **the silencer muffles engine noise** le silencieux étouffe le bruit du moteur; **we could hear muffled cries coming from the next room** on entendait des cris étouffés *ou* sourds qui venaient de la pièce voisine

▸**muffle up** **1** *vt sep* (bien) emmitoufler
2 *vi* s'emmitoufler

muffled [ˈmʌfəld] *adj* (**a**) *(sound, voice)* sourd, étouffé; *(oars)* assourdi; *(drums)* voilé; **there was a lot of muffled laughter** on entendait de nombreux rires étouffés (**b**) *(wrapped)* **muffled (up)** emmitouflé

muffler [ˈmʌflə(r)] *n* (**a**) *Old-fashioned (scarf)* écharpe *f*, cache-nez *m inv* (**b**) *Am Aut* silencieux *m* (**c**) *Mus (on piano)* étouffoir *m*

Mufti [ˈmʌftɪ] *n Rel* mufti *m*, muphti *m*

mufti [ˈmʌftɪ] *n Old-fashioned* tenue *f* civile; **wearing mufti, in mufti** en civil

mug [mʌg] (*pt & pp* **mugged**, *cont* **mugging**) **1** *n* (**a**) *(beer glass)* chope *f*; *(for tea, coffee)* grande tasse *f*; *(made of metal)* quart *m*
(**b**) *Fam (face)* gueule *f*, tronche *f*, trombine *f*; **shut your ugly mug!** ferme ta sale gueule!
(**c**) *Br Fam (dupe)* poire *f*; *(fool)* nigaud(e) *m,f*; **it's a mug's game** *(foolish)* c'est de la connerie, le jeu n'en vaut pas la chandelle; *(trap)* c'est de l'arnaque; **the lottery's a mug's game** le loto, c'est un attrape-couillon
(**d**) *Am Fam (thug)* gangster *m*, voyou *m*
(**e**) *Fam (photo)* photo *f* d'identité judiciaire ❑
2 *vt Fam (attack)* agresser ❑
▸▸ *Fam* ***mug shot*** *(of criminal)* photo *f* d'identité judiciaire ❑; *Pej Hum (passport-sized photo)* photo *f* d'identité ❑

▸**mug up** *Br Fam* **1** *vt sep* potasser, bosser
2 *vi* bûcher, boulonner; **he's mugging up for the test** il bûche ferme en prévision de son examen; **I'd better mug up on my French** je ferais mieux de potasser mon français

mugful [ˈmʌgfʊl] *n (of tea, coffee)* tasse *f* (pleine); *(of beer)* chope *f* (pleine)

mugger [ˈmʌgə(r)] *n* agresseur *m*

mugginess [ˈmʌgɪnɪs] *n Met* chaleur *f* lourde et humide

mugging [ˈmʌgɪŋ] *n* agression *f*; **he was the victim of a mugging** il a été victime d'une agression; **mugging is on the increase** il y a une augmentation des agressions

muggins [ˈmʌgɪnz] (*pl* **inv** *or* **mugginses**) *n Br Fam* mézigue; **I suppose muggins will have to go** je suppose que c'est bibi *ou* ma pomme qui devra y aller; **muggins (here) paid the bill as usual** comme d'habitude c'est mézigue qui a payé l'addition

muggy [ˈmʌgɪ] (*compar* **muggier**, *superl* **muggiest**) *adj Met* lourd et humide

mugwort [ˈmʌgwɜːt] *n Bot* armoise *f*

mugwump [ˈmʌgwʌmp] *n Am Pej Pol* indépendant(e) *m,f*

Muhammad [məˈhæmɪd] *pr n Rel* Mahomet

Muhammedan, Muhammadan [məˈhæmɪdən] *Rel*
1 *n* Mahométan(e) *m,f*
2 *adj* mahométan

mujaheddin [ˌmuːdʒəheˈdiːn] *n* moudjahid *m*

mulatto [mjuːˈlætəʊ] (*pl* **mulattos** *or* **mulattoes**) *Old-fashioned* **1** *n* mulâtre(esse) *m,f*
2 *adj* mulâtre

mulberry [ˈmʌlbərɪ] **1** *n* (**a**) *(fruit)* mûre *f*; *(tree)* mûrier *m*; **white mulberry** mûrier *m* blanc (**b**) *(colour)* violet *m* foncé
2 *adj* violet foncé *(inv)*

mulch [mʌltʃ] *Hort* **1** *n* paillis *m*
2 *vt* pailler, couvrir de paillis

mulct [mʌlkt] *Formal* **1** *n* amende *f*
2 *vt* (**a**) *(fine)* infliger une amende à (**b**) *(defraud)* escroquer; *(overcharge)* escroquer

mule [mjuːl] *n* (**a**) *(animal → male)* mulet *m*; *(→ female)* mule *f*; **(as) stubborn as a mule** têtu comme un mulet *ou* une mule (**b**) *(slipper)* mule *f* (**c**) *Fam Drugs slang (drug smuggler)* mule *f* (**d**) *Tech* mule-jenny *f*
▸▸ *Zool* ***mule deer*** cerf *m* mulet; *Fam* ***mule driver*** muletier[◻] *m*; ***mule path*** chemin *m ou* sentier *m* muletier; *Am Fam* ***mule skinner*** muletier[◻] *m*; ***mule train*** caravane *f* de mules

muleheaded [ˈmjuːlˌhedɪd] *adj* têtu comme une mule

muleteer [ˌmjuːlɪˈtɪə(r)] *n* muletier(ère) *m,f*

mulish [ˈmjuːlɪʃ] *adj* têtu, entêté

mulishly [ˈmjuːlɪʃlɪ] *adv* avec entêtement, par pure obstination

mulishness [ˈmjuːlɪʃnɪs] *n* entêtement *m*, obstination *f*

mull [mʌl] *vt (wine, beer)* chauffer et épicer
▸**mull over** *vt sep* réfléchir (longuement) à

mullah [ˈmʌlə] *n* mollah *m*

mulled [mʌld] *adj*
▸▸ ***mulled wine*** vin *m* chaud épicé

mullein [ˈmʌlɪn] *n Bot* molène *f*, cierge *m*; **great mullein** molène *f* commune, bouillon-blanc *m*
▸▸ ***mullein pink*** coquelourde *f*, passe-fleur *f*

mullet [ˈmʌlɪt] (*pl sense* (**a**) **inv** *or* **mullets,** *pl sense* (**b**) **mullets**) *n* (**a**) *Ich* mulet *m*; *(grey)* muge *m*, mulet *m* gris; *(red)* rouget *m*, mulet *m* rouge (**b**) *Fam (hairstyle)* = coupe de cheveux longue sur la nuque, courte sur les côtés et en brosse longue sur le dessus

mulligan [ˈmʌlɪgən] *n Am (of meat)* ragoût *m*; *(of fish)* fricassée *f* de poisson
▸▸ ***mulligan stew*** *(of meat)* ragoût *m*; *(of fish)* fricassée *f* de poisson

mulligatawny [ˌmʌlɪgəˈtɔːnɪ] *n Br* mulligatawny *m*, soupe *f* au curry

mullion [ˈmʌlɪən] *n Archit* meneau *m*
▸▸ ***mullion window*** fenêtre *f* à meneaux

mullioned [ˈmʌlɪənd] *adj Archit (window)* à meneaux

multiaccess [ˌmʌltɪˈækses] *adj Comput* à accès multiple

multibarrelled [ˌmʌltɪˈbærəld] *adj (gun)* multitube

multibranched [ˌmʌltɪˈbrɑːnʃt], **multibranchiate** [ˌmʌltɪˈbræŋkɪeɪt] *adj* multibranche

multibrand [ˈmʌltɪbrænd] *n Mktg* marque *f* multiple, multimarque *f*
▸▸ ***multibrand store*** point *m* de vente multimarque

multicast [ˈmʌltɪkɑːst] *n Comput* multidiffusion *f*

multicellular [ˌmʌltɪˈseljʊlə(r)] *adj* multicellulaire

multichannel [ˌmʌltɪˈtʃænəl] *adj* multicanal

multicoloured, *Am* **multicolored** [ˈmʌltɪˌkʌləd] *adj* multicolore

multicomponent [ˌmʌltɪkəmˈpəʊnənt] *adj* à composantes multiples, complexe
▸▸ *Electron* ***multicomponent signal*** signal *m* complexe

multicriterion sorting [ˌmʌltɪkraɪˈtɪərɪən-] *n Comput* classement *m* multicritère

multicultural [ˌmʌltɪˈkʌltʃərəl] *adj* multiculturel

multiculturalism [ˌmʌltɪˈkʌltʃərəlɪzəm] *n* multiculturalisme *m*

multicurrency [ˌmʌltɪˈkʌrənsɪ] *adj* multidevise

multidimensional [ˌmʌltɪdɪˈmenʃənəl] *adj* multidimensionnel

multidirectional [ˌmʌltɪdɪˈrekʃənəl] *adj* multidirectionnel

multidisciplinary [ˈmʌltɪˌdɪsɪˈplɪnərɪ] *adj Br* pluridisciplinaire, multidisciplinaire

multiethnic [ˌmʌltɪˈeθnɪk] *adj* pluriethnique

multifaceted [ˌmʌltɪˈfæsɪtɪd] *adj* présentant de multiples facettes

multifamily [ˌmʌltɪˈfæmɪlɪ] *adj Am* pour plusieurs familles

multifarious [ˌmʌltɪˈfeərɪəs] *adj (varied)* (très) divers *ou* varié; *(numerous)* (très) nombreux

multifile [ˈmʌltɪfaɪl] *adj* à fichiers multiples

multiform [ˈmʌltɪfɔːm] *adj* multiforme

multi-fuel engine *n* moteur *m* polycarburant

multifunction [ˌmʌltɪˈfʌŋkʃən] *adj* multifonction(s)

multifunctional [ˌmʌltɪˈfʌŋkʃənəl] *adj* multifonction(s)
▸▸ *Banking* ***multifunctional card*** carte *f* multifonction(s); ***multifunctional keyboard*** clavier *m* multifonction(s); ***multifunctional key*** touche *f* multifonction(s)

multigrade [ˈmʌltɪgreɪd] *adj* multigrade

multigravida [ˌmʌltɪˈgrævɪdə] *n Obst* femme *f* ayant eu plusieurs grossesses

multigym [ˈmʌltɪdʒɪm] *n* appareil *m* de musculation

multihull [ˈmʌltɪhʌl] **1** *n* multicoque *m*
2 *adj* multicoque

multilateral [ˌmʌltɪˈlætərəl] *adj* multilatéral
▸▸ ***multilateral agreement on investment*** accord *m* multilatéral sur l'investissement; ***multilateral trade agreement*** accord *m* commercial multilatéral

multilaterally [ˌmʌltɪˈlætərəlɪ] *adv* de façon multilatérale

multilayered [ˌmʌltɪˈleɪəd] *adj (cake)* à plusieurs couches; *(structure, hierarchy)* stratifié; *(film, novel)* qui fonctionne sur plusieurs niveaux

multilevel [ˌmʌltɪˈlevəl] *adj Comput* multiniveaux
▸▸ *Mktg* ***multilevel marketing*** marketing *m* de réseau, vente *f* par réseau coopté

multilingual [ˌmʌltɪˈlɪŋgwəl] *adj* multilingue

multimedia [ˌmʌltɪˈmiːdɪə] **1** *n* multimédia *m*
2 *adj* multimédia
▸▸ ***multimedia computer*** ordinateur *m* multimédia; ***multimedia group*** groupe *m* multimédia

multimeter [ˈmʌltɪˌmiːtə(r)] *n Elec* multimètre *m*

multimillion *adj* **a multimillion pound/dollar project** un projet chiffré à plusieurs millions de livres/dollars

multimillionaire [ˈmʌltɪˌmɪlɪəˈneə(r)] *n* multimillionnaire *mf*

multimodal operator [ˌmʌltɪˈməʊdəl-] *n* opérateur *m* de transport multimodal, OTM *m*

multimode [ˈmʌltɪməʊd] *adj Electron* à plusieurs modes de fonctionnement

multinational [ˌmʌltɪˈnæʃənəl] **1** *n* multinationale *f*
2 *adj* multinational
▸▸ ***multinational company*** entreprise *f* multinationale; ***multinational enterprise*** entreprise *f* multinationale; ***multinational marketing*** marketing *m* multinational

multi-ownership *n* multipropriété *f*

multipara [mʌlˈtɪpərə] *n Obst* multipare *f*

multiparous [mʌlˈtɪpərəs] *adj Zool* multipare

multipartite [ˌmʌltɪˈpɑːtaɪt] *adj* (**a**) *(talks)* multipartite, multilatéral (**b**) *(in many parts)* composé de plusieurs parties; *(with many people)* impliquant plusieurs personnes; *(with many signatories)* comportant de nombreux signataires

multiparty [ˈmʌltɪˌpɑːtɪ] *adj* multipartite, pluripartite; **the multiparty system** le multipartisme, le pluripartisme

multiphase [ˈmʌltɪfeɪz] *adj Elec (current, alternator)* polyphasé, multiphasé
▸▸ *Nucl* ***multiphase structure*** structure *f* multiphasée

multi-plate clutch *n* embrayage *m* à disques multiples

multiple [ˈmʌltɪpəl] **1** *n* (**a**) *Math* multiple *m*; **in multiples of 100** en *ou* par multiples de 100
(**b**) *Br (store)* chaîne *f* de magasins
(**c**) *Tel* multiplage *m*
2 *adj* (**a**) *(gén)* multiple; **she suffered multiple injuries** elle a été blessée en plusieurs endroits; **he died of multiple stab wounds** il a été tué de plusieurs coups de couteau
(**b**) *Elec* en parallèle
▸▸ *St Exch* ***multiple application*** application *f* multiple; ***multiple birth*** naissance *f* multiple; *Tel* ***multiple circuit*** accumulateurs *mpl* en parallèle; ***multiple collision*** collision *f* multiple; *Fin* ***multiple exchange rate*** taux *m* de change multiple; *Comput* ***multiple mailboxes*** = possibilité d'avoir plusieurs boîtes aux lettres auprès d'un fournisseur d'accès à l'internet; ***multiple occupancy*** *(by tenants)* colocation *f*; *(by owners)* copropriété *f*; *St Exch* ***multiple options facility*** ligne *f* de crédit à options multiples; ***multiple ownership*** multipropriété *f*; *Psy* ***multiple personality*** personnalité *f* multiple; *Com* ***multiple pricing*** = fait d'adapter le prix de vente d'un produit au marché où on le commercialise; *Elec & Rad* ***multiple reception*** réception *f* multiple; *Med* ***multiple sclerosis*** sclérose *f* en plaques; *Br* ***multiple shop,*** *Am* ***multiple store*** grand magasin *m* à succursales, chaîne *f* de magasins; *Tel* ***multiple switchboard*** multiple *m* (téléphonique)

multiple-access *adj Comput* à accès multiple

multiple-choice *adj* à choix multiples

multiplex [ˈmʌltɪpleks] **1** *n* (**a**) *Tel* multiplex *m* (**b**) *Cin* complexe *m* multisalles, cinéma *m* multisalle
2 *comp Tel* multiplex
3 *vt Tel* multiplexer
▸▸ *Cin* ***multiplex cinema*** complexe *m* multisalles, cinéma *m* multisalle

multiplexer [ˈmʌltɪˌpleksə(r)] *n Tel* multiplexeur *m*

multiplexing [ˈmʌltɪˌpleksɪŋ] *n Tel* multiplexage *m*

multiplexor = **multiplexer**

multipliable [ˌmʌltɪˈplaɪəbəl], **multiplicable** [ˌmʌltɪˈplɪkəbəl] *adj* multipliable

multiplicand [ˌmʌltɪplɪˈkænd] *n Math* multiplicande *m*

multiplication [ˌmʌltɪplɪˈkeɪʃən] *n (gen) & Math* multiplication *f*
▸▸ ***multiplication sign*** signe *m* de multiplication; ***multiplication table*** table *f* de multiplication

multiplicative [ˌmʌltɪˈplɪkətɪv] *adj* multiplicatif

multiplicity [ˌmʌltɪˈplɪsətɪ] *n* multiplicité *f*

multiplier [ˈmʌltɪplaɪə(r)] *n* (**a**) *Econ, Electron & Math* multiplicateur *m* (**b**) *Comput* multiplieur *m*

multiply [ˈmʌltɪplaɪ] (*pt & pp* **multiplied**) **1** *vt* multiplier; **it will multiply the costs by eight** ça va multiplier les coûts par huit
2 *vi* (**a**) *Math* faire des multiplications
(**b**) *(reproduce, increase)* se multiplier

multiply-handicapped [ˈmʌltɪplɪ-] **1** *adj* polyhandicapé
2 *npl* **the multiply-handicapped** les polyhandicapés *mpl*

multi-point fuel-injected engine *n* moteur *m* à injection multipoint

multipolar [ˌmʌltɪˈpəʊlə(r)], **multipole** [ˈmʌltɪpəʊl] *adj Elec* multipolaire
▸▸ ***multipolar moment*** moment *m* multipolaire

multiprocessing [ˌmʌltɪˈprəʊsesɪŋ] *n Comput* multitraitement *m*

multiprocessor [ˌmʌltɪˈprəʊsesə(r)] *n Comput* multiprocesseur *m*

multiprogramming [ˌmʌltɪˈprəʊgræmɪŋ] *n Comput* multiprogrammation *f*

multipurpose [ˌmʌltɪˈpɜːpəs] *adj* à usages multiples, polyvalent
▸▸ *Aut* ***multipurpose vehicle*** monospace *m*

multiracial [ˌmʌltɪˈreɪʃəl] *adj* multiracial

multiracialism [ˌmʌltɪˈreɪʃəlɪzəm] *n* multiracialisme *m*

multiscan monitor [ˈmʌltɪskæn-] *n* moniteur *m* à balayage multiple

multiscreen [ˈmʌltɪskriːn] *n* (**a**) *Cin* complexe *m* multisalles, cinéma *m* multisalle (**b**) *TV* écran-mosaïque *m*, multi-écran *m*
▸▸ *TV* ***multiscreen channel*** canal *m* mosaïque; *Cin* ***multiscreen cinema*** complexe *m* multisalles, cinéma *m* multisalle

multisector [ˈmʌltɪˌsektə(r)] *adj* multisectoriel
▸▸ ***multisector journey*** voyage *m* multi-secteur; ***multisector ticketing*** délivrance *f* de billets multi-secteurs

multiskilling [ˌmʌltɪˈskɪlɪŋ] *n* formation *f* polyvalente

multi-spreadsheet *n* multifeuille *f*

multistage [ˈmʌltɪsteɪdʒ] *adj* (**a**) *(procedure)* à plusieurs étapes (**b**) *(rocket)* à plusieurs étages

multistandard [ˌmʌltɪˈstændəd] *adj TV* multistandard

multi-station *adj Comput* multipostes

multistorey [ˌmʌltɪˈstɔːrɪ], *Am* **multistoried** [ˌmʌltɪˈstɔːrɪd] *adj*
►► ***multistorey building*** grand immeuble *m*; ***multistorey car park*** parking *m* à plusieurs niveaux

multisyllabic [ˌmʌltɪsɪˈlæbɪk] *adj* polysyllabique

multi-talented *adj* aux talents multiples

multitasking [ˌmʌltɪˈtɑːskɪŋ] *n* = capacité à mener plusieurs tâches de front; **multitasking skills** *or* **abilities** = capacité à mener plusieurs tâches de front

multitherapy [ˌmʌltɪˈθerəpɪ] *n Med* multithérapie *f*

multithreading [ˌmʌltɪˈθredɪŋ] *Comput* **1** *n* multithread *m*, multitraitement *m*
2 *adj* multithread, multitraitement

multitrack [mʌltɪtræk] *adj (recording)* multipistes

multitracking [ˌmʌltɪˈtrækɪŋ] *n (in recording)* enregistrement *m* multipistes

multitude [ˈmʌltɪtjuːd] *n* (**a**) *(large number → of people, animals)* multitude *f*; *(→ of details, reasons)* multitude *f*, foule *f*; *Fig* **it covers a multitude of sins** *(job title, definition)* ça peut vouloir dire n'importe quoi; **my new dress covers a multitude of sins!** j'ai pris une robe ample exprès pour cacher mes formes!
(**b**) *(ordinary people)* **the multitude** la multitude, la foule

multitudinous [ˌmʌltɪˈtjuːdɪnəs] *adj* innombrable

multiuser [ˌmʌltɪˈjuːzə(r)] *adj Comput* multi-utilisateur, pour utilisateurs multiples
►► ***multiuser software*** logiciel *m* multi-utilisateur; ***multiuser system*** système *m* multi-utilisateur

multivalence [ˌmʌltɪˈveɪləns] *n Chem* polyvalence *f*

multivalent [ˌmʌltɪˈveɪlənt] *adj Chem* polyvalent

multi-valve *adj* multisoupapes

multivision [ˈmʌltɪvɪʒən] *n* multivision *f*

multivitamin [*Br* ˈmʌltɪˌvɪtəmɪn, *Am* ˈmʌltɪˌvaɪtəmɪn] *n* multivitamine *f*

multiwindow [ˌmʌltɪˈwɪndəʊ] *adj Comput* multifenêtre

mum [mʌm] **1** *adj* **to keep mum** garder le silence; *Fam* **mum's the word!** motus et bouche cousue!
2 *n* (**a**) *Br (mother)* maman *f* (**b**) *Fam (chrysanthemum)* chrysanthème ❑ *m*

mumble [ˈmʌmbəl] **1** *vi* marmonner; **what are you mumbling about?** qu'est-ce que tu as à marmonner comme ça?; **to mumble to oneself** marmonner tout seul; **he mumbled on for half an hour** il a radoté pendant une demi-heure
2 *vt* marmonner; **to mumble an apology** marmonner des excuses
3 *n* paroles *fpl* indistinctes, marmonnement *m*, marmonnements *mpl*; **he replied in a mumble** il marmonna une réponse

mumbler [ˈmʌmblə(r)] *n* marmonneur(euse) *m,f*

mumbling [ˈmʌmblɪŋ] **1** *n* marmonnements *mpl*
2 *adj* qui marmonne

mumbo jumbo [ˌmʌmbəʊˈdʒʌmbəʊ] *n Pej (nonsense)* âneries *fpl*; *(words)* charabia *m*; *(ritual phrases)* bla-bla *m inv*; **it's just a load of mumbo jumbo** tout ça, c'est du charabia; **as far as I'm concerned astrology is just a load of mumbo jumbo** pour moi, l'astrologie n'est que de la superstition ridicule

mummer [ˈmʌmə(r)] *n Theat* mime *mf*

mummery [ˈmʌmərɪ] (*pl* **mummeries**) *n* (**a**) *Pej (ceremony)* cérémonie *f* pompeuse (**b**) *Theat (show)* = spectacle de danses folkloriques dans lequel les danseurs sont masqués

mummification [ˌmʌmɪfɪˈkeɪʃən] *n* momification *f*

mummify [ˈmʌmɪfaɪ] (*pt & pp* **mummified**) **1** *vt* momifier
2 *vi* se momifier

mummy [ˈmʌmɪ] (*pl* **mummies**) *n* (**a**) *(body)* momie *f* (**b**) *Br (mother)* maman *f*
►► *Br Pej* ***mummy's boy*** fils *m* à maman

mumps [mʌmps] *n (UNCOUNT)* oreillons *mpl*; **to have (the) mumps** avoir les oreillons

mumsy [ˈmʌmzɪ] *adj Fam (maternal)* maternel ❑; *Pej (frumpish)* mémère

munch [mʌntʃ] **1** *vt (crunchy food)* croquer; *(food in general)* mâcher
2 *vi* **to munch on an apple** croquer une pomme; **she was munching away at some toast** elle mâchonnait un toast; **he sat there munching away** il restait là à mâchonner; **he munched through a whole packet of biscuits** il a mangé tout un paquet de gâteaux

►**munch out** *vi Am Fam* se goinfrer, s'empiffrer

Munchausen [ˈmʌntʃaʊzən] *n Med* **Munchausen by proxy** syndrome *m* de Münchhausen par procuration
►► ***Munchausen Syndrome*** syndrome *m* de Münchhausen

munchies [ˈmʌntʃɪz] *npl Fam* (**a**) *(desire to eat)* fringale *f*; **to have the munchies** avoir la dalle; **I've got a bad case of the munchies** j'ai la dalle (**b**) *(snacks)* petites choses *fpl* à grignoter, amuse-gueule *mpl*

mundane [mʌnˈdeɪn] *adj (gen)* banal, ordinaire; *(task)* prosaïque

mundaneness [mʌnˈdeɪnnɪs], **mundanity** [mʌnˈdænɪtɪ] *n (gen)* banalité *f*; *(of task)* prosaïsme *m*

mung bean [mʌŋ-] *n* mungo *m*, ambérique *f*

Munich [ˈmjuːnɪk] *n* Munich

municipal [mjuːˈnɪsɪpəl] *adj* municipal, de la ville
►► *Am Fin* ***municipal bond*** obligation *f* de collectivité locale; ***municipal buildings*** ≃ mairie *f*; *(in large town)* hôtel *m* de ville; *Can & Austr* ***municipal district*** ≃ municipalité *f*

municipalism [mjuːˈnɪsɪpəlɪzəm] *n* municipalisme *m*

municipality [mjuːˌnɪsɪˈpælətɪ] (*pl* **municipalities**) *n* municipalité *f*

municipalization [mjuːˌnɪsɪpəlaɪˈzeɪʃən] *n* municipalisation *f*

municipally [mjuːˈnɪsɪpəlɪ] *adv* municipalement

munificence [mjuːˈnɪfɪsəns] *n* munificence *f*

munificent [mjuːˈnɪfɪsənt] *adj* munificent

muniments [ˈmjʊːnɪmənts] *npl Law* titres *mpl*

munitions [mjuːˈnɪʃənz] *npl* munitions *fpl*; **she was a munitions worker** elle travaillait dans une fabrique de munitions
►► ***munitions dump*** dépôt *m* de munitions; ***munitions factory*** fabrique *f* de munitions

Munro [mʌnˈrəʊ] *n (mountain)* = en Écosse, sommet de plus de 3000 pieds (915 mètres)

muntin [ˈmʌntɪn] *n Archit & Constr* montant *m*

muntjac, muntjak [ˈmʌntdʒæk] *n Zool* muntjac *m*

muon [ˈmjuːɒn] *n Phys* muon *m*

muppet [ˈmʌpɪt] *n Br Fam (idiot)* andouille *f*

mural [ˈmjuːərəl] **1** *n (painting)* mural *m*, peinture *f* murale
2 *adj* mural

Murcia [ˈmɜːsɪə] *n* Murcie

murder [ˈmɜːdə(r)] **1** *n* (**a**) *(killing)* meurtre *m*, assassinat *m*; **he's up on a murder charge** il est accusé de meurtre; *Fig* **he gets away with murder** il peut tout se permettre, personne ne lui dit quoi que ce soit; **their kids get away with murder** leurs gosses font absolument tout ce qu'ils veulent
(**b**) *Fam Fig (difficult task, experience)* calvaire *m*, enfer *m*; **the traffic is murder on Fridays** il y a une circulation épouvantable le vendredi; **it's murder trying to get her to agree** ce n'est pas une mince affaire que d'obtenir son consentement; **it's murder trying to park in the town centre** c'est l'enfer pour trouver à se garer dans le centre-ville; **standing all day is murder on your feet** ça fait vachement mal aux pieds de rester debout toute la journée
2 *vt* (**a**) *(kill)* tuer, assassiner; *(slaughter)* tuer, massacrer; *Fam Fig* **I'll murder you (for that)!** je vais te tuer!; *Br Fam* **I could murder a fag/beer** je me taperais bien une clope/une bière
(**b**) *Fam Fig (language, play, song)* massacrer
(**c**) *Fam Fig (defeat)* ratatiner, écraser; **the local team got murdered at the weekend** l'équipe locale s'est fait écraser ce week-end
3 *exclam* à l'assassin!
►► ***murder hunt*** chasse *f* à l'homme *(pour retrouver l'auteur d'un meurtre)*; ***murder mystery*** *(film)* ≃ film *m* policier; *(book)* ≃ roman *m* policier; ***murder mystery weekend*** = jeu de rôle étalé sur un week-end pendant lequel des gens s'amusent à jouer aux détectives après qu'un meurtre fictif a été commis; *Am Law* ***murder one*** assassinat *m*; ***murder trial*** procès *m* pour meurtre; ***murder weapon*** arme *f* du crime

'Murder considered as one of the Fine Arts' *De Quincey* 'De l'assassinat considéré comme un des beaux-arts'

'Murder on the Orient Express' *Christie, Lumet* 'Le Crime de l'Orient-Express'

'The Murders in the Rue Morgue' *Poe* 'Double Assassinat dans la rue Morgue'

murderer [ˈmɜːdərə(r)] *n* meurtrier(ère) *m,f*, assassin *m*

murderess [ˈmɜːdərɪs] *n* meurtrière *f*

murderous [ˈmɜːdərəs] *adj* (**a**) *(deadly → regime, attack, intention)* meurtrier
(**b**) *(hateful → look, expression)* meurtrier, assassin, de haine; **to give sb a murderous look** lancer un regard meurtrier à qn
(**c**) *(dangerous → road, bend)* meurtrier, redoutable
(**d**) *(hellish)* infernal, épouvantable

murderously [ˈmɜːdərəslɪ] *adv* (**a**) *(in a deadly way)* d'une manière meurtrière; **to attack sb murderously** attaquer qn dans l'intention de le tuer (**b**) *(very → difficult, complicated)* incroyablement

mure [mjʊə(r)] *n Arch or Literary (wall)* mur *m*

►**mure in** *vt sep Arch or Literary (town)* murer

►**mure up** *vt sep Arch or Literary* (**a**) *(wall up)* murer (**b**) *(confine)* cloîtrer; **to be mured up in a small room all day** être cloîtré *ou* claquemuré dans une petite chambre pendant toute la journée

murex [ˈmjʊəreks] (*pl* **murexes** *or* **murices** [-rɪsiːz]) *n* murex *m*

murine [ˈmjʊəraɪn, ˈmjʊərɪn] *adj Zool* murin

murk [mɜːk] *n (UNCOUNT)* obscurité *f*, ténèbres *fpl*

murkiness [ˈmɜːkɪnɪs] *n* obscurité *f*

murky [ˈmɜːkɪ] (*compar* **murkier**, *superl* **murkiest**) *adj* (**a**) *(dark → sky, night)* noir, sombre; *(muddy → water)* boueux, trouble; *(dirty → windows, weather)* sale (**b**) *Fig (shameful)* **a murky episode** une histoire sombre *ou* trouble; **to have a murky past** avoir un passé trouble

Murmansk [mɜːˈmænsk] *n* Mourmansk

murmur [ˈmɜːmə(r)] **1** *n* (**a**) *(sound)* murmure *m*; *(of conversation)* bruit *m*, bourdonnement *m*; **there wasn't a murmur** on aurait pu entendre une mouche voler; **without a murmur** sans broncher (**b**) *Med (of heart)* souffle *m*
2 *vt* murmurer; **to murmur excuses** murmurer des excuses
3 *vi* murmurer; **to murmur at** *or* **against sth** murmurer contre qch

murmuring [ˈmɜːmərɪŋ] **1** *n* murmure *m*
2 *adj* murmurant
3 murmurings *npl* murmures *mpl*

murphy [ˈmɜːfɪ] (*pl* **murphies**) *n Br Fam* pomme *f* de terre ❑, patate *f*

Murphy bed [ˈmɜːfɪ-] *n Am* lit *m* escamotable

Murphy's law [ˈmɜːfɪz-] *n* loi *f* de l'emmerdement maximum; **that's Murphy's law!** c'est la poisse!

murrain [ˈmʌrɪn] *n* (**a**) *Arch (plague)* peste *f*; **a murrain on him!** (la) peste soit de lui! (**b**) *Vet* épizootie *f*

Murrayfield [ˈmʌrɪfiːld] *n* = terrain de rugby d'Édimbourg où l'équipe d'Écosse dispute les rencontres internationales

Mururoa (Atoll) [ˈmʊrʊˌrəʊə-] *n* Mururoa; **on Mururoa (Atoll)** à Mururoa

MusB [ˈmʌzbiː], **MusBac** [ˈmʌzbæk] *n Univ (abbr* **Bachelor of Music***) (person)* = titulaire d'une licence de musique; *(qualification)* licence *f* de musique

Muscat [ˈmʌskət] *n* Mascate; **Muscat and Oman** Mascate et Oman

muscatel [ˌmʌskəˈtel] *n* muscat *m*

muscle [ˈmʌsəl] **1** *n* (**a**) *Anat & Zool* muscle *m*; *(strength)* muscle *m*, force *f*; **he has plenty of muscle** il est bien musclé; **she didn't move a muscle** elle est restée parfaitement immobile (**b**) *(UNCOUNT) Fam (strong men)* costauds *mpl*; **we need some muscle to help lift these shelves** on a besoin d'hommes forts pour soulever ces étagères

(**c**) *(influence, power)* puissance *f*, poids *m*; **the drink-driving laws have no muscle** les lois contre l'alcoolisme au volant n'ont aucun poids *ou* impact; **it would give our campaign more muscle** cela donnerait plus de force à notre campagne

2 *vt* muscler; **he has well-muscled arms** il a des bras bien musclés

►► ***muscle fibre*** fibres *fpl* musculaires; ***muscle power*** force *f* physique *ou* musculaire; ***muscle relaxant*** myorelaxant *m*, décontracturant *m*; *Am Fam* ***muscle shirt*** débardeur❑ *m*; *Med* ***muscle strain*** élongation *f*; ***muscle tone*** tonus *m* musculaire; **she's got excellent muscle tone** elle a les muscles très bien dessinés

►**muscle in** *vi Fam* intervenir❑; **to muscle in on sth** intervenir autoritairement dans qch❑; **to muscle one's way in** entrer par la force❑; **a lot of big companies are muscling in** de nombreuses grosses sociétés arrivent en force❑; **we don't want them muscling in** nous ne voulons pas qu'ils marchent sur nos plates-bandes

muscle-bound *adj* (**a**) *(muscular)* extrêmement musclé (**b**) *(rigid)* inflexible, rigide

muscleman ['mʌsəlmæn] *(pl* **musclemen** [-men]) *n (strongman)* hercule *m*; *(bodyguard)* garde *m* du corps, homme *m* de main

muscly ['mʌsəlɪ] *adj* musclé, plein de muscles

muscovado (sugar) [ˌmʌskə'vɑːdəʊ-] *n* cassonade *f*

Muscovite ['mʌskəvaɪt] **1** *n* Moscovite *mf*

2 *adj* moscovite

muscovite ['mʌskəvaɪt] *n Geol* muscovite *f*

Muscovy ['mʌskəvɪ] *n Hist* Moscovie *f*

►► *Orn* ***Muscovy duck*** canard *m* musqué; *Old-fashioned Miner* ***Muscovy glass*** muscovite *f*

muscular ['mʌskjʊlə(r)] *adj* (**a**) *(body, person)* musclé (**b**) *(pain, tissue)* musculaire

►► *Med* ***muscular dystrophy*** *(UNCOUNT)* myopathie *f*

muscularity [ˌmʌskjʊ'lærɪtɪ] *n* (**a**) *(of body, person)* caractère *m* musculeux; *(muscular strength)* vigueur *f* musculaire (**b**) *(of tissue)* muscularité *f*

musculature ['mʌskjʊlətʃə(r)] *n* musculature *f*

MusD ['mʌzdiː], **MusDoc** ['mʌzdɒk] *n Univ (abbr* **Doctor of Music**) *(person)* = titulaire d'un doctorat en musique; *(qualification)* doctorat *m* en musique

Muse [mjuːz] *n Myth* Muse *f*; **the (nine) Muses** les (neuf) Muses *fpl*; *Literary* **the Muse** *(poetry)* la Muse *f*, les Muses *fpl*; *(of poet)* la muse *f*; **to call on one's muse** invoquer sa muse

muse [mjuːz] **1** *vi* rêvasser, songer; **to muse on** *or* **upon** *or* **over sth** songer à qch

2 *vt* **"I wonder what happened to him", she mused** "je me demande bien ce qu'il est devenu", dit-elle d'un air songeur

museology [ˌmjuːzɪ'ɒlədʒɪ] *n* muséologie *f*

museum [mjuː'ziːəm] *n* musée *m*

►► *also Fig* ***museum piece*** pièce *f* de musée

mush¹ [mʌʃ] **1** *n* (**a**) *(food)* bouillie *f*; *Am (porridge)* bouillie *f* de maïs (**b**) *Fam Fig (sentimentality)* mièvrerie *f*

2 *vt* réduire en purée

►**mush up** *vt sep* réduire en purée

mush² [mʊʃ] *n Br Fam* (**a**) *(face)* poire *f*, trombine *f* (**b**) *(term of address)* **oi, mush!** eh, machin!

mush³ [mʌʃ] **1** *n (journey)* trajet *m* en traîneau à chiens

2 *exclam* allez, hue!, *Can* marche!

3 *vi (drive a sled)* conduire un traîneau à chiens

musher ['mʌʃə(r)] *n* (**a**) *(person)* conducteur *m* de traîneau à chiens (**b**) *(competition)* course *f* de traîneaux à chiens

mushing ['mʌʃɪŋ] *n (racing)* courses *fpl* de traîneaux à chiens

mushroom ['mʌʃrʊm] **1** *n* (**a**) *(fungus, nuclear cloud)* champignon *m*

(**b**) *Sewing* boule *f* à repriser

(**c**) *(colour)* beige *m* rosé

2 *adj (colour)* beige rosé *(inv)*

3 *comp (soup, omelette)* aux champignons

4 *vi* (**a**) *(gather mushrooms)* **to go mushrooming** aller aux champignons

(**b**) *(spring up)* pousser comme des champignons; **video shops mushroomed in almost every town** les magasins de vidéo se sont multipliés dans presque toutes les villes

(**c**) *(grow quickly)* s'étendre, prendre de l'ampleur; **the conflict mushroomed into full-scale war** le conflit a vite dégénéré en véritable guerre; **a mushrooming estate** un lotissement qui s'étend rapidement

►► ***mushroom cloud*** champignon *m* atomique; ***mushroom farm*** champignonnière *f*; ***mushroom grower*** champignonniste *mf*; *Fig* ***mushroom growth*** poussée *f ou* croissance *f* rapide; ***mushroom town*** ville *f* champignon

mushrooming ['mʌʃruːmɪŋ] *n* (**a**) *(mushroom picking)* cueillette *f* des champignons (**b**) *(rapid growth)* croissance *f* exponentielle

mushy ['mʌʃɪ] *(compar* **mushier**, *superl* **mushiest**) *adj* (**a**) *(vegetables)* en bouillie; *(fruit)* trop mûr, blet; *(ground)* détrempé (**b**) *Fam Fig (sentimental)* à l'eau de rose, mièvre

►► ***mushy peas*** purée *f* de petits pois

music ['mjuːzɪk] **1** *n* musique *f*; *(score)* partition *f*, musique *f*; **to set to music** mettre en musique; **to read music** lire une partition; **the news was music to my ears** la nouvelle m'a fait très plaisir *ou* m'a ravi

2 *comp (teacher, lesson, festival)* de musique

►► ***music box*** boîte *f* à musique; ***music case*** porte-musique *m inv*; *Old fashioned* ***music centre*** chaîne *f* (midi); ***music hall*** **1** *n (theatre)* théâtre *m* de variétés; *(entertainment)* music-hall *m* **2** *comp (song, artist)* de music-hall; ***music paper*** papier *m* à musique; ***music press*** presse *f* musicale; ***music stand*** pupitre *m* (à musique); ***music station*** station *f* musicale; ***music video*** clip *m* (vidéo)

musical ['mjuːzɪkəl] **1** *adj* (**a**) *(evening, taste, composition)* musical; *(instrument)* de musique

(**b**) *(person)* musicien; **they are a musical family** *(liking music)* c'est une famille de mélomanes; *(including musicians)* c'est une famille de musiciens; **I'm not very musical** je n'ai pas tellement l'oreille musicale

(**c**) *(pleasant → voice, chimes)* musical

2 *n* comédie *f* musicale, musical *m*

►► *Br* ***musical box*** boîte *f* à musique; *also Fig* ***musical chairs*** jeu *m* des chaises musicales; ***musical comedy*** comédie *f* musicale, musical *m*; ***musical director*** directeur(trice) *m,f* musical(e); ***musical instrument*** instrument *m* de musique

musicality [ˌmjuːzɪ'kælɪtɪ] *n* musicalité *f*

musically ['mjuːzɪklɪ] *adv (in a musical way)* musicalement; *(from a musical viewpoint)* musicalement, d'un point de vue musical

musician [mjuː'zɪʃən] *n* musicien(enne) *m,f*

musicianship [mjuː'zɪʃənʃɪp] *n* don *m* pour la musique

music-lover *n* mélomane *mf*

musicologist [ˌmjuːzɪ'kɒlədʒɪst] *n* musicologue *mf*

musicology [ˌmjuːzɪ'kɒlədʒɪ] *n* musicologie *f*

musing ['mjuːzɪŋ] **1** *n (UNCOUNT)* songes *mpl*, rêverie *f*

2 *adj* songeur, rêveur

3 **musings** *npl* songeries *fpl*

musingly ['mjuːzɪŋlɪ] *adv* pensivement; **"I don't know", she answered musingly** "je ne sais pas", répondit-elle songeuse *ou* d'un air songeur

musk [mʌsk] *n* (**a**) *(smell)* musc *m* (**b**) *Bot* mimule *m* musqué

►► *Zool* ***musk cat*** civette *f*; *Zool* ***musk deer*** porte-musc *m*; *Bot* ***musk mallow*** mauve *f* musquée; *Bot* ***musk monkeyflower*** mimule *m* musqué; *Bot* ***musk orchid*** herminium *m* à un bulbe; *Zool* ***musk ox*** bœuf *m* musqué, ovibos *m*; *Bot* ***musk rose*** *(flower)* rose *f* musquée; *(bush)* rosier *m* musqué

musket ['mʌskɪt] *n* mousquet *m*

musketeer [ˌmʌskɪ'tɪə(r)] *n* mousquetaire *m*

musketry ['mʌskɪtrɪ] *n (UNCOUNT)* (**a**) *(muskets)* mousquets *mpl* (**b**) *(musketeers)* mousquetaires *mpl*

muskiness ['mʌskɪnɪs] *n (smell)* odeur *f* de musc; *(taste)* goût *m* de musc

muskmelon ['mʌskˌmelən] *n* melon *m*

muskrat ['mʌskræt] *(pl* **inv** *or* **muskrats**) *n* (**a**) *Zool* rat *m* musqué, ondatra *m* (**b**) *(fur)* rat *m* d'Amérique, loutre *f* d'Hudson

musky ['mʌskɪ] *(compar* **muskier**, *superl* **muskiest**) *adj* musqué

Muslim ['mʊzlɪm] **1** *n* musulman(e) *m,f*

2 *adj* musulman

muslin ['mʌzlɪn] *Tex* **1** *n* mousseline *f*

2 *comp* de *ou* en mousseline

►► *Culin* ***muslin bag*** nouet *m*

muso ['mjuːzəʊ] *n Br Fam (abbr* **musician**) musico *m*

musquash ['mʌskwɒʃ] *n* (**a**) *Zool* rat *m* musqué, ondatra *m* (**b**) *(fur)* rat *m* d'Amérique, loutre *f* d'Hudson

muss [mʌs] *vt Fam (rumple)* friper❑, froisser❑; *(dirty)* salir❑; **don't muss my hair** ne me décoiffe pas❑

►**muss up** *vt sep Am Fam* (**a**) *(rumple)* friper❑, froisser❑; *(dirty)* salir❑ (**b**) *(upset → plans)* ficher par terre

mussel ['mʌsəl] *n* moule *f*

►► ***mussel bed*** parc *m* à moules; ***mussel farm*** moulière *f*

Mussorgsky [mʊ'sɔːgskɪ] *pr n* Moussorgski

MUST¹ [məs, məst, *stressed* mʌst] **1** *v aux* (**a**) *(expressing necessity, obligation)* devoir; **you must lock the door** vous devez fermer *ou* il faut que vous fermiez la porte à clé; **you must hurry up** il faut vous dépêcher; **I must go now** il faut que je parte (maintenant); **the system must change** il faut que le système change; **I must admit the idea intrigues me** je dois avouer que l'idée m'intrigue; **he is stupid, I must say** il est stupide, je dois l'avouer; *Ironic* **very clever, I must say!** je dois dire que c'est très astucieux!; **I must say I thought it was rather good** je dois dire que c'était très bien; **if I/you/***etc* **must** s'il le faut; **I can't! – you must!** je ne peux pas! – mais il le faut!; **if you must know, he's asked me out to dinner** si tu veux tout savoir, il m'a invitée à dîner; **this I must see!** il faut que je voie ça!; **you really must see his latest film** il faut vraiment que tu voies son dernier film; **must you be so rude?** es-tu obligé d'être aussi grossier?; **they told us we must leave** ils nous ont dit qu'il fallait que nous partions, ils nous ont dit que nous devions partir; **you mustn't smoke** il est interdit de fumer; **you mustn't tell anyone** vous ne devez le dire à personne, il ne faut le dire à personne; **I mustn't say any more** je n'ai pas le droit d'en dire plus; **we mustn't be late** il ne faut pas que nous soyons en retard; **they told us we mustn't come before 10 o'clock** ils nous ont dit de ne pas arriver avant 10 heures; **you mustn't forget to press this button** n'oubliez (surtout) pas d'appuyer sur ce bouton; **if you must drink so much, what do you expect?** si tu t'entêtes à boire autant, il ne faut pas t'étonner!

(**b**) *(suggesting, inviting)* **you must meet my wife** il faut que vous rencontriez *ou* fassiez la connaissance de ma femme; **you must come and see us** il faut (absolument) que vous veniez nous voir

(**c**) *(expressing likelihood)* devoir; **you must be Alison** vous devez être Alison; **you must be famished** vous devez être morts de faim; **it must be very hard for you** ça doit être très dur pour toi; **there must be thousands of them!** il doit y en avoir des milliers!; **you must be joking!** tu plaisantes!; **if he says so it must be true** s'il le dit, c'est que c'est vrai

(**d**) *(with "have" + past participle) (making assumptions, stating requirements)* **she must have forgotten** elle a dû oublier, elle a sans doute oublié; **has she forgotten? – she must have** elle a oublié? – sans doute *ou* certainement; **you must have known!** vous le saviez sûrement!; **was it her? – it must have been** est-ce que c'était elle? – oui, je pense; **there must have been at least a thousand people** il devait y avoir au moins un millier de personnes; **I saw that he must have suspected something** j'ai bien vu qu'il avait dû se douter de quelque chose; **before applying**

candidates must have successfully completed all their exams les candidats doivent avoir obtenu tous leurs examens avant de se présenter

2 *n Fam* **sunglasses are a must** les lunettes de soleil sont absolument indispensables❑; **this film/his new album is a must** il faut absolument avoir vu ce film/acheter son dernier album❑; **fake fur is a must this year** la fausse fourrure est un must cette année

---

must² [mʌst] *n* (**a**) *(mould)* moisissure *f* (**b**) *(for wine)* moût *m*

mustache ['mʌstæʃ] *Am* = **moustache**

mustached ['mʌstæʃt] *Am* = **moustached**

mustachio [mə'stɑːʃɪəʊ] *(pl* **mustachios**) *n* (longue) moustache *f*

mustachioed [mə'stɑːʃɪəʊd] *adj* moustachu

mustang ['mʌstæŋ] *n* mustang *m*

mustard ['mʌstəd] **1** *n* moutarde *f*; *Fam Fig* **to cut the mustard** se montrer à la hauteur; **mustard and cress** = mélange de cresson alénois et de pousses de moutarde blanche utilisé en salade

2 *adj (colour)* moutarde *(inv)*

►► ***mustard bath*** bain *m* sinapisé; ***mustard gas*** gaz *m* moutarde, ypérite *f*; ***mustard plaster*** sinapisme *m*; ***mustard pot*** moutardier *m*, pot *m* à moutarde; ***mustard powder*** farine *f* de moutarde; ***mustard seed*** graine *f* de moutarde

muster ['mʌstə(r)] **1** *vt* (**a**) *(gather → troops)* rassembler, réunir; *(→ courage, energy)* rassembler; *(→ finance, cash)* réunir; **they were unable to muster enough support** ils n'ont pas pu trouver suffisamment de gens pour soutenir leur initiative; **she mustered all her strength** elle a rassemblé toutes ses forces; **to muster one's courage to do sth** prendre son courage à deux mains pour faire qch

(**b**) *(take roll-call of)* faire l'appel de

2 *vi* se rassembler

3 *n* (**a**) *Mil* revue *f*, inspection *f*; *Br Fig* **to pass muster** *(in dress, appearance)* être présentable; *(in content)* être acceptable; **I don't know whether your account of the facts will pass muster** je ne sais pas si votre version des faits sera acceptée *ou* si on acceptera votre version des faits

(**b**) *(assembly)* rassemblement *m*

►► ***muster roll*** feuille *f* d'appel; ***muster station*** point *m* de ralliement

►**muster in** *vt sep Am Mil* incorporer, engager

►**muster out** *vt sep Am Mil* libérer (des obligations militaires)

►**muster up** *vt insep (courage)* rassembler; **to muster up support** chercher à obtenir un soutien *ou* un appui

must-have 1 *n* must *m*

2 *adj* **the latest must-have accessory** le must en matière d'accessoires

mustiness ['mʌstɪnɪs] *n (of smell)* odeur *f* de moisi; *(of room)* odeur *f* de renfermé

Mustique [mʊ'stiːk] *n* Moustique, l'île *f* Moustique; **in** *or* **on Mustique** à Moustique

mustn't ['mʌsənt] = **must not**

must-see 1 *n* **that film/TV programme is a must-see** il ne faut surtout pas manquer ce film/cette émission de télévision, ce film/cette émission de télévision est à voir absolument

2 *adj* **the latest must-see film/TV series** le dernier film/la dernière série télévisée à voir absolument *ou* à ne pas manquer

must've ['mʌstəv] = **must have**

musty ['mʌstɪ] *(compar* **mustier**, *superl* **mustiest**) *adj* (**a**) *(smell)* de moisi; *(books)* qui sent le moisi; *(room)* qui sent le renfermé (**b**) *Fig (old-fashioned)* suranné, vieux jeu *(inv)*; **musty ideas** idées *fpl* dépassées

mutability [,mjuːtə'bɪlətɪ] *n* mutabilité *f*

mutable ['mjuːtəbəl] *adj (gen)* mutable; *Astrol* mutable, commun

mutagen ['mjuːtədʒən] *adj Biol* mutagène

mutant ['mjuːtənt] **1** *n* mutant(e) *m,f*

2 *adj* mutant

mutase ['mjuːteɪz] *n Biol & Chem* mutase *f*

mutate [mjuː'teɪt] **1** *vt* faire subir une mutation à

2 *vi* (**a**) *(gen)* subir une mutation; **to mutate into sth** se transformer en qch (**b**) *Biol* muter

mutation [mjuː'teɪʃən] *n* mutation *f*

mute [mjuːt] **1** *adj* (**a**) *Med* muet (**b**) *Ling (vowel, letter)* muet (**c**) *(silent → person)* muet, silencieux; *(unspoken → feeling)* muet; **to stand mute** rester muet *ou* silencieux

2 *vt (sound)* amortir, atténuer; *(feelings, colour)* atténuer; **to mute the sound** *(on TV)* mettre en sourdine

3 *n* (**a**) *Med* muet(ette) *m,f* (**b**) *Mus* sourdine *f*

►► *Orn* ***mute swan*** cygne *m* muet *ou* tuberculé

muted ['mjuːtɪd] *adj* (**a**) *(sound)* assourdi, amorti, atténué; *(voice)* feutré, sourd; *(colour)* sourd; *(criticism, protest)* voilé; *(applause)* faible; **to discuss sth in muted tones** discuter qch à voix basse (**b**) *Mus* en sourdine

mutely ['mjuːtlɪ] *adv (stare, gaze)* en silence

muteness ['mjuːtnɪs] *n* (**a**) *Med* mutisme *m* (**b**) *(silence)* mutisme *m*, silence *m*

mutilate ['mjuːtɪleɪt] *vt* (**a**) *(maim → body, face)* mutiler (**b**) *(damage → property, object)* dégrader, détériorer (**c**) *(adulterate → text)* mutiler

mutilation [,mjuːtɪ'leɪʃən] *n* (**a**) *(of body, face)* mutilation *f* (**b**) *(of property, object)* détérioration *f*, dégradation *f* (**c**) *(of text)* mutilation *f*

mutineer [,mjuːtɪ'nɪə(r)] *n* mutin *m*, mutiné(e) *m,f*

mutinous ['mjuːtɪnəs] *adj* (**a**) *(rebellious → crew, soldiers)* mutiné, rebelle; **the inmates of the prison were mutinous** les détenus étaient au bord de la rébellion (**b**) *(unruly → child)* indiscipliné, rebelle

mutinously ['mjuːtɪnəslɪ] *adv (behave)* comme un rebelle; *(say)* sur un ton de rébellion

mutinousness ['mjuːtɪnəsnɪs] *n* tendance *f* à la révolte, insoumission *f*

mutiny ['mjuːtɪnɪ] *(pl* **mutinies**) **1** *n (on ship)* mutinerie *f*; *(in prison, barracks)* rébellion *f*, mutinerie *f*; *(in city)* soulèvement *m*, révolte *f*

2 *vi* se mutiner, se rebeller

'Mutiny on the Bounty' *Lloyd* 'Les Révoltés du Bounty'

'The Caine Mutiny' *Wouk, Dmytryk* 'Ouragan sur le Caine'

---

mutism ['mjuːtɪzəm] *n (gen) & Psy* mutisme *m*; *Med* mutité *f*

mutt [mʌt] *n Fam* (**a**) *(dog)* clébard *m* (**b**) *(fool)* crétin(e) *m,f*, andouille *f*

mutter ['mʌtə(r)] **1** *vt (mumble)* marmonner, grommeler; **he muttered a threat** il grommela *ou* marmonna une menace; **he muttered something and left** il marmonna quelque chose et sortit

2 *vi* (**a**) *(mumble)* marmonner, parler dans sa barbe *ou* entre ses dents; **what are you muttering about?** qu'est-ce que tu as à marmonner?; **to mutter to oneself** marmonner tout seul

(**b**) *(grumble)* grommeler, grogner

3 *n* murmure *m*, murmures *mpl*, marmonnement *m*; **this provoked mutters of discontent** cela a provoqué un murmure de mécontentement; **to speak in a mutter** marmonner dans sa barbe

muttering ['mʌtərɪŋ] *n* marmottement *m*

mutton ['mʌtən] **1** *n (meat)* mouton *m*; **she's mutton dressed as lamb** elle joue les jeunesses

2 *comp (chop, stew)* de mouton

muttonchops [,mʌtən'tʃɒps], **muttonchop whiskers** *npl* favoris *mpl (bien fournis)*

muttonhead ['mʌtənhed] *n Fam* crétin(e) *m,f*

mutual ['mjuːtʃʊəl] *adj* (**a**) *(reciprocal → admiration, help)* mutuel, réciproque; **the feeling is mutual** c'est réciproque; *Fam Pej* **a mutual admiration** *or* **appreciation society** = personnes qui passent leur temps à se faire des compliments; *Hum* **sorry to break up this mutual admiration** *or* **appreciation society, but...** désolé d'interrompre ce touchant échange de congratulations, mais...

(**b**) *(shared → friend, interest)* commun; **by mutual consent** à l'amiable, par consentement mutuel

►► *Am Nucl* ***mutual assured destruction*** destruction *f* mutuelle assurée, équilibre *m* des forces; *Fin* ***mutual benefit society*** société *f* de secours mutuel; *Am Fin* ***mutual fund*** *(unit trust)* fonds *m* commun de placement; *Fin* ***mutual insurance*** (assurance *f*) mutuelle *f*; *Fin* ***mutual insurance company*** société *f* de crédit mutuel, société *f* de mutualité

'Our Mutual Friend' *Dickens* 'Notre ami commun'

---

mutuality [,mjuːtjʊ'ælətɪ] *n* réciprocité *f*

mutually ['mjuːtʃʊəlɪ] *adv* mutuellement, réciproquement; **mutually exclusive** qui s'excluent l'un l'autre

Muzak® ['mjuːzæk] *n* musique *f* de fond, fond *m* sonore

muzziness ['mʌzɪnɪs] *n Br* (**a**) *(of mind, ideas)* confusion *f*, flou *m* (**b**) *(of picture, outline)* flou *m*, manque *m* de netteté

muzzle ['mʌzəl] **1** *n* (**a**) *(for dog, horse)* muselière *f* (**b**) *Fig (censorship)* bâillon *m*, censure *f* (**c**) *(of gun)* canon *m* (**d**) *(of animal)* museau *m*

2 *vt* (**a**) *(animal)* museler, mettre une muselière à (**b**) *Fig (speaker)* museler, empêcher de s'exprimer librement; *(press)* bâillonner, museler

►► ***muzzle velocity*** vitesse *f* initiale

muzzle-loader *n* = arme à feu dont le chargement s'opère par la bouche

muzzy ['mʌzɪ] *(compar* **muzzier**, *superl* **muzziest**) *adj Br* (**a**) *(person)* aux idées embrouillées; *(mind)* confus; *(ideas)* embrouillé, flou; **my head feels a bit muzzy** j'ai la tête qui tourne (**b**) *(picture)* flou, indistinct

MV [,em'viː] *n* (**a**) *Elec (abbr* **megavolt(s)**) MV (**b**) *Naut (abbr* **motor vessel**) bateau *m* à moteur

MVP [,emviː'piː] *n Am Sport (abbr* **most valuable player**) = titre décerné au meilleur joueur d'une équipe

MW [,em'dʌbəljuː] *n* (**a**) *Elec (abbr* **megawatt(s)**) MW (**b**) *Rad (abbr* **Medium Wave**) PO *fpl*

MX [,em'eks] *n (abbr* **missile-experimental**) = missile américain MX

my [maɪ] **1** *adj* (**a**) *(belonging to me → singular)* mon (ma); *(→ plural)* mes; **my dog/car/ear** mon chien/ma voiture/mon oreille; **my dogs/cars/ears** mes chiens/voitures/oreilles; **my hat and gloves** mon chapeau et mes gants; **I never use my own car** je n'utilise jamais ma voiture (personnelle); **I have a car of my own** j'ai une voiture (à moi); **this is MY chair** cette chaise est à moi; **one of my friends** un de mes amis, un ami à moi; **I've broken my glasses** j'ai cassé mes lunettes; **I've broken my arm** je me suis cassé le bras; **she looked into my eyes** elle m'a regardé dans les yeux; **if you don't mind my asking** si je peux me permettre de vous le demander

(**b**) *(in terms of affection)* **my dear** *or* **darling** *(to man)* mon chéri; *(to woman)* ma chérie

(**c**) *(in titles)* **my Lord** *(to judge)* Monsieur le juge; *(to nobleman)* Monsieur le Comte/le Duc; *(to bishop)* Monseigneur

(**d**) *(in exclamations)* **oh, my God!** oh! mon Dieu!

2 *exclam* oh là là!; **my, but you've grown!** oh là là! *ou* dis donc, qu'est-ce que tu as poussé!; **my, my! aren't we touchy!** oh là là! que vous êtes susceptible!

myalgia [maɪ'ældʒə] *n* myalgie *f*

myalgic encephalomyelitis [maɪ'ældʒɪken-,sefələʊ,maɪ'laɪtɪs] *n Med* encéphalomyélite *f* myalgique

Myanman [,maɪæn'mæn] **1** *n* habitant(e) *m,f* du Myanmar

2 *adj* du Myanmar

Myanmar [,maɪæn'mɑː(r)] *n* Myanmar *m*; **in Myanmar** au Myanmar

Myanmarese [,maɪænmə'riːz] *(pl* **inv**) **1** *n* habitant(e) *m,f* du Myanmar

2 *adj* du Myanmar

myasthenia [,maɪəs'θiːnɪə] *n Med* myasthénie *f*

mycelium [maɪ'siːlɪəm] *(pl* **mycelia** [-lɪə]) *n Bot* mycélium *m*, mycélion *m*

Mycenae [maɪ'siːniː] *n* Mycènes

Mycenaean [,maɪsɪ'niːən] **1** *n* Mycénien(enne) *m,f*

2 *adj* mycénien

mycologic [,maɪkə'lɒdʒɪk], **mycological** [,maɪkə-'lɒdʒɪkəl] *adj Bot* mycologique

mycologist [maɪ'kɒlədʒɪst] *n Bot* mycologue *mf*

mycology [maɪ'kɒlədʒɪ] *n Bot* mycologie *f*

mycorhiza, mycorrhiza [ˌmaɪkəˈraɪzə] *n Bot* mycorhize *f*

mycosis [maɪˈkəʊsɪs] *n* mycose *f*

mycotoxin [ˌmaɪkəʊˈtɒksɪn] *n* mycotoxine *f*

mydriasis [mɪˈdraɪəsɪs] *n Med* mydriase *f*

mydriatic [ˌmɪdrɪˈætɪk] *Pharm* **1** *n* mydriatique *m*
 2 *adj* mydriatique

myelin [ˈmaɪəlɪn] *n* myéline *f*

myelinated [ˈmaɪəlɪˌneɪtɪd] *adj* myélinisé

myelitis [ˌmaɪəˈlaɪtɪs] *n Med* myélite *f*

myeloma [ˌmaɪəˈləʊmə] *n Med* myélome *m*

mylonite [ˈmaɪlənaɪt] *n Geol* mylonite *f*

myna(h) (bird) [ˈmaɪnə-] *n Orn* martin *m*; *(Gracula religiosa)* mainate *m*

MYOB [ˌemwaɪˌəʊˈbiː] *exclam (abbr* **mind your own business**) occupez-vous de vos affaires!

myocardial [ˌmaɪəʊˈkɑːdɪəl] *adj*
 ▸▸ *Med* ***myocardial infarction*** infarctus *m* du myocarde

myocarditis [ˌmaɪəʊkɑːˈdaɪtɪs] *n Med* myocardite *f*

myocardium [ˌmaɪəʊˈkɑːdɪəm] *(pl* **myocardia** [-dɪə]) *n Anat* myocarde *m*

myocyte [ˈmaɪəʊsaɪt] *n* myocyte *m*

myofibril [ˌmaɪəʊˈfaɪbrɪl] *n Anat* myofibrille *f*

myoglobin [ˌmaɪəʊˈgləʊbɪn] *n Biol & Chem* myoglobine *f*

myologic [ˌmaɪəˈlɒdʒɪk], **myological** [ˌmaɪəˈlɒdʒɪkəl] *adj Anat* myologique

myologist [maɪˈɒlədʒɪst] *n Anat* myologiste *mf*

myology [maɪˈɒlədʒɪ] *n Anat* myologie *f*

myopathic [ˌmaɪəʊˈpæθɪk] *adj Med* myopathique

myopathy [maɪˈɒpəθɪ] *n Med* myopathie *f*

myopia [maɪˈəʊpjə] *n* myopie *f*

myopic [maɪˈɒpɪk] *adj* myope; *Fig* **they have a myopic view of things** ils ne voient pas plus loin que le bout de leur nez

myosin [maɪˈəʊsɪn] *n Biol & Chem* myosine *f*

myotonia [ˌmaɪəˈtəʊnɪə] *n* myotonie *f*

myriad [ˈmɪrɪəd] **1** *n* myriade *f*
 2 *adj Literary* innombrable

myriapod [ˈmɪrɪəpɒd] *Entom* **1** *n* myriapode *m*
 2 *adj* = relatif aux myriapodes

myrmecologist [ˌmɜːmɪˈkɒlədʒɪst] *n Zool* myrmécologiste *mf*

myrmecology [ˌmɜːmɪˈkɒlədʒɪ] *n Zool* myrmécologie *f*

myrmecophile [ˈmɜːmɪkəˌfaɪl] *n Zool* myrmécophile *mf*

myrmecophilous [ˌmɜːmɪkəˈfɪləs] *adj Zool* myrmécophile

Myrmidon [ˈmɜːmɪdən] *n* (**a**) *Myth* Myrmidon *m* (**b**) *Fig (follower)* acolyte *m*

myrrh [mɜː(r)] *n* myrrhe *f*

myrtle [ˈmɜːtəl] *n* myrte *m*

myself [maɪˈself] *pron* (**a**) *(reflexive use)* **may I help myself?** puis-je me servir?; **I knitted myself a cardigan** je me suis tricoté un gilet; *Hum* **it doesn't taste bad, though I say so** *or* **it myself** sans fausse modestie, ça n'est pas mauvais; **I can see myself reflected in the water** je vois mon reflet dans l'eau; **I can't see myself going on holiday this year** je ne crois pas que je pourrai partir en vacances cette année; **I took it upon myself to answer** j'ai pris sur moi de répondre
 (**b**) *(replacing "me")* **the group included myself and Liz** Liz et moi faisions partie du groupe; **it is meant for people like myself** c'est fait pour les gens comme moi; **I'm not (feeling) myself today** je ne me sens pas très bien *ou* je ne suis pas dans mon assiette aujourd'hui
 (**c**) *(emphatic use)* **I'm not a great fan of opera myself** personnellement, je ne suis pas un passionné d'opéra; **I'm a stranger here myself** je ne suis pas d'ici non plus; **I myself saw him leave** je l'ai vu partir de mes propres yeux; **I myself** *or* **myself, I don't believe him** pour ma part, je ne le crois pas; **I was left all by myself** on m'a laissé tout seul
 (**d**) *(unaided, alone)* moi-même; **I can do it myself** je peux le faire moi-même *ou* tout seul; **I made the pattern myself** j'ai fait le patron moi-même

mysterious [mɪˈstɪərɪəs] *adj* mystérieux

mysteriously [mɪˈstɪərɪəslɪ] *adv* mystérieusement

mysteriousness [mɪˈstɪərɪəsnɪs] *n* caractère *m* mystérieux, mystère *m*

mystery [ˈmɪstərɪ] *(pl* **mysteries**) **1** *n* (**a**) *(strange or unexplained event)* mystère *m*; **it's a mystery to me why she came** la raison de sa venue est un mystère pour moi, je n'ai aucune idée de la raison pour laquelle elle est venue; **his past is a mystery** son passé est bien mystérieux; **there's no mystery about that** ça n'a rien de mystérieux, cela n'est un mystère pour personne
 (**b**) *(strangeness)* mystère *m*; **she has a certain mystery about her** il se dégage de sa personne une impression de mystère
 (**c**) *(story)* histoire *f* policière
 (**d**) *Theat & Rel* mystère *m*
 2 *comp (man, voice)* mystérieux
 ▸▸ *Theat* ***mystery play*** mystère *m*; *Mktg* ***mystery shopper*** client(e) *m,f* mystère; *Mktg* ***mystery shopping*** pseudo-achat *m*; ***mystery story*** histoire *f* policière; ***mystery tour*** = excursion dont la destination est inconnue des participants

mystic [ˈmɪstɪk] **1** *n* mystique *mf*
 2 *adj* mystique

mystical [ˈmɪstɪkəl] *adj* (**a**) *Phil & Rel* mystique (**b**) *(occult)* occulte

mystically [ˈmɪstɪkəlɪ] *adv* mystiquement, avec mysticisme

mysticism [ˈmɪstɪsɪzəm] *n* mysticisme *m*

mystification [ˌmɪstɪfɪˈkeɪʃən] *n* mystification *f*

mystified [ˈmɪstɪfaɪd] *adj* perplexe

mystify [ˈmɪstɪfaɪ] *(pt & pp* **mystified**) *vt (puzzle)* déconcerter, laisser *ou* rendre perplexe; *(deceive)* mystifier

mystifying [ˈmɪstɪfaɪɪŋ] *adj* inexplicable, déconcertant

mystique [mɪˈstiːk] *n* mystique *f*, côté *m* mystique

myth [mɪθ] *n* mythe *m*

mythical [ˈmɪθɪkəl] *adj* mythique

mythicize, -ise [ˈmɪθɪsaɪz] *vt* (**a**) *(natural phenomenon)* donner un caractère mythique à (**b**) *(Holy Scripture)* interpréter mythologiquement

mythmaker [ˈmɪθˌmeɪkə(r)] *n* créateur(trice) *m,f* de mythes

mythographer [mɪˈθɒgrəfə(r)] *n* mythographe *mf*

mythography [mɪˈθɒgrəfɪ] *n* mythographie *f*

mythological [ˌmɪθəˈlɒdʒɪkəl] *adj* mythologique

mythologically [ˌmɪθəˈlɒdʒɪkəlɪ] *adv* mythologiquement

mythologize, -ise [mɪˈθɒlədʒaɪz] **1** *vt (event)* donner un caractère mythique à; *(person)* transformer en personnage mythique
 2 *vi* créer des mythes

mythology [mɪˈθɒlədʒɪ] *(pl* **mythologies**) *n* mythologie *f*

mythomania [ˌmɪθəˈmeɪnɪə] *n* mythomanie *f*

mythomaniac [ˌmɪθəˈmeɪnɪæk] **1** *n* mythomane *mf*
 2 *adj* mythomane

mythopoeic [ˌmɪθəʊˈpiːɪk], **mythopoetic** [ˌmɪθəʊpəʊˈetɪk] *adj* qui crée des mythes

myxoedema, *Am* **myxedema** [ˌmɪksɪˈdiːmə] *n Med* myxœdème *m*

myxoma [mɪkˈsəʊmə] *n Biol & Med* myxome *m*

myxomatosis [ˌmɪksəməˈtəʊsɪs] *n Vet* myxomatose *f*

myxomycete [ˌmɪksəʊmaɪˈsiːt] *n* myxomycète *m*

myxovirus [ˈmɪksəʊvaɪrəs] *n* myxovirus *m*

N

N¹, n¹ [en] *n (letter)* N, n *m inv*; **two n's** deux n; **N for Norman** ≃ N comme Nicolas

N² *(written abbr* **North***)* N

n² [en] *n Math* n *m*; **x to the power of n** x puissance n; **there are n possible solutions** il y a trente-six solutions possibles

'n' [ən] *conj Fam (abbr* **and***)* et❑; **fish 'n' chips** poisson-frites❑ *m*

n/a, N/A *(written abbr* **not applicable***)* s.o.

NA [ˌen'eɪ] *n Am (abbr* **Narcotics Anonymous***)* = association américaine d'aide aux toxicomanes

NAACP [ˌeneɪˌeɪsiː'piː] *n Am (abbr* **National Association for the Advancement of Colored People***)* = ligue américaine pour la défense des droits de la population noire

Naafi ['næfɪ] *n Br Mil (abbr* **Navy, Army, and Air Force Institutes***) (organization)* = organisme approvisionnant les forces armées britanniques en biens de consommation; *(canteen)* cantine *f* militaire; *(shop)* magasin *m* réservé aux militaires

naan [nɑːn] *n* = pain plat indien
►► ***naan bread*** = pain plat indien

nab [næb] *(pt & pp* **nabbed,** *cont* **nabbing***) vt Fam* (**a**) *(catch, arrest)* pincer, alpaguer; **they got nabbed as they were leaving the building** ils se sont fait pincer alors qu'ils sortaient du bâtiment (**b**) *(catch → to speak to)* coincer, agrafer (**c**) *(steal, take)* piquer, faucher; *(→ seat)* prendre❑, accaparer❑; *(→ parking place)* piquer

nabla ['næblə] *n* (**a**) *Mus* nabla *m* (**b**) *Math* (opérateur) nabla *m*

nabob ['neɪbɒb] *n* nabab *m*

nacelle [næ'sel] *n* (**a**) *(of aircraft)* carlingue *f*, habitacle *m* (**b**) *(of airship, balloon)* nacelle *f*

nachos ['nætʃəʊz] *npl Culin* nachos *mpl*

nacre ['neɪkə(r)] *n* nacre *f*

nacreous ['neɪkrɪəs] *adj* nacré

NACU [ˌeneɪsiː'juː] *n Am (abbr* **National Association of Colleges and Universities***)* = association des établissements d'enseignement supérieur américains

nadir ['neɪdɪə(r)] *n* (**a**) *Astron* nadir *m* (**b**) *Fig (lowest point)* point *m* le plus bas *ou* profond; **to reach a nadir** être au plus bas, toucher le fond, atteindre le niveau le plus bas

naevus, *Am* **nevus** ['niːvəs] *(Br pl* **naevi,** *Am pl* **nevi** [-vaɪ]*) n Med* nævus *m*

naff [næf] *Br Fam* **1** *adj (clothes, place, person)* ringard; *(comment, behaviour)* débile
2 *adj* **naff all** que dalle; **I've got naff all money** j'ai que dalle comme argent

►**naff off** *vi Br Fam* s'arracher, se casser; **naff off!** *(go away)* tire-toi!, casse-toi!; *(as refusal)* arrête ton char!; *(expressing contempt, disagreement)* va te faire voir!

naffing ['næfɪŋ] *Br Fam* **1** *adj (for emphasis)* foutu, sacré; **shut your naffing mouth!** fermela!, ferme ton clapet!; **naffing hell!** putain!
2 *adv (for emphasis)* vachement; **you're so naffing stupid!** t'es vraiment débile!; **you're naffing well coming with me!** tu viens avec moi, un point c'est tout!

NAFTA ['næftə] *n (abbr* **North American Free Trade Agreement***)* ALENA *m*

nag [næg] *(pt & pp* **nagged,** *cont* **nagging***)* **1** *vt* (**a**) *(pester)* houspiller, harceler; **she's always nagging him** elle est toujours après lui; **he nags her to death** il la harcèle sans pitié; **he nagged me into buying him a hi-fi** il m'a harcelé jusqu'à ce que je lui achète une chaîne stéréo
(**b**) *(of pain, sorrow)* ronger, travailler; *(of doubt)* tourmenter, ronger; **his conscience nagged him perpetually** sa conscience ne cessait de le tourmenter *ou* ne lui accordait pas de répit
2 *vi* trouver à redire, maugréer; **to nag at sb** harceler qn; **his children nagged at him to buy a camcorder** ses enfants lui ont cassé les pieds pour qu'il achète un caméscope®; **he's always nagging** il n'arrête pas de me/te/*etc* casser les pieds *ou* harceler
3 *n Fam* (**a**) *(person)* enquiquineur(euse) *m,f*; **he's an awful nag** *(pesterer)* il se pose là comme enquiquineur; *(complainer)* il est toujours en train de rouspéter, c'est un affreux râleur; **his wife's a real nag** sa femme est toujours sur son dos *ou* ne lui laisse pas une seconde de répit
(**b**) *(horse)* rosse *f*

nagana [nə'gɑːnə] *n Vet* nagana *m*

Nagari ['nɑːgərɪ] *n Ling* nagari *f*

Nagasaki [ˌnægə'sɑːkɪ] *n* Nagasaki

nagger ['nægə(r)] *n* enquiquineur(euse) *m,f*

nagging ['nægɪŋ] **1** *adj* (**a**) *(wife, husband)* grincheux, acariâtre
(**b**) *(doubt, feeling)* tenace, harcelant; *(pain)* tenace; **I have a nagging suspicion he won't come** je reste persuadé qu'il ne viendra pas; **I've still got this nagging doubt about him** je n'arrête pas de me poser des questions à son sujet
2 *n (UNCOUNT)* plaintes *fpl* continuelles; **I've had enough of your nagging!** j'en ai assez que tu me harcèles!

Nahuatl [nɑː'wɑːtəl] *n* nahuatl *m*

naiad ['naɪæd] *n* naïade *f*

nail [neɪl] **1** *n* (**a**) *(pin)* clou *m*; **it's another nail in his coffin** *(ruin)* pour lui, c'est un pas de plus vers la ruine; *(death)* pour lui, c'est un pas de plus vers la tombe
(**b**) *(on finger)* ongle *m*; **to do one's nails** se faire les ongles
2 *vt* (**a**) *(attach)* clouer; **nail the planks together** clouez les planches l'une à l'autre; **nailed to the door** cloué sur la porte; **the windows are nailed shut** les fenêtres ont été clouées *ou* sont condamnées; *Fig* **he stood nailed to the spot** il est resté cloué sur place; **to nail one's colours to the mast** exprimer clairement son opinion
(**b**) *Fam (catch, trap → person)* pincer, coincer
(**c**) *Fam (expose → rumour)* démentir❑; *(→ lie)* dénoncer❑, révéler❑; **we should nail the lie that unemployment is falling** nous devrions démontrer que la soi-disant baisse du chômage n'est qu'un tissu de mensonges
(**d**) *Fam (shoot)* descendre
(**e**) *Fam (stare at)* fixer (des yeux)❑
(**f**) *Fam (hit)* **to nail sb with sth** balancer qch sur qn; **we got nailed with a bill for twenty dollars** on nous a balancé une note de vingt dollars
►► ***nail bomb*** bombe *f* à fragmentation *(bourrée de clous)*; ***nail clippers*** coupe-ongles *m inv*, pince *f* à ongles; *Am* ***nail enamel*** vernis *m* à ongles; ***nail file*** lime *f* à ongles; ***nail polish*** vernis *m* à ongles; ***nail polish remover*** dissolvant *m*; ***nail punch*** chasse-clou *m*; ***nail scissors*** ciseaux *mpl* à ongles; *Tech* ***nail set*** chasse-clou *m*, chasse-pointe *m*; *Br* ***nail varnish*** vernis *m* à ongles; *Br* ***nail varnish remover*** dissolvant *m* (pour vernis à ongles)

►**nail down** *vt sep* (**a**) *(fasten)* clouer, fixer avec des clous
(**b**) *(make definite → details, date)* fixer (définitivement); *(→ agreement)* parvenir à, arriver à; *(→ person)* amener à se décider; **try to nail her down to a definite date** essayez de faire en sorte qu'elle vous fixe une date précise; **he's difficult to nail down** il est difficile d'obtenir une réponse précise de sa part

►**nail up** *vt sep* (**a**) *(shut → door, window)* condamner *(en fixant avec des clous)*; *(→ box)* clouer; *(→ items in box)* **the pictures were nailed up in a crate** les tableaux étaient placés dans une caisse fermée par des clous
(**b**) *(fix to wall, door → picture, photo etc)* fixer (avec un clou); *(→ notice)* clouer, afficher

nailbed ['neɪlbed] *n* lit *m* de l'ongle

nail-biter *n* (**a**) *(person)* personne *f* qui se ronge les ongles (**b**) *Fig (situation)* situation *f* au suspense insoutenable

nail-biting **1** *n (habit)* manie *f* de se ronger les ongles; *Fig (nervousness)* nervosité *f*, inquiétude *f*
2 *adj (situation)* angoissant, stressant; *(finish)* haletant

nailbrush ['neɪlbrʌʃ] *n* brosse *f* à ongles

nailhead ['neɪlhed] *n* (**a**) *(head of nail)* tête *f* de clou (**b**) *Archit* pointe *f* de diamant

nainsook ['neɪnsʊk] *n Tex* nansouk *m*

naira ['naɪərə] *n* naira *m*

Nairobi [naɪ'rəʊbɪ] *n* Nairobi

naive, naïve [naɪ'iːv] *adj* naïf
►► *Art* ***naive art*** l'art *m* naïf

naively, naïvely [naɪ'iːvlɪ] *adv* naïvement, avec naïveté

naïveté, naivety [naɪ'iːvtɪ] *n* naïveté *f*

naked ['neɪkɪd] *adj* (**a**) *(unclothed → person, body, leg)* nu; *Fig* **the naked ape** l'homme *m*, l'espèce *f* humaine
(**b**) *(bare → tree)* nu, dénudé, sans feuilles; *(→ landscape)* nu, dénudé; *(→ wall, room)* nu
(**c**) *(unprotected → flame, light, sword)* nu; *(→ wire)* nu, dénudé; **a naked lightbulb lit the room** une simple ampoule électrique éclairait la pièce
(**d**) *(undisguised → reality, truth)* tout nu, tout cru; *(→ facts)* brut; *(→ fear)* pur et simple; *(→ aggression)* délibéré; **an expression of naked terror** une expression de pure terreur
(**e**) *(eye)* nu; **visible to the naked eye** visible à l'œil nu
(**f**) *Bot & Zool* nu
(**g**) *Fin* sans garantie
►► *Fin* ***naked debenture*** obligation *f* chirographaire *ou* sans garantie; *Bot* ***naked lady*** colchique *m* d'automne; *St Exch* ***naked option*** option *f* d'achat vendue à découvert; ***naked sale*** vente *f* nue

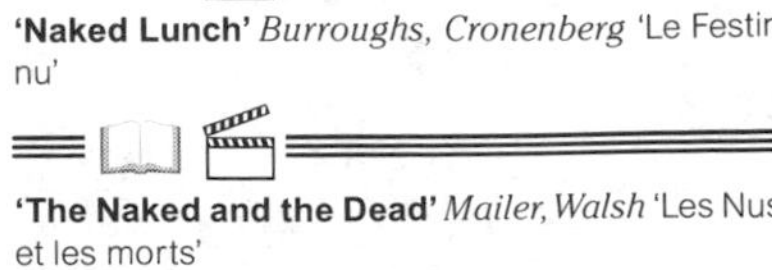

'Naked Lunch' *Burroughs, Cronenberg* 'Le Festin nu'

'The Naked and the Dead' *Mailer, Walsh* 'Les Nus et les morts'

nakedly ['neɪkɪdlɪ] *adv (expose oneself)* sans voiles, à nu; *(state facts)* nûment, simplement

nakedness ['neɪkɪdnɪs] *n* nudité *f*

NALGO ['nælgəʊ] *n Br Formerly (abbr* **National and Local Government Officers' Association***)* = ancien syndicat de la fonction publique en Grande-Bretagne

NAM [ˌeneɪ'em] *n Am (abbr* **National Association of Manufacturers***)* = organisation patronale américaine

Nam [næm] *n Am Fam Mil slang (Vietnam)* le Viêtnam❑

namable = **nameable**

namby-pamby [ˌnæmbɪ'pæmbɪ] *Fam* **1** *adj (person)* gnangnan *(inv)*, cucul *(inv)*; *(remark, attitude)* faiblard; *(style)* à l'eau de rose, fadasse

2 *n* lavette *f*, gnangnan *mf*

NAME [neɪm]

nom	► **1 (a) – (d)**
réputation	► **1 (c)**
personnage	► **1 (d)**
nommer	► **3 (a) – (c)**
désigner	► **3 (b), (c)**
citer	► **3 (b)**

1 *n* (**a**) *(of person, animal)* nom *m*; *(of company)* raison *f* sociale; *Fin (of account)* intitulé *m*; *(of ship)* devise *f*, nom *m*; *(of play, novel etc)* titre *m*; **full name** nom et prénoms *mpl*; **what's your name?** quel est votre nom?, comment vous appelez-vous?; **my name's Richard** je m'appelle Richard; **what name shall I say?** *(to caller)* qui dois-je annoncer?; **the house is in his wife's name** la maison est au nom de sa femme; **I know her only by name** je ne la connais que de nom; **she knows all the children by name** elle connaît le nom de tous les enfants; **to mention sb/sth by name** nommer qn/qch; **the shares are in my name** les actions sont à mon nom; **he is known** *or* **he goes by the name of Penn** il est connu sous le nom de Penn, il se fait appeler Penn; **someone by** *or* **of the name of Penn** quelqu'un du nom de *ou* qui s'appelle Penn; *Am Fam* **a guy name of Jones** un type du nom de Jones; **I know it by** *or* **under a different name** je le connais sous un autre nom; **he writes novels under the name of A.B. Alderman** il écrit des romans sous le pseudonyme de A.B. Alderman; **our dog answers to the name of Oscar** notre chien répond au nom d'Oscar; **to put a name to a face** mettre un nom sur un visage; **have you put your name down for evening classes?** est-ce que vous vous êtes inscrit aux cours du soir?; **she was his wife in all but name** ils n'étaient pas mariés, mais c'était tout comme; **to take sb's name** *(of police officer)* prendre le nom de qn; *Ftbl* donner un carton jaune à qn; *Ftbl* **he had his name taken** il a eu un carton jaune; **he is president in name only** il n'a de président que le nom, c'est un président sans pouvoir; **Cannon Gait is a huge name in the publishing business** Cannon Gait est une entreprise très importante dans le monde de l'édition; **what's in a name?** on n'a pas toujours le nom que l'on mérite; **to call sb names** injurier *ou* insulter qn; **she called me a rude name** elle m'a insulté; **money is the name of the game** c'est une affaire d'argent; **ah well, that's the name of the game** c'est comme ça!, c'est la vie!; **not to have a penny/a decent pair of shoes to one's name** ne pas avoir un centime/une paire de chaussures convenable à soi; **to have several books to one's name** être l'auteur de plusieurs livres; **the company trades under the name of Scandia** la société a pour dénomination Scandia

(**b**) *(sub: authority)* nom *m*; **in the name of freedom** au nom de la liberté; **in God's name!, in the name of God!** pour l'amour de Dieu!; *Fam* **what in the name of God** *or* **Heaven are you doing?** que diable faites-vous là?; **in the name of the law** au nom de la loi; **halt in the name of the King!** halte-là, au nom du Roi!

(**c**) *(reputation → professional or business)* nom *m*, réputation *f*; **to make** *or* **to win a name for oneself** se faire un nom *ou* une réputation; **we have the company's (good) name to think of** il faut penser au renom de la société; **they have a name for efficiency** ils ont la réputation d'être efficaces; **to have a good/bad name** avoir (une) bonne/mauvaise réputation; **to get a bad name** se faire une mauvaise réputation

(**d**) *(famous person)* nom *m*, personnage *m*; **he's a big name in the art world** c'est une figure de proue du monde des arts; **all the great political names were there** tous les ténors de la scène politique étaient présents; **famous name** *(person)* célébrité *f*

2 *comp Com (product)* de marque

3 *vt* (**a**) *(give name to → person, animal)* nommer, appeler, donner un nom à; *(→ ship, discovery)* baptiser; **they named the baby Felix** ils ont appelé *ou* prénommé le bébé Felix; **she wanted to name her son after the President** elle voulait donner à son fils le prénom du président, elle voulait que son fils porte le prénom du président; *Am* **the building is named for Abraham Lincoln** on a donné au bâtiment le nom d'Abraham Lincoln; **the guy named Chip** le dénommé Chip

(**b**) *(give name of)* désigner, nommer; *(cite)* citer, mentionner; **the journalist refused to name his source** le journaliste a refusé de révéler *ou* de donner le nom de son informateur; **whatever you need, just name it** vos moindres désirs seront exaucés; **you name it, we've got it** demandez-nous n'importe quoi, nous l'avons; **name the books of the Old Testament** citez les livres de l'Ancien Testament; **to name names** donner des noms; **let us name no names** ne nommons personne; **he is named as one of the consultants** son nom est cité *ou* mentionné en tant que consultant; *Law* **to name sb as a beneficiary** *(in one's will)* désigner qn comme bénéficiaire; *Law* **to name sb as a witness** citer qn comme témoin; **to name and shame** dénoncer publiquement les responsables

(**c**) *(appoint)* nommer, désigner; **she has been named as president** elle a été nommée présidente; **she was named (as) best supporting actress** elle a été élue pour le meilleur second rôle féminin; **22 June has been named as the date for the elections** la date du 22 juin a été retenue *ou* choisie pour les élections; **name your price** votre prix sera le mien, dites votre prix; **they've finally named the day** ils ont enfin fixé la date de leur mariage

(**d**) *Br Pol* **to name an MP** ≃ suspendre un député

4 Name *n* = titre réservé aux membres investissant leur fortune personnelle dans la compagnie d'assurances Lloyd's et s'engageant à avoir une responsabilité illimitée en cas de sinistre

►► *Mktg* ***name brand*** marque *f*; ***name day*** *(of person)* fête *f*; *St Exch* deuxième jour *m* de liquidation; **today is his name day** c'est aujourd'hui sa fête; *Mktg* ***name licensing*** cession *f* de licence de nom; *Br Cin & Theat* ***name part*** vrai rôle *m*; *(title role)* = rôle qui donne son titre à la pièce ou au film; *Mktg* ***name product*** marque *f*

---

nameable ['neɪməbəl] *adj* que l'on peut nommer

nameboard ['neɪmbɔːd] *n Naut* tableau *m*

name-calling *n (UNCOUNT)* insultes *fpl*, injures *fpl*

-named [neɪmd] *suff* nommé; **first-named** premier nommé

name-dropper *n* **she's an awful name-dropper** à la croire, elle connaît tout le monde

name-dropping *n* = allusion fréquente à des personnes connues dans le but d'impressionner

nameless ['neɪmlɪs] *adj* (**a**) *(anonymous, unmentioned)* sans nom, anonyme; *(unknown → grave, victim)* anonyme, inconnu; **someone who shall remain nameless** quelqu'un que je ne nommerai pas; **to remain nameless** garder l'anonymat (**b**) *(indefinable → fear, regret)* indéfinissable, indicible (**c**) *(atrocious → crime)* innommable, sans nom, inouï

namely ['neɪmlɪ] *adv* c'est-à-dire, à savoir

nameplate ['neɪmpleɪt] *n* plaque *f*; **manufacturer's nameplate** plaque *f* du fabricant *ou* du constructeur

namesake ['neɪmseɪk] *n* homonyme *m*; **she's my namesake** nous portons toutes les deux le même nom

nametape ['neɪmteɪp] *n* nom *m (du propriétaire, sur ses vêtements)*

Namib Desert [nə'mɪb-] *n* **the Namib Desert** le désert du Namib

Namibia [nə'mɪbɪə] *n* Namibie *f*; **in Namibia** en Namibie

Namibian [nə'mɪbɪən] **1** *n* Namibien(enne) *m,f*

2 *adj* namibien

3 *comp (embassy)* de Namibie; *(history)* de la Namibie

naming ['neɪmɪŋ] *n* (**a**) *(gen)* attribution *f* d'un nom; *(of ship)* baptême *m* (**b**) *(citing)* mention *f*, citation *f* (**c**) *(appointment)* nomination *f*

Namurian [næ'mjuːrɪən] *Geol* **1** *n* namurien *m*

2 *adj* namurien

nan¹ [næn] *n Br Fam (grandmother)* grand-mère ❑ *f*; *(term of address)* mémé *f*, mamie *f*

nan² = **naan**

nana¹ ['nænə] *n Br Fam (grandmother)* grand-mère ❑ *f*; *(term of address)* mémé *f*, mamie *f*

nana² ['nɑːnə] *n Fam (banana)* banane ❑ *f*

nancy (boy) ['nænsɪ-] *Fam* **1** *n (effeminate man)* chochotte *f*; *(homosexual man)* homo *m*

2 *adj (effeminate)* de chochotte, de tapette

nandrolone ['nændrɪləʊn] *n Pharm* nandrolone *f*

Nanjing [ˌnæn'dʒɪŋ] *n* Nanjing, Nankin

nankeen [næŋ'kiːn] *n* (**a**) *(cloth)* nankin *m* (**b**) *(colour)* nankin *m*, jaune *m* clair

Nanking [ˌnæn'kɪŋ] *n* Nanjing, Nankin

nanna ['nænə] *n Br Fam (grandmother)* mémé *f*, mamie *f*

nannoplankton = **nanoplankton**

nanny ['nænɪ] *n* (*pl* **nannies**) *n* (**a**) *(child carer → nowadays)* garde *mf* d'enfants; *(→ formerly)* nurse *f*, bonne *f* d'enfants (**b**) *Br Fam (grandmother)* grand-mère ❑ *f*; *(term of address)* mémé *f*, mamie *f*

►► ***nanny goat*** chèvre *f*; ***the nanny state*** l'État *m* paternaliste

nano- ['nænəʊ] *pref* nano-

nanoengineering [ˌnænəʊendʒɪ'nɪərɪŋ] *n* nano-ingénierie *f*

nanometre ['nænəʊˌmiːtə(r)] *n* nanomètre *m*

nanoplankton ['nænəʊˌplæŋktən] *n (UNCOUNT)* = organismes microscopiques du plancton

nanosecond ['nænəʊˌsekənd] *n* nanoseconde *f*

nanotechnology ['nænəʊˌteknɒlədʒɪ] *n* nanotechnologie *f*

Nantucket [næn'tʌkɪt] *n* = île au large de la côte du Massachusetts, lieu de villégiature de riches Américains

nap [næp] (*pt & pp* **napped**, *cont* **napping**) **1** *n* (**a**) *(sleep)* somme *m*; **to take** *or* **to have a nap** faire un (petit) somme; **to take an afternoon nap** faire la sieste

(**b**) *Tex* poil *m*; **against the nap** à rebrousse-poil, à rebours

(**c**) *(card game)* = jeu de cartes ressemblant au whist; **to go nap** demander les cinq levées; *Old-fashioned Fig* risquer le tout pour le tout; *Br* **to have** *or* **to hold a nap hand** avoir tous les atouts en main

(**d**) *(in horseracing)* tuyau *m* sûr

2 *vi (sleep → gen)* faire un (petit) somme; *(→ in afternoon)* faire la sieste; *Fig* **to be caught napping** *(off guard)* être pris au dépourvu

3 *vt* (**a**) *Tex (cloth)* lainer, gratter; *(velvet)* brosser

(**b**) *(in horseracing)* désigner comme favori, donner gagnant

NAPA [ˌeneɪˌpiː'eɪ] *n Am* (*abbr* **National Association of Performing Artists**) = syndicat américain des gens du spectacle

napa ['næpə] *n* nappa *m*

napalm ['neɪpɑːm] **1** *n* napalm *m*

2 *vt* bombarder au napalm

►► ***napalm bomb*** bombe *f* au napalm

nape [neɪp] *n* **nape (of the neck)** nuque *f*

napery ['neɪpərɪ] *n Scot Arch* linge *m* de table, nappage *m*

naphtha ['næfθə] *n Chem* naphta *m*

naphthalene, naphthaline ['næfθəliːn] *n Chem* naphtalène *m*; *(for mothballs)* naphtaline *f*

naphthol ['næfθɒl] *n Chem* naphtol *m*

napkin ['næpkɪn] *n* (**a**) *(on table)* serviette *f* (de table) (**b**) *Br Formal (for baby)* couche *f*

►► ***napkin ring*** rond *m* de serviette

Naples ['neɪpəlz] *n* Naples

Napoleon [nə'pəʊlɪən] *pr n* Napoléon; **Napoleon Bonaparte** Napoléon Bonaparte

napoleon [nə'pəʊlɪən] *n* (**a**) *(coin)* napoléon *m* (**b**) *Am Culin* mille-feuille *m* (**c**) *(card game)* = jeu de cartes ressemblant au whist

Napoleonic [nəˌpəʊlɪ'ɒnɪk] *adj* napoléonien

►► ***the Napoleonic Code*** le Code Napoléon; ***the Napoleonic Wars*** les guerres *fpl* napoléoniennes

napoleonite [nə'pəʊlɪənaɪt] *n Geol* napoléonite *f*

nappe [næp] *n* (**a**) *Geol* nappe *f* (**b**) *Math* nappe *f*

napper ['næpə(r)] *n* (**a**) *Tex* laineur(euse) *m,f* (**b**) *Br Fam (head)* caboche *f*

nappy ['næpɪ] (*pl* **nappies**) **1** *n Br* couche *f* (pour bébé)

2 *adj Am (fabric)* feutré

▸▸ *Br* ***nappy liner*** change *m* (jetable); *Br* ***nappy rash*** érythème *m* fessier; **babies often get nappy rash** les bébés ont souvent les fesses rouges et irritées

narc [nɑːk] *n Am Fam (narcotics agent)* agent *m* de la brigade des stups

narceine ['nɑːsiːn] *n Chem* narcéine *f*

narcissi [nɑː'sɪsaɪ] *pl of* **narcissus**

narcissism ['nɑːsɪsɪzəm] *n* narcissisme *m*

narcissist ['nɑːsɪsɪst] *n* narcissique *mf*

narcissistic [ˌnɑːsɪ'sɪstɪk] *adj* narcissique

Narcissus [nɑː'sɪsəs] *pr n Myth* Narcisse

narcissus [nɑː'sɪsəs] (*pl* **inv** *or* **narcissuses** *or* **narcissi** [-aɪ]) *n* narcisse *m*

narcoanalysis [ˌnɑːkəʊə'nælɪsɪs] *n Med* narcoanalyse *f*

narcodollars ['nɑːkəʊˌdɒləz] *npl* narcodollars *mpl*

narcolepsy ['nɑːkəlepsɪ] *n Med* narcolepsie *f*

narcoleptic [ˌnɑːkə'leptɪk] *Med* **1** *n* narcoleptique *m*

2 *adj* narcoleptique

narcosis [nɑː'kəʊsɪs] *n* narcose *f*

narcosynthesis [ˌnɑːkəʊ'sɪnθɪsɪs] *n Psy* narcosynthèse *f*

narcoterrorism [ˌnɑːkəʊ'terərɪzəm] *n* narcoterrorisme *m*

narcotherapy [ˌnɑːkəʊ'θerəpɪ] *n Med* narcothérapie *f*

narcotic [nɑː'kɒtɪk] **1** *adj* narcotique

2 *n* (**a**) *Pharm* narcotique *m* (**b**) *Am (illegal drug)* stupéfiant *m*

▸▸ *Am* ***Narcotics Anonymous*** = association américaine d'aide aux toxicomanes; ***narcotics agent*** agent *m* de la brigade des stupéfiants; ***narcotics squad*** brigade *f* des stupéfiants

narcotism ['nɑːkətɪzəm] *n* (**a**) *Med* narcotisme *m* (**b**) *(effect)* influence *f* narcotique

narcotization [ˌnɑːkətaɪ'zeɪʃən] *n* action *f* narcotique (**of** sur)

narcotize, -ise ['nɑːkətaɪz] *vt* soumettre à un traitement aux narcotiques

nard [nɑːd] *n Bot* nard *m*, spicanard *m*

nardoo [nɑː'duː] *n Bot* = fougère australienne dont les spores sont comestibles

nares ['neəriːz] *npl Anat* narines *fpl*

nark [nɑːk] *Fam* **1** *n* (**a**) *Crime slang (informer)* mouchard(e) *m,f*

(**b**) *Br (grumbler)* râleur(euse) *m,f*

(**c**) *Am (narcotics agent)* agent *m* de la brigade des stups

2 *vt Br (annoy)* foutre en rogne *ou* en boule

3 *vi* (**a**) *Crime slang (inform)* moucharder; **to nark on sb** balancer qn

(**b**) *Br Fam (grumble)* rouspéter, grogner

narked [nɑːkt] *adj Br Fam* en rogne

narky ['nɑːkɪ] (*compar* **narkier**, *superl* **narkiest**) *adj Br Fam* ronchon

narrate [*Br* nə'reɪt, *Am* 'næreɪt] *vt* (**a**) *(relate → story)* raconter, *Literary* narrer; *(→ event)* faire le récit de, relater (**b**) *(read commentary for)* lire *ou* dire le commentaire de; **the film was narrated by an American actor** le commentaire du film a été lu *ou* dit par un acteur américain

narration [*Br* nə'reɪʃən, *Am* næ'reɪʃən] *n* (**a**) *(narrative)* narration *f* (**b**) *(commentary)* commentaire *m* (**c**) *Fin* = note explicative dans un livre de commerce justifiant une écriture

narrative ['nærətɪv] **1** *adj* narratif

2 *n* (**a**) *Literature* narration *f* (**b**) *(story)* histoire *f*, récit *m* (**c**) *Fin* = note explicative dans un livre de commerce justifiant une écriture

narrator [*Br* nə'reɪtə(r), *Am* 'næreɪtə(r)] *n* narrateur(trice) *m,f*

narrow ['nærəʊ] **1** *adj* (**a**) *(not wide → street, passage, valley)* étroit; *(tight → skirt, shoe)* étroit, serré; *(long → nose)* mince; *(→ face)* allongé; **to grow** *or* **to become narrow** se rétrécir; **to have narrow shoulders** être petit de carrure, ne pas être large d'épaules; **to have a narrow face** être mince de visage; **to have a narrow waist** avoir la taille fine

(**b**) *(scant, small → advantage, budget, majority)* petit, faible; *(close → result)* serré; **it was another narrow victory/defeat for the French side** l'équipe française l'a encore emporté de justesse/a encore perdu de peu; **we had a narrow escape** on l'a échappé belle; **to win/lose by the narrowest of margins** gagner/perdre de très peu

(**c**) *(restricted → scope, field, research)* restreint, limité; *(strict → sense, interpretation)* restreint, strict; **in the narrowest sense of the word** au sens strict du mot

(**d**) *(bigoted, illiberal → mind, attitude)* borné, étroit; *(→ person)* borné; **to take a narrow view of sth** adopter un point de vue étroit sur qch

(**e**) *Formal (detailed → search)* minutieux, détaillé; **we were subjected to narrow scrutiny** nous avons été soumis à un examen minutieux

(**f**) *Ling (vowel)* tendu

(**g**) *Fin (market)* étroit

2 *vt* (**a**) *(make narrow → road)* rétrécir; **to narrow one's eyes** plisser les yeux

(**b**) *(reduce → difference, gap)* réduire, restreindre; *(limit → search)* limiter, restreindre; **the police have narrowed their search to a few streets in central Leeds** la police concentre ses recherches sur quelques rues du centre de Leeds

3 *vi* (**a**) *(become narrow → road, space)* se rétrécir, se resserrer; **the old man's eyes narrowed** le vieil homme plissa les yeux

(**b**) *(be reduced → difference, choice)* se réduire, se limiter; *(→ number, majority)* s'amenuiser, se réduire; **the gap between rich and poor has narrowed** l'écart entre les riches et les pauvres s'est resserré

4 *n (usu pl) (gen)* passage *m* étroit; *(pass)* col *m*; *(strait)* détroit *m*

▸▸ ***narrow boat*** péniche *f* (étroite); ***narrow gauge*** voie *f* étroite; *Fin* ***narrow money*** = ensemble des billets et pièces de monnaie en circulation; *Ling* ***narrow transcription*** transcription *f* étroite

▸**narrow down 1** *vt sep (limit → choice, search)* limiter, restreindre; *(reduce → majority, difference)* réduire

2 *vi (search)* se limiter, se restreindre; **the choice narrowed down to just two people** il ne restait que deux personnes en lice

narrow-band *adj* à bande étroite

narrow-bodied aircraft *n* avion *m* petit porteur

narrowcast ['nærəʊkɑːst] **1** *vt* diffuser localement

2 *vi* diffuser des émissions destinées à un public spécialisé

narrow-gauge *adj Rail (track, line)* à voie étroite

narrowing ['nærəʊɪŋ] *adj* (**a**) *(making narrow)* qui resserre, qui rétrécit; *Fig (influence)* qui restreint, qui limite (**b**) *(becoming narrow)* qui se resserre, qui se rétrécit

narrowly ['nærəʊlɪ] *adv* (**a**) *(barely)* de justesse, de peu; **he narrowly avoided capture** il s'en est fallu de peu qu'il (ne) soit capturé; **she narrowly escaped with her life** elle a échappé à la mort de justesse; **he narrowly missed being run over** il a failli se faire écraser

(**b**) *(closely)* de près, étroitement; **he watched her narrowly** il la surveillait de près

(**c**) *Formal (strictly)* de manière stricte, rigoureusement

narrow-minded *adj (person)* étroit d'esprit, borné; *(attitude, opinions)* borné

narrow-mindedly [-'maɪndɪdlɪ] *adv* de façon bornée

narrow-mindedness [-'maɪndɪdnɪs] *n (of person)* étroitesse *f* d'esprit; *(of attitude, opinions)* caractère *m* borné

narrowness ['nærəʊnɪs] *n* (**a**) *(of path, shoulders, passage etc)* étroitesse *f*; *(of someone's nose, waist)* minceur *f*; *(of space)* exiguïté *f* (**b**) *(of majority, advantage)* faiblesse *f* (**c**) *(of intelligence)* faiblesse *f*; **narrowness of mind** étroitesse *f* d'esprit

narrow-shouldered [-'ʃəʊldəd] *adj* étroit de carrure *ou* d'épaules; **he's rather narrow-shouldered** il n'est pas très large d'épaules

narthex ['nɑːθeks] *n Archit* narthex *m*

narwal, narwhal, narwhale ['nɑːwəl] *n Zool* narval *m*

nary ['neərɪ] *adj Fam* **nary a** pas un seul ❑, aucun ❑; **he said nary a word** il n'a pas dit un mot ❑

NAS [ˌeneɪ'es] *n Am* (*abbr* **National Academy of Sciences**) = académie américaine des sciences

NASA ['næsə] *n Am* (*abbr* **National Aeronautics and Space Administration**) NASA *f*

nasal ['neɪzəl] **1** *adj* (**a**) *Anat & Ling* nasal; **the nasal cavities** les fosses *fpl* nasales (**b**) *(voice, sound)* nasillard

2 *n Ling* nasale *f*

nasality [neɪ'zælɪtɪ] *n Ling* nasalité *f*

nasalization [ˌneɪzəlaɪ'zeɪʃən] *n Ling* nasalisation *f*

nasalize, -ise ['neɪzəlaɪz] *vt Ling* nasaliser

nasally ['neɪzəlɪ] *adv Ling* de manière nasale; *(speak)* d'une voix nasillarde

nascent ['neɪsənt] *adj* (**a**) *(in early stages)* naissant; **a nascent rebellion** un début de rébellion

(**b**) *Chem* naissant

Nasdaq ['næzdæk] *n St Exch* (*abbr* **National Association of Securities Dealers Automated Quotation**) le Nasdaq *(Bourse américaine des valeurs technologiques)*

nasion ['neɪzɪən] *n Anat* nasion *m*, point *m* nasal

nasopharyngeal [ˌneɪzəʊfə'rɪndʒɪəl] *adj Anat* rhino-pharyngien

nasopharyngitis [ˌneɪzəʊfærɪn'dʒaɪtɪs] *n Med* rhino-pharyngite *f*

nasopharynx [ˌneɪzəʊ'færɪnks] *n Anat* rhinopharynx *m*, nasopharynx *m*

nastic ['næstɪk] *adj*

▸▸ *Bot* ***nastic movement*** nastie *f*

nastily ['nɑːstɪlɪ] *adv* (**a**) *(unpleasantly → answer, remark)* méchamment, avec méchanceté (**b**) *(seriously → burnt, bitten)* gravement; **she cut herself nastily on the knife** elle s'est fait une vilaine blessure avec le couteau

nastiness ['nɑːstɪnɪs] *n* (**a**) *(of person)* méchanceté *f*; *(of remark, behaviour)* méchanceté *f*, malveillance *f*; **the nastiness of the weather** le mauvais temps

(**b**) *(unpleasantness)* caractère *m* très désagréable

(**c**) *(of injury)* gravité *f*

(**d**) *(obscenity)* obscénité *f*, indécence *f*

nasturtium [nəs'tɜːʃəm] *n* capucine *f*

nasty ['nɑːstɪ] (*compar* **nastier**, *superl* **nastiest**, *pl* **nasties**) **1** *adj* (**a**) *(mean, spiteful → person)* mauvais, méchant; *(→ remark, rumour)* désagréable, désobligeant; **to be nasty to sb** être méchant avec qn; **to turn nasty** devenir méchant; **that was a nasty thing to do** c'était vraiment méchant de faire ça; **he's got a nasty temper** il a un sale caractère; **what a nasty man!** quel homme désagréable *ou* déplaisant!; **nasty trick** vilain tour, *Fam* sale tour; *Fam* **he's a nasty piece of work** c'est un sale individu *ou* un sale type

(**b**) *(unpleasant → smell, taste, impression, surprise)* mauvais, désagréable; *(→ weather, job)* sale; *(→ crime)* atroce; **a nasty war** une sale guerre; **to give sb a nasty fright** faire une peur bleue à qn; **it was a very nasty moment!** on a passé un mauvais moment!; **things started to turn nasty** la situation a pris une vilaine tournure; **the weather turned nasty** le temps s'est dégradé

(**c**) *(in children's language) (dragon, giant, wolf)* vilain, méchant

(**d**) *(ugly, in bad taste)* vilain, laid; **nasty plastic flowers** d'horribles fleurs artificielles

(**e**) *(serious → sprain, burn, disease)* grave; **a nasty cold** un gros rhume; **she had a nasty accident** elle a eu un grave accident; **she's had a nasty attack of bronchitis** elle a fait une mauvaise bronchite; **he's had quite a nasty blow to the head** il a pris un mauvais coup sur la tête

(**f**) *(dangerous → bend, junction)* dangereux

(**g**) *(difficult → problem, question)* difficile, épineux

(**h**) *(book, film, scene → violent)* violent, dur; *(→ obscene)* obscène, indécent

(**i**) *Am Fam (excellent)* super, génial; **she makes a nasty pizza** elle fait super bien la pizza

2 *n* (**a**) *(person)* méchant(e) *m,f*

(**b**) *Fam (obscene film)* film *m* porno; *(violent film)* film *m* violent ❑

NAS/UWT [ˌeneɪ'esˌjuːdʌbəljuː'tiː] *n Br* (*abbr* **National Association of Schoolmasters/Union of Women Teachers**) = syndicat d'enseignants et de chefs d'établissement en Grande-Bretagne

Natal [nə'tæl] *n* Natal *m*; **in Natal** au Natal

natal ['neɪtəl] *adj* natal

▸▸ *Psy* ***natal therapy*** = thérapie cathartique fondée sur l'expérience vécue lors de la naissance

natality [neɪ'tæləti] (*pl* **natalities**) *n* (taux *m* de) natalité *f*

natatorial [,neɪtə'tɔːrɪəl] *adj* natatoire

natatorium [,neɪtə'tɔːrɪəm] *n Am* piscine *f*

natatory ['neɪtətəri] *adj* natatoire

natch [nætʃ] *Fam* **1** *adv* bien sûr ❑, bien entendu ❑

2 *exclam* bien sûr! ❑

nates ['neɪtiːz] *npl Anat* fesses *fpl*

Nathan ['neɪθən] *pr n Bible* Nathan

nation ['neɪʃən] *n* (**a**) *(country)* pays *m*, nation *f*; **the British nation** la nation britannique

(**b**) *(people)* nation *f*; **to address the nation** s'adresser à la nation; **the whole nation mourned** la nation tout entière était en deuil; *Br Pol* **to go to the nation** en appeler au peuple

▸▸ ***Nation of Islam*** Nation *f* de l'islam *(organisation américaine de défense des droits des Noirs musulmans)*; ***nation state*** État-nation *m*

national ['næʃənəl] **1** *adj* national; **the national newspapers** la presse nationale; **he became a national hero** il est devenu un héros national; **the country's national sport** le sport national du pays; **a source of national pride** une source de fierté nationale; **the killings caused a national outcry** les assassinats ont scandalisé le pays; **on a national scale** à l'échelle nationale; **they won 38 percent of the national vote** ils ont remporté 38 pour cent des voix sur l'ensemble du pays; **it's not in the national interest** ce n'est pas dans l'intérêt du pays

2 *n* (**a**) *(person)* ressortissant(e) *m,f*; **all EU nationals** tous les ressortissants des pays de l'Union européenne; **Irish nationals** ressortissants *mpl* de la République d'Irlande

(**b**) *(newspaper)* journal *m* national

▸▸ ***national accounting*** comptabilité *f* nationale; ***national anthem*** hymne *m* national; *Can* ***national assembly*** *(in Quebec)* Assemblée *f* nationale; *Br Old-fashioned* ***national assistance*** assistance *f* publique; *Am* ***National Association of Colleges and Universities*** = association des établissements d'enseignement supérieur américains; *Br* ***the National Audit Office*** ≃ la Cour des comptes; ***national bank*** = banque agréée par le gouvernement américain et qui doit faire partie du système bancaire fédéral; ***the National Cancer Institute*** = organisme américain de recherche sur le cancer; ***the National Childbirth Trust*** = organisme d'information et d'éducation des jeunes parents en Grande-Bretagne; *Austr* ***national code*** football *m* australien; *Am* ***the National Collegiate Athletic Association*** = association interuniversitaire traitant des questions sportives; *Am Pol* ***National Convention*** = grande réunion du parti démocrate ou républicain pour choisir le "ticket" (candidats à la présidence et à la vice-présidence); ***national costume*** costume *m* national; ***the National Council for Civil Liberties*** = en Grande-Bretagne, ligue de défense des droits du citoyen luttant contre toute forme de discrimination; ***the National Council for Vocational Qualifications*** = organisme britannique responsable de la formation professionnelle; ***the National Curriculum*** = programme introduit en 1988 définissant au niveau national (Angleterre et pays de Galles) le contenu de l'enseignement primaire et secondaire; *Fin* ***national debt*** dette *f* publique, dette *f* de l'État; ***national dress*** costume *m* national; ***the National Endowment for the Arts*** = organisme américain accordant des bourses à des artistes, des musées ou des compagnies théâtrales; ***the National Endowment for the Humanities*** = organisme américain accordant des bourses à des écrivains ou à des chercheurs; ***the National Endowment for Science, Technology and the Arts*** = organisme indépendant d'aide financière, à partir de fonds provenant de la Loterie nationale, aux artistes, inventeurs et scientifiques; *Press* ***National Enquirer*** = hebdomadaire américain à sensation; *Br* ***the National Enterprise Board*** ≃ Agence *f* nationale pour le développement industriel; *Br Pol* ***the National Executive Committee*** = comité chargé de définir la ligne d'action du parti travailliste; ***the National Exhibition Centre*** = centre de conférences et d'expositions à Birmingham (Angleterre); ***National Express***® = société d'autocars reliant les principales villes de Grande-Bretagne; *Br* ***National Extension College*** centre *m* d'enseignement à distance; ***the National Farmers' Union*** = syndicat britannique d'exploitants agricoles; ***the National Film Theatre*** = cinémathèque à Londres; ***the National Foundation of the Arts and Humanities*** = organisme public américain d'aide à l'action culturelle; ***the National Front*** = parti d'extrême droite britannique, ≃ le Front national; ***the National Gallery*** la National Gallery *(principal musée de peinture du Royaume-Uni, situé à Londres)*; ***national government*** gouvernement *m* de coalition; *Fin* ***National Giro*** = service britannique de chèques postaux; ***the National Graphical Association*** = syndicat britannique d'imprimeurs; ***national grid*** *Br Elec* réseau *m* national d'électricité; *Geog* réseau *m*; ***the National Guard*** *(in the US)* la Garde nationale *(armée nationale américaine composée de volontaires)*; ***National Guardsman*** membre *m* de la Garde nationale; ***the National Health (Service)*** = système créé en 1946 en Grande-Bretagne et financé par l'État, assurant la gratuité des soins et des services médicaux, ≃ la Sécurité sociale; **to get treatment on the National Health (Service)** se faire soigner sous le régime de la Sécurité sociale; *Br* ***National Health Service glasses*** = modèle de lunettes remboursé par la Sécurité sociale; ***National Heritage*** = organisme ayant pour mission la conservation du patrimoine; ***national hunt (racing)*** courses *fpl* d'obstacles; ***national income*** revenu *m* national; *Br* ***national insurance*** = système britannique de sécurité sociale (maladie, retraite) et d'assurance chômage; ***national insurance contributions*** cotisations *fpl* à la Sécurité sociale; ***national insurance number*** numéro *m* de Sécurité sociale; *Am* ***the National Labor Relations Board*** = organisme américain de conciliation et d'arbitrage des conflits du travail, ≃ conseil *m* de prud'hommes; *Press* ***National Lampoon*** = revue satirique américaine; ***National League*** = l'une des deux ligues professionnelles de base-ball aux États-Unis; ***the National Lottery*** = loterie nationale britannique; ***the National Liberation Front*** le Front de libération nationale; ***the National Maritime Museum*** = musée de la mer situé à Greenwich; ***National Missile Defence System*** projet *m* NMD *(programme de défense antimissiles américain)*; ***National Organization for Women*** = organisation de lutte pour les droits de la femme; ***national park*** parc *m* national; ***the National Portrait Gallery*** = musée londonien entièrement consacré aux portraits; ***National Power*** = entreprise privée de production d'électricité en Angleterre et au pays de Galles; *Fin* ***national product*** produit *m* national; ***National Public Radio*** = réseau américain de stations de radio libres; ***national readership survey*** étude *f* nationale sur le lectorat; ***the National Rifle Association*** = association américaine défendant le droit au port d'armes; *Br* ***National Savings Bank*** ≃ Caisse *f* nationale d'épargne; ***National Savings certificate*** bon *m* de caisse d'épargne; *Ir* ***national school*** école *f* primaire; *Am* ***the National Science Foundation*** = organisme d'aide à la recherche scientifique; ***national security*** sécurité *f* nationale; *Am Pol* ***National Security Adviser*** = conseiller du président américain sur les questions de sécurité nationale; *Pol* ***the National Security Council*** le Conseil de sécurité nationale; *Br* ***national service*** service *m* militaire; *Br* ***national serviceman*** appelé *m*, militaire *m* du contingent; ***national socialism*** national-socialisme *m*; ***national socialist*** **1** *n* national-socialiste *mf* **2** *adj* national-socialiste; ***the National Society for the Prevention of Cruelty to Children*** = association britannique de protection de l'enfance; *Ir* ***national teacher*** instituteur(trice) *m,f*; ***the National Theatre*** *(in London)* = important centre dramatique à Londres, siège de la Royal National Theatre Company; *Am* ***the National Transportation Safety Board*** = agence du gouvernement américain chargée des questions de sécurité dans le domaine des transports; *Br* ***the National Trust*** = organisme non gouvernemental britannique assurant la conservation de certains paysages et monuments historiques; ***National Trust property*** ≃ site *m* protégé; ***the National Trust for Scotland*** = organisme non gouvernemental assurant la conservation de certains paysages et monuments historiques écossais; ***National Vocational Qualification*** = diplôme britannique professionnel national; ***the National Weather Service*** = les services météorologiques américains

NATIONAL HEALTH SERVICE

Le "National Health Service" ou "NHS" fut créé par le gouvernement travailliste en 1946, donnant accès à chacun aux soins médicaux gratuits. Cependant, au cours des années 80, le gouvernement de Margaret Thatcher voulut encourager le public à souscrire des assurances médicales privées, et le "NHS" subit des coupes budgétaires importantes. Au cours de ces dernières années, la polémique autour du "National Health Service" s'est intensifiée. Le "NHS" connaît en effet de nombreuses difficultés.

nationalism ['næʃənəlɪzəm] *n* nationalisme *m*

nationalist ['næʃənəlɪst] **1** *n* nationaliste *mf*

2 *adj* nationaliste; **Nationalist China** la Chine nationaliste

nationalistic [,næʃənə'lɪstɪk] *adj* nationaliste

nationality [,næʃə'nælətɪ] (*pl* **nationalities**) *n* nationalité *f*; **what nationality are you?** de quelle nationalité êtes-vous?, quelle est votre nationalité?; **to take** *or* **adopt British nationality** se faire naturaliser britannique

nationalization [,næʃənəlaɪ'zeɪʃən] *n* nationalisation *f*

nationalize, -ise ['næʃənəlaɪz] *vt* nationaliser

nationalized ['næʃənəlaɪzd] *adj* nationalisé

nationally ['næʃənəlɪ] *adv* nationalement; **nationally renowned** connu dans *ou* à travers tout le pays; **nationally recognized qualification** un diplôme reconnu dans tout le pays; **a nationally televised speech** un discours retransmis sur les chaînes nationales; **nationally, men still outnumber women in these sectors** sur l'ensemble du pays, les hommes sont toujours plus nombreux que les femmes dans ces secteurs

nationhood ['neɪʃənhʊd] *n* statut *m* de nation; **to attain nationhood** être reconnu en tant que nation

nationwide ['neɪʃənwaɪd] **1** *adj* national; **a nationwide strike** une grève nationale; **nationwide survey** une enquête à l'échelle nationale

2 *adv* à l'échelle nationale, dans tout le pays; **the speech was broadcast nationwide** le discours a été diffusé dans tout le pays

native ['neɪtɪv] **1** *n* (**a**) *(of country)* natif(ive) *m,f*, autochtone *mf*; *(of town)* natif(ive) *m,f*; **I'm a native of Portland** je suis originaire de Portland, je suis né à Portland; **she's a native of Belgium** elle est belge de naissance, elle est née en Belgique; **she speaks English like a native** elle parle anglais comme si c'était sa langue maternelle *ou* comme les Anglais; *Hum Pej* **the natives** les autochtones *mpl*

(**b**) *Pej (of colony)* indigène *mf*

(**c**) *Bot (plant)* plante *f* indigène; *Zool (animal)* animal *m* indigène; *(species)* espèce *f* indigène; **this plant/animal is a native of southern Europe** c'est une plante/un animal indigène au sud de l'Europe

2 *adj* (**a**) *(of birth → country)* natal; *(→ language)* maternel; **our native soil** *or* **clay** notre sol natal; **his native London** Londres, sa ville natale; **he always writes in his native Russian** il écrit toujours en russe, sa langue maternelle

(**b**) *(by birth)* natif

(**c**) *(indigenous → resources)* du pays; *(→ tribe, customs, labour)* indigène; *(→ costume)* du pays, national; **to go native** adopter les us et coutumes locaux

(**d**) *(innate → ability, attraction)* inné, naturel

(**e**) *Bot & Zool* indigène, originaire; **native to India** originaire de l'Inde

(**f**) *Miner (ore, silver)* natif

nat–nat

▸▸ ***Native American*** Indien(enne) *m,f* d'Amérique, Amérindien(enne) *m,f*; ***Native Australian*** aborigène *mf*; *Austr* ***native bear*** koala *m*; ***native Indians*** Indiens *mpl* de naissance *ou* de souche; ***native land*** pays *m* natal; ***native son*** enfant *m* du pays; **Portland honours its native sons** Portland rend hommage à ses enfants; *Ling* ***native speaker*** locuteur(trice) *m,f* natif(ive); **a native speaker of Polish, a Polish native speaker** une personne de langue maternelle polonaise; **a native speaker of French/German, a French/German native speaker** un francophone/germanophone, une personne de langue maternelle française/allemande; **I'm not a native speaker** ce n'est pas ma langue maternelle; ***native wit*** esprit *m* naturel

native-born *adj* indigène, natif; **a native-born German** un(e) Allemand(e) de naissance

nativism ['neɪtɪvɪzəm] *n* (**a**) *esp Am Pol* exclusivisme *m* en faveur des natifs (**b**) *Phil* innéisme *m* (**c**) *Psy* nativisme *m*

nativist ['neɪtɪvɪst] *n* (**a**) *esp Am Pol* partisan(e) *m,f* de l'exclusivisme en faveur des natifs (**b**) *Phil* nativiste *mf*

nativistic [,neɪtɪ'vɪstɪk] *adj Psy* nativiste

nativity [nə'tɪvətɪ] (*pl* **nativities**) *n* (**a**) *Rel* **the Nativity** la Nativité (**b**) *(birth)* horoscope *m*

▸▸ ***Nativity play*** = pièce jouée par des enfants et représentant l'histoire de la Nativité; ***Nativity scene*** crèche *f*; *Art* nativité *f*

NATO ['neɪtəʊ] *n* (*abbr* **North Atlantic Treaty Organization**) l'OTAN *f*

natrolite ['nætrəlaɪt] *n Geol* natrolite *f*

natron ['neɪtrən] *n Chem* natron *m*

natter ['nætə(r)] *Fam* **1** *n Br* causerie *f*, causette *f*; **to have a natter** tailler une bavette, faire la causette

2 *vi* papoter; **what were you two nattering about?** de quoi étiez-vous en train de parler, tous les deux?❑

natterer ['nætərə(r)] *n Br Fam* bavard(e)❑ *m,f*; **what a natterer!** quel moulin à paroles!

natterjack ['nætədʒæk] *n Zool* **natterjack (toad)** crapaud *m* des roseaux, calamite *m*

nattily ['nætɪlɪ] *adv* **nattily dressed** sur son trente et un

nattiness ['nætɪnɪs] *n Fam* (**a**) *(smartness → of person)* élégance *f* vestimentaire❑; *(→ of dress)* élégance❑ *f* (**b**) *(cleverness → of device)* caractère *m* astucieux❑

natty ['nætɪ] (*compar* **nattier**, *superl* **nattiest**) *adj Fam* (**a**) *(smart, neat → person)* bien sapé; *(→ dress)* chic❑, qui a de l'allure❑; **he's a natty dresser** il est toujours très bien sapé (**b**) *(clever → device)* astucieux❑

natural ['nætʃərəl] **1** *adj* (**a**) *(created by or existing in nature → scenery, environment, light, resources, process)* naturel; **a natural harbour** un port naturel; **in a natural state** à l'état naturel; **the natural world** la nature

(**b**) *(not artificial → wood, finish)* naturel; **she's a natural redhead** c'est une vraie rousse

(**c**) *(normal → explanation, desire, wish)* naturel, normal; **it's only natural for her to be worried** *or* **that she should be worried** il est tout à fait normal *ou* il est tout naturel qu'elle se fasse du souci; **I'm sure there's a perfectly natural explanation for it** je suis sûr qu'on peut l'expliquer de façon tout à fait naturelle; **death from natural causes** mort *f* naturelle; **in the natural course of events** dans le cours normal des choses; **one's** *or* **the natural reaction is to...** la réaction instinctive est de...; **as is (only) natural** comme de juste

(**d**) *(unaffected → person, manner)* naturel, simple

(**e**) *(innate → talent)* inné, naturel; **she's a natural organizer** c'est une organisatrice-née, elle a un sens inné de l'organisation

(**f**) *(free of additives)* naturel

(**g**) *(child)* naturel

(**h**) *(real → parents)* naturel

(**i**) *Mus* naturel; *(after accidental)* bécarre (*inv*); **G natural** sol bécarre

(**j**) *Math* naturel

2 *adv Fam* **try to act natural!** soyez naturel!❑

3 *n* (**a**) *Fam (gifted person)* **she's a natural** elle a ça dans le sang; **he's a natural for the job** il a le profil de l'emploi❑; **she's a natural for the part** elle est faite pour ce rôle❑

(**b**) *Mus* bécarre *m*

▸▸ ***natural break*** *(in film, text)* coupure *f* qui va de soi; **they reached a natural break in the meeting** ils arrivèrent à une étape de la réunion où il était naturel de faire une pause; ***natural childbirth*** accouchement *m* naturel; ***natural disaster*** catastrophe *f* naturelle; ***natural economy*** économie *f* non monétaire; ***natural family planning*** = contraception par des moyens naturels; *Phys & Elec* ***natural frequency*** fréquence *f* propre; ***natural gas*** gaz *m* naturel; ***natural historian*** naturaliste *mf*; ***natural history*** histoire *f* naturelle; ***natural immunity*** immunité *f* naturelle; ***natural justice*** droits *mpl* naturels; ***natural language*** langage *m* naturel, langue *f* naturelle; ***natural language processing*** traitement *m* (automatique) du langage naturel; ***natural law*** loi *f* naturelle; ***natural life*** *(of person, animal, company)* durée *f* de vie; *(of product)* durée *f* utile; **for the rest of his/her natural life** *(sentenced)* à perpétuité; *Math* ***natural logarithm*** logarithme *m* naturel *ou* népérien; ***natural medicine*** médecine *f* douce *ou* naturelle, physiothérapie *f*; ***natural number*** nombre *m* naturel; *Law* ***natural person*** personne *f* physique *ou* naturelle; *Old-fashioned Phys* ***natural philosophy*** physique *f*; ***natural resources*** ressources *fpl* naturelles; ***natural science*** *(UNCOUNT)* sciences *fpl* naturelles; **botany is a natural science** la botanique fait partie des sciences naturelles; ***natural selection*** sélection *f* naturelle; ***the Natural State*** = surnom donné à l'Arkansas; ***natural theology*** théologie *f* naturelle; *Econ & Ind* ***natural wastage*** départs *mpl* volontaires et en retraite; ***natural yoghurt*** yaourt *m* nature

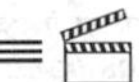

'Natural Born Killers' *Stone* 'Tueurs-nés'

natural-born *adj (singer, leader etc)* né; **natural-born Frenchwoman** Française *f* de naissance

naturalism ['nætʃərəlɪzəm] *n* naturalisme *m*

naturalist ['nætʃərəlɪst] *n* naturaliste *mf*

naturalistic [,nætʃərə'lɪstɪk] *adj* naturaliste

naturalization [,nætʃərəlaɪ'zeɪʃən] *n* (**a**) *(of alien, foreign word)* naturalisation *f* (**b**) *(of plant, animal)* acclimatation *f*

naturalize, -ise ['nætʃərəlaɪz] **1** *vt* (**a**) *(person, expression, custom)* naturaliser; **to become naturalized** *(person)* se faire naturaliser (**b**) *(plant, animal)* acclimater

2 *vi Biol* s'acclimater

naturalized ['nætʃərəlaɪzd] *adj (person)* naturalisé

naturally ['nætʃərəlɪ] *adv* (**a**) *(of course)* naturellement, bien sûr, bien entendu; **you have got the money? – naturally!** tu as l'argent? – bien sûr!; **I was naturally surprised** évidemment, cela m'a surpris; **she naturally assumed that he was joking** naturellement, elle a cru qu'il plaisantait; **these questions were naturally somewhat embarrassing for me** ces questions, comme vous le pensez bien, n'étaient pas sans m'embarrasser

(**b**) *(by nature → lazy)* de nature, par tempérament; *(→ difficult)* naturellement, par sa nature; **skiing comes naturally to her** on dirait qu'elle a fait du ski toute sa vie; **it comes naturally to him** c'est un don chez lui; **although it didn't come naturally, he forced himself to ask questions** bien que cela ne lui vienne pas naturellement, il se forçait à poser des questions; *Ironic* **punctuality doesn't come naturally to him** la ponctualité n'est pas son fort

(**c**) *(unaffectedly)* naturellement, de manière naturelle; **you answered very naturally** vous avez répondu très naturellement *ou* de manière très naturelle

(**d**) *(in natural state → occur)* naturellement, à l'état naturel; **naturally occurring** présent à l'état naturel

naturalness ['nætʃərəlnɪs] *n* (**a**) *(unaffectedness)* naturel *m*, simplicité *f*; **he behaved with great naturalness** il s'est comporté avec beaucoup de naturel; **his acting was impressive for its naturalness** le naturel de cet acteur était remarquable (**b**) *(natural appearance)* naturel *m*

nature ['neɪtʃə(r)] *n* (**a**) *(the natural world)* nature *f*; **Nature can be cruel** la nature peut être cruelle; **the wildest landscapes in nature** les paysages les plus sauvages que la nature puisse offrir; **to go back** *or* **to return to nature** retourner à la nature; **in a state of nature** à l'état de nature; *Hum (naked → man)* en costume d'Adam; *(→ woman)* en costume d'Ève; **the nature-nurture debate** le débat sur l'inné et l'acquis; **to let nature take its course** laisser faire la nature; **to draw/paint from nature** dessiner/peindre d'après nature; **to go against nature** aller contre la nature; **one of nature's gentlemen** un gentleman-né

(**b**) *(character)* nature *f*, caractère *m*; **he has such a kind nature** il a une si bonne nature *ou* un si bon caractère; **it's not in her nature to struggle** ce n'est pas dans sa nature de lutter; **lazy by nature** paresseux de nature; **to appeal to sb's better nature** faire appel aux bons sentiments de qn; **it's in the nature of volcanoes to erupt** il est dans la nature des volcans d'entrer en éruption; **human beings are by nature gregarious** l'homme est, par nature, un être sociable; **war is by its very nature destructive** la guerre est destructrice de par sa nature même; **in the nature of things** dans la nature des choses

(**c**) *(type)* nature *f*, type *m*, genre *m*; **books of a serious nature** des livres sérieux; **an incident of a serious nature** un incident grave; **questions of a personal nature** des questions à caractère personnel; **do you sell chocolates or anything of that nature?** est-ce que vous vendez des chocolats ou ce genre de choses?; **something in the nature of a...** une espèce *ou* une sorte de...; *Admin* **nature of contents** *(on parcel)* désignation du contenu

▸▸ ***the Nature Conservancy Council*** = organisme britannique de protection de la nature; ***nature cure*** naturopathie *f*, naturothérapie *f*; **to go on a nature cure** suivre une naturothérapie; ***nature lover*** amoureux(euse) *m,f* de la nature; *Am* ***nature preserve***, *Br* ***nature reserve*** réserve *f* naturelle; *Austr* ***nature strip*** bande *f* d'herbe; *Sch* ***nature study*** sciences *fpl* naturelles, histoire *f* naturelle; ***nature trail*** sentier *m* écologique

-natured ['neɪtʃəd] *suff* d'une nature..., d'un caractère...; **she's good/ill-natured** elle a bon/mauvais caractère; **gentle-natured** d'une nature douce

nature-loving *adj* qui adore la nature

naturism ['neɪtʃərɪzəm] *n Br* naturisme *m*

naturist ['neɪtʃərɪst] *Br* **1** *n* naturiste *mf*

2 *adj* naturiste

naturopath ['neɪtʃərəpæθ] *n* naturopathe *mf*

naturopathy [,neɪtʃə'rɒpəθɪ] *n* naturothérapie *f*, naturopathie *f*

Naugahyde® ['nɔːgəhaɪd] *n Am* ≃ Skaï®

naught [nɔːt] **1** *n* (**a**) *esp Am* = **nought** (**a**)

(**b**) *Arch or Literary (nothing)* **their plans came to naught** leurs projets ont échoué *ou* n'ont pas abouti; **they set my ideas at naught** ils ne font aucun cas *ou* ils ne tiennent aucun compte de mes idées

2 *adv Arch or Literary* nullement; **it matters naught** cela n'a aucune importance; **it serves you naught** cela ne vous sert nullement

naughtily ['nɔːtɪlɪ] *adv* (**a**) *(mischievously)* avec malice, malicieusement; **you have behaved very naughtily** tu as été très vilain (**b**) *(suggestively)* avec grivoiserie

naughtiness ['nɔːtɪnɪs] *n* (**a**) *(disobedience)* désobéissance *f*; *(mischievousness)* malice *f*; **she will be punished for her naughtiness** elle sera punie pour avoir désobéi (**b**) *(indecency)* grivoiserie *f*, gaillardise *f*

naughty ['nɔːtɪ] (*compar* **naughtier**, *superl* **naughtiest**) *adj* (**a**) *(child → badly behaved)* méchant, désobéissant, vilain; *(→ mischievous)* coquin, malicieux; **that was very naughty of you** ce que tu as fait était très vilain; **you naughty boy!** petit vilain! (**b**) *(indecent → joke, story, postcard)* paillard, osé; *(→ word)* vilain, gros (grosse) (**c**) *(sexy)* coquin; **naughty underwear** dessous *mpl* coquins

▸▸ *Br Euph* ***naughty bits*** parties *fpl* honteuses; ***the naughty nineties*** ≃ la Belle Époque *(1890–1900)*

nauplius ['nɔːplɪəs] *(pl* **nauplii** [-lɪaɪ]) *n Zool* nauplius *m*

Nauru [nɑː'uːruː] *n* Nauru *f*

nausea ['nɔːzɪə] *n* (**a**) *(sickness)* nausée *f*; **to be overcome with nausea** avoir mal au cœur, avoir des nausées (**b**) *Fig (disgust)* dégoût *m*, nausée *f*, écœurement *m*

nauseate ['nɔːzɪeɪt] *vt also Fig* donner la nausée à, écœurer; **the sight of blood nauseated him** en voyant le sang, il eut un haut-le-cœur

nauseating ['nɔːzɪeɪtɪŋ] *adj (food, sight, idea)* écœurant, qui donne la nausée; *(smell)* écœurant, nauséabond; *(person, behaviour)* écœurant, dégoûtant, répugnant; **the stench was nauseating** la puanteur vous levait *ou* soulevait le cœur

nauseatingly ['nɔːzɪeɪtɪŋlɪ] *adv* à vous donner la nausée, à vous écœurer; **she was nauseatingly smug** elle prenait des airs écœurants de supériorité, elle était d'une supériorité écœurante

nauseous [*Br* 'nɔːzɪəs, *Am* 'nɔːʃəs] *adj* (**a**) *(revolting → smell)* nauséabond, qui donne la nausée, écœurant (**b**) *(queasy → person)* **to feel nauseous** avoir mal au cœur, avoir des nausées; **it made me feel nauseous** cela m'a levé *ou* soulevé le cœur (**c**) *Am Fam (disgusting)* dégueulasse

Nausicaa [nɔː'sɪkɪə] *pr n Myth* Nausicaa

nautical ['nɔːtɪkəl] *adj* nautique, marin; *(term, expression)* de navigation, de marine

▸▸ ***nautical almanac*** éphémérides *fpl* nautiques; ***nautical club*** club *m* nautique; ***nautical mile*** mille *m* marin

nautilus ['nɔːtɪləs] *n Zool* nautile *m*

NAV [,eneɪ'viː] *n Fin (abbr* **net asset value**) valeur *f* d'actif net

navaid ['næveɪd] *n* radioguidage *m*, aide *f* à la navigation

Navajo ['nævəhəʊ] *(pl* **inv** *or* **Navajos** *or* **Navajoes**) **1** *n* (**a**) *(person)* Navajo *mf*; **the Navajo** les Navajos *mpl* (**b**) *Ling* navajo *m*

2 *adj* navajo

naval ['neɪvəl] *adj (gen)* naval; *(power)* maritime

▸▸ ***naval academy*** école *f* navale; ***naval architect*** architecte *m* naval, architecte *f* navale; *(for warships)* ingénieur *m* du génie maritime *ou* en construction navale; ***naval architecture*** construction *f* navale; *Mil* ***Naval Aviation*** = l'aéronavale américaine; ***naval base*** base *f* navale; ***naval college*** école *f* navale; ***naval dockyard*** arsenal *m* maritime; ***naval forces*** forces *fpl* navales; ***naval officer*** officier *m* de marine; ***naval stores*** *(depot)* entrepôts *mpl* maritimes; *(supplies)* approvisionnements *mpl ou* matériel *m ou* fournitures *fpl* de navires; ***naval surveyor*** (ingénieur *m*) hydrographe *m*; ***naval warfare*** guerre *f* navale

Navarre [nə'vɑː(r)] *n* Navarre *f*

Navarrese [nævə'riːz] **1** *n (person)* Navarrais(e) *m,f*

2 *adj* navarrais

nave [neɪv] *n* (**a**) *(of church)* nef *f* (**b**) *(hub)* moyeu *m*

navel ['neɪvəl] *n* nombril *m*; *Fig* **to contemplate one's navel** se regarder le nombril, faire du nombrilisme

▸▸ ***navel orange*** navel *f*

navel-gazing [-,geɪzɪŋ] *n* nombrilisme *m*

navelwort ['neɪvəlwɜːt] *n Bot* ombilic *m*

navicular [nə'vɪkjʊlə(r)] **1** *adj* (**a**) *Anat* naviculaire (**b**) *Bot* naviculaire

2 *n* (**a**) *Anat* os *m* naviculaire (**b**) *Vet* maladie *f* naviculaire, encastelure *f*

▸▸ *Anat* ***navicular bone*** os *m* naviculaire; ***navicular disease*** maladie *f* naviculaire, encastelure *f*; *Anat* ***navicular fossa*** *(in ear)* fossette *f* de l'anthélix; *(in urethra)* fosse *f* naviculaire

navigability [nævɪgə'bɪlɪtɪ] *n (of river, vessel)* navigabilité *f*; *(of balloon)* dirigeabilité *f*

navigable ['nævɪgəbəl] *adj (water)* navigable; *(craft)* dirigeable

navigate ['nævɪgeɪt] **1** *vt* (**a**) *(seas)* naviguer dans *ou* sur; **to navigate a ship** *(steer)* gouverner *ou* diriger un navire; *(plot path of)* calculer le parcours d'un navire; **they navigated the seven seas** ils naviguaient sur *ou* parcouraient toutes les mers du globe; **to navigate the Atlantic** traverser l'Atlantique (en bateau); **this river is difficult to navigate** la navigation est difficile sur ce fleuve; **she navigated us successfully through Bombay** *(in car)* elle nous a fait traverser Bombay sans problèmes; **he navigated the plane to the nearest airport** il dirigea l'avion sur l'aéroport le plus proche

(**b**) *Fig* **the stairs are difficult to navigate in the dark** cet escalier est difficile à monter/descendre dans l'obscurité; **she navigated her way across the crowded room** elle se fraya un chemin à travers la salle bondée

(**c**) *Comput (Web site)* naviguer sur; **to navigate the Net** naviguer sur l'Internet

2 *vi* (**a**) *(gen)* naviguer; **to navigate by the stars** naviguer aux étoiles; **can you navigate for me?** *(in car)* peux-tu m'indiquer la route *ou* me piloter?; **you drive and I'll navigate** toi tu conduis et moi je prends la carte routière

(**b**) *Comput (around Web site)* naviguer

navigating officer ['nævɪgeɪtɪŋ-] *n* officier *m* de navigation, officier *m* navigateur

navigation [,nævɪ'geɪʃən] *n* (**a**) *(act, skill of navigating)* navigation *f* (**b**) *Am (shipping)* navigation *f*, trafic *m* (maritime) (**c**) *Comput (around Web site)* navigation *f*

▸▸ ***navigation aids*** aides *fpl* à la navigation; ***navigation bar*** barre *f* de navigation; ***navigation button*** bouton *m* de navigation; ***navigation dues*** droits *mpl* de navigation; ***navigation lights*** *Aviat* feux *mpl* de position; *Naut* fanaux *mpl*, feux *mpl* de bord *ou* de route; ***navigation officer*** officier *m* de navigation, officier *m* navigateur

navigational [,nævɪ'geɪʃənəl] *adj* de (la) navigation; **his navigational skills** ses talents de navigateur

▸▸ ***navigational aid*** aide *f* à la navigation

navigator ['nævɪgeɪtə(r)] *n* navigateur(trice) *m,f*; *(in a car)* copilote *mf*

navvy ['nævɪ] *(pl* **navvies**) *n Br Fam* terrassier *m*

navy ['neɪvɪ] *(pl* **navies**) **1** *n* (**a**) *(service)* marine *f* (nationale); **to be** *or* **to serve in the navy** être dans la marine (**b**) *(warships collectively)* marine *f* de guerre; *(fleet)* flotte *f* (**c**) *(colour)* bleu *m* marine *(inv)*

2 *adj* (**a**) *(gen)* de la marine (**b**) *(colour)* bleu marine *(inv)*

▸▸ ***navy blue*** bleu *m* marine; *Br* ***Navy Cut***® tabac *m* haché fin; *Br* ***Navy List***, *Am* ***Navy Register*** ≃ liste *f* navale; ***Navy Seal*** = commando de la marine américaine; ***navy yard*** arsenal *m* maritime

navy-blue *adj* bleu marine *(inv)*

naw [nɔː] *exclam Am & Scot Fam* non!

nawab [nə'wɑːb] *n* nabab *m*

nay [neɪ] **1** *adv Arch or Hum* voire, que dis-je; **I was asked, nay ordered to come** on m'a demandé, ou plutôt donné l'ordre, de venir; **for a few dollars, nay a few cents** pour quelques dollars, voire quelques cents

2 *n* vote *m* défavorable; **the nays have it** les non l'emportent

3 *exclam (in oral vote)* non

naysayer ['neɪ,seɪə(r)] *n* = personne qui a l'esprit de contradiction

Nazarene [,næzə'riːn] **1** *n* Nazaréen(enne) *m,f*

2 *adj* nazaréen

Nazareth ['næzərəθ] *n* Nazareth

Nazarite ['næzəraɪt] *n Hist (in ancient Israel)* Naziréen(enne) *m,f*, Nazaréen(enne) *m,f*

Nazi ['nɑːtsɪ] **1** *n* nazi(e) *m,f*

2 *adj* nazi

Nazification [,nɑːtsɪfɪ'keɪʃən] *n* nazification *f*

Nazism ['nɑːtsɪzəm], **Naziism** ['nɑːtsɪ,ɪzəm] *n* nazisme *m*

NB (**a**) *(written abbr* **nota bene**) NB (**b**) *(written abbr* **New Brunswick**) Nouveau-Brunswick *m*

NBA [,enbiː'eɪ] *n* (**a**) *Am (abbr* **National Basketball Association**) = fédération américaine de basket-ball

(**b**) *Am (abbr* **National Boxing Association**) = fédération américaine de boxe

(**c**) *Formerly Com (abbr* **net book agreement**) = accord entre maisons d'édition et libraires stipulant que ces derniers n'ont le droit de vendre aucun ouvrage à un prix inférieur à celui fixé par l'éditeur

NBC [,enbiː'siː] **1** *n TV (abbr* **National Broadcasting Company**) = chaîne de télévision américaine

2 *adj (abbr* **nuclear, biological and chemical**) NBC

▸▸ ***NBC suit*** survêtement *m* de protection NBC; ***NBC weapons*** armes *fpl* NBC

nbg [,enbiː'dʒiː] *adj Br Fam (abbr* **no bloody good**) nul

NBS [,enbiː'es] *n Am (abbr* **National Bureau of Standards**) = service américain des poids et mesures

NBV [,enbiː'viː] *n Fin (abbr* **net book value**) valeur *f* comptable nette

NC (**a**) *(written abbr* **no charge**) gratuit (**b**) *(written abbr* **North Carolina**) Caroline *f* du Nord

NCAA [,ensiː,eɪ'eɪ] *n Am (abbr* **National Collegiate Athletic Association**) = association interuniversitaire traitant des questions sportives, aux États-Unis

NCB [,ensiː'biː] *n Br Formerly (abbr* **National Coal Board**) = ancien nom des charbonnages britanniques

NCC [,ensiː'siː] *n* (**a**) *Br Ecol (abbr* **Nature Conservancy Council**) = organisme britannique de protection de la nature (**b**) *(abbr* **National Curriculum Council**) = conseil responsable de l'établissement des programmes scolaires en Angleterre et au pays de Galles

NCCL [,ensiː,siː'el] *n (abbr* **National Council for Civil Liberties**) = en Grande-Bretagne, ligue de défense des droits du citoyen luttant contre toute forme de discrimination

NCO [,ensiː'əʊ] *n Mil (abbr* **non-commissioned officer**) sous-officier *m*

NCT [,ensiː'tiː] *n (abbr* **National Childbirth Trust**) = organisation de conseil aux femmes enceintes

NCU [,ensiː'juː] *n (abbr* **National Communications Union**) = syndicat des salariés qui travaillent dans les télécommunications

NCVQ [,ensiː,viː'kjuː] *n (abbr* **National Council for Vocational Qualifications**) = organisme britannique responsable de la formation professionnelle

ND *(written abbr* **North Dakota**) Dakota *m* du Nord

N'Djamena [əndʒɑː'meɪnə] *n* N'Djamena

NDP [,endiː'piː] *n Fin (abbr* **net domestic product**) produit *m* intérieur net

NDPB [,endiː,piː'biː] *n Br Pol (abbr* **non-departmental public body**) = organisme semi-public

NE (**a**) *(written abbr* **Nebraska**) Nebraska *m*

(**b**) *(written abbr* **New England**) Nouvelle-Angleterre *f*

(**c**) *(written abbr* **north-east**) NE

Neanderthal, neanderthal [nɪ'ændətɑːl] **1** *n* (**a**) *(during Stone Age)* néandertalien *m* (**b**) *Fig Pej (uncouth man)* primate *m*

2 *adj* (**a**) *(during Stone Age)* néandertalien (**b**) *Fig Pej (primitive → man)* fruste, primaire; *(→ method, system)* primitif; *(→ attitude)* primaire

▸▸ ***Neanderthal man*** l'homme *m* de Neandertal

neap [niːp] **1** *n* morte-eau *f*

2 *adj* faible

▸▸ ***neap tide*** marée *f* de morte-eau

Neapolitan [,nɪə'pɒlɪtən] **1** *n* Napolitain(e) *m,f*

2 *adj* napolitain

▸▸ ***Neapolitan ice cream*** tranche *f* napolitaine

NEAR [nɪə(r)]

près de	▸ 1 (a) – (c), (e); 6 (a), (c) – (e)
proche de	▸ 1 (b); 6 (b), (c)
au bord de	▸ 1 (e)
près	▸ 2 (a), (b)
proche	▸ 2 (b); 3 (a), (b), (e)
quasi	▸ 2 (c)
approcher de	▸ 4
approcher	▸ 5

(compar **nearer**, *superl* **nearest**) **1** *prep* (**a**) *(in space)* près de; **near Paris** près de Paris; **don't go near the fire** ne t'approche pas du feu; **is there a chemist's near here?** est-ce qu'il y a un pharmacien près d'ici *ou* dans le coin?; **she likes to have her family near her** elle aime avoir sa famille près d'elle *ou* auprès d'elle; **near the end of the book** vers la fin du livre; **I haven't been near a horse since the accident** je n'ai pas approché un cheval depuis l'accident; **you can't trust him near a gun** il est dangereux avec

une arme à feu; **she wouldn't let anyone near her** *(physically)* elle ne voulait pas qu'on l'approche; *(emotionally)* elle ne voulait être proche de personne

(**b**) *(in time)* près de, proche de; **it's getting near Christmas** c'est bientôt Noël; **ask me nearer the time** repose-moi la question quand l'heure viendra; **near the end of the film** vers la fin du film

(**c**) *(similar to)* près de; **that would be nearer the truth** ce serait plus près de la vérité; **nobody can come anywhere near her** il n'y a personne à son niveau; **he's nowhere near it!** *(with guess, calculation)* il n'y est pas du tout!

(**d**) *(in amount or number)* **profits were near the 30 percent mark** les bénéfices approchaient la barre des 30 pour cent; **it took us nearer three hours to finish** en fait, nous avons mis presque trois heures à finir; **it will cost nearer £5,000** ça coûtera plutôt dans les 5000 livres

(**e**) *(on the point of)* près de, au bord de; **the country's economy is near ruin** le pays est au bord de la faillite; **to be near tears** être au bord des larmes; **near death** sur le point de mourir; **it's near freezing** il ne fait pas loin de zéro, la température avoisine zéro degré

2 *adv* (**a**) *(in space)* près, à côté, à proximité; **to draw near** s'approcher; **come nearer** venez plus près, approchez-vous; **to bring sth nearer (to)** rapprocher qch (de); **the heat was too great for us to get near** la chaleur était trop intense pour que l'on puisse s'approcher; **so near and yet so far!** c'est dommage, si près du but!; **near at hand** tout près, à proximité

(**b**) *(in time)* proche, près; **as the time grew** *or* **drew near** à mesure que le moment approchait; **midnight drew near** minuit approchait, on approchait de minuit

(**c**) *(with adjective)* quasi; **a near impossible task** une tâche quasi *ou* quasiment *ou* pratiquement impossible; **the show went ahead with near tragic consequences** le spectacle a continué avec des conséquences quasi tragiques

(**d**) *(idioms)* **as near as makes no difference** à peu de chose près, à quelque chose près; *Fam* **£50 or as near as dammit** 50 livres à peu de chose près ❑; **as near as I can remember** autant que je puisse m'en souvenir; **it's near enough** ça va comme ça; **it's near enough 50 lbs** ça pèse dans les 50 livres; **it's nowhere near good enough** c'est loin d'être suffisant; **she's nowhere near finished** elle est loin d'avoir fini; **there weren't anywhere near enough people** il y avait bien trop peu de gens

3 *adj* (**a**) *(in space)* proche; **the near edge** le bord le plus proche; **our near neighbours** nos proches voisins; **I knew you were near** je savais que vous étiez dans les environs *ou* parages; **the nearest post office** le bureau de poste le plus proche; **the near front wheel** *(driving on left)* la roue avant gauche; *(driving on right)* la roue avant droite

(**b**) *(in time)* proche; **when the time is near** quand le moment approchera; **in the near future** dans un proche avenir

(**c**) *(virtual)* **it was a near disaster** on a frôlé la catastrophe; **he found himself in near darkness** il s'est retrouvé dans une obscurité quasi totale; **it was a near thing** on l'a échappé belle, il était moins une; **I caught the train, but it was a near thing** j'ai eu mon train de justesse; **I missed the train, but it was a near thing** j'ai manqué mon train de peu; **he's the nearest thing we have to a national hero** il est ce que nous avons de mieux en matière de héros national; **it's the nearest you'll get to a bookshop in these parts** c'est ce que vous trouverez de mieux en matière de librairie par ici

(**d**) *(in amount, number)* **to the nearest £10** à 10 livres près; **round it up/down to the nearest 10 francs** arrondissez aux 10 francs supérieurs/inférieurs

(**e**) *(closely related)* proche; **her nearest relatives** ses parents les plus proches; *Hum* **your nearest and dearest** vos proches

4 *vt* *(approach → place, date, event)* approcher de; *(→ state)* être au bord de; **the train was nearing the station** le train approchait de la gare; **he was nearing seventy when he got married** il allait sur ses soixante-dix ans quand il s'est marié; **the book is nearing completion** le livre est sur le point d'être terminé; **we are nearing our goal** nous touchons au but; **he seemed to be nearing a crisis** il semblait au bord d'une crise; **we're nearing the point of no return** il sera bientôt trop tard pour faire marche arrière, on atteindra bientôt le point de non-retour

5 *vi* *(date, place)* approcher

6 near to *prep* (**a**) *(in space)* près de; **they live near to us** ils habitent près de *ou* à côté de chez nous

(**b**) *(emotionally)* proche de; **those near and dear to him** ceux qui le touchent de près, ses proches

(**c**) *(in time)* près de, proche de; **it's getting near to Christmas** Noël approche

(**d**) *(in similarity)* près de

(**e**) *(on the point of)* près de, au bord de; **to be near to death** être sur le point de mourir; **to be near to tears** être au bord des larmes; **I came near to leaving several times** j'ai failli partir plusieurs fois

►► *Am* ***near beer*** bière *f* sans alcool; ***the Near East*** le Proche-Orient; **in the Near East** au Proche-Orient; ***near gale*** *(on Beaufort scale)* grand frais *m*; *Comput* ***near letter quality*** qualité *f* courrier; ***near letter quality printer*** imprimante *f* de qualité courrier; ***near miss*** *(gen)* & *Sport* coup *m* qui a raté de peu; *(between planes, vehicles etc)* collision *f* évitée de justesse; **it was a near miss** *(answer)* la réponse était presque bonne; *(accident)* on a frôlé l'accident; **that was a near miss!** *(escape)* on l'a échappé belle!; **the two cars had a near miss** les deux voitures ont bien failli se rentrer dedans; ***near money*** quasi-monnaie *f*; *St Exch* ***near month*** échéance *f* proche

---

near- [nɪə(r)] *pref* **near-perfect** pratiquement *ou* quasi parfait; **near-complete** pratiquement *ou* quasi complet

nearby 1 *adv* [ˌnɪə'baɪ] *(near here)* près d'ici; *(near there)* près de là; **I live just nearby** j'habite tout près d'ici; **is there a station nearby?** est-ce qu'il y a une gare près d'ici *ou* à proximité?

2 *adj* ['nɪəbaɪ] **we stopped at a nearby post office** nous nous sommes arrêtés dans un bureau de poste situé non loin de là; **he threw it into a nearby dustbin** il l'a jeté dans une poubelle non loin de là

Nearctic [nɪ'ɑːktɪk] *adj* néartique

near-death experience *n* expérience *f* aux frontières de la mort

near-earth asteroid *n Astron* géocroiseur *m*

nearly ['nɪəlɪ] *adv* (**a**) *(almost)* presque, à peu près; **I'm nearly ready** je suis presque prêt; **we're nearly there** on y est presque; **he's nearly eighty** il a près de *ou* presque quatre-vingts ans; **it's nearly 8 o'clock** il est presque 8 heures; **I nearly fell** j'ai failli tomber; **I very nearly didn't come** j'ai bien failli ne pas venir; **I can nearly reach the shelf** j'arrive presque à atteindre l'étagère; **she nearly went bankrupt** elle a failli faire faillite; **he was nearly crying** *or* **in tears** il était au bord des larmes; **I'm nearly as tall as my brother** je suis presque aussi grand que mon frère; **nearly new** d'occasion

(**b**) *(with negative)* **I didn't buy nearly enough food for everyone** je suis loin d'avoir acheté assez de provisions pour tout le monde; **he's not nearly as important as he likes to think** il est loin d'être aussi important qu'il le croit; **it's not nearly as difficult as I thought** c'est bien moins difficile que je ne l'imaginais

►► *Fam* ***nearly man*** espoir *m* raté

nearness ['nɪənɪs] *n* proximité *f*

near-shore *adj* à proximité des côtes

nearside ['nɪəsaɪd] *Br* **1** *n* *(when driving on right)* côté *m* droit; *(when driving on left)* côté *m* gauche; **get out on the nearside** descendez côté trottoir

2 *adj* *(when driving on right)* (du côté) droit, du côté trottoir; *(when driving on left)* (du côté) gauche, du côté trottoir

nearsighted [ˌnɪə'saɪtɪd] *adj Am* myope

nearsightedness [ˌnɪə'saɪtɪdnɪs] *n Am* myopie *f*

neat [niːt] **1** *adj* (**a**) *(tidy → person)* ordonné, qui a de l'ordre; *(→ in one's appearance)* net, soigné; *(→ work, handwriting)* soigné; *(→ exercise book)* bien tenu, propre; *(→ desk, room)* net, bien rangé; *(→ garden)* bien tenu *ou* entretenu, soigné; **her clothes are always neat** ses vêtements sont toujours impeccables; **to do a neat job** faire un travail soigné; **she made a neat job of it** elle a fait du bon travail; **the surgeon made a neat job of those stitches** le chirurgien a très bien fait ces points de suture; **as neat as a new pin** tiré à quatre épingles

(**b**) *(smart, pretty)* joli; **a neat little house** une gentille petite maison

(**c**) *(trim → nose)* petit; *(→ waist, figure)* mince

(**d**) *(skilful, clever → turn of phrase, answer etc)* bien tourné, adroit; *(→ solution)* ingénieux; **that's a neat trick** c'est malin

(**e**) *(effective → organization)* net, efficace; *(→ system, plan)* bien conçu

(**f**) *Am Fam (great)* chouette; **what a neat outfit!** chouettes fringues!; **that's really neat** c'est vraiment chouette, c'est super

(**g**) *(undiluted → spirits)* sec (sèche), sans eau; **to take** *or* **drink one's whisky neat** boire son whisky sec

(**h**) *(tax-free)* **we made a neat £100** on a fait 100 livres net

2 *exclam Am Fam* super!, chouette!

neaten ['niːtən] *vt* *(room, house)* remettre en ordre, ranger; *(garden)* ranger; *(clothing)* arranger, ajuster; *(hair)* arranger, mettre en ordre; *(presentation)* fignoler, peaufiner; **you ought to neaten (up) the place before they arrive** tu devrais mettre un peu d'ordre dans la maison avant qu'ils arrivent; **go and neaten your hair** va te recoiffer

'neath, neath [niːθ] *Literary* = **beneath**

neat-handed *adj Literary* aux mains adroites

neat-looking *adj Am Fam* chouette; **a neat-looking guy** un mec super mignon

neatly ['niːtlɪ] *adv* (**a**) *(tidily)* avec soin *ou* ordre; *(carefully → write, work)* avec soin, soigneusement; **put the papers neatly on the desk** posez les papiers soigneusement sur le bureau; **to dress neatly** s'habiller avec soin; **the desk fits neatly into the corner of the room** le bureau rentre pile dans le coin de la pièce

(**b**) *(skilfully)* habilement, adroitement; **neatly phrased** bien tourné; **to solve a problem neatly** résoudre un problème avec élégance; **you put that very neatly** vous l'avez très bien dit *ou* exprimé; **he neatly avoided the issue** il a habilement évité le sujet; **you got out of that situation very neatly** vous vous en êtes tiré très habilement *ou* très adroitement

neatness ['niːtnɪs] *n* (**a**) *(tidiness → of dress)* aspect *m* soigné, netteté *f*; *(→ of room)* ordre *m*; *(→ of work)* aspect *m* soigné; *(→ of exercise book)* propreté *f*; **a passion for neatness** la passion de l'ordre; **the neatness of her writing** l'élégance *f* de son écriture (**b**) *(skilfulness → of phrase)* tournure *f* adroite; *(→ of solution, idea)* ingéniosité *f*; *(→ of scheme)* habileté *f* (**c**) *(prettiness → of figure, legs)* finesse *f*

Nebraska [nɪ'bræskə] *n* le Nebraska; **in Nebraska** dans le Nebraska

Nebuchadnezzar [ˌnebjʊkəd'nezə(r)] **1** *n* *(bottle)* nabuchodonosor *m*

2 *pr n Bible* Nabuchodonosor

Nebuchadrezzar [ˌnebjʊkə'drezə(r)] *pr n Bible* Nabuchodonosor

nebula ['nebjʊlə] *(pl* **nebulas** *or* **nebulae** [-liː]) *n* (**a**) *Astron* nébuleuse *f* (**b**) *Med (of cornea)* nébulosité *f*; *(of urine)* aspect *m* trouble

nebular ['nebjʊlə(r)] *adj* (**a**) *Astron* nébulaire (**b**) *Med (cornea)* nébuleux; *(urine)* trouble

nebulize, -ise ['nebjʊlaɪz] *vt* nébuliser

nebulizer ['nebjʊˌlaɪzə(r)] *n Med* nébuliseur *m*

nebulosity [ˌnebjʊ'lɒsətɪ] *(pl* **nebulosities**) *n* nébulosité *f*

nebulous ['nebjʊləs] *adj* (**a**) *(vague)* vague, flou, nébuleux (**b**) *Astron* nébulaire (**c**) *Med (of cornea)* nébuleux (**d**) *Literary (misty)* brumeux

nebulously ['nebjʊləslɪ] *adv* nébuleusement

nebulousness ['nebjʊləsnɪs] *n* nébulosité *f*

NEC [ˌeniː'siː] *n Br* (*abbr* **National Exhibition Centre**) = parc d'expositions près de Birmingham en Angleterre

necessarian [ˌnesə'seərɪən] *Phil* **1** *n* nécessarien(enne) *m,f*, déterministe *mf*

2 *adj* nécessarien, déterministe

necessarianism [ˌnesəˈseərɪənɪzəm] *n Phil* doctrine *f* des nécessariens, déterminisme *m*

necessarily [ˌnesəˈserɪlɪ] *adv* (**a**) *(gen)* nécessairement, forcément; **we don't necessarily have to go** rien ne nous oblige à partir, nous ne sommes pas forcés de partir; **not necessarily** pas forcément (**b**) *(inevitably)* inévitablement, forcément

necessary [ˈnesəsrɪ] *(pl* **necessaries***)* **1** *adj* (**a**) *(essential)* nécessaire, essentiel; *(indispensable)* indispensable; *(compulsory)* obligatoire; **water is necessary to** *or* **for life** l'eau est indispensable à la vie; **is this visit really necessary?** est-ce que cette visite est vraiment indispensable?; **it is necessary for him to come** il est nécessaire qu'il vienne, il faut qu'il vienne; **to make it necessary for sb to do sth** obliger qn à faire qch; **circumstances made it necessary to delay our departure** les circonstances nous ont obligés à retarder notre départ; **I'll do everything necessary to make her agree** je ferai tout pour qu'elle accepte; **he did no more than was necessary** il n'a fait que le strict nécessaire; **if necessary** *(if forced)* s'il le faut; *(if need arises)* le cas échéant, si besoin est; **a necessary condition** *(gen)* une condition nécessaire *ou* sine qua non; *Phil* une condition nécessaire; **will you make the necessary arrangements?** pouvez-vous prendre les dispositions nécessaires?; **he took the necessary measures** il a pris les mesures nécessaires *ou* qui s'imposaient

(**b**) *(inevitable)* nécessaire, inéluctable; **a necessary evil** un mal nécessaire; **you can draw the necessary conclusion yourself** vous pouvez vous-même tirer les conclusions qui s'imposent

2 *n* (**a**) *Br Fam* **to do the necessary** faire le nécessaire □

(**b**) *Br Fam (cash)* **have you got the necessary?** tu as de quoi payer? □

(**c**) **the necessaries** *(food, money etc)* ce qu'il faut pour vivre; *Law (means to live)* le nécessaire

necessitate [nɪˈsesɪteɪt] *vt Formal* nécessiter, rendre nécessaire; **family problems have necessitated his resignation** des problèmes familiaux l'ont obligé *ou* contraint à démissionner

necessitous [nɪˈsesɪtəs] *adj Formal* nécessiteux, démuni, pauvre

necessity [nɪˈsesətɪ] *(pl* **necessities***)* **1** *n* (**a**) *(need)* nécessité *f*, besoin *m*; **there is no necessity for drastic measures** il n'y a pas lieu de prendre des mesures draconiennes; **there's no real necessity for us to go** nous n'avons pas vraiment besoin d'y aller, il n'est pas indispensable que nous y allions; **the necessity for** *or* **of keeping careful records** la nécessité de prendre des notes détaillées; **if the necessity should arise** si le besoin se faisait sentir; **in case of absolute necessity** en cas de force majeure; **out of** *or* **by** *or* **through necessity** par nécessité, par la force des choses; *Prov* **necessity has no law** nécessité fait loi; *Prov* **necessity is the mother of invention** = en cas de besoin on trouve toujours une solution

(**b**) *Formal (poverty)* besoin *m*, nécessité *f*

(**c**) *(essential)* chose *f* nécessaire *ou* essentielle; **the basic** *or* **bare necessities of life** les choses qui sont absolument essentielles *ou* indispensables à la vie; **a car is not one of life's necessities** une voiture n'est pas indispensable; **it's one of life's necessities** c'est un élément vital

(**d**) *Phil* nécessité *f*

2 of necessity *adv* nécessairement

neck [nek] **1** *n* (**a**) *(part of body)* cou *m*; **he threw his arms round her neck** il s'est jeté à son *ou* il lui a sauté au cou; **the cat had a collar round its neck** le chat avait un collier au cou; **water was dripping down my neck** l'eau me coulait dans le cou; **to get a stiff neck** attraper le torticolis; *Fig* **he's always breathing down my neck** il est tout le temps sur mon dos; **to be up to one's neck in work** avoir du travail par-dessus la tête, être débordé de travail; **they were up to their necks in debt** ils étaient endettés jusqu'au cou; **I'm up to my neck in trouble** j'ai des ennuis par-dessus la tête; **the problem is still hanging round my neck** je n'ai toujours pas résolu ce problème; **to risk one's neck** risquer sa peau; *Br Fam* **she'll get it in the neck** ça va chauffer pour son matricule; *Br* **he was thrown out neck and crop** *or* **on his neck** il a été mis à la porte avec pertes et fracas; *Br Fam* **it's neck or nothing** ça passe ou ça casse; *Fig* **to stick one's neck out** prendre des risques; *(commit oneself)* s'engager

(**b**) *Culin (of lamb)* collet *m*; *(of beef)* collier *m*

(**c**) *Sport* **to win by a neck** gagner d'une encolure; **to be neck and neck** être à égalité; **the two candidates are neck and neck** les deux candidats sont au coude à coude

(**d**) *(narrow part or extremity → of bottle, flask)* goulot *m*, col *m*; *(→ of pipe)* tuyau *m*; *(→ of womb, femur)* col *m*; *(→ of violin)* manche *m*; *(→ of bolt, tooth)* collet *m*

(**e**) *Geog (peninsula)* péninsule *f*, presqu'île *f*; *(strait)* détroit *m*; **a neck of land** une langue de terre; **in our neck of the woods** par chez nous; **what are you doing in this neck of the woods?** qu'est-ce que tu fais dans le coin?

(**f**) *(of dress, pullover)* col *m*, encolure *f*; **a low neck** un décolleté; **a dress with a low neck** une robe décolletée; **high neck** col *m* montant; **what neck size** *or* **what size neck do you take?** combien faites-vous de tour de cou?

(**g**) *Br Fam (cheek)* toupet *m*, culot *m*; **you've got a neck!** tu ne manques pas de culot!; **she's got some neck!** elle a un sacré culot!

2 *vi Fam (couple)* se peloter

neckband [ˈnekbænd] *n* (**a**) *(on garment)* bande *f* d'encolure; **a lace neckband** un col en dentelle (**b**) *(piece of jewellery)* tour *m* de cou

neckcloth [ˈnekklɒθ] *n Hist* foulard *m*, cravate *f*

-necked [nekt] *suff* à col; **swan-necked** en col de cygne; **a V-/round-necked pullover** un pull en V/ras du cou

neckerchief [ˈnekətʃɪf] *n* foulard *m*

necking [ˈnekɪŋ] *n* (**a**) *Fam (sexual)* pelotage *m* (**b**) *Archit (of column)* gorge *f*

necklace [ˈneklɪs] *n* collier *m*

►► ***necklace killing*** supplice *m* du collier *(consistant à placer un pneu enflammé autour du cou de la victime)*

necklet [ˈneklɪt] *n* collier *m*

neckline [ˈneklaɪn] *n* col *m*, encolure *f*; **her dress had a low/plunging neckline** elle avait une robe décolletée/très décolletée

necktie [ˈnektaɪ] *n Am* cravate *f*

►► *Fam* ***necktie party*** lynchage □ *m*

neckwear [ˈnekweə(r)] *n Com* = cravates et foulards

necro- [ˈnekrəʊ] *pref* nécro-

necrobiosis [ˌnekrəbaɪˈəʊsɪs] *n Med* nécrobiose *f*

necrological [ˌnekrəˈlɒdʒɪkəl] *adj* nécrologique

necrologist [neˈkrɒlədʒɪst] *n* nécrologue *mf*

necrology [neˈkrɒlədʒɪ] *n* nécrologie *f*

necromancer [ˈnekrəˌmænsə(r)] *n* nécromancien(enne) *m,f*

necromancy [ˈnekrəˌmænsɪ] *n* nécromancie *f*

necromantic [ˌnekrəˈmæntɪk] *adj* nécromantique

necrophagous [neˈkrɒfəgəs] *adj Zool* nécrophage

necrophilia [ˌnekrəˈfɪlɪə] *n* nécrophilie *f*

necrophiliac [ˌnekrəˈfɪlɪæk] *n* nécrophile *mf*

necrophilic [ˌnekrəˈfɪlɪk] **1** *n* nécrophile *mf* **2** *adj* nécrophile

necrophobia [ˌnekrəˈfəʊbɪə] *n* nécrophobie *f*

necropolis [neˈkrɒpəlɪs] *n* nécropole *f*

necropsy [neˈkrɒpsɪ] *n* autopsie *f*

necrosis [neˈkrəʊsɪs] *(pl* **necroses** [-siːz]*)* *n Med* nécrose *f*

necrotic [neˈkrɒtɪk] *adj Med* nécrotique

nectar [ˈnektə(r)] *n Bot & Fig* nectar *m*

nectarean [nekˈteərɪən], **nectareous** [nekˈteərɪəs] *adj Bot* nectaréen

nectariferous [ˌnektəˈrɪfərəs] *adj Bot* nectarifère

nectarine [ˈnektərɪn] *n* nectarine *f*

nectarous [ˈnektərəs] *adj Bot* nectaréen

nectary [ˈnektərɪ] *n Bot* nectaire *m*

ned [ned] *n esp Scot Fam* voyou □ *m*

NEDC [ˌeniːdiːˈsiː] *n Br Formerly (abbr* **National Economic Development Council***)* = agence nationale britannique de développement économique supprimée en 1992

neddy [ˈnedɪ] *(pl* **neddies***)* *Fam* **1** *n* (**a**) *Br (donkey)* baudet *m* (**b**) *Austr (horse)* canasson *m*; **to go to the neddies** aller aux courses

2 Neddy *n* = surnom de la NEDC

née, nee [neɪ] *adj Formal* **Evelyn Mulwray, née Cross** Evelyn Mulwray, née Cross

NEED [niːd] **1** *vt* (**a**) *(as basic requirement)* avoir besoin de; **have you got everything you need?** est-ce que tu as tout ce qu'il te faut?; **she needs rest** elle a besoin de repos *ou* de se reposer; **I need more money/time** j'ai besoin de plus d'argent/de temps; **you take the car, I won't be needing it this evening** prends la voiture, je n'en aurai pas besoin ce soir; **he likes to feel needed** il aime se sentir indispensable; **a lot of money is needed if we are to save the company** il va falloir beaucoup d'argent pour empêcher l'entreprise de couler; **you only need to ask** vous n'avez qu'à demander; **you don't need me to tell you that** vous devez le savoir mieux que moi; **the carpet needs cleaning** la moquette a besoin d'être nettoyée; **these facts need no (further) comment** ces faits se passent de commentaire; **it needs a great deal of skill to do it properly** il faut beaucoup d'habileté pour le faire correctement

(**b**) *(would benefit from)* **I need a drink/a shower** j'ai besoin de boire quelque chose/de prendre une douche; **what he needs is a good hiding** ce qu'il lui faut, c'est une bonne correction; **this soup needs more salt** cette soupe manque de sel; **it's just what I need** c'est exactement ce qu'il me faut; *Ironic* **that's all we need!** il ne nous manquait plus que ça!; **the last thing we need is someone like him snooping about the place** la dernière chose qu'il nous faut c'est bien que quelqu'un comme lui vienne fouiner par ici; **who needs money anyway?** de toute façon, l'argent n'a aucune importance; **your hair needs combing** vos cheveux ont besoin d'un coup de peigne; **I gave the car a much-needed wash** j'ai lavé la voiture, elle en avait bien besoin; **liquid nitrogen needs careful handling** *or* **to be handled with care** l'azote liquide demande à être manié avec précaution; **there are still a few points that need to be made** il reste encore quelques questions à soulever

(**c**) *(expressing obligation)* **to need to do sth** avoir besoin de *ou* être obligé de faire qch; **I need to be home by ten** il faut que je sois rentré *ou* je dois être rentré pour dix heures; **you need to try harder** tu vas devoir faire *ou* il va falloir que tu fasses un effort supplémentaire; **he didn't need to be told twice** il ne se l'est pas fait dire deux fois; **I'll help you – you don't need to** je vais t'aider – tu n'es pas obligé

2 *modal aux v*

> La forme modale de **need** est la même à toutes les personnes, et s'utilise sans **do/does**. (**he need only worry about himself**; **need she go?**; **it needn't matter**.)

you needn't come if you don't want to vous n'avez pas besoin de *ou* vous n'êtes pas obligé de venir si vous n'en avez pas envie; **you needn't wait** il est inutile que vous attendiez, inutile (pour vous) d'attendre; **I needn't tell you how important it is** je n'ai pas besoin de vous dire *ou* vous savez à quel point c'est important; **I needn't have bothered** je me suis donné bien du mal pour rien, ce n'était pas la peine que je me donne autant de mal; **the accident need never have happened** cet accident aurait pu être évité; **I need hardly tell you how grateful I am** il n'est pas besoin de vous dire combien je vous suis reconnaissant; **no-one else need ever know** ça reste entre nous; **need I say more?** ai-je besoin d'en dire davantage *ou* plus?; **need that be the case?** est-ce nécessairement *ou* forcément le cas?; **adults only need apply** les adultes seuls peuvent postuler

3 *n* (**a**) *(necessity)* besoin *m*; **I have no need of your sympathy** je n'ai que faire de votre sympathie; **I feel the need of some fresh air** *or* **to get some fresh air** j'ai besoin d'air; **phone me if you feel the need for a chat** appelle-moi si tu as besoin de parler; **there's no need to adopt that tone** inutile d'employer ce ton; **there's no need to hurry** rien ne presse, inutile de se presser;

nec–nee

there's no need to panic *or* **for any panic** inutile de paniquer; **I'll help with the dishes – no need, I've done them already** je vais vous aider à faire la vaisselle – inutile, c'est terminé; **to be in need of sth, to have need of sth** avoir besoin de qch; **I'm in need of help** j'ai besoin d'aide *ou* qu'on m'aide; **Eleanor is in urgent need of cash** Eleanor a un besoin urgent d'argent; **the ceiling is in need of repair** le plafond a besoin d'être réparé; **should the need arise** si cela s'avérait nécessaire, si le besoin s'en faisait sentir; *Hum* **your need is greater than mine** vous en avez plus besoin que moi

(**b**) *(requirement)* besoin *m*; **their needs can be easily satisfied** leurs besoins sont faciles à satisfaire; **he saw to her every need** il subvenait à ses moindres besoins; **that will meet my needs** cela fera mon affaire; **£1,000 should be enough for our immediate needs** 1000 livres devraient suffire pour répondre à nos besoins immédiats; *Mktg* **needs and wants** besoins *mpl* et désirs *mpl*

(**c**) *(poverty)* besoin *m*, nécessité *f*; *(adversity)* adversité *f*, besoin *m*; **to be in need** être dans le besoin; **in my hour of need** au moment où j'en ai eu besoin

4 needs *adv Prov* **needs must when the devil drives** nécessité fait loi; *Fam* **needs must** il le faut❑, c'est indispensable❑; **if needs must, I'll go** s'il le faut absolument *ou* si c'est indispensable, j'irai

5 if need be, if needs be *adv* si besoin est, le cas échéant

►► *Mktg* ***needs analysis*** analyse *f* des besoins; *Mktg* ***needs assessment*** estimation *f* des besoins; *Mktg* ***need identification*** identification *f* des besoins; *Mktg* ***need level*** niveau *m* des besoins; *Mktg* ***need market*** marché *m* des besoins; *Mktg* ***need recognition*** reconnaissance *f* des besoins; *Mktg* ***need set*** ensemble *m* de besoins; *Mktg* ***needs study*** étude *f* des besoins; *Br Admin* ***needs test*** examen *m* des conditions de vie *(pour bénéficier d'une aide de l'État)*; *Mktg* ***needs and wants exploration*** exploration *f* des besoins et des désirs

---

needful ['niːdfʊl] **1** *adj Formal* nécessaire, requis

2 *n Br Fam (what is necessary)* **to do the needful** faire le nécessaire❑; **to find the needful** *(money)* trouver le fric

neediness ['niːdɪnɪs] *n* indigence *f*

needle ['niːdəl] **1** *n* (**a**) *Med & Sewing* aiguille *f*; *(for record player)* pointe *f* de lecture, saphir *m*; *(of pine tree)* aiguille *f*; *(spine → of hedgehog)* piquant *m*; **it's like looking for a needle in a haystack** autant chercher une aiguille dans une botte de foin; *Fam* **I hate needles** j'ai horreur des piqûres!❑; *Fam Drugs slang* **to be on the needle** *(take drugs)* se piquer

(**b**) *(as indicator → in compass, on dial)* aiguille *f*

(**c**) *Art* **engraving needle** pointe *f* pour taille douce, pointe *f* sèche

(**d**) *Geol (rocky outcrop)* aiguille *f*, pic *m*

(**e**) *(monument)* obélisque *m*; *(on top of building)* aiguille *f*, flèche *f*

(**f**) *Fam* **to get the needle** *(become annoyed)* se foutre en boule *ou* en rogne; **to give sb the needle** foutre qn en boule *ou* rogne; *Br* **a bit of needle has crept into the match** les joueurs commencent à s'énerver *ou* disputent le match avec plus d'âpreté

2 *vt* (**a**) *(irritate)* foutre en boule *ou* en rogne; **he's always needling her about her weight** il passe son temps à la charrier à propos de son poids; **they needled him into retaliating** à force d'être asticoté, il a fini par riposter

(**b**) *Am (drink)* corser

(**c**) *Sewing* coudre

3 *vi Fam Drugs slang (inject drugs)* se shooter, se piquer

►► *Br* ***needle bank*** distributeur-échangeur *m* de seringues; ***needle exchange scheme*** programme *m* d'échange de seringues; *Br Fam* ***needle match*** match *m* âprement disputé❑; ***needle valve*** soupape *f* à pointeau

needlecord ['niːdəlkɔːd] **1** *n* velours *m* mille-raies

2 *comp (trousers, skirt)* en velours mille-raies

needlecraft ['niːdəlkrɑːft] *n* travaux *mpl* d'aiguille

needlefish ['niːdəlfɪʃ] *n Ich* aiguille *f* de mer

needle-nosed pliers *n* pince *f* à bec fin

needlepoint ['niːdəlpɔɪnt] *n (embroidery)* broderie *f*, tapisserie *f*; *(lace)* dentelle *f* à l'aiguille

►► ***needlepoint lace*** dentelle *f* brodée

needle-sharp *adj (point)* acéré; *(eyes)* de lynx; *(mind)* fin, perspicace

needless ['niːdlɪs] *adj (unnecessary → expense, effort, fuss)* superflu, inutile; *(→ remark)* inopportun, déplacé; **needless to say I won't go** il va sans dire que je n'irai pas; **the war was a needless waste of lives** la guerre a provoqué beaucoup de morts inutiles

needlessly ['niːdlɪslɪ] *adv (be rude, pedantic, worry)* inutilement; *(die, suffer, work)* pour rien

needlessness ['niːdlɪsnɪs] *n (of expense, effort, fuss)* inutilité *f*; *(of remark)* caractère *m* déplacé

needlestick injury ['niːdəlstɪk-] *n* piqûre *f* d'aiguille

needle-threader *n* enfile-aiguilles *m inv*

needletime ['niːdəltaɪm] *n (for broadcasting records)* durée *f* de passage à l'antenne

needlewoman ['niːdəlˌwʊmən] (*pl* **needlewomen** [-ˌwɪmɪn]) *n* couturière *f*; **she's a good needlewoman** elle sait manier l'aiguille, c'est une bonne couturière

needlework ['niːdəlwɜːk] *n (UNCOUNT)* travaux *mpl* d'aiguille

needling ['niːdəlɪŋ] *n (UNCOUNT)* taquineries *fpl*

needn't ['niːdənt] = **need not**

needs-based *adj* fondé sur les besoins; **the grant is needs-based** le montant de la bourse est établi selon les besoins du demandeur

►► *Mktg* ***needs-based market*** marché *m* fondé sur les besoins; *Mktg* ***needs-based segmentation*** segmentation *f* fondée sur les besoins

need-to-know *adj* **information is given on a need-to-know basis** les renseignements ne sont donnés qu'aux personnes concernées

needy ['niːdɪ] (*compar* **needier**, *superl* **neediest**) **1** *adj (financially)* nécessiteux, indigent; *(emotionally)* en manque d'affection

2 *npl* **the needy** les nécessiteux *mpl*

neem [niːm] *n Bot* margousier *m*

neep [niːp] *n Scot (swede)* rutabaga *m*, chou-navet *m*; *(turnip)* navet *m*

ne'er [neə(r)] *Literary* = **never** *adv*

ne'er-do-well 1 *n* bon (bonne) *m,f* à rien

2 *adj* bon à rien; **my ne'er-do-well cousins** mes bons à rien de cousins

nefarious [nɪ'feərɪəs] *adj* infâme, vil

nefariously [nɪ'feərɪəslɪ] *adv* d'une manière infâme

nefariousness [nɪ'feərɪəsnɪs] *n (of deed, crime, behaviour)* infâmie *f*; *(of person)* scélératesse *f*

Nefertiti [ˌnefə'tiːtɪ] *pr n* Néfertiti

neg (*written abbr* **negotiable**) négociable, à débattre

negate [nɪ'geɪt] *vt* (**a**) *(nullify → law)* abroger; *(→ order)* annuler; *(→ efforts)* réduire à néant; *(→ argument, theory)* invalider, rendre non valide

(**b**) *(deny)* réfuter, nier; *Literary* **if you negate the soul** si vous niez l'existence de l'âme

negation [nɪ'geɪʃən] *n* (**a**) *(denial → of fact, proposition)* négation *f* (**b**) *(nullification → of someone's work, efforts)* anéantissement *m*

negative ['negətɪv] **1** *adj* négatif; **a negative answer** une réponse négative; **he's a very negative sort of person** c'est quelqu'un de très négatif; **she's always so negative about my plans** elle trouve toujours quelque chose à redire à mes projets; **the result of the test was negative** le résultat de l'examen était négatif

2 *n* (**a**) *Gram* négation *f*; **in the negative** à la forme négative; **double negative** double négation

(**b**) *(answer)* réponse *f* négative, non *m inv*; **to reply in the negative** répondre négativement *ou* par la négative

(**c**) *Phot* négatif *m*

(**d**) *Elec & Phys* (pôle *m*) négatif *m*

3 *vt* (**a**) *(cancel → instruction)* annuler; *(nullify → effect)* neutraliser, réduire à néant

(**b**) *(reject → proposition, evidence)* rejeter, repousser

(**c**) *(deny)* nier, réfuter

►► *Fin* ***negative amortization*** amortissement *m* négatif; *Fin* ***negative amortization loan*** prêt *m* à amortissement négatif; *Elec & Phys* ***negative earth*** négatif *m*, terre *f* reliée au moins; *Fin* ***negative equity*** *(UNCOUNT)* plus-value *f* immobilière négative, = situation où l'acquéreur d'un bien immobilier reste redevable de l'emprunt contracté alors que son logement enregistre une moins-value; ***negative feedback*** *(in electronic circuit)* contre-réaction *f*, réaction *f* négative; *(in mechanical or cybernetic system)* feed-back *m* négatif, rétroaction *f* négative; *Fig* **we got a lot of negative feedback from the questionnaire** ce questionnaire a révélé de nombreuses réactions négatives; *Austr Fin* ***negative gearing*** = dégrèvement fiscal accordé à une personne qui a réalisé un investissement à perte; *Br Fin* ***negative income tax*** impôt *m* négatif sur le revenu; *Fin* ***negative interest*** intérêt *m* négatif; *Med* ***negative ion therapy*** ionisation *f ou* aéroionisation *f* négative; *Fin* ***negative pledge*** clause *f* de nantissement négative; ***negative pole*** *(of magnet)* pôle *m* sud; *Fin* ***negative prescription*** prescription *f* extinctive; *Psy* ***negative reinforcement*** renforcement *m* négatif; ***negative sign*** signe *m* moins *ou* négatif

negatively ['negətɪvlɪ] *adv* (**a**) *(in the negative)* négativement; **she replied negatively** sa réponse a été négative (**b**) *Elec & Phys* **negatively charged** chargé négativement

negativism ['negətɪvɪzəm] *n* négativisme *m*

negativity [ˌnegə'tɪvɪtɪ] *n* négativité *f*; **because of the negativity of his attitude** à cause de son attitude négative; **to feel a lot of negativity towards sb** avoir beaucoup de sentiments négatifs contre qn

negator [nɪ'geɪtə(r)] *n* (**a**) *(gen)* négateur(trice) *m,f* (**b**) *Electron* inverseur *m*

neglect [nɪ'glekt] **1** *n* (**a**) *(lack of attention, care → of building, garden)* abandon *m*, manque *m* de soins *ou* d'entretien; *(→ of child, invalid)* manque *m* de soins *ou* d'attention; *(→ of people's demands, needs)* manque *m* d'égards; **through neglect** par négligence; **many people fall ill through neglect** bien des gens tombent malades par négligence *ou* par manque de précautions; **the roof fell in through neglect** le toit s'est effondré faute d'entretien; **to suffer from neglect** *(person)* souffrir d'un manque de soins; *(building, garden)* être laissé à l'abandon; **his neglect of his appearance** le peu d'intérêt qu'il accorde à son apparence

(**b**) *(bad condition → of building, garden)* délabrement *m*; **to be in a state of neglect** être à l'abandon; **the buildings fell into neglect** les bâtiments sont tombés en ruine; **the apparatus fell into neglect** on cessa d'entretenir les appareils

(**c**) *(disregard → of duty, promise, rules)* manquement *m*; **he was reprimanded for neglect of duty** il a été réprimandé pour avoir manqué à ses devoirs

2 *vt* (**a**) *(fail to attend to, to care for → building, garden)* négliger, laisser à l'abandon; *(→ work)* négliger; *(→ child, invalid, friend)* délaisser, négliger; **he neglects himself** *or* **his appearance** il se néglige *ou* se laisse aller; **you shouldn't neglect your health** vous devriez vous soucier un peu plus de votre santé; **the house has been neglected for years** la maison est à l'abandon depuis des années; **he neglected his wife all evening** il n'a pas prêté la moindre attention à sa femme de toute la soirée; **governments have neglected the needs of the disabled for long enough** il est temps que les gouvernements cessent d'ignorer les besoins des invalides

(**b**) *(disregard → duty, promise)* manquer à; *(→ advice)* ignorer; **they neglect elementary rules** ils ne respectent pas les règles élémentaires

(**c**) *Formal (omit, overlook)* omettre, oublier; **to neglect to do sth** oublier *ou* omettre de faire qch; **they neglected to lock the door when they went out** ils ont oublié de fermer la porte à clé en sortant

neglected [nɪ'glektɪd] *adj* (**a**) *(uncared for → garden)* (laissé) à l'abandon, mal entretenu; *(→ building)* (laissé) à l'abandon, délabré; *(→ appearance)* négligé, peu soigné

(**b**) *(emotionally → child, pet)* délaissé, abandonné; **to feel neglected** se sentir abandonné, avoir l'impression d'être délaissé

(**c**) *St Exch (shares)* négligé

neglectful [nɪ'glektfʊl] *adj (person, attitude)*

négligent; **it's very neglectful of me** c'est très négligent de ma part; **to be neglectful of one's duty** négliger ses devoirs; **to be neglectful of one's responsibilities/obligations** manquer à ses responsabilités/obligations; **he's very neglectful of his appearance** il ne prend aucun soin de sa tenue; *Literary* **to be neglectful to do sth** omettre de faire qch

neglectfully [nɪ'glektfʊlɪ] *adv (behave)* négligemment, avec négligence

negligee, negligée, neglige ['neglɪʒeɪ] *n* négligé *m*, déshabillé *m*

negligence ['neglɪdʒəns] *n* (**a**) *(inattention)* négligence *f*; *(of duties, rules)* négligence *f*, manquement *m*; **due to** *or* **through negligence** par négligence; **negligence of basic precautions can be fatal** le non-respect des précautions élémentaires peut se révéler fatal (**b**) *Br (nonchalance)* nonchalance *f*
 ▸▸ *Ins* ***negligence clause*** clause *f* de négligence

negligent ['neglɪdʒənt] *adj* (**a**) *(neglectful)* négligent; **to be negligent of one's duties** manquer à *ou* négliger ses devoirs; **teenagers are often negligent of their appearance** les adolescents négligent souvent leur mise (**b**) *(nonchalant → attitude, manner)* nonchalant, négligent

negligently ['neglɪdʒəntlɪ] *adv* (**a**) *(carelessly)* négligemment, avec négligence; **he acted negligently** il a fait preuve de légèreté; **they behaved negligently towards their children** ils ont négligé leurs enfants (**b**) *(nonchalantly)* négligemment, nonchalamment; **she leaned negligently against the car** elle s'appuya nonchalamment contre la voiture

negligible ['neglɪdʒəbəl] *adj* négligeable, insignifiant

negligibly ['neglɪdʒɪblɪ] *adv* d'une manière négligeable

negotiability [nɪˌgəʊʃə'bɪlɪtɪ] *n Fin* négociabilité *f*

negotiable [nɪ'gəʊʃəbəl] *adj* (**a**) *Fin (bonds, bill, document)* négociable; *(price, salary, fee)* négociable, à débattre; **not negotiable** non négociable; *Fin (on cheque)* non à ordre (**b**) *(road)* praticable; *(river → navigable)* navigable; *(→ crossable)* franchissable; **the path was not easily negotiable** le chemin n'était guère praticable
 ▸▸ *Fin* ***negotiable instrument*** instrument *m* négociable; *Fin* ***negotiable paper*** papier *m* négociable; *Fin* ***negotiable stock*** titres *mpl* négociables

negotiate [nɪ'gəʊʃɪeɪt] **1** *vt* (**a**) *(gen)* négocier; *Fin (business deal)* négocier, traiter; *(bill, document)* négocier, trafiquer; **price to be negotiated** prix *m* à débattre
 (**b**) *(manoeuvre round → bend)* négocier; *(→ rapids, obstacle)* franchir; *Fig (→ difficulty)* franchir, surmonter
 2 *vi* négocier; **the unions will have to negotiate with the management for higher pay** il faudra que les syndicats négocient une augmentation de salaire auprès de la direction; **we should negotiate instead of preparing for war** nous ferions mieux de négocier au lieu de nous préparer à la guerre; **to negotiate for peace** entreprendre des pourparlers de paix

negotiating table [nɪ'gəʊʃɪeɪtɪŋ-] *n* table *f* des négociations

negotiation [nɪˌgəʊʃɪ'eɪʃən] *n* (**a**) *(discussion)* négociation *f*, pourparlers *mpl*; **to be in negotiation with sb** être en pourparler(s) avec qn; **to enter into negotiation** *or* **negotiations with sb** entamer des négociations avec qn; **to break off/resume negotiations** rompre/reprendre les négociations; **pay/redundancy negotiations** négociations *fpl* sur les salaires/les licenciements; **peace negotiations** pourparlers *mpl* de paix; **the project is under negotiation** le projet est en négociation; **the pay deal is subject to negotiation** l'accord salarial est sujet à négociation; **your salary is a matter of negotiation** nous devons débattre du montant de votre salaire
 (**b**) *(of bend, obstacle)* franchissement *m*

negotiator [nɪ'gəʊʃɪeɪtə(r)] *n* négociateur(trice) *m,f*

Negress ['ni:grɪs] *n Old-fashioned* négresse *f*

negritude ['negrɪtju:d] *n* négritude *f*

Negro ['ni:grəʊ] *(pl* **Negroes**) *Old-fashioned* **1** *n* nègre *m*
 2 *adj* nègre
 ▸▸ ***Negro spiritual*** (negro) spiritual *m*

negroid ['ni:grɔɪd] **1** *n* négroïde *mf*
 2 *adj* négroïde

Nehemiah [ˌni:ɪ'maɪə] *pr n Bible* Néhémie

Nehru jacket ['neəru:-] *n* veste *f* à col officier

neigh [neɪ] **1** *n* hennissement *m*
 2 *vi* hennir

neighbor, neighborhood *etc Am* = **neighbour, neighbourhood** *etc*

neighbour, *Am* **neighbor** ['neɪbə(r)] **1** *n* (**a**) *(who lives nearby)* voisin(e) *m,f*; **what will the neighbours say?** que vont dire les voisins?; **Britain's nearest neighbour is France** la France est le plus proche voisin de la Grande-Bretagne (**b**) *(fellow man)* prochain(e) *m,f*; **love thy neighbour as thyself** aime ton prochain comme toi-même
 2 *vt Am* avoisiner; **their farm neighbors mine** nos fermes sont voisines
 ▸▸ ***neighbour states*** pays *mpl* voisins

▸**neighbour on** *vt insep (adjoin)* avoisiner, être contigu à; *(of country)* être limitrophe à

▸**neighbor with** *vt insep Am* vivre en bon voisinage avec, entretenir des relations de bon voisinage avec

neighbourhood, *Am* **neighborhood** ['neɪbəhʊd] **1** *n* (**a**) *(district)* voisinage *m*, quartier *m*; **I was in the neighbourhood** j'étais dans le coin *ou* dans le quartier *ou* dans le voisinage; **a very friendly neighbourhood** un quartier très sympa; **the whole neighbourhood's talking about it** tout le quartier en parle
 (**b**) *(vicinity)* **in the neighbourhood of** *(place)* aux alentours de, dans les environs de; **there's some nice scenery in the neighbourhood** il y a de jolis paysages dans les environs
 (**c**) *Fig* **it'll cost you in the neighbourhood of $1,000** cela vous coûtera dans les *ou* environ 1000 dollars
 2 *comp (police, shop, school)* du quartier
 ▸▸ ***Neighbourhood Watch*** = système par lequel les habitants d'un quartier s'entraident pour en assurer la surveillance et la sécurité

neighbouring, *Am* **neighboring** ['neɪbərɪŋ] *adj* avoisinant, voisin

neighbourliness, *Am* **neighborliness** ['neɪbəlɪnɪs] *n* **(good) neighbourliness** (bons) rapports *mpl* de voisinage

neighbourly, *Am* **neighborly** ['neɪbəlɪ] *adj (person)* amical; *(relations, visit)* de bon voisinage; **to be neighbourly** être bon voisin, entretenir de bonnes relations avec ses voisins; **people used to be more neighbourly** autrefois les gens entretenaient de meilleurs rapports avec leurs voisins

neighing ['neɪɪŋ] **1** *n (UNCOUNT)* hennissement(s) *m(pl)*
 2 *adj (horse)* hennissant

neither ['ni:ðə(r), *Br* 'naɪðə(r)] **1** *pron* **neither of us** aucun de nous (deux); **neither (of them) eats fish** aucun des deux *ou* ni l'un ni l'autre ne mange de poisson; **which do you prefer? – neither!** lequel des deux préfères-tu? – ni l'un ni l'autre!
 2 *conj* **neither ... nor ...** ni... ni...; **it's neither good nor bad** ce n'est ni bon ni mauvais; **I like neither tea nor coffee** je n'aime ni le thé ni le café; **that's neither here nor there** *(unimportant)* c'est sans importance; *(irrelevant)* là n'est pas la question; **I neither know nor care** c'est vraiment le cadet de mes soucis
 3 *adv* non plus; **I don't like coffee, and neither does my wife** je n'aime pas le café, (et) ma femme non plus; **Sandra can't swim and neither can I** Sandra ne sait pas nager, (et) moi non plus; **neither did/do/were we** (et) nous non plus; *Fam* **me neither!** moi non plus!
 4 *adj* aucun (des deux), ni l'un ni l'autre; **neither bottle is big enough** aucune des deux bouteilles n'est assez grande; **neither one of them has accepted** ni l'un ni l'autre n'a accepté

nekton ['nektɒn] *n Zool* necton *m*

nelly ['nelɪ] *n Fam* (**a**) *Br* **not on your nelly!** des clous! (**b**) *Am (effeminate man)* lopette *f*

nelson ['nelsən] *n (in wrestling)* double clé *f*; **full nelson** nelson *m*
 ▸▸ ***Nelson's Column*** = monument érigé en l'honneur de l'amiral Nelson, à Trafalgar Square (Londres)

nematic [nɪ'mætɪk] *adj Phys & Chem* nématique

nematocyst ['nemətəsɪst] *n Biol* nématocyste *m*, cnidocyste *m*

nematode ['nemətəʊd] *n* nématode *m*

nem con [ˌnem'kɒn] *adv* unanimement, à l'unanimité

nemesia [nɪ'mi:ʒə] *n Bot* némésia *m*

nemesis ['neməsɪs] **1** *n Literary* (**a**) *(retribution)* **it's nemesis** c'est un juste retour des choses (**b**) *(person, organisation)* **she saw the British press as her nemesis** elle voyait dans la presse britannique l'instrument de sa perte; **to meet one's nemesis** *(be vanquished)* être vaincu; *(meet one's match)* trouver son maître
 2 Nemesis *pr n Myth* Némésis

nemoral ['nemərəl] *adj Literary* némoral

neo- ['ni:əʊ] *pref* néo-

neo-Babylonian 1 *adj Hist* néo-babylonien
 2 *n Ling* chaldéen *m*

Neocene ['ni:əʊsi:n] *Geol* **1** *n* néogène *m*
 2 *adj* néogène

neoclassical [ˌni:əʊ'klæsɪkəl] *adj* néoclassique

neoclassicism [ˌni:əʊ'klæsɪsɪzəm] *n* néoclassicisme *m*

neocolonial [ˌni:əʊkə'ləʊnɪəl] *adj* néocolonial

neocolonialism [ˌni:əʊkə'ləʊnɪəlɪzəm] *n* néocolonialisme *m*

neocolonialist [ˌni:əʊkə'ləʊnɪəlɪst] **1** *n* néocolonialiste *mf*
 2 *adj* néocolonialiste

Neo-Confucian [ˌni:əʊkən'fju:ʃən] *adj* néo-confucéen

neo-Darwinian *adj* néodarwinien

neo-Darwinism *n* néodarwinisme *m*

neodymium [ˌni:əʊ'dɪmɪəm] *n Chem* néodyme *m*

neofascism [ˌni:əʊ'fæʃɪzəm] *n* néofascisme *m*

neofascist [ˌni:əʊ'fæʃɪst] **1** *n* néofasciste *mf*
 2 *adj* néofasciste

Neogene ['ni:əʊdʒi:n] **1** *n* néogène *m*
 2 *adj* néogène

neogothic [ˌni:əʊ'gɒθɪk] *Archit* **1** *n* néogothique *m*
 2 *adj* néogothique

neo-impressionism *n Art* néo-impressionnisme *m*

neo-impressionist *Art* **1** *n* néo-impressionniste *mf*
 2 *adj* néo-impressionniste

Neo-Latin 1 *n* latin *m* scientifique
 2 *adj* (**a**) *(New Latin)* du latin scientifique (**b**) *(Romance)* néo-latin

neo-liberal 1 *n* néolibéral(e) *m,f*
 2 *adj* néolibéral

neo-liberalism *n* néolibéralisme *m*

neolith ['ni:əʊlɪθ] *n* (objet *m* de) pierre *f* polie

neolithic, Neolithic [ˌni:əʊ'lɪθɪk] **1** *adj* néolithique; **the Neolithic age** le néolithique
 2 *n* néolithique *m*

neologism [ni:'ɒlədʒɪzəm] *n* néologisme *m*

neologistic [ni:ˌɒlə'dʒɪstɪk] *adj* néologique

neology [ni:'ɒlədʒɪ] *(pl* **neologies**) *n* néologisme *m*

neomycin [ˌni:əʊ'maɪsɪn] *n* néomycine *f*

neon ['ni:ɒn] **1** *n* néon *m*
 2 *comp (lamp)* au néon
 ▸▸ ***neon lights*** néons *mpl*; ***neon sign*** enseigne *f* lumineuse (au néon); ***neon tube*** tube *m* fluorescent *ou* au néon

neonatal [ˌni:əʊ'neɪtəl] *adj* néonatal

neonate ['ni:əʊneɪt] *n* nouveau-né(e) *m,f*

neo-Nazi 1 *n* néonazi(e) *m,f*
 2 *adj* néonazi

neophobia [ˌni:əʊ'fəʊbɪə] *n* néophobie *f*

neophyte ['ni:əʊfaɪt] *n* néophyte *mf*

neoplasm ['ni:əʊˌplæzəm] *n* néoplasme *m*

Neoplatonic [ˌni:əʊplə'tɒnɪk] *adj* néoplatonicien

Neoplatonism [ˌni:əʊ'pleɪtənɪzəm] *n* néoplatonisme *m*

neoprene ['ni:əʊpri:n] *n* néoprène *m*

neorealism [ˌni:əʊ'ri:əlɪzəm] *n* néoréalisme *m*

neorealist [ˌnɪəʊ'ri:əlɪst] *adj* néoréaliste

neo-romantic 1 *n* néoromantique *mf*
 2 *adj* néoromantique

neo-romanticism *n* néoromantisme *m*

neoteinic, neotenic [ˌni:əʊ'ti:nɪk], **neotenous** [ni:'ɒtənəs] *adj Biol* néoténique

neoteny [niː'ɒtənɪ] *n Biol* néoténie *f*
neoteric [ˌniːəʊ'terɪk] *adj* récent, moderne
neotropical [ˌniːəʊ'trɒpɪkəl] *adj* néotropical
Neozoic [ˌniːəʊ'zəʊɪk] **1** *n* néozoïque *m*
2 *adj* néozoïque
Nepal [nɪ'pɔːl] *n* Népal *m*; **in Nepal** au Népal
Nepalese [ˌnepə'liːz] (*pl* **inv**) **1** *n* Népalais(e) *m,f*
2 *adj* népalais
Nepali [nɪ'pɔːlɪ] (*pl* **inv** *or* **Nepalis**) **1** *n* (**a**) *(person)* Népalais(e) *m,f* (**b**) *(language)* népalais *m*
2 *adj* népalais
3 *comp (embassy, history)* du Népal; *(teacher)* de népalais
nepenthe [nɪ'penθɪ] *adj Literary* népenthès *m*
neper ['niːpə(r)] *n* néper *m*
nephelometer [ˌnefɪ'lɒmɪtə(r)] *n* néphélémètre *m*
nephelometry [ˌnefɪ'lɒmɪtrɪ] *n* néphélémétrie *f*
nephew ['nefjuː] *n* neveu *m*
nephology [nɪ'fɒlədʒɪ] *n* science *f* des nuages
nephralgia [nɪ'frældʒə] *n (UNCOUNT) Med* néphralgie *f*
nephralgic [nɪ'frældʒɪk] *adj Med* néphralgique
nephrectomy [nɪ'frektəmɪ] (*pl* **nephrectomies**) *n Med* néphrectomie *f*
nephrite ['nefraɪt] *n Miner* néphrite *f*
nephritic [nɪ'frɪtɪk] *adj Med* néphrétique
nephritis [nɪ'fraɪtɪs] *n (UNCOUNT) Med* néphrite *f*; **to have nephritis** avoir une néphrite
nephrologist [nɪ'frɒlədʒɪst] *n Med* néphrologue *mf*
nephrology [nɪ'frɒlədʒɪ] *n Med* néphrologie *f*
nephron ['nefrɒn] *n* néphron *m*
nephropathy [nɪ'frɒpəθɪ] *n Med* néphropathie *f*
nephrosclerosis [ˌnefrəʊsklə'rəʊsɪs] *n Med* néphrosclérose *f*
nepotism ['nepətɪzəm] *n* népotisme *m*
Neptune ['neptjuːn] **1** *pr n Myth* Neptune
2 *n Astron* Neptune *f*
neptune-grass *n Bot* posidonie *f*
neptunium [nep'tjuːnɪəm] *n Chem* neptunium *m*
nerd [nɜːd] *n Fam (stupid)* crétin *m*; *(unfashionable)* ringard *m*
nerdy ['nɜːdɪ] *adj Fam (unfashionable)* ringard
Nereid ['nɪərɪɪd] (*pl* **Nereides** [nə'riːədiːz]) *n* (**a**) *Astron* Néréide *f* (**b**) *Myth* Néréide *f*
nerine [ne'raɪnɪ] *n Bot* nérine *f*
neritic [ne'rɪtɪk] *adj* néritique
nerka ['nɜːkə] *n Ich* saumon *m* rouge
Nero ['nɪərəʊ] *pr n Antiq* Néron
neroli [nɪ'rəʊlɪ] *n* néroli *m*
▸▸ ***neroli oil*** néroli *m*
Neronian [nɪə'rəʊnɪən] *adj* néronien
nerve [nɜːv] **1** *n* (**a**) *(in body)* nerf *m*; **to take the nerve out of a tooth** *(dentist)* dévitaliser une dent; *Fig* **to touch a raw nerve** toucher une corde sensible; *Fig Literary* **to strain every nerve to do sth** mettre toute sa force à faire qch
(**b**) *(courage)* courage *m*; *(boldness)* audace *f*; *(self-control)* assurance *f*, sang-froid *m*; **it takes nerve to say no to him** il faut du courage *ou* il faut avoir les nerfs solides pour lui dire non; **he didn't have the nerve to say no** il n'a pas osé dire non, il n'a pas eu le courage de dire non; **to get up enough nerve to jump** trouver le courage de sauter; **his nerve failed him, he lost his nerve** *(backed down)* le courage lui a manqué; *(panicked)* il a perdu son sang-froid
(**c**) *(cheek, audacity)* culot *m*; **he had the nerve to refuse** il a eu le culot de refuser; *Fam* **you've got a nerve coming here!** tu es gonflé de venir ici!; *Fam* **what a nerve!** quel culot *ou* toupet!
(**d**) *(vein → in leaf, marble)* veine *f*, nervure *f*
2 *vt Formal* **to nerve oneself to do sth** s'armer de courage pour faire qch; **to nerve sb to do sth** encourager *ou* inciter qn à faire qch
3 nerves *npl* (**a**) *(agitated state)* nerfs *mpl*; *(anxiety)* nervosité *f*; *(before concert, exam, interview)* trac *m*; **to have a fit of nerves** avoir le trac; **to be in a state of nerves** être sur les nerfs; **to live on one's nerves** vivre sur les nerfs; **she suffers from (her) nerves** elle a les nerfs fragiles; **I'm a bundle of nerves** je suis un paquet de nerfs; **I need a drink to steady my nerves** il faut que je boive un verre pour me calmer
(**b**) *(self-control)* nerfs *mpl*; **to have strong nerves/nerves of steel** avoir les nerfs solides/des nerfs d'acier; **working in casualty requires strong nerves** il faut avoir les nerfs solides pour travailler aux urgences; *Fam* **he gets on my nerves** il me tape sur les nerfs *ou* sur le système
▸▸ ***nerve cell*** cellule *f* nerveuse; ***nerve centre*** *Anat* centre *m* nerveux; *Fig (headquarters)* centre *m* névralgique; ***nerve ending*** terminaison *f* nerveuse; ***nerve fibre*** fibre *f* nerveuse; ***nerve gas*** gaz *m* neurotoxique; ***nerve impulse*** influx *m* nerveux; *Med* ***nerve specialist*** neurologue *mf*
nerveless ['nɜːvlɪs] *adj* (**a**) *(numb)* engourdi, inerte; **the revolver fell from his nerveless fingers** le revolver tomba de ses doigts inertes (**b**) *(weak)* sans force, mou (molle) (**c**) *(calm)* impassible, imperturbable; *(fearless)* intrépide
nerve-racking, nerve-wracking [-ˌrækɪŋ] *adj (experience)* éprouvant; *(suspense)* angoissant; **after a nerve-racking wait he was shown in** après une attente qui mit ses nerfs à rude épreuve, on le fit entrer
nerviness ['nɜːvɪnɪs] *n Fam* (**a**) *Br (tension)* nervosité ❑ *f* (**b**) *Am (impudence)* culot *m*
nervous ['nɜːvəs] *adj* (**a**) *(anxious, worried)* anxieux, appréhensif; *(shy)* timide, intimidé; *(uneasy)* mal à l'aise; *(agitated)* agité, tendu; *(tense)* tendu; **to be nervous** *(before a performance, an exam etc)* avoir le trac; *(before going to the dentist etc)* avoir peur; **to be nervous about sth** s'inquiéter à propos de qch; **I'm always nervous** *or* **I always feel nervous when he's around** je suis toujours tendu lorsqu'il est dans les parages; **don't be nervous** détendez-vous, n'ayez pas peur; **you're making me nervous** vous m'intimidez, vous me faites perdre mes moyens; **you don't need to be nervous on my account** vous n'avez pas besoin de vous inquiéter pour moi; **he is nervous of Alsatians** les bergers allemands lui font peur; **he is nervous of failure** il a peur de l'échec; **I'm nervous about speaking in public** j'ai peur *ou* j'appréhende de parler en public; **the bank was nervous about granting the loan** la banque hésitait à accorder le prêt; **I'm always nervous before exams** j'ai toujours le trac avant un examen; **airports make me nervous** je me sens mal à l'aise dans les aéroports; *Fam* **he's a nervous wreck** il est à bout de nerfs ❑, il est à cran; **not for those of a nervous disposition** à déconseiller aux âmes sensibles
(**b**) *Anat (strain, illness)* nerveux
▸▸ ***nervous breakdown*** dépression *f* nerveuse; **to have a nervous breakdown** avoir *ou* faire une dépression nerveuse; ***nervous energy*** énergie *f* nerveuse; *Am Fam Pej* ***nervous Nellie*** poule *f* mouillée; ***the nervous system*** le système nerveux; ***nervous tension*** tension *f* nerveuse
nervously ['nɜːvəslɪ] *adv (anxiously)* anxieusement, avec inquiétude; *(tensely)* nerveusement; **he wondered nervously if...** il se demanda, avec une certaine nervosité, si...
nervousness ['nɜːvəsnɪs] *n* (**a**) *(worry)* anxiété *f*, inquiétude *f*; *(before exam)* trac *m* (**b**) *(agitation)* nervosité *f*, agitation *f* (nerveuse), fébrilité *f* (**c**) *(of writing, speech)* nervosité *f*
nervure ['nɜːvjə(r)] *n Bot & Zool* nervure *f*
nervy ['nɜːvɪ] (*compar* **nervier**, *superl* **nerviest**) *adj Fam* (**a**) *Br (tense)* énervé ❑, excité ❑ (**b**) *Am (cheeky)* culotté
nescience ['nesɪəns] *n Formal* nescience *f*
nescient ['nesɪənt] *adj Formal* nescient
Nessie ['nesɪ] *n Fam* = surnom du monstre du Loch Ness
nest [nest] **1** *n* (**a**) *(for birds, wasps, snakes etc)* nid *m*; *(nestful → of fledgelings)* nichée *f*, couvée *f*; *(→ of eggs)* couvée *f*; *Fig (den → of brigands)* nid *m*, repaire *m*; *(→ for machine guns)* nid *m*; **the children have all left** *or* **flown the nest** les enfants ont tous quitté le nid familial
(**b**) *(set)* **nest of tables** (série *f ou* ensemble *m* de) tables *fpl* gigognes
2 *vi* (**a**) *(bird)* (se) nicher, faire son nid
(**b**) *(person)* **to go nesting** *(find nests)* aller chercher des nids; *(steal young)* aller dénicher des oisillons; *(steal eggs)* aller dénicher des œufs
(**c**) *(fit together)* s'emboîter; **the boxes nest together neatly** les cartons s'emboîtent bien (les uns dans les autres)
3 *vt* (**a**) *(animal, bird)* servir de nid à
(**b**) *(tables, boxes)* emboîter
▸▸ ***nest box*** *(in henhouse)* pondoir *m*; *(in birdhouse)* nichoir *m*; ***nest egg*** économies *fpl*, bas *m* de laine, pécule *m*; **I've got a nice little nest egg put by for when I retire** j'ai mis de côté un bon petit pécule en prévision de ma retraite
NESTA ['nestə] *n* (*abbr* **National Endowment for Science, Technology and the Arts**) = organisme indépendant d'aide financière aux artistes, inventeurs et scientifiques, à partir de fonds provenant de la Loterie nationale
nested ['nestɪd] *adj Comput & Typ* imbriqué
nestful ['nestfʊl] *n (of fledgelings)* nichée *f*, couvée *f*; *(of eggs)* couvée *f*
nesting ['nestɪŋ] **1** *n (building nests)* nidification *f*
2 *comp (bird)* nicheur; *(time, instinct)* de (la) nidification
▸▸ ***nesting box*** *(in henhouse)* pondoir *m*; *(in birdhouse)* nichoir *m*
nestle ['nesəl] **1** *vt* blottir
2 *vi* (**a**) *(against person)* se blottir; *(in comfortable place)* se pelotonner; **she nestled (up) against me** elle s'est blottie contre moi; **to nestle down in bed** se pelotonner dans son lit
(**b**) *(land, house)* être niché *ou* blotti; **a village nestling in a valley** un village blotti *ou* tapi dans une vallée
nestling ['neslɪŋ] *n* oisillon *m*
Nestor ['nestɔː(r)] *pr n* Nestor
Nestorian [nes'tɔːrɪən] *Rel* **1** *n* Nestorien(enne) *m,f*
2 *adj* nestorien
Nestorianism [nes'tɔːrɪənɪzəm] *n Rel* nestorianisme *m*
net [net] (*pt & pp* **netted**, *cont* **netting**) **1** *n* (**a**) *(gen)* filet *m*; *Fig (trap)* filet *m*, piège *m*; **to fall into the net** tomber dans le piège; **to slip through the net** glisser *ou* passer à travers les mailles du filet
(**b**) *Sport* filet *m*; **to come (up) to the net** *(in tennis)* monter au filet; **to practise in the nets** *(in cricket)* = s'entraîner, un filet entourant les piquets; *Ftbl* **to put the ball in the (back of the) net** marquer un but, envoyer la balle au fond des filets
(**c**) *(for hair)* filet *m* à cheveux, résille *f*
(**d**) *Tex* tulle *m*, filet *m*
(**e**) *(network)* réseau *m*; **radio net** ensemble *m* du réseau radiophonique
(**f**) *(income, profit, weight)* net *m*; **net payable** net *m* à payer
2 *vt* (**a**) *(catch → fish, butterfly)* prendre *ou* attraper (au filet); *(→ terrorist, criminal)* arrêter; **the police have netted the gang leaders** la police a mis la main sur les chefs de la bande
(**b**) *(acquire → prize)* ramasser, gagner; *(→ fortune)* amasser
(**c**) *Sport* **to net the ball** *(in tennis)* envoyer la balle dans le filet; **he netted his service** *(in tennis)* son service échoua dans le filet; *Ftbl* **to net a goal** marquer un but
(**d**) *(fruit tree)* recouvrir de filets *ou* d'un filet
(**e**) *(of person, company)* gagner net; *(profit)* rapporter net; *(of sale)* produire net; **we netted over $10,000** nous avons réalisé un bénéfice net de plus de 10 000 dollars; **he nets £20,000 a year** il gagne 20 000 livres net par an
3 *vi Ftbl* **Barnes netted from 5 yards out** ≃ Barnes a marqué un but (depuis la ligne) des 6 mètres
4 *adj* (**a**) *(amount, weight)* net; **to earn £500 net** gagner 500 livres net; **terms strictly net** sans déduction
(**b**) *(result)* final
5 *adv* **net of tax** net d'impôt; **net of VAT** hors TVA
6 Net *n Comput* **the Net** le Net, l'Internet *m*
▸▸ *Fin* ***net amount*** somme *f* nette, montant *m* net; *Fin* ***net assets*** actif *m* net; *Fin* ***net asset value*** valeur *f* d'actif net; *Br Formerly* ***the Net Book Agreement*** = accord entre maisons d'édition et libraires stipulant que ces derniers n'ont le droit de vendre aucun ouvrage à un prix inférieur à celui fixé par l'éditeur; *Fin* ***net book value*** valeur *f* comptable nette; *Fin* ***net capital expenditure*** mise *f* de fonds nette, dépenses *fpl* nettes d'investissement; *Fin* ***net cash flow*** cash-flow *m* net; *Fin* ***net change*** écart *m* net; ***net cord*** *(in tennis → part of net)* corde *f* de filet; *(→ shot)* let *m*, net *m*, filet *m*; ***net cord judge*** juge *m* de filet; *Fin* ***net cost*** prix *m* de revient; *Fin* ***net current assets*** actif *m* circulant net; ***net curtain*** rideau *m* (de tulle *ou* en filet), voilage *m*; *Fin* ***net***

discounted cash flow cash-flow *m* actualisé net, flux *mpl* de trésorerie actualisés nets; *Fin* ***net dividend*** dividende *m* net; *Fin* ***net domestic product*** produit *m* intérieur net; *Fin* ***net earnings*** *(of company)* bénéfices *mpl* nets; *(of worker)* salaire *m* net; *Fin* ***net income*** *(in accounts)* produit *m* net; *(of individual)* revenu *m* net; *Fin* ***net interest income*** net *m* financier; *Fin* ***net loss*** perte *f* nette; *Fin* ***net margin*** marge *f* nette; *Fin* ***net national income*** revenu *m* national net; *Fin* ***net national product*** produit *m* national net; *Sport* ***net play*** jeu *m* au filet; *Fin* ***net operating profit*** rentabilité *f* nette d'exploitation; *Fin* ***net present value*** valeur *f* actuelle nette; *Fin* ***net present value rate*** taux *m* d'actualisation; *Fin* ***net price*** prix *m* net; *Fin* ***net profit*** bénéfice *m* net, net *m* commercial; *Fin* ***net profit margin*** marge *f* commerciale nette; *Fin* ***net profit ratio*** ratio *m* de rentabilité nette, taux *m* de profit net; *Fin* ***net realizable value*** valeur *f* réalisable nette; *Fin* ***net receipts*** recettes *fpl* nettes; *Fin* ***net residual value*** valeur *f* résiduelle nette; *Fin* ***net result*** résultat *m* final; *Fin* ***net return*** rendement *m* net, résultat *m* net; *Fin* ***net salary*** salaire *m* net; *Fin* ***net tangible assets*** actif *m* corporel net; *Fin* ***net total*** montant *m* net; *Fin* ***net variance*** écart *m* net; *Fin* ***net working capital*** fonds *m* de roulement net; *Fin* ***net worth*** situation *f* nette, valeur *f* nette

.net *n Comput* = abréviation désignant les organismes officiels de l'Internet dans les adresses électroniques

netball ['netbɔːl] *n* net-ball *m (sport féminin proche du basket-ball)*

nethead ['nethed] *n Fam Comput* accro *mf* de l'Internet

nether ['neðə(r)] *adj Arch or Literary* bas, inférieur; *(lip)* inférieur; **the nether regions** les enfers *mpl*; *Hum (of body)* les parties *fpl* basses; *Hum (of building)* les profondeurs *fpl*

Netherlander ['neðə,lændə(r)] *n* Néerlandais(e) *m,f*

Netherlands ['neðələndz] *npl* **the Netherlands** les Pays-Bas *mpl*; **in the Netherlands** aux Pays-Bas; **the Netherlands Antilles** les Antilles *fpl* néerlandaises

nethermost ['neðəməʊst] *adj Literary* le plus bas *ou* profond

netiquette ['netɪket] *n Fam Comput* netiquette *f*

netizen ['netɪzən] *n Comput* internaute *mf*

netspeak ['netspiːk] *n* langage *m* du Net, cyberjargon *m*

netsuke ['netsʊkɪ] *n* netsuke *m*

nett [net] **1** *n (income, profit, weight)* net *m*; **net payable** net *m* à payer

2 *adj (amount, weight)* net; **to earn £500 nett** gagner 500 livres net; **terms strictly nett** sans déduction

3 *vt (of person, company)* gagner net; *(profit)* rapporter net; *(of sale)* produire net; **we netted over $10,000** nous avons réalisé un bénéfice net de plus de 10 000 dollars; **he nets £20,000 a year** il gagne 20 000 livres net par an

Nettie ['netɪ] *n Fam* fana *mf* de l'Internet

netting ['netɪŋ] *n (UNCOUNT)* (**a**) *(for strawberries, trees)* filet *m*, filets *mpl*; *(fencing)* treillis *m* (métallique), grillage *m* (**b**) *Tex (for curtains)* tulle *m*, filet *m* (**c**) *(of fish, butterfly)* prise *f* au filet

nettle ['netəl] **1** *n* ortie *f*; *Br* **to grasp the nettle** prendre le taureau par les cornes

2 *vt Br* agacer, énerver

3 *comp (soup)* aux orties

▸▸ ***nettle rash*** urticaire *f*

nettled ['netəld] *adj* agacé; **don't get nettled** ne t'énerve pas

netware loadable module ['netweə(r)-] *n Comput* module *m* logiciel téléchargeable

network ['netwɜːk] **1** *n* (**a**) *(gen), Elec & Rail* réseau *m*; *(of shops, hotels)* réseau *m*, chaîne *f*; *(of streets)* lacis *m*; *Mktg (for distribution, sales)* réseau *m*; **road network** réseau *m* routier

(**b**) *TV (national)* réseau *m*; *(channel)* chaîne *f*

(**c**) *Comput* réseau *m*

2 *vt* (**a**) *TV (broadcast)* diffuser sur l'ensemble du réseau *ou* sur tout le territoire; **the programme wasn't networked** le programme n'a pas été diffusé (sur la chaîne nationale)

(**b**) *Comput* mettre en réseau

3 *vi* (**a**) *Comput* faire partie du/d'un réseau, être raccordé au *ou* à un réseau

(**b**) *(make contacts)* établir un réseau de contacts professionnels

▸▸ *Comput* ***network administrator*** administrateur(trice) *m,f* de réseau; *Comput* ***network card*** carte *f* réseau; *Comput* ***network computer*** ordinateur *m* de réseau; *Comput* ***network driver, network manager*** gestionnaire *mf* de réseau; *Comput* ***network operating system*** système *m* d'exploitation réseau; *Comput* ***network server*** serveur *m* de réseau; *Comput* ***network software*** logiciel *m* de réseau; *Comput* ***networked systems*** systèmes *mpl* en réseau; *Comput* ***network traffic*** trafic *m* de réseau; ***network TV*** réseau *m* (de télévision) national

networking ['netwɜːkɪŋ] *n* (**a**) *Comput (working method)* travail *m* en réseau; *(of computer system)* mise *f* en réseau; **to have networking capabilities** *(terminal)* offrir la possibilité d'intégration à un réseau (**b**) *(gen) & Com* établissement *m* d'un réseau de liens *ou* de contacts

neum, neume [njuːm] *n Mus* neume *m*

neural ['njʊərəl] *adj* neural

▸▸ *Comput* ***neural network*** réseau *m* neuronal

neuralgia [njʊ'rældʒə] *n (UNCOUNT) Med* névralgie *f*

neuralgic [njʊ'rældʒɪk] *adj Med* névralgique

neurasthenia [,njʊərəs'θiːnjə] *n (UNCOUNT) Old-fashioned* neurasthénie *f*

neurasthenic [,njʊərəs'θenɪk] *adj Old-fashioned* neurasthénique

neuritis [,njʊə'raɪtɪs] *n (UNCOUNT) Med* névrite *f*

neuroanatomist [,njʊərəʊə'nætəmɪst] *n* neuroanatomiste *mf*

neuroanatomy [,njʊərəʊə'nætəmɪ] *n* neuroanatomie *f*

neurobiology [,njʊərəʊbaɪ'ɒlədʒɪ] *n* neurobiologie *f*

neurodegenerative [,njʊərəʊdɪ'dʒenərətɪv] *adj* neurodégénératif

neuroendocrine [,njʊərəʊ'endəʊ,kraɪn] *adj* neuroendocrinien

neuroendocrinology [,njʊərəʊ,endəʊkrɪ'nɒlədʒɪ] *n* neuroendocrinologie *f*

neurogenesis [,njʊərəʊ'dʒenəsɪs] *n* neurogenèse *f*, névrogenèse *f*

neurogenic [,njʊərəʊ'dʒenɪk] *adj* neurogénique

neuroleptic [,njʊərəʊ'leptɪk] **1** *n* neuroleptique *m*

2 *adj* neuroleptique

neurolinguistic [,njʊərəʊlɪŋ'gwɪstɪk] *adj* neurolinguistique

neurolinguistics [,njʊərəʊlɪŋ'gwɪstɪks] *n (UNCOUNT)* neurolinguistique *f*

neurological [,njʊərəʊ'lɒdʒɪkəl] *adj* neurologique

neurologist [,njʊə'rɒlədʒɪst] *n* neurologue *mf*

neurology [,njʊə'rɒlədʒɪ] *n* neurologie *f*

neuroma [,njʊə'rəʊmə] *(pl* **neuromas** *or* **neuromata** [-mətə]) *n* névrome *m*

neuromuscular [,njʊərəʊ'mʌskjʊlə(r)] *adj* neuromusculaire

neuron ['njʊərɒn], **neurone** ['njʊərəʊn] *n Biol* neurone *m*

neuropath ['njʊərəʊpæθ] *n* névropathe *mf*

neuropathic [,njʊərəʊ'pæθɪk] *adj* neuropathique

neuropathology [,njʊərəʊpə'θɒlədʒɪ] *n* neuropathologie *f*

neuropathy [,njʊə'rɒpəθɪ] *n* neuropathie *f*

neurophysiological ['njʊərəʊ,fɪzɪə'lɒdʒɪkəl] *adj* neurophysiologique

neurophysiology ['njʊərəʊ,fɪzɪ'ɒlədʒɪ] *n* neurophysiologie *f*

neuropsychiatric ['njʊərəʊ,saɪkɪ'ætrɪk] *adj* neuropsychiatrique

neuropsychiatrist [,njʊərəʊsaɪ'kaɪətrɪst] *n* neuropsychiatre *mf*

neuropsychiatry [,njʊərəʊsaɪ'kaɪətrɪ] *n* neuropsychiatrie *f*

neuropsychological [,njʊərəʊsaɪkə'lɒdʒɪkəl] *adj* neuropsychologique

neuropsychologist [,njʊərəʊsaɪ'kɒlədʒɪst] *n* neuropsychologue *mf*

neuropsychology [,njʊərəʊsaɪ'kɒledʒɪ] *n* neuropsychologie *f*

neuroscience ['njʊərəʊsaɪəns] *n* neurosciences *fpl*

neuroscientist [,njʊərəʊ'saɪəntɪst] *n* spécialiste *mf* en neurosciences

neurosis [,njʊə'rəʊsɪs] *(pl* **neuroses** [-siːz]) *n* névrose *f*

neurosurgeon ['njʊərəʊ,sɜːdʒən] *n* neurochirurgien(enne) *m,f*

neurosurgery [,njʊərəʊ'sɜːdʒərɪ] *n* neurochirurgie *f*

neurosurgical [,njʊərəʊ'sɜːdʒɪkəl] *adj* neurochirurgical

neurotic [,njʊə'rɒtɪk] **1** *n* névrosé(e) *m,f*

2 *adj (person)* névrosé; *(disease, behaviour)* névrotique; **a neurotic obsession** une névrose; *Fig* **he's positively neurotic about it** c'est une obsession chez lui; **don't be so neurotic about it!** tu ne vas pas en faire tout un plat *ou* une maladie!

neurotically [,njʊə'rɒtɪkəlɪ] *adv* de façon obsessionnelle; **to be neurotically obsessed with sth** avoir une obsession névrotique de qch

neuroticism [,njʊə'rɒtɪsɪzəm] *n* neurasthénie *f*

neurotoxic [,njʊərəʊ'tɒksɪk] *adj* neurotoxique

neurotoxin [,njʊərəʊ'tɒksɪn] *n* neurotoxine *f*

neurotransmitter [,njʊərəʊtrænz'mɪtə(r)] *n* neurotransmetteur *m*

neurovascular [,njʊərəʊ'væskjʊlə(r)] *adj* neurovasculaire

neurovegetative [,njʊərəʊ'vedʒɪtətɪv] *adj* neurovégétatif

neuston ['njuːstən] *n* neuston *m*

Neustria ['njuːstrɪə] *n Hist* Neustrie *f*

Noustrian ['njuːstrɪən] *Hist* **1** *n* Neustrien(enne) *m,f*

2 *adj* neustrien

neuter ['njuːtə(r)] **1** *n* (**a**) *Gram* neutre *m*; **in the neuter** au neutre (**b**) *(animal → asexual)* animal *m* asexué; *(→ castrated)* animal *m* châtré; *(insect, plant)* neutre *m*

2 *adj* neutre

3 *vt* châtrer

neutral ['njuːtrəl] **1** *n* (**a**) *Aut* point *m* mort; **in neutral** au point mort (**b**) *Pol (person)* ressortissant(e) *m,f* d'un État neutre; *(state)* État *m ou* pays *m* neutre

2 *adj* neutre; *(policy)* de neutralité; **to remain neutral** garder la neutralité, rester neutre

neutralism ['njuːtrəlɪzəm] *n* neutralisme *m*

neutralist ['njuːtrəlɪst] **1** *n* neutraliste *mf*

2 *adj* neutraliste

neutrality [njuː'trælətɪ] *n* neutralité *f*

neutralization [,njuːtrəlaɪ'zeɪʃən] *n* neutralisation *f*

neutralize, -ise ['njuːtrəlaɪz] *vt* neutraliser; **to neutralize one another** *(chemical agents)* se neutraliser; *(forces)* se neutraliser, s'annuler

neutralizing ['njuːtrə,laɪzɪŋ] **1** *n* neutralisation *f*

2 *adj* (**a**) *Chem & Phys* neutralisant, de neutralisation (**b**) *Elec* isolant, de neutralisation

▸▸ *Chem* ***neutralizing agent*** neutralisant *m*; ***neutralizing condenser*** condensateur *m* de neutralisation, condensateur *m* neutrodyne; *Mil* ***neutralizing fire*** tir *m* de neutralisation; ***neutralizing tool*** outil *m* isolant

neutrally ['njuːtrəlɪ] *adv* neutrement

neutrino [njuː'triːnəʊ] *(pl* **neutrinos**) *n Phys* neutrino *m*

neutron ['njuːtrɒn] *n Phys* neutron *m*

▸▸ ***neutron bomb*** bombe *f* à neutrons; ***neutron star*** étoile *f* à neutrons

neutropenia [,njuːtrəʊ'piːnɪə] *n Med* neutropénie *f*

neutrophil ['njuːtrəfɪl], **neutrophile** ['njuːtrəfaɪl] *Med* **1** *n* neutrophile *m*

2 *adj* neutrophile

neutrophilic [,njuːtrə'fɪlɪk] *adj Med* neutrophile

Nevada [nɪ'vɑːdə] *n* le Nevada; **in Nevada** dans le Nevada

névé [neveɪ] *n* névé *m*

never ['nevə(r)] **1** *adv* (**a**) *(not ever)* jamais; **I've never been there** je n'y suis jamais allé; **I never saw her again** je ne l'ai plus jamais *ou* jamais plus revue; **never in (all) my life, never in all my born days** jamais de la vie; **you never know** on ne sait jamais; **never before** *(until that moment)* jamais auparavant *ou* avant *ou* jusque-là; *(until now)* jamais jusqu'ici *ou* jusqu'à présent; **he's never yet been wrong** jusqu'ici *ou*

net–nev

jusqu'à présent, il ne s'est jamais trompé; **I'll never ever speak to him again** plus jamais de ma vie je ne lui adresserai la parole; **never ever do that again!** ne refais jamais cela!; **Darren, never one to complain, said nothing** Darren, qui ne se plaint jamais, n'a rien dit; **never again did he make the same mistake** il n'a plus jamais fait la même erreur; **never again!** plus jamais ça!

(**b**) *(used instead of "did not")* **she never turned up** elle n'est pas venue; **they never said a word about it** ils n'en ont jamais dit mot; **I never knew you cared** je ne savais pas que tu m'aimais

(**c**) *(as intensifier)* **never a one** pas même un seul; **I never even asked if you wanted something to drink** je ne vous ai même pas offert (quelque chose) à boire; **he never so much as blinked** il n'a même pas cillé; **never fear** ne craignez rien, n'ayez crainte; **that will never do!** *(it is unacceptable)* c'est inadmissible!; *(it is insufficient)* ça ne va pas!; *Literary* **he answered never a word** il ne répondit pas un (seul) mot

(**d**) *(in surprise, disbelief)* **you never did!** vous n'avez pas fait ça!; **you never asked him to dinner!** vous ne l'avez quand même pas *ou* tout de même pas invité à dîner!; **you've never lost your purse again!** ne me dis pas que tu as encore perdu ton porte-monnaie!; **she's never fifty!** ce n'est pas possible, elle ne peut pas avoir cinquante ans!; *Br Fam* **well I never (did)!** ça alors!, par exemple!; **well I never, look who's coming!** ça alors *ou* par exemple, regarde qui arrive!

2 *exclam* (ce n'est) pas possible!

never-ending *adj (complaints, noise)* incessant; *(task, sermon, evening)* interminable, qui n'en finit pas; **my problems seem to be never-ending** mes problèmes semblent ne pas en finir; **a never-ending supply of funny stories** un stock inépuisable d'histoires drôles; **housework is never-ending** le ménage n'est jamais fini

never-failing *adj* (**a**) *(infallible)* infaillible (**b**) *(enduring)* inépuisable, intarissable

nevermind ['nevəmaɪnd] *n Am* **it makes no nevermind** *(to me)* ça m'est égal; *(in general)* ça n'a pas d'importance

nevermore [ˌnevə'mɔː(r)] *adv Literary* jamais plus, plus jamais

never-never *Fam* **1** *n* (**a**) *Br & Austr (hire purchase)* **to buy sth on the never-never** acheter qch à crédit ❏ *ou* à tempérament ❏ (**b**) *Austr* **the never-never** *(desert)* = les endroits les plus reculés du désert

2 *adj* imaginaire, chimérique

▸▸ ***never-never land*** pays *m* de cocagne; **you're living in never-never land if you believe that…** tu rêves si tu crois que…

nevertheless [ˌnevəðə'les] *adv* (**a**) *(gen)* néanmoins; **a small, but nevertheless significant increase** une augmentation faible mais néanmoins significative; **we shall press on nevertheless and hope things get better** nous poursuivrons néanmoins nos efforts en espérant que les choses s'amélioreront; **she'd not skied before but she insisted on coming with us nevertheless** elle n'avait jamais fait de ski mais elle a quand même tenu à nous accompagner

(**b**) *(at start of clause or sentence)* cependant; **he says he never wants to see her again, nevertheless, I think he still loves her** il dit qu'il ne veut plus jamais la revoir, cependant je crois qu'il l'aime encore

never-to-be-forgotten *adj* inoubliable

Nevis ['niːvɪs] *n (island)* Nevis

NEW [njuː]

nouveau	▸ 1 (a) – (e); 2
neuf	▸ 1 (a)
autre	▸ 1 (a)

(*compar* **newer,** *superl* **newest**) **1** *adj* (**a**) *(gen)* nouveau(elle); *(different)* nouveau(elle), autre; *(unused)* neuf, nouveau(elle); **a new tablecloth** *(brand new)* une nouvelle nappe, une nappe neuve; *(fresh)* une nouvelle nappe, une nappe propre; **new evidence** de nouvelles preuves; **he's wearing his new suit for the first time** il porte son nouveau costume *ou* son costume neuf pour la première fois; **I don't want to get my new gloves dirty** je ne veux pas salir mes nouveaux gants *ou* gants neufs; **this dress isn't new** ce n'est pas une robe neuve *ou* une nouvelle robe, cette robe n'est pas neuve; **have you seen their new house yet?** est-ce que tu as vu leur nouvelle maison?; **she needs a new sheet of paper** il lui faut une autre feuille de papier; **we need some new ideas** il nous faut de nouvelles idées *ou* des idées neuves; **a new application of an old theory** une nouvelle application d'une vieille théorie; **there are new people in the flat next door** il y a de nouveaux occupants dans l'appartement d'à côté; **she likes her new boss** elle aime bien son nouveau patron; **new members are always welcome** nous sommes toujours ravis d'accueillir de nouveaux adhérents; **to look for new business** faire de la prospection; **America was a new country** *(just developing)* l'Amérique était un pays neuf; **under new management** *(sign)* changement de propriétaire; **as** *or* **like new** comme neuf; *(in advertisement)* état neuf; **as good as new (again)** *(clothing, carpet)* (à nouveau) comme neuf; *(watch, electrical appliance)* (à nouveau) en parfait état de marche; **to feel like a new woman/man** se sentir revivre; **to make a new woman/man of sb** transformer qn complètement; *Prov* **there's nothing new under the sun** il n'y a rien de nouveau sous le soleil

(**b**) *(latest, recent → issue, recording, baby)* nouveau(elle); **the newest fashions** la dernière mode; **is there anything new on the catastrophe?** est-ce qu'il y a du nouveau sur la catastrophe?; *Fam* **what's new?** quoi de neuf?; *Fam* **(so) what's new!, what else is new!** *(dismissive)* quelle surprise!; **that's nothing new!** rien de nouveau à cela!

(**c**) *(unfamiliar → experience, environment)* nouveau(elle); **everything's still very new to me here** tout est encore tout nouveau pour moi ici; *Fam* **that's a new one on me!** *(joke)* celle-là, on ne me l'avait jamais faite!; *(news)* première nouvelle!; *(experience)* on en apprend tous les jours!

(**d**) *(recently arrived)* nouveau(elle); *(novice)* novice; **you're new here, aren't you?** vous êtes nouveau ici, n'est-ce pas?; **those curtains are new in this room** ces rideaux n'étaient pas dans cette pièce; **she's new to the job** elle débute dans le métier; **we're new to this area** nous venons d'arriver dans la région

(**e**) *Culin (wine, potatoes, carrots)* nouveau(elle)

2 *n* nouveau *m*; **the cult of the new** le culte du nouveau

▸▸ *Fam* ***new blood*** sang *m* neuf; *Fin* ***new borrowings*** nouveaux emprunts *mpl*; ***new boy*** *Sch* nouveau *m*, nouvel élève *m*; *(in office, team etc)* nouveau *m*; ***New Britain*** Nouvelle-Bretagne *f*; ***New Brunswick*** le Nouveau-Brunswick; **in New Brunswick** dans le Nouveau-Brunswick; *Archit* ***new brutalism*** brutalisme *m*; *Mktg* ***new buy situation*** situation *f* de nouvel achat; ***New Caledonia*** Nouvelle-Calédonie *f*; **in New Caledonia** en Nouvelle-Calédonie; ***New Caledonian*** **1** *n* Néo-Calédonien(enne) *m,f* **2** *adj* néo-calédonien; *Fin* ***new capital*** capitaux *mpl* frais; ***the New Deal*** (**a**) *Hist* le New Deal *(programme de réformes sociales mises en place aux États-Unis par le président Roosevelt au lendemain de la grande dépression des années 30)* (**b**) *Br Pol* = programme du gouvernement Blair destiné à aider les jeunes à trouver un emploi; ***New Delhi*** New Delhi; *Can* ***New Democratic Party*** Nouveau Parti *m* démocratique; ***new economy*** nouvelle économie *f*; ***New England*** Nouvelle-Angleterre *f*; **in New England** en Nouvelle-Angleterre; ***New Englander*** habitant(e) *m,f* de la Nouvelle-Angleterre; ***the New English Bible*** = texte de la Bible révisé dans les années 60; ***New Forest*** = région forestière dans le sud de l'Angleterre; ***New Forest pony*** New Forest *m (cheval)*; ***new girl*** *Sch* nouvelle (élève) *f*; *(in office, team)* nouvelle *f*; ***new grammar*** la nouvelle grammaire; ***New Guinea*** Nouvelle-Guinée *f*; **in New Guinea** en Nouvelle-Guinée; ***New Hampshire*** le New Hampshire; **in New Hampshire** dans le New Hampshire; ***New Hebridean*** **1** *n* Néo-Hébridais(e) *m,f* **2** *adj* néo-hébridais; ***New Hebrides*** Nouvelles-Hébrides *fpl*; **in the New Hebrides** aux Nouvelles-Hébrides; ***New Ireland*** Nouvelle-Irlande *f*; **in New Ireland** en Nouvelle-Irlande; *St Exch* ***new issue*** nouvelle émission *f*; *St Exch* ***new issue market*** marché *m* des nouvelles émissions, marché *m* primaire; ***New Jersey*** le New Jersey; **in New Jersey** dans le New Jersey; ***New Labour*** = nouveau nom donné au parti travailliste britannique vers le milieu des années quatre-vingt-dix dans le souci d'en moderniser l'image; *Br Fam* ***new lad*** jeune homme *m* moderne ❏ *(qui boit avec modération et n'est pas sexiste)*; ***New Latin*** latin *m* scientifique; *Br Pol* ***the New Left*** la nouvelle gauche; ***new look*** nouvelle image *f*; ***the New Look*** *(in post-war fashion)* le new-look; ***New Man*** homme *m* moderne *(qui participe équitablement à l'éducation des enfants et aux tâches ménagères)*; *Am* ***new math,*** *Br* ***new maths*** les maths *fpl* modernes; ***the new media*** les nouveaux médias *mpl*; ***New Mexico*** le Nouveau-Mexique; **in New Mexico** au Nouveau-Mexique; *Br Hist* ***the New Model Army*** = nom donné à l'armée anglaise après la révolte du Parlement en 1645; ***new money*** *(after decimalization)* système *m* monétaire décimal; *Fin* crédit *m* de restructuration; **what's ten shillings in new money?** ten shillings, ça fait combien en système décimal?; **she married into new money** *(wealth)* elle s'est mariée avec un homme issue d'une famille enrichie de fraîche date; *Pej* elle s'est mariée avec un nouveau riche; ***new moon*** nouvelle lune *f*; *Press* ***New Musical Express*** = hebdomadaire anglais de musique rock; ***New Orleans*** La Nouvelle-Orléans; ***new potato*** pomme *f* de terre nouvelle; *Com & Mktg* ***new product*** nouveau produit *m*; *Com & Mktg* ***new product development*** développement *m* de nouveaux produits; *Com & Mktg* ***new product marketing*** marketing *m* de nouveaux produits; ***New Providence*** île *f* de la Nouvelle-Providence; ***New Quebec*** Nouveau-Québec *m*; **in New Quebec** au Nouveau-Québec; ***the new rich*** les nouveaux riches *mpl*; ***New Right*** nouvelle droite *f*; *Press* ***the New Scientist*** = hebdomadaire scientifique britannique; ***New Scotland Yard*** = siège de la police à Londres; ***New South Wales*** la Nouvelle-Galles du Sud; **in New South Wales** en Nouvelle-Galles du Sud; *Fin* ***new shares*** actions *fpl* nouvelles; *Press* ***the New Statesman*** = hebdomadaire britannique de gauche; ***new technology*** nouvelle technologie *f*, technologie *f* de pointe; ***the New Territories*** les Nouveaux Territoires *mpl (de Hong Kong)*; *Bible* ***New Testament*** Nouveau Testament *m*; *Br* ***new town*** ville *f* nouvelle; ***new wave*** *(in cinema)* nouvelle vague *f*; *(in pop music)* new wave *f*; ***the New World*** le Nouveau Monde; ***New Year*** Nouvel An *m*; **happy New Year!** bonne année!; **to see in the New Year** réveillonner *(le 31 décembre)*; ***New Year's resolutions*** résolutions *fpl* pour la nouvelle année; **have you made any New Year's resolutions?** tu as des résolutions pour la nouvelle année?; *Am* ***New Year's*** *(day)* le premier de l'an; *(eve)* le soir du réveillon *ou* du 31 décembre; ***New Year's Day*** jour *m* de l'an; ***New Year's Eve*** Saint-Sylvestre *f*; ***the New Year's Honours List*** = titres et distinctions honorifiques décernés par la Reine à l'occasion de la nouvelle année et dont la liste est établie officieusement par le Premier ministre; ***New York (City)*** New York; ***New Yorker*** New-Yorkais(e) *m,f*; *Press* ***the New Yorker*** = hebdomadaire culturel et littéraire new-yorkais; *St Exch* ***New York Mercantile Exchange*** = marché à terme des produits pétroliers de New York; ***New York (State)*** l'État *m* de New York; **in (the State of) New York, in New York (State)** dans l'État de New York; ***the New York subway*** le métro new-yorkais; *Press* ***the New York Times*** = quotidien américain de qualité; ***New Zealand*** Nouvelle-Zélande *f*; **in New Zealand** en Nouvelle-Zélande; ***New Zealand butter*** beurre *m* néo-zélandais; ***New Zealander*** Néo-Zélandais(e) *m,f*

'New World Symphony' *or* **'From the New World'** *Dvořák* 'La Symphonie du Nouveau Monde'

NEW LABOUR

Après dix-huit ans de gouvernement conservateur, les élections de mai 1997 propulsèrent les travaillistes au pouvoir avec une écrasante majorité. Convaincus par plusieurs défaites électorales de l'inéligibilité du parti travailliste traditionnel dans une Grande-Bretagne bouleversée par le thatchérisme, les nouveaux dirigeants décidèrent de réorganiser et de renommer le parti afin d'élargir leur électorat aux classes moyennes. Les "nouveaux travaillistes" établirent des liens étroits avec le patronat et promurent une "troisième voie" comme alternative à la traditionnelle idéologie de gauche du parti. Cependant, les fidèles du parti commencèrent très vite à souhaiter un retour aux valeurs traditionnelles de la gauche.

new- [nju:] *pref* **new-won freedom** une liberté toute neuve; **new-built** nouvellement construit

New Age *adj* New Age *(inv)*
▸▸ ***New Age traveller*** marginal(e) *m,f* itinérant *(vivant dans une communauté New Age)*

newbie ['njʊ:bɪ] *n Fam* (**a**) *Am (new recruit)* bleu(e) *m,f* (**b**) *Comput (Internet user)* internaute *mf* novice, cybernovice *mf*

newborn ['nju:bɔ:n] **1** *adj* nouveau-né; **a newborn baby girl** une (petite fille) nouveau-née
2 *npl* **the newborn** les nouveau-nés *mpl*

Newcastle ['nju:,kɑ:səl-] *n* Newcastle
▸▸ *Vet* ***Newcastle disease*** pseudo-peste *f* aviaire, maladie *f* de Newcastle

newcomer ['nju:,kʌmə(r)] *n* (**a**) *(new arrival)* nouveau(elle) venu(e) *m,f*; **she's a newcomer to the town** elle vient d'arriver dans la ville (**b**) *(beginner)* novice *mf*; **a good book for newcomers to computing** un bon livre pour les débutants en informatique; **I'm a newcomer to all this** tout cela est nouveau pour moi

new-edge *adj*
▸▸ ***new-edge technology*** technologie *f* de pointe

newel ['nju:əl] *n* (**a**) *(on ordinary staircase)* pilastre *m* (**b**) *(in spiral staircase)* noyau *m* (d'escalier)
▸▸ ***newel post*** pilastre *m*

newfangled [,nju:'fæŋgəld] *adj Pej (idea, device)* nouveau(elle), dernier cri *(inv)*

Newfie ['nju:fɪ] *n Fam* Terre-Neuvien(enne) ❑ *m,f*

new-found *adj* nouveau(elle), récent; **her new-found friends** ses amis de fraîche date

Newfoundland ['nju:fəndlənd] *n* (**a**) *Geog* Terre-Neuve *f*; **in Newfoundland** à Terre-Neuve (**b**) *(dog)* terre-neuve *m inv*

Newfoundlander ['nju:fəndləndə(r)] *n* Terre-Neuvien(enne) *m,f*

Newgate ['nju:gɪt] *n* = prison londonienne, fermée vers 1900, connue dans l'histoire pour avoir accueilli de grands criminels

newish ['nju:ɪʃ] *adj* assez neuf *ou* nouveau(elle)

new-laid *adj Br* **a new-laid egg** un œuf extra-frais

new-look *adj* new-look *(inv)*

newly ['nju:lɪ] *adv* nouvellement, récemment; **newly arrived** récemment arrivé, arrivé de fraîche date; **the gate has been newly painted** la barrière vient d'être peinte; **newly dug** fraîchement creusé; **newly elected** nouvellement élu; **a newly discovered galaxy** une galaxie qu'on vient de découvrir *ou* récemment découverte; **their newly won independence** leur indépendance récemment conquise
▸▸ ***newly industrialized country*** pays *m* en voie d'industrialisation

newlyweds ['nju:lɪwedz] *npl* jeunes mariés *mpl*

newmarket ['nju:,mɑ:kɪt] **1** *n Br* = jeu de cartes où on joue de l'argent
2 Newmarket *n* = ville du Suffolk célèbre pour son hippodrome

new-mown *adj Br (grass)* fraîchement coupé; *(lawn)* fraîchement tondu; *(hay)* fraîchement fauché

newness ['nju:nɪs] *n* (**a**) *(of building)* nouveauté *f*; *(of shoes, carpet)* état *m* neuf (**b**) *(of ideas, experience, fashion)* nouveauté *f*, originalité *f*

news [nju:z] *n (UNCOUNT)* (**a**) *(information)* nouvelles *fpl*, informations *fpl*; **a piece of news** une nouvelle, une information; **an interesting piece of news** une nouvelle intéressante; **is there any more news about** *or* **on the explosion?** est-ce qu'on a plus d'informations sur l'explosion?; **the news that they had been found alive** la nouvelle selon laquelle ils avaient été retrouvés vivants; **that's good/bad news** c'est une bonne/mauvaise nouvelle; **to have news of sb** avoir des nouvelles de qn; **have you had any news of her?** avez-vous eu de ses nouvelles?; **what's your news?** quoi de neuf (chez vous)?; **have I got news for you!** j'ai du nouveau (à vous annoncer)!; **it's news to me!** première nouvelle!, je l'ignorais!; **famine isn't news any more** la famine ne fait plus la une (des journaux); **to be in the news, to make news** faire parler de soi; **a city that is in the news a lot these days** une ville dont on parle beaucoup ces jours-ci; **he's always in the news** on parle toujours de lui dans la presse; **she's no longer news** on ne parle plus d'elle; **to break the news (of sth) to sb** annoncer la nouvelle (de qch) à qn; **bad news travels fast** les mauvaises nouvelles vont vite; *Ironic* **good news travels fast!** je vois, les nouvelles circulent vite!; *Fam* **he's bad news** on a toujours des ennuis avec lui; *Prov* **no news is good news** pas de nouvelles, bonnes nouvelles
(**b**) *Rad & TV* actualités *fpl*, informations *fpl*; *(bulletin)* journal *m*; *TV* **the 9 o'clock news** le journal (télévisé) *ou* les informations de 21 heures; *Rad* le journal (parlé) *ou* les informations de 21 heures; **news in brief** *(main headlines → on news bulletin)* titres *mpl*; *(→ in newspaper)* actualité *f* en résumé; *(miscellaneous news items)* faits *mpl* divers; **I heard it on the news** je l'ai entendu aux informations; **the sports/financial news** la page *ou* chronique sportive/financière
▸▸ ***news agency*** agence *f* de presse; *Am Rad & TV* ***news analyst*** commentateur(trice) *m,f*; ***news blackout*** black-out *m inv* sur l'actualité, censure *f* de l'actualité; **to impose a news blackout on sth** empêcher la divulgation de qch; **the government has imposed a news blackout** le gouvernement a fait le black-out; ***news broadcasting*** diffusion *f* des informations; ***news bulletin*** bulletin *m* d'informations; ***news centre*** salle *f* de rédaction télévision; ***news channel*** chaîne *f* d'information continue; ***news conference*** conférence *f* de presse; ***News Corporation*** = grand groupe international de médias; ***news desk*** (salle *f* de) rédaction *f*; ***news editor*** rédacteur(trice) *m,f* en chef des actualités; ***news film*** film *m* d'actualités; ***news gathering*** collecte *f* de l'information; ***news headlines*** titres *mpl* de l'actualité; ***news item*** nouvelle *f*, information *f*; ***news magazine*** news-magazine *m*; ***news programme*** magazine *m* d'actualités; *Comput* ***news reader*** logiciel *m* de lecture de nouvelles; ***news report*** bulletin *m* d'informations; ***news reporter*** reporter *m*; *Comput* ***news server*** serveur *m* de nouvelles; *Am* ***news service*** = agence de presse qui publie ses informations par le biais d'un syndicat de distribution; ***news story*** sujet *m*; ***news value*** intérêt *m* médiatique; ***news writer*** rédacteur(trice) *m,f* d'actualités

newsagent ['nju:z,eɪdʒənt] *n Br* marchand(e) *m,f* de journaux; *(shopkeeper also selling papers)* dépositaire *mf* de journaux; **at the newsagent's** chez le marchand de journaux

newsboy ['nju:zbɔɪ] *n (in street)* crieur *m* de journaux; *(delivery boy)* livreur *m* de journaux

newscast ['nju:zkɑ:st] *n* bulletin *m* d'informations; *TV* journal *m* télévisé, informations *fpl*

newscaster ['nju:z,kɑ:stə(r)] *n* présentateur(trice) *m,f* du journal

newscasting ['nju:z,kɑ:stɪŋ] *n Rad & TV* présentation *f* du journal

newsdealer ['nju:z,di:lə(r)] *n Am* marchand(e) *m,f* de journaux

newsflash ['nju:zflæʃ] *n* flash *m* d'informations

newsgroup ['nju:zgru:p] *n Comput* forum *m* de discussion, newsgroup *m*

newshawk ['nju:zhɔ:k], **newshound** ['nju:zhaʊnd] *n Fam* reporter ❑ *m*, journaliste ❑ *mf*

newsie ['nju:zɪ] *n Am Fam* (**a**) *(newspaper vendor)* vendeur(euse) *m,f* de journaux ❑ (**b**) *(journalist)* journaleux(euse) *m,f*

newsletter ['nju:z,letə(r)] *n* lettre *f*, bulletin *m*; **monthly newsletter** bulletin *m* mensuel

newsman ['nju:zmən] *(pl* **newsmen** [-mən]) *n* journaliste *m*

newsmonger ['nju:z,mʌŋgə(r)] *n Pej* pipelet(ette) *m,f*

newsocracy [,nju:z'ɒkrəsɪ] *n* = aux États-Unis, ensemble de la presse et du réseau télévisé à audience nationale

newspaper ['nju:z,peɪpə(r)] **1** *n* (**a**) *(publication)* journal *m*; **in the newspaper** dans le journal; **an evening newspaper** un journal du soir; **a daily newspaper** un quotidien (**b**) *(paper)* **wrapped in newspaper** enveloppé dans du papier journal
2 *comp (article, report)* de journal
▸▸ ***newspaper advertisement*** publicité *f* presse; ***newspaper advertising*** publicité *f* presse; ***newspaper clipping, newspaper cutting*** coupure *f* de presse; ***newspaper rack*** porte-journaux *m*; ***newspaper reporter*** reporter *m* (de la presse écrite)

newspaperman ['nju:z,peɪpəmæn] *(pl* **newspapermen** [-men]) *n* journaliste *m* (de la presse écrite)

newspaperwoman ['nju:zpeɪpə,wʊmən] *(pl* **newspaperwomen** [-,wɪmɪn]) *n* journaliste *f* (de la presse écrite)

newspeak ['nju:spi:k] *n* jargon *m* bureaucratique, ≃ langue *f* de bois

newsprint ['nju:zprɪnt] *n* papier *m* journal; **I got my hands covered in newsprint** *(ink)* je me suis mis de l'encre plein les mains

newsreader ['nju:z,ri:də(r)] *n* présentateur(trice) *m,f* du journal

newsreel ['nju:zri:l] *n* film *m* d'actualités

newsroom ['nju:zru:m] *n* (**a**) *Press* salle *f* de rédaction (**b**) *Rad & TV* studio *m*

newssheet ['nju:zʃi:t] *n* lettre *f*, bulletin *m*

newsstand ['nju:zstænd] *n* kiosque *m* (à journaux)

newsvendor ['nju:z,vendə(r)] *n Br (gen)* marchand(e) *m,f* de journaux; *(in street)* crieur(euse) *m,f* de journaux

Newsweek ['nju:zwi:k] *n Press* = hebdomadaire d'actualité américain

newswoman ['nju:z,wʊmən] *(pl* **newswomen** [-,wɪmɪn]) *n* journaliste *f*

newsworthiness ['nju:z,wɜ:ðɪnɪs] *n* intérêt *m* médiatique

newsworthy ['nju:z,wɜ:ðɪ] *adj* **it's not newsworthy** cela n'a aucun intérêt médiatique; **political scandal is always newsworthy** les médias sont toujours friands *ou* la presse est toujours friande de scandales politiques

newsy ['nju:zɪ] *(compar* **newsier,** *superl* **newsiest**) *adj Fam (letter)* plein de nouvelles ❑

newt [nju:t] *n Zool* triton *m*; *Br very Fam* **pissed as a newt** soûl comme une bourrique, beurré comme un petit lu

newton ['nju:tən] *n* newton *m*

Newtonian [nju:'təʊnɪən] *adj* newtonien

new-to-the-company product *n Mktg* produit *m* nouveau dans la société

new-to-the-world product *n Mktg* produit *m* nouveau dans le monde

new-wave *adj (cinema)* nouvelle vague *(inv)*; *(pop music)* new-wave *(inv)*

NEXT [nekst]

prochain	▸ **1 (a) – (c); 3**
suivant	▸ **1 (a) – (c)**
ensuite	▸ **2 (a)**
la prochaine fois	▸ **2 (b)**
la fois suivante	▸ **2 (b)**
à côté de	▸ **5 (a)**
après	▸ **5 (c)**
presque	▸ **5 (d)**

1 *adj* (**a**) *(in time → coming)* prochain; *(→ already past)* suivant; **keep quiet about it for the next few days** n'en parlez pas pendant les quelques jours qui viennent; **I had to stay in**

bed for the next ten days j'ai dû garder le lit pendant les dix jours qui ont suivi; **(the) next day** le lendemain; **(the) next morning/evening** le lendemain matin/soir; **next Sunday, Sunday next** dimanche prochain; **the next Sunday** le dimanche suivant; **next year** l'année prochaine; **the next year** l'année suivante; **this time next year** d'ici un an; **the week/year after next** dans deux semaines/ans; *Fam* **next minute she was dashing off out again** une minute après, elle repartait; **the situation's changing from one moment to the next** la situation change sans arrêt; **(the) next time I see him** la prochaine fois que je le vois *ou* verrai; **(the) next time I saw him** quand je l'ai revu; **you may not be so lucky next time** tu pourrais avoir moins de chance la *ou* une prochaine fois; **there isn't going to be a next time** il n'y aura pas de prochaine fois

(**b**) *(in series → in future)* prochain; *(→ in past)* suivant; **the next episode** *(in future)* le prochain épisode; *(in past)* l'épisode suivant; **the next size up/down** la taille au-dessus/au-dessous; **translate the next sentence** traduisez la phrase suivante; **their next child was a girl** ensuite, ils eurent une fille; **they want their next child to be a girl** ils veulent que leur prochain enfant soit une fille, la prochaine fois ils veulent une fille; **your name is next on the list** votre nom est le suivant *ou* prochain sur la liste; **the next ten pages** les dix pages suivantes; **the next before last** l'avant-dernier; **your train is the next but one** ton train n'est pas le prochain, mais celui d'après; **ask the next person you meet** demandez à la première personne que vous rencontrez; **(the) next to arrive was Tanya** Tanya est arrivée à la suite; **the next world** l'au-delà *m inv*; **this life and the next** ce monde et l'autre; **(the) next thing** ensuite; **and (the) next thing I knew, I woke up in hospital** et l'instant d'après je me suis réveillé à l'hôpital; **next thing, they'll be melting the polar ice!** un de ces quatre (matins), ils vont se mettre à faire fondre les glaces du pôle!

(**c**) *(in space → house, street)* prochain, suivant; **the next room/house** *(next to this one)* la pièce/maison voisine *ou* d'à côté; **take the next street on the left** prenez la prochaine à gauche; **after the kitchen, it's the next room on your right** après la cuisine, c'est la première pièce à votre droite; **they live next door to us** ils habitent à côté de chez nous, ce sont nos voisins; **I'm just going next door** je vais juste chez les voisins; **the house next door** la maison d'à côté *ou* des voisins; **the girl/boy next door** la fille/le garçon d'à côté; *Fig* **she was just the girl next door** c'était une fille simple; **he's the boy-next-door type** c'est un garçon très simple; *Fig* **that's next door to madness/absurdity** ça frise la folie/l'absurde; **next door's children** les enfants qui habitent à côté *ou* des voisins; **it's the man from next door** c'est le voisin

(**d**) *(in queue, line)* **I'm next** c'est (à) mon tour, c'est à moi; **who's next?** à qui le tour?; **I'm next after you** je suis (juste) après vous; **Helen is next in line for promotion** Helen est la suivante sur la liste des promotions; **I can take a joke as well as the next person, but...** j'aime plaisanter comme tout le monde, mais...

2 *adv* (**a**) *(afterwards)* ensuite, après; **what did you do with it next?** et ensuite, qu'en avez-vous fait?; **what shall we do next?** qu'est-ce que nous allons faire maintenant?; **next on the agenda is the question of finance** la question suivante à l'ordre du jour est celle des finances; **next came Henry VII** puis vint *ou* il y eut Henri VII; *Hum* **what will they think of next?** qu'est-ce qu'ils vont bien pouvoir inventer maintenant?; **what** *or* **whatever next?** *(indignantly or in mock indignation)* et puis quoi encore?; *Fam* **you'll be asking me to give up my job (for you) next!** tu n'as qu'à me demander de laisser tomber mon travail pendant que tu y es!

(**b**) *(next time → in future)* la prochaine fois; *(→ in past)* la fois suivante *ou* d'après; **when we next meet, when next we meet** la prochaine fois que nous nous verrons, lors de notre prochaine rencontre; **when we next met** quand nous nous sommes revus

(**c**) *(with superlative adj)* **the next youngest/oldest child** l'enfant le plus jeune/le plus âgé ensuite; **who is the next oldest/youngest after Mark?** qui est le suivant *ou* le prochain par ordre d'âge après Mark?; **the next largest size** la taille juste au-dessus; **the next highest building in the world is...** le deuxième immeuble dans le monde pour la hauteur, c'est...; **you'll have to make do with the next best** il faudra vous contenter de la qualité en dessous; **the next best thing would be to...** à défaut, le mieux serait de...; **watching the match on TV was the next best thing to actually being there** l'idéal aurait été de pouvoir assister au match, mais ce n'était déjà pas mal de le voir à la télé

(**d**) *Am Fam* **to get next to sb** *(ingratiate oneself with)* faire de la lèche à qn; *(become emotionally involved with)* se lier avec qn; *(have sex with)* coucher avec qn

3 *pron (next train, person, child)* prochain(e) *m,f*; **next please!** au suivant, s'il vous plaît!

4 *prep Am* = **next to**

5 next to *prep* (**a**) *(near)* à côté de; **they live next to a hospital** ils habitent à côté d'un hôpital; **come and sit next to me** venez vous asseoir à côté de *ou* près de moi; **I love the feel of silk next to my skin** j'adore le contact de la soie sur ma peau; **next to him, everybody looks tiny** à côté de lui, tout le monde a l'air minuscule

(**b**) *(in series)* **next to last** avant-dernier; **the next to bottom shelf** la deuxième étagère en partant du bas

(**c**) *(in comparisons)* après; **next to red, Lisa prefers white** après le rouge, Lisa préfère le blanc; **next to you, he was the smartest** après vous, c'était lui le plus élégant

(**d**) *(almost)* presque; **next to impossible** presque *ou* quasiment impossible; **I bought it for next to nothing** je l'ai acheté pour trois fois rien *ou* presque rien; **they have next to no proof** ils n'ont pratiquement aucune preuve; **in next to no time** en un rien de temps

---

next-day delivery *n Com* livraison *f* lendemain

next-door *adj* **the next-door garden** le jardin des voisins

►► ***next-door neighbour*** *(in private house)* voisin(e) *m,f* (de la maison d'à côté); *(in apartment building)* voisin(e) *m,f* de palier

next-of-kin *n (relative)* parent *m* le plus proche; *(family)* famille *f*; **to inform the next-of-kin** prévenir la famille

nexus ['neksəs] *(pl* **inv** *or* **nexuses**) *n* lien *m*, liaison *f*

NF[1] [ˌen'ef] *n (abbr* **National Front**) = parti britannique d'extrême droite, ≃ Front *m* national

NF[2] *(written abbr* **Newfoundland**) Terre-Neuve *f*

NFL [ˌenef'el] *n (abbr* **National Football League**) = fédération nationale de football américain

NFP [ˌenef'piː] *n (abbr* **natural family planning**) = contraception par des moyens naturels

NFT [ˌenef'tiː] *n (abbr* **National Film Theatre**) = cinéma d'art et d'essai londonien qui fait partie du "British Film Institute"

NFU [ˌenef'juː] *n (abbr* **National Farmers' Union**) = syndicat britannique d'exploitants agricoles

NG [ˌen'dʒiː] *n (abbr* **National Guard**) Garde *f* nationale *(milice nationale américaine composée de volontaires)*

NGA [ˌendʒiː'eɪ] *n (abbr* **National Graphical Association**) = syndicat britannique d'imprimeurs

ngaio ['naɪəʊ] *n Bot* = arbre de Nouvelle-Zélande à feuilles persistantes et bois blanc

NGO [ˌendʒiː'əʊ] *n (abbr* **non-governmental organization**) ONG *f*

NG take [ˌen'dʒiː-] *n TV & Cin* mauvaise prise *f*

NH *(written abbr* **New Hampshire**) New Hampshire *m*

NHI [ˌeneɪtʃ'aɪ] *n Br (abbr* **National Health Insurance**) = système britannique de sécurité sociale

NHL [ˌeneɪtʃ'el] *n (abbr* **National Hockey League**) = fédération nationale américaine de hockey sur glace

NHS [ˌeneɪtʃ'es] *n Br (abbr* **National Health Service**) ≃ Sécurité *f* sociale

►► ***NHS number*** numéro *m* de Sécurité sociale

NI[1] [ˌen'aɪ] *n Br (abbr* **national insurance**) = système britannique de sécurité sociale

NI[2] *(written abbr* **Northern Ireland**) Irlande *f* du Nord

niacin ['naɪəsɪn] *n Biol* acide *m* nicotinique

Niagara [naɪ'ægərə] *n*

►► ***Niagara Falls*** les chutes *fpl* du Niagara

nib [nɪb] *n* (**a**) *(of fountain pen)* (bec *m* de) plume *f*; *(of ballpoint, tool)* pointe *f*; **broad nib** grosse plume *f*, plume *f* à gros bec; **fine nib** plume *f* fine, plume *f* à bec fin (**b**) *Tech (of tool)* pointe *f*

nibbed [nɪbd] *adj (crushed)* concassé

-nibbed [nɪbd] *suff* **gold-nibbed** avec une plume en or; **fine-nibbed** *(fountain pen)* à plume fine; *(ballpoint)* à pointe fine

nibble ['nɪbəl] **1** *vt* (**a**) *(of person, caterpillar)* grignoter; *(of rodent)* grignoter, ronger; *(of goat, sheep)* brouter; **I'm not hungry, I'll just nibble a piece of bread** je n'ai pas faim, je vais juste grignoter un morceau de pain; **the mice have nibbled the telephone wire** les souris ont rongé *ou* grignoté le fil du téléphone; **the fish nibbled the bait** le poisson a mordu à l'hameçon

(**b**) *(playfully → ear)* mordiller

2 *vi* (**a**) *(cat)* **to nibble at** *or* **on sth** grignoter qch; **she nibbled nervously at her food** elle mangeait nerveusement du bout des dents; **the mice have nibbled through the wire** les souris ont entièrement rongé le fil

(**b**) *(bite)* **to nibble at sth** mordiller qch; **the cat likes to nibble at my toes** le chat aime bien me mordiller les orteils; *also Fig* **to nibble at the bait** mordre à l'hameçon

(**c**) *Fig (show interest)* **to nibble at an offer** être tenté par une offre

3 *n* (**a**) *Fishing* touche *f*

(**b**) *(snack)* **to have a nibble** grignoter quelque chose; **nibbles** amuse-gueules *mpl*

nibbler ['nɪblə(r)] *n (person)* grignoteur(euse) *m,f*

nibbling ['nɪblɪŋ] *n* grignotage *m*

niblick ['nɪblɪk] *n* niblick *m*

nibs [nɪbz] *n Br Fam* **his/her nibs** son altesse, cézigue

NIC [ˌenaɪ'siː] *n* (**a**) *(abbr* **newly-industrialized country**) pays *m* en voie d'industrialisation, NPI *m* (**b**) *(abbr* **national insurance contributions**) cotisations *fpl* à la Sécurité sociale

Nicad battery [nɪ'kæd-] *n* batterie *f* au nickel cadmium

Nicaea [naɪ'siːə] *n Hist* Nicée

NICAM ['naɪkæm] *n (abbr* **near-instantaneous companded audio multiplex**) Nicam *m*

Nicaragua [ˌnɪkə'rægjʊə] *n* Nicaragua *m*; **in Nicaragua** au Nicaragua

Nicaraguan [ˌnɪkə'rægjʊən] **1** *n* Nicaraguayen(enne) *m,f*

2 *adj* nicaraguayen

3 *comp (embassy, history)* du Nicaragua

niccolite ['nɪkəlaɪt] *n Miner* niccolite *f*, nickéline *f*

NICE [naɪs]

bien	► **1 (a), (b), (d)**
beau	► **1 (a)**
bon	► **1 (a)**
joli	► **1 (a)**
agréable	► **1 (b)**
sympathique	► **1 (b)**
gentil	► **1 (c)**
subtil	► **1 (f)**

1 *adj* (**a**) *(expressing approval → good)* bien; *(→ attractive)* beau (belle); *(→ pretty)* joli; *(→ car, picture)* beau (belle); *(→ food)* bon; *(→ idea)* bon; *(→ weather)* beau (belle); **they have a nice house** ils ont une belle maison; **very nice** *(visually)* très joli; *(food)* très bon; **to taste nice** avoir bon goût; **to smell nice** sentir bon; **she was wearing a very nice hat** elle portait un très joli chapeau; **she always looks nice** elle est toujours bien habillée *ou* mise; **we had a nice meal** on a bien mangé; **it's turned out nice again** *(weather)* il fait encore beau

(**b**) *(pleasant → gen)* agréable, bien; *(→ person)* bien, sympathique; **she's very nice** elle est très sympa; **have a nice time** amusez-vous bien; **have a nice day!** bonne journée!; **it's nice to be back again** cela fait plaisir d'être de retour; **(it was) nice meeting you** (j'ai été) ravi de faire votre connaissance; **it's not a nice thing to** happen to anyone ce n'est pas agréable quand ça arrive; **nice work!** beau travail!; *Hum* **nice work if you can get it** c'est un travail agréable, encore faut-il le décrocher; *Br Fam* **nice one!** bravo!❑

(**c**) *(kind)* gentil, aimable; **to be nice to sb** être gentil avec qn; **that's nice of her** c'est gentil *ou* aimable de sa part; **she said some nice things** elle a dit des choses gentilles *ou* aimables; **it's nice of you to say so** vous êtes bien aimable de le dire; **he was nice enough to carry my case** il a eu la gentillesse *ou* l'obligeance de porter ma valise

(**d**) *(respectable)* bien (élevé), convenable; **nice people don't blow their noses at table** les gens bien élevés ne se mouchent pas à table

(**e**) *Ironic* **he made a nice mess of the job** il a fait un travail de cochon; **we're in a nice mess** nous sommes dans de beaux draps *ou* un beau pétrin; **you're a nice one to talk!** toi, tu peux parler!; **that's a nice way to talk (to your father)!** en voilà une façon de parler (à ton père)!

(**f**) *Formal (subtle → distinction, point)* subtil, délicat; **that's a very nice point** voilà une question délicate

2 *adv* (**a**) *(as intensifier)* **nice long holidays** des vacances longues et agréables; **a nice cold drink** une boisson bien fraîche; **to have a nice long nap** faire une bonne sieste; **take it nice and easy** allez-y doucement; **nice and warm** bien chaud; **it's nice and warm in here** il fait bon ici; **it's nice and cool** il fait bien frais

(**b**) *(idiom) Am* **to make nice (to sb)** être gentil (avec qn)

---

nice-looking *adj* joli, beau (belle)

nicely ['naɪslɪ] *adv* (**a**) *(well)* bien; **to be coming along** *or* **doing nicely** *(people)* bien progresser; *(garden)* commencer à prendre tournure; *(investments)* bien se porter; **it fits her nicely** cela lui va bien; **nicely dressed** bien habillé; **nicely done!** bien joué!, beau travail!; **nicely put!** bien dit!; **this bag will do nicely** ce sac fera très bien l'affaire; **he's doing nicely** *(at school)* il travaille bien; *(after illness)* il se remet bien; *(financially)* il s'en sort bien, il n'est pas à plaindre

(**b**) *(pleasantly)* gentiment, agréablement; **she smiled at me nicely** elle me sourit gentiment

(**c**) *(politely → behave, eat)* bien, comme il faut; **ask nicely** demandez gentiment

(**d**) *(exactly)* exactement, avec précision; *(subtly)* avec précision; **they judged it nicely** ils ne se sont pas trompés dans leur appréciation

Nicene [naɪ'si:n] *adj* **the Nicene Creed** le symbole de Nicée

niceness ['naɪsnɪs] *n* (**a**) *(of person → kindness)* gentillesse *f*, amabilité *f*; *(→ pleasantness)* caractère *m* agréable; *(of house, hotel etc)* caractère *m* agréable; **the niceness of the weather** le temps agréable (**b**) *Formal (subtlety)* subtilité *f*

nicety ['naɪsətɪ] *(pl* **niceties***)* *n* (**a**) *(precision)* justesse *f*, précision *f*; **to a nicety** exactement, à la perfection (**b**) *(usu pl) (subtlety)* subtilité *f*, finesse *f*; **a distinction of some nicety** une distinction assez subtile *ou* fine; **the niceties of chess** les subtilités *fpl* des échecs; **diplomatic/legal niceties** des subtilités *fpl* diplomatiques/légales; **social niceties** *(etiquette)* règles *fpl* de la politesse; *(customs, refinements)* mondanités *fpl*

(**c**) *(refinement)* raffinement *m*, agrément *m*; **the niceties of a life of leisure** les agréments d'une vie de loisirs

niche [ni:ʃ] *n* (**a**) *(recess → in church, cliff)* niche *f*; *Fig* **to find one's niche** trouver sa voie (**b**) *Com & Mktg* créneau *m*

►► *Com & Mktg* ***niche market*** niche *f*, créneau *m* spécialisé; *Com & Mktg* ***niche marketing*** marketing *m* de créneau, marketing *m* ciblé; *Com & Mktg* ***niche player*** acteur *m* sur un segment de marché; *Com & Mktg* ***niche product*** produit *m* ciblé

nicher ['ni:ʃə(r)] *n Mktg* spécialiste *mf* dans une niche

niching ['ni:ʃɪŋ] *n Mktg* segmentation *f* en niches

nichrome ['naɪkrəʊm] *n Metal* nichrome *m*

nick [nɪk] **1** *n* (**a**) *(notch → in wood)* encoche *f*, entaille *f*; *(chip → in crockery)* ébréchure *f*; *(cut → on skin)* (petite) coupure *f*

(**b**) *Br Fam (police station)* poste *m* (de police)❑; *(prison)* taule *f*, bloc *m*; **in the nick** en taule, au bloc; **down the nick** au poste

(**c**) *Br Fam (condition)* condition❑ *f*, état❑ *m*; **in good/bad nick** en bon/mauvais état; **he's in pretty good nick for his age** il est en bonne forme pour son âge

(**d**) *(idiom)* **in the nick of time** juste à temps

2 *vt* (**a**) *(cut → deliberately)* faire une entaille *ou* une encoche sur; *(accidentally → crockery)* ébrécher; *(→ metal, paint)* faire des entailles dans; *(→ skin, face)* entailler, couper (légèrement); **he nicked his chin shaving** il s'est légèrement coupé le menton en se rasant

(**b**) *Br Fam (arrest)* agrafer, alpaguer; **he got nicked outside the bank** il s'est fait épingler *ou* pincer devant la banque; **he got nicked for stealing a car** il s'est fait arrêter pour vol de voiture

(**c**) *Br Fam (steal)* piquer, faucher

(**d**) *Am Fam (cheat)* arnaquer; **they nicked him for $1,000** il s'est fait arnaquer de 1000 dollars

nickel ['nɪkəl] *(Br pt & pp* **nickelled,** *cont* **nickelling,** *Am pt & pp* **nickeled,** *cont* **nickeling***)* **1** *n* (**a**) *(metal)* nickel *m* (**b**) *Am (coin)* pièce *f* de cinq cents; **it only costs a nickel** ça ne coûte que cinq cents; **to do sth on one's own nickel** payer qch de sa poche; *Fam* **it's not worth a plugged nickel** ça vaut pas un clou (**c**) *Am Fam (five dollars)* cinq dollars❑ *mpl*; **to buy a nickel of weed** acheter pour cinq dollars d'herbe

2 *vt* nickeler

►► ***nickel silver*** argentan *m*, maillechort *m*

nickel-and-dime *Am* **1** *vt* **to nickel-and-dime sb** *(give small amount of money to)* donner des sommes d'argent insignifiantes à qn; *(make pay money)* faire payer de nombreuses petites sommes à qn

2 *adj* de peu d'envergure

►► ***nickel-and-dime store*** = magasin à prix unique

nickel-cadmium battery *n* batterie *f* au nickel-cadmium

nickeliferous [,nɪkə'lɪfərəs] *adj Miner* nickélifère

nickelodeon [,nɪkə'ləʊdɪən] *n Am Old-fashioned* (**a**) *(jukebox)* juke-box *m* (**b**) *(cinema)* cinéma *m* bon marché

nickel-plated *adj* nickelé

nickel-plating *n* nickelage *m*

nicker ['nɪkə(r)] *(pl* **inv***)* *Br* **1** *n Fam* livres *fpl* (sterling❑); **five nicker** cinq livres

2 *vi* (**a**) *(neigh)* hennir doucement (**b**) *(snigger)* ricaner

nick-nack = **knick-knack**

nickname ['nɪkneɪm] **1** *n (gen)* surnom *m*, sobriquet *m*; *(short form)* diminutif *m*; *Comput* surnom *m*

2 *vt* surnommer

Nicodemus [,nɪkə'di:məs] *pr n Bible* Nicodème

Nicomachus [nɪ'kɒməkəs] *pr n* Nicomaque

Nicosia [,nɪkə'si:ə] *n* Nicosie

nicotiana [nɪ,kəʊʃɪ'ɑ:nə] *n Bot* nicotiane *f*

nicotinamide [,nɪkəʊ'ti:nəmaɪd] *n Biol & Chem* nicotinamide *f*

nicotine ['nɪkəti:n] *n* nicotine *f*

►► ***nicotine addiction*** tabagisme *m*; ***nicotine patch*** patch *m ou* timbre *m* anti-tabac; ***nicotine poisoning*** tabagisme *m*, intoxication *f* nicotinique; ***nicotine replacement therapy*** thérapie *f* de désaccoutumance à la nicotine *(patch, gomme nicotinique etc)*

nicotine-stained *adj* jauni par la nicotine

nicotinic [,nɪkə'tɪnɪk] *adj Chem* nicotinique

►► ***nicotinic acid*** acide *m* nicotinique

nicotinism ['nɪkəti:nɪzəm] *n Med* nicotinisme *m*, tabagisme *m*

nicotinize, -ise ['nɪkəti:naɪz] *vt* nicotiniser, nicotiser

nictate ['nɪkteɪt], **nictitate** ['nɪktɪteɪt] *vi Formal* cligner des yeux

nictitating membrane ['nɪktɪteɪtɪŋ-] *n Zool* membrane *f* nictitante

nidation [naɪ'deɪʃən] *n Physiol* nidation *f*

nidicolous [nɪ'dɪkələs] *adj Orn* nidicole

nidification [,nɪdɪfɪ'keɪʃən] *n Orn* nidification *f*

nidifugous [nɪ'dɪfjʊgəs] *adj Orn* nidifuge

niece [ni:s] *n* nièce *f*

niello [nɪ'eləʊ] *(pl* **nielli** [-lɪ] *or* **niellos***)* *n (substance for inlay)* nielle *m*; **to inlay with niello** nieller; **inlaying with niello** niellage *m*

►► ***niello enamels*** émaux *mpl* de niellure; ***niello work*** niellure *f*, niellage *m*; ***niello worker*** nielleur(euse) *m,f*

Nielsen Ratings ['ni:lsən-] *npl Am TV* ≃ l'audimat *m*

Nietzschean ['ni:tʃɪən] **1** *n* nietzschéen(enne) *m,f*

2 *adj* nietzschéen

NIF [,enaɪ'ef] *n Fin (abbr* **note issue facility***)* autorisation *f* d'émettre les billets de banque

niff [nɪf] *Br Fam* **1** *n* mauvaise odeur❑ *f*, puanteur❑ *f*; **what a niff!** ça schlingue!

2 *vi* refouler, schlinguer, fouetter

niffy ['nɪfɪ] *(compar* **niffier,** *superl* **niffiest***)* *adj Br Fam* qui fouette *ou* refoule

nifty ['nɪftɪ] *(compar* **niftier,** *superl* **niftiest***)* *adj Fam* (**a**) *(stylish)* chouette, classe *(inv)*; **they've got a nifty house** ils ont une chouette baraque; **that's a nifty sweater** il est chouette, ce pull (**b**) *(clever → solution, idea)* astucieux❑; *(→ person)* adroit❑, débrouillard; **a nifty little gadget** un petit gadget très astucieux; **a nifty piece of footwork** un beau jeu de jambes; **a nifty piece of work** du bon travail (**c**) *(quick)* rapide❑; *(agile)* agile❑

nigella [naɪ'dʒelə] *n Bot* nigelle *f*

Niger *n* (**a**) [ni:'ʒeə(r)] *(country)* Niger *m*; **in Niger** au Niger (**b**) ['naɪdʒə(r)] *(river)* **the (River) Niger** le Niger

Nigeria [naɪ'dʒɪərɪə] *n* Nigeria *m*; **in Nigeria** au Nigeria

Nigerian [naɪ'dʒɪərɪən] **1** *n* Nigérian(e) *m,f*

2 *adj* nigérian

3 *comp (embassy, history)* du Nigeria

Nigerien [ni:'ʒeərɪən] **1** *n* Nigérien(enne) *m,f*

2 *adj* nigérien

3 *comp (embassy, history)* du Niger

nigga ['nɪgə] *n Fam Black Am slang* nègre (négresse) *m,f*

niggard ['nɪgəd] *n Old-fashioned* pingre *mf*, avare *mf*

niggardliness ['nɪgədlɪnɪs] *n (of person)* pingrerie *f*, avarice *f*; *(of sum, budget, salary)* maigreur *f*; *(of quantity)* caractère *m* minuscule

niggardly ['nɪgədlɪ] **1** *adj (person)* pingre, avare; *(sum, budget, salary)* maigre; *(quantity)* minime

2 *adv* parcimonieusement, avec parcimonie

nigger ['nɪgə(r)] *n Fam* nègre (négresse) *m,f*, = terme raciste désignant un Noir; *Br Old-fashioned* **there's a nigger in the woodpile** *(problem)* il y a un hic; *(person)* il y a un empêcheur de tourner en rond; *(secret)* il y a anguille sous roche

niggle ['nɪgəl] **1** *n* (**a**) *(small criticism)* objection *f* mineure; **I've got one slight niggle** il y a un point de détail sur lequel je ne suis pas d'accord

(**b**) *(small worry, doubt)* tracasserie *f*, léger doute *m*

(**c**) *(complaint)* protestation *f*; **to have a niggle about sth** ronchonner à propos de qch

2 *vt* (**a**) *(worry → of conscience)* harceler, travailler

(**b**) *(nag)* harceler

3 *vi* (**a**) *(fuss over details)* ergoter, couper les cheveux en quatre; **to niggle over** *or* **about sth** ergoter sur qch; **don't niggle about details** ne chipote pas sur les détails

(**b**) *(nag)* trouver à redire

►**niggle at** *vt insep* **it's been niggling at me all day** ça me travaille depuis ce matin

niggler ['nɪgələ(r)] *n (who annoys people)* enquiquineur(euse) *m,f*; *(who worries about details)* coupeur(euse) *m,f* de cheveux en quatre, pinailleur(euse) *m,f*

niggling ['nɪgəlɪŋ] **1** *adj* (**a**) *(petty → person)* tatillon; *(→ details)* insignifiant (**b**) *(fastidious → job)* fastidieux (**c**) *(nagging → pain, doubt)* tenace; **I've got a niggling feeling that something is wrong** je n'arrive pas à m'ôter de l'idée que quelque chose ne va pas

2 *n* chicanerie *f*, pinaillerie *f*

niggly ['nɪgəlɪ] *(compar* **nigglier,** *superl* **niggliest***)* *adj Fam* pinailleur

nigh [naɪ] *Literary* **1** *adv* **well nigh eighty years** près de quatre-vingts ans; **well nigh impossible** presque impossible

2 *adj* proche; **the end is nigh!** la fin est proche!; **the hour is nigh** c'est bientôt *ou* presque l'heure; *Arch* **to be nigh unto death** être à l'article de la mort

3 *prep* près de, proche de

4 **nigh on** *adv* presque; **nigh on six o'clock** presque six heures; **it's nigh on sundown** le soleil se couchera d'ici peu

night [naɪt] **1** *n* (**a**) *(evening)* soir *m*; *(late)* nuit *f*; **at night** *(evening)* le soir; *(late)* la nuit; **ten o'clock at night** dix heures du soir; **all night (long)** toute la nuit; **by night** de nuit; **during** *or* **in the night** pendant la nuit; **(on) Tuesday night** *(evening)* mardi soir; *(during night)* dans la nuit de mardi à mercredi; **last night** *(evening)* hier soir; *(during night)* cette nuit; **the night before** *(evening)* la veille au soir; *(late)* la nuit précédente; **far** *or* **late into the night** jusqu'à une heure avancée de la nuit; **it's weeks since we had a night out** ça fait des semaines que nous ne sommes pas sortis le soir; **to work day and night** *or* **night and day** travailler nuit et jour; **to have a night off** avoir une soirée libre; **it's the au pair's night off** c'est la soirée libre de la jeune fille au pair; **to have a late night** se coucher tard; **too many late nights can be bad for you** se coucher tard trop souvent peut nuire à la santé; **this has been going on night after night** cela s'est prolongé des nuits durant; **what you need is a good night's sleep** ce qu'il vous faut, c'est une bonne nuit de sommeil *ou* de repos; **I had a bad night** j'ai passé une mauvaise nuit, j'ai mal dormi; *Hist* **the night of the long knives** la nuit des longs couteaux; **the night is young** la nuit n'est pas très avancée, *Hum* on a toute la nuit devant nous

(**b**) *(evening's entertainment)* soirée *f*; **to have a night out** sortir; **that was a great night last night** on a passé une super soirée hier; **Tuesday's our poker night** le mardi, c'est notre soirée poker, le mardi soir, nous faisons un poker; **to make a night of it** faire la fête toute la nuit

(**c**) *(darkness)* obscurité *f*; *Fig* ténèbres *fpl*; **as night was falling** alors que la nuit tombait; **night falls early** il fait nuit tôt, la nuit tombe tôt; **dark night of the soul** période *f* de désespoir profond; *Literary* **to go forth into the night** s'en aller dans les ténèbres *ou* dans l'obscurité

(**d**) *Theat* soirée *f*; **gala night** soirée *f* de gala; **poetry night** soirée *f* poésie

2 *comp (duty, flight, train, boat, sky)* de nuit

3 **nights** *adv* de nuit; **how can you sleep nights not knowing where he is?** comment arrives-tu à dormir sans même savoir où il est?; **to work nights** travailler de nuit; **I'm on nights next week** je suis de nuit la semaine prochaine; *Am* **to lie awake nights** ne pas dormir la nuit

▸▸ ***night bird*** *Orn* oiseau *m* nocturne *ou* de nuit; *Fig (person)* noctambule *mf*, oiseau *m* de nuit; ***night blindness*** *(UNCOUNT)* héméralopie *f*; ***night clerk*** *(in hotel)* réceptionniste *mf* de nuit; *Am* ***night crawler*** = gros ver de terre; *Banking* ***night depository*** coffre(-fort) *m* de nuit; ***night driving*** conduite *f* de nuit; ***night editor*** rédacteur(trice) *m,f* de nuit *(dans un journal)*; *Mil & Aviat* ***night fighter*** chasseur *m* de nuit; *Orn* ***night heron*** (héron *m*) bihoreau *m*; *Am* ***night letter*** télégramme *m (à tarif réduit, livré le lendemain matin)*; ***night manager*** directeur(trice) *m,f* de nuit; ***night nurse*** infirmier(ère) *m,f* de nuit; ***night nursery*** chambre *f* d'enfants; *Fam* ***night owl*** couche-tard *mf inv*, oiseau *m* de nuit; ***night porter*** portier(ère) *m,f* de nuit; *Fin* ***night rate*** tarif *m* de nuit; *Banking* ***night safe*** coffre(-fort) *m* de nuit; ***night school*** cours *mpl* du soir; **to go to night school** suivre des cours du soir; *Br* **at** *or Am* **in night school** aux cours du soir; ***night shift*** *(work force)* équipe *f* de nuit; *(period of duty)* poste *m* de nuit; **to be on the night shift** être de nuit; ***night soil*** fumier *m (d'excréments humains)*; ***night storage heater*** radiateur *m* à accumulation; *Am* ***night table*** table *f* de chevet; ***night vision*** vision *f* nocturne; **to have good/bad night vision** avoir une bonne/mauvaise vision nocturne; ***night watch*** *(period, guards)* garde *f* de nuit; *Naut* quart *m* de nuit; ***night watchman*** veilleur *m* de nuit; ***night work*** travail *m* de nuit

'The Night of the Hunter' *Laughton* 'La Nuit du chasseur'

'The Night Watch' *Rembrandt* 'La Ronde de nuit'

nightcap ['naɪtkæp] *n* (**a**) *(drink → gen)* boisson *f (que l'on prend avant d'aller se coucher)*; *(→ alcoholic)* dernier verre *m (avant d'aller se coucher)*; **would you like a nightcap?** prendrez-vous quelque chose avant de vous coucher? (**b**) *(headgear)* bonnet *m* de nuit

nightclothes ['naɪtkləʊðz] *npl (pyjamas)* pyjama *m*; *(nightdress)* chemise *f* de nuit; **the children were in their nightclothes** les enfants étaient en pyjama

nightclub ['naɪtklʌb] *n* night-club *m*, boîte *f* de nuit, *Can* club *m* de nuit

nightclubber ['naɪtˌklʌbə(r)] *n* **he's a bit of a nightclubber** c'est un vrai pilier de boîte de nuit

nightclubbing ['naɪtˌklʌbɪŋ] *n* **to go nightclubbing** sortir en boîte

nightdress ['naɪtdres] *n* chemise *f* de nuit

nightfall ['naɪtfɔːl] *n* tombée *f* de la nuit *ou* du jour; **at nightfall** à la tombée de la nuit *ou* du jour; **we must get there by nightfall** il faut que nous y arrivions avant la tombée de la nuit *ou* du jour

nightgown ['naɪtgaʊn] *n* chemise *f* de nuit

nighthawk ['naɪthɔːk] *n* (**a**) *Orn* engoulevent *m* (d'Amérique) (**b**) *Fam (person)* couche-tard *mf inv*, oiseau *m* de nuit

nightie ['naɪtɪ] *n Fam* chemise *f* de nuit ❑

nightingale ['naɪtɪŋgeɪl] *n Orn* rossignol *m*

nightjar ['naɪtdʒɑː(r)] *n Orn* engoulevent *m* (d'Europe)

nightlife ['naɪtlaɪf] *n* vie *f* nocturne; **what's the nightlife like round here?** qu'est-ce qu'on peut faire le soir, ici?

nightlight ['naɪtlaɪt] *n* veilleuse *f*

nightlong ['naɪtlɒŋ] **1** *adj* qui dure toute la nuit; **a nightlong vigil** une nuit de veille

2 *adv* pendant toute la nuit, la nuit durant

nightly ['naɪtlɪ] **1** *adj (happening every night → late)* de chaque nuit; *(→ in the evening)* de tous les soirs; **he made his nightly call home** comme chaque soir/nuit, il téléphona chez lui; **he would take his nightly stroll** il faisait sa promenade nocturne; **to make a nightly TV appearance** passer tous les soirs à la télévision

2 *adv (late)* toutes les nuits, chaque nuit; *(in the evening)* tous les soirs, chaque soir; *Theat* **appearing nightly at the Odeon** tous les soirs sur la scène de l'Odeon

▸▸ ***nightly performance*** *(sign)* représentation tous les soirs

nightmare ['naɪtmeə(r)] **1** *n also Fig* cauchemar *m*; **I had a nightmare** j'ai fait un cauchemar; **to give sb nightmares** donner des cauchemars à qn; **everybody's worst nightmare** le cauchemar *ou* la hantise de tout un chacun; **the first day of the sales was a nightmare** la première journée de soldes fut un cauchemar; **it was a nightmare scenario** c'était un vrai cauchemar

2 *comp (vision, experience)* cauchemardesque, de cauchemar

nightmarish ['naɪtˌmeərɪʃ] *adj* cauchemardesque, de cauchemar

night-night *exclam Fam* bonne nuit! ❑

nightrobe ['naɪtrəʊb] *n Am* chemise *f* de nuit

nightshade ['naɪtʃeɪd] *n Bot* morelle *f*

nightshirt ['naɪtʃɜːt] *n* chemise *f* de nuit

nightspot ['naɪtspɒt] *n Fam* boîte *f* (de nuit) ❑

nightstand ['naɪtstand] *n Am* table *f* de nuit

nightstick ['naɪtstɪk] *n Am* matraque *f (de policier)*

night-time *n* nuit *f*; **at night-time** la nuit

nightwear ['naɪtweə(r)] *n (UNCOUNT) (pyjamas)* pyjama *m*; *(nightdress)* chemise *f* de nuit; *(department in store)* vêtements *mpl* de nuit

nighty *(pl* **nighties)** = **nightie**

nighty-night *exclam Fam* bonne nuit! ❑

nigrescence [ˌnaɪ'gresəns] *n* teinte *f* noirâtre; *(of skin)* noirceur *f*

nigrescent [ˌnaɪ'gresənt] *adj* noirâtre, qui tire sur le noir

NIH [ˌenaɪ'eɪtʃ] *n Am (abbr* **National Institutes of Health)** = ensemble de centres de recherche médicale aux États-Unis

nihilism ['naɪɪlɪzəm] *n* nihilisme *m*

nihilist ['naɪɪlɪst] **1** *n* nihiliste *mf*

2 *adj* nihiliste

nihilistic [ˌnaɪɪ'lɪstɪk] *adj* nihiliste

Nijinsky [nɪ'dʒɪnskɪ] *pr n* Nijinski

Nike ['naɪkiː] *pr n Myth* Nikê

Nikkei Index ['nɪkeɪ-] *n St Exch* indice *m* Nikkei

nil [nɪl] **1** *n (gen) & Br Sport* zéro *m*; *(on written form)* néant *m*; *Br* **they won three nil** ils ont gagné par trois à zéro; *Med* **nil by mouth** *(on patient's chart)* ≃ ne rien administrer par voie orale; *Fin* **the balance is nil** le solde est nul

2 *adj* nul, zéro *(inv)*

▸▸ *Fin* ***nil growth*** croissance *f* zéro; *Fin* ***nil profit*** bénéfice *m* nul; *Fin* ***nil return*** état *m* néant

Nile [naɪl] *n Br* **the (River) Nile,** *Am* **the Nile River** le Nil; **the Blue Nile** le Nil Bleu; **the White Nile** le Nil Blanc

nilgai, nilghai ['nɪlgaɪ] *n Zool* nilgau *m*

Nilot ['naɪlɒt], **Nilote** ['naɪləʊt] *n* Nilotique *mf*

Nilotic [naɪ'lɒtɪk] *adj* nilotique

nimbi ['nɪmbaɪ] *pl of* **nimbus**

nimble ['nɪmbəl] *adj* (**a**) *(agile → person, body)* agile, souple; *(→ leap, movement)* leste, agile; *(→ fingers)* adroit, habile; **she's very nimble for (someone of) her age** elle est très alerte pour (quelqu'un de) son âge; **a nimble climber/dancer** un grimpeur/un danseur agile; **a nimble seamstress** une habile couturière; **he soon got to be nimble on his crutches** il eut tôt fait d'apprendre à se déplacer avec ses béquilles

(**b**) *(quick → thought, mind)* vif, prompt

nimble-fingered *adj* aux doigts agiles, habile de ses doigts

nimble-footed *adj* au pied agile

nimbleness ['nɪmbəlnɪs] *n (of person, body)* agilité *f*, souplesse *f*; *(of leap, movement)* agilité *f*; *(of thought, mind)* vivacité *f*

nimble-witted *adj* vif (d'esprit), à l'esprit vif *ou* rapide

nimbly ['nɪmblɪ] *adv* agilement, lestement; **he leapt nimbly over the wall** il sauta lestement par-dessus le mur; **she nimbly unpicked the knot** elle a défait le nœud de ses doigts agiles *ou* souples

nimbostratus [ˌnɪmbəʊ'streɪtəs] *(pl* **nimbostrati** [-taɪ]) *n Met* nimbo-stratus *m inv*

nimbus ['nɪmbəs] *(pl* **nimbi** [-baɪ] *or* **nimbuses)** *n* (**a**) *Met* nimbus *m* (**b**) *(halo)* nimbe *m*, auréole *f*

Nimby ['nɪmbɪ] *n Fam (abbr* **not in my backyard)** = personne qui, tout en se montrant d'accord sur le principe, est peu encline à voir un projet (de construction le plus souvent) se réaliser à proximité de chez elle

niminy-piminy [ˌnɪmɪnɪ'pɪmɪnɪ] *adj Br Fam* cucul *(inv)*

nincompoop ['nɪŋkəmpuːp] *n Fam* cruche *f*, nigaud(e) *m,f*; **don't be such a nincompoop** ne sois pas si nigaud

nine [naɪn] **1** *n* (**a**) *(number)* neuf *m inv*; **he was dressed up to the nines** il s'était mis sur son trente et un

(**b**) *Am Sport* équipe *f* (de base-ball)

(**c**) *Golf* **the front nine** l'aller *m*, les neuf premiers trous; **the back nine** les neuf derniers trous

2 *pron* neuf

3 *adj* neuf; **a nine-hole golf course** un (parcours de) neuf trous; **nine times out of ten** neuf fois sur dix; **to have nine lives** *(cat)* avoir neuf vies; *(person)* avoir l'âme chevillée au corps; *Br* **a nine day wonder** un feu de paille; **to dial** *Br* **999** *or Am* **911** appeler les urgences; *see also* **five**

ninefold ['naɪnfəʊld] **1** *adj* **there was a ninefold increase in casualties** le nombre de victimes fut multiplié par neuf

2 *adv* neuf fois; **to increase ninefold** (se) multiplier par neuf

ninepin ['naɪnpɪn] **1** *n (skittle)* quille *f*; *Br* **to go down like ninepins** tomber comme des mouches

2 **ninepins** *n (game)* quilles *fpl*

nineteen [ˌnaɪn'tiːn] **1** *n* dix-neuf *m inv*; *Br* **she talks nineteen to the dozen** elle n'arrête pas de parler; *Br* **they were talking nineteen to the dozen** ils étaient intarissables, il n'y avait pas moyen de les faire taire

2 *pron* dix-neuf

3 *adj* dix-neuf; *see also* **five**

nineteenth [,naɪn'ti:nθ] **1** *n* (**a**) *(fraction)* dix-neuvième *m* (**b**) *(in series)* dix-neuvième *mf* (**c**) *(of month)* dix-neuf *m inv*

2 *adj* dix-neuvième; *Hum* **the nineteenth hole** *(in golf)* le bar (du club)

3 *adv* dix-neuvièmement; *(in contest)* en dix-neuvième position, à la dix-neuvième place; *see also* **fifth**

ninetieth ['naɪntɪəθ] **1** *n* (**a**) *(fraction)* quatre-vingt-dixième *m* (**b**) *(in series)* quatre-vingt-dixième *mf*

2 *adj* quatre-vingt-dixième

3 *adv* quatre-vingt-dixièmement; *(in contest)* en quatre-vingt-dixième position, à la quatre-vingt-dixième place; *see also* **fifth**

nine-to-five 1 *adv* de neuf heures du matin à cinq heures du soir; **to work nine-to-five** avoir des horaires de bureau

2 *adj* (**a**) *(job)* routinier (**b**) *(mentality, attitude)* de gratte-papier

ninety ['naɪntɪ] *(pl* **nineties***)* **1** *n* quatre-vingt-dix *m inv, Belg & Suisse* nonante *m inv*

2 *pron* quatre-vingt-dix, *Belg & Suisse* nonante

3 *adj* quatre-vingt-dix, *Belg & Suisse* nonante

4 *comp* **ninety-one** quatre-vingt-onze; **ninety-two** quatre-vingt-douze; **ninety-nine** quatre-vingt-dix-neuf; *Law* **ninety-nine-year lease** bail *m* emphytéotique de quatre-vingt-dix-neuf ans; **ninety-first** quatre-vingt-onzième; **ninety-second** quatre-vingt-douzième; *see also* **fifty**

Nineveh ['nɪnɪvə] *n* Ninive

ninja ['nɪndʒə] *n* ninja *m*

ninjitsu [,nɪn'dʒɪtsu:] *n Sport* nin jitsu *m*

ninny ['nɪnɪ] *(pl* **ninnies***)* *n Fam* niais(e) *m,f*, nigaud(e) *m,f*

ninon ['ni:nɒn] *n* crêpe *m* Ninon

ninth [naɪnθ] **1** *adj* neuvième

2 *n* (**a**) *(ordinal)* neuvième *mf*

(**b**) *(fraction)* neuvième *m*

3 *adv (in contest)* en neuvième position, à la neuvième place

▸▸ *Am Sch* ***ninth grade*** = classe de lycée pour les 13–14 ans

ninthly ['naɪnθlɪ] *adv* neuvièmement, en neuvième lieu

niobium [naɪ'əʊbɪəm] *n Chem* niobium *m*

Nip [nɪp] *n very Fam* Jap *mf*, = terme injurieux désignant un Japonais

nip [nɪp] *(pt & pp* **nipped**, *cont* **nipping***)* **1** *n* (**a**) *(pinch)* pincement *m*; *(bite)* morsure *f*; **that dog gave me a nip on the leg** ce chien m'a mordu la jambe

(**b**) *(cold)* froid *m* piquant; **there's a nip in the air** l'air est piquant

(**c**) *(in taste)* goût *m* piquant; **I like cheese with a nip to it** j'aime le fromage un peu relevé *ou* fort

(**d**) *(of alcohol)* goutte *f*

(**e**) *Ir Fam* **in the nip** *(naked)* à poil

(**f**) *(idioms) Fam Hum* **nip and tuck** *(plastic surgery)* chirurgie *f* esthétique ❑; **to be nip and tuck** être au coude à coude

2 *vt* (**a**) *(pinch)* pincer; *(bite)* mordre (légèrement), mordiller; **she nipped her finger in the door** elle s'est pincé le doigt dans la porte; **the puppy nipped my leg** le chiot m'a mordu la jambe

(**b**) *Hort (plant, shoot)* pincer; *Fig* **to nip sth in the bud** tuer *ou* écraser *ou* étouffer qch dans l'œuf

(**c**) *(numb, freeze)* geler, piquer; **the cold nipped our ears** le froid nous piquait les oreilles; **the vines were nipped by the frost** les vignes ont été grillées *ou* brûlées par le gel

(**d**) *Am Fam (steal)* piquer, faucher

3 *vi* (**a**) *(try to bite)* **the dog nipped at my ankles** le chien m'a mordillé les chevilles

(**b**) *Br Fam (go)* faire un saut; **to nip (across** *or* **along** *or* **over) to the butcher's** faire un saut chez le boucher; **she nipped in to say hello** elle est passée en vitesse dire bonjour ❑; **could I just nip in in front of you?** *(in queue)* pourrais-je passer devant vous? ❑; **he always nips into the pub on the way home** il fait toujours un petit détour par le pub en rentrant chez lui ❑; **to nip in and out of the traffic** se faufiler entre les voitures ❑; **we just nipped out for a drink** on est sortis prendre un pot en vitesse

▸**nip in** *vt sep (garment)* cintrer; **a dress nipped in at the waist** une robe cintrée

▸**nip off 1** *vt sep (cut off)* couper; *Hort* pincer

2 *vi Br Fam* filer; **she nipped off home** elle a filé chez elle

nipper ['nɪpə(r)] **1** *n* (**a**) *(of crab, lobster)* pince *f* (**b**) *Br Fam (child)* gosse *mf*, môme *mf*

2 nippers *npl (tool)* pince *f*, tenailles *fpl*; **a pair of nippers** une pince, des tenailles *fpl*

nipple ['nɪpəl] *n* (**a**) *(on breast)* mamelon *m*; *(on animal)* tétine *f*, mamelle *f*

(**b**) *(teat → on feeding bottle)* tétine *f*

(**c**) *Am (baby's dummy)* tétine *f*

(**d**) *Tech (of pump)* embout *m*; *(for greasing)* graisseur *m*; *(connector)* raccord *m*

(**e**) *Geog* mamelon *m*

nipplewort ['nɪpəlwɜ:t] *n Bot* lampsane *f*

nippy ['nɪpɪ] *(compar* **nippier**, *superl* **nippiest***)* *adj* (**a**) *(weather)* frisquet; *(cold)* piquant; **it's nippy (out) this morning** il fait frisquet ce matin (**b**) *Br Fam (quick)* vif ❑, rapide ❑; **a nippy little car** une petite voiture nerveuse (**c**) *Br (odour, flavour)* piquant, âpre

nirvana [,nɪə'vɑ:nə] *n* nirvana *m*

Nisei [nɪ'seɪ] *n Am* Japonais(e) *m,f* de la deuxième génération

nisi ['naɪsaɪ] *adj Law (rule, order)* provisoire; *(decision)* rendu sous condition; *see also* **decree**

Nissen hut ['nɪsən-] *n Br Mil* abri *m (en tôle ondulée)*

nit [nɪt] *n* (**a**) *Entom* lente *f*; *(in hair)* lente *f*; **to have nits** avoir des poux (**b**) *Br Fam (idiot)* andouille *f*, courge *f*

niter *Am* = **nitre**

nitery ['naɪtərɪ] *n Am Fam* boîte *f* de nuit ❑

nitpick ['nɪtpɪk] *vi Fam* couper les cheveux en quatre, chercher la petite bête, pinailler

nitpicker ['nɪt,pɪkə(r)] *n Fam* chipoteur(euse) *m,f*

nitpicking ['nɪt,pɪkɪŋ] *Fam* **1** *n* chipotage *m*

2 *adj* chipoteur

nitrate ['naɪtreɪt] *n* (**a**) *Chem* nitrate *m*; **potassium nitrate** nitrate *m* de potassium, salpêtre *m* (**b**) *(fertilizer)* engrais *m* azoté

nitration [naɪ'treɪʃən] *n* nitration *f*

nitrazepam [naɪ'træzəpæm] *n* nitrazépam *m*

nitre, *Am* **niter** ['naɪtə(r)] *n Chem* nitrate *m* de potassium

nitric ['naɪtrɪk] *adj Chem*

▸▸ ***nitric acid*** acide *m* nitrique; ***nitric oxide*** oxyde *m* nitrique

nitride ['naɪtraɪd] *n Chem* nitrure *m*

nitrification [,naɪtrɪfɪ'keɪʃən] *n Chem* nitrification *f*

nitrify ['naɪtrɪfaɪ] *(pt & pp* **nitrified***)* *vt* (**a**) *Chem* nitrifier (**b**) *Agr* fertiliser avec des nitrates

nitrile ['naɪtraɪl] *n Chem* nitrile *m*

nitrite ['naɪtraɪt] *n Chem* nitrite *m*

nitro ['naɪtrəʊ] *n Fam Chem* nitroglycérine ❑ *f*

nitro- ['naɪtrəʊ] *pref* nitro-

nitrobenzene [,naɪtrəʊ'benzi:n] *n Chem* nitrobenzène *m*, nitrobenzine *f*

nitrocellulose [,naɪtrəʊ'seljʊləʊs] *n Chem* nitrocellulose *f*

▸▸ ***nitrocellulose finish*** enduit *m* cellulosique; ***nitrocellulose product*** produit *m* cellulosique

nitrogen ['naɪtrədʒən] *n Chem* azote *m*

▸▸ ***nitrogen cycle*** cycle *m* de l'azote; ***nitrogen dioxide*** dioxyde *m* d'azote; ***nitrogen fixation*** fixation *f* de l'azote; ***nitrogen monoxide*** oxyde *m* nitrique; ***nitrogen peroxide*** protoxyde *m* d'azote

nitrogenase [naɪ'trɒdʒəneɪz] *n Chem* nitrogénase *f*

nitrogenize, -ise [,naɪ'trɒdʒənaɪz] *vt Chem* azoter

nitrogenous [naɪ'trɒdʒɪnəs] *adj Chem* azoté

nitroglycerin, nitroglycerine [,naɪtrəʊ'glɪsəri:n] *n Chem* nitroglycérine *f*

nitromethane [,naɪtrəʊ'mi:θeɪn] *n Chem* nitrométhane *m*

nitrophenol [,naɪtrəʊ'fi:nɒl] *n Chem* nitrophénol *m*

nitrous ['naɪtrəs] *adj Chem* nitreux, azoteux

▸▸ ***nitrous acid*** acide *m* nitreux; ***nitrous oxide*** oxyde *m* azoteux, protoxyde *m* d'azote

nitty-gritty [,nɪtɪ-] *n Fam* essentiel ❑ *m*; **let's get down to the nitty-gritty** passons aux choses sérieuses; **the nitty-gritty of government** le gouvernement au quotidien ❑

nitwit ['nɪtwɪt] *n Br Fam* andouille *f*, courge *f*

nitwitted ['nɪtwɪtɪd] *adj Br Fam* idiot

nix [nɪks] *Am Fam* **1** *exclam* (**a**) *(no)* non ❑; **to say nix to** *or* **on sth** dire non à qch (**b**) *(watch out)* attention! ❑

2 *n* que dalle, rien ❑; **we got nix out of the deal** l'affaire ne nous a pas rapporté un radis

3 *vt (refuse)* rejeter ❑, refuser ❑; *(veto)* opposer un veto à ❑

NJ *(written abbr* **New Jersey***)* New Jersey *m*

NLF [,enel'ef] *n (abbr* **National Liberation Front***)* FLN *m*

NLM [,enel'em] *n Comput (abbr* **netware loadable module***)* module *m* logiciel téléchargeable

NLP [,enel'pi:] *n (abbr* **natural language processing***)* TALAN *m*

NLQ [,enel'kju:] *n Comput (abbr* **near letter quality***)* = qualité quasi-courrier

NLRB [,enel,ɑ:'bi:] *n Am (abbr* **National Labor Relations Board***)* = organisme américain de conciliation et d'arbitrage des conflits du travail

NM *(written abbr* **New Mexico***)* Nouveau-Mexique *m*

NMD [,emem'di:] *n (abbr* **National Missile Defence***)* projet *m* NMD *(programme de défense antimissiles américain)*

NME [,enem'i:] *n Press (abbr* **New Musical Express***)* = hebdomadaire anglais de musique rock

NMR [,ene'mɑ:(r)] *n Med (abbr* **nuclear magnetic resonance***)* RMN *f*

NNE *(written abbr* **north-north-east***)* N-NE

NNP [,enen'pi:] *n (abbr* **net national product***)* produit *m* national net

NNW *(written abbr* **north-north-west***)* N-NW

No., no. *(written abbr* **number***)* No, no

NO [nəʊ]

non	▸ **1 (a); 3; 4**
ne... pas	▸ **1 (b)**
ne... pas de	▸ **2 (a), (b)**
ne... aucun	▸ **2 (a)**

(pl **noes** *or* **nos***)* **1** *adv* (**a**) *(expressing refusal, disagreement)* non; **do you like spinach? – no, I don't** aimez-vous les épinards? – non; **oh no you don't!** *(forbidding, stopping)* oh que non!; **to say no** dire non; **the answer's no** la réponse est non; **they won't take no for an answer** ils n'accepteront aucun refus

(**b**) *(with comparative adj or adv)* **I can go no further** je ne peux pas aller plus loin; **we'll go no further than three million** on n'ira pas au-delà de *ou* nous ne dépasserons pas les trois millions; **you're no better than he is** vous ne valez pas mieux que lui; **call me, if you're (feeling) no better in the morning** appelez-moi si vous ne vous sentez pas mieux demain matin; **this car is no more expensive than the other one** cette voiture ne coûte pas plus cher que l'autre

(**c**) *Literary (not)* **whether you wish it or no** que vous le vouliez ou non

(**d**) *Scot Fam (not)* **it's no bad** c'est pas mal; **I'm no going** j'y vais pas

2 *adj* (**a**) *(not any, not one)* **I have no family** je n'ai pas de famille; **she has no intention of leaving** elle n'a aucune intention de partir; **there are no letters for you today** il n'y a pas de courrier *ou* aucune lettre pour toi aujourd'hui; **no sensible person would dispute this** quelqu'un de raisonnable ne discuterait pas; **no other washing powder gets clothes so clean** aucune autre lessive ne laisse votre linge aussi propre; **it's of no importance/interest** ça n'a aucune importance/aucun intérêt; **no one company can handle all the orders** une seule entreprise ne pourra jamais s'occuper de toutes les commandes; **no two experts ever come up with the same answer** il n'y a pas deux experts qui soient d'accord; **you tell us who did it and we'll let you go, no questions asked** tu nous dis qui l'a fait et t'es libre, on t'embêtera plus; **there's no telling** nul ne peut le dire; **there's no denying it** c'est indéniable; **there's no pleasing him** il n'y a pas moyen de le satisfaire; **it's no distance** ce n'est pas loin

(**b**) *(not a)* **I'm no expert, I'm afraid** malheureusement, je ne suis pas un expert; **she's no friend of mine** ce n'est pas une amie à moi; **this**

is no time for arguments ce n'est pas le moment de se disputer; **it will be no easy task persuading them** ce ne sera pas une tâche facile que de les persuader; **that's no bad thing** ce n'est pas une mauvaise chose

(**c**) *(introducing a prohibition)* **no left turn** *(sign)* interdiction de tourner à gauche; **no smoking** *(sign)* défense de fumer; **no swimming** *(sign)* baignade interdite; **no nonsense!** pas de bêtises!

3 *n* non *m inv*; **the noes have it** les non l'emportent

4 *exclam* non; **I'm getting married – no!** *(surprise, dismay)* je me marie – non!

---

no-account *Am Fam* **1** *n* bon (bonne) *m,f* à rien

2 *adj* bon à rien; **her no-account husband** son bon à rien de mari

Noah ['nəʊə] *pr n Bible* Noé

►► ***Noah's Ark*** l'arche *f* de Noé

nob [nɒb] *n Fam* (**a**) *Br (wealthy person)* rupin(e) *m,f*, richard(e) *m,f*; **the nobs** les rupins *mpl*, les richards *mpl* (**b**) *(head)* caboche *f*

no-ball *n (in cricket)* balle *f* nulle

nobble ['nɒbəl] *vt Br Fam* (**a**) *(jury, witness → bribe)* graisser la patte à; *(→ threaten)* manipuler (avec des menaces)□

(**b**) *(racehorse)* mettre hors d'état de courir□; *(with drugs)* droguer□

(**c**) *(grab, catch → person)* accrocher (au passage), agrafer; **he nobbled me as I arrived** il m'a accroché au moment où je suis arrivé

(**d**) *(steal)* faucher, barboter, chiper

(**e**) *(kidnap)* kidnapper□, enlever□

Nobel [nəʊ'bel] *pr n*

►► ***Nobel laureate*** lauréat(e) *m,f* du prix Nobel; ***Nobel Peace Prize*** prix *m* Nobel de la paix; ***Nobel prize*** prix *m* Nobel; **Nobel prize for Literature** prix *m* Nobel de littérature; ***Nobel prizewinner*** lauréat(e) *m,f* du prix Nobel

nobelium [nəʊ'biːlɪəm] *n Chem* nobélium *m*

nobility [nə'bɪlətɪ] (*pl* **nobilities**) *n* (**a**) *(aristocracy)* noblesse *f*, aristocratie *f*

(**b**) *(loftiness)* noblesse *f*, majesté *f*, grandeur *f*

noble ['nəʊbəl] **1** *adj* (**a**) *(aristocratic)* noble; **of noble birth** de haute naissance, de naissance noble

(**b**) *(fine, distinguished → aspiration, purpose)* noble, élevé; *(→ bearing, manner, proportions, building)* noble, majestueux; *(→ mountain)* altier, imposant; *(→ person, animal)* noble; *(→ wine)* grand

(**c**) *(generous → gesture)* généreux, magnanime; *Hum* **that's very noble of you** c'est très généreux de votre part

(**d**) *(brave → deed, feat)* noble, héroïque; **the noble art** *or* **science** le noble art

(**e**) *(impressive → monument)* noble, majestueux

(**f**) *Chem (gas, metal)* noble

2 *n* noble *mf*, aristocrate *mf*

►► ***noble rot*** pourriture *f* noble; ***noble savage*** bon sauvage *m*

nobleman ['nəʊbəlmən] (*pl* **noblemen** [-mən]) *n* noble *m*, aristocrate *m*

noble-minded *adj* magnanime, généreux

nobleness ['nəʊbəlnɪs] *n* (**a**) *(of birth)* noblesse *f* (**b**) *(of mind, action)* noblesse *f*; *(of soul)* grandeur *f* (**c**) *(of statue, horse)* proportions *fpl* superbes *ou* magnifiques; *(of building)* aspect *m* majestueux

noblewoman ['nəʊbəl,wʊmən] (*pl* **noblewomen** [-,wɪmɪn]) *n* noble *f*, aristocrate *f*

nobly ['nəʊblɪ] *adv* (**a**) *(by birth)* noblement; **nobly born** de haute naissance

(**b**) *(majestically, superbly)* majestueusement, superbement; **nobly proportioned** aux proportions majestueuses

(**c**) *(generously)* généreusement, magnanimement; **she nobly offered him the last piece of cake** elle lui a généreusement offert le dernier morceau de gâteau

(**d**) *(bravely)* noblement, courageusement

nobody ['nəʊbədɪ] (*pl* **nobodies**) **1** *pron* (**a**) *(no person, no one)* personne; **nobody came** personne n'est venu; **nobody knows better than I do** personne ne sait mieux que moi; **nobody else** personne d'autre; **there was nobody there** il n'y avait personne; **they found nobody** ils n'ont trouvé personne; **nobody who was there heard anything** aucun de ceux *ou* personne parmi tous ceux qui étaient là n'a entendu quoi que ce soit; **who was at the party? – nobody you know** qui était à la fête? – personne que tu connais; **nobody famous** personne de célèbre; **nobody is perfect** nul *ou* personne n'est parfait; **she's nobody's fool** elle n'est pas née d'hier *ou* de la dernière pluie; *Fam* **like nobody's business** vachement bien; *Fam* **to work like nobody's business** travailler comme un fou; *Fam* **to run like nobody's business** courir ventre à terre; *Fam* **the dogs were barking like nobody's business** les chiens aboyaient à vous rompre les tympans

(**b**) *(obscure, insignificant)* **when he was nobody** alors qu'il était encore inconnu; **as far as they're concerned, if you don't have money, you're nobody** pour eux si tu n'as pas d'argent tu es un zéro *ou* un moins que rien

2 *n (insignificant person)* zéro *m*; **he's just a nobody** c'est un zéro

no-brainer [-'breɪnə(r)] *n Am Fam* truc *m* pour débiles

NOC [,enəʊ'siː] *n* (*abbr* **National Olympic Committee**) Comité *m* olympique national

nociceptive [,nəʊsɪ'septɪv] *adj Physiol* nociceptif

nock [nɒk] *n (on arrow, bow)* encoche *f*, coche *f*

no-claim(s) bonus *n Br Ins* bonus *m*

noctambulation [nɒk,tæmbjʊ'leɪʃən], **noctambulism** [nɒk'tæmbjʊlɪzəm] *n Formal* somnambulisme *m*

noctambulist [,nɒk'tæmbjʊlɪst] *n Formal* somnambule *mf*

noctilucent [,nɒktɪ'luːsənt] *adj* (**a**) *Zool* noctiluque (**b**) *Met* visible la nuit

noctuid ['nɒktjuːɪd] *n Entom* noctuelle *f*

noctule ['nɒktjuːl] *n Zool* noctule *f*

►► ***noctule bat*** noctule *f*

nocturnal [nɒk'tɜːnəl] *adj* nocturne

►► *Med* ***nocturnal emission*** pollution *f* nocturne

nocturne ['nɒktɜːn] *n* nocturne *m*

nod [nɒd] (*pt & pp* **nodded**, *cont* **nodding**) **1** *vt* **to nod one's head** *(as signal)* faire un signe de (la) tête; *(in assent)* faire oui de la tête, faire un signe de tête affirmatif; *(in greeting)* saluer d'un signe de tête; *(with fatigue)* dodeliner de la tête; **she nodded her head in approval** *or* **nodded her approval** elle manifesta son approbation d'un signe de tête; **the boss nodded him into the office** le chef lui fit signe (de la tête) d'entrer dans le bureau

2 *vi* (**a**) *(as signal)* faire un signe de (la) tête; *(in assent, approval)* faire un signe de tête affirmatif, faire oui de la tête; *(in greeting)* saluer d'un signe de tête; **she nodded at** *or* **to him through the window** elle lui fit un signe de tête de derrière la fenêtre

(**b**) *(doze)* somnoler; **he was nodding in his chair** il somnolait dans son fauteuil

(**c**) *Fig (flowers)* danser, se balancer; *(crops, trees)* se balancer, onduler

3 *n* (**a**) *(sign)* signe *m* de (la) tête; **to give sb a nod** *(as signal)* faire un signe de tête à qn; *(in assent)* faire un signe de tête affirmatif à qn; *(in greeting)* saluer qn d'un signe de tête; **to answer with a nod** répondre d'un signe de tête; **a nod in sb's direction** un signe de tête à l'intention de qn; **a nod is as good as a wink (to a blind man)** inutile d'en dire plus; **to get** *Br* **the nod** *or Am* **a nod** *(gen)* obtenir le feu vert; *(in boxing)* gagner aux points; **to give sb** *Br* **the nod** *or Am* **a nod** donner le feu vert à qn; *Br* **to approve sth on the nod** *(without formality)* approuver qch d'un commun accord

(**b**) *(sleep)* **the land of Nod** le pays des rêves; *Hum* **to be in the land of Nod** être dans les bras de Morphée

►**nod off** *vi Fam* s'assoupir□, s'endormir□

►**nod out** *vi Fam* (**a**) *(faint)* tomber dans les vapes (**b**) *Drugs slang* planer

nodal ['nəʊdəl] *adj* nodal

nodding ['nɒdɪŋ] *adj Br* **to have a nodding acquaintance with sb** connaître qn de vue *ou* vaguement; *Fig* **I have a nodding acquaintance with marketing techniques** j'ai quelques notions des techniques de marketing; **we're on nodding terms** nous nous saluons

►► *Am Fam* ***nodding donkey*** pompe *f* à pétrole□

noddle ['nɒdəl] *n Br Fam (head)* caboche *f*, ciboulot *m*; **use your noddle!** fais marcher ton ciboulot *ou* tes méninges!

noddy ['nɒdɪ] (*pl* **noddies**) **1** *n Br Fam* bêta(asse) *m,f*

2 Noddy *pr n (in children's stories)* Oui-Oui

node [nəʊd] *n (gen)* nœud *m*; *Anat* nodosité *f*, nodule *m*

nodose [nəʊ'dəʊs, 'nəʊdəʊs] *adj* noueux

nodular ['nɒdjʊlə(r)] *adj* nodulaire

nodule ['nɒdjuːl] *n* nodule *m*

nodus ['nəʊdəs] (*pl* **nodi** [-'daɪ]) *n Literary (gen)* nœud *m*; *Anat* nodosité *f*, nodule *m*

Noel, Noël [nəʊ'el] *n Literary (Christmas)* Noël *m*

noesis [nəʊ'iːsɪs] *n Phil* noèse *f*

no-fault *adj*

►► ***no-fault divorce*** divorce *m* par consentement mutuel; *Am Law* ***no-fault insurance*** assurance *f* à remboursement automatique

no-fly zone *n Mil* zone *f* d'exclusion aérienne

no-frills *adj (airline, travel)* sans prestation de services; *(insurance policy)* de base; *(car, bicycle)* sans gadgets; *(service, wedding)* sans chichis, tout simple; **a no-frills hotel** un hôtel sans confort superflu

noggin ['nɒgɪn] *n* (**a**) *(measure)* quart *m* de pinte (**b**) *Fam (drink)* pot *m* (**c**) *Fam (head)* caboche *f*, ciboulot *m*; **use your noggin!** fais marcher tes méninges!, sers-toi de ta cervelle!

no-go area *n* zone *f* interdite; **this neighbourhood is a no-go area for the police** la police n'ose pas s'aventurer dans ce quartier

no-good *Fam* **1** *n* bon (bonne) *m,f* à rien□

2 *adj* bon à rien□

no-goodnik [-'gʊdnɪk] *n Am Fam* bon (bonne) *m,f* à rien□

no-holds-barred *adj (contest, fight)* où tous les coups sont permis; *(report, documentary)* sans fard

no-hoper [-'həʊpə(r)] *n Fam* raté(e) *m,f*, minable *mf*

nohow ['nəʊhaʊ] *adv Fam* aucunement□, en aucune façon□

noirish ['nwɑːrɪʃ] *adj Cin* qui rappelle les films noirs

noise [nɔɪz] **1** *n* (**a**) *(sound)* bruit *m*; **a loud noise** un gros bruit; **the clock is making a funny noise** la pendule fait un drôle de bruit; **I thought I heard a noise downstairs** j'ai cru entendre du bruit en bas; **the humming noise of the engine** le ronronnement du moteur; *Theat* **noises off** bruitage *m*

(**b**) *(din)* bruit *m*, tapage *m*, tintamarre *m*; *(very loud)* vacarme *m*; **to make a noise** faire du bruit; **do you call that noise music?** pour vous, ce vacarme c'est de la musique?; *Br Fam* **shut your noise!** ferme-la!

(**c**) *Elec & Tel* parasites *mpl*; *(on line)* friture *f*, sifflement *m*

(**d**) *Fam (idiom)* **to make a noise about sth** faire du tapage *ou* beaucoup de bruit autour de qch; **the critics made a lot of noise about the film** les critiques ont fait beaucoup de bruit autour de ce film; **they made a lot of noise about banning the march** ils ont remué ciel et terre pour faire interdire la manifestation

2 *vt* **to noise sth about** *or* **abroad** ébruiter qch

3 noises *npl Fam (indication of intentions)* **she made vague noises about emigrating** elle a vaguement parlé d'émigrer□; **to make encouraging noises** dire des choses encourageantes□; **to make sympathetic noises** compatir□; **he started making placatory noises** il se mit à marmonner quelques paroles d'apaisement□; **they made all the right noises, but...** ils ont fait semblant de marcher à fond *ou* d'être tout à fait d'accord, mais...□

►► ***noise abatement*** lutte *f* contre le bruit; ***noise abatement campaign*** campagne *f ou* lutte *f* contre le bruit; ***noise level*** niveau *m* de bruit; ***noise pollution*** nuisances *fpl* sonores, pollution *f* sonore

noiseless ['nɔɪzlɪs] *adj* silencieux

noiselessly ['nɔɪzlɪslɪ] *adv* silencieusement, sans faire de bruit

noiselessness ['nɔɪzlɪsnɪs] *n* silence *m*

noisemaker ['nɔɪz,meɪkə(r)] *n Am (rattle)* crécelle *f*; *(trumpet)* trompe *f*

noisette [nwæ'zet] *n (of lamb)* médaillon *m*

noisily [ˈnɔɪzɪlɪ] *adv* bruyamment

noisiness [ˈnɔɪzɪnɪs] *n* caractère *m* bruyant; **because of the noisiness of the street** à cause du bruit qu'il y a dans la rue; **I can't stand their noisiness** je ne peux pas supporter le bruit qu'ils font

noisome [ˈnɔɪsəm] *adj Literary (repellent)* répugnant, repoussant; *(smelly)* méphitique; *(noxious)* nocif, nuisible; **a noisome smell** une odeur infecte *ou* pestilentielle

noisy [ˈnɔɪzɪ] *(compar* **noisier,** *superl* **noisiest)** *adj* (**a**) *(machine, engine, person)* bruyant; **my typewriter is very noisy** ma machine à écrire est très bruyante *ou* fait beaucoup de bruit; **London was too noisy for him** Londres était trop bruyant à son goût (**b**) *(colour)* criard

nolens volens [ˌnəʊlenzˈvəʊlenz] *adv* bon gré mal gré, de gré ou de force

no-load fund *n St Exch* fonds *m* sans frais d'acquisition, fonds *m* qui ne prélève pas une commission

nomad [ˈnəʊmæd] *n* nomade *mf*

nomadic [nəʊˈmædɪk] *adj* nomade; *Fig* **a nomadic existence** une existence de nomade/nomades

nomadism [ˈnəʊmædɪzəm] *n* nomadisme *m*

nomadization [ˌnəʊmædaɪˈzeɪʃən] *n* nomadisation *f*

nomadize, -ise [ˈnəʊmædaɪz] **1** *vi* nomadiser

2 *vt* **the desert has nomadized them** le désert les a contraints à se nomadiser *ou* à la nomadisation

no-man's-land *n also Fig* no man's land *m inv*

nom de plume [ˌnɒmdəˈpluːm] *n* pseudonyme *m*, nom *m* de plume

nomenclature [*Br* ˌnəʊˈmenklətʃə(r), *Am* ˈnəʊmənˌkleɪtʃər] *n* nomenclature *f*

nomenklatura [ˌnəʊmenkləˈtʃʊrə] *n* nomenklatura *f*

nominal [ˈnɒmɪnəl] **1** *adj* (**a**) *(in name only → owner, leader)* de nom (seulement), nominal; *(→ ownership, leadership)* nominal; **he was the nominal president of the company** il n'était le président de la société que de nom

(**b**) *(negligible)* insignifiant, nominal; *(rent)* insignifiant; **a nominal amount** une somme insignifiante

(**c**) *(token)* symbolique; **a nominal contribution of one pound a year** une contribution symbolique d'une livre par an

(**d**) *Gram* nominal

2 *n Gram* élément *m* nominal; *(noun phrase)* groupe *m* nominal; *(pronoun)* nominal *m*

►► *Acct* ***nominal account*** compte *m* d'exploitation générale; *Fin* ***nominal capital*** capital *m* nominal; *Law* ***nominal damages*** dommages intérêts *mpl* symboliques; *Fin* ***nominal interest rate*** taux *m* d'intérêt nominal; *Acct* ***nominal ledger*** grand-livre *m* général; *Fin* ***nominal partner*** associé(e) *m,f* fictif(ive); *Fin* ***nominal price*** prix *m* nominal; *Fin* ***nominal value*** valeur *f* nominale; *Fin* ***nominal wages*** salaire *m* nominal; *Fin* ***nominal yield*** taux *m* nominal

nominalism [ˈnɒmɪnəlɪzəm] *n Phil* nominalisme *m*

nominalist [ˈnɒmɪnəlɪst] *n Phil* nominaliste *mf*

nominalization [ˌnɒmɪnəlaɪˈzeɪʃən] *n* nominalisation *f*

nominalize, -ise [ˈnɒmɪnəlaɪz] *vt* nominaliser

nominally [ˈnɒmɪnəlɪ] *adv* (**a**) *(in name only)* nominalement (**b**) *(as token)* pour la forme (**c**) *(theoretically)* théoriquement

nominate [ˈnɒmɪneɪt] *vt* (**a**) *(propose)* proposer (la candidature de); *Cin (for award)* sélectionner, nominer; **to nominate sb for a post** proposer la candidature de qn à un poste; **the film was nominated for an Oscar** le film a été sélectionné *ou* nominé pour un oscar

(**b**) *(appoint)* nommer, désigner; **to nominate sb to a post** nommer *ou* désigner qn à un poste; **she was nominated to replace Mr Sheridan as minister** elle a été nommée ministre en remplacement de M. Sheridan; **he was nominated chairman** *or* **to the chairmanship** il fut nommé président

nomination [ˌnɒmɪˈneɪʃən] *n* (**a**) *(proposal)* proposition *f*; *Cin (for an award)* nomination *f*; **who will get the Democratic nomination (for president)?** qui obtiendra l'investiture démocrate (à l'élection présidentielle)?; **the film got three Oscar nominations** le film a obtenu trois nominations aux oscars

(**b**) *(appointment → of candidate)* nomination *f*; *(→ of president, judge)* investiture *f*

nominative [ˈnɒmɪnətɪv] **1** *n Gram* nominatif *m*; **in the nominative** au nominatif

2 *adj* (**a**) *Gram* nominatif (**b**) *(appointed)* désigné (**c**) *(namebearing)* nominatif

►► *Gram* ***the nominative case*** le nominatif

nominator [ˈnɒmɪˌneɪtə(r)] *n* présentateur(trice) *m,f (d'un candidat)*; **his nominators** ceux qui ont proposé sa nomination

nominee [ˌnɒmɪˈniː] *n* (**a**) *(proposed)* candidat(e) *m,f* (**b**) *(appointed)* personne *f* désignée *ou* nommée; **the government nominees on the commission** les membres de la commission nommés par le gouvernement

►► *St Exch* ***nominee account*** compte *m* d'intermédiaire; ***nominee company*** prête-nom *m*; *Fin* ***nominee name*** nom *m* de l'intermédiaire; *St Exch* ***nominee shareholder*** actionnaire *mf* intermédiaire; *St Exch* ***nominee shareholding*** actionnariat *m* intermédiaire

nomogram [ˈnɒməgræm], **nomograph** [ˈnɒməgrɑːf] *n* nomogramme *m*

nomography [nɒˈmɒgrəfɪ] *n* nomographie *f*

non- [nɒn] *pref* (**a**) *(not)* non-; **the non-application of this rule** la non-application de cette règle; **all non-French nationals** tous les ressortissants de nationalité autre que française; **his answers were non-answers** ses réponses n'en étaient pas (**b**) *(against)* anti-; **non-rust** antirouille *(inv)*

nonabsorbent [ˌnɒnəbˈzɔːbənt] *adj* non absorbant

nonacademic [ˌnɒnækəˈdemɪk] *adj* (**a**) *(activity) & Sch* extrascolaire; *Univ* extra-universitaire (**b**) *Sch & Univ (staff)* non enseignant (**c**) *(course)* pratique, technique

non-acceptance *n* non-acceptation *f*

non-accidental *adj*

►► ***non-accidental injury*** *(of child, woman)* blessures *fpl* dues à des mauvais traitements

non-accountable *adj (unaccountable → individual, institution)* qui n'a de comptes à rendre à personne; **to be non-accountable to sb** ne pas avoir à répondre devant qn, ne pas avoir de comptes à rendre à qn

non-accruing loan *n Fin* emprunt *m* à risques

nonachievement [ˌnɒnəˈtʃiːvmənt] *n* non-réalisation *f*

nonachiever [ˌnɒnəˈtʃiːvə(r)] *n* élève *mf* qui ne réussit pas

nonaddictive [ˌnɒnəˈdɪktɪv] *adj* qui ne crée pas de phénomène d'accoutumance

nonadmission [ˌnɒnədˈmɪʃən] *n* non-admission *f*

non-adopter *n Mktg* = consommateur qui n'essaie jamais de nouveaux produits

nonaerosol [ˌnɒnˈeərəsɒl] *adj (container)* non pressurisé

nonaffiliated [ˌnɒnəˈfɪlɪeɪtɪd] *adj* non affilié, indépendant

nonage [ˈnəʊnɪdʒ] *n* minorité *f*

nonagenarian [ˌnəʊnədʒɪˈneərɪən] **1** *n* nonagénaire *mf*

2 *adj* nonagénaire

nonaggression [ˌnɒnəˈgreʃən] *n* non-agression *f*

►► ***nonaggression pact*** pacte *m* de non-agression

nonagon [ˈnɒnəgɒn] *n* nonagone *m*

nonalcoholic [ˌnɒnælkəˈhɒlɪk] *adj* non alcoolisé, sans alcool

nonaligned [ˌnɒnəˈlaɪnd] *adj Pol* non aligné

►► ***nonaligned countries*** pays *mpl* non alignés

nonalignment [ˌnɒnəˈlaɪnmənt] *n Pol* non-alignement *m*

no-name product *n Mktg* produit *m* sans nom

nonappearance [ˌnɒnəˈpɪərəns] *n* (**a**) *(gen)* **how do you account for her nonappearance?** comment expliquez-vous le fait qu'elle ne soit pas venue? (**b**) *Law* non-comparution *f*

nonarrival [ˌnɒnəˈraɪvəl] *n* non-arrivée *f*

nonary [ˈnɒnərɪ] *adj Math* à base neuf

non-assertive *adj (person, behaviour)* peu assuré

non-ASCII character *n Comput* caractère *m* non ASCII

nonattendance [ˌnɒnəˈtendəns] *n* absence *f*; **nonattendance of lectures** absence *f* aux cours

non-attributable *adj* dont la source ne peut être révélée

nonavailability [ˈnɒnəˌveɪləˈbɪlətɪ] *n* non-disponibilité *f*

nonavailable [ˌnɒnəˈveɪləbəl] *adj* non disponible

non-bank *adj* non-banque

nonbeliever [ˌnɒnbɪˈliːvə(r)] *n* non-croyant(e) *m,f*, incroyant(e) *m,f*

nonbelligerency [ˌnɒnbɪˈlɪdʒərənsɪ] *n* non-belligérance *f*

nonbelligerent [ˌnɒnbɪˈlɪdʒərənt] *adj* non belligérant

nonbinding [ˌnɒnˈbaɪndɪŋ] *adj* sans obligation, non contraignant

nonbiodegradable [ˈnɒnˌbaɪəʊdɪˈgreɪdəbəl] *adj* non biodégradable

non-breakable *adj* incassable

non-business marketing *n Mktg* marketing *m* non commercial

non-Catholic 1 *n* non-catholique *mf*

2 *adj* non catholique

nonce [nɒns] *n* (**a**) *Literary or Hum* **for the nonce** *(for the occasion)* pour la circonstance, pour l'occasion; *(for the moment)* pour l'instant (**b**) *Br Fam Crime slang (sex offender)* délinquant *m* sexuel ☐ *(s'attaquant en particulier aux enfants)*

►► *Ling* ***nonce word*** mot *m* créé pour l'occasion

nonchalance [*Br* ˈnɒnʃələns, *Am* ˌnɒnʃəˈlɑːns] *n* nonchalance *f*

nonchalant [*Br* ˈnɒnʃələnt, *Am* ˌnɒnʃəˈlɑːnt] *adj* nonchalant

nonchalantly [*Br* ˈnɒnʃələntlɪ, *Am* ˌnɒnʃəˈlɑːntlɪ] *adv* nonchalamment, avec nonchalance

non-Christian 1 *n* non-chrétien(enne) *m,f*

2 *adj* non chrétien

non-classified *adj* non secret

non-cognizable *adj Law* = qui ne peut faire l'objet d'une enquête judiciaire

noncollegiate [ˌnɒnkəˈliːdʒɪɪt] *Univ* **1** *n* étudiant(e) *m,f* n'appartenant à aucun collège

2 *adj (student)* n'appartenant à aucun collège; *(university)* qui n'est pas divisée en collèges

noncom [ˈnɒnkɒm] *n Fam Mil* sous-off *m*

noncombatant [*Br* ˌnɒnˈkɒmbətənt, *Am* ˌnɒnkəmˈbætənt] **1** *n* non-combattant(e) *m,f*

2 *adj* non combattant

noncombustible [ˌnɒnkəmˈbʌstəbəl] *adj* incombustible

noncommissioned [ˌnɒnkəˈmɪʃənd] *adj Mil* sans brevet

►► ***noncommissioned officer*** sous-officier *m*

noncommittal [ˌnɒnkəˈmɪtəl] *adj (statement)* évasif, qui n'engage à rien; *(attitude, person)* réservé; *(gesture)* peu révélateur; **a noncommittal reply** une réponse évasive; **to be noncommittal** *(when answering)* ne pas s'engager; **he was very noncommittal about his plans** il s'est montré très évasif sur ses projets

non-competition clause *n* clause *f* de non-concurrence

noncompetitive [ˌnɒnkəmˈpetɪtɪv] *adj* qui n'est pas basé sur la compétition

noncompletion [ˌnɒnkəmˈpliːʃən] *n (of job)* non-achèvement *m*; *(of contract)* non-exécution *f*

noncompliance [ˌnɒnkəmˈplaɪəns] *n* non-respect *m*, non-observation *f* (**with** de); **noncompliance with the treaty** le non-respect du traité; **noncompliance with the orders of a superior** refus *m* d'obéir aux ordres d'un supérieur

non compos mentis [ˈnɒnˌkɒmpɒsˈmentɪs] *adj* fou (folle), dément, irresponsable

nonconductor [ˌnɒnkənˈdʌktə(r)] *n Phys* non-conducteur *m*, mauvais conducteur *m*; *Elec* isolant *m*

nonconformism [ˌnɒnkənˈfɔːmɪzəm] **1** *n (gen)* non-conformisme *m*

2 Nonconformism *n Rel* non-conformisme *m*

nonconformist [ˌnɒnkənˈfɔːmɪst] **1** *n (gen)* non-conformiste *mf*

2 *adj* non conformiste

3 Nonconformist *Rel* **1** *n* non-conformiste *mf* **2** *adj* non conformiste

nonconformity [ˌnɒnkənˈfɔːmətɪ] **1** *n (gen)* non-conformité *f*

2 Nonconformity *n Rel* non-conformisme *m*

non-contributory *adj*
►► *Br Fin* ***non-contributory pension (scheme)*** caisse *f* de retraite sans cotisations de la part des bénéficiaires

non-controversial *adj (issue, question)* qui n'est pas sujet à controverse

non-convertible *adj* inconvertible, non convertible

noncooperation ['nɒnkəʊ,ɒpə'reɪʃən] *n* refus *m* de coopérer

noncooperative [,nɒnkəʊ'ɒpərətɪv] *adj* non coopératif

non-cumulative *adj Fin* non cumulatif
►► ***non-cumulative quantity discount*** remise *f* sur quantité non cumulable

non-current liabilities *npl Acct* passif *m* non exigible

noncustodial [,nɒnkʌs'təʊdɪəl] *adj (sentence)* n'entraînant pas l'emprisonnement

non-dairy *adj* qui ne contient aucun produit laitier
►► *Am* ***non-dairy cream*** = crème liquide d'origine végétale

non-dazzle *adj* anti-éblouissement *(inv)*

nondeductible [,nɒndɪ'dʌktəbəl] *adj* non déductible

non-delivery [,nɒndɪ'lɪvərɪ] *n (of goods)* non-livraison *f*; **in the event of non-delivery** dans l'éventualité où les marchandises ne seraient pas livrées

non-democratic *adj (state)* non démocratique

non-denominational *adj (school, education)* non confessionnel

non-departmental public body *n Pol* = organisme semi-public

nondescript [*Br* 'nɒndɪskrɪpt, *Am* ,nɒndɪ'skrɪpt] *adj (person, object)* quelconque; *(colour)* neutre, *Pej* fade; **a nondescript little man** un petit homme que rien ne distingue des autres *ou* tout à fait anodin; **the street was lined with nondescript buildings** la rue était bordée de bâtiments quelconques *ou* dépourvus de caractère

nondestructive [,nɒndɪ'strʌktɪv] *adj (test, testing)* non destructif

nondetachable [,nɒndɪ'tætʃəbəl] *adj* inamovible

nondirective [,nɒndɪ'rektɪv] *adj*
►► *Psy* ***nondirective therapy*** psychothérapie *f* non directive

nondisclosure [,nɒndɪs'kləʊʒə(r)] *n* dissimulation *f*; *Law* réticence *f*

non-discriminatory *adj* non discriminatoire

non-DOS disk *n Comput* disque *m* à format incompatible avec DOS

nondrinker [,nɒn'drɪŋkə(r)] *n* abstinent(e) *m,f*; **she's a nondrinker** elle ne boit pas (d'alcool)

nondrip [,nɒn'drɪp] *adj (paint)* qui ne coule pas

nondriver [,nɒn'draɪvə(r)] *n* **I'm a nondriver** *(never learnt)* je n'ai pas mon permis; *(out of choice)* je ne conduis pas

non-dutiable *adj* exempt de droits de douane

NONE [nʌn] **1** *pron* (**a**) *(with countable nouns)* aucun(e) *m,f*; **none of the photos is** *or* **are for sale** aucune des photos n'est à vendre; **he looked for clues but found none** il chercha des indices mais n'en trouva aucun; **there are none left** il n'en reste plus; **how many cigarettes have you got? – none at all** combien de cigarettes as-tu? – aucune *ou* pas une seule

(**b**) *(with uncountable nouns)* **none of her early work has been published** aucun de ses premiers textes n'a été publié; **none of the mail is for you** il n'y a rien pour vous au courrier; **none of the milk was fresh** tout le lait avait tourné; **none of the water was left** il ne restait rien de l'eau; **how much of the wood did you use? – none of it** quelle quantité du bois avez-vous utilisée? – pas un seul morceau; **I've done a lot of work but you've done none** j'ai beaucoup travaillé, mais toi tu n'as rien fait; **she displayed none of her usual good humour** elle était loin d'afficher sa bonne humeur habituelle; **they'll get none of my money!** ils n'auront pas un centime de moi!; **more soup anyone? – none for me, thanks** encore un peu de soupe? – pas pour moi, merci; **(I'll have) none of your cheek!** je ne tolérerai pas vos insolences!; **none of that!** *(stop it)* pas de ça!; **she would have none of it** elle ne voulait rien savoir; **none of this concerns me** rien de ceci ne me regarde

(**c**) *(not one person)* aucun(e) *m,f*; **none of them works** *or* **work hard enough** aucun d'eux ne travaille suffisamment; **none of us understood his explanation** aucun de nous n'a compris son explication; *Literary* **none can tell what the future holds** nul ne sait ce que l'avenir nous réserve; *Literary* **there was none braver than her** nul n'était plus courageux qu'elle

2 *adv Am Fam (in double negatives)* **that won't change things none** ça ne changera rien ❑; **you don't scare me none** tu ne me fais pas du tout peur ❑

3 none but *adv Formal or Literary* **we use none but the finest ingredients** nous n'utilisons que les meilleurs ingrédients; **none but an expert would know the difference** seul un expert serait à même de faire la différence; **I love none but her** je n'aime qu'elle

4 none other than *prep* personne d'autre que; **he received a letter from none other than the Prime Minister himself** il reçut une lettre dont l'auteur n'était autre que le Premier ministre en personne

5 none the *adv (with comparative adj)* **I feel none the better/worse for it** je ne me sens pas mieux/plus mal pour autant; **I like them none the better/worse for it** je ne les en aime pas plus/moins; **she's none the worse for her adventure** son aventure ne lui a pas fait de mal

6 none too *adv* **he's none too bright** il est loin d'être brillant; **I was none too pleased with them** j'étais loin d'être content d'eux; **he replied none too politely** sa réponse ne fut pas particulièrement polie; **and none too soon!** ce n'est pas trop tôt!

---

non-effective *Mil* **1** *n (soldier → unfit)* soldat *m* non valide; *(→ unavailable for service)* soldat *m* non disponible

2 *adj (unfit)* non valide; *(unavailable for service)* non disponible

non-ego *n Phil* non-moi *m inv*

nonentity [nɒn'entətɪ] (*pl* **nonentities**) *n* (**a**) *(insignificant person)* personne *f* insignifiante, nullité *f*; **she's a bit of a nonentity** elle est plutôt insignifiante (**b**) *(insignificance)* inexistence *f*

non-equity share *n St Exch* action *f* sans privilège de participation

non-erasable memory *n Comput* mémoire *f* non effaçable

nones [nəʊnz] *npl (in Roman calendar)* nones *fpl*

nonessential [,nɒnɪ'senʃəl] **1** *adj* accessoire, non essentiel; **nonessential details** des détails *mpl* superflus

2 *n* **the nonessentials** l'accessoire *m*, le superflu; **leave behind all nonessentials** n'emportez que l'essentiel

nonesuch ['nʌnsʌtʃ] *n* (**a**) *Literary or Arch* personne *f ou* chose *f* incomparable (**b**) *Bot* lupuline *f*, minette *f*

nonet [nəʊ'net] *n Mus* nonet *m*, nonetto *m*

nonetheless [,nʌnðə'les] = **nevertheless**

non-Euclidian *adj*
►► ***non-Euclidian geometry*** géométrie *f* non euclidienne

non-event *n* non-événement *m*; **the press conference was pretty much a non-event** la conférence de presse ne valait pas le déplacement

non-executive director *adj* administrateur(trice) *m,f* consultant(e)

non-execution *n (of contract)* non-exécution *f*

nonexistence [,nɒnɪg'zɪstəns] *n* non-existence *f*

nonexistent [,nɒnɪg'zɪstənt] *adj* non existant, inexistant; *Fam* **his help has been almost nonexistent** il ne s'est pas beaucoup foulé pour nous aider

nonfat ['nɒn,fæt] *adj* sans matière grasse *ou* matières grasses
►► ***nonfat diet*** régime *m* sans matière grasse *ou* matières grasses

nonfattening [,nɒn'fætnɪŋ] *adj* qui ne fait pas grossir

nonfeasance [,nɒn'fi:zəns] *n Law* délit *m* par abstention

non-feminist 1 *n* non-féministe *mf*

2 *adj* non féministe

non-ferrous *adj* non ferreux

nonfiction [,nɒn'fɪkʃən] *n (UNCOUNT)* ouvrages *mpl* non romanesques
►► ***nonfiction section*** *(of bookshop)* rayon *m* des ouvrages généraux

nonfigurative [,nɒn'fɪgjʊrətɪv] *adj* non figuratif

non-finite *adj* (**a**) *(infinite)* infini (**b**) *Gram* à aspect non fini

nonflammable [,nɒn'flæməbəl] *adj* ininflammable

non-forfeiture *n Law* non-déchéance *f*
►► *Ins* ***non-forfeiture clause*** clause *f* de reconduction automatique

non-fulfilment *n (of contract)* non-exécution *f*

non-governmental organization *n* organisation *f* non gouvernementale

non-greasy *adj (lotion, moisturizer)* non gras

non-habit-forming *adj* qui ne crée pas de phénomène d'accoutumance

nonhuman [,nɒn'hju:mən] *adj* non humain

nonillion [nəʊ'nɪlɪən] *n* nonillion *m*

non-impact printer *n* imprimante *f* sans impact

noninfectious [,nɒnɪn'fekʃəs] *adj* qui n'est pas infectieux

noninflammable [,nɒnɪn'flæməbəl] *adj* ininflammable

noninterference [,nɒnɪntə'fɪərəns] *n* non-intervention *f*, non-ingérence *f*

non-interlaced display *n Comput* affichage *m* non entrelacé

nonintervention [,nɒnɪntə'venʃən] *n* non-intervention *f*, non-ingérence *f*

noninterventionist [,nɒnɪntə'venʃənɪst] **1** *n* non-interventionniste *mf*

2 *adj (policy)* non interventionniste, de non-intervention

non-invasive *adj* non invasif, non effractif

non-iron *adj* qui ne nécessite aucun repassage

non-Jew *n* non-Juif(ive) *m,f*

non-Jewish *adj* non juif

nonjudgemental, nonjudgmental [,nɒndʒʌdʒ'mentəl] *adj* neutre, impartial; **to try to be nonjudgemental** s'efforcer de ne pas porter de jugements

non-ladder *adj (stockings, tights)* infilable

non-liability *n Law* non-responsabilité *f*
►► ***non-liability clause*** clause *f* de non-responsabilité

non-linear *adj* non linéaire

non-linearity *n* non-linéarité *f*

nonmalignant [,nɒnmə'lɪgnənt] *adj* bénin(igne)

nonmember ['nɒn,membə(r)] *n* non-membre *m*; *(of a club)* personne *f* étrangère (au club); **open to nonmembers** ouvert au public

nonmetal [,nɒn'metəl] *n* non-métal *m*

nonmetallic [,nɒnmɪ'tælɪk] *adj* non métallique

nonmigrant [,nɒn'maɪgrənt], **nonmigratory** [,nɒn'maɪgrətərɪ] *adj (bird)* sédentaire

non-Muslim 1 *n* non-musulman(e) *m,f*

2 *adj* non musulman

non-native *adj* non indigène
►► ***non-native speaker*** locuteur(trice) *m,f* étranger(ère) *ou* non natif(ive)

non-negotiable *adj* non négociable

non-nuclear *adj (country)* non nucléarisé; *(war, defence, policy)* non nucléaire

no-no *n Fam* interdit ❑ *m*; **that subject is a no-no** ce sujet est tabou ❑; **dating someone from work is a no-no** sortir avec un collègue de travail, c'est l'erreur à ne pas faire ❑; **I made one no-no after another** j'ai fait gaffe sur gaffe; **asking him for more money is a definite no-no** il est hors de question de lui demander plus d'argent ❑

non-objective *adj Art* non objectif

nonobservance [,nɒnəb'zɜ:vəns] *n (of rules)* non-observation *f*; *(of treaty)* non-respect *m*; *Rel* inobservance *f*

non obst. *(written abbr* **non obstante***)* nonobstant

no-nonsense *adj (attitude, manner)* pratique; *(person)* qui va droit au but; **she's got a very no-nonsense approach** elle va droit au but; **she told him so in her usual no-nonsense way** elle le lui a dit très directement, comme à son habitude

nonoperational [,nɒnɒpə'reɪʃənəl] *adj* non opérationnel

nonpareil ['nɒnpərəl] *n Literary (person)* personne *f* incomparable *ou* unique; *(thing)* chose *f* incomparable *ou* unique

non-participant *n* non-participant(e) *m,f*

non-participating *adj* (**a**) *St Exch (share)* sans droit de participation (**b**) *(country, institution)* qui ne participe pas (**c**) *Ins (policy)* sans participation aux bénéfices

non-participation *n* non-participation *f*

nonpartisan ['nɒn,pɑːtɪ'zæn] *adj* impartial, sans parti pris

nonparty [,nɒn'pɑːtɪ] *adj* indépendant

nonpayment [,nɒn'peɪmənt] *n* non-paiement *m*, défaut *m* de paiement; **in case of nonpayment** en cas de non-paiement, à défaut de paiement

non-penetrative *adj (sex)* sans pénétration

non-performance *n (of contract)* non-exécution *f*, inexécution *f*

non-performing loan *n Banking* prêt *m* en souffrance

non-persistent *adj* qui se dégrade rapidement

nonperson [,nɒn'pɜːsən] *n* (**a**) *(stateless person)* = personne mise au ban de la société (**b**) *(insignificant person)* personne *f* insignifiante, nullité *f*; **he treats his secretary like a nonperson** il se conduit envers sa secrétaire comme si elle n'existait pas

nonplus [,nɒn'plʌs] *(Br pt & pp* **nonplussed,** *cont* **nonplussing,** *Am pt & pp* **nonplused,** *cont* **nonplusing**) *vt* déconcerter, dérouter

nonplussed [,nɒn'plʌst] *adj* dérouté, perplexe

non-poisonous *adj* non toxique; *(snake)* non venimeux; *(mushroom)* non vénéneux

nonpolluting [,nɒnpə'luːtɪŋ] *adj* non polluant, propre

nonpractising [,nɒn'præktɪsɪŋ] *adj* non pratiquant

non-prescription drug *n Pharm* médicament *m* en vente libre

non-printable character *n* caractère *m* non imprimable

non-probability *adj*

▸▸ ***non-probability method*** *(of sampling)* méthode *f* non probabiliste; ***non-probability sample*** échantillon *m* non probabiliste; ***non-probability sampling*** échantillonnage *m* non probabiliste

non-procedural language *n Comput* langage *m* non procédural

nonproductive [,nɒnprə'dʌktɪv] *adj Econ* improductif

nonprofit [,nɒn'prɒfɪt] *adj Am* à but non lucratif

non-profit-making *adj Br* à but non lucratif

▸▸ ***non-profit-making organization*** société *f* à but non lucratif

nonproliferation ['nɒnprə,lɪfə'reɪʃən] *n* non-prolifération *f*

▸▸ ***nonproliferation treaty*** traité *m* de non-prolifération

non-punitive *adj (role, approach, system)* non punitif

non-quoted *adj St Exch* non coté en Bourse

non-racial *adj (society, democracy, government)* qui ne pratique pas la discrimination raciale

non-random *adj*

▸▸ *Mktg* ***non-random sample*** échantillon *m* empirique; ***non-random sampling*** échantillonnage *m* empirique

nonreader [,nɒn'riːdə(r)] *n (who cannot read)* personne *f* qui ne sait pas lire, illettré(e) *m,f*; *(who doesn't read)* personne *f* qui ne lit pas; **half the children are nonreaders** la moitié des enfants ne savent pas lire

non-recourse finance *n Fin* financement *m* sans recours

non-recoverable *n Comput (file, data)* non récupérable

non-recurrence [,nɒnrɪ'kʌrəns] *n (of event)* non-répétition *f*; *(of disease, symptoms)* non-réapparition *f*; *(of subject, problem)* non-retour *m*

non-recurring *adj* exceptionnel, extraordinaire

▸▸ ***non-recurring expenditure*** dépenses *fpl* extraordinaires

non-reflecting *adj* antireflet *(inv)*

non-reflective *adj* (**a**) *(person, mind)* irréfléchi (**b**) *(surface, coating)* antireflet *(inv)*

nonrefundable [,nɒnrɪ'fʌndəbəl] *adj* non remboursable; *(packaging)* perdu(e)

non-religious *adj (ceremony, person, group)* non religieux

nonrenewable [,nɒnrɪ'njuːəbəl] *adj (resources)* non renouvelable

non-representational *adj Art* non figuratif

non-residence *n* (**a**) *(of priest, owner)* non-résidence *f* (**b**) *Sch* externat *m*

non-resident **1** *n* (**a**) *(of country)* non-résident(e) *m,f* (**b**) *(of hotel)* **the dining room is open/closed to nonresidents** le restaurant est ouvert au public/réservé aux clients de l'hôtel

2 *adj* non résident; *Banking & Fin* **non-resident account** compte *m* (de) non-résident

non-residential *adj (building, area)* non résidentiel; *(course)* sans hébergement; *Med* **non-residential care** soins *mpl* en hôpital de jour

nonresistance [,nɒnrɪ'zɪstəns] *n (nonviolence)* non-violence *f*

nonresistant [,nɒnrɪ'zɪstənt] *adj* non résistant

non-restrictive *adj Gram (clause)* explicatif

nonreturnable [,nɒnrɪ'tɜːnəbəl] *adj* sans réserve de retour; *(bottle, container)* non consigné; *(deposit)* non remboursable; *(packaging)* non consigné, perdu; **sales goods are nonreturnable** les articles en solde ne sont pas repris

non-return valve *n Tech* clapet *m* anti-retour

nonrigid [nɒn'rɪdʒɪd] *adj* souple

nonrun [,nɒn'rʌn] *adj* indémaillable

nonscheduled [*Br* nɒn'ʃedjuːld, *Am* nɒn'skedjuːld] *adj (flight)* spécial

▸▸ ***nonscheduled stop*** étape *f* non prévue

nonsectarian [,nɒnsek'teərɪən] *adj* tolérant, ouvert

nonsense ['nɒnsəns] **1** *n (UNCOUNT)* (**a**) *(rubbish, absurdity)* absurdités *fpl*, sottises *fpl*; **a piece of nonsense** une sottise, une absurdité; **you're talking nonsense!** tu dis des sottises!, tu racontes n'importe quoi!; **the computer is outputting nonsense** l'ordinateur sort des âneries; **his accusations are utter nonsense** ses accusations n'ont aucun sens; **it's nonsense to say that things will never improve** il est absurde de dire que les choses n'iront jamais mieux; **I've had enough of his nonsense** j'en ai assez de l'entendre raconter n'importe quoi; **what's all this nonsense about going to live in America?** qu'est-ce que c'est que cette histoire d'aller vivre en Amérique?; **to make a nonsense of sth** *(undo, go against etc)* ôter tout sens à qch

(**b**) *(foolishness)* sottises *fpl*, bêtises *fpl*, enfantillages *mpl*; **stop this** *or* **no more of this nonsense!** arrêtez de vous conduire comme des imbéciles!; **she took no nonsense from her subordinates** elle ne tolérait aucun manquement de la part de ses subordonnés, elle menait ses subordonnés à la baguette; **the maths teacher doesn't stand for any nonsense** le prof de maths ne se laisse pas marcher sur les pieds; **there's no nonsense about him** c'est un homme très carré

2 *exclam* n'importe quoi!

3 *adj* dénué de sens

▸▸ ***nonsense verse*** vers *mpl* amphigouriques; ***nonsense word*** mot *m* qui ne veut rien dire, non-sens *m*

nonsensical [,nɒn'sensɪkəl] *adj (talk, idea, action)* absurde, qui n'a pas de sens, inepte; **a nonsensical explanation** une explication incohérente *ou* incompréhensible

nonsensically [,nɒn'sensɪkəlɪ] *adv* absurdement

non sequitur [,nɒn'sekwɪtə(r)] *n Ling* illogisme *m*; **that's a non sequitur** ça manque de suite; **his argument was full of non sequiturs** son raisonnement était incohérent

nonsexist [,nɒn'seksɪst] **1** *n* non-sexiste *mf*

2 *adj* non sexiste

nonshrink [,nɒn'ʃrɪŋk] *adj* irrétrécissable

nonskid [,nɒn'skɪd] *adj* antidérapant

nonslip [,nɒn'slɪp] *adj* antidérapant

nonsmoker [,nɒn'sməʊkə(r)] *n* (**a**) *(person)* non-fumeur(euse) *m,f* (**b**) *Rail* compartiment *m* non-fumeurs

nonsmoking [,nɒn'sməʊkɪŋ] *adj (carriage, compartment, area)* non-fumeurs; *(seat)* non-fumeur; **we have a nonsmoking office** il est interdit de fumer dans notre bureau

nonspecialist [,nɒn'speʃəlɪst] **1** *n* non-spécialiste *mf*

2 *adj* non spécialiste

nonspecific [,nɒnspɪ'sɪfɪk] *adj* non spécifique

▸▸ *Med* ***nonspecific urethritis*** *(UNCOUNT)* urétrite *f* non spécifique *ou* non gonococcique

nonspherical [,nɒn'sferɪkəl] *adj* asphérique

nonstandard [,nɒn'stændəd] *adj* (**a**) *Ling (use of word)* critiqué; **in nonstandard English** *(colloquial)* en anglais familier *ou* populaire; *(dialectal)* en anglais dialectal (**b**) *(product, size, shape etc)* non standard

nonstarter [,nɒn'stɑːtə(r)] *n* (**a**) *(horse)* non-partant *m*; *(athlete, cyclist)* = athlète ou cycliste qui ne prend pas le départ (**b**) *Fam Fig* **this project is a nonstarter** ce projet est foutu d'avance

nonstick [,nɒn'stɪk] *adj (coating)* antiadhésif; *(pan)* antiadhésif, qui n'attache pas

nonstop [,nɒn'stɒp] **1** *adj (journey)* sans arrêt; *(flight)* direct, sans escale, non-stop *(inv)*; *(train)* direct; *(show, radio programme)* non-stop *(inv)*, sans interruption; **they kept up a nonstop conversation** leur conversation se poursuivit sans interruption; **nonstop music programme** programme *m* musical en continu

2 *adv* sans arrêt; **to fly nonstop from Rome to Montreal** faire Rome-Montréal sans escale

nonsuch = **nonesuch**

non-suit *Eng Law* **1** *n* ordonnance *f* de non-lieu

2 *vt* débouter (de sa demande)

nonsymmetrical [,nɒnsɪ'metrɪkəl] *adj* dissymétrique

non-tariff barrier *n Com* barrière *f* non tarifaire

non-taxable *adj* non imposable

non-threatening *adj (situation, environment)* non menaçant

nontoxic [,nɒn'tɒksɪk] *adj* non toxique

nontransferability [,nɒntrænsfərə'bɪlɪtɪ] *n (of share)* caractère *m* nominatif; *(of property, right)* incessibilité *f*

nontransferable [,nɒntræns'fɜːrəbəl] *adj (share)* nominatif; *(property, right)* incessible

non-U *adj Br Old-fashioned* = façon de désigner "ce qui ne se fait pas" selon le code des bonnes manières

nonunion [,nɒn'juːnjən], **nonunionized** [,nɒn'juːnjənaɪzd] *adj (worker, labour)* non syndiqué; *(firm)* qui n'emploie pas de personnel syndiqué

non-usage *n Law* non-usage *m*

non-user *n* (**a**) *(person)* non-utilisateur *m* (**b**) *Law* non-usage *m*

nonverbal [,nɒn'vɜːbəl] *adj* non verbal

▸▸ ***nonverbal communication*** communication *f* par les gestes

nonviability [,nɒnvaɪə'bɪlɪtɪ] *n Med (of newborn child)* non-viabilité *f*

nonvintage [nɒn'vɪntɪdʒ] *adj (wine)* non millésimé

nonviolence [,nɒn'vaɪələns] *n* non-violence *f*

nonviolent [,nɒn'vaɪələnt] *adj* non violent

non-vocational *adj* non professionnel

non-voter *n (person → not eligible to vote)* personne *f* qui n'a pas le droit de vote; *(→ not exercising the right to vote)* abstentionniste *mf*

non-voting *adj* (**a**) *(person → not eligible to vote)* qui n'a pas le droit de vote; *(→ not exercising the right to vote)* abstentionniste (**b**) *Fin (shares)* sans droit de vote

non-warranty *n* non-garantie *f*

▸▸ ***non-warranty clause*** clause *f* de non-garantie

non-wasting *adj (asset)* indéfectible

nonwhite [,nɒn'waɪt] **1** *n* personne *f* de couleur

2 *adj* de couleur; **a nonwhite neighbourhood** un quartier où vivent des gens de couleur (et très peu de Blancs)

noodle ['nuːdəl] **1** *n* (**a**) *Culin* nouille *f*; **chicken noodle soup** soupe *f* de poulet aux vermicelles (**b**) *Fam (fool)* andouille *f*, nouille *f* (**c**) *Fam (head)* tronche *f*, caboche *f*

2 noodles *npl Culin* nouilles *fpl*

nook [nʊk] *n* (**a**) *(corner)* coin *m*, recoin *m*; **nooks and crannies** coins et recoins; **in every nook and cranny** dans le moindre recoin (**b**) *Literary (secluded spot)* retraite *f*; **a shady nook** une retraite ombragée, un coin ombragé

nookie, nooky ['nʊkɪ] *n Fam Hum* partie *f* de jambes en l'air; **to have a bit of nookie** faire une partie de jambes en l'air

noon [nuːn] **1** *n* (**a**) *(midday)* midi *m*; **at twelve**

non–noo

noon à midi; **come at noon** venez à midi (**b**) *Literary (peak)* zénith *m*
2 *comp (break, heat, sun)* de midi
►► *Am* ***noon hour*** heure *f* du déjeuner

noonday ['nu:ndeɪ] **1** *n* midi *m*; *Fig Literary* **he was at the noonday of his prosperity** il était à l'apogée de sa prospérité
2 *comp (break, heat, sun)* de midi

no one, no-one = **nobody**

noontide ['nu:ntaɪd] *n Literary* midi *m*

noontime ['nu:ntaɪm] *n* midi *m*; **the noontime traffic** la circulation à l'heure du déjeuner

noose [nu:s] **1** *n (gen)* nœud *m* coulant; *(snare)* collet *m*; *(lasso)* lasso *m*; **(hangman's) noose** corde *f* (de potence); **to get the noose** être condamné à la potence; **to put one's head in the noose, to put a noose around one's neck** creuser sa (propre) tombe
2 *vt* (**a**) *(rope)* faire un nœud coulant à (**b**) *(snare)* prendre au collet; *(lasso)* attraper *ou* prendre au lasso

no-par *adj Br* sans valeur nominale

nope [nəʊp] *exclam Fam* non ❑, nan

no-place *Am* = **nowhere**

no-quibble guarantee *n* garantie *f* sans conditions

nor [nɔ:(r)] **1** *conj (following "neither", "not")* ni; **neither he nor his wife has ever spoken to me** ni lui ni sa femme ne m'ont jamais adressé la parole; **I have neither the time nor the inclination to do it** je n'ai ni le temps ni l'envie de le faire; **she neither drinks nor smokes** elle ne boit ni ne fume; *Literary* **not a wave, nor even a ripple, disturbed the surface** pas une vague ni même une ride ne troublait la surface
2 *adv* **I don't believe him, nor do I trust him** je ne le crois pas, et je n'ai pas confiance en lui non plus; **it's not the first time, nor will it be the last** ce n'est ni la première ni la dernière fois; **she couldn't see them, nor (could) they (see) her** elle ne les voyait pas, et eux non plus; **I don't like fish – nor do I** je n'aime pas le poisson – moi non plus; **she won't do it and nor will he** elle ne le fera pas et lui non plus; **I haven't read it, nor do I intend to** je ne l'ai pas lu et d'ailleurs je n'en ai pas l'intention; **nor was this all** et ce n'était pas tout

noradrenalin [ˌnɔ:rə'drenəlɪn] *n Chem* noradrénaline *f*

Nordic ['nɔ:dɪk] **1** *n* Nordique *mf*
2 *adj* nordique
►► ***Nordic skiing*** ski *m* nordique

nor'east, nor'-east [nɔ:'ri:st] **1** *n* nord-est *m*; **in the nor'east of Scotland** dans le nord-est de l'Écosse
2 *adj* (**a**) *Geog* nord-est *(inv)*, du nord-est; **in nor'east Scotland** dans le nord-est de l'Écosse (**b**) *(wind)* de nord-est, du nord-est
3 *adv* au nord-est; *(travel)* vers le nord-est, en direction du nord-est; **it's 20 miles nor'east of Birmingham** ≃ c'est à 32 kilomètres au nord-est de Birmingham

nor'easter, nor'-easter [nɔ:'ri:stə(r)] *n* vent *m* de *ou* du nord-est; *Naut* nordé *m*, nordet *m*

nor'easterly, nor'-easterly [nɔ:'ri:stəlɪ] **1** *adj* (**a**) *Geog* nord-est *(inv)*, du nord-est; **to travel in a nor'easterly direction** aller vers le nord-est; *Naut* **to steer a nor'easterly course** faire route vers le nord-est; *(when setting out)* mettre le cap au nord-est (**b**) *(wind)* de nord-est, du nord-est
2 *adv* vers le nord-est, en direction du nord-est
3 *n (pl* **nor'easterlies***)* vent *m* de *ou* du nord-est; *Naut* nordé *m*, nordet *m*

nor'eastern, nor'-eastern [nɔ:'ri:stən] *adj* nord-est *(inv)*, du nord-est; *(wind)* de nord-est, du nord-est; **the nor'eastern suburbs** la banlieue nord-est

no-return *adj Am* sans réserve de retour; *(bottle, container)* non consigné; *(deposit)* non remboursable; *(packaging)* non consigné, perdu

Norf *(written abbr* **Norfolk***)* Norfolk *m*

Norfolk ['nɔ:fək] *n* le Norfolk, = comté dans l'est de l'Angleterre; **in Norfolk** dans le Norfolk
►► ***the Norfolk Broads*** les lacs *mpl* du Norfolk; ***Norfolk jacket*** = veste d'homme à ceinture, portée à l'origine pour la chasse au canard dans le Norfolk

nori ['nɒrɪ, 'nɔ:rɪ] *n* nori *m*

noria ['nɔ:rɪə] *n* noria *f*

nork [nɔ:k] *n Br & Austr very Fam (breast)* nichon *m*

norm [nɔ:m] *n* norme *f*; **to deviate from the norm** s'écarter de la norme; **unemployment has become the norm in certain areas** dans certaines régions, le chômage est devenu la règle; **it's the norm** c'est la règle

normal ['nɔ:məl] **1** *adj* (**a**) *(common, typical, standard)* normal; **a perfectly normal baby** un bébé parfaitement normal; **under normal conditions of use** dans des conditions normales d'utilisation; **this is not normal behaviour** ce n'est pas un comportement normal; *Fam* **he's just a normal kind of bloke** c'est un type tout ce qu'il y a de (plus) banal; **it's normal for it to rain in April** il est normal *ou* naturel qu'il pleuve en avril; **any normal person would have...** toute personne normalement constituée aurait...
(**b**) *(habitual)* habituel, normal; **at the normal time** à l'heure habituelle
(**c**) *Math (in statistics, geometry)* normal
(**d**) *Chem* normal
2 *n* (**a**) *(gen)* normale *f*, état *m* normal; **temperatures above normal** des températures au-dessus de la normale; **to get back to normal** revenir à la normale, rentrer dans l'ordre; **he'll soon be back to normal** tout rentrera bientôt dans l'ordre; *(in health)* il sera bientôt remis sur pied; **things are back to normal again** tout est rentré dans l'ordre; **the situation has returned to normal** la situation est revenue à la normale
(**b**) *Geom* normale *f*
►► ***normal distribution*** distribution *f* normale; ***normal distribution curve*** courbe *f* de distribution normale

normality [nɔ:'mælətɪ], *Am* **normalcy** ['nɔ:məlsɪ] *n* normalité *f*; **everything returned to normality** tout est redevenu normal, tout est rentré dans l'ordre

normalization [ˌnɔ:məlaɪ'zeɪʃən] *n* normalisation *f*

normalize, -ise ['nɔ:məlaɪz] **1** *vt* normaliser
2 *vi* se normaliser, redevenir normal

normally ['nɔ:məlɪ] *adv* (**a**) *(in a normal manner)* normalement; **he's behaving normally** il se comporte normalement (**b**) *(ordinarily)* en temps normal, normalement; **I normally get up at 7.30** en temps normal *ou* normalement, je me lève à 7 heures 30

Norman ['nɔ:mən] **1** *n* (**a**) *(person)* Normand(e) *m,f* (**b**) *Ling* normand *m*
2 *adj* (**a**) *Geog & Hist* normand (**b**) *Archit* roman (anglais)
►► *Hist* ***the Norman Conquest*** la conquête normande *(de l'Angleterre)*; *Ling* ***Norman French*** normand *m*

THE NORMAN CONQUEST

Cette conquête militaire de l'Angleterre par Guillaume le Conquérant fut inaugurée par sa victoire sur le roi Harold à la bataille de Hastings, en 1066. Désormais gouverné et régi par des Normands, le pays subit de grands changements dans les domaines politique et social, se voyant notamment imposer le français comme langue officielle.

Normandy ['nɔ:məndɪ] *n* Normandie *f*; **in Normandy** en Normandie
►► *Hist* ***the Normandy landings*** le débarquement

normative ['nɔ:mətɪv] *adj* normatif

nor'nor'east [nɔ:nɔ:'ri:st] **1** *n* nord-nord-est *m*
2 *adj* (**a**) *Geog* nord-nord-est *(inv)*, du nord-nord-est (**b**) *(wind)* de *ou* du nord-nord-est
3 *adv* au nord-nord-est; *(travel)* vers le nord-nord-est, en direction du nord-nord-est

nor'nor'west [nɔ:nɔ:'west] **1** *n* nord-nord-ouest *m*
2 *adj* (**a**) *Geog* nord-nord-ouest *(inv)*, du nord-nord-ouest (**b**) *(wind)* de *ou* du nord-nord-ouest
3 *adv* au nord-nord-ouest; *(travel)* vers le nord-nord-ouest, en direction du nord-nord-ouest

Norse [nɔ:s] **1** *npl Hist* **the Norse** *(Norwegians)* les Norvégiens *mpl*; *(Vikings)* les Vikings *mpl*
2 *n Ling* norrois *m*, nordique *m*
3 *adj (Scandinavian)* scandinave, nordique; *(Norwegian)* norvégien
►► ***Norse legends*** légendes *fpl* scandinaves; ***Norse mythology*** mythologie *f* scandinave

Norseman ['nɔ:smən] *(pl* **Norsemen** [-mən]*)* *n* Viking *m*

north [nɔ:θ] **1** *n* (**a**) *Geog* nord *m*; **in the north** au nord, dans le nord; **the region to the north of Sydney** la région au nord de Sydney; **two miles to the north** trois kilomètres au nord; **look towards the north** regardez vers le nord; **I was born in the north** je suis né dans le Nord; **in the north of India** dans le nord de l'Inde; **the wind is in the north** le vent est au nord; **the wind is coming from the north** le vent vient *ou* souffle du nord; *Hist* **the North** *(in American Civil War)* = les États antiesclavagistes du nord des États-Unis; *(affluent countries)* le Nord; **the North-South divide** *(in Britain)* = ligne fictive de démarcation, en termes de richesse, entre le nord de l'Angleterre (plus pauvre) et le sud (plus riche); *(in global economy)* fossé *m* Nord-Sud; *SEng Fam* **north and south** *(rhyming slang* **mouth***)* bouche *f*, clapet *m*
(**b**) *Cards* nord *m*
2 *adj* (**a**) *Geog* nord *(inv)*, du nord; *(country, state)* du Nord; *(wall)* exposé au nord; **the north coast** la côte nord; **in north London** dans le nord de Londres; **in North India** en Inde du Nord; **the North Atlantic/Pacific** l'Atlantique *m*/le Pacifique Nord; **the North Atlantic Drift** le Gulf Stream
(**b**) *(wind)* de nord, du nord
3 *adv* au nord; *(travel)* vers le nord, en direction du nord; **the ranch lies north of the town** le ranch est situé au nord de la ville; **this room faces north** cette pièce est exposée au nord; **the trail heads (due) north** le chemin va *ou* mène (droit) vers le nord; **go north until you come to a village** allez vers le nord jusqu'à ce que vous arriviez à un village; **I drove north for two hours** j'ai roulé pendant deux heures en direction du nord; **we're going north for our holidays** nous allons passer nos vacances dans le Nord; **I travelled north** je suis allé vers le nord; **to sail north** naviguer cap sur le nord; **it's 20 miles north of Manchester** c'est à 32 kilomètres au nord de Manchester; **they live up north** ils habitent dans le Nord; **north by east/by west** nord-quart-nord-est/nord-quart-nord-ouest; **further north** plus au nord; **north of Watford** = façon humoristique de désigner la partie nord de l'Angleterre
►► ***North Africa*** Afrique *f* du Nord; **in North Africa** en Afrique du Nord; ***North African*** **1** *n* Nord-Africain(e) *m,f* **2** *adj* nord-africain, d'Afrique du Nord; ***North America*** Amérique *f* du Nord; ***North American*** **1** *n* Nord-Américain(e) *m,f* **2** *adj* nord-américain, d'Amérique du Nord; ***the North American Indians*** les Indiens *mpl* d'Amérique du Nord; *Econ* ***North American Free Trade Agreement*** Accord *m* de libre-échange nord-américain; ***the North Cape*** le cap Nord; ***North Carolina*** la Caroline du Nord; **in North Carolina** en Caroline du Nord; ***the North Circular*** = voie périphérique rapide au nord de Londres; ***the North Country*** *(in England)* l'Angleterre *f* du Nord; *(in America)* = l'Alaska, le Yukon et les Territoires du Nord-Ouest; **he's got a North Country accent** il a un accent du Nord; ***North Dakota*** le Dakota du Nord; **in North Dakota** dans le Dakota du Nord; ***the North Downs*** = région de collines calcaires au sud de Londres; ***North Island*** l'île *f* du Nord; **in (the) North Island** à l'île du Nord; ***North Korea*** Corée *f* du Nord; ***North Korean*** **1** *n* Nord-Coréen(enne) *m,f* **2** *adj* nord-coréen; ***the North Pole*** le pôle Nord; ***North Rhine-Westphalia*** Rhénanie-du-Nord-Westphalie *f*; **in North Rhine-Westphalia** en Rhénanie-du-Nord-Westphalie; ***North Sea, the North Sea*** la mer du Nord; ***the North Star*** l'étoile *f* Polaire; ***the North Star State*** = surnom donné au Minnesota; ***North Vietnam*** Nord Viêt Nam *m*; **in North Vietnam** au Nord Viêt Nam; ***North Vietnamese*** **1** *n* Nord-Vietnamien(enne) *m,f* **2** *adj* nord-vietnamien; ***North Wales*** nord *m* du pays de Galles; ***North Walian*** **1** *n* habitant(e) *m,f* du nord du pays de Galles **2** *adj* du nord du pays de Galles; ***North Yemen*** Yémen *m* du Nord; **in North Yemen** au

Yémen du Nord; ***North Yorkshire*** le North Yorkshire, = comté dans le nord-est de l'Angleterre; **in North Yorkshire** dans le North Yorkshire

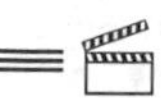

'North by Northwest' *Hitchcock* 'La Mort aux trousses'

Northamptonshire [nɔː'θæmptən,ʃɪə(r)] *n* le Northamptonshire, = comté dans le centre de l'Angleterre; **in Northamptonshire** dans le Northamptonshire

Northants *(written abbr* **Northamptonshire**) Northamptonshire *m*

northbound ['nɔːθbaʊnd] *adj (traffic)* en direction du nord; *(lane, carriageway)* du nord; *(road)* vers le nord; **northbound traffic is subject to delays** la circulation est ralentie dans le sens nord; *Br* **the northbound carriageway of the motorway is closed** l'axe nord de l'autoroute est fermé (à la circulation); **there are roadworks on the northbound carriageway of the motorway** il y a des travaux sur l'autoroute en direction du nord; **there's a jam on the northbound carriageway** il y a un bouchon en direction du nord

north-countryman *(pl* **north-countrymen** [-mən]) *n* Anglais *m* du Nord

Northd *(written abbr* **Northumberland**) Northumberland *m*

north-east 1 *n* nord-est *m*; **in the north-east of Scotland** dans le nord-est de l'Écosse

2 *adj* (**a**) *Geog* nord-est *(inv)*, du nord-est; **in north-east Scotland** dans le nord-est de l'Écosse

(**b**) *(wind)* de nord-est, du nord-est

3 *adv* au nord-est; *(travel)* vers le nord-est, en direction du nord-est; **it's 20 miles north-east of Birmingham** c'est à 32 kilomètres au nord-est de Birmingham

►► ***the North-east Corridor*** = zone fortement peuplée entre Boston et Washington

north-easter [-'iːstə(r)] *n* vent *m* de *ou* du nord-est; *Naut* nordé *m*, nordet *m*

north-easterly *(pl* **north-easterlies**) **1** *adj* (**a**) *Geog* nord-est *(inv)*, du nord-est; **to travel in a north-easterly direction** aller vers le nord-est; *Naut* **to steer a north-easterly course** faire route vers le nord-est; *(when setting out)* mettre le cap au nord-est (**b**) *(wind)* de nord-est, du nord-est

2 *adv* vers le nord-est, en direction du nord-est

3 *n* vent *m* de *ou* du nord-est; *Naut* nordé *m*, nordet *m*

north-eastern *adj* nord-est *(inv)*, du nord-est; *(wind)* de nord-est, du nord-est; **the north-eastern suburbs** la banlieue nord-est

north-eastward 1 *adj* vers le nord-est, en direction du nord-est

2 *adv* vers le nord-est, en direction du nord-est; **to sail north-eastward** naviguer cap sur le nord-est

3 *n* nord-est *m*

north-eastwardly 1 *adj* du nord-est

2 *adv* vers le nord-est, en direction du nord-est

north-eastwards *adv* vers le nord-est, en direction du nord-est; **to sail north-eastwards** naviguer cap sur le nord-est

norther ['nɔːðə(r)] *n Naut* fort vent *m* de *ou* du nord

northerly ['nɔːðəlɪ] *(pl* **northerlies**) **1** *adj* (**a**) *Geog* nord *(inv)*, du nord; **to travel in a northerly direction** aller vers le nord; **northerly point** point *m* situé au nord *ou* vers le nord; **the most northerly point of the United States** le point situé le plus au nord des États-Unis; **a room with a northerly aspect** une pièce exposée au nord; *Naut* **to steer a northerly course** faire route vers le nord; *(when setting out)* mettre le cap au nord; **in these northerly latitudes** sous ces latitudes boréales

(**b**) *(wind)* de nord, du nord

2 *adv* vers le nord, en direction du nord

3 *n* vent *m* de *ou* du nord

northern ['nɔːðən] *adj* (**a**) *Geog* nord *(inv)*, du nord; **she has a northern accent** elle a un accent du nord; **the northern wing of the castle** l'aile nord du château; **in northern Mexico** dans le nord du Mexique; **the northern migration of swallows in spring** la migration printanière des hirondelles vers le nord

(**b**) *(wind)* de nord, du nord

(**c**) *Hist (in American Civil War)* nordiste

►► ***northern hemisphere*** l'hémisphère *m* nord *ou* boréal; ***Northern Ireland*** Irlande *f* du Nord; **in Northern Ireland** en Irlande du Nord; ***Northern Ireland Assembly*** Assemblée *f* législative d'Irlande du Nord; ***northern lights*** aurore *f* boréale; *Am Orn* ***northern shrike*** pie-grièche *f* grise; *Geog* ***Northern Territory*** le Territoire du Nord; **in Northern Territory** dans le Territoire du Nord; ***northern tribes*** tribus *fpl* du nord

NORTHERN IRELAND

L'Irlande du Nord désigne la partie de l'Irlande à majorité protestante restée rattachée à la Grande-Bretagne lors de la partition du pays, en 1921. Les émeutes sanglantes qui ont éclaté à Belfast et à Londonderry en 1969 à la suite de manifestations revendiquant l'égalité des droits pour la minorité catholique ont marqué le début de trente ans de conflit entre catholiques et protestants en Irlande du Nord. Ce conflit vit s'affronter les nationalistes de l'IRA, favorables à un rattachement avec la République d'Irlande, différents groupes paramilitaires protestants anti-catholiques, et l'armée et la police, sous contrôle britannique. Le processus de paix, amorcé en 1994 et qui aboutit au **Good Friday Agreement** (voir encadré à l'entrée "good") de 1998, marqua une nouvelle étape plus optimiste dans l'histoire de l'Irlande du Nord.

Northerner, northerner ['nɔːðənə(r)] *n* (**a**) *(gen)* habitant (e) *m,f* du Nord; **she is a northerner** elle vient du Nord (**b**) *Hist (in American Civil War)* nordiste *mf*

Northernism ['nɔːðənɪzəm] *n Br* = particularité linguistique (de l'anglais) du Nord

northernmost ['nɔːðənməʊst] *adj* le plus au nord; **the northernmost island of Japan** l'île du Japon la plus au nord; **the northernmost limits of the Roman Empire** les limites septentrionales de l'Empire romain

north-facing *adj Br (house, wall)* (exposé) au nord

northing ['nɔːðɪŋ] *n Naut* chemin *m* nord

Northman ['nɔːθmən] *(pl* **Northmen** [-mən]) *n Br* Viking *m*

northmost ['nɔːθməʊst] *adj* le plus au nord

north-north-east 1 *n* nord-nord-est *m*

2 *adj* (**a**) *Geog* nord-nord-est *(inv)*, du nord-nord-est (**b**) *(wind)* de *ou* du nord-nord-est

3 *adv* au nord-nord-est; *(travel)* vers le nord-nord-est, en direction du nord-nord-est

north-north-west 1 *n* nord-nord-ouest *m*

2 *adj* (**a**) *Geog* nord-nord-ouest *(inv)*, du nord-nord-ouest (**b**) *(wind)* de *ou* du nord-nord-ouest

3 *adv* au nord-nord-ouest; *(travel)* vers le nord-nord-ouest, en direction du nord-nord-ouest

Northumb *(written abbr* **Northumberland**) Northumberland *m*

Northumberland [nɔː'θʌmbələnd] *n* le Northumberland, = comté dans le nord-est de l'Angleterre; **in Northumberland** dans le Northumberland

Northumbria [nɔː'θʌmbrɪə] *n* Northumbrie *f*

Northumbrian [nɔː'θʌmbrɪən] **1** *n Geog* habitant(e) *m,f* du Northumberland; *Hist* habitant(e) *m,f* de la Northumbrie

2 *adj Geog* du Northumberland; *Hist* northumbrien, de la Northumbrie

northward ['nɔːθwəd] **1** *adj* vers le nord, en direction du nord

2 *adv* vers le nord, en direction du nord; **to sail northward** naviguer cap sur le nord

3 *n* nord *m*

northwardly ['nɔːθwədlɪ] **1** *adj* du nord

2 *adv* vers le nord, en direction du nord

northwards ['nɔːθwədz] *adv* vers le nord, en direction du nord; **to sail northwards** naviguer cap sur le nord

north-west 1 *n* nord-ouest *m*; **in the north-west of Canada** dans le nord-ouest du Canada

2 *adj* (**a**) *Geog* nord-ouest *(inv)*, du nord-ouest; **in north-west Canada** dans le nord-ouest du Canada

(**b**) *(wind)* de nord-ouest, du nord-ouest

3 *adv* au nord-ouest; *(travel)* vers le nord-ouest, en direction du nord-ouest; **it's 20 miles north-west of London** ≃ c'est à 32 kilomètres au nord-ouest de Londres

►► ***North-west Passage*** passage *m* du Nord-Ouest; ***the North-west Territories*** les Territoires *mpl* du Nord-Ouest; **in the North-west Territories** dans les Territoires du Nord-Ouest

north-wester [-'westə(r)] *n* vent *m* de *ou* du nord-ouest; *Naut* noroît *m*

north-westerly *(pl* **northwesterlies**) **1** *adj* (**a**) *Geog* nord-ouest *(inv)*, du nord-ouest; **to travel in a north-westerly direction** aller vers le nord-ouest; *Naut* **to steer a north-westerly course** faire route vers le nord-ouest; *(when setting out)* mettre le cap au nord-ouest (**b**) *(wind)* de nord-ouest, du nord-ouest

2 *adv* vers le nord-ouest, en direction du nord-ouest

3 *n* vent *m* de *ou* du nord-ouest; *Naut* noroît *m*

north-western *adj* nord-ouest *(inv)*, du nord-ouest; **the north-western frontier** la frontière nord-ouest

north-westward 1 *adj* vers le nord-ouest, en direction du nord-ouest

2 *adv* vers le nord-ouest, en direction du nord-ouest; **to sail north-westward** naviguer cap sur le nord-ouest

3 *n* nord-ouest *m*

north-westwardly 1 *adj* du nord-ouest

2 *adv* vers le nord-ouest, en direction du nord-ouest

north-westwards *adv* vers le nord-ouest, en direction du nord-ouest; **to sail north-westwards** naviguer cap sur le nord-ouest

Norway ['nɔːweɪ] *n* Norvège *f*; **in Norway** en Norvège

►► ***Norway lobster*** langoustine *f*; ***Norway rat*** surmulot *m*; ***Norway spruce*** épicéa *m* d'Europe

Norwegian [nɔː'wiːdʒən] **1** *n* (**a**) *(person)* Norvégien(enne) *m,f* (**b**) *(language)* norvégien *m*

2 *adj* norvégien

3 *comp (embassy)* de Norvège; *(history)* de la Norvège; *(teacher)* de norvégien

nor'west, nor'-west [nɔː'west] **1** *n* nord-ouest *m*; **in the nor'west of Canada** dans le nord-ouest du Canada

2 *adj* (**a**) *Geog* nord-ouest *(inv)*, du nord-ouest; **in nor'west Canada** dans le nord-ouest du Canada

(**b**) *(wind)* de nord-ouest, du nord-ouest

3 *adv* au nord-ouest; *(travel)* vers le nord-ouest, en direction du nord-ouest; **it's 20 miles nor'west of London** c'est à 32 kilomètres au nord-ouest de Londres

nor'wester, nor'-wester [nɔː'westə(r)] *n* vent *m* de *ou* du nord-ouest; *Naut* noroît *m*

nor'westerly, nor'-westerly [nɔː'westəlɪ] **1** *adj* (**a**) *Geog* nord-ouest *(inv)*, du nord-ouest; **to travel in a nor'westerly direction** aller vers le nord-ouest; *Naut* **to steer a nor'westerly course** faire route vers le nord-ouest; *(when setting out)* mettre le cap au nord-ouest (**b**) *(wind)* de nord-ouest, du nord-ouest

2 *adv* vers le nord-ouest, en direction du nord-ouest

3 *n* *(pl* **nor'westerlies**) vent *m* de *ou* du nord-ouest; *Naut* noroît *m*

nor'western, nor'-western [nɔː'westən] *adj* nord-ouest *(inv)*, du nord-ouest; **the nor'western frontier** la frontière nord-ouest

Nos., nos. *(written abbr* **numbers**) no

nose [nəʊz] **1** *n* (**a**) *(part of body)* nez *m*; **to hold one's nose** se pincer le nez; **the dog has a wet nose** le chien a le nez *ou* la truffe humide; **your nose is bleeding** tu saignes du nez; **your nose is running** tu as le nez qui coule; **to speak through one's nose** parler du nez; **I punched him on** *or* **in the nose** je lui ai donné un coup de poing en pleine figure; **she's always got her nose in a book** elle a toujours le nez dans un livre; *Horseracing* **the favourite won by a nose** le favori a gagné d'une demi-tête; *Horseracing* **I'll have £10 on the nose** je parie 10 livres qu'il va gagner

(**b**) *(sense of smell)* odorat *m*, nez *m*; **these dogs have an excellent nose** ces chiens ont un

nor–nos

excellent flair *ou* le nez fin; *Fig* **she's got a (good) nose for a bargain** elle a le nez creux *ou* du nez pour dénicher les bonnes affaires

(**c**) *(aroma → of wine)* arôme *m*, bouquet *m*, nez *m*

(**d**) *(forward part → of aircraft, ship)* nez *m*; *(→ of car)* avant *m*; *(→ of bullet, missile, tool)* pointe *f*; *(→ of gun)* canon *m*; *Br* **the traffic was nose to tail all the way to London** les voitures étaient pare-chocs contre pare-chocs jusqu'à Londres

(**e**) *Fam (snoop)* **to have a nose around** faire un tour d'inspection ❑

(**f**) *(idioms)* **look, it's right under your nose!** regarde, il est juste sous ton nez *ou* tu as le nez dessus!; **it was (right) under my nose all the time** c'était en plein sous mon nez; *Fig* **they stole it from under the nose of the police** ils l'ont volé au nez et à la barbe de la police; **he can see no further than (the end of) his nose** il ne voit pas plus loin que le bout de son nez; *Br Fam* **to get up sb's nose** taper sur les nerfs à qn; *Fam* **he really gets** *or* **he gets right up my nose** il me tape sur les nerfs, il me pompe l'air; **you've got** *or* **hit it right on the nose** tu as mis en plein dans le mille; **to keep one's nose clean** se tenir à carreau; **try and keep your nose clean** tu ferais bien de te tenir peinard; **keep your (big) nose out of my business!** mêle-toi de ce qui te regarde!; **to keep** *or* **to have one's nose to the grindstone** bosser (dur); **to keep sb's nose to the grindstone** faire bosser *ou* trimer qn; **to lead sb by the nose** mener qn par le bout du nez; **to look down one's nose at sb/sth** traiter qn/qch avec condescendance; **to pay through the nose (for sth)** payer (qch) la peau des fesses; *Br Fam* **to put sb's nose out of joint** contrarier *ou* dépiter qn ❑; *Fam* **he's always sticking** *or* **poking his nose in** il faut qu'il fourre son nez partout; *Fam* **she's always sticking** *or* **poking her nose into our affairs** elle est toujours en train de fourrer son nez dans nos affaires; **to turn up one's nose at sth** faire la fine bouche devant qch; **that's cutting off your nose to spite your face** c'est toi le perdant; **he's always walking around with his nose in the air** il prend toujours un air hautain *ou* méprisant

2 *vt* (**a**) *(smell)* flairer, renifler

(**b**) *(push with nose)* pousser du nez; **the dog nosed the door open** le chien a ouvert la porte en la poussant du nez

3 *vi* (**a**) *(advance with care)* avancer précautionneusement; **the car nosed out into the traffic** la voiture se frayait un chemin au milieu des embouteillages

(**b**) *Fam (snoop)* fouiner; **to nose through sb's papers** fouiner *ou* mettre son nez dans les papiers de qn

▸▸ *Fam Drugs slang* ***nose candy*** *(cocaine)* coco *f*, neige *f*; ***nose cone*** *(of missile)* ogive *f*; *(of aircraft)* nez *m*; ***nose drops*** gouttes *fpl* nasales *ou* pour le nez; *Fam* ***nose job*** intervention *f* de chirurgie esthétique sur le nez ❑; **she's had a nose job** elle s'est fait refaire le nez; ***nose ring*** anneau *m* de nez; ***nose wheel*** roue *f* avant

▸**nose about, nose around** *vi Fam (snoop)* fureter, fouiner; **two men came nosing about for information** deux hommes sont venus fouiner pour avoir des renseignements; **I don't want them nosing about in here!** je ne veux pas qu'ils viennent fourrer leur nez ici!

▸**nose out** *vt sep* (**a**) *(discover → by smell)* flairer; *(→ by cunning, intuition)* dénicher, débusquer

(**b**) *Fam (beat narrowly)* battre d'une courte tête ❑; **he was nosed out of first place by an outsider** un outsider lui a soufflé la première place d'une courte tête

nosebag ['nəʊzbæg] *n (for horse)* musette *f*

noseband ['nəʊzbænd] *n (of bridle)* muserolle *f*

nosebleed ['nəʊzbli:d] *n* saignement *m* de nez, *Spec* épistaxis *f*; **I've got a nosebleed** je saigne du nez; **do you often get nosebleeds?** est-ce que vous saignez souvent du nez?

-nosed [nəʊzd] *suff* **red-nosed** au nez rouge

nosedive ['nəʊzdaɪv] **1** *n* (**a**) *(of plane, bird)* piqué *m*; **I did a nosedive onto the concrete** je suis tombé la tête la première sur le béton (**b**) *Fam Fig (sharp drop)* chute ❑ *f*, dégringolade *f*; **prices took a nosedive** les prix ont considérablement chuté; **his popularity has taken a nosedive** sa cote de popularité s'est littéralement effondrée ❑

2 *vi* (**a**) *(plane)* piquer, descendre en piqué (**b**) *Fig (drop sharply → prices, popularity)* chuter, dégringoler

no-see-um *n Am Fam* culicoïde ❑ *m*, *Can* brûlot ❑ *m*

nosegay ['nəʊzgeɪ] *n Literary* (petit) bouquet *m*

nosepiece ['nəʊzpi:s] *n* (**a**) *(of bridle)* muserolle *f* (**b**) *(of spectacles)* pont *m* (**c**) *(of microscope)* porte-objectifs *m* (**d**) *(of armour)* nasal *m*

noserag ['nəʊzræg] *n Br Fam (handkerchief)* tire-jus *m*

nose-to-tail *adj (traffic)* pare-chocs contre pare-chocs

nosey = **nosy**

nosh [nɒʃ] *Fam Old-fashioned* **1** *n* bouffe *f*

2 *vi* bouffer

no-show *n (for flight, voyage)* = passager qui ne se présente pas à l'embarquement; *(for show)* = spectateur qui a réservé sa place et qui n'assiste pas au spectacle; **there were so many no-shows that they cancelled the flight** il y a eu tellement de défections que le vol a été annulé

nosh-up *n Br Fam Old-fashioned* gueuleton *m*

no-side *n (in rugby)* fin *f* du match

nosily ['nəʊzɪlɪ] *adv Fam* indiscrètement ❑

nosiness ['nəʊzɪnɪs] *n Fam* curiosité ❑ *f*, indiscrétion ❑ *f*; **his nosiness really annoys me** il m'agace sérieusement à fourrer son nez partout

no-smoking *adj (carriage, area)* non-fumeurs; *(seat)* non-fumeur

nosocomial [nɒsəʊ'kəʊmɪəl] *adj Med* nosocomial

nosography [nɒ'sɒgrəfɪ] (*pl* **nosographies**) *n Med* nosographie *f*

nosological [,nɒsə'lɒdʒɪkəl] *adj Med* nosologique

nosologist [nɒ'sɒlədʒɪst] *n Med* nosologiste *mf*

nosology [nɒ'sɒlədʒɪ] *n Med* nosologie *f*

nostalgia [nɒ'stældʒə] *n* nostalgie *f*

nostalgic [nɒ'stældʒɪk] *adj* nostalgique; **to be** *or* **feel nostalgic for sth** avoir la nostalgie de qch

nostalgically [nɒs'tældʒɪkəlɪ] *adv* avec nostalgie, nostalgiquement

nostoc ['nɒstɒk] *n Biol* nostoc *m*, nodulaire *f*

Nostradamus [,nɒstrə'dɑ:məs] *pr n* Nostradamus

nostril ['nɒstrɪl] *n (gen)* narine *f*; *(of horse, cow etc)* naseau *m*

no-strings *adj Fam (contract, agreement)* sans pièges ❑

nostrum ['nɒstrəm] *n also Fig* panacée *f*

no-sweat *adj Am Fam (easy → exam, question)* fastoche

nosy ['nəʊzɪ] (*compar* **nosier**, *superl* **nosiest**) *adj Fam* curieux ❑, indiscret(ète) ❑; **don't be so nosy!** occupe-toi donc de tes affaires *ou* de tes oignons!; **he's very nosy** il fourre son nez partout; **I didn't mean to be nosy** je ne voulais pas être indiscret

▸▸ *Br Fam Pej* ***nosy parker*** fouine *f*

NOT [nɒt]

ne... pas	▸ (a), (b), (e), (g)
non	▸ (c), (e)
pas	▸ (c), (d), (g)
moins de	▸ (f)

À l'oral, et à l'écrit dans un style familier, on utilise généralement **not** à la forme contractée lorsqu'il suit un modal ou un auxiliaire. (**don't go!**; **she wasn't there**; **he couldn't see me**).

adv (**a**) *(after verb or auxiliary)* ne... pas; **we are not** *or* **aren't sure** nous ne sommes pas sûrs; **do not** *or* **don't believe her** ne la croyez pas; **didn't he** *or* **did he not hear you?** ne vous a-t-il pas entendu?; **is she coming? – no, she isn't** *or* **she's not** est-ce qu'elle vient? – non(, elle ne vient pas); **you've been there already, haven't you** *or Formal* **have you not?** vous y êtes déjà allé, non *ou* n'est-ce pas?; **not wishing to be seen, I drew the curtain** comme je ne désirais pas être vu, j'ai tiré le rideau

(**b**) *(with infinitive)* ne... pas; **I'll try not to cry** j'essaierai de ne pas pleurer; **I asked them not to do it** je leur ai demandé de ne pas le faire; **they were annoyed, not to say furious** ils étaient ennuyés, pour ne pas dire furieux

(**c**) *(as phrase or clause substitute)* non, pas; **we hope not** nous espérons que non; **are there any left? – I'm afraid not** est-ce qu'il en reste? – j'ai bien peur que non; *Formal* **will it rain? – I think not** est-ce qu'il va pleuvoir? – je crois que non *ou* je ne crois pas; **whether they like it or not** que ça leur plaise ou non *ou* ou pas; **not if I've got anything to do with it** pas si j'ai mon mot à dire

(**d**) *(with adjective, adverb, noun)* pas; **it's Thomas, not Jake** c'est Thomas, pas Jake; **the water is green, not blue** l'eau est verte, pas bleue; **not guilty** non coupable; **he is respected but not loved** il est respecté mais (non) pas aimé; **not a leaf stirred** pas une feuille ne bougeait; **not a word was spoken** on n'a pas dit un mot; **not all her books are good** ses livres ne sont pas tous bons, tous ses livres ne sont pas bons; **not everyone would agree with you** tout le monde ne serait pas d'accord avec toi; **who wants some more? – not me** qui en veut encore? – pas moi; *Formal* **not I** pas moi; **not any more** *or* **longer** plus maintenant; **not so** pas du tout

(**e**) *(in double negatives)* **not without some difficulty** non sans quelque difficulté; **a not insignificant amount of money** une somme non négligeable; **it's not unusual for him to be late** il n'est pas rare qu'il soit en retard; **the two events are not unconnected** les deux événements ne sont pas tout à fait indépendants l'un de l'autre

(**f**) *(less than)* moins de; **not five minutes later the phone rang** moins de cinq minutes plus tard, le téléphone a sonné; **not ten metres away** à moins de dix mètres

(**g**) **not that...** ce n'est pas que... + *subjunctive*, non (pas) que... + *subjunctive*; **not that I can remember** pas autant que je m'en souvienne

(**h**) *Arch or Literary (following the verb)* **I know not** je ne sais point

(**i**) *Fam Hum* **it was a great party, not!** c'était pas vraiment génial comme soirée!; **he's really gorgeous, not!** c'est pas exactement un Apollon!; **she really has a nice dress – not!** quelle belle robe elle a – façon de parler! *ou* faut pas être difficile!

Not!

Le film américain *Wayne's World* (1992), avec Mike Myers dans le rôle principal, est à l'origine de plusieurs expressions d'usage courant. La plus célèbre d'entre elles est sans doute le mot **not** utilisé de façon exclamative et sur le mode ironique pour exprimer exactement le contraire de ce que l'on vient de dire (voir la catégorie (**i**)).

notability [,nəʊtə'bɪlətɪ] (*pl* **notabilities**) *n* (**a**) *(importance)* importance *f* (**b**) *(important person)* notabilité *f*, notable *m*

notable ['nəʊtəbəl] **1** *adj (thing)* notable, remarquable; *(person)* notable, éminent; **it is notable that...** il faut noter que...; **with a few notable exceptions** à part quelques exceptions notables; **notable progress has been made** des progrès notables ont été accomplis; **the film was notable for its lack of violence** le film se distinguait par l'absence de scènes de violence

2 *n* notable *m*

notably ['nəʊtəblɪ] *adv* (**a**) *(particularly)* notamment, en particulier; **several officials were absent, notably the mayor** il manquait plusieurs personnalités, notamment le maire (**b**) *(markedly)* manifestement, de toute évidence

notaphily [nəʊ'tæfɪlɪ] *n* billetophilie *f*

notarial [nəʊ'teərɪəl] *adj (procedure, stamp)* notarial; *(deed)* notarié

notarize, -ise ['nəʊtəraɪz] *vt* certifier, authentifier

▸▸ ***notarized copy*** ≃ copie *f* certifiée conforme *(par un notaire)*; ***notarized deed*** acte *m* notarié

notary ['nəʊtərɪ] (*pl* **notaries**) *n* **notary (public)** notaire *m*; **signed in the presence of a notary** signé par-devant notaire

notation [nəʊ'teɪʃən] *n* (**a**) *(sign system)* notation *f*; **musical notation** notation *f* musicale; **mathematical notation** symboles *mpl* mathématiques;

in binary notation en numération binaire, en base 2 (**b**) *Am (jotting)* notation *f*, note *f*

notch [nɒtʃ] **1** *n* (**a**) *(cut → in stick)* entaille *f*, encoche *f*; *(hole → in belt, rack)* cran *m*; *(of toothed wheel)* cran *m*, dent *f*; *(in blade)* brèche *f*; *Sewing* cran *m*; *(in diskette)* encoche *f*; **he let out/took in his belt a notch** il a desserré/resserré sa ceinture d'un cran; *Fig* **a notch on the bedpost** une conquête

(**b**) *(degree)* cran *m*; **he's gone up a notch in my estimation** il est monté d'un cran dans mon estime; **turn the heating up a notch** monte un peu le chauffage; **her novel is a notch above the rest** son roman est meilleur que les autres

(**c**) *Am (gorge)* défilé *m*

2 *vt* (**a**) *(make cut in → stick)* entailler, encocher; *(→ gear wheel)* cranter, denteler; *(damage → blade)* ébrécher

(**b**) *Fig (point)* marquer; *(victory)* remporter

▸**notch up** *vt sep (point)* marquer; *(victory)* remporter; **they've notched up six wins in a row** ils ont six victoires consécutives à leur palmarès

NOTE [nəʊt]

note	▸ **1 (a), (c), (d), (f), (g), (h)**
mot	▸ **1 (b)**
billet (de banque)	▸ **1 (e), (i)**
ton	▸ **1 (f)**
remarquer	▸ **2 (a), (c)**
noter	▸ **2 (a), (b)**
observer	▸ **2 (c)**

1 *n* (**a**) *(record, reminder)* note *f*; **to take** *or* **to make notes** prendre des notes; **she spoke from/without notes** elle a parlé en s'aidant/sans s'aider de notes; **make a note of everything you spend** notez toutes vos dépenses; *Fig* **I must make a note to myself to ask her about it** il faut que je pense à le lui demander; **he made a mental note to look for it later** il se promit de le chercher plus tard; **they have no note of any such meeting** ils n'ont aucune trace de cette réunion; *Fig* **to compare notes** échanger ses impressions; *Univ* **lecture notes** notes *fpl* (de cours)

(**b**) *(short letter)* mot *m*; **she left a note to say she'd call back later** elle a laissé un mot pour dire qu'elle repasserait plus tard

(**c**) *(formal communication)* note *f*; **diplomatic note** note *f* diplomatique; **a doctor's** *or* **sick note** un certificat *ou* une attestation du médecin (traitant); *Sch* un certificat (médical)

(**d**) *(annotation, commentary)* note *f*, annotation *f*; **notes in the margin** notes *fpl* dans la *ou* en marge; **editor's note** note *f* de la rédaction; **see note 6** voir note 6; **programme notes** notes *fpl* sur le programme

(**e**) *Br (banknote)* billet *m* (de banque); **ten pound note** billet *m* de dix livres

(**f**) *(sound, tone)* ton *m*, note *f*; *Fig (feeling, quality)* note *f*; **the piercing note of the siren** le son strident de la sirène; **there was a note of contempt in her voice** il y avait du mépris dans sa voix; **the meeting began on a promising note** la réunion débuta sur une note optimiste; **on a more serious/a happier note** pour parler de choses plus sérieuses/plus gaies; **the flowers add a note of colour** les fleurs apportent une touche de couleur; **her speech struck a warning note** son discours était un signal d'alarme; **to strike the right/a false note** *(speech)* sonner juste/faux; *(behaviour)* être/ne pas être dans le ton; *Literary* **to sound the note of war** parler de guerre

(**g**) *Mus* note *f*; *Br (piano key)* touche *f*; **to hit a high note** sortir un aigu; **the black notes** les touches *fpl* noires

(**h**) *(notice, attention)* **to take note of sth** prendre (bonne) note de qch

(**i**) *Com* **(promissory) note, note of hand** billet *m* à ordre

2 *vt* (**a**) *(observe, notice)* remarquer, noter; **he noted that the window was open** il remarqua que la fenêtre était ouverte; **we have noted several omissions** nous avons relevé plusieurs oublis; **note that she didn't actually refuse** notez (bien) qu'elle n'a pas vraiment refusé; **please note that payment is now due** veuillez effectuer le règlement dans les plus brefs délais; **it should be noted that...** il est à noter que...

(**b**) *(write down)* noter, écrire; **I noted her address** j'ai noté son adresse; **all sales are noted in this book** toutes les ventes sont enregistrées *ou* consignées dans ce carnet

(**c**) *(mention)* (faire) remarquer *ou* observer; **as I noted earlier** comme je l'ai fait remarquer précédemment

3 of note *adj* **a musician of note** un musicien éminent *ou* renommé; **a musician of some note** un musicien d'une certaine renommée; **everyone of note was there** tous les gens importants *ou* qui comptent étaient là; **nothing of note has happened** il ne s'est rien passé d'important, aucun événement majeur ne s'est produit; **we have achieved little of note** nous n'avons pas fait grand-chose d'important

▸▸ *Fin* ***note issue*** émission *f* fiduciaire; ***note issue facility*** autorisation *f* d'émettre les billets de banque

▸**note down** *vt sep (write down)* noter, écrire; **I'd better note down your e-mail address** je vais prendre votre adresse électronique

notebook [ˈnəʊtbʊk] *n* carnet *m*, calepin *m*; *Sch* cahier *m*, carnet *m*; *Comput* agenda *m*

▸▸ ***notebook (computer)*** portable *m*, ordinateur *m* bloc-notes

notecase [ˈnəʊtkeɪs] *n Br Old-fashioned* portefeuille *m*

noted [ˈnəʊtɪd] *adj (person)* éminent, célèbre; *(place, object)* réputé, célèbre; *(fact, idea)* reconnu; **to be noted for one's integrity** être connu pour son intégrité; **he's not noted for his subtlety** il ne passe pas pour quelqu'un de particulièrement subtil; **a city noted as a centre of culture** une ville réputée pour sa vie culturelle; **a region noted for its lakes** une région réputée *ou* connue pour ses lacs

notelet [ˈnəʊtlɪt] *n Br* carte-lettre *f*

notepad [ˈnəʊtpæd] *n (for notes)* bloc-notes *m*; *(for letters)* bloc *m* de papier à lettres

▸▸ ***notepad computer*** ardoise *f* électronique

notepaper [ˈnəʊtpeɪpə(r)] *n* papier *m* à lettres

note-taking *n* prise *f* de notes

noteworthiness [ˈnəʊtˌwɜːðɪnɪs] *n* importance *f*

noteworthy [ˈnəʊtˌwɜːðɪ] *adj* notable, remarquable; **it is noteworthy that...** il convient de noter que...

not-for-profit *adj Am* à but non lucratif

▸▸ ***not-for-profit organization*** société *f* à but non lucratif

NOTHING [ˈnʌθɪŋ] **1** *pron* ne... rien; **she forgets nothing** elle n'oublie rien; **nothing has been decided** rien n'a été décidé; **nothing can beat French cooking** il n'y a rien de mieux que la cuisine française; **I have nothing to drink** je n'ai rien à boire; **what are you doing? – nothing** que faites-vous? – rien; **it's better than nothing** c'est mieux que rien; **to have nothing to do with sb/sth** n'avoir rien à voir avec qn/qch; **it's got nothing to do with you** ça ne te concerne absolument pas; **I told them nothing at all** je ne leur ai rien dit du tout; **I have nothing else to say** je n'ai rien d'autre à dire; **it looks like nothing on earth** c'est ridicule; **nothing serious** rien de grave; **that's nothing new** ce n'est pas nouveau; **that's nothing unusual** cela n'a rien d'anormal; **there's nothing exceptional about him arriving late** il n'y a rien d'exceptionnel à ce qu'il arrive en retard; **nothing much** pas grand-chose; **there is nothing more to be said** il n'y a plus rien à dire; **nothing could be simpler** rien de plus simple, c'est tout ce qu'il y a de plus simple; **they're always fighting over nothing** ils passent leur temps à se disputer pour des broutilles *ou* des riens; **she gets angry about nothing** elle se fâche pour un rien; **reduced to nothing** réduit à néant; **you can't live on nothing** on ne peut pas vivre de rien; **there's nothing to cry/worry about** il n'y a pas de quoi pleurer/s'inquiéter; **there's nothing for it but to start again** il n'y a plus qu'à recommencer; **there's nothing in it** *(no difference)* il n'y a aucune différence; *(in choosing between two candidates)* ils se valent, il n'y a aucune différence entre eux; *(in race)* ils sont à égalité; **there's nothing in** *or* **to these rumours** ces rumeurs sont dénuées de tout fondement; **there's nothing to it!** *(it's easy)* c'est simple (comme bonjour)!; **there's nothing like a nice hot bath** rien de tel qu'un bon bain chaud; **she says he's nothing** *or* **he means nothing to her** elle dit qu'il n'est rien pour elle; **the name means nothing to me** le nom ne me dit rien; **a thousand pounds is nothing to her** mille livres, ce n'est rien pour elle; **it's nothing to me either way** cela m'est égal; **that's nothing to what mum will say** ce n'est rien par rapport à ce que maman va dire; **in those days it was nothing to see...** en ce temps-là on voyait facilement...; **to think nothing of doing sth** *(not hesitate to do)* ne pas hésiter à faire qch; **she thinks nothing of walking 10 kilometres** pour elle 10 kilomètres à pied, ce n'est rien; **I can make nothing of it** je n'y comprends rien du tout; **I'll take what's due to me, nothing more, nothing less** je prendrai mon dû, ni plus ni moins; **to have nothing on** *(no engagement)* être libre; *(no clothes)* être tout nu; *Fam* **what a physique! Charles Atlas has got nothing on you!** quel physique! tu n'as rien à envier à Charles Atlas *ou* Charles Atlas peut aller se rhabiller!; *Literary* **our sacrifices were as nothing compared to his** nos sacrifices ne furent rien auprès des siens; *Fam* **nothing doing!** pas question!

2 *n* (**a**) *(trifle)* rien *m*, vétille *f*; **$500 may be a mere nothing to you** 500 dollars ne représentent peut-être pas grand chose pour vous

(**b**) *Fam (person)* nullité *f*, zéro *m*

(**c**) *Math* zéro *m*

3 *adj Fam (worthless)* nul; **it's a nothing play!** c'est une pièce nulle!

4 for nothing *adv* (**a**) *(gratis)* pour rien; **I got it for nothing at the flea market** je l'ai eu pour (trois fois) rien aux puces

(**b**) *(for no purpose)* pour rien; **all that work for nothing!** tout ce travail pour rien *ou* en pure perte!; **are you telling me I gave up my day off for nothing?** est-ce que tu veux dire que j'ai sacrifié ma journée de vacances pour rien?; **to count for nothing** ne compter pour rien

(**c**) *(for no good reason)* pour rien; **the police say they don't arrest people for nothing** la police dit qu'elle n'arrête personne sans raison; **it's not for nothing that...** ce n'est pas pour rien que...; **they don't call him Einstein for nothing** ce n'est pas pour rien qu'on le surnomme Einstein

5 nothing but *adv* **that car's been nothing but trouble** cette voiture ne m'a attiré que des ennuis; **nothing but a miracle can save us** seul un miracle pourrait nous sauver; **she wants nothing but the best** elle ne veut que ce qu'il y a de meilleur; **they do nothing but sleep** ils ne font que dormir

6 nothing if not *adv* rien de moins que; **she's nothing if not honest** elle n'est rien de moins qu'honnête

7 nothing less than *adv* (**a**) *(undoubtedly)* rien de moins que, tout bonnement; **it was nothing less than miraculous/a miracle** c'était tout simplement miraculeux/un miracle; **he was nothing less than overjoyed at the news** il fut absolument ravi de la nouvelle

(**b**) *(only)* seul; **nothing less than outright victory would satisfy him** seule une victoire écrasante le satisferait

8 nothing like 1 *prep* (**a**) *(completely unlike)* **she's nothing like her mother** elle ne ressemble en rien à sa mère (**b**) *(nothing as good as)* **there's nothing like a nice cup of tea!** rien de tel qu'une bonne tasse de thé!; **there's nothing like a cold shower for freshening** *or* **to freshen you up** rien de tel qu'une douche froide pour se rafraîchir **2** *adv Fam (nowhere near)* **this box is nothing like big enough** cette boîte est beaucoup trop *ou* bien trop petite ❑; **nothing like as big** loin d'être aussi grand ❑; **London is nothing like as near as that** Londres est bien plus loin que ça ❑

9 nothing more than *adv* **I want nothing more than a word of thanks from time to time** tout ce

not–not

que je demande, c'est un petit mot de remerciement de temps à autre; **he's nothing more than a petty crook** il n'est rien d'autre qu'un vulgaire escroc

nothingness ['nʌθɪŋnɪs] *n* néant *m*; **he stared out into the nothingness** il avait le regard perdu dans le vide

NOTICE ['nəʊtɪs]

annonce	▸ **1 (a)**
écriteau	▸ **1 (a)**
affiche	▸ **1 (a)**
attention	▸ **1 (b)**
avis	▸ **1 (c), (d)**
préavis	▸ **1 (c)**
congé	▸ **1 (e)**
démission	▸ **1 (e)**
critique	▸ **1 (f)**
remarquer	▸ **2 (a)**
faire attention à	▸ **2 (b)**

1 *n* (**a**) *(written announcement)* annonce *f*; *(sign)* écriteau *m*, pancarte *f*; *(poster)* affiche *f*; *(in newspaper → article)* entrefilet *m*; *(→ advertisement)* annonce *f*; **a notice was pinned to the door** il y avait une notice sur la porte; **notices went up telling people to stay indoors** on placarda des affiches pour demander aux gens de rester chez eux

(**b**) *(attention)* attention *f*; **to take notice of** faire *ou* prêter attention à; **to take not the slightest notice of sth** ne pas prêter la moindre attention à qch; **take no notice (of him)!** ne faites pas attention (à lui)!; **you never take any notice of what I say!** tu ne fais jamais attention à ce que je dis!; *Formal* **she considers it beneath her notice** elle considère que ça ne vaut pas la peine qu'elle s'y arrête; **to bring sth to sb's notice** faire remarquer qch à qn, attirer l'attention de qn sur qch; **certain facts have come to** *or* **been brought to our notice** on a attiré notre attention sur certains faits; **it has come to my notice that...** il est venu à ma connaissance que...; **her book attracted a great deal of/little notice** son livre a suscité beaucoup/peu d'intérêt; **to escape** *or* **to avoid notice** passer inaperçu; **my mistake did not escape his notice** mon erreur ne lui a pas échappé; **has it escaped their notice that something is seriously wrong?** ne se sont-ils pas aperçus qu'il y a quelque chose qui ne va pas du tout?

(**c**) *(notification, warning)* avis *m*, notification *f*; *(advance notification)* préavis *m*; **please give us notice of your intentions** veuillez nous faire part préalablement de vos intentions; *Formal* **he was given notice** *or* **notice was served on him to quit** on lui a fait savoir qu'il devait partir; **give me more notice next time you come up** préviens-moi plus tôt la prochaine fois que tu viens; **legally, they must give you a month's notice** d'après la loi, ils doivent vous donner un préavis d'un mois *ou* un mois de préavis; **we require five days' notice** nous demandons un préavis de cinq jours; **give me a few days' notice** prévenez-moi quelques jours à l'avance; **without previous** *or* **prior notice** sans prévenir; **he turned up without any notice** il est arrivé à l'improviste; **at a moment's notice** sur-le-champ, immédiatement; **at short notice** très rapidement; **it's impossible to do the work at such short notice** c'est un travail impossible à faire dans un délai aussi court; **that's rather short notice** c'est un peu court comme délai; **until further notice** jusqu'à nouvel ordre *ou* avis; **deposit at seven days' notice** dépôt *m* à sept jours de préavis

(**d**) *(notifying document)* avis *m*, notification *f*; *(warning document)* avertissement *m*; **they sent three notices before cutting off the water** ils ont envoyé trois avertissements avant de couper l'eau; **notice to pay** avertissement *m*

(**e**) *(intent to terminate contract → by employer, landlord, tenant)* congé *m*; *(→ by employee)* démission *f*; **fifty people have been given their notice** cinquante personnes ont été licenciées; **to give in** *or* **to hand in one's notice** remettre sa démission; **has the landlord given you notice?** le propriétaire vous a-t-il donné congé?; **to give sb a week's notice** donner ses huit jours à qn; **we are under notice to quit** nous avons reçu notre congé; **what notice do you require?** quel est le terme du congé?; **employees must give three months' notice** les employés doivent donner trois mois de préavis

(**f**) *(review)* critique *f*; **the film got excellent notices** le film a eu d'excellentes critiques

2 *vt* (**a**) *(spot, observe)* remarquer, s'apercevoir de; **he noticed a scratch on the table** il remarqua que la table était rayée; **surely you noticed her?** ne me dis pas que tu ne l'as pas vue!; **hello, Sam, I didn't notice you in the corner** bonjour, Sam, je ne t'avais pas vu dans le coin; **so I've noticed!** c'est ce que j'ai remarqué!; **he noticed that his watch was gone** il s'est aperçu que sa montre avait disparu; **try and slip in without her noticing** essayez d'entrer sans qu'elle s'en aperçoive; **nobody will ever notice** personne ne s'en apercevra *ou* ne le remarquera jamais; **what happened? – I don't know, I didn't notice** qu'est-ce qui s'est passé? – je ne sais pas, je ne m'en suis pas rendu compte; **I noticed her smiling** j'ai remarqué qu'elle souriait

(**b**) *(take notice of)* faire attention à; **he never notices what I wear!** il ne fait jamais attention à ce que je porte!

►► *Law* ***notice of appeal*** intimation *f* d'appel; *Com* ***notice period*** période *f* de préavis; *Com* ***notice of receipt*** accusé *m* de réception; *Banking & Fin* ***notice of withdrawal*** avis *m* de retrait de fonds

noticeable ['nəʊtɪsəbəl] *adj (mark, defect)* visible; *(effect, change, improvement)* sensible; **the stain is barely noticeable** la tache est à peine visible *ou* se voit à peine

noticeably ['nəʊtɪsəblɪ] *adv* sensiblement; **to be noticeably absent** briller par son absence; **to be noticeably lacking in good manners** manquer totalement de savoir-vivre; **students did noticeably less well in these subjects** les étudiants ont obtenu des résultats nettement inférieurs dans ces matières

noticeboard ['nəʊtɪsbɔːd] *n Br* panneau *m* d'affichage

notifiable ['nəʊtɪfaɪəbəl] *adj (disease)* à déclaration obligatoire

notification [ˌnəʊtɪfɪ'keɪʃən] *n* notification *f*, avis *m*; **you will receive notification by mail** vous serez averti par courrier

notify ['nəʊtɪfaɪ] *(pt & pp* **notified**) *vt* notifier, avertir; **to notify sb of sth** avertir qn de qch, notifier qch à qn; **have you notified the authorities?** avez-vous averti *ou* prévenu les autorités?; **winners will be notified within ten days** les gagnants seront avisés dans les dix jours

notion ['nəʊʃən] **1** *n* (**a**) *(concept)* notion *f*, concept *m*; **the notion of evil** la notion du mal; **to have no notion of sth** ne pas avoir la moindre notion de qch; **to have no notion of time** n'avoir pas la notion *ou* le sens de l'heure; **I lost all notion of time** j'ai perdu la notion du temps

(**b**) *(vague idea)* notion *f*, idée *f*; **have you any notion of what it will cost?** avez-vous une idée de ce que cela va coûter?; **where did she get the notion** *or* **whatever gave her the notion that we don't like her?** où est-elle allée chercher que nous ne l'aimions pas?

(**c**) *(thought, whim)* idée *f*; **she has some pretty strange notions** elle a de drôles d'idées; **he hit upon the notion of buying a houseboat** il eut soudain l'idée d'acheter une péniche aménagée; **to give sb notions** mettre des idées dans la tête à qn

(**d**) *(urge)* envie *f*, désir *m*; **I've got a notion to paint it red** j'ai envie de le peindre en rouge

2 notions *npl Am (haberdashery)* mercerie *f*

notional ['nəʊʃənəl] *adj* (**a**) *Br (hypothetical)* théorique, notionnel; **let's put a notional price of $2 a kilo on it** pour avoir un ordre d'idées, fixons-en le prix à 2 dollars le kilo

(**b**) *(imaginary)* imaginaire

(**c**) *Am (fanciful)* capricieux

(**d**) *Ling (word)* sémantique, plein

(**e**) *(income)* fictif

►► ***notional grammar*** grammaire *f* notionnelle; ***notional income*** revenu *m* fictif; ***notional rent*** loyer *m* insignifiant

notochord ['nəʊtəkɔːd] *n Zool* notocorde *m*, notochorde *m*

notoriety [ˌnəʊtə'raɪətɪ] *(pl* **notorieties**) *n* triste notoriété *f*; **these measures brought** *or* **gained him notoriety** ces mesures l'ont rendu tristement célèbre

notorious [nəʊ'tɔːrɪəs] *adj Pej (ill-famed → person)* tristement célèbre; *(→ crime)* célèbre; *(→ place)* mal famé; **a notorious miser/spy/murderer** un avare/espion/meurtrier notoire; **she's notorious for being late** elle est connue pour ne jamais être à l'heure; **his notorious past** son passé chargé; **a city notorious for its slums** une ville connue *ou* célèbre pour ses bidonvilles; **the junction is a notorious accident spot** ce croisement est réputé pour être très dangereux; **the area is notorious for muggings** il est bien connu que c'est un quartier où il y a beaucoup d'agressions

notoriously [nəʊ'tɔːrɪəslɪ] *adv* notoirement; **the trains here are notoriously unreliable** tout le monde sait qu'on ne peut pas se fier aux horaires des trains ici

no-trump, no-trumps *n* sans-atout *m inv*

Nottinghamshire ['nɒtɪŋəmˌʃə] *n* le Nottinghamshire, = comté dans le centre de l'Angleterre; **in Nottinghamshire** dans le Nottinghamshire

Notting Hill ['nɒtɪŋ-] *n* Notting Hill

►► ***the Notting Hill Carnival*** = carnaval afro-antillais qui se tient chaque année à Londres

not-too-distant *adj* **in the not-too-distant future** dans un avenir proche

Notts *(written abbr* **Nottinghamshire**) Nottinghamshire *m*

notwithstanding [ˌnɒtwɪθ'stændɪŋ] *Formal* **1** *prep* en dépit de; **notwithstanding the agreement, the agreement notwithstanding** en dépit de l'accord; **this notwithstanding, his accent betrayed him** nonobstant cela, son accent le trahissait

2 *adv* malgré tout, néanmoins

nougat ['nuːgɑː] *n* nougat *m*

nought [nɔːt] *n* (**a**) *Br (zero)* zéro *m*; **nought point five** zéro virgule cinq (**b**) *Arch* = **naught** *adv*

►► *Br* ***noughts and crosses*** *(UNCOUNT)* ≃ morpion *m (jeu)*; **to play (at) noughts and crosses** jouer au morpion

noumenon ['nuːmənən] *(pl* **noumena** [-nə]) *n* noumène *m*

noun [naʊn] *n* nom *m*, substantif *m*; **common/proper noun** nom *m* commun/propre

►► ***noun clause*** proposition *f*; ***noun phrase*** groupe *m ou* syntagme *m* nominal

nourish ['nʌrɪʃ] *vt* (**a**) *(feed)* nourrir; **nourished on grain** nourri au grain (**b**) *(entertain, foster)* nourrir, entretenir

nourishing ['nʌrɪʃɪŋ] *adj* nourrissant, nutritif

nourishment ['nʌrɪʃmənt] *n (UNCOUNT)* (**a**) *(food)* nourriture *f*, aliments *mpl*; **the patient has taken no nourishment** le malade ne s'est pas alimenté; **brown rice is full of nourishment** le riz complet est très nourrissant; **it's full of nourishment** c'est très nourrissant *ou* nutritif (**b**) *(act of nourishing)* alimentation *f*

nous [naʊs] *n* (**a**) *Fam* bon sens❑ *m*, jugeote *f*; **she's got a lot of nous** elle a beaucoup de bon sens, elle est très sensée❑; **anyone with any nous** n'importe qui doté d'un minimum de bon sens (**b**) *Phil* esprit *m*, intellect *m*

nouveau riche [ˌnuːvəʊ'riːʃ] *(pl* **nouveaux riches** [ˌnuːvəʊ'riːʃ]) *n* nouveau riche *m*

nouvelle cuisine [ˌnuːvelkwiː'ziːn] *n* nouvelle cuisine *f*

Nov. *(written abbr* **November**) nov

nova ['nəʊvə] *(pl* **novas** *or* **novae** [-viː]) *n* nova *f*

Nova Scotia [ˌnəʊvə'skəʊʃə] *n* la Nouvelle-Écosse; **in Nova Scotia** en Nouvelle-Écosse

Nova Scotian [ˌnəʊvə'skəʊʃən] **1** *n* Néo-Écossais(e) *m,f*

2 *adj* néo-écossais

novation [nə'veɪʃən] *n Law* novation *f*

Novaya Zemlya [ˌnɒvəjəzem'ljɑː] *n* Nouvelle-Zemble *f*; **in Novaya Zemlya** en Nouvelle-Zemble

novel ['nɒvəl] **1** *n* roman *m*; **detective/spy novel** roman *m* policier/d'espionnage

2 *adj* nouveau(elle), original; **what a novel idea!** quelle idée originale!; **it was a novel experience for me** ce fut une expérience nouvelle pour moi

novelese [nɒvə'li:z] *n* mauvaise littérature *f*

novelette [ˌnɒvə'let] *n* (**a**) *(short novel)* nouvelle *f* (**b**) *Pej (easy reading)* roman *m* de hall de gare; *(love story)* roman *m* à l'eau de rose

novelettish [ˌnɒvə'letɪʃ] *adj Pej (sentimental)* à l'eau de rose

novelist ['nɒvəlɪst] *n* romancier(ère) *m,f*

novelistic [nɒvə'lɪstɪk] *adj* romanesque

novella [nə'velə] *(pl* **novellas** *or* **novelle** [-leɪ]) *n* ≃ nouvelle *f (texte plus court qu'un roman et plus long qu'une nouvelle)*

novelty ['nɒvəltɪ] *(pl* **novelties**) **1** *n* (**a**) *(newness)* nouveauté *f*, originalité *f*; **the novelty soon wore off** l'attrait de la nouveauté n'a pas duré (**b**) *(thing, idea)* innovation *f*, nouveauté *f*; **it was a real novelty** c'était une nouveauté, c'était tout nouveau; **as the only Chinese child, he was something of a novelty** seul enfant chinois, il faisait figure de nouveauté (**c**) *(trinket)* nouveauté *f*, article *m* fantaisie; *(gadget)* gadget *m*

2 *comp (object)* fantaisie *(inv)*

►► ***novelty jewellery*** bijoux *mpl* fantaisie; ***novelty value*** attrait *m* de la nouveauté

November [nəʊ'vembə(r)] *n* novembre *m*; *see also* **February**

novena [nəʊ'vi:nə] *(pl* **novenae** [-ni:]) *n* neuvaine *f*

novice ['nɒvɪs] *n* (**a**) *(beginner)* débutant(e) *m,f*, novice *mf*; **I'm still a novice at golf** en matière de golf, je ne suis encore qu'un novice; **a novice at skiing, a novice skier** un skieur débutant (**b**) *Rel* novice *mf*

novitiate, noviciate [nə'vɪʃɪət] *n Rel* (**a**) *(period)* noviciat *m*; *Fig* noviciat *m*, apprentissage *m* (**b**) *(place)* noviciat *m*

Novocaine® ['nəʊvəkeɪn] *n Pharm* Novocaïne® *f*, procaïne *f*

NOW [naʊ] *n Am (abbr* **National Organization for Women**) = organisation féministe américaine

---

NOW [naʊ]

maintenant	► **1 (a) – (c)**
aujourd'hui	► **1 (b)**
alors	► **1 (c)**
or	► **1 (d)**
maintenant que	► **2**
tantôt... tantôt	► **5**

1 *adv* (**a**) *(at this time)* maintenant; **what shall we do now?** qu'est-ce qu'on fait maintenant?; **he hasn't seen her for a week now, it's a week now since he's seen her** ça fait maintenant une semaine qu'il ne l'a pas vue; **she'll be here any moment** *or* **any time now** elle va arriver d'un moment *ou* instant à l'autre; **don't stop now!** n'arrête pas maintenant!; **we are now entering enemy territory** nous sommes désormais en territoire ennemi; **it's now or never** c'est le moment ou jamais; **now is the time to invest, the time to invest is now** c'est maintenant le moment d'investir; *Hum* **now she tells me!** c'est maintenant qu'elle me le dit!; **(and) now for something completely different** (et) voici à présent quelque chose de tout à fait différent; **as of now** désormais; **I'd never met them before now** je ne les avais jamais rencontrés auparavant; **between now and next August/next year** d'ici le mois d'août prochain/l'année prochaine; **they must have got the letter by now** ils ont dû recevoir la lettre à l'heure qu'il est; **he ought to be here by now, he ought to have been here before now** il devrait déjà être arrivé; **that's all for now** c'est tout pour le moment; **from now until Monday/next year** d'ici (à) lundi prochain/l'année prochaine; **in a few years from now** d'ici quelques années; **from now on** désormais, dorénavant, à partir de maintenant; **from now on you do as you're told!** à partir de maintenant, tu vas obéir!; **we've had no problems till now** *or* **until now** *or* **up to now** nous n'avons eu aucun problème jusqu'ici

(**b**) *(nowadays)* maintenant, aujourd'hui, actuellement; **he lives in London now** il habite (à) Londres maintenant; **her now famous first novel** son premier roman, aujourd'hui célèbre

(**c**) *(marking a specific point in the past)* maintenant, alors, à ce moment-là; **they were singing now** ils chantaient maintenant; **by now we were all exhausted** nous étions alors tous épuisés; **up to now I'd never agreed with him** jusque-là *ou* jusqu'alors, je n'avais jamais été d'accord avec lui; **he was even now on his way** il était déjà en route

(**d**) *(introducing information)* or; **now a Jaguar is a very fast car** or, la Jaguar est une voiture très rapide

(**e**) *(before statement, argument)* **now that's what I call a car!** voilà ce que j'appelle une voiture!; **well now!** ça alors!; **now, what was I saying?** voyons, où en étais-je?; **now let me see** voyons voir; **there now** *or* **now, now, you mustn't cry** allons, allons, il ne faut pas pleurer; **now then, it's time to get up!** allons, il est l'heure de se lever!; **you be careful now!** fais bien attention, hein!; **now then...!** attention, hein...!; **now, now! stop quarrelling!** voyons, voyons! assez de querelles!; **now that's just silly!** arrête tes bêtises!

2 *conj* maintenant que, à présent que; **she's happier now (that) she's got a job** elle est plus heureuse depuis qu'elle travaille; **now you come to mention it** maintenant que tu le dis

3 *adj Fam* (**a**) *(current)* actuel ☐; **the now president** le président actuel

(**b**) *(fashionable)* branché; **a now style** un style branché; **she's a now person** c'est une branchée; **golf is the now thing to do** pour être branché, il faut se mettre au golf

4 now and again, now and then *adv* de temps en temps, de temps à autre; **we still see them (every) now and again** nous les voyons encore de temps en temps *ou* de temps à autre

5 now... now *conj* tantôt... tantôt; **now happy, now sad** tantôt gai, tantôt triste

---

nowadays ['naʊədeɪz] *adv* aujourd'hui, de nos jours; **nowadays there is much more job insecurity** la précarité de l'emploi est un phénomène beaucoup plus courant de nos jours; **where's she working nowadays?** où travaille-t-elle actuellement?

noway ['nəʊweɪ], **noways** ['nəʊweɪz] *adv Am Fam* pas du tout ☐

nowhere ['nəʊweə(r)] *adv* (**a**) *(no place)* nulle part; **he goes nowhere without her** il ne va nulle part sans elle; **I've got nowhere to go** je n'ai nulle part où aller; **there's nowhere to hide** il n'y a pas d'endroit où se cacher; **nowhere else** nulle part ailleurs; **where are you going? – nowhere in particular** où vas-tu? – je ne sais pas exactement; **it's nowhere on the map** cela ne figure pas sur la carte; **she's nowhere in the building** elle n'est pas dans l'immeuble; **my watch is nowhere to be found** impossible de retrouver ma montre, ma montre est introuvable; **she/the book was nowhere to be seen** elle/le livre avait disparu; *Fig* **a small place in the middle of nowhere** un petit trou perdu; **he appeared from nowhere** *or* **out of nowhere** il est apparu comme par enchantement; **she rose to fame from nowhere** elle est devenue célèbre du jour au lendemain; **without your help we would be nowhere** sans votre aide nous serions perdus; **the horse I backed came nowhere** le cheval sur lequel j'ai parié est arrivé bon dernier *ou* loin derrière; **lying will get you nowhere** mentir ne nous servira à rien *ou* ne mènera à rien; **I got nowhere trying to convince him** mes tentatives pour le convaincre sont restées vaines *ou* se sont soldées par un échec; *Fam* **we're getting nowhere fast** on pédale dans la choucroute *ou* la semoule; **he's going nowhere fast** il n'ira pas loin; **that kind of attitude will get you nowhere fast** ce genre d'attitude ne t'avancera *ou* ne te servira à rien du tout; **the investigation is going nowhere** l'enquête n'avance pas *ou* piétine

(**b**) *(idioms)* **the hotel was nowhere near the beach** l'hôtel était bien loin de la plage; **dinner is nowhere near ready** le dîner est loin d'être prêt; **I've nowhere near enough time** je suis loin d'avoir assez de temps

no-win situation *n* situation *f* sans issue

nowise ['nəʊwaɪz] *adv Am Fam* pas du tout ☐

nowt [naʊt] *pron NEng Fam (nothing)* rien ☐, que dalle; **have you nowt to say?** tu n'as rien à dire?

noxious ['nɒkʃəs] *adj (gas, substance)* nocif; *(influence)* néfaste

noxiousness ['nɒkʃənɪs] *n (of gas, substance)* nocivité *f*; *(of influence)* nature *f* néfaste

nozzle ['nɒzəl] *n (gen)* bec *m*, embout *m*; *(for hose, paint gun)* jet *m*, buse *f*; *(of bellows)* bec *m*, tuyau *m*, buse *f*; *(in carburettor)* gicleur *m*; *(in turbine)* tuyère *f*; *(of vacuum cleaner)* suceur *m*; *(for icing)* douille *f*

NP[1] [ˌen'pi:] *(written abbr* **notary public**) notaire *m*

NP[2] *n (abbr* **New Providence**) île *f* de la Nouvelle-Providence

NPD [ˌenpi:'di:] *n Mktg (abbr* **new product development**) développement *m* de nouveaux produits

NPV [ˌenpi:'vi:] *n Acct (abbr* **net present value**) VAN *f*, valeur *f* actuelle nette

►► ***NPV rate*** taux *m* d'actualisation

nr *(written abbr* **near**) près de

NRA [ˌenɑ:'reɪ] *n* (**a**) *Am (abbr* **National Rifle Association**) = association américaine défendant le droit au port d'armes (**b**) *Br (abbr* **National Rivers Authority**) = organisme britannique chargé de veiller à la propreté des cours d'eau en Angleterre et au pays de Galles

NRC [ˌenɑ:'si:] *n (abbr* **Nuclear Regulatory Commission**) = agence américaine chargée de veiller au respect des normes de sécurité dans le convoyage et l'utilisation de matériaux radioactifs

NREM [ˌenɑ:ˌri:'em] *n (abbr* **non-rapid eye movement**) **NREM sleep** sommeil *m* lent

NRS [ˌenɑ:'res] *n (abbr* **national readership survey**) étude *f* nationale sur le lectorat

NRT [ˌenɑ:'ti:] *n (abbr* **nicotine replacement therapy**) thérapie *f* de désaccoutumance à la nicotine *(patch, gomme nicotinique etc)*

NRV [ˌenɑ:'vi:] *n Fin (abbr* **net realizable value**) valeur *f* réalisable nette

NS (**a**) *(written abbr* **Nova Scotia**) Nouvelle-Écosse *f* (**b**) *Ir (written abbr* **national school**) école *f* primaire

NSAID [ˌenes,eɪaɪ'di:] *n Med (abbr* **non-steroidal anti-inflammatory drug**) anti-inflammatoire *m* non stéroïde

NSC [ˌenes'si:] *n Am (abbr* **National Security Council**) = organisme chargé de superviser la politique militaire de défense du gouvernement des États-Unis

NSF[1] [ˌenes'ef] *n (abbr* **National Science Foundation**) = organisme indépendant américain d'aide à la recherche scientifique

NSF[2] *(written abbr* **not sufficient funds**) fonds *mpl* insuffisants

NSPCC [ˌenes,pi:si:'si:] *n Br (abbr* **National Society for the Prevention of Cruelty to Children**) = association britannique de protection de l'enfance

NSU [ˌenes'ju:] *n Med (abbr* **nonspecific urethritis**) urétrite *f* non spécifique

NSW *(written abbr* **New South Wales**) Nouvelle-Galles *f* du Sud

NT [ˌen'ti:] *n* (**a**) *(abbr* **New Testament**) NT *m* (**b**) *Ir (abbr* **national teacher**) instituteur(trice) *m,f* (**c**) *(abbr* **National Trust**) = organisme non gouvernemental britannique assurant la conservation de certains paysages et monuments historiques (**d**) *(abbr* **(Royal) National Theatre**) = grand théâtre londonien subventionné par l'État

nth [enθ] *adj* (**a**) *Math* **to the nth power** à la puissance n (**b**) *Fam (umpteenth)* énième; **for the nth time** pour la énième fois; **to the nth degree** au énième degré

NTS [ˌenti:'es] *n (abbr* **National Trust for Scotland**) = organisme non gouvernemental assurant la conservation du patrimoine naturel et historique écossais

NTSB [ˌenti:,es'bi:] *n (abbr* **National Transportation Safety Board**) = agence du gouvernement américain chargée des questions de sécurité dans le domaine des transports

NUAAW [ˌenju:,eɪeɪ'dʌbəlju:] *n Br (abbr* **National Union of Agricultural and Allied Workers**) = syndicat britannique des employés du secteur agricole

nuance ['nju:ɒns] *n* nuance *f*

nuanced ['nju:ɒnst] *adj* nuancé; **finely nuanced** subtilement nuancé

nub [nʌb] *n* (**a**) *(crux)* essentiel *m*, cœur *m*; **the**

nub of the problem le cœur *ou* le nœud du problème; **to get to the nub of the matter** entrer dans le vif du sujet (**b**) *(small piece)* petit morceau *m*, (petit) bout *m*; *(small bump)* petite bosse *f*; **coal nubs** noisettes *fpl* de charbon

nubbin ['nʌbɪn] *n Am (gen)* (petit) bout *m*; *(of corn)* épi *m* (de maïs) rachitique

nubby ['nʌbɪ] *adj Am* couvert de peluches

Nubia ['nju:bjə] *n* Nubie *f*

Nubian ['nju:bjən] **1** *n* Nubien(enne) *m,f*

2 *adj* nubien; **the Nubian Desert** le désert de Nubie

nubile [*Br* 'njubaɪl, *Am* 'nu:bəl] *adj* (**a**) *(sexually attractive)* désirable (**b**) *Formal (marriageable)* nubile

nubility ['nju:bɪlətɪ] *n* nubilité *f*

nucellus [nju:'seləs] (*pl* **nucelli** [-laɪ]) *n Bot* nucelle *f*

nucha ['nju:kə] *n Anat* nuque *f*

nuciferous [nju:'sɪfərəs] *adj Bot* nucifère

nucivorous [nju:'sɪvərəs] *adj Zool* nucivore

nuclear ['nju:klɪə(r)] *adj* (**a**) *Phys* nucléaire (**b**) *Mil* nucléaire; **France's nuclear deterrent** la force de dissuasion nucléaire française (**c**) *Biol* nucléaire

▸▸ ***nuclear bomb*** bombe *f* atomique; ***nuclear capability*** puissance *f ou* potentiel *m* nucléaire; ***nuclear capacity*** puissance *f* nucléaire; ***nuclear chemistry*** chimie *f* nucléaire; ***nuclear disarmament*** désarmement *m* nucléaire; ***nuclear energy*** énergie *f* nucléaire; ***nuclear family*** famille *f* nucléaire; ***nuclear fission*** fission *f* nucléaire; ***nuclear fuel*** combustible *m* nucléaire; ***nuclear fusion*** fusion *f* nucléaire; ***nuclear industry*** industrie *f* nucléaire; ***nuclear magnetic resonance*** résonance *f* magnétique nucléaire; ***nuclear medicine*** médecine *f* nucléaire; ***Nuclear Non-Proliferation Treaty*** traité *m* de non-prolifération nucléaire; ***nuclear physicist*** physicien(enne) *m,f* nucléaire; ***nuclear physics*** *(UNCOUNT)* physique *f* nucléaire; ***nuclear power*** nucléaire *m*, énergie *f* nucléaire; ***nuclear powers*** puissances *fpl* nucléaires; ***nuclear power station*** centrale *f* nucléaire *ou* atomique; ***nuclear reaction*** réaction *f* nucléaire; ***nuclear reactor*** réacteur *m* nucléaire; ***Nuclear Regulatory Commission*** = commission américaine contrôlant la sécurité des centrales nucléaires; ***nuclear reprocessing*** retraitement *m* (des déchets nucléaires); ***nuclear reprocessing plant*** usine *f* de retraitement (des déchets nucléaires); ***nuclear scientist*** physicien(enne) *m,f* nucléaire; ***nuclear shelter*** abri *m* antiatomique *ou* antinucléaire; ***nuclear submarine*** sous-marin *m* nucléaire; ***nuclear testing*** essais *mpl* nucléaires; ***nuclear umbrella*** parapluie *m* atomique *ou* nucléaire; ***nuclear war*** guerre *f* atomique; ***nuclear warhead*** ogive *f ou* tête *f* nucléaire; ***nuclear waste*** déchets *mpl* nucléaires; ***nuclear weapons*** armes *fpl* nucléaires; ***nuclear winter*** hiver *m* nucléaire

nuclear-free zone *n* = périmètre dans lequel une collectivité locale interdit l'utilisation, le stockage ou le transport des matières radioactives

nuclearize, -ise ['nju:klɪəraɪz] *vt* nucléariser

nuclear-powered *adj* à propulsion nucléaire

▸▸ ***nuclear-powered submarine*** sous-marin *m* nucléaire

nuclease ['nju:klɪeɪz] *n Biol* nucléase *f*

nucleate *Biol* **1** *adj* ['nju:klɪət] nucléé

2 *vt* ['nju:klɪeɪt] former en noyau; *(several things)* assembler en noyau

3 *vi* ['nju:klɪeɪt] se former en noyau; *(several things)* s'assembler en noyau

nucleated ['nju:klɪeɪtɪd] *adj Biol* nucléé

nuclei ['nju:klɪaɪ] *pl of* **nucleus**

nucleic acid [nju:'klɪɪk-] *n Biol* acide *m* nucléique

nuclein ['nju:klɪɪn] *n Biol* nucléine *f*

nucleolar [,nju:klɪ:'əʊlə(r)] *adj Biol* nucléolaire

nucleole ['nju:klɪəʊl], **nucleolus** [,nju:klɪ'əʊlʌs] *n Biol* nucléole *m*

nucleon ['nju:klɪɒn] *n* nucléon *m*

nucleonics [,nju:klɪ'ɒnɪks] *n (UNCOUNT)* nucléonique *f*

nucleophilic [,nju:klɪəʊ'fɪlɪk] *adj Chem* nucléophile

nucleoproteid [,nju:klɪəʊ'prəʊti:d], **nucleoprotein** [,nju:klɪəʊ'prəʊti:n] *n Biol & Chem* nucléoprotéide *m*, nucléoprotéine *f*

nucleoside ['nju:klɪəʊsaɪd] *n Biol & Chem* nucléoside *m*

nucleotide ['nju:klɪəʊtaɪd] *n Biol & Chem* nucléotide *m*

nucleus ['nju:klɪəs] (*pl* **nucleuses** *or* **nuclei** [-klɪaɪ]) *n* (**a**) *Biol & Phys* noyau *m* (**b**) *Fig (of organization etc)* noyau *m*; *(of argument etc)* cœur *m*; **they form the nucleus of the team** ils forment le noyau de l'équipe; **we have the nucleus of an idea** nous avons un début d'idée; **a nucleus for regional development** un centre de développement régional

nuclide ['nju:klaɪd] *n Phys* nuclide *m*, nucléide *m*

NUCPS [,enju:,si:pi:'es] *n Br (abbr* **National Union of Civil and Public Servants**) = syndicat britannique des employés de la fonction publique

nuddy ['nʌdɪ] *n Br Fam Hum* **in the nuddy** à poil

nude [nju:d] **1** *adj (naked)* nu; **there are several nude scenes in the film** il y a plusieurs scènes déshabillées dans le film; **to sunbathe nude** faire du bronzage intégral; **is nude sunbathing common here?** est-ce qu'il y a beaucoup de nudistes par ici?; **nude photos** nus *mpl*; *(soft pornography)* photos *fpl* érotiques

2 *n* (**a**) *Art* nu *m*; **a Matisse nude** un nu de Matisse (**b**) **in the nude** nu; **I was in the nude** j'étais (tout) nu; **to pose in the nude** poser nu

nudge [nʌdʒ] **1** *vt* (**a**) *(with elbow)* pousser du coude, donner un coup de coude à; **she nudged her friend to wake her up** elle donna un petit coup de coude à son amie pour la réveiller; *Br Hum* **he didn't come home last night, nudge nudge, wink wink** il n'est pas rentré hier soir, si tu vois ce que je veux dire

(**b**) *(push)* pousser; **he cautiously nudged the door open** il poussa tout doucement la porte (pour l'ouvrir); **the truck nudged its way through the crowd** le camion se fraya un passage à travers la foule

(**c**) *(encourage)* encourager, pousser; **to nudge sb into doing sth** encourager *ou* pousser qn à faire qch; *Br* **to nudge sb's memory** rafraîchir la mémoire de qn

(**d**) *(approach)* approcher de; **he must be nudging fifty** il doit approcher de la cinquantaine; **temperatures nudging 40° C** des températures proches de 40° C

2 *n* (**a**) *(with elbow)* coup *m* de coude; *(with foot, stick etc)* petit coup *m (de pied, de bâton etc)*; **to give sb a nudge** pousser qn du coude

(**b**) *(encouragement)* **she agreed with a nudge from her friends** ses amis l'ont encouragée à dire oui; **he needs a nudge in the right direction** il a besoin qu'on le pousse dans la bonne direction

nudibranch ['nju:dɪbræŋk] *n Zool* nudibranche *m*

nudie ['nju:dɪ] *adj Fam* porno

▸▸ ***nudie book*** magazine *m* porno

nudism ['nju:dɪzəm] *n* nudisme *m*, naturisme *m*

nudist ['nju:dɪst] **1** *n* nudiste *mf*, naturiste *mf*

2 *adj* nudiste, naturiste

▸▸ ***nudist beach*** plage *f* de nudistes; ***nudist colony*** camp *m* de nudistes

nudity ['nju:dətɪ] *n* nudité *f*

nudnik ['nʌdnɪk] *n Am Fam* emmerdeur(euse) *m,f*

nugatory ['nju:gətrɪ] *adj Formal* (**a**) *(trifling)* insignifiant, sans valeur (**b**) *(not valid)* non valable; *(ineffective)* inopérant, inefficace

nugget ['nʌgɪt] *n* (**a**) *(piece)* pépite *f*; **gold nugget** pépite *f* d'or (**b**) *Fig* **nuggets of wisdom** des trésors *mpl* de sagesse; **an interesting nugget of information** un (petit) renseignement intéressant (**c**) *Culin* **chicken nuggets** morceaux *mpl* de poulet

nuggety ['nʌgɪtɪ] *adj Miner* en pépites; **nuggety gold** or *m* en pépites

nuisance ['nju:səns] *n* (**a**) *(annoying thing, situation)* **that noise is a nuisance** ce bruit est énervant; **it's (such) a nuisance having to attend all these meetings** c'est (vraiment) pénible de devoir assister à toutes ces réunions; **what a nuisance!** c'est énervant!; **it's a nuisance having to commute every day** c'est pénible de devoir faire le trajet tous les jours; **they are not politically important but they have a certain nuisance value** ils n'ont pas un grand poids politique, mais ils ont le mérite de déranger

(**b**) *(annoying person)* casse-pieds *m inv*; **he's nothing but a nuisance** c'est un véritable empoisonneur; **to make a nuisance of oneself** embêter *ou* empoisonner le monde; **stop being a nuisance** arrête de nous embêter

(**c**) *(hazard)* nuisance *f*; **that rubbish dump is a public nuisance** cette décharge est une calamité

(**d**) *Law* préjudice *m*

▸▸ *Tel* ***nuisance call*** appel *m* anonyme; *Tel* ***nuisance caller*** auteur *m* d'appels anonymes

NUJ [,enju:'dʒeɪ] *n Br (abbr* **National Union of Journalists**) = syndicat britannique des journalistes

nuke [nju:k] *Fam* **1** *n* (**a**) *(weapon)* arme *f* nucléaire❑ (**b**) *Am (power plant)* centrale *f* nucléaire❑

2 *vt* (**a**) *(bomb)* atomiser❑ (**b**) *(microwave)* faire cuire au four à micro-ondes❑ (**c**) *(defeat)* ratatiner, battre à plates coutures

null [nʌl] *adj* (**a**) *Law (invalid)* nul; *(lapsed)* caduc (caduque); **null and void** nul et non avenu; **the contract was rendered null (and void)** le contrat a été annulé *ou* invalidé (**b**) *(insignificant)* insignifiant, sans valeur; *(amounting to nothing)* nul; **the effect of the embargo was null** l'embargo n'eut aucun effet (**c**) *Math* nul

▸▸ *Comput* ***null modem cable*** câble *m* de connexion sans modem; ***null set*** ensemble *m* vide; *Comput* ***null string*** chaîne *f* vide

nullification [,nʌlɪfɪ'keɪʃən] *n* annulation *f*, invalidation *f*

nullify ['nʌlɪfaɪ] (*pt & pp* **nullified**) *vt* (**a**) *Law (claim, contract, election)* annuler, invalider (**b**) *(advantage)* neutraliser

nullity ['nʌlətɪ] (*pl* **nullities**) *n* (**a**) *(worthlessness)* nullité *f* (**b**) *Law* nullité *f* (**c**) *(person)* nullité *f*

▸▸ ***nullity suit*** demande *f* en nullité de mariage

NUM [,enju:'em] *n (abbr* **National Union of Mineworkers**) = syndicat britannique des mineurs

numb [nʌm] **1** *adj* engourdi; **we were numb with cold** nous étions transis de froid; **my arm has gone numb** mon bras est tout engourdi; **is your jaw still numb?** *(anaesthetized)* ta mâchoire est-elle encore anesthésiée?; *Fig* **numb with terror** paralysé par la peur; *Fig* **he was numb with shock** il était sous le choc

2 *vt (person, limbs, senses)* engourdir; *(pain)* atténuer, apaiser; **opium numbs the senses** l'opium engourdit les sens; **the cold numbed my ears** il faisait tellement froid que je ne sentais plus mes oreilles; **she was numbed by her father's death** elle était sous le choc après la mort de son père, la mort de son père l'a laissée sous le choc

numbat ['nʌmbæt] *n Zool* fourmilier *m* marsupial rayé

NUMBER ['nʌmbə(r)]

nombre	▸ **1 (a), (c)**
chiffre	▸ **1 (a)**
numéro	▸ **1 (b), (e), (g)**
numéroter	▸ **2 (a)**
compter	▸ **2 (b) – (d)**

1 *n* (**a**) *(gen) & Math* nombre *m*; *(figure, numeral)* chiffre *m*; **a six-figure number** un nombre de six chiffres; **the numbers on the keyboard** les chiffres sur le clavier; **in round numbers** en chiffres ronds; **to do sth by numbers** faire qch en suivant des instructions précises; **she taught him his numbers** elle lui a appris à compter; **even/odd/rational/whole number** nombre *m* pair/impair/rationnel/entier

(**b**) *(as identifier)* numéro *m*; **have you got my work number?** avez-vous mon numéro (de téléphone) au travail?; **you're number six** vous êtes (le) numéro six; **the winning number** le numéro gagnant; **we live at number 80** nous habitons au (numéro) 80; **he's the President's number two** il est le bras droit du président; *Mil* **name, rank and number!** nom, grade et matricule!; **did you get the car's (registration) number?** tu as relevé le numéro d'immatriculation de la voiture?; *Fam* **I've got your number!** toi, je te vois venir!, j'ai repéré ton manège!; *Fam* **his number's up** son compte est bon

(**c**) *(quantity)* nombre *m*; **the number of tourists is growing** le nombre de touristes va en augmentant; **any number can participate** le nombre de participants est illimité; **they were eight in number** ils étaient (au nombre de) huit; **in equal numbers** en nombre égal; **to be equal in number** être à nombre égal; **we were many/ few in number** nous étions nombreux/en petit nombre; **a number of people** un certain nombre de gens; **a (certain) number of you** un certain nombre d'entre vous; **a large number of people** un grand nombre de gens, de nombreuses personnes; **a small number of people** un petit nombre de gens, peu de gens; **any number of...** un grand nombre de..., bon nombre de...; **she is one of a number of people who...** elle figure parmi les personnes qui...; **to be present in small numbers/in (great) numbers** être présents en petit nombre/en grand nombre; **in a good** *or* **fair number of cases** dans bon nombre de cas; **times without number** à maintes (et maintes) reprises; **they defeated us by force of** *or* **by sheer weight of numbers** ils l'ont emporté sur nous parce qu'ils étaient plus nombreux

(**d**) *(group)* **one of their/our number** un des leurs/des nôtres; **she was not of our number** elle n'était pas des nôtres *ou* avec nous

(**e**) *(issue → of magazine, paper)* numéro *m*; **did you read last week's number?** avez-vous lu le numéro de la semaine dernière?

(**f**) *Fam (job)* boulot *m*; **a cushy number** une planque

(**g**) *(song, dance, act)* numéro *m*; **a dance number** un numéro de danse; **for my next number I'd like to sing...** j'aimerais vous chanter maintenant...; **they played some new numbers** ils ont joué de nouveaux morceaux; **they sang some new numbers** ils ont chanté de nouvelles chansons; **they only danced to the slow numbers** ils n'ont dansé que les slows

(**h**) *Fam (thing, person)* **this number is a hot seller** ce modèle se vend comme des petits pains; **she was wearing a little black number** elle portait une petite robe noire ❑; **he was driving a little Italian number** il était au volant d'un de ces petits bolides italiens; **who's that blonde number?** qui est cette belle blonde?; ❑ **to do** *or* **to pull a number on sb** rouler qn; *Am* **to do a number on sth** *(spoil, ruin)* bousiller qch

(**i**) *Gram* nombre *m*

(**j**) *Fam (cannabis cigarette)* joint *m*

2 *vt* (**a**) *(assign number to)* numéroter; **don't forget to number the pages** n'oubliez pas de numéroter les pages

(**b**) *(include)* compter; **I number him among the best jazz musicians** je le compte parmi les meilleurs musiciens de jazz; **I'm glad to number her among my closest friends** je suis heureux de la compter parmi mes meilleurs amis

(**c**) *(total)* compter; **each team numbers six players** chaque équipe est composée de *ou* compte six joueurs; **the crowd numbered 5,000** il y avait une foule de 5000 personnes

(**d**) *(count)* compter; *Literary* **who can number the stars?** qui peut dire combien il y a d'étoiles?; **now their options are numbered** désormais, leur choix est assez restreint; **his days are numbered** ses jours sont comptés

3 *vi* **she numbers among the great writers of the century** elle compte parmi les grands écrivains de ce siècle; **did he number among the ringleaders?** faisait-il partie des meneurs?; **the crowd numbered in thousands** il y avait des milliers de gens

4 any number of *adj* **there were any number of different dishes to choose from** un très grand nombre de plats différents furent présentés

►► *Banking* ***numbered account*** compte *m* numéroté; *Am* ***numbers game*** loterie *f* clandestine; *Comput* ***number key*** touche *f* numérique; *Comput* ***number lock*** verrouillage *m* du pavé numérique; *Comput* ***number lock key*** touche *f* de verrouillage du clavier numérique; ***number one*** **1** *n Fam (boss)* boss *m*, patron(onne) ❑ *m,f*; *Fam* **to look out for** *or* **to take care of number one** penser d'abord à soi ❑; **her record got to number one** son disque a été classé numéro un au hit-parade; *Sport* **the world number one** le numéro un mondial; *Fam (in children's language)* **to do a number one** *(urinate)* faire pipi

2 *adj* premier; **it's our number one priority** c'est la première de nos priorités; **the number one oil exporter** le premier exportateur de pétrole; **my number one choice** mon tout premier choix; **the number one hit in the charts** le numéro un au hit-parade; **the world's number one golfer** le numéro un mondial du golf; *Br Aut* ***number plate*** plaque *f* minéralogique *ou* d'immatriculation; **the lorry had a foreign number plate** le camion était immatriculé à l'étranger; *Am* ***number shop*** ≃ kiosque *m* de loterie; ***Number Ten (Downing Street)*** = résidence officielle du Premier ministre britannique; *Math* ***number theory*** théorie *f* des nombres; ***number two*** *(assistant)* numéro *m* deux; *Fam (in children's language)* **to do a number two** *(defecate)* faire la grosse commission

►**number off** *vi* se numéroter; **number off from the left** numérotez-vous en partant de la gauche

---

number-coded *adj* codé en chiffres

number-cruncher [-krʌntʃə(r)] *n Fam* ordinateur *m* puissant ❑ *(pour le traitement de données numériques)*

number-crunching [-krʌntʃɪŋ] *n Fam* traitement *m* en masse des chiffres

numbering ['nʌmbərɪŋ] *n* numérotation *f*, numérotage *m*

numberless ['nʌmbəlɪs] *adj* (**a**) *Formal (countless)* innombrable, sans nombre (**b**) *(without a number)* sans numéro, qui ne porte pas de numéro, non numéroté

Numbers ['nʌmbəz] *n Bible* Nombres *mpl*; **the book of Numbers** le livre des Nombres

numbfish ['nʌmfɪʃ] *n Ich* torpille *f*, crampe *f*

numbhead ['nʌmhed] *n Am Fam* crétin(e) *m,f*, andouille *f*

numbly ['nʌmlɪ] *adv (react, say)* mollement; *(look, stare)* d'un air engourdi

numbness ['nʌmnɪs] *n (physical)* engourdissement *m*; *(mental)* torpeur *f*, engourdissement *m*

numbskull [ˌnʌmskʌl] *n Fam* crétin(e) *m,f*, andouille *f*

numen ['nju:men] *n* numen *m*

numerable ['nju:mərəbəl] *adj* nombrable

numeracy ['nju:mərəsɪ] *n (UNCOUNT) Br* aptitudes *fpl* en calcul; **a high level of numeracy** un bon niveau en calcul

numeral ['nju:mərəl] **1** *n* chiffre *m*, nombre *m*; **in Roman numerals** en chiffres romains

2 *adj* numéral

numerate ['nju:mərət] *adj Br (skilled)* bon en mathématiques; *(having basics)* sachant compter; **to be barely numerate** savoir à peine compter; **applicants should be highly numerate** les candidats doivent avoir des compétences élevées en calcul

numeration [ˌnju:mə'reɪʃən] *n Math* numération *f*; **binary numeration** numération *f* binaire

numerator ['nju:məreɪtə(r)] *n Math* numérateur *m*

numeric [nju:'merɪk] *Comput* **1** *adj* numérique

2 numerics *npl* chiffres *mpl ou* caractères *mpl* numériques

►► ***numeric coding*** codage *m* numérique; ***numeric field*** champ *m* numérique; ***numeric keypad, numeric pad*** pavé *m* numérique

numerical [nju:'merɪkəl] *adj* numérique; **to have a numerical advantage** avoir l'avantage du nombre; **in numerical order** par ordre numérique

►► ***numerical analysis*** analyse *f* numérique; ***numerical control*** contrôle *m* numérique; ***numerical data*** données *fpl* numériques; *Mktg* ***numerical distribution*** distribution *f* numérique; *Comput* ***numerical keypad*** pavé *m* numérique

numerically [nju:'merɪkəlɪ] *adv* numériquement

numerologist [ˌnju:mə'rɒlədʒɪst] *n* numérologue *mf*

numerology [ˌnju:mə'rɒlədʒɪ] *n* numérologie *f*, arithmosophie *f*

numero uno [ˌnu:mərəʊ'u:nəʊ] *Am Fam* **1** *n* numéro un ❑ *m*; **don't forget who's numero uno around here** n'oublie pas qui commande *ou* qui est le patron ici

2 *adj* **he's the numero uno coke dealer** c'est le principal dealer de coke

numerous ['nju:mərəs] *adj* nombreux; **for numerous reasons** pour de nombreuses raisons; **a numerous group** un groupe important

numinous ['nju:mɪnəs] *adj (awe-inspiring)* terrifiant

numismatic [ˌnju:mɪz'mætɪk] *adj* numismatique

numismatics [ˌnju:mɪz'mætɪks] *n (UNCOUNT)* numismatique *f*

numismatist [nju:'mɪzmətɪst] *n* numismate *mf*

numismatology [ˌnju:mɪzmə'tɒlədʒɪ] *n* numismatique *f*

num lock ['nʌm-] *n Comput (abbr* **number lock**) verr num; **the num lock is on** le pavé numérique est verrouillé

►► ***num lock key*** touche *f* de verrouillage du pavé numérique

numskull = **numbskull**

nun [nʌn] *n* religieuse *f*; **to become a nun** prendre le voile

nunatak ['nʌnətæk] *n Geol* nunatak *m*

nunciature ['nʌnsɪətʃə(r)] *n* nonciature *f*

nuncio ['nʌnsɪəʊ] *(pl* **nuncios**) *n* nonce *m*

nunnery ['nʌnərɪ] *(pl* **nunneries**) *n* couvent *m ou* monastère *m* (de femmes)

> **Get thee to a nunnery**
> Ce sont les mots que prononce Hamlet dans l'œuvre éponyme de Shakespeare, lorsqu'il rejette Ophélia.
> Aujourd'hui cette phrase ("retire-toi dans un couvent") est utilisée de manière allusive et non sans un certain sexisme lorsqu'un homme demande à une femme de partir, ou encore pour conseiller à quelqu'un de pratiquer l'abstinence sexuelle.

NUPE ['nju:pɪ] *n Formerly (abbr* **National Union of Public Employees**) = ancien syndicat britannique des employés de la fonction publique

nuptial ['nʌpʃəl] *Literary or Hum* **1** *adj* nuptial

2 nuptials *npl* noce *f*, noces *fpl*

►► ***the nuptial bed*** le lit conjugal; ***nuptial blessing*** bénédiction *f* nuptiale; ***nuptial vows*** vœux *mpl* du mariage

NUR [ˌenju:'ɑ:(r)] *n Formerly (abbr* **National Union of Railwaymen**) = ancien syndicat britannique des employés des chemins de fer

nurd *Am* = **nerd**

Nuremberg ['njʊərəmbɜ:g] *n* Nuremberg

►► ***the Nuremberg Trials*** le procès de Nuremberg

Nureyev ['njʊərɪef] *pr n* **Rudolph Nureyev** Rudolph Noureïev

NURMTW [ˌenju:ɑ:ˌremti:'dʌbəlju:] *n (abbr* **National Union of Rail, Maritime and Transport Workers**) = syndicat britannique des cheminots, gens de mer et routiers

nurse [nɜ:s] **1** *n* (**a**) *Med (in hospital)* infirmier(ère) *m,f*; *(privately employed)* infirmier(ère) *m,f*, garde-malade *mf*; **male nurse** infirmier *m*

(**b**) *Br (nanny)* nurse *f*, bonne *f* d'enfants

(**c**) *(wet nurse)* nourrice *f*

2 *vt* (**a**) *(care for)* soigner; **he nursed her through the worst of it** il l'a soignée pendant qu'elle était au plus mal; **she nursed me back to health** elle a pris soin de moi jusqu'à ce que je guérisse; *Fig* **he was nursing a bad hangover** il essayait de faire passer sa gueule de bois; **to nurse one's pride** panser ses blessures (d'amour-propre); **she nursed the boat back into harbour** elle ramena le bateau au port sans encombre; **he nursed the company through the crisis** il a permis à l'entreprise de traverser la crise

(**b**) *(harbour, foster → grudge, hope, desire)* entretenir; *(→ scheme)* mijoter, couver

(**c**) *(breast-feed)* allaiter

(**d**) *(hold)* bercer (dans ses bras); **he sat nursing his fourth whisky** il sirotait son quatrième whisky

3 *vi* (**a**) *(as profession)* être infirmier(ère); **she spent a few years nursing** elle a travaillé pendant quelques années comme infirmière

(**b**) *(infant)* téter

►► *Am* ***nurse's aide*** aide-soignant (aide-soignante) *m,f*; ***nurse shark*** requin-tapis *m*, requin-nourrice *m*

nursehound ['nɜ:shaʊnd] *n Ich* = type de roussette

nurseling = **nursling**

nursemaid ['nɜːsmeɪd] *n* nurse *f*, bonne *f* d'enfants; *Fig* **to play nursemaid to sb** tenir qn par la main

nursery ['nɜːsərɪ] (*pl* **nurseries**) *n* (**a**) (*room → in house*) nursery *f*, chambre *f* d'enfants (**b**) (*day-care centre*) crèche *f*, garderie *f* (**c**) (*school*) école *f* maternelle; **they go to the local nursery** ils vont à l'école maternelle du quartier (**d**) (*for plants, trees*) & *Fig* pépinière *f*

►► ***nursery education*** enseignement *m* de l'école maternelle; ***nursery garden*** pépinière *f*; ***nursery nurse*** puéricultrice *f*; ***nursery rhyme*** comptine *f*; ***nursery school*** (école *f*) maternelle *f*; ***nursery school teacher*** instituteur(trice) *m,f* de maternelle; *Br* ***nursery slopes*** pistes *fpl* pour débutants; *Horseracing* ***nursery stakes*** course *f* pour chevaux de deux ans; ***nursery teacher*** instituteur(trice) *m,f* de maternelle

nurserymaid ['nɜːsərɪmeɪd] *n* nurse *f*, bonne *f* d'enfants

nurseryman ['nɜːsərɪmən] (*pl* **nurserymen** [-mən]) *n* pépiniériste *m*

nursing ['nɜːsɪŋ] **1** *n* (**a**) (*profession*) profession *f* d'infirmier; **when did she take up nursing?** quand a-t-elle commencé ses études d'infirmière? (**b**) (*care*) soins *mpl*; **she needs constant nursing** elle a besoin de soins constants (**c**) (*breast-feeding*) allaitement *m*

2 *adj* (**a**) *Med* d'infirmier; **the nursing staff** le personnel soignant (**b**) (*suckling*) allaitant

►► ***nursing auxiliary*** aide-soignant (aide-soignante) *m,f*; *Am* ***nursing bottle*** biberon *m*; ***nursing bra*** soutien-gorge *m* d'allaitement; ***nursing home*** (*for aged*) maison *f* de retraite; (*for convalescents*) maison *f* de repos; (*for mentally ill*) maison *f* de santé; *Br* (*private clinic*) hôpital *m* privé, clinique *f* privée; ***nursing mother*** mère *f* qui allaite; *Br* ***nursing officer*** infirmier(ère) *m,f* en chef; ***nursing order*** ordre *m* de sœurs infirmières

nursling ['nɜːslɪŋ] *n* nourrisson *m*

nurture ['nɜːtʃə(r)] **1** *n* (**a**) (*upbringing*) éducation *f* (**b**) (*food*) nourriture *f*

2 *vt* (**a**) (*bring up*) élever, éduquer; (*nourish*) nourrir; **a philosophy nurtured on revolutionary principles** une philosophie nourrie de principes révolutionnaires (**b**) (*foster → hope, desire*) entretenir; (*→ plan, scheme*) mijoter, couver

nurturing ['nɜːtʃərɪŋ] *adj* attentionné, maternel

NUS [ˌenjuː'es] *n Br* (*abbr* **National Union of Students**) ≃ UNEF *f*

NUT [ˌenjuː'tiː] *n* (*abbr* **National Union of Teachers**) = syndicat britannique d'enseignants

nut [nʌt] (*pt & pp* **nutted**, *cont* **nutting**) **1** *n* (**a**) *Bot & Culin* = terme générique pour les amandes, noisettes, noix etc; **nuts and raisins** mélange *m* de différents fruits secs (cacahouètes, noisettes, etc) et de raisins secs; *Fam* **she's a hard** *or* **tough nut to crack** elle n'est pas commode ❑; **it's a hard** *or* **tough nut to crack** (*problem*) c'est difficile à résoudre ❑; *Fam* **the American market will be a hard** *or* **tough nut to crack** ça ne sera pas facile de pénétrer le marché américain ❑

(**b**) *Tech* écrou *m*; **nuts and bolts** des écrous *mpl* et des boulons *mpl*; *Fig* **the nuts and bolts of the problem** les détails pratiques du problème; **the nuts and bolts of a language** les éléments de base d'une langue; **to learn the nuts and bolts of a business** apprendre à connaître le fonctionnement d'une entreprise

(**c**) *Fam* (*crazy person*) cinglé(e) *m,f*, dingue *mf*; **what a nut!** il est complètement cinglé *ou* dingue!

(**d**) *Fam* (*enthusiast*) fana *mf*; **she's a golf nut** c'est une fana de golf

(**e**) *Fam* (*head*) caboche *f*, cafetière *f*; **it hit him right on the nut** il l'a reçu en pleine caboche; **to be off one's nut** (*mad*) être dingue *ou* cinglé; **to go off one's nut** (*go insane*) perdre la boule, devenir cinglé; (*get angry*) péter les plombs, piquer une crise; *Br* **to do one's nut** (*get angry*) péter les plombs, piquer une crise; **she really did her nut** elle a piqué une de ces crises

(**f**) (*small lump of coal*) noix *f*, tête-de-moineau *f*

2 *vt Fam* donner un coup de boule à

►► ***nut oil*** (*from walnuts*) huile *f* de noix; (*from hazelnuts*) huile *f* de noisettes

nutant ['njuːtənt] *adj Bot* nutant

nutation [njuː'teɪʃən] *n Astron, Bot & Med* nutation *f*

nut-brown *adj* (couleur) noisette (*inv*); (*hair*) châtain; (*skin*) brun

nutcase ['nʌtkeɪs] *n Fam* cinglé(e) *m,f*, dingue *mf*; **he's a complete nutcase** il est complètement dingue *ou* cinglé *ou* timbré

nutcracker ['nʌtˌkrækə(r)] **1** *n Orn* casse-noix *m inv*

2 nutcrackers *npl* casse-noix *m inv*, casse-noisettes *m inv*

'The Nutcracker (Suite)' *Tchaikovsky* 'Casse-Noisette'

nuthatch ['nʌthætʃ] *n Orn* sittelle *f*

nuthouse ['nʌthaʊs, *pl* -haʊzɪz] *n Fam* maison *f* de fous; **in the nuthouse** chez les fous

nutmeg ['nʌtmeg] **1** *n* (**a**) *Bot* (*nut*) (noix *f* de) muscade *f*; (*tree*) muscadier *m* (**b**) (*in football*) petit pont *m*

2 *vt* (*in football*) **to nutmeg sb** faire un petit pont à qn

nutraceutical [ˌnjuːtrə'sjuːtɪkəl] **1** *n* alicament *m*, aliment *m* nutraceutique

2 *adj* (*foodstuff, product*) nutraceutique

nutria ['njuːtrɪə] *n Zool* ragondin *m*

nutrient ['njuːtrɪənt] **1** *n* substance *f* nutritive

2 *adj* nutritif

nutriment ['njuːtrɪmənt] *n* (*food*) nourriture *f*

nutrition [njuː'trɪʃən] *n* nutrition *f*; **cereals have a high nutrition content** les céréales sont très nourrissantes *ou* nutritives

nutritional [njuː'trɪʃənəl] *adj* (*disorder, process, value*) nutritif; (*science, research*) nutritionnel

►► *Com* ***nutritional labelling*** étiquetage *m* de l'apport nutritionnel

nutritionist [njuː'trɪʃənɪst] *n* nutritionniste *mf*

nutritious [njuː'trɪʃəs] *adj* nutritif, nourrissant

nutritiousness [njuː'trɪʃəsnɪs] *n* nutritivité *f*

nutritive ['njuːtrətɪv] *adj* nutritif

nuts [nʌts] **1** *adj Fam* dingue, cinglé, timbré; **that noise is driving me nuts** ce bruit me rend dingue; **to go nuts** (*go insane*) devenir cinglé, perdre la boule; (*get angry*) péter les plombs, piquer une crise; **to be nuts about sb/sth** être dingue de qn/qch; **to drive sb nuts** rendre qn chèvre

2 *npl very Fam* (*testicles*) couilles *fpl*, roupettes *fpl*

3 *exclam Fam* mince!; *Am* **nuts to them!** oh et puis qu'ils aillent se faire voir!; **nuts to that!** plutôt crever!

nutshell ['nʌtʃel] *n* coquille *f* de noix (*de noisette etc*); **in a nutshell** en un mot; **to put it in a nutshell** pour résumer l'histoire (en un mot)

nutso ['nʌtsəʊ] *adj Am Fam* dingue, cinglé, timbré; **to go nutso** (*go insane*) devenir cinglé, perdre la boule; (*get angry*) péter les plombs, péter une durite; **to be nutso about sb/sth** être dingue de qn/qch; **to drive sb nutso** rendre qn chèvre

nutter ['nʌtə(r)] *n Br Fam* cinglé(e) *m,f*, dingue *m,f*

nuttiness ['nʌtɪnɪs] *n* (**a**) (*taste*) goût *m* de noix (*de noisette etc*) (**b**) *Fam* (*madness*) loufoquerie *f*

nutty ['nʌtɪ] (*compar* **nuttier**, *superl* **nuttiest**) *adj* (**a**) (*tasting of or containing nuts*) aux noix (*aux amandes, aux noisettes etc*); **a nutty flavour** un goût de noix (*de noisette etc*) (**b**) *Fam* (*mad*) dingue, cinglé, timbré; **what a nutty idea!** c'est complètement débile comme idée!; *Hum* **as nutty as a fruitcake** complètement ravagé; **to be nutty about sb/sth** raffoler de qn/qch

nuzzle ['nʌzəl] **1** *vt* (*push with nose*) pousser du nez; (*sniff at*) renifler; (*of animal*) pousser du museau; **to nuzzle sb's hand** fourrer son nez dans la paume de la main de qn; **he nuzzled her neck** il lui caressait le cou de ses lèvres

2 *vi* (**a**) **to nuzzle up against, to nuzzle at** (*push with nose*) pousser du nez; (*sniff at*) renifler; (*of animal*) pousser du museau (**b**) (*nestle*) se blottir; **they nuzzled (up) against their mother** ils se blottirent contre leur mère

NV (*written abbr* **Nevada**) Nevada *m*

NVQ [ˌenviː'kjuː] *n* (*abbr* **National Vocational Qualification**) = diplôme britannique professionnel national

NW (*written abbr* **north-west**) N-O

NWT (*written abbr* **Northwest Territories**) Territoires *mpl* du Nord-Ouest

NY (*written abbr* **New York**) (*city*) New York *m*; (*state*) État *m* de New York

nyala ['njɑːlə] *n Zool* nyala *m*

Nyasaland [naɪ'æsəlænd] *n* Nyassaland *m*

NYC (*written abbr* **New York City**) New York *m*

nyctalopia [ˌnɪktə'ləʊpɪə] *n Med* héméralopie *f*

nyctalopic [ˌnɪktə'ləʊpɪk] *adj Med* héméralope, héméralopique

nyctophobia [ˌnɪktə'fəʊbɪə] *n* nyctophobie *f*, scotophobie *f*

nylon ['naɪlɒn] **1** *n* nylon *m*

2 *comp* (*thread, shirt, stockings*) de *ou* en nylon

3 nylons *npl* (*stockings*) bas *mpl* nylon

NYMEX [ˌenwaɪˌemiː'eks] *n St Exch* (*abbr* **New York Mercantile Exchange**) = marché à terme des produits pétroliers de New York

nymph [nɪmf] *n Myth & Zool* nymphe *f*; **sea nymph** néréide *f*; **tree** *or* **wood nymph** hamadryade *f*; **water nymph** naïade *f*

nymphet ['nɪmfət] *n* nymphette *f*

nympho ['nɪmfəʊ] *n Fam* (*abbr* **nymphomaniac**) nympho *f*

nymphomania [ˌnɪmfə'meɪnɪə] *n* nymphomanie *f*

nymphomaniac [ˌnɪmfə'meɪnɪæk] **1** *n* nymphomane *f*

2 *adj* nymphomane

NYSE [ˌenwaɪˌes'iː] *n St Exch* (*abbr* **New York Stock Exchange**) = la bourse de New York

nystagmus [nɪ'stægməs] *n* nystagmus *m*

nystatin ['nɪstətɪn] *n Biol* nystatine *f*

NZ (*written abbr* **New Zealand**) Nouvelle-Zélande *f*

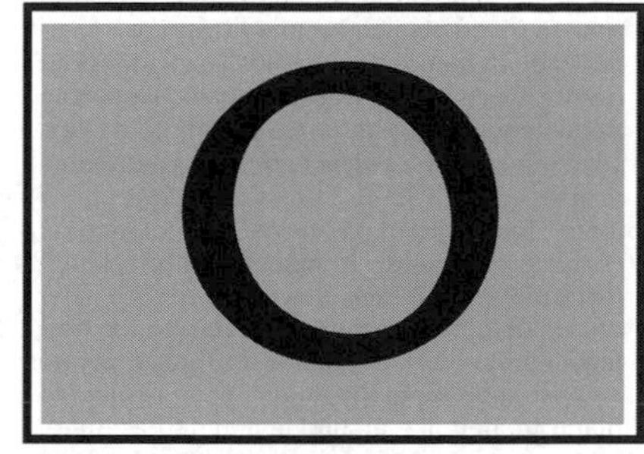

O[1], o[1] [əʊ] *n* (**a**) *(letter)* O, o *m inv*; **two O's** deux O; **O for orange** ≃ O comme Oscar
(**b**) *(zero)* zéro *m*

O[2] *(written abbr* **Ohio**) Ohio *m*

o[2] *exclam* (**a**) *Literary (as vocative)* ô; **o God!** ô mon Dieu! (**b**) *(as exclamation)* oh, ah; **o, what a surprise!** oh, quelle surprise!; **o no!** oh non!

o' [ə] *prep (of)* de

oaf [əʊf] *n (clumsy man)* lourdaud *m*; *(uncouth man)* rustre *m*, mufle *m*; **get out of the way, you great oaf!** pousse-toi, gros lourdaud!

oafish ['əʊfɪʃ] *adj (clumsy)* lourdaud, balourd; *(uncouth)* rustre, mufle

oafishly ['əʊfɪʃlɪ] *adv (clumsily)* d'un air lourdaud; *(uncouthly)* comme un rustre *ou* un mufle

oafishness ['əʊfɪʃnɪs] *n (clumsiness)* balourdise *f*; *(uncouthness)* muflerie *f*

oak [əʊk] **1** *n* (**a**) *(tree, wood)* chêne *m*
(**b**) *(colour)* chêne *m*
(**c**) *Br Old-fashioned Univ* = porte extérieure d'un appartement dans les universités d'Oxford et Cambridge; **to sport one's oak** fermer sa porte aux visiteurs
2 *comp (furniture, door, panelling)* de *ou* en chêne
3 *adj (oak-coloured)* couleur chêne *(inv)*
4 Oaks *n* **the Oaks** = course de plat pour pouliches qui se tient chaque année à Epsom
▸▸ ***oak apple*** noix *f* de galle; ***Oak Apple Day*** = le 29 mai, anniversaire de la Restauration en 1660 de Charles II d'Angleterre qui, dit-on, s'était caché dans un chêne creux pour échapper à Cromwell lors de sa défaite de 1651 face à ce dernier; ***oak forest*** forêt *f* de chênes, chênaie *f*; ***oak tree*** chêne *m*

oaken ['əʊkən] *adj Literary* de *ou* en chêne

oak-leaf cluster *n Am Mil* = barrette portée sur une première décoration en témoignage de mérite renouvelé

oakum ['əʊkəm] *n* étoupe *f*, filasse *f*; **to pick oakum** démêler *ou* tirer l'étoupe

O & M [ˌəʊənd'em] *n (abbr* **organization and methods**) O et M *f*

OAP [ˌəʊeɪ'piː] *n Br (abbr* **old age pensioner**) retraité(e) *m,f*; **students and OAPs half price** *(sign)* ≃ étudiants et carte vermeille demi-tarif

oar [ɔː(r)] **1** *n* (**a**) *(for rowing)* rame *f*, aviron *m*; *Br Fam* **to stick** *or* **to put one's oar in** ramener sa fraise; **to rest on one's oars** lever les rames; *Fig* se reposer sur ses lauriers (**b**) *(person)* rameur(euse) *m,f*
2 *vt Literary* ramer
3 *vi Literary* ramer

oarfish ['ɔːfɪʃ] *n Ich* régalec *m*

oarlock ['ɔːlɒk] *n (U-shaped)* dame *f* de nage; *(pin)* tolet *m*

oarsman ['ɔːzmən] *(pl* **oarsmen** [-mən]) *n* rameur *m*

oarsmanship ['ɔːzmənʃɪp] *n (UNCOUNT)* compétences *fpl* de rameur

oarswoman ['ɔːzˌwʊmən] *(pl* **oarswomen** [-ˌwɪmɪn]) *n* rameuse *f*

OAS [ˌəʊeɪ'es] *n* (**a**) *(abbr* **Organization of American States**) OÉA *f* (**b**) *(abbr* **Organisation armée secrète**) OAS *f*

Oasis® [əʊ'eɪsɪs] *n (for flowers)* mousse *f* florale

oasis [əʊ'eɪsɪs] *(pl* **oases** [-siːz]) *n also Fig* oasis *f*; **an oasis of calm** une oasis *ou* un havre de paix

oast [əʊst] *n Br* (**a**) *(kiln)* séchoir *m* à houblon (**b**) *(building)* sécherie *f* (de houblon)

oasthouse ['əʊsthaʊs, *pl* -haʊzɪz] *n* sécherie *f* (de houblon)

oat [əʊt] **1** *n (plant)* avoine *f*
2 oats *npl* avoine *f*; **a field of oats** un champ d'avoine; *Am Fam* **to be feeling one's oats** *(be self-important)* ne plus se sentir, faire l'important ❑; *(be full of energy)* être en pleine forme ❑; *(be cheerful)* avoir la pêche; *Br Fam* **to be off one's oats** *(be off form)* se sentir patraque, ne pas être dans son assiette; *(have no appetite)* avoir perdu l'appétit ❑; *Br Fam* **to get one's oats** *(have sex)* tirer un coup; **is he getting his oats?** est-ce qu'il a ce qu'il lui faut au lit?; *Fam Fig* **to sow one's (wild) oats** jeter sa gourme ❑
▸▸ ***oat grass*** fromental *m*, avoine *f* élevée

oatcake ['əʊtkeɪk] *n* gâteau *m* sec (d'avoine)

oaten ['əʊtən] *adj* d'avoine

oatflakes ['əʊtfleɪks] *npl* flocons *mpl* d'avoine

oath [əʊθ, *pl* əʊðz] *n* (**a**) *(vow)* serment *m*; **he took** *or* **swore an oath never to return** il fit le serment *ou* il jura de ne jamais revenir; **to take the oath of allegiance** faire (le) serment d'allégeance; **to swear on oath** jurer (sous serment); **it's true, on my oath!** c'est vrai, je vous le jure!; *Law* **to be on** *or* **under oath** être sous serment, être assermenté; *Law* **to put sb on** *or* **under oath** faire prêter serment à qn; **she swore/testified under oath that...** elle a juré/témoigné sous serment que...
(**b**) *(swearword)* juron *m*; **he let out a string of oaths** il a laissé échapper un torrent d'injures

oatmeal ['əʊtmiːl] **1** *n (UNCOUNT)* (**a**) *(flakes)* flocons *mpl* d'avoine; *(flour)* farine *f* d'avoine (**b**) *(colour)* beige *m* naturel
2 *adj (colour)* beige naturel
▸▸ ***oatmeal porridge*** bouillie *f* d'avoine, porridge *m*

OAU [ˌəʊeɪ'juː] *n (abbr* **Organization of African Unity**) OUA *f*

OB [ˌəʊ'biː] *n TV (abbr* **outside broadcast**) émission *f* réalisée en dehors des studios

Obadiah [ˌəʊbə'daɪə] *pr n Bible* Abdias

obbligato = **obligato**

obconic [ɒb'kɒnɪk], **obconical** [ɒb'kɒnɪkəl] *adj Bot* obconique

obcordate [ɒb'kɔːdeɪt] *adj Bot* obcordiforme, obcordé

obduracy ['ɒbdjʊrəsɪ] *n Formal* (**a**) *(obstinacy)* obstination *f*, entêtement *m*; *(inflexibility)* inflexibilité *f*, intransigeance *f* (**b**) *(hardheartedness)* dureté *f* (de cœur), insensibilité *f*

obdurate ['ɒbdjʊrət] *adj Formal* (**a**) *(obstinate)* obstiné, entêté; *(unyielding)* inflexible; **to remain obdurate** ne pas fléchir, rester inflexible; **we met with an obdurate refusal** on nous opposa un refus catégorique (**b**) *(hardhearted)* insensible, dur

obdurately ['ɒbdjʊrətlɪ] *adv Formal (obstinately)* avec entêtement; *(to resist)* inflexiblement; **to remain obdurately silent** garder un silence obstiné *ou* têtu; **to refuse obdurately** refuser obstinément, s'entêter à refuser

obdurateness ['ɒbdjʊrətnɪs] *n Formal* (**a**) *(obstinacy)* obstination *f*, entêtement *m*; *(inflexibility)* inflexibilité *f*, intransigeance *f* (**b**) *(hard-heartedness)* dureté *f* (de cœur), insensibilité *f*

OBE [ˌəʊbiː'iː] *n (abbr* **Officer of the Order of the British Empire**) = distinction honorifique britannique

obedience [ə'biːdjəns] *n* (**a**) *(gen)* obéissance *f*; **to show obedience to sb** obéir à qn; *Literary* **to owe obedience to sb** devoir obédience à qn; **in obedience to her wishes** conformément à ses vœux; **in obedience to his conscience** obéissant à sa conscience; **to command obedience** savoir se faire obéir (**b**) *Rel* obédience *f*

obedient [ə'biːdjənt] *adj* obéissant, docile; **to be obedient to sb** obéir à qn, être obéissant envers qn; *Formal Old-fashioned* **your obedient servant** *(in letters)* votre humble serviteur

obediently [ə'biːdjəntlɪ] *adv* docilement; **they followed him obediently** ils le suivirent docilement *ou* sans discuter

obeisance [əʊ'beɪsəns] *n Literary* (**a**) *(homage)* hommage *m*; **to make** *or* **to pay obeisance to sb** rendre hommage à qn (**b**) *(bow)* révérence *f*; *(sign)* geste *m* de respect

obelisk ['ɒbəlɪsk] *n* (**a**) *(column)* obélisque *m* (**b**) *Typ* croix *f*, obel *m*, obèle *m*

obelus ['ɒbələs] *(pl* **obeli** [-laɪ]) *n (in paleography)* obel *m*, obèle *m*

Oberon ['əʊbərɒn] *pr n Myth* Oberon

obese [əʊ'biːs] *adj* obèse

obesity [əʊ'biːsətɪ], **obeseness** [əʊ'biːsnɪs] *n* obésité *f*

obey [ə'beɪ] **1** *vt* obéir à; **he always obeyed his mother/his intuition/the law** il a toujours obéi à sa mère/à son intuition/aux lois; **an order which he refused to obey** un ordre auquel il refusa d'obéir; **the plane is no longer obeying the controls** l'avion ne répond plus; **I want these instructions obeyed to the letter** je veux que ces instructions soient suivies à la lettre
2 *vi* obéir, obtempérer

obfuscate ['ɒbfʌskeɪt] *vt Formal (obscure → issue)* obscurcir, embrouiller; *(→ mind)* embrouiller; *(perplex → person)* embrouiller, dérouter

obfuscation [ˌɒbfʌs'keɪʃən] *n Formal (of issue)* obscurcissement *m*, embrouillement *m*; *(of mind)* embrouillement *m*; *(of person)* confusion *f*, embrouillement *m*

Obie Award ['əʊbɪ-] *n* = prix d'art dramatique accordé à une mise en scène "off-Broadway"

obit ['əʊbɪt] *n Fam* nécrologie ❑ *f*

obiter dictum [ˌɒbɪtə'dɪktəm] *(pl* **obiter dicta** [-'dɪktə]) *n Law* opinion *f* judiciaire incidente; *Literature* **obiter dicta** *(of writer)* opinions *fpl* et propos *mpl*

obituarist [ə'bɪtʃʊərɪst] *n* nécrologue *mf*

obituary [ə'bɪtʃʊərɪ] *(pl* **obituaries**) **1** *n* nécrologie *f*, notice *f* nécrologique; **the obituary column, the obituaries** la rubrique nécrologique
2 *adj* nécrologique

object[1] ['ɒbdʒɪkt] *n* (**a**) *(thing)* objet *m*, chose *f*; **an unidentified object** un objet non identifié
(**b**) *(aim)* objet *m*, but *m*, fin *f*; **the real object of his visit** le véritable objet de sa visite; **with the sole object of pleasing you** dans le seul but de *ou* à seule fin de vous plaire; **with this object in mind** *or* **in view** dans ce but, à cette fin; **that's the (whole) object of the exercise** c'est (justement là) le but de l'opération; **money is no object** peu importe le prix, le prix est sans importance; **money is no object to them** ils n'ont pas de problèmes d'argent; **time is no object** peu importe le temps que cela prendra
(**c**) *(focus)* objet *m*; **an object of ridicule/interest** un objet de ridicule/d'intérêt; **the object of his love** l'objet *m* de son amour; **object of study** objet *m ou* sujet *m* d'étude
(**d**) *Gram (of verb)* complément *m* d'objet; *(of preposition)* objet *m*; **direct/indirect object** complément *m* d'objet direct/indirect
(**e**) *Comput (in document)* objet *m*
▸▸ ***object ball*** *(in snooker, pool, billiards)* bille *f* visée; ***object glass*** objectif *m*; ***object language*** *Ling (metalanguage)* métalangage *m*; *Comput* langage *m* objet; ***object lesson*** *(example)* démonstration *f*, illustration *f (d'un principe)*; *Sch*

leçon *f* de choses; **it was an object lesson in how to lose votes** ce fut une illustration (parfaite) de la façon dont il faut s'y prendre pour perdre des voix; **it was an object lesson in persistence** ce fut un parfait exemple de persévérance; *Comput* ***object program*** programme *m* objet

object[2] [əb'dʒekt] **1** *vi* élever une objection; *(stronger)* protester; **to object to sth** faire objection à qch; *(of demonstrators etc)* protester contre qch; **many groups objected to the new law** de nombreux groupes ont protesté contre *ou* se sont opposés à la nouvelle loi; **I object to being treated like a child** je n'aime pas qu'on me prenne pour un gamin; **they object to working overtime** ils ne sont pas d'accord pour faire des heures supplémentaires; **if you don't object** si vous n'y voyez pas d'inconvénient; **you know how your father objects to it!** tu sais combien ton père y est opposé!; **I object!** je proteste!; **I object strongly to that remark!** je proteste vigoureusement contre cette remarque!; **I object strongly to your attitude** je trouve votre attitude proprement inadmissible; **I wouldn't object to a cup of tea** je ne dirais pas non à *ou* je prendrais volontiers une tasse de thé; **he objects to her smoking** il désapprouve qu'elle fume; **she objects to his coming** elle n'est pas d'accord pour qu'il vienne; **why do you object to all my friends?** pourquoi cette hostilité à l'égard de tous mes amis?; **it's not her I object to but her husband** ce n'est pas elle qui me déplaît, c'est son mari; **if no one objects** si personne n'y voit d'objection(s); *Law* **to object to a witness** récuser un témoin

2 *vt* objecter; **I objected that it was too late** j'ai objecté qu'il était trop tard

objectification [əb,dʒektɪfɪ'keɪʃən] *n* objectivation *f*

objectify [əb'dʒektɪfaɪ] *vt* objectiver

objection [əb'dʒekʃən] *n* **(a)** *(protest, argument against)* objection *f*; **are there any objections?** y a-t-il des objections?; **to make** *or* **to raise an objection** faire *ou* soulever une objection; **I have no objection to his coming** je ne vois pas d'objection à ce qu'il vienne; **I have no objection to his friends** je n'ai rien contre ses amis; **if you have no objection** si vous n'y voyez pas d'inconvénient; *Law* **objection!** objection!; *Law* **objection sustained/overruled!** objection retenue/rejetée!

(b) *(reason for objecting)* inconvénient *m*; **the chief objection to your plan is its cost** le plus grand inconvénient de votre projet, c'est son coût

objectionable [əb'dʒekʃənəbəl] *adj (unpleasant)* désagréable; *(blameworthy)* répréhensible; **a highly objectionable smell/man** une odeur/un homme insupportable; **to use objectionable language** parler vulgairement; **I find his views objectionable** je n'aime pas sa façon de penser; **what is so objectionable about her behaviour?** qu'est-ce qu'on peut lui reprocher?

objectionableness [əb'dʒekʃənəbəlnɪs] *n (unpleasantness)* caractère *m* désagréable; *(blameworthiness)* caractère *m* répréhensible

objectionably [əb'dʒekʃənəblɪ] *adv (unpleasantly)* désagréablement; *(in a blameworthy manner)* de façon répréhensible

objective [əb'dʒektɪv] **1** *adj* **(a)** *(unbiased)* objectif, impartial; **an objective observer** un observateur impartial

(b) *(real, observable)* objectif

(c) *Gram* objectif

2 *n* **(a)** *(aim)* objectif *m*, but *m*; **to achieve** *or* **to reach one's objective** atteindre son but; **the committee has set out its objectives** le comité a fixé ses objectifs; **our objective for this year is to increase sales by 10 percent** nous avons pour objectif d'augmenter nos ventes de 10 pour cent au cours de l'année prochaine

(b) *Gram* accusatif *m*, cas *m* objectif

(c) *Phot* objectif *m*

►► *Gram* ***the objective case*** le cas objectif; ***objective genitive*** génitif *m* objectif; ***objective reality*** la réalité objective; *Med* ***objective symptoms*** signes *mpl*; ***objective test*** test *m* objectif

objectively [əb'dʒektɪvlɪ] *adv* **(a)** *(unbiasedly)* objectivement, impartialement **(b)** *(really, externally)* objectivement

objectivism [əb'dʒektɪvɪzəm] *n* objectivisme *m*

objectivist [əb'dʒektɪvɪst] **1** *n* objectiviste *mf*

2 *adj* objectiviste

objectivity [,ɒbdʒek'tɪvətɪ] *n* objectivité *f*

objectivize, -ise [əb'dʒektɪvaɪz] *vt* objectiver

objector [əb'dʒektə(r)] *n* opposant(e) *m,f*; **are there many objectors to the proposal?** y a-t-il beaucoup de gens contre la proposition?

object-orientated *adj Comput* orienté objet

►► ***object-orientated language*** langage *m* à objets; ***object-orientated programming*** programmation *f* par objets

objet d'art [,ɒbʒeɪ'dɑː(r)] *n* objet *m* d'art

objurgate ['ɒbdʒəgeɪt] *vt* accabler de reproches

objurgation [,ɒbdʒə'geɪʃən] *n* objurgation *f*, réprimande *f*

oblate ['ɒbleɪt] **1** *adj Geom* aplati (aux pôles)

2 *n Rel* oblat(e) *m,f*

oblation [ə'bleɪʃən] *n Rel (ceremony)* oblation *f*; *(thing offered)* oblation *f*, oblats *mpl*

oblative ['ɒblətɪv] *adj Psy* oblatif

obligate ['ɒblɪgeɪt] *vt* **(a)** *Am Formal or Br (compel)* obliger, contraindre; **to be/to feel obligated to do sth** être/se sentir obligé de faire qch **(b)** *Am Fin (funds, credits)* affecter

obligation [,ɒblɪ'geɪʃən] *n* obligation *f*; **to be under an obligation to do sth** être dans l'obligation de faire qch; **you are under no obligation to reply** vous n'êtes pas tenu de répondre, rien ne vous oblige à répondre; **to be under an obligation to sb** avoir une dette de reconnaissance envers qn; **I am under a great obligation to him** je lui suis redevable de beaucoup; **to put** *or* **to place sb under an obligation to do sth** mettre qn dans l'obligation de faire qch; **it is my obligation to inform you that...** il est de mon devoir de *ou* je suis tenu de vous informer que...; **family obligations** obligations *fpl* familiales; **moral obligations compel me to refuse** je suis moralement obligé de refuser; **to meet one's obligations** satisfaire à ses obligations, assumer ses engagements

obligato [,ɒblɪ'gɑːtəʊ] *adj Mus* obligé

obligatory [ə'blɪgətrɪ] *adj* obligatoire; **attendance is obligatory** la présence est obligatoire

oblige [ə'blaɪdʒ] **1** *vt* **(a)** *(constrain)* obliger; **to oblige sb to do sth** obliger qn à faire qch; **you're not obliged to come** tu n'es pas obligé de venir

(b) *(do a favour to)* rendre service à, *Formal* obliger; *Formal* **I would be obliged if you would refrain from smoking** vous m'obligeriez beaucoup en ne fumant pas; *Formal* **I would be obliged if you could send me the relevant details** je vous serais reconnaissant de bien vouloir m'envoyer les renseignements nécessaires; *Formal* **could you oblige me with a match?** auriez-vous l'amabilité *ou* l'obligeance de me donner une allumette?; **much obliged!** merci beaucoup!; **to be obliged to sb for sth** être reconnaissant à qn pour qch, savoir gré à qn de qch; **she obliged the guests with a song** elle a consenti à chanter pour les invités

2 *vi* **always ready to oblige!** toujours prêt à rendre service!; **I would be only too glad to oblige** je serais ravi de vous rendre service

obligee [,ɒblɪ'dʒiː] *n Com* **(a)** *(creditor)* créancier(ère) *m,f* **(b)** *(bondholder)* obligataire *mf*

obliging [ə'blaɪdʒɪŋ] *adj* serviable, obligeant; **our neighbours are very obliging** nos voisins sont très serviables; **it was very obliging of him** c'était très aimable à lui *ou* de sa part

obligingly [ə'blaɪdʒɪŋlɪ] *adv* aimablement, obligeamment; **the letter you obligingly sent me** la lettre que vous avez eu l'obligeance de m'envoyer; **"any time", he said obligingly** "je vous en prie", dit-il aimablement

oblique [ə'bliːk] **1** *adj* **(a)** *Geom (slanted)* oblique **(b)** *(indirect → reference, hint etc)* indirect; **oblique glance** regard *m* en biais; **an oblique reference** une référence indirecte **(c)** *Bot* oblique **(d)** *Gram* oblique

2 *n* **(a)** *Geom* oblique *f*; *Anat* oblique *m* **(b)** *Typ & Comput* barre *f* oblique

►► ***oblique angle*** angle *m* oblique; **at an oblique angle to the road** en biais par rapport à la route

obliquely [ə'bliːklɪ] *adv* **(a)** *Geom* obliquement, en biais **(b)** *(indirectly → refer)* indirectement; *(→ glance)* de *ou* en biais

obliqueness [ə'bliːknɪs], **obliquity** [ə'blɪkwətɪ] *(pl* **obliquities***)* *n* **(a)** *Astron & Geom* obliquité *f*

(b) *(indirectness → of reference, hint)* caractère *m* indirect

obliterate [ə'blɪtəreɪt] *vt* **(a)** *(destroy, erase → figures, footprints, traces etc)* effacer; *(→ the past, a culture)* annihiler; *(→ buildings, town, evidence)* détruire; **the town was all but obliterated during the war** la ville a été quasiment rayée de la carte pendant la guerre; **to obliterate the past** faire table rase du passé **(b)** *(cancel → stamp)* oblitérer

obliteration [ə,blɪtə'reɪʃən] *n* **(a)** *(destruction, erasure → of figures, footprints, traces etc)* effacement *m*; *(of the past, a culture)* anéantissement *m*; *(of buildings, town, evidence)* destruction *f* **(b)** *(of stamp)* oblitération *f*

oblivion [ə'blɪvɪən] *n* **(a)** *(being forgotten)* oubli *m*; **to fall** *or* **to sink into oblivion** tomber dans l'oubli; **to consign to oblivion** condamner à l'oubli; **to save sb/sth from oblivion** tirer qn/qch de l'oubli, sauver qn/qch de l'oubli **(b)** *(unconsciousness)* inconscience *f*, oubli *m*; **he had drunk himself into oblivion** il était abruti par l'alcool

oblivious [ə'blɪvɪəs] *adj* inconscient; **she was oblivious of** *or* **to what was happening** elle n'avait pas conscience de *ou* n'était pas consciente de ce qui se passait; **he remained oblivious to our comments** il est resté sourd à nos remarques; **he is oblivious to the fact that millions of people are starving** il n'est pas conscient du fait que des millions de gens meurent de faim

obliviously [ə'blɪvɪəslɪ] *adv* en toute inconscience

obliviousness [ə'blɪvɪəsnɪs] *n* inconscience *f*

oblong ['ɒblɒŋ] **1** *n (rectangle)* rectangle *m*

2 *adj (rectangular)* rectangulaire; *(elongated)* allongé, oblong

obloquy ['ɒbləkwɪ] *(pl* **obloquies***)* *n (UNCOUNT) Formal* **(a)** *(abuse)* insultes *fpl*, injures *fpl*; *(defamation)* diffamation *f* **(b)** *(disgrace)* opprobre *m*

obnoxious [əb'nɒkʃəs] *adj (person)* odieux, ignoble; *(behaviour)* odieux; *(smell)* ignoble, infect

obnoxiously [əb'nɒkʃəslɪ] *adv (behave)* de façon odieuse

obnoxiousness [əb'nɒkʃəsnɪs] *n (of behaviour)* caractère *m* odieux; *(of smell)* caractère *m* infect

obnubilation [ɒb,njuːbɪ'leɪʃən] *n Literary* obnubilation *f*

o.b.o. *(written abbr* **or best offer***)* à déb.

oboe ['əʊbəʊ] *n* hautbois *m*

►► ***oboe d'amore*** hautbois *m* d'amour

oboist ['əʊbəʊɪst] *n* hautbois *m (musicien)*, hautboïste *mf*

obscene [əb'siːn] *adj* obscène; *Fig (profits, prices, demands etc)* scandaleux, indécent; **an obscene gesture** un geste obscène; **an obscene publication** une publication obscène; *Fig* **it's obscene to earn so much money** c'est indécent de gagner autant d'argent

obscenely [əb'siːnlɪ] *adv* d'une manière obscène; **she gestured obscenely** elle fit un geste obscène; *Fig* **he's obscenely rich** il est tellement riche que c'en est dégoûtant

obscenity [əb'senətɪ] *(pl* **obscenities***)* *n* **(a)** *(UNCOUNT) (obscene language)* obscénité *f*, obscénités *fpl* **(b)** *(obscene word)* obscénité *f*, grossièreté *f*; **to shout obscenities** crier des obscénités **(c)** *Fig* obscénité *f*; **the obscenity of war** l'obscénité *f* de la guerre; **war is an obscenity** la guerre est une chose obscène

►► ***obscenity laws*** lois *fpl* concernant les outrages à la pudeur

obscurantism [,ɒbskjʊə'ræntɪzəm] *n Formal* obscurantisme *m*

obscurantist [,ɒbskjʊə'ræntɪst] *Formal* **1** *n* obscurantiste *mf*

2 *adj* obscurantiste

obscuration [,ɒbskjʊ'reɪʃən] *n* **(a)** *(darkening)* obscurcissement *m* **(b)** *Astron* obscuration *f*, éclipse *f*

obscure [əb'skjʊə(r)] **1** *adj* **(a)** *(not clear)* obscur; **the meaning is rather obscure** le sens n'est pas très clair; **an obscure feeling of unease** un obscur *ou* vague sentiment de malaise; **for some obscure reason he thought it would help** il pensait, pour d'obscures raisons, que ça serait utile; **of obscure birth** de naissance obscure

(**b**) *(little-known → writer, actor)* obscur; *(→ place)* perdu; **she comes from an obscure little village** elle vient d'un petit village perdu

(**c**) *(dark)* obscur, sombre; **to grow** *or* **become obscure** s'obscurcir, s'assombrir

2 *vt* (**a**) *(hide)* cacher; **that building obscures the view** ce bâtiment cache la vue; **to obscure the truth** cacher *ou* dissimuler la vérité

(**b**) *(confuse)* obscurcir, embrouiller; **to obscure the facts/the issue** embrouiller les faits/la question

(**c**) *(darken)* obscurcir, assombrir

obscurely [əb'skjʊəlɪ] *adv* (**a**) *(feel, see)* vaguement, obscurément (**b**) *(speak)* de façon obscure *ou* mystérieuse

obscurity [əb'skjʊərətɪ] *(pl* **obscurities***)* *n* (**a**) *(insignificance)* obscurité *f*; **to rise from obscurity to fame** passer de l'anonymat à la célébrité; **to fall into obscurity** sombrer dans l'oubli (**b**) *(difficulty)* obscurité *f* (**c**) *(darkness)* obscurité *f*, ténèbres *fpl*

obsequent ['ɒbsɪkwənt] *adj Formal* obséquent

obsequies ['ɒbsɪkwɪz] *npl Formal* obsèques *fpl*

obsequious [əb'siːkwɪəs] *adj Formal* obséquieux

obsequiously [əb'siːkwɪəslɪ] *adv Formal* obséquieusement

obsequiousness [əb'siːkwɪəsnɪs] *n Formal* obséquiosité *f*

observable [əb'zɜːvəbəl] *adj (visible)* observable, visible; *(discernible)* perceptible, appréciable; **behaviour observable in humans** un comportement observable *ou* que l'on peut observer chez les humains

observably [əb'zɜːvəblɪ] *adv* perceptiblement, visiblement

observance [əb'zɜːvəns] *n* (**a**) *(recognition → of custom, law etc)* observation *f*, observance *f*; *(→ of anniversary)* célébration *f* (**b**) *Rel (rite, ceremony)* observance *f*

observant [əb'zɜːvənt] *adj (alert)* observateur; **how observant of him!** comme il est observateur!, rien ne lui échappe!

observantly [əb'zɜːvəntlɪ] *adv* perspicacement

observation [ˌɒbzə'veɪʃən] *n* (**a**) *(study)* observation *f*, surveillance *f*; **the observation of nature** l'observation *f* de la nature; **to be under observation** *(patient)* être en observation; *(by police)* être surveillé par la police *ou* sous surveillance policière; **they are keeping the house under observation** ils ont placé la maison sous surveillance; **this fact has not escaped his observation** ce fait n'a pas échappé à sa vigilance

(**b**) *(comment)* observation *f*, remarque *f*; **I have a few observations to make** j'ai quelques remarques à faire

(**c**) *(perception)* observation *f*; **to have great powers of observation** avoir de grandes facultés d'observation

(**d**) *Naut* relèvement *m*

▸▸ ***observation aircraft*** avion *m* de reconnaissance; ***observation balloon*** ballon *m* d'observation; *Rail* ***observation car*** voiture *f* panoramique; ***observation deck*** terrasse *f* panoramique; ***observation point*** point *m* d'observation; *Mil* ***observation post*** poste *m* d'observation; ***observation satellite*** satellite *m* d'observation; ***observation tower*** tour *f* de guet, mirador *m*; *Med* ***observation ward*** salle *f* d'observation

observational [ˌɒbzə'veɪʃənəl] *adj (faculties, powers)* d'observation; *(technique, research, data, study)* qui repose sur l'observation

observatory [əb'zɜːvətrɪ] *(pl* **observatories***)* *n* observatoire *m*

observe [əb'zɜːv] *vt* (**a**) *(see, notice)* observer, remarquer; **did you observe anything strange?** tu as remarqué quelque chose d'anormal?

(**b**) *(study, pay attention to)* observer; **he likes observing human behaviour** il aime observer *ou* étudier le comportement humain; **the police are observing his movements** la police surveille ses allées et venues

(**c**) *(comment, remark)* (faire) remarquer, (faire) observer; **"she seems worried", he observed** "elle a l'air inquiet", fit-il remarquer

(**d**) *(abide by, keep → the law, the proprieties, a fast)* observer; *(→ the Sabbath)* respecter, observer; *(→ order)* se conformer à; **to fail to observe the law** ne pas observer la loi; **to observe a minute's silence** observer une minute de silence

observer [əb'zɜːvə(r)] *n* (**a**) *(watcher)* observateur(trice) *m,f*; **to the casual observer** pour un non-initié (**b**) *(at official ceremony, election)* observateur(trice) *m,f*; **he attended as an observer** il était présent en tant qu'observateur (**c**) *(commentator)* spécialiste *mf*, expert *m*; **political observers** experts *mpl ou* spécialistes *mfpl* en politique; *Press* **The Observer** = journal britannique de centre gauche, paraissant le dimanche

obsess [əb'ses] **1** *vt* obséder; **he's obsessed with punctuality** c'est un maniaque de la ponctualité; **she's obsessed with the idea of becoming an actress** elle n'a qu'une idée, devenir actrice; **he became obsessed by the horrific image** cette vision d'horreur se mit à le hanter; **to be obsessed with death** être obsédé par la mort

2 *vi* **to obsess about sth** être obsédé par qch

obsession [əb'seʃən] *n (fixed idea)* obsession *f*, idée *f* fixe; *(obsessive fear)* hantise *f*; **it's becoming an obsession with him** ça devient une idée fixe *ou* une obsession chez lui; **she has an obsession about punctuality** c'est une maniaque de la ponctualité; **because of his obsession with death** à cause de la fascination que la mort exerce sur lui

obsessional [əb'seʃənəl] *adj* obsessionnel

obsessive [əb'sesɪv] **1** *adj* (**a**) *(person, behaviour, jealousy)* obsessionnel; **he's obsessive about cleanliness** c'est un maniaque de la propreté; **he has an obsessive interest in sex** c'est un obsédé sexuel; **he was becoming quite obsessive about it** ça devenait une obsession chez lui; **his obsessive fear of failure/death** sa hantise de l'échec/de la mort

(**b**) *(thought, image)* obsédant

2 *n* obsessionnel(elle) *m,f*; **you're turning into an obsessive** ça tourne à l'obsession chez toi

obsessive-compulsive disorder *n Psy* névrose *f* obsessionnelle

obsessively [əb'sesɪvlɪ] *adv* d'une manière obsessionnelle; **he's obsessively cautious** il est d'une prudence obsessionnelle; **he is obsessively tidy** c'est un maniaque de la propreté; **he is obsessively attached to the toy** il a un attachement maladif pour ce jouet; **she is obsessively attached to her mother** elle fait une fixation sur sa mère

obsidian [ɒb'sɪdɪən] *n* obsidienne *f*

obsolescence [ˌɒbsə'lesəns] *n (of equipment, consumer goods)* obsolescence *f*; *Com* **planned** *or* **built-in obsolescence** obsolescence *f* planifiée, désuétude *f* calculée; **to fall into obsolescence** tomber en désuétude

▸▸ *Ins* ***obsolescence clause*** clause *f* de vétusté

obsolescent [ˌɒbsə'lesənt] *adj* qui tombe en désuétude; *(equipment, consumer goods)* obsolescent

obsolete ['ɒbsəliːt] *adj* (**a**) *(practice, idea)* démodé, désuet(ète); *(law, idea)* dépassé; *(machinery)* dépassé, obsolète; *(institution)* archaïque, caduc (caduque); **those machines have been obsolete for years** ces machines sont dépassées depuis des années (**b**) *Ling* obsolète (**c**) *Biol* atrophié

obsoleteness ['ɒbsəliːtnɪs] *n* (**a**) *(of practice, idea, law)* caractère *m* désuet; *(of machinery)* obsolescence *f*; *(of institution)* caractère *m* archaïque (**b**) *Ling* caractère *m* obsolète

obstacle ['ɒbstəkəl] *n* obstacle *m*; **what are the obstacles to free trade?** qu'est-ce qui fait obstacle au libre-échange?; **to put obstacles in sb's way** mettre des bâtons dans les roues à qn

▸▸ ***obstacle course*** parcours *m* d'obstacles; *Fig* parcours *m* du combattant; ***obstacle race*** course *f* d'obstacles

obstetric [ɒb'stetrɪk] *adj* obstétrical; *(nurses)* en obstétrique

obstetrical [ɒb'stetrɪkəl] *adj* obstétrical

obstetrician [ˌɒbstə'trɪʃən] *n* obstétricien(enne) *m,f*, médecin *m* accoucheur

obstetrics [ɒb'stetrɪks] *n (UNCOUNT)* obstétrique *f*

obstinacy ['ɒbstɪnəsɪ] *n* (**a**) *(stubbornness)* obstination *f*, entêtement *m*; *(tenacity)* opiniâtreté *f*, ténacité *f* (**b**) *(persistence)* persistance *f*; **the obstinacy of an infection** le caractère persistant d'une infection

obstinate ['ɒbstənət] *adj* (**a**) *(stubborn)* obstiné, entêté, têtu; *(tenacious)* obstiné, tenace, acharné; **an obstinate refusal** un refus obstiné; **to meet with obstinate resistance** se heurter à une résistance obstinée *ou* acharnée (**b**) *(persistent → cold, illness)* persistant, tenace; *(→ stain, grease)* rebelle; **an obstinate fever** une fièvre persistante

obstinately ['ɒbstənətlɪ] *adv (stubbornly)* obstinément, avec acharnement; **to behave obstinately** se montrer obstiné

obstreperous [əb'strepərəs] *adj Formal or Hum (noisy)* bruyant; *(disorderly)* turbulent, indiscipliné; *(recalcitrant)* récalcitrant; **to get obstreperous about sth** faire du scandale à propos de qch; **don't (you) get obstreperous with me!** tu ne vas pas me faire des histoires!; **a class of obstreperous children** une classe d'enfants indisciplinés *ou* turbulents

obstreperously [əb'strepərəslɪ] *adv Formal or Hum (noisily)* bruyamment; *(in a disorderly manner)* avec turbulence; *(recalcitrantly)* à contrecœur

obstreperousness [əb'strepərəsnɪs] *n Formal or Hum (of crowd, children)* caractère *m* tapageur; *(of someone's tone)* agressivité *f*; **I won't put up with your obstreperousness any longer** j'en ai assez de ton agressivité

obstruct [əb'strʌkt] *vt* (**a**) *(block → passage, road, traffic)* bloquer, obstruer; *(→ pipe)* boucher; *(→ vein, artery)* obstruer, boucher; **don't obstruct the exits** ne bloquez pas les sorties; **the lane was obstructed by** *or* **with fallen trees** le chemin était bloqué par des arbres déracinés; **her hat obstructed my view** son chapeau me cachait la vue

(**b**) *(impede → progress, measures)* faire obstruction *ou* obstacle à, entraver; **to obstruct progress/justice** entraver la marche du progrès/le cours de la justice; **he was arrested for obstructing a policeman in the course of his duty** on l'a arrêté pour avoir entravé un agent dans l'exercice de ses fonctions

(**c**) *Sport (opponent)* faire obstruction à

obstruction [əb'strʌkʃən] *n* (**a**) *(impeding → of progress, measures)* obstruction *f*; **a policy of obstruction** une politique d'obstruction

(**b**) *(blockage, obstacle → gen)* obstacle *m*; *(→ in vein, artery)* obstruction *f*; *(→ in pipe)* bouchon *m*; **the accident caused an obstruction in the road** l'accident a bloqué la route; *Med* **bowel obstruction, obstruction of the bowel** occlusion *f* intestinale

(**c**) *Sport* obstruction *f*

(**d**) *Law* obstruction *f* de la voie publique

▸▸ ***obstruction lights*** feux *mpl* d'obstacle

obstructionism [əb'strʌkʃənɪzəm] *n Pol* obstructionnisme *m*

obstructionist [əb'strʌkʃənɪst] *Pol* **1** *n* obstructionniste *mf*

2 *adj* obstructionniste

obstructive [əb'strʌktɪv] *adj (person)* qui fait de l'obstruction, qui met des bâtons dans les roues; *(tactic, attitude)* d'obstruction; *Med* obstructif, obstruant; **they are being very obstructive** ils nous mettent constamment des bâtons dans les roues; *Pol* **to use obstructive tactics** user de tactiques obstructionnistes

obstructively [əb'strʌktɪvlɪ] *adv (act)* pour faire de l'obstruction

obstructiveness [əb'strʌktɪvnɪs] *n* tactique *f* d'obstruction

obstructor [əb'strʌktə(r)] *n* empêcheur(euse) *m,f*

obstruent ['ɒbstrʊənt] **1** *adj* (**a**) *Med* obstruant (**b**) *Ling (vowel)* obstruante

2 *n* (**a**) *Med* obstruant *m* (**b**) *Ling* obstruante *f*

obtain [əb'teɪn] **1** *vt* obtenir; *(for oneself)* se procurer; **to obtain sth for sb** obtenir qch pour qn, procurer qch à qn; **to obtain sth from sb**

obs–obt

obtenir qch de qn; **the book may be obtained from the publisher** on peut se procurer le livre chez l'éditeur; **the party which obtains an absolute majority wins** le parti qui obtient la majorité absolue l'emporte

2 *vi Formal (practice)* avoir cours; *(rules)* être en vigueur; **this custom still obtains in Europe** cette coutume persiste en Europe; **the situation obtaining in Somalia** la situation (qui règne) en Somalie; **practices obtaining in British banking** des pratiques courantes dans le système bancaire britannique; **this new system will obtain as from next week** ce nouveau système entrera en vigueur dès la semaine prochaine

obtainable [əb'teɪnəbəl] *adj* **where is this drug obtainable?** où peut-on se procurer ce médicament?; **the catalogue is obtainable in our branches** le catalogue est disponible dans nos agences; **obtainable from your local supermarket** en vente dans votre supermarché; **this result is easily obtainable** ce résultat est facile à obtenir

obtaining [əb'teɪnɪŋ], **obtainment** [əb'teɪnmənt], **obtention** [əb'tenʃən] *n* obtention *f*

obtrude [əb'tru:d] *Formal* **1** *vt* (**a**) *(impose)* imposer; **to obtrude itself** s'imposer (**b**) *(stick out)* sortir

2 *vi* (**a**) *(impose oneself)* s'imposer (**b**) *(stick out)* dépasser

obtrusion [əb'tru:ʒən] *n Formal* intrusion *f*

obtrusive [əb'tru:sɪv] *adj (intrusive → decor, advertising, hoarding, architecture)* trop voyant; *(→ smell)* envahissant, pénétrant; *(→ person, behaviour)* envahissant, importun

obtrusively [əb'tru:sɪvlɪ] *adv* importunément

obtrusiveness [əb'tru:sɪvnɪs] *n* (**a**) *(of behaviour, presence)* importunité *f* (**b**) *(of smell)* caractère *m* pénétrant

obtuse [əb'tju:s] *adj* (**a**) *Formal (slow-witted)* obtus; **you're being deliberately obtuse** tu fais exprès de ne pas comprendre; **stop being so obtuse!** ne sois pas si borné! (**b**) *Geom (angle)* obtus; *(triangle)* obtusangle (**c**) *(indistinct)* vague, sourd; **an obtuse pain** une douleur sourde

obtusely [əb'tju:slɪ] *adv Formal (slow-wittedly)* stupidement

obtuseness [əb'tju:snɪs] *n Formal (slow-wittedness)* lenteur *f* d'esprit; *(stupidity)* stupidité *f*

obverse ['ɒbvɜ:s] **1** *n* (**a**) *(of coin)* avers *m*, face *f* (**b**) *(of opinion, argument etc)* contraire *m*, opposé *m*

2 *adj* **the obverse side** *(of coin)* le côté face *ou* l'avers *m*; *Fig (of opinion, argument etc)* le contraire

obviate ['ɒbvɪeɪt] *vt Formal (difficulty, need)* obvier à; **this obviates the need for further action** cela rend toute autre démarche inutile

obvious ['ɒbvɪəs] **1** *adj* (**a**) *(evident)* évident, clair; **it's obvious that he's wrong** il est évident *ou* clair qu'il a tort; **don't always go for the obvious solution** n'opte pas toujours pour la solution qui semble la plus évidente; **the obvious choice** le choix évident *ou* qui s'impose; **an obvious comparison would be with the French Revolution** la première comparaison qui vient à l'esprit est la révolution française; **her obvious innocence** son innocence manifeste; **for obvious reasons** pour des raisons évidentes; **the obvious thing to do is to leave** la seule chose à faire, c'est de partir; **it was obvious that he was going to resign** il était clair qu'il allait démissionner; **there was a very obvious stain in the middle** il y avait une tache bien visible en plein milieu

(**b**) *Pej (predictable)* prévisible; **his symbolism is too obvious** son symbolisme manque de subtilité; **you were too obvious about it** *(unsubtle)* tu n'as pas été très subtil; **the ending was a bit obvious** la fin était prévisible

2 *n* **to state the obvious** enfoncer une porte ouverte; **it would be stating the obvious to say that** cela va sans dire

obviously ['ɒbvɪəslɪ] *adv* (**a**) *(of course)* évidemment, de toute évidence; **she's obviously not lying** il est clair *ou* évident qu'elle ne ment pas; **obviously not!** il semble que non!; **he obviously got the wrong number** de toute évidence, il s'est trompé de numéro; **they were obviously ill** on voyait tout de suite qu'ils étaient malades

(**b**) *(plainly, visibly)* manifestement; **she's not obviously lying** il n'est pas sûr qu'elle mente

(**c**) *(beginning a sentence)* il va de soi; **obviously, we won't break even until next year** il va de soi que nous ne rentrerons pas dans nos frais avant un an

obviousness ['ɒbvɪəsnɪs] *n* (**a**) *(evident nature)* évidence *f*, clarté *f*; *(of lie)* caractère *m* manifeste; **the obviousness of his displeasure** son mécontentement manifeste (**b**) *Pej (predictability)* caractère *m* trop prévisible

OC [,əʊ'si:] *n Mil* (*abbr* **Officer Commanding**) chef *m* de corps

ocarina [,ɒkə'ri:nə] *n* ocarina *m*

OCAS [,əʊsi:,eɪ'es] *n* (*abbr* **Organization of Central American States**) ODEAC *f*

Occam's razor ['ɒkəmz-] *n Phil* le rasoir d'Occam *ou* d'Ockham, le principe de parcimonie

occasion [ə'keɪʒən] **1** *n* (**a**) *(circumstance, time)* occasion *f*; **on this/that occasion** cette fois-ci/là; **I am prepared to overlook it on this occasion, but...** je veux bien fermer les yeux cette fois-ci, mais...; **he was perfectly charming on that occasion** cette fois-là, il fut tout à fait charmant; **on the occasion of her wedding** à l'occasion de son mariage; **on one occasion** une fois; **on another occasion** une autre fois; **I have been there on quite a few occasions** j'y suis allé à plusieurs occasions *ou* à plusieurs reprises; **on great occasions** dans les grandes occasions; **if the occasion arises, should the occasion arise** si l'occasion se présente, le cas échéant; **it wasn't a suitable occasion** les circonstances n'étaient pas favorables; **this is no occasion for an argument** ce n'est pas le moment de se disputer; **to rise to the occasion** se montrer à la hauteur (de la situation)

(**b**) *(special event)* événement *m*; **his birthday is always a big occasion** son anniversaire est toujours un événement important; **to have a sense of occasion** savoir marquer le coup

(**c**) *(reason, cause)* motif *m*, raison *f*, occasion *f*; **I had no occasion to suspect her** je n'avais aucune raison de la soupçonner; **there is no occasion for worry** il n'y a pas lieu de s'inquiéter; **her return was the occasion for great rejoicing** son retour donna lieu à de grandes réjouissances

2 *vt* occasionner, provoquer

3 on occasion, on occasions *adv* de temps en temps, de temps à autre

occasional [ə'keɪʒənəl] *adj* (**a**) *(occurring from time to time)* occasionnel, épisodique; **he's an occasional visitor/golfer** il vient/joue au golf de temps en temps; **during his occasional visits to her** lorsqu'il allait la voir *ou* lui rendait visite; **I like an** *or* **the occasional cigar** j'aime (fumer) un cigare à l'occasion *ou* de temps en temps; **she writes me the occasional postcard** elle m'envoie une carte postale de temps à autre; **there will be occasional showers** il y aura quelques averses *ou* pluies intermittentes

(**b**) *(music, play)* de circonstance

►► ***occasional chair*** chaise *f* volante; *Br* ***occasional table*** table *f* d'appoint

occasionalism [ə'keɪʒənəlɪzəm] *n Phil* occasionnalisme *m*

occasionally [ə'keɪʒənəlɪ] *adv* de temps en temps, quelquefois, occasionnellement; **I smoke only very occasionally** je ne fume que très rarement

occident ['ɒksɪdənt] **1** *n Literary* occident *m*, couchant *m*

2 Occident *n* **the Occident** l'Occident *m*

occidental [,ɒksɪ'dentəl] **1** *adj Literary* occidental

2 Occidental 1 *adj* occidental **2** *n* Occidental(e) *m,f*

occidentalism [,ɒksɪ'dentəlɪzəm] *n* occidentalisme *m*

occidentalist [,ɒksɪ'dentəlɪst] *n (lover of western culture)* occidentaliste *mf*; *(student of western languages)* étudiant(e) *m,f* des langues occidentales

occidentalize, -ise [,ɒksɪ'dentəlaɪz] *vt* occidentaliser

occipital [ɒk'sɪpɪtəl] *Anat* **1** *n* os *m* occipital

2 *adj* occipital

►► ***occipital bone*** os *m* occipital; ***occipital lobe*** lobe *m* occipital

occiput ['ɒksɪpʌt] (*pl* **occiputs** *or* **occipita** [ɒk'sɪpɪtə]) *n* occiput *m*

occlude [ɒ'klu:d] *vt* occlure

occluded front [ɒ'klu:dɪd-] *n Met* front *m* occlus

occlusal [ɒ'klu:səl] *adj Anat* occlusal

►► ***occlusal surface*** *(of tooth)* surface *f* occlusale *ou* triturante

occlusion [ɒ'klu:ʒən] *n* occlusion *f*

occlusive [ɒ'klu:sɪv] **1** *n Ling* (consonne *f*) occlusive *f*

2 *adj* occlusif

occult [ɒ'kʌlt] **1** *n* **the occult** *(supernatural)* le surnaturel; *(mystical skills)* les sciences *fpl* occultes

2 *adj* occulte

occultation [,ɒkʌl'teɪʃən] *n Astron* occultation *f*, obscuration *f*

occultism ['ɒkʌltɪzəm] *n* occultisme *m*

occultist ['ɒkʌltɪst] **1** *n* occultiste *mf*

2 *adj* occultiste

occupancy ['ɒkjʊpənsɪ] (*pl* **occupancies**) *n* (**a**) occupation *f (d'un appartement etc)*; **hotel occupancy levels** *or* **rates** taux *m* d'occupation des hôtels (**b**) *Law* possession *f* à titre de premier occupant

occupant ['ɒkjʊpənt] *n* (**a**) occupant(e) *m,f*; *(tenant)* locataire *mf*; *(of job)* titulaire *mf* (**b**) *Law* premier(ère) occupant(e) *m,f*

occupation [,ɒkjʊ'peɪʃən] **1** *n* (**a**) *(employment)* emploi *m*, travail *m*; **what's his occupation?** qu'est-ce qu'il fait comme travail *ou* dans la vie?; **please state your name and occupation** veuillez indiquer votre nom et votre profession; **I'm not an actor by occupation** je ne suis pas acteur de métier; **raising a family is a full-time occupation** élever des enfants, c'est un travail à plein temps

(**b**) *(activity, hobby)* occupation *f*; **a leisure occupation** un loisir; **his favourite occupation is listening to music** ce qu'il aime faire pardessus tout, c'est écouter de la musique; **the TV provides some occupation for the children** la télévision est un moyen d'occuper les enfants

(**c**) *(of building, offices etc)* occupation *f*; **during Mr Gray's occupation of the premises** lorsque M. Gray occupait les locaux; **the offices are ready for occupation** les bureaux sont prêts à être occupés

(**d**) *Mil & Pol* occupation *f*; **army of occupation** armée *f* d'occupation; **the students have voted to continue their occupation** les étudiants ont voté la poursuite de l'occupation des locaux; **under French occupation** sous occupation française

2 Occupation *n Hist* **the Occupation** l'Occupation *f*

occupational [,ɒkjʊ'peɪʃənəl] *adj* professionnel

►► ***occupational accident*** accident *m* du travail; ***occupational disease*** maladie *f* professionnelle; ***occupational hazard*** risque *m* professionnel *ou* du métier; ***occupational medicine*** médecine *f* du travail; *Br* ***occupational pension*** retraite *f* complémentaire; ***occupational pension scheme*** caisse *f* de retraite complémentaire; ***occupational psychology*** psychologie *f* du travail; *Am* ***Occupational Safety and Health Administration*** = aux États-Unis, direction de la sécurité et de l'hygiène au travail; ***occupational therapist*** ergothérapeute *mf*; ***occupational therapy*** ergothérapie *f*

occupied ['ɒkjʊpaɪd] *adj (country, town, territory)* occupé; **this seat is occupied** cette place est prise; *Hist* **in occupied France** dans la France occupée; *Pol* **the occupied territories** les territoires *mpl* occupés

occupier ['ɒkjʊpaɪə(r)] *n* occupant(e) *m,f*; *(tenant)* locataire *mf*; **to the occupier** *(on letter)* à l'attention de l'occupant

occupy ['ɒkjʊpaɪ] (*pt & pp* **occupied**) *vt* (**a**) *(house, room etc)* occuper; **is this seat occupied?** est-ce que cette place est prise?

(**b**) *(keep busy → person, mind)* occuper; **she occupies herself by doing crosswords** elle s'occupe en faisant des mots croisés; **to be occupied in** *or* **with sth/doing sth** être occupé à qch/faire qch; **try to keep them occupied for a few minutes** essaie de les occuper quelques minutes; **to keep one's mind occupied** s'occuper l'esprit; **find something to occupy your mind** trouvez quelque chose qui vous occupe l'esprit; **reading keeps him occupied** ça l'occupe de lire

(**c**) *(fill, take up → time, space)* occuper; **the sofa occupies half the room** le canapé occupe *ou* prend la moitié de la pièce; **how do you occupy your evenings?** comment *ou* à quoi occupez-vous vos soirées?

(**d**) *Mil & Pol (enemy country)* occuper; *(strategic point)* s'emparer de; **occupying army** armée *f* d'occupation; **the workers have occupied the building** les ouvriers ont occupé le bâtiment

(**e**) *(hold → office, role, rank)* occuper

occur [ə'kɜː(r)] *(pt & pp* **occurred,** *cont* **occurring**) *vi* (**a**) *(happen → event)* avoir lieu, arriver; *(→ opportunity, vacancy)* se présenter; *(→ accident)* avoir lieu, se produire; **this seldom occurs** cela arrive rarement; **misunderstandings often occur over the phone** il y a souvent des malentendus au téléphone; **many changes have occurred since then** beaucoup de choses ont changé depuis ce temps-là; **if a difficulty/the opportunity occurs** si une difficulté/l'occasion se présente; **I promise it won't occur again** je promets que ça ne se reproduira pas; **whatever occurs** quoi qu'il arrive

(**b**) *(exist, be found)* se trouver, se rencontrer; **the mistake occurs at the end** l'erreur se trouve à la fin; **such phenomena often occur in nature** on rencontre souvent de tels phénomènes dans la nature

(**c**) *(come to mind)* **to occur to sb** venir à l'esprit de qn; **another thought occurred to me** autre chose m'est venu à l'esprit; **it occurred to me later that he was lying** j'ai réalisé plus tard qu'il mentait; **it occurs to me now that something wasn't quite right** je réalise seulement maintenant que quelque chose n'allait pas; **didn't it occur to you to call me?** ça ne t'est pas venu à l'idée de m'appeler?; **it would never occur to me to use violence** il ne me viendrait jamais à l'idée d'avoir recours à la violence

occurrence [ə'kʌrəns] *n* (**a**) *(incident)* événement *m*; **this was the first occurrence of its kind** c'était la première fois qu'un événement de cette espèce se produisait; **it's an everyday occurrence** ça arrive *ou* ça se produit tous les jours

(**b**) *(fact or instance of occurring)* **the increasing occurrence of racial attacks** le nombre croissant d'agressions racistes; **the occurrence of leukaemia in this community is twice...** le nombre des cas de leucémie dans cette communauté est le double de...; **this explains the higher occurrence of the disease in urban areas** ceci explique l'incidence accrue de la maladie dans les zones urbaines; **the occurrence of the disease in adults is more serious** lorsqu'elle se déclare chez l'adulte, la maladie est plus grave; **of rare occurrence** qui arrive *ou* se produit rarement

(**c**) *Ling* occurrence *f*

ocean ['əʊʃən] *n* (**a**) *(body of water)* océan *m*; *Am* **the ocean** la mer (**b**) *Fig* **oceans of** beaucoup de; **we've got oceans of time** nous avons beaucoup de temps

►► ***ocean bed*** fond *m* de l'océan; ***ocean current*** courant *m* océanique; ***ocean floor*** fond *m* de l'océan; ***ocean liner*** paquebot *m*; ***the Ocean State*** = surnom donné au Rhode Island

oceanarium [ˌəʊʃə'neərɪəm] *(pl* **oceanariums** *or* **oceanaria** [-ɪə]) *n* aquarium *m* d'eau de mer (naturelle)

oceanfront ['əʊʃənfrʌnt] *Am* **1** *n* bord *m* de mer

2 *adj* au bord de la mer, en bord de mer

oceangoing ['əʊʃənˌgəʊɪŋ] *adj* de haute mer

Oceania [ˌəʊʃɪ'ɑːnɪə] *n* Océanie *f*; **in Oceania** en Océanie

Oceanian [ˌəʊʃɪ'ɑːnɪən] **1** *n* Océanien(enne) *m,f*

2 *adj* océanien

oceanic [ˌəʊʃɪ'ænɪk] *adj* (**a**) *(marine)* océanique (**b**) *Fig (huge)* immense

Oceanid [əʊ'sɪənɪd] *(pl* **Oceanids** *or* **Oceanides** [-'ænɪdiːz]) *n Myth* Océanide *f*

oceanographer [ˌəʊʃə'nɒgrəfə(r)] *n* océanographe *mf*

oceanographic [ˌəʊʃənə'græfɪk], **oceanographical** [ˌəʊʃənə'græfɪkəl] *adj* océanographique

oceanography [ˌəʊʃə'nɒgrəfɪ] *n* océanographie *f*

oceanology [ˌəʊʃə'nɒlədʒɪ] *n* océanologie *f*

Oceanus [əʊ'sɪənəs] *pr n Myth* Océan

oceanward ['əʊʃənwəd], **oceanwards** ['əʊʃənwədz] *adv* vers l'océan

ocellus [əʊ'seləs] *n Zool* ocelle *f*

ocelot ['əʊsɪlɒt] *n Zool* ocelot *m*

och [ɒ] *exclam Scot & Ir* oh!; **och aye!** eh oui! *(parfois employé pour parodier les Écossais)*

oche ['ɒkɪ] *n Br Sport (in darts)* pas *m* de tir; **on** *or* **at the oche** sur le pas de tir

ocher *Am* = **ochre**

ochlocracy [ɒk'lɒkrəsɪ] *n Pol* ochlocratie *f*

ochlophobia [ˌɒklə'fəʊbɪə] *n Med* phobie *f* des foules

ochre, *Am* **ocher** ['əʊkə(r)] **1** *n (ore)* ocre *f*; *(colour)* ocre *m*; **red ochre** ocre *m* rouge; **yellow ochre** jaune *m* d'ocre, ocre *m* jaune

2 *adj* ocre *(inv)*

3 *vt* ocrer

ochrea ['ɒkrɪə] *(pl* **ochreae** [-rɪiː]) *n Bot* ocréa *f*, gaine *f*

ochreous ['əʊkrɪəs] *adj* ocreux, de couleur ocre

ocker ['ɒkə(r)] *Austr* **1** *n (boor)* beauf *m*

2 *adj (boorish)* rustre

o'clock [ə'klɒk] *adv* (**a**) *(time)* **it's one/two o'clock** il est une heure/deux heures; **at precisely 9 o'clock** à 9 heures précises; **a flight at 4 o'clock in the afternoon** un vol à 16 heures; **the 8 o'clock bus** le bus de 8 heures; **at 12 o'clock** *(midday)* à midi; *(midnight)* à minuit (**b**) *(position)* **enemy fighter at 7 o'clock** chasseur ennemi à 7 heures

OCR [ˌəʊsiː'ɑː(r)] *n Comput* (**a**) *(abbr* **optical character reader**) lecteur *m* (à reconnaissance) optique de caractères (**b**) *(abbr* **optical character recognition**) OCR *f*

►► ***OCR software*** logiciel *m* d'OCR

Oct. *(written abbr* **October**) oct.

octachord ['ɒktəkɔːd] *Mus* **1** *n* instrument *m* à huit cordes

2 *adj* à huit cordes

octad ['ɒktæd] *n* groupe *m* de huit

octagon ['ɒktəgən] *n* octogone *m*

octagonal [ɒk'tægənəl] *adj* octogonal

octahedral [ˌɒktə'hiːdrəl] *adj* octaédrique

octahedron [ˌɒktə'hiːdrən] *n* octaèdre *m*

octal ['ɒktəl] **1** *n* octal *m*

2 *adj* octal

octameter [ɒk'tæmɪtə(r)] *n Literature* vers *m* de huit pieds, octosyllabe *m*

octane ['ɒkteɪn] *n* octane *m*; **high-octane** *Br* **petrol** *or Am* **gas** super *m*, supercarburant *m*; **low-octane** *Br* **petrol** *or Am* **gas** ordinaire *m*, essence *f* ordinaire

►► ***octane number, octane rating*** indice *m* d'octane

octant ['ɒktənt] *n Math & Astron* octant *m*

octave ['ɒktɪv] *n Fencing, Mus & Rel* octave *f*; *Literature* huitain *m*; *Mus* **an octave apart** à une octave de différence

Octavian [ɒk'teɪvɪən] *pr n* Octave

octavo [ɒk'teɪvəʊ] *(pl* **octavos**) *n* in-octavo *m inv*

octennial [ɒk'tenɪəl] *adj* (**a**) *(happening every eight years)* qui a lieu tous les huit ans (**b**) *(lasting eight years)* qui dure huit ans

octet [ɒk'tet] *n* (**a**) *(group)* octuor *m* (**b**) *Mus* octuor *m* (**c**) *Literature* huitain *m* (**d**) *Chem* octet *m*

octillion [ɒk'tɪlɪən] *n* (**a**) *Br (10^{48})* octillion *m*

(**b**) *Am (10^{27})* mille quatrillions *m*

October [ɒk'təʊbə(r)] *n* octobre *m*; *see also* **February**

►► ***the October Revolution*** la révolution d'octobre

octocentenary [ˌɒktəʊsən'tiːnərɪ] *n* huitième centenaire *m*

octogenarian [ˌɒktəʊdʒɪ'neərɪən] **1** *n* octogénaire *mf*

2 *adj* octogénaire

octogynous [ɒk'tɒdʒɪnəs] *adj Bot* octogyne

octopod ['ɒktəpɒd] **1** *n* octopode *m*

2 *adj* octopode

octopus ['ɒktəpəs] *(pl* **octopuses** *or* **octopi** [-paɪ]) *n* (**a**) *Zool* pieuvre *f*, poulpe *m*; *Culin* poulpe *m* (**b**) *Fig* pieuvre *f*

octopush ['ɒktəpʊʃ] *n* hockey *m* subaquatique

octoroon [ˌɒktə'ruːn] *n* octavon(onne) *m,f*

octosyllabic [ˌɒktəʊsɪ'læbɪk] *adj* octosyllabique, octosyllabe; **in octosyllabic verse** en octosyllabes, en vers octosyllabiques

octosyllable [ˌɒktəʊ'sɪləbəl] *n* (**a**) *(in poetry → line)* octosyllabe *m*, vers *m* octosyllabique (**b**) *(word)* mot *m* octosyllabique *ou* octosyllabe

octuple ['ɒktjuːpəl] **1** *n* octuple *m*

2 *adj* octuple

3 *vt* octupler

octuplet ['ɒktjʊplət] *n (child)* octuplé *m*

ocular ['ɒkjʊlə(r)] **1** *n* oculaire *m*

2 *adj* oculaire

ocularist ['ɒkjʊlərɪst] *n* oculariste *mf*

oculate ['ɒkjʊleɪt], **oculated** ['ɒkjʊleɪtɪd] *adj Bot & Zool* oculé, ocellé

oculist ['ɒkjʊlɪst] *n* oculiste *mf*

oculomotor [ˌɒkjʊləʊ'məʊtə(r)] *adj Anat (nerve)* oculogyre

oculus ['ɒkjʊləs] *(pl* **oculi** [-laɪ]) *n Archit* oculus *m*

OD [ˌəʊ'diː] *(pt & pp* **OD'd,** *cont* **OD'ing**) **1** *n* (**a**) *Fam (abbr* **overdose**) overdose❑ *f* (**b**) *(abbr* **overdraft**) découvert *m*

2 *adj (abbr* **overdrawn**) à découvert

3 *vi Fam* faire une overdose (**on** de); **I've OD'd on pizzas/soap operas lately** j'ai tellement mangé de pizzas/regardé de feuilletons télé ces derniers temps que j'en suis dégoûté

ODA [ˌəʊdiː'eɪ] *n Br Formerly (abbr* **Overseas Development Administration**) = ancien nom du secrétariat d'État à la Coopération

odalisk, odalisque ['əʊdəlɪsk] *n* odalisque *f*

odd [ɒd] *adj* (**a**) *(weird)* bizarre, curieux; **he's an odd character** c'est un drôle d'individu; **the odd thing is that the room was empty** ce qui est bizarre *ou* curieux, c'est que la pièce était vide; **it felt odd seeing her again** ça m'a fait (tout) drôle de la revoir; **it's odd your not knowing about it** c'est drôle *ou* bizarre que vous n'en sachiez rien; **an odd way of saying sorry** une drôle de manière de s'excuser; **(well,) that's odd!** (tiens,) c'est bizarre *ou* curieux!; *Fam* **he's a bit odd in the head** il lui manque une case

(**b**) *(occasional, incidental)* **at odd moments** de temps en temps; **he has his odd moments of depression** il lui arrive d'avoir ses moments de déprime; **I smoke the odd cigarette** il m'arrive de fumer une cigarette de temps en temps; **we took the odd photo** nous avons pris deux ou trois photos; **we did get the odd enquiry** on a bien eu une ou deux demandes de renseignements; **nobody, apart from the odd anthropologist,...** personne, à part quelques (rares) anthropologues,...; **just add any odd carrots** ajoute simplement quelques carottes; **she gives him a few odd jobs from time to time** de temps en temps, elle lui donne une ou deux choses à faire

(**c**) *(not matching)* dépareillé; **he was wearing odd socks** ses chaussettes étaient dépareillées, il portait des chaussettes dépareillées

(**d**) *(not divisible by two)* impair; **the odd pages of a book** les pages impaires d'un livre

(**e**) *Fam (or so)* **twenty odd** vingt et quelques❑; **thirty-odd pounds** trente livres et quelques, trente et quelques livres❑; **he must be forty odd** il doit avoir la quarantaine *ou* dans les quarante ans

(**f**) *(idioms)* **the odd one/man/woman out** l'exception *f*; **everyone else was in evening dress, I was the odd one out** ils étaient tous en tenue de soirée sauf moi; **which of these drawings is the odd one out?** parmi ces dessins, lequel est l'intrus?; **when they chose the two teams, Jill was the odd one out** lorsqu'ils ont formé les deux équipes, Jill s'est retrouvée toute seule; **they all knew each other so well that I felt the odd one out** ils se connaissaient tous si bien que j'avais l'impression d'être la cinquième roue du carrosse

►► *Br Fam* ***odd bod*** allumé(e) *m,f*, farfelu(e) *m,f*; *Math* ***odd function*** fonction *f* impaire; ***odd jobs*** *(casual jobs)* petits boulots *mpl*; **to do odd jobs around the house** bricoler dans la maison; ***odd lot*** *Com* lot *m* dépareillé; *St Exch (of shares)* lot *m* de moins de cent actions; ***odd number*** nombre *m* impair

oddball [ˈɒdbɔːl] *Fam* **1** *n* allumé(e) *m,f*, farfelu(e) *m,f*; **he's a real oddball** c'est un drôle de numéro

2 *adj* loufoque, farfelu

odd-even *adj*

►► *Comput* ***odd-even check*** contrôle *m* de parité; *Mktg* ***odd-even price*** prix *m* magique; *Mktg* ***odd-even pricing*** fixation *f* des prix magiques

oddish [ˈɒdɪʃ] *adj* un peu bizarre

oddity [ˈɒdɪtɪ] (*pl* **oddities**) *n* (**a**) *(strange person)* excentrique *mf*, original(e) *m,f*; *(strange thing)* curiosité *f*; **she's a bit of an oddity** elle est un peu bizarre; **being the only woman there makes her something of an oddity** on la remarque du simple fait qu'elle est la seule femme; **this movie is an oddity** *(weird)* c'est un film bizarre; *(unusual)* ce film est une curiosité; **he has some little oddities** il a des côtés un peu bizarres

(**b**) *(strangeness)* étrangeté *f*, bizarrerie *f*

odd-jobber, odd-job man *n* homme *m* à tout faire

odd-looking *adj* à l'air bizarre

odd-lot *adj*

►► *St Exch* ***odd-lot order*** ordre *m* de moins de cent actions; ***odd-lot trading*** achats *mpl* et ventes *fpl* de lots de moins de cent actions

odd-lotter [-ˈlɒtə(r)] *n Am St Exch* petit(e) actionnaire *mf*

oddly [ˈɒdlɪ] *adv* bizarrement, curieusement; **oddly shaped** d'une forme bizarre; **oddly enough, he didn't recognize me** chose curieuse, il ne m'a pas reconnu

oddment [ˈɒdmənt] *n Com (of matched set)* article *m* dépareillé; *(of lot, line)* fin *f* de série; *(of fabric)* coupon *m*

oddness [ˈɒdnɪs] *n* bizarrerie *f*

odd-numbers *adj*

►► *Mktg* ***odd-numbers price*** prix *m* magique; *Mktg* ***odd-numbers pricing*** fixation *f* des prix magiques

odds [ɒdz] **1** *npl* (**a**) *(in betting)* cote *f*; **the odds are ten to one against** la cote est de dix contre un; **the odds are ten to one on** la cote est de un contre dix; **they're offering long/short odds against Jackson** Jackson a une bonne/faible cote; **I'll lay** *or* **give you odds of twenty to one that she'll leave him** je te parie à vingt contre un qu'elle le quittera; *Br* **I ended up paying over the odds** en fin de compte, je l'ai payé plus cher qu'il ne valait *ou* que sa valeur

(**b**) *(chances)* chances *fpl*; **what are the odds on his getting the job?** quelles chances a-t-il d'avoir le poste?; **the odds are she's been lying to us all along** il y a de fortes chances qu'elle nous ait menti depuis le début; **the odds are on/against her accepting** il y a de fortes chances/il y a peu de chances (pour) qu'elle accepte; **the odds are that he'll succeed** il y a gros à parier qu'il réussira; **the odds are in favour of the socialists winning** il y a de fortes chances pour que les socialistes l'emportent

(**c**) *(great difficulties)* **against all the odds** contre toute attente; **they won against overwhelming odds** ils ont gagné alors que tout était contre eux

(**d**) *Br Fam (difference)* **it makes no odds** ça ne change rien ❑; **it makes no odds to me** ça m'est égal ❑; **it makes no odds what I say** ce que je dis ne sert à rien; **what's the odds?** *(what does it matter?)* qu'est-ce que ça peut faire? ❑

(**e**) *(idioms)* **odds and ends** *(miscellaneous objects)* objets *mpl* divers, bric-à-brac *m inv*; *(leftovers)* restes *mpl*; *Br Fam* **odds and sods** *(miscellaneous objects)* objets *mpl* divers ❑, bric-à-brac ❑ *m inv*; *(people)* gens *mpl* divers ❑; **her desk is always covered with odds and ends** son bureau est toujours encombré de tout un bric-à-brac; **I've still a few odds and ends to do** j'ai encore quelques bricoles *ou* petites choses à faire

2 at odds *adj* **to be at odds with sb (over sth)** *(be in disagreement)* ne pas être d'accord avec qn (à propos de qch); *(be on bad terms)* être brouillé avec qn (à propos de qch); **to be at odds with oneself** être mal dans sa peau; **to be at odds with the world** en vouloir au monde entier; **his latest statement is at odds with his earlier account** sa dernière déposition ne concorde pas avec son premier récit des faits; **the way she was dressed was completely at odds with her personality** ce qu'elle portait ne correspondait pas du tout à sa personnalité; **the minister is at odds with the government on this issue** le ministre est en conflit avec son gouvernement sur ce point; **his lavish lifestyle is totally at odds with his professed political beliefs** son train de vie luxueux est en contradiction avec les convictions politiques qu'il affiche

odds-on *adj Br* **it's odds-on that he'll win** il y a tout à parier qu'il gagnera

►► ***odds-on favourite*** grand favori *m*

ode [əʊd] *n* ode *f*

'Ode to Joy' *Beethoven* 'Hymne à la joie'

'Ode To a Nightingale' *Keats* 'Ode à un rossignol'

Odessa [əʊˈdesə] *n* Odessa

Odin [ˈəʊdɪn] *pr n* Odin

odious [ˈəʊdɪəs] *adj* odieux

odiously [ˈəʊdɪəslɪ] *adv* odieusement

odiousness [ˈəʊdɪəsnɪs] *n* caractère *m* odieux

odium [ˈəʊdjəm] *n Formal (condemnation)* réprobation *f*; *(hatred)* haine *f*; **to bring** *or* **cast odium upon sb** *(condemnation)* attirer à qn la réprobation générale; *(hatred)* rendre qn odieux (aux yeux des autres)

odometer [əʊˈdɒmɪtə(r)] *n Am Aut* compteur *m* kilométrique

odontalgia [ˌɒdɒnˈtældʒɪə] *n Med* odontalgie *f*

odontalgic [ˌɒdɒnˈtældʒɪk] *Med* **1** *n* odontalgique *m*

2 *adj* odontalgique

odontoblast [ɒˈdɒntəblæst] *n Anat* odontoblaste *m*

odontogeny [ˌɒdɒnˈtɒdʒənɪ] *n Biol* odontogenèse *f*, odontogénie *f*

odontoid [əˈdɒntɔɪd] *Anat & Zool* **1** *n* apophyse *f* odontoïde

2 *adj* odontoïde

►► ***odontoid peg, odontoid process*** apophyse *f* odontoïde

odontologic [ˌɒdɒntəˈlɒdʒɪk], **odontological** [ˌɒdɒntəˈlɒdʒɪkəl] *adj* odontologique

odontologist [ˌɒdɒnˈtɒlədʒɪst] *n* odontologiste *mf*

odontology [ˌɒdɒnˈtɒlədʒɪ] *n* odontologie *f*

odor, odorless *Am* = **odour, odourless**

odoriferous [ˌəʊdəˈrɪfərəs] *adj Formal* odoriférant

odorous [ˈəʊdərəs] *adj (fragrant)* odorant; *(malodorous)* malodorant

odour, *Am* **odor** [ˈəʊdə(r)] *n* (**a**) *(smell)* odeur *f*; **guaranteed to get rid of unpleasant odours!** fini les mauvaises odeurs! (**b**) *(pervasive quality)* odeur *f*, parfum *m*, arôme *m*; *Rel* **odour of sanctity** odeur *f* de sainteté (**c**) *Br (idiom) Formal* **to be in good/bad odour with sb** être bien/mal vu de qn; **you're not in good odour with the boss** tu n'es pas en odeur de sainteté auprès du patron

odourless, *Am* **odorless** [ˈəʊdəlɪs] *adj* inodore

Odysseus [əˈdiːsɪəs] *pr n Myth* Ulysse

odyssey [ˈɒdɪsɪ] *n* odyssée *f*; *Fig* **a spiritual odyssey** une odyssée spirituelle

'The Odyssey' *Homer* 'L'Odyssée'

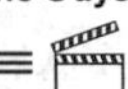

'2001: A Space Odyssey' *Kubrick* '2001: l'odyssée de l'espace'

OECD [ˌəʊiːˌsiːˈdiː] *n* (*abbr* **Organization for Economic Cooperation and Development**) OCDE *f*

oecology [iːˈkɒlədʒɪ] *n* œcologie *f*, bionomie *f*

oecumenical, oecumenicalism *etc* = **ecumenical, ecumenicalism** *etc*

oedema, *Am* **edema** [ɪˈdiːmə] (*Br pl* **oedemata** [-mətə], *Am pl* **edemata** [-mətə]) *n Med* œdème *m*

oedematose, *Am* **edematose** [ɪˈdiːmətəʊs], **oedematous,** *Am* **edematose** [ɪˈdemətəs] *adj Med* œdémateux

Oedipal [ˈiːdɪpəl] *adj* œdipien

Oedipus [ˈiːdɪpəs] *pr n Myth* Œdipe

►► ***Oedipus complex*** complexe *m* d'Œdipe

'Oedipus Rex' *Sophocles* 'Œdipe roi'

OEEC [ˌəʊiːˌiːˈsiː] *n Formerly* (*abbr* **Organization for European Economic Cooperation**) OECE *f*

OEM [ˌəʊiːˈem] *n* (*abbr* **original equipment manufacturer**) constructeur *m* de systèmes originaux, OEM *m*

oenological, *Am* **enological** [ˌiːnəˈlɒdʒɪkəl] *adj* œnologique

oenologist, *Am* **enologist** [iːˈnɒlədʒɪst] *n* œnologue *mf*

oenology, *Am* **enology** [iːˈnɒlədʒɪ] *n* œnologie *f*

oenophile, *Am* **enophile** [ˈiːnəfaɪl] *n* œnophile *mf*

o'er [ˈəʊə(r)] *Literary* = **over** *adv & prep*

oersted [ˈɜːsted] *n Phys* œrsted *m*

oesophageal, *Am* **esophageal** [iːˌsɒfəˈdʒiːəl] *adj Anat & Med* œsophagien

oesophagectomy, *Am* **esophagectomy** [iːˌsɒfəˈdʒektəmɪ] *n Med* œsophagectomie *f*

oesophagitis, *Am* **esophagitis** [iːˌsɒfəˈdʒaɪtɪs] *n Med* œsophagite *f*

oesophagoscope, *Am* **esophagoscope** [iːˈsɒfəgəskəʊp] *n Med* œsophagoscope *m*

oesophagoscopy, *Am* **esophagoscopy** [iːˌsɒfəˈgɒskəpɪ] *n Med* œsophagoscopie *f*

oesophagus, *Am* **esophagus** [iːˈsɒfəgəs] (*Br pl* **oesophaguses** *or* **oesophagi** [-gaɪ], *Am pl* **esophaguses** *or* **esophagi** [-gaɪ]) *n* œsophage *m*

oestradiol, *Am* **estradiol** [ˌiːstrəˈdaɪɒl] *n Biol & Chem* œstradiol *m*

oestrogen, *Am* **estrogen** [ˈiːstrədʒən] *n* œstrogène *m*

oestrogenic, *Am* **estrogenic** [ˌiːstrəˈdʒenɪk] *adj* œstrogénique

oestrone, *Am* **estrone** [ˈiːstrəʊn] *n Biol & Chem* œstrone *f*

oestrous, *Am* **estrous** [ˈiːstrəs] *adj* œstral

►► ***oestrous cycle*** cycle *m* œstral

oestrus, *Am* **estrus** [ˈiːstrəs] *n* œstrus *m*

OF [əv, *stressed* ɒv] *prep* (**a**) *(after nouns expressing quantity, number, amount)* de; **a pound of onions** une livre d'oignons; **a loaf of bread** un pain; **a piece of cake** un morceau de gâteau; **a bottle of wine** une bouteille de vin; **a pair of trousers** un pantalon; **there are six of us** nous sommes six; **thousands of mosquitos** des milliers de moustiques; **some/many/few of us were present** quelques-uns/beaucoup/peu d'entre nous étaient présents; **half of them failed** la moitié d'entre eux ont échoué; **how much of it do you want?** combien en voulez-vous?

(**b**) *(indicating age)* de; **a boy/a girl of three** un garçon/une fille de trois ans; **at the age of nineteen** à dix-neuf ans, à l'âge de dix-neuf ans; **his wife of twenty years** la femme avec qui il est marié depuis vingt ans

(**c**) *(indicating composition, content)* de; **a photo of Lily** une photo de Lily; **a map of Spain** une carte d'Espagne; **a report of events in Parliament** un compte rendu de ce qui se passe au Parlement; **a rise of 25 percent** une augmentation de 25 pour cent; **a team of cricketers** une équipe de cricket; **a city of 120,000** une ville de 120 000 habitants; **a series of programmes on Italy** une série d'émissions sur l'Italie

(**d**) *(created by)* de; **the poems of Byron** les poèmes de Byron

(**e**) *(with words expressing attitude or emotion)* de; **I'm ashamed of it** j'en ai honte; **I'm proud of it** j'en suis fier; *Fam* **I'm sick of it** j'en ai assez; **I'm afraid of the dark** j'ai peur du noir; **she dreamt of one day becoming Prime Minister** elle rêvait de devenir Premier ministre un jour; **I have no intention of leaving** je n'ai aucune intention de partir; **the fear of God** la crainte de Dieu

(**f**) *(indicating possession, relationship)* de; **he's a friend of mine** c'est un ami à moi; **a friend of mine saw me** un de mes amis m'a vu; **I'd like a home of my own** j'aimerais avoir mon chez-moi; **the corner of the street** le coin de la

odd–of

rue; **the subject of the lecture** le sujet du cours; **cancer of the bowel** cancer des intestins; **the love of a mother** l'amour d'une mère; **the rights of man** les droits de l'homme; **she's head of department** elle est chef de service; **doctor of medicine** docteur en médecine

(**g**) *(indicating subject of action)* **it was kind/mean of him** c'était gentil/méchant de sa part; **how clever of her** comme c'est intelligent de sa part

(**h**) *(with names of places)* de; **the city of New York** la ville de New York; **the people of Chile** le peuple *ou* les habitants du Chili; **the University of Cambridge** l'université de Cambridge; **the village of Carlton** le village de Carlton

(**i**) *(after nouns derived from verbs)* de; **the arrival/departure of Flight 556** l'arrivée/le départ du vol 556; **we need the approval of the committee** nous devons obtenir l'autorisation du comité; **a lover of fine wine** un amateur de bons vins; **the success of the meeting** le succès de la réunion; **an outbreak of cholera** une épidémie de choléra

(**j**) *(describing a particular feeling or quality)* de; **a feeling of relief** un sentiment de soulagement; **she has the gift of mimicry** elle a un talent d'imitatrice; **a man of courage** un homme de courage; **people of foreign appearance** gens à l'air étranger; **a coat of many colours** un manteau multicolore; **a sort** *or* **kind** *or* **type of tree** un type d'arbre; *Formal* **to be of sound mind** être sain d'esprit; **to be of a nervous disposition** avoir une prédisposition à la nervosité; **that fool of a sergeant** cet imbécile de sergent

(**k**) *(made from)* **a ring of solid gold** une bague en or massif; **a heart of stone** un cœur de pierre; **made of wood** fait de *ou* en bois

(**l**) *(after nouns of size, measurement etc)* de; **a width/length of sixty feet** une largeur/longueur de soixante pieds; **they reach a height of ten feet** ils atteignent une hauteur de dix pieds

(**m**) *(indicating cause, origin, source)* de; **the consequence/the effects of the explosion** la conséquence/les effets de l'explosion; **to die of cancer** mourir du *ou* d'un cancer; **of royal descent** de lignée royale; **of which/whom** dont

(**n**) *(indicating likeness, similarity)* de; **the colour of blood/of grass** la couleur du sang/de l'herbe; **the size of a tennis ball** de la taille d'une balle de tennis; **he reminds me of John Wayne** il me rappelle John Wayne; **it smells of coffee** ça sent le café; **a giant of a man** un homme très grand; **a huge barn of a house** une énorme bâtisse

(**o**) *(indicating specific point in time or space)* de; **the 3rd of May** le 3 mai; **in the middle of August** à la mi-août; **the crash of 1929** le krach de 1929; **the day of our wedding** le jour de notre mariage; **it was the high point of the week** ça a été le point culminant de la semaine; *Am* **a quarter of nine** neuf heures moins le quart; **in the middle of the road** au milieu de la chaussée; **at the far end of the room** à l'autre bout de la pièce; **south of** au sud de; **within a mile of** à moins d'un mil(l)e de

(**p**) *(indicating deprivation or absence)* **a lack of food** un manque de nourriture; **to get rid of sth** se débarrasser de qch; **to be cured of sth** être guéri de qch; **to rob sb of sth** voler qch à qn

(**q**) *(indicating information received or passed on)* **I've never heard of him** je n'ai jamais entendu parler de lui; **to learn of sth** apprendre qch; **her knowledge of French** sa connaissance du français; **of President Nixon it was said that...** il a été dit du président Nixon que...

(**r**) *(as intensifier)* **the best/the worst of all** le meilleur/le pire de tout; **today of all days!** il fallait que ça arrive aujourd'hui!; **he, of all men** *or* **people** lui entre tous; **you, of all people, should know...** toi, plus que quiconque, devrais savoir que...

(**s**) *Old-fashioned or Hum* **I like to listen to the radio of a morning/an evening** j'aime écouter la radio le matin/le soir

ofay [ɔʊ'feɪ] *n Am Fam* sale Blanc (Blanche) *m,f,* = terme injurieux désignant un Blanc

OFF [ɒf] **1** *adv* (**a**) *(indicating removal)* **to take sth off** enlever *ou* ôter qch; **to come off** *(sticker, handle)* se détacher; *(lipstick, paint)* partir; **you can leave your jacket off** ce n'est pas la peine de remettre votre veste; **with his jacket off** sans sa veste; **she kicked off her shoes** elle ôta ses chaussures d'un coup de pied; **the knob had broken off** la poignée était cassée; **peel off the wallpaper** décollez le papier peint; **she cut off her hair** elle s'est coupé les cheveux; **could you take two centimetres off?** *(off sleeves, hemline)* est-ce que vous pourriez enlever deux centimètres?; **off with those wet clothes!** retire(-moi) *ou* enlève(-moi) ces vêtements humides!; **off with his head!** coupez-lui la tête!

(**b**) *(indicating departure)* **the truck drove off** le camion démarra; **to run off** partir en courant; **when are you off to Dublin?** quand partez-vous pour Dublin?; **we'd better be off** on doit partir; *Sport* **they're off!** ils sont partis!; *Fam* **I'm off!** j'y vais!□; **off you go, you'll be late!** sauve-toi *ou* vas-y, tu vas être en retard!; **off we go!** c'est parti!; **off to bed with you!** au lit!; **isn't it time you were off to bed?** n'est-il pas l'heure que tu ailles te coucher?; *Fam* **be off with you!** va-t'en!□; **(get) off!** enlevez-vous de là!; *Hum* **oh no, he's off again!** ça y est, ça le reprend!

(**c**) *(indicating movement away from a surface)* **the ball hit the wall and bounced off** la balle a heurté le mur et a rebondi; **I knocked the glass off with my elbow** j'ai fait tomber le verre d'un coup de coude

(**d**) *(indicating location)* **it's off to the right** c'est sur la droite; **she's off playing tennis** elle est partie jouer au tennis

(**e**) *(indicating disembarkment, dismounting etc)* **to get off** descendre; **to jump off** sauter

(**f**) *(indicating absence, inactivity)* **to take a week off** prendre une semaine de congé; **Monday's my day off** le lundi est mon jour de congé; **have you any time off during the week?** avez-vous des heures libres pendant la semaine?; **I get two hours off for lunch** j'ai deux heures de libres pour le déjeuner

(**g**) *(indicating distance in time or space)* **Paris/Christmas is still a long way off** Paris/Noël est encore loin; **it's a few miles off** c'est à quelques kilomètres d'ici

(**h**) *Theat* off; **voice off** voix *f* off; **noises/voices off** bruits *mpl*/voix *fpl* en coulisses

(**i**) *(indicating disconnection)* **to put** *or* **switch** *or* **turn the light off** éteindre la lumière; **to turn the tap off** fermer le robinet; **leave the lights off** n'allume pas

(**j**) *(indicating separation, partition)* **the playing area is divided off by a low wall** l'aire de jeu est délimitée par un petit mur; **to fence off land** clôturer un terrain; **the police have cordoned off the area** la police a bouclé le quartier

(**k**) *(indicating price reduction)* **special offer: £5 off** *(sign)* offre spéciale: 5 livres de réduction; **the salesman gave me $20/20 percent off** le vendeur m'a fait une remise de 20 dollars/20 pour cent

(**l**) *(indicating relief from discomfort)* **to sleep/to walk sth off** faire passer qch en dormant/marchant

2 *prep* (**a**) *(indicating movement away from)* de; **he fell off his chair** il est tombé de sa chaise; **she knocked the vase off the table** elle a fait tomber le vase de la table; **take your elbows off the table** enlève tes coudes de la table; **off the sofa!** *(don't stand on it)* descends du canapé!; *(don't sit on it)* lève-toi du canapé!; **couples started drifting off the dance floor** les couples commencèrent à quitter la piste de danse; **drinks must not be taken off the premises** *(sign)* les boissons doivent être consommées sur place; *Fig* **it'll take your mind off it** ça te changera les idées

(**b**) *(indicating removal)* de; **take the top off the bottle** enlève le bouchon de la bouteille; **to cut a slice off sth** couper une tranche de qch; **I've stripped the wallpaper off the walls** j'ai décollé le papier peint des murs; **get that knife off him!** prends-lui son couteau!; **off the peg** en confection, en prêt-à-porter

(**c**) *(from)* **to buy sth off sb** acheter qch à qn; **I bought it off a stall** je l'ai acheté sur le marché; **can I borrow £5 off you?** je peux t'emprunter 5 livres?; **I caught a cold off my brother** mon frère m'a passé son rhume

(**d**) *(from the direction of)* de; **a cool breeze off the sea** une brise fraîche venant du large

(**e**) *(indicating location)* **a few miles off the coast** à quelques kilomètres de la côte; **off the coast of Spain** au large de la côte espagnole; **most students live off campus** la plupart des étudiants vivent à l'extérieur du campus; **we ate in a small restaurant off the main road** nous avons mangé dans un petit restaurant à l'écart de la grand-route; **the bathroom's off the bedroom** la salle de bains donne dans la chambre; **an alley off Oxford Street** une ruelle qui part d'Oxford Street; **just off Oxford Street there's a pretty little square** à deux pas d'Oxford Street il y a une petite place ravissante

(**f**) *(absent from)* **Mr Dale is off work today** M. Dale est absent aujourd'hui; **you need a few days off work** vous avez besoin de quelques jours de congé; **Wayne's off school with the flu** Wayne est à la maison avec la grippe; **I've been off work for over a year now** voilà un an que je ne travaille plus

(**g**) *(by means of)* **it runs off gas/electricity/solar power** ça marche au gaz/à l'électricité/à l'énergie solaire; **the radio works off the mains** la radio fonctionne sur secteur

(**h**) *(indicating source of nourishment)* de; **to live off vegetables** vivre de légumes; **to live off the land** vivre (des produits) de la terre; **we dined off a leg of lamb** nous avons dîné d'une tranche de gigot

(**i**) *(reduced from)* **I can get $20/20 percent off the list price** je peux avoir une remise de 20 dollars/20 pour cent sur le prix de vente; *Fam* **they'll knock** *or* **take something off it if you pay cash** ils vous feront une remise si vous payez en liquide□; **that's 2 seconds off the record** c'est 2 secondes de moins que le record

(**j**) *Fam (no longer wanting or needing)* **to be off one's food** ne pas avoir faim□; **I'm off whisky** je n'aime plus le whisky□; **I'm off him at the moment** j'en ai marre de lui en ce moment; **she's off antibiotics now** elle ne prend plus d'antibiotiques maintenant□; **he's off heroin now** il ne touche plus à l'héroïne maintenant□

3 *adj* (**a**) *(not working → electricity, light, radio, TV)* éteint; *(→ tap)* fermé; *(→ engine, machine)* arrêté, à l'arrêt; *(→ handbrake)* desserré; **the gas is off** *(at mains)* le gaz est fermé; *(under saucepan)* le gaz est éteint; *(for safety reasons)* le gaz est coupé; **off** *(on switch, appliance)* arrêt; **make sure the switches are in the off position** vérifiez que les interrupteurs sont sur (la position) arrêt; **the off button** le bouton d'arrêt

(**b**) *(bad, tainted)* mauvais, avarié; **the milk is off** le lait a tourné; **this beer's off** cette bière est éventée; **it smells/tastes off** on dirait que ce n'est plus bon

(**c**) *(cancelled)* annulé; **tonight's match is off** le match de ce soir est annulé; **if that's your attitude, the deal's off!** si c'est comme ça que vous le prenez, ma proposition ne tient plus!

(**d**) *(on vacation, not working)* en congé, en vacances; **to be off sick** être absent parce qu'on est malade, être malade; **he's off today** il n'est pas là aujourd'hui; **are you off tomorrow?** tu travailles demain?; *(no school)* tu (n')as (pas d')école demain?; *(no college)* tu (n')as (pas) cours demain?; **I'm off from 3 to 5** je ne travaille pas entre 3 et 5 heures

(**e**) *Br (not available)* **I'm afraid the salmon's off** je regrette, mais il n'y a plus de saumon

(**f**) *(unwell)* **I felt decidedly off the next morning** le lendemain matin, je ne me sentais vraiment pas bien; **everyone has their off days** on a tous nos mauvais jours

(**g**) *(inaccurate)* **his timing was a bit off** *(when he asked for a rise etc)* il n'a pas choisi un très bon moment

(**h**) *Fam (unacceptable)* **that's a bit off!** vous y allez un peu fort!; **I thought it was a bit off the way she just ignored me** je n'ai pas apprécié qu'elle m'ignore comme ça□

(**i**) *Br Aut (when driving on right)* (du côté) gauche; *(when driving on left)* (du côté) droit

ofa–off

(**j**) *(having a certain amount of)* **how are we off for milk?** combien de lait nous reste-t-il?

4 *n Fam (start)* départ ❑ *m*; **they're ready for the off** ils sont prêts à partir ❑; **right from the off** dès le départ

5 *vt Am Fam (kill)* buter, refroidir, zigouiller

6 off chance *n* **on the off chance** au cas où, à tout hasard; **I called by just on the off chance** je suis passé au cas où *ou* à tout hasard; **I phoned on the off chance of catching him at home** j'ai appelé en espérant qu'il serait chez lui; **she kept it on the off chance (that) it might prove useful** elle l'a gardé pour le cas où cela pourrait servir

7 off and on *adv* par intervalles; **we lived together off and on for three years** on a plus ou moins vécu ensemble pendant trois ans

►► *Cin & TV* ***off camera*** hors champ, off; *Br* ***off sales*** = vente à emporter de boissons alcoolisées

---

off-air 1 *adj* hors-antenne

2 *adv* hors antenne

offal ['ɒfəl] *n (UNCOUNT)* (**a**) *Br Culin* abats *mpl* (**b**) *(refuse)* ordures *fpl*, déchets *mpl* (**c**) *(carrion)* charogne *f*

Offaly ['ɒfəlɪ] *n* le comté d'Offaly, = comté dans le centre de la République d'Irlande; **in Offaly** dans le comté d'Offaly

Offa's Dyke ['ɒfəz-] *n* = levée de terre entre le pays de Galles et la Mercie construite au VIIIème siècle par le roi Offa

off-balance 1 *adj* déséquilibré

2 *adv* **to throw** *or* **to knock sb off-balance** faire perdre l'équilibre à qn; *Fig* couper le souffle à *ou* désarçonner qn; **her question caught me off-balance** sa question m'a pris au dépourvu

►► *Acct* ***off-balance sheet*** hors bilan; ***off-balance sheet item*** poste *m ou* élément *m* hors bilan; ***off-balance sheet transactions*** opérations *fpl* de hors bilan

offbeat ['ɒfbiːt] **1** *adj (unconventional)* original, excentrique

2 *n Mus* temps *m* faible

off-Broadway *adj Am* **an off-Broadway show** = spectacle new-yorkais non conventionnel qui se démarque du style de ceux de Broadway, et qui n'est pas présenté dans un "Broadway Theatre"; **an off-Broadway director** un metteur en scène de pièces d'avant-garde

off-campus *adv Univ* en dehors du campus; **I prefer to live off-campus** je préfère habiter en dehors du campus

off-centre, *Am* **off-center 1** *adj* (**a**) *(painting on wall)* décentré; *(rotation)* excentrique; *(gun sights)* désaligné; **the title is off-centre** le titre n'est pas centré (**b**) *Fig (imprecise → analysis, description)* légèrement inexact, pas tout à fait exact; *(unconventional → humour, style)* original

2 *adv* de côté; **aim slightly off-centre** visez légèrement de côté

off-colour, *Am* **off-color** *adj* (**a**) *Br (unwell)* **to be** *or* **feel off-colour** ne pas se sentir dans son assiette; **to look off-colour** ne pas avoir l'air dans son assiette (**b**) *Old-fashioned (joke)* d'un goût douteux

off-course *adj (bet)* effectué hors des champs de course

offcut ['ɒfkʌt] *n (of cloth, wood, paper)* chute *f*; *(for animals)* rognures *fpl*; **offcuts** *(of meat)* restes *mpl* du découpage

off-day *n* **he was having an off-day** il n'était pas en forme; **everyone has their off-days** il y a des jours "avec" et des jours "sans"

off-duty *adj (policeman, soldier, nurse)* qui n'est pas de service; **I'm off duty at 6** je finis mon service à 6 heures

offence, *Am* **offense** [ə'fens] *n* (**a**) *Law (minor)* infraction *f*; *(more serious)* délit *m*; **it's his first offence** c'est la première fois qu'il commet un délit; **second** *or* **subsequent offence** récidive *f*; **to commit a second** *or* **subsequent offence** récidiver; **arrested for drug offences** *(dealing)* arrêté pour trafic de drogue; *(use)* arrêté pour consommation de drogue; **indictable/nonindictable offence** infraction *f* majeure/mineure; **motoring** *or* **driving offence** infraction *f* au code de la route; **parking offence** contravention *f* au stationnement; **sex offence** ≃ attentat *m* à la pudeur

(**b**) *(displeasure, hurt)* **to give** *or* **to cause offence to sb** *(person, personal remarks)* blesser *ou* offenser qn; *(film, book, programme)* heurter la sensibilité de qn; **to take offence at sth** s'offenser *ou* s'offusquer de qch; **he's very quick to take offence** il se vexe pour un rien; **I meant no offence** je ne voulais pas vous blesser; **no offence meant – none taken!** je n'avais pas l'intention de te vexer – il n'y a pas de mal!; **no offence!** il n'y a pas de mal!; **the factory is an offence to the eye** l'usine est une insulte au regard; **it's an offence against good taste** c'est un outrage au bon goût

(**c**) *Mil (attack)* attaque *f*, offensive *f*

(**d**) *Sport (attackers)* attaque *f*

offend [ə'fend] **1** *vt (person)* offenser, blesser; *(eyes, senses, reason)* choquer; **to be offended at** *or* **by sth** se froisser *ou* s'offenser de qch; **she's easily offended** elle est susceptible, elle se vexe pour un rien; **I hope you won't be offended if I…** j'espère que vous ne vous froisserez *ou* offenserez pas si je…; **to offend the eye** choquer les regards *ou* la vue; **the film contains scenes which could offend some viewers** le film contient des scènes pouvant choquer certains spectateurs; **his behaviour offends my sense of fair play** son comportement choque mon sens du fair-play

2 *vi Law* violer la loi, commettre un délit; **he is liable to offend again** il risque de récidiver

►**offend against** *vt insep* (**a**) *(law, regulation)* enfreindre, violer; *(custom)* aller à l'encontre de; *(good manners, good taste)* être un outrage à (**b**) *(cause offence)* **I didn't mean to offend** *(give offence to the general public)* je ne voulais offenser personne; *(give offence to you)* je ne voulais pas t'offenser *ou* te froisser

offended [ə'fendɪd] *adj* (**a**) *(insulted)* froissé, blessé; **don't be offended if I leave early** ne le prends pas mal si je pars de bonne heure; **she was very offended when he didn't come to her party** elle a été extrêmement vexée qu'il ne vienne pas à sa soirée (**b**) *Law* **the offended party** l'offensé(e) *m,f*

offendedly [ə'fendɪdlɪ] *adv (say)* d'un ton froissé

offender [ə'fendə(r)] *n* (**a**) *Law* délinquant(e) *m,f*; **first offender** délinquant(e) *m,f* primaire; **13 percent of convicted offenders return to crime** 13 pour cent des condamnés récidivent; **drug offender** *(dealer)* trafiquant(e) *m,f* de drogue; *(user)* toxicomane *mf*; **traffic offenders** contrevenants *mpl* au code de la route

(**b**) *(gen → culprit)* coupable *mf*; **the chemical industry is the worst offender** l'industrie chimique est la première responsable

offending [ə'fendɪŋ] *adj* gênant; **the offending word was omitted** le mot gênant *ou* qui posait problème a été enlevé; **the offending object/article** l'objet/l'article incriminé; **the offending smell was traced to the drains** l'odeur suspecte venait des canalisations

offense *Am* = **offence**

offensive [ə'fensɪv] **1** *adj* (**a**) *(causing indignation, anger)* offensant, choquant; **to find sth offensive** être choqué par qch; **to be offensive to sb** *(person)* injurier *ou* insulter qn; **an offensive remark** une remarque blessante; **this advertisement is offensive to Muslims/women** cette publicité porte atteinte à la religion musulmane/à la dignité de la femme

(**b**) *(disgusting → smell)* nauséabond

(**c**) *(aggressive)* offensif; **they took immediate offensive action** ils sont immédiatement passés à l'offensive

2 *n Mil, Sport & Fig* offensive *f*; **to go on the offensive** passer à l'offensive; **to take the offensive** prendre l'offensive; **to be on the offensive** attaquer; **a military offensive** une offensive militaire; **a diplomatic/peace offensive** une offensive diplomatique/de paix

►► ***offensive language*** propos *mpl* choquants; ***offensive weapon*** arme *f* offensive

offensively [ə'fensɪvlɪ] *adv* (**a**) *(behave, speak)* d'une manière offensante *ou* blessante

(**b**) *Mil & Sport* offensivement; **offensively, theirs is the stronger team** en attaque, c'est leur équipe qui est la plus forte

offensiveness [ə'fensɪvnɪs] *n (of sight, behaviour)* nature *f* offensante *ou* choquante; *(of smell)* nature *f* nauséabonde; *(of remark)* nature *f* injurieuse; **the offensiveness of her tone** son ton injurieux

Offer ['ɒfə(r)] *n Br Formerly* (*abbr* **Office of Electricity Regulation**) = organisme britannique chargé de contrôler les activités des compagnies régionales de distribution d'électricité

offer ['ɒfə(r)] **1** *vt* (**a**) *(present)* offrir; *(excuses)* présenter; **to offer sth to sb, to offer sb sth** offrir qch à qn; **she offered me £800 for my car** elle m'a proposé 800 livres pour ma voiture; **he offered her a chair/his arm** il lui offrit une chaise/son bras; **can I offer you a drink?** puis-je vous offrir un verre?; **to offer advantages** présenter des avantages; **to offer sb one's sympathy** présenter ses condoléances à qn; **to have a lot to offer** *(town, person)* avoir beaucoup à offrir; **the town has little to offer in the way of entertainment** la ville n'a pas grand-chose à offrir pour ce qui est des divertissements; **candidates may offer one of the following foreign languages** les candidats peuvent présenter une des langues étrangères suivantes; **to offer goods for sale** mettre des marchandises en vente

(**b**) *(propose)* proposer; **to offer to do sth** s'offrir pour faire qch, proposer de faire qch; **I offered to help them** je leur ai proposé mon aide; **it was kind of you to offer** c'est gentil de me l'avoir proposé; **to offer a suggestion** faire une suggestion; **to offer an opinion** émettre une opinion; **to offer sb advice** donner des conseils à qn; **may I offer a little advice?** puis-je vous donner un petit conseil?; **nobody bothered to offer any explanation** personne ne s'est soucié de fournir une explication

2 *n* offre *f*; **job offers** offres *fpl* d'emploi; **offer of marriage** demande *f* en mariage; **offers of help are pouring in** les offres d'aide affluent; **I had several offers of help** plusieurs personnes m'ont proposé de m'aider; **we need somebody to help, any offers?** nous avons besoin de quelqu'un pour nous aider, est-ce qu'il y a des volontaires?; **£500 or near** *or* **nearest offer** 500 livres, à débattre; **she wants £500, but she's open to offers** elle veut 500 livres, mais elle est prête à négocier; **make me an offer!** faites-moi une offre!; **I'll make you a final offer** je vous ferai une dernière offre; **I made him an offer he couldn't refuse** je lui ai fait une offre qu'il ne pouvait pas refuser; **special offer** offre *f* spéciale, promotion *f*; **to be under offer** faire l'objet d'une proposition d'achat; **the house is under offer** on a reçu une offre pour la maison; *Fin* **offer of cover** appel *m* de marge; **offer by prospectus** offre *f* publique de vente; **offer to purchase** offre *f* publique d'achat; **offer for sale** mise *f* sur le marché; **offers in the region of £100** 100 livres à débattre

3 on offer *adv (on sale)* en vente; **these goods are on special offer this week** ces articles sont en promotion cette semaine; **there aren't many jobs on offer** les offres d'emploi sont peu nombreuses; **what is on offer in the negotiations?** qu'est-ce qui est proposé dans les négociations?

►► ***offer price*** *St Exch* cours *m ou* prix *m* vendeur; *Mktg* prix *m* vendeur, prix *m* offert

►**offer up** *vt sep (hymn, sacrifice)* offrir

offeree [ɒfə'riː] *n Fin & Law* destinataire *mf* de l'offre

offering ['ɒfərɪŋ] *n* (**a**) *(action)* offre *f*; **the offering of gifts** le fait de s'offrir des cadeaux

(**b**) *(thing offered)* offre *f*, don *m*; *Fig* **his latest offering is a novel set in Ireland** le dernier roman qu'il nous propose se déroule en Irlande; *Ironic* **let's hope this essay is better than your last offering** espérons que cette dissertation sera meilleure que votre dernier chef-d'œuvre

(**c**) *Rel* offrande *f*

(**d**) *St Exch (of new shares)* mise *f* sur le marché

►► *Fin* ***offering circular*** note *f* d'information

offeror ['ɒfərə(r)] *n Fin & Law* = personne qui fait une offre

offertory ['ɒfətrɪ] (*pl* **offertories**) *n* (**a**) *(prayers, ritual)* offertoire *m*

(**b**) *(collection)* quête *f*

►► ***offertory box*** tronc *m*

off-exchange *adj St Exch (transaction, contract, market)* hors Bourse, hors cote

off-guard *adj (moment)* **in an off-guard moment** dans un moment d'inattention

offhand [ˌɒf'hænd] **1** *adj (nonchalant)* désinvolte, cavalier; *(abrupt)* brusque; **to be offhand with sb** se montrer désinvolte *ou* cavalier à l'égard de qn

2 *adv* spontanément, au pied levé; **offhand I'd say it'll take a week** à première vue, je dirais que cela prendra une semaine; **I can't give you the figures offhand** je ne peux pas vous citer les chiffres de mémoire *ou* de tête; **I don't know offhand** comme ça de but en blanc, je ne le sais pas

offhanded [ˌɒf'hændɪd] *adj (nonchalant)* désinvolte, cavalier; *(abrupt)* brusque; **to be offhanded with sb** se montrer désinvolte *ou* cavalier à l'égard de qn

offhandedly [ˌɒf'hændɪdlɪ] *adv (nonchalantly)* de façon désinvolte *ou* cavalière, avec désinvolture; *(with abruptness)* brusquement, sans ménagement

offhandedness [ˌɒf'hændɪdnɪs] *n (casualness)* désinvolture *f*; *(brusqueness)* brusquerie *f*

off-highway 1 *adj (driving)* hors route *(inv)*

2 *adv (drive, cycle)* hors route

off-hook, offhook *adj*

►► *Comput* ***off-hook signal*** signal *m* de réponse *ou* de décrochage

off-hours *npl Am Fam* heures *fpl* creuses ❑

office ['ɒfɪs] **1** *n* (**a**) *(of firm)* bureau *m*; *(of solicitor)* étude *f*; *(of barrister)* cabinet *m*; *Am (of doctor, dentist)* cabinet *m* (de consultation); **people who work in offices** les gens qui travaillent dans les bureaux; **the whole office knows** tout le bureau est au courant; **she's been transferred to the Paris office** elle a été mutée au bureau de Paris; **he's out of the office at the moment** il n'est pas dans le bureau en ce moment; **office space is cheaper in the suburbs** les bureaux sont moins chers en banlieue; **for office use only** *(on form)* (cadre) réservé à l'administration

(**b**) *(government department)* bureau *m*, département *m*; **I have to send this to the tax office** je dois envoyer ça au centre des impôts

(**c**) *(position, power)* fonction *f*; **public office** fonction *f* publique; **a woman in high office** une femme haut placée; **to rise to/hold high office** être promu à/détenir un poste élevé; **he's one of the candidates seeking office** c'est l'un des candidats qui se présentent aux élections; **to be in** *or* **to hold office** *(political party)* être au pouvoir; *(mayor, minister, official)* être en fonction(s); **to be out of office** avoir quitté ses fonctions; **to take office** *(political party)* arriver au pouvoir; *(mayor, minister, official)* entrer en fonctions; **to resign/to leave office** se démettre de/quitter ses fonctions; **to run for** *or* **to seek office** se présenter aux élections; **elected to the office of president** élu à la présidence

(**d**) *Rel* office *m*; **office for the dead** office *m* des morts; **last offices** *(for the dead)* derniers devoirs *mpl*; *(funeral)* obsèques *fpl*

2 *comp (furniture, job, staff)* de bureau

3 offices *npl* (**a**) *(help, actions)* **I got the job through the (good) offices of Mrs Katz** j'ai obtenu ce travail grâce aux bons offices de Mme Katz

(**b**) *Br (of large house, estate)* communs *mpl*, **the usual offices** les sanitaires *mpl*

►► *Fin* ***office account*** compte *m* commercial; ***office automation*** bureautique *f*; *Br* ***office bearer*** *(in club, association)* membre *m* du bureau; *Br* ***office block*** immeuble *m* de bureaux; *Old-fashioned* ***office boy*** garçon *m* de bureau; ***office building*** immeuble *m* de bureaux; ***office equipment*** matériel *m* de bureau; ***the Office of Fair Trading*** = organisme britannique de défense des consommateurs et de régulation des pratiques commerciales; ***office hours*** heures *fpl* de bureau; **during office hours** pendant les heures de bureau; *Comput* ***office IT*** bureautique *f*; ***office junior*** stagiaire *mf (en secrétariat)*; ***the Office of Management and Budget*** = service administratif américain dont le rôle principal est d'aider le président à préparer le budget; ***office manager*** chef *m* de bureau; ***office party*** = réception organisée dans un bureau à l'occasion des fêtes de fin d'année; ***office space*** locaux *mpl* pour bureaux; ***office staff*** personnel *m* de bureau; ***office supplies*** articles *mpl* de bureau; ***office work*** travail *m* de bureau; ***office worker*** employé *m* de bureau

officeholder ['ɒfɪsˌhəʊldə(r)] *n* (**a**) *Pol* titulaire *mf* d'une fonction (**b**) *Am (in club, association)* membre *m* du bureau

officer ['ɒfɪsə(r)] **1** *n* (**a**) *Mil* officier *m*

(**b**) *(policeman)* agent *m* de police; *(as form of address → to policeman)* monsieur l'agent; *(→ to policewoman)* madame l'agent

(**c**) *(official → in local government)* fonctionnaire *mf*; *(→ of trade union)* représentant(e) *m,f* permanent(e); *(→ of company)* membre *m* de la direction; *(→ of association, institution)* membre *m* du bureau; **the officers of the association meet every month** le bureau de l'association se réunit tous les mois

2 *vt Mil* encadrer; **they were officered by young recruits** ils étaient encadrés par de jeunes recrues

►► *Mil* ***officer of the day*** officier *m* de permanence; *Mil* ***officer of the guard*** officier *m* de la garde; *Mil* ***officers' mess*** mess *m*; *Br Mil* ***Officers' Training Corps*** = organisme fournissant une préparation militaire aux étudiants souhaitant devenir officiers; *Naut* ***officer of the watch*** officier *m* du quart

official [ə'fɪʃəl] **1** *adj* (**a**) *(formal)* officiel; **she's here on official business** elle est ici en visite officielle; **I can't understand this official language** je ne comprends rien à ce jargon administratif; **the official organist** le/la titulaire de l'orgue; **it's official, they're getting a divorce** c'est officiel, ils divorcent; **it's not official yet** ce n'est pas encore officiel; **his appointment will be made official tomorrow** sa nomination sera (rendue) officielle demain; **we decided to make it official (and get married)** nous avons décidé de rendre notre liaison officielle (en nous mariant); **to act in one's official capacity** agir dans l'exercice de ses fonctions; **she was speaking in her official capacity as General Secretary** elle parlait en sa qualité de secrétaire général; **to go through the official channels** suivre la filière (habituelle); **Spanish is the official language of Mexico** l'espagnol est la langue officielle du Mexique

(**b**) *(alleged)* officiel; **the official reason for his visit is to discuss trade** officiellement, il est là pour des discussions ayant trait au commerce

2 *n (representative)* officiel *m*; *(civil servant)* fonctionnaire *mf*; *(subordinate employee)* employé(e) *m,f*; *Sport (referee)* arbitre *m*; *(linesman)* juge *m* de touche; *Sport* **the officials** l'arbitre *m* et les juges *mpl* de touche; **the official at the entrance** le préposé à l'entrée; **a bank/club/union official** un représentant de la banque/du club/du syndicat; **a government official** un haut fonctionnaire; **minor officials** petits fonctionnaires *mpl*

►► ***official biography*** biographie *f* officielle; ***the Official Birthday*** = jour de célébration officielle de l'anniversaire du souverain britannique (deuxième samedi de juin); ***official document*** document *m* officiel; *Fin* ***official exchange rate*** cours *m* officiel; ***official letter*** pli *m* officiel *ou* de service; *St Exch* ***Official List*** cote *f* officielle; *Fin* ***official market*** marché *m* officiel; ***official opening*** *(of new factory, museum etc)* inauguration *f*; *St Exch* ***official quotation*** cours *m* officiel; *Banking* ***official rate*** taux *m* officiel d'escompte; *Br* ***official receiver*** administrateur(trice) *m,f* judiciaire; **the official receiver has been called in** on a fait appel à l'administration judiciaire; *Br* ***official receivership*** liquidation *f* judiciaire; ***the Official Secrets Act*** = loi britannique sur le secret Défense; ***official strike*** = grève soutenue par la direction du syndicat

officialdom [ə'fɪʃəldəm] *n (officials)* administration *f*; *Pej (bureaucracy)* bureaucratie *f*, fonctionnarisme *m*

officialese [əˌfɪʃə'liːz] *n Pej* jargon *m* administratif

officialism [ə'fɪʃəlɪzəm] *n* (**a**) *(of civil service etc)* bureaucratie *f*, fonctionnarisme *m*

(**b**) *(of bureaucrat)* suffisance *f*, fatuité *f*

officially [ə'fɪʃəlɪ] *adv* (**a**) *(formally)* officiellement; **he's now been officially appointed** sa nomination est désormais officielle; **we now have it officially** la nouvelle est maintenant officielle

(**b**) *(allegedly)* théoriquement, en principe; **officially, he's at the dentist's** en principe, il est chez le dentiste

officiant [ə'fɪʃɪənt] *n Rel* officiant *m*, célébrant *m*

officiate [ə'fɪʃɪeɪt] *vi* (**a**) *(gen)* **to officiate as** remplir les fonctions de; **she officiated at the ceremony** elle a présidé la cérémonie; **the mayor will officiate at the opening of the stadium** le maire inaugurera le stade (**b**) *Rel* officier; **officiating minister** (pasteur *m*) officiant *m*

officinal [ɒ'fɪsɪnəl] *adj* officinal

officious [ə'fɪʃəs] *adj* (**a**) *(over-zealous)* zélé, empressé; *(interfering)* importun; *(overbearing)* impérieux, autoritaire; **to be officious** faire du zèle (**b**) *(in diplomacy → unofficial)* officieux

►► ***officious talks*** pourparlers *mpl* officieux

officiously [ə'fɪʃəslɪ] *adv (over-zealously)* avec zèle, avec empressement; *(interferingly)* d'une manière importune; *(overbearingly)* impérieusement, de manière autoritaire; **to behave officiously towards sb** faire l'empressé auprès de qn

officiousness [ə'fɪʃəsnɪs] *n (over-zealousness)* zèle *m*, empressement *m*; *(interfering manner)* caractère *m* importun; *(overbearing manner)* autoritarisme *m*; **a letter that smacks of officiousness** une lettre rédigée sur un ton impérieux

offie ['ɒfɪ] *n Br Fam (abbr* **off-licence**) = magasin autorisé à vendre des boissons alcoolisées à emporter

offing ['ɒfɪŋ] *n* (**a**) *Naut* large *m* (**b**) *(idioms)* **to be in the offing** être imminent, être dans l'air; **a confrontation had long been in the offing** une confrontation couvait depuis longtemps; **there could be some changes in the offing** il se pourrait qu'il y ait des changements en perspective

offish ['ɒfɪʃ] *adj Br Fam (aloof)* plutôt distant *ou* froid ❑

off-key 1 *adj* (**a**) *Mus* faux (fausse); **he was off-key** il n'était pas dans le ton, il jouait/chantait faux (**b**) *Fig (remark)* hors de propos, sans rapport

2 *adv* faux; **to play/to sing off-key** jouer/chanter faux

off-licence *n Br* (**a**) *(shop)* = magasin autorisé à vendre des boissons alcoolisées à emporter; **at the off-licence** chez le marchand de vins (**b**) *(licence)* licence *f (autorisant la vente de boissons alcoolisées à emporter)*

off-limits 1 *adj* interdit; *Fam* **the bar is off-limits to non-coms** le bar est interdit aux sous-offs

2 *adv* en dehors des limites autorisées; **to go off-limits** sortir des limites autorisées

off-line, offline 1 *adj* (**a**) *Comput* non connecté; *(processing)* en différé; *(printer)* déconnecté; **to be off-line** ne pas être connecté; **to go off-line** se déconnecter (**b**) *Ind (production)* hors ligne

2 *adv* hors ligne, hors connexion; **to work off-line** travailler sans se connecter à l'Internet

►► ***off-line mode*** mode *m* autonome; ***off-line reader*** lecteur *m* non connecté

offload [ɒf'ləʊd] *vt* (**a**) *(unload → passengers)* débarquer; *(→ cargo)* décharger (**b**) *(dump → work, blame)* **she tends to offload responsibility onto other people** elle a tendance à se décharger de ses responsabilités sur les autres; **to offload the blame onto sb** rejeter la faute sur qn

off-message *adj Br Pol* = qui ne respecte pas scrupuleusement la ligne du parti

off-off-Broadway *adj Am* à l'avant-garde de l'avant-garde; **off-off-Broadway show** spectacle *m* d'avant-garde

off-peak 1 *adj (consumption, train)* aux heures creuses, en dehors des périodes de pointe

2 *adv* pendant les heures creuses

►► ***off-peak electricity*** électricité *f* consommée pendant les heures creuses; ***off-peak hours*** heures *fpl* creuses; *Elec* ***off-peak rate*** tarif *m* de nuit; ***off-peak times*** heures *fpl* creuses

off-piste *Ski* **1** *adj* hors-piste(s)

2 *adv* hors piste(s)

offprint ['ɒfprɪnt] **1** *n* tiré *m* à part

2 *vt* **to offprint an article** faire un tiré à part
off-putting [-pʊtɪŋ] *adj Br (smell)* repoussant; *(manner)* rébarbatif; *(person, description)* peu engageant; *(experience)* démoralisant; **the idea of a five-hour stopover is very off-putting** l'idée d'une escale de cinq heures n'a rien d'enthousiasmant *ou* de réjouissant
off-ramp *n* sortie *f* d'autoroute
off-road 1 *adj (driving)* hors route *(inv)*
2 *adv (drive, cycle)* hors route
▸▸ ***off-road vehicle*** véhicule *m* tout-terrain
off-roader [-'rəʊdə(r)] *n Aut* tout-terrain *m inv*
offscourings ['ɒf,skaʊərɪŋz] *npl (dregs)* lie *f*; *(scum)* écume *f*
off-screen *Cin & TV* **1** *adj* (**a**) *(out of sight)* hors champ, off (**b**) *(romance, persona)* dans la vie; **their off-screen relationship mirrored their love affair in the film** la liaison qu'ils entretenaient dans la vie reflétait celle du film
2 *adv* (**a**) *(out of sight)* hors champ, off (**b**) *(in real life)* dans la réalité; **he's less handsome off-screen** il est moins séduisant dans la réalité
▸▸ ***off-screen narration*** commentaire *m* en voix off
off-season 1 *n* morte-saison *f*
2 *adj* hors saison *(inv)*
3 *adv* pendant la morte-saison
▸▸ ***off-season tariff*** tarif *m* hors saison
offset ['ɒfset] *(pt & pp* **offset**, *cont* **offsetting**) **1** *n* (**a**) *(counterbalance)* contrepoids *m*
(**b**) *Acct (compensation)* compensation *f*, dédommagement *m*
(**c**) *Typ* offset *m*
(**d**) *Bot (shoot)* rejeton *m*
(**e**) *Constr* ressaut *m*
(**f**) *Tech (of wheel)* désaxage *m*, décentrement *m*, déport *m*
2 *vt* (**a**) *(make up for)* contrebalancer, compenser; **the advantages tend to offset the difficulties** les avantages compensent presque les inconvénients; **to offset losses against tax** déduire le montant de ses pertes de ses impôts; **any wage increase will be offset by inflation** avec l'inflation, les augmentations de salaire n'en seront plus vraiment; **we'll have to offset our research investment against long-term returns** nous devons amortir notre investissement dans la recherche en faisant des bénéfices à long terme; **his faults are offset by his enthusiasm** son enthousiasme fait oublier ses défauts
(**b**) *Typ* imprimer en offset
(**c**) *Tech (wheel)* désaxer, décentrer; *(part)* déporter, décaler
▸▸ *Acct* ***offset agreement*** accord *m* de compensation
offsetting entry ['ɒfsetɪŋ-] *n Acct* écriture *f* de compensation
offshoot ['ɒfʃuːt] *n* (**a**) *(of organization, political party, movement)* ramification *f*; *(of family)* branche *f*; *(spin-off)* application *f* secondaire; *consequence → of decision etc)* retombée *f*; **it's an offshoot of space technology** c'est une application secondaire de la technologie spatiale; **French and Spanish are offshoots of Latin** le français et l'espagnol sont issus *ou* dérivent du latin; **the company has offshoots in Asia** *(subsidiaries)* la société a des succursales en Asie
(**b**) *Bot* rejeton *m*
offshore ['ɒfʃɔː(r)] **1** *adj* (**a**) *(in or on sea)* marin; *(near shore → shipping, fishing, waters)* côtier; *(→ island)* près de la côte; *Petr (installation, platform)* offshore *(inv)*, marin
(**b**) *(towards open sea → current, direction)* vers le large; *(→ wind)* de terre
(**c**) *Fin (investment, company)* offshore *(inv)*, *Offic* extraterritorial
2 *adv Petr (live, drill etc)* en mer, au large; *Fin* **to keep sth offshore** garder qch offshore
▸▸ ***offshore banking*** opérations *fpl* bancaires offshore; ***offshore company*** société *f* offshore; ***offshore fund*** fonds *m* offshore; ***offshore investment*** placement *m* offshore; *Petr* ***offshore oilfield*** champ *m* (pétrolifère) en mer *ou* offshore; ***offshore rig*** plate-forme *f* offshore
off-shot *TV & Cin* **1** *adj* hors plan
2 *adv* hors plan
offside 1 *n* ['ɒfsaɪd] *Br Aut (when driving on right)* côté *m* gauche, côté *m* rue; *(when driving on left)* côté *m* droit, côté *m* rue
2 *adj* [,ɒf'saɪd] *Sport* hors jeu *(inv)*; **to play the offside trap** jouer le hors-jeu
3 *adv* [,ɒf'saɪd] *Sport* hors jeu
▸▸ ***the offside law*** *or* ***rule*** la règle du hors-jeu
offspring ['ɒfsprɪŋ] *(pl* **inv**) **1** *n* (**a**) *Arch or Hum (son or daughter)* rejeton *m* (**b**) *Fig (consequence)* retombée *f*, conséquence *f*
2 *npl (descendants)* progéniture *f*; **none of her offspring were there** aucun de ses rejetons n'était là
offstage 1 *adv* [,ɒf'steɪdʒ] (**a**) *Theat* dans les coulisses; **she ran offstage** elle quitta la scène en courant (**b**) *Fig (in private life)* en privé; **offstage, she was surprisingly reserved** en privé, elle était étonnamment réservée
2 *adj* ['ɒf,steɪdʒ] (**a**) *Theat* dans les coulisses; **an offstage row** une querelle de coulisses (**b**) *Fig (life)* privé
off-street *adj*
▸▸ ***off-street parking*** place *f* de parking *(située ailleurs que dans la rue)*
off-the-cuff 1 *adj* impromptu, improvisé
2 *adv* au pied levé, à l'improviste
off-the-peg, *Am* **off-the-rack** *adj* de prêt-à-porter
▸▸ ***off-the-peg clothes*** prêt-à-porter *m*; *Mktg* ***off-the-peg research*** = étude de marché utilisant des données déjà rassemblées
off-the-record *adj (not to be made public)* confidentiel; *(not to be put in minutes)* à ne pas faire figurer dans le compte rendu; **on the understanding that it is strictly off-the-record** à titre strictement officieux
off-the-shelf *adj (goods)* prêt(e) à l'usage
▸▸ ***off-the-shelf company*** société *f* tiroir
off-the-shoulder *adj* qui dégage les épaules
off-the-wall *adj Fam (crazy)* loufoque, bizarroïde; *(unexpected)* original ❑, excentrique ❑
off-white 1 *n* blanc *m* cassé
2 *adj* blanc cassé *(inv)*
off-year *n Pol* = année présidentielle sans élection aux États-Unis
Ofgas ['ɒf,gæs] *n Formerly (abbr* **Office of Gas Supply**) = organisme britannique chargé de contrôler les activités des compagnies régionales de distribution de gaz
Ofgem ['ɒf,dʒem] *n (abbr* **Office of the Gas and Electricity Markets**) = nouvel organisme britannique qui a remplacé les anciens "Ofgas" et "Offer"
Oflot ['ɒf,lɒt] *n (abbr* **Office of the National Lottery**) = organisme britannique chargé de contrôler la loterie nationale
Ofsted ['ɒf,sted] *n (abbr* **Office for Standards in Education**) = organisme britannique chargé de contrôler le système d'éducation nationale
OFT [,əʊef'tiː] *n (abbr* **Office of Fair Trading**) = organisme britannique de défense des consommateurs et de régulation des pratiques commerciales
oft [ɒft] *adv Literary* maintes fois, souvent
oft- [ɒft] *pref* **oft-repeated** *(warning)* réitéré; *(argument)* ressassé; **oft-quoted** souvent cité
Oftel ['ɒf,tel] *n Br (abbr* **Office of Telecommunications**) = organisme britannique chargé de contrôler les activités des sociétés de télécommunications
often ['ɒfən, 'ɒftən] **1** *adv* souvent; **I've often thought of leaving** j'ai souvent pensé à partir; **I don't see her very often** je ne la vois pas très souvent; **it's not often you get an offer like that** ce n'est pas souvent qu'on vous fait une offre pareille; **do you come here often?** = expression toute faite dont l'équivalent français est "vous habitez chez vos parents?"; **how often?** *(how many times)* combien de fois?; *(at what intervals)* tous les combien?; **how often do I have to tell you?** combien de fois faudra-t-il que je te le répète?; **how often does he write to you?** est-ce qu'il t'écrit souvent?; **all too often the money goes to the wrong people** trop souvent, l'argent va à ceux qui n'en ont pas besoin; **it cannot be repeated too often** on ne saurait trop le répéter; **once too often** une fois de trop
2 as often as not *adv* la plupart du temps
3 every so often *adv* de temps en temps, de temps à autre
4 more often than not *adv* la plupart du temps
oftentimes ['ɒfəntaɪmz] *adv* (**a**) *Br Arch* souventes fois
(**b**) *Am* souvent
ofttimes ['ɒftaɪmz] *adv Arch* souventes fois
Ofwat ['ɒf,wɒt] *n (abbr* **Office of Water Supply**) = organisme britannique chargé de contrôler les activités des compagnies régionales de distribution des eaux
ogam, ogham ['ɒgəm] *n* ogham *m*
▸▸ ***ogam alphabet*** ogham *m*
ogival [əʊ'dʒaɪvəl] *adj* ogival, en ogive
ogive ['əʊdʒaɪv] *n Archit & Math* ogive *f*
ogle ['əʊgəl] *vt* lorgner
ogler ['əʊglə(r)] *n* lorgneur(euse) *m,f*
ogling ['əʊglɪŋ] *adj* qui lorgne, lorgnant
O grade *n Scot Formerly Sch* = premier diplôme dans l'enseignement secondaire écossais
ogre ['əʊgə(r)] *n* ogre *m*
ogreish = **ogrish**
ogress ['əʊgrɪs] *n* ogresse *f*
ogrish ['əʊgərɪʃ] *adj* = qui ressemble à un ogre; **an ogrish mouth** une bouche d'ogre
OH *(written abbr* **Ohio**) Ohio *m*
oh [əʊ] *exclam* oh!, ah!; **oh, what a surprise!** oh, quelle surprise!; **oh really?** vraiment?, ah bon?; **oh no!** oh non!; **oh yes you will!** ah si!
O'Hare [əʊ'heə(r)] *n* = l'aéroport international de Chicago
oh arr [-ɑː(r)] *exclam* = expression humoristique dénotant un parler paysan
ohc [,əʊeɪtʃ'siː] *n (abbr* **overhead camshaft**)
▸▸ ***ohc engine*** moteur *m* ACT
Ohio [əʊ'haɪəʊ] *n* l'Ohio *m*; **in Ohio** dans l'Ohio
ohm [əʊm] *n Elec* ohm *m*
ohmage ['əʊmɪdʒ] *n Elec* résistance *f* (en ohms)
ohmmeter ['əʊm,miːtə(r)] *n Elec* ohmmètre *m*
OHMS *(written abbr* **On His/Her Majesty's Service**) = tampon apposé sur le courrier administratif britannique
Ohm's law [əʊmz-] *n Phys* loi *f* d'Ohm
oho [ə'həʊ] *exclam (expressing surprise)* oh!; *(expressing satisfaction)* ah!
OHP [,əʊeɪtʃ'piː] *n (abbr* **overhead projector**) rétroprojecteur *m*
OI [,əʊ'aɪ] *n (abbr* **opportunistic infection**) infection *f* opportuniste
oi [ɔɪ] *exclam Fam* hé!
OID [,əʊaɪ'diː] *n Fin (abbr* **original issue discount bond**) obligation *f* à prime d'émission
oidium [əʊ'ɪdɪəm] *n Bot (fungus, disease)* oïdium *m*; *(spore)* oïdie *f*
oik [ɔɪk] *n Br Fam Pej* pignouf *m*, plouc *mf*
oil [ɔɪl] **1** *n* (**a**) *(petroleum)* pétrole *m*; **to drill for oil** effectuer des forages pour trouver du pétrole
(**b**) *(in food, as lubricant)* huile *f*; *(as fuel)* mazout *m*, fuel *m ou* fioul *m* domestique; **sardines in oil** sardines *fpl* à l'huile; *Aut* **to change the oil** faire la vidange; **lubricating oil** huile *f* lubrifiante; **oil of lavender/turpentine** essence *f* de lavande/de térébenthine; *Fig* **to pour oil on troubled waters** ramener le calme
(**c**) *Art (paint)* (peinture *f* à l') huile *f*; *(picture)* huile *f*; **a portrait in oils** un portrait (peint) à l'huile; **she works in oils** elle travaille avec de la peinture à l'huile
2 *comp* (**a**) *(industry, production, corporation)* pétrolier; *(deposit, reserves)* de pétrole; *(magnate, sheikh)* du pétrole
(**b**) *(level, pressure)* d'huile; *(filter)* à huile; *(heating, burner)* à mazout
3 *vt (machine, engine)* lubrifier, graisser; *(hinge, wood, skin)* huiler; *Fig* **it will help to oil the wheels** cela facilitera les choses, cela mettra de l'huile dans les rouages
4 oils *npl St Exch* (valeurs *fpl*) pétrolières *fpl*
▸▸ ***oil bath*** bain *m* d'huile; ***oil cake*** tourteau *m* (pour bétail); ***oil change*** vidange *f*; ***oil cooling*** refroidissement *m* par huile; ***oil crisis*** choc *m* pétrolier; ***oil drum*** bidon *m* à pétrole; ***oil gland*** glande *f* uropygienne; ***oil gauge*** *(for measuring level)* jauge *f ou* indicateur *m* de niveau d'huile; *(for measuring pressure)* indicateur *m* de pression d'huile; ***oil kingdom*** pétromonarchie *f*; ***oil lamp*** *(burning oil)* lampe *f* à huile; *(burning paraffin)* lampe *f* à pétrole; ***oil paint*** peinture *f* à l'huile *(substance)*; ***oil painting*** peinture *f* à l'huile; *Br Fam* **he's no oil painting** ce n'est pas une beauté; ***oil palm*** éléis *m*; *Am Aut* ***oil pan***

carter *m*; ***oil pressure switch*** manocontact *m* d'huile; ***oil pressure warning light*** témoin *m* d'alerte de pression d'huile moteur; ***oil prices*** prix *mpl* pétroliers; ***oil refinery*** raffinerie *f* de pétrole; ***oil rig*** *(onshore)* derrick *m*; *(offshore)* plate-forme *f* pétrolière; *Fin* ***oil royalty*** redevance *f* pétrolière; ***oil shale*** schiste *m* bitumineux; ***oil slick*** *(on sea)* nappe *f* de pétrole; *(on beach)* marée *f* noire; ***oil spill*** *(event)* marée *f* noire; *(result)* nappe *f* de pétrole; *Br* ***oil stove*** *(using fuel oil)* poêle *m* à mazout; *(using paraffin, kerosene)* réchaud *m* à pétrole; ***oil sump*** carter *m* d'huile; ***oil tanker*** *(ship)* pétrolier *m*, tanker *m*; *(lorry)* camion-citerne *m* *(pour le pétrole)*; ***oil temperature gauge*** indicateur *m* de température d'huile; ***oil terminal*** terminal *m* (pétrolier); ***oil well*** puits *m* de pétrole

oil-bearing *adj* pétrolifère

oilbird ['ɔɪlbɜːd] *n Orn* guacharo *m*

oil-burning *adj* à mazout

oilcan ['ɔɪlkæn] *n (drum)* bidon *m* d'huile; *(oiler)* burette *f* (à huile)

oilcloth ['ɔɪlklɒθ] *n* toile *f* cirée

oil-cooled ['ɔɪlkuːld] *adj* refroidi par huile

oiled [ɔɪld] *adj* (**a**) *(machine)* lubrifié, graissé; *(hinge, silk)* huilé (**b**) *Fam (drunk)* bourré, beurré, pété; **to be well oiled** être complètement bourré (**c**) *esp Am (area, beach, animal)* mazouté

oiler ['ɔɪlə(r)] *n* (**a**) *(person)* graisseur(euse) *m,f* (**b**) *(tanker)* pétrolier *m* (**c**) *(can)* burette *f* (à huile) (**d**) *(well)* puits *m* de pétrole

oilfield ['ɔɪlfiːld] *n* gisement *m* de pétrole *ou* pétrolier

oil-fired *adj* à mazout

oil-fuelled [-fjʊəld] *adj (ship)* qui fonctionne au mazout

oiliness ['ɔɪlɪnɪs] *n* (**a**) *(greasiness)* nature *f* huileuse; **the oiliness of the dish makes it rather indigestible** ce plat contient tellement d'huile qu'il en devient indigeste (**b**) *Fig (obsequiousness)* obséquiosité *f*, patelinerie *f*

oilman ['ɔɪlmən] *(pl* **oilmen** [-mən]) *n* pétrolier *m* *(personne)*

oilpaper ['ɔɪlpeɪpə(r)] *n* papier *m* huilé

oil-producing *adj* (**a**) *(shale etc)* pétrolifère; *(country)* producteur de pétrole; **the oil-producing countries** les pays producteurs de pétrole (**b**) *(plant)* oléifère; *(substance etc)* oléifiant

oilrich ['ɔɪl,rɪtʃ] *adj* (**a**) *(made rich by oil trade)* enrichi par le pétrole (**b**) *(rich in oil resources)* riche en gisements pétrolifères

oilseed ['ɔɪlsiːd] *n* (**a**) *(linseed)* graine *f* de lin (**b**) *(from castor-oil plant)* semence *f* de ricin (**c**) *(any oil-yielding seed)* graine *f* oléagineuse, oléagineux *m*

►► ***oilseed rape*** colza *m*

oilskin ['ɔɪlskɪn] **1** *n* (**a**) *(cloth)* toile *f* cirée (**b**) *(garment)* ciré *m*

2 *comp* en toile cirée

oilstone ['ɔɪlstəʊn] *n (for sharpening)* pierre *f* à huile

oily ['ɔɪlɪ] *(compar* **oilier,** *superl* **oiliest**) *adj* (**a**) *(substance)* huileux; *(rag, fingers)* graisseux; *(hair, skin)* gras (grasse); *(salad dressing, sauce)* à base d'huile; **an oily stain** une tache de graisse (**b**) *Pej (smile, person)* mielleux, doucereux

oink [ɔɪŋk] **1** *n* grognement *m*, grommellement *m*

2 *onomat* krouik-krouik

ointment ['ɔɪntmənt] *n* pommade *f*, onguent *m*

Oireachtas [ə'rɒχtəs] *n Ir* (**a**) *(festival)* = festival gaélique qui se tient chaque année en Irlande (**b**) *Pol* = parlement irlandais

Oirish ['ɔɪrɪʃ] *adj* = terme humoristique décrivant le caractère irlandais folklorique et artificiel d'un film, d'un pub etc

oiro *(written abbr* **offers in the region of**) oiro **£100** 100 livres à débattre

OJ ['əʊ,dʒeɪ] *n Fam (abbr* **orange juice**) jus *m* d'orange ❑

OJT [,əʊdʒeɪ'tiː] *n Am (abbr* **on-the-job training**) formation *f* en entreprise

OK¹ [,əʊ'keɪ] *(pt & pp* **OKed** [,əʊ'keɪd], *cont* **OKing** [,əʊ'keɪɪŋ]) *Fam* **1** *exclam* OK, d'accord ❑, d'ac; **well OK, I'm not a specialist, but...** bon, d'accord, je ne suis pas spécialiste, mais...; **in five minutes, OK?** dans cinq minutes, ça va? **OK yah** = expression humoristique dénotant les milieux BCBG

2 *adj* (**a**) *(in order, fine)* correct ❑, exact ❑; **everything's OK** tout est en règle ❑ *ou* OK; **to be OK** *(unhurt)* aller bien ❑; **are you OK?, did I hurt you/are you upset?** ça va?, je ne t'ai pas fait mal/tu es fâché?; **I'll be OK when I get home** ça ira une fois que je serai à la maison; **but is the car OK?** mais est-ce que la voiture n'a rien? ❑; **that's OK by** *or* **with me** d'accord! ❑; **is that OK by** *or* **with your mother?** est-ce que ta mère est d'accord?; **is it OK to bring my friend?** est-ce que ça vous dérange si je viens avec mon ami? ❑; **no, it is NOT OK** pas question; **clothes like that are OK for a party** des vêtements comme ça, ça va bien pour aller à une soirée ❑

(**b**) *(acceptable → meal, film)* pas mal; *(→ candidate, singer)* pas mauvais, pas mal; **how are things? – OK** comment ça va? – ça peut aller; **the meal/her performance was more than OK** le repas/sa prestation était au-dessus de la moyenne ❑; **was I OK?** comment j'étais? ❑; **an OK computer** un ordinateur pas mal

(**c**) *(understanding)* **she was OK about it** elle n'a pas fait d'histoires; **are you sure he'll be OK about letting us use the car?** tu es sûr qu'il ne fera pas d'histoires pour nous laisser la voiture?

(**d**) *(likeable → person)* **he's an OK sort of guy** c'est un type plutôt bien; **she's OK but I wouldn't want to live with her** elle est assez sympa mais je n'aimerais pas vivre avec elle

(**e**) **to be OK for work/money** *(have enough of)* avoir assez de travail/d'argent ❑; **is everybody OK for drink?** est-ce que tout le monde a à boire? ❑

3 *adv* bien ❑; **is the engine working OK?** le moteur, ça va?; **everything is going OK** tout marche bien *ou* va bien; **you're doing OK!** tu t'en tires bien!

4 *vt (approve)* approuver ❑; *(initial)* parafer ❑, parapher ❑; **his plan has been OKed** son projet a reçu le feu vert ❑

5 *n (agreement)* accord ❑ *m*; *(approval)* approbation ❑ *f*; **I gave him the OK** je lui ai donné le feu vert ❑; **did you get her OK on the new plan?** elle est d'accord pour le nouveau projet? ❑

OK² *(written abbr* **Oklahoma**) Oklahoma *m*

okapi [əʊ'kɑːpɪ] *(pl* **inv** *or* **okapis**) *n Zool* okapi *m*

okay = **OK**

okay-dokay, okey-doke(y) [,əʊkɪ'dəʊk(ɪ)] *exclam Fam* OK, d'ac

Okie ['əʊkɪ] *n Am Fam Pej* (**a**) *(inhabitant)* habitant(e) *m,f* de l'Oklahoma ❑

(**b**) *Hist* **the Okies** = habitants de l'Oklahoma qui se sont déplacés vers la Californie dans les années 30 pour échapper à la pauvreté du "Dust Bowl"

Okla *(written abbr* **Oklahoma**) Oklahoma *m*

Oklahoma [,əʊklə'həʊmə] *n* l'Oklahoma *m*; **in Oklahoma** dans l'Oklahoma

okra ['əʊkrə] *n* gombo *m*

ol' [əʊl] *Fam* = **old** *adj*

OLD [əʊld]

vieux	► 1 (a), (b), (e); 2
âgé de	► 1 (c)
ancien	► 1 (d)

(compar **older**, *superl* **oldest**) **1** *adj* (**a**) *(not new or recent)* vieux (vieille); **the old traditions of the countryside** les vieilles traditions campagnardes; **there's an old saying that...** il y a un vieux dicton qui dit que...; **it's hard to shake off old habits** on ne se débarrasse pas facilement de ses vieilles habitudes; **not that old excuse again!** tu ne vas pas/il ne va pas/*etc* ressortir encore une fois la même excuse!; **they're old friends** ce sont de vieux amis *ou* des amis de longue date; **he's an old friend of mine** c'est un de mes vieux amis; **to go over old ground** revenir sur un terrain déjà parcouru; **an old debt** une dette de longue date; **that's an old dodge** c'est un coup classique; **the old country** la mère patrie

(**b**) *(not young)* vieux (vieille); **an old man** un vieil homme; **an old woman** une vieille femme; **I don't like that old man/woman** je n'aime pas ce vieux/cette vieille; **old people** personnes *fpl* âgées; **the old people next door** le couple âgé qui habite à côté, *Fam* les vieux qui habitent à côté; **to get** *or* **grow old** vieillir; **who will look after me in my old age?** qui s'occupera de moi quand je serai vieux?; **I've got a little money put aside for my old age** j'ai quelques économies de côté pour mes vieux jours; **old people's home** maison *f* de retraite

(**c**) *(referring to a particular age)* **how old is she?** quel âge a-t-elle?; **to be old enough to do sth** être en âge de faire qch; **she's old enough to know better** elle ne devrait plus faire ce genre de chose à son âge; **he's old enough to look after himself** il est (bien) assez grand pour se débrouiller tout seul; **he's old enough to be my father!** il pourrait être mon père!; **you're as old as you feel** on a l'âge de ses artères; **she is older than I am** elle est plus âgée *ou* vieille que moi; **she's two years older than him** elle a deux ans de plus que lui; **my boy wants to be a soldier when he's older** mon fils veut être soldat quand il sera grand; **the older generation** la vieille génération; **my older sister** ma sœur aînée; **the oldest of the tribe** l'aîné(e) *m,f* de la tribu; **she's six months/twenty-five years old** elle a six mois/vingt-cinq ans, elle est âgée de six mois/vingt-cinq ans; **at six years old** à (l'âge de) six ans; **they have a fourteen-year-old boy** ils ont un garçon de quatorze ans; **a three-day-old baby** un bébé de trois jours

(**d**) *(former)* ancien; **that's my old address** c'est mon ancienne adresse; **an old admirer of hers** un de ses anciens admirateurs; **an old Etonian** un ancien élève d'Eton; **in the old days** autrefois, jadis; **the good old days** le bon vieux temps; **he went to my old school** il a fréquenté mon ancienne école; **of the old school** de la vieille école; **a writer of the old school** un écrivain de la vieille école

(**e**) *Fam (expressing familiarity or affection)* vieux (vieille), brave; **old Jimmy wants to speak to you** le vieux Jimmy veut te parler; **good old Frank!** ce (bon) vieux Frank!; *Old-fashioned* **hello, old thing** *or* **chap!** salut, mon vieux *ou* ma vieille branche!

(**f**) *Fam (as intensifier)* **it's a funny old life!** la vie est drôle, quand même!; *very Fam* **you old bastard!** espèce de salaud!; **silly old bat** espèce de vieille folle!; **we had a fine old time** nous avons passé un sacré bon moment; **any old bit of wood will do** n'importe quel vieux bout de bois fera l'affaire ❑; **any old how** n'importe comment ❑; **I just wear any old thing to do the gardening** je porte n'importe quel vieux truc pour jardiner; **he's not just any old scientist, he's a Nobel prizewinner** ce n'est pas n'importe quel scientifique, c'est un prix Nobel ❑

2 *npl* **the old** les vieux *mpl*

3 of old *adv* (**a**) *Literary (of former times)* **in days of old** autrefois, jadis; **the knights of old** les chevaliers du temps jadis *ou* de jadis

(**b**) *(for a long time)* **I know them of old** je les connais depuis longtemps

►► *Br* ***old age pension*** (pension *f* de) retraite *f*; *Br* ***old age pensioner*** retraité(e) *m,f*; ***the Old Bailey*** = la cour d'assises de Londres; *Br* ***old boy*** *(former pupil)* ancien élève *m*; *Fam (old man)* vieux *m*; *Fam Old-fashioned (form of address)* mon vieux; **he's a nice old boy** c'est un vieux monsieur charmant; *Br Fam* ***old boy network*** = contacts privilégiés entre anciens élèves d'un même établissement privé; **he got the job through the old boy network** il a obtenu ce poste en faisant jouer ses relations ❑; *Br Fam* ***old dear*** *(elderly woman)* grand-mère *f*; *(mother)* vieille *f*; ***the Old Dominion State*** = surnom donné à la Virginie; ***old gold*** *(colour)* vieil or *m inv*; ***Old English*** vieil anglais *m*; ***Old English sheepdog*** bobtail *m*; ***Old Faithful*** = geyser naturel dans le parc national de Yellowstone; *Br Fam* ***the Old Firm*** = appellation collective des deux grandes équipes de football de Glasgow, Celtic et Rangers; ***old flame*** ancien béguin *m*; ***Old French*** ancien français *m*; *Br* ***old girl*** *(former pupil)* ancienne élève *f*; *Fam (old woman)* vieille *f*; *Fam Old-fashioned (form of address)* ma chère, chère amie; **she's a nice old girl** c'est une vieille dame charmante; *Am* ***Old Glory*** = surnom du drapeau américain; ***old guard*** vieille garde *f*; ***old hand*** vieux routier *m*, vétéran *m*; **he's an old hand at flying these planes** cela fait des années qu'il pilote ces avions; *Fam* **old hat** dépassé□, vieux (vieille)□; **Old High German** ancien haut allemand *m*; **Old Labour** = appellation populaire du parti travailliste avant le passage au New Labour, insistant sur le fait qu'il se situait alors plus à gauche sur l'échiquier politique; *Fam* **old lady** *(wife)* bourgeoise *f*; *(mother)* vieille *f*; *Br Fam* **old lag** truand *m*; **the Old Line State** = surnom donné au Maryland; **old maid** vieille fille *f*; *Fam* **old man** *(husband)* homme *m*, jules *m*; *(father)* vieux *m*; *Br Old-fashioned (form of address)* mon cher, cher ami; *Am* **Old Man River** = surnom donné au Mississippi; *Bot* **old man's beard** *(Clematis vitalba)* clématite *f* des haies, clématite *f* vigne blanche; **old master** *(painter)* grand maître *m* (de la peinture); *(painting)* tableau *m* de maître; **old money** *(before decimalization)* ancien système *m* monétaire; **10 shillings in old money** 10 shillings dans l'ancien système monétaire; **he married into old money** *(wealth)* il a épousé une riche héritière; **old moon** vieille lune *f*; *Fam* **Old Nick** Satan□ *m*, Lucifer□ *m*; *Ling* **Old Norse** vieux norrois *m*; *Ling* **Old Persian** vieux perse *m*; *Br Hist* **the Old Pretender** le Prétendant *(surnom de Jacques Édouard Stuart (1688–1766), fils du roi Jacques II d'Angleterre, qui lutta en vain pour devenir roi de Grande-Bretagne)*; *Br* **old school tie** *(garment)* cravate *f* aux couleurs de son ancienne école; *Fig Pej* = attitudes et système de valeurs typiques des anciens élèves des écoles privées britanniques; **old stager** vieux routier *m*, vétéran *m*; *Bible* **Old Testament** Ancien Testament *m*; **Old Trafford** *(cricket ground)* = terrain de cricket à Manchester; *(football ground)* = terrain de football à Manchester; **Old Vic** = surnom du Royal Victoria Theatre à Londres; **old wives' tale** conte *m* de bonne femme; *Fam* **old woman** *(wife)* patronne *f*, bourgeoise *f*; *(mother)* vieille *f*; *Fig Pej (timid, fussy man)* chochotte *f*; **he's such an old woman** il est comme une petite vieille; **the Old World** l'Ancien Monde *m*

'The Old Curiosity Shop' *Dickens* 'Le Magasin d'antiquités'

---

olde [əʊld, 'əʊldɪ] *adj (in name of inn, shop)* d'antan, d'autrefois; **Ye Olde Sweet Shoppe** Aux Douceurs d'Autrefois

olden ['əʊldən] *adj Arch or Literary* d'autrefois, d'antan; **in olden times** *or* **days** autrefois, jadis

old-established *adj* ancien, établi depuis longtemps

olde-worlde [,əʊldɪ'wɜːldɪ] *adj Br Fam* pseudo-ancien

old-fashioned [-'fæʃənd] **1** *adj* (**a**) *(out-of-date)* suranné, désuet(ète), démodé; *(idea)* périmé, démodé; **he's a bit old-fashioned** il est un peu vieux jeu; **you can call me old-fashioned but...** tu vas peut-être me trouver vieux jeu, mais...

(**b**) *(of the past)* d'autrefois, ancien; *Fam Hum* **he needs a good old-fashioned kick in the pants** ce qu'il lui faudrait, c'est un bon coup de pied aux fesses

(**c**) *(quizzical)* **to give sb an old-fashioned look** jeter un regard dubitatif à qn

2 *n Am* old-fashioned *m (cocktail composé de whisky, d'amers, de sucre et d'eau de Seltz)*

old-growth *adj (timber)* vieux (vieille); **old-growth forest** vieux peuplement *m*

oldie ['əʊldɪ] *n Fam* (**a**) *(show, song)* vieux succès□ *m*; *(pop song)* vieux tube *m*; *(film)* classique *m* du cinéma populaire□; **that's a real oldie!** *(song, joke etc)* il ne date pas d'aujourd'hui celui-là! (**b**) *(old person)* petit(e) vieux (vieille) *m,f*

oldish ['əʊldɪʃ] *adj* vieillot

old-line *adj Am (conservative)* conservateur

old-maidish [-'meɪdɪʃ] *adj (habits)* de vieille fille; **to become old-maidish** *(man)* prendre des habitudes de vieux garçon

oldster ['əʊldstə(r)] *n Am Fam* ancien(enne)□ *m,f*, vieillard(e)□ *m,f*

old-style *adj* à l'ancienne (mode); *Hist* **the old-style calendar** le calendrier ancien style

old-time *adj* d'autrefois, ancien

►► **old-time dancing** danses *fpl* anciennes

old-timer *n Fam* (**a**) *(old person)* ancien(enne) *m,f*, vieillard(e) *m,f*; *(veteran)* vétéran *m*, vieux *m* de la vieille (**b**) *Fam (form of address)* vieux *m*

old-womanish *adj Br Fam (habits)* de vieille femme□; **he's rather old-womanish** il a des manies de petite vieille

old-world *adj* (**a**) *(of the past)* d'antan, d'autrefois; *(quaint)* pittoresque; **a village full of old-world charm** un village au charme suranné

(**b**) *(of the Old World)* de l'Ancien Monde *ou* Continent

OLE [,əʊel'iː] *n Comput (abbr* **object linking and embedding**) OLE *m*

ole [əʊl] *Fam* = **old** *adj*

oleaceous [,əʊlɪ'eɪʃəs] *adj Bot* oléacé

oleaginous [,əʊlɪ'ædʒɪnəs] *adj* oléagineux

oleander [,əʊlɪ'ændə(r)] *n Bot* laurier-rose *m*

oleaster [,əʊlɪ'æstə(r)] *n Bot* oléastre *m*

oleate ['əʊlɪeɪt] *n Chem* oléate *m*

olefin ['əʊlɪfɪn] *n Chem* oléfine *f*

oleic acid [əʊ'liːɪk-] *n* acide *m* oléique

oleiferous [,əʊlɪ'ɪfərəs] *adj* oléifère

olein ['əʊliːɪn] *n Chem* oléine *f*

oleo ['əʊlɪəʊ] *n Am* margarine *f*

oleograph ['əʊlɪəʊgrɑːf] *n* oléographie *f*

oleomargarine [,əʊlɪəʊ'mɑːdʒəriːn] *n Am* margarine *f*

oleophilic [,əʊlɪəʊ'fɪlɪk] *adj* oléophile

oleraceous [,ɒlə'reɪʃəs] *adj Bot* oléracé

olestra® [əʊ'lestrə] *n* olestra *m*

oleum ['əʊlɪəm] *n Chem* oléum *m*

O level *n Formerly Sch (in England, Wales, Northern Ireland)* = examen qui sanctionnait autrefois la fin des études au niveau de la seconde, ≃ BEPC *m*

olfaction [ɒl'fækʃən] *n* olfaction *f*

olfactory [ɒl'fæktərɪ] *adj* olfactif

►► **olfactory nerve** nerf *m* olfactif

olibanum [ɒ'lɪbənəm] *n* oliban *m*

oligarch ['ɒlɪgɑːk] *n* oligarque *m*

oligarchical [,ɒlɪ'gɑːkɪkəl] *adj* oligarchique

oligarchy ['ɒlɪgɑːkɪ] *(pl* **oligarchies**) *n* oligarchie *f*

Oligocene [ɒ'lɪgəsiːn] **1** *n* oligocène *m*

2 *adj* oligocène

oligomer ['ɒlɪgəʊmə(r)] *n Chem* oligomère *m*

oligomeric [,ɒlɪgəʊ'merɪk] *adj Chem* oligomère

oligopolist [,ɒlɪ'gɒpəlɪst] *n Econ* oligopoliste *mf*

oligopolistic [,ɒlɪ,gɒpə'lɪstɪk] *adj Econ* oligopolistique

oligopoly [,ɒlɪ'gɒpəlɪ] *n Econ* oligopole *m*

oligopsony [,ɒlɪ'gɒpsənɪ] *n* oligopsone *m*

oligosaccharide [,ɒlɪgəʊ'sækəraɪd] *n Biol & Chem* oligosaccharide *m*

oligotrophic [,ɒlɪgə'trɒfɪk] *adj Ecol* oligotrophe

oliphant ['ɒlɪfənt] *n Literary* olifant *m*

olivaceous [,ɒlɪ'veɪʃəs] *adj* olivacé, olivâtre

►► *Orn* **olivaceous warbler** hypolaïs *f* pâle

olive ['ɒlɪv] **1** *n* (**a**) *(fruit)* olive *f*; *(tree)* olivier *m*; *(wood)* (bois *m* d')olivier *m* (**b**) *(colour)* vert *m* olive

2 *adj (colour)* (vert) olive *(inv)*; **he has an olive complexion** il a le teint olive

►► **olive branch** rameau *m* d'olivier; *Fig* **to hold out an olive branch to sb** proposer à qn de faire la paix; *Am* **olive drab** *(colour)* gris-vert *m* (olive); *(cloth)* toile *f* gris-vert (olive); *(uniform)* uniforme *m* gris-vert *(surtout celui de l'armée des États-Unis)*; **olive green** vert *m* olive; **olive grove** olivaie *f*, oliveraie *f*; **olive oil** huile *f* d'olive; **olive wood** (bois *m* d')olivier *m*

olive-drab *adj Am* gris-vert (olive) *(inv)*

olive-green *adj* vert olive *(inv)*

Olivier Award [ɒ'lɪvɪe-] *n Br Theat* Olivier Award *m (distinction honorifique décernée chaque année en Grande-Bretagne dans le domaine du théâtre)*

olivin ['ɒlɪvɪn], **olivine** [,ɒlɪ'viːn] *n Miner* olivine *f*, péridot *m* (granulaire)

olm [ɒlm, əʊlm] *n Zool* protée *m*, anguillard *m*

Olympia [ə'lɪmpɪə] *n* (**a**) *Geog* Olympie

(**b**) *(in London)* = salle d'expositions à Londres

Olympiad [ə'lɪmpɪæd] *n* olympiade *f*

Olympian [ə'lɪmpɪən] **1** *n* (**a**) *Myth* Olympien(enne) *m,f* (**b**) *Am Sport* athlète *mf* olympique

2 *adj* olympien; *Fig* **it was an Olympian task** cela représentait un travail phénoménal

Olympic [ə'lɪmpɪk] **1** *adj* olympique; **an Olympic champion** un champion olympique

2 Olympics *npl* **the Olympics** les jeux *mpl* Olympiques

►► **the Olympic flame** la flamme olympique; **the Olympic Games** les jeux *mpl* Olympiques

Olympus [ə'lɪmpəs] *n* **(Mount) Olympus** l'Olympe *m*

OM [,əʊ'em] *n (abbr* **Order of Merit**) ordre *m* du Mérite

Oman [əʊ'mɑːn] *n* Oman; **in Oman** à Oman

Omani [əʊ'mɑːnɪ] **1** *n* Omanais(e) *m,f*

2 *adj* omanais

omasum [əʊ'meɪsəm] *(pl* **omasa** [-sə]) *n Zool* omasum *m*, feuillet *m*

OMB [,əʊem'biː] *n (abbr* **Office of Management and Budget**) = organisme fédéral américain chargé de préparer le budget

ombudsman ['ɒmbʊdzmən] *(pl* **ombudsmen** [-mən]) *n* ombudsman *m*, médiateur *m*; *(in Quebec)* protecteur *m* du citoyen

ombudswoman ['ɒmbʊdz,wʊmən] *(pl* **ombudswomen** [-,wɪmɪn]) *n* médiatrice *f*; *(in Quebec)* protectrice *f* du citoyen

omega ['əʊmɪgə] *n* oméga *m*

omelette, *Am* **omelet** ['ɒmlɪt] *n* omelette *f*; **plain/mushroom omelette** omelette *f* nature/aux champignons; *Prov* **you can't make an omelette without breaking eggs** on ne fait pas d'omelette sans casser des œufs

omen ['əʊmen] *n* augure *m*, présage *m*; **a good/bad omen** un bon/mauvais présage; **the omens aren't good** cela ne laisse rien présager de bon; **a bird of ill omen** un oiseau de mauvaise augure

omentum [əʊ'mentəm] *(pl* **omenta** [-tə]) *n Anat* épiploon *m*

omerta [əʊ'mɜːtə] *n* omerta *f*

omicron [əʊ'maɪkrɒn] *n* omicron *m*

ominous ['ɒmɪnəs] *adj (threatening)* menaçant, inquiétant; *(boding ill)* de mauvais augure, de sinistre présage; **an ominous silence** un silence lourd de menaces; **an ominous sign** un signe inquiétant *ou* alarmant; **ominous black clouds** des nuages menaçants; **an emergency meeting? – that sounds ominous** une réunion d'urgence? – ça ne présage rien de bon

ominously ['ɒmɪnəslɪ] *adv* de façon inquiétante *ou* menaçante; **the sea was ominously calm** la mer était étrangement calme; **he looked at her ominously** il lui jeta un regard inquiétant; **ominously, there was no answer when they rang** le téléphone ne répondait pas, ce qui ne présageait rien de bon; **the deadline was drawing ominously close** la date limite se rapprochait dangereusement

ominousness ['ɒmɪnəsnɪs] *n* caractère *m* inquiétant

omissible [ə'mɪsɪbəl] *adj* facultatif; **these details are omissible** on peut omettre ces détails

omission [ə'mɪʃən] *n* (**a**) *(exclusion → accidental)* omission *f*, oubli *m*; *(→ deliberate)* exclusion *f*; **their mistakes were sins of omission** ils ont péché par omission; **there are several major omissions in his report** il y a plusieurs oublis importants dans son rapport (**b**) *Typ* bourdon *m*

omit [ə'mɪt] *(pt & pp* **omitted**, *cont* **omitting**) *vt* (**a**) *(leave out)* omettre; **a name was omitted from the list** un nom a été omis sur la liste (**b**) *(fail)* **to omit to do sth** omettre de faire qch; **she omitted to say where she had been** elle a omis de dire où elle était allée

ommateum [ɒmə'tiːəm] *(pl* **ommatea** [-'tiːə]) *n Zool* œil *m* composé

omni- ['ɒmnɪ] *pref* omni-

omnibus ['ɒmnɪbəs] *n* (**a**) *Old-fashioned (bus)* omnibus *m* (**b**) *TV & Rad* = rediffusion hebdomadaire des épisodes d'un feuilleton diffusés pendant la semaine (**c**) *(book)* recueil *m*; **an Edgar Allan Poe omnibus** un recueil d'œuvres d'Edgar Allan Poe

►► *Am* **omnibus bill** = projet de loi englobant des mesures diverses; **omnibus edition** *TV & Rad* = rediffusion hebdomadaire des épisodes d'un feuilleton diffusés pendant la semaine; *(of stories, poems)* gros recueil *m*; *Mktg* **omnibus survey** enquête *f* omnibus; **omnibus volume** *(of stories, poems etc)* gros recueil *m*

omnicompetence [,ɒmnɪ'kɒmpɪtəns] *n Law*

compétence *f* en toute matière, compétence *f* générale

omnicompetent [ˌɒmnɪˈkɒmpɪtənt] *adj Law (judge)* compétent en toute matière, de droit commun

omnidirectional [ˌɒmnɪdɪˈrekʃənəl] *adj* omnidirectionnel

omnifarious [ˌɒmnɪˈfeərɪəs] *adj* de toutes sortes, très varié

omnipotence [ɒmˈnɪpətəns] *n* omnipotence *f*

omnipotent [ɒmˈnɪpətənt] **1** *adj* omnipotent, tout-puissant

2 *n* **the Omnipotent** le Tout-Puissant

omnipresence [ˌɒmnɪˈprezəns] *n* omniprésence *f*

omnipresent [ˌɒmnɪˈprezənt] *adj* omniprésent

omnirange [ˈɒmnɪˌreɪndʒ] *n* radiophare *m* omnidirectionnel

omniscience [ɒmˈnɪsɪəns] *n* omniscience *f*

omniscient [ɒmˈnɪsɪənt] *adj* omniscient

omnium [ˈɒmnɪəm] *n St Exch* omnium *m*

omnivore [ˈɒmnɪvɔː(r)] *n Zool* omnivore *m*

omnivorous [ɒmˈnɪvərəs] *adj* (**a**) *Zool* omnivore

(**b**) *Fig* insatiable, avide; *(reader)* qui lit de tout

omnivorously [ɒmˈnɪvərəslɪ] *adv Zool* **to eat omnivorously** se nourrir de tout; *Fig* **to read omnivorously** lire de tout

Omov, OMOV [ˈəʊmɒv] *n* (*abbr* **one member one vote**) = système de scrutin "un homme, une voix"

omphalos [ˈɒmfəlɒs] (*pl* **omphali** [-laɪ]) *n* (**a**) *Antiq (stone at Delphi, boss on shield)* omphalos *m* (**b**) *Fig (centre → of empire etc)* centre *m*, pivot *m* (**c**) *Anat* ombilic *m*

ON (*written abbr* **Ontario**) Ontario *m*

ON [ɒn]

sur	▶ **1A (a) – (d), (f); B (a); C (a), (d); D (a) – (c), (j)**
à	▶ **1A (c); D (f), (h), (i), (j); F (c), (f)**
en	▶ **1A (c); F (g)**
par rapport à	▶ **1C (e)**
selon	▶ **1D (d)**
de	▶ **1F (d)**
allumé	▶ **3 (a)**
ouvert	▶ **3 (a)**
en marche	▶ **3 (a)**
de garde	▶ **3 (c)**
de service	▶ **3 (c)**

1 *prep* **A.** (**a**) *(specifying position)* sur; **the vase is on the shelf** le vase est sur l'étagère; **put it on the shelf** mets-le sur l'étagère; **on the floor** par terre; **on the ceiling** au plafond; **there are posters on the walls** il y a des affiches aux *ou* sur les murs; **there was blood on the walls** il y avait du sang sur les murs; **a coat was hanging on the hook** un manteau était accroché à la patère; **the post with the seagull on it** le poteau sur lequel il y a la mouette; **he has a ring on his finger** il a une bague au doigt; **to lie on one's back/side** être allongé sur le dos/côté; **on this side** de ce côté; **on the other side of the page** de l'autre côté de la page; **on page four** à la quatrième page, à la page quatre; **on the left/right** à gauche/droite

(**b**) *(indicating writing or painting surface)* sur; **I had nothing to write on** je n'avais rien sur quoi écrire; **red on a green background** rouge sur un fond vert

(**c**) *(indicating general location, area)* **he works on a building site** il travaille sur un chantier; **they live on a farm** ils habitent une ferme; **there's been an accident on the M1** il y a eu un accident sur la M1; **room on the second floor** chambre au second (étage); **on Arran/the Isle of Wight** sur Arran/l'île de Wight; **on Corsica/Crete** en Corse/Crète; **on Majorca/Minorca** à Majorque/Minorque

(**d**) *(indicating part of body touched)* sur; **I kissed him on the cheek** je l'ai embrassé sur la joue; **someone tapped me on the shoulder** quelqu'un m'a tapé sur l'épaule

(**e**) *(close to)* **the village is right on the lake/sea** le village est juste au bord du lac/de la mer

(**f**) *(indicating movement, direction)* **the mirror fell on the floor** la glace est tombée par terre; **to climb on(to) a wall** grimper sur un mur; **they marched on the capital** ils marchèrent sur la capitale; **don't tread on it** ne marchez pas dessus

B. (**a**) *(indicating thing carried)* sur; **I only had £10 on me** je n'avais que 10 livres sur moi; **she's got a gun on her** elle est armée

(**b**) *(indicating facial expression)* **he had a scornful smile on his face** il affichait un sourire plein de mépris

C. (**a**) *(indicating purpose of money, time, effort spent)* sur; **I spent hours on that essay** j'ai passé des heures sur cette dissertation; **she spent £1,000 on her new stereo** elle a dépensé 1000 livres pour acheter sa nouvelle chaîne hi-fi; **to put money on a horse** parier *ou* miser sur un cheval; **what are you working on at the moment?** sur quoi travaillez-vous en ce moment?

(**b**) *(indicating activity undertaken)* **I am here on business** je suis ici pour affaires; **to be on strike** être en grève; **he's off on a trip to Brazil** il part pour un voyage au Brésil; **to go on safari** faire un safari; **she was sent on a course** on l'a envoyée suivre des cours; **I'm on nights next week** je suis de nuit la semaine prochaine; **he's on lunch/a break** il est en train de déjeuner/faire la pause; **she's been on the committee for years** ça fait des années qu'elle siège au comité

(**c**) *(indicating special interest, pursuit)* **she's keen on music** elle a la passion de la musique; **he's good on modern history** il excelle en histoire moderne; **she's very big on equal opportunities** l'égalité des chances, c'est son cheval de bataille

(**d**) *(indicating scale of activity)* **on a large/small scale** sur une grande/petite échelle

(**e**) *(compared with)* par rapport à; **imports are up/down on last year** les importations sont en hausse/en baisse par rapport à l'année dernière; **it's an improvement on the old system** c'est une amélioration par rapport à l'ancien système

D. (**a**) *(about, on the subject of)* sur; **a book/film on the French Revolution** un livre/film sur la Révolution française; **we all agree on that point** nous sommes tous d'accord sur ce point; **I need some advice on a legal matter** j'ai besoin de conseils sur un point légal; **could I speak to you on a matter of some delicacy?** pourrais-je vous parler d'une affaire assez délicate?; **the police have nothing on him** la police n'a rien sur lui

(**b**) *(indicating person, thing affected)* sur; **it has no effect on them** cela n'a aucun effet sur eux; **a tax on alcohol** une taxe sur les boissons alcoolisées; **try it on your parents** essaie-le sur tes parents; **the government must act on inflation** le gouvernement doit prendre des mesures contre l'inflation; **he has survived two attempts on his life** il a échappé à deux tentatives d'assassinat; **it's unfair on women** c'est injuste envers les femmes; **the joke's on you!** c'est toi qui as l'air ridicule!

(**c**) *(indicating cause of injury)* **I cut my finger on a piece of glass** je me suis coupé le doigt sur un morceau de verre

(**d**) *(according to)* selon; **everyone will be judged on their merits** chacun sera jugé selon ses mérites; **candidates are selected on their examination results** les candidats sont choisis en fonction des résultats qu'ils ont obtenus à l'examen

(**e**) *(indicating reason, motive for action)* **on impulse** sur un coup de tête; **the police acted on information from abroad** la police est intervenue après avoir reçu des renseignements de l'étranger; **I shall refuse on principle** je refuserai par principe

(**f**) *(included in, forming part of)* **your name isn't on the list** votre nom n'est pas sur la liste; **the books on the syllabus** les livres au programme; **on the agenda** à l'ordre du jour

(**g**) *(indicating method, system)* **they work on a rota system** ils travaillent par roulement; **reorganized on a more rational basis** réorganisé sur une base plus rationnelle

(**h**) *(indicating means of transport)* **on foot/horseback** à pied/cheval; **on the bus/train** dans le bus/train; **she arrived on the midday bus/train** elle est arrivée par le bus/train de midi; **on a bicycle** à bicyclette

(**i**) *(indicating instrument played)* **to play a tune on the flute** jouer un air à la flûte; **who's on guitar/on drums?** qui est à la guitare/à la batterie?

(**j**) *Rad, TV & Theat* **I heard it on the radio/on television** je l'ai entendu à la radio/à la télévision; **it's the first time she's been on television** c'est la première fois qu'elle passe à la télévision; **what's on the other channel** *or* **side?** qu'est-ce qu'il y a sur l'autre chaîne?; **on stage** sur scène

(**k**) *(indicating where information is stored)* **it's all on computer** tout est sur ordinateur; **on file** sur fichier

E. *INDICATING DATE, TIME ETC* **on the 6th of July** le 6 juillet; **on or about the 12th** vers le 12; **on Christmas Day** le jour de Noël; **I'll see her on Monday** je la vois lundi; **on Monday morning** lundi matin; **I don't work on Mondays** je ne travaille pas le lundi; **on a Monday morning in February** un lundi matin (du mois) de février; **on a fine day in June** par une belle journée de juin; **on time** à l'heure; **every hour on the hour** à chaque heure; **it's just on five o'clock** il est cinq heures pile; **just on a year ago** *(approximately)* il y a près d'un an

F. (**a**) *(indicating source of payment)* **have a drink on me** prenez un verre, c'est moi qui offre; **the drinks are on me/the house!** c'est ma tournée/la tournée du patron!; **you can get it on the National Health** ≃ c'est remboursé par la Sécurité sociale

(**b**) *(indicating source or amount of income)* **to live on one's private income/a student grant** vivre de ses rentes/d'une bourse d'études; **you can't live on such a low wage** on ne peut pas vivre avec des revenus aussi modestes; *Fam* **they're on the dole** *or* **on unemployment benefit** ils vivent du chômage *ou* des allocations de chômage □; **to retire on a pension of £5,000 a year** prendre sa retraite avec une pension de 5000 livres par an

(**c**) *(indicating source of power)* à; **it works on electricity** ça marche à l'électricité

(**d**) *(indicating source of nourishment)* de; **they live on cereals** ils se nourrissent de céréales; **we dined on oysters and champagne** nous avons dîné d'huîtres et de champagne

(**e**) *(indicating drugs, medicine prescribed)* **is she on the pill?** est-ce qu'elle prend la pilule?; **I'm still on antibiotics** je suis toujours sous antibiotiques; **the doctor put her on tranquillizers** le médecin lui a prescrit des tranquillisants; **he's on insulin/heroin** il prend de l'insuline/de l'héroïne; **he's on drugs** il se drogue; *Fam Fig* **what's he on?** il se sent bien?

(**f**) *(at the same time as)* à; **he'll deal with it on his return** il s'en occupera à son retour; **looters will be shot on sight** les pillards seront abattus sans sommation; **on the death of his mother** à la mort de sa mère; **on my first/last visit** lors de ma première/dernière visite; **on the count of three** à trois

(**g**) *(with present participle)* en; **on hearing the news** en apprenant la nouvelle; **on completing the test candidates should...** quand ils auront fini l'examen les candidats devront...

2 *adv* (**a**) *(in place)* **the lid wasn't on** le couvercle n'était pas mis; **put the top back on afterwards** remets le capuchon ensuite

(**b**) *(referring to clothes)* **why have you got your gloves on?** pourquoi as-tu mis tes gants?; **the woman with the blue dress on** la femme en robe bleue; **what had she got on?** qu'est-ce qu'elle portait?, comment était-elle habillée?; **he's got nothing on** il est nu

(**c**) *(indicating continued action)* **to read on** continuer à lire; **the car drove on** la voiture ne s'est pas arrêtée; **they walked on** ils poursuivirent leur chemin; **from now** *or* **this moment** *or* **this time on** désormais; **from that day on** à partir *ou* dater de ce jour; **well on in years** d'un âge avancé; **earlier/later/further on** plus tôt/tard/loin; **on with the show!** que le spectacle continue!

(**d**) *(indicating activity)* **I've got a lot on this week** je suis très occupé cette semaine; **have you got anything on tonight?** tu fais quelque chose ce soir?

(**e**) *(functioning, running)* **put** *or* **turn** *or* **switch**

the television on allume la télévision; **turn the tap on** ouvre le robinet; **the lights had been left on** les lumières étaient restées allumées; **the tap had been left on** le robinet était resté ouvert; **the car had its headlights on** les phares de la voiture étaient allumés

(**f**) *(in betting)* **I have a bet on** j'ai fait un pari

(**g**) *Fam (idiom)* **to be** *or* **go on about sth** parler de qch sans arrêt ☐; **he's on about his new car again** le voilà reparti sur sa nouvelle voiture; **what's she on about?** qu'est-ce qu'elle raconte?; **he's always on about the war/teenagers** il n'arrête pas de déblatérer sur la guerre/les adolescents; **my parents are always on at me about my hair** mes parents n'arrêtent pas de m'embêter avec mes cheveux; **I've been on at them for months to get it fixed** cela fait des mois que je suis sur leur dos pour qu'ils le fassent réparer

3 *adj* (**a**) *(working → electricity, light, radio, TV)* allumé; *(→ gas, tap)* ouvert; *(→ engine, machine)* en marche; *(→ handbrake)* serré; *(→ alarm)* enclenché; **the radio was on very loud** la radio hurlait; **make sure the switches are in the "on" position** vérifiez que les interrupteurs sont sur (la position) "marche"; **the "on" button** le bouton de mise en marche

(**b**) *(happening, under way)* **to be on** *(actor)* être en scène; **we're on in ten minutes** c'est à nous dans dix minutes; **there's a conference on next week** il y a une conférence la semaine prochaine; **the meeting is on right now** la réunion est en train de se dérouler; **the match is still on** *(on TV)* le match n'est pas terminé; *(going ahead)* le match n'a pas été annulé; **it's on at the local cinema** ça passe au cinéma du quartier; **the play was on for weeks** la pièce a tenu l'affiche pendant des semaines; **your favourite TV programme is on tonight** il y a ton émission préférée à la télé ce soir; **there's nothing good on** *(on TV, radio)* il n'y a rien de bien; **is the party still on?** est-ce que la soirée se fait toujours?; **is our deal still on?** est-ce que notre affaire tient toujours?; **the kettle's on for tea** j'ai mis de l'eau à chauffer pour le thé; **hurry up, your dinner's on** dépêche-toi, ton dîner va être prêt

(**c**) *(on duty → in hospital, surgery)* de garde; *(→ in shop, administration)* de service; **I'm on at three o'clock, then off at nine o'clock** je commence à trois heures et je finis à neuf heures

(**d**) *(in betting)* **the odds are twenty to one on** la cote est de vingt contre un

(**e**) *Fam (unacceptable)* **such behaviour just isn't on!** une telle conduite est tout à fait inadmissible! ☐; *Br* **it's not on!** ça va pas du tout!

(**f**) *Fam (feasible, possible)* **we'll never be ready by tomorrow, it just isn't on** nous ne serons jamais prêts pour demain, c'est tout bonnement impossible

(**g**) *Fam (in agreement)* **are you still on for dinner tonight?** ça marche toujours pour le dîner de ce soir?; **shall we say £10? – you're on!** disons 10 livres? – d'accord *ou* tope là!; **if you wash the dishes, I'll dry them – you're on!** si tu fais la vaisselle, je l'essuie – ça marche!

(**h**) *Br Fam* **to be on** *(menstruating)* avoir ses ragnagnas

4 on and off *adv* **we went out together on and off for a year** on a eu une relation irrégulière pendant un an

5 on and on *adv* sans arrêt; **he goes on and on about his minor ailments** il nous rebat les oreilles avec ses petits problèmes de santé; **the play dragged on and on** la pièce n'en finissait plus

onager ['ɒnədʒə(r)] *(pl* **onagers** *or* **onagri** [-graɪ]) *n* (**a**) *Zool* onagre *m* (**b**) *Hist* **(siege) onager** onagre *m*

on-air *TV & Rad* **1** *adj* à l'antenne

2 *adv* à l'antenne

►► ***on-air (warning) light*** voyant *m* de passage à l'antenne

onanism ['əʊnənɪzəm] *n* onanisme *m*

onanist ['əʊnənɪst] **1** *n* onaniste *mf*

2 *adj* onaniste

onanistic [,əʊnə'nɪstɪk] *adj* onaniste

on-board *adj Comput (built-in)* intégré

►► *Fin* ***on-board surcharge*** surcharge *f* "onboard"

ONC [,əʊen'siː] *n (abbr* **Ordinary National Certificate**) = brevet de technicien en Grande-Bretagne

on-camera *TV & Cin* **1** *adj* à l'image

2 *adv* à l'image

once [wʌns] **1** *adv* (**a**) *(on a single occasion)* une fois; **I've been there once before** j'y suis déjà allé une fois; **he's never once said he was sorry** il ne s'est jamais excusé, il ne s'est pas excusé une seule fois; **more than once** plus d'une fois; **once or twice** une ou deux fois; **once a week/month/year** une fois par semaine/mois/an; **I see her once every three months** je la vois tous les trois mois; **once in a while** occasionnellement, une fois de temps en temps; **once more** *or* **again** encore une fois, une fois de plus; **for once he isn't late** pour une fois, il n'est pas en retard; **once a liar always a liar** qui a menti mentira; **I'll try anything once** il faut bien tout essayer

(**b**) *(formerly)* jadis, autrefois; **people once believed that the world was flat** autrefois, on croyait que la terre était plate; **once it would have all been so easy** il fut un temps où ça aurait été si facile; **a once famous poet** un poète autrefois célèbre; **once upon a time there was a princess, there was once a princess** il était une fois une princesse; **once (upon a time) children used to respect their elders** il fut un temps où les enfants respectaient leurs aînés

2 *conj* une fois que, dès que; **it'll be easy once we've started** une fois qu'on aura commencé, ce sera facile; **give me a call once you get there** passe-moi un coup de fil quand tu arrives *ou* seras arrivé; **once you've told her the truth there'll be no turning back** une fois que tu lui auras dit la vérité, il ne te sera plus possible de faire marche arrière; **once he reached home, he collapsed** une fois arrivé chez lui, il s'effondra

3 *n* **(just) this once** (juste) pour cette fois-ci, (juste) pour une fois; **she did it just the once** elle ne l'a fait qu'une seule fois

4 at once *adv* (**a**) *(at the same time)* à la fois, en même temps; **it was at once fascinating and terrifying** c'était à la fois fascinant et terrifiant; **to do several things at once** faire plusieurs choses à la fois *ou* en même temps; **it all happened at once** tout est arrivé en même temps

(**b**) *(immediately)* tout de suite; **come here at once!** viens ici tout de suite *ou* immédiatement!

5 once and for all *adv* une fois pour toutes; **let's settle this matter once and for all!** réglons cette affaire une (bonne) fois pour toutes!

'Once upon a time in the West' *Leone* 'Il était une fois dans l'Ouest'

once-over *n Fam* (**a**) *(glance)* coup *m* d'œil ☐; **I gave the morning paper the once-over** j'ai jeté un coup d'œil sur le journal du matin; **I could see her giving me the once-over** je la voyais qui me regardait des pieds à la tête

(**b**) *(clean)* **give the stairs/the bookcase a quick once-over** passe un coup dans l'escalier/sur la bibliothèque

(**c**) *(beating)* raclée *f*; **to give sb the** *or* **a once-over** donner une bonne raclée à qn

oncer ['wʌnsə(r)] *n Fam Old-fashioned* = personne qui ne va qu'une fois à l'église le dimanche

onchocerciasis [,ɒŋkəʊsə'kaɪəsɪs], **onchocercosis** [,ɒŋkəʊsə'kəʊsɪs] *n Med* onchocercose *f*

oncogenesis [,ɒŋkəʊ'dʒenɪsɪs] *n Med* oncogenèse *f*

oncogenic [,ɒŋkəʊ'dʒenɪk] *adj Med* oncogène

oncologist [ɒŋ'kɒlədʒɪst] *n Med* oncologue *mf*, oncologiste *mf*

oncology [ɒŋ'kɒlədʒɪ] *n Med* oncologie *f*

oncoming ['ɒn,kʌmɪŋ] **1** *adj* (**a**) **the oncoming traffic** *(for vehicle)* les véhicules venant en sens inverse; *(for pedestrian)* les véhicules qui approchent (**b**) *(year, season)* qui arrive, qui approche; **the oncoming generation of school-leavers** les jeunes qui vont quitter l'école à la fin de cette année scolaire

2 *n* approche *f*

►► *Ind* ***oncoming shift*** poste *m* entrant

oncosts ['ɒnkɒsts] *npl Com* frais *mpl* généraux

oncotic [ɒn'kɒtɪk] *adj Med & Phys* oncotique

OND [,əʊen'diː] *n (abbr* **Ordinary National Diploma**) = brevet de technicien en Grande-Bretagne

ONE [wʌn]

un/une	► **1 (a), (b), (e) – (h)**
seul	► **1 (c)**
même	► **1 (d)**
on	► **2 B**

1 *adj* (**a**) *(in expressions of age, date, measurement etc)* un (une); **one dollar** un dollar; **one pound** une livre; **one and a half kilos** un kilo et demi; **twenty-one apples** vingt et une pommes; **one million** un million; **one thousand** mille; **at one o'clock** à une heure; **he'll be one (year old) in June** il aura un an en juin; **on page one** *(of book)* (à la) page un; *(of newspaper)* à la une; **one fifty** *(a hundred and fifty)* cent cinquante; *(one pound and fifty pence)* une livre cinquante (pence); *(one dollar fifty cents)* un dollar cinquante (cents); *(time)* deux heures moins dix, une heure cinquante; **one or two** *(a few)* un/une ou deux; **a million** *or* **a thousand and one** *(a lot)* un millier de; **the odds are (at) ten to one** la cote est à dix contre un; **it's ten to one that** *or Am* **one will get you ten that he's at the office** je parie (à) dix contre un qu'il est au bureau

(**b**) *(referring to a single object or person)* un (une); **one American in two** un Américain sur deux; **only one answer is correct** il n'y a qu'une seule bonne réponse; **at any one time** au même moment; **one car looks much like another to me** pour moi, toutes les voitures se ressemblent; **take one half and give him the other** prends-en une moitié et donne-lui l'autre; **one member one vote** = système de scrutin "un homme, une voix"

(**c**) *(only, single)* seul, unique; **my one mistake** ma seule erreur; **the one woman who knows** la seule femme qui soit au courant; **no one man should have that responsibility** c'est trop de responsabilité pour un seul homme; **not one family was spared** pas une (seule) famille ne fut épargnée

(**d**) *(same)* même; **they all arrived on the one day** ils sont tous arrivés le même jour; **the two wanted men are in fact one and the same person** les deux hommes recherchés sont en fait une seule et même personne; **to be of one mind (with sb on sth)** être du même avis (que qn sur qch); **it's all one to me** ça m'est égal

(**e**) *(instead of "a")* **if there's one thing I hate it's rudeness** s'il y a une chose que je n'aime pas, c'est bien la grossièreté; **for one thing it's too late** d'abord, c'est trop tard; **one thing at a time** chaque chose en son temps; **one thing you'll need to know is...** il y a quelque chose qu'il vous faudra savoir...; **we had one customer once who wouldn't leave** une fois on a eu un client qui ne voulait pas partir

(**f**) *(a certain)* **I was introduced to one Ian Bell** on m'a présenté un certain Ian Bell

(**g**) *(indicating indefinite time)* **one day you'll understand** un jour, tu comprendras; **one evening in July** un soir de juillet; **early one morning** un matin de bonne heure

(**h**) *Fam (as intensifier)* **that's one fine car!** c'est une sacrée bagnole!; **the room was one big mess!** il y avait une de ces pagailles dans la pièce!; **it's been one hell of a day!** quelle journée! ☐

2 *pron* **A.** (**a**) *(person, thing)* **which one** lequel (laquelle) *m,f*; **this one** celui-ci (celle-ci) *m,f*; **that one** celui-là (celle-là) *m,f*; **the other one** l'autre *mf*; **the right one** le (la) bon (bonne); **the wrong one** le (la) mauvais(e); **which one do you prefer?** lequel (laquelle) préférez-vous?; **which ones?** lesquels?; **these ones** ceux-ci (celles-ci) *mpl,fpl*; **those ones** ceux-là (celles-là) *mpl,fpl*; **which dog? – the one that's barking** quel chien? – celui qui aboie; **which cars? – the ones you like** quelles voitures? – celles que tu aimes; **the one I spoke of** celui dont j'ai parlé; **he's the one who did it** c'est lui qui l'a fait; **one of my colleagues is sick** (l')un de mes collègues est malade; **one of the bulbs has fused**

(l')une des ampoules a grillé; **one of them** l'un d'entre eux, l'un d'eux; **give me one of them** donnez-m'en un; **she's one of us** elle est des nôtres; **any one of us** n'importe lequel d'entre nous; **that's one of my favourite restaurants** c'est (l')un de mes restaurants préférés; **he's one of my many admirers** c'est un de mes nombreux admirateurs; **I've only got one** je n'en ai qu'un; **there's only one left** il n'en reste qu'un; **I was the only one there** j'étais le seul à me trouver là; **have you seen one?** en avez-vous vu un?; **two for the price of one** deux pour le prix d'un; **one or other** l'un d'eux; **one after the other** l'un après l'autre; **you can't have one without the other** l'un ne va pas sans l'autre; **take the new one** prends le nouveau; **the scheme was a good one on paper** le plan était excellent en théorie; **she's eaten all the ripe ones** elle a mangé tous ceux qui étaient mûrs/ toutes celles qui étaient mûres; **our loved** *or* **dear ones** ceux qui nous sont chers; **the mother and her little ones** la mère et ses petits; **she's my littlest one** c'est ma plus jeune *ou* ma petite dernière; **he's a strange one, that boy** il est bizarre, ce garçon; *Br Fam* **ooh, you are a one!** toi, alors!; *Br Fam* **he's a right one he is!** lui alors!; *Fam* **I'm not much of a one** *or* **I'm not a great one for cheese** je ne raffole pas du fromage; **she's a great one for computers** c'est une mordue d'informatique; **she's one in a million** *or* **thousand** c'est une perle rare; **I'm not one to gossip but...** je ne suis pas du genre commère mais...; **I want the opinion of one better able to judge** je voudrais avoir l'opinion de quelqu'un qui soit plus capable de juger; *Fam* **there's one born every minute!** comment peut-on être aussi stupide!❑; **one and all** tous (sans exception); **one at a time** un à la fois; *Prov* **one for all and all for one** un pour tous et tous pour un; *Fam* **to get one over on sb** avoir l'avantage sur qn❑

(**b**) *(joke, story, question etc)* **have you heard the one about the two postmen?** tu connais celle des deux facteurs?; **that's a good one!** elle est bien bonne celle-là!; **that's a hard one** *(a difficult question)* vous me posez une colle; **that's an easy one** c'est facile; **the question is one of great importance** cette question est d'une grande importance; **you'll have to solve this one yourself** il faudra que tu règles ça tout seul

(**c**) *Fam (drink)* **do you fancy a quick one?** on prend un verre en vitesse?❑; **to have had one too many** avoir bu un coup de trop

(**d**) *Fam (blow)* **to hit** *or* **thump** *or* **belt sb one** en coller une à qn

(**e**) *Br Fam* **to go into one** *(lose one's temper)* péter les plombs, péter une durite

(**f**) *very Fam* **to give sb one** *(have sex with)* en glisser une paire à qn

(**g**) *Knitting* **to make one** faire une augmentation, augmenter d'une maille

(**h**) *St Exch* unité *f*; **to issue shares in ones** émettre des actions en unités

B. (**a**) *Formal (as subject)* on; *(as object or after preposition)* vous; **if one loses one's** *or Am* **his temper** si on se met en colère; **one can only do one's** *or Am* **his best** on fait ce qu'on peut; **it is enough to make one weep** il y a de quoi vous faire pleurer; **it certainly makes one think** ça fait réfléchir, c'est sûr

(**b**) *(with infinitive forms)* **to wash one's hands** se laver les mains; **to put one's hands in one's pockets** mettre ses *ou* les mains dans les poches

3 at one *adv Formal* **to be at one with sb/sth** être en harmonie avec qn/qch; **she felt at one with the world** elle se sentait en harmonie avec le monde

4 for one *adv* **I for one am disappointed** pour ma part, je suis déçu; **I know that Gillian for one is against it** je sais que Gillian est contre en tout cas

5 in one *adv* (**a**) *(combined)* **all in one** à la fois; **she's a writer, actress and director (all) in one** elle est à la fois scénariste, actrice et metteur en scène; **two volumes in one** deux volumes en un; **a useful three-in-one kitchen knife** un couteau de cuisine très utile avec ses trois fonctions

(**b**) *(at one attempt)* du premier coup; **he did it in one** il l'a fait en un seul coup; *Fam* **got it in one!** du premier coup!❑

6 in ones and twos *adv* **they arrived in ones and twos** ils arrivèrent les uns après les autres; **people stood around in ones and twos** les gens se tenaient là par petits groupes

7 one another *pron (two people)* l'un l'autre (l'une l'autre) *m,f*; *(more than two people)* les uns les autres (les unes les autres) *mpl, fpl*; **they didn't dare talk to one another** ils n'ont pas osé se parler; **we love one another** nous nous aimons; **the group meet in one another's homes** le groupe se réunit chez l'un ou chez l'autre; **they respect one another** *(two people)* ils ont du respect l'un pour l'autre; *(more than two people)* ils se respectent les uns les autres; **you can copy one another's notes** *(two people)* vous pouvez copier vos notes l'un sur l'autre; *(more than two people)* vous pouvez copier vos notes les uns sur les autres

8 one by one *adv* un par un (une par une)

►► ***the One Thousand Guineas*** = course de chevaux qui se déroule à Newmarket en Angleterre

---

one-act *adj*

►► ***one-act play*** pièce *f* en un (seul) acte

one-and-one *n (in basketball)* entre-deux *m inv*

one-armed *adj* manchot (d'un bras); **a one-armed man** un manchot

►► ***one-armed bandit*** machine *f* à sous

one-day *adj* d'une journée

►► ***one-day match*** *(of cricket)* = match de cricket joué sur une journée

one-dimensional *adj* unidimensionnel

one-eyed *adj* borgne

one-handed 1 *adj (shot, catch)* fait d'une (seule) main; *(tool)* utilisable d'une seule main

2 *adv* d'une (seule) main

one-hit wonder *n* = groupe ou chanteur qui n'a eu qu'un seul tube

one-horse *adj* (**a**) *(carriage)* à un cheval (**b**) *Fam (idiom)* **a one-horse town** un (vrai) trou, un bled paumé

oneiric [əʊ'naɪrɪk] *adj* onirique

oneiromancy [əʊ'naɪrəmænsɪ] *n* oniromancie *f*

one-legged *adj* unijambiste; **a one-legged man** un unijambiste

one-level distribution channel *n Mktg* canal *m* de distribution court

one-liner *n (quip)* bon mot *m*; **she has some very good one-liners** ses boutades sont très drôles; **there are some great one-liners in the film** il y a de très bonnes répliques dans ce film

one-man *adj (vehicle, canoe)* monoplace; *(task)* pour un seul homme; *(expedition)* en solitaire; **I'm a one-man woman** je suis fidèle en amour

►► ***one-man band*** homme-orchestre *m*; *Fig* **the company is very much a one-man band** c'est une seule personne qui fait marcher cette entreprise; ***one-man show*** *(by artist)* exposition *f* individuelle; *(by performer)* spectacle *m* solo, one-man-show *m inv*

oneness ['wʌnnɪs] *n* (**a**) *(singleness)* unité *f*; *(uniqueness)* unicité *f* (**b**) *(agreement)* accord *m* (**c**) *(wholeness)* intégrité *f* (**d**) *(sameness)* identité *f*

one-night stand *n* (**a**) *Mus & Theat* représentation *f* unique (**b**) *Fam (sexual encounter)* aventure *f* (sans lendemain)❑

one-off 1 *adj (order, job)* unique; *(article)* spécial, hors-série *(inv)*; **he wants a one-off payment** il veut être payé en une seule fois; **I'll do it if it's a one-off job** je veux bien le faire mais seulement à titre exceptionnel; *Am* **this trip is definitely a one-off deal** c'est la première et dernière fois que je fais ce voyage

2 *n (original)* **he's a complete one-off** il n'y en a pas deux comme lui; **it's a one-off** *(object)* c'est unique; *(situation)* c'est exceptionnel; **the mistake was a one-off** cette erreur ne se reproduira pas; **her success was a one-off** son succès sera sans lendemain; **I promise you, this is a one-off** c'est exceptionnel, je vous le promets

►► *Com* ***one-off order*** commande *f* ponctuelle

one-on-one 1 *adv Sport* **he was one-on-one with the goalkeeper** il était seul face au gardien de but

2 *adj Am* = **one-to-one**

one-parent family *n* famille *f* monoparentale

one-party *adj Pol* à parti unique

one-piece 1 *adj* une pièce *(inv)*; *Tech (casting)* monobloc

2 *n* vêtement *m* une pièce

►► ***one-piece swimsuit*** maillot *m* une pièce

oner ['wʌnə(r)] *n Br Fam* **to do sth in a oner** faire qch d'un seul coup❑; **to down a drink in a oner** faire cul sec; **he got it in a oner** *(understood)* il a tout de suite pigé; *(got answer)* il a tout de suite trouvé la solution❑

one-room *adj* à une (seule) pièce; **a one-room** *Br* **flat** *or Am* **apartment** un studio

onerous ['əʊnərəs] *adj Formal* lourd, pénible

onerously ['əʊnərəslɪ] *adv Formal* péniblement

onerousness ['əʊnərəsnɪs] *n Formal* pénibilité *m*

oneself [wʌn'self] *pron* (**a**) *(reflexive)* se; *(after preposition)* soi, soi-même; *(emphatic)* soi-même; **to wash oneself** se laver; **to enjoy oneself** s'amuser; **to live for oneself** vivre pour soi; **to be pleased with oneself** être content de soi *ou* soi-même (**b**) *(one's normal self)* soi-même; **it's enough to be oneself** il suffit d'être soi-même (**c**) *(idiom)* **to be (all) by oneself** être tout seul

one-shot *adj Am Fam* = **one-off**

one-sided *adj* (**a**) *(unequal)* inégal; *Sport* **a one-sided match** un match inégal; **conversations with him tend to be pretty one-sided** avec lui, ce n'est pas une conversation, il n'y a que lui qui parle (**b**) *(biased)* partial (**c**) *(unilateral)* unilatéral

one-sidedness [-'saɪdɪdnɪs] *n* (**a**) *(inequality)* inégalité *f* (**b**) *(bias)* partialité *f* (**c**) *(unilateral nature)* caractère *m* unilatéral

one-stop *adj*

►► *Com & Mktg* ***one-stop buying*** achats *mpl* regroupés; *Comput* ***one-stop desktop connection*** connexion *f* directe à un ordinateur de bureau; *Com & Mktg* ***one-stop shop, one-stop store*** magasin *m* où l'on trouve de tout; *Com & Mktg* ***one-stop shopping*** achats *mpl* regroupés (dans un seul magasin)

one-time *adj* ancien; **a one-time actor turned director** un ancien acteur devenu metteur en scène

one-to-one 1 *adj* (**a**) *(discussion, meeting)* seul à seul, en tête à tête; *(relationship between people)* exclusif; **I'd prefer to talk to you on a one-to-one basis** je préférerais vous parler seul à seul; **students receive one-to-one instruction** le professeur travaille individuellement avec chaque étudiant (**b**) *(comparison, relationship)* terme à terme

2 *adv (talk, meet)* seul à seul, en tête à tête; *(correspond)* de manière univoque, exclusivement

►► ***one-to-one marketing*** marketing *m* one to one; ***one-to-one tuition*** cours *mpl* particuliers

one-track *adj* (**a**) *Rail* à voie unique (**b**) *Fam (idiom)* **he's got a one-track mind** *(thinks only of one thing)* c'est une obsession chez lui❑; *(thinks only of sex)* il ne pense qu'à ça

one-two *n* (**a**) *Boxing* = direct suivi d'un crochet de l'autre main (**b**) *Ftbl* une-deux *m inv*

one-up *(pt & pp* **one-upped,** *cont* **one-upping**) **1** *adj* **we're one-up on our competitors** nous avons pris l'avantage sur nos concurrents

2 *vt Am Fam* marquer un point sur❑

one-upmanship [-'ʌpmənʃɪp] *n* = comportement d'une personne qui ne supporte pas de voir d'autres faire mieux qu'elle; **it's pure one-upmanship on her part** elle veut uniquement prouver qu'elle est la meilleure; **this is no time for one-upmanship** ce n'est pas le moment d'essayer de démontrer sa supériorité

one-way *adj* (**a**) *(street)* à sens unique; *(traffic)* en sens unique (**b**) *(ticket)* simple; **a one-way ticket to Rome** un aller simple pour Rome (**c**) *(mirror)* sans tain (**d**) *(reaction, current)* irréversible; *(decision)* unilatéral (**e**) *(relationship, feeling)* à sens unique (**f**) *(packaging)* perdu

►► ***one-way street*** (rue *f* à) sens *m* unique; **he went the wrong way up a one-way street** il a pris un sens interdit

one-woman *adj* **I'm a one-woman man** je suis fidèle en amour

►► ***one-woman show*** *(by artist)* exposition *f* individuelle; *(by performer)* spectacle *m* solo, one-woman-show *m inv*

one–one

ongoing [ˈɒn,gəʊɪŋ] *adj* (**a**) *(continuing)* continu; **it's an ongoing state of affairs** c'est une situation courante *ou* habituelle
(**b**) *(current, in progress)* en cours; **the ongoing debate between supporters and adversaries of the system** le débat en cours entre partisans et adversaires du système

on-hook, onhook *adj*
▸▸ *Comput* ***on-hook signal*** signal *m* de fin de communication *ou* de raccrochage

onion [ˈʌnjən] **1** *n* oignon *m*; *Br Fam* **he knows his onions** il connaît son affaire ❑
2 *comp (soup)* à l'oignon
▸▸ *Archit* ***onion dome*** bulbe *m* (byzantin); ***onion rings*** rondelles *fpl* d'oignons frites

onionskin [ˈʌnjənskɪn] *n (paper)* pelure *f* d'oignon
▸▸ ***onionskin paper*** pelure *f* d'oignon

oniony [ˈʌnjənɪ] *adj (in smell)* qui sent l'oignon; *(in taste)* qui a un goût d'oignon

on-licence *n* licence *f (autorisant la consommation de boissons alcoolisées sur place)*

on-line, online **1** *adj Comput* en ligne; **to be on-line** *(person)* être connecté; **the disk contains all you need to get on-line** cette disquette contient tout ce qu'il vous faut pour vous connecter; **to go on-line** *(for the first time)* se raccorder à l'Internet; **to put the printer on-line** connecter l'imprimante
2 *adv* en ligne; **to buy/order on-line** acheter/commander en ligne; **to shop on-line** faire un achat/des achats en ligne; **to work on-line** travailler en étant connecté à l'Internet
▸▸ ***on-line bank*** banque *f* en ligne; ***on-line banking*** transactions *fpl* bancaires en ligne; *St Exch* ***on-line broker*** courtier(ère) *m,f* électronique; ***on-line cashdesk terminal*** terminal *m* de paiement connecté; *Mktg* ***on-line catalogue*** catalogue *m* en ligne; *Comput* ***on-line help*** aide *f* en ligne; *Fin* ***on-line investing*** investissement *m* en ligne; *Fin* ***on-line investor*** investisseur *m* en ligne; ***on-line marketing*** marketing *m* électronique; *Comput* ***on-line mode*** mode *m* connecté; *Comput* ***on-line registration*** inscription *f* en ligne; ***on-line retailer*** société *f* de commerce en ligne; ***on-line retailing*** commerce *m* électronique; ***on-line selling*** vente *f* en ligne, vente *f* électronique; *Comput* ***on-line service*** service *m* en ligne; ***on-line shop*** magasin *m* électronique; ***on-line shopping*** achats *mpl* par Internet; ***on-line terminal*** terminal *m* de paiement connecté; *Comput* ***on-line time*** durée *f* de connexion; *St Exch* ***on-line trading*** transactions *fpl* boursières électroniques

onlooker [ˈɒn,lʊkə(r)] *n (during event)* spectateur(trice) *m,f*; *(after accident)* badaud(e) *m,f*, curieux(euse) *m,f*

onlooking [ˈɒn,lʊkɪŋ] *adj* **the onlooking crowd** *(at state occasion, sporting event etc)* la foule des spectateurs; *(after accident)* les badauds, la foule des badauds

ONLY [ˈəʊnlɪ]

seul	▸ **1**
unique	▸ **1**
seulement	▸ **2 (a), (b); 3 (b)**
ne… que	▸ **2 (b), (c)**
mais	▸ **3 (a), (b)**

1 *adj* seul, unique; **he's/she's an only child** il est fils/elle est fille unique; **she was the only woman there** c'était la seule femme; **the only coat I possess** le seul manteau que je possède; **he's the only one who believes me** il est le seul à me croire; **we are the only people who know it** nous sommes les seuls à le savoir; **I'm fed up! – you're not the only one!** j'en ai assez! – tu n'es pas le seul!; **her only answer was to shrug her shoulders** pour toute réponse, elle a haussé les épaules; **it's our only chance** c'est notre seule chance; **the only thing is, I won't be there** le seul problème, c'est que je ne serai pas là; **the only way I'll go is if it's free** je n'irai que si c'est gratuit; **her one and only friend** son seul et unique ami; **the one and only Billy Shears!** le seul, l'unique Billy Shears!; **Edinburgh is the only place to live** Édimbourg est la ville idéale pour vivre
2 *adv* (**a**) *(exclusively)* seulement; **only if you agree** seulement si tu es d'accord; **she has only one brother** elle n'a qu'un (seul) frère; **there are only two people I trust** il n'y a que deux personnes en qui j'aie confiance; **only an expert could advise us** seul un expert pourrait nous conseiller; **you'll only get him to come if you offer him a lift** tu ne le feras venir que si tu lui proposes de l'amener; **staff only** *(sign)* réservé au personnel
(**b**) *(just, merely)* **he's only a child!** ce n'est qu'un enfant!; **it's only a scratch** c'est seulement une égratignure, ce n'est (rien) qu'une égratignure; **after all, it's only money** après tout, ce n'est que de l'argent; **it's only me!** c'est moi!; **I only touched it** je n'ai fait que le toucher; **you've only ruined my best silk shirt (, that's all)!** tu n'as fait qu'abîmer ma plus belle chemise en soie(, c'est tout)!; **go on, ask him, he can only say no** vas-y, demande-lui, ce qui peut t'arriver de pire c'est qu'il refuse; **I was only trying to help** je cherchais seulement à être utile; **it will only make him sad** ça ne fera que l'attrister; **it's only natural she should want to see him** c'est tout naturel qu'elle veuille le voir; **I shall be only too pleased to come** je ne serai que trop heureux de venir; **I only hope we're not too late** j'espère seulement que nous n'arrivons pas trop tard; **if only they knew!, if they only knew!** si (seulement) ils savaient!; **he has only to ask for it** il n'a qu'à le demander; **you only have to look at him to see he's guilty** il suffit de le regarder pour voir qu'il est coupable; **I will only say that I disagree** je me bornerai à dire que je ne suis pas de cet avis; **only think what pleasure it gave me** imaginez un peu le plaisir que cela m'a fait; **be quiet, you stupid dog, it's only the postman!** tais-toi donc, le chien, ce n'est que le facteur!; **you're only young once** il faut profiter de sa jeunesse
(**c**) *(to emphasize smallness of amount, number etc)* ne… que; **it only cost me £5** ça ne m'a coûté que 5 livres; **it only took me half an hour** je n'ai mis qu'une demi-heure
(**d**) *(to emphasize recentness of event)* **it seems like only yesterday** c'est comme si c'était hier; **I saw her/used it only yesterday** je l'ai vue/m'en suis servi pas plus tard qu'hier; **I only found out this morning** je n'ai appris ça que ce matin; **only last week he appeared to be quite happy** la semaine dernière encore, il semblait parfaitement heureux
(**e**) *(with infinitive)* **I awoke only to find he was gone** à mon réveil, il était parti
3 *conj Fam* (**a**) *(but, except)* mais ❑; **it's like Spain, only cheaper** c'est comme l'Espagne, mais en moins cher; **go on then, only hurry!** vas-y alors, mais dépêche-toi!
(**b**) *(were it not for the fact that)* mais, seulement; **I'd do it, only I don't have the time** je le ferais bien, seulement je n'ai pas le temps
4 not only *conj* **she's not only bright, she's funny too** elle est non seulement intelligente, mais en plus elle est drôle; **not only… but also** non seulement… mais aussi
5 only if, only… if *conj* seulement si; **I'll do it, but only if you say sorry first** je le ferai, mais seulement si vous vous excusez d'abord; **he'll only agree if the money's good enough** il n'acceptera que si on lui propose assez d'argent
6 only just *adv* (**a**) *(not long before)* **I've only just woken up** je viens (tout) juste de me réveiller
(**b**) *(barely)* tout juste; **I only just finished in time** je n'ai fini qu'au dernier moment; **did she win? – yes, but only just** a-t-elle gagné? – oui, mais de justesse; **I've only just got enough** j'en ai tout juste assez
7 only too *adv* **I was only too aware of my own shortcomings** je n'étais que trop conscient de mes propres imperfections; **I'd be only too delighted to come** je ne serai que trop heureux de venir; **I remember her only too well** je ne risque pas de l'oublier

only-begotten *adj Rel* **the only-begotten Son of the Father** le Fils unique du Père

on-message *adj Br Pol* = qui respecte scrupuleusement la ligne du parti

o.n.o. [,əʊenˈəʊ] *adv Br (abbr* **or near/nearest offer)** **£100 o.n.o.** 100 livres à débattre

on-off *adj (intermittent)* **they have a very on-off relationship** ils ont une relation très peu suivie
▸▸ *Elec* ***on-off button, on-off switch*** bouton *m* (de) marche-arrêt

onomastic [,ɒnəˈmæstɪk] *adj* onomastique

onomasticon [,ɒnəˈmæstɪkɒn] *n* onomasticon *m*

onomastics [,ɒnəˈmæstɪks] *n (UNCOUNT)* onomastique *f*

onomatopoeia [ˈɒnə,mætəˈpiːə] *n* onomatopée *f*

onomatopoeic [ˈɒnə,mætəˈpiːɪk], **onomatopoetic** [ˈɒnə,mætəpəʊˈetɪk] *adj* onomatopéique

on-pack *adj*
▸▸ *Mktg* ***on-pack offer*** prime *f* différée; ***on-pack promotion*** promotion *f* on-pack

on-ramp *n (to motorway)* bretelle *f* d'accès

onrush [ˈɒn,rʌʃ] *n (of attackers, army)* attaque *f*, assaut *m*; *(of emotion, tears)* crise *f*; *(of anger)* accès *m*

on-screen **1** *adj* (**a**) *Comput* à l'écran (**b**) *Cin & TV* à l'écran; **her on-screen character bears a close resemblance to her real-life personality** le personnage qu'elle joue à l'écran ressemble beaucoup à ce qu'elle est en réalité
2 *adv* (**a**) *Comput* sur (l')écran; **to work on-screen** travailler sur écran (**b**) *Cin & TV* à l'écran
▸▸ *Comput* ***on-screen help*** aide *f* en ligne

onset [ˈɒn,set] *n* (**a**) *(assault)* attaque *f*, assaut *m* (**b**) *(beginning)* début *m*, commencement *m*; **the onset of winter** le début de l'hiver

onshore [ˈɒn,ʃɔː(r)] *adj (on land)* sur terre, terrestre
▸▸ ***onshore oil production*** production *f* pétrolière à terre; ***onshore wind*** *(moving towards land)* vent *m* de mer

onside [,ɒnˈsaɪd] *Sport* **1** *adj* qui n'est pas hors jeu *ou* en position de hors-jeu
2 *adv* **to stay onside** ne pas se mettre en position de hors-jeu

on-site *adj Comput* sur place
▸▸ ***on-site guarantee*** maintenance *f* sur site; ***on-site service*** maintenance *f* sur site; ***on-site warranty*** maintenance *f* sur site

onslaught [ˈɒnslɔːt] *n* attaque *f*, assaut *m*; **the opposition's onslaught on government policy** l'attaque violente de l'opposition contre la politique du gouvernement

onstage [ˈɒnsteɪdʒ] **1** *adj* sur scène
2 *adv* sur scène

on-stream *adv* en service; **to come on-stream** être mis en service

Ont. *(written abbr* **Ontario)** Ontario *m*

on-target earnings *npl Com & Mktg* salaire *m* de base plus commissions

Ontario [ɒnˈteərɪəʊ] *n* l'Ontario *m*; **in Ontario** dans l'Ontario; **Lake Ontario** le lac Ontario

on-the-job *adj (training)* en entreprise; *(experience)* sur le tas

on-the-spot *adj (fine)* immédiat; *(report)* sur place, sur le terrain

onto [ˈɒntuː] *prep* (**a**) *(gen)* sur; **the bedroom looks out onto a garden** la chambre donne sur un jardin; **let's move onto the next point** passons au point suivant; **get onto the bus** montez dans le bus
(**b**) *(indicating discovery)* **let's just hope the authorities don't get onto us** espérons qu'on ne sera pas découverts par les autorités; **we're onto something big** nous sommes sur le point de faire une importante découverte; **is he onto the fact that they're having an affair?** est-il au courant de leur liaison?; **he'd better watch out, I'm onto him!** qu'il fasse attention, je l'ai dans mon *ou* le collimateur!
(**c**) *(in contact with)* **you should get onto head office about this** vous devriez contacter le siège à ce sujet; **she's been onto me about my poor marks** elle m'a enguirlandé à cause de mes mauvaises notes

ontogenesis [,ɒntəˈdʒenəsɪs] *n* ontogénie *f*, ontogenèse *f*

ontogenetic [,ɒntədʒɪˈnetɪk], **ontogenic** [,ɒntəˈdʒenɪk] *adj* ontogénétique, ontogénique

ontogeny [ɒnˈtɒdʒənɪ] *n* ontogénie *f*, ontogenèse *f*

ontological [,ɒntəˈlɒdʒɪkəl] *adj* ontologique

ontologically [,ɒntəˈlɒdʒɪkəlɪ] *adv* ontologiquement

ontology [ɒnˈtɒlədʒɪ] *n* ontologie *f*

onus ['əʊnəs] *n (responsibility)* responsabilité *f*; *(burden)* charge *f*; **the onus is on you to make good the damage** c'est à vous qu'il incombe de réparer les dégâts; **the onus is now on United to attack** United se doit maintenant d'attaquer; **the onus is on you to lodge a complaint** il tient à toi de déposer une plainte

onward ['ɒnwəd] **1** *adj* **the onward journey** la suite du voyage; **there is an onward flight to Chicago** il y a une correspondance pour Chicago; **the onward march of time** la fuite du temps

2 *adv Am* = **onwards**

3 *exclam* en avant!

onwards ['ɒnwədz] **1** *adv (forwards)* en avant; *(further on)* plus loin; **to go onwards** avancer; **a trip to Europe, and onwards into Asia** un voyage en Europe, qui se poursuit en Asie; **onwards and upwards!** en avant!

2 from... onwards *adv* à partir de; **from next July onwards** à partir de juillet prochain; **from her childhood onwards** dès *ou* depuis son enfance; **from now onwards** désormais, dorénavant, à partir de maintenant; **from then onwards** à partir de ce moment-là

onyx ['ɒnɪks] **1** *n* onyx *m*

2 *comp* en onyx, d'onyx

oo = **ooh**

oocyte ['əʊəsaɪt] *n Biol* ovocyte *m*

oodles ['u:dəlz] *npl Fam* des masses *fpl*, des tas *mpl*; **there's oodles of food left** il reste un tas de bouffe; **to have oodles of money** avoir un paquet de fric, être plein aux as; **to have oodles of time** avoir vachement de temps

oogamy [əʊ'ɒgəmɪ] *n Biol* oogamie *f*

oogenesis [,əʊə'dʒenɪsɪs] *n Biol* ovogenèse *f*

oogonium [,əʊə'gəʊnɪəm] *(pl* **oogoniums** *or* **oogonia** [-nɪə]) *n* (**a**) *Bot* oogone *f* (**b**) *Anat* ovogonie *f*

ooh [u:] **1** *exclam* oh!

2 *vi* **they were all oohing and aahing over her baby** ils poussaient tous des cris d'admiration devant son bébé

oolite ['əʊəlaɪt] *n Geol* oolite *m or f*, oolithe *m or f*

oolitic [,əʊə'lɪtɪk] *adj Geol* oolithique

oology [əʊ'ɒlədʒɪ] *n* oologie *f*

oolong ['u:lɒŋ] *n* (thé *m*) oolong *m*

oompah ['u:mpɑ:] *n* flonflon *m*

oomph [ʊmf] *n Fam* (**a**) *(energy)* punch *m*, pêche *f*; **he's certainly got plenty of oomph!** en tout cas, il a un sacré punch!; **their new album lacks the oomph of the last one** leur nouvel album n'a pas la pêche du précédent (**b**) *(sex appeal)* sex-appeal ▫ *m*; **she's got plenty of oomph** elle est vachement sexy

oophorectomy [,əʊəfə'rektəmɪ] *n Med* oophorectomie *f*, ovariectomie *f*

oophoritis [,əʊəfə'raɪtɪs] *n Med* oophorite *f*, ovarite *f*

oops [ʊps, u:ps], **oops-a-daisy** ['ʊpsə,deɪzɪ] *exclam Fam* (**a**) *(when stumbling, dropping something etc)* houp-là! (**b**) *(after someone has made a mistake)* oh là là!

oosphere ['əʊəsfɪə(r)] *n* oosphère *f*

oospore ['əʊəspɔ:(r)] *n Bot* oospore *f*

ootid ['əʊətɪd] *n Biol* ovotide *m*

ooze [u:z] **1** *vi* suinter; **the mud oozed up between her toes** la boue lui passait entre les orteils; **blood oozed from the wound** du sang coulait de la blessure; *Fig* **the new father fairly oozed with pride** le nouveau père débordait de fierté; *Fig* **her courage was oozing slowly away** son courage l'abandonnait peu à peu

2 *vt* **the wound was oozing pus/blood** du pus/sang suintait de la plaie; **the walls ooze moisture** l'humidité suinte des murs; *Fig* **to ooze confidence** déborder d'assurance; **to ooze charm** exsuder un charme mielleux; *Fig* **this place just oozes wealth** cet endroit sue l'opulence

3 *n* (**a**) *(mud)* boue *f*, vase *f*

(**b**) *(flow → of liquid)* suintement *m*

oozy ['u:zɪ] *adj* (**a**) *(muddy)* vaseux, bourbeux; **oozy bank** banc *m* de vase

(**b**) *(oozing liquid)* suintant

OP [,əʊ'pi:] *adj Typ (abbr* **out of print**) épuisé

op [ɒp] *n Fam Med & Mil (abbr* **operation**) opération ▫ *f*; **she has to have an op on her knee** il faut qu'elle se fasse opérer le genou ▫

op. *(written abbr* **opus**) op.

opacify [əʊ'pæsɪfaɪ] **1** *vt* opacifier

2 *vi* s'opacifier

opacity [ə'pæsətɪ] *n* opacité *f*; *Fig (of text)* inintelligibilité *f*, obscurité *f*; *(of person)* stupidité *f*

opah ['əʊpə] *n Ich* opah *m*

opal ['əʊpəl] **1** *n* opale *f*

2 *comp (brooch, ring)* en opale

opalescence [,əʊpə'lesəns] *n* opalescence *f*

opalescent [,əʊpə'lesənt] *adj* opalescent, opalin

opaline ['əʊpəlaɪn] **1** *adj* opalin

2 *n (glass)* opaline *f*

opaque [əʊ'peɪk] *adj* opaque; *Fig (text)* inintelligible, obscur; *(person)* stupide

►► *Am* ***opaque projector*** épiscope *m*, épidiascope *m*

opaqueness [əʊ'peɪknɪs] *n* opacité *f*; *Fig (of text)* inintelligibilité *f*, obscurité *f*; *(of person)* stupidité *f*

op art *n* op art *m*

op. cit. [,ɒp'sɪt] *(abbr* **opere citato**) op. cit.

OPEC ['əʊpek] *n (abbr* **Organization of Petroleum Exporting Countries**) OPEP *f*; **the OPEC countries** les pays *mpl* membres de l'OPEP

op-ed *n (in newspaper)* page *f* face éditoriale; **an op-ed piece** article *m* d'opinion *(situé sur la page faisant face à l'éditorial)*

OPEIC [,əʊpi:,i:aɪ'si:] *n Fin (abbr* **open-ended investment company**) SICAV *f*, société *f* d'investissement à capital variable

OPEN ['əʊpən]

ouvert	► **1 (a) – (d); (n), (o), (q) – (s)**
découvert	► **1 (e)**
dégagé	► **1 (g)**
vacant	► **1 (h)**
libre	► **1 (h)**
non résolu	► **1 (k)**
franc	► **1 (n)**
ouvrir	► **2 (a) – (g); 3 (d)**
déboucher	► **2 (a)**
commencer	► **2 (e); 3 (e)**
engager	► **2 (e)**
dégager	► **2 (g)**
s'ouvrir	► **3 (a) – (c)**

1 *adj* (**a**) *(not shut → window, cupboard, suitcase, jar, box, sore, valve)* ouvert; **her eyes were slightly open/wide open** ses yeux étaient entrouverts/grands ouverts; **he kicked the door open** il a ouvert la porte d'un coup de pied; **the panels slide open** les panneaux s'ouvrent en coulissant; **to smash/lever sth open** ouvrir qch en le fracassant/à l'aide d'un levier; **I can't get the bottle open** je n'arrive pas à ouvrir la bouteille; **there's a bottle already open in the fridge** il y a une bouteille entamée dans le frigo; **you won't need the key, the door's open** tu n'auras pas besoin de la clef, la porte est ouverte

(**b**) *(not fastened → coat, fly, packet)* ouvert; **his shirt was open to the waist** sa chemise était ouverte *ou* déboutonnée jusqu'à la ceinture; **his shirt was open at the neck** le col de sa chemise était ouvert; **her blouse hung open** son chemisier était déboutonné; **the wrapping had been torn open** l'emballage avait été arraché *ou* déchiré

(**c**) *(spread apart, unfolded → arms, book, magazine, umbrella)* ouvert; *(→ newspaper)* ouvert, déplié; *(→ legs, knees)* écarté; **the book lay open at page 6** le livre était ouvert à la page 6; **I dropped the coin into his open hand** *or* **palm** j'ai laissé tomber la pièce de monnaie dans le creux de sa main; **the seams had split open** les coutures avaient craqué; **he ran into my open arms** il s'est précipité dans mes bras

(**d**) *(for business)* ouvert; **I couldn't find a bank open** je n'ai pas pu trouver une banque qui soit ouverte; **are you open on Saturdays?** ouvrez-vous le samedi?; **we're open for business as usual** nous sommes ouverts comme à l'habitude; **open to the public** *(museum etc)* ouvert *ou* accessible au public; **open late** ouvert en nocturne

(**e**) *(not covered → carriage, wagon, bus)* découvert; *(→ car)* décapoté; *(→ grave)* ouvert; *(→ boat)* ouvert, non ponté; *(→ courtyard, sewer)* à ciel ouvert; **the passengers sat on the open deck** les passagers étaient assis sur le pont; **the wine should be left open to breathe** il faut laisser la bouteille ouverte pour que le vin puisse respirer

(**f**) *(not enclosed → hillside, plain)* **the shelter was open on three sides** l'abri était ouvert sur trois côtés; **the hill was open to the elements** la colline était exposée à tous les éléments; **our neighbourhood lacks open space** notre quartier manque d'espaces verts; **the wide open spaces of Texas** les grands espaces du Texas; **shanty towns sprang up on every scrap of open ground** des bidonvilles ont surgi sur la moindre parcelle de terrain vague; **they were attacked in open country** ils ont été attaqués en rase campagne; **open countryside stretched away to the horizon** la campagne s'étendait à perte de vue; **open grazing land** pâturages *mpl* non clôturés; **ahead lay a vast stretch of open water** au loin s'étendait une vaste étendue d'eau; **in the open air** en plein air; **nothing beats life in the open air** il n'y a rien de mieux que la vie au grand air; **he took to the open road** il a pris la route; **it'll do 150 on the open road** elle monte à 150 sur l'autoroute; **the open sea** la haute mer, le large

(**g**) *(unobstructed → road, passage)* dégagé; *(→ mountain pass)* ouvert, praticable; *(→ waterway)* ouvert à la navigation; *(→ view)* dégagé; **only one lane on the bridge is open** il n'y a qu'une voie ouverte à la circulation sur le pont

(**h**) *(unoccupied, available → job)* vacant; *(→ period of time)* libre; **we have two positions open** nous avons deux postes à pourvoir; **I'll keep this Friday open for you** je vous réserverai ce vendredi; **she likes to keep her weekends open** elle préfère ne pas faire de projets pour le week-end; **it's the only course of action open to us** c'est la seule chose que nous puissions faire; **she used every opportunity open to her** elle a profité de toutes les occasions qui se présentaient à elle; **he wants to keep his options open** il ne veut pas s'engager

(**i**) *(unrestricted → competition)* ouvert (à tous); *(→ meeting, trial)* public; *(→ society)* ouvert, démocratique; **the contest is not open to company employees** le concours n'est pas ouvert au personnel de la société; **club membership is open to anyone** aucune condition particulière n'est requise pour devenir membre du club; **a career open to very few** une carrière accessible à très peu de gens *ou* très fermée; **there are few positions of responsibility open to immigrants** les immigrés ont rarement accès aux postes de responsabilité; **the field is wide open for someone with your talents** pour quelqu'un d'aussi doué que vous, ce domaine offre des possibilités quasi illimitées; **to extend an open invitation to sb** inviter qn à venir chez soi quand il le souhaite; **it's an open invitation to tax-dodgers/thieves** c'est une invitation à la fraude fiscale/aux voleurs; *Am Fam* **Reno was a pretty open town in those days** à cette époque, Reno était aux mains des hors-la-loi ▫; **they have an open marriage** ils forment un couple très libre

(**j**) *(unprotected, unguarded → flank, fire)* ouvert; *(→ wiring)* non protégé; **the two countries share miles of open border** les deux pays sont séparés par des kilomètres de frontière non matérialisée; *Sport* **he missed an open goal** il n'y avait pas de défenseurs, et il a raté le but; **to lay oneself open to criticism** prêter le flanc à la critique

(**k**) *(undecided → question)* non résolu, non tranché; **the election is still wide open** l'élection n'est pas encore jouée; **it's still an open question whether he'll resign or not** on ne sait toujours pas s'il va démissionner; **I prefer to leave the matter open** je préfère laisser cette question en suspens; **he wanted to leave the date open** il n'a pas voulu fixer de date

(**l**) *(liable)* **his speech is open to misunderstanding** son discours peut prêter à confusion; **the prices are not open to negotiation** les prix ne sont pas négociables; **the plan is open to modification** le projet n'a pas encore été finalisé; **it's open to debate whether she knew about it or not** on peut se demander si elle était au courant; **open to doubt** douteux

(**m**) *(receptive)* **to be open to suggestions** être ouvert aux suggestions; **I don't want to go but**

onu–ope

I'm open to persuasion je ne veux pas y aller mais je pourrais me laisser persuader; **I try to keep an open mind about such things** j'essaie de ne pas avoir de préjugés sur ces questions; **open to any reasonable offer** disposé à considérer toute offre raisonnable

(**n**) *(candid → person, smile, countenance)* ouvert, franc (franche); *(→ discussion)* franc (franche); **let's be open with each other** soyons francs l'un avec l'autre; **they weren't very open about their intentions** ils se sont montrés assez discrets en ce qui concerne leurs intentions; **he is open about his homosexuality** il ne cache pas son homosexualité

(**o**) *(blatant → contempt, criticism, conflict, disagreement)* ouvert; *(→ attempt)* non dissimulé; *(→ scandal)* public; *(→ rivalry)* déclaré; **her open dislike** son aversion déclarée; **the country is in a state of open civil war** le pays est en état de véritable guerre civile; **they are in open revolt** ils sont en révolte ouverte; **they acted in open violation of the treaty** ce qu'ils ont fait constitue une violation flagrante du traité; **they showed an open disregard for the law** ils ont fait preuve d'un manque de respect flagrant face à la loi; **it's an open admission of guilt** cela équivaut à un aveu

(**p**) *(loose → weave)* lâche

(**q**) *Sport (play → free-flowing)* ouvert, dégagé

(**r**) *Ling (vowel, syllable)* ouvert

(**s**) *Elec (circuit)* ouvert

(**t**) *Br Fin (cheque)* non barré

(**u**) *Mus (string)* à vide

2 *vt* (**a**) *(window, lock, shop, eyes, border)* ouvrir; *(wound)* rouvrir; *(bottle, can)* ouvrir, déboucher; *(wine)* déboucher; **open quotations** *or* **inverted commas** ouvrez les guillemets; **she opened her eyes very wide** elle ouvrit grand les yeux, elle écarquilla les yeux; **they plan to open the border to refugees** ils projettent d'ouvrir la frontière aux réfugiés; *Phot* **open the aperture one more stop** ouvrez d'un diaphragme de plus; *Fig* **to open one's heart to sb** se confier à qn; **we must open our minds to new ideas** nous devons être ouverts aux idées nouvelles

(**b**) *(unfasten → coat, envelope, gift, collar)* ouvrir

(**c**) *(unfold, spread apart → book, umbrella, penknife, arms, hand)* ouvrir; *(→ newspaper)* ouvrir, déplier; *(→ legs, knees)* écarter

(**d**) *(pierce → hole)* percer; *(→ breach)* ouvrir; *(→ way, passage)* ouvrir, frayer; **to open a road through the jungle** ouvrir une route à travers la jungle; **the agreement opens the way for peace** l'accord va mener à la paix

(**e**) *(start → campaign, discussion, account, trial)* ouvrir, commencer; *(→ negotiations)* ouvrir, engager; *(→ conversation)* engager, entamer; *Banking & Fin (→ account, loan)* ouvrir; **her new film opened the festival** son dernier film a ouvert le festival; **to open a file on sb** ouvrir un dossier sur qn; **to open fire (on** *or* **at sb)** ouvrir le feu (sur qn); **to open the bidding** *(in bridge)* ouvrir (les enchères); **to open the betting** *(in poker)* lancer les enchères; *Fin* **to open a line of credit** ouvrir un crédit; **to open Parliament** ouvrir la session du Parlement; *Law* **to open the case** exposer les faits

(**f**) *(set up → shop, business)* ouvrir; *(inaugurate → hospital, airport, library)* ouvrir, inaugurer

(**g**) *(clear, unblock → road, lane, passage)* dégager; *(→ mountain pass)* ouvrir

3 *vi* (**a**) *(door, window)* (s')ouvrir; *(suitcase, valve, padlock, eyes)* s'ouvrir; **the window opens outwards** la fenêtre (s')ouvre vers l'extérieur; **open wide!** ouvrez grand!; **to open, press down and twist** pour ouvrir, appuyez et tournez; **both rooms open onto the corridor** les deux chambres donnent *ou* ouvrent sur le couloir; *Fig* **the heavens opened and we got drenched** il s'est mis à tomber des trombes d'eau et on s'est fait tremper

(**b**) *(unfold, spread apart → book, umbrella, parachute)* s'ouvrir; *(→ bud, leaf)* s'ouvrir, s'épanouir; **a new life opened before her** une nouvelle vie s'ouvrait devant elle

(**c**) *(gape → chasm)* s'ouvrir

(**d**) *(for business)* ouvrir; **what time do you open on Sundays?** à quelle heure ouvrez-vous le dimanche?; **the doors open at 8 p.m.** les portes ouvrent à 20 heures; **to open late** ouvrir en nocturne

(**e**) *(start → campaign, meeting, discussion, concert, play, story)* commencer; **the book opens with a murder** le livre commence par un meurtre; **the hunting season opens in September** la chasse ouvre en septembre; **she opened with a statement of the association's goals** elle commença par une présentation des buts de l'association; **the film opens next week** le film sort la semaine prochaine; *Theat* **when are you opening?** quand aura lieu la première?; **when it opened on Broadway, the play flopped** lorsqu'elle est sortie à Broadway, la pièce a fait un four; **the Dow Jones opened at 2461** le Dow Jones a ouvert à 2461; **to open with two clubs** *(in bridge)* ouvrir de deux trèfles

4 *n* (**a**) *(outdoors, open air)* **(out) in the open** *(gen)* en plein air, dehors; *(in countryside)* au grand air; **eating (out) in the open gives me an appetite** manger au grand air me donne de l'appétit; **to sleep in the open** dormir à la belle étoile

(**b**) *(public eye)* **to bring sth (out) into the open** exposer *ou* étaler qch au grand jour; **the riot brought the instability of the regime out into the open** l'émeute a révélé l'instabilité du régime; **the conflict finally came out into the open** le conflit a finalement éclaté au grand jour

(**c**) *Sport* open *m*; **the British Open** *(golf)* l'open *m ou* le tournoi open de Grande-Bretagne; **the French Open** *(tennis)* Roland-Garros

►► *Banking* ***open account*** compte *m* ouvert; ***open bar*** buvette *f* gratuite, bar *m* gratuit; *Banking* ***open cheque*** chèque *m* ouvert *ou* non barré; *Mil & Pol* ***open city*** ville *f* ouverte; *Sch* ***open classroom*** classe *f* primaire à activités libres; *St Exch* ***open contract*** position *f* ouverte; *Fin* ***open credit*** crédit *m* à découvert; *Br* ***open day*** journée *f* portes ouvertes; *Econ* ***open economy*** économie *f* ouverte; ***open house*** *Am (open day)* journée *f* portes ouvertes; *(party)* grande fête *f*; *Br* **to keep open house** tenir table ouverte; ***open inquiry*** enquête *f* publique; *Br* ***open learning*** enseignement *m* à la carte *(par correspondance ou à temps partiel)*; ***open letter*** lettre *f* ouverte; **an open letter to the President** une lettre ouverte au Président; ***open market*** marché *m* libre; **to buy sth on the open market** acheter qch sur le marché libre; *St Exch* **to buy shares on the open market** acheter des actions en Bourse; ***open mike*** = période pendant laquelle les clients d'un café-théâtre ou d'un bar peuvent chanter ou raconter des histoires drôles au micro; ***open mesh*** mailles *fpl* lâches; *St Exch* ***open money market*** marché *m* libre des capitaux; *St Exch* ***open outcry*** criée *f*; *St Exch* ***open outcry system*** système *m* de criée; ***open pattern*** motif *m* aéré; *Ins* ***open policy*** police *f* flottante; *St Exch* ***open position*** position *f* ouverte; *Am Pol* ***open primary*** = élection primaire américaine ouverte aux non-inscrits d'un parti; ***open prison*** prison *f* ouverte; ***open sandwich*** *(gen)* tartine *f*; *(cocktail food)* canapé *m*; ***open season*** saison *f*; **the open season for hunting** la saison de la chasse; *Fig* **the tabloid papers have declared open season on the private lives of rock stars** les journaux à scandale se sont mis à traquer les stars du rock dans leur vie privée; *Aviat & Theat* ***open seating*** places *fpl* non réservées; *Br* ***open secret*** secret *m* de Polichinelle; **it's an open secret that Alison will get the job** c'est Alison qui aura le poste, ce n'est un secret pour personne; ***open sesame*** **1** *exclam* sésame, ouvre-toi! **2** *n Br (means to success)* sésame *m*; **good A level results aren't necessarily an open sesame to university** de bons résultats aux "A levels" n'ouvrent pas forcément la porte de l'université; *Ind* ***open shop*** *Br (open to non-union members)* = entreprise ne pratiquant pas le monopole d'embauche; *Am (with no union)* établissement *m* sans syndicat; ***open ticket*** billet *m* open; *Sport* ***open tournament*** (tournoi *m*) open *m*; *Br* ***Open University*** = enseignement universitaire par correspondance doublé d'émissions de télévision ou de radio; *Law* ***open verdict*** verdict *m* de décès sans cause déterminée

►**open out 1** *vi* (**a**) *(unfold → bud, petals)* s'ouvrir, s'épanouir; *(→ parachute)* s'ouvrir; *(→ sail)* se gonfler; **the sofa opens out into a bed** le canapé est convertible en lit; **the doors open out onto a terrace** les portes donnent *ou* s'ouvrent sur une terrasse

(**b**) *(lie → vista, valley)* s'étendre, s'ouvrir; **miles of wheatfields opened out before us** des champs de blé s'étendaient devant nous à perte de vue

(**c**) *(widen → path, stream)* s'élargir; **the river opens out into a lake** la rivière se jette dans un lac; **the trail finally opens out onto a plateau** la piste débouche sur un plateau

(**d**) *Br Fig (become less reserved)* s'ouvrir; **he opened out after a few drinks** quelques verres ont suffi à le faire sortir de sa réserve

2 *vt sep (unfold → newspaper, deck chair, fan)* ouvrir; **the peacock opened out its tail** le paon a fait la roue

►**open up 1** *vi* (**a**) *(unlock the door)* ouvrir; **open up or I'll call the police!** ouvrez, sinon j'appelle la police!; **open up in there!** ouvrez, là-dedans!

(**b**) *(become available → possibility)* s'ouvrir; **we may have a position opening up in May** il se peut que nous ayons un poste disponible en mai; **new markets are opening up** de nouveaux marchés sont en train de s'ouvrir

(**c**) *(for business → shop, branch etc)* (s')ouvrir; **a new hotel opens up every week** un nouvel hôtel ouvre ses portes chaque semaine

(**d**) *(start firing → guns)* faire feu, tirer; *(→ troops, person)* ouvrir le feu, se mettre à tirer

(**e**) *(become less reserved → person)* s'ouvrir; *(→ discussion)* s'animer; **he won't open up even to me** il ne s'ouvre pas, même à moi; **he needs to open up about his feelings** il a besoin de dire ce qu'il a sur le cœur *ou* de s'épancher; **I got her to open up about her doubts** j'ai réussi à la convaincre de me faire part de ses doutes

(**f**) *(become interesting)* devenir intéressant; **things are beginning to open up in my field of research** ça commence à bouger dans mon domaine de recherche; **the game opened up in the last half** le match est devenu plus ouvert après la mi-temps

2 *vt sep* (**a**) *(crate, gift, bag, tomb)* ouvrir; **we're opening up the summer cottage this weekend** nous ouvrons la maison de campagne ce week-end; **the sleeping bag will dry faster if you open it up** le sac de couchage séchera plus vite si tu l'ouvres

(**b**) *(for business)* ouvrir; **each morning, Lucy opened up the shop** chaque matin, Lucy ouvrait la boutique; **he wants to open up a travel agency** il veut ouvrir une agence de voyages

(**c**) *(for development → isolated region)* désenclaver; *(→ quarry, oilfield)* ouvrir, commencer l'exploitation de; *(→ new markets)* ouvrir; **irrigation will open up new land for agriculture** l'irrigation permettra la mise en culture de nouvelles terres; **the airport opened up the island for tourism** l'aéroport a ouvert l'île au tourisme; **a discovery which opens up new fields of research** une découverte qui crée de nouveaux domaines de recherche; **the policy opened up possibilities for closer cooperation** la politique a créé les conditions d'une coopération plus étroite

(**d**) *Fam (accelerate)* **he opened it** *or* **her up** il a accéléré à fond

---

openable ['əʊpənəbəl] *adj* que l'on peut ouvrir; *Theat (door, window)* praticable

open-air *adj (market, concert)* en plein air; *(sports)* de plein air

►► ***open-air museum*** écomusée *m*; ***open-air restaurant*** restaurant *m* en terrasse; ***open-air swimming pool*** piscine *f* découverte

open-and-shut *adj* **it's an open-and-shut case** la solution est évidente *ou* ne fait pas l'ombre d'un doute

opencast ['əʊpənkɑːst] *adj Br Mining* à ciel ouvert

►► ***opencast mining*** extraction *f* à ciel ouvert

open-door *adj (policy)* de la porte ouverte

open-ended [-'endɪd] *adj (flexible → offer)* flexible; *(→ plan)* modifiable; *(→ question)* ouvert; *(→ mortgage)* sans date limite; **could we keep**

the arrangement open-ended? pourrions-nous garder une certaine flexibilité au niveau de notre arrangement?; **it's a bit too open-ended** c'est un peu trop vague; **an open-ended discussion** une discussion libre

►► *Fin* ***open-ended contract*** contrat *m* à durée indéterminée; *Fin* ***open-ended credit*** crédit *m* à durée indéterminée; *Fin* ***open-ended investment company, open-ended trust*** société *f* d'investissement à capital variable, SICAV *f*

opener ['əʊpənə(r)] *n* (**a**) *(tool)* outil *m ou* dispositif *m* servant à ouvrir; *(for cans)* ouvre-boîtes *m inv*; **you need a special opener for these tins** il faut un ouvre-boîtes spécial pour ces boîtes

(**b**) *(person → in cards, games)* ouvreur(euse) *m,f*

(**c**) *(first song, act etc)* lever *m* de rideau; **she chose her latest hit single as an opener for the show** elle a choisi son dernier tube pour ouvrir le spectacle

(**d**) *Sport (in cricket)* premier batteur *m*

(**e**) *(idiom) Br Fam* **for openers** pour commencer ❑; **I'm sacking the whole staff, and that's just for openers** je licencie toute l'équipe et ce n'est qu'un début ❑; **well, let's offer £100 for openers** eh bien, proposons 100 livres pour commencer ❑

open-eyed 1 *adj* (qui a) les yeux ouverts; **they watched in open-eyed amazement** ils ouvraient de grands yeux

2 *adv* **to stare open-eyed** regarder les yeux écarquillés

open-faced *adj*

►► *Am* ***open-faced sandwich*** *(gen)* tartine *f*; *(cocktail food)* canapé *m*

open-field *adj*

►► *Hist* ***the open-field system*** l'openfield *m*

open-handed *adj* généreux

open-hearted [-'hɑːtɪd] *adj* (**a**) *(candid)* franc (franche), sincère (**b**) *(kind)* bon, qui a bon cœur

open-hearth *adj*

►► *Metal* ***open-hearth furnace*** four *m* Martin; ***open-hearth process*** procédé *m* Martin

open-heart surgery *n* chirurgie *f* à cœur ouvert

opening ['əʊpənɪŋ] **1** *adj (part, chapter)* premier; *(day, hours)* d'ouverture; *(ceremony)* d'ouverture, d'inauguration; *(remark)* préliminaire, préalable; *Theat* **the opening lines** les premières lignes; **the play's opening scene** la première scène de la pièce

2 *n* (**a**) *(act of opening)* ouverture *f*; **the opening of a new supermarket** l'ouverture *f* d'un nouveau supermarché; **at the play's New York opening** lors de la première de la pièce à New York; **the opening of negotiations has been postponed** l'ouverture *f* des négociations a été ajournée; **the opening of Parliament** l'ouverture *f* du Parlement

(**b**) *(gap, hole, entrance)* ouverture *f*; **we came to an opening in the fence** nous avons trouvé un passage *ou* une ouverture dans la clôture; **an opening in the clouds** une trouée *ou* une percée dans les nuages; **the opening to the mine** l'entrée *f* de la mine

(**c**) *Am (in forest)* clairière *f*

(**d**) *(start, first part)* ouverture *f*, début *m*; *Law (speech by lawyer)* exposition *f* des faits; **the opening of the film is in black and white** le début du film est en *ou* les premières scènes du film sont en noir et blanc

(**e**) *(opportunity → gen)* occasion *f*; *(→ for employment)* débouché *m*; *Mktg (→ in market)* débouché *m*, ouverture *f*; **we have exploited an opening in the market** nous avons exploité une ouverture sur le marché; **her remarks about the company gave me the opening I needed** ses observations au sujet de l'entreprise m'ont fourni le prétexte dont j'avais besoin; **there are lots of good openings in industry** l'industrie offre de nombreux débouchés intéressants; **there's an opening with Smith & Co** il y a un poste vacant chez Smith & Co

►► *Acct* ***opening balance*** solde *m* d'ouverture; *Acct* ***opening balance sheet*** bilan *m* d'ouverture; ***opening batsman*** *(in cricket)* premier batteur *m*; *Cards* ***opening bid*** annonce *f* d'entrée *ou* d'indication; ***opening bracket*** parenthèse *f* ouvrante; *St Exch* ***opening day*** jour *m* d'ouverture; *Acct* ***opening entry*** écriture *f* d'ouverture; *Com* ***opening hours*** heures *fpl* d'ouverture; *Chess* ***opening gambit*** gambit *m*; *Fig* premier pas *m*; *St Exch* ***opening price*** *(at start of trading)* cours *m* d'ouverture, premier cours *m*; *(of new shares)* cours *m* d'introduction; ***opening quotation marks*** guillemets *mpl* ouvrants; *Fin* ***opening session*** séance *f* d'ouverture; *Fin* ***opening stock*** stock *m* initial *ou* d'ouverture; *Theat* ***opening night*** première *f*; *Comput* ***opening tag*** balise *f* de début; *Com* ***opening time*** heure *f* d'ouverture

open-jaw *adj (ticket)* open *(inv)*

openly ['əʊpənlɪ] *adv* visiblement; **drugs are on sale openly** la drogue est en vente libre; **she was openly distressed about it** ça l'avait visiblement bouleversée; **to weep openly** pleurer sans retenue

open-minded *adj (receptive)* ouvert (d'esprit); *(unprejudiced)* sans préjugés; **my parents are pretty open-minded about mixed marriages** mes parents n'ont aucun a priori contre les mariages mixtes

open-mindedness [-'maɪndɪdnɪs] *n* ouverture *f* d'esprit

open-mouthed [-'maʊðd] **1** *adj (person)* stupéfait, interdit; **he was sitting there in open-mouthed astonishment** il était assis là, béant d'étonnement

2 *adv* **to watch open-mouthed** regarder bouche bée

open-necked *adj* à col ouvert

openness ['əʊpənnɪs] *n* (**a**) *(candidness)* franchise *f*; **she spoke with refreshing openness about her career** elle parlait de son métier avec une franchise qui faisait plaisir

(**b**) *(receptivity)* ouverture *f*; **I admire her for her openness** ce que j'admire chez elle, c'est qu'elle est très ouverte

(**c**) *(spaciousness)* largeur *f*; **the picture window gives a feeling of openness to the room** la baie vitrée agrandit la pièce

(**d**) *(of coastline)* situation *f* exposée; *(of terrain)* aspect *m* découvert

open-plan *adj Archit (design, house)* à plan ouvert, sans cloisons

►► ***open-plan kitchen*** cuisine *f* américaine; ***open-plan office*** bureau *m* paysager

open-skies [-skaɪz], **open-sky** *adj* (**a**) *Mil* = qui autorise l'autre partie à effectuer des survols aériens d'installations militaires (**b**) *Aviat* = qui autorise le survol du territoire à tous

open-toe, open-toed [-təʊd] *adj (shoe)* ouvert

open-top *adj* décapotable

open-topped bus *n* autobus *m* à impériale

openwork ['əʊpənwɜːk] *n (UNCOUNT)* (**a**) *Sewing* jours *mpl*, ajours *mpl* (**b**) *Archit* claire-voie *f*, ajours *mpl*

opera ['ɒpərə] **1** *pl of* **opus**

2 *n* (**a**) *(musical play)* opéra *m* (**b**) *(art)* opéra *m*; **she adores (the) opera** elle adore l'opéra (**c**) *(opera house)* opéra *m*

►► ***opera cloak*** (grande) cape *f*; ***opera glasses*** jumelles *fpl* de théâtre; *Br* ***opera hat*** gibus *m*, (chapeau *m*) claque *m*; ***opera house*** (théâtre *m* de l')opéra *m*; ***opera singer*** chanteur(euse) *m,f* d'opéra

operable ['ɒprəbəl] *adj* (**a**) *Med (disease, tumour)* opérable (**b**) *(system)* utilisable

operagoer ['ɒprəˌgəʊə(r)] *n* amateur *m* d'opéra

operand ['ɒpərænd] *n Math* opérande *m*

operate ['ɒpəreɪt] **1** *vt* (**a**) *(machine, device)* faire fonctionner, faire marcher; **my husband doesn't even know how to operate the toaster!** mon mari ne sait même pas se servir du grille-pain!; **is it possible to operate the radio off the mains?** peut-on brancher cette radio sur le secteur?; **this clock is battery-operated** cette horloge fonctionne avec des piles; **a circuit-breaker operates the safety mechanism** un disjoncteur actionne *ou* déclenche le système de sécurité

(**b**) *(business)* gérer, diriger; *(mine)* exploiter; *(drug ring)* contrôler; **they operate several casinos** ils tiennent plusieurs casinos; **she operates her business from her home** elle fait marcher son affaire depuis son domicile; **they operate a protection racket in the neighbourhood** ils rackettent les gens du quartier; **they operate a system of rent rebates for poorer families** ils ont un système de loyers modérés pour les familles les plus démunies

2 *vi* (**a**) *(machine, device)* marcher, fonctionner; *(system, process, network)* fonctionner; **it operates by itself** ça fonctionne tout seul; **this is how colonialism operates** voici comment fonctionne le colonialisme; **the factory is operating at full capacity** l'usine tourne à plein rendement

(**b**) *Med* opérer; **to operate on sb (for sth)** opérer qn (de qch); **he was operated on for cancer** on l'a opéré *ou* il a été opéré d'un cancer; **we'll have to operate** il va falloir opérer

(**c**) *(be active)* opérer; **military patrols operate along the border** des patrouilles militaires opèrent le long de la frontière; **many crooks operate in this part of town** de nombreux malfaiteurs sévissent dans ce quartier; **the company operates out of Chicago** le siège de la société est à Chicago; **the company operates in ten countries** la société est implantée dans dix pays

(**d**) *(produce an effect)* opérer, agir; **the drug operates on the nervous system** le médicament agit sur le système nerveux; **the decision has operated against us** la décision a joué contre nous; **two elements operate in our favour** deux éléments jouent en notre faveur

(**e**) *(be operative)* s'appliquer; **the rule doesn't operate in such cases** la règle ne s'applique pas à de tels cas; **the wage increase will operate from 1 January** l'augmentation des salaires prendra effet à partir du 1er janvier

operatic [ˌɒpə'rætɪk] **1** *adj* d'opéra

2 operatics *npl (amateur)* opéra *m* d'amateurs

►► ***operatic repertoire*** répertoire *m* lyrique; ***operatic role*** rôle *m* lyrique; ***operatic society*** groupe *m* d'opéra d'amateurs

operating ['ɒpəreɪtɪŋ] *adj (costs, methods etc)* d'exploitation; **the factory has reached full operating capacity** l'usine a atteint sa pleine capacité de production

►► *Am Fin* ***operating account*** compte *m* d'exploitation; *Acct* ***operating assets*** actif *m* d'exploitation; *Acct* ***operating budget*** budget *m* d'exploitation, budget *m* de fonctionnement; *Am* ***operating capital*** capital *m* d'exploitation, capital *m* de roulement; *Acct* ***operating cash flow*** cash-flow *m* disponible; *Acct* ***operating costs*** frais *mpl ou* coûts *mpl* d'exploitation; *Acct* ***operating costs analysis*** comptabilité *f* analytique d'exploitation; *Fin* ***operating deficit*** déficit *m* d'exploitation; *Acct* ***operating expenses*** frais *mpl* d'exploitation; ***operating income*** produits *mpl* d'exploitation; ***operating instructions*** mode *m* d'emploi; *Fin* ***operating leverage*** levier *m* d'exploitation; *Acct & Fin* ***operating loss*** perte *f* d'exploitation; *Acct* ***operating margin*** marge *f* (nette) d'exploitation; *Acct & Fin* ***operating profit*** bénéfice *m* d'exploitation; *Acct* ***operating ratio*** coefficient *m ou* ratio *m* d'exploitation; *Am* ***operating room*** salle *f* d'opération; *Fin* ***operating statement*** compte *m ou* rapport *m* d'exploitation; *Comput* ***operating system*** système *m* d'exploitation; ***operating table*** table *f* d'opération; *Br* ***operating theatre*** salle *f* d'opération

operation [ˌɒpə'reɪʃən] *n* (**a**) *(functioning → of machine, device)* fonctionnement *m*, marche *f*; *(→ of process, system)* fonctionnement *m*; *(→ of drug, market force)* action *f*; **to be in operation** *(machine, train service)* être en service; *(firm, group, criminal)* être en activité; *(law)* être en vigueur; **bus services are in operation until midnight** les lignes de bus sont en service jusqu'à minuit; **the pit has been in operation for two years** le puits est exploité depuis deux ans; **the plant is in operation round the clock** l'usine fonctionne 24 heures sur 24; **to put into operation** *(machine, train service)* mettre en service; *(plan)* mettre en application *ou* en œuvre; *(law)* faire entrer en vigueur; **to come into operation** *(machine, train service)* entrer en service; *(law)* entrer en vigueur; **the old machines have been taken out of operation** les vieilles machines ont été retirées du service

(**b**) *(running, management → of firm)* gestion *f*; *(→ of mine)* exploitation *f*; *(→ of process, system)* application *f*; (→ *of machine*) fonctionnement *m*

(**c**) *(act, activity, deal etc)* opération *f*; *Mil* opération *f*; **a police/rescue operation** une opération de police/de sauvetage; **they are to close down their operations in Mexico** ils vont mettre un terme à leurs opérations *ou* activités au Mexique; **peace-keeping operations** opérations *fpl* de pacification

(**d**) *(company)* entreprise *f*, société *f*; **she works for a mining operation** elle travaille pour une exploitation minière

(**e**) *Med* opération *f*, intervention *f*; **she had an operation for cancer** elle s'est fait opérer d'un cancer; **he had a heart operation** il a subi une opération *ou* il a été opéré du cœur; **to perform an operation** réaliser une intervention; **to perform an operation on sb (for sth)** opérer qn (de qch)

(**f**) *Comput & Math* opération *f*

(**g**) *Mktg (campaign)* opération *f*

►► ***operations breakdown*** décomposition *f* des tâches; ***operations management*** gestion *f* des opérations; ***operations manager*** directeur(trice) *m,f* des exploitations; *Hist & Mil* ***Operation Omega*** Opération *f* Oméga; *Hist & Mil* ***Operation Overlord*** = nom de code du débarquement de juin 1944; ***operations research*** recherche *f* opérationnelle; ***operations room*** base *f* d'opérations

operational [ˌɒpəˈreɪʃənəl] *adj* (**a**) *Mil (gen)* opérationnel; **the design team was operational within six months** en l'espace de six mois, l'équipe de dessinateurs fut opérationnelle

(**b**) *(equipment, engine, system)* opérationnel; **the new missiles are not yet operational** les nouveaux missiles ne sont pas encore opérationnels; **as soon as the engine is operational** dès que le moteur sera en état de marche; **operational difficulties** difficultés *fpl* d'ordre pratique; **we have an operational malfunction** nous avons un problème de fonctionnement

(**c**) *(costs, requirements)* d'exploitation

►► *Acct* ***operational audit*** audit *m* opérationnel; *Acct* ***operational cost accounting*** comptabilité *f* analytique d'exploitation; *Acct* ***operational cost accounts*** comptes *mpl* analytiques d'exploitation; *Acct* ***operational cost centre*** centre *m* d'analyse opérationnel; *Acct* ***operational costs*** frais *mpl ou* coûts *mpl* d'exploitation, frais *mpl* opérationnels; *Acct* ***operational efficiency*** efficacité *f* opérationnelle; ***operational marketing*** marketing *m* opérationnel; *Com* ***operational planning*** planification *f* des opérations; *Mktg* ***operational research*** recherche *f* opérationnelle

operationalism [ˌɒpəˈreɪʃənəlɪzəm] *n Phil* opérationnalisme *m*

operationism [ˌɒpəˈreɪʃənɪzəm] *n Phil* opérationnisme *m*

operative [ˈɒprətɪv] **1** *adj* (**a**) *(law)* en vigueur; **to become operative** entrer en vigueur, prendre effet; **parking restrictions became operative last year** les limitations de stationnement ont pris effet l'an dernier

(**b**) *(operational* → *system, scheme, skill)* opérationnel; **the system will soon be operative** le système sera bientôt opérationnel

(**c**) *Med* opératoire

(**d**) *(idiom)* **the operative word** le mot qui convient

2 *n* (**a**) *(worker)* ouvrier(ère) *m,f*; *(of machine)* opérateur(trice) *m,f*; **machine operative** conducteur(trice) *m,f* de machine; **textile operative** ouvrier(ère) *m,f* du textile

(**b**) *Am (secret agent)* agent *m* secret; *(detective)* (détective *m*) privé *m*

operator [ˈɒpəreɪtə(r)] *n* (**a**) *(technician)* opérateur(trice) *m,f*; **radio operator** radio *m*

(**b**) *Tel* opérateur(trice) *m,f*; **(switchboard) operator** standardiste *mf*

(**c**) *Com (director)* directeur(trice) *m,f*, dirigeant(e) *m,f*; *(organizer)* organisateur(trice) *m,f*; **there are too many small operators in real estate** l'immobilier compte trop de petites entreprises; **he's a big drug operator** c'est un grand caïd de la drogue; *Fam Pej* **he's a smooth operator** il sait s'y prendre *ou* se débrouiller, c'est un petit malin

(**d**) *Math* opérateur *m*

(**e**) *Am (in bus)* machiniste *mf*

(**f**) *St Exch* opérateur *m*; **operator for a fall/rise** opérateur *m* à la baisse/hausse

operculum [əʊˈpɜːkjʊləm] (*pl* **operculums** *or* **opercula** [-lə]) *n Bot & Zool* opercule *m*

operetta [ˌɒpəˈretə] *n* opérette *f*

operon [ˈɒpərɒn] *n Biol* opéron *m*

Ophelia [əˈfiːlɪə] *pr n* Ophélie

ophidian [ɒˈfɪdɪən] *Zool* **1** *n* ophidien *m*, serpent *m*

2 *adj* ophidien

ophite [ˈɒfaɪt] *n Miner* ophite *m*, marbre *m* serpentin

ophthalmia [ɒfˈθælmɪə] *n Med* ophtalmie *f*

ophthalmic [ɒfˈθælmɪk] *adj Anat (nerve)* ophtalmique; *Med (hospital, surgery)* ophtalmologique

►► ***ophthalmic optician*** opticien(enne) *m,f* (optométriste)

ophthalmologic [ɒfˌθælməˈlɒdʒɪk], **ophthalmological** [ɒfˌθælməˈlɒdʒɪkəl] *adj* ophtalmologique

ophthalmologist [ˌɒfθælˈmɒlədʒɪst] *n* oculiste *mf*, ophtalmologiste *mf*, ophtalmologue *mf*

ophthalmology [ˌɒfθælˈmɒlədʒɪ] *n* ophtalmologie *f*

ophthalmoscope [ɒfˈθælməskəʊp] *n* ophtalmoscope *m*

ophthalmoscopy [ˌɒfθælˈmɒskəpɪ] *n* ophtalmoscopie *f*

opiate [ˈəʊpɪət] **1** *n Pharm* opiacé *m*; *(soporific)* somnifère *m*

2 *adj* opiacé

opine [əʊˈpaɪn] *vt Formal or Literary* (faire) remarquer

opinion [əˈpɪnjən] *n* (**a**) *(estimation)* opinion *f*, avis *m*; *(viewpoint)* point *m* de vue; **in my opinion** à mon avis; **in the opinion of her teachers** de l'avis de ses professeurs, selon ses professeurs; **I am of the opinion that we should wait** je suis d'avis que l'on attende; **what is your opinion on** *or* **about the elections?** que pensez-vous des élections?; **everyone should be free to express an opinion** chacun devrait être libre d'exprimer son opinion; **my personal opinion is that...** je suis d'avis que..., pour ma part, je pense que...; **well, if you want my honest opinion, I'll tell you** puisque tu veux savoir le fond de ma pensée, je vais te le dire; **can you give us your opinion on the festival?** pouvez-vous nous dire ce que vous pensez du festival?; **I'd like your opinion** j'aimerais avoir ton opinion *ou* savoir ce que tu en penses; **to form an opinion of sb/sth** se faire une opinion sur *ou* de qn/qch; **to have a good/bad opinion of sth** avoir une bonne/mauvaise opinion de qch; **I have a rather low opinion of him** je n'ai pas beaucoup d'estime pour lui; **he has too high an opinion of himself** il a une trop haute opinion de lui-même

(**b**) *(conviction, belief)* opinion *f*; **to have strong opinions** avoir des opinions bien arrêtées *ou* tranchées; **world/international opinion** l'opinion *f* mondiale/internationale; **a matter of opinion** une affaire d'opinion; **public opinion is against them** ils ont l'opinion publique contre eux

(**c**) *Law* avis *m*; **it is the opinion of the court that...** la cour est d'avis que...

(**d**) *(advice)* opinion *f*, avis *m*; **a medical/legal opinion** un avis médical/juridique

►► *Mktg* ***opinion former, opinion leader*** leader *m* d'opinion, préconisateur *m*; *Mktg* ***opinion measurement*** sondage *m* d'opinion; *Mktg* ***opinion measurement technique*** technique *f* de sondage d'opinion; *Mktg* ***opinion poll*** sondage *m* (d'opinion), enquête *f* (d'opinion); *Mktg* ***opinion pollster*** sondeur(euse) *m,f* (d'opinion); *Mktg* ***opinion survey*** sondage *m* d'opinion (publique), enquête *f* (d'opinion)

opinionated [əˈpɪnjəneɪtɪd] *adj Pej (tone)* dogmatique; *(person)* qui a des idées très arrêtées

opium [ˈəʊpjəm] *n* opium *m*

►► ***opium addict*** opiomane *mf*; ***opium addiction*** opiomanie *f*; ***opium den*** fumerie *f* d'opium; ***opium dream*** rêve *m* d'opium; ***opium poppy*** pavot *m* (somnifère)

opopanax [əˈpɒpənæks] *n Bot & Pharm* opopanax *m*

Oporto [əˈpɔːtəʊ] *n* Porto

opossum [əˈpɒsəm] (*pl* **inv** *or* **opossums**) *n Zool* opossum *m*

►► ***opossum shrimp*** mysidacé *m*

opp (*written abbr* **opposite**) en face

opponent [əˈpəʊnənt] **1** *n* (**a**) *(gen)* adversaire *mf*; *(rival)* rival(e) *m,f*; *(competitor)* concurrent(e) *m,f*; *(in debate)* adversaire *mf*; **political opponent** *(democratic)* adversaire *mf* politique; *(of regime)* opposant(e) *m,f* politique; **she has always been an opponent of blood sports** elle a toujours été contre les sports sanguinaires; **opponents of the new marina held a rally** les opposants à la construction de la nouvelle marina ont organisé un meeting

(**b**) *Anat* antagoniste *m*

2 *adj Anat (muscle)* antagoniste

opportune [ˈɒpətjuːn] *adj* (**a**) *(coming at the right time)* opportun; **a very opportune remark** une remarque tout à fait opportune

(**b**) *(suitable for a particular purpose)* propice; **the opportune moment** le moment opportun *ou* propice; **this seems an opportune moment to break for coffee** le moment semble propice pour faire une pause-café

opportunely [ˈɒpətjuːnlɪ] *adv* opportunément, au moment opportun

opportuneness [ˈɒpətjuːnnɪs] *n* opportunité *f*

opportunism [ˌɒpəˈtjuːnɪzəm] *n* opportunisme *m*

opportunist [ˌɒpəˈtjuːnɪst] **1** *n* opportuniste *mf*

2 *adj* opportuniste

opportunistic [ˌɒpətjuːˈnɪstɪk] *adj* opportuniste

►► *Med* ***opportunistic infection*** infection *f* opportuniste

opportunity [ˌɒpəˈtjuːnətɪ] (*pl* **opportunities**) *n* (**a**) *(chance)* occasion *f*; **to have an opportunity to do** *or* **of doing sth** avoir l'occasion de faire qch; **we don't have much opportunity of practising hang-gliding** nous avons rarement l'occasion de faire du deltaplane; **if ever you get the opportunity** si jamais vous en avez l'occasion; **to give sb an opportunity of doing sth** *or* **the opportunity to do sth** donner à qn l'occasion de faire qch; **should the opportunity arise** si l'occasion se présente; **I took every opportunity of travelling** je n'ai manqué aucune occasion de *ou* j'ai saisi toutes les occasions de voyager; **I'd like to take this opportunity to thank everyone** j'aimerais profiter de cette occasion pour remercier tout le monde; **you missed a golden opportunity** vous avez manqué *ou* laissé passer une occasion en or; **I'll leave at the first** *or* **earliest opportunity** je partirai à la première occasion *ou* dès que l'occasion se présentera; **at every opportunity** à la moindre occasion; **opportunity knocks!** voilà ta chance!

(**b**) *(prospect)* perspective *f*; **the opportunities for advancement are excellent** les perspectives d'avancement sont excellentes; **job opportunities** perspectives *fpl* d'emploi

(**c**) *Mktg* opportunité *f*; **opportunities and threats** opportunités *fpl* et menaces *fpl*; **opportunity to hear** occasion *f* d'entendre; **opportunity to see** occasion *f* de voir; **opportunity and threat analysis** analyse *f* des opportunités et des menaces

►► *Econ* ***opportunity cost*** coût *m* d'opportunité *ou* de renoncement

opposable [əˈpəʊzəbəl] *adj* opposable

oppose [əˈpəʊz] *vt* (**a**) *(decision, plan, bill etc)* s'opposer à, être hostile à; *(verbally)* parler contre; **the family opposed their marriage** la famille s'opposa à leur mariage; **the construction of the power station was opposed by local people** la construction de la centrale s'est heurtée à l'hostilité de la population locale; **40 percent of voters are strongly opposed to the plan** 40 pour cent des votants sont farouchement opposés au projet

(**b**) *(in contest, fight)* s'opposer à; *(combat)* combattre

(**c**) *(contrast)* opposer; **the social sciences are often opposed to pure science** on oppose souvent les sciences humaines aux sciences pures

opposed [əˈpəʊzd] **1** *adj* opposé, hostile; **to be opposed to sth** être opposé *ou* hostile à qch; **she is very much opposed to the idea** c'est une idée à laquelle elle est totalement opposée; **his**

views are diametrically opposed to mine il a des idées radicalement opposées aux miennes

2 as opposed to *prep* par opposition à, plutôt que; **we will propose more science as opposed to arts courses** nous proposons de renforcer l'enseignement des sciences plutôt que celui des matières littéraires

opposing [ə'pəʊzɪŋ] *adj* (**a**) *(army, team)* adverse; *(factions)* qui s'opposent; *(party, minority)* d'opposition; **they're on opposing sides** ils sont adversaires, ils ne sont pas du même côté (**b**) *(contrasting → views)* opposé, qui s'oppose

opposite ['ɒpəzɪt] **1** *adj* (**a**) *(facing)* d'en face, opposé; **the opposite side of the road** l'autre côté de la rue; **see illustration on opposite page** *(in book, magazine)* voir illustration ci-contre

(**b**) *(opposing → direction, position)* inverse, opposé; *(rival → team)* adverse; **the letter-box is at the opposite end of the street** la boîte à lettres se trouve à l'autre bout de la rue; **in the opposite direction** en sens inverse, dans le sens opposé; **they went in opposite directions** ils ont pris des directions opposées

(**c**) *(conflicting → attitude, character, opinion)* contraire, opposé; **I take the opposite view** je suis de l'avis contraire; **his words had just the opposite effect** ses paroles eurent exactement l'effet contraire

(**d**) *Bot* opposé

(**e**) *Math* opposé

2 *adv* en face; **the houses opposite** les maisons d'en face; **they live just opposite** ils habitent juste en face; **the lady opposite** la dame qui habite en face

3 *prep* (**a**) *(across from)* en face de; **he lives opposite us** il habite en face de chez nous; **our houses are opposite each other** nos maisons se font face *ou* sont en face l'une de l'autre; **they sat opposite each other** ils étaient assis l'un en face de l'autre; **we have a park opposite our house** nous avons un parc en face de chez nous; **the church is right opposite the school** l'église se trouve juste en face de l'école; **put a tick opposite the correct answer** mettre une croix en face de la bonne réponse, cocher la bonne réponse

(**b**) *Cin & Theat* **to play opposite sb** donner la réplique à qn; **she played opposite Richard Burton in many films** elle fut la partenaire de Richard Burton dans de nombreux films

(**c**) *Naut* en face de, à la hauteur de; **the ship was lying opposite Tobruk** le navire se trouvait à la hauteur de Tobrouk

4 *n* opposé *m*, contraire *m*; **I understood quite the opposite** j'ai compris exactement le contraire; **she always does the opposite of what she's told** elle fait toujours le contraire de ce qu'on lui dit de faire; **Jill is the complete opposite of her sister** Jill est tout à fait l'opposé de sa sœur; **what's the opposite of "optimistic"?** quel est le contraire de "optimistic"?

►► ***opposite number*** homologue *mf*; ***opposite sex*** sexe *m* opposé; **a person** *or* **member of the opposite sex** une personne du sexe opposé

opposition [,ɒpə'zɪʃən] **1** *n* (**a**) *(physical)* opposition *f*, résistance *f*; *(moral)* opposition *f*; **the army met with fierce opposition** l'armée se heurta à une vive résistance; **the besieged city put up little opposition** la ville assiégée n'oppose guère de [illegible] opposition avec; **the plans met with some opposition** les projets suscitèrent une certaine opposition *ou* hostilité

(**b**) *Pol* **the Opposition** l'opposition *f*; **Labour spent the 1980s in Opposition** les travaillistes furent dans l'opposition pendant toutes les années 80; **the Opposition was** *or* **were unable to decide** l'opposition fut incapable de prendre une décision; **the Opposition benches** les bancs *mpl* de l'opposition

(**c**) *(rivals → in sport)* adversaires *mpl*; *Com* concurrents *mpl*, concurrence *f*; **don't underestimate the opposition** *(in sport)* ne sous-estimez pas vos adversaires; *(in commerce, business)* ne sous-estimez pas vos concurrents *ou* la concurrence

(**d**) *(contrast)* (mise *f* en) opposition *f*

2 *comp Pol (committee, spokesperson etc)* de l'opposition

oppress [ə'pres] *vt* (**a**) *(tyrannize)* opprimer (**b**) *Literary (torment → of anxiety, atmosphere)* accabler, oppresser

oppressed [ə'prest] **1** *adj (people)* opprimé

2 *npl* **the oppressed** les opprimés *mpl*

oppression [ə'preʃən] *n* (**a**) *(persecution)* oppression *f*; **the oppression of women** l'oppression *f* des femmes

(**b**) *(sadness)* angoisse *f*, malaise *m*

oppressive [ə'presɪv] *adj* (**a**) *Pol (regime, government)* oppressif; *(tax)* accablant (**b**) *(hard to bear → debt, situation)* accablant (**c**) *(weather, atmosphere)* lourd; **the heat was oppressive** il faisait une chaleur accablante *ou* étouffante

oppressively [ə'presɪvlɪ] *adv* d'une manière oppressante *ou* accablante; **it was oppressively hot** il faisait une chaleur étouffante *ou* accablante

oppressiveness [ə'presɪvnɪs] *n* (**a**) *(of regime, government)* caractère *m* oppressif (**b**) *(of debt, situation)* caractère *m* accablant (**c**) *(of weather, atmosphere)* lourdeur *f*; **the oppressiveness of the heat** la chaleur accablante *ou* étouffante

oppressor [ə'presə(r)] *n* oppresseur *m*

opprobrious [ə'prəʊbrɪəs] *adj Formal* (**a**) *(scornful)* méprisant (**b**) *(shameful)* honteux, scandaleux

opprobrium [ə'prəʊbrɪəm] *n Formal* opprobre *m*

oppugn [ə'pju:n] *vt Formal* mettre en doute

opt [ɒpt] *vi* **to opt for sth** opter pour qch, choisir qch; **she opted to study maths** elle a choisi d'étudier les maths

►**opt in** *vi (join)* choisir de participer

►**opt into** *vt insep (join)* **to opt into an association/the EU** entrer dans une association/l'Union européenne

►**opt out** *vi* (**a**) *(gen)* se désengager, retirer sa participation; **to opt out of society** rejeter la société; **I'm opting out!** ne comptez plus sur moi!, je me retire de la partie!; **many opted out of joining the union** beaucoup ont choisi de ne pas adhérer au syndicat; **you can't just opt out of paying bills** il faudra bien que vous payiez vos factures un jour ou l'autre (**b**) *Pol (school, hospital)* = choisir l'autonomie vis-à-vis des pouvoirs publics

optative ['ɒptətɪv] **1** *n* optatif *m*

2 *adj* optatif

Optic® ['ɒptɪk] *n Br* mesure *f* transparente *(utilisée dans les bars)*

optic ['ɒptɪk] *adj* optique

►► *Anat* ***optic nerve*** nerf *m* optique

optical ['ɒptɪkəl] *adj (lens)* optique; *(instrument)* optique

►► ***optical activity*** activité *f* optique; ***optical art*** art *m* optique; ***optical axis*** axe *m* optique; ***optical brightener*** azurant *m*; *Comput* ***optical character reader*** lecteur *m* optique de caractères; *Comput* ***optical character recognition*** reconnaissance *f* optique de caractères; ***optical centre*** centre *m* optique; *Comput* ***optical disk*** disque *m* optique; *Comput* ***optical drive*** lecteur *m* optique; ***optical fibre*** fibre *f* optique; ***optical fibre cable*** câble *m* à fibre optique; ***optical fibre technology*** fibre *f* optique; ***optical glass*** verre *m* optique; ***optical illusion*** illusion *f* ou effet *m* d'optique; *Comput* ***optical mouse*** souris *f* optique; *Comput* ***optical resolution*** résolution *f* optique; *Comput* [illegible] optique; ***optical scanning device*** lecteur *m* optique

optically ['ɒptɪkəlɪ] *adv* optiquement

optician [ɒp'tɪʃən] *n* opticien(enne) *m,f*; **at the optician's** chez l'opticien

optics ['ɒptɪks] *n (UNCOUNT)* optique *f*

optimal ['ɒptɪməl] *adj* optimal, optimum

►► *Mktg* ***optimal price*** prix *m* optimum; *Mktg* ***optimal psychological price*** prix *m* psychologique optimum; *Fin* ***optimal resource allocation*** répartition *f* optimale des ressources

optimality [,ɒptɪ'mælɪtɪ] *n* optimalité *f*; **principle of optimality** principe *m* d'optimalité

optimally ['ɒptɪməlɪ] *adv* de façon optimale

optimism ['ɒptɪmɪzəm] *n* optimisme *m*

optimist ['ɒptɪmɪst] *n* optimiste *mf*

optimistic [,ɒptɪ'mɪstɪk] *adj (person, outlook)* optimiste; *(period)* d'optimisme; **things are looking quite optimistic** les choses se présentent plutôt bien

optimistically [,ɒptɪ'mɪstɪklɪ] *adv* avec optimisme, d'une manière optimiste; **they optimistically predicted record profits** ils se sont montrés optimistes et ont prédit des bénéfices record

optimization [,ɒptɪmaɪ'zeɪʃən] *n* optimisation *f*, optimalisation *f*

optimize, -ise ['ɒptɪmaɪz] *vt* optimiser, optimaliser

optimizer ['ɒptɪmaɪzə(r)] *n Comput* optimiseur *m*

optimum ['ɒptɪməm] *(pl* **optimums** *or* **optima** [-mə]) **1** *n* optimum *m*

2 *adj* optimum, optimal

►► ***optimum employment of resources*** emploi *m* optimum des ressources

option ['ɒpʃən] *n* (**a**) *(alternative)* choix *m*; **he has no option** il n'a pas le choix; **I have no option but to refuse** je ne peux faire autrement que de refuser; **we have the option of staying here** nous avons la possibilité de rester ici; **they were given the option of adopting a child** on leur a proposé d'adopter un enfant; **you leave me no option** vous ne me laissez pas le choix; **he didn't give me much option** il ne m'a pas vraiment donné le choix; **she was given the option of bail** elle a pu être libérée sous caution

(**b**) *(possible choice)* option *f*, possibilité *f*; *(accessory)* option *f*; *Sch & Univ* (matière *f* à) option *f*; **to keep** *or* **leave one's options open** ne pas prendre de décision, ne pas s'engager; **she has to choose between three foreign language options** elle doit choisir une option parmi trois langues étrangères; **economics is an option in the third year** en troisième année, l'économie politique est une option; **power steering is an option** la direction assistée est en option

(**c**) *Com* option *f*; *St Exch* option *f*, (marché *m* à) prime *f*; *St Exch* **to take up an option** lever une option; **to take an option on sth** prendre une option sur qch; **the agency allowed her to take out an option on the house until Monday** l'agence lui a laissé une option sur la maison jusqu'à lundi; **to declare an option** répondre à une option; **option on shares** option *f* sur actions; **option to double** option *f* du double; **Air France have an option to buy 15 planes** Air France a une option d'achat sur 15 appareils

(**d**) *Comput* option *f*

►► *Comput* ***option box*** case *f* d'option; *Comput* ***option button*** case *f* d'option; ***option date*** jour *m* d'option; *St Exch* ***option day*** (jour *m* de la) réponse *f* des primes, ***option deal*** opération *f* à prime; ***options desk*** desk *m* d'options; *Comput* ***option key*** touche *f* Option; ***options market*** marché *m* à options *ou* à primes; *Comput* ***options menu*** menu *f* des options; ***option money*** (montant *m* de la) prime *f*; *St Exch* ***option price*** prix *m* de l'option; *St Exch* ***option spread*** écart *m* de prime; *St Exch* ***options trading*** négociations *fpl* à prime, opérations *fpl* à option

optional ['ɒpʃənəl] *adj* facultatif; *Sch & Univ (subject)* facultatif, optionnel; **evening dress is optional** la tenue de soirée n'est pas de rigueur; **the tinted lenses are optional** les verres teintés sont en option; **German is an optional subject** l'allemand est une matière optionnelle; **linguistics is optional** la linguistique est facultative

►► ***optional extra*** option *f*; **the radio is an optional extra** la radio est en option *ou* en supplément

optional-feature pricing *n Mktg* fixation *f* du prix en fonction des options

optionally ['ɒpʃənəlɪ] *adv* facultativement

optionee ['ɒpʃəni:] *n St Exch* bénéficiaire *mf* d'options

optoelectronics [,ɒptəʊɪlek'trɒnɪks] *n (UNCOUNT)* optoélectronique *f*

optomagnetic [,ɒptəmæg'netɪk] *adj* magnéto-optique

optometer [ɒp'tɒmɪtə(r)] *n* optomètre *m*

optometrist [ɒp'tɒmətrɪst] *n* optométriste *mf*, réfractionniste *mf*

optometry [ɒp'tɒmətrɪ] *n* optométrie *f*

optophone ['ɒptəfəʊn] *n* optophone *m*

opt-out 1 *adj (clause, provisions)* de désengagement

2 *n* (**a**) *(gen)* désengagement *m* (**b**) *Pol (of* *school, hospital)* = décision de choisir l'autonomie vis-à-vis des pouvoirs publics; **Britain's opt-out from the Social Chapter** la décision de la Grande-Bretagne de ne pas souscrire au chapitre social européen

opulence ['ɒpjʊləns] *n* opulence *f*

opulent ['ɒpjʊlənt] *adj (lifestyle, figure)* opulent; *(abundant)* abondant, luxuriant; *(house, clothes)* somptueux

opulently ['ɒpjʊləntlɪ] *adv (dress, decorate, dine)* avec opulence; *(live)* dans l'opulence

opuntia [əʊ'pʌntɪə] *n* opuntia *m*, oponce *m*

opus ['əʊpəs] *(pl* **opuses** *or Formal* **opera** ['ɒpərə]) *n* opus *m*

OR[1] [,əʊ'ɑ:(r)] *n Am Fam (abbr* **operating room**) salle *f* d'op

OR[2] *(written abbr* **Oregon**) Oregon

or [ɔ:(r)] **1** *conj* (**a**) *(in positive statements)* ou; *(in negative statements)* ni; **in New York or (in) London** à New York ou à Londres; **I can go today or tomorrow** je peux y aller aujourd'hui ou demain; **have you got any brothers or sisters?** avez-vous des frères et sœurs?; **he never laughs or smiles** il ne rit ni ne sourit jamais; **in a day or two** dans un ou deux jours; **I go two or three times a week** j'y vais deux ou trois fois par semaine; **Norma Jean Baker, or Marilyn Monroe as she became known** Norma Jean Baker ou Marilyn Monroe, puisque c'est le nom sous lequel elle est devenue célèbre; **or so I thought** du moins c'est ce que je pensais; **did she do it or not?** est-ce qu'elle l'a fait ou pas?; **...or not, as the case may be** ...ou non, peut-être

(**b**) *(otherwise → in negative statements)* ou; *(→ in positive statements)* sinon; **don't hit it too hard or it'll break** ne tape pas trop fort dessus ou ça va casser; **she must have some talent or they wouldn't have chosen her** elle doit avoir un certain talent sinon ils ne l'auraient pas choisie

2 or else 1 *conj* (**a**) *(otherwise)* sinon; **I'd better rush, or else I'll be late** je ferais mieux de me dépêcher, sinon je serai en retard (**b**) *(offering an alternative)* ou bien; **Monday, or else Tuesday** lundi, ou bien mardi **2** *adv Fam* **give us the money, or else!** donne-nous l'argent, sinon!

3 or no *conj* ou pas; **I'm taking a holiday, work or no work** travail ou pas, je prends des vacances

4 or other *adv* **we stayed at San something or other** on s'est arrêté à San quelque chose; **somehow or other we made it home** on a fini par réussir à rentrer, Dieu sait comment; **somebody or other said that...** quelqu'un, je ne sais plus qui, a dit que...; **one or other of us will have to go** il faudra bien que l'un de nous s'en aille; **some actress or other** une actrice (quelconque)

5 or so *adv* environ; **ten minutes or so** environ dix minutes; **50 kilos or so** 50 kilos environ, dans les 50 kilos; **ten dollars or so** dix dollars environ, à peu près dix dollars

6 or something *adv Fam* ou quelque chose comme ça; **she's a lawyer or something** elle est avocate ou quelque chose comme ça; **are you deaf or something?** t'es sourd ou quoi?

7 or what *adv Fam* ou quoi; **are you stupid or what?** t'es bête ou quoi?

oracle ['ɒrəkəl] *n* oracle *m*; **the Delphic oracle** l'oracle de Delphes; **to consult the oracle** consulter les oracles; *Br Fam* **to work the oracle** réaliser un exploit ▫

oracular [ɒ'rækjʊlə(r)] *adj* (**a**) *(relating to an oracle)* oraculaire (**b**) *Fig (wise)* prophétique; *(mysterious)* sibyllin

oracularly [ɒ'rækjʊləlɪ] *adv* en (style d')oracle

oracy ['ɔ:rəsɪ] *n Formal* facultés *fpl* orales

oral ['ɔ:rəl] **1** *adj* (**a**) *(spoken)* oral

(**b**) *Anat (of mouth)* buccal, oral; *Pharm (medicine)* à prendre par voie orale; *Psy* **the oral stage** le stade oral

(**c**) *Ling (in phonetics)* oral

2 *n* (examen *m*) oral *m*

►► ***oral contraceptive*** contraceptif *m* oral; ***oral exam*** (examen *m*) oral *m*; ***oral literature*** littérature *f* orale; *Med* ***oral rehydration therapy*** = réhydratation par ingestion d'une solution d'eau, de glucose et de sel; ***oral sex*** rapports *mpl* bucco-génitaux; *(fellatio)* fellation *f*; *(cunnilingus)* cunnilingus *m*; ***oral surgeon*** chirurgien-dentiste *m*; ***oral tradition*** tradition *f* orale

orality [ɒ'rælɪtɪ] *n* oralité *f*

orally ['ɔ:rəlɪ] *adj* (**a**) *(verbally)* oralement, verbalement, de vive voix (**b**) *Sch* oralement; *Med* par voie orale; **to be taken orally** *(on packaging)* par voie orale; **not to be taken orally** *(on packaging)* ne pas avaler

Orange ['ɒrɪndʒ] **1** *n* (**a**) *Geog* **the Orange (River)** l'Orange *m* (**b**) *Hist* **the Prince of Orange** le prince d'Orange; **William of Orange** Guillaume d'Orange

2 *adj* (**a**) *Hist (relating to the House of Orange)* de la maison d'Orange; *(supporting the House of Orange)* orangiste (**b**) *(in Ireland)* orangiste *(protestant)*

►► ***Orange Lodge*** association *f* d'orangistes; ***Orange march*** défilé *m* des orangistes; ***Orange Order*** Ordre *m* des orangistes; ***Orange Walk*** = défilé *m* des orangistes, le 12 juillet

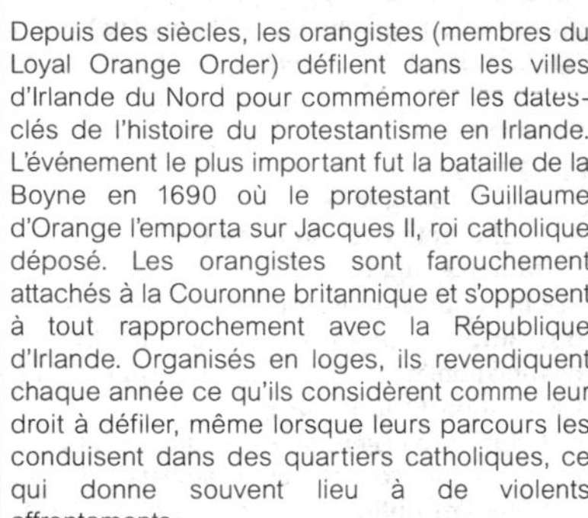

ORANGE MARCHES

Depuis des siècles, les orangistes (membres du Loyal Orange Order) défilent dans les villes d'Irlande du Nord pour commémorer les dates-clés de l'histoire du protestantisme en Irlande. L'événement le plus important fut la bataille de la Boyne en 1690 où le protestant Guillaume d'Orange l'emporta sur Jacques II, roi catholique déposé. Les orangistes sont farouchement attachés à la Couronne britannique et s'opposent à tout rapprochement avec la République d'Irlande. Organisés en loges, ils revendiquent chaque année ce qu'ils considèrent comme leur droit à défiler, même lorsque leurs parcours les conduisent dans des quartiers catholiques, ce qui donne souvent lieu à de violents affrontements.

orange ['ɒrɪndʒ] **1** *n* (**a**) *(fruit)* orange *f* (**b**) *(drink)* boisson *f* à l'orange; **vodka and orange** vodka-orange *f* (**c**) *(colour)* orange *m*

2 *adj* (**a**) *(colour)* orange *(inv)*, orangé (**b**) *(taste)* d'orange; *(liqueur, sauce, drink)* à l'orange

►► ***orange blossom*** fleur *f ou* fleurs *fpl* d'oranger; ***Orange Bowl*** = match de football américain opposant deux équipes universitaires, qui se tient chaque année à Miami; ***Orange Free State*** l'État *m* libre d'Orange; **in Orange Free State** dans l'État libre d'Orange; ***orange grove*** orangeraie *f*; ***orange juice*** jus *m* d'orange; ***orange marmalade*** marmelade *f* d'orange, confiture *f* d'orange *ou* d'oranges; ***orange peel*** écorce *f ou* peau *f* d'orange; *Fig (cellulite)* peau *f* d'orange; ***orange pekoe*** pekoe *m* orange; ***the Orange prize*** = prix accordé chaque année au meilleur roman d'expression anglaise écrit par une femme; ***orange squash*** boisson *f* à l'orange; ***orange stick*** bâtonnet *m* (de) manucure; ***orange tip*** *(butterfly)* aurore *f*; ***orange tree*** oranger *m*

orangeade [,ɒrɪndʒ'eɪd] *n* *(still)* orangeade *f*; *(fizzy)* soda *m* à l'orange

orange-flower water *n* eau *f* de fleur d'oranger

Orangeism ['ɒrɪndʒɪzəm] *n Pol* orangisme *m*

Orangeman ['ɒrɪndʒmən] *(pl* **Orangemen** [-mən]) *n* (**a**) *Br Hist* Orangiste *m (partisan de la maison d'Orange)* (**b**) *(in Ireland)* Orangiste *m (Protestant)*

►► ***Orangeman's Day*** fête annuelle des orangistes *(le 12 juillet)*

orange-peel skin *n* peau *f* d'orange

orangery ['ɒrɪndʒərɪ] *(pl* **orangeries**) *n* orangerie *f*

Orangewoman ['ɒrɪndʒ,wʊmən] *(pl* **Orangewomen** [-,wɪmɪn]) *n* orangiste *f*

orangewood ['ɒrɪndʒwʊd] *n* (bois *m* d') oranger *m*

orangey ['ɒrɪndʒɪ] *adj* (**a**) *(taste)* qui a un goût d'orange; *(perfume)* qui sent l'orange (**b**) *(colour)* orangé

orang-outang [ɒ,ræŋu:'tæŋ], **orang-utan** [ɒ,ræŋu:'tæn] *n* orang-outan(g) *m*

orangy = **orangey**

orate [ɒ'reɪt] *vi Formal (make speech)* prononcer un discours; *(pompously)* pérorer, discourir

oration [ɒ'reɪʃən] *n* (long) discours *m*, allocution *f*; **funeral oration** oraison *f* funèbre

orator ['ɒrətə(r)] *n* orateur(trice) *m,f*

oratorial [,ɒrə'tɔ:rɪəl], **oratorical** [,ɒrə'tɒrɪkəl] *adj Formal* oratoire

oratorically [,ɒrə'tɒrɪkəlɪ] *adv Formal* oratoirement, dans un style d'oration

oratorio [,ɒrə'tɔ:rɪəʊ] *(pl* **oratorios**) *n Mus* oratorio *m*

oratory ['ɒrətrɪ] *n* (**a**) *(eloquence)* art *m* oratoire, éloquence *f*; **a superb piece of oratory** un superbe morceau de rhétorique (**b**) *Rel* oratoire *m*

orb [ɔ:b] *n* (**a**) *(sphere)* globe *m* (**b**) *Astron & Literary* orbe *m*

orbed [ɔ:bd] *adj Literary* rond, sphérique

orbicular [ɔ:'bɪkjʊlə(r)] *adj* orbiculaire

orbiculate [ɔ:'bɪkjʊlət] *adj* orbiculaire

orbit ['ɔ:bɪt] **1** *n* (**a**) *Astron* orbite *f*; **to enter** *or* **to go into orbit** se mettre *ou* se placer en orbite; *Fam Fig* **to go into orbit** *(get angry)* piquer une crise; **to put** *or* **to send a satellite into orbit** mettre un satellite sur *ou* en orbite; **in orbit** en orbite

(**b**) *(domain)* orbite *f*; **the countries within Washington's orbit** les pays qui se situent dans la sphère d'influence de Washington; **that's not within the orbit of my responsibility** cela n'est pas de mon ressort, cela ne relève pas de ma responsabilité

(**c**) *Anat & Phys (of eye, electron)* orbite *f*

2 *vt (of planet, comet)* graviter *ou* tourner autour de; **the first man to orbit the Earth** le premier homme à être placé *ou* mis en orbite autour de la Terre

3 *vi* décrire une orbite

orbital ['ɔ:bɪtəl] **1** *adj* (**a**) *Astron* orbital (**b**) *Anat (cavity)* orbitaire

2 *n Br (road)* périphérique *m*

►► *Br* ***orbital motorway*** (autoroute *f*) périphérique *m*; *Br* ***orbital road*** périphérique *m*; ***orbital sander*** ponceuse *f* à disque, ponceuse *f* orbitale; ***orbital velocity*** velocité *f* orbitale; *Tech* ***orbital welding*** soudure *f* orbitale

orbiter ['ɔ:bɪtə(r)] *n Astron* orbiteur *m*

orbiting ['ɔ:bɪtɪŋ] *adj (satellite, spacecraft)* en *ou* sur orbite

orc [ɔ:k] *n Zool* orque *f*, épaulard *m*

Orcadian [ɔ:'keɪdɪən] **1** *n (inhabitant)* habitant(e) *m,f* des Orcades; *(native)* natif(ive) *m,f* des Orcades

2 *adj* des Orcades

orchard ['ɔ:tʃəd] *n* verger *m*

orchestra ['ɔ:kɪstrə] *n* (**a**) *(band)* orchestre *m* (**b**) *(in theatre, cinema)* fauteuils *mpl* d'orchestre, parterre *m*

►► ***orchestra pit*** fosse *f* d'orchestre; *Am* ***orchestra stalls*** *(in theatre, cinema)* fauteuils *mpl* d'orchestre, parterre *m*

orchestral [ɔ:'kestrəl] *adj* d'orchestre, orchestral

►► ***orchestral music*** musique *f* orchestrale

orchestrate ['ɔ:kɪstreɪt] *vt Mus & Fig* orchestrer; **a superbly orchestrated advertising campaign** une campagne publicitaire remarquablement orchestrée

orchestrater = **orchestrator**

orchestration [,ɔ:ke'streɪʃən] *n Mus & Fig* orchestration *f*

orchestrator ['ɔ:kɪstreɪtə(r)] *n Mus* orchestrateur(trice) *m,f*; *Fig* **he was the orchestrator of the campaign** c'est lui qui a orchestré la campagne

orchid ['ɔ:kɪd] *n* orchidée *f*

orchidaceous [,ɔ:kɪ'deɪʃəs] *adj* (**a**) *Bot* relatif aux orchidées (**b**) *Fam Old-fashioned (style)* fleuri ▫; *(woman)* d'une grande beauté ▫

orchidectomy [,ɔ:kɪ'dektəmɪ] *n Med* orchidectomie *f*

orchis ['ɔ:kɪs] *n* orchis *m*

orchitis [ɔ:'kaɪtɪs] *n* orchite *f*

ordain [ɔ:'deɪn] *vt* (**a**) *Rel* ordonner; **to be ordained** être ordonné, recevoir les ordres; **to be ordained priest** être ordonné prêtre

(**b**) *(order)* ordonner, décréter; *(decide)* dicter, décider; **the judge ordained that the prisoner should be released** le juge ordonna que le prisonnier soit relâché; **fate ordained that they should meet** le destin a voulu qu'ils se rencontrent

(**c**) *(declare)* décréter, déclarer; **it is ordained in the Bible** c'est la Bible qui le dit

ordainment [ɔː'deɪnmənt] *n Rel* ordination *f*

ordeal [ɔː'diːl] *n* (**a**) *(difficult experience)* épreuve *f*, calvaire *m*; **to go through an ordeal** subir une épreuve; **she has been through some terrible ordeals** elle a traversé des moments très difficiles; **it was quite an ordeal for him** ce fut une épreuve assez pénible pour lui; **it is an ordeal for me to make a speech** je suis au supplice quand je dois faire un discours; **I always find family reunions an ordeal** j'ai toujours considéré les réunions de famille comme un (véritable) calvaire

(**b**) *Hist* ordalie *f*, épreuve *f* judiciaire; **ordeal by fire** épreuve *f* du feu

ORDER ['ɔːdə(r)]

ordre	▸ **1 (a) – (c), (g), (h), (j) – (m)**
instruction	▸ **1 (c)**
commande	▸ **1 (d)**
mandat	▸ **1 (e)**
ordonnance	▸ **1 (f)**
état	▸ **1 (i)**
classe	▸ **1 (j)**
espèce	▸ **1 (j)**
ordonner	▸ **2 (a)**
commander	▸ **2 (b); 3**
organiser	▸ **2 (c)**
classer	▸ **2 (d)**
afin que	▸ **6**
afin de	▸ **7**

1 *n* (**a**) *(sequence, arrangement)* ordre *m*; **in alphabetical/chronological order** par ordre alphabétique/chronologique; **in ascending order of importance** par ordre croissant d'importance; **can you put the figures in the right order?** pouvez-vous classer les chiffres dans le bon ordre?; **let's do things in order** faisons les choses en ordre; **what was the order of events?** dans quel ordre les événements se sont-ils déroulés?; **they have two boys and a girl, in that order** ils ont deux garçons et une fille, dans cet ordre; *Theat* **in order of appearance** par ordre d'entrée en scène; *Cin & TV* par ordre d'apparition à l'écran; **in order of age** par rang d'âge; **we were called to the platform, in order of precedence** on était appelés à la tribune par ordre de préséance; **battle order** ordre *m* de bataille

(**b**) *(organization, tidiness)* ordre *m*; **to put one's affairs/books in order** mettre de l'ordre dans ses affaires/livres, ranger ses affaires/livres; **the magazines are all out of order** les magazines sont tous dérangés; **to get one's ideas in order** mettre de l'ordre dans ses idées; **she needs to get some order into her life** elle a besoin de mettre un peu d'ordre dans sa vie; *Fig* **to set one's house in order** remettre de l'ordre dans ses affaires

(**c**) *(command)* ordre *m*; *(instruction)* instruction *f*; *Mil* ordre *m*, consigne *f*; **to give sb orders to do sth** ordonner à qn de faire qch; **to give the order to open fire** donner l'ordre d'ouvrir le feu; **the Queen gave the order for the prisoner to be executed** la reine ordonna que le prisonnier soit exécuté; **Harry loves giving orders** Harry adore donner des ordres; **we have orders to wait here** on a reçu l'ordre d'attendre ici; **our orders are to...** nous avons l'ordre de...; **I'm just following orders** je ne fais qu'exécuter les ordres; **and that's an order!** et c'est un ordre!; **I don't have to take orders from you** je n'ai pas d'ordres à recevoir de vous; **orders are orders** les ordres sont les ordres; **on my order, line up in twos** à mon commandement, mettez-vous en rangs par deux; **on doctor's orders** sur ordre du médecin; **to be under sb's orders** être sous les ordres de qn; **I am under orders to say nothing** j'ai reçu l'ordre de ne rien dire; **by order of the King** par ordre du roi, de par le roi; **until further orders** jusqu'à nouvel ordre; *Fin* **order to sell** ordre *m* de vente; *Fin* **order to pay** mandat *m ou* ordonnance *f* de paiement

(**d**) *Com (request for goods)* commande *f*; *(goods ordered)* marchandises *fpl* commandées; *Am (portion)* part *f*; **to place an order for sth** passer (une) commande de qch; **to place an order with sb, to give sb an order** passer une commande à qn, commander qch à qn; **another firm got the order** ils ont passé la commande auprès d'une autre compagnie; **the books are on order** les livres ont été commandés; **your order has now arrived** votre commande est arrivée; **to fill an order** exécuter une commande; **as per order** conformément à votre commande; **can I take your order?** *(in restaurant)* avez-vous choisi?; **have you given your order?** *(in restaurant)* est-ce que vous avez commandé?; *Am* **an order of French fries** une portion de frites

(**e**) *Fin* **(money) order** mandat *m*; **pay to the order of A. Jones** payez à l'ordre de A. Jones; **pay A. Jones or order** payer à A. Jones ou à son ordre; **by order and for account of A. Jones** d'ordre et pour compte de A. Jones; **cheque to order** chèque *m* à ordre

(**f**) *Law* ordonnance *f*, arrêté *m*; **he was served with an order for the seizure of his property** il a reçu une ordonnance pour la saisie de ses biens

(**g**) *(discipline, rule)* ordre *m*, discipline *f*; **to keep order** *(police)* maintenir l'ordre; *Sch* maintenir la discipline; **children need to be kept in order** les enfants ont besoin de discipline; **to restore order** rétablir l'ordre; *(in meeting)* ordre *m*; **to call sb to order** rappeler qn à l'ordre; **to be ruled out of order** être en infraction avec le règlement; **order!** de l'ordre!; **he's out of order** ce qu'il a dit/fait était déplacé

(**h**) *(system)* ordre *m* établi; **the old order** l'ordre ancien; **in the order of things** dans l'ordre des choses; *Pol* **order of the day** ordre *m* du jour; **to be the order of the day** *(common)* être à l'ordre du jour; *(fashionable)* être au goût du jour

(**i**) *(functioning state)* **in working order** en état de marche *ou* de fonctionnement; **in good/perfect order** en bon/parfait état

(**j**) *(class)* classe *f*, ordre *m*; *(rank)* ordre *m*; *(kind)* espèce *f*, genre *m*; **the lower orders** les ordres inférieurs; **research work of the highest order** un travail de recherche de tout premier ordre; *Br* **a crook of the first order** un escroc de grande envergure; **questions of a different order** des questions d'un autre ordre; **order of magnitude** ordre de grandeur; **a disaster/a project/an investment of this order (of magnitude)** un désastre/un projet/des investissements de cette envergure

(**k**) *(decoration)* ordre *m*

(**l**) *Rel* ordre *m*; **the Order of St Benedict** l'ordre de saint Benoît

(**m**) *Archit, Bot & Zool* ordre *m*

2 *vt* (**a**) *(command)* ordonner; **to order sb to do sth** ordonner à qn de faire qch; **the Queen ordered that the prisoner (should) be executed** la reine donna l'ordre d'exécuter le prisonnier; **the doctor ordered him to rest for three weeks** le médecin lui a prescrit trois semaines de repos; **the government ordered an inquiry into the disaster** le gouvernement a ordonné l'ouverture d'une enquête sur la catastrophe; *Law* **he was ordered to pay costs** il a été condamné aux dépens; **the minister ordered the drug to be banned** le ministre a ordonné de faire retirer le médicament de la vente; **to order sb back/in/out** donner à qn l'ordre de reculer/d'entrer/de sortir; **we were ordered out of the room** on nous a ordonné de quitter la pièce; **she ordered the children to bed** elle a ordonné aux enfants d'aller se coucher; *Mil* **to order sb to do sth** donner l'ordre à qn de faire qch; **they were ordered (to return) home** on leur donna *ou* ils reçurent l'ordre de regagner leurs foyers; **the troops were ordered to the Mediterranean** les troupes ont reçu l'ordre de gagner la Méditerranée

(**b**) *Com (meal, goods)* commander; **he ordered himself a beer** il a commandé une bière

(**c**) *(organize → society)* organiser; *(→ ideas, thoughts)* mettre de l'ordre dans; *(→ affairs)* régler, mettre en ordre; **a peaceful, well-ordered existence** une existence paisible et bien réglée

(**d**) *Bot & Zool* classer

3 *vi* commander, passer une commande; **would you like to order now?** *(in restaurant)* voulez-vous commander maintenant?

4 by order of *prep* par ordre de; **by order of the Court** sur décision du tribunal

5 in order *adj* (**a**) *(valid)* en règle (**b**) *(acceptable)* approprié, admissible; **it is quite in order for you to leave** rien ne s'oppose à ce que vous partiez; **I think lunch is in order** je pense qu'il est temps de faire une pause pour le déjeuner; **an apology is in order** des excuses s'imposent

6 in order that *conj* afin que; **in order that no one goes home empty-handed** afin que nul ne rentre chez soi les mains vides

7 in order to *conj* afin de; **in order to simplify things** afin de simplifier les choses; **in order not to upset you** pour éviter de vous faire de la peine

8 in the order of, of the order of, *Am* **on the order of** *prep* de l'ordre de; **a sum** *Br* **in** *or* **of** *or Am* **on the order of £500** une somme de l'ordre de 500 livres

9 out of order *adj (machine, TV)* en panne; *(phone)* en dérangement; **out of order** *(sign)* hors service, en panne

10 to order *adv* sur commande; *Br* **she's one of these people who can cry to order** elle fait partie de ces gens qui arrivent à pleurer sur commande; **I can't do it to order** ça ne se commande pas; *also Fig* **to be made to order** être fait sur commande; **he had a suit made to order** il s'est fait faire un costume sur mesures

▸▸ ***the Order of the Bath*** l'ordre *m* du Bain; ***order book*** carnet *m* de commandes; **our order books are empty/full** nos carnets de commandes sont vides/pleins; *Mktg* ***order cycle*** cycle *m* de commande; ***order cycle time*** durée *f* du cycle de commande; ***order form*** bon *m* de commande; ***the Order of the Garter*** l'ordre *m* de la Jarretière; ***the Order of Merit*** l'ordre *m* du Mérite; ***order number*** numéro *m* de commande; *Pol* ***order paper*** (feuille *f* de l') ordre *m* du jour; ***the Order of the Thistle*** l'ordre *m* du Chardon

▸**order about, order around** *vt sep* commander; **he likes ordering people about** il adore régenter son monde; **I refuse to be ordered about!** je n'ai pas d'ordres à recevoir!

▸**order in** *vt sep* (**a**) *(supplies)* commander (**b**) *(troops)* faire intervenir

▸**order off** *vt sep Sport* expulser

order-driven *adj St Exch (market)* dirigé par les ordres

ordered ['ɔːdəd] *adj* ordonné; *(in good order)* en bon ordre; **an ordered life** une vie régulière *ou* réglée

orderer ['ɔːdərə(r)] *n* **France is the biggest orderer of these parts** la France est le principal acheteur de ces pièces détachées

orderliness ['ɔːdəlɪnɪs] *n* (**a**) *(of room, desk)* (bon) ordre *m* (**b**) *(of person, lifestyle, behaviour)* méticulosité *f* (**c**) *(of crowd, pupils)* discipline *f*, bonne conduite *f*

orderly ['ɔːdəlɪ] (*pl* **orderlies**) **1** *adj* (**a**) *(tidy → room)* ordonné, rangé; **a very orderly kitchen** une cuisine très bien rangée

(**b**) *(organized → person, mind, lifestyle)* ordonné, méthodique; **try to work in an orderly way** essayez de travailler méthodiquement; **an orderly retreat/withdrawal** une retraite/un repli ordonné(e)

(**c**) *(well-behaved)* ordonné, discipliné; **an orderly crowd** une foule disciplinée; **in case of fire, leave the building in an orderly fashion** en cas d'incendie, quitter les lieux sans précipitation

2 *n* (**a**) *Mil* officier *m* d'ordonnance

(**b**) *Med* aide-infirmier *m*

▸▸ *Br Mil* ***orderly officer*** officier *m* de permanence

order-to-remittance cycle *n Mktg* cycle *m* commande-livraison-facturation

ordinal ['ɔːdɪnəl] **1** *n* ordinal *m*

2 *adj* ordinal

▸▸ ***ordinal number*** nombre *m* ordinal

ordinance ['ɔːdɪnəns] *n Formal* ordonnance *f*, décret *m*

ordinand ['ɔːdɪnænd] *n Rel* ordinand *m*

ordinarily ['ɔːdənrəlɪ, *Am* ˌɔːrdən'erəlɪ] *adv* (**a**) *(in an ordinary way)* ordinairement, d'ordinaire; **a more than ordinarily gifted child** un enfant d'une intelligence supérieure à la normale; **the questions were more than ordinarily difficult**

les questions étaient plus difficiles que d'ordinaire *ou* qu'à l'accoutumée
(**b**) *(normally)* normalement, en temps normal; **isn't she due at 5 o'clock? – well, ordinarily, she would be** ne doit-elle pas être là *ou* arriver à 5 heures? – oui, normalement

ordinariness ['ɔːdənrɪnɪs] *n* caractère *m* ordinaire

ordinary ['ɔːdənrɪ] **1** *adj* (**a**) *(usual)* ordinaire, habituel; *(normal)* normal; **the ordinary run of things** le cours ordinaire *ou* normal des événements; **she remembered it as just an ordinary day** elle s'en souvenait comme d'un jour ordinaire;
(**b**) *(average)* ordinaire, moyen; *Fam* **Ewan was just an ordinary guy before he got involved in films** Ewan était un type comme les autres avant de faire du cinéma; **Miss Brodie was no ordinary teacher** Miss Brodie était un professeur peu banal *ou* qui sortait de l'ordinaire
(**c**) *(commonplace)* ordinaire; *Pej* quelconque; **they're very ordinary people** ce sont des gens très ordinaires; **it's a very ordinary-looking car** c'est une voiture qui n'a rien de spécial; **she's a very ordinary-looking girl** c'est une fille quelconque
2 *n* (**a**) *Rel* **the Ordinary of the mass** l'ordinaire *m* de la messe
(**b**) *Admin Br* **physician in ordinary to the king** médecin *m* (attitré) du roi
(**c**) *Her* pièce *f* honorable
3 out of the ordinary *adj* **as a pianist, she's really out of the ordinary** c'est vraiment une pianiste exceptionnelle *ou* hors du commun; **nothing out of the ordinary ever happens here** il ne se passe jamais rien de bien extraordinaire ici
►► ***ordinary activities*** *Com* activités *fpl* ordinaires; *Acct (balance sheet item)* opérations *fpl* courantes; *Fin* ***ordinary creditor*** créancier(ère) *m,f* ordinaire; *Br* ***ordinary degree*** ≃ licence *f* sans mention *ou* avec mention passable; *Scot Formerly Sch* ***Ordinary grade*** = premier diplôme de l'enseignement secondaire écossais; *Formerly Sch* ***Ordinary level*** *(in England, Wales, Northern Ireland)* = examen qui sanctionnait autrefois la fin des études au niveau de la seconde, ≃ BEPC *m*; ***Ordinary National Certificate*** = brevet de technicien en Grande-Bretagne; *Naut* ***Ordinary National Diploma*** = brevet de technicien en Grande-Bretagne; ***ordinary seaman*** matelot *m* breveté; *Br St Exch* ***ordinary share*** action *f* ordinaire; *Br St Exch* ***ordinary share capital*** capital *m* en actions ordinaires

ordinate ['ɔːdənət] *n* ordonnée *f*

ordination [,ɔːdɪ'neɪʃən] *n* ordination *f*

ordnance ['ɔːdnəns] *n* (**a**) *(supplies)* (service *m* de l') équipement *m* militaire; *Br* **Royal Army Ordnance Corps,** *Am* **Ordnance Service** Service *m* du Matériel
(**b**) *(artillery)* artillerie *f*; **piece of ordnance** bouche *f* à feu, pièce *f* d'artillerie
►► ***ordnance corps*** service *m* du matériel, ≃ train *m*; ***ordnance datum*** = niveau de la mer mesuré par l'Ordnance Survey et servant de référence aux altitudes indiquées sur les cartes; ***ordnance factory*** usine *f* d'artillerie; *Br* ***Ordnance Survey*** service *m* national de cartographie, ≃ IGN *m*; *Br* ***Ordnance Survey map*** carte *f* d'état-major

Ordovician [,ɔːdəʊ'vɪʃɪən] *adj Geol* ordovicien

ordure ['ɔːdjʊə(r)] *n Literary* excrément *m*

Ore *(written abbr* **Oregon**) Oregon *m*

ore [ɔː(r)] *n* minerai *m*; **copper ore** minerai de cuivre
►► ***ore deposit*** gisement *m* de minerai

Oreg *(written abbr* **Oregon**) Oregon *m*

oregano [*Br* ,ɒrɪ'gɑːnəʊ, *Am* ə'regənəʊ] *n Bot & Culin* origan *m*

Oregon ['ɒrɪgən] *n* l'Oregon *m*; **in Oregon** dans l'Oregon
►► *Am Hist* ***the Oregon Trail*** = itinéraire suivi par les colons américains dans leur marche vers le nord-ouest

Oreo ['ɔːrɪəʊ] *n Am* (**a**) **Oreo (cookie)**® = biscuit au chocolat fourré à la crème (**b**) *very Fam* = terme injurieux désignant un Noir qui fréquente les Blancs

Orestes [ɒ'restiːz] *pr n Myth* Oreste

orfe [ɔːf] (*pl* **inv**) *n Ich* ide *m*, mélanote *m*; **golden orfe** ide rouge, orfe *m*

orfray ['ɔːfreɪ] *n* orfroi *m*, parement *m* (de chasuble)

.org [ɔːg] *Comput* = abréviation désignant les organisations à but non lucratif dans les adresses électroniques

organ ['ɔːgən] *n* (**a**) *Mus* orgue *m*; *(large)* (grandes) orgues *fpl*
(**b**) *Anat* organe *m*; **the organs of speech** les organes phonatoires *ou* de la parole
(**c**) *Euph or Hum (penis)* membre *m*
(**d**) *Fig (means)* organe *m*, instrument *m*; *(mouthpiece)* organe *m*, porte-parole *m inv*; **the courts are the organs of justice** les tribunaux sont les organes *ou* les instruments de la justice; **the official organ of the Party** le porte-parole officiel du Parti
►► ***organ builder*** facteur *m* d'orgues; ***organ donor*** donneur *m* d'organes; ***organ grinder*** joueur(euse) *m,f* d'orgue de Barbarie; *Br Fam* **I want to speak to the organ grinder, not the monkey!** je veux parler au responsable, pas au sous-fifre!; ***organ loft*** tribune *f* d'orgue; ***organ pipe*** tuyau *m* d'orgue; ***organ screen*** jubé *m*; ***organ stop*** jeu *m* d'orgue; ***organ transplant*** transplantation *f* d'organe

organdie, organdy ['ɔːgəndɪ] (*pl* **organdies**) **1** *n* organdi *m*
2 *comp* d'organdi, en organdi

organelle [,ɔːgə'nel] *n Biol* organite *m*

organic [ɔː'gænɪk] *adj* (**a**) *Biol & Chem* organique
(**b**) *(natural* → *food, produce)* biologique
(**c**) *(structural)* organique; *(fundamental)* organique, fondamental; **an organic part** une partie intégrante; **an organic whole** un ensemble systématique, un tout intégré
►► ***organic architecture*** architecture *f* organique; ***organic change*** changement *m* organique; ***organic chemist*** organicien(enne) *m,f*; ***organic chemistry*** chimie *f* organique; ***organic compound*** composé *m* organique; ***organic disease*** maladie *f* organique; ***organic farm*** ferme *f* biologique; ***organic farming*** culture *f* biologique; ***organic fertilizer*** engrais *m* organique; ***organic life*** vie *f* organique

organically [ɔː'gænɪklɪ] *adv* (**a**) *Biol & Chem* organiquement (**b**) *(naturally* → *farm, garden)* avec des engrais organiques; **organically grown** cultivé sans engrais chimiques, biologique (**c**) *(structurally)* organiquement; **the two ideas are organically linked** les deux idées sont organiquement liées

organicism [ɔː'gænɪsɪzəm] *n* organicisme *m*

organicist [ɔː'gænɪsɪst] *n* (**a**) *Biol* organiciste *mf*
(**b**) *Med* organicien(enne) *m,f*

organigram [ɔː'gænɪgræm] *n* organigramme *m*

organism ['ɔːgənɪzəm] *n Biol* organisme *m*

organist ['ɔːgənɪst] *n* organiste *mf*

organization [,ɔːgənaɪ'zeɪʃən] *n* (**a**) *(organizing)* organisation *f*; **to have a flair for organization** avoir le sens de l'organisation; **we are unhappy with the organization of the company** l'organisation de la firme ne nous satisfait pas; *Ind* **organization and method** organisation *f* scientifique du travail, OST *f*
(**b**) *(association)* organisation *f*, association *f*; *(official body)* organisme *m*, organisation *f*; **a political organization** une organisation politique; **a charitable organization** une œuvre de bienfaisance
(**c**) *Admin (personnel)* cadres *mpl*
(**d**) *Ind (of labour)* syndicalisation *f*
►► ***Organization of American States*** Organisation *f* des États américains; ***organization chart*** organigramme *m*; ***organization man*** = employé ou cadre qui se dévoue entièrement à la société pour laquelle il travaille; ***organization tree*** organigramme *m* en arborescence

organizational [,ɔːgənaɪ'zeɪʃənəl] *adj (skills, methods)* organisationnel, d'organisation; *(expenses)* d'organisation; *(change)* dans l'organisation, structurel; **the concert turned out to be an organizational nightmare** l'organisation du concert fut un véritable cauchemar
►► *Econ* ***organizational behaviour*** comportement *m* de l'individu au sein d'une organisation; ***organizational buyer*** acheteur *m* (pour une organisation); ***organizational chart*** organigramme *m*; ***organizational marketer*** mercaticien *m* au sein d'une organisation

organizationally [ɔːgənaɪ'zeɪʃənəlɪ] *adv* du point de vue de l'organisation; **he doesn't get involved organizationally in the project** il n'est pas impliqué au niveau de l'organisation du projet

organize, -ise ['ɔːgənaɪz] **1** *vt* (**a**) *(sort out, put into groups)* organiser; **to get organized** s'organiser; **he doesn't know how to organize himself** il ne sait pas s'organiser; **to organize one's thoughts** mettre de l'ordre dans ses idées; **she's good at organizing people** elle est douée pour la gestion du personnel
(**b**) *(arrange, bring about* → *concert, party etc)* organiser; *(*→ *transport, food, accommodation)* s'occuper de; *(*→ *money)* s'occuper de trouver; **her colleagues organized a farewell dinner for her** ses collègues ont organisé un dîner d'adieu en son honneur; **I've organized a visit to a dairy for them** j'ai organisé la visite d'une laiterie à leur intention; **who's organizing the drinks?** qui est-ce qui s'occupe des boissons?; **she organized it so that we got in free** elle s'est arrangée pour que nous puissions entrer sans payer; **don't worry, it's all organized** ne t'inquiète pas, tout est organisé
(**c**) *Ind* syndiquer
2 *vi Ind* se syndiquer

organized ['ɔːgənaɪzd] *adj* (**a**) *(trip)* organisé; **we went on an organized tour of Scottish castles** nous avons visité les châteaux écossais en voyage organisé (**b**) *(unionized)* syndiqué (**c**) *(orderly)* organisé; *(methodical)* méthodique
►► ***organized crime*** le crime organisé; ***organized labour*** main-d'œuvre *f* syndiquée

organizer ['ɔːgənaɪzə(r)] *n* (**a**) *(person)* organisateur(trice) *m,f*; **she's a born organizer** elle a le sens de l'organisation, c'est une organisatrice née (**b**) *(diary)* organiseur *m*; *(electronic)* agenda *m* électronique (**c**) *Biol* organisateur *m* (**d**) *Comput (software)* organiseur *m*

organizing *n* organisation *f*
►► ***organizing committee*** comité *m* d'organisation

organogenesis [,ɔːgənəʊ'dʒenɪsɪs] *n* organogenèse *f*

organoleptic [,ɔːgənəʊ'leptɪk] *adj* organoleptique

organometallic [ɔː,gænəʊmɪ'tælɪk] *adj Chem* organométallique

organotherapy [,ɔːgənəʊ'θerəpɪ] *n Med* opothérapie *f*

organza [ɔː'gænzə] *n* organza *m*

organzine ['ɔːgənziːn] *n* organsin *m*

orgasm ['ɔːgæzəm] *n* orgasme *m*; **to have an orgasm** avoir un orgasme; *Fam Fig* **they were having orgasms about it** ils ont trouvé ça jouissif

orgasmic [ɔː'gæzmɪk] *adj* orgasmique, orgastique; *Fam Fig (food, experience etc)* jouissif

orgiast ['ɔːdʒɪæst] *n* orgiaste *mf*

orgiastic [,ɔːdʒɪ'æstɪk] *adj* orgiaque

orgy ['ɔːdʒɪ] (*pl* **orgies**) *n* orgie *f*; **a drunken orgy** une beuverie; **orgies** *(in ancient Greece, Rome)* orgies, bacchanales *fpl*; *Fig* **an orgy of killing** une orgie de meurtres

oribi ['ɒrɪbɪ] *n Zool* oribi *m*

oriel ['ɔːrɪəl] *n* oriel *m*
►► ***oriel window*** oriel *m*

Orient ['ɔːrɪənt] *n* **the Orient** l'Orient *m*
►► ***the Orient Express*** l'Orient-Express *m*

orient ['ɔːrɪənt] *vt* orienter; **to orient oneself** s'orienter; **our firm is very much oriented towards the American market** notre société est très orientée vers le marché américain

oriental [,ɔːrɪ'entəl] **1** *adj* oriental
2 Oriental *n* Asiatique *mf*
►► ***oriental rug*** tapis *m* d'Orient

orientalism [,ɔːrɪ'entəlɪzəm] *n* orientalisme *m*

orientalist [,ɔːrɪ'entəlɪst] *n* orientaliste *mf*

orientalize, -ise [,ɔːrɪ'entəlaɪz] **1** *vt* orientaliser
2 *vi* s'orientaliser

orientate ['ɔːrɪenteɪt] *vt Br* orienter; **to orientate oneself** s'orienter; **the course is very much orientated towards the sciences** le cours est très orienté vers *ou* axé sur les sciences

-orientated ['ɔːrɪenteɪtɪd] *Br* = **-oriented**

orientation [ˌɔːrɪen'teɪʃən] *n* orientation *f*; **James is in charge of student orientation** James est responsable de l'orientation des étudiants; **she's found a new orientation in life** elle a trouvé une orientation nouvelle à sa vie

oriented ['ɔːrɪentɪd] *adj* orienté

-oriented ['ɔːrɪentɪd] *suff* orienté vers..., axé sur...; **ours is a money-oriented society** c'est l'argent qui mène notre société; **she's very work-oriented** elle est très axée sur son travail; **pupil-oriented teaching** enseignement adapté aux besoins des élèves; **profit-oriented** axé sur le profit; **youth-oriented** qui s'adresse à la jeunesse

orienteer [ˌɔːrɪen'tɪə(r)] *n* orienteur(euse) *m,f*

orienteering [ˌɔːrɪen'tɪərɪŋ] *n* course *f* d'orientation

orifice ['ɒrɪfɪs] *n* orifice *m*

oriflamme ['ɒrɪflæm] *n Hist & Fig* oriflamme *f*

origami [ˌɒrɪ'gɑːmɪ] *n* origami *m*

origan ['ɒrɪgən], **origanum** [ə'rɪgənəm] *n Bot* origan *m*

origin ['ɒrɪdʒɪn] *n* (**a**) *(source)* origine *f*; **the origin of the Nile** la source du Nil; **what's the origin of that word?** quelle est l'origine de ce mot?; **country of origin** pays *m* d'origine; **of unknown origin** d'origine inconnue; **this wine is of Australian origin** ce vin est d'origine australienne; **the present troubles have their origin in the proposed land reform** le projet de réforme agraire est à l'origine des troubles actuels; **the song is Celtic in origin** la chanson est d'origine celte

(**b**) *(ancestry)* origine *f*; **he is of Canadian origin** il est d'origine canadienne; **to be of humble origins** avoir des origines modestes; **they can trace their origins back to the time of the Norman conquest** ils ont réussi à remonter dans leur arbre généalogique jusqu'à l'époque de la conquête normande

(**c**) *Anat (of muscle)* attache *f*

►► *Mktg* ***origin of goods label*** marque *f* d'origine

'The Origin of Species' *Darwin* 'De l'origine des espèces'

original [ɒ'rɪdʒɪnəl] **1** *adj* (**a**) *(initial)* premier, d'origine, initial; **the original inhabitants of the country** les premiers habitants du pays; **the original meaning of the word** le sens originel du mot; **my original intention was to drive there** ma première intention *ou* mon intention initiale était d'y aller en voiture; **the fabric has lost its original lustre** l'étoffe a perdu son éclat d'origine; **most of the original 600 copies have been destroyed** la plupart des 600 exemplaires originaux ont été détruits; **to translate from the original German** traduire d'après le texte allemand original; **the original portrait by Rubens** le portrait original peint par Rubens

(**b**) *(unusual, innovative)* original; *(strange)* singulier; **based on an original idea by Sam Ford** d'après une idée originale de Sam Ford; **he has some original ideas** il a des idées originales; **she has an original approach to child-rearing** sa conception de l'éducation est originale

(**c**) *(new → play, writing)* original, inédit; *TV & Cin* **based on an original idea by...** d'après une idée originale de...

2 *n* (**a**) *(painting, book, document)* original *m*; *Fin (of bill of exchange)* primata *m*; **the film was shown in the original** le film a été projeté en version originale; **I prefer to read Proust in the original** je préfère lire Proust dans le texte

(**b**) *(model → of hero, character)* **Catherine was the original of the novel's heroine** Catherine inspira le personnage de l'héroïne du roman

(**c**) *(unusual person)* original(e) *m,f*, excentrique *mf*; **she's a real original** elle est vraiment spéciale *ou* originale

►► *Fin* ***original capital*** capital *m* d'origine; *Fin* ***original cost*** coût *m* initial; *Acct* ***original document*** pièce *f* comptable; ***original edition*** édition *f* originale; *St Exch* ***original issue discount bond*** obligation *f* à prime d'émission; *Mktg* ***original packaging*** emballage *m* d'origine; *Rel* ***original sin*** péché *m* originel; *Fin* ***original value*** valeur *f* initiale *ou* d'origine

originality [əˌrɪdʒɪ'nælətɪ] *(pl* **originalities***)* *n* originalité *f*

originally [ə'rɪdʒɪnəlɪ] *adv* (**a**) *(initially)* à l'origine, au début, initialement; **this room was originally the kitchen** à l'origine, cette pièce servait de cuisine; **originally, I had planned to go to Greece** initialement *ou* au début, j'avais l'intention d'aller en Grèce; **originally we come from Hampshire** nous sommes originaires du Hampshire; **where do you come from originally?** d'où êtes-vous originaire?; **that's what I originally thought** c'est ce que je pensais au début *ou* au départ; **I originally heard about it in Spain** c'est en Espagne que j'en ai entendu parler pour la première fois

(**b**) *(unusually, inventively)* d'une façon *ou* d'une manière originale, originalement

originate [ə'rɪdʒɪneɪt] **1** *vi* (**a**) *(idea, rumour)* **to originate in** avoir *ou* trouver son origine dans; **to originate from** tirer son origine de; **where did the rumour originate from?** qu'est-ce qui a donné naissance à cette rumeur?; **this concept originates from Freudian psychology** ce concept est issu de la psychologie freudienne; **the conflict originated in the towns** le conflit est né dans les villes; **this information originates from an official source** le renseignement émane d'une source officielle; **I wonder how that saying originated** je me demande d'où vient ce dicton

(**b**) *(goods)* provenir; **the cocaine originates from South America** la cocaïne provient d'Amérique du Sud

(**c**) *(person)* **he originates from Sydney** il est originaire de Sydney

2 *vt (give rise to)* être à l'origine de, donner naissance à; *(be author of)* être l'auteur de; **the experience originated the story of the invisible man** cette expérience donna naissance à l'histoire de l'homme invisible

origination [əˌrɪdʒɪ'neɪʃən] *n* création *f*

originator [ə'rɪdʒɪneɪtə(r)] *n (of crime)* auteur *m*; *(of idea)* initiateur(trice) *m,f*, auteur *m*

O-ring *n Tech* joint *m* torique

Orinoco [ˌɒrɪ'nəʊkəʊ] *n* **the (River) Orinoco** l'Orénoque *m*

oriole ['ɔːrɪəʊl] *n Orn* (**a**) *(European)* loriot *m* (**b**) *(North American)* troupiale *m*, *Can* oriole *m*

Orion [ə'raɪən] **1** *pr n Myth* Orion

2 *Astron* Orion *f*

orison ['ɒrɪzən] *n Literary* oraison *f*

Orkney Islands ['ɔːknɪ-], **Orkneys** ['ɔːknɪz] *npl* **the Orkney Islands** les Orcades *fpl*; **in the Orkney Islands** dans les Orcades

Orlando [ɔː'lændəʊ] *pr n* Orlando

Orleanist [ɔː'liːənɪst] *Hist* **1** *n* orléaniste *mf*

2 *adj* orléaniste

Orlon® ['ɔːlɒn] **1** *n* Orlon® *m*

2 *comp* en Orlon

orlop ['ɔːlɒp] *n Naut* faux-pont *m*

►► ***orlop deck*** faux-pont *m*

ormer ['ɔːmə(r)] *n Zool* ormeau *m*

ormolu ['ɔːməluː] **1** *n* chrysocale *m*, bronze *m* doré

2 *comp (clock)* en chrysocale, en bronze doré

Ormuz [ɔː'muːz] *n* Hormuz, Ormuz

ornament 1 *n* ['ɔːnəmənt] (**a**) *(decorative object)* objet *m* décoratif, bibelot *m*; *(jewellery)* colifichet *m*

(**b**) *(embellishment)* ornement *m*; **rich in ornament** richement orné

(**c**) *Mus* ornement *m*

2 *vt* ['ɔːnəment] orner; **the dress was ornamented with gold braid** la robe était ornée d'un liseré d'or; **the ceiling was ornamented with frescoes** le plafond était orné de fresques; **his style is highly ornamented** il a un style très fleuri

ornamental [ˌɔːnə'mentəl] *adj (decorative)* ornemental, décoratif; *(plant)* ornemental; *(garden)* d'agrément; **ornamental lake** pièce *f* d'eau

ornamentally [ˌɔːnə'mentəlɪ] *adv (use)* pour décorer

ornamentation [ˌɔːnəmen'teɪʃən] *n* ornementation *f*

ornate [ɔː'neɪt] *adj (decoration)* (très) orné; *(style)* orné, fleuri; *(lettering)* orné

ornately [ɔː'neɪtlɪ] *adv* d'une façon très ornée; **ornately decorated room** pièce richement décorée; **ornately carved furniture** meubles ornés *ou* rehaussés de nombreuses sculptures

ornateness [ɔː'neɪtnɪs] *n* ornementation *f* très riche

ornery ['ɔːnərɪ] *adj Am Fam* (**a**) *(nasty)* méchant; **an ornery trick** un sale tour (**b**) *(stubborn)* obstiné, entêté (**c**) *(bad-tempered)* rouspéteur

ornithischian [ˌɔːnɪ'θɪskɪən] *adj* ornithischien

ornithological [ˌɔːnɪθə'lɒdʒɪkəl] *adj* ornithologique

ornithologist [ˌɔːnɪ'θɒlədʒɪst] *n* ornithologiste *mf*, ornithologue *mf*

ornithology [ˌɔːnɪ'θɒlədʒɪ] *n* ornithologie *f*

ornithomancy ['ɔːnɪθəʊˌmænsɪ] *n* ornithomancie *f*

ornithophily [ˌɔːnɪ'θɒfɪlɪ] *n* (**a**) *(love of birds)* ornithophilie *f* (**b**) *Bot* ornithogamie *f*

ornithorhynchus [ˌɔːnɪθəʊ'rɪŋkəs] *n* ornithorynque *m*

ornithosis [ˌɔːnɪ'θəʊsɪs] *n Med* ornithose *f*

orogen ['ɒrəʊdʒen] *n Geol* orogène *m*

orogenesis [ˌɒrəʊ'dʒenɪsɪs] *n Geol* orogénèse *f*

orogenetic [ˌɒrəʊdʒɪ'netɪk], **orogenic** [ˌɒrəʊ'dʒenɪk] *adj Geol* orogénique

orogenics [ˌɒrə'dʒenɪks], **orogeny** [ɒ'rɒdʒənɪ] *n (UNCOUNT)* orogénie *f*, orogenèse *f*

orographic [ɒrə'græfɪk] *adj* orographique

orography [ɒ'rɒgrəfɪ] *n* orographie *f*

oroide ['ɔːrəʊaɪd] *n* similor *m*, chrysocale *m*

orology [ɒ'rɒlədʒɪ] *n* orologie *f*

oropharynx [ˌɔːrəʊ'færɪŋks] *n Anat* oropharynx *m*

orotund ['ɒrətʌnd] *adj Formal (voice)* sonore; *(style)* ampoulé

orphan ['ɔːfən] **1** *n* (**a**) *(person)* orphelin(e) *m,f*; **to be left an orphan** se retrouver *ou* devenir orphelin

(**b**) *Typ & Comput* (ligne *f*) orpheline *f*

2 *adj* orphelin; **an orphan child** un orphelin, une orpheline

3 *vt* **to be orphaned** se retrouver *ou* devenir orphelin; **he had been orphaned at the age of six** il est devenu orphelin à l'âge de six ans; **they were orphaned by the war** ils ont perdu leurs parents pendant la guerre

►► *Pharm* ***orphan drug*** médicament *m* orphelin

orphanage ['ɔːfənɪdʒ] *n* orphelinat *m*

Orpheus ['ɔːfɪəs] *pr n Myth* Orphée

Orphean ['ɔːfɪən] *adj* (**a**) *(relating to Orpheus)* d'Orphée (**b**) *(mysterious, entrancing)* enchanteur

Orphic ['ɔːfɪk] *adj* orphique

Orphism ['ɔːfɪzəm] *n Art & Hist* orphisme *m*

orphrey ['ɔːfrɪ] *n* orfroi *m*, parement *m* (de chasuble)

orpiment ['ɔːpɪmənt] *n Miner* orpiment *m*, orpin *m*

orpine ['ɔːpaɪn] *n Bot* grand orpin *m*, orpin reprise

orrery ['ɒrərɪ] *(pl* **orreries***)* *n* planétaire *m*

orris ['ɒrɪs] *n* (**a**) *Bot* iris *m* (**b**) **orris (root)** rhizome *m* d'iris; *(in perfumery)* essence *f* de violette

ORT [ˌəʊɑː'tiː] *n Med* (*abbr* **oral rehydration therapy**) = réhydratation par ingestion d'une solution d'eau, de glucose et de sel

ortanique [ɔːtə'niːk] *n* ortanique *f*

orthicon ['ɔːθɪkɒn] *n* orthicon *m*

orthocentre ['ɔːθəsentə(r)] *n Geom* orthocentre *m*

orthochromatic [ˌɔːθəʊkrə'mætɪk] *adj* orthochromatique

orthoclase ['ɔːθəʊkleɪs] *n Miner* orthoclase *f*

orthodontic [ˌɔːθə'dɒntɪk] *adj* orthodontique

orthodontics [ˌɔːθə'dɒntɪks] *n (UNCOUNT)* orthodontie *f*

orthodontist [ˌɔːθə'dɒntɪst] *n* orthodontiste *mf*

orthodox ['ɔːθədɒks] *adj* orthodoxe

►► ***the Orthodox Church*** l'Église *f* orthodoxe

orthodoxy ['ɔːθədɒksɪ] *(pl* **orthodoxies***)* *n* orthodoxie *f*

orthoepic [ˌɔːθəʊ'epɪk], **orthoepical** [ˌɔːθəʊ'epɪkəl] *adj* orthoépique

orthoepy ['ɔːθəʊepɪ] *n* orthoépie *f*

orthogenesis [ˌɔːθə'dʒenɪsɪs] *n* orthogenèse *f*

orthogenic [ˌɔːθə'dʒenɪk] *adj* orthogénique

orthogonal [ɔː'θɒgənəl] *adj Math* orthogonal

►► ***orthogonal projection*** projection *f* orthogonale

orthographer [ɔːˈθɒɡrəfə(r)] *n* orthographiste *mf*
orthographic [ˌɔːθəˈɡræfɪk], **orthographical** [ˌɔːθəˈɡræfɪkəl] *adj* orthographique
orthographically [ˌɔːθəˈɡræfɪkəlɪ] *adv* orthographiquement
orthographist [ɔːˈθɒɡrəfɪst] *n* orthographiste *mf*
orthography [ɔːˈθɒɡrəfɪ] *n* (**a**) *(spelling)* orthographe *f* (**b**) *Math* projection *f* orthogonale
orthokeratology [ˌɔːˌəʊkərəˈtɒlədʒɪ] *n* orthokératologie *f*
orthomorphic [ˌɔːθəʊˈmɔːfɪk] *adj (map projection)* orthomorphique, conforme
orthopaedic, orthopaedics *etc Br* = **orthopedic, orthopedics** *etc*
orthopedic [ˌɔːθəˈpiːdɪk] *adj* orthopédique
►► ***orthopedic surgeon*** chirurgien(enne) *m,f* orthopédiste; ***orthopedic surgery*** chirurgie *f* orthopédique
orthopedics [ˌɔːθəˈpiːdɪks] *n (UNCOUNT)* orthopédie *f*
orthopedist [ˌɔːθəˈpiːdɪst] *n* orthopédiste *mf*
orthopteran [ɔːˈθɒptərən] *Entom* **1** *n* orthoptère *m*
2 *adj* orthoptère
orthoptic [ɔːˈθɒptɪk] *adj* orthoptique
orthoptics [ɔːˈθɒptɪks] *n (UNCOUNT)* orthoptique *f*
orthoptist [ɒːˈθɒptɪst] *n* orthoptiste *mf*
orthorhombic [ˌɔːθəʊˈrɒmbɪk] *adj (in crystallography)* orthorhombique
►► ***orthorhombic system*** système *m* orthorhombique *ou* terbinaire
orthoscopic [ˌɔːθəˈskɒpɪk] *adj* orthoscopique
orthosis [ɔːˈθəʊsɪs] *n Med* orthèse *f*
orthotic [ɔːˈθɒtɪk] *adj Med* orthétique
orthotics [ɔːˈθɒtɪks] *n (UNCOUNT) Med* orthétique *f*
ortolan [ˈɔːtələn] *n Orn* ortolan *m*
Orwellian [ɔːˈwelɪən] *adj* orwellien
oryx [ˈɒrɪks] (*pl* **inv** *or* **oryxes**) *n Zool* oryx *m*
OS[1] [ˌəʊˈes] *n* (**a**) (*abbr* **ordinary seaman**) matelot *m* breveté (**b**) *Comput* (*abbr* **operating system**) système *m* d'exploitation (**c**) (*abbr* **Ordnance Survey**) ≃ IGN *m* (**d**) *Austr* (*abbr* **overseas**) à l'étranger
OS[2] (*written abbr* **outsize**) grande taille *f*
O/S (*written abbr* **out of stock**) épuisé
Osaka [əʊˈsɑːkə] *n* Osaka
Oscar[1] [ˈɒskə(r)] *n Cin* oscar *m*
Oscar[2] *n Fam* (**a**) *Austr & NZ* (*rhyming slang* **Oscar Asche** = **cash**) pognon *m*, fric *m* (**b**) *Scot* (*rhyming slang* **Oscar Slater** = **later**) **see you Oscar!** à la revoyure!
Oscar-winning *adj* **an Oscar-winning picture** un film primé aux oscars; **in her Oscar-winning role** dans le rôle qui lui a valu l'oscar; *Fam Fig* **she really put on an Oscar-winning performance!** elle a vraiment fait un numéro d'anthologie!
OSCE [ˌəʊesˌsiːˈiː] *n* (*abbr* **Organization for Security and Cooperation in Europe**) OSCE *f*
oscillate [ˈɒsɪleɪt] **1** *vi* (**a**) *Elec & Phys* osciller (**b**) *(person)* osciller; **his mood oscillated between gloom and elation** son humeur oscillait entre la mélancolie et l'exultation
2 *vt* faire osciller
oscillating [ˈɒsɪleɪtɪŋ] *adj (electron)* oscillateur
oscillation [ˌɒsɪˈleɪʃən] *n* oscillation *f*
oscillator [ˈɒsɪleɪtə(r)] *n* oscillateur *m*
oscillatory [ɒˈsɪlətrɪ] *adj* oscillatoire
oscillogram [ɒˈsɪləɡræm] *n* oscillogramme *m*
oscillograph [ɒˈsɪləɡraf] *n* oscillographe *m*
oscilloscope [ɒˈsɪləskəʊp] *n* oscilloscope *m*
oscine [ˈɒsaɪn] *adj* oscine
osculate [ˈɒskjʊleɪt] **1** *vt Br Hum (kiss)* donner un baiser à, embrasser
2 *vi* (**a**) *Br Hum (kiss)* s'embrasser (**b**) *Math* **a curve that osculates with a line** une courbe osculatrice à une ligne
osculation [ˌɒskjʊˈleɪʃən] *n* (**a**) *Br Hum (kiss)* baiser *m* (**b**) *Math* osculation *f*
osculatory [ˈɒskjʊlətərɪ] *adj Math* osculateur(trice) *m,f*
►► *Arch Hum* ***osculatory demonstrations*** épanchements *m* en embrassades
osculum [ˈɒskjʊləm] (*pl* **oscula** [-lə]) *n Zool* oscule *m*
OSD [ˌəʊesˈdiː] *n* (*abbr* **optical scanning device**) lecteur *m* optique
OSHA [ˌəʊesˌeɪtʃˈeɪ] *n* (*abbr* **Occupational Safety and Health Administration**) = aux États-Unis, direction de la sécurité et de l'hygiène au travail
osier [ˈəʊzɪə(r)] **1** *n* osier *m*
2 *comp (basket)* d'osier
►► ***osier bed*** oseraie *f*
Osiris [əʊˈsaɪərɪs] *pr n Myth* Osiris
Oslo [ˈɒzləʊ] *n* Oslo
►► ***the Oslo Agreement*** l'accord *m* d'Oslo, les accords *mpl* d'Oslo
osmiridium [ˌɒzmɪˈrɪdɪəm] *n Chem* osmiridium *m*
osmium [ˈɒzmɪəm] *n Chem* osmium *m*
osmolarity [ˌɒzməʊˈlærɪtɪ] *n Biol & Chem* osmolarité *f*
osmometer [ɒzˈmɒmɪtə(r)] *n Biol & Chem* osmomètre *m*
osmoregulation [ˌɒzməʊregjʊˈleɪʃən] *n Biol* osmorégulation *f*
osmose [ˈɒzməʊs] *vi Chem* subir une osmose
osmosis [ɒzˈməʊsɪs] *n Chem & Fig* osmose *f*
osmotic [ɒzˈmɒtɪk] *adj Chem* osmotique
►► ***osmotic pressure*** pression *f* osmotique
osprey [ˈɒsprɪ] *n Br* (**a**) *Orn* balbuzard *m*, *Can* aigle *m* pêcheur (**b**) *(feather)* aigrette *f*
osseous [ˈɒsɪəs] *adj Anat* osseux
Ossianic [ˌɒsɪˈænɪk] *adj Literature* ossianique, inspiré de la poésie d'Ossian
Ossianism [ˈɒsɪənɪzəm] *n Literature* ossianisme *m*
Ossianist [ˈɒsɪənɪst] *n Literature* ossianiste *mf*
ossicle [ˈɒsɪkəl] *n Anat & Zool* osselet *m*
ossiferous [ɒˈsɪfərəs] *adj* ossifère
ossification [ˌɒsɪfɪˈkeɪʃən] *n* ossification *f*
ossified [ˈɒsɪfaɪd] *adj (cartilage)* ossifié; *Fig (mind, ideas, social system)* sclérosé; *(person)* à l'esprit sclérosé; **the ossified old fools who run this country** les vieux fossiles abrutis qui dirigent ce pays
ossifrage [ˈɒsɪfreɪdʒ] *n* (**a**) *(osprey)* balbuzard *m*; *Can* aigle *m* pêcheur (**b**) *(vulture)* gypaète *m* barbu, vautour *m* barbu
ossify [ˈɒsɪfaɪ] (*pt & pp* **ossified**) **1** *vt* ossifier
2 *vi (cartilage)* s'ossifier; *Fig (government, mind)* se scléroser
ossuary [ˈɒsjʊərɪ] (*pl* **ossuaries**) *n (vault)* ossuaire *m*; *(urn)* urne *f* (funéraire)
osteal [ˈɒstɪəl] *adj* ostéal, ostéique
osteitis [ˌɒstɪˈaɪtɪs] *n Med* ostéite *f*
Ostend [ɒsˈtend] *n* Ostende
ostensible [ɒˈstensəbəl] *adj (apparent)* apparent; *(pretended)* prétendu; *(so-called)* soi-disant *(inv)*; **her ostensible reason for not coming was illness** elle a prétendu être malade pour éviter de venir
ostensibly [ɒˈstensəblɪ] *adv (apparently)* apparemment; *(supposedly)* prétendument, soi-disant; **ostensibly they are diplomats** ils se font passer pour des diplomates; **he left early, ostensibly because he was sick** il est parti tôt, prétextant une indisposition *ou* soi-disant parce qu'il était souffrant
ostensive [ɒˈstensɪv] *adj* ostensible, manifeste
ostentation [ˌɒstənˈteɪʃən] *n* ostentation *f*
ostentatious [ˌɒstənˈteɪʃəs] *adj* (**a**) *(showy → display, appearance, decor)* ostentatoire, plein d'ostentation; *(→ manner, behaviour)* prétentieux, ostentatoire (**b**) *(exaggerated)* exagéré, surfait; **with ostentatious dislike** avec un mépris exagéré
ostentatiously [ˌɒstənˈteɪʃəslɪ] *adv* avec ostentation; **to display sth ostentatiously** faire ostentation de qch; **to be ostentatiously rich** faire ostentation de sa richesse
ostentatiousness [ˌɒstənˈteɪʃəsnɪs] *n* ostentation *f*
osteoarthritis [ˌɒstɪəʊɑːˈθraɪtɪs] *n Med* ostéoarthrite *f*
osteoarthrosis [ˌɒstɪəʊɑːˈθrəʊsɪs] *n Med* ostéoarthrose *f*
osteoblast [ˈɒstɪəʊblæst] *n Biol* ostéoblaste *m*
osteoclasis [ˌɒstɪəʊˈkleɪsɪs] *n Med* ostéoclasie *f*
osteoclast [ˈɒstɪəʊklæst] *n Biol & Med* ostéoclaste *m*
osteoclastoma [ˌɒstɪəʊklæsˈtəʊmə] *n Med* ostéoclastome *m*
osteogenesis [ˌɒstɪəʊˈdʒenɪsɪs], **osteogeny** [ˌɒstɪˈɒdʒɪnɪ] *n Biol* ostéogénèse *f*, ostéogénie *f*
osteologist [ˌɒstɪˈɒlədʒɪst] *n* ostéologiste *mf*
osteology [ˌɒstɪˈɒlədʒɪ] *n* ostéologie *f*
osteolysis [ˌɒstɪˈɒlɪsɪs] *n Med* ostéolyse *f*
osteoma [ˌɒstɪˈəʊmə] (*pl* **osteomas** *or* **osteomata** [-mətə]) *n Med* ostéome *m*
osteomalacia [ˌɒstɪəʊməˈleɪʃɪə] *n Med* ostéomalacie *f*
osteomyelitis [ˌɒstɪəʊmaɪˈlaɪtɪs] *n Med* ostéomyélite *f*
osteopath [ˈɒstɪəpæθ] *n* ostéopathe *mf*
osteopathic [ˌɒstɪəˈpæθɪk] *adj* ostéopathique
osteopathist [ˌɒstɪˈɒpəθɪst] *n Am* ostéopathe *mf*
osteopathy [ˌɒstɪˈɒpəθɪ] *n* ostéopathie *f*
osteoplasty [ˈɒstɪəʊˌplæstɪ] *n Med* ostéoplastie *f*
osteoporosis [ˌɒstɪəʊpəˈrəʊsɪs] *n Med* ostéoporose *f*
osteosarcoma [ˌɒstɪəʊsɑːˈkəʊmə] (*pl* **osteosarcomas** *or* **osteosarcomata** [-mətə]) *n Med* ostéosarcome *m*
ostinato [ˌɒstɪˈnɑːtəʊ] *Mus* **1** *n* **(basso) ostinato** basse *f* contrainte
2 *adj* ostinato
ostler [ˈɒslə(r)] *n Br Arch* valet *m* d'écurie
ostracism [ˈɒstrəsɪzəm] *n* ostracisme *m*
ostracize, -ise [ˈɒstrəsaɪz] *vt* frapper d'ostracisme, ostraciser; **he was ostracized by his workmates** ses collègues l'ont mis en quarantaine
ostrich [ˈɒstrɪtʃ] *n Orn* autruche *f*
►► ***ostrich farm*** élevage *m* d'autruches; ***ostrich feather*** plume *f* d'autruche
Ostrogoth [ˈɒstrəɡɒθ] *n* **the Ostrogoths** les Ostrogoths *mpl*
OT [ˌəʊˈtiː] *n* (**a**) (*abbr* **Old Testament**) AT *m* (**b**) (*abbr* **occupational therapy**) ergothérapie *f*
otalgia [əʊˈtældʒə] *n Med* otalgie *f*
OTC [ˌəʊtiːˈsiː] **1** *n Br Sch* (*abbr* **Officer Training Corps**) corps *m* de formation des officiers
2 *adj St Exch* (*abbr* **over the counter**) hors cote
OTE [ˌəʊtiːˈiː] *npl Mktg* (*abbr* **on-target earnings**) salaire *m* de base plus commissions
OTH [ˌəʊtiːˈeɪtʃ] *n Mktg* (*abbr* **opportunity to hear**) ODE *f*
Othello [əˈθeləʊ] *pr n* Othello

OTHER [ˈʌðə(r)] **1** *adj* (**a**) *(different)* autre, différent; **it's the same in other countries** c'est la même chose dans les autres pays; **I had no other choice** je n'avais pas le choix *ou* pas d'autre solution; **any other book** tout autre livre; **by other means** par d'autres moyens; **he doesn't respect other people's property** il ne respecte pas le bien d'autrui; **it always happens to other people** cela n'arrive qu'aux autres; **can't we discuss it some other time?** on ne peut pas en parler plus tard?; **for this reason, if for no other** pour cette raison, à défaut d'une autre; **in other times** autrefois, à une autre époque; **the other world** l'autre monde *m*, l'au-delà *m*
(**b**) *(second of two)* autre; **give me the other one** donnez-moi l'autre; **the other woman/man** *(in relationship)* l'autre
(**c**) *(additional)* autre; **can you get some other cups?** pouvez-vous aller chercher d'autres tasses?; **some other people came** d'autres personnes sont arrivées; **they have two other daughters** ils ont deux autres filles
(**d**) *(remaining)* autre; **the other three men** les trois autres hommes
(**e**) *(in expressions of time)* autre; **the other day/morning/month/week** l'autre jour/matin/mois/semaine
(**f**) *(opposite)* **on the other side of the room/of the river** de l'autre côté de la pièce/de la rivière; **a voice at the other end (of the telephone)** une voix à l'autre bout (du fil)
2 *pron* (**a**) *(additional person, thing)* autre; **he and two others got the sack** lui et deux autres ont été renvoyés; **some succeed, others fail** certains réussissent, d'autres échouent; **have you got any others?** *(any more)* en avez-vous encore?; *(any different ones)* en avez-vous d'autres?; **can you show me some others?** pouvez-vous m'en montrer d'autres?; **I have no other** je n'en ai pas d'autre
(**b**) *(opposite, far end)* autre; **I stood at this end of the room and she stood at the other** j'étais à

ce bout-ci de la pièce et elle était à l'autre (bout)

(**c**) *(related person)* autre; **each thought the other the better writer** chacun trouvait que l'autre était meilleur écrivain

3 *n (person, thing)* autre *mf*; *Phil* **the other** l'autre; **the three others** les trois autres; **wait for the others** attendez les autres; **politicians, industrialists and others** les hommes politiques, les industriels et les autres; **she cares nothing for others** elle ne se soucie pas du tout des autres; **the property of others** le bien d'autrui; **to talk about this, that and the other** parler de ci et ça; *Fam Hum* **to have a bit of the other** *(sex)* prendre un peu son pied

4 other than 1 *conj* (**a**) *(apart from, except)* autrement que; **she had never seen him other than on the screen** elle ne l'avait jamais vu autrement qu'à l'écran; **we had no alternative other than to accept their offer** nous n'avions pas d'autre possibilité que celle d'accepter leur offre (**b**) *(differently from)* différemment de; **I think she should have behaved other than she did** je pense qu'elle aurait dû se comporter différemment *ou* d'une autre façon; **she can't be other than she is** elle est comme ça, c'est tout **2** *prep* sauf, à part; **other than that** à part cela; **somebody other than me/you/her/***etc* quelqu'un d'autre; **all verbs other than those in -er** tous les verbes autres que ceux en -er

otherness ['ʌðənɪs] *n (difference)* altérité *f*, différence *f*; *(strangeness)* étrangeté *f*

otherwhere ['ʌðəweə(r)] *adv Literary* ailleurs

otherwise ['ʌðəwaɪz] **1** *adv* (**a**) *(differently)* autrement; **I think otherwise** *(in a different way)* je ne vois pas les choses de cette façon; *(don't agree)* je ne suis pas d'accord; **she is otherwise engaged** elle a d'autres engagements; **we'll have to invite everyone, we can hardly do otherwise** nous devrons inviter tout le monde, il nous serait difficile de faire autrement; **except where otherwise stated** *(on form)* sauf indication contraire

(**b**) *(in other respects)* autrement, à part cela; *(in other circumstances)* sinon, autrement; **an otherwise excellent performance** une interprétation par ailleurs excellente; **it's a bit small, but otherwise it's a very nice house** c'est un peu petit, mais à part cela, c'est une maison très agréable; **the weather was bad, otherwise he might have stayed longer** il faisait mauvais, sans cela *ou* sinon il aurait pu rester plus longtemps

(**c**) *(in other words)* autrement; **Louis XIV, otherwise known as the Sun King** Louis XIV, surnommé le Roi-Soleil

(**d**) *(in contrast, opposition)* **through diplomatic channels or otherwise** par voie diplomatique ou autre

2 *conj (or else)* sinon, autrement; **you'd better phone your father, otherwise he'll worry** tu devrais appeler ton père, sinon il va s'inquiéter

3 *adj* autre; **the facts are otherwise** les faits sont autres

4 or otherwise *adv* **it is of no interest, financial or otherwise** ça ne présente aucun intérêt, que ce soit financier ou autre; **she appeared to have no feelings about it, jealous or otherwise** elle ne semblait rien éprouver, que ce soit de la jalousie ou autre chose

otherworldliness [ˌʌðəˈwɜːldlɪnɪs] *n* (**a**) *(remoteness from worldly matters)* détachement *m* (des choses de ce monde) (**b**) *(mystical quality)* caractère *m* mystique (**c**) *(ethereal or exotic quality)* caractère *m* irréel

otherworldly [ˌʌðəˈwɜːldlɪ] *adj* (**a**) *(remote from worldly matters)* détaché du monde (**b**) *(mystical)* mystique (**c**) *(ethereal, exotic)* irréel

otic ['əʊtɪk] *adj Anat* otique

otiose ['əʊtɪəʊs] *adj Formal* oiseux, inutile

otitis [əʊ'taɪtɪs] *n (UNCOUNT) Med* otite *f*

otolaryngologist [ˌəʊtəʊˌlærɪŋ'gɒlədʒɪst] *n Med* oto-rhino-laryngologiste *mf*

otolaryngology [ˌəʊtəʊˌlærɪŋ'gɒlədʒɪ] *n Med* oto-rhino-laryngologie *f*

otolith ['əʊtəlɪθ] *n Zool* otolithe *f*, otolite *f*

otology [əʊ'tɒlədʒɪ] *n Med* otologie *f*

otorhinolaryngologist [ˌəʊtəʊraɪnəʊˌlærɪŋ'gɒlədʒɪst] *n Med* oto-rhino-laryngologiste *mf*

otorhinolaryngology [ˌəʊtəʊraɪnəʊˌlærɪŋ'gɒlədʒɪ] *n Med* oto-rhino-laryngologie *f*

otosclerosis [ˌəʊtəʊsklə'rəʊsɪs] *n Med* otosclérose *f*

otoscope ['əʊtəʊskəʊp] *n Med* otoscope *m*

otoscopic [ˌəʊtəʊ'skɒpɪk] *adj Med* otoscopique

otoscopy [əʊ'tɒskəpɪ] *n Med* otoscopie *f*

OTS [ˌəʊtiː'es] *n Mktg* (*abbr* **opportunity to see**) ODV *f*

OTT [ˌəʊtiː'tiː] *adj Br Fam* (*abbr* **over-the-top**) **that's a bit OTT!** c'est un peu exagéré!; **there was no need to be quite so OTT about it** ce n'était pas la peine d'en faire toute une histoire; **the house is nice, but the decor's a bit OTT** la maison est bien, mais la décoration est un peu lourdingue; **it's a bit OTT to call him a fascist** c'est un peu exagéré de le traiter de fasciste; **he went completely OTT when he heard what she'd said** il a pété les plombs quand il a appris ce qu'elle avait dit

Ottawa ['ɒtəwə] *n* Ottawa

otter ['ɒtə(r)] *n Zool* loutre *f*

▸▸ ***otter hound*** chien *m* pour la chasse aux loutres; ***otter shell*** lutraire *m*; ***otter shrew*** potamogale *m*

ottoman ['ɒtəmən] **1** *n* (**a**) *(seat)* ottomane *f* (**b**) *(fabric)* ottoman *m*

2 Ottoman 1 *n* Ottoman(e) *m,f* **2** *adj* ottoman

OU [ˌəʊ'juː] *n Br Univ* (*abbr* **Open University**) = organisme d'enseignement universitaire par correspondance doublé d'émissions de télévision et de radio

oubliette [ˌuːblɪ'et] *n Hist* oubliettes *fpl*

ouch [aʊtʃ] *exclam* aïe!, ouille!, ouïe!

ought[1] [ɔːt]

> La forme négative **ought not** s'écrit **oughtn't** en forme contractée.

v aux (**a**) *(indicating morally right action)* **you ought to tell her** vous devriez le lui dire; **you ought to talk to him** tu devrais lui parler, il faudrait que tu lui parles; **she thought she ought to tell you** elle a pensé qu'il valait mieux te le dire

(**b**) *(indicating sensible or advisable action)* **perhaps we ought to discuss this further** peut-être devrions-nous en discuter plus longuement; **I really ought to be going** il faut vraiment que je m'en aille; *Formal* **do you think I ought?** pensez-vous que je doive le faire?; **he ought to know better** il devrait être plus sensé; **that's a nice car – it ought to be, it cost me a fortune!** c'est une belle voiture – j'espère bien, elle m'a coûté une fortune!

(**c**) *(expressing expectation, likelihood)* **they ought to be home now** à l'heure qu'il est, ils devraient être rentrés; **it ought to be good** ça devrait être bien; **she ought to beat him easily** elle devrait le battre facilement *ou* sans difficulté; **that oughtn't to be too difficult** ça ne devrait pas être trop difficile

(**d**) *(followed by "to have")* **you ought to have told me!** vous auriez dû me le dire!; **you ought to have seen her!** si vous l'aviez vue!, il fallait la voir!; **they ought not to have been allowed in** on n'aurait pas dû les laisser entrer

ought[2] = **aught**

oughta ['ɔːtə] *Am Fam* = **ought to**

oughtn't ['ɔːtənt] = **ought not**

Ouija® ['wiːdʒə] *n* **Ouija**® **(board)** oui-ja *m inv*

oul' [aʊl] *Ir Fam* = **old** *adj*

ounce [aʊns] *n* (**a**) *(weight)* once *f* (**b**) *Fig* **there isn't an ounce of truth in what she says** il n'y a pas une once de vérité dans ce qu'elle raconte; **you haven't got an ounce of common sense** tu n'as pas (pour) deux sous de bon sens; **it took every ounce of strength she had** cela lui a demandé toutes ses forces (**c**) *Zool* once *f*

our ['aʊə(r)] *adj (singular)* notre; *(plural)* nos; **our house** notre maison; **this is OUR house** cette maison est à nous; **we have a car of our own** nous avons une voiture à nous; **how's our little boy, then?** alors, comment va notre petit garçon?; *Fam* **our Debbie will be sixteen next week** notre (petite) Debbie aura seize ans la semaine prochaine; *Fam* **have you seen our Ricky?** avez-vous vu Ricky?; **she's one of our finest poets** c'est un de nos meilleurs poètes

▸▸ ***Our Father*** *(prayer)* Notre Père *m*

> **'Our Man in Havana'** *Greene* 'Notre agent à La Havane'

ours ['aʊəz] *pron* (**a**) *(gen → singular)* le (la) nôtre *m,f*; *(→ plural)* les nôtres *mfpl*; **that house is ours** *(we live there)* cette maison est la nôtre; *(we own it)* cette maison est à nous *ou* nous appartient; **those books are ours** ces livres sont à nous; **it's ours to spend as we like** nous pouvons le dépenser comme nous voulons; **it's all ours!** tout cela nous appartient!; **ours was a curious relationship** nous avions des rapports assez bizarres; **ours is a big family** nous sommes une grande famille; **it must be one of ours** ce doit être un des nôtres; **she's a friend of ours** c'est une de nos amies; **a friend of ours told us** c'est un ami à nous qui nous l'a dit; *Fam* **those damned neighbours of ours** nos fichus voisins; **that wretched dog of ours** notre saleté de chien

(**b**) *Fam (our house, flat)* chez nous

ourself [aʊə'self] *pron Formal (regal or editorial plural)* nous-même

ourselves [aʊə'selvz] *pron* (**a**) *(reflexive use)* nous; **we enjoyed ourselves** nous nous sommes bien amusés; **we built ourselves a log cabin** nous avons construit une cabane en rondins; **we said to ourselves, why not wait here?** nous nous sommes dit *ou* on s'est dit: pourquoi ne pas attendre ici?

(**b**) *(emphatic use)* nous-mêmes; **we welcomed him ourselves** nous l'avons accueilli nous-mêmes; **we'd love to help him, but we're not in very good health ourselves** nous aimerions beaucoup l'aider mais nous ne sommes pas en très bonne santé nous-mêmes *ou* non plus; **we were able to visit the caves ourselves** nous avons eu la chance de pouvoir visiter les grottes; **we ourselves have much to learn** nous-mêmes avons beaucoup à apprendre; **we want to see for ourselves** nous avons envie de nous en rendre compte (par) nous-mêmes; **(all) by ourselves** tout seuls; **we had the flat to ourselves** nous avions l'appartement pour nous tout seuls

(**c**) *(replacing "us")* nous-mêmes; **apart from our parents and ourselves, everyone was Russian** en dehors de nos parents et de nous-mêmes, tout le monde était russe

oust [aʊst] *vt* (**a**) *(opponent, rival)* évincer, chasser; **the president was ousted from power** le président a été évincé du pouvoir; **she has ousted her sister in Arthur's affections** elle a pris la place de *ou* a supplanté sa sœur dans le cœur d'Arthur (**b**) *(tenant, squatter)* déloger, expulser; *(landowner)* déposséder

ouster ['aʊstə(r)] *n* (**a**) *Law* dépossession *f*, éviction *f* illicite (**b**) *Am (from country)* expulsion *f*; *(from office)* renvoi *m*

OUT [aʊt] **1** *adv* **A.** (**a**) *(indicating movement from inside to outside)* dehors; **to go out** sortir; **she ran/limped/strolled out** elle est sortie en courant/en boitant/sans se presser; **I met her on my way out** je l'ai rencontrée en sortant; **out you go!** sortez!, hors d'ici!, allez, hop!; **the cork popped out** le bouchon sauta; **she took out a gun** elle a sorti un révolver; **I had my camera out ready** j'avais sorti mon appareil; **he drew out £50** *(from bank)* il a retiré 50 livres; *(from pocket)* il a sorti 50 livres; *Fam* **I'm out of here** je me casse; *Fam* **let's get out of here** allez, on se casse

(**b**) *(away from home, office etc)* **Mr Powell's out, do you want to leave a message?** M. Powell est sorti, voulez-vous laisser un message?; **she's out a lot in the daytime** elle est souvent absente pendant la journée; **she's out picking mushrooms** elle est sortie (pour aller) cueillir des champignons; **a search party is out looking for them** une équipe de secours est partie à leur recherche; **to eat out** aller au restaurant; **it's a long time since we had an evening out** ça fait longtemps que nous ne sommes pas sortis; **he stayed out all night** il n'est pas rentré de la nuit; **the children are playing out in the street** les enfants jouent dans la rue; *Fam* **to be out to lunch** *(out of touch with reality)* être à côté de la plaque

oth–out

(**c**) *(no longer attending hospital, school etc)* sorti; **she's out of hospital now** elle est sortie de l'hôpital maintenant; **what time do you get out of school?** à quelle heure sors-tu de l'école?; **he's out in September** *(of prisoner)* il sort en septembre
(**d**) *(indicating view from inside)* **he was looking out at the people in the street** il regardait les gens qui passaient dans la rue; **I stared out of the window** je regardais par la fenêtre; **the bedroom looks out onto open fields** la chambre donne sur les champs
(**e**) *(in the open air)* dehors; **to sleep out** dormir dehors; **it's cold out** il fait froid dehors; **it's colder inside than out** il fait plus froid à l'intérieur qu'à l'extérieur
(**f**) *(indicating distance from land, centre, town etc)* **we were two days out from Portsmouth** nous étions à deux jours de Portsmouth; **on the trip out** à l'aller; **they live a long way out** ils habitent loin du centre; **out in the country** dans la campagne; **she's out in Africa** elle est en Afrique; **out there** là-bas
(**g**) *(indicating extended position)* **she stuck her tongue out at me** elle m'a tiré la langue; **he lay stretched out on the bed** il était allongé (de tout son long) sur le lit; **hold your arms/your hand out** tendez les bras/la main
B. (**a**) *(indicating distribution)* **she handed out some photocopies** elle a distribué des photocopies; **the letter was sent out yesterday** la lettre a été postée hier; **the book is out** *(borrowed from library)* le livre est en prêt
(**b**) *(indicating source of light, smell, sound etc)* **it gives out a lot of heat** ça dégage beaucoup de chaleur; **music blared out from the radio** la radio hurlait
(**c**) *(loudly, audibly)* **read out the first paragraph** lisez le premier paragraphe à haute voix; **I was thinking out loud** je pensais tout haut
C. (**a**) *(indicating exclusion or rejection)* **keep out** *(sign)* défense d'entrer, entrée interdite; **traitors out!** les traîtres, dehors!; **throw him out!** jetez-le dehors!
(**b**) *(indicating abandonment of activity)* **get out before it's too late** abandonne avant qu'il ne soit trop tard; **you can count me out** ne comptez plus sur moi; *Fam* **I want out!** je laisse tomber!
(**c**) *(extinguished)* **put** *or* **turn the lights out** éteignez les lumières; **to stub out a cigarette** écraser une cigarette
(**d**) *(unconscious)* **to knock sb out** assommer qn, mettre qn K-O; **several people passed out** plusieurs personnes se sont évanouies
(**e**) *(indicating disappearance)* **the stain will wash out** la tache partira au lavage
D. (**a**) *(revealed, made public)* **the secret is out** le secret a été éventé; **word is out that he's going to resign** le bruit court qu'il va démissionner; **the truth will out** la vérité se saura; **we must stop the news getting out** nous devons empêcher la nouvelle de s'ébruiter; *Fam* **out with it!** alors, t'accouches?
(**b**) *(published, on sale)* **is her new book/film/record out?** est-ce que son nouveau livre/film/disque est sorti?; **the new model will be** *or* **come out next month** le nouveau modèle sort le mois prochain
(**c**) *(with superlative) Fam (in existence)* **it's the best computer out** c'est le meilleur ordinateur qui existe ❑; **she's the biggest liar out** c'est la pire menteuse qui soit ❑
E. *(of tide)* **the tide's on its way out** la mer se retire, la marée descend
2 *adj* (**a**) *(flowering)* en fleurs; **the daffodils/cherry trees are out** les jonquilles/cerisiers sont en fleurs
(**b**) *(shining)* **the sun is out** il y a du soleil; **the moon is out** la lune s'est levée; **the stars are out** on voit les étoiles
(**c**) *(finished)* **before the year is out** avant la fin de l'année
(**d**) *(on strike)* en grève; **the dockers have been out for a month** les dockers sont en grève depuis un mois; **everybody out!** tout le monde en grève!
(**e**) *Sport* **if you score less than 3 points you're out** si on marque moins de 3 points on est éliminé; **the ball was out** la balle était dehors *ou* sortie, la balle était faute; **she went out in the first round** elle a été éliminée au premier tour; **not out** *(in cricket)* = encore au guichet *(à la fin de l'innings, de la journée)*
(**f**) *(tide)* bas; **the tide's out** la marée est basse
(**g**) *(wrong)* **your calculations are (way) out, you're (way) out in your calculations** vous vous êtes (complètement) trompé dans vos calculs; **I've checked the figures but I'm still £50 out** j'ai vérifié les chiffres mais il manque toujours 50 livres; **it's a few inches out** *(too long)* c'est trop long de quelques centimètres; *(too short)* c'est trop court de quelques centimètres; **it's only a few inches out** c'est bon à quelques centimètres près; **the shot was only a centimetre out** le coup n'a manqué le but que d'un centimètre
(**h**) *Fam (impossible)* **that plan's out because of the weather** ce projet est à l'eau à cause du temps
(**i**) *Fam (unfashionable)* démodé ❑; **long hair's (right) out** les cheveux longs c'est (carrément) dépassé
(**j**) *(indicating aim, intent)* **to be out to do sth** avoir l'intention de faire qch; **we're out to win** nous sommes partis pour gagner; **to be out to get sb** en avoir après qn; **to be out for sth** vouloir qch; **she was out for a good time** elle cherchait à s'amuser; **she's out for the presidency** elle vise le poste de président; **he's just out for himself** il ne s'intéresse qu'à lui-même; **he's only out for what he can get** il ne cherche qu'à servir ses propres intérêts
(**k**) *Fam (unconscious)* **to be out** être K-O
(**l**) *(extinguished)* éteint; **the fire was out** le feu était éteint
(**m**) *Fam (openly gay)* qui ne cache pas son homosexualité ❑, ouvertement homosexuel ❑
3 *n* (**a**) *(way of escape)* échappatoire *f*
(**b**) *Typ* bourdon *m*
(**c**) *Am Fam* **to be on the outs** être brouillé avec qn
4 *exclam* (**a**) *(leave)* dehors!
(**b**) *Tel* **(over and) out!** terminé!
(**c**) *Sport (in tennis)* faute!, out!
5 *prep Fam* hors de; **she went out that door** elle est sortie par cette porte; **look out the window** regarde par la fenêtre
6 *vt (expose)* dénoncer; **to out sb** *(reveal to be homosexual)* révéler que qn est homosexuel; **to out sb as a spy** dénoncer qn en tant qu'espion
7 out and about *adv* **where have you been? – oh, out and about** où étais-tu? – oh, je suis allé faire un tour; **out and about in Amsterdam** dans les rues d'Amsterdam
8 out of *prep* (**a**) *(indicating movement from inside to outside)* hors de; **she came out of the office** elle est sortie du bureau; **he ran/limped/strolled out of the office** il est sorti du bureau en courant/en boitant/sans se presser; **to look/to fall out of a window** regarder/tomber par une fenêtre; **take your hands out of your pockets!** sors *ou* ôte tes mains de tes poches!; **hardly were the words out of my mouth** à peine avais-je prononcé ces mots
(**b**) *(indicating location)* **we drank out of china cups** nous avons bu dans des tasses de porcelaine; **to drink out of the bottle** boire à (même) la bouteille; **she works out of York** elle opère à partir de York; **the company is out of Oxford** l'entreprise est basée à Oxford; **he's out of town** il n'est pas en ville; **she's out of the country** elle est à l'étranger; **it's a long way out of town** c'est loin de la ville; **there was a wind out of the Southwest** il y avait du vent de sud-ouest
(**c**) *(indicating source → of feeling, profit, money etc)* **she did well out of the deal** elle a trouvé son compte dans l'affaire; **what pleasure do they get out of it?** quel plaisir en tirent-ils?; **you won't get anything out of him** vous ne tirerez rien de lui; **she paid for it out of company funds/out of her own pocket** elle l'a payé avec l'argent de la société/payé de sa poche; **to copy sth out of a book** copier qch dans un livre
(**d**) *(indicating raw material)* **it's made out of mahogany** c'est en acajou; **plastic is made out of petroleum** on obtient le plastique à partir du pétrole; **hut made out of a few old planks** cabane faite de quelques vieilles planches
(**e**) *(indicating motive)* par; **he refused out of sheer spite** il a refusé par pur dépit; **to act out of fear** *(habitually)* agir sous l'emprise de la peur; *(on precise occasion)* agir sous le coup de la peur
(**f**) *(indicating previous tendency, habit)* **I've got out of the habit** j'en ai perdu l'habitude; **try and stay out of trouble** essaie d'éviter les ennuis
(**g**) *(lacking)* **I'm out of cigarettes** je n'ai plus de cigarettes; *Com* **I am out of this item** je n'ai plus cet article pour le moment; **out of work** au chômage
(**h**) *(in proportions, marks etc)* sur; **he got nine out of ten in maths** il a eu neuf sur dix en maths; **ninety-nine times out of a hundred** quatre-vingt-dix-neuf fois sur cent; **choose one out of these ten** choisissez-en un parmi les dix; **three days out of four** trois jours sur quatre; **one out of every three** un sur trois; **out of all the people there, only one spoke German** parmi toutes les personnes présentes, une seule parlait allemand
(**i**) *(indicating similarity to book, film etc)* **it was like something out of a Fellini film** on se serait cru dans un film de Fellini
(**j**) *(indicating exclusion or rejection)* **he's out of the race** il n'est plus dans la course; **you keep out of this!** mêlez-vous de ce qui vous regarde!
(**k**) *(indicating avoidance)* **come in out of the rain** ne reste pas dehors sous la pluie; **stay out of the sun** ne restez pas au soleil; **is there a way out of it?** y a-t-il (un) moyen d'en sortir?
(**l**) *(indicating recently completed activity)* **a young girl just out of university** une jeune fille tout juste sortie de l'université
(**m**) *(in breeding)* **Gladiator by Monarch out of Gladia** Gladiateur par *ou* issu de Monarch et Gladia
(**n**) *(idiom) Fam* **to be out of it** *(unaware of situation)* être à côté de la plaque; *(drunk, on drugs)* être raide; **I felt a bit out of it** *(excluded)* je me sentais un peu de trop
►► *Acct* **out book** livre *m* du dehors; *Comput* **out box** *(for e-mail)* corbeille *f* de départ; **out tray** corbeille *f* sortie

---

'Out of Africa' *Blixen* 'La Ferme africaine'

---

out- [aʊt] *pref* **the Opposition are attempting to out-Tory the Tories** l'opposition essaie d'être plus conservatrice que les conservateurs eux-mêmes
outa ['aʊtə] *Am Fam* = **out of**
outage ['aʊtɪdʒ] *n* (**a**) *(breakdown)* panne *f*; *Elec* coupure *f ou* panne *f* de courant (**b**) *(of service)* interruption *f* (**c**) *Com (missing goods)* marchandises *fpl* perdues *(pendant le stockage ou le transport)*
out-and-out *adj* complet(ète), total; **it was an out-and-out disaster** ce fut un désastre complet; **that's out-and-out madness!** c'est de la folie pure!; **he's an out-and-out crook** c'est un véritable escroc
out-and-outer *n Am Fam* jusqu'au-boutiste *mf*
out-argue *vt* mettre à bout d'arguments
outasight [,aʊtə'saɪt] *adj Am Fam Old-fashioned* extra, super, génial
outback ['aʊtbæk] *n* **the outback** l'arrière-pays *m inv*, l'intérieur *m* du pays
outbalance [,aʊt'bæləns] *vt* peser plus lourd que; *Fig* dépasser
outbid [,aʊt'bɪd] (*pt* **outbid**, *pp* **outbid** *or* **outbidden** [-'bɪdn], *cont* **outbidding**) *vt* enchérir sur; **we were outbid for the Renoir** nous voulions acheter le Renoir mais il est allé à plus offrant
outbidding [,aʊt'bɪdɪŋ] *n* surenchère *f*
outboard ['aʊtbɔːd] **1** *n (boat, motor)* hors-bord *m inv*
2 *adj (position, direction)* hors-bord
►► **outboard motor** moteur *m* hors-bord
outbound ['aʊtbaʊnd] *adj* en partance
►► *Com* **outbound freight** fret m de sortie; **outbound tourism** tourisme *m* émetteur
outbox [,aʊt'bɒks] *vt* boxer mieux que; **he was completely outboxed** il a été complètement dominé

outbreak ['aʊtbreɪk] *n* (**a**) *(of fire, storm, war)* début *m*; *(of violence, disease, epidemic)* éruption *f*; **there have been outbreaks of violence throughout the country** il y a eu des explosions de violence dans tout le pays; **at the outbreak of war** au début de la guerre, lorsque la guerre a éclaté; **at the outbreak of the strike** dès le début de la grève; **there's been an outbreak of flu** il y a eu de nombreux cas de grippe; **doctors fear an outbreak of meningitis** les médecins redoutent une épidémie de méningite; **to have an outbreak of spots** avoir une éruption de boutons

(**b**) *Met (sudden shower)* **there will be outbreaks of rain/snow in many places** il y aura des chutes de pluie/de neige un peu partout

outbreeding ['aʊt,bri:dɪŋ] *n* élevage *m* sans consanguinité

outbuilding ['aʊt,bɪldɪŋ] *n Br* (bâtiment *m*) annexe *f*; *(shed)* remise *f*; **the outbuildings** *(on farm, estate)* les dépendances *fpl*

outburst ['aʊtbɜ:st] *n* accès *m*, explosion *f*; **a sudden outburst of violence** *(from a group)* une soudaine explosion de violence; *(from an individual)* un accès de brutalité; **a sudden outburst of temper** un accès de mauvaise humeur; **you must control these outbursts** il faut que vous appreniez à garder votre sang-froid; **he apologized for his outburst** il s'est excusé de s'être remporté

outcast ['aʊtkɑ:st] **1** *n* paria *m*

2 *adj* proscrit, banni

outcaste ['aʊtkɑ:st] **1** *n* hors-caste *mf*

2 *adj* hors caste

outclass [,aʊt'klɑ:s] *vt* surclasser, surpasser; **she outclassed all of the other athletes** elle a surclassé tous les autres athlètes

outcome ['aʊtkʌm] *n (of election, competition)* résultat *m*; *(of sequence of events)* conséquence *f*; **the outcome of it all was that they never visited us again** résultat, ils ne sont jamais revenus chez nous; **I don't know what the outcome will be** je ne sais pas ce qui en résultera

outcrop *(pt & pp* **outcropped**, *cont* **outcropping**) **1** *n* ['aʊtkrɒp] *Geol* affleurement *m*

2 *vi* [,aʊt'krɒp] affleurer

outcropping ['aʊtkrɒpɪŋ] *Geol* **1** *n* affleurement *m*

2 *adj (seam)* affleurant au jour *ou* à la surface

outcross ['aʊtkrɒs] *n* mélange *m* d'individus sans consanguinité

outcry ['aʊtkraɪ] *(pl* **outcries**) *n* tollé *m*; **the government's decision was greeted by public outcry** la décision du gouvernement fut accueillie par un tollé général

out-cue *n TV & Cin* signal *m* de sortie; *(on video)* point *m* de sortie

outdated [,aʊt'deɪtɪd] *adj (idea, attitude)* démodé, dépassé; *(clothes)* démodé; *(expression)* désuet(ète) *m,f*

outdid [,aʊt'dɪd] *pt of* **outdo**

outdistance [,aʊt'dɪstəns] *vt* laisser derrière soi; **she was easily outdistanced by the Nigerian** elle fut facilement distancée par la Nigérienne

outdo [,aʊt'du:] *(pt* **outdid** [-'dɪd], *pp* **outdone** [-'dʌn]) *vt* surpasser, faire mieux que, l'emporter sur; **he's not easily outdone in an argument** il n'est pas facile d'avoir le dernier mot quand on discute avec lui; **Mark, not to be outdone, decided to be ill as well** Mark, pour ne pas être en reste, décida d'être malade lui aussi; **she wasn't to be outdone** *(in contest)* elle refusait de s'avouer vaincue; **she outdid all the other competitors** elle l'a emporté sur tous les autres concurrents

outdoor ['aʊtdɔ:(r)] *adj* (**a**) *(open-air → games, sports)* de plein air; *(→ work)* d'extérieur; *(→ swimming pool)* en plein air, découvert

(**b**) *(clothes)* d'extérieur

(**c**) *(person, lifestyle)* **to lead an outdoor life** vivre au grand air; **Kate is a real outdoor type** Kate aime la vie au grand air

▸▸ ***outdoor advertising*** publicité *f* extérieure; ***outdoor aerial*** antenne *f* extérieure; *Mktg* ***outdoor network*** réseau *m* d'affichage; *Cin* ***outdoor set*** décor *m* en extérieur; ***outdoor shoes*** *(warm)* grosses chaussures *fpl*; *(waterproof)* chaussures *fpl* imperméables; *(for walking)* chaussures *fpl* de marche

outdoors [,aʊt'dɔ:z] **1** *n* **the great outdoors** les grands espaces naturels

2 *adv* dehors, au dehors; **the scene takes place outdoors** la scène se déroule à l'extérieur; **to sleep outdoors** coucher à la belle étoile; **we were outdoors for most of the holiday** nous avons passé la plus grande partie de nos vacances au grand air

3 *adj (activity)* en *ou* de plein air; **she's an outdoous person** c'est une personne qui aime le grand air *ou* qui aime être dehors

outdoorsman [,aʊt'dɔ:zmən] *(pl* **outdoorsmen** [-mən]) *n* **to be an outdoorsman** aimer la nature

outer ['aʊtə(r)] **1** *adj* (**a**) *(external)* extérieur, externe; **the outer man** l'homme dans son apparence extérieure

(**b**) *(peripheral)* périphérique; **outer London** la banlieue londonienne

(**c**) *(furthest → limits)* externe; *(→ planets)* extérieur

2 *n (of target)* cercle *m* extérieur

▸▸ *Eng Law* ***outer bar*** = ensemble des avocats débutants qui ne plaident pas à la barre; *Archit* ***outer door*** avant-portail *m*; ***outer ear*** oreille *f* externe; ***outer garments*** vêtements *mpl* de dessus; ***the Outer Hebrides*** = archipel à l'ouest de l'Écosse; ***Outer Mongolia*** Mongolie-Extérieure *f*; **in Outer Mongolia** en Mongolie-Extérieure; ***outer space*** espace *m* intersidéral, cosmos *m*

outermost ['aʊtəməʊst] *adj* (**a**) *(closest to outside)* le plus (à l') extérieur; **the outermost layer was waterproofed** la première couche était imperméable; **make sure the coloured side is outermost** assure-toi que le côté coloré se trouve à l'extérieur (**b**) *(most isolated)* le plus reculé *ou* isolé; **the outermost limits of the galaxy** les limites les plus reculées de la galaxie

outerwear ['aʊtəweə(r)] *n* vêtements *mpl* d'extérieur

outface [,aʊt'feɪs] *vt* (**a**) *(outstare)* faire baisser les yeux à *(en dévisageant)*; *Fig* décontenancer (**b**) *(defy)* tenir tête à, défier

outfall ['aʊtfɔ:l] *n (of pipe)* embouchure *f*

outfield ['aʊtfi:ld] *Sport n* (**a**) *(part of field)* champ *m ou* terrain *m* extérieur (**b**) *(players)* joueurs *mpl* de champ

▸▸ ***outfield player*** joueur *m* de champ

outfielder ['aʊt,fi:ldə(r)] *n* joueur *m* de champ *(au baseball, au cricket)*

outfit ['aʊtfɪt] *(pt & pp* **outfitted**, *cont* **outfitting**) **1** *n* (**a**) *(clothes)* ensemble *m*, tenue *f*; **she appears in a new outfit every day** elle porte une tenue différente chaque jour; **riding/travelling outfit** tenue d'équitation/de voyage; **you should have seen the outfit he had on!** tu aurais dû voir comment il était attifé *ou* fagoté!

(**b**) *(child's disguise)* panoplie *f*; **cowboy's/nurse's outfit** panoplie *f* de cowboy/d'infirmière

(**c**) *(equipment, kit → for camping, fishing)* matériel *m*, équipement *m*; *(tools)* outils *mpl*, outillage *m*; *(case)* trousse *f*; **repair outfit** trousse *f* de réparation; **camera cleaning outfit** nécessaire *m* de nettoyage pour appareil photo

(**d**) *Fam (group)* équipe *f*, bande *f*; **the whole outfit was there** toute la bande *ou* l'équipe était là; *Am* **the Outfit** *(the Mafia)* la Mafia

(**e**) *Mil* équipe *f*

2 *vt (with equipment)* équiper

outfitter ['aʊt,fɪtə(r)] *n* (**a**) *esp Br (for clothes)* spécialiste *mf* de la confection; **school outfitter** *or* **outfitter's** = magasin qui vend des uniformes et autres vêtements scolaires; **sports outfitter** *or* **outfitter's** magasin de vêtements de sport; **(gentlemen's) outfitter** *or* **outfitter's** magasin de vêtements d'homme (**b**) *Am (for hunting equipment)* fournisseur *m*

outflank [,aʊt'flæŋk] *vt* (**a**) *Mil* déborder (**b**) *Fig (rival)* déjouer les manœuvres de

outflow ['aʊtfləʊ] *n* (**a**) *(of fluid)* écoulement *m*; *(of lava)* coulée *f* (**b**) *(place)* décharge *f* (**c**) *(of capital)* sorties *fpl*, fuite *f*; *(of gold, currency)* sortie *f*; *(of population)* exode *m*, sorties *fpl*, fuite *f*; **the institute's aim is to ensure the continuous outflow of new ideas** l'institut a pour but d'assurer un flux continu d'idées nouvelles; **outflow per hour** débit *m* par heure

outflowing ['aʊtfləʊɪŋ] *adj (current etc)* effluent, de sortie

▸▸ ***outflowing stream*** émissaire *m*

outfox [,aʊt'fɒks] *vt* se montrer plus rusé que

out-front *adj Am Fam* ouvert[❑], franc[❑]

outgassing [,aʊt'gæsɪŋ] *n Electron (of valve)* dégazage *m*

outgeneral [,aʊt'dʒenərəl] *vt* se montrer meilleur tacticien *ou* stratège que

outgoing ['aʊt,gəʊɪŋ] *adj* (**a**) *(departing → government, minister, tenant)* sortant; *(→ following resignation)* démissionnaire

(**b**) *(train, ship, plane)* en partance; *(letters)* à expédier; *(telephone call)* sortant

(**c**) *(tide)* descendant

(**d**) *(extrovert)* extraverti, plein d'entrain; **she's a very outgoing person** elle a une personnalité très ouverte

▸▸ *Mktg* ***outgoing inventory*** inventaire *m* de sortie; *Ind* ***outgoing shift*** équipe *f* sortante *ou* relevée

outgoings ['aʊt,gəʊɪŋz] *npl Br* dépenses *fpl*, frais *mpl*; *Fin* dépenses *fpl*, décaissements *mpl*; **the outgoings exceed the incomings** les dépenses excèdent les recettes

outgrow [,aʊt'grəʊ] *(pt* **outgrew** [-'gru:], *pp* **outgrown** [-'grəʊn]) *vt* (**a**) *(game, habit, hobby)* ne plus s'intéresser à *(en grandissant)*; *(attitude, behaviour, phase)* abandonner (en grandissant *ou* en prenant de l'âge); **Abby has outgrown dolls** Abby est devenue trop grande pour s'intéresser aux poupées; **they soon outgrew their first computer** ils ont vite eu fait le tour (des possibilités) de leur premier ordinateur; **he has outgrown his protest phase** il a dépassé le stade de la contestation; **I think I simply outgrew our friendship** je crois qu'avec l'âge, notre amitié a tout simplement perdu son intérêt pour moi; **he has outgrown his reputation as a romantic** il a fini par se défaire de sa réputation de romantique

(**b**) *(clothes)* devenir trop grand pour; **she has outgrown three pairs of shoes this year** elle a pris quatre pointures cette année

(**c**) *(grow faster than)* grandir plus (vite) que; **that boy is outgrowing his strength** ce garçon a une croissance beaucoup trop rapide pour sa constitution; **the world is outgrowing its resources** la population mondiale croît plus vite que les ressources dont elle dispose

outgrowth ['aʊtgrəʊθ] *n* excroissance *f*; *Fig (consequence)* conséquence *f*

outguess [aʊt'ges] *vt (person)* déjouer les intentions de

outgun [,aʊt'gʌn] *(pt & pp* **outgunned**, *cont* **outgunning**) *vt Mil* avoir une puissance de feu supérieure à; *Fig* vaincre, l'emporter sur

outhaul ['aʊthɔ:l] *n Naut* drisse *f*; **jib outhaul** hale-dehors *m inv*

out-Herod *vt (idiom)* **to out-Herod Herod** en rajouter *(dans la cruauté, la violence etc)*

outhouse ['aʊthaʊs, *pl* -haʊzɪz] *n* (**a**) *Br (outbuilding)* remise *f* (**b**) *Am (toilet)* toilettes *fpl* extérieures

outing ['aʊtɪŋ] *n* (**a**) *(trip)* sortie *f*, *(organized)* excursion *f*; **to go on an outing** faire une excursion; **to go for an outing in the car** partir faire une balade en voiture; **it was an outing for them** cela leur a fait une sortie; **school outing** sortie scolaire; **his first outing this season** *(of horse)* son premier concours de la saison

(**b**) *(of homosexual)* – dénonciation des homosexuels dans le monde de la politique et du spectacle

outjockey [,aʊt'dʒɒkɪ] *vt* rouler

outjump [,aʊt'dʒʌmp] *vt (competitor → in high jump)* sauter plus haut que; *(→ in long jump, triple jump, ski jump)* sauter plus loin que

outlandish [,aʊt'lændɪʃ] *adj (eccentric → appearance, behaviour, idea)* bizarre, excentrique; *Pej (language, style)* barbare

outlandishness [,aʊt'lændɪʃnɪs] *n (of appearance, behaviour, idea)* bizarrerie *f*, excentricité *f*; *Pej (of language, style)* caractère *m* barbare

outlast [,aʊt'lɑ:st] *vt (of person)* survivre à; *(of machine)* durer plus longtemps que; **the new exhaust will outlast the car** le nouveau pot d'échappement durera plus longtemps que la voiture; **it has outlasted ten centuries of war, weather and vandalism** cela a résisté à dix siècles de guerres, d'intempéries et de vandalisme; **the theory has outlasted all its critics**

cette théorie a résisté à l'assaut de tous les critiques

outlaw ['aʊtlɔː] **1** *n* hors-la-loi *m inv*

2 *vt (person)* mettre hors la loi; *(behaviour)* proscrire, interdire; *(organization)* interdire

outlay (*pt & pp* **outlaid** [-'leɪd]) **1** *n* ['aʊtleɪ] *(expense)* dépenses *fpl*, frais *mpl*; *(investment)* investissement *m*, mise *f* de fonds; **to get back** *or* **recover one's outlay** rentrer dans ses fonds

2 *vt* [aʊt'leɪ] *(spend)* dépenser; *(invest)* investir; **to outlay $10,000 capital** faire une mise de fonds de 10 000 dollars

outlet ['aʊtlet] **1** *n* (**a**) *(for liquid, air, smoke)* bouche *f*; *(in reservoir, lock)* déversoir *m*, dégorgeoir *m*; *(tap)* vanne *f* d'écoulement; **air outlet** bouche *f* d'aération; **the pipe/channel provides an outlet for excess water** le tuyau/le canal permet l'écoulement du trop-plein d'eau

(**b**) *(mouth of river)* embouchure *f*

(**c**) *(for feelings, energy)* exutoire *m*; **children need an outlet for their energies** les enfants ont besoin de se défouler; **writing is an outlet for me** l'écriture est pour moi un exutoire

(**d**) *(for talent)* débouché *m*; **the programme provides an outlet for young talent** l'émission permet à de jeunes talents de se faire connaître

(**e**) *Com (market)* débouché *m*; *(sales point)* point *m* de vente; **there are not many sales outlets in Japan** le Japon offre peu de débouchés commerciaux; **our North American outlets** notre réseau (de distribution) en Amérique du Nord

(**f**) *Am Elec* prise *f* (de courant)

2 *comp (for liquid)* d'écoulement; *(for gas, smoke)* d'échappement

►► *Com* ***outlet village*** = centre commercial spécialisé dans les marques à prix réduit

outlier ['aʊtlaɪə(r)] *n* (**a**) *Geol* avant-butte *f*, butte *f* témoin (**b**) *(person)* = personne qui habite loin de son lieu de travail

outline ['aʊtlaɪn] **1** *n* (**a**) *(contour, shape)* silhouette *f*, contour *m*; *(of building, of mountains)* silhouette *f*; *(of face, figure)* profil *m*; *Art (sketch)* esquisse *f*, ébauche *f*; **to draw sth in outline** faire un croquis de qch

(**b**) *(plan → of project, essay)* plan *m* d'ensemble, esquisse *f*; *(→ of book, play)* canevas *m*; **I've only written a rough outline of the chapter** je n'ai écrit que les grandes lignes du chapitre

(**c**) *(general idea)* idée *f* générale, grandes lignes *fpl*; *(overall view)* vue *f* d'ensemble; **to give sb an outline of sth** expliquer les grandes lignes de qch à qn; **she gave us an outline of** *or* **she explained to us in outline what she intended to do** elle nous a expliqué dans les grandes lignes ce qu'elle avait l'intention de faire; **An Outline of Modern History** *(title)* Éléments d'histoire moderne

2 *vt* (**a**) *(plan, theory)* expliquer dans les grandes lignes; *(facts)* résumer, passer en revue; **he outlined the situation briefly** il dressa un bref bilan de la situation; **could you outline your basic reasons for leaving?** pourriez-vous exposer brièvement les principales raisons de votre départ?

(**b**) *(person, building, mountain)* **the trees were outlined against the blue sky** les arbres se détachaient sur le fond bleu du ciel

(**c**) *Art* esquisser (les traits de), tracer; **to outline sth in pencil** faire le croquis de qch; **the figures are outlined in charcoal** les personnages sont esquissés au fusain; **to outline one's eyes in black** souligner le contour de ses yeux en noir

3 *adj* **an outline history of Greece** un précis d'histoire grecque

►► ***outline agreement*** protocole *m* d'accord; ***outline drawing*** dessin *m* au trait; *Comput* ***outline font*** police *f* vectorielle; ***outline plan*** plan *m* schématique *ou* d'ensemble; ***outline script*** scénario *m* indicatif

outliner ['aʊtlaɪnə(r)] *n Comput* outliner *m*

outlive [ˌaʊt'lɪv] *vt* survivre à; **she outlived her husband by only six months** elle n'a survécu à son mari que six mois; **he'll outlive us all at this rate** au train où il va, il nous enterrera tous; **the measures have outlived their usefulness** les mesures n'ont plus de raison d'être

outlook ['aʊtlʊk] *n* (**a**) *(prospect)* perspective *f*; *Econ & Pol* horizon *m*, perspectives *fpl* (d'avenir); **the outlook for the New Year is promising** cette nouvelle année s'annonce prometteuse; **it's a bleak outlook for the unemployed** pour les sans-emploi, les perspectives d'avenir ne sont guère réjouissantes; **the outlook for the future is grim** l'avenir est sombre

(**b**) *Met* prévision *f*, prévisions *fpl*; **the outlook for March is cold and windy** pour mars, on prévoit un temps froid avec beaucoup de vent

(**c**) *(viewpoint)* point de vue *m*, conception *f*; **what's your outlook on life?** quelle est votre conception de la vie?; **she has a pessimistic outlook** elle voit les choses en noir *ou* de manière pessimiste

(**d**) *(view → from window)* perspective *f*, vue *f*; **we have a pleasant outlook onto a small park** nous avons une vue agréable sur un petit parc

outlying ['aʊtˌlaɪɪŋ] *adj (remote → area, village)* isolé, à l'écart; *(far from centre → urban areas)* périphérique; **the outlying suburbs** la grande banlieue

outmanoeuvre, *Am* **outmaneuver** [ˌaʊtmə'nuːvə(r)] *vt Mil* se montrer meilleur tacticien que; *Fig* déjouer les manœuvres de; **we were outmanoeuvred by the opposition** l'opposition nous a pris de vitesse

outmatch [ˌaʊt'mætʃ] *vt* surclasser, dominer

outmoded [ˌaʊt'məʊdəd] *adj (custom, beliefs)* désuet(ète), démodé; *(furniture, theory, word)* démodé

outnumber [ˌaʊt'nʌmbə(r)] *vt* être plus nombreux que; **they were outnumbered by the enemy** l'ennemi était supérieur en nombre; **women outnumber men by two to one** il y a deux fois plus de femmes que d'hommes

out-of-body experience *n* expérience *f* hors du corps, EHC *f*, autoscopie *f*

out-of-bounds *adj* (**a**) *(barred)* interdit; **out-of-bounds to civilians** interdit aux civils (**b**) *Am Sport* hors (du) terrain

out-of-court *adj*

►► ***out-of-court settlement*** arrangement *m* à l'amiable

out-of-date *adj* (**a**) *(outdated → idea, attitude)* démodé, dépassé; *(→ clothes)* démodé; *(→ expression)* désuet(ète) (**b**) *(expired)* périmé; **your passport is out of date** votre passeport est périmé

out-of-door *Br* = **outdoor**

out-of-doors *Br* **1** *adj* = **outdoor**

2 *adv* = **outdoors**

out-of-focus *adj* flou

out-of-hand *adj Am Fam (extraordinary)* génial, géant

out-of-phase *adj TV & Cin* déphasé

out-of-pocket expenses *npl Fin* menues dépenses *fpl*

out-of-shot *adj TV & Cin* en dehors du champ

out-of-sync *adj* désynchronisé, hors synchronisation

out-of-the-money option *n St Exch* option *f* en dehors

out-of-the-ordinary *adj* insolite

out-of-the-way *adj* (**a**) *(isolated)* écarté, isolé; *(unknown to most people)* peu connu; *(not popular)* peu fréquenté (**b**) *(uncommon)* insolite

out-of-town *adj (shopping centre, retail park)* situé à la périphérie d'une ville

out-of-towner [-'taʊnə(r)] *n Am Fam* étranger(ère) *m,f* à la ville ❑; **he's an out-of-towner** il n'est pas d'ici ❑

outpace [ˌaʊt'peɪs] *vt (run faster than)* courir plus vite que; *(overtake)* dépasser, devancer; **demand has outpaced production** la demande a dépassé la production

outpatient ['aʊtˌpeɪʃənt] *n* malade *mf* en consultation externe; **he was being treated as an outpatient** il était traité en consultation externe

►► ***outpatients' clinic, outpatients' department*** service *m* de consultation externe

outperform [ˌaʊtpə'fɔːm] *vt* avoir de meilleures performances que, être plus performant que

outplacement ['aʊtpleɪsmənt] *n Com* outplacement *m*

outplay [ˌaʊt'pleɪ] *vt* jouer mieux que, dominer (au jeu); **she was outplayed** son adversaire a joué mieux qu'elle

outpoint 1 *n* ['aʊtpɔɪnt] *(on tape, film)* point *m* de sortie

2 *vt* [ˌaʊt'pɔɪnt] *(in boxing)* battre aux points

outport ['aʊtpɔːt] *n* (**a**) *(additional to main port)* avant-port *m* (**b**) *(port of embarkation)* port *m* de partance (**c**) *Can (in Newfoundland)* petit village *m* de pêcheurs

outpost ['aʊtpəʊst] *n* avant-poste *m*; **the last outposts of civilization** les derniers bastions de la civilisation

outpouring ['aʊtˌpɔːrɪŋ] *n (of feelings)* épanchement *m*, effusion *f*; *(of ideas, creativity)* déluge *m*, flux *m*; **outpourings** effusions *fpl*

output ['aʊtpʊt] (*pt & pp* **output**, *cont* **outputting**) **1** *n* (**a**) *(production)* production *f*; *(productivity)* rendement *m*; **our output is not keeping pace with demand** notre production est insuffisante pour répondre à la demande; **his writing output is phenomenal** c'est un auteur très prolifique

(**b**) *(power → of machine)* rendement *m*, débit *m*; **this machine has an output of 6,000 items an hour** cette machine débite 6000 pièces à l'heure

(**c**) *Elec* puissance *f*; *(of amplifier)* puissance *f* (de sortie); **output voltage** tension *f* de sortie

(**d**) *Comput (device)* sortie *f*; *(printout)* sortie *f* papier, tirage *m*

2 *vt* (**a**) *(of factory etc)* produire

(**b**) *Comput (data)* sortir (**to** sur)

3 *vi Comput* sortir des données

►► ***output bonus*** prime *f* de rendement; ***output buffer*** mémoire *f* tampon de sortie; ***output card*** carte *f* sortie, carte *f* résultat; ***output ceiling*** plafond *m* de la production; *Comput* ***output device*** périphérique *m* de sortie; ***output file*** fichier *m* de sortie; ***output formatting*** mise *f* en forme de sortie; ***output port*** port *m* de sortie; *Acct* ***output ratio*** coefficient *m* de capital; *Tech* ***output shaft*** arbre *m* de sortie; *Elec* ***output signal*** signal *m* de sortie; *Acct* ***output tax*** TVA *f* encaissée, impôt *m* à la consommation; *Tech* ***output torque*** couple *m* en sortie

outrage ['aʊtreɪdʒ] **1** *n* (**a**) *(affront)* outrage *m*, affront *m*; **it's an outrage against public decency** c'est un outrage aux bonnes mœurs; **it's an outrage against humanity/society** c'est un affront à l'humanité/la société

(**b**) *(scandal)* scandale *m*; **it's an outrage that no one came to their aid** c'est un scandale *ou* il est scandaleux que personne ne soit venu à leur secours

(**c**) *(indignation)* indignation *f*

(**d**) *(brutal act)* atrocité *f*, acte *m* de brutalité *ou* de violence; *Br* **bomb outrage** *(in headline)* attentat à la bombe

2 *vt* (**a**) *(person)* scandaliser

(**b**) *(moral sensibility, feelings)* outrager, faire outrage à

outraged ['aʊtreɪdʒd] *adj* outré, scandalisé; **to be outraged at** *or* **by sth** être outré *ou* scandalisé par qch

outrageous [aʊt'reɪdʒəs] *adj* (**a**) *(scandalous → behaviour, manners)* scandaleux; *(atrocious → crime, attack etc)* monstrueux, atroce; **an outrageous violation of human rights** une violation scandaleuse des droits de l'homme; **it's outrageous that anyone should believe him guilty!** il est scandaleux qu'on puisse le croire coupable!

(**b**) *(slightly offensive → humour, style)* choquant; *(→ joke, remark)* outrageant

(**c**) *(extravagant → person, colour)* extravagant; **he wears the most outrageous clothes** il porte les vêtements les plus extravagants

(**d**) *(price)* exorbitant

outrageously [aʊt'reɪdʒəslɪ] *adv* (**a**) *(scandalously)* de façon scandaleuse, scandaleusement; *(atrociously)* atrocement, monstrueusement; **they behaved outrageously** ils se sont comportés de façon scandaleuse; **we have been treated outrageously** on nous a traités d'une façon scandaleuse

(**b**) *(extravagantly)* de façon extravagante; **she was outrageously dressed** elle était habillée de façon extravagante; **the shop is outrageously expensive** les prix pratiqués dans ce magasin sont exorbitants

outrageousness [aʊt'reɪdʒəsnɪs] *n (of behaviour)* caractère *m* scandaleux *ou* outrageant; *(of crime, torture)* atrocité *f*; *(of dress, hairstyle)* extravagance *f*; *(of language)* outrance *f*; *(of prices)* exagération *f*

outran [ˌaʊt'ræn] *pt of* **outrun**

outrank [ˌaʊt'ræŋk] *vt* (**a**) *(be of higher rank than)* avoir un rang plus élevé que; *Mil* être supérieur en grade à; **he was outranked by most of those present** la plupart des personnes présentes avaient un grade supérieur au sien (**b**) *(take precedence over)* avoir *ou* prendre le pas sur; **to be outranked by** donner *ou* céder le pas à

outré ['u:treɪ] *adj Br Formal or Hum* outrancier

outreach 1 *vt* [ˌaʊt'ri:tʃ] (**a**) *(exceed)* dépasser (**b**) *(in arm length)* avoir le bras plus long que; *(in boxing)* avoir l'allonge supérieure à

2 *n* ['aʊtri:tʃ] *Admin* = recherche des personnes qui ne demandent pas l'aide sociale dont elles pourraient bénéficier

▸▸ ***outreach worker*** = employé ou bénévole dans un bureau d'aide sociale

outrider ['aʊtˌraɪdə(r)] *n Br (motorcyclist)* motard *m* (d'escorte); *(horseman)* cavalier *m*

outrigger ['aʊtˌrɪgə(r)] *n Naut (gen)* balancier *m*; *(on racing boat)* portant *m*, outrigger *m*

outright 1 *adj* ['aʊtraɪt] (**a**) *(absolute, utter → dishonesty, hypocrisy)* pur (et simple), absolu; *(→ liar)* fieffé; *(→ ownership)* total, absolu; *(frank → denial, refusal)* net, catégorique; **he's an outright fascist!** c'est un vrai fasciste!; **she's an outright opponent of capital punishment** c'est une adversaire inconditionnelle de la peine de mort; **it was outright blackmail** c'était purement et simplement du chantage, c'était du chantage, ni plus ni moins

(**b**) *(clear → win, winner)* incontesté; **it's an outright win for New Zealand** la victoire revient incontestablement à la Nouvelle-Zélande

(**c**) *Com (purchase, sale → for cash)* au comptant; *(→ total)* en bloc

2 *adv* [aʊt'raɪt] (**a**) *(frankly → refuse)* net, carrément; *(→ ask)* carrément, franchement

(**b**) *(totally → oppose)* absolument; *(→ own)* totalement

(**c**) *(clearly → win)* nettement, haut la main

(**d**) *Com (buy, sell → for cash)* au comptant; *(→ totally)* en bloc

(**e**) *(instantly)* **they were killed outright** ils ont été tués sur le coup

outrival [ˌaʊt'raɪvəl] *vt (person)* surpasser, l'emporter sur

outro ['aʊtrəʊ] *n Fam (of song)* fin ☐ *f*

outrun [ˌaʊt'rʌn] *(pt* **outran** [-'ræn], *pp* **outrun**, *cont* **outrunning**) *vt* (**a**) *(run faster than)* courir plus vite que; *(pursuer)* distancer

(**b**) *(ability, energy, resources)* excéder, dépasser; **our enthusiasm outran our financial resources** notre enthousiasme dépassait nos ressources financières; **his zeal outruns his discretion** son ardeur l'emporte sur son jugement

outs [aʊts] *npl Am Fam* **to be on the outs with sb** être brouillé avec qn; **they're on the outs** ils sont brouillés

outsell [ˌaʊt'sel] *(pt & pp* **outsold** [-'səʊld]) *vt (of article)* se vendre mieux que; *(of company)* vendre davantage que, vendre plus que; **the brand of cigarettes that outsells all the others** la marque de cigarettes la plus vendue; **her book outsold all of this week's other publications** son livre a été la meilleure vente de la semaine

outset ['aʊtset] *n* **at the outset** au début, au départ; **from the outset** dès le début, d'emblée

outshine [ˌaʊt'ʃaɪn] *(pt & pp* **outshone** [-'ʃɒn]) *vt* (**a**) *(shine brighter than)* briller plus que (**b**) *Fig (surpass)* surpasser, éclipser; **I don't like being outshone** je n'aime pas qu'on m'éclipse *ou* me surpasse

OUTSIDE

dehors	▸ **1 (a) – (c); 4 (a)**
à l'extérieur de	▸ **2 (a)**
devant	▸ **2 (c)**
en dehors de	▸ **2 (d)**
extérieur	▸ **3 (a), (b), (e); 4 (a), (d)**
faible	▸ **3 (c)**
maximum	▸ **3 (d)**

1 *adv* [aʊt'saɪd] (**a**) *(outdoors)* dehors, à l'extérieur; **it's cold outside** il fait froid dehors; **put the box outside** mettez la boîte dehors; **to go outside** sortir; **to run/to dash outside** sortir en courant/à toute vitesse; **seen from outside** vu de l'extérieur; **the car is waiting outside** la voiture attend dehors; **you'll have to park outside** il faudra vous garer dans la rue

(**b**) *(on other side of door)* dehors; **can you wait outside?** pouvez-vous attendre dehors?; **there's a woman outside in the hall** il y a une femme dehors dans le vestibule

(**c**) *(out of prison)* dehors; **after ten years, it's hard to imagine life outside** après dix ans, c'est dur d'imaginer la vie dehors

2 *prep* [aʊt'saɪd, 'aʊtsaɪd] (**a**) *(on or to the exterior)* à l'extérieur de, hors de; **nobody is allowed outside the house** personne n'a le droit de quitter la maison; **outside my bedroom** *(at the door)* à la porte de ma chambre; *(below the windows)* sous les fenêtres de ma chambre; **your front foot must remain outside the base line** votre pied d'appel doit rester derrière la *ou* ne doit pas mordre sur la ligne; **put the eggs outside the window/the door** mettez les œufs sur le rebord de la fenêtre/devant la porte; **she was wearing her shirt outside her trousers** elle portait sa chemise par-dessus son pantalon; **nobody outside the office must know** personne ne doit être mis au courant en dehors du bureau; *Fig* **the troublemakers were people from outside the group** les fauteurs de troubles ne faisaient pas partie du groupe

(**b**) *(away from)* **we live some way outside the town** nous habitons assez loin de la ville; **I don't think anybody outside France has heard of him** je ne pense pas qu'il soit connu ailleurs qu'en France

(**c**) *(in front of)* devant; **they met outside the cathedral** *(by chance)* ils se sont rencontrés devant la cathédrale; *(by arrangement)* ils se sont retrouvés devant la cathédrale

(**d**) *(beyond)* en dehors de, au-delà de; **it's outside his field** ce n'est pas son domaine; **it's outside my experience** ça ne m'est jamais arrivé; **the matter is outside our responsibility** la question ne relève pas de notre responsabilité; **outside office hours** en dehors des heures de bureau

3 *adj* ['aʊtsaɪd] (**a**) *(exterior)* extérieur; **the outside world** le monde extérieur; **she has few outside interests** elle s'intéresse à peu de choses à part son travail; **an outside toilet** des toilettes (situées) à l'extérieur; **the outside edge** le bord extérieur

(**b**) *(from elsewhere → help, influence)* extérieur; **to get an outside opinion** demander l'avis d'un tiers

(**c**) *(poor → possibility)* faible; **she has only an outside chance of winning** elle n'a que très peu de chances de gagner

(**d**) *(maximum → price)* maximum; **the outside odds are 6 to 1** la cote maximum est de 6 contre 1

(**e**) *(not belonging to a group)* extérieur, indépendant; **an outside body** un organisme indépendant

4 *n* [aʊt'saɪd, 'aʊtsaɪd] (**a**) *(exterior → of building, container)* extérieur *m*, dehors *m*; **the outside of the house needs repainting** l'extérieur de la maison a besoin d'être repeint; **on the outside of sth** à l'extérieur de qch; **the fruit is yellow on the outside** le fruit est jaune à l'extérieur; **the door opens from (the) outside** la porte s'ouvre de l'extérieur *ou* du dehors; **the arms were flown in from outside** les armes ont été introduites dans le pays par avion; *Fig* **looking at the problem from (the) outside** quand on considère le problème de l'extérieur

(**b**) *(out of prison)* **I've almost forgotten what life is like on the outside** j'ai presque oublié ce qu'est la vie dehors *ou* de l'autre côté des barreaux

(**c**) *Aut* **to overtake on the outside** *(driving on left)* doubler à droite; *(driving on right)* doubler à gauche; *Sport* **to come up on the outside** *(in race)* arriver sur l'extérieur

(**d**) *(outer edge)* extérieur *m*; **begin at the outside and work in** commencez par les bords et allez vers l'intérieur

5 at the outside *adv* (**a**) *(in number)* tout au plus, au maximum; **twenty people at the outside** vingt personnes tout au plus

(**b**) *(in time)* au plus tard; **6:30 at the outside** 6 heures 30 au plus tard

6 outside of *prep esp Am* (**a**) = **outside** *prep*

(**b**) *(except for)* en dehors de; **nobody, outside of a few close friends, was invited** personne, en dehors de *ou* à part quelques amis intimes, n'était invité

(**c**) *(more than)* au-delà de; **an offer outside of 10 million** une offre de plus de *ou* supérieure à 10 millions

▸▸ *TV* ***outside broadcast*** émission *f* réalisée en dehors des studios; *TV* ***outside broadcasting*** émissions *fpl* réalisées en dehors des studios; *TV* ***outside broadcasting vehicle*** car *m* régie, unité *f* mobile de tournage; *St Exch* ***outside broker*** courtier(ère) *m,f* marron *ou* libre; *Fin* ***outside brokerage*** affaires *fpl* de banque; ***outside half*** *(in rugby)* demi *m* d'ouverture; ***outside lane*** *(driving on left)* file *f ou* voie *f* de droite; *(driving on right)* file *f ou* voie *f* de gauche; *Sport* couloir *m* extérieur; *Ftbl* ***outside left*** ailier *m* gauche; *Tel* ***outside line*** ligne *f* extérieure; *St Exch* ***outside market*** marché *m* hors cote *ou* en coulisse; *St Exch* ***outside price*** prix *m* maximum; *Ftbl* ***outside right*** ailier *m* droit

outsider [ˌaʊt'saɪdə(r)] *n* (**a**) *(person)* étranger(ère) *m,f*; **he's always been a bit of an outsider** il a toujours été plutôt marginal; **I'd be glad to have an outsider's viewpoint** je serais heureux d'avoir un point de vue extérieur (**b**) *Sport* outsider *m* (**c**) *St Exch* courtier(ère) *m,f* marron

outsize ['aʊtsaɪz] *Br* **1** *n (gen)* grande taille *f*, grandes tailles *fpl*; *(for men)* très grand patron *m*

2 *adj* (**a**) *(large)* énorme, colossal (**b**) *(in clothes sizes)* grande taille *(inv)*

outsized ['aʊtsaɪzd] *adj* énorme, colossal

outskirts ['aʊtskɜ:ts] *npl (of town)* banlieue *f*, périphérie *f*; *(of forest)* orée *f*, lisière *f*; **we live on the outskirts of Copenhagen** nous habitons la banlieue de Copenhague

outsmart [ˌaʊt'smɑ:t] *vt Fam* se montrer plus malin(igne) que

outsource ['aʊtsɔ:s] *vt Com* externaliser; **computer maintenance has been outsourced to another company** l'entretien du matériel informatique a été externalisé

outsourcing ['aʊtsɔ:sɪŋ] *n Com* externalisation *f*

outspend [ˌaʊt'spend] *(pt & pp* **outspent** [-'spent]) *vt* dépenser plus que

outspoken [ˌaʊt'spəʊkən] *adj* franc (franche); **to be outspoken** parler franchement, avoir son franc-parler; **she was outspoken in her criticism of the project** elle a ouvertement critiqué le projet; **he has always been an outspoken critic of the reforms** il a toujours ouvertement critiqué les réformes

outspokenly [ˌaʊt'spəʊkənlɪ] *adv* franchement, carrément

outspokenness [ˌaʊt'spəʊkənnɪs] *n* franc-parler *m*

outspread [ˌaʊt'spred] *adj* écarté; **with outspread arms** les bras écartés; **with outspread wings** les ailes déployées; **with outspread fingers** les doigts écartés; **an outspread newspaper** un journal déplié

outstanding [ˌaʊt'stændɪŋ] *adj* (**a**) *(remarkable → ability, performance)* exceptionnel, remarquable; *(notable → event, feature)* marquant, mémorable; **an outstanding politician** un politicien hors pair *ou* exceptionnel; **she plays outstanding tennis** c'est une joueuse de tennis exceptionnelle *ou* remarquable

(**b**) *(unresolved → problem)* non résolu, en suspens; **there is still one outstanding matter** il reste encore un problème à régler

(**c**) *(unfinished → business, work)* inachevé, en cours; *Admin* en souffrance, en attente; **there are about 20 pages outstanding** il reste environ 20 pages à faire

(**d**) *Fin (amount, account)* impayé(e), dû (due); *(bill)* impayé; *(payment)* en retard; *(invoice)* en souffrance; *(interest)* échu(e)

(**e**) *St Exch (shares)* en cours, en circulation

▸▸ *Fin* ***outstanding balance*** solde *m* à découvert; *Banking* ***outstanding cheque*** chèque *m* en circulation; *Fin* ***outstanding credits*** encours *m* de crédit; *Fin* ***outstanding debts*** créances *fpl* (à recouvrer); ***outstanding rent*** arriérés *mpl* de loyer

outstandingly [ˌaʊt'stændɪŋlɪ] *adv* exceptionnellement, remarquablement

outstare [ˌaʊt'steə(r)] *vt* faire baisser les yeux à *(en dévisageant)*

outstation ['aʊtsteɪʃən] *n* (**a**) *(in colony, isolated region)* avant-poste *m* (**b**) *Rad* station *f* extérieure *ou* satellite

outstay [ˌaʊt'steɪ] *vt* (**a**) *(of guests)* rester plus longtemps que; **to outstay one's welcome** abuser de l'hospitalité de ses hôtes (**b**) *Br Sport (competitor)* tenir plus longtemps que

outstretched [ˌaʊt'stretʃt] *adj (limbs, body)* étendu, allongé; *(wings)* déployé; **to lie outstretched** s'allonger; **with arms outstretched, with outstretched arms** *(gen)* les bras écartés; *(in welcome)* à bras (grand) ouverts; **the beggar stood outside the church with outstretched hands** le mendiant se tenait devant l'église, la main tendue

outstrip [ˌaʊt'strɪp] *Br* (*pt & pp* **outstripped,** *cont* **outstripping**) *vt Br* dépasser, surpasser; **they outstripped all their rivals** ils l'ont emporté sur tous leurs concurrents

out-supplier *n Com* fournisseur *m* potentiel

outta ['aʊtə] *Fam* = **out of**

outtake ['aʊtteɪk] *n Cin & TV* coupure *f*

outvote [ˌaʊt'vəʊt] *vt* (**a**) *(bill, reform)* rejeter (à la majorité des voix); **the bill was outvoted** une majorité a voté contre le projet de loi (**b**) *(person)* mettre en minorité; **I wanted to go to the cinema, but I was outvoted** je voulais aller au cinéma, mais les autres ont voté contre

outward ['aʊtwəd] **1** *adj* (**a**) *(external)* extérieur, externe; *(apparent)* apparent; **to (all) outward appearances, she's very successful** selon toute apparence, elle réussit très bien; **an outward show of wealth** un étalage de richesses; **she showed no outward signs of fear** elle ne montrait aucun signe de peur

(**b**) *(in direction)* vers l'extérieur; **the outward journey** le voyage aller, l'aller *m*

2 *adv* vers l'extérieur; **outward bound** *(ship, train)* en partance

►► *Com* ***outward bill of lading*** connaissement *m* de sortie; ***outward bound course*** école *f* d'endurcissement (en plein air); ***outward cargo*** cargaison *f* d'aller; *Econ* ***outward investment*** investissement *m* à l'étranger; ***outward mail*** courrier *m* (en partance) pour l'étranger

outwardly ['aʊtwədlɪ] *adv* en apparence; **she remained outwardly calm** elle est restée calme en apparence; **outwardly they seem to get on** ils donnent l'impression de bien s'entendre

outwards ['aʊtwədz] *adv* vers l'extérieur; **his feet turn outwards** il marche les pieds en dehors; **the door opens outwards** la porte s'ouvre vers l'extérieur

outwear [aʊt'weə(r)] *vt* (**a**) *(wear away)* user (**b**) *(last longer than)* durer plus longtemps que; **the system has outworn its usefulness** le système est désormais périmé

outweigh [ˌaʊt'weɪ] *vt* (**a**) *(be more important than)* l'emporter sur; **the advantages easily outweigh the disadvantages** les avantages l'emportent largement sur les inconvénients (**b**) *(weigh more than)* peser plus que

outwit [ˌaʊt'wɪt] (*pt & pp* **outwitted,** *cont* **outwitting**) *vt* se montrer plus malin(igne) que; **we've been outwitted** on nous a eus

outwith [ˌaʊt'wɪð] *prep Scot* (**a**) *(beyond)* en dehors de, au-delà de; **it's outwith his field** ce n'est pas son domaine; **it's outwith my experience** ça ne m'est jamais arrivé; **the matter is outwith our responsibility** la question ne relève pas de notre responsabilité; **outwith office hours** en dehors des heures de bureau

(**b**) *(away from)* **we live some way outwith the town** nous habitons assez loin de la ville; **I don't think anybody outwith France has heard of him** je ne pense pas qu'il soit connu ailleurs qu'en France

outwork ['aʊtwɜːk] **1** *n Br (work)* travail *m* fait à l'extérieur

2 outworks *npl Mil* ouvrage *m* défensif avancé

outworker ['aʊtˌwɜːkə(r)] *n Br* travailleur(euse) *m,f* à domicile

outworn ['aʊtˌwɔːn] *adj (clothes)* usé; *(custom, idea)* dépassé, vieux-jeu *(inv)*

ouzel ['uːzəl] *n Orn* (**a**) **ring ouzel** merle *m* à plastron *ou* à collier; **water ouzel** cincle *m* plongeur, merle *m* d'eau (**b**) *Arch or Literary* merle *m* (noir)

ouzo ['uːzəʊ] *n* ouzo *m*

ova ['əʊvə] *pl of* **ovum**

oval ['əʊvəl] **1** *adj* (en) ovale

2 *n* ovale *m*

3 Oval *n* **the Oval** = célèbre terrain de cricket dans le centre de Londres

►► ***the Oval Office*** *(office)* le Bureau ovale; *(authority)* la présidence des États-Unis

Ovaltine® ['əʊvəltiːn] *n* = boisson chaude instantanée, surtout consommée le soir

ovarian [əʊ'veərɪən] *adj* ovarien

►► ***ovarian cancer*** cancer *m* des ovaires; ***ovarian cyst*** kyste *m* de l'ovaire

ovariectomy [ˌəʊvərɪ'ektəmɪ] (*pl* **ovariectomies**) *n Med* ovariectomie *f*

ovaritis [ˌəʊvə'raɪtɪs] *n Med* ovarite *f*

ovary ['əʊvərɪ] (*pl* **ovaries**) *n* ovaire *m*

ovate ['əʊveɪt] *adj* oviforme

ovation [əʊ'veɪʃən] *n* ovation *f*; **to give sb an ovation** faire une ovation à qn

oven ['ʌvən] *n* four *m*; **to cook sth in the oven** faire cuire qch au four; **cook in a hot/medium oven** faire cuire à four chaud/à four moyen; **to put one's head in the oven** se suicider (au gaz); *Fig* **Athens is like an oven in summer** Athènes est une vraie fournaise en été

►► ***oven glove*** gant *m* isolant

ovenable ['ʌvənəbəl] *adj* allant au four

oven-baked *adj Ind* cuit au four

►► ***oven-baked enamel*** émail *m* (cuit) au four

ovenbird ['ʌvənbɜːd] *n Orn* (**a**) *(North American)* fauvette *f* (d'Amérique) couronnée (**b**) *(South American)* fournier *m*

ovenproof ['ʌvənpruːf] *adj* allant *ou* qui va au four

oven-ready *adj* prêt à cuire *ou* à mettre au four; *(chicken, meat)* prêt à rôtir

ovenware ['ʌvənweə(r)] *n* plats *mpl* allant au four

OVER ['əʊvə(r)]

au-dessus de	► **1A (a)**
sur	► **1A (b); B (a), (b)**
par-dessus	► **1A (b), (c)**
plus de	► **1C (a)**
au sujet de	► **1D (a)**
plus	► **2B (b)**
encore	► **2B (d)**
fini	► **3**

1 *prep* **A.** (**a**) *(above)* au-dessus de; **a bullet whistled over my head** une balle siffla au-dessus de ma tête; **they live over the shop** ils habitent au-dessus du magasin; **the plane came down over France** l'avion s'est écrasé en France

(**b**) *(on top of, covering)* sur, par-dessus; **put a lace cloth over the table** mets une nappe en dentelle sur la table; **she wore a cardigan over her dress** elle portait un gilet par-dessus sa robe; **she wore a black dress with a red cardigan over it** elle avait une robe noire avec un gilet rouge par-dessus; **I put my hand over my mouth** j'ai mis ma main devant ma bouche; **he had his jacket over his arm** il avait sa veste sur le bras; **with his hat over his eyes** le chapeau enfoncé jusqu'aux yeux; **we painted over the wallpaper** nous avons peint par-dessus la tapisserie; **she was hunched over the wheel** elle était penchée sur la roue

(**c**) *(across the top or edge of)* par-dessus; **he was watching me over his newspaper** il m'observait par-dessus son journal; **I peered over the edge** j'ai jeté un coup d'œil par-dessus le rebord; **he fell/jumped over the cliff** il est tombé/a sauté du haut de la falaise

(**d**) *(across the entire surface of)* **to cross over the road** traverser la rue; **they live over the road from me** ils habitent en face de chez moi; **there's a fine view over the valley** on a une belle vue sur la vallée; **the bridge over the river** le pont qui enjambe la rivière; **he ran his eye over the article** il a parcouru l'article des yeux; **she ran her hand over the smooth marble** elle passa la main sur le marbre lisse; **we travelled for days over land and sea** nous avons voyagé pendant des jours par terre et par mer; **a strange look came over her face** son visage prit une expression étrange

(**e**) *(on the far side of)* **the village over the hill** le village de l'autre côté de la colline; **they must be over the border by now** ils doivent avoir passé la frontière maintenant

B. (**a**) *(indicating position of control)* **to rule over a country** régner sur un pays; **I have no control/influence over them** je n'ai aucune autorité/influence sur eux; **she has some kind of hold over him** elle a une certaine emprise sur lui; **she watched over her children** elle surveillait ses enfants

(**b**) *(indicating position of superiority, importance)* sur; **a victory over the forces of reaction** une victoire sur les forces réactionnaires; **our project takes priority over the others** notre projet a priorité sur les autres

C. (**a**) *(with specific figure or amount → more than)* plus de; **it took me well/just over an hour** j'ai mis bien plus/un peu plus d'une heure; **he must be over thirty** il doit avoir plus de trente ans; **children over (the age of) 7** les enfants (âgés) de plus de 7 ans; **think of a number over 100** pensez à un chiffre supérieur à 100; **not over 250 grams** *(in post office)* jusqu'à 250 grammes

(**b**) *(louder than)* **his voice rang out over the others** sa voix dominait toutes les autres; **I couldn't hear what she was saying over the music** la musique m'empêchait d'entendre ce qu'elle disait

(**c**) *Math (divided by)* **eight over two** huit divisé par deux

(**d**) *(during)* **I've got a job over the long vacation** je vais travailler pendant les grandes vacances; **I'll do it over the weekend** je le ferai pendant le week-end; **what are you doing over Easter?** qu'est-ce que tu fais pour Pâques?; **it's improved over the years** ça s'est amélioré au cours *ou* au fil des années; **over the next few decades** au cours des prochaines décennies; **over a period of several weeks** pendant plusieurs semaines; **we discussed it over a drink/over lunch/over a game of golf** nous en avons discuté autour d'un verre/pendant le déjeuner/en faisant une partie de golf

D. (**a**) *(concerning)* au sujet de; **a disagreement over working conditions** un conflit portant sur les conditions de travail; **they're always quarrelling over money** ils se disputent sans cesse pour des questions d'argent; **to laugh over sth** rire (à propos) de qch; **there's a big question mark over his future** nous n'avons aucune idée de ce qu'il va devenir

(**b**) *(by means of, via)* **they were talking over the telephone** ils parlaient au téléphone; **I heard it over the radio** je l'ai entendu à la radio

(**c**) *(recovered from)* **are you over your bout of flu?** est-ce que tu es guéri *ou* est-ce que tu t'es remis de ta grippe?; **he's over the shock now** il s'en est remis maintenant; **we'll soon be over the worst** le plus dur sera bientôt passé; **it took her a long time to get over his death** elle a mis longtemps à se remettre de sa mort; **don't worry, you'll be** *or* **get over her soon** ne t'en fais pas, bientôt tu n'y penseras plus

2 *adv* **A.** (**a**) *(indicating movement or location, across distance or space)* **an eagle flew over** un aigle passa au-dessus de nous; **she walked over to him and said hello** elle s'approcha de lui pour dire bonjour; **he led me over to the window** il m'a conduit à la fenêtre; **he must have seen us, he's coming over** il a dû nous voir, il vient vers nous *ou* de notre côté; **pass my cup over, will you** tu peux me passer ma tasse?; **throw it over!** *(over the wall etc)* lance-le par-dessus!; *(throw it to me)* lance-le moi!; **she glanced over at me** elle jeta un coup d'œil dans ma direction; **she leaned over to whisper to him** elle se pencha pour lui chuchoter quelque chose à l'oreille; **over in the States** aux États-Unis; **over there** là-bas; **come over here!** viens (par) ici!; **has Colin been over?** est-ce que Colin est passé?; **she drove over to meet us** elle est venue nous rejoindre en voiture; **let's have**

or **invite them over for dinner** si on les invitait à dîner?; **we have guests over from Morocco** nous avons des invités qui viennent du Maroc

(**b**) *(everywhere)* **she's travelled the whole world over** elle a voyagé dans le monde entier; **people the world over are watching the broadcast live** des téléspectateurs du monde entier assistent à cette retransmission en direct

(**c**) *(indicating movement from a higher to a lower level)* **I fell over** je suis tombé (par terre); **she knocked her glass over** elle a renversé son verre; **he flipped the pancake over** il a retourné la crêpe; *Am Fam* **over easy** *(egg)* cuit sur les deux côtés; **they rolled over and over in the grass** ils se roulaient dans l'herbe; **and over I went** et me voilà par terre

(**d**) *(so as to cover)* **we just whitewashed it over** nous l'avons simplement passé à la chaux; **the bodies were covered over with blankets** les corps étaient recouverts avec des couvertures

(**e**) *(into the hands of another person, group etc)* **he's gone over to the other side/to the opposition** il est passé de l'autre côté/dans l'opposition; **they handed him over to the authorities** ils l'ont remis aux autorités *ou* entre les mains des autorités; *Rad & TV* **and now over to Kirsty Jones in Paris** nous passons maintenant l'antenne à Kirsty Jones à Paris; **over to you** *(it's your turn)* c'est votre tour, c'est à vous; *Tel* **over (to you)!** à vous!; **over and out!** terminé!

B. (**a**) *(left, remaining)* **there were/I had a few pounds (left) over** il restait/il me restait quelques livres; **you will keep what is (left) over** vous garderez l'excédent *ou* le surplus; **seven into fifty-two makes seven with three over** cinquante-deux divisé par sept égale sept, il reste trois

(**b**) *(with specific figure or amount → more)* plus; **men of 30 and over** les hommes âgés de 30 ans et plus; **articles costing £100 or over** les articles de 100 livres et plus

(**c**) *(through)* **read it over carefully** lisez-le attentivement; **do you want to talk the matter over?** voulez-vous en discuter?

(**d**) *(again, more than once)* encore; *Am* **I had to do the whole thing over** j'ai dû tout refaire; **she won the tournament five times over** elle a gagné le tournoi à cinq reprises

3 *adj* fini; **the party's over** la fête est finie; **the danger is over** le danger est passé; **the war was just over** la guerre venait de finir *ou* de s'achever; **I'm glad that's over (with)!** je suis bien content que ça soit fini!; **that's over and done with** voilà qui est fini et bien fini

4 *n (in cricket)* série *f* de six balles

5 overs *npl Typ (extra paper)* main *f* de passe, simple passe *f*; *(extra books)* exemplaires *mpl* de passe

6 over and above *prep* en plus de; **over and above what we've already paid** en plus de ce que nous avons déjà payé; **and over and above that, he was banned from driving for life** en plus, on lui a retiré son permis (de conduire) à vie

7 over and over *adv* **I've told you over and over (again)** je te l'ai répété je ne sais combien de fois; **he did it over and over (again) until...** il a recommencé des dizaines de fois jusqu'à ce que...

They think it's all over (...it is now)

Ces mots, précédés de la phrase **some people are on the pitch...** ("il y a quelques personnes sur le terrain"), furent prononcés par Kenneth Wolstenholme, commentateur sportif de la BBC, au moment où Geoff Hurst marqua un dernier but pour l'Angleterre dans les dernières secondes de la finale de la Coupe du monde de football de 1966, qui vit l'Angleterre l'emporter face à la République fédérale d'Allemagne.

Aujourd'hui on utilise cette expression ("ils croient que c'est terminé,... maintenant, c'est terminé") en anglais britannique lorsque quelqu'un s'imagine à tort qu'une chose est terminée, ou bien au moment même où cette chose s'achève.

over- [ˈəʊvə(r)] *pref* (**a**) *(excessive)* **over-activity** suractivité *f*; **over-cautious** trop prudent, d'une prudence excessive (**b**) *(more than)* **a club for the over-fifties** un club pour les plus de cinquante ans

overabundance [ˌəʊvərəˈbʌndəns] *n* surabondance *f*

overabundant [ˌəʊvərəˈbʌndənt] *adj* surabondant

overachieve [ˌəʊvərəˈtʃiːv] *vi* réussir brillamment; **children who overachieve** les enfants surdoués

overachiever [ˌəʊvərəˈtʃiːvə(r)] *n* surdoué(e) *m,f*

overact [ˌəʊvərˈækt] *vi* forcer la note, en faire trop

overacting [ˌəʊvərˈæktɪŋ] *n* exagération *f*, jeu *m* outré

overactive [ˌəʊvərˈæktɪv] *adj* **to have an overactive imagination** avoir une imagination débordante; *Med* **to have an overactive thyroid** faire de l'hyperthyroïdie

overactivity [ˌəʊværækˈtɪvɪtɪ] *n* suractivité *f*

overage [ˈəʊvərɪdʒ] *n Am (surplus)* surplus *m*, excédent *m*

over-age *adj (too old)* trop âgé

overall 1 *adv* [ˌəʊvərˈɔːl] (**a**) *(in general → consider, examine)* en général, globalement

(**b**) *(measure)* de bout en bout, d'un bout à l'autre; *(cost, amount)* en tout

(**c**) *(in competition, sport)* au classement général; **Britain finished third overall** la Grande-Bretagne a fini troisième au classement général

2 *adj* [ˈəʊvərɔːl] (**a**) *(general)* global, d'ensemble; **my overall impression** mon impression d'ensemble; **overall control of the region has fallen into the hands of the rebels** la plus grande partie de la région est désormais aux mains des rebelles; **she has overall responsibility for sales** elle est responsable de l'ensemble du service des ventes

(**b**) *(total → cost, amount)* total; *(→ measurement)* total, hors tout

3 *n* [ˈəʊvərɔːl] *(protective coat)* blouse *f*; *Am (boiler suit)* bleu *m* de travail

4 overalls *npl* [ˈəʊvərɔːlz] *Br (boiler suit)* bleu *m* de travail; *Am (dungarees)* salopette *f*

►► ***overall budget*** budget *m* global; ***overall consumption*** consommation *f* totale; ***overall demand*** demande *f* globale; *Pol* ***overall majority*** majorité *f* absolue

overambitious [ˌəʊværæmˈbɪʃəs] *adj* trop ambitieux

overanxiety [ˌəʊværæŋˈzaɪɪtɪ] *n* (**a**) *(worry)* vives inquiétudes *fpl*, inquiétude *f* extrême (**b**) *(keenness)* **his overanxiety to please worked against him** son trop grand souci de plaire a joué contre lui

overanxious [ˌəʊvərˈæŋkʃəs] *adj* (**a**) *(worried)* trop inquiet(ète); **don't be overanxious about the exam** ne vous inquiétez pas trop au sujet de l'examen (**b**) *(keen)* **he did not seem overanxious to meet her** il n'avait pas l'air tellement pressé de faire sa connaissance; **she is overanxious to please** elle est trop désireuse *ou* soucieuse de plaire

overarch [ˌəʊvəˈrɑːtʃ] *Literary* **1** *vt* former une arche au-dessus de

2 *vi* former une arche

overarm [ˈəʊvərɑːm] *adv (serve, bowl)* par-dessus l'épaule; **to throw a ball overarm** lancer une balle par-dessus sa tête; **to swim overarm** nager à l'indienne

►► *Sport* ***overarm bowling*** *(in cricket)* service *m* au-dessus de la tête; *Sport* ***overarm service*** *(in tennis, badminton)* service *m* au-dessus de la tête; *Swimming* ***overarm stroke*** brasse *f* indienne, nage *f* (à l')indienne

overassess [ˌəʊvərəˈses] *vt Fin (for tax)* surimposer

overassessment [ˌəʊvərəˈsesmɪnt] *n Fin (for tax)* surimposition *f*

overate [ˌəʊvərˈeɪt] *pt of* **overeat**

overawe [ˌəʊvərˈɔː] *vt* intimider; *(of prospect, difficulty, surroundings)* impressionner; **don't be overawed by what you are about to hear** ne vous laissez pas impressionner par ce que vous allez entendre

overbalance [ˌəʊvəˈbæləns] **1** *vt (person)* faire perdre l'équilibre à; *(pile, vehicle)* renverser, faire basculer

2 *vi (person)* perdre l'équilibre; *(load, pile)* basculer, se renverser; *(car)* capoter; *(boat)* chavirer

overbear [ˌəʊvəˈbeə(r)] *(pt* **overbore** [-ˈbɔː(r)], *pp* **overborne** [-ˈbɔːn]) *vt Formal (rival, victim)* dominer, triompher de, vaincre; *(objection, proposal)* l'emporter sur, prévaloir contre

overbearing [ˌəʊvəˈbeərɪŋ] *adj* autoritaire, impérieux

overbearingly [ˌəʊvəˈbeərɪŋlɪ] *adv* autoritairement

overbid *(pt & pp* **overbid**, *cont* **overbidding**) **1** *n* [ˈəʊvəbɪd] surenchère *f*

2 *vt* [ˌəʊvəˈbɪd] enchérir sur

3 *vi* [ˌəʊvəˈbɪd] surenchérir

overblown [ˌəʊvəˈbləʊn] *adj* (**a**) *(flower)* trop épanoui *ou* ouvert; *(beauty)* qui commence à se faner (**b**) *Pej (prose, style)* ampoulé, pompier

overboard [ˈəʊvəbɔːd] *adv Naut* par-dessus bord; **to fall overboard** passer par-dessus bord; **to jump overboard** sauter à la mer; **man overboard!** un homme à la mer!; **to throw sb/sth overboard** jeter qn/qch par-dessus bord; *Fig* se débarrasser de qn/qch; *Fam* **to go overboard** dépasser la mesure, exagérer; **he has really gone overboard with his latest film** il a vraiment dépassé les bornes avec son dernier film; **the critics went overboard about her first novel** les critiques se sont enthousiasmés *ou* emballés pour son premier roman

overbook [ˌəʊvəˈbʊk] **1** *vt (hotel, flight)* surbooker, surréserver; **the flight was overbooked** le vol était surbooké

2 *vi (airline, hotel)* surbooker, surréserver

overbooking [ˌəʊvəˈbʊkɪŋ] *n* surréservation *f*, surbooking *m*

overboot [ˈəʊvəbuːt] *n* couvre-chaussure *m*

overbore [ˌəʊvəˈbɔː(r)] *pt of* **overbear**

overborne [ˌəʊvəˈbɔːn] *pp of* **overbear**

overborrow [ˌəʊvəˈbɒrəʊ] *vi Fin (of company)* emprunter de façon excessive

overborrowed [ˌəʊvəˈbɒrəʊd] *adj Fin (company)* surendetté

overborrowing [ˌəʊvəˈbɒrəʊɪŋ] *n Fin (of company)* surendettement *m*

overbought [ˌəʊvəˈbɔːt] *adj St Exch (market)* surévalué, suracheté

overbridge [ˈəʊvəbrɪdʒ] *n* passage *m* en dessus, passage *m* supérieur

overbudgeted [ˌəʊvəˈbʌdʒɪtɪd] *adj Am (project, product, film)* qui dépasse le budget alloué

overbuilt [ˌəʊvəˈbɪlt] *adj* **overbuilt areas** localités *fpl* aux constructions trop denses

overburden [ˌəʊvəˈbɜːdən] *vt* surcharger, accabler; **overburdened with work/worries** accablé de travail/de soucis; **overburdened with debts** criblé de dettes; **he is not overburdened with principles** ce ne sont pas les principes qui l'étouffent

overcall 1 *n* [ˈəʊvəkɔːl] *(in bridge)* surenchère *f*

2 *vt* [ˌəʊvəˈkɔːl] *(in bridge)* surenchérir sur

overcame [ˌəʊvəˈkeɪm] *pt of* **overcome**

overcapacity [ˌəʊvəkəˈpæsɪtɪ] *n Econ* surcapacité *f*

overcapitalization [ˌəʊvəˌkæpɪtəlaɪˈzeɪʃən] *n Fin* surcapitalisation *f*

overcapitalize, -ise [ˌəʊvəˈkæpɪtəlaɪz] *vt Fin* surcapitaliser

overcast *(pt & pp* **overcast**) **1** *vt* [ˌəʊvəˈkɑːst] *Sewing* surfiler

2 *adj* [ˈəʊvəkɑːst] *(sky)* sombre, couvert; *(weather)* couvert; **it's getting overcast** le temps se couvre; **the sky became overcast** le ciel s'assombrit

overcautious [ˌəʊvəˈkɔːʃəs] *adj* trop prudent, prudent à l'excès

overcautiously [ˌəʊvəˈkɔːʃəslɪ] *adv* avec trop de prudence, avec une prudence excessive

overcharge [ˌəʊvəˈtʃɑːdʒ] **1** *vt* (**a**) *(customer)* faire payer trop cher à; *(goods)* survendre; **I've been overcharged!** on m'a fait payer trop cher!; **they overcharged me for the coffee** ils m'ont fait payer le café trop cher; **they overcharged me for the repair** ils m'ont pris trop cher pour la réparation

(**b**) *Elec (circuit)* surcharger

(**c**) *Br (description, picture)* surcharger; **the painting was overcharged with detail** le tableau était surchargé de détails

2 *vi* faire payer trop cher; **they overcharged for**

the tomatoes ils ont fait payer les tomates trop cher

overcloud [ˌəʊvəˈklaʊd] **1** *vt* **the sky became overclouded** le ciel se couvrit de nuages

2 *vi* se couvrir, devenir nuageux

overcoat [ˈəʊvəkəʊt] *n* manteau *m*, pardessus *m*

overcome [ˌəʊvəˈkʌm] (*pt* **overcame** [-ˈkeɪm], *pp* **overcome**) **1** *vt* (**a**) *(vanquish → enemy, opposition)* vaincre, triompher de; *(→ difficulty, shyness)* surmonter; *(→ fear, repulsion, prejudice)* vaincre, surmonter, maîtriser; *(master → nerves)* maîtriser, contrôler

(**b**) *(debilitate, weaken)* accabler; **the heat overcame me** la chaleur finit par me terrasser; **she was overcome by the fumes** les émanations lui ont fait perdre connaissance; *Literary* **he felt sleep overcome him** il sentait le sommeil le gagner

(**c**) *(usu passive) (overwhelm)* **to be overcome by the enemy** succomber à l'ennemi; **to be overcome by fear** être paralysé par la peur; **to be overcome with joy** être comblé de joie; **to be overcome with grief** être accablé par la douleur; **I was overcome by the news** la nouvelle m'a bouleversé; **in a voice overcome with emotion** d'une voix tremblante d'émotion

2 *vi* vaincre; **"We Shall Overcome"** "Nous triompherons" *(célèbre chanson du mouvement américain des droits civiques)*

overcompensate [ˌəʊvəˈkɒmpənseɪt] **1** *vt* (**a**) *Psy* surcompenser

(**b**) *Law* verser des dommages-intérêts excessifs à

2 *vi* (**a**) *Psy* surcompenser; **to overcompensate for sth** surcompenser qch

(**b**) *(make amends)* **she feels guilty about being away so much and overcompensates by showering her children with gifts** elle se sent coupable d'être si souvent absente et essaie de se faire pardonner en couvrant ses enfants de cadeaux

overcompensation [ˈəʊvəˌkɒmpənˈseɪʃən] *n* (**a**) *Psy* surcompensation *f* (**b**) *Law* versement *m* de dommages-intérêts excessifs à

overcomplicated [ˌəʊvəˈkɒmplɪkeɪtɪd] *adj* trop *ou* excessivement compliqué

overconfidence [ˌəʊvəˈkɒnfɪdəns] *n* (**a**) *(arrogance)* suffisance *f*, présomption *f* (**b**) *(trust)* confiance *f* aveugle *ou* excessive

overconfident [ˌəʊvəˈkɒnfɪdənt] *adj* (**a**) *(arrogant)* suffisant, présomptueux; **you're being overconfident about the exam** tu présumes un peu trop de ta réussite à l'examen (**b**) *(trusting)* trop confiant; **I'm not overconfident of his chances of recovery** je ne crois pas trop en ses chances de guérison

overconsume [ˌəʊvəkənˈsjuːm] *vt* consommer trop de

overconsumption [ˌəʊvəkənˈsʌmpʃən] *n* surconsommation *f*

overcook [ˌəʊvəˈkʊk] **1** *vt* faire trop cuire; **the vegetables are overcooked** les légumes sont trop cuits

2 *vi* trop cuire

over-correction *n (of air/fuel ratio etc)* sur-correction *f*

overcritical [ˌəʊvəˈkrɪtɪkəl] *adj* trop critique

overcrop [ˌəʊvəˈkrɒp] *vt* surexploiter

overcropping [ˌəʊvəˈkrɒpɪŋ] *n* surexploitation *f*

overcrowd [ˌəʊvəˈkraʊd] *vt (bus, train, room)* remplir au maximum, bourrer; *(city, streets, prison)* surpeupler; *(class)* surcharger

overcrowded [ˌəʊvəˈkraʊdɪd] *adj (bus, train, room)* bondé, comble; *(city, country, prison)* surpeuplé; *(streets)* plein de monde; *(class)* surchargé; **Paris is overcrowded with tourists in summer** en été, Paris est envahi par les touristes; **they live in very overcrowded conditions** ils vivent très à l'étroit

overcrowding [ˌəʊvəˈkraʊdɪŋ] *n* surpeuplement *m*, surpopulation *f*; *(in housing)* entassement *m*; *(in bus, train etc)* entassement *m* des voyageurs, affluence *f*; *(in schools)* effectifs *mpl* surchargés; *(in prisons)* surpeuplement *m*; **overcrowding on trains means you sometimes have to stand** les trains sont tellement bondés qu'on est parfois contraint de voyager debout; **prison overcrowding is a growing problem** le surpeuplement des prisons est un problème croissant

overdemand [ˌəʊvədɪˈmɑːnd] *n* demande *f* excédentaire

overdetermined [ˌəʊvədɪˈtɜːmɪnd] *adj Psy (symbol etc)* surdéterminé

overdevelop [ˌəʊvədɪˈveləp] *vt (gen) & Phot* surdévelopper; **parts of the coastline have been overdeveloped** par endroits, le littoral est trop construit

overdeveloped [ˌəʊvədɪˈveləpt] *adj (gen) & Phot* surdéveloppé

overdevelopment [ˌəʊvədɪˈveləpmənt] *n* surdéveloppement *m*

overdo [ˌəʊvəˈduː] (*pt* **overdid** [-ˈdɪd], *pp* **overdone** [-ˈdʌn]) *vt* (**a**) *(exaggerate)* exagérer, pousser trop loin; **he rather overdoes the penniless student (bit)** il joue un peu trop l'étudiant pauvre; **the battle scenes are a bit overdone** les scènes de combat sont un peu exagérées; **all that jewellery is really overdoing it!** tous ces bijoux? c'est vraiment un peu trop!; **Maxine rather overdoes the make-up** Maxine se maquille un peu trop; **you've overdone the curry powder** tu as eu la main un peu lourde avec le curry; **she overdoes the jogging** elle force un peu trop sur le jogging

(**b**) *(eat, drink too much of)* **don't overdo the whisky** n'abuse pas du whisky

(**c**) *(idiom)* **to overdo it, to overdo things** se surmener; **I've been overdoing it again** j'ai de nouveau un peu trop forcé; *Ironic* **don't overdo it!** surtout ne te surmène pas!

(**d**) *Culin* trop cuire

overdone [ˌəʊvəˈdʌn] **1** *pp of* **overdo**

2 *adj* (**a**) *(exaggerated)* exagéré, excessif (**b**) *Culin* trop cuit

overdoor [ˈəʊvədɔː(r)] *n Art* dessus *m* de porte

overdosage [ˌəʊvəˈdəʊsɪdʒ] *n* dosage *m* excessif, surdosage *m*

overdose 1 *n* [ˈəʊvədəʊs] (**a**) *(of drugs)* dose *f* massive *ou* excessive; *(of hard drugs)* overdose *f*, surdose *f*; **to take an overdose** *(of hard drugs)* faire une overdose; **an overdose of sleeping pills** une dose massive de somnifères; **she died from a drugs overdose** elle est morte d'une overdose

(**b**) *Fig* dose *f*; *Hum* **I think I've had an overdose of culture today** je crois que j'ai eu ma dose de culture pour aujourd'hui

2 *vi* [ˈəʊvədəʊs] prendre une dose massive; *(on hard drugs)* prendre une overdose; **he overdosed on heroin/LSD** il a pris une overdose d'héroïne/de LSD; *Hum* **I've been overdosing on chocolate recently** j'ai trop forcé sur le chocolat ces derniers temps

3 *vt* [ˌəʊvəˈdəʊs] *(patient)* administrer une dose excessive à; *(drug)* prescrire une dose excessive de

overdraft [ˈəʊvədrɑːft] *n* découvert *m* (bancaire); **to have an overdraft** avoir un découvert; **to allow** *or* **to give sb an overdraft** accorder à qn un découvert; **the bank gave me a £100 overdraft** la banque m'a accordé un découvert de 100 livres; **to pay off one's overdraft** rembourser son découvert; **they live off an overdraft** ils sont en permanence à découvert

►► ***overdraft facility*** autorisation *f* de découvert, facilités *fpl* de caisse; ***overdraft limit*** plafond *m* de découvert; ***overdraft loan*** prêt *m* à découvert

overdramatic [ˌəʊvədrəˈmætɪk] *adj* mélodramatique, exagéré

overdraw [ˌəʊvəˈdrɔː] (*pt* **overdrew** [-ˈdruː], *pp* **overdrawn** [-ˈdrɔːn]) **1** *vt (account)* mettre à découvert

2 *vi* tirer à découvert; **to overdraw on one's account** mettre son compte à découvert

overdrawn [ˌəʊvəˈdrɔːn] *adj* à découvert; **to be overdrawn** avoir un découvert, être à découvert; **to go overdrawn** se mettre à découvert; **my account is overdrawn** mon compte est à découvert; **I'm overdrawn by £100, I'm £100 overdrawn** j'ai un découvert de 100 livres

overdress 1 *vi* [ˌəʊvəˈdres] *Pej* s'habiller avec trop de recherche

2 *n* [ˈəʊvədres] robe-chasuble *f*

overdressed [ˌəʊvəˈdrest] *adj Pej* trop habillé; **to be overdressed** être trop habillé pour la circonstance

overdrew [ˌəʊvəˈdruː] *pt of* **overdraw**

overdrive [ˈəʊvədraɪv] *n Aut* (vitesse *f*) surmultipliée *f*, overdrive *m*; **in overdrive** en surmultipliée; *Fig* **to go into overdrive** mettre les bouchées doubles

overdub (*pt & pp* **overdubbed**, *cont* **overdubbing**) **1** *vt* [ˌəʊvəˈdʌb] *(in recording)* ajouter une piste/plusieurs pistes à, ajouter un overdub/des overdubs à

2 *n* [ˈəʊvədʌb] overdub *m*

overdubbing [ˌəʊvəˈdʌbɪŋ] *n* overdubbing *m*, ajout *m* de pistes

overdue [ˌəʊvəˈdjuː] *adj* (**a**) *(bus, flight, person)* en retard; *(amount, bill)* impayé, en souffrance; *(payment, rent)* en retard, impayé; *(library book)* non retourné; **she is long overdue** elle devrait être là depuis longtemps; **the flight from Panama is half an hour overdue** le vol de Panama a une demi-heure de retard; **our repayments are two months overdue** nous avons un retard de deux mois dans nos remboursements

(**b**) *(apology)* tardif; *(change, reform)* qui tarde, qui se fait attendre; **an explanation is overdue** le moment semble venu de donner une explication, il est temps de donner une explication; **this reform is long overdue** cette réforme aurait dû être appliquée il y a longtemps; **the car is overdue for a service** la voiture a besoin d'être révisée

(**c**) *(in pregnancy)* **to be overdue** avoir dépassé son terme; **the baby was two weeks overdue** le bébé avait deux semaines de retard

overeager [ˌəʊvərˈiːgə(r)] *adj* trop empressé; **he is overeager to please** il est trop soucieux *ou* désireux de plaire; **I can't say I'm overeager to go** je ne peux pas dire que j'aie une envie folle d'y aller

overeat [ˌəʊvərˈiːt] (*pt* **overate** [-ˈeɪt], *pp* **overeaten** [-ˈiːtən]) *vi (once)* trop manger, faire un repas trop copieux; *(habitually)* se suralimenter

overeating [ˌəʊvərˈiːtɪŋ] *n (habitual)* suralimentation *f*

overegg [ˌəʊvərˈeg] *vt Br Fig* **to overegg the pudding** en faire trop

overelaborate [ˌəʊvərɪˈlæbərɪt] *adj (dress, style)* trop recherché; *(ornamentation)* tarabiscoté; *(explanation, excuse)* tiré par les cheveux; *(description)* alambiqué, contourné

overemotional [ˌəʊvərɪˈməʊʃənəl] *adj* hyperémotif, trop émotif

overemphasis [ˌəʊvəˈremfəsɪs] *n* accentuation *f* excessive

overemphasize, -ise [ˌəʊvərˈemfəsaɪz] *vt* trop mettre l'accent sur, trop insister sur; **I cannot overemphasize the need for discretion** je n'insisterai jamais assez sur la nécessité de faire preuve de discrétion

overemployment [ˌəʊvərɪmˈplɔɪmənt] *n* suremploi *m*

overengineered [ˌəʊvərendʒɪˈnɪəd] *adj Tech* d'une conception très complexe

overenthusiastic [ˈəʊvərɪnˌθjuːzɪˈæstɪk] *adj* trop enthousiaste

overestimate [ˌəʊvərˈestɪmeɪt] *vt (cost, person's talent, difficulty)* surestimer; *(one's strength)* trop présumer de; *Com (assets)* majorer; **to overestimate one's own importance** surestimer sa propre importance

overexaggerate [ˌəʊvərɪgˈzædʒəreɪt] *vt* exagérer, attacher trop d'importance à

overexcite [ˌəʊvərɪkˈsaɪt] *vt* surexciter

overexcited [ˌəʊvərɪkˈsaɪtɪd] *adj* surexcité; **to become** *or* **to get overexcited** (trop) s'énerver; **don't get overexcited, they haven't arrived yet** ne vous excitez pas, ils ne sont pas encore arrivés; **she got overexcited and burst into tears** elle s'est mise dans un état d'agitation extrême et a fondu en larmes

overexcitement [ˌəʊvərɪkˈsaɪtmənt] *n* surexcitation *f*

overexert [ˌəʊvərɪgˈzɜːt] *vt* surmener; **to overexert oneself** se surmener, s'éreinter

overexertion [ˌəʊvərɪgˈzɜːʃən] *n* surmenage *m*

overexpansion [ˌəʊvərekˈspænʃən] *n* expansion *f* excessive

overexploitation [ˌəʊvəreksplɔɪˈteɪʃən] *n* surexploitation *f*

overexpose [ˌəʊvərɪkˈspəʊz] *vt Phot* surexposer

overexposure [ˌəʊvərɪkˈspəʊʒə(r)] *n* (**a**) *Phot*

surexposition *f*; *Fig (on the media)* surmédiatisation *f*; **to suffer from overexposure** faire trop parler de soi; **because of people's overexposure to advertising** parce que les gens sont bombardés de publicité (**b**) *Fin* risque *m* accru

overfamiliar [ˌəʊvəfə'mɪlɪə(r)] *adj* (**a**) *(too intimate, disrespectful)* trop familier; **to be overfamiliar with sb** se montrer trop familier *ou* prendre des libertés excessives avec qn (**b**) *(conversant)* **I'm not overfamiliar with the system** je ne connais pas très bien le système

overfamiliarity [ˌəʊvəfəˌmɪlɪ'ærətɪ] *n* familiarité *f* excessive

overfed [ˌəʊvə'fed] *adj* (**a**) *(given too much food)* suralimenté (**b**) *(obese)* pansu, ventru

overfeed [ˌəʊvə'fiːd] *(pt & pp* **overfed** [-'fed]) **1** *vt* suralimenter

2 *vi* se suralimenter, trop manger

overfeeding [ˌəʊvə'fiːdɪŋ] *n* suralimentation *f*

overfill [ˌəʊvə'fɪl] *vt* trop remplir

overfish [ˌəʊvə(r)'fɪʃ] *vt (fishing ground)* surexploiter

overfishing [ˌəʊvə(r)'fɪʃɪŋ] *n* surpêche *f*

overflew [ˌəʊvə'fluː] *pt of* **overfly**

overflow 1 *vi* [ˌəʊvə'fləʊ] (**a**) *(with liquid → container, bath)* déborder; *(→ river)* déborder, sortir de son lit; *(with people → room, vehicle)* déborder, être plein à craquer; *(with objects → box, wastebin)* déborder; **the river frequently overflows onto the surrounding plain** la rivière inonde souvent la plaine environnante; **the streets were overflowing with people** les rues regorgeaient de monde; **the demonstrators overflowed into the side streets** les manifestants ont débordé dans les rues transversales; **the glass is full to overflowing** le verre est plein à ras bord; **the shop was full to overflowing** le magasin était plein à craquer; **the contents of the bin overflowed onto the floor** le contenu de la poubelle s'est répandu par terre; **her desk was overflowing with papers** son bureau disparaissait sous les papiers

(**b**) *Fig (with emotion)* déborder; **his heart was overflowing with joy** son cœur débordait de joie

2 *vt* [ˌəʊvə'fləʊ] déborder de; **the river overflowed its banks** la rivière est sortie de son lit *ou* a débordé

3 *n* ['əʊvəfləʊ] (**a**) *(drain → from sink, cistern)* trop-plein *m*; *(→ large-scale)* déversoir *m*

(**b**) *(excess → of population, production)* excédent *m*, surplus *m*; *(→ of energy, emotion)* trop-plein *m*, débordement *m*

(**c**) *(flooding)* inondation *f*; *(excess)* trop-plein *m*

(**d**) *Comput* dépassement *m* de capacité, débordement *m*

▸▸ ***overflow pipe*** *(from sink, cistern)* trop-plein *m*; *(large-scale)* déversoir *m*

overflowing [ˌəʊvə'fləʊɪŋ] *adj (water, river etc)* qui déborde; *(container)* plein à déborder; *(joy, gratitude)* débordant

overflown [ˌəʊvə'fləʊn] *pp of* **overfly**

overfly [ˌəʊvə'flaɪ] *(pt* **overflew** [-'fluː], *pp* **overflown** [-'fləʊn]) *vt* survoler

overfond [ˌəʊvə'fɒnd] *adj* **I'm not overfond of oranges** je ne raffole pas des oranges; **she's not overfond of children** on ne peut pas dire qu'elle ait une passion pour les enfants; **he's not overfond of the cinema** il n'est pas très porté sur le cinéma

overfreight [ˌəʊvə'freɪt] *n* poids *m* en excès; surcharge *f*

overfull [ˌəʊvə'fʊl] *adj* trop plein, qui déborde

overgear [ˌəʊvə'gɪə(r)] *vt Fin (company)* surendetter; **to be overgeared** être surendetté

overgearing [ˌəʊvə'gɪərɪŋ] *n Fin* surendettement *m*

overgenerous [ˌəʊvə'dʒenərəs] *adj (person, act)* (trop) généreux, prodigue; *(portion)* trop copieux, excessif

overground ['əʊvəgraʊnd] **1** *adj* à la surface du sol, en surface; **an overground rail link** une voie ferrée à l'air libre *ou* aérienne

2 *adv* à la surface du sol; **the line goes overground when it reaches the suburbs** la ligne fait surface quand elle arrive en banlieue

overgrown [ˌəʊvə'grəʊn] *adj (garden, path etc)* **overgrown with** envahi par; **the path was overgrown with weeds/brambles** le chemin était envahi par les mauvaises herbes/les ronces; **the garden has become very overgrown** le jardin est devenu une vraie jungle; **a wall overgrown with ivy** un mur recouvert de lierre; *Fig* **he's just an overgrown schoolboy** c'est un grand enfant

overgrowth ['əʊvəgrəʊθ] *n* (**a**) *(excessive growth)* surcroissance *f*, croissance *f* excessive (**b**) *(covering → of weeds, brambles, hairs etc)* couverture *f*

overhand ['əʊvəhænd] = **overarm**

overhang *(pt & pp* **overhung** [-'hʌŋ]) **1** *vt* [ˌəʊvə'hæŋ] (**a**) *(of cliff, ledge, balcony)* surplomber, faire saillie au-dessus de; *(of cloud, mist, smoke)* planer sur, flotter au-dessus de

(**b**) *Fig (of threat, danger)* planer sur, menacer

2 *vi* [ˌəʊvə'hæŋ] être en surplomb, faire saillie

3 *n* ['əʊvəhæŋ] surplomb *m*; *(smaller)* dévers *m*; *Constr* **to have an overhang** porter à faux

overhanging [ˌəʊvə'hæŋɪŋ] *adj* (**a**) *(cliff, ledge, balcony)* en surplomb, en saillie; **we walked under the overhanging branches** nous marchions sous un dais *ou* une voûte de branches (**b**) *Fig (threat)* imminent

overhaul 1 *n* ['əʊvəhɔːl] *(of car, machine)* révision *f*; *(of institution, system)* révision *f*, remaniement *m*; **the education system needs a complete overhaul** le système scolaire a besoin d'être complètement remanié

2 *vt* [ˌəʊvə'hɔːl] (**a**) *(car, machine)* réviser; *(system)* revoir, remanier (**b**) *(catch up)* rattraper; *(overtake)* dépasser; *Naut* gagner

overhead 1 *adv* [ˌəʊvə'hed] au-dessus; **we watched the hawk circling overhead** nous regardions le faucon tournoyer dans le ciel *ou* au-dessus de nos têtes

2 *adj* ['əʊvəhed] *(cable, railway)* aérien; *(lighting)* au plafond; *Sport (racket stroke)* smashé; *Ftbl (kick)* retourné

3 *n* ['əʊvəhed] (**a**) *(cost)* charge *f* opérationnelle

(**b**) *Am (costs)* frais *mpl* généraux

(**c**) *(in tennis, badminton)* smash *m*

4 overheads *npl Br* frais *mpl* généraux; **to reduce overheads** réduire les frais généraux

▸▸ *Acct* ***overhead absorption rate*** taux *m* d'amortissement des frais généraux; *Fin* ***overhead budget*** budget *m* des charges; *Tech* ***overhead camshaft*** arbre *m* à cames en tête; *Com* ***overhead costs*** frais *mpl* généraux; ***overhead door*** porte *f* basculante; ***overhead projector*** rétroprojecteur *m*; *Cin & TV* ***overhead shot*** plan *m* en plongée; *Fin* ***overhead variance*** variance *f* des frais généraux

overhear [ˌəʊvə'hɪə(r)] *(pt & pp* **overheard** [-'hɜːd]) *vt (gen)* entendre par hasard; *(conversation)* surprendre; **I couldn't help overhearing what you were saying** malgré moi, j'ai entendu votre conversation; **she overheard them talking about her** elle les a surpris à parler d'elle

overheat [ˌəʊvə'hiːt] **1** *vt* (**a**) *(oven etc)* surchauffer, trop chauffer (**b**) *(economy)* provoquer la surchauffe de

2 *vi* (**a**) *(engine etc)* chauffer (**b**) *(economy)* entrer en surchauffe

overheated [ˌəʊvə'hiːtɪd] *adj* (**a**) *(too hot → room)* surchauffé, trop chauffé; *(→ engine)* qui chauffe

(**b**) *Fig (angry)* passionné, violent, exalté; **to become** *or* **to get overheated** *(person)* s'échauffer, s'énerver; *(situation)* devenir explosif; *(discussion, conversation)* s'animer

(**c**) *(economy)* en surchauffe; **the economy is getting overheated** l'économie est en surchauffe

overheating [ˌəʊvə'hiːtɪŋ] *n* échauffement *m* excessif

overhung [ˌəʊvə'hʌŋ] *pt & pp of* **overhang**

overhype [ˌəʊvə'haɪp] *vt* faire tout un tabac sur; *(counterproductively)* faire trop de battage sur

overimpress [ˌəʊvərɪm'pres] *vt* **she wasn't overimpressed by the film** le film ne l'a pas particulièrement impressionnée

overindulge [ˌəʊvərɪn'dʌldʒ] **1** *vt* (**a**) *(appetite, desire)* céder à, succomber à, se laisser aller à; **she overindulges her passion for chocolate** elle cède *ou* succombe trop facilement à sa passion pour le chocolat

(**b**) *(person)* (trop) gâter; **she overindulges her children** elle cède à tous les caprices de ses enfants; **he has a tendency to overindulge himself** il a tendance à faire des excès *ou* à se laisser aller

2 *vi (overeat)* faire des excès de table; *(drink)* trop boire; **you mustn't overindulge** il ne faut pas abuser des bonnes choses

overindulgence [ˌəʊvərɪn'dʌldʒəns] *n* (**a**) *(in food and drink)* excès *m*, abus *m* (**b**) *(towards person)* indulgence *f* excessive, complaisance *f*

overindulgent [ˌəʊvərɪn'dʌldʒənt] *adj* (**a**) *(towards person)* trop indulgent, complaisant (**b**) *(in food and drink)* **he's overindulgent** c'est un bon vivant; **an overindulgent weekend** un week-end de bombance

overindustrialization [ˌəʊvərɪnˌdʌstrɪəlaɪ'zeɪʃən] *n* surindustrialisation *f*

overinvest [ˌəʊvərɪn'vest] *Fin* **1** *vt* trop investir (**in** dans)

2 *vi* surinvestir (**in** dans)

overinvestment [ˌəʊvərɪn'vestmənt] *n Fin* surinvestissement *m* (**in** dans)

overissue 1 *n* ['əuvərɪʃuː] *(of paper money)* surémission *f*

2 *vt* [ˌəuvə'rɪʃuː] *(paper money)* faire une surémission de

overjoyed [ˌəʊvə'dʒɔɪd] *adj* ravi, transporté, comblé; **she was overjoyed at being home again** elle était ravie d'être rentrée; **I was overjoyed at the news** cette nouvelle m'a ravi *ou* transporté; **I was overjoyed to see him after so long** j'étais ravi de le voir après si longtemps

overkeen [ˌəʊvə'kiːn] *adj* empressé (**to do** de faire); **he wasn't overkeen on her/the idea** elle/l'idée ne lui plaisait pas outre mesure

overkill ['əʊvəkɪl] *n Mil* surarmement *m*; *Fig* exagération *f*, excès *m*; **media overkill** surmédiatisation *f*, médiatisation *f* excessive

overladen [ˌəʊvə'leɪdən] **1** *pp of* **overload**

2 *adj* surchargé

overlaid [ˌəʊvə'leɪd] *pt & pp of* **overlay**

overland ['əʊvəlænd] **1** *adj* par voie de terre; **the overland route to India** le voyage en Inde par la route

2 *adv* par voie de terre

overlap *(pt & pp* **overlapped**, *cont* **overlapping**) **1** *vi* [ˌəʊvə'læp] *(gen)* (se) chevaucher, se recouvrir partiellement; *(categories etc)* avoir un domaine commun, se recouper; *(in time)* coïncider; *(of theories, evidence)* avoir des points communs, se recouper; **our visits overlapped** nos visites ont plus ou moins coïncidé; **my responsibilities overlap with hers** mes responsabilités et les siennes se recoupent; **the two systems overlap** les deux systèmes font en partie double emploi

2 *vt* [ˌəʊvə'læp] *(in space)* faire se chevaucher; **the edges/tiles overlap each other** les bords/les tuiles se chevauchent

3 *n* (**a**) ['əʊvəlæp] *(of tiles etc)* chevauchement *m*; *Fig* **there is some overlap between philosophy and religion** il y a des points communs entre la philosophie et la religion; **the overlap between two departments** les activités communes à deux services

(**b**) *Geol* nappe *f* de charriage

(**c**) *Mktg* débordement *m*

overlapping [ˌəʊvə'læpɪŋ] *adj (tiles, planks etc)* qui se chevauchent; *(responsibilities)* qui se recoupent; *(holidays)* qui coïncident

overlay *(pt & pp* **overlaid** [-'leɪd]) **1** *vt* [ˌəʊvə'leɪ] recouvrir; **the shelf is overlaid with marble** l'étagère est recouverte de marbre

2 *n* ['əʊvəleɪ] (**a**) *(covering)* revêtement *m* (**b**) *Comput* recouvrement *m*

▸▸ *Comput* ***overlay program*** programme *m* à recouvrement; ***overlay segment*** segment *m* de recouvrement

overleaf [ˌəʊvə'liːf] *adv* au dos, au verso; **see overleaf** *(in book, magazine)* voir au verso; **continued overleaf** *(in book, magazine)* suite page suivante

overlie [ˌəʊvə'laɪ] *vt (pt* **overlay** [-'leɪ], *pp* **overlain** [-'leɪn]) recouvrir, couvrir

overload *(pp sense* (**a**) **overloaded** *or* **overladen** [-'leɪdən], *pp sense* (**b**) **overloaded**) **1** *vt* [ˌəʊvə'ləʊd] (**a**) *(animal, vehicle)* surcharger; *(market)* surcharger (**b**) *(electric circuit)* surcharger; *(engine, machine)* surmener; *Fig (with*

ove–ove

work) surcharger, écraser; **she's overloaded with work** elle est surchargée *ou* débordée de travail
2 *n* ['əʊvələʊd] *Elec* surcharge *f*; *Fig* surcharge *f*

overlong [,əʊvə'lɒŋ] **1** *adj* trop *ou* excessivement long (longue)
2 *adv* trop longtemps

overlook 1 *vt* [,əʊvə'lʊk] (**a**) *(have view of)* avoir vue sur, donner sur; **villa overlooking the sea** *(in property advertisement)* villa avec vue sur la mer; **the bedroom window overlooks the garden** la fenêtre de la chambre donne sur le jardin; **the castle/hill overlooks the town** le château/la colline surplombe la ville; **our house is overlooked at the back** il y a une maison qui a vue sur l'arrière de la nôtre
(**b**) *(fail to notice* → *detail, small thing)* laisser échapper, oublier; *(neglect)* négliger, ne pas prendre en compte; **it's easy to overlook the small print** on oublie souvent de lire ce qui est en petits caractères; **they overlooked the language problem** ils n'ont pas pris en compte le problème de la langue; **he seems to have overlooked the fact that I might have difficulties** l'idée que je puisse avoir des difficultés semble lui avoir échappé; **his work has been overlooked for centuries** cela fait des siècles que ses travaux sont ignorés
(**c**) *(ignore)* laisser passer, passer sur; **I cannot overlook this insolence** je ne peux pas laisser passer cette insolence; **she decided to overlook the matter** elle décida de fermer les yeux sur l'affaire; **I'll overlook it this time** je veux bien fermer les yeux cette fois-ci
(**d**) *(supervise)* surveiller
2 *n* ['əʊvəlʊk] *Am* panorama *m*

overlord ['əʊvəlɔːd] *n* (**a**) *Hist* suzerain *m* (**b**) *Fig* grand patron *m*

overlordship [,əʊvə'lɔːdʃɪp] *n Hist* suzeraineté *f*

overly ['əʊvəlɪ] *adj* trop; **she was not overly friendly** elle ne s'est pas montrée particulièrement aimable

overlying [,əʊvə'laɪɪŋ] *adj* superposé; *(stratum)* surjacent

overman ['əʊvəmæn] (*pl* **overmen** [-men]) *n Phil* surhomme *m*

overmanned [,əʊvə'mænd] *adj (factory, production line)* en sureffectif

overmanning [,əʊvə'mænɪŋ] *n (UNCOUNT)* sureffectifs *mpl*

overmantel ['əʊvəmæntəl] *n* étagère *f* de cheminée

overmatch *Am Sport* **1** *n* ['əʊvəmætʃ] (**a**) *(superior opponent)* adversaire *m* supérieur (**b**) *(unequal contest)* partie *f* inégale
2 *vt* [,əʊvə'mætʃ] (**a**) *(be superior to)* être supérieur à (**b**) *(match with superior opponent)* mettre face à un adversaire supérieur

overmuch [,əʊvə'mʌtʃ] *Formal* **1** *adj* trop de
2 *adv* outre mesure, trop

overnice [,əʊvə'naɪs] *adj (distinction)* trop subtil; *(person)* trop méticuleux, pointilleux à l'excès

overnight 1 *adv* [,əʊvə'naɪt] (**a**) *(during the night)* pendant la nuit; *(until next day)* jusqu'au lendemain; **to drive/to fly overnight** rouler/voler de nuit; **they stopped** *or* **stayed overnight in Cork** ils ont passé la nuit à Cork; **the milk won't keep overnight** le lait ne se conservera pas jusqu'à demain
(**b**) *Fig (suddenly)* du jour au lendemain; **her hair went grey overnight** ses cheveux sont devenus gris du jour au lendemain; **the situation grew worse overnight** la situation a empiré du jour au lendemain *ou* a subitement empiré
2 *adj* ['əʊvənaɪt] (**a**) *(stay, guest)* d'une nuit; *(clothes, journey)* de nuit; **an overnight stay** une nuit; **we had an overnight stay in Paris** nous avons passé une nuit à Paris
(**b**) *Fig (sudden)* soudain, subit; **to be an overnight success** devenir célèbre du jour au lendemain; **there has been an overnight improvement in the situation** la situation s'est subitement améliorée
3 *vi* ['əʊvənaɪt] passer la *ou* une nuit
►► ***overnight bag*** sac *m ou* nécessaire *m* de voyage; *Fin* ***overnight loan*** prêt *m* du jour au lendemain; *Fin* ***overnight rate*** taux *m* de l'argent au jour le jour

overoptimism [,əʊvə'rɒptɪmɪzəm] *n* optimisme *m* exagéré; **to suffer from** *or* **to be guilty of overoptimism** être excessivement *ou* par trop optimiste

overoptimistic [,əʊvə,rɒptɪ'mɪstɪk] *adj* excessivement *ou* par trop optimiste (**about** quant à); **I am not overoptimistic about their chances** je ne crois pas qu'ils aient de grandes chances

overpaid [,əʊvə'peɪd] *pt & pp of* **overpay**

> **Overpaid, oversexed and over here**
> Cette phrase (que l'on attribue à l'artiste de music-hall anglais Tommy Trinder) était utilisée pendant la Seconde Guerre mondiale par certains Britanniques jaloux du succès que remportaient auprès des femmes les soldats américains basés en Grande-Bretagne.
> Cette formule, que l'on pourrait traduire par "surpayés, surexcités et sur place" est encore utilisée aujourd'hui à propos de certains étrangers qui séjournent en Grande-Bretagne, mais souvent avec des modifications. Ainsi on pourra dire à propos d'un boy's-band américain: **overhyped, overeager and over here** ("surfaits, trop enthousiastes et chez nous").

overpaint [,əʊvə'peɪnt] *vt* (**a**) *(paint on top of)* **to overpaint sth** peindre par-dessus qch (**b**) *Fig (description etc)* exagérer, charger

overparticular [,əʊvəpə'tɪkjʊlə(r)] *adj* (par) trop exigeant; **he's not overparticular about these things** il se moque un peu de ces choses-là

overpass ['əʊvəpɑːs] *n Aut* pont *m* routier

overpay [,əʊvə'peɪ] (*pt & pp* **overpaid** [-'peɪd]) *vt (bill, employee)* surpayer, trop payer

overpayment [,əʊvə'peɪmənt] *n* (**a**) *(of taxes, on bill)* trop-perçu *m* (**b**) *(of employee)* rémunération *f* excessive

overperform [,əʊvəpə'fɔːm] *vi St Exch (of shares)* avoir un cours anormalement élevé

overplay [,əʊvə'pleɪ] **1** *vt (importance)* exagérer; **to overplay one's hand** présumer de ses forces *ou* de ses capacités
2 *vi* exagérer son rôle

overpolite [,əʊvəpə'laɪt] *adj* trop poli

overpopulated [,əʊvə'pɒpjʊleɪtɪd] *adj* surpeuplé

overpopulation ['əʊvə,pɒpjʊ'leɪʃən] *n* surpeuplement *m*, surpopulation *f*

over-position *vt Mktg* surpositionner

over-positioning *n Mktg* surpositionnement *m*

overpower [,əʊvə'paʊə(r)] *vt* (**a**) *(physically* → *enemy, opponent)* maîtriser, vaincre (**b**) *(of smell)* suffoquer; *(of heat, emotion)* accabler; **they were overpowered by his charm** ils furent ensorcelés *ou* subjugués par son charme

overpowering [,əʊvə'paʊərɪŋ] *adj* (**a**) *(heat, sensation)* accablant, écrasant; *(smell)* suffocant; *(perfume)* entêtant (**b**) *(desire, passion)* irrésistible; *(grief)* accablant; **an overpowering sense of guilt** un sentiment irrépressible de culpabilité (**c**) *(force)* irrésistible (**d**) *(personality, charisma)* dominateur; **I find him overpowering** je le trouve trop dominateur

overprescribe [,əʊvəprɪ'skraɪb] **1** *vi Med* prescrire trop de médicaments
2 *vt (medicine, tablets)* prescrire en trop fortes quantités

overprice [,əʊvə'praɪs] *vt* vendre trop cher

overpriced [,əʊvə'praɪst] *adj* excessivement cher, trop cher; **those books are really overpriced** le prix de ces livres est vraiment excessif *ou* trop élevé

overpricing [,əʊvə'praɪsɪŋ] *n* fixation *f* d'un prix trop élevé

overprint 1 *vt* [,əʊvə'prɪnt] (**a**) *Typ (correction)* imprimer en surcharge; *Comput* surimprimer; *Phot* tirer en surimpression; **the old prices had been overprinted with new ones** les nouveaux prix avaient été imprimés sur les anciens
(**b**) *(postage stamp)* surcharger
2 *vi* [,əʊvə'prɪnt] *Comput* surimprimer
3 *n* ['əʊvəprɪnt] (**a**) *Typ* impression *f* en surcharge; *(on postage stamp etc)* surcharge *f*; *Phot* surimpression *f* (**b**) *(postage stamp)* timbre-poste surchargé

overprinting [,əʊvə'prɪntɪŋ] *n Typ* impression *f* en surcharge; *Comput* surimpression *f*; *Phot* (tirage *m* en) surimpression *f*

overproduce [,əʊvəprə'djuːs] *vt* surproduire

overproduction [,əʊvəprə'dʌkʃən] *n* surproduction *f*

overprotect [,əʊvəprə'tekt] *vt* surprotéger, trop protéger; **he was overprotected as a child** il a été trop couvé lorsqu'il était enfant

overprotective [,əʊvəprə'tektɪv] *adj* trop protecteur, protecteur à l'excès; **she is overprotective of** *or* **towards her son** elle couve trop son fils

overpublicize, -ise [,əʊvə'pʌblɪsaɪz] *vt* faire trop de publicité pour, donner trop de publicité à

overqualified [,əʊvə'kwɒlɪfaɪd] *adj* surqualifié

overran [,əʊvə'ræn] *pt of* **overrun**

overrate [,əʊvə'reɪt] *vt* (**a**) *(person, person's abilities)* surestimer; *(book, film)* surfaire (**b**) *Admin* surtaxer

overrated [,əʊvə'reɪtɪd] *adj (film, book)* surfait; **he is rather overrated as a novelist** sa réputation de romancier est assez surfaite; **I think champagne is really overrated** je pense que le champagne ne mérite pas sa réputation *ou* que la réputation du champagne est surfaite; **sex is overrated** le sexe, ce n'est pas aussi formidable qu'on le dit

overreach [,əʊvə'riːtʃ] *vt* **to overreach oneself** présumer de ses forces, viser trop haut

overreact [,əʊvərɪ'ækt] *vi (gen)* réagir de façon excessive, dramatiser; *(panic)* s'affoler; **he has a tendency to overreact** il a tendance à tout dramatiser; **I thought she overreacted to the news** j'ai pensé qu'elle réagissait de façon excessive à l'annonce de la nouvelle

overreaction [,əʊvərɪ'ækʃən] *n* réaction *f* disproportionnée *ou* excessive; *(panic)* affolement *m*

overridable [,əʊvə'raɪdəbəl] *adj Comput* annulable

override [,əʊvə'raɪd] (*pt* **overrode** [-'rəʊd], *pp* **overridden** [-'rɪdən]) *vt* (**a**) *(instruction, desire, authority)* passer outre à, outrepasser; *(decision)* annuler; *(rights)* fouler aux pieds, bafouer; **my objection was overridden** il n'a été tenu aucun compte de mon objection
(**b**) *(fact, factor)* l'emporter sur; **this duty overrode all her other commitments** cette tâche a pris la priorité sur tous ses autres engagements
(**c**) *(controls, mechanism)* annuler, neutraliser
(**d**) *(horse)* surmener

overrider ['əʊvə,raɪdə(r)] *n Br Aut* butoir *m* (de pare-chocs)

overriding [,əʊvə'raɪdɪŋ] *adj* (**a**) *(importance)* primordial, capital; *(belief, consideration, factor)* prépondérant, dominant; **our overriding desire is to avoid conflict** notre premier *ou* principal souci est d'éviter un conflit (**b**) *Law (clause)* dérogatoire
►► *Fin* ***overriding commission*** commission *f* d'arrangement

overripe [,əʊvə'raɪp] *adj (fruit)* trop mûr; *(cheese)* trop fait

overrode [,əʊvə'rəʊd] *pt of* **override**

overrule [,əʊvə'ruːl] *vt (decision)* annuler; *(claim, objection)* rejeter; **I was overruled** mon avis a été rejeté; *Am Law* **objection overruled** objection rejetée

overrun (*pt* **overran** [-'ræn], *pp* **overrun**, *cont* **overrunning**) **1** *vt* [,əʊvə'rʌn] (**a**) *(invade)* envahir; **the enemy troops overran the country** les troupes ennemies ont envahi le pays; **the garden is overrun with weeds** le jardin est envahi par les mauvaises herbes; **the building was overrun by rats** l'immeuble était infesté de rats; **the streets were overrun by holidaymakers** les rues étaient envahies par les vacanciers
(**b**) *(exceed* → *time limit)* dépasser; **the programme overran the allotted time by ten minutes** l'émission a dépassé de dix minutes le temps qui lui était imparti
(**c**) *(overshoot)* dépasser, aller au-delà de; **the plane overran the runway** l'avion a dépassé le bout de la piste d'atterrissage; *Rail* **to overrun a signal** brûler un signal
(**d**) *Typ (word, sentence* → *over line)* reporter à la ligne suivante; *(*→ *over page)* reporter à la page suivante
2 *vi* [,əʊvə'rʌn] *(programme, speech)* dépasser le temps alloué *ou* imparti; *(meeting)* dépasser l'heure prévue; **the speech overran by ten minutes** le discours a duré dix minutes de plus que prévu
3 *n* ['əʊvərʌn] (**a**) *(in time, space)* dépassement

m; *Com* **(cost) overruns** dépassement *m* du coût estimé

(**b**) *Typ (at end of line)* chasse *f*; *(at end of page)* report *m*, ligne(s) *f(pl)* à reporter

(**c**) *Ind (in production)* excédent *m*, surplus *m*

oversale ['əʊvəseɪl] *n Am* surlocation *f*

oversaw [ˌəʊvə'sɔː] *pt of* **oversee**

overscore [ˌəʊvə'skɔː(r)] *vt* barrer, rayer

overscrupulous [ˌəʊvə'skruːpjʊləs] *adj (morally)* trop scrupuleux; *(in detail)* pointilleux

overseas 1 *adv* [ˌəʊvə'siːz] à l'étranger; **to go overseas** partir à l'étranger; **she prefers to live overseas** elle préfère vivre à l'étranger; **people who come back from overseas** les gens qui reviennent de l'étranger

2 *adj* ['əʊvəsiːz] *(student, tourist, market)* étranger; *(travel, posting)* à l'étranger; *(mail → from overseas)* (en provenance) de l'étranger; *(→ to an overseas country)* pour l'étranger; *(trade)* extérieur; *(colony, possession)* d'outre-mer; **the Ministry of Overseas Development** ≃ le ministère de la Coopération et du Développement; **the French overseas territories** les Territoires *mpl* français d'outre-mer

►► *Mktg* ***overseas market*** marché *m* étranger *ou* extérieur *ou* d'outremer

oversee [ˌəʊvə'siː] *(pt* **oversaw** [-'sɔː], *pp* **overseen** [-'siːn]) *vt (watch)* surveiller, contrôler; *(supervise)* superviser

overseer ['əʊvəˌsiːə(r)] *n (foreman)* contremaître *m*, chef *m* d'équipe; *(in mine)* porion *m*; *(in printing works)* prote *m*; *Hist (of slaves)* surveillant(e) *m,f*

oversell *(pt & pp* **oversold** [-'səʊld]) **1** *vt* [ˌəʊvə'sel] (**a**) *(exaggerate → person, quality)* mettre trop en valeur, faire trop valoir; **to oversell oneself** se mettre trop en avant; **personally, I think the Costa Brava is oversold** personnellement, je pense que la Costa Brava est surfaite

(**b**) *Com* **the concert was oversold** on a vendu plus de billets pour le concert qu'il n'y avait de places

2 *n* ['əʊvəsel] *(exaggeration)* éloge *m* excessif, panégyrique *m*

oversensitive [ˌəʊvə'sensɪtɪv] *adj* trop sensible *ou* susceptible, hypersensible; **you're being oversensitive!** tu es trop susceptible!

oversew ['əʊvəsəʊ] *(pp* **oversewn** [-səʊn]) *vt* surjeter; **oversewn seam** surpiqûre *f*

oversexed [ˌəʊvə'sekst] *adj* **he's oversexed** il ne pense qu'au sexe; *Pej* c'est un obsédé sexuel

overshadow [ˌəʊvə'ʃædəʊ] *vt* (**a**) *(eclipse → person, event)* éclipser; **the peace talks were overshadowed by the presidential election** l'élection présidentielle a éclipsé les pourparlers de paix

(**b**) *(darken)* ombrager; **the house is overshadowed by a huge flyover** la maison est assombrie par un immense autopont; **the negotiations were overshadowed by gloom** une atmosphère morose planait sur les négociations; *Fig* **their lives had been overshadowed by the death of their father** leur vie avait été endeuillée par la mort de leur père

overshoe ['əʊvəˌʃuː] *n* galoche *f*; **rubber overshoes** caoutchoucs *mpl*

overshoot *(pt & pp* **overshot** [-'ʃɒt]) **1** *vt* [ˌəʊvə'ʃuːt] dépasser, aller au-delà de; **the plane overshot the runway** l'avion a dépassé la piste; **to overshoot the mark** dépasser le but; *Fig* mettre à côté de la plaque

2 *vi* [ˌəʊvə'ʃuːt] *(aircraft)* dépasser la piste

3 *n* ['əʊvəʃuːt] dépassement *m*

overshot ['əʊvəʃɒt] *adj Tech (wheel)* mû par en dessus

oversight ['əʊvəsaɪt] *n* (**a**) *(error)* omission *f*, oubli *m*; **by** *or* **through an oversight** par mégarde, par négligence; **due to an oversight your tickets have been sent to your old address** vos billets ont été envoyés par erreur à votre ancienne adresse (**b**) *(supervision)* surveillance *f*, supervision *f*

oversimplification ['əʊvəˌsɪmplɪfɪ'keɪʃən] *n* simplification *f* excessive

oversimplify [ˌəʊvə'sɪmplɪfaɪ] *(pt & pp* **oversimplified**) *vt* simplifier à l'excès

oversize(d) [ˌəʊvə'saɪz(d)] *adj* (**a**) *(very big)* énorme, démesuré (**b**) *(too big)* trop grand

overskirt ['əʊvəskɜːt] *n* jupe *f* extérieure

oversleep [ˌəʊvə'sliːp] *(pt & pp* **overslept** [-'slept]) *vi* se réveiller en retard, ne pas se réveiller à temps

oversleeve ['əʊvəsliːv] *n* manchette *f*

oversold [ˌəʊvə'səʊld] **1** *pt & pp of* **oversell**

2 *adj St Exch (market)* sousévalué(e)

oversolicitous [ˌəʊvəsə'lɪsɪtəs] *adj* trop occupé (**about** de)

overspecialization [ˌəʊvəˌspeʃəlaɪ'zeɪʃən] *n* spécialisation *f* excessive

overspeeding [ˌəʊvə'spiːdɪŋ] *n* excès *m* de vitesse, allure *f ou* vitesse *f* excessive

overspend *(pt & pp* **overspent** [-'spent]) **1** *n* ['əʊvəspend] *Fin* dépenses *fpl* excessives

2 *vi* [ˌəʊvə'spend] *(gen)* trop dépenser; *Fin* dépasser le budget; **I've been overspending recently** j'ai trop dépensé *ou* j'ai dépensé trop d'argent récemment; **I've overspent by £5** j'ai dépensé 5 livres de trop

3 *vt* [ˌəʊvə'spend] *(allowance)* dépasser; *(money)* dépenser trop de; *Fin* **to have overspent one's budget** être en dépassement budgétaire

overspending [ˌəʊvə'spendɪŋ] *n* dépense *f* excessive; *Fin* dépassement *m* budgétaire

overspill 1 *vi* [ˌəʊvə'spɪl] déborder, se répandre

2 *n* ['əʊvəspɪl] excédent *m* de population (urbaine); **the London overspill** l'excédent *m* de la population londonienne

►► ***overspill population*** excédent *m* de population; ***overspill town*** = ville servant à décongestionner une agglomération surpeuplée

overspread [ˌəʊvə'spred] *(pt & pp* **overspread**) *vt Literary* (**a**) *(cover)* (re)couvrir (**with** de); **the snow overspread the plain** la neige recouvrait la plaine; **jealousy overspread with hatred** jalousie doublée de haine (**b**) *(spread over)* se répandre sur, s'étendre sur; *(of floods, light etc)* inonder; **a mist overspread the forest** une brume planait sur la forêt

overstaffed [ˌəʊvə'stɑːft] *adj* en sureffectif; **the firm is overstaffed** le personnel de la firme est trop nombreux, la firme connaît un problème de sureffectifs

overstaffing [ˌəʊvə'stɑːfɪŋ] *n* excédents *mpl* de personnel, sureffectifs *mpl*

overstate [ˌəʊvə'steɪt] *vt* exagérer; **the importance of this factor cannot be overstated** on ne saurait insister suffisamment sur l'importance de ce facteur

overstatement [ˌəʊvə'steɪtmənt] *n* exagération *f*; **to say that he's a singer would be an overstatement** il ne mérite pas vraiment le titre de chanteur

overstay [ˌəʊvə'steɪ] *vt* **to overstay one's welcome** abuser de l'hospitalité de ses hôtes; *Mil* **to overstay one's leave** dépasser la durée de sa permission

oversteer *Aut* **1** *n* ['əʊvəstɪə(r)] survirage *m*

2 *vi* [ˌəʊvə'stɪə(r)] survirer

overstep [ˌəʊvə'step] *(pt & pp* **overstepped,** *cont* **overstepping**) *vt* dépasser, outrepasser; **to overstep one's authority** outrepasser ses pouvoirs; *Fig* **to overstep the mark** *or* **the limit** dépasser les bornes, aller trop loin

overstock [ˌəʊvə'stɒk] **1** *vt* (**a**) *Com (warehouse)* trop approvisionner; *(market)* encombrer (**with** de); *(outlet)* munir de stocks excessifs (**b**) *(farm)* mettre trop de bétail dans; *(pond, river)* mettre trop de poissons dans

2 overstocks *npl Am* surplus *m*, excédent *m*

overstocked [ˌəʊvə'stɒkt] *adj* (**a**) *Com (warehouse)* trop approvisionné; *(market)* encombré, surchargé; **to be overstocked** *(shop)* avoir des stocks excessifs; **the market is overstocked with foreign goods** le marché regorge de marchandises étrangères (**b**) *(farm)* qui a un excès de bétail; *(pond, river)* trop poissonneux

overstocking [ˌəʊvə'stɒkɪŋ] *n Com* stockage *m* excessif

overstrain [ˌəʊvə'streɪn] *vt* (**a**) *(cable etc)* surtendre (**b**) *(person, horse)* surmener; **to overstrain oneself with working** se surmener (à travailler) (**c**) *Fig* **to overstrain an argument** pousser trop loin un argument; **to overstrain the truth** donner une entorse à la vérité

overstrike *Comput* **1** *n* ['əʊvəstraɪk] *(character)* caractère *m* superposé; *(action)* frappe *f* superposée

2 *vt* [ˌəʊvə'straɪk] superposer un caractère à

overstrung [ˌəʊvə'strʌŋ] *adj* (**a**) *(person)* tendu, surexcité (**b**) *(piano)* à cordes croisées

overstuffed [ˌəʊvə'stʌft] *adj* rembourré

oversubscribe [ˌəʊvəsəb'skraɪb] *vt* **to be oversubscribed** *(concert, play)* être en surlocation; *St Exch* **the share issue was oversubscribed** l'offre d'actions a été sursouscrite; **the school trip is oversubscribed** il y a trop d'élèves inscrits à l'excursion organisée par l'école

oversubscription [ˌəuvəsəb'skrɪpʃən] *n St Exch (of loan, share issue)* sursouscription *f*

oversubtle [ˌəʊvə'sʌtəl] *adj* trop subtil

overt ['əʊvɜːt, əʊ'vɜːt] *adj* manifeste

overtake [ˌəʊvə'teɪk] *(pt* **overtook** [-'tʊk], *pp* **overtaken** [-'teɪkən]) *vt* (**a**) *(pass beyond)* dépasser, devancer; *esp Br Aut* dépasser, doubler; **he overtook all the other runners** il a dépassé tous les autres coureurs; **France has overtaken Spain as the main exporter of these products** la France a supplanté l'Espagne au rang de premier exportateur de ces produits

(**b**) *(surprise)* surprendre; *(strike)* frapper; **overtaken by events** dépassé par les événements; **catastrophe overtook the community** la catastrophe a frappé *ou* s'est abattue sur la communauté; **overtaken by** *or* **with panic** pris de panique; **their plans/we were overtaken by fate** le sort s'est joué de leurs projets/nous

(**c**) *Literary (of emotion)* s'emparer de

overtaking [ˌəʊvə'teɪkɪŋ] *n esp Br Aut* dépassement *m*; **no overtaking** *(sign)* interdiction de dépasser

►► ***overtaking lane*** *(when driving on right)* voie *f* de gauche; *(when driving on left)* voie *f* de droite

overtax [ˌəʊvə'tæks] *vt* (**a**) *Fin (person)* surimposer; *(goods)* surtaxer (**b**) *(strain → patience, hospitality)* abuser de; *(→ person, heart)* surmener; **don't overtax your strength** *or* **yourself** ne te fatigue pas inutilement, ne te surmène pas; **don't overtax his brain!** ne lui usez pas la cervelle!

overtaxation [ˌəʊvətæk'seɪʃən] *n Fin* surchargement *m* d'impôts, surimposition *f*

over-the-counter *adj* (**a**) *(medicines)* vendu sans ordonnance, en vente libre (**b**) *Am St Exch* hors cote

►► ***over-the-counter market*** marché *m* hors cote, marché *m* des transactions hors séance

over-the-top *adj Br Fam* **that's a bit over-the-top!** c'est un peu exagéré!; **there was no need to be quite so over-the-top about it** ce n'était pas la peine d'en faire toute une histoire; **the house is nice, but the decor's a bit over-the-top** la maison est bien, mais la décoration est un peu lourdingue; **it's a bit over-the-top to call him a fascist** c'est un peu exagéré de le traiter de fasciste; **he went completely over-the-top when he heard what she'd said** il a pété les plombs quand il a appris ce qu'elle avait dit; **his latest film is a bit over-the-top** il dépasse un peu la mesure dans son dernier film

over-the-transom *adj Am* non demandé

overthrow *(pt* **overthrew** [-'θruː], *pp* **overthrown** [-'θrəʊn]) **1** *vt* [ˌəʊvə'θrəʊ] *(regime, government)* renverser; *(rival, enemy army)* vaincre; *(values, standards)* bouleverser; *(plans)* réduire à néant

2 *n* ['əʊvəθrəʊ] *(of enemy)* défaite *f*; *(of regime, government)* renversement *m*, chute *f*; *(of values, standards)* bouleversement *m*

overtime ['əʊvətaɪm] *n (UNCOUNT)* (**a**) *(work)* heures *fpl* supplémentaires; **to do** *or* **to work overtime** faire des heures supplémentaires; *Fig* **he'll have to work overtime to get those two to agree!** s'il veut mettre ces deux-là d'accord, il a intérêt à se lever de bonne heure!; **your imagination seems to have been working overtime** on dirait que tu as laissé ton imagination s'emballer

(**b**) *(overtime pay)* rémunération *f* des heures supplémentaires; **after 6p.m. we're on overtime (pay)** après 18 heures, on nous paie en heures supplémentaires; **to be paid overtime** être payé en heures supplémentaires

(**c**) *Am Sport* prolongations *fpl*; **the match went into overtime** ils ont joué les prolongations

►► *Ind* ***overtime ban*** refus *m* de faire des heures supplémentaires; ***overtime pay*** rémunération *f* des heures supplémentaires; ***overtime rate*** tarif *m* des heures supplémentaires

overtire [ˌəʊvəˈtaɪə(r)] *vt (person)* surmener; **to overtire oneself** se surmener, trop se fatiguer

overtired [ˌəʊvəˈtaɪəd] *adj* surmené; **to be overtired** *(child)* être trop fatigué

overtiredness [ˌəʊvəˈtaɪədnɪs] *n* surmenage *m*

overtly [əʊˈvɜːtlɪ] *adv* franchement, ouvertement

overtness [əʊˈvɜːtnɪs] *n* franchise *f*

overtone [ˈəʊvətəʊn] *n* (**a**) *(nuance)* nuance *f*, accent *m*; **there was an overtone of aggression in what she said** il y avait une pointe d'agressivité dans ses propos; **his speech was full of racist overtones** son discours était truffé de sous-entendus racistes (**b**) *Mus* harmonique *m*

overtook [ˌəʊvəˈtʊk] *pt of* **overtake**

overtrade [ˌəʊvəˈtreɪd] *vi* avoir une marge d'exploitation trop étroite

overtrading [ˌəʊvəˈtreɪdɪŋ] *n St Exch* = emballement de l'activité d'une entreprise (au-delà des limites de son capital)

overtrick [ˈəʊvətrɪk] *n Cards (in bridge)* levée *f* de mieux

overtrump [ˌəʊvəˈtrʌmp] *vt Cards* surcouper

overture [ˈəʊvəˌtjʊə(r)] *n* (**a**) *Mus* ouverture *f* (**b**) *Fig (proposal)* ouverture *f*, avance *f*; **to make overtures to sb** *(sexually)* faire des avances à qn; *(in business, politics etc)* faire des démarches auprès de qn; *(friendly)* essayer de lier connaissance avec qn; **romantic overtures** avances *fpl* amoureuses; **peace overtures** propositions *fpl* de paix (**c**) *Fig (prelude)* prélude *m*, début *m*

overturn [ˌəʊvəˈtɜːn] **1** *vt* (**a**) *(lamp, car, furniture)* renverser; *(ship)* faire chavirer

(**b**) *(overthrow → regime, government, plans)* renverser; *Law (→ judgment, sentence)* casser; **the bill was overturned by the Senate** le projet de loi a été rejeté par le Sénat

2 *vi (lamp, furniture)* se renverser; *(car)* se retourner, capoter; *(ship)* chavirer

overuse 1 *vt* [ˌəʊvəˈjuːz] abuser de

2 *n* [ˌəʊvəˈjuːs] abus *m*, usage *m* excessif; **the phrase has become meaningless by overuse** l'expression a perdu tout son sens à force d'être trop employée

overused [ˌəʊvəˈjuːzd] *adj (expression, excuse)* usé, rebattu; *(word → that has lost its meaning)* galvaudé

overvaluation [ˌəʊvəˌvæljuːˈeɪʃən] *n (of currency)* surévaluation *f*; *(of house, painting)* surestimation *f*

overvalue [ˌəʊvəˈvæljuː] **1** *vt* (**a**) *(currency)* surévaluer; *(house, painting)* surestimer (**b**) *(overrate)* surestimer, faire trop de cas de; **his influence has been overvalued** son influence a été surestimée *ou* exagérée

2 *n (of currency)* survaleur *f*

overview [ˈəʊvəvjuː] *n* vue *f* d'ensemble, panorama *m*

overwater [ˌəʊvəˈwɔːtə(r)] *vt (plant)* trop arroser

overwatering [ˌəʊvəˈwɔːtərɪŋ] *n (of plant)* arrosage *m* excessif

overweening [ˌəʊvəˈwiːnɪŋ] *adj Br* (**a**) *(pride, ambition etc)* sans bornes, démesuré (**b**) *(person)* outrecuidant, présomptueux

overweight 1 *adj* [ˌəʊvəˈweɪt] (**a**) *(person)* (trop) gros, (trop) grosse; **overweight people are more prone to heart disease** les personnes trop grosses *ou* fortes ont plus de risques d'avoir des maladies cardiaques; **I'm a few pounds overweight** j'ai quelques kilos de trop

(**b**) *(luggage, parcel)* trop lourd

2 *n* [ˈəʊvəweɪt] excès *m* de poids

3 *vt* [ˌəʊvəˈweɪt] (**a**) *(overload)* surcharger

(**b**) *(overemphasize)* accorder trop d'importance à, trop privilégier

overwhelm [ˌəʊvəˈwelm] *vt* (**a**) *(devastate)* accabler, terrasser; *(astound)* bouleverser; *(with kindness)* combler; **overwhelmed with grief** accablé de chagrin; **grief overwhelmed us** le chagrin nous a terrassés; **your generosity overwhelms me** votre générosité me bouleverse *ou* me va droit au cœur

(**b**) *also Fig (submerge)* submerger; **our switchboard has been overwhelmed by the number of calls** notre standard a été submergé par les appels; **I'm completely overwhelmed with work** je suis débordé de travail

(**c**) *(defeat)* écraser; **the England team was finally overwhelmed** l'équipe d'Angleterre a finalement été écrasée; **we fought back but our attackers overwhelmed us** nous nous sommes débattus mais nos agresseurs ont eu le dessus

overwhelming [ˌəʊvəˈwelmɪŋ] *adj* (**a**) *(crushing → victory, defeat)* écrasant; **to win by an overwhelming majority** gagner avec une majorité écrasante; **the overwhelming majority (of people) oppose these measures** la grande majorité des gens est opposée à ces mesures

(**b**) *(extreme, overpowering → grief, heat)* accablant; *(→ joy)* extrême; *(→ love)* passionnel; *(→ desire, urge, passion)* irrésistible; **an overwhelming sense of frustration** un sentiment d'extrême frustration; **their friendliness is somewhat overwhelming** leur amabilité a quelque chose d'excessif

overwhelmingly [ˌəʊvəˈwelmɪŋlɪ] *adv* (**a**) *(crushingly)* de manière écrasante; **the House of Lords voted overwhelmingly against the bill** la Chambre des lords a voté contre le projet à une écrasante majorité (**b**) *(as intensifier)* extrêmement; *(predominantly)* surtout

overwind [ˌəʊvəˈwaɪnd] *(pt & pp* **overwound** [-ˈwaʊnd]) *vt (clock, watch)* trop remonter

overwinter [ˌəʊvəˈwɪntə(r)] *vi (birds, animals)* hiverner; *(people)* passer l'hiver

overwintering [ˌəʊvəˈwɪntərɪŋ] *n (of birds, animals)* hivernage *m*

overwork 1 *vt* [ˌəʊvəˈwɜːk] (**a**) *(person)* surmener; **he tends to overwork himself** il a tendance à se surmener; **don't overwork yourself** n'en fais pas trop; **to be overworked and underpaid** être surchargé de travail et sous-payé

(**b**) *(word)* abuser de, utiliser trop souvent; **it's one of the most overworked phrases in the English language** c'est une des expressions les plus utilisées de la langue anglaise

2 *vi* [ˌəʊvəˈwɜːk] se surmener

3 *n* [ˈəʊvəˌwɜːk] surmenage *m*

overworking [ˌəʊvəˈwɜːkɪŋ] *n* surmenage *m*

overwound [ˌəʊvəˈwaʊnd] *pt & pp of* **overwind**

overwrite [ˌəʊvəˈraɪt] *(pt* **overwrote** [-ˈrəʊt], *pp* **overwritten** [-ˈrɪtən]) **1** *vt* (**a**) *(write on top of)* écrire sur, repasser sur (**b**) *Comput (file)* écraser

2 *vi* écrire dans un style ampoulé

▸▸ *Comput* ***overwrite mode*** mode *m* de superposition

overwritten [ˌəʊvəˈrɪtən] *adj* écrit dans un style ampoulé

overwrought [ˌəʊvəˈrɔːt] *adj* sur les nerfs, à bout; **to get overwrought about sth** se mettre dans tous ses états à propos de qch

overzealous [ˌəʊvəˈzeləs] *adj* trop zélé

Ovid [ˈɒvɪd] *pr n Antiq* Ovide

oviduct [ˈəʊvɪdʌkt] *n* oviducte *m*

oviform [ˈəʊvɪfɔːm] *adj* oviforme

ovine [ˈəʊvaɪn] *adj* ovin

oviparous [əʊˈvɪpərəs] *adj* ovipare

ovipositor [ˌəʊvɪˈpɒzɪtə(r)] *n Biol* ovipositeur *m*, tarière *f*

ovoid [ˈəʊvɔɪd] **1** *n* figure *f* ovoïde

2 *adj* ovoïde, ovoïdal

ovolo [ˈəʊvələʊ] *n Archit* quart-de-rond *m*

ovoviviparous [ˌəʊvəʊvɪˈvɪpərəs] *adj* ovovivipare

ovular [ˈɒvjʊlə(r)] *adj* ovulaire

ovulate [ˈɒvjʊleɪt] *vi* ovuler

ovulation [ˌɒvjʊˈleɪʃən] *n* ovulation *f*

ovule [ˈɒvjuːl] *n* ovule *m*

ovum [ˈəʊvəm] *(pl* **ova** [-və]) *n Biol* ovule *m*

ow [aʊ] *exclam* aïe!

owe [əʊ] **1** *vt* devoir; **to owe sth to sb, to owe sb sth** devoir qch à qn; **you owe me £10** tu me dois 10 livres; **how much** *or* **what do I owe you?** combien est-ce que *ou* qu'est-ce que je vous dois?; **how much do we still owe him for** *or* **on the car?** combien nous reste-t-il à lui payer pour la voiture?; **I still owe you for the petrol** je vous dois encore l'essence; **I owe you a beer** je te dois une bière; **he thinks society owes him a living** il s'imagine avoir le droit de vivre aux crochets de la société; **I think you owe him an explanation** je pense qu'il a droit à une explication de ta part *ou* que tu lui dois une explication; **we owe them an apology** nous leur devons des excuses; **you owe it to yourself to do your best** vous vous devez à vous-même de faire de votre mieux; **we owe this discovery to a lucky accident** nous devons cette découverte à un heureux hasard; **to what do we owe the honour of your visit?** qu'est-ce qui nous vaut l'honneur de votre visite?; **I owe it all to my parents** je suis redevable de tout cela à mes parents; **to owe sb a favour** être redevable d'un service à qn; **I owe my life to you** je vous dois la vie; **he owes his good looks to his mother** il tient sa beauté de sa mère; **I owe you one!** à charge de revanche!

2 *vi* être endetté; **he still owes for** *or* **on the house** il n'a pas encore fini de payer la maison

owing [ˈəʊɪŋ] **1** *adj (after n)* dû; **the sum owing on the car** la somme qui reste due sur le prix de la voiture; **all the money owing to me** tout l'argent qui m'est dû; **to have a lot of money owing** *(to owe)* devoir beaucoup d'argent; *(to be owed)* avoir beaucoup d'argent à récupérer

2 owing to *prep* à cause de, en raison de

owl [aʊl] *n Orn* hibou *m*, chouette *f*; **he's a wise old owl** c'est la sagesse faite homme, c'est l'image même de la sagesse

owlet [ˈaʊlɪt] *n Orn* jeune hibou *m*, jeune chouette *f*

▸▸ *Entom* ***owlet moth*** noctuelle *f*

owlish [ˈaʊlɪʃ] *adj* de hibou; **those glasses give you an owlish look** tu as l'air d'un hibou avec ces lunettes

owlishly [ˈaʊlɪʃlɪ] *adv (look at)* avec des yeux de hibou

OWN [əʊn]

propre	▸ **1**
le mien/le sien/etc	▸ **2**
posséder	▸ **3 (a)**
seul	▸ **4**

1 *adj* propre; **I have my own bedroom** j'ai ma propre chambre; **I have my very own bedroom** j'ai une chambre pour moi tout seul; **a flat with its own entrance** un appartement avec une porte d'entrée indépendante; **these are my own skis** ces skis sont à moi *ou* m'appartiennent; **I'll do it (in) my own way** je le ferai à ma façon; **it's all my own work** c'est moi qui ai tout fait; **she makes all her own clothes** elle fait elle-même tous ses vêtements; **how to build your own sauna** *(title of book, article)* comment construire votre propre sauna; **it's your own fault!** tu n'as à t'en prendre qu'à toi-même!; **you'll have to make up your own mind** c'est à toi et à toi seul de décider, personne ne pourra prendre cette décision à ta place; **I saw it with my own eyes** je l'ai vu de mes propres yeux; **your own mother wouldn't recognize you!** ta propre mère ne te reconnaîtrait pas!; **to be one's own man/woman** vivre à sa façon *ou* à son idée

2 *pron* **is that car your own?** est-ce que cette voiture est à vous?; **I don't need a pen, I've brought my own** je n'ai pas besoin de stylo, j'ai apporté le mien; **if you want a car, you'll have to buy your own** si tu veux une voiture, tu n'as qu'à t'en acheter une; **her opinions are identical to my own** nous partageons exactement les mêmes opinions; **a house/a room/a garden of one's (very) own** une maison/une pièce/un jardin (bien) à soi; **their son has a car of his own** leur fils a sa propre voiture; **a child of his own** un enfant à lui; **I shan't be going for reasons of my own** je n'irai pas pour des raisons personnelles; **his ideas are his own** ses idées lui sont propres; **the town has a character of its own** *or* **all (of) its own** la ville possède un charme qui lui est propre *ou* un charme bien à elle; **my time is not my own** je ne suis pas maître de mon temps; **I haven't a single thing I can call my own** je n'ai rien à moi; **you're on your own now!** à toi de jouer maintenant!; **to come into one's own** *(show one's capabilities)* montrer de quoi on est capable; *(inherit)* toucher son héritage; **on bad roads the four-wheel-drive model really comes into its own** sur les mauvaises routes, le modèle à quatre roues motrices montre vraiment ses capacités; **to get one's own back (on sb)** se venger (de qn); **I'll get my own back on him for that** je lui revaudrai ça; **to look**

after one's own s'occuper des siens; **to make sth one's own** s'approprier qch; **she has made the role her own** elle en a fait son rôle

3 *vt* (**a**) *(possess)* posséder; **I've lost everything I own** j'ai perdu tout ce que je possède; **they own 51 per cent of the shares** ils détiennent 51 pourcent des actions; **does she own the house?** est-elle propriétaire de la maison?; **who owns this car?** à qui appartient cette voiture?; **the land owned by the Crown** les terres qui appartiennent à la Couronne; *Fam* **they walked in as if they owned the place** ils sont entrés comme (s'ils étaient) chez eux; **you don't own me!** je ne t'appartiens pas!

(**b**) *Literary (admit)* admettre, reconnaître; **she owned that I was right** elle a reconnu que j'avais raison

4 **on one's own** *adj* (tout) seul; **are you here on your own?** êtes-vous seul ici?; **he left me on my own all evening** il m'a laissé seul toute la soirée; **I'm trying to get him on his own** j'essaie de le voir seul à seul; **I did it (all) on my own** je l'ai fait tout seul; **she's setting up in business on her own** elle monte une affaire toute seule; **you're on your own!** c'est à toi de te débrouiller!

▸▸ *Mktg* ***own brand*** marque *f* de distributeur; *Ftbl* ***own goal*** but *m* marqué contre son camp, *Suisse* autogoal *m*; **to score an own goal** marquer contre son camp, *Suisse* marquer un autogoal; *Fig* agir contre ses propres intérêts

▸**own to** *vt insep Literary* avouer; **she owned to a secret passion for Damian** elle avoua une passion cachée pour Damian; **nobody owned to having taken it** personne n'a avoué l'avoir pris; **he owns to being forty** il admet qu'il a quarante ans

▸**own up** *vi* avouer, faire des aveux; **if the culprit doesn't own up...** si le coupable n'avoue pas *ou* ne passe pas aux aveux...; **to own up to sth** avouer qch; **he owned up to his mistake** il a reconnu son erreur; **to own up to having done sth** avouer avoir fait qch

---

own-brand *adj Br* **the supermarket's own-brand jam is cheaper** la confiture que le supermarché vend sous sa propre marque coûte moins cher

▸▸ *Mktg* ***own-brand label*** marque *f* de distributeur; ***own-brand product*** produit *m* à marque de distributeur

own-branding *n Mktg* apposition *f* de sa propre marque

owner ['əʊnə(r)] *n* propriétaire *mf*; **he is the rightful owner** c'est lui le propriétaire légitime; **at the owner's risk** aux risques du propriétaire; **who is the owner of this jacket?** à qui appartient cette veste?; **they are all car owners** ils possèdent *ou* ils ont tous une voiture; **dog owners should be aware that...** les propriétaires de chiens sont priés de noter que...

▸▸ *Acct* ***owner's capital account*** compte *m* de l'exploitant

owner-driver *n* conducteur(trice) *m,f* propriétaire du véhicule

ownerless ['əʊnəlɪs] *adj* sans propriétaire

owner-occupancy *n* = fait d'être propriétaire du logement qu'on occupe; **owner-occupancy has increased** de plus en plus de gens sont propriétaires de leurs logements

owner-occupied *adj* occupé par son propriétaire

owner-occupier *n* occupant(e) *m,f* propriétaire

ownership ['əʊnəʃɪp] *n* possession *f*; **we require proof of ownership** nous demandons un titre de propriété; **the government encourages home ownership** le gouvernement encourage l'accession à la propriété; **the ownership of the house is contested** les droits de propriété sont contestés; **to be in private/public ownership** appartenir au secteur privé/public; **most of the industry is in private ownership** la plus grande partie des entreprises sont aux mains du secteur privé; **change of ownership** changement de propriétaire; **under new ownership** *(sign)* changement de propriétaire

own-label *adj Mktg* à marque de distributeur

ownsome ['əʊnsəm], **owny-o** ['əʊnɪəʊ] *n Br Fam* **(all) on one's ownsome** tout seul □

owt [aʊt] *pron Fam NEng* quelque chose □; **he never said owt** il n'a rien dit □; **is there owt the matter?** il y a quelque chose qui va pas?

ox [ɒks] *(pl* **oxen** ['ɒksən]) *n* bœuf *m*; **(as) strong as an ox** fort comme un bœuf

▸▸ ***ox tongue*** langue *f* de bœuf

oxalic acid [ɒk'sælɪk-] *n Chem* acide *m* oxalique

oxalis [ɒk'sɑːlɪs] *n Bot* oxalide *f*, oxalis *m*

oxblood ['ɒksblʌd] **1** *n (colour)* rouge *m* sang

2 *adj* rouge sang *(inv)*

oxbow (lake) ['ɒksbəʊ-] *n* bras *m* mort *(d'un cours d'eau)*

Oxbridge ['ɒksbrɪdʒ] **1** *n* = désignation collective des universités d'Oxford et de Cambridge

2 *adj (graduate etc)* de l'université d'Oxford ou de Cambridge; **the privileges of an Oxbridge education** les privilèges que confère un diplôme d'Oxford ou de Cambridge

OXBRIDGE

Oxbridge désigne conjointement les universités d'Oxford et de Cambridge, les plus anciennes et les plus prestigieuses d'Angleterre. Le terme est généralement employé pour les différencier des universités de création plus récente. Oxford et Cambridge se distinguent encore des autres établissements d'enseignement supérieur, notamment de par leur structure collégiale et leurs conditions d'admission très rigoureuses. De nos jours, Oxbridge est toujours synonyme d'élitisme en dépit des efforts entrepris pour élargir le recrutement des deux universités. Jusqu'à une époque très récente, un diplôme d'Oxbridge était considéré comme indispensable pour accéder à des postes importants dans le monde de la politique ou de la diplomatie.

oxcart ['ɒkskɑːt] *n* char *m* à bœuf *ou* à bœufs

oxen ['ɒksən] *pl of* **ox**

oxeye daisy ['ɒksaɪ-] *n Bot* grande marguerite

Oxfam ['ɒksfæm] *n* (*abbr* **Oxford Committee for Famine Relief**) = association caritative britannique

▸▸ ***Oxfam shop*** = magasin où l'œuvre de bienfaisance Oxfam vend des articles d'occasion et d'artisanat au profit du tiers-monde

Oxford ['ɒksfəd] *n* Oxford

▸▸ ***Oxford bags*** *(trousers)* pantalon *m* très large; ***Oxford blue*** *(colour)* bleu *m* foncé; *(sportsperson)* = sportif qui porte ou a porté les couleurs de l'université d'Oxford ***Oxford cloth*** oxford *m*; ***Oxford English*** = l'anglais de l'université d'Oxford, servant parfois de référence pour la "bonne" prononciation; ***the Oxford Group*** = mouvement international pour un renouveau moral et spirituel fondé en 1938; ***the Oxford Movement*** le puseyisme, le mouvement d'Oxford; ***Oxford shirt*** chemise *f* en oxford; ***Oxford Street*** = une des grandes artères commerçantes de Londres

oxford-blue *adj* bleu foncé *(inv)*

oxfords ['ɒksfədz] *npl* chaussures *fpl* à lacets

Oxfordshire ['ɒksfədʃə(r)] *n* l'Oxfordshire *m*, = comté au sud du centre de l'Angleterre; **in Oxfordshire** dans l'Oxfordshire

oxhide ['ɒkshaɪd] *n* cuir *m* de bœuf

oxidant ['ɒksɪdənt] *n Chem* oxydant *m*

oxidase ['ɒksɪdeɪz] *n Biol & Chem* oxydase *f*

oxidation [ˌɒksɪ'deɪʃən] *n Chem* oxydation *f*

oxide ['ɒksaɪd] *n Chem* oxyde *m*

oxidization [ˌɒksɪdaɪ'zeɪʃən] *n Chem* oxydation *f*

oxidize, -ise ['ɒksɪdaɪz] *Chem* **1** *vt* oxyder

2 *vi* s'oxyder

oxidizer ['ɒksɪdaɪzə(r)] *n Chem* oxydant *m*

oxidizing agent ['ɒksɪdaɪzɪŋ-] *n Chem* oxydant *m*

oxidoreductase [ˌɒksɪdəʊrə'dʌkteɪz] *n Biol & Chem* oxydoréductase *f*

oxlip ['ɒkslɪp] *n Bot* primevère *f* élevée

Oxo® ['ɒksəʊ] *n* = marque anglaise de bouillon cube

Oxon *(written abbr* **Oxfordshire**) Oxfordshire *m*

Oxon. *(written abbr* **Oxoniensis**) = de l'université d'Oxford

Oxonian [ɒk'səʊnjən] **1** *n (student)* étudiant(e) *m,f* de l'université d'Oxford; *(townsperson)* Oxfordien(enne) *m,f*

2 *adj* oxfordien, d'Oxford

oxonium [ɒk'səʊnɪəm] *n Chem* oxonium *m*

oxpecker ['ɒkspekə(r)] *n Orn* pique-bœuf *m*

oxtail ['ɒksteɪl] *n* queue *f* de bœuf

▸▸ ***oxtail soup*** soupe *f* de queue de bœuf

oxter ['ɒkstə(r)] *n Scot Fam (armpit)* aisselle □ *f*

oxyacetylene [ˌɒksɪə'setɪliːn] *adj* oxyacétylénique

▸▸ ***oxyacetylene burner*** *or* ***lamp*** *or* ***torch*** chalumeau *m* oxyacétylénique

oxycarburetted [ˌɒksɪkɑːbjʊ'retɪd] *adj Chem* oxycarboné

oxychloride [ˌɒksɪ'klɔːraɪd] *n Biol & Chem* oxychlorure *m*

oxygen ['ɒksɪdʒən] *n* oxygène *m*

▸▸ ***oxygen bar*** = bar fournissant des masques pour respirer de l'oxygène pur; *Physiol* ***oxygen debt*** dette *f* d'oxygène; ***oxygen mask*** masque *m* à oxygène; ***oxygen tent*** tente *f* à oxygène

oxygenase ['ɒksɪdʒəneɪz] *n Physiol & Chem* oxygénase *f*

oxygenate ['ɒksɪdʒəneɪt] *vt Physiol & Chem* oxygéner

oxygenation [ˌɒksɪdʒə'neɪʃən] *n Physiol & Chem* oxygénation *f*

oxygenize, -ise ['ɒksɪdʒənaɪz] *vt Physiol & Chem* oxygéner

oxyhaemoglobin, *Am* **oxyhemoglobin** [ˌɒksɪˌhiːmə'gləʊbɪn] *n Physiol* oxyhémoglobine *f*

oxymoron [ˌɒksɪ'mɔːrɒn] *(pl* **oxymora** [-rə]) *n Ling* oxymoron *m*

oxysulphide, *Am* **oxysulfide** [ˌɒksɪ'sʌlfaɪd] *n Chem* oxysulfide *m*

oxytocic [ˌɒksɪ'təʊsɪk] *Med* **1** *n* oxytocine *f*

2 *adj* ocytocique

oxytocin [ˌɒksɪ'təʊsɪn] *n Med* ocytocine *f*

oxytone ['ɒksɪtəʊn] *Gram* **1** *n* oxyton *m*

2 *adj* oxyton

oyez [əʊ'jes] *exclam Arch* oyez!

oyster ['ɔɪstə(r)] **1** *n* (**a**) *(seafood)* huître *f*; **the world is her oyster** le monde lui appartient

(**b**) *(colour)* gris *m* perle *inv*

(**c**) *(part of fowl)* sot-l'y-laisse *m inv*

2 *adj (colour)* gris perle *(inv)*

▸▸ ***oyster basket*** bourriche *f*; ***oyster bed*** parc *m* à huîtres; ***oyster farm*** parc *m* à huîtres; ***oyster farmer*** ostréiculteur(trice) *m,f*; ***oyster farming*** ostréiculture *f*; ***oyster knife*** couteau *m* à huîtres; ***oyster mushroom*** pleurote *f*; ***oyster pink*** rose *m* nacré; *Culin* ***oyster sauce*** sauce *f* d'huître; ***oyster white*** blanc *m* nacré

oystercatcher ['ɔɪstəˌkætʃə(r)] *n Orn* huîtrier *m*, pie *f* de mer

oysterman ['ɔɪstəmən] *(pl* **oystermen** [-mən]) *n* (**a**) *(cultivator)* ostréiculteur(trice) *m,f*; *(seller)* écailler(ère) *m,f* (**b**) *(boat)* bateau *m* huîtrier

oyster-pink *adj* rose nacré *(inv)*

oyster-white *adj* blanc nacré *(inv)*

Oz [ɒz] *n Fam (Australia)* Australie □ *f*

oz. *(written abbr* **ounce**) once *f*

Ozalid® ['ɒzəlɪd] *n Typ* Ozalid® *m*

Ozarks ['əʊzɑːks] *n* **the Ozarks** = région naturelle de forêts dans le Missouri et l'Arkansas

ozocerite [əʊ'zɒsəraɪt], **ozokerite** [əʊ'zəʊkəraɪt] *n Miner* ozocérite *f*, ozokérite *f*

ozone ['əʊzəʊn] *n* (**a**) *(gas)* ozone *m* (**b**) *Fam (sea air)* bon air *m* marin □

▸▸ ***ozone depletion*** diminution *f* de l'ozone; ***ozone layer, ozone shield*** couche *f* d'ozone; **the hole in the ozone layer** le trou d'ozone

ozone-friendly *adj* qui préserve la couche d'ozone

ozone-safe *adj* qui préserve la couche d'ozone

ozonide ['əʊzənaɪd] *n Chem* ozonide *m*

ozonization [ˌəʊzənaɪ'zeɪʃən] *n Chem* ozonisation *f*, ozonation *f*

ozonize, -ise ['əʊzənaɪz] *vt Chem* ozoniser, ozoner

ozonizer ['əʊzənaɪzə(r)] *n Chem* ozonateur *m*

ozonosphere [əʊ'zəʊnəsfɪə(r)] *n* ozonosphère *f*

Ozzie ['ɒzɪ] *n Fam (Australian)* Australien(enne) □ *m,f*

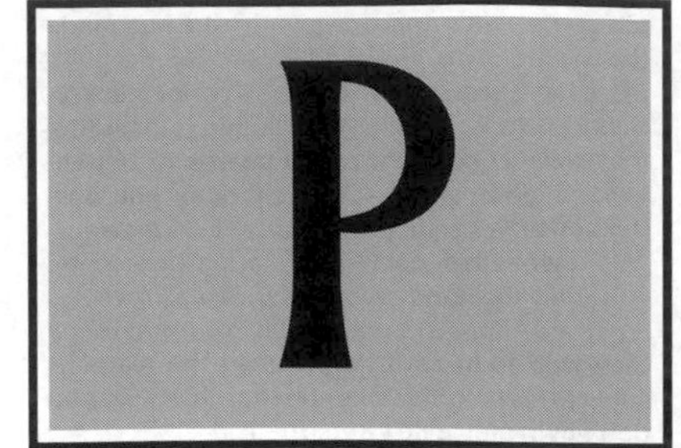

P[1], p[1] [piː] *n (letter)* P, p *m inv*; **two p's** deux p; **P for Peter** ≃ P comme Pierre; *Br* **to mind one's p's and q's** se surveiller, bien se tenir; *Mktg* **the four P's** les quatre P, le marketing mix

P[2] (**a**) (*written abbr* **president**) président *m* (**b**) (*written abbr* **prince**) Pce

p[2] *n* (**a**) (*abbr* **penny**) penny *m* (**b**) (*abbr* **pence**) pence *mpl*

p. (*written abbr* **page**) p.

P45 [ˌpiːfɔːtɪˈfaɪv] *n Br* = document administratif donné à tout employé lorsqu'il quitte un emploi et devant être présenté à tout nouvel employeur, où figurent le total des rémunérations versées par l'employeur ainsi que les sommes payées par l'employé en impôts et cotisations sociales; *Fig* **to be handed one's P45** se faire licencier

P60 [ˌpiːˈsɪkstɪ] *n Br* récapitulatif *m* annuel de paie

PA[1] [ˌpiːˈeɪ] *n* (**a**) *Br* (*abbr* **personal assistant**) (*of executive*) assistant(e) *m,f*; (*with secretarial duties*) secrétaire *mf* de direction

(**b**) (*abbr* **public address system**) système *m* de sonorisation, sono *f*; **departure times will be announced over the PA** les horaires de départ seront annoncés par haut-parleur

(**c**) *Am* (*abbr* **physician's assistant**) médecin-assistant *m*

(**d**) (*abbr* **Press Association**) = la principale agence de presse britannique

(**e**) (*abbr* **production assistant**) assistant(e) *m,f* de production

PA[2] (*written abbr* **Pennsylvania**) Pennsylvanie *f*

pa [pɑː] *n Fam* papa *m*

p.a. (*written abbr* **per annum**) par an

pabulum [ˈpæbjʊləm] *n Literary* aliment *m*, nourriture *f*; **mental pabulum** aliment *m ou* nourriture *f* de l'esprit

PABX [ˌpiːeɪbiːˈeks] *n Tel* (*abbr* **private automatic branch exchange**) = autocommutateur privé

PAC [ˌpiːeɪˈsiː] *n Am* (*abbr* **political action committee**) = comité qui réunit des fonds pour soutenir une cause politique

paca [ˈpɑːkə] *n Zool* paca *m*

pace[1] [peɪs] **1** *n* (**a**) (*speed*) allure *f*, vitesse *f*, train *m*; **she quickened her pace** elle pressa le pas; **she slackened her pace** elle ralentit le pas; **at a good** *or* **brisk** *or* **smart pace** à vive allure; **at a slow pace** à petite allure; **at walking pace** au pas; **the slower pace of country life** le rythme plus paisible de la vie à la campagne; **don't walk so fast, I can't keep pace with you** ne marche pas si vite, je n'arrive pas à te suivre; **to keep pace with new developments** se tenir au courant des derniers développements; **output is keeping pace with demand** la production se maintient au niveau de *ou* répond à la demande; **our incomes haven't kept pace with inflation** nos revenus n'ont pas augmenté au même rythme que l'inflation; **it's all happened so fast I can barely keep pace with it** tout est arrivé si vite que j'ai du mal à suivre le rythme; **he couldn't stand** *or* **take the pace** il n'arrivait pas à suivre le rythme; **do it at your own pace** faites-le à votre propre rythme; **to force the pace** forcer l'allure; **to make** *or* **to set the pace** *Sport* donner l'allure, mener le train; *Fig* donner le ton

(**b**) (*step*) pas *m*; **take two paces to the left** faites deux pas à gauche; **he was a few paces from me** il était à quelques pas de moi; *Br* **to put sb through his/her paces** mettre qn à l'épreuve; **to put a horse through its paces** faire passer un cheval à la montre; **to put a car/machine through its paces** mettre une voiture/une machine à l'épreuve; **to go through** *or* **to show one's paces** montrer ce dont *ou* de quoi on est capable

2 *vi* marcher (à pas mesurés); **he paced up and down the corridor** il arpentait le couloir

3 *vt* (**a**) (*corridor, cage, room*) arpenter

(**b**) (*regulate*) régler l'allure de; (*runner*) tirer; **she paced the first two laps well** elle a trouvé le bon rythme pour les deux premiers tours de piste; **the action is well paced** le suspense ne faiblit pas; **to pace oneself** (*when running, drinking*) trouver son rythme; (*when eating*) garder de la place pour la suite

▸▸ ***pace bowler*** (*in cricket*) lanceur *m* rapide *or* puissant; ***pace car*** (*in motor racing*) pace-car *m or f*

▸ **pace off, pace out** *vt sep* mesurer en pas; **she paced out ten steps** elle compta dix pas

pace[2] [ˈpɑːtʃeɪ] *prep Formal* n'en déplaise à

pacemaker [ˈpeɪsˌmeɪkə(r)] *n* (**a**) *Med* pacemaker *m*, stimulateur *m* cardiaque (**b**) *Sport* meneur(euse) *m,f* de train; *Fig* (*leader*) leader *m*; **they've become the pacemakers in their field** ils sont devenus les leaders dans leur domaine

pacer [ˈpeɪsə(r)] *n Sport* meneur(euse) *m,f* de train

pacesetter [ˈpeɪsˌsetə(r)] *n Sport* meneur(euse) *m,f* de train; *Fig* (*leader*) leader *m*; **they've become the pacesetters in their field** ils sont devenus les leaders dans leur domaine

pacey [ˈpeɪsɪ] (*compar* **pacier**, *superl* **paciest**) *adj* (*vehicle, runner, horse*) rapide; (*story, film*) mouvementé, vivant

pacha = **pasha**

pachyderm [ˈpækɪdɜːm] *n* pachyderme *m*

Pacific [pəˈsɪfɪk] **1** *n* (*ocean*) **the Pacific** le Pacifique, l'océan *m* Pacifique

2 *adj* du Pacifique

▸▸ ***Pacific Daylight Time*** heure *f* d'été du Pacifique; ***the Pacific Islands*** les îles *fpl* du Pacifique; **in the Pacific Islands** dans les îles du Pacifique; ***the Pacific Northwest*** = région naturelle de l'ouest des États-Unis; ***the Pacific Ocean*** le Pacifique, l'océan *m* Pacifique; ***the Pacific Rim*** = groupe de pays situés au bord du Pacifique, particulièrement les pays industrialisés d'Asie; ***Pacific (Standard) Time*** heure *f* d'hiver du Pacifique

pacific [pəˈsɪfɪk] *adj Formal* pacifique

pacifically [pəˈsɪfɪklɪ] *adv Formal* pacifiquement

pacification [ˌpæsɪfɪˈkeɪʃən] *n* (**a**) (*of anger, person*) apaisement *m* (**b**) (*of crowd, country, region*) pacification *f*

pacificatory [ˌpæsɪfɪˈkeɪtərɪ] *adj* pacificateur

pacifier [ˈpæsɪfaɪə(r)] *n* (**a**) (*person*) pacificateur(trice) *m,f* (**b**) *Am* (*for baby*) tétine *f*, sucette *f*

pacifism [ˈpæsɪfɪzəm] *n* pacifisme *m*

pacifist [ˈpæsɪfɪst] **1** *adj* pacifiste

2 *n* pacifiste *mf*

pacify [ˈpæsɪfaɪ] (*pt & pp* **pacified**) *vt* (**a**) (*anger, person*) apaiser, calmer; **she refused to be pacified** elle n'a jamais voulu se calmer (**b**) (*crowd, country, region*) pacifier

pacifying [ˈpæsɪfaɪɪŋ] *adj* pacificateur

PACK [pæk]

remplir	▸ 1 (a)
bourrer	▸ 1 (a), (c)
emballer	▸ 1 (b)
tasser	▸ 1 (d)
charger	▸ 1 (e)
faire sa valise	▸ 2 (a)
rentrer	▸ 2 (b)
s'entasser	▸ 2 (c)
sac a dos	▸ 3 (a)
paquet	▸ 3 (b)
bande	▸ 3 (d)
meute	▸ 3 (d)

1 *vt* (**a**) (*fill*) remplir, bourrer (**with** de); *Constr & Mining* (*trench*) remblayer; **to pack one's case/one's bags** faire sa valise/ses bagages; *Fig* **to pack one's bags** (*leave*) plier bagages; **we're not packed** nous n'avons pas fait nos bagages; *Theat* **she packs the house every night** elle fait salle comble chaque soir

(**b**) (*put into box, carton etc*) emballer, empaqueter; (*put into suitcase, bag, trunk etc*) mettre dans sa valise/son sac/sa malle/*etc*; **I've already packed the towels** j'ai déjà mis les serviettes dans la valise; **shall I pack the camera?** est-ce que j'emporte *ou* je prends l'appareil photo?; **I've packed a lunch for you** je t'ai préparé de quoi déjeuner; **the equipment is packed in polystyrene** le matériel est emballé dans du polystyrène; *esp Am* **shall I pack these for you?** (*in supermarket*) je vous emballe vos achats?

(**c**) (*cram tightly* → *cupboard, container*) bourrer; (→ *belongings, people*) entasser; **he packed his pockets with sweets, he packed sweets into his pockets** il a bourré ses poches de bonbons; **commuters pack the morning trains** les banlieusards s'entassent dans les trains du matin; *Fig* **we managed to pack a lot into a week's holiday** on a réussi à faire énormément de choses en une semaine de vacances

(**d**) (*compress* → *soil*) tasser; **the wind had packed the snow against the wall** le vent avait tassé la neige contre le mur

(**e**) (*load* → *horse, donkey*) charger

(**f**) (*rig*) **to pack a jury** se composer un jury favorable; **to pack a meeting** s'assurer un nombre prépondérant de partisans à une réunion; *Cards* **to pack the cards** apprêter les cartes

(**g**) *Tech* (*packing box*) garnir, étouper

(**h**) *Comput* (*database*) condenser, compacter

(**i**) *Am* (*carry in a backpack*) transporter dans un sac à dos

(**j**) (*idioms*) **he packs a lot of influence in cabinet/ministerial circles** il a beaucoup d'influence au conseil des ministres/dans les milieux ministériels; *Fam* **to pack a punch** (*person*) cogner dur; (*drink*) donner un coup de fouet; *Am Fam* **to pack a gun** être armé ❑, être chargé

2 *vi* (**a**) (*for journey*) faire sa valise *ou* ses bagages; **have you finished packing?** as-tu fini tes bagages?

(**b**) (*fit* → *into container*) rentrer; **the keyboard will pack easily into a briefcase** on peut facilement faire tenir le clavier dans un attaché-case; **this dress packs well** cette robe ne se froisse pas (même dans une valise)

(**c**) (*crowd together* → *spectators, passengers*) s'entasser; **we all packed into her car** nous nous sommes tous entassés dans sa voiture

(**d**) (*in rugby*) former une mêlée

3 *n* (**a**) (*rucksack*) sac *m* à dos; (*bundle*) ballot *m*; (*bale*) balle *f*; (*on animal*) charge *f*; **parachute pack** sac *m* à parachute

(**b**) (*packet*) paquet *m*; *Br* **a pack of washing powder** un paquet de lessive; *Am* **a pack of cigarettes** un paquet de cigarettes; **a four-/six-pack of beer** un pack de quatre/six

(**c**) *Br* (*deck of cards*) jeu *m*

(**d**) *(group → of people)* bande *f*; *(→ of cub scouts)* meute *f*; *(→ of hunting hounds)* meute *f*; *(→ of wolves)* meute *f*, bande *f*; *(→ of runners, cyclists)* peloton *m*; **wolves hunt in packs** les loups chassent en meute; *Fig* **press photographers often hunt in packs** les photographes de presse se déplacent souvent en bande; **a pack of fools** une bande *ou* un tas d'imbéciles; *Br* **that's a pack of lies!** c'est un tissu de mensonges!
(**e**) *(in rugby)* pack *m*
(**f**) *Med* compresse *f*; **wet/cold pack** enveloppement *m* humide/froid
(**g**) *(pack ice)* pack *m*, banquise *f*
(**h**) *(in snooker)* = triangle formé par les boules rouges
▸▸ ***pack animal*** bête *f* de somme; *Mil* ***pack drill*** exercice *m* avec paquetage *(à titre de punition)*; **no names, no pack drill** je ne citerai pas de noms; ***pack ice*** pack *m*, banquise *f*; ***pack leader*** *(in rugby)* responsable *m* des avants; *Am Zool* ***pack rat*** rat *m* des bois, néotome *m*; *Fam Fig* **to be a pack rat** *(person)* avoir la manie de tout garder ❑; *TV & Cin* ***pack shot*** pack shot *m*; ***pack train*** convoi *m* de bêtes de somme

▸**pack away 1** *vt sep* (**a**) *(tidy up)* ranger; *(bed, folding table, chair)* replier
(**b**) *Fam (eat)* bouffer; **he really packs it away!** qu'est-ce qu'il bouffe!; **she can really pack away the food when she gets going** ce qu'elle peut engouffrer quand elle s'y met
(**c**) *Fam (send away)* expédier ❑; **I packed the kids away to bed/school** j'ai envoyé les gosses au lit/à l'école
2 *vi (of bed, folding table, chair)* se replier; **this tent packs away easily** cette tente se replie *ou* se range facilement

▸**pack down 1** *vt sep (soil, snow)* tasser
2 *vi (in rugby)* former une mêlée

▸**pack in 1** *vt sep Br* (**a**) *(cram in)* entasser; **I couldn't pack anything more in** je ne pouvais pas en faire rentrer plus; **the play is packing them in** la pièce fait salle comble; **we were packed in like sardines** nous étions serrés comme des harengs (en caque) *ou* comme des sardines
(**b**) *Fam (task)* laisser tomber; *(job, boyfriend, girlfriend)* plaquer; **you should pack in smoking** tu devrais arrêter de fumer ❑; **pack it in!** arrête! ❑, ça suffit! ❑
2 *vi* (**a**) *(crowd in)* s'entasser (à l'intérieur)
(**b**) *Br Fam (break down → machine, engine)* tomber en panne ❑; **the photocopier's just packed in on me** la photocopieuse vient de me lâcher

▸**pack off** *vt sep Fam* expédier ❑; **I packed the kids off to bed/school** j'ai envoyé les gosses au lit/à l'école

▸**pack on** *vt insep Naut* **to pack on all sail** mettre toutes voiles dehors

▸**pack out** *vt sep Fam (fill completely → room)* remplir à craquer; **the hall was packed out** la salle était pleine à craquer *ou* comble *ou* bondée; **the theatre had been packed out for weeks** le théâtre faisait salle comble depuis des semaines; **the show was completely packed out** il n'y avait plus un seul billet pour ce spectacle ❑

▸**pack up 1** *vi* (**a**) *(pack one's suitcase)* faire sa valise *ou* ses bagages
(**b**) *(tidy up)* ranger
(**c**) *Br Fam (break down)* tomber en panne ❑; **my car's packed up** ma voiture m'a lâché; **her heart has packed up** son cœur a lâché *ou* cédé
(**d**) *Br Fam (stop work)* dételer; **I'm packing up for today** j'arrête pour aujourd'hui ❑
2 *vt sep* (**a**) *(suitcase, bags)* faire
(**b**) *(tidy up → clothes, belongings, tools)* ranger; **help me pack up the tent** aide-moi à plier la tente

---

package ['pækɪdʒ] **1** *n* (**a**) *(small parcel)* paquet *m*, colis *m*; *Am (packet)* paquet *m*
(**b**) *(set of proposals, items)* ensemble *m*; **financial package** ensemble *m* de mesures financières; **aid package** ensemble *m* de mesures d'aide; **the offer is part of a larger package** l'offre fait partie d'un ensemble plus important; **the package includes a company car** l'offre comprend une voiture de société; **a new package of measures to halt inflation** un nouvel ensemble *ou* un nouveau train de mesures visant à stopper l'inflation; **you get all these services in a complete package** vous obtenez tous ces services selon un marché global; **we offered them a generous package** nous leur avons proposé un contrat global très avantageux
(**c**) *(holiday)* voyage *m* organisé *ou* à prix forfaitaire
(**d**) *Comput* **(software) package** logiciel *m*
(**e**) *(on TV or radio)* sujet *m*
(**f**) *Fam (male genitals)* service *m* trois-pièces
2 *vt* (**a**) *(wrap)* emballer, conditionner; **each item is individually packaged** chaque article est conditionné *ou* emballé séparément
(**b**) *(pop star, candidate etc)* créer l'image de marque de; **she has packaged herself as a sex symbol** elle s'est créé *ou* fabriqué une image de sex-symbol
▸▸ ***package deal*** transaction *f* globale, accord *m* global; **the package deal put forward by the management** l'ensemble des mesures proposées par la direction; **we bought up the lot in a package deal** nous avons tout acheté en un seul lot; ***package holiday, package tour*** voyage *m* organisé *or* à prix forfaitaire

packaged ['pækɪdʒd] *adj Com* emballé, conditionné

packager ['pækɪdʒə(r)] *n (in advertising, publishing)* packager *m*, packageur *m*

packaging ['pækɪdʒɪŋ] *n* (**a**) *(wrapping materials)* emballage *m*, conditionnement *m* (**b**) *(in advertising, publishing)* packaging *m*; **the packaging of the project is all wrong** la façon dont on a présenté le projet ne marche pas du tout
▸▸ *Com* ***packaging charges, packaging costs*** frais *mpl* d'emballage

packed [pækt] *adj* (**a**) *(crowded → train, room)* bondé; *(→ theatre)* comble; *Br* **the cinema was packed** la salle était comble *ou* pleine à craquer; *Theat etc* **to play to a packed house** faire salle comble; **the meeting was packed** la réunion a fait salle comble; **the book was packed with information** le livre était truffé *ou* bourré de renseignements
(**b**) *(packaged)* emballé, conditionné
(**c**) *(jury)* favorable
▸▸ ***packed lunch*** panier-repas *m*, casse-croûte *m inv*

-packed [pækt] *suff (full of)* **a fun-packed evening** une soirée pleine de divertissements; **an action-packed first half** une première moitié pleine d'action

packer ['pækə(r)] *n (worker)* emballeur(euse) *m,f*, conditionneur(euse) *m,f*; *(machine)* emballeuse *f*, conditionneuse *f*

packet ['pækɪt] *n* (**a**) *(box)* paquet *m*; *(bag, envelope)* sachet *m*; *Br* **a packet of cigarettes** un paquet de cigarettes; **a packet of soup/seeds** un sachet de soupe/graines; *Br Hum* **a packet of three** *(condoms)* une boîte de trois préservatifs
(**b**) *(parcel)* paquet *m*, colis *m*
(**c**) *Br Fam (lot of money)* paquet *m*; **that must have cost you a packet** ça a dû te coûter les yeux de la tête *ou* un paquet d'argent; **to earn** *or* **make a packet** gagner des mille et des cents
(**d**) *Naut (boat, steamer)* paquebot *m*
(**e**) *Comput (of data)* paquet *m*
(**f**) *Fam (male genitals)* service *m* trois-pièces; **what a packet!** quel entrejambe!
▸▸ *Naut* ***packet boat*** paquebot *m*; ***packet soup*** soupe *f* en sachet; *Naut* ***packet steamer*** paquebot *m*; *Comput* ***packet switching*** commutation *f* de paquets

packhorse ['pækhɔːs, *pl* -hɔːsɪz] *n* cheval *m* de bât

packing ['pækɪŋ] *n (UNCOUNT)* (**a**) *(of personal belongings)* **have you done your packing?** as-tu fait tes bagages?; **there isn't much packing (to do)** il n'y a pas beaucoup de bagages à faire; **the removal men will do the packing** les déménageurs se chargeront de l'emballage
(**b**) *(of parcel)* emballage *m*; *(of commercial goods)* emballage *m*, conditionnement *m*; **the fish/meat packing industry** les conserveries *fpl* de poisson/viande
(**c**) *(wrapping material)* emballage *m*
(**d**) *Tech (of piston, joint)* garniture *f*
▸▸ ***packing case*** caisse *f* d'emballage; *Com* ***packing charges, packing costs*** frais *mpl* d'emballage; *Am* ***packing house*** usine *f* de conditionnement; ***packing list*** liste *f* de colisage; ***packing materials*** matériaux *mpl* d'emballage; *Tech* ***packing ring*** *(of cylinder)* rondelle *f ou* bague de garniture; *(of piston)* segment *m*, bague *f*, garniture *f*; *Com* ***packing slip*** bon *m* de livraison

packsaddle ['pækˌsædəl] *n* bât *m*

packthread ['pækθred] *n* fil *m* d'emballage, ficelle *f*

pact [pækt] *n* pacte *m*; **we made a pact to stop smoking** nous avons convenu de nous arrêter de fumer; **to make a pact with the Devil** faire un pacte *ou* pactiser avec le Diable

pacy = **pacey**

pad [pæd] (*pt & pp* **padded**, *cont* **padding**) **1** *n* (**a**) *(to cushion shock)* coussinet *m*; *(for brake)* plaquette *f*; **the skaters wear pads on their knees and elbows** les patineurs portent des genouillères et des protège-coudes
(**b**) *(for absorbing liquid, polishing etc)* tampon *m*; **a pad of cotton wool** un tampon de coton hydrophile
(**c**) *(on body → of finger, toe)* pulpe *f*; *(→ of dog, fox, hare etc)* coussinet *m*
(**d**) *(of paper)* bloc *m*; *(on desktop)* sous-main *m inv*; **(inking) pad** tampon *m* encreur
(**e**) *Aviat & Astron* aire *f*; **helicopter pad** aire *f* d'atterrissage pour hélicoptères
(**f**) *Fam (home)* casbah *f*; **let's go to my pad** allons chez moi ❑; **you can crash at my pad** tu peux pieuter chez moi
(**g**) *Bot (leaf)* feuille *f*; **(water) lily pad** feuille *f* de nénuphar
(**h**) *(noise → of animal)* pas *mpl* sourds; *(→ of person)* pas *mpl* feutrés; **the pad of footsteps behind me** des pas feutrés derrière moi; **the pad of bare feet on marble** le bruit sourd de pieds nus sur le marbre
(**i**) *Fam (sanitary towel)* serviette *f* hygiénique ❑
2 *vt (clothing)* matelasser; *(shoulder)* rembourrer; *(armchair, door, wall)* capitonner
3 *vi (walk)* avancer à pas feutrés; **he padded downstairs in his slippers** il descendit l'escalier en pantoufles; **the dog padded along beside the cyclist** le chien trottinait à côté du cycliste

▸**pad out** *vt sep (essay, article, speech)* étoffer; **he padded out the talk with anecdotes** il a étoffé son discours en le truffant d'anecdotes; **they included two old songs to pad the album out** ils ont inclu deux vieilles chansons pour étoffer l'album; **they padded out the meal with some rice** ils ont complété le repas avec du riz

padauk = **padouk**

padded ['pædɪd] *adj* (**a**) *(door, bench, wall, steering wheel)* capitonné; *(garment, envelope, oven glove)* matelassé; *(sofa)* bien rembourré (**b**) *(fat)* **he's well padded** il est bien en chair
▸▸ ***padded bra*** soutien-gorge *m* à bonnets renforcés; ***padded cell*** cellule *f* capitonnée; ***padded shoulders*** *(of dress, jacket)* épaulettes *fpl*

padding ['pædɪŋ] *n* (**a**) *(material) (for cushion etc)* bourre *f*, rembourrage *m*; *(for seat, jacket etc)* rembourrage *m*; *(on walls, door)* capitonnage *m* (**b**) *(in speech, essay etc)* délayage *m*

paddle ['pædəl] **1** *n* (**a**) *(for boat, canoe)* pagaie *f*
(**b**) *(of waterwheel, paddleboat)* palette *f*, aube *f*
(**c**) *Am (table tennis bat)* raquette *f* (de ping-pong)
(**d**) *(of turtle, penguin, seal)* nageoire *f*; *(of duck)* patte *f*
(**e**) *(walk in water)* **to go for** *or* **to have a paddle** aller patauger
2 *vi* (**a**) *(in canoe)* pagayer; *(in rowing boat)* tirer en douce; *(duck)* nager; **he paddled across the lake** il a traversé le lac en pagayant
(**b**) *(walk in water)* patauger
3 *vt* (**a**) *(boat)* **to paddle a canoe** pagayer; *Fig* **to paddle one's own canoe** se débrouiller tout seul, mener sa barque
(**b**) *Am Fam (spank)* donner une fessée à ❑; *very Fam* **I'll paddle your ass!** tu vas prendre une fessée!

pac–pad

►► *Austr* **paddle pop** glace *f* à l'eau; **paddle steamer** bateau *m* à aubes *ou* à roues; *Naut* **paddle wheel** roue *f* à aubes

paddleboat ['pædəlbəʊt] *n* (**a**) *(boat)* bateau *m* à aubes *ou* à roues (**b**) *(pedalo)* Pédalo® *m*

paddlefish ['pædəlfɪʃ] *(pl* **inv** *or* **paddlefishes**) *n Ich* spatule *f*

paddler ['pædlə(r)] **1** *n (person)* pagayeur(euse) *m,f*

2 paddlers *npl (garment)* barboteuse *f*

paddling pool ['pædəlɪŋ-] *n Br* pataugeoire *f*, *Can* barboteuse *f*

paddock ['pædək] *n* (**a**) *(gen)* enclos *m*; *(at racetrack)* paddock *m* (**b**) *Austr (field)* champ *m*

Paddy ['pædɪ] *(pl* **Paddies**) *n Br Fam (Irishman)* Irlandais❑ *m*, = terme injurieux désignant un Irlandais; **hey, Paddy!** hé, l'Irlandais!

paddy ['pædɪ] *(pl* **paddies**) *n* (**a**) *(field)* rizière *f* (**b**) *(rice)* paddy *m*, riz *m* non décortiqué (**c**) *Br Fam (fit of temper)* **to be/get in a paddy (about)** être/se mettre en rogne (pour)

►► *Am Fam* **paddy wagon** panier *m* à salade

paddyfield ['pædɪfi:ld] *n* rizière *f*

►► *Orn* **paddyfield warbler** rousserolle *f* isabelle

pademelon ['pædɪ,melən] *n Zool* thylogale *m*

padlock ['pædlɒk] **1** *n (for door, gate)* cadenas *m*; *(for bicycle)* antivol *m*

2 *vt (door, gate)* cadenasser; *(bicycle)* mettre un antivol à; **she padlocked her bicycle to a lamppost** elle a attaché sa bicyclette à un réverbère avec son antivol

padouk [pə'du:k] *n (tree)* padouk *m*; *(wood)* bois *m* de corail

padre ['pɑ:drɪ] *n* (**a**) *(gen → Catholic)* prêtre *m*, curé *m*; *(→ Protestant)* pasteur *m*; *(term of address)* (mon) Père *m* (**b**) *Mil* aumônier *m*

padsaw ['pædsɔ:] *n* scie *f* à guichet démontable

Padua ['pædjʊə] *n* Padoue

Paduan ['pædjʊən] **1** *n* Padouan(e) *m,f*

2 *adj* padouan

paean ['pi:ən] *n* (**a**) *Hist* péan *m* (**b**) *Literary (expressing praise)* dithyrambe *m*

paederast, paederastic *etc Br* = **pederast, pederastic** *etc*

paediatric, *Am* **pediatric** [,pi:dɪ'ætrɪk] *adj* pédiatrique

paediatrician, *Am* **pediatrician** [,pi:dɪə'trɪʃən] *n* pédiatre *mf*

paediatrics, *Am* **pediatrics** [,pi:dɪ'ætrɪks] *n* pédiatrie *f*

paedology *Br* = **pedology²**

paedophile ['pi:dəʊ,faɪl] *n* pédophile *m*

paedophilia [,pi:dəʊ'fɪlɪə] *n* pédophilie *f*

paeds, *Am* **peds** [pi:dz] *n Fam (subject)* pédiatrie❑ *f*; *(department)* service *m* de pédiatrie❑

paella [paɪ'elə] *n* paella *f*

paeon ['pi:ən] *n Literature* péon *m*

paeony = **peony**

pagan ['peɪgən] **1** *n* païen(enne) *m,f*

2 *adj* païen

paganism ['peɪgənɪzəm] *n* paganisme *m*

paganize, -ise ['peɪgənaɪz] **1** *vt* paganiser

2 *vi* vivre en païen

page [peɪdʒ] **1** *n* (**a**) *(of book, newspaper, Web site etc)* page *f*; **on page two** *(of book)* (à la) page deux; *(of newspaper)* (en) page deux; **page one** *(of newspaper)* la une; **the sports/business pages** *(in newspaper)* la section sport/économie; *Fig* **a glorious page in our history** une page glorieuse de l'histoire de notre pays

(**b**) *(at court)* page *m*; *(in hotel)* chasseur *m*, groom *m*; *(at wedding)* page *m*; *(in legislative body)* (jeune) huissier *m*

2 *vt* (**a**) *Typ (paginate)* paginer

(**b**) *(call → of pageboy)* appeler; *(→ with loudspeaker)* appeler par haut-parleur; *(→ by sending messenger)* envoyer chercher par un chasseur; *(→ with pager)* biper; **I'm having her paged** je la fais appeler; **paging Mrs Clark!** on demande Mme Clark!

►► *Comput* **page break** saut *m* de page; *Typ* **page depth** hauteur *f* de page; *Comput* **page description language** langage *m* de description de page; *Typ & Comput* **page design** mise *f* en page; *Comput* **page down** page suivante; *Comput* **page down key** touche *f* page suivante; *Typ & Comput* **page format** format *m* de page; *Comput* **page layout** mise *f* en page; *Typ* **page length** longueur *f* de page; *Typ* **page make-up** mise *f* en pages; **page number** numéro *m* de page; *Typ* **page numbering** numérotage *m* des pages, pagination *f*; *Typ* **page plan** plan *m* de mise en page, chemin *m* de fer; *Comput* **page preview** aperçu *m* avant l'impression; *Comput* **page printer** imprimante *f* page par page, imprimante *f* par pages; *Comput* **page printer language** langage *m* d'imprimante par pages; *Typ* **page proofs** épreuves *fpl* en pages; *Comput* **page scanner** lecteur *m* de pages; *Comput* **page setup** format *m* de page; *Press* **page three** = page sur laquelle une femme pose seins nus dans certains quotidiens de la presse populaire britannique; *Press* **page three girl** = jeune femme posant seins nus dans certains quotidiens de la presse populaire britannique; *Comput* **page up** page précédente; *Comput* **page up key** touche *f* page précédente

►**page down** *vi Comput* feuilleter en avant

►**page off** *vt sep Typ* paginer

►**page through** *vt insep* feuilleter

►**page up** *vi Comput* feuilleter en arrière

pageant ['pædʒənt] *n (display)* spectacle *m* grandiose *ou* majestueux; *(of historical events)* cortège *m* historique; *Fig* **the rich pageant of our country's history** la riche galerie de tableaux de l'histoire de notre pays

pageantry ['pædʒəntrɪ] *n* apparat *m*, pompe *f*

pageboy ['peɪdʒ,bɔɪ] *n* (**a**) *(servant)* page *m*; *(in hotel)* chasseur *m*, groom *m*; *(at wedding)* garçon *m* d'honneur (**b**) *(hairstyle)* coupe *f* à la Jeanne d'Arc

►► **pageboy cut** coupe *f* à la Jeanne d'Arc

pager ['peɪdʒə(r)] *n* pager *m*, bip *m*

page-turner *n Fam (book)* livre *m* passionnant❑, livre *m* captivant❑

paginate ['pædʒɪneɪt] *vt Typ & Comput (make into pages)* mettre en pages; *(number pages in)* paginer

pagination [,pædʒɪ'neɪʃən] *n Typ & Comput (page make-up)* mise *f* en pages; *(numbering)* pagination *f*

paging ['peɪdʒɪŋ] *n Typ* pagination *f*

pagoda [pə'gəʊdə] *n* pagode *f*

pah [pɑ:] *exclam* pouah!

paid [peɪd] **1** *pt & pp of* **pay**

2 *adj* (**a**) *(person, work)* payé, rétribué, rémunéré; **to get paid maternity leave** avoir droit aux congés de maternité; **to get paid sick leave** avoir droit aux congés de maladie

(**b**) *Com (goods, bill)* payé; **paid** *(on bill)* pour acquit

(**c**) **to put paid to sb's chances/hopes** réduire les chances/espoirs de qn en poussière; **well, that's put paid to that!** et voilà, tout tombe à l'eau!

►► **paid holidays** congés *mpl* payés; *Am* **paid political broadcast** = émission d'un parti politique

paid-out *adj Com & Fin*

►► **paid-out form** bon *m* de décaissement; **paid-out voucher** bon *m* de débours

paid-up *adj* (**a**) *(member)* à jour de ses cotisations; *Fig* **he's a (fully) paid-up member of the Communist Party** *(committed)* il a sa carte au Parti Communiste (**b**) *Fin (capital)* versé; *(shares)* libéré; **fully paid-up policy** police *f* d'assurance dont les primes sont à jour

►► **paid-up share capital** capital *m* appelé et libéré

pail [peɪl] *n* (**a**) *(bucket)* seau *m* (**b**) *(bucketful)* plein seau *m*

pailful ['peɪlfʊl] *n* plein seau *m*; **a pailful of water** un plein seau d'eau

paillasse = **palliasse**

pain [peɪn] **1** *vt* (**a**) *(mentally)* faire de la peine à, peiner, attrister; **it pained her to see them quarrel** ça lui faisait de la peine *ou* ça la peinait de les voir se disputer; **it pains me to have to tell you that...** je regrette infiniment d'avoir à vous dire que...

(**b**) *Old-fashioned (physically)* faire souffrir, faire mal à; **the wound still pained her** la blessure la faisait encore souffrir *ou* lui faisait encore mal

2 *n* (**a**) *(physical)* douleur *f*; **he has a pain in his ear** il a mal à l'oreille; **I have a pain in my side** j'ai une douleur au côté; **are you in pain?** avez-vous mal?, est-ce que vous souffrez?; **to be in great pain** souffrir beaucoup; **he was carried from the field in great pain** il souffrait beaucoup quand on l'a transporté hors du terrain; **the pain was unbearable** la douleur était insupportable; **to put a wounded animal out of its pain** achever un animal blessé; **to cry out in pain** crier *ou* hurler de douleur; **to cause sb pain** faire mal à qn; **shooting pains** élancements *mpl*, douleurs *fpl* lancinantes; **labour pains** douleurs *fpl* de l'accouchement

(**b**) *(emotional)* peine *f*, douleur *f*, souffrance *f*; **to cause sb pain** faire de la peine à qn; **he went through a lot of pain when his son left home** il a eu beaucoup de peine quand son fils a quitté la maison; **I can't bear the pain of losing her** je ne supporterai pas de la perdre

(**c**) *Fam (annoying person or thing)* **what a pain he is!** qu'est-ce qu'il est enquiquinant!; **it's a (real) pain** *or* **such a pain trying to cross London during the rush hour** traverser Londres aux heures de pointe, c'est la galère; **to be a pain (in the neck)** être casse-pieds; **to give sb a pain (in the neck)** taper sur le système à qn; *very Fam* **to be a pain in the** *Br* **arse** *or Am* **ass** être casse-couilles *ou* chiant; *very Fam* **it's a real pain in the** *Br* **arse** *or Am* **ass having to get up so early** ça fait vraiment chier de devoir se lever si tôt

(**d**) *Law* **on pain of death** sous peine de mort

3 pains *npl (efforts)* peine *f*, mal *m*; **he went to great pains to help us** il s'est donné beaucoup de mal pour nous aider; **she took great pains over her work/the dinner** elle s'est donné beaucoup de mal pour son travail/pour ce dîner; **is that all we get for our pains?** c'est comme cela que nous sommes récompensés de nos efforts?; **he was at** *or* **he took pains to avoid her** il a tout fait pour l'éviter

►► **pain barrier** seuil *m* de douleur; **pain relief** soulagement *m*; **aspirin for fast pain relief** aspirine pour soulager rapidement la douleur

pained [peɪnd] *adj* peiné, affligé; **to look pained** avoir l'air affligé *ou* peiné

painful ['peɪnfʊl] *adj* (**a**) *(sore)* douloureux; **my burns are still painful** mes brûlures me font toujours mal; **these shoes are really painful** ces chaussures me font vraiment mal; **is your back still painful?** avez-vous toujours mal au dos?; **that looked painful!** ça a dû faire mal!

(**b**) *(unpleasant → spectacle, effort, subject)* pénible; **a painful memory** un souvenir désagréable; **it was painful to see (it)** c'était pénible à voir; **it's painful to have to admit it** c'est dur à admettre; **the expensive shops were a painful reminder of their poverty** les boutiques chères leur rappelaient péniblement leur pauvreté

(**c**) *(laborious → task)* pénible, difficile, laborieux

(**d**) *Fam (bad → performance, singing)* atroce❑

painfully ['peɪnfʊlɪ] *adv* (**a**) *(hit, strike, rub)* durement; *(move, walk)* péniblement; **her head throbbed painfully** elle sentait une douleur lancinante à la tête; **she fell painfully** elle s'est fait mal en tombant

(**b**) *(laboriously)* laborieusement, avec difficulté

(**c**) *(as intensifier)* horriblement, atrocement; **a painfully slow journey** un voyage horriblement *ou* atrocement long; **a painfully boring speech** un discours mortellement ennuyeux; **it was painfully obvious that he didn't understand** il n'était que trop évident qu'il ne comprenait pas; **she's painfully shy** elle est d'une timidité maladive

painfulness ['peɪnfʊlnɪs] *n* (**a**) *(soreness)* nature *f* douloureuse (**b**) *(unpleasantness)* nature *f* pénible, pénibilité *f*

painkiller ['peɪn,kɪlə(r)] *n* analgésique *m*, calmant *m*

painkilling ['peɪn,kɪlɪŋ] *adj* analgésique, calmant; **to give sb a painkilling injection** injecter un analgésique à qn

painless ['peɪnləs] *adj* (**a**) *(injection, operation)* sans douleur, indolore; *(death)* sans souffrance (**b**) *(unproblematic)* facile; **it was a painless decision** la décision n'a pas été dure à prendre; **the painless way to pay your bills** la manière commode de payer vos factures

painlessly ['peɪnləslɪ] *adv* (**a**) *(without hurting)* sans douleur (**b**) *(unproblematically)* sans peine, sans mal

painlessness ['peɪnləsnɪs] *n* absence *f* de douleur

painstaking ['peɪnz,teɪkɪŋ] *adj (research, investigation, care)* rigoureux, méticuleux; *(worker)* assidu, soigneux; *(accuracy, attention to detail)* extrême

painstakingly ['peɪnz,teɪkɪŋlɪ] *adv* soigneusement, méticuleusement; **to be painstakingly accurate in one's work** faire preuve d'une extrême minutie dans son travail

paint [peɪnt] **1** *n* (**a**) *(gen)* peinture *f*; *Art* couleur *f*; **a set** *or* **box of paints** une boîte de couleurs; **the paint was beginning to flake off** la peinture commençait à s'écailler; **oil/acrylic paint** peinture *f* à l'huile/acrylique
(**b**) *Fam (make-up)* peinture *f*
(**c**) *Med* badigeon *m*
2 *vt* (**a**) *(gen)* peindre; **the door was painted yellow** la porte était peinte en jaune; **the kitchen needs painting** la cuisine a besoin d'être repeinte; *Theat* **to paint the scenery for a play** brosser les décors d'une pièce; **to paint a picture** peindre un tableau; **to paint (a picture of) sb** faire le portrait de qn; *Literary* **spring paints the fields with a thousand hues** le printemps diapre les champs de mille couleurs; **to paint one's nails** se vernir les ongles; **to paint one's face** se peindre le visage; *(with make-up)* se maquiller; **the kids had their faces painted** les enfants se sont fait maquiller; *Fam* **to paint the town red** faire la noce *ou* la foire; *Fig* **to paint oneself into a corner** se mettre dans une impasse
(**b**) *(apply → varnish)* appliquer (au pinceau)
(**c**) *Med (throat)* badigeonner
(**d**) *Fig (describe)* dépeindre, décrire; **the author paints a bleak picture of suburban life** l'auteur dresse un sombre portrait *ou* brosse un sombre tableau de la vie des banlieusards; **to paint everything in rosy colours** peindre tout en rose
3 *vi* peindre, faire de la peinture; **to paint in oils** faire de la peinture à l'huile; **to paint in watercolours** faire de l'aquarelle; **I've always wanted to paint** j'ai toujours voulu faire de la peinture; **I wish I could paint like that!** si seulement je pouvais peindre comme cela!
►► ***paint gun*** pistolet *m* à peinture; *Br* ***paint pot*** pot *m* de peinture; *Comput* ***paint program*** programme *m* de dessin bitmap; *Ind* ***paint shop*** atelier *m* de peinture; ***paint stripper*** décapant *m*

►**paint out, paint over** *vt sep* recouvrir (d'une couche) de peinture

paintball ['peɪntbɔːl] *n* paintball *m*

paintbox ['peɪntbɒks] *n* boîte *f* de couleurs

paintbrush ['peɪntbrʌʃ] *n* pinceau *m*

painted ['peɪntɪd] *adj* (**a**) *(with paint)* peint; **painted blue** peint en bleu (**b**) *Pej (with make-up)* maquillé, fardé
►► *Orn* ***painted bunting*** pape *m* de la Louisiane; ***the Painted Desert*** = région de l'Arizona célèbre pour ses rochers colorés; *Entom* ***painted lady*** belle-dame *f*

painter ['peɪntə(r)] *n* (**a**) *(artist, decorator)* peintre *m*; **landscape painter** paysagiste *mf*; **portrait painter** portraitiste *mf*; **painter and decorator** peintre-décorateur(trice) *m,f* (**b**) *Naut (rope)* bosse *f*; **to cut the painter** couper l'amarre

painterly ['peɪntəlɪ] *adj (skills)* de peintre; *Fig (quality)* pictural

painting ['peɪntɪŋ] *n* (**a**) *(activity)* peinture *f*; **to study painting** étudier la peinture; **landscape/portrait painting** peinture *f* de paysages/portraits (**b**) *(picture)* peinture *f*, tableau *m*

paint-spattered *adj* maculé de peinture

paintstick ['peɪntstɪk] *n* palette *f* de bois *(utilisée pour mélanger la peinture)*

paintwork ['peɪntwɜːk] *n (UNCOUNT)* peinture *f*; **the house with the white paintwork** la maison peinte en blanc

pair [peə(r)] **1** *n* (**a**) *(two related objects or people)* paire *f*; **a pair of shoes/gloves** une paire de chaussures/de gants; **these two pictures are a pair** *(match)* ces deux tableaux se font pendant; **an odd-looking pair** un drôle de tandem; **where's the pair to this sock?** où est la chaussette qui va avec celle-ci?; **to work in pairs** travailler par deux; **line up in pairs!** mettez-vous en rang (deux) par deux!; **the pair of you** vous deux; **they can go to bed without their supper, the pair of them!** qu'ils aillent au lit sans manger tous les deux!; **what a pair!** *(two people)* quelle paire!; **you're a pair of idiots!** vous faites une belle paire d'imbéciles!; **I've only got one pair of hands!** je n'ai que deux mains!
(**b**) *(single object in two parts)* **a pair of trousers/shorts/tights** un pantalon/short/collant; **a pair of pliers** une pince; **a pair of scissors** une paire de ciseaux
(**c**) *(husband and wife)* couple *m*
(**d**) *(in rowing)* deux *m*
(**e**) *(of animals)* paire *f*; *(of horses)* attelage *m*; *(of birds)* couple *m*
(**f**) *Math* paire *f*; **ordered pair** paire *f* ordonnée
(**g**) *Br Pol* = deux membres de partis adverses qui se sont entendus pour ne pas participer à un vote ou pour s'abstenir de voter durant une période déterminée
(**h**) *(in cards, dice)* paire *f*; **a pair of kings/sevens** une paire de rois/de sept; *Fam* **two pair** deux paires ❑
2 *vt (socks)* assortir; *(animals, birds)* apparier, accoupler
3 *vi (animals, birds)* s'apparier, s'accoupler
►► ***pair bond*** *(between animals)* monogamie *f*; ***pair bonding*** *(between animals)* monogamie *f*; *Cards* ***pair royal*** brelan *m*

►**pair off 1** *vt sep (arrange in couples → dancers)* répartir en couples; *(→ team members, children in class)* mettre deux par deux; **I got paired off with Roger** on m'a mis avec Roger; **he's trying to pair them off** *(in a relationship)* il essaie de les mettre ensemble
2 *vi (dancers)* former des couples; *(team members, children in class)* se mettre deux par deux

►**pair up 1** *vt sep (socks)* assortir
2 *vi (people)* se mettre par deux; **to pair up with sb** s'associer avec qn, se mettre avec qn; **he paired up with Bob for the car rally** il a choisi Bob comme équipier pour le rallye

paired [peəd] *adj* (**a**) *(in sets of two)* deux par deux, par paires, par couples; *(guns, machines)* jumelés, conjugués
(**b**) *(matching)* appareillé, apparié
►► ***paired cable*** câble *m* à paires; *Mktg* ***paired comparison*** *(in market research)* comparaison *f* par paire; *Tech* ***paired cylinders*** cylindres *mpl* accouplés; *Aviat* ***paired engines*** moteurs *mpl* jumelés; ***paired floats*** flotteurs *mpl* (disposés) en catamaran; *Nucl* ***paired lattices*** réseaux *mpl* appariés

paisley ['peɪzlɪ] *n (pattern)* (impression *f*) cachemire *m*; *(material)* tissu *m* cachemire; **a paisley tie** une cravate impression cachemire

Paiute [paɪ'uːt] *n* (**a**) **the Paiute** *(tribe)* les Paiute *mpl* (**b**) *(member of tribe)* Paiute *mf inv*

pajama *Am* = **pyjama**

pak choi [pæk'tʃɔɪ] *n* pak choi *m*

Paki ['pækɪ] *n Br Fam (abbr* **Pakistani**) = terme raciste désignant une personne d'origine pakistanaise
►► ***Paki shop*** = épicerie de quartier tenue par une personne d'origine pakistanaise

Paki-basher *n Br Fam* = individu qui attaque des personnes d'origine pakistanaise

Paki-bashing *n Br Fam* = violences à l'encontre de personnes d'origine pakistanaise

Pakistan [*Br* ,pɑːkɪ'stɑːn, *Am* 'pækɪstæn] *n* Pakistan *m*; **in Pakistan** au Pakistan

Pakistani [*Br* ,pɑːkɪ'stɑːnɪ, *Am* ,pækɪ'stænɪ] **1** *n* Pakistanais(e) *m,f*
2 *adj* pakistanais
3 *comp (embassy, history)* du Pakistan

pakora [pə'kɔːrə] *n* = spécialité indienne de beignets de légumes, de poulet etc

PAL [pæl] *n TV (abbr* **phase alternation line**) PAL *f*

pal [pæl] *(pt & pp* **palled**, *cont* **palling**) *n Fam* (**a**) *(friend)* copain (copine) *m,f*; **we're great pals** on est très copains; **be a pal and fetch my coat** sois sympa, va me chercher mon manteau
(**b**) *(term of address)* **watch it, pal!** fais gaffe, mec!; **watch where you're going pal!** hé, regarde où tu vas!; **thanks, pal** *(to friend)* merci, vieux; *(to stranger)* merci, chef

►**pal about, pal around** *vi Fam* **to pal about** *or* **around with sb** copiner avec qn, être pote avec qn; **they pal about together** ils sont toujours fourrés ensemble; **they palled around for a while at school** il y a un moment où ils étaient potes au lycée

►**pal up** *vi Br Fam (two people)* devenir copains (copines); **to pal up with sb** devenir copain (copine) avec qn

palace ['pælɪs] *n* palais *m*; **royal/bishop's palace** palais *m* royal/épiscopal; *Br* **the Palace** *(Buckingham Palace)* le palais de Buckingham *(et par extension ses habitants)*; *Br* **the Palace raised no objections to the visit** Buckingham n'a élevé aucune objection concernant la visite
►► ***palace guard*** *(person)* garde *m* du palais; *(all guards)* garde *f* du palais; ***palace revolution*** révolution *f* de palais; *Br* ***Palace spokesman*** porte-parole *mf* (du palais) de Buckingham; *Br* ***Palace spokesperson*** porte-parole *mf* (du palais) de Buckingham; ***the Palace of Westminster*** le palais de Westminster *(siège du Parlement britannique)*

paladin ['pælədɪn] *n* paladin *m*

palaeo-, palaeoanthropology *etc Br* = **paleo-, paleoanthropology** *etc*

palanquin [,pælən'kiːn] *n* palanquin *m*

palatability [,pælətə'bɪlɪtɪ] *n* (**a**) *(of food)* sapidité *f* (**b**) *Fig (of idea, doctrine)* caractère *m* acceptable

palatable ['pælətəbəl] *adj* (**a**) *(food)* savoureux; *(wine)* qui se laisse boire (**b**) *Fig (idea, doctrine)* acceptable

palatal ['pælətəl] **1** *adj* (**a**) *Anat* palatin (**b**) *Ling* palatal
2 *n Ling* palatale *f*

palatalization [,pælətəlaɪ'zeɪʃən] *n* palatalisation *f*

palatalize, -ise ['pælətəlaɪz] *vt* palataliser

palate ['pælət] *n* (**a**) *Anat* palais *m* (**b**) *(sense of taste)* palais *m*; **to have a good palate** avoir le palais fin; **to have a delicate palate** avoir du palais

palatial [pə'leɪʃəl] *adj* grandiose, magnifique; **she lives alone in a palatial house** elle vit toute seule dans un véritable palais *ou* palace

palatinate [pə'lætɪnət] **1** *n* palatinat *m*
2 Palatinate *n* **the Palatinate** le Palatinat

palatine ['pælətaɪn] **1** *adj* (**a**) *Hist* palatin (**b**) *Anat* palatin
2 *n Hist* palatin *m*
►► ***the Palatine Hill*** le mont Palatin

palato-alveolar ['pælətəʊ-] *Ling* **1** *n* alvéo-palatale *f*, consonne *f* post-alvéolaire
2 *adj* alvéo-palatal, post-alvéolaire

palatography [,pælə'tɒgrəfɪ] *n* palatographie *f*

palaver [pə'lɑːvə(r)] *Br* **1** *n (UNCOUNT)* (**a**) *Fam (fuss)* histoires *fpl*; **what a palaver!** quelle histoire!; **it was a real palaver getting a work permit** ça a été la croix et la bannière pour obtenir un permis de travail; **we had the usual palaver about who was going to pay** ça a été le cirque habituel pour décider qui allait payer
(**b**) *Old-fashioned (discussion)* palabre *m ou f*; *(tedious)* palabres *mpl ou fpl*
2 *vi* palabrer

palazzo [pæ'lætsəʊ] *(pl* **palazzos** *or* **palazzi** [-tsiː]) *n* palais *m (italien)*
►► ***palazzo pants*** pantalon *m* ample

pale [peɪl] **1** *adj* (**a**) *(face, complexion)* pâle; *(from fright, shock, sickness)* blême, blafard; **to grow** *or* **become pale** pâlir; **to turn pale with fright** pâlir de terreur; **(as) pale as death** blanc comme un linge
(**b**) *(colour)* pâle, clair; *(light)* pâle, blafard; **a pale blue dress** une robe bleu pâle
(**c**) *(feeble)* pâle; **it was a pale imitation of the real thing** c'était une pâle copie de l'original
2 *vi (person, face)* pâlir, blêmir; *(sky, colour)* pâlir; **my adventures pale beside yours** mes aventures semblent bien pâles auprès des vôtres; **our problems pale into insignificance beside hers** nos problèmes sont insignifiants comparés aux siens *ou* à côté des siens
3 *n* (**a**) *(post)* pieu *m*
(**b**) *(fence)* palissade *f*; *Br Fig* **he's beyond the pale** il n'est pas fréquentable; **I find such behaviour beyond the pale** je trouve un tel comportement inadmissible
►► ***pale ale*** pale-ale *f*, bière *f* blonde légère

'Pale Fire' *Nabokov* 'Feu pâle'

paleface [ˈpeɪlfeɪs] *n Pej or Hum* Visage *m* pâle
palefaced [ˈpeɪlfeɪst] *adj* (au teint) pâle
paleness [ˈpeɪlnɪs] *n* pâleur *f*
paleo- [ˈpælɪəʊ] *pref* paléo-
paleoanthropology [ˌpælɪəʊænθrəˈpɒlədʒɪ] *n* paléoanthropologie *f*
paleobiogeography [ˌpælɪəʊbaɪəʊdʒɪˈɒgrəfɪ] *n* paléobiogéographie *f*
paleobiology [ˌpælɪəʊbaɪˈɒlədʒɪ] *n* paléobiologie *f*
paleobotany [ˌpælɪəʊˈbɒtənɪ] *n* paléobotanique *f*
Paleocene [ˈpælɪəʊsiːn] *Geol* **1** *adj* paléocène
2 *n* **the Paleocene** le paléocène
paleoclimate [ˈpælɪəʊklaɪmət] *n* paléoclimat *m*
paleoclimatology [ˌpælɪəʊklaɪməˈtɒlədʒɪ] *n* paléoclimatologie *f*
paleoecology [ˌpælɪəʊɪˈkɒlədʒɪ] *n* paléoécologie *f*
paleoenvironment [ˌpælɪəʊɪnˈvaɪrənmənt] *n* paléoenvironnement *m*
Paleogene [ˈpælɪəʊgiːn] *Geol* **1** *adj* paléogène
2 *n* **the Paleogene** le paléogène
paleogeography [ˌpælɪəʊdʒiːˈɒgrəfɪ] *n* paléogéographie *f*
paleographer [ˌpælɪˈɒgrəfə(r)] *n* paléographe *mf*
paleographic [ˌpælɪəʊˈgræfɪk] *adj* paléographe
paleography [ˌpælɪˈɒgrəfɪ] *n* paléographie *f*
paleohistology [ˌpælɪəʊhɪˈstɒlədʒɪ] *n* paléohistologie *f*
paleolith [ˈpælɪəʊlɪθ] *n* outil *m* paléolithique
Paleolithic [ˌpælɪəʊˈlɪθɪk] **1** *adj* paléolithique
2 *n* **the Paleolithic** le paléolithique
paleomagnetism [ˌpælɪəʊˈmægnətɪzəm] *n* paléomagnétisme *m*
paleontological [ˌpælɪɒntəˈlɒdʒɪkəl] *adj* paléontologique
paleontologist [ˌpælɪɒnˈtɒlədʒɪst] *n* paléontologiste *mf*, paléontologue *mf*
paleontology [ˌpælɪɒnˈtɒlədʒɪ] *n* paléontologie *f*
paleo-oceanography *n* paléo-océanographie *f*
paleorelief [ˌpælɪəʊrəˈliːf] *n* paléorelief *m*
paleosol [ˈpælɪəʊsɒl] *n* paléosol *m*
paleotemperature [ˌpælɪəʊˈtempərətʃə(r)] *n* paléotempérature *f*
Paleozoic [ˌpælɪəʊˈzəʊɪk] *Geol* **1** *adj* paléozoïque
2 *n* **the Paleozoic** le paléozoïque
Palermitan [pəˈlɜːmɪtən] **1** *n* Palermitain(e) *m,f*
2 *adj* palermitain
Palermo [pəˈlɜːməʊ] *n* Palerme
Palestine [ˈpæləˌstaɪn] *n* Palestine *f*; **in Palestine** en Palestine
▸▸ ***Palestine Liberation Organization*** Organisation *f* de libération de la Palestine
Palestinian [ˌpæləˈstɪnɪən] **1** *n* Palestinien(enne) *m,f*
2 *adj* palestinien
palestra [pæˈlestrə] *n Antiq* palestre *f*
palette [ˈpælət] *n Art & Comput* palette *f*
▸▸ ***palette knife*** *Art* couteau *m* (à palette); *Culin* spatule *f*
palfrey [ˈpɔːlfrɪ] *n Arch* palefroi *m*
Pali [ˈpɑːlɪ] *n (language)* pali *m*
palimony [ˈpælɪmənɪ] *n* pension *f* alimentaire *(accordée à un ex-concubin ou une ex-concubine)*
palimpsest [ˈpælɪmpsest] *n* palimpseste *m*
palindrome [ˈpælɪndrəʊm] *n Literature* palindrome *m*
palindromic [ˌpælɪnˈdrɒmɪk] *adj Literature* palindrome
paling [ˈpeɪlɪŋ] **1** *n (stake)* pieu *m*; *(fence)* palissade *f*
2 palings *npl (fence)* palissade *f*
palingenesis [ˌpælɪnˈdʒenəsɪs] *n Phil* palingénésie *f*
palinode [ˈpælɪnəʊd] *n Literature* palinodie *f*
palisade [ˌpælɪˈseɪd] **1** *n (fence)* palissade *f*
2 palisades *npl Am (cliffs)* ligne *f* de falaises
▸▸ *Bot* ***palisade layer*** tissu *m* palissadique
palish [ˈpeɪlɪʃ] *adj* pâlot
pall [pɔːl] **1** *n* (**a**) *(over coffin)* drap *m* mortuaire, poêle *m* (**b**) *(of smoke)* voile *m*; *(of snow, darkness, gloom)* manteau *m*; **a pall of silence hung over the room** il régnait dans la pièce un silence profond (**c**) *Am (coffin)* cercueil *m*
2 *vi Br* perdre son charme; **it began to pall on me** j'ai commencé à m'en lasser
Palladian [pəˈleɪdɪən] *adj Archit* palladien
Palladianism [pəˈleɪdɪənɪzəm] *n Archit* palladianisme *m*
palladium [pəˈleɪdɪəm] *n Chem & Myth* palladium *m*
Pallas [ˈpæləs] *pr n* Pallas
pallbearer [ˈpɔːlˌbeərə(r)] *n* porteur *m (du cercueil)*; **the pallbearers** *(accompanying coffin)* le cortège funèbre
pallet [ˈpælɪt] *n* (**a**) *(bed)* grabat *m*; *(mattress)* paillasse *f* (**b**) *(for loading, transportation)* palette *f* (**c**) *(potter's instrument)* palette *f* (**d**) *Art & Comput* palette *f*
▸▸ ***pallet truck*** chariot *m* élévateur, transpalette *m*
palletizable [ˌpælɪˈtaɪzɪbəl] *adj Com* palettisable
palletization [ˌpælɪtaɪˈzeɪʃən] *n Com* palettisation *f*
palletize, -ise [ˈpælɪtaɪz] *vt Com* palettiser
palletizer [ˈpælɪtaɪzə(r)] *n Com* palettiseur *m*
palliasse [ˈpælɪæs] *n* paillasse *f*
palliate [ˈpælɪeɪt] *vt* (**a**) *Med* pallier, lénifier (**b**) *Formal (fears)* apaiser; *(fault, offence)* pallier, atténuer; **her words had a palliating effect** ses paroles ont eu un effet lénifiant
palliative [ˈpælɪətɪv] **1** *adj* palliatif; **to have a palliative effect** *(medicine)* avoir un effet palliatif *ou* lénifiant; *(words)* avoir un effet lénifiant
2 *n* palliatif *m*
pallid [ˈpælɪd] *adj* (**a**) *(person, face, complexion)* pâle, blême, blafard; *(skin, hands)* pâle; *(light, moon)* blafard (**b**) *(performance)* insipide
▸▸ *Orn* ***pallid swift*** martinet *m* pâle
pallidly [ˈpælɪdlɪ] *adv* pâlement
pallidness [ˈpælɪdnɪs] *n* pâleur *f*
pallium [ˈpælɪəm] *n Antiq & Rel* pallium *m*
Pall Mall [pæl mæl] *n* = grande avenue londonienne, entre Trafalgar Square et St James's Palace
pallor [ˈpælə(r)] *n* pâleur *f*
pally [ˈpælɪ] *(compar* **pallier**, *superl* **palliest**) *adj Br Fam* **to be pally with sb** être pote avec qn; **he's really pally with all the shopkeepers** il est à tu et à toi avec tous les commerçants; **they're very pally all of a sudden** ils sont très potes tout d'un coup
palm [pɑːm] **1** *n* (**a**) *(of hand)* paume *f*; *(of glove)* empaumure *f*; **to have sweaty palms** avoir les mains moites; **to read sb's palm** lire les lignes de la main à qn; **he had them in the palm of his hand** il les tenait à sa merci *ou* sous sa coupe; **to grease sb's palm** graisser la patte à qn
(**b**) *(tree)* palmier *m*
(**c**) *(branch)* palme *f*; *Rel* rameau *m*; *Br Fig* **the winner's palm** la palme du vainqueur; *Br* **to carry off the palm** remporter la palme
(**d**) *Arch (measure)* palme *m*
2 *vt (coin)* cacher dans le creux de la main; **to palm a card** *(in conjuring)* filer une carte
▸▸ *Zool* ***palm civet*** civette *f* des palmiers; ***palm grove*** palmeraie *f*; ***palm house*** serre *f* à palmiers, palmarium *m*; ***palm leaf*** feuille *f* de palmier; ***palm oil*** huile *f* de palme; ***palm plantation*** palmeraie *f*; *Zool* ***palm squirrel*** rat *m* palmiste; ***palm sugar*** sucre *m* de palme; *Rel* ***Palm Sunday*** le dimanche des Rameaux, les Rameaux *mpl*; ***palm tree*** palmier *m*; ***palm wine*** vin *m* de palme
▸**palm off** *vt sep Fam (unwanted objects)* refiler; *(inferior goods)* fourguer; **to palm sb off with sth, to palm sth off on sb** refiler qch à qn; **they're palming the children off on us for the weekend** ils vont nous refiler les enfants pour le week-end; **when I complained, they palmed me off with a standard letter** quand je me suis plaint, ils m'ont refilé une lettre toute faite; **she tried to palm me off with some ridiculous excuse** elle a essayé de me faire avaler une excuse ridicule
Palma [ˈpælmə] *n* **Palma (de Mallorca)** Palma (de Majorque)
palmaceous [pælˈmeɪʃəs] *adj Bot* de la famille des Palmacées
palmar [ˈpælmɑː(r)] *adj Anat* palmaire
palmate [ˈpælmeɪt] *adj Bot & Zool* palmé
palmatifid [ˌpælməˈtɪfɪd] *adj Bot* palmatifide
palmatisect [ˌpælmətɪˈsekt] *adj Bot* palmatiséqué
palmer [ˈpɑːmə(r)] *n* (**a**) *(pilgrim → gen)* pèlerin *m*; *(→ returning from Holy Land)* pèlerin *m* de retour de la Terre Sainte *(en foi de quoi il portait un rameau)* (**b**) *Entom* chenille *f* poilue *ou* velue
▸▸ *Entom* ***palmer worm*** chenille *f* poilue *or* velue
palmetto [pælˈmetəʊ] *(pl* **palmettos** *or* **palmettoes**) *n Bot (dwarf fan palm)* palmier *m* nain; *(sabal)* chou *m* palmiste *m*
▸▸ ***the Palmetto State*** = surnom donné à la Caroline du Sud
palmist [ˈpɑːmɪst] *n* chiromancien(enne) *m,f*
palmistry [ˈpɑːmɪstrɪ] *n* chiromancie *f*
palmitate [ˈpælmɪteɪt] *n Chem* palmitate *m*
palmitic acid [pælˈmɪtɪk-] *n Chem* acide *m* palmitique
palmitin [ˈpælmɪtɪn] *n Chem* palmitine *f*
palmtop [ˈpɑːmtɒp] *n (computer)* ordinateur *m* de poche
▸▸ ***palmtop computer*** ordinateur *m* de poche
palmy [ˈpɑːmɪ] *(compar* **palmier**, *superl* **palmiest**) *adj* (**a**) *(pleasant)* agréable, doux (douce); **in the palmy days of our youth** aux jours heureux de notre jeunesse (**b**) *(beach, coast)* bordé de palmiers
Palmyra [pælˈmaɪrə] *n* Palmyre
palomino [ˌpæləˈmiːnəʊ] *(pl* **palominos**) *n* palomino *m*
palooka [pəˈluːkə] *n Am Fam* (**a**) *(clumsy man)* manche *m*; *(stupid man)* andouille *f*, crétin *m* (**b**) *(inept fighter)* mauvais boxeur[□] *m*
palp [pælp] *n Zool* palpe *f*
palpability [ˌpælpəˈbɪlɪtɪ], **palpableness** [ˈpælpəbəlnɪs] *n* (**a**) *(tangibility)* palpabilité *f* (**b**) *(obviousness)* évidence *f*
palpable [ˈpælpəbəl] *adj* (**a**) *(tangible)* palpable, tangible (**b**) *(obvious)* évident, manifeste, flagrant; **a palpable lie** un mensonge grossier
palpably [ˈpælpəblɪ] *adv* (**a**) *(tangibly)* tangiblement (**b**) *(obviously)* manifestement
palpate [ˈpælpeɪt] *vt Med* palper
palpation [pælˈpeɪʃən] *n Med* palpation *f*, palper *m*
palpebral [ˈpælpəbrəl] *adj Anat* palpebral
palpitate [ˈpælpɪteɪt] *vi* palpiter
palpitating [ˈpælpɪteɪtɪŋ] *adj Med* palpitant
palpitation [ˌpælpɪˈteɪʃən] *n* palpitation *f*; *Med* **to have** *or* **to get palpitations** avoir des palpitations; *Hum* **I get palpitations whenever I see her** mon cœur bat la chamade *ou* s'emballe chaque fois que je la vois
palpus [ˈpælpəs] *n Zool* palpe *f*
palsied [ˈpɔːlzɪd] *adj* (**a**) *(paralysed)* paralysé (**b**) *Literary (trembling)* tremblant, tremblotant
palsy [ˈpɔːlzɪ] *n* paralysie *f*; **shaking palsy** maladie *f* de Parkinson
palsy-walsy [ˈpælzɪˈwælzɪ] *adj Fam* **to be palsy-walsy with sb** être comme cul et chemise avec qn, être à tu et à toi avec qn; **they're very palsy-walsy all of a sudden** ils sont très potes ou copain-copain tout d'un coup
paltriness [ˈpɔːltrɪnɪs] *n* (**a**) *(of sum)* caractère *f* dérisoire (**b**) *(of excuse)* faiblesse *f*
paltry [ˈpɔːltrɪ] *adj* (**a**) *(meagre → wage, sum)* misérable, dérisoire; **it'll cost you a paltry $100** ça vous coûtera cent malheureux dollars (**b**) *(worthless → person, attitude)* insignifiant, minable; **a paltry excuse** une piètre excuse
paludal [pəˈluːdəl] *adj* (**a**) *(marshy)* marécageux, paludéen; *(plant)* des marais, marécageux (**b**) *Med* paludéen
paludina [ˌpæljʊˈdiːnə] *n Zool* paludine *f*
paludism [ˈpæljʊdɪzəm] *n Med* paludisme *m*
palynology [ˌpælɪˈnɒlədʒɪ] *n* palynologie *f*, pollénographie *f*
Pamirs [pəˈmɪəz] *npl* **the Pamirs** le Pamir; **in the Pamirs** au Pamir
pampas [ˈpæmpəz] *npl* pampa *f*
▸▸ ***pampas grass*** herbe *f* de la pampa
pamper [ˈpæmpə(r)] *vt* choyer, dorloter; **a hotel where you will be pampered** un hôtel où l'on sera à vos petits soins; **to pamper oneself** se dorloter; **pamper yourself with a bubble bath** faites-vous plaisir, prenez un bain moussant
pampered [ˈpæmpəd] *adj* choyé, dorloté; **pampered tastes** goûts *mpl* exigeants *ou* luxueux
pampero [pæmˈpeərəʊ] *n* pampero *m*

pal–pam

pamphlet ['pæmflɪt] *n (gen)* brochure *f*; *(literary, scientific)* opuscule *m*; *Pol* pamphlet *m*

pamphleteer [,pæmflə'tɪə(r)] *n* auteur *m* de brochures; *Pol* pamphlétaire *mf*

Pamplona [pæm'pləʊnə] *n* Pampelune

Pan [pæn] *pr n Myth* Pan

pan [pæn] *(pt & pp* **panned,** *cont* **panning) 1** *n* **(a)** *Culin* casserole *f*; *Am* **cake pan** moule *m* à gâteau
(b) *Mining (for gold)* batée *f*
(c) *(of scales)* plateau *m*
(d) *Br (toilet bowl)* **(lavatory) pan** cuvette *f* de W-C; *Fam Fig* **to go down the pan** être foutu en l'air; *Fam* **that's six months' work down the pan!** voilà six mois de travail qui s'en vont en fumée!; **that's our holidays down the pan!** on peut faire une croix sur nos vacances!
(e) *TV & Cin* panoramique *m*; **pan down** panoramique *m* vers le bas; **pan up** panoramique *m* vertical
(f) *Geol* cuvette *f*, bassin *m* de déposition *ou* de sédimentation; **salt pan** marais *m* salant, saline *f*, salin *m*
(g) *Fam (face)* bouille *f*
2 *vi* **(a)** *Mining* laver le gravier à la batée; **to pan for gold** chercher de l'or
(b) *TV & Cin* faire un panoramique; **the camera pans around the bay** la caméra prend la baie en panoramique *ou* fait un panoramique de la baie; **to pan across the room** prendre la salle en panoramique, faire un panoramique de la salle
3 *vt* **(a)** *TV & Cin* **to pan the camera** faire un panoramique, *Spec* panoramiquer
(b) *Mining (gravel etc)* laver à la batée
(c) *Fam (criticize)* descendre (en flammes), éreinter; **the movie was panned by the critics** le film a été descendu par les critiques
▸▸ ***pan scourer, pan scrubber*** tampon *m* à récurer

▸**pan down** *vi TV & Cin* faire un panoramique vers le bas

▸**pan in** *vt sep Scot Fam* **to pan sb's face in** casser la figure à qn; **somebody's panned my windows in** quelqu'un a pété mes fenêtres

▸**pan out** *vi Br Fam (work out)* se dérouler❑, marcher❑; *(succeed)* réussir❑; **if things pan out as planned** si tout marche comme prévu; **our strategy is not panning out** notre stratégie ne donne pas de résultats❑; **it depends how things pan out** ça dépend de comment les choses vont s'arranger❑

▸**pan up** *vi TV & Cin* faire un panoramique vertical

pan- [pæn] *pref* pan-; **Pan-Asian** panasiatique

panacea [,pænə'sɪə] *n* panacée *f*

panache [pə'næʃ] *n* panache *m*

Pan-African 1 *adj* panafricain
2 *n* partisan(e) *m,f* du panafricanisme

Pan-Africanism *n* panafricanisme *m*

Panama ['pænəmɑː] *n* **(a)** *Geog* Panama *m*; **in Panama** au Panama; **the Isthmus of Panama** l'isthme *m* de Panama **(b)** *(hat)* panama *m*
▸▸ ***the Panama Canal*** le canal de Panama; ***Panama City*** Panama; ***Panama hat*** panama *m*

Panamanian [,pænə'meɪnɪən] **1** *n* Panaméen(-enne) *m,f*
2 *adj* panaméen
3 *comp (embassy, history)* du Panama

Pan-American *adj* panaméricain
▸▸ ***the Pan-American Games*** les jeux *mpl* Panaméricains; ***the Pan-American Highway*** la route panaméricaine

Pan-Americanism *n* panaméricanisme *m*

Pan-Arab *adj* panarabe

Pan-Arabism [-'ærəbɪzəm] *n* panarabisme *m*

Pan-Arabist *n* partisan(e) *m,f* du panarabisme

panary ['pænərɪ] *adj* panaire

Pan-Asian, pan-Asiatic *adj* panasiatique

panatella [,pænə'telə] *n* panatela *m*, panatella *m*

panax ['pænæks] *n Bot* **panax (ginseng)** panax *m*

pancake ['pæŋkeɪk] **1** *n* **(a)** *Culin (thin)* crêpe *f*; *(thick)* = sorte de petite galette épaisse servie au petit déjeuner; **(as) flat as a pancake** plat comme une galette
(b) *(make-up)* fond *m* de teint solide
(c) *Aviat* atterrissage *m* à plat *or* brutal
2 *vi Aviat* atterrir sur le ventre
▸▸ *Br* ***Pancake Day*** mardi gras *m*; ***pancake ice*** glace *f* en crêpes; *Aviat* ***pancake landing*** atterrissage *m* à plat *or* brutal; ***pancake race*** = course traditionnelle du mardi gras britannique consistant à courir avec une poêle dans laquelle se trouve une crêpe qu'il faut retourner; ***pancake roll*** rouleau *m* de printemps; *Br* ***Pancake Tuesday*** mardi gras *m*

pancetta [pæn'tʃetə] *n Culin* pancetta *f*

panchax ['pæntʃæks] *n Ich* panchax *m*

Panchen Lama ['pæntʃən-] *n* panchen-lama *m*

panchromatic [,pænkrəʊ'mætɪk] *adj Phot* panchromatique

panchronic [,pæn'krɒnɪk] *adj Ling* panchronique

pancreas ['pæŋkrɪəs] *n Anat* pancréas *m*

pancreatic [,pæŋkrɪ'ætɪk] *adj Anat* pancréatique
▸▸ ***pancreatic cancer*** cancer *m* du pancréas; ***pancreatic juice*** suc *m* pancréatique

pancreatin ['pæŋkrɪətɪn] *n Pharm* pancréatine *f*

pancreatitis [,pæŋkrɪə'taɪtəs] *n Med* pancréatite *f*

panda ['pændə] *n* **(a)** *Zool* panda *m* **(b)** *Br (car)* voiture *f* de police
▸▸ *Br* ***panda car*** voiture *f* de police

pandanus [pæn'deɪnəs] *n Bot* pandanus *m*

Pandean [,pæn'dɪən] *adj Myth* de Pan
▸▸ ***Pandean pipes*** flûte *f* de Pan

pandects ['pændekts] *npl Hist* pandectes *fpl*

pandemic [,pæn'demɪk] **1** *adj* **(a)** *Med* pandémique **(b)** *(universal)* universel, général
2 *n Med* pandémie *f*

pandemonium [,pændɪ'məʊnɪəm] *n (UNCOUNT) (chaos)* chaos *m*, *Literary* pandémonium *m*; *(uproar)* tumulte *m*, tohu-bohu *m*; **pandemonium broke out** cela a déclenché un véritable tumulte; **the whole office is in pandemonium** le bureau est sens dessus dessous

pander ['pændə(r)] **1** *vi* **these films pander to our worst instincts** ces films font appel à nos pires instincts; **to pander to sb** encourager bassement qn; **to pander to a vice** encourager un vice; **to pander to sb's whims** se prêter aux exigences de qn
2 *n (pimp)* entremetteur(euse) *m,f*, proxénète *mf*

panderer ['pændərə(r)] *n (pimp)* entremetteur(-euse) *m,f*, proxénète *mf*

p & h *(written abbr* **postage and handling**) frais *mpl* de port et d'emballage

pandit ['pændɪt] *n* pandit *m*

P & L [,piːən'el] *n* **(a)** *(abbr* **profit and loss**) pertes *fpl* et profits *mpl*
(b) *(abbr* **profit and loss account, profit and loss statement**) compte *m* de résultat; **we can see from the P&L that developing the product is not a viable option** le compte de résultat montre clairement qu'il ne serait pas rentable de développer ce produit
(c) *(abbr* **profit and loss form**) compte *m* d'exploitation
▸▸ ***P & L account*** compte *m* de résultat; ***P & L form*** compte *m* d'exploitation; ***P & L statement*** compte *m* de résultat

Pandora [pæn'dɔːrə] *pr n Myth* Pandore
▸▸ ***Pandora's box*** la boîte de Pandore

p & p [,piːən'piː] *n Br (abbr* **postage and packing**) frais *mpl* de port et d'emballage

pane [peɪn] *n* vitre *f*, carreau *m*; **a pane of glass** un carreau
▸▸ *Am* ***pane glass window*** fenêtre *f* panoramique

panegyric [,pænɪ'dʒɪrɪk] *n Formal* panégyrique *m*; **he launched into a panegyric of** *or* **about French cuisine** il s'est lancé dans un éloge dithyrambique de la cuisine française

panegyrical [,pænɪ'dʒɪrɪkəl] *adj Formal* panégyrique

panegyrist [,pænɪ'dʒɪrɪst] *n Formal* panégyriste *mf*

panegyrize, -ise ['pænɪdʒɪraɪz] *vt Formal* faire le panégyrique de

panel ['pænəl] *(Br pt & pp* **panelled,** *cont* **panelling,** *Am pt & pp* **paneled,** *cont* **paneling) 1** *n* **(a)** *(flat section → of wood, glass etc)* panneau *m*; *(in ceiling)* caisson *m*; *(of cartoon strip)* case *f*; *(in book, magazine)* encadré *m*; **sliding panel** panneau *m* coulissant
(b) *(group, committee → gen)* comité *m*; *(→ to judge exam, contest)* jury *m*; *(→ in radio or TV quiz)* invités *mpl*; *(→ in public debate)* panel *m*; *(→ in public inquiry)* commission *f* (d'enquête); **a panel of experts** un comité d'experts; **our panel for tonight's show** nos invités à l'émission de ce soir; **the panel were unanimous in awarding her top marks** le jury lui a accordé à l'unanimité la plus haute note
(c) *Mktg (for market research)* panel *m*
(d) *(set of controls)* **(control) panel** tableau *m* de bord; *Aviat & Aut* **(instrument) panel** tableau *m* de bord
(e) *Sewing* panneau *m*, lé *m*
(f) *Law (selection list)* liste *f* de jurés
(g) *Art (backing)* panneau *m*; *(picture)* (peinture *f* sur) panneau *m*
2 *vt (wall, hall)* lambrisser, revêtir de panneaux; *(surface)* plaquer; **a panelled door** une porte à panneaux; **the room is in panelled oak** la pièce est lambrissée de chêne; **one wall was panelled in pine** un des murs était lambrissé de pin
▸▸ *Br Aut* ***panel beater*** carrossier *m*, tôlier *m*; ***panel discussion*** débat *m*, table *f* ronde; *Br Old-fashioned* ***panel doctor*** ≃ médecin *m* conventionné; *Br* ***panel game*** *Rad* jeu *m* radiophonique; *TV* jeu *m* télévisé; ***panel heating*** chauffage *m* à panneaux; ***panel member*** *(jury member)* juré *m*; *(in radio or TV quiz)* invité(e) *m,f*; *(in public debate)* panéliste *mf*; *(of committee)* membre *m* du comité; *Br* ***panel pin*** pointe *f* à tête d'homme, clou *m* à panneau; ***panel research*** recherches *fpl* par panel; *Am* ***panel truck,*** *Austr* ***panel van*** camionnette *f*

panelling, *Am* **paneling** ['pænəlɪŋ] *n (UNCOUNT)* **(a)** *(wall covering)* lambris *m*, boiseries *fpl*, placage *m*; **oak panelling** lambris *mpl* de chêne
(b) *(material)* panneaux *mpl*

panellist, *Am* **panelist** ['pænəlɪst] *n (jury member)* juré *m*; *(in radio or TV quiz)* invité(e) *m,f*; *(in public debate)* panéliste *mf*; *(of committee)* membre *m* du comité

Pan-European *adj* paneuropéen

pan-fries *npl Am* pommes *fpl* (de terre) sautées

pan-fry *vt* (faire) sauter; **pan-fried chicken** poulet *m* sauté

pang [pæŋ] *n* **(a)** *(of emotion)* coup *m* au cœur, pincement *m* de cœur; **I felt a pang of sadness** j'ai eu un serrement de cœur; **a pang of conscience** un soubresaut de conscience, **to feel pangs of conscience** *or* **guilt** éprouver des remords; **he resigned without a pang of regret** il a démissionné sans l'ombre d'un remords *ou* regret **(b)** *(of pain)* élancement *m*; **hunger pangs** tiraillements *mpl* d'estomac

Pangaea [pæn'dʒiːə] *n* Pangée *f*

pan-German, pan-Germanic *adj* pangermanique

pan-Germanism [-'dʒɜːmənɪzəm] *n* pangermanisme *m*

pan-Germanist *n* pangermaniste *mf*

pangolin [pæŋ'gəʊlɪn] *n Zool* pangolin *m*

pangram ['pæŋgræm] *n Gram* pangramme *m*

panhandle ['pæn,hændəl] *Am* **1** *n Geog* langue *f* de terre; **the Alaska panhandle** la région sud de l'Alaska; **the Texas panhandle** = la langue de terre correspondant à la partie nord-ouest du Texas
2 *vi Fam* faire la manche
3 *vt Fam* **to panhandle money from sb, to panhandle sb** taper qn

panhandler ['pæn,hændlə(r)] *n Am Fam* mendiant(e)❑ *m,f*

Panhellenic [,pænhe'lenɪk] *adj* panhellénique, panhellénien

Panhellenism [,pæn'helənɪzəm] *n* panhellénisme *m*

panic ['pænɪk] *(pt & pp* **panicked,** *cont* **panicking) 1** *n* **(a)** *(alarm)* panique *f*, affolement *m*; **she was close to panic** elle était au bord de l'affolement; **to get into a panic over** *or* **about sth** s'affoler à cause de qch; **it started a panic on the stock exchange** cela a semé la panique à la Bourse; **to throw sb into a panic** affoler qn; *Fam* **it was panic stations!** ça a été la panique générale!
(b) *Fam (rush)* hâte❑ *f*; **I was in a mad panic to get to the airport** c'était la panique pour aller à l'aéroport❑; **what's the panic?** ne vous affolez pas!❑; **there's no panic!** il n'y a pas le feu!
(c) *Am Fam (funny thing)* **it was a panic!** c'était à hurler de rire!
2 *vi* s'affoler; **don't panic!** ne vous affolez pas!;

he's starting to panic about the wedding il commence à s'affoler à la perspective de ce mariage

3 *vt* affoler; **the news panicked the government into action** la panique provoquée par cette nouvelle a poussé le gouvernement à l'action; **she was panicked into accepting** sous le coup de la panique, elle a accepté

►► ***panic attack*** crise *f* de panique; ***panic bolt*** barre *f* antipanique; ***panic button*** signal *m* d'alarme; *Fam* **to hit the panic button** paniquer[□], flipper; ***panic buying*** *(gén)* = achats massifs provoqués par la crainte de la pénurie; *St Exch* achats *mpl* de précaution; *Bot* ***panic grass*** panic *m*; ***panic measures*** mesures *fpl* dictées par la panique; ***panic reaction*** réaction *f* de panique; *St Exch* ***panic selling*** ventes *fpl* de précaution

panicky ['pænɪkɪ] *adj (person, crowd)* paniqué; *(voice, answer, message)* affolé; *(feeling, reaction)* de panique; *(giggle)* nerveux; *(market)* enclin à la panique; **I get panicky every time I have to speak to him** je panique chaque fois que je dois lui parler

panicle ['pænɪkəl] *n Bot* panicule *f*

panicmonger ['pænɪk,mʌŋgə(r)] *n* semeur(-euse) *m,f* de panique

panic-stricken *adj* affolé, pris de panique; *(reaction, answer, look)* affolé

paniculate [pə'nɪkjʊlət] *adj Bot* paniculé

panini [pæ'ni:ni:] *(pl* **inv** *or* **paninis***) n* panini *m*

Pan-Islamic *adj* panislamique

Pan-Islamism *n* panislamisme *m*

panjandrum [,pæn'dʒændrəm] *n Fam* grand manitou *m*, ponte *m*

panmixia [,pæn'mɪksɪə] *n* panmixie *f*

panne [pæn] *n Tex* panne *f*

panniculus [pæ'nɪkjʊləs] *n Anat* pannicule *m*

pannier ['pænɪə(r)] *n* (**a**) *(bag → on bicycle, motorbike)* sacoche *f*; *(→ on donkey)* panier *m* de bât (**b**) *(basket)* panier *m*, corbeille *f*

panning ['pænɪŋ] *n* (**a**) *TV & Cin* panoramique *m* (**b**) *Mining* lavage *m* (**c**) *Fam (criticism)* descente *f* en flammes; **the movie got a real panning** le film s'est fait descendre (en flammes)

►► *TV & Cin* ***panning handle*** poignée *f* de panoramique; *TV & Cin* ***panning shot*** prise *f* panoramique

pannose ['pænəʊs] *adj Bot* duveteux

panophthalmitis [,pænɒfθæl'maɪtəs] *n Med* panophtalmie *f*

panoply ['pænəplɪ] *n* panoplie *f*; *Literary* **pomp and panoply** grand apparat *m*

panoptic [pæn'ɒptɪk] *adj (gospels, survey)* panoptique

panorama [,pænə'rɑ:mə] *n also Fig* panorama *m*

panoramic [,pænə'ræmɪk] *adj* panoramique

►► ***panoramic photograph*** photo *f* panoramique; *Cin* ***panoramic screen*** écran *m* panoramique; ***panoramic sight*** viseur *m* panoramique; ***panoramic view*** vue *f* panoramique

panpipes ['pænpaɪps] *npl* flûte *f* de Pan

Pan-Serbian *adj* panserbe

Pan-Slav *adj* panslave, panslaviste

Pan-Slavism *n* panslavisme *m*

panspermatism [pæn'spɜ:mətɪzəm], **panspermism** [pæn'spɜ:mɪzəm] *n* panspermie *f*

pansy ['pænzɪ] *(pl* **pansies***) n* (**a**) *Bot* pensée *f* (**b**) *Br Fam Pej (sissy)* poule *f* mouillée, femmelette *f*; *(effeminate man)* chochotte *f*; *(homosexual)* tante *f*

pant [pænt] **1** *vi* (**a**) *(puff)* haleter, souffler; *(of animal)* battre du flanc; **he panted up the stairs** il monta l'escalier en soufflant; **to pant for breath** chercher son souffle

(**b**) *Fam (be eager)* **he's panting to do it** il meurt d'envie de le faire; **he's panting at the prospect** il ne se tient plus d'impatience à cette perspective[□]

2 *vt (say)* dire en haletant *ou* d'une voix haletante

3 *n (breath)* halètement *m*

►**pant out** *vt sep (say)* dire en haletant

Pantaloon [,pæntə'lu:n] *pr n Theat* Pantalon

pantaloons [,pæntə'lu:nz] *npl* pantalon *m* bouffant

pantechnicon [pæn'teknɪkən] *n Br Old-fashioned* (**a**) *(van)* camion *m* de déménagement (**b**) *(warehouse)* garde-meubles *m*

pantheism ['pænθi:ɪzəm] *n* panthéisme *m*

pantheist ['pænθi:ɪst] *n* panthéiste *mf*

pantheistic [,pænθi:'ɪstɪk] *adj* panthéiste

pantheon ['pænθɪən] *n* panthéon *m*; **he belongs in the pantheon of great movie stars** il mérite de figurer au panthéon des stars du cinéma

panther ['pænθə(r)] *(pl* **inv** *or* **panthers***) n* (**a**) *(leopard)* panthère *f* (**b**) *Am (puma)* puma *m*; **the (Black) Panthers** = mouvement politique fondé par des militants noirs américains dans les années soixante

pantheress ['pænθərɪs] *n* panthère *f* (femelle)

pantie = **panty**

panties ['pæntɪz] *npl* (petite) culotte *f*; **a pair of panties** un slip, une culotte; *Am Fam Hum* **don't get your panties in a wad!** *(don't panic)* ne t'affole pas![□]; *(don't get angry)* du calme![□], calme-toi![□]

pantihose ['pæntɪ,həʊz] *n Am* collant *m*, collants *mpl*

pantile ['pæntaɪl] *n* tuile *f* en S

panting ['pæntɪŋ] **1** *adj (person, dog)* haletant

2 *n* halètement *m*

panto ['pæntəʊ] *(pl* **pantos***) n Br Fam (Christmas show)* = spectacle de Noël pour enfants

pantograph ['pæntəgrɑ:f] *n* pantographe *m*

pantomime ['pæntəmaɪm] *n* (**a**) *Br (Christmas show)* = spectacle de Noël pour enfants (**b**) *(mime)* pantomime *f* (**c**) *Br Fam Fig* comédie *f*, cirque *m*; **there was a bit of a pantomime over who should pay** ça a été tout un cirque pour savoir qui devait payer

►► ***pantomime dame*** = rôle travesti outré et ridicule dans la "pantomime"; ***pantomime horse*** = personnage de cheval joué par deux comédiens dans la "pantomime"

> **PANTOMIME**
>
> Le genre typiquement britannique de la "pantomime" est très conventionnel; certains personnages-types ("pantomime dame", "principal boy") et certaines rengaines ("Behind you!", "Oh yes he is! – Oh no he isn't!") apparaissent dans toutes les pièces. Ces pièces, qui se jouent au moment des fêtes de fin d'année, sont généralement inspirées d'un conte de fées.

pantomimic [,pæntə'mɪmɪk] *adj* pantomimique

pantothenic acid [,pæntəʊ'θi:nɪk-] *n* acide *m* pantothénique

pantoum [pæn'tu:m] *n Literature* pantoum *m*, pantoun *m*

pantry ['pæntrɪ] *(pl* **pantries***) n (cupboard)* garde-manger *m inv*; *(walk-in cupboard)* cellier *m*, office *m*

pants [pænts] **1** *npl* (**a**) *Br* **(pair of) pants** slip *m*, culotte *f*; *(boxer shorts)* caleçon *m*

(**b**) *esp Am (trousers)* **(pair of) pants** pantalon *m*; **a kick in the pants** un coup de pied aux fesses; **he's still in short pants** il est encore à l'âge des culottes courtes

(**c**) *Fam (idioms)* **to beat the pants off sb** battre qn à plates coutures; **to scare the pants off sb** foutre une trouille pas possible à qn; **to bore the pants off sb** ennuyer qn à mourir; **to be caught with one's pants down** être pris sur le fait en train de faire une bêtise[□]; **it's clear who wears the pants around here** il n'y a pas de doute sur qui porte le pantalon ici; **he charmed the pants off my parents** il a conquis mes parents[□]

2 *adj Br Fam Hum (of poor quality)* nul

3 *exclam Br Fam Hum* zut!, mince!

►► *esp Am* ***pants leg*** jambe *f* de pantalon

pantsuit ['pæntsu:t] *n Am* tailleur-pantalon *m*

panty ['pæntɪ-] *comp*

►► ***panty girdle*** gaine-culotte *f*; *Br* ***panty hose*** collant *m*, collants *mpl*; ***panty liner*** protège-slip *m*

pantywaist ['pæntɪweɪst] *n Am Fam Old-fashioned* poule *f* mouillée, femmelette *f*

panzer ['pænzə(r)] *n* panzer *m*, blindé *m*

►► ***panzer division*** division *f* blindée

Pap [pæp] *adj*

►► *Med* ***Pap smear, Pap test*** frottis *m* vaginal

pap [pæp] *n* (**a**) *(mush)* bouillie *f* (**b**) *(UNCOUNT) Fig (nonsense)* bêtises *fpl*, imbécillités *fpl*; **his films are pap** ses films sont stupides; **what a load of pap!** n'importe quoi! (**c**) *Arch or Scot & NEng (nipple)* mamelon *m*, téton *m* (**d**) *(hill)* mamelon *m*, monticule *m*

papa [pə'pɑ:] *n Old-fashioned or Hum* papa *m*

papacy ['peɪpəsɪ] *(pl* **papacies***) n (system, institution)* papauté *f*; *(term of office)* pontificat *m*

papadum = **popadum**

papaine [pə'peɪn] *n Chem* papaïne *f*

papal ['peɪpəl] *adj* papal

►► ***papal bull*** bulle *f* papale; ***papal cross*** croix *f* papale; ***papal interdict*** interdit *m* papal; ***papal nuncio*** nonce *m* du Pape; ***papal throne*** trône *m* pontifical

paparazzi [,pæpə'rætsɪ] *npl* paparazzi *mpl*

papaverin, papaverine [pæ'peɪvəraɪn] *n Pharm* papavérine *f*

papaw [pə'pɔ:] *n* (**a**) *(asimina triloba → fruit)* asimine *f*, pomme-cannelle *f*; *(→ tree)* asiminier *m* (**b**) *(carica papaya → fruit)* papaye *f*; *(→ tree)* papayer *m*

papaya [pə'paɪə] *n (fruit)* papaye *f*; *(tree)* papayer *m*

paper ['peɪpə(r)] **1** *n* (**a**) *(UNCOUNT) (material)* papier *m*; **a piece/sheet of paper** un bout/une feuille de papier; **the paper industry** l'industrie *f* papetière, la papeterie; **he wants it on paper** il veut que ce soit écrit; **to put sth down on paper** mettre qch par écrit; **on paper, they're by far the better side** sur le papier *ou* a priori, c'est de loin la meilleure équipe; **it's a good plan on paper** ce projet est excellent en théorie

(**b**) *(newspaper)* journal *m*; **it's in all the morning papers** c'est dans tous les journaux du matin; *Am Fam* **go peddle your papers!** va voir ailleurs si j'y suis!

(**c**) *(usu pl) (document)* papier *m*, document *m*; **could you fill out this paper?** pourriez-vous remplir ce formulaire?; **once you've got the necessary papers together** une fois que vous aurez réuni les pièces nécessaires; **Virginia Woolf's private papers** les écrits *mpl* personnels de Virginia Woolf; **(identity) papers** papiers *mpl* (d'identité); **ship's papers** papiers *mpl* de bord

(**d**) *Sch & Univ (exam paper)* épreuve *f*; *(questions)* questions *fpl* d'examen; *(answer)* copie *f*; **you have an hour for each paper** vous avez une heure pour chaque épreuve; **hand in your papers** rendez vos copies

(**e**) *(academic treatise → published)* article *m*; *(→ oral)* communication *f*; **to write a paper** écrire un article; **to give** *or* **to read a paper on sth** faire un exposé sur qch

(**f**) *(wallpaper)* papier *m* peint

(**g**) *Fin* papier *m* valeur; *(banknotes)* billets *mpl* de banque; **long/short paper** papier *m* à long/court terme

2 *adj* (**a**) *(napkin, towel)* en *ou* de papier

(**b**) *(theoretical)* sur le papier, théorique

(**c**) *Pej (worthless)* sans valeur

3 *vt (room, walls)* tapisser

►► *Comput* ***paper advance*** *(on printer)* entraînement *m* du papier; ***paper aeroplane*** avion *m* en papier; ***paper bag*** sac *m* en papier; ***paper chains*** guirlandes *fpl* de papier; ***paper chase*** rallye-papier *m*, ≃ jeu *m* de piste; *Fig* **education has become an academic paper chase** l'éducation est devenue une véritable course aux diplômes; ***paper clip*** trombone *m*; *Fin* ***paper company*** société *f* d'investissement; ***paper copy*** copie *f* sur papier, sortie *f* papier; ***paper cup*** gobelet *m* en carton; ***paper currency*** papier-monnaie *m*; ***paper dart*** avion *m* en papier; *Comput & Typ* ***paper feed*** alimentation *f* du papier; *Comput & Typ* ***paper format*** format *m* de papier; ***paper handkerchief,*** *Fam* ***paper hankie*** mouchoir *m* en papier[□]; *Comput* ***paper jam*** bourrage *m* de papier; ***paper knife*** coupe-papier *m inv*; *Fin* ***paper loss*** moins-value *f*; *Fin* ***paper money*** papier-monnaie *m*, monnaie *f* fiduciaire; ***paper nautilus*** argonaute *f*; ***paper plate*** assiette *f* en carton; ***paper profits*** profits *mpl* fictifs; ***paper qualifications*** diplômes *mpl*; ***paper round*** livraison *f* de journaux; **to have** *or* **do a paper round** distribuer les journaux; *Fin* ***paper securities*** titres *mpl* fiduciaires, papiers *mpl* valeurs; *Br* ***paper shop*** *(commerce)* marchand *m* de journaux; **to go to the paper shop** aller chez le marchand de journaux; **he works**

in a paper shop il travaille dans un magasin de journaux; ***paper shredder*** broyeur *m*; *Comput* ***paper tape*** bande *f* perforée; ***paper tiger*** tigre *m* de papier; ***paper tissue*** mouchoir *m* en papier; ***paper towel*** serviette *f* en papier; ***paper transaction*** jeu *m* d'écritures; *Comput* ***paper tray*** bac *m* à feuilles; ***paper victory*** victoire *f* inutile

▶**paper over** *vt sep* (**a**) *(with wallpaper)* recouvrir de papier peint (**b**) *Fig (dispute, facts)* dissimuler; **to paper over the cracks** *(disguise faults)* masquer les défauts; *(disguise disagreements)* masquer les mésententes

'The Pickwick Papers' *Dickens* 'Les Aventures de M. Pickwick'

paperback ['peɪpəbæk] **1** *n* livre *m* de poche; **it's in paperback** c'est en (édition de) poche
2 *adj (book, edition)* de poche

paperbacked ['peɪpəbækt] *adj* broché

paperboard ['peɪpəbɔːd] *n* carton *m*, carton-pâte *m*

paperbound ['peɪpəbaʊnd] *adj* broché

paperboy ['peɪpəbɔɪ] *n (delivering papers)* livreur *m* de journaux; *(selling papers)* vendeur *m* de journaux

paper-clip *vt* attacher avec un trombone

papergirl ['peɪpəgɜːl] *n (delivering papers)* livreuse *f* de journaux; *(selling papers)* vendeuse *f* de journaux

paperhanger ['peɪpə,hæŋə(r)] *n* (**a**) *(decorator)* peintre-décorateur(trice) *m,f* (**b**) *Am Fam (counterfeiter)* faux-monnayeur ❑ *m*

paperhanging ['peɪpə,hæŋɪŋ] *n* pose *f* de papiers peints

paperless ['peɪpəlɪs] *adj (electronic → communication, record-keeping)* informatique
▶▶ ***paperless office*** bureau *m* entièrement informatisé; *St Exch* ***paperless trading*** marché *m* *ou* cotation *f* électronique

papermill ['peɪpəmɪl] *n* papeterie *f*, usine *f* à papier

paper-thin *adj* extrêmement mince *ou* fin

paperweight ['peɪpəweɪt] *n* presse-papiers *m inv*

paperwork ['peɪpəwɜːk] *n* travail *m* de bureau, *Pej* paperasserie *f*; **to do the paperwork** s'occuper du travail de bureau; **I'm drowning in paperwork** je suis dans la paperasserie jusqu'au cou

papery ['peɪpərɪ] *adj* qui ressemble à du papier; *(thin)* mince comme du papier; **papery skin** peau *f* parcheminée

Papiamento [,pæpɪə'mentəʊ] *n* papiamento *m*

papier-mâché [,pæpjeɪ'mæʃeɪ] *n* papier *m* mâché

papilla [pə'pɪlə] (*pl* **papillae** [-liː]) *n Anat, Zool & Bot* papille *f*

papillary [pə'pɪlərɪ] *adj Anat, Zool & Bot* papillaire

papilloma [,pæpɪ'ləʊmə] *n Med* papillome *m*

papillon ['pæpɪjɔ̃] *n (dog)* papillon *m*

papist ['peɪpɪst] *Pej* **1** *adj* papiste
2 *n* papiste *mf*

papistry ['peɪpɪstrɪ] *n Pej* papisme *m*

papoose [pə'puːs] *n* papoose *m*

pappus ['pæpəs] *n Bot* pappe *m*, aigrette *f*

nappy[1] ['pæpɪ] (*pl* **pappies**) *n Am Fam* papa ❑ *m*

pappy[2] (*compar* **pappier**, *superl* **pappiest**) *adj* gluant

paprika ['pæprɪkə] *n* paprika *m*

Papua ['pæpjʊə] *n* Papouasie *f*; **in Papua** en Papouasie
▶▶ ***Papua New Guinea*** Papouasie-Nouvelle-Guinée *f*; **in Papua New Guinea** en Papouasie-Nouvelle-Guinée

Papuan ['pæpjʊən] **1** *n* (**a**) *(person)* Papou(e) *m,f* (**b**) *Ling* langue *f* papoue
2 *adj* papou

papyrologist [,pæpɪ'rɒlədʒɪst] *n* papyrologue *mf*

papyrology [,pæpɪ'rɒlədʒɪ] *n* papyrologie *f*

papyrus [pə'paɪrəs] (*pl* **papyruses** *or* **papyri** [-raɪ]) *n* papyrus *m*

par [pɑː(r)] (*pt & pp* **parred**, *cont* **parring**) **1** *n* (**a**) *(equality)* égalité *f*; **to be on a par (with sb/sth)** être au même niveau (que qn/qch); **you can't put him on a par with Mozart!** tu ne peux pas le comparer à Mozart!
(**b**) *(normal, average)* normale *f*, moyenne *f*; **I'm feeling a bit below** *or* **under par these days** je ne me sens pas en forme ces jours-ci; **the film isn't really up to par** le film n'est pas aussi bon qu'on aurait pu s'y attendre
(**c**) *Golf* par *m*; **a par-three (hole)** un par trois; **she got a par 4** elle a fait un par 4; **she was two under/over par** elle était à deux coups en-dessous/au-dessus du par; **the par for the course is 72** le par du parcours est de 72; *Fam Fig* **that's about par for the course** c'est ce à quoi il faut s'attendre ❑; **his behaviour was about par for the course** son comportement n'a rien eu de vraiment surprenant ❑
(**d**) *Fin & St Exch (of bills, shares)* pair *m*; **above/below par** au-dessus/au-dessous du pair; **at par** au pair; **close to par** au voisinage de la parité; **to issue shares at par** émettre des actions au pair
2 *vt Golf (hole)* faire le par à
▶▶ *Fin & St Exch* ***par bond*** obligation *f* émise au pair; *Fin & St Exch* ***par of exchange*** pair *m* du change; *Fin & St Exch* ***par value*** valeur *f* au pair *ou* nominale

para ['pærə] *n* (**a**) *(abbr* **paragraph***)* par. (**b**) *Fam Mil (abbr* **paratrooper***)* para *m*

para- ['pærə] *pref* para-

parabasis [pə'ræbəsɪs] *n Literature* parabase *f*

parabiosis [,pærəbaɪ'əʊsɪs] *n Biol* parabiose *f*

parablast ['pærəblæst] *n Biol* parablaste *m*

parable ['pærəbəl] *n Rel & Fig* parabole *f*

parabola [pə'ræbələ] *n Math* parabole *f*

parabolic [,pærə'bɒlɪk] *adj Math & Literature* parabolique
▶▶ *TV* ***parabolic dish*** antenne *f* parabolique, parabole *f*

parabolically [,pærə'bɒlɪklɪ] *adv Math & Literature* paraboliquement

parabolist [pə'ræbəlɪst] *n* paraboliste *mf*

paraboloid [pə'ræbəlɔɪd] *n Geom* paraboloïde *m*

parabrake ['pærəbreɪk] *n* parachute *m* de freinage

Paracelsus [,pærə'selsəs] *pr n* Paracelse

paracentesis [,pærəsen'tiːsɪs] *n Med* paracentèse *f*

paracetamol [,pærə'siːtəmɒl] *n* paracétamol *m*; **take two paracetamol** *or* **paracetamols** prenez deux cachets de paracétamol

parachronism [pæ'rækrənɪzəm] *n* parachronisme *m*

parachute ['pærəʃuːt] **1** *n* parachute *m*; **to drop sb/sth by parachute** larguer qn/qch par parachute, parachuter qn/qch
2 *comp (harness)* de parachute; *(troops, regiment)* de parachutistes
3 *vt* parachuter
4 *vi* sauter en parachute; **they parachuted into occupied France** ils se sont fait parachuter en France occupée
▶▶ *Can Pol* ***parachuted candidate*** candidat *m* parachuté; ***parachute drop*** parachutage *m*; ***parachute jump*** saut *m* en parachute; **to make a parachute jump** sauter en parachute; ***parachute landing*** technique *f* d'atterrissage *(en parachutisme)*; ***parachute pack*** *(parachute)* parachute *m* (plié et prêt à servir); *(container)* enveloppe *f ou* sac *m* de parachute

▶**parachute in 1** *vt sep (troops, supplies etc)* parachuter, envoyer par parachute
2 *vi* descendre en parachute

parachuting ['pærəʃuːtɪŋ] *n (of person, supplies)* parachutage *m*; *Sport* parachutisme *m*; **to go parachuting** faire du parachutisme

parachutist ['pærəʃuːtɪst] *n* parachutiste *mf*

Paraclete ['pærəkliːt] *n Rel* **the Paraclete** le Paraclet

paraclinical [,pærə'klɪnɪkəl] *adj* paraclinique

parade [pə'reɪd] **1** *n* (**a**) *(procession)* défilé *m*; **fashion parade** défilé *m* de mode
(**b**) *Mil (on parade ground)* exercice *m*; *(procession)* défilé *m*, parade *f*; **to be on parade** *(on parade ground)* à l'exercice; **to go on parade** *(in procession)* défiler
(**c**) *(along beach)* boulevard *m*; **a parade of shops** une rangée de magasins
(**d**) *(show, ostentation)* étalage *m*; **to make a parade of one's grief** faire étalage de son chagrin; **a parade of force** une démonstration de force; **a street where you'll see all the new fashions on parade** une rue où l'on arbore toutes les dernières créations de la mode; **all the world leaders were on parade** il y avait tout une panoplie de chefs d'états
(**e**) *(in fencing)* parade *f*
(**f**) *(at a racecourse)* terrain *m* de manœuvres
2 *vi* (**a**) *(march → gen) & Mil* défiler; **supporters paraded through the streets** les supporters défilaient dans les rues
(**b**) *(show off)* se pavaner, parader; **the cockerel was parading up and down** le coq allait et venait en se pavanant; **he was parading up and down as if he owned the place** il se pavanait comme s'il était chez lui
3 *vt* (**a**) *(troops, prisoners etc)* faire défiler; **the prisoners were paraded through the streets** on fit défiler les prisonniers dans les rues
(**b**) *(streets)* défiler dans
(**c**) *(show off)* faire étalage de; **he likes to parade his knowledge** il aime faire étalage de ses connaissances
▶▶ *Horseracing* ***parade ring*** terrain *m* de manœuvres

paradigm ['pærədaɪm] *n* paradigme *m*
▶▶ ***paradigm shift*** changement *m* radical

paradigmatic [,pærədɪg'mætɪk] *adj* paradigmatique

paradisaical [,pærədɪ'seɪkəl] *adj* paradisiaque, édénique

paradise ['pærədaɪs] *n* (**a**) *(heaven)* paradis *m*; *(Eden)* le paradis terrestre; **to go to Paradise** aller *ou* monter au paradis
(**b**) *Fig* paradis *m*; **it's paradise (here) on earth** c'est le paradis sur terre; **a whole week away from the kids was paradise!** une semaine entière loin des enfants, quel paradis!; **this river is a fisherman's paradise** cette rivière est le paradis des pêcheurs
▶▶ *Ich* ***paradise fish*** paradisier *m*, poisson-paradis *m*

'Paradise Lost' *Milton* 'Le Paradis perdu'

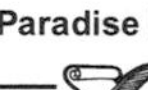

'Paradise Regained' *Milton* 'Le Paradis reconquis'

paradisiac [,pærə'dɪsɪæk], **paradisiacal** [,pærədɪ'saɪəkəl] *adj* paradisiaque, édénique

paradoctor ['pærədɒktə(r)] *n* = médecin qui atteint des endroits isolés en s'y faisant parachuter

parados ['pærədɒs] *n Archit* parados *m*

paradox ['pærədɒks] *n* paradoxe *m*

paradoxical [,pærə'dɒksɪkəl] *adj* paradoxal
▶▶ ***paradoxical sleep*** sommeil *m* paradoxal

paradoxically [,pærə'dɒksɪklɪ] *adv* paradoxalement

paraesthesia, *Am* **paresthesia** [,pærɪs'θiːʒə] *n Med* paresthésie *f*

paraffin ['pærəfɪn] **1** *n* (**a**) *Br (fuel → for lamp)* pétrole *m*; *(→ for stove)* mazout *m*; *(→ for aircraft)* kérosène *m* (**b**) *Chem (alkane)* paraffine *f*, alcane *m* (**c**) *(paraffin wax)* paraffine *f*
2 *vt* paraffiner
3 *comp (heater)* à mazout
▶▶ ***paraffin lamp*** lampe *f* à pétrole; ***paraffin stove*** poêle *m* à mazout; ***paraffin wax*** paraffine *f*

paraform ['pærəfɔːm] *n Chem* paraforme *m*

paraformaldehyde [,pærəfɔː'mældɪhaɪd] *n Chem* paraformaldéhyde *m*

paragenesis [,pærə'dʒenɪsɪs] *n Geol* paragénèse *f*

paraglider ['pærəglaɪdə(r)] *n* (**a**) *(person)* parapentiste *mf* (**b**) *(parachute)* parapente *m*

paragliding ['pærə,glaɪdɪŋ] *n* parapente *m*; **to go paragliding** faire du parapente

paragon ['pærəgən] *n* modèle *m*; **a paragon of virtue** un modèle *ou* un parangon de vertu

paragraph ['pærəgrɑːf] **1** *n* (**a**) *(in writing)* paragraphe *m*, alinéa *m*; **new paragraph** *(when dictating)* (allez) à la ligne; **to start a new paragraph** aller à la ligne; **section A, paragraph 3 (of the contract)** article A, alinéa 3 (du contrat)
(**b**) *(short article)* entrefilet *m*
(**c**) *Typ (mark)* pied *m* de mouche, alinéa *m*
2 *vt* diviser en paragraphes *ou* en alinéas

►► *Comput* ***paragraph break*** fin *f* de paragraphe; ***paragraph format*** format *m* de paragraphe; *Typ* ***paragraph mark*** pied *m* de mouche, alinéa *m*

paragraphia [ˌpærəˈgræfɪə] *n Psy* paragraphie *f*

Paraguay [ˈpærəgwaɪ] *n* Paraguay *m*; **in Paraguay** au Paraguay

Paraguayan [ˌpærəˈgwaɪən] **1** *n* Paraguayen(-enne) *m,f*

2 *adj* paraguayen

3 *comp (embassy, history)* du Paraguay

parahydrogen [ˌpærəˈhaɪdrədʒən] *n Chem* parahydrogène *m*

parakeet [ˈpærəkiːt] *n Orn* perruche *f*

paralalia [ˌpærəˈleɪlɪə] *n Med* paralalie *f*

paralanguage [ˈpærəˌlæŋgwɪdʒ] *n* paralangage *m*

paraldehyde [pəˈrældɪhaɪd] *n Chem* paraldéhyde *m*

paralegal [ˈpærəˌliːgəl] *n Am* assistant(e) *m,f (d'un avocat)*

paraleipsis [ˌpærəˈlaɪpsɪs] *n Literature* paralipse *f*

paralexia [ˌpærəˈleksɪə] *n Med* paralexie *f*

paralinguistic [ˌpærəlɪŋˈgwɪstɪk] *adj* paralinguistique

paralinguistics [ˌpærəlɪŋˈgwɪstɪks] *n (UNCOUNT)* paralinguistique *f*

paralipsis [ˌpærəˈlɪpsɪs] *(pl* **paralipses** [-siːz]) *n Literature* paralipse *f*

parallactic [ˌpærəˈlæktɪk] *adj Astron, Geom & Phot* parallactique

parallax [ˈpærəlæks] *n Astron, Geom & Phot* parallaxe *f*

parallel [ˈpærəlel] **1** *adj* (**a**) *(gen) & Math* parallèle (**to** *ou* **with** à); **there is a ditch parallel with** *or* **to the fence** il y a un fossé qui longe la clôture; **to run parallel to sth** longer qch

(**b**) *(analogous)* pareil, semblable; *(case, situation)* analogue (**to** *ou* **with** à); **a parallel investigation was mounted in England and Scotland** une enquête a été menée simultanément en Angleterre et en Écosse

(**c**) *Comput* parallèle

2 *n* (**a**) *(equivalent)* équivalent *m*; *(similarity)* ressemblance *f*, similitude *f*; **there are obvious parallels between the two cases** les deux cas présentent des similitudes frappantes; **a tradition which has no parallel in our own culture** une tradition qui n'a pas d'équivalent dans notre culture; **the two industries have developed in parallel** ces deux industries se sont développées en parallèle; **the disaster is without parallel** une telle catastrophe est sans précédent; **in parallel to** *or* **with sth** parallèlement à qch

(**b**) *(comparison)* parallèle *m*; **to draw a parallel between** faire *ou* établir un parallèle entre

(**c**) *Math (ligne f)* parallèle *f*

(**d**) *Geog & Astron* parallèle *m*; **the 48th parallel** le 48ème parallèle

(**e**) *Elec* parallèle *m*; **in parallel** en parallèle; **out of parallel** déphasé, hors de phase

(**f**) *Mil (trench) (tranchée f)* parallèle *f*

3 *vt* (**a**) *(run parallel to)* être parallèle à, longer

(**b**) *(be similar to)* être analogue à; **his career has paralleled his father's** sa carrière a suivi une trajectoire semblable à celle de son père

(**c**) *(equal)* égaler; **the victory has not been paralleled** cette victoire est restée sans égal

4 *adv* **to ski parallel, to parallel ski** skier parallèle; **to parallel park** faire un créneau

►► ***parallel bars*** barres *fpl* parallèles; *Elec* ***parallel circuit*** circuit *m* en parallèle; ***parallel computer*** ordinateur *m* à traitement parallèle; *Elec* ***parallel connection*** couplage *m ou* montage *m* en parallèle *ou* en dérivation; ***parallel importing*** importations *fpl* parallèles; *Comput* ***parallel interface*** interface *f* parallèle; ***parallel lines*** lignes *fpl* parallèles; *Fin* ***parallel market*** marché *m* parallèle; ***parallel parking*** stationnement *m* en créneau; *Comput* ***parallel port*** port *m* parallèle; ***parallel printer*** imprimante *f* en parallèle; *Comput* ***parallel processing*** traitement *m* en parallèle *or* en simultanéité; *Fin* ***parallel rate of exchange*** cours *m* parallèle; ***parallel ruler*** règle *f* parallèle, règles *fpl* parallèles; *Mktg* ***parallel selling*** vente *f* parallèle; *Ski* ***parallel slalom*** slalom *m* parallèle; *Ski* ***parallel turn*** virage *m* en parallèle

parallelepiped [ˌpærəleləˈpaɪped] *n Geom* parallélépipède *m*

parallelepipedal [ˌpærəleləˈpaɪpedəl] *adj Geom* parallélépipédique

parallelism [ˈpærəlelɪzəm] *n* parallélisme *m*

parallelogram [ˌpærəˈleləgræm] *n Geom* parallélogramme *m*

paralogism [ˈpærələdʒɪzəm] *n* paralogisme *m*

Paralympics [ˌpærəˈlɪmpɪks] *npl* **the Paralympics** les jeux *mpl* Paralympiques

paralysation, *Am* **paralyzation** [ˌpærəlaɪˈzeɪʃən] *n (of city, industry etc)* paralysie *f*, immobilisation *f*

paralyse, *Am* **paralyze** [ˈpærəlaɪz] *vt* (**a**) *Med* paralyser (**b**) *Fig (city, industry etc)* paralyser, immobiliser; *(person)* paralyser, pétrifier

paralysed, *Am* **paralyzed** [ˈpærəlaɪzd] *adj* (**a**) *Med* paralysé; **both his legs are paralysed, he's paralysed in both legs** il est paralysé des deux jambes, il a les deux jambes paralysées (**b**) *Fig (city, industry etc)* paralysé, immobilisé; *(person)* paralysé, pétrifié; **paralysed with** *or* **by shyness** paralysé par la timidité; **paralysed with fear** paralysé par l'effroi, glacé d'effroi

paralyser, *Am* **paralyzer** [ˈpærəˌlaɪzə(r)] *n Med* agent *m* paralysateur

paralysing, *Am* **paralyzing** [ˈpærəˌlaɪzɪŋ] *adj Med & Fig* paralysant

paralysis [pəˈrælɪsɪs] *n* (**a**) *Med* paralysie *f* (**b**) *Fig (of industry, business)* immobilisation *f*; *(of government)* paralysie *f*

paralytic [ˌpærəˈlɪtɪk] **1** *adj* (**a**) *Med* paralytique (**b**) *Br Fam (very drunk)* pété à mort, bourré comme un coing

2 *n Med* paralytique *mf*

►► ***paralytic stroke*** attaque *f* de paralysie

paralytically [ˌpærəˈlɪtɪklɪ] *adv Br Fam* **paralytically drunk** pété à mort, bourré comme un coing

paralyze, paralyzed *etc Am* = **paralyse, paralysed** *etc*

paramagnetic [ˌpærəmægˈnetɪk] *adj Phys* paramagnétique; **nuclear paramagnetic resonance** résonance *f* paramagnétique nucléaire

paramagnetism [ˌpærəˈmægnɪtɪzəm] *n Phys* paramagnétisme *m*

paramatta [ˌpærəˈmætə] *n Tex* paramatta *m*

paramecium [ˌpærəˈmiːsɪəm] *n Zool* paramécie *f*

paramedic [ˌpærəˈmedɪk] **1** *n* auxiliaire *mf* médical(e); *Am* **the paramedics** les services *mpl* de secours, ≃ le SAMU

2 *adj* paramédical

paramedical [ˌpærəˈmedɪkəl] *adj* paramédical

parameter [pəˈræmɪtə(r)] *n (gen) & Ling, Math & Comput* paramètre *m*; **to set the parameters of sth** paramétrer qch; **we must take all the parameters into account** il faut prendre en compte tous les paramètres; **within the parameters of the enquiry** dans les limites fixées par les paramètres de l'enquête

paramilitary [ˌpærəˈmɪlɪtrɪ] *(pl* **paramilitaries**) **1** *adj* paramilitaire

2 *n (group)* formation *f* paramilitaire; *(person)* membre *m* d'une formation paramilitaire

3 *npl* **the paramilitary** la milice

paramnesia [ˌpæræmˈniːzɪə] *n Med* paramnésie *f*

paramount [ˈpærəmaʊnt] *adj* (**a**) *(asset, necessity, concern)* primordial; **it is of paramount importance** c'est d'une importance primordiale; **it is paramount that we do this** il est primordial que nous fassions ceci; **the children's interests are paramount** l'intérêt des enfants passe avant tout (**b**) *(ruler)* suprême

paramour [ˈpærəˌmʊə(r)] *n Literary or Hum (man)* amant *m*; *(woman)* maîtresse *f*

paraneoplastic [ˌpærəniːəʊˈplæstɪk] *adj Med* paranéoplasique

►► ***paraneoplastic syndrome*** syndrome *m* paranéoplasique

parang [ˈpɑːræŋ] *n* couteau *m* malais

paranoia [ˌpærəˈnɔɪə] *n (UNCOUNT)* paranoïa *f*

paranoiac [ˌpærəˈnɔɪæk], **paranoic** [ˌpærəˈnəʊɪk] **1** *adj* paranoïaque

2 *n* paranoïaque *mf*

paranoid [ˈpærənɔɪd] **1** *adj (disorder, delusion)* paranoïde; *(person)* paranoïaque; *Fig* **he's paranoid about being cheated** il est obsédé par l'idée qu'on cherche à l'avoir; **you're being paranoid** tu es parano; **I know it'll sound paranoid, but...** je suis sûr que tu vas me trouver parano mais...

2 *n* paranoïaque *mf*

paranormal [ˌpærəˈnɔːməl] **1** *adj* paranormal

2 *n* **the paranormal** le paranormal

paranym [ˈpærənɪm] *n Ling* quasi-synonyme *m*

parapenting [ˈpærəˌpentɪŋ] *n* parapente *f*

parapet [ˈpærəpet] *n* (**a**) *Mil (in fortress)* parapet *m*; *(of trench)* berge *f* (**b**) *(wall)* parapet *m*; *(railing)* garde-fou *m*; *(of bridge)* garde-corps *m inv*

paraph [ˈpærəf] *n* paraphe *m (en fin de signature)*

paraphasia [ˌpærəˈfeɪzɪə] *n Med* paraphasie *f*

paraphernalia [ˌpærəfəˈneɪlɪə] *n (UNCOUNT)* (**a**) *(equipment)* attirail *m*; *(belongings)* fourbi *m*; **his skis, poles and other paraphernalia** ses skis, ses bâtons et le reste de son attirail (**b**) *Fam (trappings)* tralala *m*; **it was a society wedding with all the paraphernalia** ce fut un mariage mondain avec tout le tralala (**c**) *Law* biens *mpl* paraphernaux

paraphimosis [ˌpærəfɪˈməʊsɪs] *n Med* paraphimosis *m*

paraphrase [ˈpærəfreɪz] **1** *n* paraphrase *f*

2 *vt* paraphraser

paraphrastic [ˌpærəˈfræstɪk] *adj* paraphrastique

paraphrenia [ˌpærəˈfriːnɪə] *n Psy* paraphrénie *f*

paraplegia [ˌpærəˈpliːdʒə] *n Med* paraplégie *f*

paraplegic [ˌpærəˈpliːdʒɪk] *Med* **1** *adj* paraplégique

2 *n* paraplégique *mf*

parapodium [ˌpærəˈpəʊdɪəm] *n Zool* parapode *m*

parapraxis [ˌpærəˈpræksɪs] *n Psy* acte *m* manqué

parapsychological [ˌpærəsaɪkəˈlɒdʒɪkəl] *adj* parapsychique, parapsychologique

parapsychologist [ˌpærəsaɪˈkɒlədʒɪst] *n* parapsychologue *mf*

parapsychology [ˌpærəsaɪˈkɒlədʒɪ] *n* parapsychologie *f*

Paraquat® [ˈpærəkwɒt] *n* Paraquat® *m*

parasailing [ˈpærəˌseɪlɪŋ] *n* parachute *m ou* parachutisme *m* ascensionnel *(tracté par bateau)*

parascending [ˈpærəˌsendɪŋ] *n* parachute *m ou* parachutisme *m* ascensionnel *(tracté par véhicule)*

parascience [ˈpærəˌsaɪəns] *n (UNCOUNT)* études *fpl* parascientifiques

paraselene [ˌpærəsəˈliːnɪ] *n Astron* parasélène *f*

parasexuality [ˌpærəseksjʊˈælɪtɪ] *n Biol* parasexualité *f*

parasite [ˈpærəsaɪt] *n* (**a**) *Biol* parasite *m* (**b**) *Fig (person)* parasite *m*; **he's such a parasite!** c'est un vrai parasite!; **to be a parasite on society** *(person)* parasiter la société

parasitic [ˌpærəˈsɪtɪk], **parasitical** [ˌpærəˈsɪtɪkəl] *adj* (**a**) *Biol* parasite; **to be parasitic on an organism** parasiter un organisme (**b**) *Fig (person)* parasite; *(existence)* de parasite (**c**) *(illness → caused by parasites)* parasitaire

►► ***parasitic disease*** maladie *f* parasitaire

parasiticidal [ˌpærəsɪtɪˈsaɪdəl] *adj Biol* parasiticide

parasiticide [ˌpærəˈsɪtɪsaɪd] *n Biol* parasiticide *m*

parasitism [ˈpærəsaɪˌtɪzəm] *n Biol* parasitisme *m*

parasitize, -ise [ˈpærəsɪtaɪz] *vt Biol* parasiter

parasitologist [ˌpærəsaɪˈtɒlədʒɪst] *n Biol* parasitologue *mf*

parasitology [ˌpærəsaɪˈtɒlədʒɪ] *n Biol* parasitologie *f*

parasitosis [ˌpærəsɪˈtəʊsɪs] *n Med* parasitose *f*

parasol [ˈpærəsɒl] *n (for woman)* ombrelle *f*; *(for beach, table)* parasol *m*

►► *Bot* ***parasol mushroom*** coulemelle *f*, lépiote *f*; ***parasol pine*** pin *m* parasol

parasuicide [ˌpærəˈsuːɪsaɪd] *n (act)* pseudo-tentative *f* de suicide; *(person)* = personne qui fait une pseudo-tentative de suicide

parasympathetic [ˈpærəˌsɪmpəˈθetɪk] *Med* **1** *adj* parasympathique

2 *n* **the parasympathetic** le parasympathique

►► ***parasympathetic nerve*** nerf *m* parasympathique

parasympatholytic [ˈpærəˌsɪmpæθeˈlɪtɪk] *Med* **1** *adj* parasympatholytique

2 *n* parasympatholytique *m*

parasympathomimetic [ˈpærəˌsɪmpæθemɪˈmetɪk] *Med* **1** *adj* parasympathomimétique

2 *n* parasympathomimétique *m*

par-par

parasynthesis [ˌpærə'sɪnθəsɪs] *n Ling* dérivation *f* parasynthétique

parasynthetic [ˌpærəsɪn'θetɪk] *adj Ling* parasynthétique

parasyntheton [ˌpærə'sɪnθətɒn] *n Ling* parasynthétique *m*

paratactic [ˌpærə'tæktɪk] *adj Gram* paratactique

parataxis [ˌpærə'tæksɪs] *n Gram* parataxe *f*, juxtaposition *f*

paratha [pə'rɑːtə] *n Culin* paratha *m*

parathormone [ˌpærə'θɔːməʊn] *n Physiol* parathormone *f*

parathyroid [ˌpærə'θaɪrɔɪd] *Anat* **1** *adj* parathyroïdien
2 *n* parathyroïde *f*
►► ***parathyroid gland*** parathyroïde *f*

paratroop ['pærətruːp] *Mil* **1** *comp* de parachutistes; *(regiment)* parachutiste, de parachutistes; *(commander)* parachutiste
2 paratroops *npl* parachutistes *mpl*

paratrooper ['pærətruːpə(r)] *n Mil* parachutiste *m*

paratyphoid [ˌpærə'taɪfɔɪd] *Med* **1** *n* paratyphoïde *f*
2 *adj (bacillus)* paratyphique
►► ***parathyroid fever*** paratyphoïde *f*

paravane ['pærəveɪn] *n Naut* paravane *m*, appareil *m* pare-mines; **to get in/out the paravanes** rentrer/mettre à l'eau les paravanes

parawalker ['pærəwɔːkə(r)] *n* parawalker *m (orthèse permettant aux paraplégiques de se déplacer)*

paraxial [pæ'ræksɪəl] *adj Opt* paraxial

parboil ['pɑːbɔɪl] *vt Culin* faire bouillir pendant quelques minutes

Parcae ['pɑːsaɪ] *npl Myth* **the Parcae** les Parques *fpl*

parcel ['pɑːsəl] (*Br pt & pp* **parcelled,** *cont* **parcelling,** *Am pt & pp* **parceled,** *cont* **parceling**) **1** *n* (**a**) *(package)* colis *m*, paquet *m*; **to send sth by parcel post** envoyer qch par colis postal *or* en paquet-poste
(**b**) *(portion of land)* parcelle *f*
(**c**) *(group → gen)* groupe *m*, lot *m*; *(→ of shares)* paquet *m*; **a parcel of rogues** une bande de gredins
(**d**) *(integral part)* partie *f* (intégrante)
(**e**) *Culin* chausson *m*
2 *vt* (**a**) *(wrap up)* emballer, faire un colis de
(**b**) *(divide up)* diviser en parcelles
►► ***parcel bomb*** colis *m* piégé; ***parcel delivery*** livraison *f* de colis à domicile; ***parcel(s) office*** bureau *m* des messageries, messageries *fpl*; ***parcel rates*** tarif *m* colis postal; *Aut* ***parcel shelf*** tablette *f*

►**parcel out** *vt sep* (**a**) *(share out)* distribuer, partager
(**b**) *(divide up → land)* diviser en parcelles, lotir

►**parcel up** *vt sep* emballer, mettre en colis

parch [pɑːtʃ] *vt* (**a**) *(scorch)* dessécher, brûler; **the sun had parched the hills** le soleil avait brûlé les collines (**b**) *(usu passive) (make thirsty)* assoiffer (**c**) *Culin* griller légèrement

parched [pɑːtʃt] *adj* (**a**) *(grass, earth)* desséché; *(throat, lips)* sec (sèche) (**b**) *Fam (person)* **I'm parched** je crève de soif

Parcheesi® [pɑː'tʃiːzɪ] *n Am* ≃ (jeu *m* des) petits chevaux *mpl*

parchment ['pɑːtʃmənt] *n (material, document)* parchemin *m*; **skin like parchment** peau *f* parcheminée

pard [pɑːd], **pardner** ['pɑːdnə(r)] *n Am Fam* copain (copine) *m,f*

pardon ['pɑːdən] **1** *vt* (**a**) *(forgive → fault)* pardonner; *(→ person)* pardonner à; **to pardon sb for sth** pardonner qch à qn; **please pardon my rudeness** veuillez excuser mon impolitesse; **pardon me for asking, but...** excusez-moi de vous poser cette question, mais...; *Ironic* **pardon me for speaking!** hou là là, excuse-moi d'avoir osé m'exprimer!; **pardon me for breathing!** excuse-moi d'avoir osé ouvrir la bouche!; **you could be pardoned for thinking so** il est facile de croire cela
(**b**) *Law* gracier
(**c**) *Rel (person)* absoudre; *(sin)* pardonner; **to pardon sb sth** absoudre qn de qch
2 *n* (**a**) *(forgiveness)* pardon *m*
(**b**) *Law* grâce *f*; *(document)* lettre *f* de grâce; **free pardon** grâce *f*; **he was granted a pardon** il fut gracié
(**c**) *Rel* indulgence *f*
3 *exclam* **pardon (me)?** *(what?)* pardon?, comment?; **pardon (me)!** *(sorry)* pardon!, excusez-moi!

pardonable ['pɑːdənəbəl] *adj* (**a**) *(forgivable)* pardonnable, excusable (**b**) *Law* graciable

pardonably ['pɑːdənəblɪ] *adv* de façon bien pardonnable *ou* excusable

pardoner ['pɑːdənə(r)] *n* (**a**) *(person who pardons)* pardonneur(euse) *mf* (**b**) *Hist* vendeur *m* d'indulgences

pare [peə(r)] *vt* (**a**) *(fruit, vegetable)* peler, éplucher; *(nails)* ronger, couper; *(horseshoe)* parer; **pare the rind off the cheese** enlever la croûte du fromage
(**b**) *(reduce → budget)* réduire; **staff levels have already been pared to the bone** on a déjà réduit les effectifs au minimum

►**pare down** *vt sep (expenses, activity)* réduire; *(text, speech)* raccourcir; **we've got to pare the report down to fifty pages** il va falloir ramener le rapport à cinquante pages; **the budget has been pared down to the bone** le budget a été réduit *ou* ramené au strict minimum

paregoric [ˌpærɪ'gɒrɪk] **1** *n* parégorique *m*
2 *adj* parégorique

parencephalon [ˌpæren'sefəlɒn] *n Anat* cervelet *m*

parenchyma [pə'reŋkɪmə] *n Anat & Bot* parenchyme *m*

parenchymal [pə'reŋkɪməl] *adj Anat & Bot* parenchymal

parent ['peərənt] **1** *n* (**a**) *(mother)* mère *f*; *(father)* père *m*; **parents** parents *mpl*; **when you first become a parent** quand on devient père/mère; **Janet and Angus have become parents** Janet et Angus ont eu un enfant; **the parent-child relationship** la relation parents-enfant; **each parent should...** le père et la mère devraient...; **if neither parent can attend the meeting** si ni le père ni la mère ne peuvent assister à la réunion
(**b**) *Phys* parent *m*
2 *comp* (**a**) *(cooperation, participation)* des parents, parental
(**b**) *(organization)* mère
(**c**) *(animal)* parent; **one of the parent birds/seals** un des parents de l'oiseau/du phoque
►► ***parent act*** loi-cadre *f*; *Com* ***parent company*** société *f ou* maison *f* mère; ***parent plant*** plante *f* mère; **cuttings from the parent plant** des boutures *fpl* de la plante mère; ***parent tree*** arbre *m* d'origine

parentage ['peərəntɪdʒ] *n* origine *f*; **a child of unknown parentage** un(e) enfant de père et mère inconnus; **children of racially mixed parentage** des enfants *mpl* issus de mariages mixtes

parental [pə'rentəl] *adj* parental, des parents
►► ***parental guidance*** contrôle *m* parental

parentally [pə'rentəlɪ] *adv* comme des parents

parenteral [pə'rentərəl] *adj Med* parentéral

parenthesis [pə'renθɪsɪs] (*pl* **parentheses** [-siːz]) *n* parenthèse *f*; **in parentheses** entre parenthèses

parenthesize, -ise [pə'renθɪsaɪz] *vt (word, explanation)* mettre entre parenthèses

parenthetic [ˌpærən'θetɪk], **parenthetical** [ˌpærən'θetɪkəl] *adj* entre parenthèses
►► *Gram* ***parenthetic clause*** incidente *f*

parenthetically [ˌpærən'θetɪklɪ] *adv* entre parenthèses

parenthood ['peərənthʊd] *n (fatherhood)* paternité *f*; *(motherhood)* maternité *f*; **the responsibilities of parenthood** les responsabilités *fpl* parentales

parenting ['peərəntɪŋ] *n (art)* art *m* d'être parent; *(activity)* métier *m* de parent; **the problems of parenting** les problèmes qu'on a quand on est parent *ou* quand on a des enfants; **I put it down to bad parenting** d'après moi, c'est parce que les parents remplissent mal leur rôle
►► ***parenting skills*** capacités *fpl* à élever des enfants

parentless ['peərəntlɪs] *adj* sans père ni mère, orphelin

parent-teacher association *n* = association regroupant les parents d'élèves et les enseignants

pareo [pæ'reɪəʊ] *n* paréo *m*

parer ['peərə(r)] *n* économe *m*

paresis [pæ'riːsɪs] *n Med* parésie *f*; **(general) paresis** paralysie *f* générale

paresthesia *Am* = **paraesthesia**

parfait ['pɑːfeɪ] *n Culin* parfait *m*

parget ['pɑːdʒɪt] *Constr* **1** *n (plaster)* plâtre *m*; *(ornamental)* crépi *m*
2 *vt (cover)* plâtrer; *(with ornamental plasterwork)* crépir

parheliacal [ˌpɑːhɪ'laɪəkəl], **parhelic** [pɑː'hiːlɪk] *adj Met* parélique, parhélique

parhelion [pɑː'hiːlɪən] (*pl* **parhelia** [-lɪə]) *n Met* parélie *m*, parhélie *m*

pariah [pə'raɪə] *n* paria *m*
►► ***pariah dog*** (chien *m*) paria *m*

Parian ['peərɪən] **1** *n (person)* Parien(ienne) *mf*
2 *adj* parien
►► *Cer* ***Parian biscuit*** parian *m*; ***Parian marble*** marbre *m* de Paros

parietal [pə'raɪɪtəl] **1** *adj Anat & Bot* pariétal
2 *n Anat* pariétal *m*

paring ['peərɪŋ] **1** *n (activity → of fruit, vegetables)* épluchage *m*; *(→ of nails)* fait *m* de ronger
2 parings *npl (of fruit, vegetables)* épluchures *fpl*, pelures *fpl*; *(of nails)* rognures *fpl*; *(of metal)* cisaille *f*
►► ***paring knife*** couteau *m* à légumes

pari passu [ˌpærɪ'pæsʊ] *adv* (**a**) *Literary* **to go pari passu with sth** marcher de pair avec qch (**b**) *Fin & St Exch* pari passu (**with** avec)

paripinnate [ˌpærɪ'pɪnət] *adj Bot* paripenné

Paris ['pærɪs] *n* (**a**) *(city)* Paris *m* (**b**) *Myth* Pâris
►► ***the Paris Basin*** le Bassin parisien; ***Paris green*** vert *m* de Scheele *(employé comme insecticide)*

parish ['pærɪʃ] **1** *n* (**a**) *Rel* paroisse *f*
(**b**) *Pol* ≃ commune *f (en Angleterre)*
2 *comp (funds) & Rel* paroissial
►► ***parish church*** église *f* paroissiale; ***parish clerk*** bedeau *m*; ***parish council*** ≃ conseil *m* municipal *(d'une petite commune, en Angleterre)*; ***parish hall*** salle *f* paroissiale; ***parish priest*** *(Catholic)* curé *m*; *(Protestant)* pasteur *m*; ***parish register*** registre *m* paroissial; ***parish school*** école *f* communale

parishioner [pə'rɪʃənə(r)] *n* paroissien(enne) *m,f*

parish-pump *adj Br Pej (parochial → issue)* d'intérêt purement local; *(→ outlook, mentality, quarrel)* de clocher

Parisian [pə'rɪzɪən] **1** *n* Parisien(enne) *m,f*
2 *adj* parisien

parison ['pærɪsən] *n* paraison *f*

parisyllabic [ˌpærɪsɪ'læbɪk] *adj* parisyllabe, parisyllabique

parity ['pærətɪ] (*pl* **parities**) *n* (**a**) *(equality)* égalité *f*, parité *f*; **we have achieved parity of productivity with Japan** nous avons atteint le niveau de productivité du Japon; **ambulance staff want parity with firemen** les ambulanciers veulent obtenir l'égalité de statut avec les pompiers
(**b**) *Econ & Fin* parité *f*; **the two currencies were at parity** les deux monnaies étaient à parité; **franc-dollar parity** parité *f* franc-dollar
(**c**) *(analogy)* **parity of reasoning** raisonnement *m* analogue
(**d**) *Comput, Math & Phys* parité *f*
►► *Comput* ***parity bit*** bit *m* de parité; ***parity error*** erreur *f* de parité; *Econ & Fin* ***parity of exchange*** parité *f* de change; ***parity ratio*** rapport *m* de parité; ***parity table*** table *f* des parités; ***parity value*** valeur *f* au pair

park [pɑːk] **1** *n* (**a**) *(public → large)* parc *m*; *(→ smaller)* jardin *m* public; *(private estate)* parc *m*, domaine *m*
(**b**) *Aut (on automatic gearbox)* position *f* (de) stationnement; **leave the car in park** laisse la voiture en position (de) stationnement
(**c**) *Br Fam Sport* **the park** le terrain
2 *vt* (**a**) *(car)* garer; **where can I park my car?** où est-ce que je peux garer ma voiture *ou* me garer?
(**b**) *Fam (dump → person, box)* laisser; **she parked her bags in the hall** elle a laissé ses sacs dans l'entrée; **to park oneself beside sb/on sth** se poser *ou* poser ses fesses à côté de qn/sur qch; **park your** *Br* **bum** *or Am* **butt over here**

par–par

beside me! pose tes fesses ici, à côté de moi!
(**c**) *(sheep)* parquer
(**d**) *Mil (artillery etc)* mettre en parc
(**e**) *Comput (hard disk)* parquer, effectuer le parcage de
(**f**) *St Exch* mettre en attente
3 *vi Aut* se garer, stationner; **I couldn't find anywhere to park** je n'ai pas trouvé à me garer
▸▸ *Br* ***park keeper*** *(of large park)* gardien(enne) *m,f* de parc; *(of smaller park)* gardien(enne) *m,f* de jardin public; ***Park Lane*** = avenue résidentielle très chic à Londres; ***park officer*** gardien(-enne) *m,f* de parc

parka [ˈpɑːkə] *n* parka *m*

park-and-ride *n* = système de contrôle de la circulation qui consiste à garer les voitures à l'extérieur des grandes villes, puis à utiliser les transports en commun

parked [pɑːkt] *adj (vehicle)* en stationnement, garé; **he was parked by a fire hydrant** il s'était garé devant une bouche d'incendie; **behind the parked coaches** derrière les cars en stationnement

parker [ˈpɑːkə(r)] *n* **she's a good parker** elle sait très bien faire les créneaux

Parkhurst [ˈpɑːkhɜːst] *n* **Parkhurst (prison)** = prison pour condamnés de longue durée située sur l'île de Wight

parkie [ˈpɑːkɪ] *n Br Fam (of large park)* gardien(-enne) *m,f* de parc □; *(of smaller park)* gardien(-enne) *m,f* de jardin public □

parkin [ˈpɑːkɪn] *n Br* ≃ pain *m* d'épice *ou* d'épices

parking [ˈpɑːkɪŋ] **1** *n* (**a**) *(of vehicle)* stationnement *m*; **no parking** *(sign)* stationnement interdit, défense de stationner; **parking is a problem in town** il est difficile de se garer *ou* de stationner en ville; **there's plenty of underground parking** il y a de nombreuses places dans les parkings souterrains; **I'm not very good at parking** je ne suis pas très doué pour me garer
(**b**) *St Exch* mise *f* en attente
2 *comp* de stationnement
▸▸ ***parking area*** aire *f* de stationnement, parking *m*; ***parking attendant*** *(in car park)* gardien(-enne) *m,f*; *(at hotel)* voiturier *m*; ***parking bay*** aire *f* de stationnement; *Am* ***parking brake*** frein *m* à main; ***parking fine*** amende *f* de stationnement; *Am* ***parking garage*** parking *m* couvert; ***parking light*** feu *m* de position; *Am* ***parking lot*** parking *m*, parc *m* de stationnement; ***parking meter*** parcmètre *m*, parcomètre *m*, *Can* compteur *m* de stationnement; *Astron* ***parking orbit*** orbite *f* d'attente; ***parking place, parking space*** place *f* de stationnement, *Suisse* place *f* de parc; **to look for/to find a parking place** chercher/trouver à se garer; ***parking ticket*** contravention *f (pour stationnement irrégulier)*, P-V *m*

parkinsonian [ˌpɑːkɪnˈsəʊnɪən] *adj Med* parkinsonien

parkinsonism [ˈpɑːkɪnsənɪzəm] *n Med* parkinsonisme *m*

Parkinson's disease, Parkinson's [ˈpɑːkɪnsənz-] *n* maladie *f* de Parkinson; **to have Parkinson's disease** avoir la maladie de Parkinson *ou* un parkinson

Parkinson's law *n Hum* principe *m* de Parkinson; **it's a case of Parkinson's law** plus on a de temps, plus on met de temps

parkland [ˈpɑːklænd] *n (UNCOUNT)* espace *m* vert, espaces *mpl* verts

parkway [ˈpɑːkweɪ] *n Am* grand boulevard *m* bordé d'arbres

parky [ˈpɑːkɪ] *(compar* **parkier**, *superl* **parkiest**) *adj Br Fam (cold)* frisquet; **it's parky today** il fait frisquet aujourd'hui

parlance [ˈpɑːləns] *n Formal* langage *m*, parler *m*; **in common parlance** dans la langue de tous les jours, en langage courant; **in legal parlance** en langage juridique; **in the parlance of the EU** dans le langage de l'Union européenne, selon les termes de l'Union européenne

parlay [ˈpɑːlɪ] *vt Am* (**a**) *(winnings)* remettre en jeu; **he parlayed everything on the red** il a tout misé sur le rouge (**b**) *Fig (talent, project)* mener à bien; *(money)* faire fructifier; **she parlayed the local newspapers into a press empire** elle a bâti un empire de presse à partir des journaux locaux

parley [ˈpɑːlɪ] **1** *vi* parlementer
2 *n* conférence *f*; *(with enemy)* pourparlers *mpl*

parleyvoo [ˌpɑːlɪˈvuː] *Fam Old-fashioned* **1** *n* (**a**) *(French language)* français □ *m* (**b**) *(person)* Français(e) □ *m,f*
2 *vi* **I don't parleyvoo** je ne parle pas français □

parliament [ˈpɑːləmənt] *n* parlement *m*; **Parliament has decided that...** le Parlement a décidé que...; **in Parliament** au Parlement; **she was elected to Parliament in 2001** elle a été élue député en 2001; **the French Parliament** l'Assemblée nationale (française)

parliamentarian [ˌpɑːləmenˈteərɪən] **1** *adj* parlementaire
2 *n* parlementaire *mf*

parliamentarianism [ˌpɑːləmenˈteərɪənɪzəm] *n* parlementarisme *m*

parliamentary [ˌpɑːləˈmentərɪ] *adj (system, debate, democracy)* parlementaire
▸▸ ***parliamentary candidate*** candidat *m* aux (élections) législatives; *Br* ***Parliamentary Commissioner (for Administration)*** médiateur(-trice) *m,f*; *Br* ***Parliamentary committee*** commission *f* parlementaire; ***parliamentary correspondent*** journaliste *mf* parlementaire; ***parliamentary elections*** élections *fpl* législatives; *Br* ***Parliamentary Labour Party*** députés *mpl* du Parti travailliste; ***parliamentary private secretary*** = en Grande-Bretagne, député qui assure la liaison entre un ministre et la Chambre des communes; ***parliamentary privilege*** immunité *f* parlementaire; ***parliamentary procedure*** procédure *f* parlementaire; *Br* ***parliamentary secretary*** ≃ sous-secrétaire *m* d'État

parlour, *Am* **parlor** [ˈpɑːlə(r)] *n* (**a**) *Old-fashioned (in house)* salon *m* (**b**) *Old-fashioned (in hotel, club)* salon *m*; *(in pub)* arrière-salle *f* (**c**) *(in convent)* parloir *m* (**d**) *Am Com* **beer parlour** bar *m*; **billiard parlour** salle *f* de billard; **ice-cream parlour** salon *m* de dégustation de glaces
▸▸ *Am Rail* ***parlor car*** pullman *m (dans un train)*; *Br* ***parlour game*** jeu *m* de société

parlourmaid [ˈpɑːləmeɪd] *n* bonne *f (affectée au service de table)*

parlous [ˈpɑːləs] *adj Arch or Literary (state)* précaire; *(situation)* périlleux

Parma [ˈpɑːmə] *n* Parme
▸▸ ***Parma ham*** jambon *m* de Parme; ***Parma violet*** violette *f* de Parme

Parmesan (cheese) [ˌpɑːmɪˈzæn-] *n* parmesan *m*

Parnassian [pɑːˈnæsɪən] **1** *adj* parnassien
2 *n* parnassien(enne) *m,f*

Parnassus [pɑːˈnæsəs] *n* Parnasse *m*; **(Mount) Parnassus** le (mont) Parnasse

paroccipital [pærɒkˈsɪpɪtəl] *adj Anat* situé près de l'occiput

parochial [pəˈrəʊkɪəl] *adj* (**a**) *Rel* paroissial (**b**) *Pej* borné; **parochial attitudes** attitudes *fpl* de clocher *ou* bornées
▸▸ *Am* ***parochial school*** école *f* religieuse

parochialism [pəˈrəʊkɪəlɪzəm] *n Pej* esprit *m* de clocher, étroitesse *f* d'esprit

parodist [ˈpærədɪst] *n* parodiste *mf*

parodontal [ˌpærəˈdɒntəl] *adj* parodontal
▸▸ *Anat* ***parodontal tissue*** parodonte *m*

parody [ˈpærədɪ] *(pl* **parodies**, *pt & pp* **parodied**) **1** *n* parodie *f*, pastiche *m*; *(of truth)* travestissement *m*
2 *vt* parodier, pasticher

parole [pəˈrəʊl] **1** *n* (**a**) *Law* liberté *f* conditionnelle *ou* sur parole; **to be released** *or* **put on parole** être mis en liberté conditionnelle, être libéré conditionnellement; **to break one's parole** manquer à sa parole; **he's up for parole next year** il devrait être mis en liberté conditionnelle l'année prochaine
(**b**) *Am Mil (password)* mot *m* de passe
(**c**) *Ling* parole *f*
2 *vt* mettre en liberté conditionnelle, libérer sur parole
▸▸ ***parole board*** ≃ comité *m* de probation et d'assistance aux libérés

parolee [pərəʊˈliː] *n Am* prisonnier(ère) *m,f* en liberté conditionnelle

paronomasia [ˌpærənəˈmeɪzɪə] *n* paronomase *f*

paronym [ˈpærənɪm] *n* paronyme *m*

parotid [pəˈrɒtɪd] *Med* **1** *adj* parotidien *m*
2 *n* (glande *f*) parotide *f*
▸▸ ***parotid gland*** (glande *f*) parotide *f*

Parousia [pəˈruːzɪə] *n Rel* Parousie *f*, second avènement *m*

paroxysm [ˈpærəksɪzəm] *n* (**a**) *(of rage, despair)* accès *m*; *(of jealousy, grief, tears)* crise *f*; **to be in paroxysms of laughter** avoir le fou rire; **to send sb into paroxysms of laughter** donner le fou rire à qn; **to be in a paroxysm of delight** être absolument ravi (**b**) *Med* paroxysme *m*

paroxysmal [ˌpærəkˈsɪzməl], **paroxysmic** [ˌpærəkˈsɪzmɪk] *adj* paroxysmique, paroxysmal, paroxystique

parquet [ˈpɑːkeɪ] **1** *n* (**a**) *Constr (floor)* parquet *m* (**b**) *Am Theat* parterre *m*
2 *vt* parqueter
▸▸ ***parquet floor, parquet flooring*** parquet *m*

parqueted [ˈpɑːkɪtɪd] *adj* parqueté

parquetry [ˈpɑːkɪtrɪ] *n* parquetage *m*

parr [pɑː(r)] *(pl* **inv** *or* **parrs**) *n Ich* saumoneau *m*, parr *m*

parrakeet = **parakeet**

parricidal [ˌpærɪˈsaɪdəl] *adj* parricide

parricide [ˈpærɪsaɪd] *n* (**a**) *(crime)* parricide *m* (**b**) *(person)* parricide *mf*

parrot [ˈpærət] **1** *n Orn* perroquet *m*; *Fam* **I was as sick as a parrot** *(disappointed)* ça m'a rendu malade; **to repeat sth parrot fashion** répéter qch comme un perroquet; **to learn sth parrot fashion** *(by repetition)* apprendre qch en le répétant; **he learnt it parrot fashion** *(by mimicking sounds)* il est capable de le répéter comme un perroquet
2 *vt (words)* répéter comme un perroquet; *(person, actions)* imiter
▸▸ ***parrot disease*** psittacose *f*; ***parrot fever*** psittacose *f*; *Ich* ***parrot fish*** perroquet *m* de mer, poisson-perroquet *m*

parry [ˈpærɪ] *(pt & pp* **parried**, *pl* **parries**) **1** *vt* (**a**) *(in fencing, boxing)* parer; **to parry a blow** parer un coup (**b**) *(problem)* tourner, éviter; *(question)* éluder; *(manoeuvre)* parer à, contrer
2 *vi (in fencing, boxing)* parer; **he parried with his right** il a paré l'attaque *ou* le coup d'une droite; **to parry and thrust** parer et tirer
3 *n (in fencing, boxing)* parade *f*

parse [pɑːz] *vt* (**a**) *Gram (word)* faire l'analyse (grammaticale) de; *(sentence)* faire l'analyse logique de (**b**) *Comput* analyser

parsec [ˈpɑːsek] *n Astron* parsec *m*

Parsee, Parsi [ˌpɑːˈsiː] **1** *n* Parsi(e) *m,f*
2 *adj* parsi

parser [ˈpɑːzə(r)] *n Comput* analyseur *m* syntaxique

Parsifal [ˈpɑːsɪfæl] *pr n* Parsifal

parsimonious [ˌpɑːsɪˈməʊnɪəs] *adj Formal* parcimonieux; **to be parsimonious with one's money** dépenser son argent avec parcimonie

parsimoniously [ˌpɑːsɪˈməʊnɪəslɪ] *adv Formal* avec parcimonie, parcimonieusement

parsimony [ˈpɑːsɪmənɪ] *n Formal* parcimonie *f*

parsing [ˈpɑːzɪŋ] *n* (**a**) *Gram (of word)* analyse *f* grammaticale; *(of sentence)* analyse *f* logique (**b**) *Comput* analyse *f* syntaxique

parsley [ˈpɑːslɪ] **1** *n* persil *m*; **Chinese parsley** coriandre *f*
2 *comp (sauce, butter)* au persil

parsnip [ˈpɑːsnɪp] *n* panais *m*; *Prov* **fine words butter no parsnips!** ce n'est pas avec de belles paroles que nous ferons avancer les choses!

parson [ˈpɑːsən] *n (gen)* ecclésiastique *m*; *(Protestant)* pasteur *m*
▸▸ *Culin* ***parson's nose*** croupion *m*

parsonage [ˈpɑːsənɪdʒ] *n* presbytère *m*

Parsons table [ˈpɑːsəns-] *n Am* = type de table basse

PART [pɑːt]

partie	▸ **1 (a)**
rôle	▸ **1 (b)**
pièce	▸ **1 (c)**
quartier	▸ **1 (d)**
episode	▸ **1 (e)**
mesure	▸ **1 (f)**
s'entrouvrir	▸ **3 (a)**
s'ouvrir	▸ **3 (a)**
se quitter	▸ **3 (b)**
entrouvrir	▸ **4 (a)**
écarter	▸ **4 (a)**
séparer	▸ **4 (b)**

1 *n* (**a**) *(gen → portion, subdivision)* partie *f*; **the exam is in two parts** l'examen est en deux parties; **see part one, section two** voir première partie, section deux; **the parts of the body** les parties *fpl* du corps; **(a) part of the garden is flooded** une partie du jardin est inondée; **(a) part of me strongly agrees with them** sur un certain plan, je suis tout à fait d'accord avec eux; **that's only part of the problem** ce n'est qu'un des aspects du problème; **it's very much part of the game/of the process** ça fait partie du jeu/du processus; **it's all part of growing up** c'est ce qui se passe quand on grandit; **we've finished the hardest part** nous avons fait le plus dur; **I haven't told you the best part yet** je ne t'ai pas encore dit le plus beau *ou* la meilleure; **the best/worst part was when he started laughing** le mieux/le pire ça a été quand il s'est mis à rire; **in the early part of the week** au début *ou* dans les premiers jours de la semaine; **for the best** *or* **greater part of five years** *(to wait, last etc)* presque cinq ans; **the greater part of the population** la plus grande partie de la population; **to be (a) part of sth** *(be involved with)* faire partie de qch; **he desperately wants to be a part of her organization** il veut à tout prix faire partie de son organisme; **to form part of sth** faire partie de qch; **to be part and parcel of sth** faire partie (intégrante) de qch

(**b**) *(role)* rôle *m*; **who played the part of Hamlet?** qui a joué le rôle de Hamlet?; *Fig* **he's just playing a part** il joue la comédie; **to know one's part** connaître son texte; **work plays a large part in our lives** le travail joue un rôle important dans notre vie; **she played a large part in persuading the company to relocate** c'est surtout elle qui a persuadé l'entreprise de se relocaliser; **to take part (in sth)** prendre part *ou* participer (à qch); **she takes an active part in decision-making** elle participe activement au processus de prise de décision; **I had no part in that affair** je n'ai joué aucun rôle dans cette affaire; **he has no part in the running of the company** il ne participe pas à *ou* il n'intervient pas dans la gestion de la société; **Joe had no part in it** Joe n'y était pour rien; **I want no part in** *or* **of their schemes** je ne veux pas être mêlé à leurs projets; **to do one's part** y mettre du sien; **to dress the part** se mettre en tenue de circonstance; **to look the part** avoir la tenue de circonstance; **for my/his part** pour ma/sa part

(**c**) *(component → of machine)* pièce *f*; **spare parts** pièces *fpl* détachées *ou* de rechange; **parts and labour warranty** garantie *f* pièces et main-d'œuvre

(**d**) *(area → of country, town etc)* **which part of England are you from?** vous êtes d'où en Angleterre?, de quelle région de l'Angleterre venez-vous?; **in some parts of Sydney/Australia** dans certains quartiers de Sydney/certaines régions de l'Australie; **it's a dangerous part of town** c'est un quartier dangereux; **are you new to these parts?** vous êtes nouveau ici?; **they are not from our part of the world** ils ne sont pas de chez nous; **she's travelling in foreign parts** elle est en voyage à l'étranger

(**e**) *(instalment → of encyclopedia)* fascicule *m*; *(→ of serial)* épisode *m*; **don't miss part two!** *(of serial)* ne manquez pas le deuxième épisode!; *(of programme in two parts)* ne manquez pas la deuxième partie!

(**f**) *(measure)* mesure *f*; **one part of pastis and four parts of water** une mesure de pastis et quatre mesures d'eau; *Chem* **a concentration of six parts per million** une concentration de six pour un million; **the bottle was three parts empty** la bouteille était aux trois quarts vide

(**g**) *(side)* parti *m*, part *f*; **he always takes his mother's part** il prend toujours le parti de sa mère; **to take sth in good part** bien prendre qch

(**h**) *Am (in hair)* raie *f*

(**i**) *Gram* partie *f*

(**j**) *Mus* partie *f*; **the vocal/violin part** la partie vocale/(pour) violon; **to sing in three parts** chanter à trois voix

2 *adv* en partie, partiellement; **the jacket is part cotton, part polyester** la veste est un mélange de coton et de polyester *ou* un mélange coton-polyester; **he's part English, part Chinese** il est moitié anglais, moitié chinois; **a mythical creature, part woman, part fish** une créature mythique mi-femme, mi-poisson

3 *vi* (**a**) *(move apart → lips, curtains)* s'entrouvrir; *(→ legs)* s'écarter, s'ouvrir; *(→ crowd)* s'ouvrir; *(disengage → fighters)* se séparer; **the clouds parted** il y eut une éclaircie

(**b**) *(leave one another)* se quitter; **they parted good friends** ils se sont quittés bons amis

(**c**) *(break → rope)* se casser; *(tear → fabric)* se déchirer

4 *vt* (**a**) *(move apart, open → curtains)* entrouvrir; *(→ branches, legs)* écarter; **her lips were slightly parted** ses lèvres étaient entrouvertes

(**b**) *(separate)* séparer (**from** de); **the children were parted from their parents** les enfants ont été séparés de leurs parents; *Hum* **he's not easily parted from his cash** il ne se sépare pas facilement de son argent

(**c**) *(hair)* faire une raie à; **her hair's parted in the middle** elle a la raie au milieu

5 parts *npl (talents)* talents *mpl*; **a man/woman of many parts** un homme/une femme de talent

6 for the most part *adv* dans l'ensemble; **the day will be sunny for the most part** la journée sera ensoleillée dans l'ensemble; **for the most part we get along pretty well** dans l'ensemble, nous nous entendons assez bien

7 in part *adv* en partie; **it's true in part** c'est en partie vrai; **it's in large part true** c'est en grande partie vrai; **the problem stems in part from a misunderstanding** le problème vient en partie d'un malentendu

8 in parts *adv* par endroits; **the book is good in parts** le livre est bon par endroits, certains passages du livre sont bons; **in parts the text is almost illegible** le texte est presque illisible par endroits

9 on the part of *prep* de la part de; **it was negligence on the part of the landlord** c'était une négligence de la part du propriétaire

►► *Com* ***part consignment*** expédition *f* partielle; *Com* ***part exchange*** reprise *f*; **they'll take your old TV set in part exchange** ils vous font une reprise sur *or* ils reprennent votre ancien téléviseur; **will you take it in part exchange?** voulez-vous le reprendre?; *Com* ***part load*** chargement *m* partiel; ***part music*** musique *f* d'ensemble; ***part owner*** copropriétaire *mf*; ***part ownership*** copropriété *f*; ***part payment*** acompte *m*, paiement *m* partiel; **I received £500 in part payment for the car** j'ai reçu un acompte de 500 livres pour la voiture; *Com* ***part shipment*** expédition *f* partielle; ***part singing*** chant *m* polyphonique *or* à plusieurs voix; ***part song*** chant *m* polyphonique *or* à plusieurs voix; ***part of speech*** partie *f* du discours; *Br* ***part work*** ouvrage *m* à fascicules; **they published it as a part work** ils l'ont publié sous forme de fascicules

►**part with** *vt insep* se séparer de; **we'll have to part with most of the furniture** nous devrons nous séparer de presque tous les meubles; **he hates parting with his money** il a horreur de dépenser son argent

---

> **Reaches the parts that other beers can't reach**
>
> Il s'agit du slogan d'une série de publicités pour la bière Heineken pendant les années 70 dans lesquelles la bière était censée conférer des pouvoirs spéciaux à ceux qui la consommaient. Aujourd'hui on utilise encore cette formule ("atteint les parties que les autres bières ne peuvent atteindre"), en remplaçant le mot **beers** par un autre pour décrire les qualités de quelque chose de façon humoristique. On dira par exemple **she makes tea that reaches the parts that other tea cannot reach** ("elle fait du thé vraiment excellent"), ou **this tour reaches the parts of Scotland that others don't** ("ce circuit touristique explore les coins d'Écosse que les autres ignorent").

partake [pɑːˈteɪk] (*pt* **partook** [-ˈtʊk], *pp* **partaken** [-ˈteɪkən]) *vi Arch or Formal* (**a**) *(eat, drink)* **to partake of sth** prendre qch; **to partake of a meal** prendre un repas; **I no longer partake** *(don't drink)* je ne bois plus; *Rel* **to partake of the Sacrament** s'approcher des sacrements, fréquenter les sacrements

(**b**) *(participate)* **to partake in** *(event)* participer à; *(joy, grief)* partager

(**c**) *(share quality)* **to partake of** relever de, tenir à; **it partakes of a certain grandeur** c'est empreint d'une certaine grandeur

partaker [pɑːˈteɪkə(r)] *n* participant(e) *mf* (**in** à); *Rel* **to be a regular partaker of the Sacrament** s'approcher des sacrements, fréquenter les sacrements

parterre [pɑːˈteə(r)] *n Am (in theatre)* parterre *m*

parthenogenesis [ˌpɑːθənəʊˈdʒenɪsɪs] *n Biol* parthénogenèse *f*

parthenogenetic [ˌpɑːθənəʊdʒəˈnetɪk], **parthenogenic** [ˌpɑːθənəʊˈdʒenɪk], **parthenogenous** [ˌpɑːθəˈnɒdʒənəs] *adj Biol & Zool* parthénogénétique, parthénogénésique

Parthenon [ˈpɑːθɪnən] *n* **the Parthenon** le Parthénon

Parthia [ˈpɑːθɪə] *n* Parthie *f*

Parthian [ˈpɑːθɪən] *n* Parthe *mf*

►► ***Parthian shot*** flèche *f* du Parthe

partial [ˈpɑːʃəl] **1** *adj* (**a**) *(incomplete)* partiel; **a partial loss of hearing** une perte partielle de l'ouïe; **the exhibition was only a partial success** l'exposition n'a connu qu'un succès mitigé

(**b**) *(biased)* partial (**towards** envers)

(**c**) *(fond)* **to be partial to sth** avoir un penchant *ou* un faible pour qch; **I am rather partial to a spot of whisky after dinner** je bois volontiers un petit verre de whisky après dîner

2 *n Mus* ton *m* partiel

►► *Banking* ***partial acceptance*** *(of bill)* acceptation *f* partielle; *Math* ***partial derivative*** dérivée *f* partielle; ***partial eclipse*** éclipse *f* partielle; ***partial fraction*** petite partie *f* d'une fraction; *Ins* ***partial loss*** perte *f* partielle, sinistre *m* partiel; *Fin* ***partial payment*** paiement *m* partiel; *Mus* ***partial tone*** ton *m* partiel

partiality [ˌpɑːʃɪˈælətɪ] (*pl* **partialities**) *n* (**a**) *(bias)* partialité *f* (**towards** envers); *(favouritism)* favoritisme *m* (**b**) *(fondness)* faible *m*, penchant *m* (**for** pour)

partially [ˈpɑːʃəlɪ] *adv* (**a**) *(partly)* en partie, partiellement (**b**) *(in biased way)* partialement, avec partialité

partially-sighted **1** *adj* malvoyant

2 *npl* **the partially sighted** les malvoyants *mpl*

participant [pɑːˈtɪsɪpənt] *n* participant(e) *m,f*; **the participants in the debate** les participants au débat

participate [pɑːˈtɪsɪpeɪt] *vi* participer, prendre part; **to participate in** *(race, discussion)* prendre part à, participer à; *Literary* **to participate in sb's joy** s'associer à la joie de qn

participating interest [pɑːˈtɪsɪpeɪtɪŋ-] *n Fin* intérêt *m* de participation; **to hold a participating interest in a company** avoir un intérêt de participation dans une société

participation [pɑːˌtɪsɪˈpeɪʃən] *n* participation *f* (**in** à); **they should encourage greater student participation** ils devraient encourager les étudiants à participer plus activement

►► *St Exch* ***participation certificate*** titre *m ou* bon *m* de participation; *St Exch* ***participation rate*** taux *m* d'activité

participative [pɑːˈtɪsɪpətɪv] *adj* participatif

participator [pɑːˈtɪsɪpeɪtə(r)] *n* participant(e) *m,f* (**in** de)

participatory [pɑːˌtɪsɪˈpeɪtərɪ] *adj* participatif

participial [ˌpɑːtɪˈsɪpɪəl] *adj Gram* participial

participle [ˈpɑːtɪsɪpəl] *n Gram* participe *m*

particle [ˈpɑːtɪkəl] *n* (**a**) *(tiny piece → gen)* particule *f*, parcelle *f*; *(→ of blood)* goutte *f*; *(→ of metal)* paillette *f*; *(→ of dust, sand)* grain *m*; *Fig (jot)* brin *m*, grain *m*; **food particles** particules *fpl* de nourriture; **there's not a particle of truth in the story** il n'y a pas une ombre de vérité dans ce récit

(**b**) *Gram* particule *f*

(**c**) *Phys* particule *f*

(**d**) *Rel* hostie *f*

►► *Phys* ***particle accelerator*** accélérateur *m* de particules; *Phys* ***particle beam*** faisceau *m* de particules; *Constr* ***particle board*** panneau *m* d'aggloméré, panneau *m* de particules; ***particle physics*** physique *f* des particules

parti-coloured ['pɑːtɪ-] *adj* bariolé, bigarré
particular [pə'tɪkjʊlə(r)] **1** *adj* (**a**) *(specific)* particulier; **that particular book** ce livre-là, ce livre en particulier; **for no particular reason** sans raison particulière *ou* précise; **do you have a particular day in mind?** est-ce que vous avez un jour précis *ou* particulier en tête?; **only that particular colour will do** il n'y a que cette couleur-là qui fasse l'affaire; **why did you insist on this particular one?** pourquoi as-tu insisté sur celui-là en particulier?; **my own particular feelings** mes sentiments personnels; **I've got no particular place to go** je ne vais nulle part en particulier, je n'ai pas de destination précise; **the problem is not particular to this region** le problème n'est pas particulier à *ou* spécifique à *ou* ne se limite pas à cette région
(**b**) *(special)* particulier, spécial; **it's an issue of particular importance to us** c'est une question qui revêt une importance toute particulière à nos yeux; **this one is a particular favourite of mine** j'affectionne tout particulièrement celui-ci; **to take particular care to do sth** mettre un soin (tout) particulier à faire qch
(**c**) *(person → exacting)* méticuleux, minutieux, soigneux; *(→ about rules etc)* pointilleux; *(→ about choice of friends, methods used etc)* difficile, exigeant; **I have to be quite particular about what I eat** je dois faire très attention à ce que je mange; **it had to be pure silk, he was most particular about it** il fallait que ce soit de la soie pure, il a insisté; **to be particular about one's food** *(demanding)* être exigeant pour la nourriture; *(difficult)* être difficile pour la nourriture; **to be particular about one's dress** soigner sa mise *ou* sa tenue; *Fam* **I'm not particular (about it)** *(I don't care)* je n'y tiens pas plus que ça; *Fam* **he's not particular about where the goods come from** l'origine des marchandises lui importe peu ❑
(**d**) *Formal (detailed → description, account)* détaillé
2 *n* (**a**) *(specific)* **from the general to the particular** du général au particulier
(**b**) *(detail)* détail *m*; **alike in every particular** semblables en tout point; **they differ in several particulars** ils diffèrent en plusieurs points; **to go into particulars** entrer dans les détails; **to give particulars of sth** donner les détails de qch; **to ask for fuller particulars about sth** demander des précisions *ou* des détails supplémentaires sur qch; **to take down sb's particulars** prendre les coordonnées de qn; **for further particulars apply to...** pour plus amples détails *ou* renseignements s'adresser à...
3 in particular *adv* en particulier; **what are you thinking about? – nothing in particular** à quoi penses-tu? – à rien en particulier; **what happened? – nothing in particular** que s'est-il passé? – rien de particulier *ou* rien de spécial; **no one in particular** personne en particulier; **where are you going? – nowhere in particular** où vas-tu? – je vais juste faire un tour
►► *Fin* ***particular lien*** privilège *m* spécial
particularism [pə'tɪkjʊlərɪzəm] *n* particularisme *m*
particularist [pə'tɪkjʊlərɪst] **1** *n* particulariste *mf*
2 *adj* particulariste
particularity [pəˌtɪkjʊ'lærətɪ] *(pl* **particularities**) *n* (**a**) *(special quality)* particularité *f* (**b**) *(exacting nature)* méticulosité *f* (**c**) *(detailed nature → of description)* minutie *f*
particularization [pəˌtɪkjʊləraɪ'zeɪʃən] *n* fait *m* de spécifier
particularize, -ise [pə'tɪkjʊləraɪz] **1** *vt* spécifier
2 *vi* entrer dans les détails, préciser
particularly [pə'tɪkjʊləlɪ] *adv* particulièrement; **it's cold here, particularly at night** il fait froid ici, particulièrement *ou* spécialement la nuit; **I don't know him particularly well** je ne le connais pas spécialement bien; **it was a particularly vicious murder** ce fut un meurtre extrêmement *ou* particulièrement sauvage; **I was surprised he wasn't there, particularly as he'd received an official invitation** son absence m'a surpris, d'autant plus qu'il avait reçu une invitation officielle; **not particularly** pas particulièrement *ou* spécialement; **she's not particularly rich** elle n'est pas tellement riche

particulate [pə'tɪkjʊlɪt] **1** *adj* particulaire
2 *n* particule *f*
►► ***particulate emissions*** émissions *fpl* de particules
partied out ['pɑːtɪd-] *adj Fam* **I'm partied out!** *(exhausted)* j'ai trop fait la fête, je suis crevé!; *(had enough of parties)* ras-le-bol de faire la fête!
parting ['pɑːtɪŋ] **1** *n* (**a**) *(leave-taking)* séparation *f*; **they had a tearful parting at the station** ils se quittèrent en larmes à la gare; **parting from his family was hard** il a eu du mal à quitter sa famille
(**b**) *(division)* séparation *f*; *Fig* **to be at** *or* **to have come to the parting of the ways** être à la croisée des chemins; **we came to a parting of the ways** nous sommes arrivées à la croisée des chemins
(**c**) *(opening → in clouds)* trouée *f*; *Bible* **the parting of the Red Sea** le partage des eaux de la mer Rouge
(**d**) *Br (in hair)* raie *f*; **centre/side parting** raie *f* au milieu/sur le côté
2 *adj Literary (words, kiss)* d'adieu; **the parting day** le jour qui tombe; **he gave me a parting handshake** il m'a serré la main en partant
►► *Fig* ***parting shot*** flèche *f* du Parthe; **that was his parting shot** et sur ces mots, il s'en alla
partisan [ˌpɑːtɪ'zæn] **1** *adj* partisan; **a very partisan audience** un auditoire très partisan
2 *n* (**a**) *(supporter)* partisan *m*; **to act in a partisan spirit** *(politician etc)* faire preuve d'esprit de parti; *(be prejudiced)* faire preuve de parti pris (**b**) *Mil* partisan *m*
►► ***partisan politics*** politique *f* partisane
partisanship [ˌpɑːtɪ'zænʃɪp] *n* partialité *f*; *(of politician etc)* esprit *m* de parti
partita [pɑː'tiːtə] *n Mus* partita *f*
partition [pɑː'tɪʃən] **1** *n* (**a**) *(screen)* paravent *m*; *(wall)* cloison *f*; *(of ship's hold etc)* compartiment *m*; **metal partitions** cloisons *fpl* métalliques
(**b**) *(dividing → of country)* partition *f*; *(→ of room)* séparation *f*; *(→ of property)* division *f*; *(→ of power)* répartition *f*, morcellement *m*
(**c**) *Comput (of hard disk)* partition *f*
2 *vt* (**a**) *(country, property)* diviser, partager
(**b**) *(room)* séparer en deux
(**c**) *(power)* partager
(**d**) *Comput (hard disk)* diviser en partitions
►► ***partition wall*** cloison *f*
►**partition off** *vt sep (room)* cloisonner; *(part of a room)* séparer par une cloison; **a small office had been partitioned off** on avait aménagé un petit bureau derrière une cloison
partitioned [pɑː'tɪʃənd] *adj* cloisonné; *(ship's hold)* à compartiments
partitive ['pɑːtɪtɪv] *Gram* **1** *adj* partitif
2 *n* partitif *m*
partly ['pɑːtlɪ] *adv* en partie, partiellement; **wholly or partly** en tout ou en partie; **partly by force, partly by persuasion** moitié par la force, moitié par la persuasion; **a partly eaten sandwich** un sandwich à moitié mangé; **she was only partly convinced** elle n'était qu'à moitié convaincue; **it's partly because of the view that I like this room so much** c'est en partie à cause de la vue que j'aime tant cette pièce
►► *Fin* ***partly paid-up capital*** capital *m* non entièrement versé; *St Exch* ***partly paid-up shares*** actions *fpl* non entièrement libérées; *Fin* ***partly secured creditor*** créancier(ère) *m,f* partiellement nanti(e)
partner ['pɑːtnə(r)] **1** *n* (**a**) *(spouse)* époux (épouse) *m,f*, conjoint(e) *m,f*; *(boyfriend, girlfriend)* ami(e) *m,f*; **sexual partner** partenaire *mf* (sexuel(elle))
(**b**) *(in game, dance)* partenaire *mf*; **his partner in the waltz** sa partenaire *ou* sa cavalière pour la valse; *Cards* **to cut** *or* **draw for partners** = faire les rois
(**c**) *Com* associé(e) *m,f*
(**d**) *(in common undertaking)* partenaire *mf*; *(of cowboy, bank robber etc)* acolyte *m*; **our European partners** nos partenaires européens; **to be partners in crime** être complices dans le crime; *Hum* **here he comes, with his partner in crime** le voilà qui arrive avec son acolyte
2 *vt* (**a**) *(be the partner of)* être partenaire de

(**b**) *(dance with)* danser avec; *(in games)* faire équipe avec, être le partenaire de; **she partnered him in a foxtrot** elle a dansé un fox-trot avec lui; **Wilson partnered Bailey to victory in the men's doubles** Wilson et Bailey ont remporté le double messieurs
partnership ['pɑːtnəʃɪp] *n* (**a**) *(gen)* association *f*; **to work in partnership with sb/sth** travailler en association avec qn/qch; **we work in partnership with relief organizations** nous travaillons en association avec des organisations humanitaires; **a winning doubles partnership** une équipe de double gagnante; **their relationship has lasted so long because they're a partnership** s'ils sont ensemble depuis si longtemps, c'est qu'ils ont une vraie relation de partenariat
(**b**) *Com (association)* association *f*; *(company)* ≃ société *f* en nom collectif; **to go into partnership with sb** s'associer avec qn; **to dissolve a partnership** dissoudre une association; **they've gone into partnership together** ils se sont associés; **they offered him a partnership** ils lui ont proposé de devenir leur associé
►► ***partnership agreement*** accord *m* de partenariat; *St Exch* ***partnership share*** part *f* d'association
parton ['pɑːtɒn] *n Phys* parton *m*
partook [pɑː'tʊk] *pt of* **partake**
partridge ['pɑːtrɪdʒ] *(pl* **inv** *or* **partridges**) *n* perdrix *f*; *(immature)* perdreau *m*
part-singing *n* chant *m* polyphonique *ou* à plusieurs voix
part-time 1 *adj* à temps partiel; **a part-time teacher** un professeur à temps partiel; **on a part-time basis** à temps partiel; **she's got a part-time job** elle travaille à temps partiel
2 *adv* à temps partiel
part-timer *n* travailleur(euse) *m,f* à temps partiel
parturient [pɑː'tjʊrɪənt] **1** *n* parturiente *f*
2 *adj* (**a**) *(woman)* sur le point d'accoucher; *(animal)* sur le point de mettre bas (**b**) *Fig (mind)* en train de faire naître une idée
parturition [ˌpɑːtjʊ'rɪʃən] *n* parturition *f*
partway ['pɑːtweɪ] *adv* en partie, partiellement; **partway through the year, she resigned** elle a démissionné en cours d'année; **I'm only partway through the book** je n'ai pas fini le livre; **I was partway down the stairs when the phone rang** j'étais dans l'escalier quand le téléphone a sonné; **they had gone partway towards an agreement** ils s'acheminaient vers un accord; **we were partway there** *(in project etc)* nous en avions fait une bonne partie; **this will go partway towards covering the costs** cela couvrira une bonne partie des coûts
party ['pɑːtɪ] *(pl* **parties**, *pt & pp* **partied**) **1** *n* (**a**) *(social event)* fête *f*; *(more formal)* soirée *f*, réception *f*; **to give a party** *(formal)* donner une réception *ou* une soirée; *(informal)* faire une fête; **to have** *or* **to throw a party for sb** organiser une fête en l'honneur de qn; **I'm having a little cocktail party on Friday** je fais un petit cocktail vendredi; **he's caught the party spirit** il s'est abandonné aux joies de la fête; **he's a real party person** il adore faire la fête; **New Year's Eve party** réveillon *m* de fin d'année
(**b**) *Pol* parti *m*; **the Conservative/Democratic Party** le parti conservateur/démocrate; **he joined the Socialist Party in 1936** il est entré au parti socialiste en 1936
(**c**) *(group → of tourists, climbers)* groupe *m*; *(→ of miners, workers etc)* brigade *f*, équipe *f*, groupe; *Mil* détachement *m*; **will you join our party?** voulez-vous être des nôtres?; **we're a small party** nous sommes peu nombreux; **I was one of the party** j'étais de la partie; **a tour party** un groupe de touristes; **the funeral party** le cortège funèbre; **the rescue party** l'équipe *f* de secours; **the wedding party** les invités *mpl (à un mariage)*; **to make dinner reservations for a party of six** réserver une table pour six personnes; **a reservation for the Miller party** une réservation au nom de Miller
(**d**) *Formal or Law (participant)* partie *f*; **to be a party to** *(conversation)* prendre part à; *(crime)* être complice de; *(conspiracy, enterprise)* être mêlé à, tremper dans; *also Fig* **the guilty party** le (la) coupable; *Fig* **this broken wire is the guilty**

party c'est à cause de ce fil coupé; **the injured party** la partie lésée; *Law* **the contracting parties** les parties *fpl* contractantes; *Law* **(the) interested parties** les intéressés *mpl*; **I would never be (a) party to such a thing** je ne me ferais jamais complice d'une chose pareille, je ne m'associerais jamais à une chose pareille

(**e**) *(person)* individu *m*

2 *comp* (**a**) *(atmosphere, clothes)* de fête

(**b**) *Pol (leader, leadership, funds)* du parti; *(system)* des partis

3 *vi Fam* faire la fête; **let's party!** faisons la fête!; **we partied all night** nous avons fait la fête toute la nuit; **she's a great one for partying** elle adore faire la fête

►► *Fam* ***party animal*** fêtard(e) *m,f*; **she's a real party animal** elle adore faire la fête, c'est une sacrée fêtarde; *Pol* ***Party Conference*** Congrès *m* du parti; ***party dress*** robe *f* habillée; ***party games*** = jeux auxquels on joue dans les soirées ou les fêtes; ***party invitations*** invitations *fpl*; ***party line*** *Tel* ligne *f* commune *(à plusieurs abonnés)*; *Pol* ligne *f* du parti; **to toe** *or* **follow the party line** suivre la ligne du parti; *Pol* ***party machine*** machine *f* du parti; *Pol* ***party man*** homme *m* de parti; *Pol* ***party member*** membre *m* du parti; *Br Fam* ***party piece*** numéro *m (à l'occasion d'une fête)*; *Ironic* **that's his party piece** c'est son numéro habituel; *Pol* ***party politics*** politique *f* de parti; *Pej* politique *f* politicienne; *Fam* ***party pooper*** rabat-joie *m inv*; ***party snacks*** amuse-gueule(s) *mpl*; ***party wall*** mur *m* mitoyen

partygoer ['pɑːtɪgəʊə(r)] *n* fêtard(e) *m,f*, *(more formal)* habitué(e) *m,f* des soirées; **the streets were full of partygoers** les rues étaient pleines de gens se rendant à des soirées

party-plan selling *n Mktg* vente *f* domiciliaire

party political *adj (broadcast)* réservé à un parti politique; *(issue)* de parti politique; **that was a party political broadcast on behalf of the Liberal Party** vous venez de voir/d'entendre une émission du parti libéral; **he's just making a party political point** son argument ne relève que de la politique politicienne

parvenu ['pɑːvənjuː] **1** *n* parvenu(e) *m,f*

2 *adj* parvenu

parvis ['pɑːvɪs] *n Archit* parvis *m*

parvovirus ['pɑːvəʊvaɪrəs] *n Vet* parvovirus *m*

PASCAL [pæ'skæl] *n Comput* PASCAL *m*

pascal ['pæskəl] *n Phys* pascal *m*

►► ***Pascal's triangle*** le triangle *m* de Pascal

Pasch [pæsk] *n* (**a**) *(Passover)* la Pâque (juive), Pesah *m* (**b**) *Arch (Easter)* Pâques *m*

paschal, Paschal ['pæskəl] *adj* pascal

►► ***Paschal candle*** cierge *m* pascal; ***Paschal Lamb*** agneau *m* pascal

pash [pæʃ] *n Fam Old-fashioned* **to have a pash on** *or* **for sb** avoir le béguin pour qn

pasha ['pæʃə] *n* pacha *m*

pashmina [pæʃ'miːnə] *n (wool, garment)* pashmina *m*

Pashto ['pæʃtəʊ] *n Ling* pachto *m*, pachtou *m*

Pasiphae [pə'sɪfaɪ] *pr n Myth* Pasiphaé

paso doble [ˌpæsəʊ'dəʊbleɪ] *n* paso doble *m inv*

pasqueflower ['pæskflaʊə(r)] *n Bot (European)* pulsatille *f* vulgaire, anémone *f* pulsatille

pasquinade [ˌpæskwɪ'neɪd] *n* pasquin *m*, pasquinade *f*

PASS [pɑːs]

col	►1 (a)
laissez-passer	►1 (b)
moyenne	►1 (c)
passe	►1 (e) – (g)
passer devant	►2 (a)
dépasser	►2 (a)
passer	►2 (b) – (e), (j); 3 (a), (b), (d), (e), (g), (h)
être reçu à	►2 (f)
voter	►2 (g)
se passer	►3 (d), (f)
être voté	►3 (i)

1 *n* (**a**) *(in mountains)* col *m*, défilé *m*; **the Brenner Pass** le col du Brenner

(**b**) *(authorization → for worker, visitor)* laissez-passer *m inv*; *Theat* invitation *f*, billet *m* de faveur; *Mil (→ for leave of absence)* permission *f*; *(→ for safe conduct)* sauf-conduit *m*; **rail/bus pass** carte *f* d'abonnement (de train)/de bus

(**c**) *Sch & Univ (in exam)* moyenne *f*, mention *f* passable; **to get a pass** être reçu; **I got three passes** j'ai été reçu dans trois matières

(**d**) *(state of affairs)* **things have come to a pretty pass** on est dans une bien mauvaise passe, la situation s'est bien dégradée; **things came to such a pass that...** les choses en vinrent à ce point *ou* à tel point que...

(**e**) *Sport (with ball, puck)* passe *f*; *(in fencing)* botte *f*; *(in bullfighting)* passe *f*; **to make a pass at** *(in fencing)* porter une botte à

(**f**) *(by magician)* passe *f*

(**g**) *Comput* passe *f*

(**h**) *Aviat (overflight)* survol *m*; *(attack)* attaque *f*

(**i**) *Fam* **to make a pass at sb** *(sexual advances)* faire du plat à qn

2 *vt* (**a**) *(move past, go by → building, window)* passer devant; *(→ person)* croiser; *(overtake)* dépasser, doubler; **if you pass a chemist's, get some aspirin** si tu passes devant une pharmacie, achète de l'aspirine; **he passed my table without seeing me** il est passé devant ma table sans me voir; **I passed her on the stairs** je l'ai croisée dans l'escalier; **the ships passed each other in the fog** les navires se sont croisés dans le brouillard

(**b**) *(go beyond → finishing line, frontier)* passer; **we've passed the right exit** nous avons dépassé la sortie que nous aurions dû prendre; **contributions have passed the $100,000 mark** les dons ont franchi la barre des 100 000 dollars; **we've passed a major turning point** nous avons franchi un cap important; **not a word about it had passed her lips** elle n'en avait pas dit un mot; **to pass understanding** dépasser l'entendement

(**c**) *(move, run)* passer; **to pass one's hand between the bars** passer *ou* glisser sa main à travers les barreaux; **to pass a rope round sth** passer une corde autour de qch; **to pass a sponge over sth** passer l'éponge sur qch; **she passed her hand over her hair** elle s'est passé la main dans les cheveux

(**d**) *(hand)* passer; *(transmit → message)* transmettre; **to pass sth from hand to hand** passer qch de main en main; **pass me the sugar, please** passez-moi le sucre, s'il vous plaît; **pass the list around the office** faites passer *ou* circuler la liste dans le bureau; **can you pass her the message?** pourriez-vous lui transmettre *ou* faire passer le message?

(**e**) *(spend → life, time, visit)* passer; **it passes the time** cela fait passer le temps

(**f**) *(succeed in → exam, driving test)* être reçu à, réussir; **he didn't pass his history exam** il a échoué *ou* il a été recalé à son examen d'histoire; **to pass a test** *(vehicle, product)* passer une épreuve avec succès

(**g**) *(approve → bill, law)* voter; *(→ motion, resolution)* adopter; *Sch & Univ (→ student)* recevoir, admettre; **the drug has not been passed by the Health Ministry** le médicament n'a pas reçu l'autorisation de mise sur le marché du ministère de la Santé; **the censor has passed the film** le film a obtenu son visa de censure; *Typ* **to pass for press** donner le bon à tirer pour; *Mil etc* **to be passed fit** être reconnu apte

(**h**) *(pronounce → verdict, sentence)* prononcer, rendre; *(→ remark, compliment)* faire; **he declined to pass comment** il s'est refusé à tout commentaire; *Law* **to pass sentence** prononcer le jugement; **to pass judgement on sb** porter un jugement sur qn, juger qn

(**i**) *(counterfeit money, stolen goods)* écouler

(**j**) *Sport (ball, puck)* passer

(**k**) *(in games)* **to pass one's turn** passer *ou* sauter son tour

(**l**) *Physiol* **to pass blood** avoir du sang dans les urines; **to pass water** uriner

(**m**) *Mil* **to pass troops in review** passer des troupes en revue

(**n**) *Fin* **to pass a dividend** conclure un exercice sans payer de dividende

3 *vi* (**a**) *(move in specified direction)* passer; **a cloud passed across the moon** un nuage est passé devant la lune; **the wires pass under the floorboards** les fils passent sous le plancher; **alcohol passes rapidly into the bloodstream** l'alcool passe rapidement dans le sang; **his life passed before his eyes** il a vu sa vie défiler devant ses yeux; **to pass into history/legend** entrer dans l'histoire/la légende; **the expression has passed into the language** l'expression est passée dans la langue

(**b**) *(move past, go by)* passer; **let me pass** laissez-moi passer; **the road was too narrow for two cars to pass** la route était trop étroite pour que deux voitures se croisent; **the procession passed slowly** le cortège passa *ou* défila lentement; **everyone smiles as he passes** tout le monde sourit à son passage; **I happened to be passing, so I thought I'd call in** il s'est trouvé que je passais, alors j'ai eu l'idée de venir vous voir

(**c**) *(overtake)* dépasser, doubler; **no passing** défense de doubler

(**d**) *(elapse → months, years)* (se) passer, s'écouler; *(→ holiday)* se passer; **the weekend passed uneventfully** le week-end s'est passé sans surprises; **time passed rapidly** le temps a passé très rapidement; **when five minutes had passed** au bout de cinq minutes; **it seemed like no time at all had passed since I had last seen her** on aurait dit que pas une minute ne s'était écoulée depuis la dernière fois que je l'avais vue

(**e**) *(be transformed)* passer, se transformer; **it then passes into a larval stage** il se transforme par la suite en larve; **the oxygen then passes to a liquid state** ensuite l'oxygène passe à l'état liquide; **to pass from joy to despair** passer de la joie au désespoir

(**f**) *(take place)* se passer, avoir lieu; **harsh words passed between them** ils ont eu des mots; **I don't know what passed between them** je ne sais pas ce qui s'est passé entre eux; **the party, if it ever comes to pass, should be quite something** la fête, si elle a jamais lieu, sera vraiment un grand moment; *Bible* **and it came to pass that...** et il advint que...

(**g**) *(end, disappear → pain, crisis, fever)* passer; *(→ anger, desire)* disparaître, tomber; *(→ dream, hope)* disparaître; **the moment of tension passed** le moment de tension est passé; **I was about to say something witty, but the moment passed** j'allais dire quelque chose de spirituel, mais j'ai laissé passer l'occasion; **to let the opportunity pass** laisser passer l'occasion

(**h**) *(be transferred → power, responsibility)* passer; *(→ inheritance)* passer, être transmis; **authority passes to the Vice-President when the President is abroad** c'est au vice-président que revient la charge du pouvoir lorsque le président se trouve à l'étranger; **the turn passes to the player on the left** c'est ensuite au tour du joueur placé à gauche

(**i**) *(get through, be approved → proposal)* être approuvé; *(→ bill, law)* être voté; *(→ motion)* être adopté; *Sch & Univ (→ student)* être reçu *ou* admis

(**j**) *(go unchallenged)* passer; **the insult passed unnoticed** personne ne releva l'insulte; **he let the remark/mistake pass** il a laissé passer la remarque/l'erreur sans la relever; **I don't like it, but I'll let it pass** je n'aime pas ça, mais je préfère ne rien dire *ou* me taire; **let it pass!** passe pour cela!

(**k**) *(be adequate, acceptable → behaviour)* convenir, être acceptable; *(→ repair job)* passer; **in a grey suit you might just pass** avec ton costume gris, ça peut aller

(**l**) *(substitute)* **don't try to pass as an expert** n'essaie pas de te faire passer pour un expert; **you could easily pass for your sister** on pourrait très bien te prendre pour ta sœur; **he could pass for thirty** on lui donnerait trente ans; **she could pass for a Scandinavian** on pourrait la prendre pour une Scandinave

(**m**) *Sport* faire une passe

(**n**) *Cards* passer; *(at dominoes)* bouder; **(I) pass!** *(in cards, quiz)* je passe!; *Fig* aucune idée!; *Fig* **I'll pass on that** *(declining offer)* non merci; *(declining to answer question)* je préfère ne pas répondre à cette question

►► *Banking* ***pass book*** livret *m* de banque; ***pass laws*** = lois qui anciennement restreignaient la

par–pas

liberté de mouvement de la population noire en Afrique du Sud; *Br Sch* **pass mark** moyenne *f*

►**pass around** *vt sep (cake, cigarettes)* (faire) passer; *(petition)* (faire) circuler; *(supplies)* distribuer; **he passed around the tray of champagne** il a fait passer le plateau avec les coupes de champagne; *Fig* **to pass around the hat** faire une quête

►**pass away 1** *vt sep (while away)* passer; **she passed away the morning painting** elle a passé la matinée à peindre; **we read to pass the time away** nous avons lu pour tuer *ou* passer le temps

2 *vi* (**a**) *Euph (die)* s'éteindre

(**b**) *(elapse → time)* passer, s'écouler

►**pass back** *vt sep* (**a**) *(give back)* rendre; **pass the book back when you've finished** rendez-moi/-lui/*etc* le livre quand vous aurez fini

(**b**) *Rad & TV* **I'll now pass you back to the studio** je vais rendre l'antenne au studio

(**c**) *Sport (return to team mate)* repasser; *(backwards)* passer en arrière

►**pass by 1** *vt sep (disregard)* ignorer, négliger; **life is passing me by** je n'ai pas l'impression de vivre; **life has passed her by** elle n'a pas vraiment vécu; **whenever a chance comes, don't let it pass you by** quand une occasion se présente, ne la laissez pas échapper

2 *vt insep (go past → house etc)* passer devant

3 *vi* (**a**) *(go past)* passer; *(carry on without stopping)* continuer son chemin; **luckily a taxi was passing by** heureusement un taxi passait par là; **he passed by without a word!** il est passé à côté de moi sans dire un mot!

(**b**) *(visit)* passer; **she passed by to say hello** elle est passée dire bonjour

(**c**) *(of time)* passer

►**pass down** *vt sep* (**a**) *(reach down)* passer; **he passed me down my suitcase** il m'a tendu *ou* passé ma valise

(**b**) *(transmit → inheritance, disease, tradition)* transmettre, passer; **the songs were passed down from generation to generation** les chansons ont été transmises de génération en génération

►**pass off 1** *vt sep (represent falsely)* faire passer; **she passed him off as a duke** elle l'a fait passer pour un duc; **to pass oneself off as an artist** se faire passer pour (un) artiste; **to pass sth off as a joke** *(accept as a joke)* prendre qch en riant *ou* comme une plaisanterie; *(claim to be a joke)* dire qu'on a fait/dit qch pour rire

2 *vi* (**a**) *(take place → conference, attack)* se passer, se dérouler; **the meeting passed off without incident** la réunion s'est déroulée sans incident; **everything passed off well** tout s'est bien passé

(**b**) *(end → fever, fit)* passer; **the effects of the drug had passed off** les effets du médicament s'étaient dissipés

►**pass on 1** *vt sep* (**a**) *(hand on → box, letter)* (faire) passer; **read this and pass it on** lisez ceci et faites circuler

(**b**) *(transmit → disease, message, tradition)* transmettre; **they pass the costs on to their customers** ils répercutent les coûts sur leurs clients; **these cost reductions have been passed on to the consumer** le consommateur a bénéficié de ces réductions des coûts; **we meet at eight o'clock, pass it on** nous avons rendez-vous à huit heures, fais passer (la consigne)

2 *vi* (**a**) *Euph (die)* trépasser, s'éteindre

(**b**) *(proceed → on journey)* continuer son chemin *ou* sa route; **to pass on to another subject** passer à un autre sujet; **passing on to the question of cost,...** si nous passons maintenant à la question du coût,...

►**pass out 1** *vt sep* (**a**) *(hand out)* distribuer

(**b**) *Ir Aut (overtake)* dépasser

2 *vi* (**a**) *(faint)* s'évanouir, perdre connaissance; *(from drunkenness)* tomber ivre mort; *(go to sleep)* s'endormir

(**b**) *Mil (cadet)* ≃ finir ses classes

►**pass over 1** *vt sep (overlook → person)* ne pas prendre en considération; **he was passed over for promotion** on ne lui a pas accordé la promotion qu'il attendait

2 *vt insep* (**a**) *(ignore)* passer sous silence; *(difficulty etc)* passer sur, glisser sur; **they passed over the subject in silence** ils ont passé la question sous silence

(**b**) *(cross → river etc)* traverser, franchir; *(→ obstacle)* franchir, passer sur

3 *vi* (**a**) *(end → storm)* se dissiper, finir

(**b**) *(defect)* **to pass over to the enemy** passer à l'ennemi

►**pass round** = **pass around**

►**pass through 1** *vt insep (country, area, difficult period)* traverser; *(barrier)* franchir; **the bullet passed through his shoulder** la balle lui a traversé l'épaule; **you pass through a small village** vous traversez un petit village; **he passed through the checkpoint without any trouble** il a passé le poste de contrôle sans encombre

2 *vi* passer; **I'm not staying in Boston, I'm just passing through** je ne reste pas à Boston, je suis juste de passage

►**pass up** *vt sep* (**a**) *(hand up)* passer; **pass me up the light bulb** passe-moi l'ampoule

(**b**) *(not take → opportunity)* laisser passer; *(→ job)* refuser; **I'll have to pass up their invitation** je vais devoir décliner leur invitation

---

passable ['pɑːsəbəl] *adj* (**a**) *(acceptable)* passable, acceptable; **it's passable** ce n'est pas trop mal; **he does a passable impression of the boss** il imite plutôt bien le chef; **a very passable little restaurant** un petit restaurant très honnête *ou* correct (**b**) *(road)* praticable; *(river, canyon)* franchissable; **the road is passable with difficulty** la route est difficilement praticable (**c**) *(currency)* ayant cours

passably ['pɑːsəblɪ] *adv* passablement, pas trop mal; **to perform passably** offrir une performance passable

passacaglia [,pæsə'kɑːlɪə] *n Mus* passacaille *f*

passage ['pæsɪdʒ] *n* (**a**) *(way through)* passage *m*; **they cleared a passage through the crowd** ils ouvrirent un passage à travers la foule

(**b**) *(corridor)* passage *m*, couloir *m*; *(alley)* ruelle *f*; **an underground passage** un passage souterrain

(**c**) *(from book, music)* passage *m*; **selected passages from Churchill's speeches** morceaux *mpl* choisis des discours de Churchill; **the most touching passage in the book** l'endroit le plus touchant du livre

(**d**) *Anat & Tech* conduit *m*; **nasal passages** conduits *mpl* nasaux; *Anat* **air passage** conduit *m* aérifère

(**e**) *(passing → gen)* passage *m*; *Pol (→ of bill)* adoption *f*; **the trench did not block the passage of the tanks** la tranchée n'a pas empêché les chars de passer; **with the passage of time** avec le temps; **their friendship has survived the passage of time** leur amitié a survécu au temps; **the bill had an uninterrupted passage through parliament** la loi a été adoptée sans encombre par le Parlement

(**f**) *(voyage)* voyage *m*; *(crossing)* traversée *f*; *Naut* **to work one's passage** gagner son passage (en travaillant à bord)

(**g**) *Formal (access)* libre passage *m*; **to grant sb safe passage through a country** accorder à qn le libre passage à travers un pays; *Arch or Fig* **passage of** *or* **at arms** passe *f* d'armes

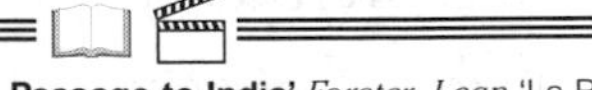

'A Passage to India' *Forster, Lean* 'La Route des Indes'

---

passageway ['pæsɪdʒweɪ] *n* (**a**) *(space)* passage *m*; **to leave a passageway** laisser le passage libre (**b**) *(corridor)* passage *m*, couloir *m*; *(alleyway)* ruelle *f*; **don't block the passageway!** n'obstruez pas le passage!, laissez le passage libre!

passata [pə'sɑːtə] *n Culin* sauce *f* tomate épaisse

passbook ['pɑːsbʊk] *n* (**a**) *(bankbook)* livret *m* (d'épargne), livret *m* de banque (**b**) *SAfr Formerly (identity document)* laissez-passer *m inv*

passé [*Br* 'pæseɪ, *Am* pæ'seɪ] *adj Pej* dépassé, vieillot, désuet(ète)

passenger ['pæsɪndʒə(r)] *n* (**a**) *(in car, bus, aircraft, ship)* passager(ère) *m,f*; *(in train)* voyageur(euse) *m,f*

(**b**) *Br Pej (worker, team member)* poids *m* mort; **we can't carry passengers** on ne peut pas traîner de poids morts

►► **passenger and cargo plane** avion *m* mixte; **passenger and cargo ship** bateau *m* mixte; *Rail Am* **passenger car,** *Br* **passenger coach** wagon *m ou* voiture *f* de voyageurs; *Br* **passenger carrying vehicle** véhicule *m* de transport en commun; **passenger compartment** *(of car)* habitacle *m*; **passenger list** liste *f* des passagers; **passenger mile** *Aviat* ≃ kilomètre-passager *m*; *Rail* ≃ kilomètre-voyageur *m*; **passenger pigeon** pigeon-voyageur *m*; *Aut* **passenger seat** *(in front)* siège *m* du passager; *(in back)* siège *m* arrière; **passenger train** train *m* de voyageurs; *Aut* **passenger wagon** voiture *f* familiale

passe-partout [,pæspɑː'tuː] *n* (**a**) *(card, gummed paper)* passe-partout *m inv* (**b**) *(key)* passe-partout *m inv*

passer ['pɑːsə(r)] *n Sport* passeur(euse) *m,f*; **he's a good passer of the ball** c'est un bon passeur

passer-by [,pɑːsə'baɪ] *(pl* **passers-by***)* *n* passant(e) *m,f*

passerine ['pæsəraɪn] *Orn* **1** *n* passereau *m*

2 *adj* des passereaux

passim ['pæsɪm] *adv* passim

passing ['pɑːsɪŋ] **1** *adj* (**a**) *(going by)* qui passe; **she watched the passing crowd** elle regardait la foule qui passait; **she flagged down a passing car** elle a fait signe à une voiture qui passait de s'arrêter; **with each passing day he grew more worried** son inquiétude croissait de jour en jour; *Literary* **the passing hour** l'heure *f* fugitive

(**b**) *(fancy, infatuation)* éphémère, passager; **a passing whim** un caprice passager; **he didn't give her absence a passing thought** c'est tout juste s'il a remarqué son absence, il a à peine remarqué son absence; **he made only a passing reference to her absence** il a fait mention de son absence en passant

(**c**) *(slight)* **to have a passing acquaintance with sb** connaître qn de vue; **to bear a passing resemblance to sb** ressembler vaguement à qn

2 *n* (**a**) *(of train, birds etc)* passage *m*; *(overtaking → of another car)* dépassement *m*, doublement *m*

(**b**) *(of time)* écoulement *m*; *(of beauty)* disparition *f*; **with the passing of time** avec le temps

(**c**) *(approval → of bill, resolution)* adoption *f*; *(→ of law)* vote *m*; *Fin & Com (→ of accounts)* approbation *f*; *Fin (→ of dividend)* passation *f*

(**d**) *(giving → of message etc)* transmission *f*; *(→ of judgement)* prononcé *m*

(**e**) *Sport* passes *fpl*; **he is renowned for his passing** il est célèbre pour (la qualité de) ses passes; **his passing of the ball is excellent** ses passes sont excellentes

(**f**) *Euph (death)* trépas *m*, mort *f*

3 *adv Arch* fort, extrêmement; **passing fair** de toute beauté

4 in passing *adv* en passant; **I'd like to say in passing...** ...soit dit en passant

►► *Literary* **passing bell** glas *m*; **passing customer** client(e) *m,f* de passage; *Am* **passing lane** voie *f* de dépassement; **passing place** *Aut (on narrow road)* aire *f* de croisement; *(in general)* endroit *m* pour doubler; *Rail* voie *f* d'évitement *ou* de dédoublement; **passing shot** *(in tennis)* passing-shot *m*; *Com* **passing trade** clients *mpl ou* clientèle *f* de passage

passing-out parade *n Mil* défilé *m* de promotion

passion ['pæʃən] **1** *n* (**a**) *(love)* passion *f*; **to have a passion for sb** aimer qn passionnément; *Fig* **to have a passion for music/painting/cars** avoir la passion de la musique/de la peinture/des voitures; **to have a passion for Chinese cooking** adorer la cuisine chinoise; **crime of passion** crime *m* passionnel; **his latest passion is Faulkner** sa dernière passion, c'est Faulkner

(**b**) *(emotion)* passion *f*; **to play with great passion** jouer avec beaucoup d'enthousiasme *ou* d'ardeur; **passions are running high on this issue** ce sujet déchaîne les passions; **she sings with great passion** elle chante avec beaucoup de passion; **nationalist passions** passions *fpl* nationalistes; **to hate sb/sth with a passion** avoir horreur de qn/qch

(**c**) *Literary (fit of anger)* (accès *m* de) colère *f*; **he tore it up in a (fit of) passion** il l'a déchiré dans un accès de colère; **to be in a passion**

about sth être fou de colère à cause de qch; **to fly into a passion** s'emporter

2 **Passion** *n Mus & Rel* **the Passion** la Passion

►► ***Passion play*** mystère *m* de la Passion; ***Passion Sunday*** le dimanche de la Passion; ***Passion Week*** la semaine de la Passion

'St Matthew Passion' *Bach* 'La Passion selon saint Matthieu'

passional ['pæʃənəl] *n Rel* passionnaire *m*

passionate ['pæʃənɪt] *adj* (**a**) *(love, lover)* passionné, ardent; *(embrace, kiss)* passionné; *(relationship)* passionnel; **to make passionate love** faire l'amour avec passion; **a passionate weekend** un week-end de passion

(**b**) *(speech)* véhément; *(advocate, believer)* fervent, ardent; **it was a passionate performance by the team** l'équipe a joué avec beaucoup d'enthousiasme *ou* d'ardeur; **he is passionate in his commitment to peace** c'est un fervent *ou* ardent défenseur de la paix; **a passionate plea for justice** un véhément appel à la justice; **she's passionate about human rights** elle est dévouée à la cause des droits de l'homme

►► ***passion fruit*** fruit *m* de la Passion

passionately ['pæʃənɪtlɪ] *adv* (**a**) *(love, kiss)* passionnément; **to be passionately in love with sb** aimer qn passionnément (**b**) *(believe, committed)* ardemment, avec ferveur; *(speak, argue)* avec passion, avec véhémence; *(sing)* avec passion; **to be passionately fond of sth/doing sth** adorer qch/faire qch; **he is passionately devoted to the cause** il est dévoué à la cause corps et âme

passionflower ['pæʃən,flaʊə(r)] *n* passiflore *f*, fleur *f* de la Passion

Passionist ['pæʃənɪst] *n Rel* passionniste *m*

passion-killer *n Fam* **it was a real passion-killer** ça m'a/l'a/*etc* complètement refroidi □

passionless ['pæʃənlɪs] *adj* sans passion

Passiontide ['pæʃəntaɪd] *n Rel* = la semaine de la Passion et la semaine sainte

passivation [,pæsɪ'veɪʃən] *n Tech* passivation *f*

passive ['pæsɪv] **1** *adj* (**a**) *(gen) & Chem & Electron* passif

(**b**) *Gram* passif; **the passive voice** la voix passive

2 *n Gram* passif *m*; **in the passive** au passif

►► *Med* ***passive immunity*** immunité *f* passive; *Comput* ***passive matrix screen*** écran *m* à matrice passive; ***passive resistance*** résistance *f* passive; ***passive smoker*** = non-fumeur dans un environnement fumeur; ***passive smoking*** tabagisme *m* passif

passively ['pæsɪvlɪ] *adv* (**a**) *(gen)* passivement (**b**) *Gram* au passif

passiveness ['pæsɪvnɪs], **passivity** [pæ'sɪvətɪ] *n* passivité *f*

passivization [,pæsɪvaɪ'zeɪʃən] *n Gram* mise *f* au passif; **the verb can undergo passivization** on peut mettre le verbe au passif

passivize, -ise ['pæsɪvaɪz] *vt Gram* passiver

passkey ['pɑːskiː] *n* passe-partout *m inv*

Passover ['pɑːs,əʊvə(r)] *n* la Pâque (juive), Pesah *m*

passport ['pɑːspɔːt] *n* (**a**) *(document)* passeport *m*; **British passport holders** les détenteurs *mpl* de passeports britanniques (**b**) *Fig* clé *f*; **the passport to happiness** la clé du bonheur; **this job was her passport to fame** ce travail a été son passeport pour la célébrité

►► ***passport control*** contrôle *m* des passeports; ***passport number*** numéro *m* de passeport; ***passport photo*** photo *f* d'identité

passport-sized photograph *n* photo *f* d'identité

pass-the-parcel *n Br* = jeu où l'on se passe un cadeau emballé dans plusieurs épaisseurs de papier, le but étant d'en enlever une lorsque la musique s'arrête et que l'on est en possession du paquet, le gagnant étant celui qui retire la dernière épaisseur de papier

pass-through *n Am (serving hatch)* passe-plats *m*

►► *Am Fin* ***pass-through securities*** titres *mpl* garantis par des créances hypothécaires; *Am Fin* ***pass-through tax entity*** = société fiscalement opaque

password ['pɑːswɜːd] *n* mot *m* de passe

►► *Comput* ***password protection*** protection *f* par mot de passe

password-protected *adj Comput* protégé par mot de passe

past [pɑːst] **1** *n* (**a**) *(former time)* passé *m*; **to live in the past** vivre dans le passé; **the great empires of the past** les grands empires de l'histoire; **it is a thing of the past** *(institution, custom)* ça n'existe plus; *(relationship)* c'est du passé; *(is old-fashioned)* c'est périmé; **those days are a thing of the past** cette époque est révolue; **politeness seems to have become a thing of the past** la politesse semble être une chose démodée

(**b**) *(background → of person)* passé *m*; **woman with a past** femme *f* qui a vécu *ou* qui a un passé chargé; **town with a past** ville *f* historique; **our country's glorious past** le glorieux passé de notre pays

(**c**) *Gram* passé *m*; **in the past** au passé

2 *adj* (**a**) *(former, gone by → life)* antérieur; *(→ quarrels, differences)* vieux (vieille), d'autrefois; *(→ generation, centuries, mistakes, event)* passé; **in centuries past** autrefois; **the time for negotiating is past** l'heure n'est plus à la négociation; **those days are past** ces temps sont révolus; **from past experience** par expérience; **in past time** *or* **times past** autrefois, (au temps) jadis; **to be past** *(ended)* être passé *ou* terminé; **the crisis is now past** la crise est maintenant passée; **the past mayors of the town** les anciens maires de la ville

(**b**) *(last)* dernier; **the past week** la semaine dernière *ou* passée; **the past two months** les deux derniers mois; **this past month has been very busy** le mois qui vient de s'achever a été très chargé; **I've not been feeling well for the past few days** ça fait quelques jours que je ne me sens pas très bien; **he has spent the past five years in China** il a passé ces cinq dernières années en Chine

(**c**) *Gram* passé

3 *prep* (**a**) *(in time)* après; **it's ten/quarter/half past six** il est six heures dix/et quart/et demie; **it is past four (o'clock)** il est quatre heures passées; **it's quarter past the hour** il est le *ou* et quart; **it's already past midnight** il est déjà plus de minuit *ou* minuit passé; **it's long** *or* **way past my bedtime** je devrais être au lit depuis longtemps; **he's past fifty** il a plus de cinquante ans, il a dépassé la cinquantaine; **she's past the adolescent stage** ce n'est plus une adolescente; **these beans are past their best** ces haricots ne sont plus très frais

(**b**) *(further than)* plus loin que, au-delà de; **just past the bridge** un peu plus loin que le pont, un peu au-delà du pont; **turn right just past the school** prenez à droite juste après l'école; **he can't count past ten** il ne sait compter que jusqu'à dix; **I didn't manage to get past the first page** je n'ai pas réussi à lire plus d'une page; **he knocked the ball past the defender** il a envoyé la balle derrière le défenseur

(**c**) *(in front of)* devant; **he walked right past my table** il est passé juste devant ma table; **he walked past me without saying hello** il est passé devant moi sans me saluer

(**d**) *(beyond scope of)* au-delà de; **it's past all understanding** ça dépasse l'entendement; **their demands are past all reason** leurs exigences sont totalement démesurées; **past endurance** insupportable; **that's past all belief** c'est incroyable

(**e**) *(incapable of)* **I'm past caring** ça ne me fait plus ni chaud ni froid; **I'm past work** *(too old)* je ne suis plus d'âge à travailler; *(too ill)* je ne peux plus travailler; *Fam* **to be past it** *(person)* avoir passé l'âge □; *(car, machine)* avoir fait son temps □; **I wouldn't put it past him** il en est bien capable; **I wouldn't put anything past this government** ce gouvernement est capable de tout *ou* du pire

4 *adv* (**a**) *(by)* **to go past** passer; **they ran past** ils passèrent en courant; **the years flew past** les années passaient à une vitesse prodigieuse

(**b**) *(ago)* **one night about three years past** une nuit il y a environ trois ans; **it had long past struck midnight** minuit avait sonné depuis longtemps

5 **in the past** *adv* autrefois, dans le temps

►► ***past master*** expert *m*; *Hum* **he's a past master at doing as little as possible** il est passé maître dans l'art d'en faire le moins possible; *Gram* ***past participle*** participe *m* passé; *Gram* ***past perfect*** plus-que-parfait *m*; *Gram* ***past tense*** passé *m*; **in the past tense** au passé

pasta ['pæstə] *n (UNCOUNT)* pâtes *fpl* (alimentaires)

►► ***pasta machine*** machine *f* à fabriquer les pâtes; ***pasta salad*** salade *f* de pâtes; ***pasta sauce*** sauce *f* pour pâtes

paste [peɪst] **1** *n* (**a**) *(smooth substance)* pâte *f*; *Cer* **hard/soft paste** pâte *f* dure/tendre

(**b**) *Culin (dough)* pâte *f*; **fish/meat paste** = pâte à tartiner à base de poisson/viande; **tomato paste** concentré *m* de tomate

(**c**) *(glue)* colle *f*

(**d**) *(for jewellery)* strass *m*, stras *m*; **paste necklace/diamonds** collier *m*/diamants *mpl* en strass *ou* strass

2 *vt* (**a**) *(stick → stamp, poster)* coller; *(→ wallpaper)* encoller; **paste the labels on the parcel** collez les étiquettes sur le colis

(**b**) *(cover → wall)* recouvrir; **the crate was pasted with stickers** la caisse était couverte d'autocollants

(**c**) *Comput (text)* coller (**into/onto** dans)

(**d**) *Fam (beat up)* tabasser, casser la figure à; *(defeat)* battre à plate(s) couture(s), mettre la pâtée à; **to get pasted** *(beaten up)* se faire tabasser; *(defeated)* être battu à plate(s) couture(s)

►**paste up** *vt sep (poster)* coller; *(notice, list)* afficher; *(wallpaper)* poser

pasteboard ['peɪstbɔːd] **1** *n* (**a**) *(cardboard)* carton *m* (**b**) *Am (for pastry)* planche *f* à pâtisserie

2 *comp* de *ou* en carton-pâte

pastel ['pæstəl] **1** *n (crayon)* pastel *m*; *(drawing)* (dessin *m* au) pastel *m*; **a portrait in pastels** un portrait au pastel; **pastels suit her** les couleurs *ou* teintes pastel lui vont bien

2 *adj* pastel *(inv)*; **pastel pink skirts** des jupes *fpl* rose pastel

►► ***pastel drawing*** (dessin *m* au) pastel *m*; ***pastel shade*** ton *m ou* teinte *f* pastel

pastelist, pastellist ['pæstəlɪst] *n Art* pastelliste *mf*

paste-on *n Typ* becquet *m*, béquet *m*

►► ***paste-on label*** applique *f*

pastern ['pæstɜːn] *n* paturon *m*

paste-up *n Typ* maquette *f*

pasteurization [,pɑːstʃəraɪ'zeɪʃən] *n* pasteurisation *f*

pasteurize, -ise ['pɑːstʃəraɪz] *vt* pasteuriser

pasteurized ['pɑːstʃəraɪzd] *adj* (**a**) *(milk, beer)* pasteurisé (**b**) *Pej (version, description)* édulcoré, aseptisé

pastiche [pæ'stiːʃ] *n* pastiche *m*

pastille, pastil ['pæstɪl] *n* pastille *f*; **cough pastilles** pastilles *fpl* pour *ou* contre la toux

pastime ['pɑːstaɪm] *n* passe-temps *m*

pastiness ['peɪstɪnɪs] *n* (**a**) *(of face)* teint *m* terreux (**b**) *(of bread etc)* consistance *f* pâteuse

pasting ['peɪstɪŋ] *n* (**a**) *(gluing → of poster etc)* collage *m*; *(→ of wallpaper)* encollage *m* (**b**) *Fam (beating)* rossée *f*, raclée *f*; **to give sb a pasting** *(beat up)* tabasser qn, mettre une raclée à qn; *(defeat)* battre qn à plate(s) couture(s); **to** *Br* **get** *or Am* **take a pasting** *(be beaten up)* se faire tabasser; *(be defeated)* être battu à plate(s) couture(s)

pastor ['pɑːstə(r)] *n Rel* pasteur *m*

pastoral ['pɑːstərəl] **1** *adj* (**a**) *(gen) & Art, Literature & Mus* pastoral; **they are a pastoral people** c'est un peuple de bergers; **a pastoral idyll** une idylle pastorale

(**b**) *Rel* pastoral; *Fig* **teachers also have a pastoral role** les enseignants ont également un rôle de conseillers

2 *n* (**a**) *Art, Literature & Mus* pastorale *f*

(**b**) *Rel* (lettre *f*) pastorale *f*

►► *Sch* ***pastoral care*** ≃ tutorat *m*; ***pastoral land*** pâturages *mpl*; *Rel* ***pastoral letter*** (lettre *f*) pastorale *f*; *Rel* ***pastoral staff*** crosse *f* (d'évêque); *Rel* ***pastoral visit*** visite *f* pastorale

'The Pastoral Symphony' *Beethoven* 'La (Symphonie) pastorale'

pastorale [pæstə'rɑːl] *n Mus* pastorale *f*

pastoralism ['pæstərəlɪzəm] *n* pastoralisme *m*, économie *f* pastorale

pastoralist ['pɑːstərəlɪst] *n* (**a**) *Austr & NZ (farmer)* éleveur *m* de bétail (**b**) *Art, Literature & Mus* pastoraliste *mf*

pastorally ['pɑːstərəlɪ] *adv Rel* pastoralement

pastorate ['pɑːstərɪt] *n Rel (office)* pastorat *m*; *(pastors)* pasteurs *mpl*

pastrami [pə'strɑːmɪ] *n* pastarmi *m*, pastermi *m*

pastry ['peɪstrɪ] (*pl* **pastries**) *n* (**a**) *(dough)* pâte *f* (**b**) *(cake)* pâtisserie *f*, gâteau *m*

▸▸ ***pastry board*** planche *f* à pâtisserie; ***pastry brush*** pinceau *m* (à pâtisserie); ***pastry case*** croûte *f*; ***pastry chef*** pâtissier(ère) *m,f*; ***pastry cream, pastry custard*** crème *f* pâtissière; ***pastry cutter*** emporte-pièce *m inv*; ***pastry shell*** fond *m* de tarte

pasturage ['pɑːstjʊrɪdʒ] *n* pâturage *m*

pasture ['pɑːstʃə(r)] **1** *n* pâture *f*, pâturage *m*; **to put out to pasture** *(animal)* mettre au pâturage; *Hum (person)* mettre au vert; *Hum (car)* mettre à la casse; **he left for greener pastures** *or* **pastures new** il est parti vers des horizons plus favorables

2 *vt (animal)* faire paître

3 *vi* paître, pâturer, pacager

pastureland ['pɑːstʃəlænd] *n* herbages *mpl*, pâturages *mpl*

pasty[1] ['peɪstɪ] (*compar* **pastier**, *superl* **pastiest**) *adj* (**a**) *(face, complexion)* terreux; *(person)* qui a le teint terreux (**b**) *(texture)* pâteux

pasty[2] ['pæstɪ] (*pl* **pasties**) *n Br Culin* ≃ petit pâté *m (en croûte)*

pasty-faced ['peɪstɪ-] *adj* au teint terreux

pat [pæt] (*pt & pp* **patted**, *cont* **patting**) **1** *vt* tapoter; *(animal)* caresser, flatter (de la main); **"sit here", she said, patting the place beside her** "assieds-toi ici", dit-elle, désignant la place à côté d'elle; **pat the fish/vegetables dry** séchez le poisson/les légumes avec de l'essuie-tout; **she patted her hair** elle se tapota les cheveux; **to pat sb on the back** donner une tape dans le dos à qn; *Fig (congratulate)* féliciter qn; *Fig* **to pat oneself on the back** se féliciter

2 *n* (**a**) *(tap)* (légère) tape *f*; **he gave me a friendly pat on the shoulder** il m'a donné une tape amicale sur l'épaule; **to give sb a pat on the back** donner une tape dans le dos à qn; *Fig (congratulate)* féliciter qn; *Fig* **to give oneself a pat on the back** se féliciter

(**b**) *(lump)* **a pat of butter** une noix de beurre

3 *adj* (**a**) *(glib → remark)* tout fait; *(→ answer)* tout prêt; **his story is a little too pat** son histoire colle un peu trop bien

(**b**) *(in poker)* **a pat hand** une main servie

4 *adv* (**a**) *(exactly)* parfaitement, avec facilité; **to know** *or* **have sth off pat** savoir qch par cœur; **he had his explanation off pat** il avait une explication toute prête

(**b**) *Am* **to stand pat** *(on decision)* rester intraitable; **dealer stands pat** *(in poker)* pas de cartes pour le donneur, donneur servi

▸**pat down** *vt sep (soil, sand etc)* tasser (doucement)

Patagonia [,pætə'gəʊnɪə] *n* Patagonie *f*; **in Patagonia** en Patagonie

Patagonian [,pætə'gəʊnɪən] **1** *n* Patagon(onne) *m,f*

2 *adj* patagon

patch [pætʃ] **1** *n* (**a**) *(of fabric)* pièce *f*; *(on garment)* pièce *f* (rapportée); *(on sail)* placard *m*; *(on inner tube)* Rustine® *f*; **a jacket with suede patches on the elbows** une veste avec des pièces en daim aux coudes; *Fam Fig* **he's not a patch on you** il ne t'arrive pas à la cheville; **his last novel isn't a patch on the others** son dernier roman est loin de valoir les autres ❑

(**b**) *(over eye)* bandeau *m*; **he wore a black eye patch** il avait un bandeau noir sur l'œil

(**c**) *(sticking plaster)* pansement *m* (adhésif)

(**d**) *(beauty spot)* mouche *f*

(**e**) *Mil (on uniform)* insigne *m*

(**f**) *(plot of land)* parcelle *f*, lopin *m*; **cabbage/strawberry patch** carré *m* de choux/de fraises; **cotton patch** champ *m* de coton; **vegetable patch** carré *m* de légumes

(**g**) *(of light, colour, grease, dampness)* tache *f*; *(of fog, mist)* nappe *f*; *(of oil)* flaque *f*; *(of ice)* plaque *f*; **there were damp patches on the ceiling** il y avait des taches d'humidité au plafond; **patch of blue sky** pan *m ou* coin *m ou* échappée *f* de ciel bleu; **snow still lay in patches on the slopes** les pistes étaient encore enneigées par endroits; **we crossed a rough patch of road** nous sommes passés sur un tronçon de route défoncé; **a bald patch** une (petite) tonsure

(**h**) *Br (period)* période *f*, moment *m*; **to go through a bad** *or* **sticky** *or* **rough patch** traverser une période difficile *ou* une mauvaise passe; **the company had a bad patch in 1998** la firme a connu des moments difficiles en 1998

(**i**) *Br (of prostitute, salesperson, police officer)* secteur *m*; *Fam* **keep off my patch!** ne mets pas les pieds sur mon territoire!

(**j**) *Comput* modification *f* (de programme); *(correction)* correction *f*

(**k**) *Med (for administering substance through skin)* patch *m*, timbre *m*

2 *vt* (**a**) *(mend → clothes)* rapiécer; *(→ tyre, canoe)* réparer; *Naut (→ sail)* placarder; **his jeans were patched at the knees** son jean avait des pièces *ou* était rapiécé aux genoux; **they patched the hole in the roof** ils ont colmaté *ou* bouché le trou dans la toiture

(**b**) *Comput (program)* modifier

(**c**) *Tel* raccorder; **I'll patch you through** je vous passe votre communication; **patch me through to headquarters** passez-moi le siège social

▸▸ *Tel* ***patch board*** tableau *m* de raccordement; *Sewing* ***patch pocket*** poche *f* plaquée; *Med* ***patch test*** test *m* cutané

▸**patch together** *vt sep Fam (temporary shelter, broken object)* assembler ❑; *(business plan, team, government)* mettre sur pied ❑; **they patched together a documentary** ils ont monté un documentaire tant bien que mal; **we are beginning to patch together an understanding of...** petit à petit nous commençons à nous faire une idée de... ❑; *Pej* **the whole thing is a bit patched together** tout est un peu mal fichu

▸**patch up** *vt sep Fam* (**a**) *(repair → clothes)* rapiécer ❑; *(→ car, boat)* réparer ❑; *(→ in makeshift way)* rafistoler; **they patched him up in hospital** ils l'ont rafistolé à l'hôpital

(**b**) *(relationship)* **he's trying to patch things up with his wife** il essaie de se rabibocher avec sa femme; **they patched up their differences** ils ont réglé leurs différends ❑

patchiness ['pætʃɪnɪs] *n* (**a**) *(of performance, novel)* manque *m* d'unité (**b**) *(of paintwork)* effet *m* de teintes *ou* de couleurs mal fondues (**c**) *(of knowledge)* **the patchiness of his knowledge of...** sa connaissance imparfaite en matière de...

patching ['pætʃɪŋ] *n (of piece of clothing)* rapiéçage *m*, rapiècement *m*; **we can use that old jacket for patching** nous pouvons utiliser cette vieille veste pour faire du rapiècement *ou* rapiéçage

patchouli ['pætʃʊlɪ] *n* patchouli *m*

▸▸ ***patchouli oil*** patchouli *m*

patchwork ['pætʃwɜːk] *n* (**a**) *Sewing* patchwork *m*; *Fig (of colours, fields)* mosaïque *f* (**b**) *(collection)* collection *f*; **the book is a patchwork of previously published writings** le livre rassemble des écrits déjà publiés; **a patchwork team** une équipe disparate *ou* hétéroclite

▸▸ ***patchwork quilt*** couverture *f* en patchwork

patchy ['pætʃɪ] (*compar* **patchier**, *superl* **patchiest**) *adj* (**a**) *(performance, novel, TV coverage)* inégal

(**b**) *(paintwork)* inégal, irrégulier; **patchy fog** des nappes *fpl* de brouillard; **patchy rain** des averses *fpl* éparses; **patchy cloud** nuages *mpl* épars

(**c**) *(evidence)* incomplet(ète); *(knowledge)* imparfait; **our knowledge of that period of history is very patchy** nous n'avons qu'une connaissance imparfaite de cette période de l'histoire

pate [peɪt] *n Arch or Hum* tête *f*; **bald pate** crâne *m* chauve

pâté ['pæteɪ] *n* pâté *m*; **liver pâté** pâté *m* de foie

patella [pə'telə] (*pl* **patellas** *or* **patellae** [-liː]) *n* (**a**) *Anat* rotule *f* (**b**) *Archeol* patelle *f*

paten ['pætən] *n Rel* patène *f*

patency ['peɪtənsɪ] *n* (**a**) *(obviousness)* évidence *f* (**b**) *(openness)* état *m* ouvert

patent [*Br* 'peɪtənt, *Am* 'pætənt] **1** *n* (**a**) *(on invention)* brevet *m* (d'invention); *(thing patented)* invention *f*/fabrication *f* brevetée; **to take out a patent on sth** prendre un brevet sur qch, faire breveter qch; **patent pending** *(on packaging)* demande de brevet déposée

(**b**) *(leather)* cuir *m* verni, vernis *m*

(**c**) *Am (on land)* concession *f*

2 *adj* (**a**) *(product, procedure)* breveté

(**b**) *Law* **letters patent** lettres *fpl* patentes

(**c**) *(evident → lack of concern, disrespect)* manifeste; *(→ fact)* évident; **that's a patent lie!** c'est un mensonge éhonté!

(**d**) *(open)* ouvert

3 *vt (of authorities)* protéger par un brevet, breveter; *(of inventor)* faire breveter, prendre un brevet pour

▸▸ ***patent agent*** agent *m* en brevets; ***patent application*** demande *f ou* dépôt *m* de brevet; *Am* ***patent attorney*** conseil *m* en matière de brevets; ***patent goods*** articles *mpl* brevetés; ***patent leather*** cuir *m* verni, vernis *m*; ***patent leather boots*** bottes *fpl* vernies *or* en cuir verni; ***patent medicine*** médicament *m* vendu sans ordonnance; *Pej (cure-all)* élixir *m* universel, remède *m* de charlatan; ***Patent Office*** ≃ Institut *m* national de la propriété industrielle; ***patent rights*** propriété *f* industrielle

patentability [*Br* ,peɪtəntə'bɪlɪtɪ, *Am* ,pætəntə'bɪlɪtɪ] *n* brevetabilité *f*

patentable [*Br* 'peɪtəntəbəl, *Am* 'pætəntəbəl] *adj* brevetable

patented [*Br* 'peɪtəntɪd, *Am* 'pætəntɪd] *adj (product, procedure)* breveté

patentee [*Br* ,peɪtən'tiː, *Am* ,pætən'tiː] *n* détenteur(trice) *m,f ou* titulaire *mf* d'un/du brevet (d'invention)

patently [*Br* 'peɪtəntlɪ, *Am* 'pætəntlɪ] *adv* manifestement, de toute évidence; **he was patently lying** il était manifeste qu'il mentait; **it was patently obvious that...** il était absolument évident que... + *indicative*

patentor [*Br* 'peɪtəntə(r), *Am* 'pætəntə(r)] *n* organisme *m* délivrant un brevet

pater ['peɪtə(r)] *n Br Fam Old-fashioned* pater *m*, paternel *m*

paterfamilias [,peɪtəfə'mɪlɪæs] *n Formal* paterfamilias *m*

paternal [pə'tɜːnəl] *adj* (**a**) *(fatherly → love, instinct)* paternel; *(→ role, responsibilities)* de père (**b**) *(related through father)* paternel

▸▸ ***paternal grandparents*** grands-parents *mpl* paternels

paternalism [pə'tɜːnəlɪzəm] *n* paternalisme *m*

paternalist [pə'tɜːnəlɪst] **1** *n* = personne qui fait preuve de paternalisme

2 *adj* paternaliste

paternalistic [pə,tɜːnə'lɪstɪk] *adj* paternaliste

paternalistically [pə,tɜːnə'lɪstɪklɪ] *adv (govern)* avec paternalisme; *(say)* d'un ton paternaliste; *(smile)* d'un air paternaliste

paternally [pə'tɜːnəlɪ] *adv* paternellement

paternity [pə'tɜːnətɪ] *n* paternité *f*; **there are doubts about his paternity** on n'est pas sûr de l'identité de son père

▸▸ ***paternity leave*** congé *m* de paternité; *Law* ***paternity order*** (ordonnance *f* de) reconnaissance *f* de paternité; *Law* ***paternity suit*** action *f* en recherche de paternité; ***paternity test*** test *m* de recherche de paternité

paternoster [,pætə'nɒstə(r)] **1** *n* (**a**) *(rosary bead)* pater *m* (**b**) *(fishing tackle, lift)* pater-noster *m*

2 Paternoster *n (prayer)* Pater *m*

path [pɑːθ, *pl* pɑːðz] *n* (**a**) *(in garden, park)* allée *f*; *(in country)* chemin *m*, sentier *m*; *(pavement)* trottoir *m*

(**b**) *(way ahead or through)* chemin *m*, passage *m*; *(of inquiry, investigation)* ligne *f*; **his career path** son choix de carrière; **to cut a path through sth** se tailler *ou* se frayer un chemin à travers qch; **a tree blocked his path** un arbre lui bloquait le passage *ou* chemin; **he stepped into the path of an oncoming vehicle** il est allé sur la chaussée au moment où arrivait un véhicule; **the hurricane destroyed everything in its path** l'ouragan a tout détruit sur son passage; *Fig* **the**

path to fame *or* **glory** la route *ou* le chemin qui mène à la gloire

(**c**) *(trajectory → of moving body)* trajet *m*, course *f*; *(→ of projectile, planet)* trajectoire *f*; *(→ of ray of light)* passage *m*, trajet *m*; *(→ of sun)* route *f*; **their paths had crossed before** leurs chemins s'étaient déjà croisés; **our paths first crossed in 1985** nos chemins se sont croisés *ou* nous nous sommes rencontrés pour la première fois en 1985

(**d**) *Comput* chemin *m* (d'accès)

'Paths of Glory' *Kubrick* 'Les Sentiers de la gloire'

Pathan [pə'tɑːn] **1** *n* Pathan(e) *m,f*

2 *adj* pathan

pathetic [pə'θetɪk] *adj* (**a**) *(pitiable → lament, waif, smile, story)* pitoyable; **it was pathetic to see how they lived** cela serrait le cœur *ou* c'était un crève-cœur de voir dans quelles conditions ils vivaient; **a pathetic story** une histoire pitoyable *ou* pathétique

(**b**) *Fam (poor, useless → excuse, game, person etc)* lamentable, pitoyable; **you're pathetic!** tu es lamentable!; **how pathetic!, it's pathetic!** c'est (vraiment) lamentable!

►► *Literature* ***pathetic fallacy*** = attribution à la nature de sentiments humains

pathetically [pə'θetɪklɪ] *adv* (**a**) *(touchingly)* pitoyablement; **they wept pathetically** ils pleuraient d'une façon pitoyable; **she looked at him pathetically** elle lui jeta un regard pitoyable; **he used to be pathetically shy** autrefois, il était d'une timidité qui faisait peine à voir

(**b**) *Fam (atrociously)* lamentablement; **pathetically bad** *(performance, speech etc)* lamentable; **pathetically easy** si facile que c'en est ridicule; **that's a pathetically weak excuse** c'est une excuse lamentable; **they performed pathetically** ils ont offert une performance lamentable *ou* pitoyable

pathfinder ['pɑːθ,faɪndə(r)] *n* (**a**) *(scout)* éclaireur *m* (**b**) *Fig (pioneer)* pionnier *m* (**c**) *(aircraft)* avion *m* éclaireur

pathless ['pɑːθlɪs] *adj* sans chemin frayé *ou* battu; *(land)* vierge

pathname ['pɑːθneɪm] *n Comput* chemin *m* d'accès

patho- ['pæθəʊ] *pref* patho-

pathogen ['pæθədʒən] *n Med* pathogéne *m*

pathogenesis [,pæθə'dʒenɪsɪs] *n Med* pathogénie *f*

pathogenetic [,pæθəʊdʒɪ'netɪk], **pathogenic** [,pæθəʊ'dʒenɪk], **pathogenous** [,pæ'θɒdʒɪnəs] *adj Med* pathogène, pathogénique

pathogeny [pə'θɒdʒənɪ] *n Med* pathogénie *f*

pathognomic [,pæθɒg'nɒmɪk], **pathognomonic** [,pæθɒgnəʊ'mɒnɪk] *adj Med* pathognomonique

pathological [,pæθə'lɒdʒɪkəl] *adj* pathologique; **he's a pathological liar** il ne peut pas s'empêcher de mentir

pathologically [,pæθə'lɒdʒɪklɪ] *adv* pathologiquement; **to be pathologically afraid of sth** avoir une peur pathologique de qch

pathologist [pə'θɒlədʒɪst] *n* pathologiste *mf*; **(forensic) pathologist** médecin *m* légiste

pathology [pə'θɒlədʒɪ] (*pl* **pathologies**) *n* pathologie *f*

pathos ['peɪθɒs] *n* pathétique *m*

pathway ['pɑːθweɪ] *n (in garden)* allée *f*; *(in country)* chemin *m*, sentier *m*; *(pavement)* trottoir *m*

patience ['peɪʃəns] *n* (**a**) *(tolerance)* patience *f*; **to lose patience (with sb)** perdre patience (avec qn); **(have) patience!** (prenez) patience!; **I haven't the patience to redo it** je n'ai pas la patience de le refaire; **he has no patience with children** les enfants l'exaspèrent; **don't try my patience any further!** ne mets pas davantage ma patience à l'épreuve!, n'abuse pas davantage de ma patience!; **my patience is wearing thin** ma patience a des limites, je suis à bout de patience

(**b**) *Br (card game)* réussite *f*; **she was playing patience** elle faisait des réussites

patient ['peɪʃənt] **1** *adj* patient; **to be patient** *(naturally)* être patient, avoir de la patience; *(on specific occasion)* être patient, patienter, prendre patience; **be patient!** (un peu de) patience!, soyez patient!; **if you'll be patient a few moments longer** veuillez patienter encore quelques instants; **with a patient smile** avec un sourire empreint d'une grande patience

2 *n Med* malade *mf*, patient(e) *m,f*; *(after operation)* opéré(e) *m,f*

►► ***patient care*** soins *mpl* administrés aux patients; ***Patient's Charter*** = la charte officielle du National Health Service

patiently ['peɪʃəntlɪ] *adv* patiemment; **a long illness, patiently borne** une longue maladie, endurée avec patience

patina ['pætɪnə] (*pl* **patinas** *or* **patinae** [-niː]) *n* patine *f*

patinated ['pætɪneɪtɪd] *adj* couvert d'une patine; *(bronze)* patiné

patio ['pætɪəʊ] (*pl* **patios**) *n* patio *m*

►► ***patio doors*** porte-fenêtre *f*; ***patio furniture*** meubles *mpl* de jardin

Patna rice ['pætnə-] *n* = variété de riz long

patois ['pætwɑː] (*pl* **inv** [-wɑːz]) *n* patois *m*

patrial ['peɪtrɪəl] *n Formerly* = personne ayant automatiquement le droit de résider au Royaume-Uni, notamment parce que ses parents ou ses grands-parents y sont nés

patriarch ['peɪtrɪɑːk] *n* patriarche *m*

patriarchal [,peɪtrɪ'ɑːkəl] *adj* patriarcal

►► ***patriarchal cross*** croix *f* patriarcale

patriarchally [,peɪtrɪ'ɑːkəlɪ] *adv* patriarcalement, en patriarche

patriarchate ['peɪtrɪɑːkɪt] *n Rel* patriarcat *m*

patriarchy ['peɪtrɪɑːkɪ] (*pl* **patriarchies**) *n* patriarcat *m*

patrician [pə'trɪʃən] **1** *adj* patricien

2 *n* patricien(enne) *m,f*

patricide ['pætrɪsaɪd] *n* (**a**) *(crime)* parricide *m* (**b**) *(person)* parricide *mf*

patrilineage [,pætrɪ'lɪnɪɪdʒ] *n* descendance *f* par la ligne paternelle

patrilineal [,pætrɪ'lɪnɪəl] *adj* patrilinéaire

patrimonial [,pætrɪ'məʊnɪəl] *adj* patrimonial

patrimonially [,pætrɪ'məʊnɪəlɪ] *adv* patrimonialement

patrimony [*Br* 'pætrɪmənɪ, *Am* 'pætrɪməʊnɪ] (*pl* **patrimonies**) *n* (**a**) *(inheritance)* patrimoine *m* (**b**) *(of church)* biens-fonds *mpl*, revenu *m*

patriot [*Br* 'pætrɪət, *Am* 'peɪtrɪət] *n* patriote *mf*

patriotic [*Br* ,pætrɪ'ɒtɪk, *Am* ,peɪtrɪ'ɒtɪk] *adj (person)* patriote; *(song, action, speech)* patriotique

patriotically [*Br* ,pætrɪ'ɒtɪklɪ, *Am* ,peɪtrɪ'ɒtɪklɪ] *adv* patriotiquement, en patriote

patriotism [*Br* 'pætrɪətɪzəm, *Am* 'peɪtrɪətɪzəm] *n* patriotisme *m*

patristic [pə'trɪstɪk] *Rel* **1** *adj* patristique, des Pères de l'Église

2 patristics *n (UNCOUNT)* patristique *f*, patrologie *f*

patrol [pə'trəʊl] (*pt & pp* **patrolled**, *cont* **patrolling**) **1** *n* (**a**) *(group)* patrouille *f*; **the patrol is** *or* **are on the way** la patrouille est en route; *Am* **highway patrol** police *f* des autoroutes

(**b**) *(task → gen)* patrouille *f*; *(→ of nightwatchman, police officer on foot)* ronde *f*; **to be on patrol** être de patrouille, patrouiller; **they were sent out on patrol** ils ont été envoyés en patrouille

2 *vi* patrouiller, être en patrouille

3 *vt (town, streets)* patrouiller dans; **the border is patrolled by armed guards** des gardes armés patrouillent le long de la frontière

►► ***patrol boat*** patrouilleur *m*; ***patrol car*** voiture *f* de police; ***patrol leader*** chef *m* de patrouille; *Am, Austr & NZ* ***patrol wagon*** fourgon *m* cellulaire

patrolman [pə'trəʊlmən] (*pl* **patrolmen** [-mən]) *n* (**a**) *Am (policeman)* agent *m* de police *(qui fait sa ronde)* (**b**) *Br (from motoring organization)* = dépanneur employé par une association d'automobilistes

patrology [pæ'trɒlədʒɪ] *n Rel* patrologie *f*, patristique *f*

patrolwoman [pə'trəʊl,wʊmən] (*pl* **patrolwomen** [-,wɪmɪn]) *n Am* femme *f* agent de police *(qui fait sa ronde)*

patron ['peɪtrən] *n* (**a**) *(sponsor → of the arts)* mécène *m*; *(→ of festival)* parrain *m*, sponsor *m*; *(→ of charity)* patron(onne) *m,f*; **he's a patron of the arts** c'est un mécène *ou* un protecteur des arts; **many multinational companies are becoming patrons of the arts** de nombreuses multinationales se lancent dans le mécénat; **the mayor is one of the patrons of our association** *(supporter)* le maire est une des personnes qui ont accordé leur patronage à notre association

(**b**) *(customer → of restaurant, hotel, shop)* client(e) *m,f*; *(→ of library)* usager *m*; *(→ of museum)* visiteur(euse) *m,f*; *(→ of theatre, cinema)* spectateur(trice) *m,f*; **patrons only** *(sign)* réservé aux clients

(**c**) *(in ancient Rome)* patron *m*

►► ***patron saint*** (saint(e) *m,f*) patron(onne) *m,f*

patronage ['peɪtrənɪdʒ] *n* (**a**) *(support → gen)* patronage *m*, parrainage *m*; *(→ of art)* mécénat *m*; *(→ of charity)* patronage *m*

(**b**) *Com (custom)* clientèle *f*; **I shall take my patronage elsewhere** j'irai me fournir ailleurs

(**c**) *Pol* pouvoir *m* de nomination; *Pej* népotisme *m*; **he got the promotion through the Minister's patronage** il a obtenu de l'avancement grâce à l'influence du ministre

(**d**) *(sponsorship)* mécénat *m*

(**e**) *(condescension)* condescendance *f*

(**f**) *(in Church of England)* droit *m* de présentation (à un bénéfice)

patronal [pə'trəʊnəl] *adj Rel* patronal

patroness ['peɪtrənɪs] *n Old-fashioned (of the arts)* protectrice *f*, mécène *m*; *(of charity)* (dame *f*) patronnesse *f*

patronize, -ise ['pætrənaɪz] *vt* (**a**) *(business)* donner *ou* accorder sa clientèle à; *(cinema)* être un(e) habitué(e) de, fréquenter; **a restaurant patronized by the famous** un restaurant fréquenté par des gens célèbres; **we no longer patronize the local shops** nous ne faisons plus nos courses dans le quartier, nous ne nous fournissons plus dans les magasins du quartier

(**b**) *(condescend to)* traiter avec condescendance; **don't patronize me!** ne prenez pas ce ton condescendant avec moi!

(**c**) *(sponsor → gen)* parrainer; *(→ artist)* soutenir

patronizing ['pætrənaɪzɪŋ] *adj* condescendant; **to be patronizing towards sb** se montrer condescendant envers qn, traiter qn avec condescendance

patronizingly ['pætrənaɪzɪŋlɪ] *adv (smile)* avec condescendance; *(say)* d'un ton condescendant

patronymic [,pætrə'nɪmɪk] **1** *n* patronyme *m*

2 *adj* patronymique

patsy ['pætsɪ] (*pl* **patsies**) *n Am Fam (gullible person)* pigeon *m*, gogo *m*; *(scapegoat)* bouc *m* émissaire ❑

patten ['pætən] *n* socque *m (pour protéger les chaussures contre la boue)*

patter ['pætə(r)] **1** *n* (**a**) *(sound → of footsteps)* petit bruit *m*; *(→ of mice)* trottinement *m*; *(→ of rain)* crépitement *m*; *(gentler)* tambourinement *m*; **the patter of rain on the windows** le crépitement de la pluie sur les fenêtres; *Hum* **we'll soon be hearing the (pitter) patter of tiny feet** nous attendons un heureux événement

(**b**) *Fam (of entertainer)* bavardage *m*, baratin *m*; *Pej (of salesman)* baratin *m*, boniment *m*

(**c**) *Fam (jargon)* jargon ❑ *m*

2 *vi* (**a**) *(raindrops)* crépiter; *(more gently)* tambouriner

(**b**) *(person, mouse)* trottiner; **she pattered down the corridor in her slippers** elle trottinait dans le couloir en pantoufles

(**c**) *Fam (talk)* bavarder, baratiner

pattern ['pætən] **1** *n* (**a**) *(design → decorative)* motif *m*; *(→ natural)* dessin *m*; *(→ on animal)* marques *fpl*; **a geometric/herringbone pattern** un motif géométrique/à chevrons

(**b**) *(physical arrangement)* disposition *f*, configuration *f*; **to form a pattern** former un motif *ou* un dessin; **the pattern of light and shade on the ground** le dessin que forment les effets d'ombre et de lumière sur le sol; **the pattern of footprints on the sand** la disposition des empreintes de pas sur le sable

(**c**) *(standard way of occurring or being arranged)* système *m*, configuration *f*; **pattern of events** cheminement *m* des événements; **sometimes there seems to be no pattern to** our lives notre existence semble parfois être régie par le hasard; **all the different elements fell into a pattern** tous les éléments ont fini par s'emboîter les uns dans les autres *ou* s'articuler les uns aux autres; **research has established that there is a pattern in** *or* **to the data** la recherche a établi que les données ne sont pas aléatoires; **such incidents are part of a wider pattern of abuse** de tels incidents s'inscrivent dans un contexte de violence plus large; **some clear patterns emerge from the statistics** des tendances nettes ressortent des statistiques; **behaviour patterns in monkeys** types *mpl* de comportement chez les singes; **weather patterns** grandes tendances *fpl* climatiques; **there is a definite pattern to the burglaries** on observe une constante bien précise dans les cambriolages; **the pattern of TV viewing in the average household** les habitudes *fpl* du téléspectateur moyen; **to follow a set pattern** se dérouler toujours de la même façon; **the evening followed the usual pattern** la soirée s'est déroulée selon le schéma habituel; **economic growth on the Japanese pattern** croissance économique à la japonaise; **pattern of trade** structure *f* des échanges; **voice pattern** empreintes *fpl* vocales

(**d**) *(diagram, shape which guides)* & *Tech* modèle *m*, gabarit *m*; *Sewing* patron *m*; **dress pattern** patron *m* de robe; **to cut out a shirt from a pattern** tailler une chemise sur un patron

(**e**) *Fig (example)* exemple *m*, modèle *m*; **to set a pattern for** *(of company, method, work)* servir de modèle à; *(of person)* instaurer un modèle pour; **their methods set the pattern for other companies** leurs méthodes ont servi de modèle à d'autres sociétés; **this opening debate set the pattern for what followed** ce débat d'ouverture a donné le ton de ce qui allait suivre

(**f**) *Mktg (sample)* échantillon *m*

2 *vt* (**a**) *(mark → fabric)* décorer d'un motif

(**b**) *(copy)* modeler; **to pattern oneself on** *or* **after sb** prendre modèle *ou* exemple sur qn; **their quality control is patterned on Japanese methods** leur contrôle de qualité est calqué sur les méthodes japonaises

►► *Mil* ***pattern bombing*** bombardement *m* systématique; ***pattern book*** livre *m* d'échantillons; *(for dressmaking)* catalogue *m* de patrons; *Ind* ***pattern designer*** dessinateur(trice) *m,f* de patrons

patterned ['pætənd] *adj* à motifs; **patterned wallpaper** papier *m* peint à motifs

patterning ['pætənɪŋ] *n* (**a**) *Psy & (in sociology)* acquisition *f* des structures de pensée (**b**) *Zool (markings)* marques *fpl*, taches *fpl*

pattie, patty ['pætɪ] (*pl* **patties**) *n* (**a**) *Am* **(hamburger) pattie** = portion de steak haché (**b**) *(pasty)* ≃ (petit) pâté *m*

pattypan ['pætɪpæn] *n Culin* petit moule *m* à pâté

►► ***pattypan squash*** pâtisson *m*

pauciloquent [pɔː'sɪləkwənt] *adj Literary* peu disert

paucity ['pɔːsətɪ] *n Formal* pénurie *f*; *(of information, proof, evidence)* manque *m*

Pauline ['pɔːlaɪn] *adj Rel* paulinien

►► ***the Pauline Epistles*** les épîtres *fpl* de saint Paul

paulownia [pɔː'lɒvnɪə] *n Bot* paulownia *m*

Paul Revere [,pɔːlrɪ'vɪə(r)] *pr n* = héros de la révolution américaine qui prévint les habitants du Massachusetts de l'arrivée des soldats britanniques

paunch [pɔːntʃ] *n* (**a**) *Pej or Hum (stomach)* (gros) ventre *m*, bedaine *f*; **he's getting a paunch** il prend du ventre (**b**) *Zool* panse *f*

paunchiness ['pɔːntʃɪnɪs] *n Pej or Hum* corpulence *f*

paunchy ['pɔːntʃɪ] (*compar* **paunchier**, *superl* **paunchiest**) *adj Pej or Hum* ventru, pansu, bedonnant; **he's getting paunchy** il prend du ventre

pauper ['pɔːpə(r)] *n (man)* pauvre *m*, indigent *m*; *(woman)* pauvre *f*, pauvresse *f*, indigente *f*; **to die a pauper** mourir dans l'indigence

►► ***pauper's grave*** fosse *f* commune

pauperdom ['pɔːpədəm] *n* (**a**) *(poverty)* indigence *f* (**b**) *(paupers)* indigents *mpl*

pauperism ['pɔːpərɪzəm] *n* paupérisme *m*

pauperization [,pɔːpəraɪ'zeɪʃən] *n* paupérisation *f*

pauperize, -ise ['pɔːpəraɪz] *vt* paupériser

pause [pɔːz] **1** *n* (**a**) *(break)* pause *f*, temps *m* d'arrêt; **pause** *(on tape recorder, video etc)* 'pause'; **there will be a ten-minute pause after the second lecture** il y aura *ou* nous ferons une pause de dix minutes après le deuxième cours; **without a pause** sans s'arrêter, sans interruption; **there was a long pause before she answered** elle garda longtemps le silence avant de répondre; *Formal* **to give sb pause, to give pause to sb** donner à réfléchir à qn

(**b**) *Mus* point *m* d'orgue

(**c**) *Literature* césure *f*

(**d**) *Comput* pause *f*

2 *vi* faire *ou* marquer une pause; **the speaker paused while the latecomer took his seat** le conférencier fit une pause pendant que le retardataire prenait place; **he paused in the middle of his explanation** il s'arrêta *ou* s'interrompit au milieu de son explication; **I signed it without pausing to read the details** je l'ai signé sans prendre le temps d'en lire les détails; **without pausing for breath** sans même reprendre son souffle; **she paused on the doorstep** elle hésita sur le pas de la porte

►► ***pause button*** *(on cassette player, video etc)* bouton *m* pause; *Comput* ***Pause key*** touche *f* Pause

pavan, pavane [pæ'væn] *n* pavane *f*

pave [peɪv] *vt (street, floor → with flagstones, tiles)* paver; *(→ with concrete, asphalt)* revêtir; **bricks paved the courtyard** la cour était pavée de briques; *Fig* **to pave the way for sth** ouvrir la voie à *ou* préparer le terrain pour qch

paved [peɪvd] *adj* **paved in** *or* **with** *(flagstones, tiles)* pavé de; *(concrete, asphalt)* revêtu de; **the road isn't paved yet** la route n'est pas encore goudronnée; *Fig* **her career was paved with success** sa carrière fut jalonnée de succès; *Fig* **they say the streets are paved with gold there** ils disent que c'est un véritable eldorado là-bas

pavement ['peɪvmənt] *n* (**a**) *Br (footpath)* trottoir *m*

(**b**) *Am (roadway)* chaussée *f*

(**c**) *(surfaced area → of cobbles)* pavé *m*; *(→ of stones, marble, granite)* dallage *m*; *(→ of concrete)* (dalle *f* de) béton *m*; *(→ of mosaic)* pavement *m*

►► *Br* ***pavement artist*** artiste *mf* de rue *(qui dessine sur les trottoirs)*; ***pavement café*** café *m*, terrasse *f* d'un café; **we sat at a pavement café** on s'est assis à une terrasse de café; ***pavement light*** = blocs de verre encastrés dans un trottoir pour éclairer une cave se trouvant au-dessous

paver ['peɪvə(r)] *n* (**a**) *(person)* paveur *m*; *(tile layer)* carreleur *m* (**b**) *(machine)* bétonnière *f* motorisée (**c**) *(paving stone)* pavé *m*

pavilion [pə'vɪljən] *n* (**a**) *(building)* pavillon *m*; *(at sports ground)* vestiaires *mpl*; **the Japanese pavilion at the exhibition** le pavillon du Japon à l'exposition; **(cricket) pavilion** = bâtiment abritant les vestiaires et parfois le bar sur un terrain de cricket (**b**) *(tent)* pavillon *m*, tente *f*

paving ['peɪvɪŋ] **1** *n (cobbles)* pavage *m*; *(flagstones)* dallage *m*; *(tiles)* carrelage *m*; *(concrete)* dallage *m*, béton *m*

2 *adj (measure, legislation)* préparatoire

►► ***paving stone*** pavé *m*; ***paving tile*** carreau *m* (de pavage); *(bigger)* dalle *f* (de pavage)

paviour, *Am* **pavior** ['peɪvjə(r)] *n* (**a**) *(person)* paveur *m*; *(tile layer)* carreleur *m* (**b**) *(paving stone)* pavé *m*

pavlova [pæv'ləʊvə] *n Culin* vacherin *m*; **raspberry pavlova** vacherin *m* à la framboise

Pavlovian [pæv'ləʊvɪən] *adj* pavlovien

paw [pɔː] **1** *n* (**a**) *(of animal)* patte *f*

(**b**) *Fam (hand)* pogne *m*, patte *f*; *Br* **paws off!**, *Am* **keep your (big) paws off!** bas les pattes!; **you're not getting your dirty** *or* **sweaty paws on my new bike!** il n'est pas question que tu touches à mon nouveau vélo!

2 *vt* (**a**) *(of animal)* donner un coup de patte à; **the horse pawed the ground** le cheval piaffait

(**b**) *Fam (touch, maul)* tripoter; *(sexually)* peloter

3 *vi* **the dog pawed at the door** le chien grattait à la porte

pawky ['pɔːkɪ] *adj Scot* pince-sans-rire *(inv)*

pawl [pɔːl] *n* cliquet *m*

pawn [pɔːn] **1** *n* (**a**) *(in chess)* pion *m*; *Fig* **to be sb's pawn** être le jouet de qn; **they are mere pawns in the hands of the politicians** ils ne sont que des pions sur l'échiquier politique

(**b**) *(at pawnbroker's)* **my watch is in pawn** ma montre est en gage; **to put sth in pawn** mettre qch en gage; **I got my watch out of pawn** j'ai dégagé ma montre (du mont-de-piété)

2 *vt* engager au mont-de-piété; *Fig (one's life, honour)* engager

►► ***pawn ticket*** reconnaissance *f* du mont-de-piété

►**pawn off** *vt sep Am Fam* **to pawn sth off on sb** refiler qch à qn

pawnable ['pɔːnəbəl] *adj* engageable

pawnbroker ['pɔːn,brəʊkə(r)] *n* prêteur *m* sur gages; **at the pawnbroker's** au mont-de-piété

pawnbroking ['pɔːn,brəʊkɪŋ] *n* prêt *m* sur gages

Pawnee [pɔː'niː] *n* Paunie *mf*, Pawnee *mf*

pawning ['pɔːnɪŋ] *n* mise *f* en gage

pawnshop ['pɔːnʃɒp] *n* boutique *f* de prêteur sur gages, mont-de-piété *m*

pawpaw ['pɔːpɔː] = **papaw**

PAX [,piːeɪ'eks] *n Tel (abbr* **private automatic exchange**) central *m* automatique privé

pax [pæks] **1** *n Rel (tablet)* paix *f*; *(kiss)* baiser *m* de paix; *Pol* **Pax Americana/Britannica** pax americana/britannica *f*; *Hist* **Pax Romana** pax romana *f*

2 *exclam Br Fam School slang* pouce!

PAY [peɪ]

payer	► **1 (a); 2**
régler	► **1 (a); 2**
rapporter à	► **1 (b)**
salaire	► **3**
paie	► **3**
traitement	► **3**

(*pt & pp* **paid** [peɪd]) **1** *vt* (**a**) *(person)* payer; *(bill, debt)* payer, régler; *(fine, taxes, fare, sum of money)* payer; *St Exch (dividend)* distribuer; *(premium)* verser, acquitter; **she's paid £2,000 a month** elle est payée *ou* elle touche 2000 livres par mois; **you should pay someone to do it for you** vous devriez payer quelqu'un pour le faire à votre place; **to be paid by the hour/the week** être payé à l'heure/la semaine; **badly paid job** travail *m* mal payé; **I wouldn't do it if you paid me** je ne le ferais pas même si on me payait; **I paid her £20** je lui ai payé 20 livres; *Fam* **shut up and pay the man!** ferme-la et casque!; **you pay £100 now, the rest later** vous payez 100 livres maintenant, le solde plus tard; **he paid £20 for the watch** il a payé la montre 20 livres; **to pay cash (down)** payer en liquide *ou* en espèces; **have you paid your union dues?** avez-vous payé vos cotisations syndicales?; **the rent is paid up until the end of May** le loyer est payé jusqu'à la fin mai; **they've paid their debt to society** ils ont payé leur dette envers la société **to pay one's way** payer sa part; **is the business paying its way?** cette affaire est-elle rentable?; **it's a small price to pay for peace of mind** c'est faire un bien petit sacrifice pour avoir sa tranquillité d'esprit

(**b**) *Fig (benefit)* rapporter à; **it pays them to use immigrant labour** cela leur rapporte d'utiliser la main-d'œuvre immigrée; **it'll pay you to start now** vous avez intérêt à commencer tout de suite; **it'll pay you to keep quiet!** tu as intérêt à tenir ta langue!

(**c**) *(give)* **pay attention!** faites attention!; **nobody pays any attention to me** personne ne m'écoute; **to pay a call on sb, to pay sb a visit** rendre visite à qn; **to pay one's respects to sb** présenter ses respects à qn; **to pay one's (last) respects to sb** rendre les derniers devoirs à qn; **to pay tribute** *or* **homage to sb** rendre hommage à qn

2 *vi* payer, régler; **to pay by cheque** payer *ou* régler par chèque; **to pay in cash** payer en liquide *ou* en espèces; **how would you like to pay?** comment souhaitez-vous régler? **to pay on delivery** payer à la livraison; **to pay in advance** payer d'avance; **to pay in full** payer intégralement *ou* en totalité; **to pay on demand**

pat–pay

or **on presentation** payer à vue *ou* à présentation; *Fin* **pay to bearer** payez au porteur; *Fin* **pay to bearer clause** clause *f* au porteur; **the job pays very well** le travail est très bien payé; **to pay on the nail** payer rubis sur ongle; **after two years the business was beginning to pay** après deux ans, l'affaire était devenue rentable; *Fig* **it pays to be honest** l'honnêteté est toujours récompensée; **crime doesn't pay** le crime ne paie pas

3 *n (gen)* salaire *m*, paie *f*; *(of domestic staff)* gages *mpl*; *(of civil servant)* traitement *m*; *Mil* solde *f*; **my first month's pay** ma première paie, mon premier salaire; **the pay is good** c'est bien payé; **he's in the pay of the enemy** il est à la solde de l'ennemi

4 *comp* (**a**) *(demand, negotiations)* salarial; *(increase, cut)* de salaire

(**b**) *(not free)* payant

(**c**) *Mining (deposit)* exploitable

►► ***pay advice slip*** fiche *f* de paie; ***pay award*** augmentation *f* de salaire; *Br* ***pay bed*** lit *m* payant; *Br* ***pay cheque,*** *Am* ***pay check*** chèque *m* de salaire; ***pay day*** jour *m* de paie; ***pay dirt*** *(earth)* gisement *m*; *Fam (discovery)* trouvaille *f*; **to hit pay dirt** trouver un bon filon; *Am* ***pay envelope*** *(envelope)* enveloppe *f* contenant le salaire; *(money)* paie *f*, salaire *m*; ***pay formula*** formule *f* de paie; ***pay freeze*** gel *m ou* blocage *m* des salaires; ***pay increase*** augmentation *f* de salaire; ***pay ledger*** livre *m* de paie; *Br* ***pay packet*** *(envelope)* enveloppe *f* contenant le salaire; *(money)* paie *f*, salaire *m*; ***pay rise*** augmentation *f* de salaire; ***pay slip*** bulletin *m* de paie; *Am* ***pay station*** téléphone *m* public; ***pay television, pay TV*** chaîne *f* à péage

►**pay back** *vt sep* (**a**) *(loan, lender)* rembourser; **she paid her father back the sum she had borrowed** elle remboursa à son père la somme qu'elle avait empruntée

(**b**) *(retaliate against)* rendre la monnaie de sa pièce à; **I'll pay you back for that!** tu me le paieras!

►**pay for** *vt insep* (**a**) *(item, task)* payer; **who paid for the drinks?** qui est-ce qui a payé les consommations?; **I paid good money for that!** ça m'a coûté cher!; **you get what you pay for** la qualité est en rapport avec le prix (que vous payez); **it's all paid for** *(someone has paid for everything)* tout a été réglé; *(I've paid for everything)* c'est à mes frais; **a free holiday with everything paid for** des vacances gratuites tout compris; **the ticket pays for itself after two trips** le billet est amorti dès le deuxième voyage

(**b**) *(crime, mistake)* payer; **he'll pay for this!, I'll make him pay for this!** il me le paiera!; **you'll pay for this tomorrow** *(for drinking too much etc)* tu vas en subir les conséquences demain; **to pay dearly for sth** payer chèrement qch; **he paid for his mistake with his life** il a payé son erreur de sa vie

►**pay in** *vt sep Br (cheque)* déposer sur un compte; *(money)* verser sur un compte; **I'd like to pay this cheque in** j'aimerais déposer ce chèque sur mon compte

►**pay into 1** *vt sep* **to pay money into an account** alimenter un compte, approvisionner un compte; **to pay money into sb's account** verser de l'argent au compte de qn; **to pay a cheque into the bank** déposer un chèque à la banque; **I'd like to pay this cheque into my account** j'aimerais déposer ce chèque sur mon compte

2 *vt insep* **to pay into a pension scheme** cotiser à un plan de retraite

►**pay off 1** *vt sep* (**a**) *(debt)* payer, régler, s'acquitter de; *(loan)* rembourser; **it takes years to pay off a mortgage** il faut des années pour rembourser un emprunt-logement

(**b**) *(dismiss, lay off)* licencier, congédier; **he threatened to pay us all off** il a menacé de nous mettre tous à la porte

(**c**) *Fam (bribe)* acheter□; **they paid off the police chief** ils ont acheté le chef de la police

2 *vi* être payant, porter ses fruits; **moving the company out of London really paid off** le transfert de la société hors de Londres a été bénéfique; **all these years of work have paid off at last** nous sommes enfin récompensés après toutes ces années de travail

►**pay out** *vt sep* (**a**) *(money)* payer, débourser

(**b**) *(rope)* laisser filer

►**pay up 1** *vi* payer; **pay up or else!** payez, sinon...!

2 *vt sep (sum)* payer

---

payable ['peɪəbəl] **1** *adj* payable; **payable in 24 monthly instalments/in advance** payable en 24 mensualités/d'avance; **refunds are payable in certain cases** vous pouvez être remboursé sous certaines conditions; **to make a cheque payable to sb** faire *ou* libeller un chèque à l'ordre de qn; **cheque payable to bearer** chèque *m* payable au porteur; **cheques should be made payable to Mr Brown** les chèques devraient être libellés *ou* établis à l'ordre de M. Brown; **payable at sight** payable à vue; **payable to order** payable à ordre; **payable in cash** payable comptant; **payable on delivery/with order** payable à la livraison/à la commande; **the interest payable on the loan** les intérêts *mpl* à payer sur le prêt

2 payables *npl Am* factures *fpl* à payer

pay-and-display *adj*

►► ***pay-and-display car park*** parking *m* à horodateur; ***pay-and-display machine*** horodateur *m*

pay-as-you-earn, *Am* **pay-as-you-go** *n Fin* prélèvement *m* de l'impôt à la source

payback ['peɪbæk] *n* (**a**) *Fin* récupération *f* du capital investi (**b**) *esp Am (revenge)* revanche *f*; **it's payback time** c'est le moment de la revanche

►► ***payback period*** délai *m* de récupération, période *f* de remboursement

payday ['peɪdeɪ] *n* jour *m* de paie; **tomorrow is payday** nous sommes payés demain

PAYE [,piːeɪ,waɪ'iː] *n Br Fin (abbr* **pay-as-you-earn**) prélèvement *m* de l'impôt à la source

payee [peɪ'iː] *n (of postal order, cheque)* bénéficiaire *mf*; *Fin (of bill)* porteur *m*, preneur *m*

payer ['peɪə(r)] *n* (**a**) *(gen)* payeur(euse) *m,f*; **a good/bad payer** un bon/mauvais payeur (**b**) *(of cheque)* tireur(euse) *m,f*

paying ['peɪɪŋ] **1** *n* paiement *m*

2 *adj* (**a**) *(who pays)* payant (**b**) *(profitable)* payant, rentable; **it's not a paying proposition** cette proposition n'est pas avantageuse *ou* profitable

►► *Fin* ***paying bank*** domiciliataire *m*, établissement *m* payeur, domiciliation *f* bancaire; ***paying guest*** hôte *m* payant, pensionnaire *mf*

paying-in *adj*

►► *Br* ***paying-in book*** carnet *m* de versements; *Br* ***paying-in slip*** bordereau *m ou* feuille *f* de versement

payload ['peɪləʊd] *n* (**a**) *(gen)* chargement *m*; **he was transporting a payload of cement** il transportait un chargement de ciment (**b**) *Tech (of vehicle, aircraft)* charge *f* payante; *(of rocket)* charge *f* utile; *(of missile, warhead)* charge *f* marchande

paymaster ['peɪ,mɑːstə(r)] *n (gen)* payeur(euse) *m,f*, intendant(e) *m,f*; *(in school, institution)* économe *mf*; *(in army)* trésorier *m*; *Naut* commissaire *m*; *(in administration)* trésorier-payeur *m*; *Pej (of criminals, terrorists)* commanditaire *mf*; **the World Bank acts as paymaster of the project** la Banque mondiale fait office de bailleur de fonds pour ce projet

►► ***the Paymaster General*** le Trésorier-payeur-général britannique

payment ['peɪmənt] *n* (**a**) *(sum paid, act of paying)* paiement *m*; *(when paying in instalments)* versement *m*; **48 monthly payments** 48 versements mensuels, 48 mensualités; **on payment of £100** contre paiement de 100 livres; **on payment of a deposit** moyennant des arrhes; **in payment of your invoice** en règlement de votre facture; **to make a payment** effectuer un versement; **to present a bill for payment** présenter un effet au paiement *ou* à l'encaissement; **she would not accept payment** elle n'a pas voulu qu'on la paie; **they offered their services without payment** ils ont offert leurs services à titre gracieux; **to stop payment on a cheque** faire opposition à un chèque; **payment by instalments** paiement *m* échelonné *ou* par versements, paiement *m* à tempérament; **in easy payments** avec facilités de paiement; **payment on account** paiement *m* partiel; **payment in advance** paiement *m* d'avance, paiement *m* par anticipation; **payment in arrears** paiement *m* arriéré; **payment in cash** paiement *m* en espèces; **payment by cheque** paiement *m* par chèque; **payment on delivery** livraison *f* contre remboursement; **payment in full** paiement *m* intégral; **payment in kind** paiement *m ou* avantages *mpl* en nature

(**b**) *(reward, compensation)* récompense *f*

►► ***payment advice*** avis *m* de paiement; ***payment card*** carte *f* de paiement; ***payment day*** jour *m* de paiement, jour *m* de règlement; ***payment facilities*** facilités *fpl* de paiement; ***payment order*** ordre *m* de paiement; ***payment schedule*** échéancier *m* de paiement

paynim ['peɪnɪm] *n Arch or Literary* (**a**) *(heathen)* païen(enne) *m,f* (**b**) *(Muslim)* musulman(e) *m,f*

payoff ['peɪɒf] *n* (**a**) *(act of paying off)* paiement *m*; **the payoff is set for tomorrow night** *(gen)* le paiement sera effectué demain soir; *(ransom)* la remise de la rançon est fixée à demain soir

(**b**) *(profit)* bénéfice *m*, profit *m*

(**c**) *(consequence)* conséquence *f*, résultat *m*; *(reward)* récompense *f*; **it's an unexpected but welcome payoff of this policy** ceci est une conséquence inattendue mais heureuse de cette politique

(**d**) *Fam (climax)* dénouement□ *m*

(**e**) *Fam (bribe)* pot-de-vin□ *m*

payola [peɪ'əʊlə] *n (UNCOUNT) Am Fam* pots-de-vin *mpl*, dessous-de-table *mpl*

payout ['peɪaʊt] *n (payment → gen)* paiement *m*; *(→ in compensation)* dédommagement *m*; *(award in competition)* prix *m*

pay-per-view *TV* **1** *n* système *m* de télévision à la carte

2 *adj* à la carte

►► ***pay-per-view television*** télévision *f* à la carte

pay-per-visit *adj Comput (Web site)* à consultation payante

payphone ['peɪfəʊn] *n* téléphone *m* public; **I'm calling from a payphone** j'appelle d'une cabine

payroll ['peɪrəʊl] *n* (**a**) *(list of employees)* liste *f* du personnel, registre *m* des salaires; *(employees collectively)* personnel *m*; **he's been on our payroll for years** il fait partie du personnel depuis des années; **they've added 500 workers to their payroll** ils ont embauché 500 travailleurs supplémentaires; **to be taken off the payroll** *(voluntarily)* quitter l'entreprise; *(be laid off)* être licencié; **to do the payroll** faire la paie, établir les bulletins de paie

(**b**) *(money paid)* masse *f* salariale

►► *Fin* ***payroll ledger*** journal *m ou* livre *m* de paie; *Fin* ***payroll tax*** impôt *m* sur la masse salariale

payslip ['peɪslɪp] *n* fiche *f* de paie

paystub ['peɪstʌb] *n* bulletin *m* de salaire

PB [,piː'biː] *n Sport (abbr* **personal best**) record *m* personnel; **he ran a PB in the 200 m** il a battu son propre record *ou* son record personnel sur 200 m

PBS [,piːbiː'es] *n Am (abbr* **Public Broadcasting Service**) = société américaine de production télévisuelle

PBX [,piːbiː'eks] *n Br Tel (abbr* **private branch exchange**) = autocommutateur privé

pc^{1}, PC^{1} [,piː'siː] *n* (**a**) *Comput (abbr* **personal computer**) PC *m*, micro *m*; **available for the PC** disponible en version PC (**b**) *(abbr* **postcard**) carte *f* postale

►► *Comput* ***PC disk*** disquette *f* pour PC

PC^{2} 1 *n* (**a**) *(abbr* **police constable**) agent *m* de police (**b**) *(abbr* **privy councillor**) = membre du Conseil privé

2 *adj (abbr* **politically correct**) politiquement correct

p/c *(written abbr* **petty cash**) petite caisse *f*

pc^{2} *(written abbr* **per cent**) pc

PCAS ['piːkæs] *n Br Formerly (abbr* **Polytechnics Central Admissions System**) = organisme britannique autrefois responsable des entrées dans les "polytechnics"

PCB [,piːsiː'biː] *n* (**a**) *Electron (abbr* **printed circuit board**) carte *f* de *ou* à circuits imprimés (**b**) *Chem (abbr* **polychlorinated biphenyl**) PCB *m*

PC-compatible *adj* compatible PC

PCI [,piːsiː'aɪ] *n Comput (abbr* **peripheral component interface**) PCI *m*

pcm (*written abbr* **per calendar month**) par mois

PCMCIA [ˌpiːsiːˈemˌsiːaɪˈeɪ] *n Comput* (*abbr* **PC memory card international association**) PCMCIA *m*

PCN [ˌpiːsiːˈen] *n Tel* (*abbr* **personal communications network**) réseau *m* de téléphonie mobile

PCP [ˌpiːsiːˈpiː] *n Chem* (*abbr* **phencyclidine**) PCP *f*

PCR [ˌpiːsiːˈɑː(r)] *n* (*abbr* **polymerase chain reaction**) réaction *f* en chaîne par polymérase, amplification *f* génique

PCV [ˌpiːsiːˈviː] *n Br* (*abbr* **passenger carrying vehicle**) véhicule *m* de transport en commun

PD [ˌpiːˈdiː] *n Am* (*abbr* **police department**) service *m* de police

pd (*written abbr* **paid**) payé

PDA [ˌpiːdiːˈeɪ] *n Comput* (*abbr* **personal digital assistant**) agenda *m* électronique de poche, assistant *m* numérique de poche

PDF [ˌpiːdiːˈef] *n Comput* (*abbr* **portable document format**) (format *m*) PDF *m*

pdq [ˌpiːdiːˈkjuː] *adv Fam* (*abbr* **pretty damn quick**) illico presto

PDSA [ˌpiːdiːˌesˈeɪ] *n Br* (*abbr* **People's Dispensary for Sick Animals**) = association de soins aux animaux malades

PDT [ˌpiːdiːˈtiː] *n Am* (*abbr* **Pacific Daylight Time**) heure *f* d'été du Pacifique

PE [ˌpiːˈiː] *n* (*abbr* **physical education**) EPS *f*

pea [piː] *n Bot* pois *m*; *Culin* (petit) pois *m*; **frozen peas** petits pois *mpl* surgelés; **they are as alike as two peas in a pod** ils se ressemblent comme deux gouttes d'eau

▸▸ ***pea green*** vert *m* pomme; ***pea jacket pea soup*** soupe *f* aux pois; ***pea souper*** *Fam (fog)* purée *f* de pois; *Can very Fam (Quebecker)* = terme injurieux désignant un Québécois

peace [piːs] *n* (**a**) *(not war)* paix *f*; *(treaty)* (traité *m* de) paix *f*; **in time of peace** en temps de paix; **the country is at peace now** la paix est maintenant rétablie dans le pays; **I come in peace** je viens en ami; **to make peace** faire la paix; *Fig* **he made (his) peace with his father** il a fait la paix *ou* il s'est réconcilié avec son père; **they wanted to sign a separate peace with the invaders** ils voulaient conclure *ou* signer une paix séparée avec les envahisseurs

(**b**) *(tranquillity)* paix *f*, tranquillité *f*; **to be at peace with oneself/the world** être en paix avec soi-même/le reste du monde; **to be at peace** *(dead person)* reposer en paix; **we haven't had a moment's peace all morning** nous n'avons pas eu un moment de tranquillité de toute la matinée; **all I want is a bit of peace and quiet** tout ce que je veux, c'est un peu de tranquillité; **peace of mind** tranquillité *f* d'esprit; **to have peace of mind** avoir l'esprit tranquille; **he'll give you no peace until you pay him** tant que tu ne l'auras pas payé, il ne te laissera pas tranquille; **leave us in peace!** laisse-nous tranquilles!, laisse-nous en paix!; *Rel* **peace be with you!** que la paix soit avec vous!; **go in peace!** allez en paix!

(**c**) *(silence)* **to hold** *or* **to keep one's peace** garder le silence, se taire; **hold your peace!** silence!

(**d**) *(law and order)* paix *f*, ordre *m* public; **to disturb the peace** troubler l'ordre public; **to keep the peace** *(army, police)* maintenir l'ordre

▸▸ ***peace camp*** = camp installé près d'une base militaire en signe de protestation contre les activités qui s'y déroulent; *Br* ***peace campaigner*** militant(e) *m,f* pour la paix; ***Peace Corps*** = organisation américaine de coopération avec les pays en voie de développement; ***peace dividend*** dividende *m* de paix; ***peace formula*** formule *f* de paix; ***the Peace Garden State*** = surnom donné au Dakota du Nord; ***peace initiative*** initiative *f* de paix; ***peace movement*** mouvement *m* pour la paix; ***peace negotiations*** négociations *fpl* pour la paix; ***peace offensive*** offensive *f* de paix; ***peace offering*** offrande *f* de paix; ***peace pipe*** calumet *m* (de la paix); ***peace process*** processus *m* de paix; ***peace sign*** signe *m* de la paix; ***peace studies*** = discipline universitaire consistant à étudier les rapports stratégiques entre pays, le rôle de l'armée et la promotion de la paix dans le monde; ***peace talks*** pourparlers *mpl* de paix; ***peace treaty*** traité *m* de paix

peaceable [ˈpiːsəbəl] *adj* (**a**) *(peace-loving → nation, person)* pacifique; **a peaceable man** un homme de paix (**b**) *(calm → atmosphere)* paisible, tranquille; *(→ demonstration, methods)* pacifique; *(→ discussion)* calme

peaceably [ˈpiːsəblɪ] *adv (live)* paisiblement, tranquillement; *(discuss, listen)* calmement, paisiblement; *(assemble, disperse)* pacifiquement, sans incident

peaceful [ˈpiːsfʊl] *adj* (**a**) *(calm, serene)* paisible, tranquille; **it's so peaceful in the country!** la campagne est si paisible!; **he had a peaceful death** il n'a pas souffert, il est mort sans souffrir

(**b**) *(non-violent → solution, protest, means)* pacifique; **we are a peaceful nation** nous sommes une nation pacifique; **a peaceful transition to independence** une transition pacifique vers l'indépendance; **the peaceful settlement of a dispute** le règlement pacifique d'un litige; **the peaceful uses of nuclear energy** les utilisations pacifiques de l'énergie nucléaire

peacefully [ˈpiːsfʊlɪ] *adv (live, rest)* paisiblement, tranquillement; *(protest)* pacifiquement; **the rally went off peacefully** le meeting s'est déroulé dans le calme *ou* sans incident; **he died peacefully** il est mort sans souffrir; **peacefully, at home** *(in death notice)* survenu à son domicile

peacefulness [ˈpiːsfʊlnɪs] *n* paix *f*, calme *m*, tranquillité *f*

peacekeeper [ˈpiːsˌkiːpə(r)] *n (soldier)* soldat *m* de la paix; *(of United Nations)* casque *m* bleu

peacekeeping [ˈpiːsˌkiːpɪŋ] **1** *n* maintien *m* de la paix

2 *adj* de maintien de la paix; **a United Nations peacekeeping force** des forces des Nations unies pour le maintien de la paix

peace-loving *adj* pacifique

peacemaker [ˈpiːsˌmeɪkə(r)] *n* pacificateur(-trice) *m,f*, conciliateur(trice) *m,f*; *Bible* **blessed are the peacemakers** bienheureux sont ceux qui procurent la paix

peacenik [ˈpiːsnɪk] *n Fam Pej* pacifiste[❑] *mf*

peacetime [ˈpiːstaɪm] *n* temps *m* de paix; **in peacetime** en temps de paix

peach [piːtʃ] **1** *n* (**a**) *(fruit)* pêche *f*; **she has a peaches and cream complexion** elle a un teint de pêche

(**b**) *(tree)* pêcher *m*

(**c**) *(colour)* couleur *f* pêche

(**d**) *Fam (expressing approval)* **he played a peach of a shot** il a joué un coup superbe[❑]; **a peach of a goal/dress** un but/une robe magnifique[❑]; **she's a peach** elle est jolie comme un cœur; **thanks, you're a peach!** merci, tu es adorable!

2 *comp (yoghurt)* aux pêches; *(jam)* de pêches

3 *adj (colour)* pêche *(inv)*

4 *vt Fam (inform on)* cafarder, moucharder

5 *vi Fam (inform)* cafarder; **to peach on sb** cafarder qn

▸▸ ***peach blossom*** fleurs *mpl* de pêcher; ***peach melba*** pêche *f* melba; ***peach schnapps*** schnapps *m* aux pêches; ***the Peach State*** = surnom donné à la Géorgie; ***peach tree*** pêcher *m*

peachy [ˈpiːtʃɪ] (*compar* **peachier**, *superl* **peachiest**) **1** *adj* (**a**) *(taste, flavour, complexion)* de pêche (**b**) *esp Am Fam* **peachy (keen)** *(excellent)* chouette, super; **everything's just peachy!** tout baigne (dans l'huile)!

2 *adv Am Fam (well)* super

peacoat [ˈpiːkəʊt] *n* caban *m*

peacock [ˈpiːkɒk] (*pl* **inv** *or* **peacocks**) **1** *n* (**a**) *Orn* paon *m* (bleu) (**b**) *(colour)* bleu *m* canard

2 *adj* bleu canard *(inv)*

▸▸ ***peacock blue*** bleu *m* canard; ***peacock butterfly*** paon *m* de jour

peacock-blue *adj* bleu canard *(inv)*

peafowl [ˈpiːfaʊl] (*pl* **inv** *or* **peafowls**) *n Orn* paon *m*

pea-green *adj* vert pomme *(inv)*

peahen [ˈpiːhen] *n* paonne *f*

peak [piːk] **1** *n* (**a**) *(mountain top)* pic *m*, sommet *m*; *(mountain)* pic *m*; **the highest peaks** les plus hauts sommets; **snowy peaks** pics *mpl ou* sommets *mpl* enneigés

(**b**) *(pointed part → of roof)* faîte *m*; **beat the egg whites until they form peaks** battez les blancs d'œuf en neige très ferme

(**c**) *(high point → of fame, career)* sommet *m*, apogée *m*; *(→ on graph)* sommet *m*; **emigration was at its peak in the 1890s** l'émigration a atteint son point culminant *ou* son sommet dans les années 1890; **the gardens are at their peak in July** c'est en juillet que les jardins sont au faîte *ou* à l'apogée de leur splendeur; **the team will be at its peak in a few weeks** l'équipe sera à son top niveau dans quelques semaines; **the party was at its peak** la fête battait son plein; **sales have reached a new peak** les ventes ont atteint un nouveau record

(**d**) *(of cap)* visière *f*

2 *vi (production, demand)* atteindre un maximum; **his popularity peaked just before the elections** sa cote a atteint un *ou* son maximum juste avant les élections; **she peaked in time for the Olympics** *(athlete)* elle a atteint le maximum de sa forme juste à temps pour les Jeux olympiques; **she peaked too soon** *(athlete)* elle s'est lancée trop tôt; *(musician, actress)* elle a donné le maximum trop tôt

3 *adj* maximum; **the team is in peak condition** l'équipe est à son top niveau

▸▸ ***peak demand*** demande *f* maximum; ***the Peak District*** = région de moyenne montagne dans le nord de l'Angleterre; ***peak experience*** summum *m*; *Med* ***peak flow*** débit *m* expiratoire de pointe; *Med* ***peak flow meter*** débitmètre *m ou* spiromètre *m* de pointe; ***peak hours, peak period*** *(of electricity use)* période *f* de pointe; *(of traffic)* heures *fpl* de pointe *or* d'affluence; *(in restaurant)* coup *m* de feu; *St Exch* ***peak price*** prix *m* maximum; ***peak rate*** tarif *m* heures pleines; ***peak season*** haute saison *f*; *Br TV* ***peak time*** heures *fpl* de grande écoute, prime time *m*; *Br TV* ***peak time advertisement*** publicité *f* aux heures de grande écoute *ou* en prime time; *Br TV* ***peak time advertising*** publicité *f* aux heures de grande écoute *ou* en prime time; *Br TV* ***peak viewing hours*** heures *fpl* de grande écoute; ***peak year*** année-record *f*

▸**peak out** *vi (reach top limit)* atteindre son maximum

peaked [piːkt] *adj (roof)* pointu; *(cap)* à visière

peakiness [ˈpiːkɪnɪs] *n Br Fam* pâleur[❑] *f*

peaky [ˈpiːkɪ] (*compar* **peakier**, *superl* **peakiest**) *adj Br Fam (unwell)* patraque; *(tired)* fatigué[❑]; **I feel a little peaky this morning** je ne me sens pas en forme *ou* je ne me sens pas dans mon assiette ce matin

peal [piːl] **1** *n* (**a**) *(sound → of bells)* carillonnement *m*; *(→ of doorbell)* sonnerie *f*; *(→ of organ)* grondement *m*; **the peal of bells** la sonnerie de cloches; **a peal of thunder** un coup de tonnerre; **peals of laughter came from the living room** des éclats de rire s'échappaient du salon; **they burst into peals of laughter** ils ont éclaté de rire

(**b**) *(set of bells)* carillon *m*

2 *vi (bells → chime)* carillonner; *(→ ring out loudly)* sonner à toute volée; *(thunder, organ)* retentir, gronder; *(laughter)* résonner

3 *vt (bells)* sonner à toute volée

▸**peal out** *vi (bells → chime)* carillonner; *(→ ring out loudly)* sonner à toute volée; *(thunder, organ)* retentir, gronder; *(laughter)* résonner

peanut [ˈpiːnʌt] *n (nut)* cacahouète *f*, cacahuète *f*; *(plant)* arachide *f*; *Fam* **peanuts** *(small sum)* clopinettes *fpl*, cacahuètes *fpl*; **to work for peanuts** travailler pour des clopinettes; **it's worth peanuts** ça ne vaut pas un clou; **£100 is peanuts for a return ticket** 100 livres, ce n'est rien pour un billet aller-retour[❑]; *Hum* **if you pay peanuts, you get monkeys** il ne faut pas s'attendre à grand chose lorsqu'on paye ses employés au lance-pierre

▸▸ ***peanut butter*** beurre *m* de cacahuètes; *Am Fam* ***peanut gallery*** *(in theatre)* poulailler *m*; ***peanut oil*** huile *f* d'arachide

peapod [ˈpiːpɒd] *n* cosse *f* de pois

pear [peə(r)] **1** *n* (**a**) *(fruit)* poire *f* (**b**) *(tree, wood)* poirier *m*

2 *comp (yoghurt, tart)* aux poires

peardrop [ˈpeədrɒp] *n Br* = bonbon parfumé à la poire

pearl [pɜːl] **1** *n* (**a**) *(gem)* perle *f*; **to cast pearls**

before swine donner de la confiture aux cochons, donner des perles aux cochons; *Fig* **pearls of dew** perles *fpl* de rosée
(**b**) *(mother-of-pearl)* nacre *f*
(**c**) *Fig* perle *f*; **Hong Kong, pearl of the East** Hongkong, perle de l'Orient; *Literary* **a pearl amongst women** une perle; **pearls of wisdom** trésors *mpl* de sagesse; *Ironic* inepties *fpl*; *also Ironic* **he comes out with some real pearls** il sort de vraies perles
2 *adj* (**a**) *(made of pearls)* de perles; **pearl earrings** perles *fpl* montées en boucles d'oreilles; **a pearl necklace** un collier de perles
(**b**) *(made of mother-of-pearl)* de *ou* en nacre; **pearl buttons** boutons *mpl* en nacre
3 *vt Literary (make pearly)* nacrer; **dawn was pearling the sky** l'aurore nacrait le ciel
4 *vi* (**a**) *(form drops)* perler
(**b**) *(search for pearls)* pêcher des perles
►► ***pearl barley*** orge *m* perlé; ***pearl diver*** pêcheur(euse) *m,f* de perles; ***pearl diving*** pêche *f* aux perles; ***pearl grey*** gris *m* perle; ***Pearl Harbor*** Pearl Harbor; ***pearl lightbulb*** ampoule *f* opale; ***pearl mussel*** mulette *f*, moule *f* d'eau douce *ou* de rivière; ***pearl onion*** = petit oignon blanc; ***pearl oyster*** huître *f* perlière; *Geol* ***pearl spar*** spath *m* perlé

PEARL HARBOR

Importante base navale américaine située à Hawaii, elle fut attaquée le 7 décembre 1941 par l'aviation japonaise, qui infligea de lourdes pertes humaines et matérielles aux États-Unis. Le lendemain, en déclarant la guerre au Japon, les États-Unis firent leur entrée dans le conflit mondial.

pearl-grey *adj* gris perle *(inv)*
pearl-handled *adj (knife, cutlery)* à manche de nacre; *(revolver)* à crosse de nacre
pearliness ['pɜːlɪnɪs] *n* tons *mpl* nacrés
pearlite ['pɜːlaɪt] *n Metal* perlite *f*
pearlize, -ise ['pɜːlaɪz] *vt* nacrer
pearlized ['pɜːlaɪzd] *adj* nacré; **pearlized nail polish** vernis *m* à ongles nacré
pearlweed ['pɜːlwiːd], **pearlwort** ['pɜːlwɜːt] *n Bot* sagine *f*
pearly ['pɜːlɪ] *(compar* **pearlier**, *superl* **pearliest**) *adj* (**a**) *(pearl-like)* nacré; **pearly pink nail polish** vernis *m* à ongles rose nacré; **pearly white teeth** dents *fpl* de perle *ou* éclatantes
(**b**) *(decorated with pearls)* perlé; *(made of mother-of-pearl)* en *ou* de nacre
►► *Fam* ***the Pearly Gates*** les portes *fpl* du paradis ❑; ***pearly king*** = marchand des quatre-saisons "cockney" dont les vêtements sont ornés d'une profusion de boutons de nacre; *Zool* ***pearly nautilus*** *(mollusc)* nautile *m*, nautilus *m*; ***pearly queen*** = marchande des quatre-saisons "cockney" dont les vêtements sont ornés d'une profusion de boutons de nacre
pearmain ['peəmeɪn] *n* permaine *f*
pear-shaped 1 *adj* en forme de poire, *Spec* piriforme; *(female figure)* plus fort au niveau des hanches
2 *adv Br Fam Fig* **to go pear-shaped** *(go wrong)* partir en eau de boudin; **it all went pear-shaped after they wouldn't lend us the money** ça s'est gâté quand ils ont refusé de nous prêter l'argent ❑
peasant ['pezənt] **1** *n* (**a**) *(from the country)* paysan(anne) *m,f* (**b**) *Fam Pej (uncouth person)* péquenaud(e) *m,f*, plouc *m*
2 *adj* paysan; **peasant life** la vie des paysans; **peasant dress** des vêtements *mpl* de paysans
►► ***peasant farmer*** paysan *m*; ***peasant farming*** petite agriculture *f*; *Br Hist* ***the Peasants' Revolt*** la guerre des Gueux

THE PEASANTS' REVOLT 

Il s'agit de la première grande révolte populaire de l'histoire d'Angleterre (en 1381), provoquée par la mise en vigueur de la capitation. Son meneur, Wat Tyler, fut assassiné lors de pourparlers avec le roi Richard II et la révolte s'éteignit sans avoir apporté de changements.

peasantry ['pezəntrɪ] *n* paysannerie *f*, paysans *mpl*
pease [piːz] *(pl* **inv**) *n Br Arch* (petit) pois *m*
►► *Culin* ***pease pudding*** = purée de pois au jambon
peashooter ['piːˌʃuːtə(r)] *n* sarbacane *f*
peat [piːt] *n* tourbe *f*; **turf** *or* **sod** *or* **block of peat** motte *f* de tourbe; **to cut** *or* **dig peat** tourber
►► ***peat bog*** tourbière *f*; *Bot* ***peat moss*** sphaigne *f*
peaty ['piːtɪ] *(compar* **peatier**, *superl* **peatiest**) *adj (soil, water, stream)* tourbeux; *(taste)* de fumée de tourbe
pebble ['pebəl] **1** *n* (**a**) *(stone)* caillou *m*; *(water-worn)* galet *m*; **a pebble beach** une plage de galets; **he's not the only pebble on the beach** un de perdu, dix de retrouvés
(**b**) *Opt (lens)* lentille *f* en cristal de roche
2 *vt* (**a**) *(road, path)* caillouter; **a pebbled drive** une allée de gravillons
(**b**) *(leather)* greneler
►► *Fam* ***pebble glasses*** lunettes *fpl* à verres très épais ❑
pebbledash ['pebəldæʃ] *Br* **1** *n* crépi *m (incrusté de cailloux)*
2 *vt* crépir
pebbly ['peblɪ] *(compar* **pebblier**, *superl* **pebbliest**) *adj* (**a**) *(stony → soil, path)* caillouteux; **a pebbly beach** une plage de galets (**b**) *(grainy)* grené, grenu
pecan [*Br* 'piːkən, *Am* pɪ'kæn] **1** *n* (**a**) *(nut)* (noix *f* de) pecan *m*, (noix *f* de) pacane *f* (**b**) *(tree)* pacanier *m*
2 *adj (pie, ice cream)* à la noix de pecan
peccable ['pekəbəl] *n Formal* peccable
peccadillo [ˌpekə'dɪləʊ] *(pl* **peccadillos** *or* **peccadilloes**) *n* peccadille *f*
peccary ['pekərɪ] *(pl* **inv** *or* **peccaries**) *n Zool* pécari *m*
peck [pek] **1** *vt* (**a**) *(pick up)* picorer, picoter; *(strike with beak)* donner un coup de bec à; **chickens were pecking the ground** des poulets picoraient le sol; **be careful, it'll peck you!** fais attention, tu vas recevoir un coup de bec!
(**b**) *(kiss)* faire une bise à
2 *n* (**a**) *(with beak)* coup *m* de bec
(**b**) *(kiss)* bise *f*, (petit) baiser *m*; **she gave me a peck on the cheek** elle m'a fait une bise
(**c**) *(measure)* picotin *m*
►► *also Fig Am* ***peck order***, *Br* ***pecking order*** hiérarchie *f*
►**peck at** *vt insep* (**a**) *(pick up)* picorer, picoter; *(strike with beak)* donner un coup de bec à
(**b**) **to peck at one's food** *(person)* manger du bout des dents
pecker ['pekə(r)] *n* (**a**) *Br Fam (spirits)* **to keep one's pecker up** ne pas se laisser abattre ❑; **keep your pecker up!** (du) courage! ❑ (**b**) *Am very Fam (penis)* queue *f*, quéquette *f*
peckerwood ['pekəwuːd] *n Fam Black Am slang* **to be a peckerwood** être génial *ou* super
peckish ['pekɪʃ] *adj esp Br Fam* **to be** *or* **to feel peckish** avoir un petit creux; **it made me feel quite peckish** ça m'a donné bien faim *ou* bien ouvert l'appétit ❑
pecs [peks] *npl Fam (abbr* **pectoral muscles**) pectoraux ❑ *mpl*; **he's got a great set of pecs** il a des super pectoraux
pecten ['pektɪn] *n Anat & Zool* peigne *m*
pectic ['pektɪk] *adj* pectique
►► ***pectic acid*** acide *m* pectique
pectin ['pektɪn] *n* pectine *f*
pectoral ['pektərəl] **1** *adj Mil & Rel* pectoral
2 *n Anat, Mil & Rel* pectoral *m*
►► ***pectoral cross*** *(of bishop)* croix *f* pectorale; *Ich* ***pectoral fin*** nageoire *f* pectorale; *Anat* ***pectoral muscle*** muscle *m* pectoral
pectose ['pektəʊs] *n Chem* pectose *f*
peculate ['pekjʊleɪt] *Formal* **1** *vi* détourner les fonds *ou* deniers publics
2 *vt (funds)* détourner
peculation [ˌpekjʊ'leɪʃən] *n Formal* détournement *m* de fonds publics
peculiar [pɪ'kjuːlɪə(r)] *adj* (**a**) *(strange)* étrange, bizarre; **he/she is a little peculiar** il/elle est un peu bizarre; **well, that's peculiar** tiens, c'est bizarre *ou* curieux!, voilà qui est singulier!; **I feel a bit peculiar** je me sens un peu bizarre
(**b**) *(specific, exclusive)* particulier; **to be peculiar to** être spécifique *ou* particulier à; **this species is peculiar to Scandinavia** cette espèce n'existe qu'en Scandinavie; **such phenomena are not peculiar to this country** de tels phénomènes ne sont pas spécifiques à ce pays, il n'y a pas que dans ce pays que de tels phénomènes se produisent; **it has a peculiar taste** ça a un goût spécial; **a detail of peculiar significance** un détail particulièrement significatif
peculiarity [pɪˌkjuːlɪ'ærətɪ] *(pl* **peculiarities**) *n* (**a**) *(oddness)* étrangeté *f*, bizarrerie *f*; **I should explain the peculiarity of my situation** il faut que je vous explique ce qu'il y a d'étrange dans ma situation; **we all have our little peculiarities** nous avons tous nos petites manies (**b**) *(specific characteristic)* particularité *f*; **each region has its own peculiarities** chaque région a son particularisme *ou* ses particularités
peculiarly [pɪ'kjuːlɪəlɪ] *adv* (**a**) *(oddly)* étrangement, bizarrement (**b**) *(especially)* particulièrement, singulièrement; **a peculiarly French institution/obsession** une institution/obsession bien française
pecuniary [pɪ'kjuːnɪərɪ] *adj Formal* pécuniaire
pedagogic [ˌpedə'gɒdʒɪk], **pedagogical** [ˌpedə'gɒdʒɪkəl] *adj* pédagogique
pedagogically [ˌpedə'gɒdʒɪkəlɪ] *adv* pédagogiquement
pedagogue ['pedəgɒg] *n* pédagogue *mf*
pedagogy ['pedəgɒdʒɪ] *n* pédagogie *f*
pedal ['pedəl] *(Br pt & pp* **pedalled**, *cont* **pedalling**, *Am pt & pp* **pedaled**, *cont* **pedaling**) **1** *n* pédale *f*; **clutch/brake pedal** pédale *f* d'embrayage/de frein; **loud/soft pedal** *(of piano)* pédale *f* droite *ou* forte/gauche *ou* douce
2 *vi* pédaler; **we pedalled along the back roads** nous roulions (à bicyclette) sur les routes de l'arrière-pays; **it's hard pedalling uphill** c'est dur de grimper une côte à bicyclette *ou* à vélo; **he pedalled off** il est parti (à vélo)
3 *vt* faire avancer en pédalant; **he pedalled his bike up the hill** il a pédalé jusqu'en haut de la côte sur son vélo
►► *Br* ***pedal bin*** poubelle *f* à pédale; ***pedal boat*** pédalo *m*; ***pedal car*** voiture *f* à pédales; ***pedal cycle*** bicyclette *f*; ***pedal keyboard*** *(of organ)* pédalier *m*; *Mus* ***pedal point*** pédale *f*; ***pedal pushers*** (pantalon *m*) corsaire *m*; ***pedal steel (guitar)*** guitare *f* hawaïenne, pedal-steel *f*
pedalo ['pedələʊ] *(pl* **pedalos** *or* **pedaloes**) *n* pédalo *m*
pedal-operated *adj* commandé par pédale(s)
pedant ['pedənt] *n* pédant(e) *m,f*
pedantic [pɪ'dæntɪk] *adj* pédant
pedantically [pɪ'dæntɪklɪ] *adv* de manière pédante; *(say)* d'un ton pédant
pedantry ['pedəntrɪ] *(pl* **pedantries**) *n* (**a**) *(behaviour)* pédantisme *m*, pédanterie *f* (**b**) *(remark)* pédanterie *f*
pedate ['pedeɪt] *adj* (**a**) *Bot* palmilobé, pédalé (**b**) *Zool* pourvu de pattes
peddle ['pedəl] **1** *vt* (**a**) *Old-fashioned (wares)* colporter; **he didn't want to peddle encyclopedias all his life** il ne voulait pas passer sa vie à faire du porte à porte pour vendre des encyclopédies (**b**) *(drugs)* revendre, faire le trafic de; **drug peddling** trafic *m* de drogue (**c**) *Pej (promote → idea, opinion)* propager; *(→ gossip, scandal)* colporter
2 *vi* faire du colportage
peddler ['pedlə(r)] *n* (**a**) *(seller)* colporteur(-euse) *m,f* (**b**) *(drug pusher)* trafiquant(e) *m,f* (de drogue), revendeur(euse) *m,f* (**c**) *Pej (promoter → of ideas, opinions)* propagateur(trice) *m,f*; *(→ of gossip, scandal)* colporteur(euse) *m,f*; **peddlers of dreams** marchands *mpl* de rêves
pederast ['pedəræst] *n* pédéraste *m*
pederastic [ˌpedə'ræstɪk] *adj* pédérastique
pederasty ['pedəræstɪ] *n* pédérastie *f*
pedestal ['pedɪstəl] *n* piédestal *m*, socle *m*; *Fig* piédestal *m*; **to place** *or* **to put sb on a pedestal** mettre qn sur un piédestal; **that knocked him off his pedestal** cela l'a fait tomber de son piédestal
►► ***pedestal basin*** lavabo *m* sur colonne; ***pedestal desk*** bureau *m* ministre; ***pedestal table*** guéridon *m*
pedestrian [pɪ'destrɪən] **1** *n* piéton *m*; **pedestrians only** *(sign)* réservé aux piétons
2 *comp (street, area)* piéton, piétonnier

3 *adj* (**a**) *(prosaic)* prosaïque; *(commonplace)* banal; **a pedestrian style** un style prosaïque
(**b**) *(done on foot → exercise, outing)* pédestre, à pied
▸▸ *Br* ***pedestrian crossing*** passage *m* clouté *ou* piétons; ***pedestrian overpass*** passerelle *f*; *Br* ***pedestrian precinct,*** *Am* ***pedestrian zone*** zone *f* piétonnière *ou* piétonne

pedestrian-controlled crossing *n* passage *m* pour piétons à bouton d'appel

pedestrianism [pɪ'destrɪənɪzəm] *n* (**a**) *Sport* pédestrianisme *m* (**b**) *(prosaicness)* prosaïsme *m*

pedestrianization [pə,destrɪənaɪ'zeɪʃən] *n* transformation *f* en zone piétonne *ou* piétonnière

pedestrianize, -ise [pə'destrɪənaɪz] *vt* transformer en zone piétonne *ou* piétonnière
▸▸ ***pedestrianized streets*** rues *fpl* piétonnes *or* piétonnières

pediatric, pediatrician *etc Am* = **paediatric, paediatrician** *etc*

pediatrist [,pi:dɪ'ætrɪst] *n* pédiatre *mf*

pediatry ['pi:dɪætrɪ] *n* pédiatrie *f*

pedicab ['pedɪkæb] *n* cyclo-pousse *m inv*

pedicel ['pedɪsel] *n Bot & Biol* pédicule *m*; *Entom* pédicelle *m*

pedicle ['pedɪkəl] *n Bot & Biol* pédicule *m*

pediculosis [,pedɪkjʊ'ləʊsɪs] *n Med* pédiculose *f*

pedicure ['pedɪ,kjʊə(r)] *n (treatment)* soins *mpl* des pieds; **to have a pedicure** se faire soigner les pieds, aller chez le/la pédicure

pedigree ['pedɪgri:] 1 *n* (**a**) *(descent → of animal)* pedigree *m*; *(→ of person)* ascendance *f*, lignée *f*; *Fig (background → of person)* origine *f*; **she had an impeccable political pedigree** ses antécédents politiques étaient irréprochables (**b**) *(document for animal)* pedigree *m* (**c**) *(genealogical table)* arbre *m* généalogique
2 *adj (horse, cat, dog)* de (pure) race

pediment ['pedɪmənt] *n* (**a**) *Archit* fronton *m* (**b**) *Geol* pédiment *m*

pedimented ['pedɪmentɪd] *adj Archit* à fronton

pediplain ['pedɪpleɪn] *n Geol* pédiplaine *f*

pediplanation [,pedɪplə'neɪʃən] *n Geol* pédiplanation *f*

pediplane = **pediplain**

pedlar = **peddler**

pedologic [,pedəʊ'lɒdʒɪk], **pedological** [,pedəʊ'lɒdʒɪkəl] *adj Geol* pédologique

pedologist [pɪ'dɒlədʒɪst] *n Geol* pédologue *mf*

pedology[1] [pɪ'dɒlədʒɪ] *n Geol* pédologie *f*

pedology[2] *n (study of child growth, development etc)* pédologie *f*

pedometer [pɪ'dɒmɪtə(r)] *n* pédomètre *m*, podomètre *m*

pedophile = **paedophile**

pedophilia = **paedophilia**

peds *Am* = **paeds**

peduncle [pɪ'dʌŋkəl] *n* pédoncule *m*

pedunculate [pɪ'dʌŋkjʊleɪt] *adj* pédonculé
▸▸ ***pedunculate oak*** chêne *m* pédonculé, rouvre *m*

ped Xing *Am (written abbr* **pedestrian crossing***)* passage *m* clouté *ou* piétons

pee [pi:] *Fam* 1 *n* pipi *m*; **to have** *or* **to take a pee** faire pipi; **to go for a pee** aller faire pipi
2 *vi* faire pipi; **it's peeing down** *(raining)* il pleut comme vache qui pisse
3 *vt* **to pee oneself** *or Br* **one's pants** faire pipi dans sa culotte; **to pee oneself (laughing)** rire à en faire dans sa culotte

▸**pee off** *vt sep very Fam (annoy)* **to pee sb off** faire chier qn; **to be peed off** être fumasse *ou* furibard; **to be peed off at sb/about sth** être en pétard contre qn/à cause de qch; **to be peed off with sb/sth** *(have had enough of)* en avoir ras le bol de qn/qch

peek [pi:k] 1 *vi (glance)* jeter un coup d'œil; *(look furtively)* regarder furtivement; **to peek at sth** jeter un coup d'œil à *ou* sur qch; **someone was peeking through the keyhole** quelqu'un regardait par le trou de la serrure; **turn around and no peeking!** retourne-toi et n'essaie pas de voir ce que je fais!
2 *n* coup *m* d'œil; **to have** *or* **to take a peek at sth** jeter un coup d'œil à *ou* sur qch

peekaboo ['pi:kəbu:] *Fam* 1 *exclam* coucou!
2 *n* **to play peekaboo** jouer à faire coucou
3 *adj (see-through)* transparent❑; *(with holes)* avec *ou* en broderie(s) ajourée(s)❑

peel [pi:l] 1 *n* (**a**) *(of banana)* peau *f*; *(of orange, lemon)* écorce *f*; *(of apple, onion, potato)* pelure *f*; **add a twist of lemon peel** ajouter un zeste de citron
(**b**) *(UNCOUNT) (peelings)* épluchures *fpl*
2 *vt (fruit, vegetable)* peler, éplucher; *(boiled egg)* écaler, éplucher; *(shrimp)* décortiquer; *(twig)* écorcer; *(skin, bark)* enlever; **to keep one's eyes peeled** ouvrir l'œil; **we were all keeping our eyes peeled for a pub** nous guettions tous un pub, nous étions tous à l'affût d'un pub
3 *vi* (**a**) *(fruit, vegetable)* se peler
(**b**) *(plaster on wall, ceiling etc)* s'écailler, se craqueler; *(paint, varnish)* s'écailler; *(wallpaper)* se décoller
(**c**) *(skin on back, face etc)* peler; **I'm peeling all over** je pèle de partout

▸**peel away** 1 *vi (plaster on wall, ceiling etc)* s'écailler, se craqueler; *(paint, varnish)* s'écailler; *(wallpaper)* se décoller
2 *vt sep (label, wallpaper)* détacher, décoller; *(bandage)* enlever, ôter

▸**peel back** *vt sep (label, wallpaper)* détacher, décoller; **peel back the plastic backing** décoller la pellicule de protection en plastique

▸**peel off** 1 *vi* (**a**) *(plaster on wall, ceiling etc)* s'écailler, se craqueler; *(paint, varnish)* s'écailler; *(wallpaper)* se décoller
(**b**) *Fam (undress)* se déshabiller❑
(**c**) *(turn away)* se détacher; **two aircraft peeled off from the main group** deux avions se détachèrent du gros de l'escadre
2 *vt sep* (**a**) *(label, wallpaper)* détacher, décoller; *(bandage)* enlever, ôter
(**b**) *(item of clothing)* enlever; **to peel off one's clothes** se déshabiller

peeler ['pi:lə(r)] *n* (**a**) *(device)* éplucheur *m*; *(electric)* éplucheuse *f*; **potato peeler** économe *m* (**b**) *Am Fam (stripper)* effeuilleuse *f* (**c**) *Br Fam Old-fashioned (policeman)* flic *m*

peelie-wally [,pi:lɪ'wælɪ] *adj Scot Fam* pâlot❑

peeling ['pi:lɪŋ] 1 *n* (**a**) *Med (of skin)* desquamation *f* (**b**) **peelings** *(of potato etc)* épluchures *fpl*, pelures *fpl*
2 *adj (nose, back etc)* qui pèle/pelait

peen [pi:n] *n (of hammer)* panne *f*

peep [pi:p] 1 (**a**) *(glance)* coup *m* d'œil; **to have a peep at sth** jeter un coup d'œil à qch; **I got a peep at the file before he came in** j'ai réussi à jeter un coup d'œil sur le dossier avant qu'il arrive
(**b**) *(of bird)* pépiement *m*; *Fam Fig* **any news from him? – not a peep!** tu as eu de ses nouvelles? – pas un mot *ou* que dalle!; *Fam* **one more peep out of you and you've had it!** encore un mot et ton compte est bon!
2 *vi* (**a**) *(glance)* jeter un coup d'œil; **to peep at/over/under sth** jeter un coup d'œil (furtif) à/par-dessus/sous qch; **the children were peeping through the keyhole** les enfants épiaient à travers le trou de la serrure; **someone was peeping at her from behind the curtains** quelqu'un l'observait, caché derrière les rideaux; **shut your eyes and don't peep!** ferme les yeux et n'essaie pas de voir ce que je fais!; **no peeping!** on ne regarde pas!
(**b**) *(emerge)* se montrer; **snowdrops were beginning to peep through** des perce-neiges commençaient à pointer
(**c**) *(bird)* pépier; *(of mouse)* couiner

▸**peep out** *vi (be visible)* se laisser entrevoir, se montrer; *(flower)* percer, pointer; **the moon peeped out through the clouds** la lune a percé *ou* est apparue à travers les nuages; **his feet were peeping out from beneath the curtains** ses pieds dépassaient de derrière les rideaux; **his big toe was peeping out through a hole in his sock** son gros doigt de pied pointait par un trou de sa chaussette; **a handkerchief peeped out from his pocket** la pointe d'un mouchoir dépassait de sa poche; **her nose peeped out over her scarf** le bout de son nez pointait *ou* apparaissait par-dessus son écharpe

peepbo ['pi:p,bəʊ] *Fam* 1 *exclam* coucou!
2 *n* **to play peepbo** jouer à faire coucou

pee-pee *n Am Fam (in children's language)* **to go pee-pee** faire pipi

peeper ['pi:pə(r)] *Fam* 1 *n Am (detective)* privé *m*
2 **peepers** *npl (eyes)* mirettes *fpl*

peephole ['pi:phəʊl] *n* trou *m*; *(in house door, cell)* judas *m*

peeping Tom [,pi:pɪŋ'tɒm] *n* voyeur *m*

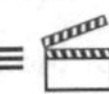

'Peeping Tom' *Powell* 'Le Voyeur'

peepshow ['pi:pʃəʊ] *n (device)* stéréoscope *m (pour images érotiques)*; *(pictures)* vues *fpl* stéréoscopiques; *(form of entertainment)* peep-show *m*

peep-toe(d) shoes *npl* escarpins *mpl* à bout découpé

peer [pɪə(r)] 1 *n* (**a**) *(noble)* pair *m*, noble *mf*; **he was made a peer** il a été élevé à la pairie; *Pol* **the Conservative Peers** les pairs *mpl* conservateurs *(en Grande-Bretagne)*; **peer of the realm** pair *m* du royaume
(**b**) *(equal)* pair *m*; **a jury of one's peers** un jury formé *ou* composé de ses pairs; **as a negotiator she has no peer** c'est une négociatrice hors pair, comme négociatrice elle n'a pas son pareil
2 *vi (look → intently)* regarder attentivement; *(→ with difficulty)* s'efforcer de voir; **to peer at sb/sth** scruter qn/qch du regard; **she peered out into the darkness** elle scruta l'obscurité; **he peered at the suspects' faces** il dévisagea les suspects; **she peered at the small print** elle s'efforça de lire ce qui était écrit en petits caractères
▸▸ ***peer group*** pairs *mpl*; ***peer pressure*** influence *f* des pairs *ou* du groupe; ***peer review*** révision *f* par un collègue

peerage ['pɪərɪdʒ] *n* (**a**) *(title)* pairie *f*; **he was given a peerage** *or* **raised to the peerage** il a été élevé à la pairie (**b**) *(body of peers)* pairs *mpl*, noblesse *f* (**c**) *(book)* nobiliaire *m*

peeress ['pɪərɪs] *n* pairesse *f*

peerless ['pɪəlɪs] *adj* sans pareil, incomparable

peerlessly ['pɪəlɪslɪ] *adv* incomparablement

peeve [pi:v] *vt Fam* mettre en rogne; **it really peeves me that he got the job** ça me met en rogne qu'il ait eu le poste

peeved [pi:vd] *adj Fam (person)* en rogne; *(expression)* irrité❑; **to be peeved at sb** être en rogne contre qn; **to get peeved** se mettre en rogne

peevish ['pi:vɪʃ] *adj (person)* irritable, grincheux; *(child)* grognon; *(report, expression)* irrité; **in a peevish mood** de mauvaise humeur

peevishly ['pi:vɪʃlɪ] *adv (say, refuse)* d'un ton irrité; *(behave)* de façon désagréable; **to complain peevishly** ronchonner

peevishness ['pi:vɪʃnɪs] *n* mauvaise humeur *f*, irritabilité *f*

peewee ['pi:,wi:] *Am Fam* 1 *n* moustique *m (personne très petite)*
2 *adj* riquiqui

peewit ['pi:wɪt] *n Orn* vanneau *m*

peg [peg] *(pt & pp* **pegged,** *cont* **pegging***)* 1 *n* (**a**) *(for hat, coat)* patère *f*; *Fig* **a peg to hang an argument on** un prétexte de dispute, une excuse pour se disputer
(**b**) *Br (clothespeg)* pince *f* à linge
(**c**) *(dowel → wooden)* cheville *f*; *(→ metal)* fiche *f*
(**d**) *(for tent)* piquet *m*
(**e**) *(in mountaineering)* piton *m*
(**f**) *(in croquet)* piquet *m*
(**g**) *(of barrel)* fausset *m*, fosset *m*
(**h**) *Mus (on string instrument)* cheville *f*
(**i**) *Fig (degree, notch)* degré *m*, cran *m*; **she's gone down a peg (or two) in my estimation** elle a baissé d'un cran dans mon estime; **to bring** *or* **to take sb down a peg or two** rabattre le caquet à qn, remettre qn à sa place
(**j**) *Br Fam (of spirits)* petit verre❑ *m*
2 *vt* (**a**) *(fasten → gen)* attacher; *(→ with dowels)* cheviller; *(insert → stake)* enfoncer, planter; *(in mountaineering)* pitonner; **he was pegging the washing on the line** il accrochait le linge à la corde avec des pinces; **to peg a tent** fixer une tente avec des piquets
(**b**) *(set → price, increase)* fixer; *(tie → currency)* indexer; **oil was pegged at $20 a barrel** le prix du pétrole était fixé à 20 dollars le baril; **to peg sth to the rate of inflation** indexer qch sur le taux de l'inflation; **countries which have**

pegged their currencies to the euro les pays qui ont indexé leur monnaie sur l'euro; **export earnings are pegged to the exchange rate** le revenu des exportations varie en fonction du taux de change

(**c**) *Fam (throw)* balancer

(**d**) *Am Fam (classify)* classer □

►► *Fam* ***peg leg*** *(wooden leg)* jambe *f* de bois □, pilon □ *m*; *(artificial leg)* jambe *f* artificielle □; *(person)* = personne qui a une jambe de bois ou une jambe artificielle

►**peg away** *vi Br Fam* travailler sans relâche □; *(student)* bûcher; **she pegged away at her Latin** elle bûchait son latin; **we're pegging away at the backlog** petit à petit, nous rattrapons notre retard □

►**peg down** *vt sep (fasten down)* fixer *ou* attacher (avec des piquets); **he pegged the tarpaulin down** il fixa la bâche au sol avec des piquets

►**peg out 1** *vt sep* (**a**) *(hang out → washing)* étendre

(**b**) *(mark out with pegs)* piqueter

2 *vi* (**a**) *Fam (die)* crever, claquer

(**b**) *Fam (give up)* laisser tomber □, abandonner □

(**c**) *(in croquet)* toucher le piquet final *(et se retirer de la partie)*

Pegasus ['pegəsəs] *n* (**a**) *Myth* Pégase; *Literary* **to mount one's Pegasus** monter sur Pégase (**b**) *Astron* Pégase *m*

pegboard ['pegbɔːd] *n* plaquette *f* perforée *(utilisée dans certains jeux)*

pegmatite ['pegmətaɪt] *n Miner* pegmatite *f*

peg-top trousers *npl* (pantalon *m*) fuseau *m*

PEI *(written abbr* **Prince Edward Island***)* l'île *f* du Prince-Édouard

pein = **peen**

pejoration [,piːdʒə'reɪʃən] *n Ling* péjoration *f*

pejorative [pɪ'dʒɒrətɪv] **1** *adj* péjoratif

2 *n* péjoratif *m*

pejoratively [pɪ'dʒɒrətɪvlɪ] *adv* péjorativement

peke [piːk] *n Fam* pékinois □ *m (chien)*

peke-faced *adj (cat)* à museau aplati *(comme un pékinois)*

Pekinese [,piːkə'niːz], **Pekingese** [,piːkɪŋ'iːz] **1** *n* (**a**) *(person)* Pékinois(e) *m,f* (**b**) *Ling* pékinois *m* (**c**) *(dog)* pékinois *m*

2 *adj* pékinois

Peking [,piː'kɪŋ] *n* Pékin

►► ***Peking duck*** canard *m* laqué

pekoe ['piːkəʊ] *n* pekoe *m*

pelagic [pe'lædʒɪk] *adj* (**a**) *(fauna, sediment)* pélagique (**b**) *(not coastal)* hauturier, de haute mer

pelargonium [,pelə'gəʊnɪəm] *n* pélargonium *m*

pelf [pelf] *n Pej* lucre *m*

pelham ['peləm] *n* pelham *m*

pelican ['pelɪkən] *n Orn* pélican *m*

►► *Br* ***pelican crossing*** = passage piétons à commande manuelle; ***the Pelican State*** = surnom donné à la Louisiane

pelite ['piːlaɪt] *n Geol* pélite *f*

pellagra [pə'lægrə] *n Med* pellagre *f*

pellet ['pelɪt] *n* (**a**) *(small ball)* boulette *f*; **wax/paper pellets** boulettes *fpl* de cire/de papier; **pellets of rabbit dung** crottes *fpl* de lapin (**b**) *(for gun)* (grain *m* de) plomb *m* (**c**) *(pill)* pilule *f* (**d**) *Zool (regurgitated food of owl etc)* pelote *f* de régurgitation

►► ***pellet gun*** fusil *m* à plombs

pellitory-of-the-wall ['pelɪtərɪ-] *n Bot* pariétaire *f*

pell-mell [,pel'mel] *adv Br (pile, throw)* pêle-mêle; **the crowd ran pell-mell into the square** la foule s'est ruée sur la place dans une cohue indescriptible

pellucid [pe'luːsɪd] *adj (membrane, zone)* pellucide; *(water)* limpide; *Fig (prose, style)* clair, limpide

pelmanism ['pelmənɪzəm] *n Cards (game)* paires *fpl*

pelmet ['pelmɪt] *n (for curtains)* cantonnière *f*; *(wood, board)* lambrequin *m*

Peloponnese [,peləpə'niːz] *n* **the Peloponnese** le Péloponnèse

Peloponnesian [,peləpə'niːzɪən] *adj* péloponnésien, du Péloponnèse

►► ***the Peloponnesian War*** la guerre du Péloponnèse

Pelops ['piːlɒps] *pr n Myth* Pélops

pelorus [pe'lɔːrəs] *n* alidade *f*

pelota [pə'lɒtə] *n* pelote *f* basque

►► ***pelota court*** fronton *m*

pelotherapy [piːləʊ'θerəpɪ] *n* pélothérapie *f*

pelt [pelt] **1** *vt (person, target)* bombarder; **they were pelting each other with snowballs** ils se bombardaient de boules de neige; **the speaker was pelted with eggs** l'orateur a été bombardé d'œufs

2 *vi Fam* (**a**) *(rain)* **it was pelting with rain** il pleuvait à verse □, il tombait des cordes; **I changed the tyre in the pelting rain** j'ai changé le pneu sous la pluie battante □

(**b**) *(run)* courir à fond de train *ou* à toute allure; **she came pelting up the stairs** elle grimpa l'escalier quatre à quatre; **she came pelting down the stairs** elle dévala l'escalier

3 *n* (**a**) *(skin)* peau *f*; *(fur)* fourrure *f*

(**b**) *Ir Fam* **in one's pelt** *(naked)* à poil

(**c**) *Br (idiom)* **at full pelt** à fond de train

►**pelt down** *vi Fam (rain)* tomber à verse □; **the rain** *or* **it was pelting down** la pluie tombait à verse, il pleuvait à verse □; **the hail pelted down** la grêle tombait dru □

peltate ['pelteɪt] *adj Bot* pelté, en forme de bouclier

peltry ['peltrɪ] *n* peaux *fpl*

pelvic ['pelvɪk] *adj* pelvien

►► ***pelvic bone*** ilion *m*; *Ich* ***pelvic fins*** pelviennes *fpl*; ***pelvic floor*** plancher *m* pelvien; ***pelvic floor exercises*** exercices *mpl* de musculation du plancher pelvien; ***pelvic girdle*** ceinture *f* pelvienne; ***pelvic inflammatory disease*** syndrome *m* inflammatoire pelvien

pelvis ['pelvɪs] *(pl* **pelvises** *or* **pelves** ['-viːz]*)* *n* bassin *m*, pelvis *m*

pemmican ['pemɪkən] *n* pemmican *m*

pen [pen] *(pt & pp* **penned**, *sense* (**b**) *also* **pent** [pent], *cont* **penning**) **1** *n* (**a**) *(for writing)* stylo *m*; **fountain pen** stylo *m* à plume, stylo-plume *m*; **ball(point) pen** stylo *m* à bille, stylo-bille *m*; **felt(-tip) pen** (crayon *m ou* stylo *m*) feutre *m*; **to put pen to paper** écrire, prendre sa plume; **another novel from the pen of Muriel Spark** un nouveau roman de la plume de Muriel Spark; **she lives by her pen** elle vit de sa plume; **a slip of the pen** un lapsus; *Prov* **the pen is mightier than the sword** un coup de langue est pire qu'un coup de lance

(**b**) *(of squid)* plume *f*

(**c**) *(female swan)* cygne *m* femelle

(**d**) *(for animals)* enclos *m*, parc *m*; **sheep pen** parc *m* à moutons

(**e**) *(for submarines)* **(submarine) pen** bassin *m* protégé

(**f**) *Am Fam (penitentiary)* taule *f*, tôle *f*; **in the pen** en taule, en cabane; **he spent ten years in the pen** il a passé dix ans en taule, il a fait dix ans de taule

(**g**) *Br Fam Ftbl (penalty)* péno *m*

2 *vt* (**a**) *(write)* écrire; **a letter penned in a childish hand** une lettre d'une écriture enfantine

(**b**) *(enclose)* **to pen in** *or* **up** *(livestock)* parquer, enfermer dans un enclos; *(dog)* enfermer; *(person)* enfermer, cloîtrer, claquemurer

►► *Br* ***pen friend*** correspondant(e) *m,f (épistolaire)*; ***pen name*** nom *m* de plume, pseudonyme *m*; ***pen nib*** plume *f (de stylo)*; *Fam* ***pen pal*** correspondant(e) □ *m,f (épistolaire)*; *Fam Pej* ***pen pusher*** gratte-papier *m inv*; *Fam Pej* ***pen pushing*** travail *m* de bureau □

penal ['piːnəl] *adj* (**a**) *(law)* pénal; *(establishment)* pénitentiaire

(**b**) *(severe → taxation, fine)* écrasant

►► ***penal code*** code *m* pénal; ***penal colony*** colonie *f* pénitentiaire, bagne *m*; *Fin* ***penal interest*** intérêts *mpl* moratoires; *Hist* ***the Penal Laws*** = lois adoptées aux XVIIème et XVIIIème siècles par le gouvernement britannique, privant les catholiques irlandais de certains droits essentiels; ***penal offence*** infraction *f* pénale; *Fin* ***penal rate*** taux *m* d'usure; ***penal servitude*** travaux *mpl* forcés, bagne *m*; ***penal settlement*** colonie *f* pénitentiaire, bagne *m*

penalization [,piːnəlaɪ'zeɪʃən] *n* pénalisation *f*, sanction *f*

penalize, -ise ['piːnəlaɪz] *vt* (**a**) *(punish)* pénaliser, sanctionner (**b**) *(disadvantage)* pénaliser, défavoriser, désavantager; **the new tax penalizes large families** le nouvel impôt pénalise les familles nombreuses

penally ['piːnəlɪ] *adv* pénalement

penalty ['penəltɪ] *(pl* **penalties**) *n* (**a**) *Law (punishment)* peine *f*; *(fine)* amende *f*; **on penalty of** sous peine de; **under penalty of death** sous peine de mort; **they advocate stiffer penalties for drunk driving** ils préconisent des peines plus lourdes pour conduite en état d'ivresse; **the penalty for that offence is six months' imprisonment** la peine encourue pour ce délit est de six mois d'emprisonnement; **penalty for improper use: £25** *(sign)* tout abus est passible d'une amende de 25 livres

(**b**) *Admin & Com (for breaking contract)* pénalité *f*, sanction *f*

(**c**) *Fig (unpleasant consequence)* **to pay the penalty (for sth)** subir les conséquences (de qch); **that's the penalty for being famous** c'est la rançon de la gloire

(**d**) *Sport (gen)* pénalisation *f*; *(kick → in football)* penalty *m*; *(→ in rugby)* pénalité *f*; **to award a penalty** *(in football)* accorder un penalty; *(in rugby)* accorder une pénalité; **to score (from) a penalty** *(in football)* marquer un penalty; **a two-minute (time) penalty** *(in ice hockey)* une pénalité de deux minutes

►► *Ftbl* ***penalty area*** surface *f* de réparation; ***penalty bench*** *(in ice hockey)* banc *m* de pénalité; ***penalty box*** *Ftbl* surface *f* de réparation; *(in ice hockey)* banc *m* de pénalité; *Law* ***penalty clause*** clause *f* pénale; ***penalty corner*** *(in hockey)* coup *m* de coin de pénalité; ***penalty double*** *(in bridge)* contre *m* de pénalité; *Sport* ***penalty goal*** but *m* sur pénalité; *Fin* ***penalty interest*** pénalité *f* de retard, intérêts *mpl* moratoires; ***penalty kick*** *(in football)* penalty *m*; *(in rugby)* (coup *m* de pied de) pénalité *f*; ***penalty points*** *(in quiz, game)* gage *m*; *(for drivers)* points *mpl* de pénalité *(dans le système du permis à points)*; ***penalty rate*** *(of taxation)* taux *m* de pénalité; *Am, Austr & Can (for overtime)* tarif *m* des heures supplémentaires; *Ftbl* ***penalty shootout*** épreuve *f* des penalties; ***penalty shot*** *(in ice hockey)* pénalité *f*; *Ftbl* ***penalty spot*** point *m* de réparation; *Golf* ***penalty stroke*** coup *m* d'amende; *Sport* ***penalty throw*** penalty *m*; ***penalty try*** *(in rugby)* essai *m* de pénalité

penance ['penəns] *n* pénitence *f*; **to do penance for one's sins** faire pénitence; **to do sth as a penance** faire qch par pénitence

pen-and-ink 1 *comp (drawing)* à la plume

2 *vi SEng Fam (rhyming slang* **stink***)* schlinguer, fouetter

penannular [,pen'ænjʊlə(r)] *adj* à peu près annulaire, approximativement en forme d'anneau

pence [pens] *npl (pl of* **penny***)* pence *mpl*

penchant [*Br* 'pɑ̃ʃɑ̃, *Am* 'pentʃənt] *n* penchant *m*, goût *m*; **to have a penchant for sth** avoir un penchant *ou* un faible pour qch

pencil ['pensəl] *(Br pt & pp* **pencilled,** *cont* **pencilling**, *Am pt & pp* **penciled,** *cont* **penciling**) **1** *n* (**a**) *(for writing, makeup)* crayon *m*; **a box of coloured pencils** une boîte de crayons de couleur; **the corrections are in pencil** les corrections sont (faites) au crayon

(**b**) *Fig (narrow beam)* **a pencil of light** un pinceau de lumière

(**c**) *Zool (tuft)* houppe *f*

2 *comp (drawing)* au crayon

3 *vt* écrire au crayon; *(hastily)* crayonner; **question marks were pencilled in the margin** on avait mis des points d'interrogation au crayon dans la marge; **to pencil one's eyebrows** se dessiner les sourcils (au crayon)

►► ***pencil box*** plumier *m*; ***pencil case*** trousse *f*; ***pencil holder*** porte-crayon *m*; *Am Fam Pej* ***pencil pusher*** gratte-papier *m inv*; ***pencil sharpener*** taille-crayon *m*; ***pencil sketch*** croquis *m* au crayon

►**pencil in** *vt sep (date, name, address)* noter *ou* inscrire au crayon; *Fig* fixer provisoirement; **I'll pencil the meeting/you in for 6 June** retenons provisoirement la date du 6 juin pour la réunion/notre rendez-vous

pencilled ['pensəld] *adj* (**a**) *(written in pencil)* écrit au crayon (**b**) *(marked with pencil)* marqué au crayon; **pencilled eyebrows** sourcils

peg–pen

mpl dessinés *ou* tracés au crayon; **delicately pencilled eyebrows** sourcils *mpl* d'un tracé délicat (**c**) *Zool* à houppe

pendant ['pendənt] **1** *n* (**a**) *(necklace)* pendentif *m* (**b**) *(piece of jewellery → on necklace)* pendentif *m*; *(→ on earring)* pendeloque *f* (**c**) *(chandelier)* lustre *m*

2 *adj* (**a**) *(hanging)* pendant, qui pend (**b**) *(overhanging)* en surplomb, en saillie

▸▸ ***pendant earrings*** pendants *mpl* d'oreille

pendency ['pendənsɪ] *n Law* litispendance *f*

pendent ['pendənt] *adj Formal* (**a**) *(hanging)* pendant, qui pend (**b**) *(overhanging)* en surplomb, en saillie

pendentive [,pen'dentɪv] *n Archit* pendentif *m*, trompe *f*

pending ['pendɪŋ] **1** *adj* (**a**) *(waiting to be settled → gen)* en attente; *Law* en instance, pendant; *(→ documents)* en souffrance; **a pending court case** une affaire en instance *ou* en cours (**b**) *(imminent)* imminent; **a merger is pending** une fusion est imminente

2 *prep* en attendant

▸▸ *Br* ***pending tray*** corbeille *f* des dossiers en attente; **mail is piling up in the pending tray** le courrier en attente s'accumule

penduline tit ['pendjʊlaɪn-] *n Orn* mésange *f* rémiz, (rémiz *m*) penduline *f*

pendulous ['pendjʊləs] *adj* (**a**) *(sagging → breasts)* tombant; *(→ lips)* pendant (**b**) *(swinging)* oscillant

pendulum ['pendjʊləm] *n* pendule *m*; *(in clock)* balancier *m*; *Fig* **a swing of the pendulum sent the president's popularity plummeting** un revirement de l'opinion a fait chuter la cote de popularité du président; **the pendulum of fashion has swung back to a sixties look** la mode des années soixante est revenue au goût du jour

▸▸ ***pendulum bob*** lentille *f* de pendule *ou* de balancier; ***pendulum clock*** horloge *f* à pendule *ou* à balancier

Penelope [pə'neləpɪ] *pr n Myth* Pénélope

peneplain ['pi:nɪpleɪn] *n Geol* pénéplaine *f*

peneplanation [,pi:nɪplə'neɪʃən] *n Geol* pénéplanation *f*

peneplane = **peneplain**

penetrability [,penɪtrə'bɪlɪtɪ] *n* pénétrabilité *f*; *Petr* **worked/unworked penetrability** pénétrabilité *f* après/sans malaxage

penetrable ['penɪtrəbəl] *adj* (**a**) *(material, defences)* pénétrable; **easily penetrable** facile à pénétrer (**b**) *(prose, style)* **barely penetrable** difficilement compréhensible

penetrameter [,penɪ'træmɪtə(r)] = **penetrometer**

penetrance ['penɪtrəns] *n Biol* pénétrance *f*

penetrant ['penɪtrənt] *n Chem* fluide *m* pénétrant

penetrate ['penɪtreɪt] **1** *vt* (**a**) *(find way into or through → jungle, region)* pénétrer dans; *(→ blockade, enemy defences)* pénétrer; **they penetrated unknown territory** ils ont pénétré en territoire inconnu; **it's not easy to penetrate those kinds of social circles** il n'est pas facile de s'introduire dans ce genre de milieux

(**b**) *(infiltrate → party, movement)* s'infiltrer dans, noyauter; **penetrated by an informer** infiltré par un indicateur

(**c**) *(pierce → of missile)* percer, transpercer; **the bullet penetrated his right lung** la balle lui a perforé le poumon droit

(**d**) *(pass through → of sound, light etc)* traverser, transpercer; **the child's cries penetrated the silence** les cris de l'enfant déchiraient le silence; **the cold wind penetrated her clothing** le vent glacial passait à travers ses vêtements; **the ship's lights failed to penetrate the fog** les lumières du bateau ne parvenaient pas à percer le brouillard

(**e**) *(see through → darkness, disguise, mystery)* percer; **to penetrate sb's thoughts** lire dans les pensées de qn

(**f**) *Mktg (market)* pénétrer

(**g**) *(sexually)* pénétrer

2 *vi* (**a**) *(break through)* pénétrer; **the troops penetrated deep into enemy territory** les troupes ont pénétré très avant en territoire ennemi

(**b**) *(ideas, beliefs)* s'implanter; **the custom has not penetrated to this part of the country** cette coutume n'est pas parvenue jusqu'à cette partie du pays

(**c**) *(sink in)* **I heard what you said but it didn't penetrate at the time** j'ai entendu ce que tu as dit, mais je n'ai pas saisi sur le moment; **I had to explain it to him several times before it finally penetrated** j'ai dû le lui expliquer plusieurs fois avant que ça (ne) rentre

penetrating ['penɪtreɪtɪŋ] *adj* (**a**) *(sound → pleasant)* pénétrant; *(→ unpleasant)* perçant (**b**) *(cold)* pénétrant, perçant; *(rain, wind)* pénétrant (**c**) *(look)* pénétrant, perçant; *(mind, question)* pénétrant; **she had penetrating eyes** elle avait un regard pénétrant

▸▸ ***penetrating oil*** dégrippant *m*

penetratingly ['penɪtreɪtɪŋlɪ] *adv* (**a**) *(loudly)* **to scream penetratingly** pousser un cri perçant; **to whistle penetratingly** émettre un sifflement strident (**b**) *Fig* avec perspicacité; **she looked at him penetratingly** elle lui lança un regard pénétrant *ou* aigu

penetration [,penɪ'treɪʃən] *n* (**a**) *(gen) & Mktg* pénétration *f* (**b**) *Mil* percée *f* (**c**) *Phot* profondeur *f* de champ

▸▸ *Mktg* ***penetration price*** prix *m* de pénétration

penetrative ['penɪtrətɪv] *adj (force)* de pénétration

▸▸ ***penetrative sex*** relations *fpl* sexuelles avec pénétration

penetrometer [,penɪ'trɒmɪtə(r)] *n Tech* pénétromètre *m*, pénétramètre *m*

penfold ['penfəʊld] *n* enclos *m*

penguin ['peŋgwɪn] *n* manchot *m*

▸▸ *Br Fam* ***penguin suit*** costard *m* chic

penguinery ['peŋgwɪnərɪ] *n* colonie *f* de manchots

penholder ['pen,həʊldə(r)] *n* porte-plume *m inv*

penicillate [penɪ'sɪlɪt] *adj Biol* pénicillé

penicillin [,penɪ'sɪlɪn] *n* pénicilline *f*

penicillium [,penɪ'sɪlɪəm] *n* pénicillium *m*

penile ['pi:naɪl] *adj* pénien

peninsula [pə'nɪnsjʊlə] *n (large)* péninsule *f*; *(small)* presqu'île *f*

peninsular [pə'nɪnsjʊlə(r)] **1** *adj* péninsulaire

2 Peninsular *adj* **the Peninsular War** la guerre d'Espagne *(1808-1814)*

penis ['pi:nɪs] *(pl* **penises** *or* **penes** [-ɪz]) *n* pénis *m*

▸▸ *Psy* ***penis envy*** envie *f* du pénis

penitence ['penɪtəns] *n* pénitence *f*, repentir *m*

penitent ['penɪtənt] **1** *adj* (**a**) *(gen)* contrit (**b**) *Rel* pénitent

2 *n Rel* pénitent(e) *m,f*

penitential [,penɪ'tenʃəl] **1** *adj* pénitentiel

2 *n (book)* pénitentiel *m*

penitentiary [,penɪ'tenʃərɪ] *(pl* **penitentiaries**) **1** *n* (**a**) *Am (prison)* prison *f*

(**b**) *Rel (priest)* pénitencier *m*

2 *adj* (**a**) *Am (life, conditions)* pénitentiaire; *(offence)* passible d'une peine de prison

(**b**) *(penitential)* pénitentiel

3 Penitentiary *n Rel* **the Penitentiary** *(cardinal)* le grand pénitencier; *(tribunal)* la Sacrée Pénitencerie, la Pénitencerie apostolique

▸▸ *Am* ***penitentiary guard*** gardien(enne) *m,f* de prison

penitently ['penɪtəntlɪ] *adv (say)* d'un ton contrit; *(submit, kneel)* avec contrition

penknife ['pennaɪf] *(pl* **penknives** [-naɪvz]) *n* canif *m*

penlight ['penlaɪt] *n* lampe-stylo *f*, minitorche *f*

penmanship ['penmənʃɪp] *n* calligraphie *f*

Penn, Penna *(written abbr* **Pennsylvania**) Pennsylvanie *f*

penna ['penə] *(pl* **pennae** [-ni:]) *n Orn* penne *f*

pennant ['penənt] *n* (**a**) *(flag → gen)* fanion *m* (**b**) *Naut (for identification)* flamme *f*; *(for signalling)* pavillon *m* (**c**) *Am Sport* = drapeau servant de trophée dans certains championnats; **to win the pennant** remporter le championnat

pennate ['peneɪt] *adj Bot* penné, pinné

penniless ['penɪlɪs] *adj* sans le sou; **they're absolutely penniless** ils n'ont pas un sou; **the stock market crash left him penniless** le krach boursier l'a mis sur la paille

Pennines ['penaɪnz] *npl* **the Pennines** les Pennines *fpl*

Pennine Way ['penaɪn-] *n* **the Pennine Way** = sentier de grande randonnée qui suit la crête des Pennines

pennon ['penən] *n* (**a**) *(flag → gen)* fanion *m*; *(→ on lance)* pennon *m* (**b**) *Naut (for identification)* flamme *f*; *(for signalling)* pavillon *m*

Pennsylvania [,pensɪl'veɪnɪə] *n* la Pennsylvanie; **in Pennsylvania** dans la Pennsylvanie; **1600 Pennsylvania Avenue** = adresse de la Maison Blanche, utilisée par les médias américains pour faire référence au gouvernement

▸▸ ***Pennsylvania Dutch*** = communauté protestante fondée aux États-Unis par les colons allemands aux XVIIème et XVIIIème siècles (dont font partie les Amish et les Mennonites)

Pennsylvanian [,pensɪl'veɪnɪən] **1** *n* Pennsylvanien(enne) *m,f*

2 *adj* pennsylvanien

penny ['penɪ] *(pl sense* (**a**) **pence** [pens], *pl sense* (**b**) **pennies**) *n* (**a**) *(unit of currency → in Britain, Ireland)* penny *m*; **it cost me 44 pence** ça m'a coûté 44 pence

(**b**) *(coin → in Britain, Ireland)* penny *m*, pièce *f* d'un penny; *(→ in US)* cent *m*, pièce *f* d'un cent; **it was expensive, but it was worth every penny** c'était cher, mais j'en ai vraiment eu pour mon argent; **it won't cost you a penny** ça ne vous coûtera pas un centime *ou* un sou; **every penny counts** un sou est un sou; **they haven't got a penny to their name** *or* **two pennies to rub together** ils n'ont pas un sou vaillant; **to earn** *or Am* **turn an honest penny** gagner honnêtement sa vie; *Br Fam* **people like him are two** *or* **ten a penny** des gens comme lui, ce n'est pas ça qui manque; **a penny for your thoughts** à quoi penses-tu?; *Br Fam* **suddenly the penny dropped** d'un seul coup ça a fait tilt; *Br Fam* **he keeps turning up like a bad penny** c'est un vrai pot de colle; *Br* **penny for the guy** = phrase rituelle des enfants qui font la quête la veille de "Guy Fawkes Day"; *Prov* **in for a penny in for a pound** quand le vin est tiré, il faut le boire; *Br Prov* **take care of the pennies and the pounds will take care of themselves** les petits ruisseaux font les grandes rivières; **to be penny wise and pound foolish** chipoter sur les petites dépenses sans regarder aux grandes

▸▸ *Am* ***penny arcade*** galerie *f* de jeux; ***Penny Black*** = premier timbre-poste britannique; *Br Fam Old-fashioned* ***penny dreadful*** *(novel)* = roman d'amour ou d'aventures à quatre sous; *(magazine)* magazine *m* à sensation; *Br St Exch* ***penny shares*** actions *fpl* d'une valeur de moins d'une livre sterling; *Am St Exch* ***penny stocks*** actions *fpl* d'une valeur de moins d'un dollar; ***penny whistle*** pipeau *m*

penny-cress *n Bot* thlaspi *m*

penny-farthing *n Br* bicycle *m*, vélocipède *m*

penny-in-the-slot machine *n Old-fashioned* machine *f* à sous

penny-pincher [-,pɪntʃə(r)] *n Fam* pingre *mf*, radin(e) *m,f*

penny-pinching [-,pɪntʃɪŋ] *Fam* **1** *n (UNCOUNT)* économies *fpl* de bouts de chandelle; **government penny-pinching will ruin the education system** à force de serrer les cordons de la bourse, le gouvernement finira par étrangler le système éducatif

2 *adj (person)* radin, pingre, qui fait des économies de bouts de chandelle; *(action, step)* mesquin; *(lifestyle, measures)* de lésine, d'économie de bouts de chandelle

pennyroyal [,penɪ'rɔɪəl] *n Bot* pouliot *m*

pennyweight ['penɪweɪt] *n Br* = 1,5 grammes

pennywort ['penɪwɜ:t] *n Bot* (**a**) **(wall) pennywort** cotylédon *m*, nombril *m* de Vénus, gobelets *mpl* (**b**) **(marsh) pennywort** hydrocotyle *f*, écuelle *f* d'eau

pennyworth ['penɪwɜ:θ, 'penəθ] *(pl* **inv** *or* **pennyworths**) *n Br* (**a**) *Old-fashioned* **she asked for a pennyworth of toffees** elle demanda pour un penny de caramels (**b**) *Fig (small quantity)* **if he had a pennyworth of sense** s'il avait une once de bon sens

penologist [pi:'nɒlədʒɪst] *n (gen)* criminologiste *mf*; *(person studying prison systems)* spécialiste *mf* de l'étude des régimes pénitentiaires

penology [pi:'nɒlədʒɪ] *n* pénologie *f*

pen-pushing *adj Fam Pej (job)* de gratte-papier

pensile ['pensaɪl] *adj* (**a**) *(hanging, suspended)* suspendu (**b**) *Orn (bird)* qui bâtit un nid suspendu

pension ['penʃən, *sense* (**b**) *also* 'pɑ̃sjɔ̃] **1** *n* (**a**) *(for retired people)* retraite *f*; *(for disabled people)* pension *f*; **to draw a pension** *(retired person)* toucher une retraite; *(disabled person)* toucher une pension, être pensionné; **to pay sb a pension** verser une pension à qn; **disability pension** pension *f* d'invalidité; **widow's pension** *(before retiring age)* allocation *f* de veuvage; *(at retiring age)* pension *f* de réversion

(**b**) *(small hotel)* pension *f* de famille

2 *vt (for retirement)* verser une pension de retraite à; *(for disability)* pensionner, verser une pension à

►► *Br* ***pension book*** ≃ titre *m* de pension *(carnet permettant de retirer sa pension de retraite)*; ***pension fund*** caisse *f* de retraite, fonds *m* de pension; ***pension plan, pension scheme*** plan *m ou* régime *m* de retraite

►**pension off** *vt sep Br* (**a**) *(person)* mettre à la retraite

(**b**) *Hum (old car, machine)* mettre au rancart

pensionable ['penʃənəbəl] *adj* (**a**) *(person → gen)* qui a droit à une pension; *(→ for retirement)* qui a atteint l'âge de la retraite (**b**) *(job)* qui donne droit à une retraite

►► ***pensionable age*** âge *m* de la mise à la retraite; **teachers of pensionable age** les enseignants qui ont atteint l'âge de la retraite

pensionary ['penʃənərɪ] **1** *n* (**a**) *(person receiving a pension → gen)* pensionné(e) *m,f*; *(→ old age pensioner)* retraité(e) *m,f* (**b**) *(hireling)* mercenaire *m* (**c**) *Hist* **the Grand Pensionary** le Grand Pensionnaire

2 *adj (receiving a pension → gen)* pensionné; *(→ old age pension)* retraité

pensioned ['penʃənd] *adj* retraité

pensioner ['penʃənə(r)] *n Br* **(old age) pensioner** retraité(e) *m,f*; **war pensioner** ancien combattant *m (titulaire d'une pension militaire d'invalidité)*

pensive ['pensɪv] *adj* pensif, méditatif, songeur

pensively ['pensɪvlɪ] *adv* pensivement

pensiveness ['pensɪvnɪs] *n* air *m* pensif, songerie *f*

penstemon [,pen'sti:mən] *n Bot* penstémon *m*

penstock ['penstɒk] *n* (**a**) *(sluice)* vanne *f* d'écluse (**b**) *(in hydro-electric power station)* conduite *f* forcée

pent [pent] *pt & pp of* **pen**

pentachord ['pentəkɔ:d] *n Mus* pentacorde *m*

pentacle ['pentəkəl] *n* pentacle *m*

pentad ['pentæd] *n* (**a**) *(group of five)* groupe *m* de cinq (**b**) *(five years)* période *f* de cinq ans; *(five days)* période *f* de cinq jours

pentadactyl [,pentə'dæktɪl] *Zool* **1** *n* pentadactyle *m*

2 *adj* pentadactyle

pentagon ['pentəgən] **1** *n Geom* pentagone *m*

2 Pentagon *n Pol* **the Pentagon** le Pentagone

►► ***the Pentagon papers*** = documents secrets détenus par le Pentagone, portant sur l'intervention des États-Unis au Viêt-nam, publiés par le 'New York Times' en 1971 et objet d'un procès qui établit le droit du public américain à l'information

PENTAGON

Le Pentagone, immense bâtiment à cinq façades situé à Arlington, en Virginie, abrite le ministère américain de la Défense; plus généralement, le terme désigne le pouvoir militaire américain.

pentagonal [pen'tægənəl] *adj* pentagonal

pentagram ['pentəgræm] *n* (**a**) *Geom* pentagone *m* étoilé (**b**) *(in occultism)* pentagramme *m*

pentahedral [,pentə'hi:drəl] *adj Geom* pentaèdre

pentahedron [,pentə'hi:drən] (*pl* **pentahedrons** *or* **pentahedra** [-drə]) *n Geom* pentaèdre *m*

pentamerous [pen'tæmərəs] *adj Biol* pentamère

pentameter [pen'tæmɪtə(r)] *Literature* **1** *n* pentamètre *m*

2 *adj* pentamètre

pentametric [,pentə'metrɪk] *adj Literature* pentamétrique

pentane ['penteɪn] *n Chem* pentane *m*

pentangle ['pentæŋgəl] *n* pentacle *m*

pentanoic acid [,pentə'nəʊɪk-] *n Chem* acide *m* valérique

pentaprism ['pentəprɪzəm] *n Phot* pentaprisme *m*

Pentateuch ['pentətju:k] *n* **the Pentateuch** le Pentateuque

pentathlete [pen'tæθli:t] *n* pentathlonien(enne) *m,f*

pentathlon [pen'tæθlən] *n* pentathlon *m*

pentatonic [,pentə'tɒnɪk] *adj Mus (scale)* pentatonique

pentavalent [,pentə'veɪlənt] *adj Chem* pentavalent, quintivalent

Pentecost ['pentɪkɒst] *n* Pentecôte *f*

pentecostal [pentɪ'kɒstəl] *adj Rel* de la Pentecôte

►► ***the Pentecostal Church*** l'église *f* pentecôtiste

Pentecostalism [,pentɪ'kɒstəlɪzəm] *n* pentecôtisme *m*

Pentecostalist [,pentɪ'kɒstəlɪst] **1** *adj* pentecôtiste

2 *n* pentecôtiste *mf*

penthouse ['penthaʊs, *pl* -haʊzɪz] *n* (**a**) *(flat)* = appartement de luxe avec terrasse, généralement au dernier étage d'un immeuble (**b**) *(on roof)* **elevator penthouse** machinerie *f* d'ascenseur *(installée sur un toit)* (**c**) *(doorway shelter)* auvent *m*; *(shed)* appentis *m*

►► ***penthouse suite*** *(in hotel)* suite *f* avec terrasse

pentode ['pentəʊd] *n Electron* pentode *f*

Pentonville ['pentənvɪl] *n (prison)* = grande prison dans le nord de Londres

►► ***Pentonville Prison*** = grande prison dans le nord de Londres

pentose ['pentəʊz] *n Biol & Chem* pentose *m*

pentoxide [pen'tɒksaɪd] *n Chem* pentoxyde *m*

pent-up *adj (emotion)* refoulé, réprimé; *(force)* contenu, réprimé; **his anger is a product of pent-up frustration** sa colère vient de ce qu'il est frustré; **to get rid of pent-up energy** se défouler; **the children are full of pent-up energy** les enfants débordent d'énergie

penult [pe'nʌlt] *n* pénultième *f*

penultimate [pe'nʌltɪmət] **1** *adj* (**a**) *(gen)* avant-dernier (**b**) *Ling* pénultième

2 *n* (**a**) *(gen)* avant-dernier(ère) *m,f* (**b**) *Ling* pénultième *f*

penumbra [pɪ'nʌmbrə] (*pl* **penumbras** *or* **penumbrae** [-bri:]) *n Astron & Phys* pénombre *f*

penurious [pɪ'njʊərɪəs] *adj Formal* (**a**) *(impoverished)* indigent, sans ressources (**b**) *(miserly)* parcimonieux, avare

penury ['penjʊrɪ] *n Formal* (**a**) *(poverty)* indigence *f*, dénuement *m* (**b**) *(scarcity)* pénurie *f*

penwiper ['penwaɪpə(r)] *n* essuie-plume(s) *m inv*

peon ['pi:ən] *n* (**a**) *Agr (in Latin America)* péon *m* (**b**) *Mil (in India, Sri Lanka)* fantassin *m* (**c**) *Am Fam (worker)* prolo *mf*

peonage ['pi:ənɪdʒ] *n Agr* péonage *m*

peony ['pi:ənɪ] (*pl* **peonies**) *n* pivoine *f*

PEOPLE ['pi:pəl]

personnes	► **1 (a)**
gens	► **1 (a), (c)**
on	► **1 (b)**
peuple	► **1 (d); 2 (a)**
nation	► **2 (a)**
population	► **2 (b)**
peupler	► **3**

1 *npl* (**a**) *(gen)* personnes *fpl*, gens *mpl*; **500 people** 500 personnes; **there were people everywhere** il y avait des gens *ou* du monde partout; **how many people were there?** combien de personnes y avait-il?; **there were a lot of people there** il y avait beaucoup de monde; **some people think it's true** certaines personnes *ou* certains pensent que c'est vrai; **a lot of people think that...** beaucoup de gens pensent que...; **some people will believe anything!** il y a des gens qui croiraient n'importe quoi!; **I've talked to several people about it** j'en ai parlé à plusieurs personnes; **to have people skills** avoir le sens du contact; **she's a real people person** elle a vraiment le sens du contact; **many/most people disagree** beaucoup de gens/la plupart des gens ne sont pas d'accord; **really, some people!** il y a des gens, je vous jure!; **are you people coming or not?** et vous (autres), vous venez ou pas?; **it's Meg, of all people!** ça alors, c'est Meg!; **you of all people should know that!** si quelqu'un doit savoir ça, c'est bien toi!

(**b**) *(in indefinite uses)* on; **people say it's impossible** on dit que c'est impossible; **I don't want people to know about this** je ne veux pas qu'on le sache *ou* que cela se sache; **people won't like it** les gens ne vont pas aimer ça

(**c**) *(with qualifier)* gens *mpl*; **clever/sensitive people** les gens *mpl* intelligents/sensibles; **rich/poor/blind people** les riches/pauvres/aveugles *mpl*; **young people** les jeunes *mpl*; **old people** les personnes *fpl* âgées; **city/country people** les citadins/campagnards *mpl*; **people who know her** ceux qui la connaissent; **people like you** les gens comme toi; **people of taste** les gens *mpl* de goût; **people with large cars** ceux qui ont de grandes voitures; **they are nice people** ce sont des gens sympathiques; **nice people don't do that!** les gens bien *ou* comme il faut ne font pas ce genre de chose!; **they are theatre/circus people** ce sont des gens de théâtre/du cirque; **Danish people** les Danois *mpl*; **the people of Brazil** les Brésiliens *mpl*; **the people of Glasgow** les habitants *mpl* de Glasgow; **the people of Yorkshire** les gens *mpl* du Yorkshire; **I'll call the electricity/gas people tomorrow** je téléphonerai à la compagnie d'électricité/de gaz demain; **the President's financial people** les conseillers *mpl* financiers du Président

(**d**) *Pol* **the people** le peuple; **the people are behind her** le peuple la soutient *ou* est avec elle; **power to the people!** le pouvoir au peuple!; **a people's government/democracy** un gouvernement/une démocratie populaire

(**e**) *Old-fashioned (family)* famille *f*, parents *mpl*; **her people emigrated in 1801** sa famille a émigré en 1801

2 *n* (**a**) *(nation)* peuple *m*, nation *f*; **a seafaring people** un peuple de marins

(**b**) *(ethnic group)* population *f*; **the native peoples of Polynesia** les populations *fpl* indigènes *ou* autochtones de Polynésie; **the French-speaking peoples** les populations *fpl* francophones

3 *vt (usu passive) (inhabit)* peupler; **peopled by** peuplée de, habité par; *Fig* **the monsters that people his dreams** les monstres qui hantent ses rêves

►► ***people carrier*** *(car)* monospace *m*; ***people mover*** *(car)* monospace *m*; *(transport)* système *m* de transport automatique; *(moving pavement)* trottoir *m* roulant; ***people power*** pouvoir *m* populaire; ***the People's Republic of China*** la République populaire de Chine

PEP [pep] *n Br Formerly Fin (abbr* **personal equity plan**) ~ PEA *m*

pep [pep] (*pt & pp* **pepped**, *cont* **pepping**) *n Fam* punch *m*; **to have a lot of** *or* **to be full of pep** avoir du punch

►► ***pep pill*** stimulant□ *m*, excitant□ *m*; *Am* ***pep rally*** = rassemblement des élèves d'un lycée avant une compétition sportive afin de les encourager; ***pep talk*** discours *m* d'encouragement□; **their boss gave them a pep talk** leur patron leur a dit quelques mots pour leur remonter le moral□

►**pep up** *vt sep Fam* (**a**) *(person → depressed)* remonter le moral à□; *(→ ill, tired)* requinquer, retaper; **a cup of tea will soon pep you up** une tasse de thé aura vite fait de te ravigoter *ou* retaper

(**b**) *(business)* faire repartir□, dynamiser□; *(party)* dynamiser□, remettre de l'entrain dans□; *(conversation)* égayer□, ranimer□, relancer□

Pepin ['pepɪn] *pr n Hist* **Pepin the Short** Pépin le Bref

pepino [pe'pi:nəʊ] (*pl* **pepinos**) *n* pepino *m*

peplum ['pepləm] (*pl* **peplums** *or* **pepla** [-lə]) *n* (**a**) *(on jacket)* basque *f* (**b**) *(Roman tunic)* peplum *m*

pepper ['pepə(r)] **1** *n* (**a**) *(condiment)* poivre *m*; **black/white pepper** poivre *m* noir/blanc

(**b**) *(vegetable → sweet)* poivron *m*; *(→ hot)* piment *m*; **green/red/yellow pepper** poivron vert/rouge/jaune

2 *vt* (**a**) *Culin* poivrer

pen–pep

(**b**) *(scatter, sprinkle)* émailler, parsemer; **her text was peppered with quotations** son texte était émaillé de citations

(**c**) *(pelt)* **the walls were peppered with lead shot** les murs étaient criblés d'impacts de balles; **they peppered the houses with machine-gun fire** ils ont mitraillé les maisons

►► ***pepper mill*** moulin *m* à poivre; ***pepper pot*** poivrier *m*, poivrière *f*; ***pepper sauce*** sauce *f* au poivre; *Br Culin* ***pepper steak*** steak *m* au poivre

pepper-and-salt *adj* (**a**) *(hair, beard)* poivre et sel *(inv)* (**b**) *(jacket)* marengo *(inv)*

►► ***pepper-and-salt cloth*** marengo *m*

pepperbox ['pepəbɒks] *n Am* poivrier *m*

peppercorn ['pepəkɔːn] *n* grain *m* de poivre

►► *Br* ***peppercorn rent*** loyer *m* modique

peppered ['pepəd] *adj*

►► *Entom* ***peppered moth*** phalène *f* du bouleau; *Culin* ***peppered steak*** steak *m* au poivre

peppermint ['pepəmɪnt] **1** *n* (**a**) *Bot* menthe *f* poivrée (**b**) *(sweet)* bonbon *m* à la menthe

2 *adj* à la menthe; **peppermint** *or* **peppermint-flavoured toothpaste** dentifrice *m* au menthol

►► ***peppermint cream*** bonbon *m* à la crème de menthe; ***peppermint tea*** thé *m* à la menthe

pepperoni [pepə'rəʊnɪ] *n* pepperoni *m*

peppery ['pepərɪ] *adj* (**a**) *Culin* poivré (**b**) *(quick-tempered)* coléreux, irascible (**c**) *(incisive)* mordant, piquant

peppy ['pepɪ] *(compar* **peppier**, *superl* **peppiest**) *adj Fam (person)* qui a du punch

pepsin ['pepsɪn] *n Biol & Chem* pepsine *f*

peptic ['peptɪk] *adj* peptique

►► ***peptic ulcer*** ulcère *m* gastro-duodénal *ou* de l'estomac

peptide ['peptaɪd] *n Biol & Chem* peptide *m*

peptone ['peptəʊn] *n Biol & Chem* peptone *f*

per [pɜː(r)] **1** *prep (for each)* par; **per person** par personne; **per head** par tête; **per day/week/month/year** par jour/semaine/mois/an; **we need five litres of water per person per day** il nous faut cinq litres d'eau par personne et par jour; **they are paid £6 per hour** ils sont payés 6 livres de l'heure; **100 miles per hour** ≃ 160 kilomètres à l'heure; **it costs £8 per kilo** ça coûte 8 livres le kilo; **output per worker has increased** la production individuelle des ouvriers a augmenté; **per annum** par an, annuellement; **$5,000 per annum** 5000 dollars par an; *Formal* **per capita** par personne, par tête; **per capita consumption** consommation *f* par tête; **per capita income is higher in the south** le revenu par habitant est plus élevé dans le sud; *Formal* **per diem** par jour; *(expenses)* dépenses *fpl* journalières

2 as per *prep* suivant, selon; **as per specifications** *(on bill)* conformément aux spécifications requises; **as per your instructions/letter** conformément à vos instructions/votre lettre; **the work is going ahead as per schedule** le travail avance selon le calendrier prévu; *Fam* **as per normal** *or* **usual** comme d'habitude ❑

peradventure [pərəd'ventʃə(r)] *adv Arch* par hasard, d'aventure

perambulate [pə'ræmbjʊleɪt] *Literary or Hum* **1** *vi* se promener, (se) baguenauder

2 *vt* (**a**) *(estate, boundary)* inspecter (**b**) *(sea, region)* parcourir

perambulation [pəˌræmbjʊ'leɪʃən] *n Literary or Hum (stroll)* promenade *f*

perambulator [pə'ræmbjʊleɪtə(r)] *n Old-fashioned* landau *m*

p/e ratio [ˌpiː'iː-] *n St Exch (abbr* **price-earnings ratio**) ratio *m ou* rapport *m* cours-bénéfices, PER *m*

percale [pə'keɪl] *n Tex* percale *f*

►► ***percale sheets*** des draps *mpl* en percale

perceive [pə'siːv] *vt* (**a**) *(see)* distinguer; *(hear, smell etc)* percevoir; **he was unable to perceive colours** il était incapable de distinguer les couleurs

(**b**) *(notice)* s'apercevoir de, remarquer; **few people perceived the differences** peu de gens ont remarqué les différences

(**c**) *(conceive, understand)* percevoir, comprendre; **their presence is perceived as a threat** leur présence est perçue comme une menace

(**d**) *Mktg (product, brand)* percevoir

perceived [pə'siːvd] *adj* perçu; **public reaction to perceived injustice in the trial** la réaction du public à ce qu'il a perçu comme une injustice au cours du procès; **the government's perceived failure to resolve the conflict** ce qui est perçu comme l'incapacité du gouvernement à résoudre le conflit

►► ***perceived noise decibel*** perceived noise decibel *m*; *Mktg* ***perceived performance*** résultats *mpl* perçus; *Mktg* ***perceived quality*** qualité *f* perçue; ***perceived risk*** risque *m* perçu; *Mktg* ***perceived service*** service *m* perçu; *Mktg* ***perceived value*** valeur *f* perçue; *Mktg* ***perceived value pricing*** tarification *f* en fonction de la valeur perçue

percent [pə'sent] *(pl* **inv**) **1** *adv* pour cent; **prices went up (by) 10 percent** les prix ont augmenté de 10 pour cent; **it's 50 percent cotton** il y a 50 pour cent de coton, c'est du coton à 50 pour cent; **a 9 percent interest rate** un taux d'intérêt à 9 pour cent; **I'm 99 percent certain** j'en suis à 99 pour cent sûr

2 *n (percentage)* pourcentage *m*; **what percent of people own a mobile phone?** quel est le pourcentage des propriétaires de téléphones portables?

percentage [pə'sentɪdʒ] **1** *n* (**a**) *(proportion)* proportion *f*; *(expressed in %)* pourcentage *m*; **to express sth as a percentage** exprimer qch en pourcentage; **in a high/tiny percentage of cases** dans une vaste/petite proportion des cas; **a high percentage of the staff** une grande partie du personnel

(**b**) *(share of profits, investment)* pourcentage *m*; **his manager takes a percentage of his winnings** son directeur prend un pourcentage sur ses gains; **to get a percentage on sth** toucher un pourcentage sur qch

(**c**) *Br Fam (advantage)* avantage ❑ *m*, intérêt ❑ *m*; **there's no percentage in kicking up a fuss** ça ne sert à rien de faire des histoires

2 *adj Am (profitable)* payant

►► ***percentage increase*** augmentation *f* en pourcentage; ***percentage point*** point *m*; ***percentage reduction*** réduction *f* en pourcentage;

percentile [pə'sentaɪl] *n* centile *m*

perceptibility [pəˌseptə'bɪlɪtɪ] *n* perceptibilité *f*

perceptible [pə'septəbəl] *adj* perceptible; *(difference, change)* sensible

perceptibly [pə'septəblɪ] *adv (diminish, change)* sensiblement; *(move)* de manière perceptible; **she was perceptibly thinner** elle avait sensiblement maigri

perception [pə'sepʃən] *n* (**a**) *(faculty)* perception *f*; **visual/aural perception** perception *f* visuelle/auditive; **organs of perception** organes *mpl* percepteurs; **powers of perception** facultés *fpl* perceptives

(**b**) *(notion, conception)* perception *f*, conception *f*; *Mktg (of product, brand)* perception *f*; **her perception of the problem is different from mine** sa façon de voir le problème diffère de la mienne; **the general public's perception of the police** l'image que le grand public a de la police, la façon dont le grand public perçoit la police

(**c**) *(insight)* perspicacité *f*, intuition *f*; **a man of great perception** un homme très perspicace

perceptive [pə'septɪv] *adj* (**a**) *(observant → person)* perspicace; *(→ remark)* judicieux; *(analysis, article)* tout en finesse (**b**) *(sensitive)* sensible (**c**) *(organ)* sensoriel

perceptively [pə'septɪvlɪ] *adv* avec perspicacité

perceptiveness [pə'septɪvnɪs] *n* perspicacité *f*, pénétration *f*

perceptual [pə'septjʊəl] *adj* (**a**) *(organ)* percepteur (**b**) *Mktg* perceptuel

►► ***perceptual map*** carte *f* perceptuelle

perch [pɜːtʃ] *(pl sense* (**d**) **inv** *or* **perches**) **1** *n* (**a**) *(for bird → in cage)* perchoir *m*; *(→ on tree)* branche *f*; **the bird flew from its perch on the roof** l'oiseau s'envola du toit où il était perché

(**b**) *Fam (for person → seat)* perchoir *m*; **to knock sb off his/her perch** *(depose)* détrôner qn ❑; *(force to abandon pretensions)* rabattre son caquet à qn; *Hum* **to fall** *or* **drop off one's perch** *(die)* passer l'arme à gauche

(**c**) *(linear or square measure)* ≃ perche *f*

(**d**) *Ich* perche *f*

2 *vi (bird, person)* se percher; **he perched on the edge of the table** il se percha *ou* se jucha sur le bord de la table

3 *vt (person, object)* percher, jucher; **she was perched on a stool/on the arm of the chair** elle était juchée sur un tabouret/sur le bras du fauteuil; **castle perched on a hill** château perché sur (le sommet d')une colline; **with his glasses perched on the end of his nose** avec ses lunettes perchées sur le bout du nez

perchance [pə'tʃɑːns] *adv Arch or Literary* (**a**) *(perhaps)* peut-être (**b**) *(by accident)* par hasard, fortuitement

perchlorate [pɜː'klɔːreɪt] *n Chem* perchlorate *m*

perchloric [pɜː'klɒrɪk] *adj Chem* perchlorique

percipience [pə'sɪpɪəns], **percipiency** [pə'sɪpɪənsɪ] *n Formal* perception *f*

percipient [pə'sɪpɪənt] *adj* (**a**) *Formal (person)* perspicace (**b**) *Anat (organ)* sensoriel

percoid ['pɜːkɔɪd] *adj Zool* percoïde

percolate ['pɜːkəleɪt] **1** *vi* (**a**) *(liquid)* filtrer, s'infiltrer; *(coffee)* passer; **toxic chemicals had percolated through the soil** des produits chimiques toxiques s'étaient infiltrés dans le sol

(**b**) *(ideas, news)* filtrer; **his ideas percolated through to the rank and file** ses idées ont gagné la base

(**c**) *Am Fam (be excited)* être (tout) excité ❑; **he is percolating with joy** il déborde de joie ❑; **she percolates with ideas** elle bouillonne d'idées

2 *vt (coffee)* préparer, faire *(dans une cafetière à pression)*; **I'll just percolate some coffee** je vais faire du café

►► ***percolated coffee*** café *m* fait avec une cafetière à pression

percolation [ˌpɜːkə'leɪʃən] *n (gen)* filtration *f*, filtrage *m*; *Petr & Chem* percolation *f*

percolator ['pɜːkəleɪtə(r)] *n* cafetière *f* à pression; *(for large quantities)* percolateur *m*

percuss [pə'kʌs] *vt (gen) & Med* percuter

percussion [pə'kʌʃən] *n* (**a**) *Mus* percussion *f*; **Jane Stowell on percussion** aux percussions, Jane Stowell

(**b**) *(collision, shock)* percussion *f*, choc *m*

(**c**) *Med & Mil* percussion *f*

►► *Mil* ***percussion cap*** amorce *f* fulminante; ***percussion drill*** perceuse *f* à percussion; *Mus* ***percussion instrument*** instrument *m* à percussion; *Mil* ***percussion lock*** percuteur *m*; *Mus* ***percussion player*** percussionniste *mf*; *Mus* ***the percussion section*** les percussions *fpl*; ***percussion tool*** outil *m* à percussion

percussionist [pə'kʌʃənɪst] *n Mus* percussionniste *mf*

percussive [pə'kʌsɪv] *adj (instrument)* à percussion; *(force)* de percussion

percutaneous [ˌpɜːkjuː'teɪnɪəs] *adj Med* percutané; *(injection)* hypodermique, sous-cutané

►► ***percutaneous reaction*** percuti-réaction *f*

perdition [pə'dɪʃən] *n* (**a**) *Literary (spiritual ruin)* perdition *f*; *(hell)* enfer *m*, damnation *f* (**b**) *Arch (ruin)* perte *f*, ruine *f*

perdurable [pɜː'djʊərəbəl] *adj Arch or Literary* (**a**) *(friendship)* durable; *(peace)* durable, stable, permanent; *Rel (life, bliss)* éternel (**b**) *(rock, material)* résistant

peregrinate ['perɪgrɪneɪt] *vi Formal* voyager

peregrination [ˌperɪgrɪ'neɪʃən] *n Formal* pérégrination *f*; *also Hum* **peregrinations** pérégrinations *fpl*

peregrine ['perɪgrɪn] *n Orn* **peregrine (falcon)** (faucon *m*) pèlerin *m*

peremptorily [pə'remptərəlɪ] *adv* de façon péremptoire, impérieusement

peremptoriness [pə'remptərɪnɪs] *n* caractère *m* péremptoire *ou* impérieux

peremptory [pə'remptərɪ] *adj (tone, manner, person)* péremptoire, impérieux; **there was a peremptory knock at the door** on a frappé à la porte de façon péremptoire

►► *Br Law* ***peremptory writ*** assignation *f* à comparaître en personne

perennial [pə'renɪəl] **1** *adj* (**a**) *Bot* vivace (**b**) *Fig (everlasting)* éternel; *(recurrent, continual)* perpétuel, sempiternel; **a perennial subject of debate** un éternel *ou* perpétuel sujet de discussion

2 *n Bot* plante *f* vivace

perennially [pə'renıəlı] *adv (everlastingly)* éternellement; *(recurrently, continually)* perpétuellement, continuellement

perestroika [,perə'strɔıkə] *n* perestroïka *f*

perfect **1** *adj* ['pɜ:fıkt] (**a**) *(flawless → person, performance etc)* parfait; **a perfect circle** un cercle parfait; **to be in perfect condition** *(engine, appliance)* être en parfait état de marche; *(painting, antique, teeth)* être en parfait état; **in perfect health** en excellente *ou* parfaite santé; **her hearing is still perfect** elle entend encore parfaitement; **her English is perfect** son anglais est impeccable *ou* parfait; **try it yourself, since you think you're (so) perfect!** essaie toi-même, puisque tu te crois *ou* tu es si fort!; **nobody's perfect** personne n'est parfait

(**b**) *(complete → agreement, mastery etc)* parfait, complet(ète); *(as intensifier)* véritable, parfait; **there was perfect silence** il y avait un silence total; **you have a perfect right to be here** vous avez parfaitement *ou* tout à fait le droit d'être ici; **it makes perfect sense (to me)** ça me semble tout à fait logique; **it was a perfect disaster!** ce fut un véritable désastre!; **he's a perfect idiot** c'est un parfait imbécile

(**c**) *(fine, lovely → conditions)* parfait, idéal; *(→ weather)* idéal, superbe; **it was a perfect day** *(weather)* il faisait un temps magnifique; *(activities)* nous avons passé une excellente journée

(**d**) *(fitting, right → example)* parfait, approprié; **the perfect gift** le cadeau idéal; **the perfect opportunity** l'occasion idéale *ou* rêvée; **tonight at 7? – that will be perfect** ce soir à 7 heures? – c'est parfait; **Monday is perfect for me** lundi me convient parfaitement; **the colour is perfect on you** cette couleur te va à merveille *ou* à la perfection

(**e**) *(exemplary → gentleman, host)* parfait, exemplaire

(**f**) *Mus* **to have perfect pitch** avoir l'oreille absolue

2 *n* ['pɜ:fıkt] *Gram* parfait *m*; **in the perfect** au parfait

3 *vt* [pə'fekt] (**a**) *(improve → knowledge, skill)* perfectionner, parfaire

(**b**) *(bring to final form → plans, method)* mettre au point

(**c**) *Typ* imprimer en retiration

►► *Mus* ***perfect cadence*** cadence *f* parfaite; *Econ* ***perfect competition*** concurrence *f* parfaite; *Mus* ***perfect fifth*** quinte *f* juste; *Mus* ***perfect fourth*** quarte *f* juste; *Math* ***perfect number*** nombre *m* parfait; *Gram* ***perfect participle*** participe *m* passé; *Gram* ***the perfect tense*** le parfait

perfecta [pə'fektə] *n* pari *m* couplé gagnant, pari *m* jumelé gagnant *(où l'on spécifie l'ordre d'arrivée)*

perfectibility [pə'fektəbılıtı] *n* perfectibilité *f*

perfectible [pə'fektəbəl] *adj* perfectible

perfection [pə'fekʃən] *n* (**a**) *(quality)* perfection *f*; **to attain perfection** atteindre la perfection; **this cake is perfection!** ce gâteau est un vrai délice!; **to do sth to perfection** faire qch à la perfection (**b**) *(perfecting → of skill, knowledge)* perfectionnement *m*; *(→ of plans, method)* mise *f* au point

perfectionism [pə'fekʃənızəm] *n* perfectionnisme *m*

perfectionist [pə'fekʃənıst] **1** *adj* perfectionniste

2 *n* perfectionniste *mf*

perfective [pə'fektıv] *adj Gram* perfectif

perfectly ['pɜ:fıktlı] *adv* (**a**) *(speak, understand)* parfaitement; **perfectly formed** d'une forme parfaite

(**b**) *(as intensifier)* tout à fait, parfaitement; **you are perfectly right** vous avez parfaitement *ou* tout à fait raison; **to be perfectly honest/frank with you** pour être tout à fait honnête/franc avec vous; **you know perfectly well** *(what I mean)* tu le sais parfaitement bien *ou* très bien; **it's a perfectly good raincoat** cet imperméable est tout à fait mettable

perfecto [pɜ:'fektəʊ] *(pl* **perfectos***) n Am (cigar)* = cigare effilé aux deux bouts

perfervid [pɜ:'fɜ:vıd] *adj Literary* chaleureux, ardent, exalté

perfidious [pə'fıdıəs] *adj Literary* perfide

►► ***perfidious Albion*** la perfide Albion

perfidiously [pə'fıdıəslı] *adv Literary* perfidement

perfidiousness [pə'fıdıəsnıs], **perfidy** ['pɜ:fıdı] *(pl* **perfidies***) n Literary* perfidie *f*

perfluorocarbon [,pɜ:flʊərəʊ'kɑ:bən] *n Chem* perfluorocarbone *m*

perfoliate [pɜ:'fəʊlıət] *adj Bot* perfolié

perforate ['pɜ:fəreıt] *vt* (**a**) *(pierce)* perforer, percer (**b**) *Tech (punch holes in)* perforer

perforated ['pɜ:fəreıtıd] *adj* perforé, percé; *Med* **to have a perforated eardrum** avoir un tympan perforé *ou* crevé; **tear along the perforated line** *(on form)* détacher suivant les pointillés

►► *Comput* ***perforated paper*** papier *m* à bandes perforées; *Comput* ***perforated tape*** bande *f* perforée; *Med* ***perforated ulcer*** perforation *f* ulcéreuse

perforation [,pɜ:fə'reıʃən] *n* perforation *f*

perforce [pə'fɔ:s] *adv Literary* forcément, nécessairement

perform [pə'fɔ:m] **1** *vt* (**a**) *(carry out → manoeuvre, task)* exécuter, accomplir; *(→ calculation)* effectuer, faire; *(→ miracle)* accomplir; *(→ wedding, ritual)* célébrer; **the robot can perform complex movements** le robot peut exécuter des mouvements complexes; *Med* **to perform an operation** opérer

(**b**) *(fulfil → function, duty)* remplir; **the agency performs a vital service** l'agence remplit une fonction vitale

(**c**) *(stage → play)* jouer, donner; *(→ ballet, opera)* interpréter, jouer; *(→ concert)* donner; *(→ piece of music)* exécuter; **to perform a part** *Theat* jouer *ou* interpréter un rôle; *(in ballet)* danser un rôle

2 *vi* (**a**) *(actor, comedian, musician)* jouer; *(dancer)* danser; *(singer)* chanter; **the Berlin Philharmonic is performing tonight** l'Orchestre philharmonique de Berlin donne un concert *ou* joue ce soir; **she performed superbly in the role of Lady Bracknell** elle a magnifiquement interprété le rôle de Lady Bracknell

(**b**) *(person → in job, situation)* se débrouiller; **to perform well/badly** bien/ne pas bien s'en tirer; **he'd never spoken in public before, but he performed well** il n'avait jamais parlé en public avant, mais il s'en est bien tiré *ou* il s'est bien débrouillé; **how does she perform under pressure?** comment réagit-elle lorsqu'elle est sous pression?; **I couldn't perform** *(sexually)* je n'ai pas pu

(**c**) *(company, business)* fonctionner; *(shares, investment, currency)* se comporter; **to perform well/badly** *(company)* avoir de bons/mauvais résultats; **the Miami branch is not performing well** les résultats de la succursale de Miami ne sont pas très satisfaisants; **how did the company perform in the first quarter?** comment la société a-t-elle fonctionné au premier trimestre?; **shares performed well yesterday** les actions se sont bien comportées hier

(**d**) *(function → vehicle, machine)* marcher, fonctionner; **the car performs well/badly in wet conditions** cette voiture a une bonne/mauvaise tenue de route par temps de pluie

performance [pə'fɔ:məns] *n* (**a**) *(show)* spectacle *m*, représentation *f*; *Cin* séance *f*; **afternoon performance** matinée *f*; **there is no performance on Mondays** il n'y a pas de représentation le lundi, le lundi est jour de relâche

(**b**) *(rendition → by actor, musician, dancer)* interprétation *f*; **he gave an excellent performance in the role of Othello** son interprétation du rôle d'Othello fut remarquable

(**c**) *(showing → by sportsman, politician etc)* performance *f*, prestation *f*; *(→ by pupil, economy, exports, company)* résultats *mpl*, performances *fpl*; *(→ by employee)* rendement *m*, performance *f*; *(→ by shares, investment, currency)* performance *f*; **to put up a good performance** *(team, athlete etc)* accomplir une bonne performance; *(in exam, interview, court case)* bien s'en tirer; **the Prime Minister gave the performance of his career** le Premier ministre n'a jamais été aussi bon de toute sa carrière; **another poor performance by the French team** encore une contre-performance de l'équipe française; **the country's poor economic performance** les mauvais résultats économiques du pays; **sterling's performance on the Stock Exchange** le comportement en Bourse de la livre sterling; **sexual performance** prouesses *fpl* sexuelles

(**d**) *(of machine, computer, car)* performance *f*

(**e**) *(carrying out → of task, manoeuvre)* exécution *f*; *(→ of miracle, duties)* accomplissement *m*; *(→ of ritual)* célébration *f*; **she has always been painstaking in the performance of her duties** elle s'est toujours montrée consciencieuse dans l'accomplissement de ses devoirs

(**f**) *Fam (rigmarole)* histoire *f*, cirque *m*; **it's such a performance getting a visa!** quelle histoire *ou* quel cirque pour avoir un visa!; **what a performance!** quel cirque!

(**g**) *Ling* performance *f*

►► ***performance appraisal*** *(system)* système *m* d'évaluation; *(individual)* évaluation *f*; ***performance art*** performance *f*, action *f*; ***performance artist*** = artiste spécialisé dans la performance; *Fin* ***performance bond*** garantie *f* de bonne fin *ou* de bonne exécution; *Aut* ***performance car*** voiture *f* puissante, voiture *f* haute performance; ***performance indicator*** indice *m* de performance; ***performance pay*** prime *f* de mérite *or* de résultat; *Fin* ***performance ratio*** coefficient *m* *ou* ratio *m* d'exploitation; *Psy & Mktg* ***performance test*** test *m* de performance

performance-related *adj* en fonction du mérite *ou* résultat

►► ***performance-related pay*** salaire *m* au mérite

performative [pə'fɔ:mətıv] **1** *adj Ling & Phil* performatif

2 *n Ling (verb)* performatif *m*; *(utterance)* énoncé *m* performatif

performer [pə'fɔ:mə(r)] *n (singer, dancer, actor)* interprète *mf*; **nightclub performer** artiste *mf* de cabaret; **he's a good stage performer but awful on camera** il est très bon sur la scène mais il ne passe pas du tout à l'écran; **he has been a consistent performer** *(in sport)* il a toujours été régulier

performing [pə'fɔ:mıŋ] *adj (bear, dog etc)* savant

►► ***performing arts*** arts *mpl* du spectacle; ***performing rights*** *Theat* droits *mpl* de représentation; *Mus* droits *mpl* d'exécution

perfume ['pɜ:fju:m] **1** *n* (**a**) *(bottled)* parfum *m*; **I don't usually wear perfume** d'habitude je ne me parfume pas; **what perfume does she wear** *or* **use?** quel parfum met-elle?, quel est son parfum? (**b**) *(smell)* parfum *m*

2 *vt* [pə'fju:m] parfumer

►► ***perfume counter*** *(in shop)* rayon *m* parfumerie; ***perfume spray*** atomiseur *m* de parfum

perfumed [*Br* 'pɜ:fju:md, *Am* pɜ:'fju:md] *adj* parfumé

perfumer [pə'fju:mə(r)] *n* parfumeur(euse) *m,f*

perfumery [pə'fju:mərı] *(pl* **perfumeries***) n* parfumerie *f*

perfunctorily [pə'fʌŋktərəlı] *adv (wave, greet)* machinalement; *(explain, apologize, search)* sommairement; *(read out, announce)* sans conviction

perfunctoriness [pə'fʌŋktərınıs] *n (of greeting, gesture)* caractère *m* machinal; *(of manner)* brusquerie *f*

perfunctory [pə'fʌŋktərı] *adj (greeting, gesture)* machinal; *(explanation, apology, letter)* sommaire; *(effort)* de pure forme; *(interrogation, search)* fait pour la forme; *(manner)* brusque; **he greeted me with a perfunctory nod** il me salua machinalement d'un signe de la tête

perfusion [pə'fju:ʒən] *n* (**a**) *(pouring)* aspersion *f* (**b**) *Med* perfusion *f*

Pergamum ['pɜ:gəməm] *n* Pergame

pergola ['pɜ:gələ] *n* pergola *f*

perhaps [pə'hæps] *adv* peut-être; **perhaps he's forgotten** peut-être qu'il a oublié, il a peut-être oublié; **perhaps not** peut-être que non; **there were perhaps 200 people there** il y avait peut-être 200 personnes; **perhaps you'd be kind enough to close the door** peut-être aurais-tu la gentillesse de fermer la porte; **a glass of something, perhaps?** un verre de quelque chose, peut-être?

perianal [,perı'eınəl] *adj Anat* périanal

perianth ['perıænθ] *n Bot* périanthe *m*

periastron [,perı'æstrɒn] *n Astron* périastre *m*

pericardial [,perı'kɑ:dıəl] *adj Anat* péricardique

pericarditis [,perıkɑ:'daıtıs] *n Med* péricardite *f*

pericardium [ˌperɪˈkɑːdɪəm] *n Anat* péricarde *m*
pericarp [ˈperɪkɑːp] *n Bot* péricarpe *m*
perichondrium [ˌperɪˈkɒndrɪəm] *n Anat* périchondre *m*
periclase [ˈperɪkleɪz] *n Chem* périclase *m*
Pericles [ˈperɪkliːz] *pr n Antiq* Périclès
periclinal [ˌperɪˈklaɪnəl] *adj Geol & Bot* périclinal
pericranium [ˌperɪˈkreɪnɪəm] *n Anat* péricrâne *m*
peridot [ˈperɪdɒt] *n Miner* péridot *m*
peridotite [ˌperɪˈdəʊtaɪt] *n Miner* péridotite *f*
perigee [ˈperɪdʒiː] *n Astron* périgée *m*
periglacial [ˌperɪˈgleɪʃəl] *adj* périglaciaire
perihelion [ˌperɪˈhiːlɪən] *n Astron* périhélie *m*
perihepatic [ˌperɪhəˈpætɪk] *adj Anat* périhépatique
perihepatitis [ˌperɪhepəˈtaɪtɪs] *n Med* périhépatite *f*
perikaryon [ˌperɪˈkærɪɒn] *n Anat* périkaryon *m*
peril [ˈperɪl] *n* péril *m*, danger *m*; **the perils of hard drugs** le danger des drogues dures; **to be in peril** être en péril *ou* danger; **in peril of one's life** en danger de mort; *Br* **you do it at your peril** c'est à vos risques et périls
perilous [ˈperɪləs] *adj* périlleux, dangereux
perilously [ˈperɪləslɪ] *adv* périlleusement, dangereusement; **he came perilously close to defeat/drowning** il s'en est fallu d'un cheveu qu'il ne perde/qu'il ne se noie; **to come perilously close to disaster** frôler la catastrophe
perilousness [ˈperɪləsnɪs] *n* caractère *m* dangereux; *(of undertaking)* danger *m*
perilune [ˈperɪluːn] *n Astron* périlune *m*
perimeter [pəˈrɪmɪtə(r)] *n* périmètre *m*
►► *Mktg* ***perimeter advertising*** publicité *f* périphérique; *Mktg* ***perimeter board*** panneau *m* publicitaire *(autour d'un terrain de sport)*; ***perimeter fence*** grillage *m*
perimysium [ˌperɪˈmɪzɪəm] *n Anat* périmysium *m*
perinatal [ˌperɪˈneɪtəl] *adj* périnatal
perineal [ˌperɪˈniːəl] *adj Anat* périnéal
perinephrium [perɪˈnefrɪəm] *n Anat* enveloppe *f* adipeuse du rein
perinephritis [ˌperɪneˈfraɪtɪs] *n Med* périnéphrite *f*
perineum [ˌperɪˈniːəm] *(pl* **perinea** [-ˈniːə]*) n Anat* périnée *m*
period [ˈpɪərɪəd] **1** *n* (**a**) *(length of time)* période *f*; *(historical epoch)* période *f*, époque *f*; **within a period of a few months** en l'espace de quelques mois; **we have a two-month period in which to do it** nous avons un délai de deux mois pour le faire; **he's going through a difficult period** il traverse une période difficile; **he found a job after a long period of unemployment** il a trouvé un emploi après avoir été au chômage pendant longtemps; **a period of colonial expansion** une période d'expansion coloniale; **the Elizabethan period** l'époque élisabéthaine; **at that period in her life** à cette époque de sa vie; **his cubist/jazz period** sa période cubiste/jazz; **there will be a question/discussion period after the lecture** un moment sera consacré aux questions/au débat après la conférence
(**b**) *Geol* période *f*; **the Jurassic period** la période jurassique
(**c**) *Sch (lesson)* cours *m*; **during the Latin period** pendant le cours de latin; **a free period** *(for pupil)* une heure de permanence; *(for teacher)* une heure de battement
(**d**) *(in ice hockey)* période *f*
(**e**) *Astron* **period of rotation** période *f* de rotation
(**f**) *(menstruation)* règles *fpl*; **I've got my period** j'ai mes règles; **my periods have stopped** je n'ai plus mes règles
(**g**) *Am (full stop)* point *m*
(**h**) *(sentence)* période *f*
(**i**) *Chem (in periodic table)* période *f*
(**j**) *Mus* période *f*
2 *comp (furniture, costume)* d'époque; *(novel)* historique; **the play has a definite period flavour** la pièce nous transporte vraiment dans une autre époque
3 *adv Fam* **you're not going out alone, period!** tu ne sortiras pas tout seul, un point c'est tout!; **I said no, period** j'ai dit non, point final
►► *Fin* ***period bill*** effet *m* à terme; ***period detail*** détail *m* historique; *Fin* ***period of grace*** délai *m* de grâce; ***period pains*** règles *fpl* douloureuses; ***period piece*** *(object, antique)* objet *m* d'époque; *(film)* film *m* historique; *(play)* pièce *f* historique
periodic [ˌpɪərɪˈɒdɪk] *adj* (**a**) *(gen)* périodique (**b**) *Chem & Math* périodique
►► ***periodic function*** fonction *f* périodique; *Fin* ***periodic inventory*** inventaire *m* périodique; ***periodic law*** loi *f* périodique; *Fin* ***periodic payments*** paiements *mpl* périodiques; *Chem* ***periodic table*** classification *f* périodique (des éléments), tableau *m* de Mendeleïev
periodical [ˌpɪərɪˈɒdɪkəl] **1** *n (publication)* périodique *m*
2 *adj* périodique
periodically [ˌpɪərɪˈɒdɪklɪ] *adv* périodiquement, de temps en temps
periodicity [ˌpɪərɪəˈdɪsətɪ] *n* périodicité *f*
periodontal [ˌperɪəˈdɒntəl] *adj Med* parodontal
periodontics [ˌperɪəˈdɒntɪks] *n (UNCOUNT) Med* = branche de la stomatologie qui s'occupe du parodonte
periodontist [ˌperɪəˈdɒntɪst] *n Med* parodontiste *mf*
periodontitis [ˌperɪəʊdɒnˈtaɪtɪs] *n Med* parodontite *f*
periodontoclasia [ˌperɪədɒntəʊˈkleɪzɪə] *n Med* parodontopathie *f*
periodontology [ˌperɪədɒnˈtɒlədʒɪ] *n Med* parodontologie *f*
periodontitis [ˌperɪəʊdɒnˈtəʊsɪs] *n Med* parodontolyse *f*, parodontose *f*
periodontum [ˌperɪəˈdɒntəm] *n Anat* parodonte *m*
periosteum [ˌperɪˈɒstɪəm] *(pl* **periostea** [-stɪə]*) n Anat* périoste *m*
periostitis [ˌperɪəˈstaɪtɪs] *n Med* périostite *f*
Peripatetic [ˌperɪpəˈtetɪk] *Antiq* **1** *adj* péripatéticien
2 *n* péripatéticien(enne) *m,f*
peripatetic [ˌperɪpəˈtetɪk] *adj (itinerant)* itinérant
►► *Br Sch* ***peripatetic teacher*** = professeur qui enseigne dans plusieurs établissements scolaires
peripatus [peˈrɪpətəs] *n Zool* péripate *m*
peripeteia [perɪpəˈtaɪə, perɪpəˈtiːə] *n Literature* péripétie *f*
peripheral [pəˈrɪfərəl] **1** *adj* (**a**) *(gen)* périphérique
(**b**) *Fig (unimportant)* secondaire; **of purely peripheral importance** d'une importance tout à fait secondaire; **this issue is peripheral to the central debate** ce problème est accessoire au débat principal
2 *n Comput* périphérique *m*
►► *Comput* ***peripheral device, peripheral unit*** unité *f* périphérique *m*; ***peripheral vision*** vue *f* périphérique
periphery [pəˈrɪfərɪ] *(pl* **peripheries***) n* (**a**) *(of circle, vision, city etc)* périphérie *f*; **on the periphery** à la périphérie (**b**) *(of group, movement)* frange *f*; **on the periphery of society** en marge de la société
periphlebitis [ˌperɪflɪˈbaɪtɪs] *n Med* paraphlébite *f*
periphrasis [pəˈrɪfrəsɪs] *(pl* **periphrases** [-siːz]*) n* périphrase *f*, circonlocution *f*
periphrastic [ˌperɪˈfræstɪk] *adj* périphrastique
periplus [ˈperɪplʌs] *n Literary* périple *m*, circumnavigation *f*
perirenal [ˌperɪˈriːnəl] *adj Anat* périnéphrétique
periscope [ˈperɪskəʊp] *n* périscope *m*; **up periscope!** sortez le périscope!
perish [ˈperɪʃ] **1** *vi* (**a**) *Br (rot → rubber, leather etc)* s'abîmer, se détériorer; *(→ food)* se gâter, pourrir
(**b**) *Literary (die)* périr; **perish the thought!** loin de moi cette pensée!; **you're not pregnant, are you? – perish the thought!** tu n'es pas enceinte au moins? – tu veux rire *ou* j'espère bien que non!; **if, perish the thought, he were to die** si, Dieu nous en préserve, il venait à mourir; **and that, perish the thought, would mean giving up your weekends** et pour ça, comble de l'horreur, tu devrais renoncer à tes week-ends
2 *vt (rubber, leather)* abîmer, détériorer; *(food)* gâter
perishability [ˌperɪʃəˈbɪlɪtɪ] *n Com* périssabilité *f*
perishable [ˈperɪʃəbəl] **1** *adj* périssable
2 **perishables** *npl* denrées *fpl* périssables
perished [ˈperɪʃt] *adj Br Fam (very cold)* frigorifié; **I'm perished** je meurs de froid, je suis frigorifié
perisher [ˈperɪʃə(r)] *n Br Fam* galopin *m*
perishing [ˈperɪʃɪŋ] *adj Br Fam* (**a**) *(very cold → person, hands)* frigorifié; **it's perishing (cold)** il fait un froid de canard *ou* de loup (**b**) *Old-fashioned (as intensifier)* sacré, fichu, foutu; **that perishing telephone** ce fichu téléphone; **what a perishing nuisance!** c'est vraiment casse-pied!
perishingly [ˈperɪʃɪŋlɪ] *adv Br Fam* **it's perishingly cold** il fait un froid de canard *ou* de loup
perisperm [ˈperɪspɜːm] *n Bot* périsperme *m*
perissodactyl [ˌpərɪsəʊˈdæktɪl] *n Zool* périssodactyle *m*
peristalith [pəˈrɪstəlɪθ] *n Archeol* péristalithe *m*
peristalsis [ˌperɪˈstælsɪs] *(pl* **peristalses** [-siːz]*) n Physiol* péristaltisme *m*
peristaltic [ˌperɪˈstæltɪk] *adj Physiol* péristaltique
peristyle [ˈperɪstaɪl] *n Archit* péristyle *m*
peritendinitis [ˌperɪtendɪˈnaɪtɪs] *n Med* péritendinite *f*
peritoneal [ˌperɪtəˈniːəl] *adj Anat* péritonéal
►► *Med* ***peritoneal lavage*** lavage *m* du péritoine
peritoneum [ˌperɪtəˈniːəm] *(pl* **peritoneums** *or* **peritonea** [-ˈniːə]*) n Anat* péritoine *m*
peritonitis [ˌperɪtəˈnaɪtɪs] *n (UNCOUNT) Med* péritonite *f*; **to have peritonitis** avoir une péritonite
periwig [ˈperɪwɪg] *n Hist* perruque *f*
periwigged [ˈperɪwɪgd] *adj Arch* coiffé d'une perruque, en perruque, emperruqué
periwinkle [ˈperɪˌwɪŋkəl] *n* (**a**) *Bot* pervenche *f* (**b**) *Zool* bigorneau *m*
►► ***periwinkle blue*** bleu *m* pervenche
periwinkle-blue *adj* bleu pervenche *(inv)*
perjure [ˈpɜːdʒə(r)] *vt* **to perjure oneself** faire un faux témoignage
perjured [ˈpɜːdʒəd] *adj* **his evidence was perjured** il a fait un faux témoignage
►► ***perjured evidence*** faux témoignage *m*
perjurer [ˈpɜːdʒərə(r)] *n* faux témoin *m*
perjury [ˈpɜːdʒərɪ] *(pl* **perjuries***) n* faux témoignage *m*; **to commit perjury** faire un faux témoignage
perk [pɜːk] *Fam* **1** *n (from job)* avantage *m* en nature ❑; *(advantage)* avantage ❑ *m*; **cheap air travel is one of the perks of his job** un des avantages de son boulot, c'est qu'il peut prendre l'avion pour trois fois rien
2 *vt (coffee)* passer ❑
3 *vi (coffee)* passer ❑
►**perk up** **1** *vt sep (cheer up)* remonter, ragaillardir, revigouer; *(liven up)* revigorer; **the news really perked me up** la nouvelle m'a vraiment remonté le moral; **some wine will perk you up** un peu de vin te remontera
2 *vi* (**a**) *(cheer up)* se ragaillardir, retrouver le moral; **he perked up in the afternoon** il a retrouvé son entrain l'après-midi
(**b**) *(become interested)* dresser l'oreille *ou* la tête; **she perked up when money was mentioned** elle a dressé l'oreille quand on a parlé d'argent
(**c**) *(ears, head)* se dresser
perkily [ˈpɜːkɪlɪ] *adv (in a lively manner)* d'un air animé; *(answer, say)* d'un ton dégagé *ou* désinvolte
perkiness [ˈpɜːkɪnɪs] *n* entrain *m*; *(of voice)* ton *m* guilleret
perky [ˈpɜːkɪ] *(compar* **perkier,** *superl* **perkiest***) adj (lively)* plein d'entrain, animé; *(cheerful)* guilleret; *(tone)* dégagé, désinvolte
Perl [pɜːl] *n Comput (abbr* **practical extraction and report language***)* langage *m* Perl
perlite [ˈpɜːlaɪt] *n Miner* perlite *f*
perlocution [pɜːləˈkjuːʃən] *n Phil* perlocution *f*
perm [pɜːm] **1** *vt (hair)* permanenter; **her hair is permed** elle a les cheveux permanentés; **I've had my hair permed** je me suis fait faire une permanente
2 *n* (**a**) *(in hair)* permanente *f*; **to have a perm** se faire faire une permanente (**b**) *Br (permutation)* = combinaison jouée dans les paris sur les matches de football en Grande-Bretagne
permaculture [ˈpɜːməkʌltʃə(r)] *n Ecol* permaculture *f*
permafrost [ˈpɜːməfrɒst] *n* permagel *m*, permafrost *m*, pergélisol *m*

permalloy [ˈpɜːmælɔɪ] *n Metal* permalloy *m*

permanence [ˈpɜːmənəns] *n* permanence *f*, caractère *m* permanent

permanency [ˈpɜːmənənsɪ] (*pl* **permanencies**) *n* (**a**) *(person, thing)* **they predicted that computers would be a permanency in every office** ils avaient prévu que les ordinateurs deviendraient indispensables dans tous les bureaux (**b**) *(state, quality)* permanence *f*, caractère *m* permanent

permanent [ˈpɜːmənənt] **1** *adj* permanent; **no permanent damage was caused** aucun dégât irréparable n'a été occasionné; **are you here on a permanent basis?** êtes-vous ici à titre définitif?; **she has taken up permanent residence abroad** elle s'est installée définitivement à l'étranger
2 *n Am (in hair)* permanente *f*
►► ***permanent address*** domicile *m*; *Fin* ***permanent assets*** actif *m* immobilisé; *Fin* ***permanent credit*** accréditif *m* permanent; *Ins* ***permanent health insurance*** assurance *f* longue maladie; ***permanent ink*** encre *f* indélébile; ***permanent magnet*** aimant *m* permanent; ***permanent post*** *(gen)* emploi *m* permanent; *(in public service)* poste *f* de titulaire; *Br* ***Permanent Secretary*** chef *m* de cabinet; ***permanent staff*** *(gen)* personnel *m* permanent; *(in public service)* personnel *m* titulaire; ***permanent tooth*** dent *f* permanente; *Br* ***Permanent Undersecretary*** ≃ secrétaire *mf* général(e) *(dans la fonction publique)*; ***permanent wave*** permanente *f*; *Br* ***permanent way*** voie *f* ferrée

permanently [ˈpɜːmənəntlɪ] *adv* (**a**) *(constantly)* en permanence, constamment; **he's permanently drunk** il ne dessoûle jamais (**b**) *(definitively)* définitivement, à titre définitif; **they came to live here permanently** ils sont venus s'installer ici définitivement

permanent-press *adj*
►► ***permanent-press skirt*** jupe *f* à pli permanent; ***permanent-press trousers*** pantalon *m* à pli permanent

permanganate [pɜːˈmæŋgəneɪt] *n Chem* permanganate *m*

permanganic [ˌpɜːmæŋˈgænɪk] *adj Chem* permanganique

permeability [ˌpɜːmɪəˈbɪlətɪ] *n* perméabilité *f*

permeable [ˈpɜːmɪəbəl] *adj* perméable

permeate [ˈpɜːmɪeɪt] **1** *vt* (**a**) *(of gas, smell)* se répandre dans; **a lovely smell permeated the kitchen** une merveilleuse odeur emplissait la cuisine
(**b**) *(of liquid)* s'infiltrer dans; **damp had permeated the floorboards** le plancher était imprégné *ou* gorgé d'humidité; **the sand is permeated with oil** le sable est imbibé de pétrole
(**c**) *Fig (of ideas)* imprégner; *(of feelings)* envahir, emplir; **an atmosphere of gloom permeates his novels** ses romans sont empreints d'une mélancolie profonde; **the optimism that permeated the sixties** l'optimisme qui prévalait *ou* dominait dans les années soixante
2 *vi* (**a**) *(gas)* se répandre, se diffuser; *(smell)* se répandre
(**b**) *(liquid)* filtrer; **rain water had permeated through the walls** les eaux de pluie avaient filtré à travers les murs
(**c**) *Fig (ideas, feelings)* se répandre, se propager

Permian [ˈpɜːmɪən] *Geol* **1** *adj* permien
2 *n* permien *m*

permissible [pəˈmɪsəbəl] *adj Formal* (**a**) *(allowed)* permis, autorisé; **is it permissible for him to take two days off?** est-ce qu'il est autorisé à prendre deux jours de congé? (**b**) *(tolerable → behaviour)* admissible, acceptable; **degree of permissible error** marge *f* d'erreur admissible *ou* admise

permission [pəˈmɪʃən] *n* permission *f*, autorisation *f*; **to ask for permission to do sth** demander la permission *ou* l'autorisation de faire qch; **to have permission to do sth** avoir la permission *ou* l'autorisation de faire qch; **to give sb permission to do sth** donner à qn la permission de faire qch; **who gave them permission?** qui le leur a permis?; **who gave him permission to go out?** qui lui a permis de *ou* l'a autorisé à sortir?; **with your permission** avec votre permission, si vous le permettez; **without my/your/her permission** sans ma/votre/sa permission; **photos published by kind permission of Larousse** photos publiées avec l'aimable autorisation de Larousse; **you need written permission to work at home** il faut une autorisation écrite pour travailler chez soi; *St Exch* **permission to deal** visa *m (de la COB)*

permissive [pəˈmɪsɪv] *adj* (**a**) *(tolerant → behaviour, parent etc)* permissif; **the permissive society** la société permissive (**b**) *Arch (optional)* facultatif
►► ***permissive path*** = sentier privé dont le propriétaire autorise l'accès au public

permissively [pəˈmɪsɪvlɪ] *adv* de manière permissive

permissiveness [pəˈmɪsɪvnɪs] *n* (**a**) *(morally)* permissivité *f* (**b**) *(of legislation)* caractère *m* facultatif

permit (*pt & pp* **permitted**, *cont* **permitting**) **1** *vt* [pəˈmɪt] (**a**) *(allow)* permettre, autoriser; **to permit sb to do sth** permettre à qn de faire qch, autoriser qn à faire qch; **she was permitted to take two weeks off** on l'a autorisée à prendre deux semaines de congé; **permit me to inform you that...** laissez-moi vous apprendre que...; **he won't permit it** il ne le permettra pas; **you are not permitted to enter the building** vous n'avez pas le droit de pénétrer dans l'immeuble; **smoking is not permitted upstairs** il est interdit de fumer à l'étage; **the hotel won't permit animals in the bedrooms** l'hôtel n'autorise pas la présence d'animaux dans les chambres; **he permits far too much rudeness from his children** il tolère trop de grossièreté chez ses enfants
(**b**) *(enable)* permettre; **the computer permits her to take more time off** l'ordinateur lui laisse plus de temps libre; **the statistics permit the following conclusions** les statistiques permettent (de tirer) les conclusions suivantes
2 *vi* [pəˈmɪt] permettre; **weather permitting** si le temps le permet; **if time permits** si j'ai/nous avons/*etc* le temps
3 *n* [ˈpɜːmɪt] *(authorization)* autorisation *f*, permis *m*; *(pass)* laissez-passer *m inv*; **export/drinks permit** licence *f* d'exportation/pour la vente de boissons alcoolisées; **permit holders only** *(on sign)* réservé aux personnes autorisées
►► *Br Admin* ***permitted hours*** *(for selling alcohol)* = heures légales de vente des boissons alcoolisées

▸**permit of** *vt insep Formal (admit possibility of)* admettre; **this permits of only one explanation** ceci n'admet qu'une explication

permittivity [ˌpɜːmɪˈtɪvɪtɪ] *n Elec* permittivité *f*, constante *f* diélectrique

permutable [pɜːˈmjuːtəbəl] *adj* permutable

permutate [ˈpɜːmjʊteɪt] *vt* permuter

permutation [ˌpɜːmjuːˈteɪʃən] *n Math* permutation *f*

permute [pəˈmjuːt] *vt* permuter

pernicious [pəˈnɪʃəs] *adj* (**a**) *(harmful)* pernicieux (**b**) *(malicious → gossip, lie)* malveillant
►► *Med* ***pernicious anaemia*** anémie *f* pernicieuse

perniciously [pəˈnɪʃəslɪ] *adv* pernicieusement

perniciousness [pəˈnɪʃəsnɪs] *n* perniciosité *f*, effet *m* pernicieux

pernickety [pəˈnɪkətɪ], *Am* **persnickety** [pəˈsnɪkɪtɪ] *adj Fam* (**a**) *Pej (person → fussy)* tatillon, chipoteur; *(→ hard to please)* difficile □; **to be pernickety about one's food** être difficile sur la nourriture; **she's very pernickety about punctuality** elle ne plaisante pas avec *ou* elle est très à cheval sur la ponctualité (**b**) *(fiddly → job)* délicat □, minutieux □

peroneal [ˌperəˈniːəl] *adj Anat* péronier

perorate [ˈperəreɪt] *vi Formal* (**a**) *(conclude speech)* faire la péroraison (**b**) *(speak at length)* discourir longuement, pérorer

peroration [ˌperəˈreɪʃən] *n Formal* (**a**) *(conclusion)* péroraison *f* (**b**) *(long speech)* long discours *m*, discours *m* de longue haleine

peroxidase [pəˈrɒksɪdeɪs] *n Biol & Chem* peroxydase *f*

peroxidate [pəˈrɒksɪdeɪt] *vt Chem* peroxyder

peroxidation [pəˌrɒksɪˈdeɪʃən] *n Chem* péroxydation *f*

peroxide [pəˈrɒksaɪd] **1** *n* (**a**) *Chem* peroxyde *m* (**b**) *(for hair)* eau *f* oxygénée
2 *vt (bleach → hair)* décolorer, *Spec* oxygéner
►► *Pej* ***peroxide blonde*** *(woman)* blonde *f* décolorée

peroxidize, -ise [pəˈrɒksɪdaɪz] *vt Chem* peroxyder

perp [pɜːp] *n Am Fam Crime slang (abbr* **perpetrator***)* auteur □ *m*

perpendicular [ˌpɜːpənˈdɪkjʊlə(r)] **1** *adj* (**a**) *Geom* perpendiculaire (**to** à); **the line AB is perpendicular to the line CD** la ligne AB est perpendiculaire à la ligne CD (**b**) *(vertical → cliff)* escarpé, abrupt, à pic; *(→ slope)* raide, à pic
2 *n* perpendiculaire *f*; **the tower is out of (the) perpendicular** la tour n'est pas verticale *ou Spec* est hors d'aplomb
3 Perpendicular *adj Archit* perpendiculaire

perpendicularly [ˌpɜːpənˈdɪkjʊləlɪ] *adv* perpendiculairement; *(rise, fall, drop)* verticalement, à la verticale; *(be built)* d'aplomb; **the cliff rose perpendicularly** la falaise s'élevait tout droit

perpetrate [ˈpɜːpɪtreɪt] *vt Formal (commit → crime)* commettre, *Literary* perpétrer; *(→ error)* commettre; **she perpetrated several frauds** elle a escroqué plusieurs personnes; **to perpetrate a hoax** être l'auteur d'une farce

perpetration [ˌpɜːpɪˈtreɪʃən] *n Formal* perpétration *f*

perpetrator [ˈpɜːpɪtreɪtə(r)] *n Formal* auteur *m*; **the perpetrator of the crime** l'auteur du délit

perpetual [pəˈpetʃʊəl] *adj* (**a**) *(state, worry)* perpétuel; *(noise, questions)* continuel, incessant; **her perpetual coughing kept me awake all night** sa toux incessante m'a gardé éveillé toute la nuit; **it's a perpetual worry to us** c'est pour nous un sujet d'inquiétude *ou* un souci permanent; **perpetual snows** neiges *fpl* éternelles
(**b**) *Hort* perpétuel
►► ***perpetual calendar*** calendrier *m* perpétuel; *Chess* ***perpetual check*** échec *m* perpétuel; *Fin* ***perpetual inventory*** stock *m* stratégique; *Fin* ***perpetual loan*** emprunt *m* perpétuel; ***perpetual motion*** mouvement *m* perpétuel

perpetually [pəˈpetʃʊəlɪ] *adv* perpétuellement, sans cesse; **they're perpetually complaining** ils sont toujours à se plaindre, ils se plaignent sans arrêt

perpetuate [pəˈpetʃʊeɪt] *vt* perpétuer

perpetuation [pəˌpetʃʊˈeɪʃən] *n* perpétuation *f*; **this leads to the perpetuation of this type of situation** c'est ce qui permet à ce type de situation de se perpétuer

perpetuity [ˌpɜːpɪˈtjuːətɪ] (*pl* **perpetuities**) *n* (**a**) *(eternity)* perpétuité *f*; **in** *or* **for perpetuity** à perpétuité (**b**) *(annuity)* rente *f* perpétuelle

perplex [pəˈpleks] *vt* (**a**) *(puzzle)* rendre *ou* laisser perplexe; **his questions perplexed us** ses questions nous ont laissés perplexes *ou* nous ont plongés dans la perplexité (**b**) *(complicate)* compliquer

perplexed [pəˈplekst] *adj* perplexe; **I'm perplexed about what to do** je ne sais pas trop quoi faire

perplexedly [pəˈpleksɪdlɪ] *adv* avec perplexité; **he looked at me perplexedly** il me regarda d'un air perplexe, il me lança un regard perplexe

perplexing [pəˈpleksɪŋ] *adj* inexplicable, incompréhensible; **I find their silence rather perplexing** je me demande bien ce que peut signifier leur silence; **he asked us some perplexing questions** il a posé des questions qui nous ont laissés perplexes

perplexity [pəˈpleksətɪ] *n* (**a**) *(confusion)* perplexité *f*; **you could see the perplexity on his face** la perplexité se lisait sur son visage (**b**) *(complexity → of problem)* complexité *f*

perquisite [ˈpɜːkwɪzɪt] *n Formal (from job)* avantage *m* en nature; *(advantage)* avantage *m*

perron [ˈperən] *n Archit* perron *m*

perry [ˈperɪ] (*pl* **perries**) *n* poiré *m*

per se [pɜːˈseɪ] *adv (as such)* en tant que tel; *(in itself)* en soi

persecute [ˈpɜːsɪkjuːt] *vt* (**a**) *(oppress)* persécuter; **they were persecuted for their religious beliefs** ils ont été persécutés à cause de leurs convictions religieuses (**b**) *(pester)* persécuter, harceler; **they persecuted her with questions** ils l'ont harcelée de questions

persecution [,pɜːsɪ'kjuːʃən] *n* persécution *f*

►► ***persecution complex*** délire *m* de persécution; ***persecution mania*** manie *f* de la persécution

persecutor ['pɜːsɪkjuːtə(r)] *n* persécuteur(trice) *m,f*

Persephone [pɜː'sefənɪ] *pr n Myth* Perséphone

Persepolis [pɜː'sepəlɪs] *n* Persépolis *f*

Perseus ['pɜːsjuːs] *pr n Myth* Persée

perseverance [,pɜːsɪ'vɪərəns] *n* persévérance *f*

persevere [,pɜːsɪ'vɪə(r)] *vi* persévérer; **persevere in your efforts** persévérez dans vos efforts; **you must persevere with your studies** il faut persévérer dans vos études

persevering [,pɜːsɪ'vɪərɪŋ] *adj* persévérant, obstiné

perseveringly [,pɜːsɪ'vɪərɪŋlɪ] *adv* avec persévérance

Persia ['pɜːʃə] *n* Perse *f*; **in Persia** en Perse

Persian ['pɜːʃən] **1** *n* (**a**) *(person)* Persan(e) *m,f*; *Antiq* Perse *mf* (**b**) *Ling (modern)* persan *m*; *(ancient)* perse *m*

2 *adj* persan; *Antiq* perse

►► ***Persian blinds*** persiennes *fpl*; ***Persian carpet*** tapis *m* persan; ***Persian cat*** chat *m* persan; ***the Persian Gulf*** le golfe Persique; ***persian lamb*** *(animal, fur)* karakul *m*, caracul *m*

persicaria [,pɜːsɪ'keərɪə] *n Bot* persicaire *f*

persiflage [,pɜːsɪ'flɑːʒ] *n Literary (banter)* badinage *m*; *(frivolous talk)* propos *mpl* frivoles

persimmon [pə'sɪmən] *n* (**a**) *(fruit)* plaquemine *f*, kaki *m* (**b**) *(tree)* plaqueminier *m*

persist [pə'sɪst] *vi* (**a**) *(person)* persister; **to persist in doing sth** persister *ou* s'obstiner à faire qch; **he persists in the belief that...** il persiste à croire que... (**b**) *(weather, problem etc)* persister; **rain will persist in the north** la pluie persistera dans le nord; **if the fever persists** si la fièvre persiste

persistence [pə'sɪstəns], **persistency** [pə'sɪstənsɪ] *n* (**a**) *(perseverance)* persistance *f*, persévérance *f*; *(insistence)* persistance *f*, insistance *f*; *(obstinacy)* obstination *f*; **his persistence finally paid off** sa persévérance a fini par porter ses fruits; **his persistence in asking awkward questions** son obstination à poser des questions embarrassantes (**b**) *(continuation → of rain, problem, belief etc)* persistance *f*

persistent [pə'sɪstənt] *adj* (**a**) *(continual → demands, rain etc)* continuel, incessant (**b**) *(lingering → smell, fever, pain etc)* persistant, tenace (**c**) *(persevering)* persévérant; **you must be more persistent in your efforts** il faut être plus persévérant (**d**) *Bot* persistant

►► ***persistent offender*** récidiviste *mf*; *Med* ***persistent vegetative state*** état *m* végétatif chronique

persistently [pə'sɪstəntlɪ] *adv* (**a**) *(continually)* continuellement, sans cesse; **I've warned you persistently** je me suis acharné à vous prévenir; **they persistently insult him** ils ne cessent de l'insulter (**b**) *(perseveringly)* avec persévérance *ou* persistance, obstinément

persnickety [pə'snɪkɪtɪ] *Am* = **pernickety**

person ['pɜːsən] *(pl* **people** ['piːpəl] *or Formal* **persons**) **1** *n* (**a**) *(individual)* personne *f*; **he's just the person we need** c'est exactement la personne qu'il nous faut; **a young person** *(female)* une jeune personne; *(male)* un jeune homme; *Law* **by a person or persons unknown** par des personnes inconnues *ou* non identifiées; **she is a nice/strange person** c'est une personne gentille/étrange, c'est quelqu'un de gentil/d'étrange; **I like him as a person** je l'aime bien en tant que personne; **he's a good worker, but I don't really like him as a person** au travail il est bien, mais je n'aime pas trop sa personnalité *ou* mais sur le plan personnel je ne l'aime pas trop; **he's not that sort of person** ce n'est pas du tout son genre; *Fam* **I'm not a great eating-out person** je n'aime pas beaucoup manger au restaurant❑; *Fam* **are you a cat person or a dog person?** est-ce que tu préfères les chats ou chiens?❑; **in the person of** en la personne de

(**b**) *Formal (body)* personne *f*; **to have sth on** *or* **about one's person** avoir qch sur soi; **she had the wallet concealed about her person** le portefeuille était caché sur elle

(**c**) *Gram* personne *f*; **in the first person plural** à la première personne du pluriel

(**d**) *Rel* personne *f*

2 in person *adv* en personne; **she came in person** elle est venue en personne; **this letter must be delivered to him in person** cette lettre doit lui être remise en mains propres

persona [pə'səʊnə] *(pl* **personas** *or* **personae** [-niː]) *n Literature & Psy* personnage *m*; **to take on a new persona** se créer un personnage

personable ['pɜːsənəbəl] *adj* plaisant, charmant; **he's a very personable young man** c'est un jeune homme qui présente très bien

personage ['pɜːsənɪdʒ] *n Formal* personnage *m* *(individu)*; **an important personage** un personnage important

persona grata [pə'səʊnə'grɑːtə] *(pl* **personae gratae** [pə'səʊniː'grɑːtiː]) *n* **to be persona grata** être persona grata

personal ['pɜːsənəl] **1** *adj* (**a**) *(individual → experience, belief etc)* personnel; **she tries to give her work a personal touch** elle essaie de donner une touche personnelle à son travail; **my personal opinion is that he drowned** personnellement, je crois qu'il s'est noyé; **you get more personal attention in small shops** on s'occupe mieux de vous dans les petits magasins; **will you do me a personal favour?** pourriez-vous m'accorder une faveur?

(**b**) *(in person)* personnel; **under the personal supervision of the author** supervisé personnellement par l'auteur; **the boss made a personal visit to the scene** le patron est venu lui-même *ou* en personne sur les lieux; **we were expecting a personal appearance by the Prime Minister** nous pensions que le Premier ministre ferait une apparition en personne; **personal callers welcome** *(sign)* vente en gros et au détail

(**c**) *(private → message, letter)* personnel; **personal and private** *(on letter)* strictement confidentiel

(**d**) *(for one's own use)* personnel; **to be careless about one's personal appearance** négliger sa tenue; **this is for my personal use** ceci est destiné à mon usage personnel

(**e**) *(intimate → feelings, reasons, life)* personnel; **for personal reasons** pour des raisons personnelles; **I'd like to see her on a personal matter** je voudrais la voir pour des raisons personnelles; **just a few personal friends** rien que quelques amis intimes

(**f**) *(offensive)* désobligeant; **personal remark** remarque *f* désobligeante; **there's no need to be so personal!** ce n'est pas la peine de t'en prendre à moi!; **nothing personal!** ne le prenez pas pour vous!, n'y voyez rien de personnel!; **it's nothing personal but...** ça n'a rien de personnel mais...; **the discussion was getting rather personal** la discussion prenait un tour un peu trop personnel

(**g**) *Gram* personnel; **personal pronoun** pronom *m* personnel

2 *n Am (advert)* petite annonce *f (pour rencontres)*

►► ***personal accident insurance*** assurance *f* contre les accidents corporels; ***personal account*** *Banking* compte *m* personnel; *St Exch* compte *m* de tiers; *Acct* compte *m* propre; *Fam* ***personal ad*** petite annonce❑ *f (pour rencontres)*; *Fin* ***personal allowance*** abattement *m (sur l'impôt sur le revenu)*; *Banking* ***personal assets*** patrimoine *m*; *Banking* ***personal assets profile*** profil *m* patrimonial; ***personal assistant*** *(of executive)* assistant(e) *m,f*; *(with secretarial duties)* secrétaire *mf* de direction; ***personal belongings*** objets *mpl* personnels, affaires *fpl*; *Sport* ***personal best*** record *m* personnel; **he ran a personal best in the 200 m** il a battu son propre record *or* record personnel sur 200 m; *Tel* ***personal call*** appel *m* personnel *ou* privé; **is this a personal call?** c'est personnel?; ***personal column*** petites annonces *fpl (pour rencontres)*; **to put an ad in the personal column** passer une petite annonce; *Comput* ***personal computer*** ordinateur *m* individuel *ou* personnel, PC *m*; ***personal computing*** informatique *f* individuelle; ***personal credit*** crédit *m* personnel; *Comput* ***personal digital assistant*** agenda *m* électronique de poche, assistant *m* numérique de poche; ***personal effects*** effets *mpl* personnels; ***personal estate*** biens *mpl* mobiliers personnels; *Br Formerly Fin* ***personal equity plan*** ≃ plan *m* d'épargne en actions; ***personal foul*** *(in basketball)* faute *f* personnelle; *Comput* ***personal home page*** page *f* personnelle, page *f* perso; ***personal hygiene*** hygiène *f* corporelle; **he has a personal hygiene problem** il ne doit pas se laver bien souvent; *Banking* ***personal identification number*** code *m* confidentiel *(d'une carte bancaire)*; *Br Fin* ***Personal Investment Authority*** = organisme chargé de surveiller les activités des conseillers financiers indépendants et de protéger les petits investisseurs; ***personal loan*** prêt *m* personnel, prêt *m* personnalisé; ***personal maid*** femme *f* de chambre; *Mktg* ***personal observation*** observation *f* en situation; ***personal organizer*** organiseur *m*; *(electronic)* agenda *m* électronique, organiseur *m*; *Fin* ***personal pension plan*** retraite *f* personnelle; ***personal possessions*** objets *mpl* personnels, affaires *fpl*; ***personal property*** biens *mpl* mobiliers personnels; *Mktg* ***personal selling*** ventes *fpl* personnelles; ***personal shopper*** acheteur(euse) *m,f* personnel(elle); ***personal stereo*** Walkman® *m*, *Offic* baladeur *m*; ***personal trainer*** entraîneur(euse) *m,f* personnel(elle); *Am* ***personal watercraft*** scooter *m* des mers, jet-ski *m*; *Banking* ***personal withdrawal*** levée *f* de compte

personality [,pɜːsə'nælətɪ] *(pl* **personalities**) **1** *n* (**a**) *(character → of person)* personnalité *f*, caractère *m*; *(→ of thing, animal etc)* caractère *m*; **a woman with a lot of personality** une femme dotée d'une forte personnalité; **he's got no personality** il n'a aucune personnalité; **he was an interesting personality** il avait une personnalité intéressante

(**b**) *(famous person)* personnalité *f*; *Cin & TV* vedette *f*; **sports personality** vedette *f* du monde du sport; **media personality** vedette *f* des médias

(**c**) *Psy* personnalité *f*

2 personalities *npl Old-fashioned (offensive remarks)* propos *mpl* désobligeants

►► ***personality cult*** culte *m* de la personnalité; ***personality disorder*** trouble *m* de la personnalité; **he has a serious personality disorder** il a de graves problèmes psychologiques; ***personality profile*** profil *m* de personnalité; *Mktg* ***personality promotion*** promotion *f* par une personnalité; ***personality test*** test *m* de personnalité, *Spec* test *m* projectif; ***personality type*** configuration *f* psychologique

personalization [,pɜːsənəlaɪ'zeɪʃən] *n* (**a**) *(making personal)* personnalisation *f* (**b**) *(personification)* personnification *f*

personalize, -ise ['pɜːsənəlaɪz] *vt* (**a**) *(make personal → gen)* personnaliser; *(→ luggage, clothes)* marquer (à son nom) (**b**) *(argument, campaign)* donner un tour personnel à; **I don't want to personalize the issue** je ne veux pas donner un tour personnel à cette question (**c**) *(personify)* personnifier

personalized ['pɜːsənəlaɪzd] *adj (individually tailored)* personnalisé; **his personalized luggage** ses bagages marqués à son nom

►► ***personalized number plate*** plaque *f* d'immatriculation personnalisée; ***personalized stationery*** papier *m* à lettres à en-tête

personally ['pɜːsnəlɪ] *adv* (**a**) *(speaking for oneself)* personnellement, pour ma/sa/*etc* part; **personally (speaking), I think it's a silly idea** pour ma part *ou* en ce qui me concerne, je trouve que c'est une idée stupide

(**b**) *(in person, directly)* en personne, personnellement; **I was not personally involved in the project** je n'ai pas participé directement au projet; **I want to speak to him personally** j'aimerais lui parler personnellement; **deliver the letter to the director personally** remettez la lettre en mains propres au directeur

(**c**) *(not officially)* sur le plan personnel

(**d**) *(individually)* personnellement; **I was talking about the whole team, not you personally** je parlais de toute l'équipe, pas de toi personnellement *ou* en particulier; **to take things personally** prendre les choses trop à cœur; **don't take it personally** *(what was said, done)* n'en faites pas une affaire personnelle; **don't**

take it personally, but... ne vous sentez pas visé, mais...; **I didn't mean it personally** ma remarque n'avait rien de personnel

personalty ['pɜːsənəltɪ] (*pl* **personalties**) *n Law* biens *mpl* mobiliers; **to convert realty into personalty** ameublir un bien

persona non grata [pə'səʊnənɒn'grɑːtə] (*pl* **personae non gratae** [pə'səʊniːnɒn'grɑːtiː]) *n* **to be persona non grata** être persona non grata; **to be persona non grata with sb** ne pas être dans les petits papiers de qn; **he's definitely persona non grata in this house** il n'est absolument pas le bienvenu dans cette maison

personate ['pɜːsəneɪt] *vt* (**a**) *Law* se faire passer pour (**b**) *Theat* jouer le rôle de

personation [,pɜːsə'neɪʃən] *n* (**a**) *Law* **(false) personation** usurpation *f* de nom *ou* d'état civil (**b**) *Theat* représentation *f*

personification [pə,sɒnɪfɪ'keɪʃən] *n* personnification *f*; **he is the personification of evil** c'est le mal personnifié *ou* en personne

personify [pə'sɒnɪfaɪ] (*pt & pp* **personified**) *vt* personnifier; **he is evil personified** c'est le mal personnifié *ou* incarné

personnel [,pɜːsə'nel] *n* (**a**) *(staff)* personnel *m*
(**b**) *(department)* service *m* du personnel; **she works in personnel** elle travaille au service du personnel
(**c**) *Mil (troops)* troupes *fpl*
▸▸ *Mil* ***personnel carrier*** (véhicule *m* de) transport *m* de troupes; ***personnel consultant*** conseiller(ère) *m,f* du travail; ***personnel department*** service *m* du personnel; ***personnel management*** direction *f ou* administration *f* du personnel; ***personnel officer*** responsable *mf* du personnel; ***personnel resource management*** gestion *f* des ressources humaines

person-to-person 1 *adv* **I'd like to speak to her person-to-person** je voudrais lui parler en particulier *ou* seule à seul
2 *adj (conversation)* personnel
▸▸ *Mktg* ***person-to-person approach*** approche *f* personnalisée; *Tel* ***person-to-person call*** communication *f* avec préavis *(se dit d'un appel téléphonique où la communication n'est établie et facturée que lorsque la personne à qui l'on veut parler répond)*

perspective [pə'spektɪv] 1 *n* (**a**) *Archit & Art* perspective *f*; **to draw sth in perspective** dessiner qch en perspective; **the houses are out of perspective** la perspective des maisons est fausse; **perspective made it look smaller** l'effet de perspective le faisait paraître plus petit
(**b**) *(opinion, viewpoint)* perspective *f*, optique *f*; **it gives you a different perspective on the problem** cela vous permet de voir le problème sous un angle *ou* un jour différent; **from a psychological perspective** d'un point de vue psychologique; **the latest developments put a new perspective on the case** les derniers événements éclairent l'affaire d'un jour nouveau
(**c**) *(proportion)* **we must try to keep our (sense of) perspective** *or* **to keep things in perspective** nous devons nous efforcer de garder notre sens des proportions; **to get things out of perspective** perdre le sens des proportions; **it should help us to get** *or* **to put the role she played into perspective** cela devrait nous aider à mesurer le rôle qu'elle a joué; **the figures must be looked at in (their proper) perspective** il faut étudier les chiffres dans leur contexte
(**d**) *Formal (view, vista)* perspective *f*, panorama *m*, vue *f*; **a fine perspective opened out before his eyes** une belle perspective s'ouvrit devant ses yeux
(**e**) *(prospect)* perspective *f*; **the perspective of higher inflation** la perspective d'une hausse du taux d'inflation
2 *adj (drawing)* perspectif

perspectivism [pə'spektɪvɪzəm] *n Phil* perspectivisme *m*

perspectivist [pɜː'spektɪvɪst] *n Art* perspectiviste *mf*

Perspex® ['pɜːspeks] *Br* 1 *n* Plexiglas® *m*
2 *comp (window, windscreen etc)* en Plexiglas®

perspicacious [,pɜːspɪ'keɪʃəs] *adj Formal (person)* perspicace; *(remark, judgment)* pénétrant, lucide

perspicaciously [,pɜːspɪ'keɪʃəslɪ] *adv Formal* avec perspicacité

perspicacity [,pɜːspɪ'kæsətɪ] *n Formal* perspicacité *f*

perspicuity [,pɜːspɪ'kjuːətɪ] *n Formal* clarté *f*, lucidité *f*

perspicuous [pə'spɪkjʊəs] *adj Formal* clair, lucide

perspicuously [pə'spɪkjʊəslɪ] *adv Formal* clairement, nettement

perspicuousness [pɜː'spɪkjʊəsnɪs] *n Formal* clarté *f*, lucidité *f*

perspiration [,pɜːspə'reɪʃən] *n* (**a**) *(sweat)* transpiration *f*, sueur *f*; **beads of perspiration** des perles *fpl* de sueur; **bathed in** *or* **dripping with perspiration** trempé de sueur, en nage (**b**) *(act)* transpiration *f*, perspiration *f*

perspire [pə'spaɪə(r)] *vi* transpirer; **his hands were perspiring** il avait les mains moites; **she was perspiring freely** *or* **heavily** elle transpirait à grosses gouttes

persuadable [pə'sweɪdəbəl] *adj* facile à persuader

persuade [pə'sweɪd] *vt* persuader, convaincre; **to persuade sb to do sth** persuader *ou* convaincre qn de faire qch; **to persuade sb not to do sth** persuader qn de ne pas faire qch, dissuader qn de faire qch; **I managed to persuade him (that) I was right** j'ai réussi à le persuader *ou* convaincre que j'avais raison; **I let myself be persuaded into coming** je me suis laissé convaincre qu'il fallait venir; **she persuaded herself that everything would work out** elle s'est persuadée *ou* convaincue elle-même que tout marcherait bien; *Fig* **she finally persuaded the car to start** elle a réussi à faire démarrer la voiture; *Formal* **I was persuaded of her innocence** j'étais convaincu *ou* persuadé qu'elle était innocente

persuasion [pə'sweɪʒən] *n* (**a**) *(act of convincing)* persuasion *f*; **persuasion works better than force** la persuasion est plus efficace que la force; **the art of gentle persuasion** l'art de convaincre en douceur; **powers of persuasion** force *f ou* pouvoir *m* de persuasion; **I used all my powers of persuasion on him** j'ai fait tout mon possible *ou* tout ce qui était en mon pouvoir pour le convaincre; **I wouldn't need much persuasion to give it up** il ne faudrait pas insister beaucoup pour que j'abandonne; **to be open to persuasion** être disposé à se laisser convaincre
(**b**) *(belief) & Rel* confession *f*, religion *f*; *Pol* tendance *f*; **men and women of many persuasions** des hommes et des femmes de nombreuses confessions; **people, regardless of their political persuasion** les gens, quelles que soient leurs convictions politiques
(**c**) *Formal (conviction)* conviction *f*

persuasive [pə'sweɪsɪv] *adj (manner, speaker)* persuasif, convaincant; *(argument)* convaincant

persuasively [pə'sweɪsɪvlɪ] *adv* de façon convaincante *ou* persuasive; **she argues persuasively** elle emploie des arguments convaincants

persuasiveness [pə'sweɪsɪvnəs] *n (of person)* force *f* persuasive *ou* de persuasion; *(of argument)* caractère *m* convaincant

pert [pɜːt] *adj* (**a**) *(cheeky → person, reply)* effronté (**b**) *(stylishly neat → garment, hat)* coquet (**c**) *(nose)* mutin; *(bottom)* (petit et) ferme

pertain [pə'teɪn] *vi* (**a**) *(apply)* s'appliquer (**b**) **to pertain to** *(concern)* avoir rapport à, se rapporter à; *Law (of land, property)* se rattacher à, dépendre de; **the evidence pertaining to the case** les témoignages se rattachant *ou* se rapportant à l'affaire; **books pertaining to photography** des livres sur la photographie

Perth [pɜːθ] *n* Perth

pertinacious [,pɜːtɪ'neɪʃəs] *adj Formal* opiniâtre

pertinaciously [,pɜːtɪ'neɪʃəslɪ] *adv Formal* opiniâtrement

pertinacity [,pɜːtɪ'næsətɪ] *n Formal* opiniâtreté *f*

pertinence ['pɜːtɪnəns] *n* pertinence *f*, à-propos *m*; **I don't see the pertinence of that remark** cette remarque ne me semble pas pertinente

pertinent ['pɜːtɪnənt] *adj* pertinent, à propos; **a very pertinent question** une question très pertinente

pertinently ['pɜːtɪnəntlɪ] *adv* pertinemment, avec justesse *ou* à-propos

pertly ['pɜːtlɪ] *adv (reply)* avec effronterie; *(dress)* coquettement

pertness ['pɜːtnɪs] *n (of reply, manner)* effronterie *f*; *(of garment, hat)* coquetterie *f*

perturb [pə'tɜːb] *vt* (**a**) *(worry)* inquiéter, troubler; **they were very perturbed by his disappearance** sa disparition les a beaucoup inquiétés (**b**) *Astron & Electron* perturber

perturbation [,pɜːtə'beɪʃən] *n* (**a**) *Formal (anxiety)* trouble *m*, inquiétude *f* (**b**) *Astron & Electron* perturbation *f*

perturbed [pə'tɜːbd] *adj* troublé, inquiet(ète); **I was perturbed to hear that he is ill** ça m'a troublé *ou* inquiété d'apprendre qu'il est malade

perturbing [pə'tɜːbɪŋ] *adj* inquiétant, troublant

pertussis [pə'tʌsɪs] *n Med* coqueluche *f*

Peru [pə'ruː] *n* Pérou *m*; **in Peru** au Pérou

Perugia [pə'ruːdʒə] *n* Pérouse

Perugino [peruː'dʒiːnəʊ] *pr n* **Il Perugino** le Pérugin; **a painting by Il Perugino** un tableau du Pérugin

perusal [pə'ruːzəl] *n (thorough reading)* lecture *f* approfondie, examen *m*; *(quick reading)* lecture *f* sommaire, survol *m*; **he left the document for her perusal** il lui a laissé le document pour information

peruse [pə'ruːz] *vt (read thoroughly)* lire attentivement, examiner; *(read quickly)* parcourir, survoler

Peruvian [pə'ruːvɪən] 1 *n* Péruvien(enne) *m,f*
2 *adj* péruvien
3 *comp (embassy, history)* du Pérou

perv [pɜːv] *n Br & Austr Fam* pervers(e)❑ *m,f*, détraqué(e) *m,f*

pervade [pə'veɪd] *vt* (**a**) *(of gas, smell)* se répandre dans
(**b**) *(of ideas)* se répandre dans, se propager à travers; *(of feelings)* envahir; **the scent of pine trees pervaded the air** l'air était embaumé de l'odeur des pins; **the fundamental error that pervades their philosophy** l'erreur fondamentale qui imprègne leur philosophie; **such attitudes pervade British business** ces attitudes sont omniprésentes dans *ou* se retrouvent à tous les niveaux de l'entreprenariat britannique; **a feeling of mistrust pervaded their relationship** il y avait toujours entre eux une certaine défiance

pervading [pə'veɪdɪŋ] *adj (smell)* pénétrant; *(influence, feeling, idea)* dominant; **all-pervading** qui se répand partout; **the pervading nostalgia of his work** la nostalgie qui est omniprésente dans son œuvre

pervasive [pə'veɪsɪv] *adj (feeling)* envahissant; *(influence)* omniprésent; *(effect)* général; *(smell)* envahissant, omniprésent; **the pervasive influence of television** l'omniprésence *f* de la télévision; **a pervasive atmosphere of pessimism** une atmosphère de pessimisme général

pervasiveness [pɜː'veɪsɪvnɪs] *n* tendance *f* à se répandre

perverse [pə'vɜːs] *adj* (**a**) *(stubborn → person)* têtu, entêté; *(→ desire)* tenace; *(contrary, wayward)* contrariant; **he felt a perverse urge to refuse** il lui prit une envie de refuser simplement pour le plaisir; **she takes a perverse delight in doing this** elle y prend un malin plaisir; **you're just being perverse!** tu fais ça juste pour embêter le monde! (**b**) *(sexually deviant)* pervers

perversely [pə'vɜːslɪ] *adv (stubbornly)* obstinément; *(unreasonably, contrarily)* par esprit de contradiction; **to perversely believe that...** s'entêter à croire que...

perverseness [pə'vɜːsnɪs] *n (stubbornness)* entêtement *m*, obstination *f*; *(unreasonableness, contrariness)* esprit *m* de contradiction

perversion [*Br* pə'vɜːʃən, *Am* pə'vɜːrʒən] *n* (**a**) *(sexual abnormality)* perversion *f* (**b**) *(distortion → of truth)* déformation *f*

perversity [pə'vɜːsətɪ] (*pl* **perversities**) *n* (**a**) *(stubbornness)* entêtement *m*, obstination *f*; *(unreasonableness, contrariness)* esprit *m* de contradiction (**b**) *(sexual abnormality)* perversité *f*

pervert 1 *vt* [pə'vɜːt] (**a**) *(corrupt morally → person)* pervertir, corrompre; *Psy* pervertir (**b**) *(distort → truth)* déformer; *(→ words)* dénaturer; **our old ideals have been perverted** nos vieux idéaux ont été déformés; *Law* **to pervert the course of justice** entraver le cours de la justice

2 *n* ['pɜːvɜːt] pervers(e) *m,f*; *Hum* **you pervert!** espèce d'obsédé!

perverted [pə'vɜːtɪd] *adj Psy* pervers

perverter [pə'vɜːtə(r)] *n* pervertisseur(euse) *m,f*

pervertible [pə'vɜːtɪbəl] *adj* pervertissable

pervious ['pɜːvɪəs] *adj* (**a**) *Geol (permeable)* perméable (**b**) *Literary (receptive)* ouvert, perméable

pervy ['pɜːvɪ] *adj Br Fam* pervers❑

peseta [pə'seɪtə] *n* peseta *f*

pesky ['peskɪ] (*compar* **peskier**, *superl* **peskiest**) *adj esp Am Fam* fichu; **pesky weather!** fichu temps!; **pesky flies!** maudites *ou* satanées mouches!

peso ['peɪsəʊ] (*pl* **pesos**) *n* peso *m*

pessary ['pesərɪ] (*pl* **pessaries**) *n Med* pessaire *m*

pessimism ['pesɪmɪzəm] *n* pessimisme *m*; **there is growing pessimism about the prospects for peace** on est de plus en plus pessimiste quant aux chances de paix

pessimist ['pesɪmɪst] *n* pessimiste *mf*

pessimistic [,pesɪ'mɪstɪk] *adj* pessimiste; **I feel very pessimistic about her chances of getting the job** je doute fort qu'elle obtienne ce poste; **don't be so pessimistic about your future** ne regarde pas l'avenir d'un œil si sombre, ne sois pas si pessimiste quant à l'avenir

pessimistically [,pesɪ'mɪstɪklɪ] *adv* avec pessimisme; **he viewed the future somewhat pessimistically** il avait une vision de l'avenir plutôt pessimiste

PEST [pest] *n Mktg* (*abbr* **political, economic, sociological, technological**) = facteurs politiques, économiques, sociaux et technologiques

pest [pest] *n* (**a**) *(insect)* insecte *m* nuisible; *(animal)* animal *m* nuisible

(**b**) *Fam (nuisance)* plaie *f*, peste *f*; **what a pest he is!** quelle plaie!, qu'est-ce qu'il est casse-pieds!; **that dog is a real pest** ce chien est une véritable plaie; **look what she's done, the little pest!** regarde un peu ce qu'elle a fait, la petite peste!; **having to take the dog for a walk every day is a real pest** c'est vraiment empoisonnant *ou* embêtant d'avoir à promener le chien tous les jours

►► ***pest control*** *(action → of rats)* dératisation *f*; *(→ of insects)* désinsectisation *f*; *(department → for rats)* service *m* de dératisation; *(→ for insects)* service de désinsectisation

pester ['pestə(r)] *vt* importuner, harceler; **to pester sb with questions** importuner *ou* assommer *ou* harceler qn de (ses) questions; **stop pestering your mother!** arrête d'embêter ta mère!; **they're always pestering me for money** ils sont toujours à me réclamer de l'argent; **the children pestered me to tell them a story** les enfants n'ont eu de cesse que je leur raconte une histoire; **he pestered me into buying him a computer** il m'a harcelé jusqu'à ce que je lui achète un ordinateur

pestering ['pestərɪŋ] *adj* importun

pesticidal [,pestɪ'saɪdəl] *adj* pesticide

pesticide ['pestɪsaɪd] *n* pesticide *m*

pestiferous [pe'stɪfərəs] *adj* (**a**) *Literary (unhealthy)* pestilentiel (**b**) *(pernicious → doctrine)* pernicieux (**c**) *Fam (annoying)* enquiquinant

pestilence ['pestɪləns] *n Literary* pestilence *f*

pestilent ['pestɪlənt] *adj Literary* (**a**) *(harmful, destructive)* nocif, nuisible (**b**) *(annoying)* agaçant

pestilential [,pestɪ'lenʃəl] *adj* (**a**) *Med* pestilentiel (**b**) *Literary (annoying)* agaçant

pestle ['pesəl] *n Culin* pilon *m*

pesto ['pestəʊ] *n Culin* pistou *m*

pestology [pes'tɒlədʒɪ] *n* étude *f* des insectes nuisibles

PET [pet] *n Med* (*abbr* **positron emission tomography**) tomographie *f* par émission de positrons

pet [pet] (*pt & pp* **petted**, *cont* **petting**) **1** *n* (**a**) *(animal)* animal *m* domestique *ou* familier *ou* de compagnie; **we don't keep pets** nous n'avons pas d'animaux à la maison; **he keeps a snake as a pet** il a un serpent apprivoisé; **sorry, no pets** *(sign, in advertisement)* les animaux ne sont pas admis

(**b**) *(favourite)* favori(ite) *m,f*, *Pej* chouchou(oute) *m,f*; **the teacher's pet** le (la) chouchou(oute) du prof

(**c**) *Fam (term of endearment)* chéri(e)❑ *m,f*; **how are you, pet?** comment ça va, mon chou?; **be a pet and close the door** tu seras un chou de fermer la porte; **she's a real pet** elle est adorable❑

(**d**) *Fam (temper)* crise *f* de colère❑; **to be in a pet** être de mauvais poil *ou* en rogne

2 *adj* (**a**) *(hawk, snake etc)* apprivoisé; **they have a pet budgerigar/hamster** ils ont une perruche/un hamster chez eux

(**b**) *Fam (favourite → project, theory)* favori❑; **it's my pet ambition to write a novel** ma grande ambition, c'est d'écrire un roman❑; **Lauren is the teacher's pet pupil** Lauren est la chouchoute du prof; **his pet subject** *or* **pet topic** son dada

3 *vt* (**a**) *(pamper)* chouchouter

(**b**) *(stroke → animal)* câliner, caresser

(**c**) *Fam (caress sexually)* caresser❑

4 *vi Fam (sexually)* se caresser❑

►► ***pet food*** aliments *mpl* pour animaux (domestiques); ***pet hate*** bête *f* noire; ***pet name*** surnom *m* affectueux; **her pet name for him was "honeybun"** elle l'appelait "honeybun"; *Am* ***pet peeve*** bête *f* noire; ***pet shop*** magasin *m* d'animaux domestiques, animalerie *f*; ***pet sitter*** garde *mf* d'animaux familiers

PETA ['petə] *n Am* (*abbr* **People for the Ethical Treatment of Animals**) = association américaine de défense des droits des animaux, opposée notamment à la vivisection

petal ['petəl] *n* (**a**) *(of flower)* pétale *m* (**b**) *Br Fam (term of affection)* mon chou; **thanks, petal** merci, mon chou

-petalled, *Am* **-petaled** ['petəld] *suff* **five-petalled** à cinq pétales; **large-petalled** à grands pétales

petard [pə'tɑːd] *n* pétard *m*; *Fig* **to be hoist with one's own petard** être pris à son propre piège

Pete [piːt] *pr n Fam* **for Pete's sake!** mais nom d'un chien!, mais bon sang!

petechia [pe'tiːkɪə] *n Med* pétéchie *f*

Peter ['piːtə(r)] *pr n* Pierre

►► ***Peter the Great*** Pierre le Grand; *Br Hist* ***Peter's Pence*** = impôt annuel (originellement d'un penny) payé en Angleterre par certains propriétaires au siège papal jusqu'à la Réforme; ***the Peter Principle*** le principe de Peter *(théorie humoristique selon laquelle tout employé finit par être promu à un poste au-dessus de ses compétences)*

'Peter and the Wolf' *Prokofiev* 'Pierre et le loup'

peter ['piːtə(r)] *n* (**a**) *Fam (safe)* coffiot *m* (**b**) *Am very Fam (penis)* quéquette *f*, zizi *m*

►**peter out** *vi* (**a**) *(run out → supplies, money)* s'épuiser; *(come to end → path)* se perdre; *(→ stream)* tarir; *(→ line)* s'estomper, s'évanouir; *(→ conversation)* tarir (**b**) *(die away → voice)* s'éteindre; *(→ fire)* s'éteindre, mourir (**c**) *(come to nothing → plan)* tomber à l'eau

peterman ['piːtəmæn] (*pl* **petermen** [-mən]) *n Fam Crime slang (safe-breaker)* perceur *m* de coffres-forts❑

Peter Pan *pr n* **he's a real Peter Pan** c'est un vrai gosse

►► ***Peter Pan collar*** col *m* Claudine

petersham ['piːtəʃəm] *n Tex* gros-grain *m*

Peters' projection *n (map)* projection *f* de Peters

pethidine ['peθɪdiːn] *n Pharm* péthidine *f*

petiole ['petɪəʊl] *n Bot* pétiole *m*

petit bourgeois ['petɪ-] (*pl* **petits bourgeois** ['petɪ-]) **1** *n* petit-bourgeois (petite-bourgeoise) *m,f*

2 *adj* petit-bourgeois

petite [pə'tiːt] **1** *adj (woman)* menue

2 *n (clothing size)* petites tailles *fpl (pour adultes)*

petit four [,petɪ'fɔː] (*pl* **petits fours** [,petɪ'fɔːz]) *n* petit-four

petition [pɪ'tɪʃən] **1** *n* (**a**) *(with signatures)* pétition *f*; **to hand in/sign a petition** remettre/signer une pétition; **they got up a petition against the council's plans** ils ont préparé une pétition pour protester contre les projets de la municipalité; **there were 5,000 signatures on the petition for his release** la pétition demandant sa libération a recueilli 5000 signatures

(**b**) *(request)* requête *f*; *Br Hist* **the Petition of Right** la Pétition de droit

(**c**) *Law* requête *f*, pétition *f*; **petition for divorce** demande *f* de divorce; **petition in bankruptcy** demande *f* de mise en liquidation judiciaire; **to file a petition in bankruptcy** déposer son bilan; **petition for mercy** recours *m* en grâce

(**d**) *Rel* prière *f*

2 *vt* (**a**) *(court, sovereign etc)* adresser une pétition à; **they petitioned the government for the release of** *or* **to release the political prisoners** ils ont adressé une pétition au gouvernement pour demander la libération des prisonniers politiques; **we are going to petition to have the wall demolished** nous allons demander que le mur soit démoli

(**b**) *Formal (beg)* **they petitioned the king to save them** ils ont imploré le roi de les sauver

(**c**) *Law* **to petition the court** déposer une requête auprès du tribunal

3 *vi* (**a**) *(with signatures)* faire signer une pétition; **they petitioned for his release** ils ont fait circuler une pétition demandant sa libération

(**b**) *(take measures)* **why don't you petition against the plan?** pourquoi n'engagez-vous pas un recours contre le projet?

(**c**) *Law* **to petition for divorce** faire une demande de divorce

THE PETITION OF RIGHT

Charles Ier, pressé par des besoins d'argent, fut forcé d'accepter cette pétition rédigée en 1628 par le Parlement anglais à l'encontre de l'autorité royale. Ce document devint un symbole de la limitation du pouvoir monarchique.

petitionary [pɪ'tɪʃənərɪ] *adj* de pétition

petitioner [pɪ'tɪʃənə(r)] *n* (**a**) *Law* pétitionnaire *mf*; *(in divorce)* demandeur(eresse) *m,f* de divorce (**b**) *(on petition)* signataire *mf* d'une/de la pétition

petit mal [,petɪ'mæl] *n Med* petit mal *m*

Petra ['petrə] *n* Pétra

Petrarch ['petrɑːk] *pr n* Pétrarque

petrel ['petrəl] *n Orn* pétrel *m*

Petri dish ['piːtrɪ-] *n* boîte *f* de Petri

petrifaction [,petrɪ'fækʃən] *n* (**a**) *(fossilization)* pétrification *f* (**b**) *(shock)* ébahissement *m*, *Literary* pétrification *f*

petrified ['petrɪfaɪd] *adj* (**a**) *(fossilized)* pétrifié (**b**) *(terrified)* paralysé *ou* pétrifié de peur; *(weaker use)* terrifié

►► ***petrified forest*** forêt *f* pétrifiée

petrify ['petrɪfaɪ] (*pt & pp* **petrified**) *vt* (**a**) *(fossilize)* pétrifier (**b**) *(terrify)* paralyser *ou* pétrifier de peur; *(weaker use)* terrifier; **the noise petrified me** le bruit me glaça le sang

petrifying ['petrɪfaɪɪŋ] *adj Fam (frightening)* paralysant

Petrine ['petriːn] *adj* pétrinien

petrochemical [,petrəʊ'kemɪkəl] **1** *adj (industry etc)* pétrochimique

2 petrochemicals *npl* produits *mpl* pétrochimiques

petrochemistry [,petrəʊ'kemɪstrɪ] *n* pétrochimie *f*

petrocurrency [,petrəʊ'kʌrənsɪ] (*pl* **petrocurrencies**) *n* devise *f* pétrolière, pétromonnaies *fpl*

petrodollar ['petrəʊ,dɒlə(r)] *n* pétrodollar *m*

petroglyph ['petrəʊglɪf] *n Geol* pétroglyphe *f*

Petrograd ['petrəgræd] *n* Petrograd

petrographer [pə'trɒgrəfə(r)] *n* pétrographe *mf*

petrographic [,petrəʊ'græfɪk], **petrographical** [,petrəʊ'græfɪkəl] *adj* pétrographique

petrography [pə'trɒgrəfɪ] *n* pétrographie *f*

petrol ['petrəl] *Br* **1** *n* essence *f*; **to fill up with petrol** faire le plein d'essence; **to run out of petrol** tomber en panne d'essence

2 *comp (fumes, rationing, shortage)* d'essence

►► ***petrol blue*** bleu *m* pétrole; ***petrol bomb***

per–pet

cocktail *m* Molotov; ***petrol bomber*** lanceur(-euse) *m,f* de cocktail Molotov; ***petrol can*** bidon *m* d'essence; ***petrol cap*** bouchon *m* d'essence; ***petrol coupon*** bon *m* d'essence; ***petrol engine*** moteur *m* à essence; ***petrol filler cap*** bouchon *m* d'essence; ***petrol filler pipe*** tuyau *m* de remplissage d'essence; ***petrol gauge*** jauge *f* à essence; ***petrol pump*** *(at service station)* pompe *f* à essence; **prices at the petrol pump have risen** le prix de l'essence à la pompe a augmenté; ***petrol station*** station-service *f*; *Aut* ***petrol tank*** réservoir *m* (d'essence); ***petrol tanker*** *(lorry)* camion-citerne *m*; *(ship)* pétrolier *m*, tanker *m*

petrolatum [ˌpetrəˈleɪtəm] *n Am* vaseline *f*

petrol-blue *adj Br* bleu pétrole *(inv)*

petrol-bomb *vt Br* attaquer au cocktail Molotov, lancer un cocktail Molotov contre *ou* sur; **the police station was petrol-bombed during the night** le commissariat a été attaqué à coups de cocktails Molotov pendant la nuit

petrol-driven *adj Br (engine)* à essence

petroleum [pɪˈtrəʊlɪəm] **1** *n* pétrole *m*
2 *comp (industry)* du pétrole, pétrolier; *(imports)* de pétrole
▸▸ *Br* ***petroleum jelly*** vaseline *f*

petrologic [ˌpetrəˈlɒdʒɪk], **petrological** [ˌpetrəˈlɒdʒɪkəl] *adj* pétrologique

petrology [peˈtrɒlədʒɪ] *n* pétrologie *f*

petrous [ˈpetrəs] *adj* pierreux

Petrushka [pəˈtruːʃkə] *pr n* Petrouchka

petticoat [ˈpetɪkəʊt] **1** *n (waist slip)* jupon *m*; *(full-length slip)* combinaison *f*
2 *comp Pej (government, politics)* de femmes
▸▸ ***Petticoat Lane*** = rue de Londres connue pour son marché du dimanche matin

pettifogger [ˈpetɪfɒgə(r)] *n Br* (**a**) *(quibbler)* chicaneur(euse) *m,f*, ergoteur(euse) *m,f* (**b**) *(lawyer)* avocat *m* marron

pettifogging [ˈpetɪfɒgɪŋ] *adj* (**a**) *(petty → person)* chicanier; *(→ details)* insignifiant (**b**) *(dishonest)* louche; **a pettifogging lawyer** un avocat marron

pettily [ˈpetɪlɪ] *adv* mesquinement, avec mesquinerie

pettiness [ˈpetɪnɪs] *n* (**a**) *(triviality → of details)* insignifiance *f*; *(→ of rules)* caractère *m* pointilleux (**b**) *(small-mindedness)* mesquinerie *f*, étroitesse *f* d'esprit

petting [ˈpetɪŋ] *n (UNCOUNT) Fam (sexual)* caresses □ *fpl*
▸▸ *Am* ***petting zoo*** = partie d'un zoo où les enfants peuvent s'approcher des animaux

pettish [ˈpetɪʃ] *adj Br (person)* grincheux, acariâtre; *(mood)* maussade; *(remark)* hargneux, désagréable

pettishly [ˈpetɪʃlɪ] *adv* avec humeur

petty [ˈpetɪ] *(compar* **pettier**, *superl* **pettiest**) *adj* (**a**) *Pej (trivial → detail)* insignifiant, mineur; *(→ difficulty)* mineur; *(→ question)* tatillon; *(→ regulation)* tracassier; *(→ ambitions)* médiocre
(**b**) *Pej (mean → behaviour, mind, spite)* mesquin
(**c**) *(minor, small-scale)* petit; **petty acts of vandalism** de petits actes *mpl* de vandalisme; **petty annoyances** tracasseries *fpl*, petits ennuis *mpl*
▸▸ ***petty bourgeois*** **1** *n* petit-bourgeois (petite-bourgeoise) *m,f* **2** *adj* petit-bourgeois; ***petty bourgeoisie*** petite bourgeoisie *f*; ***petty cash*** petite caisse *f*; **I took the money out of petty cash** j'ai pris l'argent dans la petite caisse; **they'll pay you back out of petty cash** ils vous rembourseront avec la petite caisse; ***petty cash book*** livre *m* de petite caisse; ***petty cash box*** petite caisse *f*; ***petty cash voucher*** bon *m* de petite caisse; ***petty crime*** actes *mpl* délictueux; ***petty expenses*** menues dépenses *fpl*; ***petty larceny*** larcin *m*; ***petty nobility*** petite noblesse *f*; ***petty offence*** infraction *f* mineure; ***petty official*** petit(e) fonctionnaire *mf*; *Br Naut* ***petty officer*** ≃ second maître *m*; ***petty sessions*** = en Angleterre, tribunal dépendant de la juridiction d'un juge de paix; ***petty thief*** petit(e) délinquant(e) *m,f*

petty-minded *adj* borné, mesquin

petty-mindedness [-ˈmaɪndɪdnɪs] *n* mesquinerie *f*

petulance [ˈpetjʊləns] *n* irritabilité *f*, mauvaise humeur *f*

petulant [ˈpetjʊlənt] *adj (bad-tempered → person)* irritable, acariâtre; *(→ remark)* acerbe, désagréable; *(→ behaviour)* désagréable, agressif; *(sulky)* maussade; **in a petulant mood** de mauvaise humeur

petulantly [ˈpetjʊləntlɪ] *adv (act, speak → irritably)* avec irritation; *(→ sulkily)* avec mauvaise humeur; **"no!" she said petulantly** "non!", dit-elle avec mauvaise humeur

petunia [pəˈtjuːnɪə] *n Bot* pétunia *m*

pew [pjuː] *n* banc *m* d'église; *Br Fam Hum* **take** *or* **have a pew!** pose-toi quelque-part!

pewit = **peewit**

pewter [ˈpjuːtə(r)] **1** *n* (**a**) *(metal)* étain *m* (**b**) *(UNCOUNT) (ware)* étains *mpl*, vaisselle *f* d'étain (**c**) *(colour)* gris étain *m*
2 *comp (tableware, tankard)* en étain
▸▸ ***pewter grey*** gris anthracite *m*

pewter-grey *adj* gris anthracite *(inv)*; **a pewter-grey sky** un ciel plombé

peyote [peɪˈəʊtɪ] *n* peyotl *m*

Pfc, PFC [ˌpiːefˈsiː] *n Am Mil (abbr* **private first class**) soldat *m* de première classe

pfennig [ˈfenɪg] *n* pfennig *m*

PFI [ˌpiːefˈaɪ] *n (abbr* **private finance initiative**) partenariat *m* public-privé

PFLP [ˌpiːefˌelˈpiː] *n (abbr* **Popular Front for the Liberation of Palestine**) FPLP *m*

PG [ˌpiːˈdʒiː] **1** *adj Cin (abbr* **parental guidance**) = désigne un film dont certaines scènes peuvent choquer, ≃ tous publics *(l'accord des parents étant souhaitable)*
2 *n Br (abbr* **paying guest**) pensionnaire *mf*

PGA [ˌpiːdʒiːˈeɪ] *n (abbr* **Professional Golfers Association**) PGA *f (association des golfeurs professionnels)*

PGCE [ˌpiːdʒiːˌsiːˈiː] *n Br Sch (abbr* **postgraduate certificate in education**) = diplôme d'enseignement

PGP [ˌpiːdʒiːˈpiː] *n Comput (abbr* **Pretty Good Privacy**) (logiciel *m* de chiffrement) PGP *m*

PH [ˌpiːˈeɪtʃ] *n Am Mil (abbr* **Purple Heart**) = médaille décernée aux blessés de guerre

pH [piːˈeɪtʃ] *n Chem* pH *m*; **a pH of 9** un pH de 9

PHA [ˌpiːeɪtʃˈeɪ] *n Am (abbr* **Public Housing Administration**) = services du logement social aux États-Unis

phacoid [ˈfækɔɪd] *adj* en forme de lentille

Phaedra [ˈfiːdrə] *pr n Myth* Phèdre
▸▸ *Psy* ***Phaedra complex*** complexe *m* de Phèdre

Phaëthon [ˈfeɪəθən] *pr n Myth* Phaéton

phaeton [ˈfeɪtən] *n* (**a**) *(carriage)* phaéton *m* (**b**) *Am Old-fashioned Aut* limousine *f* décapotable

phage [feɪdʒ] *n Biol* (bactério)phage *m*
▸▸ ***phage type*** lysotype *m*; ***phage typing*** lysotypie *f*; **enteric phage typing** lysotypie *f* entérique

phagocyte [ˈfægəsaɪt] *n Biol* phagocyte *m*

phagocytic [ˌfægəʊˈsɪtɪk] *adj Biol* phagocytaire

phagocytosis [ˌfægəsaɪˈtəʊsɪs] *n Biol* phagocytose *f*

phalange [ˈfælændʒ] *n Anat* phalange *f*

phalangeal [fəˈlændʒɪəl] *adj Anat* phalangien

phalanger [fəˈlændʒə(r)] *n Zool* phalanger *m*

Phalangist [fæˈlændʒɪst] **1** *adj* phalangiste
2 *n* phalangiste *mf*

phalanstery [ˈfælənstrɪ] *(pl* **phalansteries**) *n* phalanstère *m*

phalanx [ˈfælæŋks] *(pl* **phalanxes** *or* **phalanges** [-lændʒiːz]) *n* (**a**) *Antiq & Mil* phalange *f* (**b**) *Anat* phalange *f* (**c**) *Pol* phalange *f*

phalarope [ˈfælərəʊp] *n Orn* phalarope *m*

phallic [ˈfælɪk] *adj* phallique
▸▸ ***phallic symbol*** symbole *m* phallique

phallicism [ˈfælɪsɪzəm], **phallism** [ˈfælɪzəm] *n* phallisme *m*

phallocentric [ˌfæləʊˈsentrɪk] *adj* phallocentrique

phallocentrism [ˌfæləʊˈsentrɪzəm] *n* phallocentrisme *m*

phallus [ˈfæləs] *(pl* **phalluses** *or* **phalli** [-laɪ]) *n* phallus *m*

phantasm [ˈfæntæzəm] *n* fantasme *m*

phantasmagoria [ˌfæntæzməˈgɔːrɪə] *n* fantasmagorie *f*

phantasmagoric [ˌfæntæzməˈgɒrɪk], **phantasmagorical** [ˌfæntæzməˈgɒrɪkəl] *adj* fantasmagorique

phantasmal [fænˈtæzməl] *adj* fantomatique

phantasy = **fantasy**

phantom [ˈfæntəm] **1** *n* (**a**) *(ghost)* fantôme *m*, spectre *m* (**b**) *(threat, source of dread)* spectre *m* (**c**) *Literary (illusion)* illusion *f*
2 *adj* imaginaire, fantôme
▸▸ *Med* ***phantom limb*** membre *m* fantôme; *Br* ***phantom pregnancy*** grossesse *f* nerveuse; ***phantom ship*** vaisseau *m* fantôme

Pharaoh [ˈfeərəʊ] *n* pharaon *m*
▸▸ ***Pharaoh ant*** fourmi *f* de Pharaon

Pharaonic [feəˈrɒnɪk] *adj* pharaonien, pharaonique

pharisaic [ˌfærɪˈseɪk], **pharisaical** [ˌfærɪˈseɪkəl] *adj* pharisaïque

Pharisee [ˈfærɪsiː] *n* Pharisien(enne) *m,f*

pharmaceutical [ˌfɑːməˈsjuːtɪkəl] **1** *adj* pharmaceutique
2 *npl* **pharmaceuticals** *(medicines)* produits *mpl* pharmaceutiques, médicaments *mpl*; *(industry)* industrie *f* pharmaceutique
▸▸ ***pharmaceutical company*** société *f* pharmaceutique

pharmacist [ˈfɑːməsɪst] *n* pharmacien(enne) *m,f*

pharmacodynamic [ˌfɑːməkəʊdaɪˈnæmɪk] *adj* pharmacodynamique

pharmacodynamics [ˌfɑːməkəʊdaɪˈnæmɪks] *n (UNCOUNT)* pharmacodynamie *f*

pharmacogenetics [ˌfɑːməkəʊdʒɪˈnetɪks] *n (UNCOUNT)* pharmacogénétique *f*

pharmacognosy [ˌfɑːməˈkɒgnəsɪ] *n* pharmacognosie *f*

pharmacological [ˌfɑːməkəʊˈlɒdʒɪkəl] *adj* pharmacologique

pharmacologist [ˌfɑːməˈkɒlədʒɪst] *n* pharmacologiste *mf*, pharmacologue *mf*

pharmacology [ˌfɑːməˈkɒlədʒɪ] **1** *n* pharmacologie *f*
2 *comp (laboratory, studies)* de pharmacologie, pharmacologique

pharmacopoeia, *Am* **pharmacopeia** [ˌfɑːməkəʊˈpiːə] *n* pharmacopée *f*

pharmacotherapy [ˌfɑːməkəʊˈθerəpɪ] *n* pharmacothérapie *f*

pharmacy [ˈfɑːməsɪ] *(pl* **pharmacies**) *n* (**a**) *(science)* pharmacie *f* (**b**) *(dispensary, shop)* pharmacie *f*

pharyngal [fəˈrɪŋgəl], **pharyngeal** [ˌfærɪnˈdʒiːəl] *adj* (**a**) *Med (infection)* pharyngé; *(organ)* pharyngien (**b**) *Ling* pharyngal

pharyngitis [ˌfærɪnˈdʒaɪtɪs] *n (UNCOUNT)* pharyngite *f*; **to have pharyngitis** avoir une pharyngite

pharynx [ˈfærɪŋks] *(pl* **pharynxes** *or* **pharynges** [fæˈrɪndʒiːz]) *n* pharynx *m*

phase [feɪz] **1** *n* (**a**) *(period → gen)* phase *f*, période *f*; *(→ of illness)* phase *f*, stade *m*; *(→ of career, project)* étape *f*; *(→ of civilization)* période *f*; **the project is going through a critical phase** le projet traverse une phase critique; **it's still in the development phase** c'est encore en cours de développement; **the final phase of the election campaign** la dernière étape de la campagne électorale; **phase two of the government's incomes policy** la deuxième étape de la politique salariale du gouvernement; **phase two of the restoration project/rebuilding programme** la deuxième tranche des travaux de restauration/de reconstruction; **the investigation/trial has entered a new phase** l'enquête/le procès est désormais dans une nouvelle phase; **their daughter's going through a difficult phase** leur fille traverse une période difficile; **don't worry, it's just a phase she's going through** ne vous inquiétez pas, ça lui passera
(**b**) *Astron (of moon)* phase *f*
(**c**) *Chem, Elec & Phys* phase *f*; **in the solid phase** en phase *ou* à l'état solide; *also Fig* **to be in phase** être en phase; *also Fig* **to be out of phase** être déphasé; **the government is out of phase with the mood of the country** le gouvernement est en décalage complet avec les sentiments de la population
2 *vt* (**a**) *(changes, new methods)* introduire progressivement; *(project)* développer en phases successives; *(schedule, introduction of technology etc)* échelonner; **the closure of the plant will be phased over three years** la fermeture de l'usine se fera progressivement, sur trois ans

pet–pha

(**b**) *(synchronize)* synchroniser, faire coïncider; **the two operations have to be perfectly phased** les deux opérations doivent être parfaitement synchronisées

(**c**) *Am (prearrange → delivery, development)* planifier, programmer

(**d**) *Elec & Tech* mettre en phase

▸**phase in** *vt sep (new methods)* introduire progressivement *ou* par étapes; *(new systems, new equipment)* mettre progressivement en place; **the reforms will obviously have to be phased in** il est évident que les réformes devront être introduites progressivement; **the increases will be phased in over five years** les augmentations seront échelonnées sur cinq ans

▸**phase out** *vt sep (stop using → machinery, weapon)* cesser progressivement d'utiliser *(stop producing → car, model)* abandonner progressivement la production de; *(do away with → jobs, tax)* supprimer progressivement *ou* par étapes; *(→ grant)* retirer progressivement; **when the use of these pesticides has been phased out** quand ces pesticides auront cessé d'être utilisés; **the system is being phased out** ce système est en cours d'abandon

phased [feɪzd] *adj (withdrawal, development)* progressif, par étapes; *(evacuation)* progressif

phase-out *n* suppression *f* progressive

phasic ['feɪzɪk] *adj Elec* de phase

phasing ['feɪzɪŋ] *n*

▸▸ ***phasing in*** *(of new methods)* adoption *f ou* introduction *f* progressive; *(of new systems, new equipment)* mise *f* en place progressive; ***phasing out*** *(of old methods, systems, equipment etc)* abandon *m* progressif; *(of jobs)* suppression *f* progressive

phasmid ['fæzmɪd] *n Entom* phasmidé *m*

phat [fæt] *adj Am Fam* super, génial

phatic ['fætɪk] *adj* phatique

▸▸ ***phatic communicaton*** communication *f* phatique

PhD [ˌpiːeɪtʃ'diː] *n (abbr* **Doctor of Philosophy**) *(person)* = titulaire d'un doctorat de 3ème cycle; *(qualification)* = doctorat de 3ème cycle; **to have a PhD in Maths** avoir un doctorat en maths

▸▸ ***PhD student*** étudiant(e) *m,f* inscrit(e) en doctorat; ***PhD thesis*** thèse *f* de doctorat

pheasant ['fezənt] *(pl* **inv** *or* **pheasants**) *n* faisan *m*; *(hen)* (poule *f*) faisane *f*

▸▸ ***pheasant poult*** faisandeau *m*; ***pheasant shoot*** faisanderie *f*; ***pheasant shooting*** chasse *f* au faisan

pheasantry ['fezəntrɪ] *n* faisanderie *f*

phellem ['feləm] *n Bot* liège *m*

phenacetin [fə'næsɪtɪn] *n Pharm* phénacétine *f*

phencyclidine [ˌfen'saɪklɪdiːn] *n Chem* phencyclidine *f*

phenetics [fe'netɪks] *n (UNCOUNT) Biol* phénétique *f*

phenix *Am* = **phoenix**

phenobarbitone [ˌfiːnəʊ'bɑːbɪtəʊn], **phenobarbital** [ˌfiːnəʊ'bɑːbɪtəl] *n* phénobarbital *m*

phenocryst ['fiːnəkrɪst] *n Geol* phénocristal *m*

phenol ['fiːnɒl] *n Chem* phénol *m*

phenolic [fə'nɒlɪk] *adj Chem* phénolique

phenology [fə'nɒlədʒɪ] *n Met* phénologie *f*

phenolphthalein [ˌfiːnɒl'θeɪliːn] *n Chem* phénolphtaléine *f*

phenomena [fɪ'nɒmɪnə] *pl of* **phenomenon**

phenomenal [fɪ'nɒmɪnəl] *adj* phénoménal; **a phenomenal success** un immense succès

phenomenalism [fɪ'nɒmɪnəlɪzəm] *n Phil* phénoménalisme *m*, phénoménisme *m*

phenomenalist [fɪ'nɒmɪnəlɪst] *n Phil* phénoméniste *mf*

phenomenally [fɪ'nɒmɪnəlɪ] *adv* phénoménalement; **it's phenomenally expensive** ça coûte horriblement cher

phenomenological [fɪˌnɒmɪnə'lɒdʒɪkəl] *adj* phénoménologique

phenomenologist [fɪˌnɒmə'nɒlədʒɪst] *n* phénoménologue *mf*

phenomenology [fɪˌnɒmɪ'nɒlədʒɪ] *n* phénoménologie *f*

phenomenon [fɪ'nɒmɪnən] *(pl* **phenomena** [-nə]) *n* phénomène *m*; **the credit card phenomenon** le phénomène des cartes de crédit

phenothiazine [ˌfiːnəʊ'θaɪəziːn] *n Chem* thiodiphénylamine *f*, phénothiazine *f*

phenotype ['fiːnəʊtaɪp] *n Biol* phénotype *m*

phenotypic [ˌfiːnəʊ'tɪpɪk], **phenotypical** [ˌfiːnəʊ'tɪpɪkəl] *adj Biol* phénotypique

phenyl ['fiːnəl] *n Chem* phényle *m*

phenylalanine [ˌfenɪ'læləniːn] *n Chem* phénylalanine *f*

phenylketonuria [ˌfiːnɪlkiːtəʊ'njʊərɪə] *n Med* phénylcétonurie *f*

pheromone ['ferəməʊn] *n* phéromone *f*, phérormone *f*

phew [fjuː] *exclam (in relief)* ouf!; *(from heat)* pff!; *(in disgust)* berk!, beurk!

phial ['faɪəl] *n* fiole *f*

Phi Beta Kappa ['faɪˌbeɪtə'kæpə] *n* = aux États-Unis, association universitaire à laquelle ne peuvent appartenir que les étudiants émérites

Philadelphia [ˌfɪlə'delfɪə] *n* Philadelphie; **in Philadelphia** à Philadelphie

Philadelphian [ˌfɪlə'delfɪən] **1** *n* Philadelphien(-enne) *m,f*

2 *adj* philadelphien

philadelphus [ˌfɪlə'delfəs] *n Bot* philadelphus *m*; *(mock orange)* seringa *m*, seringat *m*

philander [fɪ'lændə(r)] *vi Pej* courir le jupon

philanderer [fɪ'lændərə(r)] *n Pej* coureur *m* (de jupons)

philandering [fɪ'lændərɪŋ] *Pej* **1** *n* **she had had enough of his philandering** elle en avait assez qu'il coure le jupon

2 *adj (ways, habits)* de coureur de jupon; **her philandering husband** son coureur de jupon de mari

philanthropic [ˌfɪlən'θrɒpɪk] *adj* philanthropique

philanthropically [ˌfɪlən'θrɒpɪklɪ] *adv* philanthropiquement, avec philanthropie

philanthropist [fɪ'lænθrəpɪst] *n* philanthrope *mf*

philanthropy [fɪ'lænθrəpɪ] *n* philanthropie *f*

philatelic [ˌfɪlə'telɪk] *adj* philatélique

philatelist [fɪ'lætəlɪst] *n* philatéliste *mf*

philately [fɪ'lætəlɪ] *n* philatélie *f*

-phile [faɪl] *suff* -phile; **Anglophile** anglophile *mf*; **Francophile** francophile *mf*

Philemon [fɪ'liːmɒn] *pr n Myth* Philémon

philharmonic [ˌfɪlɑː'mɒnɪk] **1** *adj* philharmonique

2 *n* orchestre *m* philharmonique

▸▸ ***philharmonic orchestra*** orchestre *m* philharmonique

philhellene [ˌfɪl'heliːn] **1** *n* philhellène *mf*

2 *adj* philhellène

philhellenic [ˌfɪlhe'liːnɪk] *adj* philhellène

philhellenism [ˌfɪl'helɪnɪzəm] *n* philhellénisme *m*

-philia ['fɪlɪə] *suff* -philie; **necrophilia** nécrophilie *f*; **anglophilia** anglophilie *f*

Philip ['fɪlɪp] *pr n Bible* Philippe

▸▸ ***Philip Augustus*** Philippe Auguste; ***Philip the Fair*** Philippe le Bel

Philippi ['fɪlɪpaɪ] *n* Philippes

Philippians [fɪ'lɪpɪənz] *npl Bible* **the Philippians** les Philippiens *mpl*

philippic [fɪ'lɪpɪk] *n* philippique *f*

Philippines ['fɪlɪpiːnz] *npl* **the Philippines** les Philippines *fpl*; **in the Philippines** aux Philippines

Philistine [*Br* 'fɪlɪstaɪn, *Am* 'fɪlɪstiːn] **1** *n* (**a**) *Hist* Philistin *m* (**b**) *Fig* béotien(enne) *m,f*

2 *adj* philistin

Philistinism ['fɪlɪstɪnɪzəm] *n* philistinisme *m*

Phillips® ['fɪlɪps] *n*

▸▸ ***Phillips® screw*** vis *f* cruciforme; ***Phillips® screwdriver*** tournevis *m* cruciforme

Philly ['fɪlɪ] *n Fam* = surnom donné à Philadelphie

philodendron [ˌfɪlə'dendrən] *(pl* **philodendrons** *or* **philodendra** [-drə]) *n Bot* philodendron *m*

philological [ˌfɪlə'lɒdʒɪkəl] *adj* philologique

philologically [ˌfɪlə'lɒdʒɪklɪ] *adv* philologiquement

philologist [fɪ'lɒlədʒɪst] *n* philologue *mf*

philology [fɪ'lɒlədʒɪ] *n* philologie *f*

philosopher [fɪ'lɒsəfə(r)] *n* philosophe *mf*; **she's a bit of a philosopher** elle est portée sur la philosophie; **the philosopher's stone** la pierre philosophale

philosophic [ˌfɪlə'sɒfɪk] *adj Phil* philosophique

philosophical [ˌfɪlə'sɒfɪkəl] *adj* (**a**) *Phil* philosophique (**b**) *(calm, resigned)* philosophe; **I feel quite philosophical about the situation** j'envisage la situation avec philosophie

philosophically [ˌfɪlə'sɒfɪklɪ] *adv* (**a**) *Phil* philosophiquement (**b**) *(calmly)* philosophiquement, avec philosophie

philosophize, -ise [fɪ'lɒsəfaɪz] *vi* philosopher; **to philosophize about sth** philosopher sur qch

philosophizing [fɪ'lɒsəfaɪzɪŋ] *n* réflexions *fpl* philosophiques; **that's enough philosophizing, we need to make a decision now!** assez philosophé, il faut se décider maintenant!

philosophy [fɪ'lɒsəfɪ] *(pl* **philosophies**) *n* philosophie *f*; **she's a philosophy student** elle est étudiante en philosophie; *Fig* **we share the same philosophy of life** nous avons la même conception de la vie; **she accepted the defeat with philosophy** elle accepta la défaite avec philosophie

philtre, *Am* **philter** ['fɪltə(r)] *n Literary* philtre *m*

phimosis [faɪ'məʊsɪs] *n Med* phimosis *m*

phiz [fɪz], **phizog** ['fɪzɒg] *n Br Fam Old-fashioned (face)* tronche *f*, poire *f*

phlebitis [flɪ'baɪtɪs] *n (UNCOUNT)* phlébite *f*

phlebography [flɪ'bɒgrəfɪ] *n Med* phlébographie *f*

phlebotomy [flɪ'bɒtəmɪ] *n Med* phlébotomie *f*

phlegm [flem] *n* (**a**) *Med (in respiratory passages)* glaire *f*; **to cough up phlegm** tousser gras (**b**) *Fig (composure)* flegme *m* (**c**) *Arch (bodily humour)* flegme *m*

phlegmatic [fleg'mætɪk] *adj* flegmatique

phlegmatically [fleg'mætɪklɪ] *adv* avec flegme, flegmatiquement

phlegmy ['flemɪ] *adj Med* flegmatique, pituiteux; **a phlegmy cough** une toux grasse

phloem ['fləʊem] *n Bot* phloème *m*

phlogiston [flɒ'dʒɪstən] *n Chem* phlogistique *m*

phlomis ['fləʊmɪs] *n Bot* phlomis *m*

phlox [flɒks] *n Bot* phlox *m inv*

phlyctena, phlyctaena [flɪk'tiːnə] *(pl* **phlyctenae, phlyctaenae** [-niː]) *n Med* phlyctène *f*, ampoule *f*

Phnom Penh [ˌnɒm'pen] *n* Phnom Penh

-phobe [fəʊb] *suff* -phobe; **xenophobe** xénophobe *mf*; **Anglophobe** anglophobe *mf*

phobia ['fəʊbɪə] *n* phobie *f*; **he has a phobia of spiders** il a la phobie des araignées; *Fam Fig* **she's got a phobia about work** elle est allergique au travail

-phobia ['fəʊbɪə] *suff* -phobie *f*; **claustrophobia** claustrophobie *f*; **xenophobia** xénophobie *f*

phobic ['fəʊbɪk] **1** *adj* phobique

2 *n* phobique *mf*

Phocaea [fəʊ'siːə] *n* Phocée

Phocaean [fəʊ'siːən] **1** *n* Phocéen(enne) *m,f*

2 *adj* phocéen

Phoebe ['fiːbɪ] *pr n Myth* Phébé

Phoebus ['fiːbəs] *pr n Myth* Phébus

Phoenicia [fɪ'nɪʃɪə] *n* Phénicie *f*

Phoenician [fɪ'nɪʃɪən] **1** *n* (**a**) *(person)* Phénicien(enne) *m,f* (**b**) *Ling* phénicien *m*

2 *adj* phénicien

phoenix, *Am* **phenix** ['fiːnɪks] *n* phénix *m*

phoenix-like 1 *adj* tel un phénix *(qui renaît de ses cendres)*

2 *adv* tel un phénix; **the new movement was born phoenix-like out of the old** le nouveau mouvement est né des cendres du précédent

phon [fɒn] *n (in acoustics)* phone *m*

phonate [fəʊ'neɪt] *vi* produire des sons

phonation [fəʊ'neɪʃən] *n* phonation *f*

phonatory ['fəʊnətrɪ] *adj* phonatoire

phone [fəʊn] **1** *n* (**a**) *(telephone)* téléphone *m*; **I answered the phone** j'ai répondu au téléphone; **just a minute, I'm on the phone** un instant, je suis au téléphone; **he was on the phone for an hour** il a passé une heure au téléphone; **we're not on the phone yet** nous n'avons pas encore le téléphone; **you're wanted on the phone** on vous demande au téléphone; **to get on the phone to sb** téléphoner à qn; **she told me the news by phone** elle m'a appris la nouvelle au téléphone; **I don't wish to discuss it over the phone** je préfère ne pas en parler au téléphone; *Fam* **to give sb a**

phone donner un coup de téléphone *ou* de fil à qn ❑; **get off the phone!** raccroche!
 (**b**) *Ling* phone *m*
 2 *comp (bill)* de téléphone; *(line, message)* téléphonique
 3 *vi Br* téléphoner; **to phone for a plumber/a taxi** appeler un plombier/un taxi *(par téléphone)*; **to phone home** téléphoner à la maison
 4 *vt Br* téléphoner à; **I'll phone him when I arrive** je lui téléphonerai à mon arrivée; **to phone Paris** téléphoner à Paris; **can you phone me the answer?** pouvez-vous me donner la réponse par téléphone?
 ►► ***phone book*** annuaire *m* (téléphonique); ***phone booth*** cabine *f* téléphonique; *Br* ***phone box*** cabine *f* téléphonique; **I'm calling from a phone box** j'appelle d'une cabine; ***phone call*** coup *m* de téléphone, appel *m* (téléphonique); ***phone number*** numéro *m* de téléphone; *Fam Comput* ***phone phreak*** pirate *m* du téléphone ❑; ***phone zap*** zapping *m (par un groupe de pression)*
►**phone up 1** *vt sep* téléphoner à
 2 *vi* téléphoner
-phone [fəʊn] *suff* -phone; **Anglophone** anglophone; **Francophone** francophone
phonecard ['fəʊnkɑːd] *n* Télécarte® *f*, carte *f* de téléphone
phone-in *n Rad & TV* **phone-in (programme)** = émission au cours de laquelle les auditeurs ou les téléspectateurs peuvent intervenir par téléphone
phoneme ['fəʊniːm] *n Ling* phonème *m*
phonemic [fə'niːmɪk] *adj Ling* phonémique, phonématique
phonemics [fə'niːmɪks] *n Ling (UNCOUNT)* phonémique *f*, phonématique *f*
phone-tapping *n (UNCOUNT)* écoute *f* téléphonique, écoutes *fpl* téléphoniques; **phone-tapping has become more widespread** la pratique de l'écoute téléphonique est de plus en plus répandue
phonetic [fə'netɪk] *adj* phonétique
 ►► ***phonetic alphabet*** alphabet *m* phonétique
phonetically [fə'netɪklɪ] *adv* phonétiquement
phonetician [,fəʊnɪ'tɪʃən] *n* phonéticien(enne) *m,f*
phonetics [fə'netɪks] *n (UNCOUNT)* phonétique *f*
phoney ['fəʊnɪ] *(compar* **phonier,** *superl* **phoniest,** *pl* **phonies)** *Fam* **1** *adj* (**a**) *(false → banknote, jewel, name)* faux (fausse) ❑; *(→ title, company, accent)* bidon; *(→ tears)* de crocodile; *(→ laughter)* qui sonne faux ❑; **his story sounds phoney** son histoire a tout l'air d'être (du) bidon; **the phoney war** la drôle de guerre
 (**b**) *(spurious → person)* bidon
 2 *n* (**a**) *(impostor)* imposteur ❑ *m*; *(charlatan)* charlatan ❑ *m*
 (**b**) *(pretentious person)* frimeur(euse) *m,f*, m'as-tu-vu *mf inv*
 (**c**) *(fake object)* faux ❑ *m*
phonic ['fəʊnɪk] *adj* phonique
phonics ['fəʊnɪks] *n (UNCOUNT) Sch* méthode *f* syllabique
 ►► ***phonics method*** méthode *f* syllabique
phonily ['fəʊnɪlɪ] *adv Fam* faussement ❑
phoniness ['fəʊnɪnɪs] *n Fam* fausseté ❑ *f*; **it was of obvious phoniness** c'était manifestement faux ❑
phonogram ['fəʊnəgræm] *n* phonogramme *m*
phonograph ['fəʊnəgrɑːf] *n* (**a**) *(early gramophone)* phonographe *m* (**b**) *Am Old-fashioned (record player)* tourne-disque *m*, électrophone *m*
phonographic [,fəʊnə'græfɪk] *adj* phonographique
phonolite ['fəʊnəlaɪt] *n Miner* phonolithe *f*, phonolite *f*
phonological [,fəʊnə'lɒdʒɪkəl] *adj* phonologique
phonologist [fə'nɒlədʒɪst] *n* phonologue *mf*
phonology [fə'nɒlədʒɪ] *(pl* **phonologies)** *n* phonologie *f*
phony = **phoney**
phooey ['fuːɪ] *exclam Fam (expressing irritation)* zut!, flûte!; *(expressing disbelief)* mon œil!
phormium ['fɔːmɪəm] *n Bot* phormium *m*, lin *m* de la Nouvelle-Zélande
phosgene ['fɒsdʒiːn] *n Chem* phosgène *m*
phosphate ['fɒsfeɪt] *n Agr & Chem* phosphate *m*; **contains no phosphates** *(on packaging)* sans phosphates
phosphatic [fɒs'fætɪk] *adj Chem* phosphatique, phosphaté
phosphatide ['fɒsfətaɪd] = **phospholipid**
phosphatize, -ise ['fɒsfətaɪz] *vt* (**a**) *(convert into phosphate)* convertir en phosphate (**b**) *(treat with phosphate → gen)* traiter au phosphate; *(→ soil)* phosphater
phosphene ['fɒsfiːn] *n* phosphène *m*
phosphide ['fɒsfaɪd] *n Chem* phosphure *m*
phosphine ['fɒsfiːn] *n* phosphine *f*, hydrogène *m* phosphoré
phosphite ['fɒsfaɪt] *n Chem* phosphite *m*
phospholipase [,fɒsfəʊ'lɪpeɪs] *n Biol & Chem* phospholipase *f*
phospholipid [,fɒsfəʊ'lɪpɪd] *n Biol & Chem* phospholipide *m*, phosphatide *m*
phosphor ['fɒsfə(r)] *n* luminophore *m*, phosphore *m (substance phosphorescente)*
phosphoresce [,fɒsfə'res] *vi* être phosphorescent
phosphorescence [,fɒsfə'resəns] *n* phosphorescence *f*
phosphorescent [,fɒsfə'resənt] *adj* phosphorescent
phosphoric [fɒs'fɒrɪk] *adj Chem* phosphorique
 ►► ***phosphoric acid*** acide *m* orthophosphorique
phosphorism ['fɒsfərɪzəm] *n Med* phosphorisme *m*
phosphorous ['fɒsfərəs] *adj Chem* phosphorique
phosphorus ['fɒsfərəs] *n Chem* phosphore *m*
phot [fɒt] *n* phot *m*
photic ['fəʊtɪk] *adj* photique
photo ['fəʊtəʊ] *(pl* **photos)** *n* photo *f*; **to take good photos** prendre de bonnes photos; **to take a good photo** *(be photogenic)* être photogénique; **it was a good photo opportunity** c'était une bonne occasion de se faire prendre en photo
 ►► ***photo album*** album *m* de photos; *Comput* ***photo CD*** CD-Photo *m*, Photo-CD *m*; *Comput* ***photo editing*** retouche *f* d'images; ***photo finish*** *Sport* arrivée *f* groupée; *Fig* partie *f* serrée; **the race was a photo finish** il a fallu départager les vainqueurs de la course avec la photo-finish; **the election is going to be a photo finish** pour les élections, la partie sera serrée; ***photo shoot*** séance *f* photos
photo- ['fəʊtəʊ] *pref* photo-
photoactive [,fəʊtəʊ'æktɪv] *adj (organism)* sensible à la lumière
photobiology [,fəʊtəʊbaɪ'ɒlədʒɪ] *n* photobiologie *f*
photobooth ['fəʊtəʊbuːð] *n* Photomaton®
photocall ['fəʊtəʊkɔːl] *n* séance *f* photo *(avec des photographes de presse)*
photocard ['fəʊtəʊkɑːd] *n* = carte portant une photo d'identité du titulaire
photocathode [,fəʊtəʊ'kæθəʊd] *n Chem* photocathode *f*
photocell ['fəʊtəʊsel] *n* cellule *f* photoélectrique
photochemical [,fəʊtəʊ'kemɪkəl] *adj* photochimique
photochemistry [,fəʊtəʊ'kemɪstrɪ] *n* photochimie *f*
photocompose [,fəʊtəʊkəm'pəʊz] *vt Typ* photocomposer
photocomposer ['fəʊtəʊ,kəm'pəʊzə(r)] *n Typ (person)* photocompositeur(trice) *m,f*
photocomposition ['fəʊtəʊ,kɒmpə'zɪʃən] *n Typ* photocomposition *f*
photocompositor ['fəʊtəʊ,kəm'pɒzɪtə(r)] *n Typ (machine)* photocomposeuse *f*
photoconductive ['fəʊtəʊ,kən'dʌktɪv] *adj Electron* photoconducteur
 ►► ***photoconductive cell*** cellule *f* photoconductrice; ***photoconductive effect*** photoconduction *f*, effet *m* photoélectrique interne
photoconductivity ['fəʊtəʊ,kɒndʌk'tɪvətɪ] *n Electron* photoconduction *f*
photoconductor [,fəʊtəʊkən'dʌktə(r)] *n Electron* photoconducteur *m*
photocopier ['fəʊtəʊ,kɒpɪə(r)] *n* photocopieur *m*, photocopieuse *f*
photocopy ['fəʊtəʊ,kɒpɪ] *(pl* **photocopies,** *pt & pp* **photocopied) 1** *n* photocopie *f*; **to take** *or* **make a photocopy of sth** faire une photocopie de qch, photocopier qch
 2 *vt* photocopier
photocopying ['fəʊtəʊ,kɒpɪɪŋ] *n (UNCOUNT)* reprographie *f*, photocopie *f*; **there's some photocopying to do** il y a des photocopies à faire
 ►► ***photocopying machine*** photocopieur *m*, photocopieuse *f*
photodegradable [,fəʊtəʊdiː'greɪdəbəl] *adj* photodégradable
photodiode [,fəʊtəʊ'daɪəʊd] *n Electron* photodiode *f*
photodisintegration ['fəʊtəʊdɪ,sɪntɪ'greɪʃən] *n Phys* photodésintégration *f*
photodissociation [,fəʊtəʊdɪsəʊsɪ'eɪʃən] *n Chem* photodissociation *f*
photodynamic [,fəʊtəʊdaɪ'næmɪk] *adj Biol* photodynamique
photodynamics [,fəʊtəʊdaɪ'næmɪks] *n (UNCOUNT) Biol* photodynamique *f*
photoelasticity [,fəʊtəʊɪlæ'stɪsətɪ] *n* photoélasticité *f*
photoelectric [,fəʊtəʊɪ'lektrɪk] *adj* photoélectrique
 ►► ***photoelectric cell*** cellule *f* photoélectrique; ***photoelectric effect*** effet *m* photoélectrique; ***photoelectric resistor*** photorésistance *f*
photoelectricity [,fəʊtəʊɪlek'trɪsətɪ] *n* photoélectricité *f*
photoelectron [,fəʊtəʊɪ'lektrɒn] *n Phys* photoélectron *m*
photoemission [,fəʊtəʊɪ'mɪʃən] *n* photoémission *f*
photoengraving [,fəʊtəʊɪn'greɪvɪŋ] *n* photogravure *f*
Photofit® ['fəʊtəʊfɪt] *n (picture)* photo-robot *f*, portrait-robot *m*
 ►► ***Photofit***® ***picture*** photo-robot *f*, portrait-robot *m*
photoflood ['fəʊtəʊflʌd] *n (lamp)* lampe *f* flood
 ►► ***photoflood lamp*** lampe *f* flood
photofluorography [,fəʊtəʊflʊə'rɒgrəfɪ] *n* radiophotographie *f*
photogenic [,fəʊtəʊ'dʒenɪk] *adj* (**a**) *(person)* photogénique (**b**) *Biol* photogène
photogeology [,fəʊtəʊdʒɪ'ɒlədʒɪ] *n* photogéologie *f*
photogram ['fəʊtəʊgræm] *n* photogramme *m*
photogrammetry [,fəʊtəʊ'græmətrɪ] *n* photogrammétrie *f*
photograph ['fəʊtəgrɑːf] **1** *n* photographie *f* *(image)*, photo *f (image)*; **to take a photograph** prendre *ou* faire une photo; **to take a photograph of sb** prendre qn en photo, photographier qn; **they took our photograph** ils nous ont pris en photo; **to have one's photograph taken** se faire photographier; **I'm in this photograph** je suis sur cette photo; **we took a lot of good photographs on holiday** nous avons pris *ou* fait beaucoup de bonnes photos pendant les vacances; **she takes a good photograph** *(is photogenic)* elle est photogénique
 2 *vt* photographier, prendre en photo; **she doesn't like being photographed** elle n'aime pas qu'on la prenne en photo
 3 *vi* **he photographs well** *(is photogenic)* il est photogénique; **the trees won't photograph well in this light** il n'y a pas assez de lumière pour faire une bonne photo des arbres
 ►► ***photograph album*** album *m* de photos
photographer [fə'tɒgrəfə(r)] *n* photographe *mf*; **I'm not much of a photographer** je ne suis pas très doué pour la photographie
photographic [,fəʊtəʊ'græfɪk] *adj* photographique; **to have a photographic memory** avoir une bonne mémoire visuelle
 ►► ***photographic library*** photothèque *f*; ***photographic shop*** magasin *m* de photo; ***photographic society*** club *m* d'amateurs de photo
photographically [,fəʊtəʊ'græfɪklɪ] *adv* photographiquement
photography [fə'tɒgrəfɪ] *n* photographie *f (art)*, photo *f (art)*; **an exhibition of French photography** une exposition de photographie française
photogravure [,fəʊtəʊgrə'vjʊə(r)] *n* photogravure *f*

pho–pho

photojournalism [ˌfəʊtəʊ'dʒɜːnəlɪzəm] *n* photojournalisme *m*

photojournalist [ˌfəʊtəʊ'dʒɜːnəlɪst] *n* reporter *m* photographe, photojournaliste *mf*

photokinesis [ˌfəʊtəʊkɪ'niːsɪs] *n Biol* photocinèse *f*

photolithograph [ˌfəʊtəʊ'lɪθəgrɑːf] *n* photolithographie *f (image)*

photolithography [ˌfəʊtəʊlɪ'θɒgrəfɪ] *n* photolithographie *f (art)*

photoluminescence ['fəʊtəʊˌluːmɪ'nesəns] *n* photoluminescence *f*

photoluminescent ['fəʊtəʊˌluːmɪ'nesənt] *adj* photoluminescent

photolysis [fəʊ'tɒlɪsɪs] *n Chem* photolyse *f*

photomap ['fəʊtəʊmæp] (*pt & pp* **photomapped,** *cont* **photomapping**) **1** *n* photocarte *f*

2 *vt* faire une photocarte de

photomechanical [ˌfəʊtəʊmɪ'kænɪkəl] *adj Typ* photomécanique

photometer [fəʊ'tɒmɪtə(r)] *n* photomètre *m*

photometric [ˌfəʊtəʊ'metrɪk] *adj* photométrique

photometry [fəʊ'tɒmɪtrɪ] *n* photométrie *f*

photomicrograph [ˌfəʊtəʊ'maɪkrəʊgræf] *n* photomicrographie *f*

photomicrographic [ˌfəʊtəʊmaɪkrəʊ'græfɪk] *adj* photomicrographique

photomicrography [ˌfəʊtəʊmaɪ'krɒgrəfɪ] *n* photomicrographie *f*

photomontage [ˌfəʊtəʊ'mɒntɑːʒ] *n* photomontage *m*

photomultiplier [ˌfəʊtəʊ'mʌltɪplaɪə(r)] *n* photomultiplicateur *m*

photon ['fəʊtɒn] *n Phys* photon *m*

photonovel ['fəʊtəʊˌnɒvəl] *n* roman-photo *m*, photo-roman *m*

photo-offset *n* offset *m*

photoperiod [ˌfəʊtəʊ'pɪərɪəd] *n Biol* photopériode *f*

photoperiodic ['fəʊtəʊˌpɪərɪ'ɒdɪk] *adj Biol* photopériodique

photoperiodism [ˌfəʊtəʊ'pɪərɪədɪzəm] *n Biol* photopériodisme *m*

photophily [fəʊ'tɒfɪlɪ] *n* photophilie *f*

photophobia [ˌfəʊtəʊ'fəʊbɪə] *n* photophobie *f*

photophobic [ˌfəʊtəʊ'fəʊbɪk] *adj* photophobique

photophore [ˌfəʊtəʊ'fɔː(r)] *n Zool* (organe *m*) photophore *m*

photopolymer [ˌfəʊtəʊ'pɒlɪmə(r)] *n* plastique *m* photopolymère

photorealism [ˌfəʊtəʊ'rɪəlɪzəm] *n* photoréalisme *m*

photoreceptor [ˌfəʊtəʊrɪ'septə(r)] *n* photorécepteur *m*

photoreconnaissance [ˌfəʊtəʊrɪ'kɒnɪsəns] *n* reconnaissance *f* photographique

photosensitive [ˌfəʊtəʊ'sensɪtɪv] *adj* photosensible

photosensitivity ['fəʊtəʊˌsensɪ'tɪvətɪ] *n* photosensibilité *f*

photosensitize, -ise [ˌfəʊtəʊ'sensɪtaɪz] *vt* rendre photosensible

photoset ['fəʊtəʊset] (*pt & pp* **photoset,** *cont* **photosetting**) *vt* photocomposer

photosetter ['fəʊtəʊˌsetə(r)] *n Br* photocomposeuse *f*, photocompositeur *m*

photosetting ['fəʊtəʊˌsetɪŋ] *n Br* photocomposition *f*

►► ***photosetting machine*** photocomposeuse *f*

photosphere ['fəʊtəʊsfɪə(r)] *n Astron* photosphère *f*

photostat ['fəʊtəʊstæt] (*pt & pp* **photostatted,** *cont* **photostatting**) **1** *vt* photocopier

2 Photostat® *n* photocopie *f*

►► ***photostat copy*** photocopie *f*; ***photostat machine*** photocopieuse *f*

photo-story *n* roman-photo *m*

photosynthesis [ˌfəʊtəʊ'sɪnθəsɪs] *n Biol* photosynthèse *f*

photosynthesize, -ise [ˌfəʊtəʊ'sɪnθəsaɪz] *vt Biol* fabriquer par photosynthèse

photosynthetic [ˌfəʊtəʊsɪn'θetɪk] *adj Biol* photosynthétique

phototaxis [ˌfəʊtəʊ'tæksɪs], **phototaxy** [ˌfəʊtəʊ'tæksɪ] *n Biol* phototaxie *f*

phototherapy [ˌfəʊtəʊ'θerəpɪ] *n Med* photothérapie *f*

phototransistor [ˌfəʊtəʊtræn'zɪstə(r)] *n* phototransistor *m*

phototropism [ˌfəʊtəʊ'trəʊpɪzəm] *n Biol* phototropisme *m*

phototype ['fəʊtəʊtaɪp] *Typ* **1** *n* (**a**) *(process)* phototypie *f* (**b**) *(print)* phototype *m*

2 *vt* faire un phototype de

phototypesetter [ˌfəʊtəʊ'taɪpsetə(r)] *n* photocompositeur *m*

phototypesetting [ˌfəʊtəʊ'taɪpsetɪŋ] *n* photocomposition *f*

phototypography [ˌfəʊtəʊtaɪ'pɒgrəfɪ] *n* photocomposition *f*

photovoltaic [ˌfəʊtəʊvɒl'teɪɪk] *adj* photovoltaïque

►► ***photovoltaic cell*** cellule *f* photovoltaïque, photopile *f*; ***photovoltaic effect*** effet *m* photovoltaïque

phrasal ['freɪzəl] *adj Gram*

►► ***phrasal conjunction*** locution *f* conjonctive; ***phrasal preposition*** locution *f* prépositive; ***phrasal verb*** verbe *m* à particule

phrase [freɪz] **1** *n* (**a**) *(expression)* expression *f*, locution *f*; **I can't find the right phrase** je ne trouve pas l'expression que je cherche

(**b**) *Ling* syntagme *m*, groupe *m*

(**c**) *Mus* phrase *f*

2 *vt* (**a**) *(letter)* rédiger, tourner; *(idea)* exprimer, tourner; **couldn't you phrase it differently?** ne pourriez-vous pas trouver une autre formule?; **how shall I phrase it?** comment dire ça?; **he phrased it very elegantly** il a trouvé une tournure très élégante (pour le dire)

(**b**) *Mus* phraser

►► *Ling* ***phrase marker*** indicateur *m* syntagmatique; *Ling* ***phrase structure*** structure *f* syntagmatique; *Ling* ***phrase structure grammar*** grammaire *f* syntagmatique; *Ling* ***phrase structure rules*** règles *fpl* syntagmatiques

phrasebook ['freɪzbʊk] *n* guide *m* de conversation

phraseogram ['freɪzɪəʊgræm] *n* sténogramme *m* *(qui représente une locution ou un groupe de mots)*

phraseology [ˌfreɪzɪ'ɒlədʒɪ] (*pl* **phraseologies**) *n* phraséologie *f*

phrasing ['freɪzɪŋ] *n* (**a**) *(expressing)* choix *m* des mots; **with careful phrasing** en choisissant ses mots avec le plus grand soin *ou* soigneusement ses mots; **the phrasing of her refusal was very elegant** son refus était formulé de manière très élégante (**b**) *Mus* phrasé *m*

phreaker ['friːkə(r)] *n Fam Comput* pirate *m* du téléphone ❑

phreatic [frɪ'ætɪk] *adj Geog* phréatique

►► ***phreatic layer*** nappe *f* phréatique

phrenetic = **frenetic**

phrenic ['frenɪk] *adj Anat* phrénique

►► ***phrenic nerve*** nerf *m* phrénique

phrenological [ˌfrenə'lɒdʒɪkəl] *adj* phrénologique

phrenologist [frɪ'nɒlədʒɪst] *n* phrénologue *mf*, phrénologiste *mf*

phrenology [frɪ'nɒlədʒɪ] *n* phrénologie *f*

Phrygia ['frɪdʒɪə] *n* Phrygie *f*

Phrygian ['frɪdʒɪən] **1** *n* Phrygien(enne) *m,f*

2 *adj* phrygien

►► ***Phrygian cap*** bonnet *m* phrygien

phthiriasis [θɪ'raɪəsɪs] *n Med* phtiriase *f*, maladie *f* pédiculaire

phthisis ['θaɪsɪs] *n (UNCOUNT) Old-fashioned* phtisie *f*

phut [fʌt] *Fam* **1** *n* **the engine made a phut and stopped** le moteur eut un hoquet puis s'arrêta

2 *adv* **to go phut** *(break down)* rendre l'âme, lâcher

phycocyanin [ˌfaɪkəʊ'saɪənɪn] *n* cyanophycée *f*

phycology [faɪ'kɒlədʒɪ] *n* phycologie *f*, algologie *f*

phycomycete [ˌfaɪkəʊ'maɪsiːt] *n Biol* phycomycète *m*

phylactery [fɪ'læktərɪ] (*pl* **phylacteries**) *n Rel* phylactère *m*

phyletic [faɪ'letɪk] *adj Biol* phylétique

phyllite ['fɪlaɪt] *n Geol* phyllite *f*.

phylloclade ['fɪləʊkleɪd] *n Bot* phylloclade *m*

phyllode ['fɪləʊd] *n Bot* phyllode *f*

phyllomania [ˌfɪləʊ'meɪnɪə] *n Bot* = production excessive de feuilles

phylloquinone [ˌfɪləʊkwɪ'nəʊn] *n Biol & Chem* phylloquinone *f*

phyllotaxis [ˌfɪləʊ'tæksɪs] *n Bot* phyllotaxie *f*

phylloxera [fɪ'lɒksərə] *n Entom* phylloxéra *m*, phylloxera *m*

phylogenesis [ˌfaɪləʊ'dʒenɪsɪs] (*pl* **phylogeneses** [-ˌsiːz]) *n Biol* phylogenèse *f*, phylogénie *f*

phylogenetic [ˌfaɪləʊdʒə'netɪk] *adj Biol* phylogénétique

phylogeny [faɪ'lɒdʒənɪ] (*pl* **phylogenies**) *n Biol* phylogenèse *f*, phylogénie *f*

phylum ['faɪləm] (*pl* **phyla** [-lə]) *n* phylum *m*

Phys Ed ['fɪzˌed] *n Am* (*abbr* **physical education**) éducation *f* physique

physiatrics [ˌfɪzɪ'ætrɪks] *n (UNCOUNT) Am* kinésithérapie *f*

physiatrist [ˌfɪzɪ'ætrɪst] *n Am* kinésithérapeute *mf*

physic ['fɪzɪk] *n Arch* médicament *m*, remède *m*

physical ['fɪzɪkəl] **1** *adj* (**a**) *(bodily)* physique; **a physical examination** un examen médical, une visite médicale; **I don't get enough physical exercise** je ne fais pas assez d'exercice (physique); **rugby is a very physical sport** le rugby est un sport dans lequel il y a beaucoup de contacts physiques; **it was a very physical match** ce fut un match très physique; **it left him a physical wreck** ça lui a détruit la santé

(**b**) *(natural, material → forces, property, presence)* physique; *(→ manifestation, universe)* physique, matériel; **it's a physical impossibility** c'est physiquement *ou* matériellement impossible

(**c**) *Chem & Phys* physique

(**d**) *Geog* physique; **the physical features of the desert** la topographie du désert

2 *n* visite *f* médicale; **to go for a physical** passer une visite médicale

►► ***physical abuse*** sévices *mpl*; ***physical access control*** contrôle *m* d'accès physique; ***physical anthropology*** anthropologie *f* physique; *Fin* ***physical assets*** immobilisations *fpl* non financières; *Fin* ***physical capital*** capital *m* existant; ***physical chemistry*** chimie *f* physique; *Comput* ***physical disk cache*** cache *m* disque physique; *Mktg* ***physical distribution*** distribution *f* physique; *Mktg* ***physical distribution management*** gestion *f* de la distribution physique; ***physical education*** éducation *f* physique; ***physical fitness*** (bonne) forme *f* physique; ***physical geography*** géographie *f* physique; ***physical handicap*** infirmité *f*; *Com* ***physical inventory*** inventaire *m* effectif; *Br Fam Old-fashioned* ***physical jerks*** mouvements *mpl* de gym ❑; **to do physical jerks** faire des mouvements de gym; ***physical presence*** présence *f* physique; ***physical property*** propriété *f* physique; ***physical sciences*** sciences *fpl* physiques; ***physical strength*** force *f* physique; ***physical therapist*** kinésithérapeute *mf*; ***physical therapy*** kinésithérapie *f*; *(after accident or illness)* rééducation *f*; ***physical training*** éducation *f* physique

physicalism ['fɪzɪkəlɪzəm] *n Phil* physicalisme *m*

physicality [ˌfɪzɪ'kælɪtɪ] *n* (**a**) *(physical quality)* caractère *m* physique (**b**) *(bodily functions)* **her disgust with physicality** le dégoût qu'elle éprouve pour tout ce qui a trait au corps

physically ['fɪzɪklɪ] *adv* physiquement; **to be physically fit** être en bonne forme physique; **she is physically handicapped** elle a un handicap physique; *Euph* **physically challenged** = terme politiquement correct qui désigne les handicapés physiques

physician [fɪ'zɪʃən] *n* médecin *m*

physicism ['fɪzɪsɪzəm] *n* physicisme *m*

physicist ['fɪzɪsɪst] *n* physicien(enne) *m,f*

physicochemical [ˌfɪzɪkəʊ'kemɪkəl] *adj* physico-chimique

physics ['fɪzɪks] *n (UNCOUNT)* physique *f*

physio ['fɪzɪəʊ] (*pl sense* (**b**) **physios**) *n Fam* (**a**) (*abbr* **physiotherapy**) kiné *f* (**b**) (*abbr* **physiotherapist**) kiné *mf*

physio- ['fɪzɪəʊ] *pref* physio-

physiocracy [ˌfɪzɪ'ɒkrəsɪ] *n Hist & Econ* physiocratie *f*

physiocrat ['fɪzɪəʊkræt] *n Hist & Econ* physiocrate *m*

physiognomic [ˌfɪzɪəʊ'nɒmɪk], **physiognomical** [ˌfɪzɪəʊ'nɒmɪkəl] *adj* morphopsychologique

pho–phy

physiognomist [ˌfɪzɪˈɒnəmɪst] *n* adepte *mf* de la morphopsychologie

physiognomy [ˌfɪzɪˈɒnəmɪ] (*pl* **physiognomies**) *n* (**a**) *(facial features)* physionomie *f* (**b**) *(art of judging character)* morphopsychologie *f* (**c**) *Geog* topographie *f*, configuration *f*; **the physiognomy of London is changing** la physionomie de Londres est en train de changer

physiographical [ˌfɪzɪəʊˈgræfɪkəl] *adj* physiographique

physiography [ˌfɪzɪˈɒgrəfɪ] *n* physiographie *f*

physiological [ˌfɪzɪəʊˈlɒdʒɪkəl] *adj* physiologique

physiologically [ˌfɪzɪəˈlɒdʒɪklɪ] *adv* physiologiquement

physiologist [ˌfɪzɪˈɒlədʒɪst] *n* physiologiste *mf*

physiology [ˌfɪzɪˈɒlədʒɪ] *n* physiologie *f*

physiopathology [ˌfɪzɪəʊpəˈθɒlədʒɪ] *n* physiopathologie *f*

physiotherapist [ˌfɪzɪəʊˈθerəpɪst] *n* kinésithérapeute *mf*

physiotherapy [ˌfɪzɪəʊˈθerəpɪ] *n* kinésithérapie *f*; *(after accident or illness)* rééducation *f*; **to go for** *or* **to have physiotherapy** faire des séances de kinésithérapie

physique [fɪˈziːk] *n* constitution *f* physique, physique *m*; **to have a fine physique** avoir un beau corps; **to have a poor physique** être chétif; **he hasn't the physique for it** il n'a pas le physique de l'emploi

physostigmine [ˌfaɪsəʊˈstɪgmaɪn] *n Chem* physostigmine *f*

phytochemical [ˌfaɪtəʊˈkemɪkəl] **1** *n* produit *m* phytochimique

2 *adj* phytochimique

phytochemistry [ˌfaɪtəʊˈkemɪstrɪ] *n* phytochimie *f*

phytogenesis [ˌfaɪtəʊˈdʒenɪsɪs], **phytogeny** [faɪˈtɒdʒənɪ] *n* phytogenèse *f*

phytogeographic [ˌfaɪtəʊdʒiːəˈgræfɪk], **phytogeographical** [ˌfaɪtəʊdʒiːəˈgræfɪkəl] *adj* phytogéographique

phytogeography [ˌfaɪtəʊdʒɪˈɒgrəfɪ] *n* phytogéographie *f*

phytohormone [ˌfaɪtəʊˈhɔːməʊn] *n* phytohormone *f*

phytopathology [ˌfaɪtəʊpəˈθɒlədʒɪ] *n* phytopathologie *f*

phytoplankton [ˌfaɪtəˈplæŋktən] *n* phytoplancton *m*

PI [ˌpiːˈaɪ] *n Am* (*abbr* **private investigator**) détective *m* privé

pi [paɪ] **1** *n Math* pi *m*

2 *adj Br Fam Pej* (**a**) *(pious)* bigot □ (**b**) *(self-satisfied)* suffisant □

PIA [ˌpiːaɪˈeɪ] *n Br Fin* (*abbr* **personal investment authority**) = organisme chargé de surveiller les activités des conseillers financiers indépendants et de protéger les petits investisseurs

Piacenza [pjəˈtʃentsə] *n* Plaisance

piacular [ˌpaɪˈækjʊlə(r)] *adj Literary* (**a**) *(making expiation)* piaculaire, expiatoire (**b**) *(requiring expiation)* qui demande une expiation

piaffe [pɪˈæf] *vi* piaffer

pia mater [ˈpaɪəˈmeɪtə(r)] *n Anat* pie-mère *f*

pianissimo [ˌpɪəˈnɪsɪməʊ] **1** *n* pianissimo *m*

2 *adv* pianissimo

pianist [ˈpɪənɪst] *n* pianiste *mf*

piano[1] [pɪˈænəʊ] (*pl* **pianos**) **1** *n* piano *m*

2 *comp (duet, lesson, stool, teacher, tuner)* de piano; *(music)* pour piano; *(lid, leg)* du piano

►► ***piano accordion*** accordéon *m* (à touches); ***piano concerto*** concerto *m* pour piano; ***piano key*** touche *f*; **the piano keys** le clavier (du piano); ***piano organ*** piano *m* mécanique; ***piano player*** pianiste *mf*; ***piano roll*** bande *f* perforée *(pour piano mécanique)*

'The Piano' *Campion* 'La Leçon de piano'

piano[2] [ˈpjɑːnəʊ] *Mus* **1** *adj* piano *(inv)*

2 *adv* piano

pianoforte [pɪˌænəʊˈfɔːtɪ] *n Formal* pianoforte *m*

Pianola® [ˌpɪəˈnəʊlə] *n* Pianola® *m*

piassaba [pɪəˈsɑːbə], **piassava** [pɪəˈsɑːvə] *n* piassava *m*

piastre [pɪˈæstə(r)] *n* piastre *f*

piazza [pɪˈætsə] *n* (**a**) *(square)* place *f*, piazza *f* (**b**) *Br (gallery)* galerie *f* (**c**) *Am (veranda)* véranda *f*

PIBOR [ˈpaɪbɔː(r)] *n* (*abbr* **Paris Interbank Offered Rate**) TIOP *m*, PIBOR *m*

pibroch [ˈpiːbrɒχ] *n Mus* pibroch *m*, pibrock *m* *(air de cornemuse)*

pic [pɪk] (*pl* **pics** *or* **pix** [pɪks]) *n Fam (photograph)* photo □ *f*; *(picture)* illustration □ *f*; *(film)* film □ *m*

pica [ˈpaɪkə] *n* (**a**) *Typ (unit)* pica *m* (**b**) *(on typewriter)* pica *m* (**c**) *Med* pica *m*

picador [ˈpɪkədɔː(r)] *n* picador *m*

picaninny (*pl* **picaninnies**) = **piccaninny**

Picardy [ˈpɪkədɪ] *n* Picardie *f*; **in Picardy** en Picardie

picaresque [ˌpɪkəˈresk] *adj* picaresque

picaroon [pɪkəˈruːn] *n Arch* (**a**) *(rogue)* brigand *m* (**b**) *(pirate)* pirate *m*, corsaire *m*

picayune [ˌpɪkəˈjuːn] *Am Fam* **1** *adj (unimportant)* insignifiant □; *(worthless)* sans valeur □

2 *n* pièce *f* de cinq cents □; **I don't care a picayune** je m'en fiche royalement

Piccadilly Circus [ˌpɪkəˈdɪlɪ-] *n* Piccadilly Circus; *Br Fam* **it's like Piccadilly Circus in here!** que de va-et-vient!

piccalilli [ˌpɪkəˈlɪlɪ] *n* piccalilli *m* *(pickles à la moutarde)*

piccaninny [ˌpɪkəˈnɪnɪ] (*pl* **piccaninnies**) *n Fam* négrillon(onne) *m,f*, = terme raciste désignant un enfant noir

piccolo [ˈpɪkələʊ] (*pl* **piccolos**) *n* piccolo *m*, picolo *m*

piccy [ˈpɪkɪ] (*pl* **piccies**) *n Br Fam (photograph)* photo □ *f*

pichurim [ˈpɪtʃʊrɪm] *n Bot* pichurim *m*

PICK [pɪk]

choisir	► 1 (a); 2
cueillir	► 1 (b)
enlever	► 1 (c)
gratter	► 1 (d)
crocheter	► 1 (f)
pincer	► 1 (g)
choix	► 3 (a)
meilleur	► 3 (b)
pic	► 3 (c)

1 *vt* (**a**) *(select)* choisir; **he always picks the most expensive dish** il choisit toujours le plat le plus cher; **to pick one's words (carefully)** (bien) choisir ses mots; **she's been picked for the England team** elle a été sélectionnée pour l'équipe d'Angleterre; **to pick a team** former une équipe; **to pick a winner** *(in racing)* choisir un cheval gagnant; *Fig* **we've certainly picked a winner in Paul Rodger** nous avons vraiment tiré le bon numéro avec Paul Rodger; *Ironic* **you really (know how to) pick them!** tu les choisis bien!; *Ironic* **you picked a fine time to tell me** tu as bien choisi ton moment pour me le dire

(**b**) *(gather → fruit, flowers)* cueillir; *(→ mushrooms)* ramasser; **to pick cherries/grapes** *(for pleasure)* cueillir des cerises/du raisin; *(as job)* faire la cueillette des cerises/les vendanges; **pick your own** *(sign)* cueillette à la ferme

(**c**) *(remove)* enlever; **I had to pick the cat hairs off my dress** il a fallu que j'enlève les poils de chat de ma robe

(**d**) *(poke at → spot, scab)* gratter; **to pick one's nose** se mettre les doigts dans le nez; **to pick one's teeth** se curer les dents; **they picked the bones clean** ils n'ont rien laissé sur les os; **she picked a hole in her jumper** elle a fait un trou à son pull en tirant sur la laine

(**e**) *(walk carefully)* **they picked their way along the narrow ridge** ils avancèrent prudemment le long de la crête étroite; **he picked his way through the crowd** il se fraya un chemin à travers la foule

(**f**) *(lock)* crocheter

(**g**) *(pluck → guitar string)* pincer; *(→ guitar)* pincer les cordes de

(**h**) *(idioms)* **to have a bone to pick with sb** avoir un compte à régler avec qn; **to pick sb's brains** tirer parti de l'intelligence *ou* des connaissances de qn; **can I pick your brains a minute?** est-ce que je peux faire appel à tes connaissances une minute?; **to pick a fight** chercher la bagarre; **to pick holes in sth** *(in argument, theory, book etc)* trouver des failles dans qch; **she's always picking holes (in everything)** elle n'arrête pas de chercher la petite bête; **to pick sb's pocket** faire les poches à qn; **to pick a quarrel with sb** chercher noise *ou* querelle à qn

2 *vi (choose)* choisir; **to pick and choose** *(be fussy)* faire le/la difficile, faire la fine bouche; **I like to be able to pick and choose** j'aime bien avoir le choix; **with your qualifications you can pick and choose** avec vos diplômes, toutes les portes vous sont ouvertes

3 *n* (**a**) *(choice)* choix *m*; **take your pick** faites votre choix, choisissez; **you can have your pick of them** vous pouvez choisir celui qui vous plaît; **he could have his pick of any job he wanted** il pourrait obtenir n'importe quel emploi; **we had first pick** nous avons été les premiers à choisir

(**b**) *(best)* meilleur(e) *m,f*; **the pick of France's footballers/writers** *(one)* le meilleur footballer/écrivain français; *(several)* les meilleurs footballers/écrivains français; *Fam* **the pick of the bunch** *(people)* le dessus du panier, le gratin; *(things)* ce qui se fait de mieux □

(**c**) *(tool)* pic *m*, pioche *f*; *(of miner)* pic *m* à main; *(of mason)* smille *f*; *(of climber)* piolet *m*

(**d**) *(plectrum)* plectre *m*, médiator *m*

►**pick at** *vt insep* (**a**) *(pull at → loose end)* tirer sur; *(→ flake of paint, scab)* gratter

(**b**) *(food)* manger du bout des dents; **he only picked at the fish** il a à peine touché au poisson

(**c**) *(criticize pettily)* être sur le dos de

►**pick off** *vt sep* (**a**) *(shoot)* abattre; **a marksman picked off the leaders one by one** un tireur d'élite a abattu les meneurs un à un

(**b**) *(remove → scab, paint)* gratter; *(→ flowers, leaves)* enlever, ôter; **pick those papers off the ground** ramassez ces papiers qui sont par terre; **to pick the meat off a bone** décortiquer un os; **she picked herself off the floor** elle s'est relevée

►**pick on** *vt insep* (**a**) *(victimize)* harceler, s'en prendre à; **pick on someone your own size!** ne t'en prends pas à un plus petit que toi!

(**b**) *(single out)* choisir; **why pick on today of all days?** pourquoi choisir ce jour entre tous?

►**pick out** *vt sep* (**a**) *(choose)* choisir; **he picked out the best peaches** il a choisi les meilleures pêches

(**b**) *(spot, identify → person in crowd)* repérer; *(→ person in photo)* reconnaître; *(→ person in identification parade)* identifier; *(→ landmark, object)* distinguer; **I tried to pick him out in the crowd** j'ai essayé de le repérer dans la foule; **she was easy to pick out in her orange coat** elle était facilement reconnaissable *ou* facile à repérer avec son manteau orange

(**c**) *(highlight, accentuate)* rehausser; **the stitching is picked out in bright green** un vert vif fait ressortir les coutures

(**d**) *(play)* **to pick out a tune on the piano** retrouver un air au piano

►**pick over** *vt insep (examine → fruit, vegetables etc)* trier; *(→ performance, evidence, details)* décortiquer, analyser

►**pick up** **1** *vt sep* (**a**) *(lift)* prendre; *(something from the ground)* ramasser; *(something that has fallen over)* relever; *Knitting (stitch)* relever; **pick up those books!** ramassez ces livres!; **to pick up the telephone** décrocher le téléphone; **to pick up a child** *(in one's arms)* prendre un enfant dans ses bras; *(after falling)* relever un enfant; **to pick oneself up** *(after falling)* se relever; *Fig (recover from crisis)* se remettre; **they left me to pick up the** *Br* **bill** *or Am* **tab** ils m'ont laissé l'addition; *Fig* **to pick up the pieces** recoller les morceaux

(**b**) *(collect → gen)* passer prendre; *(→ children from school, people from airport etc)* aller chercher; **I've got to pick up the children at four** il faut que j'aille chercher les enfants à quatre heures; **my father picked me up at the station** mon père est venu me chercher à la gare; **I have to pick up a parcel at the post office** je dois passer prendre un colis à la poste; **helicopters were sent to pick up the wounded** on a envoyé des hélicoptères pour ramener les blessés; **I never pick up hitchhikers** je ne prends jamais d'auto-stoppeurs

(**c**) *(acquire, come by → skill, information)* apprendre; *(→ reputation)* gagner, acquérir; *(→*

prize) gagner, remporter; **did you pick up any Greek during your stay?** avez-vous appris un peu de grec pendant votre séjour?; **to pick up bad habits** prendre de mauvaises habitudes; **I don't know where he's picking up these funny ideas from** je ne sais pas où il va chercher ces idées bizarres; **to pick up a parking ticket** attraper un PV; **our country picked up most of the medals** notre pays a remporté la plupart des médailles

(**d**) *Fam (buy cheaply)* **to pick up a bargain** dénicher une bonne affaire; **to pick sth up cheap** acheter qch bon marché❑; **I picked it up at the flea market** je l'ai trouvé au marché aux puces❑

(**e**) *(catch → illness, infection)* attraper

(**f**) *Fam (earn)* se faire; **you can pick up good money working on the rigs** on peut se faire pas mal de fric en travaillant sur les plates-formes pétrolières

(**g**) *Fam (arrest)* pincer, agrafer

(**h**) *Fam* **to pick sb up** *(sexual partner)* lever qn; **he picked her up in a bar** il l'a levée dans un bar; **he tried to pick her up** il l'a draguée; **to pick up a customer** *(of prostitute)* racoler *ou* raccrocher un client

(**i**) *(detect)* détecter; **he picked up the sound of a distant bell** il perçut le son d'une cloche dans le lointain; **the dogs picked up the scent again** les chiens ont retrouvé la piste

(**j**) *Rad & TV (receive)* capter

(**k**) *(notice)* relever; **the proofreaders pick up most of the mistakes** les correcteurs repèrent *ou* relèvent la plupart des erreurs

(**l**) *(criticize)* reprendre; **to pick sb up sharply** reprendre qn vertement; **nobody picked him up on his sexist comments** personne n'a relevé ses remarques sexistes

(**m**) *(resume)* reprendre; **we picked up the discussion where we'd left off** nous avons repris la discussion là où nous l'avions laissée

(**n**) *(return to)* revenir sur, reprendre; **I'd like to pick up a point you made earlier** j'aimerais revenir sur une remarque que vous avez faite tout à l'heure

(**o**) *(gather → speed, momentum)* prendre; **to pick up strength** *(person)* reprendre des forces

(**p**) *Fam (revive)* remonter❑, requinquer; **that will pick you up** voilà qui vous remontera

2 *vi* (**a**) *(get better → sick person)* se rétablir, se sentir mieux

(**b**) *(improve → conditions, weather)* s'améliorer; *(→ business, trade)* reprendre; **the market is picking up after a slow start** après avoir démarré doucement le marché commence à prendre; **the game certainly picked up in the second half** la partie s'est animée pendant la deuxième mi-temps

(**c**) *(resume)* reprendre; **they picked up where they had left off** *(in conversation)* ils ont repris la conversation là où ils l'avaient laissée; *(in game)* ils ont repris le jeu là où ils l'avaient laissé

(**d**) *(notice)* **she didn't pick up on the criticism** elle n'a pas relevé la critique

---

pickaback ['pɪkəbæk] **1** *adv (on one's back)* sur le dos; **to ride** *or* **to be carried pickaback** se faire porter sur le dos de qn

2 *n* **to give sb a pickaback** porter qn sur le dos; **can I have a pickaback?** est-ce que je peux monter sur ton dos?

3 *adj (ride)* sur le dos

4 *vt (carry)* porter sur son dos

pickaninny *(pl* **pickaninnies**) = **piccaninny**

pickaxe, *Am* **pickax** ['pɪkæks] *n* pic *m*, pioche *f*

picked [pɪkt] *adj (products, items)* sélectionné; *(people)* d'élite, trié sur le volet

picker ['pɪkə(r)] *n (of fruit, cotton etc)* cueilleur(-euse) *m,f*, ramasseur(euse) *m,f*; **grape-picker** vendangeur(euse) *m,f*; **strawberry-picker** cueilleur(euse) *m,f* de fraises; **mushroom-picker** ramasseur(euse) *m,f* de champignons

pickerel ['pɪkərəl] *(pl* **inv** *or* **pickerels**) *n Ich* brochet *m*

picket ['pɪkɪt] **1** *n* (**a**) *Ind (group)* piquet *m* de grève; *(individual)* gréviste *mf* (en faction); **there was a picket outside the factory** il y avait un piquet de grève devant l'usine; **to be on picket duty** faire partie d'un piquet de grève; **twenty pickets stood in front of the factory** vingt grévistes se tenaient devant l'usine

(**b**) *(outside embassy, ministry → group)* groupe *m* de manifestants; *(→ individual)* manifestant(e) *m,f*

(**c**) *Mil* piquet *m*

(**d**) *(stake)* piquet *m*

2 *vt* (**a**) *Ind (workplace, embassy)* **the strikers picketed the factory** les grévistes ont mis en place un piquet de grève devant l'usine; **demonstrators picketed the consulate at the week-end** des manifestants ont bloqué le consulat ce week-end

(**b**) *(fence)* palissader

(**c**) *(tie up)* attacher, mettre au piquet

3 *vi Ind* mettre en place un piquet de grève

►► ***picket duty*** piquet *m*; ***picket fence*** clôture *f* de piquets, palissade *f*; ***picket line*** piquet *m* de grève; **to be** *or* **to stand on a picket line** faire partie d'un piquet de grève; **to cross a picket line** franchir un piquet de grève

picketing ['pɪkətɪŋ] *n (UNCOUNT)* (**a**) *(of workplace)* piquets *mpl* de grève; **there is heavy picketing at the factory gates** les piquets de grève sont très nombreux aux portes de l'usine

(**b**) *(of ministry, embassy)* **there was picketing outside the embassy today** aujourd'hui, il y a eu des manifestations devant l'ambassade

picking ['pɪkɪŋ] **1** *n* (**a**) *(selection → of object)* choix *m*; *(→ of team)* sélection *f*

(**b**) *(of fruit, vegetables)* cueillette *f*, ramassage *m*; **cherry-/strawberry-picking** cueillette *f* des cerises/des fraises; **mushroom-/potato-picking** ramassage *m* des champignons/des pommes de terre

(**c**) *(of lock)* crochetage *m*

2 pickings *npl* (**a**) *(remains)* restes *mpl*; **you can have the pickings** vous pouvez prendre ce qui reste

(**b**) *Fam (spoils)* gratte *f*; **there are rich** *or* **easy pickings to be had** on pourrait se faire pas mal d'argent, ça pourrait rapporter gros

pickle ['pɪkəl] **1** *n* (**a**) *Am (gherkin)* cornichon *m*

(**b**) *(vinegar)* vinaigre *m*; *(brine)* saumure *f*

(**c**) *Fam (mess, dilemma)* pétrin *m*; **to be in a pickle** être dans le pétrin *ou* dans de beaux draps

(**d**) *Br Fam (mischievous child)* petit diable *m*, fripon(onne) *m,f*

(**e**) *(UNCOUNT) Br Culin (food)* pickles *mpl (petits oignons, cornichons, morceaux de chouxfleurs etc, macérés dans du vinaigre)*

2 *vt* (**a**) *Culin (in vinegar)* conserver dans le vinaigre; *(in brine)* conserver dans la saumure

(**b**) *Tech (metal)* nettoyer à l'acide *ou* dans un bain d'acide

pickled ['pɪkəld] *adj* (**a**) *Culin (in vinegar)* au vinaigre; *(in brine)* conservé dans la saumure (**b**) *Am (wood, furniture)* cérusé (**c**) *Fam (drunk)* bourré, pété

►► ***pickled cabbage*** chou *m* rouge au vinaigre; ***pickled herring*** rollmops *m inv*; ***pickled onion*** oignon *m* au vinaigre

pickling ['pɪklɪŋ] *n* saumurage *m*, conservation *f* au vinaigre

►► ***pickling onions*** petits oignons *mpl*

picklock ['pɪklɒk] *n* (**a**) *(instrument)* crochet *m*, passe-partout *m inv* (**b**) *(burglar)* crocheteur *m* (de serrures)

pick-me-up *n Fam* remontant❑ *m*

pick-'n'-mix *n (sweets, cheese etc)* assortiment *m (composé par l'acheteur lui-même)*

pickpocket ['pɪk,pɒkɪt] *n* pickpocket *m*, voleur(-euse) *m,f* à la tire

pickpocketing ['pɪk,pɒkɪtɪŋ] *n* vol *m* à la tire

pick-up **1** *n* (**a**) *Aut (vehicle)* pick-up *m inv*, camionnette *f* (découverte)

(**b**) *Fam (casual acquaintance)* partenaire *mf* de rencontre❑

(**c**) *(act of collecting)* **the truck made several pick-ups on the way** le camion s'est arrêté plusieurs fois en route pour charger des marchandises; **where will the pick-up be made?** où est-ce qu'on doit passer prendre les marchandises?

(**d**) *(on record player)* pick-up *m inv*, lecteur *m*

(**e**) *(on guitar)* micro *m*

(**f**) *(UNCOUNT) Am Aut (acceleration)* reprises *fpl*; **this car has got good pick-up** cette voiture a de bonnes reprises

(**g**) *(improvement → of business, economy)* reprise *f*; **we're hoping for a pick-up in sales** nous espérons une reprise des ventes

(**h**) *Fam (arrest)* arrestation❑ *f*

(**i**) *Tech (detector)* détecteur *m*, capteur *m*

(**j**) *Rad & TV (reception)* réception *f*

2 *adj Am (impromptu)* **sometimes I try and get a pick-up game of squash with the pro** de temps en temps j'improvise une petite partie de squash avec le pro; **a pick-up musician** un(e) musicien(enne) amateur

►► ***pick-up arm*** *(on record player)* pick-up *m inv*; ***pick-up point*** *(for cargo)* aire *f* de chargement; *(for passengers)* point *m* de ramassage, lieu *m* de rendez-vous; ***pick-up truck*** pick-up *m inv*, camionnette *f* (découverte)

picky ['pɪkɪ] *(compar* **pickier**, *superl* **pickiest**) *adj Fam* difficile❑; **she's really picky about her food** elle est très difficile pour la nourriture; **don't be so picky!** arrête de faire le/la difficile!

pick-your-own *adj (farm)* où l'on peut cueillir soi-même ses fruits et ses légumes; *(strawberries, raspberries)* cueilli à la ferme

picnic ['pɪknɪk] *(pt & pp* **picnicked**, *cont* **picnicking**) **1** *n* (**a**) *(in open air)* pique-nique *m*; **to go on** *or* **for a picnic** faire un pique-nique; **we took a picnic lunch** nous avons emporté de quoi faire un pique-nique; **let's have a picnic** faisons un pique-nique

(**b**) *Fam Fig (easy task)* **it was no picnic!** c'était pas de la tarte!; **it's no picnic showing tourists around London** ce n'est pas une partie de plaisir que de faire visiter Londres aux touristes; **it was no picnic cleaning all the pans** ça n'a pas été du gâteau de nettoyer toutes les casseroles

2 *vi* pique-niquer

►► ***picnic area*** aire *f* de pique-nique; ***picnic basket, picnic hamper*** panier *m* à pique-nique; *(filled)* panier *m* garni; ***picnic site*** aire *f* de pique-nique

picnicker ['pɪknɪkə(r)] *n* pique-niqueur(euse) *m,f*

picofarad ['pi:kə,færəd] *n* picofarad *m*

picornavirus [pɪ'kɔ:nəvaɪrəs] *n Biol* picornavirus *m*

picosecond ['pi:kə,sekənd] *n* picoseconde *f*

picot ['pi:kəʊ] *n (in embroidery)* picot *m*

picric acid ['pɪkrɪk-] *n Chem* acide *m* picrique

picrotoxin [,pɪkrəʊ'tɒksɪn] *n Chem* picrotoxine *f*

Pict [pɪkt] *n* Picte *mf*

Pictish ['pɪktɪʃ] **1** *n* langue *f* picte

2 *adj* picte

pictogram ['pɪktəgræm], **pictograph** ['pɪktəgrɑ:f] *n* (**a**) *Ling (symbol)* pictogramme *m*, idéogramme *m* (**b**) *(chart)* graphique *m*

pictographic [,pɪktə'græfɪk] *adj* pictographique

pictorial [pɪk'tɔ:rɪəl] **1** *adj* (**a**) *(in pictures)* en images; *(magazine, newspaper)* illustré (**b**) *(vivid → style)* vivant (**c**) *Art* pictural

2 *n* illustré *m*

pictorially [pɪk'tɔ:rɪəlɪ] *adv* en images

PICTURE ['pɪktʃə(r)]

image	► **1 (a), (d)**
dessin	► **1 (a)**
peinture	► **1 (a)**
tableau	► **1 (a), (c)**
photo	► **1 (a)**
film	► **1 (b)**
portrait	► **1 (c)**
situation	► **1 (e)**
s'imaginer	► **2 (a)**
dépeindre	► **2 (b)**
représenter	► **2 (b), (c)**

1 *n* (**a**) *(gen)* image *f*; *(drawing)* dessin *m*; *(painting)* peinture *f*, tableau *m*; *(in book)* illustration *f*; *(photograph)* photo *f*; **he used pictures to illustrate his talk** il a illustré sa conférence à l'aide d'images; **to draw/to paint a picture** faire un dessin/une peinture; **to draw a picture of sb/sth** dessiner qn/qch; **to paint a picture of sb** peindre le portrait de qn; **to take a picture** prendre une photo; **to take a picture of sb, to take sb's picture** prendre une photo de qn, prendre qn en photo; **to have one's picture taken** se faire prendre en photo; **I saw your picture in the paper** j'ai vu votre photo dans le journal; **the picture's blurred** *(on television)* l'image est floue

(**b**) *(film)* film *m*; **she was in several Hitchcock pictures** elle a joué dans plusieurs films de Hitchcock; *Br Fam* **the pictures** *(the cinema)* le cinoche, le ciné

(**c**) *(description)* tableau *m*, portrait *m*; **his novels give a vivid picture of the period** l'époque est peinte de façon très vivante dans ses romans, ses romans brossent un portrait très vivant de l'époque; **the TV series gives a good picture of life in a mining town** cette série télévisée donne un bon aperçu de la vie dans une ville minière; **the picture he painted was a depressing one** il a brossé *ou* fait un tableau déprimant de la situation; **to paint a bleak picture of the future** présenter une triste image de l'avenir

(**d**) *(idea, image)* image *f*; **I have a strong mental picture of what war was like** je m'imagine très bien ce qu'était la guerre; **he's the picture of health** il respire la santé, il est resplendissant de santé; **she was the picture of despair** elle était l'image vivante du désespoir; **he's the picture of his elder brother** c'est (tout) le portrait de son frère aîné

(**e**) *(situation)* situation *f*; **the economic picture is bleak** la situation économique est inquiétante

(**f**) *Fam (idioms)* **to be in the picture** être au courant ❑; **she hates being left out of the picture** elle déteste qu'on la laisse dans l'ignorance ❑; **to put sb in the picture** mettre qn au courant ❑; **I get the picture!** je pige!, j'y suis!; **doesn't she look a picture!** n'est-elle pas adorable *ou* ravissante! ❑; **you're no picture yourself!** tu n'es pas une beauté non plus!; **her face was a real picture when she heard the news!** il fallait voir sa tête quand elle a appris la nouvelle!; **the big picture** *(overview)* une vue d'ensemble ❑

2 *vt* (**a**) *(imagine)* s'imaginer, se représenter; **I can't quite picture him as a teacher** j'ai du mal à me l'imaginer comme enseignant; **picture yourself at eighty** imagine-toi à quatre-vingts ans; **just picture the scene** imaginez un peu la scène

(**b**) *(describe)* dépeindre, représenter

(**c**) *(paint, draw etc)* représenter; **the artist pictured her on horseback** l'artiste l'a représentée à cheval; **he was pictured with her on the front page of all the papers** une photo où il était en sa compagnie s'étalait à la une de tous les journaux

►► ***picture book*** livre *m* d'images; *Cards* ***picture card*** figure *f*; ***picture cheque*** image-chèque *f*; *Mktg* ***picture completion*** images *fpl* à compléter; *Journ* ***picture desk*** bureau *m* des illustrations; ***picture dictionary*** dictionnaire *m* en images; ***picture editor*** illustrateur(trice) *m,f*; ***picture frame*** cadre *m* (pour tableaux); ***picture framer*** encadreur(euse) *m,f*; ***picture gallery*** musée *m* de peinture; ***picture hat*** capeline *f*; *Br Old-fashioned* ***picture house*** cinéma *m*; ***picture library*** banque *f* d'images; *Comput* ***picture memory*** mémoire *f* d'images; *Br Old-fashioned* ***picture palace*** cinéma *m*; *Old-fashioned* ***picture postcard*** carte *f* postale (illustrée); ***picture puzzle*** rébus *m*; ***picture rail*** cimaise *f*; ***picture research*** documentation *f* iconographique; ***picture researcher*** documentaliste *mf* iconographique; ***picture restorer*** restaurateur(trice) *m,f* de tableaux; *TV* ***picture tube*** tube *m* image; ***picture window*** fenêtre *f ou* baie *f* panoramique; ***picture writing*** écriture *f* idéographique

---

'The Picture of Dorian Gray' *Wilde* 'Le Portrait de Dorian Gray'

---

picturegoer ['pɪktʃə,gəʊə(r)] *n Br Old-fashioned* cinéphile *mf*

picture-perfect *adj* parfait

picture-postcard *adj (view)* qui ressemble à une *ou* qui fait carte postale

picturesque [,pɪktʃə'resk] *adj* pittoresque

picturesquely [,pɪktʃə'resklɪ] *adv* de façon pittoresque; **the village is picturesquely situated** le village se trouve dans un site pittoresque

picturesqueness [,pɪktʃə'resknɪs] *n* pittoresque *m*

PID [,pi:aɪ'di:] *n Med (abbr* **pelvic inflammatory disease**) syndrome *m* inflammatoire pelvien

piddle ['pɪdəl] *Fam* **1** *vi* faire pipi

2 *n* pipi *m*; **to have a piddle** faire pipi; **to go for a piddle** aller faire pipi

piddling ['pɪdlɪŋ], **piddly** ['pɪdlɪ] *adj Fam (details)* insignifiant ❑; *(job, pay)* minable

piddock ['pɪdək] *n Zool* pholade *f*

pidgin ['pɪdʒɪn] *n Ling* pidgin *m*

►► *Ling* ***pidgin English*** pidgin *m*, pidgin-english *m*; *Pej* **to speak pidgin English** parler de façon incorrecte

pidginization [,pɪdʒɪnaɪ'zeɪʃən] *n Ling* pidginisation *f*

pi-dog = **pye-dog**

pie [paɪ] *n* (**a**) *Culin (with fruit)* tarte *f*; *(with meat, fish etc)* tourte *f*; **chicken pie** tourte *f* au poulet; *Fig* **I want my piece of the pie** je veux ma part du gâteau; *Fam* **it's just pie in the sky** ce sont des paroles *ou* promesses en l'air (**b**) *Typ* pâte *f*

►► ***pie chart*** graphique *m* circulaire, camembert *m*; ***pie dish*** plat *m* à tarte; *(for meat)* terrine *f*; *(oven-proof)* plat *m* allant au four; *Am* ***pie plate*** plat *m* allant au four

piebald ['paɪbɔ:ld] **1** *adj* pie *(inv)*

2 *n* cheval *m* pie

PIECE [pi:s]

morceau	► (a), (c), (e)
bout	► (a)
parcelle	► (a)
pièce	► (b) – (e), (g), (h)
pion	► (d)
article	► (f)

n (**a**) *(bit → of bread, chocolate, paper, wood)* morceau *m*, bout *m*; *(→ of cake, pie)* morceau *m*, tranche *f*; *(→ of land)* parcelle *f*, lopin *m*; *(of string, ribbon)* bout *m*; *(→ of cloth)* morceau *m*, coupon *m*; *(→ of glass)* morceau *m*, fragment *m*, éclat *m*; **a piece of advice** un conseil; **a piece of information** un renseignement; **a piece of news** une nouvelle; **that was a real piece of luck** cela a vraiment été un coup de chance; **it's a superb piece of craftsmanship** *or* **workmanship** c'est du très beau travail; **to be in pieces** *(in parts)* être en pièces détachées; *(broken)* être en pièces *ou* en morceaux; **to be in one piece** *(undamaged)* être intact; *(uninjured)* être indemne; *(safe)* être sain et sauf; **to be all of a piece** *(in one piece)* être tout d'une pièce *ou* d'un seul tenant; *(consistent)* être cohérent; *(alike)* se ressembler; *Br* **his actions are of a piece with his opinions** ses actes sont conformes à ses opinions; **to be still in one piece** *(person, car etc after accident)* être encore entier; **to break sth into pieces** mettre qch en morceaux *ou* en pièces; **to pull sth to pieces** *(doll, garment, book)* mettre qch en morceaux; *(flower)* effeuiller qch; *Fig (argument, suggestion, idea)* démolir qch; **to pull sb to pieces** descendre qn en flammes; **to come to pieces** *(into separate parts)* se démonter; *(break)* se briser; **the toy came to pieces in my hands** le jouet s'est brisé entre mes mains; **to fall to pieces** partir en morceaux; **to take sth to pieces** démonter qch; *Fam* **to go (all) to pieces** *(person)* s'effondrer ❑, craquer; *(team)* se désintégrer ❑; *(market)* s'effondrer ❑; *Fam* **it's a piece of cake** c'est du gâteau; *Br very Fam* **a piece of piss** un jeu d'enfant ❑; *Br Fam* **he's a nasty piece of work** c'est un sale type; **I gave him a piece of my mind** *(spoke frankly)* je lui ai dit ma façon de penser; *(spoke harshly)* je lui ai passé un savon; **to say one's piece** dire ce qu'on a sur le cœur

(**b**) *(item)* pièce *f*; **a piece of clothing** un vêtement; **a piece of furniture** un meuble; **a piece of luggage** *(suitcase)* une valise; *(bag)* un sac; **how many pieces of luggage do you have?** combien de bagages avez-vous?; **one piece of hand luggage** un bagage à main; **to sell sth by the piece** vendre qch à la pièce *ou* au détail; **to be paid by the piece** être payé à la pièce *ou* à la tâche

(**c**) *(part → of machine, set)* pièce *f*; *(→ of jigsaw)* pièce *f*, morceau *m*; **to put sth together piece by piece** assembler qch pièce par pièce *ou* morceau par morceau; **an 18-piece dinner service** un service de table de 18 pièces; **an 18-piece band** un orchestre de 18 musiciens

(**d**) *(for games → in chess)* pièce *f*; *(→ in draughts)* pion *m*; *(→ in backgammon)* dame *f*; *(→ in dominoes)* domino *m*

(**e**) *(performance)* morceau *m*; *(musical composition)* morceau *m*, pièce *f*; *(sculpture)* pièce *f* (de sculpture); **a piano piece** un morceau pour piano

(**f**) *(newspaper article)* article *m*; **there was a piece about it in yesterday's paper** il y a eu un article à ce sujet *ou* on en a parlé dans le journal d'hier

(**g**) *(coin)* pièce *f*; **a 50p piece** une pièce de 50 pence

(**h**) *Mil (firearm, cannon)* pièce *f*; *Fam Crime slang (gun)* flingue *m*

(**i**) *very Fam (girl)* **she's a nice** *or* **tasty piece** c'est un beau brin de fille ❑

(**j**) *Scot (sandwich)* sandwich *m*; **a piece and cheese** un sandwich au fromage

(**k**) *Am (time)* moment *m*; *(distance)* bout *m* de chemin; **he walked with me a piece** il a fait un bout de chemin avec moi

(**l**) *Metal* **punched/shaped piece** pièce *f* estampée/profilée; **to cast cylinders in one piece** couler des cylindres d'un seul jet *ou* en bloc

►► ***piece rate*** paiement *m* à la pièce; **to be on piece rate** être payé aux pièces

►**piece together** *vt sep* (**a**) *(from parts → broken object)* recoller; *(→ jigsaw)* assembler; **the collage was pieced together from scraps of material** le collage était fait *ou* constitué de petits bouts de tissu

(**b**) *(story, facts)* reconstituer; **to piece together what happened** reconstituer ce qui s'est passé; **detectives are piecing together a picture of the events** les enquêteurs sont en train de se faire une idée des événements

---

pièce de résistance [,pjesdərezɪs'tɑ̃:s] *(pl* **pièces de résistance** [,pjesdərezɪs'tɑ̃:s]) *n* pièce *f* de résistance

piecemeal ['pi:smi:l] **1** *adv (little by little)* peu à peu, petit à petit; **he told the story piecemeal** il a raconté l'histoire par bribes; **the town was rebuilt piecemeal after the war** la ville a été reconstruite par étapes après la guerre; **the collection was sold piecemeal** les pièces de la collection ont été vendues séparément

2 *adj (fragmentary)* fragmentaire, parcellaire; *(work)* fait petit à petit; *(funding, transformation)* morcelé, fragmenté

piecework ['pi:swɜ:k] *n (UNCOUNT)* travail *m* à la pièce; **to be on piecework** travailler à la pièce

pieceworker ['pi:swɜ:kə(r)] *n* travailleur(euse) *m,f* à la pièce

piecrust ['paɪkrʌst] *n* couche *f* de pâte *(pour recouvrir une tourte)*

►► ***piecrust table*** = table ronde à bord sculpté

pied [paɪd] *adj (gen)* bariolé, bigarré; *(animal)* pie *(inv)*

►► *Orn* ***pied flycatcher*** gobe-mouches *m* noir; *Orn* ***pied wagtail*** bergeronnette *f* de Yarrell

pied-à-terre [,pjeɪdæ'teə(r)] *(pl* **pieds-à-terre** [,pjeɪdæ'teə(r)]) *n* pied-à-terre *m inv*

Piedmont ['pi:dmənt] *n* Piémont *m*; **in Piedmont** dans le Piémont

Piedmontese [,pi:dmən'ti:z] **1** *n* Piémontais(e) *m,f*

2 *adj* piémontais

Pied Piper (of Hamelin) [-'hæmlɪn] *pr n* **the Pied Piper (of Hamelin)** le joueur de flûte de Hamelin

pie-eyed *adj Fam (drunk)* bourré, rond

pier [pɪə(r)] *n* (**a**) *Br (at seaside)* jetée *f* (**b**) *(jetty)* jetée *f*; *(landing stage)* embarcadère *m*; *(breakwater)* digue *f* (**c**) *(pillar)* pilier *m*, colonne *f*; *(of bridge)* pile *f*

►► ***pier glass*** trumeau *m*

pierce [pɪəs] *vt* (**a**) *(make hole in)* percer, transpercer; **to pierce a hole in sth** faire *ou* percer un trou dans qch; **the knife pierced her lung** le couteau lui a perforé *ou* transpercé le poumon; **she had her ears pierced** elle s'est fait percer les oreilles; **his words pierced my heart** ses paroles me fendirent le cœur

pic–pie

(**b**) *(of sound, scream, light)* percer; **a cry pierced the silence** un cri perça *ou* déchira le silence; **the beam pierced the darkness** le faisceau perça l'obscurité; **we were pierced (through) with cold** nous étions transis *ou* morts de froid; **the biting wind pierced his clothing** le vent glacial transperçait ses vêtements

(**c**) *(penetrate → defence, barrier)* percer; **the attack pierced (through) enemy lines** l'attaque a percé les lignes ennemies

pierced [pɪəst] *adj* percé; **to have pierced ears** avoir les oreilles percées

►► ***pierced earring*** boucle *f* d'oreille pour oreilles percées

piercing ['pɪəsɪŋ] *adj (scream, eyes, look)* perçant; *(question)* lancinant; *(wind)* glacial

piercingly ['pɪəsɪŋlɪ] *adv* **the wind is piercingly cold** il fait un vent glacial; **she looked at me piercingly** elle m'a fixé d'un regard perçant; **a piercingly loud scream** un cri perçant

pierhead ['pɪəhed] *n* musoir *m*

Pierrot ['pɪərəʊ] *pr n* Pierrot

pietà [pɪ'eɪtɑː] *n Art* pietà *f*

pietism ['paɪətɪzəm] *n* (**a**) *Rel & Hist* piétisme *m* (**b**) *(piety)* piété *f* sincère; *(exaggerated piety)* piété *f* outrée

pietist ['paɪətɪst] *n* (**a**) *Rel & Hist* piétiste *mf* (**b**) *(pious person)* personne *f* d'une piété sincère; *(exaggeratedly pious person)* personne *f* d'une piété outrée

pietistic [paɪə'tɪstɪk] *adj* (**a**) *Rel & Hist* piétiste (**b**) *(pious)* d'une piété sincère; *(exaggeratedly pious)* d'une piété outrée

piety ['paɪətɪ] *(pl* **pieties***)* *n* piété *f*

piezoelectric [ˌpiːzəʊɪ'lektrɪk] *adj* piézo-électrique

piezoelectricity [ˌpiːzəʊˌɪlek'trɪsətɪ] *n* piézo-électricité *f*

piezometer [ˌpiː'zɒmɪtə(r)] *n* piézomètre *m*

piffle ['pɪfəl] *Br Fam* **1** *n (UNCOUNT)* balivernes *fpl*, niaiseries *fpl*; **don't talk piffle!** ne dis pas de bêtises! ❑

2 *exclam* des sottises tout ça!

3 *vi* dire des bêtises ❑; **what are you piffling on about?** qu'est-ce que tu radotes?

piffling ['pɪflɪŋ] *adj Br Fam (excuse, amount, mistake)* insignifiant ❑; **a piffling little man** un moins que rien

pig [pɪg] *(pt & pp* **pigged**, *cont* **pigging***)* **1** *n* (**a**) *(animal)* cochon *m*, porc *m*; *Am (young pig)* cochonnet *m*, porcelet *m*; **pigs might fly!** quand les poules auront des dents!; *Am Fam* **in a pig's eye!** jamais de la vie! ❑; *Br Fam* **to make a pig's ear of sth** saloper qch, foirer qch; **you made a real pig's ear of that** ça, vous avez fait du beau!; **he made a pig's ear of laying the carpet** il a posé la moquette comme un vrai sagouin; *Am Fam* **to be like a pig in mud** être comme un poisson dans l'eau ❑; **to buy a pig in a poke** acheter chat en poche

(**b**) *Fam (greedy person)* goinfre *mf*; *(dirty eater)* cochon(onne) *m,f*; **to eat like a pig** manger comme un cochon *ou* un porc; **to make a pig of oneself** se goinfrer, s'empiffrer

(**c**) *Fam (dirty person)* cochon(onne) *m,f*; **to live like pigs** vivre dans une écurie *ou* porcherie

(**d**) *Fam (unpleasant person)* ordure *f*, chameau *m*; **fascist pig!** sale fasciste!; **the dirty pig!** quel chameau!; **what a selfish pig!** quel sale égoïste!

(**e**) *Br Fam (unpleasant thing, task)* truc *m* chiant; **it's a real pig of a job** ce travail est un véritable cauchemar; **cleaning the oven is a pig of a job** c'est vraiment chiant de nettoyer le four; **the filing cabinet was a pig to move** ça a été vachement difficile de déplacer le classeur

(**f**) *Fam Pej (policeman)* flic *m*, poulet *m*; **the pigs** les flics *mpl*, les poulets *mpl*

(**g**) *Metal (of casting)* gueuse *f*; *(of lead, tin etc)* saumon *m*

(**h**) *Fam (ugly person)* mocheté *f*

2 *vt Fam* (**a**) *(stuff)* **to pig oneself (on sth)** s'empiffrer (de qch), se goinfrer (de qch)

(**b**) **to pig it** *(dirty person)* vivre comme des cochons

3 *vi (sow)* mettre bas, cochonner

►► ***pig farm*** porcherie *f*, élevage *m* de porcs; ***pig iron*** fonte *f* brute; ***Pig Latin*** = argot codé utilisé en milieu scolaire, ≃ javanais *m*; *Culin* ***pig's trotter*** pied *m* de porc

► **pig out** *vi Fam* s'empiffrer, se goinfrer (**on sth** de qch)

pigeon ['pɪdʒɪn] *n* (**a**) *Orn* pigeon *m* (**b**) *Br Fam (business)* **it's not my pigeon** ce n'est pas mon problème ❑; **that's their pigeon** c'est leurs affaires *ou* leurs oignons (**c**) *Fam Fig (dupe)* pigeon *m*, poire *f*

►► ***pigeon droppings*** fiente *f* de pigeon; ***pigeon fancier*** colombophile *mf*; ***pigeon loft*** pigeonnier *m*; ***pigeon post*** transport *m* de dépêches par pigeons voyageurs; ***pigeon shooting*** tir *m ou* chasse *f* aux pigeons

pigeon-breasted [-ˌbrestɪd], **pigeon-chested** [-ˌtʃestɪd] *adj* **to be pigeon-breasted** avoir la poitrine bombée

pigeonhole ['pɪdʒɪnhəʊl] **1** *n* casier *m* (à courrier); *Fig* **he tends to put people in pigeonholes** il a tendance à étiqueter les gens *ou* à mettre des étiquettes aux gens

2 *vt* (**a**) *(file)* classer

(**b**) *(postpone)* différer, remettre (à plus tard); **the scheme had been pigeonholed until further notice** le projet avait été remis jusqu'à nouvel ordre

(**c**) *(classify)* étiqueter, cataloguer; **they pigeonholed me as a feminist** ils m'avaient étiquetée comme féministe

pigeonry ['pɪdʒɪnrɪ] *n* pigeonnier *m*

pigeon-toed *adj* **to be pigeon-toed** avoir les pieds tournés en dedans

piggery ['pɪgərɪ] *(pl* **piggeries***)* *n* (**a**) *(for pigs)* porcherie *f* (**b**) *(greediness)* gloutonnerie *f*

piggish ['pɪgɪʃ] *adj Fam Pej* (**a**) *(dirty)* cochon; *(greedy)* glouton ❑ (**b**) *Br (stubborn)* têtu ❑

piggy ['pɪgɪ] *(pl* **piggies***)* *Fam* **1** *n (in children's language → pig)* (petit) cochon ❑ *m*; *(→ toe)* doigt *m* de pied ❑; *(→ finger)* doigt ❑ *m*; **piggy in the middle** = jeu d'enfants au cours duquel deux enfants se lancent un ballon alors qu'un troisième placé au milieu essaie de l'attraper; *Fig* **I'm tired of being piggy in the middle** j'en ai assez d'être pris entre deux feux

2 *adj* (**a**) *(greedy)* glouton ❑, goinfre

(**b**) *(features)* **piggy eyes** de petits yeux *mpl* porcins ❑

piggyback ['pɪgɪbæk] **1** *adv* (**a**) *(on one's back)* sur le dos; **to ride** *or* **to be carried piggyback** se faire porter sur le dos de qn

(**b**) *Comput* **to mount sth piggyback on sth** superposer qch sur qch

2 *n* **to give sb a piggyback** porter qn sur le dos; **can I have a piggyback?** est-ce que je peux monter sur ton dos?

3 *adj (ride)* sur le dos

4 *vt* (**a**) *(carry)* porter sur son dos; *Fig* **the new music festival was piggybacked onto the main theatre festival** ils ont profité de l'existence du festival de théâtre pour lancer le nouveau festival de musique; **this provision was piggybacked onto the new legislation** cette disposition a été incorporée à la nouvelle loi

(**b**) *esp Am Transp* ferrouter

►► *Comput* ***piggyback board*** carte *f* fille; *esp Am Transp* ***piggyback traffic, piggyback transport*** ferroutage *m*

piggybacking ['pɪgɪˌbækɪŋ] *n* (**a**) *Banking* portage *m* (**b**) *(in export)* exportation *f* kangourou (**c**) *esp Am Transp* ferroutage *m*

piggybank ['pɪgɪbæŋk] *n* tirelire *f (souvent en forme de petit cochon)*, *Can* cochon *m*

pigheaded [pɪg'hedɪd] *adj* têtu, obstiné

pigheadedly [pɪg'hedɪdlɪ] *adv* obstinément, avec entêtement

pigheadedness [pɪg'hedɪdnɪs] *n* obstination *f*, entêtement *m*

piglet ['pɪglɪt] *n* cochonnet *m*, porcelet *m*

pigman ['pɪgmən] *(pl* **pigmen** [-mən]*)* *n* porcher *m*

pigmeat ['pɪgmiːt] *n* (viande *f* de) porc *m*

pigment 1 *n* ['pɪgmənt] (**a**) *Art* couleur *f*, colorant *m*, pigment *m* (**b**) *Physiol* pigment *m*

2 [pɪg'ment] *vt* pigmenter

►► ***pigment cell*** cellule *f* pigmentaire

pigmentary ['pɪgməntərɪ] *adj* pigmentaire

pigmentation [ˌpɪgmən'teɪʃən] *n* pigmentation *f*

Pigmy = **Pygmy**

pignut ['pɪgnʌt] *n* (**a**) *Bot* conopode *m* dénudé (**b**) *(earthnut)* gland *m ou* noix *f* de terre (**c**) *Am (hickory nut)* noix *f* de hickory

pigpen ['pɪgpen] *n Am also Fig* porcherie *f*

pigskin ['pɪgskɪn] **1** *n* (**a**) *(leather)* peau *f* de porc; **it's made of pigskin** c'est en (peau de) porc (**b**) *Am (football)* ballon *m (de football américain)*

2 *comp (bag, watchstrap)* en (peau de) porc

pigsticking ['pɪgˌstɪkɪŋ] *n* chasse *f* au sanglier

pigsty ['pɪgstaɪ] *(pl* **pigsties***)* *n also Fig* porcherie *f*

pigswill ['pɪgswɪl] *n Br* pâtée *f* (pour les cochons); *Fig* **our school meals are pigswill** ce qu'on (nous) sert à la cantine de l'école est bon pour les cochons

pigtail ['pɪgteɪl] *n* natte *f*

pigtailed ['pɪgteɪld] *adj* (**a**) *(girl)* qui a des nattes; *(wig)* à queue (**b**) *(with a tail like a pig's)* à queue de porc

►► ***pigtailed monkey*** singe *m* cochon

pig-thick *adj Br Fam* con comme un balai

pig-ugly *adj Br Fam* moche comme un pou

pika ['paɪkə] *n Zool* pika *m*

pike [paɪk] *(pl* **inv** *or* **pikes***)* *n* (**a**) *Ich* brochet *m* (**b**) *(spear)* pique *f* (**c**) *NEng (hill)* pic *m* (**d**) *(barrier)* barrière *f* de péage (**e**) *(in diving)* plongeon *m* groupé (**f**) *Am (idiom)* **to come down the pike** apparaître; **we're prepared for whatever happens down the pike** nous sommes parés à toute éventualité

pikeman ['paɪkmən] *(pl* **pikemen** [-mən]*)* *n* (**a**) *Hist* piquier (**b**) *(miner using a pickaxe)* piqueur

pikestaff ['paɪkstɑːf] *n* (**a**) *(weapon)* bois *m ou* hampe *f* de pique (**b**) *(for walking)* bâton *m* à pointe de fer

pilaf, pilaff ['pɪlæf] = **pilau**

pilaster [pɪ'læstə(r)] *n* pilastre *m*

pilastered [pɪ'læstəd] *adj (supported by pilasters)* supporté par des pilastres; *(built on pilasters)* bâti sur pilastres

Pilate ['paɪlət] *pr n* Pilate; **Pontius Pilate** Ponce Pilate

pilau [pɪ'laʊ] *n* pilaf *m*

►► ***pilau rice*** riz *m* pilaf

pilchard ['pɪltʃəd] *n Ich* pilchard *m*

PILE [paɪl]

pile	► **1 (a), (e) – (g)**
tas	► **1 (a), (b)**
fortune	► **1 (c)**
édifice	► **1 (d)**
pieu	► **1 (g)**
poil	► **1 (h)**
empiler	► **2**
entasser	► **2**

1 *n* (**a**) *(neat stack)* pile *f*; *(heap)* tas *m*; **to put books/magazines in a pile** empiler des livres/magazines; **she left her clothes/records in a pile on the floor** elle a laissé ses vêtements/disques en tas par terre; *Fam Fig* **to be at the top/bottom of the pile** être en haut/en bas de l'échelle ❑

(**b**) *(usu pl) Fam (large quantity)* tas *m ou mpl*, masses *fpl*; **to have piles of money** avoir plein d'argent, être plein aux as; **I've got piles of work to do** j'ai un tas de boulot *ou* un boulot dingue

(**c**) *Fam (fortune)* fortune ❑ *f*; **he made his pile in the fur trade** il a fait fortune dans le commerce de la fourrure; **she must have made a pile out of that deal** elle a dû gagner une fortune dans ce contrat

(**d**) *(large building)* édifice *m*; **she owns a huge Jacobean pile in the country** elle a un immense manoir du XVIIème siècle à la campagne

(**e**) *(battery)* pile *f*

(**f**) *Nucl* **(atomic) pile** pile *f*, réacteur *m* (atomique)

(**g**) *Constr* pieu *m*; *(for bridge)* pile *f*; **built on piles** sur pilotis

(**h**) *(UNCOUNT) Tex* fibres *fpl*, poil *m*; **a deep-pile carpet** une moquette épaisse

2 *vt (stack)* empiler; *(put in a heap)* entasser; **she piled her clothes neatly on the chair** elle empila soigneusement ses habits sur la chaise;

don't pile those records on top of one another n'empilez pas ces disques les uns sur les autres; **she piled her clothes into the suitcase** elle a mis tous ses habits pêle-mêle dans la valise; **we piled the toys into the car** on a entassé les jouets dans la voiture; **the table was piled high with papers** il y avait une grosse pile de papiers sur la table; **he piled more coal on the fire** il a remis du charbon dans le feu; **he piled spaghetti onto his plate** il a rempli son assiette de spaghettis; **a plate piled with mashed potato** une assiette remplie *ou* pleine de purée; **she wears her hair piled high on her head** ses cheveux sont ramenés en chignon au sommet de sa tête

3 *vi Fam* **they piled into the car** ils se sont entassés dans la voiture; **they all piled off the bus** ils sont tous descendus du bus en se bousculant ❏; **we piled up the stairs** nous avons monté l'escalier en nous bousculant ❏

►► *Constr* ***pile driver*** sonnette *f*; *Fam Fig (blow)* coup *m* violent ❏; ***pile dwelling*** habitation *f* lacustre *ou* sur pilotis

▸**pile in** *vi Fam (enter)* entrer en se bousculant ❏; **they opened the doors and we all piled in** ils ont ouvert les portes et nous nous sommes tous bousculés pour entrer; **pile in!** *(into car)* montez! ❏, en voiture! ❏; **once the first punch was thrown we all piled in** *(joined the fight)* après le premier coup de poing, on s'est tous lancés dans la bagarre ❏

▸**pile into** *vt insep Fam* (**a**) *(crash)* rentrer dans ❏; **the two cars piled into each other** les deux voitures se sont rentrées dedans *ou* se sont télescopées

(**b**) *(attack → physically)* rentrer dans ❏, foncer dans ❏; *(→ verbally)* rentrer dans ❏, tomber sur ❏

▸**pile off** *vi Fam (from bus, train)* descendre en se bousculant ❏

▸**pile on** *Fam* **1** *vt sep (increase → suspense)* faire durer ❏; *(→ pressure)* faire monter ❏; **to pile on the agony** forcer la dose, dramatiser (à l'excès) ❏; **to pile on the pounds** grossir ❏, prendre du poids ❏; **to pile it on** *(exaggerate)* exagérer ❏, en rajouter

2 *vi (onto bus, train)* s'entasser, monter en s'entassant

▸**pile out** *vi Fam (off bus, train)* descendre en se bousculant ❏; *(from cinema, lecture hall)* sortir en se bousculant ❏

▸**pile up 1** *vi* (**a**) *(crash → cars)* se rentrer dedans, se caramboler

(**b**) *(accumulate → work, debts)* s'accumuler, s'entasser; *(→ washing, clouds)* s'amonceler; **work was piling up on her desk** le travail s'amoncelait sur son bureau

2 *vt sep* (**a**) *(stack)* empiler; *(put in a heap)* entasser

(**b**) *(accumulate → evidence, examples)* accumuler

piles [paɪlz] *npl (haemorrhoids)* hémorroïdes *fpl*; **to have piles** avoir des hémorroïdes

pileum ['paɪlɪəm] *n Orn* pileum *m*, capuchon *m*

pile-up *n* carambolage *m*; **there was a 50-car pile-up in the fog** 50 voitures se sont télescopées *ou* carambolées dans le brouillard

pileus ['paɪlɪəs] *n Bot* pileus *m*

pilfer ['pɪlfə(r)] **1** *vt* chaparder (**from sb** à qn)

2 *vi* chaparder

pilferage ['pɪlfərɪdʒ] *n* petits vols *mpl*, larcins *mpl*; **the percentage lost through pilferage** le pourcentage perdu imputable aux petits vols

pilferer ['pɪlfərə(r)] *n* chapardeur(euse) *m,f*

pilfering ['pɪlfərɪŋ] *n* petits vols *mpl*, larcins *mpl*; **the percentage lost through pilfering** le pourcentage perdu imputable aux petits vols

pilgrim ['pɪlgrɪm] *n* pèlerin *m*

►► ***the Pilgrim Fathers*** les (Pères) Pèlerins *mpl*; ***Pilgrim's Way*** = chemin suivi par les pèlerins de Londres à Cantorbéry, dont une partie constitue aujourd'hui un chemin de randonnée

'The Pilgrim's Progress' *Bunyan* 'Le Voyage du pèlerin'

THE PILGRIM FATHERS

Puritains persécutés en Angleterre, les "Pèlerins" parvinrent en Amérique du Nord à bord du "Mayflower" et fondèrent la première colonie permanente du nouveau monde, à Plymouth (dans ce qui devait devenir l'État du Massachusetts), en 1620.

pilgrimage ['pɪlgrɪmɪdʒ] *n* pèlerinage *m*; **to make** *or* **to go on a pilgrimage** faire un pèlerinage; **they made** *or* **went on a pilgrimage to Lourdes** ils sont allés en pèlerinage à Lourdes; *Fig* **I made a pilgrimage to my childhood home** je suis retourné visiter la maison de mon enfance

piliferous [paɪ'lɪfərəs] *adj Bot* pilifère

pill [pɪl] **1** *n* (**a**) *Med* pilule *f*, comprimé *m*; *Fig* **to sugar** *or* **to sweeten the pill (for sb)** dorer la pilule (à qn) (**b**) *(contraceptive pill)* **the pill** la pilule; **to go on the pill** commencer à prendre la pilule; **to be on the pill** prendre la pilule

2 Pill *n* **the Pill** *(contraceptive)* la pilule

►► *Fam* ***pill popper*** accro *mf* aux tranquillisants; *Fam Pej* ***pill pusher*** pharmacien(enne) ❏ *m,f*

pillage ['pɪlɪdʒ] **1** *vt* mettre à sac, piller

2 *vi* se livrer au pillage

3 *n* pillage *m*

pillager ['pɪlɪdʒə(r)] *n* pilleur(euse) *m,f*, pillard(e) *m,f*

pillaging ['pɪlɪdʒɪŋ] *adj* pillard

pillar ['pɪlə(r)] *n* (**a**) *(structural support)* pilier *m*; *(ornamental)* colonne *f*; **to go from pillar to post** tourner en rond; **he was sent from pillar to post** on l'a envoyé à droite et à gauche; *Geog* **the Pillars of Hercules** les colonnes *fpl* d'Hercule

(**b**) *(of smoke)* colonne *f*; *(of water)* trombe *f*; **pillar of rock** colonne *f* rocheuse; *Bible* **a pillar of salt** une statue de sel

(**c**) *Fig (mainstay)* pilier *m*; **a pillar of society** un pilier de la société; **to be a pillar of strength** être ferme comme un roc; **you've been a real pillar of strength** vous avez été un soutien précieux

►► *Br* ***pillar box*** boîte *f* à lettres

pillar-box red *Br* **1** *n* rouge *m* vif

2 *adj* rouge vif *(inv)*

pillared ['pɪləd] *adj* à piliers, à colonnes

pillbox ['pɪlbɒks] *n* (**a**) *Med* boîte *f* à pilules (**b**) *Mil* blockhaus *m inv*, casemate *f* (**c**) *(hat)* toque *f*

pillion ['pɪljən] **1** *n* (**a**) *(on motorbike)* siège *m* arrière (**b**) *(on horse)* selle *f* de derrière

2 *adv* **to ride pillion** *(on motorbike)* voyager sur le siège arrière; *(on horse)* monter en croupe

►► ***pillion passenger, pillion rider*** passager(ère) *m,f (sur une moto)*; ***pillion seat*** siège *m* arrière

pillock ['pɪlək] *n Br Fam (idiot)* andouille *f*, courge *f*

pillory ['pɪlərɪ] (*pl* **pillories**, *pt & pp* **pilloried**) **1** *n* pilori *m*

2 *vt Hist & Fig* mettre *ou* clouer au pilori

pillow ['pɪləʊ] **1** *n* (**a**) *(on bed)* oreiller *m*

(**b**) *Tex (for lace)* carreau *m* (de dentellière)

(**c**) *Am (on chair, sofa)* coussin *m*

2 *vt (rest)* reposer; **he pillowed his head on his arms** il posa sa tête sur ses bras; **her head was pillowed on a mound of leaves** sa tête reposait sur un oreiller de feuilles

►► ***pillow fight*** bataille *f* de polochons; *Am* ***pillow sham*** taie *f* d'oreiller; ***pillow talk*** *(UNCOUNT)* confidences *fpl* sur l'oreiller

pillowcase ['pɪləʊkeɪs], *Br* **pillowslip** ['pɪləʊslɪp] *n* taie *f* d'oreiller

pilose ['paɪləʊz] *adj Bot & Zool* pileux, poilu

pilosity [paɪ'lɒsɪtɪ] *n Bot & Zool* pilosité *f*

pilot ['paɪlət] **1** *n* (**a**) *Aviat & Naut* pilote *m*; *Fig (guide)* guide *m*

(**b**) *Tech (on tool)* guidage *m*

(**c**) *(pilot light)* veilleuse *f*

(**d**) *TV* émission *f* pilote

2 *comp (error)* de pilotage

3 *vt* (**a**) *Aviat & Naut* piloter

(**b**) *(guide)* piloter, guider; **he's piloted the company through several crises** il a sorti l'entreprise de la crise *ou* de ses difficultés à plusieurs reprises; **she piloted the bill through parliament** elle s'est assurée que le projet de loi serait voté

(**c**) *(test)* tester, expérimenter; **the project was piloted at Harvard University** le projet a été testé à l'Université de Harvard

(**d**) *Mktg (study, scheme)* piloter

4 *adj (trial → study, programme, scheme)* d'essai, pilote, expérimental

►► *Met* ***pilot balloon*** ballon-sonde *m*; ***pilot boat*** bateau-pilote *m*; ***pilot burner*** veilleuse *f*; ***pilot cutter*** bateau-pilote *m*; *Rail* ***pilot engine*** locomotive *f* pilote; ***pilot film*** épisode *m* pilote; *Ich* ***pilot fish*** pilote *m*, poisson-pilote *m*; ***pilot flame*** veilleuse *f*; *Naut* ***pilot house*** poste *m* de pilotage; ***pilot jet*** veilleuse *f* (au gaz); ***pilot lamp*** veilleuse *f* (électrique); ***pilot light*** veilleuse *f*; *Br Aviat* ***pilot officer*** ≃ sous-lieutenant *m*; ***pilot project*** projet-pilote *m*; ***pilot questionnaire*** questionnaire *m* pilote; *Aviat, Ind & Com* ***pilot run*** présérie *f*; *Br* ***pilot scheme*** projet-pilote *m*; *Ind & Com* ***pilot series*** présérie *f*; ***pilot study*** étude *f* pilote, avant-projet *m*, pré-étude *f*; ***pilot survey*** enquête-pilote *f*; ***pilot waters*** zone *f* de pilotage; *Zool* ***pilot whale*** globicéphale *m*

pilotage ['paɪlətɪdʒ] *n* pilotage *m*

pilotless ['paɪlətləs] *adj* sans pilote

Pilsner, Pilsener ['pɪlznə(r)] *n* Pilsner *f (bière blonde parfumée)*

Piltdown Man ['pɪltdaʊn-] *n* l'homme *m* de Piltdown *(race préhistorique dont on crut découvrir des ossements en Angleterre en 1912, avant de découvrir qu'il s'agissait d'une mystification scientifique montée de toutes pièces)*

Pima ['piːmə] **1** *n* (**a**) *(tribe)* **the Pima** les Pima *mpl* (**b**) *(member)* Pima *mf inv*

2 *adj* pima *(inv)*

pimento [pɪ'mentəʊ] (*pl* **pimentos**) *n* piment *m*

pi-meson [paɪ'miːzɒn] *n Phys* pi *m*, pion *m*

Pimlico ['pɪmlɪkəʊ] *n* = quartier du sud de Londres

pimp [pɪmp] **1** *n* maquereau *m*, souteneur *m*

2 *vi* faire le maquereau

pimpernel ['pɪmpənel] *n Bot (scarlet)* mouron *m*; *(yellow)* lysimaque *f*

pimping ['pɪmpɪŋ] *n* maquerellage *m*, proxénétisme *m*

pimple ['pɪmpəl] *n* bouton *m*; **to come out in pimples** boutonner, bourgeonner

pimpled ['pɪmpəld] *adj* boutonneux

pimply ['pɪmplɪ] (*compar* **pimplier**, *superl* **pimpliest**) *adj* boutonneux

pimpmobile ['pɪmpməʊˌbiːl] *n Am Fam Pej* voiture *f* tape-à-l'œil

PIMS [pɪmz] *n Mktg* (*abbr* **profit impact of marketing strategy**) IRSM *m*

PIN [pɪn] *n* (*abbr* **personal identification number**) code *m* confidentiel *(d'une carte bancaire)*

►► ***PIN number*** code *m* confidentiel *(d'une carte bancaire)*

PIN [pɪn]

épingle	► **1 (a)**
punaise	► **1 (a)**
broche	► **1 (b), (e), (f)**
cheville	► **1 (d)**
épingler	► **2 (a)**
punaiser	► **2 (a)**
immobiliser	► **2 (b)**
cheviller	► **2 (c)**

(*pt & pp* **pinned**, *cont* **pinning**) **1** *n* (**a**) *(for sewing, fastening)* épingle *f*; *(drawing pin)* punaise *f*; *(hairpin)* épingle *f* à cheveux; **she took a pin from her hair** elle enleva une épingle de ses cheveux; **you could have heard a pin drop** on aurait entendu voler une mouche; **as bright** *or* **clean as a new pin** propre comme un sou neuf; **for two pins I'd let the whole thing drop** il ne faudrait pas beaucoup me pousser pour que je laisse tout tomber; **he doesn't care two pins about it** il s'en moque complètement

(**b**) *Am (brooch)* broche *f*; *(badge)* insigne *m*

(**c**) *Fam* **pins** *(legs)* cannes *fpl*, guibolles *fpl*, gambettes *fpl*; **he's a bit unsteady on his pins** il ne tient pas bien sur ses guibolles

(**d**) *(peg → in piano, violin)* cheville *f*; *(→ in hinge, pulley)* goujon *m*; *(→ in hand grenade)* goupille *f*; **(firing) pin** percuteur *m*; *Am Fam* **to pull the pin on sth** mettre un terme à qch ❏

(**e**) *Elec (on plug)* broche *f*; **two-pin plug** prise *f* à deux broches
(**f**) *Med (for broken bone)* broche *f*
(**g**) *(in skittles, bowling)* quille *f*
(**h**) *(in wrestling → gen)* prise *f*; *(→ with shoulders on floor)* tombé *m*
(**i**) *Chess* clouage *m*
(**j**) *Golf* drapeau *m*

2 *vt* (**a**) *(attach → with pin or pins)* épingler; *(→ with drawing pin or pins)* punaiser; **she had a brooch pinned to her jacket** elle portait une broche épinglée à sa veste; **there was a sign pinned to the door** un écriteau était punaisé sur la porte; *Fig* **to pin one's hopes on sb/sth** mettre tous ses espoirs dans qn/qch; **to pin one's faith on sb** placer sa foi en qn; **the crime was pinned on James** c'est James qu'on a accusé du délit, on a mis le délit sur le dos de James; **they pinned the blame on the shop assistant** ils ont rejeté la responsabilité sur la vendeuse, ils ont mis ça sur le dos de la vendeuse; **you can't pin this on me** tu ne peux pas me mettre ça sur le dos
(**b**) *(immobilize)* immobiliser, coincer; **they pinned his arms behind his back** ils lui ont coincé les bras derrière le dos; **to pin sb to the ground/against a wall** clouer qn au sol/contre un mur; **she was pinned under a boulder** elle était coincée *ou* bloquée sous un rocher
(**c**) *Tech* cheviller, goupiller, mettre une goupille à
(**d**) *Constr (wall)* étayer, étançonner
(**e**) *Chess* clouer

►► *Orn* ***pin feather*** plume *f* naissante, sicot *m*; ***pin money*** argent *m* de poche; **she works at weekends to earn a bit of pin money** elle travaille le week-end pour se faire un peu d'argent pour ses menus plaisirs; *Fam* ***pins and needles*** fourmillements ❑ *mpl*; **I've got pins and needles in my arm** j'ai des fourmis dans le bras ❑, je ne sens plus mon bras; *Am* **to be on pins and needles** trépigner d'impatience ❑, ronger son frein ❑; *Sewing* ***pin tuck*** nervure *f*; ***pin wheel*** *(on printer)* roue *f* à picots

►**pin back** *vt sep Fam* **pin back your ears!** ouvrez vos oreilles!, écoutez bien! ❑

►**pin down** *vt sep* (**a**) *(with pin or pins)* fixer avec une épingle/des épingles; *(with drawing pin or pins)* fixer avec une punaise/des punaises
(**b**) *(trap)* coincer; **his legs were pinned down by the fallen tree** ses jambes étaient coincées sous l'arbre; **he had me pinned down** il m'avait coincé; **pinned down by enemy fire** coincé par le feu de l'ennemi
(**c**) *(define clearly → difference, meaning)* mettre le doigt sur, cerner avec précision; **a feeling that's difficult to pin down** un sentiment qu'il est difficile d'isoler *ou* d'identifier; **it's difficult to pin it down** c'est difficile de mettre le doigt dessus
(**d**) *(commit)* amener à se décider; **try to pin her down to a definite schedule** essayez d'obtenir d'elle un planning définitif; **he doesn't want to be pinned down** il veut avoir les coudées franches, il tient à garder sa liberté de manœuvre

►**pin together** *vt sep* épingler, attacher avec une épingle/des épingles

►**pin up** *vt sep* (**a**) *(poster)* punaiser; *(results, names)* afficher
(**b**) *(hem)* épingler; *(hair)* relever (avec des épingles); **she wears her hair pinned up** elle porte ses cheveux relevés en chignon

---

pina colada [ˌpiːnəkə'lɑːdə] *n* piña colada *f*

pinafore ['pɪnəfɔː(r)] *Br n* (**a**) *(apron)* tablier *m* (**b**) *(dress)* robe-chasuble *f*
►► ***pinafore dress*** robe *f* chasuble

pinball ['pɪnbɔːl] *n (game)* flipper *m*; **to play pinball** jouer au flipper
►► ***pinball machine, pinball table*** flipper *m*

pince-nez ['pænsneɪ] *(pl* **inv***) n* pince-nez *m*

pincer ['pɪnsə(r)] **1** *n (of crab)* pince *f*
2 pincers *npl (tool)* tenaille *f*, tenailles *fpl*; **a pair of pincers** une tenaille, des tenailles *fpl*
►► *Mil* ***pincer movement*** manœuvre *f ou* mouvement *m* d'encerclement

pinch [pɪntʃ] **1** *vt* (**a**) *(squeeze)* pincer; **she pinched her hand in the gate** elle s'est pincé la main dans la barrière; **he pinched her cheek** il lui a pincé la joue; **I had to pinch myself to make sure I wasn't dreaming** je me suis pincé pour voir si je ne rêvais pas; **these new shoes pinch my feet** ces chaussures neuves me font mal aux pieds
(**b**) *Br Fam (steal)* piquer, faucher; **to pinch sth from sb** piquer qch à qn; **I had my stereo pinched** on m'a piqué ma chaîne stéréo; **who's pinched my pen?** qui est-ce qui m'a piqué mon stylo?
(**c**) *Am Fam (arrest)* pincer, agrafer; **they got pinched for shoplifting** ils se sont fait pincer pour vol à l'étalage
(**d**) *Hort* pincer
2 *vi* (**a**) *(shoes)* serrer, faire mal (aux pieds); *Fig* **that's where the shoe pinches** c'est là que le bât blesse
(**b**) *(economize)* **to pinch and scrape** économiser sur tout, regarder (de près) à la dépense
3 *n* (**a**) *(squeeze)* pincement *m*; **if it comes to the pinch** s'il le faut vraiment, en cas de nécessité absolue; **we're beginning to feel the pinch** nous commençons à devoir nous priver
(**b**) *(of salt, snuff)* pincée *f*
4 at a pinch, *Am* **in a pinch** *adv* à la rigueur

►**pinch back, pinch off, pinch out** *vt sep Hort* pincer

pinchbeck ['pɪntʃbek] **1** *n* (**a**) *Metal* chrysocale *m* (**b**) *Fig (sham)* toc *m*
2 *adj* (**a**) *Metal* en chrysocale (**b**) *Fig (sham)* en toc

pinched [pɪntʃt] *adj* (**a**) *(features)* tiré; **his face looked pale and pinched** il était pâle et avait les traits tirés; **pinched with cold** transi de froid (**b**) *(lacking)* **I'm a bit pinched for money** je suis à court d'argent; **I'm a bit pinched for time** je n'ai pas beaucoup de temps; **they're pinched for space in their flat** ils sont à l'étroit *ou* ils n'ont pas beaucoup de place dans leur appartement

pinch-hit *vi Am* (**a**) *Sport* remplacer un joueur (**b**) *Fig (act as replacement)* effectuer un remplacement; **he's pinch-hitting for Joe** il remplace Joe

pinch-hitter *n Am Sport* remplaçant(e) *m,f*

pinchpenny ['pɪntʃpenɪ] *(pl* **pinchpennies***)* **1** *adj* de bout de chandelle
2 *n* grippe-sou *m*

pinch-runner *n Am Sport* coureur(euse) *m,f* d'urgence *ou* suppléant

pincushion ['pɪnˌkʊʃən] *n* pelote *f* à épingles

Pindar ['pɪndə(r)] *pr n Antiq* Pindare

Pindaric [pɪn'dærɪk] *adj* pindarique

pine [paɪn] **1** *n Bot (tree, wood)* pin *m*
2 *comp (furniture)* en pin
3 *vi* (**a**) *(long)* **to pine for sth** désirer qch ardemment, soupirer après qch; **he was pining for home** il avait le mal du pays; **they're pining to be given another chance** ce qu'ils désirent par-dessus tout, c'est qu'on leur accorde une seconde chance
(**b**) *(grieve)* languir; **she was pining for her lover** elle se languissait de son amant
►► ***pine cone*** pomme *f* de pin, *Can* cocotte *f*; ***pine forest*** forêt *f* de pins, pinède *f*; *Orn* ***pine grosbeak*** dur-bec *m* des sapins; ***pine grove*** pinède *f*; ***pine kernel*** pignon *m*, pigne *f*; ***pine marten*** martre *f*; ***pine needle*** aiguille *f* de pin; ***pine nut*** pignon *m*, pigne *f*; ***the Pine Tree State*** = surnom donné au Maine

►**pine away** *vi* dépérir

pineal ['pɪnɪəl] *adj Anat* pinéal, de l'épiphyse
►► ***pineal gland*** épiphyse *f*

pineapple ['paɪnˌæpəl] **1** *n* (**a**) *(fruit)* ananas *m* (**b**) *Fam Mil slang (grenade)* ananas *m (grenade défensive)*
2 *comp (juice)* d'ananas; *(ice cream, yoghurt)* à l'ananas
►► ***pineapple chunks*** ananas *m* en morceaux; *Bot* ***pineapple weed*** matricaire *f* odorante

pinewood ['paɪnwʊd] *n* (**a**) *(group of trees)* pinède *f* (**b**) *(material)* bois *m* de pin, pin *m*

Pinewood Studios ['paɪnwʊd-] *n* = studios de cinéma à l'ouest de Londres

pinfold ['pɪnfəʊld] *n (for animals → pound)* fourrière *f*; *(→ enclosure)* parc *m*

ping [pɪŋ] **1** *onomat* ding
2 *n* tintement *m*
3 *vi* (**a**) *(make pinging sound)* faire ding; *(timer)* sonner (**b**) *Am (car engine)* cliqueter

pinger ['pɪŋə(r)] *n* minuteur *m* (de cuisine)

pinging ['pɪŋɪŋ] *Am* = **pinking¹**

pingo ['pɪŋgəʊ] *(pl* **pingos***) n* pingo *m*, hydrolaccolithe *m*

ping-pong, ping pong ['pɪŋpɒŋ] *n* ping-pong *m*
►► ***ping-pong ball*** balle *f* de ping-pong; ***ping-pong player*** pongiste *mf*; ***ping-pong table*** table *f* de ping-pong

pinhead ['pɪnhed] *n* (**a**) *(of pin)* tête *f* d'épingle (**b**) *Fam (fool)* andouille *f*, crétin(e) *m,f*

pinheaded [pɪn'hedɪd] *adj Fam (foolish)* idiot ❑

pinhole ['pɪnhəʊl] *n* trou *m* d'épingle
►► ***pinhole camera*** appareil *m* à sténopé

pining ['paɪnɪŋ] *n* langueur *f*, languissement *m*; *(strong desire)* désir *m* ardent (**for** de); *(for home)* nostalgie *f*

pinion ['pɪnjən] **1** *n* (**a**) *Orn (wing tip)* aileron *m*; *(flight feather)* penne *f*, rémige *f* (**b**) *Literary (wing)* aile *f* (**c**) *Tech* pignon *m*
2 *vt* (**a**) *(hold fast)* retenir de force; **two policemen pinioned his arms** deux policiers le retenaient par le bras; **we were pinioned against the wall by the crowd** la foule nous coinçait contre le mur (**b**) *Orn (bird)* rogner les ailes à
►► *Tech* ***pinion wheel*** roue *f* à pignon

pink [pɪŋk] **1** *n* (**a**) *(colour)* rose *m*
(**b**) *Fig* **to be in the pink (of health)** se porter à merveille; *Fam* **you're looking in the pink!** tu as l'air en pleine forme!
(**c**) *Bot* œillet *m*; **garden pink** mignardise *f*
2 *adj* (**a**) *(in colour)* rose; **to paint a room pink** peindre une pièce en rose; **the sky turned pink** le ciel vira au rose *ou* rosit; **she went** *or* **turned pink with delight** elle rosit de bonheur; **to go** *or* **to turn pink with anger/embarrassment** rougir de colère/confusion; *Hum* **to see pink elephants** voir des éléphants roses
(**b**) *Fam (left-wing)* de gauche ❑, gauchisant ❑
(**c**) *Fam (gay)* gay, homo
3 *vt* (**a**) *(wound → of marksman)* blesser (légèrement); *(→ of bullet)* érafler; **he pinked my shoulder with his sword** il m'a éraflé *ou* égratigné l'épaule d'un coup d'épée
(**b**) *Sewing* cranter
(**c**) *(punch holes in)* perforer
4 *vi Br (car engine)* cliqueter
►► ***pink champagne*** champagne *m* rosé; ***pink gin*** = cocktail à base de gin et d'angustura; ***pink lady*** = cocktail à base de gin et de grenadine; ***pink noise*** bruit *m* rose; *Br* ***pink pound*** = le pouvoir d'achat des homosexuels; *Am Fam* ***pink slip*** lettre *f ou* avis *m* de licenciement ❑; **to get a pink slip** se faire virer

pink-collar *adj*
►► *Am Fam* ***pink-collar job*** = emploi typiquement féminin; ***pink-collar workers*** employées *fpl* de bureau ❑

pinkeye ['pɪŋkaɪ] *n Med* conjonctivite *f* aiguë contagieuse; *Vet* ophtalmie *f* périodique

pink-footed goose *n Orn* oie *f* à bec court

pinkie = **pinky**

pinking¹ ['pɪŋkɪŋ] *n Br Aut* cliquetis *m*, cliquettement *m*

pinking² *adj Sewing*
►► ***pinking scissors, pinking shears*** ciseaux *mpl* à cranter

pinkish ['pɪŋkɪʃ] *adj* (**a**) *(in colour)* rosâtre, rosé (**b**) *Fam (left-wing)* gauchisant ❑

pinko ['pɪŋkəʊ] *(pl* **pinkos** *or* **pinkoes***) Fam Pej* **1** *n* gaucho *m,f*
2 *adj* gaucho

pinky ['pɪŋkɪ] *(pl* **pinkies***) n Am, Can & Scot* petit doigt *m*

pinna ['pɪnə] *n* (**a**) *Anat* pavillon *m* (**b**) *Bot* foliole *f* (**c**) *Orn (feather)* plume *f*; *(wing)* aile *f* (**d**) *Ich* nageoire *f*

pinnace ['pɪnɪs] *n* chaloupe *f*

pinnacle ['pɪnəkəl] *n* (**a**) *(mountain peak)* pic *m*, cime *f*; *(rock formation)* piton *m*, gendarme *m* (**b**) *Fig (of fame, career)* apogée *m*, sommet *m*; *(of technology)* fin *m* du fin (**c**) *Archit* pinacle *m*

pinnacled ['pɪnəkəld] *adj* (**a**) *Archit* à pinacle(s) (**b**) *Fig* porté au pinacle

pinnate ['pɪneɪt] *adj* penné

pinnatiped [pɪ'nætɪped] *adj Orn* pinnatipède

pinnule ['pɪnjuːl] *n* (**a**) *Bot* pinnule *f*, foliole *f* (**b**) *Zool* pinnule *f*

pinny ['pɪnɪ] *(pl* **pinnies***) n Fam* tablier ❑ *m*

Pinocchio [pɪ'nəʊkɪəʊ] *pr n* Pinocchio

pinocle, pinochle ['pi:nʌkəl] *n* = jeu de cartes ressemblant à la belote

pinout ['pɪnaʊt] *n Comput* broche *f* de sortie

pinpoint ['pɪnpɔɪnt] **1** *vt* (**a**) *(locate → smell, leak)* localiser; *(→ on map)* localiser, repérer
(**b**) *(identify → difficulty, source of rumour, cause of problem)* identifier
2 *n* pointe *f* d'épingle; **a pinpoint of light** un minuscule point lumineux
3 *adj* (**a**) *(precise)* très précis; **with pinpoint accuracy** avec une précision parfaite
(**b**) *(tiny)* minuscule
▸▸ *Mil* ***pinpoint bombing*** bombardement *m* de précision

pinprick ['pɪnprɪk] *n* (**a**) *(puncture)* piqûre *f* d'épingle; **a pinprick of light** un petit point lumineux (**b**) *(irritation)* agacement *m*, tracasserie *f*

pinstripe ['pɪnstraɪp] *Tex* **1** *n* rayure *f* (très fine)
2 *adj* rayé

pinstriped ['pɪnstraɪpt] *adj* rayé
▸▸ ***pinstriped suit*** costume *m* rayé

pint [paɪnt] *n* (**a**) *(measure)* pinte *f*, ≃ demi-litre *m* (**b**) *Br Fam (beer)* bière❑ *f*; **I had a few pints last night** j'ai bu quelques bières hier soir; **I'm going for a pint** je vais prendre une bière
▸▸ ***pint mug, pint pot*** chope *f* d'une pinte

pinta[1] ['pɪntə] *n Med* pinta *m*

pinta[2] ['paɪntə] *n Br Fam (pint of milk)* pinte *f* de lait❑

pintable ['pɪnteɪbəl] *n Br* flipper *m*

pintail ['pɪnteɪl] *n Orn* pilet *m*

pintle ['pɪntəl] *n Tech (bolt, pin)* broche *f*, goujon *m*

pinto ['pɪntəʊ] *(pl* **pintos** *or* **pintoes**) **1** *n Am* cheval *m* pie
2 *adj Am (gen)* tacheté; *(horse)* pie *(inv)*
▸▸ ***pinto bean*** = variété de haricot moucheté de rose

pint-sized *adj Fam Pej* tout petit❑, minuscule❑

pin-up **1** *n* pin-up *f inv*
2 *adj (photo)* de pin-up
▸▸ ***pin-up girl*** pin-up *f inv*

pinwheel ['pɪnwi:l] *n* (**a**) *(firework)* soleil *m (feu d'artifice)* (**b**) *(cogwheel)* roue *f* dentée (**c**) *Am (windmill)* moulin *m* à vent *(jouet)*

pinworm ['pɪnwɜ:m] *n* oxyure *m*

piny ['paɪnɪ] *adj (smell)* de pin; *(forest floor)* couvert d'aiguilles de pin

Pinyin [,pɪn'jɪn] *n Ling* pinyin *m*

pion ['paɪɒn] *n Phys* pion *m*

pioneer [,paɪə'nɪə(r)] **1** *n* (**a**) *(explorer, settler)* pionnier(ère) *m,f*
(**b**) *(of technique, activity)* pionnier(ère) *m,f*; **she was a pioneer in the field of psychoanalysis** elle a été une pionnière de la psychanalyse; **they were pioneers in the development of heart surgery** ils ont ouvert la voie en matière de chirurgie cardiaque
(**c**) *Mil* pionnier *m*, sapeur *m*
(**d**) *Bot* espèce *f* pionnière
2 *comp (work, research)* novateur, original; **a pioneer researcher in the field of genetics** un chercheur à l'avant-garde dans le domaine de la génétique; **her pioneer work in the study of radioactivity** ses travaux novateurs dans le domaine de la radioactivité
3 *vt* **to pioneer research in nuclear physics** être à l'avant-garde de la recherche en physique nucléaire; **the town is pioneering a job-creation scheme** la municipalité expérimente un nouveau programme de création d'emplois; **the factory pioneered the use of robots** l'usine a été la première à utiliser des robots

pioneering [,paɪə'nɪərɪŋ] *adj (work, spirit)* novateur, original; **in pioneering days** au temps des pionniers
▸▸ ***pioneering company*** entreprise *f* innovatrice

pious ['paɪəs] *adj* (**a**) *(person, act, text)* pieux (**b**) *(falsely devout)* hypocrite (**c**) *(unrealistic)* irréel; **to have pious hopes** avoir de vains espoirs, nourrir des espoirs chimériques

piously ['paɪəslɪ] *adv* pieusement

piousness ['paɪəsnɪs] *n* piété *f*

PIP [pɪp] *n Comput (abbr* **peripheral interchange program**) logiciel *m* de commutation de périphérique

pip [pɪp] *(pt & pp* **pipped**, *cont* **pipping**) **1** *n* (**a**) *(in fruit)* pépin *m*; **orange pip** pépin *m* d'orange
(**b**) *Br (sound)* bip *m*; *Tel* **the pips** *(time signal)* le signal sonore, le signal horaire
(**c**) *(on playing card, domino)* point *m*
(**d**) *(on radar screen)* spot *m*
(**e**) *Br Fam Mil slang (on uniform)* ficelle *f*; **to get one's third pip** recevoir sa troisième ficelle
(**f**) *Br Fam Old-fashioned (idiom)* **to give sb the pip** courir sur le haricot à qn
(**g**) *Vet* pépie *f*
2 *vi* (**a**) *(chirrup)* pépier
(**b**) *(hatch out)* éclore
3 *vt Br* (**a**) *(defeat)* battre, vaincre; **to pip sb at the post** coiffer qn au poteau
(**b**) *Fam (hit with bullet)* atteindre❑; **he got pipped in the leg** il a pris une balle dans la jambe❑

pipa ['pi:pə] *n Zool* pipa *m*

pipal ['pi:pəl] *n Bot* arbre *m* des conseils, figuier *m* des pagodes

pipe [paɪp] **1** *n* (**a**) *(for smoking)* pipe *f*; **he smokes a pipe** il fume la pipe; **he smokes four pipes a day** il fume quatre pipes par jour; *Fam* **put that in your pipe and smoke it!** mets ça dans ta poche et ton mouchoir par-dessus!
(**b**) *(for gas, liquid etc)* tuyau *m*, conduite *f*; *(for stove)* tuyau *m*; **to lay gas pipes** poser des conduites de gaz; **the pipes have frozen** les canalisations ont gelé
(**c**) *Mus (gen)* pipeau *m*; *(boatswain's whistle)* sifflet *m*; *(on organ)* tuyau *m*; **the pipes** *(bagpipes)* la cornemuse
(**d**) *Anat & Zool* tube *m*; **respiratory pipe** tube *m* respiratoire
(**e**) *(birdsong)* pépiement *m*, gazouillis *m*
(**f**) *Am Fam (telephone)* bigophone *m*; **get on the pipe to Heather** passe un coup de bigophone à Heather
(**g**) *Geol* **volcanic pipe** cheminée *f* volcanique
(**h**) *Comput (symbol)* barre *f* verticale
2 *comp (bowl, stem)* de pipe; *(tobacco)* à pipe
3 *vt* (**a**) *(convey → liquid)* acheminer par tuyau; **natural gas is piped to the cities** le gaz naturel est acheminé jusqu'aux villes par gazoducs; **the irrigation system will pipe water to the fields** le système d'irrigation amènera l'eau jusqu'aux champs; **untreated sewage is piped into the lake** les égouts se déversent directement dans le lac; **to pipe coolant through a system** faire circuler un produit refroidissant dans un système
(**b**) *Mus (tune)* jouer
(**c**) *Naut (order)* siffler; **to pipe sb aboard** rendre à qn les honneurs du sifflet *(quand il monte à bord)*; **to pipe sb out** saluer le départ de qn au sifflet
(**d**) *(say)* dire d'une voix flûtée
(**e**) *Sewing* passepoiler
(**f**) *Culin (cake)* décorer avec une (poche à) douille; **pipe the cream onto the sponge** avec une poche à douille, versez la crème sur le gâteau
(**g**) *Comput (commands)* chaîner
4 *vi Mus (on bagpipes)* jouer de la cornemuse; *(on simple pipe)* jouer du pipeau
▸▸ *Mus* ***pipe band*** orchestre *m* de cornemuses; ***pipe cleaner*** cure-pipe *m*; ***pipe dream*** chimère *f*; **you and your pipe dreams!** toi et tes châteaux en Espagne!; ***pipe fitter*** tuyauteur(euse) *m,f*; ***pipe major*** cornemuse *f* principale; ***pipe organ*** grandes orgues *fpl*; ***pipe of peace*** calumet *m* de la paix; ***pipe rack*** râtelier *m* à pipes

▸**pipe down** *vi Fam* (**a**) *(make less noise)* faire moins de bruit❑; **pipe down!** moins de bruit!
(**b**) *(not talk so much)* rabattre son caquet; **pipe down!** boucle-la!; **he piped down when he realized she knew a lot more about it** il a rabattu son caquet quand il s'est rendu compte qu'elle en savait bien plus que lui

▸**pipe in** *vt sep* (**a**) *(with bagpipes)* **to pipe in the guests** = jouer de la cornemuse en tête de la procession (lors de l'entrée solennelle des invités)
(**b**) *Naut* **to pipe sb in** saluer l'arrivée de qn au sifflet

▸**pipe up** *vi* (**a**) *(person)* se faire entendre; **"me too!" he piped up** "moi aussi!", dit-il, sortant de son silence
(**b**) *(band)* se mettre à jouer

pipeclay ['paɪpkleɪ] *n* terre *f* de pipe

piped music [paɪpt-] *n* musique *f* de fond, fond *m* sonore

pipefish ['paɪpfɪʃ] *(pl* **pipefish** *or* **pipefishes**) *n Ich* syngnathe *m*

pipeful ['paɪpfʊl] *n* pipe *f* (de tabac)

pipelayer ['paɪp,leɪə(r)] *n* poseur(euse) *m,f* de tuyaux

pipelaying ['paɪp,leɪɪŋ] *n* pose *f* de tuyaux

pipeline ['paɪplaɪn] *n* (**a**) *(gen)* pipeline *m*; *(for oil)* oléoduc *m*; *(for gas)* gazoduc *m*
(**b**) *Am Fam Fig* **to have a pipeline to sb** avoir l'oreille de qn❑
(**c**) *(idiom)* **they have a new model in the pipeline** ils sont en train de mettre un nouveau modèle au point; **he's got another movie/project in the pipeline** il travaille actuellement sur un autre film/projet; **changes are in the pipeline for next year** des changements sont prévus pour l'année prochaine

pipemma [,pɪp'emə] *adv Old-fashioned* de l'après-midi

piper ['paɪpə(r)] *n (gen)* joueur(euse) *m,f* de pipeau; *(of bagpipes)* joueur(euse) *m,f* de cornemuse, cornemuseur *m*; *Prov* **he who pays the piper calls the tune** celui qui paie les pipeaux commande la musique

piperidine [pɪ'perɪdi:n] *n Chem* pipéridine *f*

piperine ['pɪpəraɪn] *n Chem* pipérine *f*, pipérin *m*

pipestone ['paɪpstəʊn] *n* catlinite *f*

pipette, *Am* **pipet** [pɪ'pet] *n* pipette *f*

pipework ['paɪpwɜ:k] *n* tuyauterie *f*, canalisations *fpl*

piping ['paɪpɪŋ] **1** *n* (**a**) *(system of pipes)* tuyauterie *f*, canalisations *fpl*; **a piece of copper piping** un tuyau de cuivre
(**b**) *Sewing* passepoil *m*
(**c**) *Mus (gen)* son *m* du pipeau *ou* de la flûte; *(of bagpipes)* son *m* de la cornemuse
(**d**) *Culin* décoration *f* (appliquée à la douille)
(**e**) *Comput (of commands)* chaînage *m*
2 *adv (as intensifier)* **piping hot** très chaud, brûlant; **a cup of piping hot tea** une tasse de thé bien chaud
3 *adj (sound, voice)* flûté
▸▸ *Culin* ***piping bag*** poche *f* à douille; *Culin* ***piping nozzle*** douille *f*

pipistrelle ['pɪpɪstrel] *n Zool* pipistrelle *f*

pipit ['pɪpɪt] *n Orn* pipit *m*

pipkin ['pɪpkɪn] *n* poêlon *m*

pipless ['pɪplɪs] *adj* sans pépins

pippin ['pɪpɪn] *n* (**a**) *(apple)* (pomme *f*) reinette *f* (**b**) *Arch (seed)* pépin *m*

pip-pip *exclam Br Fam Old-fashioned (goodbye)* salut!

pipsqueak ['pɪpskwi:k] *n Fam Pej* demi-portion *f*

piquancy ['pi:kənsɪ] *n* (**a**) *(interest)* piquant *m*, piment *m*; **it adds piquancy to the situation** cela corse un peu la situation (**b**) *(taste)* goût *m* piquant

piquant ['pi:kənt] *adj* piquant

piquantly ['pi:kəntlɪ] *adv* d'une manière piquante, avec du piquant

pique [pi:k] **1** *n* dépit *m*, ressentiment *m*; **he resigned in a fit of pique** il a démissionné par pur dépit, il était tellement dépité qu'il a démissionné
2 *vt* (**a**) *(vex)* dépiter, irriter, froisser (**b**) *(arouse)* piquer, exciter; **my curiosity was piqued** cela a piqué ma curiosité (**c**) *(pride)* **to pique oneself on sth/on doing sth** se piquer de qch/de faire qch

piqued [pi:kt] *adj (resentful)* vexé, froissé

piquet [pɪ'ket] *n* piquet *m (jeu de cartes)*

piracy ['paɪrəsɪ] *(pl* **piracies**) *n* (**a**) *(of vessel)* piraterie *f*; **air piracy** piraterie *f* aérienne (**b**) *(of copyright)* atteinte *f* au droit d'auteur; *(of software, book, cassette etc)* piratage *m*; *(of idea)* copie *f*, vol *m*

Piraeus [paɪ'ri:əs] *n* Le Pirée

piranha [pɪ'rɑ:nə] *(pl* **inv** *or* **piranhas**) *n Ich* piranha *m*, piraya *m*

pirate ['paɪrət] **1** *n* (**a**) *(person → on ship, plane)* pirate *m*; *(ship)* navire *m* de pirates
(**b**) *(of software, book, cassette etc)* pirate *m*; *(of idea)* voleur(euse) *m,f*
2 *comp* (**a**) *(raid, flag)* de pirates (**b**) *(software, book, cassette etc)* pirate
3 *vt (software, book, cassette etc)* pirater; *(idea)* s'approprier, voler

pin–pir

►► ***pirate edition*** édition *f* pirate; ***pirate radio*** radio *f* pirate; ***pirate station*** poste *m ou* émetteur *m* pirate

pirated ['paɪrɪtɪd] *adj* pirate
►► ***pirated edition*** édition *f* pirate

piratical [paɪ'rætɪkəl] *adj* de pirate

piri-piri ['pɪriːpɪriː] *n Culin* pili-pili *m*

pirogue [pɪ'rəʊg] *n* pirogue *f*

pirouette [,pɪrʊ'et] **1** *n* pirouette *f*
2 *vi* pirouetter

Pisa ['piːzə] *n* Pise

Pisan ['piːzən] **1** *n* Pisan(e) *m,f*
2 *adj* pisan, de Pise

piscatorial [,pɪskə'tɔːrɪəl], **piscatory** ['pɪskətrɪ] *adj Formal* halieutique; *(tribe)* de pêcheurs

Piscean ['paɪsɪən] *Astrol* **1** *n* **to be a Piscean** être (du signe des) Poissons
2 *adj* des Poissons; **the Piscean male** l'homme *m* Poissons

Pisces ['paɪsiːz] **1** *n* **(a)** *Astron* Poissons *mpl* **(b)** *Astrol* Poissons *mpl*; **he's a Pisces** il est (du signe des) Poissons
2 *adj Astrol* des Poissons; **he's Pisces** il est (du signe des) Poissons

pisciculture ['pɪsɪkʌltʃə(r)] *n* pisciculture *f*

pisciculturist [,pɪsɪ'kʌltʃərɪst] *n* pisciculteur(-trice) *m,f*

piscina [pɪ'siːnə, pɪ'saɪnə] *n Rel* piscine *f*

piscine [pɪ'saɪn] *adj* du poisson

piscivorous [pɪ'sɪvərəs] *adj* piscivore

pish[1] [pɪʃ] *exclam Old-fashioned* peuh!

pish[2] *Scot* = **piss**

piss [pɪs] *very Fam* **1** *vi* **(a)** *(urinate)* pisser; **to piss in the wind** se fatiguer pour rien ❑; *Am* **piss on it!** *(forget it)* laisse béton!; *(I'm fed up)* j'en ai plein le cul!
(b) *(rain)* **it's pissing with rain** il pleut comme vache qui pisse
(c) to piss all over sb *(defeat)* battre qn à plates coutures
(d) *Am* **to piss and moan** geindre, pleurnicher
2 *vt* pisser; **to piss one's pants** pisser dans sa culotte; **to piss oneself** se pisser dessus; **to piss oneself (laughing)** rire à en pisser dans sa culotte
3 *n* **(a)** *(urine, act of urinating)* pisse *f*; *Br* **to have** *or Am* **to take a piss** pisser (un coup); **to go for a piss** aller pisser
(b) *Br* **to go on the piss** *(go out drinking)* aller se bourrer la gueule, aller prendre une cuite; *Br* **to be on the piss** se bourrer la gueule, prendre une cuite
(c) to take the piss out of sb *Br (mock)* se foutre de la gueule de qn; *Am (calm down)* calmer qn ❑
(d) *Br (worthless thing)* **the film/book was piss** le film/le bouquin ne valait pas un clou; **their beer is piss** leur bière, c'est du pipi de chat
4 *adv Br* **piss easy** fastoche
►► *Br* ***piss artist*** *(drunkard)* poivrot(e) *m,f*; **he's a real piss artist** *(fool)* il n'arrête pas de déconner

►**piss about, piss around** *very Fam* **1** *vi (fool around)* déconner, faire le con; *(waste time)* glander, glandouiller; **we don't have time to piss about** on n'a pas de temps à perdre en conneries; **don't piss around with my stuff** arrête de tripoter mes affaires *ou* de foutre le bordel dans mes affaires
2 *vt sep* emmerder; **to piss sb about** *(cause problems for)* se foutre de la gueule de qn; *(waste time of)* faire perdre son temps à qn

►**piss away** *vt sep very Fam* **to piss sth away** *(winnings, inheritance)* gaspiller qch ❑

►**piss down** *very Fam* **1** *vt sep* **it's pissing it down** il pleut comme vache qui pisse
2 *vi* **it's pissing down** il pleut comme vache qui pisse

►**piss off** *very Fam* **1** *vi (go away)* se casser, se tirer, foutre le camp; **piss off!** *(go away)* casse-toi!, tire-toi!, fous(-moi) le camp!; *(expressing contempt, diasgreement)* va te faire foutre!
2 *vt sep* faire chier; **to be pissed off** *(bored)* s'emmerder; *(angry)* être en rogne, être fumasse; **to be pissed off with sb/sth** *(have had enough of)* en avoir ras le bol de qn/qch; **to be pissed off at sb/about sth** être en pétard contre qn/à cause de qch

piss-ant *very Fam* **1** *n (stickler)* pinailleur(euse) *m,f*
2 *adj (niggling)* pinailleur

pissed [pɪst] *adj very Fam* **(a)** *Br (drunk)* bourré, pété; **to get pissed** se soûler *ou* se péter la gueule; **as pissed as a fart** *or* **a newt, pissed out of one's head** *or* **mind** bourré comme un coing, plein comme une barrique
(b) *Am (angry)* en rogne; **to be pissed** être fumasse; **I was pretty pissed about it** ça m'a vraiment foutu en rogne; **to be pissed at sb/about sth** être en pétard contre qn/à cause de qch; **to be pissed with sb/sth** *(have had enough of)* en avoir ras le bol de qn/qch

pissed-up *adj Br very Fam (drunk)* bourré, pété, beurré

pisser ['pɪsə(r)] *n very Fam* **(a)** *(annoying situation)* **what a pisser!** quelle merde!; **it was a real pisser that the weather wasn't better** c'était vraiment chiant qu'il fasse pas plus beau **(b)** *Am (remarkable situation)* **what a pisser!** c'est génial ou super! **(c)** *Am (annoying person)* emmerdeur(euse) *m,f* **(d)** *Am (remarkable person)* **to be a pisser** être un mec/une nana génial(e)

pisshead ['pɪshed] *n very Fam* **(a)** *Br (drunkard)* poivrot(e) *m,f*, soûlard(e) *m,f* **(b)** *Am (unpleasant person)* connard (connasse) *m,f*; *(bore)* emmerdeur(euse) *m,f*

pisshole ['pɪshəʊl] *n very Fam* **his eyes are like pissholes in the snow** il a des petits yeux ❑

piss-poor *adj very Fam* minable, nul

piss-take *n Br very Fam (mockery)* mise *f* en boîte; *(of book, film)* parodie ❑ *f*; **this is a piss-take, isn't it?** non mais tu te fous de ma gueule ou quoi?

piss-taker *n Br very Fam (mocker)* personne *f* qui se fout du monde; **he's a real piss-taker** il se fout vraiment de la gueule du monde

piss-up *n Br very Fam* beuverie *f*; **to go on** *or* **to have a piss-up** se soûler *ou* se bourrer la gueule, prendre une cuite; *Hum* **he couldn't organize a piss-up in a brewery** il n'est pas foutu d'organiser quoi que ce soit, c'est un incompétent de première

pissy ['pɪsɪ] *adj very Fam* de mauvais poil

pistachio [pɪ'stɑːʃɪəʊ] *(pl* **pistachios***)* **1** *n* **(a)** *(nut)* pistache *f*; *(tree)* pistachier *m*; **pistachio-flavoured** à la pistache **(b)** *(colour)* (vert *m*) pistache *m*
2 *comp (ice cream)* à la pistache
3 *adj (in colour)* (vert) pistache *(inv)*

piste [piːst] *n* piste *f* (de ski)

pistil ['pɪstɪl] *n Bot* pistil *m*

pistol ['pɪstəl] *n* **(a)** *(gun)* pistolet *m*; **I heard pistol shots** j'ai entendu des coups de feu; *Fig* **he's holding a pistol to her head** il lui met le couteau sur la gorge **(b)** *Tech (of pneumatic tool)* pistolet *m*
►► ***pistol grip*** *(of tool, camera)* crosse *f*

pistole [pɪ'stəʊl] *n Hist (coin)* pistole *f*

pistol-whip *vt* frapper (au visage) avec un pistolet

piston ['pɪstən] *n* piston *m*
►► ***piston dwell*** temps *m* d'immobilité du piston; ***piston engine*** moteur *m* à pistons; ***piston head*** tête *f ou* fond *m* du piston; ***piston ring*** segment *m* (de piston); ***piston rod*** tige *f* de piston, bielle *f*; ***piston walls*** parois *fpl* du piston

pit [pɪt] *(pt & pp* **pitted**, *cont* **pitting***)* **1** *n* **(a)** *(hole in ground)* fosse *f*, trou *m*; *(pothole in road)* nid *m* de poule; **to dig a pit** creuser un trou
(b) *(shallow mark → in metal)* marque *f*, piqûre *f*; *(→ on skin)* cicatrice *f*, marque *f*
(c) *(mine)* mine *f*, puits *m*; *(mineshaft)* puits *m* de mine; **to go down the pit** descendre dans la mine; *(work as miner)* travailler à la mine; **to work down the pit** travailler à la mine
(d) *(quarry)* carrière *f*
(e) *Br Theat (for orchestra)* fosse *f* (d'orchestre); *(seating section)* parterre *m*
(f) *St Exch* parquet *m*, corbeille *f*
(g) *(usu pl) (at motor-racing track)* stand *m* (de ravitaillement)
(h) *(in cockfighting)* arène *f*
(i) *Sport (for long jump)* fosse *f*
(j) *Anat* creux *m*; **the pit of the stomach** le creux de l'estomac; *Fig* **her rejection hit him in the pit of his stomach** son rejet lui a fait l'effet d'un coup de poing dans l'estomac
(k) *Br Fam (bed)* plumard *m*, pieu *m*; **in one's pit** au pieu
(l) *Fam (untidy place)* foutoir *m*
(m) *Am (in fruit)* noyau *m*
(n) *Literary (hell)* **the pit** l'enfer *m*
2 *comp (closure)* de mine; *(worker)* de fond; *(accident)* minier
3 *vt* **(a)** *(mark)* cribler; **his face was pitted with acne** son visage était criblé d'acné; **meteors have pitted the surface of the moon** la lune est criblée de cratères laissés par les météores; **a road pitted with potholes** une route criblée de nids-de-poule; **pitted with rust** piqué par la rouille
(b) *(oppose)* opposer, dresser; **she was pitted against the champion** on l'a opposée à la championne; **to pit oneself against sb** se mesurer à qn; **to pit one's wits against sb** se mesurer à *ou* avec qn
(c) *Am (fruit)* dénoyauter
4 pits *npl Fam* **to be the pits** être complètement nul; **it's the pits!** c'est l'horreur!; **this town is the pits** cette ville est un vrai trou
►► ***pit bull (terrier)*** pit bull *m*; ***pit pony*** cheval *m* de mine; ***pit prop*** poteau *m ou* étau *m* de mine, étançon *m*; ***pit stop*** *(in motor racing)* arrêt *m* au stand; **to make a pit stop** s'arrêter au stand; *Zool* ***pit viper*** *(Crotalus)* crotale *m*; *(Bothrops)* bothrops *m*

pita = **pitta**[1]

pit-a-pat = **pitter-patter**

pitch [pɪtʃ] **1** *vt* **(a)** *(throw)* lancer, jeter; *(in cricket)* lancer; *Fig* **she found herself pitched into the political arena** elle se trouva propulsée dans l'arène politique; **he pitched a great game last night** *(in baseball)* il a très bien joué hier soir
(b) *Mus (note)* donner; *(tune)* donner le ton de; *(one's voice)* poser; **I can't pitch my voice any higher** je n'arrive pas à chanter dans un ton *ou* un registre plus aigu; **the music was pitched too high/low for her** le ton était trop haut/bas pour elle
(c) *(set level of)* **we must pitch the price at the right level** il faut fixer le prix au bon niveau; **our prices are pitched too high** nos prix sont trop élevés; **he pitched his speech at the level of the man in the street** son discours était à la portée de l'homme de la rue, il avait rendu son discours accessible à l'homme de la rue; **stories pitched at older children** histoires écrites pour des enfants plus âgés
(d) *(set up → camp)* établir; **let's pitch camp here** établissons notre camp *ou* dressons nos tentes ici; **to pitch wickets** *(in cricket)* planter *ou* dresser les guichets
(e) *(in golf)* pitcher
(f) *Fam (tell)* raconter ❑
(g) *(product)* promouvoir; *(idea)* présenter, soumettre
2 *vi* **(a)** *(fall over)* tomber; **he pitched into the water** il est tombé dans l'eau; **to pitch headlong** tomber la tête la première; **the passengers pitched forwards/backwards** les passagers ont été projetés en avant/en arrière
(b) *(bounce → ball)* pitcher
(c) *Aviat & Naut* tanguer
(d) *(in baseball → player)* lancer, être lanceur; *Am Fam Fig* **to be in there pitching** y mettre du sien ❑
(e) *(slope → roof)* être incliné; **the roof pitches sharply** le toit est fortement incliné
(f) *(for contract)* faire une soumission **(for** pour)
(g) *(in golf → player)* pitcher; **she pitched to within three feet of the hole** elle a pitché à moins d'un mètre du trou
3 *n* **(a)** *(tone)* ton *m*; **the pitch of his voice grew higher and higher** sa voix devint de plus en plus aiguë; **to give the orchestra the pitch** donner le ton à l'orchestre; **to rise in pitch** monter de ton
(b) *(particular level or degree)* niveau *m*, degré *m*; *(highest point)* comble *m*; **a high pitch of excitement was reached** l'excitation était presque à son comble; **how did their relationship reach such a pitch?** comment leurs relations ont-elles pu se détériorer à ce point?; **the suspense was at its highest pitch** le suspense était à son comble
(c) *Br (sports field)* terrain *m*; **rugby pitch** terrain *m* de rugby

pir–pit

(**d**) *(act of throwing)* lancer *m*, lancement *m*; **the ball went full pitch through the window** la balle passa à travers la vitre sans rebondir
(**e**) *Br Fam (street vendor's place)* place❑ *f*, emplacement❑ *m*
(**f**) *Mktg (of product)* promotion *f*; *(of idea)* présentation *f*, soumission *f*; **the salesman's pitch** le boniment du vendeur
(**g**) *(slope → of roof)* pente *f*, inclinaison *f*; *(→ of staircase)* pente *f*, rampant *m*; *Tech (→ of plane)* inclinaison *f*, basile *f*
(**h**) *(movement → of boat, aircraft)* tangage *m*; **angle of pitch** angle *m* de tangage
(**i**) *Tech (of rivets, holes)* espacement *m*, écartement *m*; *(of screw, cogwheel, rotor)* pas *m*; *Typ (of characters)* pas *m*
(**j**) *Archit (of ceiling)* hauteur *f*
(**k**) *(in golf)* pitch *m*
(**l**) *(natural tar)* poix *f*; *(distillation residue)* brai *m*
(**m**) *(in climbing)* longueur *f*
(**n**) *Am Fam (idiom)* **to make a pitch for sth** jeter son dévolu sur qch❑; **he made a pitch at her** il lui a fait du plat, il a essayé de la draguer
►► ***pitch angle*** angle *m* de tangage; ***pitch circle*** cercle *m* primitif; *(of wheel)* ligne *f* d'engrènement; ***pitch mark*** *(in golf)* pitch *m*; ***pitch pine*** pitchpin *m*; *Mus* ***pitch pipe*** diapason *m* *(sifflet)*

►**pitch in** *vi (start work)* s'attaquer au travail; *(lend a hand)* donner un coup de main; **everybody is expected to pitch in** on attend de chacun qu'il mette la main à la pâte

►**pitch into** *vt insep (attack)* s'en prendre à; **to pitch into a task** se mettre à une tâche; **they pitched into the meal** ils ont attaqué le repas

►**pitch on** *vt insep* choisir, opter pour

►**pitch out** *vt sep (rubbish)* jeter; *(person)* expulser, mettre à la porte

pitch-and-putt *n* pitch-and-putt *m (forme simplifiée du golf)*

pitch-and-toss *n* = jeu d'adresse et de hasard utilisant des pièces de monnaie

pitch-black *adj (water)* noir comme de l'encre; **the cave was pitch-black** la caverne était plongée dans l'obscurité totale; **it's pitch-black in here** il fait noir comme dans un four ici

pitchblende ['pɪtʃblend] *n Miner* pechblende *f*

pitch-dark *adj (night)* noir; **it was pitch-dark inside** à l'intérieur, il faisait noir comme dans un four

pitched [pɪtʃt] *adj (roof)* en pente
►► *Mil & Fig* ***pitched battle*** bataille *f* rangée; ***pitched roof*** toit *m* en pente

pitcher ['pɪtʃə(r)] *n* (**a**) *(jug → earthenware)* cruche *f*; *(→ metal, plastic)* broc *m*; *Am (smaller → for milk)* pot *m*; *Prov* **little pitchers have big ears** = pas devant les enfants (**b**) *(in baseball)* lanceur *m*
►► *Sport* ***pitcher's mound*** monticule *m*; ***pitcher plant*** *(Nepenthes genus)* népenthès *m*; *(Sarracenia genus)* sarracénie *f*, sarracenia *m*

pitcherful ['pɪtʃəfʊl] *n (jugful → earthenware)* cruchée *f*; *(→ metal, plastic)* plein broc *m*

pitchfork ['pɪtʃfɔːk] **1** *n* fourche *f* (à foin)
2 *vt* (**a**) *(hay)* fourcher (**b**) *Fig (person)* propulser; **she was pitchforked into the job** elle a été parachutée à ce poste

piteous ['pɪtɪəs] *adj* pitoyable; *(situation)* triste

piteously ['pɪtɪəslɪ] *adv* pitoyablement

piteousness ['pɪtɪəsnɪs] *n* état *m* pitoyable; *(of situation)* tristesse *f*

pitfall ['pɪtfɔːl] *n* (**a**) *(hazard)* embûche *f*, piège *m*; **the pitfalls of English** les pièges *mpl* de l'anglais (**b**) *Hunt* piège *m*, trappe *f*

pith [pɪθ] *n* (**a**) *(in citrus fruit)* peau *f* blanche *(sous l'écorce des agrumes)* (**b**) *(crux)* substance *f*, moelle *f*; **this is the pith of the matter** c'est le cœur *ou* le fond du problème (**c**) *(force)* vigueur *f*, force *f*; **his argument lacks pith** son argument manque de force (**d**) *Bot (in stem)* moelle *f*
►► ***pith helmet*** casque *m* colonial

pithead ['pɪthed] *n* carreau *m* de mine
►► ***pithead ballot*** vote *m* des mineurs

pithecanthropus [ˌpɪθɪkæn'θrəʊpəs] *(pl* **pithecanthropi** [-paɪ]*) n* pithécanthrope *m*

pithily ['pɪθɪlɪ] *adv* avec concision

pithiness ['pɪθɪnɪs] *n* concision *f*

pithy ['pɪθɪ] *(compar* **pithier,** *superl* **pithiest**) *adj* (**a**) *(fruit)* couvert de peau blanche (**b**) *(style, phrase, writing etc)* concis, lapidaire (**c**) *Bot (stem)* moelleux

pitiable ['pɪtɪəbəl] *adj* (**a**) *(arousing pity)* pitoyable (**b**) *(arousing contempt)* piteux, lamentable

pitiably ['pɪtɪəblɪ] *adv* (**a**) *(touchingly)* pitoyablement (**b**) *(contemptibly)* lamentablement

pitiful ['pɪtɪfʊl] *adj* (**a**) *(arousing pity)* pitoyable; **it's pitiful to see people living on the street** cela fait pitié de voir des gens à la rue (**b**) *(arousing contempt)* piteux, lamentable; **they're paid a pitiful wage** ils touchent un salaire de misère

pitifully ['pɪtɪfʊlɪ] *adv* (**a**) *(touchingly)* pitoyablement; **she was pitifully thin** sa maigreur faisait peine à voir, elle était maigre à faire pitié (**b**) *(contemptibly)* lamentablement; **a pitifully bad performance** une prestation lamentable; **he was pitifully bad at drawing** il était lamentable en dessin; **she earns a pitifully small salary** elle gagne un salaire de misère

pitiless ['pɪtɪlɪs] *adj (person)* impitoyable, sans pitié; *(weather)* rude, rigoureux

pitilessly ['pɪtɪlɪslɪ] *adv* impitoyablement, sans pitié

pitilessness ['pɪtɪlɪsnɪs] *n* manque *m* de pitié

pitman ['pɪtmən] *(pl* **pitmen** [-mən]*) n Scot & NEng* mineur *m*

piton ['piːtɒn] *n* piton *m* (d'alpiniste)

Pitot tube ['piːtəʊ-] *n Aviat* tube *m* de Pitot

pitta[1] ['pɪtə] *n* **pitta (bread)** pita *m*

pitta[2] *n Orn* brève *m*

pittance ['pɪtəns] *n* somme *f* misérable *ou* dérisoire; **to work for a pittance** travailler pour un salaire de misère; **to live on a pittance** vivre de presque rien

pitted ['pɪtɪd] *adj* (**a**) *(metal etc)* piqué, alvéolé; *(surface of moon)* alvéolé; *(skin → by smallpox)* grêlé; *(→ by acne)* couvert de marques (**b**) *(fruit, olives)* dénoyauté

pitter-patter ['pɪtə-] **1** *n (of rain, hail)* crépitement *m*; *(of feet)* trottinement *m*; *(of heart)* battement *m*
2 *adv* **to go pitter-patter** *(feet)* trottiner; *(heart)* palpiter; **the rain fell pitter-patter on the leaves** la pluie tambourinait doucement sur les feuilles

pittosporum [pɪ'tɒspərəm] *n Bot* pittosporum *m*

Pittsburgh ['pɪtsbɜːg] *n* Pittsburgh

pituitary [pɪ'tjuːɪtrɪ] **1** *n (gland)* glande *f* pituitaire, hypophyse *f*
2 *adj* pituitaire
►► ***pituitary gland*** glande *f* pituitaire, hypophyse *f*

pity ['pɪtɪ] *(pl* **pities,** *pt & pp* **pitied**) **1** *n* (**a**) *(compassion)* pitié *f*, compassion *f*; **I feel great pity for them** j'ai beaucoup de pitié pour eux, je les plains énormément; **the sight moved her to pity** le spectacle l'a apitoyée *ou* attendrie; **out of pity** par pitié; **to take** *or* **to have pity on sb** avoir pitié de qn
(**b**) *(mercy)* pitié *f*, miséricorde *f*; **have pity on the children!** ayez pitié des enfants!; **he showed no pity to the traitors** il s'est montré impitoyable envers les traîtres; **for pity's sake!** *(as entreaty)* pitié!; *(in annoyance)* par pitié!
(**c**) *(misfortune, shame)* dommage *m*; **what a pity!** c'est dommage!; **it's a pity (that) she isn't here** quel dommage qu'elle ne soit pas là; **it seems a pity not to finish the bottle** ce serait dommage de ne pas finir la bouteille; **we're leaving tomorrow, more's the pity** nous partons demain, malheureusement
2 *vt* avoir pitié de, s'apitoyer sur; **he pities himself** il s'apitoie sur son sort; **they are greatly to be pitied** ils sont bien à plaindre

'Tis Pity She's a Whore' *Ford* 'Dommage qu'elle soit une putain'

pitying ['pɪtɪɪŋ] *adj (look, smile)* de pitié, compatissant

pityingly ['pɪtɪɪŋlɪ] *adv* avec compassion, avec pitié

pityriasis [ˌpɪtɪ'raɪəsɪs] *n Med* pityriasis *m*

Pius ['paɪəs] *pr n* Pie

pivot ['pɪvət] **1** *n* (**a**) *Tech* pivot *m*, axe *m*; *(of crane)* pivot *m*; *(of axle)* tourillon *m*
(**b**) *Fig (person in company etc)* pivot *m*, cheville *f* ouvrière; *Mil* pivot *m*, guide *m*, homme *m* de base
2 *vi* (**a**) *(turn)* pivoter; **pivot on your left foot** pivotez sur votre pied gauche
(**b**) *Fig* **his life pivots around his family** toute son existence tourne autour de sa famille
3 *vt* faire pivoter
►► ***pivot bridge*** pont *m* tournant; *Mil* ***pivot man*** pivot *m*, guide *m*, homme *m* de base

►**pivot on** *vt insep Fig* dépendre de; **everything pivots on her decision** tout dépend de sa décision

pivotal ['pɪvətəl] *adj (crucial)* crucial, central; **she is pivotal in their plans** elle joue un rôle central dans leurs projets

pix [pɪks] *pl of* **pic**

pixel ['pɪksəl] *n* pixel *m*
►► ***pixel density*** densité *f* en pixels

pixellated ['pɪksəleɪtɪd] *adj Comput (image)* pixélisé, bitmap, en mode point

pixelization [pɪksəlaɪ'zeɪʃən] *n TV (to hide identity)* mosaïquage *m*

pixelize, -ise ['pɪksəlaɪz] *vt TV (to hide identity)* mosaïquer

pixie ['pɪksɪ] *n* fée *f*, lutin *m*
►► ***pixie boots*** bottines *fpl* à bout pointu; ***pixie hat*** bonnet *m* pointu

pixilated ['pɪksɪleɪtɪd] *adj Am Fam (drunk)* bourré, pété

pixy *(pl* **pixies**) = **pixie**

pizazz = **pizzazz**

pizza ['piːtsə] *n* pizza *f*
►► ***pizza base*** pâte *f* à pizza; ***pizza parlour*** pizzeria *f*

pizza-face *n Fam Hum (person with acne)* calculette *f*

pizzazz [pɪ'zæz] *n Fam (dynamism)* tonus❑ *m*, punch *m*; *(panache)* panache❑ *m*

pizzeria [ˌpiːtsə'rɪə] *n* pizzeria *f*

pizzicato [ˌpɪtsɪ'kɑːtəʊ] *n Mus* pizzicato *m*

pizzle ['pɪzəl] *n Arch* verge *f* (de taureau)

PJs ['piːdʒeɪz] *npl Fam (abbr* **pyjamas**) pyjama❑ *m*

pkg *(written abbr* **package**) paquet *m*, colis *m*

pkt *(written abbr* **packet**) paquet *m*

pkwy *Am (written abbr* **parkway**) grand boulevard *m* bordé d'arbres

Pl. *(written abbr* **place**) rue *f*

pl *(written abbr* **plural**) pl

placard ['plækɑːd] **1** *n (on wall)* affiche *f*, placard *m*; *(hand-held)* pancarte *f*
2 *vt* (**a**) *(wall, town)* placarder (**b**) *(advertisement)* placarder, afficher

placate [plə'keɪt] *vt* apaiser, calmer

placating [plə'keɪtɪŋ] *adj* apaisant, lénifiant

placatory [plə'keɪtərɪ] *adj* apaisant, conciliant

PLACE [pleɪs]

endroit	►**1 (a)**
lieu	►**1 (a)**
maison	►**1 (c)**
place	►**1 (d) – (f), (h), (i)**
couvert	►**1 (g)**
poste	►**1 (h)**
avoir lieu	►**1 (k)**
placer	►**2 (a) – (d), (g)**
(se) remettre	►**2 (e)**
passer	►**2 (f)**

1 *n* (**a**) *(gen → spot, location)* endroit *m*, lieu *m*; **this is the place** c'est ici; **place of death/amusement** lieu *m* de décès/de divertissement; **the place where the accident happened** l'endroit où a eu lieu l'accident; **keep the documents in a safe place** gardez les documents en lieu sûr; **store in a cool place** *(on packaging)* à conserver au frais; **this is neither the time nor the place to discuss it** ce n'est ni le moment ni le lieu pour en discuter; **this looks like a good place to pitch the tent** l'endroit semble parfait pour monter la tente; **I had no particular place to go** je n'avais nulle part où aller; **you can't be in two places at once** on ne peut pas être en deux endroits à la fois; **her leg is fractured in two places** elle a deux fractures à la jambe; **there are still one or two places where the text needs changing** le texte doit encore être modifié en un ou deux endroits; **to go places** *(travel)*

pit–pla

aller quelque part; *Fig* **that girl will go places!** cette fille ira loin!

(**b**) *(locality)* **do you know the place well?** est-ce que tu connais bien le coin?; **she comes from a place called Barton** elle vient d'un endroit qui s'appelle Barton; **the whole place went up in flames** *(building)* tout l'immeuble s'est embrasé; *(house)* toute la maison s'est embrasée; **how long have you been working in this place?** depuis combien de temps travaillez-vous ici?; **we had lunch at a little place in the country** nous avons déjeuné dans un petit restaurant de campagne; **can you recommend a place to eat?** pouvez-vous me recommander un restaurant?; **I'm looking for a place to stay** je cherche un logement; *Fam* **to shout** *or* **to scream the place down** hurler comme un forcené; **the other place** *Br Univ (at Oxford)* Cambridge; *(at Cambridge)* Oxford; *Br Parl (in House of Commons)* la Chambre des Lords; *(in House of Lords)* la Chambre des Communes

(**c**) *(house)* maison *f*; *(flat)* appartement *m*; **they have a place in the country** ils ont une maison de campagne; *Fam* **nice place you've got here** c'est joli chez toi ❑; *Fam* **your place or mine?** on va chez toi ou chez moi? ❑; *Fam* **they met up at Ali's place** ils se sont retrouvés chez Ali ❑

(**d**) *(position)* place *f*; **take your places!** prenez vos places!; **everything is in its place** tout est à sa place; **put it back in its proper place** remets-le à sa place; **it occupies a central place in his philosophy** cela occupe une place centrale dans sa philosophie; **I lost my place in the queue** j'ai perdu ma place dans la file d'attente; **I've lost my place** *(in a book)* je ne sais plus où j'en étais; **push the lever till it clicks into place** poussez le levier jusqu'au déclic; *Fig* **suddenly everything fell** *or* **clicked into place** *(I understood)* tout à coup, ça a fait tilt; *(everything went well)* tout d'un coup, tout s'est arrangé; **what would you do (if you were) in my place?** que feriez-vous (si vous étiez) à ma place?; **try and put yourself in his place** essaie de te mettre à sa place; **I wouldn't change places with her for anything** pour rien au monde je n'aimerais être à sa place; **his anger gave place to pity** sa colère a fait place à un sentiment de pitié

(**e**) *(role, function)* place *f*; **robots took the place of human workers** des robots ont remplacé les hommes dans l'accomplissement de leur tâche; **if she leaves there's nobody to take** *or* **to fill her place** si elle part, il n'y a personne pour la remplacer; **it's not really my place to say** ce n'est pas à moi de le dire

(**f**) *(seat → on train, in theatre etc)* place *f*; *(→ on committee)* siège *m*; **she gave up her place to an old man** elle a offert sa place à un vieux monsieur; **save me a place** garde-moi une place; **there are a few places left on the next flight** il reste quelques places sur le prochain vol; **she has a place on the new commission** elle siège à la nouvelle commission; **to change places with sb** changer de place avec qn; **we changed places so that he could sit by the window** nous avons échangé nos places pour qu'il puisse s'asseoir près de la fenêtre

(**g**) *(table setting)* couvert *m*; **how many places should I set?** combien de couverts dois-je mettre?

(**h**) *(post, vacancy)* place *f*, poste *m*; **to get a place at university** être admis à l'université; **there is keen competition for university places** il y a une forte compétition pour les places en faculté

(**i**) *(ranking → in competition, hierarchy etc)* place *f*; **the prize for second place** le prix pour la deuxième place; **Brenda took third place in the race/exam** Brenda a terminé troisième de la course/a été reçue troisième à l'examen; **the team is in fifth place** l'équipe est en cinquième position; *Horseracing* **to back a horse for a place** jouer un cheval placé; **for me, work takes second place to my family** pour moi, la famille passe avant le travail; **he needs to find his place in society** il a besoin de trouver sa place dans la société; **I'll soon put him in his place** j'aurai vite fait de le remettre à sa place; **to know one's place** savoir se tenir à sa place

(**j**) *Math* **to three decimal places, to three places of decimals** jusqu'à la troisième décimale

(**k**) **to take place** *(to happen)* avoir lieu; **the meeting will take place in Geneva** la réunion aura lieu à Genève; **many changes have taken place** il y a eu beaucoup de changements; **while this was taking place** tandis que cela se passait

(**l**) *Am (in adverbial phrases)* **no place** nulle part; **I'm not going any place** je ne vais nulle part; **some place** quelque part; **I've looked every place** j'ai cherché partout

2 *vt* (**a**) *(put, set)* placer, mettre; **she placed the vase on the shelf** elle a mis le vase sur l'étagère; **to place a book back on a shelf** remettre un livre (en place) sur un rayon; **to place a book with a publisher** confier un livre à un éditeur; **he placed an ad in the local paper** il a fait passer *ou* mis une annonce dans le journal local; **the proposals have been placed before the committee** les propositions ont été soumises au comité; **to place a matter in sb's hands** mettre une affaire dans les mains de qn; **I place myself at your disposal** je me mets à votre disposition

(**b**) *(find work or a home for)* placer; **to place sb in care** placer qn; **all the refugee children have been placed** tous les enfants réfugiés ont été placés

(**c**) *(usu passive) (situate)* placer, situer; **the house is well placed** la maison est bien située; **strategically placed airfields** des terrains d'aviation stratégiquement situés; **you are better placed to judge than I am** vous êtes mieux placé que moi pour en juger; **British industry is well placed to...** l'industrie britannique est à même de...; **we met several people similarly placed** nous avons rencontré plusieurs personnes qui se trouvaient dans la même situation; **how are we placed for time?** combien de temps avons-nous?; **how are you placed for money at the moment?** quelle est ta situation financière en ce moment?

(**d**) *(usu passive) (rank → in competition, race etc)* placer, classer; **she was placed third** elle était en troisième position; **the runners placed in the first five go through to the final** les coureurs classés dans les cinq premiers participent à la finale; **the horse we bet on wasn't even placed** le cheval sur lequel nous avions parié n'est même pas arrivé placé; **I would place her amongst the best writers of our time** je la classerais parmi les meilleurs écrivains de notre époque

(**e**) *(identify)* (se) remettre; **I can't place him** je n'arrive pas à (me) le remettre

(**f**) *(order, contract)* passer (**with** à); **to place an order for sth** passer commande de qch; **to place a bet** faire un pari; **to place a bet on sb/sth** parier sur qn/qch; **place your bets!** *(in casino)* faites vos jeux!

(**g**) *(invest → funds)* placer; *(sell → goods, shares)* placer, vendre

3 *vi Am (in racing)* être placé

4 all over the place *adv Fam (everywhere)* partout ❑; *(untidy)* en désordre ❑; **you always leave your things all over the place!** tu laisses toujours traîner tes affaires partout!; **my hair's all over the place** je suis complètement décoiffé ❑; *Fig* **the team were all over the place** l'équipe a joué n'importe comment ❑; **these figures are all over the place** *(are inaccurate)* ces chiffres ont été calculés n'importe comment ❑; **at the interview he was all over the place** *(panicking, unclear)* il a raconté n'importe quoi à l'entretien ❑

5 in place *adv* (**a**) *(steady)* en place; **hold it in place while I nail it in** tiens-le en place pendant que je le cloue

(**b**) *(on the spot → run, jump)* sur place

6 in place of *prep* à la place de; **she came in place of her sister** elle est venue à la place de sa sœur

7 in places *adv* par endroits

8 in the first place *adv* **what drew your attention to it in the first place?** qu'est-ce qui a attiré votre attention à l'origine *ou* en premier lieu?; **I didn't want to come in the first place** d'abord, je ne voulais même pas venir; **in the first place, it's too big, and in the second place...** premièrement, c'est trop grand, et deuxièmement..., primo, c'est trop grand, et secundo...

9 out of place *adj* **the wardrobe looks out of place in such a small room** l'armoire n'a pas l'air à sa place dans une pièce aussi petite; **he felt out of place amongst so many young people** il ne se sentait pas à sa place parmi tous les jeunes; **he didn't look out of place** il ne déparait pas; **such remarks are out of place at a funeral** de telles paroles sont déplacées lors d'un enterrement

►► ***place of birth*** lieu *m* de naissance; ***place of business*** lieu *m* de travail; ***place card*** = carte marquant la place de chaque convive à table; *Mktg* ***place of delivery*** lieu *m* de livraison; *Fin* ***place of issue*** lieu *m* d'émission; *Sport* ***place kick*** coup *m* de pied placé; ***place mat*** set *m* (de table); ***place of residence*** résidence *f*, domicile *m* (réel); *Br Law* ***place of safety order*** = ordonnance autorisant une personne ou un organisme à garder des enfants maltraités en lieu sûr; ***place setting*** couvert *m*; ***place of work*** lieu *m* de travail; ***place of worship*** lieu *m* de culte

---

placebo [plə'siːbəʊ] (*pl* **placebos** *or* **placeboes**) *n also Fig* placebo *m*

►► *Med* ***placebo effect*** effet *m* placebo

placeman ['pleɪsmən] (*pl* **placemen** [-mən]) *n esp Br Pej* = fonctionnaire qui obtient son poste grâce à son appartenance politique, et qui ne recherche que son propre intérêt

placement ['pleɪsmənt] *n* (**a**) *(gen → act of putting, sending)* placement *m*; *(situation, position)* situation *f*, localisation *f*; *Mktg (of product)* placement *m*; *St Exch (of shares)* placement *m* (**b**) *(job-seeking)* placement *m* (**c**) *(work experience)* stage *m* (en entreprise)

►► *Am Univ* ***placement office*** centre *m* d'orientation (professionnelle); ***placement service*** agence *f* pour l'emploi

place-name *n* nom *m* de lieu

placenta [plə'sentə] (*pl* **placentas** *or* **placentae** [-tiː]) *n Anat, Zool & Bot* placenta *m*

placental [plə'sentəl] **1** *n Zool* placentaire *m*

2 *adj Anat, Zool & Bot* placentaire

►► ***placental barrier*** barrière *f* placentaire; ***placental murmur*** murmure *m* placentaire; ***placental vessels*** vaisseaux *mpl* placentaires.

placer ['pleɪsə(r)] *n Mining* (**a**) *(deposit)* placer *m* (**b**) *(place)* chantier *m* de lavage

placet ['pleɪset, 'plæket] *n* (**a**) *(vote of assent)* approbation *f* (**b**) *Hist* placet *m*

placid ['plæsɪd] *adj (person, attitude)* placide; *(lake, town)* tranquille, calme

placidity [plə'sɪdətɪ] *n (of person, attitude)* placidité *f*; *(of place)* calme *m*, tranquillité *f*

placidly ['plæsɪdlɪ] *adv* placidement

placidness ['plæsɪdnɪs] = **placidity**

placing ['pleɪsɪŋ] *n (act of putting)* placement *m*; *(situation, position)* situation *f*, localisation *f*; *(arrangement)* disposition *f*

placket ['plækɪt] *n Sewing* patte *f* (de boutonnage)

placoderm ['plækəʊdɜːm] *n* placoderme *m*

placoid ['plækɔɪd] *adj Zool* placoïde

plagal ['pleɪgəl] *adj Mus* plagal

plagiarism ['pleɪdʒərɪzəm] *n* plagiat *m*; **it's a crude piece of plagiarism** c'est un plagiat grossier

plagiarist ['pleɪdʒərɪst] *n* plagiaire *mf*

plagiarize, -ise ['pleɪdʒəraɪz] **1** *vt* plagier

2 *vi* plagier

plagioclase ['pleɪdʒɪəʊkleɪs] *n Miner* plagioclase *f*

plagiostome ['pleɪdʒɪəʊstəʊm] *n Ich* plagiostome *m*

plague [pleɪg] **1** *n* (**a**) *(bubonic)* **the plague** la peste; **to avoid sb like the plague** fuir qn comme la peste; *Hum* **he avoids work like the plague** il est allergique au travail; *Arch* **a plague on them!** qu'ils crèvent!; *Arch* **a plague on both your houses!** allez tous au diable!

(**b**) *(epidemic)* épidémie *f*; *Fig* **there's been a veritable plague of burglaries** il y a eu toute une série de cambriolages

(**c**) *(scourge)* fléau *m*; *Bible* plaie *f*; **a plague of rats** une invasion de rats

(**d**) *Fam (annoying person)* enquiquineur(-euse) *m,f*

2 *vt* (**a**) *(afflict)* tourmenter; **the region is plagued by floods** la région est en proie aux

inondations; **we are plagued with tourists in the summer** l'été, nous sommes envahis par les touristes; **we are plagued with mosquitoes in the summer** l'été, nous sommes infestés de moustiques; **it's an old injury that still plagues him** c'est une vieille blessure dont il souffre encore; **the industry has been plagued with strikes this year** l'industrie a beaucoup souffert des grèves cette année
(**b**) *(pester)* harceler; **to plague sb with telephone calls** harceler qn de coups de téléphone

plaguey, plaguy ['pleɪgɪ] *adj Fam Old-fashioned* enquiquinant

plaice [pleɪs] (*pl* **inv** *or* **plaices**) *n Ich* carrelet *m*, plie *f*

plaid [plæd, *Scot & Ir* pleɪd] **1** *n* (**a**) *(fabric, design)* tartan *m*, tissu *m* écossais (**b**) *(worn over shoulder)* plaid *m*
2 *adj* (en tissu) écossais

Plaid Cymru [ˌplaɪd'kʌmrɪ] *n* = parti nationaliste gallois

PLAIN [pleɪn]

plaine	▸ 1 (a)
simple	▸ 2 (a)
nature	▸ 2 (a)
clair	▸ 2 (b)
uni	▸ 2 (c)
franc	▸ 2 (d)
quelconque	▸ 2 (e)
pur	▸ 2 (f)

1 *n* (**a**) *Geog* plaine *f*
(**b**) *(in knitting)* maille *f* à l'endroit
2 *adj* (**a**) *(simple → style, furniture, dress)* simple; *(with nothing added → omelette, rice, yoghurt)* nature *(inv)*; **a plain dress** une robe toute simple; **he's just a plain soldier** il n'est que simple soldat; **she was just plain Sarah then** elle s'appelait tout simplement Sarah à l'époque; **I like good plain cooking** j'aime la cuisine simple; **a plain piece of bread and butter** une simple tartine beurrée; **it's plain sailing from now on** maintenant ça va marcher tout seul *or* comme sur des roulettes; **to be in** *or* **to wear plain clothes** être en civil
(**b**) *(clear, obvious)* clair, évident, manifeste; **it's plain (to see) that he's lying** il est clair *ou* évident qu'il ment; **it soon became plain that I was lost** j'ai vite réalisé *ou* je me suis vite rendu compte que j'étais égaré; **his embarrassment was plain to see** on pouvait voir qu'il était gêné, sa gêne était évidente; **the facts are plain** c'est clair, les choses sont claires; **I want to make our position absolutely plain to you** je veux que vous compreniez bien notre position; **she made her intentions plain** elle n'a pas caché ses intentions; **he made it plain to us that he wasn't interested** il nous a bien fait comprendre que cela ne l'intéressait pas; **I thought I'd made myself plain** je croyais avoir été assez clair; *Fam* **it's as plain as a pikestaff** *or* **as the nose on your face** c'est clair comme de l'eau de roche, ça saute aux yeux
(**c**) *(of one colour, not patterned)* uni; **plain blue wallpaper** papier peint bleu uni; **under plain cover, in a plain envelope** sous pli discret
(**d**) *(blunt, unambiguous)* franc (franche); **the plain truth of the matter is I'm bored** la vérité, c'est que je m'ennuie; **let me be plain with you** je vais être franc avec vous; **I want a plain yes or no answer** je veux une réponse claire et nette; **the time has come for plain words** *or* **speaking** le moment est venu de parler franchement; **in plain language** de manière claire; **I told him in plain English what I thought** je lui ai dit ce que je pensais sans mâcher mes mots
(**e**) *(unattractive)* pas très beau (belle), quelconque; **she's a bit of a plain Jane** ce n'est pas une beauté *ou* une Vénus
(**f**) *(pure, sheer)* pur (et simple); **that's just plain foolishness/ignorance** c'est de la pure bêtise/ignorance
(**g**) *Knitting* **plain one, purl two** une maille à l'endroit, deux à l'envers
3 *adv* (**a**) *(clearly)* franchement, carrément; **you couldn't have put it any plainer** tu n'aurais pas pu être plus clair
(**b**) *Fam (utterly)* complètement ❑, carrément; **he's just plain crazy** il est complètement cinglé; **he's just plain ignorant** il est tout simplement ignorant ❑; **I just plain forgot!** j'ai tout bonnement oublié! ❑
▸▸ ***plain chocolate*** chocolat *m* noir; ***plain flour*** farine *f* (sans levure); ***plain paper*** *(unheaded)* papier *m* sans en-tête; *(unruled)* papier *m* non réglé; *Knitting* ***plain row*** rang *m* à l'endroit; *Knitting* ***plain stitch*** maille *f* à l'endroit

plainchant ['pleɪntʃɑːnt] *n* plain-chant *m*

plain-clothes *adj* en civil

plainclothesman [pleɪnkləʊðzmən] (*pl* **plainclothesmen** [-mən]) *n Am* policier *m* en civil

plainly ['pleɪnlɪ] *adv* (**a**) *(manifestly)* clairement, manifestement; **you plainly weren't listening** manifestement, vous n'écoutiez pas, il est évident que vous n'écoutiez pas; **he was plainly tired** il était visiblement fatigué; **she's plainly his favourite** il est clair qu'elle est sa préférée
(**b**) *(distinctly → remember, hear)* clairement, distinctement
(**c**) *(simply → dress, lunch)* simplement
(**d**) *(bluntly, unambiguously)* franchement, carrément, sans ambages

plainness ['pleɪnnɪs] *n* (**a**) *(of clothes, cooking)* simplicité *f* (**b**) *(clarity, obviousness)* clarté *f* (**c**) *(unattractiveness)* physique *m* quelconque *ou* ingrat

plain-paper *adj (fax, printer)* à papier ordinaire

Plains Indian *n* Indien(enne) *m,f* des Plaines *ou* des Prairies

plainsman ['pleɪnzmən] (*pl* **plainsmen** [-mən]) *n (gen)* habitant *m* de la plaine; *(of Great Plains)* habitant *m* des Grandes Plaines

plainsong ['pleɪnsɒŋ] *n* plain-chant *m*

plain-spoken *adj* qui a son franc-parler

plaint [pleɪnt] *n Literary* plainte *f*, lamentation *f*

plaintiff ['pleɪntɪf] *n Law* demandeur(eresse) *m,f*, plaignant(e) *m,f*

plaintive ['pleɪntɪv] *adj (voice, sound)* plaintif

plaintively ['pleɪntɪvlɪ] *adv* plaintivement

plaintiveness ['pleɪntɪvnɪs] *n* ton *m* plaintif

plait [plæt] **1** *n (of hair)* natte *f*, tresse *f*; *(of straw)* tresse *f*
2 *vt (hair, rope, grass)* natter, tresser; *(garland)* tresser

plan [plæn] (*pt & pp* **planned**, *cont* **planning**) **1** *n* (**a**) *(strategy)* plan *m*, projet *m*; **to draw up** *or* **to make a plan** dresser *ou* établir un plan; **what's your plan of action** *or* **campaign?** qu'est-ce que vous comptez faire?; **to put a plan into operation** mettre un plan en œuvre; **to go according to plan** se dérouler comme prévu *ou* selon les prévisions; **we'll have to try plan B** il faudra qu'on essaie l'autre solution; **I've thought of a plan** j'ai un plan
(**b**) *(intention, idea)* projet *m*; **I had to change my holiday plans** j'ai dû changer mes projets de vacances; **we had made plans to stay at a hotel** nous avions prévu de descendre à l'hôtel; **what are your plans for Monday?** qu'est-ce que tu as prévu pour lundi?; **to have other plans** avoir d'autres projets; **the plan is to meet up at Rachel's** l'idée, c'est de se retrouver chez Rachel
(**c**) *(diagram, map)* plan *m*; **I'll draw you a plan of the office** je vais vous dessiner un plan du bureau
(**d**) *(outline → of book, essay, lesson)* plan *m*; **rough plan** canevas *m*, esquisse *f*
(**e**) *Archit* plan *m*; **drawn in plan and in elevation** dessiné en plan et en élévation
2 *vt* (**a**) *(organize in advance → project)* élaborer; *(→ concert, conference)* organiser, monter; *(→ crime, holiday, trip, surprise, lesson)* préparer; *(→ campaign)* organiser, preparer; *Econ* planifier; **everything had been planned down to the last detail** tout avait été planifié dans les moindres détails; **plan your time carefully** organisez votre emploi du temps avec soin; **they're planning a surprise for you** ils te préparent une surprise; **they're planning a new venture** ils ont en projet une nouvelle entreprise; **the Pope's visit is planned for March** la visite du pape doit avoir lieu en mars; **an industrial estate is planned for this site** il est prévu d'aménager un parc industriel sur ce site; **everything went as planned** tout s'est déroulé comme prévu
(**b**) *(intend)* projeter; **we're planning to go to the States** nous projetons d'aller aux États-Unis; **plan to finish it in about four hours** comptez environ quatre heures pour le terminer
(**c**) *(design → house, garden, town)* concevoir, dresser les plans de
(**d**) *(make outline of → book, essay)* faire le plan de, esquisser; *(→ lesson)* préparer
3 *vi* faire des projets; **it is important to plan ahead** il est important de faire des projets pour l'avenir

▸**plan for** *vt insep* prévoir; **to plan for the future** faire des projets d'avenir; **we didn't plan for this many people** nous n'avions pas prévu *ou* nous n'attendions pas autant de monde; **you must plan for everything** vous devez tout prévoir *ou* parer à toute éventualité

▸**plan on** *vt insep* (**a**) *(intend)* projeter; **what are you planning on doing?** qu'est-ce que vous projetez de faire *ou* vous avez l'intention de faire?; **we're planning on going to Brazil** *or* **on a trip to Brazil** nous projetons de *ou* nous avons l'intention de partir au Brésil, nous projetons un voyage au Brésil
(**b**) *(expect)* compter sur; **we hadn't planned on it raining** nous n'avions pas prévu qu'il pleuvrait; **don't plan on being able to persuade him** ne compte pas arriver à le persuader; **we hadn't planned on staying long** nous n'avions pas prévu de *ou* nous ne comptions pas rester longtemps

▸**plan out** *vt sep (make detailed plans for)* prévoir (en détail); **he had planned it all out** il avait tout prévu, il en avait établi tous les détails

planar ['pleɪnə(r)] *adj Geom* plan

planarian [plə'neərɪən] *n Zool* planaire *f*

planchet ['plɑːntʃɪt] *n* flan *m*

planchette [plæn'ʃet] *n* oui-ja *m*

Planck's constant [plæŋks-] *n Phys* constance *f* de Planck

plane [pleɪn] **1** *n* (**a**) *(aeroplane)* avion *m*; **by plane** en avion; **it's just a short plane ride** c'est un court voyage en avion
(**b**) *Archit, Art & Math* plan *m*; **vertical plane** plan *m* vertical
(**c**) *(level, degree)* plan *m*; **she's on a higher intellectual plane** elle est d'un niveau intellectuel plus élevé
(**d**) *(tool)* rabot *m*
(**e**) *(tree)* platane *m*
2 *adj (flat)* plan, plat; *Geom* plan
3 *vi (glide)* planer
4 *vt (in carpentry)* **to plane sth (down)** raboter qch
▸▸ ***plane crash*** accident *m* d'avion; ***plane geometry*** géométrie *f* plane; ***plane ticket*** billet *m* d'avion; ***plane tree*** platane *m*

planet ['plænɪt] *n* planète *f*; **the biggest country on the planet** le plus grand pays de la planète

'Planet of the Apes' *Schaffner, Burton, Boulle* 'La Planète des singes'

planetarium [ˌplænɪ'teərɪəm] (*pl* **planetariums** *or* **planetaria** [-rɪə]) *n* planétarium *m*

planetary ['plænɪtrɪ] *adj* planétaire

planetoid ['plænɪtɔɪd] *n Astron* planétoïde *m*

planetology [ˌplænɪ'tɒlədʒɪ] *n* planétologie *f*

plangency ['plændʒənsɪ] *n Literary* (**a**) *(loudness)* retentissement *m*, résonance *f* (**b**) *(plaintiveness)* caractère *m* plaintif

plangent ['plændʒənt] *adj Literary* (**a**) *(loud)* sonore, retentissant (**b**) *(plaintive)* plaintif, mélancolique

planimeter [plæ'nɪmɪtə(r)] *n* planimètre *m*; **polar planimeter** planimètre *m* polaire

planimetric [ˌplænɪ'metrɪk] *adj* planimétrique

planimetry [plæ'nɪmɪtrɪ] *n* planimétrie *f*

planing ['pleɪnɪŋ] *n (of wood)* rabotage *m*, planage *m*, aplanissage *m*; *(of metal)* planage *m*, aplanissage *m*
▸▸ ***planing machine*** raboteuse *f*

planisphere ['plænɪˌsfɪə(r)] *n* planisphère *m*

plank [plæŋk] **1** *n* (**a**) *(board)* planche *f*; **to walk the plank** subir le supplice de la planche (**b**) *Pol*

article *m*; **the main plank of their policy** la pièce maîtresse de leur politique
2 *vt* (**a**) *(floor, room)* planchéier (**b**) *Scot Fam (hide)* planquer
▸**plank down** *vt sep (put down heavily)* poser brusquement
planking ['plæŋkɪŋ] *n (UNCOUNT)* planches *fpl*, planchéiage *m*; **the floor consists of rough planking** quelques planches mal dégrossies font office de plancher
plankton ['plæŋktən] *n* plancton *m*
planktonic [plæŋk'tɒnɪk] *adj* planctonique
planned [plænd] *adj (trip)* projeté; *(murder)* prémédité; *(baby)* désiré, voulu; **news of the planned sale was leaked** le projet de vente s'est ébruité; **a demonstration against the planned nuclear power station** une manifestation contre le projet de centrale nucléaire; **Shula was a planned baby** Shula était un bébé désiré *ou* voulu
▸▸ *Econ* ***planned economy*** économie *f* planifiée; *Ind* ***planned obsolescence*** obsolescence *f* planifiée, désuétude *f* calculée; *Am* ***Planned Parenthood*** = organisme de planning familial; ***planned redundancy scheme*** plan *m* social
planner ['plænə(r)] *n* (**a**) *(gen) & Econ* planificateur(trice) *m,f*; *Rad & TV* **programme planner** programmateur(trice) *m,f*; **(town) planner** urbaniste *mf* (**b**) *(in diary, on wall)* planning *m*
planning ['plænɪŋ] *n* (**a**) *(of project)* élaboration *f*; *(of concert, conference)* organisation *f*; *(of crime, holiday, trip, surprise, lesson)* préparation *f*; *(of campaign)* organisation *f*, préparation *f*; *Econ* planification *f*; **the expedition will require careful planning** il faudra une organisation minutieuse pour mener à bien cette expédition; **the new product is still at the planning stage** le nouveau produit n'en est encore qu'au stade de projet
(**b**) *(of economy, production)* planification *f*; **demographic planning** planification *f* des naissances
(**c**) *(of town, city)* urbanisme *m*
▸▸ *Br* ***planning blight*** = effets négatifs possibles de l'urbanisation; ***planning permission*** *(UNCOUNT)* permis *m* de construire
planning-programming-budgeting system *n Fin* système *m* de planification-programmation-budgétisation, rationalisation *f* des choix budgétaires
plano-concave [ˌpleɪnəʊ-] *adj Opt* plan-concave
plano-convex [ˌpleɪnəʊ-] *adj Opt* plan-convexe
plant [plɑːnt] **1** *n* (**a**) *Bot* plante *f*
(**b**) *(factory)* usine *f*
(**c**) *(UNCOUNT) (industrial equipment)* équipement *m*, matériel *m*; *(buildings and equipment)* bâtiments *mpl* et matériel
(**d**) *Fam (thing)* = objet caché dans le but d'incriminer quelqu'un; **he claims the heroin was a plant by the police** il prétend que l'héroïne a été mise là par la police (pour le compromettre)□
(**e**) *Fam (infiltrator)* agent *m* infiltré□, taupe *f*; *(from police)* mouchard *m*; *(of magician, memory man)* compère□ *m*
(**f**) *(in snooker, pool)* = situation dans laquelle un joueur blouse une bille en en percutant une autre avec laquelle elle est en contact
2 *vt* (**a**) *(flowers, crops, seed)* planter; **fields planted with wheat** des champs (plantés) de blé
(**b**) *Fam (place firmly)* planter□; **she planted herself in the doorway** elle se planta *ou* se campa dans l'entrée□
(**c**) *Br Fam (offload)* **don't try and plant the blame on me!** n'essaie pas de me faire porter le chapeau!; **they planted their kids on us for the weekend** ils nous ont laissé leurs gosses sur les bras pour le week-end
(**d**) *Fam (give → kick, blow)* envoyer□, donner□; *(→ kiss)* planter□; **he planted a punch on his nose** il lui a mis un coup de poing sur le nez□
(**e**) *(in someone's mind)* mettre, introduire; **her talk planted doubts in their minds** son discours a semé le doute dans leur esprit; **who planted that idea in your head?** qui t'a mis cette idée dans la tête?
(**f**) *(hide → bomb)* poser; *(→ microphone)* cacher; *(infiltrate → spy)* infiltrer; **he says the weapons were planted in his flat** il prétend que les armes ont été placées dans son appartement pour le compromettre; **to plant evidence on sb** cacher un objet compromettant sur qn pour l'incriminer
▸▸ ***plant biology*** phytobiologie *f*; ***plant breeder*** phytogénéticien(enne) *m,f*; ***plant food*** engrais *m (pour plantes d'appartement)*; ***plant hire*** location *f* de matériel industriel; ***the plant kingdom*** le règne végétal; ***plant life*** flore *f*; ***plant louse*** puceron *m*; ***plant physiology*** physiologie *f* végétale; ***plant pot*** pot *m* (de fleurs); ***plant stand*** jardinière *f*
▸**plant out** *vt sep (young plants)* repiquer
Plantagenet [plæn'tædʒənɪt] *n* Plantagenêt *mf*
plantain¹ ['plæntɪn] *n (plant)* plantain *m*
plantain² *n* (**a**) *(fruit)* banane *f* plantain (**b**) *(tree)* plantain *m*
▸▸ ***plantain tree*** plantain *m*
plantar ['plæntə(r)] *adj Anat* plantaire
plantation [plæn'teɪʃən] *n* plantation *f*; **sugar plantation** plantation *f* de canne à sucre
▸▸ ***Plantation State*** = surnom donné au Rhode Island
planter ['plɑːntə(r)] *n* (**a**) *(person)* planteur(-euse) *m,f*; **tea planter** planteur(euse) *m,f* de thé (**b**) *(machine)* planteuse *f* (**c**) *(flowerpot holder)* cache-pot *m inv*; *(for several plants)* bac *m* à fleurs
▸▸ ***planter's punch*** (punch *m*) planteur *m*
plantigrade ['plæntɪgreɪd] **1** *adj* plantigrade
2 *n* plantigrade *m*
planting ['plɑːntɪŋ] *n* plantation *f*
▸▸ ***planting bed*** planche *f (de semis ou de jeunes plantes)*; ***planting out*** repiquage *m*
plantlet ['plɑːntlɪt] *n* petite plante *f*
plaque [plɑːk] *n* (**a**) *(on wall, monument)* plaque *f*
(**b**) *(on teeth)* **(dental) plaque** plaque *f* dentaire
plaquette [plæ'ket] *n* plaquette *f*
plash [plæʃ] *Literary* **1** *n (of waves, oars)* clapotement *m*, clapotis *m*; *(of stream, fountain)* murmure *m*
2 *vi (waves)* clapoter; *(oars)* frapper l'eau avec un bruit sourd; *(stream, fountain)* murmurer
plashy ['plæʃɪ] (*compar* **plashier**, *superl* **plashiest**) *adj Literary (marshy)* marécageux
plasm ['plæzəm] *n Biol* protoplasme *m*
plasma ['plæzmə] *n Med & Phys* plasma *m*
▸▸ ***plasma cell*** plasmocyte *m*; *Comput* ***plasma display*** affichage *m* à plasma; ***plasma screen*** écran *m* (à) plasma; ***plasma TV*** télévision *f* à plasma
plasmapheresis [ˌplæzmə'ferəsɪs] *n Med* plasmaphérèse *f*, échange *m* plasmatique
plasmatic [ˌplæz'mætɪk] *adj* plasmatique
plasmid ['plæzmɪd] *n Biol* plasmide *m*
plasmin ['plæzmɪn] *n Biol & Chem* plasmine *f*
plasminogen [plæz'mɪnədʒən] *n Biol* plasminogène *m*
plasmodesm ['plæzməʊdezəm] *n Bot* plasmodesme *m*
plasmodium [plæz'məʊdɪəm] (*pl* **plasmodia** [-ɪə]) *n* plasmodie *f*, plasmodium *m*
plaster ['plɑːstə(r)] **1** *n* (**a**) *(for walls, modelling)* plâtre *m*
(**b**) *(for broken limbs)* plâtre *m*; *Br* **her arm was in plaster** elle avait le bras dans le plâtre
(**c**) *Br (for cut)* **(sticking) plaster** pansement *m* (adhésif); **corn plasters** pansements *mpl* coricides
2 *comp (model, statue)* de *ou* en plâtre
3 *vt* (**a**) *Constr & Med* plâtrer
(**b**) *(smear → ointment, cream)* enduire; **she had plastered make-up on her face, her face was plastered with make-up** elle avait une belle couche de maquillage sur la figure; **they were plastered with mud** ils étaient couverts de boue
(**c**) *(make stick)* coller; **the rain had plastered his shirt to his back** la pluie lui avait plaqué la chemise sur le dos; **he tried to plaster his hair down with oil** il mit de l'huile sur ses cheveux pour essayer de les plaquer sur sa tête
(**d**) *(cover)* **to plaster sth with sth** couvrir qch de qch; **to plaster a wall with notices, to plaster notices over a wall** couvrir un mur d'affiches; **the town was plastered with election posters** les murs de la ville étaient tapissés *ou* recouverts d'affiches électorales; **her name was plastered over the front pages** son nom s'étalait en première page
(**e**) *Fam (defeat heavily)* écraser; *(beat up)* tabasser, passer à tabac
▸▸ ***plaster cast*** *Med* plâtre *m*; *Art* moule *m* (en plâtre); ***plaster of Paris*** plâtre *m* de Paris *or* à mouler
▸**plaster over, plaster up** *vt sep (hole, crack)* boucher (avec du plâtre)
plasterboard ['plɑːstəbɔːd] *n* Placoplâtre® *m*
plastered ['plɑːstəd] *adj Fam (drunk)* bourré, pété; **to get plastered** se soûler
plasterer ['plɑːstərə(r)] *n* plâtrier *m*
plastering ['plɑːstərɪŋ] *n Constr* plâtrage *m*
plasterwork ['plɑːstəwɜːk] *n (UNCOUNT) Constr* plâtre *m*, plâtres *mpl*
plastic ['plæstɪk] **1** *n* (**a**) *(material)* plastique *m*, matière *f* plastique; **the plastics industry** l'industrie *f* du plastique
(**b**) *(UNCOUNT) Fam (credit cards)* cartes *fpl* de crédit□; **she pays for everything with plastic** elle règle tous ses achats avec des cartes de crédit; **to put sth on the plastic** payer qch avec une carte de crédit; **do they take plastic?** est-ce qu'ils acceptent *ou* prennent les cartes de crédit?
2 *adj* (**a**) *(made of plastic)* en *ou* de plastique
(**b**) *(malleable)* plastique, malléable; *(adaptable)* influençable
(**c**) *Art* plastique
(**d**) *Fam Pej (artificial)* synthétique□; **the plastic rubbish they call bread** cette espèce de caoutchouc qu'ils appellent du pain
▸▸ *Art* ***the plastic arts*** les arts *mpl* plastiques; ***plastic bomb*** charge *f* de plastique, bombe *f* au plastique; ***plastic bullet*** balle *f* en plastique; ***plastic cup*** gobelet *m* en plastique; ***plastic explosive*** plastic *m*; **the laboratory was blown up with plastic explosives** le laboratoire a été plastiqué; *Fam* **plastic money** *(UNCOUNT)* cartes *fpl* de crédit□; ***plastic surgeon*** *(cosmetic)* chirurgien(enne) *m,f* esthétique; *(therapeutic)* plasticien(enne) *m,f*; ***plastic surgery*** *(cosmetic)* chirurgie *f* esthétique; *(therapeutic)* chirurgie *f* plastique *ou* réparatrice; **she had plastic surgery on her nose** elle s'est fait refaire le nez; ***plastic wrap*** film *m* alimentaire
Plasticine® ['plæstɪsiːn] *n* pâte *f* à modeler
plasticity [plæs'tɪsətɪ] *n* plasticité *f*
plasticization [ˌplæstɪsaɪ'zeɪʃən] *n* plastification *f*
plasticize, -ise ['plæstɪsaɪz] *vt* plastifier
plasticizer ['plæstɪsaɪzə(r)] *n (agent m)* plastifiant *m*
plastid ['plæstɪd] *n Bot* plaste *m*, plastide *m*
plastron ['plæstrən] *n* plastron *m*
plate [pleɪt] **1** *n* (**a**) *(for eating)* assiette *f*; *(for serving)* plat *m*; **he ate a huge plate of spaghetti** il a mangé une énorme assiette de spaghettis; *Fig* **to hand sth to sb on a plate** donner *ou* apporter qch à qn sur un plateau (d'argent); **she was handed the job on a plate** on lui a offert cet emploi sans qu'elle ait à lever le petit doigt; *Fig* **to have a lot on one's plate** avoir du pain sur la planche; **I've already got far too much on my plate** j'ai déjà beaucoup trop à faire; *Br Fam* **plates** *(rhyming slang* **plates of meat = feet***)* arpions *mpl*, panards *mpl*
(**b**) *(piece of metal, glass etc)* plaque *f*; *(rolled metal)* tôle *f*; *(for microscope)* lamelle *f*; **he has a metal plate in his thigh** il a une plaque en métal dans la cuisse
(**c**) *(with inscription)* plaque *f*; **a car with foreign plates** une voiture avec une plaque d'immatriculation étrangère *ou* immatriculée à l'étranger
(**d**) *(on cooker)* plaque *f* (de cuisson)
(**e**) *(dishes, cutlery → silver)* vaisselle *f* en argent; *(→ gold)* vaisselle *f* en or; **the burglars took all the (silver) plate** les cambrioleurs ont pris toute l'argenterie
(**f**) *(coated metal)* plaqué *m*; *(metal coating)* placage *m*; **the knives are silver plate** les couteaux sont en plaqué argent
(**g**) *Typ (for printing)* cliché *m*; *(for engraving)* planche *f*; *(illustration)* planche *f*, hors-texte *m inv*; **offset plate** plaque *f* offset
(**h**) *Phot* plaque *f* (sensible)

(**i**) *(for church collection)* plateau *m* (de quête)
(**j**) *Anat & Zool* plaque *f*
(**k**) *(denture)* dentier *m*, appareil *m ou* prothèse *f* dentaire; *(for straightening teeth)* appareil *m* (orthodontique)
(**l**) *(in earth's crust)* plaque *f*
(**m**) *(trophy, race)* trophée *m*
(**n**) *Elec & Electron* plaque *f*
(**o**) *(in baseball → home plate)* bâton *m*, = plaque qui marque le début et la fin du parcours que doit effectuer le batteur pour marquer un point
2 *vt* (**a**) *(coat with metal → gen)* plaquer; *(→ in gold)* dorer; *(→ in silver)* argenter; *(→ in nickel)* nickeler; *(→ in copper)* cuivrer
(**b**) *(cover with metal plates)* garnir de plaques; *(armour-plate)* blinder
(**c**) *Typ* clicher
3 Plate *n* **the River Plate** le Rio de la Plata
►► ***plate armour*** armure *f (en plaques de fer)*; ***plate glass*** verre *m* (à vitres); ***plate rack*** égouttoir *m*; ***plate tectonics*** *(UNCOUNT)* tectonique *f* des plaques

►**plate up** *vi (in restaurant kitchen)* disposer les aliments sur les plats

plateau ['plætəʊ] *(pl* **plateaus** *or* **plateaux** [-təʊz]) *n Geog & Fig* plateau *m*; **to reach a plateau** *(activity, process)* atteindre un palier

plated ['pleɪtɪd] *adj* (**a**) *(covered with metal plates)* recouvert *ou* garni de plaques; *(armour-plated)* blindé (**b**) *(coated with metal)* plaqué (**c**) *(wool)* vanisé

plateful ['pleɪtfʊl] *n* assiettée *f*, assiette *f*

plate-glass *adj* en verre
►► ***plate-glass window*** vitrine *f*

plate-hanger *n* accroche-plat *m*

platelayer ['pleɪt,leɪə(r)] *n Br Rail* poseur *m* de rails

plateless printing ['pleɪtlɪs-] *n Typ* impression *f* sans presse

platelet ['pleɪtlɪt] *n Anat* plaquette *f* (sanguine)

plate-making *n Typ* préparation *f* des plaques offset

platen ['plætən] *n* (**a**) *(on typewriter)* rouleau *m*, cylindre *m* (**b**) *(in printing press)* platine *f* (**c**) *(on machine tool)* table *f*, plateau *m*
►► ***platen knob*** bouton *m* (d'entraînement) du cylindre

plater ['pleɪtə(r)] *n* (**a**) *(person)* plaqueur(euse) *m,f* (**b**) *(metal)* placage *m*, revêtement *m* (**c**) *Horseracing* cheval *m* à réclamer

platewarmer ['pleɪt,wɔːmə(r)] *n* chauffe-plats *m inv*

platform ['plætfɔːm] **1** *n* (**a**) *(stage)* estrade *f*; *(for speakers)* tribune *f*; *Fig* tribune *f*; **she shared the platform with her rival** elle était à la même tribune que son rival; *Fig* **it serves as a platform for their racist views** cela sert de tribune pour propager leurs opinions racistes
(**b**) *(raised structure)* plate-forme *f*; *(of weighing machine)* tablier *m*; *(of crane)* passerelle *f*; **gun platform** plate-forme *f* de tir; **loading platform** quai *m* de chargement
(**c**) *(at station)* quai *m*; **what platform is it for York?** quel quai est-ce pour York?; **the train waiting at platform one** le train au départ voie no 1
(**d**) *Pol (programme)* plate-forme *f*; **electoral platform** plate-forme *f* électorale
(**e**) *Br (on bus)* plate-forme *f*
(**f**) *Comput (hardware standard)* plate-forme *f*; **on the Macintosh platform** sur la plate-forme Macintosh
2 platforms *npl* chaussures *fpl* à semelle compensée
►► *Am Rail* ***platform car*** (wagon *m*) plate-forme *f*; ***platform scale*** (balance *f* à) bascule *f*; ***platform shoes*** chaussures *fpl* à semelle compensée; ***platform soles*** semelles *fpl* compensées; ***platform ticket*** ticket *m* de quai

platform-soled *adj* à semelles compensées

plating ['pleɪtɪŋ] *n* (**a**) *(coating with metal → gen)* placage *m*; *(→ in gold)* dorage *m*, dorure *f*; *(→ in silver)* argentage *m*, argenture *f*; *(→ in nickel)* nickelage *m*; *(→ in copper)* cuivrage *m*
(**b**) *(covering with metal plates)* placage *m*; *(armour-plating)* blindage *m*

platinic [plə'tɪnɪk] *adj* platinique

platinization [,plætɪnaɪ'zeɪʃən] *n* platinage *m*

platinize, -ise ['plætɪnaɪz] *vt* platiner, platiniser

platinous ['plætɪnəs] *adj Chem* platineux

platinum ['plætɪnəm] **1** *n* platine *m*
2 *comp (jewellery, pen)* en platine
3 *adj (colour)* platine *(inv)*
4 *adv* **to go platinum** *(record)* devenir disque de platine
►► *Chem* ***platinum black*** noir *m* de platine; ***platinum blonde*** blonde *f* platine; *Mus* ***platinum disc, platinum record*** disque *m* de platine

platinum-blonde *adj* (blond) platine *(inv)*

platitude ['plætɪtjuːd] *n* (**a**) *(trite remark)* platitude *f*, lieu *m* commun (**b**) *(triteness)* platitude *f*

platitudinous [,plætɪ'tjuːdɪnəs] *adj Formal* banal, d'une grande platitude

Plato ['pleɪtəʊ] *pr n* Platon

platonic [plə'tɒnɪk] **1** *adj (love, relationship)* platonique
2 Platonic *adj Phil* platonicien
►► *Math* ***Platonic solid*** polyèdre *m* régulier

platonically [plə'tɒnɪklɪ] *adv* d'une manière platonique, platoniquement

Platonism ['pleɪtənɪzəm] *n* platonisme *m*

Platonist ['pleɪtənɪst] *n* platonicien(enne) *m,f*

platoon [plə'tuːn] *n Mil* section *f*; *(of bodyguards, firemen etc)* armée *f*

platter ['plætə(r)] *n* (**a**) *(for serving)* plat *m*; **seafood platter** plateau *m* de fruits de mer (**b**) *Am Fam (record)* disque ❑ *m*

platyhelminth [,plætɪ'helmɪnθ] *n Zool* plathelminthe *m*

platypus ['plætɪpəs] *n Zool* ornithorynque *m*

platyrrhine ['plætɪraɪn] *Zool* **1** *n* singe *m* platyrrhinien
2 *adj* platyrrhinien

plaudits ['plɔːdɪts] *npl Formal* (**a**) *(applause)* applaudissements *mpl* (**b**) *(praise)* éloges *mpl*; **her poetry won her plaudits from the critics** ses poésies lui ont valu les éloges de la critique

plausibility [,plɔːzə'bɪlətɪ] *n* plausibilité *f*; **the plot is lacking in plausibility** l'intrigue n'est guère plausible; **I would question the plausibility of someone doing that** il ne me semble guère plausible que quelqu'un fasse cela

plausible ['plɔːzəbəl] *adj (excuse, alibi, theory)* plausible; *(person)* crédible; **he's a very plausible liar** il ment de façon très convaincante

plausibly ['plɔːzəblɪ] *adv* de façon convaincante; **he argued his case very plausibly** il s'est défendu de façon très convaincante

Plautus ['plɔːtəs] *pr n* Plaute

PLAY [pleɪ]

jeu	► **1 (a), (e), (f), (h), (i)**
tour	► **1 (c)**
stratagème	► **1 (d)**
pièce (de théâtre)	► **1 (g)**
intérêt	► **1 (j)**
jouer à	► **2 (a), (h)**
jouer	► **2 (b), (c), (e) – (g), (i) – (k); 3 (a) – (e), (h)**
faire jouer	► **2 (d)**
jouer de	► **2 (m)**
mettre	► **2 (n)**
s'amuser	► **3 (a)**
se jouer	► **3 (f)**

1 *n* (**a**) *(fun, recreation)* jeu *m*; **I like to watch the children at play** j'aime regarder les enfants jouer; **the aristocracy at play** l'aristocratie en train de se détendre; **to say sth in play** dire qch en plaisantant *ou* pour rire; **play on words** jeu *m* de mots, calembour *m*
(**b**) *Sport* **play starts at one o'clock** le match commence à une heure; **play on the centre court is starting** le match sur le court central commence; **after some very boring play in the first half...** après une première mi-temps très ennuyeuse...; **there was some nice play from Brooks** Brooks a réussi de belles actions *ou* a bien joué; **to keep the ball in play** garder la balle en jeu; **out of play** sorti, hors jeu; **rain stopped play** la partie a été interrompue par la pluie; *Am* **she scored off a passing play** elle a marqué un but après une combinaison de passes; *Am* **the coach calls the plays** l'entraîneur choisit les combinaisons
(**c**) *(turn)* tour *m*; **whose play is it?** c'est à qui de jouer?
(**d**) *(manoeuvre)* stratagème *m*; **it was a play to get money/their sympathy** c'était un stratagème pour obtenir de l'argent/pour s'attirer leur sympathie; **he is making a play for the presidency** il se lance dans la course à la présidence; **she made a play for my boyfriend** elle a fait des avances à mon copain
(**e**) *(gambling)* jeu *m*; **I lost heavily at last night's play** j'ai perdu gros au jeu hier soir
(**f**) *(activity, interaction)* jeu *m*; **the result of a complex play of forces** le résultat d'un jeu de forces complexe; **to come into play** entrer en jeu; **to bring sth into play** mettre qch en jeu
(**g**) *Theat* pièce *f* (de théâtre); **Shakespeare's plays** les pièces *fpl ou* le théâtre de Shakespeare; **to be in a play** jouer dans une pièce; **it's been ages since I've seen** *or* **gone to see a play** ça fait des années que je ne suis pas allé au théâtre; **radio play** pièce *f* radiophonique; **television play** dramatique *f*
(**h**) *Tech (slack, give)* jeu *m*; **there's too much play in the socket** il y a trop de jeu dans la douille; **give the rope more play** donnez plus de mou à la corde; *Fig* **to give** *or* **to allow full play to sth** donner libre cours à qch
(**i**) *(of sun, colours)* jeu *m*; **I like the play of light and shadow in his photographs** j'aime les jeux d'ombre et de lumière dans ses photos
(**j**) *Fam (attention, interest)* intérêt ❑ *m*; **the summit meeting is getting a lot of media play** les médias font beaucoup de tapage *ou* battage autour de ce sommet; **in my opinion she's getting far too much play** à mon avis, on s'intéresse beaucoup trop à elle ❑; **they made a lot of play** *or* **a big play about his war record** ils ont fait tout un plat de son passé militaire
2 *vt* (**a**) *(games, cards)* jouer à; **to play football/tennis** jouer au football/tennis; **to play poker/chess** jouer au poker/aux échecs; **to play hide-and-seek** jouer à cache-cache; **the children were playing dolls/soldiers** les enfants jouaient à la poupée/aux soldats; **how about playing some golf after work?** si on faisait une partie de golf après le travail?; **do you play any sports?** pratiquez-vous un sport?; **squash is played indoors** le squash se pratique en salle; **to play the game** *Sport* jouer selon les règles; *Fig* jouer le jeu; **I won't play his game** je ne vais pas entrer dans son jeu; **she's playing games with you** elle te fait marcher; *Fam* **to play it cool** ne pas s'énerver ❑, garder son calme ❑; *Am* **to play favorites** faire du favoritisme; **to play sb for a fool** rouler qn; *Fam* **the meeting's next week, how shall we play it?** la réunion aura lieu la semaine prochaine, quelle va être notre stratégie? ❑; **to play it safe** ne pas prendre de risque, jouer la sécurité
(**b**) *(opposing player or team)* jouer contre, rencontrer; **Italy plays Brazil in the finals** l'Italie joue contre *ou* rencontre le Brésil en finale; **I played him at chess** j'ai joué aux échecs avec lui; **he will play Karpov** il jouera contre Karpov; **I'll play you for the drinks** je vous joue les consommations
(**c**) *(match)* jouer, disputer; **to play a match against sb** disputer un match avec *ou* contre qn; **how many tournaments has he played this year?** à combien de tournois a-t-il participé cette année?; **the next game will be played on Sunday** la prochaine partie aura lieu dimanche
(**d**) *(include on the team → player)* faire jouer; **the coach didn't play her until the second half** l'entraîneur ne l'a fait entrer (sur le terrain) qu'à la deuxième mi-temps
(**e**) *(card, chess piece)* jouer; **to play spades/trumps** jouer pique/atout; **how should I play this hand?** comment devrais-je jouer cette main?; **she played her ace** elle a joué son as; *Fig* elle a abattu sa carte maîtresse; *Fig* **he plays his cards close to his chest** il cache son jeu
(**f**) *(position)* jouer; **he plays winger/defence** il joue ailier/en défense
(**g**) *(shot, stroke)* jouer; **she played a chip shot to the green** elle a fait un coup coché jusque sur le green; **try playing your backhand more** essayez de faire plus de revers; **to play a six iron** *(in golf)* jouer un fer numéro six; **he played the ball to me** il m'a envoyé la balle

(**h**) *(gamble on → stock market, slot machine)* jouer à; **to play the horses** jouer aux courses; **to play the property market** spéculer sur le marché immobilier; **he played the red/the black** il a misé sur le rouge/le noir

(**i**) *(joke, trick)* **to play a trick/joke on sb** jouer un tour/faire une farce à qn; **your memory's playing tricks on you** votre mémoire vous joue des tours

(**j**) *Cin & Theat (act → role, part)* jouer, interpréter; **Cressida was played by Joan Dobbs** le rôle de Cressida était interprété par Joan Dobbs; **who played the godfather in Coppola's movie?** qui jouait le rôle du parrain dans le film de Coppola?; *Fig* **to play a part** *or* **role in sth** prendre part *ou* contribuer à qch; **an affair in which prejudice plays its part** une affaire dans laquelle les préjugés entrent pour beaucoup *ou* jouent un rôle important

(**k**) *Cin & Theat (perform at → theatre, club)* **they played Broadway last year** ils ont joué à Broadway l'année dernière; **'Othello' is playing the Strand for another week** 'Othello' est à l'affiche du Strand pendant encore une semaine; **he's now playing the club circuit** il se produit maintenant dans les clubs

(**l**) *(act as)* **to play the fool** faire l'idiot *ou* l'imbécile; **some doctors play God** il y a des médecins qui se prennent pour Dieu sur terre; **to play host to sb** recevoir qn; **to play the hero** jouer les héros; **one played the heavy while the other asked the questions** l'un jouait les méchants tandis que l'autre posait les questions; **don't play the wise old professor with me!** ce n'est pas la peine de jouer les grands savants avec moi!; *Br Fam* **play the white man!** sois sympa!

(**m**) *(instrument)* jouer de; *(note, melody, waltz)* jouer; **to play the violin** jouer du violon; **to play the blues** jouer du blues; **they're playing our song/Strauss** ils jouent notre chanson/du Strauss; **to play scales on the piano** faire des gammes au piano

(**n**) *(put on → record, tape)* passer, mettre; *(→ radio)* mettre, allumer; *(→ tapedeck, jukebox)* faire marcher; **don't play the stereo so loud** ne mets pas la chaîne si fort; **he's in his room playing records** il écoute des disques dans sa chambre; **can you play some Pink Floyd?** tu peux mettre quelque chose des Pink Floyd?; **I'll play the first side** *Br* **again** *or Am* **over for you** je vous repasse *ou* je vous fais réécouter la première face

(**o**) *(direct → beam, nozzle)* diriger (**on** sur); **he played his torch over the cave walls** il promena le faisceau de sa lampe sur les murs de la grotte

(**p**) *(fish)* fatiguer

(**q**) *Am (idiom)* **to play both ends against the middle** jouer sur les deux tableaux

3 *vi* (**a**) *(amuse oneself)* jouer, s'amuser; *(frolic → children, animals)* folâtrer, s'ébattre; **I like to work hard and play hard** quand je travaille, je travaille, quand je m'amuse, je m'amuse; **he didn't mean to hurt you, he was only playing** il ne voulait pas te faire de mal, c'était juste pour jouer; **don't play on the street!** ne jouez pas dans la rue!; **to play with dolls/with guns** jouer à la poupée/à la guerre

(**b**) *Sport* jouer; **to play well/badly/regularly** jouer bien/mal/régulièrement; **to play against sb/a team** jouer contre qn/une équipe; **to play in goal** être goal; **it's her (turn) to play** c'est à elle de jouer, c'est (à) son tour; **to play in a tournament** participer à un tournoi; **he plays in the Italian team** il joue dans l'équipe d'Italie; **she played into the left corner** elle a envoyé la balle dans l'angle gauche; **try playing to his backhand** essayez de jouer son revers; **to play high/low** *(in cards)* jouer une forte/basse carte; **do you play?** est-ce que tu sais jouer?; **to play to win** jouer pour gagner; **to play dirty** ne pas jouer franc jeu; *Fig* ne pas jouer le jeu; **to play fair** jouer franc jeu; *Fig* jouer le jeu; **to play into sb's hands** faire le jeu de qn; **you're playing right into his hands!** tu entres dans son jeu!; **to play for time** essayer de gagner du temps; **to play safe** ne pas prendre de risques, jouer la sécurité

(**c**) *(gamble)* jouer; **to play high** *or* **for high stakes** jouer gros (jeu); **to play for drinks/for money** jouer les consommations/de l'argent

(**d**) *Mus (person, band, instrument)* jouer; *(record)* passer; **I heard a guitar playing** j'entendais le son d'une guitare; **music played in the background** *(recorded)* des haut-parleurs diffusaient de la musique d'ambiance; *(band)* un orchestre jouait en fond sonore; **is that Strauss playing?** est-ce que c'est du Strauss que l'on entend?; **a radio was playing upstairs** on entendait une radio en haut; **the stereo was playing full blast** on avait mis la chaîne à fond

(**e**) *Cin & Theat (act)* jouer; **the last movie she played in** le dernier film dans lequel elle a joué

(**f**) *Cin & Theat (show, play, movie)* se jouer; **Hamlet is playing tonight** on joue Hamlet ce soir; **the movie is playing to full** *or* **packed houses** le film fait salle comble; **the same show has been playing there for five years** cela fait cinq ans que le même spectacle est à l'affiche; **now playing at all Park Cinemas** actuellement dans toutes les salles (de cinéma) Park; **what's playing at the Rex?** qu'est-ce qui passe au Rex?; **the company will be playing in the provinces** la compagnie va faire une tournée en province

(**g**) *(feign)* faire semblant; **to play dead** faire le mort; **to play innocent** *or Fam* **dumb** faire l'innocent, jouer les innocents; *Fam* **to play hard to get** se faire désirer□

(**h**) *(breeze, sprinkler, light)* **to play (on)** jouer (sur); **sun played on the water** le soleil jouait sur l'eau; **a smile played on** *or* **about** *or* **over his lips** un sourire jouait sur ses lèvres; **lightning played across the sky** le ciel était zébré d'éclairs

►► ***play area*** aire *f* de jeux

►**play about** *vi Br (have fun → children)* jouer, s'amuser; *(frolic)* s'ébattre, folâtrer; **it's time he stopped playing about and settled down** il est temps qu'il arrête de s'amuser et qu'il se fixe

►**play about with** *vt insep* (**a**) *(fiddle with, tamper with)* **to play about with sth** jouer avec *ou* tripoter qch; **stop playing about with the aerial** arrête de jouer avec *ou* de tripoter l'antenne; **I don't think we should be playing about with genes** à mon avis, on ne devrait pas s'amuser à manipuler les gènes

(**b**) *(juggle → statistics, figures)* jouer avec; *(consider → possibilities, alternatives)* envisager, considérer; **I'll play about with the figures and see if I can come up with something more reasonable** je vais jouer un peu avec les chiffres et voir si je peux suggérer quelque chose de plus raisonnable; **she played about with several endings for her novel** elle a essayé plusieurs versions pour le dénouement de son roman

(**c**) *Fam (trifle with)* **to play about with sb** faire marcher qn

►**play along 1** *vt sep (tease, deceive)* faire marcher

2 *vi (cooperate)* coopérer; **to play along with sb** *or* **with sb's plans** entrer dans le jeu de qn; **you'd better play along** tu as tout intérêt à te montrer coopératif

►**play around** *vi* (**a**) = **play about**

(**b**) *Fam (have several lovers)* coucher à droite et à gauche

►**play around with** = **play about with**

►**play at** *vt insep* (**a**) *(of child)* jouer à; **to play at cops and robbers** jouer aux gendarmes et aux voleurs; *Fam* **just what do you think you're playing at?** à quoi tu joues exactement?

(**b**) *(dabble in → politics, journalism)* faire en dilettante; **you're just playing at being an artist** tu joues les artistes; **you can't play at being a revolutionary** tu ne peux pas t'improviser révolutionnaire

►**play back** *vt sep (cassette, film)* repasser; **play the last ten frames back** repassez les dix dernières images

►**play by** *vt sep Fam* **play it by me again** reprenez votre histoire depuis le début□

►**play down** *vt sep (role, victory)* minimiser; *(problem)* dédramatiser; **we've been asked to play down the political aspects of the affair** on nous a demandé de ne pas insister sur le côté politique de l'affaire; **her book rightly plays down the conspiracy theory** son livre minimise à juste titre la thèse du complot

►**play in** *vt sep* (**a**) *(in basketball)* **to play the ball in** remettre la balle en jeu

(**b**) *Br Fig* **to play oneself in** s'habituer, se faire la main

(**c**) *(with music)* accueillir en musique

►**play off** *vi (teams, contestants)* disputer un match de barrage

►**play off against** *vt sep* **he played Neil off against his father** il a monté Neil contre son père; **he played his enemies off against each other** il a monté ses ennemis l'un contre l'autre

►**play on 1** *vt insep (weakness, naivety, trust, feelings)* jouer sur; **his political strength comes from playing on people's fears** il tire sa force politique de sa capacité à jouer sur la peur des gens; **the waiting began to play on my nerves** l'attente commençait à me porter sur les nerfs; **the title plays on a line from Shakespeare** le titre est un jeu de mots sur une phrase de Shakespeare

2 *vi* continuer à jouer; **the referee waved them to play on** l'arbitre leur fit signe de continuer à jouer

►**play out** *vt sep* (**a**) *(enact → scene)* jouer; *(→ fantasy)* satisfaire; **the events being played out on the world's stage** les événements qui se déroulent dans le monde; **the drama was played out between rioters and police** les incidents ont eu lieu entre les émeutiers et les forces de police

(**b**) *(usu passive) Fam (exhaust)* **to be played out** *(person, horse etc)* être vanné *ou* éreinté□; *(idea)* être vieux jeu□ *ou* démodé□; *(story)* avoir perdu tout intérêt□

(**c**) *(with music)* **they were played out to the strains of...** leur départ a été accompagné par l'air de...

►**play through** *vi Golf* dépasser d'autres joueurs; **may we play through?** vous permettez que nous vous dépassions?

►**play up 1** *vt sep* (**a**) *(exaggerate → role, importance)* exagérer; *(stress)* souligner, insister sur; **in the interview, play up your sales experience** pendant l'entretien, mettez en avant *ou* insistez sur votre expérience de la vente; **his speech played up his working-class background** son discours mettait l'accent sur ses origines populaires; **the press played up her divorce** la presse a monté son divorce en épingle

(**b**) *Br Fam (bother)* tracasser□; **my back is playing me up** mon dos me joue encore des tours; **don't let the kids play you up** ne laissez pas les enfants vous marcher sur les pieds

2 *vi Br Fam (car, child, TV, machine etc)* faire des siennes; **my back is playing up** mon dos me joue encore des tours

►**play up to** *vt insep Fam* **to play up to sb** *(flatter)* faire de la lèche à qn

►**play upon** *vt insep* = **play on 1**

►**play with** *vt insep* (**a**) *(toy with → pencil, hair)* jouer avec; **he was playing with the radio dials** il jouait avec les boutons de la radio; **he only played with his food** il a à peine touché à son assiette; *Fig* **to play with fire** jouer avec le feu

(**b**) *(manipulate → words)* jouer sur; *(→ rhyme, language)* manier; **she plays with language in bold and startling ways** elle manipule la langue avec une audace saisissante

(**c**) *(consider → idea)* caresser; **he played with the idea for weeks before rejecting it** il a caressé l'idée pendant des semaines avant de l'abandonner; **we're playing with the idea of buying a house** nous pensons à acheter une maison; **here are a few suggestions to play with** voici quelques suggestions que je soumets à votre réflexion

(**d**) *(treat casually)* **to play with sb's affections** jouer avec les sentiments de qn; **don't you see he's just playing with you?** tu ne vois pas qu'il se moque de toi *ou* qu'il te fait marcher?

(**e**) *(have available → money, time)* disposer de; **how much time have we got to play with?** de combien de temps disposons-nous?; **they've got $2 million to play with** ils disposent de deux millions de dollars

(**f**) *Fam* **to play with oneself** *(masturbate)* se toucher

Play it again Sam
Cette formule célèbre ("joue-le encore, Sam"), que l'on attribue au film *Casablanca*, n'est en fait pas prononcée dans le film. Le personnage incarné par Ingrid Bergman dit au pianiste du Rick's Bar **play it once Sam, for old times' sake** ("joue-le une fois, Sam, en souvenir du bon vieux temps").
Aujourd'hui on utilise cette formule en allusion au film lorsque l'on demande à quelqu'un de refaire quelque chose, et particulièrement lorsqu'il s'agit de rejouer un air de musique.

playable ['pleɪəbəl] *adj* jouable; *(sports pitch)* praticable

play-act *vi* (**a**) *Fig (pretend)* jouer la comédie; **he's not in pain, he's just play-acting!** il n'a pas mal, il joue la comédie *ou* c'est du cinéma!; **stop play-acting!** arrête ton cinéma *ou* de jouer la comédie! (**b**) *(act in plays)* faire du théâtre

play-acting *n* (**a**) *(pretence)* (pure) comédie *f*, cinéma *m* (**b**) *(acting in play)* théâtre *m*

playback ['pleɪbæk] *n* (**a**) *(replay)* enregistrement *m*; **we watched the playback after the programme** nous avons regardé l'enregistrement après l'émission (**b**) *(function)* lecture *f*; **put it on playback** mettez-le en position lecture
►► ***playback head*** tête *f* de lecture

playbill ['pleɪbɪl] *n* (**a**) *(poster)* affiche *f* (de théâtre) (**b**) *(programme)* programme *m*

playboy ['pleɪbɔɪ] *n* playboy *m*

'The Playboy of the Western World' *Synge* 'Le Baladin du monde occidental'

play-by-play *Am* **1** *n (of sporting event)* commentaire *m*
2 *adj (account, commentary)* détaillé

Play-Doh® ['pleɪˌdəʊ] *n* = sorte de pâte à modeler

player ['pleɪə(r)] *n* (**a**) *(of game, sport)* joueur(-euse) *m,f*; **bridge player** bridgeur(euse) *m,f*; **are you a poker player?** est-ce que vous jouez au poker?
(**b**) *(of musical instrument)* joueur(euse) *m,f*; **she's a piano/guitar player** elle joue du piano/de la guitare
(**c**) *(participant)* participant(e) *m,f*; *Mktg* acteur *m*; **France has been a major player in this debate** la France a eu un rôle clé dans ce débat; **the major players in the bond market** les principaux intéressés du marché obligataire; **who are the key players in this market?** qui sont les acteurs principaux sur ce marché?
(**d**) *Fam (insider)* initié(e) *m,f*
(**e**) *Arch (actor)* acteur(trice) *m,f*
►► ***player piano*** piano *m* mécanique

playfellow ['pleɪˌfeləʊ] *n Br Old-fashioned* camarade *mf* (de jeux)

playful ['pleɪfʊl] *adj (lively → person)* gai, espiègle; *(→ animal)* espiègle; *(good-natured → answer)* en forme de plaisanterie; *(→ nudge)* complice; **to be in a playful mood** être d'humeur enjouée

playfully ['pleɪfʊlɪ] *adv (answer, remark)* d'un ton taquin; *(smile)* d'un air enjoué; *(act)* avec espièglerie

playfulness ['pleɪfʊlnɪs] *n* enjouement *m*, espièglerie *f*

playgoer ['pleɪˌgəʊə(r)] *n* amateur *m* de théâtre; **disappointed playgoers were demanding their money back** des spectateurs déçus demandaient à être remboursés

playground ['pleɪgraʊnd] *n (at school)* cour *f* de récréation; *(in park)* aire *f* de jeu; *Fig* **the islands are a playground for the rich** les îles sont des lieux de villégiature pour les riches

playgroup ['pleɪgruːp] *n* = réunion régulière d'enfants d'âge préscolaire généralement surveillés par une mère

playhouse ['pleɪhaʊs, *pl* -haʊzɪz] *n* (**a**) *(theatre)* théâtre *m* (**b**) *(children's)* maison *f* de poupée

playing ['pleɪɪŋ] *n Mus* **the pianist's playing was excellent** le pianiste jouait merveilleusement bien; **guitar playing is becoming more popular** de plus en plus de gens jouent de la guitare
►► ***playing card*** carte *f* à jouer; *Br* ***playing field*** terrain *m* de sport; *Fig* **to have a level playing field** être sur un pied d'égalité; **everyone should start off on a level playing field** tout le monde devrait commencer au même niveau; **to create a level playing field** créer une situation qui n'avantage personne en particulier; **the playing field has changed** le contexte n'est plus le même

playlet ['pleɪlɪt] *n* pièce *f* en un acte

playlist ['pleɪlɪst] *n Rad* playlist *f (programme des disques à passer)*

playmaker ['pleɪmeɪkə(r)] *n Sport* meneur(euse) *m,f* de jeu

playmate ['pleɪmeɪt] *n* camarade *mf* (de jeux)

play-off *n Sport* match *m* de barrage

playpen ['pleɪpen] *n* parc *m (pour bébés)*

play-reading *n* lecture *f* d'une pièce (de théâtre)

playroom ['pleɪrʊm] *n (in house)* salle *f* de jeux

playschool ['pleɪskuːl] *n Br* = réunion régulière d'enfants d'âge préscolaire généralement surveillés par une mère

playsuit ['pleɪsuːt] *n (for child)* barboteuse *f*

play-the-ball *n (in rugby league)* dégagement *m* au talon *(après un tenu)*

plaything ['pleɪθɪŋ] *n also Fig* jouet *m*; **she's just his plaything** il se sert d'elle comme d'un jouet

playtime ['pleɪtaɪm] *n* récréation *f*; **at playtime** pendant la récréation

playtoy ['pleɪtɔɪ] *n Am also Fig* jouet *m*

playwright ['pleɪraɪt] *n* dramaturge *m*, auteur *m* dramatique

plaza ['plɑːzə] *n* (**a**) *(open square)* place *f* (**b**) *Am (shopping centre)* centre *m* commercial; **toll plaza** péage *m* (d'autoroute)

plc, PLC [ˌpiːel'siː] *n* (**a**) *Br Com (abbr* **public limited company**) ≃ SA *f*; **Scandia PLC** ≃ Scandia SA (**b**) *Mktg (abbr* **product lifecycle**) cycle *m* de vie du produit

plea [pliː] *n* (**a**) *(appeal)* appel *m*, supplication *f*; **they ignored his plea for help** ils n'ont pas répondu à son appel au secours; **she made a plea to the nation not to forget the needy** elle conjura la nation de ne pas oublier les nécessiteux
(**b**) *Law (argument)* argument *m*; *(defence)* défense *f*; **what is your plea?** plaidez-vous coupable ou non coupable?; **to enter a plea of guilty/not guilty/insanity** plaider coupable/non coupable/la démence
(**c**) *(excuse, pretext)* excuse *f*, prétexte *m*; **his plea of ill health didn't fool anyone** sa prétendue maladie n'a trompé personne; **they did not accept his plea that he had simply forgotten** ils n'ont pas accepté son excuse, à savoir qu'il avait simplement oublié
►► *Law* ***plea bargaining*** = possibilité pour un inculpé de se voir notifier un chef d'inculpation moins grave s'il accepte de plaider coupable

plead [pliːd] *(Br pt & pp* **pleaded**, *Scot & Am pt & pp* **pleaded** *or* **pled** [pled]) **1** *vi* (**a**) *(beg)* supplier; **to plead for forgiveness** implorer le pardon; **she pleaded to be given more time** elle supplia qu'on lui accorde plus de temps; **to plead with sb** supplier *ou* implorer qn; **I pleaded with her to give me a second chance** je la suppliai de me donner une deuxième chance
(**b**) *Law* plaider; **to plead in court** plaider devant le tribunal; **to plead guilty/not guilty** plaider coupable/non coupable; **to plead for the defence** plaider pour la défense; **how does the accused plead?** l'accusé plaide-t-il coupable ou non coupable?
2 *vt* (**a**) *(beg)* implorer, supplier; **"please let me go" he pleaded** "laissez-moi partir, je vous en prie" implora-t-il; **she pleaded that her son be forgiven** elle supplia que l'on pardonne à son fils
(**b**) *(gen) & Law* plaider; **to plead sb's case** *Law* défendre qn; *Fig* plaider la cause de qn; **who will plead our cause to the government?** qui plaidera notre cause auprès du gouvernement?; **to plead self-defence** plaider la légitime défense
(**c**) *(put forward as excuse)* invoquer, alléguer; *(pretend)* prétexter; **we could always plead ignorance** nous pourrions toujours prétendre que nous ne savions pas; **she pleaded a prior engagement** elle a prétendu qu'elle était déjà prise

pleader ['pliːdə(r)] *n (gen)* intercesseur *m* (**for** en faveur de); *Law* avocat(e) *m,f* plaidant(e)

pleading ['pliːdɪŋ] **1** *adj* implorant, suppliant
2 *n* (**a**) *(entreaty)* supplication *f*, prière *f*; **I couldn't resist her pleading** *or* **pleadings** je n'ai pas pu résister à ses prières (**b**) *Law (presentation of case)* plaidoyer *m*, plaidoirie *f*
3 pleadings *npl Law (written exchange of allegations)* ≃ débats *mpl* préliminaires *(visant à fixer les points de litige)*

pleadingly ['pliːdɪŋlɪ] *adv (look)* d'un air suppliant *ou* implorant; *(ask)* d'un ton suppliant *ou* implorant

pleasant ['plezənt] *adj* (**a**) *(enjoyable, attractive)* agréable, plaisant; **thank you for a most pleasant evening** merci pour cette merveilleuse soirée; **it was pleasant to be out in the countryside again** c'était agréable de se retrouver de nouveau à la campagne; **the account of the trial does not make pleasant reading** le récit du procès n'est pas une lecture des plus agréables; **pleasant dreams!** fais de beaux rêves!
(**b**) *(friendly → person, attitude, smile)* aimable, agréable; **she was very pleasant to us as a rule** elle était en général très aimable à notre égard

pleasantly ['plezəntlɪ] *adv* (**a**) *(attractively)* agréablement; **the room was pleasantly arranged** la pièce était aménagée de façon agréable (**b**) *(enjoyably)* agréablement; **pleasantly surprised** agréablement surpris, surpris en bien (**c**) *(kindly → speak, smile)* aimablement

pleasantness ['plezəntnɪs] *n* (**a**) *(attractiveness)* attrait *m*, charme *m* (**b**) *(enjoyableness)* agrément *m* (**c**) *(friendliness)* amabilité *f*, affabilité *f*

pleasantry ['plezəntrɪ] *(pl* **pleasantries**) *n (agreeable remark)* propos *m* aimable; **to exchange pleasantries** échanger des civilités

please [pliːz] **1** *adv* (**a**) *(requesting or accepting)* s'il vous/te plaît; **could you pass the salt, please?** pouvez-vous me passer le sel, s'il vous plaît?; **another cup of tea? – (yes) please!** une autre tasse de thé? – oui, s'il vous plaît! *ou* volontiers!; **may I sit beside you? – please do** puis-je m'asseoir près de vous? – mais bien sûr; **please, make yourselves at home** faites comme chez vous, je vous en prie; **please carry on** continuez, s'il vous plaît *ou* je vous en prie; **please, Miss!** s'il vous plaît, Mademoiselle!; **please ring** *(sign)* sonnez SVP, veuillez sonner; **quiet please** *(sign)* silence
(**b**) *(pleading)* **please don't hurt him** je vous en prie, ne lui faites pas de mal
(**c**) *(in indignation, disgust etc)* **(oh) please!** c'est pas vrai!
(**d**) *(remonstrating)* **Henry, please, we've got guests!** Henry, voyons *ou* je t'en prie, nous avons des invités!
(**e**) *(hoping)* **please let them arrive safely!** faites qu'ils arrivent sains et saufs!
2 *vt* (**a**) *(give enjoyment to)* plaire à, faire plaisir à; *(satisfy)* contenter; **he only did it to please his mother** il ne l'a fait que pour faire plaisir à sa mère; **he's always trying to please the boss** il passe son temps à essayer de faire plaisir au patron; **you can't please everybody** on ne peut pas faire plaisir à tout le monde; **you can't please all of the people all of the time** on ne peut pas faire plaisir à tout le monde; **to be easy/hard to please** être facile/difficile à satisfaire
(**b**) *(idioms)* **to please oneself** faire comme on veut; **please yourself!** comme tu veux!; **I can please myself what I do** je fais ce qui me plaît; **everything will be all right, please God!** tout ira bien, plaise à Dieu!
3 *vi* (**a**) *(give pleasure)* plaire, faire plaisir; **to be eager to please** chercher à faire plaisir
(**b**) *(choose)* **she does as** *or* **what she pleases** elle fait ce qu'elle veut *ou* ce qui lui plaît; **I'll talk to whoever I please!** je parlerai avec qui je veux!; *Formal* **as you please!** comme vous voudrez!, comme bon vous semblera!; *Formal* **if you please** *(requesting)* s'il vous/te plaît; **she told me I was fat, if you please!** figure-toi qu'elle m'a dit que j'étais gros!
4 *n* **without so much as a please or thank you** sans même dire merci

pleased [pliːzd] *adj (satisfied)* satisfait, content; *(happy)* heureux; **a pleased smile** un sourire satisfait; **to be pleased with sb/sth** être content de qn/qch; **to be pleased for sb** être content pour qn; **you're looking very pleased with yourself!** tu as l'air très content de toi!; **I am not at all pleased with the results** je ne suis pas du tout satisfait des résultats; **I'm very pleased to be here this evening** je suis très heureux d'être ici ce soir; *Formal* **Mr & Mrs Adams are pleased to announce...** M. et Mme Adams sont heureux de *ou* ont le plaisir de vous faire part de...; **she would be only too pleased to help us** elle ne demanderait pas mieux que de nous aider; **I'm very pleased (that) you could come** je suis ravi que tu aies pu venir; **I'm afraid they were none too pleased!** je crains qu'ils n'aient pas été très contents!; **pleased to meet you!** enchanté (de faire votre connaissance)!; **as pleased as Punch** heureux comme un roi

pleasing ['pliːzɪŋ] *adj (meal, film, conversation etc)* agréable; *(person, manner)* agréable, plaisant; *(news, result)* qui fait plaisir

pleasingly ['pliːzɪŋlɪ] *adv* agréablement, plaisamment

pleasurable ['pleʒərəbəl] *adj* agréable, plaisant

pleasurably ['pleʒərəblɪ] *adv* agréablement, plaisamment

pleasure ['pleʒə(r)] **1** *n* **(a)** *(enjoyment, delight)* plaisir *m*; **to write/to paint for pleasure** écrire/peindre pour le plaisir; **are you here on business or for pleasure?** êtes-vous là pour affaires ou pour le plaisir?; **to take** *or* **to find pleasure in doing sth** prendre plaisir *ou* éprouver du plaisir à faire qch; **I'd accept your invitation with pleasure, but...** j'accepterais votre invitation avec plaisir, seulement...; **another beer? – with pleasure!** une autre bière? – avec plaisir *ou* volontiers!; **the pleasures of country life** les plaisirs *mpl* de la vie à la campagne; **it's one of my few pleasures in life** c'est un de mes rares plaisirs dans la vie; **thank you very much – my pleasure!** *or* **it's a pleasure!** merci beaucoup – je vous en prie!; **it's a great pleasure (to meet you)** ravi de faire votre connaissance; **I haven't the pleasure of knowing her** je n'ai pas le plaisir de la connaître; *Formal* **would you do me the pleasure of having lunch with me?** me feriez-vous le plaisir de déjeuner avec moi?; *Formal* **may I have the pleasure (of this dance)?** m'accorderez-vous *ou* voulez-vous m'accorder cette danse?; *Formal* **Mr and Mrs Evans request the pleasure of your company at their son's wedding** M. et Mme Evans vous prient de leur faire l'honneur d'assister au mariage de leur fils

(b) *Formal (desire)* **at your pleasure** à votre guise; **they are appointed at the chairman's pleasure** ils sont nommés selon le bon vouloir du président; *Br Euph* **detained at His/Her Majesty's pleasure** emprisonné pour longtemps

(c) *Euph (sexual gratification)* plaisir *m*

2 *comp (boat, yacht)* de plaisance; *(park)* de loisirs; *(cruise, tour)* d'agrément

3 *vt Arch or Literary* plaire à, faire plaisir à

►► ***pleasure beach*** parc *m* d'attractions en bord de mer; ***pleasure boat*** bateau *m* de plaisance; ***the pleasure principle*** le principe de plaisir; ***pleasure trip*** excursion *f*

pleasure-seeker *n* hédoniste *mf*

pleasure-seeking [-,siːkɪŋ] *adj* hédoniste

pleat [pliːt] **1** *n* pli *m*

2 *vt* plisser

pleated ['pliːtɪd] *adj* plissé; **a pleated skirt** une jupe plissée

pleating ['pliːtɪŋ] *n (UNCOUNT) (pleats)* plis *mpl*, plissé *m*

pleb [pleb], *Am* **plebe** [pliːb] *n* **(a)** *Pej (plebeian)* plébéien(enne) *m,f*; **it's not for the plebs** ce n'est pas pour n'importe qui! **(b)** *Br Fam Pej (vulgar, uncultured person)* plouc *m*; **you pleb!** espèce de plouc! **(c)** *Antiq* **the plebs** la plèbe

plebby ['plebɪ] *adj Br Fam* prolo

plebe [pliːb] *Am* = **pleb**

plebeian [plɪ'biːən] **1** *n* plébéien(enne) *m,f*

2 *adj* **(a)** *Pej (vulgar)* plébéien; **his tastes are rather plebeian** il a des goûts plutôt vulgaires **(b)** *Antiq* plébéien

plebiscitary [plɪ'bɪsɪtərɪ] *adj* plébiscitaire

plebiscite ['plebɪsaɪt] *n* plébiscite *m*; **to hold a plebiscite** organiser un plébiscite; **to vote for sb/sth by plebiscite** plébisciter qn/qch

plectrum ['plektrəm] *(pl* **plectrums** *or* **plectra** [-trə]*) n* médiator *m*, plectre *m*

pled [pled] *Scot & Am pt & pp of* **plead**

pledge [pledʒ] **1** *vt* **(a)** *(promise)* promettre; **they have pledged £500 to the relief fund** ils ont promis 500 livres à la caisse de secours; **she pledged never to see him again** *(to herself)* elle s'est promis de ne plus jamais le revoir; *(to sb else)* elle a promis de ne plus jamais le revoir; *Formal* **her heart is pledged to another** son cœur est déjà pris

(b) *Formal (commit)* engager; **he pledged himself to fight for the cause** il s'engagea à lutter pour la cause; **I am pledged to secrecy** j'ai juré de garder le secret; **to pledge one's word** donner *ou* engager sa parole; **to pledge one's loyalty/support** accorder sa loyauté/son soutien

(c) *Fin (offer as security)* donner en gage *ou* garantie; *(pawn)* mettre en gage, engager; **to pledge one's property** engager son bien; **to pledge securities** déposer des titres en garantie

(d) *Formal (toast)* porter un toast à, boire à la santé de

(e) *Am Univ* nouveau venu *m (dans une confrérie)*

2 *n* **(a)** *(promise)* promesse *f*; **manifesto pledge** promesse *f* électorale; **a £10 pledge** un gage de 10 livres; **thousands of people phoned in with pledges of money** des milliers de personnes ont téléphoné en promettant de donner de l'argent; **you have my pledge** vous avez ma parole; **I am under a pledge of secrecy** j'ai juré de garder le secret; **she told me under a pledge of secrecy** elle me l'a dit sous le sceau du secret; **to sign** *or* **to take the pledge** *(stop drinking)* cesser de boire

(b) *Fin (security, collateral)* gage *m*, garantie *f*; **in pledge** en gage

(c) *(token, symbol)* gage *m*; **as a pledge of our sincerity** comme gage de notre sincérité

(d) *Formal (toast)* toast *m*; **let us drink a pledge to their success** portons un toast *ou* buvons à leur réussite

►► ***Pledge of Allegiance*** = serment de loyauté prononcé à l'occasion du discours d'investiture du président des États-Unis; *Fin* ***pledge holder*** détenteur(trice) *m,f* de gage(s); *Fin* ***pledged securities*** valeurs *fpl* nanties

pledgee [ple'dʒiː] *n Fin* gagiste *mf*

pledget ['pledʒɪt] *n* compresse *f*, tampon *m*

pledgor ['pledʒə(r)] *n Fin* gageur *m*

Pleiades ['plaɪədiːz] *npl Myth & Astron* **the Pleiades** les Pléiades *fpl*

Pleiocene = **Pliocene**

Pleistocene ['plaɪstəsiːn] *Geol* **1** *adj* pléistocène

2 *n* pléistocène *m*

plenary ['pliːnərɪ] **1** *adj (meeting)* plénier

2 *n (plenary meeting)* réunion *f* plénière; *(plenary session)* séance *f* plénière

►► ***plenary assembly*** assemblée *f* plénière; *Rel* ***plenary indulgence*** indulgence *f* plénière; *Pol* ***plenary powers*** pleins pouvoirs *mpl*; ***plenary session*** *(at conference)* séance *f* plénière; **in plenary session** en séance plénière

plenipotentiary [,plenɪpə'tenʃərɪ] *(pl* **plenipotentiaries***)* **1** *adj* plénipotentiaire; **ambassador plenipotentiary** ministre *m* plénipotentiaire

2 *n* plénipotentiaire *mf*

plenitude ['plenɪtjuːd] *n Literary* plénitude *f*

plenteous ['plentɪəs] *adj Literary (gen)* abondant; *(meal)* copieux

plentiful ['plentɪfʊl] *adj (gen)* abondant; *(meal)* copieux; **we have a plentiful supply of food** nous avons de la nourriture en abondance

plentifully ['plentɪfʊlɪ] *adv* abondamment, copieusement; **weeds grow plentifully there** les mauvaises herbes y poussent en abondance

plentifulness ['plentɪfʊlnɪs] *n* abondance *f*

plenty ['plentɪ] **1** *pron* **(a)** *(enough)* (largement) assez, plus qu'assez; **no thanks, I've got plenty** non merci, j'en ai (largement) assez; **£20 should be plenty** 20 livres devraient suffire (amplement); **they have plenty to live on** ils ont largement de quoi vivre; **to arrive in plenty of time** arriver de bonne heure; **we've got plenty of time** nous avons largement le temps

(b) *(a great deal)* beaucoup; **there's still plenty to be done** il y a encore beaucoup à faire; **there'll be plenty of other opportunities** il y aura beaucoup d'autres occasions; **you've got plenty of explaining to do** tu vas devoir t'expliquer; **we see plenty of Colin and Jackie** on voit beaucoup Colin et Jackie

2 *n Literary (abundance)* abondance *f*; **the years of plenty** les années *fpl* d'abondance

3 *adv Fam* **(a)** *(a lot)* beaucoup[□]; **there's plenty more food in the fridge** il y a encore plein de choses à manger dans le frigo; **there's plenty more where that came from!** *(food etc)* quand il y en a plus, il y en a encore; *Am* **he sure talks plenty** c'est un vrai moulin à paroles

(b) *(easily)* **the room is plenty big enough for two** la pièce est largement assez grande pour deux[□]

4 *adj Scot & Ir Fam (a lot of)* plein de; **there's plenty work to be done!** ce n'est pas le boulot qui manque!

5 in plenty *adv* en abondance

plenum ['pliːnəm] *n* **(a)** *(plenary meeting)* réunion *f* plénière; *(plenary session)* séance *f* plénière **(b)** *Phys* plein *m*

►► *Phys* ***plenum chamber*** chambre *f* de tranquillisation; *Phys* ***plenum system, plenum ventilation*** système *m* de ventilation par plenum

pleomorphism [,pliːəʊ'mɔːfɪzəm] *n* pléomorphisme *m*, polymorphisme *m*

pleonasm ['pliːənæzəm] *n* pléonasme *m*

pleonastic [,plɪə'næstɪk] *adj* pléonastique

pleonastically [,plɪə'næstɪklɪ] *adv* d'une manière pléonastique, par pléonasme

plesiosaur ['pliːsɪəsɔː(r)] *n* plésiosaure *m*

plessor ['plesə(r)] *n Med* percuteur *m*

Plessy vs Ferguson ['plesɪ,vɜːsəs'fɜːgəsən] *n Am Hist* = procès de 1869 par lequel la cour suprême décida que la ségrégation raciale était légale

plethora ['pleθərə] *n* pléthore *f*

plethoric [plɪ'θɒrɪk] *adj* pléthorique

pleura ['plʊərə] *(pl* **pleurae** [-riː]*) n Anat* plèvre *f*

pleural ['plʊərəl] *adj Anat* pleural

►► ***pleural membrane*** plèvre *f*

pleurisy ['plʊərəsɪ] *n (UNCOUNT)* pleurésie *f*; **to have pleurisy** avoir *ou* faire une pleurésie; **dry pleurisy** pleurite *f*

pleuritic [,plʊə'rɪtɪk] *adj* pleurétique

pleuropneumonia [,plʊərəʊnjuː'məʊnɪə] *n Med* pleuropneumonie *f*, pneumopleurésie *f*; *Vet* **contagious bovine pleuropneumonia** péripneumonie *f*

Plexiglas® ['pleksɪglɑːs] *n* Plexiglas® *m*

plexor ['pleksɔː(r)] *n Med* percuteur *m*

plexus ['pleksəs] *n* **(a)** *Anat* plexus *m* **(b)** *Formal (intricate network)* enchevêtrement *m*, dédale *m*

pliability [,plaɪə'bɪlətɪ] *n* **(a)** *(of material)* flexibilité *f* **(b)** *(of person)* malléabilité *f*, docilité *f*

pliable ['plaɪəbəl] *adj* **(a)** *(material)* flexible, pliable **(b)** *(person)* malléable, accommodant, docile

pliancy ['plaɪənsɪ] *n* **(a)** *(of material)* flexibilité *f* **(b)** *(of person)* malléabilité *f*, docilité *f*

pliant ['plaɪənt] *adj* **(a)** *(material)* flexible, pliable **(b)** *(person)* malléable, accommodant, docile

pliers ['plaɪəz] *npl* pince *f*; **a pair of pliers** une pince

plight [plaɪt] **1** *n (bad situation)* situation *f* désespérée; **the plight of the young homeless** la situation désespérée dans laquelle se trouvent les jeunes sans-abri; **to be in a sad** *or* **sorry plight** être dans une situation désespérée; **seeing my plight she stopped to help** voyant mon embarras, elle s'est arrêtée pour m'aider

2 *vt Arch (pledge)* promettre, engager; **to plight one's troth (to sb)** se fiancer (à qn); **to plight one's word** donner *ou* engager sa parole

plimsoll ['plɪmsəl] *n Br (shoe)* tennis *m*

►► *Naut* ***Plimsoll line, Plimsoll mark*** ligne *f* de flottaison en charge

Plinian ['plɪnɪən] *adj Geol* plinien

►► ***Plinian eruption*** éruption *f* plinienne

plink [plɪŋk] **1** *n* bruit *m* métallique

2 *vi* faire un bruit métallique

plinth [plɪnθ] *n (of statue)* socle *m*; *(of column, pedestal)* plinthe *f*; *Mktg (for displaying goods)* plinthe *f*

Pliny ['plɪnɪ] *pr n* **Pliny the Elder** Pline l'Ancien; **Pliny the Younger** Pline le Jeune

Pliocene ['plaɪəsiːn] *Geol* **1** *adj* pliocène

2 *n* pliocène *m*

plip key [plɪp-] *n Aut* plip *m*

PLO [ˌpiːelˈəʊ] *n (abbr* **Palestine Liberation Organization**) OLP *f*

plod [plɒd] *(pt & pp* **plodded**, *cont* **plodding**) **1** *vi* (**a**) *(walk)* marcher lourdement
(**b**) *Fam (carry on)* **he'd been plodding along in the same job for years** ça faisait des années qu'il faisait le même boulot; **she kept plodding on until it was finished** elle s'est accrochée jusqu'à ce que ce soit fini; **I plodded through the first five chapters** je me suis coltiné les cinq premiers chapitres; **I'm plodding through a rather boring book just now** j'avance péniblement dans un livre plutôt barbant en ce moment
2 *n* (**a**) *(heavy walk)* **we could hear the plod of feet** on entendait des pas lourds; **we maintained a steady plod** nous avons gardé un pas régulier
(**b**) *Br Fam (policeman)* flic *m*, poulet *m*; **the plod** *(the police)* les flics *mpl*, les poulets *mpl*

plodder [ˈplɒdə(r)] *n Fam Pej* **he's a bit of a plodder** il est plutôt lent à la tâche□

plodding [ˈplɒdɪŋ] *adj Pej (walk, rhythm, style)* lourd, pesant; *(worker)* lent

ploidy [ˈplɔɪdɪ] *n Biol* ploïdie *f*

plonk [plɒŋk] **1** *n* (**a**) *(heavy sound)* bruit *m* sourd
(**b**) *Br Fam (cheap wine)* pinard *m*, piquette *f*
2 *vt Fam (put, place)* flanquer, coller; *(put down)* poser bruyamment□; **just plonk your stuff on the table** t'as qu'à foutre tes affaires sur la table; **plonk yourself down over there** pose-toi là-bas□; **he plonked his glass down** il posa son verre bruyamment; **she plonked herself down on the sofa** elle s'est affalée sur le canapé□
3 *vi* **to plonk away on the piano** jouer du piano (mal et assez fort)

plonker [ˈplɒŋkə(r)] *n Br Fam* (**a**) *(penis)* quéquette *f*, zizi *m* (**b**) *(fool)* andouille *f*, courge *f*

plook [plʊk] *n Scot & NEng Fam (pimple)* bouton□ *m*

plop [plɒp] *(pt & pp* **plopped**, *cont* **plopping**) **1** *n* plouf *m*, floc *m*
2 *adv* **to go plop** faire plouf; **the stone landed plop in the water** le caillou a fait plouf en tombant dans l'eau
3 *vi (splash)* faire plouf *ou* floc
4 *vt (put)* poser, mettre

plosion [ˈpləʊʒən] *n Ling* occlusion *f*

plosive [ˈpləʊsɪv] *Ling* **1** *adj* occlusif
2 *n* occlusive *f*

plot [plɒt] *(pt & pp* **plotted**, *cont* **plotting**) **1** *n* (**a**) *(conspiracy)* complot *m*, conspiration *f*; **to hatch a plot** tramer *ou* ourdir un complot; **a plot to overthrow the government** un complot pour renverser le gouvernement
(**b**) *(story line → of novel, play)* intrigue *f*; **the plot thickens** l'affaire se corse
(**c**) *(piece of land)* terrain *m*; **vacant/building plot** terrain *m* vague/à bâtir; **the land has been split up into 12 plots** le terrain a été divisé en 12 lotissements; **we have a small vegetable plot** nous avons un petit potager *ou* carré de légumes
(**d**) *Am (graph)* graphique *m*
(**e**) *Am Archit* plan *m*
2 *vt* (**a**) *(conspire)* comploter; **they were accused of plotting to overthrow the government** ils ont été accusés de complot *ou* de conspiration contre le gouvernement; **I think they're plotting something** je crois qu'ils préparent quelque chose
(**b**) *(course, position)* déterminer; *Fig* **they're trying to plot the company's development over the next five years** ils essaient de prévoir le développement de la société dans les cinq années à venir
(**c**) *(curve, diagram, graph)* tracer, faire le tracé de; **to plot figures on** *or* **onto a graph** reporter des coordonnées sur un graphique
(**d**) *(map, plan)* lever
3 *vi (conspire)* comploter, conspirer; **to plot against sb** conspirer contre qn

plotter [ˈplɒtə(r)] *n* (**a**) *(conspirator)* conspirateur(trice) *m,f* (**b**) *(device)* traceur *m*

plotting [ˈplɒtɪŋ] *n (UNCOUNT)* (**a**) *(conspiring)* complots *mpl*, conspirations *fpl* (**b**) *Comput & Math* traçage *m*
▸▸ *Comput & Math* ***plotting board, plotting table*** table *f* traçante, traceur *m* de courbes

plough, *Am* **plow** [plaʊ] **1** *n* (**a**) *(farm implement)* charrue *f*; **large areas of moorland have gone under the plough** de larges portions de lande ont été labourées; *Fig* **to put one's hand to the plough** s'atteler à la tâche
(**b**) *Astron* **the Plough** la Grande Ourse
2 *vt* (**a**) *(land)* labourer; *(furrow)* creuser; *(of ship → waves)* fendre, sillonner
(**b**) *Fig (invest)* investir; **to plough money into sth** investir de l'argent dans qch
(**c**) *Br Fam Old-fashioned Sch* **to plough an exam** se planter à un examen; **to be** *or* **get ploughed in an exam** être recalé *ou* collé à un examen
3 *vi* (**a**) *Agr* labourer
(**b**) *Br Fam Old-fashioned Sch (fail exam)* se faire recaler
▸▸ *Br Old-fashioned* ***Plough Monday*** le lundi de l'Épiphanie

▸**plough back**, *Am* **plow back** *vt sep (profits)* réinvestir (**into** dans); **all the profits have been ploughed back into the business** tous les bénéfices ont été réinvestis dans l'affaire

▸**plough in**, *Am* **plow in** *vt sep* (**a**) *(earth, crops, stubble)* enfouir (en labourant)
(**b**) *(money)* investir

▸**plough into**, *Am* **plow into** *vt insep* (**a**) *(of vehicle)* rentrer dans, foncer dans
(**b**) *(attack → physically)* se jeter sur; *(→ verbally)* s'en prendre à

▸**plough on**, *Am* **plow on** *vi (continue laboriously)* **to plough on with one's work/one's book** poursuivre laborieusement son travail/sa lecture; **let's plough on another fifteen minutes** encore un petit effort d'un quart d'heure; **as negotiations plough on** tandis que les négociations se poursuivent laborieusement

▸**plough through**, *Am* **plow through** **1** *vt insep* (**a**) *(move laboriously through)* **to plough through the snow** avancer péniblement dans la neige; **the ship ploughed through the waves** le navire fendait les flots
(**b**) *(progress laboriously through)* **to plough through a book** lire laborieusement un livre; **they were ploughing through their work** ils avançaient laborieusement dans leur travail; **I've got all this to plough through** j'ai tout ça à me taper
2 *vt sep* **to plough one's way through the snow** avancer péniblement dans la neige; **to plough one's way through a book** lire un livre à grand peine; **he was ploughing his way through a huge plate of spaghetti** il s'efforçait de finir une énorme assiette de spaghettis

▸**plough under**, *Am* **plow under** *vt sep (earth, crops, stubble)* enfouir (en labourant)

▸**plough up**, *Am* **plow up** *vt sep* (**a**) *Agr (field, footpath)* labourer
(**b**) *(rip up)* labourer; **the grass had been ploughed up by the motorbikes** le gazon avait été labouré par les motos

ploughback, *Am* **plowback** [ˈplaʊbæk] *n Fin* bénéfices *mpl* réinvestis

ploughboy, *Am* **plowboy** [ˈplaʊbɔɪ] *n* garçon *m* de charrue

ploughed, *Am* **plowed** [plaʊd] *adj (field)* labouré

ploughing, *Am* **plowing** [ˈplaʊɪŋ] *n* labourage *m*

ploughland, *Am* **plowland** [ˈplaʊlænd] *n (UNCOUNT)* terre *f* de labour, labours *mpl*

ploughman, *Am* **plowman** [ˈplaʊmən] *(pl* **ploughmen** [-mən]) *n* laboureur *m*
▸▸ *Br* ***ploughman's (lunch)*** = assiette de fromage, de pain et de pickles (généralement servie dans un pub); *Bot* ***ploughman's spikenard*** inule *f* conyze

ploughshare, *Am* **plowshare** [ˈplaʊʃeə(r)] *n* soc *m*

plover [ˈplʌvə(r)] *n Orn* pluvier *m*

plow, plowback *etc Am* = **plough, ploughback** *etc*

ploy [plɔɪ] *n* (**a**) *(stratagem, trick)* ruse *f*, stratagème *m*; **it's just a ploy to get us to leave** ce n'est qu'une ruse pour nous faire partir (**b**) *Fam Old-fashioned (pastime)* passe-temps□ *m inv*; *(job)* turbin *m*

PLP [ˌpiːelˈpiː] *n Br (abbr* **Parliamentary Labour Party**) députés *mpl* du Parti travailliste

PLR [ˌpiːelˈɑː(r)] *n (abbr* **Public Lending Right**) = droit d'auteur versé pour les ouvrages prêtés par les bibliothèques

pluck [plʌk] **1** *vt* (**a**) *(pick → flower, fruit)* cueillir
(**b**) *(pull)* tirer, retirer; **to pluck sb from obscurity** arracher qn à l'obscurité; **he plucked the cigarette from my mouth** il m'a arraché la cigarette de la bouche; **the ten survivors were plucked from the sea by helicopter** les dix survivants ont été récupérés en mer par un hélicoptère; **to be plucked from the jaws of death** être arraché à la mort; **these figures have been plucked from the air** ces chiffres ne reposent sur rien de concret
(**c**) *(chicken)* plumer; *(feathers)* arracher
(**d**) *(instrument)* pincer les cordes de; *(string)* pincer
(**e**) *(eyebrow)* épiler; **to pluck one's eyebrows** s'épiler les sourcils
2 *vi* **he plucked at my sleeve** il m'a tiré par la manche; **she was plucking at (the strings of) her guitar** elle pinçait les cordes de sa guitare
3 *n* (**a**) *(courage)* courage *m*; **it takes pluck to do that** il faut du courage pour faire ça
(**b**) *(tug)* petite secousse *f*; *(at string)* pincement *m*
(**c**) *Culin* fressure *f*

▸**pluck up** *vt sep* (**a**) *(uproot)* arracher, extirper
(**b**) *Fig* **to pluck up (one's) courage** prendre son courage à deux mains; **to pluck up the courage to do sth** trouver le courage de faire qch

pluckily [ˈplʌkɪlɪ] *adv* courageusement

pluckiness [ˈplʌkɪnɪs] *n* courage *m*

plucky [ˈplʌkɪ] *(compar* **pluckier**, *superl* **pluckiest**) *adj* courageux

plug [plʌg] *(pt & pp* **plugged**, *cont* **plugging**) **1** *n* (**a**) *Elec (on appliance, cable)* fiche *f*, prise *f* (mâle); *(wall socket)* prise *f* (de courant); **to pull the plug out** *(disconnect electrical appliance)* débrancher; *Comput* **plug compatible** compatible au niveau du matériel
(**b**) *(stopper → gen)* bouchon *m*; *(→ in barrel)* bonde *f*; *(→ for nose, wound)* tampon *m*
(**c**) *(for sink, bath)* bonde *f*; **to pull the plug out** retirer la bonde; *Fig* **this will pull the plug on our competitors** cela va couper l'herbe sous le pied de nos concurrents; **he pulled the plug on our plan** *(stopped it)* il a mis le holà à notre projet; **this pulls the plug on the whole operation** ça fiche tout par terre
(**d**) *(of toilet)* chasse *f* d'eau; **to pull the plug** tirer la chasse
(**e**) *Aut* **(spark) plug** bougie *f*
(**f**) *(for fixing screws)* cheville *f*
(**g**) *Fam (advertising)* coup *m* de pub; **their products got another plug on TV** on a encore fait du battage *ou* de la pub pour leurs produits à la télé
(**h**) *(of tobacco)* carotte *f*
(**i**) *Geol* **(volcanic) plug** culot *m*
(**j**) *Am* **(fire) plug** bouche *f* d'incendie
(**k**) *Fam (blow)* beigne *f*, gnon *m*
2 *vt* (**a**) *(block → hole, gap)* boucher; *(→ leak)* colmater; *(→ wound)* tamponner; **they plugged (up) the hole in the dam** ils ont colmaté la brèche dans le barrage
(**b**) *(insert)* enficher; **plug the cable into the socket** branchez le câble sur la prise
(**c**) *Fam (advertise)* faire du battage *ou* de la pub pour; **the radio stations are continually plugging her record** les stations de radio passent son disque sans arrêt□
(**d**) *Am Fam (shoot)* flinguer
▸▸ *Aut* ***plug spanner*** clé *f* à bougies

▸**plug away** *vi* travailler dur; **he keeps plugging away at his work** il s'acharne sur son travail

▸**plug in** *vt sep* brancher

▸**plug into** **1** *vt sep (connect)* **to plug sth into sth** brancher qch sur qch
2 *vt insep* (**a**) *(connect)* **the TV plugs into that socket** la télé se branche sur cette prise; *Fig* **to plug into a computer network** avoir accès à un réseau informatique
(**b**) *(be in touch with)* **to plug into public opinion** se mettre à l'écoute de l'opinion publique; **we try to plug into people's needs** nous essayons d'être à l'écoute des besoins de la population

plug-and-play *Comput* **1** *n* plug and play *m inv*
2 *adj* plug and play *(inv)*

plugboard [ˈplʌgbɔːd] *n* tableau *m* de raccordement

plugged [plʌgd] *adj (blocked → nose, ear)* bouché

plugger [ˈplʌgə(r)] *n (dentist's tool)* fouloir *m*

plughole [ˈplʌghəʊl] *n* trou *m* d'écoulement; *Br Fam* **that's all our work gone down the plughole!** tout notre travail est fichu!; **that's £300 down the plughole!** voilà 300 livres par la fenêtre!; **his company's going down the plughole** sa société se casse la figure

plug-in **1** *adj (radio)* qui se branche sur le secteur; *(accessory for computer, stereo etc)* qui se branche sur l'appareil

2 *n Comput* module *m* d'extension, *Can* plugiciel *m*

plug-in-and-go *adj Comput* prêt à brancher

plug-ugly *Fam* **1** *adj* très moche, moche comme un pou

2 *n Am (ruffian)* voyou □ *m*, loubard *m*

plum [plʌm] **1** *n* **(a)** *(fruit)* prune *f* **(b)** *(tree)* prunier *m* **(c)** *(colour)* couleur *f* prune

2 *comp (tart)* aux prunes; *(jam)* de prunes

3 *adj* **(a)** *(colour)* prune *(inv)* **(b)** *Fam (desirable)* **it's a plum job** c'est un boulot en or

►► ***plum brandy*** (eau *f* de vie de) prune *f*; ***plum cake*** cake *m*; *Br* ***plum duff, plum pudding*** plum-pudding *m*; ***plum sauce*** sauce *f* aux prunes; ***plum tomato*** olivette *f*; ***plum tree*** prunier *m*

plumage [ˈpluːmɪdʒ] *n* plumage *m*

plumb [plʌm] **1** *n* **(a)** *(weight)* plomb *m*

(b) *(verticality)* aplomb *m*; **the wall is out of plumb** le mur n'est pas d'aplomb *ou* à l'aplomb

2 *adj* **(a)** *(vertical)* vertical, à l'aplomb

(b) *Am Fam (utter, complete)* complet(ète) □, absolu □; **it's a plumb nuisance!** c'est la barbe!

3 *adv* **(a)** *(in a vertical position)* à l'aplomb, d'aplomb; **plumb with** d'aplomb avec

(b) *Fam (exactly, right)* exactement □, en plein □; **plumb in the middle of the first act** en plein *ou* au beau milieu du premier acte □

(c) *Am Fam (utterly, completely)* complètement □, tout à fait □; **I'm plumb exhausted!** je suis complètement crevé!; **she's plumb crazy!** elle est complètement dingue!

4 *vt* **(a)** *(measure depth of)* sonder; **to plumb the depths** toucher le fond; **his films plumb the depths of bad taste** ses films sont d'un mauvais goût inimaginable

(b) *(test for verticality)* vérifier l'aplomb de; *(wall)* vérifier l'aplomb de, plomber

►► ***plumb bob*** plomb *m*; ***plumb line*** *Constr* fil *m* à plomb; *Naut* sonde *f*

►**plumb in** *vt sep* effectuer le raccordement de; *(washing machine)* raccorder

plumbago [plʌmˈbeɪgəʊ] *(pl* **plumbagos***)* *n* **(a)** *(plant)* plumbago *m* **(b)** *(graphite)* plombagine *f*

plumber [ˈplʌmə(r)] *n* plombier *m*

►► *Am* ***plumber's friend, plumber's helper*** *(tool)* ventouse *f (pour déboucher)*

plumbic [ˈplʌmbɪk] *adj Chem* plombique

plumbing [ˈplʌmɪŋ] *n* **(a)** *(job)* plomberie *f* **(b)** *(pipes)* plomberie *f*, tuyauterie *f*; *(toilets, washbasins)* installations *fpl* sanitaires **(c)** *Fam Euph (urinary system)* voies *fpl* urinaires □; **I'm having a bit of trouble with my plumbing** j'ai des problèmes de vessie □

plum-capped finch *n Orn* diamant *m* modeste

plume [pluːm] **1** *n* **(a)** *(feather)* plume *f*; **ostrich plume** plume *f* d'autruche; *Fig Literary* **in borrowed plumes** paré des plumes du paon

(b) *(on helmet)* plumet *m*, panache *m*; *(on hat)* plumet *m*; *(on woman's hat)* plume *f*

(c) *(of smoke)* volute *f*; *(of water)* jet *m*

2 *vt* **(a)** *(preen)* lisser; **the swan plumed itself** *or* **its feathers** le cygne se lissait les plumes

(b) *Fig Literary (pride)* **to plume oneself on sth** se glorifier de qch

►► *Entom* ***plume moth*** alucite *f*

plumed [pluːmd] *adj* **(a)** *(hat, helmet)* emplumé, empanaché **(b)** *(bird)* **brightly plumed peacocks** des paons au plumage éclatant

plummer-block [ˈplʌmə-] *n Tech* chaise *f* palier *m*

plummet [ˈplʌmɪt] **1** *vi* **(a)** *(plunge, dive)* tomber, plonger, piquer; **he plummeted from the roof** il est tombé du toit; **the plane plummeted towards the earth** l'avion piqua vers le sol

(b) *(drop, go down → price, rate, amount)* chuter, dégringoler; *(→ blood pressure)* tomber soudainement; **his popularity has plummeted** sa cote de popularité a beaucoup baissé; **the value of the pound plummeted** la livre a chuté; **educational standards have plummeted** le niveau d'instruction a considérablement baissé

2 *n (weight)* plomb *m*; *(plumb line)* fil *m* à plomb

plummy [ˈplʌmɪ] *(compar* **plummier,** *superl* **plummiest***)* *adj* **(a)** *Br Pej (voice, accent)* snob **(b)** *Old-fashioned (job)* agréable, bien payé **(c)** *(colour)* prune *(inv)*

plump [plʌmp] **1** *adj (person)* rondelet, dodu; *(arms, legs)* dodu, potelé; *(fowl)* dodu, bien gras; *(fruit)* charnu

2 *adv (heavily)* lourdement; *(directly)* exactement, en plein; **he ran plump into me** il m'a heurté de plein fouet; **it landed plump in the middle** ça a atterri en plein milieu

3 *vt* **(a)** *(pillow, cushion)* retaper

(b) *(fowl)* engraisser

►**plump down** **1** *vt sep* **to plump sth down** laisser tomber qch (lourdement); **she plumped herself/her bag down next to me** elle s'est affalée/a laissé tomber son sac à côté de moi

2 *vi* se laisser tomber (lourdement), s'affaler

►**plump for** *vt insep Fam* arrêter son choix sur □, opter pour □

►**plump out** *vi* s'arrondir, engraisser

►**plump up** *vt sep* **1** *vt sep (pillow, cushion)* retaper

2 *vi (become fat)* devenir dodu

plumpish [ˈplʌmpɪʃ] *adj (person)* rondelet, dodu; *(arms, legs)* dodu, potelé

plumpness [ˈplʌmpnɪs] *n* rondeur *f*, embonpoint *m*; **to be inclined to plumpness** avoir tendance à prendre de l'embonpoint

plumule [ˈpluːmjuːl] *n Bot & Zool* plumule *f*

plumy [ˈpluːmɪ] *adj* **(a)** *(covered in plumes)* couvert de plumes, emplumé **(b)** *(like a plume)* plumeux

plunder [ˈplʌndə(r)] **1** *vt* piller; *Fig (bookshelves, fridge)* faire une descente dans

2 *vi* piller

3 *n* **(a)** *(booty)* butin *m* **(b)** *(act of pillaging)* pillage *m*

plunderer [ˈplʌndərə(r)] *n* pillard(e) *m,f*

plundering [ˈplʌndərɪŋ] **1** *n* pillage *m*

2 *adj* pillard

plunge [plʌndʒ] **1** *vi* **(a)** *(dive)* plonger

(b) *(throw oneself)* se jeter, se précipiter; *(fall, drop)* tomber, chuter; **the bus plunged into the river** le bus est tombé dans la rivière; **the lorry plunged over the cliff** le camion plongea pardessus la falaise; **the helicopter plunged to the ground** l'hélicoptère piqua vers le sol; **to plunge to one's death** faire une chute mortelle; **I slipped and plunged forward** j'ai glissé et je suis tombé la tête la première *ou* la tête en avant

(c) *Fig* **he plunged into a long and complicated story** il s'est lancé dans une histoire longue et compliquée; **she plunged bravely into the discussion** elle se lança courageusement dans la discussion; **the neckline plunges deeply at the front** le devant est très décolleté

(d) *Fam (gamble)* flamber

(e) *(price, rate, currency)* chuter, dégringoler; **sales have plunged by 30 percent** les ventes ont chuté de 30 pour cent

2 *vt* **(a)** *(immerse)* plonger; **plunge the tomatoes into boiling water** plonger les tomates dans l'eau bouillante

(b) *Fig* plonger; **he plunged his hands into his pockets** il enfonça les mains dans ses poches; **he was plunged into despair by the news** la nouvelle l'a plongé dans le désespoir; **the office was plunged into darkness** le bureau fut plongé dans l'obscurité

3 *n* **(a)** *(dive)* plongeon *m*; *Fig* **to take the plunge** *(dare)* se jeter à l'eau; *(get married)* faire le grand saut, se mettre la corde au cou

(b) *(fall, drop)* chute *f*; **a ten-metre plunge** une chute de dix mètres; **prices have taken a plunge** les prix ont chuté *ou* se sont effondrés

plunger [ˈplʌndʒə(r)] *n* **(a)** *(for sinks, drains)* ventouse *f*, déboucheur *m* **(b)** *(piston → in coffee-maker, syringe)* piston *m*; *(→ of detonator)* manette *f* **(c)** *Br Fam (gambler)* flambeur(euse) *m,f*

plunging [ˈplʌndʒɪŋ] *adj* plongeant; **a plunging neckline** un décolleté plongeant

plunk [plʌŋk] *Fam* **1** *n* **(a)** *(sound)* bruit *m* sourd □; **I could hear the plunk of a guitar** j'entendais quelqu'un gratter sa guitare

(b) *Am (blow)* beigne *f*, gnon *m*

2 *vt* **(a)** *(put down)* poser lourdement □

(b) *(guitar, banjo)* gratter

(c) *Am (hit)* flanquer une beigne à; *(shoot)* flinguer

►**plunk down** *Fam* **1** *vt sep* poser lourdement □

2 *vi* se laisser tomber (lourdement) □, s'affaler □

pluperfect [ˌpluːˈpɜːfɪkt] *n Gram* plus-que-parfait *m*; **in the pluperfect** au plus-que-parfait

►► ***pluperfect subjunctive*** plus-que-parfait *m* du subjonctif; ***pluperfect tense*** plus-que-parfait *m*

plural [ˈplʊərəl] **1** *adj* **(a)** *Gram (form, ending)* pluriel, du pluriel; *(noun)* au pluriel **(b)** *(multiple)* multiple; *(heterogeneous)* hétérogène, pluriel; **a plural society** une société plurielle; **a plural system of education** un système d'éducation diversifié

2 *n Gram* pluriel *m*; **in the plural** au pluriel

►► *Pol* ***plural vote*** vote *m* plural

pluralism [ˈplʊərəlɪzəm] *n* **(a)** *(gen) & Phil* pluralisme *m* **(b)** *(holding of several offices)* cumul *m* des fonctions

pluralist [ˈplʊərəlɪst] *n (gen) & Phil* pluraliste *mf*

pluralistic [ˌplʊərəˈlɪstɪk] *adj* pluraliste

plurality [plʊəˈrælətɪ] *(pl* **pluralities***)* *n* **(a)** *(multiplicity)* pluralité *f* **(b)** *Am Pol* majorité *f* relative **(c)** *(holding of several offices)* cumul *m* des fonctions

pluralization [ˌplʊərəlaɪˈzeɪʃən] *n* pluralisation *f*

pluralize, -ise [ˈplʊərəlaɪz] **1** *vt* mettre au pluriel

2 *vi* prendre le pluriel

plurally [ˈplʊərəlɪ] *adv* **(a)** *Gram* au pluriel **(b)** *(hold offices)* par cumul

plus [plʌs] *(pl* **pluses** *or* **plusses***)* **1** *prep* **(a)** *Math* plus; **two plus two is** *or* **equals** *or* **makes four** deux plus deux *ou* deux et deux font quatre; **plus six** plus six

(b) *(as well as)* plus; **there were six of us, plus the children** nous étions six, sans compter les enfants; **£97 plus VAT** 97 livres plus la TVA; **two floors plus an attic** deux étages plus un grenier

2 *adj* **(a)** *Elec & Math* positif

(b) *(good, positive)* positif; **on the plus side, it's near the shops** un des avantages, c'est que c'est près des magasins; **it certainly is a big plus point** c'est incontestablement un gros avantage

(c) *(after n) (over, more than)* plus; **children of twelve plus** les enfants de douze ans et plus; *Fam* **we're looking for somebody with talent plus** notre candidat devra avoir plus que du talent □

3 *n* **(a)** *Math* plus *m*; **two minuses make a plus** deux moins font un plus

(b) *(bonus, advantage)* plus *m*, avantage *m*; **there are a number of pluses to the new plan** le nouveau projet comporte un certain nombre d'avantages

4 *conj Fam* (et) en plus □; **he's stupid, plus he's ugly** il est bête, et en plus il est laid

►► ***plus factor*** facteur *m* positif, plus *m*; ***plus fours*** pantalon *m* de golf; *Comput* ***plus key*** touche *f* plus; ***plus sign*** signe *m* plus, plus *m*

plush [plʌʃ] **1** *adj* **(a)** *Fam (luxurious → apartment)* luxueux □; *(→ restaurant, hotel)* de luxe □ **(b)** *(made of plush)* en peluche

2 *n* peluche *f*

plushy [ˈplʌʃɪ] *(compar* **plushier,** *superl* **plushiest***)* *adj Fam (luxurious → apartment)* luxueux □; *(→ restaurant, hotel)* de luxe □

Plutarch [ˈpluːtɑːk] *pr n* Plutarque

Pluto [ˈpluːtəʊ] *n* **(a)** *Myth* Pluton *m* **(b)** *Astron* Pluton *f*

plutocracy [pluːˈtɒkrəsɪ] *(pl* **plutocracies***)* *n* ploutocratie *f*

plutocrat [ˈpluːtəkræt] *n* ploutocrate *mf*

plutocratic [ˌpluːtəˈkrætɪk] *adj* ploutocratique

Plutonian [pluːˈtəʊnɪən] *adj* **(a)** *Myth* plutonien **(b)** *Geol* plutonique

plutonic [plu:'tɒnɪk] *Geol* **1** *adj* plutonique

2 plutonics *npl* roches *f* plutoniques

►► ***the plutonic hypothesis*** l'hypothèse *f* vulcanienne

plutonium [plu:'təʊnɪəm] *n* plutonium *m*

►► ***plutonium radiation*** radiation *f* de plutonium

pluvial ['plu:vɪəl] *adj* pluvial

pluviometer [,plu:vɪ'ɒmɪtə(r)] *n* pluviomètre *m*

pluviometric [,plu:vɪəʊ'metrɪk], **pluviometrical** [,plu:vɪəʊ'metrɪkəl] *adj* pluviométrique

pluviometry [,plu:vɪ'ɒmɪtrɪ] *n* pluviométrie *f*

ply [plaɪ] (*pl* **plies**, *pt & pp* **plied**) **1** *n* (**a**) *(thickness)* épaisseur *f*; *(layer → of plywood, tyre)* pli *m*; *(strand → of rope, wool)* brin *m*

(**b**) *Fam (plywood)* contreplaqué [□] *m*

2 *vt* (**a**) *(supply insistently)* **she plied us with food all evening** elle nous a gavés toute la soirée; **he plied us with drinks** il nous versait sans arrêt à boire; **we plied her with questions** nous l'avons assaillie de questions

(**b**) *Literary (perform, practise)* exercer; **to ply one's trade** exercer son métier

(**c**) *Literary (use → tool)* manier; *(→ needle)* faire courir

(**d**) *Literary (travel → river, ocean)* naviguer sur; **the barges that ply the Thames** les péniches qui descendent et remontent le cours de la Tamise

3 *vi* (**a**) *(seek work)* **to ply for hire** *(taxi)* prendre des clients

(**b**) *(travel → ship, boat)* **to ply between** faire la navette entre

-ply [plaɪ] *suff* **two-/three-ply toilet tissue** papier *m* hygiénique double/triple épaisseur; **five-ply wood** contreplaqué *m* en cinq épaisseurs; **three-ply wool** laine *f* trois fils

Plymouth ['plɪməθ-] *pr n*

►► ***Plymouth Brethren*** darbystes *mpl*; ***Plymouth Rock*** = rocher sur lequel débarquèrent les Pèlerins en 1620

plywood ['plaɪwʊd] *n* contreplaqué *m*

PM [,pi:'em] *n* (**a**) (*abbr* **Prime Minister**) Premier ministre *m* (**b**) (*abbr* **post mortem**) autopsie *f*

p.m. [,pi:'em] *adv* (*abbr* **post meridiem**) de l'après-midi; **3 p.m.** 3 heures de l'après-midi, 15 heures; **at 11 p.m.** à 11 heures du soir, à 23 heures

PMG [,pi:em'dʒi:] *n Br* (**a**) *Fin* (*abbr* **Paymaster General**) Trésorier-payeur-général *m* britannique (**b**) (*abbr* **Postmaster General**) ≃ ministre *m* des Postes et Télécommunications, *Can* Ministre *m* des Postes

PMS [,pi:em'es] *n Am* (*abbr* **premenstrual syndrome**) syndrome *m* prémenstruel

PMT [,pi:em'ti:] *n Br* (*abbr* **premenstrual tension**) syndrome *m* prémenstruel

P/N *Com* (*written abbr* **promissory note**) billet *m* à ordre, effet *m* à ordre

pneumatic [nju:'mætɪk] *adj* pneumatique

►► ***pneumatic brakes*** freins *mpl* à air comprimé; ***pneumatic drill*** marteau-piqueur *m*; ***pneumatic tyre*** pneu *m*

pneumatically [nju:'mætɪklɪ] *adv* pneumatiquement

pneumatics [nju:'mætɪks] *n (UNCOUNT)* pneumatique *f*

pneumococcus [,nju:məʊ'kɒkəs] (*pl* **pneumo-** [illegible]

pneumoconiosis [,nju:məʊkəʊnɪ'əʊsɪs] *n* pneumoconiose *f*

pneumoenteritis [,nju:məʊentə'raɪtɪs] *n* pneumoentérite *f*

pneumogastric [,nju:məʊ'gæstrɪk] *Anat* **1** *n* **the pneumogastric** le (nerf) pneumogastrique

2 *adj* pneumogastrique

pneumonia [nju:'məʊnɪə] *n (UNCOUNT)* pneumonie *f*; **you'll catch** *or* **get pneumonia!** tu vas attraper une pneumonie!

pneumonologist [,nju:mə'nɒlədʒɪst] *n* pneumologue *mf*

pneumonology [,nju:mə'nɒlədʒɪ] *n* pneumologie *f*

pneumothorax [,nju:məʊ'θɔ:ræks] *n* pneumothorax *m*

PO[1] [,pi:'əʊ] *n* (*abbr* **Post Office**) poste *f*

►► ***PO Box*** BP *f*, boîte *f* postale

PO[2] (**a**) (*written abbr* **postal order**) mandat *m* postal (**b**) *Naut* (*written abbr* **petty officer**) second maître *m*

Po [pəʊ] *n* **the (River) Po** le Pô

po [pəʊ] (*pl* **pos**) *n Br Fam* pot *m* (de chambre) [□]

po' [pɔ:] *adj Am Fam* **po' white trash** petits blancs *mpl*

POA [,pi:əʊ'eɪ] *n Br* (*abbr* **Prison Officers' Association**) = syndicat des agents pénitentiaires en Grande-Bretagne

poa ['pəʊə] *n Bot* pâturin *m*

poach [pəʊtʃ] **1** *vt* (**a**) *(hunt illegally)* prendre en braconnant; **all the game has been poached** les braconniers ont tué tout le gibier

(**b**) *Fig (steal → idea)* voler; *(→ employee)* débaucher; **several of our staff have been poached by a rival company** plusieurs de nos employés ont été débauchés par un de nos concurrents; **to poach sb's shots** *(in tennis)* piquer les balles de qn

(**c**) *Culin* pocher; **a poached egg** un œuf poché; **poached salmon** saumon *m* poché

2 *vi* braconner; **to poach for hare** chasser le lièvre sur une propriété privée; **to poach for salmon** prendre du saumon en braconnant; *Fig* **to poach on sb's territory** *or* **preserves** braconner sur les terres de qn, empiéter sur le territoire de qn

poacher ['pəʊtʃə(r)] *n* (**a**) *(person)* braconnier *m*

(**b**) *Culin* **(egg) poacher** pocheuse *f*

poaching ['pəʊtʃɪŋ] *n (hunting)* braconnage *m*

POB [,pi:əʊ'bi:] *n* (*abbr* **post office box**) boîte *f* postale, BP *f*

po'boy ['pəʊbɔɪ] *n Am* gros sandwich *m (typique de la Nouvelle-Orléans)*

pochard ['pəʊtʃəd] *n Orn* (fuligule *f*) milouin *m*

pock [pɒk] = **pockmark**

pocked [pɒkt] = **pockmarked**

pocket ['pɒkɪt] **1** *n* (**a**) *(on clothing)* poche *f*; *(on car door)* compartiment *m*; **it's in your coat pocket** c'est dans la poche de ton manteau; **take your hands out of your pockets!** enlève tes mains de tes poches!; **I went through his pockets** j'ai fouillé *ou* regardé dans ses poches; **he tried to pick her pocket** il a essayé de lui faire les poches; **the maps are in the pocket of the car door** les cartes sont dans (le compartiment de) la portière de la voiture; **to have sb in one's pockets** avoir qn dans sa poche; **we had the deal in our pocket** le marché était dans la poche; **they live in each other's pockets** ils sont tout le temps ensemble; **to line one's pockets** se remplir les poches, s'en mettre plein les poches; *Fig* **to put one's hand in one's pocket** mettre la main au portefeuille; **he doesn't like putting his hand in his pocket** il est du genre radin; **to be out of pocket** en être de sa poche; **how much are you out of pocket?** combien ça vous a coûté?

(**b**) *Fig (financial resources)* portefeuille *m*, porte-monnaie *m*; **we have prices to suit all pockets** nous avons des prix pour toutes les bourses

(**c**) *Mining (of ore, water, gas)* poche *f*; *(of firedamp)* nid *m*; **pockets of water** poches *fpl* d'eau; **pocket of air** trou *m* d'air

(**d**) *(small area → of resistance, rebellion, unemployment)* poche *f*

(**e**) *(of snooker or pool table)* blouse *f*

(**f**) *(bag → for hops, wool)* sac *m*

2 *comp (diary, camera, revolver etc)* de poche

3 *vt* (**a**) *(put in one's pocket)* mettre dans sa poche, empocher; **I paid up and pocketed the change** j'ai payé et j'ai mis la monnaie dans ma poche; *Fig* **to pocket one's pride** mettre son amour-propre dans sa poche; **to pocket an insult** encaisser une insulte sans rien dire

(**b**) *(steal)* voler; **somebody must have pocketed the money** quelqu'un a dû voler l'argent

(**c**) *(in snooker, pool)* mettre dans la blouse

(**d**) *Sport (another runner)* bloquer

(**e**) *Am Pol* **to pocket a bill** = garder un projet de loi sous le coude pour l'empêcher d'être adopté

►► ***pocket battleship*** cuirassé *m* de poche; *Br* ***pocket billiards*** *(pool)* billard *m* américain; *very Fam Fig Hum* **to play pocket billiards** se caresser les boules à travers sa poche de pantalon; *Hist* ***pocket borough*** = circonscription électorale contrôlée par une personne ou une famille; ***pocket calculator*** calculatrice *f* de poche; ***pocket comb*** peigne *m* de poche; ***pocket computer*** ordinateur *m* de poche; ***pocket dictionary*** dictionnaire *m* de poche; *Zool* ***pocket gopher*** gaufre *m*; ***pocket handkerchief*** mouchoir *m* de poche; *Br* ***pocket money*** argent *m* de poche; *Zool* ***pocket mouse*** souris *f* à poche; ***pocket notebook*** carnet *m*; *Am* ***pocket pool*** billard *m* américain; *very Fam Fig Hum* **to play pocket pool** se caresser les boules à travers sa poche de pantalon; ***pocket size*** *(in bookbinding)* format *m* de poche; *Am* ***pocket veto*** = refus par le Président de signer une proposition de loi, pour l'empêcher d'être adoptée

pocketbook ['pɒkɪtbʊk] *n* (**a**) *(notebook)* calepin *m*, carnet *m* (**b**) *Am (handbag)* sac *m* à main; *(wallet)* portefeuille *m*; *(purse)* porte-monnaie *m*

pocketful ['pɒkɪtfʊl] *n* poche *f* pleine; **I've got pocketfuls of small change** j'ai les poches pleines de petite monnaie

pocketknife ['pɒkɪtnaɪf] (*pl* **pocketknives** [-naɪvz]) *n* canif *m*

pocket-sized *adj* (**a**) *(book, revolver etc)* de poche (**b**) *(tiny)* tout petit, minuscule

pockmark ['pɒkmɑ:k] *n (on surface)* marque *f*, petit trou *m*; *(from smallpox)* cicatrice *f* de variole; **his face is covered with pockmarks** il a le visage grêlé *ou* variolé

pockmarked ['pɒkmɑ:kt] *adj (face)* grêlé; *(surface)* criblé de petits trous; **pockmarked with rust** piqué par la rouille

poculiform ['pɒkjʊlɪfɔ:m] *adj Biol* en forme de coupe

POD [,pi:əʊ'di:] *adv Am Com* (*abbr* **pay on delivery**) **to send sth POD** envoyer qch contre remboursement; **all goods are sent POD** toutes les marchandises doivent être payées à la livraison

pod [pɒd] (*pt & pp* **podded**, *cont* **podding**) **1** *n* (**a**) *Bot* cosse *f*; **bean pod** cosse *f* de haricot (**b**) *Zool* oothèque *f* (**c**) *Aviat* nacelle *f*; *Astron* capsule *f*

2 *vt Br (peas)* écosser

3 *vi Bot* produire des cosses

podagra [pɒ'dægrə] *n Med* podagre *f*

podded ['pɒdɪd] *adj (bearing pods)* à cosses; *(growing in pods)* en cosses

podginess ['pɒdʒɪnɪs] *n* embonpoint *m*, rondeur *f*

podgy ['pɒdʒɪ] (*compar* **podgier**, *superl* **podgiest**) *adj Br* grassouillet

podiatrist [pə'daɪətrɪst] *n* pédicure *mf*

podiatry [pə'daɪətrɪ] *n* pédicurie *f*, soin *m* des pieds

podium ['pəʊdɪəm] (*pl* **podiums** *or* **podia** [-dɪə]) *n* (**a**) *(stand)* podium *m* (**b**) *Am (desk, counter)* guichet *m*; **next podium please** *(sign)* passez au guichet suivant

podsol ['pɒdsɒl] = **podzol**

podsolic [pɒd'sɒlɪk] = **podzolic**

podzol ['pɒdzɒl] *n Geol* podzol *m*, podsol *m*

podzolic [pɒd'zɒlɪk] *adj Geol* podzolique, podsolique

POE [,pi:əʊ'i:] *n* (**a**) (*abbr* **port of embarkation**) port *m* d'embarquement (**b**) (*abbr* **port of entry**) port *m* de débarquement

poem ['pəʊɪm] *n* poème *m*

poesy ['pəʊɪzɪ] *n Arch or Literary* poésie *f*

[illegible]

►► ***Poets' Corner*** = partie de l'abbaye de Westminster où reposent plusieurs poètes anglais; ***poet laureate*** poète *m* lauréat

poetaster [,pəʊɪ'tæstə(r)] *n Pej* rimailleur(euse) *m,f*

poetess ['pəʊɪtɪs] *n Old-fashioned* poétesse *f*

poetic [pəʊ'etɪk] *adj* poétique

►► ***poetic justice*** justice *f* immanente; **it's poetic justice that they ended up losing** ce n'est que justice qu'ils aient fini par perdre; ***poetic licence*** licence *f* poétique

poetical [pəʊ'etɪkəl] *adj* poétique

poetically [pəʊ'etɪklɪ] *adv* poétiquement

poeticize, -ise [pəʊ'etɪsaɪz] *vt* poétiser

poetics [pəʊ'etɪks] *n (UNCOUNT)* poétique *f*

poetry ['pəʊɪtrɪ] *n* poésie *f*; **to write poetry** écrire des poèmes; **the art of poetry** l'art *m* poétique; **it was poetry in motion** c'était un vrai plaisir pour les yeux; *Ironic* c'était beau à voir!

►► ***poetry reading*** lecture *f* de poèmes

po-faced *adj Br Fam* à l'air pincé [□]

plu–pof

pogo ['pəʊgəʊ] **1** *n (dance)* pogo *m (danse punk)* **2** *vi (dance)* danser le pogo
►► ***pogo stick*** bâton *m* sauteur

pogrom ['pɒgrəm] *n* pogrom *m*

poignancy ['pɔɪnjənsɪ] *n* caractère *m* poignant; **a moment of great poignancy** un moment d'intense émotion

poignant ['pɔɪnjənt] *adj* poignant

poignantly ['pɔɪnjəntlɪ] *adv* de façon poignante

poikilothermic [,pɔɪkɪləʊ'θɜːmɪk] *adj Zool* poïkilotherme

poinciana [,pɔɪnsɪ'ɑːnə] *n Bot* poinciana *f*

poinsettia [pɔɪn'setɪə] *n Bot* poinsettia *m*

POINT [pɔɪnt]

pointe	► 1 (a)
point	► 1 (b), (c), (e), (f), (i) – (l), (n), (o)
endroit	► 1 (c)
moment	► 1 (d)
essentiel	► 1 (g)
but	► 1 (h)
virgule	► 1 (m)
diriger	► 2 (a)
pointer	► 2 (a)
indiquer	► 2 (b)
montrer du doigt	► 3 (a)

1 *n* (**a**) *(tip → of sword, nail, pencil etc)* pointe *f*; **trim one end of the stick into a point** taillez un des bouts de la branche en pointe; **his beard ended in a neat point** sa barbe était soigneusement taillée en pointe; **draw a star with five points** dessinez une étoile à cinq branches; **a dog with white points** un chien aux pattes et aux oreilles blanches; **an eight-point stag** un cerf huit cors; **to dance on points** faire des pointes; **on (full) point** *(ballet dancer)* sur la pointe; **on demi-point** *(ballet dancer)* sur la demi-pointe; **not to put too fine a point on it...** pour dire les choses clairement...

(**b**) *(small dot)* point *m*; **a tiny point of light** un minuscule point de lumière

(**c**) *(specific place)* point *m*, endroit *m*, lieu *m*; **intersection point** point *m* d'intersection; **meeting point** *(sign)* point rencontre; **the runners have passed the halfway point** les coureurs ont dépassé la mi-parcours; **we're back to our point of departure** *or* **our starting point** nous sommes revenus au *ou* à notre point de départ; **the point where the accident occurred** l'endroit où l'accident a eu lieu; **at that point you'll see a church on the left** à ce moment-là, vous verrez une église sur votre gauche; **the terrorists claim they can strike at any point in the country** les terroristes prétendent qu'ils peuvent frapper n'importe où dans le pays; **the bus service to Dayton and points west** le service de bus à destination de Dayton et des villes situées plus à l'ouest; **points south of here get little rainfall** les régions situées au sud d'ici n'ont pas une grande pluviosité

(**d**) *(particular moment)* moment *m*; *(particular period)* période *f*; **the country is at a critical point in its development** le pays traverse une période *ou* phase critique de son développement; **we are at a critical point** nous voici à un point critique; **there comes a point when a decision has to be made** il arrive un moment où il faut prendre une décision; **when it comes to the point of actually doing it** quand vient le moment de passer à l'acte; **when it came to the point** quand le moment critique est arrivé; **at one point in the discussion** à un moment de la discussion; **at one point in my travels** au cours de mes voyages; **at one point, I thought the roof was going to cave in** à un moment (donné), j'ai cru que le toit allait s'effondrer; **at one point in the book** à un moment donné dans le livre; **at this point the phone rang** c'est alors que le téléphone a sonné, à ce moment-là le téléphone a sonné; **at that point, I was still undecided** à ce moment-là, je n'avais pas encore pris de décision; **at that point in China's history** à ce moment précis de l'histoire de la Chine; **it's too late by this point** il est déjà trop tard à l'heure qu'il est; **by that point, I was too tired to move** j'étais alors tellement fatigué que je ne pouvais plus bouger

(**e**) *(stage in development or process)* point *m*; **she had reached the point of wanting a divorce** elle en était (arrivée) au point de vouloir divorcer; **thank God we haven't reached that point!** Dieu merci, nous n'en sommes pas (encore arrivés) là!; **to reach the point of no return** atteindre le point de non-retour; **to be at the point of death** être sur le point de mourir; **the conflict has gone beyond the point where negotiations are possible** le conflit a atteint le stade où toute négociation est impossible; **the regime is on the point of collapse** le régime est au bord de l'effondrement; **I was on the point of admitting everything** j'étais sur le point de tout avouer; **she had worked to the point of exhaustion** elle avait travaillé jusqu'à l'épuisement; **he was jealous to the point of madness** sa jalousie confinait à la folie; **he stuffed himself to the point of being sick** il s'est gavé à en être malade

(**f**) *(for discussion or debate)* point *m*; **a seven-point memorandum** un mémorandum en sept points; **let's go on to the next point** passons à la question suivante *ou* au point suivant; **on this point we disagree** sur ce point nous ne sommes pas d'accord; **I want to emphasize this point** je voudrais insister sur ce point; **are there any points I haven't covered?** y a-t-il des questions que je n'ai pas abordées?; **to make** *or* **to raise a point** faire une remarque; **to make the point that...** faire remarquer que... + *indicative*; **my point** *or* **the point I'm making is that...** là où je veux en venir c'est que...; **all right, you've made your point!** d'accord, on a compris!; **the points raised in her article** les points qu'elle soulève dans son article; **the main points to keep in mind** les principaux points à garder à l'esprit; **let me illustrate my point** laissez-moi illustrer mon propos; **to prove his point he showed us a photo** pour prouver ses affirmations, il nous a montré une photo; **I see** *or* **take your point** je vois ce que vous voulez dire *ou* où vous voulez en venir; **point taken!** c'est juste!; **he may not be home – you've got a point there!** il n'est peut-être pas chez lui – ça c'est vrai!; **the fact that he went to the police is a point in his favour/a point against him** le fait qu'il soit allé à la police est un bon/mauvais point pour lui; **I corrected her on a point of grammar** je l'ai corrigée sur un point de grammaire; **she was disqualified on a technical point** elle a été disqualifiée pour *ou* sur une faute technique; **to make a point of doing sth** tenir à faire qch; **he made a point of speaking to her** il a tenu à lui adresser la parole; **kindly make a point of remembering next time** faites-moi le plaisir de ne pas oublier la prochaine fois

(**g**) *(essential part, heart → of argument, explanation)* essentiel *m*; *(conclusion → of joke)* chute *f*; **I get the point** je comprends, je vois; **the point is (that) we're overloaded with work** le fait est que nous sommes débordés de travail; **we're getting off** *or* **away from the point** nous nous éloignons *ou* écartons du sujet; **that's the (whole) point!** *(that's the problem)* c'est là (tout) le problème!; *(that's the aim)* c'est ça, le but!; **that's not the point!** là n'est pas la question!; **the money is/your feelings are beside the point** l'argent n'a/vos sentiments n'ont rien à voir là-dedans; **get** *or* **come to the point!** dites ce que vous avez à dire!, ne tournez pas autour du pot!; **I'll come straight to the point** je serai bref; **to keep to the point** ne pas s'écarter du sujet

(**h**) *(purpose)* but *m*; *(meaning, use)* sens *m*, intérêt *m*; **the point of the game is to get rid of all your cards** le but du jeu est de se débarrasser de toutes ses cartes; **there's no point in asking him now** ça ne sert à rien *ou* ce n'est pas la peine de le lui demander maintenant; **what's the point of all this?** à quoi ça sert tout ça?; **I don't see the point (of re-doing it)** je ne vois pas l'intérêt (de le refaire); **oh, what's the point anyway!** oh, et puis à quoi bon, après tout!

(**i**) *(feature, characteristic)* point *m*; **the boss has his good points** le patron a ses bons côtés; **it's my weak/strong point** c'est mon point faible/fort; **her strong point is her sense of humour** son point fort, c'est son sens de l'humour; **tact has never been one of your strong points** la délicatesse n'a jamais été ton fort

(**j**) *(unit → in scoring, measuring)* point *m*; *Mktg (→ on customer loyalty card)* point *m*; **the Dow Jones index is up/down two points** l'indice Dow Jones a augmenté/baissé de deux points; **who scored the winning point?** qui a marqué le point gagnant?; **an ace is worth 4 points** un as vaut 4 points; **to win/to lead on points** *(in boxing)* gagner/mener aux points; *Am Fam* **to make points with sb** *(find favour with)* faire bonne impression à qn; *Sch* **merit points** bons points *mpl*; **points competition** *(in cycling)* classement *m* par points

(**k**) *(on compass)* point *m*; **the four points of the compass** les quatre points *mpl* cardinaux; **the 32 points of the compass** les 32 points *mpl* de la rose des vents; **to alter course 16 points** venir de 16 quarts; **our people were scattered to all points of the compass** notre peuple s'est retrouvé éparpillé aux quatre coins du monde

(**l**) *Geom* point *m*; **a straight line between two points** une droite reliant deux points

(**m**) *(in decimals)* virgule *f*; **five point one** cinq virgule un

(**n**) *(punctuation mark)* point *m*; **three** *or* **ellipsis points** points *mpl* de suspension

(**o**) *Typ & Comput (measurement)* point *m*; **6-point type** caractères *mpl* de 6 points

(**p**) *Geog (promontory)* pointe *f*, promontoire *m*

(**q**) *Aut* vis *f* platinée

(**r**) *Br Elec (socket)* **(power) point** prise *f* (de courant); **eight-point distributor** *(in engine)* distributeur *m* (d'allumage) à huit plots

(**s**) *Br Rail* **points** aiguillage *m*

(**t**) *(on backgammon board)* flèche *f*, pointe *f*

(**u**) *Her* point *m*

2 *vt* (**a**) *(direct, aim → vehicle)* diriger; *(→ flashlight, hose)* pointer, braquer; *(→ finger)* pointer, tendre; *(→ telescope)* diriger, braquer; **to point one's finger at sb/sth** montrer qn/qch du doigt; **he pointed his finger accusingly at Gus** il pointa un doigt accusateur vers Gus, il montra *ou* désigna Gus d'un doigt accusateur; **to point a gun at sb** braquer une arme sur qn; **he pointed the rifle/the camera at me** il braqua le fusil/l'appareil photo sur moi; **she pointed the truck towards the garage** elle tourna le camion vers le garage; **he pointed the boat out to sea** il a mis le cap vers le large; **if anybody shows up, just point them in my direction** si quelqu'un arrive, tu n'as qu'à me l'envoyer; **just point me in the right direction** dites-moi simplement quelle direction je dois prendre; **just point him to the nearest bar** tu n'as qu'à lui indiquer le chemin du bar le plus proche

(**b**) *(indicate)* **to point the way** indiquer la direction *ou* le chemin; *Fig* montrer le chemin, indiquer la direction à suivre; **he pointed the way to future success** il a montré le chemin de la réussite; **her research points the way to a better understanding of the phenomenon** ses recherches vont permettre une meilleure compréhension du phénomène; **they point the way (in) which reform must go** ils indiquent la direction dans laquelle les réformes doivent aller

(**c**) *(in dance)* **to point one's toes** tendre le pied

(**d**) *Constr (wall, building)* jointoyer

(**e**) *(sharpen → stick, pencil)* tailler

(**f**) *Ling* mettre des signes diacritiques à

3 *vi* (**a**) *(person)* **to point at** *or* **to** *or* **towards sth** montrer qch du doigt; **she pointed left** elle fit un signe vers la gauche; **he pointed back down the corridor** il fit un signe vers le fond du couloir; **he pointed at** *or* **to me with his pencil** il pointa son crayon vers moi; **he was pointing at me** son doigt était pointé vers moi; **it's rude to point** ce n'est pas poli de montrer du doigt

(**b**) *(road sign, needle on dial)* **the signpost points up the hill** le panneau est tourné vers le haut de la colline; **a compass needle always points north** l'aiguille d'une boussole indique toujours le nord; **the weather vane is pointing north** la girouette est orientée au nord; **when the big hand points to twelve** quand la grande aiguille est sur le douze

(**c**) *(be directed, face → gun, camera)* être braqué; *(→ vehicle)* être dirigé, être tourné; **hold the gun with the barrel pointing downwards** tenez le canon de l'arme pointé vers le bas; **the rifle/the camera was pointing straight at me** la carabine/la caméra était braquée sur moi; **point your flashlight over there** éclaire là-bas; **insert the disk with the arrow pointing right** insérez la disquette, la flèche pointée *ou* pointant vers la droite; **the aerial should be pointing in the direction of the transmitter** l'antenne devrait être tournée dans la direction de *ou* tournée vers l'émetteur; **he walks with his feet pointing outwards** il marche les pieds en dehors

(**d**) *(dog)* tomber en arrêt

4 at this point in time *adv* pour l'instant; **no more details are available at this point in time** pour l'instant, nous ne disposons pas d'autres détails

5 in point of fact *adv* en fait, à vrai dire

6 to the point *adj* pertinent

7 up to a point *adv* jusqu'à un certain point; **did the strategy succeed? – up to a point** est-ce que la stratégie a réussi? – dans une certaine mesure; **productivity can be increased up to a point** la productivité peut être augmentée jusqu'à un certain point; **she can be persuaded, but only up to a point** il est possible de la convaincre, mais seulement jusqu'à un certain point

►► *Mktg* ***point of delivery*** lieu *m* de livraison; *Br* ***point duty*** *(of police officer, traffic warden)* service *m* de la circulation; **to be on point duty** diriger la circulation; ***point guard*** *(in basketball)* meneur(euse) *m,f*; ***point of intersection*** point *m* d'intersection; *Br Rail* ***point lever*** levier *m* d'aiguille; ***point of order*** point *m* de procédure; **he rose on a point of order** il a demandé la parole pour soulever un point de procédure; *Am* ***point man*** *(in the forefront)* précurseur *m*; *Comput* ***point of presence*** point *m* de présence, point *m* d'accès; *Mktg* ***point of purchase*** lieu *m* d'achat, lieu *m* de vente; ***point of reference*** point *m* de référence; *Mktg* ***point of sale*** lieu *m* de vente, point *m* de vente; **at the point of sale** sur le lieu de vente; ***point shoes*** *(for ballet)* (chaussons *mpl* à) pointes *fpl*; *Typ & Comput* ***point size*** corps *m*; ***point source*** source *f* ponctuelle; ***point of view*** *TV & Cin* angle *m* du regard; *(opinion)* point *m* de vue, opinion *f*; **from my point of view, it doesn't make much difference** en ce qui me concerne, ça ne change pas grand-chose; **to consider sth from all points of view** considérer qch sous tous ses aspects; ***point work*** *(of ballet dancer)* pointes *fpl*

►**point off** *vt sep Math (decimals)* séparer par une virgule

►**point out** *vt sep* (**a**) *(indicate)* indiquer, montrer; **I'll point the church out to you as we go by** je vous montrerai *ou* vous indiquerai l'église quand nous passerons devant

(**b**) *(mention, call attention to → error)* signaler; *(→ fact)* faire remarquer; **she pointed out several mistakes to us** elle nous a signalé plusieurs erreurs, elle a attiré notre attention sur plusieurs erreurs; **I'd like to point out that it was my idea in the first place** je vous ferai remarquer que l'idée est de moi; **might I point out that...?** permettez-moi de vous faire observer ou remarquer que...; **he pointed out that two people were missing** il fit remarquer qu'il manquait deux personnes

►**point to** *vt insep* (**a**) *(signify, denote)* signifier, indiquer; *(foreshadow)* indiquer, annoncer; **the facts point to only one conclusion** les faits ne permettent qu'une seule conclusion; **all the evidence points to him** toutes les preuves indiquent que c'est lui; **everything points to CIA involvement** tout indique que la CIA est impliquée

(**b**) *(call attention to)* attirer l'attention sur; **ecologists point to the destruction of forest land** les écologistes attirent notre attention sur la destruction des forêts; **they proudly point to the government's record** ils invoquent avec fierté le bilan du gouvernement

►**point up** *vt sep (of person, report)* souligner, mettre l'accent sur; *(of event)* faire ressortir; **his account points up the irony of the defeat** son exposé met l'accent sur l'ironie de la défaite; **the accident points up the need for closer cooperation** l'accident fait ressortir le besoin d'une coopération plus étroite

point-and-shoot *adj (camera)* automatique

point-blank 1 *adj* (**a**) *(shot)* (tiré) à bout portant; **he was shot at point-blank range** on lui a tiré dessus à bout portant (**b**) *(refusal, denial)* catégorique; *(question)* (posé) de but en blanc, (posé) à brûle-pourpoint

2 *adv* (**a**) *(shoot)* à bout portant (**b**) *(refuse, deny)* catégoriquement; *(ask)* de but en blanc, à brûle-pourpoint

point-by-point *adj* méthodique

pointed ['pɔɪntɪd] *adj* (**a**) *(sharp)* pointu; *(beard)* (taillé) en pointe (**b**) *Fig (comment, remark, look)* qui en dit long, lourd de sous-entendus; *(reference)* peu équivoque

►► *Archit* ***pointed arch*** arche *f* en ogive; *Archit* ***pointed style*** style *m* gothique

-pointed ['pɔɪntɪd] *suff* **five-/six-pointed** *(gen)* à cinq/six pointes; *(star)* à cinq/six branches

pointedly ['pɔɪntɪdlɪ] *adv (comment)* de façon explicite; **she looked at me pointedly** elle m'a lancé un regard qui en disait long; **she pointedly ignored me all evening** elle m'a ostensiblement ignoré pendant toute la soirée

pointedness ['pɔɪntɪdnɪs] *n (of comment, reference)* caractère *m* explicite

pointed-nose pliers *npl* pince *f* à bec pointu

pointer ['pɔɪntə(r)] *n* (**a**) *(for pointing → stick)* baguette *f*; *(→ arrow)* flèche *f*

(**b**) *(on dial)* aiguille *f*

(**c**) *(indication, sign)* indice *m*, signe *m*; *(tip)* tuyau *m*; **there are several pointers as to what really happened** plusieurs indices nous permettent de deviner ce qui s'est réellement passé; **all the pointers indicate an impending economic recovery** tout indique que la reprise économique est imminente; **a pointer to the future** une idée de ce que l'avenir nous réserve; **he gave me a few pointers on how to use the computer** il m'a donné quelques tuyaux sur la façon d'utiliser l'ordinateur

(**d**) *Comput* pointeur *m*

(**e**) *(dog)* pointer *m*

(**f**) *Constr (bricklayer's tool)* pointe *f*

pointillism ['pɔɪntɪlɪzəm] *n Art* pointillisme *m*

pointillist ['pɔɪntɪlɪst] *Art* **1** *adj* pointilliste

2 *n* pointilliste *mf*

pointing ['pɔɪntɪŋ] *n (UNCOUNT) Constr (act, job)* jointoiement *m*; *(cement work)* joints *mpl*

►► *Comput* ***pointing device*** pointeur *m*

pointless ['pɔɪntlɪs] *adj* inutile, vain; *(crime, violence, vandalism)* gratuit; *(story, joke)* qui ne rime à rien; **all my efforts seemed pointless** tous mes efforts semblaient inutiles *ou* vains; **it's pointless trying to convince him** ça ne sert à rien *ou* il est inutile d'essayer de le convaincre

pointlessly ['pɔɪntlɪslɪ] *adv (gen)* inutilement, vainement; *(hurt, murder, vandalize)* gratuitement

pointlessness ['pɔɪntlɪsnɪs] *n (gen)* inutilité *f*; *(of remark)* manque *m* d'à-propos; *(of crime, violence, vandalism)* gratuité *f*

point-of-purchase *adj Mktg*

►► ***point-of-purchase advertising*** publicité *f* sur le lieu de vente, PLV *f*; ***point-of-purchase display*** exposition *f* sur le lieu de vente; ***point-of-purchase information*** informations *fpl* sur le lieu de vente; ***point-of-purchase material*** matériel *m* de publicité sur le lieu de vente, matériel *m* de PLV; ***point-of-purchase promotion*** promotion *f* sur le lieu de vente

point-of-sale *adj* sur le point *ou* sur le lieu de vente

►► ***point-of-sale advertising*** publicité *f* sur le lieu de vente, PLV *f*; ***point-of-sale competition*** concurrence *f* entre points de vente; ***point-of-sale display*** exposition *f* sur le lieu de vente; ***point-of-sale information*** informations *fpl* sur le lieu de vente; ***point-of-sale material*** matériel *m* de publicité sur le lieu de vente *ou* de PLV; ***point-of-sale network*** réseau *m* de points de vente; ***point-of-sale promotion*** communication *f ou* promotion *f ou* publicité *f* sur le lieu de vente, CLV *f*, PLV *f*; ***point-of-sale terminal*** terminal *m* point de vente, TPV *m*

pointsman ['pɔɪntsmən] (*pl* **pointsmen** [-mən]) *n Br Rail* aiguilleur *m*

point-to-point *n Br* rallye *m* hippique

point-to-point protocol *n Comput* protocole *m* point à point

pointy-headed [,pɔɪntɪ'hedɪd] *adj Am Fam Pej* intello

poise [pɔɪz] **1** *n* (**a**) *(composure, coolness)* calme *m*, aisance *f*, assurance *f*; **to recover one's poise** retrouver son aplomb (**b**) *(physical bearing)* port *m*, maintien *m*; *(gracefulness)* grâce *f*

2 *vt (balance)* mettre en équilibre; *(hold suspended)* tenir suspendu; **she poised herself on the arm of my chair** elle s'est assise gracieusement sur le bras de mon fauteuil

poised [pɔɪzd] *adj* (**a**) *(balanced)* en équilibre; *(suspended)* suspendu; **her hand was poised over the telephone** sa main était suspendue au-dessus du téléphone; **she held her glass poised near her lips** elle tenait son verre près de ses lèvres; **he was poised between life and death** il était entre la vie et la mort; **the cat was poised ready to spring** le chat se tenait prêt à bondir

(**b**) *(ready, prepared)* prêt; **poised for action** prêt à agir; **Rome was poised to conquer the known world** Rome se tenait prête à conquérir le monde connu

(**c**) *(composed, self-assured)* calme, assuré

poison ['pɔɪzən] **1** *n* (**a**) *(substance)* poison *m*; *(of reptile)* venin *m*

(**b**) *Fig* poison *m*, venin *m*; **the poison spreading through our society** le mal qui se propage dans notre société; **they hate each other like poison** ils se détestent cordialement; *Fam* **he's absolute poison!** c'est un vrai poison!; *Fam Hum* **name your poison**, *Br* **what's your poison?** qu'est-ce que tu bois? ❑, qu'est-ce que je t'offre? ❑

2 *comp (mushroom, plant)* vénéneux; *(gas)* toxique

3 *vt* (**a**) *(give poison to)* empoisonner; **to poison sb with sth** empoisonner qn à qch; **a poisoned arrow/drink** une flèche/boisson empoisonnée; **all these pesticides are poisoning the air** tous ces pesticides empoisonnent l'atmosphère

(**b**) *Fig* envenimer, gâcher; **his arrival poisoned the atmosphere** son arrivée rendit l'atmosphère insupportable; **they are poisoning his mind** ils sont en train de le corrompre; **he poisoned our minds against her** il nous a montés contre elle

►► *Fig* ***poisoned chalice*** cadeau *m* empoisonné; *Zool* ***poison gland*** glande *f* à venin; *Bot* ***poison ivy*** sumac *m* vénéneux, *Can* herbe *f* à puces *ou* à la puce; *Fam Fin* ***poison pill*** *(strategy)* pilule *f* empoisonnée

poisoner ['pɔɪzənə(r)] *n* empoisonneur(euse) *m,f*

poisoning ['pɔɪzənɪŋ] *n* empoisonnement *m*; **mercury poisoning** empoisonnement *m* au mercure

poisonous ['pɔɪzənəs] *adj* (**a**) *(mushroom, plant)* vénéneux; *(snake, lizard)* venimeux; *(gas, chemical)* toxique; **mercury is highly poisonous** le mercure est très toxique (**b**) *Fig (person)* malveillant, venimeux; *(remark, allegation)* venimeux; *(doctrine)* pernicieux; **he's got a poisonous tongue** il a une langue de vipère

poisonousness ['pɔɪzənəsnɪs] *n* (**a**) *(of substance)* toxicité *f* (**b**) *Fig (of person, remark)* caractère *m* venimeux; *(of doctrine)* caractère *m* pernicieux

poison-pen letter *n* lettre *f* anonyme malfaisante

Poisson Distribution ['pwæsɒn-] *n Math* distribution *f* de Poisson

poke [pəʊk] **1** *vt* (**a**) *(push, prod → gen)* donner un coup à; *(→ with elbow)* donner un coup de coude à; **somebody poked me in the back** quelqu'un m'a donné un coup dans le dos

(**b**) *(stick, insert)* enfoncer; **she poked her finger/knife into the tart** elle enfonça son doigt/son couteau dans la tarte; **to poke a hole in sth** faire un trou dans qch; **he poked his finger at the map** il a pointé le doigt vers la carte; **he poked his stick at me** il fit un mouvement avec son bâton dans ma direction; **she opened the door and poked her head in/out** elle ouvrit la porte et passa sa tête à l'intérieur/à l'extérieur; **he's always poking his nose in other people's business** il se mêle toujours de ce qui ne le regarde pas

(**c**) *(fire)* tisonner

(**d**) *Am Fam (punch)* flanquer un coup de

poing à; **I poked him in the nose** je lui ai flanqué un coup de poing sur le nez

(**e**) *Vulg (have sex with)* tirer un coup avec, tringler

(**f**) *(idiom)* **to poke fun at sb/sth** se moquer de qn/qch

2 *vi (prod)* **to poke at sth** *(with finger)* toucher qch du doigt; *(with stick)* donner un petit coup dans qch

3 *n* (**a**) *(push, prod)* poussée *f*, (petit) coup *m*; **he gave me a poke in the back** il m'a donné un (petit) coup dans le dos; **give the fire a poke** donne un coup de tisonnier dans le feu; *Fam Hum* **it's better than a poke in the eye with a sharp stick** c'est mieux que rien ☐

(**b**) *Am Fam (punch)* gnon *m*, marron *m*; **he's asking for a poke in the nose!** il va prendre un marron s'il continue!

(**c**) *Scot (bag)* sac *m*

(**d**) *Vulg (sexual intercourse)* **to have a poke** tirer un coup

▸**poke about 1** *vi* (**a**) *(search)* fouiller, fureter; **a dog was poking about in the bushes** un chien fouinait *ou* furetait dans les buissons; **she was poking about in the wardrobe for something to wear** elle fouillait dans l'armoire pour trouver quelque chose à mettre

(**b**) *(make unwanted enquiries)* fourrer son nez partout, fouiner; **that social worker is always poking about** cette assistante sociale est toujours en train de fourrer son nez partout

2 *vt insep (search in)* fouiller dans; **she loves poking about antique shops** elle adore fouiner *ou* farfouiller dans les magasins d'antiquités

▸**poke along** *vi Am* avancer lentement

▸**poke around** = **poke about**

▸**poke out 1** *vi (stick out)* dépasser; **the new shoots were just poking out of the ground** les nouvelles pousses commençaient tout juste à sortir de terre; **her umbrella was poking out of her bag** son parapluie sortait *ou* dépassait de son sac

2 *vt sep (remove)* déloger; **to poke sb's eye out** crever un œil à qn

poker ['pəʊkə(r)] *n* (**a**) *(card game)* poker *m* (**b**) *(for fire)* tisonnier *m*

▸▸ ***poker dice* 1** *n (game)* poker *m* d'as **2** *npl (set of dice)* dés *mpl* pour le poker d'as; ***poker face*** visage *m* impassible *or* impénétrable; **she kept a poker face** son visage n'a pas trahi la moindre émotion *ou* est resté totalement impassible

poker-faced *adj (person)* au visage impassible; *(reply, response)* qui ne trahit aucune émotion

pokerwork ['pəʊkəwɜːk] *n (UNCOUNT) Br (art)* pyrogravure *f*; *(objects)* pyrogravures *fpl*

pokeweed ['pəʊkwiːd] *n Bot* phytolaque *m*

pokey ['pəʊkɪ] *(compar* **pokier**, *superl* **pokiest**) *Fam* **1** *n Am (prison)* taule *f*, cabane *f*; **in (the) pokey** en taule, en cabane

2 *adj* (**a**) *Br (house, room → cramped)* exigu(uë) ☐ (**b**) *Am (slow)* lambin

pokie ['pəʊkɪ] *n Austr Fam (fruit machine)* machine *f* à sous ☐

poky ['pəʊkɪ] *(compar* **pokier**, *superl* **pokiest**) = **pokey**

Polack ['pəʊlæk] *n very Fam* Polaque *mf*, = terme injurieux désignant un Polonais

Poland ['pəʊlənd] *n* Pologne *f*; **in Poland** en Pologne

polar ['pəʊlə(r)] *adj* (**a**) *Chem, Elec, Geog & Math* polaire

(**b**) *Fig (completely different → opinions, attitudes)* diamétralement opposé; **they are polar opposites** ils sont diamétralement opposés

▸▸ *Zool **polar bear*** ours *m* polaire *ou* blanc; ***the Polar Circle*** le cercle polaire; ***polar coordinates*** coordonnées *fpl* polaires; ***the polar lights*** l'aurore *f* polaire; ***polar regions*** les régions *fpl* polaires

polarimeter [ˌpəʊlə'rɪmɪtə(r)] *n Phys* polarimètre *m*

polarimetric [ˌpəʊlərɪ'metrɪk] *adj Phys* polarimétrique

polarimetry [ˌpəʊlə'rɪmətrɪ] *n Phys* polarimétrie *f*

Polaris [pəʊ'lɑːrɪs] *n* (**a**) *Astron* l'étoile *f* Polaire, la Polaire (**b**) *(missile)* missile *m* Polaris

▸▸ ***Polaris missile*** missile *m* Polaris

polariscope [pəʊ'lærɪskəʊp] *n Opt* polariscope *m*

polarity [pəʊ'lærətɪ] *(pl* **polarities**) *n Phys* polarité *f*; *Fig* **there is a growing polarity between the two parties** les deux partis sont en opposition de plus en plus nette

polarization [ˌpəʊləraɪ'zeɪʃən] *n* polarisation *f*

polarize, -ise ['pəʊləraɪz] **1** *vt* polariser; *Fig (people, opinion)* diviser

2 *vi* se polariser; *Fig (opinion)* se diviser

polarized ['pəʊləraɪzd] *adj Phys & Opt* polarisé; **elliptically/horizontally/vertically polarized** polarisé elliptiquement/horizontalement/verticalement

▸▸ ***polarized neutron*** neutron *m* polarisé; ***polarized nucleus*** noyau *m* polarisé; ***polarized radiation*** radiation *f* polarisée; ***polarized relay*** relais *m* polarisé; ***polarized wave*** onde *f* polarisée

polarizer ['pəʊləraɪzə(r)] *n Opt* polariseur *m*

polarizing filter ['pəʊləraɪzɪŋ-] *n TV & Cin* filtre *m* polarisant

Polaroid® ['pəʊlərɔɪd] **1** *adj (camera)* Polaroid®; *(film)* pour Polaroid®; *(glasses)* à verre polarisé

2 *n (camera)* Polaroid®; *(photo)* photo *f ou* cliché *m* Polaroid®

3 Polaroids® *npl (sunglasses)* lunettes *fpl* de soleil à verre polarisé

polder ['pəʊldə(r)] *n Geog* polder *m*

Pole [pəʊl] *n* Polonais(e) *m,f*

pole [pəʊl] **1** *n* (**a**) *Elec & Geog* pôle *m*; **to travel from pole to pole** parcourir la terre entière; *Fig* **they are poles apart** ils n'ont absolument rien en commun; **their positions on disarmament are poles apart** leurs positions sur le désarmement sont diamétralement opposées

(**b**) *(rod)* bâton *m*, perche *f*; *(for tent)* montant *m*; *(in fence, construction)* poteau *m*, pieu *m*; *(for gardening)* tuteur *m*; *(for climbing plants)* rame *f*; *(for polevaulting, punting)* perche *f*; *(for skier)* bâton *m*; *(of stretcher)* bras *m*

(**c**) *(mast → for phonelines)* poteau *m*; *(→ for flags, circus tent)* mât *m*

(**d**) *(for climbing)* mât *m*; *(in fire-station)* perche *f*

(**e**) *Br Fam* **to be up the pole** *(crazy)* être cinglé *ou* dingue; **to be up the pole with worry** être fou *ou* malade d'inquiétude; **he's driving me up the pole!** il me rend dingue!

(**f**) *Am (on racecourse)* corde *f*

(**g**) *(unit of measure)* ≃ perche *f*

(**h**) *Vulg (penis)* queue *f*, bite *f*

2 *vt* (**a**) *(punt)* faire avancer (avec une perche)

(**b**) *(plants)* ramer

▸▸ *Am **pole bean*** haricot *m* à rames; ***pole jump*** saut *m* à la perche; ***pole position*** *(in motor racing)* pole position *f*; **to be in pole position** être en pole position; ***Pole Star*** (étoile *f*) Polaire *f*; ***pole vault*** saut *m* à la perche

poleaxe, *Am* **poleax** ['pəʊlæks] **1** *n* (**a**) *(weapon)* hache *f* d'armes (**b**) *(for slaughter)* merlin *m*

2 *vt (hit → person)* assommer; *(→ animal)* abattre avec un merlin; *Fig* **she was poleaxed by the news** la nouvelle l'a abasourdie *ou* assommée

poleaxed ['pəʊlækst] *adj Fam* (**a**) *(surprised)* baba, épaté (**b**) *(drunk)* bourré, beurré

polecat ['pəʊlkæt] *(pl* **inv** *or* **polecats**) *n Zool* (**a**) *(European, African)* putois *m* (**b**) *Am (skunk)* moufette *f*, mouffette *f*

polemic [pə'lemɪk] **1** *adj* polémique

2 *n (argument)* polémique *f*

3 polemics *n (UNCOUNT) (skill, practice)* art *m* de la polémique

polemical [pə'lemɪkəl] *adj* polémique

polemicist [pə'lemɪsɪst] *n* polémiste *mf*

polemicize, -ise [pə'lemɪsaɪz], **polemize, -ise** ['pɒlɪmaɪz] *vi* polémiquer

polenta [pə'lentə] *n* polenta *f*

pole-vault *vi (as activity)* faire du saut à la perche; *(on specific jump)* faire un saut à la perche

pole-vaulter [-ˌvɔːltə(r)] *n* perchiste *mf*

police [pə'liːs] **1** *npl* (**a**) *(police force)* police *f*; **the police are on their way** la police arrive, les gendarmes arrivent; **he's in the police** il est dans la police, c'est un policier; **a man is helping police with their enquiries** un homme est entendu par les policiers dans le cadre de leur enquête

(**b**) *(police officers)* policiers *mpl*; **18 police were injured** 18 policiers ont été blessés

2 *comp (vehicle, patrol, spy)* de police; *(protection, work)* de la police, policier; *(harassment)* policier; **he was taken into police custody** il a été emmené en garde à vue; **all police leave was cancelled** les permissions des policiers ont été annulées; **police powers were extended** les pouvoirs de la police ont été étendus; **there was a heavy police presence** d'importantes forces de police se trouvaient sur place

3 *vt* (**a**) *(of policemen)* surveiller, maintenir l'ordre dans; **the streets are being policed 24 hours a day** les rues sont surveillées par la police 24 heures sur 24; **the match was heavily policed** d'importantes forces de police étaient présentes lors du match

(**b**) *(of guards, vigilantes)* surveiller, maintenir l'ordre dans; **the factory is policed by security guards** l'usine est surveillée par des vigiles; **vigilante groups police the neighbourhood** des groupes d'autodéfense maintiennent l'ordre dans le quartier

(**c**) *(of army, international organization)* surveiller, contrôler; **the area is policed by army patrols** des patrouilles militaires veillent au maintien de l'ordre dans la région

(**d**) *(regulate → prices)* contrôler; *(→ agreement)* veiller à l'application *ou* au respect de; **prices are policed by consumer associations** les associations de consommateurs contrôlent les prix

(**e**) *Am (clean → military camp)* nettoyer

▸▸ *Am **police academy*** école *f* de police; *Am **police captain*** ≃ commissaire *m* de police; ***police car*** voiture *f* de police; ***police cell*** cellule *f* d'un poste de police; ***police chief*** ≃ préfet *m* de police; *Am **police commissioner*** commissaire *m* de police; *Br **Police Complaints Board*** ≃ Inspection *f* générale des services; ***police complaints procedure*** procédure *f* pour porter plainte contre la police; *Br **police constable*** ≃ gardien *m* de la paix, ≃ agent *m* (de police); ***police court*** tribunal *m* de police; *Am **police department*** service *m* de police; ***police dog*** chien *m* policier; **a *police escort*** une escorte policière; *Br* **the *Police Federation*** = le syndicat de la police britannique; ***police force*** police *f*; **the local police force** la police locale; **to join the police force** entrer dans la police; ***police informer*** indicateur(trice) *m,f*; ***police inspector*** inspecteur(trice) *m,f* de police; *Br (in the CID)* commissaire *m* de police; *Am **police line*** cordon *m* de police *(sur le lieu du crime)*; ***police officer*** policier *m*, agent *m* de police; ***police record*** casier *m* judiciaire; **she has no police record** elle n'a pas de casier judiciaire, son casier judiciaire est vierge; ***police sergeant*** ≃ brigadier *m* (de police); ***police state*** État *m ou* régime *m* policier; ***police station*** *(urban)* poste *m* de police, commissariat *m* (de police); *(rural)* gendarmerie *f*; ***police van*** *(for transporting prisoners)* voiture *f* cellulaire; *Am **police wagon*** fourgon *m* cellulaire

policeman [pə'liːsmən] *(pl* **policemen** [-mən]) *n* agent *m* (de police), policier *m*

policewoman [pə'liːsˌwʊmən] *(pl* **policewomen** [-ˌwɪmɪn]) *n* femme *f* policier

policing [pə'liːsɪŋ] *n* (**a**) *(by police)* maintien *m* de l'ordre; **the policing of the match/demonstration was inadequate** le service d'ordre du match/de la manifestation était inadéquat (**b**) *Fig* **the policing of these regulations** la responsabilité de veiller au respect de cette réglementation

▸▸ ***policing policy*** politique *f* de maintien de l'ordre

policy ['pɒləsɪ] *(pl* **policies**) **1** *n* (**a**) *Pol* politique *f*; **the government's economic policies** la politique économique du gouvernement

(**b**) *Com (of company, organization)* politique *f*, orientation *f*; **they don't know what policy to adopt** ils ne savent pas quelle politique adopter; **this is in line with company policy** ça va dans le sens de la politique de l'entreprise; **our policy is to hire professionals only** nous avons pour politique de n'engager que des professionnels; **the company's success is essentially down to their inspired marketing policy** le succès de l'entreprise est dû en grande partie à l'intelligence de leur politique de commercialisation

(**c**) *(personal principle, rule of action)* principe *m*, règle *f*; **her policy has been always to tell the truth** elle a toujours eu pour principe de dire la vérité; **it's bad policy to reveal your objectives early on** c'est une mauvaise tactique de dévoiler vos objectifs à l'avance

(**d**) *(for insurance)* police *f*; **to take out a policy** souscrire à une police d'assurance

2 *comp (decision, statement)* de principe; *(debate)* de politique générale

►► ***policy document*** document *m* de politique générale; ***policy meeting*** séance *f* de concertation; ***policy paper*** = document énonçant une position de principe; ***policy position*** position *f* de principe; ***policy statement*** déclaration *f* de principe; *Am Pej* ***policy wonk*** conseiller(ère) *m,f* politique

policyholder ['pɒləsɪˌhəʊldə(r)] *n* assuré(e) *m,f*

policymaker ['pɒləsɪˌmeɪkə(r)] *n Pol* responsable *mf* politique; *Com* décideur *m*

polio ['pəʊlɪəʊ] *n (UNCOUNT) Med* polio *f*; **to have polio** avoir la polio

poliomyelitis [ˌpəʊlɪəʊmaɪə'laɪtɪs] *n (UNCOUNT) Med* poliomyélite *f*

Polish ['pəʊlɪʃ] **1** *npl* **the Polish** les Polonais *mpl*

2 *n (language)* polonais *m*

3 *adj* polonais

4 *comp (embassy)* de Pologne; *(history)* de la Pologne; *(teacher)* de polonais

polish ['pɒlɪʃ] **1** *vt* (**a**) *(furniture, floor, tiles)* cirer, encaustiquer; *(brass, car, mirror)* astiquer; *(shoes)* cirer, brosser; *(gemstone, wood, metal)* polir; *(gold, silver)* brunir

(**b**) *Culin (rice)* décortiquer

(**c**) *Fig (perfect)* polir, perfectionner; **to polish one's prose/style** polir sa prose/son style

(**d**) *Fig (person)* parfaire l'éducation de; **his manners could do with polishing** ses manières laissent à désirer

2 *n* (**a**) *(product → for wood, furniture)* encaustique *f*, cire *f*; *(→ for shoes)* cirage *m*; *(→ for brass, car, silverware)* produit *m* d'entretien; *(→ for fingernails)* vernis *m*

(**b**) *(act of polishing)* **to give sth a polish** *(furniture, floor, tiles)* cirer qch, encaustiquer qch; *(brass, car, mirror)* astiquer qch; *(shoes)* cirer qch, brosser qch; **give your shoes a quick polish** donne un petit coup de brosse à tes chaussures; **the brass could do with a polish** les cuivres auraient besoin d'être astiqués

(**c**) *(shine, lustre)* brillant *m*, éclat *m*; **the silver has a lovely polish** l'argent a un bel éclat; **his shoes have lost their polish** ses chaussures ont perdu leur lustre; **to put a polish on sth** faire briller qch

(**d**) *Fig (of prose, style, performance)* brio *m*; **her writing lacks polish** sa prose manque de brio

(**e**) *Fig (of person)* raffinement *m*, élégance *f*; **she has a lot of polish** elle est très raffinée

►**polish off** *vt sep Fam* (**a**) *(finish → meal)* finir[❑], avaler[❑]; **they polished off half a loaf between them** ils ont avalé la moitié d'un pain à eux seuls; **they soon polished off the rest of the beer** ils ont eu vite fait de finir ce qui restait de bière

(**b**) *(complete → job)* expédier[❑]; *(→ book, essay)* en finir avec[❑]

(**c**) *(defeat)* se débarrasser de, écraser; *(kill)* liquider, descendre

►**polish up 1** *vi* **brass polishes up well** le cuivre est facile à faire briller

2 *vt sep* (**a**) *(furniture, shoes)* faire briller; *(diamond)* polir

(**b**) *Fig (perfect → maths, language)* perfectionner, travailler; *(→ technique)* parfaire, améliorer

polished ['pɒlɪʃt] *adj* (**a**) *(surface)* brillant, poli (**b**) *Culin (rice)* poli (**c**) *(person)* qui a du savoir-vivre, raffiné; *(manners)* raffiné (**d**) *(prose, style)* raffiné, élégant; *(performance)* parfait, impeccable; *(performer)* accompli

polisher ['pɒlɪʃə(r)] *n (person)* cireur(euse) *m,f*; *(machine)* polissoir *m*; *(for floors)* cireuse *f*

Politburo ['pɒlɪtˌbjʊərəʊ] *(pl* **Politburos***) n* Politburo *m*

polite [pə'laɪt] *adj* (**a**) *(person)* poli, courtois; *(refusal)* poli; *(remark, conversation)* poli, aimable; **to be polite to sb** être poli envers *ou* avec qn; **it is polite to ask first** quand on est poli, on demande d'abord; **to make polite conversation** faire la conversation; **she was very polite about my poems** elle s'est montrée très diplomate dans ses commentaires sur mes poèmes

(**b**) *(refined → manners)* raffiné, élégant

►► ***polite society*** la bonne société, le beau monde

politely [pə'laɪtlɪ] *adv* poliment, de manière courtoise

politeness [pə'laɪtnɪs] *n* politesse *f*, courtoisie *f*; **out of politeness** par politesse

politic ['pɒlətɪk] *adj Formal (shrewd)* habile, avisé; *(wise)* judicieux, sage; **it would not be politic to refuse** ce ne serait pas prudent de refuser

political [pə'lɪtɪkəl] *adj* (**a**) *(relating to politics)* politique; **political beliefs** opinions *fpl* politiques; **man is a political animal** l'homme est un animal politique; **things are getting far too political in the office** il y a vraiment trop de manigances au bureau en ce moment

(**b**) *(tactical → decision, appointment)* stratégique, tactique

(**c**) *(interested in politics)* **he's always been very political** il s'est toujours intéressé à la politique

►► ***political asylum*** asile *m* politique; **to request/be granted political asylum** demander/se voir accorder l'asile politique; ***political correctness*** le politiquement correct; ***political editor*** rédacteur(trice) *m,f* en chef politique; ***political geography*** géographie *f* politique; ***political prisoner*** prisonnier(ère) *m,f* politique; ***political science*** *(UNCOUNT)* sciences *fpl* politiques; ***political scientist*** spécialiste *mf* en sciences politiques

POLITICAL CORRECTNESS

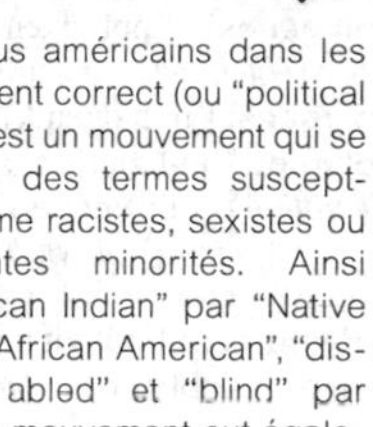

Apparu dans les campus américains dans les années 80, le politiquement correct (ou "political correctness" en anglais) est un mouvement qui se consacre à l'élimination des termes susceptibles d'être perçus comme racistes, sexistes ou injurieux par différentes minorités. Ainsi a-t-on remplacé "American Indian" par "Native American", "Black" par "African American", "disabled" par "differently abled" et "blind" par "visually challenged". Ce mouvement eut également des conséquences sur les comportements sociaux en sensibilisant la population à des problèmes comme le harcèlement sexuel. Pour les adeptes du politiquement correct, ces changements contribuent à éliminer discrimination et préjugés, mais nombreux sont ceux qui s'opposent à ce mouvement en le qualifiant de tyrannique et d'obsessionnel.

politically [pə'lɪtɪklɪ] *adv* politiquement; **politically informed** au courant des choses de la politique; **to be politically aware** avoir une conscience politique, être politisé; **politically correct** politiquement correct

politician [ˌpɒlɪ'tɪʃən] *n* (**a**) *(gen → man)* homme *m* politique, politique *m*; *(→ woman)* femme *f* politique, politique *f* (**b**) *Am Pej* politicien(-enne) *m,f*

politicization [pəˌlɪtɪsaɪ'zeɪʃən] *n* politisation *f*

politicize, -ise [pə'lɪtɪsaɪz] **1** *vt* politiser; **the whole issue has become highly politicized** on a beaucoup politisé toute cette question

2 *vi* faire de la politique

politicking ['pɒlətɪkɪŋ] *n Pej* politique *f* politicienne

politico [pə'lɪtɪkəʊ] *(pl* **politicos** *or* **politicoes***) n Fam Pej* politicard(e) *m,f*

politico- [pə'lɪtɪkəʊ] *pref* politico-

politico-economical *adj* politico-économique

politics ['pɒlətɪks] **1** *n (UNCOUNT)* (**a**) *(as a profession)* politique *f*; **to go into politics** faire de la politique; **local politics** la politique locale; **politics has never attracted her** la politique ne l'a jamais intéressée

(**b**) *(art or science)* politique *f*; **she studied politics at university** elle a étudié les sciences politiques à l'université

(**c**) *(activity)* politique *f*; **I tried not to be drawn into office politics** j'ai essayé de ne pas me laisser entraîner dans les intrigues de bureau; **sexual politics** = ensemble des idées et des problèmes touchant aux droits des femmes, des homosexuels etc

2 *npl (opinions)* idées *fpl ou* opinions *fpl* politiques; **what exactly are her politics?** quelles sont ses opinions politiques au juste?; **his politics are right of centre** politiquement parlant il se situe à droite

polity ['pɒlɪtɪ] *(pl* **polities***) n Formal (state)* État *m*; *(administration)* organisation *f* politique *ou* administrative; *(political unit)* entité *f* politique

polka ['pɒlkə] **1** *n* polka *f*

2 *vi* danser la polka

►► ***polka dot*** pois *m*

polka-dot *adj* à pois

►► ***polka-dot jersey*** *(in cycling)* maillot *m* à pois

poll [pəʊl] **1** *n* (**a**) *Pol (elections)* élection *f*, élections *fpl*, scrutin *m*; **the poll took place in June** les élections ont eu lieu en juin; **to go to the polls** voter, se rendre aux urnes; **the country will go to the polls in September** la population se rendra aux urnes en septembre, le pays votera en septembre; **the party is likely to be defeated at the polls** le parti sera probablement battu aux élections

(**b**) *(vote)* vote *m*; *(votes cast)* suffrages *mpl* (exprimés), nombre *m* de voix; **there was an unexpectedly heavy poll** contrairement aux prévisions, il y a eu un fort taux de participation au scrutin; **the ecology candidate got three percent of the poll** le candidat écologiste a obtenu *ou* recueilli trois pour cent des suffrages *ou* des voix

(**c**) *(survey → of opinion, intentions)* sondage *m* (d'opinion); **to conduct a poll (on** *or* **about sth)** faire un sondage (sur qch); **the latest poll puts the Socialists in the lead** le dernier sondage donne les socialistes en tête

(**d**) *(count, census)* recensement *m*

(**e**) *(list → of taxpayers)* rôle *m* nominatif; *(→ of electors)* liste *f* électorale

2 *vt* (**a**) *Pol (votes)* recueillir, obtenir; **the Greens polled 14 percent of the vote** les verts ont obtenu 14 pour cent des voix

(**b**) *(person)* sonder, recueillir l'opinion de; **most of those polled were in favour of the plan** la plupart des personnes interrogées *ou* sondées étaient favorables au projet

(**c**) *Am (assembly)* inscrire le vote de

(**d**) *Comput (terminal)* appeler; *(data)* recueillir

(**e**) *(tree)* étêter; *(cattle)* décorner

3 *vi* (**a**) *(cast one's vote)* voter

(**b**) *(receive votes)* **the party polled well** le parti a remporté une bonne proportion des suffrages *ou* des voix

►► ***poll tax*** *(in UK)* = impôt aboli en 1993, regroupant taxe d'habitation et impôts locaux, payable par chaque occupant adulte d'une même habitation; *(in US)* = impôt, aboli en 1964, donnant droit à être inscrit sur les listes électorales; *Hist* capitation *f*

pollack ['pɒlək] *n Ich* merlu *m*, colin *m*

pollan ['pɒlən] *n Ich* corégone *m (Coregonus pollan)*

pollard ['pɒləd] **1** *n* (**a**) *Bot* têtard *m (arbre)* (**b**) *Zool* animal *m* sans cornes

2 *vt* (**a**) *Bot* étêter (**b**) *Zool* décorner

pollen ['pɒlən] *n* pollen *m*

►► ***pollen analysis*** analyse *f* pollinique; ***pollen count*** taux *m* de pollen; ***pollen sac*** sac *m* pollinique; ***pollen tube*** tube *m* pollinique

pollex ['pɒleks] *n Anat & Zool* pollex *m*

pollie ['pɒlɪ] *n Austr Fam* politicien(enne)[❑] *m,f*

pollinate ['pɒlɪneɪt] *vt* polliniser

pollination [ˌpɒlɪ'neɪʃən] *n* pollinisation *f*

polling ['pəʊlɪŋ] *n (UNCOUNT)* (**a**) *Pol (voting)* vote *m*, suffrage *m*; *(elections)* élections *fpl*, scrutin *m*; **the result of the polling** le résultat du scrutin *ou* des élections; **polling takes place every five years** le scrutin a lieu tous les cinq ans; **the first round of polling** le premier tour de scrutin *ou* des élections; **polling is up on last year** la participation au vote est plus élevée que l'année dernière

(**b**) *(for opinion poll)* sondage *m*

(**c**) *Comput (querying)* interrogation *f*

►► ***polling booth*** isoloir *m*; ***polling company*** institut *m* de sondage; ***polling day*** jour *m* des élections *or* du scrutin; ***polling station*** bureau *m* de vote

polliwog ['pɒlɪwɒg] *n Am Zool* têtard *m*

pollo ['pɒləʊ] (*pl* **pollos**) *n Am Fam* = Mexicain qui s'introduit illégalement sur le territoire américain en ayant recours aux services d'un passeur

pollock = **pollack**

pollster ['pəʊlstə(r)] *n Fam* enquêteur(euse) *m,f*, sondeur(euse) *m,f*; **the pollsters are predicting a high turnout** les sondages prévoient un fort taux de participation

pollutant [pə'lu:tənt] *n* polluant *m*

pollute [pə'lu:t] *vt* (**a**) *(environment, river, atmosphere)* polluer; **the rivers are polluted with toxic waste** les cours d'eau sont pollués par les déchets toxiques (**b**) *(language, mind)* contaminer

polluted [pə'lu:tɪd] *adj Am Fam (drunk)* pété, bourré, rond

polluter [pə'lu:tə(r)] *n* pollueur(euse) *m,f*

pollution [pə'lu:ʃən] *n* (**a**) *(of environment, river, atmosphere)* pollution *f*; **experts are trying to identify the source of the pollution** les experts tentent de localiser la source *ou* l'origine de la pollution
(**b**) *(UNCOUNT) (pollutants)* polluants *mpl*; **volunteers are helping to clear the beach of pollution** des volontaires participent aux opérations d'assainissement de la plage
(**c**) *(of language, mind)* contamination *f*
(**d**) *Formal (emission of semen)* pollution *f* nocturne

pollution-free *adj* non pollué

Polly ['pɒlɪ] *pr n* = nom typique pour un perroquet, ≃ Jacquot

Pollyanna [,pɒlɪ'ænə] *n* = individu naïvement optimiste

pollywog = **polliwog**

polo ['pəʊləʊ] (*pl* **polos**) **1** *n* (**a**) *Sport* polo *m* (**b**) *Am (shirt)* polo *m (chemise)*
2 *comp (match, pony)* de polo
►► *Br* **polo neck** *(collar)* col *m* roulé; *(sweater)* (pull *m* à) col *m* roulé; **polo shirt** polo *m (chemise)*; *Sport* **polo stick** maillet *m*

polonaise [,pɒlə'neɪz] *n Mus & Sewing* polonaise *f*

polo-neck(ed) *adj Br* à col roulé

polonium [pə'ləʊnɪəm] *n Chem* polonium *m*

polony [pə'ləʊnɪ] (*pl* **polonies**) *n Br* salami *m*, saucisson *m* de Bologne

poltergeist ['pɒltəgaɪst] *n* esprit *m* frappeur, poltergeist *m*

poltroon [pɒl'tru:n] *n Arch* poltron(onne) *m,f*

poly ['pɒlɪ] (*pl* **polys**) *n Br Fam Formerly (polytechnic)* = en Grande-Bretagne, avant 1993, établissement d'enseignement supérieur qui appartenait à un système différent de celui des universités

poly- ['pɒlɪ] *pref* poly-

polyacide ['pɒlɪæsɪd] *n Chem* polyacide *m*

polyacrylate [,pɒlɪ'ækrɪleɪt] *n Chem* polyacrylate *m*

polyamide [,pɒlɪ'æmaɪd] *n Chem* polyamide *m*

polyamine [,pɒlɪ'æmi:n] *n Chem* polyamine *f*

polyandrous [,pɒlɪ'ændrəs] *adj* polyandre

polyandry ['pɒlɪændrɪ] *n* polyandrie *f*

polyanthus [,pɒlɪ'ænθəs] (*pl* **polyanthuses** *or* **polyanthi** [-θaɪ]) *n* (**a**) *(primrose)* primevère *f* (**b**) *(narcissus)* narcisse *m* à bouquet

polyarchy ['pɒlɪɑ:kɪ] *n* polyarchie *f*

polyarthritis [,pɒlɪɑ:θ'raɪtəs] *n Med* polyarthrite *f*

polyatomic [,pɒlɪə'tɒmɪk] *adj Chem* polyatomique

poly bag *n Br Fam* sac *m* en plastique ❑

polybasic [,pɒlɪ'beɪsɪk] *adj Chem* polybasique

polybutadiene [,pɒlɪ'bju:tədi:n] *n Chem* polybutadiène *m*

polycarbonate [,pɒlɪ'kɑ:bənət] *n Chem* polycarbonate *m*

polycarpic [,pɒlɪ'kɑ:pɪk], **polycarpous** [,pɒlɪ'kɑ:pəs] *adj Bot* polycarpique

polycentric [,pɒlɪ'sentrɪk] *adj Biol* polycentrique

polycentrism [,pɒlɪ'sentrɪzəm] *n Pol* polycentrisme *m*

polychaete ['pɒlɪki:t] *n Zool* polychète *m*

polychlorinated biphenyl [,pɒlɪ'klɔ:rɪneɪtɪd,baɪ'fi:nəl] *n Chem* polychlorobiphényle *m*

polychromatic [,pɒlɪkrəʊ'mætɪk] *adj* (**a**) *(multicoloured)* multicolore, polychrome (**b**) *Phys (light)* polychromatique

polychrome ['pɒlɪkrəʊm] **1** *adj* polychrome
2 *n* (**a**) *(object)* objet *m* polychrome (**b**) *(colouring)* polychromie *f*

polychromy ['pɒlɪkrəʊmɪ] *n* polychromie *f*

polyclinic [,pɒlɪ'klɪnɪk] *n* polyclinique *f*

polycondensate [,pɒlɪ'kɒndenseɪt] *n Chem* polycondensat *m*

polycondensation [,pɒlɪkɒnden'seɪʃən] *n Chem* polycondensation *f*

polycotyledonous [,pɒlɪkɒtə'li:dənəs] *adj Bot* polycotylédone

polycrystalline [,pɒlɪ'krɪstəlaɪn] *adj Miner* polycristallin

polycyclic [,pɒlɪ'saɪklɪk] *adj Biol & Chem* polycyclique

polydactyl [,pɒlɪ'dæktɪl] **1** *n* polydactyle *mf*
2 *adj* polydactyle

polydactylous [,pɒlɪ'dæktɪləs] *adj* polydactyle

polydipsia [,pɒlɪ'dɪpsɪə] *n Med* polydipsie *f*

Polydorus [,pɒlɪ'dɔ:rəs] *pr n Myth* Polydore

polyelectrolyte [,pɒlɪə'lektrəlaɪt] *n Chem* polyélectrolyte *m*

polyelectrolytic [,pɒlɪəlektrə'lɪtɪk] *adj Chem* polyélectrolyte

polyembryony [,pɒlɪ'embrɪənɪ] *n Biol* polyembryonie *f*

polyester [,pɒlɪ'estə(r)] *Chem* **1** *n* polyester *m*
2 *adj* (de *ou* en) polyester

polyether [,pɒlɪ'i:θə(r)] *n Chem* polyether *m*

polyethylene [,pɒlɪ'eθɪli:n] *n Chem* polyéthylène *m*, Polythène® *m*

polygala [pə'lɪgələ] *n Bot* polygale *m*

polygamist [pə'lɪgəmɪst] *n* polygame *m*

polygamous [pə'lɪgəməs] *adj* polygame

polygamy [pə'lɪgəmɪ] *n* polygamie *f*

polygene ['pɒlɪdʒi:n] *n Biol* polygène *m*

polygenesis [,pɒlɪ'dʒenɪsɪs] *n* (**a**) *Biol* polygénie *f* (**b**) *(of man)* polygénisme *m*

polygenic [,pɒlɪ'dʒenɪk] *adj Biol* polygénique

polyglot ['pɒlɪglɒt] **1** *adj (person)* polyglotte; *(edition)* multilingue
2 *n (person)* polyglotte *mf*; *(book)* édition *f* multilingue

polyglottism ['pɒlɪglɒtɪzəm] *n* multilinguisme *m*

polygon ['pɒlɪgɒn] *n Geom* polygone *m*

polygonaceous [,pɒlɪgə'neɪʃəs] *adj Bot* **polygonaceous plant** polygonacée *f*

polygonal [pɒ'lɪgənəl] *adj Geom* polygonal

polygonum [pə'lɪgənəm] *n Bot* polygonum *m*, renouée *f*

polygraph ['pɒlɪgrɑ:f] *n* (**a**) *(lie detector)* détecteur *m* de mensonges; **to take a polygraph test** subir un test au détecteur de mensonges (**b**) *(copying device)* photocopieuse *f*

polygraphic [,pɒlɪ'græfɪk] *adj* polygraphique

polygyny [pə'lɪdʒɪnɪ] *n* polygynie *f*

polyhedral [,pɒlɪ'hi:drəl] *adj Geom* polyèdre, polyédrique

polyhedron [,pɒlɪ'hi:drən] (*pl* **polyhedrons** *or* **polyhedra** [-drə]) *n Geom* polyèdre *m*

polymath ['pɒlɪmæθ] *n Formal* esprit *m* universel

polymer ['pɒlɪmə(r)] *n Chem* polymère *m*

polymerase ['pɒlɪməreɪz] *n Chem* polymérase *f*
►► **polymerase chain reaction** réaction *f* en chaîne par polymérase, amplification *f* génique

polymeric [,pɒlɪ'merɪk] *adj Chem* polymère

polymerizable ['pɒlɪməraɪzəbəl] *adj Chem* polymérisable

polymerization [,pɒlɪməraɪ'zeɪʃən] *n Chem* polymérisation *f*

polymerize, -ise ['pɒlɪməraɪz] *Chem* **1** *vt* polymériser
2 *vi* polymériser

polymetallic [,pɒlɪmə'tælɪk] *adj* polymetallique

polymorph ['pɒlɪ,mɔ:f] *n Biol* espèce *f* polymorphe; *Chem* substance *f* polymorphe

polymorphic [,pɒlɪ'mɔ:fɪk] *adj* polymorphe

polymorphism [,pɒlɪ'mɔ:fɪzəm] *n (gen)* polymorphisme *m*; *Chem* polymorphie *f*

polymorphous [,pɒlɪ'mɔ:fəs] *adj* polymorphe

polymyxin [,pɒlɪ'mɪksɪn] *n Pharm* polymyxine *f*

Polynesia [,pɒlɪ'ni:zjə] *n* Polynésie *f*; **in Polynesia** en Polynésie; **French Polynesia** la Polynésie française

Polynesian [,pɒlɪ'ni:zjən] **1** *n* (**a**) *(person)* Polynésien(enne) *m,f* (**b**) *Ling* polynésien *m*
2 *adj* polynésien

polyneuritis [,pɒlɪnjʊ'raɪtɪs] *n Med* polynévrite *f*

polynomial [,pɒlɪ'nəʊmɪəl] *Math* **1** *adj* polynomial
2 *n* polynôme *m*

polynuclear [,pɒlɪ'nju:klɪə(r)], **polynucleate** [,pɒlɪ'nju:klɪət] *adj Biol* polynucléaire

polynucleotide [,pɒlɪ'nju:klɪəʊtaɪd] *n Biol & Chem* polynucléotide *m*

polyolefin [,pɒlɪ'ɒləfɪn] *n Chem* polyoléfine *f*

polyp ['pɒlɪp] *n Med & Zool* polype *m*

polypary ['pɒlɪpərɪ] *n Zool* polypier *m*

polypeptide [,pɒlɪ'peptaɪd] *n Biol & Chem* polypeptide *m*

polyphagia [,pɒlɪ'feɪdʒɪə] *n Med & Zool* polyphagie *f*

polyphase ['pɒlɪfeɪz] *adj Elec* polyphasé

Polyphemus [,pɒlɪ'fi:məs] *pr n Myth* Polyphème

polyphone ['pɒlɪfəʊn] *n Ling* lettre *f* pouvant être prononcée de plusieurs façons

polyphonic [,pɒlɪ'fɒnɪk], **polyphonous** [pə'lɪfənəs] *adj* polyphonique

polyphony [pə'lɪfənɪ] *n* polyphonie *f*

polyploid ['pɒlɪplɔɪd] *Biol* **1** *n* polyploïde *m*
2 *adj* polyploïde
►► **polyploid cell** cellule *f* polyploïde; **polyploid complex** complexe *m* polyploïde; **polyploid series** série *f* polyploïde

polyploidy ['pɒlɪplɔɪdɪ] *n Biol* polyploïdie *f*

polypnoea [,pɒlɪp'nɪə] *n Med* polypnée *f*

polypody ['pɒlɪ,pəʊdɪ] *n Bot* polypode *m*

polypous ['pɒlɪpəs] *adj Med & Zool* polypeux

polypropylene [,pɒlɪ'prəʊpəli:n] *n* polypropylène *m*

polyptych ['pɒlɪptɪk] *n Art* polyptique *m*

polyradiculoneuritis ['pɒlɪ,rədɪkjʊləʊnjʊ'raɪtɪs] *n Med* polyradiculonévrite *f*

polyribosome [,pɒlɪ'raɪbəsəʊm] *n Biol & Chem* polyribosome *m*

polysaccharide [,pɒlɪ'sækəraɪd] *n Chem* polysaccharide *m*, polyoside *m*, polyholoside *m*

polysemous [pə'lɪsɪməs] *adj* polysémique

polysemy [pə'lɪsɪmɪ] *n* polysémie *f*

polysome ['pɒlɪsəʊm] *n Biol & Chem* polysome *m*

polysorbate [,pɒlɪ'sɔ:beɪt] *n Chem* polysorbate *m*

polystyrene [,pɒlɪ'staɪri:n] *n* polystyrène *m*
►► **polystyrene cement** colle *f* polystyrène; **polystyrene tiles** carreaux *mpl* de polystyrène

polysulphide [,pɒlɪ'sʌlfaɪd] *n Chem* polysulfure *m*

polysyllabic [,pɒlɪsɪ'læbɪk] *adj* polysyllabe, polysyllabique

polysyllable ['pɒlɪ,sɪləbəl] *n* polysyllabe *m*

polysyndeton [,pɒlɪ'sɪndətən] *n* (**a**) *(in rhetoric)* polysyndète *f*, syndèse *f* (**b**) *Gram* = phrase contenant plus de deux propositions coordonnées

polysynthetic [,pɒlɪsɪn'θetɪk] *adj Ling* polysynthétique

polytechnic [,pɒlɪ'teknɪk] *n Br Formerly* = en Grande-Bretagne, avant 1993, établissement d'enseignement supérieur qui appartenait à un système différent de celui des universités

polytetrafluoroethylène ['pɒlɪ,tetrəflʊərəʊ'eθɪli:n] *n Chem* polytétrafluoroéthylène *m*

polytheism ['pɒlɪθi:ɪzəm] *n* polythéisme *m*

polytheist [,pɒlɪ'θi:ɪst] *n* polythéiste *mf*

polytheistic [,pɒlɪθi:'ɪstɪk] *adj* polythéiste

polythene ['pɒlɪθi:n] **1** *n* polyéthylène *m*, Polythène® *m*
2 *comp* en polyéthylène, en Polythène®
►► **polythene bag** sac *m* (en) plastique

polytonal [,pɒlɪ'təʊnəl] *adj Mus* polytonal

polytonality [,pɒlɪtəʊ'nælɪtɪ], **polytonalism** [,pɒlɪ'təʊnəlɪzəm] *n Mus* polytonalité *f*

polytunnel ['pɒlɪtʌnəl] *n Agr* polytunnel *m*

polyunsaturated [,pɒlɪʌn'sætʃəreɪtɪd] *adj* polyinsaturé

polyuresis [,pɒlɪjʊə'ri:sɪs], **polyuria** [,pɒlɪ'jʊərɪə] *n Med* polyurie *f*

polyurethane [,pɒlɪ'jʊərəθeɪn], **polyurethan** [,pɒlɪ'jʊərəθæn] *n Chem* polyuréthane *m*, polyuréthanne *m*
►► **polyurethane foam** mousse *f* de polyuréthane

polyuric [,pɒlɪ'jʊərɪk] *adj Med* polyurique

polyvalence [,pɒlɪ'veɪləns], **polyvalency** [,pɒlɪ'veɪlənsɪ] *n Chem* polyvalence *f*

polyvalent [,pɒlɪ'veɪlənt] *adj Chem* polyvalent

pol–pol

polyvinyl [ˌpɒlɪˈvaɪnɪl] *adj* polyvinylique
 ►► ***polyvinyl chloride*** chlorure *m* de polyvinyle
pom [pɒm] = **pommie**
pomace [ˈpʌmɪs] *n (pulp → of apple)* pulpe *f* de pommes; *(→ of grapes)* pulpe *f* de raisin; *(residue → of apple)* marc *m* de pommes; *(→ of grapes)* marc *m* de raisin
 ►► ***pomace brandy*** eau-de-vie *f* de marc
pomade [pəˈmeɪd] **1** *n* pommade *f (pour les cheveux)*
 2 *vt* pommader
pomander [pəˈmændə(r)] *n (bag)* sachet *m* aromatique; *(orange stuck with cloves)* pomme *f* d'amour
pome [pəʊm] *n* fruit *m* à pépins
pomegranate [ˈpɒmɪˌgrænɪt] *n (fruit)* grenade *f*; *(tree)* grenadier *m*
 ►► ***pomegranate tree*** grenadier *m*
pomelo [ˈpɒmɪləʊ] *(pl* **pomelos***) n* pomelo *m*; *Am (grapefruit)* pamplemousse *m*
Pomerania [ˌpɒməˈreɪnjə] *n* Poméranie *f*; **in Pomerania** en Poméranie
Pomeranian [ˌpɒməˈreɪnjən] **1** *n* (**a**) *(person)* Poméranien(enne) *m,f* (**b**) *(dog)* loulou *m* (de Poméranie)
 2 *adj* poméranien
pommel [ˈpɒməl] *(Br pt & pp* **pommelled,** *cont* **pommelling**, *Am pt & pp* **pommeled,** *cont* **pommeling***)* **1** *n* pommeau *m*
 2 *vt* = **pummel**
 ►► ***pommel horse*** cheval-d'arçons *m inv*
pommie, pommy [ˈpɒmɪ] *(pl* **pommies***) Austr & NZ Fam* **1** *n* angliche *mf*
 2 *adj* angliche
pomological [ˌpɒməˈlɒdʒɪkəl] *adj Agr* pomologique
pomology [pɒˈmɒlədʒɪ] *n Agr* pomologie *f*
pomp [pɒmp] *n* pompe *f*, faste *m*; **with great pomp (and circumstance)** en grande pompe; **the pomp of great state occasions** le faste des grandes cérémonies nationales
pompadour [ˈpɒmpəˌdʊə(r)] *n* coiffure *f* style Pompadour
Pompeian [ˌpɒmˈpeɪən] = **Pompeiian**
Pompeii [ˌpɒmˈpeiː] *n* Pompéi
Pompeiian [pɒmˈpeɪən] **1** *n* Pompéien(enne) *m,f*
 2 *adj* pompéien
Pompey [ˈpɒmpɪ] *pr n* Pompée
pompom [ˈpɒmˌpɒm] *n (flower, bobble)* pompon *m*
pom-pom *n Mil* canon-mitrailleuse *m*
pomposity [ˌpɒmˈpɒsətɪ] *(pl* **pomposities***) n* (**a**) *(UNCOUNT) (of person)* comportement *m* pompeux, manières *fpl* pompeuses (**b**) *(of ceremony)* apparat *m*, pompe *f*; *(of style, comment)* caractère *m* pompeux
pompous [ˈpɒmpəs] *adj (pretentious)* pompeux, prétentieux
pompously [ˈpɒmpəslɪ] *adv* pompeusement; **it's rather pompously called a marina** on qualifie cela, assez pompeusement, de marina
pompousness [ˈpɒmpəsnɪs] *n* (**a**) *(of person)* comportement *m* pompeux, manières *fpl* pompeuses (**b**) *(of ceremony)* apparat *m*, pompe *f*; *(of style, comment)* caractère *m* pompeux
ponce [pɒns] *Br Fam* **1** *n* (**a**) *(pimp)* maquereau *m* (**b**) *Pej (effeminate man)* chochotte *f*
 2 *vi* (**a**) *(pimp)* faire le maquereau (**b**) *Pej (behave effeminately)* minauder, faire chochotte
►**ponce about, ponce around** *vi Br Fam* (**a**) *(waste time)* traîner, glander; **stop poncing around and get on with it** arrête un peu de traîner et dépêche-toi (**b**) *Pej (behave effeminately)* minauder, faire chochotte
poncey [ˈpɒnsɪ] *adj Br Fam Pej (effeminate)* qui fait chochotte
poncho [ˈpɒntʃəʊ] *(pl* **ponchos***) n* poncho *m*
poncy = **poncey**
pond [pɒnd] *n (small)* mare *f*; *(large)* étang *m*; *(in garden, park)* bassin *m*; *Fam* **the Pond** *(the Atlantic)* l'Atlantique □ *m*; *Fam* **across the pond** outre-Atlantique □
 ►► ***pond life*** la faune des étangs; *Fam Hum Pej (disreputable people)* minables *mpl*; *Bot* ***pond lily*** nénuphar *m*; *Entom* ***pond skater*** gerris *m*; *Zool* ***pond snail*** limnée *f*
ponder [ˈpɒndə(r)] **1** *vi (think)* réfléchir; *(meditate)* méditer; **he spent hours pondering over the meaning of it all** il passa des heures à méditer sur le sens de tout cela; **she had plenty of time to ponder on** *or* **upon the folly of her ways** elle a eu tout le temps de réfléchir à la stupidité de ses actes
 2 *vt* réfléchir à; **I sat down and pondered what to do** je m'assis et considérai ce que j'allais faire; **she retreated to her own room to ponder her next move** elle se retira dans sa chambre pour réfléchir à la décision qu'elle allait prendre
ponderable [ˈpɒndərəbəl] *Formal* **1** *adj* pondérable
 2 **ponderables** *npl* données *fpl* mesurables
ponderous [ˈpɒndərəs] *adj (heavy)* pesant, lourd; *(slow)* lent, laborieux; *(dull)* lourd; **with ponderous steps** d'un pas lourd; **a ponderous style** un style lourd *ou* laborieux; **he has a very ponderous way of speaking** il s'exprime avec difficulté *ou* laborieusement
ponderously [ˈpɒndərəslɪ] *adv (heavily)* lourdement; *(laboriously)* laborieusement; **he walked ponderously across the yard** il traversa la cour d'un pas pesant
ponderousness [ˈpɒndərəsnɪs] *n (heaviness, dullness)* lourdeur *f*; *(slowness)* lenteur *f*
Pondicherry [ˌpɒndɪˈtʃerɪ] *n* Pondichéry
pondweed [ˈpɒndwiːd] *n Bot* potamot *m*
pone [pəʊn] *n Am (bread)* pain *m* au maïs
 ►► ***pone bread*** pain *m* au maïs
pong [pɒŋ] *Br Fam* **1** *n* puanteur □ *f*; **what a pong!** ça pue! □, ça schlingue!; **there's a terrible pong of fish!** ça pue le poisson à plein nez!
 2 *vi* puer □, schlinguer; **the room still pongs of cigarettes** la pièce pue encore la cigarette
pongee [pɒnˈdʒiː] *n Tex* pongé *m*, pongée *m*
pongo [ˈpɒŋgəʊ] *(pl* **pongos***) n Zool* pongidé *m*
pongy [ˈpɒŋɪ] *adj Br Fam (smelly)* **it's a bit pongy in here** ça pue □ *ou* schlingue là-dedans
poniard [ˈpɒnjəd] **1** *n* poignard *m*
 2 *vt* poignarder
pons [pɒnz] *n Anat* **pons (Varolii)** pont *m* de Varole
Pontic [ˈpɒntɪk] *adj Antiq* pontique, du Pont
 ►► ***the Pontic Sea*** le Pont-Euxin
pontifex [ˈpɒntɪfeks] *(pl* **pontifices** [ˌpɒnˈtɪfɪsiːz]*) n Antiq* pontife *m*
 ►► ***pontifex maximus*** grand pontife *m*
pontiff [ˈpɒntɪf] *n* souverain pontife *m*, pape *m*
pontifical [pɒnˈtɪfɪkəl] **1** *adj* (**a**) *Rel* pontifical (**b**) *(pompous)* pompeux
 2 *n Rel (book)* pontifical *m*
pontificate 1 *vi* [pɒnˈtɪfɪkeɪt] *(gen) & Rel* pontifier; *Pej* **he's always pontificating about** *or* **on something or other** il faut toujours qu'il pontifie
 2 *n* [pɒnˈtɪfɪkɪt] pontificat *m*
Pontius Pilate [ˈpɒnʃəs-] *pr n* Ponce Pilate
pontoon [pɒnˈtuːn] *n* (**a**) *(float)* ponton *m*; *(on seaplane)* flotteur *m* (**b**) *(card game)* vingt-et-un *m inv*
 ►► ***pontoon bridge*** pont *m* flottant
Pontus [ˈpɒntəs] *n Antiq* le Pont
 ►► ***Pontus Euxinus*** le Pont-Euxin
pony [ˈpəʊnɪ] *(pl* **ponies***) n* (**a**) *Zool* poney *m*; *Am (small horse)* petit cheval *m*; **we went for a pony ride** nous avons fait une promenade à dos de poney
 (**b**) *Fam (glass)* verre *m* à liqueur □
 (**c**) *Br Fam (£25)* vingt-cinq livres □ *fpl*; *(bet)* pari *m* de vingt-cinq livres □
 (**d**) *Am Fam (crib)* antisèche *f*
 ►► *Br* ***Pony Club*** = club équestre pour enfants; ***pony express*** = service postal américain à cheval mis en place en 1860 et détrôné par l'apparition du télégraphe
ponytail [ˈpəʊnɪteɪl] *n* queue *f* de cheval; **she wears her hair in a ponytail** elle a *ou* se fait une queue de cheval
pony-trekking [-ˌtrekɪŋ] *n* randonnée *f* à dos de poney; **to go pony-trekking** faire une randonnée à dos de poney
poo [puː] *Fam* **1** *n* (**a**) *(excrement)* caca *m*; **to do** *or Br* **have** *or Am* **take a poo**, *Am* **to make poo** faire caca (**b**) *Br (worthless things)* **it's a load of poo** c'est de la merde; **he's talking a load of poo** il raconte n'importe quoi □
 2 *vi* faire caca
pooch [puːtʃ] *n Fam (dog)* toutou *m*
poodle [ˈpuːdəl] *n* caniche *m*; *Fig* **I'm not your poodle!** je ne suis pas ton chien!
poof[1] [pʊf] **1** *n Br very Fam* pédé *m*, tapette *f*, = terme injurieux désignant un homosexuel
poof[2] *exclam Fam* **and then it was gone, poof, just like that!** et puis hop! il a disparu d'un coup
poofter [ˈpʊftə(r)] *n Br very Fam* pédé *m*, tapette *f*, = terme injurieux désignant un homosexuel
poofy [ˈpʊfɪ] *(compar* **poofier,** *superl* **poofiest***) adj Br very Fam Pej* qui fait pédé *ou* tapette; **he's a bit poofy** il fait un peu pédé *ou* tapette
pooh [puː] *Br Fam* **1** *exclam (with disgust)* pouah!; *(with disdain)* peuh!
 2 *n (excrement)* caca *m*
 3 *vi* faire caca
Pooh-Bah [ˈpuːˈbɑː] *n Br Fam* cumulard(e) *m,f*
Pooh Bear *pr n* Winnie l'Ourson
pooh-pooh *vt Br* rire de, ricaner de
pooh-sticks *n* = jeu consistant à lancer une brindille dans l'eau du haut d'un pont, le gagnant étant la personne dont la brindille réapparaît la première de l'autre côté
pooka [ˈpuːkə] *n Ir* ≃ loup-garou *m*
pool [puːl] **1** *n* (**a**) *(pond → small)* mare *f*; *(→ large)* étang *m*; *(→ ornamental)* bassin *m*
 (**b**) *(puddle)* flaque *f*; **a pool of blood** une flaque *ou* une mare de sang; **a pool of light** un rond de lumière
 (**c**) *(swimming pool)* piscine *f*
 (**d**) *(in harbour)* bassin *m*; *(in canal, river)* plan *m* d'eau
 (**e**) *(of money)* cagnotte *f*; *(in card games)* cagnotte *f*, poule *f*
 (**f**) *(of workmen, babysitters)* groupe *m*, groupement *m*; *(of experts, advisers)* équipe *f*; *(of typists)* pool *m*; *(of company cars, computers)* parc *m*; *(of ideas)* réserve *f*; *(of talent)* pépinière *f*, réserve *f*
 (**g**) *(consortium)* cartel *m*, pool *m*; *(group of producers)* groupement *m* de producteurs
 (**h**) *Am Fin (group)* groupement *m*; *(agreement)* entente *f*, accord *m*
 (**i**) *(game)* billard *m* américain; *Br* **to have a game of pool,** *Am* **to shoot (some) pool** jouer au billard (américain)
 2 *vt (resources, cars, capital, profits)* mettre en commun; *(efforts, ideas)* unir
 ►► ***pool cue*** queue *f* de billard; ***pool hall*** salle *f* de billard; ***pool party*** = fête organisée autour d'une piscine; ***pool table*** (table *f* de) billard *m*
pooling [ˈpuːlɪŋ] *n Am Fin* **pooling of interests** (absorption-)fusion *f*, unification *f*
poolroom [ˈpuːlˌruːm] *n* salle *f* de billard
pools [puːlz] *npl Br* **the (football) pools** les concours *mpl* de pronostics (au football); **to win the (football) pools** gagner aux pronostics (au football)
 ►► ***pools coupon*** grille *f* de pronostics *(au football)*, ≃ loto *m* sportif
poon [puːn] *n esp Am Vulg* chatte *f*
Poona [ˈpuːnə] *n* Poona, Pune
poontang [ˈpuːntæŋ] *n esp Am Vulg* chatte *f*
poop [puːp] **1** *n* (**a**) *Am Fam (excrement)* caca *m*; **to take a poop** faire caca (**b**) *Naut (deck)* (pont *m* de) dunette *f*, gaillard *m* d'arrière (**c**) *Naut (raised part)* poupe *f*
 2 *vi Am Fam (defecate)* faire caca; **poop and scoop** *(sign)* nettoyer derrière votre chien!
 ►► *Naut* ***poop deck*** (pont *m* de) dunette *f*, gaillard *m* d'arrière
►**poop out** *Am Fam* **1** *vt sep (exhaust)* crever
 2 *vi (drop out)* déclarer forfait □
pooped [puːpt] *adj esp Am Fam (exhausted)* claqué, crevé
pooper-scooper [ˈpuːpəˌskuːpə(r)] *n* ramasse-crotte *m*

POOR [pʊə(r)]

pauvre	►**1** (**a**), (**f**)
faible	►**1** (**b**), (**e**)
médiocre	►**1** (**b**)
mauvais	►**1** (**c**)
peu doué	►**1** (**d**)

1 *adj* (**a**) *(not rich → person, area, country)* pauvre; **a poor man/woman** un pauvre/une pauvre; **poor people** les pauvres *mpl*; **they're too poor to own a car** ils n'ont pas les moyens d'avoir une voiture; **I'm 1,000 francs poorer, I'm**

poorer by 1,000 francs j'en suis pour 1000 francs; **the oil crisis made these countries considerably poorer** la crise du pétrole a considérablement appauvri ces pays; **poor as a church mouse** pauvre comme Job

(**b**) *(mediocre → output, sales figures)* faible, médiocre; *(→ land, soil)* maigre, pauvre; *(→ effort, excuse)* piètre; *(→ piece of work)* médiocre; *(→ results)* médiocre, piètre; *(→ weather, summer)* médiocre; *(→ quality, condition)* mauvais; **the match took place in poor light** le match a eu lieu alors qu'on n'y voyait pratiquement rien; **the joke was in extremely poor taste** la plaisanterie était du plus mauvais goût; **she has very poor taste in clothes** elle s'habille avec un goût douteux; **a poor excuse** une piètre excuse; **poor reception** *(unwelcoming)* mauvais accueil *m*; *Rad & TV* mauvaise transmission *f*; **poor performance** *(of company)* contre-performance *f*; **the team put in a poor performance** l'équipe n'a pas très bien joué; **our side put up a very poor show** notre équipe a donné un piètre spectacle; **to come a poor second** *(in race)* se classer deuxième, loin derrière le vainqueur; **in terms of exports, Britain comes a poor second to Japan** en matière d'exportations, la Grande-Bretagne est en deuxième position, loin derrière le Japon; **I come a very poor second in his affections** je n'ai qu'une misérable deuxième place dans son cœur; **it's a poor substitute for the real thing** c'est loin de valoir l'original; **he gave a poor account of himself** il ne s'en est pas très bien tiré; **there was a poor turnout** peu de gens sont venus; **his pay is very poor** il est très mal payé; **don't be such a poor loser!** *(in game)* ne sois pas si mauvais perdant!; **I have only a poor understanding of economics** je ne comprends pas grand-chose à l'économie; *Sch* **poor work** travail *m* insuffisant; **our chances of success are very poor** nos chances de réussite sont bien maigres

(**c**) *(weak → memory, sight)* mauvais; **to be in poor health** être en mauvaise santé; **I have rather poor sight** j'ai une mauvaise vue; **I have rather poor hearing** j'entends mal

(**d**) *(in ability)* peu doué; **I'm a poor cook** je ne suis pas doué pour la cuisine; **my spelling/French is poor** je ne suis pas fort en orthographe/en français; **she's a poor sailor** elle n'a pas le pied marin; **she's a poor traveller** elle supporte mal les voyages; **he is very poor at maths/at making speeches** il n'est pas doué en maths/pour les discours

(**e**) *(inadequate)* faible; **their food is poor in vitamins** leur alimentation est pauvre en vitamines

(**f**) *(pitiful)* pauvre; **poor you!, you poor thing!** *(to man)* mon pauvre (vieux)!; *(to woman)* ma pauvre (vieille)!; **the poor girl!** la pauvre (fille)!; **poor me!** pauvre de moi!; **poor (old) Bill** le pauvre Bill; **I'm so sorry for the poor man** comme je le plains, le pauvre homme; **to cut a poor figure** faire piètre figure

2 *npl* **the poor** les pauvres *mpl*; **the poor are always with us** il y a toujours des pauvres parmi nous; **the new poor** les nouveaux pauvres *mpl*

►► ***poor box*** tronc *m* des pauvres; *Hist* ***poor law*** = loi sociale dictant les conditions dans lesquelles les pauvres étaient pris en charge par les communes; ***poor relation*** parent *m* pauvre; **we're definitely considered the poor relations of the publishing world** on nous considère vraiment comme les parents pauvres de l'édition; *Am Pej* ***poor White*** petit(e) blanc (blanche) *m,f*

---

poorhouse ['pʊəhaʊs, *pl* -haʊzɪz] *n Hist* asile *m* des pauvres

poorly ['pʊəlɪ] (*compar* **poorlier**, *superl* **poorliest**) **1** *adj Br* malade, souffrant; *Med* **his condition is described as poorly** son état est considéré comme sérieux

2 *adv (badly)* mal; **poorly lit** mal éclairé; **poorly dressed** pauvrement *ou* mal vêtu; **to be poorly off** *(financially)* avoir des problèmes d'argent; **I did poorly in the maths test** je n'ai pas bien réussi à l'interrogation de maths; **the school was very poorly maintained** l'école était assez mal entretenue; **to think poorly of sb** avoir une mauvaise opinion de qn

poor-mouth *vt Am* rabaisser

poorness ['pʊənɪs] *n* (**a**) *(financially)* pauvreté *f* (**b**) *(mediocrity)* médiocrité *f*, pauvreté *f*

poor-spirited *adj* pusillanime; **it was rather poor-spirited of him** il a fait preuve d'une certaine lâcheté *ou* d'un certain manque de courage

poor-will *n Orn* engoulevent *m* de Californie

POP [,pi:əʊ'pi:] *n* (**a**) *Comput (abbr* **post office protocol**) protocole *m* POP (**b**) *Comput (abbr* **point of presence**) point *m* de présence, point *m* d'accès (**c**) *Mktg (abbr* **point of purchase**) lieu *m* d'achat, lieu *m* de vente

---

POP [pɒp]

musique pop	► **2 (a)**
bruit sec	► **2 (b)**
boisson gazeuse	► **2 (c)**
crever	► **4 (a)**
faire sauter	► **4 (a)**
mettre	► **4 (b)**
sauter	► **5 (a)**

(*pt & pp* **popped**, *cont* **popping**) **1** *onomat* pan!

2 *n* (**a**) *Mus* musique *f* pop, pop *f*

(**b**) *(sound)* bruit *m* sec; **we heard a pop** on a entendu un bruit sec; **to go pop** *(cork)* sauter; *(balloon)* éclater

(**c**) *(drink)* boisson *f* gazeuse, soda *m*; **ginger pop** boisson *f* gazeuse au gingembre

(**d**) *Am Fam (father)* papa *m*

(**e**) *Fam (idiom)* **dinner is $15 a pop** le dîner coûte 15 dollars par tête de pipe; **the treatment costs £5,000 a pop and there's no guarantee it'll work** le traitement coûte 5000 livres à chaque fois et l'efficacité n'est pas garantie □

3 *comp (singer, song)* pop *(inv)*

4 *vt* (**a**) *(balloon, bag)* crever; *(button, cork)* faire sauter; **to pop some corn** faire du pop-corn

(**b**) *Fam (put)* mettre □, fourrer; **she popped her purse into her bag** elle a fourré son porte-monnaie dans son sac; **just pop the paper through the letterbox** vous n'avez qu'à glisser le journal dans la boîte aux lettres; **she kept popping tablets into her mouth** elle n'arrêtait pas de se fourrer des comprimés dans la bouche; **to pop one's head out of the window** passer la tête par la fenêtre □; *Am* **let's pop open a bottle of beer** ouvrons une bouteille de bière □; **to pop the question** proposer le mariage □; *Br Fam* **to pop one's clogs** casser sa pipe

(**c**) *Fam (hit)* **he popped me one on the chin** il m'a fichu un coup de poing au menton

(**d**) *Fam Drugs slang* **to pop pills** prendre des pilules □ *(pour se droguer)*

(**e**) *Br Fam Old-fashioned (pawn)* mettre au clou

5 *vi* (**a**) *(cork, buttons)* sauter; *(bulb, balloon)* éclater; *(ears)* se déboucher d'un seul coup; **to make a popping noise** faire un bruit de bouchon qui saute; **champagne corks popped and the party began** les bouchons de champagne sautèrent et la fête commença; **to pop open** *(box, bag)* s'ouvrir tout d'un coup; *(buttons)* sauter

(**b**) *(eyes)* s'ouvrir tout grand; **his eyes were popping out of his head** les yeux lui sortaient de la tête

(**c**) *Br Fam (go)* **to pop into town** faire un saut en ville; **she popped into the butcher's on her way home** elle a fait un saut chez *ou* elle est passée en vitesse chez le boucher sur le chemin du retour; **they popped by** *or* **round to see us** ils sont passés nous voir □

►► ***pop art*** pop art *m*; ***pop concert*** concert *m* pop; ***pop group*** groupe *m* pop; ***pop music*** musique *f* pop, pop music *f*; ***pop poetry*** = poésie destinée à être dite en public; *Fam Old-fashioned* ***pop shop*** mont-de-piété □ *m*; ***pop star*** vedette *f* de la musique pop; ***pop video*** clip *m* (vidéo)

►**pop in** *vi Fam* passer □, faire une petite visite □; **pop in on your way home** passez chez moi en rentrant (à la maison); **to pop in to see sb** passer voir qn; **I've just popped in** je ne fais que passer; **he popped in to say hello** il est passé (me/nous/*etc*) dire bonjour

►**pop off** *vi* (**a**) *Fam (leave)* s'en aller □, filer; **he popped off home to get his tennis things** il est allé chez lui chercher ses affaires de tennis (**b**) *Br Fam (die)* casser sa pipe, calancher (**c**) *Am Fam (shout)* gueuler

►**pop out** *vi Fam* sortir un instant □; **I only popped out for five minutes** je ne suis sorti que cinq minutes; **to pop out to the tobacconist's** faire un saut au bureau de tabac

►**pop over** *vi Fam* passer □, faire une petite visite □; **she popped over to see me** elle est passée me voir

►**pop up** *vi Fam (appear suddenly)* surgir □; **a head popped up through the trap door** une tête a surgi de la trappe; **his name seems to pop up everywhere** on ne parle que de lui □; **this question has popped up again** cette question est revenue sur le tapis; **he popped up again some years later in Miami** il est réapparu quelques années après à Miami □

---

pop. *(written abbr* **population**) population *f*

popadum ['pɒpədəm] *n Culin* papadum *m*, papadam *m (galette indienne)*

popcorn ['pɒpkɔ:n] *n* pop-corn *m inv*

pope [pəʊp] *n* (**a**) *(in Catholic Church)* pape *m*; *Fam Hum* **is the Pope Catholic?** à ton avis? (**b**) *(in Eastern Orthodox Church)* pope *m*

►► *Am Culin* ***pope's nose*** croupion *m*

popemobile ['pəʊpməbi:l] *n Fam* papamobile *f*

popery ['pəʊpərɪ] *n Pej* papisme *m*

pop-eyed *adj Fam* ébahi □, aux yeux écarquillés □; **to stare pop-eyed at sth** regarder qch bouche bée □

popgun ['pɒpgʌn] *n* pistolet *m* (d'enfant) à bouchon

popinjay ['pɒpɪndʒeɪ] *n Arch Pej* fat *m*, freluquet *m*

popish ['pəʊpɪʃ] *adj Pej* papiste

►► *Br Hist* ***the Popish Plot*** le complot catholique

THE POPISH PLOT

On désigne ainsi la rumeur lancée en 1678 par Titus Oates, selon laquelle un complot catholique visait à assassiner Charles II, à massacrer les protestants et à incendier Londres. Elle sema la terreur parmi la population et fut responsable de l'assassinat de nombreux catholiques.

poplar ['pɒplə(r)] *n* peuplier *m*

poplin ['pɒplɪn] **1** *n* popeline *f*

2 *adj* en popeline

popliteal [pɒp'lɪtɪəl] *adj Anat* poplité

popover ['pɒp,əʊvə(r)] *n* (**a**) *(garment)* débardeur *m* (**b**) *Am Culin* chausson *m*; **apple popover** chausson *m* aux pommes

poppa ['pɒpə] *n Am Fam* papa *m*

poppadom, poppadum = **popadum**

popper ['pɒpə(r)] **1** *n* (**a**) *Br (press-stud)* bouton-pression *m*, pression *f* (**b**) *Am (for popcorn)* appareil *m* à pop-corn (**c**) *Fam Drugs slang* popper *m*

2 poppers *npl Fam Drugs slang* poppers *mpl*

poppet ['pɒpɪt] *n* (**a**) *Br Fam* chéri(e) □ *m,f*, mignon(onne) *m,f*; **be a poppet and fetch my bag for me** sois mignon et va me chercher mon sac; **her new puppy's an absolute poppet** son nouveau petit chien est mignon à croquer; **thanks, poppet** *(to male)* merci, mon mignon; *(to female)* merci, ma mignonne (**b**) *Tech (valve)* soupape *f* à champignon

►► ***poppet valve*** soupape *f* à champignon

popping crease ['pɒpɪŋ-] *n (in cricket)* = ligne blanche marquant la limite dans laquelle doit se tenir le batteur, au cricket

popple ['pɒpəl] **1** *n* clapotement *m*

2 *vi (water, stream)* clapoter, s'agiter

poppy ['pɒpɪ] (*pl* **poppies**) *n* (**a**) *(flower)* coquelicot *m*; *(opium poppy)* pavot *m* (**b**) *(paper flower)* coquelicot *m* en papier *(vendu à l'occasion du "Poppy Day")* (**c**) *(colour)* rouge *m* coquelicot *(inv)*

►► *Br* ***Poppy Day*** = journée de commémoration (le dimanche suivant ou précédant le 11 novembre) pendant laquelle on porte un coquelicot en papier en souvenir des soldats britanniques morts lors des guerres mondiales; ***poppy seed*** graine *f* de pavot

poppycock ['pɒpɪkɒk] *n (UNCOUNT) Br Fam Old-fashioned* sottises *fpl*, balivernes *fpl*

pops [pɒps] *n Am Fam (term of address → to father)* papa *m*; *(→ to old man)* pépé *m*

Popsicle® ['pɒpsɪkəl] *n Am* glace *f* à l'eau

popsock ['pɒpsɒk] *n Br* mi-bas *m inv*

popsy ['pɒpsɪ] *(pl* **popsies***) n Br Fam Old-fashioned* pépée *f*

pop-top *n Am* (**a**) *(car roof)* toit *m* extensible *(d'un camping-car)*; *(type of vehicle)* = camping-car doté d'un toit extensible (**b**) *(of can)* onglet *m*; *(type of can)* canette *f* à onglet

populace ['pɒpjʊləs] *n* (**a**) *(population)* population *f*; *Fig* **the whole populace is up in arms** la population entière s'est rebellée (**b**) *(masses)* peuple *m*, *Pej* masses *fpl*, populace *f*

popular ['pɒpjʊlə(r)] **1** *adj* (**a**) *(well-liked → person)* populaire; **she's very popular with her pupils** elle est très populaire auprès de ses élèves, ses élèves l'aiment beaucoup; **Britain's most popular TV personality** la personnalité la plus populaire de la télévision britannique; **he was a very popular president** ce fut un président très populaire; **to make oneself popular (with)** se rendre populaire (auprès de); **his views have not made him popular with the authorities** à cause de ses opinions, il est mal vu des autorités; **he isn't very popular with his men** il n'est pas très bien vu de ses hommes, ses hommes ne l'aiment pas beaucoup; **I'm not going to be very popular when they find out it's my fault!** je ne vais pas être bien vu quand ils découvriront que c'est de ma faute!

(**b**) *(appreciated by many → product, colour)* populaire; *(→ restaurant, resort)* très couru, très fréquenté; **the movie was very popular in Europe** le film a été un très grand succès en Europe; **the most popular book of the year** le livre le plus vendu *ou* le best-seller de l'année; **videotapes are a popular present** les vidéocassettes sont des cadeaux très appréciés; **it's very popular with the customers** les clients l'apprécient beaucoup; **a popular line** un article qui se vend bien; **it's always been a popular café with young people** ce café a toujours été très populaire auprès des jeunes

(**c**) *(common)* courant, répandu; *(general)* populaire; **contrary to popular belief** contrairement à ce que les gens croient; **a popular misconception** une erreur répandue *ou* fréquente; **on** *or* **by popular demand** à la demande générale; **it's an idea that enjoys great popular support** c'est une idée qui a l'approbation générale *ou* de tous; **popular unrest** mécontentement *m* populaire

(**d**) *(of or for the people)* populaire; **a book of popular mechanics** un livre de mécanique pour tous *ou* à la portée de tous; **quality goods at popular prices** marchandises *fpl* de qualité à des prix abordables

2 populars *npl Br Fam Journ* presse *f* à grand tirage et à sensation ❑

▸▸ *Pol* ***popular front*** front *m* populaire; ***Popular Front for the Liberation of Palestine*** Front *m* populaire de libération de la Palestine; ***popular music*** musique *f* populaire; ***the popular press*** la presse à grand tirage et à sensation

popularity [,pɒpjʊ'lærətɪ] *n* popularité *f*; **to grow/decline in popularity** devenir plus/moins populaire; **they enjoy a certain popularity with young people** ils jouissent d'une certaine popularité auprès des jeunes; **the sport has gained in popularity** le sport est de plus en plus populaire; **sociologists have failed to explain their popularity** les sociologues n'ont pas su expliquer leur popularité

popularization [,pɒpjʊləraɪ'zeɪʃən] *n* (**a**) *(of trend, activity)* popularisation *f*; *(of science, philosophy)* vulgarisation *f* (**b**) *(book)* œuvre *f* de vulgarisation

popularize, -ise ['pɒpjʊləraɪz] *vt* (**a**) *(make popular)* populariser; *(fashion)* mettre en vogue; **a sport popularized by television** un sport que la télévision a rendu populaire (**b**) *(science, philosophy, knowledge)* vulgariser

popularizer ['pɒpjʊləraɪzə(r)] *n* *(of fashion, ideas)* promoteur(trice) *m,f*

popularly ['pɒpjʊləlɪ] *adv* généralement; *(commonly)* couramment, communément; **antirrhinums are popularly known as snapdragons** les antirrhinums sont plus connus sous le nom de gueules-de-loup; **once the earth was popularly thought to be flat** autrefois tout le monde croyait que la Terre était plate

populate ['pɒpjʊleɪt] *vt (inhabit)* peupler, habiter; *(colonize)* peupler, coloniser; **a town populated by miners and their families** une ville habitée par des mineurs et leurs familles; **a densely populated country** un pays fortement peuplé *ou* à forte densité de population

population [,pɒpjʊ'leɪʃən] **1** *n* population *f*; **the whole population is in mourning** tous les habitants portent *ou* toute la population porte le deuil; **the white population of South Africa** la population blanche d'Afrique du Sud; **Edinburgh has a population of about half a million** Édimbourg compte environ un demi-million d'habitants; **the prison population** la population carcérale; **the beaver population is declining** la population de castors est en baisse; **world population figures are rising** la population mondiale augmente

2 *comp (control, fall, increase)* démographique, de la population

▸▸ ***population census*** recensement *m* démographique *ou* de la population; ***population explosion*** explosion *f* démographique; ***population growth*** croissance *f* démographique; ***population statistics*** statistiques *fpl* démographiques

populism ['pɒpjʊlɪzəm] *n* populisme *m*

populist ['pɒpjʊlɪst] *n* populiste *mf*

populous ['pɒpjʊləs] *adj* populeux

populousness ['pɒpjʊləsnɪs] *n* densité *f* de population

pop-up *adj (book, card)* en relief; *(toaster)* automatique

▸▸ *Comput* ***pop-up menu*** menu *m* local; *Aut* ***pop-up sunroof*** toit *m* ouvrant dépliant

Pop Warner [-'wɔːnə(r)] *n* = fédération de football américain pour les jeunes

porbeagle ['pɔːbiːgəl] *n Ich (shark)* taupe *f*, touille *f*

▸▸ ***porbeagle shark*** taupe *f*, requin *m* taupe, touille *f*

porcelain ['pɔːsəlɪn] **1** *n* porcelaine *f*

2 *comp (dish, vase, lamp)* en porcelaine

▸▸ ***porcelain clay*** kaolin *m*; ***porcelain manufacturer*** porcelainier(ère) *m,f*

porch [pɔːtʃ] *n* (**a**) *(entrance)* porche *m* (**b**) *Am (veranda)* véranda *f*

▸▸ ***porch roof*** auvent *m*

porchscreen ['pɔːtʃskriːn] *n Am* moustiquaire *f (autour d'une véranda)*

porchswing ['pɔːtʃswɪŋ] *n Am* balançoire *f (sur une véranda, typique de certaines maisons aux États-Unis)*

porcine ['pɔːsaɪn] *adj* porcin

porcini [pɔː'tʃiːnɪ] *n (mushroom)* cèpe *m*, bolet *m* comestible

▸▸ ***porcini mushroom*** cèpe *m*, bolet *m* comestible

porcupine ['pɔːkjʊpaɪn] *n Zool* porc-épic *m*

▸▸ *Ich* ***porcupine fish*** poisson *m* porc-épic

pore [pɔː(r)] **1** *n (in skin, plant, fungus, rock)* pore *m*

2 *vi* **to pore over sth** *(book)* être plongé dans *ou* absorbé par qch; *(picture, details)* étudier qch de près

porgy ['pɔːgɪ] *n Ich* pagre *m*

poriferan [pɒ'rɪfərən] *adj Zool* relatif aux spongiaires

pork [pɔːk] **1** *n Culin* porc *m*

2 *comp (chop, sausage)* de porc

3 *vt Vulg (have sex with)* tringler, troncher

▸▸ *Am Pol* ***pork barrel*** = projet local entrepris par un parlementaire ou un parti à des fins électorales; ***pork butcher*** ≃ charcutier(ère) *m,f*; ***pork pie*** ≃ pâté *m* en croûte *(à la viande de porc)*; *Am* ***pork rinds,*** *Br* ***pork scratchings*** = petits morceaux croustillants de couenne de porc consommés comme amuse-gueule

pork-barrel legislation *n Am Pol* = action menée par un parlementaire pour favoriser des intérêts locaux dans sa circonscription

porker ['pɔːkə(r)] *n* (**a**) *(animal)* porcelet *m (engraissé par la boucherie)* (**b**) *Fam (man)* gros lard *m*; *(woman)* grosse vache *f*

porkpie hat [,pɔːkpaɪ-] *n* = chapeau de feutre rond et aplati

porky ['pɔːkɪ] *(pl* **porkies**, *compar* **porkier**, *superl* **porkiest**) **1** *n Br Fam* **porky (pie)** *(rhyming slang* **lie**) bobard *m*, craque *f*

2 *adj* (**a**) *(resembling pork)* semblable au porc (**b**) *Fam Pej (fat)* gros (grosse) ❑, mastard

Porlock ['pɔːlɒk] *n*

The person from Porlock

Cette formule ("la personne de Porlock") est une allusion au poète anglais Samuel Taylor Coleridge. Ce dernier était dans sa maison du Somerset en train de composer son poème *Kubla Khan*, inspiré par un rêve qui lui était venu sous l'effet de l'opium, lorsqu'un visiteur (la personne de Porlock) vint l'interrompre pour une affaire sans importance. Coleridge fut dans l'incapacité de terminer son poème comme il l'espérait.

Aujourd'hui, on utilise cette formule de façon allusive pour parler d'un importun qui vient interrompre quelqu'un et lui fait perdre son inspiration. Ainsi on pourra dire **I knew that I would be alone all day and that no person from Porlock was likely to interrupt me** ("je savais que je serais seul toute la journée et que personne ne viendrait me déranger").

porn [pɔːn] *Fam* **1** *n* porno *m*; **hard porn** hard-core *m*; **soft porn** porno *m* soft

2 *adj* porno

▸▸ ***porn shop*** sex-shop *m*; *Br* ***porn squad*** = branche de la police chargée de réprimer la production et la distribution illégales de matériel pornographique

porno ['pɔːnəʊ] *adj Fam* porno

pornographer [pɔː'nɒgrəfə(r)] *n* pornographe *mf*

pornographic [,pɔːnə'græfɪk] *adj* pornographique

pornography [pɔː'nɒgrəfɪ] *n* pornographie *f*; **the customs officers impounded a large consignment of pornography** les douaniers ont saisi une grande quantité de revues pornographiques

porosity [pɔː'rɒsɪtɪ] *(pl* **porosities***) n* porosité *f*

porous ['pɔːrəs] *adj* poreux

porousness ['pɔːrəsnɪs] *n* porosité *f*

porphyrin ['pɔːfɪrɪn] *n Biol & Chem* porphyrine *f*

porphyritic [,pɔːfɪ'rɪtɪk] *adj Miner* porphyrique, porphyritique

porphyry ['pɔːfɪrɪ] *(pl* **porphyries***) n Miner* porphyre *m*

porpoise ['pɔːpəs] *(pl* **inv** *or* **porpoises***) n Zool* marsouin *m*

porridge ['pɒrɪdʒ] *n* (**a**) *Br Culin* porridge *m* (**b**) *Br Fam Crime slang (prison sentence)* peine *f* de prison ❑; **to do porridge** faire de la tôle

▸▸ ***porridge oats*** flocons *mpl* d'avoine

porringer ['pɒrɪndʒə(r)] *n* = récipient à porridge

port [pɔːt] **1** *n* (**a**) *(harbour)* port *m*; **to come into port** entrer dans le port; **we put into port at Naples** nous avons relâché dans le port de Naples; **we left port before dawn** nous avons appareillé avant l'aube; **the country's largest port** le plus grand port du pays; *Prov* **any port in a storm** nécessité fait loi

(**b**) *(wine)* porto *m*

(**c**) *(window → on ship, plane)* hublot *m*

(**d**) *(for loading)* sabord *m (de charge)*

(**e**) *Mil (in wall)* meurtrière *f*; *(in tank)* fente *f* de visée

(**f**) *Comput* port *m*; **input/output port** port *m* entrée/sortie

(**g**) *Tech (in engine)* orifice *m*; **inlet/outlet port** orifice *m* d'admission/d'échappement

(**h**) *Naut (left side)* bâbord *m*; **the ship listed to port** le navire donnait de la gîte à bâbord; **on the port side** à bâbord; **ship to port!** navire à bâbord!

(**i**) *Aviat* côté *m* gauche, bâbord *m*

2 *comp (activity, facilities)* portuaire; *(bow, quarter)* de bâbord

3 *vt* (**a**) *Comput* transférer

(**b**) *Mil* **port arms!** présentez armes!

(**c**) *Naut* **port the helm!** barre à bâbord!

▸▸ ***port of arrival*** port *m* d'arrivée; ***port authority*** autorité *f* portuaire; *Naut* ***port of call*** escale *f*; *Fig* **her last port of call was the bank** elle est passée à la banque en dernier; ***port charges*** droits *mpl* de port, frais *mpl* portuaires; ***port of***

departure port *m* de départ; ***port of discharge*** port *m* d'arrivée; ***port dues*** droits *mpl* de port, frais *mpl* portuaires; ***port of embarkation*** port *m* d'embarquement; ***port of entry*** port *m* de débarquement; ***port of loading*** port *m* d'embarquement; ***Port of London Authority*** = le port autonome de Londres; ***port of refuge*** port *m* de refuge; ***port of registry*** port *m* d'attache; ***Port Said*** Port-Saïd; ***Port of Spain*** Port of Spain; *Old-fashioned* ***port wine stain*** *(birthmark)* tache *f* de vin

portability [ˌpɔːtəˈbɪlətɪ] *n (gen) & Comput* portabilité *f*

portable [ˈpɔːtəbəl] **1** *adj* **(a)** *(easily carried, moved)* portatif, portable; *Fin (pension, mortgage)* transférable **(b)** *Comput (software, program)* compatible

2 *n (typewriter)* machine *f* portative; *(TV)* télévision *f* portative; *(computer)* ordinateur *m* portatif

▸▸ ***portable TV (set)*** télévision *f* portative

Portacrib® [ˈpɔːtəˌkrɪb] *n Am* moïse *m*, porte-bébé *m*

portage [ˈpɔːtɪdʒ] *n* **(a)** *(transport)* transport *m*; *(cost)* (frais *mpl* de) port *m* **(b)** *Naut* portage *m*

Portakabin® [ˈpɔːtəˌkæbɪn] *n Br* baraquement *m* préfabriqué

portal [ˈpɔːtəl] *n* **(a)** *Archit (of cathedral)* portail *m*; *Fig* **she found herself standing at the portals of a new life** elle se trouvait à l'aube d'une nouvelle vie **(b)** *Comput* portail *m*

▸▸ *Anat* ***portal vein*** veine *f* porte

Portaloo® [ˈpɔːtəluː] *n* toilettes *fpl* provisoires

portamento [ˌpɔːtəˈmentəʊ] *(pl* **portamenti** [-tiː]) *n Mus* glissade *f*

Port-au-Prince [ˌpɔːtəʊˈprɪns] *n* Port-au-Prince

portcullis [ˌpɔːtˈkʌlɪs] *n* herse *f (de château fort)*

portend [pɔːˈtend] *vt Literary* (laisser) présager, annoncer; **who knows what mysteries these events may portend?** qui sait quels mystères ces événements présagent?

portent [ˈpɔːtənt] *n Literary* **(a)** *(omen)* présage *m*, augure *m*; *(bad omen)* mauvais présage *m*; **a portent of evil** un très mauvais présage **(b)** *(significance)* portée *f*, signification *f*

portentous [pɔːˈtentəs] *adj Literary* **(a)** *(ominous → sign)* de mauvais présage *ou* augure **(b)** *(momentous → event)* capital, extraordinaire; **I've nothing very portentous to announce** je n'ai rien d'extraordinaire *ou* de très important à annoncer **(c)** *(serious)* grave, solennel; **her face took on a portentous air** elle prit un air solennel **(d)** *(pompous)* pompeux

portentously [pɔːˈtentəslɪ] *adv Literary* **(a)** *(ominously)* sinistrement **(b)** *(momentously)* mémorablement **(c)** *(seriously)* solennellement **(d)** *(pompously)* pompeusement

porter [ˈpɔːtə(r)] *n* **(a)** *(of luggage)* porteur(euse) *m,f* **(b)** *Br (door attendant → in hotel)* portier(ère) *m,f*; *(→ in block of flats)* concierge *mf*, gardien(enne) *m,f*; *(→ on private estate)* gardien(enne) *m,f*; *(→ in university, college)* appariteur *m* **(c)** *(in hospital)* brancardier(ère) *m,f* **(d)** *Am Rail (on train)* employé(e) *m,f* des wagons-lits **(e)** *Old-fashioned (beer)* porter *m*, bière *f* brune

porterage [ˈpɔːtərɪdʒ] *n* **(a)** *(transport)* portage *m*, transport *m* (par porteurs) **(b)** *(cost)* coût *m* du transport

▸▸ ***porterage facilities*** service *m* de porteurs

porterhouse [ˈpɔːtəhaʊs, *pl* -haʊzɪz] *n* **(a)** *(steak)* chateaubriand *m*, châteaubriant *m* **(b)** *Hist (public house)* = taverne où l'on servait de la bière et de la viande de bœuf

▸▸ *Culin* ***porterhouse steak*** chateaubriand *m*, châteaubriant *m*

portfolio [ˌpɔːtˈfəʊljəʊ] *(pl* **portfolios**) *n* **(a)** *(briefcase)* porte-documents *m inv*

(b) *(of artist → dossier)* carton *m* à dessins; *(→ collection of work)* book *m*

(c) *Pol* portefeuille *m*; **minister without portfolio** ministre *m* sans portefeuille

(d) *St Exch* portefeuille *m* (financier *ou* d'investissements); **securities in portfolio** valeurs *fpl* en portefeuille

(e) *Mktg* portefeuille *m*

▸▸ ***portfolio analysis*** analyse *f* de portefeuille; ***portfolio diversification*** diversification *f* de portefeuille; ***portfolio insurance*** assurance *f* de portefeuille; ***portfolio management*** gestion *f* de portefeuille; ***portfolio manager*** gestionnaire *mf* de portefeuille; ***portfolio mix*** portefeuille *m* d'activités; ***portfolio securities*** valeurs *fpl* de portefeuille

porthole [ˈpɔːthəʊl] *n* hublot *m*

portico [ˈpɔːtɪkəʊ] *(pl* **porticos** *or* **porticoes**) *n Archit* portique *m*

portion [ˈpɔːʃən] *n* **(a)** *(part, section)* partie *f*; **I've read only a portion of the book** je n'ai lu qu'une partie du livre; **this portion to be given up** *(on ticket)* côté *m* à détacher

(b) *(share)* part *f*; *(measure)* mesure *f*, dose *f*; *Law* **portion (of inheritance)** part *f* d'héritage; **he cut the cake into five portions** il a coupé le gâteau en cinq (parts); **three portions of flour to one portion of sugar** trois mesures *ou* doses de farine pour une mesure *ou* dose de sucre

(c) *(helping → of food)* portion *f*

(d) *Literary (fate)* sort *m*, destin *m*; **it fell to my portion to break the news to her** c'est à moi qu'échut le devoir de lui annoncer la nouvelle; **suffering is our portion here below** la souffrance est notre part ici-bas

(e) *Arch (dowry)* **(marriage) portion** dot *f*

▸**portion out** *vt sep* distribuer, répartir

Portland [ˈpɔːtlənd-] *n*

▸▸ ***Portland cement*** portland *m inv*, ciment *m* Portland; ***Portland stone*** pierre *f* de Portland

portliness [ˈpɔːtlɪnɪs] *n* corpulence *f*, embonpoint *m*

portly [ˈpɔːtlɪ] *(compar* **portlier**, *superl* **portliest**) *adj* corpulent, fort; **a portly gentleman** un monsieur corpulent

portmanteau [ˌpɔːtˈmæntəʊ] *(pl* **portmanteaus** *or* **portmanteaux** [-təʊz]) **1** *n* grande valise *f*

2 *adj* qui combine plusieurs éléments *ou* styles

▸▸ ***portmanteau word*** mot-valise *m*

portobello [ˌpɔːtəˈbeləʊ] *n* **portobello mushroom** champignon *m* portobello

Portobello Road [ˌpɔːtəˈbeləʊ-] *n* = rue de l'ouest de Londres connue pour son marché aux puces

Porton Down [ˈpɔːtən-] *n* = ville du Wiltshire

PORTON DOWN

Cette ville du sud de l'Angleterre est célèbre pour son centre de microbiologie. Ce centre a suscité des controverses pour ses recherches sur les armes bactériologiques et chimiques et pour ses expériences sur des animaux vivants.

portrait [ˈpɔːtreɪt] **1** *n* **(a)** *(gen) & Art* portrait *m*; **he had his portrait painted** il a fait faire son portrait; **a portrait of 18th century society** un portrait de la société du XVIIIème siècle

(b) *Comput & Typ (paper format)* (format *m*) portrait *m*; **to print sth in portrait** imprimer qch en portrait, imprimer qch à la française

2 *adj Typ & Comput* au format portrait, à la française

▸▸ ***portrait bust*** (portrait *m* en) buste *m*; ***portrait gallery*** galerie *f* de portraits; *Comput* ***portrait mode*** mode *m* portrait; ***portrait painter*** portraitiste *mf*; ***portrait painting*** le portrait; ***portrait photograph*** portrait *m* photographique, photoportrait *f*; ***portrait photographer*** photographe *mf* portraitiste

'(The) Portrait of a Lady' *James, Campion* 'Un Portrait de femme'

'A Portrait of the Artist as a Young Man' *Joyce* 'Portrait de l'artiste en jeune homme'

'Portrait of the Artist as a Young Dog' *Thomas* 'Portrait de l'artiste en jeune chien'

portraitist [ˈpɔːtreɪtɪst] *n* portraitiste *mf*

portraiture [ˈpɔːtrɪtʃə(r)] *n* art *m* du portrait

portray [pɔːˈtreɪ] *vt* **(a)** *(represent)* représenter; **he portrayed John as a scoundrel** il a représenté John sous les traits d'un voyou

(b) *(act role of)* jouer le rôle de; **in the movie he portrays King Richard** dans le film, il joue le rôle du roi Richard

(c) *(depict)* dépeindre; **she vividly portrays medieval life** elle fait une vivante description de la vie au Moyen Âge; **in the movie the soldiers are portrayed as monsters** dans le film, les soldats sont dépeints comme des monstres

(d) *(of artist)* peindre, faire le portrait de

portrayal [pɔːˈtreɪəl] *n* **(a)** *(description)* portrait *m*, description *f*; **he disputes the portrayal of the protesters as extremists** il conteste la façon dont les médias présentent les protestataires comme des extrémistes **(b)** *Art* portrait *m* **(c)** *Theat & Cin* interprétation *f*

portrayer [pɔːˈtreɪə(r)] *n* peintre *m (des événements)*; **a faithful portrayer of the life of his period** un peintre fidèle des mœurs de son époque

portress [ˈpɔːtrɪs] *n* portière *f*

Portugal [ˈpɔːtʃʊgəl] *n* Portugal *m*; **in Portugal** au Portugal

Portuguese [ˌpɔːtʃʊˈgiːz] **1** *npl* **the Portuguese** les Portugais *mpl*

2 *n* **(a)** *(pl* **inv**) *(person)* Portugais(e) *m,f* **(b)** *(language)* portugais *m*

3 *adj* portugais

4 *comp (embassy, history)* du Portugal; *(teacher)* de portugais

▸▸ *Zool* ***Portuguese man-of-war*** physalie *f*

Portuguese-speaking *adj* lusophone

POS [ˌpiːəʊˈes] *n Com (abbr* **point of sale**) PDV *m*

pose [pəʊz] **1** *n* **(a)** *(position → gen)* pose *f*; **to take up** *or* **to strike a pose** prendre une pose

(b) *(pretence)* façade *f*; **their puritanism is only a pose** leur puritanisme n'est qu'une façade

2 *vi* **(a)** *Art & Phot* poser; **to pose for a photograph/for an artist** poser pour une photographie/pour un artiste; **to pose in the nude** poser nu; **she posed as a nymph** elle a posé en nymphe

(b) *(masquerade)* **he posed as a hero** il s'est posé en héros, il s'est fait passer pour un héros; **a man posing as a policeman** un homme se faisant passer pour un policier

(c) *(behave affectedly)* frimer; **look at him posing in his designer suit!** regarde-le frimer avec son costume de marque!; **stop posing!** arrête de frimer!

3 *vt (constitute → problem)* poser, créer; *(→ threat)* constituer; *(set → question)* poser; *(put forward → claim, idea)* formuler

Poseidon [pɒˈsaɪdən] *pr n Myth* Poséidon

poser [ˈpəʊzə(r)] *n Br Fam* **(a)** *(question → thorny)* question *f* épineuse ❑; *(→ difficult)* colle *f*; **that's a bit of a poser!** alors ça, c'est une colle! **(b)** *Pej (show-off)* poseur(euse) *m,f*

poseur [pəʊˈzɜː(r)] *n Pej* poseur(euse) *m,f*

posey [ˈpəʊzɪ] *adj Br Fam Pej* prétentieux ❑

posh [pɒʃ] *Br Fam* **1** *adj (clothes, car, restaurant)* chic ❑ *(inv)*; *Pej (person, accent)* snob ❑; *(neighbourhood)* rupin; **he's joined a posh tennis club** il s'est inscrit à un club de tennis huppé *ou* chic; **he moves in some very posh circles** il fréquente des milieux très huppés *ou* des gens de la haute; **posh people don't usually come here** généralement les gens de la haute ne viennent pas ici

2 *adv* **to talk posh** parler avec un accent snob

▸**posh up** *vt sep Br Fam (person)* pomponner; *(town, house)* embellir; **go and posh yourself up** va te faire beau; **she was all poshed up** elle était sur son trente et un

posit [ˈpɒzɪt] *vt Formal* **(a)** *(put forward → idea)* avancer; *(→ theory)* avancer, postuler **(b)** *(put in position)* situer

POSITION [pəˈzɪʃən]

position	▸ **1 (a), (b), (d), (e), (h) – (j)**
situation	▸ **1 (a), (c), (d), (f)**
place	▸ **1 (d)**
poste	▸ **1 (f)**
guichet	▸ **1 (g)**
mettre en place	▸ **2 (a)**
placer	▸ **2 (a), (b)**
situer	▸ **2 (b)**
orienter	▸ **2 (c)**

1 *n* (**a**) *(place → gen)* position *f*; *(→ of town, house etc)* situation *f*, emplacement *m*; **in position** en place; **to put sth in(to) position** mettre qch en place; *Aviat & Naut* **to fix** *or* **work out one's position** faire le point; **you've changed the position of the lamp** vous avez changé la lampe de place; **remember the position of the cards** souvenez-vous de la position des cartes; **white is now in a strong position** *(in chess)* les blancs sont maintenant très bien placés; **they put the machine guns in** *or* **into position** ils mirent les mitrailleuses en batterie; **take up your positions!, get into position!** *(actors, dancers)* à vos places!; *(soldiers, guards)* à vos postes!

(**b**) *(posture, angle)* position *f*; **to change** *or* **to shift position** changer de position; **in a sitting position** en position assise; **hold the spray can in an upright position** tenez le vaporisateur en position verticale; **the position of the pointer on the dial** la position de l'aiguille sur le cadran; **the lever should be in the on/off position** le levier devrait être en position marche/arrêt

(**c**) *(circumstances)* situation *f*; **the position as I see it is this** voici comment je vois la situation *ou* les choses; **to be in a bad/good position** être en mauvaise/bonne posture; **you're in no position to judge** vous êtes mal placé pour (en) juger; **to be in a position to do sth** être en mesure de faire qch; **to be in a strong position** être bien placé; **put yourself in my position** mettez-vous à ma place; **it's an awkward position to be in** c'est une drôle de situation; **our financial position is improving** notre situation financière s'améliore; **the present economic position** la conjoncture économique actuelle; **the cash position is not good** la situation de la caisse laisse à désirer

(**d**) *(rank → in table, scale)* place *f*, position *f*; *(→ in hierarchy)* position *f*, situation *f*; *(social standing)* position *f*, place *f*; **they're in tenth position in the championship** ils sont à la dixième place *ou* ils occupent la dixième place du championnat; **his position in the firm is unclear** sa situation au sein de l'entreprise n'est pas claire; **what exactly is his position in the government?** quelles sont exactement ses fonctions au sein du gouvernement?; **a person in my position can't afford a scandal** une personne de mon rang ne peut se permettre un scandale; **she is concerned about her social position** elle est préoccupée par sa position sociale

(**e**) *(standpoint)* position *f*, point *m* de vue; **try to see things from my position** essayez de voir les choses de mon point de vue; **to take up a position on sth** adopter une position *ou* prendre position sur qch; **I have no position on the matter** je n'ai pas d'idée bien arrêtée sur le sujet; **could you make your position clear on this point?** pouvez-vous préciser votre position à ce sujet?; **his position on the death penalty is indefensible** son point de vue sur la peine de mort est indéfendable; **what is the American position on this issue?** quelle est la position des Américains sur ce problème?; **her position is that...** ce qu'elle pense c'est que..., son point de vue est que...

(**f**) *(job)* poste *m*, situation *f*; **there were four candidates for the position of manager** il y avait quatre candidats au poste de directeur; **it is a position of great responsibility** c'est un poste à haute responsabilité; **position of trust** poste *m* de confiance; **what was your previous position?** quel était votre poste précédent?

(**g**) *Admin (in bank, post office)* guichet *m*; **position closed** *(sign)* guichet fermé

(**h**) *Sport (in team, on field)* position *f*; **he can play in any position** il peut jouer à n'importe quelle position *ou* place; **the full back was out of position** l'arrière était mal placé

(**i**) *Mil* position *f*; **to move into position** se mettre en place *ou* en position; **the men took up position on the hill** les hommes prirent position sur la colline; **to defend a position** défendre une position; **to jockey** *or* **to jostle** *or* **to manoeuvre for position** chercher à occuper le terrain; *Fig* chercher à obtenir la meilleure place

(**j**) *St Exch* position *f*; **to take a long/short position** prendre une position longue/courte

2 *vt* (**a**) *(put in place → cameras, equipment)* mettre en place, placer, disposer; *(→ guests, officials, players)* placer; *(→ guards, police, troops)* poster, mettre en position; **the TV cameras were positioned round the square** les caméras de télé ont été disposées autour de la place; **he positioned himself on the roof** il a pris position sur le toit; **they have positioned their ships in the gulf** ils ont envoyé leurs navires dans le golfe

(**b**) *(usu passive) (situate → house, building)* situer, placer; **the school is positioned near a dangerous crossroads** l'école est située *ou* placée près d'un carrefour dangereux; **the flat is well positioned** l'appartement est bien situé; **we are well positioned to take advantage of this opportunity** nous sommes bien placés pour tirer parti de cette opportunité

(**c**) *(adjust angle of → lamp, aerial)* orienter

(**d**) *(locate)* déterminer la position de, positionner

(**e**) *Mktg (product)* positionner

►► *St Exch* ***position limit*** limite *f* de position; *Pol* ***position paper*** déclaration *f* de principe; *St Exch* ***position trader*** spéculateur(trice) *m,f* sur plusieurs positions

positional [pəˈzɪʃənəl] *adj (warfare)* de position, de positions; *Ling (variant)* contextuel; *Sport* **his positional play is excellent** il sait très bien se placer sur le terrain; **Man United were forced to make some positional changes** Manchester United a dû modifier les positions des joueurs

►► *Astron* ***positional astronomy*** astrométrie *f*, astronomie *f* de position; *Math* ***positional notation*** numération *f* positionnelle

positioning [pəˈzɪʃənɪŋ] *n* (**a**) *(putting in place)* mise *f* en place *ou* en position; **positioning and deployment of the covering forces** mise *f* en place des forces de couverture

(**b**) *(adjusting position)* positionnement *m*; *(of aerial)* orientation *f*

(**c**) *Mktg* positionnement *m*

(**d**) *Gram (of word)* **end positioning** rejet *m*

►► *Constr* ***positioning angle*** cornière *f* de mise en place *or* de centrage; *Comput* ***positioning arm*** bras *m* de positionnement *or* de lecture-écriture; *Comput* ***positioning macro*** macro-commande *f* de position; *Mil* ***positioning map*** carte *f* de positionnement; *Mktg* ***positioning strategy*** stratégie *f* de positionnement; *Mktg* ***positioning study*** étude *f* de positionnement

positive [ˈpɒzɪtɪv] **1** *adj* (**a**) *(sure)* sûr, certain; **are you positive about that?** en êtes-vous sûr?; **are you absolutely sure? – yes, positive** en êtes-vous absolument sûr? – sûr et certain; **I'm positive (that) he wasn't there** je suis absolument sûr qu'il n'y était pas; **it's absolutely positive** c'est sûr et certain

(**b**) *(constructive)* positif, constructif; **it's one of my few positive achievements** c'est une des rares choses positives *ou* constructives que j'aie faites; **haven't you got any positive suggestions?** n'avez-vous rien à proposer qui fasse avancer les choses?; **she has a very positive approach to the problem** son approche du problème est très positive *ou* constructive

(**c**) *(affirmative → reply, response)* positif, affirmatif; *(→ fact, result)* positif; **there was a tremendously positive response to this idea** cette idée a été extrêmement bien accueillie *ou* reçue

(**d**) *(definite → fact, progress)* réel, certain; *(clear → change, advantage)* réel, effectif; *(precise → instructions)* formel, clair; **we have positive evidence of his involvement** nous avons des preuves irréfutables de son implication; **his intervention was a positive factor in the release of the hostages** son intervention a efficacement contribué à la libération des otages; **the team needs some positive support** l'équipe a besoin d'un soutien réel *ou* effectif; **positive proof,** *Br* **proof positive** preuve *f* formelle

(**e**) *(as intensifier → absolute)* absolu, véritable, pur; **the whole thing was a positive nightmare** tout cela était un véritable cauchemar; **a positive delight** un pur délice; **a positive pleasure** un véritable plaisir; **it's a positive lie** c'est un mensonge, ni plus ni moins

(**f**) *(assured)* assuré, ferme; **she answered in a very positive tone** elle a répondu d'un ton très assuré *ou* très ferme

(**g**) *Elec, Math & Phot* positif

(**h**) *Am Pol (progressive)* progressiste

(**i**) *Gram* **positive degree** *(of adjective, adverb)* degré *m* positif

2 *n* (**a**) *Gram* positif *m*; **in the positive** à la forme positive

(**b**) *(answer)* réponse *f* positive *ou* affirmative, oui *m*; **to reply in the positive** répondre par l'affirmative *ou* affirmativement

(**c**) *Phot* épreuve *f* positive

(**d**) *Elec* borne *f* positive

►► ***positive discrimination*** *(UNCOUNT)* discrimination *f* positive *(mesures favorisant les membres de groupes minoritaires)*; **positive discrimination in favour of people with disabilities** mesures *fpl* en faveur des handicapés; ***positive feedback*** *(in electronic circuit)* réaction *f* positive; *(in mechanical or cybernetic system)* feed-back *m inv* positif, rétroaction *f* positive; *Fig* **I didn't get much positive feedback on my suggestion** ma proposition n'a pas enthousiasmé grand monde; *Am* ***positive ID*** papiers *mpl* d'identité *(avec photo)*; ***positive pole*** *(magnet)* pôle *m* nord; *(anode)* anode *f (pôle positif)*; *Fin* ***positive prescription*** prescription *f* acquisitive; *Phot* ***positive print*** positif *m*, épreuve *f* positive; ***positive proof*** preuve *f* formelle; *Psy* ***positive reinforcement*** renforcement *m* positif; ***positive thinking*** idées *fpl* constructives; ***positive vetting*** contrôle *m ou* enquête *f* de sécurité *(sur un candidat à un poste touchant à la sécurité nationale)*

positively [ˈpɒzɪtɪvlɪ] *adv* (**a**) *(absolutely)* absolument, positivement; *(definitely)* incontestablement, positivement; **it's positively ridiculous** c'est absolument ridicule; **her behaviour was positively disgraceful** elle s'est comportée de manière absolument scandaleuse; **smiling? – she was positively beaming!** souriante? – elle était carrément *ou* littéralement radieuse!

(**b**) *(constructively)* positivement, de façon constructive; **it's important to act positively** il est important d'agir de façon positive; **to think positively** positiver; **try to think positively about the situation** essaie de voir la situation d'une manière constructive; **people have responded quite positively to our suggestions** nos suggestions ont été fort bien accueillies

(**c**) *(affirmatively)* affirmativement; *(with certainty)* avec certitude, positivement; **the body has been positively identified** le cadavre a été formellement identifié; **he had been positively vetted on three occasions** il avait fait l'objet de trois enquêtes de sécurité qui s'étaient avérées satisfaisantes

(**d**) *Elec* positivement; **positively charged** chargé positivement

positiveness [ˈpɒzɪtɪvnɪs] *n* (**a**) *(certainty)* certitude *f*, assurance *f* (**b**) *(of reply, response)* ton *m* décisif

positivism [ˈpɒzɪtɪvɪzəm] *n* positivisme *m*

positivist [ˈpɒzɪtɪvɪst] **1** *n* positiviste *mf*

2 *adj* positiviste

positivity [ˌpɒzɪˈtɪvɪtɪ] *n* (**a**) *(certainty)* certitude *f*, assurance *f* (**b**) *(of reply, response)* ton *m* décisif

positron [ˈpɒzɪtrɒn] *n Phys* positron *m*, positon *m*

►► *Med* ***positron emission tomography*** tomographie *f* par émission de positrons

positronium [ˌpɒzɪˈtrəʊnɪəm] *n Phys* positronium *m*

posology [pəˈsɒlədʒɪ] *n Med* posologie *f*

poss [pɒs] *adj Fam* possible[❑]; **as soon as poss** dès que possible

posse [ˈpɒsɪ] *n* (**a**) *Am Hist* = autrefois, petit groupe d'hommes rassemblés par le shérif en cas d'urgence; **to round up a posse** réunir un groupe d'hommes; *Fig* **a posse of fans were in hot pursuit** des fans en détachement spécial s'étaient lancés dans une poursuite échevelée

(**b**) *Fam (group of friends)* bande *f*; **he's out with the posse** il est sorti avec ses potes *ou* avec sa bande

(**c**) *Fam Black Am slang (entourage)* clique *f*; *(criminal gang)* gang[❑] *m*

possess [pə'zes] *vt* (**a**) *(have possession of → permanently)* posséder, avoir; *(→ temporarily)* être en possession de, détenir, avoir; **I would give all I possess to be with you** je donnerais tout ce que je possède *ou* j'ai pour être avec toi; **what proof do you possess?** quelles preuves avez-vous?; **she possesses a clear understanding of the subject** elle connaît bien son sujet, elle a une bonne connaissance du sujet

(**b**) *(obsess)* obséder; **he was completely possessed by the idea of going to India** il était complètement obsédé par l'idée d'aller en Inde; **what on earth possessed him to do such a thing?** qu'est-ce qui lui a pris de faire une chose pareille?

(**c**) *Formal or Literary* **to possess oneself of sth** se munir de qch

possessed [pə'zest] *adj* (**a**) *(controlled → by an evil spirit)* possédé; **she/her soul is possessed by the devil** elle/son âme est possédée du démon; **he was shouting like one possessed** il criait comme un possédé

(**b**) *Literary (filled)* **possessed by curiosity** dévoré de *ou* en proie à la curiosité; **possessed by hatred** en proie à la haine

(**c**) *Formal or Literary* **none of her children was possessed of any great talent** aucun de ses enfants n'était particulièrement doué

possession [pə'zeʃən] **1** *n* (**a**) *(gen)* possession *f*; **to be in possession of sth** être en possession de qch; **to have sth in one's possession** avoir qch en sa possession; **he was found in possession of a flick-knife, a flick-knife was found in his possession** il a été trouvé en possession d'un couteau à cran d'arrêt; **he's been arrested for possession** *(of drugs)* il a été arrêté pour détention de drogue; **she was charged with possession of illegal substances** elle a été inculpée pour détention de stupéfiants; **the file is no longer in my possession** le dossier n'est plus en ma possession, je ne suis plus en possession du dossier; **how did the car come into your possession?** comment la voiture est-elle entrée en votre possession?; **to be in full possession of one's senses** être en pleine possession de ses moyens; *Sport* **to be in** *or* **to have possession (of the ball)** avoir le ballon; **certain documents have come into my possession** certains documents sont tombés en ma possession; **she got possession of the house two weeks ago** elle a pris possession de la maison il y a deux semaines; **do they have possession of the necessary documents?** ont-ils *ou* possèdent-ils les documents nécessaires?; **to take possession of sth** *(acquire)* prendre possession de qch; *(by force)* s'emparer de *ou* s'approprier qch; *(confiscate)* confisquer qch; *Br* **possession is nine points** *or* **parts** *or* **tenths of the law** possession vaut titre

(**b**) *Law (of property)* possession *f*, jouissance *f*; **to take possession** prendre possession; **immediate possession** jouissance *f* immédiate

(**c**) *(by evil)* possession *f*

2 possessions *npl* (**a**) *(belongings)* affaires *fpl*, biens *mpl*; **the jade vases are our most precious possessions** les vases en jade sont ce que nous possédons de plus précieux

(**b**) *(colonies)* possessions *fpl*; *(land)* terres *fpl*

possessive [pə'zesɪv] **1** *adj* (**a**) *(gen)* possessif; **he's possessive about his belongings** il a horreur de prêter ses affaires; **she's possessive about her children** c'est une mère possessive

(**b**) *Gram* possessif

2 *n Gram (case)* (cas *m*) possessif *m*; *(word)* possessif *m*

▸▸ *Gram* ***possessive adjective*** adjectif *m* possessif; *Gram* ***possessive pronoun*** pronom *m* possessif

possessively [pə'zesɪvlɪ] *adv* de manière possessive; **she clung possessively to her father's hand** elle agrippa jalousement la main de son père

possessiveness [pə'zesɪvnɪs] *n* caractère *m* possessif, possessivité *f*

possessor [pə'zesə(r)] *n* possesseur *m*, propriétaire *mf*; **I found myself the possessor of an old manor house** je me suis trouvé propriétaire d'un vieux manoir

possessory [pə'zesərɪ] *adj Law* possessoire

▸▸ ***possessory action*** action *f* possessoire; ***possessory right*** possessoire *m*

posset ['pɒsɪt] *n* = boisson d'autrefois à base de lait chaud et de bière ou de vin

possibility [,pɒsə'bɪlətɪ] *(pl* **possibilities***)* **1** *n* (**a**) *(chance)* possibilité *f*, éventualité *f*; **it's a possibility** c'est une possibilité, c'est bien possible; **within the bounds of possibility** dans la limite du possible; **the possibility of a settlement is fading fast** la perspective d'un règlement est de moins en moins probable; **is there any possibility of you coming up for the weekend?** pourriez-vous venir ce week-end?, y a-t-il des chances que vous veniez ce week-end?; **if there's any possibility of leaving early, I'll let you know** s'il y a moyen de partir de bonne heure, je vous le ferai savoir; **there's no possibility of that happening** il n'y a aucune chance *ou* aucun risque que cela se produise; **there's little possibility of any changes being made to the budget** il est peu probable que le budget soit modifié; **there's a strong possibility we'll know the results tomorrow** il est fort possible que nous connaissions les résultats demain; **they hadn't even considered the possibility that he might leave** ils n'avaient même pas envisagé qu'il puisse partir

(**b**) *(person → for job)* candidat(e) *m,f* possible; *(→ as choice)* choix *m* possible; **she's still a possibility** elle conserve toutes ses chances

(**c**) *(possible event, outcome)* éventualité *f*; **that is a distinct possibility** c'est bien possible; **to allow for all possibilities** parer à toute éventualité; **the possibilities are endless!** les possibilités sont innombrables!

2 possibilities *npl (potential)* possibilités *fpl*; **the job has a lot of possibilities** le poste offre de nombreuses perspectives; **job possibilities** possibilités *fpl* d'emploi

possible ['pɒsəbəl] **1** *adj* possible; **if possible** si possible; **I'll be there, if at all possible** j'y serai, dans la mesure du possible; **that's possible** c'est possible, ça se peut; **anything's possible** tout est possible; **it's quite possible to complete the job in two months** il est tout à fait possible de terminer le travail en deux mois; **it wasn't possible to achieve our objectives** il ne nous a pas été possible d'atteindre nos objectifs; **it isn't possible for her to come** il ne lui est pas possible *ou* il lui est impossible de venir; **it's possible (that) he won't come** il se peut qu'il ne vienne pas; **it's just possible she's forgotten** il n'est pas impossible qu'elle ait oublié; **it seems barely possible** cela semble à peine possible; **it doesn't seem possible that anyone could be so stupid** il est difficile d'imaginer que l'on puisse être aussi bête; **he comes to see me whenever possible** il vient me voir quand il le peut; **the grant made it possible for me to continue my research** la bourse m'a permis de poursuivre mes recherches; **the doctors did everything possible to save her** les médecins ont fait tout leur possible *ou* tout ce qu'ils ont pu pour la sauver; **as far as possible** *(within one's competence)* dans la mesure du possible; *(at maximum distance)* aussi loin que possible; **as long/cheap as possible** aussi longtemps/bon marché que possible; **as much** *or* **as many as possible** autant que possible; **to give as many details as possible** donner le plus de détails possible *ou* tous les détails possibles; **as soon as possible** dès que *ou* le plus tôt possible; **the best/the smallest possible** le meilleur/le plus petit possible; **the shortest possible route** l'itinéraire le plus court possible; **I mean that in the nicest possible way** je dis cela sans méchanceté (aucune); **the best of all possible worlds** le meilleur des mondes possibles; **he tried all possible means** il a essayé tous les moyens possibles (et imaginables); **there's no possible way out** il n'y a absolument aucune issue; **what possible benefit can we get from it?** quel bénéfice *ou* quel profit peut-on bien en tirer?; **we chose several possible candidates** on a choisi plusieurs candidats possibles; **it's one possible answer to the problem** c'est une solution possible au problème; **to insure against possible accidents** s'assurer contre les accidents éventuels

2 *n* (**a**) *(activity)* possible *m*; **it's in the realms of the possible** c'est dans le domaine du possible; **diplomacy is the art of the possible** la diplomatie est l'art du possible

(**b**) *(choice)* choix *m* possible; *(candidate)* candidature *f* susceptible d'être retenue; *Sport (player)* joueur(euse) *m,f* susceptible d'être choisi; **we looked at ten houses, of which two were possibles** nous avons visité dix maisons dont deux nous intéressent *ou* sont à retenir; **she is still a possible for the prize/job** elle garde toutes ses chances d'avoir le prix/d'obtenir le poste; **the England possibles** les joueurs *mpl* susceptibles de faire partie de l'équipe d'Angleterre

3 Possibles *npl Br Fam Sport* **the Possibles versus the Probables** l'équipe B contre l'équipe A

possibly ['pɒsəblɪ] *adv* (**a**) *(perhaps)* peut-être; **he is possibly the greatest musician of his time** c'est peut-être le plus grand musicien de son temps; **possibly (so)/possibly not, but he had no other choice** peut-être (bien)/peut-être pas, mais il n'avait pas le choix; **will you be there tomorrow? – possibly** vous serez là demain? – c'est possible; **could you possibly lend me £5?** vous serait-il possible de me prêter 5 livres?

(**b**) *(conceivably)* **what advantage can we possibly get from it?** quel avantage pouvons-nous espérer en tirer?; **she can't possibly get here on time** elle ne pourra jamais arriver à l'heure; **where can they possibly have got to?** où peuvent-ils bien être passés?; **run as fast as you possibly can** cours aussi vite que tu peux; **the doctors did all they possibly could to save her** les médecins ont fait tout ce qu'ils ont pu *ou* tout leur possible pour la sauver; **I'll come whenever I possibly can** je viendrai chaque fois que cela me sera possible; **I couldn't possibly accept your offer** je ne puis accepter votre proposition; **she might possibly still be here** il se pourrait qu'elle soit encore ici

possum ['pɒsəm] *n (American)* opossum *m*; *(Australian)* phalanger *m*; *Fam* **to play possum** faire le mort[□]

POST [pəʊst]

courrier	▸ **1 (a)**
poste	▸ **1 (a), (f), (g)**
poteau	▸ **1 (c) – (e)**
pieu	▸ **1 (c)**
poster	▸ **2 (a), (b)**
muter	▸ **2 (c)**
affecter	▸ **2 (c)**
afficher	▸ **2 (d)**

1 *n* (**a**) *Br (letters)* courrier *m*; *(postal service)* poste *f*, courrier *m*; *(delivery)* (distribution *f* du) courrier *m*; *(collection)* levée *f* (du courrier); **has the post come?** est-ce que le facteur est passé?; **by return of post** par retour du courrier; **there's no post today** il n'y a pas de courrier aujourd'hui; **did it come through the post** *or* **by post?** est-ce que c'est arrivé par la poste?; **I sent it by post** je l'ai envoyé par la poste; **it's in the post** c'est parti au courrier; **can you put the cheque in the post?** pouvez-vous envoyer le chèque par la poste?; **do you want the letters to go first or second class post?** voulez-vous envoyer ces lettres au tarif normal ou au tarif lent?; **a parcel came in this morning's post** un paquet est arrivé au courrier de ce matin; **I don't want to miss the post** je ne veux pas manquer la levée; **will we still catch the post?** pourrons-nous poster le courrier à temps *ou* avant la levée?; **I missed the post** quand je suis arrivé, la levée était déjà faite *ou* le courrier était déjà parti; **can you take the letters to the post?** *(post office)* pouvez-vous porter les lettres à la poste?; *(post them)* pouvez-vous poster les lettres *ou* mettre les lettres à la boîte?

(**b**) *Hist (station)* relais *m* de poste; *(rider)* courrier *m*

(**c**) *(of sign, street lamp)* poteau *m*; *(of fence)* pieu *m*; *(of four-poster bed)* colonne *f*; *(upright → of door, window)* montant *m*

(**d**) *(in racing)* poteau *m*; **starting/finishing** *or* **winning post** poteau *m* de départ/d'arrivée; *also Fig* **to be left at the post** rater le départ; *also Fam Fig* **to be beaten** *or* **pipped at the**

pos–pos

post se faire coiffer *ou* battre sur le poteau

(**e**) *Ftbl* poteau *m*, montant *m*; **the near/back post** le premier/deuxième poteau

(**f**) *(job)* poste *m*, emploi *m*; **he got a post as an economist** il a obtenu un poste d'économiste; **a university/diplomatic post** un poste universitaire/de diplomate; **a government post** un poste au gouvernement

(**g**) *Mil etc (duty station)* poste *m*; *Am (permanent station)* camp *m*, fort *m*; *(garrison)* garnison *f*; **remain at your post** restez à votre poste; **a sentry post** un poste de sentinelle; **advanced** *or* **outlying post** *(place, group of men)* poste *m* avancé; **lookout post** poste *m* de guet *ou* d'observation; **frontier post** poste *m* frontière

(**h**) *Am (trading post)* comptoir *m*

(**i**) *Mil (bugle call)* **first post** première partie *f* de la sonnerie de la retraite; **last post** *(at night)* extinction *f* des feux; *(at funeral)* sonnerie *f* aux morts; **to sound the last post (over the grave)** jouer la sonnerie aux morts

2 *vt* (**a**) *esp Br (letter → put in box)* poster, mettre à la poste; *(→ send by post)* envoyer par la poste; **to post sth to sb** envoyer qch à qn par la poste, poster qch à qn

(**b**) *Mil etc (station → guard, sentry)* poster; **they posted men all around the house** ils ont posté des hommes tout autour de la maison; *Fig* **she posted herself at the window** elle s'est postée à la fenêtre

(**c**) *(assign → gen)* muter, affecter; *Mil* affecter; **to be posted to a different branch** être muté dans une autre succursale; *Mil* **to be posted to a unit/a ship** être affecté à une unité/un navire; **to be posted overseas** être en poste à l'étranger

(**d**) *(display → on bulletin board, wall)* afficher; *(→ banns, names)* publier; **he has been posted missing** il a été porté disparu; *Am* **post no bills** *(sign)* défense d'afficher; *Fig* **to keep sb posted** tenir qn au courant

(**e**) *Acct (amount)* passer; *(ledger)* tenir à jour; **to post an entry** passer une écriture; **to post the books** passer les écritures

(**f**) *Am (issue)* **to post bail** déposer une caution

(**g**) *St Exch* **to post security** déposer des garanties

(**h**) *Comput (on Internet)* poster

▶▶ ***post chaise*** chaise *f* de poste; *Am Mil* ***post exchange*** = économat pour les militaires et leurs familles; ***post horn*** trompe *f* (de la malle-poste); ***post house*** relais *m* de poste; ***post office*** *(place)* (bureau *m* de) poste *f*; *(service)* (service *m* des) postes *fpl*, poste *f*; *Am (game)* = jeu d'enfant dans lequel un des joueurs fait semblant de distribuer des lettres, en échange desquelles il reçoit un baiser; ***the Post Office*** *(government department)* ≃ la Poste; ***post office account*** compte *m* chèque postal; ***post office box*** boîte *f* postale; ***post office and general store*** = petite épicerie de village faisant office de bureau de poste; *Comput* ***post office protocol*** protocole *m* POP; *Br* ***post office savings*** ≃ Caisse *f* (nationale) d'épargne; **we have a little money in post office savings** nous avons un peu d'argent à la Caisse d'épargne; ***the Post Office Tower*** = ancien nom de la "Telecom Tower"

▶**post on** *vt sep (letters)* faire suivre; **can you post my letters on to me?** pouvez-vous faire suivre mon courrier?

▶**post up** *vt sep* (**a**) *(notice)* afficher (**b**) *(ledger)* mettre à jour *(les écritures)*

---

postage [ˈpəʊstɪdʒ] **1** *n (UNCOUNT) (postal charges)* tarifs *mpl* postaux *ou* d'affranchissement; *(cost of posting)* frais *mpl* d'expédition *ou* d'envoi *ou* de port; **what's the postage on this parcel?** c'est combien pour envoyer ce paquet?; *Br* **postage and packing,** *Am* **postage and handling** frais *mpl* de port et d'emballage; **postage included** port compris; **postage paid** franco, port payé

2 *comp (rates)* postal

▶▶ ***postage due stamp*** timbre *m* taxe; ***postage stamp*** timbre *m*, timbre-poste *m*

postal [ˈpəʊstəl] *adj* (**a**) *(charge, district)* postal; *(administration, service, strike)* des postes; *(delivery)* par la poste

(**b**) *Am Fam* **to go postal** *(get angry)* piquer une crise

▶▶ ***postal charges*** frais *mpl* d'envoi *ou* de port; ***postal code*** code *m* postal; *Am* ***postal meter*** machine *f* à affranchir; *Br* ***postal order*** mandat *m* postal, mandat *m* poste; ***postal rates*** tarifs *mpl* postaux; *Am* ***the Postal Service*** ≃ la Poste; *Mktg* ***postal survey*** enquête *f* postale; *Br* ***postal vote*** vote *m* par correspondance; ***postal worker*** employé(e) *m,f* des postes

postbag [ˈpəʊstbæg] *n Br* (**a**) *(sack)* sac *m* postal (**b**) *(correspondence)* courrier *m*; **we've got a full postbag this morning** nous avons reçu énormément de lettres *ou* une avalanche de courrier ce matin

post-Biblical *adj* postbiblique

postbox [ˈpəʊstbɒks] *n Br* boîte *f* à *ou* aux lettres

postbus [ˈpəʊstbʌs] *n Br* = car transportant (en milieu rural) du courrier et des voyageurs

postcard [ˈpəʊstkɑːd] *n* carte *f* postale

post-classical *adj* postérieur à l'époque classique, postclassique

postcode [ˈpəʊstkəʊd] *n Br* code *m* postal

▶▶ ***postcode discrimination*** = forme d'ostracisme social qui frappe les habitants des quartiers défavorisés

postdate [ˌpəʊstˈdeɪt] *vt* (**a**) *(letter, cheque)* postdater (**b**) *(event)* assigner une date postérieure à; **historians now postdate the event by several centuries** les historiens pensent aujourd'hui que l'événement a eu lieu des siècles plus tard

post-doctoral, post-doctorate *adj Univ* postdoctoral

postedit [ˌpəʊstˈedɪt] *vt (in machine translation)* post-éditer

posted price *n Mktg* prix *m* public

poster [ˈpəʊstə(r)] *n* (**a**) *(informative)* affiche *f*; *(decorative)* poster *m* (**b**) *(idiom)* **to be a poster boy/girl for sth** incarner qch

▶▶ *Mktg* ***poster advertising*** publicité *f* par affichage, publicité *f* par voie d'affiches; ***poster art*** l'art *m* de l'affiche; *Mktg* ***poster campaign*** campagne *f* d'affichage; ***poster colour*** gouache *f*; ***poster paint*** gouache *f*; ***poster presentation*** communication *f* affichée

poste restante [ˌpəʊstresˈtɒnt] *n* poste *f* restante; **you can write to me poste restante Florence** vous pouvez m'écrire poste restante à Florence

posterior [pɒˈstɪərɪə(r)] **1** *adj* (**a**) *Formal (in time)* postérieur (**b**) *Tech (rear)* arrière

2 *n Fam Hum (of person)* postérieur *m*, arrière-train *m*

posterity [pɒˈsterɪtɪ] *n* postérité *f*; **for posterity** pour la postérité; **to go down in** *or* **to posterity** entrer dans la postérité *ou* l'histoire

postern [ˈpɒstən] *n* poterne *f*

post-feminist *adj* postféministe

post-free 1 *adj* (**a**) *Br (prepaid)* port payé (**b**) *(free of postal charge)* dispensé d'affranchissement

2 *adv* (**a**) *Br (prepaid)* en port payé (**b**) *(free of postal charge)* en franchise postale

postgrad [ˌpəʊstˈgræd] *Fam* = **postgraduate**

postgraduate [ˌpəʊstˈgrædʒʊət] **1** *n* étudiant(e) *m,f* de troisième cycle

2 *adj (diploma, studies)* de troisième cycle

posthaste [ˌpəʊstˈheɪst] *adv Literary* à toute vitesse, en toute hâte

postholder [ˈpəʊstˌhəʊldə(r)] *n* titulaire *mf*

post-horse *n* cheval *m* de poste

posthumous [illegible] *adj* posthume

posthumously [ˈpɒstjʊməslɪ] *adj* après la mort; **the poems were published posthumously** les poèmes ont été publiés après la mort de l'auteur; **the prize was awarded posthumously** le prix a été décerné à titre posthume

postiche [pɒsˈtiːʃ] *n* postiche *m*

postie [ˈpəʊstɪ] *n Br Fam (postman)* facteur[❑] *m*

post-ignition *n* auto-allumage *m*

postilion, postillion [pəˈstɪljən] *n* postillon *m*

Postimpressionism [ˌpəʊstɪmˈpreʃənɪzəm] *n* postimpressionnisme *m*

Postimpressionist [ˌpəʊstɪmˈpreʃənɪst] **1** *n* postimpressionniste *mf*

2 *adj* postimpressionniste

postindustrial [ˌpəʊstɪnˈdʌstrɪəl] *adj* postindustriel

posting [ˈpəʊstɪŋ] *n* (**a**) *Br (of diplomat)* nomination *f*, affectation *f*; *(of soldier)* affectation *f*; *(of guards)* mise *f* en faction; **to get an overseas posting** être nommé en poste à l'étranger; **he had been given a posting as sales manager in Eastern Europe** on l'avait envoyé en Europe de l'Est comme directeur des ventes

(**b**) *Com (in ledger)* inscription *f*, enregistrement *m*

(**c**) *Br (of letter) (putting in the post)* mise *f* à la boîte *ou* à la poste; *(sending by mail)* envoi *m* par la poste

▶▶ ***posting date*** date *f* de la poste

Post-it® *n* Post-it® *m*

postman [ˈpəʊstmən] (*pl* **postmen** [-mən]) *n* facteur *m*, *Admin* préposé *m*

▶▶ *Br* ***postman's knock*** = jeu d'enfant dans lequel un des joueurs fait semblant de distribuer des lettres, en échange desquelles il reçoit un baiser

'The Postman Always Rings Twice' *Cain, Garnett, Rafelson* 'Le Facteur sonne toujours deux fois'

---

postmark [ˈpəʊstmɑːk] **1** *n (on letter)* cachet *m* de la poste; **date as postmark** le cachet de la poste faisant foi

2 *vt* oblitérer; **the letter is postmarked Phoenix** la lettre vient de *ou* a été postée à Phoenix

postmaster [ˈpəʊstˌmɑːstə(r)] *n* (**a**) *Admin* receveur *m* des Postes (**b**) *Comput (for e-mail)* maître *m* de poste

▶▶ ***Postmaster General*** ≃ ministre *m* des Postes et Télécommunications, *Can* ministre *m* des Postes

post meridiem [-məˈrɪdɪəm] *adv Formal (in afternoon)* de l'après-midi; *(in evening)* du soir

postmillennial [pəʊstmɪˈlenjəl] *adj* (**a**) *Rel* qui suit le millénium (**b**) *(after the millennium)* qui suit le passage à un nouveau millénaire

postmillennialism [ˌpəʊstmɪˈlenɪəlɪzəm] *n* = croyance selon laquelle le second avènement du Christ aurait lieu après le millénium

postmillennialist [ˌpəʊstmɪˈlenɪəlɪst] *n* = partisan de la croyance selon laquelle le second avènement du Christ aurait lieu après le millénium

postmistress [ˈpəʊstˌmɪstrɪs] *n* receveuse *f* des Postes

post-modern *adj* postmoderne

post-modernism *n* postmodernisme *m*

post-modernist 1 *n* postmoderniste *mf*

2 *adj* postmoderniste

postmortem [ˌpəʊstˈmɔːtəm] **1** *n* (**a**) *Med* autopsie *f*; **to carry out a postmortem** pratiquer une autopsie (**b**) *Fig* autopsie *f*; **they held a postmortem on the game** ils ont disséqué *ou* analysé le match après coup

2 *adj* après le décès

▶▶ ***postmortem examination*** autopsie *f*

postnatal [ˌpəʊstˈneɪtəl] *adj* postnatal

▶▶ ***postnatal depression*** dépression *f* postnatale

postnuptial [ˌpəʊstˈnʌpʃəl] *adj* postérieur au mariage

post-op 1 *adj* postopératoire

2 *n* salle *f* de réveil

postoperative [ˌpəʊstˈɒpərətɪv] *adj* postopératoire

postpaid [ˌpəʊstˈpeɪd] *adj & adv* franc de port, en port payé

postpartum [ˌpəʊstˈpɑːtəm] *n Med* postpartum *m*

postponable [ˌpəʊstˈpəʊnəbəl] *adj* ajournable

postpone [ˌpəʊstˈpəʊn] *vt (meeting, holiday)* remettre (à plus tard), reporter; *(match, game)* reporter; *(decision)* différer; **the meeting was postponed for three weeks/until a later date** la réunion a été reportée de trois semaines/remise à une date ultérieure

postponement [ˌpəʊstˈpəʊnmənt] *n (of meeting, match)* renvoi *m* (à une date ultérieure), report *m*; *(of holiday)* report *m*

postposition [ˌpəʊstpəˈzɪʃən] *n Gram* postposition *f*

postpositive [ˌpəʊstˈpɒzɪtɪv] *adj Gram* postpositif

postprandial [ˌpəʊstˈprændɪəl] *adj Formal or Hum* postprandial; **I like to take a postprandial nap/walk** j'aime faire une petite sieste/promenade après le déjeuner

postproduction [ˌpəʊstprəˈdʌkʃən] *n Cin & TV* postproduction *f*

▶▶ ***postproduction editing*** montage *m* de postproduction; ***postproduction mixer*** mélangeur *m* de postproduction; ***postproduction studio*** studio *m* de postproduction

post-purchase *adj Mktg* post-achat

►► ***post-purchase behaviour*** comportement *m* post-achat; ***post-purchase dissonance*** discordance *f* post-achat; ***post-purchase evaluation*** évaluation *f* post-achat

PostScript® ['pəʊstskrɪpt] *n Comput* PostScript® *m*

►► ***PostScript® font*** police *f* de caractères PostScript®; ***Postscript® printer*** imprimante *f* PostScript®

postscript ['pəʊstskrɪpt] *n* (**a**) *(in letter)* postscriptum *m inv*; **by way of postscript** en postscriptum (**b**) *(in book)* postface *f*; *Fig (additional events)* suite *f*

post-serial *adj* postsériel

►► ***post-serial music*** musique *m* postsériel

post-structuralism *n* post-structuralisme *m*

post-synch *n Fam Cin & TV* postsynchronisation❑ *f*

post-synchronization *n Cin & TV* postsynchronisation *f*

post-test *Mktg* **1** *n* post-test *m*

2 *vt* post-tester

post-traumatic stress disorder *n (UNCOUNT)* syndrome *m* de stress post-traumatique

postulant ['pɒstjʊlənt] *n Rel* postulant(e) *m,f*

postulate *Formal* **1** *vt* ['pɒstjʊleɪt] (**a**) *(hypothesize)* poser comme hypothèse; **to postulate the existence of an underground lake** soutenir l'hypothèse d'un lac souterrain; **we postulate that a cure will soon be found** nous sommes sûrs qu'on trouvera bientôt un remède

(**b**) *(take as granted)* postuler, poser comme principe; **the charter postulates that all men are equal** la charte part du principe que tous les hommes sont égaux

(**c**) *Rel (nominate)* postuler

(**d**) *(claim)* demander

2 *n* ['pɒstjʊlət] postulat *m*

postulation [,pɒstjʊ'leɪʃən] *n* (**a**) *(assumption)* supposition *f*, postulat *m* (**b**) *Rel* postulation *f* (**c**) *(claim)* demande *f*

posture ['pɒstʃə(r)] **1** *n* (**a**) *(body position)* posture *f*, position *f*; **to keep an upright posture** se tenir droit (**b**) *Fig (attitude)* attitude *f*

2 *vi* se donner des airs, poser

posturing ['pɒstʃərɪŋ] *n* pose *f*, affectation *f*

postviral syndrome [,pəʊst'vaɪərəl-] *n Med* syndrome *m* post-viral

postvocalic [,pəʊstvə'kælɪk] *adj Ling* postvocalique

postwar [,pəʊst'wɔː(r)] *adj* d'après-guerre, après la guerre; **the postwar period** l'après-guerre *m ou f*; **in the immediate postwar period** au cours des années qui ont immédiatement suivi la guerre, tout de suite après la guerre

posy ['pəʊzɪ] (*pl* **posies**) *n* petit bouquet *m* (de fleurs)

pot [pɒt] (*pt & pp* **potted**, *cont* **potting**) **1** *vt* (**a**) *(jam)* mettre en pot *ou* pots; *(fruit)* mettre en conserve

(**b**) *(plant)* mettre en pot

(**c**) *Br (in snooker, pool, billiards)* **to pot a ball** empocher une bille

(**d**) *Br (shoot)* tuer; **she potted a partridge** elle a abattu une perdrix; **he's out potting rabbits** il est à la chasse au lapin

2 *vi* (**a**) *(do pottery)* faire de la poterie

(**b**) *Br (shoot)* **to pot at sth** tirer sur qch

3 *n* (**a**) *(container → for paint, plant, jam etc)* pot *m*; *(teapot)* théière *f*; *(coffee pot)* cafetière *f*; **a pot of paint/mustard** un pot de peinture/de moutarde; **I drank a whole pot of tea/coffee** j'ai bu une théière/une cafetière entière; **I'll make another pot of tea/coffee** je vais refaire du thé/café; **a pot of tea for two** du thé pour deux personnes; *very Fam* **he hasn't got a pot to piss in** il est complètement fauché

(**b**) *(saucepan)* casserole *f*; **pots and pans** batterie *f* de cuisine; **(cooking) pot** marmite *f*, fait-tout *m inv*; *Br Prov* **it's a case of the pot calling the kettle black** c'est l'hôpital qui se moque de la charité

(**c**) *(pottery object)* poterie *f*, pot *m*; **to throw a pot** tourner une poterie

(**d**) *Fam (trophy)* trophée❑ *m*, coupe❑ *f*

(**e**) *(in card games)* cagnotte *f*

(**f**) *Fam (belly)* bedaine *f*, brioche *f*

(**g**) *Br Fam* **to take a pot (shot) at sth** *(shoot at)* tirer à l'aveuglette sur qch❑; *(attempt)* faire qch à l'aveuglette❑

(**h**) *Fam (marijuana)* herbe *f*, beu *f*

(**i**) *Br (in snooker, pool, billiards)* blousage *m*, empochage *m*

(**j**) *Elec* potentiomètre *m*

(**k**) *Fam (idiom)* **to go to pot** *(deteriorate → country)* aller à la dérive❑; *(→ morals)* dégénérer❑; *(→ plans)* tomber à l'eau; *(→ person)* se laisser aller❑; **everything has gone to pot** tout est fichu; **his health has gone to pot** sa santé s'est délabrée❑; **her marriage has gone to pot** ça ne va plus du tout avec son mari❑

4 pots *npl Br Fam (large amount)* tas *mpl*, tonnes *fpl*; **to have pots of money** avoir plein de fric, être plein aux as

►► *Am* ***pot cheese*** fromage *m* blanc (égoutté), cottage cheese *m*; *Am* ***pot pie*** tourte *f* à la viande et aux légumes; *Br* ***pot plant*** plante *f* d'intérieur; *esp Am* ***pot roast*** rôti *m* à la cocotte

►**pot on** *vt sep (plant)* rempoter

►**pot up** *vt sep (plant)* empoter

potable ['pəʊtəbəl] *adj Literary or Hum* potable, buvable

potash ['pɒtæʃ] *n Chem (UNCOUNT)* potasse *f*

potassium [pə'tæsɪəm] *n Chem (UNCOUNT)* potassium *m*

►► ***potassium chloride*** chlorure *m* de potassium; ***potassium hydrogencarbonate*** hydrogénocarbonate *m* de potassium; ***potassium hydroxide*** hydroxyde *m* de potassium; ***potassium nitrate*** nitrate *m* de potassium; ***potassium permanganate*** permanganate *m* de potassium

potassium-argon dating *n Chem* datation *f* au potassium-argon

potation [pəʊ'teɪʃən] *n Literary or Hum (drink)* boisson *f* (alcoolisée); *(drinking)* libations *fpl*

potato [pə'teɪtəʊ] (*pl* **potatoes**) **1** *n* pomme *f* de terre

2 *comp (farming, salad, soup)* de pommes de terre

►► *Entom* ***potato beetle*** doryphore *m*, *Can* bête *f* à patates; ***potato blight*** mildiou *m* de la pomme de terre; *Entom* ***potato bug*** doryphore *m*; ***potato chip*** *Br (French fry)* (pomme *f*) frite *f*; *Am (crisp)* (pomme *f*) chips *f*; *Br* ***potato crisp*** (pomme *f*) chips *f*; *Hist* **the potato famine** la disette de la pomme de terre *(de 1845 à 1849)*; *see also box on* **The Great Famine**; ***potato masher*** presse-purée *m inv*; ***potato peeler*** *(tool)* éplucheur *m*, épluche-légumes *m inv*, (couteau *m*) économe *m*; *(machine)* éplucheuse *f*

potbellied ['pɒt,belɪd] *adj (person)* bedonnant; **to be potbellied** avoir du ventre

►► ***potbellied stove*** poêle *m*

potbelly ['pɒt,belɪ] (*pl* **potbellies**) *n* (**a**) *(stomach)* ventre *m*, bedon *m*; **to have a potbelly** avoir du ventre (**b**) *Am (stove)* poêle *m*

potboiler ['pɒt,bɔɪlə(r)] *n Fam* gagne-pain *m*; **he only writes potboilers** il n'écrit que pour faire bouillir la marmite

pot-bound *adj (plant)* à l'étroit dans son pot

potboy ['pɒtbɔɪ] *n Arch* garçon *m* de café

poteen [pɒ'tʃiːn] *n Ir* = whisky fabriqué clandestinement

potency ['pəʊtənsɪ] (*pl* **potencies**) *n* (**a**) *(strength → of spell, influence, argument)* force *f*, puissance *f*; *(→ of medicine)* efficacité *f*; *(→ of drink)* (forte) teneur *f* en alcool (**b**) *(virility)* puissance *f*, virilité *f*

potent ['pəʊtənt] *adj* (**a**) *(spell, influence)* fort, puissant; *(argument)* convaincant; *(medicine, poison, antidote)* actif; *(drink)* fort (en alcool); **potent stuff, this rum!** il est fort, ce rhum! (**b**) *(virile)* viril

potentate ['pəʊtənteɪt] *n Pol* potentat *m*; *Fig* magnat *m*

potential [pə'tenʃəl] **1** *adj* (**a**) *(possible)* possible, potentiel, éventuel; **that boy is a potential genius** ce garçon est un génie en puissance; **they're potential criminals** ce sont des criminels en puissance; **we mustn't discourage potential investors** il ne faut pas décourager les investisseurs éventuels *ou* potentiels

(**b**) *Ling* potentiel

(**c**) *Elec & Phys* potentiel

2 *n* (**a**) *(UNCOUNT) (of person)* promesse *f*, possibilités *fpl* (d'avenir); **your son has potential** votre fils a de l'avenir *ou* un avenir prometteur; **she has the potential to succeed** elle a la capacité de réussir; **they don't have much intellectual potential** ils n'ont pas de grandes capacités intellectuelles; **she has great potential as an actress** *or* **great acting potential** elle a toutes les qualités d'une grande actrice; **she has potential as an athlete** elle peut devenir une grande athlète; **to fulfil one's potential** donner toute sa mesure; **he never achieved his full potential** il n'a jamais exploité pleinement ses capacités

(**b**) *(of concept, discovery, situation)* possibilités *fpl*; **the idea has potential** l'idée a de l'avenir; **your latest invention has great potential for developing countries** votre dernière invention ouvre de grandes perspectives dans les pays en voie de développement; **the scheme has no potential** le projet n'a aucun avenir; **there is little potential for development in the firm** l'entreprise offre peu de possibilités de développement; **the country's military potential** le potentiel militaire du pays

(**c**) *(of place)* possibilités *fpl*; **the area/garden has real potential** le quartier/le jardin offre de nombreuses possibilités; **the building has a lot of potential** le bâtiment offre de grandes possibilités d'aménagement

(**d**) *Elec, Phys & Math* potentiel *m*

►► *Com & Mktg* ***potential buyer*** acheteur(euse) *m,f* éventuel(elle); *Elec & Phys* ***potential difference*** différence *f* de potentiel; *Elec & Phys* ***potential energy*** énergie *f* potentielle

potentiality [pə,tenʃɪ'ælətɪ] (*pl* **potentialities**) *n* (**a**) *(likelihood)* potentialité *f* (**b**) *(potential)* possibilités *fpl*, perspective *f* (d'avenir); **to have potentialities** offrir de nombreuses possibilités

potentialize, -ise [pə'tenʃəlaɪz] *vt Tech (energy)* convertir en énergie potentielle

potentially [pə'tenʃəlɪ] *adv* potentiellement; **she's potentially a great writer** elle pourrait être un grand écrivain; **potentially lethal poisons** des poisons *mpl* qui peuvent être mortels

potentiate [pə'tenʃɪeɪt] *vt* (**a**) *(give power to)* donner de la force à (**b**) *(make possible)* rendre possible (**c**) *Physiol (drug)* potentialiser

potentiation [pə,tenʃɪ'eɪʃən] *n Physiol* potentialisation *f*

potentilla [,pəʊtən'tɪlə] *n Bot* potentille *f*

potentiometer [pə,tenʃɪ'ɒmɪtə(r)] *n* potentiomètre *m*

potful ['pɒtfʊl] *n (volume)* (contenu *m* d'un) pot *m*; **a potful of coffee** un pot plein de café, une cafetière pleine

pothead ['pɒthed] *n Fam Drugs slang* gros (grosse) fumeur(euse) *m,f* de haschisch

potheen = **poteen**

pother ['pɒðə(r)] *n* agitation *f*; **to get into a pother over sth** se mettre dans tous ses états au sujet de qch

potherb ['pɒthɜːb] *n (as seasoning)* herbe *f* aromatique; *(as vegetable)* légume *m* vert

potholder ['pɒthəʊldə(r)] *n (in kitchen)* manique *f*, manicle *f*

pothole ['pɒthəʊl] *n* (**a**) *(in road)* fondrière *f*, nid-de-poule *m* (**b**) *(underground)* caverne *f*, grotte *f* (**c**) *(in river)* marmite *f* de géants

potholer ['pɒt,həʊlə(r)] *n Br* spéléologue *mf*

potholing ['pɒt,həʊlɪŋ] *n (UNCOUNT) Br* spéléologie *f*; **to go potholing** faire de la spéléologie

pothook ['pɒthʊk] *n* (**a**) *(in fireplace)* crémaillère *f (crochet en forme de s)* (**b**) *(in writing)* boucle *f*

pothunter ['pɒt,hʌntə(r)] *n Pej* (**a**) *Hunt* chasseur(euse) *m,f* sans scrupules (**b**) *(archaeologist)* archéologue *mf* amateur (**c**) *Sport* chasseur(euse) *m,f* de médailles

potion ['pəʊʃən] *n* (**a**) *Med* potion *f* (**b**) *Fig* potion *f*, breuvage *m*; **magic potion** potion *f* magique

potlatch ['pɒtlætʃ] *n* (**a**) *(Native American ceremony)* potlatch *m* (**b**) *Am Fam (party)* fête *f* bruyante❑

potluck [,pɒt'lʌk] *n Fam* **to take potluck** *(for meal)* manger à la fortune du pot; *(take what one finds)* s'en remettre au hasard❑; **it was just potluck** c'était un pur hasard❑

►► *Am* ***potluck lunch/supper*** déjeuner *m*/dîner *m* où chacun apporte un plat

potman ['pɒtmən] (*pl* **potmen** [-men]) *n Arch* garçon *m* de café

potoo [pɒ'tuː] *n Orn* ibijau *m*

potoroo [ˌpɒtə'ruː] *n Zool* potoroo *m*, potorou *m*

potpourri [ˌpəʊ'pʊərɪ] *n* pot-pourri *m*

potroast ['pɒtrəʊst] *vt* rôtir à la cocotte

Potsdam ['pɒtsdæm] *n* Potsdam

potshard ['pɒtʃɑːd], **potsherd** ['pɒtʃɜːd] *n Archeol* tesson *m* de poterie, fragment *m*

pottage ['pɒtɪdʒ] *n Culin* potage *m* épais

potted ['pɒtɪd] *adj* (**a**) *Hort* en pot

(**b**) *Culin (cooked)* (cuit) en terrine; *(conserved)* (conservé) en terrine *ou* en pot

(**c**) *Fam (condensed → version)* condensé ❑, abrégé ❑; **a potted history of the Second World War** un abrégé d'histoire de la Seconde Guerre mondiale; **she gave me a potted version of the truth** elle m'a donné une version sommaire des faits

(**d**) *Am Fam (drunk)* pété, bourré

►► ***potted meat*** ≃ terrine *f*; ***potted palm*** palmier *m* en pot; ***potted plant*** plante *f* verte; ***potted shrimps*** crevettes *fpl* en conserve

potter ['pɒtə(r)] **1** *n* potier(ère) *m,f*

2 *vi Br Fam* (**a**) *(do odd jobs)* bricoler; **I spent the evening just pottering** j'ai passé la soirée à bricoler

(**b**) *(move about slowly)* traîner, traînasser; **after lunch, I'll potter down to the post office** après le déjeuner, je ferai un saut à la poste

►► ***potter's clay*** argile *f* de potier, terre *f* glaise; *Am* ***potter's field*** cimetière *m* des pauvres; ***potter's wheel*** tour *m* de potier

►**potter about** *Br Fam* **1** *vi* (**a**) *(do odd jobs)* s'occuper ❑, bricoler; **to potter about in the garden** faire de petits travaux *ou* bricoler dans le jardin

(**b**) *(move about slowly)* traîner, traînasser; **pottering about in country lanes in her car** en se baladant dans les chemins de campagne au volant de sa voiture

2 *vt insep* **to potter about the house/garden** faire des petits travaux *ou* bricoler dans la maison/le jardin

►**potter along** *vi Br Fam* aller son petit bonhomme de chemin; **I'd better be pottering along now** bon, il faudrait que je commence à y aller; **I might potter along to the library later** j'irai peut-être faire un tour à la bibliothèque tout à l'heure

►**potter around** = **potter about**

Potteries ['pɒtərɪz] *npl* **the Potteries** la région des poteries dans le Staffordshire (en Angleterre)

pottery ['pɒtərɪ] (*pl* **potteries**) *n* (**a**) *(UNCOUNT) (craft)* poterie *f* (**b**) *(UNCOUNT) (earthenware)* poterie *f*, poteries *fpl*; *(ceramics)* céramiques *fpl*; **a beautiful piece of pottery** une très belle poterie (**c**) *(workshop)* atelier *m* de poterie

potting ['pɒtɪŋ] *n (UNCOUNT)* (**a**) *Hort* rempotage *m* (**b**) *(pottery)* poterie *f*

►► ***potting compost*** terreau *m*; *Br* ***potting shed*** remise *f ou* resserre *f* (de jardin)

potto ['pɒtəʊ] (*pl* **pottos**) *n Zool* potto *m*

pot-trained *adj Br* propre

Pott's disease ['pɒts-] *n Med* mal *m* de Pott

Pott's fracture ['pɒts-] *n Med* fracture *f* de Dupuytren

potty ['pɒtɪ] (*pl* **potties**, *compar* **pottier**, *superl* **pottiest**) **1** *n (for children)* pot *m* (de chambre)

2 *adj Br Fam (crazy)* timbré, dingue; **to go potty** devenir timbré *ou* dingue; **to be potty about sb/sth** être timbré *ou* dingue de qn/qch; **you're driving me potty** tu me rends dingue, tu me fais tourner en bourrique

potty-train *vt* **to potty-train a child** apprendre à un enfant à aller sur son pot

potty-trained *adj* propre

potty-training *n* apprentissage *m* de la propreté

POTUS *Am (written abbr* **President of the United States**) = président des États-Unis d'Amérique

pouch [paʊtʃ] *n* (**a**) *(bag)* (petit) sac *m*; *(for tobacco)* blague *f*; *(for money)* sac *m*, bourse *f*; *(for ammunition)* cartouchière *f*, giberne *f*; *(for gunpowder)* sacoche *f*, sac *m*; *(for mail)* sac *m* (postal) (**b**) *Zool (of rodent → in cheeks)* poche *f*, abajoue *f*; *(of marsupial → pocket of skin)* poche *f* (**c**) *Am (for diplomats)* valise *f* diplomatique

pouched [paʊtʃt] *adj Zool (gen)* à poche; *(monkey)* à abajoues

pouf, pouffe [puːf] *n Br* (**a**) *(cushion)* pouf *m* (**b**) *very Fam* pédé *m*, tapette *f*, = terme injurieux désignant un homosexuel

poulard, poularde ['puːlɑːd] *n Culin* poularde *f*

poult [pəʊlt] *n (young chicken)* (jeune) poulet *m*; *(young turkey)* dindonneau *m*; *(young pheasant, partridge)* pouillard *m*

poulterer ['pəʊltərə(r)] *n Br* volailler(ère) *m,f*

poultice ['pəʊltɪs] **1** *n Med* cataplasme *m*

2 *vt* mettre un cataplasme à

poultry ['pəʊltrɪ] **1** *n (UNCOUNT) (meat)* volaille *f*

2 *npl (birds)* volaille *f*, volailles *fpl*

►► ***poultry farm*** élevage *m* de volaille *or* de volailles; ***poultry farmer*** éleveur(euse) *m,f* de volaille *or* de volailles, aviculteur(trice) *m,f*; ***poultry farming*** élevage *m* de volaille *or* de volailles, aviculture *f*

poultryman ['pəʊltrɪmən] (*pl* **poultrymen** [-mən]) *n* (**a**) *(breeder)* éleveur *m* de volaille *ou* de volailles, aviculteur *m* (**b**) *(dealer)* marchand *m* de volaille, volailler *m*

pounce [paʊns] **1** *vi* sauter, bondir; **the cat crouched nearby, ready to pounce** le chat était tapi là, prêt à bondir; **a man pounced (out) from behind the bush** un homme a surgi de derrière le buisson

2 *n* bond *m*; **with a sudden pounce** d'un bond

►**pounce on, pounce upon** *vt insep* (**a**) *(of animal)* se jeter sur, bondir sur; *(of bird)* se jeter sur, fondre sur; *(of police)* saisir, arrêter; **the customs pounced on the drug-runners** les douaniers ont arrêté les trafiquants de drogue

(**b**) *(in criticism)* bondir sur, sauter sur; **they pounce on your slightest mistake** ils sautent *ou* bondissent sur la moindre de vos erreurs

(**c**) *(seize → opportunity)* sauter sur, saisir

POUND [paʊnd]

livre	►**1 (a), (b)**
fourrière	►**1 (c)**
broyer	►**2 (a)**
cogner (sur)	►**2 (b); 3 (a)**
taper	►**3 (a)**
battre	►**3 (b)**

1 *n* (**a**) *(unit of weight)* = 453,6 grammes, livre *f*; **to sell goods by the pound** vendre des marchandises à la livre; **three pound** *or* **pounds of apples** trois livres *fpl* de pommes; **two dollars a pound** deux dollars la livre; *Fig* **to get one's pound of flesh** obtenir ce que l'on exigeait; **he wants his pound of flesh** il veut son dû à n'importe quel prix

(**b**) *(money)* livre *f*; **have you got change for a pound?** avez-vous la monnaie d'une livre?; **two for a pound** deux pour une livre; **the pound fell yesterday against the Deutschmark** la livre est tombée hier face au Deutsche Mark; **pound coin** pièce *f* d'une livre; **the Lebanese/Maltese pound** la livre libanaise/maltaise; **the pound sterling** la livre sterling

(**c**) *(for dogs, cars)* fourrière *f*

2 *vt* (**a**) *(crush, pulverize → grain)* broyer, concasser; *(→ spices, drugs etc)* piler, broyer; *(→ rocks)* concasser, broyer, piler; **to pound sth to a powder/a paste** réduire qch en poudre/en [illegible]

(**b**) *(hammer, hit)* cogner sur, marteler; *(flatten → earth)* pilonner, tasser; **she pounded the table with her fist** elle martelait la table du poing; **the soldiers' heavy boots pounded the earth** les soldats martelaient le sol de leurs lourdes bottes; **the waves pounded the rocks/boat** les vagues battaient les rochers/venaient s'écraser violemment contre le bateau; **he began pounding the typewriter keys** il commença à taper sur *ou* à marteler le clavier de la machine à écrire

(**c**) *(bombard, shell)* bombarder, pilonner; **they pounded the enemy positions with mortar fire** ils ont bombardé les positions ennemies au mortier

(**d**) *(walk → corridor)* faire les cent pas dans, aller et venir dans; **to pound the streets** battre le pavé; **to pound the beat** *(policeman)* faire sa ronde

3 *vi* (**a**) *(hammer → on table, ceiling)* cogner, taper; *(→ on piano, typewriter)* taper; **the neighbours started pounding on the ceiling** les voisins ont commencé à cogner au plafond; **we had to pound on the door before anyone answered** il a fallu frapper à la porte à coups redoublés avant d'obtenir une réponse; **the waves pounded against the rocks** les vagues battaient les rochers; **the rain was pounding on the roof** la pluie tambourinait sur le toit

(**b**) *(rhythmically → drums)* battre; *(→ heart)* battre fort; *(→ with fear, excitement)* battre la chamade; **my head was pounding from the noise** le bruit me martelait la tête

(**c**) *(run noisily)* **he pounded up/down the stairs** il monta/descendit l'escalier bruyamment; **the horses came pounding along the track** les chevaux arrivaient au grand galop dans un bruit de tonnerre

►► *Culin* ***pound cake*** ≃ quatre-quarts *m inv*; ***pound sign*** (£) symbole *m* de la livre (sterling); *Am (on telephone)* dièse *m*

►**pound away** *vi* (**a**) *(on typewriter, piano, drums)* **he was pounding away at the piano** il martelait les touches du piano; **she's been pounding away at her typewriter since eight o'clock** elle s'acharne sur sa machine à écrire depuis huit heures; **every weekend, he pounds away on his drums** il passe ses week-ends à taper sur sa batterie; **he spent the holidays pounding away at his thesis** il a passé les vacances à travailler dur à sa thèse

(**b**) *(with artillery)* **to pound away at the enemy lines** pilonner sans arrêt les lignes ennemies; **we heard the guns pounding away** nous entendions le bruit incessant des canons

►**pound down** *vt sep* (**a**) *(crush)* piler, concasser; **pound the millet down to a fine powder** réduisez le millet en une poudre fine; **pound the mixture down to a pulp** réduisez le mélange en bouillie

(**b**) *(flatten → earth)* pilonner, tasser

►**pound out** *vt sep* (**a**) *(rhythm)* marteler; **the pianist was pounding out a tune** le pianiste martelait un air

(**b**) *(letter, document)* taper (avec fougue); **she pounds out a book a month** elle sort *ou* écrit un livre par mois

►**pound up** *vt sep* piler, concasser

Pound of flesh

Cette formule ("une livre de chair") vient du *Marchand de Venise*, de Shakespeare, pièce dans laquelle Shylock vient réclamer son dû à Antonio (une livre de la chair de ce dernier) comme dédommagement pour n'avoir pas tenu ses engagements.

Aujourd'hui on utilise cette expression pour parler des conditions exactes d'un contrat ou d'une façon plus générale en référence à une somme d'argent qu'un débiteur est dans l'incapacité de payer. On pourra dire par exemple **We're barely able to make ends meet as it is, the last thing we need is the taxman asking for his pound of flesh** ("on a déjà du mal à joindre les deux bouts, on n'a vraiment pas besoin que le percepteur vienne nous réclamer de l'argent").

poundage ['paʊndɪdʒ] *n (UNCOUNT)* (**a**) *(on weight)* droits *mpl* perçus par livre de poids (**b**) *(on value)* droits *mpl* perçus par livre de valeur (**c**) *(weight)* poids *m* (en livres)

-pounder ['paʊndə(r)] *suff* **a fifteen-pounder** *(fish)* un poisson de quinze livres; **a two-hundred-pounder** *(shell)* un obus de deux cents livres; **a six-pounder** *(gun)* un canon *ou* une pièce de six

pounding ['paʊndɪŋ] *n* (**a**) *(noise)* martèlement *m*

(**b**) *(UNCOUNT) (beating → of heart)* battements *mpl*; **I could hear the pounding of her heart** j'entendais son cœur qui battait à tout rompre

(**c**) *Fam (battering)* rossée *f*; **he took a real pounding in the first five rounds** il a pris une bonne volée *ou* il s'est drôlement fait rosser pendant les cinq premières reprises; **the jetty/harbour took a pounding in the storm** la jetée/le port en a pris un coup pendant la tempête; **the dollar took a severe pounding last week** le dollar a été sérieusement malmené la semaine dernière

(**d**) *Fam (severe defeat)* déculottée *f*, piquette *f*; **the team took a real pounding last week**

pot–pou

l'équipe a subi une lourde défaite *ou* s'est fait battre à plate couture la semaine dernière

pour [pɔː(r)] **1** *vt* (**a**) *(liquid)* verser; *(serve)* servir, verser; *Metal* couler; **to pour a drink for sb** servir à boire à qn; **pour yourself a drink** servez-vous *ou* versez-vous à boire; **may I pour you some wine?** je vous sers du vin?; **would you pour the tea?** voulez-vous servir le thé?; **she poured milk into their mugs** elle a versé du lait dans leurs tasses; **we poured the water/wine down the sink** nous avons vidé l'eau/jeté le vin dans l'évier; **pour the cider into the jug** versez le cidre dans le pichet; **her jeans were so tight she looked as if she'd been poured into them** son jean était tellement serré qu'elle semblait avoir été coulée dedans; **to pour cold water on** *or* **over sb's plans** décourager *ou* refroidir qn dans ses projets; **to pour scorn on sb** traiter qn avec mépris

(**b**) *(supply in large amounts)* **he poured all his energies into the project** il a mis toute son énergie dans le projet; **the government poured money into the industry** le gouvernement a investi des sommes énormes dans cette industrie; **I've already poured a fortune into the firm** j'ai déjà investi une fortune dans la société; **they poured reinforcements into the area** ils ont envoyé des renforts en masse dans la région

2 *vi* (**a**) *(liquid)* se déverser, couler à flots; **water poured from the gutters** l'eau débordait des gouttières; **water was pouring into the cellar** l'eau entrait à flots dans la cave; **tears poured down her face** elle pleurait à chaudes larmes; **blood poured from the wound** la blessure saignait abondamment; **the sweat was pouring off him/his back** il/son dos ruisselait de sueur; **light poured into the church** l'église était inondée de lumière; **smoke poured out of the blazing building** des nuages de fumée s'échappaient de l'immeuble en flammes

(**b**) *(rain)* pleuvoir à verse; **it's pouring (with rain)** il pleut à verse *ou* à torrents

(**c**) *(crowd)* affluer; **reporters pour into Cannes for the festival** les journalistes affluent à Cannes pour le festival; **spectators poured into/out of the cinema** une foule de spectateurs entrait dans le cinéma/sortait du cinéma; **thousands of cars poured out of Paris** des milliers de voitures se pressaient aux portes de Paris

(**d**) *(pan, jug)* **to pour well/badly** verser bien/mal

(**e**) *(serve a drink)* **shall I pour?** je fais le service?

▶**pour away** *vt sep (empty)* vider; *(throw out)* jeter

▶**pour down** *vi (rain)* tomber à verse; **it's been pouring down for days** il pleut à verse depuis des jours et des jours

▶**pour forth** *vi Literary (light, water)* se déverser; *(people)* affluer

▶**pour in** *vi* (**a**) *(rain, light, water)* entrer à flots; **rain poured in through a hole in the roof** la pluie entrait à flots par un trou dans le plafond

(**b**) *(cars, refugees, spectators)* arriver en masse; *(information, reports)* affluer, arriver en masse; **the crowd came pouring in** la foule est entrée en masse; **offers of help poured in from all sides** des offres d'aide ont afflué de toutes parts; **money poured in for the disaster victims** des milliers de dons ont été envoyés pour les victimes de la catastrophe

▶**pour off** *vt sep (liquid, excess)* vider

▶**pour on** *vt sep (cream)* verser

▶**pour out 1** *vt sep* (**a**) *(liquid)* verser

(**b**) *(information, propaganda)* répandre, diffuser; *(of chimney → clouds of smoke)* cracher, vomir; **the industry pours out tons of dangerous chemicals** l'industrie déverse des tonnes de produits chimiques dangereux

(**c**) *(emotions)* donner libre cours à; **she poured out all her troubles to me** elle m'a raconté tout ce qu'elle avait sur le cœur; **to pour out one's heart to sb** parler à qn à cœur ouvert; **to pour out a torrent of abuse at sb** déverser un torrent d'injures sur qn

2 *vi* (**a**) *(water)* jaillir, couler à flots; *(tears)* couler abondamment; *(light)* jaillir; **smoke was pouring out of the window** des nuages de fumée s'échappaient de la fenêtre; **the words just poured out** les mots sont sortis en flots; **all his feelings came pouring out** il a laissé libre cours à ses émotions

(**b**) *(people)* sortir en masse

pourer ['pɔːrə(r)] *n (gen)* verseur *m*; *Metal (ladle man)* couleur *m*; **this teapot isn't a good pourer** cette théière verse mal

pouring ['pɔːrɪŋ] *adj* (**a**) *(rain)* battant, diluvien; **we were stranded in the pouring rain** nous étions coincés sous une pluie battante (**b**) *(cream)* liquide; **the sauce should be of pouring consistency** il faut que la sauce soit bien liquide

poussin ['puːsæn] *n Br Culin* poussin *m*

pout [paʊt] *(pl sense* (**b**) **inv** *or* **pouts**) **1** *vi* faire la moue

2 *vt* dire en faisant la moue

3 *n* (**a**) *(facial expression)* moue *f*; **with a pout** en faisant la moue (**b**) *(fish → eelpout)* lycode *m*, lotte *f*; *(→ whiting)* tacaud *m*

pouter ['paʊtə(r)] *n Orn* boulant *m*

pouting ['paʊtɪŋ] *n (sulking)* moue *f*

POV [ˌpiːəʊ'viː] *n TV & Cin (abbr* **point of view**) angle *m* du regard

poverty ['pɒvətɪ] *n* (**a**) *(financial)* pauvreté *f*, misère *f*; **to live in poverty** vivre dans le besoin

(**b**) *(shortage → of resources)* manque *m*; *(→ of ideas, imagination)* pauvreté *f*, manque *m*; *(weakness → of style, arguments)* pauvreté *f*, faiblesse *f*

(**c**) *(of soil)* pauvreté *f*, aridité *f*

▶▶ ***poverty line*** seuil *m* de pauvreté; **to live on/below the poverty line** vivre à la limite/en dessous du seuil de pauvreté; ***poverty trap*** = situation inextricable de ceux qui dépendent de prestations sociales qu'ils perdent pour peu qu'ils trouvent une activité, même peu rémunérée

poverty-stricken *adj (person)* dans la misère, dans le plus grand dénuement; *(areas)* misérable, où sévit la misère

POW [ˌpiːəʊ'dʌbəljuː] *n (abbr* **prisoner of war**) PG *m*

pow [paʊ] *onomat (from collision)* vlan, v'lan; *(from gun)* pan

powan [paʊən] *n Ich* (corégone *m*) lavaret *m*

powder ['paʊdə(r)] **1** *n* (**a**) *(gen)* & *Mil* poudre *f*; **in powder form** en poudre, sous forme de poudre; **to grind sth to a powder** réduire qch en poudre, pulvériser qch; *Br Fig* **to keep one's powder dry** se tenir prêt, être aux aguets

(**b**) *(snow)* poudreuse *f*

(**c**) *(for face)* poudre *f*

(**d**) *Old-fashioned* **to take a headache powder** prendre un médicament (en sachet) contre le mal de tête

(**e**) *Am Fam (idiom)* **to take a powder** *(disappear)* ficher le camp, décamper

2 *vt* (**a**) *(crush, pulverize)* pulvériser, réduire en poudre

(**b**) *(make up)* poudrer; **to powder one's face** se poudrer le visage; *Euph* **to powder one's nose** *(go to the toilet)* aller se repoudrer le nez

(**c**) *(sprinkle)* saupoudrer; **the Christmas tree was powdered with artificial snow** le sapin de Noël était saupoudré de neige artificielle

▶▶ ***powder blue*** bleu *m* pastel; ***powder compact*** poudrier *m*; ***powder eyeshadow*** ombre *f* à paupières en poudre; ***powder horn*** corne *f*, cartouche *f* à poudre; ***powder keg*** *(of gunpowder)* baril *m* de poudre; *Fig* poudrière *f*; ***powder puff*** houppette *f*; *Euph* **powder room** toilettes *fpl* (pour dames)

powder-blue *adj* bleu pastel *(inv)*

powdered ['paʊdəd] *adj* (**a**) *(milk)* en poudre; *(coffee)* instantané (**b**) *(hair, face)* poudré

▶▶ *Am* ***powdered sugar*** sucre *m* glace

powderiness ['paʊdərɪnɪs] *n* pulvérulence *f*

powdery ['paʊdərɪ] *adj* (**a**) *(covered in powder)* couvert de poudre (**b**) *(like powder)* poudreux; **powdery snow** (neige *f*) poudreuse *f* (**c**) *(crumbling)* friable

POWER ['paʊə(r)]

puissance	▶ **1 (a), (c), (d)**
force	▶ **1 (a)**
pouvoir	▶ **1 (b), (e), (f)**
capacité	▶ **1 (e)**
faculté	▶ **1 (f)**
courant	▶ **1 (g)**
faire fonctionner	▶ **2**

1 *n* (**a**) *(strength, force → gen)* puissance *f*, force *f*; *Phys (→ of engine, lens, microscope)* puissance *f*; *(→ of magnet)* force *f*; **I underestimated the power of the explosion** j'ai sous-estimé la puissance *ou* la force de l'explosion; **they could see the power of his muscles** ils voyaient travailler ses muscles puissants; **we want greater economic and industrial power** nous voulons renforcer la puissance économique et industrielle; **at full power** à plein régime; **the vehicle moves under its own power** le véhicule se déplace par ses propres moyens *ou* de façon autonome; **sea/air power** puissance *f* maritime/aérienne; *Fam* **the holiday did me a power of good** les vacances m'ont fait un bien fou; *Br Fam* **more power to your elbow!** bonne chance! ❑, bon courage! ❑

(**b**) *(influence, control)* & *Pol* pouvoir *m*; *(authority)* autorité *f*, pouvoir *m*; **the power of the Church/of student unions** le pouvoir de l'Église/des syndicats étudiants; **to have sb in one's power** avoir qn en son pouvoir; **to be in sb's power** être à la merci de qn; **to fall into sb's power** tomber au pouvoir de qn; **to be in power** être au pouvoir; **to come (in)to/to take power** arriver au/prendre le pouvoir; **to lose power** perdre le pouvoir; **to have the power to decide/judge** avoir le pouvoir de décider/juger, avoir autorité pour décider/juger; **absolute/executive/legislative power** pouvoir absolu/exécutif/législatif; **the committee doesn't really have much power** le comité n'a pas grand pouvoir; **to act with full powers** agir de pleine autorité; **the police have been given greater powers** la police a reçu des pouvoirs plus importants; **it's beyond** *or* **outside my power(s)** cela dépasse ma compétence *ou* ne relève pas de mon autorité; **it's beyond my power to do anything** je n'ai pas compétence en la matière, je ne suis pas habilité à intervenir

(**c**) *(influential group or person)* puissance *f*; **the President is the real power in the land** c'est le président qui détient le véritable pouvoir dans le pays; **to be a power in the land** avoir une grande influence *ou* être très puissant dans un pays; **the powers of darkness** les forces *fpl* *ou* puissances *fpl* des ténèbres; **the (real) power behind the throne** *(individual)* l'éminence *f* grise, celui (celle) *m,f* qui tire les ficelles; *(group)* ceux *mpl* qui tirent les ficelles, les véritables acteurs *mpl*; *also Hum* **the powers that be** les autorités *fpl* constituées; **no power on earth will persuade me to go** rien au monde ne me persuadera d'y aller

(**d**) *Pol (state)* puissance *f*; **the great Western powers** les grandes puissances occidentales; **industrial/nuclear/world power** *(country)* puissance industrielle/nucléaire/mondiale

(**e**) *(ability, capacity)* capacité *f*, pouvoir *m*; **he has great powers as an orator** *or* **great oratorical powers** il a de grands talents oratoires; **to be at the height** *or* **peak of one's powers** être à l'apogée de sa puissance; **it's within her power to do it** c'est en son pouvoir, elle est capable de le faire; **I'll do everything in my power to help you** je ferai tout mon possible *ou* tout ce qui est en mon pouvoir pour vous aider; **magical/aphrodisiacal powers** pouvoirs *mpl* magiques/aphrodisiaques; **to have great powers of persuasion/suggestion** avoir un grand pouvoir *ou* une grande force de persuasion/suggestion; **the body's powers of resistance** la capacité de résistance du corps; **she has great intellectual powers** elle a de grandes capacités intellectuelles; *Phys & Chem* **power of absorption** capacité *f* d'absorption

(**f**) *(faculty)* faculté *f*, pouvoir *m*; **her powers are failing** ses facultés déclinent; **the power of sight** la vue; **the power of hearing** l'ouïe *f*; **the power of reason** la raison; **he lost the power of speech** il a perdu l'usage de la parole

(**g**) *Elec (current)* courant *m*; **to turn on/cut off the power** mettre/couper le courant

(**h**) *Elec & Phys (energy)* énergie *f*; **nuclear/solar power** énergie *f* nucléaire/solaire

(**i**) *Law (proxy)* pouvoir *m*

(**j**) *Math* puissance *f*; **5 to the power (of) 6** 5 puissance 6; **raised to the 5th power** élevé à la puissance 5

2 *comp (source, consumption)* d'énergie; *(cable)* électrique; *(brakes)* assisté

3 *vt (give power to)* faire fonctionner *ou* marcher; *(propel)* propulser; **powered by solar energy** fonctionnant à l'énergie solaire; **the boat is powered by gas turbines** le bateau est propulsé par des turbines à gaz

4 *vi* avancer à toute vitesse, foncer; **he powered into his opponent** il fonça sur son adversaire; **the leading cars powered down the home straight** les voitures de tête foncèrent dans la dernière ligne; **his business is powering on** son affaire monte en puissance

►► *Law* ***power of attorney*** procuration *f*; **to give sb power of attorney** donner procuration à qn; ***power base*** assise *f* politique; *Mktg* ***power brand*** marque *f* forte; ***power breakfast*** = petit déjeuner d'affaires entre personnes importantes; ***power broker*** décideur(euse) *m,f* politique; ***power cut*** coupure *f* de courant; *Aviat* ***power dive*** (descente *f* en) piqué *m*; *Br* ***power dressing*** = façon de s'habiller qu'adoptent certaines femmes cadres dans le but de projeter une image d'autorité; ***power drill*** perceuse *f* électrique; ***power failure*** panne *f* de courant; ***power game*** lutte *f* d'influence, course *f* au pouvoir; ***power line*** ligne *f* à haute tension; ***power lunch*** déjeuner *m* d'affaires entre personnes importantes; *Am* ***power outage*** rupture *f* de l'alimentation; *Elec* ***power pack*** bloc *m* d'alimentation électrique; ***power plant*** *(factory)* centrale *f* électrique; *(generator)* groupe *m* électrogène; *(engine)* groupe *m* moteur; ***power play*** *(in ice hockey)* coup *m* de force; ***power point*** prise *f* de courant; ***power politics*** *(UNCOUNT)* politique *f* du coup de force; *Math* ***power set*** ensemble *m* des sous-ensembles; *Pol* ***power sharing*** partage *m* du pouvoir; ***power shower*** douche *f* à jet puissant; ***power station*** centrale *f* (électrique); *Aut* ***power steering*** direction *f* assistée; ***power strike*** grève *f* des employés de l'électricité; ***power structure*** *(system)* hiérarchie *f*, répartition *f* des pouvoirs; *(people with power)* = ensemble des personnes qui détiennent le pouvoir; ***power struggle*** lutte *f* pour le pouvoir; ***power supply*** *Elec* alimentation *f* (électrique); *Comput* transformateur *m*; ***power tool*** outil *m* électrique; *Comput* ***power unit*** dispositif *m* d'alimentation; ***power user*** gros (grosse) utilisateur(trice) *m,f*; *Comput* = personne qui sait utiliser au mieux les ressources de son ordinateur; ***power walking*** marche *f* sportive; ***power worker*** employé(e) *m,f* de l'électricité; ***power yoga*** power yoga *m* *(forme de yoga où l'on travaille en puissance)*

►**power down, power off** **1** *vt sep* éteindre, mettre hors tension

2 *vi (computer, machine)* s'éteindre, se mettre hors tension

►**power up** **1** *vt sep* mettre sous tension, allumer

2 *vi (computer, machine)* se mettre sous tension, s'allumer

'The Power and the Glory' *Greene* 'La Puissance et la gloire'

---

power-assisted *adj* assisté

powerboat ['paʊəbəʊt] *n (outboard)* hors-bord *m inv*; *(inboard)* vedette *f* (rapide)

►► ***powerboat racing*** courses *fpl* offshore

power-down *n Comput* mise *f* hors tension

-powered ['paʊəd] *suff* **high/low-powered** de haute/faible puissance; **a high-powered executive** un cadre très haut placé; **steam/wind-powered** mû par la vapeur/le vent; **jet-powered** propulsé par un moteur à réaction

powerful ['paʊəfʊl] **1** *adj* (**a**) *(strong* → *gen)* puissant; *(*→ *smell)* fort; *(*→ *kick)* violent; *(*→ *imagination)* débordant; *(*→ *language, prose style)* vigoureux, qui a de l'impact; **a powerful swimmer** un excellent nageur; **she has a very powerful voice** elle a une voix très puissante; **the engine isn't powerful enough** le moteur n'est pas assez puissant; **powerful binoculars** jumelles *fpl* puissantes *ou* à fort grossissement; **powerful drugs** médication *f* puissante *ou* active; **he has been a powerful influence in her life** il a exercé une influence décisive dans sa vie

(**b**) *(influential* → *person)* fort, influent; *(*→ *country, firm)* puissant

2 *adv Br Fam* vachement; **to try powerful hard** faire un effort surhumain

powerfully ['paʊəfʊlɪ] *adv* puissamment; **he's powerfully built** il est d'une stature imposante

powerfulness ['paʊəfʊlnɪs] *n* puissance *f*, force *f*

Power Gen [-dʒen] *n* = entreprise privée de production d'électricité en Angleterre et au pays de Galles

powerhouse ['paʊəhaʊs, *pl* -haʊzɪz] *n* (**a**) *Elec* centrale *f* électrique (**b**) *Fig (person)* personne *f* énergique, locomotive *f*; *(place)* pépinière *f*; **she's a powerhouse of energy** elle déborde d'énergie; **the university became a powerhouse of new ideas** l'université est devenue une vraie pépinière d'idées nouvelles

powerless ['paʊəlɪs] *adj* impuissant, désarmé; **they were powerless to prevent the scandal** ils n'ont rien pu faire pour éviter le scandale; **our arguments were powerless in the face of such conviction** nos arguments sont restés lettre morte devant une telle conviction

powerlessly ['paʊəlɪslɪ] *adv* sans pouvoir rien faire; **I watched powerlessly as the dogs attacked** j'ai regardé, impuissant, les chiens attaquer

powerlessness ['paʊəlɪsnɪs] *n* impuissance *f*

power-on key *n Br Comput* touche *f* d'alimentation

powertrain ['paʊətreɪn] *n Aut* groupe *m* motopropulseur

powwow ['paʊwaʊ] **1** *n (of American Indians)* assemblée *f*; *Fam Fig (meeting)* réunion ❑ *f*; *(discussion)* discussion ❑ *f*, pourparlers ❑ *mpl*; **to have** *or* **to hold a powwow** *(American Indians)* tenir une assemblée; *Fam Fig* discuter ❑

2 *vi (American Indians)* tenir une assemblée; *Fam Fig (talk)* discuter ❑

Powys ['paʊɪs] *n* le Powys, = comté de l'est du pays de Galles; **in Powys** dans le Powys

pox [pɒks] *n Fam* vérole ❑ *f*; *Arch* **a pox on him!** qu'il aille au diable!

poxy ['pɒksɪ] *(compar* **poxier**, *superl* **poxiest**) *adj Fam* (**a**) *Med* vérolé ❑ (**b**) *Br (worthless)* minable; **he only gave me a poxy five pounds for it** il me l'a acheté (pour) cinq malheureuses livres

pozidriv® ['pɒzɪdraɪv] *n* **pozidriv**® **screw** vis *m* pozidriv®

Poznan ['pɒznən] *n* Poznan

pp [,piː'piː] *(abbr* **per procurationem**) **1** *adv* **pp Jane Smith** pp Jane Smith

2 *vt* **shall I pp it?** est-ce que je signe à votre/sa place?

pp. *(written abbr* **pages**) pp.; **see pp. 44 to 47** voir pp. 44 à 47

PPB [,piːpiː'biː] *n Acct (abbr* **planning-programming-budgeting system**) système *m* de planification-programmation-budgétisation, rationalisation *f* des choix budgétaires

PPD [,piːpiː'diː] *adj Com (abbr* **prepaid**) port payé par le destinataire

PPE [,piːpiː'iː] *n Br (abbr* **philosophy, politics and economics**) = philosophie, science politique et science économique (cours à l'université d'Oxford)

ppm (**a**) *(written abbr* **parts per million**) ppm (**b**) *(written abbr* **pages per minute**) ppm

PPP [,piːpiː'piː] *n Comput (abbr* **point-to-point protocol**) protocole *m* PPP, protocole *m* point à point

PPS [,piːpiː'es] *n* (**a**) *Br (abbr* **parliamentary private secretary**) = en Grande-Bretagne, député qui assure la liaison entre un ministre et la Chambre des communes (**b**) *(abbr* **post postscriptum**) PPS

ppsi *(written abbr* **pounds per square inch**) = livres au pouce carré (mesure de pression)

ppv [,piːpiː'viː] *TV (abbr* **pay-per-view**) **1** *n* système *m* de télévision à la carte

2 *adj* à la carte

PQ [,piː'kjuː] *n Can* (**a**) *(abbr* **Province of Quebec**) province *f* de Québec (**b**) *(abbr* **Parti québécois**) PQ *m*

PR[1] [,piː'ɑː(r)] *n* (**a**) *(abbr* **public relations**) relations *fpl* publiques, RP *fpl*; **we need better PR** il nous faut améliorer nos relations publiques; **a skilful PR man** un homme qui excelle dans les relations publiques; **who does their PR?** qui est-ce qui s'occupe de leurs relations publiques?

(**b**) *Pol (abbr* **proportional representation**) RP *f*

►► ***PR agency*** agence *f* conseil en communication; ***PR company*** société *f* conseil en communication; ***PR consultancy*** agence *f* conseil en communication; ***PR consultant*** conseil *m* en communication

PR[2] (**a**) *(written abbr* **Puerto Rico**) Porto Rico (**b**) *Am Pej (written abbr* **Puerto Rican**) Portoricain(e) *m,f*

Pr. *(written abbr* **prince**) Pce

practicability [,præktɪkə'bɪlətɪ] *n* (**a**) *(of plan, action)* faisabilité *f*, viabilité *f*; **we discussed the practicability of the project** nous avons discuté de la viabilité du projet (**b**) *(of road)* praticabilité *f*

practicable ['præktɪkəbəl] *adj* (**a**) *(feasible)* réalisable, praticable; *(possible)* possible; **as far as practicable** autant que possible, autant que faire se peut (**b**) *(road)* praticable

practical ['præktɪkəl] **1** *adj* (**a**) *(convenient, easy to use)* pratique, commode; **this electric screwdriver is very practical** ce tournevis électrique est très pratique

(**b**) *(sensible, commonsense* → *person)* (qui a le sens) pratique, doué de sens pratique; *(*→ *mind, suggestion)* pratique; **my sister's the practical one** s'il y a quelqu'un qui a le sens pratique, c'est bien ma sœur; **now, be practical, we can't afford a new car** allons, un peu de bon sens, nous n'avons pas les moyens de nous offrir une nouvelle voiture; **is white the most practical colour?** le blanc, c'est ce qu'il y a de plus pratique comme couleur?

(**c**) *(training, experience, question)* pratique, concret(ète); **does it have any practical application?** est-ce qu'il y a une application pratique?; **for all practical purposes** à toutes fins utiles; **he has a practical knowledge of German** il connaît l'allemand usuel

(**d**) *(virtual)* **it's a practical impossibility** c'est pratiquement impossible

2 *n Br Sch & Univ (class)* travaux *mpl* pratiques, TP *mpl*; *(exam)* épreuve *f* pratique

►► ***practical joke*** farce *f*; **to play a practical joke on sb** faire une farce *ou* jouer un tour à qn; ***practical joker*** farceur(euse) *m,f*; *Am* ***practical nurse*** aide-soignant(e) *m,f*

practicality [,præktɪ'kælətɪ] *(pl* **practicalities**) **1** *n (of person)* sens *m* pratique; *(of ideas)* nature *f* pratique; **I'm not too sure about the practicality of his suggestions** je doute que ses propositions puissent trouver une application pratique

2 practicalities *npl (details)* détails *mpl* pratiques; **let's get down to practicalities** venons-en aux détails pratiques

practically ['præktɪkəlɪ] *adv* (**a**) *(sensibly)* de manière pratique; **she very practically suggested telephoning home** elle a eu la bonne idée de suggérer qu'on téléphone chez elle; **to be practically dressed** être habillé de façon pratique

(**b**) *(based on practice)* pratiquement; **the whole course is very much practically based** le cours est fondé en grande partie sur la pratique

(**c**) *(almost)* presque, pratiquement; **there has been practically no snow** il n'y a presque *ou* pratiquement pas eu de neige; **practically the whole of the audience** la quasi-totalité de l'auditoire; **we're practically there** nous y sommes presque, nous sommes pratiquement arrivés

(**d**) *(in practice)* dans la pratique; **practically speaking** en fait

practical-minded *adj* **to be practical-minded** avoir le sens pratique

practicalness ['præktɪkəlnɪs] *n (of person)* sens *m* pratique; *(of ideas)* nature *f* pratique

practice ['præktɪs] **1** *n* (**a**) *(habit)* pratique *f*, habitude *f*; *(custom)* pratique *f*, coutume *f*, usage *m*; **tribal/religious practices** pratiques *fpl* tribales/religieuses; **they make a regular practice of going jogging on Sundays** ils font régulièrement du jogging le dimanche; **he makes a practice of voting against** *or* **he makes it a practice to vote against the government** il se fait une règle de voter contre le gouvernement; **they've introduced the practice of morning**

pow–pra

prayer ils ont introduit la prière du matin; **it's not company practice to refund deposits** il n'est pas dans les habitudes de la société de rembourser les arrhes; **it's normal practice among most shopkeepers** c'est une pratique courante chez les commerçants; **it's our usual practice** c'est ce que nous faisons habituellement, c'est notre politique habituelle; **it's standard practice to make a written request** la procédure habituelle veut que l'on fasse une demande par écrit

(**b**) *(exercise → of profession, witchcraft, archery)* pratique *f*

(**c**) *(training)* entraînement *m*; *(rehearsal)* répétition *f*; *(study → of instrument)* étude *f*, travail *m*; **I've had a lot of practice at** *or* **in dealing with difficult negotiations** j'ai une grande habitude des négociations difficiles; **it's good practice for your interview** c'est un bon entraînement pour votre entrevue; **to be in practice** être bien entraîné; **to be out of practice** manquer d'entraînement; **I'm getting out of practice** *(on piano)* je commence à avoir les doigts rouillés; *(at sport)* je commence à manquer d'entraînement; *(at skill)* je commence à perdre la main; **it's time for your piano practice** c'est l'heure de travailler ton piano; *Sport* **Schumacher was fastest in practice** Schumacher a été le plus rapide aux essais; *Prov* **practice makes perfect** c'est en forgeant qu'on devient forgeron

(**d**) *(training session)* (séance *f* d')entraînement *m*; *(rehearsal → of choir)* répétition *f*

(**e**) *(practical application)* pratique *f*; **to put sth in** *or* **into practice** mettre qch en pratique; **in practice** dans la pratique

(**f**) *(professional activity)* exercice *m*; **to be in practice as a doctor** exercer en tant que médecin; **to go into** *or* **to set up in practice as a doctor** s'installer comme médecin, ouvrir un cabinet de médecin; **medical/legal practice** l'exercice *m* de la médecine/de la profession d'avocat

(**g**) *(office, surgery)* cabinet *m*; *(clientele)* clientèle *f*; **he has a country practice** il est médecin de campagne

2 *comp (game, run, session)* d'entraînement

3 *vt & vi Am* = **practise**

►► *Golf* ***practice ground*** practice *m*; *Sport* ***practice match*** match *m* d'entraînement

practiced *Am* = **practised**

practicing *Am* = **practising**

practise, *Am* **practice** ['præktɪs] **1** *vt* (**a**) *(for improvement → musical instrument)* s'exercer à, travailler; *(→ song)* travailler, répéter; *(→ foreign language)* travailler, pratiquer; *(→ stroke, shot)* travailler; **she was practising a Chopin nocturne** elle travaillait un nocturne de Chopin; **can I practise my French on you?** est-ce que je peux parler français *ou* pratiquer mon français avec vous?; **to practise speaking French** s'entraîner à parler français; **you should practise your backhand** vous devriez travailler votre revers

(**b**) *(put into practice → principle, virtue)* pratiquer, mettre en pratique; **in this school, we practise self-discipline** dans cette école, on pratique l'autodiscipline; **you should practise what you preach** vous devriez donner l'exemple; **he doesn't practise what he preaches** il ne met pas en pratique ce qu'il prêche

(**c**) *(profession)* exercer, pratiquer; **he practises medicine** il pratique *ou* exerce la médecine; **to practise law** exercer le métier de notaire/d'avocat; **he studied law/medicine, but never practised it** il a étudié le droit/la médecine, mais n'a jamais exercé

(**d**) *(inflict)* infliger; **the cruelty they practised on their victims** les cruautés qu'ils infligeaient à *ou* les sévices qu'ils faisaient subir à leurs victimes

(**e**) *(customs, beliefs)* observer, pratiquer; **pagan rituals are still practised in the area** on pratique encore certains rites païens dans la région

(**f**) *Rel* pratiquer

(**g**) *(magic)* pratiquer

2 *vi* (**a**) *(gen) & Mus* s'entraîner, s'exercer; *Sport* s'entraîner; **I'm just practising** je ne fais que m'entraîner; **she practises a few hours every day** elle s'entraîne plusieurs heures par jour; **to practise on the guitar** faire des exercices à la guitare

(**b**) *(professionally)* exercer; **he practises in Edinburgh** il exerce à Édimbourg

(**c**) *Rel* être pratiquant

practised, *Am* **practiced** ['præktɪst] *adj* (**a**) *(experienced)* expérimenté, chevronné; *(skilled)* habile; **practised in the arts of seduction/deception** rompu aux arts de la séduction/tromperie

(**b**) *(expert → aim, movement)* expert; *(→ ear, eye)* exercé; **with a practised hand** d'une main exercée *ou* habile; **with practised ease** avec une grande aisance

(**c**) *(artificial → smile, charm)* factice, étudié

practising, *Am* **practicing** ['præktɪsɪŋ] *adj* (**a**) *Rel* pratiquant; **he's a practising Jew** c'est un juif pratiquant (**b**) *(professionally → doctor)* exerçant; *(→ lawyer, solicitor)* en exercice (**c**) *(homosexual)* actif

practitioner [præk'tɪʃənə(r)] *n* (**a**) *Med* **(medical) practitioner** médecin *m* (**b**) *(gen)* praticien(enne) *m,f*

praesidium = **presidium**

praetor = **pretor**

praetorian = **pretorian**

pragmatic [præg'mætɪk] *adj* pragmatique; **from a pragmatic point of view** d'un point de vue pratique

►► *Hist* ***pragmatic sanction*** pragmatique sanction *f*

pragmatically [præg'mætɪkəlɪ] *adv* pragmatiquement

pragmatics [præg'mætɪks] *n (UNCOUNT) Ling* pragmatique *f*

pragmatism ['prægmətɪzəm] *n* pragmatisme *m*

pragmatist ['prægmətɪst] *n* pragmatiste *mf*

Prague [prɑːg] *n* Prague

►► ***the Prague spring*** le printemps de Prague

prairie ['preərɪ] **1** *n* plaine *f* (herbeuse)

2 Prairie *n* **the Prairie** *or* **Prairies** *(in US)* la Grande Prairie; *(in Canada)* les Prairies *fpl*

►► *Orn* ***prairie chicken*** poule *f* des prairies; *Zool* ***prairie dog*** chien *m* de prairie; ***prairie oyster*** *(drink)* = boisson à base d'œuf cru (remède contre les excès d'alcool); *(offal)* = délices de brebis; ***Prairie Provinces*** les provinces *fpl* des Prairies *(au Canada)*; **in the Prairie Provinces** dans les (provinces des) Prairies; *Am Fam* ***prairie schooner*** petit chariot *m* (à bâche)❑; ***the Prairie State*** = surnom donné à l'Illinois; *Zool* ***prairie wolf*** coyote *m*

praise [preɪz] **1** *n* (**a**) *(compliments)* éloge *m*, louanges *fpl*; **she was full of praise for their kindness** elle ne tarissait pas d'éloges sur leur gentillesse; **he was full of our praise** *or* **praises** il ne tarissait pas d'éloges sur notre compte; **I have nothing but praise for him** je n'ai rien pour lui que des éloges *ou* louanges; **she deserves special praise** elle mérite tous les éloges *ou* toutes les louanges; **her film has received high praise from the critics** son film a été couvert d'éloges par la critique; **it is beyond praise** on ne saurait être trop élogieux

(**b**) *Rel* louange *f*, louanges *fpl*, gloire *f*; **to give praise to the Lord** rendre gloire à Dieu; **praise (be to) the Lord!** Dieu soit loué!; *Old-fashioned* **praise be!** Dieu merci!; **hymn** *or* **song of praise** cantique *m*

2 *vt* (**a**) *(gen)* louer, faire l'éloge de; **he praised her for her patience** il la loua de *ou* pour sa patience; **he praised her for having been so patient** il la loua d'avoir été si patiente; **to praise sb to high heaven** *or* **to the skies** couvrir qn d'éloges, porter qn aux nues

(**b**) *Rel* louer, glorifier, rendre gloire à

3 in praise of *prep* à la louange de; **the director spoke in praise of his staff** le directeur fit l'éloge de son personnel; **she gave a speech in praise of the institute's work** elle fit un discours à la louange des travaux de l'institut

praiseworthiness ['preɪz,wɜːðɪnɪs] *n* mérite *m*

praiseworthy ['preɪz,wɜːðɪ] *adj (person)* digne d'éloges; *(action, intention, sentiment)* louable, méritoire

Prakrit ['prɑːkrɪt] *n Ling* prakrit *m*

praline ['prɑːliːn] *n* pralin *m*

PRAM [præm] *n Comput (abbr* **programmable random access memory**) RAM *f* programmable

pram [præm] *n* (**a**) *Br (for baby)* voiture *f* d'enfant, landau *m* (**b**) *Naut* prame *f*

prance [prɑːns] **1** *vi* (**a**) *(cavort → horse)* caracoler, cabrioler; *(→ person)* caracoler, gambader; **the horses came prancing into the circus ring** les chevaux sont entrés en caracolant sur la piste du cirque (**b**) *(strut)* se pavaner, se dandiner; **he came prancing into the room** il entra dans la pièce en se pavanant

2 *n* sautillement *m*

▸**prance about** *vi (horse)* caracoler; *(person)* se pavaner

prancing ['prɑːnsɪŋ] *n (of horse)* caracoles *fpl*; *(of person)* gambades *fpl*

prandial ['prændɪəl] *adj* prandial

prang [præŋ] *Br Fam* **1** *vt (car)* esquinter; *(plane)* bousiller

2 *n* accrochage❑ *m*; **to have a prang** avoir un accrochage❑

prank [præŋk] *n* farce *f*, tour *m*; **to play a prank on sb** jouer un tour *ou* faire une farce à qn; **it's only a childish prank** c'est seulement une gaminerie; **they used to get up to all kinds of pranks when they were at school** ils faisaient toutes sortes de farces quand ils étaient à l'école

prankster ['præŋkstə(r)] *n* farceur(euse) *m,f*; **he's a little prankster** c'est un petit farceur *ou* polisson

praseodymium [,preɪzɪəʊ'dɪmɪəm] *n Chem* praséodyme *m*

prat [præt] *n Br Fam* andouille *f*, crétin(e) *m,f*; **I feel like a right prat** j'ai vraiment l'air d'une andouille

▸**prat about, prat around** *vi Br Fam (act foolishly)* faire l'idiot; *(waste time)* glander, glandouiller

prate [preɪt] *vi Old-fashioned Pej* jacasser, bavarder; **they're always prating on about their holidays** ils n'en finissent pas de raconter leurs vacances

pratfall ['prætfɔːl] *n Fam (fall)* gadin *m*, pelle *f*; *(blunder)* gaffe *f*

pratincole ['prætɪŋkəʊl] *n Orn* glaréole *f* à collier

prattish ['prætɪʃ] *adj Br Fam* crétin, idiot

prattle ['prætəl] *Br Fam Pej* **1** *vi (child)* babiller; *(adult)* jacasser; *(converse)* papoter; **she prattles away** *or* **on about her children for hours** elle radote pendant des heures au sujet de ses enfants; **they're forever prattling on about politics** ils sont toujours à discutailler politique

2 *n (babble)* babillage *m*; *(conversation)* papotage *m*, bavardage *m*

prattling ['prætəlɪŋ] *n Br Fam Pej (babbling)* babillage *m*; *(conversation)* bavardage *m*

prawn [prɔːn] *n* (**a**) *(seafood)* crevette *f* (rose); *(bigger)* bouquet *m*; **prawn curry** curry *m* de crevettes (**b**) *Fam (person)* **I felt a right prawn** je me suis senti vraiment bête❑

►► ***prawn cocktail*** cocktail *m* de crevettes; *Br* ***prawn cracker*** beignet *m* de crevette

praxis ['præksɪs] *(pl* **praxes** [-siːz]) *n* pratique *f*

Praxiteles [,præk'sɪtəliːz] *pr n* Praxitèle

pray [preɪ] **1** *vi* prier; **to pray to God** prier Dieu; **to pray for sb/for sb's soul** prier pour qn/pour l'âme de qn; **to pray over sb's grave** prier sur la tombe de qn; **she prayed to God to save her child** elle pria Dieu qu'il sauve son enfant; **to pray for sb's soul** prier pour (le repos de) l'âme de qn; **I've been praying for you to say that** j'espérais de tout mon cœur que tu dises cela; **she's past praying for** *(will die)* elle est perdue; **the country is past praying for at this stage** il n'y a plus d'espoir pour le pays à ce stade; **to pray for rain** prier pour qu'il pleuve; **let's just pray for fine weather** espérons qu'il fasse beau

2 *vt* (**a**) *Rel* **she prayed God he might live** elle pria Dieu pour qu'il vive; **I prayed that they wouldn't hear me** j'ai prié pour qu'ils ne m'entendent pas; **I pray we are on time** je prie pour que nous arrivions à l'heure; **I just pray he doesn't come back** je prie Dieu *ou* le ciel (pour) qu'il ne revienne pas

(**b**) *Arch or Formal (request)* prier; **to pray sb to do sth** prier qn de faire qch; **I pray you** je vous (en) prie

3 *exclam Arch or Formal* **pray be seated** asseyez-vous, je vous en prie; **pray, do tell me** dites-le-moi, je vous (en) prie; *Literary or Ironic* **and what, pray, would you have me say?** et que voudrais-tu donc que je dise?; *Literary or Ironic*

and what, pray, would you suggest I do? et que suggérerais-tu donc que je fasse?

prayer [preə(r)] **1** *n* (**a**) *Rel* prière *f*; **Morning/ Evening Prayer** office *m* du matin/du soir; **to be at prayer** être en prière, prier; **to kneel in prayer** prier à genoux, s'agenouiller pour prier; **they believe he can be made well through prayer** ils croient qu'on peut le guérir par la prière; **to say a prayer for sb** dire une prière pour qn; **to say one's prayers** faire sa prière; **remember me in your prayers** pensez à moi *ou* ne m'oubliez pas dans vos prières; **her prayer was granted** *or* **answered** sa prière fut exaucée; *Fam* **he doesn't have a prayer** il n'a pas la moindre chance *ou* l'ombre d'une chance ❑

(**b**) *(wish)* souhait *m*; **it is my earnest prayer that you will succeed** j'espère de tout cœur que vous réussirez, je souhaite sincèrement que vous réussissiez

2 prayers *npl (at church)* office *m* (divin), prière *f*; *Br Sch* prière *f* du matin

▸▸ ***prayer beads*** chapelet *m*; ***prayer book*** livre *m* de prières; ***prayer mat*** tapis *m* de prière; ***prayer meeting*** réunion *f* de prière; ***prayer rug*** tapis *m* de prière; ***prayer shawl*** talith *m*, tallith *m*; ***prayer stool*** prie-Dieu *m inv*; ***prayer wheel*** moulin *m* à prières

pray-in *n* prière *f* collective

praying ['preɪɪŋ] **1** *adj* en prières

2 *n* prière *f*, prières *fpl*

▸▸ *Entom* ***praying mantis*** mante *f* religieuse

pre- [priː] *pref* pré-

preach [priːtʃ] **1** *vi* (**a**) *Rel* prêcher; **to preach to sb** prêcher qn; *Fig* **to preach to the converted** prêcher un converti

(**b**) *(lecture)* prêcher, sermonner; **stop preaching at me!** arrête tes sermons *ou* de me faire la leçon!

2 *vt* (**a**) *Rel* prêcher; **to preach a sermon** prêcher, faire un sermon

(**b**) *Fig (recommend)* prêcher, prôner; **to preach a new doctrine** prêcher une doctrine nouvelle; **she preaches austerity and lives in luxury** elle prêche l'austérité mais elle vit dans le luxe

preacher ['priːtʃə(r)] *n (gen)* prédicateur(trice) *m,f*; *esp Am (minister)* pasteur *m*

preachify ['priːtʃɪfaɪ] *(pt & pp* **preachified**) *vi Fam Pej* faire la morale ❑

preaching ['priːtʃɪŋ] *n (UNCOUNT) (sermon)* prédication *f*; *Fam Pej (moralizing)* sermons *mpl*

preachy ['priːtʃɪ] *(compar* **preachier**, *superl* **preachiest**) *adj Fam Pej* prêcheur, sermonneur

preadaptation [,priːædæp'teɪʃən] *n Biol* préadaptation *f*

preadolescence [,priːædə'lesəns] *n* préadolescence *f*

preadolescent [,priːædə'lesənt] **1** *n* préadolescent(e) *m,f*

2 *adj (problems)* de la préadolescence

preamble [,priː'æmbəl] *n* (**a**) *Formal (to legal text)* préambule *m*; *(of book)* introduction *f*, préface *f*; *(of treaty)* préliminaires *mpl*; *(to speech)* préambule *m*, entrée *f* en matière; **Preamble to the Constitution** Préambule *m* de la Constitution des États-Unis (**b**) *Law (of bill)* exposé *m*

preamplifier [,priː'æmplɪfaɪə(r)] *n* préamplificateur *m*

prearrange [,priːə'reɪndʒ] *vt* fixer *ou* régler à l'avance; **at a prearranged time** à une heure fixée à l'avance *ou* au préalable

prebend ['prebənd] *n Rel* prébende *f*

prebendal [prɪ'bendəl] *adj Rel* prébendé

▸▸ ***prebendal services*** offices *mpl* canoniaux; ***prebendal stall*** stalle *f* canoniale

prebendary ['prebəndərɪ] *(pl* **prebendaries**) *n Rel* prébendier *m*

prebill [,priː'bɪl] *vt Acct* préfacturer

prebilling [,priː'bɪlɪŋ] *n Acct* préfacturation *f*

pre-board *vt* pré-embarquer

Precambrian [,priː'kæmbrɪən] *Geol* **1** *n* précambrien *m*

2 *adj* précambrien

precancerous [,priː'kænsərəs] *adj* précancéreux

precarious [prɪ'keərɪəs] *adj* précaire; **to make a precarious living** gagner sa vie précairement

precariously [prɪ'keərɪəslɪ] *adv* précairement; **precariously balanced** en équilibre précaire

precariousness [prɪ'keərɪəsnɪs] *n* précarité *f*

precast [,priː'kɑːst] *adj (concrete)* prémoulé

precaution [prɪ'kɔːʃən] *n* précaution *f*; *(attitude)* prévoyance *f*; **as a precaution** par précaution; **to take precautions** prendre des précautions; *(use contraceptive)* se protéger; **she took the precaution of informing her solicitor** elle prit la précaution d'avertir son avocat; **fire precautions** mesures *fpl* de prévention contre l'incendie

precautionary [prɪ'kɔːʃənərɪ] *adj* de précaution; **as a precautionary measure** par mesure de précaution; **to take precautionary measures** *or* **steps against sth** prendre des mesures préventives contre qch

precede [prɪ'siːd] *vt* (**a**) *(in order, time)* précéder; **during the minutes preceding the operation** pendant les minutes précédant l'opération; **the conference was preceded by a reception** une réception a eu lieu avant la conférence (**b**) *(in importance, rank)* avoir la préséance sur, prendre le pas sur (**c**) *(preface)* (faire) précéder

precedence ['presɪdəns], **precedency** ['presɪdənsɪ] *n (UNCOUNT)* (**a**) *(priority)* priorité *f*; **this job takes precedence over everything else** ce travail est à faire en priorité; **her health must take precedence over all other considerations** sa santé doit passer avant toute autre considération

(**b**) *(in rank, status)* préséance *f*; **in order of precedence** par ordre de préséance; **to have** *or* **to take precedence over sb** avoir la préséance *ou* prendre le pas sur qn

precedent ['presɪdənt] **1** *n* (**a**) *Law* précédent *m*, jurisprudence *f*; **to set a precedent** faire jurisprudence; **there is no precedent** il n'y a pas de jurisprudence; **to follow a precedent** s'appuyer sur un précédent, suivre la jurisprudence

(**b**) *(example case)* précédent *m*; **to create** *or* **to set** *or* **to establish a precedent** créer un précédent; **without precedent** sans précédent

(**c**) *(tradition)* tradition *f*; **to break with precedent** rompre avec la tradition; **the college has broken with precedent by electing a woman president** le collège a rompu avec la tradition en élisant une femme à la présidence

2 *adj* précédent

precedented ['presɪdəntɪd] *adj* ayant (un) précédent

preceding [prɪ'siːdɪŋ] *adj* précédent; **the preceding day** le jour précédent, la veille; **the preceding evening** le soir précédent, la veille au soir; **on the preceding page** à la page précédente; **the preceding week/year** la semaine/l'année *f* précédente

precentor [prɪ'sentə(r)] *n Rel* préchantre *m*

precept ['priːsept] *n* précepte *m*

preceptor [prɪ'septə(r)] *n* précepteur(trice) *m,f*

preceptorial [priːsep'tɔːrɪəl] *n Am Univ* travaux *mpl* dirigés, TD *mpl*

preceramic [,priːsə'ræmɪk] *adj* précéramique

precession [prɪ'seʃən] *n* précession *f*

▸▸ ***precession of the equinoxes*** précession *f* des équinoxes

pre-check-in *n* pré-inscription *f*

pre-Christian **1** *n* préchrétien(enne) *m,f*

2 *adj* préchrétien

precinct ['priːsɪŋkt] **1** *n* (**a**) *(area → round castle, cathedral)* enceinte *f*; **(shopping) precinct** centre *m* commercial; **(pedestrian) precinct** zone *f* piétonnière *ou* piétonne; **within the castle precincts** dans l'enceinte du château

(**b**) *(boundary)* pourtour *m*; **the question falls within the precincts of philosophy** la question est du domaine *ou* relève de la philosophie

(**c**) *Am (police district)* arrondissement *m*, circonscription *f* administrative; **7th precinct** 7ème arrondissement *m*

(**d**) *Am Pol* circonscription *f* électorale

2 precincts *npl* environs *mpl*, alentours *mpl*; **somewhere in the precincts** quelque part dans les environs *ou* alentours

▸▸ *Am* ***precinct police*** police *f* de quartier *ou* d'arrondissement; *Am* ***precinct station*** commissariat *m* de quartier *ou* d'arrondissement

preciosity [,presɪ'ɒsətɪ] *n Formal* préciosité *f*

precious ['preʃəs] **1** *adj* (**a**) *(jewel, material, object)* précieux, de grande valeur; **the world's most precious resources** les ressources les plus précieuses de la planète

(**b**) *(friend, friendship, moment)* précieux; **my time is precious** mon temps est précieux; **the ambulance lost precious minutes in a traffic jam** l'ambulance a perdu des minutes précieuses dans un embouteillage; **a few precious drops of water** quelques précieuses gouttes d'eau; **that photo is very precious to me** je tiens beaucoup à cette photo

(**c**) *(affected → style, person)* précieux

(**d**) *Fam (expressing irritation)* **I don't want your precious advice** je ne veux pas de vos fichus conseils; **here's your precious book!** le voilà ton sacré livre!

2 *adv Fam* très ❑; **there's precious little chance of that happening** il y a bien peu *ou* très peu de chances (pour) que cela se produise; **precious few of them turned up** il y en a très peu qui sont venus

3 *n (term of affection)* **(my) precious** mon trésor

▸▸ ***precious metal*** métal *m* précieux; ***precious stone*** pierre *f* précieuse

preciously ['preʃəslɪ] *adv* (**a**) *Fam (greatly)* joliment, extrêmement; **Birmingham came preciously close to winning the cup** Birmingham a bien failli gagner la coupe (**b**) *(affectedly)* avec préciosité, avec affectation

preciousness ['preʃəsnɪs] *n* (**a**) *(of jewel, material, object)* haute valeur *f* (**b**) *(affectation)* préciosité *f*

precipice ['presɪpɪs] *n* précipice *m*; *Fig* catastrophe *f*; **the car fell over the precipice** la voiture est tombée dans le précipice

precipitance [prɪ'sɪpɪtəns], **precipitancy** [prɪ'sɪpɪtənsɪ] *n Formal (hastiness)* précipitation *f*; **the precipitance of his decision** sa précipitation à prendre une décision

precipitant [prɪ'sɪpɪtənt] **1** *adj Formal (action)* précipité; *(decision, judgement)* hâtif; *(remark)* irréfléchi

2 *n Chem* précipitant *m*

precipitate **1** *vt* [prɪ'sɪpɪteɪt] (**a**) *(downfall, ruin, crisis)* précipiter, hâter

(**b**) *(person, vehicle, object)* précipiter

(**c**) *Chem* précipiter

2 *vi* [prɪ'sɪpɪteɪt] (**a**) *Chem* se précipiter

(**b**) *Met* se condenser

3 *n* [prɪ'sɪpɪteɪt] *Chem* précipité *m*

4 *adj* [prɪ'sɪpɪtət] (**a**) *Formal (hasty → action)* précipité; *(→ decision, judgement)* hâtif; *(→ remark)* irréfléchi; **let's not be precipitate** ne précipitons pas les choses

(**b**) *(steep)* abrupt, à pic

precipitately [prɪ'sɪpɪtətlɪ] *adv Formal* précipitamment, avec précipitation

precipitating [prɪ'sɪpɪteɪtɪŋ] *adj*

▸▸ ***precipitating agent*** précipitant *m*

precipitation [prɪ,sɪpɪ'teɪʃən] *n (UNCOUNT)* (**a**) *Formal (haste)* précipitation *f*; **to act with precipitation** agir avec précipitation *ou* précipitamment (**b**) *Chem* précipitation *f* (**c**) *Met* précipitations *fpl*

precipitous [prɪ'sɪpɪtəs] *adj* (**a**) *(steep → cliff)* à pic, escarpé; *(→ road, stairs)* raide; *(→ fall)* à pic (**b**) *(hasty)* précipité

precipitously [prɪ'sɪpɪtəslɪ] *adv* (**a**) *(steeply)* à pic, abruptement (**b**) *Formal (hastily)* précipitamment

précis [*Br* 'preɪsiː, *Am* 'preɪ'siː] (*pl* **inv** [*Br* 'preɪsiːz, *Am* 'preɪ'siːz]) **1** *n* précis *m*, résumé *m*

2 *vt* faire un résumé de

▸▸ ***précis writing*** compte rendu *m* de lecture

precise [prɪ'saɪs] *adj* (**a**) *(exact → amount, detail)* précis; *(→ location)* exact; *(→ pronunciation)* exact, juste; **eleven, to be precise** onze, pour être précis; **be more precise!** soyez plus précis!; **he was very precise in his description** il a donné une description très précise *ou* détaillée; **at that precise moment** à ce moment précis (**b**) *(meticulous → person, manner, mind, movement)* précis, méticuleux (**c**) *Pej (fussy)* pointilleux, maniaque

precisely [prɪ'saɪslɪ] **1** *adv (exactly → explain, cost)* précisément, exactement; *(→ describe, draw, measure)* avec précision; **that's precisely the reason (why) I'm not going** c'est précisément pourquoi je n'y vais pas; **she speaks very precisely** elle s'exprime avec beaucoup de précision; **at four o'clock precisely** à quatre heures précises

pra–pre

2 *exclam* précisément!, exactement!; **do you think it's too risky? – precisely!** pensez-vous que ce soit trop risqué? – tout à fait! *ou* exactement!
preciseness [prɪ'saɪsnɪs] *n* (**a**) *(exactness)* précision *f* (**b**) *(meticulousness)* méticulosité *f* (**c**) *(fussiness)* formalisme *m*
precision [prɪ'sɪʒən] **1** *n* précision *f*; **with mathematical precision** avec une précision (toute) mathématique
2 *comp (instrument, engineering, tool, bombing)* de précision
precision-approach radar *n Aviat* radar *m* d'approche de précision
precision-engineered *adj* de haute précision
precision-made *adj* de (haute) précision
preclassical [ˌpriː'klæsɪkəl] *adj* préclassique
preclinical [ˌpriː'klɪnɪkəl] *adj* (**a**) *(disease)* préclinique (**b**) *(training, education)* théorique
preclude [prɪ'kluːd] *vt Formal* exclure, prévenir; **this rule precludes any possibility of a misunderstanding** cette règle exclut toute possibilité de malentendu; **the crisis precludes her (from) going to Moscow** la crise rend impossible son départ pour Moscou, la crise l'empêche de partir pour Moscou; **we were precluded from making any further progress** nous ne pouvions plus avancer
precocial [prɪ'kəʊʃəl] *adj Orn* nidifuge
precocious [prɪ'kəʊʃəs] *adj* précoce
precociously [prɪ'kəʊʃəslɪ] *adv* précocement, avec précocité
precociousness [prɪ'kəʊʃəsnɪs], **precocity** [prɪ'kɒsətɪ] *n* précocité *f*
precoded [ˌpriː'kəʊdɪd] *adj Comput* préprogrammé
precognition [ˌpriːkɒg'nɪʃən] *n (gift)* prescience *f*, don *m* de seconde vue; *(knowledge)* connaissance *f* préalable
pre-Columbian *adj* précolombien
precombustion [ˌpriːkəm'bʌstʃən] *n* précombustion *f*
preconceive [ˌpriːkən'siːv] *vt* préconcevoir
preconceived [ˌpriːkən'siːvd] *adj* préconçu; **preconceived idea** idée *f* préconçue
preconception [ˌpriːkən'sepʃən] *n* préconception *f*, idée *f* préconçue; *(prejudice)* préjugé *m*; **to free oneself from all preconceptions** se libérer de toute opinion préconçue
preconceptual [ˌpriːkɒn'septjʊəl] *adj Phil* préconceptif
precondition [ˌpriːkən'dɪʃən] **1** *n* condition *f* préalable, condition *f* sine qua non; **a university degree is a precondition for a diplomatic career** il est impossible de faire carrière dans la diplomatie si l'on n'a pas un diplôme universitaire
2 *vt* conditionner
pre-configured [ˌpriːkən'fɪgəd] *adj* préconfiguré
preconize, -ise ['priːkənaɪz] *vt Formal* (**a**) *(proclaim)* préconiser, vanter (**b**) *(summon)* sommer nominativement (**c**) *Rel (proclaim election of)* préconiser
preconscious [ˌpriː'kɒnʃəs] *Psy* **1** *n* préconscient *m*
2 *adj* préconscient
precook [ˌpriː'kʊk] *vt* précuire
precooked [ˌpriː'kʊkt] *adj* précuit
precool [ˌpriː'kuːl] *vt* préréfrigérer
precursor [ˌpriː'kɜːsə(r)] *n (person)* précurseur *m*; *(invention, machine)* ancêtre *m*; *(event)* signe *m* avant-coureur *ou* précurseur; **the precursor of the modern computer** l'ancêtre *m* de l'ordinateur d'aujourd'hui; **the stock exchange crash was a precursor to worldwide recession** le krach boursier fut le signe précurseur de la récession à l'échelle mondiale
precursory [ˌpriː'kɜːsərɪ] *adj* (**a**) *(anticipatory)* précurseur, annonciateur (**b**) *(introductory)* préliminaire, préalable
precut [ˌpriː'kʌt] *adj (gen)* prédécoupé; *(ham, fish, bread)* prédécoupé, prétranché
predaceous, predacious [prɪ'deɪʃəs] *adj* prédateur
predate [ˌpriː'deɪt] *vt* (**a**) *(give earlier date to → cheque)* antidater; *(→ historical event)* attribuer une date antérieure à (**b**) *(precede)* être antérieur à
predator ['predətə(r)] *n* (**a**) *(animal, bird)* prédateur *m* (**b**) *Fig (person)* rapace *m*
predatory ['predətərɪ] *adj* (**a**) *(animal, bird)* prédateur (**b**) *Fig (person, instinct)* rapace; *(attacker)* pillard; **the predatory world of advertising** le milieu rapace de la publicité
►► *Mktg* ***predatory price*** prix *m* prédateur; *Mktg* ***predatory pricing*** fixation *f* de prix prédateurs
predecease [ˌpriːdɪ'siːs] *vt* prédécéder
predecessor ['priːdɪsesə(r)] *n (person, model)* prédécesseur *m*; *(event)* précédent *m*; **my (immediate) predecessor (in the job)** mon prédécesseur (à ce poste); **my new desk is much better than its predecessor** mon nouveau bureau est bien mieux que le précédent
predella [prɪ'delə] *n* (**a**) *Art* prédelle *f* (**b**) *(retable)* retable *m*
predestination ['priːˌdestɪ'neɪʃən] *n* prédestination *f*
predestine [ˌpriː'destɪn] *vt* prédestiner; **it was as if they were predestined to lose** on aurait dit qu'ils étaient prédestinés à perdre
predetermination ['priːdɪˌtɜːmɪ'neɪʃən] *n* prédétermination *f*
predetermine [ˌpriːdɪ'tɜːmɪn] *vt* prédéterminer
predetermined [ˌpriːdɪ'tɜːmɪnd] *adj* déterminé; **at a predetermined date** à une date déterminée *ou* arrêtée d'avance
predeterminer [ˌpriːdɪ'tɜːmɪnə(r)] *n* prédéterminant *m*
predicable ['predɪkəbəl] **1** *adj* prédicable
2 *n* prédicable *m*
predicament [prɪ'dɪkəmənt] *n* situation *f* difficile; **to be in a predicament** être dans une situation difficile; **we'll have to find some way out of this predicament** il va nous falloir trouver un moyen de nous sortir de ce mauvais pas; **this is quite a predicament you've landed us in** tu nous as fourrés dans un beau pétrin
predicate 1 *vt* ['predɪkeɪt] *Formal* (**a**) *(state)* affirmer (**b**) *(base)* **to predicate one's arguments/policy on sth** fonder ses arguments/sa politique sur qch (**c**) *Phil* **to predicate a quality of sth** attribuer une qualité à qch
2 *n* ['predɪkət] *Phil* prédicat *m*; *Gram* attribut *m*
3 *adj* ['predɪkət] prédicatif
►► *Math* ***predicate calculus*** calcul *m* fonctionnel
predication [ˌpredɪ'keɪʃən] *n* (**a**) *(in logic)* affirmation *f*, assertion *f* (**b**) *Gram* **verb of incomplete predication** verbe *m* attributif (**c**) *(preaching)* prédication *f*; *(sermon)* sermon *m*
predicative [prɪ'dɪkətɪv] *adj* prédicatif
predict [prɪ'dɪkt] *vt* prédire; **you could have predicted she would be late** il était à prévoir qu'elle serait en retard; **she predicted that he would have a long life** elle a prédit qu'il vivrait longtemps; **the weathermen are predicting rain** les météorologues annoncent de la pluie
predictability [prɪˌdɪktə'bɪlətɪ] *n* prévisibilité *f*; **there is a terrible predictability about the whole thing** tout ça est terriblement prévisible
predictable [prɪ'dɪktəbəl] *adj* prévisible; **the outcome was predictable** le résultat était prévisible; **the film was too predictable** ce film était sans surprise; *Pej* **you're so predictable!** avec toi au moins, on n'est jamais surpris!; **there was the predictable standing ovation** comme on pouvait le prévoir, le public s'est levé pour l'ovationner/les ovationner
predictably [prɪ'dɪktəblɪ] *adv (behave, happen)* de manière prévisible; **predictably, she forgot to tell him** comme on pouvait le prévoir *ou* comme on pouvait s'y attendre, elle a oublié de le lui dire; **the evening proceeded entirely predictably** la soirée s'est déroulée sans surprise aucune
prediction [prɪ'dɪkʃən] *n (gen)* prévision *f*; *(supernatural)* prédiction *f*
predictive [prɪ'dɪktɪv] *adj* prophétique; **to be predictive of sth** être annonciateur de qch; **the predictive power of the theory** la capacité de la théorie de prévoir des événements
predictor [prɪ'dɪktə(r)] *n* (**a**) *(prophet)* prophète *m* (**b**) *(in statistics)* variable *f* indépendante
predigest [ˌpriːdaɪ'dʒest] *vt* prédigérer
predigested [ˌpriːdaɪ'dʒestɪd] *adj* prédigéré; *Fig (idea)* tout fait
predikant [predɪ'kænt] *n Rel* = ministre de l'Église réformée de Hollande, en particulier en Afrique du Sud
predilection [ˌpriːdɪ'lekʃən] *n* prédilection *f* (**for** pour)
predispose [ˌpriːdɪs'pəʊz] *vt* prédisposer; **to be predisposed to do sth** être prédisposé à faire qch; **I was not predisposed in his favour** je n'étais pas prédisposé en sa faveur
predisposition ['priːˌdɪspə'zɪʃən] *n* prédisposition *f* (**to** à)
prednisone ['prednɪzəʊn] *n Pharm* prednisone *f*
predominance [prɪ'dɒmɪnəns], **predominancy** [prɪ'dɒmɪnənsɪ] *n* prédominance *f*; **there is a predominance of women in the profession** il y a une prédominance de femmes dans ce métier
predominant [prɪ'dɒmɪnənt] *adj* prédominant
predominantly [prɪ'dɒmɪnəntlɪ] *adv* principalement; **the population is predominantly English-speaking** la population est majoritairement anglophone; **cars sold here are predominantly Italian** la plupart des voitures vendues ici sont italiennes; **a predominantly Jewish area** un quartier à majorité juive; **to be predominantly concerned with a particular problem** être essentiellement préoccupé par un problème particulier
predominate [prɪ'dɒmɪneɪt] *vi* (**a**) *(be greater in number)* prédominer; **males still predominate over females in industry** les hommes continuent à être plus nombreux que les femmes dans l'industrie (**b**) *(prevail)* prédominer, prévaloir, l'emporter; **a sense of apathy predominated at the meeting** lors de la réunion, un sentiment d'apathie a prédominé
predominating [prɪ'dɒmɪneɪtɪŋ] *adj* prédominant
pre-eclampsia *n Med* pré-éclampsie *f*
pre-election 1 *n* élection *f* anticipée
2 *adj* préélectoral; **pre-election promises** promesses *fpl* préélectorales *ou* de candidature
►► ***pre-election campaign*** campagne *f* préélectorale
pre-embryo (*pl* **pre-embryos**) *n Biol & Med* pré-embryon *m*
preemie ['priːmɪ] *n Am Fam Obst (premature baby)* prématuré(e)[□] *m,f*
pre-eminence *n* prééminence *f*; **this country's sporting pre-eminence** la prééminence de ce pays sur le plan sportif; **to achieve pre-eminence in the field of ecology** obtenir une place prééminente dans le domaine de l'écologie
pre-eminent *adj* prééminent
pre-eminently *adv* essentiellement, avant tout; **the reasons are pre-eminently economic** les raisons sont avant tout économiques
pre-empt [-'empt] **1** *vt* (**a**) *(plan, decision)* anticiper, devancer; *(person)* devancer; **the Prime Minister's decision pre-empted their plans for social reform** la décision du Premier ministre a devancé leurs projets de réforme sociale (**b**) *Law (land, property)* acquérir par (droit de) préemption
2 *vi Cards (in bridge)* faire une annonce de barrage
pre-emption [-'empʃən] *n Law* préemption *f*
►► *St Exch* ***pre-emption right*** droit *m* de préemption
pre-emptive [-'emptɪv] *adj* (**a**) *Law (right)* de préemption (**b**) *(strike, attack)* préventif
►► *Cards* ***pre-emptive bid*** *(in bridge)* annonce *f* de barrage
preen [priːn] *vt* (**a**) *(plumage)* lisser; **the bird was preening its feathers** *or* **was preening itself** l'oiseau se lissait les plumes; *Fig* **to preen oneself** *(of person)* se faire beau, se pomponner (**b**) *(pride)* **to preen oneself on sth** s'enorgueillir de qch; **he preened himself on his success** il s'enorgueillissait *ou* tirait fierté de son succès
pre-establish *vt* préétablir
pre-established *adj* préétabli
pre-exist *vt* préexister
pre-existence *n* préexistence *f*
pre-existent, pre-existing *adj* préexistant
prefab ['priːfæb] *n Fam* (bâtiment *m*) préfabriqué[□] *m*; **they live in a prefab** ils habitent une maison préfabriquée
prefabricate [ˌpriː'fæbrɪkeɪt] *vt* préfabriquer
prefabricated [ˌpriː'fæbrɪkeɪtɪd] *adj (house)* en préfabriqué
preface ['prefɪs] **1** *n* (**a**) *(to text)* préface *f*,

avant-propos *m inv*; *(to speech)* introduction *f*, préambule *m*
(**b**) *Rel* préface *f*
2 *vt (book)* préfacer; *(speech)* faire précéder; **she prefaced the book with a reply to her critics** la préface de son livre est une réponse à ses critiques; **he usually prefaces his speeches with a joke** d'habitude, il commence ses discours par une histoire drôle; **the events that prefaced the crisis** les événements qui ont précédé la crise

prefade ['pri:feɪd] *n TV & Cin* pré-fondu *m*

prefaded [,pri:'feɪdɪd] *adj (fabric)* délavé

prefatory ['prefətərɪ] *adj (remarks)* préliminaire, préalable; *(note)* liminaire; *(page)* de préface

prefect ['pri:fekt] *n* (**a**) *Sch* = élève chargé de la discipline (**b**) *Admin (in France, Italy etc)* préfet *m*

prefectship ['pri:fektʃɪp] *n Sch* = responsabilité de maintenir la discipline, attribuée à un(e) élève des grandes classes

prefecture ['pri:fek,tjʊə(r)] *n Admin* préfecture *f*

prefer [prɪ'fɜ:(r)] *vt* (**a**) *(like better)* préférer, aimer mieux; **to prefer sth to sth** préférer qch à qch, aimer mieux qch que qch; **I prefer Paris to London** je préfère Paris à Londres, j'aime mieux Paris que Londres; **which would you prefer, wine or beer?** tu préfères du vin ou de la bière?; **she prefers living** *or* **to live alone** elle préfère vivre seule; **he prefers to walk rather than take the bus** il préfère marcher plutôt que prendre le bus; **I much prefer his first movie** je préfère de loin *ou* de beaucoup son premier film; **many people prefer watching TV to going out** *or* **rather than going out** beaucoup de gens préfèrent regarder la télévision plutôt que de sortir; **do you mind if I smoke? – I'd prefer (it) if you didn't** cela vous dérange si je fume? – j'aimerais mieux que vous ne le fassiez pas; **I'd prefer you not to go, I would prefer it if you didn't go** je préférerais que vous n'y alliez pas
(**b**) *Law* **to prefer charges against sb** *(civil action)* porter plainte contre qn; *(police action)* ≃ déférer qn au parquet
(**c**) *(submit → argument, petition)* présenter
(**d**) *Fin (creditor)* privilégier
(**e**) *Formal (appoint)* nommer, élever

preferable ['prefərəbəl] *adj* préférable; **it is preferable to book seats** il est préférable de *ou* il vaut mieux retenir des places

preferably ['prefərəblɪ] *adv* de préférence, préférablement; **come tomorrow, preferably in the evening** venez demain, de préférence dans la soirée; **would you like to make the presentations? – preferably not** voudriez-vous faire les présentations? – je n'y tiens pas

preference ['prefərəns] *n* (**a**) *(liking)* préférence *f*; **what is your preference?** que préférez-vous?; **this is my preference** voilà celui que je préfère; **to have** *or* **to show a preference for sth** avoir une préférence pour qch; **his preference is for Mozart** il préfère Mozart; **women will be given preference** les femmes auront la préférence; **in order of preference** par ordre de préférence; **he chose the first candidate in preference to the second** il a choisi le premier candidat plutôt que le second; **to express a preference** se prononcer
(**b**) *(priority)* préférence *f*, priorité *f*; **to have** *or* **to be given preference over** avoir la priorité sur
(**c**) *Econ* tarif *m ou* régime *m* de faveur; *(preferential treatment)* traitement *m* préférentiel *ou* de faveur; **imports entitled to preference** importations *fpl* bénéficiant d'un régime de faveur
(**d**) *St Exch* droit *m* de priorité
►► *Br St Exch* ***preference dividend*** dividende *m* privilégié *ou* prioritaire; *Br St Exch* ***preference share*** action *f* privilégiée *ou* de priorité; *Mktg* ***preference test*** test *m* de préférence

preferential [prefə'renʃəl] *adj (treatment, rate)* préférentiel, de faveur; **to get preferential treatment** *(of person)* bénéficier d'un traitement préférentiel *ou* de faveur
►► *Law* ***preferential claim*** privilège *m*; *Fin* ***preferential creditor*** créancier(ère) *m,f* privilégié(e); *Fin* ***preferential dividend*** dividende *m* privilégié *ou* de priorité; *Customs* ***preferential duty*** préférences *fpl* douanières; *Com* ***preferential price*** prix *m* de faveur *ou* préférentiel; *Fin* ***preferential rate*** tarif *m* préférentiel; *Law* ***preferential right*** privilège *m*; *Pol* ***preferential voting*** vote *m* préférentiel

preferment [prɪ'fɜ:mənt] *n (gen) & Rel* avancement *m*, promotion *f*

preferred [prɪ'fɜ:d] *adj* préféré
►► *Fin* ***preferred creditor*** créancier(ère) *m,f* privilégié; *Fin* ***preferred debt*** dette *f ou* créance *f* privilégiée; *Am St Exch* ***preferred stock*** *(UNCOUNT)* actions *fpl* privilégiées *ou* de priorité

prefiguration [,pri:,fɪgə'reɪʃən] *n* préfiguration *f*

prefigure [,pri:'fɪgə(r)] *vt* (**a**) *(foreshadow)* préfigurer (**b**) *(foresee)* se figurer *ou* s'imaginer (d'avance)

pre-financing *n Acct* préfinancement *m*

prefix ['pri:fɪks] **1** *n* préfixe *m*; *(before name)* particule *f*; *(title)* titre *m*
2 *vt* préfixer; **to prefix sth to sth** faire précéder qch de qch; **compounds prefixed with the word mega-** les composés commençant par le mot méga-; **telephone numbers prefixed with the code 0800** les numéros de téléphone commençant par le code 0800

preflight ['pri:flaɪt] *adj* préalable au décollage
►► ***preflight checks*** vérifications *fpl* avant décollage

preformation [,pri:fɔ:'meɪʃən] *n* préformation *f*

preformatted [,pri:'fɔ:mætɪd] *adj Comput (disk)* préformaté

prefrontal [,pri:'frʌntəl] *adj Anat* préfrontal

pregame ['pri:geɪm] *adj* avant le match; **a pregame interview** une interview avant le match

pregenital [,pri:'dʒenɪtəl] *adj Psy* prégénital
►► ***pregenital phase*** stade *m* prégénital

preggers ['pregəz] *adj Fam (pregnant)* en cloque

preglacial [,pri:'gleɪsɪəl] *adj Geol* préglaciaire

pregnable ['pregnəbəl] *adj Literary* prenable

pregnancy ['pregnənsɪ] (*pl* **pregnancies**) *n* (**a**) *(of woman)* grossesse *f*; *(of animal)* gestation *f* (**b**) *Literary (of pause, silence)* lourdeur *f*
►► ***pregnancy test*** test *m* de grossesse

pregnant ['pregnənt] *adj* (**a**) *(woman)* enceinte; *(animal)* pleine, grosse; **to get** *or* **to become pregnant** tomber enceinte; **to get a woman pregnant** faire un enfant à une femme; **to be six months pregnant** être enceinte de six mois; **she was pregnant with Kyle then** à cette époque, elle attendait Kyle
(**b**) *Literary (pause, silence)* lourd *ou* chargé de sens; **pregnant with meaning/tension** chargé de sens/tension; **pregnant with possibilities** riche de possibilités; **pregnant with danger** plein de danger

preheat [,pri:'hi:t] *vt* préchauffer

preheated [,pri:'hi:tɪd] *adj* préchauffé

prehensile [,prɪ'hensaɪl] *adj Zool* préhensile

prehension [,pri:'henʃən] *n* (**a**) *(act of grasping)* préhension *f* (**b**) *(mental understanding)* compréhension *f*

prehistoric [,pri:hɪ'stɒrɪk] *adj also Fig* préhistorique

prehistory [,pri:'hɪstərɪ] *n* préhistoire *f*

pre-ignition *n Aut* préallumage *m*

pre-industrial *adj* préindustriel

pre-install *vt Comput (software)* préinstaller

pre-installed *adj Comput (software)* préinstallé

pre-inventory balance *n Acct* balance *f* avant inventaire

prejudge [,pri:'dʒʌdʒ] *vt (issue, topic)* préjuger de; *(person)* porter un jugement prématuré sur

prejudice ['predʒʊdɪs] **1** *n* (**a**) *(bias)* préjugé *m*; **to have a prejudice in favour of/against** avoir un préjugé en faveur de/contre; **he's full of/without prejudice** il est plein de/sans préjugés; **racial prejudice** préjugés *mpl* raciaux, racisme *m*; **I have a certain prejudice in favour of the first solution** j'ai une petite préférence pour la première solution
(**b**) *Formal (harm)* préjudice *m*, tort *m*; **to the prejudice of sb's rights** au préjudice *ou* au détriment des droits de qn; *Law* **without prejudice to your guarantee** sans préjudice de votre garantie
2 *vt* (**a**) *(bias → person, outcome, decision)* influencer; **to prejudice sb against/in favour of sth** prévenir qn contre/en faveur de qch
(**b**) *(harm → reputation etc)* nuire à, faire du tort à, porter préjudice à; *(→ interests)* nuire à; **without prejudicing my rights** sans préjudice de mes droits

prejudiced ['predʒʊdɪst] *adj (person)* qui a des préjugés *ou* des idées préconçues; *(idea, opinion)* partial, préconçu; **to be prejudiced against sth** avoir des préjugés contre qch; **let's not be prejudiced about this** essayons de ne pas avoir d'idées préconçues là-dessus; **he is racially prejudiced** il est raciste; **her politics are prejudiced** ses idées politiques sont fondées sur des préjugés

prejudicial [,predʒʊ'dɪʃəl] *adj* préjudiciable, nuisible (**to** à); **this decision is prejudicial to world peace** cette décision risque de compromettre la paix mondiale

prejudicially [,predʒʊ'dɪʃəlɪ] *adv* d'une manière préjudiciable, nuisiblement

prelacy ['preləsɪ] (*pl* **prelacies**) *n* (**a**) *(office)* prélature *f* (**b**) *(prelates generally)* **the prelacy** les prélats *mpl*

prelapsarian [,pri:læp'seərɪən] *adj Rel* d'avant la chute; *Fig* innocent

prelate ['prelɪt] *n Rel* (**a**) *(office)* prélature *f* (**b**) *(prelates)* prélats *mpl*

prelim ['pri:lɪm] **1** *n* (*abbr* **preliminary exam**) *Univ* examen *m* préliminaire; *Scot Sch* examen *m* blanc
2 prelims *npl Typ* (*abbr* **preliminary pages**) pages *fpl* liminaires *(précédant le corps de l'ouvrage)*

preliminary [prɪ'lɪmɪnərɪ] (*pl* **preliminaries**) **1** *adj* préliminaire, préalable; **after a few preliminary remarks** après quelques remarques préliminaires; **the preliminary stages of the inquiry** les étapes préliminaires *ou* les débuts de l'enquête; *Formal* **preliminary to departure, preliminary to leaving** avant le départ, avant de partir
2 *n* (**a**) *(gen)* préliminaire *m*; **to go through all the preliminaries** passer par tous les préliminaires; **as a preliminary** en guise de préliminaire, au préalable; **the measure is seen by many as a preliminary to...** cette mesure est considérée par beaucoup comme une action préliminaire à...
(**b**) *(eliminating contest)* épreuve *f* éliminatoire
►► ***preliminary exam*** *Univ* examen *m* préliminaire; *Scot Sch* examen *m* blanc; ***preliminary expenses*** frais *mpl* d'établissement; *Law* ***preliminary hearing*** première audience *f*; *Law* ***preliminary investigation*** instruction *f* (d'une affaire); *Typ* ***preliminary pages*** pages *fpl* liminaires *(précédant le corps de l'ouvrage)*

preliterate [,pri:'lɪtərɪt] *adj (society)* ne connaissant pas l'écriture

preloaded [,pri:'ləʊdɪd] *adj Comput* préchargé

preloved [,pri:'lʌvd] *adj Austr Fam (second-hand)* d'occasion ▫

prelude ['prelju:d] **1** *n (gen) & Mus* prélude *m* (**to** à)
2 *vt* préluder à

premarital [,pri:'mærɪtəl] *adj* prénuptial, avant le mariage
►► ***premarital sex*** rapports *mpl* sexuels avant le mariage

pre-marketing *n Mktg* précommercialisation *f*, prémarketing *m*

premature ['premə,tjʊə(r)] *adj* (**a**) *(birth, child)* prématuré, avant terme; **three months premature** né trois mois avant terme, prématuré de trois mois (**b**) *(death, decision, judgement)* prématuré; *(baldness, senility, ejaculation)* précoce; **you're being a bit premature!** tu vas trop vite!; **it was a bit premature of him** c'était un peu prématuré de sa part

prematurely ['premə,tjʊəlɪ] *adv* prématurément; **he was born prematurely** il est né avant terme; **he died prematurely** il est mort prématurément; **to be prematurely senile/bald** souffrir de sénilité/calvitie précoce

prematureness [,premə'tjʊənɪs], **prematurity** [,premə'tjʊərɪtɪ] *n* prématurité *f*

premed ['pri:,med] *Fam Med* **1** *adj* ≃ de première année de médecine
2 *n* (**a**) *(medication)* prémédication ▫ *f* (**b**) *(student)* ≃ étudiant(e) *m,f* en première année de médecine (**c**) *(studies)* ≃ études *fpl* de première année de médecine

pre–pre

premedical [ˌpriːˈmedɪkəl] *adj Med (studies)* ≃ de première année de médecine; **she's a premedical student** ≃ elle est en première année de médecine

premedication [ˈpriːˌmedɪˈkeɪʃən] *n Med* prémédication *f*

premeditate [ˌpriːˈmedɪteɪt] *vt* préméditer

premeditated [ˌpriːˈmedɪteɪtɪd] *adj* prémédité

premeditation [ˈpriːˌmedɪˈteɪʃən] *n* préméditation *f*; **without premeditation** sans préméditation

premenstrual [ˌpriːˈmenstrʊəl] *adj* prémenstruel; **I think she's feeling premenstrual** je crois que ses règles ne vont pas tarder à arriver

►► *Am* ***premenstrual syndrome,*** *Br* ***premenstrual tension*** syndrome *m* prémenstruel

premier [ˈpremjə(r)] **1** *adj* (**a**) *(earliest)* premier (**b**) *(most important)* **this is our premier product** c'est notre produit haut de gamme

2 *n* Premier ministre *m*

►► *Ftbl* ***Premier Division*** = première division de football en Écosse; ***Premier League*** *(in Scotland)* = première division du football professionnel écossais; *(in England)* = ancienne appellation de la première division du football professionnel anglais

premiere [ˈpremɪeə(r)] **1** *n Cin & Theat* première *f*; **the film's London/television premiere** la première londonienne/télévisée du film

2 *vt* donner la première de; **the play was premiered in Paris** la première de la pièce a eu lieu à Paris

3 *vi* **the play premiered in New York** la première de la pièce a eu lieu à New York

premiership [ˈpremjəʃɪp] **1** *n* poste *m* de Premier ministre; **to be elected to the premiership** être élu Premier ministre; **during her premiership** alors qu'elle était Premier ministre; **elected to the premiership** choisi comme Premier ministre; **he had a successful premiership** il a rempli son mandat de Premier ministre avec succès

2 Premiership *n* **the Premiership** = première division du football professionnel anglais

premillennial [ˌpriːmɪˈlenɪəl] *adj* (**a**) *Rel* d'avant le millénium (**b**) *(preceding the millennium)* qui précède le passage à un nouveau millénaire

premillennialism [ˌpriːmɪˈlenɪəlɪzəm] *n* = croyance des millénaristes, selon laquelle le second avènement du Christ aurait lieu juste avant le millénium

premise [ˈpremɪs] **1** *n (hypothesis)* prémisse *f*; **on the premise that...** en partant du principe que...

2 *vt Formal* **to premise that...** poser en principe que...; *(in logic)* poser en prémisse que...; **to be premised on sth** être basé *ou* fondé sur qch

premises [ˈpremɪsɪz] *npl* (**a**) *(place)* locaux *mpl*, lieux *mpl*; **business premises** locaux *mpl* commerciaux; **on the premises** sur les lieux, sur place; **she's still on the premises** elle est encore dans le bâtiment (**b**) *Law* préalable *m*

premiss = **premise**

premium [ˈpriːmɪəm] *n* (**a**) *(insurance payment)* prime *f* (d'assurance); **to pay an additional premium** payer une surprime

(**b**) *(additional sum → on price)* supplément *m*; *(→ on salary)* prime *f*; *St Exch* **to pay a premium** verser *ou* acquitter un premium; **to issue shares at a premium** émettre des actions au-dessus du pair *ou* de leur valeur nominale; **to sell sth at a premium** vendre qch à prime *ou* à bénéfice; **antiques are at a premium** *(are sought after)* les antiquités sont très recherchées; *(sell at high prices)* les antiquités se vendent à prix d'or; **time is at a premium** le temps presse; **her time is at a premium** son temps est précieux; **good translators are at a premium** les bons traducteurs ne courent pas les rues *ou* sont rares; *Fig* **to put** *or* **place a premium on sth** *(of people, government etc)* accorder beaucoup d'importance à qch; *(of circumstances, nature of work etc)* mettre l'accent sur qch

(**c**) *Am (fuel)* supercarburant *m*

►► ***premium bonds*** obligations *fpl* à lots; *Com* ***premium discount*** ristourne *f* de prime; *Com* ***premium price*** prix *m* de prestige; *Mktg* ***premium product*** produit *m* de prestige; ***premium quality*** qualité *f* extra; *Com* ***premium rebate*** ristourne *f* de prime; *Fin* ***premium on redemption*** prime *f* de remboursement; *Mktg* ***premium selling*** vente *f* avec prime; *Mktg* ***premium service*** service *m* premier

premolar [ˌpriːˈməʊlə(r)] *n Anat* prémolaire *f*

►► ***premolar tooth*** prémolaire *f*

premonition [ˌpreməˈnɪʃən] *n* prémonition *f*, pressentiment *m*; **to have a premonition of sth** pressentir qch, avoir le pressentiment de qch; **I had a premonition he wouldn't come** j'avais le pressentiment qu'il ne viendrait pas

premonitory [prɪˈmɒnɪtərɪ] *adj* prémonitoire

prenatal [ˌpriːˈneɪtəl] *adj* prénatal

prenup [ˈpriːnʌp] *n Fam* contrat *m* de mariage ❑

prenuptial [ˌpriːˈnʌpʃəl] *adj* prénuptial

►► ***prenuptial agreement*** contrat *m* de mariage

preoccupation [ˈpriːˌɒkjʊˈpeɪʃən] *n* préoccupation *f*; **to have a preoccupation with sth** être préoccupé par qch; **I don't understand his preoccupation with physical fitness** je ne comprends pas qu'il soit si préoccupé par sa forme physique

preoccupied [ˌpriːˈɒkjʊpaɪd] *adj* préoccupé; **to be preoccupied by** *or* **with sth** être préoccupé par qch; **he seems preoccupied with the idea** il semble que cette idée le préoccupe; **she was too preoccupied with her work to spare a thought for me** elle était trop préoccupée par son travail pour penser à moi

preoccupy [ˌpriːˈɒkjʊpaɪ] *(pt & pp* **preoccupied***)* *vt* préoccuper

preop [ˈpriːˌɒp] *Fam Med* **1** *adj* préopératoire ❑

2 *n* examen *m* préopératoire ❑; **she's gone for a preop** elle est allée passer un examen préopératoire

►► ***preop medication*** prémédication ❑ *f*, médication *f* préopératoire ❑

preoperative [ˌpriːˈɒpərətɪv] *adj* préopératoire

preordain [ˌpriːɔːˈdeɪn] *vt (destine)* prédéterminer; **she felt preordained to be a missionary** elle se sentait prédestinée à devenir missionnaire; **our defeat was preordained** il était dit que nous perdrions

preowned [ˌpriːˈəʊnd] *adj* d'occasion

prep [prep] *Fam* **1** *n (UNCOUNT) Br* (**a**) *(homework)* devoirs ❑ *mpl* (**b**) *(study period)* étude ❑ *f (après les cours)*

2 *vt Am* préparer ❑; *Med* **to prep sb for an operation** préparer qn pour une opération

3 *vi Am* = faire ses études dans un établissement privé

►► ***prep period*** (heure *f* de) permanence ❑ *f*; ***prep room*** (salle *f* d')étude ❑ *f*; ***prep school*** *(in UK)* école *f* primaire privée ❑ *(pour enfants de sept à treize ans, préparant généralement à entrer dans une "public school")*; *(in US)* = école privée qui prépare à l'enseignement supérieur

pre-pack, pre-package *vt* préemballer, préconditionner; **the fruit is all pre-packed** les fruits sont entièrement conditionnés

pre-packaged *adj* préconditionné, préemballé

pre-packaging *n* préemballage *m*, conditionnement *m*

pre-packed *adj* préconditionné, préemballé

prepaid 1 [ˌpriːˈpeɪd] *pt & pp of* **prepay**

2 *adj* [ˈpriːpeɪd] prépayé; *Acct* payé (d'avance), constaté d'avance

►► ***prepaid card*** carte *f* prépayée; ***prepaid envelope*** enveloppe *f* affranchie; ***prepaid income*** produit *m* constaté d'avance; ***prepaid reply*** réponse *f* payée

preparation [ˌprepəˈreɪʃən] **1** *n* (**a**) *(UNCOUNT) (gen)* préparation *f*; *(of plane, car etc)* mise *f* en état; **to be in preparation** être en préparation; **in preparation for publication** en vue d'une publication; **in preparation for Christmas** pour préparer Noël; **the dish requires careful preparation** ce plat exige une préparation extrêmement délicate; **as a preparation for public life** pour préparer à la vie publique

(**b**) *Chem & Pharm* préparation *f*; **to make up a preparation** faire une préparation

(**c**) *(UNCOUNT) Br Sch (homework)* devoirs *mpl*; *(study period)* étude *f (après les cours)*

2 preparations *npl (arrangements)* préparatifs *mpl*, dispositions *fpl*; **preparations for war** préparatifs *mpl* de guerre; **she attended to the wedding preparations** elle s'est occupée des préparatifs du mariage; **to make preparations for sth** faire des préparatifs en vue de qch

preparatory [prɪˈpærətərɪ] *adj (work)* préparatoire; *(measure)* préalable, préliminaire; **the report is still at the preparatory stage** le rapport en est encore au stade préliminaire *ou* préparatoire; *Formal* **preparatory to the launch** avant le lancement; *Formal* **preparatory to travelling abroad** avant de partir en voyage à l'étranger

►► ***preparatory school*** *(in UK)* école *f* primaire privée *(pour enfants de sept à treize ans, préparant généralement à entrer dans une "public school")*; *(in US)* = école privée qui prépare à l'enseignement supérieur

prepare [prɪˈpeə(r)] **1** *vt (plan, food, lesson, person)* préparer; *(attack)* monter, préparer; *(plane, car)* mettre en état; **to prepare a meal for sb** préparer un repas à *ou* pour qn; **to prepare a surprise for sb** préparer une surprise à qn; **to prepare the ground for negotiations** préparer le terrain pour des négociations; **we are preparing to leave tomorrow** nous nous préparons à partir demain; **she's preparing them for the exam** elle les prépare à l'examen; **to prepare oneself for sth** se préparer à qch; **prepare yourself for a surprise** attendez-vous à une surprise; **prepare yourself for the worst** préparez-vous *ou* attendez-vous au pire; **you'd better prepare yourself for some bad news** préparez-vous à recevoir de mauvaises nouvelles; **their training had prepared them for most eventualities** leur entraînement les avait préparés à presque toutes les éventualités; **prepared from the finest ingredients** préparé avec les meilleurs ingrédients

2 *vi* **to prepare for sth** faire des préparatifs en vue de *ou* se préparer à qch; **to prepare to do sth** se préparer *ou* s'apprêter à faire qch; **to prepare for departure** faire des préparatifs en vue d'un départ, se préparer à partir; **the country is preparing for war** le pays se prépare à la guerre; **to prepare for a meeting/an exam** préparer une réunion/un examen; **prepare for the worst!** préparez-vous au pire!

prepared [prɪˈpeəd] *adj* (**a**) *(ready → gen)* préparé, prêt; *(→ answer, excuse)* tout prêt; **to be prepared for anything** être prêt à tout; **be prepared** *(Scout's motto)* toujours prêt; **I was prepared to leave** j'étais préparé *ou* prêt à partir; **he wasn't prepared for what he saw** *(hadn't expected)* il ne s'attendait pas à ce spectacle; *(was shocked)* il n'était pas préparé à voir cela; **a prepared statement** une déclaration préparée à l'avance; **prepared timber** bois *m* refait

(**b**) *(willing)* prêt, disposé; **I am prepared to cooperate** je suis prêt *ou* disposé à coopérer; **he was not prepared to lie** il n'était pas disposé à mentir

preparedness [prɪˈpeədnɪs] *n* état *m* de préparation; **preparedness for war** préparation *f* à la guerre; **I am unsure of their preparedness to deal with such an eventuality** je doute qu'ils soient prêts à faire face à une telle éventualité

prepay [ˌpriːˈpeɪ] *(pt & pp* **prepaid** [-ˈpeɪd]*)* *vt* payer d'avance

prepayment [ˌpriːˈpeɪmənt] *n* paiement *m* d'avance, paiement *m* préalable; *Acct* charge *f* constatée d'avance

►► *Acct* ***prepayment clause*** clause *f* de remboursement par anticipation; *Fin* ***prepayment penalty*** indemnité *f* de remboursement par anticipation

preponderance [prɪˈpɒndərəns] *n (in importance)* prépondérance *f*; *(in number)* supériorité *f* numérique; **there was a preponderance of boys in the science subjects** les garçons étaient majoritaires dans les disciplines scientifiques

preponderant [prɪˈpɒndərənt] *adj* prépondérant; **boys tend to be preponderant** il tend à y avoir une majorité de garçons

preponderantly [prɪˈpɒndərəntlɪ] *adv (in importance)* de façon prépondérante; *(especially)* surtout; **the guests were preponderantly French** les invités étaient pour la majeure partie français

preponderate [prɪˈpɒndəreɪt] *vi* être prépondérant, prédominer; **to preponderate over sth** l'emporter sur qch

preposition [ˌprepəˈzɪʃən] *n Gram* préposition *f*
prepositional [ˌprepəˈzɪʃənəl] *adj Gram* prépositionnel
▸▸ ***prepositional phrase*** locution *f* prépositive
prepositionally [ˌprepəˈzɪʃənəlɪ] *adv Gram* prépositivement
prepositive [prɪˈpɒzətɪv] *adj Gram* prépositif
prepossess [ˌpriːpəˈzes] *vt Formal* (**a**) *(engross)* préoccuper (**b**) *(influence)* influencer
prepossessing [ˌpriːpəˈzesɪŋ] *adj (person)* avenant; *(smile, behaviour)* avenant, engageant; **a most prepossessing young man** un jeune homme très présentable; **her manners are not very prepossessing** ses manières ne font pas très bon effet *ou* laissent à désirer
prepossessingly [ˌpriːpəˈzesɪŋlɪ] *adv* d'une manière avenante *ou* engageante
preposterous [prɪˈpɒstərəs] *adj* absurde, grotesque; **that's a preposterous lie!** c'est complètement absurde *ou* grotesque!
preposterously [prɪˈpɒstərəslɪ] *adv* absurdement, ridiculement; **it was preposterously easy** ça a été un jeu d'enfant
preposterousness [prɪˈpɒstərəsnɪs] *n* absurdité *f*
prepotent [ˌpriːˈpəʊtənt] *adj* (**a**) *(more influential)* prédominant (**b**) *Biol* dominant
preppie, preppy [ˈprepɪ] *(pl* **preppies**, *compar* **preppier**, *superl* **preppiest**) *Am Fam* **1** *n* BCBG *mf inv*
2 *adj* BCBG *(inv)*
preprandial [ˌpriːˈprændɪəl] *adj Literary or Hum (drink)* avant le repas
pre-press *n Typ* prépresse *m*
pre-printed form *n* pré-imprimé *m*
preprocessor [ˌpriːˈprəʊsesə(r)] *n Comput* préprocesseur *m*
preproduction [ˌpriːprəˈdʌkʃən] *n TV & Cin* préproduction *f*; **the movie is in preproduction** le film est en préproduction
preprogram [ˌpriːˈprəʊgræm] *vt Comput* préprogrammer; **humans are preprogrammed to behave in certain ways** les êtres humains sont conditionnés à se comporter d'une certaine façon
preprogrammed [ˌpriːˈprəʊgræmd] *adj Comput* préprogrammé
prepubescent [ˌpriːpjuːˈbesənt] *adj* prépubère; *Fig Pej (immature)* puéril
prepublication [ˌpriːpʌblɪˈkeɪʃən] *n* prépublication *f*
prepuce [ˈpriːˌpjuːs] *n Anat* prépuce *m*
prequel [ˈpriːkwəl] *n* = film qui reprend les thèmes et les personnages d'un film réalisé précédemment, mais dont l'action est antérieure
Pre-Raphaelism [ˌpriːˈræfəlɪzəm] *n Art* préraphaélisme *m*
Pre-Raphaelite [ˌpriːˈræfəlaɪt] *Art* **1** *adj* préraphaélite
2 *n* préraphaélite *mf*
Pre-Raphaelitism [ˌpriːˈræfəlaɪtɪzəm] *n Art* préraphaélitisme *m*
prerecord [ˌpriːrɪˈkɔːd] *vt* préenregistrer
prerecorded [ˌpriːrɪˈkɔːdɪd] *adj* préenregistré; **a prerecorded TV debate** un débat télévisé préenregistré *ou* en différé
▸▸ ***prerecorded cassette*** cassette *f* enregistrée
prerecording [ˌpriːrɪˈkɔːdɪŋ] *n* préenregistrement *m*; *TV & Rad* (émission *f* en) différé *m*
preregistration [ˌpriːredʒɪˈstreɪʃən] *n Univ* préinscription *f*
prerelease [ˌpriːrɪˈliːs] **1** *n (of film)* avant-première *f*; *(of record)* sortie *f* précommerciale
2 *vt (film, record)* faire sortir en avant-première
▸▸ ***prerelease publicity*** = publicité qui précède la sortie d'un film, d'un livre, d'un disque etc
prerequisite [ˌpriːˈrekwɪzɪt] **1** *n* (condition *f*) préalable *m*, condition *f* sine qua non; **to be a prerequisite for** *or* **of sth** être une condition préalable à qch; **a knowledge of foreign languages is not a prerequisite** la connaissance de langues étrangères n'est pas indispensable
2 *adj* préalablement nécessaire, indispensable
▸▸ ***prerequisite condition*** condition *f* préalable
prerevolutionary [ˈpriːˌrevəˈluːʃənərɪ] *adj* prérévolutionnaire; **in prerevolutionary Spain** dans l'Espagne d'avant la révolution
prerogative [prɪˈrɒgətɪv] *n* prérogative *f*, apanage *m*; **the royal prerogative** la prérogative royale; **to exercise one's prerogative** exercer ses prérogatives; **it's a woman's prerogative to be late** les femmes ont le droit d'être en retard
Pres. *(written abbr* **president**) président *m*
presage [ˈpresɪdʒ] *Literary* **1** *n (sign)* présage *m*; *(foreboding)* pressentiment *m*; **to have a presage of doom** pressentir un malheur
2 *vt* présager, annoncer
presbyopia [ˌprezbɪˈəʊpɪə] *n Opt* presbytie *f*
presbyopic [ˌprezbɪˈəʊpɪk] *adj Opt (sight)* presbytique; *(person)* presbyte
presbyter [ˈprezbɪtə(r)] *n Rel* membre *m* du conseil presbytéral
Presbyterian [ˌprezbɪˈtɪərɪən] *Rel* **1** *n* presbytérien(enne) *m,f*
2 *adj* presbytérien
Presbyterianism [ˌprezbɪˈtɪərɪənɪzəm] *n Rel* presbytérianisme *m*
presbytery [ˈprezbɪtrɪ] *n* (**a**) *(residence)* presbytère *m* (**b**) *(court)* consistoire *m* (**c**) *(part of church)* presbyterium *m*
preschool [ˌpriːˈskuːl] **1** *adj (playgroup, age)* préscolaire; *(child)* d'âge préscolaire
2 *n Am* école *f* maternelle
preschooler [ˌpriːˈskuːlə(r)] *n Am* enfant *mf* d'âge préscolaire
prescience [ˈpresɪəns] *n Formal* prescience *f*
prescient [ˈpresɪənt] *adj Formal* prescient
prescientific [ˌpriːsaɪənˈtɪfɪk] *adj* préscientifique
prescribe [prɪˈskraɪb] *vt* (**a**) *Med* prescrire; **to prescribe sth for sb** prescrire qch à qn; **the doctor prescribed her a month's rest** le médecin lui a prescrit un mois de repos; **what can you prescribe for migraine?** que prescrivez-vous contre la migraine?; **do not exceed the prescribed dose** *(on packaging)* ne pas dépasser la dose prescrite
(**b**) *(advocate)* préconiser, recommander; **what cure would you prescribe for the current economic problems?** quelles mesures préconiseriez-vous pour remédier aux problèmes économiques actuels?
(**c**) *(set → punishment)* infliger; *Br Sch & Univ (→ books)* inscrire au programme; **in the prescribed time** dans le délai prescrit
(**d**) *Law* prescrire
▸▸ *Br* ***prescribed form*** formulaire *m* prescrit; *Br* ***prescribed number*** nombre *m* prescrit
prescription [prɪˈskrɪpʃən] *n* (**a**) *Med* ordonnance *f*; **the doctor wrote out a prescription for her** le médecin lui a rédigé *ou* fait une ordonnance; **to make up a prescription for sb** exécuter *ou* préparer une ordonnance pour qn; **I'll give you a prescription for some antibiotics** je vais vous prescrire des antibiotiques; **to get sth on prescription** obtenir qch sur ordonnance; **available** *or* **obtainable only on prescription** délivré seulement sur ordonnance
(**b**) *(recommendation)* prescription *f*; **what's your prescription for a happy life?** quelle est votre recette du bonheur?
▸▸ *Br* ***prescription charge*** = partie du coût des médicaments délivrés sur ordonnance qui est à la charge du patient; ***prescription drug*** = médicament délivré seulement sur ordonnance
prescriptive [prɪˈskrɪptɪv] *adj* (**a**) *Ling (grammar, rule)* normatif (**b**) *(dogmatic)* dogmatique, [illegible]
▸▸ *Law* ***prescriptive right*** droit *m* consacré par l'usage
prescriptivism [prɪˈskrɪptɪvɪzəm] *n* normativisme *m*
preselect [ˌpriːsəˈlekt] *vt (tracks, channels)* prérégler
preselection [ˌpriːsəˈlekʃən] *n* présélection *f*
pre-selector *n Aut* présélecteur *m*
▸▸ ***pre-selector gearbox*** boîte *f* à présélection
presence [ˈprezəns] *n* (**a**) *(gen)* présence *f*; **in the presence of sb** en présence de qn; **it happened in my presence** cela s'est passé en ma présence; **don't say anything about it in his presence** n'en parlez pas devant lui; **to be aware of sb's presence** sentir la présence de qn; **your presence is requested at Saturday's meeting** vous êtes prié d'assister à la réunion de samedi; *Formal* **to be admitted to the presence of sb** être admis en présence de qn; **presence of mind** présence *f* d'esprit; **to show/to have great presence of mind** faire preuve d'une/avoir une grande présence d'esprit; **to have the presence of mind to do sth** avoir la présence d'esprit de faire qch
(**b**) *(number of people present)* présence *f*; **there was a large student/police presence at the demonstration** il y avait un nombre important d'étudiants/un important service d'ordre à la manifestation; **the police maintained a discreet presence** la police a assuré une surveillance discrète; **America has maintained a strong military presence in the area** l'Amérique a maintenu une forte présence militaire dans la région
(**c**) *(personality, magnetism)* présence *f*; **to lack presence** manquer de présence; **she has great stage presence** elle a beaucoup de présence sur scène; **to make one's presence felt** se faire remarquer, faire sentir sa présence
(**d**) *(entity)* présence *f*; **I could sense a presence in the room** je sentais comme une présence dans la pièce

PRESENT

cadeau	▸ **1 (a)**
présent	▸ **1 (b), (c); 2 (a)**
actuel	▸ **2 (b)**
donner	▸ **3 (a), (c)**
remettre	▸ **3 (a)**
présenter	▸ **3 (b), (c) – (h), (j)**

1 *n* [ˈprezənt] (**a**) *(gift)* cadeau *m*; **to give sb a present** faire un cadeau à qn; **we gave her a pony as a present** nous lui avons offert un *ou* fait cadeau d'un poney; **to make sb a present of sth** faire cadeau de qch à qn; **it's for a present** *(in shop)* c'est pour offrir
(**b**) *(in time)* présent *m*; **at present** actuellement, à présent; **that's all I can tell you at present** c'est tout ce que je peux vous dire pour l'instant *ou* pour le moment; **as things are at present** *(at this stage)* au point où en sont les choses; *(nowadays)* par les temps qui courent; **up to the present** jusqu'à présent, jusqu'à maintenant; **that's enough for the present** ça suffit pour le moment *ou* pour l'instant; **to live only in** *or* **for the present** vivre pour l'instant présent *ou* au présent
(**c**) *Gram* présent *m*; **in the present** au présent
(**d**) *Law* **by these presents** par les présentes
2 *adj* [ˈprezənt] (**a**) *(in attendance)* présent; **to be present at a meeting** être présent à *ou* assister à une réunion; **how many were present?** combien de personnes étaient là *ou* étaient présentes?; **those present were very moved** les personnes présentes étaient très émues, l'assistance était très émue; **he cannot be interviewed without a lawyer being present** on ne peut pas l'interroger sans la présence d'un avocat; **present company excepted** à l'exception des personnes présentes
(**b**) *(current → job, government, price)* actuel; **in the present case** dans le cas présent; **at the present time** actuellement, à l'époque actuelle; **up to the present day** jusqu'à présent, jusqu'à aujourd'hui; **the present year** l'année *f* en cours; *Fin* l'année *f* courante; **given the present circumstances** étant donné les circonstances actuelles, dans l'état actuel des choses; **in the present writer's opinion** de l'avis de l'auteur de ces lignes
(**c**) *Gram* au présent
3 *vt* [prɪˈzent] (**a**) *(gift)* donner, offrir; *(prize)* remettre, décerner; *(medal, diploma)* remettre; **to present sth to sb** *or* **sb with sth** donner *ou* offrir qch à qn; **they presented him with a clock** ils lui ont offert une *ou* fait cadeau d'une pendule; **he presented his collection to the museum** il a fait cadeau de sa collection au musée; **the singer was presented with a bunch of flowers** la chanteuse s'est vu offrir *ou* remettre un bouquet de fleurs; **who is going to present the prizes?** qui va procéder à la remise des prix?; **she was presented with first prize** on lui a décerné le premier prix; **the project presents us with a formidable challenge** le projet constitue pour nous un formidable défi; **he presented us with a fait accompli** il nous a mis devant le fait accompli; **they were presented with an empty goalmouth** ils se trouvèrent devant un

but vide; **this presented her with no option but to agree** ceci ne lui a pas laissé d'autre alternative que d'accepter; *Fig* **to present sb with an easy target** offrir une bonne cible à qn; **she presented him with a daughter** elle lui a donné une fille

(**b**) *Formal (introduce)* présenter; **to present sb to sb** présenter qn à qn; **allow me to present Mr Jones** permettez-moi de vous présenter M. Jones; **to be presented at Court** être présenté à la Cour

(**c**) *(put on → play, film)* donner; *(→ exhibition)* présenter, monter

(**d**) *Rad & TV* présenter; **the programme was presented by Ian King** l'émission était présentée par Ian King

(**e**) *(offer → entertainment)* présenter; **we proudly present Donna Stewart** nous avons le plaisir *ou* nous sommes heureux de vous présenter Donna Stewart; **presenting Vanessa Brown in the title role** avec Vanessa Brown dans le rôle principal; **the opera company is presenting a varied programme** la troupe de l'opéra présente un programme varié

(**f**) *(put forward → apology, view, report)* présenter; *(→ plan)* soumettre; *(orally)* exposer; **the essay is well presented** la dissertation est bien présentée; **I wish to present my complaint in person** je tiens à déposer plainte moi-même; **to present a bill in Parliament** présenter *ou* introduire un projet de loi au Parlement; *Law* **to present a plea** introduire une instance

(**g**) *(pose, offer → problem, difficulty)* présenter, poser; *(→ chance, view)* offrir; **the house presented a sorry sight** la maison offrait un triste spectacle; **if the opportunity presents itself** si l'occasion se présente; **a strange idea presented itself to her** une idée étrange lui est venue; **the case presents all the appearances of murder** tout semble indiquer qu'il s'agit d'un meurtre; **to present sb/sth in a good/bad light** présenter qn/qch sous un jour favorable/défavorable

(**h**) *(show → passport, ticket)* présenter; **you must present proof of ownership** vous devez présenter un certificat de propriété *ou* prouver que cela vous appartient; *Mil* **present arms!** présentez armes!

(**i**) *(arrive, go)* **to present oneself** se présenter; **she presented herself at 9 o'clock as instructed** elle se présenta, comme convenu, à 9 heures; **to present oneself at** *or* **for an examination** se présenter à *ou* pour un examen

(**j**) *Com (invoice)* présenter; **to present a cheque for payment** présenter un chèque à l'encaissement; **to present a bill for acceptance** présenter une traite à l'acceptation

(**k**) *Obst* **the foetus presented itself normally** la présentation (fœtale) était normale

4 *vi* [prɪ'zent] (**a**) *Obst (foetus)* se présenter

(**b**) *Med (patient)* consulter le médecin; **the patient presented with bruises and multiple fractures** cette patiente présentait des contusions et des fractures multiples

(**c**) *Med (illness, condition)* se manifester (**as** par)

►► *Fin* ***present capital*** capital *m* appelé; *Gram* ***present indicative*** présent *m* de l'indicatif; *Gram* ***present participle*** participe *m* présent; *Gram* ***present perfect*** passé *m* composé; **in the present perfect** au passé composé; *Gram* ***present subjunctive*** présent *m* du subjonctif; *Gram* ***present tense*** présent *m*; **in the present tense** au présent; *Acct* ***present value*** valeur *f* actuelle *ou* actualisée

---

presentable [prɪ'zentəbəl] *adj (person, room)* présentable; *(clothes)* présentable, mettable; **do I look presentable?** est-ce que j'ai l'air présentable?; **make yourself presentable** arrange-toi un peu; **I'm afraid the room's not very presentable** je crains que la pièce ne soit pas très présentable

presentation [,prezən'teɪʃən] *n* (**a**) *(showing)* présentation *f*; *(putting forward → of ideas, facts)* présentation *f*, exposition *f*; *(→ of petition)* présentation *f*, soumission *f*; *(talk)* exposé *m*; **to give a presentation** faire un exposé; **on presentation of this voucher** sur présentation de ce bon; **cheque payable on presentation** chèque *m* payable à vue; **he made a very clear presentation of the case** il a très clairement présenté l'affaire; **payable on presentation of the coupon** payable contre remise du coupon; **on presentation of the invoice** au vu de *ou* sur présentation de la facture

(**b**) *Com (of product, policy, invoice)* présentation *f*; *Com* **presentation for acceptance** présentation *f* à l'acceptation; *Com* **presentation for payment** présentation *f* au paiement

(**c**) *(introduction)* présentation *f*; **can you make the presentations?** pouvez-vous faire les présentations?

(**d**) *(performance → of play, film)* représentation *f*; **in a new presentation of 'Hamlet'** dans une nouvelle mise en scène de 'Hamlet'

(**e**) *(of piece of work)* présentation *f*; **she lost marks for poor presentation** elle a perdu des points parce que sa présentation n'était pas assez soignée

(**f**) *(award → of prize, medal, diploma, gift)* remise *f*; **to make sb a presentation of sth** remettre qch à qn

(**g**) *(award ceremony)* cérémonie *f* de remise *(d'un prix)*

(**h**) *Med (of foetus)* présentation *f*

►► ***presentation ceremony*** cérémonie *f* de remise *(d'un prix)*; ***presentation copy*** *(specimen)* spécimen *m* (gratuit); *(from writer)* exemplaire *m* gratuit; *Fin* ***presentation date*** date *f* de présentation; *Comput* ***presentation graphics*** graphiques *mpl* de présentation; *Mktg* ***presentation pack*** paquet *m* de présentation

present-day *adj* actuel, contemporain; **present-day London/Brazil** le Londres/Brésil d'aujourd'hui

presenteeism [prezən'tiːɪzəm] *n* zèle *m (fait de faire beaucoup d'heures, par opposition à "absenteeism")*

presenter [prɪ'zentə(r)] *n* présentateur(trice) *m,f*

presentiment [prɪ'zentɪmənt] *n* pressentiment *m*; **to have a presentiment of danger** avoir le pressentiment qu'il y a du danger

presently ['prezəntlɪ] *adv* (**a**) *(soon)* bientôt, tout à l'heure; **he will be here presently** il sera bientôt là; **presently, she got up and left** au bout de quelques minutes elle se leva et s'en alla (**b**) *(now)* à présent, actuellement; **she's presently working on a new novel** elle travaille actuellement à un nouveau roman

presentment [prɪ'zentmənt] *n* (**a**) *Law* déclaration *f* (**b**) *Fin (of bill)* présentation *f*

presents ['prezənts] *npl Law* **by these presents** par la présente (lettre)

preservation [,prezə'veɪʃən] *n* (**a**) *(maintenance → of tradition)* conservation *f*; *(→ of leather, building, wood)* entretien *m*; *(→ of peace, order, life)* maintien *m*; *(→ of specimen, plant)* naturalisation *f*; **the mummy was in a good state of preservation** la momie était en bon état de conservation *ou* était bien conservée; **to put a preservation order on a building** classer un édifice *(monument historique)*

(**b**) *(of food)* conservation *f*

(**c**) *(protection)* préservation *f*

►► ***preservation society*** = association pour la protection des sites et monuments

preservative [prɪ'zɜːvətɪv] **1** *n* conservateur *m*; *(in foods)* agent *m* de conservation, conservateur *m*, préservateur *m*; **contains no artificial preservatives** *(on packaging)* sans conservateurs

2 *adj* conservateur

preserve [prɪ'zɜːv] **1** *vt* (**a**) *(maintain → tradition, building)* conserver; *(→ leather)* conserver, entretenir; *(→ silence)* garder, observer; *(→ peace, order, life)* maintenir; *(→ dignity)* garder, conserver; *(→ specimen, plant)* naturaliser; **to be well preserved** *(building, specimen)* être en bon état de conservation; *(person)* être bien conservé; **they tried to preserve some semblance of normality** ils essayaient de faire comme si de rien n'était

(**b**) *(protect)* préserver, protéger; **Saints preserve us!** le Ciel *ou* Dieu nous préserve!

(**c**) *Culin* mettre en conserve

2 *n* (**a**) *Hunt* réserve *f* (de chasse)

(**b**) *(privilege)* privilège *m*, apanage *m*; **it's still very much a male preserve** c'est encore un domaine essentiellement réservé aux hommes; **cruises are the preserve of the rich** les croisières sont réservées aux *ou* sont le privilège des riches

(**c**) *Culin (jam)* confiture *f*; *(of vegetables)* conserve *f*

3 preserves *npl Culin (jam)* confitures *fpl*; *(vegetables, fruit)* conserves *fpl*; *(pickles)* pickles *mpl*

►► *Culin* ***preserved fruit*** fruits *mpl* en conserve

preserver [prɪ'zɜːvə(r)] *n* sauveur *m*; *(of tradition)* gardien(enne) *m,f*

preset [,priː'set] *(pt & pp* **preset**) **1** *vt* prérégler, régler à l'avance

2 *adj* préréglé, réglé d'avance; *Comput* présélectionné

preshrink [,priː'ʃrɪŋk] *vt (pt* **preshrank** [-'ʃræŋk], *pp* **preshrunk** [-'ʃrʌŋk]) *(fabric)* rendre irrétrécissable

preshrunk [,priː'ʃrʌŋk] *adj* irrétrécissable

preside [prɪ'zaɪd] *vi* présider; **to preside at a meeting/at table** présider une réunion/la table

►**preside over** *vt insep* (**a**) *(meeting)* présider; *(changes)* présider à; **the man who presided over the collapse of the company** l'homme qui était président lors de la chute de l'entreprise (**b**) *(of statue, building)* dominer; **the statue presided over the square** la statue dominait la place

presidency ['prezɪdənsɪ] *(pl* **presidencies**) *n* présidence *f*; **during his presidency** durant sa présidence; **the Clinton presidency** la présidence de Clinton; **to assume the presidency** assumer la présidence

president ['prezɪdənt] *n* (**a**) *(of state)* président(e) *m,f*; **President Simpson** le président Simpson; **Mr President** Monsieur le Président (**b**) *(of organization, club)* président(e) *m,f*; *Br Pol* **President of the Board of Trade** ministre *mf* du Commerce et de l'Industrie (**c**) *Am (of company, bank)* président-directeur général *m*, P-DG *m*

►► *Am* ***President's Day*** = jour férié en l'honneur des anniversaires des présidents Washington et Lincoln

president-elect *n Am* = titre du président des États-Unis entre son élection et son investiture

presidential [,prezɪ'denʃəl] *adj (elections, candidate)* présidentiel; *(aeroplane, suite)* présidentiel, du président; **to nurse presidential ambitions** *or* **aspirations** aspirer à *ou* ambitionner la présidence; **it's a presidential year** c'est l'année des élections présidentielles

►► ***presidential elections*** (élections *fpl*) présidentielles *fpl*; ***presidential hopeful*** présidentiable *mf*

presiding [prɪ'zaɪdɪŋ] *adj* qui préside

►► ***presiding examiner*** surveillant(e) *m,f (à un examen écrit)*; *Br* ***presiding officer*** président *m* (de bureau de vote)

presidium [prɪ'sɪdɪəm] *(pl* **presidiums** *or* **presidia** [-dɪə]) *n* praesidium *m*, présidium *m*

presoak [,priː'səʊk] *vt* faire tremper

PRESS [pres]

presse	► **1 (a) – (e)**
serrement	► **1 (i)**
appuyer (sur)	► **3 (a), (e); 4 (a)**
presser	► **3 (b), (c)**
forcer	► **3 (d)**
faire pression	► **4 (b)**

1 *n* (**a**) *(newspapers)* presse *f*; **the national/local press** la presse nationale/locale; **freedom of the press** la liberté de la presse; **they advertised in the press** ils ont fait passer une annonce dans les journaux; **reports in the press were biased** les comptes rendus parus dans la presse étaient tendancieux; **they managed to keep her name out of the press** ils ont réussi à ce que son nom ne paraisse pas dans la presse

(**b**) *(journalists)* presse *f*; **the press were there** la presse était là; **she's a member of the press** elle a une carte de presse; *Ironic* **the gentlemen of the press** ces messieurs de la presse

(**c**) *(report, opinion)* presse *f*; **to get (a) good/bad press** avoir bonne/mauvaise presse; **to give sb (a) good/bad press** faire l'éloge/la critique de qn (**d**) *(printing)* presse *f*; **to go to press** *(book)* être mis sous presse; *(newspaper)* partir à l'impression; **we go to press at 5 p.m.** on est mis sous presse à 5 heures; *(copy deadline)* on boucle à 5 heures; **in** *or* **at (the) press** sous presse; **hot** *or* **straight from the press** tout frais; **ready for press** prêt à mettre sous presse; **the proofs were passed for press** on a donné le bon à tirer; **prices correct at time of going to press** prix corrects au moment de la mise sous presse

(**e**) *(machine)* **(printing) press** presse *f*; **to set the presses rolling** mettre les presses en marche; *Fig* mettre la machine en marche

(**f**) *(publisher)* presses *fpl*

(**g**) *(for tennis racket, handicrafts, woodwork, trousers)* presse *f*; *(for cider, oil, wine)* pressoir *m*

(**h**) *(push)* **the machine dispenses hot coffee at the press of a button** il suffit d'appuyer sur un bouton pour que la machine distribue du café chaud; **give it a slight press** appuyez légèrement là-dessus

(**i**) *(squeeze)* serrement *m*; **he gave my hand a quick press** il m'a serré la main rapidement

(**j**) *(crowd)* foule *f*; *(rush)* bousculade *f*; *Literary (of battle)* mêlée *f*; **in the press for the door we became separated** dans la ruée de la foule vers la porte, nous avons été séparés; **to force one's way through the press** fendre la foule, se frayer un chemin à travers la foule

(**k**) *(ironing)* coup *m* de fer; **to give sth a press** donner un coup de fer à qch

(**l**) *Ir & Scot (cupboard)* placard *m*, armoire *f*

(**m**) *(in weightlifting)* développé *m*

(**n**) *(in basketball)* pressing *m*; **full court press** zone-presse *f* (tout terrain); *Am Fig* **it was the full court press** on faisait le maximum; **to be engaged in a full court press to do sth** faire le maximum *ou* tout son possible pour faire qch

(**o**) *Ind (forming machine)* presse *f*

(**p**) *Mil* recrutement *m* de force

(**q**) *Naut* **press of sail** *or* **canvas** pleine voilure *f*; **under press of sail** toutes voiles dehors

2 *comp (reporter, photographer)* de presse; *(advertising)* dans la presse

3 *vt* (**a**) *(push → button, bell, trigger, accelerator)* appuyer sur; **try pressing it** essayez d'appuyer dessus; **he pressed the lid shut** il a fermé le couvercle (en appuyant dessus); **to press sth flat** aplatir qch; **to press sth home** enfoncer qch; **to press sth (back) into shape** rendre sa forme à qch; **to press one's way through a crowd/to the front** se frayer un chemin à travers une foule/jusqu'au premier rang; **he was pressed (up) against the railings** il s'est trouvé coincé contre le grillage; **I pressed myself against the wall** je me suis collé contre le mur; **she pressed a note into my hand** elle m'a glissé un billet dans la main; **he pressed his nose (up) against the window** il a collé son nez à la vitre; **he pressed his hat down on his head** il rabattit *ou* enfonça son chapeau sur sa tête; **she pressed the papers down into the bin** elle a enfoncé les papiers dans la poubelle

(**b**) *(squeeze → hand, arm)* presser, serrer; *(→ grapes, lemon, olives)* presser; **she pressed her son to her** elle serra son fils contre elle

(**c**) *(urge)* presser, pousser; *(harass)* harceler, talonner; **to press sb for payment/an answer** presser qn de payer/répondre; **she pressed me to tell her the truth** elle me pressa de lui dire la vérité; **if you press her she'll tell you** si tu insistes, elle te le dira; **if pressed, he would admit...** quand on insistait *ou* le poussait, il admettait...; **his creditors were pressing him hard** ses créanciers le harcelaient *ou* ne lui laissaient pas le moindre répit; **to be pressed for time/money** être à court de temps/d'argent

(**d**) *(force)* forcer, obliger; **I was pressed into signing the contract** j'ai été obligé de signer le contrat; **don't let yourself be pressed into going** ne laissez personne vous forcer à y aller

(**e**) *(impose, push forward → claim)* appuyer, pousser; *(→ opinions)* insister sur; **can I press a cup of tea on you?** puis-je vous offrir une tasse de thé?; **to press a gift on sb** forcer qn à accepter un cadeau; **to press (home) one's advantage** profiter d'un avantage; **to press one's attentions on sb** poursuivre qn de ses assiduités; **I don't want to press the point** je ne veux pas insister; *Law* **to press charges against sb** engager des poursuites contre qn

(**f**) *(iron → shirt, tablecloth)* repasser

(**g**) *(manufacture in mould → component)* mouler; *(→ record)* presser

(**h**) *(preserve by pressing → flower)* presser, faire sécher *(dans un livre ou un pressoir)*

(**i**) *(in weightlifting)* soulever

(**j**) *Mil (enlist by force)* recruter *ou* enrôler de force; *Fig* **to press into service** réquisitionner; **the local mechanic was pressed into service** le mécanicien du coin fut réquisitionné pour la circonstance

4 *vi* (**a**) *(push)* appuyer; **press here** appuyez *ou* pressez ici; **he pressed (down) on the accelerator** il appuya sur l'accélérateur; **the crowd pressed against the barriers/round the President** la foule se pressait contre les barrières/autour du président; **they pressed forward to get a better view** ils poussaient pour essayer de mieux voir; **to press through a crowd** se frayer un chemin à travers une foule; **to press close against sb** se serrer contre qn

(**b**) *(weight, burden)* faire pression (**on** sur); *(troubles)* peser (**on** à); **the rucksack pressed on his shoulders** le sac à dos pesait sur ses épaules; **her problems pressed on her mind** ses problèmes lui pesaient; **time presses!** le temps presse!

(**c**) *(insist)* **he pressed hard to get the grant** il a fait des pieds et des mains pour obtenir la bourse; **to press for an answer** insister pour avoir une réponse immédiate; **to press for an adjournment/the law to be tightened up** exiger un ajournement/que la loi soit renforcée

(**d**) *(iron)* se repasser; **some shirts press easily** il y a des chemises qui se repassent facilement

►► ***press agency*** agence *f* de presse; ***press agent*** attaché(e) *m,f* de presse; *Br* ***the Press Association*** = la principale agence de presse britannique; ***press attaché*** attaché(e) *m,f* de presse; ***press badge*** macaron *m* de presse; ***press baron*** magnat *m* de la presse; ***press box*** tribune *f* de (la) presse; ***press button*** bouton-poussoir *m*; ***press campaign*** campagne *f* de presse; ***press card*** carte *f* de presse *ou* de journaliste; ***press clipping*** coupure *f* de presse *or* de journal; *Br* ***the Press Complaints Commission*** = organisme britannique de contrôle de la presse; ***press conference*** conférence *f* de presse; ***press copy*** *(of book)* exemplaire *m* de service de presse; ***press corps*** journalistes *mpl*; **the White House press corps** = les journalistes accrédités à la Maison-Blanche; *Br* ***the Press Council*** = organisme indépendant veillant au respect de la déontologie dans la presse britannique; ***press coverage*** couverture-presse *f*; **the resignation got a lot of press coverage** la démission a été largement couverte dans la presse; *Br* ***press cutting*** coupure *f* de presse *ou* de journal; **a collection of press cuttings** une collection de coupures de journaux, un dossier de presse; ***press gallery*** tribune *f* de (la) presse; ***press handout*** communiqué *m* de presse; ***press insert*** encart *m* presse; ***press kit*** dossier *m* de presse *(distribué aux journalistes)*; ***press lord*** magnat *m* de la presse; ***press office*** service *m* de presse; ***press officer*** responsable *mf* des relations avec la presse; ***press pack*** dossier *m* de presse; ***press pass*** carte *f* de presse; *Typ* ***press proof*** dernière épreuve *f*; ***press relations*** relations *fpl* presse; ***press release*** communiqué *m* de presse; ***press report*** reportage *m*; **press reports of the incident were inaccurate** les articles de presse relatant l'incident étaient inexacts; ***press run*** tirage *m*; *Pol* ***press secretary*** ≃ porte-parole *m inv* du gouvernement; *Br* ***press stud*** bouton-pression *m*, pression *f*

►**press ahead** = **press on**

►**press down** **1** *vt sep* appuyer sur; *(with force)* enfoncer

2 *vi* **to press down on sb** peser sur qn

►**press for** *vt insep (demand)* exiger, réclamer; **they pressed for a pay rise** ils ont réclamé *ou* exigé une augmentation de salaire; **the residents are pressing for a pedestrian zone** les résidents font pression pour obtenir une zone piétonnière; **the opposition are pressing for an enquiry** l'opposition exige une enquête *ou* insiste pour que l'on fasse une enquête

►**press in** *vt sep* enfoncer

►**press on** *vi (continue → on journey)* poursuivre *ou* continuer son chemin; *(→ with activity)* continuer; *(persevere → in enterprise, job)* poursuivre, persévérer; **the travellers pressed on in the darkness** les voyageurs poursuivirent leur chemin dans la nuit; **we must press on to York** *or* **as far as York** il faut poursuivre jusqu'à York; **we pressed on regardless** nous avons continué malgré tout

►**press on with** *vt insep (job, negotiations)* continuer, poursuivre; **they pressed on with the plan in spite of opposition** ils ont poursuivi leur projet malgré l'opposition rencontrée

►**press out** *vt sep* (**a**) *(juice etc)* exprimer (**b**) *Tech (holes)* percer; *(shapes, parts)* découper

---

press-button *adj* à touches, à boutons-poussoirs

►► *Tel* ***press-button dialling*** numérotation *f* à touches

pressed [prest] **1** *adj* (**a**) *(flower)* pressé, séché (**b**) *(hurried)* pressé; *(overworked)* débordé

2 pressed for *adj (short of)* à court de; **we're pressed for space** nous manquons de place; **we're rather pressed for time** le temps nous est compté

►► ***pressed steel*** acier *m* embouti

press-gang **1** *n Mil & Hist* racoleurs *mpl*, recruteurs *mpl*

2 *vt* (**a**) *Br (force)* **to press-gang sb into doing sth** obliger qn à faire qch (contre son gré); **I was press-ganged into taking part** on m'a obligé à participer (**b**) *Mil & Hist* racoler, recruter de force

pressie ['prezɪ] *n Br Fam* cadeau ☐ *m*

pressing ['presɪŋ] **1** *adj* (**a**) *(urgent → appointment, business, debt)* urgent; **the matter is pressing** c'est une affaire urgente; **there is a pressing need for action** il faut agir vite

(**b**) *(insistent → demand, danger, need)* pressant; **at her pressing invitation, we agreed to go** devant son insistance, nous avons accepté d'y aller

(**c**) *(imminent → danger)* imminent

2 *n* (**a**) *(gen)* pression *f*; *(of grapes)* pressurage *m*; *(with feet)* foulage *m*; *(of record)* pressage *m*

(**b**) *(ironing)* repassage *m*

(**c**) *(insistence)* insistance *f*; **after much pressing from me, he finally gave in** j'ai tellement insisté qu'il a fini par céder

pressman ['presmæn] (*pl* **pressmen** [-men]) *n* (**a**) *(journalist)* journaliste *m* (**b**) *(printer)* typographe *m*

pressmark ['presmɑːk] *n* cote *f (d'un livre)*

press-on *adj* adhésif

pressroom ['presrʊm] *n* salle *f* de presse

press-up *n Br Sport* pompe *f*; **to do press-ups** faire des pompes

pressure ['preʃə(r)] **1** *n* (**a**) *(strain, stress)* pression *f*; **the pressures of city life** le stress de la vie en ville; **I can't take all this pressure** je ne supporte pas d'être sous une telle pression; **he's been under a lot of pressure lately** il est très stressé *ou* vraiment sous pression ces derniers temps; **he pleaded pressure of work** il s'est excusé en disant qu'il était débordé de travail; **to work under pressure** travailler sous pression; **we're under pressure to finish on time** on nous presse de respecter les délais; **the pressure of work is too much for me** la charge de travail est trop lourde pour moi; **there's a lot of pressure on her to succeed** on fait beaucoup pression sur elle pour qu'elle réussisse; **the pressure's on!** il va falloir mettre les bouchées doubles!

(**b**) *Met & Phys* pression *f*; *(of blood)* tension *f*; **high/low pressure area** *(on weather chart)* zone *f* de hautes/basses pressions; **a pressure of 20 kilogrammes to the square centimetre** une pression de 20 kilogrammes au centimètre carré; *Fig* **to work at full pressure** *(person)* travailler à plein régime; *(machine, factory)* tourner à plein régime; **oil pressure** pression *f* d'huile

(**c**) *(squeezing)* pression *f*; **she could feel the pressure of his grip on her arm** elle sentait la pression de sa poigne sur son bras (**d**) *(force, influence)* pression *f*; *Formal* **to bring pressure to bear** *or* **to put pressure on sb** faire pression *ou* exercer une pression sur qn; **they put pressure on me to come** ils ont fait pression sur moi pour que je vienne; **she did it under pressure** elle l'a fait contrainte et forcée; **she came under pressure from her parents** elle est venue parce que ses parents l'y ont obligée; **there's no pressure, don't come if you don't want to** rien ne t'oblige, si tu ne veux pas venir, ne viens pas; **they're putting too much pressure on him** ils le soumettent à trop de pression; *Sport* **they came under sustained pressure in the second half** ils ont été constamment sous pression pendant la deuxième mi-temps

2 *vt* faire pression sur; **stop pressuring me!** arrête de me presser comme ça!; **they pressured him into resigning** ils l'ont contraint à démissionner

▸▸ *Med* ***pressure bandage*** bandage *m* compressif; *Aviat* ***pressure cabin*** cabine *f* pressurisée *ou* sous pression; *Tech* ***pressure chamber*** réservoir *m* d'air comprimé; ***pressure cooker*** cocotte-minute® *f*, autocuiseur *m*; *Fig* **a pressure cooker atmosphere** une ambiance lourde de tension; ***pressure feed*** alimentation *f* par pression; ***pressure gauge*** jauge *f* de pression, manomètre *m*; ***pressure group*** groupe *m* de pression; *Naut* ***pressure hull*** coque *f* intérieure; ***pressure point*** *(on artery)* point *m* de compression; ***pressure ridge*** *(in ice)* chaîne *f* de pression; *Med* ***pressure sore*** escarre *f*; ***pressure suit*** scaphandre *m* pressurisé

pressure-cook *vt* faire cuire à la cocotte-minute® *ou* à l'autocuiseur

pressurization [ˌpreʃəraɪ'zeɪʃən] *n* pressurisation *f*

pressurize, -ise ['preʃəraɪz] *vt* (**a**) *(person, government)* faire pression sur; **to pressurize sb to do sth** *or* **into doing sth** faire pression sur qn pour qu'il/elle fasse qch; **don't pressurize me** ne me force pas; **a pressurized environment** un environnement stressant (**b**) *Aviat & Astron* pressuriser

pressurized ['preʃəraɪzd] *adj (container)* pressurisé; *(liquid, gas)* sous pression

▸▸ ***pressurized cabin*** cabine *f* pressurisée *or* sous pression

pressurized-water reactor *n* réacteur *m* à eau sous pression

Prestel® ['prestel] *n* = service de vidéotexte et fournisseur d'accès à l'internet de British Telecom

prestidigitation ['prestɪˌdɪdʒɪ'teɪʃən] *n Formal or Hum* prestidigitation *f*

prestidigitator [ˌprestɪ'dɪdʒɪteɪtə(r)] *n Formal or Hum* prestidigitateur(trice) *m,f*

prestige [pre'stiːʒ] **1** *n* prestige *m*; **it would mean a loss of prestige** ce serait déchoir *ou* déroger

2 *adj* de prestige; **prestige appartments** appartements *mpl* de grand standing; **a prestige job** un poste prestigieux; **the prestige value of the address** le caractère prestigieux de l'adresse, l'adresse *f* prestigieuse; **it has prestige value** c'est prestigieux

▸▸ *Mktg* ***prestige advertising*** publicité *f* de prestige; ***prestige goods*** produits *mpl* prestigieux; ***prestige model*** modèle *m* de prestige; *Com* ***prestige price*** prix *m* de prestige; *Mktg* ***prestige product*** produit *m* de prestige; *Mktg* ***prestige promotion*** promotion *f* de prestige

prestigious [pre'stɪdʒəs] *adj* prestigieux

presto ['prestəʊ] *(pl* **prestos**) **1** *adv* (**a**) *Mus* presto (**b**) **hey presto!** et voilà, le tour est joué! (**c**) *Fam* **presto (pronto)** *(immediately)* illico presto

2 *n Mus* presto *m*

prestress [ˌpriː'stres] *vt Constr* précontraindre

prestressed concrete [ˌpriː'strest-] *n Constr* béton *m* précontraint

presumable [prɪ'zjuːməbəl] *adj* présumable

presumably [prɪ'zjuːməblɪ] *adv* vraisemblablement; **presumably, he isn't coming** apparemment, il ne viendra pas; **presumably, she married him in the end** elle a vraisemblablement *ou* sans doute fini par l'épouser; **presumably you told him that...** je suppose que vous lui avez dit que...; **have they left? – presumably** ils sont partis? – je pense *ou* vraisemblablement

presume [prɪ'zjuːm] **1** *vt* (**a**) *(suppose)* présumer, supposer; **I presume he isn't coming** je présume *ou* suppose qu'il ne viendra pas; **I presumed them to be aware** *or* **that they were aware of the difficulties** je supposais qu'ils étaient au courant des difficultés; *Mil* **missing, presumed dead** manque à l'appel *ou* porté disparu, présumé mort; **he was presumed dead** *(by family etc)* on le croyait mort; *(by authorities)* on a présumé qu'il était mort, on l'a considéré comme décédé; *Law* **every man is presumed innocent until proven guilty** tout homme est présumé innocent tant qu'il n'a pas été déclaré coupable; **I presume so** je suppose, je présume que oui

(**b**) *(take liberty)* oser, se permettre; **I wouldn't presume to contradict you** je ne me permettrais pas de vous contredire; **I wouldn't presume so far as to...** je n'aurais pas la présomption de...; **you're presuming rather a lot** tu es bien présomptueux

(**c**) *(presuppose)* présupposer; **presuming they agree** à supposer qu'ils soient d'accord

2 *vi* **I don't want to presume** je ne voudrais pas m'imposer; **to presume on** *or* **upon sb** abuser de la gentillesse de qn

> **Dr Livingstone, I presume**
> Ce sont les mots que Sir Henry Stanley aurait adressés au Docteur Livingstone lorsqu'il le retrouva dans la jungle africaine où il s'était perdu en 1871. Stanley avait été envoyé à la recherche de l'explorateur par un journal américain. Cette phrase ("Docteur Livingstone, je présume") est utilisée sur le mode humoristique lorsqu'on fait la connaissance de quelqu'un dont on a entendu parler auparavant, le plus souvent en remplaçant **Doctor Livingstone** par le nom de la personne en question.

presumption [prɪ'zʌmpʃən] *n* (**a**) *(supposition)* présomption *f*, supposition *f*; **the presumption is that he was drowned** on pense *ou* suppose qu'il s'est noyé; **there is a strong presumption that he is guilty** on le soupçonne d'être coupable; **it's only a presumption** ce n'est qu'une hypothèse; **to make a presumption that...** présumer que...; **to act on a false presumption** agir sur une *ou* à partir d'une fausse supposition; **we worked on the presumption that she would agree** nous avons agi en supposant qu'elle serait d'accord; *Law* **presumption of innocence** présomption *f* d'innocence

(**b**) *(UNCOUNT) (arrogance)* audace *f*, présomption *f*, prétention *f*; **she had the presumption to say I was lying** elle a eu l'audace de dire que je mentais; **excuse my presumption, but haven't we met somewhere?** excusez mon audace, mais est-ce que nous ne nous sommes pas déjà rencontrés quelque part?

presumptive [prɪ'zʌmptɪv] *adj (heir)* présomptif

▸▸ ***presumptive proof*** preuve *f* par déduction *or* par présomption

presumptively [prɪ'zʌmptɪvlɪ] *adv* par présomption, présomptivement

presumptuous [prɪ'zʌmptʃʊəs] *adj* présomptueux, arrogant

presumptuously [prɪ'zʌmptʃʊəslɪ] *adv* présomptueusement, avec arrogance; **she presumptuously assumed that...** elle a eu la présomption de croire que...

presumptuousness [prɪ'zʌmptʃʊəsnɪs] *n* présomption *f*, arrogance *f*

presuppose [ˌpriːsə'pəʊz] *vt* présupposer

presupposition [ˌpriːsʌpə'zɪʃən] *n* présupposition *f*

pre-tax *adj* brut, avant (le prélèvement des) impôts

▸▸ ***pre-tax profits*** bénéfices *mpl* bruts *ou* avant impôts

pre-teen **1** *adj (sizes, fashions)* pour préadolescents; *(problems)* des préadolescents

2 *n* préadolescent(e) *m,f*

▸▸ ***pre-teen child*** préadolescent(e) *m,f*

pretence, *Am* **pretense** [prɪ'tens] *n* (**a**) *(false display)* simulacre *m*, faux-semblant *m*; **to make a pretence of doing sth** faire semblant *ou* mine de faire qch; **everyone sees through her pretence of being the devoted wife** elle ne trompe personne en jouant les femmes dévouées; **he's not really ill, it's only** *or* **all (a) pretence!** il n'est pas vraiment malade, il fait seulement semblant *ou* c'est (simplement) de la comédie!; **at least SHE made some pretence of sympathy!** elle au moins, elle a fait comme si ça la touchait!; **he made no pretence of his boredom/his scepticism** il n'a pas caché son ennui/son scepticisme; **she made no pretence of being interested** elle n'a aucunement feint d'être intéressée; **a pretence of democracy** un simulacre de démocratie

(**b**) *(pretext)* prétexte *m*; **under** *or* **on the pretence of doing sth** sous prétexte de faire qch; **he criticizes her on the slightest pretence** il la critique pour un rien *ou* à la moindre occasion

(**c**) *(claim)* prétention *f*; **a woman without the slightest pretence of culture** une femme qui n'a pas la moindre prétention d'être cultivée; **he has** *or* **makes no pretence to musical taste** il ne prétend pas *ou* il n'a pas la prétention de s'y connaître en musique

(**d**) *(UNCOUNT) (arrogance)* prétention *f*

pretend [prɪ'tend] **1** *vt* (**a**) *(make believe)* **to pretend to do sth** faire semblant de faire qch, feindre de faire qch; **they pretend to be rich** ils font semblant d'être riches; **they pretended not to see** *or* **to have seen us** ils ont fait semblant *ou* mine de ne pas nous voir; **she pretended to be shocked** elle a fait semblant *ou* mine d'être choquée; **he pretended not to be interested** il a fait semblant de ne pas être intéressé, il a joué les indifférents; **they pretended to be ill** ils ont fait semblant d'être malades; **he pretended to be** *or* **that he was their uncle** il s'est fait passer pour leur oncle; **she pretends that everything is all right** elle fait comme si tout allait bien; **it's no use pretending things will improve** cela ne sert à rien de faire comme si les choses allaient s'améliorer; **I'll pretend I didn't hear that last remark** je vais faire comme si je n'avais pas entendu cette dernière remarque; **let's pretend that we're astronauts** *(children playing)* on dirait qu'on était astronautes; **you pretend to be Mummy** toi, tu serais une maman

(**b**) *(claim)* prétendre; **I don't pretend to be an expert** je ne prétends pas être un expert, je n'ai pas la prétention d'être un expert; **I don't pretend to understand** je ne prétends pas comprendre

(**c**) *(feign → indifference, ignorance)* feindre, simuler

2 *vi* (**a**) *(feign)* faire semblant; **there's no point in pretending (to me)** inutile de faire semblant (avec moi); **I'm only pretending!** c'est juste pour rire!; **stop pretending and admit the truth** arrête de faire semblant et avoue la vérité; **to play at let's pretend** *(children)* jouer à faire semblant *ou* comme si; **let's pretend** faisons semblant *ou* comme si

(**b**) *(lay claim)* prétendre; **to pretend to sth** prétendre à qch; **I don't pretend to great knowledge on the matter/any special expertise** je ne prétends pas savoir grand-chose sur la question/avoir des connaissances particulières; *Arch* **to pretend to the throne** prétendre au trône; *Arch* **he pretended to her hand** il la courtisait

3 *adj Fam (fight)* pour faire semblant❑, pour jouer❑; **it was only pretend!** c'était pour rire *ou* pour faire semblant!; **it's only pretend money/a pretend gun** ce n'est pas du vrai argent/un vrai pistolet❑

pretended [prɪ'tendɪd] *adj (emotion, interest)* feint, simulé; *(doctor, wealth, ignorance etc)* prétendu, soi-disant

pretender [prɪ'tendə(r)] *n* (**a**) *(to throne, title, right)* prétendant(e) *m,f*; *Br Hist* **the Old Pretender** le Prétendant; *Br Hist* **the Young Pretender** le Jeune Prétendant (**b**) *(impostor)* imposteur *m*

pretense *Am* = **pretence**

pretension [prɪ'tenʃən] *n* (**a**) *(claim)* prétention *f*; **to have pretensions to sth** avoir des prétentions *ou* prétendre à qch; **a film with intellectual pretensions** un film qui a des prétentions intellectuelles; **to have social pretensions** vouloir arriver; **I make no pretensions to expert knowledge** je n'ai pas la prétention *ou* je ne me flatte pas d'être expert en la matière; **he has**

literary pretensions il se prend pour un écrivain
(**b**) *(UNCOUNT) (pretentiousness)* prétention *f*; **he is devoid of pretension** il est sans prétention

pretentious [prɪ'tenʃəs] *adj* prétentieux

pretentiously [prɪ'tenʃəslɪ] *adv* prétentieusement

pretentiousness [prɪ'tenʃəsnɪs] *n (UNCOUNT)* prétention *f*

preterite, *Am* **preterit** ['pretərət] *Gram* **1** *adj (form)* du prétérit
2 *n* prétérit *m*; **in the preterite** au prétérit
▸▸ ***preterite tense*** prétérit *m*

preterm [,priː'tɜːm] **1** *adj (baby)* né avant terme; *(birth, complications etc)* ayant lieu avant la fin du terme
2 *adv (born)* avant terme; *(occur)* avant la fin du terme

preternatural [,priːtə'nætʃərəl] *Literary* **1** *adj* surnaturel
2 *n* surnaturel *m*

preternaturally [,priːtə'nætʃərəlɪ] *adv Literary* exceptionnellement

pre-test 1 *n* pré-test *m*
2 *vt* pré-tester

pretext ['priːtekst] *n* prétexte *m*; **on** *or* **under the pretext of doing sth** sous prétexte de faire qch; **it's just a pretext for avoiding work** ce n'est qu'un prétexte pour ne pas travailler

pretor ['priːtə(r)] *n Hist* préteur *m*

Pretoria [prɪ'tɔːrɪə] *n* Pretoria

pretorian [prɪ'tɔːrɪən] *adj Hist* prétorien
▸▸ *Hist & Fig* ***pretorian guard*** garde *f* prétorienne

pretreat [,priː'triːt] *vt Tech* prétraiter

pretreatment [,priː'triːtmənt] *n Tech* prétraitement *m*

prettify ['prɪtɪfaɪ] *(pt & pp* **prettified***)* *vt Pej (room, garden)* enjoliver; **to prettify oneself** se pomponner

prettily ['prɪtɪlɪ] *adv* joliment; **prettily dressed** joliment habillé; **to smile prettily** faire un/des sourire(s) charmeur(s); **she sang very prettily** elle a chanté avec beaucoup de charme

prettiness ['prɪtɪnɪs] *n* (**a**) *(of appearance)* beauté *f*; **she had a certain prettiness** elle avait une certaine beauté; **the prettiness of her smile** son joli sourire (**b**) *Pej (of style)* mièvrerie *f*

pretty ['prɪtɪ] *(compar* **prettier,** *superl* **prettiest,** *pt & pp* **prettied***)* **1** *adj* (**a**) *(attractive → clothes, girl, place, picture, song)* joli; **she's a pretty little thing** elle est mignonne comme tout; **who's a pretty boy?** *(to parrot)* le beau perroquet!; *Fam* **I'm not just a pretty face!** qu'est-ce que tu crois?, il y en a, là-dedans!; **to be as pretty as a picture** *(person)* être mignon comme tout; *(place)* être ravissant
(**b**) *Ironic* **it was not a pretty sight** ce n'était pas beau à voir; **this is a pretty state of affairs!** c'est du joli *ou* du propre!; **things have come to a pretty pass!** nous voilà bien!; **it cost a pretty penny** ça a coûté une jolie petite somme; **that'll cost me a pretty penny!** ça va me coûter cher!; **to make a pretty penny out of sth** tirer une petite fortune de qch
(**c**) *Pej (style, expression)* précieux; **it's not enough to make pretty speeches** il ne suffit pas de faire de beaux discours; *Pej* **his pretty boy good looks** son physique de jeune minet
2 *adv Fam* (**a**) *(quite)* assez □; **it's pretty good** c'est pas mal du tout □; **it's pretty important** c'est assez important □; **it's pretty difficult** c'est plutôt difficile □; **you did pretty well for a beginner** tu t'en es plutôt bien tiré pour un débutant; **we've got a pretty good idea of what she was like** nous nous imaginons assez bien comment elle était □
(**b**) *(almost)* presque □, à peu près □, pratiquement □; **I'm pretty certain I'm right** je suis presque sûr d'avoir raison; **it's pretty much the same team as last week** c'est à peu près la même équipe que la semaine dernière; **he told her pretty well everything** il lui a raconté pratiquement *ou* à peu près tout
(**c**) *(idiom)* **to be sitting pretty** ne pas avoir de souci à se faire □
3 *n Fam Old-fashioned (girl, animal)* mignon(onne) *m,f*; **come here, my pretty** viens ici, mon (ma) mignon(onne)

▸**pretty up** *vt sep* enjoliver; **to pretty oneself up** se faire beau (belle)

pretty-pretty *adj Fam Pej (person)* gentillet □, mignonnet □; *(dress)* cucul la praline *(inv)*; *(painting)* gentillet □; *(garden)* mignon, gentil □

pretzel ['pretsəl] *n Culin* bretzel *m*

prevail [prɪ'veɪl] *vi* (**a**) *(triumph)* l'emporter, prévaloir; **to prevail against sb** l'emporter *ou* prévaloir contre qn; **to prevail over sb** l'emporter *ou* prévaloir sur qn; **luckily, common sense prevailed** heureusement, le bon sens a prévalu *ou* l'a emporté
(**b**) *(exist → situation, opinion, belief)* régner, avoir cours; **the rumour which is now prevailing** le bruit qui court en ce moment; **the conditions prevailing in the Third World** les conditions que l'on rencontre le plus souvent dans le tiers monde

▸**prevail on, prevail upon** *vt insep Formal* persuader; **he was prevailed upon to accept the post** il s'est laissé persuader d'accepter le poste; **can I prevail on your good nature?** puis-je faire appel à votre bonté?; **he was not to be prevailed on** il fut impossible de le faire changer d'avis

prevailing [prɪ'veɪlɪŋ] *adj* (**a**) *(wind)* dominant (**b**) *(belief, opinion)* courant, répandu; *(fashion)* en vogue; **according to prevailing opinion** selon l'opinion la plus répandue (**c**) *(current)* actuel; **the prevailing exchange rate** le taux de change actuel; **in the prevailing conditions** *(now)* dans les conditions actuelles; *(then)* à l'époque; **the prevailing political climate** le climat politique actuel

prevalence ['prevələns] *n (widespread existence)* prédominance *f*; *(of disease)* prévalence *f*; *(frequency)* fréquence *f*; **the prevalence of rented property surprised him** il fut surpris de constater à quel point les locations étaient répandues; **the prevalence of these theories can only do harm** la popularité de ces théories ne peut qu'être nuisible

prevalent ['prevələnt] *adj* (**a**) *(widespread)* répandu, courant; *(frequent)* fréquent; **violence is prevalent in big cities** la violence est monnaie courante dans les grandes villes; **this opinion is prevalent among teenagers** cette opinion est très répandue parmi les adolescents; **to become prevalent** se généraliser (**b**) *(current)* actuel, d'aujourd'hui; *(in past)* de *ou* à l'époque

prevaricate [prɪ'værɪkeɪt] *vi* tergiverser, user de faux-fuyants; **stop prevaricating!** assez de faux-fuyants!

prevaricating [prɪ'værɪkeɪtɪŋ], **prevarication** [prɪ,værɪ'keɪʃən] *n* tergiversation *f*, faux-fuyants *mpl*; **I'm fed up with your prevaricating** j'en ai assez de tes faux-fuyants *ou* tergiversations

prevaricator [prɪ'værɪkeɪtə(r)] *n* personne *f* qui tergiverse *ou* qui use de faux-fuyants

prevenient [,priː'viːnjənt] *adj Literary* préalable, antécédent (**to** à)

prevent [prɪ'vent] *vt (accident, catastrophe, scandal)* empêcher, éviter; *(illness)* prévenir; **to prevent sb (from) doing sth** empêcher qn de faire qch; **there is nothing to prevent our going** *or* **to prevent us from going** rien ne nous empêche d'y aller; **a sudden storm prevented the match from going ahead** une tempête soudaine a empêché le déroulement du match; **to prevent a disease from spreading** empêcher une maladie de s'étendre, éviter qu'une maladie ne s'étende; **I couldn't prevent her** je n'ai pas pu l'en empêcher; **we were unable to prevent the bomb from exploding** nous n'avons rien pu faire pour empêcher la bombe d'exploser; **they couldn't prevent his departure** ils n'ont pu l'empêcher de partir

preventable [prɪ'ventəbəl] *adj* évitable; **it would have been easily preventable** ç'aurait été facile à éviter; **a preventable disease** une maladie que l'on peut prévenir

preventative [prɪ'ventətɪv] *adj* préventif; **to take preventative measures** prendre des mesures préventives

preventible = **preventable**

prevention [prɪ'venʃən] *n* prévention *f*; **the prevention of cruelty to animals** la protection des animaux; **the Prevention of Terrorism Act** = en Grande-Bretagne, loi sur la prévention du terrorisme permettant notamment la garde à vue de toute personne suspectée; *Prov* **prevention is better than cure** mieux vaut prévenir que guérir

preventionism [prɪ'venʃənɪzəm] *n* préventologie *f*

preventionist [prɪ'venʃənɪst] *n* préventologue *mf*

preventive [prɪ'ventɪv] **1** *adj (medicine)* préventif, prophylactique; *(measure)* préventif
2 *n* (**a**) *(measure)* mesure *f* préventive; **as a preventive** à titre préventif (**b**) *Med* médicament *m* préventif *ou* prophylactique
▸▸ *Br Law* ***preventive detention*** détention *f* préventive

preventively [prɪ'ventɪvlɪ] *adv* préventivement; **to act preventively against sth** prendre des mesures préventives contre qch

preverbal [,priː'vɜːbəl] *adj* (**a**) *(infant)* qui ne parle pas encore (**b**) *Gram* avant le verbe
▸▸ ***preverbal communication*** activité *f* préverbale

preview ['priːvjuː] **1** *n* (**a**) *(of movie, show, exhibition)* avant-première *f*; *(of art exhibition)* vernissage *m*; **and here is a preview of tomorrow's programmes** et voici un aperçu des programmes de demain; **can you give us a preview of what to expect?** pouvez-vous nous donner une idée de ce à quoi il faut s'attendre?
(**b**) *Am Cin (trailer)* bande-annonce *f*
(**c**) *Comput* prévisualisation *f*, aperçu *m* avant impression
2 *vt* (**a**) **to preview a movie** *(put on)* donner un film en avant-première; *(see)* voir un film en avant-première; **to preview the evening's television viewing** passer en revue les programmes télévisés de la soirée
(**b**) *Comput* prévisualiser, faire un aperçu avant impression de

previous ['priːvjəs] **1** *adj* (**a**) *(prior)* précédent; **on a previous occasion** auparavant; **on the previous occasion we had met** la dernière fois que nous nous étions rencontrés; **I have a previous engagement** j'ai déjà un rendez-vous, je suis déjà pris; **she has had several previous accidents** elle a déjà eu plusieurs accidents; **do you have any previous experience of this kind of work?** avez-vous déjà une expérience de ce genre de travail?; **the two months previous to your arrival** les deux mois précédant votre arrivée; *Law* **he has no previous convictions** il n'a pas de casier judiciaire, il a un casier judiciaire vierge; **he has had several previous convictions** il a déjà fait l'objet de plusieurs condamnations
(**b**) *(former)* antérieur; **in a previous life** dans une vie antérieure; **his previous marriages ended in divorce** ses autres mariages se sont soldés par des divorces
(**c**) *(with days and dates)* précédent; **the previous Monday** le lundi précédent; **the previous June** au mois de juin précédent; **the previous day** le jour précédent, la veille; **the previous evening** le soir précédent, la veille au soir
(**d**) *Br Fam (hasty → decision, judgement)* prématuré □, hâtif □; *(→ person)* expéditif □; **aren't you being a little previous?** n'êtes-vous pas un peu pressé? □ n'allez-vous pas un peu vite? □
2 *adv* antérieurement; *Formal* **previous to his death** avant sa mort, avant qu'il ne meure
3 *n Fam Crime slang (previous convictions)* casier □ *m*

previously ['priːvjəslɪ] *adv* (**a**) *(in the past)* auparavant, précédemment; **six weeks previously** six semaines auparavant *ou* plus tôt; **previously, the country was under British rule** auparavant, le pays était sous autorité britannique (**b**) *(already)* déjà; **we've met previously** nous nous sommes déjà rencontrés

prevocalic [,priːvə'kælɪk] *adj Ling* prévocalique

prewar [,priː'wɔː(r)] *adj* d'avant-guerre; **the prewar years** l'avant-guerre *m ou f*

prewash ['priːwɒʃ] **1** *n* prélavage *m*
2 *vt* faire un prélavage de

prey [preɪ] *n (UNCOUNT) also Fig* proie *f*; **hens are often (a) prey to foxes** les poules sont souvent la proie des renards; **the sheep fell (a) prey to some marauding beast** les moutons ont été attaqués par un animal maraudeur; **to be (a)**

prey to doubts/nightmares être en proie au doute/à des cauchemars; **she was an easy prey for** *or* **to fast-talking salesmen** elle était une proie facile pour le boniment des vendeurs; **to fall prey to temptation** tomber en proie à la tentation

►**prey on, prey upon** *vt insep* (**a**) *(of predator)* faire sa proie de; *Fig* **he preyed on her fears** il exploita ses angoisses; *Fig* **the thieves preyed upon old women** les voleurs s'en prenaient aux vieilles dames

(**b**) *(of fear, doubts)* ronger; **the thought continued to prey on his mind** l'idée continuait à lui ronger l'esprit

prez [prez] *n Fam (president)* président(e)[❑] *m,f*

prial ['praɪəl] *n Br (in cards)* brelan *m*

Priam ['praɪəm] *pr n Myth* Priam

priapic [praɪ'æpɪk] *adj* priapique

priapism ['praɪəpɪzəm] *n Med* priapisme *m*

Priapus [praɪ'eɪpəs] **1** *pr n Myth* Priape

2 *n* phallus *m*, priape *m*

PRICE [praɪs]

prix	► **1 (a), (b), (d)**
valeur	► **1 (b)**
cours	► **1 (c)**
cote	► **1 (c), (e)**
fixer le prix de	► **3 (a)**
évaluer	► **3 (a)**
marquer le prix de	► **3 (b)**
demander le prix de	► **3 (c)**

1 *n* (**a**) *(cost)* prix *m*; **what price is the clock?** quel est le prix de cette pendule?; **what is the price of petrol?** à quel prix est l'essence?; **to rise** *or* **increase** *or* **go up in price** augmenter; **the price has risen** *or* **gone up by 10 percent** le prix a augmenté de 10 pour cent; **petrol has gone down in price** le prix de l'essence a baissé; **prices are rising/falling** les prix sont en hausse/baisse; **to raise the price of sth** augmenter le prix de qch; **I paid a high price for it** je l'ai payé cher; **their prices are a bit expensive** leurs prix sont un peu chers; **he charges reasonable prices** ses prix sont raisonnables; **they pay top prices for antique china** ils achètent la porcelaine ancienne au prix fort; **if the price is right** si le prix est correct; **she got a good price for her car** elle a obtenu un bon prix de sa voiture; **to sell sth at a reduced price** vendre qch à prix réduit; **I'll let you have the carpet at a reduced price** je vous ferai un prix d'ami pour le tapis; **I got the chair at a reduced/at half price** j'ai eu la chaise à prix réduit/à moitié prix; **her jewels fetched huge prices at auction** ses bijoux ont atteint des sommes folles aux enchères; **that's my price, take it or leave it** c'est mon dernier prix, à prendre ou à laisser; **name** *or* **state your price!** votre prix sera le mien!; **every man has his price** tout homme s'achète; **he gave us a price for repairing the car** il nous a donné le prix des réparations à faire sur la voiture; *Br Fam Hum* **what's that got to do with the price of fish?** qu'est-ce que ça a à voir avec la choucroute?

(**b**) *(value)* prix *m*, valeur *f*; **to argue over the price of sth** débattre le prix de qch; **to put a price on sth** *(definite)* fixer le prix *ou* la valeur de qch; *(estimate)* évaluer le prix *ou* estimer la valeur de qch; **I wouldn't like to put a price on that fur coat** je n'ose pas imaginer le prix de ce manteau de fourrure; **to put a price on sb's head** mettre la tête de qn à prix; **there's a price on his head** sa tête a été mise à prix; **you can't put a price on love/health** l'amour/la santé n'a pas de prix; **what price all her hopes now?** que valent tous ses espoirs maintenant?; **he puts a high price on loyalty** il attache beaucoup d'importance *ou* il accorde beaucoup de valeur à la loyauté; **to be beyond** *or* **without price** être (d'un prix) inestimable *ou* hors de prix, ne pas avoir de prix

(**c**) *St Exch* cours *m*, cote *f*; **today's prices** les cours *mpl* du jour; **what is the price of gold?** quel est le cours de l'or?

(**d**) *Fig (penalty)* prix *m*; **it's a small price to pay for peace of mind** c'est bien peu de chose pour avoir l'esprit tranquille; **this must be done at any price** il faut que cela se fasse à tout prix *ou* coûte que coûte; **it's a high price to pay for independence** c'est bien cher payer l'indépendance; **you've paid a high price for success** vous avez payé bien cher votre réussite; **that's the price of** *or* **the price paid for fame** c'est la rançon de la gloire

(**e**) *(chance, odds)* cote *f*; *Horseracing* **what price are they giving on Stardust?** quelle est la cote de Stardust?; *Horseracing* **long/short price** forte/faible cote *f*; **what price he'll keep his word?** combien pariez-vous qu'il tiendra parole?; **what price peace now?** quelles sont les chances de paix maintenant?; **what price my chances of being appointed?** quelles sont mes chances d'être nommé?

(**f**) *(quotation)* devis *m*

2 *comp (bracket)* de prix; *(rise)* des prix

3 *vt* (**a**) *(set cost of)* fixer *ou* établir *ou* déterminer le prix de; *(estimate value of)* évaluer qch, estimer la valeur de qch; **the book is priced at £17** le livre coûte 17 livres; **his paintings are rather highly priced** le prix de ses tableaux est un peu élevé; **a reasonably priced hotel** un hôtel aux prix raisonnables; **how would you price that house?** à combien estimeriez-vous cette maison?

(**b**) *(indicate cost of)* marquer le prix de, mettre le prix sur; *(with label)* étiqueter; **all goods must be clearly priced** le prix des marchandises doit être clairement indiqué; **the book is priced at £10** le livre est vendu (au prix de) 10 livres; **this book isn't priced** le prix de ce livre n'est pas indiqué; **these goods haven't been priced** ces articles n'ont pas été étiquetés

(**c**) *(ascertain price of)* demander le prix de, s'informer du prix de; **she priced the stereo in several shops before buying it** elle a comparé le prix de la chaîne dans plusieurs magasins avant de l'acheter

(**d**) *Econ (quantity)* valoriser

4 at any price *adv* **she wants a husband at any price** elle veut un mari à tout prix *ou* coûte que coûte; **he wouldn't do it at any price!** il ne voulait le faire à aucun prix *ou* pour rien au monde!

5 at a price *adv* en y mettant le prix; **she'll help you, at a price** elle vous aidera, à condition que vous y mettiez le prix; **you can get real silk, but only at a price** vous pouvez avoir de la soie véritable, à condition d'y mettre le prix; **you got what you wanted, but at a price!** vous avez eu ce que vous souhaitiez, mais à quel prix! *ou* mais vous l'avez payé cher!

►► ***price agreement*** accord *m* sur les prix; *Fin* ***price bid*** offre *f* de prix; ***price break*** baisse *f* de prix; ***price ceiling*** plafond *m* de prix; ***price comparison*** comparaison *f* des prix; ***price competitiveness*** compétitivité-prix *f*; ***price control*** contrôle *m* des prix; ***price cut*** rabais *m*, réduction *f* (des prix), baisse *f* des prix; **huge price cuts!** *(in advertisement)* prix sacrifiés!; *Mktg* ***price differential*** écart *m* de prix; ***price discount*** remise *f* sur les prix; ***price discrimination*** tarif *m* discriminatoire; ***price elasticity*** élasticité *f* des prix; ***price escalation*** flambée *f* des prix; ***price ex-works*** prix *m* départ usine; ***price floor*** prix *m* plancher; ***price freeze*** blocage *m* des prix, gel *m* des prix; ***price hike*** hausse *f* de prix; *Fin* ***prices and incomes policy*** politique *f* des prix et des salaires; ***price increase*** hausse *f* des prix, augmentation *f* des prix; ***prices index*** indice *m* des prix, *Belg* index *m* des prix; *Fin* ***price inflation*** inflation *f* des prix; *Mktg* ***price label*** étiquette *f* de prix; *Mktg* ***price leader*** prix *m* directeur; *Mktg* ***price leadership*** commandement *m* des prix; ***price level*** niveau *m* de prix; ***price list*** tarif *m*, liste *f* des prix; *St Exch* ***price maker*** inflation *f* des prix; *Mktg* ***price mark-up*** majoration *f* de prix; *Fin* ***price of money*** prix *m ou* loyer *m* de l'argent; *Fin* ***price plan*** plan *m* prix; *Mktg* ***price point*** prix *m* (de référence); *Mktg* ***price policy*** politique *f* de prix; *Mktg* ***price positioning*** positionnement *m* de prix; *Mktg* ***price promotion*** promotion *f*; *Mktg* ***price proposal*** proposition *f* de prix; ***price range*** gamme *f ou* échelle *f* des prix; **what is your price range?** combien voulez-vous mettre?; **it's not in my price range** ce n'est pas dans mes prix; ***price reduction*** réduction *f* (des prix); ***price regulation*** réglementation *f* des prix; *Fin* ***price ring*** monopole *m* des prix; *Mktg* ***price scale*** barème *m* des prix, échelle *f* des prix; *Mktg* ***price sensitivity*** sensibilité *f* aux prix; *Mktg* ***price setting*** détermination *f* des prix, fixation *f* des prix; *St Exch* ***price spreads*** écarts *mpl* de cours; *Mktg* ***price stability*** stabilité *f* des prix; *Mktg* ***price step*** écart *m* de prix; *Fin* ***price structure*** structure *f* des prix; *Mktg* ***price survey*** enquête *f* sur les prix; ***price tag*** *(label)* étiquette *f* de prix; *(value)* prix *m*, valeur *f*; **what's the price tag on a Rolls these days?** combien vaut une Rolls de nos jours?; ***price ticket*** étiquette *f* de prix; *Mktg* ***price undercutting*** gâchage *m* des prix; ***price war*** guerre *f* des prix

►**price down** *vt sep Br* baisser le prix de, démarquer; **everything has been priced down by 10 percent for the sales** tous les articles ont été démarqués de 10 pour cent pour les soldes

►**price out of** *vt sep* **to price oneself** *or* **one's goods out of the market** perdre son marché *ou* sa clientèle à cause de ses prix trop élevés; **we've been priced out of the Japanese market** nous avons perdu le marché japonais à cause de nos prix; **to price competitors out of the market** éliminer la concurrence en pratiquant des prix déloyaux; **cheap charter flights have priced the major airlines out of the market** les vols charters à prix réduit ont fait perdre des parts de marché aux grandes compagnies aériennes; **imported textiles have priced ours out of the market** les importations de textiles, en cassant les prix, nous ont fait perdre toute compétitivité; **he priced himself out of the job** il n'a pas été embauché parce qu'il a demandé un salaire trop élevé

►**price up** *vt sep Br (raise cost of)* augmenter *ou* majorer le prix de, majorer; *(on label)* indiquer un prix plus élevé sur

price-conscious *adj* attentif aux prix

price-cutting *n (UNCOUNT)* réductions *fpl* de prix

-priced [praɪst] *suff* **high-priced** à prix élevé, (plutôt) cher; **low-priced** à bas prix, peu cher; **over-priced** trop cher

price-earnings ratio *n St Exch* ratio *m* cours-bénéfices, rapport *m* cours-bénéfices

price-elastic *adj Mktg* au prix élastique

price-fixing *n (control)* contrôle *m* des prix; *(rigging)* entente *f* sur les prix

price-inelastic *adj Mktg* au prix stable

priceless ['praɪslɪs] *adj* (**a**) *(precious → jewels, friendship)* d'une valeur inestimable (**b**) *Fam (funny → joke)* tordant, bidonnant; *(→ person)* impayable, crevant

pricelessness ['praɪslɪsnɪs] *n* valeur *f* inestimable

price-rigging *n* entente *f* sur les prix

price-sensitive *adj Mktg* sensible au prix

pricey ['praɪsɪ] *(compar* **pricier**, *superl* **priciest**) *adj Fam* chérot

pricing ['praɪsɪŋ] *n* détermination *f* du prix, fixation *f* du prix

►► ***pricing policy*** politique *f* de(s) prix

prick [prɪk] **1** *vt* (**a**) *(jab, pierce)* piquer, percer; **she pricked her finger/herself with the needle** elle s'est piqué le doigt/elle s'est piquée avec l'aiguille; **to prick holes in sth** faire des trous dans qch; **the kids were pricking balloons with pins** les gosses crevaient des ballons avec des épingles; **the thorns pricked their legs** les épines leur piquaient les jambes

(**b**) *(irritate)* piquer, picoter; **tears pricked his eyes** les larmes lui piquaient les yeux; **the smoke was pricking my eyes** la fumée me piquait les yeux; *Fig* **his conscience was pricking him** il n'avait pas la conscience tranquille, il avait mauvaise conscience

2 *vi* (**a**) *(pin, cactus, thorn)* piquer

(**b**) *(be irritated)* picoter; **my eyes are pricking from the smoke** j'ai les yeux qui me piquent *ou* brûlent à cause de la fumée; *Fig* **her conscience was pricking (at her)** elle n'avait pas la conscience tranquille, elle avait mauvaise conscience

3 *n* (**a**) *(from insect, pin, thorn)* piqûre *f*; **he felt a sudden prick in his finger** soudain il a senti quelque chose lui piquer le doigt; *Fig* **pricks of**

conscience remords *mpl*; **to have a prick of conscience** être titillé par sa conscience
(**b**) *Vulg (penis)* bite *f*, queue *f*
(**c**) *very Fam (man)* con *m*, connard *m*; **stop making such a prick of yourself!** arrête de faire le con!; *Vulg* **to feel like a spare prick (at a wedding)** tenir la chandelle
▸**prick out** *vt sep Hort (seedlings)* repiquer
▸**prick up 1** *vi (ears)* se dresser
2 *vt sep* dresser; **the dog pricked up its ears** le chien a dressé les oreilles; **she pricked up her ears at the sound of her name** elle a dressé *ou* tendu l'oreille en entendant son nom

pricking [ˈprɪkɪŋ] **1** *n (piercing)* piquage *m*; *(sensation)* picotement *m*; **she felt a pricking in her fingers** elle avait des picotements dans les doigts; **the prickings of conscience** les remords *mpl*
2 *adj* piquant; **a pricking sensation** un picotement, un fourmillement
▸▸ *Hort* ***pricking out*** *(of seedlings)* repiquage *m*

prickle [ˈprɪkəl] **1** *n* (**a**) *(of rose, cactus)* épine *f*, piquant *m*; *(of hedgehog, porcupine)* piquant *m* (**b**) *(sensation)* picotement *m*; *(of anticipation, excitement)* fourmillement *m*
2 *vt* piquer
3 *vi (skin)* picoter, fourmiller; **her skin prickled with excitement** elle eu un frisson d'excitation; *Fig* **to prickle with indignation** se hérisser

prickliness [ˈprɪkəlɪnɪs] *n* hérissement *m*

prickly [ˈprɪkəlɪ] *(compar* **pricklier,** *superl* **prickliest)** *adj* (**a**) *(cactus, plant)* épineux; *(hedgehog)* couvert de piquants; *(beard)* piquant; *(clothes)* qui pique; **his fingers felt prickly** il avait des fourmillements dans les doigts; **his skin felt prickly** sa peau le démangeait; **the surface felt prickly** la surface était piquante; **a prickly sensation** une sensation de picotement
(**b**) *Fam (irritable → person)* ombrageux❑, irritable❑; *(→ character)* ombrageux❑; **he's very prickly** il se froisse facilement❑, il est très susceptible❑; **she's a bit prickly today** elle est plutôt irritable aujourd'hui❑
(**c**) *(delicate → subject, topic, problem)* épineux, délicat; **it's a prickly situation** c'est une situation épineuse *ou* délicate
▸▸ *Med* ***prickly heat*** *(UNCOUNT)* fièvre *f* miliaire, miliaire *f*, suette *f* miliaire; ***prickly pear*** *(fruit)* figue *f* de Barbarie; *(tree)* figuier *m* de Barbarie; *Bot* ***prickly saltwort*** kali *m*

pricktease [ˈprɪktiːz], **prickteaser** [ˈprɪktiːzə(r)] *n Vulg* allumeuse *f*

pricy = **pricey**

pride [praɪd] **1** *n* (**a**) *(satisfaction)* fierté *f*; **she takes great pride in her son** elle est très fière de son fils; **they take pride in their town** ils sont fiers de leur ville; **to take (a) pride in one's appearance** prendre soin de sa personne; **he takes no pride in his work** il ne prend pas du tout son travail à cœur; **to take (a) pride in doing sth** mettre de la fierté à faire qch, s'enorgueillir de faire qch; **he had pride in his sister's success** il était fier de la réussite de sa sœur; **she pointed with pride to her new car** elle montra fièrement du doigt sa nouvelle voiture
(**b**) *(self-respect)* fierté *f*, amour-propre *m*; **a sense of pride** un sentiment d'amour-propre; **he has no pride** il n'a pas d'amour-propre; **I have my pride!** j'ai ma fierté!; **her pride was hurt** elle était blessée dans son amour-propre; **they have too much pride to accept charity** ils sont trop fiers *ou* ils ont trop d'amour-propre pour accepter la charité
(**c**) *Pej (arrogance)* orgueil *m*; **the sin of pride** le péché d'orgueil; *Prov* **pride comes** *or* **goes before a fall** = plus on est fier, plus dure est la chute
(**d**) *(most valuable thing)* orgueil *m*, fierté *f*; **she is her parents' pride and joy** elle fait la fierté de ses parents; **that antique table is her pride and joy** elle est très fière de cette table ancienne; **this painting is the pride of the collection** ce tableau est le joyau de la collection; **pride of place** place *f* d'honneur; **to have** *or* **to take pride of place** occuper la place d'honneur
(**e**) *(of lions)* troupe *f*
2 *vt* **to pride oneself on** *or* **upon sth** être fier *ou* s'enorgueillir de qch; **she prided herself on being the youngest member of the team** elle s'enorgueillissait *ou* était fière d'être la plus jeune de l'équipe

'Pride and Prejudice' *Austen* 'Orgueil et préjugé'

prie-dieu [priːˈdjɜː] *n* prie-dieu *m inv*

prier [ˈpraɪə(r)] *n Pej* fouineur(euse) *m,f*

priest [priːst] *n* prêtre *m*; **parish priest** *(Catholic)* curé *m*; **a Buddhist priest** un prêtre bouddhiste
▸▸ *Hist* ***priest hole*** = cachette pour les prêtres à l'époque des persécutions contre les catholiques

priestcraft [ˈpriːstkrɑːft] *n* (**a**) *(art, skills)* sacerdoce *m*; **to learn priestcraft** apprendre à être prêtre (**b**) *Pej (influence)* pouvoir *m* des curés

priestess [ˈpriːstɪs] *n* prêtresse *f*

priesthood [ˈpriːsthʊd] *n (as vocation)* prêtrise *f*; **the priesthood** *(priests)* le clergé; **to enter the priesthood** se faire prêtre

priestly [ˈpriːstlɪ] *(compar* **priestlier,** *superl* **priestliest)** *adj* sacerdotal, de prêtre

priest-ridden *adj Pej* dominé par l'Église

prig [prɪg] *n Br* **he's such a prig!** il fait toujours son petit saint!; **don't be such a prig!** ne sois pas aussi bégueule!

priggish [ˈprɪgɪʃ] *adj (prudish)* pudibond, bégueule; *(smug)* suffisant

priggishly [ˈprɪgɪʃlɪ] *adv (say, criticize)* d'un ton moralisateur; *(react)* de façon pudibonde

priggishness [ˈprɪgɪʃnɪs] *n (prudishness)* pudibonderie *f*; *(smugness)* suffisance *f*

prim [prɪm] *(compar* **primmer,** *superl* **primmest)** *adj Pej* (**a**) *(person)* collet monté *(inv)*; *(attitude, behaviour)* guindé, compassé; *(voice)* affecté; **she's very prim and proper** elle est très collet monté (**b**) *(neat → clothes)* (très) comme il faut, (très) classique; *(→ house, hedge, lawn)* impeccable; **it's too prim for my taste** c'est trop comme il faut à mon goût

prima [ˈpriːmə] *n*
▸▸ ***prima ballerina*** danseuse *f* étoile; ***prima donna*** *(opera singer)* prima donna *f*; *Pej (temperamental person)* diva *f*; **don't be such a prima donna** arrête de jouer les divas; **he's a real prima donna** c'est une vraie diva

primacy [ˈpraɪməsɪ] *(pl* **primacies)** *n* (**a**) *(preeminence)* primauté *f*, prééminence *f*; *Ling* **the primacy of speech** la primauté de la parole (**b**) *Rel* primatie *f*

primaeval = **primeval**

prima facie [ˌpraɪməˈfeɪʃiː] **1** *adv* à première vue, de prime abord
2 *adj Law* **a prima facie case** une affaire simple a priori; **it's a prima facie case of mistaken identity** a priori, il s'agit d'une erreur sur la personne; **there's a prima facie case for not acting hastily** a priori, il ne faut pas agir trop hâtivement; **prima facie evidence** commencement *m* de preuve, *Can* preuve *f* prima facie; **there is no prima facie evidence** a priori, il n'y a aucune preuve

primal [ˈpraɪməl] *adj* (**a**) *(original)* primitif, premier (**b**) *(main)* primordial, principal
▸▸ *Psy* ***primal scream*** cri *m* primal; *Psy* ***primal scream therapy*** thérapie *f* primale; *Psy* ***primal therapy*** thérapie *f* primale

primarily [*Br* ˈpraɪmərɪlɪ, *Am* praɪˈmerəlɪ] *adv* (**a**) *(mainly)* principalement, avant tout (**b**) *(originally)* primitivement, à l'origine

primary [ˈpraɪmərɪ] *(pl* **primaries)** **1** *adj* (**a**) *(main)* principal, premier; *(basic)* principal, fondamental; **our primary objective** notre premier objectif, notre objectif principal; **our primary duty** notre premier devoir *m*; **the primary meaning of this word** le sens premier de ce mot; **this question is of primary importance** cette question revêt une importance capitale; **the primary cause of the accident** la cause principale de l'accident
(**b**) *Biol, Chem & Phys* primaire
(**c**) *Sch* primaire
(**d**) *Econ* primaire
2 *n* (**a**) *Pol (in US)* (élection *f*) primaire *f*
(**b**) *(school)* école *f* primaire
(**c**) *(colour)* couleur *f* primaire
(**d**) *Zool* rémige *f*
(**e**) *Elec* bobine *f* primaire
▸▸ *Mus* ***primary accent*** accent *m* principal; *Elec* ***primary cell*** pile *f* primaire; *Elec* ***primary circuit*** circuit *m* primaire; *Elec* ***primary coil*** bobine *f* primaire; ***primary colour*** couleur *f* primaire; *Mktg* ***primary data*** informations *fpl* primaires, données *fpl* primaires; *Fin* ***primary dealer*** spécialiste *mf* en valeurs du Trésor; *Mktg* ***primary demand*** demande *f* primaire; *Am St Exch* ***primary earnings per share*** bénéfices *mpl* premiers par action; *Sch* ***primary education*** enseignement *m* primaire; *Pol* ***primary election*** *(in US)* (élection *f*) primaire *f*; *Orn* ***primary feather*** rémige *f*; ***primary health care*** soins *mpl* primaires; *Med* ***primary infection*** primo-infection *f*; *Med* ***primary lesion*** lésion *f ou* accident *m* primaire; *St Exch* ***primary market*** marché *m* primaire, marché *m* du neuf; *Astron* ***primary planet*** planète *f* principale *ou* primaire; *Com* ***primary product*** matière *f* première, produit *m* brut; ***primary production*** production *f* de matières premières; *Acct* ***primary ratio*** ratio *m* des bénéfices d'exploitation sur le capital employé; *Geol* ***primary rocks*** roches *fpl* primaires; ***primary school*** école *f* primaire; ***primary school teacher*** instituteur(trice) *m,f*; *Econ* ***primary sector*** secteur *m* primaire; *Econ* **the primary sector industries** les industries *fpl* du secteur primaire; *Ling* ***primary stress*** accent *m* principal; *Anat* ***primary tooth*** dent *f* de lait

PRIMARIES

Les élections primaires américaines (directes ou indirectes selon les États) aboutissent à la sélection des candidats qui seront en lice pour representer les deux grands partis nationaux à l'élection présidentielle.

primate [ˈpraɪmeɪt] *n* (**a**) *Zool* primate *m* (**b**) *Rel* primat *m*; **the Primate of All England** = titre officiel de l'archevêque de Cantorbéry

prime [praɪm] **1** *adj* (**a**) *(foremost)* premier, primordial; *(principal)* premier, principal; *(fundamental)* fondamental; **one of the prime causes of heart disease** une des principales causes des maladies cardiaques; **our prime concern is to avoid loss of life** notre préoccupation principale est d'éviter de faire des victimes; **of prime importance** de la plus haute importance, d'une importance primordiale
(**b**) *(perfect)* parfait; *(excellent)* excellent; **in prime condition** *(person)* en parfaite santé; *(athlete)* en parfaite condition; *(car, antique, stamp)* en parfait état; **it's a prime example of what I mean** c'est un excellent exemple de ce que je veux dire;
(**c**) *Math (number)* premier; **10 is prime to 11** 10 et 11 sont premiers entre eux
2 *n* (**a**) *(best moment)* **to be in one's prime** *or* **in the prime of life** être dans la fleur de l'âge; **the prime of youth** la fleur de la jeunesse; **I'm past my prime** je ne suis plus dans la fleur de l'âge; **these roses look a bit past their prime** ces roses sont plutôt défraîchies; **these curtains look a bit past their prime** ces rideaux ont vu des jours meilleurs; **when Romantic poetry was in its prime** lorsque la poésie romantique était à son apogée
(**b**) *Math (prime number)* nombre *m* premier; [illegible]
(**c**) *(beginning)* commencement *m*
(**d**) *Rel* prime *f*; **to say/sing the prime** dire/chanter prime; *Arch* **at prime** à l'aube, au point du jour
(**e**) *Fencing* prime *f*
(**f**) *Chem* atome *m* simple
(**g**) *Mus* son *m* fondamental
3 *vt* (**a**) *(gun, machine, pump)* amorcer; **to prime sb with drink** faire boire qn; *Fam* **he was well primed** il était bien parti; *Fig* **to prime the pump** faire repartir la machine, remettre les choses en route
(**b**) *(brief → person)* mettre au courant; **to prime sb for a meeting** préparer qn à une réunion; **he is well primed in local politics** il est bien renseigné sur la politique locale; **the witnesses had all been primed by the police** les dépositions des témoins leur avaient été suggérées par la police
(**c**) *(with paint, varnish)* apprêter
4 *vi Tech (boiler)* primer, avoir des projections d'eau

▸▸ ***prime beef*** bœuf *m* de première catégorie; *Fin* ***prime bill*** papier *m* commercial de premier ordre; *Fin* ***prime bond*** obligation *f* de premier ordre; ***prime cost*** prix *m* de revient; ***prime cut*** *(of meat)* morceau *m* de premier choix; *Fin* ***prime lending rate*** taux *m* de base bancaire; ***prime location*** site *m* idéal; ***prime meridian*** premier méridien *m*, méridien *m* origine; ***prime minister*** Premier ministre *m*; ***prime ministership, prime ministry*** fonctions *fpl* de Premier ministre; **during her prime ministership** pendant qu'elle était Premier ministre; ***prime mover*** *Phys* force *f* motrice; *Phil* cause *f* première; *Fig (person)* instigateur(trice) *m,f*; *Math* ***prime number*** nombre *m* premier; ***prime quality*** première qualité *f*; *Fin* ***prime rate*** taux *m* d'escompte bancaire préférentiel, prime rate *m*; *Am* ***prime rib*** *(UNCOUNT)* ≃ côte *f* de bœuf; *TV* ***prime time*** heures *fpl* de grande écoute, prime time *m*

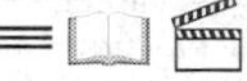

'The Prime of Miss Jean Brodie' *Spark, Neame* 'Le Bel âge de Miss Brodie' (roman), 'Les Belles années de Miss Brodie' (film)

prime-ministerial *adj* du Premier ministre

prime-quality *adj* de première qualité

primer ['praɪmə(r)] *n* (**a**) *(paint)* apprêt *m* (**b**) *(for explosives)* amorce *f* (**c**) *(book → elementary)* manuel *m* (élémentaire); *(→ for reading)* abécédaire *m*; **a Latin primer** un manuel de latin pour débutants

prime-time *adj TV* diffusé à une heure de grande écoute *ou* de prime time

▸▸ ***prime-time advertisement*** publicité *f* aux heures de grande écoute *ou* en prime time; ***prime-time advertising*** publicité *f* aux heures de grande écoute *ou* en prime time

primeval [praɪ'miːvəl] *adj* (**a**) *(prehistoric)* primitif, des premiers âges *ou* temps (**b**) *(primordial → fears, emotions)* atavique, instinctif

▸▸ ***primeval forest*** forêt *f* vierge

primigravida [,praɪmɪ'grævɪdə] *n Obst* femme *f* enceinte pour la première fois

priming ['praɪmɪŋ] *n (UNCOUNT)* (**a**) *(of pump)* amorçage *m*; *(of gun)* amorce *f* (**b**) *(of wood etc)* apprêtage *m*, apprêt *m*; *(paint)* apprêt *m*

primipara [praɪ'mɪpərə] *n Obst* primipare *f*

primitive ['prɪmɪtɪv] **1** *adj (gen)* primitif; *(manners)* grossier, rude; *(understanding)* rudimentaire

2 *n* (**a**) *(primitive person)* primitif(ive) *m,f* (**b**) *(artist, picture)* primitif *m* (**c**) *Comput & Math* primitive *f*

▸▸ ***primitive art*** art *m* primitif

primitively ['prɪmɪtɪvlɪ] *adv (gen)* primitivement; *(constructed, equipped)* de manière rudimentaire

primitiveness ['prɪmɪtɪvnɪs] *n (gen)* caractère *m* primitif; *(of plumbing, understanding)* caractère *m* rudimentaire; *(of manners)* grossièreté *f*, rudesse *f*

primitivism ['prɪmɪtɪvɪzəm] *n Art* primitivisme *m*

primitivist ['prɪmɪtɪvɪst] *Art* **1** *n* primitiviste *mf*

2 *adj* primitiviste

primly ['prɪmlɪ] *adv Pej* d'une manière guindée *ou* collet monté; **to be primly dressed** être habillé très comme il faut; **she sat primly in the corner** elle se tenait assise très sagement dans le coin; **"no thank you", he said primly** "non merci", dit-il d'une voix affectée

primness ['prɪmnɪs] *n Pej (of person)* air *m* collet monté *ou* compassé; *(of behaviour)* caractère *m* maniéré *ou* compassé; *(of dress)* aspect *m* collet monté *ou* très comme il faut; *(of voice)* caractère *m* affecté

primogenitor [,praɪməʊ'dʒenɪtə(r)] *n* (premier) ancêtre *m*

primogeniture [,praɪməʊ'dʒenɪtʃə(r)] *n* primogéniture *f*; **(right of) primogeniture** droit *m* d'aînesse

primordial [praɪ'mɔːdɪəl] *adj* primordial

▸▸ *Biol* ***primordial ooze, primordial soup*** soupe *f* primitive

primordially [praɪ'mɔːdɪəlɪ] *adv* primordialement, originellement

primp [prɪmp] *Old-fashioned* **1** *vi* se faire beau (belle)

2 *vt* **to primp oneself (up)** se faire beau (belle)

primrose ['prɪmrəʊz] **1** *n* (**a**) *Bot* primevère *f* (**b**) *(colour)* jaune *m* pâle

2 *adj* jaune pâle *(inv)*

▸▸ *Literary* ***the primrose path*** la voie de la facilité; ***primrose yellow*** jaune *m* pâle

primrose-yellow *adj* jaune pâle *(inv)*

primula ['prɪmjʊlə] *(pl* **primulas** *or* **primulae** [-liː]) *n Bot* primevère *f*

primum mobile [,praɪməm'məʊbɪlɪ] *n Antiq & Astron* premier mobile *m*

Primus® ['praɪməs] *n Br (stove)* réchaud *m* (de camping)

▸▸ ***Primus***® ***stove*** réchaud *m* (de camping)

prince [prɪns] *n also Fig* prince *m*; **Prince Rupert** le prince Rupert; **he is a prince among men** c'est un prince parmi les hommes; **to live like a prince** vivre comme un prince; *Am Fam* **thanks, you're a prince** merci, vous êtes très généreux; *Br Hist* **the Princes in the Tower** = le jeune roi Édouard V et son frère Richard, assassinés dans la Tour de Londres en 1483

▸▸ ***Prince Albert*** *(jacket)* redingote *f*; *(genital piercing)* Prince Albert *m*; ***Prince Charming*** le Prince Charmant; ***prince consort*** prince *m* consort; ***the Prince of Darkness*** le prince des ténèbres; ***Prince Edward Island*** l'île *f* du Prince-Édouard; **on Prince Edward Island** sur l'île du Prince-Édouard; ***the Prince of Peace*** le prince de la paix; ***prince regent*** prince *m* régent; ***Princes Street*** = principale rue commerçante d'Édimbourg; ***the Prince of Wales*** le prince de Galles

'The Prince' *Machiavelli* 'Le Prince'

princedom ['prɪnsdəm] *n* principauté *f*

princeling ['prɪnslɪŋ] *n* petit prince *m*

princely ['prɪnslɪ] *adj* princier

▸▸ ***princely sum*** somme *f* princière

princess [prɪn'ses] *n* princesse *f*; **Princess Anne** la princesse Anne; **the Princess of Wales** la princesse de Galles; **she's like a fairytale princess** c'est une princesse de conte de fées

▸▸ ***princess dress*** robe *f* princesse; ***the princess royal*** la princesse royale *(fille aînée du monarque)*

principal ['prɪnsɪpəl] **1** *adj* (**a**) *(gen)* principal; **the principal cause of the problem** la cause principale du problème

(**b**) *Mus (violin, oboe)* premier

2 *n* (**a**) *(head → of school)* directeur(trice) *m,f*; *(→ of university)* doyen(enne) *m,f*

(**b**) *Law (employer of agent)* mandant(e) *m,f*, commettant *m*; *St Exch* donneur(euse) *m,f* d'ordre

(**c**) *(main character → in play)* acteur(trice) *m,f* principal(e); *(→ in orchestra)* chef *m* de pupitre; *(→ in crime)* auteur *m*

(**d**) *Fin (capital → gen)* capital *m*; *(→ of debt)* principal *m*; **principal and interest** capital *m* et intérêts *mpl*

(**e**) *Constr (rafter)* poutre *f* maîtresse

▸▸ ***principal boy*** = jeune héros d'une pantomime dont le rôle est traditionnellement joué par une femme; *Gram* ***principal clause*** (proposition *f*) principale *f*; *Gram* ***principal parts*** temps *mpl* primitifs

principality [,prɪnsɪ'pælətɪ] *n* principauté *f*; **the Principality** *(Wales)* le pays de Galles

principally ['prɪnsɪpəlɪ] *adv* principalement, surtout; **principally, it's a question of money** c'est principalement *ou* essentiellement une question d'argent; **the delay was principally due to a staff shortage** le retard était dû principalement à un manque de personnel

principalship ['prɪnsɪpəlʃɪp] *n (of school)* directorat *m*; *(of university)* décanat *m*

principate ['prɪnsɪpeɪt] *n Hist* principat *m*

principle ['prɪnsɪpəl] **1** *n* (**a**) *(for behaviour)* principe *m*; **she has high principles** elle a des principes; **she was a woman of principle** c'était une femme de principes *ou* qui avait des principes; **he has no principles** il n'a pas de principes; **it's not the money, it's the principle** ce n'est pas pour l'argent, c'est pour le principe; **on principle, as a matter of principle** par principe; **it's a matter of principle, it's the principle of the thing** c'est une question de principe; **it's against my principles to eat meat** j'ai pour principe de ne pas manger de viande; **she makes it a principle never to criticize others** elle a pour principe de ne jamais critiquer les autres; **to stick to one's principles** rester fidèle à ses principes; **he's very strict in matters of principle** il est très à cheval sur les principes

(**b**) *(fundamental law)* principe *m*; **to go back to first principles** remonter jusqu'au principe; *Phil* **principle of causality** loi *f* de causalité

(**c**) *(theory)* principe *m*; **basic principle** principe *m* de base; **to be based on false principles** reposer sur de faux principes *ou* de fausses prémisses; **machines that work on the same principle** machines qui fonctionnent sur *ou* d'après le même principe; **we acted on the principle that everybody knew** nous sommes partis du principe que tout le monde était au courant

2 in principle *adv* en principe; **to reach an agreement in principle** parvenir à un accord de principe

principled ['prɪnsɪpəld] *adj (behaviour)* dicté par des principes; *(person)* qui a des principes; **to take a principled stand** adopter une position de principe; **it was very principled of her to refuse** elle a démontré de hauts principes en refusant; *Fam* **he doesn't have a principled bone in his body!** il est complètement dépourvu de principes!

prink [prɪŋk] *Old-fashioned* **1** *vi* se faire beau (belle)

2 *vt* **to prink oneself (up)** se faire beau (belle)

print [prɪnt] **1** *n* (**a**) *(of publications)* **to appear in print** *(book)* être publié *ou* imprimé; **he appeared in print for the first time in 2001** son premier ouvrage/roman a été publié en 2001; **to see oneself/one's name in print** voir ses écrits imprimés/son nom imprimé; **her work will soon be in print** son œuvre sera bientôt publiée; **to be in/out of print** *(book)* être disponible/épuisé; **his unguarded comments got into print** ses propos irréfléchis ont été publiés *ou* imprimés; **he refused to believe the story until he saw it in print** il a refusé de croire à l'histoire tant qu'il ne l'a pas vue publiée; **the newspapers had already gone to print before the news broke** les journaux étaient déjà sous presse lorsque la nouvelle est tombée

(**b**) *(UNCOUNT) (characters)* caractères *mpl*; *(text)* texte *m* (imprimé); **in large print** en gros caractères; **in bold print** en caractères gras; **I had to read through twenty pages of print** j'ai dû lire vingt pages imprimées; **the print was so small I could barely read it** il était imprimé en caractères si petits que j'avais du mal à le lire; **always read the small print** *(of contract, guarantee etc)* il faut toujours lire ce qu'il y a d'écrit en petits caractères

(**c**) *Phot* épreuve *f*, tirage *m*; **to make a print from a negative** tirer une épreuve d'un négatif

(**d**) *Art (engraving)* gravure *f*, estampe *f*; *(reproduction)* poster *m*

(**e**) *Tex (fabric)* imprimé *m*; *(dress)* robe *f* imprimée; **a floral print** un imprimé à fleurs

(**f**) *(mark → from tyre, foot)* empreinte *f*; *(fingerprint)* empreinte *f* digitale; **thumb print** empreinte *f* du pouce; **the thief left his prints all over the door handle** le voleur a laissé ses empreintes partout sur la poignée de la porte

2 *adj (dress)* en tissu imprimé

3 *vt* (**a**) *(book, newspaper, money)* imprimer; *(copies)* tirer; *(publish → story, article)* publier; **the novel is being printed** le roman est sous presse *ou* en cours d'impression; **1,000 copies of the book have already been printed** on a déjà tiré le livre à 1000 exemplaires; **the papers refused to print the story** les journaux ont refusé de publier cette histoire; **printed in France** imprimé en France

(**b**) *Comput* imprimer; **to print sth to disk** imprimer qch sur disque

(**c**) *(write)* écrire en caractères d'imprimerie; **print your name clearly** écrivez votre nom lisiblement

(**d**) *Phot* tirer

(**e**) *Tex* imprimer

(**f**) *(mark)* imprimer; *Fig (in memory)* graver, imprimer; **the mark of a man's foot was printed**

in the wet sand la trace d'un pied d'homme était imprimée dans le sable humide; **the incident remained printed in their memory** l'incident est resté gravé dans leur mémoire

4 *vi* (**a**) *(book, text)* imprimer; *Comput (document)* s'imprimer; *(printer)* imprimer; **the book is now printing** le livre est à l'impression *ou* est actuellement sous presse; **the drawing should print well** le dessin devrait bien ressortir à l'impression

(**b**) *(in handwriting)* écrire en caractères d'imprimerie

(**c**) *Phot (negative)* **to print well** sortir bien au tirage

▸▸ *Mktg* ***print ad, print advertisement*** publicité *f* presse; *Mktg* ***print advertising*** publicité *f* presse; *Comput* ***print buffer*** mémoire *f* tampon d'imprimante; *Comput* ***print cartridge*** cartouche *f*; *Comput* ***print drum*** tambour *m* d'impression; *Comput* ***print file*** fichier *m* d'impression; *Comput* ***print format*** format *m* d'impression; *Comput* ***print head*** tête *f* d'impression; *Comput* ***print job*** *(file)* fichier *m* à imprimer; *Comput* ***print list*** liste *f* de fichiers à imprimer; ***print media*** la presse écrite et l'édition; *Comput* ***print menu*** menu *m* d'impression; *Comput* ***print option*** option *f* d'impression; *Comput* ***print preview*** prévisualisation *f*, aperçu *m* avant impression; *Comput* ***print quality*** qualité *f* d'impression; *Comput* ***print queue*** liste *f* de fichiers à imprimer; *Comput* ***print queuing*** mise *f* en attente à l'impression; *Typ* ***print room*** cabinet *m* d'estampes; ***print run*** tirage *m*; **a print run of 5,000** un tirage à 5000 exemplaires; *Comput* ***print screen*** copie *f* d'écran; *Comput* ***print screen key*** touche *f* d'impression d'écran; **to do a print screen** imprimer un écran; ***print shop*** imprimerie *f*; *Comput* ***print speed*** vitesse *f* d'impression; ***print union*** syndicat *m* des typographes

▸**print off** *vt sep* (**a**) *Typ* imprimer; *(copies)* tirer (**b**) *Comput* imprimer (**c**) *Phot* tirer

▸**print out** *vt sep Comput* imprimer

▸**print up** *vt sep Typ* imprimer

printability [ˌprɪntə'bɪlɪtɪ] *n* imprimabilité *f*

printable ['prɪntəbəl] *adj* imprimable, publiable; **some of their remarks were hardly printable** certaines de leurs remarques étaient difficilement publiables; **my opinion on the matter is not printable** mon avis sur la question n'est pas très agréable à entendre

printed ['prɪntɪd] *adj* (**a**) *(gen)* imprimé; **the printed word** l'écrit *m* (**b**) *(notepaper)* à en-tête

▸▸ *Elec* ***printed circuit*** circuit *m* imprimé; *Elec* ***printed circuit board*** carte *f* de *ou* à circuits imprimés; *Tex* ***printed cotton*** coton *m* imprimé; ***printed form*** imprimé *m*, formulaire *m*; ***printed matter*** imprimés *mpl*

printer ['prɪntə(r)] *n* (**a**) *(person → gen)* imprimeur *m*; *(→ typographer)* typographe *mf*; *(→ compositor)* compositeur(trice) *m,f*; **it's at the printer's** c'est chez l'imprimeur *ou* à l'impression

(**b**) *Comput* imprimante *f*

(**c**) *Phot (person)* tireur(euse) *m,f* d'épreuves; *(machine)* tireuse *f*

▸▸ ***printer cable*** câble *m* d'imprimante; ***printer's devil*** apprenti *m* imprimeur; *Comput* ***printer driver*** programme *m* de commande d'impression; ***printer drum*** tambour *m* d'impression; ***printer's error*** coquille *f*; ***printer font*** fonte *f* d'imprimante; ***printer's ink*** encre *f* d'imprimerie; ***printer's mark*** marque *f* d'imprimeur; ***printer paper*** papier *m* d'impression; *Comput* ***printer port*** port *m* d'imprimante; ***printer's proofs*** épreuves *fpl* d'imprimerie; ***printer's reader*** correcteur(trice) *m,f* d'épreuves; ***printer ribbon*** ruban *m* d'impression; *Comput* ***printer server*** serveur *m* d'imprimante; ***printer speed*** vitesse *f* d'impression; ***printer spooler*** spouleur *m* d'imprimante, pilote *m* de mise en attente des fichiers à imprimer; ***printer spooling*** mise *f* en attente des fichiers à imprimer

printing ['prɪntɪŋ] *n* (**a**) *(industry, craft)* imprimerie *f*; **he works in printing** il travaille dans l'imprimerie

(**b**) *(process)* impression *f*

(**c**) *(copies printed)* impression *f*, tirage *m*; **fourth printing** quatrième impression *f*

(**d**) *Phot* tirage *m*

(**e**) *(UNCOUNT) (handwriting)* (écriture *f* en) caractères *mpl* d'imprimerie

▸▸ ***printing error*** erreur *f* typographique; ***printing ink*** encre *f* d'imprimerie; ***printing office*** imprimerie *f*; ***printing press*** presse *f* (d'imprimerie)

printmaker ['prɪntˌmeɪkə(r)] *n* (**a**) *Typ* typographe *mf* (**b**) *Art* graveur(euse) *m,f*

printout ['prɪntaʊt] *n (act of printing out)* tirage *m*, sortie *f* sur imprimante; *(printed version)* sortie *f* (sur) papier, tirage *m*; *(results of calculation)* listing *m*; **to do a printout** sortir un document sur imprimante, imprimer (un document); **here's the printout of the results** voici le listing des résultats

print-through paper *n Comput* papier *m* à effet d'empreinte, liasse *f* carbonnée

printwheel ['prɪntwiːl] *n* marguerite *f (d'imprimante)*

prion ['praɪɒn] *n Biol* prion *m*

prior ['praɪə(r)] **1** *adj* (**a**) *(earlier)* antérieur, précédent; **she had a prior engagement** elle était déjà prise; **to have prior knowledge of sth** être déjà au courant de qch; **without prior notice** sans préavis; **without his prior agreement** sans son accord préalable

(**b**) *(more important)* **to have a prior claim to** *or* **on sth** avoir un droit de priorité *ou* d'antériorité sur qch; **her son had a prior claim on her attention** son fils passait avant tout

2 *n Rel* (père *m*) prieur *m*

3 prior to *prep* avant, antérieurement à, préalablement à; **prior to (his) departure...** avant son départ *ou* avant de partir...; **prior to today** avant aujourd'hui; **prior to any discussion** préalablement à *ou* avant toute discussion; **prior to his winning/appointment** avant qu'il ne gagne/ne soit nommé, avant sa victoire/sa nomination; **prior to his becoming president** avant qu'il ne devienne président

prioress ['praɪərɪs] *n Rel* (mère *f*) prieure *f*

prioritization [ˌpraɪɒrɪtaɪ'zeɪʃən] *n* **the prioritization of all these jobs** la définition d'un ordre de priorité pour toutes ces tâches; **they opted for a prioritization of expansion** ils ont décidé de donner la priorité à l'expansion

prioritize, -ise [praɪ'ɒrɪtaɪz] **1** *vt* (**a**) *(give priority to)* donner *ou* accorder la priorité à; **if elected, we will prioritize health care** si nous sommes élus, nous accorderons la priorité aux services de santé; **they've prioritized those who've been waiting longest** ils ont donné la priorité à ceux qui avaient attendu le plus longtemps; **it's wrong to prioritize any one issue** c'est un tort de donner la priorité à une question plutôt qu'à une autre

(**b**) *(arrange according to priority)* donner un ordre de priorité à; **it depends how you prioritize them** tout dépend de l'ordre de priorité que tu établis; **it was wrongly prioritized** on a mal jugé de son importance

2 *vi (evaluate priorities)* établir un ordre de priorités

priority [praɪ'ɒrətɪ] (*pl* **priorities**) **1** *n* priorité *f*; **to give priority to** donner *ou* accorder la priorité à; **to have priority** *(of job etc)* être prioritaire; *(of driver)* avoir la priorité; **to have** *or* **to take priority over** avoir la priorité sur; **to do sth as a (matter of) priority** faire qch en priorité; **the matter has top priority** l'affaire a la priorité absolue *ou* est absolument prioritaire; **the library came high/low on the list of priorities** la bibliothèque venait en tête/venait loin sur la liste des priorités; **you should get your priorities right** il faudrait que tu apprennes à distinguer ce qui est important de ce qui ne l'est pas; **the government has got its priorities all wrong** le gouvernement n'accorde pas la priorité aux choses les plus importantes; **according to priority** selon l'ordre de priorité

2 *comp* **to get priority treatment** *(task)* être exécuté *ou* fait en priorité

▸▸ ***priority booking*** réservation *f* prioritaire; ***priority holder*** prioritaire *mf*; *Am* ***priority mail*** courrier *m* prioritaire; *Law* ***priority rights*** droits *mpl* de priorité *ou* de préférence; *St Exch* ***priority share*** action *f* privilégiée, action *f* de priorité

priory ['praɪərɪ] (*pl* **priories**) *n Rel* prieuré *m*

prise [praɪz] *vt Br* **to prise sth open** ouvrir qch à l'aide d'un levier; **he tried to prise open the door** il a essayé de forcer la porte; **she managed to prise her leg free** elle a réussi à dégager sa jambe; **they had to prise his hand open to get the key** ils ont dû ouvrir sa main de force pour avoir la clé; **we prised the top off with a spoon** on a enlevé le couvercle à l'aide d'une cuillère; *Fig* **we managed to prise the information out of her** on a réussi à lui arracher le renseignement; **I managed to prise £10 out of him** j'ai réussi à lui soutirer 10 livres

prism ['prɪzəm] *n* prisme *m*

prismatic [prɪz'mætɪk] *adj* prismatique

prison ['prɪzən] **1** *n* prison *f*; **to be in prison** être en prison; **he's been in prison** il a fait de la prison; **to go to prison** aller en prison, être emprisonné; **to send sb to prison, to put sb in prison** envoyer *ou* mettre qn en prison; **to be sent to** *or* **put in prison** être incarcéré; **to sentence sb to three years in prison** condamner qn à trois ans de prison; *Fig* **marriage had become a prison** le mariage était devenu une prison

2 *comp (director, warder, cell)* de prison; *(food, conditions)* en prison, dans les prisons; *(system, regulations, administration)* pénitentiaire, carcéral

▸▸ ***prison camp*** camp *m* de prisonniers; ***prison colony*** bagne *m*, colonie *f* pénitentiaire; ***prison officer*** gardien(enne) *m,f* de prison; ***prison sentence*** peine *f* de prison; **the assignment to Vladivostok had become a prison sentence** son séjour à Vladivostok, où il est en poste, est devenu un long exil; ***prison van*** fourgon *m* cellulaire; ***prison visitor*** visiteur(euse) *m,f* de prison; ***prison yard*** cour *f* de prison

prisoner ['prɪzənə(r)] *n* (**a**) *(captive)* prisonnier(ère) *m,f*; **to take sb prisoner** faire qn prisonnier; **to hold sb prisoner** retenir qn prisonnier, détenir qn; **to be taken prisoner** être fait prisonnier; **to be held prisoner** être détenu; *Fig* **she became a prisoner of her own fears** elle devint prisonnière de ses propres peurs; *Fig* **to take no prisoners** ne faire aucune concession

(**b**) *Law* détenu(e) *m,f*; *(after sentence)* détenu(e) *m,f*, prisonnier(ère) *m,f*; **he's a prisoner in Wormwood Scrubs** il est détenu à la prison de Wormwood Scrubs; **prisoner at the bar** prévenu(e) *m,f*; *(for serious crimes)* accusé(e) *m,f*; **political prisoner** prisonnier(ère) *m,f ou* détenu(e) *m,f* politique

▸▸ ***prisoner of conscience*** prisonnier(ère) *m,f* d'opinion; ***prisoner of war*** prisonnier(ère) *m,f* de guerre; ***prisoner of war camp*** camp *m* de prisonniers de guerre

prissy ['prɪsɪ] *adj (fussy)* pointilleux, maniaque; *(prudish)* bégueule

pristine ['prɪstiːn] *adj* (**a**) *(immaculate)* parfait, immaculé; **of pristine cleanliness** d'une propreté immaculée; **in pristine condition** en parfait état (**b**) *(original)* primitif, premier

prithee ['prɪðɪ] *exclam Arch* je vous prie, s'il vous plaît

privacy ['prɪvəsɪ, 'praɪvəsɪ] *n* (**a**) *(seclusion)* solitude *f*; **lack of privacy** manque *m* d'intimité; **there is no privacy here** on n'est jamais seul ici; **can I have some privacy for a few hours?** pouvez-vous me laisser seul quelques heures?; **she hates having her privacy disturbed** elle déteste qu'on la dérange chez elle

(**b**) *(private life)* vie *f* privée; **I value my privacy** je tiens à ma vie privée; **you can't have any privacy if you're a star** les stars n'ont pas de vie privée; **an intrusion on sb's privacy** une ingérence dans la vie privée de qn; **in the privacy of one's own home** dans l'intimité de son foyer; **there's no privacy in this world** tout se sait dans ce bas monde

(**c**) *(secrecy)* intimité *f*, secret *m*; **to get married in the strictest privacy** se marier dans la plus stricte intimité; **in the privacy of one's home** dans l'intimité de son foyer

▸▸ *Can* ***Privacy Commissioner*** Commissaire *m* à la protection de la vie privée

PRIVATE ['praɪvɪt]

privé	▸**1 (a) – (d), (f); 4**
personnel	▸**1 (c) – (e)**
particulier	▸**1 (e)**
intime	▸**1 (f)**
soldat	▸**2**

1 *adj* (**a**) *(not for the public)* privé; **private** *(sign)* privé, interdit au public; **the funeral will be private** les obsèques auront lieu dans la plus stricte intimité; **they want a private wedding** ils veulent se marier dans l'intimité

(**b**) *(not state-run)* privé; **they operate a private pension scheme** ils ont leur propre caisse de retraite; **the private sector** le secteur privé

(**c**) *(personal)* privé, personnel; **for private reasons** pour des raisons personnelles; **don't interfere in my private affairs** *or* **business** ne vous mêlez pas de mes affaires personnelles; **private agreement** accord *m* à l'amiable; **I thought we had a private agreement about it** je croyais que nous avions réglé ce problème entre nous; **for your private information** à titre confidentiel; **it's my private opinion** c'est mon opinion personnelle; **it's a private joke** c'est une blague entre nous/eux/*etc*; **she lives in her own private fantasy world** elle vit dans un monde imaginaire bien à elle; **she keeps her private thoughts to herself** elle garde pour elle ses opinions personnelles

(**d**) *(confidential)* privé, confidentiel, personnel; **a private conversation** une conversation privée *ou* à caractère privé; **we had a private meeting** nous nous sommes vus en privé; **I have some private information about him** j'ai des renseignements confidentiels à son sujet *ou* le concernant; **keep it private** gardez-le pour vous; **can I tell him? – no, it's private** je peux le lui dire? – non, c'est personnel; **private and confidential** secret et confidentiel; **private** *(on envelope)* personnel

(**e**) *(individual → bank account)* personnel; *(→ bathroom, lessons, tuition)* particulier; **she has private lessons in French** elle prend des cours particuliers de français; **this is a private house** c'est une maison particulière *ou* qui appartient à des particuliers; **in my private capacity** à titre personnel; **for your private use** pour votre usage personnel; **this is his own private room** c'est sa pièce à lui

(**f**) *(quiet, intimate)* intime, privé; **a private place** un endroit tranquille; **he's a very private person** c'est quelqu'un de très discret; **do you have a private room where we can talk?** avez-vous une pièce où l'on puisse parler tranquillement?

(**g**) *(ordinary)* **a private citizen** *or* **individual** un (simple) citoyen, un particulier

2 *n Mil* (simple) soldat *m*, soldat *m* de deuxième classe; **it belongs to Private Hopkins** ça appartient au soldat Hopkins; **the privates and the NCOs** la troupe et les gradés; **Private Murdoch!** soldat Murdoch!

3 **privates** *npl Fam Euph* parties *fpl* génitales □

4 **in private** *adv (confidentially)* en privé, en confidence; *(in private life)* en privé, dans la vie privée; *(with close family)* dans l'intimité; *(with friends, not in public)* dans le privé; **to sit in private** *(assembly)* se réunir en séance privée *ou* à huis clos; *Law* **to hear a case in private** juger une affaire à huis clos; **to speak to sb in private** parler à qn en privé; **in private she admitted she was worried** en privé, elle a admis qu'elle était inquiète; *(to herself)* dans son for intérieur elle a admis qu'elle était inquiète

►► ***private address*** adresse *f* personnelle, domicile *m*; *Law* ***private agreement*** acte *m* sous seing privé; *Tel* ***private automatic exchange*** central *m* automatique privé; ***private bank*** banque *f* privée; ***private bar*** = salon dans un pub; ***private car*** voiture *f* particulière; ***private citizen*** simple particulier *m*; ***private company*** entreprise *f ou* société *f* privée; ***private dance*** bal *m* sur invitation; ***private detective*** détective *m* privé; ***private education*** enseignement *m* privé; ***private enterprise*** entreprise *f* privée; *(principle)* libre entreprise *f*; *Press* ***Private Eye*** = bimensuel satirique britannique fondé en 1960, dont le ton irrévérencieux rappelle celui du 'Canard enchaîné' en France; *Fam* ***private eye*** *(private detective)* privé *m*; ***private finance initiative*** partenariat *m* public-privé; ***private fishing*** pêche *f* gardée; ***private health insurance*** assurance *f* maladie privée; *Law* ***private hearing*** audience *f* à huis clos; ***private hotel*** ≃ pension *f* de famille; ***private income*** rentes *fpl*; **to live on** *or* **off a private income** vivre de ses rentes; ***private industry*** privé *m*; ***private investigator*** détective *m* privé; *Fin* ***private investment*** investissement *m ou* placement *m* privé; *Fin* ***private investor*** investisseur(euse) *m,f* privé(e); ***private land*** terrain *m* privé; ***private life*** vie *f* privée; **in (his) private life** dans sa vie privée, en privé; **she has no private life** elle n'a pas de vie privée; *Fin* ***private limited company*** société *f* à responsabilité limitée; *Tel* ***private line*** ligne *f* privée; ***private means*** rentes *fpl*, fortune *f* personnelle; **a man of private means** un rentier; *Parl* ***private member*** = simple député *m*; *Parl* ***private member's bill*** = proposition de loi faite par un simple député; ***private ownership*** propriété *f* privée; *Fam Euph* ***private parts*** parties *fpl* génitales □; ***private party*** *(gathering)* réunion *f* privée *ou* intime; *(group)* groupe *m* de particuliers; ***private patient*** = patient d'un médecin dont les consultations ne sont pas prises en charge par les services de santé; *Fin* ***private pension*** retraite *f* complémentaire; *Theat* ***private performance*** représentation *f* privée; *Med* ***private practice*** médecine *f* privée *or* non conventionnée; **she's in private practice** elle a un cabinet (médical) privé; ***private property*** propriété *f* privée; **private property, keep out!** *(sign)* propriété privée, défense d'entrer; ***private pupil*** élève *mf (à qui l'on donne des cours particuliers)*; **he has a lot of private pupils** il donne beaucoup de cours particuliers; ***private road*** voie *f* privée; ***private room*** *(in hospital)* chambre *f* particulière; ***private sale*** vente *f* à l'amiable; ***private school*** école *f* privée; ***private secretary*** secrétaire *mf* particulier(ère); *Br Pol* = haut fonctionnaire dont le rôle est d'assister un ministre; *Cin* ***private showing*** projection *f* privée; ***private soldier*** simple soldat *m*, (soldat *m* de) deuxième classe *m*; ***private teacher*** précepteur(trice) *m,f*; *Art* ***private view*** vernissage *m*; *Law* ***private wrong*** atteinte *f* aux droits d'un individu

privateer [ˌpraɪvəˈtɪə(r)] *n* corsaire *m*

privateering [ˌpraɪvəˈtɪərɪŋ] *n* (guerre *f* de) course *f*; **to go privateering** aller en course, faire la guerre de course

private-label brand *n Mktg* marque *f* de distributeur

privately [ˈpraɪvɪtlɪ] *adv* (**a**) *(not publicly)* **a privately owned company** une entreprise privée; **I had it done privately** *(treatment at doctor's, dentist's)* je l'ai fait faire à mes frais; **she sold her house privately** elle a vendu sa maison de particulier à particulier; **they were married privately** leur mariage a eu lieu dans l'intimité; **to be privately educated** *(at school)* faire ses études dans une école privée; *(with tutor)* avoir un précepteur; **the jury's deliberations took place privately** les délibérations du jury se sont déroulées à huis clos

(**b**) *(personally)* dans *ou* en mon/son/*etc* for intérieur, en moi-même/lui-même/*etc*; **privately, he didn't agree** dans son for intérieur *ou* intérieurement, il n'était pas d'accord; **privately, I was disgusted** dans mon for intérieur, j'étais dégoûté

(**c**) *(secretly)* secrètement; **privately, he was plotting to oust his rival** il complotait secrètement *ou* en secret d'évincer son rival

(**d**) *(confidentially)* en privé; **she informed me privately that...** elle m'a informé en toute confidence que...; **we met privately** nous avons eu une entrevue privée; **can I see you privately?** puis-je vous voir en privé *ou* en tête-à-tête?; **I spoke to her privately** je lui ai parlé en tête-à-tête

(**e**) *(as a private individual)* à titre personnel; **he acted privately and not in his capacity as mayor** il a agi à titre personnel et non en tant que maire

private-sector *adj (business, pay, bosses)* privé

privation [ˌpraɪˈveɪʃən] *n* privation *f*; **to live in privation** vivre dans la privation, vivre de privations

privative [ˈprɪvətɪv] 1 *adj* privatif

2 *n* privatif *m*

privatization [ˌpraɪvɪtaɪˈzeɪʃən] *n* privatisation *f*

privatize, -ise [ˈpraɪvɪtaɪz] *vt* privatiser

privet [ˈprɪvɪt] *n Bot* troène *m*

►► ***privet hedge*** haie *f* de troènes

privilege [ˈprɪvɪlɪdʒ] 1 *n* (**a**) *(right, advantage)* privilège *m*; **the privileges of the nobility** les privilèges *mpl* de la noblesse; **to grant sb the privilege of doing sth** accorder à qn le privilège de faire qch

(**b**) *(UNCOUNT) (unfair advantage)* **a struggle against privilege** une lutte contre les privilèges

(**c**) *(honour)* honneur *m*; **it was a privilege doing business with you** ce fut un honneur de travailler avec vous; **I had the privilege of attending his wedding** j'ai eu le bonheur *ou* la chance d'assister à son mariage; **it is my privilege to introduce...** j'ai le grand honneur *ou* le privilège de vous présenter...; **it was a privilege to have known her** c'est un privilège de l'avoir connue

(**d**) *Law (of lawyer)* droit *m* de tenir une information secrète; *Pol* **parliamentary privilege** immunité *f* parlementaire

(**e**) *Comput (for access to network, database)* droits *mpl* d'accès

2 *vt* privilégier; **these tax changes privilege the rich** ces modifications fiscales privilégient les riches; **I am privileged to be able to present to you...** j'ai l'honneur *ou* le privilège de vous présenter...

privileged [ˈprɪvɪlɪdʒd] 1 *adj* (**a**) *(person)* privilégié; **he comes from a privileged background** il est issu d'un milieu privilégié; **only a privileged few were invited** seuls quelques privilégiés ont été invités; **a privileged minority** une minorité privilégiée, quelques privilégiés *mpl*; **a privileged position** une position privilégiée; **a privileged few** quelques privilégiés *mpl*

(**b**) *Law (document, information)* laissé à la discrétion du témoin; **such information is privileged** le témoin n'est pas obligé de divulguer une telle information

2 *npl* **the privileged** les privilégiés *mpl*

►► *Fin* ***privileged debt*** dette *f* privilégiée

privily [ˈprɪvɪlɪ] *adv Arch* en secret

privity [ˈprɪvɪtɪ] *n* (**a**) *(knowledge)* connaissance *f* (**to** de); **it was done with the privity of his mother** cela s'est fait au su de sa mère (**b**) *Law (relation → of blood)* lien *m*; *(→ between employer and employee)* lien *m* contractuel; **privity of contract** obligation *f* contractuelle

privy [ˈprɪvɪ] (*pl* **privies**) 1 *adj* (**a**) *Formal (informed)* **to be privy to sth** avoir connaissance de qch, être au courant de qch; **an officer who had been privy to the plot was arrested** un officier qui était au courant du complot fut arrêté

(**b**) *Arch (secret)* secret(ète), caché

2 *n Old-fashioned (toilet)* lieux *mpl* d'aisances *(souvent en dehors de la maison)*

►► ***Privy Council*** = le Conseil privé du souverain en Grande-Bretagne; ***Privy Councillor*** = membre du Conseil privé; ***Privy Purse*** cassette *f* royale; ***the Privy Seal*** le Petit Sceau

PRIVY COUNCIL

Le "Privy Council" se compose de tous les ministres présents et passés du gouvernement ainsi que d'autres personnalités du "Commonwealth" et compte environ quatre cents membres. En théorie, le "Privy Council" a pour fonction de conseiller le monarque, mais en réalité aujourd'hui son rôle est presque purement symbolique. Ses membres ne se réunissent en assemblée plénière que dans des circonstances exceptionnelles.

PRIVY SEAL

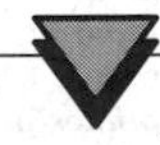

On désigne ainsi le sceau apposé sur certains documents royaux qui ne sont pas assez importants pour recevoir le Grand Sceau ("the Great Seal").

prize[1] [praɪz] 1 *n* (**a**) *(for merit)* prix *m*; **to award a prize to sb** décerner un prix à qn; **to win (the) first prize in a contest** remporter le premier prix d'un concours; **she won the prize for the best pupil** elle s'est vu décerner *ou* elle a reçu le prix d'excellence; *Fig* **no prizes for guessing who won** vous n'aurez aucun mal à deviner le nom du gagnant

(**b**) *(in game)* prix *m*; *(in lottery)* lot *m*; **to win first prize** gagner le gros lot; **the first prize is a week in London** le premier prix est une semaine à Londres

(**c**) *Naut* prise *f*

2 *vt* *(cherish → gen)* chérir, attacher une grande valeur à; *(→ for quality, rarity)* priser; **I prize his friendship very highly** son amitié m'est très précieuse; **her most prized possession** l'objet qu'elle chérit plus que tout; **original editions are highly prized** les éditions originales sont très prisées *ou* recherchées

3 *adj* (**a**) *(prizewinning)* primé, médaillé; **prize lamb** agneau *m* primé *ou* médaillé

(**b**) *(excellent)* parfait, typique; **a prize specimen of manhood** un superbe mâle; **that's a prize example of what not to do!** c'est un parfait exemple de ce qu'il ne faut pas faire!; *Fam* **a prize fool** un parfait imbécile

(**c**) *(valuable)* de valeur; *(cherished)* prisé; **it's my prize possession** c'est l'objet que je prise au-dessus de tout

►► *Fin* ***prize bond*** obligation *f* à lots, valeur *f* à lots; *Br Sch* ***prize day*** (jour *m* de la) distribution *f* des prix; ***prize draw*** tombola *f*, loterie *f*; ***prize list*** liste *f* des gagnants; ***prize money*** prix *m* *(en argent)*; *Boxing* ***prize ring*** ring *m* *(pour la boxe professionnelle)*

prize² = **prise**

prizefight ['praɪzfaɪt] *n Boxing* combat *m* professionnel

prizefighter ['praɪzfaɪtə(r)] *n Boxing* boxeur(-euse) *m,f* professionnel(elle)

prizefighting ['praɪzfaɪtɪŋ] *n Boxing* boxe *f* professionnelle

prize-giving *n* distribution *f ou* remise *f* des prix

►► ***prize-giving ceremony*** cérémonie *f* de distribution *ou* de remise des prix

prizeman ['praɪzmən] (*pl* **prizemen** [-men]) *n (of exam, essay contest)* lauréat(e) *m,f*; *(of game, lottery)* gagnant(e) *m,f*

prizewinner ['praɪzwɪnə(r)] *n (of exam, essay contest)* lauréat(e) *m,f*; *(of game, lottery)* gagnant(e) *m,f*

prizewinning ['praɪzwɪnɪŋ] *adj (novel, entry)* primé; *(ticket, number, contestant)* gagnant

PRM [,piːɑː'rem] *n* (*abbr* **personnel resource management**) GRH *f*

PRO [,piːɑː'rəʊ] *n* (**a**) (*abbr* **public relations officer**) responsable *mf* des relations publiques (**b**) *Br* (*abbr* **Public Record Office**) ≃ Archives *fpl* nationales

pro [prəʊ] (*pl* **pros**) **1** *n Fam* (**a**) (*abbr* **professional**) pro *mf*; **to turn pro** passer pro; **she was a real pro** *(actress, singer etc)* c'était une vraie pro

(**b**) (*abbr* **professional**) *(at sports club)* pro *mf*

(**c**) (*abbr* **prostitute**) professionnelle *f*

2 *adj Fam* (*abbr* **professional**) pro

3 *prep (in favour of)* pour; **he's very pro capital punishment** c'est un partisan convaincu de la peine capitale

4 **pros** *npl* **the pros and cons** le pour et le contre; **the pros and the antis** ceux qui sont pour et ceux qui sont contre

►► *Am* ***pro ball*** *(baseball)* base-ball *m* professionnel; *Golf* ***pro shop*** pro shop *m*, *Can* boutique *f* du pro

pro- [prəʊ] *pref (in favour of)* pro-; **pro-American** proaméricain; **pro-Europe** pro-européen; **pro-Bush supporters** les partisans de Bush; **they were pro-Stalin** ils étaient pour Staline, c'étaient des partisans de Staline

proactive [,prəʊ'æktɪv] *adj* (**a**) *(not reactive)* dynamique, qui prend des initiatives; **you should be more proactive** tu devrais prendre plus souvent des initiatives (**b**) *Psy* proactif

►► *Mktg* ***proactive marketing*** marketing *m* proactif; *Admin* ***proactive staffing*** dotation *f* par anticipation

proactively [,prəʊ'æktɪvlɪ] *adv* de manière dynamique

pro-am [,prəʊ'æm] *Sport* **1** *adj* professionnel et amateur

2 *n* = tournoi opposant des équipes composées chacune d'un professionnel et d'un amateur

►► ***pro-am tournament*** = tournoi opposant des équipes composées chacune d'un professionnel et d'un amateur

prob [prɒb] *n Fam (problem)* problème *m*, blème *m*; *Br* **no probs!** pas de problèmes!

probabilism ['prɒbəbɪlɪzəm] *n* probabilisme *m*

probability [,prɒbə'bɪlətɪ] (*pl* **probabilities**) *n* (**a**) *(likelihood)* probabilité *f*; **the probability is that he won't come** il est probable qu'il ne viendra pas, il y a de fortes chances (pour) qu'il ne vienne pas; **there is little** *or* **not much probability of her changing her mind** il est peu probable qu'elle *ou* il y a peu de chance (pour) qu'elle change d'avis; **there is a strong probability of that happening** il y a de fortes chances que cela se produise; **in all probability** selon toute probabilité

(**b**) *Math* probabilité *f*; **what is the probability** *or* **what are the probabilities of such a result?** quelle est la probabilité d'un tel résultat?; **what is the probability of 10 percent proving defective?** quelle probabilité y a-t-il que 10 pour cent s'avèrent défectueux?

►► ***probability method*** *(of sampling)* méthode *f* probabiliste; ***probability sample*** échantillon *m* probabiliste; ***probability sampling*** échantillonnage *m* probabiliste; *Math* ***probability theory*** théorie *f* des probabilites

probable ['prɒbəbəl] **1** *adj* (**a**) *(likely)* probable; **the most probable hypothesis** l'hypothèse la plus vraisemblable; **her success is more than probable** son succès est plus que probable; **it's highly probable that we won't arrive before 2 o'clock** il est fort probable *ou* plus que probable que nous n'arriverons pas avant 14 heures; **it's hardly probable that he will be there** il est peu probable qu'il soit là; **that's quite probable** c'est tout à fait probable; **probable cause of death** cause *f* probable de la mort

(**b**) *(plausible)* vraisemblable; **it doesn't sound very probable to me** ça ne me paraît pas très vraisemblable

2 *n* **he's a probable for the team next Saturday** il y a de fortes chances pour qu'il joue dans l'équipe samedi prochain; **she's one of the probables for the job** elle fait partie des candidats qui ont de bonnes chances

►► *Law* ***probable cause*** motif *m* raisonnable

probably ['prɒbəblɪ] *adv* probablement; **you're probably right** tu as probablement raison; **probably not** probablement pas; **will you be able to come? – probably** pourrez-vous venir? – probablement; **will he write to you? – very probably** il t'écrira? – c'est très probable; **she's probably left already** elle est probablement déjà partie, il est probable qu'elle soit déjà partie

proband ['prəʊbænd] *n Am Med* cas *m* index *(dans l'étude d'une famille donnée)*

probang ['prəʊbæŋ] *n Med* sonde *f* œsophagienne

probate ['prəʊbeɪt] *Law* **1** *n (authentification)* homologation *f*, authentification *f*, validation *f*; **to grant/to take out probate of a will** homologuer/faire homologuer un testament; **to value sth for probate** évaluer *ou* expertiser qch pour l'homologation d'un testament

2 *vt Am (will)* homologuer, faire authentifier

►► ***probate court*** tribunal *m* des successions et des tutelles

probation [prə'beɪʃən] *n* (**a**) *Law* sursis *m* avec mise à l'épreuve, *Spec* probation *f*; **to be on probation** ≃ être en sursis avec mise à l'épreuve; **to put sb on probation** ≃ condamner qn avec sursis et mise à l'épreuve

(**b**) *(trial employment)* essai *m*; **period of probation** période *f* d'essai; **to be on probation** être en période d'essai

(**c**) *Rel* probation *f*

►► ***probation hostel*** = logement temporaire destiné aux condamnés en sursis avec mise à l'épreuve; ***probation officer*** ≃ agent *m* de probation

probationary [prə'beɪʃənərɪ] *adj* (**a**) *(trial)* d'essai (**b**) *Law* de probation (**c**) *Rel* de probation, de noviciat

►► ***probationary period*** période *f* d'essai; ***probationary teacher*** professeur *m* stagiaire; *Br Sch* ***probationary year*** année *f* probatoire

probationer [prə'beɪʃənə(r)] *n* (**a**) *(employee)* employé(e) *m,f* à l'essai *ou* en période d'essai; *Br (teacher)* (professeur *m*) stagiaire *mf*; *(trainee nurse)* élève *mf* infirmier(ère) (**b**) *Law* probationnaire *mf* (**c**) *Rel* novice *mf*

probe [prəʊb] **1** *n* (**a**) *(investigation)* enquête *f*, investigation *f*; **there has been a newspaper probe into corruption** la presse a fait une enquête sur la corruption

(**b**) *(question)* question *f*, interrogation *f*; **he didn't respond to our probes into** *or* **about his past** il est resté muet lorsque nous avons essayé de l'interroger sur son passé

(**c**) *Astron, Electron & Med* sonde *f*; *Zool* trompe *f*

2 *vt* (**a**) *(investigate)* enquêter sur; **police are probing the company's accounts** la police épluche les comptes *ou* examine la comptabilité de la société

(**b**) *(examine, sound out → person, motive, reasons)* sonder; **to probe sb about sth** sonder qn sur qch

(**c**) *(explore)* explorer, fouiller, sonder; *Med* sonder; **she probed the snow with her umbrella** elle fouilla la neige avec la pointe de son parapluie; **to probe the mysteries of the mind** sonder les mystères de l'esprit

3 *vi* (**a**) *(investigate)* enquêter, faire une enquête; **the police are probing for clues** les policiers recherchent des indices; **to probe into sth** enquêter sur qch; **if you probe into his past, you'll have some surprises** si vous fouillez dans son passé, vous aurez des surprises; **to probe into people's private lives** fouiller dans la vie des gens; **if you probe a little deeper,...** si on fouille un peu plus,...

(**b**) *Med* faire un sondage

probing ['prəʊbɪŋ] **1** *adj (look)* inquisiteur, perçant; *(mind)* pénétrant, clairvoyant; *(analysis)* pénétrant; **after hours of probing questioning** après des heures d'un interrogatoire très poussé *ou* approfondi

2 *n (UNCOUNT)* (**a**) *(investigation)* enquête *f*, investigations *fpl*; *(questioning)* questions *fpl*, interrogatoire *m*; **she didn't react to my probing** je l'ai sondée, mais elle n'a pas réagi; **I'll do some probing and try to find out why she's so reluctant** je ferai ma petite enquête pour savoir pourquoi elle est si réticente; **no amount of probing will persuade him to reveal the truth** on aura beau insister, rien ne le persuadera à révéler la vérité

(**b**) *Med* sondage *m*

probity ['prəʊbətɪ] *n Formal* probité *f*

problem ['prɒbləm] **1** *n* problème *m*; **a maths problem** un problème de mathématique; **a technical/financial problem** un problème technique/financier; **to cause problems for sb** causer des ennuis *ou* poser des problèmes à qn; **to solve a problem** résoudre un problème; **he's got problems with the police** il a des problèmes *ou* ennuis avec la police; **that's your problem** ça, c'est ton problème; **their problem is that they don't have enough time** leur problème c'est qu'ils n'ont pas assez de temps; **money isn't a problem** l'argent n'est pas un problème; **and I thought I had problems!** moi qui pensais que j'avais des problèmes!; **I can't pay until next week – that's not a problem** je ne pourrai pas payer avant la semaine prochaine – pas de problème *ou* ce n'est pas un problème; *Fam* **I haven't got a car – no problem, I'll take you** je n'ai pas de voiture – pas de problème, je t'emmènerai; **the housing problem** la crise du logement; **it's a problem to know what to do** il est bien difficile de savoir quoi faire; **he's a problem** c'est un cas *ou* c'est un problème, celui-là; **I don't want to be a problem** je ne veux pas causer *ou* créer de problème(s); **what seems to be the problem?** qu'est-ce qu'il y a?, où est le problème?; **has anyone got a problem with that?** est-ce que quelqu'un a une objection?, est-ce que ça dérange quelqu'un?; *Fam* **what's your problem?** tu as un problème ou quoi?; **to have a drink/drug problem** (trop) boire/se droguer; **she has a bit of a weight problem** elle a des problèmes de poids; **it's a real problem case** c'est un cas qui pose de réels problèmes

2 *comp (family, hair)* à problèmes; *(play)* à thèse

►► ***problem area*** *(in town)* quartier *m* à problèmes; *(in project)* source *f* de problèmes; ***problem child*** *(child)* enfant *mf* à problèmes, enfant *mf* difficile; *Mktg (company, product)* dilemme *m*; *Br* ***problem page*** courrier *m* du cœur

problematic [,prɒblə'mætɪk], **problematical** [,prɒblə'mætɪkəl] *adj* problématique, incertain; **staying the night there could be a bit problematic** ça paraît compliqué d'y passer la nuit

problematically [ˌprɒbləˈmætɪkəlɪ] *adv* problématiquement

problem-solving [-ˌsɒlvɪŋ] *n* résolution *f* de problèmes; **a problem-solving test** un test par résolution de problèmes

pro bono [-bəʊnəʊ] *adj Am Law (legal work)* à titre gratuit; *(lawyer)* exerçant à titre gratuit

proboscis [prəʊˈbɒsɪs] *(pl* **proboscises** [-sɪsiːz], **proboscides** [-sɪdiːz]) *n Zool* trompe *f*; *Hum (nose)* appendice *m*

▸▸ *Zool* ***proboscis monkey*** nasique *m*

procaine [ˈprəʊkeɪn] *n* procaïne *f*

procathedral [ˌprəʊkəˈθiːdrəl] *n* = église qui tient lieu de cathédrale

procedural [prəˈsiːdʒərəl] *adj* de procédure, procédural; **the delays were merely procedural** les retards étaient dus à de simples questions de procédure

▸▸ ***procedural agreement*** accord *m* de procédure *ou* sur la procédure; ***procedural fault*** faute *f* de procédure; ***procedural motion*** motion *f* d'ordre

procedure [prəˈsiːdʒə(r)] *n* (**a**) *(course of action)* procédure *f*; **you must follow (the) normal procedure** vous devez suivre la procédure normale; **what's the correct procedure?** comment doit-on procéder?, quelle est la marche à suivre?; **what's the procedure for renewing a passport?** quelle est la marche à suivre pour faire renouveler un passeport?; **rules** *or* **order of procedure** règles *fpl* de procédure; *(of assembly)* règlement *m* intérieur; *Law* **criminal/civil (law) procedure** procédure *f* pénale/civile

(**b**) *Comput* procédure *f*, sous-programme *m*

procedure-oriented, procedure-orientated *adj Comput* orienté procédure

▸▸ ***procedure-oriented language*** langage *m* procédural

proceed [prəˈsiːd] *vi* (**a**) *(continue)* continuer, poursuivre; **you may proceed** vous pouvez poursuivre *ou* continuer; **the play proceeded without further interruption** la pièce se poursuivit sans autre interruption; **the project is proceeding well** le projet se déroule bien; **negotiations are now proceeding** des négociations sont en cours; **before proceeding any further with our investigations...** avant de poursuivre nos investigations..., avant de pousser plus avant nos investigations...; **just proceed with the announcement as usual** faites votre annonce comme à l'accoutumée; **before I proceed** avant d'aller plus loin

(**b**) *(happen)* se passer, se dérouler; **is the meeting proceeding according to plan?** est-ce que la réunion se déroule comme prévu?

(**c**) *(move on)* passer; **let's proceed to item 32** passons à la question 32; **to proceed to do sth** *(start)* se mettre à faire qch; *(do next)* passer à qch; **he proceeded to tear up my report** puis, il a déchiré mon rapport; **he immediately proceeded to say the opposite** et le voilà qui se met à dire le contraire

(**d**) *(act)* procéder, agir; **how should we proceed?** comment devons-nous procéder?, quelle est la marche à suivre?; **I'm not sure how to proceed** je ne vois pas très bien comment faire; **proceed with caution** agissez avec prudence

(**e**) *(go, travel)* avancer, aller; *(car)* avancer, rouler; **they proceeded at a slow pace** ils ont avancé lentement; **she proceeded on her way** elle a poursuivi son chemin; **they are proceeding towards Calais** ils se dirigent vers Calais; **to proceed with caution** avancer prudemment; **I then proceeded to the post office** je me suis ensuite rendu au bureau de poste; **I was proceeding along Henley Road in a westerly direction** *(policeman)* je longeais Henley Road en me dirigeant vers l'ouest; **the road proceeds along the coast** la route longe la côte

(**f**) *Law* **to proceed with charges against sb** poursuivre qn en justice, intenter un procès contre qn

(**g**) *(originate)* **to proceed from** provenir de, découler de; **smells proceeding from the kitchen** des odeurs provenant de la cuisine

(**h**) *Comput (in dialog box)* continuer

▸**proceed against** *vt insep Law* poursuivre en justice

proceeding [prəˈsiːdɪŋ] **1** *n* (**a**) *Formal (way of acting)* manière *f* de procéder, façon *f* d'agir

(**b**) *(event)* événement *m*

2 proceedings *npl* (**a**) *(events)* **proceedings were interrupted by...** le déroulement des événements a été interrompu par...; **the proceedings passed off peacefully** tout s'est déroulé sans incident; **we watched the proceedings on television** nous avons regardé la retransmission télévisée de la cérémonie

(**b**) *(meeting)* réunion *f*, séance *f*; **I missed some of the proceedings** j'ai manqué une partie de la réunion *ou* des débats

(**c**) *(records → of meeting)* compte rendu *m*, procès-verbal *m*; *(→ of conference, learned society)* actes *mpl*

(**d**) *Law (legal action)* procès *m*, poursuites *fpl*; *(legal process)* procédure *f*; **to take** *or* **to institute (legal) proceedings against sb** intenter une action (en justice) contre qn, engager des poursuites contre qn; **legal proceedings are very slow in this country** la procédure judiciaire est très lente dans ce pays

proceeds [ˈprəʊsiːdz] *npl* recette *f*, bénéfices *mpl*; **all proceeds will go to charity** tous les bénéfices seront versés aux associations caritatives

process 1 *n* [ˈprəʊses] (**a**) *(series of events, operation)* processus *m*; **the ageing process** le processus de vieillissement; **the democratic process** le processus démocratique; **the peace process** le processus de paix; **by a process of elimination** en procédant par élimination; **to be in the process of doing sth** être en train de faire qch; **in the process of speaking to him, I found out that his wife was dead** c'est en lui parlant que j'ai appris que sa femme était morte; **they're in the process of getting a divorce** ils sont en instance de divorce; **the building is in the process of being repaired** le bâtiment est en cours de réparation; **in the process of time** avec le temps, à la longue; **he lost most of his friends in the process** il a perdu presque tous ses amis en faisant cela; **but you ruined the carpet in the process** mais tu as abîmé la moquette par la même occasion; **during the process of dismantling** au cours du démontage; **the work is in process** le travail est en cours

(**b**) *Tech (industrial)* procédé *m*; *(chemical)* réaction *f*; *Typ & Phot* procédés *mpl* photomécaniques; *Comput* procédé *m*, opération *f*, traitement *m*

(**c**) *Law* procès *m*, action *f* en justice; *(summons)* sommation *f* de comparaître; **by due process of law** par voies légales

(**d**) *Biol (outgrowth)* processus *m*

2 *vt* [ˈprəʊses] (**a**) *(transform → raw materials)* traiter, transformer; *(→ cheese, meat, milk)* traiter; *(→ nuclear waste)* retraiter; *Comput (data)* traiter

(**b**) *Admin & Com (deal with → order, information, cheque)* traiter; **my insurance claim is still being processed** ma déclaration de sinistre est toujours en cours de règlement; **we process thousands of applications every week** nous traitons des milliers de demandes chaque semaine; **your request is being processed** votre demande est en cours de traitement

(**c**) *Law (person)* intenter un procès à, poursuivre (en justice)

(**d**) *Phot* développer

(**e**) *Fig (come to terms with)* faire face à

3 *vi* [prəˈses] *(march)* défiler; *Rel* défiler en procession; **the bishops processed slowly down the aisle** la procession des évêques avançait lentement dans l'allée centrale

▸▸ *Phot* ***process camera*** tireuse *f* optique; *Comput & Typ* ***process colours*** impression *f* en quadrichromie; ***process engineer*** ingénieur *m* en procédés; ***process engineering*** ingénierie *f* de procédés; ***process printing*** impression *f* en couleurs

processed [ˈprəʊsest] *adj (food)* traité, *Pej* industriel

▸▸ ***processed cheese*** *(for spreading)* fromage *m* à tartiner; *(in slices)* fromage *m* en tranches

processing [ˈprəʊsesɪŋ] *n* (**a**) *(of raw material, product)* traitement *m*, transformation *f*; *Comput (of data)* traitement *m*

(**b**) *Admin (of application)* traitement *m*

(**c**) *Phot (of film)* développement *m*, traitement *m*

▸▸ ***processing industry*** industrie *f* de transformation; *Comput* ***processing language*** langage *m* de traitement; ***processing plant*** *(for sewage, nuclear waste etc)* usine *f* de traitement; *Comput* ***processing power*** puissance *f* de traitement; *Comput* ***processing speed*** vitesse *f* de traitement; *Comput* ***processing time*** temps *m* de traitement; *Comput* ***processing unit*** unité *f* de traitement

procession [prəˈseʃən] *n* (**a**) *(ceremony)* procession *f*, cortège *m*; *Rel* procession *f*

(**b**) *(demonstration)* défilé *m*, cortège *m*; **to go** *or* **walk in procession** aller en cortège *ou* en procession, défiler

(**c**) *(continuous line)* procession *f*, défilé *m*; **the soldiers marched in procession through the town** les soldats ont défilé à travers la ville; **I've had a procession of people through my office all day** toute la journée, ça a été un défilé permanent dans mon bureau

processional [prəˈseʃənəl] **1** *adj* processionnel

2 *n Rel (hymn)* hymne *m* processionnel; *(book)* processional *m*

▸▸ ***processional march*** marche *f* processionnelle

processionary [prəˈseʃənərɪ] *adj Entom*

▸▸ ***processionary caterpillar*** processionnaire *f*; ***processionary moth*** processionnaire *f* du pin

processor [ˈprəʊsesə(r)] *n* (**a**) *Comput* processeur *m* (**b**) *Culin* robot *m* ménager

▸▸ *Comput* ***processor speed*** vitesse *f* du processeur

process-server *n Law* huissier *m (qui dresse des exploits)*

processual [prəʊˈsesjʊəl] *adj* processuel

pro-choice *adj* en faveur du droit à l'avortement, *Can* pro-choix *(inv)*

prochronism [ˈprəʊkrɒnɪzəm] *n* prochronisme *m*

proclaim [prəˈkleɪm] *vt* (**a**) *(declare)* proclamer, déclarer; **to proclaim independence** proclamer l'indépendance; **on the day that peace was proclaimed** le jour de l'armistice; **to proclaim a state of emergency** proclamer l'état d'urgence; **a holiday was proclaimed for the investiture** une journée de congé fut octroyée pour l'investiture; **many proclaimed that he was mad** *or* **proclaimed him to be mad** beaucoup de gens ont déclaré qu'il était fou; **he proclaimed himself emperor** il s'est proclamé empereur; **she proclaimed her innocence** elle a clamé son innocence

(**b**) *(reveal)* révéler, manifester, trahir; **his behaviour proclaimed his nervousness** son comportement trahissait sa nervosité; **his expression proclaimed his absolute sincerity** une sincérité totale se lisait sur son visage

proclamation [ˌprɒkləˈmeɪʃən] *n* proclamation *f*, déclaration *f*; **by public proclamation** par proclamation publique; **to issue** *or* **to make a proclamation** faire une proclamation

proclitic [ˌprəʊˈklɪtɪk] *adj Gram* proclitique

proclivity [prəˈklɪvətɪ] *(pl* **proclivities***) n Formal* propension *f*, inclination *f*, tendance *f*; **to have a proclivity to** *or* **towards sth** avoir une propension à qch; **sexual proclivities** penchant *m* pour certaines pratiques sexuelles

proconsul [ˌprəʊˈkɒnsəl] *n Hist* proconsul *m*

procrastinate [prəˈkræstɪneɪt] *vi* remettre les choses au lendemain; **he's always procrastinating** il remet toujours tout au lendemain, il fait toujours traîner les choses; **if you hadn't procrastinated** *(wasted time)* si vous n'aviez pas fait traîner les choses; *(hesitated)* si vous n'aviez pas hésité

procrastination [prəˌkræstɪˈneɪʃən] *n* tendance *f* à tout remettre au lendemain; **there's too much procrastination** on a trop tendance à remettre les choses au lendemain; *Prov* **procrastination is the thief of time** ≃ il ne faut pas remettre au lendemain ce que l'on peut faire le jour même

procrastinator [prəʊˈkræstɪneɪtə(r)] *n* indécis(e) *m,f*, velléitaire *mf*; **he's a terrible procrastinator!** il a une fâcheuse tendance à toujours tout remettre au lendemain!

procreate [ˈprəʊkrɪeɪt] *Formal* **1** *vi* procréer

2 *vt* engendrer

procreation [ˌprəʊkrɪ'eɪʃən] *n Formal* procréation *f*

procreative [ˌprəʊkrɪ'eɪtɪv] *adj Formal* procréateur

procreator [ˌprəʊkrɪ'eɪtə(r)] *n Formal* procréateur(trice) *m,f*

Procrustean [ˌprəʊ'krʌstɪən] *adj* de Procruste

proctitis [ˌprɒk'taɪtəs] *n Med* proctite *f*, rectite *f*

proctologist [ˌprɒk'tɒlədʒɪst] *n Med* proctologue *mf*

proctology [ˌprɒk'tɒlədʒɪ] *n Med* proctologie *f*

proctor ['prɒktə(r)] **1** *n* (**a**) *Law (agent)* ≃ fondé(e) *m,f* de pouvoir (**b**) *Univ (in UK)* représentant(e) *m,f* du conseil de discipline; *(in US → invigilator)* surveillant(e) *m,f* (à un examen) (**c**) *Rel* procureur *m*

2 *vt Am Univ* surveiller

3 *vi Am Univ* surveiller

procumbent [ˌprəʊ'kʌmbənt] *adj* (**a**) *Bot* procombant, rampant (**b**) *(of person)* couché sur le ventre

procurable [prə'kjʊərəbəl] *adj* que l'on peut se procurer *ou* obtenir; **these goods are procurable only from an overseas supplier** on ne peut se procurer ces denrées qu'auprès d'un fournisseur à l'étranger; **it is no longer procurable** on ne peut plus s'en procurer

procuration [ˌprɒkjʊ'reɪʃən] *n* (**a**) *(acquisition)* obtention *f*, acquisition *f* (**b**) *Law* procuration *f* (**c**) *(of prostitutes)* proxénétisme *m*

procurator ['prɒkjʊreɪtə(r)] *n* (**a**) *Law* fondé(e) *m,f* de pouvoir; *Scot* = en Écosse, magistrat qui fait office de procureur et qui remplit les fonctions du "coroner" en Angleterre (**b**) *Antiq* procurateur *m*

►► ***procurator fiscal*** = en Écosse, magistrat qui fait office de procureur et qui remplit les fonctions du "coroner" en Angleterre

procure [prə'kjʊə(r)] **1** *vt* (**a**) *Formal (obtain)* procurer, obtenir; *(buy → for oneself)* se procurer, acheter; *(→ for someone else)* procurer, acheter; **to procure sth (for oneself)** se procurer qch; **to procure sth for sb** procurer qch à qn; **the defence lawyers procured his acquittal** les avocats de la défense ont obtenu son acquittement

(**b**) *Law (prostitutes)* procurer, prostituer

(**c**) *Arch (cause)* procurer, causer, provoquer; **to procure sb's death** *(have killed)* faire assassiner qn; *(cause death)* provoquer la mort de qn

2 *vi Law* faire du proxénétisme

procurement [prə'kjʊəmənt] *n* (**a**) *Formal (acquisition)* obtention *f*, acquisition *f* (**b**) *Com (buying)* achat *m*, acquisition *f*; *Mil* acquisition *f* de matériel; *(department)* service *m* des achats

►► *Mil* ***procurement department*** service *m* des achats; *Mil* ***procurement officer*** agent *m* des achats

procurer [prə'kjʊərə(r)] *n Law* proxénète *m*

procuress [prə'kjʊərɪs] *n Law* proxénète *f*

procuring [prə'kjʊərɪŋ] *n* (**a**) *Formal (acquisition)* acquisition *f*, obtention *f* (**b**) *Law* proxénétisme *m*

Prod [prɒd] *n Ir & Scot Fam* = terme péjoratif désignant un Protestant

prod [prɒd] *(pt & pp* **prodded,** *cont* **prodding**) **1** *n* (**a**) *(with finger)* petit coup *m* (avec le doigt); *(with stick)* petit coup *m* de bâton; **I gave him a prod with my walking stick** je lui ai donné un petit coup avec ma canne; **he gave the sausages a prod with his fork** il a piqué les saucisses avec sa fourchette

(**b**) *Fig (urging)* **to give sb a prod** pousser qn; **he needs an occasional prod** il a besoin qu'on le pousse de temps en temps

(**c**) *(stick)* bâton *m*, pique *f*; *(for cattle)* aiguillon *m*

2 *vt* (**a**) *(with finger)* donner un coup avec le doigt à, pousser (du doigt); *(with stick)* pousser avec la pointe d'un bâton; **he prodded me in the back with his pen** il m'a donné un (petit) coup dans le dos avec son stylo; **he prodded the sausages with a fork** il a piqué les saucisses avec une fourchette

(**b**) *Fig (urge)* pousser, inciter; **to prod sb into doing sth** pousser *ou* inciter qn à faire qch; **to prod sb into action** pousser qn à agir; **she prodded me in the right direction** elle m'a mis sur la voie

►**prod at** *vt insep* pousser, piquer; **she prodded at her food distractedly** elle piquait dans son assiette d'un air distrait

prodigal ['prɒdɪgəl] **1** *adj* prodigue; *Formal* **to be prodigal with** *or* **of sth** être prodigue de qch

2 *n* prodigue *mf*

►► *Bible* ***the prodigal son*** le fils prodigue

prodigality [ˌprɒdɪ'gælətɪ] *n* prodigalité *f*

prodigally ['prɒdɪgəlɪ] *adv* avec prodigalité

prodigious [prə'dɪdʒəs] *adj* prodigieux; **a prodigious reader** un lecteur avide

prodigiously [prə'dɪdʒəslɪ] *adv* prodigieusement

prodigiousness [prə'dɪdʒəsnɪs] *n* prodigiosité *f*

prodigy ['prɒdɪdʒɪ] *(pl* **prodigies**) *n* (**a**) *(person)* prodige *m*; **child** *or* **infant prodigy** enfant *mf* prodige (**b**) *(marvel)* prodige *m*

prodrome ['prəʊdrəʊm] *(pl* **prodromes** *or* **prodromata** [-'drəʊmətə]) *n Med* prodrome *m*

PRODUCE

produits	►1
produire	►2 (a) – (c), (f), (g)
rapporter	►2 (b)
donner naissance à	►2 (d)
causer	►2 (e)
provoquer	►2 (e)

1 *n* ['prɒdju:s] *(UNCOUNT)* produits *mpl* (alimentaires); **agricultural/dairy produce** produits *mpl* agricoles/laitiers; **farm produce** produits *mpl* agricoles *ou* de la ferme; **home produce** produits *mpl* du pays; **they eat their own produce** ils mangent ce qu'ils produisent; **produce of Spain** *(on packaging)* produit en Espagne

2 *vt* [prə'dju:s] (**a**) *(manufacture, make)* produire, fabriquer; **we aren't producing enough spare parts** nous ne produisons pas assez de pièces détachées; **our factory produces spare parts for washing machines** notre usine fabrique des pièces détachées pour machines à laver; **Denmark produces dairy products** le Danemark est un pays producteur de produits laitiers; **we have produced three new models this year** nous avons sorti trois nouveaux modèles cette année

(**b**) *(yield → minerals, crops)* produire; *(→ interest, profit)* rapporter; **this mine is producing less and less coal** la production de charbon de cette mine est en déclin; **this region produces good wine** cette région produit du bon vin; **halogen lamps produce a lot of light** les lampes halogènes donnent beaucoup de lumière; **my investments produce a fairly good return** mes investissements sont d'un assez bon rapport; **this account produces a high rate of interest** ce compte rapporte des intérêts élevés

(**c**) *(bring out → book, record)* produire, sortir; *(publish)* publier, éditer; **he hasn't produced a new painting for over a year now** cela fait maintenant plus d'un an qu'il n'a rien peint; **she has produced a lot of poetry** elle a publié de nombreux poèmes; **the publishers produced a special edition** les éditeurs ont publié *ou* sorti une édition spéciale

(**d**) *Biol (give birth to → of woman)* donner naissance à; *(→ of animal)* produire, donner naissance a; *(secrete → saliva, sweat etc)* secréter; **she produced many children** elle a eu de nombreux enfants

(**e**) *(bring about → situation, problem)* causer, provoquer, créer; *(→ illness, death)* causer, provoquer; *(→ anger, pleasure, reaction)* susciter, provoquer; *(→ effect)* provoquer, produire; **the first candidate produced a favourable impression on the panel** le premier candidat a fait une impression favorable sur le jury; **the team has produced some good results/some surprises this season** l'équipe a obtenu quelques bons résultats/provoqué quelques surprises cette saison; **she can produce a meal from nothing** il lui suffit d'un rien pour cuisiner un bon repas; **to produce a sensation** *(of book etc)* faire sensation; **the drug produces a sensation of well-being** cette drogue procure une sensation de bien-être

(**f**) *(present, show → evidence, documents)* présenter, produire; **he produced a £5 note from his pocket** il a sorti un billet de 5 livres de sa poche; **you have to be able to produce identification** vous devez pouvoir présenter une pièce d'identité; **the defendant was unable to produce any proof** l'accusé n'a pu fournir *ou* apporter aucune preuve; **to produce a witness** faire comparaître un témoin; **they produced some excellent arguments** ils ont avancé d'excellents arguments; **she is continually producing new ideas** elle ne cesse d'avoir des idées nouvelles; **he finally managed to produce the money** il a enfin réussi à trouver l'argent *ou* réunir la somme nécessaire

(**g**) *(finance → film, play, programme)* produire; *(make → documentary, current affairs programme)* réaliser; **a well-produced play** une pièce bien montée

(**h**) *Geom (line)* prolonger, continuer

(**i**) *Chem, Elec & Phys (reaction, spark)* produire; *(discharge)* produire, provoquer; *(vacuum)* faire, créer

3 *vi* [prə'dju:s] (**a**) *(yield → factory, mine)* produire, rendre

(**b**) *(organize production of a film, play, radio or TV programme)* assurer la production; *(make film or programme)* assurer la réalisation

producer [prə'dju:sə(r)] *n* (**a**) *Agr & Ind* producteur(trice) *m,f*; **the country is a major producer of coffee** *or* **coffee producer** ce pays est un important producteur de café; **this region is Europe's biggest wine producer** cette région est la plus grande productrice de vin d'Europe

(**b**) *(of film)* producteur(trice) *m,f*; *(of play, of TV or radio programme → organizer, financer)* producteur(trice) *m,f*; *(→ director)* réalisateur(trice) *m,f*

►► ***producer gas*** gaz *m* de gazogène; ***producer goods*** biens *mpl* de production

producible [prə'dju:səbəl] *adj* (**a**) *(that can be made)* productible; *(that can be shown)* présentable (**b**) *Geom (line)* prolongeable

-producing [prə'dju:sɪŋ] *suff* producteur de; **oil-producing** producteur de pétrole; *Anat* **tear/sweat-producing glands** glandes *fpl* lacrymales/sudoripares

product ['prɒdʌkt] *n* (**a**) *Agr, Chem, Com & Ind* produit *m*; **finished product** *Ind* produit *m* fini; *(piece of work)* résultat *m* final; **food products** produits *mpl* alimentaires, denrées *fpl* alimentaires; **product of India** *(on packaging)* produit d'Inde

(**b**) *(result)* produit *m*, résultat *m*; **this book is the product of many years' hard work** ce livre est le fruit de longues années d'un travail acharné; **she's the product of an unhappy childhood** elle est le produit d'une enfance malheureuse; **the product of our labour** le résultat *ou* le fruit de notre travail; **that's the product of a lively imagination** c'est le produit d'une imagination débordante; **she was a product of her age** c'était un pur produit de son époque

(**c**) *Math* produit *m*; **the product of x and y** le produit de x par y

►► ***product advertising*** publicité *f* de produit; ***product attribute*** attribut *m* du produit; ***product augmentation*** amélioration *f* du produit; ***product awareness*** notoriété *f* du produit, mémorisation *f* du produit; ***product awareness advertising*** publicité *f* de sensibilisation au produit; ***product awareness level*** degré *m* de mémorisation d'un produit; ***product bundling*** groupage *m* de produits; ***product bundling pricing*** fixation *f* des prix par lot; ***product champion*** champion *m* de produit; ***product depth*** profondeur *f* de produit; ***product design*** conception *f* du produit; ***product development*** élaboration *f* du produit; ***product development cost*** coût *m* de l'élaboration du produit; ***product development programme*** programme *m* de mise au point du produit; ***product differentiation*** différenciation *f* du produit; ***product display*** présentation *f* du produit; ***product diversification*** diversification *f* des produits; ***product features*** caractéristiques *fpl* du produit; ***product group manager*** directeur(trice) *m,f* de groupe de produits; ***product hierarchy*** hiérarchie *f* des produits; ***product image*** image *f* de produit; ***product information sheet*** fiche *f* technique; ***product innovation***

innovation *f* de produit; *EU* ***product liability*** responsabilité *f* du produit; ***product liability insurance*** assurance *f* de responsabilité du produit; ***product lifecycle*** cycle *m* de vie du produit; ***product lifecycle curve*** courbe *f* du cycle *m* de vie du produit; ***product line*** ligne *f* de produits; ***product line manager*** directeur(-trice) *m,f* de ligne de produits; ***product management*** gestion *f* de produits; ***product manager*** chef *m ou* directeur(trice) *m,f* de produit, responsable *mf* produit; ***product mapping*** carte *f* perceptuelle de produits; ***product market*** marché *m* de produits; ***product marketing*** marketing *m* du produit; ***product mix*** assortiment *m ou* mix *m* de produits; ***product mix depth*** profondeur *f* de l'assortiment de produits; ***product mix width*** largeur *f* de l'assortiment de produits; ***product orientation*** optique *f* produit; ***product placement*** placement *m* de produit; ***product planning*** plan *m* de développement des produits; ***product policy*** politique *f* de lancement de produit; ***product portfolio*** portefeuille *m* de produits; ***product positioning*** positionnement *m* du produit; ***product positioning map*** carte *f* de positionnement des produits, carte *f* de l'univers des produits; ***product promotion*** communication *f* produit; ***product range*** gamme *f* de produits; ***product specialist*** spécialiste *mf* produit; ***product test*** test *m* de produit, essai *m* de produits; ***product testing*** essais *mpl ou* tests *mpl* de produit; ***product testing panel*** panel *m* d'essayeurs de produits

production [prəˈdʌkʃən] *n* (**a**) *(process of producing → of goods)* production *f*, fabrication *f*; *(→ of crops, electricity, heat)* production *f*; **the workers have halted production** les travailleurs ont arrêté la production; **to go into/out of production** être/ne plus être fabriqué; **the model is now in production** le modèle est en cours de production; **this model went into/out of production in 1999** on a commencé la fabrication de ce modèle/ce modèle a été retiré de la production en 1999; **is it in production yet?** est-ce qu'on en a commencé la production?; **to move** *or* **shift production** relocaliser son unité de production

(**b**) *(amount produced)* production *f*; **an increase/fall in production** une hausse/baisse de la production *ou* du rendement; **wine production has increased** la production viticole a augmenté

(**c**) *(of film)* production *f*; *(of play, of radio or TV programme → organization, financing)* production *f*; *(→ artistic direction)* réalisation *f*, mise *f* en scène

(**d**) *(show, work of art)* & *Cin, Rad, Theat* & *TV* production *f*; *Art & Literature* œuvre *f*; **the RSC's production of 'Macbeth'** le 'Macbeth' de la RSC; *Fam Fig* **there's no need to make such a (big) production out of it!** il n'y a pas de quoi en faire un plat *ou* toute une histoire!; *Cin* **a film with high/low production values** un film à gros/petit budget

(**e**) *(presentation → of document, passport, ticket)* présentation *f*; **on production of this voucher** sur présentation de ce bon

►► *Cin, Rad, TV & Theat* ***production assistant*** assistant(e) *m,f* de production; *Cin, Rad, TV & Theat* ***production associate*** producteur(trice) *m,f* associé(e); *Ind* ***production budget*** budget *m* de production; *Cin, Rad, TV & Theat* ***production buyer*** responsable *mf* des achats; ***production capacity*** capacité *f* de production; ***production car*** voiture *f* de série; *Cin, Rad, TV & Theat* ***production company*** société *f* de production; *Cin, Rad, TV & Theat* ***production control*** direction *f* de la production; *Cin, Rad, TV & Theat* ***production control room*** salle *f* de contrôle de production; ***production cost*** coût *m* de production; ***production department*** service *m* (de) production; ***production director*** directeur(trice) *m,f* de production; *Journ* directeur(trice) *m,f* de la fabrication; *TV* administrateur(trice) *m,f* de la production; ***production editor*** rédacteur(trice) *m,f* en chef technique; ***production flowchart*** organigramme *m* de production; ***production leadtime*** délai *m* de production; ***production line*** chaîne *f* de fabrication; **to work on the production line** travailler à la chaîne; ***production manager*** directeur(trice) *m,f* de la production; ***production meeting*** conférence *f* de production; ***production mixer*** mélangeur *m* (de production); ***production overheads*** frais *mpl* généraux de production; ***production platform*** plate-forme *f* de production; ***production secretary*** secrétaire *mf* de production; ***production switcher*** mélangeur *m* (de production); ***production talkback system*** réseau *m* d'ordres, intercom *m* de production; ***production team*** équipe *f* de production

productive [prəˈdʌktɪv] *adj* (**a**) *(gen)* productif; *Formal* **to be productive of sth** engendrer qch, créer qch; **such methods are productive of stress** de telles méthodes favorisent le stress

(**b**) *(land)* fertile; *(imagination)* fertile, fécond; *(writer, artist)* prolifique

(**c**) *(useful)* fructueux, utile; **our visit/meeting has been very productive** notre visite/réunion a été très fructueuse

(**d**) *Econ* productif; **the productive forces** les forces *fpl* productives *ou* de production

(**e**) *Ling* productif

►► *Econ* ***productive labour*** travail *m* productif; ***productive life*** *(of machine)* vie *f* physique

productively [prəˈdʌktɪvlɪ] *adv* (**a**) *Econ* d'une manière productive (**b**) *(usefully)* utilement; *(fruitfully)* fructueusement, profitablement; **to use one's time productively** employer son temps de façon efficace

productivity [ˌprɒdʌkˈtɪvətɪ] **1** *n* productivité *f*, rendement *m*; **productivity is up/down** la productivité est en augmentation/en baisse

2 *comp (fall, rise, level)* de productivité

►► ***productivity agreement*** contrat *m* de productivité; ***productivity bargaining*** négociation *f* syndicale d'un contrat de productivité; ***productivity bonus*** prime *f* de rendement; ***productivity deal*** contrat *m* de productivité; ***productivity drive*** campagne *f* de productivité

product/market pair *n Mktg* couple *m* produit/marché

product/price policy *n Mktg* politique *f* de produit/prix

proem [ˈprəʊem] *n* préface *f*

proembryo [ˌprəʊˈembrɪəʊ] (*pl* **proembryos**) *n Biol* proembryon *m*

Prof. *(written abbr* **professor***)* Pr

prof [prɒf] *n Fam (abbr* **professor***)* prof *mf*

profanation [ˌprɒfəˈneɪʃən] *n Rel* profanation *f*

profanatory [prəˈfænətərɪ] *adj Rel* profanateur

profane [prəˈfeɪn] **1** *adj* (**a**) *(irreligious)* sacrilège (**b**) *(secular)* profane, laïque; **things sacred and profane** le sacré et le profane (**c**) *(uninitiated)* profane (**d**) *(language → vulgar)* vulgaire, grossier; *(→ blasphemous)* blasphématoire; *(person)* qui blasphème à tout propos

2 *vt* profaner; **to profane the name of God** blasphémer le saint nom de Dieu

profanely [prəˈfeɪnlɪ] *adv* (**a**) *(irreligiously)* d'une manière profane, avec impiété (**b**) *(blasphemously)* en blasphémant

profanity [prəˈfænətɪ] (*pl* **profanities**) *n* (**a**) *(profane nature → of text)* nature *f ou* caractère *m* profane; *(→ of action)* impiété *f*; **an act of profanity** une profanation (**b**) *(oath)* grossièreté *f*, juron *m*; **to utter profanities** *(swear)* proférer des grossièretés; *(blaspheme)* blasphémer

profess [prəˈfes] **1** *vt* (**a**) *(declare)* déclarer, proclamer, *Literary* professer; **to profess hatred for** *or* **of sb** professer sa haine pour qn; **to profess oneself satisfied** se déclarer satisfait; **to profess ignorance** avouer son ignorance; **to profess an opinion** professer *ou* proclamer une opinion; *Rel* **to profess Catholicism/Islam** être catholique/musulman

(**b**) *(claim)* prétendre, déclarer; **he professes to be a socialist** il se prétend *ou* se déclare socialiste; **I don't profess to be an expert (in the subject)** je ne prétends pas être expert en la matière

(**c**) *(profession)* exercer; **to profess medicine** exercer la profession de médecin

2 *vi Rel* prononcer ses vœux, faire sa profession

professed [prəˈfest] *adj* (**a**) *(avowed)* déclaré; **a professed Marxist** un marxiste déclaré; **that is my professed aim** c'est mon but avoué (**b**) *(alleged)* supposé, prétendu; **a professed friend** un soi-disant ami; **she's a professed expert in the field** elle se dit experte en la matière (**c**) *Rel* profès; **a professed nun** une religieuse professe

professedly [prəˈfesɪdlɪ] *adv* (**a**) *(avowedly)* **they are professedly anarchists** de leur propre aveu, ce sont des anarchistes; **she has professedly killed three people** d'après elle *ou* d'après ses dires, elle aurait tué trois personnes (**b**) *(allegedly)* soi-disant, prétendument; **he came here professedly to help me** à l'en croire, il est venu pour m'aider; **she's professedly rich** c'est une femme prétendument riche

profession [prəˈfeʃən] *n* (**a**) *(occupation)* profession *f*, métier *m*; **what's your profession?** quelle est votre profession *ou* métier?; **she's a lawyer by profession** elle exerce la profession d'avocat, elle est avocate (de profession); **I'm not an artist by profession** je ne suis pas un artiste professionnel; **the (liberal) professions** les professions *fpl* libérales; **learned profession** profession *f* intellectuelle; *Hum* **the oldest profession (in the world)** le plus vieux métier du monde

(**b**) *(body)* (membres *mpl* d'une) profession *f*, corps *m*; **those in the profession think that...** les membres de la profession pensent que...; **the teaching profession** le corps enseignant, les enseignants *mpl*

(**c**) *(declaration)* profession *f*, déclaration *f*; **professions of love** des déclarations *fpl* d'amour

(**d**) *Rel* **profession of faith** profession *f* de foi; **the novice made his professions** le novice a fait sa profession *ou* a prononcé ses vœux

professional [prəˈfeʃənəl] **1** *adj* (**a**) *(relating to a profession)* professionnel; **the surgeon demonstrated his great professional skill** le chirurgien a montré ses grandes compétences professionnelles; **a lawyer is a professional man** un avocat exerce une profession libérale; **a club for professional people** un club réservé aux membres des professions libérales; **professional person wanted for flat share** *(in advertisement)* recherchons personne avec emploi pour partager un appartement; **to take a professional interest in sth** s'intéresser professionnellement à qch; **it would be against professional etiquette to tell you** vous le dire serait contraire aux usages *ou* à la déontologie de la profession; **may I give you some professional advice?** puis-je vous donner l'avis d'un professionnel?; **to take** *or* **to get professional advice** *(gen)* consulter un professionnel; *(from doctor, lawyer)* consulter un médecin/un avocat; **his work is not up to professional standards** son travail n'est pas ce qu'on peut attendre d'un professionnel; *Euph* **I think she needs professional help** je pense qu'elle a besoin d'aller voir un psychiatre

(**b**) *(as career, full-time)* professionnel, de profession; *(soldier, diplomat)* de carrière; **she's a professional writer/photographer** elle est écrivain professionnel/photographe professionnelle; **he's a professional painter** il vit de sa peinture; *Fig* **he's a professional drunk** il passe son temps à boire

(**c**) *Sport* professionnel; **to go** *or* **to turn professional** passer professionnel; **professional golf** le golf professionnel

(**d**) *(in quality, attitude)* professionnel; **a professional piece of work** un travail de professionnel; **they made a very professional job of the repair** la réparation qu'ils ont faite est digne de professionnels; **she is very professional in her approach to the problem** elle aborde le problème de façon très professionnelle; **he works in a very professional manner** il travaille en professionnel

2 *n* professionnel(elle) *m,f*; **it's best to leave such work to the professionals** il vaut mieux laisser ce genre de travail à des professionnels *ou* à des gens du métier; **a golf/rugby professional** un golfeur/rugbyman professionnel

►► ***professional army*** armée *f* de métier; ***professional association*** association *f* professionnelle; ***professional body*** organisme *m* professionnel; ***professional code of ethics*** déontologie *f*; *Ftbl* ***professional foul*** faute *f* délibérée; ***professional hospitality*** industrie *f* de l'hôtellerie; ***professional indemnity insurance*** assurance *f* d'indemnisation professionnelle; ***professional misconduct*** faute *f* professionnelle

professionalism [prə'feʃənəlɪzəm] *n* professionnalisme *m*; **nobody would doubt her professionalism** personne ne remettrait en question son professionnalisme; **this burglary shows great professionalism** ce cambriolage est l'œuvre d'un professionnel

professionalize, -ise [prə'feʃənəlaɪz] *vt* professionnaliser

professionalization [prə,feʃənəlaɪ'zeɪʃən] *n* professionnalisation *f*

professionally [prə'feʃənəlɪ] *adv* (**a**) *(as profession)* professionnellement; **he writes professionally** il vit de sa plume; **she's a professionally qualified doctor** elle est médecin diplômé; *Sport* **he plays professionally** c'est un joueur professionnel; **I've only ever met her professionally** mes seuls rapports avec elle ont été d'ordre professionnel *ou* ont été des rapports de travail; **we had the house painted professionally** on a fait peindre la maison par un professionnel *ou* un homme de métier

(**b**) *(skilfully, conscientiously)* de manière professionnelle, comme un professionnel; **this work has been done very professionally** c'est le travail d'un professionnel; **she works very professionally** elle travaille en vraie professionnelle, elle fait un vrai travail de professionnel

professor [prə'fesə(r)] *n Univ (in UK → head of department)* titulaire *mf* d'une chaire, professeur *m*; *(in US → lecturer)* enseignant(e) *m,f* (de faculté) *ou* d'université; **professor of sociology** *(in UK)* titulaire *mf* de la chaire de sociologie, professeur *m* responsable du département de sociologie; *(in US)* professeur *m* de sociologie; **Professor Colin Appleton** le professeur Colin Appleton; **Dear Professor Appleton** Monsieur le Professeur; *(less formally)* (Cher) Monsieur

professorial [,prɒfɪ'sɔːrɪəl] *adj* professoral

professorship [prə'fesəʃɪp] *n* chaire *f*; **she has a professorship in French at Durham** elle occupe la chaire *ou* est titulaire de la chaire de français à l'Université de Durham

proffer ['prɒfə(r)] *vt Formal* (**a**) *(offer, present → drink, present)* offrir, tendre; *(→ resignation)* remettre; *(→ advice)* donner; *(→ excuses)* présenter, offrir; **we all proffered our excuses to her** nous lui avons tous offert *ou* présenté nos excuses; **to proffer one's hand to sb** tendre la main à qn (**b**) *(put forward → idea, opinion)* émettre; *(→ remark, suggestion)* émettre, faire

proficiency [prə'fɪʃənsɪ] *n* compétence *f*, maîtrise *f*; **she attained a high degree of proficiency in French** elle a acquis une grande maîtrise du français; **proficiency in driving is essential** une maîtrise de la conduite (automobile) est indispensable

proficient [prə'fɪʃənt] *adj (worker)* compétent, expérimenté; *(driver)* expérimenté, chevronné; **she's a very proficient pianist** c'est une excellente pianiste; **to be proficient at German** avoir une bonne maîtrise de l'allemand; **to be a proficient liar** avoir le mensonge facile

proficiently [prə'fɪʃəntlɪ] *adv* de façon (très) compétente, avec (beaucoup de) maîtrise; **she speaks French proficiently** elle parle couramment le français; **to swim proficiently** être un excellent nageur; **to lie proficiently** avoir le mensonge facile

profile ['prəʊfaɪl] **1** *n* (**a**) *Art & Archit* profil *m*; **to look at/to draw sb in profile** regarder/dessiner qn de profil

(**b**) *(description → of person)* profil *m*, portrait *m*; **psychiatrists came up with a profile of the killer** les psychiatres ont établi un profil du tueur

(**c**) *(of candidate, employee, company, product etc)* profil *m*; **to have the right profile for the job** avoir le bon profil pour le poste; **to keep a high profile** occuper le devant de la scène, faire parler de soi; **the President has been keeping a high profile recently** le président a occupé le devant de la scène ces derniers temps; **to raise one's profile** se mettre plus en vue; **to keep a low profile** adopter un profil bas, se faire tout petit; **when the boss is in a bad mood I keep a low profile** lorsque le patron est de mauvaise humeur, je me fais tout petit *ou* je ne me fais pas remarquer

(**d**) *(graph)* profil *m*

(**e**) *Geog & Geol* profil *m*; **a soil profile** le profil d'un sol

(**f**) *Tech* profil *m*

2 *vt* (**a**) *(show in profile)* profiler; **his shadow was profiled against the wall** son ombre se profilait *ou* se découpait sur le mur

(**b**) *(write profile of)* brosser le portrait de; **she was profiled in a recent TV programme** une émission télévisée récente a présenté son portrait

3 *vi Fam Black Am slang (show off)* frimer, crâner

▸▸ *Phys* ***profile drag*** traînée *f* de profil

profit ['prɒfɪt] **1** *n* (**a**) *(financial gain)* profit *m*, bénéfice *m*; **to make a profit out of sth** faire un bénéfice sur qch; **we made a £200 profit on the sale** nous avons réalisé un bénéfice de 200 livres sur cette vente; **to be in profit** être bénéficiaire; **to move into profit** *(business)* devenir rentable; **to make** *or* **to turn out a profit** réaliser *ou* faire un bénéfice *ou* des bénéfices; **£100 clear profit** 100 livres de bénéfice net; **to show a profit** rapporter (un bénéfice *ou* des bénéfices); **the fair didn't show much of a profit** la foire n'a pas beaucoup rapporté (de bénéfices); **profits were down/up this year** les bénéfices ont diminué/augmenté cette année; **to sell sth at a profit** vendre qch à profit, faire un bénéfice sur la vente de qch; **he only writes for profit** il n'écrit que pour l'argent; **I don't do it for profit** je ne le fais pas dans un but lucratif; *Com* **profit and loss** pertes *fpl* et profits *mpl*; *Fin* **profit and loss account, profit and loss form, profit and loss statement** compte *m* de résultat; **profit before tax** bénéfices *mpl* avant impôts

(**b**) *Formal (advantage)* profit *m*, avantage *m*; **to turn sth to one's profit, to gain profit from sth** tirer profit *ou* avantage de qch; **to do sth for profit** faire qch dans un but intéressé; **what profit is there in it for her?** quel avantage cela présente-t-il pour elle?, qu'est-ce que cela peut lui rapporter?

2 *vt Formal or Arch* profiter à, bénéficier à; **it won't profit you to tell lies** cela ne vous servira à rien de mentir

3 *vi* profiter, tirer un profit *ou* avantage; **to profit from** *or* **by sth** tirer profit *ou* avantage de qch, profiter de qch; **to profit from others' misfortunes** tirer profit du malheur des autres; **you could well profit by being more careful** vous avez tout intérêt à faire plus attention

▸▸ *Acct* ***profit balance*** solde *m* bénéficiaire; *Acct* ***profit centre*** centre *m* de profit; *Fin* ***profit equation*** équation *f* de bénéfice; *Fin* ***profit indicator*** indice *m* de profit; *Fin* ***profit margin*** marge *f* bénéficiaire; *Fin* ***profit motive*** motivation *f* par le profit; *Fin* ***profit optimization*** optimisation *f* du *ou* des profits; *Fin* ***profit outlook*** perspectives *fpl* de profit; *Fin* ***profit rate*** taux *m* de profit *ou* de bénéfice; *Fin* ***profit squeeze*** compression *f* des bénéfices, étranglement *m* des marges; *Fin* ***profit tax*** impôt *m* sur les bénéfices; *Fin* ***profit warning*** = annonce d'une baisse prochaine des bénéfices d'une entreprise

profitability [,prɒfɪtə'bɪlətɪ] *n Fin* rentabilité *f*; *(of ideas, action)* caractère *m* profitable *ou* fructueux

▸▸ ***profitability index*** indice *m* de rentabilité; ***profitability value*** *(of a company)* valeur *f* de rendement

profitable ['prɒfɪtəbəl] *adj* (**a**) *(lucrative)* rentable, lucratif; **this shop is no longer profitable** ce magasin n'est plus rentable; **a profitable investment** un investissement rentable *ou* lucratif; **it wouldn't be very profitable for me to sell** cela ne me rapporterait pas grand-chose de vendre

(**b**) *(beneficial)* profitable, fructueux; **we had a very profitable discussion** nous avons eu une discussion très fructueuse; **this is the most profitable way to do it** c'est la manière la plus avantageuse de le faire; **it would be a more profitable use of your time** ça serait pour vous une meilleure manière d'utiliser votre temps

profitably ['prɒfɪtəblɪ] *adv* (**a**) *Fin* avec profit, d'une manière rentable; **we sold it very profitably** on l'a vendu en faisant un bénéfice confortable (**b**) *(usefully)* utilement, avec profit, profitablement; **use your time profitably** ne gaspillez pas votre temps

profit-centre accounting *n Acct* = comptabilité par centres de profits

profit-driven *adj Com* poussé par les profits

profiteer [,prɒfɪ'tɪə(r)] **1** *n* profiteur(euse) *m,f*

2 *vi* faire des bénéfices exorbitants

profiteering [,prɒfɪ'tɪərɪŋ] *n* **they were accused of profiteering** on les a accusés de profiter de la situation pour faire des bénéfices excessifs

profiterole [prɒ'fɪtərəʊl] *n Culin* profiterole *f*

profitless ['prɒfɪtlɪs] *adj* sans profit; **it would be absolutely profitless to do such a silly thing** il ne servirait à rien de faire quelque chose d'aussi stupide; **we spent a profitless afternoon** nous avons perdu *ou* gaspillé notre après-midi

profit-making *adj* (**a**) *(aiming to make profit)* à but lucratif; **non profit-making organization** association *f* à but non lucratif (**b**) *(profitable)* rentable

profit-sharing *n* participation *f ou* intéressement *m* aux bénéfices; **we have a profit-sharing agreement/scheme** nous avons un accord/un système de participation (aux bénéfices)

profit-taking *n* prise *f* de bénéfices

profit-volume ratio *n Fin* rapport *m* profit sur ventes

profligacy ['prɒflɪgəsɪ] *n Formal* (**a**) *(dissoluteness)* débauche *f*, licence *f* (**b**) *(extravagance)* (extrême) prodigalité *f*

profligate ['prɒflɪgət] *Formal* **1** *adj* (**a**) *(dissolute)* débauché, dévergondé; **to behave in a profligate manner** se comporter en débauché; **a profligate way of life** une vie dissolue *ou* de débauche

(**b**) *(extravagant)* (très) prodigue, dépensier; *(wasteful)* (très) gaspilleur; **the profligate use of natural resources** le gaspillage des ressources naturelles; **she's profligate with her riches** elle gaspille ses richesses; **he's got profligate tastes** il a des goûts dispendieux

2 *n* (**a**) *(dissolute person)* débauché(e) *m,f*, libertin(e) *m,f*

(**b**) *(spendthrift)* dépensier(ère) *m,f*

profligately ['prɒflɪgɪtlɪ] *adv (dissolutely)* dans la débauche, sans mœurs

pro-form *n* proforme *f*

pro forma [-fɔːmə] **1** *adj* pro forma *(inv)*

2 *adv* pour la forme

3 *n (invoice)* facture *f* pro forma

▸▸ *Fin* ***pro forma bill*** traite *f* pro forma; ***pro forma invoice*** facture *f* pro forma

profound [prə'faʊnd] *adj* profond

profoundly [prə'faʊndlɪ] *adv* profondément; **the profoundly deaf** les sourds *mpl* profonds

profundity [prə'fʌndətɪ] (*pl* **profundities**) *n Formal* profondeur *f*

profuse [prə'fjuːs] *adj* (**a**) *(copious)* abondant, *Literary* profus; **profuse vegetation** végétation *f* abondante; **profuse sweating** transpiration *f* profuse (**b**) *(generous → praise, apologies)* prodigue, profus; **to be profuse in one's praise** se répandre en compliments; **to be profuse in one's apologies** se confondre en excuses

profusely [prə'fjuːslɪ] *adv* (**a**) *(copiously)* abondamment, profusément; **to sweat profusely** transpirer abondamment (**b**) *(generously)* **they thanked her profusely** ils la remercièrent avec effusion; **to praise sb profusely** se répandre en éloges sur qn; **she was profusely apologetic** elle s'est confondue en excuses

profuseness [prə'fjuːsnɪs] *n* profusion *f*

profusion [prə'fjuːʒən] *n* profusion *f*, abondance *f*; **in profusion** à profusion, en abondance

prog [prɒg] *n Fam TV & Rad* émission *f*

progenitor [prəʊ'dʒenɪtə(r)] *n Formal* (**a**) *(ancestor)* ancêtre *m* (**b**) *(originator)* auteur *m*; *(precursor)* précurseur *m*; *Hum (parent)* géniteur(trice) *m,f*

progenitress [prəʊ'dʒenɪtrɪs], **progenitrix** [prəʊ'dʒenɪtrɪks] *n* ancêtre *f*

progeny ['prɒdʒənɪ] *n Formal (offspring)* progéniture *f*; *(descendants)* descendants *mpl*, lignée *f*

progesterone [prə'dʒestərəʊn] *n Physiol* progestérone *f*
progestogen [prə'dʒestədʒən] *n Physiol* progestatif *m*
prognathism ['prɒgnəθɪzəm], **prognathy** ['prɒgnəθɪ] *n Zool* prognathisme *m*, prognathie *f*
prognathous [prɒg'neɪθəs] *adj Zool* prognathe
prognosis [prɒg'nəʊsɪs] (*pl* **prognoses** [-siːz]) *n* (**a**) *Med* pronostic *m*; *(art)* prognose *f* (**b**) *(forecast)* prévision(s) *f(pl)*, pronostic *m*; **to make a prognosis** faire un pronostic *ou* des prévisions
prognostic [prɒg'nɒstɪk] **1** *n* (**a**) *Med (symptom)* signe *m* pronostique (**b**) *Formal (sign)* présage *m*; *(forecast)* pronostic *m*
2 *adj Med* pronostique
prognosticate [prɒg'nɒstɪkeɪt] *vt Formal (foretell)* pronostiquer, présager, prédire; *(foreshadow)* annoncer, présager
prognostication [prɒg,nɒstɪ'keɪʃən] *n Formal* pronostic *m*
program¹ ['prəʊgræm] (*pt & pp* **programmed** *or* **programed,** *cont* **programming** *or* **programing**) *Comput* **1** *n* programme *m*
2 *vt* programmer; **to program a computer to do sth** programmer un ordinateur pour qu'il fasse qch; **to be programmed to do sth** être programmé pour faire qch
3 *vi* programmer; **to program in assembly language** programmer en assembleur
►► ***program card*** carte *f* programme; ***program disk*** disquette *f* programme; ***program error*** erreur *f* de programmation; ***program file*** fichier *m* programme; ***program language*** langage *m* de programmation; ***program library*** bibliothèque *f* de programmes; ***program manager*** gestionnaire *m* de programmes
program² *Am* = **programme**
programable, programer *Am* = **programmable, programmer**
programmable, *Am* **programable** [,prəʊ'græməbəl] *adj Comput* programmable
►► ***programmable function key*** touche *f* de fonction programmable; ***programmable ROM*** mémoire *f* morte programmable
programme, *Am* **program** ['prəʊgræm] **1** *n* (**a**) *Mus, Pol & Theat* programme *m*; **the programme of the day's events** le programme des manifestations de la journée; **there's a change in the programme** il y a un changement de programme; **the programme includes three pieces by Debussy** il y a trois morceaux de Debussy au programme; *esp Am* **an election programme** un programme électoral; **a research programme** un programme de recherches; **training programme** programme *m* d'instruction *ou* de formation; **the party has adopted a new programme** le parti a adopté un nouveau programme; **what's (on) the programme for next week?** quel est l'emploi du temps prévu pour la semaine prochaine?; *Am Fam* **get with the program!** un peu d'attention!
(**b**) *(booklet)* programme *m*; *(syllabus)* programme *m*; *(timetable)* emploi *m* du temps; **to draw up a programme** arrêter un programme; **programme of study** programme *m*
(**c**) *Rad & TV (broadcast)* émission *f*; **there's a good programme about** *or* **on opera on TV tonight** il y a une bonne émission sur l'opéra à la télévision ce soir
(**d**) *(TV station)* chaîne *f*; *(radio station)* station *f*; **to change programme** *TV* changer de chaîne; *Rad* changer de station
2 *vt* programmer; **the heating is programmed to switch itself off at night** le chauffage est programmé pour s'arrêter la nuit; **the documentary was programmed for nine o'clock** le documentaire était programmé pour neuf heures; **his arrival wasn't programmed** son arrivée n'était pas prévue; **all children are programmed to learn language** chez les enfants, la capacité d'apprentissage du langage est innée
►► *TV & Rad* ***programme controller*** directeur(trice) *m,f* des programmes *ou* d'antenne; ***programme grid*** grille *f* de programmes; ***programmed learning*** enseignement *m* programmé; *Mus* ***programme music*** musique *f* à programme; *Theat* ***programme notes*** notes *fpl* sur le programme; **the programme notes are very useful** les commentaires donnés dans le programme sont très utiles; ***programme schedule*** grille *f* de programmes; *Theat* ***programme seller*** vendeur(euse) *m,f* de programmes; ***programme supervisor*** chef *m* d'antenne; ***programme trail*** annonce *f* de programme
programme-maker, *Am* **program-maker** *n TV & Rad* réalisateur(trice) *m,f*
programmer, *Am* **programer** ['prəʊgræmə(r)] *n Comput* (**a**) *(person)* programmeur(euse) *m,f* (**b**) *(device)* programmateur *m*
programming, *Am* **programing** ['prəʊgræmɪŋ] *n* (**a**) *Comput* programmation *f* (**b**) *TV & Rad* programmation *f*
►► *Comput* ***programming error*** erreur *f* de programmation; *Comput* ***programming language*** langage *m* de programmation
progress 1 *n (UNCOUNT)* ['prəʊgres] (**a**) *(headway)* progrès *mpl*; **they have made fast progress** ils ont avancé *ou* ils ont progressé rapidement; **it was slow progress** ça n'avançait pas vite; **to make good progress** *(in journey, process)* bien avancer; **negotiations are making good progress** les négociations sont en bonne voie; **the patient is making good progress** le patient donne de bons signes de récupération; **he is making progress in English** il fait des progrès en anglais; **we'll never make any progress this way** nous ne ferons jamais de progrès *ou* jamais aucun progrès de cette façon
(**b**) *(evolution)* progrès *m*; **to hinder progress** entraver *ou* freiner le progrès; **she believes in the progress of mankind** elle croit au progrès de l'humanité; **you can't stop progress** on ne peut arrêter le progrès; *Ironic* **that's progress for you!** c'est ça le progrès!
(**c**) *(forward movement)* progression *f*; *(of time, disease etc)* marche *f*; *(of events)* cours *m*; *(of plan, project)* déroulement *m*; **we watched the progress of the boat along the canal** nous avons regardé le bateau avancer le long du canal; *Chess* **the knight's progress** la marche du cavalier
(**d**) *Arch (journey)* voyage *m*
2 *vi* [prə'gres] (**a**) *(make headway* → *negotiations, research)* progresser, avancer; *(*→ *situation)* progresser, s'améliorer; *(*→ *patient)* aller mieux; *(*→ *student)* progresser, faire des progrès; **the talks are progressing well** les pourparlers sont en bonne voie; **the patient is progressing satisfactorily** le malade fait des progrès satisfaisants
(**b**) *(move forward)* avancer; **to progress towards a place/an objective** se rapprocher d'un lieu/d'un objectif; **as the day progressed** à mesure que la journée avançait; **to progress onto more difficult tasks** passer à des tâches plus difficiles; **I never progressed beyond the first lesson** je ne suis jamais allé au-delà de la première leçon
3 *vt* [prə'gres] *Com (advance)* faire progresser; **we need to progress this issue as quickly as possible** il nous faut accélérer les choses le plus possible
4 in progress *adj* **to be in progress** être en cours; **work in progress** travaux *mpl* en cours; **while the exam is in progress** pendant l'examen; **service in progress** *(in cathedral)* office en cours; **the meeting is in progress** la réunion est en cours
►► *Ind* ***progress chart*** diagramme *m* de l'avancement des travaux; ***progress chaser*** responsable *mf* du (suivi d'un) planning; *Ind* ***progress payment*** paiement *m* proportionnel (à l'avancement des travaux); ***progress report*** compte-rendu *m*; *(on work)* rapport *m* sur l'avancement des travaux; *(on patient)* bulletin *m* de santé; *(on pupil)* bulletin *m* scolaire
progression [prə'greʃən] *n* (**a**) *(advance* → *of disease, army)* progression *f* (**b**) *Math & Mus* progression *f*; *Mus* **melodic progression** progression *f* mélodique (**c**) *(series)* série *f*, suite *f*; **I watched the endless progression of suburban houses from the taxi** du taxi, j'ai regardé la succession sans fin des pavillons de banlieue
(**d**) *(of star)* marche *f*
progressive [prə'gresɪv] **1** *adj* (**a**) *(forward-looking* → *idea, teacher, politician, jazz)* progressiste; *(*→ *education, method)* nouveau(elle), moderne; **he has a very progressive outlook** sa vision des choses est très moderne; **to be progressive** *(person)* avoir des idées progressistes
(**b**) *(gradual* → *change)* progressif; **to do sth in progressive steps** *or* **stages** faire qch par étapes successives
(**c**) *Med (disease)* progressif; **progressive hardening of the arteries** artériosclérose *f* progressive
(**d**) *Gram (aspect)* progressif
2 *n* (**a**) *Pol* progressiste *mf*
(**b**) *Gram* forme *f* progressive, progressif *m*; **in the progressive** à la forme progressive
►► *Fin* ***progressive tax*** impôt *m* progressif
progressively [prə'gresɪvlɪ] *adv* (**a**) *Pol & Sch* d'une manière progressiste; **to think progressively** avoir des idées progressistes (**b**) *(gradually)* progressivement, graduellement, petit à petit; **taxes were progressively increased** les impôts ont augmenté progressivement
progressiveness [prə'gresɪvnɪs] *n* (**a**) *(of ideas, teaching)* caractère *m* progressiste (**b**) *(gradualness)* progressivité *f*
prohibit [prə'hɪbɪt] *vt* (**a**) *(forbid)* interdire, défendre, prohiber; **to prohibit sb from doing sth** défendre *ou* interdire à qn de faire qch; **drinking alcohol at work is prohibited** il est interdit de boire de l'alcool sur le lieu de travail; **smoking is strictly prohibited** il est formellement interdit de fumer; **smoking prohibited** *(sign)* défense de fumer; **parking prohibited** *(sign)* stationnement interdit
(**b**) *(prevent)* interdire, empêcher; **to prohibit sb from doing sth** empêcher qn de faire qch; **his pacifism prohibits him from joining the army** son pacifisme lui interdit *ou* l'empêche de s'engager dans l'armée; **my promise to her prohibits me from saying more** la promesse que je lui ai faite m'interdit *ou* m'empêche d'en dire plus
prohibition [,prəʊɪ'bɪʃən] **1** *n* interdiction *f*, prohibition *f*; **the prohibition of alcohol** la prohibition de l'alcool; **there should be a prohibition on the sale of such goods** il devrait y avoir une loi qui interdise la vente de ce genre de marchandises
2 Prohibition *n Am Hist* la Prohibition

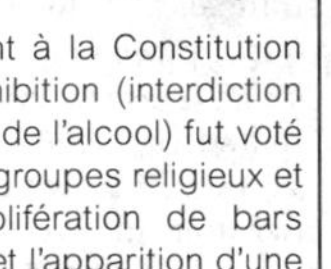

PROHIBITION

Le dix-huitième amendement à la Constitution américaine instituant la Prohibition (interdiction de consommer et de vendre de l'alcool) fut voté en 1919 sous la pression de groupes religieux et conservateurs; mais la prolifération de bars clandestins ("speakeasies") et l'apparition d'une guerre des gangs (les "bootleggers") pour le monopole de la vente d'alcool incitèrent le Congrès à voter l'annulation de cette mesure en 1933, et les États l'abandonnèrent un à un.

prohibitionism [,prəʊɪ'bɪʃənɪzəm] *n* prohibitionnisme *m*
prohibitionist [,prəʊɪ'bɪʃənɪst] **1** *adj* prohibitionniste
2 *n* prohibitionniste *mf*
prohibitive [prə'hɪbətɪv] *adj* prohibitif; **the price of flowers is prohibitive** les fleurs sont hors de prix
►► ***prohibitive price*** prix *m* prohibitif *ou* inabordable
prohibitively [prə'hɪbətɪvlɪ] *adv* **prohibitively expensive** d'un coût prohibitif
prohibitory [prə'hɪbətərɪ] *adj* prohibitif

PROJECT

projet	► **1 (a)**
travaux pratiques	► **1 (b)**
étude	► **1 (c)**
prévoir	► **2 (a), (b)**
projeter	► **2 (c) – (e), (g)**
présenter	► **2 (d)**
dépasser	► **3 (a)**

1 *n* ['prɒdʒekt] (**a**) *(plan)* projet *m*; *(enterprise, undertaking)* opération *f*, entreprise *f*; **they're working on a new building project** ils travaillent sur un nouveau projet de construction; **the start of the project has been delayed** le début de l'opération a été retardé; **a fund-raising**

project to save *or* **for saving the shipyard** une collecte de fonds pour sauver le chantier naval

(**b**) *Sch (class work)* travaux *mpl* pratiques; *(individual work)* dossier *m*; **the class has just finished a nature project** la classe vient de terminer des travaux pratiques de sciences naturelles; **Tina's project was the best in the whole class** le dossier de Tina était le meilleur de toute la classe

(**c**) *(study, research)* étude *f*; **a mining project** une étude minière

(**d**) *Am* **(housing) project** cité *f* HLM

2 *vt* [prə'dʒekt] (**a**) *(plan)* prévoir; **two new airports are projected for the next decade** il est prévu de construire deux nouveaux aéroports durant la prochaine décennie

(**b**) *(forecast → figures, output)* prévoir; **he's projecting a 40 percent slide in May** il prévoit une baisse de 40 pour cent au mois de mai

(**c**) *(send forth → gen)* projeter, envoyer; *(→ film, slide etc)* projeter; **to project one's voice** projeter sa voix; **the missile was projected into space** le missile a été envoyé dans l'espace; **the explosion projected debris high into the air** l'explosion a projeté des débris très haut dans les airs; *Art* **projected shadow** ombre *f* portée; *Fig* **try to project yourself forward into the 25th century** essayez d'imaginer que vous êtes au 25ème siècle

(**d**) *(present)* présenter, projeter; **football hooligans project a poor image of our country abroad** les hooligans donnent une mauvaise image de notre pays à l'étranger; **she projects an image of self-confidence** elle donne d'elle-même l'image d'une personne pleine d'assurance; **to project one's personality** mettre sa personnalité en avant; **he tries to project himself as a great humanist** il essaie de se faire passer pour un grand humaniste

(**e**) *Psy (transfer)* projeter; **to project one's feelings onto sb** projeter ses sentiments sur qn

(**f**) *(cause to jut out)* faire dépasser

(**g**) *Geom* projeter; **to project a cylinder on** *or* **onto a plane** projeter un cylindre sur un plan

3 *vi* [prə'dʒekt] (**a**) *(protrude, jut out)* faire saillie, dépasser; **the barrel of his gun projected from his overcoat** le canon de son revolver dépassait de son pardessus; **the balcony projects over the pavement** le balcon surplombe le trottoir

(**b**) *Psy* se projeter

(**c**) *(show personality)* **she doesn't project well** elle présente mal

(**d**) *(with voice)* projeter sa voix

►► ***project analysis*** étude *f* de projet; ***project management*** gestion *f* de projets; ***project manager*** *(gen)* chef *m* de projet; *Constr* maître *m* d'œuvre; ***project milestone*** étape *f* principale du projet

projected [prə'dʒektɪd] *adj* (**a**) *(planned → undertaking, visit)* prévu; **they are opposed to the projected building scheme** ils sont contre le projet de construction (**b**) *(forecast → figures, production)* prévu; **the projected growth of the economy** la croissance économique prévue, les prévisions de croissance économique; *Fin* **projected turnover** chiffre *m* d'affaires prévisionnel

►► *Geom* ***projected angle*** angle *m* projeté

projectile [prə'dʒektaɪl] *n* **1** *adj (force)* impulsif, projectif

2 *n* projectile *m*

►► ***projectile vomiting*** vomissements *mpl* violents; *Mil* ***projectile weapons*** armes *fpl* de jet

projecting [prə'dʒektɪŋ] *adj (roof, balcony etc)* saillant, en saillie, qui fait saillie; *(teeth)* en avant

projection [prə'dʒekʃən] *n* (**a**) *Cin, Geom & Psy* projection *f*

(**b**) *(estimate)* projection *f*, prévision *f*; **here are my projections for the next ten years** voici mes prévisions pour les dix années à venir; **demographic projections** projections *fpl* démographiques

(**c**) *(of missile)* lancement *m*, envoi *m*; *(of one's voice)* projection *f*

(**d**) *(protrusion)* saillie *f*, avancée *f*; *(overhang)* surplomb *m*

►► *Cin* ***projection room*** cabine *f* de projection

projectionist [prə'dʒekʃənɪst] *n Cin* projectionniste *mf*

projective [prə'dʒektɪv] *adj Math (plane)* de projection

►► *Math* ***projective geometry*** géometrie *f* projective; *Psy* ***projective psychology*** psychologie *f* projective; ***projective test*** test *m* projectif

projector [prə'dʒektə(r)] *n* projecteur *m*

prokaryote [prəʊ'kærɪɒt] *n Biol* procaryote *m*

Prokofiev [prə'kɒfɪef] *pr n* Prokofiev

prolactin [prəʊ'læktɪn] *n Physiol* prolactine *f*

prolapse ['prəʊlæps] *Med* **1** *n* prolapsus *m*, ptôse *f*; **prolapse (of the uterus)** prolapsus *m ou* descente *f* de l'utérus

2 *vi* descendre, tomber

prolapsed ['prəʊlæpst] *adj Med* prolabé

prolate ['prəʊleɪt] *adj Geom* oblong

prole [prəʊl] *Fam Pej* **1** *adj* prolo

2 *n* prolo *mf*

prolegomenon [,prəʊle'gɒmɪnən] *(pl* **prolegomena** [-nə]*)* *n Literature* prolégomènes *mpl*

prolepsis [prəʊ'lepsɪs] *(pl* **prolepses** [-si:z]*)* *n Ling* prolepse *f*

proleptic [prəʊ'leptɪk] *adj* proleptique, avant-coureur

►► *Med* ***proleptic fever*** fièvre *f* proleptique *ou* subintrante; ***proleptic year*** année *f* proleptique

proletarian [,prəʊlɪ'teərɪən] **1** *n* prolétaire *mf*

2 *adj* prolétarien; *Pej* de prolétaire

proletarianization [,prəʊlɪ,teərɪənaɪ'zeɪʃən] *n* prolétarisation *f*

proletarianize, -ise [,prəʊlɪ'teərɪənaɪz] *vt* prolétariser

proletariat [,prəʊlɪ'teərɪət] *n* prolétariat *m*

pro-life *adj* contre l'interruption volontaire de grossesse

►► ***pro-life movement*** mouvement *m* pour le respect de la vie

pro-lifer *n Fam* = adversaire de l'interruption volontaire de grossesse

proliferate [prə'lɪfəreɪt] *vi* proliférer

proliferation [prə,lɪfə'reɪʃən] *n* (**a**) *(rapid increase)* prolifération *f* (**b**) *(large amount or number)* grande quantité *f*

proliferative [prə'lɪfərətɪv] *adj Med* (**a**) *(tending to proliferate)* capable de proliférer (**b**) *(increasing)* en cours de prolifération

prolific [prə'lɪfɪk] *adj* prolifique, fécond; **the country has been a prolific producer of inventors** le pays a été fécond en inventeurs; **a prolific goalscorer** un gros buteur

prolifically [prə'lɪfɪkəlɪ] *adv (write, compose)* abondamment; *(grow)* en abondance; **she is a prolifically productive writer** c'est un écrivain prolifique *ou* fécond; **he has been a prolifically successful goalscorer** il a marqué énormément de buts

prolin, proline ['prəʊlɪn] *n Biol & Chem* proline *f*

prolix ['prəʊlɪks] *adj Formal* prolixe

prolixity [prəʊ'lɪksətɪ] *n Formal* prolixité *f*

prologue, *Am* **prolog** ['prəʊlɒg] *n* (**a**) *also Fig* prologue *m*, prélude *m* (**to** de); **her arrival was the prologue to yet another row** son arrivée allait être le prélude d'une *ou* préluder à une nouvelle querelle (**b**) *(in cycling)* prologue *m*

prolong [prə'lɒŋ] *vt* prolonger; *Fig Hum* **to prolong the agony** faire durer le suspense

prolongation [,prəʊlɒŋ'geɪʃən] *n (in time)* prolongation *f*; *(in space)* prolongement *m*, extension *f*

prolonged [prə'lɒŋd] *adj* long (longue); **after a prolonged absence** après une longue absence

PROM [prɒm] *n Comput (abbr* **programmable read-only memory***)* PROM *f inv*

prom [prɒm] **1** *n* (**a**) *Br Fam (at seaside)* front *m* de mer[□], promenade[□] *f*

(**b**) *Br Fam Mus (concert)* concert-promenade[□] *m*

(**c**) *Am (dance)* bal[□] *m (de lycéens ou d'étudiants)*

2 Proms *npl* **the Proms** = série de concerts-promenades, qui a lieu au mois de juillet au Albert Hall de Londres; **the Last Night of the Proms** = le dernier des concerts-promenades de la saison londonienne, au cours duquel le public se joint aux musiciens pour chanter des airs très connus

►► *Am Sch & Univ* ***prom queen*** reine *f* du bal

promenade [,prɒmə'nɑ:d] **1** *n* (**a**) *Br (at seaside)* front *m* de mer, promenade *f*

(**b**) *Br Mus* concert-promenade *m*

(**c**) *(walk)* promenade *f*

(**d**) *Am (dance)* bal *m (de lycéens ou d'étudiants)*

2 *comp (performance)* = où les auditeurs doivent se déplacer pour suivre l'action de la pièce

3 *vi* (**a**) *Formal or Hum (walk)* se promener

(**b**) *(in dancing)* marcher

4 *vt* (**a**) *Formal or Hum (walk in)* se promener dans

(**b**) *(show off)* faire parade de, exhiber

►► ***promenade concert*** concert-promenade *m*; *Naut* ***promenade deck*** pont *m* promenade

promenader [,prɒmə'nɑ:də(r)] *n Mus* auditeur(trice) *m,f* d'un concert-promenade

Promethean [prə'mi:θjən] *adj* prométhéen

Prometheus [prə'mi:θɪəs] *pr n Myth* Prométhée

'Prometheus Unbound' *Shelley* 'Prométhée délivré'

promethium [prə'mi:θɪəm] *n Chem* prométhéum *m*

prominence ['prɒmɪnəns] *n* (**a**) *(importance)* importance *f*; *(fame)* célébrité *f*; **to rise to prominence** se hisser au premier rang; **to come into** *or* **to prominence** *(become important)* prendre de l'importance; *(become famous)* devenir célèbre; **she came to international prominence with that song** c'est grâce à cette chanson qu'elle a percé au niveau international; **to give prominence to sth** faire ressortir qch, donner une place importante à qch; **to bring sb/sth into prominence** attirer l'attention sur qn/qch; **to occupy a position of prominence** *(politician etc)* occuper une position éminente; *(house)* être situé sur une éminence

(**b**) *(of land, feature etc)* proéminence *f*; *(part sticking up)* saillie *f*, protubérance *f*; **the prominence of his ears was very noticeable** on ne voyait que ses oreilles décollées; **a rocky prominence** une saillie rocheuse

(**c**) *Astron* protubérance *f* solaire

prominent ['prɒmɪnənt] *adj* (**a**) *(well-known)* célèbre; *(eminent)* éminent; *(obvious)* saillant, frappant; **she's a very prominent individual** c'est un personnage très en vue; **a scandal involving a prominent politician** un scandale impliquant un éminent homme politique; **he has a prominent position in the government** il est très haut placé au gouvernement; **he was very prominent in the campaign** il a joué un rôle très important dans la campagne; **rice is prominent in Eastern cuisine** le riz est l'un des principaux ingrédients de la cuisine asiatique; **to play a prominent part** *or* **role in sth** jouer un rôle important *ou* de tout premier plan dans qch

(**b**) *(striking → detail, difference)* frappant, remarquable; *(→ fact, feature)* saillant, marquant; **put that poster in a prominent position** mettez cette affiche (dans un endroit) bien en vue; **the title needs to be more prominent** il faut que le titre ressorte plus

(**c**) *(projecting)* saillant, en saillie, proéminent; *(land, structure, nose)* proéminent; *(teeth)* qui avance, proéminent

prominently ['prɒmɪnəntlɪ] *adv* bien en vue; **he figures prominently in French politics** il occupe une position importante *ou* de premier plan dans la vie politique française; **the medal was prominently displayed** la médaille était mise en évidence

promiscuity [,prɒmɪ'skju:ətɪ] *n* promiscuité *f* sexuelle

promiscuous [prə'mɪskjʊəs] *adj* (**a**) *(sexually)* **to be promiscuous** *(person)* avoir des mœurs dissolues; *(society, group)* être permissif; **he's very promiscuous** il couche avec n'importe qui; **promiscuous behaviour** promiscuité *f* sexuelle (**b**) *Formal (mixed)* confus, mêlé; *(crowd)* hétérogène

promiscuously [prə'mɪskjʊəslɪ] *adv* (**a**) *(sexually)* **to behave promiscuously** avoir des mœurs dissolues (**b**) *Formal (in a random or confused way)* confusément

promiscuousness [prəˈmɪskjʊəsnɪs] *n* promiscuité *f* sexuelle

promise [ˈprɒmɪs] **1** *n* (**a**) *(pledge)* promesse *f*; **to make** *or* **to give sb a promise** faire une promesse à qn, donner sa parole à qn; **to keep a promise** respecter *ou* tenir une promesse; **she always keeps her promises** elle tient toujours ses promesses, elle tient toujours (sa) parole; **don't make promises if you can't keep them** on ne fait pas de promesses quand on ne peut pas les tenir; **I'm not making any promises but I'll try my best** je ne promets rien, mais je ferai de mon mieux; **I kept** *or* **held him to his promise** j'ai fait en sorte qu'il tienne parole; **to break one's promise** manquer à sa parole, ne pas tenir ses promesses; **these are empty promises** ce sont de vaines promesses; **a promise of help** une promesse d'assistance; **to hold out the promise of sth to sb** laisser espérer qch à qn, faire miroiter qch à qn; **he did it under (the) promise of a Parliamentary seat** il l'a fait parce qu'on lui a promis un siège de député; **I'm under a promise of secrecy** j'ai promis de garder le secret *ou* de ne rien dire; **a promise is a promise** chose promise, chose due; **promises, promises!** toujours des promesses!

(**b**) *(potential)* promesse *f*; **she is full of promise, she shows promise** elle est pleine de promesse *ou* promesses; **an artist of promise** un artiste qui promet; **a young man with every promise of a brilliant future** un jeune homme promis à un brillant avenir

2 *vt* (**a**) *(pledge)* promettre; **to promise sth to sb, to promise sb sth** promettre qch à qn; **to promise (sb) to do sth** promettre (à qn) de faire qch; **I can't promise (you) anything** je ne peux rien vous promettre; **he promised himself a good meal** il se promit mentalement de faire un bon repas; **she promised him (that) she would come** elle lui a promis de venir *ou* qu'elle viendrait; **you'll get into trouble, I promise you!** tu auras des ennuis, je te le promets *ou* tu verras ce que je te dis!; **the weather forecast promised us three days of good weather** la météo nous a promis *ou* annoncé trois jours de beau temps

(**b**) *(indicate)* promettre, annoncer; **it promises to be hot today** le temps promet d'être *ou* s'annonce chaud aujourd'hui; **the clouds promised a thunderstorm** les nuages annonçaient de l'orage; **next week already promises to be difficult** la semaine prochaine promet déjà d'être difficile *ou* s'annonce déjà difficile

(**c**) *(in marriage)* **she was promised to the King's son at birth** dès sa naissance, elle fut promise au fils du roi

3 *vi* (**a**) *(gen)* promettre; **he wanted to come but he couldn't promise** il espérait pouvoir venir mais ne pouvait rien promettre; **I'll wait for you – (do you) promise?** je t'attendrai – tu le promets? *ou* promis?; **OK, I promise!** d'accord, c'est promis!; **but you promised!** mais tu avais promis!

(**b**) **to promise well** *(enterprise)* promettre, s'annoncer bien; *(person)* être prometteur *ou* plein de promesses; *(results, harvest, negotiations)* s'annoncer bien; **his first article promises well** son premier article promet *ou* est prometteur

▸▸ *Am Rel* ***Promise Keepers*** = mouvement intégriste chrétien américain exclusivement composé d'hommes; *Bible & Fig* ***Promised Land*** Terre *f* promise

promising [ˈprɒmɪsɪŋ] *adj* (**a**) *(full of potential → person)* prometteur, qui promet, plein de promesses; **she's a promising actress** c'est une actrice pleine de promesses *ou* qui promet

(**b**) *(encouraging)* prometteur, qui promet; **these are promising signs** ce sont des signes prometteurs; **she got off to a promising start** elle a fait des débuts prometteurs; **her work is very promising** son travail est très prometteur; **the forecast isn't very promising for tomorrow** les prévisions météo n'annoncent rien de bon pour demain

promisingly [ˈprɒmɪsɪŋlɪ] *adv* d'une façon prometteuse; **he began his acting career promisingly** il a débuté sa carrière d'acteur de façon prometteuse; **France started the match promisingly** la France a bien débuté la partie

promisor [ˈprɒmɪsɔː(r)] *n Law* = personne qui a fait une promesse

promissory note [ˈprɒmɪsərɪ-] *n Com* billet *m* à ordre, effet *m* à ordre

promo [ˈprəʊməʊ] (*pl* **promos**) *n Fam* (**a**) *(video)* vidéo *f* promotionnelle[❑]; *(for record)* clip[❑] *m* (**b**) *(sales promotion)* promo *f*

promontory [ˈprɒməntərɪ] (*pl* **promontories**) *n* promontoire *m*

promote [prəˈməʊt] *vt* (**a**) *(in profession, army)* promouvoir; **to be** *or* **to get promoted** être promu, monter en grade, obtenir de l'avancement; **Blyth has been promoted to (the rank of) captain** Blyth a été promu (au grade de) capitaine; **she's been promoted to regional manager** elle a été promue (au poste de) directrice régionale

(**b**) *Sport* **to be promoted to the first division** passer *ou* monter en première division; **to get** *or* **be promoted** passer *ou* monter dans la division supérieure

(**c**) *(encourage → peace, growth, justice, cause)* promouvoir; *(→ the arts, a project)* encourager; *(→ success)* favoriser; *(→ person's interests)* servir; **to promote international cooperation** promouvoir *ou* favoriser *ou* encourager la coopération internationale; **cleanliness promotes health** la propreté est un facteur de santé; **to promote economic growth** promouvoir *ou* favoriser la croissance économique; *Parl* **to promote a bill** prendre l'initiative d'un projet de loi

(**d**) *Com (advertise, publicize)* promouvoir, faire la promotion de; **to promote a new product** faire la promotion d'un nouveau produit; **she's in England to promote her new record** elle est en Angleterre pour faire la promotion de son nouveau disque

(**e**) *(in chess)* promouvoir

promoter [prəˈməʊtə(r)] *n* (**a**) *Com* promoteur(trice) *m,f* (des ventes) (**b**) *(organizer → of match, concert)* organisateur(trice) *m,f*; *(sponsor)* parrain *m* (**c**) *(of peace, scheme)* promoteur(trice) *m,f*; **to be a promoter of sth** *(theory, idea, cause)* promouvoir qch

promotion [prəˈməʊʃən] *n* (**a**) *(advancement)* promotion *f*, avancement *m*; **to get promotion** être promu, obtenir de l'avancement; **there are good prospects of promotion in this company** il y a de réelles possibilités de promotion *ou* d'avancement dans cette société

(**b**) *Sport* promotion *f*; **the team won promotion to the first division** l'équipe a gagné sa place en première division; **to get** *or* **win promotion** passer *ou* monter dans la division supérieure

(**c**) *(encouragement)* promotion *f*, développement *m*; **the promotion of good international relations** le développement de bonnes relations internationales

(**d**) *Com & Mktg* promotion *f*; **this week's promotion** la promotion de la semaine; **I helped in the promotion of her new book** j'ai contribué à la promotion *ou* au lancement de son nouveau livre

(**e**) *(in chess)* promotion *f*

▸▸ ***promotions agency*** agence *f* de promotion; ***promotion budget*** budget *m* promotionnel; ***promotion campaign*** campagne *f* de promotion; ***promotion team*** équipe *f* promotionnelle; ***promotion techniques*** techniques *fpl* de promotion des ventes

promotional [prəˈməʊʃənəl] *adj Com & Mktg* promotionnel, publicitaire

▸▸ ***promotional campaign*** campagne *f* de promotion; ***promotional costs*** coûts *mpl* de promotion; ***promotional discount*** remise *f* promotionnelle; ***promotional literature*** prospectus *mpl* promotionnels; ***promotional material*** matériel *m* de promotion; ***promotional offer*** offre *f* promotionnelle; ***promotional policy*** politique *f* de communication, politique *f* de promotion; ***promotional price*** prix *m* promotionnel; ***promotional sample*** échantillon *m* promotionnel; ***promotional target*** cible *f* de communication; ***promotional video*** (cassette *f*) vidéo *f* promotionnelle

prompt [prɒmpt] **1** *adj* (**a**) *(quick)* rapide, prompt; **a prompt answer/decision** une réponse/décision rapide; **to be prompt to take offence** être prompt à s'offenser; **Carrie was prompt to answer our letter** Carrie a répondu rapidement *ou* sans attendre à notre lettre; **to take prompt action** prendre des mesures immédiates; **her prompt action saved his life** la rapidité de sa réaction lui a sauvé la vie; **you should give this matter prompt attention** vous devriez vous occuper de cette question sans (plus) attendre *ou* le plus rapidement possible; **to be prompt in paying one's debts** être prompt à payer ses dettes

(**b**) *(punctual)* exact, à l'heure

2 *adv (exactly)* **at nine o'clock prompt** à neuf heures précises

3 *vt* (**a**) *(provoke → person)* pousser, inciter; *(→ reaction, reply)* provoquer; **to prompt sb to do sth** pousser *ou* porter qn à faire qch; **he's shy and needs to be prompted to speak up** il est timide, il faut l'encourager à s'exprimer; **I felt prompted to intervene** je me suis senti obligé d'intervenir; **the wave of strikes has prompted the Government to step up its reform programme** la vague de grèves a incité le gouvernement à accélérer son programme de réformes; **his letter prompts me to think that he's mad** sa lettre m'incite à penser qu'il est fou; **what prompted you to suggest such a thing?** qu'est-ce qui vous a incité à proposer une chose pareille?; **the scandal prompted his resignation** le scandale a provoqué sa démission

(**b**) **to prompt sb** *(actor)* souffler sa réplique à qn; *(speaker, pupil)* souffler à qn; **she needed no prompting when asked her opinion on the subject** elle n'avait pas besoin d'encouragement pour donner son opinion sur le sujet; **the teacher prompted him with another question** le professeur lui posa une autre question pour le mettre sur la voie

4 *n* (**a**) *Theat* **to give an actor a prompt** souffler une réplique à un acteur

(**b**) *Comput* invite *f*; *(with wording)* message *m* d'invite *ou* d'attente; **DOS prompt** invite *f* du DOS; **return to the C:\ prompt** revenir au message d'attente du DOS

(**c**) *Fin (for payment)* délai *m* (de paiement)

▸▸ *Theat* ***prompt box*** trou *m* (du souffleur); *Fin* ***prompt day*** jour *m* de paiement; *Fin* ***prompt note*** rappel *m* d'échéance; *Com* ***prompt payment*** paiement *m* dans les délais; *Theat* ***prompt side*** *(in UK)* côté *m* cour; *(in US)* côté *m* jardin; **opposite prompt side** *(in UK)* côté *m* jardin; *(in US)* côté *m* cour

promptbook [ˈprɒmptbʊk] *n Theat* manuscrit *m* (du souffleur)

prompter [ˈprɒmptə(r)] *n Theat* souffleur(euse) *m,f*; *TV* téléprompteur *m*

prompting [ˈprɒmptɪŋ] *n* (**a**) *(persuasion)* incitation *f*; **no amount of prompting will induce me to go there** rien ne pourra me décider à y aller; **they will not do it without the prompting of the international community** ils ne le feront pas si la communauté internationale ne les y pousse pas; **to do sth at sb's prompting** faire qch sur les instances *ou* à l'instigation de qn; **the promptings of conscience** l'aiguillon *m* de la conscience; **he needed no prompting** il n'a pas été nécessaire de le pousser

(**b**) *(of actor, pupil, speaker)* **he needed a lot of prompting** *(actor)* on devait lui souffler tout le temps; **to answer a question without prompting** répondre à une question sans que personne ne souffle; *Sch* **no prompting!** ne soufflez pas!

promptitude [ˈprɒmptɪtjuːd] *n Formal* (**a**) *(quickness)* promptitude *f*, rapidité *f* (**b**) *(punctuality)* ponctualité *f*

promptly [ˈprɒmptlɪ] *adv* (**a**) *(quickly)* promptement, rapidement; **he promptly sent off the telegram** il a rapidement envoyé le télégramme; **he paid up promptly** il a payé immédiatement (**b**) *(punctually)* ponctuellement; **he always gets up promptly at seven o'clock** il se lève toujours à sept heures précises (**c**) *(immediately)* aussitôt, tout de suite; **I promptly forgot what I was meant to do** j'ai aussitôt oublié ce que j'étais supposé faire

promptness [ˈprɒmptnɪs] *n* (**a**) *(quickness)* promptitude *f*, rapidité *f* (**b**) *(punctuality)* ponctualité *f*

promulgate [ˈprɒməlgeɪt] *vt Formal* (**a**) *(decree, law)* promulguer (**b**) *(belief, idea, opinion)* répandre, diffuser

promulgation [ˌprɒməl'geɪʃən] *n Formal* (**a**) *(of decree, law)* promulgation *f* (**b**) *(of belief, idea, opinion)* diffusion *f*, dissémination *f*

promulgator ['prɒməlgeɪtə(r)] *n Formal* (**a**) *(of decree, law)* promulgateur(trice) *m,f* (**b**) *(of belief, idea, opinion)* diffuseur *m*, propagateur(trice) *m,f*

pronation [prəʊ'neɪʃən] *n Anat* pronation *f*

pronator [prəʊ'neɪtə(r)] *n Anat* pronateur *m*

prone [prəʊn] *adj* (**a**) *(inclined)* sujet, enclin; **to be prone to do sth** être sujet *ou* enclin à faire qch; **prone to a disease** prédisposé à une maladie (**b**) *(prostrate)* à plat ventre; **in a prone position** couché sur le ventre

-prone [prəʊn] *suff* **to be accident/disaster-prone** être enclin aux accidents/désastres; **a strike-prone industry** une industrie sujette aux grèves

proneness ['prəʊnnɪs] *n* tendance *f*, prédisposition *f*; **he has a certain proneness to accidents/to letting himself be influenced** il est assez enclin aux accidents/à se laisser influencer

prong [prɒŋ] *n (of fork)* dent *f*; *(of tuning fork)* branche *f*; *(of antler)* pointe *f*; *(of attack, argument)* pointe *f*

pronged [prɒŋd] *adj* à dents, à pointes

-pronged [prɒŋd] *suff* **two-pronged** *(fork)* à deux dents; *Mil (attack)* sur deux fronts; *(argument)* double

pronghorn ['prɒŋhɔ:n] *n Zool* antilope *f* d'Amérique

pronominal [prə'nɒmɪnəl] *adj* pronominal

pronominalize, -ise [prə'nɒmɪnəlaɪz] *vt* pronominaliser

pronominally [prə'nɒmɪnəlɪ] *adv* pronominalement

pronoun ['prəʊnaʊn] *n* pronom *m*

pronounce [prə'naʊns] **1** *vt* (**a**) *(say)* prononcer; **his name is hard to pronounce** son nom est difficile à prononcer; **how's it pronounced?** comment est-ce que ça se prononce?; **you don't pronounce the "p" in "psalm"** on ne prononce pas le "p" de "psalm", le "p" de "psalm" est muet

(**b**) *Formal (declare)* déclarer, prononcer; **the doctor pronounced him dead** le médecin l'a déclaré mort; **judgment has not yet been pronounced** le jugement n'est pas encore prononcé *ou* rendu; **I now pronounce you man and wife** *(in marriage service)* je vous déclare mari et femme

2 *vi* (**a**) *(articulate)* prononcer

(**b**) *(declare)* se prononcer; **to pronounce for/against sth** se prononcer pour/contre qch; *Law* prononcer pour/contre qch; **to pronounce on** *or* **upon sth** se prononcer sur qch; *Law* statuer *ou* prononcer sur qch

pronounceable [prə'naʊnsəbəl] *adj* prononçable

pronounced [prə'naʊnst] *adj (squint, accent, liking)* prononcé, marqué; *(features)* accusé; *(views, opinions)* arrêté; **the change is becoming more pronounced** le changement s'accentue; **he walks with a pronounced limp** il boite de façon prononcée

pronouncedly [prə'naʊnsɪdlɪ] *adv* d'une manière prononcée *ou* marquée

pronouncement [prə'naʊnsmənt] *n* déclaration *f*

pronouncing [prə'naʊnsɪŋ] *n Law (of sentence)* prononcé *m*

▸▸ ***pronouncing dictionary*** dictionnaire *m* de prononciation

pronto ['prɒntəʊ] *adv Fam* illico (presto), pronto

pronuclear [ˌprəʊ'nju:klɪə(r)] *adj (policy, statement)* en faveur du nucléaire; **he is pronuclear** il est pour le nucléaire

pronucleus [ˌprəʊ'nju:klɪəs] *(pl* **pronuclei** [-klɪaɪ]) *n Biol* pronucléus *m*

pronunciation [prəˌnʌnsɪ'eɪʃən] *n* prononciation *f*; **his French pronunciation was good** il avait une bonne prononciation en français

proof [pru:f] **1** *n* (**a**) *(UNCOUNT) (evidence)* preuve *f*; **to show** *or* **to give proof of sth** faire *ou* donner la preuve de qch; **do you have any proof?** vous en avez la preuve *ou* des preuves?; **you need proof of identity** vous devez fournir une pièce d'identité; **can you produce any proof for your accusations?** avez-vous des preuves pour justifier vos accusations?; **we have written proof of it** nous en avons la preuve écrite *ou* par écrit; **that's no proof!** ce n'est pas une preuve!; **by way of proof** comme *ou* pour preuve; **he cited several other cases in proof of his argument** il a cité plusieurs autres cas pour défendre sa thèse; **he gave her a locket as proof of his love** il lui a offert un médaillon comme preuve de son amour pour elle *ou* en gage d'amour; *Prov* **the proof of the pudding is in the eating** il faut juger sur pièces

(**b**) *Phot & Typ* épreuve *f*; **to correct** *or* **to read the proofs** corriger les épreuves; **to pass the proofs** donner le bon à tirer; **at the proof stage** à la correction des épreuves

(**c**) *(of alcohol)* teneur *f* (en alcool); **45 percent proof brandy** ≃ cognac *m* à 45 degrés

2 *adj Br* **to be proof against** *(fire, acid, rust)* être à l'épreuve de; *(danger, temptation)* être à l'abri de *ou* insensible à

3 *vt* (**a**) *(fabric)* imperméabiliser

(**b**) *Typ (proofread)* corriger les épreuves de; *(produce proof of)* préparer les épreuves de

▸▸ ***proof of delivery*** bordereau *m* de livraison; ***proof of payment*** justificatif *m* de paiement; ***proof of postage*** certificat *m* d'expédition; ***proof of purchase*** reçu *m*; ***proof spirit*** *(in UK)* alcool *m* à 57°; *(in US)* alcool *m* à 50°

-proof [pru:f] *suff* à l'épreuve de; **acid-proof** à l'épreuve des acides; **an idiot-proof mechanism** un mécanisme (totalement) indéréglable

proofing ['pru:fɪŋ] *n* (**a**) *(action → of fabric)* imperméabilisation *f* (**b**) *(coating)* enduit *m* imperméable (**c**) *Typ (reading)* correction *f* des épreuves; *(production)* tirage *m* des épreuves

proofread ['pru:fri:d] *(pt & pp* **proofread** [-red]) *vt* corriger (les épreuves de)

proofreader ['pru:fˌri:də(r)] *n* correcteur(trice) *m,f* (d'épreuves *ou* d'imprimerie)

proofreading ['pru:fˌri:dɪŋ] *n* correction *f* (d'épreuves)

▸▸ ***proofreading mark, proofreading symbol*** signe *m* de correction

prop [prɒp] *(pt & pp* **propped**, *cont* **propping**) **1** *n* (**a**) *(gen)* support *m*; *Constr (for tunnel, wall)* étai *m*, étançon *m*; *(in pit)* étai *m*

(**b**) *(pole, stick → for plant, flowers)* tuteur *m*; *(→ for beans, peas)* rame *f*; *(→ for vines)* échalas *m*; *(→ for washing line)* perche *f*

(**c**) *Sport (in rugby)* pilier *m*

(**d**) *Fig* soutien *m*; **he uses alcohol as a prop** il boit pour se donner du courage; **he was the prop of his father's old age** il était le bâton de vieillesse de son père

(**e**) *Theat (property)* accessoire *m*

(**f**) *Fam (propeller)* hélice ❑ *f*

2 *vt* (**a**) *(lean)* appuyer; **she propped her bike (up) against the wall** elle a appuyé son vélo contre le mur; **prop yourself** *or* **your back against these cushions** calez-vous contre *ou* adossez-vous à ces coussins; **he was propping his head (up) in his hands** il tenait sa tête calée entre ses mains

(**b**) *(support)* **to prop (up)** *(wall, tunnel)* étayer, étançonner, consolider; *(plants)* mettre un tuteur à; *(peas, beans)* ramer; **I propped the door open with a chair** j'ai maintenu la porte ouverte avec une chaise

▸▸ *Sport* ***prop forward*** *(in rugby)* pilier *m*; *Aut* ***prop shaft*** arbre *m* de transmission

▸**prop up** *vt sep (regime, family, business, currency)* soutenir; **the government stepped in to prop up the franc** le gouvernement est intervenu pour soutenir le franc; *Fam Hum* **he's always propping up the bar** c'est un vrai pilier de bar *ou* de bistro

prop. *(written abbr* **proprietor**) propriétaire *mf*

propaganda [ˌprɒpə'gændə] **1** *n* propagande *f*

2 *comp (film, machine, material, exercise)* de propagande

propagandist [ˌprɒpə'gændɪst] **1** *adj* propagandiste

2 *n* propagandiste *mf*

propagandize, -ise [ˌprɒpə'gændaɪz] **1** *vi* faire de la propagande

2 *vt (ideas, views)* faire de la propagande pour *ou* en faveur de; *(person, masses)* faire de la propagande auprès de

propagate ['prɒpəgeɪt] **1** *vt Bot & Phys* propager; *Fig (ideas etc)* propager, disséminer

2 *vi* se propager

propagation [ˌprɒpə'geɪʃən] *n Bot, Phys & Fig* propagation *f*

propagator ['prɒpəgeɪtə(r)] *n* (**a**) *(gen)* propagateur(trice) *m,f* (**b**) *Bot* germoir *m*

propane ['prəʊpeɪn] *n Chem* propane *m*

propanoic acid [ˌprəʊpə'nəʊɪk-] *n Chem* acide *m* propanoïque

propanol ['prəʊpənɒl] *n Chem* propanol *m*, alcool *m* propylique

propel [prə'pel] *(pt & pp* **propelled**, *cont* **propelling**) *vt* (**a**) *(machine, vehicle etc)* propulser, faire avancer

(**b**) *(person)* propulser, pousser; **she was propelled along the road by the crowd** elle fut poussée par la foule sur toute la longueur de la rue; **the sudden stop propelled us all forward** l'arrêt subit nous a tous propulsés vers l'avant; **he was propelled into the position of manager** on l'a bombardé directeur

propellant, propellent [prə'pelənt] **1** *n (for rocket)* propergol *m*; *(for gun)* poudre *f* propulsive; *(in aerosol)* (agent *m*) propulseur *m*; **liquid/solid (rocket) propellant** propergol *m* liquide/solide

2 *adj* propulsif, propulseur

propeller [prə'pelə(r)] *n* hélice *f*

▸▸ ***propeller shaft*** *Aviat* arbre *m* porte-hélice; *Naut* arbre *m* d'hélice; *Aut* arbre *m* de transmission

propelling pencil [prə'pelɪŋ-] *n Br* portemine *m*

propene ['prəʊpi:n] *n Chem* propène *m*

propensity [prə'pensətɪ] *(pl* **propensities**) *n Formal* propension *f*, tendance *f*, penchant *m*; **he has a propensity for** *or* **towards drink** il a tendance à boire (plus que de raison); **my propensity not to trust** *or* **for not trusting other people** ma propension *ou* ma tendance à ne pas faire confiance aux autres

PROPER ['prɒpə(r)]

bon	▸ **1 (a)**
correct	▸ **1 (a), (c)**
convenable	▸ **1 (a), (c)**
vrai	▸ **1 (b), (d)**
proprement dit	▸ **1 (e)**

1 *adj* (**a**) *(correct)* bon, juste, correct; *(appropriate)* convenable, approprié; **the proper answer** la bonne réponse, la réponse correcte; **what is the proper use of the imperfect?** quand doit-on utiliser l'imparfait?; **you're not doing it in the proper way** vous ne vous y prenez pas comme il faut; **to apply to the proper person** s'adresser à qui de droit; **to put sth in the proper place** mettre qch à sa place; **John wasn't waiting at the proper place** John n'attendait pas au bon endroit *ou* là où il fallait; **she didn't come at the proper time** elle s'est trompée d'heure; **to think it proper to do sth** juger bon de faire qch; **do as you think proper** faites comme bon vous semble; **that wasn't the proper thing to say/to do** ce n'était pas ce qu'il fallait dire/faire; **she thanked him, as is only proper** elle l'a remercié, comme il se devait; **that noisy pub isn't a proper place for a meeting** ce pub bruyant n'est pas un endroit approprié pour tenir une réunion; **paid at the proper rate** payé au taux *ou* au prix convenable; **he wasn't wearing the proper clothes** il n'était pas vêtu pour la circonstance; **you must go through the proper channels** il faut suivre la filière officielle; **evening dress is the proper thing to wear for a ball** porter une tenue de soirée est de circonstance pour aller au bal; **I don't have the proper tools for this engine** je n'ai pas les outils appropriés pour *ou* qui conviennent pour ce moteur; **I can't find the proper word to describe him** je n'arrive pas à trouver le mot juste *ou* qui convient pour le décrire; *Old-fashioned or Hum* **he did the proper thing by her** *(he married her)* il a réparé

(**b**) *(real)* vrai, véritable; **I haven't had a proper meal in ages** il y a une éternité que je n'ai pas fait un vrai repas; **we must give the President a proper welcome** nous devons réserver au président un accueil digne de ce nom; **it's a toy, not a proper rifle** c'est un jouet, pas un vrai fusil; **they call him Tommy but his proper name's Thomas** on l'appelle Tommy mais son vrai nom c'est Thomas; **he's not a**

proper doctor ce n'est pas un vrai docteur; **in the proper sense of the word** au sens propre du mot; **putting letters in envelopes isn't a proper job** mettre des lettres dans des enveloppes n'a rien d'un vrai travail

(**c**) *(respectable)* correct, convenable, comme il faut; **that's not proper behaviour** ce n'est pas convenable, cela ne se fait pas; **she's a very proper young woman** c'est une jeune femme très bien; **she's a bit too proper** elle est un peu trop comme il faut; **may I take my shoes off? – no, that's not the proper thing to do here** puis-je ôter mes chaussures? – non, ça ne se fait pas *ou* ce serait déplacé ici

(**d**) *Br Fam (as intensifier)* vrai❑, véritable❑, complet(ète)❑; **it's a proper catastrophe** c'est une vraie *ou* véritable catastrophe; **you're a proper idiot** tu es un parfait imbécile *ou* un imbécile fini; **he made a proper fool of himself** il s'est couvert de ridicule❑; **a proper little madam** une vraie petite madame; **we're in a proper mess** nous voilà dans de beaux draps!; **her room was in a proper mess** il y avait un vrai bazar dans sa chambre; **I gave him a proper telling-off** je lui ai passé un bon savon

(**e**) *(predicative use → specifically)* proprement dit; **he lives outside the city proper** il habite en dehors de la ville même *ou* proprement dite

(**f**) *(characteristic)* **proper to** propre à, typique de; **illnesses proper to tropical climates** maladies propres aux climats tropicaux

2 *adv Br Fam* **they got it good and proper** ils ont reçu ce qu'ils méritaient❑; **to talk proper** parler correctement❑; *NEng* **he was proper angry with me** il était très *ou* vraiment en colère contre moi❑

3 *n Rel* propre *m*

►► *Math* ***proper fraction*** fraction *f* inférieure à l'unité; *Astron* ***proper motion*** mouvement *m* propre; ***proper name*** nom *m* propre; ***proper noun*** nom *m* propre

---

properly ['prɒpəlɪ] *adv* (**a**) *(well, correctly)* bien, juste, correctement; **the lid isn't on properly** le couvercle n'est pas bien mis; **the engine isn't working properly** le moteur ne marche pas bien; **for once they pronounced my name properly** pour une fois, ils ont prononcé mon nom correctement *ou* ils ont bien prononcé mon nom; **I haven't slept properly in weeks** ça fait des semaines que je n'ai pas bien dormi; **she quite properly intervened** c'est avec raison *ou* à juste titre qu'elle est intervenue

(**b**) *(decently, suitably)* correctement, convenablement; *(correctly in behaviour)* comme il faut; **patrons must be properly dressed** une tenue vestimentaire correcte est exigée de nos clients; **eat properly!** mange proprement *ou* comme il faut!; **he didn't behave properly towards her** il ne s'est pas comporté correctement envers elle; **I haven't thanked you properly** je ne vous ai pas remercié comme il faut *ou* comme il convient

(**c**) *(strictly)* proprement; **he isn't properly speaking an expert** il n'est pas à proprement parler un expert

(**d**) *Br Fam (as intensifier)* vraiment❑, complètement❑, tout à fait❑; **I'm properly exhausted** je suis complètement crevé; **he looks properly idiotic in those trousers** il a l'air complètement *ou* parfaitement idiot dans ce pantalon; **they were properly told off** ils en ont pris pour leur grade

propertied ['prɒpətɪd] *adj Formal* possédant; **a propertied gentleman** un homme fortuné; **the propertied classes** les classes *fpl* possédantes

property ['prɒpətɪ] (*pl* **properties**) *n* (**a**) *(UNCOUNT) (belongings)* propriété *f*, biens *mpl*; *(objects)* objets *mpl*; *Law* biens *mpl*; **hands off! that's my property!** n'y touchez pas, c'est à moi *ou* ça m'appartient!; **this book is the property of Theresa Lloyd** ce livre appartient à Theresa Lloyd; **government property** propriété *f* de l'État; **she left him all her property** elle lui a laissé tous ses biens; **this is stolen property** ce sont des objets volés

(**b**) *(UNCOUNT) (buildings)* propriété *f*; *(real estate)* biens *mpl* immobiliers, immobilier *m*; *(land)* terres *fpl*, propriété *f* (foncière); **Smythe is investing his money in property** Smythe investit son argent dans l'immobilier; **they own a lot of property in the country** *(houses)* ils ont de nombreuses propriétés à la campagne; *(land)* ils ont de nombreuses terres à la campagne; **a man of property** un homme qui possède des biens immobiliers *ou* une fortune personnelle; **to get a foot on the property ladder** accéder à la propriété, devenir propriétaire

(**c**) *(plot of land)* terrain *m*; *(house, building)* propriété *f*; **to be on sb's property** être dans la propriété de qn; **get off my property!** sortez de chez moi!

(**d**) *(quality)* propriété *f*; **what are the chemical properties of cobalt?** quelles sont les propriétés chimiques du cobalt?; **healing properties** vertus *fpl* thérapeutiques *ou* curatives

(**e**) *Law (right)* (droit *m* de) propriété *f*; **literary/intellectual property** propriété *f* littéraire/intellectuelle

(**f**) *Theat* accessoire *m*

►► *Br* ***property assets*** patrimoine *m* immobilier; ***property centre*** centre *m* de vente immobilière; ***property developer*** promoteur(trice) *m,f* (immobilier(ère)); ***property development*** promotion *f* immobilière; *Br* ***property loan*** prêt *m* immobilier; *Theat* ***property man*** accessoiriste *m*; ***property market*** marché *m* immobilier; *Theat* ***property mistress*** accessoiriste *f*; ***property owner*** propriétaire *mf*; ***property shares*** valeurs *fpl* immobilières; ***property speculation*** spéculation *f* immobilière; ***property speculator*** spéculateur(trice) *m,f* immobilier(ère); ***property surveyor*** (architecte *mf*) expert(e) *m,f*; ***property tax*** impôt *m* foncier

propfan ['prɒpfæn] *n* propfan *m*

prophase ['prəʊfeɪz] *n Biol* prophase *f*

prophecy ['prɒfɪsɪ] (*pl* **prophecies**) *n* prophétie *f*

prophesy ['prɒfɪsaɪ] (*pt & pp* **prophesied**) **1** *vt* prophétiser, prédire; **scaremongers prophesied the end of the world** des alarmistes ont annoncé la fin du monde; **to prophesy that sth will happen** prédire que qch va arriver

2 *vi* faire des prophéties

prophet ['prɒfɪt] **1** *n* prophète *m*; **the Prophet** *(in Islam)* le Prophète (Mahomet); **a prophet of doom** un prophète de malheur

2 Prophets *n Bible* **(the Book of) Prophets** le livre des Prophètes

prophetess ['prɒfɪtɪs] *n* prophétesse *f*

prophetic [prə'fetɪk] *adj* prophétique

prophetically [prə'fetɪkəlɪ] *adv* prophétiquement

prophylactic [ˌprɒfɪ'læktɪk] **1** *adj* prophylactique

2 *n* (**a**) *(drug)* médicament *m* prophylactique (**b**) *(condom)* préservatif *m*

prophylaxis [ˌprɒfɪ'læksɪs] (*pl* **prophylaxes** [-siːz]) *n* prophylaxie *f*

propinquity [prə'pɪŋkwətɪ] *n Formal* (**a**) *(in space, time)* proximité *f* (**b**) *(in kinship)* consanguinité *f*

propionic acid [ˌprəʊpɪ'ɒnɪk-] *n Chem* acide *m* propionique

propitiate [prə'pɪʃɪeɪt] *vt Formal* apaiser

propitiation [prəˌpɪʃɪ'eɪʃən] *n Formal* propitiation *f*

propitiatory [prə'pɪʃɪətrɪ] *adj Formal* propitiatoire

propitious [prə'pɪʃəs] *adj Formal* propice, favorable (**for** à); **it wasn't really a propitious moment to ask for a rise** le moment était plutôt mal choisi pour demander une augmentation

propitiously [prə'pɪʃəslɪ] *adv Formal* d'une manière propice

propman ['prɒpmæn] (*pl* **propmen** [-mən]) *n Theat* accessoiriste *m*

proponent [prə'pəʊnənt] *n* avocat(e) *m,f*, partisan(e) *m,f*

proportion [prə'pɔːʃən] **1** *n* (**a**) *(gen) & Math (ratio)* proportion *f*, rapport *m*; **in the proportion of 6 parts water to 1 part shampoo** dans la proportion de 6 mesures d'eau pour 1 mesure de shampooing; **the sentence is out of all proportion to the crime** la peine est disproportionnée par rapport au *ou* est sans commune mesure avec le délit; **the price bears little proportion to its real value** le prix n'a guère de rapport avec sa véritable valeur; **the proportion of income to *or* over expenditure** le rapport entre les revenus et les dépenses

(**b**) *(perspective)* proportion *f*; **to have a sense of proportion** avoir le sens des proportions; **he has no sense of proportion** il n'a pas le sens de la mesure; **you seem to have got *or* blown the problem out of (all) proportion** vous semblez avoir exagéré *ou* grossi le problème; **you must try to see things in proportion** vous devez essayer de ramener les choses à leur juste valeur; **the artist has got the tree out of proportion** l'artiste n'a pas respecté les proportions de l'arbre

(**c**) *(dimension)* proportion *f*, dimension *f*; **a ship of vast proportions** un navire de grande dimension; **the affair has assumed worrying proportions** l'affaire a pris des proportions alarmantes; **the disease has reached epidemic proportions** la maladie est devenue une véritable épidémie; **the problem has reached epidemic proportions** le problème s'est étendu tel une épidémie

(**d**) *(part)* partie *f*; **a large proportion of the staff/population** une grande partie du personnel/de la population; **she only got a small proportion of the profits** elle n'a touché qu'une petite part *ou* partie des bénéfices; **what proportion of your income do you spend on tobacco?** quel pourcentage de vos revenus dépensez-vous en tabac?

2 *vt* proportionner; **to proportion one's expenditure to one's resources** proportionner ses dépenses à ses ressources, calculer ses dépenses en fonction de ses ressources

3 in proportion to, in proportion with *prep* par rapport à; **the office block is huge in proportion to the houses around it** l'immeuble de bureaux est énorme par rapport aux maisons qui l'entourent; **the job is badly paid in proportion to the effort required** cet emploi est mal payé vu le travail exigé; **his salary is in proportion to his experience** son salaire correspond à son expérience; **the monthly payments are calculated in proportion to your income** les mensualités sont calculées en fonction de *ou* sont proportionnelles à vos revenus; **inflation may increase in proportion with wage rises** l'inflation risque d'augmenter proportionnellement aux augmentations de salaire

proportional [prə'pɔːʃənəl] *adj* proportionnel, en proportion; **proportional to** proportionnel à; **her income is proportional to the work she puts in** ses revenus sont proportionnels au travail effectué

►► *Pol* ***proportional representation*** représentation *f* proportionnelle; *Typ* ***proportional spacing*** espacement *m* proportionnel

proportionally [prə'pɔːʃənəlɪ] *adv* proportionnellement; **they spend proportionally more of their budget on research than does Chemco** ils accordent à la recherche une proportion de leur budget supérieure à celle que dépense Chemco

proportionate 1 *adj* [prə'pɔːʃənət] proportionné

2 *vt* [prə'pɔːʃəneɪt] proportionner

proportionately [prə'pɔːʃənətlɪ] *adv* proportionnellement, en proportion

proportioned [prə'pɔːʃənd] *adj* **well/badly proportioned** bien/mal proportionné

proposal [prə'pəʊzəl] *n* (**a**) *(offer)* proposition *f*, offre *f*; **to make a proposal** faire *ou* formuler une proposition

(**b**) *(of marriage)* demande *f* en mariage; **she refused his proposal** elle a rejeté sa demande en mariage, elle a refusé de l'épouser

(**c**) *(suggestion)* proposition *f*, suggestion *f*; **he accepted her proposal to go on holiday** il a accepté de partir en vacances, comme elle l'avait suggéré

(**d**) *(plan, scheme)* proposition *f*, projet *m*, plan *m*; **the proposal for a car park/to build a car park** le projet de parking/de construction d'un parking

propose [prə'pəʊz] **1** *vt* (**a**) *(suggest)* proposer, suggérer; **to propose sth to sb** proposer qch à qn; **to propose doing sth** proposer de faire qch; **it was proposed that we might like to stay a few days longer** on nous a proposé de rester quelques jours de plus; **I propose (that) we all go for a drink** je propose *ou* suggère que nous allions tous prendre un verre (**b**) *(present → policy, resolution, scheme)* proposer, présenter, soumettre; **to propose sb's health, to propose a toast to sb** porter un toast à (la santé de) qn; **I propose Jones as** *or* **for treasurer** je propose Jones comme trésorier; **to propose (marriage to sb)** demander qn en mariage, faire une demande en mariage à qn

(**c**) *(intend)* se proposer, avoir l'intention, compter; **I propose taking** *or* **to take a few days off work** je me propose de prendre quelques jours de congé; **they propose leaving early** ils ont l'intention de partir de bonne heure

2 *vi* (**a**) *(offer marriage)* faire une demande en mariage; **to propose to sb** demander qn en mariage

(**b**) *(idiom)* **man proposes, God disposes** l'homme propose, Dieu dispose

proposed [prəˈpəʊzd] *adj* projeté; **the proposed visit** la visite prévue; **the building of the proposed car park has been delayed** le projet de construction d'un parking a été suspendu

proposer [prəˈpəʊzə(r)] *n* (**a**) *(of motion)* auteur *m* (d'une proposition) (**b**) *(of candidate → man)* parrain *m*; *(→ woman)* marraine *f*

proposition [ˌprɒpəˈzɪʃən] **1** *n* (**a**) *(proposal, statement)* proposition *f*; **Proposition 13** = loi adoptée en Californie en 1978 par référendum, et qui fut suivie par d'autres lois visant à réduire les impôts et les taxes

(**b**) *(task)* affaire *f*; **that's quite a proposition** c'est une tout autre affaire; **climbing that mountain will be no easy proposition** ce ne sera pas une petite *ou* mince affaire que de gravir cette montagne; **that's a tough proposition you're making** ce n'est pas rien, ce que vous demandez là; *Fig* **the boss is a tough proposition** le patron n'est pas quelqu'un de commode *ou* facile, le patron est du genre coriace

(**c**) *(available choice)* solution *f*; **solar power is not an economic proposition** l'énergie solaire n'est pas une solution rentable; **the deal wasn't a paying proposition** l'affaire n'était pas rentable

(**d**) *(offer of sex)* proposition *f*; **to make sb a proposition** faire des propositions (malhonnêtes) *ou* des avances à qn

(**e**) *Math* proposition *f*

2 *vt* faire des propositions (malhonnêtes) *ou* des avances à

propositional [ˌprɒpəˈzɪʃənəl] *adj* propositionnel, de la proposition; **the two propositional terms** les deux prémisses

►► ***propositional theology*** théologie *f* par syllogismes

propositus [ˌprəʊˈpɒzɪtəs] *n Med* cas *m* index *(dans l'étude d'une famille donnée)*

propound [prəˈpaʊnd] *vt Formal (argument, theory)* avancer, mettre en avant; *(opinion)* avancer, émettre; *(problem)* poser

proprietary [prəˈpraɪətərɪ] *adj* (**a**) *Com* de marque déposée

(**b**) *(attitude, behaviour, function)* de propriétaire; **his manner towards her was rather proprietary** il était plutôt possessif avec elle

►► *Com* ***proprietary article*** article *m* de marque (déposée); *Com* ***proprietary brand*** marque *f* déposée; *Hist* ***proprietary colony*** = aux États-Unis, colonie octroyée à un propriétaire par la Couronne anglaise au XVIIème siècle; *Am* ***proprietary hospital*** hôpital *m* privé, clinique *f* privée; ***proprietary information*** informations *fpl* confidentielles, informations *fpl* exclusives à la société; *Pharm* ***proprietary medicine*** spécialité *f* pharmaceutique; *Com* ***proprietary name*** marque *f* déposée; *Com* ***proprietary process*** processus *m* breveté

proprietor [prəˈpraɪətə(r)] *n* propriétaire *mf*

proprietorial [prəˌpraɪəˈtɔːrɪəl] *adj* de propriétaire; **he's very proprietorial about it** il est très possessif avec ça

proprietorship [prəˈpraɪətəʃɪp] *n* propriété *f*, possession *f*; *Law* (droit *m* de) propriété *f*; **under new proprietorship** *(sign)* changement de propriétaire

proprietress [prəˈpraɪətrɪs] *n* propriétaire *f*

propriety [prəˈpraɪətɪ] *(pl* **proprieties***)* *n Formal* (**a**) *(decorum)* bienséance *f*, convenance *f*; **the rules of propriety require you to write to her** les règles de la bienséance vous obligent à lui écrire; **his behaviour is lacking in propriety** son comportement est tout à fait inconvenant *ou* déplacé; **to have a sense of propriety** avoir le sens des convenances; **contrary to the proprieties** contraire aux bienséances *ou* convenances

(**b**) *(suitability → of action, measure)* opportunité *f*; *(→ of word, remark)* justesse *f*, propriété *f*

(**c**) *(rectitude)* rectitude *f*; **to behave with propriety** respecter les convenances

proprioception [ˌprəʊprɪəʊˈsepʃən] *n Physiol* proprioception *f*

proprioceptive [ˌprəʊprɪəʊˈseptɪv] *adj Physiol* proprioceptif

proprioceptor [ˌprəʊprɪəʊˈseptə(r)] *n Physiol* propriocepteur *m*

propshaft [ˈprɒpʃɑːft] *n Tech* arbre *m* de transmission

propulsion [prəˈpʌlʃən] *n* propulsion *f*

propulsive [prəˈpʌlsɪv] *adj* propulseur, propulsif

propyl [ˈprɒpɪl] *n Chem* propyle *m*

►► ***propyl alcohol*** alcool *m* propylique

propylaeum [ˌprɒpɪˈlɪəm] *n Archit* propylée *m*

propylene [ˈprɒpɪliːn] *n Chem* propylène *m*

pro rata [-ˈrɑːtə] **1** *adj* au prorata

2 *adv* au prorata

prorate [ˈprəʊreɪt] *vt Am* distribuer au prorata *ou* de façon proportionnelle

prorogation [ˌprəʊrəˈgeɪʃən] *n* prorogation *f*

prorogue [prəˈrəʊg] *vt* proroger

prosaic [ˌprəʊˈzeɪɪk] *adj* prosaïque

prosaically [ˌprəʊˈzeɪɪklɪ] *adv* prosaïquement

prosaicalness [ˌprəʊˈzeɪɪkəlnɪs], **prosaicness** [ˌprəʊˈzeɪɪknɪs] *n* prosaïsme *m*

Pros. Atty *Am Law (written abbr* **prosecuting attorney***)* ≃ procureur *m*

proscenium [prəˈsiːnjəm] *(pl* **prosceniums** *or* **proscenia** [-njə]*)* *n Theat* avant-scène *f*; *Antiq* proscenium *m*

►► *Theat* ***proscenium arch*** ≃ manteau *m* d'Arlequin

prosciutto [prɒˈʃuːtəʊ] *n Culin* prosciutto *m*

proscribe [prəʊˈskraɪb] *vt* proscrire

proscription [prəʊˈskrɪpʃən] *n* proscription *f*

proscriptive [prəʊsˈkrɪptɪv] *adj (law)* de proscription; *(decree)* prohibitif

prose [prəʊz] *n* (**a**) *Literature* prose *f*; **to write in prose** écrire en prose, faire de la prose; **the writer's elegant/rhythmic prose style** la prose élégante/rythmée de l'auteur (**b**) *Br Sch & Univ (translation)* thème *m*

►► ***prose poem*** poème *m* en prose; ***prose poetry*** poésie *f* en prose

prosecutable [ˌprɒsɪˈkjuːtəbəl] *adj* (**a**) *(person)* poursuivable (**b**) *(action)* que l'on peut intenter; *(claim)* que l'on peut déposer

prosecute [ˈprɒsɪkjuːt] **1** *vt* (**a**) *Law* poursuivre (en justice), engager des poursuites contre; **to prosecute sb for sth** poursuivre qn (en justice) pour qch; **he was prosecuted for disturbing the peace** il a été poursuivi pour tapage nocturne

(**b**) *Formal (pursue → war, investigation)* poursuivre

2 *vi Law (lawyer → in civil case)* représenter la partie civile; *(→ in criminal case)* représenter le ministère public *ou* le parquet; **to decide to prosecute** décider d'engager des poursuites judiciaires

prosecuting attorney [ˈprɒsɪkjuːtɪŋ-] *n Am Law* ≃ procureur *m*

prosecution [ˌprɒsɪˈkjuːʃən] *n* (**a**) *Law (proceedings)* poursuites *fpl* (judiciaires); *(indictment)* accusation *f*; **to be liable to prosecution** s'exposer à des poursuites (judiciaires); **to bring a prosecution against sb** poursuivre qn en justice, engager des poursuites judiciaires contre qn; **this is her second prosecution** c'est la deuxième fois qu'elle est poursuivie

(**b**) *Law (lawyer → in civil case)* avocat *m* ou avocats *mpl* représentant les plaignants *ou* la partie plaignante; *(→ in criminal case)* ministère *m* public, accusation *f*; **witness for the prosecution** témoin *m* à charge

(**c**) *Formal (pursuit)* poursuite *f*; **the prosecution of the war** la poursuite de la guerre; **in the prosecution of his duties** dans l'exercice *ou* l'accomplissement de ses fonctions

prosecutor [ˈprɒsɪkjuːtə(r)] *n Law* (**a**) *(person bringing case)* plaignant(e) *m,f* (**b**) *(lawyer)* **(public) prosecutor** procureur *m*

proselyte [ˈprɒsəlaɪt] **1** *n* prosélyte *mf*

2 *vi* faire du prosélytisme

3 *vt* faire un prosélyte de

proselytism [ˈprɒsəlɪtɪzəm] *n* prosélytisme *m*

proselytize, -ise [ˈprɒsəlɪtaɪz] **1** *vi* faire du prosélytisme

2 *vt* faire un prosélyte de

proselytizer [ˈprɒsəlɪtaɪzə(r)] *n* personne *f* animée de prosélytisme

proselytizing [ˈprɒsəlɪtaɪzɪŋ] *n* prosélytisme *m*

Proserpina [ˌprɒsəˈpiːnə] *pr n Myth* Proserpine

prosimian [prəʊˈsɪmɪən] *n Zool* prosimien *m*

prosodic [prəˈsɒdɪk] *adj* prosodique

prosody [ˈprɒsədɪ] *n* prosodie *f*

prosopopoeia [ˌprɒsəʊpəˈpiːə] *n Ling* prosopopée *f*

prospect **1** *n* [ˈprɒspekt] (**a**) *(possibility)* chance *f*, perspective *f*; **what are his prospects of success?** quelles chances a-t-il de réussir?; **there's little prospect of their winning the match** ils ont peu de chances de remporter *ou* il y a peu d'espoir (pour) qu'ils remportent le match; **we had given up all prospect of hearing from you** nous avions renoncé à tout espoir d'avoir *ou* nous pensions ne jamais plus recevoir de vos nouvelles

(**b**) *(impending event, situation)* perspective *f*; **I don't relish the prospect of working for him** la perspective de travailler pour lui ne m'enchante guère; **to have sth in prospect** avoir qch en vue *ou* en perspective; **he has a bright future in prospect** il a un bel avenir en perspective *ou* devant lui; **what are the weather prospects for tomorrow?** quelles sont les prévisions météorologiques pour demain?

(**c**) *(usu pl) (chance of success)* perspectives *fpl* d'avenir; **the prospects are not very good** les choses se présentent plutôt mal; **the prospect(s) for the automobile industry** les perspectives d'avenir de l'industrie automobile; **her prospects are bleak** ses perspectives d'avenir sont sombres; **she's a woman with good prospects** c'est une femme qui a de l'avenir *ou* une femme d'avenir; **this company has good prospects/no prospects** cette entreprise a un bel avenir devant elle/n'a pas d'avenir; **a job with prospects** un poste qui offre des perspectives d'avenir; **it's a job without any prospects of promotion** c'est un poste qui n'offre aucune perspective d'avancement; **this job has good promotion prospects** ce poste offre de réelles possibilités d'avancement

(**d**) *(person → customer)* client(e) *m,f* potentiel(elle) *ou* éventuel(elle), prospect *m*; *(→ candidate)* espoir *m*; *Old-fashioned (→ marriage partner)* parti *m*; **he's a good prospect for the manager's job** c'est un candidat potentiel au poste de directeur; **there are two young prospects in the team** l'équipe compte deux joueurs prometteurs *ou* qui ont un bel avenir devant eux; **Robbins is a good prospect** Robbins a un bel avenir devant lui

(**e**) *(view)* perspective *f*, vue *f*

2 *vi* [prəˈspekt] prospecter; **to prospect for oil** chercher du pétrole; *Mktg* **to prospect for new customers** prospecter la clientèle

3 *vt* [prəˈspekt] *(area, land)* prospecter

►► *Mktg* ***prospect pool*** groupe *m* de prospects

prospecting [prəˈspektɪŋ] *n* prospection *f*; *Mining & Petr* **oil/gold prospecting** prospection *f* pétrolière/d'or

prospective [prəˈspektɪv] *adj* (**a**) *(future)* futur; **my prospective mother-in-law** ma future belle-mère (**b**) *(possible → customer)* potentiel, éventuel; *(→ candidate)* éventuel; **he's a prospective customer** c'est un client potentiel (**c**) *(intended, expected)* en perspective; **my prospective trip to Ireland** le voyage que je projette de faire en Irlande

prospector [prəˈspektə(r)] *n* prospecteur(trice) *m,f*, chercheur(euse) *m,f*; **gold prospectors** chercheurs *mpl* d'or

prospectus [prəˈspektəs] *n* prospectus *m*; *Mktg (about company, product)* prospectus *m*; *St Exch (about share issue)* appel *m* à la souscription publique

prosper [ˈprɒspə(r)] **1** *vi* prospérer

2 *vt Literary* faire prospérer, faire réussir; **(may) God prosper you!** Dieu vous fasse prospérer!

prosperity [prɒ'sperətɪ] *n* prospérité *f*

prosperous ['prɒspərəs] *adj (business, area, family)* prospère; *(period)* prospère, de prospérité; *Literary* **prosperous winds** vents *mpl* favorables

prosperously ['prɒspərəslɪ] *adv* de manière prospère; **they live prosperously** ils vivent dans la prospérité

prosperousness ['prɒspərəsnɪs] *n* prospérité *f*

prostaglandin [,prɒstə'glændɪn] *n Physiol* prostaglandine *f*

prostate ['prɒsteɪt] *n (gland)* prostate *f*
►► ***prostate cancer*** cancer *m* de la prostate; ***prostate gland*** prostate *f*

prostatic [prɒs'tætɪk] *adj* prostatique

prostatitis [,prɒstə'taɪtɪs] *n Med* prostatite *f*

prosthesis [prɒs'θi:sɪs] (*pl* **prostheses** [-si:z]) *n* (**a**) *Med* prothèse *f* (**b**) *Ling* prosthèse *f*

prosthetic [prɒs'θetɪk] *adj* (**a**) *Med* prothétique (**b**) *Ling* prosthétique
►► *Biol* ***prosthetic group*** groupement *m* prosthétique

prosthetics [prɒs'θetɪks] *n (UNCOUNT) Med* prothétique *f*

prosthodontics [,prɒsθə'dɒntɪks] *n Med* prothèse *f* dentaire *(technique)*

prosthodontist [,prɒsθə'dɒntɪst] *n Med* prothésiste *mf* dentaire

prostitute ['prɒstɪtju:t] **1** *n* prostituée *f*; **male prostitute** prostitué *m*
2 *vt also Fig* prostituer; **to prostitute oneself** se prostituer

prostitution [,prɒstɪ'tju:ʃən] *n* prostitution *f*

prostrate 1 *adj* ['prɒstreɪt] (**a**) *(lying flat)* (couché) à plat ventre; *(in submission)* prosterné; **to lie prostrate before sb** être prosterné devant qn
(**b**) *(exhausted)* épuisé, abattu; *(overwhelmed)* prostré, accablé, atterré; **prostrate with grief** accablé de chagrin
2 *vt* [prɒ'streɪt] (**a**) *(in obedience, respect)* **to prostrate oneself before sb** se prosterner devant qn
(**b**) *(overwhelm)* accabler, abattre; **to be prostrated by illness** être accablé *ou* abattu par la maladie; **to be prostrated with grief** être accablé de chagrin

prostration [prɒ'streɪʃən] *n* (**a**) *(lying down)* prosternement *m*; *Rel* prostration *f* (**b**) *(exhaustion)* prostration *f*, épuisement *m*; **the country was in a state of economic prostration** l'économie du pays était en ruine

prostyle ['prəʊstaɪl] *Archit* **1** *n* prostyle *m*
2 *adj* prostyle

prosy ['prəʊzɪ] (*compar* **prosier**, *superl* **prosiest**) *adj (dull)* ennuyeux, prosaïque; *(long-winded)* verbeux

protactinium [,prəʊtæk'tɪnɪəm] *n Chem* protactinium *m*

protagonist [prə'tægənɪst] *n* protagoniste *mf*

protasis ['prɒtəsɪs] *n Gram* protase *f*

protea ['prəʊtɪə] *n Bot* protée *f*

protean [prəʊ'ti:ən] *adj Literary* changeant

protease ['prəʊtɪeɪz] *n Physiol* protéase *f*
►► *Pharm* ***protease inhibitor*** antiprotéase *f*, inhibiteur *m* de protéase

protect [prə'tekt] *vt* protéger; **to protect sb/sth from** *or* **against sth** protéger qn/qch de *ou* contre qch; **she protected her eyes from the sun** elle se protégea les yeux du soleil; **to protect oneself from sth** se protéger de *ou* contre qch; **it is important to protect your civil rights** il est important de veiller à ce que vos droits civiques ne soient pas bafoués

protected [prə'tektɪd] *adj* protégé
►► ***protected industries*** industries *fpl* protégées; ***protected species*** espèce *f* protégée

protection [prə'tekʃən] *n* (**a**) *(safeguard)* protection *f*; **this drug offers protection against** *or* **from the virus** ce médicament vous protège *ou* vous immunise contre le virus; **cyclists often wear face masks for protection against car fumes** les cyclistes portent souvent des masques pour se protéger des gaz d'échappement des voitures; **to be under sb's protection** être sous la protection de qn; **she travelled under police protection** elle a voyagé sous la protection de la police; **environmental protection** protection *f* de l'environnement; **society for the protection of birds** société *f* protectrice des oiseaux
(**b**) *(insurance)* protection *f*; **protection against fire and theft** protection *f* contre l'incendie et le vol
(**c**) *(run by gangsters)* argent *m* versé aux racketteurs; **all the shopkeepers have to pay protection (money)** tous les commerçants sont rackettés
►► ***protection factor*** *(of suntan lotion)* indice *m* de protection; ***protection money*** argent *m* versé aux racketteurs; ***protection racket*** racket *m*; **to run a protection racket** être à la tête d'un racket

protectionism [prə'tekʃənɪzəm] *n Econ* protectionnisme *m*

protectionist [prə'tekʃənɪst] *Econ* **1** *adj* protectionniste
2 *n* protectionniste *mf*

protective [prə'tektɪv] *adj* (**a**) *(person)* protecteur; *(behaviour, attitude)* protecteur, de protection; **to be protective towards sb** avoir une attitude protectrice envers qn; **she's too protective towards her children** elle a trop tendance à couver ses enfants; **he put a protective arm around her** il l'a entourée d'un bras protecteur; **to be protective of one's interests** sauvegarder ses intérêts
(**b**) *(material, clothes)* de protection; *(cover)* protecteur, de protection
(**c**) *Econ (duty, measure)* protecteur
►► *Aut* ***protective cage*** cage *f* de sécurité; *Zool* ***protective coloration*** homochromie *f*; *Law* ***protective custody*** détention *f* dans l'intérêt de la personne

protectively [prə'tektɪvlɪ] *adv (behave, act)* de façon protectrice; *(speak)* d'un ton protecteur, d'une voix protectrice; *(look)* d'un œil protecteur; **he put an arm protectively around her shoulder** il entoura son épaule d'un bras protecteur

protectiveness [prə'tektɪvnɪs] *n* attitude *f* protectrice

protector [prə'tektə(r)] **1** *n* (**a**) *(person)* protecteur(trice) *m,f* (**b**) *(on machine)* dispositif *m* de protection, protecteur *m*
2 Protector *n Br Hist* **the Protector** le Protecteur

protectorate [prə'tektərət] **1** *n* protectorat *m*
2 Protectorate *n Br Hist* **the Protectorate** le Protectorat

> **THE PROTECTORATE**
>
> Il s'agit de la période allant de 1653 à 1658, succédant à la guerre civile, pendant laquelle Oliver Cromwell, se proclamant "Lord Protector", exerça son autorité sur l'Angleterre. Son fils Richard lui succéda jusqu'en 1659. En dépit de l'existence du Parlement, le gouvernement de Cromwell était quasiment dictatorial et s'appuyait avant tout sur l'armée. Le Protectorat, qui vit l'essor du puritanisme dans la société anglaise, prit fin en 1659 lorsqu'un nouveau Parlement rétablit la monarchie.

protectress [prə'tektrɪs] *n* protectrice *f*

protégé, protégée ['prɒteʒeɪ] *n* protégé(e) *m,f*

protein ['prəʊti:n] *n* protéine *f*
►► ***protein deficiency*** carence *f* en protéines

proteinaceous [,prəʊti:'neɪʃəs] *adj Med* protéique

proteinuria [,prəʊti:'njʊərɪə] *n Med* protéinurie *f*

pro tem [-'tem], **pro tempore** [-'tempərɪ] **1** *adv* temporairement
2 *adj* intérimaire, temporaire

proteolysis [,prəʊtɪ'ɒlɪsɪs] *n Biol & Chem* protéolyse *f*

proteolytic [,prəʊtɪəʊ'lɪtɪk] *adj Biol & Chem* protéolytique

Proterozoic [,prəʊtərəʊ'zəʊɪk] *Geol* **1** *n* protérozoïque *m*
2 *adj* protérozoïque

protest 1 *n* ['prəʊtest] (**a**) *(gen)* protestation *f*; **to make a protest against** *or* **about sth** élever une protestation contre qch, protester contre qch; **to register** *or* **to lodge a protest with sb** protester auprès de qn; **in protest against** *or* **at sth** en signe de protestation contre qch; **they did it without the slightest protest** ils l'ont fait sans élever la moindre protestation *ou* sans protester le moins du monde; **despite their protests, the children had to go to school** malgré leurs protestations, les enfants ont dû aller à l'école; **to stage a protest** *(complaint)* organiser une protestation; *(demonstration)* organiser une manifestation; **she resigned in protest (at this decision)** elle a démissionné en signe de protestation (contre cette décision); **to do sth under protest** faire qch en protestant
(**b**) *Com & Law* protêt *m*
2 *comp* ['prəʊtest] *(letter, meeting)* de protestation; *(singer)* engagé
3 *vt* [prə'test] (**a**) *(innocence, love etc)* protester de; **"no one told me", she protested** "personne ne me l'a dit", protesta-t-elle; **she protested that it was unfair** elle déclara que ce n'était pas juste
(**b**) *Am (measures, law etc)* protester contre
4 *vi* [prə'test] protester; **to protest at** *or* **against/about sth** protester contre qch; **I must protest in the strongest terms at** *or* **about...** je m'élève avec la dernière energie *ou* énergiquement contre...; **really, I protest, that's too much!** non, vraiment, je proteste, c'est trop!
►► ***protest demonstration, protest march*** manifestation *f*; ***protest marcher*** manifestant(e) *m,f*; ***protest song*** chanson *f* engagée; ***protest vote*** vote *m* de protestation

> **The lady protests too much, methinks**
>
> Cette phrase ("la dame fait trop de serments, me semble-t-il") vient de *Hamlet* de Shakespeare, et est prononcée par Gertrude lorsqu'elle assiste à la représentation de la *Souricière*, la pièce écrite par son fils Hamlet, et dans laquelle le personnage de la reine, calqué sur la reine Gertrude elle-même, jure de ne jamais se remarier après la mort de son mari.
>
> On utilise cette expression en plaçant **methinks** en début de phrase et en ajoutant la forme archaïque **doth** avant le verbe, lorsqu'on estime que quelqu'un proteste trop de son innocence pour être honnête. On se sert souvent de l'expression à propos de l'attitude de personnes de sexe féminin, mais pas exclusivement; ainsi on pourra dire **the minister has spoken loudly on the issue, but methinks he doth protest too much** ("le ministre a beaucoup parlé du problème, et son insistance même me semble suspecte").

Protestant ['prɒtɪstənt] **1** *adj* protestant
2 *n* Protestant(e) *m,f*
►► ***the Protestant Church*** l'Église *f* protestante; ***the Protestant (work) ethic*** l'éthique *f* protestante (du travail)

Protestantism ['prɒtɪstən,tɪzəm] *n* protestantisme *m*

Protestantize, -ise ['prɒtɪstəntaɪz] *vt* convertir au protestantisme

protestation [,prɒte'steɪʃən] *n* protestation *f*; **in spite of his protestations of innocence** en dépit de ses protestations d'innocence

protester [prə'testə(r)] *n (demonstrator)* manifestant(e) *m,f*; *(complainer)* protestataire *mf*; **anti-nuclear/peace protester** manifestant(e) *m,f* contre le nucléaire/pour la paix

protestingly [prə'testɪŋlɪ] *adv* en protestant

protestor = **protester**

Proteus ['prəʊtɪəs] *pr n Myth* Protée

prothalamion [,prəʊθə'leɪmɪən], **prothalamium** [,prəʊθə'leɪmɪəm] *n Literature* prothalame *m*

prothallus [,prəʊ'θæləs] *n Bot* prothallium *m*, prothalle *m*

prothesis [,prəʊ'θi:sɪs] *n* (**a**) *Ling* prosthèse *f* (**b**) *Rel (preparation)* prothèse *f*; *(table)* autel *m* de la prothèse

prothrombin [,prəʊ'θrɒmbɪn] *n Physiol* prothrombine *f*

protist ['prəʊtɪst] (*pl* **protista** [-tə]) *n Biol* protiste *m*

protium ['prəʊtɪəm] *n Chem* protium *m*

proto- ['prəʊtəʊ] *pref* proto-

protococcus [,prəʊtəʊ'kɒkəs] *n Bot* protococcus *m*

protocol ['prəʊtəkɒl] *n (gen) & Comput* protocole *m*

protogalaxy [,prəʊtəʊ'gæləksɪ] *n Astron* protogalaxie *f*

protogyny [ˌprəʊˈtɒdʒənɪ] *n Bot* protogynie *f*

protohistoric [ˌprəʊtəʊhɪsˈtɒrɪk] *adj* protohistorique

protohistory [ˈprəʊtəʊˌhɪstərɪ] *n* protohistoire *f*

Proto-Indo-European [ˌprəʊtəʊ-] *n Ling* proto-indo-européen *m*

proton [ˈprəʊtɒn] *n Phys* proton *m*
▸▸ ***proton microscope*** microscope *m* protonique; ***proton number*** numéro *m* atomique

protonema [ˌprəʊtəʊˈniːmə] *n Bot* protonéma *m*

protonic [ˌprəʊˈtɒnɪk] *adj Chem* protonique

protoplasm [ˈprəʊtəʊplæzəm] *n Biol* protoplasme *m*, protoplasma *m*

protoplasmic [ˌprəʊtəʊˈplæzmɪk] *adj Biol* protoplasmique

protoplast [ˈprəʊtəʊplæst] *n* (**a**) *(original person or thing)* prototype *m* (**b**) *Biol* protoplaste *m*

protostar [ˈprəʊtəʊstɑː(r)] *n Astron* protoétoile *f*

prototherian [ˌprəʊtəʊˈθɪərɪən] *n Zool* protothérien *m*

prototype [ˈprəʊtətaɪp] *n* prototype *m*

prototypic [ˌprəʊtəʊˈtɪpɪk], **prototypical** [ˌprəʊtəʊˈtɪpɪkəl] *adj* prototypique

prototyping [ˈprəʊtəʊˌtaɪpɪŋ] *n Comput* prototypage *m*

protoxide [ˌprəʊˈtɒksaɪd] *n Chem* protoxyde *m*

protozoal [ˌprəʊtəˈzəʊəl] *adj Zool* protozoaire

protozoan [ˌprəʊtəˈzəʊən] (*pl* **protozoans** *or* **protozoa** [-ˈzəʊə]) *n Zool* protozoaire *m*

protozoic [ˌprəʊtəˈzəʊɪk] *adj Zool* protozoaire

protozoon [ˌprəʊtəˈzəʊən] (*pl* **protozoa** [-ˈzəʊə]) *n Zool* protozoaire *m*

protract [prəˈtrækt] *vt (prolong)* prolonger, faire durer

protracted [prəˈtræktɪd] *adj (stay)* prolongé; *(argument, negotiations)* qui dure, (très) long (longue); *(illness)* long (longue); **a protracted death** une longue agonie

protractile [prəˈtræktaɪl] *adj* protractile

protraction [prəˈtrækʃən] *n* (**a**) *(of trial etc)* prolongation *f*; *(of procedure etc)* longueur *f* (**b**) *Anat (of muscle)* protraction *f*

protractor [prəˈtræktə(r)] *n* (**a**) *Geom* rapporteur *m* (**b**) *Anat (muscle)* (muscle *m*) protracteur *m*
▸▸ *Anat* ***protractor muscle*** (muscle *m*) protracteur *m*

protrude [prəˈtruːd] **1** *vi (rock, ledge)* faire saillie, dépasser; *(eyes, chin)* saillir; *(teeth)* avancer; **the promontory protrudes into the sea** le promontoire s'avance dans la mer; **his belly protruded over his trousers** son ventre débordait de son pantalon; **his feet protruded from under the bedclothes** ses pieds dépassaient de sous les couvertures
2 *vt* avancer, pousser en avant

protruding [prəˈtruːdɪŋ] *adj (ledge)* en saillie; *(chin, ribs)* saillant; *(eyes)* globuleux; *(teeth)* proéminent, protubérant; *(belly)* protubérant; **the protruding end of the nail** le bout du clou qui dépasse

protrusion [prəˈtruːʒən] *n (ledge)* saillie *f*; *(bump)* bosse *f*, protrusion *f*

protrusive [prəˈtruːsɪv] = **protruding**

protuberance [prəˈtjuːbərəns] *n Formal* protubérance *f*

protuberant [prəˈtjuːbərənt] *adj Formal* protubérant

proud [praʊd] **1** *adj* (**a**) *(pleased)* fier; **to be proud of sb/sth** être fier de qn/qch; **to be proud of oneself** être fier de soi; *Ironic* **I hope you're proud of yourself!** tu peux être fier de toi!; **he was proud to have won** *or* **of having won** il était fier d'avoir gagné; **I'm proud (that) you didn't give up** je suis fier que tu n'aies pas abandonné; **it's nothing to be proud of!** il n'y a vraiment pas de quoi être fier!; **she was too proud to accept** elle était trop fière pour accepter; **I'll do anything, I'm not proud** je ferai n'importe quoi, je ne suis pas fier; **they are now the proud parents of a daughter** ils sont désormais les heureux parents d'une petite fille; **a picture of the proud parents** une photo des parents, débordants de fierté; **we are proud to present this concert** nous sommes heureux de vous présenter ce concert; **it was a proud moment for me** pour moi, ce fut un moment de grande fierté; **it was her proudest possession** c'était son bien le plus précieux
(**b**) *(arrogant)* fier, orgueilleux; **he's a proud man** c'est un orgueilleux; **as proud as a peacock** fier comme un coq *ou* comme Artaban
(**c**) *Literary (stately → tree, mountain)* majestueux, altier; *(→ bearing, stallion, eagle)* fier, majestueux
(**d**) *Br (protruding)* qui dépasse; **it's a few millimetres proud** ça dépasse de quelques millimètres; **to stand proud** faire saillie
2 *adv Fam* **to do sb proud** *(entertain lavishly)* recevoir qn comme un roi/une reine; *(honour)* faire honneur à qn; **the caterers did us proud** les traiteurs nous ont fait un festin de rois; **to do oneself proud** se dépasser
▸▸ *Med* ***proud flesh*** bourgeon *m* conjonctif *ou* charnu

proudly [ˈpraʊdlɪ] *adv* (**a**) *(with pride)* fièrement, avec fierté; **we proudly present...** nous avons le plaisir de vous présenter... (**b**) *(arrogantly)* orgueilleusement (**c**) *(majestically)* majestueusement

Proustian [ˈpruːstɪən] *adj* proustien

provable [ˈpruːvəbəl] *adj* prouvable, démontrable

prove [pruːv] (*Br pt & pp* **proved**, *Am pt* **proved**, *pp* **proved** *or* **proven** [ˈpruːvən]) **1** *vt* (**a**) *(verify, show)* prouver; *(by demonstration, argument)* démontrer; *(one's identity)* justifier de; **the facts prove her (to be) guilty** les faits prouvent qu'elle est coupable; **the autopsy proved that it was suicide** l'autopsie prouva que c'était un suicide; **the evidence goes to prove that...** les témoignages concourent à prouver que...; **the accused is innocent until proved** *or* **proven guilty** l'accusé est innocent jusqu'à preuve du contraire *ou* tant que sa culpabilité n'est pas prouvée; **to prove sb right/wrong** donner raison/tort à qn; **they can't prove anything against us** ils n'ont aucune preuve contre nous; **to do sth to prove a point** faire qch pour prouver qu'on a raison; **after their relegation last season, the team will be out to prove a point** après sa relégation de la saison dernière, l'équipe tâchera de montrer de quoi elle est capable; **I think I've proved my point** je crois avoir apporté la preuve de ce que j'avançais; **it remains to be proved whether the decision was correct** rien ne prouve que cette décision était la bonne; **she quickly proved herself indispensable** elle s'est vite montrée indispensable; **he has already proved his loyalty** il a déjà prouvé sa fidélité, sa fidélité n'est plus à prouver
(**b**) *(proposition, theorem → in maths, logic)* démontrer
(**c**) *(put to the test)* mettre à l'épreuve; **the method has not yet been proved** la méthode n'a pas encore fait ses preuves; **to prove oneself** faire ses preuves
(**d**) *Law (will)* homologuer
(**e**) *Arch (experience)* éprouver
2 *vi* (**a**) *(turn out)* s'avérer, se révéler; **your suspicions proved (to be) well-founded** vos soupçons se sont avérés fondés; **the arrangement proved (to be) unworkable** cet arrangement s'est révélé impraticable; **the hotel proved to be open** l'hôtel s'avéra être ouvert; **he may prove (to be) of help to you** il pourrait bien vous être utile; **it has proved impossible to find him** il a été impossible de le retrouver; **if that proves to be the case** s'il s'avère que tel est le cas
(**b**) *Culin (dough)* lever

▸**prove out** *Am* **1** *vt sep* mettre à l'épreuve
2 *vi* faire ses preuves

proven 1 [ˈpruːvən] *pp of* **prove**
2 *adj* (**a**) [ˈpruːvən] *(tested)* éprouvé; **a woman of proven courage** une femme qui a fait preuve de courage; **a candidate with proven experience** un candidat qui a déjà fait ses preuves; **a proven method** une méthode qui a fait ses preuves (**b**) [ˈprəʊvən] *Scot Law* **a verdict of not proven** ≃ un non-lieu

provenance [ˈprɒvənəns] *n* provenance *f*

Provençal [ˌprɒvɒnˈsɑːl] **1** *n* (**a**) *(person)* Provençal(e) *m,f* (**b**) *Ling* provençal *m*
2 *adj* provençal

Provence [prɒˈvɑːns] *n* Provence *f*; **in Provence** en Provence

provender [ˈprɒvɪndə(r)] *n* (**a**) *(fodder)* fourrage *m*, provende *f* (**b**) *(food)* nourriture *f*

proverb [ˈprɒvɜːb] **1** *n* proverbe *m*
2 Proverbs *n Bible* **(the Book of) Proverbs** le Livre des Proverbes

proverbial [prəˈvɜːbjəl] *adj* proverbial, légendaire

proverbially [prəˈvɜːbjəlɪ] *adv* proverbialement

provide [prəˈvaɪd] **1** *vt* (**a**) *(supply)* fournir; **to provide sth for sb, to provide sb with sth** fournir qch à qn; **who provided them with that information?** qui leur a fourni *ou* transmis ces renseignements?; **to provide jobs** fournir des emplois; **this factory will provide 500 new jobs** cette usine créera 500 emplois; **they provide a car for her use** ils mettent une voiture à sa disposition; **the plane is provided with eight emergency exits** l'avion dispose de huit sorties de secours; **write the answers in the spaces provided** écrivez les réponses dans les blancs prévus à cet effet
(**b**) *(offer)* offrir; **a small summerhouse provides some privacy** un petit pavillon dans le jardin offre une certaine intimité; **I want to provide my children with a good education** je veux pouvoir offrir *ou* donner une bonne éducation à mes enfants; **the book provides a good introduction to maths** ce livre est une bonne introduction aux maths; **milk provides a good source of protein** le lait constitue un bon apport en protéines
(**c**) *(stipulate → of contract, law)* stipuler; **the rules provide that...** le règlement stipule que...
2 *vi* **to provide against sth** se prémunir contre qch; **the Lord will provide** Dieu y pourvoira

▸**provide for** *vt insep* (**a**) *(support)* **to provide for sb** pourvoir *ou* subvenir aux besoins de qn; **I have a family to provide for** j'ai une famille à nourrir; **an insurance policy that will provide for your children's future** une assurance qui subviendra aux besoins de vos enfants; **his widow was left well provided for** sa veuve était à l'abri du besoin
(**b**) *(prepare)* **to provide for sth** se préparer à qch; **they hadn't provided for the drop in demand** la baisse de la demande les a pris au dépourvu; **expenses provided for in the budget** dépenses *fpl* prévues au budget; **we try to provide for all eventualities** nous nous efforçons de parer à toute éventualité
(**c**) *(contract, law)* **to provide for sth** stipuler *ou* prévoir qch; **the bill provides for subsidies to be reduced** le projet de loi prévoit une baisse des subventions

provided [prəˈvaɪdɪd] *conj* **provided (that)** pourvu que, à condition que; **I'll wait for you provided (that) it doesn't take too long** je t'attendrai à condition que ce ne soit pas trop long; **you can leave early provided (that) you finish your work** vous pouvez partir plus tôt à condition d'avoir fini votre travail

providence [ˈprɒvɪdəns] **1** *n* (**a**) *(fate)* la providence (**b**) *Old-fashioned (foresight)* prévoyance *f*; *(thrift)* économie *f*
2 Providence *n (fate)* la Providence; **Providence smiled on us** la Providence nous a souri

provident [ˈprɒvɪdənt] *adj (foresighted)* prévoyant; *(thrifty)* économe
▸▸ *Br* ***provident club*** = système d'achat à tempérament organisé par certains grands magasins; *Fin* ***provident fund*** caisse *f* de prévoyance; *Br* ***provident society*** société *f* de prévoyance

providential [ˌprɒvɪˈdenʃəl] *adj* providentiel

providentially [ˌprɒvɪˈdenʃəlɪ] *adv* providentiellement

providently [ˈprɒvɪdəntlɪ] *adv* avec prévoyance, prudemment

provider [prəˈvaɪdə(r)] *n* (**a**) *(person)* pourvoyeur(euse) *m,f*; *Com* fournisseur(euse) *m,f*; **she's the family's sole provider** elle subvient seule aux besoins de la famille (**b**) *Comput* fournisseur *m* d'accès à l'Internet

providing [prəˈvaɪdɪŋ] = **provided**

province [ˈprɒvɪns] **1** *n* (**a**) *(region, district)* province *f*; **the Province of Ontario/Ulster** la province d'Ontario/d'Ulster; **the Maritime/Prairie Provinces** *(of Canada)* les provinces *fpl* maritimes/des prairies
(**b**) *(field, sphere → of activity)* domaine *m*; *(→ of responsability)* compétence *f*; **politics was once the sole province of men** autrefois, la politique

était un domaine exclusivement masculin; **staff supervision is not within my province** la gestion du personnel n'est pas de mon ressort (**c**) *Rel* province *f* ecclésiastique

2 provinces *npl Br (not the metropolis)* **the provinces** la province; **in the provinces** en province

provincial [prəˈvɪnʃəl] **1** *adj* provincial

2 *n* (**a**) *(from provinces)* provincial(e) *m,f* (**b**) *Rel* provincial *m*

provincialism [prəˈvɪnʃəlɪzəm] *n* provincialisme *m*

provincialize, -ise [prəˈvɪnʃəlaɪz] *vt* rendre provincial; **to become provincialized** se provincialiser

proving [ˈpruːvɪŋ] *n (of truth of something)* preuve *f*, démonstration *f*; *(of fact)* constatation *f*; *Law (of a will)* homologation *f*; **the proving of a theory/a hypothesis** la démonstration d'une théorie/d'une hypothèse

▸▸ ***proving ground*** terrain *m* d'essai

provirus [ˈprəʊvaɪrəs] *n Med* provirus *m*

provision [prəˈvɪʒən] **1** *vt* approvisionner, ravitailler

2 *n* (**a**) *(act of supplying)* approvisionnement *m*, fourniture *f*, ravitaillement *m*; **provision of supplies in wartime is a major problem** le ravitaillement en temps de guerre pose de graves problèmes; **one of their functions is the provision of meals for the homeless** un de leurs rôles est de distribuer des repas aux sans-abri; **the provision of new jobs** la création d'emplois

(**b**) *(stock, supply)* provision *f*, réserve *f*; **to lay in provisions for the winter** faire des provisions pour l'hiver; **the US sent medical provisions** les États-Unis envoyèrent des stocks de médicaments; **I have a week's provision of firewood left** il me reste du bois *ou* assez de bois pour une semaine

(**c**) *(arrangement)* disposition *f*; **they are making provisions for a crisis** ils prennent des dispositions en vue d'une crise; **no provision had been made for the influx of refugees** aucune disposition n'avait été prise pour faire face à l'afflux de réfugiés; **social service provision has been cut again** les services sociaux ont à nouveau connu des compressions budgétaires; **to make provisions for one's family** pourvoir aux besoins de sa famille; **you should think about making provisions for the future** vous devriez penser à assurer votre avenir; **having a lot of children was a provision for old age** le fait d'avoir de nombreux enfants constituait pour les parents une sorte d'assurance vieillesse

(**d**) *Fin (allowance)* provision *f*; **to make provision for sth** prévoir qch

(**e**) *(condition, clause)* disposition *f*, clause *f*; **under the provisions of the UN charter/his will** selon les dispositions de la charte de l'ONU/de son testament; **a 4 percent increase is included in the budget's provisions** une augmentation de 4 pour cent est prévue dans le budget; *Law* **notwithstanding any provision to the contrary** nonobstant toute clause contraire

3 provisions *npl (food)* vivres *mpl*, provisions *fpl*

▸▸ *Acct* ***provision for bad debts*** provision *f* pour créances douteuses; *Fin* ***provision of capital*** prestation *f* de capitaux; *Acct* ***provision for depreciation*** provision *f* pour dépréciation *ou* amortissement; *Acct* ***provision for liabilities*** provision *f* pour sommes exigibles

provisional [prəˈvɪʒənəl] **1** *adj* provisoire

2 Provisional *n* membre *m* de l'IRA provisoire

▸▸ *Fin* ***provisional budget*** budget *m* prévisionnel; *Br* ***provisional (driving) licence*** permis *m* de conduire provisoire *(autorisation que l'on doit obtenir avant de prendre des leçons)*; *Pol* ***the Provisional IRA*** l'IRA *f* provisoire *(branche de l'IRA favorable à la lutte armée)*

provisionally [prəˈvɪʒənəlɪ] *adv* provisoirement

proviso [prəˈvaɪzəʊ] *(pl* **provisos** *or* **provisoes***) n* stipulation *f*, condition *f*; **with the proviso that the goods be delivered** à la condition expresse *ou* sous réserve que les marchandises soient livrées; **they accept, with one proviso** ils acceptent, à une condition

provisory [prəˈvaɪzərɪ] *adj* (**a**) *(conditional)* conditionnel (**b**) *(provisional)* provisoire

provitamin [*Br* ˌprəʊˈvɪtəmɪn, *Am* ˌprəʊˈvaɪtəmɪn] *n* provitamine *f*

Provo [ˈprəʊvəʊ] *(pl* **Provos***) n Fam* = membre de l'IRA provisoire, la branche de l'IRA favorable à la lutte armée

provocation [ˌprɒvəˈkeɪʃən] *n* provocation *f*; **he loses his temper at** *or* **given the slightest provocation** il se met en colère à la moindre provocation; **the crime was committed under provocation** ce crime a été commis en réponse à une provocation

provocative [prəˈvɒkətɪv] *adj* (**a**) *(challenging)* provocateur, provocant; **his early films were very provocative** ses premiers films étaient très provocants; **she doesn't really think that, she was just being provocative** elle ne le pense pas vraiment, c'est simplement de la provocation (**b**) *(sexually → behaviour, dress, person)* provocant; *(→ smile, look)* aguichant (**c**) *(obscene)* **a provocative gesture** un geste obscène

provocatively [prəˈvɒkətɪvlɪ] *adv (write, dress)* d'une manière provocante; *(say)* sur un ton provocateur *ou* provocant

provoke [prəˈvəʊk] *vt* (**a**) *(goad)* provoquer; *(infuriate)* enrager; *(vex)* exaspérer; **to provoke sb into doing sth** pousser qn à faire qch; **they'll shoot if in any way provoked** ils tireront à la moindre provocation; **I was provoked** on m'a provoqué; **the dog is dangerous when provoked** le chien devient méchant si on le provoque *ou* l'excite

(**b**) *(cause → accident, quarrel, anger)* provoquer; **to provoke a reaction** provoquer une réaction; **the revelations provoked a public outcry** les révélations ont soulevé un tollé général

provoking [prəˈvəʊkɪŋ] *adj (situation)* contrariant; *(person, behaviour)* exaspérant

provokingly [prəˈvəʊkɪŋlɪ] *adv* par provocation

provost *n* (**a**) [ˈprɒvəst] *Univ Br* ≃ recteur *m*; *Am* ≃ doyen *m* (**b**) [ˈprɒvəst] *Rel* doyen *m* (**c**) [ˈprɒvəst] *Scot* maire *m* (**d**) [prəˈvəʊ] *Mil* ≃ gendarme *m* (**e**) [ˈprɒvəst] *Hist* prévôt *m*

▸▸ *Mil* ***provost court*** tribunal *m* prévôtal; *Am Mil* ***provost guard*** ≃ prévôté *f*; *Mil* ***provost marshal*** prévôt *m*

provostship [ˈprɒvəstʃɪp] *n* (**a**) *Univ Br* ≃ rectorat *m*; *Am* ≃ décanat *m* (**b**) *Rel* décanat *m* (**c**) *Scot* mairie *f*, charge *f* de maire (**d**) *Hist* prévôté *f*

prow [praʊ] *n Naut* proue *f*

prowess [ˈpraʊɪs] *n (UNCOUNT)* (**a**) *(skill)* (grande) habileté *f*; **prowess in negotiating** habileté *f ou* savoir-faire *m inv* en matière de négociations; **he showed great prowess on the sports field** il s'est révélé d'une adresse remarquable sur le terrain de sport; **sexual prowess** prouesses *fpl* sexuelles (**b**) *Literary (bravery)* vaillance *f*

prowl [praʊl] **1** *vi* rôder

2 *vt (street, jungle)* rôder dans; **cats prowled the rooftops** des chats rôdaient sur les toits

3 *n* **to be on the prowl** rôder; **to be on the prowl for sth** être en quête *ou* à la recherche de qch; *also Fig* **to go on the prowl** partir en chasse

▸▸ *Am* ***prowl car*** voiture *f* de police en patrouille

▸ **prowl about, prowl around 1** *vi* rôder

2 *vt insep* rôder dans; **to prowl about the streets** rôder dans les rues

prowler [ˈpraʊlə(r)] *n* rôdeur(euse) *m,f*

prowling [ˈpraʊlɪŋ] *adj* rôdeur

prox *Old-fashioned (written abbr* **proximo***)* du mois prochain

proxemics [prɒkˈsiːmɪks] *n (UNCOUNT)* proxémique *f*

proximal [ˈprɒksɪməl] *adj Biol* proximal

proximity [prɒkˈsɪmətɪ] *n* proximité *f*; **its proximity to London** sa situation à proximité de Londres; **in proximity to, in the proximity of** à proximité de; **in close proximity to** juste à proximité *ou* tout près de

▸▸ *Mil* ***proximity fuse*** fusée *f* à influence, fusée *f* de proximité; *Pol* ***proximity talks*** négociations *fpl* rapprochées

proximo [ˈprɒksɪməʊ] *adv Old-fashioned Admin* du mois prochain; **the 4th proximo** le 4 du mois prochain

proxy [ˈprɒksɪ] *(pl* **proxies***) n (person)* mandataire *mf*, fondé(e) *m,f* de pouvoir; *(authorization)* procuration *f*, mandat *m*; *Comput* mandataire *m*; **to vote by proxy** voter par procuration

▸▸ ***proxy bomb*** = bombe amenée sur les lieux par une personne agissant sous la contrainte; *Comput* ***proxy server*** serveur *m* proxy, serveur *m* mandataire *ou* de procuration; ***proxy vote*** vote *m* par procuration

Prozac® [ˈprəʊzæk] *n Pharm* Prozac® *m*

PRP [ˌpiːɑːˈpiː] *n (abbr* **performance-related pay***)* salaire *m* au mérite

prude [pruːd] *n* prude *mf*, bégueule *mf*; **don't be such a prude!** ne sois pas si prude *ou* bégueule!

prudence [ˈpruːdəns] *n* prudence *f*, circonspection *f*

▸▸ *Acct* ***prudence concept*** principe *m* de prudence

prudent [ˈpruːdənt] *adj* prudent, circonspect

prudential [pruːˈdenʃəl] *adj*

▸▸ *Am* ***prudential committee*** *(of municipality, company)* = comité de surveillance

prudently [ˈpruːdəntlɪ] *adv* prudemment

prudery [ˈpruːdərɪ] *n* pruderie *f*, pudibonderie *f*

prudish [ˈpruːdɪʃ] *adj* prude, pudibond

prudishness [ˈpruːdɪʃnɪs] *n* pruderie *f*, pudibonderie *f*

prune [pruːn] **1** *n* (**a**) *(fruit)* pruneau *m*; **stewed prunes** pruneaux *mpl* cuits; *Fam Fig* **to look like an old prune** être ridé comme une vieille pomme (**b**) *Br Fam (fool)* patate *f*, ballot *m*

2 *vt* (**a**) *(hedge, tree)* tailler; *(branch)* élaguer (**b**) *Fig (text, budget)* élaguer, faire des coupes sombres dans; **to prune (back** *or* **down) expenditure** réduire les dépenses

prunella [pruːˈnelə] *n Tex* prunelle *f*

pruner [ˈpruːnə(r)] *n* tailleur *m* d'arbres, élagueur *m*

pruning [ˈpruːnɪŋ] *n (of hedge, tree)* taille *f*; *(of branches)* élagage *m*; *Fig (of budget, staff)* élagage *m*; **there will have to be some pruning in this department** il va falloir faire du nettoyage dans ce service

▸▸ ***pruning hook*** ébranchoir *m*; ***pruning knife*** serpette *f*

prurience [ˈprʊərɪəns] *n* lubricité *f*, lascivité *f*

prurient [ˈprʊərɪənt] *adj* lubrique, lascif

prurigo [prʊˈraɪgəʊ] *n Med* prurigo *m*

pruritus [prʊˈraɪtəs] *n Med* prurit *m*

Prussia [ˈprʌʃə] *n* Prusse *f*; **in Prussia** en Prusse

Prussian [ˈprʌʃən] **1** *n* Prussien(enne) *m,f*

2 *adj* prussien

▸▸ ***Prussian blue*** bleu *m* de Prusse

Prussian-blue *adj* bleu de Prusse

prussic acid [ˈprʌsɪk-] *n* acide *m* prussique

pry[1] [praɪ] *(pt & pp* **pried***) vi* fouiller, fureter; **I didn't mean to pry** je ne voulais pas être indiscret; **I told him not to pry into my affairs** je lui ai dit de ne pas venir mettre le nez dans mes affaires; **he doesn't like people prying into his past** il n'aime pas qu'on aille fouiller dans son passé

pry[2] *Am* = **prise**

prying [ˈpraɪɪŋ] *adj* indiscret(ète); **away from prying eyes** à l'abri des regards indiscrets

PS [ˌpiːˈes] *n (abbr* **postscript***)* PS *m*

psalm [sɑːm] *n* psaume *m*; **(the Book of) Psalms** (le livre des) Psaumes

psalmbook [ˈsɑːmbʊk] *n* livre *m* de psaumes, psautier *m*

psalmist [ˈsɑːmɪst] *n* psalmiste *m*; **the Psalmist** le Psalmiste

psalmodic [sælˈmɒdɪk] *adj* psalmodique

psalmody [ˈsælmədɪ] *(pl* **psalmodies***) n* psalmodie *f*

psalter [ˈsɔːltə(r)] *n* psautier *m*

psaltery [ˈsɔːltərɪ] *n Hist & Mus* psaltérion *m*

PSAT [ˌpiːesˌeɪˈtiː] *n Am Sch (abbr* **Preliminary Scholastic Aptitude Test***)* = examen blanc préparant au "SAT"

PSB [ˌpiːesˈbiː] *n Rad & TV (abbr* **public-service broadcasting***)* émissions *fpl* de service public

PSBR [ˌpiːesˌbiːˈɑː(r)] *n Br Fin (abbr* **public sector borrowing requirement***)* = besoins d'emprunt du secteur public non couverts par les rentrées fiscales

psephological [ˌsefəˈlɒdʒɪkəl] *adj* = relatif à

l'étude statistique et sociologique des élections

psephologist [se'fɒlədʒɪst] *n* spécialiste *mf* des élections

psephology [se'fɒlədʒɪ] *n* = étude statistique et sociologique des élections

pseud [sju:d] *n Fam* poseur(euse) ❑ *m,f*, prétentieux(euse) ❑ *m,f*

►► ***Pseud's Corner*** = section de la revue humoristique 'Private Eye' où des articles prétentieux sont publiés pour l'amusement général

pseudo ['sju:dəʊ] *adj Fam (kindness, interest)* prétendu; *(person)* faux (fausse)

pseudo- ['sju:dəʊ] *pref* pseudo-

pseudocarp ['sju:dəʊ,kɑ:p] *n Bot* pseudocarpe *m*

pseudocyesis [,sju:dəʊsaɪ'i:sɪs] *n Med* grossesse *f* nerveuse

pseudohermaphroditism [,sju:dəʊhɜ:'mæfrədɪtɪzəm] *nm* pseudohermaphrodisme *m*

pseudointellectual [,sju:dəʊ'intəlektjʊəl] **1** *n* pseudo-intellectuelle(elle) *m,f*

2 *adj* soi-distant intellectuel

pseudomembrane [,sju:dəʊ'membreɪn] *n Med* pseudomembrane *f*

pseudomorph ['sju:dəʊ,mɔ:f] *n Miner* pseudomorphe *m*

pseudonym ['sju:dəʊnɪm] *n* pseudonyme *m*; **to write under a pseudonym** écrire sous un pseudonyme *ou* sous un nom d'emprunt

pseudonymous [sju:'dɒnɪməs] *adj (writer)* qui écrit sous un pseudonyme; *(column, article)* écrit sous un pseudonyme

pseudopodium [,sju:dəʊ'pəʊdɪəm] *(pl* **pseudopodia** [-dɪə]) *n Biol* pseudopode *m*

pseudoscience [,sju:dəʊ'saɪəns] *n* pseudoscience *f*

pseudy ['sju:dɪ] *adj Fam Pej* prétentieux ❑

pshaw [(p)ʃɔ:] *exclam Old-fashioned* peuh!

psi [,pi:es'aɪ] *n Phys (abbr* **pounds per square inch**) = livres au pouce carré (mesure de pression)

psilocybin [,saɪlə'saɪbɪn] *n Bot* psilocybine *f*

psittacine ['sɪtəsaɪn] *adj* psittacin, psittaciné

psittacosis [,sɪtə'kəʊsɪs] *n (UNCOUNT)* psittacose *f*

psoriasis [sɒ'raɪəsɪs] *n (UNCOUNT)* psoriasis *m*

psst [pst] *exclam (to attract attention)* psitt!, pst!; *(to warn)* chut!

PST [,pi:es'ti:] *n Am (abbr* **Pacific Standard Time**) heure *f* du Pacifique

PSTN [,pi:es,ti:'en] *n Tel (abbr* **Public Switched Telephone Network**) RTC *m*

PSV [,pi:es'vi:] *n Br Formerly (abbr* **public service vehicle**) véhicule *m* de transport en commun

psych [saɪk] *vt Fam* (**a**) *(psychoanalyse)* psychanalyser ❑

(**b**) *Am (excite)* **I'm really psyched about my vacation** je suis surexcité à l'idée de partir en vacances ❑

►**psych out** *vt sep Fam* (**a**) *(sense → someone's motives)* deviner ❑; *(→ situation)* comprendre ❑, piger

(**b**) *(intimidate)* **he soon psyched out his opponent and the game was his** très vite il a décontenancé son adversaire et il a gagné ❑

►**psych up** *vt sep Fam (motivate)* **to psych oneself up for sth/to do sth** se préparer psychologiquement à qch/à faire qch ❑; **he had to psych himself up to tell her** il a dû prendre son courage à deux mains pour arriver à le lui dire ❑; **she psyched herself up before the race** elle s'est concentrée avant la course ❑; **they're all psyched up and raring to go** ils rongent leur frein

Psyche ['saɪkɪ] *pr n Myth* Psyché

psyche¹ ['saɪkɪ] *n (mind)* psyché *f*, psychisme *m*

psyche² [saɪk] = **psych**

psychedelia [,saɪkə'di:lɪə] *npl (objects)* objets *mpl* psychédéliques; *(dress, music etc)* univers *m* psychédélique

psychedelic [,saɪkə'delɪk] *adj* psychédélique

psychiatric [,saɪkɪ'ætrɪk] *adj* psychiatrique; **he needs psychiatric help** il devrait consulter un psychiatre

►► ***psychiatric nurse*** infirmier(ère) *m,f* psychiatrique; ***psychiatric patient*** patient(e) *m,f* en psychiatrie; *Br* ***psychiatric social worker*** assistant(e) *m,f* social(e) en psychiatrie

psychiatrist [saɪ'kaɪətrɪst] *n* psychiatre *mf*

psychiatry [saɪ'kaɪətrɪ] *n* psychiatrie *f*

psychic ['saɪkɪk] **1** *adj* (**a**) *(supernatural)* parapsychique; **to be psychic, to have psychic powers** avoir le don de double vue *ou* un sixième sens; *Hum* **I'm not psychic!** je ne suis pas devin! (**b**) *(mental)* psychique

2 *n* médium *m*

►► ***psychic research*** parapsychologie *f*

psychical ['saɪkɪkəl] = **psychic** *adj*

psycho ['saɪkəʊ] *(pl* **psychos**) *Fam* **1** *n* psychopathe ❑ *mf*, cinglé(e) *m,f*

2 *adj* psychopathe ❑

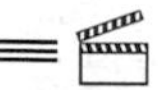

'Psycho' *Hitchcock* 'Psychose'

psychoactive [,saɪkəʊ'æktɪv] *adj* psychotrope

psychoanalyse, *Am* **psychoanalyze** [,saɪkəʊ'ænəlaɪz] *vt* psychanalyser

psychoanalysis [,saɪkəʊə'næləsɪs] *n* psychanalyse *f*; **to undergo psychoanalysis** suivre une psychanalyse, se faire psychanalyser; **he spent five years in psychoanalysis** il a été en psychanalyse pendant cinq ans

psychoanalyst [,saɪkəʊ'ænəlɪst] *n* psychanalyste *mf*

psychoanalytic ['saɪkəʊ,ænə'lɪtɪk], **psychoanalytical** ['saɪkəʊ,ænə'lɪtɪkəl] *adj* psychanalytique

psychoanalyze *Am* = **psychoanalyse**

psychobabble ['saɪkəʊ,bæbəl] *n Fam Pej* jargon *m* des psychologues ❑

psychobiological [,saɪkəʊbaɪə'lɒdʒɪkəl] *adj* psychobiologique

psychobiology [,saɪkəʊbaɪ'ɒlədʒɪ] *n* psychobiologie *f*

psychodrama ['saɪkəʊ,drɑ:mə] *n* psychodrame *m*

psychodynamic [,saɪkəʊdaɪ'næmɪk] *adj* psychodynamique

psychodynamics [,saɪkəʊdaɪ'næmɪks] *n (UNCOUNT)* psychodynamisme *m*

psychogenesis [,saɪkəʊ'dʒenəsɪs] *n* psychogénie *f*, psychogenèse *f*

psychogenic [,saɪkəʊ'dʒenɪk] *adj* psychogène

psychogeriatric [,saɪkəʊdʒerɪ'ætrɪk] *adj* psychogériatrique

psychographic [,saɪkəʊ'græfɪk] *n* psychographique

psychographics [,saɪkəʊ'græfɪks] *n (UNCOUNT)* psychographie *f*

psychokinesis [,saɪkəʊkɪ'ni:sɪs] *n* psychokinèse *f*, psychokinésie *f*

psycholinguistic [,saɪkəʊlɪŋ'gwɪstɪk] *adj* psycholinguistique

psycholinguistics [,saɪkəʊlɪŋ'gwɪstɪks] *n (UNCOUNT)* psycholinguistique *f*

psychological [,saɪkəʊ'lɒdʒɪkəl] *adj* psychologique

►► ***psychological block*** blocage *m* psychologique; **I have a psychological block about driving** je fais un blocage quand il s'agit de conduire; ***psychological contract*** contrat *m* psychologique; ***the psychological moment*** le bon moment, le moment favorable *or* psychologique; *Mktg* ***psychological price*** prix *m* psychologique *ou* d'acceptabilité; ***psychological profile*** profil *m* psychologique; ***psychological warfare*** guerre *f* psychologique

psychologically [,saɪkəʊ'lɒdʒɪkəlɪ] *adv* psychologiquement; **inflation has fallen below the psychologically important 5 percent level** l'inflation est passée sous le seuil psychologique de 5 pour cent

psychologism [saɪ'kɒlədʒɪzəm] *n* psychologisme *m*

psychologist [saɪ'kɒlədʒɪst] *n* psychologue *mf*

psychologistic [saɪ,kɒlə'dʒɪstɪk] *adj* psychologiste

psychology [saɪ'kɒlədʒɪ] *n* psychologie *f*; **it would be good/bad psychology to tell them** ce serait faire preuve de psychologie/d'un manque de psychologie que de le leur dire

psychometric [,saɪkəʊ'metrɪk] *adj* psychométrique

psychometrics [,saɪkəʊ'metrɪks] *n (UNCOUNT)* psychométrie *f*

psychometry [saɪ'kɒmɪtrɪ] *n* psychométrie *f*

psychomotor [,saɪkəʊ'məʊtə(r)] *adj* psychomoteur

psychoneurosis [,saɪkəʊnjʊə'rəʊsɪs] *(pl* **psychoneuroses** [-si:z]) *n* psychonévrose *f*

psychopath ['saɪkəʊpæθ] *n* psychopathe *mf*

psychopathic [,saɪkəʊ'pæθɪk] *adj (person)* psychopathe; *(disorder, personality)* psychopathique

psychopathological [,saɪkəʊpæθə'lɒdʒɪkəl] *adj* psychopathologique

psychopathology [,saɪkəʊpə'θɒlədʒɪ] *n* psychopathologie *f*

psychopathy [saɪ'kɒpəθɪ] *n* psychopathie *f*

psychopharmacology [,saɪkəʊ,fɑ:mə'kɒlədʒɪ] *n* psychopharmacologie *f*

psychophysical [,saɪkəʊ'fɪzɪkəl] *adj* psychophysique

psychophysiologist [,saɪkəʊfɪzɪ'ɒlədʒɪst] *n* psychophysiologiste *mf*, psychophysiologue *mf*

psychophysiology [,saɪkəʊfɪsɪ'ɒlədʒɪ] *n* psychophysiologie *f*

psychosexual [,saɪkəʊ'sekʃʊəl] *adj* psychosexuel

psychosis [saɪ'kəʊsɪs] *(pl* **psychoses** [-si:z]) *n* psychose *f*

psychosocial [,saɪkəʊ'səʊʃəl] *adj* psychosocial

psychosomatic [,saɪkəʊsə'mætɪk] *adj* psychosomatique

psychosurgery [,saɪkəʊ'sɜ:dʒərɪ] *n* psychochirurgie *f*

psychotherapeutic [,saɪkəʊθerə'pju:tɪk] *adj* psychothérapeutique

psychotherapist [,saɪkəʊ'θerəpɪst] *n* psychothérapeute *mf*

psychotherapy [,saɪkəʊ'θerəpɪ] *n* psychothérapie *f*

psychotic [saɪ'kɒtɪk] **1** *adj* psychotique

2 *n* psychotique *mf*

psychotropic [,saɪkəʊ'trɒpɪk] *adj* psychotrope

PT¹ [,pi:'ti:] *n* (**a**) *(abbr* **physical training**) EPS *f* (**b**) *Am (abbr* **physical therapy**) kinésithérapie *f*

►► ***PT instructor*** professeur *mf* d'éducation physique

PT² *n (abbr* **patrol torpedo**)

►► ***PT boat*** = vedette rapide utilisée par les forces américaines pendant la Seconde Guerre mondiale

pt (**a**) *(written abbr* **pint**) pinte *f* (**b**) *(written abbr* **point**) point *m*

Pt. *(written abbr* **point**) *(on map)* Pte

PTA [,pi:ti:'eɪ] *n Sch (abbr* **parent-teacher association**) = association de parents d'élèves et de professeurs

ptarmigan ['tɑ:mɪgən] *(pl* **inv** *or* **ptarmigans**) *n Orn* lagopède *m* des Alpes, ptarmigan *m*, perdrix *f* des neiges

Pte. *Br Mil (written abbr* **private**) soldat *m* de deuxième classe

pterodactyl [,terə'dæktɪl] *n* ptérodactyle *m*

pteropod ['terəʊpɒd] *n Zool* ptéropode *m*

pterosaur ['terəʊsɔ:(r)] *n* ptérosaurien *m*

PTO¹ [,pi:ti:'əʊ] *n Am Sch (abbr* **parent-teacher organization**) = association de parents d'élèves et de professeurs

PTO² *Br (written abbr* **please turn over**) TSVP

Ptolemaic [,tɒlə'meɪɪk] *adj* (**a**) *Antiq* ptolémaïque (**b**) *Astron* de Ptolémée

►► *Astron* ***Ptolemaic system*** système *m* de Ptolémée

Ptolemy ['tɒləmɪ] *pr n* Ptolémée

ptomaine ['təʊmeɪn] *n* ptomaïne *f*

►► ***ptomaine poisoning*** intoxication *f* alimentaire

ptosis ['təʊsɪs] *(pl* **ptoses** [-si:z]) *n Med (of organ)* ptôse *f*; *(of eyelid)* ptôsis *m*, blépharoptôse *f*

PTV [,pi:ti:'vi:] *n* (**a**) *(abbr* **pay television**) = télévision à péage (**b**) *(abbr* **public television**) = programmes télévisés éducatifs

Pty *(written abbr* **proprietary company**) SARL *f*

ptyalin ['taɪəlɪn] *n Biol & Chem* ptyaline *f*

pub [pʌb] *n* pub *m*; **we had a pub lunch** nous avons déjeuné dans un pub

►► *Br Fam* ***pub crawl*** tournée *f* des bars ❑; **to go on a pub crawl** faire la tournée des bars; *Br Fam* ***pub grub*** = nourriture (relativement simple) servie dans un pub; ***pub quiz*** jeu *m* de culture générale dans un pub

PUB

Dans l'ensemble des îles Britanniques, le pub est un des grands foyers de la vie locale, mais son rôle varie selon les régions et selon qu'il se trouve en ville ou dans un village. Ces établissements – interdits aux personnes de moins de seize ans – étaient soumis à des horaires sévèrement réglementés, qui se sont beaucoup assouplis récemment (voir encadré à **licensing hours**). De même, le pub a cessé d'être un simple débit de boissons pour devenir de plus en plus une sorte de brasserie-restaurant, servant des repas légers.

pub. (*written abbr* **published**) publié

pub-crawl *vi Br Fam* faire la tournée des bars❑, aller de bar en bar❑

pube [pju:b] *n Fam* poil *m* pubien❑

puberty ['pju:bətɪ] *n* puberté *f*; **to reach puberty** atteindre l'âge de la puberté

pubes ['pju:bi:z] (*pl* **inv**) *n* (*region*) pubis *m*, région *f* pubienne; (*hair*) poils *mpl* pubiens; (*bones*) (os *m* du) pubis *m*

pubescence [pju:'besəns] *n* (**a**) (*puberty*) (âge *m* de la) puberté *f* (**b**) (*of plant, animal*) pubescence *f*

pubescent [pju:'besənt] *adj* (**a**) (*at puberty*) pubère (**b**) (*plant, animal*) pubescent

pubic ['pju:bɪk] *adj* pubien

▸▸ ***pubic bone*** symphyse *f* pubienne; ***pubic hair*** poils *mpl* pubiens *ou* du pubis; (*single*) poil *m* pubien *ou* du pubis; ***pubic louse*** pou *m* du pubis

pubis ['pju:bɪs] (*pl* **pubes** [-bi:z]) *n* pubis *m*

public ['pʌblɪk] **1** *adj* (**a**) (*of, by the state* → *education, debt*) public; **built at public expense** construit aux frais du contribuable; **to hold public office** avoir des fonctions officielles

(**b**) (*open or accessible to all* → *place, meeting*) public; **was it a public trial?** le public pouvait-il assister au procès?; **let's talk somewhere less public** allons discuter dans un endroit plus tranquille; **these gardens are public property!** ces jardins appartiennent à tout le monde!

(**c**) (*of, by the people*) public; **the public interest** *or* **good** le bien *ou* l'intérêt *m* public; **in the public interest** dans l'intérêt du public; **public interest in the matter was flagging** le public manifestait de moins en moins d'intérêt pour cette affaire; **to make a public protest** protester publiquement; **the increase in crime is generating great public concern** la montée de la criminalité inquiète sérieusement la population; **to restore public confidence** regagner la confiance de la population; **to be in the** *Br* **public** *or Am* **public's eye** être très en vue; **to disappear from the** *Br* **public** *or Am* **public's eye** tomber dans les oubliettes; **a public outcry** un tollé général; **it created a public scandal** ça a provoqué un scandale retentissant; **public awareness of the problem has increased** le public est plus sensible au problème maintenant; **the bill has public support** l'opinion publique est favorable au projet de loi

(**d**) (*publicly known, open*) public; **to make sth public** rendre qch public; **to make a public appearance** paraître en public; **to go into public life** se lancer dans les affaires publiques; **she's active in public life** elle prend une part active aux affaires publiques; **the contrast between his public and his private life** le contraste entre sa vie publique et sa vie privée; **his first public statement** sa première déclaration publique; **he made a public denial of the rumours** il a démenti publiquement les rumeurs, il a apporté un démenti public aux rumeurs; **it's public knowledge that...** il est de notoriété publique que...

2 *adv* **to go public** (*company*) s'introduire en Bourse; (*reveal information*) tout dire *ou* raconter; **the company is going public** la société va être cotée en Bourse; **to go public with the story** raconter toute l'histoire

3 *n* public *m*; **the (general) public** le (grand) public; **in public** en public, publiquement; **the public is** *or* **are tired of political scandals** la population est lasse des scandales politiques; *Fin* **to issue shares to the public** placer des actions dans le public; **her books reach a wide public** ses livres touchent un public très large; **the movie-going public** les amateurs de *ou* les gens qui vont au cinéma; **the viewing public** les téléspectateurs; **your public awaits** *or* **await you** votre public vous attend

4 in public *adv* en public

▸▸ *Am TV* ***public access channel*** = chaîne du réseau câblé sur laquelle des particuliers peuvent diffuser leurs propres émissions; *Am TV* ***public access television*** = chaînes télévisées câblées non commerciales; ***public affairs*** affaires *fpl* publiques; *Am* ***public assistance*** aide *f* sociale; ***public authorities*** pouvoirs *mpl* publics; *Br* ***public bar*** salle *f* de bar (*dans un pub qui contient deux bars séparés, l'expression désigne le plus populaire des deux*); ***public baths*** bains *mpl* publics; *Br Pol* ***public bill*** ≃ projet *m* de loi d'intérêt général; ***public body*** corporation *f* de droit public; *Br* ***public call box*** cabine *f* (téléphonique) publique; ***public company*** ≃ société *f* anonyme; *Br* ***public convenience*** toilettes *fpl* publiques; *Br & Can* ***public corporation*** entreprise *f* publique; *Fin* ***public debt*** dette *f* publique *ou* de l'État; *Am Law* ***public defender*** avocat *m* commis d'office; *Fin* ***public deposits*** = avoirs des différents services du gouvernement britannique à la Banque d'Angleterre; ***public domain*** domaine *m* public; **to be in the public domain** (*publication*) être dans le domaine public; *Comput* ***public domain software*** logiciel *m* (du domaine) public, *Can* publiciel *m*; ***public enemy*** ennemi *m* public; **public enemy number one** ennemi *m* public numéro un; *Fin* ***public enterprise*** (*company*) entreprise *f* publique; ***public examination*** examen *m* national de l'enseignement public; ***public expenditure*** dépenses *fpl* publiques; ***public figure*** personnalité *f* très en vue; ***public finance*** finances *fpl* publiques; *Br* ***public footpath*** sentier *m* public; ***public funds*** fonds *mpl* publics; ***public gallery*** tribune *f* réservée au public; ***public health*** santé *f* publique; ***the public health authorities*** = administration régionale des services publics de santé; ***public health clinic*** centre *m* d'hygiène publique; ***public health hazard*** risque *m* pour la santé publique; *Old-fashioned* ***public health inspector*** inspecteur(trice) *m,f* sanitaire; ***public health official*** représentant(e) *m,f* de la santé publique; ***public holiday*** jour *m* férié, fête *f* légale; ***public house*** *Br* (*pub*) pub *m*, bar *m*; *Am* (*inn*) auberge *f*; *Am* ***public housing*** logements *mpl* sociaux, ≃ HLM *f inv*; *Am* ***Public Housing Administration*** = services du logement social aux États-Unis; *Am* ***public housing project*** ≃ cité *f* HLM; *Law* ***public indecency*** outrage *m* public à la pudeur; **to be arrested for public indecency** se faire arrêter pour outrage public à la pudeur; ***public inquiry*** enquête *f* officielle; **to hold a public inquiry** faire une enquête officielle; *Br* ***public lavatory*** toilettes *fpl* publiques; ***public law*** droit *m* public; ***public lending right*** = droits que touche un auteur ou un éditeur pour le prêt de ses livres en bibliothèque; ***public liability*** responsabilité *f* civile; ***public liability insurance*** assurance *f* responsabilité civile; ***public library*** bibliothèque *f* municipale; ***public limited company*** ≃ société *f* anonyme; ***public loan*** emprunt *m* public; ***public money*** deniers *mpl ou* fonds *mpl* publics; ***public monies*** deniers *mpl* de l'État; ***public nuisance*** (*person*) fléau *m* public, empoisonneur(euse) *m,f*; **the pub's late opening hours were creating a public nuisance** (*act*) les heures d'ouverture tardives du pub portaient atteinte à la tranquillité générale; *St Exch* ***public offering*** offre *f* publique; ***public official*** fonctionnaire *mf*; ***public opinion*** opinion *f* publique; ***public opinion poll*** sondage *m* (d'opinion); ***public ownership*** nationalisation *f*, étatisation *f*; **most airports are under public ownership** la plupart des aéroports appartiennent à l'État; ***public park*** jardin *m* public; *Law* ***public prosecutor*** ≃ procureur *m* général, ≃ ministère *m* public; *Br* ***the public purse*** le Trésor (public); *Br* ***Public Record Office*** ≃ Archives *fpl* nationales; ***public relations*** relations *fpl* publiques; **giving them a free meal was great public relations** en leur offrant le repas, nous avons fait un excellent travail de relations publiques; ***public relations agency, public relations consultancy*** agence *f* conseil en communication; ***public relations consultant*** conseil *m* en relations publiques, conseil *m* en communication; ***public relations exercise*** opération *f* de relations publiques; **it was a good public relations exercise** ce fut une réussite pour ce qui est des relations publiques; ***public relations manager*** directeur(trice) *m,f* des relations publiques; ***public relations officer*** responsable *mf* des relations publiques; ***public room*** (*in hotel, institution*) salle *f* de réception; *Scot* (*in house*) salon *m*; ***public school*** (*in UK*) public school *f*, école *f* privée (*prestigieuse*); (*in US*) école *f* publique; *Br* ***public schoolboy*** = élève d'une "public school"; *Br* ***public schoolgirl*** = élève d'une "public school"; ***public sector*** secteur *m* public; *Br Fin* ***public sector borrowing requirement*** = besoins d'emprunt du secteur public non couverts par les rentrées fiscales; *Fin* ***public sector deficit*** déficit *m* du secteur public; *Fin* ***public sector earnings*** revenus *mpl* du secteur public; ***public servant*** fonctionnaire *mf*; ***public service*** (*amenity*) service *m* public *ou* d'intérêt général; *Br* (*civil service*) fonction *f* publique; **she's in public service** elle est fonctionnaire; *Admin* **our organization performs a public service** notre association assure un service d'intérêt général; *St Exch* ***public share offer*** offre *f* publique de vente; ***public speaker*** orateur(trice) *m,f*; **he's a very good public speaker** c'est un excellent orateur; ***public speaking*** art *m* oratoire; *Hum* **unaccustomed as I am to public speaking** bien que je n'aie pas l'habitude de prendre la parole en public; *Sch* ***public speaking contest*** concours *m* d'éloquence; *Fin* ***public spending*** (*UNCOUNT*) dépenses *fpl* publiques *ou* de l'État; ***public spirit*** sens *m* civique, civisme *m*; *Am* ***public television*** (télévision *f* du) service *m* public; ***public transport*** (*UNCOUNT*) transports *mpl* en commun; **he went by public transport** (*bus*) il est allé en bus; (*train*) il est allé en train; ***public transport users*** usagers *mpl* des transports en commun; ***public utility*** *Am* (*company*) = société privée assurant un service public et réglementée par une commission d'État; *Br* (*amenity*) service *m* public; *Br* ***public utility company*** société *f* d'utilité publique; ***public works*** travaux *mpl* publics

PUBLIC ACCESS TELEVISION

Aux États-Unis, on appelle "public access television" les chaînes télévisées câblées non commerciales mises à la disposition d'organisations à but non lucratif et des citoyens. En 1984, le Congrès adopta le "Cable Communications Policy Act" afin de faire face au problème de la monopolisation des chaînes par un nombre réduit de cablo-opérateurs. Cette loi exige des propriétaires de chaînes câblées qu'ils mettent une chaîne à la disposition des communautés locales ainsi qu'un studio et du matériel d'enregistrement, et qu'ils fournissent également une assistance technique si nécessaire.

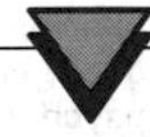

PUBLIC SCHOOL

En Angleterre et au pays de Galles, le terme "public school" désigne une école privée de type traditionnel. Certaines de ces écoles (Eton et Harrow, par exemple) sont très prestigieuses et élitistes. Les "public schools" sont censées former l'élite de la nation. Aux États-Unis et parfois en Écosse, le terme désigne une école publique.

public-address system *n* (système *m* de) sonorisation *f*

publican ['pʌblɪkən] *n* (**a**) *Br* (*pub owner*) patron(onne) *m,f* de pub; (*manager*) tenancier(ère) *m,f* de pub (**b**) *Bible* (*tax collector*) publicain *m*

publication [,pʌblɪ'keɪʃən] *n* (**a**) (*of book, statistics, banns*) publication *f*; (*of edict*) promulgation *f*; **her article has been accepted for publication** son article va être publié; **this isn't for publication** ceci n'est pas destiné à la publication (**b**) (*work*) publication *f*, ouvrage *m* publié

▸▸ ***publication date*** (*of book*) date *f* de parution

ou de publication; **what's the book's publication date?** quelle est la date de publication *ou* de parution du livre?

publicist ['pʌblɪsɪst] *n* (**a**) *(press agent)* (agent *m*) publicitaire *mf* (**b**) *(journalist)* journaliste *mf* (**c**) *Law* publiciste *mf*

publicity [pʌb'lɪsɪtɪ] *n* (**a**) *(media interest, exposure)* publicité *f*; **it'll give us free publicity for the product** ça fera de la publicité gratuite pour notre produit; **she/her movie is getting** *or* **attracting a lot of publicity** c'est un procès/un film dont on a beaucoup parlé; **there's no such thing as bad publicity** on ne fait jamais trop parler de soi; **the incident will mean bad publicity for us** cet incident va être mauvais pour *ou* va faire du tort à notre image de marque; **an actress who shuns publicity** une actrice qui fuit les médias; **they don't want any publicity** ils ne veulent pas faire parler d'eux

(**b**) *(advertising material, information)* matériel *m* publicitaire; **have you seen any of their publicity?** avez-vous vu leur matériel publicitaire?; **advance publicity** promotion *f*

►► ***publicity brochure*** brochure *f* publicitaire; ***publicity budget*** budget *m* publicitaire; ***publicity campaign*** *(for new product)* campagne *f* publicitaire, campagne *f* de publicité; *(by government)* campagne *f* d'information; ***publicity department*** service *m* de publicité; ***publicity expenses*** dépenses *fpl* de la publicité; ***publicity gimmick*** astuce *f* publicitaire; ***publicity manager*** chef *m* de (la) publicité; ***publicity photograph*** photographie *f* publicitaire; *Cin* ***publicity still*** photo *f* publicitaire; ***publicity stunt*** coup *m* de pub

publicity-seeking [-si:kɪŋ] **1** *n* **he accused the minister of publicity-seeking** il a accusé le ministre de vouloir se faire de la publicité; **some people interpreted her trips to the Third World as publicity-seeking** certains ont interprété ses voyages dans les pays du tiers-monde comme une manœuvre publicitaire

2 *adj (person)* qui cherche à se faire de la publicité; *(operation, manoeuvre)* publicitaire

publicize, -ise ['pʌblɪsaɪz] *vt* (**a**) *(make known)* faire connaître (au public); **her father is a minister, but she doesn't publicize the fact** son père est ministre, mais elle ne tient pas spécialement à ce que cela se sache *ou* elle ne le crie pas sur les toits; **his much publicized blunders don't help his image** ses célèbres gaffes ne font rien pour arranger son image de marque; **the government's environmental reforms have been well publicized in the press** la presse a beaucoup parlé des réformes du gouvernement en matière d'environnement

(**b**) *Mktg (advertise → product, event)* faire de la publicité pour; **the festival was well publicized** le festival a été annoncé à grand renfort de publicité; **the launch of the their new product has been widely publicized** leur nouveau produit a été lancé à grand renfort de publicité

publicly ['pʌblɪklɪ] *adv* publiquement, en public; **his publicly declared intentions** les intentions qu'il avait affichées; *Econ* **publicly owned** nationalisé; **the company is 51 percent publicly controlled** la compagnie est contrôlée à 51 pour cent par des capitaux publics

public-service *adj*

►► *Rad & TV* ***public-service announcement*** communiqué *m* (d'un ministère); *Rad & TV* ***public-service broadcasting*** émissions *fpl* de service public; *Am* ***public-service Commission*** = commission chargée de la réglementation des sociétés privées assurant des services publics; *Am* ***public-service corporation*** = société privée assurant un service public et réglementée par une commission d'État; *Rad & TV* ***public-service message*** communiqué *m* (d'un ministère); *Br Formerly* ***public-service vehicle*** véhicule *m* de transport en commun

public-spirited *adj (gesture)* d'esprit civique; *(person)* **to be public-spirited** faire preuve de civisme

publish ['pʌblɪʃ] **1** *vt* (**a**) *(book, journal)* publier, éditer; *(author)* éditer; *Comput (Web page)* publier; **her latest novel has just been published** son dernier roman vient de paraître; **he's a published author** ses livres sont publiés; **it's published by Harrap** c'est édité chez Harrap; **the magazine is published quarterly** la revue paraît tous les trois mois; **the newspaper published my letter** le journal a publié ma lettre

(**b**) *(of author)* **he's published poems in several magazines** ses poèmes ont été publiés dans plusieurs revues

(**c**) *(make known → statistics, statement, banns)* publier; **the price index which was published on Monday** l'indice des prix publié lundi

2 *vi (newspaper)* paraître; *(author)* être publié; **she publishes regularly in women's magazines** ses articles sont régulièrement publiés dans la presse féminine; **the pressure on academics to publish** l'obligation pour les universitaires de publier des articles

> **Publish and be damned**
> Il s'agit de la réponse que fit Lord Wellington à une femme qui menaçait de révéler qu'elle avait eu une aventure avec lui.
> On utilise couramment cette formule lorsque, comme Wellington, on défie quelqu'un de publier une information ("publiez si vous voulez et allez au diable!"), ou pour afficher son indifférence quant aux conséquences que pourrait avoir une révélation: **we're going to publish and be damned** ("on publiera, advienne que pourra").

publishable ['pʌblɪʃəbəl] *adj* publiable; **her remarks aren't publishable!** ses commentaires sont impubliables!, on ne peut pas publier ses commentaires!

publisher ['pʌblɪʃə(r)] *n* (**a**) *(person)* éditeur(trice) *m,f*; *(company)* maison *f* d'édition (**b**) *(newspaper owner)* patron *m* de presse

publishing ['pʌblɪʃɪŋ] *n* (**a**) *(industry)* édition *f*; **she's** *or* **she works in publishing** elle travaille dans l'édition; **a publishing giant** un géant de l'édition; **a publishing empire** un empire de l'édition (**b**) *(of book, journal)* publication *f*

►► ***publishing company*** maison *f* d'édition; ***publishing house*** maison *f* d'édition

Publius ['pʌblɪəs] *pr n* Publius

puce [pju:s] **1** *n* couleur *f* puce

2 *adj* puce *(inv)*

puck [pʌk] *n* (**a**) *(in ice hockey)* palet *m* (**b**) *(sprite)* lutin *m*, farfadet *m*

pucker ['pʌkə(r)] **1** *vi (face, forehead)* se plisser; *(fabric, collar)* goder, godailler

2 *vt (face, forehead)* plisser; *(fabric, collar)* faire goder, faire godailler; **to pucker one's lips** faire une bouche en cul de poule; **she puckered her lips at the sour taste** elle fit la grimace en sentant le goût acide; **the seam/hem is puckered** la couture/l'ourlet fait des plis

3 *n (crease)* pli *m*

►**pucker up** **1** *vi* (**a**) *(face, forehead)* se plisser; *(fabric, collar)* goder, godailler (**b**) *Fam (for kiss)* avancer les lèvres ❑

2 *vt sep (face, forehead)* plisser; *(fabric, collar)* faire goder, faire godailler

puckered ['pʌkəd] *adj (brow)* plissé; *(skin)* ridé; *(fabric)* godé, godaillé

puckish ['pʌkɪʃ] *adj* espiègle

pud [pʊd] *n* (**a**) *Br Fam (abbr* **pudding***)* dessert ❑ *m* (**b**) *Am Vulg (penis)* bite *f*

pudding ['pʊdɪŋ] *n* (**a**) *(cooked sweet dish)* **jam pudding** pudding *m ou* pouding *m* à la confiture; **rice/tapioca pudding** riz *m*/tapioca *m* au lait

(**b**) *Br (part of meal)* dessert *m*; **what are we having for pudding?** qu'est-ce qu'il y a comme dessert?

(**c**) *Br (savoury dish)* = tourte cuite à la vapeur

(**d**) *Br (sausage)* boudin *m*; **white pudding** boudin *m* blanc

(**e**) *Br Fam (podgy person)* patapouf *m*

(**f**) *Br Fam (idiom)* **to be in the pudding club** avoir un polichinelle dans le tiroir

►► *Br* ***pudding basin, pudding bowl*** = jatte dans laquelle on fait cuire le pudding; ***pudding basin haircut*** coupe *f* au bol; *Br Fam* ***pudding face*** visage *m* empâté ❑; *Br Fam* ***pudding head*** *(idiot)* andouille *f*, patate *f*; ***pudding rice*** riz *m* rond; *Geol* ***pudding stone*** poudingue *m*

puddle ['pʌdəl] **1** *n (of water, oil)* flaque *f*; *(small pool)* petite mare *f*; *Fam* **the dog's made a puddle on the carpet** le chien a fait pipi sur le tapis

2 *vt (clay)* malaxer

►**puddle about, puddle around** *vi* (**a**) *(wade)* patauger, barboter (**b**) *Am Fam (laze)* flemmarder, traîner (**c**) *Am Fam (tinker, potter)* faire des bricoles

pudency ['pju:dənsɪ] *n Literary* pudicité *f*

pudendum [pju:'dendəm] *(pl* **pudenda** [-də]) *n (usu pl)* parties *fpl* génitales

pudgy ['pʌdʒɪ] *(compar* **pudgier,** *superl* **pudgiest***) adj Br Fam* grassouillet

pudicity [pju:'dɪsɪtɪ] *n Literary* pudicité *f*

pudu ['pu:du:] *n Zool* pudu *m*

Pueblo ['pwebləʊ] *(pl* **inv** *or* **Pueblos***) n* (**a**) *(group of tribes)* **the Pueblo** les Pueblo *mpl* (**b**) *(member of tribe)* Pueblo *mf inv*

pueblo ['pwebləʊ] *(pl* **pueblos***) n Am* village *m* pueblo

puerile ['pjʊəraɪl] *adj* puéril

puerility [pjʊə'rɪlətɪ] *n* puérilité *f*

puerperal [pju:'ɜ:pərəl] *adj Med* puerpéral

►► ***puerperal fever*** fièvre *f* puerpérale

puerperium [pjuə'pɪərɪəm] *n Med* puerpéralité *f*

Puerto Rican [,pwɜ:təʊ'ri:kən] **1** *n* Portoricain(e) *m,f*

2 *adj* portoricain

3 *comp (embassy, history)* du Puerto Rico

Puerto Rico [,pwɜ:təʊ'ri:kəʊ] *n* Porto Rico, Puerto Rico; **in Puerto Rico** à Porto Rico, à Puerto Rico

puff[1] [pʌf] **1** *vt* (**a**) *(smoke → cigar, pipe)* tirer des bouffées de

(**b**) *(emit, expel)* **to puff (out) smoke/steam** envoyer des nuages de fumée/des jets de vapeur; **he sat opposite me puffing smoke in my face!** il était assis en face de moi et m'envoyait sa fumée en pleine figure!

(**c**) *(pant)* **"I can't go on", he puffed** "je n'en peux plus", haleta-t-il

(**d**) *(swell → sail, parachute)* gonfler

(**e**) *Fam Old-fashioned (laud)* vanter ❑, faire mousser

2 *vi* (**a**) *(blow → person)* souffler; *(→ wind)* souffler en bourrasques; **to puff (away) at one's pipe** tirer sur sa pipe, tirer des bouffées de sa pipe

(**b**) *(pant)* haleter; *(breathe heavily)* souffler; **I was puffing as I climbed the stairs** je haletais en montant l'escalier; **he was puffing and panting** il soufflait comme un phoque; **I puffed along beside her** je courais, tout essoufflé, à ses côtés

(**c**) *(smoke)* **to puff on one's cigar** tirer sur son cigare

(**d**) *(issue → smoke, steam)* sortir

(**e**) *(train)* **the train puffed into the station** le train entra en gare dans un nuage de fumée; **the steam engine puffed into view** la fumée indiqua l'arrivée du train

3 *n* (**a**) *(gust, whiff)* bouffée *f*; *(gasp)* souffle *m*; **her breath came in short puffs** elle haletait; **a puff of dust/smoke on the horizon** un nuage de poussière/fumée à l'horizon; *Fig* **all our plans went up in a puff of smoke** tous nos projets sont partis en fumée *ou* se sont évanouis

(**b**) *(on cigarette, pipe)* bouffée *f*; **to have** *or* **to take a puff** tirer une bouffée; **give me a puff** *(of your cigarette)* passe-moi une bouffée

(**c**) *(sound → of train)* teuf-teuf *m*

(**d**) *Br Fam (breath)* souffle ❑ *m*; **to be out of puff** être à bout de souffle *ou* essoufflé ❑

(**e**) *(fluffy mass)* **puffs of cloud in the sky** des moutons *mpl ou* des petits nuages *mpl* dans le ciel

(**f**) *(for make-up)* **(powder) puff** houppe *f* (à poudrer), houpette *f*

(**g**) *(pastry)* chou *m*; **cream puff** chou *m* à la crème

(**h**) *Am (eiderdown)* édredon *m*

(**i**) *Fam Old-fashioned (free publicity)* publicité *f* gratuite ❑; *(favourable publicity)* battage *m*; **to give sth a puff** faire de la réclame *ou* du battage pour qch

(**j**) *Br Fam Drugs slang (marijuana)* herbe *f*, beu *f*; *(cannabis)* shit *m*, hasch *m*

►► *Zool* ***puff adder*** vipère *f* heurtante; *Culin Am* ***puff paste,*** *Br* ***puff pastry*** pâte *f* feuilletée; ***puff sleeves*** manches *fpl* ballon

▸**puff out** **1** *vt sep* (**a**) *(extinguish)* souffler, éteindre (en soufflant)
(**b**) *(inflate, make rounded → cheeks, sail)* gonfler; *(→ chest)* bomber; *(→ cushion, hair)* faire bouffer; **the pigeon puffed out its feathers** le pigeon fit gonfler ses plumes; **the wind puffed out the sails** les voiles se gonflèrent
(**c**) *(emit)* **to puff out smoke/steam** envoyer des nuages de fumée/de vapeur
2 *vi* (**a**) *(parachute, sail)* se gonfler
(**b**) *(be emitted → smoke)* s'échapper

▸**puff up** **1** *vt sep* (**a**) *(inflate, make rounded → cheeks, sail)* gonfler; *(→ cushion, hair)* faire bouffer
(**b**) *(usu passive) (swell → lip, ankle etc)* enfler; **her eyes were puffed up** elle avait les yeux bouffis; *Fig* **to be puffed up with pride** être bouffi d'orgueil
2 *vi (lip, ankle etc)* enfler, bouffir

puff² [pʊf] = **poof**

Puffa jacket® [ˈpʌfə-] *n* blouson *m* de rappeur

puffball [ˈpʌfbɔːl] *n Bot* vesse-de-loup *f*; **giant puffball** vesse-de-loup *f* géante
▸▸ ***puffball skirt*** = jupe plus évasée en bas qu'en haut

puffed [pʌft] *adj* (**a**) *(rice, oats)* soufflé (**b**) *Br Fam (out of breath)* **puffed (out)** essoufflé ❑, à bout de souffle ❑; **we were puffed (out) after the climb** la montée nous a essoufflés
▸▸ ***puffed rice*** riz *m* gonflé; ***puffed sleeves*** manches *fpl* ballon; ***puffed wheat*** blé *m* soufflé

puffed-up *adj* (**a**) *(swollen)* boursouflé, enflé (**b**) *(conceited)* suffisant, content de soi; **puffed-up with pride** bouffi d'orgueil

puffer [ˈpʌfə(r)] *n* (**a**) *Ich* **puffer (fish)** poisson-globe *m* (**b**) *Br Fam (train)* train ❑ *m* (**c**) *Scot Hist (boat)* petit vapeur *m (pour le transport de marchandises sur la côte et les îles de l'ouest de l'Écosse)*

puffin [ˈpʌfɪn] *n Orn* macareux *m*

puffiness [ˈpʌfɪnɪs] *n* boursouflure *f*

puff-puff *Fam* **1** *n (in children's language)* teuf-teuf *m*
2 *onomat* teuf-teuf

puffy [ˈpʌfɪ] *(compar* **puffier**, *superl* **puffiest**) *adj (face)* bouffi, boursouflé; *(lip, cheek)* enflé; *(eye)* bouffi; **puffy clouds** moutons *mpl*

pug [pʌg] *n* (**a**) *(dog)* carlin *m* (**b**) *Fam (pugilist)* boxeur(euse) ❑ *m,f*
▸▸ ***pug nose*** nez *m* camus

Puget Sound [ˈpjuːdʒɪt-] *n* Puget Sound *m*

pugilism [ˈpjuːdʒɪlɪzəm] *n Literary* pugilat *m*, boxe *f*

pugilist [ˈpjuːdʒɪlɪst] *n Literary* pugiliste *mf*, boxeur(euse) *m,f*

pugilistic [ˌpjuːdʒɪˈlɪstɪk] *adj Literary* pugilistique, de boxeur

pugnacious [pʌgˈneɪʃəs] *adj Formal* pugnace, agressif

pugnaciously [pʌgˈneɪʃəslɪ] *adv Formal* avec pugnacité *ou* agressivité

pugnacity [pʌgˈnæsətɪ] *n Formal* pugnacité *f*

pug-nosed *adj (face, person)* au nez camus; **to be pug-nosed** avoir le nez camus

puisne [ˈpjuːnɪ] *adj Law (judge)* subalterne

puissance [ˈpwiːsɒns] *n (in show jumping)* puissance *f*

puke [pjuːk] *Fam* **1** *vt* dégueuler, gerber
2 *vi* dégueuler, gerber; *Fig* **you make me puke!** tu me dégoûtes!
3 *n* dégueulis *m*

▸**puke up** *Fam* **1** *vt sep* rendre
2 *vi* dégueuler, gerber

pukey [ˈpjuːkɪ] *adj Fam* dégueulasse

pukka [ˈpʌkə] *adj Br Old-fashioned or Hum* (**a**) *(genuine)* réglo *(inv)*, régulier, **a pukka sahib** un vrai gentleman; **pukka information** des renseignements *mpl* exacts (**b**) *(done well)* bien fait, très correct; *(excellent)* de premier ordre, super *(inv)* (**c**) *(socially acceptable)* (très) comme il faut

pulchritude [ˈpʌlkrɪtjuːd] *n Literary* beauté *f*, splendeur *f*

pule [pjuːl] *vi* gémir, geindre

puling [ˈpjuːlɪŋ] *adj (baby, child)* vagissant

Pulitzer Prize [ˈpʊlɪtsə-] *n* **the Pulitzer Prize** le prix Pulitzer

PULL [pʊl]

fait de tirer	▸ **1 (a)**
traction	▸ **1 (b)**
résistance	▸ **1 (c)**
attrait	▸ **1 (d)**
influence	▸ **1 (e)**
tirer	▸ **2 (a) – (c); 3 (a)**
traîner	▸ **2 (a)**
arracher	▸ **2 (d)**
se déchirer	▸ **2 (e)**
réussir	▸ **2 (f)**

1 *n* (**a**) *(tug, act of pulling)* **to give sth a pull, to give a pull on sth** tirer (sur) qch; **give it a hard** *or* **good pull!** tirez fort!; **give it one more pull** tire encore un coup; **we'll need a pull to get out of the mud** nous aurons besoin que quelqu'un nous remorque *ou* nous prenne en remorque pour nous désembourber; **with a pull the dog broke free** le chien tira sur sa laisse et s'échappa; **she felt a pull at** *or* **on her handbag** elle a senti qu'on tirait sur son sac à main; **I felt a pull on the fishing line** ça mordait
(**b**) *(physical force → of machine)* traction *f*; *(→ of sun, moon, magnet)* (force *f*) d'attraction *f*; **the winch applies a steady pull** le treuil exerce une traction continue; **the gravitational pull is stronger on Earth** la gravitation est plus forte sur Terre; **we fought against the pull of the current** nous luttions contre le courant qui nous entraînait
(**c**) *(resistance → of bowstring)* résistance *f*; **adjust the trigger if the pull is too stiff for you** réglez la détente si elle est trop dure pour vous
(**d**) *(psychological, emotional attraction)* attrait *m*; **the pull of city life** l'attrait *m* de la vie en ville; **he resisted the pull of family tradition and went his own way** il a résisté à l'influence de la tradition familiale pour suivre son propre chemin
(**e**) *Fam (influence, power)* influence ❑ *f*, piston *m*; **to have a lot of pull** avoir le bras long; **he has a lot of pull with the Prime Minister** il a beaucoup d'influence sur le Premier ministre; **his money gives him a certain political pull** son argent lui confère une certaine influence *ou* un certain pouvoir politique; **his father's pull got him in** son père l'a pistonné
(**f**) *(prolonged effort)* **it'll be a long pull to the summit** la montée sera longue (et difficile) pour atteindre le sommet; **it will be a hard pull upstream** il faudra ramer dur pour remonter le courant; **it's going to be a long uphill pull to make the firm profitable** ça sera difficile de remettre l'entreprise à flot
(**g**) *(in rowing → stroke)* coup *m* de rame *ou* d'aviron; **with another pull he was clear of the rock** d'un autre coup de rame, il évita le rocher
(**h**) *(at cigar)* bouffée *f*; *(at drink, bottle)* gorgée *f*; **to take a pull at** *or* **on one's beer** boire *ou* prendre une gorgée de bière; **to take a pull at** *or* **on one's cigarette/pipe** tirer sur sa cigarette/pipe
(**i**) *(usu in cpds) (knob, handle)* poignée *f*; *(cord)* cordon *m*; *(strap)* sangle *f*
(**j**) *(snag → in sweater)* accroc *m*; **my cardigan has a pull in it** j'ai fait un accroc à mon cardigan
(**k**) *Typ* épreuve *f*
(**l**) *Fam* **to be on the pull** *(man)* chercher à lever une nana; *(woman)* chercher à lever un mec
2 *vt* (**a**) *(object → yank, tug)* tirer; *(→ drag)* traîner; *(person)* tirer, entraîner; **she pulled my hair** elle m'a tiré les cheveux; **to pull the blinds** baisser les stores; **to pull the** *Br* curtains *or Am* **drapes** tirer *ou* fermer les rideaux; **we pulled the heavy log across to the fire** nous avons traîné la lourde bûche jusqu'au feu; **pull the lamp towards you** tirez la lampe vers vous; **he pulled his chair closer to the fire** il approcha sa chaise de la cheminée; **she pulled the hood over her face** elle abaissa le capuchon sur son visage; **he pulled his hat over his eyes** il enfonça *ou* rabattit son chapeau sur ses yeux; **he pulled the steering wheel to the right** il a donné un coup de volant à droite; **to pull a drawer open** ouvrir un tiroir; **she came in and pulled the door shut behind her** elle entra et ferma la porte derrière elle; **pull the rope taut** tendez la corde; **pull the knot tight** serrez le nœud; **pull the tablecloth straight** tendez la nappe; **he pulled the wrapping from the package** il arracha l'emballage du paquet; **he pulled the sheets off the bed** il enleva les draps du lit; **she pulled her hand from mine** elle retira (brusquement) sa main de la mienne; **she pulled the box from his hands** elle lui a arraché la boîte des mains; **he was pulling her towards the exit** il l'entraînait vers la sortie; **he pulled her closer (to him)** il l'a attirée plus près de lui; **the current pulled us into the middle of the river** le courant nous a entraînés au milieu de la rivière; **he pulled himself onto the riverbank** il se hissa sur la berge; *Fig* **the sound of the doorbell pulled him out of his daydream** le coup de sonnette l'a tiré de *ou* arraché à ses rêveries; *Fig* **he was pulled off the first team** on l'a écarté *ou* exclu de la première équipe; *Br Fam* **pull the other one (it's got bells on)!** mon œil!, à d'autres!; **to pull to bits** *or* **pieces** *(toy, appliance)* démolir, mettre en morceaux; *(book, flower)* déchirer; *Fig (book, play, person)* démolir
(**b**) *(operate → lever, handle)* tirer; **pull the trigger** appuyez *ou* pressez sur la détente
(**c**) *(tow, draw → load, trailer, carriage, boat)* tirer, remorquer; **carts pulled by mules** des charrettes tirées par des mules; **a suitcase with wheels that you pull behind you** une valise à roulettes qu'on tire *ou* traîne derrière soi; **the barges were pulled along the canals** les péniches étaient halées le long des canaux
(**d**) *(take out → tooth)* arracher, extraire; *(→ weeds)* arracher; *(→ weapon)* tirer, sortir; **he pulled a dollar bill from his wad/wallet** il a tiré un billet d'un dollar de sa liasse/sorti un billet d'un dollar de son portefeuille; **he pulled a gun on me** il a braqué un revolver sur moi; **to pull a cork** déboucher une bouteille; **to have a tooth pulled** se faire arracher une dent; **it was like pulling teeth** c'était pénible comme tout; **getting him to talk is like pulling teeth!** il faut lui arracher les mots de la bouche!; *Fam* **can you pull that file for me?** pourriez-vous me sortir ce dossier? ❑
(**e**) *(strain → muscle, tendon)* se déchirer; **she pulled a muscle** elle s'est déchiré un muscle, elle s'est fait un claquage; **a pulled muscle** un claquage; **my shoulder feels as if I've pulled something** j'ai l'impression que je me suis froissé un muscle de l'épaule
(**f**) *Fam (bring off)* réussir ❑; **she has pulled several daring financial coups** elle a réussi plusieurs opérations financières audacieuses; **he pulled a big bank job in Italy** il a réussi un hold-up de première dans une banque italienne; **to pull a trick on sb** jouer un tour à qn ❑; **what are you trying to pull?** qu'est-ce que tu es en train de combiner *ou* manigancer? ❑; **don't try and pull anything!** n'essayez pas de jouer au plus malin!; **don't ever pull a stunt like that again** ne me/nous/*etc* refais jamais un tour comme ça ❑; **to pull a fast one on sb** avoir qn, rouler qn; *Am* **I pulled an all-nighter** j'ai bossé toute la nuit
(**g**) *(hold back) Horseracing* **to pull a horse** retenir un cheval; *also Fig* **to pull one's punches** retenir ses coups, ménager son adversaire; *Fig* **she didn't pull any punches** elle n'y est pas allée de main morte
(**h**) *(in golf, tennis → ball)* puller; **to pull a shot** puller
(**i**) *(in rowing → boat)* faire avancer à la rame; **he pulls a good oar** c'est un bon rameur; **the boat pulls eight oars** c'est un bateau à huit avirons
(**j**) *Typ (proof)* tirer
(**k**) *Comput* extraire
(**l**) *(gut → fowl)* vider
(**m**) *Fam (withdraw)* retirer ❑; **people complained and they had to pull the commercial** ils ont dû retirer la pub suite à des plaintes
(**n**) *Fam (attract → customers, spectators)* attirer ❑; **the festival pulled a big crowd** le festival a attiré beaucoup de monde; **how many votes will he pull?** combien de voix va-t-il récolter? ❑
(**o**) *Br (serve → draught beer)* tirer; **he pulls pints at the Crown** il est barman au Crown
(**p**) *Fam (sexual partner)* lever, emballer

3 *vi* (**a**) *(exert force, tug)* tirer; **pull harder!** tirez plus fort!; **to pull on** *or* **at a rope** tirer sur un cordage; **the bandage may pull when I take it off** le pansement risque de vous tirer la peau quand je l'enlèverai; **the steering pulls to the right** la direction tire à droite; *Aut* **the 2-litre model pulls very well** le modèle 2 litres a de bonnes reprises; *Fig* **they're pulling in different directions** ils tirent à hue et à dia

(**b**) *(rope, cord)* **the rope pulled easily** la corde filait librement

(**c**) *(go, move)* **pull into the space next to the Mercedes** mettez-vous *ou* garez-vous à côté de la Mercedes; **he pulled into the right-hand lane** il a pris la file de droite; **pull into the garage** entrez dans le garage; **when the train pulls out of the station** quand le train quitte la gare; **she pulled clear of the pack** elle s'est détachée du peloton; **he pulled clear of the traffic and sped on** il est sorti du flot de la circulation et a accéléré; **he pulled sharply to the left** il a viré brutalement sur la gauche; **the lorry pulled slowly up the hill** le camion gravissait lentement la côte

(**d**) *(strain, labour → vehicle)* peiner; *(→ horse)* tirer sur le mors; **the engine's pulling** le moteur fatigue *ou* peine

(**e**) *Fam (exert influence, give support)* **the head of personnel is pulling for you** *or* **on your behalf** vous avez le chef du personnel derrière vous❑

(**f**) *(snag → sweater)* filer; **my sweater's pulled in a couple of places** mon pull a plusieurs mailles filées

(**g**) *(row)* ramer; **to pull for shore** ramer vers la côte; **to pull with a long stroke** ramer à grands coups d'aviron

(**h**) *Fam (find sexual partner)* **did you pull last night?** t'as levé une nana/un mec hier soir?

►► *Am* ***pull date*** date *f* limite de vente; *Mktg* ***pull strategy*** stratégie *f* pull; ***pull tab*** *(on can)* anneau *m*, bague *f*

►**pull about** *vt sep (handle roughly → person)* malmener; *(→ object)* tirer dans tous les sens, tirailler; **stop pulling me about!** mais lâche-moi donc!

►**pull ahead** *vi* prendre de l'avance; **to pull ahead of sb** prendre de l'avance sur qn

►**pull along** *vt sep (load, vehicle)* tirer; *(person)* entraîner; **he was pulling the suitcase along by the strap** il tirait la valise derrière lui par la sangle; **she pulled me along by my arm** elle m'entraînait en me tirant par le bras

►**pull apart 1** *vt sep* (**a**) *(take to pieces → machine, furniture)* démonter; **now you've pulled it all apart, are you sure you can fix it?** maintenant que tu as tout démonté, es-tu sûr de pouvoir le réparer?

(**b**) *(destroy, break → object)* mettre en morceaux *ou* en pièces; *(→ clothing)* déchirer; *(body, flesh)* déchiqueter; **the wreck was pulled apart by the waves** les vagues ont disloqué l'épave; **tell him where it's hidden or he'll pull the place apart** dites-lui où c'est (caché) sinon il va tout saccager

(**c**) *(criticize → essay, performance, theory)* démolir; *(→ person)* éreinter

(**d**) *(separate → fighters, dogs)* séparer; *(→ papers)* détacher, séparer

(**e**) *(make suffer)* déchirer

2 *vi (furniture)* se démonter, être démontable; **the shelves simply pull apart** les étagères se démontent sans outils

►**pull around** *vt sep* (**a**) *(cart, toy, suitcase)* tirer derrière soi

(**b**) *(make turn)* tourner, faire pivoter; **he pulled the horse around** il fit faire demi-tour à son cheval

►**pull at** *vt insep* (**a**) *(strain at, tug at)* tirer sur; **the dog pulled at the leash** le chien tira sur la laisse; **we pulled at the rope** nous avons tiré sur la corde; **I pulled at his sleeve** je l'ai tiré par la manche; **each pulled at an oar** chacun tirait sur un aviron; **the wind pulled at her hair** le vent faisait voler ses cheveux

(**b**) *(suck → pipe, cigar)* tirer sur; *(→ bottle)* **he pulled at his bottle of beer** il a bu une gorgée de bière

►**pull away 1** *vt sep (withdraw → covering, hand)* retirer; *(grab)* arracher; **she pulled her hand away** elle retira *ou* ôta sa main; **he pulled me away from the window** il m'éloigna de la fenêtre; **she pulled the book away from him** elle lui arracha le livre

2 *vi* (**a**) *(withdraw → person)* s'écarter; **I put out my hand but she pulled away** j'ai tendu la main vers elle mais elle s'est détournée; **he had me by the arm but I managed to pull away** il me tenait par le bras mais j'ai réussi à me dégager

(**b**) *(move off → vehicle, ship)* démarrer; *(→ train, convoy)* s'ébranler; **the boat pulled away from the bank** le bateau quitta la rive; **the train pulled away from the station** le train a quitté la gare; **as the train began to pull away** alors que le train s'ébranlait

(**c**) *(get ahead → runner, competitor)* prendre de l'avance; **she's pulling away from the pack** elle prend de l'avance sur le peloton, elle se détache du peloton

►**pull back 1** *vt sep* (**a**) *(draw backwards or towards one)* retirer; **he pulled his hand back** il retira *ou* ôta sa main; **she pulled back the curtains** elle ouvrit les rideaux; **pull the lever back** tirez le levier (vers l'arrière); **he pulled me back from the railing** il m'a éloigné de la barrière; **to pull sb/a company back from the brink** faire refaire surface à qn/une entreprise, tirer qn/une entreprise d'affaire

(**b**) *(withdraw → troops)* retirer

2 *vi* (**a**) *(withdraw → troops, participant)* se retirer; **it's too late to pull back now** il est trop tard pour se retirer *ou* pour faire marche arrière maintenant; **they pulled back from committing themselves fully** ils ont renoncé à s'engager complètement

(**b**) *(step backwards)* reculer; **to pull back involuntarily** avoir un mouvement de recul involontaire

(**c**) *(jib → horse, person)* regimber

►**pull down 1** *vt sep* (**a**) *(lower → lever, handle)* tirer (vers le bas); *(→ trousers, veil)* baisser; *(→ suitcase, book)* descendre; *(→ blind, window)* baisser; **pull the blind/the window down** baissez le store/la vitre; **with his hat pulled down over his eyes** son chapeau rabattu sur les yeux; **she pulled her skirt down over her knees** elle ramena sa jupe sur ses genoux; **I pulled him down onto the chair** je l'ai fait asseoir sur la chaise; **he's pulling the whole team down** il fait baisser le niveau de toute l'équipe; **my marks in the oral exam will pull me down** mes notes à l'oral vont baisser *ou* descendre ma moyenne

(**b**) *(demolish → house, wall)* démolir, abattre; **they're pulling down the whole neighbourhood** ils démolissent tout le quartier; *Fig* **it'll pull down the government** ça va renverser le gouvernement

(**c**) *Fam (weaken → of illness)* affaiblir❑, abattre❑; *(depress)* déprimer❑, abattre❑

(**d**) *Am Fam (earn)* gagner❑, se faire

(**e**) *Comput (menu)* dérouler

2 *vi (blind)* descendre

►**pull in 1** *vt sep* (**a**) *(line, fishing net)* ramener; **they pulled the rope in** ils tirèrent la corde à eux; **to pull sb in** *(into building, car)* tirer qn à l'intérieur, faire entrer qn; *(into water)* faire tomber qn à l'eau

(**b**) *(stomach)* rentrer; **to pull oneself in** rentrer son ventre

(**c**) *(attract → customers, investors, investment)* attirer; **the show's really pulling them in** le spectacle attire les foules

(**d**) *Fam (earn → of person)* gagner❑, se faire; *(→ of business)* rapporter❑

(**e**) *Fam (arrest)* arrêter❑, embarquer; **they pulled him in for questioning** ils l'ont arrêté pour l'interroger

(**f**) *(stop → horse)* retenir, tirer les rênes de; **to pull one's car in to the kerb** se ranger près du trottoir; **to be pulled in for speeding** être arrêté pour excès de vitesse

2 *vi (vehicle, driver → stop)* s'arrêter; *(→ park)* se garer; *(→ move to side of road)* se rabattre; *(arrive → train)* entrer en gare; **I pulled in for petrol** je me suis arrêté pour prendre de l'essence; **the car in front pulled in to let me past** la voiture devant moi s'est rabattue pour me laisser passer; **pull in here** arrête-toi là; **to pull in to the kerb** se ranger près du trottoir; **the express pulled in two hours late** l'express est arrivé avec deux heures de retard

►**pull off 1** *vt sep* (**a**) *(clothes, boots, ring)* enlever, retirer; *(cover, bandage, knob, wrapping)* enlever; *(page from calendar, sticky backing)* détacher; **to pull the sheets off the bed** retirer *ou* enlever les draps du lit; **I pulled her hat off** je lui ai enlevé son chapeau; *(more violently)* je lui ai arraché son chapeau

(**b**) *Fam (accomplish → deal, stratagem, mission, shot)* réussir❑; *(→ press conference, negotiations)* mener à bien❑; *(→ plan)* réaliser❑; *(→ prize)* décrocher, gagner❑; **the deal will be difficult to pull off** cette affaire ne sera pas facile à négocier; **will she (manage to) pull it off?** est-ce qu'elle va y arriver?; **he pulled it off** il a réussi

(**c**) *Vulg (masturbate)* **to pull sb off** branler qn; **to pull oneself off** se branler

2 *vi* (**a**) *(move off)* démarrer; *(after halt)* redémarrer

(**b**) *(stop)* s'arrêter; *(leave main road)* quitter la route; **he pulled off onto a side road** il bifurqua sur une petite route; **there's no place to pull off** il n'y a pas de place pour s'arrêter

(**c**) *(come off)* **the lid simply pulls off** il suffit de tirer pour enlever le couvercle; **the top pulls off to reveal...** le dessus se retire et on peut voir...

►**pull on 1** *vt sep (clothes, boots, pillow slip)* mettre, enfiler

2 *vt insep* (**a**) *(tug at → rope, handle etc)* tirer sur

(**b**) *(draw on → cigarette, pipe)* tirer sur

►**pull out 1** *vt sep* (**a**) *(remove → tooth, hair, weeds)* arracher; *(→ splinter, nail)* enlever; *(→ plug, cork)* ôter, enlever; *(produce → wallet, weapon)* sortir, tirer; **she pulled a map out of her bag** elle a sorti une carte de son sac; **he pulled a page out of his notebook** il a déchiré une feuille de son carnet; **pull the paper gently out of the printer** retirez doucement le papier de l'imprimante; **to pull a nail out of a plank** arracher un clou d'une planche; **the tractor pulled us out of the mud/ditch** le tracteur nous a sortis de la boue/du fossé; **to pull the country out of recession** (faire) sortir le pays de la récession; **to pull sb out of a tight spot** tirer qn d'un mauvais pas; *Fam* **to pull out all the stops (to do sth)** faire le maximum (pour faire qch)

(**b**) *(draw towards one → drawer, leaf of table, shelf)* tirer; *(unfold)* déplier; **pull the bed out from the wall** écartez le lit du mur; **he pulled a chair out from under the table** il a écarté une chaise de la table

(**c**) *(withdraw → troops, contestant)* retirer; **the battalion was pulled out of the border area** le bataillon a été retiré de la région frontalière; **he threatened to pull the party out of the coalition** il menaça de retirer le parti de la coalition

(**d**) *Comput (select, produce → data)* sortir

2 *vi* (**a**) *(withdraw → troops, ally, participant)* se retirer; *(→ company from project, buyer)* se désister; *(→ company from place)* quitter une/la région/ville/*etc*; **when they pulled out of Vietnam** quand ils se sont retirés du Viêt-nam; **she's pulling out of the election** elle retire sa candidature; **they've pulled out of the deal** ils se sont retirés de l'affaire

(**b**) *(move off → car, ship)* démarrer; *(→ train, convoy)* s'ébranler; *(move out to overtake)* déboîter; **she was pulling out of the garage** elle sortait du garage; **he pulled out to overtake** il a déboîté pour doubler; **a truck suddenly pulled out in front of me** soudain, un camion m'a coupé la route; **to pull out into traffic** s'engager dans la circulation; *Aviat* **to pull out of a dive** sortir d'un piqué, se rétablir

(**c**) *(economy)* **to pull out of a recession/a crisis** sortir de la récession/d'une crise

(**d**) *(be extendible or detachable → drawer)* s'ouvrir; *(→ handle)* s'allonger; *(→ map)* se déplier; **the sofa pulls out into a bed** le canapé se transforme en lit; **the shelves pull out** on peut retirer les étagères; **the table top pulls out** c'est une table à rallonges

►**pull over 1** *vt sep* (**a**) *(draw into specified position)* tirer, traîner; **pull the chair over to the window** amenez la chaise près de la fenêtre; **she pulled the dish over and helped herself** elle a tiré le plat vers *ou* à elle et s'est servie

pul–pul

(**b**) *(make fall → pile, person, table)* faire tomber, renverser; **watch out you don't pull that lamp over** fais attention de ne pas faire tomber cette lampe

(**c**) *(usu passive) (stop → vehicle, driver)* arrêter; **I got pulled over for speeding** je me suis fait arrêter pour excès de vitesse

2 *vi (vehicle, driver → stop)* s'arrêter; *(→ move to side of road)* se ranger, se rabattre; **pull over and let the fire engine past** rangez-vous *ou* rabattez-vous sur le côté et laissez passer les pompiers

▶**pull round** *Br* **1** *vt sep* (**a**) = **pull around**

(**b**) *(revive)* ranimer; **a drop of brandy will pull her round** un peu de cognac la remettra *ou* remontera

2 *vi (regain consciousness)* revenir à soi, reprendre connaissance; *(recover)* se remettre

▶**pull through 1** *vt sep* (**a**) *(draw through → rope, thread)* faire passer; **pull the needle through to the other side** faites sortir l'aiguille de l'autre côté

(**b**) *(help survive or surmount)* tirer d'affaire; **he says his faith pulled him through** il dit que c'est sa foi qui lui a permis de s'en sortir

2 *vi (recover)* s'en sortir, s'en tirer

▶**pull to** *vt sep (shut → door, gate)* fermer

▶**pull together 1** *vt sep* (**a**) *(place together, join)* joindre

(**b**) *(organize → demonstration, rescue team)* organiser; *(prepare)* préparer; **I've pulled together a few suggestions** j'ai préparé *ou* noté quelques propositions

(**c**) **to pull oneself together** se reprendre, se ressaisir; **pull yourself together!** ressaisissez-vous!, ne vous laissez pas aller!

2 *vi* (**a**) *(on rope)* tirer ensemble; *(on oars)* ramer à l'unisson; **pull together!** *(in rowing)* avant partout!

(**b**) *(combine efforts, cooperate)* concentrer ses efforts, agir de concert; **we've all got to pull together on this one** il faut que nous nous y mettions tous ensemble, il faut que nous nous attelions tous ensemble à la tâche

▶**pull up 1** *vt sep* (**a**) *(draw upwards → trousers, sleeve, blanket, lever)* remonter; *(→ blind)* hausser, lever; *(→ skirt)* retrousser, relever; *(hoist oneself)* hisser; **they pulled the boat up onto the beach** ils ont tiré le bateau sur la plage; **she pulled herself up onto the ledge** elle s'est hissée sur le rebord; **to pull one's socks up** tirer *ou* remonter ses chaussettes; *Fam Fig* se remuer, s'activer

(**b**) *(move closer → chair)* approcher; **I pulled a chair up to the desk** j'ai approché une chaise du bureau; **why don't you pull up a chair and join us?** prenez donc une chaise et joignez-vous à nous!; **he pulled the crate up to the scales** il a traîné la caisse jusqu'à la balance

(**c**) *(uproot → weeds)* arracher; *(→ bush, stump, tree)* arracher, déraciner; *(rip up → floorboards)* arracher

(**d**) *(stop → person, vehicle, horse)* arrêter; *(check → person)* retenir; **to be pulled up (by the police)** se faire arrêter (par un agent); **his warning pulled me up short** je me suis arrêté net lorsqu'il m'a crié de faire attention; **he was about to tell them everything but I pulled him up (short)** il était sur le point de tout leur dire mais je lui ai coupé la parole

(**e**) *Fam (improve → score, mark)* améliorer❑; *(→ average)* remonter❑; **his good marks in maths pulled him up again** ses bonnes notes en maths ont remonté sa moyenne

(**f**) *Br Fam (rebuke)* réprimander❑, enguirlander; **he was pulled up for being late** il s'est fait enguirlander pour être arrivé en retard; **if your work is sloppy, they'll pull you up on it** si ton travail est bâclé, tu vas te faire taper sur les doigts

2 *vi* (**a**) *(stop)* s'arrêter; **as I was pulling up at the red light** alors que j'allais m'arrêter au feu rouge; **pull up at** *or* **outside the main entrance** arrêtez-vous devant l'entrée principale; **to pull up short** s'arrêter net *ou* brusquement

(**b**) *Fam (ease up)* se détendre❑, se relâcher❑

(**c**) *(draw even)* rattraper; **to pull up with sb** rattraper qn; **Sun Boy is pulling up on the outside!** Sun Boy remonte à l'extérieur!

(**d**) *(improve → student, athlete, performance)* s'améliorer

pull-back *n Mil* repli *m*, retraite *f*

pull-down *adj (bench, counter)* à abattant

▸▸ *Comput* ***pull-down menu*** menu *m* déroulant; ***pull-down seat*** strapontin *m*; *Comput* ***pull-down window*** fenêtre *f* déroulante

pullet [ˈpʊlɪt] *n Orn* poulette *f*

pulley [ˈpʊlɪ] *n (wheel, device)* poulie *f*; *Tech (set of parallel wheels)* molette *f*

▸▸ ***pulley block*** palan *m*, moufle *f*; ***pulley wheel*** réa *m*, rouet *m*

pull-in *n Br Aut (café)* café *m* au bord de la route, ≃ restaurant *m* routier

pulling power [ˈpʊlɪŋ-] *n Br Fam* pouvoir *m* de séduction❑; **he thinks this new sports car will do wonders for his pulling power** il croit que sa nouvelle voiture de sport l'aidera à lever les nanas

Pullman [ˈpʊlmən] *(pl* **Pullmans**) *n* (**a**) *(sleeping car)* (voiture *f*) pullman *m* (**b**) *(train)* rapide *m* de nuit

▸▸ ***Pullman car, Pullman carriage*** voiture *f* pullman

pull-off *n Am Aut (rest area)* aire *f* de repos

pull-on *adj*

▸▸ ***pull-on boots*** bottes *fpl* (sans lacets); ***pull-on skirt*** jupe *f* à taille élastique

pull-out 1 *n* (**a**) *(magazine supplement)* supplément *m* détachable

(**b**) *(fold-out)* hors-texte *m inv (qui se déplie)*

(**c**) *(withdrawal → gen) & Mil* retrait *m*; *(→ of candidate)* désistement *m*; *(evacuation)* évacuation *f*; *Fin* **investment pull-out** désinvestissement *m*

(**d**) *Aviat* rétablissement *m*

2 *adj (magazine section)* détachable; *(map, advertising page)* hors texte *(inv)*; *(legs, shelf)* rétractable

▸▸ ***pull-out bed*** canapé-lit *m*; ***pull-out leaf*** *(on desk, table)* rallonge *f*

pullover [ˈpʊlˌəʊvə(r)] *n* pullover *m*, pull *m*

pullulate [ˈpʌljʊleɪt] *vi* (**a**) *Literary (teem, breed)* pulluler (**b**) *Bot (germinate)* germer

pull-up *n* (**a**) *Sport* traction *f (sur une barre ou sur des anneaux)*; **to do pull-ups** faire des tractions (**b**) *Br Aut (café)* café *m* au bord de la route, ≃ restaurant *m* routier

pulmonary [ˈpʌlmənərɪ] *adj Med* pulmonaire

▸▸ *Med* ***pulmonary embolism*** embolie *f* pulmonaire; *Med* ***pulmonary emphysema*** emphysème *m* pulmonaire; *Med* ***pulmonary oedema*** œdème *m* pulmonaire

pulp [pʌlp] **1** *n* (**a**) *(in fruit)* pulpe *f*

(**b**) *(for paper)* pâte *f* à papier, pulpe *f*; **pulp and paper mill** fabrique *f* de papier

(**c**) *(in tooth)* pulpe *f*

(**d**) *(mush)* bouillie *f*; **to beat** *or* **to smash to a pulp** réduire en bouillie *ou* en marmelade

(**e**) *Mining* pulpe *f*

2 *vt* (**a**) *(crush → wood)* réduire en pâte; *(→ fruit, vegetables)* réduire en pulpe; *(→ book)* mettre au pilon

(**b**) *(remove pulp from)* ôter la pulpe de

(**c**) *Anat (cavity, canal)* pulpaire

▸▸ ***pulp fiction*** romans *mpl* de gare; ***pulp magazine*** magazine *m* à sensation; ***pulp writer*** auteur *m* de romans de gare

pulped [pʌlpt] *adj (wood)* réduit en pâte; *(fruit, vegetables)* réduit en pulpe; *(book)* mis au pilon

pulpiness [ˈpʌlpɪnɪs] *n (of fruit)* nature *f* pulpeuse

pulpit [ˈpʊlpɪt] *n Rel* chaire *f*; *Fig* **the pulpit** *(clergy)* le clergé, les ecclésiastiques *mpl*

pulpwood [ˈpʌlpwʊd] *n* bois *m* à pâte

pulpy [ˈpʌlpɪ] *(compar* **pulpier**, *superl* **pulpiest**) *adj* (**a**) *(fruit, tissue)* pulpeux (**b**) *Fam Pej (novel, magazine)* à sensation❑

pulsar [ˈpʌlsɑː(r)] *n Astron* pulsar *m*

pulsate [pʌlˈseɪt] *vi* (**a**) *(throb → heart)* battre fort, palpiter; *(→ music, room)* vibrer; **the pulsating rhythm of jazz** le rythme syncopé du jazz; **the pulsating beat of the drums** le rythme lancinant des tambours (**b**) *Phys* subir des pulsations; *Astron (variable star)* pulser

pulsating [pʌlˈseɪtɪŋ] *adj* (**a**) *Physiol* battant, palpitant (**b**) *Elec* pulsatoire

▸▸ *Aviat* ***pulsating de-icer*** dégivreur *m* à impulsions; *Astron* ***pulsating star*** étoile *f* pulsante *ou* variable, céphéide *f*; *Biol* ***pulsating vacuole*** vacuole *f* contractile

pulsation [pʌlˈseɪʃən] *n (of heart, arteries)* battement *m*, pulsation *f*; *Astron & Phys* pulsation *f*

pulsatory [ˈpʌlsətərɪ] *adj (gen)* pulsatoire; *(insect, organ)* pulsatile

pulse [pʌls] **1** *n* (**a**) *Med* pouls *m*; *(single throb)* pulsation *f*; **he took my pulse** il m'a pris le pouls, il a pris mon pouls; **her pulse (rate) is a hundred** son pouls est à cent (pulsations par minute); **my pulse quickens when I see her** quand je la vois, j'ai le cœur qui bat plus fort; *Fig* **to have one's finger on the pulse** être à la page; *Fig* **to keep one's finger on the pulse** se tenir au courant

(**b**) *Electron & Phys (series)* série *f* d'impulsions; *(single)* impulsion *f*

(**c**) *(vibration)* rythme *m* régulier; **I felt the pulse of the ship's motors** je sentais le rythme régulier des moteurs du navire

(**d**) *(bustle, life)* animation *f*

(**e**) *Bot (plant)* légumineuse *f*; *Culin* **(dried) pulses** légumes *mpl* secs

2 *vi (blood)* battre; *(music, room)* vibrer; **a vein pulsed in his temple** une veine palpitait sur sa tempe; **the whole place pulsed with life** il y avait partout une animation extraordinaire; **the music pulsed inside my head** la musique résonnait dans ma tête

▸▸ *Electron* ***pulse modulation*** *(of one parameter)* modulation *f* d'impulsions; *(by pulse series)* modulation *f* par impulsions; ***pulse rate*** fréquence *f* du pouls; **an exercise that increases the pulse rate** un exercice qui fait accélérer le rythme cardiaque

pulse-jet engine *n Aviat* pulsoréacteur *m*

pulverization [ˌpʌlvəraɪˈzeɪʃən] *n* pulvérisation *f*

pulverize, -ise [ˈpʌlvəraɪz] *vt also Fig* pulvériser

puma [ˈpjuːmə] *(pl* **inv** *or* **pumas**) *n Zool* puma *m*

pumice [ˈpʌmɪs] **1** *n* ponce *f*

2 *vt* poncer, passer à la pierre ponce

▸▸ ***pumice stone*** pierre *f* ponce

pummel [ˈpʌməl] *(Br pt & pp* **pummelled**, *cont* **pummelling**, *Am pt & pp* **pummeled**, *cont* **pummeling**) *vt* (**a**) *(punch)* donner des coups de poing à, marteler à coups de poing; *Fig (thrash)* battre à plate(s) couture(s); **she pummelled his chest** elle lui martelait la poitrine à coups de poings *ou* de ses poings; **to be pummelled by artillery** être pilonné par les tirs d'artillerie

(**b**) *(in massage)* masser, palper

(**c**) *(knead → dough)* pétrir

pummelling, *Am* **pummeling** [ˈpʌməlɪŋ] *n* volée *f* de coups, raclée *f*; **to give sb a good pummelling** donner une bonne raclée à qn; **to get a pummelling** *(boxer)* se faire taper dessus; *Fig (team)* se faire battre à plate(s) couture(s)

pump [pʌmp] **1** *n* (**a**) *Tech* pompe *f*; **hand/water pump** pompe *f* à main/à eau

(**b**) *(shoe → for dancing)* chausson *m*; *(→ for gym)* (chaussure *f* de) tennis *m*

(**c**) *Am Fam (heart)* cœur❑ *m*, palpitant *m*

2 *vt* (**a**) *(liquid, gas)* pomper; **to pump sth out of sth** pomper *ou* aspirer qch de qch; **the water is pumped into a tank** l'eau est acheminée dans un réservoir au moyen d'une pompe; **to pump water into a cavity** amener de l'eau à la pompe dans une cavité; **the factory pumps its waste directly into the river** l'usine déverse ses déchets directement dans la rivière; **they pumped air into the football** ils ont gonflé le ballon de foot; **the heart's function is to pump blood around the body** le cœur a pour fonction de pomper le sang dans tout le corps; **coolant is pumped through the system** une pompe fait circuler le liquide de refroidissement dans le système; *Am* **to pump gas** travailler comme pompiste

(**b**) *Med* **to pump sb's stomach** faire un lavage d'estomac à qn; **he had to have** *or* **to get his stomach pumped** on a dû lui faire un lavage d'estomac

(**c**) *(inflate → tyre, ball etc)* gonfler

(**d**) *(move back and forth → pedal, handle)* appuyer sur *ou* actionner (plusieurs fois); **pump the brakes or they'll lock** freinez progressivement ou les freins se bloqueront; *Fig* **to pump sb's hand** secouer vigoureusement la main de qn; *Fam* **to pump iron** faire de la gonflette

(**e**) *Fam (shoot)* **to pump sb full of lead** cribler qn de plomb
(**f**) *Fam (money)* investir ❑; **he pumped a fortune into the business** il a investi une fortune dans cette affaire; **public money is being pumped into the area** la région reçoit d'importantes subventions du gouvernement ❑; **the government has pumped money into the project** le gouvernement a injecté des capitaux dans ce projet ❑
(**g**) *Fam (interrogate)* interroger ❑, tirer les vers du nez à; **they pumped her for information** ils l'ont cuisinée
(**h**) *Vulg (have sex with)* baiser, tringler
3 *vi* (**a**) *(machine, person)* pomper; *(heart)* battre fort
(**b**) *(liquid)* couler à flots, jaillir; **blood pumped from the wound** du sang coulait de la blessure
►► ***pump attendant*** pompiste *mf*; ***pump gun*** fusil *m* à pompe; *Econ* ***pump priming*** = relance de l'économie par injection de fonds publics; ***pump room*** *(building)* pavillon *m*; *(room)* buvette *f (dans une station thermale)*

►**pump in** *vt sep* (**a**) *(liquid, gas)* refouler; **the village pumps in water from the river** l'eau du village est amenée de la rivière à l'aide d'un système de pompage
(**b**) *Fam (funds, capital)* investir ❑, injecter ❑

►**pump out** **1** *vt sep* (**a**) *(liquid, gas)* pomper; *(stomach)* vider; **it took two hours to pump the bilge out** il a fallu deux heures pour pomper *ou* écoper l'eau de la cale
(**b**) *Fam Pej (mass-produce → music, graduates, products)* produire ❑; *(→ books, essays)* produire à la chaîne ❑, pondre en série ❑
2 *vi (liquid, blood)* couler à flots

►**pump up** *vt sep* (**a**) *(liquid, mixture)* pomper
(**b**) *(inflate)* gonfler
(**c**) *Am Fam (excite)* **to be all pumped up** être tout excité ❑

pump-action shotgun *n* fusil *m* à pompe

pumped [pʌmpt] *adj* (**a**) *(gen)* pompé; *Electron (vacuum tube)* **pumped (out)** vidé (**b**) *Fam (exhausted)* **pumped (out)** épuisé ❑, éreinté, pompé (**c**) *Am Fam (excited)* surexcité ❑; *(enthusiastic)* emballé
►► *Electron* ***pumped rectifier*** redresseur *m* à vide entretenu

pumpernickel ['pʌmpənɪkəl] *n* ≃ pain *m* noir, pumpernickel *m*

pump-handle *vt Fam (shake hand of)* serrer vigoureusement la main à ❑

pumping station ['pʌmpɪŋ-] *n (building)* station *f* de pompage; *(machinery)* installation *f* de pompage

pumpkin ['pʌmpkɪn] **1** *n* potiron *m*; *(smaller)* citrouille *f*
2 *comp (soup)* au potiron
►► ***pumpkin pie*** tarte *f* au potiron

pumpkinseed ['pʌmpkɪn,siːd] *n* (**a**) *Bot* graine *f* de potiron (**b**) *Ich* perche-soleil *f*, calicoba *m*

pun [pʌn] (*pt & pp* **punned,** *cont* **punning**) **1** *n* calembour *m*, jeu *m* de mots
2 *vi* faire des calembours, faire des jeux de mots;

Punch [pʌntʃ] *pr n* = Polichinelle; **Punch-and-Judy show** ≃ (spectacle *m* de) guignol *m*; **as pleased as Punch** heureux comme un roi

PUNCH AND JUDY

En Grande-Bretagne, le "Punch and Judy show" est un spectacle pour enfants semblable aux Guignols en France. Il est souvent présenté dans un jardin public ou sur une plage. On y retrouve Punch le bossu, sa femme Judy avec laquelle il se querelle constamment, et leur chien Toby.

punch [pʌntʃ] **1** *n* (**a**) *(blow)* coup *m* de poing; **he gave him a punch on the chin/in the stomach** il lui a donné un coup de poing dans le menton/dans l'estomac; *Fam* **to pack a powerful** *or* **mean punch** *(hit hard)* cogner dur ❑; *Boxing* avoir du punch ❑; *(drink, cocktail)* être costaud; *(film)* être percutant ❑
(**b**) *Fig (effectiveness → of person)* punch *m inv*; *(of speech, cartoon, play)* mordant *m*; **find a slogan with a bit more punch** trouvez un slogan un peu plus accrocheur
(**c**) *(for holes → in paper)* perforateur *m inv*; *(→ in metal)* poinçonneuse *f*; *(for tickets → by hand)* poinçonneuse *f*; *(→ machine)* composteur *m*; *(steel rod, die)* poinçon *m*
(**d**) *(for stamping design)* machine *f* à estamper
(**e**) *(for nails, bolts)* chasse-clou *m*
(**f**) *(drink)* punch *m*
2 *vt* (**a**) *(hit → once)* donner un coup de poing à; *(→ repeatedly)* marteler à coups de poing; **he punched him on the chin/nose** il lui a donné un coup de poing au menton/sur le nez; **he punched him in** *or* **on the jaw** il lui a donné un coup de poing dans les gencives; **he punched the door** il a martelé la porte à coups de poing; **to punch the air** lever le bras en signe de victoire
(**b**) *(key, button)* appuyer sur; **I punched the return key** j'ai appuyé sur la touche retour
(**c**) *(pierce → ticket)* poinçonner; *(→ in machine)* composter; *(→ paper, computer card)* perforer; *(→ sheet metal)* poinçonner; **to punch a hole in sth** faire un trou dans qch; **to punch the time clock** *or* **one's time card** pointer
(**d**) *(stamp)* estamper
(**e**) *Am* **to punch cattle** être cowboy
3 *vi (strike)* frapper; **no punching!** pas de coups de poing!; **they were punching away at each other** ils se donnaient des coups de poing
►► ***punch bowl*** *(container)* coupe *f* à punch; *Br Geog (between two hills)* cuvette *f*; *Am Comput* ***punch card*** carte *f* perforée; ***punch line*** chute *f (d'une histoire drôle)*; **I've forgotten the punch line** j'ai oublié la chute *ou* comment ça finit

►**punch in** **1** *vt sep* (**a**) *(enter → code, number)* taper, composer; *(→ figures, data)* introduire; **punch your number in** composez votre numéro
(**b**) *(knock in → door)* défoncer (à coups de poing); *(→ nails)* enfoncer; *Fam* **I'll punch your face** *or* **head** *or* **teeth in!** je vais te casser la figure!
2 *vi Am (on time clock)* pointer (en arrivant)

►**punch out** **1** *vt sep* (**a**) *(enter → code, number)* taper, composer
(**b**) *(cut out → form, pattern)* découper; **the holes are punched out by a machine** les trous sont faits par une machine
(**c**) *(remove → nail, bolt)* enlever au chasse-clou
(**d**) *(stamp)* estamper, emboutir
(**e**) *Fam Br* **to punch sb's lights out,** *Am* **to punch sb out** *(beat up)* tabasser qn, amocher qn; *Am* **to get punched out** se faire tabasser *ou* amocher; *Am* **to punch it out with sb** échanger des coups de poing avec qn ❑
2 *vi* (**a**) *Am (on time clock)* pointer (en partant)
(**b**) *Fam (pilot)* s'éjecter

punchbag ['pʌntʃbæg] *n Br Sport* sac *m* de sable, punching-bag *m*; *Fig (victim)* souffre-douleur *m inv*

punchball ['pʌntʃbɔːl] *n Sport* (**a**) *Br (used for training)* punching-ball *m* (**b**) *Am (game)* = version simplifiée du base-ball, qui se joue sans batte et avec une balle moins dure

punch-drunk *adj (boxer)* groggy *(inv)*; *Fig* abruti, sonné; **I was punch-drunk after seeing four films in a row** après avoir vu quatre films d'affilée, j'étais complètement abruti

punched card [pʌntʃt-] *n Br* carte *f* perforée

puncher ['pʌntʃə(r)] *n* (**a**) *Tech (person → of sheet metal)* poinçonneur(euse) *m,f*, perceur(euse) *m,f*; *(→ in metalworking)* estampeur(euse) *m,f* (**b**) *Tech (device → for sheet metal)* poinçonneuse *f*; *(→ for cardboard, leather)* emporte-pièce *m inv*; *Comput (for cards, tapes)* perforatrice *f* (**c**) *Boxing* puncheur *m* (**d**) *Am* **cow puncher** cow-boy *m*

Punchinello [,pʌntʃɪ'neləʊ] *pr n* Polichinelle

punching ['pʌntʃɪŋ] *n*
►► *Am* ***punching bag*** *Sport* sac *m* de sable, punching-bag *m*; *Fig (victim)* souffre-douleur *m inv*; *Am Sport* ***punching ball*** punching-ball *m*

punchtape reader ['pʌntʃteɪp-] *n* lecteur *m* de ruban perforé

punch-up *n Fam* bagarre ❑ *f*; **they had a punch-up** ils se sont bagarrés

punchy ['pʌntʃɪ] (*compar* **punchier,** *superl* **punchiest**) *adj Fam* (**a**) *(slogan, speech, novel)* percutant ❑; **he produced a punchy piece of writing on the election campaign** il a écrit un texte percutant sur la campagne électorale (**b**) *(boxer)* groggy ❑ *(inv)*; *Fig* abruti, sonné

punctilio [pʌŋk'tɪlɪəʊ] (*pl* **punctilios**) *n* (**a**) *(attitude)* formalisme *m* (**b**) *(point)* formalité *f*

punctilious [pʌŋk'tɪlɪəs] *adj* pointilleux, méticuleux

punctiliously [pʌŋk'tɪlɪəslɪ] *adv* pointilleusement, de façon pointilleuse

punctiliousness [pʌŋk'tɪlɪəsnɪs] *n* grande attention *f* portée aux détails, méticulosité *f*

punctual ['pʌŋktʃʊəl] *adj (bus)* à l'heure; *(person)* ponctuel; **be punctual for the interview** soyez à l'heure pour l'entretien

punctuality [,pʌŋktʃʊ'ælətɪ] *n* ponctualité *f*, exactitude *f*

punctually ['pʌŋktʃʊəlɪ] *adv (begin, arrive)* à l'heure; *(pay)* ponctuellement; **the flight left punctually at nine/at noon** le vol est parti à neuf heures pile/à midi juste

punctuate ['pʌŋktʃʊeɪt] *vt* (**a**) *(sentence etc)* ponctuer (**b**) *Fig* **a speech punctuated with anecdotes/applause** un discours ponctué *ou* agrémenté d'anecdotes/entrecoupé d'applaudissements; **a landscape punctuated with clumps of trees** un paysage avec ça et là un bouquet d'arbres

punctuation [,pʌŋktʃʊ'eɪʃən] *n* ponctuation *f*
►► ***punctuation mark*** signe *m* de ponctuation

puncture ['pʌŋktʃə(r)] **1** *n* (**a**) *(in tyre, ball, balloon)* crevaison *f*; **one of the front tyres had a puncture** un des pneus avant était crevé; **I had a puncture on the way to work** j'ai crevé en allant travailler; **the garage has repaired the puncture** le garage a réparé le pneu crevé
(**b**) *(gen → hole)* perforation *f*
(**c**) *Med* ponction *f*
2 *vt* (**a**) *(gen)* perforer; **the bullet punctured his lung** la balle lui a perforé le poumon
(**b**) *(tyre, ball, balloon)* crever
(**c**) *Fig (pride, self-esteem)* blesser, porter atteinte à
3 *vi* crever
►► ***puncture patch*** *(for repairing inner tube)* rustine® *f*; ***puncture repair kit*** trousse *f* de réparation pour crevaisons; *Med* ***puncture wound*** blessure *f* pénétrante

pundit ['pʌndɪt] *n* (**a**) *(expert)* expert *m (qui pontifie)* (**b**) *(Brahmin)* pandit *m*

Pune = **Poona**

pungency ['pʌndʒənsɪ] *n* (**a**) *(of smell, taste, food → sourness)* âcreté *f*; *(→ spiciness)* piquant *m* (**b**) *(of wit, remark)* causticité *f*, mordant *m*

pungent ['pʌndʒənt] *adj* (**a**) *(smell, taste → sour)* âcre; *(→ spicy)* piquant (**b**) *(wit, remark)* caustique, mordant

pungently ['pʌndʒəntlɪ] *adv* d'une manière piquante

Punic ['pjuːnɪk] *adj* punique
►► *Hist* ***the Punic Wars*** les guerres *fpl* puniques

puniness ['pjuːnɪnɪs] *n* faiblesse *f*

punish ['pʌnɪʃ] *vt* (**a**) *(person, crime)* punir; **to punish sb for having done sth** *or* **for doing sth** punir qn pour avoir fait qch; **they will be punished for their mistakes** ils seront punis pour leurs erreurs; **such offences are punished by imprisonment** ce genre de délit est passible d'une peine de prison
(**b**) *Fam Fig (opponent, enemy)* malmener ❑; *(engine)* fatiguer ❑, forcer ❑; **they punished the French defence** ils ont malmené *ou* mis à mal la défense française; **he really punishes himself in training** il se donne à fond à l'entraînement ❑; *Hum* **to punish a bottle of wine/whisky** faire un sort à une bouteille de vin/de whisky

punishable ['pʌnɪʃəbəl] *adj* punissable; **punishable by prison/a £50 fine** passible d'emprisonnement/d'une amende de 50 livres
►► ***punishable offence*** délit *m*

punisher ['pʌnɪʃə(r)] *n* punisseur(euse) *m,f*; *Fam Boxing* boxeur(euse) *m,f* qui frappe dur ❑

punishing ['pʌnɪʃɪŋ] **1** *n* (**a**) *(punishment)* punition *f*
(**b**) *Fam Fig* **to take a punishing** *(opponent, team)* se faire malmener ❑; *Hum (bottle)* en prendre un coup; **the car's suspension/this bottle of wine has taken a punishing** la suspension de la voiture/cette bouteille de vin en a pris un coup
2 *adj (heat, climb, effort)* exténuant; *(defeat)*

écrasant; **a punishing race** une course exténuante; **a punishing schedule** un emploi du temps très éprouvant

punishment ['pʌnɪʃmənt] *n* (**a**) *(act of punishing)* punition *f*, châtiment *m*

(**b**) *(means of punishment)* punition *f*, châtiment *m*, sanction *f*; *Law* peine *f*; **I had to dig the garden as a punishment** comme punition, j'ai dû bêcher le jardin; **to take one's punishment like a man** recevoir sa punition sans broncher; **no punishment is harsh enough for them** aucune peine n'est assez sévère pour eux; **to make the punishment fit the crime** adapter le châtiment au délit

(**c**) *Fam Fig* **to take a lot of punishment** *(boxer)* encaisser; *(army, warship, tank, car, boat etc)* être malmené❑; *(shoes, clothes)* être soumis à rude épreuve; **the landing gear can take a lot of punishment** même soumis à rude épreuve, le train d'atterrissage tiendra le coup

punitive ['pju:nɪtɪv] *adj* (**a**) *(expedition, method)* punitif (**b**) *(measures, tax)* écrasant; **to take punitive action** avoir recours à des sanctions

►► *Law* ***punitive damages*** dommages et intérêts *mpl* dissuasifs; ***punitive raid*** expédition *f* punitive

Punjab [,pʌn'dʒɑ:b] *n* **the Punjab** le Pendjab; **in the Punjab** au Pendjab

Punjabi [,pʌn'dʒɑ:bɪ] **1** *n* (**a**) *(person)* Pendjabi *mf* (**b**) *Ling* pendjabi *m*

2 *adj* pendjabi, du Pendjab

punk [pʌŋk] **1** *n* (**a**) *(music, fashion)* punk *m* (**b**) *(punk rocker)* punk *mf* (**c**) *Am very Fam (worthless person)* vaurien(enne)❑ *m,f*; *(hoodlum)* voyou❑ *m*

2 *adj* (**a**) *(music, fashion)* punk *(inv)* (**b**) *Am Fam (worthless)* nul (**c**) *Am very Fam (ill)* **he's feeling kind of punk** il se sent un peu nase

►► ***punk rock*** punk *m*; ***punk rocker*** punk *mf*

punka, punkah ['pʌŋkə] *n (in India)* panca *m*, panka *m*, punka *m*

►► ***punka wallah*** tireur *m* de panca

punky ['pʌŋkɪ] *adj* punk *(inv)*

punnet ['pʌnɪt] *n Br* barquette *f*

punster ['pʌnstə(r)] *n* faiseur(euse) *m,f* de calembours *ou* de jeux de mots

punt¹ [pʌnt] **1** *n* (**a**) *(boat)* = longue barque à fond plat manœuvrée à la perche (**b**) *Sport (kick)* coup *m* de pied de volée (**c**) *Br Fam (bet)* **to have a punt (on sth)** parier (sur qch)❑

2 *vt* (**a**) *(boat)* faire avancer à la perche (**b**) *Sport (kick)* envoyer d'un coup de pied de volée

3 *vi* (**a**) *(in boat)* **to go punting** faire un tour en barque (**b**) *Br Fam (gamble)* jouer❑

►► ***punt pole*** perche *f (pour la conduite d'un bateau à fond plat)*

punt² [pʊnt] *n (currency)* livre *f* irlandaise

punter ['pʌntə(r)] *n Br Fam* (**a**) *(gambler)* parieur(euse)❑ *m,f* (**b**) *(consumer, customer)* client(e)❑ *m,f*; **the average punter** *(typical customer)* le client type *ou* moyen; *(typical person)* l'homme *m* de la rue❑; **the punters** le public❑ (**c**) *St Exch (speculator)* boursicoteur(euse)❑ *m,f*, boursicotier(ère)❑ *m,f* (**d**) *(prostitute's client)* micheton *m*

puny ['pju:nɪ] *(compar* **punier**, *superl* **puniest**) *adj* (**a**) *(frail → person, animal, plant)* malingre, chétif; *(→ arms, legs)* maigre, grêle (**b**) *(feeble → effort)* pitoyable; *(→ argument, excuse)* piètre

pup [pʌp] *(pt & pp* **pupped**, *cont* **pupping**) **1** *n* (**a**) *(young dog)* chiot *m*; *(young animal)* jeune animal *m*; **spaniel pup** jeune *ou* petit épagneul *m*; **seal pup** jeune *ou* bébé phoque *m*; **to be in pup** *(bitch)* être pleine; *Br Fam Fig* **to be sold a pup** se faire avoir

(**b**) *Fam (youth → self-important)* freluquet *m*; *(→ inexperienced)* blanc-bec *m*; **you cheeky young pup!** espèce de petit impertinent!

2 *vi* mettre bas

►► ***pup tent*** canadienne *f*

pupa ['pju:pə] *(pl* **pupas** *or* **pupae** [-pi:]) *n Entom* nymphe *f*, chrysalide *f*, pupe *f*

pupal ['pju:pəl] *adj Entom* de nymphe, de chrysalide, de pupe

pupate [pju:'peɪt] *vi Entom* se métamorphoser (en nymphe *ou* en chrysalide)

pupation [pju:'peɪʃən] *n Entom* nymphose *f*, pupation *f*, pupaison *f*

pupil ['pju:pəl] **1** *n* (**a**) *Sch* élève *mf* (**b**) *Law (minor ward)* pupille *mf* (**c**) *Anat* pupille *f*

2 *comp Sch (participation, power)* des élèves

pupilage, pupillage ['pju:pɪlɪdʒ] *n Law* pupillarité *f*; **a child in pupilage** un enfant en pupille *ou* en tutelle

pupilometer [,pju:pɪ'lɒmɪtə(r)] *n* pupillomètre *m*

puppet ['pʌpɪt] **1** *n* (**a**) *(gen)* marionnette *f*; *(string puppet)* fantoche *m*, pantin *m* (**b**) *Fig* pantin *m*, fantoche *m*

2 *comp Pol (government, president)* fantoche

►► ***puppet show*** (spectacle *m* de) marionnettes *fpl*; ***puppet theatre*** théâtre *m* de marionnettes

puppeteer [,pʌpɪ'tɪə(r)] *n* marionnettiste *mf*

puppetry ['pʌpɪtrɪ] *n (art → of making)* fabrication *f* de marionnettes; *(→ of manipulating)* art *m* du marionnettiste

puppy ['pʌpɪ] *(pl* **puppies**) *n* chiot *m*

►► ***puppy farm*** chenil *m*, élevage *m* de chiens; *Br* ***puppy fat*** *(UNCOUNT)* rondeurs *fpl* de l'adolescence; ***puppy love*** amourette *f*, amour *m* d'adolescent; **it's only puppy love** ce n'est qu'une amourette *ou* qu'un amour de jeunesse

puppyish ['pʌpɪɪʃ] *adj* impertinent, fat

Purana [pʊ'rɑ:nə] *n Literature* Purana *m*

purblind ['pɜ:blaɪnd] *adj* (**a**) *(poorly sighted)* malvoyant (**b**) *Literary (obtuse)* obtus, borné

purchasable ['pɜ:tʃəsəbəl] *adj* achetable

purchase ['pɜ:tʃəs] **1** *vt* acheter; **to purchase sth from sb** acheter qch à qn; **to purchase sth for sb, to purchase sb sth** acheter qch à *ou* pour qn; **to purchase sth on credit** acheter qch à crédit; *Acct* **to purchase a debt** racheter une créance

2 *n* (**a**) *(act of buying, thing bought)* achat *m*; **to make a purchase** faire un achat; **date of purchase** date *f* d'achat

(**b**) *(of company)* rachat *m*

(**c**) *(grip)* prise *f*; **she managed to gain (a) purchase on a small ledge** elle parvint à trouver une prise sur une petite corniche

3 *vi* acheter; **now is the time to purchase** c'est maintenant qu'il faut acheter

►► *Acct* ***purchase account*** compte *m* d'achats; *Am Acct* ***purchase accounting*** = méthode de comptabilité utilisée lors de l'acquistion d'une entreprise, dans laquelle les résultats de la filiale n'apparaissent pas dans le bilan de la société mère; *Mktg* ***purchase behaviour*** comportement *m* d'achat; *Acct* ***purchase budget*** budget *m* des approvisionnements; ***purchase cost*** coût *m* d'achat; *Acct* ***purchase of debts*** rachat *m* des créances; *Mktg* ***purchase decision*** décision *f* d'achat; *Mktg* ***purchase diary*** relevé *m* d'achat journalier; *Acct* ***purchase entry*** écriture *f* d'achats; *Mktg* ***purchase environment*** environnement *m* d'achat; *Mktg* ***purchase frequency*** fréquence *f* d'achat; *Acct* ***purchase invoice*** facture *f* d'achat; *Acct* ***purchase invoice ledger*** journal *m* factures-fournisseurs; *Acct* ***purchase ledger*** (grand-) livre *m* d'achats, journal *m* des achats; *Acct* ***purchase method*** méthode *f* d'achat; *Fin* ***purchase note*** bordereau *m* d'achat; ***purchase order*** *Fin (for goods, service)* bon *m* de commande; *St Exch (for shares)* ordre *m* d'achat; ***purchase price*** prix *m* d'achat; *Fin* ***purchase tax*** taxe *f* à l'achat; *Fin* ***purchase value*** valeur *f* d'achat; *Mktg* ***purchase volume*** volume *m* d'achat

purchaser ['pɜ:tʃəsə(r)] *n* acheteur(euse) *m,f*

►► *Mktg* ***purchaser behaviour*** comportement *m* de l'acheteur

purchasing ['pɜ:tʃəsɪŋ] *n* achat *m*; *(of company)* rachat *m*

►► *Am* ***purchasing agent*** acheteur(euse) *m,f*; *Mktg* ***purchasing behaviour*** comportement *m* d'achat; *Mktg* ***purchasing behaviour model*** modèle *m* de comportement d'achat; ***purchasing costs*** frais *mpl* de passation de commande; *Mktg* ***purchasing decision*** décision *f* d'achat; ***purchasing department*** service *m* des achats; ***purchasing manager*** chef *m* des achats; *Mktg* ***purchasing motivator*** mobile *m* d'achat; *Fin* ***purchasing power*** capacité *f* d'achat, pouvoir *m* d'achat; *Mktg* ***purchasing process*** processus *m* d'achat; ***purchasing rights*** droits *mpl* d'achat

purdah ['pɜ:də] *n* = chez certains peuples hindous et musulmans, système qui astreint les femmes à une vie retirée; **to be in purdah** être reclus; *Fig* vivre en reclus

pure [pjʊə(r)] *adj* (**a**) *(unadulterated, untainted)* pur; **a pure silk tie** une cravate (en) pure soie; **pure new wool** laine *f* vierge; **pure air** air *m* pur; **pure water** eau *f* pure; **pure white** blanc *m* immaculé; **the pure tones of the flute** le son clair *ou* pur de la flûte

(**b**) *(chaste → person, mind, life)* pur; **pure thoughts** pensées *fpl* pures; *Bible* **the pure in heart** ceux qui ont le cœur pur; **as pure as the driven snow** *(not guilty)* blanc (blanche) comme neige; *(chaste)* innocent comme l'enfant *ou* l'agneau qui vient de naître

(**c**) *(science, maths, research)* pur

(**d**) *(as intensifier)* pur; **by pure chance** par (un) pur hasard; **it's the truth, pure and simple** c'est la vérité pure et simple

►► *Mktg* ***pure competition*** concurrence *f* pure

pure-blood 1 *adj (horse)* pur-sang *inv*

2 *n (horse)* pur-sang *m inv*

pure-blooded *adj* pur-sang *(inv)*

purebred ['pjʊəbred] *adj* de race (pure); *(horse)* pur-sang *(inv)*

puree, purée ['pjʊəreɪ] *(pt & pp* **pureed** *or* **puréed**, *cont* **pureeing** *or* **puréeing**) **1** *n* purée *f*; **tomato puree** *(gen)* purée *f* de tomates; *(in tube)* concentré *m* de tomates

2 *vt* réduire en purée; **pureed carrots** purée *f* de carottes

purely ['pjʊəlɪ] *adj* purement; **purely and simply** purement et simplement; **ours is a purely professional relationship** nos rapports sont purement *ou* strictement professionnels; **it was purely by chance that we met** notre rencontre n'était qu'un pur hasard; **purely routine questioning** interrogatoire *m* de simple routine

pureness ['pjʊənɪs] *n* pureté *f*

purfle ['pɜ:fəl] **1** *n Sewing* bordure *f* brodée, liseré *m*

2 *vt* (**a**) *Sewing (garment)* orner d'une bordure brodée, liserer (**b**) *Archit* orner, embellir (**with** de)

purfling ['pɜ:flɪŋ] *n (on violin)* filet *m*

purgation [pɜ:'geɪʃən] *n* (**a**) *Med (of intestine)* purge *f* (**b**) *Rel (in purgatory)* purgation *f* de l'âme

purgative ['pɜ:gətɪv] **1** *n* purgatif *m*

2 *adj* purgatif

purgatorial [pɜ:gə'tɔ:rɪəl] *adj Rel* du purgatoire; *(purifying)* purificateur, purifiant

purgatory ['pɜ:gətərɪ] *n Rel* purgatoire *m*; *Fig* enfer *m*; **the souls in purgatory** les âmes du purgatoire, les âmes en peine; **rush hour is absolute purgatory!** les heures de pointe sont un véritable enfer!

purge [pɜ:dʒ] **1** *vt* (**a**) *Pol (party, organization)* purger, épurer; *(undesirable elements)* éliminer; **the extreme right was purged from the party** le parti s'est débarrassé de son extrême droite

(**b**) *(free, rid)* débarrasser, délivrer; **purge your mind of such morbid ideas** chassez ces idées morbides de votre esprit; *Rel* **to purge oneself of** *or* **from sin** se laver de ses péchés

(**c**) *Law (clear)* disculper, innocenter; *Am Law* **to purge one's contempt** faire amende honorable *(pour outrage aux magistrats)*

(**d**) *Med (bowels)* purger

2 *n* (**a**) *(gen) & Pol* purge *f*, épuration *f*; **he carried out a purge of the army** il procéda à une purge au sein de l'armée

(**b**) *Med* purge *f*

purging ['pɜ:dʒɪŋ] *n Med (of body)* purge *f*, purification *f*; *Pol (of party, organization)* épuration *f*

purification [,pjʊərɪfɪ'keɪʃən] *n* (**a**) *(of water, oil)* épuration *f* (**b**) *Rel* purification *f*; **the Purification (of the Virgin Mary)** la Purification (de la Vierge Marie)

purifier ['pjʊərɪfaɪə(r)] *n (device → for water, oil)* épurateur *m*; *(→ for air, atmosphere)* purificateur *m*, assainisseur *m*

purify ['pjʊərɪfaɪ] *(pt & pp* **purified**) *vt (water, oil)* épurer; *(air, soul, mind)* purifier; *(blood)* dépurer

purifying ['pjʊərɪfaɪɪŋ] *adj* purifiant, purificatoire, purificateur

purine ['pjʊəri:n] *n Chem* purine *f*

►► ***purine base*** base *f* purique

purism ['pjʊərɪzəm] *n* purisme *m*

purist ['pjʊərɪst] **1** *adj* puriste

2 *n* puriste *mf*; **a linguistic purist** un (une) puriste en matière de linguistique

puritan ['pjʊərɪtən] **1** *n* puritain(e) *m,f*

2 *adj* puritain

3 Puritan *Rel* **1** *n* puritain(e) *m,f* **2** *adj* puritain

THE PURITANS

Protestants anglais radicaux apparus au XVIème siècle, dont beaucoup se réclamaient du calvinisme, les puritains souhaitaient purger l'Église anglicane de tout rite catholique. Soutenus par la Chambre des communes mais rejetés par Elizabeth Ière, ils réussirent à s'imposer pendant la période du Protectorat de Cromwell.

puritanical [,pjʊərɪ'tænɪkəl] *adj* puritain, de puritain

puritanism ['pjʊərɪtənɪzəm] **1** *n* puritanisme *m*

2 Puritanism *n Rel* puritanisme *m*

purity ['pjʊərɪtɪ] *n* pureté *f*; **degree of purity** *(of water etc)* (degré *m* de) pureté *f*; *(of gold)* titre *m*

purl[1] [pɜːl] *Knitting* **1** *n* maille *f* à l'envers

2 *vt* tricoter à l'envers; **knit one, purl one** une maille à l'endroit, une maille à l'envers

►► ***purl stitch*** maille *f* à l'envers

purl[2] *Literary* **1** *n (of stream, brook)* doux murmure *m*, gazouillement *m*, gazouillis *m*

2 *vi (stream, brook)* murmurer, gazouiller

purler ['pɜːlə(r)] *n Br Fam Old-fashioned* **to come** *or* **to take a purler** se casser la figure

purlieus ['pɜːljuːz] *npl Literary* alentours *mpl*, environs *mpl*; **in the purlieus of** aux alentours de, dans les environs de

purlin ['pɜːlɪn] *n Constr* panne *f*, ventrière *f*

purloin [pɜː'lɔɪn] *vt Formal or Hum* dérober, voler

purple ['pɜːpəl] **1** *n* (**a**) *(colour → gen)* violet *m*; *(→ reddish)* pourpre *m*

(**b**) *(dye, cloth)* pourpre *f*

(**c**) *(high rank)* **the purple** la pourpre

2 *adj* (**a**) *(in colour → gen)* violet; *(→ reddish)* pourpre; **he turned** *or* **went purple (with rage)** il est devenu cramoisi (de rage)

(**b**) *(prose)* emphatique, ampoulé

►► *Entom* ***purple emperor*** grand mars *m* (changeant); *Orn* ***purple gallinule*** poule *f* sultane; *Mil* ***Purple Heart*** = médaille décernée aux blessés de guerre de l'armée américaine; *Fam Drugs slang* ***purple heart*** pilule *f* d'amphétamine; *Am Orn* ***purple heron*** héron *m* pourpre; *Orn* ***purple martin*** hirondelle *f* pourprée; *Br* ***purple passage, purple patch*** *(of writing)* morceau *m* de bravoure; *(period of success)* **he's been going through a purple patch recently: he's won five out of the last six tournaments he's entered** il est dans une bonne période: il a gagné cinq des six tournois auxquels il a participé; *Orn* ***purple sandpiper*** bécasseau *m* maritime

purplish ['pɜːpəlɪʃ], **purply** ['pɜːpəlɪ] *adj (gen)* violacé, violâtre; *(reddish)* pourpré, purpurin; *(of the face)* cramoisi; **purplish red** rouge violacé; **purplish blue** hyacinthe *(inv)*

purport *Formal* **1** *vt* [pə'pɔːt] *(claim)* prétendre; *(of film, book)* se vouloir; **he purports to be an expert** il prétend être un expert, il se fait passer pour un expert; **her book purports to be the definitive work on the French Revolution** son livre se veut la somme de ce qui a été écrit sur la Révolution française

2 *n* ['pɜːpɔːt] signification *f*, teneur *f*

purported [pə'pɔːtɪd] *adj Formal* prétendu

purportedly [pə'pɔːtɪdlɪ] *adv Formal* prétendument

purpose ['pɜːpəs] **1** *n* (**a**) *(objective, reason)* but *m*, objet *m*; **what's the purpose of your visit?** quel est le but *ou* l'objet de votre visite?; **for** *or* **with the purpose of doing sth** dans l'intention *ou* le but de faire qch; **he buys real estate for tax purposes** il investit dans l'immobilier pour des raisons fiscales; **it suits my purposes to stay here** j'ai de bonnes raisons de rester ici; **to do sth with a purpose in mind** *or* **for a purpose** faire qch dans un but précis; **for this purpose** dans ce but, à cet effet; **but that's the whole purpose of the exercise!** mais tout l'intérêt de l'exercice est là!; **to have a sense of purpose** être motivé; **to give sb a sense of purpose** motiver qn; **his life lacked any real sense of purpose** sa vie était dépourvue de but précis; **to have a purpose in life** avoir un but dans la vie; **her remarks were to the purpose/not to the purpose** ses remarques étaient pertinentes/hors de propos

(**b**) *(use, function)* usage *m*; *(end, result)* fin *f*; **what is the purpose of this room/object?** à quoi sert cette pièce/cet objet?; **the hangar wasn't built for that purpose** le hangar n'était pas destiné à cet usage; **for all purposes** à toutes fins, à tous usages; **intended for practical purposes** destiné à des usages pratiques; **for our purposes** pour ce que nous voulons faire; **for the purposes of this demonstration** pour les besoins de cette démonstration; **for the purpose of this article...** *(in lease, contract etc)* au sens du présent article...; **£5,000 will be enough for present purposes** 5000 livres suffiront à couvrir nos besoins actuels; **the funds are to be used for humanitarian purposes** les fonds seront utilisés à des fins humanitaires; **intended purpose** *(of building, amount of money)* destination *f*, affectation *f*; **they were never used for their intended purpose** ils n'ont jamais servi à l'usage auquel on les destinait; **does it serve any useful purpose?** est-ce que ça sert à quelque chose?; **to serve no purpose** ne servir à rien; **this will suit** *or* **serve your purpose** cela fera votre affaire; **once she had served her purpose they abandoned her** une fois qu'elle eut tenu son rôle, ils l'abandonnèrent; **the money will be put** *or* **used to good purpose** l'argent sera bien employé; **he will use his knowledge to good purpose there** il pourra y mettre à profit ses connaissances; **we are arguing to no purpose** nous discutons inutilement; **my efforts had been to no purpose** mes efforts étaient restés vains; **the negotiations have been to little purpose** les négociations n'ont pas abouti à grand-chose

(**c**) *(determination)* résolution *f*, détermination *f*; **she has great strength of purpose** elle a une volonté de fer, c'est quelqu'un de très déterminé

2 *vt Literary* **to purpose to do sth** *or* **doing sth** se proposer de faire qch

3 on purpose *adv* exprès; **I did it on purpose** je l'ai fait exprès; **I avoided the subject on purpose** j'ai fait exprès d'éviter *ou* j'ai délibérément évité la question

purpose-built *adj Br* construit *ou* conçu pour un usage spécifique; **a purpose-built conference centre** un centre de conférence entièrement conçu pour cet usage

►► ***purpose-built flat*** = appartement dans un immeuble (par opposition à une "conversion"); **purpose-built flats for the disabled** appartements *mpl* spécialement adaptés aux besoins des handicapés

purposeful ['pɜːpəsfʊl] *adj (person)* résolu, déterminé; *(look, walk)* résolu, décidé; *(act)* réfléchi

purposefully ['pɜːpəsfʊlɪ] *adv (for a reason)* dans un but précis, délibérément; *(determinedly)* d'un air résolu; **she walked forward purposefully** elle avança d'un pas résolu

purposefulness ['pɜːpəsfʊlnɪs] *n* détermination *f*

purposeless ['pɜːpəslɪs] *adj (life)* sans but, vide de sens; *(act, violence)* gratuit

purposelessness ['pɜːpəslɪsnɪs] *n (of life)* absence *f* de but; *(of act, violence)* gratuité *f*

purposely ['pɜːpəslɪ] *adv* exprès, délibérément; **they purposely didn't invite her** ils ont fait exprès de ne pas l'inviter

purposive ['pɜːpəsɪv] *adj Formal* délibéré

►► *Mktg* ***purposive sample*** échantillon *m* empirique; *Mktg* ***purposive sampling*** échantillonnage *m* empirique

purpurin ['pɜːpjʊrɪn] *n Chem* purpurine *f*

purr [pɜː(r)] **1** *vi (cat, engine)* ronronner

2 *vt* susurrer; **"do have another drink," she purred** "vous prendrez bien encore un verre," susurra-t-elle

3 *n (of cat)* ronronnement *m*, ronron *m*; *(of engine)* ronronnement *m*

purring ['pɜːrɪŋ] **1** *n (UNCOUNT) (of cat)* ronronnement *m*, ronron *m*; *(of engine)* ronronnement *m*

2 *adj* qui ronronne

purse [pɜːs] **1** *n* (**a**) *Br (for coins)* porte-monnaie *m inv*

(**b**) *Am (handbag)* sac *m* à main

(**c**) *Fig (wealth, resources)* bourse *f*; **to hold** *or* **to control the purse strings** tenir les cordons de la bourse; **the public purse** le Trésor public; *Old-fashioned* **it is beyond my purse** c'est au-dessus de mes moyens

(**d**) *Sport (prize money)* prix *m*

2 *vt* **to purse (up) one's lips** *or* **mouth** pincer les lèvres; **she pursed her lips in disapproval** elle pinça les lèvres en signe de désapprobation

►► *Zool* ***purse crab*** crabe *m* des cocotiers; ***purse net*** bourse *f*; *Fishing* ***purse seine*** bourse *f*; *Am* ***purse snatching*** vol *m* à l'arraché

purser ['pɜːsə(r)] *n Naut* commissaire *m* du bord

purslane ['pɜːslɪn] *n Bot* pourpier *m*

pursuance [pə'sjʊəns] *n Formal* exécution *f*, accomplissement *m*; **in (the) pursuance of his duties** dans l'exercice de ses fonctions; *Law* **in pursuance of this contract/clause** conformément au présent contrat/à la présente clause

pursuant [pə'sjʊənt] **pursuant to** *prep Formal (following)* à la suite de, suivant; *(in accordance with)* conformément à

pursue [pə'sjuː] *vt* (**a**) *(chase, follow)* poursuivre; *Fig* suivre, poursuivre; **he was being pursued by dogs** il était poursuivi par des chiens; *Literary* **she was pursued by ill fortune/ill health** elle était poursuivie par la malchance/la maladie

(**b**) *(strive for → pleasure, happiness)* rechercher; *(→ aim)* poursuivre; **we are all pursuing the same goals** nous poursuivons tous les mêmes buts

(**c**) *(studies)* poursuivre; *(course of action)* suivre; *(policy)* mener; **I have no time to pursue any hobbies** je n'ai pas de temps à consacrer à des hobbies; **to pursue a career in law/journalism** faire carrière dans le droit/le journalisme

(**d**) *(take further → enquiry, matter)* poursuivre; **he became so upset that she decided not to pursue the matter** il s'est mis dans un état tel qu'elle a préféré ne pas insister; **if I may pursue that line of argument** si je peux me permettre de pousser plus loin *ou* de développer ce raisonnement; **to pursue a point** insister sur *ou* revenir sur un point

pursuer [pə'sjuːə(r)] *n* poursuivant(e) *m,f*

pursuit [pə'sjuːt] *n* (**a**) *(chasing)* poursuite *f*; **they went out in pursuit of the vandals** ils se sont lancés à la poursuite des vandales; **with a pack of dogs in hot pursuit** avec une meute de chiens à leurs trousses

(**b**) *(of pleasure, knowledge etc)* quête *f*, recherche *f*; **the pursuit of knowledge/happiness** la quête du savoir/du bonheur; **in pursuit of fame/glory** en quête de renommée/de gloire

(**c**) *(pastime)* occupation *f*; **leisure pursuits** loisirs *mpl*, passe-temps *mpl*

(**d**) *Sport (in cycling)* poursuite *f*

►► *Mil & Aviat* ***pursuit plane*** avion *m* de chasse; *Cycling* ***pursuit race*** poursuite *f*

pursuivant ['pɜːsɪvənt] *n* (**a**) *Her* poursuivant *m* d'armes (**b**) *Hist (follower)* suivant *m*

purulence ['pjʊərʊləns] *n* purulence *f*

purulent ['pjʊərʊlənt] *adj* purulent

purvey [pə'veɪ] *vt* (**a**) *(sell)* vendre, fournir; **to purvey sth to sb** fournir qch à qn, approvisionner qn en qch (**b**) *(communicate → information, news)* communiquer; *(→ lies, rumours)* colporter

purveyance [pə'veɪəns] *n* fourniture *f*, approvisionnement *m*

purveyor [pə'veɪə(r)] *n Formal* (**a**) *(supplier)* fournisseur(euse) *m,f*; **purveyors of marmalade to HM the Queen** fournisseurs en confiture de Sa Majesté la Reine (**b**) *(spreader → of gossip, lies)* colporteur(euse) *m,f*

purview ['pɜːvjuː] *n* (**a**) *Formal (scope)* champ *m*, domaine *m*; **the matter falls within/outside the purview of the committee** la question relève/ne relève pas de la compétence du comité (**b**) *Law (body of statute)* texte *m*

pus [pʌs] *n* pus *m*

PUSH [pʊʃ]

poussée	▸ **1 (a)**
mot d'encouragement	▸ **1 (b)**
effort	▸ **1 (e)**
pousser	▸ **2 (a), (d); 3 (a)**
enfoncer	▸ **2 (a)**
appuyer (sur)	▸ **2 (b); 3 (b)**
forcer	▸ **2 (d)**
prôner	▸ **2 (e)**
avancer	▸ **3 (c)**

1 *n* (**a**) *(shove)* poussée *f*; **to give sb/sth a push** pousser qn/qch; **the door opens at the push of a button** il suffit d'appuyer sur un bouton pour que la porte s'ouvre; **he expects these things to happen at the push of a button** il s'attend à ce que ça se fasse sur commande

(**b**) *(encouragement)* mot *m* d'encouragement; **he'll do it, but he needs a little push** il le fera, mais il a besoin qu'on le pousse un peu; **he just needs a push in the right direction** il a juste besoin qu'on le mette sur la bonne voie

(**c**) *Br Fam* **to give sb the push** *(from job)* virer qn; *(in relationship)* plaquer qn; **he got the push** *(from job)* il s'est fait virer; *(from relationship)* il s'est fait plaquer

(**d**) *Fam (critical moment)* **when it comes to the push, when push comes to shove** au moment critique *ou* crucial ❑; **I can lend you the money if it comes to the push** au pire, je pourrai vous prêter l'argent ❑; **if it comes to the push, he'll choose Sarah not Gillian** s'il fallait qu'il choisisse, il prendrait Sarah et pas Gillian ❑; **at a push** à la limite ❑; **I can do it at a push** je peux le faire si c'est vraiment nécessaire ❑

(**e**) *(effort)* effort *m*, coup *m* de collier; *(campaign)* campagne *f*; **the final push for the summit** le dernier effort pour atteindre le sommet; **to make a push for change** lutter pour le changement; **the club's push for promotion** les efforts soutenus du club pour être promu; **a sales push** une campagne de promotion des ventes; **the push towards protectionism is gathering strength** la tendance au protectionnisme se renforce

(**f**) *Mil (advance)* poussée *f*; **the platoon made a push to capture the airfield** la section a fait une poussée pour s'emparer de l'aérodrome

(**g**) *(drive, dynamism)* dynamisme *m*; **he has a lot of push** il est très dynamique

(**h**) *(billiards)* coup *m* queuté

(**i**) *Austr Fam (gang)* bande *f*, clique *f*

2 *vt* (**a**) *(shove, propel)* pousser; *(thrust)* enfoncer; **she pushed the door open/shut** elle ouvrit/ferma la porte (en la poussant); **he pushed her onto the chair/into the room** il la poussa sur la chaise/(pour la faire entrer) dans la pièce; **to push sb into a corner** acculer qn; **to push sb out of the way** écarter qn; **don't push (me)!** ne (me) poussez pas!, ne (me) bousculez pas!; **a man was pushed out of the window** quelqu'un a poussé un homme par la fenêtre; *Fig* **did he fall or was he pushed?** il est tombé ou on l'a poussé?; **did he leave or was he pushed?** *(from job)* il est parti de lui-même ou on l'y a poussé?; **push all that mess under the bed** pousse tout ce bazar sous le lit; **he pushed the branches apart** il a écarté les branches; **she pushed her way to the bar** elle se fraya un chemin jusqu'au bar; **push one tube into the other** enfoncez un tube dans l'autre; **he pushed a gun into my ribs** il m'enfonça un revolver dans les côtes; **she pushed the cork into the bottle** elle enfonça le bouchon dans la bouteille; **he pushed his hands into his pockets** il enfonça ses mains dans ses poches; **to push an attack home** pousser à fond une attaque; **to push home one's advantage** tirer le meilleur parti possible de son avantage

(**b**) *(press → doorbell, pedal, button)* appuyer sur

(**c**) *(cause to move in specified direction)* **it will push inflation upwards** cela va relancer l'inflation; **the crisis is pushing the country towards chaos** la crise entraîne le pays vers le chaos; **he is pushing the party to the right** il fait glisser le parti vers la droite; **buying the car will push us even further into debt** en achetant cette voiture, nous allons nous endetter encore plus; **economic conditions have pushed the peasants off the land** les paysans ont été chassés des campagnes par les conditions économiques

(**d**) *(pressurize)* pousser; *(force)* forcer, obliger, contraindre; **to push sb to do sth** pousser qn à faire qch; **to push sb into doing sth** forcer *ou* obliger qn à faire qch; **his parents pushed him to become a doctor** ses parents l'ont poussé à devenir médecin; **her teacher pushed her in Latin** son professeur l'a poussée à travailler en latin; **he needs pushing** il faut toujours le pousser; **their coach doesn't push them hard enough** leur entraîneur ne les pousse pas assez; **I like to push myself hard** j'aime me donner à fond; **he pushed the car to its limits** il a poussé la voiture à la limite de ses possibilités; **you're still weak, so don't push yourself** tu es encore faible, vas-y doucement; **he won't do it if he's pushed too hard** il ne le fera pas si l'on insiste trop; **don't push him too far** ne le poussez pas à bout; **I won't be pushed, I need time to think it over!** je ne me laisserai pas bousculer, j'ai besoin de temps pour y réfléchir!; **when I pushed her, she admitted it** quand j'ai insisté, elle a avoué; **he keeps pushing me for the rent** il me relance sans cesse au sujet du loyer; *Fam* **don't push your luck!** n'exagère pas!

(**e**) *(advocate, argue for → idea, method)* prôner, préconiser; *(promote → product)* promouvoir; **he's trying to push his own point of view** il essaie d'imposer son point de vue personnel; **the mayor is pushing his town as the best site for the conference** le maire présente sa ville comme le meilleur endroit pour tenir la conférence; **the government is pushing the idea of people setting up small businesses** le gouvernement favorise la création de petites entreprises; **he's pushing himself as a compromise candidate** il se présente comme le candidat du compromis; **there are so many adverts pushing beauty products** il y a tellement de publicités pour des produits de beauté

(**f**) *(stretch, exaggerate → argument, case)* présenter avec insistance, insister sur; **if we push the comparison a little further** si on pousse la comparaison un peu plus loin; *Fam* **that's pushing it a bit!** *(going too far)* c'est un peu exagéré!; **I'll try to arrive by 7 p.m. but it's pushing it a bit** je tâcherai d'arriver à 19 heures, mais ça va être juste ❑

(**g**) *Fam (sell → drugs)* revendre ❑, dealer

(**h**) *Fam (approach)* friser; **to be pushing thirty** friser la trentaine; **the car was pushing 100 mph** ≃ la voiture frisait les 160

(**i**) *St Exch* **to push shares** placer des valeurs douteuses

3 *vi* (**a**) *(shove)* pousser; **to push against sth** pousser qch; **no pushing please!** ne poussez pas, s'il vous plaît!; **push** *(on door)* poussez; **people were pushing to get in** les gens se bousculaient pour entrer; **he pushed through the crowd to the bar** il s'est frayé un chemin jusqu'au bar à travers la foule; **somebody pushed past me** quelqu'un est passé en me bousculant; **we'll have to get out and push** il va falloir descendre pousser

(**b**) *(press → on button, bell, knob)* appuyer

(**c**) *(advance)* avancer; **the army pushed towards the border** l'armée a avancé jusqu'à la frontière; **the country is pushing towards democracy** le pays évolue vers la démocratie

(**d**) *(extend → path, fence)* s'étendre; **the road pushed deep into the hills** la route s'enfonçait dans les collines

▸▸ ***push button*** bouton-poussoir *m*; *Com* ***push money*** prime *f* au vendeur; *Mktg* ***push strategy*** stratégie *f* push; ***push stroke*** *(in billiards, snooker)* coup *m* queuté; *Comput* ***push technology*** technologie *f* du push de données

▸**push about** *vt sep* (**a**) *(physically)* malmener; **he didn't hit her but he was pushing her about** il ne l'a pas frappée mais il la malmenait

(**b**) *Fam (bully)* marcher sur les pieds à; **I won't be pushed about!** je ne vais pas me laisser marcher sur les pieds!

▸**push ahead** *vi* (**a**) *(continue)* continuer, persévérer; **to push ahead with the work** poursuivre les travaux; **they decided to push ahead with the plans to extend the school** ils ont décidé d'activer les projets d'extension de l'école

(**b**) *(advance)* avancer, progresser (**with** dans); **research is pushing ahead** les recherches avancent

▸**push along 1** *vt sep (trolley, pram)* pousser (devant soi)

2 *vi Fam (leave)* filer; **I'll be pushing along now** bon, il est temps que je file

▸**push around** = **push about**

▸**push aside** *vt sep* (**a**) *(objects)* pousser, écarter

(**b**) *(reject → proposal)* écarter, rejeter; **issues which have been pushed aside** des questions qui ont été volontairement écartées; **you can't just push aside the problem like that** vous ne pouvez pas faire comme si le problème n'existait pas; **I pushed my doubts aside** je n'ai pas tenu compte de mes doutes

▸**push away** *vt sep* repousser; **she pushed my hand away** elle repoussa ma main; **he pushed his chair away from the fire** il éloigna sa chaise du feu

▸**push back** *vt sep* (**a**) *(person)* repousser (en arrière); *(crowd)* faire reculer, refouler; *(curtains)* écarter; *(bedclothes)* rejeter, repousser; **he pushed me back from the door** il m'a éloigné de la porte

(**b**) *(repulse → troops)* repousser; **the enemy was pushed back ten miles/to the river** l'ennemi a été repoussé d'une quinzaine de kilomètres/jusqu'à la rivière

(**c**) *(postpone)* repousser; **the meeting has been pushed back to Friday** la réunion a été repoussée à vendredi

▸**push down 1** *vt sep* (**a**) *(lever, handle, switch)* abaisser; *(pedal)* appuyer sur; **she pushed the clothes down in the bag** elle a tassé les vêtements dans le sac; **he pushed down the lid but it wouldn't shut** il a appuyé sur le couvercle mais il ne voulait pas fermer

(**b**) *(knock over)* renverser, faire tomber

(**c**) *(prices)* faire baisser

2 *vi (pedal, lever)* s'abaisser; *(person → on pedal, lever)* appuyer (**on** sur)

▸**push for** *vt insep (argue for)* demander; *(campaign for)* faire campagne pour; **some ministers were pushing for more monetarist policies** certains ministres demandaient une politique plus monétariste; **to push for a 35-hour week** demander la semaine de 35 heures; **I'm going to push for a bigger budget** je vais faire tout ce qui est en mon pouvoir pour obtenir un budget plus important; **the unions are pushing for 10 percent** les syndicats font pression pour obtenir 10 pour cent; **to push for a decision** exiger qu'une décision soit prise

▸**push forward 1** *vt sep* pousser (en avant); **he was pushed forward by the crowd** la foule l'a poussé en avant; *Fig* **to push oneself forward** se mettre en avant, se faire valoir

2 *vi* (**a**) *(advance → person, car)* avancer; *(→ crowd, herd)* se presser en avant

(**b**) = **push ahead**

▸**push in 1** *vt sep* (**a**) *(drawer)* pousser; *(electric plug, key)* enfoncer, introduire; *(disk)* insérer; *(knife, stake, spade)* enfoncer; *(button, switch)* appuyer sur; **push the button right in** appuyer à fond sur le bouton

(**b**) *(person)* **they pushed me in the water** ils m'ont poussé dans l'eau; **he opened the door and pushed me in** il ouvrit la porte et me poussa à l'intérieur

(**c**) *(break down → panel, cardboard)* enfoncer; **the door had been pushed in** la porte avait été enfoncée

2 *vi (in queue)* **to push in ahead of sb** doubler qn; **no pushing in!** faites la queue!; **she's always pushing in where she's not wanted** il faut toujours qu'elle s'immisce *ou* s'impose là où on ne veut pas d'elle

▸**push off 1** *vt sep* (**a**) *(knock off)* faire tomber; **they pushed me off the ladder** ils m'ont fait tomber de l'échelle; **I pushed him off the chair** je l'ai fait tomber de sa chaise

(**b**) *(boat)* déborder

(**c**) *(remove)* pousser; **push the lid off** soulève le couvercle; **they tried to push her (car) off the road** ils ont essayé de faire sortir sa voiture de la route; **to push sb off a committee** exclure *ou* écarter qn d'un comité

2 *vi* (**a**) *Fam (go away)* filer, mettre les bouts; **time for me to push off** il faut que je file; **push off!** de l'air!, dégage!

(**b**) *(in boat)* pousser au large

►**push on 1** *vt sep (urge on)* **to push sb on to do sth** pousser *ou* inciter qn à faire qch

2 *vi (on journey → set off again)* reprendre la route, se remettre en route; *(→ continue)* poursuivre *ou* continuer son chemin; *(keep working)* continuer, persévérer; **let's push on to Dundee** poussons jusqu'à Dundee; **they're pushing on with the reforms** ils poursuivent leurs efforts pour faire passer les réformes

►**push out 1** *vt sep* (**a**) *(person, object)* pousser dehors; **they pushed the car out of the mud** ils ont désembourbé la voiture en la poussant; **the bed had been pushed out from the wall** le lit avait été écarté du mur; **to push one's way out** se frayer un chemin vers la sortie; **to push the boat out** déborder l'embarcation; *Fig* faire la fête

(**b**) *(stick out → hand, leg)* tendre

(**c**) *(grow → roots, shoots)* faire, produire

(**d**) *(oust)* évincer; *(dismiss from job)* mettre à la porte; **we've been pushed out of the Japanese market** nous avons été évincés du marché japonais

(**e**) *Fam (churn out → articles, books)* produire à la chaîne ❑, pondre en série ❑

2 *vi (appear → roots, leaves)* pousser; *(→ snowdrops, tulips)* pointer

►**push over** *vt sep* (**a**) *(pass → across table, floor)* pousser; **he pushed the book over to me** il poussa le livre vers moi

(**b**) *(knock over)* faire tomber, renverser; *(from ledge, bridge)* pousser, faire tomber; **many cars had been pushed over onto their sides** beaucoup de voitures avaient été renversées sur le côté

►**push through 1** *vt sep* (**a**) *(project, decision)* faire accepter; *(deal)* conclure; *(bill, budget)* réussir à faire voter *ou* passer

(**b**) *(thrust → needle)* passer; **she eventually managed to push her way through (the crowd)** elle réussit finalement à se frayer un chemin (à travers la foule)

2 *vi (car, person)* se frayer un chemin; *(troops, army)* avancer

►**push to** *vt sep (door, drawer)* fermer

►**push up** *vt sep* (**a**) *(push upwards → handle, lever)* remonter, relever; *(→ sleeves)* remonter, retrousser; **she pushed herself up onto her feet** elle se releva; *Fam* **he's pushing up (the) daisies** il mange les pissenlits par la racine

(**b**) *(increase → taxes, sales, demand)* augmenter; *(→ prices, costs, statistics)* faire monter; **the effect will be to push interest rates up** cela aura pour effet de faire grimper les taux d'intérêt

---

pushbike ['pʊʃbaɪk] *n Br Fam* vélo ❑ *m*, bécane *f*

push-broom *n Am* (grand) balai *m*

push-button *adj (telephone)* à touches, à boutons-poussoirs; *(car window)* à commande automatique

►► ***push-button controls*** commandes *fpl* automatiques; ***push-button warfare*** guerre *f* presse-bouton

pushcart ['pʊʃkɑːt] *n Am* charrette *f* à bras

pushchair ['pʊʃtʃeə(r)] *n Br* poussette *f*

pushed [pʊʃt] *adj* (**a**) *Fam (lacking → money, time)* **to be pushed for sth** manquer de *ou* être à court de qch ❑; **we're really pushed for time** nous n'avons que très peu de temps ❑; **I'd like to stay longer, but I'm a bit pushed** j'aimerais rester plus longtemps, mais je suis assez pressé ❑

(**b**) *(in difficulty)* **to be hard pushed to do sth** avoir du mal à faire qch; **a lot of them would be hard pushed to name the President of France** beaucoup d'entre eux auraient du mal à dire qui est le président de la République française

pusher ['pʊʃə(r)] *n* (**a**) *Fam (drug dealer)* trafiquant(e) *m,f* (de drogue) ❑, dealer *m* (**b**) *Aviat* hélice *f* propulsive

pushiness ['pʊʃɪnɪs] *n Fam (ambitiousness)* arrivisme ❑ *m*; *(forwardness)* insistance ❑ *f*; **I can't stand his pushiness** je ne supporte pas sa façon de s'imposer ❑

pushing ['pʊʃɪŋ] *n* bousculade *f*; **no pushing!** ne poussez pas!; **there was a lot of pushing and shoving** ça poussait et ça se bousculait dans tous les sens

Pushkin ['pʊʃkɪn] *pr n* Pouchkine

pushover ['pʊʃˌəʊvə(r)] *n* (**a**) *Fam (easy thing)* jeu *m* d'enfant; **the exam was a pushover** l'examen était un jeu d'enfant; **the match will be a pushover** le match, c'est du tout cuit *ou* ça va être du gâteau; **that team are no pushover** cette équipe n'est pas du genre à se laisser battre

(**b**) *Fam (gullible person)* poire *f*, pigeon *m*; **he's no pushover** il ne se laisse pas avoir facilement; **when it comes to flattery, I'm a complete pushover** la flatterie marche à tous les coups avec moi

►► ***pushover try*** *(in rugby)* essai *m* collectif (par les avants)

pushpin ['pʊʃpɪn] *n Am* punaise *f*

push-pull *adj*

►► *Elec* ***push-pull amplifier*** amplificateur *m* push-pull; ***push-pull circuit*** montage *m* symétrique, push-pull *m inv*; *Aut* ***push-pull hand control*** *(for disabled driver)* commande *f* manuelle pousser-tirer; ***push-pull train*** train *m* réversible

pushrod ['pʊʃrɒd] *n Aut* tige *f* de poussoir, tige *f* de culbuteur

push-start 1 *n Aut* **to give sb a push-start** pousser la voiture de qn pour la faire démarrer

2 *vt* faire démarrer en poussant

push-up *n* pompe *f (exercice physique)*; **to do push-ups** faire des pompes

pushy ['pʊʃɪ] *(compar* **pushier**, *superl* **pushiest**) *adj Fam* (**a**) *Pej (ambitious)* arriviste ❑; *(self-serving)* qui cherche à se faire mousser, qui se met en avant ❑; **don't be so pushy** arrête de te faire valoir comme ça! ❑ (**b**) *(self-assertive)* **you have to be pretty pushy in this work** il faut savoir s'imposer dans ce travail ❑

pusillanimity [ˌpjuːsɪlə'nɪmətɪ] *n Formal* pusillanimité *f*

pusillanimous [ˌpjuːsɪ'lænɪməs] *adj Formal* pusillanime

pusillanimously [ˌpjuːsɪ'lænɪməslɪ] *adv Formal* avec pusillanimité

puss [pʊs] *n* (**a**) *Fam (cat)* minou *m*, minet(ette) *m,f* (**b**) *Fam (mouth, face)* gueule *f*, binette *f* (**c**) *Fam (girl, woman)* belette *f*

►► *Entom* ***puss moth*** grande queue *f* fourchue

'Puss in Boots' *Perrault* 'Le Chat botté'

---

pussy ['pʊsɪ] *(pl* **pussies**) *n* (**a**) *Fam (cat)* minou *m*, minet(ette) *m,f* (**b**) *Vulg (female sex organs)* chatte *f*, chagatte *f* (**c**) *Vulg (women)* nanas *fpl*, cuisse *f*; **they're looking out for pussy** ils cherchent des meufs (**d**) *very Fam (weak, cowardly man)* lavette *f*

►► *Bot* ***pussy willow*** saule *m* blanc

pussycat ['pʊsɪkæt] *n Fam* minou *m*

pussyfoot ['pʊsɪfʊt] *vi Fam* ne pas se mouiller; **stop pussyfooting (about** *or* **around)!** assez tergiversé!

pussyfooting ['pʊsɪfʊtɪŋ] *n Fam* l'art *m* de ne pas se mouiller; **to speak out with no pussyfooting** se déclarer [illegible]

pussy-whipped *adj very Fam* dominé par sa femme ❑; **he's totally pussy-whipped** c'est sa femme qui porte la culotte

pustular ['pʌstjʊlə(r)] *adj Med & Bot* pustuleux, pustulé

pustule ['pʌstjuːl] *n* pustule *f*

PUT [pʊt]

mettre	► 1 (a), (c) – (f), (i)
dire	► 1 (g)
soumettre	► 1 (h)
placer	► 1 (i), (l)
investir	► 1 (k), (l)
miser	► 1 (m)

(pt & pp **put**, *cont* **putting**) **1** *vt* (**a**) *(into specified place or position)* mettre; **put the saucepan on the shelf** mets la casserole sur l'étagère; **she put her hand on my shoulder** elle a mis sa main sur mon épaule; **put the chairs nearer the table** approche les chaises de la table; **he put his arm around my shoulders** il passa son bras autour de mes épaules; **she put her arms around him** elle l'a pris dans ses bras; **to put one's head round the door/through the window** passer la tête par la porte/par la fenêtre; **did you put any salt in?** as-tu mis du sel (dedans)?; **put some more water on to boil** remettez de l'eau à chauffer; **he put another brick on the pile** il a mis une autre brique sur la pile; **to put a coin/a letter/a gun into sb's hand** glisser *ou* mettre une pièce/une lettre/un revolver dans la main de qn; **she put a match to the wood** elle a allumé le bois; **to put an advert in the paper** mettre une annonce dans le journal; **they want to put me in an old folks' home** ils veulent me mettre dans une maison pour les vieux; **to put a child to bed** mettre un enfant au lit, coucher un enfant; **to put a man on the moon** envoyer un homme sur la lune; **he put the telescope to his eye** il a porté la longue-vue à son œil; **to put honour before riches** préférer l'honneur à l'argent; **to put a play on the stage** monter une pièce; **to put a guard on the door** faire surveiller la porte; *Fig* **I didn't know where to put myself!** je ne savais plus où me mettre!; **put yourself in my position** *or* **place** mettez-vous à ma place; **to put oneself into sb's hands** s'en remettre à qn; **put it out of your mind** *or* **head** sors-le-toi de la tête; **I had long put this thought out of my mind** ça faisait longtemps que je m'étais sorti cette idée de la tête; **we put a lot of emphasis on creativity** nous mettons beaucoup l'accent sur la créativité; **don't put too much trust in what he says** ne te fie pas trop à ce qu'il dit; *Fam* **put it there!** *(shake hands)* tope-là!, serrons-nous la pince!

(**b**) *(push or send forcefully)* **he put his fist through the window** il a passé son poing à travers le carreau; **he put a bullet through his head** il s'est mis une balle dans la tête; **she put her pen through the whole paragraph** elle a rayé tout le paragraphe d'un coup de stylo

(**c**) *(impose → limit, responsibility, tax)* mettre; **to put a ban on sth** interdire qch; **it puts an extra burden on our department** c'est un fardeau de plus pour notre service; **the new tax will put 5p on a packet of cigarettes** la nouvelle taxe augmentera de 5 pence le prix d'un paquet de cigarettes

(**d**) *(into specified state)* mettre; **you're putting me in an awkward position** vous me mettez dans une situation délicate; **I hope I've not put you to too much trouble** j'espère que je ne vous ai pas trop dérangé; **music always puts him in a good mood** la musique le met toujours de bonne humeur; **the new rules will be put into effect next month** le nouveau règlement entrera en vigueur le mois prochain; **to put sb out of a job** mettre qn au chômage; **to put a prisoner on bread and water** mettre un prisonnier au pain sec et à l'eau; **the money will be put to good use** l'argent sera bien employé; **to put sb to sleep** endormir qn; *Euph* **the dog had to be put to sleep** il a fallu piquer le chien

(**e**) *(write down)* mettre, écrire; **I forgot to put my address** j'ai oublié de mettre mon adresse; **what date shall I put?** quelle date est-ce que je mets?

(**f**) *(bring about)* **to put an end or a stop to sth** mettre fin *ou* un terme à qch

(**g**) *(say, express)* dire, exprimer; **I wouldn't put it quite like that** je ne dirais pas cela; **I don't know how to put it** je ne sais comment dire; **to put one's thoughts into words** exprimer sa pensée, s'exprimer; **let me put it this way** laissez-moi l'exprimer ainsi; **it was, how shall I put it, rather long** c'était, comment dirais-je, un peu long; **to put it another way,...** en d'autres termes,...; **he put it better than that** il l'a dit *ou* formulé mieux que ça; **you could have put that better** tu aurais pu tourner cela un peu mieux; **she put it politely but firmly** elle l'a dit poliment mais clairement; **as Churchill once put it** comme l'a dit Churchill un jour; **to put it briefly** *or* **simply, they refused** bref *ou* en un mot, ils ont refusé; **to put it bluntly** pour parler franc; **putting it in terms you'll understand...** plus simplement, pour que vous compreniez...

(**h**) *(present, submit → suggestion, question)* soumettre; *(→ motion)* proposer, présenter; **to**

pus–put

put a proposal to the board présenter une proposition au conseil d'administration; **he put his case very well** il a très bien présenté son cas; **I have a question to put to the Prime Minister** j'ai une question à soumettre au Premier ministre; *Law* **I put it to you that...** n'est-il pas vrai que...?; **I put it to the delegates that now is the time to act** je tiens à dire aux délégués que c'est maintenant qu'il faut agir

(**i**) *(class, rank)* placer, mettre; **I wouldn't put them in the same class as the Beatles** je ne les mettrais *ou* placerais pas dans la même catégorie que les Beatles; **I put my family above my job** je fais passer ma famille avant mon travail

(**j**) *(set to work)* **to put sb to work** mettre qn au travail; **they put her on the Jones case** ils l'ont mise sur l'affaire Jones

(**k**) *(devote → effort)* investir, consacrer; **to put a lot of time/energy into sth** consacrer beaucoup de temps/d'énergie à qch, investir beaucoup de temps/d'énergie dans qch; **she puts more into their relationship than he does** elle s'investit plus que lui dans leur relation; **to put a lot of work into sth/doing sth** beaucoup travailler à qch/pour faire qch; *Sport* **he put everything he had into his first service** il a tout mis dans son premier service

(**l**) *(invest → money)* placer, investir; **she had put all her savings into property** elle avait investi *ou* placé toutes ses économies dans l'immobilier

(**m**) *(bet)* miser, parier; **to put money on a horse** miser *ou* parier sur un cheval; **he put all his winnings on the red** il misa tous ses gains sur le rouge

(**n**) *Sport* **to put the shot** lancer le poids

(**o**) *Naut* **to put a ship into port** rentrer un bateau au port

2 *vi Naut* **to put to sea** lever l'ancre, appareiller; **they had to put back into harbour** ils ont dû rentrer au port; **we put into port at Bombay** nous avons relâché *ou* fait relâche à Bombay

3 *n* (**a**) *Sport* lancer *m* (du poids); **his third put** son troisième lancer

(**b**) *St Exch* option *f* de vente, put *m*; **put and call** stellage *m*, double option *f*

►► *St Exch* ***put band*** période *f* de validité d'une option de vente; *St Exch* ***put bond*** emprunt *m* à fenêtre; *St Exch* ***put option*** option *f* de vente; *St Exch* ***put warrant*** warrant *m* à la vente

►**put about** **1** *vt sep* (**a**) *(spread → gossip, story)* faire courir; *(→ rumour)* faire circuler; **to put it about that...** faire circuler le bruit que...; **it is being put about that he intends resigning** le bruit court qu'il a l'intention de démissionner

(**b**) *Naut* **to put a boat about** virer de bord

(**c**) *Fam* **to put it** *or* **oneself about** *(be promiscuous)* coucher à droite à gauche

2 *vi Naut* virer de bord

►**put across** *vt sep* (**a**) *(communicate → gen)* faire comprendre; *(→ feeling)* communiquer; **to put sth across to sb** faire comprendre qch à qn; **I don't know how to put the argument across to them** je ne sais pas comment leur faire comprendre cet argument; **she knows how to put her ideas across** elle sait bien faire passer ses idées; **she's good at putting herself across** elle sait se mettre en valeur

(**b**) *Br Fam* **to put one across on sb** avoir qn, rouler qn; **don't try putting anything across on me!** ne me prends pas pour un imbécile!

►**put around** *vt sep* = **put about** *vt sep* (**a**)

►**put aside** *vt sep* (**a**) *(book, piece of work)* mettre de côté, poser

(**b**) *(disregard, ignore)* écarter, laisser de côté; **let's put aside our differences of opinion for the moment** laissons nos différends de côté pour le moment; **put aside all gloomy thoughts** oublie toutes ces pensées maussades

(**c**) *(save, keep)* mettre de côté; **we have a little money put aside** nous avons un peu d'argent de côté

►**put at** *vt sep (estimate)* estimer; **they put the cost of repairs to the bridge at around $10,000** ils estiment le montant des réparations du pont à environ 10 000 dollars; **I wouldn't have put her (age) at more than twenty-five** je ne lui aurais pas donné plus de vingt-cinq ans; **what would you put it at?** quelle est votre estimation?

►**put away** *vt sep* (**a**) *(tidy)* ranger; *(return to its place)* remettre à sa place; *(car)* garer; **put your toys away!** range tes jouets!; **put your money/wallet away** *(I'm paying)* range ton argent/ton portefeuille

(**b**) *(save)* mettre de côté; **I have a few pounds put away** j'ai un peu d'argent de côté, j'ai quelques économies; **to put something away for one's old age** mettre quelque chose de côté pour sa retraite

(**c**) *Fam (lock up → in prison)* coffrer; *(→ in mental home)* enfermer[□]

(**d**) *Fam (eat)* enfourner, s'envoyer; *(drink)* descendre, écluser; **he can really put it away!** *(food)* il a un sacré appétit!; *(drink)* qu'est-ce qu'il descend!

►**put back** **1** *vt sep* (**a**) *(replace, return)* remettre; **put that record back where you found it!** remets ce disque où tu l'as trouvé!

(**b**) *(postpone)* remettre; **the meeting has been put back to Thursday** la réunion a été repoussée *ou* remise à jeudi

(**c**) *(slow down, delay)* retarder; **the strike has put our schedule back at least a month** la grève nous a fait perdre au moins un mois sur notre planning

(**d**) *(turn back → clock)* retarder; **we put the clocks back next weekend** le week-end prochain, on passe à l'heure d'hiver; *Fig* **this decision has put the clock back** cette décision nous a ramenés en arrière

(**e**) *Fam (drink)* descendre, écluser

2 *vi Naut* **to put back (to port)** rentrer au port

►**put by** *vt sep (save → money)* mettre de côté; *(→ supplies)* mettre en réserve; **have you got anything put by?** avez-vous un peu d'argent de côté?

►**put down** **1** *vt sep* (**a**) *(on table, floor etc)* poser; **put that knife down at once!** pose ce couteau tout de suite!; **put me down!** lâche-moi!; **put that down!** laisse (ça)!; **to put the phone down** raccrocher; **he put the phone down on me** il m'a raccroché au nez; **it's one of those books you just can't put down** c'est un de ces livres que tu ne peux pas poser avant de l'avoir fini; **I couldn't put it down** *(book)* je l'ai lu d'un trait

(**b**) *(drop off → passenger)* déposer, laisser

(**c**) *(write down)* écrire, inscrire; *(enrol, enter on list)* inscrire; **put down your name and address** écrivez votre nom et votre adresse; **she put us down as Mr and Mrs Smith** elle nous a inscrits sous le nom de M. et Mme Smith; **it's never been put down in writing** ça n'a jamais été mis par écrit; **I can put it down as expenses** je peux le faire passer dans mes notes de frais

(**d**) *(on agenda)* inscrire à l'ordre du jour; **to put down a motion of no confidence** déposer une motion de censure

(**e**) *(quell)* réprimer, étouffer; **the revolt was put down by armed police** la révolte a été réprimée par les forces de police

(**f**) *(belittle)* rabaisser, critiquer; **he's always putting students down** il passe son temps à critiquer les étudiants; **you shouldn't put yourself down** tu ne devrais pas te sous-estimer

(**g**) *Br Euph (kill)* **to have a cat/dog put down** faire piquer un chat/chien

(**h**) *(pay as deposit)* verser; **I've already put £50 down on the sofa** j'ai déjà versé 50 livres pour le canapé

(**i**) *(store → wine)* mettre en cave

(**j**) *(put to bed → baby)* coucher

(**k**) *(land → plane)* poser

(**l**) *(close → umbrella)* fermer

2 *vi (land → plane, pilot)* atterrir, se poser

►**put down as** *vt sep* classer parmi; **I think they'd put me down as a mere amateur** je crois qu'ils me classeraient parmi les simples amateurs

►**put down for** *vt sep* inscrire pour; **put me down for £20** inscrivez-moi pour 20 livres; **I'll put you down for Thursday at three o'clock** je vous mets jeudi à trois heures; **they've already put their son down for public school** ils ont déjà inscrit leur fils dans une école privée

►**put down to** *vt sep* mettre sur le compte de; **you can't put all the country's problems down to inflation** vous ne pouvez pas mettre tous les problèmes du pays sur le compte de l'inflation; **I put it down to her stubbornness** je mets ça sur le compte de son entêtement; **we'll have to put it down to experience** au moins on a appris quelque chose

►**put forth** *vt insep* (**a**) *Literary (sprout → shoots, leaves)* produire

(**b**) *Formal (state → argument, reason)* avancer

►**put forward** *vt sep* (**a**) *(suggest → proposal, idea, hypothesis)* avancer; *(→ candidate)* proposer; **she put her name forward for the post of treasurer** elle a posé sa candidature au poste de trésorière; **to put one's best foot forward** *(walk faster)* presser le pas; *Fig* se mettre en devoir de faire de son mieux

(**b**) *(turn forward → clock, hands of clock)* avancer; **we put the clocks forward next weekend** le week-end prochain, on passe à l'heure d'été

(**c**) *(bring forward)* avancer; **the meeting has been put forward to early next week** la réunion a été avancée au début de la semaine prochaine

►**put in** **1** *vt sep* (**a**) *(place inside bag, container, cupboard etc)* mettre dans; **he put the eggs in the fridge** il a mis les œufs dans le réfrigérateur; **to put one's contact lenses in** mettre ses lentilles de contact; **to put one's head in at the window** passer la tête par la fenêtre; *Sport (in rugby)* **to put the ball in** remettre la balle en jeu

(**b**) *(insert, include)* insérer, inclure; **have you put in the episode about the rabbit?** as-tu inclus l'épisode du lapin?

(**c**) *(interject)* placer; **her name was Alicia, the woman put in** elle s'appelait Alicia, ajouta la femme

(**d**) *(install)* installer; **we're having central heating put in** nous faisons installer le chauffage central; **the voters put the Tories in** les électeurs ont mis les conservateurs au pouvoir; **they've put in a new manager at the factory** ils ont nommé un nouveau directeur à l'usine

(**e**) *(devote → time)* passer; **I've put in a lot of work on that car** j'ai beaucoup travaillé sur cette voiture; **I put in a few hours' revision before supper** j'ai passé quelques heures à réviser avant le dîner; **to put in an hour's work** faire une heure de travail; **to put in a full day at the office** passer toute la journée au bureau; **you only get out what you put in** on ne récolte que ce qu'on sème

(**f**) *(submit → request, demand)* déposer, soumettre; **they put in a claim for a 10 percent pay rise** ils ont déposé une demande d'augmentation de salaire de 10 pour cent; **to put in an application for a job** déposer sa candidature pour *ou* se présenter pour un emploi

2 *vi Naut* relâcher, faire relâche; **we put in at Wellington** nous avons relâché *ou* fait relâche à Wellington

►**put in for** **1** *vt sep* présenter; **we're putting him in for the 500 metres** nous le présentons pour le 500 mètres; **to put pupils in for an examination** présenter des élèves à un examen

2 *vt insep* **to put in for sth** *(post)* poser sa candidature pour qch; *(leave, promotion)* faire une demande de qch, demander qch; **she put in for a transfer to Florida** elle a demandé à être mutée en Floride

►**put off** **1** *vt sep* (**a**) *(drop off → passenger)* déposer, laisser; **just put me off at the corner** vous n'avez qu'à me laisser *ou* me déposer au coin

(**b**) *(postpone → meeting, appointment)* remettre à plus tard, repousser; *(→ decision, payment)* remettre à plus tard, différer; *(→ work)* remettre à plus tard; *(→ guests)* décommander; **the meeting has been put off until tomorrow** la réunion a été renvoyée *ou* remise à demain; **I kept putting off telling him the truth** je continuais à repousser le moment de lui dire la vérité; **I can't put him off again** je ne peux pas encore annuler un rendez-vous avec lui

(**c**) *(dissuade)* **once he's made up his mind nothing in the world can put him off** une fois qu'il a pris une décision, rien au monde ne peut le faire changer d'avis

(**d**) *(distract)* déranger, empêcher de se concentrer; **he deliberately tries to put his opponent off** il fait tout pour empêcher son

adversaire de se concentrer; **the noise put her off her service** le bruit l'a gênée *ou* dérangée pendant son service
(**e**) *(repel)* dégoûter, rebuter; **it's the smell that puts me off** c'est l'odeur qui me rebute; **don't be put off by his odd sense of humour** ne te laisse pas rebuter par son humour un peu particulier; **it put me off skiing for good** ça m'a définitivement dégoûté du ski; **it put me off my dinner** ça m'a coupé l'appétit
(**f**) *(switch off → television, radio etc)* éteindre
2 *vi Naut* déborder du quai, pousser au large; **to put off from the shore** quitter la côte, prendre le large

►**put on** *vt sep* (**a**) *(clothes, make-up, ointment)* mettre; **put your hat on** mets ton chapeau; **to put on one's make-up** se maquiller
(**b**) *(present, stage → play, opera)* monter; *(→ poetry reading, slide show etc)* organiser; **why can't they put something decent on for a change?** *(on TV, radio)* ils ne pourraient pas passer quelque chose d'intéressant pour une fois?
(**c**) *(lay on, provide → train)* mettre en service; **they put on excellent meals on Sundays** ils servent d'excellents repas le dimanche; **they have put on twenty extra trains** ils ont ajouté vingt trains
(**d**) *(gain → speed, weight)* prendre; **I've put on a few pounds** j'ai pris quelques kilos
(**e**) *(turn on, cause to function → light, radio, gas)* allumer; *(→ record, tape)* mettre; *(→ handbrake)* mettre, serrer; **put the heater on** mets *ou* allume le chauffage; **he put on some Vivaldi/the news** il a mis du Vivaldi/les informations; **I've put the kettle on for tea** j'ai mis de l'eau à chauffer pour le thé; **to put on the brakes** freiner
(**f**) *(start cooking)* mettre (à cuire); **I forgot to put the peas on** j'ai oublié de mettre les petits pois à cuire
(**g**) *(bet)* parier; **I put £10 on the favourite** j'ai parié 10 livres sur le favori
(**h**) *(assume)* prendre; **to put on airs** prendre des airs; **he put on a silly voice** il a pris une voix ridicule; **to put on an act** jouer la comédie; *Fam* **don't worry, he's just putting it on** ne t'inquiète pas, il fait du cinéma *ou* du chiqué
(**i**) *Fam (tease)* faire marcher; **you're putting me on!** là, tu me fais marcher!
(**j**) *(apply → pressure)* exercer
(**k**) *(add)* ajouter; **the tax increase will put another 10p on a gallon of petrol** l'augmentation de la taxe va faire monter le prix du gallon d'essence de 10 pence
(**l**) *(impose)* imposer; **new restrictions have been put on bringing animals into the country** de nouvelles restrictions ont été imposées à l'importation d'animaux dans le pays
(**m**) *(attribute)* **it's hard to put a price on it** c'est difficile d'en évaluer *ou* estimer le prix
(**n**) *(advance → clock)* avancer
(**o**) *(on telephone)* **could you put him on, please?** pouvez-vous me le passer, s'il vous plaît?

►**put onto** *vt sep (help find)* indiquer à; **I'll put you onto a good solicitor** je vous donnerai le nom d'un *ou* je vous indiquerai un bon avocat; **she's put me onto quite a few bargains** elle m'a indiqué plusieurs bonnes affaires; **to put the police/taxman onto sb** dénoncer qn à la police/au fisc; **what put you onto the butler, detective inspector?** qu'est-ce qui vous a amené à soupçonner le maître d'hôtel, commissaire?

►**put out 1** *vt sep* (**a**) *(place outside)* mettre dehors, sortir; **have you put the dustbin out?** as-tu sorti la poubelle?; **I'll put the washing out (to dry)** je vais mettre le linge (dehors) à sécher; **to put a cow out to grass** mettre une vache en pâture
(**b**) *(remove)* **to put sb's eye out** éborgner qn; **you almost put my eye out!** tu as failli m'éborgner!
(**c**) *(issue → apology, announcement)* publier; *(→ story, rumour)* faire circuler; *(→ new record, edition, model etc)* sortir; *(→ appeal, request)* faire; *(broadcast)* émettre; **police have put out a description of the wanted man** la police a publié une description de l'homme qu'elle recherche; **to put out an SOS** lancer un SOS
(**d**) *(extinguish → fire, light, candle)* éteindre; *(→ cigarette)* éteindre, écraser; *(→ gas)* fermer; **don't forget to put the light out when you leave** n'oubliez pas d'éteindre (la lumière) en partant
(**e**) *(lay out, arrange)* sortir; **the valet had put out a suit for me** le valet de chambre m'avait sorti un costume
(**f**) *(stick out, stretch out → arm, leg)* étendre, allonger; *(→ hand)* tendre; *(→ tongue)* tirer; **she walked up to me and put out her hand** elle s'approcha de moi et me tendit la main; **she put out a foot to trip him up** elle a mis un pied en avant pour le faire trébucher
(**g**) *(dislocate)* **to put one's back/shoulder out** se démettre le dos/l'épaule; **I've put my back out** je me suis déplacé une vertèbre
(**h**) *(annoy, upset)* **to be put out about sth** être fâché à cause de qch; **he seems quite put out about it** on dirait que ça l'a vraiment contrarié
(**i**) *(inconvenience)* déranger; **I hope I haven't put you out** j'espère que je ne vous ai pas dérangé; **she's always ready to put herself out for other people** elle est toujours prête à rendre service
(**j**) *(sprout → shoots, leaves)* produire
(**k**) *(make unconscious → with drug, injection)* endormir
(**l**) *(subcontract)* sous-traiter; **we put most of our work out** nous confions la plus grande partie de notre travail à des sous-traitants
(**m**) *Hort (plant out)* repiquer
2 *vi* (**a**) *Naut* prendre le large; **to put out to sea** faire appareiller
(**b**) *Am Fam (woman)* accepter de coucher (**for** avec); **everyone knows she puts out** tout le monde sait qu'elle est prête à coucher; **did she put out?** est-ce qu'elle a bien voulu coucher?; **she'd put out for anybody** elle coucherait avec le premier venu

►**put over** = **put across**

►**put round** *vt sep (spread → gossip, story)* faire courir

►**put through** *vt sep* (**a**) *Tel (connect)* passer la communication à; **hold on, I'll try to put you through** ne quittez pas, je vais essayer de vous le/la passer; **put the call through to my office** passez-moi la communication dans mon bureau; **I'll put you through to Mrs Powell** je vous passe Mme Powell
(**b**) *(carry through, conclude)* conclure; **we finally put through the necessary reforms** nous avons fini par faire passer les réformes nécessaires
(**c**) *(subject to)* soumettre à; **he was put through a whole battery of tests** on l'a soumis à toute une série d'examens; **I'm sorry to put you through this** je suis désolé de vous imposer ça; **have you any idea what you're putting him through?** as-tu la moindre idée de ce que tu lui fais subir?; *Fam* **to put sb through it** en faire voir de toutes les couleurs à qn; *(at interview)* faire passer un mauvais quart d'heure à qn; **he really put me through it** il m'en a vraiment fait voir (de toutes les couleurs)
(**d**) *(pay for)* **he put himself through college** il a payé ses études

►**put together** *vt sep* (**a**) *(place side by side → two objects)* mettre côte à côte; *(→ facts)* rapprocher, comparer; **he's more trouble than the rest of them put together** il nous crée plus de problèmes à lui seul que tous les autres réunis
(**b**) *(kit, furniture, engine)* monter, assembler; *(meal)* préparer, confectionner; *(menu)* élaborer; *(dossier)* réunir; *(proposal, report)* préparer; *(story, facts)* reconstituer; *(show, campaign)* organiser, monter; **to put sth (back) together again** remonter qch; **we're trying to put together enough evidence to convict him** nous essayons de réunir assez de preuves pour le faire condamner; **to put together a convincing picture of what happened** reconstituer une idée convaincante de ce qui s'est passé; **the programme is nicely put together** ce programme est bien fait; **I'll just put a few things together (in my bag)** je vais faire rapidement ma valise

►**put under** *vt sep (with drug, injection)* endormir

►**put up 1** *vt sep* (**a**) *(raise → hand)* lever; *(→ flag)* hisser; *(→ hood)* relever; *(→ umbrella)* ouvrir; *(→ one's hair, coat collar)* relever; **could all those going put up their hands?** que tous ceux qui y vont lèvent la main; **put your hands up!** haut les mains!; *Fam* **put 'em up!** *(in surrender)* haut les mains!; *(to fight)* défends-toi!; **I'm going to put my feet up for a few minutes** je vais me reposer un peu
(**b**) *(erect → tent)* dresser, monter; *(→ house, factory)* construire; *(→ monument, statue)* ériger; *(→ scaffolding)* installer, monter; *(→ ladder)* dresser; **they put up a statue to her** ils érigèrent une statue en son honneur
(**c**) *(install, put in place)* mettre; *(curtains)* poser, accrocher; *(wallpaper)* poser; **they've already put up the Christmas decorations** ils ont déjà installé les décorations de Noël; **the shopkeeper put up the shutters** le commerçant a baissé le rideau de fer
(**d**) *(send up → rocket, satellite)* lancer
(**e**) *(display → sign)* mettre; *(→ poster)* afficher; **the results will be put up tomorrow** les résultats seront affichés demain
(**f**) *(show → resistance)* offrir, opposer; **to put up a good show** bien se défendre; **to put up a struggle** se défendre, se débattre
(**g**) *(present → argument, proposal)* présenter; **he puts up a good case for abstention** il a des arguments convaincants en faveur de l'abstention
(**h**) *(offer for sale)* **to put sth up for sale/auction** mettre qch en vente/aux enchères
(**i**) *(put forward → candidate)* présenter; *(→ person, name)* proposer (comme candidat); **we are not putting up any candidates** nous ne présentons aucun candidat
(**j**) *Fam (provide → capital)* fournir; **who's putting the money up for the new business?** qui finance la nouvelle entreprise?; **we put up our own money** nous sommes auto-financés
(**k**) *(increase)* faire monter, augmenter; **this will put up the price of meat** ça va faire augmenter *ou* monter le prix de la viande
(**l**) *(give hospitality to)* loger, héberger; **to put sb up for the night** coucher qn
(**m**) *(urge, incite)* **to put sb up to (doing) sth** pousser qn à (faire) qch
(**n**) *Arch (put away → sword, pistol)* rengainer
2 *vi* (**a**) *Br* **to put up at a hotel** descendre dans un hôtel; **where are you putting up?** où est-ce que tu loges?; *(in hotel)* où es-tu descendu?; **I'm putting up at Gary's for the moment** je loge chez Gary pour le moment
(**b**) *(stand → in election)* se présenter, se porter candidat; **she put up as a Labour candidate** elle s'est présentée comme candidate du parti travailliste
(**c**) *Fam* **put up or shut up!** assez parlé, agissez!

►**put upon** *vt insep (usu passive)* **to put upon sb** *(abuse)* abuser de qn; *(exploit)* exploiter qn; **you shouldn't let yourself be put upon like that!** tu ne devrais pas te laisser marcher sur les pieds comme ça!

►**put up with** *vt insep* supporter, tolérer; **I refuse to put up with this noise any longer!** je ne supporterai pas ce bruit une minute de plus!; **we'll have to put up with it** il faut l'accepter *ou* nous y résigner

'Put Out More Flags' *Waugh* 'Hissez le grand pavois'

putative ['pjuːtətɪv] *adj Formal* présumé, putatif
putatively ['pjuːtətɪvlɪ] *adv Law* putativement
put-down *n Fam (snub)* rebuffade *f*
Putin ['puːtɪn] *pr n* Poutine
put-in *n Sport (in rugby)* introduction *f*
put-off *n Am Fam (evasion)* faux-fuyant *m*; *(excuse)* prétexte *m*
put-on 1 *adj* affecté, simulé
2 *n Fam* (**a**) *(pretence)* simulacre *m*; **it's just a put-on** c'est du chiqué, c'est de la comédie; **the whole thing was a put-on to gain sympathy** toute l'histoire n'était qu'un subterfuge pour s'attirer de la sympathie (**b**) *(hoax)* canular *m* (**c**) *Am (charlatan)* charlatan *m*
put-put ['pʌt,pʌt] *(pt & pp* **put-putted**, *cont* **put-putting***) Br Fam* **1** *n* teuf-teuf *m*

2 *vi* **to put-put along** avancer en faisant teuf-teuf

putrefaction [ˌpju:trɪˈfækʃən] *n* putréfaction *f*

putrefy [ˈpju:trɪfaɪ] (*pt & pp* **putrefied**) **1** *vi* se putréfier

2 *vt* putréfier

putrefying [ˈpju:trɪfaɪɪŋ] *adj* en putréfaction; **putrefying corpses** des cadavres en état de putréfaction *ou* de décomposition

putrescence [pju:ˈtresəns] *n Formal* putrescence *f*

putrescent [pju:ˈtresənt] *adj Formal* putrescent

putrid [ˈpju:trɪd] *adj* (**a**) *(decaying)* putride; **a putrid smell** une odeur nauséabonde (**b**) *Fam (awful)* dégueulasse

putsch [pʊtʃ] *n* putsch *m*, coup *m* d'État

putt [pʌt] *Golf* **1** *n* putt *m*; **to hole a long putt** rentrer un long putt

2 *vt* putter

3 *vi* putter

puttee [ˈpʌtɪ] *n* bande *f* molletière

putter¹ [ˈpʌtə(r)] **1** *n Golf* (**a**) *(club)* putter *m* (**b**) *(person)* **he's a good putter** il putte bien

2 *vi (vehicle)* avancer en faisant teuf-teuf

putter² *Am* = **potter** *vi*

putting [ˈpʌtɪŋ] *n Golf* putting *m*

▸▸ ***putting green*** green *m*

putto [ˈpʊtəʊ] (*pl* **putti** [-ti:]) *n Art* putto *m*

putty [ˈpʌtɪ] (*pt & pp* **puttied**) **1** *n* (**a**) *(for cracks, holes)* mastic *m*; *(for walls)* enduit *m*; **my legs feel like putty** j'ai les jambes en coton; **Max is putty in her hands** elle fait de Max (tout) ce qu'elle veut, Max ne sait pas lui résister (**b**) *(colour)* (couleur *f*) mastic *m*

2 *vt* mastiquer

▸▸ ***putty knife*** couteau *m* à mastiquer, spatule *f* de vitrier

put-up job *n Br Fam* coup *m* monté

put-upon *adj Br* exploité; **he's very put-upon** tout le monde l'exploite; **his poor put-upon wife** sa pauvre femme qui lui sert de bonne à tout faire; **she was feeling put-upon** elle avait l'impression qu'on abusait de sa gentillesse; **a put-upon expression** une tête de martyr

put-you-up *n Br* canapé-lit *m*

putz [ˈpʌts] *n Am Fam* andouille *f*, truffe *f*

▸**putz around** *vi Am Fam* (**a**) *(act foolishly)* faire l'idiot, faire l'imbécile (**b**) *(waste time)* glander, glandouiller

puzzle [ˈpʌzəl] **1** *n* (**a**) *(game → gen)* jeu *m* de patience; *(→ jigsaw)* puzzle *m*; *(→ brainteaser)* casse-tête *m inv*; *(→ riddle)* devinette *f*

(**b**) *(problem)* question *f* (difficile); *(enigma, mystery)* énigme *f*, mystère *m*; **how he escaped remains a puzzle** la façon dont il s'y est pris pour s'évader reste un mystère *ou* une énigme

(**c**) *(perplexity)* perplexité *f*; **he was in a puzzle about what to do** il ne savait pas trop quoi faire

2 *vt* laisser *ou* rendre perplexe; **you puzzle me, Mr Cox** je ne suis pas sûr de vous suivre, M. Cox; **he puzzles me** il m'intrigue, c'est une énigme pour moi; **I'm still puzzled to know how he got out** j'essaie toujours de comprendre comment il s'y est pris pour sortir; **don't puzzle your head over** *or* **about it** ne vous tracassez pas pour ça

3 *vi (wonder)* se poser des questions; *(ponder)* réfléchir; **to puzzle about sth** chercher à comprendre qch

▸▸ ***puzzle book*** *(gen)* livre *m* de jeux; *(of crosswords)* livre *m* de mots croisés

▸**puzzle out** *vt sep Br (meaning, solution, route, way)* trouver, découvrir; *(code, enigma, handwriting)* déchiffrer; *(problem)* résoudre; *(behaviour, intentions)* comprendre; **I'm still trying to puzzle out how he did it** je cherche toujours à comprendre comment il l'a fait; **I was never able to puzzle her out** je ne suis jamais arrivé *ou* parvenu à la comprendre

▸**puzzle over** *vt insep (answer, explanation)* essayer de trouver; *(absence, letter, theory)* essayer de comprendre; *(enigma, crossword)* essayer de résoudre; *(code, handwriting)* essayer de déchiffrer; **we're still puzzling over why he did it** nous nous demandons toujours ce qui a bien pu le pousser à faire cela; *Br* **he puzzled over the list of figures** la liste des chiffres le laissait perplexe; *Br* **that'll give you something to puzzle over!** cela vous donnera de quoi réfléchir!

puzzled [ˈpʌzəld] *adj* perplexe; **you look puzzled** tu as l'air perplexe; **the public are puzzled** les gens sont perplexes *ou* ne savent pas quoi penser

puzzlement [ˈpʌzəlmənt] *n* perplexité *f*; **to look at sb in puzzlement** regarder qn d'un air perplexe

puzzler [ˈpʌzlə(r)] *n* énigme *f*, casse-tête *m inv*; **his statement is a real puzzler** sa déclaration est des plus ambiguës

puzzling [ˈpʌzlɪŋ] *adj (behaviour, remark)* curieux, qui laisse perplexe; *(symbol, machine)* incompréhensible; **it's puzzling that he hasn't sent word** c'est curieux qu'il n'ait pas donné signe de vie; **it remains a puzzling phenomenon** c'est un phénomène encore inexpliqué; **it's a puzzling affair** c'est une affaire difficile à éclaircir

P/V *Fin (written abbr* **profit-volume ratio**) rapport *m* profit sur ventes, ratio *m* de volume de bénéfices

PVC [ˌpi:vi:ˈsi:] *n (abbr* **polyvinyl chloride**) PVC *m*

PVS [ˌpi:vi:ˈes] *n Med (abbr* **persistent vegetative state**) état *m* végétatif chronique

Pvt. *(written abbr* **private**) soldat *m* de deuxième classe

PW [ˌpi:ˈdʌbəlju:] *n Br (abbr* **policewoman**) femme *f* policier

pw *(written abbr* **per week**) p.sem

PWA [ˌpi:dʌbəlju:ˈeɪ] *n (abbr* **person with AIDS**) sidéen(enne) *m,f*

PWR [ˌpi:dʌbəlju:ˈɑ:(r)] *n Nucl & Phys (abbr* **pressurized-water reactor**) REP *m*

PX [ˌpi:ˈeks] *n Am Mil (abbr* **post exchange**) = économat pour les militaires et leurs familles

pyaemia [paɪˈi:mɪə] *n Med* py(o)hémie *f*, pyémie *f*

pycnogonid [pɪkˈnɒgənɪd] *n Zool* pycnogonide *m*

pye-dog [ˈpaɪ-] *n* chien *m* errant *(en Asie)*

pyelonephritis [ˌpaɪləʊneˈfraɪtɪs] *n Med* pyélonéphrite *f*

pyemia = **pyaemia**

Pygmalion [pɪgˈmeɪlɪən] *pr n Myth* Pygmalion

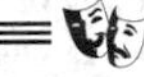

'Pygmalion' *Shaw* 'Pygmalion'

pygmy [ˈpɪgmɪ] (*pl* **pygmies**) **1** *n* (**a**) *Zool (small animal)* nain(e) *m,f* (**b**) *Fig Pej (person)* nain(e) *m,f*; **he's a political pygmy** c'est un homme politique sans importance

2 *adj Zool* nain

3 Pygmy 1 *n* Pygmée *mf* **2** *adj* pygmée

▸▸ *Orn* ***pygmy owl*** chevêchette *f*

pyjama, *Am* **pajama** [pəˈdʒɑ:mə] **1** *comp (jacket, trousers)* de pyjama

2 pyjamas, *Am* **pajamas** *npl* pyjama *m*; **a pair of pyjamas** un pyjama; **he was in his pyjamas** il était en pyjama; *Br* **(lounging) pyjamas** pyjama *m* d'intérieur *(pour femmes)*

▸▸ ***pyjama party*** = fête où l'on doit venir en pyjama; ***pyjama top*** *(jacket)* veste *f* de pyjama; *(pull-on type)* haut *m* de pyjama

pyknic [ˈpɪknɪk] *adj* pycnique

pylon [ˈpaɪlən] *n (gen) & Archeol* pylône *m*

pyloric [paɪˈlɒrɪk] *adj Anat* pylorique

pylorus [paɪˈlɔ:rəs] *n Anat* pylore *m*

PYO *(written abbr* **pick your own**) *(sign)* cueillette à la ferme

pyogenic [ˌpaɪəʊˈdʒenɪk] *adj Med* pyogène

Pyongyang [ˌpjɒŋˈjæŋ] *n* Pyongyang

pyorrhoea, *Am* **pyorrhea** [ˌpaɪəˈrɪə] *n Med* pyorrhée *f*

pyracanth [ˈpaɪərəˌkænθ], **pyracantha** [ˌpaɪərəˈkænθə] *n Bot* pyracanthe *f*, buisson *m* ardent

pyramid [ˈpɪrəmɪd] **1** *n* pyramide *f*; **age** *or* **population pyramid** pyramide *f* des âges

2 *vt* (**a**) *(build in pyramid form)* ériger en forme de pyramide (**b**) *Fin (companies)* structurer en holdings

▸▸ *Com* ***pyramid scheme*** plan *m* commercial en cascade; *Com* ***pyramid selling*** vente *f* pyramidale

pyramidal [pɪˈræmɪdəl], **pyramidical** [ˌpɪrəˈmɪdɪkəl] *adj* pyramidal

▸▸ *Bot* ***pyramidal orchid*** orchis *m* pyramidal

pyre [ˈpaɪə(r)] *n* **(funeral) pyre** bûcher *m* funéraire

Pyrenean [ˌpɪrəˈni:ən] *adj* pyrénéen, des Pyrénées

▸▸ ***Pyrenean mountain dog*** chien *m ou* berger *m* des Pyrénées

Pyrenees [ˌpɪrəˈni:z] *npl* **the Pyrenees** les Pyrénées *fpl*

pyrethrum [paɪˈri:θrəm] *n Bot* pyrèthre *m*

pyretic [paɪˈretɪk] *adj Med* pyrétique

Pyrex® [ˈpaɪreks] **1** *n* Pyrex® *m*

2 *comp (dish)* en Pyrex®

pyrexia [paɪˈreksɪə] *n Med* pyrexie *f*

pyridin, pyridine [ˈpaɪərɪdɪn] *n Chem* pyridine *f*

pyridoxin, pyridoxine [pɪrɪˈdɒksɪn] *n Biol & Chem* pyridoxine *f*

pyrimidin, pyrimidine [pɪˈrɪmɪdɪn] *n Chem* pyrimidine *f*

pyrite [ˈpaɪˌraɪt], **pyrites** [ˌpaɪˈraɪti:z] *n Miner* pyrite *f*

pyritic [paɪˈrɪtɪk] *adj Miner* pyriteux

pyro- [ˈpaɪərəʊ] *pref* pyro-

pyroclast [ˈpaɪərəˌklæst] *n Geol* dépôt *m* pyroclastique

pyroclastic [ˌpaɪərəˈklæstɪk] *adj Geol* pyroclastique

pyroelectricity [ˈpaɪərəʊɪˌlekˈtrɪsətɪ] *n Phys* pyroélectricité *f*

pyrogallol [ˌpaɪərəˈgælɒl] *n Chem* pyrogallol *m*

pyrogenic [ˌpaɪərəˈdʒenɪk] *adj Geol* igné

pyrography [paɪˈrɒgrəfɪ] *n* pyrogravure *f*

pyrolusite [ˌpaɪərəˈlu:saɪt] *n Geol* pyrolusite *f*

pyrolysis [paɪˈrɒləsɪs] *n* pyrolyse *f*

pyromancy [ˈpaɪərəˌmænsɪ] *n* pyromancie *f*

pyromania [ˌpaɪərəˈmeɪnɪə] *n* pyromanie *f*

pyromaniac [ˌpaɪrəˈmeɪnɪæk] *n* pyromane *mf*

pyrometer [ˌpaɪəˈrɒmɪtə(r)] *n Phys & Metal* pyromètre *m*; **dial pyrometer** pyromètre *m* à cadran; **optical pyrometer** pyromètre *m* à lunette; **radiation pyrometer** pyromètre *m* à radiation totale

▸▸ *Cer* ***pyrometer cone*** cône *m* pyrométrique

pyrometric [ˌpaɪərəʊˈmetrɪk], **pyrometrical** [ˌpaɪərəʊˈmetrɪkəl] *adj Phys* pyrométrique

▸▸ *Cer* ***pyrometric cone*** cône *m* pyrométrique

pyrometry [paɪəˈrɒmɪtrɪ] *n Phys* pyrométrie *f*

▸▸ ***pyrometry wire*** fil *m* pyrométrique

pyrope [ˈpaɪərəʊp] *n Miner* pyrope *m*

pyrostat [ˈpaɪərəʊˌstæt] *n* pyrostat *m*

pyrotechnic [ˌpaɪərəʊˈteknɪk] *adj* pyrotechnique

pyrotechnics [ˌpaɪrəʊˈteknɪks] **1** *n (UNCOUNT) (process)* pyrotechnie *f*

2 *npl* (**a**) *(display)* feu *m* d'artifice (**b**) *Fig (display of skill)* performance *f* éblouissante

pyroxene [ˈpaɪərɒksi:n] *n Miner* pyroxène *m*

Pyrrhic victory [ˈpɪrɪk-] *n* victoire *f* à la Pyrrhus

pyrrhotine [ˈpɪrətaɪn], **pyrrhotite** [ˈpɪrətaɪt] *n Miner* pyrrhotine *f*, pyrrhotite *f*, magnétopyrite *f*

Pyrrhus [ˈpɪrəs] *pr n* Pyrrhus

pyrrol, pyrrole [ˈpɪrəʊl] *n Chem* pyrrol(e) *m*

pyrrolidin, pyrrolidine [pɪˈrəʊlɪdɪn] *n Chem* pyrrolidine *f*

Pythagoras [paɪˈθægərəs] *pr n* Pythagore

▸▸ ***Pythagoras' theorem*** théorème *m* de Pythagore

Pythagorean [paɪˌθægəˈri:ən] **1** *adj (relating to Pythagoras)* pythagoricien; *(relating to Pythagoras' theorem)* pythagorique

2 *n* pythagoricien(enne) *m,f*

▸▸ ***Pythagorean numbers*** nombres *mpl* pythagoriques

python [ˈpaɪθən] **1** *n Zool* python *m*

2 Python *pr n Myth* Python

Pythonesque [ˌpaɪθəˈnesk] *adj* à la Monty Python

pythoness [ˈpaɪθənes] *n Antiq (gen)* pythonisse *f*; *(in Delphi)* pythie *f*

pyx [pɪks] *n Rel* ciboire *m*

pyxis [ˈpɪksɪs] (*pl* **pyxides** [-ˈdi:z]) *n* (**a**) *Bot* pyxide *f* (**b**) *Anat* cavité *f* cotyloïde

pzazz [pəˈzæz] *n Fam (flair)* punch *m inv*

Q¹, q¹ [kjuː] *n (letter)* Q, q *m inv*; **two q's** deux q; **Q for Quentin** ≃ Q comme quintal

Q² *(written abbr* **Queen**) *(in chess)* D

q² *(written abbr* **quart**) ≃ litre *m*

QA *(written abbr* **quality assurance**) garantie *f* de qualité

qat [kæt] *n (shrub, drug)* qat *m*, khat *m*

Qatar, Qatari = **Katar, Katari**

QC [ˌkjuːˈsiː] *n* (**a**) *Br Law (abbr* **Queen's Counsel**) ≃ bâtonnier *m* de l'ordre (**b**) *(abbr* **quality control**) contrôle *m* de (la) qualité

QE2 [ˌkjuːiːˈtuː] *n Br Naut (abbr* **Queen Elizabeth II**) = grand paquebot de luxe

QED [ˌkjuːiːˈdiː] *adv (abbr* **quod erat demonstrandum**) CQFD

Q-fever *n Med* fièvre *f* Q

QIP [ˌkjuːaɪˈpiː] *n (abbr* **quality improvement programme**) programme *m* d'amélioration de la qualité

QM [ˌkjuːˈem] *n Mil (abbr* **Quartermaster**) (**a**) *(in army)* commissaire *m*; *Hist* intendant *m* (**b**) *(in navy)* officier *m* de manœuvre

QMG [ˌkjuːemˈdʒiː] *n Mil (abbr* **Quartermaster General**) ≃ Directeur *m* de l'Intendance (militaire)

Qom, Qum [kʊm] *n* Qom, Qum

QSO [ˌkjuːesˈəʊ] *n Astron (abbr* **quasi-stellar object**) objet *m* quasistellaire, QSO *m*

qt¹ *(written abbr* **quart**) ≃ litre *m*

qt², QT [ˌkjuːˈtiː] **1** *adv Br Fam* en douce

2 on the qt *adv* **this is strictly on the qt** c'est confidentiel

Q-tip® *n Am* coton-tige® *m*

qty *(written abbr* **quantity**) qté

qua [kweɪ] *prep Formal* en tant que; **alcohol qua alcohol** l'alcool en tant que tel; **money qua money does not interest us** l'argent en lui-même ne nous intéresse pas

quack [kwæk] **1** *vi (duck)* cancaner, faire coin-coin

2 *n* (**a**) *(of duck)* cancanement *m*, coin-coin *m inv* (**b**) *(charlatan)* charlatan *m* (**c**) *Br & Austr Fam Hum (doctor)* toubib *m*

3 *adj (medicine, method, remedy)* de charlatan

4 *onomat* **quack (quack)!** coin-coin!

►► ***quack doctor*** charlatan *m*

quackery [ˈkwækərɪ] *n* charlatanisme *m*

quacking [ˈkwækɪŋ] *n* cancanement *m*, coin-coin *m inv*

quackish [ˈkwækɪʃ] *adj* de charlatan, charlatanesque

quad [kwɒd] *n* (**a**) *(abbr* **quadruplet**) quadruplé(e) *m,f* (**b**) *(abbr* **quadrangle**) cour *f* (**c**) *Typ* cadrat *m* (**d**) *Elec* quarte *f*

►► ***quad bike*** quad *m*; ***quad biking*** quad *m*; **to go quad biking** faire du quad

quadragenarian [ˌkwɒdrədʒəˈneərɪən] **1** *n* quadragénaire *mf*

2 *adj* quadragénaire

Quadragesima [ˌkwɒdrəˈdʒesɪmə] *n* **Quadragesima (Sunday)** quadragésime *f*

quadragesimal [ˌkwɒdrəˈdʒesɪməl] *adj* quadragésimal

quadrangle [ˈkwɒdræŋgəl] *n* (**a**) *Geom* quadrilatère *m*; **complete quadrangle** quadrangle *m* (**b**) *(courtyard)* cour *f* carrée

quadrangular [kwɒˈdræŋgjʊlə(r)] *adj* quadrangulaire

quadrant [ˈkwɒdrənt] *n* (**a**) *Geom* quadrant *m* (**b**) *Astron & Naut* quart-de-cercle *m*, quadrant *m*

quadrantal [kwɒˈdræntəl] *adj Geom* quadrantal

►► *Aviat* ***quadrantal altitude*** altitude *f* quadrantale; ***quadrantal deviation*** déviation *f* quadrantale (de l'aiguille aimantée); *Math* ***quadrantal triangle*** triangle *m* quadrantal

quadraphonic [ˌkwɒdrəˈfɒnɪk] *adj* quadriphonique, tétraphonique; **in quadraphonic sound** en quadriphonie

quadraphonics [ˌkwɒdrəˈfɒnɪks], **quadraphony** [kwɒˈdrɒfənɪ] *n (UNCOUNT)* quadriphonie *f*, quadri *f*, tétraphonie *f*

quadrasonic [ˌkwɒdrəˈsɒnɪk] *adj* quadriphonique, tétraphonique

quadrat [ˈkwɒdrət] *n Typ* cadrat *m*, quadrat *m*; **em-quadrat** cadratin *m*; **en-quadrat** demi-cadratin *m*

quadrate [ˈkwɒdreɪt] **1** *n* (**a**) *(square)* carré *m*; *(cube)* cube *m* (**b**) *Anat* muscle *m* carré *m*; *Zool* os *m* carré *(de la tête)*

2 *adj* carré

►► *Zool* ***quadrate bone*** os *m* carré *(de la tête)*; *Anat* ***quadrate muscle*** muscle *m* carré

quadratic [kwɒˈdrætɪk] *Math* **1** *adj* quadratique

2 *n* équation *f* quadratique *ou* du second degré

►► ***quadratic equation*** équation *f* quadratique *ou* du second degré

quadrature [ˈkwɒdrətʃə(r)] *n Geom & Astron* quadrature *f*

quadrennial [kwɒˈdrenɪəl] *adj* quadriennal

quadrennially [kwɒˈdrenɪəlɪ] *adv* tous les quatre ans

quadri- [ˈkwɒdrɪ] *pref* quadri-

quadric [ˈkwɒdrɪk] *Math* **1** *adj* quadrique

2 *n* quadrique *f*

quadricentennial [ˌkwɒdrɪsenˈtenɪəl] *n* quadricentenaire *m*

quadriceps [ˈkwɒdrɪseps] *(pl* **inv** *or* **quadricepses** [-sɪz]) *n Anat* quadriceps *m*

quadrifid [ˈkwɒdrɪfɪd] *adj Bot* quadrifide

quadriga [kwɒˈdriːgə] *n Antiq* quadrige *m*

quadrilateral [ˌkwɒdrɪˈlætərəl] *Geom* **1** *adj* quadrilatère, quadrilatéral

2 *n* quadrilatère *m*

quadrilingual [ˌkwɒdrɪˈlɪŋgwəl] *adj (text)* (écrit) en quatre langues; *(person)* qui parle quatre langues

quadrille [kwəˈdrɪl] *n* quadrille *m*

quadrillion [kwɒˈdrɪlɪən] *n Br* quatrillion *m* (10^{24}); *Am* mille billions *mpl* (10^{15})

quadrinomial [ˌkwɒdrɪˈnəʊmɪəl] *adj Math* quadrinôme

quadripartite [ˌkwɒdrɪˈpɑːtaɪt] *adj (gen) & Bot* quadripartite

quadriplegia [ˌkwɒdrɪˈpliːdʒə] *n Med* tétraplégie *f*, quadriplégie *f*

quadriplegic [ˌkwɒdrɪˈpliːdʒɪk] *Med* **1** *adj* tétraplégique

2 *n* tétraplégique *mf*

quadripolar [ˌkwɒdrɪˈpəʊlə(r)] *adj Elec* quadripolaire

quadripole [ˈkwɒdrɪpəʊl] *n Elec* quadripôle *m*

quadrisyllabic [ˌkwɒdrɪsɪˈlæbɪk] *adj* quadrisyllabique

quadrisyllable [ˈkwɒdrɪˌsɪləbəl] *n* quadrisyllabe *m*

quadrivalent [ˌkwɒdrɪˈveɪlənt] *adj Chem* quadrivalent, tétravalent

quadroon [kwɒˈdruːn] *n* quarteron(onne) *m,f*

quadrophonic = **quadraphonic**

quadrumanous [kwɒˈdruːmənəs] *adj Zool* quadrumane

quadruped [ˈkwɒdrʊped] **1** *adj* quadrupède

2 *n* quadrupède *m*

quadrupedal [kwɒˈdruːpɪdəl] *adj* quadrupède

quadruple [kwɒˈdruːpəl] **1** *adj* quadruple

2 *n* quadruple *m*

3 *vt* quadrupler

4 *vi* quadrupler

►► ***quadruple scull*** *(in rowing)* quatre *m* de couple

quadruplet [ˈkwɒdrʊplɪt] *n* quadruplé(e) *m,f*

quadruplicate 1 *adj* [kwɒˈdruːplɪkət] quadruple

2 *n* [kwɒˈdruːplɪkət] **in quadruplicate** en quatre exemplaires

3 *vt* [kwɒˈdruːplɪkeɪt] (**a**) *(multiply by four)* quadrupler, multiplier par quatre (**b**) *(make four copies of → letter etc)* faire *ou* tirer quatre exemplaires de

quadruplication [ˌkwɒdruːplɪˈkeɪʃən] *n* quadruplication *f*

quaestorial [kwiːsˈtɔːrɪəl] *adj Antiq* questorien

quaff [kwɒf] *vt (wine)* boire à longs traits; *(glass)* vider d'un trait

quagga [ˈkwægə] *n Zool* couagga *m*

quagmire [ˈkwægmaɪə(r)] *n* marécage *m*; *Fig* bourbier *m*

quahog [ˈkwɑːhɒg] *n Am* = grand clam (spécialité de la Nouvelle-Angleterre)

quaich [kweɪχ] *n Scot (drinking cup)* coupe *f (en bois cerclé)*

quail [kweɪl] *(pl* **inv** *or* **quails**) **1** *n Orn* caille *f*

2 *vi (feel afraid)* trembler; *(give way, lose heart)* fléchir, faiblir; **to quail before sb/sth** trembler devant qn/qch; **he quailed at the thought of having to talk to her** il tremblait à l'idée d'avoir à lui parler; **I quailed before the enormity of the task** j'ai fléchi devant l'énormité de la tâche

quaint [kweɪnt] *adj* (**a**) *(picturesque)* pittoresque; *(old-fashioned)* au charme désuet; **a quaint little cottage** un mignon petit cottage; **the quaint narrow streets of the old town** les rues étroites et pittoresques de la vieille ville; **she made a quaint curtsey** elle exécuta une révérence au charme désuet; **a quaint old lady** une vieille dame aux manières désuètes (**b**) *(odd)* bizarre, étrange; **what a quaint idea!** quelle drôle d'idée!

quaintly [ˈkweɪntlɪ] *adv* (**a**) *(picturesquely)* de façon pittoresque; **the quaintly old-fashioned villages** les vieux villages pittoresques; **quaintly dressed** habillé à l'ancienne; **rather quaintly worded** formulé de façon assez désuète (**b**) *(oddly)* bizarrement, étrangement

quaintness [ˈkweɪntnɪs] *n* (**a**) *(picturesqueness)* pittoresque *m*; *(old-fashioned charm)* charme *m* vieillot *ou* démodé (**b**) *(oddness)* bizarrerie *f*, étrangeté *f*

quake [kweɪk] **1** *vi* (**a**) *(person)* trembler, frémir; **to quake with fear** trembler de peur; **he was quaking in his boots** il était mort de peur; **I was quaking at the thought of having to confront her** je tremblais à l'idée d'avoir à lui faire face (**b**) *(earth)* trembler

2 *n Fam* tremblement *m* de terre ❑

Quaker [ˈkweɪkə(r)] *Rel* **1** *n* quaker(eresse) *m,f*

2 *adj* des quakers

Quakeress [ˈkweɪkəres] *n Rel* quakeresse *f*

Quakerish [ˈkweɪkərɪʃ] *adj* de quaker, des quakers; **Quakerish dress** costume *m* sobre digne d'un quaker

Quakerism [ˈkweɪkərɪzəm] *n Rel* quakerisme *m*

quaking [ˈkweɪkɪŋ] *adj* tremblant

►► *Bot* ***quaking ash*** tremble *m*; *Bot* ***quaking grass*** brize *f*, amourette *f*

qualifiable [ˌkwɒlɪˈfaɪəbəl] *adj* qualifiable

qualification [ˌkwɒlɪfɪˈkeɪʃən] *n* (**a**) *(diploma, degree)* diplôme *m*; **candidates with formal**

qualifications in translating des candidats possédant un diplôme de traducteur; **list your academic qualifications** indiquez vos diplômes scolaires et universitaires; **he has no academic or professional qualifications** il n'a ni diplôme universitaire ni qualification professionnelle

(**b**) *(ability, quality)* aptitude *f*, compétence *f*; *(for job)* qualification *f*; **one of the qualifications for this job is a sense of humour** une des qualités requises pour ce poste est le sens de l'humour

(**c**) *(restriction)* réserve *f*; **they accepted the idea with some/without qualification** ils acceptèrent l'idée avec quelques réserves/sans réserve

(**d**) *(graduation)* **most of our students find jobs after qualification** la plupart de nos étudiants trouvent du travail dès qu'ils ont obtenu leur diplôme

(**e**) *(act of qualifying)* qualification *f*; **her qualification for the semi-final** sa qualification pour la demi-finale

qualificatory [ˌkwɒlɪfɪˈkeɪtərɪ] *adj* qualificatif

qualified [ˈkwɒlɪfaɪd] *adj* (**a**) *(trained)* qualifié, diplômé; **qualified teachers** professeurs *mpl* qualifiés *ou* diplômés; **our staff are highly qualified** notre personnel est hautement qualifié; **applications are invited from suitably qualified persons for appointment to the position of lecturer in French** nous recherchons des personnes qualifiées pour un poste d'assistant de français

(**b**) *(able, competent)* compétent, qualifié; **a respected journalist, he is well qualified to write about this issue** en tant que journaliste éminent, il est à même d'écrire *ou* il est bien placé pour écrire un article à ce sujet; **I don't feel qualified to discuss such matters** je ne suis pas à même de discuter de cela

(**c**) *(limited, conditional)* mitigé; **their efforts met with qualified praise** leurs efforts ont recueilli des louanges mitigées *ou* réservées

►► *Banking* ***qualified acceptance*** acceptation *f* conditionnelle *ou* sous condition; *Banking* ***qualified approval*** approbation *f* avec réserve; *Acct* ***qualified report*** rapport *m* réservé; ***qualified success*** demi-succès *m*

qualifier [ˈkwɒlɪfaɪə(r)] *n* (**a**) *Sport (person)* qualifié(e) *m,f*; *(contest)* (épreuve *f*) éliminatoire *f* (**b**) *Gram* qualificatif *m*

qualify [ˈkwɒlɪfaɪ] *(pt & pp* **qualified**) **1** *vi* (**a**) *(pass exams, complete training)* obtenir son diplôme; **only 10 percent of the students go on to qualify** seuls 10 pour cent des étudiants finissent par obtenir leur diplôme; **to qualify as an accountant/a vet** obtenir son diplôme de comptable/vétérinaire; **to qualify as a pilot** obtenir son brevet de pilote

(**b**) *(be eligible)* **to qualify for a pension** avoir droit à la retraite; **none of the candidates really qualifies for the post** aucun candidat ne répond véritablement aux conditions requises pour ce poste; **you don't qualify for a grant** vous ne remplissez pas les conditions requises pour recevoir une bourse; *Fig* **it hardly qualifies as a mountain** on ne peut pas vraiment appeler cela une montagne, ça ne mérite pas le nom de montagne

(**c**) *(in competition)* se qualifier; **he qualified for the finals** il s'est qualifié pour la finale

2 *vt* (**a**) *(make able or competent)* qualifier, habiliter; **to qualify sb for sth/for doing** *or* **to do sth** *(of course, training etc)* donner à qn les compétences voulues pour qch/pour faire qch, qualifier qn pour qch/pour faire qch; *Law* donner qualité à qn pour qch/pour faire qch; **her experience qualifies her for the post** son expérience lui permet de prétendre à ce poste; **this diploma qualifies you to practise acupuncture** par ce diplôme, vous êtes habilité à pratiquer l'acupuncture; **what qualifies him to talk about French politics?** en quoi est-il qualifié pour parler de la politique française?

(**b**) *(modify → statement, criticism)* mitiger, atténuer; *(put conditions on)* poser des conditions à; **they qualified their acceptance of the plan** ils ont accepté le projet sous conditions

(**c**) *(describe)* qualifier; **I wouldn't qualify the play as a masterpiece** je n'irai pas jusqu'à qualifier cette pièce de chef-d'œuvre

(**d**) *Gram* qualifier

qualifying [ˈkwɒlɪfaɪɪŋ] *adj* (**a**) *Gram* qualificatif (**b**) *(modifying)* modificateur

►► ***qualifying examination*** *(at end of course)* examen *m* de fin d'études; *(to get onto course)* examen *m* d'entrée; *Sport* ***qualifying heat*** (épreuve *f*) éliminatoire *f*; *Br Sch* ***qualifying mark*** moyenne *f*; *Sport* ***qualifying round*** (épreuve *f*) éliminatoire *f*; ***qualifying statement*** déclaration *f* corrective

qualitative [ˈkwɒlɪtətɪv] *adj* qualitatif

►► ***qualitative analysis*** analyse *f* qualitative; *Mktg* ***qualitative forecasting*** prévisions *fpl* qualitatives; *Mktg* ***qualitative research*** études *fpl* qualitatives; *Mktg* ***qualitative study*** étude *f* qualitative

qualitatively [ˈkwɒlɪtətɪvlɪ] *adv* qualitativement

quality [ˈkwɒlɪtɪ] *(pl* **qualities**) **1** *n* (**a**) *(standard, nature)* qualité *f*; **the high/poor quality of the workmanship** la bonne/mauvaise qualité du travail; **the quality of life** la qualité de la vie

(**b**) *(high standard, excellence)* qualité *f*; **quality matters more than quantity** la qualité importe plus que la quantité; **never mind the price, I'm only interested in quality** peu importe le prix, ce que je recherche, c'est la qualité; **we have a reputation for quality** nous sommes réputés pour la qualité de nos produits

(**c**) *(feature, attribute)* qualité *f*; **these are the qualities we are looking for in our candidates** voici les qualités que nous recherchons chez nos candidats; **he has a lot of good qualities** il a de nombreuses qualités; **I don't doubt her intellectual qualities** je ne doute pas de ses capacités intellectuelles; **these tyres have superior road-holding qualities** ces pneus offrent une meilleure adhérence au sol

(**d**) *Br (newspaper)* = quotidien ou journal du dimanche de qualité (par opposition à la presse populaire)

(**e**) *Arch (high social status)* qualité *f*; **a gentleman of quality** un homme de qualité; **the quality** les gens *mpl* de qualité, *Pej* le beau linge

(**f**) *(tone)* timbre *m*

(**g**) *Ling (in phonetics)* qualité *f*

2 *comp (goods, work, shop)* de qualité; **I only spend an hour in the evening with my kids, but it's quality time** je ne passe qu'une heure avec mes gosses le soir, mais je profite bien d'eux

►► ***quality assurance*** garantie *f* de qualité; ***quality audit*** audit *m* de qualité; *Br* ***quality circle*** cercle *m* de qualité; ***quality control*** contrôle *m* de (la) qualité; ***quality controller*** responsable *mf* du contrôle de (la) qualité, qualiticien(enne) *m,f*; ***quality improvement*** l'amélioration *f* de la qualité; ***quality label*** label *m* de qualité; ***quality management*** gestion *f* qualité; *Br* ***quality newspaper*** = quotidien ou journal du dimanche de qualité (par opposition à la presse populaire); *Mktg* ***quality positioning*** positionnement *m* par la qualité

quality-assurance manager *n* directeur(trice) *m,f* de l'assurance-qualité

quality-price ratio *n Mktg* rapport *m* qualité-prix

qualm [kwɑːm] *n* (**a**) *(scruple)* scrupule *m*; *(misgiving)* appréhension *f*, inquiétude *f*; **I occasionally have qualms about the job I do** il m'arrive d'avoir des scrupules à faire le travail que je fais; **he had no qualms about laying off his staff** il n'avait aucun scrupule à licencier ses employés; **she has no qualms about going out alone** elle ne craint pas de sortir seule (**b**) *(pang of nausea)* haut-le-cœur *m inv*, nausée *f*

quandary [ˈkwɒndərɪ] *(pl* **quandaries**) *n* dilemme *m*; **I'm in a dreadful quandary** je suis confronté à un terrible dilemme; **she was in a quandary over** *or* **about whether or not to tell him** elle ne parvenait pas à décider si elle devait le lui dire

quango [ˈkwæŋgəʊ] *(pl* **quangos**) *n Br (abbr* **quasiautonomous non-governmental organization**) = organisme semi-public

> **QUANGO**
>
> En Grande-Bretagne, un "quango" est un organisme semi-public principalement financé par l'État mais disposant d'une certaine autonomie. Certains de ces organismes ont un rôle purement consultatif. D'autres sont habilités à prendre des décisions, notamment au niveau local, et c'est pourquoi au cours de ces dernières années les "quangos" ont fait l'objet de critiques, car leurs membres sont nommés par le gouvernement et non pas élus.

quant [kwɒnt] *n (for punting)* perche *f* de bachot

quanta [ˈkwɒntə] *pl of* **quantum**

quantic [ˈkwɒntɪk] *n Math* fonction *f* homogène à plusieurs variables

quantifiable [ˌkwɒntɪˈfaɪəbəl] *adj* quantifiable

quantification [ˌkwɒntɪfɪˈkeɪʃən] *n (in logic)* quantification *f*

quantifier [ˈkwɒntɪfaɪə(r)] *n* (**a**) *Gram* quantificateur *m*, quantifieur *m* (**b**) *(in logic) & Math* quantificateur *m*

quantify [ˈkwɒntɪfaɪ] *(pt & pp* **quantified**) *vt* (**a**) *(estimate)* quantifier, évaluer quantitativement; **it is hard to quantify the damage** il est difficile d'évaluer l'ampleur des dégâts (**b**) *(in logic)* quantifier

quantitative [ˈkwɒntɪtətɪv] *adj* quantitatif

►► ***quantitative analysis*** analyse *f* quantitative; ***quantitative forecasting*** prévisions *fpl* quantitatives; ***quantitative research*** études *fpl* quantitatives; ***quantitative study*** étude *f* quantitative

quantitatively [ˈkwɒntɪtətɪvlɪ] *adv* quantitativement

quantitive [ˈkwɒntɪtɪv] = **quantitative**

quantity [ˈkwɒntɪtɪ] *(pl* **quantities**) *n (gen) & Ling & Math* quantité *f*; **what quantity of sugar do you need for the cake?** de quelle quantité de sucre avez-vous besoin pour le gâteau?; **in quantity** en (grande) quantité; **large quantities of** de grandes quantités de; **to buy sth in large quantities** acheter qch en grande quantité

►► ***quantity discount*** remise *f ou* escompte *m* sur la quantité *ou* sur les achats en gros; ***quantity mark*** signe *m* de quantité; ***quantity rebate*** remise *f* sur la quantité; ***quantity surveying*** métrage *m*; ***quantity surveyor*** métreur(euse) *m,f*; *Econ* ***quantity theory*** théorie *f* quantitative

quantization [ˌkwɒntaɪˈzeɪʃən] *n Phys* quantification *f*

►► ***quantization distortion*** distorsion *f* de quantification

quantize, -ise [ˈkwɒntaɪz] *vt Phys* quantifier

quanton [ˈkwɒntən] *n Phys* quanton *m*

quantum [ˈkwɒntəm] *(pl* **quanta** [-tə]) *n Math & Phys* quantum *m*

►► ***quantum jump, quantum leap*** progrès *m* énorme, bond *m* en avant; *Fig* **the new model represents a quantum jump** le nouveau modèle représente un grand bond en avant; ***quantum mechanics*** *(UNCOUNT)* (mécanique *f*) quantique *f*; ***quantum number*** nombre *m* quantique; ***quantum theory*** théorie *f* des quanta *ou* quantique

quaquaversal [ˌkweɪkwəˈvɜːsəl] *adj Geol* quaquaversal

quarantine [ˈkwɒrəntiːn] **1** *n Med & Vet* quarantaine *f*; **our dog is in quarantine** notre chien est en quarantaine

2 *vt* mettre en quarantaine

3 *comp (laws, regulations)* sur la quarantaine; *(period)* de quarantaine

►► ***quarantine flag*** pavillon *m* de quarantaine

quark [kwɑːk] *n* (**a**) *Phys* quark *m* (**b**) *(cheese)* fromage *m* blanc

quarrel [ˈkwɒrəl] *(Br pt & pp* **quarrelled**, *cont* **quarrelling**, *Am pt & pp* **quarreled**, *cont* **quarreling**) **1** *n* (**a**) *(dispute)* querelle *f*, dispute *f*; **they had a quarrel over money** ils se sont disputés pour des histoires d'argent; **are you trying to start a quarrel?** tu cherches la dispute?; **to pick a quarrel with sb** chercher querelle à qn

(**b**) *(cause for complaint)* **I have no quarrel with him** je n'ai rien à lui reprocher; **my only quarrel with the plan is its cost** la seule chose que je reproche à ce projet, c'est son coût; **I have no quarrel with her proposal** je n'ai rien contre sa proposition

2 *vi* (**a**) *(argue)* se disputer, se quereller; **I don't want to quarrel with you over** *or* **about this** je ne veux pas me disputer avec toi à ce sujet *ou* à propos de cela; **they're always quarrelling over money** ils se disputent sans cesse pour des histoires d'argent

(**b**) *(take issue)* **I can't quarrel with your figures** je ne peux pas contester vos chiffres; **I**

can't quarrel with that je n'ai rien à redire à cela; **critics might quarrel with parts of the introduction** les critiques pourraient trouver à redire à certains passages de l'introduction

quarreller, *Am* **quarreler** ['kwɒrələ(r)] *n* querelleur(euse) *m,f*

quarrelling, *Am* **quarreling** ['kwɒrəlɪŋ] **1** *n (UNCOUNT)* disputes *fpl*, querelles *fpl*

2 *adj (children, parents, lovers)* qui se disputent

quarrelsome ['kwɒrəlsəm] *adj* querelleur

quarrelsomeness ['kwɒrəlsəmnɪs] *n* humeur *f* querelleuse

quarrier ['kwɒrɪə(r)] *n* carrier *m*

quarry ['kwɒrɪ] *(pl* **quarries,** *pt & pp* **quarried) 1** *n* (**a**) *(for stone, slate, sand, marble etc)* carrière *f* (**b**) *(prey)* proie *f*

2 *vt* (**a**) *(stone, slate, sand, marble etc)* extraire (**b**) *(land, mountain)* exploiter; **the hills have been extensively quarried** de nombreuses carrières ont été ouvertes dans les collines

3 *vi* exploiter; **they are quarrying for marble** ils exploitent une carrière de marbre

▸▸ ***quarry tile*** carreau *m*

quarrying ['kwɒrɪɪŋ] *n* (**a**) *(of stone, slate, sand, marble etc)* extraction *f* (**b**) *(of land, mountain)* exploitation *f*; **the countryside has been spoilt by quarrying** les carrières ont défiguré *ou* massacré le paysage

quarryman ['kwɒrɪmən] *(pl* **quarrymen** [-mən]) *n* carrier *m*

quart [kwɔ:t] *n (liquid measurement) Br* = 1,136 l; *Am* = 0,946 l; *Br Prov* **you can't fit a quart into a pint pot** à l'impossible nul n'est tenu

quarte [kɑ:t] *n Fencing* quarte *f*

quarter ['kwɔ:tə(r)] **1** *adj* **a quarter hour/century/pound** un quart d'heure/de siècle/de livre

2 *vt* (**a**) *(divide into four)* diviser en quatre; *(beef etc)* diviser par quartiers, équarrir; **to quarter a cake** couper un gâteau en quatre parts égales

(**b**) *(divide by four)* diviser par quatre; **prices have been quartered** les prix ont été divisés par quatre

(**c**) *(lodge)* loger; *Mil* cantonner; **the troops are quartered in the town** les soldats sont logés en ville

(**d**) *Hist (dismember)* écarteler

(**e**) *(of hunting dog)* **to quarter the ground** quêter

3 *n* (**a**) *(one fourth)* quart *m*; *(portion → of apple, circle, century etc)* quart *m*; *(→ of orange, moon)* quartier *m*; **during the first quarter of the century** au cours du premier quart de ce siècle; **a quarter of a century/of an hour** un quart de siècle/d'heure; **a quarter century** un quart de siècle; **a ton and a quarter, one and a quarter tons** une tonne un quart; **he ate a quarter/three quarters of the cake** il a mangé le quart/les trois quarts du gâteau; **it's a quarter/three quarters empty** c'est au quart/aux trois quarts vide; **we've only done (a) quarter of the work** nous n'avons fait que le quart du travail

(**b**) *(in telling time)* quart *m*; *Br* **(a) quarter to six,** *Am* **(a) quarter of six** six heures moins le quart; *Br* **(a) quarter past six,** *Am* **(a) quarter after six** six heures et quart; **it's a quarter past** il est le quart

(**c**) *(three-month period)* trimestre *m*; **published every quarter** publié tous les trimestres *ou* tous les trois mois; **to be paid by the quarter** être payé par trimestre; **profits were up during the last quarter** les bénéfices ont augmenté au cours du dernier trimestre

(**d**) *(US and Canadian money)* (pièce *f* de) vingt-cinq cents *mpl*

(**e**) *(unit of weight → quarter of hundredweight)* = 12 kg; *(→ quarter pound)* = 113 g

(**f**) *Naut (direction)* **the wind is in the port/starboard quarter** le vent souffle par la hanche de bâbord/tribord

(**g**) *(milieu)* **the decision has been criticized in certain quarters** la décision a été critiquée dans certains milieux; **in well-informed quarters** dans les milieux bien informés; **offers of help poured in from all quarters** des offres d'aide affluèrent de tous côtés

(**h**) *(part of town)* quartier *m*; **the residential quarter** le quartier résidentiel

(**i**) *(phase of moon)* quartier *m*; **the moon is in the first/last quarter** la lune est dans le premier/dernier quartier

(**j**) *Sport (period of play)* quart-temps *m inv*

(**k**) *(part of butchered animal)* quartier *m*

(**l**) *(usu neg) Literary (mercy)* quartier *m*; **they gave no quarter** ils ne firent pas de quartier; **there was no quarter given or asked** on ne fit pas de quartier

4 quarters *npl (accommodation)* domicile *m*, résidence *f*; *Mil* quartiers *mpl*, cantonnement *m*, logement *m*; **the servants' quarters** les appartements *mpl* des domestiques; **married quarters** logement *m* pour couples mariés; **she took up quarters in central London** elle a élu domicile *ou* s'est installée dans le centre de Londres; **many families live in very cramped quarters** de nombreuses familles vivent dans des conditions de surpeuplement

▸▸ ***quarter binding*** *(in bookbinding)* demi-reliure *f*; *Br Fin* ***quarter day*** (jour *m* du) terme *m*; *Am Mus* ***quarter note*** noire *f*; *Law* ***quarter sessions*** *(in England and Wales)* ≃ cour *f* d'assises *(remplacée en 1972 par la "Crown Court")*; *(in US)* = dans certains États, tribunal local à compétence criminelle, pouvant avoir des fonctions administratives; *Mus* ***quarter tone*** quart *m* de ton

quarterage ['kwɔ:tərɪdʒ] *n (payment)* paiement *m* trimestriel

quarterback ['kwɔ:tə,bæk] **1** *n Sport* quarterback *m*, *Can* quart-arrière *m*

2 *vt Am* (**a**) *Sport (team)* jouer quarterback dans (**b**) *Fig* être le stratège de, diriger la stratégie de

quarterdeck ['kwɔ:tə,dek] *n* (**a**) *Naut (part of ship)* plage *f* arrière (**b**) *(personnel)* **the quarterdeck** les officiers *mpl*

quarterfinal [,kwɔ:tə'faɪnəl] *n* quart *m* de finale; **knocked out in the quarterfinals** éliminé en quart de finale

quarterfinalist [,kwɔ:tə'faɪnəlɪst] *n* quart-de-finaliste *mf*

quarter-hourly 1 *adj* tous les quarts d'heure

2 *adv* tous les quarts d'heure

quartering ['kwɔ:tərɪŋ] *n* (**a**) *(dividing up)* division *f* en quatre (**b**) *Mil (billeting)* cantonnement *m*

quarterlight ['kwɔ:tə,laɪt] *n Br Aut* déflecteur *m*

quarterly ['kwɔ:təlɪ] **1** *adj* trimestriel

2 *n* publication *f* trimestrielle

3 *adv* trimestriellement, tous les trimestres

quartermaster ['kwɔ:tə,mɑ:stə(r)] *n* (**a**) *(in army)* commissaire *m*; *Hist* intendant *m* (**b**) *(in navy)* officier *m* de manœuvre

▸▸ *Mil* ***Quartermaster General*** Directeur *m* de l'Intendance *(militaire)*

quartern ['kwɔ:tən] *n (of pint, stone, ounce etc)* quart *m*

▸▸ ***quartern loaf*** pain *m* de quatre livres

quarter-pounder *n* gros hamburger *m*

quarterstaff ['kwɔ:tə,stɑ:f] *n Hist* bâton *m (utilisé comme arme)*

quartet, quartette [kwɔ:'tet] *n* (**a**) *Mus (players → classical)* quatuor *m*; *(→ jazz)* quartette *m* (**b**) *Mus (piece of music)* quatuor *m* (**c**) *(group of four people)* quatuor *m*

quartic ['kwɔ:tɪk] *n Math* quartique *f*

quartile ['kwɔ:taɪl] *n Math* quartile *m*

quarto ['kwɔ:təʊ] *(pl* **quartos) 1** *n* in-quarto *m inv*

2 *adj* in-quarto *(inv)*

quartz [kwɔ:ts] *Miner* **1** *n* quartz *m*

2 *comp (clock, watch)* à quartz

▸▸ ***quartz crystal*** cristal *m* de quartz

quartz-halogen *n* halogène *m* à quartz

quartziferous [,kwɔ:t'sɪfərəs] *adj Miner* quartzifère

quartz-iodine lamp *n* lampe *f* à iode

quartzite ['kwɔ:tsaɪt] *n Miner* quartzite *m*

quasar ['kweɪzɑ:(r)] *n Astron* quasar *m*

quash [kwɒʃ] *vt Br* (**a**) *(annul → verdict, decision)* casser, annuler (**b**) *(suppress → revolt)* étouffer, écraser; *(→ emotion)* réprimer, refouler; *(→ suggestion)* rejeter, repousser; **their creativity is quashed at an early age** leur créativité est étouffée dès leur jeune âge

quashing ['kwɒʃɪŋ] *n* (**a**) *Law (of verdict, decision)* cassation *f*, annulation *f* (**b**) *(of revolt)* écrasement *m*

quasi- ['kweɪzaɪ] *pref* quasi-; **a quasi-official organization** une organisation quasi officielle

quasi-contract *n Law* quasi-contrat *m*

quasi-crystal *n Phys* quasi-cristal *m*

quasi-money *n Fin* quasi-monnaie *f*

quasi-stellar *adj Astron* quasistellaire

▸▸ ***quasi-stellar object*** objet *m* quasistellaire

quassia ['kwɒʃɪə, 'kwɒsɪə] *n* (**a**) *Bot* quassier *m*, quassia *m* (**b**) *Pharm* quassia *m*

▸▸ *Bot* ***quassia tree*** quassier *m*, quassia *m*

quatercentenary [,kwætəsen'ti:nərɪ] *(pl* **quatercentenaries)** *n* quatrième centenaire *m*

quaternary [kwə'tɜ:nərɪ] **1** *adj Chem & Math* quaternaire

2 *n (set of four)* ensemble *m* de quatre (éléments)

3 Quaternary *Geol* **1** *adj* quaternaire **2** *n* **the Quaternary** le quaternaire

quaternion [kwə'tɜ:nɪən] *n* (**a**) *(set of four)* ensemble *m* de quatre (éléments) (**b**) *Typ* cahier *m* de quatre feuilles (**c**) *Math* quaternion *m*

quatrain ['kwɒtreɪn] *n Literature* quatrain *m*

quatrefoil ['kætrəfɔɪl] *n Archit* quadrilobe *m*, quatre-feuilles *m inv*

quattrocentist [,kwætrəʊ'tʃentɪst] *Art & Literature* **1** *n* quattrocentiste *mf*

2 *adj* des quattrocentistes

quattrocento [,kwætrəʊ'tʃentəʊ] *n Art & Literature* quattrocento *m*

quaver ['kweɪvə(r)] **1** *vi (voice)* trembloter, chevroter; *(person)* parler d'une voix tremblotante *ou* chevrotante

2 *n* (**a**) *(of sound, in voice)* chevrotement *m*, tremblement *m* (**b**) *Br Mus* croche *f*

quavering ['kweɪvərɪŋ] **1** *adj* tremblotant, chevrotant

2 *n* tremblement *m*, chevrotement *m*

quaveringly ['kweɪvərɪŋlɪ] *adv* d'une voix tremblotante *ou* chevrotante, avec des trémolos dans la voix

quavery ['kweɪvərɪ] *adj* tremblotant, chevrotant

quay [ki:] *n* quai *m*

quayage ['ki:ɪdʒ] *n* (**a**) *(area)* quais *mpl* (**b**) *(charges)* droits *mpl* de quai

quayside ['ki:saɪd] *n* quai *m*; **we walked along the quayside** nous nous sommes promenés le long du quai; **she was waiting at the quayside** elle attendait sur le quai

queasiness ['kwi:zɪnɪs] *n (UNCOUNT)* (**a**) *(nausea)* nausée *f* (**b**) *(uneasiness)* scrupules *mpl*

queasy ['kwi:zɪ] *(compar* **queasier,** *superl* **queasiest)** *adj* (**a**) *(nauseous)* nauséeux; **I** *or* **my stomach felt a little queasy** j'avais un peu mal au cœur; **the drugs make him queasy** les médicaments lui donnent des nausées; **the very sight of meat makes her feel queasy** la simple vue de la viande lui donne la nausée; **she was looking rather queasy** elle avait l'air d'avoir mal au cœur (**b**) *(uneasy)* mal à l'aise, gêné

Quebec [kwɪ'bek] *n* (**a**) *(city)* Québec (**b**) *(province)* le Québec; **in Quebec** au Québec

Quebecker, Quebecer [kwɪ'bekə(r)] *n* Québécois(e) *m,f*

Quebecois, Québecois [,kebe'kwɑ:] *(pl* **Quebecois)** *n* Québécois(e) *m,f*

quebracho [keɪ'brɑ:tʃəʊ] *(pl* **quebrachos)** *n Bot* quebracho *m*

Quechua ['ketʃwɑ:] *n* (**a**) *(person)* Quechua *mf* (**b**) *(language)* quechua *m*

queen [kwi:n] **1** *n* (**a**) *(sovereign, king's wife)* reine *f*; **the Queen of Spain/Belgium** la reine d'Espagne/de Belgique; **Queen Elizabeth II** la reine Élisabeth II; **she was queen to Charles II** elle fut la reine *ou* l'épouse de Charles II; *Br* **the Queen's Christmas message** = discours télévisé et radiodiffusé de la reine le jour de Noël

(**b**) *(woman, place, thing considered best)* reine *f*; **the queen of the blues** la reine du blues; **the rose is the queen of flowers** la rose est la reine des fleurs

(**c**) *Cards & Chess* dame *f*, reine *f*; **he played his queen of clubs** il joua sa dame de trèfle

(**d**) *(of bees, ants)* reine *f*

(**e**) *Fam Pej (any homosexual)* pédé *m*, tantouze *f*; *(effeminate homosexual)* folle *f*

2 *vt* (**a**) *Chess* **to queen a pawn** aller à dame

(**b**) *Br Fam (idiom)* **to queen it** prendre des airs de (grande) marquise; **she thinks she can**

qua–que

queen it over us! elle s'imagine qu'elle est supérieure à nous!□

3 *vi Chess (pawn)* aller à dame

►► *Queen Anne* = style d'architecture et de mobilier du XVIIIème siècle caractérisé par des lignes sobres; *Bot* **Queen Anne's lace** carotte *f* sauvage; *Entom* **queen bee** reine *f* des abeilles; *Fam Fig* **she's the queen bee round here** c'est elle la patronne ici; *Law* **Queen's Bench (Division)** = en Angleterre et au pays de Galles, l'une des trois divisions de la "High Court", ≃ tribunal *m* de grande instance; *Am Culin* **queen cake** = petit gâteau aux raisins secs; **queen consort** reine *f (épouse du roi)*; **Queen's Counsel** avocat(e) *m,f* de la Couronne *(en Grande-Bretagne)*; **Queen Elizabeth Islands** les îles *fpl* de la Reine-Élisabeth; **Queen's English** = l'anglais britannique correct; **she speaks the Queen's English** elle s'exprime dans un anglais très soigné; *Br* **the Queen's highway** la voie publique; **Queen Mother** reine *f* mère; *Br Fam* **the Queen Mum** la reine mère□; *Archit* **queen post** clef *f* pendante latérale; *Culin* **queen of puddings** = dessert à base de mie de pain, d'œufs, de confiture et de lait, garni de meringue; **queen regent** reine *f* régente; *Br* **Queen's Regulations** règlement *m* militaire; **queen scallop** vanneau *m (mollusque)*; **Queen's Speech** *(in UK)* = allocution prononcée par la reine (mais préparée par le gouvernement) lors de la rentrée parlementaire et dans laquelle elle définit les grands axes de la politique gouvernementale

queenie ['kwi:nɪ] *n (scallop)* vanneau *m (mollusque)*

queenliness ['kwi:nlɪnɪs] *n* majesté *f*

queenly ['kwi:nlɪ] *adj* royal, majestueux

Queens [kwi:nz] *n* = quartier de New York

Queensberry ['kwi:nzbərɪ] *pr n*

►► *Boxing* **the Queensberry Rules** = réglementations régissant les matches de boxe

queen-size bed *n* grand lit *m* double *(de 2 mètres sur 1,50 mètre)*

Queensland ['kwi:nzlənd] *n* le Queensland; **in Queensland** dans le Queensland

Queenslander ['kwi:nzləndə(r)] *n* habitant(e) *m,f* du Queensland, originaire *mf* du Queensland

queer [kwɪə(r)] **1** *adj* **(a)** *(strange)* étrange, bizarre; **he's a queer fish!** c'est un drôle d'individu!; **he's got some queer ideas** il a de drôles d'idées, il a des idées bizarres; **she's a queer-looking person** elle a une drôle de tête; **she has a queer-sounding name** elle a un drôle de nom

(b) *(suspicious)* suspect, louche; **there've been some queer goings-on around here** il s'est passé des choses bizarres ici

(c) *Fam (queasy)* mal fichu, patraque

(d) *Fam (crazy)* timbré, cinglé; **he's a bit queer in the head** il lui manque une case

(e) *very Fam (homosexual)* homo, pédé; *Am Pej* **as queer as a three-dollar bill** pédé comme un phoque

(f) *Br Fam Old-fashioned (difficult position)* **to be in queer street** être dans une mauvaise passe

2 *n very Fam (homosexual)* pédé *m*, pédale *f*

3 *vt Fam* gâter□, gâcher□; *Br* **to queer sb's pitch** couper l'herbe sous les pieds de qn

►► *Am Fam* **queer money** *(counterfeit)* fausse monnaie□ *f*

queer-basher *n Br very Fam* = individu qui se livre à des violences à l'encontre d'homosexuels

queer-bashing *n Br very Fam* = violences à l'encontre d'homosexuels

queerly ['kwɪəlɪ] *adv* étrangement, bizarrement; **she looked at me queerly** elle me regarda d'un drôle d'air

queerness ['kwɪənɪs] *n* **(a)** *(strangeness)* étrangeté *f*, bizarrerie *f* **(b)** *(queasiness)* nausée *f*

quelea ['kwi:lɪə] *n Orn* quéléa *m*

quell [kwel] *vt* **(a)** *(quash → revolt, opposition)* réprimer, étouffer **(b)** *(overcome → emotion)* dompter, maîtriser **(c)** *(allay → pain)* apaiser, soulager; *(→ doubts, fears)* dissiper

quench [kwentʃ] *vt* **(a) to quench one's thirst** étancher sa soif, se désaltérer **(b)** *(fire)* éteindre **(c)** *Metal* tremper **(d)** *Fig (enthusiasm)* atténuer; *(desire)* réprimer, étouffer

quenchless ['kwentʃlɪs] *adj Literary* inextinguible

quercetin, quercitin ['kwɜ:sɪtɪn] *n Chem* quercétine *f*

quercitrin [,kwɜ:'sɪtrɪn] *n Chem* quercitrin *m*, quercitrine *f*

querist ['kwɪərɪst] *n* questionneur(euse) *m,f*

quern [kwɜ:n] *n* moulin *m* à céréales *(à meules de pierre)*

querulous ['kwerʊləs] *adj (person)* pleurnicheur; *(voice, tone)* plaintif, gémissant

querulously ['kwerʊləslɪ] *adv* d'un ton plaintif

querulousness ['kwerʊləsnɪs] *n (of person)* disposition *f* à se plaindre, habitude *f* de se plaindre; *(of voice, words)* ton *m* plaintif

query ['kwɪərɪ] *(pl* **queries**, *pt & pp* **queried**) **1** *n* **(a)** *(question)* question *f*; *(doubt)* doute *m*; **I have a query** j'ai une question; **she accepted my explanation without a query** elle a accepté mon explication sans poser de questions; **the latest facts to come to light raise a query about his honesty** les derniers faits qui ont été mis au jour jettent un doute sur son honnêteté; **there was a note of query in her voice** il y avait une note d'interrogation dans sa voix

(b) *Br (question mark)* point *m* d'interrogation

(c) *Comput* interrogation *f*

2 *vt* **(a)** *(express doubt about)* mettre en doute; **it is not for me to query their motives** ce n'est pas à moi de mettre en doute leurs mobiles; **the accountant queried the figures** le comptable posa des questions sur les chiffres; **I would query it if I were you** à votre place je le vérifierais

(b) *(ask)* demander; **"how much is it?" she queried** "combien est-ce?" demanda-t-elle

(c) *(mark with question mark)* marquer d'un point d'interrogation

(d) *Am (interrogate)* interroger; **he queried me about my trip** il m'a posé des questions sur mon voyage

(e) *Comput (database)* interroger

►► *Comput* **query language** langage *m* d'interrogation; *Am* **query mark** point *m* d'interrogation

quest [kwest] **1** *n* quête *f*; **to go in quest of sb/sth** se mettre *ou* aller *ou* partir à la recherche de qn/qch *ou* en quête de qn/qch; **her quest for justice** sa bataille pour que justice soit faite; **in quest of the truth** en quête de *ou* à la recherche de la vérité

2 *vi Literary* **to quest for** *or* **after sth** se mettre en quête de qch

QUESTION ['kwestʃən]

question	► **1 (a), (b), (d), (e)**
doute	► **1 (c)**
interroger	► **2 (a)**
mettre en doute	► **2 (b)**

1 *n* **(a)** *(query)* question *f*; **to ask sb a question** poser une question à qn; **I wish to put a question to the chairman** j'aimerais poser une question au président; *Parl* **to put down a question for sb** adresser une interpellation à qn; **you haven't answered my question** vous n'avez pas répondu à ma question; **they obeyed without question** ils ont obéi sans poser de questions; **a question and answer session** une séance questions-réponses; **what a question!** quelle question!; *Gram* **direct/indirect question** interrogation *f* directe/indirecte; *Br Parl* **(Prime Minister's) Question Time, Prime Minister's Questions** = session hebdomadaire du Parlement britannique réservée aux questions des députés au Premier ministre

(b) *(matter, issue)* question *f*; *(problem)* problème *m*; **her article raises some important questions** son article soulève d'importantes questions *ou* d'importants problèmes; **it raises the question of how much teachers should be paid** cela soulève *ou* pose le problème du salaire des enseignants; **the place/time in question** le lieu/l'heure en question; **the person in question is away at the moment** la personne en question est absente en ce moment; **the Jewish question** la question juive; **the question is, will he do it?** toute la question est de savoir s'il le fera; **that is the question** voilà la question; **that's another** *or* **a different question** c'est une autre histoire; **but that's not the question, that's beside the question** mais là n'est pas la question, il ne s'agit pas de cela; **it's not a question of who's right** la question n'est pas de savoir qui a raison; **it's a question of how much you want to spend** tout dépend de la somme que vous voulez mettre; **it's only a question of money/time** ce n'est qu'une question d'argent/de temps; **it's only a question of time before it happens** ça arrivera tôt ou tard

(c) *(UNCOUNT) (doubt)* doute *m*; **there's no question about it, he was murdered** il a été assassiné, cela ne fait aucun doute; **his honesty was never in question** son honnêteté n'a jamais été mise en doute *ou* remise en question; **to bring** *or* **to call sth into question** remettre qch en question; **she is without** *or* **beyond question the best** elle est incontestablement la meilleure; **they know beyond question where their interests lie** ils savent parfaitement (bien) où est leur intérêt; **whether they are happier now is open to question** sont-ils plus heureux maintenant? on peut se le demander; **the wisdom of this decision is open to question** le bien-fondé de la décision est discutable

(d) *(possibility)* **there was some question of...** il a été question de...; **there's no question of our making the same mistake again** nous ne sommes pas près de refaire la même erreur; **there is no question of going back now** il n'est pas question de revenir en arrière; **there's no question of his coming with us, it's out of the question that he should come with us** il est hors de question qu'il vienne avec nous; **there was never any question of his coming with us** il n'a jamais été question qu'il nous accompagne; **I'm sorry, you can't go, it's out of the question!** je regrette, vous ne pouvez pas y aller, c'est hors de question!

(e) *Hist* **to put sb to the question** *(torture)* mettre qn à la question, appliquer la question à qn

2 *vt* **(a)** *(interrogate)* interroger, poser des questions à; *(of police)* interroger; *Sch* interroger; *Mktg (consumer)* interroger; **to be questioned** être interrogé; *(suspect)* subir un interrogatoire; **the people questioned in the survey** les personnes interrogées dans le cadre du sondage; **she was questioned on her views** on l'a interrogée sur ses opinions

(b) *(doubt → motives, honesty, wisdom)* mettre en doute, mettre en question; *(→ statement, claim)* mettre en doute, contester; **nobody is questioning your motives** personne ne met en doute *ou* en question vos motivations; **I questioned whether it was wise to continue** je me suis demandé s'il était bien sage de continuer

►► *Gram* **question form** forme *f* interrogative; **question mark** *(punctuation mark)* point *m* d'interrogation; *Mktg (product)* point *m* d'interrogation, dilemme *m*; *Fig* **a question mark hangs over the future of this country** il est impossible de prédire quel sort attend ce pays *ou* sera réservé à ce pays; **there is a question mark over her reasons for leaving** on ignore les raisons qui l'ont poussée à partir; **question master** meneur(euse) *m,f* de jeu; *Rad & TV* animateur(trice) *m,f (d'un jeu)*; *Ling* **question tag** question tag *m*, = tournure interrogative en fin de phrase, équivalent du "n'est-ce pas" français

'A Question of Upbringing' *Powell* 'Une Question d'éducation'

questionable ['kwestʃənəbəl] *adj* **(a)** *(doubtful)* contestable, douteux; **his involvement in the affair is questionable** sa participation dans cette affaire reste à démontrer *ou* à prouver; **it is questionable whether she knew** rien ne prouve qu'elle était au courant; **this is the most democratic country – that's very questionable** c'est le pays le plus démocratique – c'est très discutable

(b) *(suspicious → motives)* douteux, louche; *(→ behaviour)* louche

(c) *(strange → taste, style)* douteux

questionably ['kwestʃənəblɪ] *adv* d'une manière

contestable; **secondly, and more questionably, he argues that...** deuxièmement, et ce qui est plus discutable, il affirme que...

questioner ['kwestʃənə(r)] *n (gen, in quiz show)* animateur(trice) *m,f*; *Law* interrogateur(trice) *m,f*; **she sent her questioners away** elle renvoya ceux qui l'interrogeaient; *Rad & TV* **our next questioner is from Belfast** la question suivante nous vient de Belfast

questioning ['kwestʃənɪŋ] **1** *adj* interrogateur; **to have a questioning mind** avoir un esprit curieux

2 *n* interrogation *f*; *Law* **he was taken in for questioning** il a été interpellé pour être interrogé

questioningly ['kwestʃənɪŋlɪ] *adv* de manière interrogative

questionnaire [ˌkwestʃə'neə(r)] *n* questionnaire *m*

►► ***questionnaire analysis*** dépouillement *m* de questionnaire; ***questionnaire construction*** construction *f* de questionnaire; ***questionnaire survey*** enquête *f* par questionnaire

questor ['kwestə(r)] *n Antiq* questeur *m*

quetzal ['ketsəl] *n* (**a**) *Orn* quetzal *m* (**b**) *(currency)* quetzal *m*

queue [kju:] **1** *n* (**a**) *Br* queue *f*, file *f* d'attente; **they were standing in a queue** ils faisaient la queue; **to form a queue** former une queue; **a long queue of cars** une longue file de voitures; **I was first in the queue** j'étais le premier de la file; **we joined the queue for foreign exchange** nous avons fait la queue devant le bureau de change

(**b**) *Comput* file *f* d'attente

(**c**) *Arch (of hair, wig)* queue *f*

2 *vt Comput (print jobs)* mettre en file d'attente

3 *vi Br* faire la queue; **I spent ages queuing for a bus** j'ai passé des heures à attendre le bus; **queue here for tickets** *(sign)* file d'attente pour les billets

►**queue up** *vi Br* faire la queue; **people queued up to shake his hand** les gens faisaient la queue pour lui serrer la main; **people are queuing up for a job like yours** les gens se battent pour décrocher un emploi comme le vôtre

queue-jump *vi Br* essayer de passer avant son tour, resquiller

queue-jumper *n Br* resquilleur(euse) *m,f (qui n'attend pas son tour)*

quibble ['kwɪbəl] **1** *vi* chicaner; **to quibble over details** chicaner sur des détails; **he didn't quibble about the price** il n'a pas chipoté sur le prix

2 *n* chicane *f*; **I have one small quibble** il y a juste une petite chose qui me gêne

quibbler ['kwɪblə(r)] *n* chicaneur(euse) *m,f*, chicanier(ère) *m,f*

quibbling ['kwɪblɪŋ] **1** *adj* chicaneur, chicanier

2 *n* chicanerie *f*

Quiberon ['ki:brɔ̃] *pr n*

►► ***the Quiberon peninsula*** la presqu'île de Quiberon

quiche [ki:ʃ] *n* quiche *f*

quick [kwɪk] **1** *adj* (**a**) *(rapid)* rapide; *(easy → profits)* rapide, facile; **he's a quick worker** il travaille vite; *Fig* il ne perd pas de temps; **be quick (about it)!** faites vite!, dépêchez-vous!; **I need a quick answer** j'ai besoin d'une réponse rapide; **to have a quick look** jeter un rapide coup d'œil; **can I have a quick word?** est-ce que je peux vous parler un instant?; **we had a quick lunch** nous avons déjeuné sur le pouce; *Fam* **let's have a quick one** *or* **a quick drink** prenons un verre en vitesse❑; **she did the job in double quick time** elle a fait le travail en deux temps, trois mouvements *ou* en un rien de temps; **the questions came in quick succession** les questions se sont succédé à un rythme très rapide; **quick crossword** mots *mpl* croisés faciles; **quick march** marche *f* rapide *ou* au pas accéléré; **(as) quick as lightning** *or* **as a flash** rapide *ou* vif comme l'éclair

(**b**) *(sharp)* alerte, éveillé, vif; **he is quick to learn** il apprend vite; **she has a quick ear** elle a l'oreille fine; **she has a quick eye for detail** aucun détail ne lui échappe; **thanks to his quick eye for bargains** grâce au chic qu'il a pour dénicher *ou* pour faire de bonnes affaires; **I was quick to notice the difference** j'ai tout de suite remarqué la différence; **she's too quick for me** elle est trop rapide pour moi; **she's quick on the uptake** elle comprend vite; *Br* **they were very quick off the mark** ils n'ont pas perdu de temps; **he wasn't exactly quick off the mark when it came to ordering drinks** il était plutôt lent à la détente quand il s'agissait de commander les boissons

(**c**) *(hasty → judgment)* hâtif, rapide; **he has a quick temper** il s'emporte facilement; **he is quick to take offence** il est prompt à s'offenser, il se vexe pour un rien

(**d**) *Arch or Literary* **to be quick with child** être dans un état de grossesse assez avancé

2 *adv Fam* rapidement❑; **as quick as possible** aussi vite que possible; **come quick!** venez vite!; **to get rich quick** s'enrichir rapidement

3 *n (of fingernail)* vif *m*; **his nails were bitten to the quick** il s'était rongé les ongles jusqu'au sang; **her remark cut him to the quick** sa remarque l'a piqué au vif

4 *npl Arch (living)* **the quick and the dead** les vivants *mpl* et les morts *mpl*

►► *Acct* ***quick assets*** liquidités *fpl*, actif *m* liquide; ***quick fix*** solution *f* miracle; *Comput* ***quick launch bar*** barre *f* de lancement rapide; *Acct* ***quick ratio*** ratio *m* de liquidité immédiate

quick- [kwɪk] *pref* **quick-dry** *or* **quick-drying paint** peinture *f* à séchage rapide; **quick-setting cement** ciment *m* à prise rapide

quick-acting, quick-action *adj (mechanism)* à action rapide *ou* immédiate; *(drug, medication)* à action rapide

quick-change artist *n* = artiste qui change plusieurs fois de costume au cours d'un spectacle

quickdraw ['kwɪkdrɔ:] *n (in mountaineering)* dégaine *f*

quicken ['kwɪkən] **1** *vt* (**a**) *(hasten)* accélérer, hâter; *(→ pulse)* accélérer; *Mus (→ tempo)* presser; **to quicken one's pace** *or* **step** hâter *ou* presser le pas

(**b**) *(stir → imagination, appetite, interest)* stimuler; *(→ hatred, desire)* exciter; *(→ resolve)* hâter; **the incident quickened his sense of injustice** l'incident a aiguisé son sentiment d'injustice

2 *vi* (**a**) *(step, pulse)* s'accélérer; **my heart** *or* **pulse quickened** mon cœur se mit à battre plus vite

(**b**) *Literary (hopes, fire)* se ranimer

(**c**) *(foetus)* commencer à bouger

quickening ['kwɪkənɪŋ] **1** *adj* (**a**) *(pace, pulse)* qui s'accélère (**b**) *Literary (hopes, fire)* qui se ranime

2 *n* (**a**) *(of pace, pulse)* accélération *f* (**b**) *(of foetus)* premiers mouvements *mpl*

quickfire ['kwɪkfaɪə(r)] *adj* **he directed quickfire questions at me** il m'a mitraillé de questions; **a series of quickfire questions** un feu roulant de questions

quick-freeze (*pt* **quick-froze,** *pp* **quick-frozen**) *vt* surgeler

quickie ['kwɪkɪ] *n Fam* (**a**) *(gen)* truc *m* vite fait; *(question)* question *f* rapide❑

(**b**) *(sex)* coup *m* en vitesse *ou* entre deux portes; **to have a quickie** tirer un coup vite fait

(**c**) *(drink)* pot *m* rapide; **to have a quickie** prendre un pot en vitesse; **we stopped at a pub for a quickie** on s'est arrêtés dans un bar pour prendre un pot en vitesse

►► ***quickie divorce*** divorce *m* express❑

quicklime ['kwɪklaɪm] *n* chaux *f* vive

quickly ['kwɪklɪ] *adv* rapidement, vite; **come as quickly as possible** venez aussi vite que possible; **he quickly telephoned the doctor** il se dépêcha d'appeler le médecin

quickness ['kwɪknɪs] *n* (**a**) *(rapidity → of movement, pulse)* rapidité *f*; *(→ of thought, reaction)* rapidité *f*, vivacité *f* (**b**) *(acuteness → of wit)* vivacité *f*; *(→ of sight)* acuité *f*; *(→ of hearing)* finesse *f* (**c**) *(hastiness)* **his quickness of temper** sa promptitude à s'emporter

quicksand ['kwɪksænd] **1** *n* sables *mpl* mouvants; **to get caught** *or* **stuck in quicksand** être pris dans des sables mouvants

2 quicksands *npl* sables *mpl* mouvants

quickset hedge ['kwɪkset-] *n Br* haie *f* vive

quicksilver ['kwɪkˌsɪlvə(r)] **1** *n* vif-argent *m*, mercure *m*

2 *adj (mind)* très vif, comme du vif-argent

quickstep ['kwɪkstep] *n* quickstep *m*

quick-tempered *adj* emporté, coléreux; **to be quick-tempered** s'emporter facilement

quick-witted *adj* à l'esprit vif; **she is very quick-witted** *(in answers)* elle a de la repartie; *(in intelligence)* elle a l'esprit vif

quick-wittedness [-'wɪtɪdnɪs] *n* vivacité *f* d'esprit

quid [kwɪd] (*pl sense* (**a**) **inv**) *n* (**a**) *Br Fam (pound sterling)* livre *f* sterling❑; **could you lend me ten quid?** t'as pas dix livres à me prêter? (**b**) *(tobacco)* chique *f* (**c**) *Br Fam (idiom)* **to be quids in** être à l'aise, avoir du fric

quiddity ['kwɪdətɪ] (*pl* **quiddities**) *n Phil* quiddité *f*

quid pro quo [ˌkwɪdprəʊ'kwəʊ] (*pl* **quid pro quos**) *n* contrepartie *f*, récompense *f*; **what did she get as a quid pro quo for her silence?** qu'est-ce qu'elle a reçu en contrepartie de son silence?

quiescence [kwaɪ'esəns] *n* (**a**) *Literary* tranquillité *f*, quiétude *f* (**b**) *Biol* quiescence *f*

quiescent [kwaɪ'esənt] *adj* (**a**) *Literary (passive)* passif; *(peaceful)* tranquille (**b**) *Biol* quiescent

QUIET ['kwaɪət]

tranquillité	►1
calme	►1; 2 (b), (c)
silence	►1
tranquille	►2 (a), (b)
silencieux	►2 (a), (c)
doux	►2 (a)
docile	►2 (c)
dans l'intimité	►2 (d)
discret	►2 (e)
calmer	►3

1 *n (calm)* tranquillité *f*, calme *m*; *(silence)* silence *m*; **to ask for quiet** demander le silence; **a minute's quiet** une minute de silence; **to enjoy perfect peace and quiet** jouir d'une parfaite tranquillité; *Br Fam* **on the quiet** *(in secrecy)* en douce, en cachette❑; *(discreetly)* discrètement❑, en douceur❑; *(in confidence)* en confiance❑

2 *adj* (**a**) *(silent)* tranquille, silencieux; *(not loud → music)* doux (douce); *(→ voice)* bas, doux (douce); **be** *or* **keep quiet!** taisez-vous!; **could you try to keep them quiet?** pourriez-vous essayer de les faire taire?; **quiet please!** silence, s'il vous plaît!; **you're very quiet** vous ne dites pas grand-chose; **keep quiet about what you've seen** ne dites rien de ce que vous avez vu; **it was as quiet as the grave** il régnait un silence de mort; **she was as quiet as a mouse** elle ne faisait pas le moindre bruit; **the wind grew quiet** le vent s'est apaisé; **we were having a quiet conversation** nous bavardions tranquillement; **in a quiet voice** d'une voix douce

(**b**) *(calm, tranquil)* calme, tranquille, paisible; *Fin (market, business)* calme; **to lead a quiet life** mener une vie paisible *ou* tranquille; **the TV keeps the children quiet** pendant qu'ils regardent la télé, les enfants se tiennent tranquilles; **sit quiet for ten minutes** restez assis tranquillement pendant dix minutes; **he's a very quiet kind of chap** c'est un type très tranquille; **quiet disposition** caractère *m* doux *ou* calme; **to have a quiet drink** boire un verre tranquillement; **we had a quiet Christmas** nous avons passé un Noël tranquille; **it's very pretty countryside, in a quiet sort of way** c'est un très joli paysage, dans le genre paisible; **she had a quiet night** elle a passé une nuit tranquille *ou* paisible; **all is quiet** tout va bien, rien à signaler; **anything for a quiet life** tout pour avoir la paix

(**c**) *(docile → animal)* docile; *(easy → baby)* calme; *(uncommunicative)* silencieux, peu communicatif; **you're very quiet, is anything wrong?** tu es drôlement silencieux, il y a quelque chose qui ne va pas?

(**d**) *(private → wedding)* dans l'intimité; *(→ party)* avec quelques intimes, avec peu d'invités; *(secret)* secret(ète), dissimulé; **can I have a quiet word with you?** est-ce que je peux vous dire un mot en particulier?; **keep the news** quiet gardez la nouvelle pour vous; **she was very quiet about her background** elle n'a pas dit grand-chose de ses antécédents

(**e**) *(subtle, discreet → irony)* voilé, discret(ète); *(→ optimism)* discret(ète); *(→ anger)* sourd; *(→ despair, resentment)* secret(ète); **he had a quiet smile on his lips** il avait un petit sourire aux lèvres

(**f**) *(muted → colour, style)* sobre; **he's a quiet dresser** il s'habille sobrement *ou* sans ostentation

3 *vt (calm)* calmer; *(silence)* faire taire

▸**quiet down** *vi Am* se calmer

'The Quiet American' *Greene* 'Un Américain bien tranquille'

All quiet on the Western front
Il s'agit du titre anglais du roman *À l'Ouest rien de nouveau* de l'écrivain allemand Erich Maria Remarque ainsi que du film de Lewis Milestone. Aujourd'hui on utilise cette phrase de façon allusive et sur le mode humoristique (et en la modifiant si nécessaire) à propos d'une période d'accalmie dans une situation de crise, ou bien pour dire qu'il ne se passe grand-chose comme dans l'exemple suivant: **How's things up there in Helsinki? – Oh, you know, all quiet on the Northern front** ("comment ça va, là-haut, à Helsinki? – rien à signaler").

quieten ['kwaɪətən] **1** *vt Br (child, audience)* calmer, apaiser; *(conscience)* tranquilliser, apaiser; *(doubts)* dissiper; **does that quieten your fears?** est-ce que cela dissipe vos craintes?

2 *vi (child)* se calmer; *(music)* devenir plus doux (douce)

▸**quieten down** **1** *vi* (**a**) *(become quiet → person)* se calmer; *(→ storm, wind)* se calmer, s'apaiser; **the meeting gradually quietened down** peu à peu, l'assemblée s'est calmée (**b**) *(become reasonable)* s'assagir; **he's quietened down a lot since he got married** il s'est beaucoup assagi depuis son mariage

2 *vt sep (calm)* calmer, apaiser; *(shut up)* faire taire

quietism ['kwaɪətɪzəm] *n* quiétisme *m*

quietist ['kwaɪətɪst] **1** *adj* quiétiste

2 *n* quiétiste *mf*

quietly ['kwaɪətlɪ] *adv* (**a**) *(silently)* silencieusement, sans bruit

(**b**) *(calmly)* doucement, calmement; **a quietly flowing river** une rivière au cours paisible; **to be quietly determined to do sth** être froidement décidé à faire qch

(**c**) *(peacefully)* tranquillement, paisiblement; **sit quietly** restez assis tranquillement

(**d**) *(discreetly)* simplement, discrètement; **they got married quietly** ils se sont mariés dans l'intimité

quietness ['kwaɪətnɪs] *n* (**a**) *(silence)* silence *m* (**b**) *(calmness, tranquillity)* tranquillité *f*, calme *m* (**c**) *(of colour, style)* caractère *m* sobre

quietude ['kwaɪətju:d] *n Literary* quiétude *f*

quietus [kwaɪ'i:təs] *(pl* **quietuses** [-si:z] *n* (**a**) *Literary (death)* trépas *m* (**b**) *Law (settlement of debt)* règlement *m*

quiff [kwɪf] *n (hairstyle)* banane *f*

quill [kwɪl] *n* (**a**) *(feather)* penne *f*; *(shaft of feather)* tuyau *m*; *(of hedgehog, porcupine)* piquant *m* (**b**) *(pen)* plume *f* (d'oie)

▸▸ ***quill pen*** plume *f* d'oie

quillwort ['kwɪlwɜ:t] *n Bot* isoète *m*

quilt [kwɪlt] *n (eiderdown)* édredon *m*; *(bedspread)* dessus-de-lit *m inv*; *(duvet)* couette *f*, *Suisse* duvet *m*

▸▸ ***quilt cover*** housse *f* de couette

quilted ['kwɪltɪd] *adj* matelassé

quilting ['kwɪltɪŋ] *n* (**a**) *(fabric)* tissu *m* matelassé; *(on furniture)* capitonnage *m* (**b**) *(of clothing)* ouatinage *m*; *(of furniture covering)* capitonnage *m* (**c**) *(hobby)* = réalisation d'ouvrages (vêtements, dessus-de-lit) en tissu matelassé

quim [kwɪm] *n Br Vulg* con *m*, chatte *f*

quin [kwɪn] *n Br (abbr* **quintuplet**) quintuplé(e) *m,f*

quinary ['kwɪnərɪ] *adj Math* quinaire

quinate ['kwɪneɪt] *adj Bot* quiné

quince [kwɪns] **1** *n (fruit)* coing *m*; *(tree)* cognassier *m*

2 *comp (jam, jelly)* de coings

quincentenary [,kwɪnsen'ti:nərɪ] *(pl* **quincentenaries**) *n* cinq-centième anniversaire *m*

quincentennial [,kwɪnsen'tenɪəl] **1** *n* cinq-centième anniversaire *m*

2 *adj* cinq-centième

quincunx ['kwɪnkʌnks] *n* quinconce *m*

quindecemvir [,kwɪn'desəmvɪə(r)] *n Antiq* quindécemvir *m*

quine [kwaɪn] *n (in N Scotland) (girl)* jeune fille *f*

quinella [kwɪ'nelə] *n* pari *m* couplé gagnant, pari *m* jumelé gagnant *(où l'on ne spécifie pas l'ordre d'arrivée)*

quinidine ['kwɪnɪdaɪn] *n Chem* quinidine *f*

quinine [kwɪ'ni:n] *n* quinine *f*

quinoa [ki:'nəʊə] *n Bot* quinoa *m*

quinol ['kwɪnɒl] *n Chem* hydroquinone *f*

quinoline ['kwɪnəʊlaɪn] *n Chem* quinoléine *f*

quinolone ['kwɪnələʊn] *n Pharm* quinolone *f*

quinone ['kwɪnəʊn] *n Chem* quinone *f*

quinquagenarian [,kwɪŋkwədʒə'neərɪən] **1** *n* quinquagénaire *mf*

2 *adj* quinquagénaire

Quinquagesima [,kwɪŋkwə'dʒesɪmə] *n Rel* Quinquagésime *f*

quinquennial [kwɪŋ'kwenɪəl] *adj* quinquennal

quinquennium [kwɪŋ'kwenɪəm] *(pl* **quinquenniums** *or* **quinquennia** [-nɪə]) *n* quinquennat *m*

quinquereme ['kwɪŋkwɪri:m] *n Antiq* quinquérème *f*

quinsy ['kwɪnzɪ] *n Old-fashioned* amygdalite *f* purulente

quint[1] [kwɪnt] *n Am (abbr* **quintuplet**) quintuplé(e) *m,f*

quint[2] [kɪnt] *n Cards* quinte *f*

quintal ['kwɪntəl] *n* quintal *m*

quinte [kænt] *n Fencing* quinte *f*

quintessence [kwɪn'tesəns] *n Literary* quintessence *f*

quintessential [,kwɪntɪ'senʃəl] *adj* typique, type; **she's the quintessential Parisian** c'est la Parisienne type; **he's the quintessential English gentleman** c'est le gentleman anglais typique

quintessentially [,kwɪntɪ'senʃəlɪ] *adv* fondamentalement

quintet, quintette [kwɪn'tet] *n* (**a**) *(players → classical)* quintette *m*; *(→ jazz)* quintet *m* (**b**) *(piece of music)* quintette *m*

Quintilian [,kwɪn'tɪlɪən] *pr n* Quintillien

quintillion [,kwɪn'tɪlɪən] *n Br* quintillion *m* (10^{30}); *Am* trillion *m* (10^{18})

quintuple [,kwɪn'tju:pəl] **1** *adj* quintuple

2 *n* quintuple *m*

3 *vt* quintupler

4 *vi* quintupler

quintuplet [,kwɪn'tju:plɪt] *n* quintuplé(e) *m,f*

quintuplicate **1** *adj* [,kwɪn'tju:plɪkət] quintuple

2 *n* [,kwɪn'tju:plɪkət] **in quintuplicate** en cinq exemplaires

3 *vt* [,kwɪn'tju:plɪkeɪt] (**a**) *(multiply by five)* quintupler, multiplier par cinq (**b**) *(make five copies of → letter etc)* faire *ou* tirer cinq exemplaires de

quip [kwɪp] *(pt & pp* **quipped**, *cont* **quipping**) **1** *n (remark → witty)* bon mot *m*, mot *m* d'esprit; *(→ sarcastic)* sarcasme *m*; *(gibe)* quolibet *m*; **to make a quip** faire un bon mot *ou* de l'esprit; **he made a nasty quip about her humble origins** il a fait une remarque désobligeante sur ses origines modestes

2 *vt (say sarcastically)* dire de façon sarcastique; *(say wittily)* dire avec esprit; **"only if I'm asked", he quipped** "seulement si on me le demande", lança-t-il d'un air malicieux

quipster ['kwɪpstə(r)] *n Fam* plaisantin ❏ *m*

quire ['kwaɪə(r)] *n (in bookbinding)* cahier *m*; *(of paper)* main *f* (de papier)

Quirinal ['kwɪrɪnəl] *n* mont *m* Quirinal

quirk [kwɜ:k] *n* (**a**) *(idiosyncrasy)* manie *f*, excentricité *f*; **he's got a lot of little quirks** il y a plein de choses bizarres chez lui (**b**) *(accident)* bizarrerie *f*, caprice *m*; **by a strange quirk of fate we met in Sydney** par un caprice du destin, nous nous sommes rencontrés à Sydney (**c**) *(flourish)* fioriture *f*

quirky ['kwɜ:kɪ] *(compar* **quirkier**, *superl* **quirkiest**) *adj* bizarre, original

quirt [kwɜ:rt] *Am* **1** *n* cravache *f*

2 *vt* cravacher

quisling ['kwɪzlɪŋ] *n Pej* collaborateur(trice) *m,f*

quit [kwɪt] *(pt & pp* **quit** *or* **quitted**, *cont* **quitting**) **1** *vt* (**a**) *(leave)* quitter; **we have to quit the premises by the end of the month** nous devons quitter les lieux avant la fin du mois

(**b**) *Am (give up, stop)* quitter, cesser; **he quit school at 15** il a quitté l'école à 15 ans; **he quit his job** il a quitté son travail; **I quit work at 4 o'clock** je quitte le travail à 16 heures; **I've quit smoking** j'ai arrêté *ou* cessé de fumer; **quit it!** arrête!, ça suffit!

(**c**) *Comput (database, program)* sortir de, quitter

2 *vi* (**a**) *(give up)* renoncer, abandonner; *(resign)* démissionner; *Fam* **I quit!** j'abandonne!; **I want to quit** j'ai envie de tout laisser tomber; **you shouldn't quit so easily** vous ne devriez pas abandonner la partie si facilement

(**b**) *(leave)* partir; **to receive notice to quit** *(tenant)* recevoir son congé

(**c**) *Comput* sortir

3 *adj Formal* **to be quit of sb/sth** être débarrassé de qn/qch

QUITE [kwaɪt]

assez	▸ **1 (a)**
tout à fait	▸ **1 (b), (c); 2**
exactement	▸ **1 (c)**

1 *adv* (**a**) *(moderately)* assez; **the movie is quite good** le film est assez bon; **it's quite cold today** il fait assez froid aujourd'hui; **quite frequently/recently** assez fréquemment/récemment; **I'd quite like to go** ça me plairait assez d'y aller; **quite a difficult job** un travail assez difficile; **quite a good job** un assez bon emploi; **quite a lot of people seem to believe it** un bon nombre de gens semblent le croire; **there were quite a few good paintings** il y avait un assez grand nombre de bons tableaux; **there was quite a crowd** il y avait pas mal de monde; **I've been here for quite some time** je suis ici depuis un bon moment *ou* depuis assez longtemps; **he was in France for quite some time** il a passé pas mal de temps en France

(**b**) *(completely, absolutely)* tout à fait; **she's quite right** elle a tout à fait *ou* parfaitement raison; **the story isn't quite true** l'histoire n'est pas tout à fait *ou* entièrement vraie; **I quite understand** je comprends tout à fait *ou* parfaitement; **she's quite brilliant** elle est vraiment très brillante; **we've always been quite happy together** nous avons toujours été parfaitement heureux ensemble; **he's quite happy to let others do the work** ça ne le dérange absolument pas de laisser les autres faire le travail; **he was quite obviously drunk** il était manifestement ivre; **if you've quite finished** si vous avez terminé; **that's quite another matter!** ça, c'est autre chose!; **quite the opposite** bien au contraire; **in quite another tone** sur un tout autre ton; **not quite a month ago** il y a un peu moins d'un mois; **not quite 300** pas tout à fait 300; **it's not quite 2 o'clock** il n'est pas tout à fait 2 heures; **you've had quite enough** vous en avez eu largement assez; **that's quite enough (of that)!** ça suffit comme ça!; **I'm afraid I'll be a bit late – that's quite all right** je crains d'être un peu en retard – ce n'est pas grave; **quite apart from the fact that...** en dehors du fait que...; **quite the best story of its kind** sans aucun doute la meilleure histoire de ce genre; **he's quite the young gentleman** c'est le parfait jeune homme

(**c**) *(exactly)* exactement, tout à fait; **that wasn't quite what I had in mind** ce n'est pas exactement ce que j'avais en tête; **I don't quite know what he will do** je ne sais pas trop ce qu'il fera; **I'm not quite sure what you mean** je ne vois pas très bien ce que vous voulez dire; **I can't quite remember when it happened** je ne me souviens pas bien *ou* tout à fait quand ça s'est passé

(**d**) *(expressing approval, appreciation)* **that was quite a party!** ça a été une sacrée soirée!;

it's been quite a day quelle journée!; **she's quite a girl** elle est formidable; **that movie was quite something** ce film, c'était vraiment quelque chose; **his speech was quite something** son discours était tout à fait remarquable
2 *exclam* **quite (so)!** tout à fait!, parfaitement!

Quito ['ki:təʊ] *n* Quito
quits [kwɪts] *adj* quitte; **I'm quits with her now** maintenant, je suis quitte envers elle; **now we're quits** maintenant nous sommes quittes; **double or quits** quitte ou double; **let's call it quits** *(financially)* disons que nous sommes quittes; *(in fight, argument)* restons-en là
quittance ['kwɪtəns] *n Fin & Law* quittance *f*
quitter ['kwɪtə(r)] *n Fam* dégonflé(e) *m,f*
quiver ['kwɪvə(r)] **1** *vi* (**a**) *(tremble → person)* frémir, trembler; *(→ lips, hands, voice)* trembler; *(→ flesh)* palpiter, frémir; **to quiver with fear/rage** trembler de peur/de rage; **to quiver with emotion** frissonner d'émotion; **the quivering tones of the violin** les trémolos *mpl* du violon
(**b**) *(flutter → heart)* trembler, frémir; *(→ leaves)* frémir, frissonner; *(→ flame)* trembler, vaciller
2 *n* (**a**) *(tremble)* tremblement *m*; *(of violin)* trémolo *m*, frémissement *m*; **a quiver of fear went down my spine** un frisson de peur me parcourut le dos; **he had a quiver in his voice** sa voix tremblait d'émotion; **her heart gave a quiver** son cœur fit un bond dans sa poitrine
(**b**) *(for arrows)* carquois *m*
quivering ['kwɪvərɪŋ] **1** *adj (person)* frémissant, tremblant; *(lips, voice)* tremblant; *(flesh)* palpitant, frémissant; *(leaves)* frémissant, frissonnant; *(flame)* tremblant, vacillant; **the experience had reduced him to a quivering mass** *or* **jelly** l'épreuve l'avait réduit à l'état de loque
2 *n (UNCOUNT) (gen)* tremblement *m*; *(of flesh)* palpitation *f*, frémissement *m*
qui vive [ˌki:'vi:v] *n Br* **on the qui vive** sur le qui-vive
Quixote ['kwɪksət] *pr n* **Don Quixote** Don Quichotte
quixotic [kwɪk'sɒtɪk] *adj (idealistic)* idéaliste, chimérique; *(chivalrous)* généreux, chevaleresque
quixotically [kwɪk'sɒtɪklɪ] *adv* à la (manière de) Don Quichotte
quixotism ['kwɪksətɪzəm], **quixotry** ['kwɪksətrɪ] *n* don-quichottisme *m*
quiz [kwɪz] *(pl* **quizzes,** *pt & pp* **quizzed,** *cont* **quizzing) 1** *n* (**a**) *(game → on TV)* jeu *m* télévisé; *(→ on radio)* jeu *m* radiophonique; *(→ in newspaper)* quiz *m*, questionnaire *m*; **quiz shows** *or* **programmes** les jeux *mpl* télévisés/radiophoniques (**b**) *Am Sch (test)* interrogation *f* écrite
2 *vt* (**a**) *(question)* interroger, questionner; **to quiz sb about sth** interroger qn au sujet de qch
(**b**) *Am Sch (test)* interroger
quizmaster ['kwɪzˌmɑ:stə(r)] *n Rad & TV* animateur(trice) *m,f (d'un jeu)*
quizzical ['kwɪzɪkəl] *adj (questioning)* interrogateur; *(ironic)* ironique, narquois; **to give sb a quizzical look** lancer un regard narquois à qn
quizzically ['kwɪzɪklɪ] *adv (questioningly)* d'un air interrogateur; *(ironically)* d'un air ironique *ou* narquois
Qum = **Qom**
quod [kwɒd] *n Br Fam (jail)* tôle *f*; **he's in quod** il est en tôle
quoin [kɔɪn] *n (cornerstone)* pierre *f* d'angle; *(keystone)* clef *f* de voûte
quoit [kɔɪt] *n (in game)* anneau *m*; **to play quoits** jouer aux anneaux
quokka ['kwɒkə] *n Zool* quokka *m*
quondam ['kwɒndæm] *adj Literary* ancien; **her quondam suitor** son ancien prétendant
Quonset hut® ['kwɒnsɪt-] *n Am* abri *m* préfabriqué *(en tôle ondulée)*
quorate ['kwɔ:reɪt] *adj Br Formal* **to be quorate** être en nombre
Quorn® [kwɔ:n] *n* = aliment aux protéines végétales servant de substitut à la viande
quorum ['kwɔ:rəm] *n* quorum *m*; **to have a quorum** être en nombre; **we don't have a quorum** le quorum n'est pas atteint; **to form a quorum** constituer un quorum
quota ['kwəʊtə] *n* (**a**) *(limited quantity)* quota *m*, contingent *m*; **they are admitted on a quota system** il y a un numerus clausus *ou* un quota pour les admissions; **to apportion** *or* **to fix quotas for import** déterminer les quotas d'importation
(**b**) *(share)* part *f*, quota *m*; **I've had my quota of bad luck** j'ai eu ma dose *ou* ma part de malchance; **we've had more than our quota of rain recently** nous avons eu plus que notre quota *ou* notre dose de pluie dernièrement
►► *Mktg* ***quota method*** *(of sampling)* méthode *f* des quotas; *Mktg* ***quota sample*** échantillon *m* par quotas; *Mktg* ***quota sampling*** échantillonnage *m* par quotas
quotable ['kwəʊtəbəl] *adj* (**a**) *(worth quoting)* digne d'être cité; **an eminently quotable phrase** une phrase tout à fait digne d'être citée; **the press find him very quotable** les journalistes adorent ses petites phrases
(**b**) *(on the record)* que l'on peut citer; **are these figures quotable?** peut-on citer ces chiffres?; **what he said is not quotable** ce qu'il a dit ne peut être répété
(**c**) *St Exch* cotable
quotation [kwəʊ'teɪʃən] *n* (**a**) *(remark, sentence)* citation *f*
(**b**) *St Exch* cours *m*, cotation *f*; **the latest quotations** les derniers cours; **to seek a share quotation** faire une demande d'admission *ou* d'inscription à la cote
(**c**) *Com (estimate)* devis *m*; *(for insurance)* cotation *f*; **to get a quotation** faire faire un devis; **they gave me a quotation of £500** ils m'ont fait un devis de 500 livres
►► ***quotation marks*** guillemets *mpl*; **in quotation marks** entre guillemets
quotation-driven *adj St Exch (market)* à prix affichés
quote [kwəʊt] **1** *vt* (**a**) *(cite → words, example, statistics)* citer; **can I quote you on that?** vous me permettez de citer ce que vous venez de dire?; **don't quote me on that** *(don't repeat it)* ne le répétez pas; *(don't say who told you)* ne dites pas que c'est moi qui vous l'ai dit; **she quoted several passages from the book** elle cita plusieurs passages du livre; **he said, quote, get lost, unquote** il a dit, je cite, allez vous faire voir; **their leader was quoted as denying the allegation** leur leader aurait rejeté l'accusation; **you are quoted as saying he's mad** vous auriez dit qu'il était fou
(**b**) *Admin & Com* **please quote this reference (number)** prière de mentionner cette référence; **in reply please quote this number** prière de rappeler ce numéro dans toute correspondance ultérieure
(**c**) *(specify → price)* indiquer; *St Exch (→ shares)* coter; **gold prices were quoted at £500** l'or a été coté à 500 livres; **quoted on the Stock Exchange** coté en Bourse; *St Exch* **to quote an expiry** coter une échéance; **can you quote me a price?** pouvez-vous me donner *ou* m'indiquer un prix?
2 *vi* (**a**) *(cite)* faire des citations; **to quote from Yeats** citer Yeats
(**b**) *Com* **to quote for a job** faire un devis pour un travail
3 *n* (**a**) *(quotation)* citation *f*; *(statement)* déclaration *f*; **a quote from Shakespeare** une citation de Shakespeare
(**b**) *(estimate)* devis *m*
(**c**) *(quotation mark)* guillemet *m*; **in quotes** entre guillemets
►► *Br St Exch* ***quoted company*** société *f* cotée en Bourse; *Fin* ***quoted investment*** valeurs *fpl* mobilières de placement; *Fin* ***quoted price*** cours *m* inscrit à la cote officielle; *Fin* ***quoted securities*** valeurs *fpl* de Bourse; *St Exch* ***quoted share*** action *f* cotée, action *f* inscrite à la cote officielle
quote-driven *adj St Exch (market)* à prix affichés
quoteworthy ['kwəʊtwɜ:ðɪ] *adj* digne d'être cité
quoth [kwəʊθ] *vt Arch* **"nay", quoth the King** "non", fit *ou* dit le roi
quotidian [kwɒ'tɪdɪən] *adj Formal* quotidien
quotient ['kwəʊʃənt] *n* quotient *m*
Qur'an, Qur'anic = **Koran, Koranic**
qv *(written abbr* **quod vide)** = expression renvoyant le lecteur à une autre entrée dans une encyclopédie
qwerty, Qwerty ['kwɜ:tɪ] *n*
►► ***qwerty keyboard*** clavier *m* QWERTY
qwertz, Qwertz [kwɜ:ts] *n*
►► ***qwertz keyboard*** clavier *m* QWERTZ

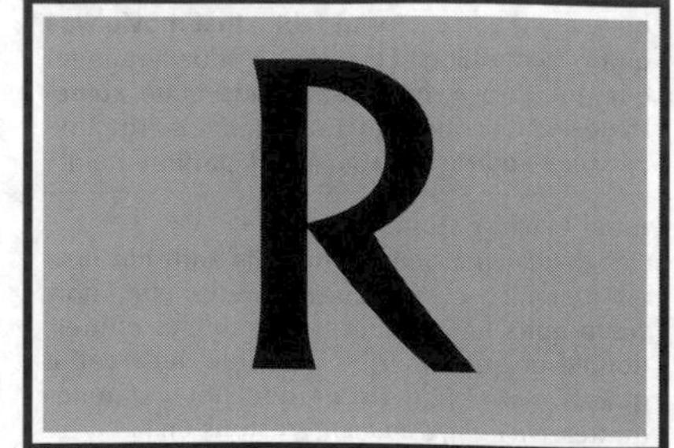

R[1], **r** [ɑː(r)] *n (letter)* R, r *m inv*; **two r's** deux r; **R for Robert** ≃ R comme Raoul; *Br Sch* **the three Rs** = la lecture, l'écriture et l'arithmétique *(qui constituent les fondements de l'enseignement primaire)*

R[2] [ɑː(r)] *adj Am (abbr* **restricted***)* = indique qu'un film est interdit aux moins de 17 ans

R[3] **(a)** *(written abbr* **right***)* dr **(b)** *(written abbr* **river***)* rivière *f* **(c)** *(written abbr* **Réaumur***)* R **(d)** *Am (written abbr* **Republican***)* républicain **(e)** *Br (written abbr* **Rex***)* = suit le nom d'un roi **(f)** *Br (written abbr* **Regina***)* = suit le nom d'une reine **(g)** *Geom (written abbr* **radius***)* R **(h)** *(written abbr* **road***)* rue *f* **(i)** *(written abbr* **rand***)* R

RA [ɑː'reɪ] *n* **(a)** *(abbr* **rear admiral***)* contre-amiral *m* **(b)** *(abbr* **Royal Academician***)* = membre de la "Royal Academy" **(c)** *(abbr* **Royal Academy***)* Académie *f* royale britannique *(académie des beaux-arts)*

RAAF [ræf] *n Austr (abbr* **Royal Australian Air Force***)* = armée de l'air australienne

Rabat [rə'bɑːt] *n* Rabat

rabbet ['ræbɪt] *Carp* **1** *n (groove)* feuillure *f*
2 *vt* feuiller
▸▸ ***rabbet plane*** feuilleret *m*

rabbi ['ræbaɪ] *n* rabbin *m*; **chief rabbi** grand rabbin *m*

rabbinate ['ræbɪnət] *n* rabbinat *m*

rabbinic [rə'bɪnɪk] **1** *adj* rabbinique
2 Rabbinic *n* hébreu *m* rabbinique

rabbinical [rə'bɪnɪkəl] *adj* rabbinique

rabbinism ['ræbɪnɪzəm] *n* rabbinisme *m*

rabbit ['ræbɪt] **1** *n* **(a)** *(animal)* lapin(e) *m,f*; **doe rabbit** lapine *f*; **young rabbit** lapereau *m*; **wild rabbit** lapin *m* de garenne; *Fig* **they breed like rabbits** ils se reproduisent comme des lapins; **to produce a rabbit out of a hat** *(conjuror)* faire sortir un lapin d'un chapeau; *Fig* trouver une solution miracle
(b) *Br Fam Old-fashioned (poor player)* **I'm a bit of a rabbit at chess** je ne suis pas très bon aux échecs ❑
2 *comp (coat)* en (peau de) lapin
3 *vi* **to go rabbiting** chasser le lapin
▸▸ ***rabbit burrow*** terrier *m* (de lapin); *Am* ***rabbit ears*** antenne *f* télescopique; ***rabbit food*** aliments *mpl* pour lapins; *Fam Hum Pej (salad, green vegetables)* verdure ❑ *f*; ***rabbit hole*** terrier *m* de lapin; ***rabbit hutch*** clapier *m*, cage *f ou* cabane *f* à lapins; *Br Fam Fig (accommodation)* cage *f* à lapins; ***rabbit punch*** coup *m* du lapin; ***rabbit stew*** ragoût *m ou* gibelote *f* de lapin; ***rabbit warren*** garenne *f*; *Fig* labyrinthe *m*, dédale *m*

▸**rabbit on** *vi Br Fam (talk)* jacasser, bavasser (**about** à propos de); **what's she rabbiting on about?** qu'est-ce qu'elle raconte *ou* bave?; **do stop rabbiting on** tais-toi un peu; **he's been rabbiting on about his money problems** il me rebat les oreilles de ses problèmes d'argent; **he's always rabbiting on at me about it** il me serine cette histoire à longueur de journée

rabble ['ræbəl] *n* **(a)** *(disorderly mob)* foule *f* **(b)** *Old-fashioned Pej (lower classes)* **the rabble** la populace, la canaille **(c)** *Tech (in foundry)* râble *m*

rabble-rouser [-raʊzə(r)] *n* agitateur(trice) *m,f*

rabble-rousing 1 *n* incitation *f* à la révolte
2 *adj (speech)* incendiaire; *(leader)* qui incite à la révolte

Rabelaisian [,ræbə'leɪzɪən] *adj* rabelaisien

rabic ['ræbɪk] *adj Med* rabique

rabid ['ræbɪd, 'reɪbɪd] *adj* **(a)** *Med (animal)* enragé; *(person)* atteint de la rage **(b)** *Fig (extremist, revolutionary)* enragé; *(hatred)* farouche; *(anger)* féroce

rabidity [ræ'bɪdɪtɪ] *n* **(a)** *Med* rage *f* **(b)** *(extremity → of feelings, opinions)* violence *f*

rabidly ['ræbɪdlɪ, 'reɪbɪdlɪ] *adv* férocement, farouchement

rabidness ['ræbɪdnɪs] = **rabidity**

rabies ['reɪbiːz] *n (UNCOUNT)* rage *f*; **the dog is a rabies carrier** le chien est porteur de la rage
▸▸ ***rabies vaccine*** vaccin *m* contre la rage

RAC [,ɑːreɪ'siː] *n Br (abbr* **Royal Automobile Club***)* **the RAC** = automobile club britannique et compagnie d'assurances qui garantit le dépannage de ses adhérents et propose des services touristiques et juridiques, ≃ ACF *m*, ≃ TCF *m*

raccoon [rə'kuːn] **1** *n Zool* raton *m* laveur
2 *comp (coat, stole)* en (fourrure de) raton laveur

race [reɪs] **1** *n* **(a)** *(competition)* course *f*; **an 800-metre race** une course de *ou* sur 800 mètres; **the 100 metres race** le 100 mètres, la course de 100 mètres; **to run a race** courir, participer à une course; **it's anybody's race** il n'y a pas de favori; *Horseracing* **a day at the races** une journée aux courses; **a race against time** une course contre la montre; **it'll be a race to finish on time** il faudra se dépêcher pour finir à temps; **the race for the Presidency** la course à la présidence
(b) *(ethnic group)* race *f*; *(in anthropology)* ethnie *f*; **the human race** la race humaine; *Fig* **he belongs to the race of poets** il est de la race des poètes
(c) *Literary (passing → of sun, moon)* course *f*; *(→ of life)* cours *m*
(d) *(swift current)* fort courant *m*; *(in sea)* raz *m*
(e) *Aviat (slipstream)* sillage *m*; *(turbulence)* turbulence *f*
(f) *Tech (for ball bearings)* voie *f* de roulement
2 *comp (discrimination, hatred, prejudice)* racial
3 *vt* **(a)** *(compete against)* faire la course avec; **(I'll) race you there!** à qui y arrivera le premier!; **I'll race you home!** le premier arrivé à la maison a gagné!; **he raced me round the block** il a fait la course avec moi autour du pâté de maisons; **the car raced the bus to the traffic lights** la voiture a fait la course avec le bus pour arriver les première aux feux
(b) *(rush)* **he raced me to the airport** il m'a emmené à l'aéroport à toute vitesse; **the casualties were raced to hospital** les blessés ont été transportés d'urgence à l'hôpital; **to race a bill through Parliament** faire adopter un projet de loi en toute hâte
(c) *(put into a race)* **to race a horse** faire courir un cheval; **this colt hasn't been raced yet** ce poulain n'a pas encore couru; **to race pigeons** faire des courses de pigeons
(d) *Aut* **to race the engine** accélérer; *(excessively)* faire s'emballer le moteur
4 *vi* **(a)** *(compete)* courir; **the cars/drivers were racing against each other** les voitures/les conducteurs faisaient la course; **his horse will be racing at Ascot** son cheval courra à Ascot
(b) *(go fast, rush)* aller à toute allure *ou* vitesse; **to race in/out/past** entrer/sortir/passer à toute allure; **they raced out of the café** ils se précipitèrent hors du café; **to race for a bus** courir pour attraper un bus; **she raced downstairs** elle a dévalé l'escalier; **she raced up the stairs** elle a monté les escaliers quatre à quatre; **you'll have to race to catch your train** tu vas devoir te dépêcher si tu veux avoir ton train; **he raced through his meal** il a avalé son repas à toute vitesse; **my pulse was racing** mon cœur battait à tout rompre; **the ambulance raced to the scene of the accident** l'ambulance fonça sur les lieux de l'accident; **the car was racing along** la voiture allait à toute vitesse; **a thousand ideas raced through her mind** mille idées lui sont passées par la tête; **the work is racing ahead** le travail avance très vite; **the competition is racing ahead of us** nous sommes en train de nous faire dépasser par la concurrence; **the clouds are racing across the sky** les nuages filent dans le ciel
(c) *(engine)* s'emballer
▸▸ *Am* ***race car*** voiture *f* de course; ***race card*** programme *m* (des courses); *Am* ***race driver*** pilote *m* de course; ***race meeting*** courses *fpl*; **there is a race meeting at Newmarket tomorrow** on court *ou* il y a des courses demain à Newmarket; ***race norming*** égalité *f* des chances; ***race relations*** relations *fpl* interraciales; ***the Race Relations Act*** *(in the UK)* = loi de 1976 sur le respect des minorités ethniques; *Br* ***race relations body*** *or* ***board*** = organisme luttant contre la discrimination raciale; ***race riot*** émeute *f* raciale; ***race walking*** marche *f* (athlétique)

▸**race by** *vi (time)* filer; **the weekend just raced by** le weekend a passé très vite

racecourse ['reɪskɔːs] *n* **(a)** *(for horses)* champ *m* de courses, hippodrome *m* **(b)** *Am (for cars, motorbikes)* circuit *m*; *(for runners, cycles)* piste *f*

racegoer ['reɪs,gəʊə(r)] *n* turfiste *mf*

racehorse ['reɪshɔːs, *pl* -hɔːsɪz] *n* cheval *m* de course

racemate ['ræsɪmət] *n Chem* mélange *m* racémique

raceme ['ræsiːm] *n Bot* grappe *f (inflorescence)*

racemic [rə'siːmɪk] *adj Chem* racémique

racer ['reɪsə(r)] *n (runner)* coureur(euse) *m,f*; *(horse)* cheval *m* de course; *(car)* voiture *f* de course; *(cycle)* vélo *m* de course

racetrack ['reɪstræk] *n (gen)* piste *f*; *(for horses)* champ *m* de courses, hippodrome *m*

raceway ['reɪsweɪ] *n* **(a)** *(channel for water)* canal *m* **(b)** *esp Am Elec* conduite *f* pour câbles **(c)** *Am (for car racing)* circuit *m* **(d)** *esp Am Horseracing* champ *m* de courses, hippodrome *m* **(e)** *esp Am Tech (for ball bearings)* chemin *m* de roulement à billes

Rachel ['reɪtʃəl] *pr n Bible* Rachel

rachis ['reɪkɪs] *n Anat, Bot & Orn* rachis *m*

rachitic [rə'kɪtɪk] *adj Med* rachitique; **rachitic rosary** nouure *f*

rachitis [rə'kaɪtɪs] *n Med* rachitisme *m*

Rachmaninoff [ræk'mænɪnɒf] *pr n* Rachmaninov

Rachmanism ['rækmənɪzəm] *n* = pressions exercées par un propriétaire sur ses locataires pour obtenir leur éviction

racial ['reɪʃəl] *adj* **(a)** *(concerning a race)* racial, ethnique
(b) *(between races)* racial
▸▸ ***racial discrimination*** discrimination *f* raciale; ***racial engineering*** = pratiques visant à favoriser l'égalité des races dans l'emploi, l'éducation etc; ***racial harmony*** harmonie *f ou* entente *f* raciale; *Am* ***racial profiling*** = pratique policière qui consiste à contrôler l'identité des membres de la communauté noire américaine en priorité; ***racial violence*** violence *f* raciale

racialism ['reɪʃəlɪzəm] *n* racisme *m*

racialist ['reɪʃəlɪst] **1** *adj* raciste

2 *n* raciste *mf*

racially ['reɪʃəlɪ] *adv* du point de vue racial; **a racially motivated attack** une agression raciste; **the characteristic is not racially determined** cette caractéristique n'est pas déterminée par l'appartenance à une race; **racially prejudiced** raciste

racily ['reɪsɪlɪ] *adv (in a lively manner)* avec verve

raciness ['reɪsɪnɪs] *n* (**a**) *(liveliness)* verve *f* (**b**) *(suggestiveness)* grivoiserie *f*

racing ['reɪsɪŋ] **1** *n (of horses)* courses *fpl* de chevaux

2 *comp (bicycle, yacht)* de course

►► ***racing car*** voiture *f* de course; *Horseracing* ***racing colours*** couleurs *fpl* de l'écurie; ***racing cyclist*** coureur(euse) *m,f* cycliste; ***racing driver*** coureur(euse) *m,f* automobile, pilote *mf* (de course); ***racing pigeon*** pigeon *m* voyageur *(de compétition)*; ***racing stable*** écurie *f* de courses; ***racing tip*** pronostic *m*

racism ['reɪsɪzəm] *n* racisme *m*

racist ['reɪsɪst] **1** *adj* raciste

2 *n* raciste *mf*

rack [ræk] **1** *n* (**a**) *(shelf)* étagère *f*; *(in shop)* présentoir *m*; *(on cycle)* porte-bagages *m inv*; *(for cooling, drying)* grille *f*, claie *f*; *(for fodder, bicycles, test tubes, pipes)* râtelier *m*; *(for bottles)* casier *m*; **(luggage) rack** *(in train, bus)* filet *m* (à bagages); **(tool) rack** porte-outils *m inv*; **(clothes) rack** triangle *m* (à vêtements); **to buy a suit off the rack** acheter un costume en prêt-à-porter

(**b**) *Hist* chevalet *m*; **to put sb on the rack** faire subir à qn le supplice du chevalet; *Fig* mettre qn au supplice; **that question put him on the rack** cette question l'a mis dans une position très difficile

(**c**) *Tech* crémaillère *f*

(**d**) *Culin* **rack of lamb** carré *m* d'agneau

(**e**) *Br Fam (woman's breasts)* nénés *mpl*

(**f**) *Am Fam* **to hit the rack** *(go to bed)* se pieuter, se bâcher

(**g**) *(idiom)* **to go to rack and ruin** *(house)* tomber en ruine; *(garden)* être à l'abandon; *(person)* dépérir; *(company)* péricliter; *(country, institution)* aller à vau-l'eau

2 *vt* (**a**) *(torture)* faire subir le supplice du chevalet à; *Fig* tenailler, ronger; **to be racked with pain** être perclus de douleur; **racked by guilt** tenaillé par un sentiment de culpabilité; **her body was racked with sobs** son corps était secoué de sanglots; **to rack one's brains** se creuser la tête

(**b**) *(wine)* soutirer

►► ***rack and pinion*** crémaillère *f*; ***rack and pinion railway*** chemin *m* de fer à crémaillère; ***rack railway*** chemin *m* de fer à crémaillère; *Br* ***rack rent*** loyer *m* exorbitant

► **rack back** *vt sep Am Fam* **to rack sb back** passer un savon à qn, remonter les bretelles à qn

► **rack up** *vt sep (points)* marquer

racket ['rækɪt] **1** *n* (**a**) *Sport (bat)* raquette *f*

(**b**) *(snowshoe)* raquette *f*

(**c**) *Fam (din)* boucan *m*, barouf *m*; **to make a racket** faire du boucan *ou* du barouf; **the neighbours are making a terrible racket** les voisins font un boucan épouvantable; **will you turn that racket off!** arrêtez ce boucan!

(**d**) *Fam (extortion)* racket ❑ *m*; *(fraud)* escroquerie ❑ *f*; *(traffic)* trafic ❑ *m*; **protection racket** racket *m*; **drugs racket** trafic *m* de drogue; **this lottery is such a racket** cette loterie, c'est de l'arnaque; **he's involved in some money-laundering racket** il trempe dans des affaires de blanchiment d'argent

(**e**) *Fam (job)* boulot *m*; **what's your racket?** vous travaillez dans quoi?; **is she still in the teaching/publishing racket?** est-ce qu'elle est encore dans l'enseignement/dans l'édition? ❑

2 *vi Fam (be noisy)* faire du boucan

3 rackets *n (UNCOUNT) (game)* racquet-ball *m*

►► *Sport* ***racket cover*** housse *f* de raquette; *Sport* ***racket-press*** presse-raquette *m*

► **racket about, racket around** *vi Fam Old-fashioned (enjoy oneself)* faire la bombe

racketeer [,rækə'tɪə(r)] **1** *n* racketteur(euse) *m,f*

2 *vi* racketter

racketeering [,rækə'tɪərɪŋ] *n* racket *m*

rackety ['rækɪtɪ] *adj (noisy)* tapageur, bruyant

racking ['rækɪŋ] *adj (pain)* atroce, déchirant

raconteur [,rækɒn'tɜː(r)] *n* raconteur(euse) *m,f*

racoon = **raccoon**

racquet ['rækət] *n Sport (bat)* raquette *f*

racquetball ['rækɪtbɔːl] *n* racquet-ball *m*

racy ['reɪsɪ] *(compar* **racier**, *superl* **raciest)** *adj* (**a**) *(lively)* plein de verve *ou* de brio (**b**) *(suggestive)* osé (**c**) *(wine)* racé

rad [ræd] **1** *n Phys* rad *m*

2 *adj Am Fam* génial, géant

RADA ['rɑːdə] *n Br (abbr* **Royal Academy of Dramatic Art)** = conservatoire britannique d'art dramatique

radar ['reɪdɑː(r)] **1** *n* radar *m*; **to navigate by radar** naviguer au radar

2 *comp (image)* radar

►► ***radar astronomy*** radarastronomie *f*; ***radar beacon*** radiophare *m*; ***radar blip*** top *m* d'écho (radar); ***radar detection*** détection *f* radar; ***radar gun*** radar gun *m*; *Am* ***radar man***, *Br* ***radar operator*** radariste *mf*; ***radar scanner*** antenne *f* radar; ***radar screen*** écran *m* (de) radar; ***radar speed trap*** contrôle *m* radar; ***radar station*** station *f* radar; ***radar trap*** contrôle *m* radar

radarscope ['reɪdɑːskəʊp] *n* écran *m* de radar

raddle ['rædəl] **1** *n* ocre *f* rouge

2 *vt (face)* maquiller avec du rouge; *(sheep)* marquer à l'ocre

raddled ['rædəld] *adj* ravagé

radial ['reɪdɪəl] **1** *adj* (**a**) *Tech & Math* radial

(**b**) *Anat (artery etc)* radial

2 *n* (**a**) *(tyre)* pneu *m* radial *ou* à carcasse radiale

(**b**) *(line)* rayon *m*

►► ***radial engine*** moteur *m* en étoile; ***radial roads*** routes *fpl* en étoile; ***radial symmetry*** symétrie *f* radiée *ou* radiaire; ***radial tyre*** pneu *m* radial *ou* à carcasse radiale; *Astron* ***radial velocity*** vitesse *f* radiale

radially ['reɪdɪəlɪ] *adv* radialement

radial-ply *adj Aut* à carcasse radiale

radian ['reɪdɪən] *n Geom* radian *m*

radiance ['reɪdɪəns], **radiancy** ['reɪdɪənsɪ] *n* (**a**) *(of light, sun)* éclat *m*, rayonnement *m*; *Fig (beauty, happiness)* éclat *m* (**b**) *Phys* exitance *f*

radiant ['reɪdɪənt] **1** *adj* (**a**) *Literary (bright)* radieux; *Fig* **her radiant beauty** sa beauté éclatante

(**b**) *(happy)* radieux, rayonnant; **the bride was radiant** la mariée était radieuse; **he was radiant with joy** il rayonnait de joie

(**c**) *Phys* radiant, rayonnant

(**d**) *Bot* rayonnant

2 *n* (**a**) *Phys* point *m* radiant

(**b**) *Astron* radiant *m*

►► *Phys* ***radiant energy*** énergie *f* de rayonnement; *Phys* ***radiant flux*** flux *m* de rayonnement; *Phys* ***radiant heat*** chaleur *f* rayonnante; ***radiant heating*** chauffage *m* par rayonnement

radiantly ['reɪdɪəntlɪ] *adv (shine, glow)* avec éclat; *(smile)* d'un air radieux; **radiantly beautiful** d'une beauté éclatante

radiate ['reɪdɪeɪt] **1** *vi* (**a**) *(emit energy)* émettre de l'énergie; *(be emitted)* rayonner, irradier; **heat radiates from the centre** le centre dégage de la chaleur

(**b**) *(spread)* rayonner; **the roads which radiate from Chicago** les routes qui partent de Chicago

2 *vt* (**a**) *(heat)* émettre, dégager; *(light)* émettre

(**b**) *Fig* **the children radiate good health/happiness** les enfants respirent la santé/rayonnent de bonheur; **his manner radiated confidence** il semblait très sûr de lui

radiation [,reɪdɪ'eɪʃən] *n* (**a**) *Phys (act of radiating)* rayonnement *m*; *(energy radiated)* rayonnement(s) *m(pl)*, rayons *mpl*; **low-level radiation** radiations *fpl* de faible intensité; **ultraviolet radiation** rayons *mpl* ultraviolets

(**b**) *Nucl* radiation *f*; **atomic radiation** radiations *fpl* (atomiques); **low-level radiation** radiations *fpl* de faible intensité; **to be exposed to radiation** être exposé à des radiations

(**c**) *Med* rayons *mpl*

►► ***radiation sickness*** mal *m* des rayons; ***radiation therapy*** radiothérapie *f*

radiative ['reɪdɪeɪtɪv] *adj Phys* radiatif

►► ***radiative capture*** capture *f* radiative; ***radiative equilibrium*** équilibre *m* radiatif

radiator ['reɪdɪeɪtə(r)] *n (gen) & Aut* radiateur *m*

►► ***radiator cap*** bouchon *m* du radiateur; ***radiator core*** faisceau *m* de radiateur; ***radiator grille*** calandre *f*; ***radiator key*** = petite clé servant à purger les radiateurs; ***radiator matrix*** faisceau *m* de radiateur

radical ['rædɪkəl] **1** *adj* (**a**) *(gen)* radical (**b**) *Am Fam (excellent)* génial, géant

2 *n* (**a**) *Pol* radical(e) *m,f* (**b**) *Ling, Math & Chem* radical *m*

►► ***radical chic*** ≃ socialisme *m* de salon

'Radical Chic' *Wolfe* 'Le Gauchisme de Park Avenue'

radicalism ['rædɪkəlɪzəm] *n* radicalisme *m*

radicalize, -ise ['rædɪkəlaɪz] *vt* radicaliser

radically ['rædɪkəlɪ] *adv* radicalement

radicand ['rædɪkænd] *n Math* quantité *f* radicale

radicchio [rə'diːkɪəʊ] *(pl* **radicchios)** *n* trévise *f*

radices ['reɪdɪsiːz] *pl of* **radix**

radicle ['rædɪkəl] *n* (**a**) *Bot (part of plant embryo)* radicule *f*; *(rootlet)* radicelle *f* (**b**) *Chem* radical *m*

radii ['reɪdɪaɪ] *pl of* **radius**

radio ['reɪdɪəʊ] *(pl* **radios)** **1** *n* (**a**) *(apparatus)* radio *f*; **to turn the radio on/off** allumer/éteindre la radio

(**b**) *(system, industry, activity)* radio *f*; **by radio** par radio; **I heard it on the radio** je l'ai entendu à la radio; **to be on the radio** passer à la radio; **Radio Birmingham** Radio Birmingham; *Br Press* **the Radio Times** = magazine de radio et de télévision

2 *comp (broadcast, play, programme)* radiophonique; *(contact, link, silence)* radio *(inv)*; *(announcer, technician)* à la radio

3 *vt* (**a**) *(person)* appeler *ou* contacter par radio

(**b**) *(message)* envoyer par radio; *(position, movement)* signaler par radio

4 *vi* envoyer un message radio; **to radio for a doctor** demander un médecin par radio; **she radioed for help/instructions** elle demanda de l'aide/des instructions par radio

►► *Mktg* ***radio advertising*** publicité *f* à la radio; ***radio alarm (clock)*** radio-réveil *m*; ***radio astronomer*** radioastronome *mf*; ***radio astronomy*** radioastronomie *f*; ***radio beacon*** radiobalise *f*; ***radio beam*** faisceau *m* hertzien; ***radio broadcast*** émission *f* de radio; ***radio button*** bouton *m* radio, bouton *m* d'option; ***radio car*** voiture *f* radio; ***radio cassette*** radiocassette *f*; ***radio communication*** contact *m* radio, liaison *f* radio, radiocommunications *fpl*; ***radio compass*** radiocompas *m*; ***radio control*** télécommande *f* (par) radio, radiocommande *f*; ***radio data system*** *(for motorists)* système *m* radio de transmission de données; ***radio engineer*** ingénieur *m* radio; ***radio frequency*** fréquence *f* radioélectrique, radiofréquence *f*; *Astron* ***radio galaxy*** radiogalaxie *f*; ***radio ham*** radioamateur *m*; ***radio journalism*** journalisme *m* de radio; ***radio listener*** auditeur(trice) *m,f*; ***radio microphone*** microphone *m* sans fil; ***radio navigation*** radionavigation *f*; ***radio officer*** radionavigant *m*; ***radio operator*** *(on plane)* radio *m*; *(on ship)* radionavigant *m*; ***radio producer*** producteur(trice) *m,f* d'émissions de radio; ***radio receiver*** radiorécepteur *m*; *Naut* ***radio room*** poste *m* radio de bord; ***radio satellite*** satellite *m* radio; ***radio source*** radiosource *f*; ***radio spectrum*** spectre *m* radio *ou* radioélectrique *ou* des fréquences radioélectriques; ***radio star*** radiosource *f*; ***radio station*** station *f* de radio; ***radio taxi*** radio-taxi *m*; ***radio telescope*** radiotélescope *m*; ***radio transmitter*** (poste *m*) émetteur *m*; ***radio vehicle*** véhicule *m* radio; ***radio waves*** ondes *fpl* hertziennes

RADIO

Les principales stations de radio de la BBC sont: Radio 1 (bulletins d'information, musique pop et rock); Radio 2 (variétés); Radio 3 (musique classique); Radio 4 (actualités, reportages, théâtre, programmes éducatifs); Radio 5 Live (sports, programmes éducatifs, musique pop et rock). La BBC comprend également trente-neuf stations locales. Il existe d'autre part plus de cent stations indépendantes.

radioactive [ˌreɪdɪəʊ'æktɪv] *adj* radioactif
►► ***radioactive dating*** datation *f* au carbone 14; ***radioactive decay*** désintégration *f* radioactive; ***radioactive dust*** poussières *fpl* radioactives; ***radioactive fallout*** retombées *fpl* radioactives; ***radioactive tracer*** traceur *m* radioactif; ***radioactive waste*** déchets *mpl* radioactifs *ou* nucléaires

radioactivity [ˌreɪdɪəʊæk'tɪvɪtɪ] *n* radioactivité *f*

radiobiological [ˌreɪdɪəʊbaɪə'lɒdʒɪkəl] *adj* radiobiologique

radiobiology [ˌreɪdɪəʊbaɪ'ɒlədʒɪ] *n* radiobiologie *f*

radiocarbon [ˌreɪdɪəʊ'kɑːbən] *n* radiocarbone *m*, carbone *m* 14
►► ***radiocarbon dating*** datation *f* au carbone 14

radiocast ['reɪdɪəʊkɑːst] *vt Am* radiodiffuser

radiochemical [ˌreɪdɪəʊ'kemɪkəl] *adj* radiochimique

radiochemist [ˌreɪdɪəʊ'kemɪst] *n* radiochimiste *mf*

radiochemistry [ˌreɪdɪəʊ'kemɪstrɪ] *n* radiochimie *f*

radiocommunication ['reɪdɪəʊkəˌmjuːnɪ'keɪʃən] *n* radiocommunication *f*

radio-controlled *adj* radioguidé

radioelement [ˌreɪdɪəʊ'elɪmənt] *n* radioélément *m*

radiogenic [ˌreɪdɪəʊ'dʒenɪk] *adj* (**a**) *(produced by radioactive decay)* radiogène (**b**) *(suitable for broadcasting)* radiogénique, qui rend bien à la radio

radiogram ['reɪdɪəʊgræm] *n* (**a**) *Old-fashioned (radio and record player)* radio *f* avec pick-up (**b**) *(message)* radiogramme *m* (**c**) *(radiograph)* radiographie *f*

radiograph ['reɪdɪəʊgrɑːf] *n* radiographie *f*

radiographer [ˌreɪdɪ'ɒgrəfə(r)] *n* radiologue *mf*, radiologiste *mf*

radiographic [ˌreɪdɪəʊ'græfɪk] *adj* radiographique

radiography [ˌreɪdɪ'ɒgrəfɪ] *n* radiographie *f*

radioimmunoassay [ˌreɪdɪəʊˌɪmjuːnəʊ'æseɪ] *n Biol* dosage *m* radio-immunologique

radioisotope [ˌreɪdɪəʊ'aɪsətəʊp] *n* radio-isotope *m*, isotope *m* radioactif

radiolabelled ['reɪdɪəʊˌleɪbəld] *adj* marqué par traceur radioactif

radiolocation ['reɪdɪəʊləkeɪʃən] *n* radiorepérage *m*

radiological [ˌreɪdɪəʊ'lɒdʒɪkəl] *adj* radiologique

radiologist [ˌreɪdɪ'ɒlədʒɪst] *n* radiologue *mf*, radiologiste *mf*

radiology [ˌreɪdɪ'ɒlədʒɪ] *n* radiologie *f*

radioluminescence [ˌreɪdɪəʊluːmɪ'nesəns] *n* radioluminescence *f*

radiolysis [ˌreɪdɪ'ɒləsɪs] *n* radiolyse *f*

radiometer [ˌreɪdɪ'ɒmɪtə(r)] *n* radiomètre *m*

radiometric [ˌreɪdɪəʊ'metrɪk] *adj* radiométrique

radiometry [ˌreɪdɪ'ɒmɪtrɪ] *n* radiométrie *f*

radionuclide [ˌreɪdɪəʊ'njuːklaɪd] *n* nucléide *m* radioactif

radiopager ['reɪdɪəʊˌpeɪdʒə(r)] *n* récepteur *m* d'appel *ou* de poche

radiopaging ['reɪdɪəʊˌpeɪdʒɪŋ] *n* radiomessagerie *f*

radiopaque [ˌreɪdɪəʊ'peɪk] *adj* radio-opaque

radiophone ['reɪdɪəʊfəʊn] *n* radiotéléphone *m*

radioscopic [ˌreɪdɪəʊ'skɒpɪk] *adj*
►► ***radioscopic image*** radiophotographie *f*

radioscopy [ˌreɪdɪ'ɒskəpɪ] *n* radioscopie *f*

radiosensitive [ˌreɪdɪəʊ'sensɪtɪv] *adj Biol* radiosensible; *Med* radiosensible, radiolabile

radiosensitivity [ˌreɪdɪəʊsensɪ'tɪvɪtɪ] *n* radiosensibilité *f*

radiosonde ['reɪdɪəʊsɒnd] *n* radiosonde *f*

radiotelegram [ˌreɪdɪəʊ'telɪgræm] *n* radiotélégramme *m*, radiogramme *m*

radiotelegraph [ˌreɪdɪəʊ'telɪgrɑːf] **1** *n* radiotélégraphie *f*
2 *vt* envoyer par radiotélégraphie

radiotelegraphy [ˌreɪdɪəʊtɪ'legrəfɪ] *n* radiotélégraphie *f*

radiotelephone [ˌreɪdɪəʊ'telɪfəʊn] *n* radiotéléphone *m*

radiotelephony [ˌreɪdɪəʊtɪ'lefənɪ] *n* radiotéléphonie *f*

radiotherapist [ˌreɪdɪəʊ'θerəpɪst] *n* radiothérapeute *mf*

radiotherapy [ˌreɪdɪəʊ'θerəpɪ] *n* radiothérapie *f*

radish ['rædɪʃ] *n* radis *m*

radium ['reɪdɪəm] *n Chem* radium *m*
►► ***radium therapy, radium treatment*** curiethérapie *f*

radius ['reɪdɪəs] (*pl* **radiuses** *or* **radii** [-dɪaɪ]) *n* (**a**) *(gen)* & *Math* rayon *m*; **within** *or* **in a radius of 20 km** dans un rayon de 20 km (**b**) *Anat* radius *m* (**c**) *(of crane)* portée *f*
►► *Mil* ***radius of action*** rayon *m* d'action; *Math* ***radius vector*** rayon *m* vecteur

radix ['reɪdɪks] (*pl* **radices** [-dɪsiːz]) *n* (**a**) *Math* base *f* (**b**) *Ling* radical *m*

radome ['reɪdəʊm] *n* radôme *m*

radon ['reɪdɒn] *n Chem* radon *m*

radula ['raedjʊlə] (*pl* **radulae** [-iː]) *n Zool* radula *f*, radule *f*

radwaste ['rædweɪst] *n Am* déchets *mpl* radioactifs

RAF [ˌɑːreɪ'ef] *n Br* (*abbr* **Royal Air Force**) = armée de l'air britannique

raffia ['ræfɪə] *n* raphia *m*

raffish ['ræfɪʃ] *adj* dissolu

raffishly ['ræfɪʃlɪ] *adv* d'un air dissolu

raffle ['ræfəl] **1** *n* tombola *f*; **I won it in a raffle** je l'ai gagné dans une tombola
2 *vt* **to raffle (off)** mettre en tombola
►► ***raffle ticket*** billet *m* de tombola

rafflesia [ræ'fliːzɪə] *n Bot* rafflesia *m*, rafflésie *f*

raft [rɑːft] **1** *n* (**a**) *(craft → gen)* radeau *m*; *(→ inflatable)* matelas *m* pneumatique; *Sport* raft *m*
(**b**) *(logs)* train *m* de flottage
(**c**) *Fam (large amount)* tas *m*, flopée *f*; **we've got rafts of** *or* **a raft of mail** nous avons reçu des tas de lettres
(**d**) *Constr* radier *m*
2 *vt* **they raft wood down the river** ils envoient le bois en aval dans des trains de flottage
3 *vi* voyager en radeau

rafter ['rɑːftə(r)] *n Constr* chevron *m*; **main rafter** arbalétrier *m*; **the rafters** le chevronnage; *Fam* **to raise the rafters** *(make noise)* faire un foin d'enfer *ou* un boucan de tous les diables

raftered ['rɑːftəd] *adj* à chevrons

rafting ['rɑːftɪŋ] *n* (**a**) *Sport* rafting *m*; **to go rafting** faire du rafting (**b**) *(of wood)* flottage *m* (de bois) en trains

rag [ræg] (*pt & pp* **ragged**, *cont* **ragging**) **1** *n* (**a**) *(cloth)* chiffon *m*; **he wiped his hands on a rag** il s'essuya les mains avec un chiffon; **a piece of rag** un bout de chiffon; *Fam* **to chew the rag** discuter le bout de gras; *Fam* **to feel like** *Br* **a wet rag** *or Am* **a dish rag** *(physically)* être crevé; *(emotionally)* être vidé; *Br Fam* **to lose one's** *or* **the rag** piquer une crise, péter les plombs; **when he said that to her it was like a red rag to a bull** elle a vu rouge après ce qu'il lui a dit
(**b**) *(worn-out garment)* loque *f*; **this old dress is an absolute rag** cette vieille robe est une vraie loque
(**c**) *(shred, scrap)* lambeau *m*; **torn to rags** mis en lambeaux
(**d**) *Fam Pej (newspaper)* feuille *f* de chou, torchon *m*; **the local rag** la feuille de chou locale
(**e**) *Br very Fam (sanitary towel)* serviette *f* hygiénique; **to be on the rag** avoir ses ragnagnas
(**f**) *Br Univ* = semaine pendant laquelle les étudiants préparent des divertissements, surtout au profit d'œuvres charitables
(**g**) *Br (joke)* farce *f*, canular *m*
(**h**) *Mus* ragtime *m*
(**i**) *Geol* calcaire *m* oolithique
(**j**) *Constr* pierre *f* bourrue, bourru *m*
2 *vt (tease)* taquiner; **they ragged her about her accent** ils la taquinaient au sujet de son accent
3 rags *npl (worn-out clothes)* guenilles *fpl*, haillons *mpl*, loques *fpl*; *Am Fam (clothes)* fringues *fpl*; **a tramp dressed in rags** un clochard vêtu de haillons; **in rags and tatters** en loques; **to go from rags to riches** passer de la misère à la richesse; **a rags-to-riches story** un véritable conte de fées
►► ***rag book*** livre *m* en tissu; ***rag content*** *(of paper)* pourcentage *m* de peille; ***rag doll*** poupée *f* de chiffon; *Br Univ* ***rag mag*** = magazine humoristique publié pendant "rag week"; ***rag paper*** papier *m* à base de peille; ***rag picker*** chiffonnier(ère) *m,f*; ***rag rug*** catalogne *f*; *Fam* ***rag trade*** confection ▫ *f*; **he's in the rag trade** il est *or* travaille dans les fringues; ***rag week*** = semaine pendant laquelle les étudiants préparent des divertissements, surtout au profit d'œuvres charitables

raga ['rɑːgə] *n Mus* raga *m inv*

ragamuffin ['rægəˌmʌfɪn] *n* *(vagrant)* va-nu-pieds *m inv*, gueux (gueuse) *m,f*; *(urchin)* galopin *m*, polisson(onne) *m,f*

rag-and-bone man *n Br* chiffonnier *m*

ragbag ['rægbæg] *n Br Fig* ramassis *m*, bric-à-brac *m inv*, fouillis *m*; **a ragbag of ideas** un fouillis d'idées (confuses); **they were a ragbag team** ils formaient une équipe hétéroclite

rage [reɪdʒ] **1** *n* (**a**) *(anger)* rage *f*, fureur *f*; **the boss was in a rage** le patron était furieux; **to fly into a rage** entrer dans une rage folle; **a fit of rage** un accès *ou* une crise de rage
(**b**) *Fam (fashion)* **to be all the rage** faire fureur
(**c**) *(of sea, elements)* furie *f*
2 *vi* (**a**) *(person)* être furieux, s'emporter; **he was raging against the Government** il pestait contre le gouvernement
(**b**) *(sea, river)* se déchaîner; *(fire, storm, war)* faire rage; **a gun battle was raging in the valley** une fusillade faisait rage dans la vallée; **the plague was raging throughout Europe** la peste ravageait l'Europe; **the argument still rages** la question est toujours très controversée

ragga ['rægə] *n Mus* ragga *m*

raggamuffin ['rægəˌmʌfɪn] *n* (**a**) *(black youth)* raggamuffin *m (jeune noir branché)* (**b**) *Mus* raggamuffin *m*

ragged ['rægɪd] *adj* (**a**) *(tattered → clothes)* en lambeaux, en loques, en haillons; *(→ person)* loqueteux, vêtu de loques *ou* de haillons; **she was beginning to look rather ragged** elle commençait à avoir l'air dépenaillé
(**b**) *(uneven)* irrégulier; **the ragged coastline** la côte échancrée; **a ragged edge** un bord irrégulier; **they formed a ragged line** ils se mirent en file irrégulière
(**c**) *(erratic → performance)* inégal, décousu
(**d**) *Typ* **ragged right/left** non-justifié à droite/à gauche; *Typ* **to print sth ragged** imprimer qch sans justification
(**e**) *Fam (idiom)* **to run sb ragged** éreinter *ou* crever qn; **to run oneself ragged** s'éreinter; **I've been running myself ragged for you!** je me suis vraiment décarcassé pour toi!
►► *Bot* ***ragged robin*** fleur *f* de coucou *(lychnis)*; *Br Formerly* ***ragged school*** = école primaire pour les pauvres

raggedly ['rægɪdlɪ] *adv* (**a**) *(dressed)* de guenilles, de haillons (**b**) *(erratically)* **the grass grew raggedly** l'herbe poussait irrégulièrement; **to play raggedly** *(team)* manquer d'ensemble

raggedness ['rægɪdnɪs] *n* (**a**) *(of person)* déguenillement *m*, guenilles *fpl*; *(of garment)* délabrement *m* (**b**) *(unevenness)* inégalités *fpl*, rugosités *fpl* (**c**) *(of performance, piece of work)* inégalité *f*, rudesse *f*; *(of team, orchestra)* manque *m* d'ensemble

raggedy ['rægɪdɪ] *adj Fam* en loques

ragging ['rægɪŋ] *n* *(teasing)* taquineries *fpl*; **to give sb a ragging** mettre qn en boîte, taquiner qn; **he took a lot of ragging** on l'a beaucoup taquiné

raggle ['rægəl] *n* *(for roof flashing)* rainure *f*

raggle-taggle [-ˌtægəl] *adj Br Fam (band, army)* disparate ▫; *(person)* débraillé ▫, dépenaillé ▫

raghead ['ræghed] *n Am Fam* (**a**) *(Arab)* raton *m*, bicot *m*, = terme injurieux désignant un Arabe du Proche-Orient (**b**) *(gypsy)* romanichel(elle) *m,f*, = terme injurieux désignant un Tsigane

raging ['reɪdʒɪŋ] *adj* (**a**) *(intense → pain)* insupportable, atroce; *(→ fever)* violent; **I had a raging headache** j'avais affreusement mal à la tête; **I've got a raging thirst** je meurs de soif;

raging anticlericalism un anticléricalisme virulent; **raging toothache** rage *f* de dents
(**b**) *(storm)* déchaîné, violent; *(sea)* démonté; *(torrent)* furieux
(**c**) *(person)* furieux; **to be in a raging temper** être furieux

raglan ['ræglən] **1** *n* raglan *m*
2 *adj* raglan *(inv)*

raglet ['ræglɪt] *n (for roof flashing)* rainure *f*

ragman ['rægmən] *(pl* **ragmen** [-mən]*) n* chiffonnier *m*

ragout ['rægu:] *n* ragoût *m*

rag-roll *vt* peindre au chiffon

rag-rolling *n* peinture *f* au chiffon

ragstone ['rægstəʊn] *n* (**a**) *Geol* calcaire *m* oolithique (**b**) *Constr* pierre *f* bourrue, bourru *m*

ragtag ['rægtæg] *Br Fam* **1** *adj (band, army)* disparate ❑; *(person)* débraillé ❑, dépenaillé ❑
2 *n* **the ragtag and bobtail** la racaille, la populace

ragtime ['rægtaɪm] *n Mus* ragtime *m*

ragtop ['rægtɒp] *n Am Fam Aut* décapotable ❑ *f*

ragweed ['rægwi:d] *n Bot* ambroisie *f*, ambrosia *f*

ragworm ['rægwɜ:m] *n Br* néréide *f*, néréis *m*

ragwort ['rægwɜ:t] *n Bot* jacobée *f*, herbe *f* de Saint-Jacques

rah [rɑ:] *exclam Am* hourra!

raid [reɪd] **1** *n* (**a**) *Mil* raid *m*, incursion *f*; **they made a raid over the border** ils ont fait une incursion de l'autre côté de la frontière; **bombing raid** raid *m* aérien; **they fear a terrorist raid on the palace** ils craignent une attaque terroriste contre le palais
(**b**) *(by police)* descente *f*, rafle *f*; **a police raid** une descente de police; **a drugs raid** une descente de police (pour saisir de la drogue)
(**c**) *(robbery)* hold-up *m inv*, braquage *m*; **a raid on a bank** un hold-up dans une banque; *Hum* **a raid on the fridge** une razzia dans le frigo
(**d**) *St Exch* raid *m*
2 *vt* (**a**) *Mil (of army)* faire un raid *ou* une incursion dans; *(of airforce)* bombarder
(**b**) *(of police)* faire une descente *ou* une rafle dans
(**c**) *(of thieves)* **to raid a bank** dévaliser une banque; **somebody's raided my locker** quelqu'un a fouillé dans mon casier; *Hum* **to raid the fridge** dévaliser le frigo
(**d**) *St Exch* **to raid the bears** chasser le découvert

raider ['reɪdə(r)] *n* (**a**) *Mil (soldier)* membre *m* d'un commando; *(boat)* raider *m*; *(plane)* bombardier *m*; **the raiders were repelled** le commando a été repoussé (**b**) *(thief)* voleur(euse) *m,f*; **the bank raiders have all been arrested** les auteurs du hold-up (de la banque) ont tous été arrêtés (**c**) *St Exch* **(corporate) raider** raider *m*

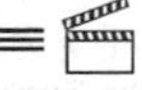

'Raiders of the Lost Ark' *Spielberg* 'Les Aventuriers de l'arche perdue'

raiding party ['reɪdɪŋ-] *n* commando *m*

rail [reɪl] **1** *n* (**a**) *(bar → gen)* barre *f*; *(→ in window, on bridge)* garde-fou *m*; *(→ on ship)* bastingage *m*; *(→ on balcony)* balustrade *f*; *(→ on stairway)* rampe *f*; *(→ for carpet)* tringle *f*; **towel rail** porte-serviettes *m inv*
(**b**) *(for train, tram)* rail *m*; **the live rail** le rail sous tension; **to travel by rail** voyager en train; **to send goods by rail** envoyer des marchandises par chemin de fer; **it's quicker by rail!** c'est plus rapide en train!; **to go off the rails** *(train)* dérailler; *Br Fig (person)* perdre la tête *ou* le nord; **to get the economy back on the rails** remettre l'économie sur les rails; **I did my best to get him back on the rails after his breakdown** j'ai fait de mon mieux pour le remettre sur pieds après sa dépression nerveuse
(**c**) *Orn* râle *m*
2 *comp (traffic, link, tunnel)* ferroviaire; *(ticket, fare)* de train; *(journey, travel)* en train; *(employee, union)* des chemins de fer
3 *vt (enclose)* clôturer
4 *vi (complain bitterly)* **to rail against** *or* **at** pester contre; **she railed against her fate** elle fulminait contre son sort
5 rails *npl (fencing)* grille *f*; *(in horseracing)* corde *f*; **he was pushed to the rails by the other jockeys** il a été forcé de tenir la corde par les autres jockeys; *Fig* **to be on the rails** *(in difficult situation)* être sur la corde raide
►► ***rail network*** réseau *m* ferroviaire *ou* de chemin de fer; ***rail strike*** grève *f* des chemins de fer; **the rail strike has affected the whole of France** la grève SNCF a touché la France entière; ***rail transport*** transport *m* par chemin de fer *ou* par train; ***rail worker*** *(gen)* employé(e) *m,f* des chemins de fer; *(for track, rolling stock)* cheminot *m*

►**rail in** *vt sep* clôturer

►**rail off** *vt sep* fermer (au moyen d'une barrière); **the end of the hall was railed off** une barrière interdisait l'accès au fond de la salle

railcar ['reɪlkɑ:(r)] *n* autorail *m*

railcard ['reɪlkɑ:d] *n Br* = carte permettant de bénéficier de tarifs avantageux sur les chemins de fer britanniques; **student railcard** carte *f* de réduction pour étudiant

railee ['reɪlɪ] *n Austr Fam* cheminot ❑ *m*

railhead ['reɪlhed] *n* tête *f* de ligne

railing ['reɪlɪŋ] **1** *n* (**a**) *(barrier → gen)* barrière *f*; *(→ on bridge)* garde-fou *m*; *(→ on balcony)* balustrade *f* (**b**) *(upright bar)* barreau *m* (**c**) *(fence)* grille *f*
2 railings *npl (fence)* grille *f*; **she squeezed through the railings** elle se glissa entre les barreaux de la grille

raillery ['reɪlərɪ] *(pl* **railleries***) n* raillerie *f*

railman ['reɪlmən] *(pl* **railmen** [-men]*) n Br & Can (gen)* employé(e) *m,f* des chemins de fer; *(technical employee)* cheminot *m*

railroad ['reɪlrəʊd] **1** *n Am (system)* chemin *m* de fer; *(track)* voie *f* ferrée; **to travel by railroad** voyager en chemin de fer
2 *vt* (**a**) *Fam (force acceptance of)* **to railroad a bill through Parliament** imposer un projet de loi au Parlement ❑
(**b**) *Fam (force into action)* **to railroad sb into doing sth** faire pression sur qn pour qu'il fasse qch ❑; **to be railroaded into doing sth** être forcé à faire qch ❑; **I don't want to railroad you, but...** je ne voudrais pas te forcer mais...; **she was railroaded into this job** on a fait pression sur elle pour qu'elle prenne ce poste
(**c**) *esp Am Fam Law (convict by false charges)* condamner à l'aide de fausses inculpations ❑; *(hastily)* juger sommairement ❑
(**d**) *Am (transport)* transporter par chemin de fer
►► *Am* ***railroad apartment*** = appartement dont les pièces sont en enfilade; ***railroad car*** wagon *m*

railroader ['reɪl,rəʊdə(r)] *n Am (gen)* employé(e) *m,f* des chemins de fer; *(for track, rolling stock)* cheminot *m*

railway ['reɪlweɪ] **1** *n* (**a**) *(system, organization)* chemin *m* de fer; **I'd never travelled by Russian railway** *or* **on the Russian railways** je n'avais jamais pris le train en Russie; **he works on the railways** il est cheminot
(**b**) *(track)* voie *f* ferrée
2 *comp (bridge, traffic, link, tunnel)* ferroviaire; *(company)* ferroviaire, de chemin de fer; *(journey, travel)* en train; *(employee, union)* des chemins de fer
►► ***railway carriage*** wagon *m*, voiture *f*; ***railway crossing*** passage *m* à niveau; ***railway cutting*** traversée *f* en déblai; ***railway embankment*** remblai *m*; ***railway engine*** locomotive *f*; ***railway engineer*** ingénieur *m* des chemins de fer; ***railway guide*** indicateur *m* des chemins de fer; ***railway line*** *(route)* ligne *f* de chemin de fer; *(track)* voie *f* ferrée; *(rail)* rail *m*; ***railway network*** réseau *m* ferroviaire *ou* de chemin de fer; ***railway signal*** signal *m* ferroviaire; ***railway station*** *(gen)* gare *f* (de chemin de fer); *(in France)* gare *f* SNCF; ***railway strike*** grève *f* des chemins de fer; ***railway system*** réseau *m* ferroviaire *ou* de chemin de fer; ***railway ticket*** billet *m* de train; ***railway timetable*** horaires *mpl* des chemins de fer; ***railway track*** voie *f* ferrée; ***railway worker*** *(gen)* employé(e) *m,f* des chemins de fer; *(for track, rolling stock)* cheminot *m*; ***railway yard*** dépôt *m*

railwayman ['reɪlweɪmən] *(pl* **railwaymen** [-mən]*) n Br & Can (gen)* employé(e) *m,f* des chemins de fer; *(technical employee)* cheminot *m*; *Br Formerly* **National Union of Railwaymen** = syndicat des employés de chemins de fer

raiment ['reɪmənt] *n (UNCOUNT) Literary* atours *mpl*

rain [reɪn] **1** *n* (**a**) *(precipitation)* pluie *f*; **it was pouring with rain** il pleuvait à verse; **the rain was heavy** il pleuvait beaucoup; **we had some rain yesterday** il a plu hier; **a light rain was falling** il tombait une pluie fine; **come in out of the rain** rentre, ne reste pas sous la pluie; **it looks like rain** on dirait qu'il va pleuvoir; **Venice in the rain** Venise sous la pluie; **the rains** la saison des pluies; **come rain or shine** *(whatever the weather)* qu'il pleuve ou qu'il vente; *(whatever the circumstances)* quoiqu'il arrive; *Fam* **don't worry, you'll be as right as rain in a minute** ne t'inquiète pas, ça va passer ❑
(**b**) *Fig (of projectiles, blows)* pluie *f*
2 *vi* pleuvoir; **it's raining** il pleut; *Fig* **arrows rained from the sky** des flèches pleuvaient du ciel; *Fam* **it's raining cats and dogs** il pleut des cordes, il tombe des hallebardes; *Prov Br* **it never rains but it pours,** *Am* **when it rains, it pours** = tout arrive en même temps
3 *vt* faire pleuvoir; **they rained blows on his head** ils firent pleuvoir des coups sur sa tête
►► *Am* ***rain check*** = bon pour un autre match (ou spectacle) donné par suite d'une annulation à cause de la pluie; *Fam Fig* **I'll take a rain check on that** ça sera pour une autre fois ❑; ***rain cloud*** nuage *m* de pluie; ***rain dance*** danse *f* de la pluie; ***rain gauge*** pluviomètre *m*; ***rain shadow*** région *f* sous le vent *(dans les montagnes)*

►**rain down 1** *vi (projectiles, blows etc)* pleuvoir
2 *vt sep (projectiles, blows etc)* faire pleuvoir

►**rain off** *vt sep Br* **the game was rained off** *(cancelled)* la partie a été annulée à cause de la pluie; *(abandoned)* la partie a été abandonnée à cause de la pluie

►**rain out** *vt sep* (**a**) *(campers)* **to be rained out** être chassé par la pluie
(**b**) *Am* **the game was rained out** *(cancelled)* la partie a été annulée à cause de la pluie; *(abandoned)* la partie a été abandonnée à cause de la pluie

rainbelt ['reɪnbelt] *n* zone *f* des pluies

rainbow ['reɪnbəʊ] *n* arc-en-ciel *m*; **all the colours of the rainbow** toutes les couleurs de l'arc-en-ciel; *Fig* **it's at the end of the rainbow** c'est un mirage; *Fig* **to chase rainbows** se bercer d'illusions
►► ***rainbow coalition*** = coalition représentant un large éventail de tendances; ***rainbow trout*** truite *f* arc-en-ciel

'The Rainbow' *Lawrence* 'l'Arc-en-ciel'

rainbow-coloured *adj* arc-en-ciel *(inv)*, multicolore

raincoat ['reɪnkəʊt] *n* imperméable *m*

raindrop ['reɪndrɒp] *n* goutte *f* de pluie

rainfall ['reɪnfɔ:l] *n (amount of rain)* pluviosité *f*; **the average annual rainfall in the region** la pluviosité annuelle de la région; **after three days of heavy rainfall** après trois jours de fortes pluies

rainforest ['reɪn,fɒrɪst] *n* forêt *f* pluviale, forêt *f* tropicale humide

rainhat ['reɪnhæt] *n* capuche *f* en plastique

rainhood ['reɪnhʊd] *n* capuche *f*; *(attached to anorak, jacket etc)* capuchon *m*, capuche *f*

raininess ['reɪnɪnɪs] *n* caractère *m* pluvieux; **the raininess of the weather** le temps pluvieux

rainless ['reɪnlɪs] *adj* sans pluie

rainmaker ['reɪn,meɪkə(r)] *n* (**a**) *(in tribe)* faiseur *m* de pluie (**b**) *Fam (in company)* cadre *m* hyperperformant

rainmaking ['reɪn,meɪkɪŋ] *adj (ritual, dance)* pour faire pleuvoir

rainout ['reɪnaʊt] *n* (**a**) *(UNCOUNT) (pollution)* = retombées entraînées par la pluie (**b**) *Am Sport* = match annulé à cause du mauvais temps

rainproof ['reɪnpru:f] **1** *adj* imperméable
2 *vt* imperméabiliser

rainslicker ['reɪnslɪkə(r)] *n Am* ciré *m*

rainstorm ['reɪnstɔ:m] *n* pluie *f* torrentielle

raintight ['reɪntaɪt] *adj* imperméable *(à la pluie)*

raintree ['reɪntri:] *n Bot* pithecolobium *m*

rainwater ['reɪn,wɔ:tə(r)] *n* eau *f* de pluie *ou* pluviale

rainwear ['reɪnweə(r)] *n (UNCOUNT)* vêtements *mpl* de pluie

rainy ['reɪnɪ] *(compar* **rainier,** *superl* **rainiest)** *adj* pluvieux; **a rainy day** un jour de pluie; *Fig* **to save sth for a rainy day** garder qch pour les mauvais jours

►► ***rainy season*** saison *f* des pluies

RAISE [reɪz]

augmentation	► **1 (a)**
lever	► **2 (a), (e), (f), (n)**
soulever	► **2 (a), (k)**
remonter	► **2 (a), (c)**
relever	► **2 (a), (b)**
augmenter	► **2 (b)**
élever	► **2 (c), (d), (i), (j), (l), (r)**

1 *n* **(a)** *Am (pay increase)* augmentation *f* (de salaire); **to get a raise** être augmenté, avoir une augmentation

(b) *Cards (in bridge)* enchère *f*; *(in poker)* relance *f*

2 *vt* **(a)** *(lift, move upwards → gen)* lever; *(→ burden, lid)* soulever; *(→ veil)* relever; *(→ weight)* lever, soulever; *(→ blind)* remonter; *(→ flag)* hisser; *(→ sunken ship)* renflouer; **to raise one's head** *(from lowered position)* lever la tête; *(hold erect)* dresser la tête; **she didn't raise her eyes from her book** elle n'a pas levé les yeux de son livre; **he tried to raise himself from the sofa** il essaya de se lever du canapé; **she raised herself to her full height** elle se dressa de toute sa hauteur; **to raise a patient to a sitting position** soulever un malade pour l'asseoir; **to raise one's glass (to sb)** lever son verre (à la santé de qn); **to raise one's glass to one's lips** porter son verre à ses lèvres; **to raise one's fist to sb** menacer qn du poing; **to raise sb's hackles** hérisser qn; **to raise one's hand to sb** lever la main sur qn; **to raise one's hat to sb** soulever son chapeau pour saluer qn; *Fig* tirer son chapeau à qn; **to raise a cloud of dust** soulever un nuage de poussière; *Mil & Fig* **to raise one's sights** viser plus haut

(b) *(increase → offer, price, tax, salaries)* augmenter; *(→ interest rates)* relever; *(→ temperature, tension)* faire monter; *(→ volume)* augmenter; **the speed limit has been raised to 150 km/h** la limitation de vitesse est passée à 150 km/h; **the age limit has been raised to 18** la limite d'âge a été repoussée à 18 ans; **to raise the school-leaving age** prolonger la scolarité; **to raise a credit limit** déplafonner un crédit; **to raise the ceiling on wage increases** augmenter le plafond des salaires; **to raise production to a maximum** porter la production au maximum; **to raise the stakes** faire monter les enjeux; **to raise the pass mark** élever le niveau requis; **to raise (the level of) a wall** rehausser *ou* surélever un mur; **to raise the level of the ground** rehausser le niveau du sol; **to raise one's voice** *(speak more loudly)* élever la voix; *(speak in anger)* hausser le ton; **no one raised their voice (to answer** *or* **to speak)** personne ne souffla mot

(c) *(boost, improve)* remonter, élever; **to raise standards** *(of education, morality)* élever le niveau; *(of cleanliness, safety)* améliorer les conditions; **to raise the standard of living** améliorer le niveau de vie; **our aim is to raise overall standards** notre but est d'élever le niveau global; **to raise sb's spirits** remonter le moral à qn; **to raise sb's hopes** donner des espoirs à qn; **to raise the tone** *or* **the level of the conversation** élever le niveau de la conversation

(d) *(promote)* élever, promouvoir; *Mil & Fig* **to raise sb from the ranks** promouvoir qn; **raised to the rank of colonel** élevé au rang de colonel; **the Queen raised him to the peerage** la reine l'éleva à la pairie

(e) *(collect together → support)* réunir; *(→ army)* lever; **we have raised over a million signatures** nous avons recueilli plus d'un million de signatures

(f) *(obtain → money)* trouver, obtenir; *(→ capital)* mobiliser, procurer; *(→ taxes)* lever; **he wanted a new motorbike but couldn't raise the money** il voulait une moto neuve mais il n'a pas pu trouver l'argent nécessaire; **we have to raise $10,000 by Friday** il faut que nous trouvions 10 000 dollars d'ici vendredi; **to raise funds (for)** *(for charity)* collecter des fonds (pour *ou* au profit de); *(for business, government programme)* se procurer des fonds (pour *ou* au profit de); **to raise a loan (on)** *(of government)* émettre *ou* lancer un emprunt (sur); *(of individual)* faire un emprunt (sur)

(g) *(make, produce)* **they raised a cheer when she came in** ils ont poussé des bravos quand elle est entrée; **he managed to raise a smile when he saw us** il a réussi à sourire en nous voyant

(h) *(cause as reaction → laugh, welt, blister, rebellion)* provoquer; **his jokes didn't even raise a smile** ses plaisanteries n'ont même pas fait sourire; **to raise a storm of laughter/protest** déclencher *ou* soulever une tempête de rires/de protestations

(i) *(rear → children, family)* élever

(j) *(breed → livestock)* élever; *(grow → crops)* cultiver

(k) *(introduce, bring up → point, subject, question)* soulever; *(→ doubts)* soulever, susciter; **she raised several objections** elle souleva plusieurs objections; **this might raise doubts as to his competence** ça pourrait soulever *ou* susciter des doutes quant à ses compétences; **his attitude raises certain questions** son attitude pose *ou* soulève certaines questions; **his attitude raises questions about his loyalty** son attitude remet en question sa loyauté

(l) *(erect)* élever, ériger; **to raise a statue to sb** élever une statue à qn

(m) *(resuscitate)* ressusciter; *(evoke → spirit)* évoquer; **they were making enough noise to raise the dead** ils faisaient un bruit à réveiller les morts

(n) *(end → ban, embargo, siege)* lever

(o) *(contact)* contacter; **the radio officer was trying to raise Boston** le radio essayait de contacter Boston

(p) *(in bridge)* monter sur; *(in poker)* relancer; **I'll raise you £5** je relance de 5 livres

(q) *Culin (dough, bread)* faire lever

(r) *Math* élever; **to raise a number to the power of n** élever un nombre à la puissance n

(s) *Naut* **to raise land** arriver en vue de terre

(t) *(cheque)* faire

3 *vi (in bridge)* monter, enchérir; *(in poker)* relancer

►**raise up** *vt sep* **to raise oneself up** se soulever; **she raised herself up onto the chair** elle se hissa sur la chaise

raised [reɪzd] *adj* **(a)** *(elevated → ground, platform, jetty etc)* surélevé **(b)** *(embossed → pattern, letter, motif)* en relief **(c)** *Am Culin* levé, à la levure **(d)** *Ling (vowel)* haut **(e)** *Tex* lainé, gratté

►► *Geog* ***raised beach*** plage *f* soulevée

raiser ['reɪzə(r)] *n (of livestock)* éleveur(euse) *m,f*; *(of crops)* cultivateur(trice) *m,f*

raisin ['reɪzən] *n* raisin *m* sec

►► ***raisin bread*** pain *m* aux raisins *(miche)*

raising ['reɪzɪŋ] *n* **(a)** *(lifting → of curtain)* lever *m*; *(→ of sunken ship)* renflouage *m*; *(→ of standards)* élévation *f*

(b) *(of offer, price, tax, salaries)* augmentation *f*; **raising of the school-leaving age** prolongation *f* de la scolarité

(c) *(of army)* levée *f*; *(collecting → of funds for charity)* collecte *f*; *(→ of taxes)* levée *f*

(d) *(of barn, building)* construction *f*; *(of monument, statue)* érection *f*

(e) *(of animals)* élevage *m*; *(of children)* éducation *f*; *(of crops)* culture *f*

(f) *(of blockade, embargo, siege)* levée *f*

(g) raising of the dead résurrection *f* des morts

►► *Culin* ***raising agent*** levure *f*

raita [rɑ:'i:tə] *n Culin* raita *m*

Raj [rɑ:dʒ] *n* **the Raj** l'empire *m* britannique (en Inde)

raja, rajah ['rɑ:dʒə] *n* raja *m*, rajah *m*, radjah *m*

rake [reɪk] **1** *n* **(a)** *(in garden, casino)* râteau *m*; **as thin as a rake** maigre comme un clou

(b) *(libertine)* roué *m*, libertin *m*

(c) *(slope → of seating, terrace)* pente *f*

(d) *Naut (of mast, funnel)* quête *f*

2 *vt* **(a)** *(soil, lawn, path)* ratisser, râteler; **she raked the leaves into a pile** elle ratissa les feuilles en tas

(b) *(search)* fouiller (dans); **to rake one's memory** fouiller dans ses souvenirs

(c) *(scan)* balayer; **his eyes raked the audience** son regard parcourut l'assistance; **a searchlight raked the darkness** un projecteur fouilla l'obscurité

(d) *(strafe)* balayer; **machine-gun fire raked the trench** le feu d'une mitrailleuse balaya la tranchée

3 *vi* **(a)** *(search)* **to rake among** *or* **through** fouiller dans

(b) *(slope)* être en pente, être incliné

►**rake about, rake around** *vi (search)* fouiller (**among** *or* **in** dans)

►**rake in** *vt sep Fam (money)* amasser ❑; **that shop is raking in a fortune** ce magasin ramasse une fortune; **they must be raking it in** ils doivent s'en mettre plein les poches

►**rake off** *vt sep Fam (share of profits)* empocher ❑, ramasser ❑; **he was raking off 10 percent of the profits** il empochait *ou* ramassait 10 pour cent des bénéfices

►**rake out** *vt sep* **(a)** *(fire)* enlever les cendres de; *(ashes)* enlever **(b)** *(search out)* dénicher

►**rake over** *vt sep* **(a)** *(soil, lawn, path)* ratisser **(b)** *Fig* remuer; **why rake over the past?** pourquoi remuer le passé?

►**rake up** *vt sep* **(a)** *(collect together → leaves, weeds)* ratisser; *(→ people)* réunir, rassembler **(b)** *(dredge up)* déterrer; **to rake up sb's past** fouiller dans le passé de qn; **to rake up an old quarrel** raviver une ancienne querelle

'The Rake's Progress' *Hogarth, Stravinsky* 'La Carrière du roué' (tableau), 'Le Libertin' (opéra)

raked [reɪkt] *adj (inclined)* incliné

rake-off *n Fam* ristourne ❑*f*, petit profit ❑*m*; **to get a rake-off on each sale** toucher un pourcentage *ou* une commission sur chaque vente

raki ['rɑ:ki:, 'rækɪ] *n (drink)* raki *m*

rakish ['reɪkɪʃ] *adj* **(a)** *(dissolute)* débauché; *(jaunty)* désinvolte, insouciant; **he wore his hat at a rakish angle** il portait son chapeau avec désinvolture **(b)** *(boat)* à la forme élancée, allongé

rakishly ['reɪkɪʃlɪ] *adv (dissolutely)* d'un air débauché; *(jauntily)* d'un air désinvolte

rale [rɑ:l] *n Med* râle *m*

rallentando [,rælən'tændəʊ] *adv Mus* rallentando

rally ['rælɪ] *(pl* **rallies,** *pt & pp* **rallied) 1** *n* **(a)** *(gathering → gen)* rassemblement *m*; *Mil (during battle)* ralliement *m*; *Pol* rassemblement *m*, (grand) meeting *m*

(b) *(recovery → gen)* amélioration *f*; *(→ of prices, shares, business)* reprise *f*; **the England team staged a rally in the second half** l'équipe anglaise s'est reprise au cours de la deuxième mi-temps

(c) *Aut* rallye *m*; **the Monte Carlo rally** le rallye de Monte-Carlo

(d) *Sport (in tennis, squash etc)* long échange *m*

2 *vi* **(a)** *(assemble, gather → gen)* se rassembler; *(→ troops, supporters)* se rallier; **they rallied to the party/to the defence of their leader** ils se sont ralliés au parti/pour défendre leur chef

(b) *(recover → gen)* s'améliorer; *(→ sick person)* aller mieux, reprendre des forces; *(→ currency, prices, shares, business)* se redresser, reprendre; *(→ stock market)* se reprendre; **the pound rallied in the afternoon** la livre est remontée dans l'après-midi; **the market rallied** les cours ont repris

(c) *Aut* faire des rallyes

3 *vt* **(a)** *(gather)* rallier, rassembler; **she's trying to rally support for her project** elle essaie de rallier des gens pour soutenir son projet

(b) *(summon up)* reprendre; *(boost)* ranimer; **to rally one's spirits** reprendre ses esprits; **the news rallied their morale** la nouvelle leur a remonté le moral

(c) *Arch (tease)* taquiner

►► ***rally driver*** pilote *m* de rallye

▸**rally round** 1 *vi* **all her family rallied round** toute sa famille est venue lui apporter son soutien
 2 *vt insep* **they rallied round her** ils lui ont apporté leur soutien

rallycross ['rælɪkrɒs] *n Br* rallye-cross *m*

rallyer ['rælɪə(r)] *n Sport* concurrent(e) *m,f* d'un rallye

rallying ['rælɪɪŋ] **1** *n Sport* rallyes *mpl*; **to go rallying** faire un rallye
 2 *adj* de ralliement
 ▸▸ ***rallying cry*** cri *m* de ralliement; ***rallying point*** point *m* de ralliement

rallyist ['rælɪɪst] *n Sport* concurrent(e) *m,f* d'un rallye

ralph [rælf] *vi Fam (vomit)* gerber, dégueuler

RAM[1] [ræm] *n Comput* (*abbr* **random-access memory**) RAM *f*, mémoire *f* vive
 ▸▸ ***RAM chip*** puce *f* de mémoire vive; ***RAM disk*** mémoire *f* à disque

RAM[2] [,ɑːreɪ'em] *n* (*abbr* **Royal Academy of Music**) = conservatoire national de musique de Londres

ram [ræm] (*pt & pp* **rammed**, *cont* **ramming**) **1** *n*
 (**a**) *Zool* bélier *m*
 (**b**) *Hist (for breaking doors, walls)* bélier *m*
 (**c**) *Tech (piston)* piston *m*; *(flattening tool)* hie *f*, dame *f*; *(pile driver)* mouton *m*; *(lifting pump)* bélier *m* hydraulique
 2 *vt* (**a**) *(bang into)* percuter; *Naut* aborder; *(in battle)* éperonner; **the police car rammed them twice** la voiture de police les a percutés deux fois; **he rammed the trolley into my ankles** il m'a heurté les chevilles avec son caddie®
 (**b**) *(push)* pousser (violemment); **a table had been rammed up against the door** une table avait été poussée contre la porte; **she rammed the bolt home** elle repoussa le verrou (violemment); **she rammed the papers into her bag** elle fourra les papiers dans son sac; **he rammed his pipe with tobacco** il bourra sa pipe; *Fig* **in order to ram home the point** pour enfoncer le clou; **she's always ramming religion down my throat** elle me rebat toujours les oreilles avec sa religion
 3 *vi* **to ram into sth** entrer dans *ou* percuter qch; **a Jag rammed into the back of me** une Jaguar a embouti l'arrière de ma voiture
 ▸▸ *Aut* ***ram air*** air *m* forcé; *Aut* ***ram air induction*** introduction *f* d'air par forçage; ***ram cylinder*** vérin *m*

Ramadan [,ræmə'dæn] *n Rel* ramadan *m*; **during Ramadan** pendant ramadan

Raman effect ['rɑːmən-] *n Phys* effet *m* Raman

ramble ['ræmbəl] **1** *n (hike)* randonnée *f* (pédestre); *(casual walk)* promenade *f*; **to go for a ramble** aller faire un tour
 2 *vi* (**a**) *(hike)* faire une randonnée
 (**b**) *(wander)* se balader
 (**c**) *(talk)* divaguer, radoter; **he rambled on and on about nothing** il n'arrêtait pas de parler pour ne rien dire; **what are you rambling on about now?** qu'est-ce que tu racontes maintenant?
 (**d**) *(be delirious)* divaguer
 (**e**) *(plant)* pousser à tort et à travers
 (**f**) *(path, stream)* serpenter

rambler ['ræmblə(r)] *n* (**a**) *(hiker)* randonneur(euse) *m,f* (**b**) *(in speech)* **he's a bit of a rambler** il est du genre radoteur (**c**) *Bot* plante *f* sarmenteuse

rambling ['ræmblɪŋ] **1** *adj* (**a**) *(building)* plein de coins et de recoins; *(path, stream)* sinueux
 (**b**) *(conversation, style)* décousu; *(ideas, book, thoughts)* incohérent, sans suite; *(person)* qui divague, qui radote
 (**c**) *(plant)* sarmenteux
 2 *n* (**a**) *(hiking)* randonnée *f*; **to go rambling** aller en randonnée
 (**b**) **ramblings** *(delirium)* divagations *fpl*; **the ramblings of old age** les radotages *mpl* de la vieillesse
 ▸▸ ***rambling rose*** rosier *m* sarmenteux

rambunctious [ræm'bʌŋkʃəs] *adj Fam* (**a**) *(boisterous)* turbulent❏, chahuteur, tapageur (**b**) *(noisy)* bruyant❏

rambutan ['ræmbuːtən] *n Bot* ramboutan *m*

RAMC [,ɑːreɪ,em'siː] *n Br* (*abbr* **Royal Army Medical Corps**) = service de santé des armées britanniques

ramekin ['ræmɪkɪn] *n* ramequin *m*

ramen ['rɑːmən] *n Culin* soupe *f* aux nouilles *(spécialité japonaise)*

ramequin = **ramekin**

Rameses ['ræmɪsiːz] = **Ramses**

ramie ['ræmɪ] *n Tex* ramie *f*

ramification [,ræmɪfɪ'keɪʃən] *n* (**a**) *(implication)* implication *f*; **I'm not sure if you understand all the ramifications of this decision** je ne suis pas sûr que vous compreniez toutes les conséquences qu'aura cette décision (**b**) *(branching)* ramification *f*

ramiform ['ræmɪfɔːm] *adj* ramifié

ramify ['ræmɪfaɪ] (*pt & pp* **ramified**) **1** *vt* ramifier
 2 *vi* se ramifier

ramjet ['ræmdʒet] *n (engine)* statoréacteur *m*, tuyère *f* thermopropulsive; *(aircraft)* avion *m* à statoréacteur

rammer ['ræmə(r)] *n (for road-making)* dame *f*; *(for metal-working)* fouloir *m*, batte *f*; *(for civil engineering)* engin *m* de compactage du sol

ramp [ræmp] *n* (**a**) *(slope)* rampe *f* (**b**) *Aut (in garage)* pont *m* élévateur (**c**) *Am (connecting road)* bretelle *f* (d'accès) (**d**) *(bump on road)* dos *m* d'âne; *(difference in level)* dénivellation *f*, dénivellement *m*; *(to slow traffic down)* ralentisseur *m*

▸**ramp up** *vt sep (increase)* gonfler

rampage [ræm'peɪdʒ] **1** *n* fureur *f*; **to be on the rampage** être déchaîné; **to go on the rampage** se livrer à des actes de violence; **football fans went on the rampage through the town** des supporters de football ont saccagé la ville; **the headmaster's on the rampage!** le directeur est déchaîné!
 2 *vi* se déchaîner; **a herd of elephants rampaged through the bush** un troupeau d'éléphants avançait dans la brousse en balayant tout sur son passage; **they rampaged through the town** ils ont saccagé la ville

rampaging [ræm'peɪdʒɪŋ] *adj* déchaîné

rampancy ['ræmpənsɪ] *n (of corruption, vice)* prolifération *f*; *(of plant)* exubérance *f*

rampant ['ræmpənt] *adj* (**a**) *(unrestrained)* déchaîné, effréné; *(plant)* exubérant, luxuriant; **they're rampant Marxists** ce sont des marxistes purs et durs; **corruption is rampant** la corruption sévit, **the disease is rampant** la maladie fait des ravages; *Fam* **he's a bit rampant tonight** *(sexually)* il est émoustillé ce soir
 (**b**) *(exuberant → vegetation)* exubérant, foisonnant
 (**c**) *(after n) Her* rampant; **the Lion Rampant** le Lion rampant

rampantly ['ræmpəntlɪ] *adv* (**a**) *(without restraint)* violemment, sans frein (**b**) *(in abundance)* surabondamment

rampart ['ræmpɑːt] **1** *n also Fig* rempart *m*; *Literary* **the ramparts of liberty** les remparts *mpl* de la liberté
 2 *vt* fortifier

rampion ['ræmpjən] *n Bot* raiponce *f*

ramraid ['ræmreɪd] *vt Br* cambrioler *(en enfonçant la vitrine avec un véhicule)*

ramraider ['ræm,reɪdə(r)] *n Br* = personne qui cambriole les magasins en fracassant les vitrines avec sa voiture

RAM-resident [ræm-] *adj Comput* résident en mémoire vive

ramrod ['ræmrɒd] **1** *n (for cleaning rifle)* écouvillon *m*; *(for loading cannon)* refouloir *m*; **to sit/to stand as stiff as a ramrod** être assis/se tenir raide comme un piquet
 2 *adv* **the sentry stood ramrod straight** la sentinelle se tenait debout, raide comme un piquet

Ramses ['ræmsiːz] *pr n* Ramsès

ramshackle ['ræm,ʃækəl] *adj* délabré

ramshorn snail ['ræmz,hɔːn-] *n* planorbe *f*

ramsons ['ræmsənz] *n Bot* ail *m* des ours

RAN [,ɑːreɪ'en] *n Austr* (*abbr* **Royal Australian Navy**) = marine de guerre australienne

ran [ræn] *pt of* **run**

ranch [rɑːntʃ] **1** *n* ranch *m*; **chicken ranch** élevage *m* de poulets
 2 *vi* exploiter un ranch
 3 *vt* **to ranch cattle** élever du bétail (sur un ranch)
 ▸▸ *Culin* ***ranch dressing*** = mayonnaise crémeuse à l'ail; ***ranch hand*** ouvrier(ère) *m,f* agricole; ***ranch house*** *(bungalow)* maison *f* sans étage; *(on ranch)* maison *f*; *Am* ***ranch mink*** vison *m* d'élevage

rancher ['rɑːntʃə(r)] *n (owner)* propriétaire *mf* de ranch; *(manager)* exploitant(e) *m,f* de ranch; *(worker)* garçon *m* de ranch, cow-boy *m*

ranchero [rɑːn'tʃeərəʊ] (*pl* **rancheros**) *n Am* rancher *m*

ranching ['rɑːntʃɪŋ] *n* exploitation *f* d'un ranch; **cattle/chicken ranching** élevage *m* de bétail/de poulets

rancid ['rænsɪd] *adj* rance; **to go** *or* **to turn rancid** rancir

rancidity [ræn'sɪdɪtɪ], **rancidness** ['rænsɪdnɪs] *n* rancidité *f*, rancissure *f*

rancor *Am* = **rancour**

rancorous ['ræŋkərəs] *adj* rancunier

rancorously ['ræŋkərəslɪ] *adv* avec haine *ou* rancune

rancour, *Am* **rancor** ['ræŋkə(r)] *n* rancœur *f*, rancune *f*

rand [rænd] (*pl* **inv**) *n (money)* rand *m*

R & B [,ɑːrən'biː] *n* (*abbr* **rhythm and blues**) rhythm and blues *m inv*

R & D [,ɑːrən'diː] *n* (*abbr* **research and development**) recherche *f* et développement *m*, R-D *f*
 ▸▸ ***R & D department*** bureau *m* d'études; ***R & D director*** directeur(trice) *m,f* de recherche et développement; ***R & D expenditure*** dépenses *fpl* pour la recherche et le développement

randem ['rændəm] **1** *n* voiture *f* à trois chevaux en flèche
 2 *adv* **to drive randem** conduire à trois chevaux en flèche

random ['rændəm] **1** *adj (choice)* fait au hasard; *(pattern)* irrégulier; *Math (error, number)* aléatoire; **the arrangement of the dots seems completely random** la disposition des points semble complètement aléatoire; **I just made a random guess** j'ai deviné tout à fait par hasard; **a random selection of people were asked if...** on a demandé à des gens choisis au hasard si...; **a random selection of goods** des marchandises prises au hasard, une sélection arbitraire de marchandises; **a random shot** une balle perdue
 2 **at random** *adv* au hasard; **chosen at random** choisi au hasard; **to lash out at random** distribuer des coups à l'aveuglette
 ▸▸ *Comput* ***random access*** accès *m* aléatoire; *Mktg* ***random check*** contrôle *m* par sondage(s); *Comput* ***random error*** erreur *f* aléatoire; ***random killings*** tuerie *f* aveugle *ou* au hasard; *Mktg* ***random sample*** échantillon *m* aléatoire; *Mktg* ***random sampling*** échantillonnage *m* aléatoire; *Mktg* ***random selection*** sélection *f* au hasard; *Math* ***random variable*** variable *f* aléatoire; ***random violence*** violence *f* aveugle; *Math & St Exch* ***random walk*** marche *f* aléatoire

random-access *adj Comput* à accès aléatoire *ou* direct
 ▸▸ ***random-access file*** fichier *m* à accès aléatoire; ***random-access memory*** mémoire *f* vive

randomization [,rændəmaɪ'zeɪʃən] *n* randomisation *f*

randomize, -ise ['rændəmaɪz] *vt* randomiser

randomly ['rændəmlɪ] *adv* au hasard

randomness ['rændəmnɪs] *n* aspect *m ou* caractère *m* aléatoire

R and R, R&R [,ɑːrən'ɑː(r)] *n Am Mil* (*abbr* **rest and recreation**) permission *f*; *Fam Fig* **she went on holiday for some R and R** elle est allée en vacances pour se reposer un peu❏

randy ['rændɪ] (*compar* **randier**, *superl* **randiest**) *adj Fam* excité❏; **to get** *or* **to become randy** commencer à s'exciter; **he's a randy devil** c'est un chaud lapin; **a randy old man** un vieux satyre

ranee = **rani**

rang [ræŋ] *pt of* **ring**

RANGE [reɪndʒ]

portée	▸ **1 (a)**
échelle	▸ **1 (b)**
gamme	▸ **1 (c)**
champ	▸ **1 (d)**
étendue	▸ **1 (d)**
parcourir	▸ **2 (a); 3 (b)**
ranger	▸ **2 (b), (c)**
aller de...à	▸ **3 (a)**

ral–ran

1 *n* **(a)** *(of missile, sound, transmitter, telescope)* portée *f*; *(of vehicle, aircraft)* autonomie *f*; **medium-range** *or* **intermediate-range missiles** missiles *mpl* à portée intermédiaire; **short/medium/long-range aircraft** court-/moyen-/long-courrier *m*; *Met* **short/long-range forecast** prévisions *fpl* météorologiques à court/long terme; **at long/short range** à longue/courte portée; **out of range** hors de portée; **within (firing) range** à portée de tir; **to be within hearing range** être à portée de voix; **it can kill a man at a range of 800 metres** ça peut tuer un homme à une distance de 800 mètres; **at point blank range** à bout portant; **range of vision** champ *m* visuel; **it gives you some idea of the range of their powers** ça vous donne une petite idée de l'étendue de leurs pouvoirs

(b) *(scale → of prices, salaries)* échelle *f*, éventail *m*; *(of instrument, voice)* tessiture *f*; **there is a wide range of temperatures in these parts** il existe de très grands écarts de température dans ces régions; **children in the same age range** les enfants dans la même tranche d'âge; **beyond one's range** *(note)* hors de son registre; **within one's range** *(note)* dans son registre; **it's within my price range** c'est dans mes prix; **what is your price range?** quel prix voulez-vous mettre?; *St Exch* **opening/closing range** fourchette *f* de cours d'ouverture/de clôture

(c) *(series, selection → of colours, feelings, products)* gamme *f*; *(→ of patterns, sizes)* choix *m*; **we stock a wide range of office materials** nous avons en stock une large gamme de matériels de bureaux; **the new autumn range** *(of clothes)* la nouvelle collection d'automne; **this car is (at) the top/bottom of the range** cette voiture est le modèle haut/bas de gamme; **the coat comes in a wide range of colours/sizes** le manteau existe dans une gamme variée de couleurs/un grand choix de tailles; **an actor with a wide range of expressions** un acteur qui a une gamme d'expressions très variée; **we talked on a wide range of topics** nous avons discuté de sujets très divers; **she has a wide range of interests** elle s'intéresse à beaucoup de choses; **to experience the full range of emotions** passer par toute la gamme des émotions; **the range of possibilities is almost infinite** l'éventail des possibilités est presque infini

(d) *(scope → of activity)* champ *m*; *(→ of knowledge, research)* étendue *f*; *(→ of inquiry, investigation)* domaine *m*; *Mktg (→ of advertising campaign)* rayon *m* d'action; **that is beyond the range of the present inquiry** cela ne relève pas de cette enquête; **that lies outside the range of my responsibility** ça dépasse les limites de ma responsabilité

(e) *(of mountains)* chaîne *f*

(f) *(territory → of animal, plant)* habitat *m*; *Am (prairie)* prairie *f*

(g) *(for target practice)* champ *m* de tir; **missile range** champ *m* de tir de missiles

(h) *(cooker)* fourneau *m* (de cuisine)

(i) *(row, line)* rang *m*, rangée *f*

(j) *(in surveying)* alignement *m*, direction *f*

2 *vt* **(a)** *(roam over)* parcourir

(b) *(put in a row or in rows)* ranger, mettre *ou* disposer en rang *ou* en rangs; **the troops ranged themselves in front of the embassy** les troupes se rangèrent devant l'ambassade; **the desks are ranged in threes** les pupitres sont en rangées de trois

(c) *(join, ally)* ranger, rallier; **to range oneself with sb** se ranger du côté de qn; *(ideologically)* s'aligner sur la position de qn; **to range oneself against sb** s'opposer à qn; **the forces ranged against them** les forces ralliées contre eux

(d) *(aim → cannon, telescope)* braquer (**on** sur)

(e) *Typ* aligner, justifier; **ranged left/right** justifié à gauche/à droite

(f) *(classify)* classer, ranger

(g) *Am* **to range cattle** élever du bétail dans la prairie

3 *vi* **(a)** *(extend, vary)* aller (**from…to** de…à), varier (**from…to** entre…et); **prices range from £15 to £150** les prix vont de 15 à 150 livres; **incomes ranging from £12,000 to £15,000** *or* **between £12,000 and £15,000** revenus de l'ordre de 12 000 à 15 000 livres; **their ages range from 5 to 12** *or* **between 5 and 12** ils ont de 5 à 12 *ou* entre 5 et 12 ans; **the quality ranges from mediocre to excellent** la qualité varie de médiocre à excellent; **the survey ranged over the whole country** l'enquête couvrait la totalité du pays; **our conversation ranged over a large number of topics** nous avons discuté d'un grand nombre de sujets

(b) *(roam)* **to range over sth** parcourir qch; **they range over the countryside** ils parcourent la campagne; **thugs range through the city streets** des voyous rôdent dans les rues de la ville; **his eyes ranged over the audience** il parcourut l'auditoire des yeux

(c) *(gun, missile)* **to range over** avoir une portée de

►► *Mktg* ***range addition*** ajout *m* à la gamme; *Am* ***range cattle*** bétail *m* élevé dans la prairie; ***range pole, range rod*** *(surveying instrument)* jalon *m*; *Mktg* ***range stretching*** extension *f* de la gamme

---

rangefinder ['reɪndʒˌfaɪndə(r)] *n* télémètre *m*

rangeland ['reɪndʒlænd] *n Am* prairie *f*

ranger ['reɪndʒə(r)] **1** *n* **(a)** *(in park, forest)* garde *m* forestier **(b)** *Am (lawman)* ≃ gendarme *m* **(c)** *Am Mil* ranger *m*

2 Ranger (Guide) *n* guide *m*

ranging ['reɪndʒɪŋ] *adj*

►► *Mil* ***ranging fire*** tir *m* de réglage; ***ranging pole, ranging rod*** *(surveying instrument)* jalon *m*

Rangoon [ræŋ'guːn] *n* Rangoon

rangy ['reɪndʒɪ] *(compar* **rangier**, *superl* **rangiest**) *adj* **(a)** *(tall and thin)* grand et élancé **(b)** *(roomy)* spacieux

rani ['rɑːnɪ] *n* rani *f*

rank [ræŋk] **1** *n* **(a)** *(grade)* rang *m*, grade *m*; **promoted to the rank of colonel** promu (au rang de *ou* au grade de) colonel; **the rank of manager** le titre de directeur; **to pull rank** faire valoir sa supériorité hiérarchique; **I don't want to have to pull rank on you** je ne veux pas avoir à user de mon autorité sur vous

(b) *(quality)* rang *m*; **we have very few players in the first** *or* **top rank** nous avons très peu de joueurs de premier ordre

(c) *(social class)* rang *m*, condition *f* (sociale); **the lower ranks of society** les couches inférieures de la société

(d) *(row, line)* rang *m*, rangée *f*; *(on chessboard)* rangée *f*; **a double rank of policemen** une double rangée de policiers; **to break ranks** *Mil* rompre les rangs; *Fig* se désolidariser; *Mil & Fig* **to close ranks** serrer les rangs; *Mil* **close ranks!** serrez!

(e) *Br* **(taxi) rank** station *f* (de taxis)

(f) *Math (in matrix)* rang *m*

(g) *Fin (of debt, mortgage)* rang *m*

2 *vt* **(a)** *(rate)* classer; **she is ranked among the best contemporary writers** elle est classée parmi les meilleurs écrivains contemporains; **I rank this as one of our finest performances** je considère que c'est une de nos meilleures représentations; **he is ranked number 3** il est classé numéro 3

(b) *(arrange)* ranger

(c) *Am (outrank → in army)* avoir un grade supérieur à; *(→ in office, organization etc)* être le supérieur de; **a general ranks a captain** un général est au-dessus d'un capitaine

3 *vi* **(a)** *(rate)* figurer; **to rank above sb** être le supérieur de *ou* occuper un rang supérieur à qn; **to rank below sb** occuper un rang inférieur à qn; **to rank equally (with sb)** être au même niveau (que qn); **it ranks high/low on our list of priorities** c'est/ce n'est pas une de nos priorités; **he hardly ranks as an expert** on ne peut guère le qualifier d'expert; *Chess* **a castle ranks above a bishop** la tour est plus forte que le fou

(b) *Fin (creditor, claimant)* **to rank before/after sb** prendre rang *ou* passer avant/après qn; **to rank equally (with sb)** prendre *ou* avoir le même rang (que qn)

(c) *Fin (share)* **to rank after sth** être primé par qch; **to rank before sth** avoir la priorité sur qch

(d) *Am Mil* être officier supérieur; *Fig* **he doesn't rank** ce n'est pas quelqu'un d'important

4 *adj* **(a)** *(as intensifier)* complet(ète), véritable; **it's a rank injustice** c'est une injustice flagrante; **he is a rank outsider in this competition** il fait figure d'outsider dans cette compétition

(b) *(foul-smelling)* infect, fétide; *(rancid)* rance; **to smell rank** sentir fort; **his shirt was rank with sweat** sa chemise empestait la sueur

(c) *Br Fam (worthless)* merdique; **his last film was totally rank!** son dernier film était complètement merdique!

(d) *(coarse → person, language)* grossier

(e) *Literary (profuse → vegetation)* luxuriant; *(→ weeds)* prolifique

5 ranks *npl* **(a)** *(members)* rangs *mpl*; **to join the ranks of the opposition/unemployed** rejoindre les rangs de l'opposition/des chômeurs

(b) *Mil (rank and file)* **the ranks, other ranks** les hommes *mpl* du rang; **to have served in the ranks** avoir servi comme simple soldat; **to come up through** *or* **to rise from the ranks** sortir du rang; **to reduce an officer to the ranks** dégrader un officier

►**rank on** *vt insep Am Fam* **to rank on sb** agonir qn d'injures ❑, traiter qn de tous les noms

-rank [ræŋk] *suff* **top-rank** grand, majeur; **second-rank** petit, mineur

rank and file *n* **(a)** *Mil (soldiers)* simples soldats *mpl*; **ten officers and two hundred rank and file** dix officiers et deux cents hommes **(b)** *(ordinary members → in political party, union)* base *f*; **we'll have to consult the rank and file** il faudra que nous consultions la base

rank-and-file *adj (party member)* de la base; **rank-and-file soldiers** simples soldats *mpl*; **to protect rank-and-file interests** protéger les intérêts de la base

rank-and-filer *n (in army)* simple soldat *m*; *(in political party, union)* membre *m* de la base

ranker ['ræŋkə(r)] *n Br Mil (private)* homme *m* du rang; *(officer)* officier *m* sorti du rang

ranking ['ræŋkɪŋ] **1** *n* classement *m*; **his ranking is number four** il est classé quatrième

2 *adj Am (prominent)* de premier ordre

►► *Am Mil* ***ranking officer*** officier *m* responsable

-ranking ['ræŋkɪŋ] *suff* **high-ranking** de haut rang *ou* grade; **low-ranking** de bas rang *ou* grade

rankle ['ræŋkəl] *vi* rester sur le cœur; **it rankled with me** je ne l'ai pas digéré; **what they did still rankles (with her)** elle n'a toujours pas digéré ce qu'ils ont fait

rankly ['ræŋklɪ] *adv* **(a)** *(grossly)* grossièrement; **rankly cheated** grossièrement abusé **(b)** *(with a foul smell)* avec une odeur fétide **(c)** *Literary (abundantly → grow)* surabondamment, à profusion

rankness ['ræŋknɪs] *n* **(a)** *(smell)* puanteur *f*; *(taste)* rance *m* **(b)** *Literary (luxuriance → of vegetation)* luxuriance *f*, profusion *f*

ransack ['rænsæk] *vt* **(a)** *(plunder)* saccager, mettre à sac; **the burglars had ransacked his flat** les cambrioleurs avaient saccagé son appartement **(b)** *(search)* mettre sens dessus dessous; **he ransacked the wardrobe for his tie** il mit l'armoire sens dessus dessous pour trouver sa cravate

ransacking ['rænsækɪŋ] *n* **(a)** *(plundering)* pillage *m* **(b)** *(searching)* fouille *f*

ransom ['rænsəm] **1** *n* rançon *f*; **the family paid the ransom (money)** la famille a payé la rançon; **they held her to ransom** ils l'ont kidnappée pour avoir une rançon; *Fig* **they're holding the country to ransom** ils tiennent le pays en otage; *Fig* **a king's ransom** une fortune

2 *vt (hold to ransom)* rançonner; *(pay ransom for release of)* racheter

rant [rænt] *vi* fulminer; **they ranted on and on** ils n'arrêtaient pas de fulminer; **to rant at sb** fulminer contre qn; **to rant and rave** tempêter, tonitruer

ranter ['ræntə(r)] *n* énergumène *mf*, exalté(e) *m,f*

ranting ['ræntɪŋ] **1** *n (UNCOUNT)* vociférations *fpl* **2** *adj* déclamatoire

ranunculus [rə'nʌŋkjʊləs] *n Bot* renoncule *f*

rap [ræp] *(pt & pp* **rapped**, *cont* **rapping**) **1** *vt* **(a)** *(strike)* frapper sur, cogner sur; **she rapped the desk** elle frappa sur le bureau; *Fig* **to rap sb's knuckles, to rap sb over the knuckles** sermonner qn

(b) *(in newspaper headlines)* réprimander

(c) *Am Fam (criticize)* éreinter, descendre

2 *vi* **(a)** *(knock)* frapper, cogner; **somebody rapped on the door** quelqu'un a frappé (à la porte) (**b**) *Am Fam (chat)* bavarder❑, discuter le bout de gras; **what's he rapping about now?** qu'est-ce qu'il raconte maintenant?

(**c**) *Mus* faire du rap

3 *n* (**a**) *(blow, sound)* coup *m* (sec); **I heard a rap at the door** j'ai entendu frapper à la porte; *Fig* **to be given a rap over** *or* **on the knuckles** se faire taper sur les doigts

(**b**) *Fam (blame)* **to take the rap (for sth)** écoper (pour qch)

(**c**) *Am Fam (legal charge)* accusation❑ *f*; **he's up on a murder/drugs rap** il est accusé de meurtre/dans une affaire de drogue❑; **to beat the rap** échapper à la justice❑, échapper à la condamnation❑, être acquitté❑

(**d**) *Am Fam (speech)* **don't give me that rap!** raconte pas n'importe quoi!; **he was laying down some rap about the new model** il était en train de faire un baratin sur le nouveau modèle

(**e**) *Mus* rap *m*

(**f**) *Br Fam (idiom)* **I don't care a rap!** je m'en fiche (pas mal)!

►► *Mus* ***rap artist*** chanteur(euse) *m,f* de rap; *Mus* ***rap music*** rap *m*; ***rap session*** bavardage *m*; **we had a good rap session** on a discuté pendant un bon bout de temps; *Am Fam* ***rap sheet*** casier *m* judiciaire❑

►**rap out** *vt sep* (**a**) *(say sharply)* lancer, lâcher; **she rapped out an order** elle lança un ordre (**b**) *(tap out → message)* taper

rapacious [rə'peɪʃəs] *adj* rapace

rapaciously [rə'peɪʃəslɪ] *adv* avec rapacité *ou* avidité

rapaciousness [rə'peɪʃəsnɪs], **rapacity** [rə'pæsɪtɪ] *n* rapacité *f*

rape[1] [reɪp] **1** *n* (**a**) *(sex crime)* viol *m*; **to commit rape** perpétrer un viol; *Fig* **the rape of the countryside** la dévastation de la campagne (**b**) *Arch (abduction)* rapt *m*, enlèvement *m*

2 *vt* violer

►► ***rape crisis centre*** centre *m* d'accueil pour femmes violées; ***rape suite*** pièce *f* réservée aux victimes de viols *(dans un commissariat)*; ***rape victim*** personne *f* violée, victime *f* d'un viol

'The Rape of the Lock' *Pope* 'La Boucle dérobée'

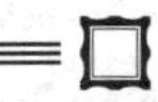

'The Rape of the Sabine Women' *Poussin* 'L'Enlèvement des Sabines'

rape[2] *n* (**a**) *Bot (crop)* colza *m* (**b**) *(remains of grapes)* marc *m* (de raisin)

►► ***rape oil*** huile *f* de colza

rapeseed ['reɪpsiːd] *n* graine *f* de colza

►► ***rapeseed oil*** huile *f* de colza

Raphael ['ræfeɪəl] *pr n* Raphaël

raphia ['ræfɪə] **1** *n Bot* raphia *m*

2 *adj* en raphia

rapid ['ræpɪd] **1** *adj* rapide; **in rapid succession** en une succession rapide; **a rapid pulse** un pouls rapide; *Fig* **we are making rapid strides towards a cure for cancer** la recherche contre le cancer fait des progrès rapides

2 rapids *npl* rapide *m*, rapides *mpl*; **to shoot the rapids** franchir le rapide *ou* les rapides

►► *Mil* ***rapid deployment force*** force *f* d'intervention rapide; ***rapid eye movement*** mouvements *mpl* oculaires rapides; ***rapid reaction force*** forces *fpl* d'action rapide; *Am* ***rapid transit*** transport *m* urbain rapide; *Am* ***rapid transit chess*** échecs *mpl* rapides

rapid-fire *adj Mil* à tir rapide; *Fig (questions, jokes)* qui se succèdent à toute allure

rapidity [rə'pɪdɪtɪ] *n* rapidité *f*

rapidly ['ræpɪdlɪ] *adv* rapidement

rapidness ['ræpɪdnɪs] *n* rapidité *f*

rapier ['reɪpjə(r)] *n* rapière *f*

►► ***rapier thrust*** coup *m* de rapière; ***rapier wit*** esprit *m* acerbe

rapine ['ræpaɪn] *n Literary* rapine *f*

rapist ['reɪpɪst] *n* violeur *m*

rappel [rə'pel] *(in mountaineering)* **1** *vi* descendre en rappel

2 *n* (descente *f* en) rappel *m*

►**rappel down** *vi* descendre en rappel

rappeling [rə'pelɪŋ] *n* rappel *m*

rapper ['ræpə(r)] *n* (**a**) *(on door)* heurtoir *m* (**b**) *Mus* chanteur(euse) *m,f* de rap, rappeur(euse) *m,f*

rapport [ræ'pɔː(r)] *n* rapport *m*; **I have a good rapport with him** j'ai de bons rapports avec lui; **there was an instant rapport between them** ils ressentirent une sympathie immédiate

rapprochement [ræ'prɒʃmɑ̃] *n* rapprochement *m*

rapscallion [ræp'skæljən] *n Arch* fripon(onne) *m,f*, gredin(e) *m,f*

rapt [ræpt] *adj* (**a**) *(engrossed)* absorbé, captivé; **the clown held the children rapt** le clown fascinait les enfants; **with rapt attention** complètement absorbé; **to be rapt in contemplation** être plongé dans ses pensées (**b**) *(delighted)* ravi; **rapt with joy** transporté de joie; **a rapt smile** un sourire ravi

raptly ['ræptlɪ] *adv (listen)* avec une attention profonde

raptor ['ræptə(r)] *n* rapace *m*

rapture ['ræptʃə(r)] *n* ravissement *m*, extase *f*; **he was filled with rapture at the thought/the idea** il était en extase à cette pensée/cette idée; **to go into raptures over** *or* **about sth** s'extasier sur qch; **they were in raptures about their presents** leurs cadeaux les ont ravis

rapturous ['ræptʃərəs] *adj (feeling)* intense, profond; *(gaze)* ravi, extasié; *(praise, applause)* enthousiaste; **the champions were given a rapturous welcome** on a réservé un accueil délirant aux champions; **they were rapturous about their daughter's success** le succès de leur fille les rendait fous de joie

rapturously ['ræptʃərəslɪ] *adv (watch)* d'un air ravi, avec ravissement; *(praise, applaud)* avec enthousiasme

rara avis [ˌreərə'eɪvɪs] *n* oiseau *m* rare, rara avis *m*

ra-ra skirt ['rɑːrɑː-] *n Br* mini-jupe *f* plissée

rare [reə(r)] *adj* (**a**) *(uncommon)* rare; **a rare stamp** un timbre rare; **it's rare to see such marital bliss nowadays** un tel bonheur conjugal est rare de nos jours; **on rare occasions** en de rares occasions; **on the rare occasions when I've seen him angry** les rares fois où je l'ai vu en colère; **a rare opportunity** une occasion exceptionnelle; **that rare bird, the man who does the housework** cet oiseau rare qu'est l'homme qui fait le ménage

(**b**) *(exceptional)* rare, exceptionnel; **she has a rare gift** elle a un don exceptionnel

(**c**) *Fam (extreme)* énorme❑; **you gave me a rare fright!** tu m'as fait une peur bleue *ou* une de ces peurs!

(**d**) *(excellent)* fameux, génial; **we had a rare old time** on s'est amusés comme des fous

(**e**) *(meat)* saignant; **very rare** bleu

(**f**) *(rarefied → air, atmosphere)* raréfié

►► *Chem* ***rare earth*** terre *f* rare

rarebit ['reəbɪt] *n* ≃ toast *m* au fromage

rarefaction [ˌreərɪ'fækʃən] *n* raréfaction *f*

rarefied ['reərɪfaɪd] *adj* (**a**) *(air, atmosphere)* raréfié; **to become rarefied** se raréfier (**b**) *(refined)* raffiné; **the rarefied circles in which she moves** les milieux raffinés dans lesquels elle évolue

rarefy ['reərɪfaɪ] *(pt & pp* **rarefied***)* **1** *vt* raréfier

2 *vi* se raréfier

rarely ['reəlɪ] *adv* rarement; **rarely have I** *or* **I have rarely encountered anyone like him** j'ai rarement rencontré quelqu'un comme lui

rareness ['reənɪs] *n* rareté *f*

raring ['reərɪŋ] *adj Fam* impatient❑; **to be raring to go** ronger son frein

rarity ['reərɪtɪ] *(pl* **rarities***)* *n* (**a**) *(uncommon person, thing)* rareté *f*; **a foreigner's a rarity in these parts** les étrangers sont rares par ici (**b**) *(scarcity)* rareté *f*

rasbora [ræz'bɔːrə] *n Ich* rasbora *m*

rascal ['rɑːskəl] *n* (**a**) *(naughty child)* coquin(e) *m,f*, polisson(onne) *m,f* (**b**) *(rogue)* vaurien *m*, gredin *m*

rascally ['rɑːskəlɪ] *adj (person)* coquin; *(deed)* de coquin

rash [ræʃ] **1** *n* (**a**) *Med* rougeur *fpl*, éruption *f*; **to come out in a rash** avoir une éruption; **oysters bring me out in a rash** les huîtres me donnent des éruptions; **I've got a rash on my face** j'ai des rougeurs sur le visage

(**b**) *(wave, outbreak)* vague *f*; **a rash of strikes** une vague de grèves; **last summer's rash of air disasters** la série noire de catastrophes aériennes de l'été dernier

2 *adj* imprudent; **it was rash of her to walk out** c'était imprudent de sa part de partir comme ça; **that was a bit rash of you** c'était un peu risqué de ta part; **don't do anything rash** ne faites pas de bêtises; **don't make any rash promises!** ne faites pas de promesses en l'air!; **I bought it in a rash moment** je l'ai acheté dans un moment de folie *ou* sur un coup de tête; **rash words** des paroles *fpl* irréfléchies

rasher ['ræʃə(r)] *n* tranche *f (de bacon)*

rashly ['ræʃlɪ] *adv* imprudemment; **I rather rashly offered to drive her home** dans un moment de folie, j'ai offert de la reconduire chez elle

rashness ['ræʃnɪs] *n* imprudence *f*; **I paid for my rashness** j'ai payé cher mes imprudences

rasp [rɑːsp] **1** *n* (**a**) *(file)* râpe *f*

(**b**) *(sound)* bruit *m* de râpe; **the rasp in his voice** sa voix rauque

(**c**) *Scot Fam (raspberry)* framboise❑ *f*

2 *vt* (**a**) *(scrape, file)* râper; *Fig* **the cat rasped its tongue over my face** le chat m'a léché la figure de sa langue râpeuse; **he rasped his hand over his unshaven chin** il frotta sa main sur son menton râpeux

(**b**) *(say)* dire d'une voix rauque; **to rasp out an answer/a plea** répondre/supplier d'une voix rauque

3 *vi (make rasping noise)* grincer, crisser; **her breath rasped in her lungs** elle avait une respiration sifflante

►**rasp out** *vt sep* crier d'une voix rauque

raspatory ['rɑːspətərɪ] *(pl* **raspatories***)* *n Med* raspatoire *m*, rugine *f*

raspberry ['rɑːzbərɪ] *(pl* **raspberries***)* **1** *n* (**a**) *(fruit)* framboise *f*

(**b**) *Fam (noise)* **to blow a raspberry** faire pfft *(en signe de dérision)*; **the announcement was greeted with a chorus of raspberries** la nouvelle fut accueillie par des sifflements❑

2 *comp (jam)* de framboises; *(tart, ice-cream)* aux framboises

3 *adj (colour)* framboise *(inv)*

►► ***raspberry bush, raspberry cane*** framboisier *m*; ***raspberry vinegar*** vinaigre *m* de framboise

rasping ['rɑːspɪŋ] **1** *adj (noise)* grinçant, crissant; *(voice)* rauque, grinçant

2 *n (noise)* grincement *m*, crissement *m*

raspingly ['rɑːspɪŋlɪ] *adv* d'une voix rauque

raspings ['rɑːspɪŋz] *npl Culin (breadcrumbs)* chapelure *f*

Rasputin [ræ'spjuːtɪn] *pr n* Raspoutine

raspy ['rɑːspɪ] *(compar* **raspier**, *superl* **raspiest***)* *adj* (**a**) *(noise)* grinçant, crissant; *(voice)* rauque, grinçant (**b**) *(surface)* râpeux (**c**) *(person → irritable)* de mauvaise humeur

Rasta ['ræstə] *(abbr* **Rastafarian***)* **1** *n* rasta *mf*

2 *adj* rasta *(inv)*

Rastafarian [ˌræstə'feərɪən] **1** *n* rastafari *mf*

2 *adj* rastafari *(inv)*

Rastafarianism [ˌræstə'feərɪənɪzəm] *n* rastafarisme *m*

Rastaman ['ræstəmæn] *n (pl* **Rastamen** [-men]*)* rasta *m*

raster ['ræstə(r)] *n Comput, Typ & TV* trame *m*

►► *Comput & Typ* ***raster image*** image *f* tramée; *Comput & Typ* ***raster image processor*** processeur *m* d'image tramée; *Comput & Typ* ***raster scan*** balayage *m* de trame

rasterize, -ise ['ræstəraɪz] *vt Comput, Typ & TV* rastériser

rat [ræt] *(pt & pp* **ratted**, *cont* **ratting***)* **1** *n* (**a**) *Zool* rat *m*; **female rat, she-rat** rate *f*; **baby rat** raton *m*; **black rat** rat *m* noir; **grey** *or* **sewer rat** rat *m* d'égout, surmulot *m*; **to look like a drowned rat** avoir l'air d'un chien mouillé; **to be caught like a rat in a trap** être fait comme un rat; **with her hair all in rats' tails** avec ses mèches collées; *Am very Fam* **I don't give a rat's ass** je m'en fous pas mal, je m'en balance

(**b**) *Fam (despicable person)* ordure *f*; **you dirty rat!** espèce d'ordure!

(**c**) *Am Fam Pej (informer)* mouchard(e) *m,f*, indic *m* (**d**) *Fam Pej (strikebreaker)* jaune *mf*, briseur(euse) *m,f* de grève ❑

(**e**) *Br Fam Old-fashioned* **rats!** zut!

2 *vi Fam Fig* retourner sa veste

►► *Zool* ***rat kangaroo*** rat-kangourou *m*; ***rat pack*** *(paparazzi)* paparazzi(s) *mpl*; ***rat poison*** mort-aux-rats *f inv*; ***rat race*** foire *f* d'empoigne; **she dropped out of the rat race to live in the country** elle quitta le monde impitoyable du travail et partit vivre à la campagne; ***rat run*** = rue résidentielle empruntée par les automobilistes qui veulent éviter les bouchons aux heures de pointe; *Zool* ***rat snake*** serpent *m* ratier; ***rat trap*** *(for rats)* piège *m* à rats, ratière *f*; *Am (building)* taudis *m*

►**rat on** *vt insep Fam* (**a**) *(betray)* vendre; *(inform on)* moucharder (**b**) *(go back on)* revenir sur❑; **they ratted on our deal** ils nous ont laissé tomber dans cette affaire

►**rat out** *vt sep Am Fam* **to rat sb out** balancer qn, moucharder qn

ratable = **rateable**

ratafia [,rætəˈfɪə] *n* (**a**) *(liqueur)* ratafia *m* (**b**) *(biscuit)* macaron *m*

►► ***ratafia biscuit*** macaron *m*

ratal [ˈreɪtəl] *n Br Admin (of building)* valeur *f* locative imposable; *(of site)* évaluation *f* cadastrale (d'impôts locaux)

rat-arsed [-ɑːst] *adj Br very Fam* bourré comme un coing, pété à mort; **to get rat-arsed** se bourrer la gueule

rat-a-tat(-tat) [ˈrætə,tæt(ˈtæt)] *n (on door)* toc-toc *m*; *(of machine gun)* pétarade *f*; *(of typewriter)* tac-tac-tac *m*

ratatouille [,rætəˈtuːiː] *n Culin* ratatouille *f*

ratbag [ˈrætbæg] *n Br Fam* peau *f* de vache, ordure *f*; **the old ratbag!** la vieille chouette!

ratcatcher [ˈræt,kætʃə(r)] *n (gen)* chasseur(euse) *m,f* de rats; *(official)* agent *m* de la dératisation

ratchet [ˈrætʃɪt] *n* rochet *m*; *Fig* **this had a ratchet effect on prices** cela a entraîné une augmentation irréversible des prix

►► ***ratchet mechanism*** (dispositif *m* d')encliquetage *m*; ***ratchet screwdriver*** tournevis *m* à cliquet; ***ratchet wheel*** roue *f* à rochet; ***ratchet wrench*** clé *f* à rochet

►**ratchet up** *vt sep (prices, inflation)* faire augmenter de façon irréversible

rate [reɪt] **1** *n* (**a**) *(ratio, level)* taux *m*; **the birth/death/divorce/suicide rate** le taux de natalité/de mortalité/de divorce/de suicide; **the success rate is falling** le taux de réussite est en baisse; **how do you explain the high suicide rate?** comment expliquez-vous le nombre élevé de suicides?; **the hourly rate is going to be increased** le taux horaire va être augmenté

(**b**) *(cost, charge)* tarif *m*; **his rates have gone up** ses prix ont augmenté; **to strike for higher rates of pay** faire la grève pour obtenir une augmentation de salaire; **the rate is 60p in the pound** le taux est de 60 pence par livre; **postal** *or* **postage rate** tarifs *mpl* postaux; **standard/reduced rate** tarif *m* normal/réduit; **the going rate** le tarif courant

(**c**) *(speed)* vitesse *f*, train *m*; **at the rate we're going** *or* **at this rate we'll never get there** au rythme où nous allons, nous n'y arriverons jamais; **she shot past at a terrific rate** elle est passée comme une flèche; *Fam* **at a rate of knots** à toute allure

(**d**) *(idiom) Fam* **any rate** enfin bref

2 *vt* (**a**) *(reckon, consider)* considérer; **she's rated as one of the best players in the world** elle est classée parmi les meilleures joueuses du monde; **I rate him among my closest friends** je le compte au nombre de *ou* le considère comme un de mes amis les plus proches; **to rate sb/sth highly** avoir une haute opinion de qn/qch, faire grand cas de qn/qch

(**b**) *(deserve)* mériter; **her film rates better reviews** son film mérite de meilleures critiques; **a battle that didn't rate a mention in the history books** une bataille qui n'a pas mérité d'apparaître dans les livres d'histoire; **that performance should rate him third place** cette prestation devrait lui assurer la troisième place

(**c**) *Fam (have high opinion of)* **I don't rate him as an actor** à mon avis, ce n'est pas un bon acteur❑; **I don't rate their chances much** je ne pense pas qu'ils aient beaucoup de chance❑

(**d**) *Br (fix rateable value of)* fixer la valeur locative imposable de; **their house has been rated higher this year** leur maison a été classée dans la tranche supérieure cette année

(**e**) *Literary (scold)* tancer

3 *vi (rank high)* se classer; **he rates highly in my estimation** je le tiens en très haute estime; **in terms of efficiency, she rates higher than anyone else** en ce qui concerne l'efficacité, elle bat tout le monde

4 rates *npl Br Formerly* impôts *mpl* locaux

5 at any rate *adv* de toute façon, de toute manière, en tout cas

►► *Mktg* ***rate of adoption*** *(of product)* taux *m* d'adoption; *Mktg* ***rate of awareness*** taux *m* de notoriété; *Fin* ***rate band*** plage *f ou* fourchette *f* de taux; *Mktg* ***rate of churn*** taux *m* de clients passés à la concurrence; *Br Formerly* ***rate collector*** receveur(euse) *m,f* municipal(e); *Fin* ***rate of depreciation*** taux *m* d'amortissement; ***rate of exchange*** cours *m ou* taux *m* de change; *Fin* ***rate of growth*** taux *m* d'accroissement *ou* de croissance; *Fin* ***rate of increase*** taux *m* d'accroissement; *Fin & Econ* ***rate of inflation*** taux *m* d'inflation; *Br Formerly* ***rates office*** recette *f* municipale; *Mktg* ***rate of penetration*** taux *m* de pénétration; *Chem* ***rate of reaction*** vitesse *f* de réaction; *Br Formerly* ***rate rebate*** dégrèvement *m* d'impôts locaux; *Mktg* ***rate of renewal*** taux *m* de renouvellement; *Fin* ***rate of return*** *(on investment)* taux *m* de rendement; *Fin* ***rate of return pricing*** fixation *f* de prix au taux de rendement établi; *Br* ***rate support grant*** = subvention à une collectivité locale; ***rate of taxation*** taux *m* d'imposition; ***rate of uptake*** taux *m* de succès

►**rate up** *vt sep Ins* **to rate sb up** faire payer à qn une prime plus élevée

-rate [reɪt] *suff* **first-rate** de premier ordre; **second-rate** de deuxième ordre

rateable [ˈreɪtəbəl] *adj*

►► *Br* ***rateable value*** ≃ valeur *f* locative imposable

rate-cap *vt Br Admin (local authority)* fixer un taux plafond pour les impôts locaux de

rate-capping [-,kæpɪŋ] *n Br Admin* plafonnement *m* des impôts locaux

rated [ˈreɪtɪd] *adj Tech (load, speed, voltage)* nominal

ratel [ˈreɪtəl] *n Zool* ratel *m*

ratepayer [ˈreɪt,peɪə(r)] *n Br Formerly* contribuable *mf*

ratfink [ˈrætfɪŋk] *n Am very Fam* salaud *m*, salopard *m*

rathe [reɪð] *adj Arch or Literary (flower, fruit)* hâtif, précoce

rather [ˈrɑːðə(r)] **1** *adv* (**a**) *(slightly, a bit)* assez, un peu; **I was rather tired** j'étais assez fatigué; **it's rather too small for me** c'est un peu trop petit pour moi; **she cut me a rather large slice** elle m'a coupé une tranche plutôt grande; **it tastes rather like honey** ça a un peu le goût du miel; **I am rather inclined to agree with you** je suis plutôt de votre avis; **I rather rashly volunteered** j'ai offert mes services un peu rapidement

(**b**) *Br (as intensifier)* **I rather like this town** je trouve cette ville plutôt agréable; **she's rather nice** elle est plutôt sympa

(**c**) *(expressing preference)* plutôt; **I'd** *or* **I would rather go by car** je préférerais *ou* j'aimerais mieux y aller en voiture; **I'd rather not do it today** je préférerais *ou* j'aimerais mieux ne pas le faire aujourd'hui; **would you rather go to Scotland?** préféreriez-vous aller en Écosse?; **I would rather that you came** je préférerais que vous veniez; **I'd rather you didn't do it** je préférerais que tu ne le fasses pas; **shall we go out tonight? – I'd rather not** si on sortait ce soir? – je n'ai pas très envie; **rather you than me!** plutôt toi que moi!

(**d**) *(more exactly)* plutôt, plus exactement; **my parents, or rather my mother and stepfather** mes parents, ou plutôt ma mère et mon beau-père; **bring some wine, or rather some champagne** apportez du vin, ou mieux *ou* plutôt du champagne

2 *predet* plutôt; **it was rather a long film** le film était plutôt long

3 *exclam Br Old-fashioned* et comment!; **cold, isn't it? – rather!** il fait froid, n'est-ce pas? – plutôt!; **fancy a drink? – rather!** tu veux boire quelque chose? – je ne dis pas non! *ou* ce n'est pas de refus!

4 rather than 1 *prep* plutôt que; **you should congratulate his wife rather than him** c'est sa femme que tu devrais féliciter, pas lui; **it's a melodrama rather than a tragedy** c'est un mélodrame plus qu'une tragédie **2** *conj* plutôt que; **rather than walk I took the bus** plutôt que d'y aller à pied, j'ai pris le bus

ratification [,rætɪfɪˈkeɪʃən] *n* ratification *f*

ratify [ˈrætɪfaɪ] *(pt & pp* **ratified***) vt* ratifier

ratine [ræˈtiːn] *n Tex* ratine *f*

rating [ˈreɪtɪŋ] **1** *n* (**a**) *(ranking)* classement *m*; *Fin (of bank, company)* notation *f*; **popularity rating** cote *f* de popularité

(**b**) *(appraisal)* évaluation *f*, estimation *f*

(**c**) *Br Naut* matelot *m*; **the ratings** les matelots *mpl* et gradés *mpl*

(**d**) *(scolding) Literary* réprimande *f*, admonestation *f*

2 ratings *npl Rad & TV* indice *m* d'écoute; **to boost the ratings** améliorer l'indice d'écoute; **to be high in the ratings** avoir un fort indice d'écoute

►► ***rating agency*** agence *f* de notation *ou* de rating; *Rad & TV* ***ratings battle*** course *f* à l'Audimat®; *Mktg* ***rating scale*** *(in market research)* échelle *f* de classement; *Rad & TV* ***ratings war*** course *f* à l'Audimat®

ratio [ˈreɪʃɪəʊ] *(pl* **ratios***) n* (**a**) *(proportion)* proportion *f*, rapport *m*; **in the ratio of 6 to 1** dans la proportion de 6 contre 1; **the teacher-student ratio is 1 to 10** le rapport enseignants-étudiants est de 1 pour 10 (**b**) *Math* raison *f*, proportion *f* (**c**) *Econ* ratio *m*

ratiocinate [,rætɪˈɒsɪneɪt] *vi Formal* raisonner

ratiocination [,rætɪɒsɪˈneɪʃən] *n Formal* raisonnement *m*

ration [ˈræʃən] **1** *n also Fig* ration *f*; **I've had my ration of television for today** j'ai eu ma dose de télévision pour aujourd'hui

2 *vt* (**a**) *(food)* rationner; **they are rationed to one pound of meat a week** ils sont rationnés à une livre de viande par semaine; **I've rationed myself to five cigarettes a day** je me suis rationné à cinq cigarettes par jour

(**b**) *(funds)* limiter; **arts subsidies are being rationed because of the recession** les subventions à la culture sont limitées du fait de la récession

3 rations *npl (food)* vivres *mpl*; **to be on double/short rations** toucher une ration double/réduite; *Mil* **to draw rations** toucher sa ration; **full rations** rations *fpl* complètes; **half rations** demi-rations *fpl*

►► ***ration book*** carnet *m* de tickets de rationnement; ***ration card*** carte *f* de rationnement

►**ration out** *vt sep* rationner

rational [ˈræʃənəl] **1** *adj* (**a**) *(capable of reason)* doué de raison, raisonnable; **a rational being** un être doué de raison

(**b**) *(reasonable, logical → person)* raisonnable; *(→ behaviour, explanation)* rationnel; **it seemed like the rational thing to do** il me semblait que c'était ce qu'il y avait de plus logique à faire; **he is incapable of rational thought** il est incapable de raisonner logiquement

(**c**) *(of sound mind, sane)* lucide

(**d**) *Math* rationnel

2 *n* rationnel *m*

►► ***rational number*** nombre *m* rationnel

rationale [,ræʃəˈnɑːl] *n* (**a**) *(underlying reason)* logique *f*; **what is the rationale for** *or* **behind their decision?** quelle logique sous-tend leur décision? (**b**) *(exposition)* exposé *m*

rationalism [ˈræʃənəlɪzəm] *n* rationalisme *m*

rationalist [ˈræʃənəlɪst] **1** *adj* rationaliste

2 *n* rationaliste *mf*

rationalistic [,ræʃənəˈlɪstɪk] *adj* rationaliste

rationality [,ræʃəˈnælɪtɪ] *n* (**a**) *(of belief, system etc)* rationalité *f* (**b**) *(faculty)* raison *f*

rationalization [,ræʃənəlaɪˈzeɪʃən] *n* rationalisation *f*

rationalize, -ise [ˈræʃənəlaɪz] *vt* (**a**) *(gen) & Com* rationaliser (**b**) *Math* rendre rationnel

rationally [ˈræʃənəlɪ] *adv* rationnellement

rationing ['ræʃənɪŋ] *n* (**a**) *(of food)* rationnement *m* (**b**) *(of funds)* rationnement *m*; **banks are warning of mortgage rationing** les banques annoncent qu'elles vont limiter le nombre de prêts immobiliers

Ratisbon ['rætɪzbɒn] *n* Ratisbonne

ratite ['rætaɪt] *n Orn* ratite *m*

►► ***ratite bird*** ratite *m*

ratlin, ratline ['rætlɪn] *n* enfléchure *f*

ratrack ['rætræk] *n Ski* ratrack *m*

rattan [rə'tæn] **1** *n Bot* rotang *m*; *(substance)* rotin *m*

2 *comp (furniture)* en rotin

rat-tat ['ræt,tæt] = **rat-a-tat(-tat)**

ratteen = **ratine**

ratter ['rætə(r)] *n (dog, cat)* chasseur *m* de rats

rattiness ['rætɪnɪs] *n Br Fam (irritability)* irritabilité *f* ❑

ratting ['rætɪŋ] *n* **to go ratting** faire la chasse aux rats

rattle ['rætəl] **1** *vi (gen)* faire du bruit; *(car, engine)* faire un bruit de ferraille; *(chain, machine, dice)* cliqueter; *(gunfire, hailstones)* crépiter; *(door, window)* vibrer; **the trains make the windows rattle** les trains font vibrer les fenêtres; **somebody was rattling at the door** quelqu'un secouait la porte; **an old car came rattling down the hill** une vieille voiture descendait la côte dans un bruit de ferraille

2 *vt* (**a**) *(box)* agiter *(en faisant du bruit)*; *(key)* faire cliqueter; *(chain, dice)* agiter, secouer; *(door, window)* faire vibrer; *Fam* **who rattled your cage?** quelle mouche te pique?

(**b**) *(disconcert)* ébranler, secouer; **to get rattled** perdre son sang froid; **don't get rattled!** pas de panique!

3 *n* (**a**) *(noise → of chains)* bruit *m*; *(→ of car, engine)* bruit *m* de ferraille; *(→ of coins, keys)* cliquetis *m*; *(→ of gunfire, hailstones)* crépitement *m*; *(→ of window, door)* vibration *f*, vibrations *fpl*

(**b**) *(for baby)* hochet *m*; *(for sports fan)* crécelle *f*

(**c**) *Zool (of rattlesnake)* cascabelle *f*

►**rattle around** *vi* **you'll be rattling around in that big old house!** tu seras perdu tout seul dans cette grande maison!

►**rattle off** *vt sep (speech, list)* débiter, réciter à toute allure; *(piece of work)* expédier; *(letter, essay)* écrire en vitesse

►**rattle on** *vi* jacasser

►**rattle through** *vt insep (speech, meeting etc)* expédier

rattlebrain ['rætəlbreɪn] *n Fam Old-fashioned* écervelé(e) *m,f*

rattlebrained ['rætəlbreɪnd] *adj Fam Old-fashioned (person)* écervelé, qui a un pois chiche à la place du cerveau; *(idea)* stupide ❑

rattler ['rætlə(r)] *n Am Fam* serpent *m* à sonnettes ❑, crotale ❑ *m*

rattlesnake ['rætəlsneɪk] *n* serpent *m* à sonnettes, crotale *m*

rattletrap ['rætəltræp] *n Br Fam Old-fashioned (car)* tacot *m*

rattling ['rætəlɪŋ] **1** *n (noise → of chains)* bruit *m*; *(→ of car, engine)* bruit *m* de ferraille; *(→ of coins, keys)* cliquetis *m*; *(→ of gunfire, hailstones)* crépitement *m*; *(→ of window, door)* vibration *f*, vibrations *fpl*

2 *adj* (**a**) *(sound)* **there was a rattling noise** on entendait un cliquetis; *Fam* **her rattling old banger** son vieux tacot bringuebalant

(**b**) *(fast)* rapide; **at a rattling pace** à vive allure

3 *adv Fam Old-fashioned* **we had a rattling good time** on s'est drôlement amusés; **this book is a rattling good read** ce livre est vraiment formidable ❑

ratty ['rætɪ] *(compar* **rattier,** *superl* **rattiest)** *adj Fam* (**a**) *(irritable)* de mauvais poil, râleur; **don't get ratty!** ne commence pas à râler! (**b**) *Am (shabby)* miteux

raucous ['rɔːkəs] *adj* (**a**) *(noisy)* bruyant; **raucous laughter** rires *mpl* gras; **a raucous party** une soirée tapageuse *ou* bruyante; **things got a bit raucous as the evening wore on** la soirée est devenue de plus en plus bruyante (**b**) *(hoarse)* rauque

raucously ['rɔːkəslɪ] *adv* (**a**) *(noisily)* bruyamment (**b**) *(hoarsely)* d'une voix rauque

raucousness ['rɔːkəsnɪs] *n* (**a**) *(noisiness)* tapage *m* (**b**) *(hoarseness)* ton *m* rauque

raunchiness ['rɔːntʃɪnɪs] *n* sensualité *f*

raunchy ['rɔːntʃɪ] *(compar* **raunchier,** *superl* **raunchiest)** *adj Fam* (**a**) *(lewd)* cochon; *(in more light-hearted way)* grivois; **that's much too raunchy for our viewers** c'est beaucoup trop grivois pour nos téléspectateurs (**b**) *(sexy)* sexy; **there is something a little raunchy about her** elle a un petit quelque chose de sexy (**c**) *Am (slovenly)* négligé ❑

rauwolfia [rɔː'wɒlfɪə] *n* (**a**) *Bot* rauwolfia *f* (**b**) *Pharm* réserpine *f*

ravage ['rævɪdʒ] **1** *vt* ravager, dévaster; **the invading army ravaged the land** l'armée ennemie a mis le pays à feu et à sang; **the city had been ravaged by war** la ville avait été ravagée par la guerre

2 ravages *npl* **the ravages of time/passion** les ravages *mpl* du temps/des passions

ravaged ['rævɪdʒd] *adj* ravagé

rave [reɪv] **1** *vi* (**a**) *(be delirious)* délirer

(**b**) *(talk irrationally)* divaguer

(**c**) *(shout)* se déchaîner; **she started raving at me** elle a commencé à vitupérer

(**d**) *Fam (praise)* s'extasier ❑; **to rave about sb/sth** s'extasier sur qn/qch

(**e**) *Br Fam (at party)* faire la bringue *ou* la fête

2 *n Fam* (**a**) *(praise)* critique *f* élogieuse ❑

(**b**) *(fashion, craze)* mode ❑ *f*; **the latest rave** la dernière mode, le dernier cri

(**c**) *Br (party)* rave *f*

3 *adj Fam* (**a**) *(enthusiastic)* élogieux ❑; **the play got rave notices or reviews** les critiques de la pièce furent très élogieuses

(**b**) *(trendy)* branché

►**rave up** *vt sep Br Fam Old-fashioned* **to rave it up** faire la bringue *ou* la fête

ravel ['rævəl] *(Br pt & pp* **ravelled,** *cont* **ravelling,** *Am pt & pp* **raveled,** *cont* **raveling)** **1** *vt* (**a**) *(entangle)* emmêler, enchevêtrer (**b**) *(cloth)* effilocher; *(threads)* démêler (**c**) *Literary (mystery)* éclaircir; *(difficulty)* démêler

2 *vi* (**a**) *(tangle up)* s'emmêler, s'enchevêtrer (**b**) *(fray)* s'effilocher (**c**) *Constr (road surface)* se détériorer

►**ravel out 1** *vt sep* (**a**) *(cloth)* effilocher, *(threads)* démêler (**b**) *Literary (mystery)* éclaircir; *(difficulty)* démêler

2 *vi* s'effilocher

raven¹ ['reɪvən] **1** *n Orn* (grand) corbeau *m*

2 *adj* noir comme un corbeau *ou* comme du jais

'The Raven' *Poe* 'Le Corbeau'

raven² *Literary* **1** *vt (prey)* ravir, dévorer

2 *vi (animal)* chercher sa proie; *Fig* **to raven for sth** être affamé de qch

raven-haired *adj* aux cheveux de jais; **a raven-haired beauty** une beauté aux cheveux noirs de jais

ravening ['rævənɪŋ] *adj Literary* vorace

Ravenna [rə'venə] *n* Ravenne *f*

ravenous ['rævənəs] *adj* (**a**) *(hungry)* affamé; **I was ravenous!** j'avais une faim de loup!; *Fig* **to be ravenous for sth** *(fame, power)* être assoiffé *ou* avide de qch (**b**) *(rapacious)* vorace

ravenously ['rævənəslɪ] *adv* voracement; **to be ravenously hungry** avoir une faim de loup

ravenousness ['rævənəsnɪs] *n* (**a**) *(voracity)* voracité *f* (**b**) *(hunger)* faim *f* dévorante *ou* de loup

raver ['reɪvə(r)] *n Br* (**a**) *Fam (socially active person)* fêtard(e) *m,f*, noceur(euse) *m,f*; **he's a bit of a raver** il est noceur (**b**) *(who goes to raves)* raver *mf*

rave-up *n Br Fam Old-fashioned* fête ❑ *f*; **to have a rave-up** faire une fête; **the neighbours had a right old rave-up last night** les voisins ont fait une de ces fiestas *ou* noubas hier soir

ravine [rə'viːn] *n* ravin *m*

raving ['reɪvɪŋ] **1** *adj* (**a**) *(mad)* délirant

(**b**) *(as intensifier)* **she is a raving beauty** elle est d'une grande beauté; **she's no raving beauty** elle n'est pas d'une beauté éblouissante; *Fam* **he's a raving lunatic** c'est un fou furieux, il est fou à lier

2 *adv Fam* **raving mad** fou à lier

3 ravings *npl* divagations *fpl*; **the ravings of a madman** les divagations *fpl* d'un fou

ravioli [,rævɪ'əʊlɪ] *n (UNCOUNT)* ravioli *mpl*, raviolis *mpl*

ravish ['rævɪʃ] *vt* (**a**) *Literary (delight)* ravir, transporter de joie (**b**) *Arch or Literary (abduct)* ravir, enlever; *(rape)* violer

ravisher ['rævɪʃə(r)] *n Arch or Literary (abductor)* ravisseur *m*, voleur *m*; *(rapist)* ravisseur *m*, violateur *m*

ravishing ['rævɪʃɪŋ] *adj* ravissant, éblouissant

ravishingly ['rævɪʃɪŋlɪ] *adv* de façon ravissante; **ravishingly beautiful** d'une beauté éblouissante

ravishment ['rævɪʃmənt] *n* (**a**) *Literary (delight)* ravissement *m* (**b**) *Arch or Literary (abduction)* enlèvement *m*; *(rape)* viol *m*

raw [rɔː] **1** *adj* (**a**) *(uncooked)* cru; **raw vegetables** légumes *mpl* crus; *(as hors d'oeuvre)* crudités *fpl*

(**b**) *(untreated → sugar, latex, leather)* brut; *(→ milk)* cru; *(→ spirits)* pur; *(→ cotton, linen)* écru; *(→ silk)* grège, écru; *(→ sewage)* non traité

(**c**) *(unprocessed → data, statistics)* brut

(**d**) *(sore → gen)* sensible, irrité; *(→ wound, blister)* à vif; *(→ nerves)* à fleur de peau; **her hands were raw with the cold** ses mains étaient rougies par le froid; *Fig* **the remark touched a raw nerve (in him)** la remarque l'a touché *ou* piqué au vif; **my nerves are raw** j'ai les nerfs à vif *ou* à fleur de peau

(**e**) *(emotion, power, energy)* brut

(**f**) *(inexperienced)* inexpérimenté; **a raw recruit** un bleu

(**g**) *(weather)* rigoureux, rude; **a raw wind** un vent âpre *ou* pénétrant; **a raw February night** une froide nuit de février

(**h**) *(forthright)* franc (franche), direct

(**i**) *Am (rude, coarse)* grossier, cru; **the movie paints a raw picture of penitentiary life** le film peint la vie carcérale de façon crue *ou* brutale *ou* réaliste

(**j**) *(idioms)* **to give sb a raw deal** traiter qn de manière injuste; **he got a raw deal from his last job** il n'était pas gâté dans son dernier emploi; **the unemployed get a raw deal** les chômeurs n'ont pas la part belle; **he's had a raw deal out of life** il n'a pas été gâté par la vie; *Austr Fam* **don't come the raw prawn with me!** n'essaie pas de m'embobiner!

2 *n (idioms) Fam* **in the raw** à poil; *Br* **to touch sb on the raw** toucher *ou* piquer qn au vif

►► ***raw edge*** *(of material)* bord *m* coupé; ***raw material*** matière *f* première; **her marriage provided her with raw material for her novel** son mariage lui a servi de matière première pour son roman

rawboned ['rɔːbəʊnd] *adj* décharné

rawhide ['rɔːhaɪd] *n* (**a**) *(skin)* cuir *m* vert *ou* brut (**b**) *(whip)* fouet *m* (de cuir)

Rawlplug® ['rɔːlplʌg] *n* cheville *f*, fiche *f*

rawly ['rɔːlɪ] *adv* **the wind blew rawly** le vent soufflait aigrement *ou* âprement

rawness ['rɔːnɪs] *n* (**a**) *(natural state)* nature *f* brute (**b**) *(soreness)* irritation *f* (**c**) *(inexperience)* inexpérience *f*, manque *m* d'expérience (**d**) *(of weather)* rigueur *f*, rudesse *f* (**e**) *(frankness)* franchise *f* (**f**) *Am (coarseness → of language)* grossièreté *f*

ray [reɪ] *n* (**a**) *(of light)* rayon *m*; **a ray of sunlight** un rayon de soleil; **ultraviolet rays** rayons *mpl* ultraviolets

(**b**) *Fig (of hope, intelligence)* lueur *f*; **a ray of comfort** une petite consolation; **a ray of hope** une lueur d'espoir; **that child has brought a ray of sunshine into my life** cet enfant, c'est mon rayon de soleil; *Ironic* **he's a little ray of sunshine** il est de charmante humeur

(**c**) *Ich* raie *f*

(**d**) *Mus* ré *m inv*

►► ***ray gun*** pistolet *m* à rayons

Ray-Bans® ['reɪbænz] *npl* Ray-Bans® *fpl*

Raynaud's disease ['reɪnəʊz-] *n Med* maladie *f* de Raynaud

rayon ['reɪɒn] *Tex* **1** *n* rayonne *f*

2 *comp* en rayonne

raze [reɪz] *vt* raser; **the village was razed to the ground** le village fut entièrement rasé

razor ['reɪzə(r)] **1** *n* rasoir *m*; **electric/safety razor**

rasoir *m* électrique/de sûreté; **the company is on a** *or* **the razor's edge** l'entreprise est sur le fil du rasoir; **these people are living on the razor's edge** ces gens vivent dans la peur et l'incertitude; **her life was on a razor's edge for days** sa vie n'a tenu qu'à un fil pendant plusieurs jours

2 *vt* raser

►► ***razor blade*** lame *f* de rasoir; *Am Zool* ***razor clam*** couteau *m*; ***razor cut*** *(hairstyle)* coupe *f* au rasoir; *Am* ***razor ribbon*** *(UNCOUNT)* barbelés *mpl* tranchants; *Br Zool* ***razor shell*** couteau *m*; ***razor wire*** *(UNCOUNT)* barbelés *mpl* tranchants

'The Razor's Edge' *Maugham* 'Le Fil du rasoir'

razorback ['reɪzəbæk] *n* (**a**) *(whale)* balénoptère *m*, rorqual *m* (**b**) *Am (pig)* sanglier *m*

razorbill ['reɪzəbɪl] *n Orn* petit pingouin *m*, (pingouin *m*) torda *m*

razor-cut *vt (hair)* couper au rasoir

razor-sharp *adj* (**a**) *(blade)* tranchant comme un rasoir *ou* comme une lame de rasoir; *(nails)* acéré (**b**) *(person, mind)* vif

razz [ræz] *vt Am Fam (jeer at)* chambrer

razzle ['ræzəl] *n Br Fam* **to be** *or* **to go on the razzle** faire la bringue *ou* la nouba

razzle-dazzle *n Fam (flashy display)* tape-à-l'œil *m inv*, clinquant *m*; *Br* **to be** *or* **to go on the razzle-dazzle** faire la bringue *ou* la fête *ou* la nouba

razzmatazz ['ræzmə͵tæz] *n Fam (flashy display)* tape-à-l'œil *m inv*, clinquant *m*; **the razzmatazz of Hollywood** le côté tape-à-l'œil de Hollywood

RBI [͵ɑːbiː'aɪ] *n Am Sport (abbr* **runs batted in**) = points marqués par le batteur

RC [͵ɑː'siː] *n* (**a**) *(abbr* **Roman Catholic**) catholique *mf* (**b**) *(abbr* **Red Cross**) Croix-Rouge *f*

RCA [͵ɑːsiː'eɪ] *n (abbr* **Royal College of Art**) = école de beaux-arts, à Londres

RCAF [͵ɑːsiː͵eɪ'ef] *n Can (abbr* **Royal Canadian Air Force**) = armée de l'air canadienne

RCCh *(written abbr* **Roman Catholic Church**) Église *f* catholique

RCMP [͵ɑːsiː͵em'piː] *n Can (abbr* **Royal Canadian Mounted Police**) Gendarmerie *f* royale du Canada

RCN [͵ɑːsiː'en] *n Can (abbr* **Royal Canadian Navy**) = marine de guerre canadienne

Rd *(written abbr* **road**) rue *f*

RDA [͵ɑːdiː'eɪ] *n (abbr* **recommended daily allowance**) recommandation *f* quotidienne officielle *(en vitamines, sels minéraux etc)*

RDBMS [͵ɑːdiː͵biːem'es] *n Comput (abbr* **relational database management system**) SGBDR *m*

RE[1] [͵ɑː'riː] *n (abbr* **religious education**) éducation *f* religieuse

RE[2] *(written abbr* **Royal Engineers**) génie *m* militaire britannique

re[1] [reɪ] *n Mus* ré *m inv*

re[2] [riː] *prep* (**a**) *Admin & Com* **re your letter of 6 June** en réponse à *ou* suite à votre lettre du 6 juin; **Re: job application** *(in letter heading)* Objet: demande d'emploi (**b**) *Law* **(in) re** en l'affaire de

reabsorb [͵riːəb'sɔːb] *vt* réabsorber

reabsorption [͵riːəb'sɔːpʃən] *n* réabsorption *f*

reacclimate [rɪ'æklɪmeɪt] *vt Am* **I was getting reacclimated** j'étais en train de retrouver mes repères

reaccustom [riːə'kʌstəm] *vt* réhabituer, réaccoutumer (**to** à)

REACH [riːtʃ]

portée	► **1 (a), (e)**
extension	► **1 (b)**
arriver à	► **2 (a), (c), (d)**
atteindre	► **2 (a) – (c)**
parvenir à	► **2 (a), (d)**
passer	► **2 (e)**
joindre	► **2 (f)**
tendre la main	► **3 (a)**
s'étendre	► **3 (b)**

1 *n* (**a**) *(range)* portée *f*, atteinte *f*; **within (arm's) reach** à portée de la main; **within reach of** à la portée de; *(of place)* à proximité de, proche de; **the house is within easy reach of the shops** la maison est à proximité des magasins; **within everyone's reach** *(affordable by all)* à la portée de toutes les bourses; **out of** *or* **beyond reach** hors de portée; **out of reach of** hors de (la) portée de; **keep out of the reach of children** *(on packaging)* ne pas laisser à la portée des enfants; **nuclear physics is beyond my reach** la physique nucléaire, ça me dépasse complètement; **beyond the reach of the authorities** à l'abri des *ou* hors de la portée des autorités

(**b**) *(arm's length)* extension *f*; *(in boxing)* allonge *f*; **a good** *or* **long reach** une bonne allonge

(**c**) *(action)* **she made a reach for the gun** elle étendit la main pour prendre le revolver

(**d**) *Naut* bordée *f*, bord *m*

(**e**) *TV & Rad (audience size)* portée *f*

2 *vt* (**a**) *(arrive at → destination)* arriver à, atteindre; *(of letter, news, parcel)* parvenir à; **we'll never reach Las Vegas by nightfall** nous n'arriverons jamais à Las Vegas avant la tombée de la nuit; **they reached port** ils arrivèrent au *ou* gagnèrent le port; **to reach the end of one's journey** arriver au bout de son voyage; **easy/difficult to reach** facile/difficile d'accès; **which page have you reached?** à quelle page en es-tu?; **I've reached the end of chapter one** je suis arrivé à la fin du premier chapitre; **the letter hasn't reached him yet** la lettre ne lui est pas encore parvenue; **it has reached my ears that...** j'ai entendu dire *ou* appris que... + *indicative;* **the sound of laughter reached their ears** des rires parvenaient à leurs oreilles

(**b**) *(get as far as → age, goal, point, level)* atteindre; **to reach the age of eighty** atteindre l'âge de quatre-vingts ans; **to reach the semi-finals** atteindre les demi-finales; **contributions have reached the million-pound mark** le montant des contributions a atteint un million de livres; **inflation has reached record levels** l'inflation a atteint des niveaux record; **production has reached rock bottom** *or* **an all time low** la production est descendue à son niveau le plus bas; **to reach a ceiling** *(imports, wages)* plafonner; **to reach a younger/wider audience** toucher un public plus jeune/large

(**c**) *(extend to)* arriver (jusqu')à; *(be able to touch)* atteindre; **the water reached my knees** l'eau m'arrivait aux genoux; **she reaches his shoulders** elle lui arrive à l'épaule; **can you reach the top shelf?** est-ce que tu peux atteindre la dernière étagère?; **the ladder doesn't quite reach the roof** l'échelle n'atteint pas tout à fait le toit; **are the curtains long enough to reach the floor?** est-ce que les rideaux sont suffisamment longs pour descendre jusqu'au sol?; **his feet don't reach the floor** ses pieds ne touchent pas par terre

(**d**) *(come to → agreement, decision, conclusion)* arriver à, parvenir à; *(→ compromise)* arriver à, aboutir à; *(→ verdict)* parvenir à

(**e**) *(pass, hand)* passer; **could you reach me that book?** pourriez-vous me passer ce livre?

(**f**) *(contact)* joindre; **to reach sb by telephone** joindre qn par *ou* au téléphone; **you can always reach me at this number** vous pouvez toujours me joindre à ce numéro

(**g**) *Am (bribe → witness)* soudoyer

3 *vi* (**a**) *(with hand)* **to reach for sth** *or* **to get sth** tendre la main pour prendre qch; **she reached for her glass** elle tendit la main pour prendre son verre; **he reached across the table for the mustard** il allongea le bras par-dessus la table pour prendre la moutarde; **the policeman reached for his gun** l'agent de police mit la main sur son revolver; **to reach into sth (for sth)** mettre la main dans qch (pour prendre qch); **reach for the sky!** haut les mains!; **to reach for the stars** viser haut

(**b**) *(forest, property etc)* s'étendre (**to** jusqu'à); *(noise, voice)* porter (**to** jusqu'à)

(**c**) *(be long enough)* **it won't reach** ce n'est pas assez long

(**d**) *Naut* faire une bordée

4 reaches *npl* étendue *f*; **vast reaches of water/moorland** de vastes étendues *fpl* d'eau/de lande; **the upper/the lower reaches of a river** l'amont *m*/l'aval *m* d'une rivière; **the upper reaches of society** les échelons *mpl* supérieurs de la société; **in the further reaches of the empire** au fin fond de l'empire

►**reach back** *vi (in time)* remonter; **a family reaching back to the 16th century** une famille qui remonte au XVIème siècle

►**reach down 1** *vt sep* descendre; **can you reach me down that saucepan?** est-ce que tu peux me passer la casserole là-haut?

2 *vi* (**a**) *(coat, hair)* descendre; **her skirt reached down to her ankles** sa jupe lui descendait jusqu'aux chevilles

(**b**) *(person)* tendre *ou* étendre le bras (**for** pour prendre)

►**reach out 1** *vt sep (arm, hand)* tendre, étendre; **he reached out his hand and took the money** il étendit la main et prit l'argent

2 *vi* tendre *ou* étendre le bras; **to reach out to people in need** venir en aide aux nécessiteux; **reach out for Jesus!** tendez la main vers le Seigneur!

►**reach up** *vi* (**a**) *(raise arm)* lever le bras (**for** pour prendre)

(**b**) *(rise → water, snow)* **to reach up to** arriver à; **the water reached up to my waist** l'eau m'arrivait à la taille; **her boots reached halfway up her legs** ses bottes lui montaient à mi-jambe

reachable ['riːtʃəbəl] *adj* (**a**) *(town, destination)* accessible; **is it reachable by boat?** peut-on y aller *ou* accéder par bateau? (**b**) *(person)* joignable; **he's reachable at the following number** on peut le joindre au numéro suivant

reach-me-down *n Br Fam* vieux vêtement ❑ *m (que les aînés passent aux cadets)*

reacquire [͵riːə'kwaɪə(r)] *vt* réacquérir; *(regain possession of)* rentrer en possession de

react [rɪ'ækt] **1** *vi* réagir; **to react to sth** réagir à qch; **the patient is reacting well to the treatment** le malade réagit bien au traitement; **to be slow to react** *(chemical)* avoir une réaction lente; *(person)* être lent à réagir; **to react against sb/sth** réagir contre qn/qch; **the acid reacts with the metal** l'acide réagit avec le métal

2 *vt Chem* faire réagir (**sth with sth** qch avec qch)

reactance [rɪ'æktəns] *n* réactance *f*

reactant [rɪ'æktənt] *n* réactif *m*

reaction [rɪ'ækʃən] *n* (**a**) *(gen)* réaction *f*; *Mktg (of consumer to product)* réaction *f*; **their reaction to the news was unexpected** ils ont réagi à la nouvelle de façon inattendue; **what was her reaction?** quelle a été sa réaction?, comment a-t-elle réagi?; **her work is a reaction against abstract art** son œuvre est une réaction par rapport à l'art abstrait; **public reaction to the policy has been mixed** la réaction du public face à cette mesure a été mitigée

(**b**) *(reflex)* réflexe *m*; **it slows down your reactions** cela ralentit vos réflexes

(**c**) *Pol* réaction *f*; **the forces of reaction** les forces *fpl* réactionnaires

►► *Tech* ***reaction engine, reaction motor*** moteur *m* à réaction, réacteur *m*; ***reaction time*** temps *m* de réaction; *Tech* ***reaction turbine*** turbine *f* à réaction

reactionary [rɪ'ækʃənrɪ] *(pl* **reactionaries**) **1** *adj* réactionnaire

2 *n* réactionnaire *mf*

reactivate [rɪ'æktɪveɪt] *vt* (**a**) *(start again → group, club)* reconstituer, reformer; *(→ economy)* relancer; *(revive → feelings, memories)* raviver, réveiller (**b**) *Chem, Electron & Med* réactiver (**c**) *Comput* relancer (**d**) *esp Am Mil (return to active status → ship)* remettre en service

reactivation [͵rɪæktɪ'veɪʃən] *n* (**a**) *(of group, club)* reconstitution *f*; *(of economy)* relance *f*; *(of feelings, memories)* réveil *m* (**b**) *Chem, Electron & Med* réactivation *f* (**c**) *Comput* relance *f* (**d**) *esp Am Mil (of ship)* remise *f* en service

reactive [rɪ'æktɪv] *adj (gen) & Chem & Phys* réactif; *Psy* réactionnel

►► ***reactive current*** courant *m* réactif; ***reactive marketing*** marketing *m* réactif

reactiveness [rɪ'æktɪvnɪs], **reactivity** [͵riːæk'tɪvɪtɪ] *n* réactivité *f*

reactor [rɪ'æktə(r)] *n* réacteur *m*

READ¹ [ri:d]

lire	► 1 (a), (b); 2 (a), (b), (f), (j); 3 (a), (b)
interpréter	► 2 (c)
comprendre	► 2 (c)
recevoir	► 2 (d)
étudier	► 2 (e)
indiquer	► 2 (g)
annoncer	► 2 (h)

(*pt & pp* **read** [red]) **1** *n* (**a**) *(act of reading)* **to have a read** lire; **I enjoy a good read** j'aime lire; **he was having a quiet read** il lisait tranquillement; **can I have a read of your paper?** est-ce que je peux jeter un coup d'œil sur ton journal?

(**b**) *(reading matter)* **it's an easy read** c'est facile à lire; **her books are a good read** ses livres se lisent bien

2 *vt* (**a**) *(book, magazine etc)* lire; *(bad handwriting, music)* lire, déchiffrer; **I read it in the paper** je l'ai lu dans le journal; **have you got anything to read?** avez-vous de quoi lire *ou* quelque chose à lire?; **to read sth over and over (again)** lire et relire qch; **everything I've read about the subject** tout ce que j'ai lu à ce sujet; **she read herself to sleep** elle a lu jusqu'à ce qu'elle s'endorme; **for "Barry" read "Harry"** lire "Harry" à la place de "Barry"; **can you read music/braille/Italian?** savez-vous lire la musique/le braille/l'italien?; **to read sb's lips** lire sur les lèvres de qn; *Fig* **read my lips!** écoutez-moi bien!; *Admin* **read and approved** *(stamp on document)* lu et approuvé; **to take sth as read** *(evident)* considérer qch comme allant de soi; *(agreed upon)* considérer qch comme entendu

(**b**) *(aloud)* lire (à haute voix); **to read sb sth, to read sth to sb** lire qch à qn; **read me a story** lis-moi une histoire; **to read a paper at a conference** présenter un exposé à une conférence; *Rel* **to read the lesson** lire un passage de l'Évangile; **to read the news** *Rad* lire les informations; *TV* présenter le journal; *Law* **to read a will** exécuter la lecture d'un testament

(**c**) *(interpret → situation, behaviour)* interpréter; *(understand → person, mood)* comprendre; **I read it this way** c'est comme ça que je l'interprète; **to read sb's mind** *or* **thoughts** lire dans les pensées de qn; **to read sb's palm** *or* **hand** lire les lignes de la main à qn; **I can read him like a book!** je sais comment il fonctionne!; *Sport* **he reads the game very well** c'est un très bon stratège; **he read that well** il a bien anticipé

(**d**) *(via radio)* recevoir; **do you read me?** est-ce que vous me recevez?; *Fig* est-ce que tu me comprends?; **reading you loud and clear** je vous reçois cinq sur cinq; *Fig* oui, oui j'ai compris

(**e**) *Br (at university)* étudier; **he read history** il a étudié l'histoire, il a fait des études d'histoire; **to read law/medicine** faire son droit/sa médecine, faire des études de droit/de médecine

(**f**) *(temperature, thermometer, barometer)* lire; **to read the meter** relever le compteur

(**g**) *(register → of gauge, dial, barometer)* indiquer; **the thermometer is reading 40° le thermomètre indique 40°**

(**h**) *(announce → of notice)* annoncer; **a sign on the door read "staff only"** un écriteau sur la porte indiquait "réservé au personnel"; **the inscription on the monument reads...** on peut lire sur le monument...

(**i**) *(proofs)* corriger

(**j**) *Comput (data, disk)* lire; **this computer only reads double-density disks** cet ordinateur ne lit que les disquettes (à) double densité

3 *vi* (**a**) *(person)* lire; **she's learning to read** elle apprend à lire; **to read to sb** faire la lecture à qn; **to read aloud** lire à haute voix; **to read to oneself** lire; **read quietly to yourselves** lisez en silence; **I enjoy reading** j'aime beaucoup lire *ou* la lecture; **I'd read about it in the papers** je l'avais lu dans les journaux; **we read of his death in the newspaper** nous avons appris sa mort dans le journal; **we've all read about** *or* **of such phenomena** nous avons tous lu des textes qui traitent de tels phénomènes

(**b**) *(interpret)* **to read between the lines** lire entre les lignes; **she read in the cards that I would be famous** elle a lu dans les cartes que je serais célèbre

(**c**) *(text)* **her article reads well/badly** son article est bien/mal écrit; **the table reads from left to right** le tableau se lit de gauche à droite; **the book reads like a translation** à la lecture, on sent que ce roman est une traduction; **article 22 reads as follows** voici ce que dit l'article 22; **her life story reads like a fairytale** sa vie ressemble à un conte de fées

(**d**) *(gauge, meter etc)* **the dials read differently** les cadrans n'indiquent pas le même chiffre

(**e**) *Br (at university)* **what's he reading?** qu'est-ce qu'il fait comme études?; *Br* **I'm reading history** je fais des études d'histoire; **to read for a degree** préparer un diplôme; **to read for the Bar** faire des études de droit

►► *Comput* ***read head*** tête *f* de lecture

► **read back** *vt sep (dictated letter)* relire

► **read in** *vt sep Comput (data)* lire (en mémoire)

► **read into** *vt sep* **you shouldn't read too much into their silence** vous ne devriez pas accorder trop d'importance à leur silence; **you're reading far too much into it** tu interprètes beaucoup trop

► **read off** *vt sep* (**a**) *(names etc)* énumérer (**from** sur) (**b**) *(figure on dial, scale etc)* relever

► **read on** *vi* lire la suite

► **read out** *vt sep* (**a**) *(aloud)* lire (à haute voix) (**b**) *Comput (data)* sortir, extraire de la mémoire (**c**) *Am (expel)* expulser

► **read over** *vt sep (quickly)* parcourir; *(with special care)* examiner; *esp Am (read again)* relire

► **read through** *vt sep (skim)* parcourir; *(examine closely)* lire en détail, examiner; *Theat* **to read through a play** faire la lecture d'une pièce

► **read up** *vt sep* étudier

► **read up on** *vt insep* étudier

Read my lips

Il s'agit d'un extrait de la formule utilisée par George Bush lors de sa campagne électorale de 1988, avant son élection à la présidence des États-Unis. La formule complète était: **read my lips, no new taxes** (regardez bien mes lèvres: pas d'augmentation des impôts). Aujourd'hui on utilise cette expression pour insister sur le fait que ce que l'on dit est vrai.

---

read² [red] **1** *pt & pp of* **read**

2 *adj* **he's widely read** c'est un homme cultivé; **her books are widely read** ses livres sont très lus

readability [ˌri:də'bɪlɪtɪ] *n* lisibilité *f*

readable ['ri:dəbəl] *adj* (**a**) *(handwriting, disk)* lisible (**b**) *(book)* qui se laisse lire

readdress [ˌri:ə'dres] *vt (mail, e-mail)* faire suivre

reader ['ri:də(r)] *n* (**a**) *(of book)* lecteur(trice) *m,f*; *Am (company librarian)* documentaliste *mf*; **she's an avid reader** c'est une passionnée de lecture; **I'm not a fast reader** je ne lis pas vite; **he's not a great reader** il ne lit pas beaucoup; **publisher's reader** lecteur(trice) *m,f* de manuscrits *(dans une maison d'édition)*

(**b**) *Comput* lecteur *m*; **optical character reader** lecteur *m* optique

(**c**) *(reading book)* livre *m* de lecture; *(anthology)* recueil *m* de textes; **German reader** recueil *m* de textes allemands

(**d**) *Br Univ* ≃ maître-assistant(e) *m,f*

(**e**) *Am Univ* ≃ assistant(e) *m,f*; *Can Univ* chargé(e) *m,f* de cours

(**f**) *Rel (Protestant)* lecteur(trice) *m,f*; *(Jewish)* chantre *m*

readership ['ri:dəʃɪp] *n* (**a**) *(of newspaper, magazine)* nombre *m* de lecteurs, lectorat *m*; **what is their readership (figure)?** combien ont-ils de lecteurs?; **this book should attract a wide readership** ce livre devrait intéresser un grand nombre de lecteurs (**b**) *Br Univ* ≃ poste *m* de maître-assistant (**c**) *Am Univ* ≃ fonction *f* d'assistant(e); *Can Univ* fonction *f* de chargé(e) de cours

readies ['redɪz] *npl Br Fam (cash)* fric *m*, liquide *m*; **£500 in readies** 500 livres en liquide; **I want the readies first** je veux le fric d'abord

readily ['redɪlɪ] *adv* (**a**) *(willingly)* volontiers (**b**) *(with ease)* facilement, aisément; **readily understandable ideas** des idées qu'on comprend facilement; **our products are readily available** nos produits sont en vente partout

readiness ['redɪnɪs] *n* (**a**) *(preparedness)* **to be in readiness for sth** être préparé à qch; **to be in a state of readiness** être fin prêt (**b**) *(willingness)* empressement *m*; **their readiness to assist us** leur empressement à nous aider

reading ['ri:dɪŋ] *n* (**a**) *(activity)* lecture *f*; **reading, writing and arithmetic** la lecture, l'écriture et le calcul; **reading is not his favourite activity** a lecture n'est pas son passe-temps favori; **I have a lot of reading to catch up on** j'ai beaucoup de retard à rattraper dans mes lectures; **take some reading matter** emmenez de quoi lire; **the reading public** le public des lecteurs

(**b**) *(reading material)* lecture *f*; **light reading** lecture *f* facile *ou* distrayante; **his autobiography makes fascinating/dull reading** son autobiographie est passionnante/ennuyeuse à lire

(**c**) *(recital)* lecture *f*; **the reading of the will** la lecture du testament

(**d**) *(from instrument, gauge)* relevé *m*; **the reading on the dial was wrong** les indications qui apparaissaient sur le cadran étaient fausses; **to take a reading** faire un relevé

(**e**) *Pol* lecture *f*; **to give a bill its first/second reading** examiner un projet de loi en première/deuxième lecture

(**f**) *(interpretation)* interprétation *f*; **my reading of the situation** la manière dont j'interprète la situation; **a new reading of Dante** une nouvelle lecture de Dante

(**g**) *(variant)* variante *f*

►► *Br* ***reading age*** niveau *m* de lecture; **she has a reading age of eleven** elle a le niveau de lecture d'un enfant de onze ans; **she has a reading age well in advance of her years** elle est très en avance sur son âge pour ce qui est de la lecture; **children of reading age** des enfants en âge de lire; ***reading book*** livre *m* de lecture; ***reading desk*** pupitre *m*; *Rel* lutrin *m*; ***reading glass*** *(magnifying glass)* loupe *f (pour lire)*; ***reading glasses*** *(spectacles)* lunettes *fpl* pour lire; *Comput* ***reading head*** tête *f* de lecture; ***reading lamp*** lampe *f* de bureau; *(by bed)* lampe *f* de chevet; ***reading light*** liseuse *f*; ***reading list*** *(syllabus)* liste *f* des ouvrages au programme; *(for further reading)* liste *f* des ouvrages recommandés; ***reading room*** salle *f* de lecture

readjust [ˌri:ə'dʒʌst] **1** *vt* (**a**) *(readapt)* **to readjust oneself** se réadapter (**b**) *(alter → controls, prices, clothing)* rajuster, réajuster

2 *vi* se réadapter; **to readjust to sth** se réadapter à qch

readjustment [ˌri:ə'dʒʌstmənt] *n* (**a**) *(readaptation)* réadaptation *f* (**b**) *(alteration)* rajustement *m*, réajustement *m*

read-me document *n Comput* (fichier *m*) lisez-moi *m*, ouvrez-moi *m*

read-me file *n Comput* (fichier *m*) lisez-moi *m*, ouvrez-moi *m*

readmission [ˌri:əd'mɪʃən] *n (to political party)* réintégration *f*; *(to hospital)* réadmission *f*; **no readmission** *(on ticket)* ce ticket ne sera accepté qu'une seule fois à l'entrée

readmit [ˌri:əd'mɪt] *vt (to political party)* réintégrer; *(to hospital)* réadmettre; **she has been readmitted to hospital** elle a été réadmise à l'hôpital; **he was readmitted to the concert** on l'a relaissé passer à l'entrée du concert

read-only *adj Comput* (à) lecture seule; **that file is read-only** ce fichier est protégé en écriture; **to make a file read-only** mettre un fichier en lecture seule

►► ***read-only disk*** *(hard)* disque *m* en lecture seule; *(floppy)* disquette *f* en lecture seule; ***read-only file*** fichier *m* en lecture seule; ***read-only memory*** mémoire *f* morte; ***read-only mode*** mode *m* lecture seule

readopt [ˌri:ə'dɒpt] *vt* réadopter

readoption [ˌri:ə'dɒpʃən] *n* réadoption *f*

readout ['ri:daʊt] *n Comput (gen)* lecture *f*; *(on screen)* affichage *m*; *(on paper)* sortie *f* papier *ou* sur imprimante, listing *m*

►► ***readout device*** unité *f* d'affichage

read-through *n (of script)* lecture *f* du scénario; **we'll have a read-through this afternoon** nous lirons la pièce cet après-midi; **to give sth a quick read-through** parcourir qch rapidement

readvertise [ˌriːˈædvətaɪz] **1** *vt* repasser une annonce de

2 *vi* repasser une annonce

readvertisement [ˌriːədˈvɜːtɪsmənt] *n* deuxième annonce *f*; **this is a readvertisement** *(in job advertisement)* deuxième annonce d'offre d'emploi

read-write *adj Comput*

▸▸ ***read-write head*** tête *f* de lecture-écriture; ***read-write memory*** mémoire *f* lecture-écriture; ***read-write protection notch*** encoche *f* de protection lecture-écriture

ready [ˈredɪ] *(compar* **readier**, *superl* **readiest**, *pl* **readies**, *pt & pp* **readied**) **1** *adj* (**a**) *(prepared)* prêt; **are you ready?** êtes-vous prêt?; **he's just getting ready** il est en train de se préparer; **to be ready to do sth** être prêt à faire qch; **to be ready for anything** être prêt à tout; **he's not ready for such responsibility** il n'est pas prêt pour affronter une telle responsabilité; **she's always ready with an answer, she always has an answer ready** elle a toujours réponse à tout; **to get sth ready** préparer qch; **I'll get the room/the dinner ready** je vais préparer la chambre/le dîner; **to get ready to do sth** se préparer *ou* s'apprêter à faire qch; **to get ready for bed** s'apprêter à aller au lit; **we're ready when you are** nous n'attendons que toi; **ready when you are!** quand tu veux!; *Arch or Literary* **to make ready** se préparer; **dinner's ready!** c'est prêt!; **are you ready to order?** vous avez choisi?; **the tomatoes are ready for eating** les tomates sont bonnes à manger; **ready, steady, go!** à vos marques, prêts, partez!; *Com* **ready for delivery** livrable; *Com* **ready for shipping** sous palan; **ready for use** prêt à l'usage

(**b**) *(willing)* prêt, disposé; **to be ready to do sth** être prêt à faire qch; **she's always ready to lend a hand** elle est toujours prête à donner un coup de main; **I'm ready to agree with you on that point** je suis entièrement d'accord avec vous sur ce point-là; **they are always ready to find fault** ils sont toujours prêts à critiquer; **don't be so ready to believe him** ne le crois pas systématiquement; **we're ready to negotiate** nous sommes prêts *ou* disposés à négocier; **you know me, I'm ready for anything** tu me connais, je suis toujours partant; **I'm ready for bed!** j'ai envie d'aller me coucher

(**c**) *(quick)* prompt; **to be always ready with an answer** avoir la réplique prompte; **you're always a bit too ready with advice** tu donnes toujours trop de conseils; **he's very ready with his fists** il est prompt à se battre; **don't be too ready to condemn him** ne le condamnez pas trop rapidement, ne soyez pas trop prompt à lui jeter la pierre; **she has a ready wit** elle a l'esprit d'à-propos; **she has a ready tongue** elle n'a pas la langue dans sa poche; **he had a ready smile** il souriait facilement

(**d**) *(likely)* **to be ready to do sth** être sur le point de faire qch; **she looks ready to explode** on dirait qu'elle va exploser; **I'm ready to collapse!** je suis à bout de forces!, je suis épuisé!

(**e**) *(easily accessible)* **a ready market for our products** un marché tout trouvé pour nos produits; **ready to hand** *(within reach)* à portée de main; *(available)* à disposition; **ready cash** *or* **money** argent *m* comptant *ou* liquide; **to pay in ready cash** *or* **money** payer (au) comptant;

2 *n Br Fam (money)* **the ready** le fric, le pognon

3 *adv Br* **ready cut ham** jambon *m* prétranché; **ready salted crisps** chips *fpl* nature

4 *vt* préparer; **to ready oneself for sth** se préparer pour qch

5 at the ready *adj* (tout) prêt; **the reporter had her notebook at the ready** la journaliste avait son carnet tout prêt; **with their guns at the ready** prêts à tirer

▸▸ ***ready meal*** plat *m* cuisiné; *Br* ***ready reckoner*** barème *m*

ready-cooked *adj* précuit

ready-made **1** *adj* (**a**) *(clothes)* de prêt-à-porter; *(food)* précuit; *(curtains)* tout fait (**b**) *(excuse, solution, argument)* tout prêt

2 *n (garment)* vêtement *m* de prêt-à-porter

ready-mix *adj (cake)* fait à partir d'une préparation; *(concrete)* prémalaxé

ready-to-serve *adj* prêt à l'emploi

ready-to-wear *adj*

▸▸ ***ready-to-wear clothing*** prêt-à-porter *m*

reaffirm [ˌriːəˈfɜːm] *vt* réaffirmer

reaffirmation [ˌriːæfəˈmeɪʃən] *n* réaffirmation *f*

reafforest [ˌriːəˈfɒrɪst] *vt* reboiser

reafforestation [ˈriːəˌfɒrɪˈsteɪʃən] *n* reboisement *m*, reforestation *f*

Reaganite [ˈreɪgənaɪt] **1** *n* partisan *m* de Reagan

2 *adj* reaganien; **Reaganite budget/programme** budget *m*/programme *m* reaganien

Reaganomics [ˌreɪgəˈnɒmɪks] *n* = politique reaganienne selon laquelle l'argent des riches finit par profiter aux pauvres

reagent [riːˈeɪdʒənt] *n Chem* réactif *m*

real [rɪəl] **1** *adj* (**a**) *(authentic)* vrai, véritable; *(not imitation → diamond, pearl)* vrai; *(→ gold, leather)* véritable; *(→ silk, flowers)* naturel; **a real friend/idiot** un véritable ami/idiot; **a real disaster/shock** un véritable *ou* vrai désastre/choc; **a real man** un vrai homme; **I don't know his real name** je ne connais pas son vrai nom; **my first real job** mon premier vrai travail; **we have no real cause for concern** nous n'avons aucune raison de nous inquiéter; **we'll never know her real feelings** nous ne saurons jamais quels étaient vraiment ses sentiments; **she has no real feeling for poetry** elle n'a pas le sens de la poésie; **he's made a real effort** il a fait un véritable effort, il a fait un effort réel; **they're real silver** ils sont en argent véritable; **are her pearls real?** ses perles sont-elles vraies?; **that's what I call a real cup of tea!** ça, c'est ce que j'appelle une tasse de thé!; **it's the real thing** *(authentic object)* c'est du vrai de vrai; *(true love)* c'est le grand amour; **this orange drink is not bad but it's poor stuff compared to the real thing** cette boisson à l'orange n'est pas mauvaise, mais ça ne vaut pas le vrai jus d'orange; **this is not a drill, it's the real thing** ce n'est pas un exercice, c'est pour de vrai; *Fam* **get real!** arrête de délirer *ou* de rêver!, redescends sur terre!

(**b**) *(actual)* réel; **the real world** le monde réel; **the threat is a very real one** la menace est bien réelle; **what does that mean in real terms?** qu'est-ce que ça signifie au bout du compte?; **salaries have fallen in real terms** les salaires ont baissé en termes réels; **in real life** dans la réalité, dans la vie

(**c**) *Fin (cost, income, profit, salary)* réel

(**d**) *(as intensifier)* vrai, véritable; **it was a real surprise** ce fut une vraie surprise; **she's a real pain** elle est vraiment rasante

(**e**) *Comput, Math, Phil & Phys* réel

2 *adv Am Fam (very)* vachement; **you were real lucky** t'as eu une sacré veine; **it's real hot** il fait vachement chaud; **we had a real good time** on s'est vachement bien amusés; **that's real nice of you** c'est vraiment *ou* très gentil de votre part ❑; **I'll see you real soon** à très bientôt ❑

3 *n Phil* **the real** le réel

4 for real *adj & adv Fam* pour de vrai ❑, pour de bon; **this time it's for real** cette fois-ci c'est la bonne; **is he for real?** d'où il sort, celui-là?; **is that for real?** c'est vrai?

▸▸ *Fin* ***real accounts*** comptes *mpl* de valeur; *Br* ***real ale*** bière *f* artisanale; *Fin* ***real assets*** biens *mpl* immobiliers; ***real estate*** *(UNCOUNT) Br Law* biens *mpl* fonciers; *Am (property)* biens *mpl* immobiliers; **he works in real estate** il travaille dans l'immobilier; ***real estate agent*** agent *m* immobilier; *Fin* ***real estate mortgage investment conduit*** obligation *f* garantie par hypothèque; ***real estate leasing*** crédit-bail *m* immobilier; ***real estate office*** agence *f* immobilière; *Comput, Math, Phil & Phys* ***real image*** image *f* réelle; *Math* ***real number*** nombre *m* réel; *Comput* ***Real Player*** lecteur *m* Real Media; *Mktg* ***real repositioning*** repositionnement *m* réel; ***real property*** *(UNCOUNT)* biens *mpl* immobiliers *ou* immeubles; ***real tennis*** jeu *m* de paume; **to play real tennis** jouer à la paume; *Comput* ***real time*** temps *m* réel; ***real value*** valeur *f* effective

realgar [rɪˈælgə(r)] *n Miner* réalgar *m*

realia [ˌriːˈeɪlɪə] *npl* = textes ou objets authentiques utilisés par les enseignants pour animer leurs cours

realign [ˌriːəˈlaɪn] **1** *vt* aligner (de nouveau); *Fin (currencies)* réaligner; *Pol* regrouper

2 *vi* s'aligner (de nouveau); *Pol* se regrouper

realignment [ˌriːəˈlaɪnmənt] *n* (nouvel) alignement *m*; *Fin* réalignement *m*; *Pol* regroupement *m*

▸▸ ***realignment of currencies*** réalignement *m* monétaire

realism [ˈrɪəlɪzəm] *n* réalisme *m*

realist [ˈrɪəlɪst] **1** *adj* réaliste

2 *n* réaliste *mf*

realistic [ˌrɪəˈlɪstɪk] *adj* (**a**) *(reasonable)* réaliste (**b**) *(lifelike)* ressemblant

realistically [ˌrɪəˈlɪstɪklɪ] *adv* de façon réaliste; **they can't realistically expect us to do all this** ils ne peuvent pas s'attendre sérieusement à ce que nous fassions tout cela

reality [rɪˈælətɪ] *(pl* **realities**) **1** *n* réalité *f*; **the reality** *or* **realities of living in today's Britain** les réalités de la vie dans la Grande-Bretagne d'aujourd'hui; **will our dream ever become (a) reality?** notre rêve deviendra-t-il un jour réalité?; **you have to face reality** il faut que tu regardes la réalité en face; **it was a reality check for him** ça l'a ramené à la réalité

2 in reality *adv* en réalité

▸▸ *Am TV* ***reality show*** reality show *m*

realizable [ˈrɪəlaɪzəbəl] *adj also Fin* réalisable

▸▸ ***realizable assets*** actif *m* réalisable; ***realizable securities*** valeurs *fpl* réalisables

realization [ˌrɪəlaɪˈzeɪʃən] *n* (**a**) *(awareness)* **this sudden realization left us speechless** cette découverte nous a laissés sans voix; **there has been a growing realization on the part of the government that...** le gouvernement s'est peu à peu rendu compte que...+ *indicative*; **his realization that he was gay** la prise de conscience de son homosexualité

(**b**) *(of aim, dream, project)* réalisation *f*

(**c**) *Fin (of assets)* réalisation *f*

realize, -ise [ˈrɪəlaɪz] **1** *vt* (**a**) *(be or become aware of)* se rendre compte de; **I don't think you realize the work involved** je ne crois pas que tu te rendes compte de tout le travail que ça représente; **do you realize what time it is?** tu te rends compte de *ou* tu as vu l'heure qu'il est?; **I didn't realize how late it was** je ne m'étais pas rendu compte qu'il était si tard; **it made me realize what a fool I had been** cela m'a fait comprendre quel imbécile j'avais été; **I realize you're busy, but...** je sais que tu es occupé mais...

(**b**) *(achieve)* réaliser; **will we ever realize our goal of unity?** parviendrons-nous un jour à réaliser notre objectif d'unité?; **my worst fears were realized** ce que je craignais le plus s'est produit *ou* est arrivé; **a job where you could realize your full potential** un travail qui te permettrait de te réaliser complètement

(**c**) *Fin (yield financially)* rapporter; *(convert into cash)* réaliser; **to realize a high price** *(goods)* atteindre un prix élevé; *(seller)* obtenir un prix élevé; **how much did they realize on the sale?** combien est-ce qu'ils ont gagné sur la vente?; **these shares cannot be realized** il n'y a pas de marché pour ces titres

2 *vi* **I'm sorry, I didn't realize** je suis désolé, je ne m'en étais pas rendu compte

real-life *adj* vrai; **the real-life drama of her battle against illness** le drame affreux de sa lutte contre la maladie

reallocate [ˌriːˈæləkeɪt] *vt (tasks, duties)* redistribuer; *(funds, resources)* réaffecter, réattribuer; *Fin (shares)* attribuer *ou* répartir à nouveau

reallocation [ˌriːæləˈkeɪʃən] *n (of tasks, duties)* redistribution *f*; *(of funds, resources)* réaffectation *f*; *Fin (of shares)* nouvelle répartition *f*; *Law* réadjudication *f*

reallot [ˌriːəˈlɒt] *vt Fin (shares)* attribuer *ou* répartir à nouveau; *Mil (troops)* affecter à nouveau

reallotment [ˌriːəˈlɒtmənt] *n Fin (of shares)* nouvelle répartition *f*; *Mil (of troops)* nouvelle affectation *f*

really [ˈrɪəlɪ] **1** *adv* (**a**) *(actually)* vraiment, réellement; **did you really say that?** as-tu vraiment dis ça?; **what's she really like?** comment estelle vraiment?; **here's what really happened** voilà ce qui s'est vraiment passé; **things that**

really exist des choses qui existent réellement; **that's really a matter for the manager** c'est là proprement l'affaire du gérant

(**b**) *(as intensifier)* vraiment; **these cakes are really delicious** ces gâteaux sont vraiment délicieux; **he really likes you** il t'aime beaucoup; **you really ought to see it** il faut vraiment que vous le voyiez; **it really doesn't matter** ce n'est vraiment pas important; **you really shouldn't be here** vous ne devriez vraiment pas être ici; **now you're really being silly!** tu es vraiment ridicule!

(**c**) *(softening negative statements)* **it doesn't really matter** ce n'est pas vraiment important; **you shouldn't really be here** vous ne devriez pas vraiment être ici; **I don't really know** je ne sais pas vraiment

(**d**) *(tentative use)* **he's quite nice, really** il est plutôt sympa, en fait; **do you want to go? – I suppose I do, really** tu veux y aller? – pourquoi pas, après tout

2 *exclam* (**a**) *(in irritation)* **(well) really!** enfin!

(**b**) *(in surprise, interest)* **(oh) really?** oh, vraiment?, c'est pas vrai?

realm [relm] *n* (**a**) *(field, domain)* domaine *m*; **the realm of the supernatural** le domaine du surnaturel; **it is within the realms of possibility** c'est du domaine du possible; **health is no longer exclusively the realm of doctors** la santé n'est plus l'apanage du médecin (**b**) *Literary (kingdom)* royaume *m*; **the realms of heaven** le royaume des cieux; **the realm of the dead** l'empire *m* des morts

realpolitik [reɪ'ɑ:lpɒlɪˌti:k] *n* realpolitik *f*

real-time *adj (system, control, processing)* en temps réel

▸▸ ***real-time clock*** horloge *f* (en) temps réel; ***real-time graphics*** graphiques *mpl* en temps réel; ***real-time management*** gestion *f* en temps réel; ***real-time operating system*** système *m* d'exploitation en temps réel; *St Exch* ***real-time trading*** cotation *f* en temps réel

realtor ['rɪəltə(r)] *n Am* agent *m* immobilier

realty ['rɪəltɪ] *n (UNCOUNT) Am* biens *mpl* immobiliers

ream [ri:m] **1** *n (of paper)* rame *f*; *Fam Fig* **to write reams** écrire des tartines; *Fam* **reams of statistics/information** des quantités *fpl* de statistiques/d'informations

2 *vt* (**a**) *Tech* fraiser (**b**) *Am (lemon)* presser (**c**) *Am Fam (person)* rouler

▸**ream out** *vt sep Am Fam* **to ream sb out** *(scold)* passer un savon à qn, remonter les bretelles à qn

reamer ['ri:mə(r)] *n* (**a**) *Tech* fraise *f* (**b**) *(juice extractor)* presse-citron *m inv*

reanimate [ˌri:'ænɪmeɪt] *vt* réanimer

reanimation [ˌri:ænɪ'meɪʃən] *n* réanimation *f*

reap [ri:p] **1** *vt* (**a**) *(crop)* moissonner, faucher (**b**) *Fig* récolter, tirer; **to reap the benefit** *or* **the benefits of sth** récolter les bénéfices de qch; **she reaped a rich reward** elle a été bien récompensée

2 *vi* moissonner, faire la moisson

reaper ['ri:pə(r)] *n* (**a**) *(machine)* moissonneuse *f*; **reaper and binder** moissonneuse-lieuse *f* (**b**) *(person)* moissonneur(euse) *m,f*; *Literary* **the (Grim) Reaper** la Faucheuse

reaping ['ri:pɪŋ] *n* moisson *f*

▸▸ ***reaping hook*** faucille *f*; ***reaping machine*** moissonneuse *f*

reappear [ˌri:ə'pɪə(r)] *vi (person, figure, sun)* réapparaître; *(lost object)* refaire surface

reappearance [ˌri:ə'pɪərəns] *n* réapparition *f*

reapply [ˌri:ə'plaɪ] *(pt & pp* **reapplied**) **1** *vt (cream, lotion etc)* réappliquer

2 *vi* **to reapply for a job** poser de nouveau sa candidature à un poste; **to reapply for a grant/loan** faire une nouvelle demande de bourse/de prêt; **previous applicants need not reapply** les personnes ayant déjà posé leur candidature n'ont pas besoin de le faire à nouveau

reappoint [ˌri:ə'pɔɪnt] *vt* réengager, rengager

reappointment [ˌri:ə'pɔɪntmənt] *n* **since her reappointment as minister for the arts** depuis qu'elle a été nommée à nouveau ministre de la Culture

reapportion [ˌri:ə'pɔ:ʃən] *vt* redistribuer, répartir à nouveau

reappraisal [ˌri:ə'preɪzəl] *n* (**a**) *Fin (of property)* réévaluation *f* (**b**) *(of policy)* réexamen *m*

reappraise [ˌri:ə'preɪz] *vt* (**a**) *Fin (property)* réévaluer (**b**) *(policy)* réexaminer

rear [rɪə(r)] **1** *n* (**a**) *(of place)* arrière *m*; **at the rear of the bus** à l'arrière du bus; **the garden** *Br* **at the rear** *or Am* **in the rear of the house** le jardin qui est derrière la maison; **they attacked them from the rear** ils les ont attaqués par derrière

(**b**) *Mil* arrière *m*, arrières *mpl*; *Mil & Fig* **to bring up the rear** fermer la marche; **to protect one's rear** *Mil* protéger ses arrières; *Fig* assurer ses arrières

(**c**) *Fam* **rear (end)** *(buttocks)* arrière-train *m*

2 *adj (door, wheel)* arrière *(inv)*, de derrière; *(engine)* arrière *(inv)*; *(carriages)* de queue; **is there a rear entrance?** est-ce qu'il y a une entrée par derrière?

3 *vt* (**a**) *(children, animals)* élever; *(plants)* cultiver

(**b**) *(head, legs)* lever, relever; *Fig* **racism has reared its ugly head again** le spectre du racisme a refait son apparition

4 *vi* (**a**) *(horse)* **to rear (up)** se cabrer

(**b**) *(mountain, skyscraper)* **to rear (up)** se dresser

▸▸ ***rear admiral*** contre-amiral *m*; ***rear drive axle*** pont *m* arrière; ***rear gunner*** mitrailleur *m* arrière; *Br Aut* ***rear lamp, rear light*** feu *m* arrière; ***rear spoiler*** aileron *m ou* spoiler *m* arrière; ***rear window*** lunette *f* arrière

'Rear Window' *Hitchcock* 'Fenêtre sur cour'

rear-drive *adj* à traction arrière

rear-end *vt Am (drive into back of)* emboutir à l'arrière

rear-engined *adj* avec moteur à l'arrière

rearguard ['rɪəgɑ:d] *n* arrière-garde *f*

▸▸ ***rearguard action*** combat *m* d'arrière-garde; *also Fig* **to fight a rearguard action** mener un combat d'arrière-garde

rearing ['rɪərɪŋ] *n* (**a**) *(of children)* éducation *f*; *(of animals)* élevage *m*; *(of plants)* culture *f* (**b**) **rearing (up)** *(of horse)* cabrage *m*

rearm [ˌri:'ɑ:m] **1** *vt (nation, ship)* réarmer

2 *vi* réarmer

rearmament [ˌri:'ɑ:məmənt] *n* réarmement *m*

rearmost ['rɪəməʊst] *adj* dernier

rear-mounted *adj* monté à l'arrière

rearrange [ˌri:ə'reɪndʒ] *vt* (**a**) *(arrange differently* → *furniture, objects)* réarranger, changer la disposition de; *(*→ *flat, room)* réaménager

(**b**) *(put back in place)* réarranger; **she rearranged her hair** elle se recoiffa

(**c**) *(reschedule)* changer la date/l'heure de; **the meeting has been rearranged for Monday** la réunion a été remise à lundi; **we'll have to rearrange our schedule** il faudra réaménager notre programme

rearrangement [ˌri:ə'reɪndʒmənt] *n* (**a**) *(different arrangement)* réarrangement *m*, réaménagement *m* (**b**) *(rescheduling)* changement *m* de date/d'heure

rearrest [ˌri:ə'rest] *vt* arrêter de nouveau

rear-view mirror ['rɪəvju:-] *n* rétroviseur *m*

rearward ['rɪəwəd] **1** *adj (part, end)* arrière *(inv)*; *(motion)* en arrière, vers l'arrière

2 *adv* en arrière, vers l'arrière

3 *n* arrière *m*

rearwards ['rɪəwədz] *adv* en arrière, vers l'arrière

rear-wheel *adj Aut*

▸▸ ***rear-wheel drive*** traction *f* arrière; ***rear-wheel steering*** roues *fpl* arrière directrices

REASON ['ri:zən]

raison	▸ **1 (a), (b)**
maintenir	▸ **2 (a)**
calculer	▸ **2 (a)**
conclure	▸ **2 (a)**
persuader	▸ **2 (b)**
raisonner	▸ **3**

1 *n* (**a**) *(cause, motive)* raison *f* (**for** de); **what is the reason for his absence?** quelle est la raison de son absence?; **there is a reason for his doing that** il y a une raison pour qu'il fasse ça; **did he give a reason for being so late?** a-t-il donné la raison d'un tel retard?; **what reason could they give for such inhuman acts?** comment peuvent-ils justifier des actes d'une telle cruauté?; **I (can) see no reason for disagreeing** *or* **to disagree** je ne vois pas pourquoi je ne serais pas d'accord; **all the more reason for trying again** *or* **to try again** raison de plus pour réessayer; **to have reason enough (to do sth)** avoir de bonnes raisons (de faire qch); **you have every reason** *or* **good reason to be angry** vous avez de bonnes raisons d'être en colère; **that's no reason to get annoyed** ce n'est pas une raison pour s'énerver; **we have/there is reason to believe he is lying** nous avons de bonnes raisons de croire/il y a lieu de croire qu'il ment; **the reason (why) they refused** la raison de leur refus, la raison pour laquelle ils ont refusé; **she wouldn't tell me the reason why** elle ne voulait pas me dire pourquoi; **give me one good reason why I should believe you!** donne-moi une bonne raison de te croire!; **I chose him for the simple reason I liked him** je l'ai choisi pour la simple (et bonne) raison qu'il me plaisait; **reasons of state** la raison d'État; **for reasons of health** pour raisons de santé; **for reasons best known to herself** pour des raisons qu'elle est seule à connaître; **for some reason (or other), for one reason or other** pour une raison ou pour une autre; **for no other reason than that I forgot** pour la simple raison que j'ai oublié; **for no particular reason** sans raison particulière; **why do you ask? – oh, no particular reason** pourquoi est-ce que tu me demandes ça? – oh, comme ça; **for no reason at all** sans aucune raison; **but that's the only reason I came!** mais c'est pour ça que je suis venue!; **they were upset, and with (good) reason** ils étaient bouleversés, et pour cause; **to give sb good reason for doing sth** donner de bonnes raisons à qn de faire qch; **give me one good reason why I should!** donne-moi une raison valable pour que je le fasse!; **she's my reason for living** elle est ma raison de vivre

(**b**) *(common sense, rationality)* raison *f*; **he lost his reason** il a perdu la raison; **he won't listen to reason** il refuse d'entendre raison; **I can't make her listen to reason** je n'arrive pas à lui faire entendre raison *ou* à la raisonner; **at last he saw reason** il a fini par entendre raison; **your demands are beyond all reason** vos exigences dépassent les limites du raisonnable; **it stands to reason (that...)** il va de soi *ou* sans dire (que... + *indicative*); **that stands to reason** c'est logique, ça va de soi; **man has the power of reason** l'homme est doué de raison

2 *vt* (**a**) *(maintain)* maintenir, soutenir; *(work out)* calculer, déduire; *(conclude)* conclure; **they reasoned that the fault must be in the cooling system** ils en ont déduit que la défaillance devait provenir du système de refroidissement

(**b**) *(persuade)* **I reasoned him out of the idea** je l'ai persuadé *ou* convaincu d'abandonner son idée; **she reasoned me into/out of going** elle m'a persuadé/dissuadé d'y aller

3 *vi* raisonner; **to reason with sb** raisonner qn; **I tried to reason with them** j'ai essayé de les raisonner *ou* de leur faire entendre raison; *Hum* **ours is not to reason why** il ne faut pas chercher à comprendre

4 by reason of *prep* en raison de; **to be found not guilty by reason of insanity** être déclaré non-coupable pour cause de démence

5 for reasons of *prep* **for reasons of space/national security** pour des raisons de place/de sécurité nationale

6 within reason *adv* dans la limite du raisonnable; **you can do what you like, within reason** vous pouvez faire ce que vous voulez, dans la limite du raisonnable

▸**reason out** *vt sep (maths problem)* résoudre; *(one's differences)* résoudre en discutant

reasonable ['ri:zənəbəl] *adj* (**a**) *(sensible* → *person, behaviour, attitude)* raisonnable; *(*→ *explanation, decision)* raisonnable, sensé; **be reasonable!** soyez raisonnable!; **you must be reasonable in your demands** vos revendications doivent être raisonnables

(**b**) *(moderate* → *price)* raisonnable, correct; *(*→

restaurant) qui pratique des prix raisonnables; **with a reasonable amount of luck** avec un peu de chance

(**c**) *(fair, acceptable → offer, suggestion)* raisonnable, acceptable; **we've had quite a reasonable day** nous avons passé une journée plutôt agréable; **beyond all reasonable doubt** indubitablement

reasonableness ['riːzənəbəlnɪs] *n* (**a**) *(of person, behaviour)* caractère *m* raisonnable (**b**) *(of price)* modération *f*

reasonably ['riːzənəblɪ] *adv* (**a**) *(behave, argue)* raisonnablement; **one can reasonably expect...** on est en droit d'attendre...; **reasonably priced at $100** au prix raisonnable *ou* modéré de 100 dollars (**b**) *(quite, rather)* assez; **reasonably good** assez bien, pas mal; **reasonably fit** en assez bonne forme

reasoned ['riːzənd] *adj (argument, decision)* raisonné

reasoning ['riːzənɪŋ] *n* raisonnement *m*; **the reasoning behind the decision** les raisons de cette décision; **such reasoning is dangerous** un tel raisonnement est dangereux

reassemble [ˌriːə'sembəl] **1** *vt* (**a**) *(people, arguments)* rassembler (**b**) *(machinery)* remonter; *(frame)* réassembler

2 *vi* se rassembler; **Parliament/school reassembles in September** la rentrée parlementaire/des classes a lieu en septembre

reassembly [ˌriːə'semblɪ] *n* (**a**) *(of group)* rassemblement *m*; *Pol* rentrée *f* (**b**) *(of machine)* remontage *m*; *(of frame)* réassemblage *m*

reassert [ˌriːə'sɜːt] *vt (authority)* réaffirmer; **you'll have to reassert yourself** vous devrez imposer à nouveau *ou* réaffirmer votre autorité; **her self-confidence reasserted itself** sa confiance est revenue

reassertion [ˌriːə'sɜːʃən] *n* réaffirmation *f*

reassess [ˌriːə'ses] *vt* (**a**) *(position, opinion)* réexaminer (**b**) *Fin (damages)* réévaluer; *(taxation)* réviser; **you have been reassessed** votre situation fiscale a été réexaminée

reassessment [ˌriːə'sesmənt] *n* (**a**) *(of position, opinion)* réexamen *m* (**b**) *Fin (of damages)* réévaluation *f*; *(of taxes)* révision *f*

reassign [ˌriːə'saɪn] *vt (employee)* muter (**to** à); *(work, project)* confier (**to** à); *(funds)* réaffecter (**to** à); **the work's been reassigned** le travail a été confié à quelqu'un d'autre

reassignment [ˌriːə'saɪnmənt] *n (transfer)* mutation *f*; *(duties)* nouveau poste *m*, nouvelles fonctions *fpl*; *(of funds)* réaffectation *f*

reassume [ˌriːə'sjuːm] *vt (one's duties)* reprendre

reassurance [ˌriːə'ʃɔːrəns] *n* (**a**) *(comforting)* réconfort *m*; **she turned to me for reassurance** elle s'est tournée vers moi *ou* est venue à moi pour que je la rassure

(**b**) *(guarantee)* assurance *f*, confirmation *f*; **despite his reassurance** *or* **reassurances that the contract is still valid** bien qu'il affirme que le contrat est toujours valable; **the government has given reassurances that...** le gouvernement a assuré que...+ *indicative*

(**c**) *Br Fin* réassurance *f*

reassure [ˌriːə'ʃɔː(r)] *vt* (**a**) *(gen)* rassurer; **I feel reassured now** je me sens rassuré maintenant (**b**) *Br Fin* réassurer

reassuring [ˌriːə'ʃɔːrɪŋ] *adj* rassurant

reassuringly [ˌriːə'ʃɔːrɪŋlɪ] *adv* d'une manière rassurante; **he smiled at me reassuringly** il me fit un sourire pour me rassurer; **reassuringly simple** d'une grande simplicité

reawake [ˌriːə'weɪk] (*pt* **reawoke** [-'wəʊk] *or* **reawaked,** *pp* **reawoken** [-'wəʊkən] *or* **reawaked**) *vi* se réveiller de nouveau

reawaken [ˌriːə'weɪkən] **1** *vt (person, interest)* réveiller; *(feelings)* faire renaître, raviver

2 *vi (person)* se réveiller de nouveau; *(feelings, interest)* se raviver

reawakening [ˌriːə'weɪkənɪŋ] *n (of person, interest)* regain *m*; **the reawakening of national pride** le réveil de l'orgueil national

rebarbative [rɪ'bɑːbətɪv] *adj Formal* rébarbatif

rebate ['riːbeɪt] **1** *n* (**a**) *(reduction → on goods)* remise *f*, ristourne *f*; *(→ on tax)* dégrèvement *m* (**b**) *(refund)* remboursement *m* (**c**) *(groove)* feuillure *f*

2 *vt* feuiller

Rebecca [rɪ'bekə] *pr n Bible* Rébecca

rebel (*pt & pp* **rebelled,** *cont* **rebelling**) **1** *n* ['rebəl] *(in revolution)* rebelle *mf*, insurgé(e) *m,f*; *Fig* rebelle *mf*; *Am Hist* **the Rebels** les confédérés *mpl*

2 *adj* ['rebəl] *(soldier)* rebelle; *(camp, territory)* des rebelles; *(attack)* de rebelles

3 *vi* [rɪ'bel] se rebeller; **to rebel against sb/sth** se révolter contre qn/qch; *Hum* **my stomach rebelled** mon estomac a protesté

►► ***rebel forces*** forces *fpl* rebelles; ***rebel leader*** chef *m* des rebelles; ***rebel MP*** parlementaire *m* rebelle

'Rebel Without a Cause' *Ray* 'La Fureur de vivre'

Rebel without a cause
Il s'agit du titre original de *La Fureur de vivre*, un film de Nicholas Ray de 1955 dans lequel James Dean joue le rôle d'un fils de bonne famille. L'interprétation de James Dean et son personnage de jeune rebelle ténébreux a fait de l'acteur l'incarnation d'une jeunesse inquiète et en rupture avec son milieu.
Aujourd'hui, on utilise cette formule à propos du type de personnage interprété par James Dean dans ce film.

rebellion [rɪ'beljən] *n* rébellion *f*, révolte *f*; **in open rebellion** en rébellion ouverte; **to rise (up) in rebellion against sb/sth** se révolter contre qn/qch

rebellious [rɪ'beljəs] *adj (behaviour, child, hair)* rebelle; *(troops)* insoumis; **a rebellious act** un acte de rébellion

rebelliously [rɪ'beljəslɪ] *adv (reply)* d'un ton de défi; *(act)* en rebelle

rebelliousness [rɪ'beljəsnɪs] *n (of child, politician)* esprit *m* de rébellion; *(of soldier)* insoumission *f*; *(of inhabitants)* disposition *f* à la rébellion

rebind [ˌriː'baɪnd] *vt* (*pt & pp* **rebound** [-'baʊnd]) (**a**) *(book)* relier de nouveau *ou* à neuf (**b**) *(wheel)* recercler

rebirth [ˌriː'bɜːθ] *n* renaissance *f*

rebirthing [ˌriː'bɜːθɪŋ] *n Psy* rebirth *m*, rebirthing *m*, respiration *f* consciente

reboot [ˌriː'buːt] *Comput* **1** *vt* réamorcer

2 *vi* se réamorcer

rebore 1 [ˌriː'bɔː(r)] *vt* réaléser

2 ['riːbɔː(r)] *n* réalésage *m*; **my car needs a rebore** le cylindre de ma voiture a besoin d'être réalésé *ou* d'un réalésage

reborn [ˌriː'bɔːn] *adj* réincarné; **to be reborn** renaître; **I feel reborn** je me sens renaître

rebound 1 *vi* [rɪ'baʊnd] (**a**) *(ball)* rebondir; **the ball rebounded against the wall/into the road** le ballon a rebondi contre le mur/sur la route

(**b**) *Fig* **to rebound on sb** se retourner contre qn; **the situation rebounded on us** la situation s'est retournée contre nous

(**c**) *(recover → business)* reprendre, repartir; *(→ prices)* remonter

2 *n* ['riːbaʊnd] (**a**) *(of ball)* rebond *m*; **to catch a ball on the rebound** attraper une balle au rebond; **he headed in the rebound** il a marqué un but de la tête en prenant la balle au rebond

(**b**) *(idioms)* **to be on the rebound** *(after relationship)* être sous le coup d'une déception sentimentale; *(after setback)* être sous le coup d'un échec; **he married her on the rebound** il l'a épousée à la suite d'une déception sentimentale; **he caught her on the rebound** il a commencé à la fréquenter au moment où elle sortait d'une déception amoureuse

rebrand [ˌriː'brænd] *vt Mktg (product)* changer la marque de

rebranding [ˌriː'brændɪŋ] *n Mktg (of product)* changement *m* de marque

rebroadcast [ˌriː'brɔːdkɑːst] **1** *n* retransmission *f*

2 *vt* retransmettre

rebuff [rɪ'bʌf] **1** *vt (snub)* rabrouer; *(reject)* repousser

2 *n* rebuffade *f*; **to meet with** *or* **to suffer a rebuff** *(person)* essuyer une rebuffade; *(request)* être repoussé

rebuild [ˌriː'bɪld] (*pt & pp* **rebuilt** [-'bɪlt]) *vt (town, economy)* rebâtir, reconstruire; *(company, relationship, life)* reconstruire; *(confidence)* faire renaître; **we must rebuild confidence in industry** nous devons faire renaître la confiance dans l'industrie

rebuilding [ˌriː'bɪldɪŋ] **1** *n (of town, economy, relationship)* reconstruction *f*

2 *comp (project, work)* de réfection, de reconstruction

rebuke [rɪ'bjuːk] **1** *vt (reprimand)* réprimander; **to rebuke sb for sth** reprocher qch à qn; **to rebuke sb for doing** *or* **having done sth** reprocher à qn d'avoir fait qch

2 *n* reproche *m*, réprimande *f*

rebukingly [rɪ'bjuːkɪŋlɪ] *adv (look)* d'un air de reproche; *(say)* d'un ton de reproche

rebus ['riːbəs] *n* rébus *m*

rebut [rɪ'bʌt] (*pt & pp* **rebutted,** *cont* **rebutting**) *vt* réfuter

rebuttal [rɪ'bʌtəl] *n* réfutation *f*

rebuy ['riːbaɪ] *n Mktg* réachat *m*

►► ***rebuy rate*** taux *m* de réachat

rec [rek] *n Fam* (**a**) *Br (ground)* terrain *m* de jeux ❑ (**b**) *Am Sch (break)* récré *f*

►► *Br* ***rec ground*** terrain *m* de jeux ❑; *Am* ***rec room*** *(in home)* salle *f* de jeux ❑

rec. *(written abbr* **received)** reçu

recalcitrance [rɪ'kælsɪtrəns] *n Formal* caractère *m ou* esprit *m* récalcitrant

recalcitrant [rɪ'kælsɪtrənt] *adj Formal* récalcitrant

recalculate [ˌriː'kælkjʊleɪt] *vt* recalculer

recalculation [ˌriːkælkjʊ'leɪʃən] *n* recalcul *m*

recall 1 *vt* [rɪ'kɔːl] (**a**) *(remember)* se rappeler, se souvenir de; **I don't recall seeing** *or* **having seen her** je ne me rappelle pas l'avoir vue; **as far as I can recall** aussi loin que je m'en souvienne; **as I recall** si mes souvenirs sont bons; **as you may recall** comme vous vous en souvenez peut-être; **how vividly I recall the scene!** avec quelle netteté je revois ce spectacle!

(**b**) *(evoke → past)* rappeler, évoquer; **paintings that recall the past** des tableaux qui évoquent le passé

(**c**) *(summon back → ambassador, faulty goods)* rappeler; *(→ Parliament)* rappeler (en session extraordinaire); *(→ library book, hire car)* demander le retour de; **the sound of the telephone recalled her to the present** la sonnerie du téléphone la ramena à la réalité

(**d**) *Mil (troops)* rappeler; *Sport (player)* rappeler, sélectionner à nouveau

2 *n* ['riːkɔːl] (**a**) *(memory)* rappel *m*, mémoire *f*; **to have instant recall** avoir une excellente mémoire; **total recall** aptitude à se souvenir des moindres détails; **to be beyond** *or* **past recall** être oublié à tout jamais

(**b**) *Mktg (of brand name)* mémorisation *f*

(**c**) *(summoning back → of ambassador, faulty goods)* rappel *m*; *(→ of library book)* fait *m* de demander le retour de; *(→ of Parliament)* reconvocation *f*

(**d**) *Mil (of troops)* rappel *m*; *Sport (of player)* **he was expecting a recall to the team** il s'attendait à ce qu'on le rappelle dans l'équipe; **the England team announced today includes a recall for Bryson** la composition de l'équipe d'Angleterre a été annoncée aujourd'hui et Bryson en fait à nouveau partie

►► ***recall button*** *(on phone)* rappel *m* automatique; *Mktg* ***recall rate*** taux *m* de mémorisation; *Mktg* ***recall score*** score *m* de mémorisation; ***recall slip*** *(for library book)* fiche *f* de rappel; *Mktg* ***recall test*** test *m* de rappel *ou* de mémorisation

recant [rɪ'kænt] **1** *vt (religion)* abjurer; *(opinion)* rétracter

2 *vi (from religion)* abjurer; *(from opinion)* se rétracter

recantation [ˌriːkæn'teɪʃən] *n (of religion)* abjuration *f*; *(of statement)* rétractation *f*

recap ['riːkæp] (*pt & pp* **recapped,** *cont* **recapping**) **1** *n* (**a**) *(summary)* récapitulation *f* (**b**) *Am (tyre)* pneu *m* rechapé

2 *vt* (**a**) *(summarize)* récapituler; **so, to recap** donc, pour récapituler *ou* résumer (**b**) *Am (tyre)* rechaper

recapitalization ['riːˌkæpɪtəlaɪ'zeɪʃən] *n Fin (of company)* recapitalisation *f*, changement *m* de la structure financière

recapitalize, -ise [ˌriːˈkæpɪtəlaɪz] *vt Fin (company)* recapitaliser, changer la structure financière de

recapitulate [ˌriːkəˈpɪtjʊleɪt] **1** *vt* (**a**) *(summarize → discussion etc)* récapituler (**b**) *Mus (theme)* reprendre
2 *vt* récapituler; **so, to recapitulate** donc, pour récapituler *ou* résumer

recapitulation [ˌriːkəˌpɪtjʊˈleɪʃən] *n* (**a**) *(of discussion etc)* récapitulation *f* (**b**) *Mus* reprise *f*

recapture [ˌriːˈkæptʃə(r)] **1** *vt* (**a**) *(prisoner, town)* reprendre; *(animal)* capturer (**b**) *(regain → confidence)* reprendre; *(→ feeling, spirit)* retrouver; *(evoke → of film, book, play)* recréer, faire revivre (**c**) *Am Fin* saisir
2 *n* (**a**) *(of escapee, animal)* capture *f*; *(of town)* reprise *f* (**b**) *Am Fin* saisie *f*

recast [ˌriːˈkɑːst] *(pt & pp* **recast**) **1** *vt* (**a**) *(redraft)* remanier; **their policies have been recast in a more acceptable form** ils ont remanié leur politique de façon plus satisfaisante
(**b**) *(play)* changer la distribution de; *(actor)* donner un nouveau rôle à; **he was recast in the role of Prospero** on lui a donné un nouveau rôle, celui de Prospero
(**c**) *Metal* refondre
2 *n Metal* refonte *f*

recce [ˈrekɪ] *(pt & pp* **recced** *or* **recceed**) *Fam* **1** *vt* reconnaître □
2 *vi* faire une reconnaissance □
3 *n* reconnaissance □ *f*; **to go on a recce** *(gen)* faire la reconnaissance des lieux; *Mil* aller en reconnaissance

recd, rec'd *(written abbr* **received**) reçu

recede [rɪˈsiːd] **1** *vi* (**a**) *(move away → coastline, person, object)* s'éloigner; *(→ waters)* refluer; *(→ tide)* descendre; **to recede into the distance** disparaître dans le lointain
(**b**) *(fade → hopes)* s'évanouir; *(→ fears)* s'estomper; *(→ danger)* s'éloigner; **as memories of the past recede** à mesure que les souvenirs du passé s'effacent
(**c**) *(hairline)* **his hair has started to recede** son front commence à se dégarnir
(**d**) *Fin* baisser
2 *vt Law (right)* rétrocéder; *(land)* recéder

receding [rɪˈsiːdɪŋ] *adj* (**a**) *(chin, forehead)* fuyant; **to have a receding hairline** avoir le front qui se dégarnit; **to have receding gums** avoir les gencives qui s'atrophient (**b**) *Fin* en baisse

receipt [rɪˈsiːt] **1** *n* (**a**) *(for purchase, meal, taxi fare)* reçu *m* (**for** de); *(in supermarket, bar)* ticket *m* de caisse, reçu *m*; *(for bill)* acquit *m*; *(for rent, insurance)* quittance *f*; *(from customs)* récépissé *m*; *(for letter, parcel)* récépissé *m*, accusé *m* de réception
(**b**) *(reception → of letter, parcel etc)* réception *f*; **to pay on receipt** payer à la réception; **to be in receipt of sth** avoir reçu qch; *Com* **I am in receipt of the goods** j'ai bien reçu les marchandises; *Com* **to acknowledge receipt of sth** accuser réception de qch; **on receipt of your results** dès que vous aurez reçu vos résultats
2 *vt Br* acquitter, quittancer; **to receipt a bill** acquitter une facture
3 receipts *npl (takings)* recettes *fpl*, rentrées *fpl*; **receipts and expenditure** recettes *fpl* et dépenses *fpl*
►► *Fin* ***receipted bill*** facture *f* acquittée; *Fin* ***receipt book*** carnet *m* de quittances

receivable [rɪˈsiːvəbəl] **1** *adj* recevable; *Com (outstanding)* à recevoir; **accounts receivable** comptes *mpl* clients, créances *fpl*
2 receivables *npl (debts)* comptes *mpl* clients, créances *fpl*; *(bills)* effets *mpl* à recevoir

receive [rɪˈsiːv] **1** *vt* (**a**) *(gift, letter)* recevoir; *(salary, money)* toucher, recevoir; **to receive sth from sb** recevoir qch de qn; **we received your letter on Monday** nous avons reçu votre lettre *ou* votre lettre nous est parvenue lundi; **to receive a high salary** recevoir *ou* toucher un salaire élevé; *Com* **received with thanks** *(on receipt)* acquitté, pour acquit; *Law* **to receive damages** obtenir *ou* recevoir des dommages-intérêts; *Law* **she received ten years** elle a été condamnée à dix ans de réclusion; *St Exch* **to receive a premium** encaisser un premium
(**b**) *(blow)* recevoir; *(insult, refusal)* essuyer; *(criticism)* être l'objet de; **to receive treatment (for sth)** se faire soigner (pour qch); **to receive injuries** être blessé; **he has received dreadful/excellent treatment** il a été traité d'une manière épouvantable/avec beaucoup d'égards; **she received injuries from which she has since died** elle est morte des suites de ses blessures
(**c**) *(greet, welcome)* accueillir, recevoir; *(into club, organization)* admettre; **to be cordially received** *(visitor etc)* trouver un accueil chaleureux, être bien reçu; **the new movie was enthusiastically received** le nouveau film a été accueilli avec enthousiasme; **their offer was not well received** leur proposition n'a pas reçu un accueil favorable; *Formal* **will Madam receive the doctor now?** Madame recevra-t-elle le médecin maintenant?; **to be received into the Church** être reçu *ou* admis dans le sein de l'Église
(**d**) *(signal, broadcast)* recevoir, capter; **are you receiving me?** *(on radio)* est-ce que vous me recevez?; **I'm receiving you loud and clear** je vous reçois cinq sur cinq
(**e**) *Sport* **to receive service** recevoir le service
(**f**) *Law (stolen goods)* receler
(**g**) *Formal (accommodate)* recevoir, prendre; **holes were drilled to receive the pegs** des trous étaient percés pour recevoir les chevilles
2 *vi* (**a**) *Formal (have guests)* recevoir
(**b**) *Sport* relancer, être le relanceur
(**c**) *Rel* recevoir la communion
(**d**) *Law (thief)* receler; **to be accused of receiving** être accusé de recel

received [rɪˈsiːvd] *adj* **the received wisdom is that…** de l'avis général…
►► ***received idea, received opinion*** idée *f* reçue *ou* toute faite; *Br* ***Received Pronunciation*** prononciation *f* standard (de l'anglais); *Am* ***Received Standard*** prononciation *f* standard (de l'américain)

receiver [rɪˈsiːvə(r)] *n* (**a**) *(gen) & Sport* receveur(euse) *m,f*; *(of consignment)* destinataire *mf*, consignataire *mf*; *(of stolen goods)* receleur(euse) *m,f*
(**b**) *(on telephone)* combiné *m*, récepteur *m*; **to lift/to replace the receiver** décrocher/raccrocher (le téléphone)
(**c**) *TV* récepteur *m*, poste *m* de télévision; *Rad* récepteur *m*, poste *m* de radio
(**d**) *Fin* administrateur(trice) *m,f* judiciaire; **to be in the hands of the receiver(s)** être sous administration judiciaire; **they have been placed in the hands of the receiver, the receiver has been called in** ils ont été placés sous administration judiciaire
(**e**) *Chem* récipient *m*
►► *Am* ***receiver general*** receveur *m* des impôts; ***receiver rest*** *(for telephone)* berceau *m* (du combiné)

receivership [rɪˈsiːvəʃɪp] *n Fin* **to go into receivership** être placé sous administration judiciaire

receiving [rɪˈsiːvɪŋ] **1** *adj* (**a**) *(office)* de réception; *(country)* d'accueil
(**b**) *Sport* **to be at the receiving end** recevoir (le service); *Fam* **to be on the receiving end** écoper; **if anything goes wrong, you'll be on the receiving end** si ça tourne mal, c'est toi qui vas payer les pots cassés *ou* qui vas prendre; **she was on the receiving end of their bad mood** c'est sur elle qu'ils ont passé leur mauvaise humeur, c'est elle qui a fait les frais de leur mauvaise humeur
2 *n (of stolen property)* recel *m*
►► *Br Law* ***receiving order*** ordonnance *f* de mise sous administration judiciaire *ou* sous séquestre

recension [rɪˈsenʃən] *n (revision)* révision *f*; *(text)* texte *m* révisé, texte *m* revu et corrigé

recent [ˈriːsənt] *adj (new)* récent, nouveau(elle); *(modern)* récent, moderne; **in recent months** ces derniers mois; **in recent times** récemment; **one of the most charismatic leaders of recent times** l'un des dirigeants les plus charismatiques de ces dernières années; **recent developments** les derniers événements *mpl*; **her most recent novel** son dernier roman; **have you any recent news of them?** avez-vous eu de leurs nouvelles récemment?

recently [ˈriːsəntlɪ] *adv* récemment, dernièrement, ces derniers temps; **I saw her as recently as yesterday** je l'ai vue pas plus tard qu'hier; **until recently** jusqu'à ces derniers temps; **I hadn't heard of it until very recently** je n'en ai entendu parler que très récemment

recentness [ˈriːsəntnɪs] *n (of event)* date *f* récente

receptacle [rɪˈseptəkəl] *n* (**a**) *Formal (container)* récipient *m* (**b**) *Am Elec* prise *f* de courant (femelle)

reception [rɪˈsepʃən] *n* (**a**) *(welcome)* réception *f*, accueil *m*; **to get a warm reception** recevoir un accueil chaleureux; **to get a cold reception** être reçu froidement; **the movie got an enthusiastic reception from the critics** le film a été accueilli avec enthousiasme par la critique
(**b**) *(formal party)* réception *f*; *(in the evening)* réception *f*, soirée *f*; **to hold a reception** donner une réception
(**c**) *(in hotel)* réception *f*; *(in office, hospital)* accueil *m*; **at reception** à la réception
(**d**) *Rad & TV* réception *f*
(**e**) *Am Sport (of ball)* réception *f*
(**f**) *Br Sch* ≃ cours *m* préparatoire
►► *Br* ***reception centre*** centre *m* d'accueil; *Br Sch* ***reception class*** première année *f* de maternelle; *Am* ***reception clerk*** réceptionniste *mf*; *also Hum* ***reception committee*** comité *m* d'accueil; ***reception desk*** *(in hotel)* réception *f*; *(in office, hospital)* accueil *m*; ***reception order*** arrêté *m* d'internement; ***reception room*** *(in hotel)* salle *f* de réception; *Br (in house)* salon *m*

receptionist [rɪˈsepʃənɪst] *n (in hotel)* réceptionniste *mf*; *(in office)* hôtesse *f* d'accueil; **he's a receptionist at Brown's** il travaille à l'accueil chez Brown

receptive [rɪˈseptɪv] *adj* (**a**) *(open)* réceptif; **to be receptive to new ideas** être ouvert aux idées nouvelles (**b**) *(passive)* **receptive knowledge of a language** connaissance *f* passive *ou* réceptive d'une langue

receptiveness [rɪˈseptɪvnɪs], **receptivity** [ˌrɪsepˈtɪvɪtɪ] *n* réceptivité *f*

receptor [rɪˈseptə(r)] *n Phys & Physiol* récepteur *m*
►► ***receptor site*** (site *m*) récepteur *m*

recess [*Br* rɪˈses, *Am* ˈriːses] **1** *n* (**a**) *(alcove → gen)* renfoncement *m*; *(→ in bedroom)* alcôve *f*; *(→ for statue)* niche *f*; *(in doorway)* embrasure *f*; **dining recess** coin *m* repas, coin *m* salle à manger
(**b**) *(of mind, memory)* recoin *m*, tréfonds *m*; **in the innermost recesses of the soul** dans les replis *ou* les recoins les plus secrets de l'âme
(**c**) *Am Law* suspension *f* d'audience; **the court went into recess** l'audience a été suspendue
(**d**) *Am Sch* récréation *f*; **during the recess** pendant la récréation; **to go recess** aller en récréation
(**e**) *(closure → of Parliament)* vacances *fpl* parlementaires, intersession *f* parlementaire; *(→ of courts)* vacances *fpl* judiciaires, vacations *fpl*; **Parliament is in recess for the summer** le Parlement est en vacances pour l'été
2 *vi Am Law* suspendre l'audience; *Pol* suspendre la séance; **Parliament will recess next week** *(begin holiday)* les vacances parlementaires commenceront la semaine prochaine
3 *vt (lighting, switch etc)* encastrer

recessed [*Br* rɪˈsest, *Am* ˈriːsest] *adj (bookshelves, lighting)* encastré

recession [rɪˈseʃən] *n* (**a**) *Econ* récession *f*; **the economy is in recession** l'économie est en récession (**b**) *Formal (retreat)* recul *m*, retraite *f* (**c**) *Rel* sortie *f* en procession du clergé (**d**) *Law* rétrocession *f*

recessional [rɪˈseʃənəl] **1** *n Rel* = cantique de sortie en procession du clergé
2 *adj* (**a**) *(hymn)* de sortie (processionnelle) (**b**) *Econ* de (la) récession

recessionary [rɪˈseʃənərɪ] *adj Econ* de crise, de récession; **to have a recessionary effect** *(of policy etc)* entraîner une récession

recessive [rɪˈsesɪv] **1** *adj* (**a**) *(gene)* récessif (**b**) *(backward → measure)* rétrograde
2 *n (gene)* gène *m* récessif; *(organism)* sujet *m* récessif

recessiveness [rɪˈsesɪvnɪs] *n Biol* récessivité *f*

recharge 1 *vt* [ˌriːˈtʃɑːdʒ] *(battery, rifle)* recharger; **to recharge one's batteries** recharger ses batteries
2 *vi* [ˌriːˈtʃɑːdʒ] *(battery)* se recharger
3 *n* [ˈriːtʃɑːdʒ] recharge *f*

rechargeable [ˌriːˈtʃɑːdʒəbəl] *adj* rechargeable
recherché [rəˈʃeəʃeɪ] *adj (film, topic)* recherché
rechip [ˌriːˈtʃɪp] *vt (mobile phone)* reprogrammer la puce de
rechipping [rɪˈtʃɪpɪŋ] *n* reprogrammation *f* de la puce sur un téléphone portable
rechristen [riːˈkrɪsən] *vt Rel* rebaptiser; *Fig* donner un nouveau nom à, rebaptiser
recidivism [rɪˈsɪdɪvɪzəm] *n Law* récidive *f*
recidivist [rɪˈsɪdɪvɪst] *Law* **1** *adj* récidiviste
2 *n* récidiviste *mf*
Recife [reˈsiːfə] *n* Recife *f*
recipe [ˈresɪpɪ] *n Culin* recette *f*; *Fig* recette *f*, secret *m*; **a recipe for success/long life** le secret de la réussite/de la longévité; **it's a recipe for disaster** c'est le meilleur moyen d'aller droit à la catastrophe
▸▸ ***recipe book*** livre *m* de recettes; ***recipe card*** fiche-recette *f*, fiche-cuisine *f*
recipient [rɪˈsɪpɪənt] *n* **(a)** *(of letter, e-mail)* destinataire *mf*; *(of cheque, bill)* bénéficiaire *mf*; *(of award, honour)* récipiendaire *m*; **he was the proud recipient of a gold watch** il a eu la chance de se voir remettre une montre en or **(b)** *Med (of transplant)* receveur(euse) *m,f*
reciprocal [rɪˈsɪprəkəl] **1** *adj (mutual)* réciproque, mutuel; *(bilateral)* réciproque, bilatéral; *Gram* réciproque; *Math* réciproque, inverse
2 *n Math* réciproque *f*, inverse *f*
▸▸ ***reciprocal agreement*** accord *m* réciproque; *Mktg* ***reciprocal relationships model*** modèle *m* de relations réciproques; ***reciprocal trading*** commerce *m* réciproque
reciprocally [rɪˈsɪprəkəlɪ] *adv* réciproquement
reciprocate [rɪˈsɪprəkeɪt] **1** *vt* **(a)** *(favour, invitation, smile)* rendre; *(love, sentiment)* répondre à, rendre; **to reciprocate sb's kindness** payer la gentillesse de qn de retour; **he had great admiration for her but his feelings were never reciprocated** il avait beaucoup d'admiration pour elle mais ce n'était pas réciproque
(b) *Tech* actionner d'un mouvement alternatif
2 *vi* **(a)** *(in praise, compliments)* retourner le compliment; *(in fight)* rendre coup pour coup; *(in dispute)* rendre la pareille; *(in argument)* répondre du tac au tac
(b) *Tech* avoir un mouvement de va-et-vient
reciprocating [rɪˈsɪprəˌkeɪtɪŋ] *adj Tech* alternatif
▸▸ ***reciprocating engine*** moteur *m* alternatif
reciprocation [rɪˌsɪprəˈkeɪʃən] *n* **(a)** *(of feeling)* réciprocité *f*; **in reciprocation for** en retour de; **his reciprocation of her feelings was clear** il était clair que leurs sentiments étaient réciproques; **these feelings met with no reciprocation** ces sentiments n'ont pas été payés de retour **(b)** *Tech* mouvement *m* alternatif, va-et-vient *m inv*
reciprocity [ˌresɪˈprɒsɪtɪ] *n* réciprocité *f*
recirculate [ˌriːˈsɜːkjʊleɪt] **1** *vt* remettre en circulation *ou* en circuit
2 *vi (fluid, water etc)* recirculer
recirculated air [ˌriːˈsɜːkjʊleɪtɪd-] *n Aut* air *m* recyclé
recital [rɪˈsaɪtəl] **1** *n* **(a)** *Mus & Literature* récital *m*; **to give a recital** donner un récital; **piano/poetry recital** récital *m* de piano/poésie; **Bach/Verdi recital** récital *m* Bach/Verdi
(b) *(narrative)* narration *f*, relation *f*; *(of details)* énumération *f*; **she bored us with a recital of all her ills** elle nous a assommés avec une énumération de tous ses malheurs
2 recitals *npl Law* préambule *m (à un acte notarié)*
recitation [ˌresɪˈteɪʃən] *n* récitation *f*
recitative [ˌresɪtəˈtiːv] *n Mus* récitatif *m*
recite [rɪˈsaɪt] **1** *vt (play, poem)* réciter, déclamer; *(details, facts)* réciter, énumérer
2 *vi* réciter; *Am Sch* réciter sa leçon
reciter [rɪˈsaɪtə(r)] *n* **(a)** *(person)* déclamateur(trice) *m,f*, narrateur(trice) *m,f* **(b)** *(book)* livre *m* de récitations, recueil *m* de monologues
reck [rek] *vt Arch or Literary* **I reck not my life** je fais peu de cas de ma vie; **what recks it me that she is penniless?** que m'importe qu'elle est sans le sou?
reckless [ˈreklɪs] *adj (foolhardy)* téméraire; *(rash)* imprudent; *(thoughtless)* irréfléchi; **to make a reckless promise** s'engager à la légère; **to be a reckless spender** dépenser sans compter; **it would be reckless to ignore the consequences/the danger** il serait imprudent de ne pas tenir compte des conséquences/du danger
▸▸ *Admin & Law* ***reckless driver*** conducteur(trice) *m,f* imprudent(e); ***reckless driving*** conduite *f* imprudente
recklessly [ˈreklɪslɪ] *adv (fearlessly)* avec témérité; *(rashly)* imprudemment; *(thoughtlessly)* sans réfléchir; **to spend recklessly** dépenser sans compter; **they rather recklessly promised to contribute £500** ils ont promis assez imprudemment *ou* un peu hâtivement de donner 500 livres; **he drives very recklessly** il conduit dangereusement
recklessness [ˈreklɪsnɪs] *n (foolhardiness)* témérité *f*; *(rashness)* imprudence *f*; *(thoughtlessness)* insouciance *f*, étourderie *f*
reckon [ˈrekən] **1** *vt* **(a)** *(estimate)* estimer; **there were reckoned to be about fifteen hundred demonstrators** on a estimé à mille cinq cents le nombre des manifestants; **I reckon this building to be about three hundred years old** je pense que ce bâtiment a environ trois cents ans
(b) *(consider)* considérer; **I reckon this restaurant to be the best in town** je considère ce restaurant comme le meilleur de la ville; **he is reckoned to be one of the richest men in England** ce serait l'un des hommes les plus riches d'Angleterre; *Fam* **I don't reckon her chances much** je ne crois pas qu'elle ait beaucoup de chances ☐
(c) *Fam (suppose, think)* croire ☐, supposer ☐; **I reckon you're right** je crois bien que tu as raison ☐; **I reckon the omelette is ready** je crois que l'omelette est prête ☐; **how old do you reckon he is?** quel âge lui donnez-vous? ☐; **it's all over, I reckon** je suppose que tout est fini ☐; **what do you reckon?** qu'en pensez-vous? ☐
(d) *(expect)* compter, penser; **they had reckoned to make more profit from the venture** ils comptaient *ou* pensaient que l'entreprise leur rapporterait de plus gros bénéfices; **you should reckon to be there by six o'clock at the latest** il faut que tu prévois d'arriver à six heures au plus tard
(e) *Formal (calculate)* calculer
2 *vi (calculate)* calculer, compter; **reckoning from today** à partir *ou* à compter d'aujourd'hui
▸ **reckon in** *vt sep Br* compter, inclure
▸ **reckon on** *vt insep* **(a)** *(rely on)* compter sur; **you can reckon on him making a mess of it** tu peux compter sur lui pour tout gâcher; **don't reckon on it** n'y comptez pas
(b) *(expect)* s'attendre à, espérer; **I was reckoning on more** je m'attendais à plus; **she had reckoned on going next week** elle avait prévu d'y aller la semaine prochaine; **I didn't reckon on that extra cost** je n'avais pas prévu ces frais supplémentaires
▸ **reckon up** **1** *vt sep (column of figures)* additionner; *(change, coins)* compter; *(total, cost)* calculer; **to reckon up a bill** faire une facture
2 *vi* faire ses comptes; **to reckon up with sb** régler ses comptes avec qn
▸ **reckon with** *vt insep* compter avec; *(as opponent)* avoir affaire à; **they didn't reckon with the army/the opposition** ils ont compté sans l'armée/l'opposition; **we had to reckon with stiff opposition** nous avons eu affaire à une forte opposition; **you'll have to reckon with another guest/his brother** il faudra compter avec un invité supplémentaire/son frère; **he hadn't reckoned with this response** il ne s'attendait pas à cette réaction; **she's a force to be reckoned with** c'est une femme avec laquelle il faut compter
▸ **reckon without** *vt insep Br* **(a)** *(do without)* se passer de, se débrouiller sans; **you'll have to reckon without my help** il faudra vous débrouiller sans *ou* vous passer de moi
(b) *Fam (ignore, overlook)* ne pas tenir compte de ☐; **he had reckoned without his rivals** il n'avait pas tenu compte de ses rivaux; **she had reckoned without the fact that they had no car** elle n'avait pas pris en compte le fait qu'ils n'avaient pas de voiture
reckoning [ˈrekənɪŋ] *n* **(a)** *(UNCOUNT) (calculation)* calcul *m*, compte *m*; **you are way out in your reckoning** vous vous êtes complètement trompé dans vos comptes *ou* dans vos calculs; **on** *or* **by my reckoning, you owe us £50** d'après mes calculs, vous nous devez 50 livres; **in the final reckoning** en fin de compte
(b) *(estimation)* estimation *f*; *(opinion)* avis *m*; **to the best of my reckoning** pour autant que je puisse en juger; **by** *or* **on any reckoning she's a fine pianist** personne ne niera que c'est une excellente pianiste; *Rel* **day of reckoning** jour *m* du Jugement dernier
(c) *Naut* estime *f*
reclaim [rɪˈkleɪm] **1** *vt* **(a)** *(land → gen)* mettre en valeur; *(→ from undergrowth)* défricher; *(→ marsh)* assécher; **they have reclaimed 1,000 hectares of land from the forest/marshes** ils ont défriché 1000 hectares de forêt/asséché 1000 hectares de marais; **they have reclaimed 1,000 hectares of land from the sea/the desert** ils ont gagné 1000 hectares de terres sur la mer/le désert
(b) *(salvage)* récupérer; *(recycle)* recycler
(c) *(deposit, baggage)* récupérer, réclamer; *(tax, expenses)* se faire rembourser; **to reclaim sth from sb** récupérer qch auprès de qn
(d) *Literary (sinner, drunkard)* ramener dans le droit chemin
(e) *(rehabilitate → term, word)* se réapproprier
(f) *Ind (rubber etc)* régénérer; *(by-product)* récupérer
2 *n* **to be past** *or* **beyond reclaim** être irrécupérable
reclaimable [rɪˈkleɪməbəl] *adj (land)* amendable; *(waste → for salvage)* récupérable; *(→ for recycling)* recyclable
reclamation [ˌrekləˈmeɪʃən] *n* **(a)** *(of land → gen)* remise *f* en valeur; *(→ from forest)* défrichement *m*; *(→ from sea, marsh)* assèchement *m*, drainage *m*; *(→ from desert)* reconquête *f*
(b) *(salvage)* récupération *f*; *(recycling)* recyclage *m*
(c) *(of tax, expenses)* remboursement *m*
(d) *Ind (of rubber etc)* régénération *f*; *(of by-product)* récupération *f*
reclassification [ˌriːklæsɪfɪˈkeɪʃən] *n* reclassement *m*
reclassify [ˌriːˈklæsɪfaɪ] *(pt & pp* **reclassified***) vt* reclasser
reclinate [ˈreklɪneɪt] *adj Bot* récliné
recline [rɪˈklaɪn] **1** *vt* **(a)** *(head)* appuyer **(b)** *(seat)* baisser, incliner
2 *vi* **(a)** *(be stretched out)* être allongé, être étendu; *(lie back)* s'allonger; **he was reclining on the sofa** il était allongé *ou* étendu sur le canapé **(b)** *(seat)* être inclinable, avoir un dossier inclinable
recliner [rɪˈklaɪnə(r)] *n (for sunbathing)* chaise *f* longue; *(armchair)* fauteuil *m* à dossier inclinable, fauteuil *m* relax
reclining [rɪˈklaɪnɪŋ] *adj (seat)* inclinable, à dossier inclinable; **to be in a reclining position** *(person)* être en position allongée *ou* couchée; *(seat)* être incliné
▸▸ ***reclining chair*** chaise *f* longue
recluse [rɪˈkluːs] *n* reclus(e) *m,f*; **to live like a recluse** vivre en reclus *ou* en ermite; **she's a bit of a recluse** elle aime la solitude
reclusive [rɪˈkluːsɪv] *adj* reclus
recode [ˌriːˈkəʊd] *vt* recoder, rechiffrer; *Comput* reprogrammer
recognition [ˌrekəgˈnɪʃən] *n* **(a)** *(identification)* reconnaissance *f*; **she disguised her voice to avoid recognition** elle déguisa sa voix pour ne pas être reconnue; **he gave no sign of recognition** il n'a pas eu l'air de me/le/*etc* reconnaître; **the town has changed beyond** *or* **out of all recognition** la ville est méconnaissable; **she's changed him beyond** *or* **out of all recognition** elle l'a changé du tout au tout; *Comput* **optical/speech/character recognition** reconnaissance *f* optique/de la parole/de caractères
(b) *(acknowledgment, thanks)* reconnaissance *f*; **in recognition of** en reconnaissance de
(c) *(appreciation)* **to win** *or* **to achieve recognition** être (enfin) reconnu; **to seek recognition (for oneself)** chercher à être reconnu; **his play received little recognition** sa pièce est passée quasi inaperçue; **a composer who received no recognition during his lifetime** un compositeur

méconnu de son vivant; **public recognition** la reconnaissance du public

(**d**) *(realization → of problem)* reconnaissance *f*; **there is a growing recognition that this is a serious social problem** de plus en plus de gens reconnaissent qu'il s'agit là d'un grave problème social; **the report led to the recognition that there is indeed a problem** le rapport nous a amenés à reconnaître qu'il y a effectivement un problème

(**e**) *(of state, organization, trade union)* reconnaissance *f*; **to withhold recognition from** *(government)* refuser de reconnaître

►► *Mktg* ***recognition score*** score *m* de reconnaissance; *Mktg* ***recognition test*** test *m* de reconnaissance

recognizable [ˈrekəg,naɪzəbəl] *adj* reconnaissable; **she was barely recognizable as the woman he had known twenty years before** il reconnaissait à peine la femme qu'il avait rencontrée vingt ans auparavant; **his style was instantly recognizable** son style était immédiatement reconnaissable

recognizably [ˈrekəg,naɪzəblɪ] *adv* d'une manière *ou* d'une façon reconnaissable; **the car was not recognizably Japanese** on n'aurait pas dit une voiture japonaise, cette voiture ne ressemblait pas à une voiture japonaise

recognizance [rɪˈkɒgnɪzəns] *n Law (bond)* engagement *m*; *(monies)* caution *f*; **to enter into recognizances for sb** *(with money)* verser une caution pour qn; *(personally)* se porter garant de qn; **to be released on one's own recognizances** être remis en liberté sur engagement personnel

recognize, -ise [ˈrekəgnaɪz] *vt* (**a**) *(identify → person, place, voice etc)* reconnaître; **you'll recognize him by his hat** vous le reconnaîtrez à son chapeau; **they recognized him for what he was** ils le reconnurent pour ce qu'il était

(**b**) *(acknowledge → person)* reconnaître les talents de; *(→ achievement)* reconnaître; *Sport (record)* homologuer; **to recognize sb as king** reconnaître qn comme *ou* en tant que roi

(**c**) *(be aware of, admit)* reconnaître; **I recognize (that) I made a mistake** je reconnais *ou* j'admets que je me suis trompé; **the scale of the disaster has finally been recognized** on a fini par se rendre compte de l'étendue du désastre; **he can certainly recognize a good business opportunity** il sait repérer les bonnes affaires

(**d**) *Admin & Pol (state, diploma)* reconnaître

(**e**) *Am (in debate)* donner la parole à

(**f**) *Comput* reconnaître

recognized [ˈrekəgnaɪzd] *adj* (**a**) *(acknowledged)* reconnu, admis; **it is a recognized fact that...** c'est un fait avéré *ou* reconnu que...+ *indicative*; **she's a recognized authority on medieval history** c'est une autorité en histoire médiévale

(**b**) *(official)* officiel, attitré; **that's not the recognized legal term** ce n'est pas le terme juridique officiel

►► *Com* ***recognized agent*** agent *m* accrédité; *Fin* ***recognized investment exchange*** marché *m* d'investissement agréé; ***recognized professional body*** = organisme professionnel agréé

recoil 1 *vi* [rɪˈkɔɪl] (**a**) *(person)* reculer, avoir un mouvement de recul; **she recoiled in horror** horrifiée, elle recula; **to recoil from doing sth** reculer devant l'idée de faire qch

(**b**) *(firearm)* reculer; *(spring)* se détendre; *Fig* **the plan was bound to recoil on him** il était à prévoir que le plan se retournerait contre lui

2 *n* [ˈriːkɔɪl] (**a**) *(of gun)* recul *m*; *(of spring)* détente *f*

(**b**) *(of person)* mouvement *m* de recul; *Fig* répugnance *f*

recoilless, *Am* **recoiless** [ˈriːkɔɪlɪs] *adj Mil & Tech* sans recul

recollect [,rekəˈlekt] **1** *vt* (**a**) *(remember)* se souvenir de, se rappeler; **I don't recollect having asked her** je ne me rappelle pas le lui avoir demandé; **she was unable to recollect what had happened** elle était incapable de se souvenir de ce qui s'était passé

(**b**) *Literary (gather → courage)* rassembler; **to recollect oneself** se ressaisir

2 *vi* se souvenir; **as far as I (can) recollect** autant que je m'en souvienne, autant qu'il m'en souvienne

recollection [,rekəˈlekʃən] *n (memory)* souvenir *m*; **I have no recollection of it** je n'en ai aucun souvenir; **I have a slight recollection of it** je n'en ai qu'un vague souvenir; **to the best of my recollection** (pour) autant que je m'en souvienne

recolonization [,riːkɒlənaɪˈzeɪʃən] *n* établissement *m* d'une nouvelle colonie (**of** dans)

recolonize, -ise [,riːˈkɒlənaɪz] *vt* établir une nouvelle colonie dans, rétablir une colonie dans

recombinant [rɪˈkɒmbɪnənt] *adj Biol*

►► ***recombinant DNA*** ADN *m* recombinant; ***recombinant technology*** recombinaison *f* génétique

recombination [,riːkɒmbɪˈneɪʃən] *n Biol & Phys* recombinaison *f*

recommence [,riːkəˈmens] **1** *vi* recommencer

2 *vt* recommencer

recommend [,rekəˈmend] *vt* (**a**) *(speak in favour of)* recommander (**to/for** à/pour); **she recommended him for the job** elle l'a recommandé pour cet emploi; **I'll recommend you to the Minister** j'appuierai votre candidature auprès du ministre; **the book has been highly recommended to me** le livre m'a été fortement recommandé; **it's a restaurant I can thoroughly recommend** c'est un restaurant que je recommande vivement; **the town has little to recommend it** la ville est sans grand intérêt; **the proposal has a lot to recommend it** la proposition a beaucoup d'avantages *ou* d'attrait

(**b**) *(advise)* recommander, conseiller; **I recommend you (to) see the film** je vous recommande *ou* conseille d'aller voir ce film; **not (to be) recommended** à déconseiller; **recommended** *(in film or book review etc)* à voir/lire/*etc*

(**c**) *Arch or Formal (entrust)* recommander; **to recommend one's soul to God** recommander son âme à Dieu; **the orphans were recommended to the care of their grandmother** les orphelins ont été confiés à leur grand-mère

►► *Com & Mktg* ***recommended retail price*** prix *m* recommandé *ou* conseillé

recommendable [,rekəˈmendəbəl] *adj* recommandable

recommendation [,rekəmenˈdeɪʃən] *n* (**a**) *(personal)* recommandation *f*; **on your/his recommendation** sur votre/sa recommandation; **my recommendation is that...** ce que je recommande *ou* conseille c'est que...+ *subjunctive*

(**b**) *(of committee, advisory body)* recommandation *f*; **to make a recommendation** faire une recommandation

(**c**) *(commendation)* recommandation *f*; **the hotel's sole recommendation is its location** l'emplacement de l'hôtel est son seul intérêt

recommendatory [,rekəˈmendətrɪ] *adj (letter)* de recommandation

recommit [,riːkəˈmɪt] *vt* (**a**) *Am Pol (bill)* renvoyer devant une commission (**b**) *(prisoner)* réincarcérer (**c**) *(crime)* commettre une nouvelle fois

recommittal [,riːkəˈmɪtəl] *n Am Pol* renvoi *m* devant une commission

recompense [ˈrekəmpens] **1** *n* (**a**) *(reward)* récompense *f*; **in recompense for your trouble** en récompense de *ou* pour vous récompenser de votre peine (**b**) *Law (compensation)* dédommagement *m*, compensation *f*

2 *vt* récompenser; **to recompense sb for sth** *(gen)* récompenser qn de qch; *Law* dédommager qn de *ou* pour qch

recompose [,riːkəmˈpəʊz] *vt* (**a**) *(text)* réécrire; *(print)* recomposer (**b**) *(calm)* **to recompose oneself** se ressaisir

recompute [,riːkəmˈpjuːt] *vt* recalculer

reconcilable [ˈrekənsaɪləbəl] *adj (opinions)* conciliable, compatible; *(people)* compatible

reconcile [ˈrekənsaɪl] *vt* (**a**) *(people)* réconcilier; *(ideas, opposing principles)* concilier; **Peter and Jane are reconciled at last** Peter et Jane se sont enfin réconciliés; **you cannot reconcile morality with politics** on ne saurait concilier moralité et politique

(**b**) *(resign)* **to reconcile oneself** *or* **to become reconciled to sth** se résigner à qch; **she reconciled herself to the idea of going** elle s'est faite à l'idée de partir

(**c**) *(win over)* **to reconcile sb to sth** faire accepter qch à qn

(**d**) *(settle → dispute)* régler

(**e**) *Fin (figures, bank statements)* rapprocher; *Acct (accounts, entries)* faire cadrer, faire accorder

reconciliation [,rekənsɪlɪˈeɪʃən] *n* (**a**) *(between people)* réconciliation *f*; *(of ideas, opinions, principles)* conciliation *f* (**b**) *Fin (of figures, bank statements)* rapprochement *m*; *Acct (of accounts, entries)* ajustement *m*

►► *Fin* ***reconciliation account*** compte *m* collectif; *Acct* ***reconciliation statement*** état *m* de rapprochement

recondite [ˈrekəndaɪt] *adj Formal* (**a**) *(obscure → text, style)* abscons, obscur; *(→ writer)* obscur; *(→ taste)* ésotérique (**b**) *(profound)* profond

reconditeness [ˈrekəndaɪtnɪs] *n* (**a**) *(obscurity)* caractère *m* abscons, obscurité *f* (**b**) *(profundity)* profondeur *f*, sens *m* profond

recondition [,riːkənˈdɪʃən] *vt* remettre en état *ou* à neuf

reconditioned [,riːkənˈdɪʃənd] *adj* remis à neuf; *Br (tyre)* rechapé

►► *Aut* ***reconditioned engine*** (moteur *m*) échange *m* standard

reconditioning [,riːkənˈdɪʃənɪŋ] *n* remise *f* en état *ou* à neuf

reconfiguration [,riːkənfɪgəˈreɪʃən] *n Comput* reconfiguration *f*

reconfigure [,riːkənˈfɪgə(r)] *vt Comput* reconfigurer

reconfirm [,riːkənˈfɜːm] *vt (booking)* confirmer; *(opinion, decision)* réaffirmer

reconnaissance [rɪˈkɒnɪsəns] *n Mil* reconnaissance *f*; **to be on reconnaissance** être en reconnaissance; **aerial reconnaissance** reconnaissance *f* aérienne; **reconnaissance flight/mission** vol *m*/mission *f* de reconnaissance

reconnect [,riːkəˈnekt] *vt* rebrancher; **to reconnect the water supply** rétablir l'alimentation en eau; *Tel* **the operator reconnected us** l'opérateur a rétabli la communication; **the telephone company reconnected us** la compagnie de téléphone nous a reconnectés

reconnection [,riːkəˈnekʃən] *n (of cable, telephone etc)* rebranchement *m*; *(of pipe)* raccordement *m*; *(of water supply, telephone call)* rétablissement *m*

►► *Tel* ***reconnection charge*** frais *mpl* de rebranchement

reconnoitre, *Am* **reconnoiter** [,rekəˈnɔɪtə(r)] **1** *vt Mil* reconnaître

2 *vi* effectuer une reconnaissance

reconquer [,riːˈkɒŋkə(r)] *vt* reconquérir

reconquest [,riːˈkɒŋkwest] *n* reconquête *f*

reconsider [,riːkənˈsɪdə(r)] **1** *vt (decision, problem)* réexaminer; *(topic)* se repencher sur; *(judgment)* réviser, revoir

2 *vi* reconsidérer la question; **I advise you to reconsider** je vous conseille de revoir votre position

reconsideration [ˈriːkən,sɪdəˈreɪʃən] *n (reexamination)* nouvel examen *m*, nouveau regard *m*; *(of judgment)* révision *f*

reconstitute [,riːˈkɒnstɪtjuːt] *vt* reconstituer

reconstituted [,riːˈkɒnstɪtjuːtɪd] *adj* reconstitué; **reconstituted vegetable protein** protéine *f* végétale reconstituée

reconstitution [ˈriː,kɒnstɪˈtjuːʃən] *n* reconstitution *f*

reconstruct [,riːkənˈstrʌkt] *vt* (**a**) *(make again → house, bridge)* reconstruire, rebâtir (**b**) *(form picture of → crime, event)* reconstituer; *(→ government, system)* reconstituer; *(→ one's life, a country)* reconstruire

reconstructed [,riːkənˈstrʌktɪd] *adj (modern → politician, feminist, man)* moderne

reconstruction [,riːkənˈstrʌkʃən] *n* (**a**) *(of demolished building)* reconstruction *f*; *(of old building)* reconstitution *f*; *(of façade, shop)* réfection *f* (**b**) *(of crime, event, government)* reconstitution *f*; *(of economy)* restauration *f*; *Am Hist* **the Reconstruction** la Reconstruction

THE RECONSTRUCTION

On désigne ainsi la période allant de 1865 à 1876, succédant à la guerre de Sécession et pendant laquelle les États de l'ex-Confédération (États sudistes) étaient réintégrés dans l'Union à condition d'avoir adopté les trois amendements à la Constitution fédérale. Ces amendements précisaient les droits des Noirs et stipulaient l'élimination des Confédérés de toute activité politique et administrative.

reconstructive surgery [ˌriːkənˈstrʌktɪv-] *n* chirurgie *f* réparatrice

reconvene [ˌriːkənˈviːn] **1** *vt* reconvoquer

2 *vi* se réunir à nouveau; **the meeting reconvenes at three** la réunion reprend à trois heures

reconversion [ˌriːkənˈvɜːʃən] *n* reconversion *f*

reconvert [ˌriːkənˈvɜːt] *vt* reconvertir

recopy [ˌriːˈkɒpɪ] (*pt & pp* **recopied**) *vt* recopier

RECORD

rapport	► **1 (a)**
dossier	► **1 (a), (b)**
procès-verbal	► **1 (a)**
antécédents	► **1 (b)**
disque	► **1 (c)**
record	► **1 (d); 3**
noter	► **4 (a)**
enregistrer	► **4 (a) – (c); 5**
rapporter	► **4 (a)**
marquer	► **4 (b), (d)**

1 *n* [ˈrekɔːd] (**a**) *(account, report)* rapport *m*; *(file)* dossier *m*; *(note)* note *f*; *(of attendance)* registre *m*; *(of proceedings, debate)* procès-verbal *m*, compte rendu *m*; **records** *(of government, police, hospital)* archives *fpl*; *(of learned society)* actes *mpl*; **to make a record of sth** noter qch; *Law* **to strike sth from the record** rayer qch du procès-verbal; **they keep a record of all deposits/all comings and goings** ils enregistrent tous les versements/toutes les allées et venues; **there is no record of their visit** il n'existe aucune trace de leur visite; **do you have any record of the transaction?** avez-vous gardé une trace de la transaction?; **there's no record of it anywhere** ce n'est mentionné nulle part; **the apparatus gives a permanent record of ground movements** l'appareil enregistre en permanence les mouvements du sol; **the book provides a record of 19th-century Parisian society** le livre évoque la société parisienne du XIXème siècle; **the carvings are a record of civilization on the island** les sculptures témoignent de l'existence d'une civilisation sur l'île; **the wettest June since records began** le mois de juin le plus humide depuis que l'on tient des statistiques; **public records office** archives *fpl* nationales; **police accident records** liste *f* des accidents enregistrés par la police; **a newspaper of record** un journal qui fait autorité; **to put** *or* **to set the record straight** mettre les choses au clair

(**b**) *(past history)* passé *m*, antécédents *mpl*; *(reputation)* réputation *f*; *(criminal or police file)* casier *m* (judiciaire); **his past record** *(behaviour)* ses antécédents; *(achievements)* ses résultats antérieurs; **his past record with the firm** son passé dans l'entreprise; **given your record as a late payer** vu vos antécédents de mauvais payeur; **she has an excellent attendance record** elle a été très assidue, elle n'a presque jamais été absente; **the plane has a good safety record** l'avion est réputé pour sa sécurité; **the makers have an excellent record for high quality** les fabricants sont très réputés pour l'excellente qualité de leurs produits; **to have a (criminal) record** avoir un casier judiciaire; **to have a clean record** avoir un casier judiciaire vierge; **he has a record of previous convictions** il a déjà été condamné; **case record** *Med* dossier *m* médical; *Law* dossier *m* judiciaire; *Mil* **service** *or* **army record** états *mpl* de service; **school record** dossier *m* scolaire

(**c**) *(disc)* disque *m*; *(recording)* enregistrement *m*; **to play** *or* **to put on a record** mettre *ou* passer un disque; **to make** *or* **to cut a record** faire *ou* graver un disque

(**d**) *(gen) & Sport* record *m*; **to set/to break a record** établir/battre un record; **to hold the record (for)** détenir le record (de); **the 200 m record** le record du 200 m

(**e**) *Comput (in database)* article *m*, enregistrement *m*

2 *comp* [ˈrekɔːd] *(shop, collector)* de disques

3 *adj* [ˈrekɔːd] *(summer, temperature)* record *(inv)*; **in record time** en un temps record; **to reach record levels** atteindre un niveau record; **a record number of spectators** une affluence record; **a record score** un score record; **unemployment is at a record high/low** le chômage a atteint son chiffre le plus haut/bas

4 *vt* [rɪˈkɔːd] (**a**) *(take note of → fact, complaint, detail)* noter, enregistrer, consigner; *(→ in archives, on computer)* enregistrer; *(give account of → events)* attester, rapporter; *(→ thoughts, ideas)* noter (par écrit), consigner, mettre sur papier; *Law (judgment)* minuter; **your objection has been recorded** nous avons pris acte de votre objection; **to record the minutes** *or* **the proceedings of a meeting** faire le procès-verbal *ou* le compte rendu d'une réunion; **no biography records the visit** aucune biographie ne fait mention de *ou* n'atteste la visite; **the debate was recorded in the newsletter** le débat a été rapporté dans le bulletin d'informations; **their answer was not recorded** leur réponse n'a pas été enregistrée; **a photograph was taken to record the event** une photographie a été prise pour rappeler cet événement; **the book records life in medieval England** le livre dépeint *ou* évoque la vie en Angleterre au Moyen Âge; **history records that 30,000 soldiers took part** selon les livres d'histoire, 30 000 soldats y ont participé; *Parl* **to record a vote** *(MP)* voter; **how many votes were recorded?** combien de voix ont été exprimées?

(**b**) *(register → of equipment)* enregistrer; *(→ of dial, gauge)* indiquer, marquer; **the thermometer records 10°** le thermomètre marque 10°; **temperatures of 50° were recorded** on a relevé des températures de 50°

(**c**) *(music, tape, TV programme)* enregistrer; **the group are in the studio recording their new album** le groupe est dans le studio en train d'enregistrer son nouveau disque

(**d**) *Sport (score)* marquer; **he recorded a time of 10.7 seconds for the 100 metres** il a couru le 100 m en 10,7 secondes

5 *vi* [rɪˈkɔːd] *(on tape, video)* enregistrer; **leave the video, it's recording** laisse le magnétoscope, il est en train d'enregistrer; **his voice doesn't record well** sa voix ne se prête pas bien à l'enregistrement

6 for the record *adv* pour mémoire, pour la petite histoire; **just for the record, you started it!** je te signale au passage que c'est toi qui as commencé!

7 off the record 1 *adj* confidentiel; **I want these remarks to be off the record** je veux que ces remarques restent confidentielles; **the negotiations were off the record** *(secret)* les négociations étaient secrètes; *(unofficial)* les négociations étaient officieuses; *(not reported)* les négociations n'ont pas été rapportées (dans la presse); *(not recorded)* les négociations n'ont pas été enregistrées; **all this is strictly off the record** tout ceci doit rester strictement entre nous **2** *adv* **he admitted off the record that he had known** il a admis en privé qu'il était au courant

8 on record *adv* enregistré; **it's on record that you were informed** il est établi que vous étiez au courant; **we have it on record that...** il est attesté *ou* établi que... + *indicative*; **it isn't on record** il n'y en a aucune trace; **to put** *or* **to place sth on record** *(say)* dire *ou* déclarer qch officiellement; *(write)* consigner qch par écrit; **I wish to go on record as saying that...** je voudrais dire officiellement *ou* publiquement que... + *indicative*; **it's the wettest June on record** c'est le mois de juin le plus humide que l'on ait connu; **it's the only example on record** c'est le seul exemple connu

►► ***record buff*** discophile *mf*; ***record cabinet*** discothèque *f (meuble)*; ***record card*** fiche *f*; ***record company*** maison *f* de disques; ***record deck*** platine *f* (tourne-disque); ***record holder*** *(man)* recordman *m*, détenteur *m* d'un record; *(woman)* recordwoman *f*, détentrice *f* d'un record; ***record label*** label *m*; ***record library*** discothèque *f (de prêt)*; ***record player*** tourne-disque *m*, platine *f* (disques); ***record producer*** producteur *m* de disques; ***record token*** chèque-disque *m*

record-breaker *n Sport (man)* nouveau recordman *m*; *(woman)* nouvelle recordwoman *f*; *Br Fig* **the new product is a record-breaker** le nouveau produit bat tous les records

record-breaking *adj* (**a**) *Sport* **a record-breaking jump** un saut qui a établi un nouveau record (**b**) *(year, temperatures)* record *(inv)*

record-changer *n* changeur *m* de disques (automatique)

recorded [rɪˈkɔːdɪd] *adj* (**a**) *(music, message, tape)* enregistré; *(programme)* préenregistré; *(broadcast)* transmis en différé

(**b**) *(fact)* attesté, noté; *(history)* écrit; *(votes)* exprimé; **throughout recorded history** pendant toute la période couverte pour laquelle on dispose de documents écrits

►► *Br* ***recorded delivery*** recommandé *m*; **to send sth (by) recorded delivery** envoyer qch en recommandé avec accusé de réception; ***recorded highlights*** *(on TV)* extraits *mpl* préenregistrés

recorder [rɪˈkɔːdə(r)] *n* (**a**) *(apparatus)* enregistreur *m* (**b**) *(musical instrument)* flûte *f* à bec (**c**) *(keeper of records)* archiviste *mf*; *Law* **court recorder** greffier *m* (**d**) *Br Law* = avocat nommé à la fonction de magistrat (à temps partiel)

recording [rɪˈkɔːdɪŋ] **1** *n (of music, data)* enregistrement *m*; **this is a very poor recording** cet enregistrement est très mauvais; **a mono recording** un enregistrement (en) mono

2 *comp* (**a**) *Mus & TV (equipment, session)* d'enregistrement; *(company)* de disques; *(star)* du disque

(**b**) *(indicating → apparatus)* enregistreur

(**c**) *Admin & Law (official, clerk → in census)* chargé du recensement; *(→ in court of law)* qui enregistre les débats

►► *Bible & Fig* ***Recording Angel*** = l'ange qui tient le livre des actes (bons et mauvais) de chacun; ***recording artist*** musicien(enne) *m,f* qui enregistre des disques; **she's a recording artist for Phonolog** elle enregistre (des disques) chez Phonolog; ***recording engineer*** ingénieur *m* du son; ***recording head*** tête *f* d'enregistrement; ***recording studio*** studio *m* d'enregistrement; ***recording tape*** ruban *m ou* bande *f* d'enregistrement

recork [ˌriːˈkɔːk] *vt* reboucher

recount [rɪˈkaʊnt] *vt (story, experience)* raconter

re-count 1 *vt* [ˌriːˈkaʊnt] *(count again)* recompter, compter de nouveau

2 *n* [ˈriːkaʊnt] *Pol* nouveau décompte *m*; **to demand a re-count** exiger un nouveau décompte; **there were four re-counts** on a compté le nombre de bulletins de vote à quatre reprises

recoup [rɪˈkuːp] *vt* (**a**) *(get back → losses, cost)* récupérer; **to recoup one's investments** rentrer dans ses fonds; **to recoup one's costs** rentrer dans *ou* couvrir ses frais (**b**) *(pay back)* rembourser, dédommager (**c**) *Law (deduct)* défalquer, déduire

recoupment [rɪˈkuːpmənt] *n* (**a**) *(reimbursement)* dédommagement *m* (**b**) *Law (deduction)* défalcation *f*, décompte *m*

recourse [rɪˈkɔːs] *n* (**a**) *(gen)* recours *m*; **to have recourse to sth** recourir à qch, avoir recours à qch; **right of recourse** droit *m* de recours (**b**) *Fin* recours *m*; **endorsement without recourse** endossement *m* à forfait

recover [rɪˈkʌvə(r)] **1** *vt* (**a**) *(get back → property)* récupérer, retrouver; *(→ debt, loan, deposit)* récupérer, recouvrer; *(take back)* reprendre; *(regain → territory, ball)* regagner; *(→ control, hearing)* retrouver; *(→ advantage)* reprendre; **50 bodies have been recovered** 50 corps ont été retrouvés; **to recover one's breath/footing** reprendre haleine/pied; **to recover one's balance** retrouver son équilibre; **to recover one's composure** se ressaisir; **to recover consciousness** reprendre connaissance; **to recover one's health** guérir, se rétablir, recouvrer la santé; **to recover one's strength** reprendre des forces; *also Fig* **to recover lost ground** regagner du terrain; **to recover one's expenses** rentrer dans ses fonds

(**b**) *(salvage → wreck, waste)* récupérer; *(→ from water)* récupérer, repêcher

(**c**) *Law* **to recover damages** obtenir des dommages-intérêts

(**d**) *(extract → from ore)* extraire

(**e**) *Comput (file, data)* récupérer

2 *vi* (**a**) *(after accident, shock, setback)* se remettre; *(after illness)* se rétablir, guérir; **the patient is recovering in hospital** le malade se remet à l'hôpital; **to recover from sth** se remettre de qch; **to be fully recovered** être complètement guéri *ou* rétabli; **I still haven't recovered from the shock** je ne me suis pas encore remis du choc

(**b**) *(currency, economy)* se redresser; *(market)* reprendre, se redresser; *(prices, shares)* se redresser, remonter

(**c**) *Law* gagner son procès, obtenir gain de cause

re-cover [,riː'-] *vt (chair etc)* recouvrir

recoverable [rɪ'kʌvrəbəl] *adj (debt)* recouvrable; *(losses, mistake)* réparable; *(by-product)* récupérable

recovery [rɪ'kʌvərɪ] (*pl* **recoveries**) *n* (**a**) *(of lost property, wreck)* récupération *f*; *(of debt)* recouvrement *m*, récupération *f*; *(of money, deposit)* récupération *f*; **the recovery of his sight changed his life** le fait de recouvrer la vue a transformé sa vie

(**b**) *(from illness)* rétablissement *m*, guérison *f*; **to make a speedy recovery** se remettre vite; **to be on the way** *or* **road to recovery** être en voie de guérison; **she is making a good recovery** elle est en bonne voie de guérison; **he is past** *or* **beyond recovery** *(patient)* on ne peut plus rien faire pour lui, il est dans un état désespéré

(**c**) *(of economy)* relance *f*, redressement *m*; *(of prices, shares)* redressement *m*, remontée *f*; *(of currency)* redressement *m*; *(of market, business)* reprise *f*; *Sport* **to stage** *or* **to make a recovery** reprendre le dessus; **the country made a slow recovery after the war** le pays s'est rétabli lentement après la guerre; **to be past** *or* **beyond recovery** *(situation)* être irrémédiable *ou* sans espoir; *(loss)* être irrécupérable *ou* irréparable

(**d**) *(of wreck, waste)* récupération *f*; *(from water)* récupération *f*, repêchage *m*

(**e**) *Comput (of file, data)* récupération *f*

(**f**) *Law (of damages)* obtention *f*

►► ***recovery plan*** plan *m* de redressement; *Med* ***recovery position*** position *f* latérale de sécurité; *Am* ***recovery program*** = programme d'aide aux personnes souffrant d'une accoutumance; *Med* ***recovery room*** salle *f* de réanimation; *Br Aut* ***recovery service*** service *m* de dépannage; ***recovery ship*** navire *m* de récupération; *Br* ***recovery vehicle*** dépanneuse *f*; ***recovery vessel*** navire *m* de récupération

recreant ['rekrɪənt] *Arch* **1** *adj (cowardly)* lâche; *(disloyal)* perfide, déloyal

2 *n (coward)* lâche *mf*; *(turncoat)* renégat(e) *m,f*

re-create [,riː-] *vt (past event)* reconstituer; *(place, scene)* recréer

recreation [,rekrɪ'eɪʃən] **1** *n* (**a**) *(relaxation)* récréation *f*, détente *f*; **she only reads for** *or* **as recreation** elle ne lit que pour se délasser *ou* se détendre

(**b**) *Sch* récréation *f*

2 *comp (activities, facilities)* de loisirs

►► ***recreation area*** aire *f* de jeux; ***recreation centre*** centre *m* de loisirs; *Br* ***recreation ground*** terrain *m* de jeux; ***recreation room*** *(in school, hospital)* salle *f* de récréation; *(in hotel)* salle *f* de jeux; *Am (at home)* salle *f* de jeux

re-creation [,riː-] *n (of event, scene)* recréation *f*, reconstitution *f*

recreational [,rekrɪ'eɪʃənəl] *adj (activities, facilities)* de loisirs

►► ***recreational drug*** drogue *f* à usage récréatif; ***recreational therapy*** thérapie *f* par le jeu; *Am* ***recreational vehicle*** camping-car *m*

recriminate [rɪ'krɪmɪneɪt] *vt Formal* récriminer; **to recriminate against sb** récriminer contre qn

recrimination [rɪ,krɪmɪ'neɪʃən] *n (usu pl)* **recriminations** récriminations *fpl*

recriminatory [rɪ'krɪmɪnətrɪ] *adj Formal* récriminateur

recrudesce [,riːkruː'des] *vi Formal* réapparaître

recrudescence [,riːkruː'desəns] *n Formal* recrudescence *f*

recrudescent [,riːkruː'desənt] *adj Formal* recrudescent

recruit [rɪ'kruːt] **1** *n (gen) & Mil* recrue *f*

2 *vt (member, army)* recruter; *(worker)* recruter, embaucher

recruiter [rɪ'kruːtə(r)] *n* recruteur(euse) *m,f*

recruiting [rɪ'kruːtɪŋ] *n* recrutement *m*

►► ***recruiting office*** bureau *m* de recrutement; ***recruiting officer*** *Mil* recruteur(euse) *m,f*; *Hist* racoleur *m*; *Mil* ***recruiting sergeant*** sergent *m* recruteur

recruitment [rɪ'kruːtmənt] *n* recrutement *m*

►► *Br* ***recruitment agency*** cabinet *m* de recrutement; ***recruitment campaign*** campagne *f* de recrutement; ***recruitment consultant*** conseil *m* en recrutement; ***recruitment drive*** campagne *f* de recrutement; ***recruitment officer*** recruteur(euse) *m,f*

recrystallization [,riːkrɪstəlaɪ'zeɪʃən] *n* recristallisation *f*

recrystallize, -ise [,riː'krɪstəlaɪz] **1** *vt* recristalliser

2 *vi* recristalliser

rectal ['rektəl] *adj* rectal

►► ***rectal cancer*** cancer *m* du rectum; ***rectal examination*** examen *m* rectal *ou* du rectum

rectally ['rektəlɪ] *adv Med* par l'anus, par le rectum

rectangle ['rek,tæŋgəl] *n* rectangle *m*

rectangular [,rek'tæŋgjʊlə(r)] *adj* rectangulaire

rectifiable ['rektɪfaɪəbəl] *adj (gen) & Chem & Math* rectifiable, qui peut être rectifié; *Elec* qui peut être redressé

rectification [,rektɪfɪ'keɪʃən] *n* (**a**) *(correction)* rectification *f*, correction *f* (**b**) *Chem & Math* rectification *f*; *Elec* redressement *m* (**c**) *Acct (of entry)* modification *f*, rectification *f*

rectifier ['rektɪfaɪə(r)] *n* (**a**) *Elec* redresseur *m*; *Chem* rectificateur *m* (**b**) *(person)* correcteur(-trice) *m,f*

rectify ['rektɪfaɪ] (*pt & pp* **rectified**) *vt* (**a**) *(mistake)* rectifier, corriger; *(oversight)* réparer; *(situation)* redresser (**b**) *Chem & Math* rectifier; *Elec* redresser (**c**) *Acct (entry)* modifier, rectifier

rectilineal [,rektɪ'lɪnɪəl], **rectilinear** [,rektɪ'lɪnɪə(r)] *adj* rectiligne

rectitude ['rektɪtjuːd] *n* rectitude *f*; **moral rectitude** droiture *f*

recto ['rektəʊ] (*pl* **rectos**) *n Typ* recto *m*

rector ['rektə(r)] *n* (**a**) *Rel (Anglican, Presbyterian)* pasteur *m*; *(Catholic)* recteur *m* (**b**) *Scot Sch* proviseur *m*, directeur(trice) *m,f* (**c**) *Scot Univ* = personnalité élue par les étudiants pour les représenter

rectorial [rek'tɔːrɪəl] *adj (decision, duties)* rectoral

►► *Scot Univ* ***rectorial election*** = élection d'une personnalité dont le rôle est de représenter les étudiants

rectory ['rektərɪ] (*pl* **rectories**) *n* presbytère *m*

rectoscope ['rektəskəʊp] *n Med* rectoscope *m*

rectrix ['rektrɪks] *n Orn* penne *f* rectrice, rectrice *f*

rectum ['rektəm] (*pl* **rectums** *or* **recta** [-tə]) *n* rectum *m*

rectus ['rektəs] *n Anat* muscle *m* droit

recumbent [rɪ'kʌmbənt] *adj* couché, étendu, allongé

►► *Art* ***recumbent effigy*** *(on grave)* gisant *m*; *Art* ***recumbent figure*** figure *f* couchée, gisant *m*

recuperate [rɪ'kuːpəreɪt] **1** *vi* se remettre, récupérer; **to recuperate from sth** se remettre de qch; **he had gone to the South of France to recuperate** il était allé en convalescence dans le Midi; **she is still recuperating** elle est encore en convalescence

2 *vt (materials, money)* récupérer; *(loss)* compenser; *(strength)* reprendre

recuperation [rɪ,kuːpə'reɪʃən] *n* (**a**) *Med* rétablissement *m* (**b**) *(of materials)* récupération *f* (**c**) *Fin (of market)* reprise *f*

recuperative [rɪ'kuːpərətɪv] *adj (medicine)* régénérateur, reconstituant; *(rest)* réparateur; *(powers)* de récupération

recur [rɪ'kɜː(r)] (*pt & pp* **recurred**, *cont* **recurring**) *vi* (**a**) *(occur again → event)* se reproduire; *(reappear → theme, image)* réapparaître, revenir; **it's a notion which recurs every now and then** c'est une idée qui revient *ou* qu'on retrouve de temps en temps; **come back if the problem recurs** revenez si le problème réapparaît *ou* se représente

(**b**) *(to memory)* revenir à la mémoire

(**c**) *Math* se reproduire, se répéter

recurrence [rɪ'kʌrəns] *n (of mistake, notion, event)* répétition *f*; *(of disease, symptoms)* réapparition *f*; *(of theme)* répétition *f*, réapparition *f*; *(of subject, problem)* retour *m*; **there must be no recurrence of such behaviour** ce genre de comportement ne devra jamais se reproduire; **has there been any recurrence of the symptoms?** les symptômes se sont-ils manifestés à nouveau?

recurrent [rɪ'kʌrənt] *adj* (**a**) *(event)* périodique, qui revient *ou* se répète périodiquement; *(theme)* récurrent; *(dream, nightmare)* qui revient souvent; **I get recurrent headaches/bouts of flu** j'ai souvent des maux de tête/la grippe (**b**) *Anat & Med* récurrent

►► ***recurrent expenses*** *(gen)* dépenses *fpl* courantes; *Com* frais *mpl* généraux

recurring [rɪ'kɜːrɪŋ] *adj* (**a**) *(persistent → problem)* qui revient *ou* qui se reproduit souvent; *(→ dream, nightmare)* qui revient sans cesse (**b**) *Math* périodique; **2 point 7 recurring** 2 virgule 7 périodique

►► ***recurring decimal*** fraction *f* périodique

recursion [rɪ'kɜːʃən] *n* récurrence *f*

recursive [rɪ'kɜːsɪv] *adj* récursif

recusant ['rekjʊzənt] *Rel* **1** *adj* réfractaire

2 *n* rebelle *mf* à l'Église

recyclable [,riː'saɪkləbəl] *adj* recyclable

recycle [,riː'saɪkəl] *vt (materials)* recycler; *(money)* réinvestir; *(funds)* remettre en circulation

►► *Comput* **recycle bin** corbeille *f*

recycled [,riː'saɪkəld] *adj (materials)* recyclé

►► ***recycled paper*** papier *m* recyclé

recycling [,riː'saɪklɪŋ] *n* recyclage *m*; *(of funds)* remise *f* en circulation

►► ***recycling facility*** installation *f* de recyclage; ***recycling plant*** usine *f* de recyclage

red [red] (*compar* **redder**, *superl* **reddest**) **1** *adj* (**a**) *(gen)* rouge; *(hair, beard)* roux (rousse); **to turn** *or* **to go red** *(person, litmus paper)* rougir, devenir rouge; *(leaves)* roussir; *(sky)* rougeoyer; **wait till the lights turn red** attend que le feu passe au rouge; **red with anger/shame** rouge de colère/honte; **to take a red pen to sth** corriger qch à l'encre rouge; **to be red in the face** *(after effort)* avoir la figure toute rouge; *(with embarrassment)* être rouge de confusion; *(permanent state)* être rougeaud; **there will be some red faces on the Opposition benches** cela va causer de l'embarras dans les rangs de l'opposition; **to be as red as a beetroot** être rouge comme une pivoine; **to bring** *or* **to raise a metal to red heat** chauffer *ou* porter un métal au rouge; **to be as red as a lobster** *(with sunburn)* être rouge comme une écrevisse; *Prov* **red sky at night, shepherd's delight** = ciel rouge le soir est signe de beau temps; *Prov* **red sky in the morning, shepherd's warning** = ciel rouge le matin est signe de mauvais temps; *Am Fam* **it's not worth a red cent** ça ne vaut pas un clou *ou* un centime; *Literary* **hands red with the blood of martyrs** mains trempées dans le sang des martyrs

(**b**) *Fam (communist)* rouge

(**c**) *Am* **to go into red ink** *(person)* être à découvert; *(company)* être en déficit; *(account)* avoir un solde déficitaire

2 *n* (**a**) *(colour)* rouge *m*; **dressed in red** habillé en rouge; *Fam* **to see red** *(be angry)* voir rouge

(**b**) *(in roulette)* rouge *m*; *(in snooker)* (bille *f*) rouge *f*

(**c**) *(wine)* rouge *m*

(**d**) *Fam Pej (communist)* rouge *mf*, coco *mf*; **reds under the bed** = expression évoquant la psychose du communisme; **the reds-under-the-bed syndrome** la phobie anti-communiste

(**e**) *(deficit)* **to be in the red** *(person)* avoir un découvert, être dans le rouge; *(company)* être en déficit; *(account)* avoir un solde déficitaire; **to be £5,000 in the red** *(person)* avoir un découvert de 5000 livres; *(company)* avoir un déficit de 5000 livres; *(account)* avoir un solde déficitaire de 5000 livres; **to get out of the red** *(person)* combler son découvert; *(company)* sortir du rouge

►► *Entom* ***red admiral*** vulcain *m*; ***red alert*** alerte *f* rouge; **to be on red alert** être en état d'alerte maximale; *Entom* ***red ant*** fourmi *f* rouge; ***Red Army*** Armée *f* rouge; ***the Red Arrows*** = patrouille d'avions de chasse britannique spécialisée dans les spectacles de voltige aérienne; *Hist* ***the Red Baron*** le Baron rouge; ***the Red Berets*** = division des parachutistes de l'armée britannique; ***red blood cell*** globule *m* rouge, hématie *f*; *Acct & Fin* ***red bottom line*** solde *m* débiteur; ***red cabbage*** chou *m* rouge; ***red card*** *(in football, rugby)* carton *m* rouge, *Belg* carte *f* rouge; **to get** *or* **to receive the red card** recevoir le carton *ou Belg* la carte rouge; ***red carpet*** tapis *m* rouge; **to roll out the red carpet for sb** *(for VIP)* dérouler le tapis rouge en l'honneur de qn; *(for guest)* mettre les petits plats dans les grands en l'honneur de qn; **to give sb the red-carpet treatment** réserver un accueil fastueux *ou* princier à qn; *Bot* ***red cedar*** cèdre *m* rouge; ***red channel*** *(at airport etc)* file *f* pour les passagers qui ont des objets à déclarer à la douane; *Fam* ***Red China*** la Chine communiste *ou* populaire ❑; ***red corpuscle*** globule *m* rouge, hématie *f*; ***the Red Crescent*** le Croissant-Rouge; ***the Red Cross (Society)*** la Croix-Rouge; *Bot* ***red deadnettle*** ortie *f* pourpre; *Zool* ***red deer*** cerf *m* commun; ***Red Devils*** = équipe de parachutistes de l'armée britannique connue pour ses spectacles d'acrobatie aérienne; *Br Fam* ***red duster*** = pavillon de la marine marchande britannique; *Astron* ***red dwarf*** naine *f* rouge; ***Red Ensign*** = pavillon de la marine marchande britannique; *Phot* ***red eye*** *(UNCOUNT)* = phénomène provoquant l'apparition de taches rouges dans les yeux des personnes photographiées au flash; ***red flag*** drapeau *m* rouge; ***the Red Flag*** = hymne du parti travailliste britannique; *Zool* ***red fox*** renard *m* roux; *Astron* ***red giant*** géante *f* rouge; *Orn* ***red grouse*** lagopède *m* (rouge) d'Écosse; ***Red Guard*** garde *f* rouge; *Rel* ***red hat*** barrette *f (de cardinal)*; ***red herring*** *(fish)* hareng *m* saur; *Fig* diversion *f*; **it's just a red herring** ce n'est qu'un truc pour nous dépister *ou* pour brouiller les pistes; ***Red Indian*** Peau-Rouge *mf*; *Orn* ***red kite*** milan *m* royal; ***red lead*** minium *m*; *Culin* ***Red Leicester*** = fromage anglais à pâte pressée; *Aut* ***red light*** feu *m* rouge; **to go through a red light** passer au rouge, brûler le feu rouge; *Am* ***Red Light Green Light*** *(game)* ≃ 1,2,3... Soleil; ***red list*** = liste gouvernementale des produits illégaux; ***red meat*** viande *f* rouge; ***red mud*** boues *fpl* rouges; *Ich* ***red mullet*** rouget barbet *m*; ***Red Nose Day*** = au Royaume-Uni, journée d'action caritative organisée tous les deux ans par une association composée essentiellement de comiques (ainsi nommée en raison des nez rouges en plastique vendus à cette occasion); *Zool* ***red panda*** petit panda *m*; ***red pepper*** *(spice)* (poivre *m* de) cayenne *m*; *(vegetable)* poivron *m* rouge; ***the Red Planet*** *(Mars)* la planète rouge; *Bot* ***red rattle*** pédiculaire *m* des bois; ***the Red River*** la Red River; *Br* ***red route*** axe *m* rouge; *Am Hist* ***the Red Scare*** = vague de déportations d'immigrants suspectés de communisme organisée par le gouvernement américain dans les années 20; ***the Red Sea*** la mer Rouge; ***red setter*** setter *m* irlandais; *Hist* ***Red Shirts*** Chemises *fpl* rouges; *Ich* ***red snapper*** vivanneau *m*; ***red spider*** araignée *f* rouge; *Astron* ***Red Spot*** (Grande) Tache *f* rouge; ***Red Square*** la place Rouge; *Zool* ***red squirrel*** écureuil *m* roux; ***red tape*** *(bureaucracy)* paperasserie *f*; **there's too much red tape** il y a trop de paperasserie *ou* de bureaucratie; ***red tide*** marée *f* rouge

'The Red Badge of Courage' *Crane* 'La Conquête du courage'

redact [rɪ'dækt] *vt* **(a)** *(write)* rédiger **(b)** *(edit)* mettre au point

redaction [rɪ'dækʃən] *n* **(a)** *(writing)* rédaction *f* **(b)** *(editing)* mise *f* au point

redback ['redbæk] *n Entom* veuve *f* d'Australie

►► ***redback spider*** veuve *f* d'Australie

red-backed shrike [-,bækd-] *n Orn* pie-grièche *f* écorcheuse

red-billed hornbill [-,bɪld-] *n Orn* tock *m* à bec rouge

red-blooded [-'blʌdɪd] *adj* vigoureux, viril; **the average red-blooded male** n'importe quel homme digne de ce nom

redbreast ['redbrest] *n Orn* rouge-gorge *m*

red-breasted [-,brestɪd] *adj Orn*

►► ***red-breasted goose*** bernache *f* à cou roux; ***red-breasted merganser*** harle *m* huppé

red-brick *adj Br (building)* en brique rouge

redbrick university ['redbrɪk-] *n Br* = université de province (par opposition à Oxford et Cambridge) fondée à la fin du XIXème siècle

redbug ['redbʌg] *n Entom* chique *f*, puce *f* pénétrante

redcap ['redkæp] *n* **(a)** *Br Fam* policier *m* militaire ❑ **(b)** *Am Rail* porteur *m*

redcoat ['redkəʊt] *n Br* **(a)** *Hist* soldat *m* anglais **(b)** *(in holiday camp)* animateur(trice) *m,f*

red-crested pochard *n Orn* nette *f* rousse

redcurrant ['redkʌrənt] **1** *n* groseille *f* (rouge)

2 *(tart, sauce)* aux groseilles

►► ***redcurrant bush*** groseillier *m* rouge; ***redcurrant jelly*** gelée *f* de groseille

redden ['redən] **1** *vt* rougir, rendre rouge; *(hair)* teindre en roux

2 *vi (person, face)* rougir, devenir (tout) rouge; *(leaves)* devenir roux (rousse), roussir; **to redden with shame** rougir de honte

reddening ['redənɪŋ] *adj* rougissant, rougeoyant

reddish ['redɪʃ] *adj (light, colour)* rougeâtre; *(fur)* roussâtre; *(hair)* roussâtre, qui tire sur le roux

redeal *Cards* **1** *n* ['ri:di:l] redonne *f*

2 *vt* [,ri:'di:l] redonner, redistribuer

redecorate [,ri:'dekəreɪt] **1** *vt (gen → room, house)* refaire; *(repaint)* refaire les peintures de; *(re-wallpaper)* retapisser; **we're redecorating the flat** nous sommes en train de repeindre et de retapisser l'appartement

2 *vi (repaint)* refaire les peintures; *(re-wallpaper)* refaire les papiers peints

redecoration [ri:,dekə'reɪʃən] *n (painting)* remise *f* à neuf des peintures; *(wallpapering)* remise *f* à neuf des papiers peints

redeem [rɪ'di:m] *vt* **(a)** *(from pawn)* dégager, retirer

(b) *(cash → voucher)* encaisser; *(→ share)* réaliser, racheter; *(exchange → coupon, savings stamps)* échanger; *(→ banknote)* compenser

(c) *(annuity, mortgage)* rembourser; *(debt)* amortir, se libérer de; *(bill)* honorer; *(loan)* rembourser, amortir

(d) *(make up for → mistake, failure)* racheter, réparer; *(→ crime, sin)* expier; **to redeem oneself** se racheter

(e) *(save → situation, position)* sauver; *(→ loss)* récupérer, réparer; *(→ honour)* sauver; *Rel (→ sinner)* racheter

(f) *(fulfil → promise)* s'acquitter de, tenir; *(→ obligation)* satisfaire à, s'acquitter de

(g) *(free → slave)* racheter

redeemable [rɪ'di:məbəl] *adj* **(a)** *(loan, mortgage)* remboursable; *(voucher)* encaissable; *(share)* réalisable, rachetable; *(debt)* remboursable, amortissable; **the stamps are not redeemable for cash** les timbres ne peuvent être échangés contre des espèces **(b)** *(mistake)* réparable; *(sin, crime)* expiable; *(sinner)* rachetable

redeemer [rɪ'di:mə(r)] *n Rel & Fig* rédempteur *m*

redeeming [rɪ'di:mɪŋ] *adj (characteristic, feature)* qui rachète *ou* compense les défauts; **his one redeeming feature** sa seule qualité, la seule chose qui le rachète

redefine [,ri:dɪ'faɪn] *vt (restate → objectives, terms)* redéfinir; *(modify)* modifier

redefinition [,ri:defɪ'nɪʃən] *n (restatement → of objectives, terms)* redéfinition *f*; *(modification)* modification *f*

redeliver [,ri:dɪ'lɪvə(r)] *vt* **(a)** *(parcel, letter)* livrer de nouveau **(b)** *(warning)* répéter; *(speech)* prononcer de nouveau

redemption [rɪ'dempʃən] *n* **(a)** *(from pawn)* dégagement *m*

(b) *Fin (of annuity, debt, loan, mortgage)* remboursement *m*; *(of shares)* rachat *m*

(c) *(gen) & Rel* rédemption *f*, rachat *m*; **past** *or* **beyond redemption** *(person)* perdu à tout jamais, qui ne peut être racheté; *(situation, position)* irrémédiable, irrécupérable; *(book, furniture)* irréparable, irrécupérable; *Fig* **this setback proved his redemption** ce revers de fortune fut son salut

(d) *(of slave)* rachat *m*

►► *Fin* ***redemption date*** date *f* d'échéance; *Fin* ***redemption fee*** prime *f* de remboursement; *Fin* ***redemption premium*** prime *f* de remboursement; *Fin* ***redemption price*** prix *m* de rachat; *Fin* ***redemption value*** valeur *f* de remboursement *ou* de rachat; *Fin* ***redemption yield*** rendement *m* à l'échéance

'The Shawshank Redemption' *Karabont* 'Les Évadés'

redemptive [rɪ'demptɪv] *adj* rédempteur

Redemptorist [rɪ'demptərɪst] *n Rel* rédemptoriste *m*

redeploy [,ri:dɪ'plɔɪ] *vt (troops, forces, resources)* redéployer; *(workers → to new job)* reconvertir; *(→ to new location)* réaffecter

redeployment [,ri:dɪ'plɔɪmənt] *n (of troops, resources)* redéploiement *m*; *(of workers → to new job)* reconversion *f*; *(→ to new location)* réaffectation *f*

redesign [,ri:dɪ'zaɪn] *vt (plan of room, garden etc)* redessiner; *(layout of furniture, rooms etc)* réagencer; *(system)* repenser; *(book cover, poster etc)* refaire le design de

redevelop [,ri:dɪ'veləp] *vt* **(a)** *(urban area, site)* réaménager; *(region)* revaloriser; *(tourism, industry)* relancer **(b)** *(argument)* réexposer **(c)** *Phot* redévelopper

redevelopment [,ri:dɪ'veləpmənt] *n* **(a)** *(of urban area, site)* réaménagement *m*; *(of region)* revalorisation *f*; *(of tourism, industry)* relance *f*; **urban redevelopment** rénovation *f* urbaine, réaménagement *m* urbain **(b)** *Phot* redéveloppement *m*

►► ***redevelopment area*** zone *f* de réaménagement

redeye ['redaɪ] *n Am Fam* **(a)** *(whisky)* mauvais whisky ❑ *m*, ≃ gnôle *f* **(b)** *(night flight)* vol *m* de nuit

red-eyed *adj* aux yeux rouges; **she was red-eyed from crying/staying up all night** elle avait les yeux rouges d'avoir pleuré/d'avoir passé une nuit blanche

red-faced *adj (naturally)* rougeaud; *Fig (with anger, embarrassment)* rouge de confusion *ou* de honte

red-haired *adj* roux (rousse), aux cheveux roux; **a red-haired girl** une rousse

red-handed *adv* **to be caught red-handed** être pris en flagrant délit *ou* la main dans le sac

redhead ['redhed] *n* **(a)** *(person)* roux (rousse), rouquin(e) *m,f* **(b)** *Orn* fuligule *f* à tête rouge

red-headed *adj* roux (rousse), aux cheveux roux; **a red-headed girl** une rousse

red-hot **1** *adj* **(a)** *(metal)* chauffé au rouge

(b) *(very hot)* brûlant

(c) *Fam Fig (keen)* passionné ❑, enthousiaste ❑

(d) *Fam (recent → news, information)* de dernière minute ❑

(e) *Fam (sure → tip, favourite)* certain ❑, sûr ❑

(f) *Fam (expert)* calé; **he's red-hot on the best investments** c'est un expert en matière d'investissements

(g) *(strong → passion)* fort, puissant

(h) *Fam (sensational → scandal, story)* croustillant, sensationnel ❑

2 *n Am Fam (hot dog)* hot-dog *m* épicé ❑

►► *Bot* ***red-hot poker*** tritoma *m*

redial *Tel* **1** *vt* [,ri:'daɪəl] **to redial a number** refaire un numéro

2 *vi* [,ri:'daɪəl] refaire le numéro

3 *n* ['ri:daɪəl] rappel *m* du dernier numéro; **the latest model has automatic redial** le dernier modèle est muni du système de rappel du dernier numéro

►► ***redial feature*** rappel *m* du dernier numéro

redid [ˌriːˈdɪd] *pt of* **redo**

redirect [ˌriːdɪˈrekt] *vt* (**a**) *(mail)* faire suivre, réexpédier; *(telephone call etc)* réacheminer; *Comput (e-mail message)* faire suivre (**to** à); *(aeroplane, traffic)* dérouter; **the plane was redirected to Oslo** l'avion a été dérouté sur Oslo (**b**) *Fig (efforts, attentions)* réorienter

redirection [ˌriːdɪˈrekʃən] *n* (**a**) *(of letter etc)* réacheminement *m*, réexpédition *f* (**b**) *(of plane)* déroutement *m* (**c**) *Fig* **the situation demands the redirection of some of our attention to…** la situation exige que l'on réoriente nos efforts vers…

rediscount *Com* **1** *n* [ˈriːdɪskaʊnt] réescompte *m*
2 *vt* [ˌriːˈdɪskaʊnt] réescompter

rediscover [ˌriːdɪˈskʌvə(r)] *vt* redécouvrir

rediscovery [ˌriːdɪˈskʌvərɪ] (*pl* **rediscoveries**) *n* redécouverte *f*

redistribute [ˌriːdɪˈstrɪbjuːt] *vt (money, wealth, objects)* redistribuer; *(tasks)* réassigner; *Pol* **to redistribute seats** redécouper les circonscriptions électorales

redistribution [ˈriːˌdɪstrɪˈbjuːʃən] *n* redistribution *f*; **the redistribution of wealth** la redistribution *ou* la répartition des richesses; *Pol* **redistribution of seats** nouveau découpage *m* des circonscriptions

red-legged partridge *n Orn* perdrix *m* rouge

red-letter day *n* jour *m* à marquer d'une pierre blanche; **this has been a red-letter day for everyone** ceci a été un jour mémorable pour tout le monde

red-light district *n* quartier *m* chaud

red-line *vt* discriminer contre *(dans l'attribution de logements ou d'assurances)*

redneck [ˈrednek] *Am Fam Pej* **1** *n* plouc *mf*, bouseux(euse) *m,f (du Sud des États-Unis)*; **a redneck politician/cop** un homme politique/flic tout ce qu'il y a de plus réactionnaire
2 *comp (attitude)* de plouc, borné ❑

red-necked nightjar *n Orn* engoulevent *m* à collier roux

redness [ˈrednɪs] *n (UNCOUNT) (of face, sky etc)* rougeur *f*; *(of hair)* rousseur *f*; *(inflammation)* rougeurs *fpl*

red-nosed *adj* qui a le nez rouge, au nez rouge

redo [ˌriːˈduː] (*pt* **redid** [-ˈdɪd], *pp* **redone** [-ˈdʌn]) *vt* refaire; *(hair)* recoiffer; *(repaint)* refaire, repeindre; *Comput* rétablir, refaire

redolence [ˈredələns] *n* parfum *m*, odeur *f*

redolent [ˈredələnt] *adj* (**a**) *(perfumed)* **redolent of** *or* **with lemon** qui sent le citron, qui a une odeur de citron (**b**) *(evocative, reminiscent)* **the style is redolent of James Joyce** le style rappelle celui de James Joyce

redone [ˌriːˈdʌn] *pp of* **redo**

redouble [ˌriːˈdʌbəl] **1** *vt* (**a**) *(in intensity)* redoubler; **to redouble one's efforts** redoubler ses efforts *ou* d'efforts (**b**) *Cards* surcontrer
2 *vi Cards* surcontrer
3 *n Cards* surcontre *m*

redoubt [rɪˈdaʊt] *n Mil* redoute *f*; *Fig* forteresse *f*

redoubtable [rɪˈdaʊtəbəl] *adj (formidable)* redoutable, terrifiant; *(awe-inspiring)* impressionnant

redound [rɪˈdaʊnd] *vi Formal* **to redound on** *or* [illegible] *ively)* rejaillir sur qn; **to redound to sb's advantage** être *ou* rejaillir à l'avantage de qn; **her behaviour can only redound to her credit** sa conduite ne peut qu'être portée à son crédit

redox [ˈriːdɒks] *n*
▸▸ *Chem* ***redox reaction*** réaction *f* redox

red-pencil *vt (correct)* biffer au crayon rouge; *(censor)* censurer

redpoll [ˈredpəʊl] *n Orn* sizerin *m* flammé

redraft **1** *vt* [ˌriːˈdrɑːft] *(bill, contract)* rédiger de nouveau; *(demand)* reformuler; *(text)* remanier
2 *n* [ˈriːdrɑːft] *(rewriting)* nouvelle rédaction *f*; *(reformulation)* reformulation *f*

redraw [ˌriːˈdrɔː] (*pt* **redrew** [-ˈdruː], *pp* **redrawn** [-ˈdrɔːn]) *vt* redessiner; *Comput* actualiser, rafraîchir

redress [rɪˈdres] **1** *vt (grievance, errors)* réparer; *(wrong)* réparer, redresser; *(situation)* rattraper; **to redress the balance** rétablir l'équilibre
2 *n (gen) & Law* réparation *f*; **to seek redress for sth** demander réparation de qch; **there is no redress** il n'y a pas de recours

re-dress [ˌriː-] *vt* **to re-dress a wound** refaire le pansement d'une blessure

redrew [ˌriːˈdruː] *pt of* **redraw**

red-rimmed *adj* **to have red-rimmed eyes** avoir les yeux rouges

redshank [ˈredʃæŋk] *n Orn* chevalier *m* gambette

redshift [ˈredʃɪft] *n Astron* décalage *m* spectral vers le rouge

redskin [ˈredskɪn] *n Fam Old-fashioned* Peau-Rouge *mf*, = terme raciste désignant un Amérindien

redstart [ˈredstɑːt] *n Orn* rouge-queue *m*, rossignol *m* des murailles

red-throated [-ˌθrəʊtɪd] *adj Orn*
▸▸ ***red-throated diver*** plongeon *m* catmarin, plongeon *m* à gorge rousse; ***red-throated pipit*** pipit *m* à gorge rousse

redtop [ˈredtɒp] *n Br Fam* tabloïde ❑ *m*, journal *m* à sensation ❑

reduce [rɪˈdjuːs] **1** *vt* (**a**) *(risk, scale, time, workload)* réduire, diminuer; *(temperature)* abaisser; *(speed)* réduire, ralentir; *(in length)* réduire, raccourcir; *(in size)* réduire, rapetisser, diminuer; *(in weight)* réduire, alléger; *(in height)* réduire, abaisser; *(in thickness)* réduire, amenuiser; *(in strength)* réduire, affaiblir; **the record has been reduced by two seconds** le record a été amélioré de deux secondes; **I'm trying to reduce my sugar consumption by half** j'essaie de réduire ma consommation de sucre de moitié; **you must reduce the power** il faut réduire la puissance; **to reduce output** ralentir la production; **to reduce speed** *(driver)* diminuer *ou* réduire la vitesse, ralentir
(**b**) *Com & Fin (price)* baisser, réduire; *(rate, expenses, cost, investment)* réduire; *(tax)* alléger, réduire; *(goods)* solder, réduire le prix de; *(output)* ralentir; **the shirt was reduced to £15** la chemise était soldée à 15 livres
(**c**) *(render)* **to reduce sth to ashes/to a pulp** réduire qch en cendres/en bouillie; **to reduce sb to silence/to poverty/to submission** réduire qn au silence/à la pauvreté/à l'obéissance; **his words reduced her to tears** ses paroles l'ont fait fondre en larmes; **we were reduced to helpless laughter** nous riions sans pouvoir nous arrêter; **she was reduced to buying her own pencils** elle en était réduite à acheter ses crayons elle-même
(**d**) *Culin (sauce)* faire réduire
(**e**) *Chem & Math* réduire; **to reduce fractions to a common denominator** réduire des fractions à un dénominateur commun
(**f**) *Med (fracture)* réduire; *(swelling)* résorber, résoudre
(**g**) *(dilute)* diluer
(**h**) *Law* **to reduce sth to writing** consigner qch par écrit
(**i**) *Arch or Literary (subjugate)* soumettre
(**j**) *Mil* dégrader
2 *vi* (**a**) *Culin* réduire
(**b**) *(slim)* maigrir

reduced [rɪˈdjuːst] *adj (price, rate, scale)* réduit; *(goods)* soldé, en solde; **at reduced prices** à prix réduits; **to buy sth at a reduced price** acheter qch à prix réduit; **on a reduced scale** en plus petit; **reduced to clear** *(sign)* articles en solde; *Euph* **to be in reduced circumstances** être dans la gêne
▸▸ *Fin* ***reduced rate*** taux *m* réduit; **to buy/sell sth at a reduced rate** acheter/vendre qch à tarif réduit

reduced-price offer *n Mktg* offre *f* à prix réduit

reducer [rɪˈdjuːsə(r)] *n Tech* réducteur *m*; *Phot* affaiblisseur *m*; *(for slimmer)* appareil *m* d'amaigrissement

reducible [rɪˈdjuːsəbəl] *adj* réductible

reducing [rɪˈdjuːsɪŋ] *adj Chem & Tech* réducteur; *(diet)* amaigrissant
▸▸ ***reducing agent*** (agent *m*) réducteur *m*; ***reducing cream*** crème *f* amincissante

reductase [rɪˈdʌkteɪz] *n Biol & Chem* réductase *f*

reduction [rɪˈdʌkʃən] *n* (**a**) *(lessening → gen)* réduction *f*, diminution *f*; *(→ in temperature)* baisse *f*, diminution *f*; *(→ in length)* réduction *f*, raccourcissement *m*; *(→ in weight)* réduction *f*, diminution *f*; *(→ in strength)* réduction *f*, affaiblissement *m*; *(→ in speed)* réduction *f*, ralentissement *m*; **staff reductions** compression *f* de personnel; **the reduction of the argument to basic principles** la réduction du débat à des principes fondamentaux
(**b**) *Com & Fin (of price)* baisse *f*, diminution *f*; *(of rate, expenses, cost, investment)* réduction *f*; *(of taxes)* allègement *m*; *(on goods)* rabais *m*, remise *f*; **to make a 5 percent reduction on an article** faire une remise de 5 pour cent sur un article; **cash reduction** *(discount)* remise *f ou* escompte *m* au comptant; *(refund)* remise *f* en espèces; **I'll give you a reduction** *(on purchase)* je vous fais un prix; **big reductions** *(sign)* rabais, soldes
(**c**) *Chem, Math & Phot* réduction *f*
(**d**) *Tech (of gear)* démultiplication *f*
(**e**) *Med (of fracture)* réduction *f*; *(of swelling)* résorption *f*

reductionism [rɪˈdʌkʃənɪzəm] *n Phil* réductionnisme *m*

reductionist [rɪˈdʌkʃənɪst] *Phil* **1** *n* réductionniste *mf*
2 *adj* réductionniste

reductive [rɪˈdʌktɪv] *adj* réducteur

redundancy [rɪˈdʌndənsɪ] (*pl* **redundancies**) *n* (**a**) *Br (layoff)* licenciement *m*; *(unemployment)* chômage *m*; **voluntary redundancy** départ *m* volontaire; **there is a high level of redundancy here** il y a un fort taux de chômage ici; **5,000 redundancies have been announced** on a annoncé 5000 licenciements
(**b**) *(superfluousness)* caractère *m* superflu; *(tautology)* pléonasme *m*
(**c**) *Comput, Ling & Tel* redondance *f*
▸▸ *Br* ***redundancy notice*** préavis *m* de licenciement; *Br* ***redundancy payment*** indemnité *f* de licenciement

redundant [rɪˈdʌndənt] *adj* (**a**) *Br (worker)* licencié, au chômage; **to make sb redundant** *(of employer)* licencier qn, mettre qn au chômage; *(of technology etc)* entraîner le licenciement de qn; **to be made redundant** être licencié, être mis au chômage
(**b**) *(superfluous)* redondant, superflu; *(tautologous)* pléonastique; **much of what you write is redundant** il y a beaucoup de redites *ou* de répétitions dans ce que vous écrivez
(**c**) *Comput, Ling & Tel* redondant

redundantly [rɪˈdʌndəntlɪ] *adv* avec redondance

reduplicate **1** *vt* [rɪˈdjuːplɪkeɪt] redoubler; *Ling* rédupliquer
2 *vi* [rɪˈdjuːplɪkeɪt] être redoublé; *Ling* être rédupliqué
3 [rɪˈdjuːplɪkət] *adj* redoublé; *Ling* rédupliqué

reduplication [rɪˌdjuːplɪˈkeɪʃən] *n* redoublement *m*; *Ling* réduplication *f*

redwing [ˈredwɪŋ] *n Orn Br* grive *f* mauvis; *Am* carouge *m* à épaulettes rouges

redwood [ˈredwʊd] *n Bot* séquoia *m*

reebok [ˈriːbɒk] *n Zool* pélée *f*, antilope-chevreuil *f*

re-echo [ˌriːˈ-] **1** *vt* répercuter, renvoyer
2 *vi* retentir; **the wood re-echoed with his shouts** le bois retentit *ou* résonna de ses cris

reed [riːd] **1** *n* (**a**) *Bot* roseau *m*
(**b**) *Mus* anche *f*; **the reeds** les instruments *mpl* à anche
(**c**) *(idiom)* **he's a broken reed** on ne peut pas compter sur lui
2 *comp (chair, mat)* en roseau *ou* roseaux, fait de roseaux
▸▸ *Orn* ***reed bunting*** bruant *m* des roseaux; ***reed instrument*** instrument *m* à anche; ***reed organ*** harmonium *m*; ***reed pipe*** pipeau *m*, chalumeau *m*; ***reed stop*** jeu *m* d'anches; *Orn* ***reed warbler*** fauvette *f* des roseaux, rousserolle *f* effarvatte

reedbed [ˈriːdbed] *n* roselière *f*

reedbuck [ˈriːdbʌk] *n Zool* cobe *m* des roseaux

reeding [ˈriːdɪŋ] *n Archit* rudenture *f*

re-edit *vt* [ˌriːˈ-] rééditer

re-educate *vt* [ˌriːˈ-] rééduquer

re-education *n* [ˌriː-] rééducation *f*

reedy [ˈriːdɪ] (*compar* **reedier**, *superl* **reediest**) *adj* (**a**) *(place)* envahi par les roseaux (**b**) *(voice, sound)* flûté, aigu(uë)

reef [riːf] **1** *n* (**a**) *(in sea)* récif *m*, écueil *m*; *Fig* écueil *m* (**b**) *Mining* filon *m* (**c**) *Naut* ris *m*; **to hit a reef** *(ship)* faire naufrage sur un récif
2 *vt (spar)* rentrer; **to reef a sail** prendre un ris dans une voile

▸▸ ***reef aquarium*** aquarium *m* récifal; ***reef knot*** nœud *m* plat

reefer ['ri:fə(r)] *n* (**a**) *(garment)* caban *m* (**b**) *Fam (cannabis cigarette)* joint *m*, stick *m* (**c**) *Am Fam (for transporting goods → truck)* camion *m* frigorifique; *(→ ship)* navire *m* frigorifique; *(→ train compartment)* wagon *m* frigorifique; *(refrigerator)* chambre *f* frigorifique

▸▸ ***reefer jacket*** caban *m*

reek [ri:k] **1** *vi* (**a**) *(smell)* puer, empester; **it reeks of tobacco in here** ça empeste *ou* ça pue le tabac ici; **to reek of cheap perfume** *(person, room)* empester le parfum bon marché; *Fig* **the whole affair reeks of corruption** toute cette affaire sent la corruption à plein nez; *Fam Fig* **this place reeks of money** cet endroit pue le fric

(**b**) *Scot (chimney)* fumer

2 *n* puanteur *f*

reel [ri:l] **1** *n* (**a**) *(for thread, film, tape)* bobine *f*; *(for hose)* dévidoir *m*, enrouleur *m*; *(for cable)* enrouleur *m*; *(for rope-making)* caret *m*; **(fishing) reel** moulinet *m* (de pêche)

(**b**) *(film, tape)* bande *f*, bobine *f*

(**c**) *(dance)* quadrille *m (écossais ou irlandais)*; *Mus* branle *m (écossais ou irlandais)*

2 *vi* (**a**) *(stagger)* tituber; *(sway)* chanceler; **the blow sent me reeling across the room** le coup m'a envoyé valser à travers la pièce; **the force of the shock made us reel** la violence du choc nous a fait chanceler; **to reel back/down/out** reculer/descendre/sortir en chancelant; **a drunk came reeling downstairs** un ivrogne descendait l'escalier en titubant

(**b**) *Fig (whirl → head, mind)* tournoyer; **my head is reeling** j'ai la tête qui tourne; **he is still reeling from the shock** il ne s'est pas encore remis du choc; **the room started reeling before her** la pièce a commencé à tournoyer autour d'elle; **to make sb's senses reel** donner le vertige à qn

3 *vt* bobiner

▸▸ ***reel holder*** porte-bobines *m inv*

▸**reel in** *vt sep (cable, hose)* enrouler; *(fish)* remonter, ramener; *(line)* enrouler, remonter; *Fig* **he charmed her for months, then he just reeled her in** il lui a fait du charme pendant des mois, puis il l'a tout simplement cueillie

▸**reel off** *vt sep (poem, speech, story)* débiter

▸**reel out** *vt sep (thread)* dévider, dérouler; *Fishing (line)* laisser filer

▸**reel up** *vt sep* enrouler

re-elect [ˌri:-] *vt* réélire; **she is sure to be re-elected** sa réélection est assurée

re-election [ˌri:-] *n* réélection *f*; **to stand** *or* **to run for re-election** se représenter aux élections

reeling ['ri:lɪŋ] *adj (gait)* titubant

reel-to-reel 1 *adj (system, tape recorder)* à bobines

2 *n* magnétophone *m* à bobines

re-embark [ˌri:-] **1** *vt (passengers)* rembarquer

2 *vi* rembarquer; *Fig* **to re-embark on sth** recommencer qch

re-embarkation [ˌri:-] *n* rembarquement *m*

re-emerge [ˌri:-] *vi (new facts)* ressortir; *(idea, clue)* réapparaître; *(problem, question)* se reposer; *(person, sun)* réapparaître; *(from hiding, tunnel)* ressortir, ressurgir

re-emergence [ˌri:-] *n* réapparition *f*

re-emphasize, -ise [ˌri:-] *vt* insister une fois de plus sur, souligner une nouvelle fois

re-employ [ˌri:-] *vt (materials)* réemployer, remployer; *(workers)* réembaucher, rembaucher

re-employment [ˌri:-] *n (of materials)* réemploi *m*, remploi *m*; *(of workers)* réembauche *f*

re-enact [ˌri:-] *vt* (**a**) *(scene, crime)* reconstituer; **we were able to re-enact the incident in detail** nous avons pu reconstituer l'incident en détail (**b**) *Admin & Pol (legislation)* remettre en vigueur

re-enactment [ˌri:-] *n* (**a**) *(of scene, crime)* reconstitution *f* (**b**) *Admin, Law & Pol (of regulation, legislation)* remise *f* en vigueur

re-engage [ˌri:-] *vt* (**a**) *(troops)* rengager; *(employee)* réengager, rengager, réembaucher (**b**) *(mechanism)* rengrener; **to re-engage the clutch** rembrayer

re-engagement [ˌri:-] *n* (**a**) *(of troops, of worker)* réengagement *m*, rengagement *m*, réembauche *f* (**b**) *Tech* rengrènement *m*

re-enlist [ˌri:-] *Mil* **1** *vt* réengager, rengager

2 *vi* se réengager, se rengager

re-enter [ˌri:-] **1** *vi* (**a**) *(gen)* rentrer, entrer à nouveau; *Astron* rentrer dans l'atmosphère; *Theat* **re-enter Macbeth** Macbeth rentre

(**b**) *(candidate)* **to re-enter for an exam** se réinscrire à un examen

(**c**) *(job seeker)* **to re-enter the job market** se remettre à chercher du travail

2 *vt* (**a**) *(room, country)* rentrer dans, entrer à nouveau dans; *(atmosphere)* rentrer dans; **he never re-entered that house** il n'a jamais remis les pieds dans cette maison

(**b**) *(date, name)* réinscrire, inscrire de nouveau; *Comput (data)* saisir à nouveau, réintroduire

re-entrant [ˌri:-] *Math* **1** *n* angle *m* rentrant

2 *adj* rentrant

re-entry [ˌri:-] *(pl* **re-entries***)* *n* (**a**) *(gen) & Astron* rentrée *f* (**b**) *Mus (of theme)* reprise *f*

▸▸ *Astron* ***re-entry point*** point *m* de rentrée

re-equip [ˌri:-] *vt* rééquiper

re-establish [ˌri:-] *vt* (**a**) *(order)* rétablir; *(practice)* restaurer; *(law)* remettre en vigueur

(**b**) *(person)* réhabiliter, réintégrer; **the team have re-established themselves as the best in the country** l'équipe s'est imposée de nouveau comme la meilleure du pays; **to re-establish oneself** *or* **one's position** rétablir sa position

re-establishment [ˌri:-] *n* (**a**) *(of order)* rétablissement *m*; *(of practice)* restauration *f*; *(of law)* remise *f* en vigueur (**b**) *(of person)* réintégration *f*; **her re-establishment as team leader** sa réintégration en tant que chef d'équipe

re-evaluate [ˌri:-] *vt* réévaluer

re-evaluation [ˌri:-] *n* réévaluation *f*

reeve [ri:v] *(pt & pp* **reeved** *or* **rove** [rəʊv]*)* **1** *n* (**a**) *Br Hist (in town)* premier magistrat *m*; *(in manor)* intendant *m* (**b**) *Can* président *m* (du conseil municipal)

2 *vt Naut (rope → pass)* passer; *(→ fasten)* capeler

re-examination [ˌri:-] *n (of question)* réexamen *m*; *Law (of witness)* nouvel interrogatoire *m*

re-examine [ˌri:-] *vt (question, case)* réexaminer, examiner de nouveau; *(candidate)* faire repasser un examen à; *Law (witness)* réinterroger, interroger de nouveau

re-export 1 *vt* [ˌri:-] réexporter

2 *n* [ˌri:'ekspɔ:t] (**a**) *(of goods)* réexportation *f* (**b**) *(product)* marchandise *f* de réexportation

re-exportation [ˌri:-] *n* réexportation *f*

ref[1]**, ref.** *(written abbr* **reference***)* réf.; **your ref** v/réf.; **our ref** n/réf.

ref[2] [ref] *n Br Fam Sport (abbr* **referee***)* arbitre ▫ *m*

reface [ˌri:'feɪs] *vt (wall, building)* ravaler

refashion [ˌri:'fæʃən] *vt (object)* refaçonner; *(image)* reconstruire

refasten [ri:'fɑ:sən] *vt* rattacher

refectory [rɪ'fektərɪ] *(pl* **refectories***)* *n* (**a**) *(in monastery, school)* réfectoire *m* (**b**) *(university canteen)* restaurant *m* universitaire

▸▸ ***refectory table*** = table longue et étroite *(souvent en chêne massif)*

refer [rɪ'fɜ:(r)] *(pt & pp* **referred,** *cont* **referring***)* *vt* (**a**) *(submit → matter, proposal etc)* soumettre (**to** à); **the dispute has been referred to arbitration** le litige a été soumis à arbitrage *ou* à l'arbitrage d'un médiateur; **I refer the matter to you for a decision** je m'en remets à vous pour prendre une décision sur la question; **the question has been referred to Jane** la question a été soumise à Jane; **to refer a case to a higher court** renvoyer *ou* déférer une affaire à une instance supérieure; **the contract has been referred to us** le contrat nous a été soumis; *Banking* **to refer a cheque to drawer** refuser d'honorer un chèque; **refer to drawer** *(on cheque)* voir le tireur

(**b**) *(send, direct → person)* renvoyer; **my doctor referred me to the hospital/to a specialist** mon docteur m'a envoyé à l'hôpital/chez un spécialiste; **the doctor's going to refer me** le docteur va m'envoyer chez un spécialiste; **I refer you to Ludlow's book** je vous renvoie au livre de Ludlow; **here the author refers us to 'Alice in Wonderland'** ici l'auteur nous renvoie à 'Alice au pays des merveilles'

(**c**) *Law* **to refer the accused** déférer l'accusé

(**d**) *Univ (student)* refuser, recaler; *(thesis)* renvoyer pour révision

(**e**) *Med* **the pain may be referred to another part of the body** il peut y avoir irradiation de la douleur dans d'autres parties du corps

(**f**) *(attribute)* attribuer; **to refer sth to an event** attribuer qch à un événement

▸**refer back** *vt sep* (**a**) *(put off → meeting, decision)* ajourner, remettre (à plus tard)

(**b**) *(redirect → case)* renvoyer; **the case was referred back to our office** l'affaire a été renvoyée à notre service

▸**refer to** *vt insep* (**a**) *(allude to)* faire allusion *ou* référence à, parler de; **no one refers to it now** personne n'en parle plus maintenant; **I don't know what you are referring to** je ne sais pas à quoi vous faites allusion *ou* de quoi vous parlez; **we won't refer to it again** nous n'en reparlons plus; **he keeps referring to me as Dr Rayburn** il ne cesse de m'appeler Dr Rayburn; **the revolutionaries are referred to as Mantras** ces révolutionnaires sont connus sous le nom de Mantras; **that comment refers to you** cette remarque s'adresse à vous; **they refer to themselves as martyrs** ils se qualifient eux-mêmes de martyrs

(**b**) *(relate to)* correspondre à, faire référence à; *(apply, be connected to)* s'appliquer à, s'adresser à; **the numbers refer to footnotes** les chiffres renvoient à des notes en bas de page; **these measures only refer to taxpayers** ses mesures ne s'appliquent qu'aux contribuables

(**c**) *(consult → notes)* consulter; *(→ book, page, instructions)* se reporter à; *(→ person)* **I shall have to refer to my boss** je dois en référer à *ou* consulter mon patron

referable [rɪ'fɜ:rəbəl] *adj* **referable to** attribuable à, qui relève de

referee [ˌrefə'ri:] **1** *n* (**a**) *Sport* arbitre *m*; *(in tennis)* juge-arbitre *m*

(**b**) *Br (for job)* = personne pouvant fournir des références; **I was referee** *or* **I acted as his referee for his last job** je lui ai fourni des références pour son dernier emploi; **you can give my name as a referee** si vous donnez mon nom, je vous fournirai des références; **please give the names of three referees** veuillez nous donner le nom de trois personnes susceptibles de fournir des références

(**c**) *Law* conciliateur *m*, médiateur *m*

(**d**) *Fin* **referee in case of need** *(on bill of exchange)* adresse *f* au besoin

2 *vt Sport* arbitrer; **he refereed the game well** il a bien arbitré

3 *vi Sport* être arbitre; **who'll referee for us?** qui va nous servir d'arbitre?

reference ['refrəns] **1** *n* (**a**) *(allusion)* allusion *f* (**to** à); *(mention)* mention *f* (**to** de); **to make a reference to sth** faire allusion à qch; **if any reference is made to me** si on parle de moi; **a talk on the environment with particular reference to...** un exposé sur l'environnement abordant tout particulièrement...; **with reference to your request for more funding** en ce qui concerne votre demande de fonds supplémentaires; *Com* **with reference to your letter of 25 June...** suite à votre courrier du 25 juin...; **with reference to what was said at the meeting** à propos de *ou* en ce qui concerne ce qui a été dit au cours de la réunion

(**b**) *(consultation)* consultation *f*; **without reference to me** sans me consulter; **for reference only** *(on library book)* consultation sur place; *(on document etc in circulation)* pour information seulement; **to keep sth for future reference** garder qch à titre d'information; **for future reference, please note...** pour votre information à l'avenir, veuillez noter...

(**c**) *(in code, catalogue)* référence *f*; *(on map)* coordonnées *fpl*; *(in book → allusion)* référence *f*, allusion *f*; *(→ footnote, cross-reference)* renvoi *m*; **look up the reference in the dictionary** cherchez la référence dans le dictionnaire; **it's a biblical reference** c'est une allusion *ou* une référence biblique

(**d**) *Com* référence *f*; **quote this reference** rappelez cette référence; **your reference** votre référence; **our reference** notre référence

(**e**) *Banking (testimonial)* référence *f*

(**f**) *(recommendation → for job)* références *fpl*;

to give sb a reference fournir une référence à qn; **to have good references** avoir de bonnes références; **could you give me a reference please?** pouvez-vous me fournir des références, s'il vous plaît?; **I'm often asked for references** on me demande souvent de fournir des références; **to take up references** prendre contact avec *ou* contacter les personnes dont un candidat se recommande; **you can use my name as a reference** vous pouvez me citer comme référence; **banker's reference** références *fpl* bancaires

(**g**) *(remit → of commission)* compétence *f*, pouvoirs *mpl*; **the question is outside the tribunal's reference** la question n'est pas de la compétence du tribunal

(**h**) *Ling* référence *f*

(**i**) *Law (of case)* renvoi *m*

2 *comp (material, section)* de référence; *(value, quantity)* de référence, étalon

3 *vt* (**a**) *(refer to)* faire référence à

(**b**) *(thesis)* établir la liste des citations dans; *(quotation)* donner la référence de

(**c**) *Comput* référencer

►► ***reference book*** ouvrage *m* de référence; *Mktg* ***reference customer*** client(e) *m,f* de référence; *Mktg* ***reference group*** groupe *m* de référence; ***reference library*** bibliothèque *f* d'ouvrages de référence; ***reference number*** numéro *m* de référence; ***reference point*** point *m* de repère; *Fin* ***reference rate*** taux *m* de référence; ***reference room*** *(in public library)* salle *f* de lecture; *(in university)* salle *f* de consultation; *Mktg* ***reference sale*** vente *f* de référence; ***reference work*** ouvrage *m* de référence

referendum [ˌrefəˈrendəm] (*pl* **referendums** *or* **referenda** [-də]) *n* référendum *m*; **to hold a referendum** organiser un référendum

referent [ˈrefərənt] *n* référent *m*

referential [ˌrefəˈrenʃəl] *adj* référentiel

referral [rɪˈfɜːrəl] *n* (**a**) *(forwarding)* renvoi *m* (**b**) *(consultation)* consultation *f* (**c**) *Univ (of thesis)* renvoi *m* pour révision (**d**) *(person)* patient(e) *m,f (envoyé par son médecin chez un spécialiste)*

referred pain [rɪˈfɜːd-] *n* douleur *f* irradiée

refill 1 *vt* [ˌriːˈfɪl] *(glass)* remplir (à nouveau); *(lighter, canister)* recharger

2 *n* [ˈriːfɪl] *(for pen, lighter, notebook)* recharge *f*; *(for propelling pencil)* mine *f* de rechange; **do you need a refill?** *(drink)* je vous en ressers un?

3 *comp* [ˈriːfɪl] de rechange

refillable [ˌriːˈfɪləbəl] *adj* rechargeable

refinance [ˌriːˈfaɪnæns] **1** *vt (loan)* refinancer

2 *vi (company)* se refinancer

refinancing [ˌriːˈfaɪnænsɪŋ] *n Fin* refinancement *m*; **to get refinancing from a bank** se refinancer auprès d'une banque

refine [rɪˈfaɪn] *vt* (**a**) *(oil, sugar)* raffiner; *(ore, metal)* affiner; *(by distillation)* épurer (**b**) *(model, manners)* améliorer; *(judgment, taste)* affiner; *(lecture, speech)* parfaire, peaufiner

►**refine on, refine upon** *vt insep* parfaire, peaufiner; *Literary* **to refine on a question** subtiliser sur une question

refined [rɪˈfaɪnd] *adj* (**a**) *(oil, sugar)* raffiné; *(ore)* affiné; *(by distillation)* épuré (**b**) *(style, person, taste)* raffiné

refinement [rɪˈfaɪnmənt] *n* (**a**) *(of oil, sugar)* raffinage *m*; *(of metals, ore)* affinage *m*; *(by distillation)* épuration *f*

(**b**) *(of person)* délicatesse *f*, raffinement *m*; *(of taste, culture)* raffinement *m*; *(of morals)* pureté *f*; **a man of refinement** un homme raffiné; **his lack of refinement** ses manières peu raffinées

(**c**) *(of style, discourse, language)* subtilité *f*, raffinement *m*

(**d**) *(improvement)* perfectionnement *m*, amélioration *f*; **it's a refinement on an old process** c'est un processus ancien qui a été amélioré; **all the latest technical refinements** tous les derniers perfectionnements techniques

refiner [rɪˈfaɪnə(r)] *n (of oil, sugar)* raffineur(euse) *m,f*; *(of metal)* affineur(euse) *m,f*

refinery [rɪˈfaɪnərɪ] (*pl* **refineries**) *n (for oil, sugar)* raffinerie *f*; *(for metals)* affinerie *f*

refining [rɪˈfaɪnɪŋ] *n (of oil, sugar)* raffinage *m*; *(of metal)* affinage *m*

refit (*pt & pp* **refitted**, *cont* **refitting**) **1** *vt* [ˌriːˈfɪt] (**a**) *(repair)* remettre en état

(**b**) *(refurbish)* rééquiper, renouveler l'équipement de

2 *vi* [ˌriːˈfɪt] *(ship)* être remis en état

3 *n* [ˈriːfɪt] *(of plant, factory)* rééquipement *m*, nouvel équipement *m*; *(of ship)* remise *f* en état, réparation *f*; **the yacht is under refit** le yacht est en cours de réparation

reflag [riːˈflæg] *vt (ship)* changer le pays d'immatriculation de

reflate [ˌriːˈfleɪt] *vt* (**a**) *(ball, tyre)* regonfler (**b**) *Econ* relancer

reflation [ˌriːˈfleɪʃən] *n Econ* relance *f*

reflationary [ˌriːˈfleɪʃənərɪ] *adj Econ (policy)* de relance

►► *Econ* ***reflationary pressure*** pression *f* pour une relance (économique)

reflect [rɪˈflekt] **1** *vt* (**a**) *(image)* refléter; *(sound, heat)* renvoyer; *(light)* réfléchir; **her face was reflected in the mirror/the water** son visage se reflétait dans la glace/dans l'eau; **she saw herself reflected in the window** elle a vu son image dans la vitre; **the mirror reflected the light from the lamp** le miroir réfléchissait la lumière de la lampe; **the plate reflects heat (back) into the room** la plaque renvoie la chaleur dans la pièce; **the sound was reflected off the rear wall** le son était renvoyé par le mur du fond

(**b**) *Fig (credit)* faire jaillir, faire retomber; **the behaviour of a few reflects discredit on us all** le comportement de quelques-uns porte atteinte à l'honneur de tous; *Fig* **to bask** *or* **to bathe in reflected glory** se parer des plumes du paon; **he bathed in the reflected glory of his wife's achievements** il tira gloire de la réussite de sa femme

(**c**) *Fig (personality, reality)* traduire, refléter; **the graph reflects population movements** le graphique traduit les mouvements de population; **many social problems are reflected in his writing** de nombreux problèmes de société sont évoqués dans ses écrits; **her personal problems are reflected in her poor performance at school** elle a des problèmes personnels et ses résultats scolaires s'en ressentent

(**d**) *(think)* penser, se dire; *(say)* dire, réfléchir; **I often reflect that...** je me dis souvent *ou* je me fais souvent la réflexion que...; **Peter might know, she reflected** Peter saura peut-être, songeait-elle

2 *vi* (**a**) *(light)* se réfléchir

(**b**) *(think)* réfléchir; **to reflect on a question** réfléchir sur une question; **I'll reflect on it** j'y songerai *ou* réfléchirai; **after reflecting for a while...** après mûre réflexion...

►**reflect on, reflect upon** *vt insep (negatively)* porter atteinte à, nuire à; *(positively)* rejaillir sur; *(cast doubt on)* mettre en doute, jeter le doute sur; **their behaviour reflects well on them** leur comportement leur fait honneur; **this will reflect badly upon the company** ceci va porter atteinte à l'image de l'entreprise; **how is that going to reflect on the company?** quelles en seront les conséquences *ou* les répercussions pour l'image de l'entreprise?

reflectance [rɪˈflektəns] *n Phys* coefficient *m ou* facteur *m* de réflexion

reflecting [rɪˈflektɪŋ] *adj*

►► *Phys* ***reflecting factor*** coefficient *m ou* facteur *m* de réflexion; ***the Reflecting Pool*** = bassin situé devant le Lincoln Memorial de Washington; *Astron* ***reflecting telescope*** réflecteur *m*, télescope *m*

reflection [rɪˈflekʃən] *n* (**a**) *(image)* reflet *m*; **a reflection in the mirror/the window** un reflet dans la glace/la vitre; **can you see your reflection?** voyez-vous votre reflet *ou* votre image?; **there is some reflection on the screen** il y a des reflets sur l'écran; *Fig* **the result was not a fair reflection of the game** le résultat ne reflétait pas la manière dont le match s'était joué; *Fig* **an accurate reflection of reality** un reflet exact de la réalité

(**b**) *(action → of light, sound, heat)* réflexion *f*

(**c**) *(comment)* réflexion *f*, remarque *f*, observation *f*; **to make a reflection on sth** faire une réflexion sur qch; **reflections on James Joyce/on Communism** réflexions sur James Joyce/sur le communisme

(**d**) *(criticism)* critique *f*; **his book was seen as a reflection on the government** son livre a été perçu comme une critique du gouvernement; **their conduct is a (bad) reflection on all of us** leur conduite nous fait du tort à tous; **it's no reflection on their integrity** leur intégrité n'est pas en cause; **my comment was not meant to be a reflection on you** ce que j'ai dit ne vous visait pas personnellement

(**e**) *(deliberation)* réflexion *f*; *(thought)* pensée *f*; **on reflection** après *ou* à la réflexion, en y réfléchissant; **on due reflection** après mûre réflexion; **with no reflection** sans avoir réfléchi

reflective [rɪˈflektɪv] *adj* (**a**) *Opt (surface)* réfléchissant, réflecteur; *(power, angle)* réflecteur; *(light)* réfléchi (**b**) *(mind, person)* pensif, réfléchi; *(faculty)* de réflexion

reflectively [rɪˈflektɪvlɪ] *adv (speak)* d'un ton pensif; *(behave)* d'un air songeur

reflector [rɪˈflektə(r)] *n* réflecteur *m*; *Aut* catadioptre *m*

►► ***reflector board*** panneau *m* réflecteur

reflex [ˈriːfleks] **1** *n* (**a**) *(gen) & Physiol* réflexe *m*; **to have good reflexes** avoir de bons réflexes; **to test sb's reflexes** tester les réflexes de qn (**b**) *Phot* (appareil *m*) reflex *m*

2 *adj* (**a**) *Physiol* réflexe (**b**) *Opt & Phys* réfléchi (**c**) *Phot* reflex *(inv)* (**d**) *Math* rentrant

►► *Physiol* ***reflex action*** réflexe *m*; *Physiol* ***reflex arc*** arc *m* réflexe; *Phot* ***reflex camera*** (appareil *m*) reflex *m*

reflexion *Br* = **reflection**

reflexive [rɪˈfleksɪv] **1** *adj* (**a**) *Gram* réfléchi (**b**) *Physiol* réflexe (**c**) *(in logic) & Math* réflexif

2 *n Gram (verb)* verbe *m* réfléchi; *(pronoun)* pronom *m* (personnel) réfléchi

►► *Gram* ***reflexive pronoun*** pronom *m* réfléchi; *Gram* ***reflexive verb*** verbe *m* réfléchi

reflexively [rɪˈfleksɪvlɪ] *adv Gram (in meaning)* au sens réfléchi; *(in form)* à la forme réfléchie

reflexologist [ˌriːflekˈsɒlədʒɪst] *n* réflexologiste *mf*

reflexology [ˌriːflekˈsɒlədʒɪ] *n* réflexothérapie *f*

refloat [ˌriːˈfləʊt] **1** *vt* (**a**) *(ship)* renflouer, (re-)mettre à flot (**b**) *Fin (loan)* émettre de nouveau; *(company)* renflouer, remettre à flot; *(economy)* renflouer

2 *vi* être renfloué

reflux [ˈriːflʌks] *n* reflux *m*

refocus [ˌriːˈfəʊkəs] (*pt & pp* **refocused** *or* **refocussed**, *cont* **refocusing** *or* **refocussing**) **1** *vt (projector, camera)* refaire la mise au point de; *Fig* **it has refocused attention on the problem** cela a attiré une nouvelle fois l'attention sur ce problème

2 *vi* refaire la mise au point

reforest [ˌriːˈfɒrɪst] = **reafforest**

reforestation [riːˌfɒrɪˈsteɪʃən] = **reafforestation**

reform [rɪˈfɔːm] **1** *vt* (**a**) *(modify → law, system, institution)* réformer

(**b**) *(person)* faire perdre ses mauvaises habitudes à; *(drunkard)* faire renoncer à la boisson; *(habits, behaviour)* corriger; **to reform oneself** s'amender, se corriger

2 *vi* se corriger, s'amender

3 *n* réforme *f*

►► *Br Hist* ***Reform Act, Reform Bill*** = loi de réforme du système parlementaire; **the great Reform Bills** les grandes réformes *fpl*; *Br* ***Reform Club*** = club pour hommes proche du Parti libéral; ***Reform Judaism*** judaïsme *m* réformé; *Am* ***reform school*** ≃ centre *m* d'éducation surveillée

THE GREAT REFORM BILLS

Il s'agit d'une série de réformes parlementaires (1832, 1867, 1884–85) concernant le droit de vote et la représentation parlementaire. Elles ouvrirent la voie à l'adoption du suffrage universel en Grande-Bretagne.

re-form [riː-] **1** *vt* (**a**) *Mil (ranks)* remettre en rang, reformer; *(men)* rallier

(**b**) *(return to original form)* rendre sa forme primitive *ou* originale à; *(in new form)* donner une nouvelle forme à; *(form again → battalion, group etc)* reformer

2 *vi* (**a**) *Mil (men)* se remettre en rangs; *(ranks)* se reformer (**b**) *(group, band, battalion)* se reformer; **the band has re-formed for a charity concert** le groupe s'est reformé pour donner un concert de bienfaisance

reformat [ˌriːˈfɔːmæt] *(pt & pp* **reformatted,** *cont* **reformatting**) *Comput* **1** *vt* reformater

2 *vi* reformater

reformation [ˌrefəˈmeɪʃən] **1** *n* (**a**) *(of law, institution)* réforme *f* (**b**) *(of behaviour)* réforme *f*; *(of criminal, addict etc)* réinsertion *f*

2 Reformation 1 *n* **the Reformation** la Réforme

2 *comp (music, writer)* de la Réforme

reformative [rɪˈfɔːmətɪv] *adj (concerning reform)* de réforme; *(reforming)* réformateur

reformatory [rɪˈfɔːmətrɪ] **1** *adj* réformateur

2 *n Br* ≃ maison *f* de redressement, *Am* ≃ centre *m* d'éducation surveillée

reformatting [ˌriːˈfɔːmætɪŋ] *n Comput* reformatage *m*

reformed [rɪˈfɔːmd] *adj* (**a**) *(person)* qui a perdu ses mauvaises habitudes; *(prostitute, drug addict)* ancien; **he's a reformed character since his marriage** il s'est assagi depuis son mariage (**b**) *(institution, system)* réformé (**c**) *Rel (Christian)* réformé; *(Jewish)* non orthodoxe

▸▸ ***Reformed Church*** Église *f* réformée

reformer [rɪˈfɔːmə(r)] *n* réformateur(trice) *m,f*

reformism [rɪˈfɔːmɪzəm] *n* réformisme *m*

reformist [rɪˈfɔːmɪst] **1** *adj* réformiste

2 *n* réformiste *mf*

refract [rɪˈfrækt] **1** *vt* réfracter; **to be refracted** être réfracté

2 *vi* se réfracter

refracting [rɪˈfræktɪŋ] *adj (material, prism)* réfringent; *(angle)* de réfraction

▸▸ ***refracting telescope*** réfracteur *m*, lunette *f* astronomique

refraction [rɪˈfrækʃən] *n (phenomenon)* réfraction *f*; *(property)* réfringence *f*

▸▸ *Astron* ***refraction correction*** correction *f* tenant compte de la réfraction atmosphérique

refractive [rɪˈfræktɪv] *adj Phys* réfringent

▸▸ ***refractive index*** indice *m* de réfraction

refractivity [ˌriːfrækˈtɪvɪtɪ] *n Phys* réfringence *f*

refractometer [ˌriːfrækˈtɒmɪtə(r)] *n* réfractomètre *m*; **immersion** *or* **dipping refractometer** réfractomètre *m* à immersion; **parallax refractometer** réfractomètre *m* à parallaxe

refractometry [ˌriːfrækˈtɒmɪtrɪ] *n* réfractométrie *f*

refractor [rɪˈfræktə(r)] *n* (**a**) *Opt & Phys (apparatus)* appareil *m* de réfraction; *(material, medium)* milieu *m* réfringent (**b**) *Astron (telescope)* réfracteur *m*, lunette *f* astronomique

refractoriness [rɪˈfræktərɪnɪs] *n* (**a**) *Formal (of person)* récalcitrance *f*, insoumission *f* (**b**) *Tech* nature *f* réfractaire, réfractérité *f*

refractory [rɪˈfræktərɪ] *adj* (**a**) *Formal (person)* réfractaire, récalcitrant, rebelle (**b**) *Med & Tech* réfractaire

refrain [rɪˈfreɪn] **1** *vi (hold back)* **to refrain from sth/doing sth** s'abstenir de qch/de faire qch; **to refrain from comment** s'abstenir de tout commentaire; **she refrained from making a remark** elle s'est retenue *ou* abstenue de faire une remarque; **he couldn't refrain from smiling** il n'a pu s'empêcher de sourire; **please refrain from smoking** *(sign)* prière de ne pas fumer

2 *n Mus, Literature & Fig* refrain *m*

reframe [ˌriːˈfreɪm] *vt* (**a**) *(approach, point of view)* recentrer; *(argument)* remanier; *(question)* reformuler (**b**) *(picture)* réencadrer

refrangible [rɪˈfrændʒɪbəl] *adj Phys & Opt* réfrangible

refreeze [ˌriːˈfriːz] *(pt* **refroze** [-ˈfrəʊz], *pp* **refrozen** [-ˈfrəʊzən]) *vt (ice, ice-cream)* remettre au congélateur; *(food)* recongeler

refresh [rɪˈfreʃ] **1** *vt* (**a**) *(revive → of drink, shower, ice)* rafraîchir; *(→ of exercise, swim)* revigorer; *(→ of sleep)* reposer, détendre; **I feel refreshed** *(after shower, drink)* je me sens rafraîchi; *(after exercise)* je me sens revigoré; *(after rest)* je me sens reposé; **they returned refreshed** *(from rest, holiday)* ils sont revenus détendus; *(from exercise)* ils sont revenus revigorés; **they woke refreshed** ils se sont réveillés frais et dispos

(**b**) *(memory, experience)* rafraîchir; **to refresh one's memory** se rafraîchir la mémoire; **let me refresh your memory** laissez-moi vous rafraîchir la mémoire; **she wanted to refresh her German** elle voulait se remettre à niveau en allemand

(**c**) *Comput (screen)* actualiser, rafraîchir

2 *n Comput* actualisation *f*, rafraîchissement *m*

▸▸ *Comput* ***refresh rate*** taux *m* d'actualisation *ou* de rafraîchissement

refresher [rɪˈfreʃə(r)] *n* (**a**) *(drink)* boisson *f* rafraîchissante (**b**) *Br Law* honoraires *mpl* supplémentaires

▸▸ ***refresher course*** stage *m ou* cours *m* de recyclage

refreshing [rɪˈfreʃɪŋ] *adj* (**a**) *(physically → breeze)* rafraîchissant; *(→ exercise)* tonique, revigorant; *(→ bath, shower, cup of tea)* revigorant, ravigotant; *(→ sleep)* réparateur, reposant; *(→ holiday)* reposant

(**b**) *(mentally → idea)* original, stimulant; *(→ sight)* réconfortant; *(→ performance)* plein de vie; **a refreshing change** un changement agréable *ou* appréciable; **his honesty is refreshing** son honnêteté est comme une bouffée d'air frais *ou* est réconfortante

refreshingly [rɪˈfreʃɪŋlɪ] *adv* **it's refreshingly different** c'est un changement agréable; **refreshingly honest** d'une honnêteté rassurante; **she is refreshingly different from most politicians/actresses** cela fait plaisir de voir qu'elle est différente de la plupart des politiques/des actrices

refreshment [rɪˈfreʃmənt] **1** *n (of body, mind)* repos *m*, délassement *m*; **would you like some refreshment?** *(food)* voulez-vous manger un morceau?; *(drink)* voulez-vous boire quelque chose?

2 refreshments *npl (drinks)* rafraîchissements *mpl*; *(snacks)* collation *f*; **refreshments available** *(sign)* buvette

▸▸ ***refreshment bar, refreshment stall*** buvette *f*

refried beans [ˌriːˈfraɪd-] *npl Culin* haricots *mpl* rouges sautés

refrigerant [rɪˈfrɪdʒərənt] **1** *adj* réfrigérant

2 *n* (**a**) *(substance)* mélange *m* réfrigérant (**b**) *Med* réfrigérant *m*

refrigerate [rɪˈfrɪdʒəreɪt] *vt (in cold store)* frigorifier, réfrigérer; *(freeze)* congeler; *(put in fridge)* mettre au réfrigérateur; **keep refrigerated** *(on packaging)* conserver au réfrigérateur

▸▸ ***refrigerated lorry*** camion *m* frigorifique; ***refrigerated meat*** viande *f* frigorifiée *ou* réfrigérée; ***refrigerated ship*** navire *m* frigorifique

refrigeration [rɪˌfrɪdʒəˈreɪʃən] *n* réfrigération *f*; **industrial refrigeration** froid *m* industriel; **to keep sth under refrigeration** garder qch au réfrigérateur

▸▸ ***refrigeration plant*** installation *f* frigorifique

refrigerator [rɪˈfrɪdʒəreɪtə(r)] **1** *n (in kitchen)* réfrigérateur *m*, Frigidaire® *m*; *(storeroom)* chambre *f* froide *ou* frigorifique

2 *comp (ship, lorry, unit)* frigorifique

refrigerator-freezer *n Am* réfrigérateur-congélateur *m*

refringent [rɪˈfrɪndʒənt] *adj* réfringent

refroze [ˌriːˈfrəʊz] *pt of* **refreeze**

refrozen [ˌriːˈfrəʊzən] *pp of* **refreeze**

refuel [ˌriːˈfjʊəl] *(Br pt & pp* **refuelled,** *cont* **refuelling,** *Am pt & pp* **refueled,** *cont* **refueling**) **1** *vt* ravitailler (en carburant); *Fig* **to refuel speculation** alimenter les conjectures

2 *vi* se ravitailler en carburant; *Fig (eat, drink)* se restaurer; **the aeroplane refuelled in mid-flight** l'avion s'est ravitaillé en vol

refuelling, *Am* **refueling** [ˌriːˈfjʊəlɪŋ] **1** *n* ravitaillement *m* (en carburant)

2 *comp (boom, tanker)* de ravitaillement; **to make a refuelling stop** *Aut* s'arrêter pour prendre de l'essence; *Aviat* faire une escale technique

refuge [ˈrefjuːdʒ] *n* (**a**) *(shelter → gen)* refuge *m*, abri *m*; *(→ in mountains)* refuge *m*; *Br (→ for crossing road)* refuge *m*; **women's refuge** foyer *m* pour femmes battues

(**b**) *(protection → from weather)* **to take refuge from the rain** s'abriter de la pluie; **she took refuge in the tent** elle s'est réfugiée sous la tente; **to seek refuge** *(from attack, reality)* chercher refuge; **he sought refuge from his persecutors** il chercha un asile pour échapper à ses persécuteurs; **to seek refuge in drugs** chercher refuge dans la drogue; **to take refuge in fantasy** se réfugier dans l'imagination; **place of refuge** *(from rain)* abri *m*; *(from pursuit)* (lieu *m* d')asile *m*; *Literary* **God is my refuge** Dieu est mon refuge

refugee [ˌrefjʊˈdʒiː] *n* réfugié(e) *m,f*; **economic refugee** migrant(e) *m,f* économique

▸▸ ***refugee camp*** camp *m* de réfugiés; ***refugee status*** statut *m* de réfugié; **he was granted refugee status** on lui a accordé le statut de réfugié

refugium [rɪˈfjuːdʒɪəm] *n Biol* refuge *m*

refulgence [rɪˈfʌldʒəns] *n Literary* splendeur *f*, éclat *m*

refulgent [rɪˈfʌldʒənt] *adj Literary (day)* resplendissant; *(sun)* éclatant, radieux

refund 1 *vt* [rɪˈfʌnd] (**a**) *(expenses, excess, person)* rembourser; **to refund sth to sb, to refund sb sth** rembourser qch à qn; **they refunded me the postage** ils m'ont remboursé les frais de port

(**b**) *Fin & Law (monies)* restituer

2 *n* [ˈriːfʌnd] (**a**) *Com* remboursement *m*; **to get a refund** se faire rembourser

(**b**) *Fin & Law (of monies)* restitution *f*

(**c**) *Am (of tax)* bonification *f* de trop-perçu

refundable [ˌriːˈfʌndəbəl] *adj* remboursable

refunding [ˌriːˈfʌndɪŋ] *n* remboursement *m*

▸▸ *Fin* ***refunding clause*** clause *f* de remboursement; *Fin* ***refunding loan*** prêt *m* de remboursement

refurbish [ˌriːˈfɜːbɪʃ] *vt* remettre à neuf

refurbished [ˌriːˈfɜːbɪʃt] *adj (studio, apartment)* refait à neuf

refurbishment [ˌriːˈfɜːbɪʃmənt] *n* remise *f* à neuf

refurnish [ˌriːˈfɜːnɪʃ] *vt (house)* remeubler

refusal [rɪˈfjuːzəl] *n* (**a**) *(of request, suggestion)* refus *m*, rejet *m*; **to meet with a refusal** *(person)* se heurter à *ou* essuyer un refus; **my offer/invitation met with a refusal** je me suis vu refuser mon offre/mon invitation; **to receive a refusal** recevoir une réponse négative; **we don't understand your refusal to compromise** nous ne comprenons pas les raisons pour lesquelles vous vous opposez à un compromis

(**b**) *Horseriding* refus *m*

(**c**) *(denial → of justice, truth)* refus *m*, déni *m*

(**d**) *Com* **to have first refusal (on sth)** avoir la priorité (sur qch); **to give sb first refusal** donner la priorité à qn; **you promised me first refusal on the car** tu m'as promis que je serais le premier à qui tu proposerais (d'acheter) la voiture

▸▸ *Mktg* ***refusal rate*** taux *m* de refus

refuse¹ [rɪˈfjuːz] **1** *vt* (**a**) *(turn down → invitation, gift)* refuser; *(→ offer)* refuser, décliner; *(→ request, proposition)* refuser, rejeter; **to refuse to do sth** refuser de *ou Formal* se refuser à faire qch; **I refuse to accept that all is lost** je refuse de croire que tout soit perdu; **to refuse to comment** se refuser à tout commentaire; **I refused to take delivery of the parcel** j'ai refusé le paquet; **to refuse to fight** refuser le combat; **the car refuses to start** la voiture ne veut pas démarrer; **to be refused** essuyer un refus; **she refused him** *(would not marry him)* elle l'a rejeté

(**b**) *(deny → permission)* refuser (d'accorder); *(→ help, visa)* refuser; **he was refused entry** on lui a refusé l'entrée; **they were refused a loan** on leur a refusé un prêt; **we were refused permission to see him** on nous a refusé la permission de le voir; **I don't see how we can refuse them** je ne vois pas comment on peut le leur refuser

(**c**) *Horseriding* refuser; **to refuse a jump** refuser de sauter

2 *vi (person)* refuser; *(horse)* refuser l'obstacle

refuse² [ˈrefjuːs] *n Br (household)* ordures *fpl* (ménagères); *(garden)* détritus *mpl*; *(industrial)* déchets *mpl*; **no refuse** *(sign)* défense de déposer les ordures

▸▸ ***refuse bag*** sac *m* à ordures; *Br* ***refuse bin*** poubelle *f*; *Br* ***refuse chute*** vide-ordures *m inv*; *Br* ***refuse collection*** ramassage *m* d'ordures; *Br* ***refuse collector*** éboueur *m*; *Br* ***refuse disposal*** traitement *m* des ordures; ***refuse disposal unit*** broyeur *m* d'ordures; *Br* ***refuse dump*** *(public)* décharge *f* (publique), dépotoir *m*

refusenik, refusnik [rɪˈfjuːznɪk] *n* refuznik *mf*

refutable [ˈrefjʊtəbəl] *adj* réfutable

refutation [ˌrefjuːˈteɪʃən] *n* réfutation *f*

refute [rɪˈfjuːt] *vt (disprove)* réfuter; *(deny)* nier

reg[1] *(written abbr* **registered***)* **reg trademark** marque *f* déposée

reg[2] [redʒ] *Br Fam (abbr* **registration***)* immatriculation ❑ *f*; **what reg is your car?** ta voiture est de quelle année? ❑

regain [rɪˈgeɪn] *vt* **(a)** *(territory)* reconquérir; *(health)* recouvrer; *(strength)* retrouver; *(sight, composure)* retrouver, recouvrer; *(glory)* retrouver; **to regain possession of sth** rentrer en possession de qch; **to regain lost time** rattraper le temps perdu; **to regain consciousness** reprendre connaissance; **to regain one's balance** retrouver l'équilibre; **to regain one's footing** reprendre pied

(b) *Formal (get back to → road, place, shelter)* regagner

regal [ˈriːgəl] **1** *adj* royal; *Fig (person, bearing)* majestueux; *(banquet, decor)* somptueux

2 *n Mus* régale *f*

regale [rɪˈgeɪl] *vt* **to regale sb with sth** régaler qn de qch

regalia [rɪˈgeɪljə] *npl* **(a)** *(insignia)* insignes *mpl* **(b)** *(finery, robes)* accoutrement *m*, atours *mpl*; **to be in full regalia** *(judge, general)* être en grande tenue; *Fig Hum (woman)* être paré de tous ses atours

regality [rɪˈgælɪtɪ] **1** *n* royauté *f*, souveraineté *f*

2 regalities *npl* droits *mpl* régaliens

regally [ˈriːgəlɪ] *adv* royalement, majestueusement

regard [rɪˈgɑːd] **1** *vt* **(a)** *(consider)* considérer, regarder; *(treat)* traiter; **I regard him as** *or* **like a brother** je le considère comme un frère; **I regard their conclusions as correct** *or* **to be correct** je tiens leurs conclusions pour correctes; **I prefer to regard the whole thing as a joke** je préfère considérer toute l'affaire comme une plaisanterie; **we didn't regard the problem as deserving attention** nous n'avons pas considéré que le problème méritait notre attention; **he regards himself as an expert** il se considère comme *ou* il se prend pour un expert

(b) *(esteem)* estimer, tenir en estime; **to regard sb highly** tenir qn en grande estime; **highly regarded** très estimé

(c) *Formal (observe)* regarder, observer; **they regarded me with some trepidation** ils m'ont regardé avec une certaine inquiétude

(d) *(heed → advice, wishes)* tenir compte de

2 *n* **(a)** *(notice, attention)* considération *f*, attention *f*; **to pay regard to sth** tenir compte de qch, faire attention à qch; **they paid scant regard to my explanations** ils n'ont guère fait attention à mes explications; **having regard to his age** en tenant compte de *ou* eu égard à son âge; *Admin* **having regard to paragraph 24** vu le paragraphe 24

(b) *(care, respect)* souci *m*, considération *f*, respect *m*; **they have no regard for your feelings** ils ne se soucient pas de vos sentiments; **to have scant regard for human rights** se soucier peu des droits de l'homme; **they showed no regard for our wishes** ils n'ont tenu aucun compte de nos souhaits; **without regard for the difficulties** sans se soucier des difficultés; **with out regard to race or colour** sans distinction de race ni de couleur; **with no regard for his health** sans se soucier de sa santé; **out of regard for** par égard pour; **with due regard for your elders** avec les égards dus à vos aînés; **without due regard to** sans tenir compte de

(c) *(connection)* **in this regard** à cet égard

(d) *(esteem)* estime *f*, considération *f*; **to have great regard for sb** avoir beaucoup d'estime pour qn; **I hold them in high regard** je les tiens en grande estime

(e) *Formal (eyes, look)* regard *m*; **to turn one's regard on sb** tourner ses regards sur qn

3 regards *npl* **(a)** *(in letter)* **regards, Peter** bien cordialement, Peter; **kind regards, best regards** bien à vous, amitiés, bien amicalement

(b) *(in greetings)* **give them my regards** transmettez-leur mon bon souvenir; **he sends his regards** vous avez le bonjour de sa part

4 as regards *prep* en ce qui concerne, pour ce qui est de; **as regards the cost** en ce qui concerne le coût, quant au coût

5 in regard to, with regard to *prep* en ce qui concerne

regardful [rɪˈgɑːdfʊl] *adj Formal* **to be regardful of** *(needs, wishes, difficulties)* être attentif à, faire attention à; *(children, interests, image)* s'occuper de, soigner

regarding [rɪˈgɑːdɪŋ] *prep* quant à, en ce qui concerne, pour ce qui est de; **what are we going to do regarding Fred?** qu'allons-nous faire en ce qui concerne Fred?; **questions regarding management** des questions relatives à la gestion

regardless [rɪˈgɑːdlɪs] **1** *adv (in any case)* quand même, en tout cas; *(without worrying)* sans s'occuper *ou* se soucier du reste; **they carried on regardless** ils continuèrent quand même

2 regardless of *prep (consequences, danger, noise etc)* sans se soucier de; **regardless of what you think** *(without bothering)* sans se soucier de ce que vous pensez; *(whatever your opinion)* indépendamment de ce que vous pouvez penser; **regardless of the danger** sans se soucier du danger; **regardless of the expense** sans regarder à la dépense

regatta [rɪˈgætə] *n* régate *f*

regd *(written abbr* **registered***)* **regd trademark** marque *f* déposée

regency [ˈriːdʒənsɪ] *(pl* **regencies***)* **1** *n* régence *f*

2 Regency *comp (style, furniture, period)* Regency *(inv)*, de la Régence anglaise *(1811–1820)*

regenerate 1 *vt* [rɪˈdʒenəreɪt] régénérer; **to regenerate interest in sth** provoquer un regain d'intérêt pour qch, raviver l'intérêt pour qch

2 *vi* [rɪˈdʒenəreɪt] *(industry, party etc)* se régénérer; *(tail, organ etc)* repousser

3 *adj* [rɪˈdʒenərət] régénéré

regeneration [rɪˌdʒenəˈreɪʃən] *n (gen)* régénération *f*; *(of interest)* regain *m*; *(of urban area)* reconstruction *f*, rénovation *f*

regenerative [rɪˈdʒenərətɪv] *adj* régénérateur

►► *Aut* ***regenerative braking*** freinage *m* à régénération

regent [ˈriːdʒənt] *n* **(a)** *Hist* régent(e) *m,f*; **prince regent** prince *m* régent **(b)** *Am* = membre du conseil d'administration d'une université

►► ***Regent's Park*** = parc où se trouve le zoo de Londres ainsi qu'un théâtre en plein air où l'on donne des pièces de Shakespeare; ***Regent Street*** = rue commerçante dans le West End à Londres

reggae [ˈregeɪ] **1** *n* reggae *m*

2 *comp (song, group, singer)* reggae *(inv)*

regicidal [redʒɪˈsaɪdəl] *adj* régicide

regicide [ˈredʒɪsaɪd] *n (person)* régicide *mf*; *(crime)* régicide *m*

regime, régime [reɪˈʒiːm] *n* **(a)** *Pol & (in sociology)* régime *m*; **under the present regime** sous le régime actuel; **military regime** régime *m* militaire **(b)** *Med* régime *m (sous surveillance médicale)*

regimen [ˈredʒɪmen] *n* régime *m (sous surveillance médicale)*

regiment 1 *n* [ˈredʒɪmənt] *Mil & Fig* régiment *m*; **there's enough to feed a regiment** il y a de quoi nourrir un régiment

2 [ˈredʒɪment] *vt (organize)* enrégimenter; *(discipline)* soumettre à une discipline trop stricte

regimental [ˌredʒɪˈmentəl] *Mil* **1** *adj (mess, dress)* régimentaire, du régiment; *(band, mascot)* du régiment; *Fig (organization)* trop discipliné, enrégimenté

2 regimentals *npl* uniforme *m ou* tenue *f* (militaire); **in full regimentals** en grande tenue

►► ***regimental sergeant major*** ≃ adjudant-chef *m*

regimentally [redʒɪˈmentəlɪ] *adv* par régiment

regimentation [ˌredʒɪmenˈteɪʃən] *n Pej (of business, system)* organisation *f* quasi militaire; *(in school)* discipline *f* étouffante *ou* trop sévère

regimented [ˈredʒɪmentɪd] *adj Pej* strict; **a regimented lifestyle** un mode de vie strict; **it's a very regimented organization** c'est une organisation très rigide *ou* stricte

Regina [rɪˈdʒaɪnə] *n Br* **Victoria Regina** la reine Victoria; *Law* **Regina vs Smith** le ministère public contre Smith

region [ˈriːdʒən] **1** *n* **(a)** *Geog & Admin* région *f*; **in the Liverpool region** dans la région de Liverpool; *Fig* **the lower regions** les Enfers *mpl*

(b) *(in body)* région *f*; **in the region of the heart** dans la région du cœur; **in the lower back region** dans la région lombaire

(c) *(of knowledge, sentiments)* domaine *m*; **now we move into the region of mere speculation** là, nous entrons dans le domaine de la spéculation pure

2 in the region of *prep* environ; **in the region of 10 kg** dans les 10 kg (environ); **in the region of £500** aux environs de *ou* dans les 500 livres

regional [ˈriːdʒənəl] *adj* régional

►► *Br* ***regional development*** *(building, land development)* aménagement *m* du territoire; *(for jobs)* action *f* régionale; *Br* ***regional development corporation*** = organisme pour l'aménagement du territoire

regionalism [ˈriːdʒənəlɪzəm] *n* régionalisme *m*

regionalist [ˈriːdʒənəlɪst] **1** *adj* régionaliste

2 *n* régionaliste *mf*

regionalization [ˌriːdʒənəlaɪˈzeɪʃən] *n* régionalisation *f*

regionalize, -ise [ˈriːdʒənəlaɪz] *vt* régionaliser

regionally [ˈriːdʒənəlɪ] *adv* à l'échelle régionale

REGISTER [ˈredʒɪstə(r)]

registre	► **1 (a), (c) – (g)**
liste	► **1 (a)**
enregistreur	► **1 (b)**
caisse	► **1 (b)**
enregistrer	► **2 (a)**
inscrire	► **2 (a)**
indiquer	► **2 (b)**
exprimer	► **2 (b)**
s'inscrire	► **3 (a)**
donner une indication	► **3 (b)**

1 *n* **(a)** *(book)* registre *m*; *(list)* liste *f*; *Sch* registre *m* de présences, cahier *m* d'appel; *(on ship)* livre *m* de bord; **to keep a register** tenir un registre; **to enter sth in a register** inscrire qch dans un registre; *Sch* **to call** *or* **to take the register** faire l'appel; **electoral register** liste *f* électorale; **commercial** *or* **trade register** registre *m* du commerce; **register of shipping** registre *m* maritime; **register of births, deaths and marriages** registre *m* de l'état civil; *St Exch* **register of shareholders** registre *m* des actionnaires

(b) *(gauge)* enregistreur *m*; *(counter)* compteur *m*; *(cash till)* caisse *f* (enregistreuse)

(c) *(pitch → of voice)* registre *m*, tessiture *f*; *(→ of instrument)* registre *m*

(d) *Ling* registre *m*, niveau *m* de langue

(e) *Typ* registre *m*; **to be in/out of register** être/ne pas être en registre

(f) *Art* registre *m*

(g) *Comput (of memory)* registre *m*

2 *vt* **(a)** *(record → name)* (faire) enregistrer, (faire) inscrire; *(→ on list)* inscrire; *(→ birth, death)* déclarer; *(→ vehicle)* (faire) immatriculer; *(→ trademark)* déposer; *(→ request)* enregistrer; *(→ readings)* relever, enregistrer; *Fin (→ shares)* immatriculer; *(→ mortgage)* inscrire; *Comput (→ software)* inscrire; *Mil (→ recruit)* recenser; **to register a complaint** déposer une plainte; **to register a protest** protester; **to register one's vote** exprimer son vote, voter; **record wind speeds have been registered in the country** on a enregistré des vitesses record du vent dans le pays; **is the car registered in your name?** est-ce que la voiture est à votre nom?; **she is not registered at this hotel** elle n'est pas descendue à cet hôtel; **I'd like to register my disagreement officially** je voudrais exprimer officiellement mon désaccord

(b) *(indicate → of thermometer, dial etc)* indiquer; *(→ of person, face)* exprimer; **the needle is registering 700 kg** l'aiguille indique 700 kg; **the earthquake registered seven on the Richter scale** le séisme a atteint sept sur l'échelle de Richter; **winds registering 100 mph** ≃ des vents atteignant 160 km/h; **her face registered disbelief** l'incrédulité se lisait sur son visage; *Fin* **the pound has registered a fall** la livre a enregistré une baisse

(c) *(obtain → success)* remporter; *(→ defeat)* essuyer (**d**) *Fam (understand)* saisir, piger; **they don't seem to have registered (the fact) that the situation is hopeless** ils ne semblent pas se rendre compte que la situation est désespérée □

(**e**) *(parcel, letter)* envoyer en recommandé

(**f**) *(at railway station, airport etc → suitcase)* (faire) enregistrer

(**g**) *Typ* mettre en registre

(**h**) *Tech* (faire) aligner, faire coïncider

3 *vi* (**a**) *(for course)* s'inscrire, se faire inscrire; *(at hotel)* s'inscrire sur *ou* signer le registre (de l'hôtel); *(voter)* se faire inscrire sur la liste électorale; **to register at night school/for Chinese lessons** s'inscrire aux cours du soir/à des cours de chinois; **foreign nationals must register with the police** les ressortissants étrangers doivent se faire enregistrer au commissariat de police; **to register with a GP/on the electoral roll** se faire inscrire auprès d'un médecin traitant/sur les listes électorales

(**b**) *(instrument)* donner une indication; **is the barometer registering?** est-ce que le baromètre indique quelque chose?; **the current was too weak to register** le courant était trop faible pour donner une indication; **the quake was so small it barely even registered** la secousse a été à peine perceptible

(**c**) *Fam (be understood)* **maths just doesn't register with him** il ne comprend absolument rien aux maths □; **I did give them the address but I don't think it registered** je leur ai bien donné l'adresse mais je ne crois pas qu'ils l'aient retenue □; **her success didn't really register with her** elle ne s'était pas vraiment rendu compte de son succès □; **the truth slowly began to register (with me)** petit à petit, la vérité m'est apparue □; **his name doesn't register (with me)** son nom ne me dit rien □

(**d**) *Tech* coïncider, être aligné; *Typ* être en registre

►► *Admin* ***register office*** bureau *m* de l'état civil; *Naut* ***register ton*** tonneau *m* (de jauge)

---

registered ['redʒɪstəd] *adj* (**a**) *(student, elector)* inscrit; *Br (charity)* ≃ reconnu d'utilité publique; *Fin (bond, securities, stocks)* nominatif; **registered unemployed** inscrit au chômage; *Br* **to be registered disabled** avoir une carte d'invalidité

(**b**) *(letter, parcel, mail)* recommandé; *Br* **send it registered** envoyez-le en recommandé

►► *Fin* ***registered bond*** obligation *f* nominative; *Fin* ***registered capital*** capital *m* déclaré; ***registered charity*** organisme *m* de bienfaisance reconnu par l'État; ***registered childminder*** nourrice *f* agréée; ***registered company*** société *f* inscrite au registre du commerce; *Fin* ***registered debenture*** obligation *f* nominative; *Mktg* ***registered design*** modèle *m* déposé; ***Registered General Nurse*** infirmier(ère) *m,f* diplômé(e) d'État *(remplacé en 1992 par "Registered Nurse")*; ***Registered Mental Nurse*** infirmier(ère) *m,f* psychiatrique diplômé(e) d'État; ***registered name*** nom *m* déposé; ***Registered Nurse*** infirmier(ère) *m,f* diplômé(e) d'État; *Br* ***registered office*** siège *m* social; *Br* ***registered post*** envoi *m* recommandé; *Can Fin* ***registered retirement savings plan*** régime *m* enregistré d'épargne-retraite; *Fin* ***registered securities*** titres *mpl* nominatifs, valeurs *fpl* nominatives; *Fin* ***registered share certificate*** certificat *m* nominatif d'action(s); *St Exch* ***registered stock*** titres *mpl* nominatifs, valeurs *fpl* nominatives; *Naut* ***registered tonnage*** jauge *f*; ***registered trademark*** marque *f* déposée; *Comput* ***registered user*** utilisateur(trice) *m,f* disposant d'une licence

registrar [,redʒɪ'strɑː(r)] *n* (**a**) *Br Admin* officier *m* de l'état civil; **to inform the registrar's office of a death** déclarer un décès au bureau de l'état civil

(**b**) *Br & NZ Med* chef *m* de clinique

(**c**) *Law* greffier *m*

(**d**) *Am Univ* chef *m* du service *ou* du bureau des inscriptions; *Br Univ* secrétaire *m* général

(**e**) *Com & Fin* **companies' registrar** responsable *mf* du registre des sociétés

►► ***the Registrar General*** le Conservateur des actes de l'état civil

registrarship ['redʒɪstrɑːʃɪp] *n* (**a**) *Br Admin* charge *f* d'officier de l'état civil (**b**) *Br & NZ Med* charge *f* de chef de clinique (**c**) *Law* charge *f* de greffier

registration [,redʒɪ'streɪʃən] *n* (**a**) *(of name)* enregistrement *m*; *(of student)* inscription *f*; *(of voter)* inscription *f* sur la liste électorale; *(of trademark)* dépôt *m*; *(of vehicle, shares, company)* immatriculation *f*; *(of luggage)* enregistrement *m*; *(of birth, death, marriage)* déclaration *f*; *(of mortgage)* inscription *f*; **when does registration start?** *(for university, evening classes)* quand les inscriptions commencent-elles?

(**b**) *Br Sch* appel *m*

(**c**) *(of mail)* recommandation *f*

(**d**) *Mus (on organ)* registration *f*

(**e**) *Am* ≃ carte *f* grise

►► *St Exch* ***registration body*** chambre *f* d'enregistrement; ***registration card*** *(for enrolling on course etc)* fiche *f* d'inscription; *(for foreign guests)* fiche *f* voyageur; *(for non-EU guests)* fiche *f* de police; *Comput* licence *f*; ***registration certificate*** matricule *f*; *Br Aut* ***registration document*** ≃ carte *f* grise; *Fin* ***registration fees*** droits *mpl* d'inscription; ***registration number*** *Br Aut* numéro *m* d'immatriculation; *(of student)* numéro *m* d'inscription; *(of baggage)* numéro *m* d'enregistrement; *Comput* numéro *m* de licence; **the car has the registration number E123 SYK** la voiture est immatriculée E123 SYK; *Austr & NZ Aut* ***registration plate*** plaque *f* d'immatriculation *ou* minéralogique; ***registration and transfer fees*** droits *mpl* d'inscription et de transfert

registry ['redʒɪstrɪ] (*pl* **registries**) *n* (**a**) *(registration)* enregistrement *m*; *Univ* inscription *f*

(**b**) *(office)* bureau *m* d'enregistrement

(**c**) *Naut* immatriculation *f*; **a ship of Japanese registry** un navire immatriculé au Japon; **port of registry** port *m* d'attache

(**d**) *Comput (Windows® file)* registre *m*

►► *Br Admin* ***registry office*** bureau *m* de l'état civil; **to be married at a registry office** se marier civilement, ≃ se marier à la mairie

Regius professor ['riːdʒɪəs-] *n Br Univ* = professeur titulaire d'une chaire de fondation royale

reglet ['reglɪt] *n Archit* réglet *m*; *Typ* filet *m*, réglette *f*

regnal ['regnəl] *adj*

►► ***regnal year*** année *f* du règne

regnant ['regnənt] *adj* (**a**) *(after n) (queen, prince)* régnant (**b**) *Literary (idea)* répandu; *(taste)* prépondérant

regrade [,riː'greɪd] *vt (essay)* renoter, noter de nouveau; *(employee, nurse, officer, objects)* reclasser

regrading [,riː'greɪdɪŋ] *n (of employee, nurse, officer)* reclassement *m*

regress 1 *vi* [rɪ'gres] (**a**) *Biol & Psy* régresser; **to regress to childhood** régresser à un stade infantile; **to regress to an earlier stage** régresser

(**b**) *Sch (go back)* reculer, revenir en arrière

2 *n* ['riːgres] (**a**) *Biol & Psy* régression *f* (**b**) *(retreat)* recul *m*, régression *f*

regression [rɪ'greʃən] *n* (**a**) *Biol & Psy* régression *f* (**b**) *(retreat)* recul *m*, régression *f*

regressive [rɪ'gresɪv] *adj Biol, Fin & Psy* régressif; *(movement)* de recul

regressively [rɪ'gresɪvlɪ] *adv Biol, Fin & Psy* régressivement

regressiveness [rɪ'gresɪvnɪs] *n Biol, Fin & Psy* caractère régressif

regret [rɪ'gret] (*pt & pp* **regretted**, *cont* **regretting**)

1 *vt* (**a**) *(be sorry about → action, behaviour)* regretter; **I regret to say** *(apologize)* j'ai le regret de *ou* je regrette de dire; *(unfortunately)* hélas, malheureusement; **we regret to inform you...** nous avons le regret de vous informer...; **to regret doing** *or* **having done sth** regretter d'avoir fait qch; **I regret ever mentioning it** je regrette d'en avoir jamais parlé; **I regret not being able to come** je regrette *ou* je suis désolé de ne pouvoir venir; **she regrets that she never met Donovan** elle regrette de n'avoir jamais rencontré Donovan; **it is to be regretted that...** il est regrettable *ou* à regretter que... + *subjunctive*; **the accident/the error is greatly to be regretted** l'accident/l'erreur est tout à fait regrettable *ou* déplorable; **you'll live to regret this!** vous le regretterez!; **the airline regrets any inconvenience caused to passengers** la compagnie s'excuse pour la gêne occasionnée

(**b**) *Literary (lament)* regretter; **she will be much regretted** on la regrettera beaucoup; **he regrets his student days** il regrette l'époque où il était étudiant

2 *n (sorrow, sadness)* regret *m*; **with regret** avec regret; **we announce with regret the death of our chairman** nous avons le regret de vous faire part de la mort de notre directeur; **much to our regret** à notre grand regret; **to express one's regrets at** *or* **about sth** exprimer ses regrets devant qch; **I have no regrets** je n'ai pas de regrets, je ne regrette rien; **do you have any regrets about** *or* **for what you did?** regrettez-vous ce que vous avez fait?; **my only regret is that I didn't resign earlier** je n'ai qu'un regret, c'est de ne pas avoir donné ma démission plus tôt; **to send sb one's regrets** *(condolences)* exprimer ses regrets à qn; *(apologies)* s'excuser auprès de qn

regretful [rɪ'gretfʊl] *adj (person)* plein de regrets; *(expression, attitude)* de regret; **to be** *or* **to feel regretful about sth** regretter qch

regretfully [rɪ'gretfʊlɪ] *adv (sadly)* avec regret; *(unfortunately)* malheureusement

regrettable [rɪ'gretəbəl] *adj (unfortunate)* regrettable, malencontreux; *(inconvenient)* fâcheux, ennuyeux; **it is most regrettable that you were not informed** il est fort regrettable que vous n'ayez pas été informé

regrettably [rɪ'gretəblɪ] *adv (unfortunately)* malheureusement, malencontreusement; *(inconveniently)* fâcheusement; **regrettably few people were present** il est regrettable que si peu de personnes soient venues; **a joke in regrettably poor taste** une plaisanterie dont le mauvais goût est à déplorer

regroup [,riː'gruːp] **1** *vt* regrouper

2 *vi* se regrouper

regt *(written abbr* **regiment***)* régiment *m*

REGULAR ['regjʊlə(r)]

habitué	► **1 (a)**
régulier	► **2 (a) – (c), (e)**
habituel	► **2 (b)**
fidèle	► **2 (b)**
permanent	► **2 (c)**
uni	► **2 (d)**

1 *n* (**a**) *(customer → in bar, restaurant)* habitué(e) *m,f*; *(→ in shop)* client(e) *m,f* fidèle

(**b**) *(contributor, player)* **she's a regular on our column** elle contribue régulièrement à notre rubrique; **he's a regular in the team** il joue régulièrement dans l'équipe

(**c**) *Mil (soldier)* militaire *m* de carrière

(**d**) *Rel* religieux *m* régulier, régulier *m*

(**e**) *Am (fuel)* ordinaire *m*

(**f**) *Am Pol (loyal party member)* membre *m* fidèle (du parti)

2 *adj* (**a**) *(steady, even → features, footsteps, movement, sound)* régulier; *(→ breathing, pulse)* régulier, égal; *(→ meetings, service, salary)* régulier; **at regular intervals** à intervalles réguliers; **on a regular basis** régulièrement; **it's a regular occurrence** cela arrive régulièrement; **she has regular treatment** elle suit régulièrement un traitement; **he was a man of regular habits** il avait ses habitudes; **to keep regular hours** se lever et se coucher à heures régulières; **to have regular bowel movements** aller régulièrement à la selle; **bran will keep you regular** le son vous fera aller régulièrement à la selle; **to be as regular as clockwork** être réglé comme une horloge

(**b**) *(usual → brand, dentist, procedure, supplier)* habituel; *(→ customer)* régulier, fidèle; *(→ listener, reader)* fidèle; *(→ price, model)* courant; *(→ size)* courant, standard; **who is your regular doctor?** qui est votre médecin traitant?; **she's a regular reader of this paper** elle lit ce journal régulièrement; **to be in regular employment** avoir un emploi régulier; **a regular visitor to the house** un/une des habitué(e)s de la maison; **a regular Coke®** un Coca® normal; **to go through the regular channels** suivre la filière normale *ou* habituelle; **it's regular practice to pay by cheque** les paiements par chèque sont pratique courante

(**c**) *(permanent → agent)* attitré, permanent; *(→ police force)* permanent, régulier; *(→ army)* de métier; *(→ soldier)* de carrière

(**d**) *(smooth, level)* uni, égal

(**e**) *Gram & Math* régulier

(**f**) *Fam (as intensifier)* vrai ❑, véritable ❑; **a regular mess** une vraie pagaille; **a regular hero** un vrai héros

(**g**) *Am Fam (pleasant)* sympa, chouette; **a regular guy** un type sympa

(**h**) *Rel (clergy)* régulier

(**i**) *Am Pol (loyal to party)* fidèle au parti

3 *adv Fam* régulièrement ❑

►► *Journ* ***regular column*** chronique *f*; ***regular customer*** client(e) *m,f* habitué(e); *Am Aut* ***regular (grade) gas*** (essence *f*) ordinaire *m*; ***regular price*** prix *m* de règle; *Gram* ***regular verb*** verbe *m* régulier

---

regularity [ˌregjʊ'lærɪtɪ] (*pl* **regularities**) *n* régularité *f*; **to do sth with unfailing regularity** faire qch avec une régularité infaillible

regularization [ˌregjʊləraɪ'zeɪʃən] *n* régularisation *f*

regularize, -ise ['regjʊləraɪz] *vt* régulariser

regularly ['regjʊləlɪ] *adv* régulièrement

regulate ['regjʊleɪt] *vt* (**a**) *(control, adjust → machine, expenditure)* régler; *(→ flow)* réguler; **the machine is regulated by a lever** la machine se règle à l'aide d'un levier (**b**) *(organize → habit, life)* régler; *(→ with rules)* réglementer; **he followed a well regulated diet** il suivit un régime équilibré; **rules regulating the use of additives** les réglementations qui régissent l'emploi des additifs

regulating ['regjʊleɪtɪŋ] *adj (knob, switch, valve)* de réglage; *(hormone, mechanism)* régulateur; **self-regulating** à réglage automatique

regulation [ˌregjʊ'leɪʃən] **1** *n* (**a**) *(ruling)* règlement *m*; **it's contrary to** *or* **against (the) regulations** c'est contraire au règlement; **it complies with EU regulations** c'est conforme aux dispositions communautaires; **safety regulations** règles *fpl* de sécurité; **fire regulations** consignes *fpl* en cas d'incendie; **building regulations** normes *fpl* de construction; **(food) hygiene regulations** normes *fpl* d'hygiène alimentaire

(**b**) *(adjustment, control → of machine)* réglage *m*; *(→ of flow, voltage)* régulation *f*

(**c**) *(by law → of food additives etc)* réglementation *f*; *(→ of information)* contrôle *m*

2 *comp (size, haircut, issue, dress)* réglementaire; *(pistol, helmet)* d'ordonnance

regulative ['regjʊleɪtɪv] *adj* régulateur

regulator ['regjʊleɪtə(r)] *n* (**a**) *(person)* régulateur(trice) *m,f* (**b**) *(apparatus)* régulateur *m*

regulatory ['regjʊlətərɪ] *adj (framework)* réglementaire; *(authority)* de contrôle

►► ***regulatory body*** instance *f* de contrôle

regulo ['regjʊləʊ] *n Br* **regulo 4** thermostat 4

regulus ['regjʊləs] *n Metal* régule *m*

regurgitate [rɪ'gɜːdʒɪteɪt] **1** *vt (food)* régurgiter; [illegible] régurgiter, reproduire

2 *vi (bird)* dégorger

regurgitation [rɪˌgɜːdʒɪ'teɪʃən] *n* régurgitation *f*

rehab ['riːhæb] *n* **to be in rehab** faire une cure de désintoxication

►► ***rehab centre*** centre *m* de désintoxication

rehabilitate [ˌriːə'bɪlɪteɪt] *vt* (**a**) *(convict, drug addict, alcoholic)* réhabiliter; *(restore to health)* rééduquer; *(find employment for)* réinsérer (**b**) *(reinstate → idea, style)* réhabiliter (**c**) *(renovate → area, building)* réhabiliter

rehabilitation ['riːəˌbɪlɪ'teɪʃən] *n* (**a**) *(of disgraced person, memory, reputation)* réhabilitation *f*; *(of convict, alcoholic, drug addict)* réhabilitation *f*; *(of disabled person)* rééducation *f*; *(of unemployed)* réinsertion *f* (**b**) *(of idea, style)* réhabilitation *f* (**c**) *(of area, building)* réhabilitation *f*

►► ***rehabilitation centre*** *(for work training)* centre *m* de réadaptation; *(for drug addicts)* centre *m* de désintoxication

rehash *Fam Pej* **1** *vt* [ˌriː'hæʃ] (**a**) *Br (rearrange)* remanier ❑ (**b**) *(repeat → argument)* ressasser ❑; *(→ programme)* reprendre ❑; *(→ artistic material)* remanier ❑

2 *n* ['riːhæʃ] réchauffé *m*; **it's just a rehash** ce n'est que du réchauffé; **it was a rehash of her first novel** c'était une resucée de son premier roman

rehear [ˌriː'hɪə(r)] (*pt & pp* **reheard** [-'hɜːd]) *vt Law* entendre de nouveau, réviser

rehearing [ˌriː'hɪərɪŋ] *n Law* révision *f* de procès

rehearsal [rɪ'hɜːsəl] *n* (**a**) *also Fig (practice)* répétition *f*; **to have** *or* **to hold a rehearsal** faire une répétition; **when's the rehearsal?** quand est-ce qu'on répète?; **she's in rehearsal** elle est en répétition; **the play is currently in rehearsal** ils sont en train de répéter; *Fig* **the naval exercises were just a rehearsal for the real thing** les exercices navals n'étaient qu'une répétition

(**b**) *Literary (recital → of list, facts, complaints)* récit *m*, énumération *f*; *(→ of old arguments)* répétition *f*; **a rehearsal of old grievances** une énumération d'anciens griefs

►► ***rehearsal room*** salle *f* de répétition

rehearse [rɪ'hɜːs] **1** *vt* (**a**) *also Fig (play, music, speech, coup d'état)* répéter; *(actors, singers, orchestra)* faire répéter; **you'd better rehearse your speech** vous feriez bien de répéter votre discours; **well rehearsed** *(play, performance)* bien répété, répété avec soin; *(actor)* qui a bien répété son rôle, qui sait son rôle sur le bout des doigts; *(request, coup d'état, applause)* bien *ou* soigneusement préparé; **I rehearsed what I was going to say** j'ai préparé ce que j'allais dire

(**b**) *Literary (recite → list, facts, complaints)* réciter, énumérer; *(→ old arguments)* répeter, ressasser

2 *vi Mus & Theat* répéter

reheat [ˌriː'hiːt] *vt* réchauffer

re-heel [ˌriː-] *vt (shoes)* remettre des talons à

rehome [ˌriː'həʊm] *vt (child, pet)* trouver un nouveau foyer pour

Rehoboam [ˌriːə'bəʊəm] *pr n* Roboam

rehoboam [ˌriːə'bəʊəm] *n (wine bottle)* réhoboam *m*

rehouse [ˌriː'haʊz] *vt* reloger

rehousing [ˌriː'haʊzɪŋ] *n* relogement *m*

rehydrate [ˌriː'haɪdreɪt] **1** *vt* réhydrater

2 *vi* se réhydrater

rehydration [ˌriːhaɪ'dreɪʃən] *n Med* réhydratation *f*

Reichian ['raɪkɪən] *Psy* **1** *n* reichien(enne) *m,f*

2 *adj* reichien

►► ***Reichian therapy*** bioénergie *f*

reification [ˌreɪɪfɪ'keɪʃən] *n* réification *f*

reify ['reɪɪfaɪ] (*pt & pp* **reified**) *vt* réifier

reign [reɪn] **1** *n* règne *m*; **in** *or* **under the reign of** sous le règne de; **the reign of silence** le règne du silence; **reign of terror** règne *m* de terreur

2 *vi* (**a**) *(rule)* régner (**b**) *Fig (predominate)* régner; **silence reigns** le silence règne; **to reign supreme** *(monarch, champion)* régner en maître; **plague/terror reigns over the town** la peste sévit dans/la terreur règne sur la ville

►**reign over** *vt insep (of monarch, silence etc)* régner sur

reigning ['reɪnɪŋ] *adj* (**a**) *(monarch, emperor)* régnant (**b**) *(present → champion)* en titre (**c**) *(predominant* [illegible]*)* régnant, dominant

reignite [ˌriːɪg'naɪt] *vt* rallumer

Reiki ['raɪkɪ] *n* Reiki *m*

reillume [riːɪ'ljuːm] *vt Literary* éclairer de nouveau

reimbursable [ˌriːɪm'bɜːsəbəl] *adj* remboursable; **reimbursable over 25 years** remboursable sur 25 ans

reimburse [ˌriːɪm'bɜːs] *vt* rembourser; **to reimburse sb (for) sth** rembourser qch à qn *ou* qn de qch; **I was reimbursed** je me suis fait rembourser

reimbursement [ˌriːɪm'bɜːsmənt] *n* remboursement *m*

reimport 1 *vt* [ˌriːɪm'pɔːt] réimporter

2 *n* [ˌriː'ɪmpɔːt] réimportation *f*

reimportation [ˌriːɪmpɔː'teɪʃən] *n* réimportation *f*

reimpose [ˌriːɪm'pəʊz] *vt* réimposer

reimposition [ˌriːɪmpə'zɪʃən] *n* réimposition *f*

Reims [riːmz] *n* Reims *m*

rein [reɪn] **1** *n* (**a**) *(for horse)* rêne *f*

(**b**) *Fig (control)* bride *f*; **to give (a) free rein to sb** laisser à qn la bride sur le cou; **to give free rein to one's emotions/imagination** donner libre cours à ses émotions/son imagination; **to keep a rein on sth** tenir qch en bride, maîtriser qch; **to keep a tight rein on sb** tenir la bride haute à qn; **to keep a tight rein on one's emotions** ne pas se laisser aller à ses émotions, maîtriser ses émotions; **to keep a tight rein on one's spending** surveiller étroitement ses dépenses

2 reins *npl (for horse, child)* rêne *f*; *Fig* **the reins of government** les rênes du gouvernement; **to hand over the reins** passer les rênes

►**rein back 1** *vi* tirer sur les rênes, serrer la bride

2 *vt sep* faire ralentir, freiner

►**rein in 1** *vi* ralentir

2 *vt sep* (**a**) *(horse)* serrer la bride à, ramener au pas (**b**) *Fig (person)* ramener au pas; *(emotions)* maîtriser, réfréner

reincarnate 1 *vt* [riː'ɪnkɑːneɪt] réincarner

2 *adj* [ˌriːɪn'kɑːnɪt] réincarné

reincarnation [ˌriːɪnkɑː'neɪʃən] *n* réincarnation *f*

reincorporate [ˌriːɪn'kɔːpəreɪt] *vt* réincorporer

reindeer ['reɪndɪə(r)] (*pl* **inv**) *n Zool* renne *m*

►► *Bot* ***reindeer moss*** cladonie *f*

reinfect [ˌriːɪn'fekt] *vt* réinfecter

reinfection [ˌriːɪn'fekʃən] *n* réinfection *f*

reinforce [ˌriːɪn'fɔːs] *vt* (**a**) *Mil* renforcer (**b**) *(gen) & Constr (wall, heel)* renforcer (**c**) *Fig (demand)* appuyer; *(argument)* renforcer

►► ***reinforced concrete*** béton *m* armé

reinforcement [ˌriːɪn'fɔːsmənt] **1** *n* (**a**) *(strengthening → of army, wall, fabric)* renforcement *m*; *(→ of foundations)* consolidation *f*; *(→ of concrete, glass)* armature *f*

(**b**) *(gen) & Mil* renfort *m*; **reinforcements have arrived** des renforts sont arrivés

2 *comp (troops, ships, supplies)* de renfort

reinitialize, -ise [ˌriːɪ'nɪʃəlaɪz] *vt Comput* réinitialiser

reinsert [ˌriːɪn'sɜːt] *vt* réinsérer

reinstall [ˌriːɪn'stɔːl] *vt Comput* réinstaller

reinstallation [ˌriːɪnstə'leɪʃən] *n Comput* réinstallation

reinstate [ˌriːɪn'steɪt] *vt (employee)* réintégrer, rétablir (dans ses fonctions); *(idea, system)* rétablir, restaurer

reinstatement [ˌriːɪn'steɪtmənt] *n* réintégration *f*

reinstitute [ˌriː'ɪnstɪtjuːt] *vt* réintroduire

reinstitution [ˌriːɪnstɪ'tjuːʃən] *n* réintroduction *f*

reinsurance [ˌriːɪn'ʃɔːrəns] *n* réassurance *f*

reinsure [ˌriːɪn'ʃɔː(r)] *vt* réassurer

reintegrate [ˌriː'ɪntɪgreɪt] *vt* réintégrer; *(criminal, addict)* réinsérer

reintegration ['riːˌɪntɪ'greɪʃən] *n* réintégration *f*; *(of criminal, addict)* réinsertion *f*

reinter [ˌriːɪn'tɜː(r)] *vt* (*pt & pp* **reinterred**, *cont* **reinterring**) renterrer

reinterpret [ˌriːɪn'tɜːprɪt] *vt* réinterpréter

reinterpretation [ˌriːɪntɜːprɪ'teɪʃən] *n* réinterprétation *f*

reintroduce ['riːˌɪntrə'djuːs] *vt* réintroduire

reintroduction ['riːˌɪntrə'dʌkʃən] *n* réintroduction *f*

reinvent [ˌriːɪn'vent] *vt Fig* **to reinvent the wheel** refaire ce qui a déjà été fait; **to reinvent oneself** changer d'image

reinvest [ˌriːɪn'vest] *vt* réinvestir

reinvestigate [ˌriːɪn'vestɪgeɪt] *vt (question, problem)* examiner de nouveau; *(crime)* faire une nouvelle enquête sur

reinvestment [ˌriːɪn'vestmənt] *n* réinvestissement *m*

reinvigorate [ˌriːɪn'vɪgəreɪt] *vt* revigorer

reinvigoration [ˌriːɪnvɪgə'reɪʃən] *n* revigorisation *f*

reissue [ˌriː'ɪʃuː] **1** *vt* (**a**) *(book)* rééditer; *(film)* rediffuser, ressortir (**b**) *Admin & Fin (banknotes, shares, stamps)* réémettre, émettre de nouveau

2 *n* (**a**) *(of book)* réédition *f*; *(of film)* rediffusion *f* (**b**) *Admin & Fin (of banknotes, shares, stamps)* nouvelle émission *f*

reiterate [ˌriː'ɪtəreɪt] *vt* réitérer, répéter

reiteration [ˌriːɪtə'reɪʃən] *n* réitération *f*, répétition *f*

reiterative [ˌriː'ɪtərətɪv] *adj* réitératif

reject 1 *vt* [rɪ'dʒekt] (**a**) *(offer, suggestion, unwanted article)* rejeter; *(advances, demands)*

reg–rej

rejeter, repousser; *(application, manuscript)* rejeter, refuser; *(suitor)* éconduire, repousser; *(belief, system, values)* rejeter; **to feel rejected** se sentir rejeté; **the machine keeps rejecting this coin** pas moyen que la machine accepte cette *ou* ma pièce
(**b**) *Med (foreign body, transplant)* rejeter
(**c**) *Comput* rejeter
(**d**) *Mktg (goods)* refuser
2 *n* ['ri:dʒekt] (**a**) *Com (in factory)* article *m ou* pièce *f* de rebut; *(in shop)* (article *m* de) second choix *m*; *Fig (person)* personne *f* marginalisée
(**b**) *Comput* rejet *m*
3 *comp* ['ri:dʒekt] *(merchandise)* de rebut; *(for sale)* (de) second choix; *(shop)* d'articles de second choix
►► ***reject shop*** magasin *m* d'articles de second choix

rejection [rɪ'dʒekʃən] *n* (**a**) *(of offer, manuscript)* refus *m*; *(of advances, demands)* rejet *m*; **to meet with rejection** *(applicant etc)* essuyer un refus; *(offer, suggestion)* être rejeté; **her application met with rejection** sa candidature a été rejetée *ou* n'a pas été retenue; **to be afraid of rejection** *(emotional)* avoir peur d'être rejeté (**b**) *Med* rejet *m*
►► ***rejection slip*** lettre *f* de refus

rejig [,ri:'dʒɪg] *(pt & pp* **rejigged**, *cont* **rejigging**) *vt Br* (**a**) *(re-equip)* rééquiper, réaménager (**b**) *(reorganize)* réarranger, revoir

rejigger [,ri:'dʒɪgə(r)] *vt Am* (**a**) *(re-equip)* rééquiper, réaménager (**b**) *(reorganize)* réarranger, revoir

rejoice [rɪ'dʒɔɪs] **1** *vi* se réjouir; **to rejoice at** *or* **over sth** se réjouir de qch; **they rejoiced at** *or* **over the good news** ils se réjouissaient *ou* ils étaient ravis de la bonne nouvelle; *Hum* **he rejoices in the name of French-Edwardes** il a le privilège de porter le nom de French-Edwardes; **the hotel rejoices in the title "Imperial Palace"** l'hôtel porte le nom ronflant de "Palais Impérial"
2 *vt* réjouir, ravir

rejoicing [rɪ'dʒɔɪsɪŋ] *n* (**a**) *(joy)* réjouissance *f*; **it was the occasion of much rejoicing** ce fut l'occasion de grandes réjouissances (**b**) **rejoicings** *(festivities)* réjouissances *fpl*, festivités *fpl*; **there were great rejoicings on the day of the Coronation** il y a eu de grandes réjouissances le jour du couronnement

rejoin¹ [,ri:'dʒɔɪn] **1** *vt* (**a**) *(go back to)* rejoindre; *Mil* **to rejoin one's regiment** rallier *ou* rejoindre son régiment; *Naut* **to rejoin ship** rallier le bord; **we rejoined the main road a few miles later** nous avons rejoint la nationale quelques kilomètres plus loin (**b**) *(join again)* rejoindre; *(club, political party)* se réinscrire à; *Pol* **to rejoin the majority** rallier la majorité
2 *vi (roads, lines etc)* se rejoindre

rejoin² [rɪ'dʒɔɪn] **1** *vt (reply)* répliquer
2 *vi (reply)* répliquer

rejoinder [rɪ'dʒɔɪndə(r)] *n* réplique *f*

rejuvenate [rɪ'dʒu:vəneɪt] *vt* rajeunir

rejuvenating [rɪ'dʒu:vəneɪtɪŋ] *adj* rajeunissant
►► ***rejuvenating cream*** crème *f* de beauté rajeunissante

rejuvenation [rɪ,dʒu:və'neɪʃən] *n* rajeunissement *m*

rejuvenesce [,ri:dʒu:və'nes] *Biol* **1** *vt (cells)* rajeunir
2 *vi (cells)* rajeunir

rekey [,ri:'ki:] *vt Comput* refrapper

rekeying [,ri:'ki:ɪŋ] *n Comput* refrappe *f*

rekindle [,ri:'kɪndəl] **1** *vt (fire)* rallumer, attiser; *Fig (enthusiasm, desire, hatred)* raviver, ranimer
2 *vi (fire)* se rallumer; *Fig (feelings)* se ranimer

relabel [,ri:'leɪbəl] *vt* réétiqueter

relapse [rɪ'læps] **1** *n Med & Fig* rechute *f*; **to have a relapse** faire une rechute, rechuter
2 *vi* (**a**) *Med* rechuter, faire une rechute
(**b**) *(go back)* retomber; **to relapse into alcoholism** retomber dans l'alcoolisme; **to relapse into unconsciousness** reperdre connaissance; **to relapse into depression** replonger dans la dépression; **to relapse into silence** redevenir silencieux; **the country has relapsed into war** le pays est à nouveau plongé dans la guerre

relapsing fever [rɪ'læpsɪŋ-] *n* maladie *f* à fièvres intermittentes

Relate [rɪ'leɪt] *n* = organisme britannique de conseil et d'assistance aux couples en difficulté

relate [rɪ'leɪt] **1** *vt* (**a**) *(tell → events, story)* relater, raconter; *(→ details, facts)* rapporter; **strange to relate...** chose curieuse...
(**b**) *(connect → ideas, events)* rapprocher, établir un rapport *ou* un lien entre; **we can relate this episode to a previous scene in the novel** nous pouvons établir un lien entre cet épisode et une scène antérieure du roman; **she always relates everything to herself** elle ramène toujours tout à elle
2 *vi* (**a**) *(connect → idea, event)* se rapporter, se rattacher; **I don't understand how the two ideas relate** je ne comprends pas la relation entre les deux idées; **this relates to what I was just saying** ceci est lié à *ou* est en rapport avec ce que je viens de dire
(**b**) *(have relationship, interact)* **at school, they learn to relate to other children** à l'école, ils apprennent à vivre avec d'autres enfants; **I just can't relate to my parents** je n'arrive pas à communiquer avec mes parents
(**c**) *Fam (respond, appreciate)* **I can't relate to his music** je n'accroche pas à sa musique; **I can relate to that** je comprends tout à fait

related [rɪ'leɪtɪd] *adj* (**a**) *(in family)* parent; *(animal, species)* apparenté; *(language)* de même famille, proche; **we are related** nous sommes parents; **she is related to the president** elle est parente du président; **they are related on his father's side** ils sont parents par son père; **to be related by marriage to sb** être parent de qn par alliance; **they aren't related** ils n'ont aucun lien de parenté; **they are closely related** ils sont proches parents; **an animal related to the cat** un animal apparenté au *ou* de la famille du chat
(**b**) *(connected)* connexe, lié; *(neighbouring)* voisin; **psychoanalysis and other related areas** la psychanalyse et les domaines qui s'y rattachent; **problems related to health** problèmes qui se rattachent *ou* qui touchent à la santé; **the cost of the project is directly related to...** le coût du projet est directement lié à...; **the two topics are closely related** les deux sujets sont étroitement liés; **the two events are not related** les deux événements n'ont aucun rapport
(**c**) *Mus* relatif

-related [rɪ'leɪtɪd] *suff* lié à; **stress-/industry-related** lié au stress/à l'industrie; **performance-related bonus** prime *f* d'encouragement

relatedness [rɪ'leɪtɪdnɪs] *n* (**a**) *(of people)* parenté *f* (**b**) *(of ideas, subjects)* connexité *f*

relating [rɪ'leɪtɪŋ] **relating to** *prep* ayant rapport à, relatif à, concernant; *Admin & Law* afférent à

relation [rɪ'leɪʃən] **1** *n* (**a**) *(member of family)* parent(e) *m,f*; **they have relations in Paris** ils ont de la famille à Paris; **he's a relation** il est de ma famille; **she is no relation of mine** il n'y a aucun lien de parenté entre nous; **is she a relation of yours?** est-elle de votre famille?
(**b**) *(kinship)* parenté *f*; **what relation is he to you?** quelle est votre lien de parenté?
(**c**) *(connection)* rapport *m*, relation *f*; **to have** *or* **to bear a relation to sth** avoir (un) rapport à qch, être en rapport avec qch; **your answer bore no relation to the question** votre réponse n'avait rien à voir avec la question
(**d**) *(relationship, contact)* rapport *m*, relation *f*; *(between people, countries)* rapport *m*, rapports *mpl*; **to enter into relation** *or* **relations with sb** entrer *ou* se mettre en rapport avec qn; **their relations are somewhat strained** ils ont des rapports assez tendus; *Formal* **to have (sexual) relations with sb** avoir des rapports (sexuels) avec qn; **diplomatic relations** relations *fpl* diplomatiques; **to break off all relations with sb** rompre toute relation *ou* cesser tout rapport avec qn
(**e**) *Formal (narration → of events, story)* récit *m*, relation *f*; *(→ of details)* rapport *m*
2 in relation to, with relation to *prep* par rapport à, relativement à

relational [rɪ'leɪʃənəl] *adj* relationnel
►► *Comput* ***relational database*** base *f* de données relationnelle

relationship [rɪ'leɪʃənʃɪp] *n* (**a**) *(between people, countries)* rapports *mpl*, relations *fpl*; **to have a good/bad relationship with sb** *(gen)* avoir de bonnes/mauvaises relations avec qn; **our relationship is purely a business one** nos relations sont simplement des relations d'affaires; **they have a good/bad relationship** ils s'entendent bien/mal; **she has a good relationship with her class** elle a de bons rapports avec sa classe; **he has a very close relationship with his mother** il est très lié à sa mère
(**b**) *(sexual)* relation *f* amoureuse; **I'd like to talk to you about our relationship** *(as a couple)* j'aimerais qu'on parle un peu de nous deux *ou* de notre couple; **a relationship is something you have to work at** être en couple, ça demande des efforts; **to have a relationship (with)** *(affair)* avoir une liaison (avec); **I'm already in a relationship** j'ai déjà quelqu'un, je suis déjà avec quelqu'un; **she's been trying to get out of the relationship for months** elle essaye de rompre depuis des mois
(**c**) *(kinship)* **family relationship** lien *m ou* liens *mpl* de parenté; **blood relationship** parenté *f*, (degré *m* de) consanguinité *f*; **what is your exact relationship to her?** quels sont vos liens de parenté exacts avec elle?
(**d**) *(connection → between ideas, events, things)* rapport *m*, relation *f*, lien *m*
►► *Mktg* ***relationship marketing*** marketing *m* relationnel

relative ['relətɪv] **1** *adj* (**a**) *(comparative)* relatif; **to live in relative comfort** vivre dans un confort relatif; **the relative advantages of electricity as opposed to gas** les avantages relatifs de l'électricité par rapport au gaz; **taxation is relative to income** l'imposition est proportionnelle au revenu; **the relative qualities of the two candidates** les qualités respectives des deux candidats
(**b**) *(not absolute)* relatif
(**c**) *Mus* relatif
(**d**) *Gram* relatif
2 *n* (**a**) *(person)* parent(e) *m,f*; **relative by marriage** parent(e) *m,f* par alliance; **she is my closest living relative** c'est la plus proche parente qui me reste; **she has relatives in Canada** elle a de la famille au Canada; **he's a relative of mine** il fait partie de ma famille
(**b**) *Gram* relatif *m*
3 relative to *prep* relativement à
►► *Phot* ***relative aperture*** ouverture *f* relative de l'objectif; *Phys* ***relative atomic mass*** poids *m ou* masse *f* atomique; *Gram* ***relative clause*** (proposition *f*) relative *f*; *Gram* ***relative conjunction*** conjonction *f* relative; ***relative density*** densité *f* relative; ***relative humidity*** humidité *f* relative; *Mus* ***relative major*** ton *m* majeur relatif; *Mktg* ***relative market share*** part *f* de marché relative; *Mus* ***relative minor*** ton *m* mineur relatif; *Phys* ***relative molecular mass*** masse *f* moléculaire; *Gram* ***relative pronoun*** pronom *m* relatif

relatively ['relətɪvlɪ] *adv* relativement; **relatively difficult** relativement *ou* assez difficile; **relatively speaking** relativement parlant

relativism ['relətɪvɪzəm] *n* relativisme *m*

relativist ['relətɪvɪst] **1** *adj* relativiste
2 *n* relativiste *mf*

relativistic [,relətɪ'vɪstɪk] *adj* relativiste

relativity [,relə'tɪvɪtɪ] *n* relativité *f*; **theory of relativity** théorie *f* de la relativité

relativization [,relətɪvaɪ'zeɪʃən] *n* relativisation *f*

relativize, -ise ['relətɪvaɪz] *vt* relativiser

relaunch *Com & Mktg* **1** *n* ['ri:lɔ:ntʃ] *(of product, company)* relancement *m*, relance *f*
2 *vt* [,ri:'lɔ:ntʃ] *(product, company)* relancer

relax [rɪ'læks] **1** *vi* (**a**) *(person)* se détendre, se délasser; *(in comfort, on holiday)* se relaxer, se détendre; *(calm down)* se calmer, se détendre; **you need to relax** vous avez besoin de détente *ou* de vous détendre; **try and relax a bit** essayez de vous détendre un peu; **relax!** *(calm down)* du calme!; *(don't worry)* ne t'inquiète pas!
(**b**) *(grip)* se relâcher, se desserrer; *(muscle)* se relâcher, se décontracter; *Tech (spring)* se détendre; **his face relaxed into a smile** son visage s'est détendu et il a souri; **to relax in one's efforts** relâcher ses efforts
2 *vt* (**a**) *(mind)* détendre, délasser; *(muscles)* relâcher, décontracter; **the music will relax you** la musique vous détendra
(**b**) *(grip)* relâcher, desserrer; **to relax one's**

hold *or* **one's grip** relâcher son étreinte; *Fig* **to relax one's grip on** relâcher son emprise sur

(**c**) *Med (bowels)* relâcher

(**d**) *Fig (discipline, restriction)* assouplir, relâcher; *(concentration, effort)* relâcher; **the government has relaxed the laws on immigration** le gouvernement a assoupli les lois sur l'immigration; **during the holiday period, parking restrictions are relaxed** la réglementation du stationnement est plus souple pendant la période des vacances

(**e**) *(hair)* défriser; **to get one's hair relaxed** se faire défriser les cheveux

relaxant [rɪ'læksənt] **1** *n* (médicament *m*) relaxant *m*

2 *adj* relaxant

relaxation [ˌriːlæk'seɪʃən] *n* (**a**) *(rest)* détente *f*, relaxation *f*; **she needs a week of relaxation** elle a besoin d'une semaine de détente *ou* de repos; **he plays golf for relaxation** il joue au golf pour se détendre; **she finds relaxation in gardening** pour elle, le jardinage est une détente; **reading is one of my favourite forms of relaxation** lire est une de mes façons préférées de me détendre

(**b**) *(loosening → of grip)* relâchement *m*, desserrement *m*; *Fig (→ of authority, law, discipline)* relâchement *m*, assouplissement *m*

►► ***relaxation therapy*** relaxation *f*

relaxed [rɪ'lækst] *adj* (**a**) *(person, atmosphere)* détendu, décontracté; *(smile)* détendu; *(attitude)* décontracté; **to feel/to look relaxed** se sentir/avoir l'air détendu; **he's very relaxed about the whole business** cette affaire n'a pas l'air de beaucoup le perturber (**b**) *(muscle)* relâché; *(discipline)* assoupli

relaxin [re'læksɪn] *n Physiol* relaxine *f*

relaxing [rɪ'læksɪŋ] *adj (restful → atmosphere, afternoon, holiday)* reposant; *(→ bath, music)* relaxant; **she finds gardening relaxing** elle trouve le jardinage reposant; **you need a nice relaxing bath** ce qu'il te faut, c'est un bon bain pour te détendre

relay *(pt & pp senses* (**a**), (**b**) **relayed**, *pt & pp sense* (**c**) **relaid** [-leɪd]) **1** *n* ['riːleɪ] (**a**) *(team → of athletes, workers, horses)* relais *m*; *Br* **to work in relays** travailler par relais, se relayer

(**b**) *Rad & TV (transmitter)* réémetteur *m*, relais *m*; *(broadcast)* émission *f* relayée

(**c**) *Elec & Tech* relais *m*

(**d**) *Sport (race)* (course *f* de) relais *m*; **the 4 x 100 m relay** le relais 4 x 100 m

2 *vt* (**a**) ['riːleɪ] *(pass on → message, news)* transmettre

(**b**) ['riːleɪ] *Rad & TV (broadcast)* relayer, retransmettre

(**c**) [ˌriː'leɪ] *(cable, carpet)* reposer

►► *Sport* ***relay race*** course *f* de relais *m*; *Rad & TV* ***relay station*** relais *m*

relearn [ˌriː'lɜːn] *(Br pt & pp* **relearned** *or* **relearnt** [-'lɜːnt], *Am pt & pp* **relearned**) *vt* réapprendre, rapprendre

release [rɪ'liːs] **1** *n* (**a**) *(from captivity)* libération *f*; *(from prison)* libération *f*, mise *f* en liberté, *Admin* élargissment *m*; *(from custody)* mise *f* en liberté, relaxe *f*; *(from debt)* libération *f*; *(from obligation, promise)* libération *f*, dispense *f*; *(from pain, suffering)* délivrance *f*; **on his release from prison** lors de sa mise en liberté, dès sa sortie de prison; **release on bail** mise *f* en liberté provisoire (sous caution); **release on parole** libération *f* conditionnelle; **order of release** ordre *m* de levée d'écrou; **death was a release for her** pour elle, la mort a été une délivrance

(**b**) *Fin (of credits, funds)* déblocage *m*, dégagement *m*

(**c**) *Com (from bond, customs)* congé *m*

(**d**) *(distribution → of film, record)* sortie *f*; *(→ of book)* sortie *f*, parution *f*; *(→ of document)* diffusion *f*; **the film is on general release** le film est sorti

(**e**) *(new film, book, record)* nouveauté *f*; *(software)* version *f*; **her latest release is called 'Perfect Moment'** son dernier disque s'appelle 'Perfect Moment'; **it's a new release** ça vient de sortir

(**f**) *(of handle, switch)* déclenchement *m*; *(of brake)* desserrage *m*; *(of clutch)* débrayage *m*; *(of spring)* détente *f*; *(of bomb)* largage *m*; *(of balloons, pigeons)* lâcher *m*; *(of gas etc)* dégagement *m*; *(of steam)* échappement *m*; *(of pressure)* relâchement *m*; *(of energy)* libération *f*

(**g**) *Tech (lever)* levier *m*; *(safety catch)* cran *m* de sûreté

2 *comp (button, switch)* de déclenchement

3 *vt* (**a**) *(prisoner)* libérer, relâcher; *(from custody)* remettre en liberté, relâcher, relaxer; *(captive person, animal)* libérer; *(employee, schoolchild)* libérer, laisser partir; *(hospital patient)* laisser sortir; *(from obligation)* libérer, dégager; *(from promise)* dégager, relever; *(from vows)* relever, dispenser; **to release sb from captivity** libérer qn; *Law* **to be released on bail** être libéré sous caution; **the earthquake victims were released from the wreckage** les victimes du tremblement de terre ont été dégagées des décombres; **the children were released into the care of their grandparents** on a confié les enfants à leurs grands-parents; **death finally released her from her suffering** la mort a mis un terme à ses souffrances; **to release sb from a debt** remettre une dette à qn

(**b**) *(let go → from control, grasp)* lâcher; *(→ feelings)* donner *ou* laisser libre cours à; *(→ bomb)* larguer, lâcher; *(→ gas, heat)* libérer, dégager; **he released his grip on my hand** il m'a lâché la *ou* il a lâché ma main; **to release one's hold** desserrer son étreinte, lâcher prise; **the explosion released chemicals into the river** l'explosion a libéré des agents chimiques dans la rivière; **insecticides were released over the crops** des pesticides ont été répandus sur les récoltes; **playing squash is a good way of releasing tension** le squash est un bon moyen de se détendre

(**c**) *(issue → film)* sortir; *(→ book)* sortir, faire paraître, mettre en vente; *(→ record)* sortir, metter en vente; *(→ goods, new model)* mettre en vente *ou* sur le marché; *(→ stamps, coins)* émettre

(**d**) *(make public → statement)* publier; *(→ information, story)* dévoiler, annoncer; **the company refuses to release details of the contract** la compagnie refuse de divulguer *ou* de faire connaître les détails du contrat

(**e**) *(lever, mechanism)* déclencher; *(brake)* desserrer; *(jammed part etc)* dégager; *(spring)* détendre; *Aut* **to release the clutch** débrayer; *Phot* **to release the shutter** déclencher (l'obturateur); **release the catch to open the door** pour ouvrir la porte, soulever le loquet; **to release the safety catch** *(on gun)* libérer le cran de sûreté

(**f**) *Fin (credits, funds)* dégager, débloquer

(**g**) *(property, rights)* céder

(**h**) *Com (goods from bond)* dédouaner

►► *Tech* ***release lever*** *(on clutch)* levier *m* de débrayage; *(on typewriter)* levier *m* de dégagement du chariot; *Cin* ***release print*** copie *f* d'exploitation

relegate ['relɪgeɪt] *vt* (**a**) *(person, thought)* reléguer; **to relegate sb/sth to sth** reléguer qn/qch à qch; *Fig* **we relegated the old bed to the spare room** on a relégué le vieux lit dans la chambre d'amis (**b**) *Sport (team)* reléguer, déclasser; *Ftbl* **to be relegated** descendre en *ou* être relégué à la division inférieure (**c**) *(refer → issue, question)* renvoyer

relegation [ˌrelɪ'geɪʃən] *n* (**a**) *(demotion → of person, team, thing)* relégation *f* (**b**) *(referral → of issue, matter)* renvoi *m*

relent [rɪ'lent] *vi* (**a**) *(person)* se laisser fléchir, céder; **they begged him for mercy but he would not relent** ils lui ont demandé grâce mais il ne s'est pas laissé fléchir *ou* mais il n'a pas cédé; **the prime minister shows no sign of relenting** le premier ministre ne semble pas vouloir céder; **he finally relented and let us go** il a finalement accepté de nous laisser partir (**b**) *(storm)* s'apaiser, se calmer

relentless [rɪ'lentlɪs] *adj* (**a**) *(merciless)* implacable, impitoyable (**b**) *(sustained → activity, effort)* acharné, opiniâtre; *(→ noise)* ininterrompu; *(→ rain)* incessant; *(→ pain)* tenace; *(→ advance)* inexorable

relentlessly [rɪ'lentlɪslɪ] *adv* (**a**) *(mercilessly)* impitoyablement, implacablement (**b**) *(persistently)* avec acharnement *ou* opiniâtreté; **he worked relentlessly** il travailla avec acharnement; **the rain beat down relentlessly** il n'a pas cessé de pleuvoir à verse

relentlessness [rɪ'lentlɪsnɪs] *n* inflexibilité *f*, implacabilité *f*, intransigeance *f*; **relentlessness in revenge** acharnement *m* à la vengeance

relet [ˌriː'let] *vt* relouer

relevance ['reləvəns], **relevancy** ['reləvənsɪ] *n* (**a**) *(of facts, remarks etc)* pertinence *f*, intérêt *m*; **I don't see the relevance of your remark** la pertinence de votre remarque m'échappe; **what is the relevance of this to the matter under discussion?** quel est le rapport avec ce dont on parle?; **this question has little relevance for us** cette question ne nous concerne pas vraiment

(**b**) *(usefulness, significance)* intérêt *m*; **many students fail to see the practical relevance of such courses** de nombreux étudiants considèrent que ces formations n'ont pas d'intérêt *ou* d'utilité pratique

relevant ['reləvənt] *adj* (**a**) *(pertinent → comment, beliefs, ideas)* pertinent; **to be relevant (to sth)** avoir un rapport (avec qch); **such considerations are not relevant** de telles considérations sont hors de propos; **confine yourself to the relevant facts** ne vous écartez pas du sujet

(**b**) *(appropriate)* approprié; **fill in your name in the relevant space** inscrivez votre nom dans la case correspondante; **she did not have the relevant experience for the job** elle n'avait pas l'expérience requise pour le poste; **you should report the matter to the relevant department** vous devriez en référer au service compétent; **the relevant documents** les documents qui se rapportent à l'affaire; *Law* les pièces justificatives

(**c**) *(useful, significant)* **to be highly relevant (for)** *(experience, qualifications)* être très utile (pour); **to be/remain relevant** *(book, play, idea, ideology etc)* être/rester d'actualité; **her novels no longer seem relevant to modern life** ses romans ne sont plus d'actualité; **all relevant information** tous renseignements utiles

►► *Acct* ***relevant costs*** coûts *mpl* attribuables; ***relevant range*** fourchette *f* pertinente d'activité

relevantly ['reləvəntlɪ] *adv* pertinemment

reliability [rɪˌlaɪə'bɪlɪtɪ] *n* (**a**) *(of person, company)* sérieux *m*; *(of information)* sérieux *m*, fiabilité *f*; *(of memory, judgment)* sûreté *f*, fiabilité *f*; **I'm not altogether sure about the reliability of our witnesses** je ne suis pas vraiment sûr qu'on puisse faire confiance à nos témoins (**b**) *(of clock, machine, car)* fiabilité *f*

reliable [rɪ'laɪəbəl] *adj* (**a**) *(trustworthy → friend)* sur qui on peut compter, sûr; *(→ worker)* à qui on peut faire confiance, sérieux; *(→ witness)* digne de confiance *ou* de foi; *(→ information)* sérieux, sûr; *(→ memory, judgment)* fiable, auquel on peut se fier; *(→ company)* sérieux; **he's very reliable** on peut toujours compter sur lui *ou* lui faire confiance; **the news came from a reliable source** la nouvelle provenait d'une source sûre; **my memory isn't reliable** je n'ai pas bonne mémoire

(**b**) *(clock, machine, car)* fiable; **my watch isn't very reliable** ma montre n'est pas très fiable

reliably [rɪ'laɪəblɪ] *adv (operate, perform etc)* de façon fiable; **we are reliably informed that...** nous avons appris de bonne source *ou* de source sûre que...

reliance [rɪ'laɪəns] *n* (**a**) *(trust)* confiance *f*; **to place reliance in** *or* **on sb/sth** faire confiance à qn/qch (**b**) *(dependence)* dépendance *f*; **his reliance on their advice** le fait qu'il ne fasse rien sans les consulter; **her reliance on alcohol** sa dépendance vis-à-vis de l'alcool

reliant [rɪ'laɪənt] *adj* (**a**) *(dependent)* dépendant; **to be reliant on sb (for sth)** dépendre de qn (pour qch); **we are heavily reliant on your advice** vos conseils nous sont indispensables; **he is too reliant on tranquillizers** il a trop recours aux tranquillisants (**b**) *(trusting)* confiant; **to be reliant on sb** faire confiance à *ou* avoir confiance en qn

relic ['relɪk] *n* (**a**) *(reminder of past, remnant)* vestige *m*; **the last surviving relic of** les derniers vestiges de; **relics of the past** vestiges *mpl* du passé; *Hum* **their old relic of a car** leur vieille bagnole toute pourrie; *Literary* **relics** *(corpse)* dépouille *f* mortelle (**b**) *Rel* relique *f*

relict ['relɪkt] *n* (**a**) *Biol & Ecol* relique *f*; *Geol* forme *f* relique (**b**) *Arch (widow)* veuve *f*

relief [rɪ'li:f] **1** *n* (**a**) *(from anxiety, pain)* soulagement *m*; **to bring relief to sb** soulager qn, apporter un soulagement à qn; **the medicine gave** *or* **brought her little relief from the pain** le médicament ne la soulagea guère; **he finds relief in writing** ça le soulage d'écrire; **to our great relief, much to our relief** à notre grand soulagement; **it was a great relief to her when the exams ended** la fin des examens fut un grand soulagement pour elle; **that's** *or* **what a relief!** quel soulagement!

(**b**) *(aid)* secours *m*, aide *f*; **to send relief to Third-World countries** apporter de l'aide aux pays du tiers-monde; **famine relief** aide *f* aux victimes de la famine

(**c**) *Am (state benefit)* aide *f* sociale; **to be on relief** recevoir des aides sociales *ou* des allocations

(**d**) *(diversion)* divertissement *m*, distraction *f*; **he included a few comic scenes in the play for light relief** il a inclus plusieurs scènes comiques dans la pièce pour détendre l'atmosphère; **she reads detective novels for light relief** elle lit des romans policiers pour se distraire

(**e**) *(of besieged city)* libération *f*, délivrance *f*

(**f**) *(of guard, team)* relève *f*; **I've been on duty all night with only one hour's relief** j'ai été de garde toute la nuit, sauf une heure pendant laquelle j'ai été relevé; **reliefs have arrived** *(gen)* la relève *ou* l'équipe de relève est arrivée; *(troops)* les troupes de relève sont arrivées, la relève est arrivée

(**g**) *Art* relief *m*; **the inscription stood out in relief** l'inscription était en relief; **the mountains stood out in bold relief against the sky** les montagnes se détachaient *ou* se découpaient nettement sur le ciel; *Fig* **to bring** *or* **to throw sth into relief** mettre qch en relief *ou* en valeur; *Art* **high relief** haut-relief *m*; **low relief** bas-relief *m*

(**h**) *Geog* relief *m*; **an area of low relief** une zone au relief peu élevé

(**i**) *Law (redress)* réparation *f*; *(exemption)* dérogation *f*, exemption *f*

2 *comp* (**a**) *(extra → transport, service)* supplémentaire; *(replacement → worker, troops, team)* de relève; *(→ bus, machine)* de remplacement

(**b**) *(for aid → fund)* de secours

▸▸ ***relief agency*** organisme *m* d'aide humanitaire; ***relief driver*** chauffeur *m* qui assure la relève; ***relief fund*** caisse *f* de secours; ***relief map*** carte *f* en relief; ***relief organization*** organisation *f* humanitaire; ***relief printing*** impression *f* en relief; ***relief road*** itinéraire *m* bis, route *f* de délestage; ***relief valve*** soupape *f* de sûreté, clapet *m* de décharge; ***relief work*** coopération *f*; ***relief worker*** = membre d'une organisation humanitaire qui travaille sur le terrain

relieve [rɪ'li:v] *vt* (**a**) *(anxiety, distress, pain)* soulager, alléger; *(poverty)* soulager; **the good news relieved her of her anxiety** la bonne nouvelle a dissipé ses inquiétudes; *Med & Transp* **to relieve congestion** décongestionner

(**b**) *(gloom)* dissiper; *(boredom)* tromper; *(monotony)* briser; **the darkness of the room was relieved only by the firelight** la pièce n'était éclairée que par la lueur du feu; **they relieved the monotony of the evening by playing cards** pour briser la monotonie de la soirée, ils ont joué aux cartes; **black dress relieved by** *or* **with white lace** robe noire agrémentée de dentelle blanche

(**c**) *(unburden)* **to relieve sb of sth** soulager *ou* débarrasser qn de qch; **he relieved her of her suitcase/coat** il l'a débarrassée de sa valise/de son manteau; **to relieve sb of a burden** soulager qn d'un fardeau; *Hum* **to relieve sb of their wallet** délester qn de son portefeuille; **to relieve sb of an obligation** décharger *ou* dégager qn d'une obligation; **to relieve sb of his/her duties** *or* **position** relever qn de ses fonctions

(**d**) *(aid → population, refugees, country)* secourir, venir en aide à

(**e**) *(replace → worker, team)* relayer, prendre la relève de; *(→ guard, sentry)* relever

(**f**) *(liberate → fort, city)* délivrer, libérer; *(from siege)* lever le siège de

(**g**) *Euph (urinate)* **to relieve oneself** se soulager

relieved [rɪ'li:vd] *adj* soulagé; **to feel relieved** se sentir soulagé; **we were greatly relieved at the news** nous avons été très soulagés d'apprendre la nouvelle

relievo [rɪ'li:vəʊ] (*pl* **relievos**) *n Art* relief *m*

relight [ˌri:'laɪt] (*pt & pp* **relighted** *or* **relit** [-'lɪt]) *vt* rallumer

religion [rɪ'lɪdʒən] *n* (**a**) *Rel* religion *f*; *(Catholic, Protestant)* religion *f*, culte *m*; *(heading on form)* confession *f*; **the Jewish religion** la religion *ou* la confession juive; **what is your religion?** à quelle confession appartenez-vous?; **to enter religion** entrer en religion; **a man of religion** un homme de religion *ou* d'Église; **various religions were represented at the conference** diverses confessions étaient représentées à la conférence; *Am* **to get religion** découvrir Dieu; *Fig* devenir un modèle de vertu; *Hum* **it's against my religion to work on Sundays** ma religion m'interdit de travailler le dimanche

(**b**) *Fig (obsession)* religion *f*, culte *m*; **to make a religion of sth** se faire une religion de qch; **sport is a religion with him** le sport est son dieu

religiosity [rɪˌlɪdʒɪ'ɒsɪtɪ] *n* religiosité *f*

religious [rɪ'lɪdʒəs] **1** *adj* (**a**) *(authority, order, ceremony, art)* religieux; *(war)* de religion (**b**) *(devout)* pieux, croyant (**c**) *Fig (scrupulous)* religieux; **to do sth with religious care** faire qch avec un soin religieux

2 *n (monk, nun)* religieux(euse) *m,f*

▸▸ ***religious beliefs*** croyances *fpl* religieuses; ***religious education, religious instruction*** instruction *f* religieuse; ***religious persuasion*** confession *f*

religiously [rɪ'lɪdʒəslɪ] *adv also Fig* religieusement

religiousness [rɪ'lɪdʒəsnɪs] *n (of person)* piété *f*, dévotion *f*; *(of music, art)* caractère *m* religieux; *Fig (of attendance, obedience)* caractère *m* scrupuleux; *(in carrying out task)* extrême méticulosité *f*

reline [ˌri:'laɪn] *vt (garment)* mettre une nouvelle doublure à, redoubler; *(picture)* rentoiler; *Aut* **to reline the brakes** changer les garnitures de freins

relinquish [rɪ'lɪŋkwɪʃ] *vt* (**a**) *(give up → claim, hope, power)* abandonner, renoncer à; *(→ property, possessions)* se dessaisir de; *(→ right)* renoncer à; **she relinquished all hope of ever seeing him again** elle abandonna tout espoir de le revoir un jour; **he relinquished his voting rights to the chairman** il a cédé son droit de vote au président; **they are reluctant to relinquish control of monetary policy** ils sont peu enclins à laisser à d'autres le contrôle de la politique monétaire

(**b**) *(release → grip, hold)* **to relinquish one's hold of** *or* **on sth** lâcher qch; *Fig* relâcher l'étreinte que l'on a sur qch

relinquishment [rɪ'lɪŋkwɪʃmənt] *n* abandon *m*, renonciation *f*; **the relinquishment of one's rights** l'abandon de *ou* la renonciation à ses droits

reliquary ['relɪkwərɪ] (*pl* **reliquaries**) *n* reliquaire *m*

reliquiae [rə'lɪkwɪi:] *npl (fossilized remains)* restes *mpl*

relish ['relɪʃ] **1** *n* (**a**) *(pleasure, enthusiasm)* goût *m*, plaisir *m*, délectation *f*; **to do sth with relish** faire qch avec délectation *ou* avec grand plaisir, adorer faire qch; **... she said with great relish** ... dit-elle avec délectation; **he ate with relish** il mangea avec délice *ou* avec délectation; **he has lost his relish for reading** il a perdu son goût pour la lecture

(**b**) *(condiment, sauce)* condiment *m*, sauce *f*; **sweetcorn relish** condiment *m* au maïs doux

(**c**) *(flavour)* goût *m*, saveur *f*; *Fig* **life had lost its relish for her** la vie avait perdu toute saveur pour elle

2 *vt* (**a**) *(enjoy)* savourer; **to relish one's triumph** savourer son triomphe; **I bet he's relishing this moment** je parie qu'il savoure cet instant; **I don't relish the idea** *or* **the prospect** *or* **the thought of seeing them again** l'idée *ou* la perspective de les revoir ne m'enchante *ou* ne me réjouit guère

(**b**) *(savour → food, drink)* savourer, se délecter de

relit [ˌri:'lɪt] *pt & pp of* **relight**

relive [ˌri:'lɪv] *vt* revivre

reload [ˌri:'ləʊd] **1** *vt (ship, camera, rifle, software etc)* recharger

2 *vi (ship, photographer etc)* recharger; *(gun, software)* se recharger

relocate [ˌri:ləʊ'keɪt] **1** *vt* réimplanter, délocaliser; **the facilities were relocated to Scotland** les services ont été réimplantés *ou* délocalisés en Écosse

2 *vi* se réimplanter, déménager; **the company has relocated to Idaho** l'entreprise a déménagé dans l'Idaho

relocation [ˌri:ləʊ'keɪʃən] *n (of premises, industry)* délocalisation *f*, déménagement *m*; *(of population)* relogement *m*

▸▸ ***relocation allowance*** *(for employee)* indemnité *f* de déménagement; ***relocation assistance*** *(from employer)* contribution *f* aux frais de déménagement; ***relocation expenses*** *(for employee)* frais *mpl* de déménagement

reluctance [rɪ'lʌktəns] *n* (**a**) *(unwillingness)* réticence *f*, répugnance *f*; **to do sth with reluctance** faire qch à contrecœur *ou* de mauvais gré; **to show (some) reluctance to do sth** se montrer peu disposé *ou* peu empressé à faire qch; **she expressed some reluctance to get involved in the matter** elle a dit qu'elle n'avait pas envie de se laisser entraîner dans cette histoire; **to do sth with a show of reluctance** faire qch avec une réticence feinte

(**b**) *Phys* réluctance *f*

reluctant [rɪ'lʌktənt] *adj* (**a**) *(unwilling)* réticent; **to be reluctant to do sth** être peu enclin à faire qch, n'avoir pas envie de faire qch; **to feel reluctant (to do)** hésiter (à faire); **she was reluctant to admit the truth** elle ne voulait pas admettre *ou* n'avait pas envie d'admettre la vérité

(**b**) *(against one's will → commitment, promise, approval)* accordé à contrecœur; **she gave a reluctant smile** elle eut un sourire contraint; **he was a reluctant sex symbol** c'est bien malgré lui qu'il était devenu un sex-symbol

reluctantly [rɪ'lʌktəntlɪ] *adv* à contrecœur; **to do sth reluctantly** faire qch à contrecœur; **she sat down reluctantly** elle s'est assise à contrecœur

▸ **rely on, rely upon** [rɪ'laɪ] (*pp & pt* **relied**) *vt insep*

(**a**) *(count on → person's help, discretion)* compter sur; *(have confidence in → person)* compter sur, avoir confiance en; *(→ judgment, opinion etc)* avoir confiance en; *(be dependent on → person)* dépendre de (**for sth** pour qch); **she can always be relied upon to give good advice** on peut toujours compter sur elle pour donner de bons conseils; **we were relying on the weather being good** nous comptions sur du beau temps; **we can't rely on the weather** on ne peut jamais savoir quel temps il va faire; **we relied on you bringing the records** on comptait sur vous pour apporter les disques; **you can never rely on them** on ne peut jamais compter sur eux; **he can never be relied upon to keep a secret** on ne peut lui confier aucun secret; **you may rely on** *or* **upon it** vous pouvez compter dessus; **I'm relying on it** j'y compte (bien); **I rely on my daughter to drive me to the shops** je dépends de ma fille pour me conduire aux magasins; **he relies on his family for everything** il dépend de sa famille pour tout; **she relies too much on luck** elle compte trop sur la chance; **I'm relying on you to find a solution** je compte sur vous pour trouver une solution; *Ironic* **you can always rely on him to be late** tu peux compter sur lui pour arriver en retard à chaque fois

(**b**) *Law (call on)* invoquer; **the points of fact and law relied on** les arguments de fait et de droit invoqués

REM [ˌɑ:ri:'em] *n* (*abbr* **rapid eye movement**) mouvements *mpl* oculaires rapides

▸▸ ***REM sleep*** sommeil *m* paradoxal

rem [rem] *n Nucl* (*abbr* **roentgen equivalent man**) rem *m*

remailer [ˌriːˈmeɪlə(r)] *n Comput* service *m* de courrier électronique anonyme

remain [rɪˈmeɪn] *vi* (**a**) *(be left)* rester; *(doubts)* rester, subsister; **only two slices remain** il ne reste que deux tranches; **very little remains** *or* **there remains very little of the original building** il ne reste pas grand-chose du bâtiment d'origine; **much remains to be discussed** il y a encore beaucoup de choses à discuter; **that remains to be seen** cela reste à voir; **it remains to be seen whether he will agree** (il) reste à savoir s'il sera d'accord; **the fact remains that we can't afford this house** il n'en reste pas moins que *ou* toujours est-il que nous ne pouvons pas nous offrir cette maison; **all that remained to be done was to say goodbye** il ne restait plus qu'à se dire au revoir; **it only remains for me to thank you** il ne me reste plus qu'à vous remercier

(**b**) *(stay)* rester, demeurer; **please remain seated** *or* **in your seats** veuillez rester assis; **to remain faithful to sb** rester fidèle à qn; **to remain silent** garder le silence, rester silencieux; **for reasons that remain unknown** pour des raisons inconnues; **the weather remained settled** le temps est resté stable; **remain here, please** restez-là, je vous prie; **he remained behind after the meeting** il est resté après la réunion; **it remains a mystery whether...** on ignore toujours si...; **the crime remains unsolved** le crime n'a toujours pas été élucidé; **the real reasons were to remain a secret** les véritables raisons devaient demeurer secrètes; **to remain a problem** demeurer un problème; **one thing remains certain** une chose demeure certaine; **he has remained the same despite all that has happened** il n'a pas changé malgré tout ce qui s'est passé; **let things remain as they are** laissez les choses telles qu'elles sont; *Formal Old-fashioned* **I remain, Sir, your most faithful servant** veuillez agréer *ou* je vous prie d'agréer, Monsieur, l'expression de mes sentiments les plus respectueux

remainder [rɪˈmeɪndə(r)] **1** *n* (**a**) *(leftover → supplies, time)* reste *m*; *(→ money)* solde *m*; *(→ debt)* reliquat *m*; **the remainder** *(remaining people)* les autres *mfpl*; **for the remainder of his life** pour le restant de ses jours; **she spent the remainder on sweets** elle a dépensé ce qui restait en bonbons

(**b**) *Math* reste *m*

(**c**) *(unsold book)* invendu *m*; *(unsold product)* fin *f* de série

(**d**) *Law* usufruit *m* avec réversibilité

2 *vt Com* solder

remaining [rɪˈmeɪnɪŋ] *adj (food, money, wine etc)* qui reste, restant; **the only remaining member of her family** la seule personne de sa famille (qui soit) encore en vie; **the remaining guests/travellers** le reste des invités/des voyageurs; **it's our only remaining hope** c'est le seul espoir qui nous reste, c'est notre dernier espoir

remains [rɪˈmeɪnz] *npl* (**a**) *(of meal, fortune)* restes *mpl*; *(of building)* restes *mpl*, vestiges *mpl* (**b**) *Euph Formal (corpse)* restes *mpl*, dépouille *f* mortelle; **(human) remains** restes *mpl* humains (**c**) *Old-fashioned* **(literary) remains** œuvres *fpl* posthumes

'The Remains of the Day' *Ishiguro, Ivory* 'Les Vestiges du jour'

remake *(pt & pp* **remade** [-ˈmeɪd]) **1** *vt* [ˌriːˈmeɪk] refaire

2 *n* [ˈriːmeɪk] *(film)* remake *m*

remand [rɪˈmɑːnd] *Br* **1** *vt Law (case)* renvoyer; *(defendant)* déférer; **to remand sb in custody** placer qn en détention préventive; **to remand sb on bail** mettre qn en liberté *ou* libérer qn sous caution; **the magistrate remanded the case for a week** le magistrat a renvoyé l'affaire à huitaine

2 *n* renvoi *m*; **to be on remand** *(in custody)* être en détention préventive; *(on bail)* avoir été libéré sous caution

▸▸ *Br* ***remand centre*** = centre de détention préventive; *Br Old-fashioned* ***remand home*** maison *f* de correction

remanence [ˈremənəns] *n Phys* rémanence *f*

remanent [ˈremənənt] *adj* (**a**) *(remaining)* qui reste (**b**) *Phys* rémanent, résiduel

remark [rɪˈmɑːk] **1** *n* (**a**) *(comment)* remarque *f*, réflexion *f*; **to make** *or* **to pass a remark** faire une remarque; **to make** *or* **to pass remarks about sb/sth** faire des réflexions sur qn/qch; **she made the remark that no one knew the truth** elle fit remarquer *ou* observer que personne ne savait la vérité; **it was a valid remark** c'était une réflexion pertinente; **to let sth pass without remark** laisser passer qch sans faire de commentaire

(**b**) *Formal (attention)* attention *f*, intérêt *m*; **worthy of remark** digne d'attention; **his behaviour did not escape remark** son comportement n'est pas passé inaperçu

2 *vt* (**a**) *(comment)* (faire) remarquer, (faire) observer; **"the days are getting longer", she remarked** "les jours rallongent", fit-elle remarquer

(**b**) *Formal (notice)* remarquer; **it may be remarked that...** constatons que... + *indicative*

▸**remark on, remark upon** *vt insep* **to remark on** *or* **upon sth** *(comment)* faire un commentaire *ou* une observation sur qch; *(criticize)* faire des remarques sur qch; **he remarked on the lateness of the hour** il fit remarquer qu'il était tard

remarkable [rɪˈmɑːkəbəl] *adj (quality, aspect)* remarquable; *(event, figure)* remarquable, marquant; **they are remarkable for their modesty** ils sont d'une rare modestie *ou* remarquablement modestes

remarkably [rɪˈmɑːkəblɪ] *adv* remarquablement; **she was looking remarkably well** elle avait l'air très en forme; **remarkably, most of the population survived the earthquake** la majorité de la population a survécu au tremblement de terre, ce qui est remarquable

remarket [ˌriːˈmɑːkɪt] *vt Mktg* recommercialiser

remarketing [ˌriːˈmɑːkɪtɪŋ] *n Mktg* marketing *m* de relance

remarriage [ˌriːˈmærɪdʒ] *n* remariage *m*

remarry [ˌriːˈmærɪ] *(pt & pp* **remarried**) **1** *vt (first spouse)* se remarier avec, épouser de nouveau

2 *vi* se remarier

remaster [ˌriːˈmɑːstə(r)] *vt (album)* remastériser

rematch *Sport* **1** *vt* [ˌriːˈmætʃ] *(players, contestants)* opposer de nouveau

2 *n* [ˈriːmætʃ] *(return)* match *m* retour; *(second)* deuxième match *m*

Rembrandt [ˈrembrænt] *pr n* Rembrandt

remediable [rɪˈmiːdjəbəl] *adj* remédiable

remedial [rɪˈmiːdjəl] *adj* (**a**) *(measures, action)* de redressement; **to take remedial action** prendre des mesures de redressement; **the public is demanding remedial action to halt the destruction of the environment** le public demande que des mesures soient prises pour stopper la destruction de l'environnement

(**b**) *Br Sch (classes)* de rattrapage, de soutien; *(education)* spécialisé; *(pupil, student)* qui n'a pas le niveau; **she teaches remedial maths** elle donne des cours de rattrapage *ou* de soutien en maths

(**c**) *Med (treatment)* correctif, curatif

▸▸ *Med* ***remedial exercises*** gymnastique *f* corrective; *Br Sch* ***remedial teacher*** enseignant(e) *m,f* chargé(e) d'une classe de rattrapage; *Br Sch* ***remedial teaching*** rattrapage *m* scolaire

remediation [rɪˌmiːdɪˈeɪʃən] *n Am Sch* rattrapage *m* scolaire

remedy [ˈremədɪ] *(pl* **remedies,** *pt & pp* **remedied**)

1 *n* (**a**) *also Fig* remède *m*; **it's a good remedy for insomnia** c'est un bon remède contre l'insomnie; **to find a remedy for sth** trouver un remède à qch; **it's past** *or* **beyond remedy** c'est irrémédiable *ou* sans remède

(**b**) *Br Law* recours *m*; **to have no remedy at law against sb** n'avoir aucun recours légal contre qn

2 *vt Med* remédier à; *Fig* rattraper, remédier à; **the situation cannot be remedied** la situation est sans issue; **how can we remedy the loss of our three best players?** comment remédier à la perte de nos trois meilleurs joueurs?

remember [rɪˈmembə(r)] **1** *vt* (**a**) *(recollect → face, past event)* se souvenir de, se rappeler; *(→ person)* se souvenir de; **don't you remember me?** *(in memory)* vous ne vous souvenez pas de moi?; *(recognize)* vous ne me reconnaissez pas?; **I remember him as a child** je me souviens de lui enfant; **I remember her as a very elegant woman** je me souviens d'elle comme de quelqu'un de très élégant; **I remember locking the door** je me rappelle avoir *ou* je me souviens d'avoir fermé la porte à clé; **I don't remember ever going** *or* **having gone there** je ne me rappelle pas y être jamais allé; **do you remember me knocking on your door?** vous souvenez-vous que j'ai frappé à votre porte?; **I can't remember anything else** c'est tout ce dont je me souviens; **I remember when there was no such thing as a paid holiday** je me souviens de l'époque où les congés payés n'existaient pas; **I can't remember her name** son nom m'échappe, je ne me souviens pas de son nom; **I can never remember names** je n'ai aucune mémoire des noms; **I'll remember his name in a minute** son nom me reviendra dans une minute; **we have nothing to remember him by** nous n'avons aucun souvenir de lui; **she will always be remembered as a great poet** on se souviendra toujours d'elle comme d'un grand poète; **as you will remember, the door is always locked** vous savez sans doute que la porte est toujours fermée à clef; **nobody could remember such a thing happening before** personne n'avait jamais vu une chose pareille se produire

(**b**) *(not forget)* penser à, songer à; **remember my advice** n'oubliez pas mes conseils; **remember to close the door** n'oubliez pas de *ou* pensez à fermer la porte; **a night/holiday to remember** une nuit mémorable/des vacances mémorables; **you must remember (that) he's only ten years old** n'oubliez pas qu'il n'a que dix ans; **we can't be expected to remember everything** nous ne pouvons quand même pas penser à tout; **you must remember that smoking is forbidden** n'oubliez pas qu'il est interdit de fumer; **that's a date worth remembering** voilà une date qu'il faudrait ne pas oublier; **she will remember you in her prayers** elle ne vous oubliera pas *ou* elle pensera à vous dans ses prières; **remember where you are!** un peu de tenue, voyons!, **remember who you're talking to!** à qui croyez-vous parler?; **he remembered himself just in time** il s'est repris juste à temps; **let us remember them in our prayers** prions pour eux

(**c**) *(give regards to)* **remember me to your parents** rappelez-moi au bon souvenir de vos parents; **she asked to be remembered to you** elle vous envoie son meilleur souvenir

(**d**) *(give tip or present to)* **please remember the driver** n'oubliez pas le chauffeur; **she always remembers me on my birthday** elle n'oublie jamais le jour de mon anniversaire; **he remembered me in his will** il a pensé à moi dans son testament

(**e**) *(commemorate → war)* commémorer; *(→ victims)* se souvenir de

2 *vi* se souvenir; **I remember now** maintenant, je m'en souviens; **as far as I can remember** autant qu'il m'en souvienne; **not that I remember** pas que je m'en souvienne; **if I remember rightly** si je me *ou* si je m'en souviens bien, si j'ai bonne mémoire

remembrance [rɪˈmembrəns] **1** *n* (**a**) *(recollection)* souvenir *m*, mémoire *f*; **to the best of my remembrance** autant qu'il m'en souvienne; **I have no remembrance of it** je n'en ai gardé aucun souvenir

(**b**) *(memory)* souvenir *m*

(**c**) *(keepsake)* souvenir *m*; **she gave him a ring as a remembrance of her** elle lui a donné une bague en souvenir d'elle

(**d**) *(commemoration)* souvenir *m*, commémoration *f*; **remembrance service, service of remembrance** cérémonie *f* du souvenir, commémoration *f*

(**e**) *Old-fashioned (greeting)* **give my kind remembrances to him** rappelez-moi à son bon souvenir

2 in remembrance of *prep* **in remembrance of sb/sth** en souvenir *ou* en mémoire de qn/qch

▸▸ ***Remembrance Day,*** *Br* ***Remembrance Sunday*** (commémoration *f* de) l'Armistice *m (le dimanche avant ou après le 11 novembre)*

remembrancer [rɪ'membrənsə(r)] *n* (**a**) *(memento)* souvenir *m*, mémento *m*
(**b**) *(notebook)* carnet *m* (de notes)
(**c**) **King's** *or* **Queen's Remembrancer** = fonctionnaire qui perçoit les dettes dues au souverain
(**d**) **City Remembrancer** = représentant du Conseil de la City de Londres devant les commissions parlementaires

remex ['ri:meks] *n Orn* rémige *f*

REMIC [,ɑ:ri:,emaɪ'si:] *n Am Fin (abbr* **real estate mortgage investment conduit**) obligation *f* garantie par hypothèque

remilitarization [,ri:mɪlɪtəraɪ'zeɪʃən] *n* remilitarisation *f*

remilitarize, -ise [,ri:'mɪlɪtəraɪz] *vt* remilitariser

remind [rɪ'maɪnd] *vt* rappeler à; **to remind sb to do sth** rappeler à qn de faire qch, faire penser à qn qu'il faut faire qch; **to remind sb about sth** rappeler qch à qn; **he reminds me of my brother** il me fait penser à *ou* me rappelle mon frère; **the music reminded them of Greece** la musique leur rappelait la Grèce; **remind him that we're going out** rappelez-lui que nous sortons; **can you remind me about the bills/to pay the bills?** pouvez-vous me faire penser aux factures/me rappeler qu'il faut payer les factures?; **she reminded herself that he was still very young** elle se dit qu'il était encore très jeune; **do I need to remind you of the necessity for discretion?** inutile de vous rappeler que la discrétion s'impose; **how many times do they have to be reminded?** combien de fois faut-il le leur rappeler?; **I'm glad you reminded me** je suis content que vous me l'ayez rappelé; **that reminds me!** à propos!, pendant que j'y pense!; **passengers are reminded that the duty-free shop will close in five minutes** nous rappelons aux voyageurs que la boutique hors taxe ferme dans cinq minutes

reminder [rɪ'maɪndə(r)] *n (of event)* rappel *m*; *(to jog memory)* pense-bête *m*; *Admin & Com (of unpaid bill)* rappel *m*; **final reminder** dernier rappel *m*; **to give sb a reminder to do sth** rappeler à qn qu'il doit faire qch; **she tied a knot in her handkerchief as a reminder** elle a fait un nœud à son mouchoir pour ne pas oublier; **the picture was a reminder of her life in Paris** cette image lui rappelait sa vie à Paris; **their success was a reminder of his own failure** leur réussite lui rappelait son propre échec; **we gave him a gentle reminder that it's her birthday tomorrow** nous lui avons discrètement rappelé que demain, c'est son anniversaire; **the exhibition is a stark** *or* **a grim reminder of the horrors of war** l'exposition rappelle la guerre dans toute son horreur; *Fin* **reminder of account due** rappel *m* d'échéance
▸▸ *Acct* ***reminder entry*** poste *m* de mémoire

remineralize, -ise [,ri:'mɪnərəlaɪz] *Med* **1** *vt* reminéraliser
2 *vi* se reminéraliser

reminisce [,remɪ'nɪs] *vi* évoquer *ou* raconter ses souvenirs; **to reminisce about the past** évoquer le passé, parler du passé

reminiscence [,remɪ'nɪsəns] **1** *n (memory)* réminiscence *f*, souvenir *m*
2 reminiscences *npl (memoirs)* mémoires *mpl*

reminiscent [,remɪ'nɪsənt] *adj* (**a**) *(suggestive)* **reminiscent of** qui rappelle, qui fait penser à; **in a voice reminiscent of that of her mother** *or* **of her mother's** d'une voix qui fait penser à *ou* qui rappelle celle de sa mère; **parts of the book are reminiscent of Proust** on trouve des réminiscences de Proust dans certaines parties du livre, certaines parties du livre rappellent Proust
(**b**) *(nostalgic → person, smile)* nostalgique; **to be in a reminiscent mood** être enclin à *ou* d'humeur à évoquer des souvenirs

reminiscently [,remɪ'nɪsəntlɪ] *adv (smile, say)* avec nostalgie; **to talk reminiscently of sth** évoquer des souvenirs de qch

remise [rɪ'maɪz] **1** *n* (**a**) *Law* renonciation *f* (**b**) *Fencing* remise *f*
2 *vt Law (right, claim)* renoncer à
3 *vi Fencing* faire une remise

remiss [rɪ'mɪs] *adj Formal* négligent; **he is remiss in his duties** il néglige ses devoirs; **it was rather remiss of you to forget her birthday** c'était un peu négligent *ou* léger de votre part d'oublier son anniversaire

remission [rɪ'mɪʃən] *n* (**a**) *Br Law (release → from prison sentence)* remise *f* (de peine); *(→ from debt, claim)* remise *f*; *Admin (dispensation)* dispense *f*; **he was granted five years' remission for good behaviour** on lui a accordé une remise de peine de cinq ans pour bonne conduite; **he asked for the remission of a deposit** il a demandé à être dispensé de verser une caution
(**b**) *Med & Rel* rémission *f*; **to go into remission** *(disease, patient)* entrer en phase de rémission

remit (*pt & pp* **remitted,** *cont* **remitting**) **1** *vt* [rɪ'mɪt] (**a**) *(release → from penalty)* remettre; *Rel (→ from sins)* remettre, pardonner; **his sentence was remitted by five years** il a bénéficié d'une remise de peine de cinq ans; **to remit sb's debt** remettre la dette de qn, tenir qn quitte d'une dette; **to remit sb's sentence** accorder une remise de peine à qn
(**b**) *(dispense, exonerate → fees, tax)* remettre; *Fin (→ debt)* remettre, faire remise de; **to remit sb's fees** dispenser qn de ses frais; **his exam fees were remitted** il a été dispensé des droits d'examen; **to remit sb's income tax** dispenser *ou* exempter qn d'impôt
(**c**) *(send → money)* envoyer; **to remit a sum of money to sb** envoyer une somme (d'argent) à qn
(**d**) *Law (case)* renvoyer (à une instance inférieure)
(**e**) *Formal (defer)* différer, remettre
(**f**) *Formal (relax → attention, activity)* relâcher
2 *vi* [rɪ'mɪt] (**a**) *(lessen → zeal)* diminuer; *(→ attention, efforts)* se relâcher; *(→ storm)* s'apaiser, se calmer
(**b**) *Fin (pay)* régler, payer; **please remit by cheque** veuillez régler *ou* payer par chèque
(**c**) *Med (fever)* tomber, diminuer; *(disease)* régresser
3 *n* ['ri:mɪt] attributions *fpl*, pouvoirs *mpl*; **that's outside their remit** cela n'entre pas dans (le cadre de) leurs attributions; **our remit is to...** il nous incombe de...

remittal [rɪ'mɪtəl] *n* (**a**) *Fin (of debt)* remise *f* (**b**) *Law* renvoi *m*

remittance [rɪ'mɪtəns] *n* (**a**) *(payment)* versement *m*; *(settlement)* paiement *m*, règlement *m*; **to send a remittance to sb** envoyer un versement à qn; **return the form with your remittance** renvoyez le formulaire avec votre paiement *ou* votre règlement
(**b**) *(delivery → of papers, documents)* remise *f*
▸▸ *Fin* ***remittance advice*** avis *m* de remise; *Fin* ***remittance date*** date *f* de remise; *Fin* ***remittance of funds*** remise *f* de fonds; *Old-fashioned* ***remittance man*** = homme vivant à l'étranger et recevant des mandats de Grande-Bretagne

remittee [rɪ,mɪt'i:] *n Admin* destinataire *mf (d'un envoi de fonds)*

remittent [rɪ'mɪtənt] *adj Med* rémittent

remitter, remittor [rɪ'mɪtə(r)] *n Fin* remettant(e) *m,f*; *(of letter, document)* porteur *m*

remix 1 *vt* [,ri:'mɪks] *(record, recording)* remixer, refaire le mixage de
2 *n* ['ri:mɪks] remix *m*

remnant ['remnənt] **1** *n (remains → of meal, material)* reste *m*; *(vestige → of beauty, culture)* vestige *m*; **the remnants of the army/his fortune** ce qui reste de l'armée/de sa fortune
2 remnants *npl Com (unsold goods)* invendus *mpl*; *(fabric)* coupons *mpl* (de tissus); *(oddments)* fins *fpl* de série

remodel [,ri:'mɒdəl] (*Br pt & pp* **remodelled,** *cont* **remodelling,** *Am pt & pp* **remodeled,** *cont* **remodeling**) *vt (bill, draft)* remanier; *(structure, legislation)* modifier; **to have one's nose/one's chin remodelled** se faire refaire le nez/le menton

remold *Am* = **remould**

remonstrance [rɪ'mɒnstrəns] *n Formal* (**a**) *(act of remonstrating)* remontrance *f* (**b**) *(protest)* protestation *f*

remonstrant [rɪ'mɒnstrənt] *n Formal* **1** (**a**) *(protestor)* protestataire *mf* (**b**) *Rel & Hist* remontrant *m*
2 *adj* (**a**) *(tone, look, letter)* de remontrance, de protestation; *(person)* qui proteste (**b**) *Rel & Hist* de remontrant, des remontrants

remonstrate ['remənstreɪt] **1** *vi Formal* protester; **to remonstrate with sb** faire des remontrances à qn (**about** au sujet de); **to remonstrate against sth** protester contre qch
2 *vt* **to remonstrate that...** protester en disant que... + *indicative*

remonstration [,remən'streɪʃən] *n Formal* (**a**) *(act of remonstrating)* remontrance *f* (**b**) *(protest)* protestation *f*

remonstrative [rɪ'mɒnstrətɪv] *adj Formal (tone, letter)* de remontrance, de protestation

remontant [rɪ'mɒntənt] *Bot* **1** *n* plante *f* remontante
2 *adj* remontant

remora ['remərə] *n* (**a**) *Ich* rémora *m* (**b**) *(obstacle)* obstacle *m*, *Arch* rémora *m*

remorse [rɪ'mɔ:s] *n* remords *m*; **to feel remorse (for having done sth)** éprouver *ou* avoir du *ou* des remords (d'avoir fait qch); **she felt no remorse** elle n'éprouvait aucun remords; **he was filled with remorse at what he had done** il était pris de remords en songeant à ce qu'il avait fait; **without remorse** *(with no regret)* sans remords; *(pitilessly)* sans pitié; **in a fit of remorse** dans un accès de remords; **to show remorse** manifester des remords

remorseful [rɪ'mɔ:sfʊl] *adj* plein de remords

remorsefully [rɪ'mɔ:sfʊlɪ] *adv* avec remords

remorseless [rɪ'mɔ:slɪs] *adj* (**a**) *(relentless → person, wind)* impitoyable; *(→ cruelty, persecution)* incessant; *Fig (→ ambition, logic, self-interest etc)* implacable; **he was remorseless in the demands that he made on his employees** il ne laissait aucun répit à ses employés (**b**) *(with no regret)* sans remords

remorselessly [rɪ'mɔ:slɪslɪ] *adv* (**a**) *(relentlessly)* impitoyablement, implacablement (**b**) *(with no regret)* sans remords

remorselessness [rɪ'mɔ:slɪsnɪs] *n* (**a**) *(relentlessness)* acharnement *m* (**b**) *(lack of regret)* absence *f* de remords

remortgage [,ri:'mɔ:gɪdʒ] *vt (house, property)* hypothéquer de nouveau, prendre une nouvelle hypothèque sur

remote [rɪ'məʊt] *adj* (**a**) *(far away)* éloigné, lointain; *(isolated)* reculé, isolé; *(ancestor)* lointain; **in the remotest parts of the continent** au fin fond du continent; **they lived in a remote part of Scotland** ils vivaient en Écosse, dans un endroit reculé *ou* isolé; **a remote house** une maison isolée; **areas remote from the capital/coast** des régions éloignées de la capitale/de la côte; **remote from civilization** loin de la civilisation; **his plays are remote from everyday life** ses pièces sont éloignées de la vie quotidienne; **in the remote future/past** dans un avenir/un passé lointain
(**b**) *(aloof → person, manner)* distant, froid; *(faraway → look)* lointain, vague; *(→ voice)* lointain; **she seems very remote** elle semble être très distante *ou* d'un abord difficile
(**c**) *(unconnected → idea, comment)* éloigné; **your comments are rather remote from the subject** vos commentaires n'ont pas grand-chose à voir avec le sujet
(**d**) *(slight → chance)* petit, faible; *(→ resemblance)* vague, lointain; **our chances of success are rather remote** nos chances de réussite sont assez minces, nous n'avons que peu de chances de réussir; **it's a remote possibility** c'est très peu probable; **there is a remote possibility that...** il y a une vague possibilité que... + *subjunctive*; **I haven't the remotest idea** je n'en ai pas la moindre idée
(**e**) *Comput (terminal)* distant; *(user)* à distance
(**f**) *Fin (payment)* à distance
▸▸ ***remote access*** accès *m* à distance; *Tel* **this telephone has an answering machine with a remote access facility** ce répondeur est interrogeable à distance; ***remote antiquity*** la haute antiquité; *Fin* ***remote banking*** banque *f* à distance; ***remote control*** télécommande *f*, commande *f* à distance; *Comput* ***remote (data) processing*** télétraitement *m*; *Nucl* ***remote handling equipment*** équipement *m* de télémanipulation; *Comput* ***remote job entry*** télésoumission *f* de

travaux; *Comput* ***remote loading*** téléchargement *m*; *Comput* ***remote sensing*** télédétection *f*; *Comput* ***remote sensing satellite*** satellite *m* de télédétection; *Comput* ***remote server*** serveur *m* distant; *Comput* ***remote terminal*** terminal *m* distant

remote-controlled *adj* télécommandé

remotely [rɪ'məʊtlɪ] *adv* (**a**) *(slightly)* faiblement, vaguement; **the two subjects are only very remotely linked** il n'y a qu'un rapport très lointain entre les deux sujets; **it is remotely possible that I'm mistaken** il n'est pas absolument impossible que je fasse erreur; **she's not remotely interested** ça ne l'intéresse pas le moins du monde *ou* absolument pas; **I'm not even remotely tired** je ne suis pas fatigué du tout *ou* absolument pas fatigué
(**b**) *(distantly)* **the house is remotely situated** la maison se trouve dans un coin isolé; **they are remotely related** ils sont parents éloignés
(**c**) *(aloofly)* de façon distante *ou* hautaine; *(dreamily)* vaguement, de façon songeuse

remoteness [rɪ'məʊtnɪs] *n* (**a**) *(distance → in space)* éloignement *m*, isolement *m*; *(→ in time)* éloignement *m* (**b**) *(aloofness → of person)* distance *f*, froideur *f*; **her air of remoteness** *(aloofness)* son air distant; *(absent-mindedness)* son air absent (**c**) *(of resemblance)* faible degré *m*; **the remoteness of her chances of success** l'improbabilité *f* de sa réussite

remould, *Am* **remold 1** *vt* [ˌriː'məʊld] (**a**) *Art & Tech* refaçonner (**b**) *Aut (tyre)* rechaper (**c**) *Fig (person, character)* changer, remodeler
2 *n* ['riːməʊld] *(tyre)* pneu *m* rechapé

remount 1 *vt* [ˌriː'maʊnt] (**a**) *(bicycle)* remonter sur; *(hill, steps)* remonter, gravir à nouveau; *(ladder)* remonter à *ou* sur; **to remount one's horse** se remettre en selle
(**b**) *(go up again → stairs)* remonter
(**c**) *(picture)* rentoiler; *(photograph)* remplacer le support de; *(jewel)* remonter
2 *vi* [ˌriː'maʊnt] *(on horse, bicycle)* remonter à cheval/à bicyclette
3 *n* ['riːmaʊnt] *Horseriding* remonte *f*

removable [rɪ'muːvəbəl] *adj* (**a**) *(detachable → lining, cover)* amovible, détachable (**b**) *(transportable → furniture, fittings)* mobile, transportable
▸▸ *Comput* ***removable disk*** disque *m* amovible *ou* extractible

removal [rɪ'muːvəl] **1** *n* (**a**) *(of garment, stain, object)* enlèvement *m*; *(of abuse, evil, threat)* suppression *f*; *(of doubt, fear)* dissipation *f*; *Med (of organ, tumour)* ablation *f*; **for stain removal, for the removal of stains** pour enlever les taches, pour détacher; **make-up removal** démaquillage *m*; **removal of customs barriers** suppression *f* des barrières douanières
(**b**) *(change of residence)* déménagement *m*; *(transfer)* transfert *m*; **their removal from/to Dublin** leur départ de/pour Dublin; **we haven't notified them of our removal** nous ne les avons pas avertis de notre changement de domicile; **the removal of the prisoner to a safer place** le transfert *ou* le déplacement du prisonnier dans un endroit plus sûr
(**c**) *(dismissal)* renvoi *m*; *(of civil servant, judge etc)* destitution *f*; **removal from office** révocation *f*, renvoi *m*
2 *comp (expenses, firm)* de déménagement
▸▸ *Br* ***removal man*** déménageur *m*; ***removal van*** camion *m* de déménagement

remove [rɪ'muːv] **1** *vt* (**a**) *(take off, out → clothes, object)* enlever, retirer, ôter; *(→ stain)* enlever, faire partir; *Med (→ organ, tumour)* enlever, retirer; *(take or send away → rubbish, plates etc)* enlever; *(→ person)* emmener (**to** à); **to remove one's make-up** se démaquiller; **to remove hair from one's legs** s'épiler les jambes; **to have a mole/wart removed** se faire enlever un grain de beauté/une verrue; **to remove a picture from the wall** enlever un tableau du mur, décrocher un tableau; **the chairs were removed to the attic** les chaises ont été mises au grenier; **she was removed to hospital** elle a été transportée à l'hôpital *ou* hospitalisée; **to remove a child from school** retirer un enfant de l'école; **death has removed her from us** la mort nous l'a enlevée; **the soldiers were removed to the front** on envoya les soldats au front; *Formal* **she removed herself to her room** elle se retira dans sa chambre; **police removed the demonstrators** la police a fait partir les manifestants; **the judge ordered her to be removed from the court room** le juge a ordonné qu'on la fasse sortir de la salle d'audience; **remove the prisoner!** *(in courtroom)* qu'on emmène le prisonnier!
(**b**) *(suppress → clause, paragraph)* supprimer; *(→ suspicion, doubt, fear)* dissiper; *(→ worry, obstacle, threat, word)* supprimer, éliminer; **all obstacles have been removed** tous les obstacles ont été écartés; **does this remove your objection?** est-ce que cela répond à votre objection?; **to remove sb's name from a list** rayer qn d'une liste; **his name has been removed from the list** son nom ne figure plus sur la liste
(**c**) *(dismiss → employee)* renvoyer; *(→ official)* révoquer, destituer; **his opponents had him removed from office** ses opposants l'ont fait révoquer
(**d**) *Euph (kill)* faire disparaître, tuer; **I want him removed** je veux qu'on le fasse disparaître
2 *vi Formal* (**a**) *(firm, premises, family)* déménager; **our office removed to Glasgow** notre service s'est installé à Glasgow
(**b**) *(person → go)* **she removed to her room** elle se retira dans sa chambre
3 *n* (**a**) *(distance)* distance *f*; **to experience sth at one remove** faire indirectement l'expérience de qch; **at one remove from reality** en léger décalage par rapport à la réalité; **this is but one remove from blackmail** ça frôle le chantage; **her account is several removes from the truth** son récit est assez loin de la vérité; **it's several removes** *or* **a far remove from what we need** ce n'est vraiment pas ce qu'il nous faut; **it's only a slight remove from his usual themes** ça ne diffère pas beaucoup de ses thèmes habituels
(**b**) *(degree of kinship)* degré *m* de parenté

removed [rɪ'muːvd] *adj* **to be far removed from** être très éloigné *ou* loin de; **what you say is not far removed from the truth** ce que vous dites n'est pas bien éloigné de la vérité; **one stage removed from insanity** au bord de la folie; **first cousin once/twice removed** cousin(e) *m,f* au deuxième/troisième degré

remover [rɪ'muːvə(r)] *n* (**a**) *(of furniture)* déménageur *m* (**b**) *(solvent)* **paint remover** décapant *m (pour peinture)*; **stain remover** détachant *m*

remunerate [rɪ'mjuːnəreɪt] *vt* rémunérer

remuneration [rɪˌmjuːnə'reɪʃən] *n* rémunération *f* (**for** de); **to receive remuneration for sth** être rémunéré *ou* payé pour qch
▸▸ ***remuneration package*** = salaire et avantages complémentaires

remunerative [rɪ'mjuːnərətɪv] *adj* rémunérateur

renaissance [rə'neɪsəns] **1** *n* renaissance *f*; *Art & Hist* **the Renaissance** la Renaissance
2 *comp (art, painter, literature)* de la Renaissance; *(palace, architecture, style)* Renaissance *(inv)*
▸▸ ***Renaissance man*** esprit *m* universel

renal ['riːnəl] *adj* rénal
▸▸ ***renal failure*** insuffisance *f* rénale

rename [ˌriː'neɪm] *vt (person, street)* rebaptiser; *Comput (file)* changer le nom de, renommer

renascence [rɪ'næsəns] *n* renaissance *f*

renascent [rɪ'næsənt] *adj* renaissant

renationalization [riːˌnæʃənəlaɪ'zeɪʃən] *n* renationalisation *f*

renationalize, -ise [ˌriː'næʃənəlaɪz] *vt* renationaliser

rend [rend] *(pt & pp* **rent** [rent]) *vt Literary* (**a**) *(tear → fabric)* déchirer; *(→ wood, armour)* fendre; *Fig (→ silence, air)* déchirer; **the air was rent with her screams** l'air était déchiré par ses hurlements; **the country was rent in two by political strife** le pays était profondément divisé par les conflits politiques; **a flash of lightning rent the sky** un éclair déchira le ciel; **to rend sb's heart** fendre le cœur à qn
(**b**) *(wrench)* arracher; **the child was rent from its mother's arms** on a arraché l'enfant des bras de sa mère

render ['rendə(r)] *vt* (**a**) *(deliver → homage, judgment, verdict)* rendre; *(→ assistance)* prêter; *(→ help)* fournir; *(submit → bill, account)* présenter, remettre; **to render an account of sth** *(explain)* rendre compte de qch; *Com* remettre *ou* présenter le compte de qch; *Fin & Com* **account rendered** facture *f* de rappel; *Fin & Com* **as per account rendered** suivant compte remis; **to render sb a service** rendre (un) service à qn; **to render an explanation of sth** fournir une explication à qch; **to render thanks to sb** remercier qn, faire des remerciements à qn; **to render thanks to God** rendre grâce à Dieu; *Bible* **render unto Caesar the things that are Caesar's** rendez à César ce qui appartient à César
(**b**) *(cause to become)* rendre; **a misprint rendered the text incomprehensible** une coquille rendait le texte incompréhensible; **the news rendered her speechless** la nouvelle l'a laissée sans voix
(**c**) *(perform → song, piece of music)* interpréter; *(convey → atmosphere, spirit)* rendre, évoquer
(**d**) *(translate)* rendre, traduire; **rendered into English** rendu *ou* traduit en anglais
(**e**) *Culin* faire fondre
(**f**) *Constr* crépir, enduire de crépi

▸**render down** *vt sep Br Culin* faire fondre; *(reduce)* réduire

▸**render up** *vt sep Literary (fortress)* rendre; *(hostage)* libérer, rendre; *(secret)* livrer

rendering ['rendərɪŋ] *n* (**a**) *(performance → of song, play, piece of music)* interprétation *f* (**b**) *(evocation → of atmosphere, spirit)* évocation *f* (**c**) *(translation)* traduction *f* (**d**) *Constr* enduit *m* (**e**) *Comput* rendu *m* (**f**) *(of meat)* équarrissage *m*
▸▸ ***rendering plant*** usine *f* d'équarrissage

rendezvous ['rɒndɪvuː] *(pl* **inv** [-vuːz], *pp & pt* **rendezvoused** [-vuːd], *cont* **rendezvousing** [-vuːɪŋ]) **1** *n* (**a**) *(meeting)* rendez-vous *m* (**b**) *(meeting place)* lieu *m* de rendez-vous
2 *vi* (*friends*) se retrouver; *(group, party)* se réunir; **to rendezvous with sb** rejoindre qn; **the boats rendezvoused successfully after the operation** les bateaux se sont retrouvés comme prévu après l'opération

rendition [ren'dɪʃən] *n* (**a**) *(of poem, piece of music)* interprétation *f*; **to give a rendition of** *(role etc)* interpréter; **they finished with a rendition of the Marseillaise** ils ont terminé en chantant/jouant la Marseillaise (**b**) *(translation)* traduction *f* (**c**) *Arch (surrender)* reddition *f*

rendzina [rend'ziːnə] *n Geol* rendzine *f*

renegade ['renɪgeɪd] **1** *n* (**a**) *(traitor)* renégat(e) *m,f* (**b**) *(outlaw)* hors-la-loi *m inv*
2 *adj* renégat
▸▸ ***renegade priest*** prêtre *m* parjure

renege [rɪ'niːg] *vi (in cards)* faire une renonce

▸**renege on** *vt insep (responsibilities)* manquer à; *(agreement)* revenir sur; **to renege on a promise/a contract** revenir sur sa parole/un contrat

renegotiate [ˌriːnɪ'gəʊʃɪeɪt] **1** *vi* renégocier
2 *vt* renégocier

renegotiation ['riːnɪˌgəʊʃɪ'eɪʃən] *n* renégociation *f*

renegue = **renege**

renew [rɪ'njuː] *vt* (**a**) *(extend validity of → passport)* renouveler; *(→ library book)* faire prolonger; *(→ contract, lease)* renouveler, reconduire; **to renew one's subscription to sth** renouveler son abonnement *ou* se réabonner à qch; **to renew one's wardrobe** renouveler sa garde-robe
(**b**) *(repeat → attack, promise, threat)* renouveler; *(restart → correspondence, negotiations)* reprendre; *(restate → request, promise)* renouveler; **to renew one's acquaintance with sb** renouer avec qn
(**c**) *(increase → strength)* reconstituer, reprendre; **to renew one's efforts to do sth** redoubler d'efforts pour faire qch; **to renew pressure on sb (to do sth)** recommencer à faire pression sur qn (pour qu'il fasse qch)
(**d**) *(replace → supplies)* renouveler, remplacer; *(→ batteries, mechanism)* remplacer, changer

renewable [rɪ'njuːəbəl] *adj (passport etc)* renouvelable; *(lease, contract)* reconductible, renouvelable
▸▸ ***renewable energy*** énergie *f* renouvelable;

renewable resources ressources *fpl* renouvelables

renewal [rɪ'nju:əl] *n* (**a**) *(extension → of validity)* renouvellement *m*; *(restart → of negotiations, hostilities)* reprise *f*; *(→ of acquaintance)* fait *m* de renouer; *(increase → of energy, hope)* regain *m*; *(repetition → of promise, threat)* renouvellement *m*; **renewal of subscription** réabonnement *m*, renouvellement *m* d'abonnement; **renewal of activity** reprise *f ou* regain *m* d'activité
(**b**) *(renovation)* rénovation *f*
(**c**) *Rel* renouveau *m*
►► *Ins* ***renewal notice*** avis *m* de renouvellement; *Ins* ***renewal premium*** prime *f* de renouvellement

renewed [rɪ'nju:d] *adj (confidence, hope)* renouvelé; *(vigour, force)* accru; **with renewed enthusiasm** avec un regain d'enthousiasme; **renewed outbreaks of violence** une reprise des violences; **there is renewed interest in...** il y a un regain d'intérêt pour...

reniform ['renɪfɔ:m] *adj* réniforme

renin ['renɪn] *n Physiol* rénine *f*

rennet ['renɪt] *n* (**a**) *(for cheese, junket)* présure *f* (**b**) *Zool* caillette *f*

rennin ['renɪn] *n Biol & Chem* présure *f*

renormalization ['ri:ˌnɔ:məlaɪ'zeɪʃən] *n Phys* renormalisation *f*

renormalize, -ise [ˌri:'nɔ:məlaɪz] *vt Phys* renormaliser

renounce [rɪ'naʊns] **1** *vt (claim, title)* abandonner, renoncer à; *(faith, principle, habit)* renoncer à, renier; *(treaty)* dénoncer; *Law (nationality, inheritance)* répudier; **to renounce the world** renoncer au monde; *Rel* **to renounce Satan and all his works** renoncer à Satan, à ses pompes et à ses œuvres
2 *vi Cards* renoncer

renovate ['renəveɪt] *vt* remettre à neuf, rénover

renovation [ˌrenə'veɪʃən] *n (of house etc)* remise *f* à neuf, rénovation *f*; **to be under renovation** être en cours de rénovation; **closed for renovation(s)** *(sign)* fermé pour cause de travaux de rénovation; **to carry out renovations** faire des travaux de rénovation

renovator ['renəveɪtə(r)] *n* rénovateur(trice) *m,f*

renown [rɪ'naʊn] *n* renommée *f*, renom *m*; **a man of great renown** un homme de grand renom; **to win renown (as/for)** acquérir une renommée, se faire une renommée (en tant que/pour)

renowned [rɪ'naʊnd] *adj* renommé, célèbre, réputé; **to be renowned for sth** être connu *ou* célèbre pour qch; **an internationally-renowned** *or* **a world-renowned expert** un expert célèbre dans le monde entier

rent [rent] **1** *pt & pp of* **rend**
2 *vt* (**a**) *(of tenant, hirer)* louer, prendre en location; **to rent sth from sb** louer qch à qn; **they rented a car for the holidays** ils ont loué une voiture pour les vacances; **their house must be expensive to rent** le loyer de leur maison doit être élevé
(**b**) *(of owner)* louer, donner en location; **to rent sth (out) to sb** louer qch à qn
3 *vi* (**a**) *(property)* **this apartment rents easily** cet appartement se loue facilement
(**b**) *(tenant)* louer
4 *n* (**a**) *(for flat, house)* loyer *m*; *(for farm)* loyer *m*, fermage *m*; *(for car, TV)* (prix *m* de) location *f*; **for rent** à louer; **how much do you pay in rent?, how much rent do you pay?** combien est-ce que tu paies de loyer?; **to be behind with the rent** être en retard pour (payer) le loyer
(**b**) *Econ* loyer *m*
(**c**) *(tear → in clothing)* déchirure *f*; *(→ in clouds)* déchirure *f*, trouée *f*
(**d**) *(split → in movement, party)* rupture *f*, scission *f*
►► ***rent book*** carnet *m* de quittances de loyer; *Fam* ***rent boy*** jeune prostitué *m* homosexuel□; ***rent collector*** receveur(euse) *m,f* des loyers; ***rent control*** contrôle *m* des loyers; ***rent rebate*** réduction *f* de loyer; ***rent strike*** grève *f* des loyers; ***rent tribunal*** commission *f* de contrôle des loyers

rent-a-car *n Br* location *f* de voitures

rent-a-crowd, rent-a-mob *n Br Fam (protestors)* agitateurs *mpl* professionnels□; *(audience, supporters)* claque *f*

rental ['rentəl] **1** *n* (**a**) *(hire agreement → for car, house, TV, telephone)* location *f*
(**b**) *(payment → for property, land)* loyer *m*; *(→ for TV, car, holiday accommodation)* (prix *m* de) location *f*; *(→ for telephone)* abonnement *m*, redevance *f*
(**c**) *(income)* (revenu *m* des) loyers *mpl*
(**d**) *Am (apartment)* appartement *m* en location; *(house)* maison *f* en location; *(land)* terrain *m* en location
2 *adj (agency)* de location; *(property)* à louer
►► ***rental agreement*** contrat *m* de location; ***rental charge*** *(for telephone)* abonnement *m*; *(for TV, car)* prix *m* de location; ***rental income*** revenus *mpl* locatifs; *Am* ***rental library*** bibliothèque *f* de prêt

rent-controlled *adj* dont le loyer est contrôlé

rented ['rentɪd] *adj* loué, de location; **she lives in a rented house** elle habite dans une maison qu'elle loue; **the high cost of rented accommodation in London** le prix élevé des loyers londoniens

renter ['rentə(r)] *n* (**a**) *(of property → tenant)* locataire *mf*; *(→ landlord)* propriétaire *mf* (**b**) *Cin* distributeur(trice) *m,f* (de films)

rent-free 1 *adj* exempt de loyer
2 *adv* sans payer de loyer, sans avoir de loyer à payer; **to live in an apartment rent-free** habiter un appartement sans payer de loyer

rent-roll *n Br (register)* registre *m* de l'état des loyers; *(income)* revenu *m* des loyers

rents [rents] *npl Am Fam (parents)* vieux *mpl*

renumber [ˌri:'nʌmbə(r)] *vt* renuméroter

renunciation [rɪˌnʌnsɪ'eɪʃən] *n* (**a**) *(of authority, claim, title)* renonciation *f*, abandon *m*; *(of faith, religion)* renonciation *f*, abjuration *f*; *(of principle)* abandon *m*, répudiation *f*; *(of treaty)* dénonciation *f* (**b**) *Law (of nationality, inheritance)* répudiation *f*

reoccupation [ˌri:ɒkjʊ'peɪʃən] *n* réoccupation *f*

reoccupy [ˌri:'ɒkjʊpaɪ] *(pt & pp* **reoccupied***)* *vt* réoccuper

reoccur [ˌri:ə'kɜ:(r)] *(pt & pp* **reoccurred**, *cont* **reoccurring**) = **recur** (**a**), (**b**)

reoccurrence [ˌri:ə'kʌrəns] = **recurrence**

reopen [ˌri:'əʊpən] **1** *vt* (**a**) *(door, border, book, bank account)* rouvrir; *Fig* **to reopen an old wound** rouvrir une plaie (**b**) *(restart → hostilities)* reprendre; *(→ debate, negotiations)* reprendre, rouvrir
2 *vi* (**a**) *(door, wound)* se rouvrir; *(shop, theatre)* rouvrir; *(school → after holiday)* reprendre (**b**) *(negotiations)* reprendre

reopening [ˌri:'əʊpənɪŋ] *n (of shop)* réouverture *f*; *(of negotiations)* reprise *f*

reorder 1 *vt* [ˌri:'ɔ:də(r)] (**a**) *Com (goods, supplies)* commander de nouveau, faire une nouvelle commande de (**b**) *(rearrange → numbers, statistics, objects)* reclasser réorganiser
2 *n* ['ri:ɔ:də(r)] *Com* nouvelle commande *f*
►► *Com* ***reorder level*** seuil *m* de réapprovisionnement

reorganization ['ri:ˌɔ:gənaɪ'zeɪʃən] *n* réorganisation *f*

reorganize, -ise [ˌri:'ɔ:gənaɪz] **1** *vt* réorganiser
2 *vi* se réorganiser

reorient [ˌri:'ɔ:rɪənt], **reorientate** [ˌri:'ɔ:rɪənteɪt] *vt* réorienter; **to reorient oneself** se réorienter

reorientation ['ri:ˌɔ:rɪən'teɪʃən] *n* réorientation *f*

Rep *Am* (**a**) *(written abbr* **Representative***)* ≃ député *m* (**b**) *(written abbr* **Republican***)* républicain(e) *m,f*

rep [rep] *n* (**a**) *Fam (abbr* **representative***)* représentant(e)□ *m,f*, VRP□ *m*
(**b**) *Br Fam (abbr* **repertory***) (theatre)* théâtre *m* de répertoire□; **to be** *or* **to work in rep** faire partie d'une troupe de répertoire, faire du théâtre de répertoire
(**c**) *Tex* reps *m*
(**d**) *Fam (abbr* **reputation***)* réputation□ *f*
(**e**) *Fam (abbr* **repetition***) (in physical training)* mouvement□ *m*; **twenty reps on each piece of equipment** vingt mouvements sur chaque machine

repack [ˌri:'pæk] *vt (goods)* remballer, emballer de nouveau; *(suitcase)* refaire

repackage [ˌri:'pækɪdʒ] *vt (goods)* remballer; *Mktg (product)* reconditionner, repenser l'emballage de; *Fig (company, image)* redorer

repaginate [ˌri:'pædʒɪneɪt] *vt* remettre en pages; *(renumber)* repaginer

repaid [ˌri:'peɪd] *pt & pp of* **repay**

repaint [ˌri:'peɪnt] *vt* repeindre

repair [rɪ'peə(r)] **1** *vt* (**a**) *(mend → car, tyre, watch, machine)* réparer; *(→ road, roof)* réparer, refaire; *(→ clothes)* raccommoder; *(→ hull)* radouber, caréner; *(→ tights)* repriser; **he repaired the hole in his trousers** il a raccommodé son pantalon; **she repaired her tights** elle a reprisé ses bas; **to have one's shoes repaired** faire réparer ses chaussures
(**b**) *(make amends for → error, injustice)* réparer, remédier à
2 *vi Formal or Hum* aller, se rendre; **let us repair to bed** allons nous coucher
3 *n* (**a**) *(mending → of car, machine, building, roof)* réparation *f*, remise *f* en état; *(→ of clothes)* raccommodage *m*; *(→ of shoes)* réparation *f*; *(→ of road)* réfection *f*, remise *f* en état; *Naut* radoub *m*; **to carry out repairs to** *or* **on sth** effectuer des réparations sur qch; **to be under repair** être en réparation; **road under repair** *(sign)* travaux; **closed for repairs** *(sign)* fermé pour (cause de) travaux; **road repairs** *(sign)* réfection de la chaussée; **the bridge was damaged beyond repair** le pont avait subi des dégâts irréparables; **the repairs to the car cost him a fortune** les travaux de réparation *ou* les réparations de la voiture lui ont coûté une fortune
(**b**) *(condition)* état *m*; **to be in good/bad repair** être en bon/mauvais état; **to keep sth in good repair** bien entretenir qch; **the road is in a terrible state of repair** la route est très mal entretenue *ou* en très mauvais état
►► ***repair kit*** trousse *f* à outils; ***repair shop*** atelier *m* de réparations

repairable [rɪ'peərəbəl] *adj* réparable

repairer [rɪ'peərə(r)] *n* réparateur(trice) *m,f*

repairman [rɪ'peəmən] *(pl* **repairmen** [-mən]) *n* réparateur *m*

repand [rɪ'pænd] *adj Bot & Zool* aux bords dentelés

repaper [ˌri:'peɪpə(r)] *vt* retapisser

reparable ['repərəbəl] *adj* réparable

reparation [ˌrepə'reɪʃən] *n* (**a**) *Formal (amends)* réparation *f*; *Fig* **to make reparations for sth** réparer qch (**b**) *(usu pl) (damages → after war, invasion etc)* réparations *fpl*
►► ***reparation payments*** réparations *fpl*

reparative ['repərətɪv] *adj* réparateur; *(compensatory)* réparatoire

reparcelling [ˌri:'pɑ:səlɪŋ] *n (of land)* remembrement *m*

repartee [ˌrepɑ:'ti:] *n* (**a**) *(witty conversation)* esprit *m*, repartie *f*; **to be good at repartee** avoir la repartie facile, avoir de la repartie (**b**) *(witty comment)* repartie *f*, réplique *f*

repartition [ˌri:pɑ:'tɪʃən] **1** *n* répartition *f*
2 *vt* redistribuer, répartir de nouveau

repast [rɪ'pɑ:st] *n Literary* repas *m*

repatriate 1 *vt* [ˌri:'pætrɪeɪt] rapatrier (**to** vers)
2 *n* [ri:'pætrɪət] rapatrié(e) *m,f*

repatriation [ˌri:pætrɪ'eɪʃən] *n* rapatriement *m*

repave [ri:'peɪv] *vt* repaver

repay [ˌri:'peɪ] *(pt & pp* **repaid** [-'peɪd]) *vt* (**a**) *(refund → creditor, loan)* rembourser; *(→ money)* rendre, rembourser; **to repay a debt** rembourser une dette; *Fig* s'acquitter d'une dette
(**b**) *(return → visit)* rendre; *(→ hospitality, kindness)* rendre, payer de retour; **how can I ever repay you (for your kindness)?** comment pourrai-je jamais vous remercier (pour votre gentillesse)?; **to repay good for evil** rendre le bien pour le mal
(**c**) *(reward → efforts, help)* récompenser; **to be repaid for one's efforts/one's persistence** être récompensé de ses efforts/de sa persévérance; **her generosity was repaid with indifference** tout ce qu'elle a obtenu en échange de sa générosité, c'est de l'indifférence

repayable [ˌri:'peɪəbəl] *adj* remboursable; **repayable in five years** remboursable sur cinq ans *ou* en cinq annuités

repayment [ˌri:'peɪmənt] *n* (**a**) *(of money, loan)* remboursement *m*; **repayments can be spread over twelve months** les remboursements peuvent être échelonnés sur douze mois (**b**) *(reward → for kindness, effort)* récompense *f*

►► *Br* ***repayment mortgage*** prêt-logement *m (qui n'est pas lié à une assurance-vie)*; ***repayment options*** formules *fpl* de remboursement; ***repayment plan*** calendrier *m* des paiements

repeal [rɪˈpiːl] **1** *vt (law)* abroger, annuler; *(prison sentence)* annuler; *(decree)* rapporter, révoquer

2 *n (of law)* abrogation *f*; *(of prison sentence)* annulation *f*; *(of decree)* révocation *f*

repealer [rɪˈpiːlə(r)] *n* = auteur de l'ordre de révocation; *Hist* = partisan de l'abrogation de l'Acte d'union entre la Grande-Bretagne et l'Irlande

repeat [rɪˈpiːt] **1** *vt* (**a**) *(say again → word, secret, instructions, question)* répéter; *(→ demand, promise, threat)* répéter, réitérer; **you're repeating yourself** vous vous répétez; **I don't dare repeat what he said** je n'ose pas répéter ce qu'il a dit; **it can't be repeated too often** on ne saurait trop le répéter; **it doesn't bear repeating** *(rude)* c'est trop grossier pour être répété; *(trivial)* ça ne vaut pas la peine d'être répété

(**b**) *(redo, re-execute → action, attack, mistake)* répéter, renouveler; *Mus* reprendre; **I wouldn't like to repeat the experience** je n'aimerais pas renouveler l'expérience; **it's history repeating itself** c'est l'histoire qui se répète; **the same little ritual is repeated every morning** le même petit rituel se renouvelle chaque matin; **the pattern repeats itself** le motif se répète

(**c**) *Rad & TV (broadcast)* rediffuser

(**d**) *Com (order, offer)* renouveler

(**e**) *Sch & Univ (class, year)* redoubler

2 *vi* (**a**) *(say again)* répéter; **I repeat, I have never heard of him** je le répète, je n'ai jamais entendu parler de lui; **I shall never, repeat never, go there again** je n'y retournerai jamais, mais alors ce qui s'appelle jamais; *Sch* **repeat after me** répétez après moi

(**b**) *(recur)* se répéter, se reproduire; *Math* se reproduire périodiquement

(**c**) *(food)* donner des renvois; **onions always repeat on me** les oignons me donnent toujours des renvois

(**d**) *Am Pol* voter plus d'une fois *(à une même élection)*

(**e**) *(watch, clock)* être à répétition

3 *n* (**a**) *(gen)* répétition *f*

(**b**) *Mus (passage)* reprise *f*; *(sign)* signe *m* de reprise

(**c**) *Rad & TV (broadcast)* rediffusion *f*, reprise *f*

4 *comp (order, visit)* renouvelé

►► *Comput* ***repeat function*** fonction *f* de répétition; *Law* ***repeat offender*** récidiviste *mf*; *Theat* ***repeat performance*** deuxième représentation *f*; *Fig* **we don't want a repeat performance of last year's chaos** nous ne voulons pas que le désordre de l'année dernière se reproduise; *Pej* **to give a repeat performance** jouer la même comédie; ***repeat prescription*** ordonnance *f (de renouvellement d'un médicament)*; **she gave me a repeat prescription** elle a renouvelé mon ordonnance; *Mktg* ***repeat purchase*** achats *mpl* répétés; *Mktg* ***repeat sale*** ventes *fpl* répétées

repeatable [rɪˈpiːtəbəl] *adj* susceptible d'être répété; **what he said is not repeatable** je n'ose pas répéter ce qu'il a dit

repeat-action key *n Comput* touche *f* de répétition

repeated [rɪˈpiːtɪd] *adj (action)* répété; *(question, statement)* réitéré; *(effort)* renouvelé

repeatedly [rɪˈpiːtɪdlɪ] *adv* à plusieurs *ou* à maintes reprises; **you have been told repeatedly not to play by the canal** on vous a dit cent fois de ne pas jouer près du canal; **I've repeatedly said that I can't come on Mondays** j'ai répété à maintes reprises *ou* j'ai bien dit que je ne pouvais pas venir le lundi

repeater [rɪˈpiːtə(r)] *n* (**a**) *(clock)* pendule *f* à répétition; *(alarm)* réveil *m* à répétition (**b**) *(gun)* fusil *m* à répétition (**c**) *Elec* répéteur *m* (**d**) *Am Sch* redoublant(e) *m,f* (**e**) *Am Pol* électeur(trice) *m,f* qui vote plus d'une fois *(à une même élection)*

repeating [rɪˈpiːtɪŋ] *adj* (**a**) *Math* périodique (**b**) *(gun)* à répétition

►► *Math* ***repeating decimal*** fraction *f* décimale périodique

repechage [ˈrepəʃɑːʒ] *n Sport* repêchage *m*

repel [rɪˈpel] *(pt & pp* **repelled**, *cont* **repelling**) **1** *vt* (**a**) *(drive back → attacker, advance, suggestion)* repousser; **a spray that repels greenfly** un aérosol qui éloigne les pucerons; **to repel moisture** empêcher l'infiltration de l'humidité

(**b**) *(disgust → of unpleasant sight, smell etc)* rebuter, dégoûter; **the sight of blood repelled him** la vue du sang lui soulevait le cœur *ou* le dégoûtait

(**c**) *Elec & Phys* repousser

2 *vi Elec & Phys* se repousser

repellent, repellant [rɪˈpelənt] **1** *adj* repoussant, répugnant; **to find sb/sth repellent** éprouver de la répugnance pour qn/qch

2 *n* (**a**) *(for insects)* insecticide *m*; *(for mosquitoes)* anti-moustiques *m inv* (**b**) *(for waterproofing)* imperméabilisant *m*

repent [rɪˈpent] **1** *vi* se repentir; **to repent of sth** se repentir de qch

2 *vt* se repentir de

repentance [rɪˈpentəns] *n* repentir *m*; **to show no sign of repentance** ne manifester aucun signe de repentir

repentant [rɪˈpentənt] *adj* repentant

repentantly [rɪˈpentəntlɪ] *adv (say)* d'un ton repentant; *(look at)* d'un air repentant

repercussion [ˌriːpəˈkʌʃən] *n* (**a**) *(consequence)* répercussion *f*, retentissement *m*, contrecoup *m*; **to have repercussions (for** *or* **on)** avoir des répercussions (sur); **the scandal has had serious repercussions on his family life** le scandale a eu de sérieuses répercussions sur sa vie familiale; **the repercussions of the affair** les répercussions *ou* le contrecoup de l'affaire (**b**) *(echo)* répercussion *f*

repertoire [ˈrepətwɑː(r)] *n also Fig* répertoire *m*; **to have a wide/a limited repertoire** avoir un vaste répertoire/un répertoire restreint

repertory [ˈrepətərɪ] *(pl* **repertories**) *n* (**a**) *Theat* **to be** *or* **to act in repertory** faire partie d'une troupe de répertoire, faire du théâtre de répertoire; *(theatre)* théâtre *m* de répertoire (**b**) *(repertoire)* répertoire *m*

►► ***repertory company*** compagnie *f ou* troupe *f* de répertoire; ***repertory theatre*** théâtre *m* de répertoire

répétiteur [ˌrepetɪˈtɜː(r)] *n Theat* maître *m* de musique

repetition [ˌrepɪˈtɪʃən] *n* (**a**) *(of words, orders)* répétition *f* (**b**) *(of action)* répétition *f*, renouvellement *m*; **I don't want any repetition of this disgraceful behaviour** je ne veux plus vous voir vous conduire de cette façon scandaleuse (**c**) *Mus* reprise *f*

repetitious [ˌrepɪˈtɪʃəs] *adj* plein de répétitions *ou* de redites

repetitive [rɪˈpetɪtɪv] *adj (activity, work, rhythm)* répétitif, monotone; *(song, speech)* plein de répétitions

►► ***repetitive strain injury, repetitive stress injury*** lésions *fpl* attribuables au travail répétitif

repetitiveness [rɪˈpetɪtɪvnɪs] *n* caractère *m* répétitif

rephrase [ˌriːˈfreɪz] *vt* reformuler; **can you rephrase that question?** pouvez-vous formuler cette question autrement?

repine [rɪˈpaɪn] *vi Literary (be sad)* languir, dépérir; *(complain)* maugréer

replace [rɪˈpleɪs] *vt* (**a**) *(put back)* replacer, remettre (à sa place *ou* en place); **to replace the receiver** *(on telephone)* reposer le combiné, raccrocher (le téléphone)

(**b**) *(person)* remplacer; *(mechanism, tyres)* remplacer; **you can go if you find someone to replace you** vous pouvez partir si vous vous faites remplacer par quelqu'un; **she replaced him as head of department/leader** elle lui a succédé à la tête du service/en tant que leader; **to replace a worn part by** *or* **with a new one** remplacer une pièce usée par une pièce neuve

(**c**) *Comput* remplacer; **replace all** *(command)* tout remplacer

replaceable [rɪˈpleɪsəbəl] *adj* remplaçable; **he is easily replaceable** on peut le remplacer facilement

replacement [rɪˈpleɪsmənt] **1** *n* (**a**) *(putting back)* remise *f* en place

(**b**) *(substitution)* remplacement *m*; **the replacement of damaged books** le remplacement des livres endommagés

(**c**) *(person)* remplaçant(e) *m,f*; **we are looking for a replacement for our secretary** nous cherchons quelqu'un pour remplacer notre secrétaire

(**d**) *(engine or machine part)* pièce *f* de rechange; *(product)* produit *m* de remplacement

2 *comp (part)* de rechange; *(staff)* de remplacement

►► *Ins* ***replacement cost*** coût *m* de remplacement; *Med* ***replacement hip joint*** prothèse *f* de (la) hanche; *Med* ***replacement knee joint*** prothèse *f* de (la) rotule; *Sch* ***replacement teacher*** professeur *m* suppléant, suppléant(e) *m,f*, remplaçant(e) *m,f*; *Ins* ***replacement value*** valeur *f* de remplacement

replant [ˌriːˈplɑːnt] *vt* replanter

replanting [ˌriːˈplɑːntɪŋ] *n* replantage *m*, replantation *f*

replaster [ˌriːˈplɑːstə(r)] *vt* replâtrer, recrépir

replay 1 *n* [ˈriːpleɪ] (**a**) **(action) replay** *(on TV)* = répétition d'une séquence précédente; *(in slow motion)* ralenti *m*; **the replay clearly shows the foul** on voit bien la faute au ralenti (**b**) *Sport* match *m* rejoué

2 *vt* [ˌriːˈpleɪ] (**a**) *(record, piece of film, video)* repasser (**b**) *(match)* rejouer

replenish [rɪˈplenɪʃ] *vt Formal* (**a**) *(restock → cellar, stock)* réapprovisionner; **to replenish one's supplies of sth** se réapprovisionner en qch; *Banking* **to replenish an account** approvisionner un compte (**b**) *(refill → glass)* remplir de nouveau; **to replenish one's glass** se resservir à boire; **she kept his glass replenished** elle veillait à ce que son verre fût toujours plein

replenishment [rɪˈplenɪʃmənt] *n Formal (of glass)* remplissage *m*; **replenishment of supplies/stocks** réapprovisionnement *m*

replete [rɪˈpliːt] *adj Formal (full)* rempli, plein; *(person → full up)* rassasié; **to be replete with** *(food)* être repu *ou* rassasié de; *(fuel, supplies)* être (bien) ravitaillé en

repletion [rɪˈpliːʃən] *n Formal* satiété *f*; **to eat to repletion** se rassasier, manger à satiété

replica [ˈreplɪkə] **1** *n (of painting, model, sculpture)* réplique *f*, copie *f*; *(of document)* copie *f* (exacte), fac-similé *m*; **she is the exact replica of her mother** c'est la réplique vivante *ou* exacte de sa mère

2 *adj* **it's a replica aircraft/pistol** ce n'est pas un avion/pistolet d'époque, c'est une réplique; **a replica Messerschmitt** la réplique d'un Messerschmitt

replicase [ˈreplɪkeɪz] *n Biol* réplicase *f*

replicate [ˈreplɪkeɪt] **1** *vt (document)* copier; *(experiment, cell, gene)* reproduire; *Comput (in spreadsheet)* recopier à l'identique; **the gene can replicate itself** le gène peut se reproduire

2 *vi Biol* se reproduire par mitose

replication [ˌreplɪˈkeɪʃən] *n* (**a**) *(gen)* reproduction *f* (**b**) *Biol* reproduction *f* par mitose

reply [rɪˈplaɪ] *(pl* **replies**, *pt & pp* **replied**) **1** *n* (**a**) *(answer)* réponse *f*; *(retort)* réplique *f*; **he made no reply** il n'a pas répondu; **his reply to that was to march out of the room** il a réagi à cela en sortant d'un air furieux de la pièce; **there was no reply** *(to telephone call)* on n'a pas répondu, ça ne répondait pas; *(to knock on door)* on n'a pas ouvert; **what did you say in reply?** qu'est-ce que tu as répondu?; **what did you do in reply?** comment est-ce que tu as réagi?

(**b**) *Law* réplique *f*

2 *vt (answer)* répondre; *(retort)* répliquer, rétorquer; **"I don't know", she replied** "je ne sais pas", répondit-elle; **what did you reply?** qu'est-ce que tu as répondu?

3 *vi* répondre; **to reply to sb** répondre à qn; **have you replied to their offer/letter?** avez-vous répondu à leur offre/leur lettre?

4 in reply to *prep* en réponse à; **to say sth in reply to sb/sth** dire qch en réponse à qn/qch; **in reply to your letter** en réponse à votre lettre

►► *Mktg* ***reply card*** carte-réponse *f*; *Mktg* ***reply coupon*** coupon-réponse *m*; ***reply slip*** talon *m* à retourner

reply-paid *adj Br* avec réponse payée

►► *Mktg* ***reply-paid card*** carte *f* T; ***reply-paid letter*** lettre *f* avec réponse payée

repo ['ri:pəʊ] **1** *n* (**a**) *Am Fam St Exch* (*abbr* **repossession**) réméré❑ *m*

(**b**) (*abbr* **repurchase**) rachat *m*; *St Exch & Banking* réméré *m*

2 *vt Fam* (*abbr* **repossess**) saisir❑

▸▸ *St Exch & Banking* ***repo agreement*** opération *f* de réméré *ou* de prise en pension, opération *f* repo; *Am Fam* ***repo man*** ≃ huissier *m* (*chargé par une société de saisir des meubles etc non payés*); *St Exch & Banking* ***repo operation*** opération *f* de réméré *ou* de prise en pension, opération *f* repo; ***repo rate*** taux *m* de réméré *ou* de prise en pension

repoint [,ri:'pɔɪnt] *vt Constr* rejointoyer

repopulate [,ri:'pɒpjʊleɪt] *vt* repeupler

repopulation [,ri:pɒpjʊ'leɪʃən] *n* repeuplement *m*

REPORT [rɪ'pɔ:t]

rapport	▸ **1 (a)**
compte rendu	▸ **1 (a)**
procès-verbal	▸ **1 (a), (d)**
reportage	▸ **1 (b)**
bulletin	▸ **1 (b), (c)**
annoncer	▸ **2 (a), (b)**
rendre compte de	▸ **2 (a)**
faire un reportage sur	▸ **2 (b)**
signaler	▸ **2 (c)**
faire un/son rapport	▸ **3 (a)**
se présenter	▸ **2 (d); 3 (c)**

1 *n* (**a**) (*account*) rapport *m*; (*summary* → *of speech, meeting*) compte rendu *m*; (*official record*) procès-verbal *m*; *Com & Fin* (*review*) rapport *m*; (*balance sheet*) bilan *m*; **to draw up** *or* **to make a report on sth** faire *ou* rédiger un rapport sur qch; **he gave an accurate report of the situation** il a fait un rapport précis sur la situation; **official/police report** rapport *m* officiel/de police; **his report on the meeting** son compte rendu de la réunion; **report of the board of directors** (*in annual account*) rapport *m* de gestion; **sales report** rapport *m ou* bilan *m* commercial; *Sch* **book report** compte rendu *m* de lecture

(**b**) (*in media*) reportage *m*; (*investigation*) enquête *f*; (*bulletin*) bulletin *m*; (*rumour*) rumeur *f*; (*news*) nouvelle *f*; **to do a report on sth** faire un reportage *ou* une enquête sur qch; *Rad & TV* **here is a report from Keith Owen** voici le reportage de Keith Owen; **according to newspaper/intelligence reports** selon les journaux/les services de renseignements; **we have had reports of several burglaries in city stores** on nous a signalé plusieurs cambriolages dans les magasins du centre-ville; **there are reports of civil disturbances in the North** il y aurait des troubles dans le Nord; **reports are coming in of an earthquake** on parle d'un tremblement de terre; **I only know it by report** je ne le sais que par ouï-dire, j'en ai seulement entendu parler

(**c**) *Br Sch* **(school) report** bulletin *m* (scolaire); **end of term report** bulletin *m* trimestriel

(**d**) *Law* (*of court proceedings*) procès-verbal *m*; **law reports** recueil *m* de jurisprudence

(**e**) (*sound* → *of explosion, shot*) détonation *f*

(**f**) *Comput* (*of database*) état *m*

(**g**) *Formal* (*repute*) renom *m*, réputation *f*; **of good report** de bonne réputation

2 *vt* (**a**) (*announce*) annoncer, déclarer, signaler; (*give account of*) faire état de, rendre compte de; **the police have reported some progress in the fight against crime** la police a annoncé des progrès dans la lutte contre la criminalité; **to report one's findings** (*in research*) rendre compte des résultats de ses recherches; (*in inquiry, commission*) présenter ses conclusions; **the discovery of a new vaccine is reported** on annonce la découverte d'un nouveau vaccin; **it is reported from Delhi that a ten-year contract has been signed** on annonce à Delhi qu'un contrat de dix ans a été signé; **to report the position of a ship** signaler la position d'un navire; *Customs* **to report a vessel** déclarer un navire; **the company reports a profit for the first time in five years** l'entreprise annonce un bénéfice pour la première fois depuis cinq ans; **the doctors report his condition as comfortable** les médecins déclarent son état satisfaisant

(**b**) (*of press, media* → *event, match*) faire un reportage sur; (→ *winner*) annoncer; (→ *debate, speech*) faire le compte rendu de; **the newspapers report heavy casualties** les journaux font état de nombreuses victimes; **our correspondent reports that troops have left the city** notre correspondant nous signale que des troupes ont quitté la ville; **her resignation is reported in several papers** sa démission est annoncée dans plusieurs journaux; **the speech was reported in the 8 o'clock news bulletin** il y avait un compte rendu du discours dans le bulletin d'informations de 8 heures; **reporting restrictions were not lifted** l'interdiction faite aux journalistes de rapporter les débats n'a pas été levée; **it is reported that a woman drowned** une femme se serait noyée; **the plane is reported to have crashed in the jungle** l'avion se serait écrasé dans la jungle; **he is reported to have left** *or* **as having left the country** il aurait quitté le pays

(**c**) (*accident, burglary, disappearance, murder*) signaler; (*wrongdoer*) dénoncer, porter plainte contre; **I'd like to report an accident** je voudrais signaler un accident; **to report sb missing (to the police)** signaler la disparition de qn (à la police); **ten people were reported dead** on a annoncé la mort de dix personnes; **she has been reported missing** on a signalé sa disparition; **she was reported missing five years ago** elle a été portée disparue il y a cinq ans; **nothing to report** rien à signaler; **they were reported to the police for vandalism** on les a dénoncés à la police pour vandalisme; **the school reported the boy's rudeness to his parents** l'école a signalé l'insolence du garçon à ses parents

(**d**) *Formal* (*present*) **to report oneself for duty** se présenter au travail

3 *vi* (**a**) (*make a report* → *committee*) faire son rapport, présenter ses conclusions; (→ *police*) faire un rapport; (→ *journalist*) faire un reportage; **to report on sth** *Admin* faire un rapport sur qch; *Press* faire un reportage sur qch; **to report on a murder case** faire un rapport sur un meurtre; **to report on an aircraft hijacking** faire un reportage sur un détournement d'avion; **she's reporting on the train crash** elle fait un reportage sur l'accident de train; **he reports for the BBC** il est reporter *ou* journaliste à la BBC; **this is Keith Owen, reporting from Moscow for CBS** de Moscou, pour la CBS, Keith Owen

(**b**) (*in hierarchy*) **to report to sb** être sous les ordres de qn; **who do you report to?** qui est votre supérieur?; **I report directly to the sales manager** je dépends directement du chef des ventes

(**c**) (*present oneself*) se présenter; **report to my office** présentez-vous à mon bureau; **to report for duty** prendre son service, se présenter au travail; **to report sick** se faire porter malade; **report to the sergeant when you arrive** présentez-vous au sergent à votre arrivée; *Mil* **to report to base** (*go*) se présenter à la base; (*contact*) contacter la base; *Mil* **to report to barracks** *or* **to one's unit** rallier son unité

▸▸ *Sch* ***report card*** bulletin *m ou* carnet *m* scolaire; *Comput* ***report form*** rapport *m* (d'édition), fiche *f* d'état; *Comput* ***report form generator*** générateur *m* d'états; *Br Pol* ***report stage*** = examen d'un projet de loi avant la troisième lecture; **the bill has reached report stage** ≃ le projet de loi vient de passer en commission

▸**report back 1** *vi* (**a**) (*return* → *soldier*) regagner ses quartiers, rallier son régiment; (→ *journalist, salesman*) rentrer; **to report back to headquarters** *Mil* rentrer au quartier général; (*salesman, clerk*) rentrer au siège; **I have to report back to the office** il faut que je repasse au bureau; **what time did he report back?** à quelle heure est-il rentré *ou* était-il de retour?

(**b**) (*present report*) présenter son rapport; **the commission must first report back to the minister** la commission doit d'abord présenter son rapport au ministre; **can you report back on what was discussed?** pouvez-vous rapporter ce qui a été dit?; **please report back to me before you decide anything** veuillez vous en référer à moi avant de prendre une décision

2 *vt sep* (*results, decision*) rapporter, rendre compte de

▸**report out** *vt sep Am Pol* (*bill, legislation*) renvoyer après examen

reportage [,repɔ:'tɑ:ʒ] *n* reportage *m*

reported [rɪ'pɔ:tɪd] *adj* **there have been reported sightings of dolphins off the coast** on aurait vu des dauphins près des côtes; **the last reported sighting of the aircraft** la dernière fois que l'on a vu l'avion; **what was their last reported position?** où ont-ils été signalés pour la dernière fois?

▸▸ *Gram* ***reported speech*** style *m ou* discours *m* indirect; **in reported speech** en style indirect

reportedly [rɪ'pɔ:tɪdlɪ] *adv* **he is reportedly about to resign** il serait sur le point de démissionner; **three hundred people have reportedly been killed** trois cents personnes auraient été tuées

reporter [rɪ'pɔ:tə(r)] *n* (**a**) (*for newspaper*) journaliste *mf*, reporter *m*; *Rad & TV* reporter *m* (**b**) (*scribe* → *in court*) greffier(ère) *m,f*; (→ *in parliament*) sténographe *mf*

reporting [rɪ'pɔ:tɪŋ] *n* (*of news*) reportage *m*; **his reporting of the facts is always accurate** il rapporte toujours fidèlement les faits; **she is noted for her objective reporting** elle est connue pour l'objectivité de ses reportages

▸▸ *St Exch* ***reporting limit*** seuil *m* d'annonce obligatoire; ***reporting restrictions*** restrictions *fpl* journalistiques; **reporting restrictions have been imposed** on a imposé des restrictions quant aux reportages; ***reporting structure*** (*within company*) structure *f* hiérarchique

repose [rɪ'pəʊz] **1** *vt Formal* (**a**) (*rest*) **to repose oneself** se reposer

(**b**) (*place* → *confidence, trust*) mettre, placer; **to repose trust in sb** placer *ou* mettre sa confiance en qn

2 *vi* (**a**) (*rest* → *person*) se reposer; (→ *the dead*) reposer

(**b**) (*be founded* → *belief, theory*) reposer; **to repose on firm evidence** reposer sur des preuves solides

3 *n Formal or Literary* (*rest*) repos *m*; (*sleep*) sommeil *m*; **in repose** au *ou* en repos; **her face is beautiful in repose** son visage est très beau lorsqu'elle est détendue; **to pray for the repose of a soul** prier pour le repos d'une âme

reposition [,ri:pə'zɪʃən] *vt* (**a**) (*move*) **to reposition sth** changer qch de place; **she repositioned herself nearer the door** elle a changé de place pour aller se placer près de la porte (**b**) *Com* (*change image of* → *product, brand, political party*) repositionner

repositioning [,ri:pə'zɪʃənɪŋ] *n Com* (*of product, brand, political party*) repositionnement *m*

repository [rɪ'pɒzɪtərɪ] (*pl* **repositories**) *n* (**a**) (*storehouse* → *large*) entrepôt *m*; (→ *smaller*) dépôt *m* (**b**) *Literary* (*of knowledge, secret*) dépositaire *mf*; **to make sb the repository of one's sorrows** confier ses peines à qn

repossess [,ri:pə'zes] *vt* reprendre possession de; *Law* saisir; **they have been repossessed, their house has been repossessed** leur maison a été mise en saisie immobilière

repossession [,ri:pə'zeʃən] *n* reprise *f* de possession; *Law* saisie *f*

▸▸ ***repossession order*** ordre *m* de saisie

repot [,ri:'pɒt] (*pt & pp* **repotted**, *cont* **repotting**) *vt* (*plant*) rempoter

repotting [,ri:'pɒtɪŋ] *n* rempotage *m*

repp [rep] *n Tex* reps *m*

reprehend [,reprɪ'hend] *vt* (*person*) réprimander; (*conduct, action*) condamner, désavouer

reprehensible [,reprɪ'hensəbəl] *adj* répréhensible

reprehensibly [,reprɪ'hensəblɪ] *adv* de façon répréhensible

reprehension [,reprɪ'henʃən] *n Formal* (*rebuke*) réprimande *f*; (*criticism*) condamnation *f*

represent [,reprɪ'zent] *vt* (**a**) (*symbolize* → *of diagram, picture, symbol*) représenter; **the statue represents peace** la statue représente *ou* symbolise la paix; **what does the scene represent?** que représente la scène?

(**b**) (*constitute* → *achievement, change*) représenter, constituer; **this new development**

represents a danger to world peace ce fait nouveau représente un danger pour la paix mondiale; **the book represents five years' work** le livre représente cinq années de travail

(**c**) *Pol (voters, members)* représenter; **she represents Tooting** elle est député de *ou* elle représente la circonscription de Tooting

(**d**) *(be delegate for → of person)* représenter; **the President was represented by the ambassador** le Président était représenté par l'ambassadeur; **I represent the agency** je viens de la part de l'agence; **the best lawyers are representing the victims** les victimes sont représentées par les meilleurs avocats

(**e**) *(opinion)* représenter; **the voice of women is not represented on the committee** les femmes ne sont pas représentées au comité; **the government's policy does not represent my opinions** la politique du gouvernement n'est pas représentative de mes opinions

(**f**) *(in numbers)* représenter; **foreign students are well represented in the university** il y a une forte proportion d'étudiants étrangers à l'université

(**g**) *(depict)* représenter, dépeindre; *(describe)* décrire; **he represented her as a queen** il l'a peinte sous les traits d'une reine

(**h**) *Formal (express, explain → advantages, prospect, theory)* présenter; **they represented their grievances to the director** ils ont fait part de *ou* présenté leurs griefs au directeur

(**i**) *Theat (of actor)* jouer, interpréter

re-present [ˌriː-] *vt Fin* présenter de nouveau

representation [ˌreprɪzen'teɪʃən] **1** *n* (**a**) *Pol* représentation *f*; **they have increased their representation to six** le nombre de leurs délégués est passé à six; **they still lacked representation in Parliament** ils n'étaient toujours pas représentés au parlement

(**b**) *(description, presentation)* représentation *f*

(**c**) *(of facts)* exposé *m* des faits; **this is a fair representation of their point of view** cela représente bien leur point de vue

2 representations *npl (complaints)* plaintes *fpl*, protestations *fpl*; *(intervention)* démarche *f*, intervention *f*; **to make representations to sb** *(complain)* se plaindre auprès de qn; *(intervene)* faire des démarches auprès de qn

representational [ˌreprɪzen'teɪʃənəl] *adj (gen)* représentatif; *Art* figuratif

representationalism [ˌreprɪsen'teɪʃənəlɪzəm] *n Art* art *m* figuratif

representationalist [ˌreprɪzen'teɪʃənəlɪst] **1** *adj Art* (du genre) figuratif

2 *n Art* figuratif *m*

representative [ˌreprɪ'zentətɪv] **1** *adj (typical)* typique, représentatif; **to be representative of sth** être représentatif de qch; **the high rate of abstention is representative of the lack of interest in politics** le fort taux d'abstention est représentatif du manque d'intérêt pour la politique

2 *n* (**a**) *(gen)* représentant(e) *m,f*; **he is our country's representative abroad** il représente notre pays à l'étranger

(**b**) *Com* **(sales) representative** représentant(e) *m,f* (de commerce)

3 Representative *Am Pol* **1** *n* ≃ député *m* **2** *adj* représentatif

▸▸ ***representative sample*** échantillon *m* type; **is this a representative sample of your results?** est-ce un échantillon représentatif de vos résultats?

representativeness [ˌreprɪ'zentətɪvnɪs] *n* représentativité *f*

repress [rɪ'pres] *vt* (**a**) *(impulse, desire)* réprimer (**b**) *Psy* refouler

repressed [rɪ'prest] *adj* (**a**) *(gen)* réprimé (**b**) *Psy* refoulé; **she had a very repressed adolescence** elle a été refoulée à l'adolescence

repression [rɪ'preʃən] *n* (**a**) *(gen)* répression *f* (**b**) *Psy* refoulement *m*

repressive [rɪ'presɪv] *adj (authority, system, law)* répressif; *(measures)* de répression, répressif

repressiveness [rɪ'presɪvnɪs] *n (of authority, system, law, measures)* caractère *m* répressif

repressor [rɪ'presə(r)] *n Biol* répresseur *m*

reprieve [rɪ'priːv] **1** *vt* (**a**) *Law (prisoner → remit)* gracier; *(→ postpone)* accorder un sursis à

(**b**) *Fig (give respite to → company)* accorder un sursis à; **the shipyard has been reprieved** *(temporarily)* le chantier naval bénéficie d'un sursis; *(definitively)* le chantier naval a été sauvé

2 *n* (**a**) *Law (permanent)* remise *f* de peine, grâce *f*; *(temporary)* sursis *m*; **to be given a reprieve** *(permanent)* être gracié, obtenir une remise de peine; *(temporary)* obtenir un sursis

(**b**) *Fig (respite → from danger, illness)* sursis *m*, répit *m*; *(extra time)* sursis *m*, délai *m*; **this is a reprieve for the government** cela constitue un sursis pour le gouvernement

reprimand ['reprɪmɑːnd] **1** *vt (rebuke)* réprimander (**for** pour); *(employee, accused person)* blâmer (**for** pour); **the children were severely reprimanded** les enfants ont été sévèrement réprimandés; **he was reprimanded for being late** *(schoolchild)* on lui a donné un avertissement pour son retard; *(employee)* il a reçu un blâme pour son retard

2 *n (rebuke)* réprimande *f*; *(professional)* blâme *m*

reprint 1 *vt* [ˌriː'prɪnt] *(book)* réimprimer; *(article)* faire paraître *ou* publier à nouveau; **the book is being reprinted** le livre est en réimpression

2 *vi* [ˌriː'prɪnt] *(book)* être en réimpression

3 *n* ['riːprɪnt] *(of book)* réimpression *f*; *(of article)* nouvelle parution *f*, nouvelle publication *f*; **her novel is on its tenth reprint** son roman en est à sa dixième réimpression

reprisal [rɪ'praɪzəl] **1** *n* représailles *fpl*; **to take reprisals (against sb)** user de représailles *ou* exercer des représailles (contre qn); **by way of** *or* **in reprisal, as a reprisal** par représailles; **he was shot as a reprisal for yesterday's killing** on l'a fusillé en représailles de l'assassinat d'hier; **there have been threats of reprisal** il y a eu des menaces de représailles

2 *comp (attack, raid)* de représailles

reprise [rɪ'priːz] *n Mus* reprise *f*

repro ['riːprəʊ] *(pl* **repros**) *n Fam Typ (abbr* **reproduction**) (épreuve *f*) repro *f*

▸▸ ***repro head*** tête *f* de lecture

reproach [rɪ'prəʊtʃ] **1** *n* (**a**) *(criticism)* reproche *m*; **in a tone of reproach** sur un ton réprobateur *ou* de reproche; **to heap reproaches on sb** accabler qn de reproches; **above** *or* **beyond reproach** au-dessus de tout reproche, irréprochable

(**b**) *(source of shame)* honte *f*; **to be a reproach to** être la honte de; **it is a reproach to the government that...** c'est une honte pour le gouvernement que...; **things that have brought reproach upon him** des choses qui ont jeté le discrédit sur lui

2 *vt* faire des reproches à; **to reproach sb with sth** reprocher qch à qn; **she reproached him for** *or* **with having broken his promise** elle lui reprochait d'avoir manqué à sa parole; **I reproach myself for failing to warn them** je m'en veux de ne pas les avoir prévenus; **I have nothing to reproach myself for** *or* **with** je n'ai rien à me reprocher; **he was reproached for his insensitivity** on lui a reproché son manque de sensibilité

reproachful [rɪ'prəʊtʃfʊl] *adj (voice, look, attitude)* réprobateur; *(tone, words)* de reproche, réprobateur

reproachfully [rɪ'prəʊtʃfʊlɪ] *adv* avec reproche; **"why not?" she said reproachfully** "pourquoi pas?" dit-elle d'un ton de reproche; **to look at sb reproachfully** lancer des regards réprobateurs à qn

reprobate ['reprəbeɪt] **1** *adj* dépravé

2 *n Formal* réprouvé(e) *m,f*; *Hum* vaurien(-enne) *m,f*

3 *vt* réprouver

reprobation [ˌreprə'beɪʃən] *n* réprobation *f*

reprocess [ˌriː'prəʊses] *vt* retraiter

reprocessing [ˌriː'prəʊsesɪŋ] *n* retraitement *m*; **nuclear reprocessing** retraitement *m* des déchets nucléaires

▸▸ ***reprocessing plant*** usine *f* de retraitement

reproduce [ˌriːprə'djuːs] **1** *vt (painting, document)* reproduire

2 *vi* (**a**) *Biol* se reproduire (**b**) *(photocopier)* reproduire; **this print will reproduce well** cette estampe se prêtera bien à la reproduction

reproduction [ˌriːprə'dʌkʃən] **1** *n* (**a**) *Biol* reproduction *f*

(**b**) *(of painting, document)* reproduction *f*, copie *f*; **thousands of reproductions have been made of this picture** ce tableau a été reproduit à des milliers d'exemplaires; **a reproduction Regency armchair** une reproduction *ou* une copie d'un fauteuil Régence

▸▸ ***reproduction furniture*** reproduction *f ou* copie *f* de meubles d'époque; *Typ* ***reproduction proof*** contre-épreuve *f*

reproductive [ˌriːprə'dʌktɪv] *adj Biol* reproducteur, de reproduction

▸▸ ***reproductive organs*** organes *mpl* reproducteurs; ***reproductive system*** appareil *m* reproducteur

reprogram [ˌriː'prəʊgræm] *vt Comput* reprogrammer; **to reprogram a computer to do sth** reprogrammer un ordinateur pour qu'il fasse qch

reprogrammable ['riːˌprəʊ'græməbəl] *adj Comput (key)* reprogrammable

reprographic [ˌriːprəʊ'græfɪk] *adj Typ* reprographique

reprographics [ˌriːprəg'ræfɪks], **reprography** [rɪ'prɒgrəfɪ] *n* reprographie *f*

REPROM [ˌriː'prɒm] *n Comput* mémoire *f* morte reprogrammable

reproof[1] [rɪ'pruːf] *n (reproach)* réprimande *f*, reproche *m*

reproof[2] [ˌriː'pruːf] *vt (raincoat)* réimperméabiliser

reproval [rɪ'pruːvəl] *n* reproche *m*; **a look of reproval** un regard chargé de reproche

reprove [rɪ'pruːv] *vt (person)* réprimander; *(action, behaviour)* réprouver; **he was reproved for his conduct** on lui a reproché sa conduite

reproving [rɪ'pruːvɪŋ] *adj* réprobateur

reprovingly [rɪ'pruːvɪŋlɪ] *adv (look)* d'un air réprobateur *ou* de reproche; *(say)* d'un ton réprobateur *ou* de reproche

reptant ['reptənt] *adj Biol* rampant

reptile ['reptaɪl] **1** *adj* reptile

2 *n* reptile *m*

▸▸ ***reptile house*** vivarium *m*

reptilian [rep'tɪlɪən] **1** *adj* (**a**) *Zool* reptilien (**b**) *Fig Pej* reptile

2 *n* reptile *m*

reptiliferous [ˌreptɪ'lɪfərəs] *adj Geol* reptilifère

Repub. *Am (written abbr* **Republican**) républicain

republic [rɪ'pʌblɪk] *n Pol & Fig* république *f*; **the republic of letters** la république des lettres

'The Republic' *Plato* 'La République'

republican [rɪ'pʌblɪkən] **1** *adj* républicain

2 *n* républicain(e) *m,f*

3 Republican *Pol* **1** *n* républicain(e) *m,f* **2** *adj* républicain

▸▸ ***the Republican party*** le Parti républicain

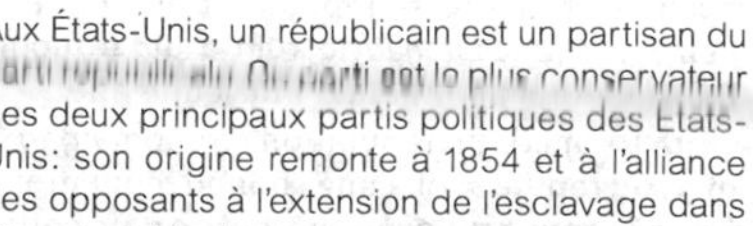

REPUBLICAN

Aux États-Unis, un républicain est un partisan du parti républicain. Ce parti est le plus conservateur des deux principaux partis politiques des États-Unis: son origine remonte à 1854 et à l'alliance des opposants à l'extension de l'esclavage dans l'Ouest américain.

En Irlande, le terme républicain désigne une personne qui souhaite le rattachement de l'Irlande du Nord à la république d'Irlande.

Au Royaume-Uni et en Australie, le terme désigne les personnes favorables à l'abolition de la monarchie et à l'établissement d'une république.

republicanism [rɪ'pʌblɪkənɪzəm] *n* républicanisme *m*

republication ['riːˌpʌblɪ'keɪʃən] *n (of book)* réédition *f*, nouvelle édition *f*; *(of banns)* nouvelle publication *f*

republish [ˌriː'pʌblɪʃ] *vt (book)* rééditer; *(banns)* republier, publier de nouveau

repudiate [rɪ'pjuːdɪeɪt] *vt* (**a**) *(reject → opinion, belief, friend)* renier, désavouer; *(→ authority, accusation, charge, evidence)* rejeter; *(→ spouse)* répudier; *(→ gift, offer)* refuser, rejeter (**b**) *(go back on → obligation, debt, treaty)* refuser d'honorer

repudiation [rɪˌpjuːdɪˈeɪʃən] *n* (**a**) *(of opinion, belief, friend)* reniement *m*, désaveu *m*; *(of spouse)* répudiation *f*; *(of authority, accusation, charge, evidence)* rejet *m*; *(of gift, offer)* refus *m*, rejet *m* (**b**) *(of obligation, debt, treaty)* refus *m* d'honorer

repugnance [rɪˈpʌgnəns] *n* répugnance *f* (**for** pour)

repugnant [rɪˈpʌgnənt] *adj* répugnant; **I find the idea repugnant** cette idée me répugne

repulse [rɪˈpʌls] **1** *vt (attack, offer)* repousser; **their avarice repulses me** je trouve leur avarice choquante; **to be repulsed by sth** *(disgusted)* être révolté par qch

2 *n Mil (defeat)* défaite *f*, échec *m*; *Fig (refusal)* refus *m*, rebuffade *f*

repulsion [rɪˈpʌlʃən] *n* (**a**) *(disgust)* répulsion *f* (**for** à l'égard de); **to feel repulsion for sb/sth** éprouver de la répulsion à l'égard de qn/qch (**b**) *Phys* répulsion *f*

repulsive [rɪˈpʌlsɪv] *adj* (**a**) *(disgusting)* répugnant, repoussant (**b**) *Phys* répulsif

repulsively [rɪˈpʌlsɪvlɪ] *adv* de façon repoussante *ou* répugnante; **repulsively ugly** d'une laideur repoussante; **repulsively dirty** d'une saleté répugnante *ou* repoussante

repulsiveness [rɪˈpʌlsɪvnɪs] *n* (**a**) *(disgusting quality)* caractère *m* repoussant *ou* répugnant (**b**) *Phys* force *f* répulsive

repurchase [ˌriːˈpɜːtʃɪs] **1** *n* rachat *m*; *Mktg* réachat *m*; *St Exch & Banking* réméré *m*; **sale with option of repurchase** vente *f* avec faculté de rachat

2 *vt* racheter; *Mktg* réacheter

▸▸ *St Exch & Banking* ***repurchase agreement*** pension *f* livrée, opération *f* de réméré *ou* de prise en pension; *Mktg* ***repurchase market*** marché *m* de renouvellement; ***repurchase period*** délai *m* de réachat; ***repurchase rate*** taux *m* de réachat; *St Exch & Banking* taux *m* de réméré *ou* de prise en pension; ***repurchase right*** droit *m* de rachat

reputable [ˈrepjʊtəbəl] *adj (person, family)* qui a bonne réputation, honorable, estimable; *(firm, tradesman)* qui a bonne réputation; *(profession)* honorable; *(source)* sûr; **they're a very reputable firm** c'est une entreprise d'excellente réputation

reputably [ˈrepjutəblɪ] *adv* honorablement

reputation [ˌrepjʊˈteɪʃən] *n* réputation *f*; **to have a good/bad reputation** avoir (une) bonne/mauvaise réputation; **to know sb by reputation** connaître qn de réputation; **his reputation had gone before him** sa réputation l'avait précédé; **she has a reputation as a cook** sa réputation de cuisinière n'est plus à faire; **they have a reputation for good service** ils sont réputés pour la qualité de leur service; **she has a reputation for being difficult** elle a la réputation d'être difficile; **to live up to one's reputation** *(person)* se montrer à la hauteur de sa réputation; *(book, restaurant etc)* être à la hauteur de sa réputation; **he lives up to his reputation as a big spender** il mérite sa réputation de grand dépensier; *Old-fashioned* **to ruin a girl's reputation** entacher l'honneur d'une jeune fille

repute [rɪˈpjuːt] **1** *n* réputation *f*, renom *m*; **to be of good repute** avoir (une) bonne réputation; **a firm of some repute** une entreprise d'un certain renom; **a wine of great repute** un vin hautement réputé *ou* de grand renom; **I only know her by repute** je ne la connais que de réputation; **she is held in high repute by all her colleagues** elle jouit d'une excellente réputation auprès de ses collègues

2 *vt (rumoured)* **she is reputed to be wealthy** elle passe pour riche; **he is reputed to be a genius** il passe pour un génie

reputed [rɪˈpjuːtɪd] *adj* réputé

▸▸ *Law* ***reputed father*** père *m* putatif

reputedly [rɪˈpjuːtɪdlɪ] *adv* d'après ce qu'on dit; **he is reputedly a millionaire** on le dit milliardaire; **she is reputedly the best heart specialist** elle a la réputation d'être la meilleure cardiologue

request [rɪˈkwest] **1** *n* (**a**) *(demand)* demande *f*, requête *f*; **to make a request** faire une demande; **to grant** *or* **to meet sb's request** accéder à la demande *ou* à la requête de qn; **at sb's request** à la demande *ou* à la requête de qn; **I did it at** *or* **on her request** je l'ai fait à sa demande *ou* à sa requête; **to do sth on request** faire qch sur simple demande; **tickets are available on request** des billets peuvent être obtenus sur simple demande; **any last requests?** quelles sont vos dernières volontés?; **by popular request** à la demande générale

(**b**) *(record → on radio)* = disque demandé par un auditeur; *(→ at dance)* = disque ou chanson demandé(e) par un membre du public; **to play a request for sb** passer un disque à l'intention de qn; **here is a birthday request for Sarah Brown** voici une chanson (qui a été demandée) pour l'anniversaire de Sarah Brown

2 *vt* demander; **to request sb to do sth** demander à qn *ou* prier qn de faire qch; **visitors are requested not to touch the objects on display** les visiteurs sont priés de ne pas toucher aux objets exposés; **Mr and Mrs Booth request the pleasure of your company** M. et Mme Booth vous prient de leur faire l'honneur de votre présence; **I enclose a postal order for £5, as requested** selon votre demande, je joins un mandat postal de 5 livres; *Formal* **to request sth of sb** demander qch à qn

▸▸ *Rad* ***request programme, request show*** programme *m* des auditeurs, émission *f* de disques à la demande; *Br* ***request stop*** arrêt *m* facultatif

requiem [ˈrekwɪəm] *n Mus* requiem *m*; *Rel (mass)* messe *f* de requiem, messe *f* des morts

▸▸ *Rel* ***requiem mass*** messe *f* de requiem, messe *f* des morts; **to have a requiem mass for sb** faire dire une messe de requiem pour qn

require [rɪˈkwaɪə(r)] *vt* (**a**) *(need → attention, care etc)* exiger, nécessiter, demander; *(→ of person)* avoir besoin de; **extreme caution is required** une extrême vigilance s'impose; **is that all you require?** c'est tout ce qu'il vous faut?, c'est tout ce dont vous avez besoin?; **if required** si besoin est, s'il le faut; **when required** quand il le faut; **your presence is urgently required** on vous réclame d'urgence

(**b**) *(demand → qualifications, standard, commitment)* exiger, requérir, réclamer; **to require sth of sb** exiger qch de qn; **to require sb to do sth** exiger que qn fasse qch; **candidates are required to provide three photographs** les candidats doivent fournir trois photographies; **the law requires you to wear seatbelts** la loi exige que vous portiez une ceinture de sécurité; **custom/tradition requires it** c'est l'usage/la tradition (qui veut cela); **this job requires skill and experience** ce travail demande *ou* requiert *ou* réclame compétence et expérience; **what do you require of me?** que voulez-vous *ou* qu'attendez-vous de moi?; **it is required that you begin work at 8 a.m. every morning** on exige de vous que vous commenciez votre travail à 8 heures tous les matins; **formal dress required** *(on invitation)* tenue correcte exigée

required [rɪˈkwaɪəd] *adj (conditions, qualifications, standard)* requis, exigé; **in** *or* **by the required time** dans les délais (prescrits); **to reach the required standard** atteindre le niveau requis

▸▸ *Sch & Univ* ***required reading*** lectures *fpl* à faire

requirement [rɪˈkwaɪəmənt] *n* (**a**) *(demand)* exigence *f*, besoin *m*; **to meet sb's requirements** satisfaire aux exigences *ou* aux besoins de qn; **this doesn't meet our requirements** ceci ne répond pas à nos exigences; **according to your requirements** selon vos besoins

(**b**) *(necessity)* besoin *m*, nécessité *f*; **energy requirements** besoins *mpl* énergétiques

(**c**) *(condition, prerequisite)* condition *f* requise; **she doesn't fulfil the requirements for the job** elle ne remplit pas les conditions requises pour le poste; **dedication is an essential requirement** le dévouement est une condition essentielle; **what are the course requirements?** *(for enrolment)* quelles conditions faut-il remplir pour s'inscrire à ce cours?; *(as student)* quel niveau doit-on avoir pour suivre ce cours?; **a qualification in Greek is no longer a requirement** un diplôme de grec n'est plus nécessaire

requisite [ˈrekwɪzɪt] **1** *n Formal* (**a**) *(for travel etc)* article *m*; **toilet requisites** articles *mpl ou* nécessaire *m* de toilette (**b**) *(condition)* condition *f* (requise); **a qualification in Greek is no longer a requisite** un diplôme de grec n'est plus nécessaire

2 *adj* requis, nécessaire; **he didn't have the requisite amount of money** il n'avait pas assez d'argent *ou* l'argent qu'il fallait

requisition [ˌrekwɪˈzɪʃən] **1** *n* (**a**) *Mil* réquisition *f*; **to make a requisition for supplies** réquisitionner des provisions

(**b**) *Com* demande *f*; **the boss put in a requisition for staplers** le patron a fait une demande d'agrafeuses

2 *vt* (**a**) *Mil & Fig* réquisitionner; *Hum* **my car was requisitioned to take the team to the match** ma voiture a été réquisitionnée pour emmener l'équipe au match

(**b**) *Com* commander, faire la demande de

▸▸ ***requisition number*** numéro *m* de référence

requisitioning [ˌrekwɪˈzɪʃənɪŋ] *n*

▸▸ *Mil* ***requisitioning officer*** officier *m* chargé des réquisitions

requital [rɪˈkwaɪtəl] *n Formal (repayment)* récompense *f*; *(retaliation)* revanche *f*; **in requital of** *or* **for sth** *(as reward)* en récompense de *ou* pour qch; *(in retaliation)* pour se venger de qch

requite [rɪˈkwaɪt] *vt Formal* (**a**) *(return → payment, kindness)* récompenser, payer de retour; **to requite sb's love** répondre à l'amour de qn (**b**) *(satisfy → desire)* satisfaire (**c**) *(avenge → injury)* venger

reran [ˌriːˈræn] *pt of* **rerun**

reread [ˌriːˈriːd] *(pt & pp* **reread** [-ˈred]*) vt* relire

rerecord [ˌriːrɪˈkɔːd] *vt* réenregistrer

reredos [ˈrɪədɒs] *n* retable *m*

rerelease [ˌriːrɪˈliːs] **1** *vt (film, record)* ressortir

2 *n (film, record)* reprise *f*

reroute [ˌriːˈruːt] *vt* dérouter, changer l'itinéraire de; **the flight was rerouted to Shannon** le vol a été dérouté sur Shannon; **the traffic was rerouted through the suburbs** la circulation a été déviée vers la banlieue

rerouting [ˌriːˈruːtɪŋ] *n (of flight etc)* déroutement *m*; *(of goods)* déroutage *m*

rerun *(pt* **reran** [-ˈræn], *pp* **rerun**, *cont* **rerunning)** **1** *n* [ˈriːrʌn] *(of film)* reprise *f*; *(of TV serial)* rediffusion *f*; *Fig* **it's just a rerun of last year's final** la finale prend la même tournure que celle de l'année dernière

2 *vt* [ˌriːˈrʌn] (**a**) *(film)* passer de nouveau; *(TV series)* rediffuser (**b**) *(race)* courir de nouveau; **the race had to be rerun** la course a dû être recourue (**c**) *Comput (program)* relancer

resale [ˈriːseɪl] *n* revente *f*; **not for resale** *(on packaging)* ne peut être vendu

▸▸ *Mktg* ***resale price maintenance*** prix *m* de vente imposé; *Am* ***resale shop*** vente *f* de charité; ***resale value*** valeur *f* à la revente

resaleable [ˌriːˈseɪləbəl] *adj Mktg* revendable

resat [ˌriːˈsæt] *pt & pp of* **resit**

rescale [ˌriːˈskeɪl] *vt Am* réviser; *(to smaller scale)* réviser à la baisse

reschedule [*Br* ˌriːˈʃedjuːl, *Am* ˌriːˈskedʒʊl] *vt* (**a**) *(appointment, meeting)* modifier l'heure/la date de; *(bus, train, flight)* modifier l'horaire de; *(planned event)* modifier le programme de; **the meeting has been rescheduled for next week** la réunion a été déplacée à la semaine prochaine (**b**) *Fin (debt)* rééchelonner

rescheduling [*Br* riːˈʃedjuːlɪŋ, *Am* ˌriːˈskedʒʊlɪŋ] *n* (**a**) *(of appointment, meeting)* modification *f* de l'heure/de la date; *(of bus, train, flight)* modification *f* de l'horaire; *(of planned event)* modification *f* du programme (**b**) *Fin (of debt)* rééchelonnement *m*

rescind [rɪˈsɪnd] *vt Formal (judgment)* casser, annuler; *(agreement)* annuler; *(law)* abroger; *(contract)* résilier

rescission [rɪˈsɪʒən] *n (of judgment)* cassation *f*, annulation *f*; *(of agreement)* annulation *f*; *(of law)* abrogation *f*; *(of contract)* résiliation *f*

rescript [ˈriːskrɪpt] *n* (**a**) *Rel & Antiq* rescrit *m* (**b**) *(rewrite)* (nouvelle) transcription *f*

rescue [ˈreskjuː] **1** *vt (from danger)* sauver; *(from captivity)* délivrer; *(from need, difficulty)* secourir, venir au secours de; **to rescue sb from drowning** sauver qn de la noyade; **they were rescued from a potentially dangerous situation**

on les a tirés d'une situation qui aurait pu être dangereuse; **the survivors were waiting to be rescued** les survivants attendaient des secours; *Fig* **thanks for rescuing me from that boring conversation** merci de m'avoir délivré, cette conversation m'assommait; **to rescue sb's name from oblivion** arracher le nom de qn à l'oubli; **to rescue sb from poverty** tirer qn de la misère

2 *n (from danger, drowning)* sauvetage *m*; *(from captivity)* délivrance *f*; *(from need, difficulty)* secours *m*; **to go/to come to sb's rescue** aller/venir au secours *ou* à la rescousse de qn; **rescue was impossible** toute opération de sauvetage était impossible

3 *comp (attempt, mission, operation, party, team)* de sauvetage, de secours

►► ***rescue services*** services *mpl* de secours; ***rescue worker*** sauveteur *m*

rescuer ['reskjʊə(r)] *n* sauveteur *m*

reseal [ˌriː'siːl] *vt (envelope)* recacheter; *(jar)* refermer hermétiquement

resealable [ˌriː'siːləbəl] *adj* qui peut être recacheté

research [rɪ'sɜːtʃ] **1** *n (UNCOUNT) (concept, activity)* recherche *f*; *(work involved)* recherches *fpl*; **to do research into sth** faire des recherches sur qch; **she's engaged in research into rare viruses** elle fait des recherches sur les virus rares; **what kind of research do you do?** quel type de recherches faites-vous?; **when I finish my degree I'd like to do research** quand j'aurai mon diplôme, j'aimerais faire de la recherche *ou* devenir chercheur; **research into the problem revealed a worrying trend** les recherches sur le problème ont révélé une tendance inquiétante; **an excellent piece of research** un excellent travail de recherche; **scientific research** la recherche scientifique

2 *comp (establishment, work)* de recherche

3 *vt (article, book, problem, subject)* faire des recherches sur; **your essay is not very well researched** votre travail n'est pas très bien documenté

4 *vi* faire des recherches *ou* de la recherche

►► ***research assistant*** assistant(e) *m,f* de recherche; ***research budget*** budget *m* consacré à la recherche; ***research department*** service *m* de recherche; ***research and development*** recherche *f* et développement *m*, recherche-développement *f*; *Mktg* ***research and development manager*** directeur(trice) *m,f* de recherche et développement; ***research fellow*** chercheur(euse) *m,f (qui a reçu une bourse)*; *Petr* ***research octane number*** indice *m* d'octane recherche; ***research programme*** programme *m* de recherche; ***research scientist*** chercheur(euse) *m,f*; ***research student*** étudiant(e) *m,f* qui fait de la recherche *(après la licence)*; ***research technique*** technique *f* de recherche; ***research tool*** outil *m* de recherche; ***research worker*** *(scientific)* chercheur(euse) *m,f*; *Am (literary)* documentaliste *mf*

researcher [rɪ'sɜːtʃə(r)] *n* chercheur(euse) *m,f*

reseat [ˌriː'siːt] *vt* (**a**) *(person → sit again)* faire rasseoir; *(→ change place)* assigner une nouvelle place à; **to reseat oneself** *(sit down)* se rasseoir; *(change place)* changer de place (**b**) *(chair)* refaire le fond de; *(trousers)* remettre un fond à (**c**) *Tech (valve)* roder

resect [rɪ'sekt] *vt Med* réséquer

resection [riː'sekʃən] *n Med* résection *f*

reseda ['resɪdə] **1** *n* (**a**) *Bot* réséda *m* (**b**) *(colour)* vert *m* réséda

2 *adj* (vert) réséda *(inv)*

reseed [ˌriː'siːd] *Bot* **1** *vt* ressemer

2 *vi* se ressemer

reselect [ˌriːsɪ'lekt] *vt* sélectionner de nouveau

resell [ˌriː'sel] *(pt & pp* **resold** [-'səʊld]*) vt* revendre

resemblance [rɪ'zembləns] *n* ressemblance *f*; **to bear a resemblance to sb/sth** ressembler à qn/qch; **the brothers show a strong family resemblance** les frères se ressemblent beaucoup; **any resemblance to persons living or dead is purely accidental** toute ressemblance avec des personnes existantes ou ayant existé ne peut être que fortuite; **the newspaper account bears little resemblance to the actual interview** il n'y a qu'une vague ressemblance entre l'article du journal et l'interview proprement dite

resemble [rɪ'zembəl] *vt* ressembler à; **they resemble each other greatly** ils se ressemblent beaucoup

resent [rɪ'zent] *vt (person)* en vouloir à, éprouver du ressentiment à l'égard de; *(remark, criticism)* ne pas apprécier; **to resent sth strongly** avoir beaucoup de mal à supporter *ou* à accepter qch; **he resented their criticism** il n'a pas apprécié leurs critiques; **I resent their presence** le fait qu'ils soient là me déplaît; **I resent that remark!** je n'apprécie pas du tout cette remarque!; **I resent that!** je n'apprécie pas du tout!; **her presence in the country was strongly resented** sa présence dans le pays a été très mal acceptée; **I resent them taking over** *or* **the fact that they have taken over** je leur en veux de prendre tout en charge; **they resent her enjoying herself** ils lui en veulent de s'amuser, ils supportent mal qu'elle s'amuse; **he resents having to take orders from a woman** il accepte mal d'avoir une femme comme supérieur

resentful [rɪ'zentfʊl] *adj* plein de ressentiment *ou* d'amertume; **to feel resentful about** *or* **at sth** mal supporter *ou* accepter qch; **to be resentful about** *or* **of sb's achievements** en vouloir à qn parce qu'il a réussi; **don't be so resentful!** ne soyez pas si rancunier!

resentfully [rɪ'zentfʊlɪ] *adv* avec ressentiment

resentment [rɪ'zentmənt] *n* ressentiment *m*

reservation [ˌrezə'veɪʃən] **1** *n* (**a**) *(doubt)* réserve *f*, restriction *f*; **to have reservations about sth** faire *ou* émettre des réserves sur qch; **I have reservations about letting them go abroad** j'hésite à les laisser partir à l'étranger; **without reservation** *or* **reservations** sans réserve; **to accept sth without reservation** approuver qch sans réserve; **with (some) reservations** avec certaines réserves; **he expressed some reservations about the plan** il a émis quelques doutes à propos *ou* au sujet du projet

(**b**) *(booking)* réservation *f*; **to make a reservation** *(on train)* réserver une *ou* sa place; *(in hotel)* réserver *ou* retenir une chambre; *(in restaurant)* réserver une table; **the secretary made all the reservations** la secrétaire s'est occupée de toutes les réservations; **I have a reservation** *(at hotel)* j'ai une réservation, j'ai réservé une chambre

(**c**) *(enclosed area)* réserve *f*; **Indian reservation** réserve *f* indienne

(**d**) *Rel* **the Reservation (of the sacrament)** la Sainte Réserve

2 *comp* des réservations

►► ***reservation agent*** agent *m* de réservation; *Am* ***reservation clerk*** préposé(e) *m,f* aux réservations; ***reservation desk*** bureau *m* des réservations; ***reservation sheet*** feuille *f* de réservation, bordereau *m* de réservations; ***reservation ticket*** coupon *m* de réservation

reserve [rɪ'zɜːv] **1** *vt* (**a**) *(keep back)* réserver, mettre de côté; **to reserve one's strength** garder *ou* ménager ses forces; **to reserve the right to do sth** se réserver le droit de faire qch; **to reserve (one's) judgment about sth** ne pas se prononcer sur qch

(**b**) *(book)* réserver, retenir; **these seats are reserved for VIPs** ces places sont réservées aux personnalités

2 *n* (**a**) *(store → of energy, money, provisions)* réserve *f*; **to draw on one's reserves** puiser dans ses réserves; **the body's food reserves** les réserves nutritives du corps; **the nation's coal reserves** les réserves de charbon du pays; **he has great reserves of energy** il a beaucoup d'énergie en réserve *ou* de grandes réserves d'énergie; **cash reserves** réserves *fpl* de caisse

(**b**) *(storage)* réserve *f*; **to have** *or* **to keep in reserve** avoir *ou* garder en réserve; **luckily, they have some money in reserve** heureusement, ils ont (mis) un peu d'argent de côté

(**c**) *Br (doubt, qualification)* réserve *f*; **without reserve** sans réserve, sans restriction; **with all proper reserves** sous toutes réserves

(**d**) *(reticence)* réserve *f*, retenue *f*; **to break through sb's reserve** amener qn à sortir de sa réserve

(**e**) *Mil* réserve *f*; **to call up the reserve** *or* **reserves** faire appel à la réserve *ou* aux réservistes

(**f**) *(area of land)* réserve *f*; *Can* **Indian reserve** réserve *f* indienne

(**g**) *Sport* remplaçant(e) *m,f*; **to play for the reserves** jouer dans l'équipe de réserve

(**h**) *(at auction)* prix *m* minimum; **to put a reserve on sth** fixer un prix minimum à qch; **the item did not reach its reserve** l'article n'a pas atteint le prix minimum fixé

3 *comp* (**a**) *Fin (funds, resources)* de réserve

(**b**) *Sport* remplaçant; **the reserve goalkeeper** le gardien de but remplaçant

►► *Fin* ***reserve account*** compte *m* de réserve; ***reserve bank*** banque *f* de réserve; *Fin* ***reserve capital*** capital *m* de réserve; *Fin* ***reserve currency*** monnaie *f* de réserve; *Acct* ***reserve fund*** fonds *m* de réserve; ***Reserve Officer Training Corps*** = préparation militaire proposée par l'armée de terre américaine aux étudiants désireux de se faire payer leur études, en échange de quoi ces derniers s'engagent à passer quatre ans dans l'armée; ***reserve price*** prix *m* minimum; *Fin* ***reserve ratio*** taux *m* de mise en réserve; *Aut* ***reserve tank*** réservoir *m* de secours; *Sport* ***reserve team*** équipe *f* de réserve

reserved [rɪ'zɜːvd] *adj* (**a**) *(shy → person)* timide, réservé; **she is very reserved** elle est très réservée

(**b**) *(doubtful)* **to be reserved in one's opinion about sth** ne pas se prononcer sur qch; **he has always been rather reserved about the scheme** il a toujours exprimé des doutes sur ce projet

(**c**) *(room, seat)* réservé; **all rights reserved** tous droits réservés

►► *Mil* ***reserved list*** cadre *m* de réserve; ***reserved occupation*** = secteur professionnel essentiel dont les membres ne sont pas mobilisés en temps de guerre

reservedly [rɪ'zɜːvɪdlɪ] *adv* avec réserve, avec retenue

reservist [rɪ'zɜːvɪst] *n* réserviste *m*

reservoir ['rezəvwɑː(r)] *n also Fig* réservoir *m*

reset *(pt & pp* **reset**, *cont* **resetting**) **1** *vt* [ˌriː'set] (**a**) *(jewel)* remonter (**b**) *(watch, clock)* remettre à l'heure; *(alarm)* réenclencher; *(stopwatch, counter)* remettre à zéro (**c**) *Comput* réinitialiser (**d**) *(limb)* remettre en place; *(fracture)* réduire (**e**) *Typ* recomposer (**f**) *(lay)* **to reset the table** *(in restaurant)* remettre le couvert; *(in home)* remettre la table

2 *n* ['riːset] *Comput* réinitialisation *f*

►► *Comput* ***reset button, reset switch*** bouton *m* de remise à zéro, bouton *m* de réinitialisation

resettle [ˌriː'setəl] **1** *vt (refugees, population)* établir *ou* implanter (dans une nouvelle région); *(territory)* repeupler

2 *vi* se réinstaller (**in** dans)

resettlement [ˌriː'setəlmənt] *n (of refugees, population)* établissement *m ou* implantation *f* (dans une nouvelle région); *(of territory)* repeuplement *m*

reshape [ˌriː'ʃeɪp] *vt* (**a**) *(clay, material)* refaçonner (**b**) *(novel, policy, industry, company, department)* réorganiser, remanier; *(garment)* redonner sa forme à

reshuffle [ˌriː'ʃʌfəl] **1** *vt* (**a**) *Pol (cabinet)* remanier (**b**) *(cards)* rebattre, battre de nouveau

2 *n* (**a**) *Pol* remaniement *m*; **a Cabinet reshuffle** un remaniement ministériel (**b**) *(in cards)* **to have a reshuffle** battre les cartes à nouveau

reside [rɪ'zaɪd] *vi Formal* (**a**) *(live)* résider; **they reside in New York** ils résident *ou* ils sont domiciliés à New York (**b**) *Fig (be located)* **authority resides in** *or* **with the Prime Minister** c'est le Premier ministre qui est investi de l'autorité; **the problem resides in the fact that...** le problème est dû au fait que... + *indicative*

residence ['rezɪdəns] *n* (**a**) *(home)* résidence *f*, demeure *f*; **town/country residence** résidence *f* en ville/à la campagne; **official summer residence** résidence *f* officielle d'été; **desirable residence for sale** *(in advertisement)* belle demeure *ou* demeure de caractère à vendre; *Formal* **Lord Bellamy's residence** la résidence de Lord Bellamy; *Hum* **the Hancock residence** la résidence des Hancock; **to be in residence** *(monarch)* être en résidence; **writer/artist in residence** écrivain *m*/artiste *mf* en résidence; **place of residence** *(on form)* domicile *m*; **I gave**

res–res

London as my place of residence j'ai mis Londres comme lieu de résidence

(**b**) *Univ* **(university) residence** résidence *f* (universitaire)

(**c**) *(period of stay)* résidence *f*, séjour *m*; **a short period of residence in Spain** un bref séjour en Espagne; **after three years' residence abroad** après avoir résidé pendant trois ans à l'étranger; **to take up residence in a new house** s'installer *ou* s'établir dans une nouvelle maison; **they took up residence in Oxford** ils se sont installés *ou* ils ont élu domicile à Oxford

►► *Am* ***residence hall*** résidence *f* (universitaire); ***residence permit*** ≃ permis *m* de séjour; *Am* ***residence tax*** taxe *f* de séjour

residency ['rezɪdənsɪ] (*pl* **residencies**) *n* (**a**) *Formal (home)* résidence *f* officielle (**b**) *Am Med* = période d'études spécialisées après l'internat (**c**) *Mus & Theat (engagement)* contrat *m* (à long terme)

resident ['rezɪdənt] **1** *n* (**a**) *(of town)* habitant(e) *m,f*; *(of street)* riverain(e) *m,f*; *(in hotel, hostel)* pensionnaire *mf*; *(foreigner)* résident(e) *m,f*; **(local) residents' association** *(in building)* association *f* des copropriétaires; *(in neighbourhood)* association *f* de riverains; **are you a resident of an EU country?** êtes-vous ressortissant d'un pays membre de l'Union européenne?; **residents only** *(sign → in street)* interdit sauf aux riverains; *(→ in hotel)* réservé à la clientèle de l'hôtel

(**b**) *Am Med* interne *mf (qui poursuit une spécialité)*

(**c**) *Zool* résident *m*

2 *adj* (**a**) *(as inhabitant)* résidant; **to be resident in a country** résider dans un pays; **to have permanent resident status** avoir le statut de résident permanent; **the swallow is resident to the area** l'hirondelle réside dans la région

(**b**) *(staff)* qui habite sur place, à demeure; **our resident interpreter** notre interprète; **our resident pianist** notre pianiste attitré; **he's our resident expert on football** c'est notre expert attitré pour le football

(**c**) *Comput* résident

►► *Am* ***resident alien*** résident(e) *m,f* étranger(-ère); ***residents' association*** association *f* de locataires; ***resident population*** population *f* résidante *ou* fixe

residential [,rezɪ'denʃəl] *adj* (**a**) *(district, accommodation)* résidentiel; *(status)* de résident; **the building is reverting to residential use** l'édifice va être à nouveau utilisé comme habitation (**b**) *(course)* avec résidence sur place; **a residential post** un travail qui oblige à rester sur les lieux

►► ***residential care*** = mode d'hébergement supervisé pour handicapés, délinquants etc; *Am Formal* ***residential treatment facility*** hôpital *m* psychiatrique

residual [rɪ'zɪdjʊəl] **1** *adj* (**a**) *(gen)* restant (**b**) *Chem & Geol* résiduel; *Phys (magnetism)* rémanent

2 *n Math* reste *m*; *Chem & Geol* résidu *m*

3 residuals *npl Cin & TV (repeat fees)* droits *mpl* de seconde diffusion

►► *Elec* ***residual current device*** coupe-circuit *m*; *Fin* ***residual income*** revenu *m* résiduel

residuary [rɪ'zɪdjʊərɪ] *adj (gen)* restant; *Chem* résiduaire; *Geol* résiduel

►► *Law* ***residuary legatee*** légataire *mf* universel(elle)

residue ['rezɪdju:] *n* (**a**) *(leftovers)* reste *m*, restes *mpl*; *(of money)* reliquat *m* (**b**) *Chem & Phys* résidu *m*; *Math* reste *m*, reliquat *m*

residuum [rɪ'zɪdjʊəm] (*pl* **residua** [-dʊə]) *n Chem* résidu *m*

resign [rɪ'zaɪn] **1** *vi* (**a**) *(from post)* démissionner, donner sa démission; **she resigned from her job/from the committee** elle a démissionné de son emploi/du comité; **he has resigned as Prime Minister** il a démissionné de son poste de Premier ministre

(**b**) *Chess* abandonner

2 *vt* (**a**) *(give up → advantage)* renoncer à; *(→ job)* démissionner de; *(→ function)* se démettre de, démissionner de; **she was forced to resign the party leadership** elle a dû démissionner de la tête du parti

(**b**) *(give away)* céder; **to resign sth to sb** céder qch à qn; **I resigned my voting rights to the chairman** j'ai cédé mon droit de vote au président

(**c**) *(reconcile)* **to resign oneself to sth/to doing sth** se résigner à qch/à faire qch; **to resign oneself to one's fate** se résigner à son sort; **I had resigned myself to going alone** je m'étais résigné à y aller seul

re-sign [,ri:-] *vt (document)* signer une nouvelle fois

resignation [,rezɪg'neɪʃən] *n* (**a**) *(from job)* démission *f*; *Formal* **to hand in** *or* **to tender one's resignation** donner sa démission (**b**) *(acceptance → of fact, situation)* résignation *f*

resigned [rɪ'zaɪnd] *adj* résigné; **to become resigned to sth/to doing sth** se résigner à qch/à faire qch; **she is resigned to her fate** elle s'est résignée à son sort; **she gave me a resigned look/smile** elle m'a regardé/souri avec résignation

resignedly [rɪ'zaɪnɪdlɪ] *adv* avec résignation

resile [rɪ'zaɪl] *vi Formal* (**a**) *(draw back → from contract, agreement)* se désister (**b**) *(recoil)* avoir un mouvement de recul (**c**) *(of object)* reprendre sa forme

resilience [rɪ'zɪlɪəns] *n* (**a**) *(of rubber, metal → springiness)* élasticité *f*; *(→ toughness)* résistance *f* (**b**) *(of character, person)* énergie *f*, ressort *m*; *(of institution)* résistance *f*

resilient [rɪ'zɪlɪənt] *adj* (**a**) *(rubber, metal → springy)* élastique; *(→ tough)* résistant (**b**) *(person → in character)* qui a du ressort, qui ne se laisse pas abattre *ou* décourager; *(→ in health, condition)* très résistant; **children are more resilient than adults** les enfants se remettent plus vite que les adultes; **the economy is proving remarkably resilient** l'économie fait preuve d'une remarquable capacité de reprise

resin ['rezɪn] *n* résine *f*

resinate ['rezɪneɪt] **1** *n* résinate *m*

2 *vt* résiner

resinated ['rezɪneɪtɪd] *adj (wine)* résiné

resiniferous [,rezɪ'nɪfərəs] *adj* résinifère

resinify ['rezɪnɪfaɪ] (*pt & pp* **resinified**) **1** *vt* résinifier

2 *vi* se résinifier

resinous ['rezɪnəs] *adj* résineux

resist [rɪ'zɪst] **1** *vt (temptation, attack, change, pressure)* résister à; *(reform, influence, attempt)* s'opposer à; **I can't resist chocolates** je ne peux pas résister aux chocolats; **he couldn't resist having just one more drink** il n'a pas pu résister à l'envie de prendre un dernier verre; **nobody can resist her** personne ne peut lui résister; **I can't resist it!** c'est plus fort que moi!; *Formal* **he was charged with resisting arrest** il a été inculpé de résistance aux forces de l'ordre

2 *vi* résister, offrir de la résistance

resistance [rɪ'zɪstəns] **1** *n* résistance *f*; **their resistance to all reform** leur opposition (systématique) à toute réforme; **they offered no resistance to the new measures** ils ne se sont pas opposés aux nouvelles mesures; **they put up fierce resistance to their attackers** ils opposèrent une vive résistance à leurs agresseurs; **her resistance to infection is low** elle offre peu de résistance à l'infection; *Fig* **to take the line of least resistance** aller au plus facile, choisir la facilité; **air/wind resistance** résistance *f* de l'air/du vent; *Hist* **the (French) Resistance** la Résistance (française)

2 *comp (movement)* de résistance; *(group)* de résistants

►► ***resistance coupling*** couplage *m* par résistance; ***resistance fighter*** résistant(e) *m,f*; ***resistance thermometer*** thermomètre *m* à résistance; ***resistance welding*** soudure *f* électrique par résistance

resistant [rɪ'zɪstənt] **1** *adj* résistant; **she is very resistant to change** elle est très hostile au changement; **resistant to antibiotics** résistant aux antibiotiques

2 *n* résistant(e) *m,f*

-resistant [rɪ'zɪstənt] *suff* **heat-resistant** qui résiste à la chaleur; **water-resistant** résistant à l'eau; **flame-resistant** ignifugé

resistor [rɪ'zɪstə(r)] *n Elec* résistance *f (objet)*

resit (*pt & pp* **resat** [-'sæt], *cont* **resitting**) *Br* **1** *vt* [,ri:'sɪt] *(exam, driving test)* repasser

2 *n* ['ri:sɪt] examen *m* de rattrapage; **the resits are scheduled for August** la session de rattrapage est prévue pour le mois d'août; **how many resits do you have?** combien d'examens est-ce que tu as à repasser?; **the French resit is on Monday** la deuxième session de l'examen de français a lieu lundi

resize [,ri:'saɪz] *vt Comput (window)* redimensionner

►► ***resize box*** case *f* de redimensionnement

resold [,ri:'səʊld] *pt & pp of* **resell**

resole [,ri:'səʊl] *vt* ressemeler

resolute ['rezəlu:t] *adj (determined → person, expression, jaw)* résolu; *(steadfast → faith, courage, refusal)* inébranlable; **he is resolute in his decision** il est inébranlable dans sa décision; **to be resolute in one's efforts** être déterminé dans ses efforts

resolutely ['rezəlu:tlɪ] *adv (oppose, struggle, believe)* résolument; *(refuse)* fermement; **she marched forward resolutely** elle avança d'un pas résolu

resoluteness ['rezəlu:tnɪs] *n* résolution *f*, détermination *f*

resolution [,rezə'lu:ʃən] *n* (**a**) *(decision)* résolution *f*, décision *f*; **to be full of good resolutions** être plein de bonnes résolutions; **she made a resolution to stop smoking** elle a pris la résolution d'arrêter de fumer

(**b**) *(formal motion)* résolution *f*; **they passed/adopted/rejected a resolution to limit the budget** ils ont voté/adopté/rejeté une résolution pour limiter le budget; **to put a resolution to the meeting** soumettre *ou* proposer une résolution à l'assemblée; **the statutes can only be changed by resolution** les statuts ne peuvent être modifiés que par l'adoption d'une résolution

(**c**) *(determination)* résolution *f*; **to say/to act with resolution** dire/agir avec fermeté; **a note of resolution entered her voice** sa voix a pris un ton résolu; **he always showed resolution** il a toujours fait preuve de résolution

(**d**) *(settling, solving)* résolution *f*; **in Act V we see the resolution of the tragedy** au cinquième acte, nous assistons au dénouement de la tragédie

(**e**) *Comput, Opt & TV (of image)* résolution *f*; **high resolution screen** écran *m* à haute résolution *ou* définition

(**f**) *Med (of tumour)* résolution *f*

(**g**) *Mus* résolution *f*

resolvable [rɪ'zɒlvəbəl] *adj* résoluble, soluble

resolve [rɪ'zɒlv] **1** *vt* (**a**) *(work out → quarrel, difficulty, dilemma)* résoudre; *(→ doubt)* dissiper; *Math (→ equation)* résoudre; **there are a few points left to resolve** il nous reste encore quelques petits problèmes à résoudre; **have you resolved your difficulties yet?** avez-vous résolu vos difficultés?

(**b**) *(decide)* (se) résoudre; **to resolve to do sth** décider de *ou* se résoudre à faire qch; **I resolved to resign** j'ai pris la décision de démissionner; **she had resolved that he would have to leave** elle avait décidé qu'il devrait partir; **it was resolved that a final decision would be taken later** il a été résolu *ou* on a décidé qu'une décision finale serait prise ultérieurement

(**c**) *(break down, separate)* résoudre, réduire; **the problem can be resolved into three simple questions** le problème peut se résoudre en *ou* être ramené à trois questions simples

(**d**) *Opt & Phys (parts, peaks)* distinguer; *(image)* résoudre

(**e**) *Med* résoudre, faire disparaître

(**f**) *Mus* résoudre

2 *vi* (**a**) *(separate, break down)* se résoudre

(**b**) *Mus (chord)* être résolu

3 *n* (**a**) *(determination)* résolution *f*; **it only strengthened our resolve** ça n'a fait que renforcer notre détermination

(**b**) *(decision)* résolution *f*, décision *f*; **to make a resolve to do sth** prendre la résolution de faire qch

resolved [rɪ'zɒlvd] *adj* résolu, décidé, déterminé; **I was firmly resolved to go** j'étais fermement décidé à partir

resolvent [rɪ'zɒlvənt] *Med* **1** *n* résolutif *m*

2 *adj* résolutif

resolving [rɪ'zɒlvɪŋ] *n*

►► *Opt* ***resolving power*** *(of lens)* pouvoir *m* de résolution

resonance ['rezənəns] *n* résonance *f*; *(of voice)* sonorité *f*

►► *Aut* ***resonance chamber*** *(in silencer)* pot *m* de résonance; *Electron* ***resonance curve*** courbe *f* de résonance

resonant ['rezənənt] *adj* (**a**) *(loud, echoing)* retentissant, sonore (**b**) *Mus & Phys* résonant, résonnant

►► *Mus & Phys* ***resonant cavity*** cavité *f* résonante; *Mus & Phys* ***resonant frequency*** fréquence *f* de résonance

resonantly ['rezənəntlɪ] *adv* d'une voix retentissante

resonate ['rezəneɪt] *vi (noise, voice, laughter, place)* résonner, retentir; **the valley resonated with their cries** la vallée retentissait de leurs cris

resonating ['rezəneɪtɪŋ] *adj* qui résonne

►► ***resonating chamber*** caisse *f* de résonance

resonator ['rezəneɪtə(r)] *n* résonateur *m*

resorb [rɪ'sɔːb] **1** *vt* (**a**) *Med* résorber (**b**) *(absorb again)* réabsorber

2 *vi Med* se résorber

resorcin [rɪ'zɔːsɪn] *n Chem* résorcine *f*

resorption [rɪ'sɔːpʃən] *n Med* résorption *f*

resort [rɪ'zɔːt] *n* (**a**) *(recourse)* recours *m*; **without resort to threats** sans avoir recours aux menaces; **the doctor is our last resort** le médecin est notre dernier recours; **as a last resort** en dernier ressort; **call me only as a last** *or* **in the last resort** ne m'appelez qu'en dernier ressort; **flight was the only resort left to me** *or* **my only resort** il ne me restait plus qu'à fuir

(**b**) *(for holidays)* lieu *m* de villégiature; **ski resort** station *f* de sports d'hiver

(**c**) *(haunt, hang-out)* repaire *m*

►► ***resort development*** aménagement *m* touristique; ***resort hotel*** hôtel *m* de tourisme; ***resort tax*** taxe *f* sur l'hôtellerie

►**resort to** *vt insep* (**a**) *(violence, sarcasm etc)* avoir recours à, recourir à; **to resort to doing sth** en venir à faire qch; **you resorted to lying to your wife** vous en êtes venu à mentir à votre femme (**b**) *Arch or Literary (town)* se rendre à

resound [rɪ'zaʊnd] *vi* (**a**) *(noise, words, explosion)* retentir, résonner; **the trumpet resounded through the barracks** le son de la trompette retentissait dans toute la caserne

(**b**) *(hall, cave, hills, room)* retentir; **the woods resounded with birdsong** les bois étaient pleins de chants d'oiseaux

(**c**) *Formal or Literary (spread → rumour)* se propager; **the declaration resounded throughout the country** la déclaration a eu un retentissement national

resounding [rɪ'zaʊndɪŋ] *adj* (**a**) *(loud → noise, blow, wail)* retentissant; *(→ voice)* sonore, claironnant; *(→ explosion)* violent; **with a resounding splash** avec un grand plouf; **greeted with resounding applause** accueilli par des applaudissements retentissants

(**b**) *(unequivocal)* retentissant, éclatant; **it was a resounding failure** ce fut un échec retentissant; **he was met with a resounding refusal** on lui a opposé un refus catégorique; **her first novel was a resounding success** son premier roman a connu un succès retentissant

resoundingly [rɪ'zaʊndɪŋlɪ] *adv* (**a**) *(loudly)* bruyamment (**b**) *(unequivocally → win)* d'une manière retentissante *ou* décisive; *(→ criticize, condemn)* sévèrement; **to be resoundingly successful** connaître un succès retentissant; **the measure was resoundingly unpopular** cette mesure fut extrêmement impopulaire; **the team was resoundingly beaten** l'équipe a été battue à plate couture

resource [rɪ'sɔːs] **1** *n* (**a**) *(asset)* ressource *f*; **there's a limit to the resources we can invest** il y a une limite à la somme que nous pouvons investir; **your health is a precious resource** ta santé est un précieux capital; **natural/energy resources** ressources *fpl* naturelles/énergétiques

(**b**) *(human capacity)* ressource *f*; **the task called for all my resources of tact** cette tâche a demandé toute ma diplomatie; **after lunch I'll leave you to your own resources** après le déjeuner, je vous laisserai vous débrouiller tout seul; **left to their own resources, they're likely to mess everything up** livrés à eux-mêmes, ils risquent de tout gâcher

(**c**) *(ingenuity)* ressource *f*; **a man of resource** un homme plein de ressource *ou* de ressources

2 *vt (project)* accorder les ressources nécessaires à

►► ***resource allocation*** allocation *f* des ressources; *Sch & Univ* ***resource*** *or* ***resources centre*** centre *m* de documentation; ***resource management*** gestion *f* des ressources; ***resource market*** marché *m* de ressources; ***resource materials*** *(written)* documentation *f*; *(audio-visual)* aides *fpl* pédagogiques; ***resource person*** *(in career centre)* conseiller(ère) *m,f* d'orientation; *(in library)* bibliothécaire *mf (chargé d'orienter les usagers et d'entreprendre certaines recherches bibliographiques)*; *Sch & Univ* ***resource*** *or* ***resources room*** salle *f* de documentation

resourceful [rɪ'sɔːsfʊl] *adj (person)* ingénieux, plein de ressource *ou* de ressources; *(solution etc)* habile, ingénieux; **that was very resourceful of you** tu as fait preuve de beaucoup de débrouillardise

resourcefully [rɪ'sɔːsfʊlɪ] *adv* ingénieusement; **he acted resourcefully in a difficult situation** dans cette situation difficile, il s'est montré très ingénieux

resourcefulness [rɪ'sɔːsfʊlnɪs] *n* ressource *f*, ingéniosité *f*

resourceless [rɪ'sɔːslɪs] *adj* sans ressources

resourcing [rɪ'sɔːsɪŋ] *n* financement *m*

►► ***resourcing officer*** agent *m* de financement

respect [rɪ'spekt] **1** *vt* (**a**) *(esteem → person, judgment, right, authority)* respecter; **I respect him for his efficiency** je le respecte pour son efficacité; **if you don't respect yourself, no one else will** si vous ne vous respectez pas vous-même, personne ne vous respectera

(**b**) *(comply with → rules, customs, wishes)* respecter; **to respect sb's wishes** respecter les volontés de qn; **we don't have to respect his wishes** nous ne sommes pas tenu de faire ce qu'il veut; **you should respect the laws of any country you visit** il faut respecter les lois des pays dans lesquels on va

2 *n* (**a**) *(esteem)* respect *m*, estime *f*; **I have (an) enormous respect for her competence** je respecte infiniment sa compétence; **I don't have much respect for his methods** je n'ai pas beaucoup de respect pour ses méthodes; **she is held in great respect by her colleagues** elle est très respectée *ou* elle est tenue en haute estime par ses collègues; **you have to get** *or* **to gain the children's respect** il faut savoir se faire respecter par les enfants; **you have lost all my respect** je n'ai plus aucun respect pour toi; **he has no respect for authority/money** il méprise l'autorité/l'argent

(**b**) *(care, politeness)* respect *m*, égard *m*; **show a little respect!** un peu de respect!; **he should show more respect for local customs** il devrait se montrer plus respectueux des coutumes locales; **they have no respect for public property** ils n'ont aucun respect pour le bien public; **to do sth out of respect for sb/sth** faire qch par respect pour qn/qch; **I stood up in respect** je me suis levé respectueusement; **treat those plates with respect** *(they are fragile)* fais attention à ces assiettes; **treat mountains with respect** *(be careful)* soyez prudent en montagne; **guns should be treated with respect** les armes à feu doivent être maniées avec précaution; **with (all due) respect, Mr Clark...** avec tout le respect que je vous dois, M. Clark...; **with the utmost** *or* **greatest respect to Boyd, his figures aren't conclusive** malgré tout le respect que je dois à Boyd, ses chiffres ne sont guère concluants

(**c**) *(regard, aspect)* égard *m*; **in every respect** à tous les égards; **in some/other respects** à certains/d'autres égards; **in many respects** à bien des égards

(**d**) *(compliance, observance)* respect *m*, observation *f*; **his strict respect of the letter of the law** son strict respect de la loi

3 respects *npl (salutations)* respects *mpl*, hommages *mpl*; **give my respects to your father** présentez mes respects à votre père; **to pay one's respects to sb** présenter ses respects *ou* ses hommages à qn; **I went to the funeral to pay my last respects** je suis allé à l'enterrement pour lui rendre un dernier hommage

4 with respect to *prep* quant à, en ce qui concerne

respectability [rɪˌspektə'bɪlɪtɪ] *n* respectabilité *f*

respectable [rɪ'spektəbəl] *adj* (**a**) *(socially proper, worthy)* respectable, convenable, comme il faut; **a thoroughly respectable part of town** un quartier tout à fait comme il faut; **I'm a respectable married woman!** je suis une femme mariée et respectable!; **that's not done in respectable society** ça ne se fait pas dans la bonne société; **to be outwardly respectable** avoir l'apparence de la respectabilité; **I'm sure he had a very respectable reason** je suis sûr qu'il avait une raison tout à fait respectable *ou* honorable; **to make oneself (look) respectable** se préparer; **I'm not respectable, YOU answer the door** va ouvrir, je ne suis pas présentable

(**b**) *(fair → speech, athlete)* assez bon; *(→ amount, wage etc)* respectable, correct; **a respectable actor** un acteur qui n'est pas dénué de talent; **a respectable first novel** un premier roman qui n'est pas dénué d'intérêt; **I play a respectable game of golf** je joue passablement bien au golf; **a respectable number of people** un bon nombre de gens; **he left a respectable tip** il a laissé un pourboire correct

respectably [rɪ'spektəblɪ] *adv (properly)* convenablement, comme il faut; **he's respectably married** il est convenablement marié; **she has to dress respectably for work** elle doit s'habiller correctement pour son travail

respected [rɪ'spektɪd] *adj* respecté; **she's a highly respected researcher** c'est une chercheuse très respectée

respecter [rɪ'spektə(r)] *n* **she is no respecter of tradition** elle ne fait pas partie de ceux qui respectent la tradition; **disease is no respecter of class** nous sommes tous égaux devant la maladie

respectful [rɪ'spektfʊl] *adj* respectueux

respectfully [rɪ'spektfʊlɪ] *adv* respectueusement; *Old-fashioned* **(I remain,) yours respectfully** *(at end of letter)* veuillez agréer l'expression de mes sentiments respectueux

respectfulness [rɪ'spektfʊlnɪs] *n* respect *m*; **the respectfulness of his answer** le respect avec lequel il a répondu

respecting [rɪ'spektɪŋ] *prep Formal* concernant, en ce qui concerne

respective [rɪ'spektɪv] *adj* respectif

respectively [rɪ'spektɪvlɪ] *adv* respectivement

respiration [ˌrespə'reɪʃən] *n* respiration *f*

respirator ['respəreɪtə(r)] *n (mask, machine)* respirateur *m*; **to be on a respirator** être sous respirateur

respiratory [*Br* rɪ'spɪrətərɪ, *Am* 'respərətɔːrɪ] *adj* respiratoire

►► ***respiratory failure*** insuffisance *f* respiratoire; ***respiratory problems*** troubles *mpl* respiratoires; ***respiratory quotient*** quotient *m* respiratoire; ***respiratory system*** système *m* respiratoire

respirometer [ˌrespɪ'rɒmɪtə(r)] *n* respiromètre *m*

respire [rɪ'spaɪə(r)] **1** *vi* respirer

2 *vt* respirer

respite ['respaɪt] **1** *n* (**a**) *(pause, rest)* répit *m*; **without respite** sans répit *ou* relâche; **there wasn't a moment's respite from the noise** il y avait un bruit ininterrompu; **the weekend was a welcome respite** le weekend a constitué un répit bienvenu; **he never has any respite from the pain** la douleur ne lui laisse aucun répit

(**b**) *(delay)* répit *m*, délai *m*; *(stay of execution)* sursis *m*; **we've been given a week's respite before we need to pay** on nous a accordé un délai d'une semaine pour payer

2 *vt Formal* accorder un sursis à

►► ***respite care*** *(UNCOUNT)* = accueil temporaire, dans un établissement médicalisé, de personnes malades, handicapées etc, destiné à prendre le relais des familles

resplendence [rɪ'splendəns] *n Literary (splendour)* splendeur *f*; *(brightness)* resplendissement *m*

resplendent [rɪ'splendənt] *adj (splendid)* magnifique, splendide; *(bright)* resplendissant; **Joe,**

res–res

resplendent in his new suit Joe, resplendissant *ou* magnifique dans son nouveau costume; **her face was resplendent with joy/with health** son visage resplendissait de joie/de santé

resplendently [rɪ'splendəntlɪ] *adv (dress, decorate)* somptueusement; *(shine)* avec éclat

respond [rɪ'spɒnd] **1** *vi* (**a**) *(answer → person, guns)* répondre; **to respond to a request** répondre à une demande; **she responded with a smile** elle a répondu par un sourire

(**b**) *(react)* répondre, réagir; **the steering is slow to respond** la direction ne répond pas bien; **the cells respond by producing enzymes** les cellules réagissent en produisant des enzymes; **the patient is responding** le malade réagit positivement; **her condition isn't responding to treatment** le traitement ne semble pas agir sur sa maladie; **syphilis responds to antibiotics** les antibiotiques sont efficaces contre la syphilis; **they'll respond to the crisis by raising taxes** ils répondront à la crise en augmentant les impôts; **are people responding to the candidate's message?** l'opinion publique réagit-elle favorablement au message du candidat?; **he doesn't respond well to criticism** il réagit mal à la critique; **to respond to flattery** être sensible à la flatterie

2 *vt* répondre; **"who cares?" he responded angrily** "qu'est-ce que ça peut bien faire?", répondit-il avec colère

3 *n* (**a**) *Archit (for arch)* pilier *m* butant; *(ending colonnade)* colonne *f* engagée

(**b**) *Rel* répons *m*

respondent [rɪ'spɒndənt] **1** *n* (**a**) *Law* défendeur(eresse) *m,f* (**b**) *(in survey)* sondé(e) *m,f*, répondant(e) *m,f*; **10 percent of the respondents** 10 pour cent des personnes interrogées (**c**) *Psy (reflex)* répondant *m*

2 *adj Psy* répondant

response [rɪ'spɒns] **1** *n* (**a**) *(answer)* réponse *f*; **have you had any response to your request yet?** avez-vous obtenu une réponse à votre demande?; **when asked, she gave** *or* **made no response** quand on lui a posé la question, elle n'a pas répondu; **he smiled in response** il a répondu par un sourire; **in response to your question** en réponse à votre question, pour répondre à votre question; **in response to your letter** suite à votre lettre

(**b**) *(reaction)* réponse *f*, réaction *f*; **their response to the rioting was harsh** ils ont sévèrement réprimé les émeutes; **their proposals met with a favourable/lukewarm response** leurs propositions ont été accueillies favorablement/ont reçu un accueil mitigé; **response from the public was disappointing** la réponse du public a été décevante

(**c**) *(in bridge)* réponse *f*

(**d**) *Rel* répons *m*; **to make the responses at Mass** répondre la messe

(**e**) *Med* réaction *f*

2 in response to *prep* en réponse à; **he resigned in response to the party's urging/to the pressure** il a démissionné, cédant à l'insistance du parti/à la pression

▸▸ *Mktg* ***response rate*** *(to questionnaire)* taux *m* de réponse; ***response time*** *Comput* temps *m* de réponse; *Med & Psy* temps *m* de réaction

responsibility [rɪˌspɒnsə'bɪlɪtɪ] *(pl* **responsibilities**) *n* (**a**) *(control, authority)* responsabilité *f*; **responsibility for the campaign has been transferred to her** c'est à elle qu'incombe désormais la responsabilité de la campagne; **to have responsibility for sth** avoir la charge *ou* la responsabilité de qch; **a position of great responsibility** un poste à haute responsabilité; **how much responsibility for the operation did the president really have?** jusqu'à quel point le président était-il responsable de l'opération?; **can he handle all that responsibility?** est-il capable d'assumer toutes ces responsabilités?; **he authorized it on his own responsibility** il l'a autorisé de son propre chef, il a pris sur lui de l'autoriser

(**b**) *(accountability)* responsabilité *f*; **he has no sense of responsibility** il n'a aucun sens des responsabilités; **to accept** *or* **to assume responsibility for one's mistakes** assumer la responsabilité de ses erreurs; **I take full responsibility for the defeat** je prends (sur moi) l'entière responsabilité de la défaite; **we accept no responsibility for lost or stolen items** *(sign)* nous déclinons toute responsabilité pour les objets perdus ou volés; **no one has yet claimed responsibility for the attack** personne n'a encore revendiqué l'attaque

(**c**) *(task, duty)* responsabilité *f*; **responsibilities include product development** vous assurerez entre autres le développement des nouveaux produits; **answering the phone is your responsibility, not mine** c'est à toi de répondre au téléphone, pas à moi; **it's his responsibility!** c'est son affaire!; **to have a responsibility to sb** avoir une responsabilité envers qn; **they have a responsibility to the shareholders/the electors** ils ont une responsabilité envers les actionnaires/les électeurs; **to shirk one's responsibilities** fuir ses responsabilités; **children are a big responsibility** c'est une lourde responsabilité que d'avoir des enfants

▸▸ *Acct* ***responsibility accounting*** comptabilité *f* par centres de responsabilité

responsible [rɪ'spɒnsəbəl] *adj* (**a**) *(in charge, in authority)* responsable; **who's responsible for research?** qui est chargé de la recherche?; **he was responsible for putting the children to bed** c'était lui qui couchait les enfants; **a responsible position** un poste à responsabilité

(**b**) *(accountable)* responsable (**for** de); **he's not responsible for her behaviour** il n'est pas responsable de ses actes; **human error/a malfunction was responsible for the disaster** la catastrophe était due à une erreur humaine/à une défaillance technique; **who's responsible for this mess?** qui est responsable de ce désordre?; **he can be held legally responsible for the accident** il peut être tenu légalement responsable de l'accident; **I hold you personally responsible** je vous tiens personnellement responsable; **he is responsible only to the managing director** il n'est responsable que devant le directeur général

(**c**) *(serious, trustworthy)* sérieux, responsable; **it wasn't very responsible of him** ce n'était pas très sérieux de sa part; **responsible newspapers won't print the story** les journaux sérieux ne publieront pas cet article; **the chemical industry has become more environmentally responsible** l'industrie chimique se préoccupe davantage de l'environnement; **they aren't responsible parents** ce ne sont pas des parents dignes de ce nom; **our bank makes responsible investments** notre banque a une politique d'investissement responsable

responsibly [rɪ'spɒnsɪblɪ] *adv* de manière responsable; **to behave responsibly** avoir un comportement responsable

responsion [rɪ'spɒnʃən] *n Arch or Literary* réponse *f*

responsive [rɪ'spɒnsɪv] *adj* (**a**) *(person → sensitive)* sensible; *(→ receptive)* ouvert; *(→ enthusiastic)* enthousiaste; *(→ affectionate)* affectueux; **I asked him for advice, but he wasn't very responsive** je lui ai demandé des conseils mais il semblait peu disposé à me répondre; **to be responsive to praise** être sensible aux compliments; **he is very responsive to my needs** il est très attentif à mes besoins; **management should be responsive to suggestions** la direction devrait être ouverte aux suggestions; **the play opened to a responsive audience** la première a eu lieu devant un public enthousiaste

(**b**) *(brakes, controls, keyboard)* sensible; **the patient isn't proving responsive to treatment** le malade ne réagit pas au traitement; **most allergies are responsive to this treatment** on peut guérir la plupart des allergies avec ce traitement; **the industry is not responsive to market signals** l'industrie ne réagit *ou* ne répond pas aux sollicitations du marché

(**c**) *(answering → smile, nod)* en réponse

responsively [rɪ'spɒnsɪvlɪ] *adv* avec sympathie; **she glanced at him and he smiled responsively** elle lui lança un coup d'œil auquel il répondit par un sourire

responsiveness [rɪ'spɒnsɪvnɪs] *n* (**a**) *(of person → sensitivity)* sensibilité *f*; *(→ receptiveness)* ouverture *f*; *(→ enthusiasm)* enthousiasme *m*; *(→ affection)* affection *f*, tendresse *f* (**b**) *(of brakes, controls, keyboard)* sensibilité *f*

responsor [rɪ'spɒnsə(r)] *n* récepteur *m* de réponses

responsory [rɪ'spɒnsərɪ] *(pl* **responsories**) *n Rel* répons *m*

respray 1 *vt* [ˌriː'spreɪ] *(car)* repeindre

2 *n* ['riːspreɪ] **I took the car in for a respray** j'ai donné la voiture à repeindre

REST [rest]

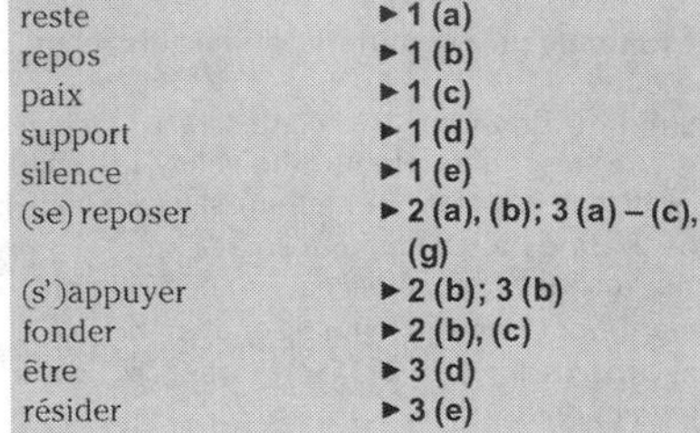

reste	▸ **1 (a)**
repos	▸ **1 (b)**
paix	▸ **1 (c)**
support	▸ **1 (d)**
silence	▸ **1 (e)**
(se) reposer	▸ **2 (a), (b); 3 (a) – (c), (g)**
(s')appuyer	▸ **2 (b); 3 (b)**
fonder	▸ **2 (b), (c)**
être	▸ **3 (d)**
résider	▸ **3 (e)**

1 *n* (**a**) **the rest (of)** *(remainder)* le reste (de); *(others)* les autres *mfpl*; **take the rest of the cake** prenez le reste *ou* ce qui reste du gâteau; **take the rest of the cakes** prenez les autres gâteaux *ou* les gâteaux qui restent; **I'm keeping the rest of it for tomorrow** je garde le reste *ou* le restant pour demain; **the rest of the time they watch television** le reste du temps, ils regardent la télévision; **he's the only amateur, the rest of them are professionals** c'est le seul amateur, les autres sont professionnels; **the rest of the group disagreed** le reste du groupe n'était pas d'accord; **the rest of us** nous autres, le reste (d'entre nous); **it's just another day like all the rest** c'est un jour comme un autre; **(as) for the rest** pour le reste, quant au reste; **and all the rest (of it), and the rest** et tout le reste *ou* tout le tralala

(**b**) *(relaxation)* repos *m*; *(pause)* repos *m*, pause *f*; **(a) rest will do him good** un peu de repos lui fera du bien; **try to get some rest** essayez de vous reposer (un peu); **I had** *or* **I took a ten-minute rest** je me suis reposé pendant dix minutes, j'ai fait une pause de dix minutes; **you need a week's rest/a good night's rest** vous avez besoin d'une semaine de repos/d'une bonne nuit de sommeil; **my arms need a rest** j'ai besoin de me reposer les bras; **after a moment's rest** après s'être reposé quelques instants; **after her afternoon rest** après sa sieste; **a day of rest** une journée de repos; **she had to take several rests while climbing the stairs** en montant l'escalier, elle a été obligée de s'arrêter à plusieurs reprises; **he needs a rest from the pressure/the children** il a besoin de se détendre/d'un peu de temps sans les enfants; **he gave her no rest until she consented** il ne lui a pas laissé une minute de répit jusqu'à ce qu'elle accepte; **his conscience gave him no rest** sa conscience ne lui laissait pas de répit; **you'd better give the skiing a rest** vous feriez mieux de ne pas faire de ski pendant un certain temps; *Fam* **give it a rest!** arrête, tu veux?; **rest and recuperation** *Am Mil* permission *f*, *Hum* vacances *fpl*; **to put** *or* **to set sb's mind at rest** tranquilliser *ou* rassurer qn; **the machines are at rest** les machines sont au repos; **her hands were rarely at rest** ses mains restaient rarement inactives; **to come to rest** *(vehicle, pendulum, ball)* s'immobiliser, s'arrêter; *(bird, falling object)* se poser

(**c**) *Euph (death)* paix *f*; **eternal rest** repos *m* éternel; **he's finally at rest** il a finalement trouvé la paix; **to lay sb to rest** porter qn en terre; **to lay** *or* **to put sth to rest** *(doubts, rumour, suspicions)* dissiper qch; *(allegation, notion)* abandonner qch; **perhaps we could lay the matter to rest** *(not discuss any further)* peut-être qu'on pourrait arrêter de parler de cette affaire une bonne fois pour toutes; **the matter should be laid to rest as quickly as possible** *(resolved)* cette affaire doit être résolue au plus vite

(**d**) *(support)* support *m*, appui *m*; *(in snooker)* chevalet *m*; **she used it as a rest for her camera** elle s'en est servie comme appui pour son appareil photo (**e**) *Mus* silence *m*; *Br* **minim** *or Am* **half rest** demi-pause *f*; *Br* **crotchet** *or Am* **quarter rest** soupir *m*; *Br* **quaver** *or Am* **eighth rest** demi-soupir *m*

(**f**) *(in poetry)* césure *f*

2 *vt* (**a**) *(allow to relax)* laisser se reposer; **to rest oneself** se reposer; **they had to stop to rest the camels** ils ont dû s'arrêter pour laisser se reposer les chameaux; **sit down and rest your legs** assieds-toi et repose-toi les jambes; *Agr* **to rest a field** mettre un champ en jachère; **(God) rest his soul!** que Dieu ait son âme!, qu'il repose en paix!; **I rest my case** *Law* j'ai conclu mon plaidoyer; *Fig* je n'ai rien d'autre à ajouter

(**b**) *(support, lean → gen)* appuyer; *(→ one's head)* reposer (**on** sur); *(→ one's hopes, confidence etc)* fonder (**on** sur); **she rested her bicycle against a lamppost** elle appuya sa bicyclette contre un réverbère; **I rested my suitcase on the step** j'ai posé ma valise sur la marche; **he rested his arm on the back of the sofa** son bras reposait sur le dossier du canapé

(**c**) *(base → argument, theory)* fonder (**on** sur)

3 *vi* (**a**) *(relax)* se reposer; **they set off again after resting for an hour** ils se sont remis en route après s'être reposés pendant une heure; **horses resting in the shade** des chevaux qui se reposent à l'ombre; **to be resting** *(actor)* = se trouver sans engagement; **we shall not rest until the fight is won** nous n'aurons de cesse que la lutte ne soit gagnée

(**b**) *(be held up or supported)* reposer; *(lean → person)* s'appuyer; *(→ bicycle, ladder)* être appuyé; **the buildings rest on solid foundations** les bâtiments reposent sur des fondations solides; **his arm rested on the back of the sofa** son bras reposait sur le dossier du canapé; **his head was resting on her shoulder** il avait la tête appuyée contre son épaule; **she was resting on her broom** elle était appuyée sur son balai; **the skis were resting against the wall** les skis étaient appuyés contre le mur

(**c**) *(be based)* **to rest on** *(argument, hope)* reposer sur; **the theory rests on a false assumption** la théorie repose sur une hypothèse fausse; **the whole problem rests on a misunderstanding** tout le problème repose sur un malentendu

(**d**) *(be, remain)* être; **rest assured we're doing our best** soyez certain que nous faisons de notre mieux; **their fate rests in your hands** leur sort est entre vos mains; **that's how things rest between us** voilà où en sont les choses entre nous; **can't you let the matter rest?** ne pouvez-vous pas abandonner cette idée?; **I won't let it rest at that** cela ne se passera pas ainsi; **he just won't let it rest** il y revient sans cesse

(**e**) *(reside, belong)* résider; **power rests with the committee** c'est le comité qui détient le pouvoir; **the choice rests with you** c'est à vous de choisir; **the decision doesn't rest with me** la décision ne dépend pas de moi

(**f**) *(alight → eyes, gaze)* se poser (**on** sur)

(**g**) *Euph (lie dead)* reposer; **may they rest in peace!** qu'ils reposent en paix!; **rest in peace** *(on gravestone)* repose en paix *(épitaphe)*

(**h**) *Law* **the defence/the prosecution rests** = formule de fin de plaidoyer ou de réquisitoire

(**i**) *Agr (lie fallow)* être en repos *ou* en jachère; **to let a field rest** laisser un champ en repos *ou* en jachère

►► *Aut* ***rest area*** aire *f* de repos; ***rest cure*** cure *f* de repos; *Fig* **this job is no rest cure** ce travail n'est pas une sinécure; ***rest day*** jour *m* de repos; ***rest home*** *(for convalescents)* maison *f* de repos; *(for elderly)* maison *f* de retraite; *Am* ***rest room*** toilettes *fpl*; *Am Aut* ***rest stop*** aire *f* de stationnement *ou* de repos; **to make a rest stop** faire une pause pour se détendre

► **rest up** *vi Fam* se reposer (un peu)❑, prendre un peu de repos❑

---

restage [ˌriːˈsteɪdʒ] *vt* remettre en scène

restart 1 *vt* [ˌriːˈstɑːt] (**a**) *(activity)* reprendre, recommencer; *(engine, mechanism)* remettre en marche

(**b**) *Comput (system)* relancer, redémarrer; *(program)* reprendre

2 *vi* [ˌriːˈstɑːt] (**a**) *(job, project)* reprendre, recommencer; *(engine, mechanism)* redémarrer

(**b**) *Comput (system)* redémarrer; *(program)* reprendre

3 *n* [ˈriːstɑːt] (**a**) *(of engine, mechanism)* remise *f* en marche

(**b**) *Comput (of system)* redémarrage *m*; *(of program)* reprise *f*; **warm/cold restart** redémarrage *m* à chaud/à froid

4 Restart *n* [ˈriːstɑːt] = organisme britannique d'aide et de formation pour chômeurs de longue durée

►► *Comput* ***restart point*** point *m* de reprise

restate [ˌriːˈsteɪt] *vt* (**a**) *(reiterate → argument, case, objection)* répéter, réitérer; *(→ one's intentions, innocence, faith)* réaffirmer; **the unions restated their position** les syndicats ont réaffirmé leur position (**b**) *(formulate differently)* reformuler

restatement [ˌriːˈsteɪtmənt] *n* (**a**) *(repetition → of argument, case, objection)* répétition *f*, réitération *f*; *(→ of intentions, innocence, faith)* réaffirmation *f* (**b**) *(different formulation)* reformulation *f*; **a restatement of our objectives is perhaps necessary at this stage** à ce stade, nous devrions peut-être reformuler nos objectifs

restaurant [ˈrestrɒnt] *n* restaurant *m*

►► *Br* ***restaurant car*** wagon-restaurant *m*, voiture-restaurant *f*; ***restaurant chain*** chaîne *f* de restaurants; ***restaurant manager*** gérant(e) *m,f* de restaurant

restaurateur [ˌrestərəˈtɜː(r)] *n* restaurateur(-trice) *m,f (tenant un restaurant)*

rested [ˈrestɪd] *adj* reposé; **to feel rested** se sentir (bien) reposé

restful [ˈrestfʊl] *adj* reposant, délassant, paisible

restfully [ˈrestfʊlɪ] *adv* paisiblement

restfulness [ˈrestfʊlnɪs] *n* tranquillité *f*

restharrow [ˌrestˈhærəʊ] *n Bot* bugrane *f*

resting [ˈrestɪŋ] *n*

►► ***resting place*** lieu *m* de repos; *Fig Literary (grave)* dernière demeure *f*; *Physiol* ***resting potential*** potentiel *m* de repos

restitution [ˌrestɪˈtjuːʃən] *n Formal (of stolen property)* restitution *f*; *(compensation)* réparation *f*; **the company was ordered to make full restitution of the monies** la société a été sommée de restituer l'intégralité de la somme

restive [ˈrestɪv] *adj* (**a**) *(nervous, fidgety)* nerveux, agité (**b**) *(unmanageable)* rétif, difficile

restively [ˈrestɪvlɪ] *adv* nerveusement

restiveness [ˈrestɪvnɪs] *n* (**a**) *(of person)* nervosité *f*, agitation *f* (**b**) *(of horse)* caractère *m* rétif

restless [ˈrestlɪs] *adj* (**a**) *(fidgety)* nerveux, agité; *(impatient)* impatient; **I get restless after a few days in the country** après quelques jours à la campagne, je ne tiens plus en place; **the audience was beginning to grow restless** le public commençait à s'impatienter; **to be a restless sleeper** avoir un *ou* le sommeil agité

(**b**) *(constantly moving)* agité; **her restless mind** son esprit en ébullition

(**c**) *(giving no rest)* **a restless night** une nuit agitée

restlessly [ˈrestlɪslɪ] *adv* (**a**) *(nervously)* nerveusement; *(impatiently)* impatiemment, avec impatience; **to pace restlessly up and down** faire les cent pas (**b**) *(sleeplessly)* **she tossed restlessly all night** elle a eu une nuit très agitée

restlessness [ˈrestlɪsnɪs] *n (fidgeting, nervousness)* nervosité *f*, agitation *f*; *(impatience)* impatience *f*; **the audience began showing signs of restlessness** le public a commencé à montrer des signes d'impatience

restock [ˌriːˈstɒk] **1** *vt* (**a**) *(with food, supplies)* réapprovisionner; **to restock a freezer** regarnir un congélateur (**b**) *Com (shop)* réassortir (**c**) *(with fish)* empoissonner; *(with game)* réapprovisionner en gibier

2 *vi (shop)* se réapprovisionner

restocking [ˌriːˈstɒkɪŋ] *n Com (of shop)* réassortiment *m*

restoration [ˌrestəˈreɪʃən] **1** *n* (**a**) *(giving back)* restitution *f*

(**b**) *(re-establishment)* restauration *f*, rétablissement *m*; *(of law and order, monarchy)* restauration *f*

(**c**) *(repairing, cleaning → of work of art, building)* restauration *f*

2 Restoration *Hist* **1** *n* **the Restoration** la Restauration anglaise **2** *comp (literature, drama)* de (l'époque de) la Restauration (anglaise)

►► ***Restoration comedy*** *(genre)* théâtre *m* de la Restauration anglaise *(caractérisé par la satire des mœurs du temps)*; *(play)* comédie *f* de l'époque de la Restauration anglaise *(caractérisée par la satire des mœurs du temps)*; *Fin* ***restoration fund*** caisse *f* de restauration; ***restoration project*** projet *m* de restauration; ***restoration work*** travail *m* de restauration

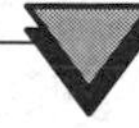

THE RESTORATION

En 1660, la restauration de la monarchie britannique par l'avènement de Charles II mit fin à la période d'austérité du Protectorat de Cromwell.

restorative [rɪˈstɒrətɪv] **1** *adj* fortifiant, remontant

2 *n* fortifiant *m*, remontant *m*

restore [rɪˈstɔː(r)] **1** *vt* (**a**) *(re-establish → peace, confidence etc)* restaurer, rétablir; *(→ monarchy)* restaurer; *(→ monarch)* remettre sur le trône; **to restore sb's sight/hearing** rendre la vue/l'ouïe à qn; **restored to his former post** rétabli *ou* réintégré dans ses anciennes fonctions; **if the left-wing government is restored to power** si le gouvernement de gauche revient au pouvoir; **it restored my faith in human nature** cela m'a redonné confiance en la nature humaine; **the treatment should soon restore his health** *or* **him to health** le traitement devrait très vite le remettre sur pied; **she managed to restore the company to profitability** grâce à elle, l'entreprise fait de nouveau des profits

(**b**) *(repair, clean → work of art, building)* restaurer; **to restore sth to its former glory** redonner son éclat d'antan à qch; **to be restored to its former glory** retrouver son éclat d'antan

(**c**) *Comput (file, text, data)* restaurer

(**d**) *(give back)* rendre, restituer; **the jewels have been restored to their rightful owners** les bijoux ont été rendus *ou* restitués à leurs propriétaires légitimes

2 *n Comput* restauration *f*

restorer [rɪˈstɔːrə(r)] *n (of work of art, building)* restaurateur(trice) *m,f*

restrain [rɪˈstreɪn] *vt* (**a**) *(hold back, prevent)* retenir, empêcher; **restrain him from spending so much money** empêchez-le de dépenser tant d'argent; **I couldn't restrain myself from making a remark** je n'ai pas pu m'empêcher de faire une remarque; **I had to restrain an impulse to laugh out loud** il a fallu que je me retienne pour ne pas rire tout haut

(**b**) *(overpower, bring under control → person)* maîtriser; **it took four policemen to restrain him** il a fallu quatre policiers pour le maîtriser; **he had to be forcibly restrained** il a fallu le retenir de force

(**c**) *(repress → emotion, anger, laughter)* contenir, réprimer

(**d**) *(imprison)* interner, emprisonner

restrained [rɪˈstreɪnd] *adj* (**a**) *(person)* retenu, réservé; *(emotion)* contenu, maîtrisé; *(tone, terms)* mesuré; **they sat in restrained silence** ils étaient assis ensemble et se retenaient de parler; **her manner was very restrained** son attitude était très réservée (**b**) *(colour, style)* sobre, discret(ète)

restraining order [rɪˈstreɪnɪŋ-] *n Law* injonction *f*

restraint [rɪˈstreɪnt] *n* (**a**) *(self-control)* retenue *f*; **with remarkable restraint** avec une retenue remarquable

(**b**) *(restriction)* restriction *f*, contrainte *f*; **to put a restraint on sb** contraindre qn; **certain restraints should be put on the committee's powers** il faudrait restreindre les pouvoirs du comité; **the right to travel without restraint** le droit de se déplacer en toute liberté *ou* librement; *Law* **to place** *or* **to keep sb under restraint** interner qn

(**c**) *(control)* contrôle *m*; **a policy of price restraint** une politique de contrôle des prix

restrict [rɪˈstrɪkt] *vt* restreindre, limiter; **I restrict myself to ten cigarettes a day** je me limite à dix cigarettes par jour; **fog is restricting visibility** le brouillard limite la visibilité; **airlines restrict the amount of luggage you can take** les lignes aériennes limitent la quantité de bagages qu'on peut emporter

restricted [rɪ'strɪktɪd] *adj* (**a**) *(limited)* limité, restreint; **the choice is too restricted** le choix est trop restreint; **to be on a restricted diet** suivre un régime sévère *ou* strict; **she feels less restricted wearing trousers** elle se sent plus libre de ses mouvements lorsqu'elle porte un pantalon; **restricted access** *(sign)* accès réservé; **restricted area** *(out of bounds)* zone *f* interdite; *Br Aut (with parking restrictions)* zone *f* à stationnement réglementé; *(with speed limit)* zone *f* à vitesse limitée

(**b**) *Admin (secret → document, information)* secret(ète), confidentiel

(**c**) *(narrow → ideas, outlook)* étroit, borné

►► *Comput* ***restricted users group*** = nombre restreint d'utilisateurs ayant accès à des informations confidentielles

restriction [rɪ'strɪkʃən] *n* (**a**) *(limitation)* restriction *f*, limitation *f*; **they'll accept no restriction of their liberty** ils n'accepteront pas qu'on restreigne leur liberté; **to put** *or* **to place** *or* **to impose restrictions on sth** imposer des restrictions sur qch; **speed restriction** limitation *f* de vitesse (**b**) *(in logic) & Math* condition *f*

►► *Biol & Chem* ***restriction enzyme*** enzyme *f* de restriction

restrictive [rɪ'strɪktɪv] *adj* (**a**) *(clause, list)* restrictif, limitatif; *(interpretation)* strict (**b**) *Ling (clause)* déterminatif

►► ***restrictive clause*** clause *f* restrictive; *Law* ***restrictive covenant*** clause *f* restrictive; ***restrictive practice*** *(by union)* pratique *f* syndicale restrictive; *(by traders)* atteinte *f* à la libre concurrence

restrictively [rɪ'strɪktɪvlɪ] *adv* d'une façon restrictive, avec des restrictions

restring [,riː'strɪŋ] *(pt & pp* **restrung** [-'strʌŋ]) *vt (bow)* remplacer la corde de; *(musical instrument)* remplacer les cordes de; *(tennis racket)* recorder; *(beads)* renfiler

restructure [,riː'strʌktʃə(r)] *vt* restructurer

restructuring [,riː'strʌktʃərɪŋ] *n* restructuration *f*

restrung [,riː'strʌŋ] *pt & pp of* **restring**

restyle [,riː'staɪl] *vt (car)* changer le design de; *(hair, clothes)* changer le style de; *(magazine)* changer la présentation de

result [rɪ'zʌlt] **1** *n* (**a**) *(consequence)* résultat *m*, conséquence *f*; **with disastrous results** avec des conséquences désastreuses; **this paint gives excellent results** cette peinture donne d'excellents résultats; **the net result** le résultat final; **these problems are the result of a misunderstanding** ces problèmes sont dus à un malentendu; **I overslept, with the result that I was late for work** je ne me suis pas réveillé à temps, et du coup, je suis arrivé à mon travail en retard

(**b**) *(success)* résultat *m*; **our policy is beginning to get** *or* **to show results** notre politique commence à porter ses fruits; **they're looking for sales staff who can get results** ils cherchent des vendeurs capables d'obtenir de bons résultats; *Fam* **we need a result** *(a successful outcome)* il faut qu'on fasse un résultat; *Br Fam* **he had a result last night, he pulled some gorgeous bird** il a fait fort hier soir, il a levé une super nana; *Fam* **a 20 percent pay rise? what a result!** 20 pour cent d'augmentation? tu as fait fort!

(**c**) *(of match, exam, election)* résultat *m*; **the football results** les résultats des matches de football; *Br* **she got good A-level results** ≃ elle a obtenu de bons résultats au baccalauréat; *Br Fam* **to get a result** *(in sport)* gagner ❑, l'emporter ❑; *Fam* **our team needs a result next week** *(win)* notre équipe a besoin de gagner la semaine prochaine ❑; *Fin* **the company's results are down on last year** les résultats financiers de l'entreprise sont moins bons que (ceux de) l'année dernière

(**d**) *Math (of sum, equation)* résultat *m*

2 *vi* résulter; **who knows what will result from such a step?** qui sait ce qui résultera d'une telle démarche?; **the fire resulted from a short circuit** c'est un court-circuit qui a provoqué l'incendie; **a price rise would inevitably result** il en résulterait *ou* il s'ensuivrait inévitablement une augmentation des prix; **to result in** avoir pour résultat; **the dispute resulted in her resigning** la dispute a entraîné sa démission; **the attack resulted in heavy losses on both sides** l'attaque s'est soldée par d'importantes pertes des deux côtés; **the resulting protests** les protestations qui s'ensuivirent

3 as a result *adv* **as a result, I missed my flight** à cause de cela, j'ai manqué mon avion

4 as a result of *prep* à cause de; **I was late as a result of the strike** j'ai été en retard en raison de la grève

resultant [rɪ'zʌltənt] **1** *adj (gen) & Math & Mus* résultant

2 *n Math & Phys* résultante *f*

►► ***resultant tone*** son *m* résultant

resultative [rɪ'zʌltətɪv] *adj Ling* résultatif

resume [rɪ'zjuːm] **1** *vt* (**a**) *(activity, duties, negotiations, speech, discussions)* reprendre; *(trip, journey, walk)* continuer, poursuivre; *(relations)* renouer; *Comput* reprendre; **after he left, we resumed our discussion** après son départ, nous avons repris notre discussion; *Formal* **kindly resume your seats** veuillez regagner vos places *ou* vous rasseoir; **to resume work** se remettre au travail; **she resumed her maiden name** elle a repris son nom de jeune fille

(**b**) *Arch (sum up)* résumer

2 *vi* reprendre, continuer; **when everyone's ready, we can resume** quand tout le monde sera prêt, nous pourrons continuer *ou* poursuivre; **the meeting will resume after lunch** la réunion reprendra après le déjeuner; **play resumed at four** le match a repris à quatre heures

résumé ['rezjuːmeɪ] *n* (**a**) *(summary)* résumé *m*; **to give a résumé of sth** faire un résumé de qch (**b**) *Am (curriculum vitae)* curriculum vitae *m inv*

resumption [rɪ'zʌmpʃən] *n* reprise *f*

resupinate [rɪ'suːpɪneɪt] *adj Bot* résupiné

resupply [,riːsə'plaɪ] *(pt & pp* **resupplied**) *vt* réapprovisionner (**with** de)

resurface [,riː'sɜːfɪs] **1** *vi also Fig* refaire surface; **the stolen jewels resurfaced in Australia** les bijoux volés ont refait surface en Australie

2 *vt (road)* refaire

resurgence [rɪ'sɜːdʒəns] *n (of ideology, party, trend)* résurgence *f*, réapparition *f*; *(of disease)* réapparition *f*; *(of interest)* renouveau *m*; *(of company)* reprise *f*

resurgent [rɪ'sɜːdʒənt] *adj (ideology, trend, party)* qui connaît un nouvel essor; *(interest)* renaissant; **the threat of resurgent nationalism** la menace du nationalisme renaissant

resurrect [,rezə'rekt] *vt also Fig* ressusciter; **resurrected from the dead** ressuscité des *ou* d'entre les morts; **they've resurrected this old tradition** ils ont ressuscité cette vieille tradition; **the minister succeeded in resurrecting his career** le ministre réussit à faire redémarrer sa carrière

resurrection [,rezə'rekʃən] *n also Fig* résurrection *f*; **the Resurrection (of Christ)** la résurrection du Christ, la Résurrection

►► *Bot* ***resurrection plant*** rose *f* de Jéricho

resuscitate [rɪ'sʌsɪteɪt] *vt Med* réanimer; *(company)* faire repartir

resuscitation [rɪ,sʌsɪ'teɪʃən] *n Med* réanimation *f*; **all attempts at resuscitation failed** toutes les tentatives de réanimation ont échoué

resuscitator [rɪ'sʌsɪteɪtə(r)] *n (apparatus)* respirateur *m*; *(person)* réanimateur(trice) *m,f*

retable [rɪ'teɪbəl] *n* retable *m*

retail ['riːteɪl] **1** *n* (vente *f* au) détail *m*

2 *adj* de détail; **they run a retail hi-fi business** ils ont un magasin de matériel hi-fi; *Hum* **I indulged in a little retail therapy this weekend** j'ai fait un peu de shopping pour me remonter le moral ce week-end; **a wholesale and retail business** un commerce de gros et de détail

3 *adv* au détail

4 *vt* (**a**) *(goods)* vendre au détail

(**b**) *Formal (story, event, experience)* raconter; *(gossip, scandal)* répandre, *Pej* colporter

5 *vi (goods)* se vendre (au détail); **they retail at £10 each** ils se vendent à 10 livres la pièce

►► ***retail audit*** audit *m* des détaillants; ***retail auditor*** audit *m* des détaillants, auditeur(trice) *m,f* des détaillants; ***retail bank*** banque *f* de détail; ***retail banking*** banque *f* de détail; ***retail chain*** chaîne *f* de vente au détail, chaîne *f* de détail; ***retail customer*** client(e) *m,f* qui achète au détail; ***retail dealer*** détaillant(e) *m,f*; *Am Pej* ***retail elephant*** magasin *m* de grande distribution *(qui domine une zone donnée)*; ***retail goods*** marchandises *fpl* vendues au détail, marchandises *fpl* au détail; ***retail outlet*** magasin *m* de (vente au) détail, point *m* de (vente au) détail; ***retail panel*** panel *m* de détaillants; *Br* ***retail park*** zone *f* commerciale; ***retail price*** prix *m* de *ou* au détail; *Br Fin* ***Retail Price Index*** indice *m* des prix de détail; ***retail price maintenance*** prix *m* imposé; ***retail sales*** ventes *fpl* au détail; ***retail shipment*** expédition *f* de détail; ***retail shop*** magasin *m* de (vente au) détail; ***retail trade*** commerce *m* (de détail)

retailer ['riːteɪlə(r)] *n* détaillant(e) *m,f*

►► ***retailer brand*** marque *f* de revendeur *ou* de détaillant *ou* de distributeur; ***retailer co-operative*** groupe *m* de détaillants; ***retailers' group*** groupement *m* de détaillants; ***retailer margin*** marge *f* du détaillant

retailing ['riːteɪlɪŋ] *n* vente *f* au détail

►► *Com & Mktg* ***retailing mix*** marchéage *m* de distribution

retain [rɪ'teɪn] *vt* (**a**) *(keep)* garder; **the village has retained its charm** le village a conservé son charme (**b**) *(hold, keep in place)* retenir; **to retain heat** retenir la chaleur (**c**) *(remember)* retenir, garder en mémoire; **I just can't retain dates** je suis tout à fait incapable de retenir les dates (**d**) *(reserve → place, hotel room)* retenir, réserver (**e**) *(engage → solicitor)* engager; **to retain sb's services** s'assurer les services de qn

retained [rɪ'teɪnd] *adj Acct*

►► ***retained earnings*** revenu *m* non distribué; ***retained profit*** bénéfices *mpl* non distribués

retainer [rɪ'teɪnə(r)] *n* (**a**) *(retaining fee)* provision *f*; **to pay sb a retainer** verser une provision à qn (**b**) *(servant)* domestique *mf*, *Arch* serviteur *m* (**c**) *(nominal rent)* loyer *m* nominal

retaining [rɪ'teɪnɪŋ] *n*

►► ***retaining fee*** provision *f ou* avance *f* sur honoraires; ***retaining wall*** mur *m* de soutènement

retake *(pt* **retook** [-'tʊk], *pp* **retaken** [-'teɪkən]) **1** *vt* [,riː'teɪk] (**a**) *(town, fortress)* reprendre (**b**) *(exam)* repasser (**c**) *Cin (shot)* reprendre, refaire; *(scene)* refaire une prise (de vues) de

2 *n* ['riːteɪk] (**a**) *(exam)* examen *m* à repasser; **how many retakes did you have?** combien d'examens est-ce que tu as dû repasser? (**b**) *Cin* nouvelle prise *f* (de vues); **it took several retakes** il a fallu plusieurs prises

retaliate [rɪ'tælɪeɪt] *vi* se venger, riposter; **the government retaliated by banning all foreign coal imports** le gouvernement a riposté en interdisant toutes les importations de charbon; **the goalkeeper was sent off for retaliating** le gardien de but a été expulsé pour avoir riposté à l'agression; **she retaliated against her critics** elle a riposté à l'attaque de ses critiques

retaliation [rɪ,tælɪ'eɪʃən] *n (UNCOUNT)* représailles *fpl*, vengeance *f*; **in retaliation (for sth)** en *ou* par représailles (contre qch)

retaliatory [rɪ'tælɪətərɪ] *adj* de représailles, de rétorsion; **to take retaliatory measures** exercer des représailles, riposter

►► ***retaliatory attack*** riposte *f*; ***retaliatory bombing*** des représailles *fpl* sous forme de bombardements

retard [rɪ'tɑːd] **1** *vt* retarder

2 *n Fam* débile *mf* mental(e) ❑, demeuré(e) ❑ *m,f*

retardant [rɪ'tɑːdənt] **1** *n* retardateur *m*

2 *adj* retardateur

retardation [,riːtɑː'deɪʃən] *n* (**a**) *(mental)* arriération *f* (**b**) *(delaying)* retardement *m*

retarded [rɪ'tɑːdɪd] **1** *adj* (**a**) *(mentally)* arriéré (**b**) *(delayed)* retardé

2 *npl Old-fashioned* **the (mentally) retarded** les arriérés *mpl* mentaux; **a school for the retarded** une école pour enfants arriérés

retch [retʃ] **1** *vi* avoir un *ou* des haut-le-cœur; **the smell made me retch** l'odeur m'a donné des haut-le-cœur *ou* m'a soulevé l'estomac

2 *n* haut-le-cœur *m inv*

retching [ˈretʃɪŋ] *n* haut-le-cœur *m inv*

retd (*written abbr* **retired**) à la retraite

retell [ˌriːˈtel] (*pt & pp* **retold** [-ˈtəʊld]) *vt* raconter de nouveau

retelling [ˌriːˈtelɪŋ] *n* nouvelle version *f*; **the story gained in the retelling** l'histoire gagnait à être racontée de nouveau

retention [rɪˈtenʃən] *n* (**a**) *(keeping)* conservation *f*; *(of authority, provisions, restrictions)* maintien *m*; *(of fact, impression etc)* mémoire *f*; *Com* **retention of title** réserve *f* de propriété (**b**) *Med (holding)* rétention *f*; **fluid retention** rétention *f* d'eau; **urine retention** rétention *f* d'urine (**c**) *(memory)* rétention *f*

retentive [rɪˈtentɪv] *adj (memory)* qui retient bien; **she's a very retentive pupil** c'est une élève qui a une très bonne mémoire

retentiveness [rɪˈtentɪvnɪs] *n* mémoire *f*

retexture [ˌriːˈtekstʃə(r)] *vt* apprêter de nouveau

rethink (*pt & pp* **rethought** [-ˈθɔːt]) **1** *vt* [ˌriːˈθɪŋk] repenser; **we'll have to rethink our strategy** il faudra repenser *ou* revoir notre stratégie

2 *n* [ˈriːθɪŋk] **to have a rethink (about sth)** réfléchir de nouveau (à qch); **a rethink of the whole project is necessary** il faut repenser le projet dans son ensemble; **we need a complete rethink of our strategy** il nous faut revoir entièrement notre stratégie

reticence [ˈretɪsəns] *n (on one occasion)* réticence *f*; *(character trait)* réserve *f*; **this reticence isn't like her** elle n'est pas aussi réservée d'habitude

reticent [ˈretɪsənt] *adj* réticent; **he's reticent about explaining his reasons** il hésite *ou* est peu disposé à expliquer ses raisons

reticently [ˈretɪsəntlɪ] *adv* avec réticence

reticle [ˈretɪkəl] *n Opt* réticule *m*

reticular [rɪˈtɪkjʊlə(r)] *adj* réticulé

reticulate 1 *adj* [rɪˈtɪkjʊlət] réticulé

2 *vt* [rɪˈtɪkjʊleɪt] *(surface)* couvrir d'un réseau; **reticulated structure** *f* maillée

3 *vi* [rɪˈtɪkjʊleɪt] former un réseau

reticulation [rɪˌtɪkjʊˈleɪʃən] *n* réticulation *f*

reticule [ˈretɪkjuːl] *n* (**a**) *Hist (bag)* réticule *m* (**b**) *Opt* réticule *m*

reticulin [rɪˈtɪkjʊlɪn] *n Physiol* réticuline *f*

reticulum [rɪˈtɪkjʊləm] (*pl* **reticula** [-lə]) *n* réticulum *m*

retiform [ˈriːtɪfɔːm] *adj* rétiforme

retile [ˌriːˈtaɪl] *vt (roof)* renouveler les tuiles de; *(room, floor)* recarreler

retina [ˈretɪnə] (*pl* **retinas** *or* **retinae** [-niː]) *n* rétine *f*

retinal [ˈretɪnəl] *adj* rétinien

▸▸ *Med* ***retinal detachment*** décollement *m* de la rétine

retinitis [ˌretɪˈnaɪtəs] *n Med* rétinite *f*

retinopathy [ˌretɪnˈɒpəθɪ] *n Med* rétinopathie *f*; **diabetic retinopathy** rétinopathie *f* diabétique

retinoscope [ˈretɪnəskəʊp] *n Opt* skiascope *m*

retinoscopy [ˌretɪˈnɒskəpɪ] *n Opt* skiascopie *f*

retinue [ˈretɪnjuː] *n* suite *f*, cortège *m*

retire [rɪˈtaɪə(r)] **1** *vi* (**a**) *(from job)* prendre sa retraite; *(from business, politics)* se retirer; **to retire at sixty-five** prendre sa retraite à soixante-cinq ans; **to have retired** être à la retraite; **to retire from the political scene** se retirer de la scène politique; **to retire from boxing/from motor racing** abandonner la boxe/la course automobile; **to retire early** prendre une retraite anticipée

(**b**) *Formal or Hum (go to bed)* aller se coucher

(**c**) *(leave)* se retirer; **the jury retired to consider its verdict** les jurés se sont retirés pour délibérer; **shall we retire to the lounge?** si nous passions au salon?; **to retire to a monastery** se retirer dans un monastère; *Sport* **to retire hurt** abandonner à la suite d'une blessure

(**d**) *Mil (pull back)* se replier

2 *vt* (**a**) *(employee)* mettre à la retraite

(**b**) *Mil (troops)* retirer

(**c**) *Fin (coins, bill, bonds, shares)* retirer

retired [rɪˈtaɪəd] *adj* (**a**) *(from job)* retraité, à la retraite; **to be retired** être à la retraite; *Mil* **to put** *or* **to place sb on the retired list** mettre qn à la retraite; **Admiral James Walker, retired** Amiral James Walker, retraité (**b**) *Fin (coins, bill, bonds, shares)* retiré (**c**) *(secluded)* retiré; **to live a retired life** mener une vie retirée; **a retired spot** un endroit retiré *ou* isolé

retiree [ˌrɪtaɪəˈriː] *n Am* retraité(e) *m,f*

retirement [rɪˈtaɪəmənt] *n* (**a**) *(from job)* retraite *f*; **how do you plan to spend your retirement?** comment comptez-vous passer votre retraite?; **to take early retirement** prendre une retraite anticipée; **to come out of retirement** reprendre sa carrière

(**b**) *(seclusion)* isolement *m*, solitude *f*

(**c**) *Mil (withdrawal)* repli *m*

(**d**) *Sport (from match, competition)* abandon *m*

(**e**) *Fin (of coins, bill, bonds, shares)* retrait *m*

▸▸ ***retirement age*** âge *m* de la retraite; **to reach retirement age** atteindre l'âge de la retraite; ***retirement benefit*** indemnité *f* de départ en retraite, prime *f* de mise à la retraite; ***retirement community*** résidence *f* pour retraités; *Br* ***retirement flat*** appartement *m* pour retraités; ***retirement pay*** retraite *f*; ***retirement pension*** (pension *f* de) retraite *f*; *Am* ***retirement plan*** régime *m* de retraite; *Fin* ***retirement savings plan*** plan *m* d'épargne retraite

retiring [rɪˈtaɪərɪŋ] *adj* (**a**) *(reserved)* réservé (**b**) *(leaving → official, MP)* sortant (**c**) *(employee)* qui part à la retraite; **to reach retiring age** atteindre l'âge de la retraite

retiringly [rɪˈtaɪərɪŋlɪ] *adv* modestement, en s'effaçant

retold [ˌriːˈtəʊld] *pt & pp of* **retell**

retook [ˌriːˈtʊk] *pt of* **retake**

retool [ˌriːˈtuːl] **1** *vt* (**a**) *Ind* rééquiper (**b**) *Am Fam (company)* réorganiser ❑

2 *vi* (**a**) *Ind* se rééquiper (**b**) *Am (company)* se réorganiser

retort [rɪˈtɔːt] **1** *vi* rétorquer, riposter

2 *vt* rétorquer, riposter

3 *n* (**a**) *(reply)* riposte *f*, réplique *f* (**b**) *Chem & Ind* cornue *f*

retouch [ˌriːˈtʌtʃ] **1** *n (of photograph)* retouche *f*

2 *vt (photograph)* retoucher

retouching [ˌriːˈtʌtʃɪŋ] *n (of photograph)* retouche *f*

retrace [rɪˈtreɪs] *vt* (**a**) *(go back over → route)* refaire; **to retrace one's steps** rebrousser chemin, revenir sur ses pas (**b**) *(reconstitute → past events, someone's movements)* reconstituer

retract [rɪˈtrækt] **1** *vt* (**a**) *(withdraw → statement, confession)* retirer, rétracter; *(go back on → promise, agreement)* revenir sur (**b**) *(draw in → claws, horns)* rétracter, rentrer; *Aviat (→ wheels, undercarriage)* escamoter, rentrer

2 *vi* (**a**) *(recant)* se rétracter, se désavouer (**b**) *(be drawn in → claws, horns)* se rétracter; *Aviat (→ wheels, undercarriage)* rentrer, s'escamoter

retractable [rɪˈtræktəbəl] *adj* (**a**) *(aerial, undercarriage, handle)* escamotable; *(ballpoint pen)* à pointe rétractable (**b**) *(statement)* que l'on peut rétracter *ou* désavouer

retractile [rɪˈtræktaɪl] *adj* rétractile

retraction [rɪˈtrækʃən] *n (of statement)* rétractation *f*; *(of opinion)* désaveu *m*, reniement *m*; **to publish a retraction** *(newspaper)* publier un désaveu

retractor [rɪˈtræktə(r)] *n* (**a**) *Anat* (muscle *m*) releveur *m* (**b**) *Med (instrument → gen)* rétracteur *m*, écarteur *m*; *(→ for eyelid)* releveur *m*

retrain [ˌriːˈtreɪn] **1** *vt* recycler

2 *vi* se recycler

retraining [ˌriːˈtreɪnɪŋ] *n* recyclage *m*

▸▸ ***retraining programme*** programme *m* de recyclage

retransmission [ˌriːtrænsˈmɪʃən] *n TV* retransmission *f*; *(of telegram)* réexpédition *f*

retransmit [ˌriːtrɑːnsˈmɪt] (*pt & pp* **retransmitted**) *vt TV* retransmettre; *(telegram)* réexpédier

retread (*pt* **retrod** [-ˈtrɒd], *pp* **retrodden** [-ˈtrɒdən] *or* **retrod** [-ˈtrɒd]) *Aut* **1** *vt* [ˌriːˈtred] rechaper

2 *n* [ˈriːtred] pneu *m* rechapé

retreat [rɪˈtriːt] **1** *vi* (**a**) *Mil* battre en retraite, se replier; *Fig* **the management was forced to retreat on this point** la direction a été obligée de céder sur ce point

(**b**) *(gen)* se retirer; **we retreated towards the back of the room** nous nous sommes retirés au fond de la salle; **to retreat to the country** se retirer à la campagne; **to retreat into a world of one's own** s'isoler dans son petit monde (à soi); **to retreat from the public eye** se retirer du monde

(**c**) *(flood waters)* reculer

2 *n* (**a**) *Mil & (withdrawal)* retraite *f*, repli *m*; **to beat/to sound the retreat** battre/sonner la retraite; **this is a retreat from the unions' original position** les syndicats ont fait là des concessions par rapport à leur position initiale; **to beat a hasty retreat** prendre ses jambes à son cou

(**b**) *(refuge)* refuge *m*, asile *m*; **a mountain retreat** un refuge de montagne; **a holiday/a weekend retreat** un lieu paisible pour les vacances/le week-end

(**c**) *Rel* retraite *f*; **to go on** *or* **into retreat** faire une retraite

(**d**) *(of flood waters)* retrait *m*, recul *m*

retrench [ˌriːˈtrentʃ] **1** *vt* (**a**) *(costs, expenses)* réduire, restreindre (**b**) *(literary work)* faire des coupures dans; *(passage)* supprimer

2 *vi (economize)* faire des économies, restreindre ses dépenses

retrenchment [ˌriːˈtrentʃmənt] *n* (**a**) *(of costs, expenses)* réduction *f*, compression *f*; **a policy of retrenchment** une politique d'économies (**b**) *(of literary passage)* suppression *f*

retrial [ˌriːˈtraɪəl] *n* nouveau procès *m*

retribution [ˌretrɪˈbjuːʃən] *n* punition *f*, châtiment *m*; **in retribution for sth** comme châtiment pour qch; **it is divine retribution** c'est le châtiment de Dieu

retributive [rɪˈtrɪbjʊtɪv], **retributory** [rɪˈtrɪbjʊtərɪ] *adj (involving punishment)* de punition, de châtiment; *(avenging)* vengeur; **they have no retributive powers** ils n'ont pas le pouvoir de punir; **retributive measures will be taken against the culprits** les coupables seront punis

retrievable [rɪˈtriːvəbəl] *adj (object)* récupérable; *(fortune, health)* recouvrable; *(error, loss)* réparable; *(situation)* rattrapable; *Comput (data, file)* accessible; *(lost file)* récupérable

retrieval [rɪˈtriːvəl] *n* (**a**) *(getting back → of object)* récupération *f*; *(→ of fortune, health)* recouvrement *m* (**b**) *Comput (of data, file)* recherche *f*; *(of lost data)* récupération *f* (**c**) *(making good → of error, loss)* réparation *f*; **the situation is beyond retrieval** il n'y a plus rien à faire (pour sauver la situation)

▸▸ *Comput* ***retrieval system*** système *m* de recherche

retrieve [rɪˈtriːv] **1** *vt* (**a**) *(get back → lost object)* récupérer; *(→ fortune, health)* recouvrer, retrouver; **I retrieved my bag from the lost property office** j'ai récupéré mon sac au bureau des objets trouvés

(**b**) *(save)* sauver; **she managed to retrieve her coat from the fire** elle réussit à sauver son manteau du feu

(**c**) *(of dog → ball, stick, game bird)* rapporter

(**d**) *Comput (data, file)* rechercher; *(lost data)* récupérer

(**e**) *(make good → error, loss)* réparer; *(→ situation)* rattraper, sauver

2 *vi Hunt (dog)* rapporter le gibier

retriever [rɪˈtriːvə(r)] *n (dog)* retriever *m*

retro [ˈretrəʊ] *adj* rétro *(inv)*

▸▸ ***retro chic*** la mode rétro

retro- [ˈretrəʊ] *pref* rétro-

retroact [ˌretrəʊˈækt] *vi* (**a**) *(have retroactive effect)* avoir un effet rétroactif, *Literary* rétroagir (**b**) *(act in opposition)* réagir

retroaction [ˌretrəʊˈækʃən] *n* rétroaction *f*

retroactive [ˌretrəʊˈæktɪv] *adj* rétroactif; **the increase is retroactive to last January** l'augmentation a un effet rétroactif à compter de janvier dernier

retroactively [ˌretrəʊˈæktɪvlɪ] *adv* rétroactivement

retroactivity [ˌretrəʊækˈtɪvɪtɪ] *n* rétroactivité *f*

retrocede [ˌretrəʊˈsiːd] **1** *vt (territory)* rétrocéder, recéder, rendre

2 *vi* rétrograder, reculer

retrocession [ˌretrəʊˈseʃən], **retrocedence** [ˌretrəʊˈsiːdəns] *n* rétrocession *f*

retrod [ˌriːˈtrɒd] *pt of* **retread**

retrofit [ˈretrəʊfɪt] (*pt & pp* **retrofitted**) *vt* moderniser

retroflex [ˈretrəʊfleks], **retroflexed** [ˈretrəʊflekst] *adj* (**a**) *Ling* rétroflexe (**b**) *Anat* rétrofléchi

▸▸ *Ling* ***retroflex consonant*** rétroflexe *f*

retroflexion [ˌretrəʊˈflekʃən] *n Ling* rétroflexion *f*

retrogradation [ˌretrəʊgrəˈdeɪʃən] *n Astron* rétrogradation *f*

ret–ret

retrograde [ˈretrəʊgreɪd] **1** *adj* rétrograde
2 *vi* (**a**) *(gen)* rétrograder (**b**) *Am Mil (retreat)* battre en retraite

retrogress [ˈretrəʊgres] *vi Formal* (**a**) *(degenerate)* régresser (**b**) *(move backwards)* rétrograder

retrogression [ˌretrəʊˈgreʃən] *n* rétrogression *f*, rétrogradation *f*

retrogressive [ˌretrəʊˈgresɪv] *adj* rétrogressif, régressif

retropack [ˈretrəʊpæk] *n* système *m* de rétrofusées

retrorocket [ˈretrəʊˌrɒkɪt] *n* rétrofusée *f*

retrorse [rɪˈtrɔːs] *adj Bot & Zool* recourbé, retourné

retrospect [ˈretrəʊspekt] **in retrospect** *adv* rétrospectivement, avec le recul

retrospection [ˌretrəʊˈspekʃən] *n* rétrospection *f*

retrospective [ˌretrəʊˈspektɪv] **1** *adj (fear, analysis)* rétrospectif; *(law, effect)* rétroactif
2 *n Art & Cin* rétrospective *f*

retrospectively [ˌretrəʊˈspektɪvlɪ] *adv (wonder, acknowledge)* rétrospectivement; *(apply, increase)* rétroactivement; **the law will not be applied retrospectively** la loi n'aura pas d'effet rétroactif

retrosynthetic [ˌretrəʊsɪnˈθetɪk] *adj Chem*
►► ***retrosynthetic analysis*** analyse *f* rétrosynthétique

retroussé [rəˈtruːseɪ] *adj (nose)* retroussé

retroversion [ˌretrəʊˈvɜːʃən] *n Med* rétroversion *f*, renversement *m*

retroverted [ˌretrəʊˈvɜːtɪd] *adj Med (uterus)* rétroversé

retrovirus [ˈretrəʊˌvaɪrəs] *n Med* rétrovirus *m*

retry [ˌriːˈtraɪ] *(pt & pp* **retried***)* **1** *vt Law* refaire le procès de, juger à nouveau
2 *vi Comput* réessayer

retsina [retˈsiːnə] *n* retsina *m*

retune [ˌriːˈtjuːn] **1** *vt* (**a**) *Mus* réaccorder (**b**) *Rad* régler (**c**) *(engine)* régler
2 *vi Rad* **to retune to medium wave** régler son poste sur ondes moyennes; **don't forget to retune tomorrow to the same wavelength** n'oubliez pas de reprendre l'écoute demain sur la même longueur d'ondes
3 *n (of engine)* réglage *m*; **the engine needs a retune** il faut faire régler le moteur

RETURN [rɪˈtɜːn]

retour	► **1 (a), (b), (e), (h) – (j)**
renvoi	► **1 (b)**
rendu	► **1 (c)**
aller et retour	► **1 (d)**
réapparition	► **1 (e)**
rendement	► **1 (f)**
rendre	► **2 (a), (c), (d), (h)**
rapporter	► **2 (a), (i)**
renvoyer	► **2 (a), (e)**
remettre	► **2 (b)**
retourner	► **3**
revenir	► **3**
réapparaître	► **3**

1 *n* (**a**) *(going or coming back)* retour *m*; **on her return** à son retour; **on his return to France** à son retour en France; **the point of no return** le point de non-retour; *Br* **by return (of post)** par retour du courrier; **a return to normal** un retour à la normale; **a return to traditional methods** un retour aux méthodes traditionnelles; **the strikers' return to work** la reprise du travail par les grévistes; **return to office** *(of politician)* reprise *f* de fonctions
(**b**) *(giving or taking back)* retour *m*; *(sending back)* renvoi *m*, retour *m*; *(of stolen property)* restitution *f*; *(of overpayment)* remboursement *m*; **on return of this coupon** sur renvoi de ce bon; **on sale or return** *(goods)* vendu avec possibilité de retour; **no deposit, no return** *(on bottle)* ni retour, ni consigne; **it's a small return for all your kindness** c'est une modeste récompense pour votre bonté
(**c**) *(returned article)* rendu *m*; *(library book)* livre *m* (de bibliothèque) que l'on rapporte; *Theat* **returns may be available on the day of the performance** des places peuvent se libérer le jour de la représentation
(**d**) *Br (round trip, ticket)* aller et retour *m*; **two returns to Edinburgh, please** deux allers et retours pour Édimbourg, s'il vous plaît
(**e**) *(reappearance → of fever, pain, good weather)* réapparition *f*, retour *m*
(**f**) *Fin (yield)* rendement *m*, rapport *m*; **a 10 percent return on investment** un rendement de 10 pour cent sur la somme investie; **how much return do you get on your investment?** combien est-ce que ton investissement te rapporte?; **to bring a good return** être d'un bon rapport; **return on capital** retour *m* sur capital; **return on capital employed** retour *m* sur capital permanent; **return on capital invested** retour *m* sur capitaux investis; **return on equity** rendement *m* sur fonds propres; **return on investment** retour *m* sur investissements; **return on net assets** rendement *m* de l'actif net; **return on sales** retour *m* sur ventes
(**g**) *(for income tax)* (formulaire *m* de) déclaration *f* d'impôts
(**h**) *Sport (in tennis)* retour *m*; **return of service** retour *m* de service; **to make a good return (of service)** bien renvoyer le service; **what a brilliant return!** ce retour est superbe!
(**i**) *Archit* retour *m*
(**j**) *(on keyboard)* touche *f* retour
2 *vt* (**a**) *(give back)* rendre; *(take back)* rapporter; *(send back)* renvoyer, retourner; *Mktg (goods)* renvoyer; **the jewels have been returned to their rightful owners** les bijoux ont été rendus à leurs propriétaires légitimes; **I have to return the library books today** il faut que je rapporte les livres à la bibliothèque aujourd'hui; **return this coupon for your fabulous free gift** renvoyez ce bon pour obtenir votre magnifique cadeau; **return to sender** *(on envelope)* retour à l'expéditeur; **she returned my look** elle me regarda à son tour; **the soldiers returned our fire** les soldats répondirent à notre tir; *Tel* **to return a call** rappeler
(**b**) *(replace, put back)* remettre; **she returned the file to the drawer** elle remit le dossier dans le tiroir; **to return an animal to the wild** remettre un animal en liberté
(**c**) *(repay → kindness, compliment)* rendre (en retour); **how can I return your favour?** comment vous remercier?; **to return sb's greeting** rendre un salut à qn; **they returned our visit the following year** ils sont venus nous voir à leur tour l'année suivante
(**d**) *(reciprocate → affection)* rendre; **she did not return his love** l'amour qu'il éprouvait pour elle n'était pas partagé
(**e**) *Sport (in tennis → serve)* renvoyer; **to return (the) service** renvoyer le service
(**f**) *Br (elect)* élire; **she was returned as member for Tottenham** elle a été élue député de Tottenham
(**g**) *(reply)* répondre
(**h**) *Law (pronounce → verdict)* rendre, prononcer; **the jury returned a verdict of guilty/not guilty** le jury a déclaré l'accusé coupable/non coupable
(**i**) *Fin (yield → profit, interest)* rapporter
(**j**) *Cards (in bridge)* rejouer; **East returns clubs for dummy's ace** Est rejoue pique pour l'as du mort
3 *vi (go back)* retourner; *(come back)* revenir; *(reappear → fever, pain, good weather, fears)* revenir, réapparaître; **they've returned to Australia** *(speaker is in Australia)* ils sont revenus en Australie; *(speaker is elsewhere)* ils sont retournés *ou* repartis en Australie; **as soon as she returns** dès son retour; **to return home** rentrer (à la maison *ou* chez soi); **let's return to your question** revenons à votre question; **when I returned to consciousness** quand j'ai repris connaissance, quand je suis revenu à moi; **to return to work** reprendre le travail; **she returned to her reading** elle reprit sa lecture; **he soon returned to his old ways** il est vite retombé dans *ou* il a vite repris ses anciennes habitudes; **the situation should return to normal next week** la situation devrait redevenir normale la semaine prochaine; **her colour returned** elle a repris des couleurs; *Naut* **to return to port** rentrer au port; **to return from the dead** ressusciter d'entre les morts
4 returns *npl* (**a**) *(results)* résultats *mpl*; *(statistics)* statistiques *fpl*, chiffres *mpl*; **the election returns** les résultats *mpl* des élections; **first returns indicate a swing to the left** les premiers résultats du scrutin indiquent un glissement à gauche
(**b**) *Fin (profit)* bénéfices *mpl*
(**c**) *(birthday greetings)* **many happy returns (of the day)!** bon *ou* joyeux anniversaire!
5 in return *adv* en retour, en échange; **in return, he's letting me use his car** en retour *ou* en échange, il me laisse utiliser sa voiture; **if you will do sth in return** si vous voulez bien faire qch en retour; **you must expect the same treatment in return** il faut vous attendre à la pareille
6 in return for *prep* en échange de; **in return for which...** moyennant quoi...; **in return for this service...** en récompense de ce service...
►► ***return address*** adresse *f* de l'expéditeur; *Br* ***return air fare*** tarif *m* aérien aller-retour; *Acct* ***returns book*** journal *m* des rendus; ***return cargo*** cargaison *f* de retour; ***returned cheque*** chèque *m* retourné; *Br* ***return fare*** tarif *m* aller (et) retour; ***return flight*** vol *m* de retour; ***return freight*** fret *m* de retour; ***return journey*** (voyage *m* du) retour *m*; *Comput* ***return key*** touche *f* retour; *Acct* ***returns ledger*** journal *m* des rendus; *Sport* ***return match*** match *m* retour; *Br* ***return ticket*** (billet *m* d')aller (et) retour *m*

'The Return of the Native' *Hardy* 'Le Retour au pays natal'

returnable [rɪˈtɜːnəbəl] *adj* (**a**) *(container, bottle)* consigné; *(purchase, ticket)* qui peut être rendu; **sale items are not returnable** *(sign)* les articles en solde ne sont ni échangés ni repris (**b**) *(document)* à retourner; **returnable by 1 July** à renvoyer avant le 1er juillet
►► *Com* ***returnable packaging*** emballage *m* consigné

returner [rɪˈtɜːnə(r)] *n* (**a**) *(person returning to work)* = personne réintégrant la vie professionnelle après une période d'inactivité volontaire (**b**) *(in tennis)* **she's a very good returner (of the ball)** ses retours de service sont excellents

returning officer [rɪˈtɜːnɪŋ-] *n* président(e) *m,f* du bureau de vote

return-to-base warranty *n* garantie *f* retour atelier

retuse [rɪˈtjuːs] *adj Bot* rétus

retype [ˌriːˈtaɪp] *vt (document, text)* retaper

reuben [ˈruːbɪn] *n Am Culin* = sandwich chaud au pastrami, corned beef, fromage et choucroute

reunification [ˈriːˌjuːnɪfɪˈkeɪʃən] *n* réunification *f*

reunify [ˌriːˈjuːnɪfaɪ] *(pt & pp* **reunified***)* *vt* réunifier

Réunion [ˌriːˈjuːnjən] *n (island)* (l'île *f* de) la Réunion; **in Réunion** à la Réunion
►► ***Réunion Island*** l'île *f* de la Réunion

reunion [ˌriːˈjuːnjən] *n* réunion *f*; **a family reunion** une réunion familiale; **reunion celebration** célébration *f* de retrouvailles; **reunion dinner** dîner *m* de retrouvailles

reunite [ˌriːjuːˈnaɪt] **1** *vt* réunir; **when the hostages were reunited with their families** quand les otages ont retrouvé leur famille; **he reunited the band for one last gig** il a reformé le groupe pour un ultime concert
2 *vi* se réunir; *(band)* se reformer

re-up [ˌriː-] *vi Am Fam (re-enlist)* rempiler

reupholster [ˌriːʌpˈhəʊlstə(r)] *vt (furniture)* refaire

reusable [riːˈjuːzəbəl] *adj* réutilisable, recyclable

re-use 1 *vt* [ˌriːˈjuːz] réutiliser, remployer, recycler
2 *n* [ˌriːˈjuːs] réutilisation *f*, remploi *m*, recyclage *m*

Rev. *(written abbr* **Reverend***)* révérend *m*

rev [rev] *(pt & pp* **revved,** *cont* **revving***)* *Fam* **1** *n Aut (abbr* **revolution***)* tour □ *m*; **3,000 revs per minute** 3000 tours par minute
2 *vt (engine)* faire monter le régime de □
3 *vi (driver)* appuyer sur l'accélérateur □; *(engine)* monter en régime □
►► ***rev counter*** compte-tours □ *m inv*

►**rev up 1** *vt sep (engine)* faire monter le régime de

2 *vi (driver)* appuyer sur l'accélérateur; *(engine)* monter en régime

revaccinate [ˌriːˈvæksɪneɪt] *vt* revacciner

revalidate [rɪˈvælɪdeɪt] *vt* revalider

▸▸ ***revalidate sticker*** autocollant *m* de revalidation

revaluate [ˌriːˈvæljʊeɪt] *vt Am (currency)* réévaluer; *(property)* réévaluer, estimer à nouveau la valeur de

revaluation [ˌriːvæljʊˈeɪʃən] *n (of currency, property)* réévaluation *f*

revalue [ˌriːˈvæljuː] *vt (currency)* réévaluer; *(property)* réévaluer, estimer à nouveau la valeur de

revamp *Fam* **1** *n* [ˈriːvæmp] *(of method, play)* remaniement❑ *m*; *(of policy)* modification❑ *f*, remaniement❑ *m*; *(of company)* réorganisation❑ *f*, restructuration❑ *f*; *(of house, furniture, room)* retapage *m*

2 *vt* [ˌriːˈvæmp] *(method, play)* remanier❑; *(policy)* modifier❑, remanier❑; *(company)* réorganiser❑, restructurer❑; *(house, furniture)* retaper; *(room)* donner un coup de frais à

revanchism [rɪˈvæntʃɪzəm] *n* revanchisme *m*

revanchist [rɪˈvæntʃɪst] **1** *adj* revanchiste

2 *n* revanchiste *mf*

Revd *(written abbr* **reverend***)* révérend *m*

reveal [rɪˈviːl] *vt* (**a**) *(disclose, divulge)* révéler; **the press revealed he had accepted bribes** la presse révéla qu'il avait accepté des pots-de-vin; **to reveal a secret** révéler *ou* divulguer un secret; **the police do not want to reveal the identity of the victim** la police ne veut pas révéler l'identité de la victime

(**b**) *(show)* révéler, découvrir, laisser voir; **she removed the veil to reveal her face** elle enleva son voile pour découvrir son visage; **he tried hard not to reveal his true feelings** il s'efforça de ne pas révéler ses vrais sentiments; **the undertaking revealed itself to be impossible** l'entreprise s'est révélée impossible; **a medical examination revealed two cracked ribs** un examen médical a permis de découvrir deux côtes fêlées

revealing [rɪˈviːlɪŋ] *adj* (**a**) *(experience, action, comment)* révélateur (**b**) *(dress)* décolleté, qui ne cache rien; *(neckline)* décolleté

revealingly [rɪˈviːlɪŋlɪ] *adv* (**a**) *(significantly)* **revealingly, not one of them speaks a foreign language** il est révélateur qu'aucun d'entre eux ne parle une langue étrangère (**b**) *(exposing the body)* **a revealingly short dress** une robe courte qui laisse tout voir

reveille [*Br* rɪˈvælɪ, *Am* ˈrevəlɪ] *n Mil* réveil *m*; **sound the reveille!** sonnez le réveil!

revel [ˈrevəl] *(Br pt & pp* **revelled,** *cont* **revelling,** *Am pt & pp* **reveled,** *cont* **reveling)** **1** *vi* (**a**) *(bask, wallow)* se délecter; **to revel in sth/in doing sth** se délecter de *ou* à qch/à faire qch; **to revel in one's freedom** savourer pleinement sa liberté (**b**) *(make merry)* s'amuser

2 revels *npl* festivités *fpl*

revelation [ˌrevəˈleɪʃən] *n* révélation *f*; **divine revelation** révélation *f* divine; **her talent was a revelation to me** son talent a été une révélation pour moi; *Bible* **the Revelation (of Saint John the Divine), Revelations** l'Apocalypse *f* (de saint Jean l'Évangéliste)

revelatory [ˌrevəˈleɪtərɪ] *adj* révélateur

reveller, *Am* **reveler** [ˈrevələ(r)] *n* fêtard(e) *m,f*, noceur(euse) *m,f*; **there were no taxis left for the late-night revellers** il n'y avait plus de taxis pour les oiseaux de nuit

revelry [ˈrevəlrɪ] *(pl* **revelries***)* *n* festivités *fpl*, réjouissances *fpl*; **they could hear the sound of revelry in the streets** ils pouvaient entendre le bruit des festivités dans les rues; **a night of revelry** *or* **revelries** une nuit de réjouissances

revenge [rɪˈvendʒ] **1** *n* (**a**) *(vengeance)* vengeance *f*, revanche *f*; **revenge is sweet** c'est bon de se venger; **revenge is a dish best eaten cold** la vengeance est un plat qui se mange froid; **I'll get** *or* **I'll take my revenge on him for this!** il va me le payer!; **she did it out of revenge** elle l'a fait pour se venger *ou* par vengeance

(**b**) *Sport* revanche *f*; **Liverpool got their revenge for last week's defeat** Liverpool a pris la revanche de sa défaite de la semaine dernière

2 *vt* venger; **to revenge oneself, to be revenged (on/for)** se venger (sur/de); **how can I revenge myself on them for this insult?** comment leur faire payer cette insulte?

revengeful [rɪˈvendʒfʊl] *adj* vengeur, vindicatif

revengefully [rɪˈvendʒfʊlɪ] *adv* vindicativement, par vengeance; *(say)* d'un ton vengeur

revenger [rɪˈvendʒə(r)] *n* vengeur(eresse) *m,f*

'The Revenger's Tragedy' *Tourneur* 'La Tragédie du vengeur'

revenue [ˈrevənjuː] **1** *n* revenu *m*; *(from land, property)* revenu *m*, rentes *fpl*; *(from sales)* recettes *fpl*; **advertising revenue** recettes *fpl* de publicité; **oil revenue** revenu *m* pétrolier; **state revenue** *or* **revenues** les recettes *fpl* publiques *ou* de l'État

2 *comp (department, official)* du fisc

3 Revenue *n Br Fam Fin* **the Revenue** ≃ le fisc❑

▸▸ *Fin* ***revenue account*** *(from land, property)* compte *m* de recettes; *(profit and loss account)* compte *m* d'exploitation; *Am Fin* ***revenue bond*** obligation *f* à intérêt conditionnel; *Fin* ***revenue centre*** centre *m* de revenus *ou* de profit; ***revenue cutter*** vedette *f* des garde-côtes; ***revenue expenditure*** dépenses *fpl* de fonctionnement; ***revenue man*** agent *m* du fisc; ***revenue stamp*** timbre *m* fiscal; ***revenue tariff*** tarif *m* douanier fiscal

reverb [ˈriːvɜːb] *n Fam Mus* réverbération❑ *f*; *(unit)* réverbérateur❑ *m*

▸▸ ***reverb unit*** réverbérateur❑ *m*

reverberate [rɪˈvɜːbəreɪt] **1** *vi* (**a**) *(sound)* résonner, retentir; **the building reverberated with their cries** l'immeuble retentissait de leurs cris (**b**) *(light)* se réverbérer (**c**) *Fig (spread)* retentir; **the scandal reverberated through the country** ce scandale a secoué tout le pays

2 *vt* (**a**) *(sound)* renvoyer, répercuter (**b**) *(light)* réverbérer

reverberation [rɪˌvɜːbəˈreɪʃən] *n* (**a**) *(of sound, light)* réverbération *f* (**b**) *Fig (repercussion)* retentissement *m*, répercussion *f*; **the crisis had reverberations in neighbouring countries** la crise a eu des répercussions dans les pays voisins

reverberator [rɪˈvɜːbəreɪtə(r)] *n* réflecteur *m*

revere [rɪˈvɪə(r)] *vt* révérer, vénérer; **she was a much revered figure** c'était une personnalité très respectée

reverence [ˈrevərəns] **1** *n* (**a**) *(respect)* révérence *f*, vénération *f*; **they hold her in reverence** ils la révèrent *ou* vénèrent (**b**) *(term of address)* **Your Reverence** mon révérend (père); **His Reverence the Archbishop** Son Excellence l'archevêque

2 *vt* révérer, vénérer

reverend [ˈrevərənd] **1** *adj* (**a**) *Rel* **a reverend gentleman** un révérend père; **the Reverend Paul James** le révérend Paul James; *Br* **the Right Reverend James Brown** *(bishop → Protestant)* le très révérend James Brown; *(→ Catholic)* monseigneur Brown; **Very Reverend** *(dean)* très révérend; **Most Reverend** *(archbishop)* révérendissime

(**b**) *(gen → respected)* vénérable, révéré

2 *n (Protestant)* pasteur *m*; *(Catholic)* curé *m*; **yes, reverend** *(Protestant)* oui, Monsieur le pasteur; *(Catholic)* oui, Monsieur le curé

▸▸ ***Reverend Mother*** révérende mère *f*

reverent [ˈrevərənt] *adj* respectueux, *Literary* révérencieux

reverential [ˌrevəˈrenʃəl] *adj* respectueux, *Literary* révérencieux

reverentially [ˌrevəˈrenʃəlɪ] *adv* avec révérence

reverently [ˈrevərəntlɪ] *adv* avec révérence

reverie [ˈrevərɪ] *n (gen) & Mus* rêverie *f*

revers [rɪˈvɪə(r)] *(pl* **inv** [-ˈvɪəz]*)* *n* revers *m*

reversal [rɪˈvɜːsəl] *n* (**a**) *(change → of situation)* retournement *m*; *(→ of opinion)* revirement *m*; *(→ of order, roles)* interversion *f*, inversion *f*; *(→ of policy)* changement *m* (**b**) *(setback)* revers *m*; **reversal of fortune** revers *m* de fortune; **the patient has suffered a reversal** le malade a fait une rechute (**c**) *Law (annulment)* annulation *f* (**d**) *Phot* inversion *f*

▸▸ ***reversal film*** film *m* inversible

REVERSE [rɪˈvɜːs]

marche arrière	▸ 1 (a)
contraire	▸ 1 (b)
envers	▸ 1 (c)
revers	▸ 1 (c), (d)
échec	▸ 1 (d)
inverse	▸ 2
renverser	▸ 3 (a)
retourner	▸ 3 (a), (b)
inverser	▸ 3 (a)
mettre en/faire marche arrière	▸ 3 (d)

1 *n* (**a**) *Aut* marche *f* arrière; **in reverse** en marche arrière; **he put the bus into reverse** le conducteur de l'autobus passa en marche arrière; *Fig* **the company's fortunes are going into reverse** l'entreprise connaît actuellement un revers de fortune

(**b**) *(contrary)* contraire *m*, inverse *m*, opposé *m*; **unfortunately, the reverse is true** malheureusement, c'est le contraire qui est vrai; **did you enjoy it? – quite the reverse** cela vous a-t-il plu? – pas du tout; **she is the reverse of shy** elle est tout sauf timide; **try to do the same thing in reverse** essayez de faire la même chose dans l'ordre inverse

(**c**) *(other side → of cloth, leaf)* envers *m*; *(→ of sheet of paper)* verso *m*; *(→ of coin, medal)* revers *m*

(**d**) *(setback)* revers *m*, échec *m*; *(defeat)* échec *m*, défaite *f*; **to suffer a reverse** essuyer un revers de fortune; *(be defeated)* essuyer un échec; **his condition has suffered a reverse** il a rechuté

(**e**) *Typ* noir *m* au blanc; **in reverse** inversé (en noir au blanc)

2 *adj (opposite, contrary)* inverse, contraire, opposé; *(turned around)* inversé; **we are now experiencing the reverse trend** actuellement, c'est l'inverse qui se produit; **in reverse order** dans l'ordre inverse; **in the reverse direction** en sens inverse; **the reverse side** *(of cloth, leaf)* l'envers; *(of sheet of paper)* le verso; *(of coin, medal)* le revers

3 *vt* (**a**) *(change → process, trend)* renverser; *(→ situation)* retourner; *(→ order, roles, decline)* inverser; **this could reverse the effects of all our policies** ceci pourrait annuler les effets de toute notre politique; **the unions have reversed their policy** les syndicats ont fait volte-face; **I had to reverse my opinion of him** j'ai dû réviser complètement l'opinion que j'avais de lui; **it reversed all our plans** cela a bouleversé tous nos projets; *Mil* **to reverse arms** renverser les fusils; *Tech* **to reverse steam** renverser la vapeur

(**b**) *(turn around → garment)* retourner; *(→ photo)* inverser

(**c**) *(annul → decision)* annuler; *Law* casser, annuler

(**d**) *(cause to go backwards → car)* mettre en marche arrière; *(→ machine)* renverser la marche de; **this lever reverses the belt** ce levier permet d'inverser la marche de la courroie; **she reversed the car up the street/out of the garage** elle remonta la rue/elle sortit du garage en marche arrière; **he reversed the truck into a lamppost** en faisant marche arrière avec le camion, il est rentré dans un réverbère

(**e**) *Br Tel* **to reverse the charges** appeler en PCV, faire un appel en PCV; **she always reverses the charges when she phones her parents** elle appelle toujours ses parents en PCV

(**f**) *Acct (entry)* contre-passer

(**g**) *Typ* **reversed out** inversé (en noir au blanc)

4 *vi Aut (car, driver)* faire marche arrière; **she reversed up the street** elle remonta la rue en marche arrière; **the driver in front reversed into me** la voiture qui était devant moi m'est rentrée dedans en marche arrière

▸▸ *TV & Cin* ***reverse cut*** contrechamp *m*; ***reverse discrimination*** = discrimination à l'encontre d'un groupe normalement privilégié; ***reverse engineering*** ingénierie *f* inverse; *Acct* ***reverse entry*** écriture *f* inverse; *Aut* ***reverse gear*** marche *f* arrière; *Comput* ***reverse mode*** inversion *f* vidéo; *St Exch* ***reverse repo operation*** opération *f* de mise en pension; *Comput* **reverse slash** barre *f* oblique inversée; *Comput* **reverse sort** tri *m* en ordre décroissant; *Fin* **reverse takeover** contre-OPA *f*; *Aviat* **reverse thrust** poussée *f* inversée; *Biol* **reverse transcriptase** transcriptase *f* inverse; *Aut* **reverse turn** virage *m* en marche arrière; **to do** *or* **to make a reverse turn** faire un virage en marche arrière; **reverse video** vidéo *f* inverse

▸**reverse out** *vt sep Typ* inverser

---

reverse-charge call *n Br* communication *f* en PCV, *Can* appel *m* à frais virés

reverser [rɪ'vɜːsə(r)] *n Tech* inverseur *m*; **thrust reverser** inverseur *m* de poussée

reversi [rɪ'vɜːsɪ] *n* reversi *m* (sur échiquier)

reversibility [rɪˌvɜːsə'bɪlɪtɪ] *n* réversibilité *f*

reversible [rɪ'vɜːsəbəl] *adj (garment, process)* réversible; *(decision, decree, judgement, sentence)* révocable; *Phot (film)* inversible

▸▸ *Chem* **reversible reaction** réaction *f* réversible

reversing light [rɪ'vɜːsɪŋ-] *n Br* feu *m* de recul

reversion [rɪ'vɜːʃən] *n* (**a**) *(to former condition, practice)* retour *m*; **a reversion to anarchy** un retour à l'anarchie (**b**) *Law* réversion *f*; **right of reversion** réversion *f*; **estate in reversion** bien *m* grevé d'une réversion (**c**) *Biol* réversion *f*; **reversion to type** retour *m* au type primitif; *Fig* **this was a not unexpected reversion to type** comme on s'y attendait, le naturel a repris le dessus

reversionary [rɪ'vɜːʃənərɪ] *adj* (**a**) *Law (right)* de réversion, réversible (**b**) *Biol (characteristic, organ)* atavique

▸▸ *Ins* **reversionary annuity** rente *f* réversible; *Fin* **reversionary bonus** prime *f* d'intéressement; *Fin* **reversionary owner** nu-propriétaire *m*; *Fin* **reversionary ownership** nue-propriété *f*

revert [rɪ'vɜːt] *vi* (**a**) *(gen)* retourner, revenir; **they reverted to barbarism** ils ont à nouveau sombré dans la barbarie; **he soon reverted to his old ways** il est vite retombé dans *ou* il a vite repris ses anciennes habitudes; **to revert to childhood** retomber en enfance; **the field has reverted to a wild meadow** le champ est retourné à l'état de prairie

(**b**) *Law* **the property reverts to the spouse** les biens reviennent à l'époux

(**c**) *Biol* **to revert to type** revenir *ou* retourner au type primitif; *Fig* **he soon reverted to type and started drinking again** le naturel a vite repris le dessus et il s'est remis à boire

(**d**) *Comput (undo)* défaire; **to revert to the previous settings** rétablir les paramètres précédents

revet [rɪ'vet] *(pt & pp* **revetted***) vt Constr* revêtir, garnir d'un revêtement

revetment [rɪ'vetmənt] *n* revêtement *m*

review [rɪ'vjuː] **1** *n* (**a**) *(critical article)* critique *f*; **the play got good/bad reviews** la pièce a eu de bonnes/de mauvaises critiques; **he gave it a good review** il en a fait une bonne critique

(**b**) *(magazine)* revue *f*; *(radio or TV programme)* magazine *m*

(**c**) *(assessment → of situation, conditions)* étude *f*, examen *m*, bilan *m*; **the annual review of expenditure** le bilan annuel des dépenses; **she first gave us a brief review of the situation** elle nous a d'abord présenté un court bilan de la situation; **pollution controls are under review** on est en train de réexaminer la réglementation en matière de pollution; **a review of the year** une rétrospective des événements de l'année

(**d**) *(reassessment → of salary, prices, case)* révision *f*; **all our prices are subject to review** tous nos prix sont susceptibles d'être révisés; **my salary comes** *or* **is up for review next month** mon salaire doit être révisé le mois prochain; *Law* **he asked for a review of his case** il a demandé la révision de son procès

(**e**) *Mil (inspection)* revue *f*; **to hold a review** passer une revue; **to pass troops in review** passer des troupes en revue

(**f**) *Am Sch & Univ (revision)* révision *f*

(**g**) *Theat* revue *f*

2 *vt* (**a**) *(write critical article on)* faire la critique de; **she reviews books for an Australian paper** elle est critique littéraire pour un journal australien

(**b**) *(assess)* examiner, étudier, faire le bilan de; *(reassess)* réviser, revoir; *Law (case)* réviser; **they should review their security arrangements** ils devraient revoir leurs dispositifs de sécurité; **to review a decision** reconsidérer une décision

(**c**) *(go back over, look back on)* passer en revue; **we shall be reviewing the events of the past year** nous passerons en revue les événements qui se sont produits au cours de l'année passée

(**d**) *Mil (troops)* passer en revue

(**e**) *(revise)* réviser; **she quickly reviewed her notes before the speech** elle jeta un dernier coup d'œil sur ses notes avant le discours; *Am* **he's reviewing his French** il révise son français

2 *vi* (**a**) *(write reviews)* **he reviews for the Sunday Times** il rédige des critiques pour le Sunday Times

(**b**) *Am (revise for exam, test)* réviser, faire des révisions

▸▸ **review board** commission *f* d'étude; **review copy** exemplaire *m* de service de presse; *TV* **review screen** écran *m* de vision

reviewer [rɪ'vjuːə(r)] *n (of film, play etc)* critique *m*; **book reviewer** critique *m* littéraire

revile [rɪ'vaɪl] *vt* vilipender, injurier; **our much reviled education system** notre système scolaire tellement décrié *ou* dont on dit tant de mal

revilement [rɪ'vaɪlmənt] *n (insults)* injures *fpl*; *(speech)* discours *m* injurieux

revise [rɪ'vaɪz] **1** *vt* (**a**) *(alter → policy, belief, offer, price)* réviser; **to revise one's opinion of sb** changer d'opinion à l'égard de qn

(**b**) *(read through → text, manuscript)* revoir, corriger

(**c**) *(update)* mettre à jour, corriger; **our dictionaries are revised regularly** nos dictionnaires sont régulièrement mis à jour

(**d**) *Br Sch & Univ* réviser; **have you revised your geography?** as-tu révisé ta géographie?

2 *vi Br Sch & Univ* réviser; **she's revising for her end-of-year exams** elle révise pour ses examens de fin d'année

3 *n Typ* deuxième épreuve *f*

revised [rɪ'vaɪzd] *adj* (**a**) *(figures, estimate)* révisé (**b**) *(edition)* revu et corrigé

▸▸ **Revised Standard Version** = traduction américaine de la Bible établie en 1952; **Revised Version** = traduction anglaise de la Bible faite en 1885

reviser [rɪ'vaɪzə(r)] *n (gen)* réviseur(euse) *m,f*; *Typ* correcteur(trice) *m,f*

revision [rɪ'vɪʒən] *n* (**a**) *(alteration etc)* révision *f*; **the book has undergone several revisions** ce livre a été révisé *ou* remanié plusieurs fois (**b**) *Br Sch & Univ* révision *f*; **to do some revision** faire des révisions

revisional [rɪ'vɪʒənəl], **revisionary** [rɪ'vɪʒənərɪ] *adj* de révision

revisionism [rɪ'vɪʒənɪzəm] *n* révisionnisme *m*

revisionist [rɪ'vɪʒənɪst] **1** *adj* révisionniste

2 *n* révisionniste *mf*

revisit [ˌriː'vɪzɪt] *vt (place)* revisiter; *(person)* retourner voir; *Fig* **Dickens revisited** Dickens revisité

'Brideshead Revisited' *Waugh, Sturridge & Lindsay-Hogg* 'Le Retour au château'

---

revitalize, -ise [ˌriː'vaɪtəlaɪz] *vt (person)* revigorer; *(economy)* relancer; *(industry, arts, trade unionism)* donner un nouvel essor à

revival [rɪ'vaɪvəl] *n* (**a**) *(resurgence)* renouveau *m*, renaissance *f*; **a revival of interest in Latin poets** un regain d'intérêt pour les poètes latins; **a religious revival** un renouveau de la religion

(**b**) *(bringing back → of custom, language)* rétablissement *m*; *(→ of fashion)* réapparition *f*, renouveau *m*; **they would like to see a revival of Victorian values** ils souhaitent le retour aux valeurs de l'époque victorienne

(**c**) *(of play, TV series)* reprise *f*

(**d**) *(recovery → from a faint)* reprise *f* de connaissance; *(→ from illness)* récupération *f*; *(resuscitation)* réanimation *f*; **all attempts at revival failed** toutes les tentatives de réanimation ont échoué

▸▸ *Am* **revival tent** = chapiteau sous lequel se tiennent des réunions religieuses

revivalism [rɪ'vaɪvəlɪzəm] *n* (**a**) *Rel* revivalisme *m* (**b**) *(of past)* passéisme *m*

revivalist [rɪ'vaɪvəlɪst] **1** *n* (**a**) *Rel* revivaliste *mf*; **Hindu revivalists** des revivalistes *mpl* hindous (**b**) *(of past)* traditionaliste *mf*

2 *adj Rel* revivaliste; **a revivalist meeting** une réunion revivaliste

revive [rɪ'vaɪv] **1** *vi* (**a**) *(regain consciousness)* reprendre connaissance, revenir à soi; *(regain strength or form)* récupérer

(**b**) *(flourish again → business, economy)* reprendre; *(→ movement, group)* renaître, ressusciter; *(→ custom, expression)* réapparaître; **their interest revived when the clowns came on** ils ont recommencé à trouver le spectacle intéressant quand les clowns sont entrés en scène; **interest in her work is beginning to revive** on assiste à un renouveau *ou* un regain d'intérêt pour son œuvre; **hopes have revived of finding the miners alive** l'espoir renaît de trouver les mineurs vivants

2 *vt* (**a**) *(restore to consciousness)* ranimer; *Med* réanimer; *(restore strength to)* remonter; **this will revive you!** *(drink)* voilà qui te remontera!

(**b**) *(make flourish again → discussion, faith etc)* ranimer, raviver; *(→ business, economy)* relancer, faire redémarrer; *(→ interest, hope etc)* raviver, faire renaître; **a plan to revive the city centre** un projet destiné à dynamiser le centre-ville; **revived interest in the art of this period** un renouveau *ou* un regain d'intérêt pour l'art de cette époque; **this role could revive his flagging career** ce rôle pourrait faire redémarrer sa carrière sur le déclin

(**c**) *(bring back → law)* remettre en vigueur; *(→ fashion)* relancer; *(→ style, look)* remettre en vogue; *(→ custom, language, movement)* raviver, ressusciter; **prewar fashions have been revived** on est revenu à la mode de l'avant-guerre

(**d**) *(play, TV series)* reprendre

revivification ['riːˌvɪvɪfɪ'keɪʃən] *n* revivification *f*

revivify [ˌriː'vɪvɪfaɪ] *(pt & pp* **revivified***) vt* revivifier

revocability [rɪˌvəʊkə'bɪlɪtɪ] *n Law* révocabilité *f*

revocable [rɪ'vəʊkəbəl] *adj Law (contract, law, will)* révocable; *(decision)* sur laquelle on peut revenir; *(order)* que l'on peut annuler

▸▸ **revocable letter of credit** crédit *m* documentaire révocable

revocation [ˌrevə'keɪʃən] *n Law (of decision)* annulation *f*; *(of measure, law)* abrogation *f*, annulation *f*, révocation *f*; *(of will)* révocation *f*, annulation *f*; *(of title, diploma, permit)* retrait *m*

re-voice [ˌriː-] *vt TV & Cin* doubler

revoke [rɪ'vəʊk] *vt Law (decision)* annuler; *(measure, law)* abroger, annuler, révoquer; *(will)* révoquer, annuler; *(title, diploma, permit)* retirer

revolt [rɪ'vəʊlt] **1** *vi (rise up)* se révolter, se rebeller, se soulever; **they revolted against the tyrant** ils se soulevèrent contre le tyran

2 *vt* dégoûter; **she is revolted by the idea** l'idée la dégoûte *ou* la révolte; **the sight of food revolts me at the moment** la vue de la nourriture m'écœure *ou* me dégoûte en ce moment

3 *n* (**a**) *(uprising)* révolte *f*, rébellion *f*; **the peasants rose up in revolt** les paysans se sont révoltés *ou* soulevés; **they are in revolt against the system** ils se rebellent contre le système

(**b**) *(disgust)* dégoût *m*; *(indignation)* indignation *f*

revolting [rɪ'vəʊltɪŋ] *adj* (**a**) *(disgusting → story, scene)* dégoûtant; *(→ person, act)* ignoble; *(→ food, mess)* écœurant, immonde; *(→ taste, smell)* infect, écœurant; **that sounds revolting!** ça semble répugnant (**b**) *Fam (nasty)* affreux ▫

revoltingly [rɪ'vəʊltɪŋlɪ] *adv* (**a**) *(disgustingly)* de façon dégoûtante; **he's revoltingly ugly/dirty** il est d'une laideur/d'une saleté repoussante (**b**) *Fam (as intensifier)* **she's so revoltingly clever!** ça m'écœure qu'on puisse être aussi intelligent!

revolution [ˌrevə'luːʃən] *n* (**a**) *Pol & Fig* révolution *f*; **a revolution in computer technology** une révolution dans le domaine de l'informatique (**b**) *(turn → of wheel)* révolution *f*, tour *m*; *(→ of record, turntable, propeller)* tour *m*; *(→ of planet)* révolution *f*; *Tech* **100 revolutions per minute** 100 tours *ou* révolutions par minute (**c**) *(turning)* révolution *f*

revolutionary [ˌrevəˈluːʃənərɪ] (*pl* **revolutionaries**) **1** *adj* révolutionnaire
2 *n* révolutionnaire *mf*
▸▸ ***Revolutionary Calendar*** calendrier *m* républicain

revolutionism [ˌrevəˈluːʃənɪzəm] *n* révolutionnarisme *m*

revolutionist [ˌrevəˈluːʃənɪst] = **revolutionary**

revolutionize, -ise [ˌrevəˈluːʃənaɪz] *vt* (**a**) *(change radically)* révolutionner (**b**) *Pol (country)* faire une révolution dans; *(people)* insuffler des idées révolutionnaires à

revolve [rɪˈvɒlv] **1** *vi* (**a**) *(rotate)* tourner; **the moon revolves around** *or* **round the earth** la Lune tourne autour de la Terre; **couples revolved slowly on the dance floor** des couples évoluaient *ou* tournaient lentement sur la piste de danse
(**b**) *(centre, focus)* tourner; **their conversation revolved around** *or* **round two main points** leur conversation tournait autour de deux points principaux; **everything revolves around your decision** tout dépend de votre décision; **his whole life revolves around his work** sa vie tout entière est centrée *ou* axée sur son travail
(**c**) *(recur)* revenir; **the seasons revolve** les saisons se succèdent; **ideas revolved in her mind** elle tournait et retournait des idées dans sa tête
2 *vt* (**a**) *(rotate)* faire tourner
(**b**) *Formal (ponder)* considérer, ruminer; **he revolved the arguments in his mind** il passait mentalement les différents arguments en revue

revolver [rɪˈvɒlvə(r)] *n* revolver *m*
▸▸ *Am Fin* ***revolver credit*** crédit *m* renouvelable, crédit *m* revolving

revolving [rɪˈvɒlvɪŋ] *adj (gen)* tournant; *(chair)* pivotant; *Tech* rotatif; *Astron* en rotation
▸▸ ***revolving credit*** crédit *m* renouvelable, crédit *m* revolving; ***revolving door*** tambour *m (porte)*; *Am Fig* = le va-et-vient de fonctionnaires haut-placés entre les services publics et le secteur privé; *Fin* ***revolving fund*** fonds *m* de roulement; *Fin* ***revolving letter of credit*** crédit *m* documentaire renouvelable, crédit *m* revolving; ***revolving light*** *(on ambulance, police car)* gyrophare *m*; ***revolving stand*** *(to display goods)* tourniquet *m*

revue [rɪˈvjuː] *n Theat* revue *f*

revulsion [rɪˈvʌlʃən] *n* (**a**) *(disgust)* répulsion *f*, dégoût *m*; **she turned away in revulsion** elle s'est détournée, dégoûtée (**b**) *(recoiling)* (mouvement *m* de) recul *m* (**c**) *Med* révulsion *f*

reward [rɪˈwɔːd] **1** *n* récompense *f*; **they're offering a $500 reward** ils offrent 500 dollars de récompense *ou* une récompense de 500 dollars; **as a reward for his efforts** en récompense de ses efforts; **I do everything for him, and what do I get in reward?** je fais tout pour lui, et tu vois comment il me remercie?; **she gave it to me as a reward for helping her** elle me l'a donnée pour me remercier de l'avoir aidée
2 *vt* récompenser; **he was handsomely rewarded with a cheque for £1,000** on l'a généreusement récompensé par un chèque de 1000 livres; **our patience has finally been rewarded** notre patience est enfin récompensée; **I'm sure the book will reward your attention** je suis sûr que la lecture de ce livre vous sera profitable; **his alibi might reward investigation** ça vaut peut-être la peine d'enquêter sur son alibi

rewarding [rɪˈwɔːdɪŋ] *adj (job, career)* gratifiant; *(experience, conference)* enrichissant; **financially rewarding** rémunérateur, lucratif; **a rewarding book** un livre qui vaut la peine d'être lu

rewind (*pt & pp* **rewound** [-ˈwaʊnd]) **1** *vt* [ˌriːˈwaɪnd] rembobiner
2 *vi* [ˌriːˈwaɪnd] se rembobiner
3 *n* [ˈriːwaɪnd] rembobinage *m*; **it has automatic rewind** ça se rembobine automatiquement
▸▸ ***rewind button*** bouton *m* de rembobinage

rewire [ˌriːˈwaɪə(r)] *vt (house)* refaire l'électricité dans; *(machine)* refaire les circuits électriques de; **we had to get the place rewired** nous avons dû faire refaire l'électricité

reword [ˌriːˈwɜːd] *vt* reformuler; **let me reword that** je vais essayer de m'exprimer autrement

rework [ˌriːˈwɜːk] *vt* (**a**) *(speech, text)* retravailler; **his last novel reworks the same theme** son dernier roman reprend le même thème (**b**) *Ind* retraiter

reworking [ˌriːˈwɜːkɪŋ] *n* reprise *f*; **the movie is a reworking of the "doppelgänger" theme** le film reprend le thème du double

rewound [ˌriːˈwaʊnd] *pt & pp of* **rewind**

rewrap [ˌriːˈræp] (*pt & pp* **rewrapped**, *cont* **rewrapping**) *vt* remballer

rewritable [ˌriːˈraɪtəbəl] *adj Comput* réinscriptible

rewrite (*pt* **rewrote** [-ˈrəʊt], *pp* **rewritten** [-ˈrɪtən]) **1** *vt* [ˌriːˈraɪt] récrire, réécrire; *(for publication)* récrire, rewriter; *Fig* **to rewrite history** réécrire l'histoire
2 *n* [ˈriːraɪt] (**a**) *(act)* réécriture *f*, rewriting *m*; **can you do a rewrite of this?** pouvez-vous me récrire *ou* rewriter ça?
(**b**) *(text)* nouvelle version *f*; **it's a modern rewrite of 'Romeo and Juliet'** c'est une version moderne de 'Roméo et Juliette'
▸▸ ***rewrite rule*** règle *f* de réécriture

rewriter [ˌriːˈraɪtə(r)] *n Journ* réviseur *m*, rewriter *m*

rewriting [ˌriːˈraɪtɪŋ] *n Journ* récriture *f*, rewriting *m*

rewritten [ˌriːˈrɪtən] *pp of* **rewrite**

rewrote [ˌriːˈrəʊt] *pt of* **rewrite**

REX [ˌɑːriːˈeks] *n* (*abbr* **real-time executive routine**) = superviseur en temps réel

Rex [reks] *n Br* **Edward/George Rex** le roi Édouard/Georges, Édouard/Georges Roi; *Law* **Rex v Gibson** la Couronne contre Gibson

Reye's syndrome [ˈraɪz-, ˈreɪz-] *n* syndrome *m* de Reye

Reykjavik [ˈrekjəvɪk] *n* Reykjavik

Reynolds number [ˈrenəldz-] *n Tech* nombre *m* de Reynolds

RF [ˌɑːˈref] *n* (*abbr* **radio frequency**) fréquence *f* radio

RFC (*written abbr* **Rugby Football Club**) = club de rugby

RFU [ˌɑːrefˈjuː] *n Br Sport* (*abbr* **Rugby Football Union**) = fédération anglaise de rugby

RGB [ˌɑːdʒiːˈbiː] *n Comput* (*abbr* **red, green and blue**) RVB *m*

RGN [ˌɑːdʒiːˈen] *n Br Formerly* (*abbr* **registered general nurse**) infirmier(ère) *m,f* diplômé(e) d'État *(remplacé en 1992 par "RN")*

Rgt (*written abbr* **regiment**) rég

Rh (*written abbr* **rhesus**) Rh
▸▸ ***Rh factor*** (facteur *m*) rhésus *m*

rhabdomancy [ˈræbdəmænsɪ] *n* rhabdomancie *f*, divination *f* à la baguette

Rhaetian [ˈriːʃən] *Ling* **1** *n* rhétique *m*
2 *adj* rhétique

rhagades [ˈrægədiːz] *npl Med* rhagades *fpl*

rhapsode [ˈræpsəʊd] *n Antiq* rhapsode *m*

rhapsodic [ræpˈsɒdɪk] *adj* (**a**) *(ecstatic)* extatique; *(full of praise)* dithyrambique (**b**) *Mus* rhapsodique, rapsodique

rhapsodist [ˈræpsədɪst] *n* (**a**) *Antiq* rhapsode *m* (**b**) *(reciter of poems)* déclamateur(trice) *m,f* de vers (**c**) *(person using rhapsodic language)* rhapsodiste *mf*, enthousiaste *mf*

rhapsodize, -ise [ˈræpsədaɪz] *vi* s'extasier; **to rhapsodize about sth** s'extasier sur qch

rhapsody [ˈræpsədɪ] (*pl* **rhapsodies**) *n* (**a**) *(ecstasy)* extase *f*; **to go into rhapsodies about sth** s'extasier sur qch; **to send sb into rhapsodies** rendre qn extatique (**b**) *Mus & Literature* rhapsodie *f*, rapsodie *f*

rhatany [ˈrætənɪ] *n Bot* ratanhia *m*

rhea [rɪə] *n Orn* nandou *m*

Rheims = **Reims**

rheme [riːm] *n Ling* rhème *m*

Rhenish [ˈriːnɪʃ] **1** *adj* rhénan, du Rhin
2 *n* vin *m* du Rhin
▸▸ ***Rhenish wine*** vin *m* du Rhin

rhenium [ˈriːnɪəm] *n Chem* rhénium *m*

rheobase [ˈrɪəʊbeɪs] *n Physiol* rhéobase *f*

rheological [ˌrɪəʊˈlɒdʒɪkəl] *adj Phys* rhéologique

rheologist [rɪˈɒlədʒɪst] *n Phys* rhéologue *mf*

rheology [rɪˈɒlədʒɪ] *n Phys* rhéologie *f*

rheometer [rɪˈɒmɪtə(r)] *n Med* rhéomètre *m*

rheostat [ˈriːəʊstæt] *n Elec* rhéostat *m*

rhesus [ˈriːsəs] *n Zool (monkey)* rhésus *m*; **rhesus positive/negative** Rhésus positif/négatif; **I'm rhesus negative** je suis Rhésus négatif
▸▸ ***rhesus baby*** = enfant rhésus positif souffrant d'incompatibilité avec le rhésus négatif de la mère; *Physiol* ***rhesus factor*** (facteur *m*) rhésus *m*; *Zool* ***rhesus monkey*** (macaque *m*) rhésus *m*

rhetor [ˈretə(r)] *n Antiq* rhéteur *m*

rhetoric [ˈretərɪk] *n* (**a**) *Pej (bombast)* emphase *f*, rhétorique *f*; **his speech contained nothing but rhetoric** son discours ne consistait qu'en de belles phrases vides de sens; **it's just empty rhetoric** ce ne sont que des mots (**b**) *(art of speaking)* rhétorique *f*

rhetorical [rɪˈtɒrɪkəl] *adj (question)* rhétorique; *(term)* de rhétorique; **his question was purely rhetorical** sa question était purement rhétorique
▸▸ ***rhetorical question*** question *f* posée pour la forme

rhetorically [rɪˈtɒrɪklɪ] *adv* en rhétoricien; **"who knows?" she asked rhetorically** "qui sait?", demanda-t-elle sans vraiment attendre de réponse; **I was only asking rhetorically** je demandais ça simplement pour la forme

rhetorician [ˌretəˈrɪʃən] *n* (**a**) *(speaker)* rhétoricien(enne) *m,f*; *Pej (who uses over-elaborate language)* rhéteur *m* (**b**) *(teacher of rhetoric)* rhéteur *m*

rheum [ruːm] *n* chassie *f*

rheumatic [ruːˈmætɪk] **1** *adj (pain, symptom)* rhumatismal; *(person)* rhumatisant; *(finger, joint, limb)* atteint de rhumatismes; **his rheumatic fingers** ses doigts déformés par les rhumatismes; **he suffered from a rheumatic condition** il souffrait de rhumatismes
2 *n* rhumatisant(e) *m,f*
▸▸ ***rheumatic fever*** rhumatisme *m* articulaire aigu

rheumatically [ruːˈmætɪklɪ] *adv* **rheumatically affected** souffrant de rhumatisme; **to walk rheumatically** avoir une allure de rhumatisant

rheumaticky [ruːˈmætɪkɪ] *adj Br Fam (person)* rhumatisant ❑; *(finger, joint, limb)* atteint de rhumatismes ❑

rheumatics [ruːˈmætɪks] *npl Fam* rhumatismes ❑ *mpl*; **to have** *or* **to suffer from rheumatics** avoir des *ou* souffrir de rhumatismes ❑

rheumatism [ˈruːmətɪzəm] *n* rhumatisme *m*

rheumatoid [ˈruːmətɔɪd] *adj* rhumatoïde
▸▸ ***rheumatoid arthritis*** polyarthrite *f* rhumatoïde

rheumatologist [ˌruːməˈtɒlədʒɪst] *n* rhumatologue *mf*

rheumatology [ˌruːməˈtɒlədʒɪ] *n* rhumatologie *f*

rheumy [ˈruːmɪ] (*compar* **rheumier**, *superl* **rheumiest**) *adj* chassieux

Rhine [raɪn] *n* **the (River) Rhine** le Rhin
▸▸ ***Rhine wine*** vin *m* du Rhin

Rhineland [ˈraɪnlænd] *n* Rhénanie *f*

Rhinelander [ˈraɪnlændə(r)] *n* Rhénan(e) *m,f*

Rhineland-Palatinate *n* Rhénanie-Palatinat *f*

rhinestone [ˈraɪnstəʊn] **1** *n* faux diamant *m*; *(smaller)* strass *m*
2 *comp* en strass

rhinitis [rɪˈnaɪtɪs] *n Med* rhinite *f*; **chronic rhinitis** coryza *m* chronique

rhino [ˈraɪnəʊ] (*pl* **inv** *or* **rhinos**) *n Zool* rhinocéros *m*
▸▸ ***rhino bars*** pare-buffles *m inv*

rhinoceros [raɪˈnɒsərəs] (*pl* **inv** *or* **rhinoceroses** *or* **rhinoceri** [-raɪ]) *n Zool* rhinocéros *m*; *Fig* **to have skin** *or* **a hide like a rhinoceros** manquer totalement de *ou* être complètement dépourvu de sensibilité

rhinology [raɪˈnɒlədʒɪ] *n Med* rhinologie *f*

rhinoplasty [ˈraɪnəʊˌplæstɪ] *n Med* rhinoplastie *f*

rhinoscopy [raɪˈnɒskəpɪ] *n Med* rhinoscopie *f*

rhizobium [raɪˈzəʊbɪəm] *n* rhizobium *m*

rhizocarp [ˈraɪzəʊkɑːp] *n Bot* rhizocarpée *f*

rhizocarpian [ˌraɪzəʊˈkɑːpɪən], **rhizocarpic** [ˌraɪzəʊˈkɑːpɪk], **rhizocarpous** [ˌraɪzəʊˈkɑːpəs] *adj Bot* rhinzocarpé, rhizocarpique, rhizocarpien

rhizoid [ˈraɪzɔɪd] *n Bot* rhizoïde *f*

rev–rhi

rhizome ['raɪzəʊm] *n Bot* rhizome *m*

rhizopod ['raɪzəʊpɒd] *n Bot* rhizopode *m*

rhizosphere ['raɪzəʊsfiːə(r)] *n Bot* rhizosphère *f*

Rh-negative *adj* rhésus négatif

rhodamin, rhodamine ['rəʊdəmɪn] *n Chem* rhodamine *f*

Rhode Island [rəʊd-] *n* le Rhode Island; **in Rhode Island** dans le Rhode Island

►► ***Rhode Island Red*** poule *f* Rhode-Island

Rhodes [rəʊdz] *n* Rhodes; **in Rhodes** à Rhodes; **the Colossus of Rhodes** le colosse de Rhodes

►► ***Rhodes scholar*** = titulaire d'une "Rhodes Scholarship"; ***Rhodes Scholarship*** = bourse permettant à certains étudiants étrangers d'étudier à l'université d'Oxford

Rhodesia [rəʊ'diːʃə] *n Formerly* Rhodésie *f*; **in Rhodesia** en Rhodésie; **Northern/Southern Rhodesia** Rhodésie *f* du Nord/du Sud

Rhodesian [rəʊ'diːʃən] **1** *n* Rhodésien(enne) *m,f*

2 *adj* rhodésien

►► ***Rhodesian man*** l'homme *m* de Rhodésie

Rhodian ['rəʊdɪən] **1** *n* Rhodien(enne) *m,f*

2 *adj* rhodien

rhodium ['rəʊdɪəm] *n Chem* rhodium

rhodochrosite [,rəʊdə'krəʊsaɪt] *n Miner* rhodochrosite *f*

rhododendron [,rəʊdə'dendrən] *n Bot* rhododendron *m*

►► ***rhododendron bush*** rhododendron *m*

rhodolite ['rəʊdəlaɪt] *n Miner* rhodolite *f*

rhodonite ['rəʊdənaɪt] *n Miner* rhodonite *f*

rhodopsin [rəʊ'dɒpsɪn] *n Biol & Chem* rhodopsine *f*

rhomb [rɒm] *n* **(a)** *Geom (rhombus)* losange *m*
(b) *(in crystallography)* rhomboèdre *m*

rhombic ['rɒmbɪk] *adj* **(a)** *Geom* rhombique **(b)** *(in crystallography)* orthorhombique

►► ***rhombic aerial*** antenne *f* rhombique

rhombohedral [,rɒmbəʊ'hiːdrəl] *adj (in crystallography)* rhomboédrique

rhombohedron [,rɒmbəʊ'hiːdrən] *(pl* **rhombohedra** [-drə]*)* *n (in crystallography)* rhomboèdre *m*

rhomboid ['rɒmbɔɪd] *Geom* **1** *n* parallélogramme *m (dont les côtés adjacents sont inégaux)*

2 *adj* rhomboïdal, rhombiforme

rhomboidal [rɒm'bɔɪdəl] *adj Geom* rhomboïdal

rhombus ['rɒmbəs] *(pl* **rhombuses** *or* **rhombi** [-baɪ]*)* *n Geom* losange *m*

rhonchus ['rɒŋkəs] *n Med* rhoncus *m*

Rhône [rəʊn] *n* **the (River) Rhône** le Rhône

►► ***the Rhône glacier*** le glacier du Rhône

rhotacism ['rəʊtəsɪzəm] *n Ling* rhotacisme *m*

Rh-positive *adj* rhésus positif

rhubarb ['ruːbɑːb] **1** *n* **(a)** *Bot* rhubarbe *f* **(b)** *Theat* brouhaha *m*, murmures *mpl* **(c)** *Am Fam Old-fashioned (squabble)* chamailleries *fpl*, engueulade *f*

2 *comp (jam)* de rhubarbe; *(tart)* à la rhubarbe

rhumb [rʌm] *n* rhumb *m*, rumb *m*

rhumbatron ['rʌmbətrɒn] *n Electron* rhumbatron *m*

rhyme [raɪm] **1** *n* **(a)** *(sound)* rime *f*; **the use of rhyme** l'emploi de la rime; **give me a rhyme for "mash"** trouve-moi un mot qui rime avec "mash"; *Fig* **without rhyme or reason** sans rime ni raison; **their demands have neither rhyme nor reason** leurs revendications ne riment à rien
(b) *(UNCOUNT) (poetry)* vers *mpl*; **in rhyme** en vers
(c) *(poem)* poème *m*; **I've made up a rhyme about you** j'ai composé un petit poème sur toi

2 *vi* **(a)** *(word, lines)* rimer; **what rhymes with "orange"?** qu'est-ce qui rime avec "orange"?
(b) *(write verse)* écrire *ou* composer des poèmes

3 *vt* faire rimer; **you can't rhyme "lost" with "host"** on ne peut pas faire rimer "lost" avec "host"

►► ***rhyme royal*** septain *m (combinaison ABABBCC)*; ***rhyme scheme*** combinaison *f* de rimes

rhymed [raɪmd] *adj* rimé

►► ***rhymed verse*** vers *mpl* rimés

rhymer ['raɪmə(r)], **rhymester** ['raɪmstə(r)] *n Pej* rimeur(euse) *m,f*, rimailleur(euse) *m,f*

rhyming ['raɪmɪŋ] *adj*

►► ***rhyming couplet*** distique *m*; ***rhyming dictionary*** dictionnaire *m* de rimes; ***rhyming slang*** = sorte d'argot qui consiste à remplacer un mot par un groupe de mots choisis pour la rime

RHYMING SLANG

Il s'agit d'un procédé complexe consistant à remplacer un mot par une expression dont le dernier terme rime avec le mot en question; bien souvent n'est prononcé que le premier terme de l'expression, à savoir celui qui ne rime pas avec le mot remplacé. Exemple: kids = dustbin lids = dustbins; head = loaf of bread = loaf. À l'origine ce type d'argot était pratiqué par les Cockneys (habitants de l'est de Londres) mais certains termes sont maintenant passés dans la langue courante et sont connus de la plupart des Britanniques.

rhyolite ['raɪəʊlaɪt] *n Miner* rhyolit(h)e *f*, liparite *f*

rhythm ['rɪðəm] *n* rythme *m*; **she's got (a sense of) rhythm** elle a le sens du rythme

►► ***rhythm and blues*** rhythm and blues *m inv*; ***rhythm guitar*** guitare *f* rythmique; ***rhythm method*** *(of contraception)* méthode *f* des températures; ***rhythm section*** section *f* rythmique

rhythmic ['rɪðmɪk], **rhythmical** ['rɪðmɪkəl] *adj (pattern, exercice)* rythmique; *(music, noise)* rythmé; **rhythmical structure/movement** structure *f*/mouvement *m* rythmique; **the rhythmical rattling of the train** le bruit régulier du train; **Greek music is less rhythmic** la musique grecque est moins rythmée

►► ***rhythmic gymnastics*** gymnastique *f* rythmique, GRS *f*

rhythmically ['rɪðmɪklɪ] *adv* rythmiquement; **they swayed rhythmically with the music** ils se balançaient au rythme de la musique

rhytidectomy [,raɪtɪ'dektəmɪ] *n (facelift)* lifting *m*; *(dermabrasion)* dermabrasion *f*

RI[1] [,ɑː'raɪ] *n (abbr* **religious instruction***)* instruction *f* religieuse

RI[2] *(written abbr* **Rhode Island***)* Rhode Island *m*

ria ['riːə] *n Geog* ria *f*

►► ***ria coast*** côte *f* à rias

rial [rɪ'ɑːl] *n* rial *m*

rib [rɪb] *(pt & pp* **ribbed**, *cont* **ribbing***)* **1** *n* **(a)** *Anat* côte *f*; **he dug** *or* **he poked her in the ribs** il lui a donné un petit coup de coude; **his ribs stick out** on lui voit les côtes; **floating rib** côte *f* flottante; **true/false rib** vraie/fausse côte *f*; *Fam* **this soup will stick to your ribs!** *(is very thick)* cette soupe vous tiendra bien au corps!
(b) *Culin* côte *f*; **rib of beef** côte *f* de bœuf
(c) *(of vault, leaf, aircraft or insect wing)* nervure *f*; *(of ship's hull)* couple *m*, membre *m*; *(of umbrella)* baleine *f*
(d) *Knitting* côte *f*; **knit fifteen rows in rib** tricotez quinze rangs en côtes
(e) *(on mountain → spur)* éperon *m*; *(→ crest)* arête *f*
(f) *(vein of ore)* veine *f*, filon *m*

2 *vt Fam (tease)* taquiner, mettre en boîte

3 *vi Knitting* **rib for fifteen rows** tricotez quinze rangs en côtes

RIBA [,ɑːraɪ,biː'eɪ] *n Br (abbr* **Royal Institute of British Architects***)* = institut d'architectes, à Londres

ribald ['rɪbəld, 'raɪbəld] *adj Literary (joke, language)* grivois, paillard; *(laughter)* égrillard

ribaldry ['rɪbəldrɪ, 'raɪbəldrɪ] *n Literary* paillardises *fpl*, grivoiserie *f*

riband, ribband ['rɪbənd] *n* **(a)** *(award)* ruban *m*, décoration *f* **(b)** *Arch (in hair)* ruban *m*

ribbed [rɪbd] *adj* **(a)** *(vault, leaf)* à nervures **(b)** *(garment, fabric)* à côtes

►► *Bot* ***ribbed melilot*** mélilot *m* officinal

ribbing ['rɪbɪŋ] *n* **(a)** *(UNCOUNT) (of fabric, knitting)* côtes *fpl* **(b)** *Fam (teasing)* taquinerie *f*, mise *f* en boîte; **to get a ribbing from sb** être mis en boîte par qn

ribbon ['rɪbən] **1** *vt* **(a)** *(adorn with ribbon)* enrubanner
(b) *Fig (streak)* sillonner, zébrer
(c) *(cut)* couper en rubans; *(shred)* mettre en lambeaux

2 *n* **(a)** *(for hair, typewriter, parcel etc)* ruban *m*; *Horseriding* **ribbons** *(reins)* guides *fpl*; **it washes like a ribbon** ça se lave facilement
(b) *(on medal)* ruban *m*; *(of order)* cordon *m*
(c) *Fig (of road)* ruban *m*; *(of land)* bande *f*; *(of cloud)* traînée *f*; *(of smoke)* filet *m*; **her dress hung in ribbons** sa robe était en lambeaux *ou* en loques; **to tear sth to ribbons** mettre qch en lambeaux; **I've cut my hand to ribbons** je me suis charcuté la main
(d) *Comput (under menu bar)* ruban *m*, barre *f* d'outils

►► ***ribbon cartridge*** ruban *m* encreur; ***ribbon cassette*** cassette *f* de ruban; *Br* ***ribbon development*** croissance *f* urbaine linéaire *(le long des grands axes routiers)*; ***ribbon guide*** *(on printer)* guide-ruban *m*; ***ribbon microphone*** microphone *m* à ruban; *Zool* ***ribbon worm*** némerte *f*

ribboned ['rɪbənd] *adj* **(a)** *(decorated with ribbons)* orné *ou* garni de rubans, enrubanné **(b)** *Anat & Zool* rubané, rubanaire

ribcage ['rɪbkeɪdʒ] *n* cage *f* thoracique

Ribena® [raɪ'biːnə] *n* sirop *m* de cassis

rib-eye *n* **rib-eye (steak)** faux-filet *m*

riboflavin [,raɪbəʊ'fleɪvɪn], **riboflavine** [,raɪbəʊ'fleɪviːn] *n* riboflavine *f*

ribonuclease [,raɪbəʊ'njuːklɪeɪs] *n Chem* ribonucléase *f*

ribonucleic acid [,raɪbəʊnjuː'kliːɪk-] *n Chem* acide *m* ribonucléique

ribonucleotide [,raɪbəʊ'njuːklɪətaɪd] *n Chem* ribonucléotide *m*

ribose ['raɪbəʊs] *n Chem* ribose *m*

ribosomal [,raɪbəʊ'səʊməl] *adj Chem* ribosomal

ribosome ['raɪbəʊsəʊm] *n Chem* ribosome *m*

rib-tickler *n Fam Hum* plaisanterie ❑ *f*

ribwort ['rɪbwɜːt] *n Bot* plantain *m* lancéolé

rice [raɪs] **1** *n* riz *m*

2 *vt Am (potatoes)* faire une purée de

►► ***rice bowl*** *(dish)* bol *m* à riz; *Fig (region)* région *f* productrice de riz; **this province was the rice bowl of Burma** cette province était le grenier à riz de la Birmanie; ***rice grower*** riziculteur(trice) *m,f*; ***rice growing*** riziculture *f*; ***rice paddy*** rizière *f*; ***rice paper*** papier *m* de riz; ***rice pudding*** riz *m* au lait; ***rice water*** eau *f* de riz; ***rice wine*** alcool *m* de riz, saké *m*

riced [raɪst] *adj*

►► ***riced potatoes*** purée *f* (de pommes de terre)

ricefield ['raɪsfiːld] *n* rizière *f*

rice-growing *adj (country, region)* rizicole

ricer ['raɪsə(r)] *n* presse-purée *m inv*

rich [rɪtʃ] **1** *adj* **(a)** *(wealthy, affluent)* riche; **it doesn't affect rich people** ça ne touche pas les riches; **they want to get rich quick** ils veulent s'enrichir très vite; **the rich part of town** les quartiers riches, les beaux quartiers; **I'm a hundred pounds richer** j'ai une centaine de livres de plus
(b) *(elegant, luxurious)* riche, luxueux, somptueux; **rich tapestries** des tapisseries somptueuses
(c) *(abundant, prolific)* riche, abondant; **rich in vitamins/in proteins** riche en vitamines/en protéines; **rich vegetation** végétation *f* luxuriante; *also Fig* **there are rich pickings to be had** ça peut rapporter gros
(d) *(fertile)* riche, fertile; **rich soil** sol *m* fertile *ou* riche; **a rich imagination** une imagination fertile
(e) *(full, eventful)* riche; **she led a very rich life** elle a eu une vie bien remplie; **their culture was extremely rich** ils avaient une culture extrêmement riche
(f) *(strong, intense → colour)* riche, chaud, vif; *(→ voice, sound)* chaud, riche; *(→ smell)* fort
(g) *Culin (food)* riche; *(meal)* lourd; **your diet is too rich** vous mangez trop d'aliments riches
(h) *(funny)* drôle; **rich humour** humour *m* très drôle; *Fam Ironic* **that's rich coming from you!** venant de toi, c'est un peu fort!

2 *npl* **the rich** les riches *mpl*

3 riches *npl* richesses *fpl*

►► *Aut & Tech* ***rich mixture*** *(in engine)* mélange *m* riche

-rich [rɪtʃ] *suff* riche en...; **vitamin-rich foods** aliments *mpl* riches en vitamines

Richard ['rɪtʃəd] **1** *pr n* **Richard the Lionheart** Richard Cœur de Lion

2 *n Br very Fam (rhyming slang* **Richard the Third = turd***)* étron *m*

richly ['rɪtʃlɪ] *adv* **(a)** *(handsomely, generously)*

rhi–ric

largement, richement; **they will be richly rewarded** ils seront largement *ou* généreusement récompensés

(**b**) *(thoroughly)* largement, pleinement; **the punishment she so richly deserved** le châtiment qu'elle méritait amplement

(**c**) *(abundantly)* abondamment, richement; **the region is richly provided with arable land** la région est riche en terres arables; **richly illustrated** richement illustré

(**d**) *(elegantly, luxuriously)* somptueusement, luxueusement; **richly dressed/furnished** somptueusement habillé/meublé

(**e**) *(vividly)* **richly coloured** aux couleurs riches *ou* vives

richness ['rɪtʃnɪs] *n* (**a**) *(wealth, affluence)* richesse *f*

(**b**) *(elegance, luxury)* luxe *m*, richesse *f*

(**c**) *(abundance)* abondance *f*, richesse *f*; **an amazing richness of detail** une étonnante abondance de détails

(**d**) *(fertility)* richesse *f*, fertilité *f*; **the richness of the soil/of her imagination** la richesse du sol/de son imagination

(**e**) *(fullness, eventfulness)* richesse *f*; **the richness of his experience** la richesse de son expérience

(**f**) *(strength, intensity → of colour, sound)* richesse *f*; *(→ of smell)* intensité *f*

Richter scale ['rɪktə-] *n* échelle *f* de Richter; **it measured six on the Richter scale** il mesurait six sur l'échelle de Richter

rick [rɪk] **1** *n* (**a**) *Agr* meule *f (de foin etc)* (**b**) *(in ankle, wrist)* entorse *f*; *(in neck)* torticolis *m*

2 *vt* (**a**) *Agr* mettre en meules (**b**) *Br (sprain)* se faire une entorse à; **to rick one's neck** attraper un torticolis; **to rick one's back** se donner un tour de reins

ricketiness ['rɪkətɪnɪs] *n* manque *m* de solidité, état *m* branlant

rickets ['rɪkɪts] *n (UNCOUNT) Med* rachitisme *m*; **to have rickets** souffrir de rachitisme, être rachitique

rickettsia [rɪ'ketsɪə] *n Med & Biol* rickettsie *f*

rickety ['rɪkətɪ] *adj* (**a**) *(shaky → structure)* branlant; *(→ chair)* bancal; *(→ vehicle)* (tout) bringuebalant (**b**) *(feeble → person)* frêle, chancelant (**c**) *Med* rachitique

rickrack ['rɪkræk] *n (UNCOUNT)* croquet *m*, galon *m* en zigzag

rickshaw ['rɪkʃɔː] *n (pulled)* pousse *m inv*, pousse-pousse *m inv*; *(pedalled)* cyclo-pousse *m inv*

ricochet ['rɪkəʃeɪ] *(pt & pp* **ricocheted** [-ʃeɪd] *or* **ricochetted** [-ʃetɪd], *cont* **ricocheting** [-eɪɪŋ] *or* **ricochetting** [-ʃetɪŋ]) **1** *n* ricochet *m*; **he was injured by a ricochet** il a été blessé par une balle qui a ricoché

2 *vi* ricocher; **to ricochet off sth** ricocher sur qch

ricotta [rɪ'kɒtə] *n* ricotta *f*

ricrac = **rickrack**

rictus ['rɪktəs] *n* rictus *m*

rid [rɪd] *(pt & pp* **rid** *or* **ridded**, *cont* **ridding**) **1** *vt* débarrasser; **to rid a house of rats** débarrasser une maison de ses rats, dératiser une maison; **to rid the world of poverty** délivrer le monde de la pauvreté; **we must rid the country of corruption** il faut débarrasser le pays de la corruption; **you should rid yourself of such illusions!** arrêtez de vous bercer d'illusions!

2 *adj* **to get rid of** se débarrasser de; **how can we get rid of all this rubbish?** comment nous débarrasser de tout ce bazar?; **I'll get rid of it for you** je vais t'en débarrasser; **I can't seem to get rid of this cold** je n'arrive pas à me débarrasser de ce rhume; **I thought we were never going to get rid of them!** *(guests)* j'ai cru que nous n'allions jamais arriver à nous en débarrasser *ou* à nous débarrasser d'eux!; **we can't get rid of the house** nous n'arrivons pas à vendre la maison; **to be rid of** être débarrassé de; **I was glad to be rid of them** j'étais content d'être débarrassé d'eux; **to be well rid of sb/sth** être bien débarrassé de qn/qch; **you're well rid of him!** tu en es bien débarrassé!

riddance ['rɪdəns] *n* débarras *m*; *Fam* **good riddance (to bad rubbish)!** bon débarras!

ridden ['rɪdən] **1** *pp of* **ride**

2 *adj* affligé, atteint; **to be ridden with** *or* **by guilt** être bourrelé de remords *ou* accablé par le remords

-ridden ['rɪdən] *suff* **flea-ridden** infesté de puces; **disease-ridden** infesté de maladies; **debt-ridden** criblé de dettes

riddle ['rɪdəl] **1** *n* (**a**) *(poser)* devinette *f*; **to ask sb a riddle** poser une devinette à qn (**b**) *(mystery)* énigme *f*; **to talk** *or* **to speak in riddles** parler par énigmes (**c**) *(sieve)* crible *m*, tamis *m*

2 *vt* (**a**) *(pierce)* cribler; **they riddled the car with bullets** ils criblèrent la voiture de balles (**b**) *(sift)* passer au crible, cribler

3 *vi Literary* parler par énigmes

riddled ['rɪdəld] *adj* plein (**with** de); **a wall riddled with holes** un mur plein de trous; **his letter is riddled with spelling mistakes** sa lettre est pleine de fautes d'orthographe; **his whole body is riddled with cancer** il a un cancer généralisé; **the department is riddled with corruption** la corruption règne dans le département

RIDE [raɪd]

tour	▸ 1 (a)
promenade	▸ 1 (a)
parcours	▸ 1 (b)
monter à	▸ 2 (a)
monter sur	▸ 2 (b)
parcourir	▸ 2 (c)
faire	▸ 2 (c), (d)
faire un tour de	▸ 2 (e)
faire du cheval	▸ 3 (a)
aller	▸ 3 (b)
voguer	▸ 3 (c)
dépendre	▸ 3 (d)

(pt **rode** [rəʊd], *pp* **ridden** ['rɪdən]) **1** *n* (**a**) *(trip → on bicycle, motorbike, in car)* tour *m*, promenade *f*; *(→ in taxi)* course *f*; *(→ on horse)* promenade *f*; *(→ in train)* voyage *m*; *(→ in boat, helicopter, plane)* tour *m*; **to go for a car ride** *or* **a ride in a car** (aller) faire un tour *ou* une promenade en voiture; **we went on long bicycle/horse rides** nous avons fait de longues promenades à bicyclette/à cheval; **a donkey ride** une promenade à dos d'âne; **to go for a ride** *(on horse)* faire une promenade à cheval; **he saddled up and went for his morning ride** il sella son cheval et partit faire sa promenade matinale; **he's got a ride in the 3:00 at Sandown** *(jockey)* il monte dans la course de 15 heures à Sandown; **how about a ride in my new car?** et si on faisait un tour dans ma nouvelle voiture?; **give Tom a ride** *or* **let Tom have a ride on your tricycle** laisse Tom monter sur ton tricycle; **give me a ride on your back** porte-moi sur ton dos; **his sister came along for the ride** sa sœur est venue faire un tour avec nous; **this type of suspension gives a smoother ride** ce type de suspension est plus confortable; **we're in for a bumpy ride** *(in plane, car etc)* ça va secouer; *Fig* ça promet!; **the journalists gave her a rough ride** *or* **didn't give her an easy ride** les journalistes ne l'ont pas ménagée; *Fam* **to take sb for a ride** *(deceive)* faire marcher qn; *(cheat)* arnaquer *ou* rouler qn; *Am (kill)* descendre *ou* liquider qn; *Fam* **you've been taken for a ride** tu t'es fait avoir; *Am Fam* **take a ride!** fous-moi la paix!

(**b**) *(distance)* parcours *m*, trajet *m*; **she has a long car/bus ride to work** elle doit faire un long trajet en voiture/en bus pour aller travailler; **allow an hour for the bus ride** comptez une heure de trajet en bus; **it's a long bus ride to Mexico** c'est long d'aller en car au Mexique; **it's only a short ride away by car** il n'y en a pas pour longtemps en voiture; **it's a thirty-minute ride by bus/train/car** il faut trente minutes en bus/train/voiture; **how much will the ride cost?** combien le voyage va-t-il coûter?; **it's a 70p ride on the bus** il y en a pour 70 pence en autobus

(**c**) *Am (lift → in car)* **can you give me a ride to the station?** peux-tu me conduire à la gare?; **I have a ride coming** on vient me chercher; **I waited for my ride for half an hour** j'ai attendu une demi-heure qu'on passe me prendre; **get a ride to the party with Ewan** demande à Ewan s'il peut t'emmener à la fête; **don't accept rides from strangers** ne montez pas dans la voiture de quelqu'un que vous ne connaissez pas; **we got from New York to Chicago in one ride** nous sommes allés de New York jusqu'à Chicago dans la même voiture

(**d**) *Am Fam (car)* bagnole *f*, caisse *f*

(**e**) *(in fairground → attraction)* manège *m*; *(→ turn)* tour *m*; **he wanted to go on all the rides** il a voulu faire un tour sur chaque manège; **it's 50p a ride** c'est 50 pence le tour; **to have a ride on the big wheel** faire un tour sur la grande roue

(**f**) *(bridle path)* piste *f* cavalière; *(wider)* allée *f* cavalière

(**g**) *(passenger in taxi)* client(e) *m,f*

(**h**) *Vulg (sexual partner)* **to be a good ride** être un bon coup

2 *vt* (**a**) *(horse)* monter à; *(camel, donkey, elephant)* monter à dos de; **I don't know how to ride a horse** je ne sais pas monter à cheval; **they were riding horses/donkeys/camels** ils étaient à cheval/à dos d'âne/à dos de chameau; **she rode her mare in the park each day** elle montait sa jument chaque jour dans le parc; **Razzle, ridden by Jo Burns** Razzle, monté par Jo Burns; **he rode Prince into town** il a pris Prince pour aller en ville; **she rode her horse back** elle est revenue à cheval; **she rode her horse at the fence** elle a dirigé son cheval sur la barrière; **they rode their horses across the river** ils ont traversé la rivière sur leurs chevaux; **he rode his horse down the lane** il descendit le chemin à cheval; **to ride a horse into the ground** monter un cheval jusqu'à l'épuisement; **witches ride broomsticks** les sorcières chevauchent des balais *ou* des manches à balai

(**b**) *(bicycle, motorcycle)* monter sur; **he won't let me ride his bike** il ne veut pas que je monte sur *ou* que je me serve de son vélo; **I don't know how to ride a bike/a motorbike** je ne sais pas faire du vélo/conduire une moto; **she was riding a motorbike** elle était à *ou* en moto; **she rides her bicycle everywhere** elle se déplace toujours à bicyclette; **he rides his bike to work** il va travailler à vélo, il va au travail à vélo; **a gang of youths riding racers** une bande de jeunes (montés) sur des vélos de course; **he's riding his tricycle in the yard** il fait du tricycle dans la cour

(**c**) *(go about → fields, valleys)* parcourir; *(cover → distance)* faire; **when the Sioux rode the prairies** à l'époque où les Sioux parcouraient *ou* sillonnaient la prairie; *Am* **you can ride this highway to Tucson** vous pouvez prendre *ou* suivre cette route jusqu'à Tucson

(**d**) *(participate in → race)* faire; **she's ridden four races this year** elle a fait quatre courses cette année; **he rode a good race** *(jockey, horse)* il a fait une bonne course

(**e**) *Am (have a go on → roundabout, fairground attraction)* faire un tour de; *(use → bus, lift, subway, train)* prendre; **do you want to ride the rollercoaster?** veux-tu faire un tour sur les montagnes russes?; **he rode the chairlift to the top of the slope** il a pris le télésiège jusqu'au sommet de la piste; **she wanted to ride the miniature train** elle voulait monter dans le petit train; **do you ride this line often?** est-ce que vous prenez souvent cette ligne?; **she rides a bus to work** elle prend le bus pour aller travailler, elle va travailler en bus; **he spent three hours riding the subway** il a passé trois heures dans le métro

(**f**) *(move with)* **to ride the waves** *(ship)* voguer sur les flots; *(surfer)* glisser sur les vagues; **to ride the rapids** descendre les rapides; **hang-gliders were riding the updrafts** des deltaplanes se laissaient porter par les courants ascendants; **the candidate is riding a surge of popularity** le candidat est porté par une vague de popularité; **to ride one's luck** compter sur sa chance; **to ride the storm** *Naut* étaler la tempête; *Fig* surmonter la crise

(**g**) *(take, recoil with → punch, blow)* encaisser

(**h**) *Am Fam (nag)* harceler ❑; **stop riding her!** laisse-la tranquille!; **you ride the kids too hard** tu es trop dur avec les gosses; **you're always riding me about being late** tu me reproches sans arrêt d'être en retard ❑

(**i**) *Am Fam (tease)* taquiner, mettre en boîte; **we were riding him about his accent** nous le

ric–rid

taquinions au sujet de son accent; **my colleagues are really going to ride me!** je vais être la risée de mes collègues!

(**j**) *(copulate with → of animal)* monter

(**k**) *Vulg (have sex with)* **to ride sb** se faire qn

(**l**) *Am (give a lift to)* amener; **hop in and I'll ride you home** monte, je te ramène chez toi; **to ride sb out of town** *(drive out)* chasser qn de la ville; *(ridicule)* tourner qn en ridicule *ou* en dérision; **the sheriff was ridden out of town** ils ont chassé le shérif de la ville

3 *vi* (**a**) *(ride a horse)* monter (à cheval), faire du cheval; **can you ride?** est-ce que vous savez monter à cheval *ou* faire du cheval; **she learnt to ride very young** elle a appris à faire du cheval *ou* à monter à cheval très jeune; **he rides well** il monte bien (à cheval), il est bon cavalier; **I like to ride on the beach in the morning** j'aime faire du cheval le matin sur la plage; **I was stiff after riding all day** j'avais des courbatures après avoir chevauché toute la journée *ou* après une journée entière à cheval; **he's riding in the 3:30** *(in horserace)* il dispute la course de 3 h 30; **to ride to hounds** faire de la chasse à courre; *Hum* **Zorro rides again!** Zorro est de retour!

(**b**) *(go → on horseback)* aller (à cheval); *(→ by bicycle)* aller (à bicyclette); *(→ by car)* aller (en voiture); **we rode along the canal and over the bridge** nous avons longé le canal et traversé le pont; **he rode by on a bicycle/on a white horse/on a donkey** il passa à bicyclette/sur un cheval blanc/monté sur un âne; **they ride to work on the bus/the train** ils vont travailler en autobus/en train; **I want to ride in the front seat/in the first carriage** je veux monter à l'avant/dans la voiture de tête; **she was riding in the back seat** elle était assise à l'arrière; **have you ever ridden in a rickshaw?** avez-vous jamais pris un pousse-pousse?; **I'll ride up/down in the lift** je monterai/descendrai en ascenseur; **they rode to the top in the cable car** ils ont pris la télécabine pour aller au sommet; **you can ride on the handlebars/on my shoulders** tu peux monter sur le guidon/sur mes épaules; **to ride on an elephant** aller à dos d'éléphant; **to ride off** *(leave)* partir; *(move away)* s'éloigner; **he rode off into the sunset** il s'éloigna vers le soleil couchant

(**c**) *(float, sail)* voguer; **to ride with the current** voguer au fil de l'eau; **the raft will ride over the reef** le radeau franchira le récif; **to ride at anchor** être ancré; **the buoy rode with the swell** la bouée se balançait au gré de la houle; **the moon was riding high in the sky** la lune était haut dans le ciel

(**d**) *(depend)* dépendre; **everything rides on whether the meeting is successful** tout dépend de la réussite de la réunion; **my reputation is riding on the outcome** ma réputation est en jeu

(**e**) *(money in bet)* miser; **I've $5 riding on the favourite** j'ai misé 5 dollars sur le favori; **they have a fortune riding on this project** ils ont investi une fortune dans ce projet

(**f**) *(idioms)* **to be riding high** avoir le vent en poupe; **to be riding for a fall** courir à l'échec; **we'll have to ride with it** il faudra faire avec; **to ride with the punches** encaisser (les coups); **he decided to let the matter ride** il a décidé de laisser courir; **let it ride!** laisse tomber!; **she was riding on a wave of popularity** elle était portée par une vague de popularité; **he rode to victory on a policy of reform** il a obtenu la victoire grâce à son programme de réformes; **he's riding on his reputation** il vit sur sa réputation

▸**ride about, ride around** *vi* **she rides about** *or* **around in a limousine** elle se déplace en limousine; **I saw him riding about in a brand new sports car** je l'ai vu passer dans une voiture de sport toute neuve

▸**ride down** *vt sep* (**a**) *(knock over)* renverser; *(trample)* piétiner

(**b**) *(catch up with)* rattraper; **they rode the wounded doe down** ils ont poursuivi la biche blessée jusqu'à ce qu'ils la rattrapent

▸**ride in** *vt sep (horse)* préparer *(pour un concours)*

▸**ride out 1** *vt insep (difficulty, crisis)* surmonter; *(recession)* survivre à; **if we can ride out the next few months** si nous pouvons tenir *ou* nous maintenir à flot encore quelques mois; **they managed to ride out a bad stretch** ils ont réussi à se tirer d'une mauvaise passe; **to ride out the storm** *Naut* étaler la tempête; *Fig* surmonter la crise, tenir

2 *vi* sortir *(à cheval, à bicyclette etc)*

▸**ride up** *vi (garment)* remonter

---

ride-on mower *n* mototondeuse *f*

rider ['raɪdə(r)] *n* (**a**) *(of horse, donkey)* cavalier(ère) *m,f*; *(of racehorse)* jockey *m*; *(of bicycle)* cycliste *mf*; *(of motorcycle)* motocycliste *mf*

(**b**) *(proviso)* condition *f*, stipulation *f*; **he agrees, with the rider that he won't have to pay for it** il est d'accord à condition que ce ne soit pas lui qui paie; **I'd like to add one small rider to what my colleague said** j'aimerais apporter une petite précision à ce qu'a dit mon collègue

(**c**) *(annexe → to contract)* annexe *f*; *Br Law (jury recommendation)* recommandation *f*

(**d**) *(on scales)* curseur *m*

▸▸ ***rider mower*** mototondeuse *f*

riderless ['raɪdəlɪs] *adj (horse)* sans cavalier; *(racehorse)* sans jockey

ridership ['raɪdəʃɪp] *n Am* nombre *m* de voyageurs

ridesharing ['raɪd,ʃeərɪŋ] *n Am* = partage d'un véhicule pour se rendre sur son lieu de travail

ridge [rɪdʒ] **1** *n* (**a**) *(of mountains)* crête *f*, ligne *f* de faîte; *(leading to summit)* crête *f*, arête *f*

(**b**) *(raised strip or part)* arête *f*, crête *f*; *(on sand)* ride *f*; *Agr (in ploughed field)* crête *f*; **the wet sand formed ridges** le sable mouillé était couvert de petites rides; *Met* **a ridge of high pressure** une crête de haute pression, *Spec* une dorsale barométrique

(**c**) *(of roof)* faîte *m*

2 *vt (crease)* sillonner, rider; **you should ridge the roof with new tiles** vous devriez poser de nouvelles faîtières sur votre toit

▸▸ ***ridge tent*** tente *f* à faîtière; ***ridge tile*** (tuile *f*) faîtière *f*

ridgeboard ['rɪdʒbɔːd] *n* faîtage *m*

ridged [rɪdʒd] *adj* ridé; **her brow was ridged with worry** l'inquiétude se lisait sur son visage

ridgepiece ['rɪdʒpiːs] *n Archit* panne *f* faîtière

ridgepole ['rɪdʒpəʊl] *n (of roof)* panne *f* faîtière; *(of tent)* mât *m* de faîte

ridgetree ['rɪdʒtriː] *n (of roof)* panne *f* faîtière

ridgeway ['rɪdʒweɪ] *n* = chemin de randonnée qui suit une ligne de faîte

ridicule ['rɪdɪkjuːl] **1** *n* ridicule *m*; **to pour ridicule on sth, to hold sth up to ridicule** tourner qch en ridicule; **to lay oneself open to ridicule** s'exposer au ridicule

2 *vt* ridiculiser, tourner en ridicule

ridiculous [rɪ'dɪkjʊləs] **1** *adj* ridicule; **you look ridiculous in that hat** tu as l'air ridicule avec ce chapeau; **it's ridiculous that I should have to pay a fine** il est absurde que j'aie à payer une amende; **£500? don't be ridiculous!** 500 livres? vous plaisantez!; **to make sb/sth look ridiculous** rendre qn/qch ridicule, ridiculiser qn/qch; **to make oneself look ridiculous** se ridiculiser, se couvrir de ridicule

2 *n* **the ridiculous** le ridicule; **to verge on the ridiculous** friser le ridicule

ridiculously [rɪ'dɪkjʊləslɪ] *adv* ridiculement; **it's ridiculously expensive** *(price)* c'est un prix exorbitant; *(article, shop)* c'est beaucoup trop cher; **it's ridiculously cheap** *(price)* c'est un prix dérisoire; *(article, shop)* c'est très bon marché

ridiculousness [rɪ'dɪkjʊləsnɪs] *n* ridicule *m*; **the ridiculousness of the situation** le (côté) ridicule de la situation

riding ['raɪdɪŋ] **1** *n* (**a**) *Horseriding* **(horse) riding** équitation *f*; **to go riding** faire de l'équitation *ou* du cheval; **do you like riding?** aimez-vous l'équitation *ou* monter à cheval?

(**b**) *(in Yorkshire)* division *f* administrative

(**c**) *(in Canada, New Zealand)* circonscription *f* électorale

2 *comp (boots, jacket)* de cheval; *(lesson, techniques)* d'équitation

▸▸ ***riding breeches*** culotte *f* de cheval; ***riding crop*** cravache *f*; ***riding habit*** tenue *f* d'amazone; ***riding instructor*** professeur *m* d'équitation; ***riding kit*** tenue *f* de cheval; ***riding school*** école *f* d'équitation

RIE [,ɑːraɪ'iː] *n Fin (abbr* **recognized investment exchange**) marché *m* d'investissement agréé

riel ['riːəl] *n* riel *m*

Riesling ['riːslɪŋ] *n* riesling *m*

rife [raɪf] *adj* (**a**) *(widespread)* répandu; **corruption is rife** la corruption est chose commune

(**b**) *(full)* **rife with** abondant en; **the garden is rife with caterpillars** le jardin est envahi par les chenilles; **the office is rife with rumour** les langues vont bon train au bureau; **the city was rife with disease** la ville était en proie à la maladie, la maladie régnait dans la ville

riff [rɪf] *n* riff *m*

riffle ['rɪfəl] **1** *vt* (**a**) *(magazine, pages)* feuilleter

(**b**) *(cards)* battre (**c**) *Am (water, lake)* rider

2 *n Am* (**a**) *(rapids)* rapide *m*, rapides *mpl* (**b**) *(on surface of water)* ride *f*, ondulation *f*

▸**riffle through** *vt insep* feuilleter

riffraff ['rɪfræf] *n* racaille *f*

rifle ['raɪfəl] **1** *vt* (**a**) *(search)* fouiller (dans); **I caught him rifling my desk** je l'ai surpris en train de fouiller dans mon bureau

(**b**) *(rob)* dévaliser; **they rifled the safe** ils ont dévalisé le coffre-fort

(**c**) *(steal)* voler; **all the money had been rifled** tout l'argent avait été volé

(**d**) *(gun barrel)* rayer

2 *vi* **to rifle through sth** fouiller dans qch

3 *n (gun)* fusil *m*

4 *comp (bullet, butt, shot)* de fusil

5 rifles *npl Mil (unit)* fusiliers *mpl*

▸▸ ***rifle club*** société *f* de tir; *Mil* ***Rifle Corps*** corps *m* des fusiliers *ou* des chasseurs à pied; ***rifle grenade*** grenade *f* à fusil; *TV & Rad* ***rifle mike*** micro *m* canon; ***rifle practice*** (exercice *m* de) tir *m* au fusil; ***rifle range*** *Mil (for practice)* champ *m* de tir; *(at funfair)* stand *m* de tir; **within rifle range** *(distance)* à portée de tir *ou* de fusil

rifleman ['raɪfəlmən] *(pl* **riflemen** [-mən]) *n* fusilier *m*

rifling ['raɪflɪŋ] *n (UNCOUNT) (in gun barrel)* rayures *fpl*

rift [rɪft] **1** *n* (**a**) *(gap, cleavage)* fissure *f*, crevasse *f*; *Geol (fault)* faille *f*; **a rift in the clouds** une trouée dans les nuages

(**b**) *Fig (split)* cassure *f*, faille *f*; *Pol* scission *f*; *(quarrel)* désaccord *m*, querelle *f*; **in order to prevent a rift in our relationship** pour éviter une rupture; **there is a deep rift between them** un abîme les sépare; **she hasn't seen her family since that rift** elle n'a pas vu sa famille depuis cette dispute; **a rift in the opposition** une scission au sein de l'opposition

2 *vt* scinder

3 *vi* se scinder

▸▸ ***rift valley*** fossé *m* d'effondrement; ***the Rift Valley*** la Rift Valley

rig [rɪg] *(pt & pp* **rigged**, *cont* **rigging**) **1** *vt* (**a**) *(fiddle)* truquer; *(prices)* fixer illégalement; **they were accused of rigging the match/the elections** on les a accusés d'avoir truqué le match/les élections; **the dice were rigged** les dés étaient truqués *ou* pipés; **the whole affair was rigged!** c'était un coup monté du début jusqu'à la fin!; **to rig a jury** manipuler un jury; *St Exch* **to rig the market** manipuler la Bourse

(**b**) *Naut* gréer

(**c**) *(install)* monter, bricoler

2 *n* (**a**) *(gen → equipment)* matériel *m*

(**b**) *Naut* gréement *m*

(**c**) *Petr (on land)* derrick *m*; *(offshore)* plate-forme *f*

(**d**) *Fam (clothes)* tenue❑ *f*, fringues *fpl*

(**e**) *Fam (large truck)* semi-remorque❑ *m*, gros-cul *m*

(**f**) *St Exch (rise)* hausse *f* factice; *(fall)* baisse *f* factice

▸**rig down 1** *vt sep* dégréer

2 *vi* dégréer

▸**rig out** *vt sep* (**a**) *Fam (clothe)* habiller❑; **he was rigged out in a cowboy costume** il était habillé *ou* déguisé en cowboy; *Pej* **look at the way she's rigged out!** regarde comme elle est fagotée! (**b**) *(equip)* équiper

▸**rig up** *vt sep (install)* monter, installer

Riga ['riːgə] *n* Riga *m*

rigadoon [ˌrɪgəˈduːn] *n* rigodon *m*
rigamarole [ˈrɪgəmərəʊl] *Am* = **rigmarole**
-rigged [rɪgd] *suff* gréé
rigger [ˈrɪgə(r)] *n* (**a**) *Naut* gréeur *m* (**b**) *Petr* = personne qui travaille sur un chantier de forage
rigging [ˈrɪgɪŋ] *n* (**a**) *Naut* gréement *m* (**b**) *Theat* machinerie *f* (**c**) *(fiddling)* trucage *m*; *(of market)* hausse *f ou* baisse *f* factice; *(of prices)* fixation *f* illégale
►► ***rigging loft*** *Naut* (atelier *m* de) garniture *f*; *Theat* cintre *m*

RIGHT [raɪt]

droite	► **1 (a) – (c)**
droit	► **1 (d); 2 (a), (b); 3 (a), (i)**
bien	► **1 (e); 3 (e) – (h); 7 (b), (c), (h)**
bon	► **3 (b), (c)**
juste	► **3 (b), (d); 7 (b), (e)**
vrai	► **3 (j)**
redresser	► **4 (a), (b)**
se redresser	► **5**
à droite	► **7 (a)**
tout de suite	► **7 (g)**

1 *n* (**a**) *(in directions)* droite *f*; **look to the** *or* **your right** regardez à droite *ou* sur votre droite; **keep to the** *or* **your right** restez à droite; **take a right** tournez à droite; **he was seated on your right** il était assis à ta droite; **from right to left** de droite à gauche

(**b**) *Pol* **the right** la droite; **the right is** *or* **are divided** la droite est divisée; **to be to** *or* **on the right** être à droite; **he's to the right of the party leadership** il est plus à droite que les dirigeants du parti

(**c**) *(in boxing)* droite *f*; **with a right to the jaw** d'une droite à la mâchoire

(**d**) *(entitlement)* droit *m*; **to have a right to sth** avoir droit à qch; **she has a right to half the profits** elle a droit à la moitié des bénéfices; **to have a** *or* **the right to do sth** avoir le droit de faire qch; **you've no right to talk to me like that!** tu n'as pas le droit de me parler ainsi!; **you have every right to be angry** tu as toutes les raisons d'être en colère; **by what right?** de quel droit?; **what right have you to do that?** de quel droit faites-vous cela?; **right of abode** droit *m* de séjour; **right of asylum** droit *m* d'asile; **the right to vote/to know** le droit de vote/de savoir; **the right to life** le droit à la vie; **right of reply** droit *m* de réponse *ou* de rectification; **he's American by right of birth** il est américain de naissance; **as of right** de (plein) droit; **I know my rights** je connais mes droits; **the rights of man** les droits *mpl* de l'homme; **you'd be within your rights to demand a refund** vous seriez dans votre (bon) droit si vous réclamiez un remboursement; *Am* **read him his rights** *(on arresting a suspect)* prévenez-le de ses droits; **she's rich in her own right** elle a une grande fortune personnelle; **he became a leader in his own right** il est devenu leader par son seul talent

(**e**) *(what is good, moral)* bien *m*; **to know right from wrong** faire la différence entre le bien et le mal; **to be in the right** être dans le vrai, avoir raison; **he put himself in the right by apologizing** il s'est racheté en s'excusant

2 *npl* (**a**) *Com & Law* **rights** droits *mpl*; **mineral rights** droits *mpl* miniers; **film/distribution rights** droits *mpl* d'adaptation cinématographique/de distribution; **to hold the translation rights to a book** détenir les droits de traduction d'un livre; **all rights reserved** tous droits réservés

(**b**) *St Exch* **(application** *or* **subscription) rights** droits *mpl* de souscription

(**c**) *(proper order)* **to put** *or* **to set to rights** *(room)* mettre en ordre; *(firm, country)* redresser; *(situation)* arranger; **I'll soon have this kitchen set to rights** j'aurai vite fait de remettre de l'ordre dans la cuisine; **to put** *or* **to set the world to rights** refaire le monde

3 *adj* (**a**) *(indicating location, direction)* droit; **raise your right hand** levez la main droite; **he's my right hand** c'est mon bras droit; **the right side of the stage** le côté droit de *ou* la droite de la scène; **take the next right turn** prenez la prochaine à droite; **would you like to try the right shoe?** *(in shop)* vous voulez essayer le pied droit?

(**b**) *(accurate, correct → answer, address)* bon; *(→ prediction)* juste, exact; **the weather forecasts are never right** les prévisions météo ne sont jamais exactes; **he didn't give me the right change** il ne m'a pas rendu la monnaie exacte; **have you got the right change?** avez-vous le compte exact?; **is this the right house?** est-ce la bonne maison?, est-ce bien la maison?; **the station clock is right** l'horloge de la gare est juste *ou* à l'heure; **have you got the right time?** est-ce que vous avez l'heure (exacte)?; **that can't be right** ça ne peut pas être ça, ça ne peut pas être juste; **the sentence doesn't sound/look quite right** la phrase sonne/a l'air un peu bizarre; **there's something not quite right in what he says** il y a quelque chose qui cloche dans ce qu'il dit; **to be right** *(person)* avoir raison; **you're quite right!** vous avez bien raison!; **the customer is always right** le client a toujours raison; **you were right about the bus schedules/about him/about what she would say** vous aviez raison au sujet des horaires de bus/à son sujet/sur ce qu'elle dirait; **I was right in thinking he was an actor** j'avais raison de penser que c'était un acteur; **am I right in thinking you're German?** vous êtes bien allemand, ou est-ce que je me trompe?; **you're the eldest, am I right** *or* **is that right?** c'est (bien) toi l'aîné, ou est-ce que je me trompe?; **I owe you $5, right?** je te dois 5 dollars, c'est (bien) ça?; **and I'm telling you you still owe me £10, right!** et moi je te dis que tu me dois encore 10 livres, vu?; **he's sick today, right?** il est malade aujourd'hui, non?; **that's right** c'est juste, oui; **he got the pronunciation/spelling right** il l'a bien prononcé/épelé; **she got the answer right** elle a donné la bonne réponse; **I never get those quadratic equations right** je me trompe toujours avec ces équations quadratiques; **he got the time right but the date wrong** il ne s'est pas trompé d'heure mais de date; **make sure you get your figures/her name right** faites attention de ne pas vous tromper dans vos calculs/sur son nom; **place the document right side down/up** placez le document face en bas/vers le haut; **the right side of the material** l'endroit *m* du tissu; **turn the socks right side in/out** mettez les chaussettes à l'envers/à l'endroit; **he's on the right side of forty** il n'a pas encore quarante ans; **to get on the right side of sb** s'insinuer dans les bonnes grâces de qn; **to keep on the right side of the law** respecter la loi; **you're not doing it the right way!** ce n'est pas comme ça qu'il faut faire *ou* s'y prendre!; **there's no one right way to go about it** il n'y a pas qu'une façon de s'y prendre; **that's the right way to approach the problem** c'est comme ça qu'il faut aborder la question; **get your facts right!** vérifiez vos renseignements!; **he got it right this time** il ne s'est pas trompé cette fois-ci; **let's get this right** mettons les choses au clair; **time proved her right** le temps lui a donné raison; **how right you are!** vous avez cent fois raison!; **to put sb right (about sb/sth)** détromper qn (au sujet de qn/qch); **he thought he could get away with it, but I soon put him right** il croyait qu'il pourrait s'en tirer comme ça mais je l'ai vite détrompé; **to put** *or* **to set right** *(fallen or upright object)* redresser, remettre d'aplomb; *(clock)* remettre à l'heure; *(machine, mechanism)* réparer; *(text, mistake, record)* corriger; *(oversight, injustice)* réparer; **to put things** *or* **matters right** *(politically, financially etc)* redresser *ou* rétablir la situation; *(in relationships)* arranger les choses; **he made a mess of it and I had to put things right** il a raté son coup et j'ai dû réparer les dégâts

(**c**) *(most appropriate → diploma, tool, sequence, moment)* bon; *(→ choice, decision)* meilleur; **I think it's the right strategy** je crois que c'est la bonne stratégie; **when the time is right** au bon moment, au moment voulu; **you'll know when the time is right** tu sauras quand ce sera le bon moment; **to be in the right place at the right time** être là où il faut quand il faut; **I can't find the right word** je ne trouve pas le mot juste; **are we going in the right direction?** est-ce que nous allons dans le bon sens?; **we're on the right road** nous sommes sur le bon chemin *ou* la bonne route; **if the price is right** si le prix est intéressant; **the colour is just right** la couleur est parfaite; **the magazine has just the right mix of news and commentary** la revue a juste ce qu'il faut d'informations et de commentaires; **she's the right woman for the job** c'est la femme qu'il faut pour ce travail; **the right holiday for your budget** les vacances qui conviennent le mieux à votre budget; **the frame is right for the picture** le cadre convient tout à fait au tableau; **her hairdo isn't right for her** sa coiffure ne lui va pas; **teaching isn't right for you** l'enseignement n'est pas ce qu'il vous faut; **she's the right person to talk to** c'est à elle qu'il faut s'adresser; **is this the right sort of outfit to wear?** est-ce la bonne tenue?; **it wasn't the right thing to say** ce n'était pas la chose à dire; **you've done the right thing to tell us about it** vous avez bien fait de nous en parler; **he did the right thing, but for the wrong reasons** il a fait le bon choix mais pour de mauvaises raisons

(**d**) *(fair, just)* juste, équitable; *(morally good)* bien *(inv)*; *(socially correct)* correct; **it's not right to separate the children** ce n'est pas bien de séparer les enfants; **I don't think capital punishment is right** je ne crois pas que la peine de mort soit juste; **it is only right and proper for the father to be present** il est tout à fait naturel que le père soit présent; **do you think it's right for them to sell arms?** est-ce que vous croyez qu'ils ont raison de vendre des armes?; **I can't accept the money, it wouldn't look right** je ne peux pas accepter cet argent, ça ferait mauvais effet; **I thought it right to ask you first** j'ai cru bon de vous demander d'abord; **I don't feel right leaving you alone** ça me gêne de te laisser tout seul; **it's only right that you should know** il est juste que vous le sachiez; **I only want to do what is right** je ne cherche qu'à bien faire; **to do the right thing (by sb)** bien agir (avec qn); *Br Old-fashioned* **I hope he's going to do the right thing by you** *(marry you)* j'espère qu'il va agir honorablement à ton égard (et demander ta main)

(**e**) *(healthy)* bien *(inv)*; **I don't feel right** je ne me sens pas très bien, je ne suis pas dans mon assiette; **my knee doesn't feel right** j'ai quelque chose au genou; **a rest will put** *or* **set you right again** un peu de repos te remettra; **nobody in their right mind would refuse such an offer!** aucune personne sensée ne refuserait une telle offre!; *Fam* **he's not quite right in the head** ça ne va pas très bien dans sa tête

(**f**) *(functioning properly)* **the window is still not right** la fenêtre ne marche pas bien encore; **there's something not quite right with the motor** le moteur ne marche pas très bien

(**g**) *(satisfactory)* bien *(inv)*; **things aren't right between them** ça ne va pas très bien entre eux; **does the hat look right to you?** le chapeau, ça va?; **I can't get this hem right** je n'arrive pas à faire un bel ourlet; *Fam* **to come right** s'arranger ❑

(**h**) *(indicating social status)* bien *(inv)*, comme il faut; **she took care to be seen in all the right places** elle a fait en sorte d'être vue partout où il fallait; **you'll only meet her if you move in the right circles** vous ne la rencontrerez que si vous fréquentez le beau monde; **to know the right people** connaître des gens bien placés; **he went to the right school and belonged to the right clubs** il a fréquenté une très bonne école et a appartenu aux meilleurs clubs

(**i**) *Geom (angle, line, prism, cone)* droit

(**j**) *Br Fam (as intensifier)* vrai ❑, complet(-ète) ❑; **I felt like a right idiot** je me sentais vraiment bête ❑; **the government made a right mess of it** le gouvernement a fait un beau gâchis; **there was a right one in here this morning!** on a eu un vrai cinglé ce matin!

(**k**) *Am Fam* **a right guy** un chic type

(**l**) *Scot & Ir Fam (ready)* prêt ❑

4 *vt* (**a**) *(set upright again → chair, ship)* redresser; **the crane righted the derailed carriage** la grue a redressé le wagon qui avait déraillé; **the raft will right itself** le radeau se redressera (tout seul)

(**b**) *(redress → situation)* redresser, rétablir; *(→ damage, injustice)* réparer; *(→ mistake)* corriger, rectifier; **to right a wrong** redresser un tort;

rig–rig

to right the balance rétablir l'équilibre; **the problem won't just right itself** ce problème ne va pas se résoudre de lui-même *ou* s'arranger tout seul

5 *vi (car, ship)* se redresser

6 *exclam* **come tomorrow – right (you are)!** venez demain – d'accord!; **right, let's get to work!** bon *ou* bien, au travail!; **right (you are) then, see you later** bon alors, à plus tard; *Fam* **too right!** tu l'as dit!; *Fam* **right on!** bravo!

7 *adv* (**a**) *(in directions)* à droite; **turn right at the traffic lights** tournez à droite au feu (rouge); **look right** regardez à droite; **the party is moving further right** le parti est en train de virer plus à droite; *Fam* **right, left and centre** *(everywhere)* de tous les côtés; *Fam* **he owes money right and left** *or* **right, left and centre** il doit de l'argent à droite et à gauche; *Fam* **they're giving out gifts right and left** *or* **right, left and centre** ils distribuent des cadeaux à tour de bras

(**b**) *(accurately, correctly → hear)* bien; *(→ guess)* juste; *(→ answer, spell)* bien, correctement; **if I remember right** si je me rappelle bien; **he predicted the election results right** il a vu juste en ce qui concernait les résultats des élections

(**c**) *(properly)* bien, comme il faut; **the door doesn't shut right** la porte ne ferme pas bien; **nothing works right in this house!** rien ne marche comme il faut dans cette maison!; **you're not holding the saw right** tu ne tiens pas la scie comme il faut; **the top isn't on right** le couvercle n'est pas bien mis; **if we organize things right, there'll be enough time** si nous organisons bien les choses, il y aura assez de temps; **I hope things go right for you** j'espère que tout ira bien pour toi; **nothing is going right today** tout va de travers aujourd'hui; **he can't do anything right** il ne peut rien faire correctement *ou* comme il faut; **do it right the next time!** ne vous trompez pas la prochaine fois!; **the roast is done just right** le rôti est cuit à la perfection

(**d**) *(emphasizing precise location)* **the lamp's shining right in my eyes** j'ai la lumière de la lampe en plein dans les yeux *ou* en pleine figure; **it's right opposite the post office** c'est juste en face de la poste; **it's right in front of/behind you** c'est droit devant vous/juste derrière vous; **he parked right in front of the gate** il s'est garé en plein devant le portail; *Fig* **I'm right behind you there** je suis entièrement d'accord avec vous là-dessus; **I stepped right in it** j'ai marché en plein dedans; **he shot him right in the forehead** il lui a tiré une balle en plein front; **the hotel was right on the beach** l'hôtel donnait directement sur la plage; **it broke right in the middle** ça a cassé juste au milieu; **I left it right here** je l'ai laissé juste ici; **stay right there** ne bougez pas

(**e**) *(emphasizing precise time)* juste, exactement; **I arrived right at that moment** je suis arrivé juste à ce moment-là; **right in the middle of the fight** au beau milieu de la bagarre

(**f**) *(all the way)* **it's right at the back of the drawer/at the front of the book** c'est tout au fond du tiroir/juste au début du livre; **right down to the bottom** jusqu'au fond; **right at the top** tout en haut; **a wall right round the house** un mur tout autour de la maison; **he turned right round** il a fait un tour complet; **right from the start** dès le début; **move right over** allez jusqu'au fond; **his shoes were worn right through** ses chaussures étaient usées jusqu'à la corde; **the car drove right through the roadblock** la voiture est passée à travers le barrage; **the path leads right to the lake** le sentier va jusqu'au lac; **the water came right up to the window** l'eau est montée jusqu'à la fenêtre; **she walked right up to me** elle se dirigea tout droit vers moi; **we worked right up until the last minute** nous avons travaillé jusqu'à la toute dernière minute; *Fig* **that girl is going right to the top** cette fille ira loin; *Fig* **you have to go right to the top if you want to get anything done** il faut aller tout en haut de la hiérarchie pour arriver à quelque chose

(**g**) *(immediately)* tout de suite; **I'll be right back** je reviens tout de suite; **I'll be right over** je viens tout de suite; **I'll be right with you** je suis à vous tout de suite; **let's talk right after the meeting** parlons-en juste après la réunion

(**h**) *(justly, fairly)* bien; *(decently, fittingly)* correctement; **you did right** tu as bien fait; **to see sb right** *(financially)* veiller à ce que qn ne soit pas à court d'argent; **to do right by sb** agir correctement envers qn

(**i**) *Br (in titles)* **the Right Reverend William Walker** le très révérend William Walker

(**j**) *Br Fam (for emphasis)* vachement, drôlement; **I was right angry** j'étais vachement en colère; **it's a right cold day** ça pince drôlement aujourd'hui, il fait drôlement frisquet aujourd'hui; **she was right nice** elle était bien aimable; **I was right glad to hear it** j'étais très heureux de l'apprendre

8 **by right, by rights** *adv* en principe; **she ought, by rights, to get compensation** en principe, elle devrait toucher une compensation

9 **right away** *adv (at once)* tout de suite, aussitôt; *(from the start)* dès le début; *(first go)* du premier coup; **right away, sir!** tout de suite, monsieur!; **I knew right away there'd be trouble** j'ai su tout de suite *ou* dès le début qu'il y aurait des problèmes

10 **right now** *adv* (**a**) *(at once)* tout de suite (**b**) *(at the moment)* pour le moment

11 **right off** *Am* = **right away**

▸▸ ***right angle*** angle *m* droit; **the corridors are at right angles** les couloirs sont perpendiculaires; **a line at right angles to the base** une ligne perpendiculaire à la base; **the path made a right angle** le sentier formait un coude; *Comput* ***right arrow*** flèche *f* vers la droite; *Comput* ***right arrow key*** touche *f* de déplacement vers la droite; *Br* ***Right Honourable*** = titre utilisé pour s'adresser à certains hauts fonctionnaires ou à quelqu'un ayant un titre de noblesse; **my Right Honourable Friend** *(form of address in Parliament)* mon distingué collègue; **the Right Honourable Member for Edinburgh West** le député de la circonscription "Edinburgh West"; *Fin* ***rights issue*** émission *f* de nouvelles actions à taux préférentiel; *Typ* ***right justification*** justification *f* à droite; *Br* ***right to roam*** = droit d'emprunter des sentiers sur des terres appartenant à de grands propriétaires terriens; *Am Geom* ***right triangle*** triangle *m* rectangle; ***right of way*** *Aut* priorité *f*; *(right to cross land)* droit *m* de passage; *(path, road)* chemin *m*; *Am (for power line, railroad etc)* voie *f*; **it's your right of way** vous avez (la) priorité; **to have (the) right of way** avoir (la) priorité; *Zool* ***right whale*** baleine *f* franche; ***right wing*** *Pol* droite *f*; *Sport (position)* aile *f* droite; *(player)* ailier *m* droit; **the right wing of the party** l'aile droite du parti

'The Rights of Man' *Paine* 'Les Droits de l'homme'

'The Right Stuff' *Wolfe* 'L'Étoffe des héros'

RIGHT TO ROAM

Depuis toujours, une très grande partie des plus beaux endroits de la campagne britannique est interdite au public et pendant des siècles, les propriétaires terriens ont tout fait pour que la situation reste inchangée. Cependant, en mai 2000, le gouvernement travailliste introduisit le "right to roam" qui devrait ouvrir aux promeneurs plus d'1,6 million d'hectares de campagne et environ 6400 kilomètres de droits de passage. De nombreux propriétaires terriens ont exprimé leur mécontentement car ils estiment que les promeneurs abîment les cultures et perturbent le bétail mais avec les nouvelles propositions de loi, ils ne pourraient interdire le passage sur leurs terres que 28 jours par an au maximum.

right-about turn *n* demi-tour *m*

right-angled *adj (hook, turn)* à angle droit

▸▸ *Br* ***right-angled triangle*** triangle *m* rectangle

right-click *Comput* **1** *vt* cliquer avec le bouton droit de la souris sur

2 *vi* cliquer avec le bouton droit de la souris (**on** sur); **right-click on the icon to start the program** cliquez sur l'icône avec le bouton droit de la souris pour faire démarrer le programme

righten ['raɪtən] **1** *vt* redresser

2 *vi* se redresser

righteous ['raɪtʃəs] **1** *adj* (**a**) *(just)* juste; *(virtuous)* vertueux (**b**) *Pej (self-righteous)* suffisant; **righteous indignation** colère *f* indignée (**c**) *Fam Black Am slang (genuine)* authentique[❑]; *(excellent)* génial, super *inv*

2 *npl* **the righteous** les bons *mpl*, les justes *mpl*

righteously ['raɪtʃəslɪ] *adv* (**a**) *(virtuously)* vertueusement (**b**) *Pej (self-righteously)* avec suffisance

righteousness ['raɪtʃəsnɪs] *n* vertu *f*, rectitude *f*

right-footed [-'fʊtɪd] *adj* qui se sert de son pied droit

right-footer *n* (**a**) *Sport* joueur(euse) *m,f* qui joue du pied droit (**b**) *Ir & Scot Fam Pej (Protestant)* protestant(e)[❑] *m,f*

rightful ['raɪtfʊl] *adj* légitime; *(inheritance)* auquel on a droit; **to have one's rightful share** avoir sa juste part; **she insisted on being given her rightful share** elle insista pour qu'on lui donne la part à laquelle elle avait droit

▸▸ ***rightful owner*** propriétaire *mf* légitime

rightfully ['raɪtfʊlɪ] *adv* légitimement

right-hand *adj* droit; **on the right-hand side** à droite; **the right-hand side of the road** le côté droit de la route; **it's in the right-hand drawer** c'est dans le tiroir de droite; **a right-hand bend** un virage à droite; **my right-hand glove** mon gant droit

▸▸ *Aut* ***right-hand drive*** conduite *f* à droite; **a right-hand drive vehicle** un véhicule avec la conduite à droite; ***right-hand man*** bras *m* droit

right-handed *adj* (**a**) *(person)* droitier (**b**) *(punch)* du droit (**c**) *(scissors, golf club)* pour droitiers; *(screw)* fileté à droite

right-handedly [-'hændɪdlɪ] *adj (play, hit, kick)* de la main droite

right-handedness [-'hændɪdnɪs] *n* dextralité *f*

right-hander *n* (**a**) *(person)* droitier(ère) *m,f* (**b**) *(blow)* coup *m* du droit

right-ho *exclam Br Fam* OK!, d'ac!

rightism ['raɪtɪzəm] *n* idées *fpl* de droite

rightist ['raɪtɪst] **1** *n* homme *m*/femme *f* de droite; **they're rightists** ils sont de droite

2 *adj* de droite

rightly ['raɪtlɪ] *adv* (**a**) *(correctly)* correctement, bien; **rightly dressed for the occasion** habillé pour la circonstance; *Fam* **I don't rightly know** je ne sais pas bien[❑] (**b**) *(with justification)* à juste titre, avec raison; **he was rightly angry, he was angry and rightly so** il était en colère à juste titre

right-minded *adj* raisonnable, sensé; **every right-minded citizen/Christian** tout citoyen/chrétien honnête

rightness ['raɪtnɪs] *n* (**a**) *(accuracy → of answer)* exactitude *f*, justesse *f*; *(→ of guess)* justesse *f* (**b**) *(justness → of decision, judgment)* équité *f*; *(→ of claim)* légitimité *f* (**c**) *(appropriateness → of tone, dress)* justesse *f*, caractère *m* approprié

righto ['raɪtəʊ] *exclam Br Fam* OK!, d'ac!

right-of-centre *adj* centre droit

right-on *adj Fam (socially aware)* politiquement correct[❑]

rightsize ['raɪtsaɪz] *vt* dégraisser

rightsizing ['raɪt,saɪzɪŋ] *n* dégraissage *m*

right-thinking *adj* raisonnable, sensé

right-to-lifer *n* adversaire *mf* de l'avortement

right-to-work *adj Am (law, legislation)* qui rend illégal le fait de n'embaucher que des travailleurs syndiqués

▸▸ ***right-to-work movement*** = mouvement s'opposant à la pratique du "syndicat unique" aux États-Unis

rightward ['raɪtwəd] **1** *adj* de droite

2 *adv Am* à droite

rightwards ['raɪtwədz] *adv* à droite

right-wing *adj Pol* de droite; **she's more right-wing than the others** elle est plus à droite que les autres

right-winger *n* (**a**) *Pol* homme *m*/femme *f* de droite; **he's a right-winger** il est de droite; **measures unpopular with right-wingers** mesures peu appréciées par la droite (**b**) *Sport* ailier *m* droit

righty-ho [ˌraɪtɪ'həʊ] *exclam Br Fam* OK!, d'accord!

rigid ['rɪdʒɪd] *adj* (**a**) *(structure, material)* rigide; *(body, muscle)* raide; **he was rigid with fear** il était paralysé par la peur; *Fam* **it shook me rigid!** ça m'a fait un de ces coups! (**b**) *(person, ideas, policy)* rigide, inflexible; *(discipline)* strict, sévère; **she's very rigid in her ideas** elle a des idées très rigides *ou* inflexibles; *Br Fam* **to be bored rigid** s'ennuyer ferme
 ▸▸ ***rigid disk*** disque *m* dur

rigidify [rɪ'dʒɪdɪfaɪ] *(pt & pp* **rigidified***) vt* rigidifier

rigidity [rɪ'dʒɪdɪtɪ] *n* (**a**) *(of structure, material)* rigidité *f*; *(of body, muscle)* raideur *f* (**b**) *(of person, ideas, policy)* rigidité *f*, inflexibilité *f*; *(of discipline)* sévérité *f*

rigidly ['rɪdʒɪdlɪ] *adv* rigidement, avec raideur; **the rules are rigidly applied** le règlement est rigoureusement appliqué

rigmarole ['rɪgmərəʊl], *Am* **rigamarole** ['rɪgəmərəʊl] *n* (**a**) *(procedure)* cirque *m*; **I don't want to go through all the rigmarole of applying for a licence** je ne veux pas m'embêter à déposer une demande de permis (**b**) *(talk)* charabia *m*, galimatias *m*

rigor[1] ['rɪgə(r)] *n (UNCOUNT) Med (before fever)* frissons *mpl*; *(in muscle)* crampe *f*

rigor[2] *Am* = **rigour**

rigorism ['rɪgərɪzəm] *n* rigorisme *m*, austérité *f*; *Rel* rigorisme *m*

rigorist ['rɪgərɪst] **1** *n* rigoriste *mf*
 2 *adj* rigoriste

rigor mortis [ˌrɪgə'mɔːtɪs] *n* rigidité *f* cadavérique

rigorous ['rɪgərəs] *adj* rigoureux
 ▸▸ *Math* ***rigorous proof*** preuve *f* rigoureuse

rigorously ['rɪgərəslɪ] *adv* rigoureusement, avec rigueur

rigorousness ['rɪgərəsnɪs] *n* rigueur *f*

rigour, *Am* **rigor** ['rɪgə(r)] *n* rigueur *f*

rigout ['rɪgaʊt] *n Fam* accoutrement ❑ *m*; **you can't go in that rigout!** tu ne peux pas y aller accoutré comme ça!

rile [raɪl] *vt* (**a**) *(person)* agacer, énerver; **don't get riled!** ne t'énerve pas! (**b**) *Am (water)* troubler

Riley ['raɪlɪ] *n Fam* **to live the life of Riley** se la couler douce, avoir la belle vie

rill [rɪl] *n* (**a**) *Literary (brook)* ruisselet *m* (**b**) *(on moon)* vallée *f* (**c**) *(from erosion)* ravine *f* (**d**) *Ling* fricative *f*

rille [rɪl] *n (on moon)* vallée *f*

rim [rɪm] *(pt & pp* **rimmed,** *cont* **rimming**) **1** *n* (**a**) *(of bowl, cup)* bord *m*; *(of eye, lake)* bord *m*, pourtour *m*; *(of well)* margelle *f*
 (**b**) *(of spectacles)* monture *f*
 (**c**) *(of wheel)* jante *f*
 (**d**) *(of dirt)* marque *f*; **a rim of coffee left in the cup** des traces de café à l'intérieur de la tasse; **there was a black rim around the bath** il y avait une trace de crasse tout autour de la baignoire
 2 *vt* border; **trees rim the lake** le lac est bordé *ou* entouré d'arbres
 ▸▸ ***rim brake*** frein *m* sur jante; *TV & Cin* ***rim light*** éclairage *m* rasant

rime[1] [raɪm] *Literary* **1** *n (frost)* givre *m*, gelée *f* blanche
 2 *vt* givrer

rime[2] *Arch* = **rhyme**

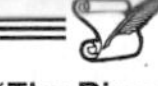

'The Rime of the Ancient Mariner' *Coleridge* 'La Chanson du vieux marin'

Rimini ['rɪmɪnɪ] *n* Rimini *m*

rimless ['rɪmlɪs] *adj (spectacles)* sans monture

-rimmed [rɪmd] *suff* **gold/steel-rimmed spectacles** lunettes *fpl* à monture en or/d'acier; **to have red-rimmed eyes** avoir les yeux rouges

rimming ['rɪmɪŋ] *n TV & Cin* éclairage *m* frisant

Rimsky-Korsakov [ˌrɪmskɪ'kɔːsəkɒf] *pr n* Rimski-Korsakov

rimy ['raɪmɪ] *(compar* **rimier,** *superl* **rimiest**) *adj Literary* givré

rind [raɪnd] *n (on bacon)* couenne *f*; *(on cheese)* croûte *f*; *(on fruit)* écorce *f*; *(of bark)* couche *f* extérieure

rinderpest ['rɪndəpest] *n Vet* peste *f* bovine

rindless ['raɪndlɪs] *adj (bacon)* sans couenne

RING [rɪŋ]

sonnerie	▸ 1 (a)
tintement	▸ 1 (a)
coup de fil	▸ 1 (b)
anneau	▸ 1 (d) – (f)
bague	▸ 1 (d), (e)
cercle	▸ 1 (f), (i)
sonner	▸ 2 (a); 3 (a), (c)
téléphoner (à)	▸ 2 (b); 3 (d)
entourer	▸ 2 (c), (d)
tinter	▸ 3 (a)
résonner	▸ 3 (b)

(senses **2** (**a**), (**b**), **3** *pt* **rang** [ræŋ], *pp* **rung** [rʌŋ], *senses* **2** (**c**) – (**f**) *pt & pp* **ringed**) **1** *n* (**a**) *(sound → of bell, telephone)* sonnerie *f*; *(→ of small bell, coins)* tintement *m*; **there was a ring at the door** on a sonné (à la porte); **she answered the phone after just one ring** le téléphone n'avait sonné qu'une fois quand elle a décroché; **give two long rings and one short one** sonnez trois fois, deux coups longs et un coup bref; **the ring of the church bells** le carillonnement des cloches de l'église; **the ring of their voices in the empty warehouse** leurs voix qui résonnaient dans l'entrepôt vide; *Fig* **it has a hollow ring** cela sonne creux; **his words had a ring of truth** il y avait un accent de vérité dans ses paroles; **the name has a familiar ring** ce nom me dit quelque chose; **that excuse has got a familiar ring!** j'ai déjà entendu ça quelque part!
 (**b**) *Br Fam (telephone call)* coup *m* de fil ❑; **give me a ring tomorrow** passe-moi un coup de fil *ou* appelle-moi demain
 (**c**) *(set of bells)* jeu *m* de cloches
 (**d**) *(on finger)* anneau *m*; *(with stone)* bague *f*; *(in nose, ear)* anneau *m*; **a diamond ring** une bague de diamant(s); **a wedding ring** une alliance, un anneau de mariage
 (**e**) *(round object)* anneau *m*; *(for serviette)* rond *m*; *(for swimmer)* bouée *f*; *(for identifying bird)* bague *f*; *(of piston)* segment *m*; **moor the boat to that ring** amarrez le bateau à cet anneau; *Tech* **retaining ring** plaquette *f* de fixation; **the rings** *(in gym)* les anneaux *mpl*
 (**f**) *(circle → of people, chairs)* cercle *m*; *(→ in water, of smoke)* rond *m*; *(→ in or around tree trunk, around planet)* anneau *m*; *(→ around sun, moon)* halo *m*; **they formed a ring round her** ils ont formé un cercle autour d'elle; **all stand in a ring** mettez-vous tous en cercle *ou* en rond; **sitting in a ring** assis en cercle *ou* en rond; **she looked round the ring of faces** elle regarda les visages tout autour d'elle; **the glasses left rings on the piano** les verres ont laissé des ronds *ou* des marques sur le piano; **the rings of Saturn** les anneaux de Saturne; **there's a ring around the moon** la lune est cernée d'un halo; **he has rings round his eyes** il a les yeux cernés; *Fam* **to run rings round sb** éclipser *ou* écraser qn
 (**g**) *(for boxing, wrestling)* ring *m*; *(in circus)* piste *f*; *(for bullfight)* arène *f*; *(for showjumping)* enceinte *f*; **the ring** *(boxing as sport)* la boxe; *St Exch* **the Ring** le Parquet
 (**h**) *Br (for cooking → electric)* plaque *f*; *(→ gas)* feu *m*, brûleur *m*
 (**i**) *(group → of people)* cercle *m*; *(→ gang)* bande *f*; *(→ of spies, drug traffickers)* réseau *m*; [illegible] cartel *m*; **price-fixing ring** cartel *m*; **spy/drug ring** réseau *m* d'espions/de trafiquants de drogue; **paedophile ring** réseau *m* pédophile
 (**j**) *Chem (of atoms)* chaîne *f* fermée
 2 *vt* (**a**) *(bell, alarm)* sonner; **I rang the doorbell** j'ai sonné à la porte; **the church clock rings the hours** l'horloge de l'église sonne les heures; **the name/title rings a bell** ce nom/titre me dit quelque chose; *Fam* **to ring the bell** *(succeed)* décrocher le pompon; **to ring the changes** *(on church bells)* carillonner; *Fig* changer; **to ring the changes on sth** apporter des changements à qch
 (**b**) *Br (phone)* téléphoner à, appeler
 (**c**) *(surround)* entourer, encercler; **a lake ringed with trees** un lac entouré *ou* bordé d'arbres
 (**d**) *(draw circle round)* entourer d'un cercle; **ring the right answer** entourez la bonne réponse
 (**e**) *(bird)* baguer; *(bull, pig)* anneler
 (**f**) *(in quoits, hoop-la → throw ring round)* lancer un anneau sur
 3 *vi* (**a**) *(chime, peal → bell, telephone, alarm)* sonner; *(→ with high pitch)* tinter; *(→ long and loud)* carillonner; **to ring at the door** sonner à la porte; **the doorbell rang** on a sonné (à la porte); **the bell is ringing for dinner** on sonne pour le dîner; **the line is ringing for you** ne quittez pas, je vous le/la passe
 (**b**) *(resound → gen)* résonner, retentir; *(→ ears)* bourdonner; **their laughter rang through the house** leurs rires résonnaient dans toute la maison; **the theatre rang with applause** la salle retentissait d'applaudissements; **my ears are ringing** j'ai les oreilles qui bourdonnent; **her words still ring in my ears** ses paroles résonnent encore à mes oreilles; **to ring true/false/hollow** sonner vrai/faux/creux
 (**c**) *(summon)* sonner; **to ring for the maid** sonner la bonne; **I rang for a glass of water** j'ai sonné pour qu'on m'apporte un verre d'eau; **you rang, Sir?** Monsieur a sonné?
 (**d**) *Br (phone)* téléphoner
 ▸▸ ***ring binder*** classeur *m* (à anneaux); ***ring circuit*** circuit *m* de bouclage; *Mus* ***the Ring Cycle*** la Tétralogie; ***ring finger*** annulaire *m*; ***ring main*** conducteur *m* de bouclage; *Comput* ***ring network*** réseau *m* en anneau; *Orn* ***ring ouzel*** merle *m* à plastron *ou* à collier; ***ring road*** périphérique *m*; *Br* ***ring spanner*** clé *f* polygonale

▸**ring around** = **ring round**

▸**ring back** *Br* **1** *vt sep (phone back)* rappeler
 2 *vi (phone back)* rappeler

▸**ring down** *vt sep Theat* **to ring down the curtain** baisser le rideau; *Fig* **to ring down the curtain on sth** marquer la fin de qch

▸**ring in** **1** *vt sep* (**a**) **to ring the new year in** sonner les cloches pour annoncer la nouvelle année
 (**b**) *Austr & NZ (rope in)* enrôler
 2 *vi Br* téléphoner; **listeners are encouraged to ring in** on encourage les auditeurs à téléphoner (au studio); **to ring in sick** téléphoner pour dire qu'on est malade

▸**ring off** *vi Br* raccrocher

▸**ring out** **1** *vt sep* **to ring out the old year** sonner les cloches pour annoncer la fin de l'année; *Fig* **to ring out the old and ring in the new** se débarrasser du vieux pour faire place au neuf
 2 *vi (bell, telephone)* sonner; *(voice, shot)* retentir

▸**ring round** *Br* **1** *vt insep* téléphoner à, appeler; **if you ring round everybody, I'm sure you'll find someone to help** si tu appelles tout le monde, tu trouveras bien quelqu'un pour t'aider
 2 *vi* passer une série de coups de fil

▸**ring up** *Br* **1** *vt sep* (**a**) *(phone)* téléphoner à, appeler (**b**) *(on cash register → sale, sum)* enregistrer; **to ring up a profit** réaliser un bénéfice (**c**) *Theat* **to ring up the curtain** lever le rideau; *Fig* **to ring up the curtain on sth** marquer le début de qch
 2 *vi* téléphoner

'The Ring of the Nibelung' *Wagner* 'L'Anneau des Nibelung'

ring-a-ring-a-roses *n* = chanson que chantent les enfants en faisant la ronde

ringbark ['rɪŋbɑːk] *vt (tree)* baguer, cerner

ringbolt ['rɪŋbəʊlt] *n* boulon *m* à anneau de levage

ring-bound *adj (notebook, file)* à anneaux

ringdove ['rɪŋdʌv] *n Orn* (pigeon *m*) ramier *m*, palombe *f*

ringed [rɪŋd] *adj (bird → wearing ring)* bagué; *(→ with marking)* à collier
 ▸▸ *Orn* ***ringed plover*** grand gravelot *m*, grand pluvier *m* à collier

ringer ['rɪŋə(r)] *n* (**a**) *(of bells)* sonneur *m*, carillonneur(euse) *m,f* (**b**) *Fam (double)* sosie ❑ *m*; **he's a (dead) ringer for you** vous vous ressemblez comme deux gouttes d'eau (**c**) *Am Fam Sport (horse)* = cheval qui participe frauduleusement à une course; *(player)* = joueur participant frauduleusement à un match (**d**) *Austr Fam (expert)* as *m*, crack *m*

ring-fence *vt Br (money)* allouer *(à des fins préétablies par le gouvernement)*

ringhals ['rɪŋhæls] *n Zool* sépédon *m*

ringing ['rɪŋɪŋ] **1** *adj* sonore, retentissant; **I still have a ringing sound in my ears** j'ai encore les oreilles qui sifflent; **in ringing tones** d'une voix vibrante

2 *n* (**a**) *(of doorbell, phone, alarm)* sonnerie *f*; *(of cowbell)* tintement *m*; *(of church bells)* carillonnement *m* (**b**) *(of cries, laughter)* retentissement *m*; *(in ears)* bourdonnement *m*

►► *Br Tel* ***ringing tone*** sonnerie *f*, signal *m* d'appel

ringleader ['rɪŋ,liːdə(r)] *n* meneur(euse) *m,f*

ringlet ['rɪŋlɪt] *n (curl)* anglaise *f*, boucle *f* (de cheveux); **to wear one's hair in ringlets** porter les cheveux en boucles, porter des anglaises

ringmaster ['rɪŋ,mɑːstə(r)] *n* ≃ Monsieur Loyal *m*

ringnecked ['rɪŋnekt] *adj (bird, snake)* à collier

►► *Orn* ***ringnecked dove*** pigeon *m* ramier, palombe *f*; *Orn* ***ringnecked pheasant*** faisan *m* de chasse, faisan *m* à collier; *Orn* ***ringnecked plover*** pluvier *m* à collier

ring-pull *n Br* anneau *m*, bague *f (sur une boîte de conserve, de boisson etc)*

►► ***ring-pull can*** cannette *f*, boîte *f (qu'on ouvre en tirant sur une bague)*

ringside ['rɪŋsaɪd] *n (UNCOUNT) Sport* premiers rangs *mpl*; **at the ringside** au premier rang; **to have a ringside seat** *(at circus, boxing match)* avoir une place au premier rang; *Fig* être aux premières loges; **to have a ringside view of sth** être bien placé pour voir qch

ring-tailed lemur *n Zool* maki *m*

ringway ['rɪŋweɪ] *n Br* périphérique *m*

ringworm ['rɪŋwɜːm] *n* teigne *f*

rink [rɪŋk] *n (for ice-skating)* patinoire *f*; *(for roller-skating)* piste *f*

rinky-dink ['rɪŋkɪdɪŋk] *adj Am Fam (goods)* merdique; *(business, businessman)* minable

rinse [rɪns] **1** *vt* rincer; **she rinsed her hands/her mouth** elle se rinça les mains/la bouche; **rinse the soap out of the clothes** rincez les vêtements

2 *n* (**a**) *(gen)* rinçage *m*; **I gave the shirt a good rinse** j'ai bien rincé la chemise; **put the washing machine on rinse** mettez le lave-linge sur rinçage

(**b**) *(for hair)* rinçage *m*; **to put a rinse through one's hair** se faire une couleur

▸**rinse out** **1** *vt sep (cup, bucket)* rincer; **to rinse out the dirt/the soap** rincer pour enlever la saleté/le savon; *Fig* **go and rinse your mouth out!** va te laver la bouche!

2 *vi (stain, dye)* partir à l'eau

Rio ['riːəʊ] *n* Rio de Janeiro *m*

►► ***the Rio Grande*** le Rio Grande; ***Rio de Janeiro*** Rio de Janeiro *m*; ***the Rio Negro*** le Rio Negro; ***the Rio Summit*** le sommet de Rio

Rioja [rɪ'ɒkə] *n* rioja *m*

riot ['raɪət] **1** *n* (**a**) *(civil disturbance)* émeute *f*; **race riots** émeutes *fpl* raciales

(**b**) *Fam (entertaining person, event, situation)* **the party was a riot** on s'est éclatés à la fête, la soirée était vraiment démente; **Alex is a riot** Alex est tordant *ou* impayable

(**c**) *(profusion)* profusion *f*; **the garden is a riot of colour** le jardin offre une véritable débauche de couleurs

2 *vi (gen)* se livrer à de violentes manifestations; *(at football match)* se battre; *(in prison)* se mutiner; **they are afraid the people will riot** ils craignent des émeutes populaires

3 *adv* **to run riot** *(people)* se déchaîner; *(imagination)* se débrider; *(plant)* proliférer, envahir le terrain; **a group of youths ran riot through the streets** un groupe de jeunes a semé la panique dans les rues; **the team ran riot in the second half** l'équipe s'est déchaînée au cours de la seconde mi-temps; **when she heard the news her imagination ran riot** *(anxiously)* quand elle a entendu la nouvelle, elle s'est mise à imaginer toutes sortes de choses

►► *Br Hist* ***the Riot Act*** loi *f* antiémeutes, loi *f* contre les rasssemblements séditieux; *Fam Fig* **to read the riot act** faire acte d'autorité❑; *Fam Fig* **to read sb the riot act** souffler dans les bronches à qn, passer un savon à qn; ***riot gear*** matériel *m* antiémeutes; ***riot police*** police *f ou* forces *fpl* antiémeutes; ***riot shield*** bouclier *m* antiémeutes; ***riot squad*** brigade *f* antiémeutes

rioter ['raɪətə(r)] *n* émeutier(ère) *m,f*

rioting ['raɪətɪŋ] *n (UNCOUNT)* émeutes *fpl*

riotous ['raɪətəs] *adj* (**a**) *(mob)* déchaîné; *(behaviour)* séditieux

(**b**) *(debauched)* débauché; *(exuberant, noisy)* tapageur, bruyant; **to lead a riotous life** mener une vie déréglée *ou* dissolue; **a riotous party was going on upstairs** à l'étage au-dessus, des fêtards s'en donnaient à cœur joie; **bursts of riotous laughter** des éclats de rire bruyants; **we had a riotous time** on a bien rigolé

(**c**) *(funny)* désopilant, tordant

►► *Law* ***riotous assembly*** attroupement *m* séditieux

riotously ['raɪətəslɪ] *adv* (**a**) *(seditiously)* de façon séditieuse (**b**) *(noisily)* bruyamment (**c**) *(as intensifier) Fam* **it's riotously funny** c'est à mourir *ou* à hurler de rire

riotousness ['raɪətəsnɪs] *n* (**a**) *(of crowd)* turbulence *f* (**b**) *(debauchery)* dérèglement *m*

RIP [,ɑːraɪ'piː] *n* (**a**) *(abbr* **rest in peace**) RIP (**b**) *Comput & Typ (abbr* **Raster Image Processor**) processeur *m* d'image tramée, RIP *m*

rip [rɪp] *(pt & pp* **ripped**, *cont* **ripping**) **1** *vt* (**a**) *(tear)* déchirer (violemment); **he ripped the envelope open** il déchira l'enveloppe; **to rip sth to shreds** *or* **to pieces** *(garment, letter)* mettre qch en morceaux *ou* en lambeaux; *Fig (criticize)* éreinter

(**b**) *(snatch)* arracher; **she ripped the book from my hands** elle m'arracha le livre des mains

(**c**) *Am Fam (rob)* voler❑; **she ripped him for all he had** elle lui a piqué tout ce qu'il avait

2 *vi* (**a**) *(tear)* se déchirer

(**b**) *Fam (go fast)* aller à fond de train *ou* à fond la caisse; **a motorbike ripped past** une moto est passée à toute allure❑; *Old-fashioned* **let it rip!** *(accelerate)* appuie sur le champignon!

(**c**) *Br Fam* **to let rip** *(behave unrestrainedly)* se déchaîner; *(pass wind)* larguer une caisse; **now they're gone we can really let rip** maintenant qu'ils sont partis, on va pouvoir s'éclater; **to let rip at sb** se mettre en pétard contre qn; *Old-fashioned* **let it rip!** *(go ahead)* vas-y!❑

3 *n* (**a**) *(tear)* déchirure *f* (**in** à)

(**b**) *(ocean current)* zone *f* de forts courants

▸**rip apart** **1** *vt sep* déchirer; *Fig* éreinter, mettre en pièces

2 *vi* se déchirer

▸**rip off** *vt sep* (**a**) *(tear off)* arracher; **the binding had been ripped off the book** la reliure du livre avait été arrachée

(**b**) *Fam (cheat, overcharge)* arnaquer; **they rip off tourists** ils arnaquent les touristes

(**c**) *Fam (rob)* dévaliser❑; *(steal)* faucher, piquer; **they ripped off a bank** ils ont braqué une banque; **my wallet was ripped off** je me suis fait faucher mon portefeuille; **he ripped off our idea** il nous a piqué notre idée

▸**rip out** *vt sep* arracher

▸**rip through** *vt insep* **the explosion ripped through the building** *(shook the building)* le choc de l'explosion a ébranlé tout le bâtiment; *(gutted the building)* l'explosion a éventré le bâtiment; **the fire ripped through the town** le feu s'est rapidement propagé dans toute la ville; *Fig* **we ripped through the work in no time** on a expédié le travail en un rien de temps

▸**rip up** *vt sep (paper, cloth)* déchirer *(violemment)*, mettre en pièces; *(road surface, street)* éventrer

riparian [rɪ'peərɪən] *Formal* **1** *adj (person, property)* riverain; *(rights)* des riverains

2 *n* riverain(e) *m,f*

ripcord ['rɪpkɔːd] *n* poignée *f* d'ouverture *(de parachute)*

ripe [raɪp] *adj* (**a**) *(fruit, vegetable)* mûr; *(cheese)* fait, à point

(**b**) *(age)* **to live to a ripe old age** vivre jusqu'à un âge avancé; **he married at the ripe old age of eighty** il s'est marié au bel âge de quatre-vingts ans

(**c**) *(ready)* prêt, mûr; **the country is ripe for a change of regime** le pays est mûr pour un changement de régime; **this land is ripe for development** ce terrain ne demande qu'à être aménagé; **the company is ripe for takeover** la société est prête pour être rachetée; **the time is ripe to sell** c'est le moment de vendre; **the time is not yet ripe** le temps n'est pas encore venu

(**d**) *(full → lips)* sensuel, charnu; *(→ breasts)* plantureux

(**e**) *(pungent → smell)* âcre

(**f**) *Fam (vulgar)* égrillard

ripen ['raɪpən] **1** *vi (gen)* mûrir; *(cheese)* se faire; **her feelings for him had ripened over the years** ses sentiments pour lui avaient mûri avec le temps

2 *vt (of sun)* mûrir; *(of farmer)* (faire) mûrir; **sun-ripened oranges** oranges *fpl* mûries au soleil

ripeness ['raɪpnɪs] *n* maturité *f*

ripening ['raɪpənɪŋ] **1** *n (of fruit, grain)* maturation *f*, mûrissage *m*, mûrissement *m*; *(of cheese)* affinage *m*

2 *adj* (**a**) *Literary (sun)* qui fait mûrir (**b**) *(fruit, grain)* mûrissant, qui mûrit; *(cheese)* qui se fait

rip-off *n Fam* (**a**) *(swindle)* escroquerie❑ *f*, arnaque❑ *f*; **that restaurant's a rip-off** ce restaurant est une arnaque; **what a rip-off!** quelle arnaque! (**b**) *(theft)* vol❑ *m*, fauche *f*; **it's a rip-off from an Osborne play** ils ont pompé l'idée dans une pièce d'Osborne

riposte [*Br* rɪ'pɒst, *Am* rɪ'pəʊst] **1** *n* (**a**) *(retort)* riposte *f*, réplique *f* (**b**) *Fencing* riposte *f*

2 *vi* riposter

ripped [rɪpt] *adj Fam (drunk)* bourré, pété; *(on drugs)* raide, défoncé; *Br very Fam* **ripped to the tits** *(drunk)* bourré comme un coing, plein comme une barrique; *(on drugs)* complètement raide *ou* défoncé

ripper ['rɪpə(r)] **1** *n* (**a**) *(criminal)* éventreur *m*; **Jack the Ripper** Jack l'Éventreur (**b**) *(machine)* scarificateur *m* (**c**) *Austr Fam* **he's a ripper** c'est quelqu'un de super; **it's a ripper** c'est super *ou* génial

2 *adj Austr Fam (excellent)* super *(inv)*, génial

ripping ['rɪpɪŋ] *adj Br Fam Old-fashioned* épatant, sensass *(inv)*; **a ripping yarn** une histoire épatante

ripple ['rɪpəl] **1** *n* (**a**) *(on water)* ride *f*, ondulation *f*; *(on wheatfield, hair, sand)* ondulation *f*

(**b**) *(sound → of waves)* clapotis *m*; *(→ of brook)* gazouillis *m*; *(→ of conversation)* murmure *m*; *Fig* **a ripple of excitement ran through the crowd** un murmure d'excitation parcourut la foule; **a ripple of laughter ran through the audience** des rires discrets parcoururent l'assistance

(**c**) *(repercussion)* répercussion *f*, vague *f*; **her resignation hardly caused a ripple** sa démission a fait très peu de bruit

(**d**) *Culin* **strawberry/chocolate ripple (ice cream)** glace *f* marbrée à la fraise/au chocolat

(**e**) *Electron* oscillation *f*

2 *vi* (**a**) *(undulate → water)* se rider; *(→ wheatfield, hair)* onduler; **moonlight rippled on the surface of the lake** le clair de lune scintillait sur la surface du lac; **the muscles rippled in his back** ses muscles se dessinaient sous la peau de son dos; **rippling muscles** muscles *mpl* saillants *ou* puissants

(**b**) *(murmur → water, waves)* clapoter

(**c**) *(resound, have repercussions)* se répercuter; **the scandal rippled through the whole department** le scandale s'est répercuté à travers *ou* a fait des vagues dans tout le service

3 *vt (water, lake)* rider

►► *TV & Cin* ***ripple dissolve*** fondu *m* par ondulation; ***ripple effect*** répercussions *fpl*; *Phys* ***ripple tank*** bac *m* à ondes

ripple-mark *n Geol* ripple-mark *f*

rip-rap *n Carp* enrochement *m*

rip-roaring *adj Fam (noisy)* bruyant❑, tapageur; *(great, fantastic)* génial, super *(inv)*; **we had a rip-roaring time** on s'est amusés comme des fous; **a rip-roaring success** un succès monstre

ripsaw ['rɪpsɔː] *n* scie *f* à refendre

ripsnorter ['rɪp,snɔːtə(r)] *n Fam* petite merveille *f*; **his new film's a ripsnorter** son nouveau film est vraiment génial

riptide ['rɪptaɪd] *n* contre-courant *m*, turbulence *f*

Rip Van Winkle ['rɪpvæn'wɪŋkəl] *pr n* = désigne

une personne déphasée par rapport aux réalités contemporaines (du nom du personnage d'un conte de Washington Irving, qui s'endormit sous un arbre et se réveilla vingt ans plus tard)

RISC [rɪsk] *n Comput* (*abbr* **reduced instruction set chip** *or* **computer**) RISC *m*

RISE [raɪz]

hauteur	►**1 (a)**
lever	►**1 (b)**
montée	►**1 (b)**
hausse	►**1 (c)**
se lever	►**2 (a), (b)**
se relever	►**2 (a)**
s'élever	►**2 (b), (f)**
augmenter	►**2 (c)**
monter	►**2 (c), (g)**

(*pt* **rose** [rəʊz], *pp* **risen** ['rɪzən]) **1** *n* (**a**) *(high ground)* hauteur *f*, éminence *f*; *(slope)* pente *f*; *(hill)* côte *f*; **we reached the top of a steep rise** nous sommes arrivés au sommet d'une côte raide

(**b**) *(of moon, sun, curtain)* lever *m*; *(to power, influence)* montée *f*, ascension *f*; *(in rank)* avancement *m*, promotion *f*; *(of industry, technology)* essor *m*; **the rise and fall of the tide** le flux et le reflux de la marée; **the rise and fall of the Roman Empire** la croissance et la chute *ou* la grandeur et la décadence de l'Empire romain; **the rise and fall of the fascist movement** la montée et la chute du mouvement fasciste; **her rise to fame came overnight** elle est devenue célèbre du jour au lendemain; *Br Fam* **to get** *or* **to take a rise out of sb** faire marcher qn, faire enrager qn

(**c**) *(increase → of price, cost of living, crime, accidents)* hausse *f*, augmentation *f*; *(→ in bank rate, interest)* relèvement *m*, hausse *f*; *(→ of temperature, pressure)* hausse *f*; *(→ in level of river)* crue *f*; *(→ of affluence, wealth)* augmentation *f*; *Br (→ in salary)* augmentation *f* (de salaire); **to be on the rise** être en hausse; **there has been a steep rise in house prices** les prix de l'immobilier ont beaucoup augmenté; **the rise in the price of petrol** la hausse du prix de l'essence; **there was a 10 percent rise in the number of visitors** le nombre de visiteurs a augmenté de 10 pour cent; **there has been a steady rise in the number of accidents** les accidents sont en augmentation régulière; **rise in value** appréciation *f*; *St Exch* **to speculate on a rise** jouer à la hausse; *Br* **to be given a rise** être augmenté

(**d**) *(origin → of river)* source *f*; *Fig* **to give rise to sth** donner lieu à qch, entraîner qch; **it gave rise to a lot of hostility/difficulties** cela a provoqué une forte hostilité/beaucoup de difficultés; **their disappearance gave rise to great scandal/suspicion** leur disparition a provoqué un énorme scandale/éveillé de nombreux soupçons

2 *vi* (**a**) *(get up → from chair, bed)* se lever; *(→ from knees, after fall)* se relever; **he rose (from his chair) to greet me** il s'est levé (de sa chaise) pour me saluer; **to rise to one's feet** se lever, se mettre debout; **he rises late every morning** il se lève tard tous les matins; **all rise!** *(in courtroom)* levez-vous s'il vous plaît!; *Horseriding* **to rise in the saddle** faire du trot enlevé; **the horse rose on its hind legs** le cheval s'est cabré; **rise and shine!** debout!; *Rel* **to rise from the dead** ressusciter d'entre les morts; **he looked as if he'd risen from the grave** il avait une mine de déterré

(**b**) *(sun, moon, star, fog)* se lever; *(smoke, balloon)* s'élever, monter; *(land)* s'élever; *(fish)* mordre; *Theat (curtain)* se lever; **to rise into the air** *(bird, balloon)* s'élever (dans les airs); *(plane)* monter *ou* s'élever (dans les airs); **the birds rose above our heads** les oiseaux se sont envolés au-dessus de nos têtes; **to rise to the surface** *(swimmer, whale)* remonter à la surface; *(anger)* faire surface; *(doubts, conflict)* se faire jour; *also Fig* **to rise to the bait** mordre à l'hameçon; **the colour rose in** *or* **to her cheeks** le rouge lui est monté aux joues; **his eyebrows rose in surprise** il leva les sourcils de surprise; **laughter/cheers rose from the crowd** des rires/des hourras montèrent de la foule; **a feeling of panic rose in me** un sentiment de panique s'est emparé de moi; **disturbing images rose into my mind** des images troublantes me vinrent à l'esprit; **to rise to the occasion** se montrer à la hauteur de la situation; *Fig* **to rise from the ashes** renaître de ses cendres

(**c**) *(increase → value)* augmenter; *(→ number, amount)* augmenter, monter; *(→ prices, costs)* monter, augmenter, être en hausse; *(→ temperature, pressure)* monter; *(→ barometer)* monter, remonter; *(→ wind)* se lever; *(→ tide, river level)* monter; *(→ tension, tone)* monter; *(→ voice)* s'élever; **gold has risen in value by 10 percent** la valeur de l'or a augmenté de 10 pour cent; **to rise by 10 dollars/by 10 percent** augmenter de 10 dollars/de 10 pour cent; **the pound has risen against the dollar** la livre s'est appréciée vis-à-vis du dollar; **to make prices rise** faire monter les prix; **prices are rising** les prix montent *ou* sont à la *ou* en hausse; **rents are rising fast** les loyers augmentent rapidement; **the river has risen by two metres** la rivière est montée de deux mètres; **the wind has risen to gale force** le vent se mit à souffler en tempête; **his voice rose above the noise of the crowd** sa voix s'élevait au-dessus du bruit de la foule; **his spirits rose when he heard the news** il a été soulagé *ou* heureux d'apprendre la nouvelle

(**d**) *Culin (dough)* lever; *(soufflé)* monter

(**e**) *(become erect → hair)* se hérisser; **the dog's hackles rose** le chien s'est hérissé de colère; **the hair on the back of her neck rose** ses poils se sont hérissés

(**f**) *(mountains, buildings)* se dresser, s'élever; **the trees rose above our heads** les arbres se dressaient au-dessus de nos têtes; **the mountain rises to 2,500 m** la montagne a une altitude de *ou* culmine à *ou* s'élève à 2500 m; **the steeple rises 200 feet into the air** le clocher a *ou* fait 60 mètres de haut; **many new apartment blocks have risen in the past ten years** de nombreux immeubles neufs ont été construits au cours des dix dernières années

(**g**) *(socially, professionally)* monter, réussir; **to rise in society** réussir socialement; **to rise in the world** faire son chemin dans le monde; **to rise to fame** devenir célèbre; **to rise to power** accéder au pouvoir; **to rise in sb's esteem** monter dans l'estime de qn; **to rise to the rank of colonel** monter jusqu'au grade de colonel; **to rise through the ranks** monter les échelons un à un; **to rise from the ranks** sortir du rang; **she rose to the position of personnel manager** elle a réussi à devenir chef du personnel

(**h**) *(revolt)* se soulever, se révolter (**against** contre); **to rise in arms** prendre les armes; **to rise in protest against sth** se soulever contre qch

(**i**) *(adjourn → assembly, meeting)* lever la séance; *(→ Parliament, court)* clore la session; **Parliament rose for the summer recess** la session parlementaire est close pour les vacances d'été

(**j**) *(originate → river)* prendre sa source

►► *Comput* ***rise time*** temps *m* de montée

►**rise above** *vt insep (obstacle, fear)* surmonter; *(figure)* dépasser; **this book never rises above the level of potboiler** ce livre n'est que de la littérature alimentaire; **she seems to rise above that kind of petty jealousy** elle semble être au-dessus de ce genre de jalousie mesquine; **try to rise above it** tâche de rester au-dessus de la mêlée; **politics should rise above the level of personal attacks** le débat politique ne devrait pas se situer au niveau des attaques personnelles

►**rise up** *vi* (**a**) *(get up)* se lever; **to rise up from one's chair** se lever de sa chaise

(**b**) *(go up)* monter, s'élever; **the smoke/the balloon rose up into the sky** la fumée/le ballon s'élevait dans le ciel

(**c**) *(revolt)* se soulever, se révolter; **to rise up against an oppressor** se soulever contre un oppresseur

(**d**) *Rel* ressusciter; **to rise up from the dead** ressusciter d'entre les morts

(**e**) *(appear)* apparaître; **a strange sight rose up before his eyes** un spectacle étrange s'offrit alors à son regard; **a shadowy figure rose up out of the mist** une ombre surgit de la brume

risen ['rɪzən] **1** *pp of* **rise**

2 *adj* ressuscité; **Christ is risen** le Christ est ressuscité

riser ['raɪzə(r)] *n* (**a**) *(person)* **to be an early/late riser** être un(e) lève-tôt *(inv)*/lève-tard *(inv)*

(**b**) *(of step)* contremarche *f* (**c**) *(in plumbing)* conduite *f* montante

risibility [ˌrɪzə'bɪlətɪ] (*pl* **risibilities**) *n Formal* caractère *m* risible *ou* ridicule

risible ['rɪzəbəl] *adj Formal* risible, ridicule

rising ['raɪzɪŋ] **1** *n* (**a**) *(revolt)* insurrection *f*, soulèvement *m*

(**b**) *(of sun, moon, theatre curtain)* lever *m*

(**c**) *(of prices)* augmentation *f*, hausse *f*

(**d**) *(of river)* crue *f*; *(of ground)* élévation *f*; *(of sap)* montée *f*

(**e**) *(from dead)* résurrection *f*

(**f**) *(of Parliament, an assembly)* ajournement *m*, clôture *f* de séance

2 *adj* (**a**) *(sun)* levant; **they were up early to see the rising sun** ils se levèrent de bonne heure pour voir le soleil se lever *ou* le soleil levant; **the land of the rising sun** *(Japan)* l'empire *m* du Soleil-Levant

(**b**) *(tide)* montant; *(water level)* ascendant

(**c**) *(ground, road)* qui monte

(**d**) *(increasing → temperature, prices)* en hausse; *Fin (→ market)* orienté à la hausse; **the rising number of homeless people/tourists** le nombre croissant de sans-logis/de touristes

(**e**) *(up-and-coming)* qui monte; **the rising generation** la nouvelle génération, la génération montante; **he's a rising celebrity** c'est une étoile montante

(**f**) *(emotion)* croissant

3 *adv Br Fam* **she's rising forty** elle va sur ses quarante ans

►► ***rising damp*** humidité *f* ascensionnelle *ou* par capillarité; *Br* ***rising fives*** = enfants allant sur leurs cinq ans (âge où ils doivent commencer l'école); ***rising star*** *Astron* étoile *f* montante; *Mktg (product)* produit *m* d'avenir; *Horseriding* ***rising trot*** trot *m* enlevé *ou* à l'anglaise

risk [rɪsk] **1** *n* (**a**) *(gen)* risque *m*; **to take a risk** prendre un risque; **to run the risk** courir le risque; **the government runs the risk of losing support** le gouvernement (court le) risque de ne plus être soutenu; **if you don't leave now there's a risk of you not arriving on time** si vous ne partez pas maintenant, vous risquez de ne pas arriver à temps; **is there any risk of him making another blunder?** est-ce qu'il risque de commettre un nouvel impair?; **there's no risk of that happening** pas de danger que ça se passe, ça ne risque pas d'arriver; **it's not worth the risk** c'est trop risqué; **that's a risk we'll have to take** c'est un risque à courir; **I'm not taking any risks** je ne veux prendre aucun risque, je ne veux rien risquer; **I'll take that risk** j'en prends le risque; **do it at your own risk** faites-le à vos risques et périls; **cars may be parked here at the owner's risk** *(sign)* les automobilistes peuvent stationner ici à leurs risques (et périls); **at the risk of one's life** au péril de sa vie; **at the risk of sounding ignorant, how does one open this box?** au risque de passer pour un idiot, j'aimerais savoir comment on ouvre cette boîte?

(**b**) *(in insurance)* risque *m*; **to underwrite a risk** souscrire un risque; **fire risk** risque *m* d'incendie; **he's a bad risk** c'est un client à risques; **risks and perils at sea** fortune *f* de mer

2 *vt* (**a**) *(endanger → life, reputation, job)* risquer, hasarder; **don't risk your career/reputation on a shady deal** ne risquez pas votre carrière/réputation sur une affaire louche; **you're risking an accident when you drive so fast** vous risquez un accident en conduisant si vite; **to risk one's neck** *or* **skin, to risk life and limb** risquer sa peau

(**b**) *(take the chance of → defeat, failure)* courir le risque de; **to risk sb's anger** s'exposer à la colère de qn; **she won't risk leaving** elle ne se risquera pas à partir; **to risk breaking one's leg** risquer de *ou* courir le risque de se casser une jambe

3 at risk *adj* **to place** *or* **put sth at risk** risquer qch; **to place** *or* **put sb at risk** faire courir un danger à qn; **there's too much at risk** les risques *ou* les enjeux sont trop importants; **our children are at risk from all kinds of violence** nos enfants ont toutes sortes de violences à craindre; **all our jobs are at risk** tous nos emplois sont menacés; *Med & Admin* **to be at risk** être vulnérable, être une personne à risque

▸▸ ***risk analysis*** analyse *f* des risques; *Am St Exch* ***risk arbitrage*** arbitrage *m* risque; ***risk assessment*** évaluation *f* des risques; *Acct* ***risk asset ratio*** coefficient *m* de solvabilité; *Br Fin* ***risk capital*** *(UNCOUNT)* capital *m* à risque; ***risk factor*** facteur *m* de risque; ***risk management*** gestion *f* des risques; ***risk management tool*** instrument *m* de maîtrise du risque; ***risk monitoring*** suivi *m ou* surveillance *f* des risques; *St Exch* ***risk premium*** prime *f* de risque de marché; *St Exch* ***risk-reward ratio*** ratio *m* risque-rentabilité; ***risk spreading*** répartition *f* des risques; *St Exch* ***risk warning*** = avertissement donné aux personnes désirant investir dans les produits dérivés, les renseignant sur les risques inhérents à ce genre d'investissement

riskily [ˈrɪskɪlɪ] *adv* d'une manière hasardeuse *ou* chanceuse

riskiness [ˈrɪskɪnɪs] *n (UNCOUNT)* risques *mpl*

risk-taker *n* = personne qui aime prendre des risques

risk-taking *n (UNCOUNT)* = fait de prendre des risques; **we knew there would be some risk-taking involved** nous savions que ce ne serait pas sans risques

risky [ˈrɪskɪ] *(compar* **riskier**, *superl* **riskiest**) *adj (hazardous)* risqué, hasardeux; **risky business** entreprise *f* hasardeuse

risorius [rɪˈsɔːrɪəs] *n Anat* muscle *m* risorius

▸▸ ***risorius muscle*** muscle *m* risorius

risotto [rɪˈzɒtəʊ] *(pl* **risottos**) *n Culin* risotto *m*

risqué [ˈriːskeɪ] *adj (story, joke)* risqué, osé, scabreux

rissole [ˈrɪsəʊl] *n Culin* rissole *f*

Ritalin® [ˈrɪtəlɪn] *n Pharm* Ritaline® *f*

ritardando [ˌrɪtɑːˈdændəʊ] *adv Mus* ritardando

rite [raɪt] *n* rite *m*; **initiation/fertility rites** rites *mpl* d'initiation/de fertilité; **rite of passage** cérémonie *f* d'initiation

'The Rite of Spring' *Stravinsky* 'Le Sacre du printemps'

ritornello [ˌrɪtɔːˈneləʊ] *(pl* **ritornellos** *or* **ritornelli** [-liː]) *n Mus* ritournelle *f*

ritual [ˈrɪtʃʊəl] **1** *n* rituel *m*; **to make a ritual of sth** (se) faire un rituel de qch; **it's become a bit of a ritual** c'est devenu comme un rituel; **he went through his nightly ritual of locking the doors** il a verrouillé les portes selon son rituel de tous les soirs; **everyone has to go through the ritual of official receptions** nul ne peut échapper au cérémonial des réceptions officielles

2 *adj* rituel; *Fig* **we all had to sit down to the ritual Sunday lunch** dimanche, nous avons tous dû prendre part au déjeuner rituel; **there was ritual condemnation of him in the press** la presse l'a condamné pour la forme

ritualism [ˈrɪtʃʊəlɪzəm] *n* ritualisme *m*

ritualist [ˈrɪtʃʊəlɪst] *n* ritualiste *mf*

ritualistic [ˌrɪtʃʊəˈlɪstɪk] *adj* ritualiste

ritualize, -ise [ˈrɪtʃʊəlaɪz] *vt* ritualiser

ritually [ˈrɪtʃʊəlɪ] *adv* rituellement

ritz [rɪts] *n Am Fam* tape-à-l'œil *m inv*; **to put on the ritz** se mettre sur son trente et un, *Pej* faire du tape-à-l'œil

ritzy [ˈrɪtsɪ] *(compar* **ritzier**, *superl* **ritziest**) *adj Fam* tape-à-l'œil *inv*, clinquant

rival [ˈraɪvəl] *(Br pt & pp* **rivalled**, *cont* **rivalling**, *Am pt & pp* **rivaled**, *cont* **rivaling**) **1** *n (gen)* rival(e) *m,f*; *Com* rival(e) *m,f*, concurrent(e) *m,f*; **rivals in business/love** rivaux *mpl* en affaires/amour

2 *adj (gen)* rival; *Com* concurrent, rival

3 *vt (gen)* rivaliser avec; *Com* être en concurrence avec; **his talent doesn't rival hers** il n'est pas aussi doué qu'elle; **no one can rival her when it comes to business acumen** son sens des affaires n'a pas d'égal; **it rivals anything to be seen in Paris** ça vaut largement tout ce que l'on peut voir à Paris; **New York cannot rival London for historic interest** New York ne vaut pas Londres du point de vue de l'intérêt historique; **your stubbornness is rivalled only by your narrow-mindedness** votre entêtement n'a d'égal que votre étroitesse d'esprit

'The Rivals' *Sheridan* 'Les Rivaux'

rivalry [ˈraɪvəlrɪ] *(pl* **rivalries**) *n* rivalité *f*; **there's a lot of rivalry between the two brothers** il y a une forte rivalité entre les deux frères; **the party is torn by personal rivalries** le parti est divisé par des rivalités d'ordre personnel; **in rivalry with sb** en concurrence *ou* rivalité avec qn

riven [ˈrɪvən] *adj* déchiré, divisé; **the party was riven by deep ideological divisions** le parti était déchiré par de profondes divergences idéologiques

river [ˈrɪvə(r)] **1** *n* (**a**) *(as tributary)* rivière *f*; *(flowing to sea)* fleuve *m*; **we sailed up/down the river** nous avons remonté/descendu la rivière; *Am Fam* **to be up the river** *(in prison)* être en taule *ou* en cabane; *Am Fam* **to send sb up the river** *(to prison)* mettre qn en taule *ou* en cabane; *Fam* **to sell sb down the river** trahir qn ❑, vendre qn ❑

(**b**) *Fig (of mud, lava)* coulée *f*; **a river of blood** un fleuve de sang

2 *comp (port, system, traffic)* fluvial; *(fish)* d'eau douce

▸▸ ***river basin*** bassin *m* fluvial; *Med* ***river blindness*** cécité *f* des rivières; *Zool* ***river dolphin*** dauphin *m* d'eau douce; ***river mouth*** *(of tributary)* embouchure *f* de la rivière *ou* du fleuve; ***river police*** police *f* fluviale

riverbank [ˈrɪvəbæŋk] *n* rive *f*, berge *f*; **on the riverbank** sur la rive (de la rivière *ou* du fleuve)

riverbed [ˈrɪvəbed] *n* lit *m* de rivière *ou* de fleuve

riverine [ˈrɪvəraɪn] *adj (fluvial)* fluvial; *(riverside)* riverain

riverside [ˈrɪvəsaɪd] **1** *n* bord *m* d'une rivière *ou* d'un fleuve, rive *f*; **we walked along the riverside** nous nous sommes promenés le long de la rivière

2 *adj* au bord d'une rivière *ou* d'un fleuve; **a riverside park** un parc situé au bord de l'eau *ou* d'une rivière

▸▸ ***riverside properties*** propriétés *fpl* riveraines

rivet [ˈrɪvɪt] **1** *n* rivet *m*

2 *vt* (**a**) *Tech* riveter, river (**b**) *Fig* **to be riveted to the spot** rester cloué *ou* rivé sur place; **the children were riveted to the television set** les enfants étaient rivés au poste de télévision (**c**) *(fascinate)* fasciner

▸▸ ***rivet gun*** pistolet *m* à river; ***rivet head*** tête *f* de rivet; ***rivet hole*** trou *m* de rivet

riveter [ˈrɪvɪtə(r)] *n (person)* riveur(euse) *m,f*; *(machine)* riveteuse *f*

riveting [ˈrɪvɪtɪŋ] **1** *n* rivetage *m*

2 *adj Fig (fascinating)* fascinant, passionnant, captivant

▸▸ ***riveting machine*** riveteuse *f*

Riviera [ˌrɪvɪˈeərə] *n* **the French Riviera** la Côte d'Azur; **on the French Riviera** sur la Côte d'Azur; **the Italian Riviera** la Riviera italienne; **on the Italian Riviera** sur la Riviera italienne

rivière [ˌrɪvɪˈeə(r)] *n (of precious stones)* rivière *f*

rivulet [ˈrɪvjʊlɪt] *n* (petit) ruisseau *m*, *Literary* ru *m*

Riyadh [ˈriːæd] *n* Riyad, Riad

riyal [rɪˈjæl] *n* rial *m*

RMT [ˌɑːremˈtiː] *n Br (abbr* **National Union of Rail, Maritime and Transport Workers**) = syndicat britannique des cheminots et des gens de mer

RN [ˌɑːˈren] *n Br* (**a**) *(abbr* **Royal Navy**) marine *f* nationale britannique (**b**) *(abbr* **registered nurse**) *(nurse)* infirmier(ère) *m,f* diplômé(e) (d'État) (**c**) *(qualification)* diplôme *m* (d'État) d'infirmier

RNA [ˌɑːrenˈeɪ] *n Biol (abbr* **ribonucleic acid**) ARN *m*

RNIB [ˌɑːrenˌaɪˈbiː] *n (abbr* **Royal National Institute for the Blind**) = institution britannique pour les aveugles

RNLI [ˌɑːrenˌelˈaɪ] *n (abbr* **Royal National Lifeboat Institution**) = société britannique de sauvetage en mer

RNZAF [ˌɑːrenˌzedeɪˈef] *n (abbr* **Royal New Zealand Air Force**) = armée de l'air néo-zélandaise

RNZN [ˌɑːrenˌzedˈen] *n (abbr* **Royal New Zealand Navy**) = marine de guerre néo-zélandaise

roach [rəʊtʃ] *(pl sense* (**a**) **inv** *or* **roaches**) *n* (**a**) *Ich* gardon *m* (**b**) *Am (cockroach)* cafard *m*, cancrelat *m* (**c**) *Fam Drugs slang (of cannabis cigarette)* mégot ❑ *m (d'une cigarette de marijuana)*

▸▸ *Fam Drugs slang* ***roach clip*** fume-joint *m*; *Am Fam* ***roach motel*** piège *m* à cafards; ***roach powder*** poudre *f* pour tuer les cafards

road [rəʊd] **1** *n* (**a**) *(gen)* route *f*; *(small)* chemin *m*; **minor road** route *f* secondaire; **by road** par la route; **the Liverpool road** la route de Liverpool; **is this the (right) road for** *or* **to Liverpool?** est-ce la (bonne) route pour Liverpool?; **are we on the right road?** sommes-nous sur la bonne route?; **on the road to Liverpool, the car broke down** en allant à Liverpool, la voiture est tombée en panne; **we took the road from Manchester to Liverpool** on a pris la route qui va de Manchester à Liverpool *ou* qui relie Manchester à Liverpool; **to take to the road** *(driver)* prendre la route *ou* le volant; *(tramp)* partir sur les routes; **to be on the road** *(travelling)* être en route *ou* chemin *ou* voyage; *(salesman)* être sur la route; *(pop star, troupe)* être en tournée; **we've been on the road since six o'clock this morning** nous roulons depuis six heures ce matin; **his car shouldn't be on the road** sa voiture devrait être retirée de la circulation; **someone of his age shouldn't be on the road** une personne de son âge ne devrait pas prendre le volant; *Br* **the price on the road excludes number plates and delivery** le prix clés en mains ne comprend pas les frais de livraison et d'immatriculation; **my car is off the road at the moment** ma voiture est en panne *ou* chez le garagiste

(**b**) *(street)* rue *f*; **a road of shops/of houses** une rue de magasins/de maisons, une artère commerçante/résidentielle; **he lives just down the road** il habite un peu plus loin dans la même rue; **Mr James from across the road** M. James qui habite en face; **he lives across the road from us** il habite en face de chez nous

(**c**) *(roadway)* route *f*, chaussée *f*; **to stand in the middle of the road** se tenir au milieu de la route *ou* de la chaussée; *Fig* **let's get this show on the road!** bon, on y va!; *Fam* **one for the road** un petit coup avant de partir; *Prov* **the road to hell is paved with good intentions** l'enfer est pavé de bonnes intentions

(**d**) *Fig (path)* chemin *m*, voie *f*; **if we go down that road** si nous nous engageons sur cette voie; **we don't want to go down the road of military intervention** nous ne voulons pas nous engager dans la voie d'une intervention armée; **to be on the right road** être sur la bonne voie; **to be on the road to success/recovery** être sur le chemin de la réussite/en voie de guérison; **he is on the road to an early death** il est (bien) parti pour mourir jeune; **down the road** *(in the future)* à l'avenir; **no one can see what is down the road** personne ne peut savoir ce que l'avenir réserve; **a few years down the road** dans quelques années; **yes, when I'm seventy, but that's a long way down the road (yet)** oui, quand j'aurai soixante-dix ans, mais ce n'est pas pour tout de suite; *Br Fam* **you're in my road!** *(I can't pass)* vous me bouchez le passage! ❑; *(I can't see)* vous me bouchez la vue! ❑; *Br Fam* **get out (of) my road!** poussez-vous! ❑, dégagez!; *Fam* **it was getting in the road of solving the problem** cela empêchait de résoudre le problème ❑; *Prov* **all roads lead to Rome** tous les chemins mènent à Rome

(**e**) *Am (railway)* chemin *m* de fer, voie *f* ferrée

(**f**) *(usu pl) Naut* rade *f*

(**g**) *(in mine)* galerie *f*

(**h**) *NEng Fam (idiom)* **any road (up)** de toute façon ❑; **it's too late, any road** de toute façon, c'est trop tard

2 *comp (traffic, bridge)* routier; *(accident)* de la route; *(conditions, construction, repairs)* des routes

▸▸ *Am Fam* ***road apple*** *(dung)* crottin ❑ *m*; ***road atlas*** atlas *m* routier; ***road book*** guide *m* routier; *Am Theat* ***road company*** troupe *f* itinérante; ***road haulage*** camionnage *m*, transports *mpl* routiers; ***road haulage company*** entreprise *f* de transports routiers; ***road haulage forwarding agent*** groupeur *m* routier; ***road haulier*** transporteur *m* routier, affréteur *m* routier; *Fam* ***road kill*** = animaux écrasés par des voitures; ***road maintenance*** voirie *f*; ***road manager*** responsable *mf* de tournée *(d'un chanteur ou d'un groupe pop)*; ***road map*** carte *f* routière; ***road metal*** *(for road)* empierrement *m*; *Rail* terre-plein *m*, ballast *m*; ***road movie*** road-movie *m*; ***road pricing*** = instauration d'un système de routes à péage; ***road race*** *(in cycling)* course *f* cycliste sur route; ***road racer*** *(bicycle)* bicyclette *f* de compétition; *(cyclist)* routier(ère) *m,f*; ***road racing*** *(cycling)* cyclisme *m* sur route; *(motor racing)* compétition *f* automobile *(sur route)*; ***road rage*** = accès de colère provoqué par la conduite des autres automobilistes; ***road roller*** rouleau *m* compresseur; ***road safety*** sécurité *f* routière; ***road sense*** *(for driver)* sens *m* de la conduite; **children have to be taught road sense** on doit apprendre aux enfants à faire attention à la circulation; ***road sign*** panneau *m* de signalisation; *Br* ***road tax*** taxe *f* sur les automobiles; **have you paid your road tax?** ≃ est-ce que tu as acheté ta vignette?; ***road tax disc*** ≃ vignette *f* (automobile); ***road test*** essai *m* sur route; ***road train*** train *m* *ou* convoi *m* routier; ***road transport*** transports *mpl* routiers; ***road transport company*** entreprise *f* de transport routier; *Am Fam* ***road warrior*** = homme d'affaires constamment en déplacement; ***road works*** travaux *mpl* (d'entretien des routes)

'On the Road' *Kerouac* 'Sur la route'

roadbed ['rəʊdbed] *n Constr* empierrement *m*; *Rail* ballast *m*

roadblock ['rəʊdblɒk] *n* barrage *m* routier

roadbuilding ['rəʊd,bɪldɪŋ] *n* construction *f* de routes

►► ***roadbuilding programme*** programme *m* pour construire des routes

road-fund *adj Br*

►► ***road-fund licence*** ≃ vignette *f*; ***road-fund tax*** taxe *f* routière

roadhog ['rəʊdhɒg] *n Fam (man)* chauffard *m*, écraseur *m*; *(woman)* écraseuse *f*

roadholding ['rəʊd,həʊldɪŋ] *n Aut* tenue *f* de route

roadhouse ['rəʊdhaʊs, *pl* -haʊzɪz] *n* relais *m* routier

roadie ['rəʊdɪ] *n Fam* = technicien qui accompagne les groupes de rock en tournée

roadman ['rəʊdmən] (*pl* **roadmen** [-mən]) *n* cantonnier *m*

roadrunner ['rəʊd,rʌnə(r)] *n Orn* coucou *m* terrestre de Californie

roadshow ['rəʊdʃəʊ] *n (gen)* tournée *f*; *(radio show)* = animation en direct proposée par une station de radio en tournée; *Mktg* tournée *f* de présentation

roadside ['rəʊdsaɪd] **1** *n* bord *m* de la route, bas-côté *m*; **we stopped the car by the roadside** nous avons arrêté la voiture au bord *ou* sur le bord de la route

2 *adj* au bord de la route

►► ***roadside advertising*** affichage *m* routier; *Aut* ***roadside assistance*** assistance *f* technique aux véhicules, assistance *f* dépannage; ***roadside camera*** caméra *f* en bord de route; ***roadside inn*** auberge *f* située au bord de la route; ***roadside repairs*** *(by driver)* réparations *fpl* de fortune; *(by mechanic)* dépannage *m*

roadstead ['rəʊdsted] *n Naut* rade *f*

roadster ['rəʊdstə(r)] *n* (**a**) *(car)* roadster *m* (**b**) *(bicycle)* bicyclette *f* (de tourisme)

roadsweeper ['rəʊd,swiːpə(r)] *n (person)* balayeur(euse) *m,f*; *(vehicle)* balayeuse *f*

road-test *vt* essayer sur route; *Fig* tester

road-testing *n* essai *m* routier; *Fig* tests *mpl*

roadtrip ['rəʊdtrɪp] *n Am (short)* promenade *f* en voiture; *(longer)* voyage *m* en voiture

road-user *n* usager(ère) *m,f* de la route

roadway ['rəʊdweɪ] *n* chaussée *f*

roadwork ['rəʊdwɜːk] *n (by boxer, athlete etc)* entraînement *m* consistant à courir le long de la route; **to do roadwork** courir le long de la route

roadworthiness ['rəʊd,wɜːðɪnɪs] *n* état *m* général *(d'un véhicule)*

roadworthy ['rəʊd,wɜːðɪ] *adj (vehicle)* en état de rouler

roam [rəʊm] **1** *vt* (**a**) *(travel → world)* parcourir; *(→ streets)* errer dans; **to roam the seven seas** aller aux quatre coins du monde (**b**) *(hang about → streets)* traîner dans

2 *vi* (**a**) *(wander)* errer, voyager sans but; **to roam about the world** courir le monde; *Fig* **he allowed his imagination/his thoughts to roam** il a laissé vagabonder son imagination/ses pensées (**b**) *Tel (mobile phone user)* itinérer

►**roam about, roam around** *vi* (**a**) *(travel)* vagabonder, bourlinguer (**b**) *(aimlessly)* errer, traîner

roamer ['rəʊmə(r)] *n* vagabond(e) *m,f*

roaming ['rəʊmɪŋ] **1** *adj* vagabond, errant

2 *n* (**a**) *(wandering)* vagabondage *m* (**b**) *Tel (of mobile phone)* roaming *m*, itinérance *f*; *Comput (on Internet)* roaming *m*

roan [rəʊn] **1** *adj* rouan

2 *n (horse)* (cheval *m*) rouan *m*; *(cow)* vache *f* rouanne

roar [rɔː(r)] **1** *vi (lion)* rugir; *(bull)* beugler, mugir; *(elephant)* barrir; *(person, crowd)* hurler; *(radio, music)* beugler, hurler; *(sea, wind)* mugir; *(storm, thunder)* gronder; *(fire, furnace)* ronfler; *(cannon)* tonner, gronder; *(car, motorcycle, engine)* vrombir; **to roar with anger** rugir *ou* hurler de colère; **to roar with laughter** rire aux éclats, rire à gorge déployée; **to roar with pain** hurler de douleur; **it made everyone roar (with laughter)** ça a déclenché un tonnerre d'hilarité *ou* l'hilarité générale; **the car roared past** *(noisily)* la voiture est passée en vrombissant; *(fast)* la voiture est passée à toute allure; **the leading car roared into the pits** la voiture de tête est arrivée à toute allure à son stand; **he roared up to us on his motorbike** il est venu vers nous à toute allure en faisant vrombir sa moto

2 *vt (feelings, order)* hurler; **the sergeant roared (out) an order to the men** le sergent a hurlé un ordre aux hommes; **he roared something at me** il m'a hurlé quelque chose; **the crowd roared their delight** la foule hurlait de joie; **they roared their team on** *(encouraged)* ils ont crié de toutes leurs forces pour encourager leur équipe

3 *n (of lion)* rugissement *m*; *(of bull)* mugissement *m*, beuglement *m*; *(of elephant)* barrissement *m*; *(of sea, wind)* mugissement *m*; *(of thunder, storm, cannons)* grondement *m*; *(of fire, furnace)* ronflement *m*; *(of crowd)* clameur *f*; *(hostile)* grondement *m*; *(of engine)* vrombissement *m*; **to give a roar** *(person)* hurler; *(lion)* rugir; **roars of laughter** gros *ou* grands éclats *mpl* de rire; **the roar of the traffic outside my window is awful** le vacarme de la circulation sous ma fenêtre est épouvantable

roaring ['rɔːrɪŋ] **1** *adj* (**a**) *(lion)* rugissant; *(bull)* mugissant, beuglant; *(elephant)* qui barrit; *(person, crowd)* hurlant; *(sea, wind)* mugissant; *(thunder, storm)* qui gronde; *(engine)* vrombissant; **a roaring fire** une bonne flambée

(**b**) *Fig (excellent)* **a roaring success** un succès fou; *Br* **to do a roaring trade** faire des affaires en or; **they did a roaring trade in pancakes** ils ont vendu énormément de crêpes

2 *adv Fam* **roaring drunk** ivre mort, complètement bourré

►► *Naut* ***Roaring Forties*** quarantièmes *mpl* rugissants; ***Roaring Twenties*** les Années *fpl* folles

roast [rəʊst] **1** *vt* (**a**) *(meat)* rôtir, faire rôtir; *(peanuts, almonds, chestnuts)* griller, faire griller; *(coffee)* griller, torréfier; **I decided to roast a chicken for dinner** j'ai décidé de faire un poulet rôti pour le dîner

(**b**) *(minerals)* calciner

(**c**) *Fig (by sun, fire)* griller, rôtir; **I sat roasting my toes by the fire** j'étais assis devant le feu pour me réchauffer les pieds

(**d**) *Fam (criticize → book, film)* éreinter

(**e**) *Am Fam (tease → person)* railler[□], mettre en boîte

2 *vi* (**a**) *(meat)* rôtir

(**b**) *Fig (person)* avoir très chaud; **we spent a week roasting in the sun** nous avons passé une semaine à nous rôtir au soleil

3 *adj* rôti; **medium roast coffee** café *m* torréfié; **high roast coffee** café *m* torréfié à cœur

4 *n* (**a**) *(joint of meat)* rôti *m*; **a pork roast, a roast of pork** un rôti de porc

(**b**) *Am (barbecue)* barbecue *m*; **to have a roast** faire un barbecue

(**c**) *Am Fam (of celebrity)* = soirée ou émission en l'honneur d'une vedette, et au cours de laquelle cette dernière fait l'objet de taquineries et de flatteries

►► ***roast beef*** rôti *m* de bœuf, rosbif *m*; ***roast chestnuts*** marrons *mpl* chauds; ***roast chicken*** poulet *m* rôti; ***roast pork*** rôti *m* de porc; ***roast potatoes*** pommes *fpl* de terre rôties au four; ***roast veal*** rôti *m* de veau

roaster ['rəʊstə(r)] *n* (**a**) *Br Culin (chicken)* volaille *f* à rôtir; *(pan)* cocotte *f* (**b**) *(for coffee)* brûloir *m*, torréfacteur *m*

roasting ['rəʊstɪŋ] **1** *n* (**a**) *(of meat)* rôtissage *m*; *(of coffee)* torréfaction *f*

(**b**) *Br Fam Fig* **to give sb a roasting** *(tell off)* souffler dans les bronches à qn, passer un savon à qn; *(criticize)* éreinter qn; **to get a roasting** *(get told off)* se faire souffler dans les bronches, prendre *ou* se faire passer un savon; *(get criticized)* se faire éreinter

2 *adj Fam (weather)* torride[□]; **it was roasting in her office** il faisait une chaleur à crever dans son bureau; **I'm roasting!** je crève de chaud!

►► ***roasting pan*** plat *m* à rôtir; ***roasting spit*** tournebroche *m*; ***roasting tin*** plat *m* à rôtir

rob [rɒb] (*pt & pp* **robbed**, *cont* **robbing**) **1** *vt* (**a**) *(person)* voler; *(bank)* dévaliser; *(house)* cambrioler; **to rob sb of sth** voler *ou* dérober qch à qn; *(deprive)* priver qn de qch; **when we got back we found that we had been robbed** en rentrant, on a découvert qu'on avait été cambriolés; **I've been robbed of my wallet!** on m'a volé mon portefeuille!; **someone has robbed the till!** on a volé l'argent de la caisse!

(**b**) *Fig (deprive)* priver; **to rob sb of sth** priver qn de qch; **the immigrants were robbed of their rights** les immigrés ont été privés de leurs droits; **the illness had robbed him of his good looks** la maladie lui avait fait perdre sa beauté; **the team was robbed of its victory** l'équipe s'est vue ravir la victoire; **we were robbed!** *(after match)* on nous a volé la victoire!; **to rob Peter to pay Paul** déshabiller Pierre pour habiller Paul

2 *n Br Fam* **to go on the rob** aller chaparder

robber ['rɒbə(r)] *n (of property)* voleur(euse) *m,f*

►► ***robber baron*** *Hist* baron *m* pillard; *Fig (tough businessman)* requin *m* de l'industrie; *Zool* ***robber crab*** crabe *m* des cocotiers, crabe *m* voleur; *Entom* ***robber fly*** asile *m*

robbery ['rɒbərɪ] (*pl* **robberies**) *n* (**a**) *(of property)* vol *m*; *(of bank)* hold-up *m inv*; *(of house)* cambriolage *m*; **robbery with violence** vol *m* avec coups et blessures, *Spec* vol *m* qualifié (**b**) *Fam (overcharging)* vol *m*; **it's highway** *or* **daylight robbery!** c'est du vol (organisé)!, c'est de l'arnaque!; **it's nothing short of robbery!** c'est du vol!

robe [rəʊb] **1** *n* (**a**) *(dressing gown → heavy)* robe *f* de chambre; *(→ light, for women)* peignoir *m*; *(→ bathrobe)* sortie *f* de bain, peignoir *m* (de bain)

(**b**) *(long garment → gen)* robe *f*; *(→ for judge, [illegible])* toge *f*; **magistrate in his robes** magistrat *m* en robe

(**c**) *Am (blanket)* couverture *f*

2 *vt (dress → gen)* habiller, vêtir; *(→ in robe)* vêtir d'une robe; **robed in red** vêtu de rouge; **to robe oneself** se vêtir

3 *vi (judge)* revêtir sa robe

Robert the Bruce [,rɒbətðə'bruːs] *pr n Hist* Robert Bruce

robin ['rɒbɪn] *n Orn* (**a**) *(European)* rouge-gorge *m* (**b**) *(American)* merle *m* américain; **robin's-egg blue** *(colour)* bleu-vert *m inv* pâle

►► ***Robin Hood*** Robin des bois; *Orn* ***robin redbreast*** rouge-gorge *m*

robing room ['rəʊbɪŋ-] *n (of judge)* vestiaire *m*

robinia [rɒ'bɪnɪə] *n Bot* robinier *m*

Robinson Crusoe [,rɒbɪnsən'kruːsəʊ] *pr n* Robinson Crusoé

robot ['rəʊbɒt] **1** *n* (**a**) *also Fig (automaton)* robot *m*, automate *m* (**b**) *SAfr (traffic lights)* feux *mpl* de circulation

2 *comp (pilot, vehicle, system)* automatique
▸▸ **robot bomb** bombe *f* volante

robotic [rəʊ'bɒtɪk] *adj* robotique

robotics [rəʊ'bɒtɪks] *n* (**a**) *(UNCOUNT) (science)* robotique *f* (**b**) *(dancing)* = danse des années 80 caractérisée par des mouvements saccadés

robotization [ˌrəʊbətaɪ'zeɪʃən] *n* robotisation *f*

robotize, -ise ['rəʊbətaɪz] *vt* robotiser

robust [rəʊ'bʌst] *adj (person)* robuste, vigoureux, solide; *(health)* solide; *(appetite)* robuste, solide; *(wine)* robuste, corsé; *(structure)* solide; *(economy, style, car)* robuste; *(response, defence)* vigoureux, énergique

robusta [rəʊ'bʌstə] *n (coffee)* robusta *m*

robustly [rəʊ'bʌstlɪ] *adv (built, constructed)* solidement; *(defend, reply)* avec force

robustness [rəʊ'bʌstnɪs] *n (of person)* robustesse *f*, vigueur *f*; *(of appetite)* robustesse *f*, solidité *f*; *(of furniture, health)* solidité *f*; *(of economy, style, car)* robustesse *f*; *(of response, defence)* vigueur *f*

roc [rɒk] *n Myth (bird)* rock *m*

rocaille [rəʊ'kaɪ] *n* rocaille *f*

rocambole ['rɒkəmbəʊl] *n Bot* rocambole *f*, ail *m* d'Espagne

ROCE [ˌɑːrəʊˌsiː'iː] *n Fin (abbr* **return on capital employed**) retour *m* sur capital immobilisé

Roche limit ['rəʊʃ-] *n Astron* limite *f* de Roche

rochet ['rɒtʃɪt] *n Rel* rochet *m*

rock [rɒk] **1** *n* (**a**) *(substance → gen)* roche *f*; *(→ hard)* roc *m*; **the lighthouse is built on rock** le phare est construit sur le roc; **a layer of rock** une couche rocheuse
(**b**) *(boulder, rock face)* rocher *m*; *Am (stone)* pierre *f*; **to run onto the rocks** *(ship)* s'échouer sur des rochers; *Fig* **she was an absolute rock during the crisis** elle nous a été d'un grand secours pendant cette épreuve; *Fig* **to be as solid as a rock** être solide comme le roc; *Fig* **to see the rocks ahead** anticiper les difficultés futures; *Fam* **to be on the rocks** *(person)* être dans la dèche; *(company)* être en faillite ❑; *(relationship, marriage)* mal tourner ❑, tourner à la catastrophe ❑; **this time last year the firm seemed to be on the rocks** l'an dernier à cette époque, l'entreprise semblait être au bord de la faillite; **on the rocks** *(drink)* avec des glaçons, *Can* sur glace; **to be between a rock and a hard place** être pris entre deux feux, être entre le marteau et l'enclume; *Am Fam* **to have rocks in one's head** être bête comme ses pieds
(**c**) *(music)* rock *m*; **rock and roll** rock *m* (and roll)
(**d**) *(in place names)* rocher *m*, roche *f*; **the Rock** *(Gibraltar)* le rocher de Gibraltar; *(Alcatraz)* = surnom donné à la prison d'Alcatraz
(**e**) *Br (sweet)* ≃ sucre *m* d'orge; **a stick of rock** un bâton de sucre d'orge *(parfumé à la menthe)*
(**f**) *Rel (stronghold)* rocher *m*, roc *m*; **Rock of Ages** Jésus-Christ
(**g**) *Fam (diamond)* diam *m*
(**h**) *very Fam* **rocks** *(testicles)* couilles *fpl*, boules *fpl*; **to get one's rocks off** *(have sex)* baiser, s'envoyer en l'air; *(have orgasm)* prendre son pied, jouir; *(enjoy oneself)* s'éclater, prendre son pied; **to get one's rocks off doing sth** s'éclater *ou* prendre son pied en faisant qch
(**i**) *Fam Drugs slang (crack cocaine)* crack *m*; *Br (cocaine)* coco *f*, neige *f*
2 *comp (film)* rock *(inv)*; *(band, record, concert, guitarist)* (de) rock *(inv)*
3 *vt* (**a**) *(swing to and fro → baby)* bercer; *(→ chair, cradle)* balancer; *(→ lever)* basculer; **to rock a baby to sleep** bercer un bébé pour l'endormir; **he rocked himself in the rocking chair** il se balançait dans le fauteuil à bascule; **the boat was rocked by the waves** *(gently)* le bateau était bercé par les flots; *(violently)* le bateau était ballotté par les vagues; *Fig* **to rock the boat** jouer les trouble-fête, semer le trouble; **don't rock the boat** ne fais pas de vagues; **now you've settled in, you must be careful not to rock the boat** maintenant que tu es bien adapté, essaie de ne pas nous causer d'ennuis
(**b**) *(shake)* secouer, ébranler; **the village was rocked by an explosion/an earthquake** le village fut secoué par une explosion/un tremblement de terre; **the Government has been rocked by the latest sex scandal** le gouvernement a été secoué par la dernière histoire de mœurs; **she was rocked by the news** elle a été bouleversée par la nouvelle
4 *vi* (**a**) *(sway)* se balancer; **to rock on a chair** se balancer sur une chaise; **to rock with laughter** se tordre de rire
(**b**) *(building, ground)* trembler
(**c**) *(jive)* danser le rock
(**d**) *Fam (be excellent)* **his new girlfriend really rocks!** sa nouvelle copine est vraiment géniale!; **the party was really rocking** *(animated)* il y avait une ambiance d'enfer à la soirée
5 *adv (idiom)* **to hit rock bottom** *(person, morale)* avoir le moral à zéro, toucher le fond; *(firm, funds)* atteindre le niveau le plus bas
▸▸ *Ich* **rock bass** achigan *m* de roche; **rock boots** chaussures *fpl* d'escalade; *Zool* **rock borer** pholade *f*; *Culin* **rock bun, rock cake** rocher *m (gâteau)*; *Am* **rock candy** sucre *m* d'orge; *Fam* **rock chick** mordue *f* de hard rock; **rock climber** varappeur(euse) *m,f*; **rock climbing** escalade *f* (de rochers), varappe *f*; **to go rock climbing** faire de l'escalade *ou* de la varappe; **rock crystal** cristal *m* de roche; *Am Constr* **rock dash** crépi *m*; *Orn* **rock dove** (pigeon *m*) biset *m*; **rock face** paroi *f* rocheuse; **rock garden** (jardin *m* de) rocaille *f*; *Orn* **rock hopper** gorfou *m*, manchot *m* sauteur; *Am Fam* **rock hound** *(professional)* géologue ❑ *mf*; *(amateur)* collectionneur(euse) *m,f* de pierres ❑; *Zool* **rock lobster** langouste *f*; *Am, Austr & NZ* **rock melon** cantaloup *m*; **rock music** rock *m*; **rock oil** pétrole *m*; *Orn* **rock partridge** bartavelle *f*; *Orn* **rock pigeon** (pigeon *m*) biset *m*; *Orn* **rock pipit** pipit *m* maritime, pipit *m* obscur; *Bot* **rock plant** plante *f* de rocaille; **rock pool** flaque *f* dans les rochers; *Bot* **rock rose** hélianthème *m*; *Ich* **rock salmon** roussette *f*; **rock salt** sel *m* gemme; **rock slide** *(action)* éboulement *m* de rochers; *(result)* éboulis *m*; *Orn* **rock sparrow** moineau *m* soulcie; **rock star** rock star *f*; *Orn* **rock thrush** merle *m* de roche; **blue rock thrush** merle *m* bleu; *Constr* **rock wool** laine *f* minérale

'Brighton Rock' *Greene, Boulting* 'Le Rocher de Brighton'

rockabilly ['rɒkəˌbɪlɪ] *n* rockabilly *m*

rock-and-roll facility *n TV & Cin (for dubbing)* dispositif *m* de marche avant-arrière synchronisé

rock-bottom *adj (price)* défiant toute concurrence, le plus bas, sacrifié

rock-bound *adj* encerclé de rochers

rock-climb *vi* faire de la varappe

rocker ['rɒkə(r)] *n* (**a**) *(of cradle, chair)* bascule *f*; *Fam* **to be off one's rocker** être cinglé, débloquer; *Fam* **to go off one's rocker** *(go mad)* devenir dingue *ou* cinglé, perdre la boule; *(lose one's temper)* péter une durit, piquer une crise
(**b**) *(rocking chair)* fauteuil *m* à bascule, *Can* berçante *f*
(**c**) *Mus (person)* rocker *m*, rockeur(euse) *m,f*
(**d**) *Aut & Tech* culbuteur *m*
(**e**) *Br (youth)* rocker *m*, rockeur(euse) *m,f*; **the Rockers** = jeunes motards aux cheveux longs qui rivalisaient avec les "Mods" dans les années 60
▸▸ *Aut & Tech* **rocker arm** culbuteur *m*

rockery ['rɒkərɪ] *(pl* **rockeries**) *n* (jardin *m* de) rocaille *f*

rocket ['rɒkɪt] **1** *n* (**a**) *Aviat & Astron* fusée *f*; **to fire** *or* **launch a rocket** lancer une fusée; **to go off like a rocket** partir comme une fusée
(**b**) *Mil (missile)* roquette *f*; **to fire a rocket** lancer une roquette
(**c**) *(signal, firework)* fusée *f*
(**d**) *Br Fam (telling off)* engueulade *f*; **to get a rocket (from sb)** se faire engueuler (par qn), prendre *ou* se faire passer un savon (par qn); **to give sb a rocket** engueuler qn, passer un savon à qn
(**e**) *Bot & Culin* roquette *f*
2 *comp (propulsion)* par fusée; *(engine)* de fusée
3 *vt* (**a**) *(missile, astronaut)* lancer (dans l'espace); **the spacecraft was rocketed to the moon** le vaisseau spatial a été lancé en direction de la lune
(**b**) *(record, singer)* faire monter en flèche; **the record rocketed the group into the top 10** grâce à ce disque, le groupe est monté en flèche jusqu'au top 10
4 *vi (price, sales)* monter en flèche; **to rocket to fame** devenir célèbre du jour au lendemain; **the group rocketed up the charts** le groupe est monté dans le hit-parade comme une flèche; **the car rocketed down the road/round the track** la voiture a descendu la rue/fait le tour de la piste à une vitesse incroyable
▸▸ *Mil* **rocket attack** attaque *f* à la roquette; *Mil* **rocket bomb** roquette *f*; **rocket fuel** *Aviat & Astron* propergol *m*; *Fig (strong drink)* dynamite *f*; **rocket gun** fusil *m* lance-roquettes; **rocket launcher** *Aviat & Astron* lance-fusées *m inv*; *Mil* lance-roquettes *m inv*; *Mil* **rocket range** base *f* de lancement de missiles; **rocket science** fuséologie *m*; *Fam Fig* **it's not exactly rocket science** ce n'est pas sorcier; **rocket scientist** spécialiste *mf* de fuséologie; *Fam St Exch* = personne qui spécule sur le cours des monnaies; *Fam Fig* **she's no rocket scientist** elle n'a pas inventé la poudre

rocketry ['rɒkɪtrɪ] *n* (**a**) *(science)* fuséologie *f* (**b**) *(rockets collectively)* arsenal *m* de fusées

rockfall ['rɒkfɔːl] *n* chute *f* de pierres *ou* de rochers, éboulement *m*

rockfish ['rɒkfɪʃ] *(pl* **rockfish** *or* **rockfishes**) *n Ich* gobie *m*, rascasse *f*

rock-hard *adj* dur comme le roc

rockhouse ['rɒkhaʊs, *pl* -haʊzɪz] *n Am Fam Drugs slang* = lieu où l'on achète, vend et consomme du crack

Rockies ['rɒkɪz] *npl* **the Rockies** les Rocheuses *fpl*

rocking ['rɒkɪŋ] **1** *adj (movement)* oscillant; *(building)* branlant; **a rocking movement** des oscillations *fpl*
2 *n* (**a**) *(of chair, boat, cradle)* balancement *m*; *(of baby)* bercement *m*; *(of head → to rhythm)* balancement *m* (**b**) *Tech* oscillation *f*
▸▸ **rocking chair** fauteuil *m* à bascule, rocking-chair *m*, *Can* berçante *f*; **rocking horse** cheval *m* à bascule; *Geol* **rocking stone** rocher *m* branlant

rock-like *adj* comme un *ou* le roc

rockling ['rɒklɪŋ] *n Ich* loche *f*

rock'n'roll [ˌrɒkən'rəʊl] *n* rock *m* (and roll)

rock-solid *adj* inébranlable

rocksteady [ˌrɒk'stedɪ] *n Mus* rocksteady *m*

rocky ['rɒkɪ] **1** *(compar* **rockier**, *superl* **rockiest**) *adj* (**a**) *(seabed, mountain, shoreline)* rocheux; *(path, track)* rocailleux; *(soil)* rocailleux, pierreux; **rocky outcrop** affleurement *m* rocheux; *Culin* **rocky road** *(ice cream, confectionery)* = au chocolat, avec de la guimauve et des morceaux de noix
(**b**) *(unstable → situation)* précaire, instable; *(→ government)* peu stable; *(relationship, marriage)* difficile; **it's been a rocky year for the oil industry** ça a été une année difficile pour l'industrie pétrolière; **to have a rocky road ahead** avoir des problèmes en perspective; **to go through a rocky patch** traverser une période difficile
2 *n Br Fam Drugs slang (cannabis)* marocain *m*
▸▸ **the Rocky Mountains** les montagnes *fpl* Rocheuses; *Zool* **Rocky Mountain goat** chèvre *f* des montagnes Rocheuses; *Med* **Rocky Mountain spotted fever** fièvre *f* pourprée des montagnes Rocheuses

rococo [rə'kəʊkəʊ] **1** *adj* rococo *(inv)*
2 *n* rococo *m*

rod [rɒd] *n* (**a**) *(of metal)* tige *f*; *(of wood)* baguette *f*; *(for curtains, carpet)* tringle *f*; *(for fishing)* canne *f*; *(for punishment → stiff)* baguette *f*; *(→ flexible)* verge *f*; *Sch (pointer)* baguette *f*; **to be beaten with a rod** recevoir des coups de baguette; **to fish with rod and line** pêcher à la ligne; **rod fishing** pêche *f* à la ligne; **rods** *(mechanism)* tringlerie *f*, timonerie *f*; *Fig* **to rule with a rod of iron** gouverner d'une main *ou* poigne de fer; *Fig* **to make a rod for one's own back** s'attirer des ennuis; *Fig* **a rod to beat oneself with** des verges pour se faire battre; **that would be giving them a rod to beat us with**

ce serait leur donner des bâtons pour nous faire battre

(**b**) *(of uranium)* barre *f*

(**c**) *(symbol of office)* verge *f*

(**d**) *(for surveying)* mire *f*

(**e**) *Anat (in eye)* bâtonnet *m*

(**f**) *(linear or square measure)* ≃ perche *f*

(**g**) *Am Fam (gun)* flingue *m*

(**h**) *Fam (car)* voiture *f* gonflée

(**i**) *Vulg (penis)* bite *f*, tige *f*

rode [rəʊd] *pt of* **ride**

rodent ['rəʊdənt] **1** *adj* rongeur; **rodent characteristics/habitat** caractéristiques *fpl*/habitat *m* des rongeurs

2 *n* rongeur *m*

►► ***rodent control*** dératisation *f*; *Br Admin* ***rodent operative*** spécialiste *mf* de la dératisation; *Med* ***rodent ulcer*** carcinome *m* basocellulaire ulcéreux

rodenticide [rəʊ'dentɪsaɪd] *n* rodenticide *m*

rodent-like *adj* qui fait penser à un rongeur

rodeo ['rəʊdɪəʊ] *(pl* **rodeos***) n* rodéo *m*

►► ***Rodeo Drive*** = luxueuse rue commerçante à Hollywood; ***rodeo rider*** cavalier(ère) *m,f* pratiquant le rodéo

rodomontade [,rɒdəmɒn'teɪd] *n Literary* rodomontade *f*

roe [rəʊ] *(pl sense* (**b**) **inv** *or* **roes***) n* (**a**) *(UNCOUNT) (eggs)* œufs *mpl* de poisson; *(sperm)* laitance *f*; **cod roe** œufs *mpl* de cabillaud (**b**) *(deer)* chevreuil *m*

►► *Zool* ***roe deer*** chevreuil *m*

roebuck ['rəʊbʌk] *n Zool* chevreuil *m* mâle

Roedean ['rəʊdiːn] *n* **Roedean (School)** = célèbre école privée pour jeunes filles en Angleterre

roentgen ['rɜːntgən] *n Phys* röntgen *m*, rœntgen *m*

►► ***roentgen equivalent man*** = unité employée pour évaluer l'effet biologique d'un rayonnement radioactif; **measurements are given in roentgen equivalent man** les mesures sont données en "Rœntgen Equivalent Man"; ***roentgen rays*** rayons *mpl* X

roentgenotherapy [,rɒntjənəʊ'θerəpɪ] *n Phys* radiothérapie *f*

Roe vs Wade ['rəʊvɜːsəs'weɪd] *n Am Law* = procès de 1973 reconnaissant le droit à l'avortement dans tous les États américains

rogation [rəʊ'geɪʃən] *n (usu pl)* rogations *fpl*

►► ***Rogation Days*** rogations *fpl*; ***Rogation Sunday*** dimanche *m* des rogations; ***Rogation Week*** la semaine des Rogations

rogatory ['rɒgətərɪ] *adj Law* rogatoire; **letters rogatory** commission *f* rogatoire

roger ['rɒdʒə(r)] **1** *exclam Tel* reçu et compris, d'accord; **roger and out** message reçu, terminé

2 *vt Br very Fam (have sex with)* baiser, sauter

Rogerian [rɒ'dʒeərɪən] *adj* = inspiré de la méthode du psychothérapeute Carl Rogers

rogue [rəʊg] **1** *n* (**a**) *(scoundrel)* escroc *m*, filou *m*; *(mischievous child)* polisson(onne) *m,f*, coquin(e) *m,f*; *(maverick)* franc-tireur *m*

(**b**) *(animal)* solitaire *m*

2 *adj* (**a**) *(animal)* solitaire; **a rogue elephant** un éléphant solitaire

(**b**) *Am (delinquent)* dévoyé

►► ***rogues' gallery*** *(in police files)* photographies *fpl* de repris de justice; *Fig Hum* **they're a real rogues' gallery!** ils ont des mines patibulaires!; *Biol* ***rogue gene*** gène *m* aberrant; ***rogue policeman*** policier *m* corrompu; ***rogue state*** État *m* voyou, État *m* paria; *St Exch* ***rogue trader*** opérateur(trice) *m,f* peu scrupuleux(euse)

roguery ['rəʊgərɪ] *(pl* **rogueries***) n (dishonesty)* malhonnêteté *f*; *(mischievousness)* côté *m* farceur; *(of child)* espièglerie *f*

roguish ['rəʊgɪʃ] *adj (mischievous)* espiègle, malicieux, coquin

roguishly ['rəʊgɪʃlɪ] *adv (smile, wink)* avec espièglerie, d'un air coquin

roguishness ['rəʊgɪʃnɪs] *n (dishonesty)* malhonnêteté *f*; *(mischievousness)* côté *m* farceur; *(of child)* espièglerie *f*

ROI [,ɑːrəʊ'aɪ] *n Fin (abbr* **return on investment***)* retour *m* sur investissement(s)

roid [rɔɪd] *n Am Fam (abbr* **steroid***)* **roids** stéroïdes ❑ *mpl*

►► ***roid rage*** = état d'agressivité extrême causé par l'absorption de stéroïdes

roil [rɔɪl] *vt* (**a**) *(liquid)* troubler (**b**) *Am Fam (annoy)* embêter

roister ['rɔɪstə(r)] *vi* faire la fête

roisterer ['rɔɪstərə(r)] *n* noceur(euse) *m,f*

roistering ['rɔɪstərɪŋ] **1** *n* tapage *m*

2 *adj (behaviour)* tapageur; *(crowd)* bruyant

roisterous ['rɔɪstərəs] *adj (behaviour)* tapageur; *(crowd)* bruyant

Roland ['rəʊlənd] *n* **a Roland for an Oliver** un prêté rendu; **to give sb a Roland for an Oliver** rendre à qn la monnaie de sa pièce

role, rôle [rəʊl] *n* rôle *m*; **to have** *or* **to play the leading role** jouer le rôle principal; **she had** *or* **she played an important role in this project** elle a joué un rôle important dans ce projet; **his role (in the project) was to keep everyone happy** son rôle (dans le projet) était de s'assurer qu'il n'y ait pas de mécontents; **to have a role in life** avoir un rôle dans la vie; **his role in life seems to be to annoy as many people as possible** on dirait que son rôle dans la vie est d'embêter le plus de monde possible

►► ***role model*** modèle *m*; **children need a role model** les enfants ont besoin de quelqu'un à qui s'identifier; ***role play*** *(gén)* jeu *m* de rôles; *Psy* psychodrame *m*; ***role playing*** *(UNCOUNT) (gén)* jeux *mpl* de rôles; *Psy* psychodrames *mpl*; ***role reversal*** inversion *f* des rôles

rolf [rɒlf] *vi Am very Fam (vomit)* dégueuler

Rolfing ['rɒlfɪŋ] *n* rolfing *m*

ROLL [rəʊl]

rouleau	► **1 (a)**
petit pain	► **1 (b)**
roulement	► **1 (c)**
liste	► **1 (d)**
rouler	► **2 (a), (b); 3 (a)**
avoir du roulis	► **3 (b)**
tourner	► **3 (c)**

1 *n* (**a**) *(of carpet, paper)* rouleau *m*; *(of banknotes)* liasse *f*; *(of tobacco)* carotte *f*; *(of butter)* coquille *f*; *(of fat, flesh)* bourrelet *m*; *(of tools)* trousse *f*; **a roll of film** une pellicule photo

(**b**) *(bread)* petit pain *m*; **ham/cheese roll** sandwich *m* au jambon/fromage

(**c**) *(movement → of ball)* roulement *m*; *(→ of dice)* lancement *m*; *(→ of car, ship)* roulis *m*; *(→ of plane) (in turbulence)* roulis *m*; *(in aerobatics)* tonneau *m*; *(→ of hips, shoulders)* balancement *m*; *(→ of sea)* houle *f*; *(somersault)* galipette *f*; **to have a roll on the ground** *(horse)* se rouler par terre; **to do a roll** *(in high jump)* sauter en rouleau; **to walk with a roll** se balancer *ou* se dandiner en marchant; *Literary* **the roll of the ages** le déroulement des époques; *Fam* **to have a roll in the hay** *(have sex)* se rouler dans le foin, se faire une partie de jambes en l'air; *Fam* **to be on a roll** être bien parti

(**d**) *(list → of members)* liste *f*, tableau *m*; *Admin & Naut* rôle *m*; *Sch* liste *f* des élèves; **to call the roll** faire l'appel; **to be on the roll** *(of club)* être membre; *Br Sch* faire partie des élèves; *Law* **to strike sb off** *or* **from the rolls** rayer qn du tableau; **falling rolls** baisse *f* d'effectifs; **nominal roll** liste *f* nominative; **roll of honour** *Mil* liste *f* des combattants morts pour la patrie; *Sch* tableau *m* d'honneur

(**e**) *(noise → of drum)* roulement *m*; *(→ of thunder)* grondement *m*; **I can hear the rolls of thunder/the far-off roll of a drum** j'entends gronder le tonnerre/le roulement lointain d'un tambour

(**f**) *Am Fam Drugs slang (ecstasy pill)* ecsta *f*

2 *vt* (**a**) *(ball)* (faire) rouler; *(dice)* jeter, lancer; *(cigarette, paper, carpet, umbrella)* rouler; *(coil)* enrouler; **to roll sth along the ground** faire rouler qch sur le sol; **to roll yarn into a ball** faire des pelotes de laine; **she rolled the child in a blanket** elle a enroulé *ou* enveloppé l'enfant dans une couverture; **the hedgehog rolled itself into a tight ball** le hérisson s'est mis en boule; **the dog rolled itself in the mud** le chien s'est roulé dans la boue; **to roll sth in** *or* **between one's fingers** rouler qch entre ses doigts; **the boy rolled the modelling clay into a long snake** le garçon roula la pâte à modeler pour en faire un long serpent; **he rolled his sleeves above his elbows** il a roulé *ou* retroussé ses manches au-dessus du coude; **to roll the presses** faire tourner les presses; **to roll dice** *(to play)* jouer aux dés; **to roll one's r's** rouler les r; **to roll one's hips/shoulders** rouler les hanches/épaules; **to roll one's eyes in fright** rouler les yeux de frayeur; *Br* **to roll one's own** *(cigarettes)* se rouler ses cigarettes; **she's a company executive, wife and housekeeper all rolled into one** elle cumule les rôles de cadre dans sa société, d'épouse et de ménagère; **this room is a bedroom and study rolled into one** cette pièce sert à la fois de chambre et de bureau

(**b**) *(flatten → grass)* rouler; *(→ pastry, dough)* étendre; *(→ gold, metal)* laminer; *(→ road)* cylindrer

(**c**) *Cin (camera)* faire tourner; **roll 'em!** moteur!

(**d**) *Am Fam (rob)* dévaliser ❑, faire les poches à *(une personne ivre ou endormie)*

3 *vi* (**a**) *(ball, coin etc)* rouler; **to roll on the ground/in the grass** *(person, animal)* se rouler par terre/dans l'herbe; **to roll in the mud** *(gen)* se rouler dans la boue; *(wallow)* se vautrer dans la boue; **his eyes rolled in horror** il roulait des yeux horrifiés; **the ball rolled under the car/down the stairs** la balle roula sous la voiture/en bas de l'escalier; **the boulders rolled down the mountainside** les rochers dévalaient la montagne; **the car rolled down the hill/the slope** la voiture dévalait la colline/la pente; **the ball rolled along the floor** la balle roulait sur le sol; **the parade rolled slowly past the window** le défilé passait lentement devant la fenêtre; **the bus rolled into the yard** le bus est entré dans la cour; **the car rolled to a halt** la voiture s'est arrêtée lentement; **tears rolled down her face** des larmes roulaient sur ses joues; **sweat rolled off his back** la sueur lui dégoulinait dans le dos; **to roll with the punches** *(boxer)* encaisser les coups de l'adversaire; *Fig* encaisser; *Fam* **to be rolling in money** *or* **rolling in it** rouler sur l'or, être plein aux as; **he had them rolling in the aisles** il les faisait mourir de rire

(**b**) *(ship)* avoir du roulis; *(plane → with turbulence)* avoir du roulis; *(→ in aerobatics)* faire un tonneau *ou* des tonneaux; *Astron* tourner sur soi-même

(**c**) *(camera, machine)* tourner; **to keep the cameras/the presses rolling** laisser tourner les caméras/les presses; *TV & Cin* **roll!** moteur!; **the credits started to roll** *(of film)* le générique commença à défiler; *Fig* **the wheels never stop rolling** les roues ne s'arrêtent jamais de tourner; *Fig* **OK, we're ready to roll!** bon, on est prêt, allons-y!; *Fig* **to get** *or* **to start things rolling** mettre les choses en marche; *Theat* **to keep the show rolling** faire en sorte que le spectacle continue; **let the good times roll** que la fête continue

(**d**) *(drums)* rouler; *(thunder)* gronder; *(voice)* retentir; *(music)* retentir, résonner; *(organ)* résonner, sonner

(**e**) *Am Fam Drugs slang* **to be rolling** être sous ecsta

►► *Aut* ***roll bar*** arceau *m* de sécurité; ***roll call*** appel *m*; **to take (the) roll call** faire l'appel; ***roll collar*** col *m* roulé; ***roll film*** pellicule *f* en bobine; ***roll neck*** col *m* roulé

►**roll about 1** *vt sep* **to roll sth about** faire rouler qch

2 *vi (marble, ball etc)* rouler ça et là; *(ship)* rouler; **to roll about on the floor** *or* **ground/grass** *(person)* se rouler par terre/dans l'herbe; **to roll about with laughter** se tordre de rire, se tenir les côtes

►**roll along 1** *vt sep (hoop, ball)* faire rouler; *(car, wheelbarrow)* pousser

2 *vi* (**a**) *(river)* couler; *(car)* rouler; **the car was rolling along at 140 km/h** la voiture roulait à 140 (**b**) *(project)* avancer (**c**) *Fam (visit)* passer ❑, se pointer; **let's roll along to Jake's place** si on se pointait chez Jake?, si on débarquait chez Jake?

►**roll around** = **roll about**

►**roll away 1** *vt sep (take away)* emmener; *(put away)* ranger

2 *vi (car, clouds)* s'éloigner; *(marble, ball etc)* rouler au loin; *(mist)* se retirer; **the hills rolled**

away into the distance les collines disparaissaient au loin; **the ball rolled away into the street** la balle a roulé jusque dans la rue; **suddenly all my troubles simply rolled away** subitement tous mes ennuis s'éloignèrent

►**roll back 1** *vt sep* (**a**) *(push back → carpet)* rouler, enrouler; *(→ blankets)* replier; *(→ enemy, difficulties)* faire reculer; *(→ trolley, wheelchair)* reculer; **the doctor rolled the wheelchair back against the wall** le médecin recula la chaise roulante contre le mur; **to roll back the frontiers of science** faire reculer les frontières de la science

(**b**) *(time)* faire reculer; **it would be nice to roll back the years** ce serait bien de revenir des années en arrière

(**c**) *Am (prices)* casser

(**d**) *(bring back)* ramener

2 *vi (waves)* se retirer; *(car)* reculer, rouler en arrière; *(memories, time)* revenir; **her eyes rolled back in her head** ses yeux se révulsèrent

►**roll by** *vi* (**a**) *(time)* s'écouler, passer (**b**) *(car)* passer

►**roll down 1** *vt sep (blind, car window)* baisser; *(sleeves)* redescendre; *(blanket)* replier

2 *vi (tears, sweat)* couler; **to roll down a hill** *(car, children)* débouler une pente; **the tears rolled down his cheeks** les larmes coulaient le long de ses joues

►**roll in 1** *vt sep (bring in)* faire entrer; *(barrel, car)* faire entrer en roulant; **to roll the ball in** *(in hockey)* remettre la balle en jeu

2 *vi* (**a**) *(car)* entrer; *(waves)* déferler; *(mist, clouds, train)* arriver

(**b**) *(pour in → money, crowds)* affluer

(**c**) *Fam (person → arrive)* se pointer; *(→ come back)* rentrer ❑; **they finally rolled in at three o'clock in the morning** ils sont finalement rentrés à trois heures du matin; **she rolled in to work three hours late** elle s'est amenée au travail avec trois heures de retard

(**d**) *(in hockey)* remettre la balle en jeu

►**roll off 1** *vt sep Typ (print)* imprimer

2 *vt insep Typ* **to roll off the presses** sortir des presses

3 *vi (fall on floor)* rouler par terre; **the top rolled off into the bath** le bouchon a roulé dans la baignoire; **to roll off the shelf/the table** rouler de l'étagère/de la table; **sweat was rolling off his back** la sueur lui coulait dans le dos; **cars are rolling off the production line** les voitures sortent de la chaîne de production

►**roll on 1** *vt sep* (**a**) *(paint)* appliquer au rouleau; *(deodorant)* appliquer (**b**) *(stockings)* enfiler

2 *vi* (**a**) *(ball)* continuer à rouler (**b**) *(time)* s'écouler (**c**) *Br Fam* **roll on Christmas!** vivement (qu'on soit à) Noël! ❑; **roll on the day when I'm my own boss!** vivement que je sois mon propre patron! ❑

►**roll out 1** *vt sep* (**a**) *(ball)* rouler (dehors); *(car)* rouler *ou* pousser dehors; *(map)* dérouler; *(pastry)* étendre (au rouleau); **we rolled the lawnmower out into the garden** nous avons sorti la tondeuse dans le jardin

(**b**) *(produce → goods, speech)* débiter

(**c**) *(launch → product)* lancer; *(extend → new scheme)* étendre; *(→ production)* accroître; **the new scheme will be rolled out nationwide** le nouveau système s'étendra à tout le pays

2 *vi* sortir; **to roll out of bed** *(person)* sortir du lit; **the ball rolled out from under the sofa** la balle est sortie de sous le canapé; **the train rolled out of the station** le train quitta la gare; *Fam* **we rolled out of the pub at midnight** nous sommes sortis du pub à minuit ❑

►**roll over 1** *vt sep* (**a**) *(person, animal, object)* retourner (**b**) *Fin (credit, interest rates)* renouveler

2 *vt insep* rouler sur; *(of car)* écraser

3 *vi (person, animal)* se retourner; *(car)* faire un tonneau; **to roll over and over** *(in bed)* se retourner plusieurs fois; *(car)* faire une série de tonneaux

►**roll past 1** *vt insep* passer devant

2 *vi* passer

►**roll round** *vi (season etc)* arriver

►**roll up 1** *vt sep (map, carpet)* rouler; *(sleeves)* retrousser; *(trousers)* remonter, retrousser; *(blind, car window)* remonter; **to roll sth up in a blanket** enrouler *ou* envelopper qch dans une couverture

2 *vi* (**a**) *(carpet)* se rouler; *(blind)* remonter; **the map keeps rolling up on its own** impossible de faire tenir cette carte à plat; **to roll up into a ball** se rouler en boule

(**b**) *Fam (arrive → guests)* rappliquer, se pointer, s'amener; *(→ customers, spectators)* rappliquer en foule; **roll up! roll up!** approchez! ❑

rollaway ['rəʊləweɪ] *adj* à roulettes

►► ***rollaway bed*** lit *m* pliant sur roulettes

rollback ['rəʊlbæk] *n Am* réduction *f*, baisse *f*

rolled [rəʊld] *adj* (**a**) *(paper)* en rouleau; *(carpet, umbrella)* roulé (**b**) *(iron, steel)* laminé (**c**) *(tobacco)* en carotte

►► ***rolled gold*** plaqué *m* or; **a rolled gold bracelet** un bracelet en plaqué or; ***rolled oats*** flocons *mpl* d'avoine; *Constr* ***rolled steel joist*** solive *f* en I

rolled-up *adj* roulé, enroulé

Roller [ˌrəʊlə(r)] *n Br Fam (Rolls-Royce®)* Rolls Royce® ❑ *f*

roller ['rəʊlə(r)] *n* (**a**) *(cylinder → for paint, pastry, garden, hair)* rouleau *m*; *(→ for blind)* enrouleur *m*; *(→ of typewriter)* rouleau *m*, cylindre *m*; *Tex* calandre *f*; *Metal* laminoir *m*; **to put rollers in (one's hair), to put one's hair in rollers** se mettre des rouleaux *ou* des bigoudis; **my hair's in rollers** j'ai des rouleaux *ou* des bigoudis sur la tête

(**b**) *(wheel → for marking, furniture)* roulette *f*; *(→ in machine)* galet *m*; **the piano is on rollers** le piano est sur roulettes

(**c**) *(wave)* rouleau *m*

(**d**) *Orn (pigeon)* pigeon *m* culbutant, (pigeon *m*) rouleur *m*; *(European)* rollier *m* d'Europe

►► ***roller bandage*** bandage *m* enroulé; ***roller bearing*** roulement *m* à rouleaux; ***roller blind*** store *m* à enrouleur; *TV* ***roller caption*** déroulant *m*; ***roller derby*** course *f* en patins à roulettes; ***roller disco*** = discothèque où l'on tourne en patins à roulettes sur une piste; ***roller hockey*** hockey *m* sur patins à roulettes; ***roller map*** carte *f* sur rouleau; *TV* ***roller prompter*** prompteur *m* déroulant; ***roller skate*** patin *m* à roulettes; ***roller towel*** essuie-mains *m inv (monté sur un rouleau)*

rollerblader ['rəʊləˌbleɪdə(r)] *n* patineur(euse) *m,f* en rollers

rollerblades ['rəʊləˌbleɪdz] *npl* patins *mpl* en ligne, rollerblades *mpl*, rollers *mpl*

rollerblading ['rəʊləˌbleɪdɪŋ] *n* roller *m*; **to go rollerblading** faire du roller

rollercoaster ['rəʊləˌkəʊstə(r)] **1** *n* montagnes *fpl* russes, grand huit *m*; **the rollercoaster fortunes of a company/a party** les hauts et les bas que connaît une société/un parti; **to be on an emotional rollercoaster** être ballotté par ses émotions

2 *vi esp Am (road)* faire des montagnes russes; *(economy)* connaître des hauts et des bas prononcés

►► *St Exch* ***rollercoaster market*** marché *m* volatile

roller-skate *vi* faire du patin à roulettes

roller-skater *n* patineur(euse) *m,f* (à roulettes)

roller-skating *n* patinage *m* à roulettes; **to go roller-skating** aller faire du patin à roulettes

rollick ['rɒlɪk] *Fam* **1** *vi (romp)* s'ébattre ❑; *(celebrate)* faire la noce

2 *vt Br* engueuler, remonter les bretelles à

3 *n* ébats ❑ *mpl*

►**rollick about** *vi Br Fam* s'ébattre ❑, faire le fou (la folle)

rollicking ['rɒlɪkɪŋ] *Fam* **1** *adv* **to get rollicking drunk** se soûler; **it's a rollicking good read!** *(book)* c'est un livre excellent! ❑; **to have a rollicking good time** s'amuser comme des fous

2 *adj (joyful)* joyeux ❑; *(noisy)* bruyant ❑; **to lead a rollicking life** mener une vie de patachon; **we had a rollicking time** on s'est amusé comme des fous

3 *n Br (scolding)* **to get a rollicking** se faire engueuler, se faire remonter les bretelles; **to give sb a rollicking** engueuler qn, remonter les bretelles à qn

rolling ['rəʊlɪŋ] **1** *adj* (**a**) *(object)* roulant, qui roule; *Culin* **bring to a rolling boil** maintenir à ébullition

(**b**) *(countryside, hills)* ondulant; **to have a rolling gait** rouler les hanches

(**c**) *(sea)* houleux; *(boat)* qui a du roulis

(**d**) *(fog)* enveloppant; *(thunder)* grondant

(**e**) *(mobile → target)* mobile, mouvant; **a rolling plan for development** un plan de développement constamment remis à jour

2 *n* (**a**) *(of ball, marble)* roulement *m*; *(of dice)* lancement *m*

(**b**) *(of boat)* roulis *m*

(**c**) *(of drum)* roulement *m*; *(of thunder)* grondement *m*

(**d**) *(of shoulders)* roulement *m*

(**e**) *(of road, lawn)* cylindrage *m*

(**f**) *Metal* laminage *m*

3 *adv Br Fam* **to be rolling drunk** être complètement soûl ❑

►► *Acct* ***rolling budget*** budget *m* glissant; ***rolling mill*** *(factory)* usine *f* de laminage; *(equipment)* laminoir *m*; ***rolling pin*** rouleau *m* à pâtisserie; *Acct* ***rolling plan*** plan *m* glissant; *Rail* ***rolling stock*** matériel *m* roulant; ***rolling stone*** *(person)* vadrouilleur(euse) *m,f*; **to be a rolling stone** rouler sa bosse, avoir une âme de vagabond; *Prov* **a rolling stone gathers no moss** pierre qui roule n'amasse pas mousse; ***rolling strikes*** grèves *fpl* tournantes

rollmop ['rəʊlmɒp] *n* rollmops *m*

roll-neck(ed) *adj* à col roulé

roll-on *n* (**a**) *(deodorant)* déodorant *m* à bille (**b**) *(corset)* gaine *f*, corset *m*

►► ***roll-on deodorant*** déodorant *m* à bille; ***roll-on lip-gloss*** brillant *m* à lèvres

roll-on/roll-off 1 *n (ship)* (navire *m*) transbordeur *m*, ferry-boat *m*; *(system)* roll on-roll off *m inv*, manutention *f* par roulage

2 *adj (ferry)* transbordeur, ro-ro *(inv)*; *(port)* à roulage direct

roll-out *n* (**a**) *Aviat (of new aircraft)* sortie *f* d'usine (**b**) *Aviat (after touching down)* roulage *m* au sol (**c**) *Mktg (of product)* lancement *m*

►► ***roll-out marketing*** marketing *m* expansionniste

rollover ['rəʊlˌəʊvə(r)] **1** *n* (**a**) *Br (in National Lottery)* = à la loterie nationale, situation où, personne n'ayant gagné le gros lot, celui-ci est ajouté à l'enjeu du tirage suivant

(**b**) *Fin (in taxation)* (disposition *f* de) roulement *m*; *(of loan)* reconduction *f*

2 *adj Am (renewable)* renouvelable; *(renegotiable)* renégociable; *(credit, loan)* à taux révisable

►► *Fin* ***rollover credit*** crédit *m* renouvelable; *Br* ***rollover jackpot*** *(in National Lottery)* = gros lot composé de l'enjeu de plusieurs semaines successives; *Fin* ***rollover loan*** prêt *m* renouvelable; *Br* ***rollover week*** *(in National Lottery)* = tirage dont le gros lot est composé de l'enjeu de plusieurs semaines successives

Rolls [rəʊlz] *n Br Fam (Rolls-Royce®)* Rolls Royce® ❑ *f*

rolltop ['rəʊltɒp] *n* bureau *m* à cylindre

►► ***rolltop desk*** bureau *m* à cylindre

roll-up 1 *adj (map)* qui s'enroule

2 *n Br Fam* cigarette *f* roulée à la main ❑; **she smokes roll-ups** elle roule elle-même ses cigarettes

roll-your-own *n Fam* cigarette *f* roulée à la main ❑

roly-poly [ˌrəʊlɪ'pəʊlɪ] *(pl* **roly-polies***)* **1** *adj Fam* grassouillet, rondelet

2 *n* (**a**) *Fam (plump person)* **she's a real roly-poly** elle est vraiment grassouillette (**b**) *Culin* gâteau *m* roulé à la confiture

►► *Culin* ***roly-poly pudding*** gâteau *m* roulé à la confiture

ROM [rɒm] *n Comput (abbr* **read-only memory***)* mémoire *f* morte, (mémoire *f*) ROM *f*

Romagna [rəʊ'mɑːnɪə] *n Hist* **the Romagna** la Romagne

romaine [rəʊ'meɪn] *n Am (lettuce)* romaine *f*

►► ***romaine lettuce*** laitue *f* romaine

Roman ['rəʊmən] **1** *n* (**a**) *(person from Rome)* Romain(e) *m,f*; *Bible* **the Epistle of Paul to the Romans** l'Épître de saint Paul aux Romains

(**b**) *Typ* romain *m*

2 *adj* (**a**) *(gen) & Typ & Rel* romain

(**b**) *(nose)* aquilin

►► ***Roman alphabet*** alphabet *m* romain; *Hist* ***Roman Britain*** = période de domination romaine en Grande-Bretagne allant du Ier siècle av. J.-C. au IVème siècle ap. J.-C.; ***Roman calendar*** calendrier *m* romain; ***Roman candle*** chandelle *f* romaine; *Rel* ***Roman Catholic*** **1** *adj* catholique **2** *n* catholique *mf*; *Rel* ***Roman Catholicism*** catholicisme *m*; *Hist* ***Roman Empire*** l'Empire *m* romain; ***Roman holiday*** = plaisir tiré du malheur des autres; ***Roman law*** droit *m* romain; ***Roman numeral*** chiffre *m* romain; ***Roman road*** voie *f* romaine

roman ['rəʊmən] *Typ* **1** *n* romain *m*; **in roman** en romain

2 *adj* romain; **Roman type** caractères *mpl* romains

romance [rəʊ'mæns] **1** *n* (**a**) *(love affair)* liaison *f* (amoureuse); **to have a romance with sb** *(affair)* avoir une liaison avec qn; *(idyll)* vivre un roman d'amour avec qn; **a holiday romance** un amour de vacances

(**b**) *(love)* amour *m* (romantique); **romance is in the air** il y a de l'amour dans l'air; **everyone dreams of romance** tout le monde rêve d'un grand amour

(**c**) *(romantic novel)* roman *m* d'amour; *(film)* film *m* romantique; **historical romance** = roman d'amour situé à une époque ancienne

(**d**) *(charm)* charme *m*, poésie *f*; *(excitement)* attrait *m*; **after a while the romance wore off** après quelque temps, le charme s'estompa

(**e**) *(fantasy)* fantaisie *f*; *(invention)* invention *f*; **most of what he says is just romance** il invente presque tout ce qu'il raconte

(**f**) *Literature* roman *m* de chevalerie *ou* d'aventures

(**g**) *Mus* romance *f*

2 *vi* laisser vagabonder son imagination, fabuler; **to romance on** *or* **about sth** fabuler *ou* broder sur qch

3 *vt (person)* courtiser

4 Romance 1 *n Ling* roman *m* **2** *adj* **the Romance languages** les langues *fpl* romanes; **student of Romance languages** romaniste *mf*

►► ***romance writer*** romancier(ère) *m,f*, auteur *m* d'histoires romanesques

romancer [rəʊ'mænsə(r)] *n* (**a**) *(writer)* = auteur d'œuvres romanesques (**b**) *(fantasizer)* fabulateur(trice) *m,f*

romancing [rəʊ'mænsɪŋ] *n (invention)* fabulations *fpl*, affabulations *fpl*; *(exaggeration)* exagérations *fpl*

Romanesque [ˌrəʊmə'nesk] *Archit* **1** *adj* roman

2 *n* roman *m*

Romani = **Romany**

Romania [ru:'meɪnɪə] *n* Roumanie *f*; **in Romania** en Roumanie

Romanian [ru:'meɪnɪən] **1** *n* (**a**) *(person)* Roumain(e) *m,f* (**b**) *(language)* roumain *m*

2 *adj* roumain

3 *comp (embassy)* de Roumanie; *(history)* de la Roumanie; *(teacher)* de roumain

Romanic [rəʊ'mænɪk] **1** *adj* romain, des Romains

2 *n Ling* roman *m*

Romanism ['rəʊmənɪzəm] *n* (**a**) *esp Pej Rel* romanisme *m*, catholicisme *m* (**b**) *Hist* influence *f* de Rome *ou* des Romains

Romanist ['rəʊmənɪst] **1** *n* (**a**) *esp Pej Rel* romaniste *mf*, catholique *mf* (**b**) *Ling, Law & Art* romaniste *mf*

2 *adj esp Pej Rel* romaniste, catholique

Romanization [ˌrəʊmənaɪ'zeɪʃən] *n* (**a**) *Hist* romanisation *f* (**b**) *Rel* conversion *f* au catholicisme

romanization [ˌrəʊmənaɪ'zeɪʃən] *n Typ* transcription *f* en caractères romains

Romanize, -ise ['rəʊmənaɪz] *vt Hist* romaniser

romanize ['rəʊmənaɪz] *vt Typ* transcrire en caractères romains

Romansch, Romansh [rəʊ'mænʃ] **1** *n* romanche *m*

2 *adj* romanche

romantic [rəʊ'mæntɪk] **1** *adj* (**a**) *(relating to romance, love)* romantique; **they had a romantic attachment** ils ont eu une liaison amoureuse; **a romantic dinner for two** un dîner romantique *ou* en tête à tête; **to play the romantic lead** *(in film, play)* être le (la) jeune premier(ère)

(**b**) *(unrealistic)* romanesque; **she still has some romantic ideas about life** elle a encore des idées romanesques sur l'existence

2 *n* romantique *mf*; **he's an incurable romantic** c'est un éternel romantique

3 Romantic *adj Art, Literature & Mus* romantique; **the French Romantic poets** les poètes *mpl* romantiques français

►► ***romantic adventure*** aventure *f* romanesque; ***romantic comedy*** comédie *f* romantique; ***romantic love*** l'amour *m* romantique; ***romantic novelist*** auteur *m* de romans d'amour; ***romantic play*** pièce *f* romantique

romantically [rəʊ'mæntɪkəlɪ] *adv* de manière romantique; **to be romantically involved with sb** avoir des relations amoureuses avec qn; **the two celebrities have been romantically linked** les deux célébrités ont eu une liaison amoureuse; **a hotel set romantically by the side of a lake** un hôtel situé dans un cadre romantique tout près d'un lac

romanticism [rəʊ'mæntɪsɪzəm] **1** *n* romantisme *m*

2 Romanticism *n Art, Literature & Mus* romantisme *m*

romanticist [rəʊ'mæntɪsɪst] *n* romantique *mf*

romanticize, -ise [rəʊ'mæntɪsaɪz] **1** *vt (idea, event)* idéaliser; **to romanticize war** glorifier la guerre; **they have a romanticized view of life in Britain** ils ont une vision très romantique de la vie en Grande-Bretagne

2 *vi* donner dans le romanesque

Romany ['rəʊmənɪ] *(pl* **Romanies**) **1** *n* (**a**) *(person)* Bohémien(enne) *m,f*, Rom *mf inv* (**b**) *Ling* rom *m*

2 *adj* bohémien, rom *(inv)*

Rome [rəʊm] *n* (**a**) *(city)* Rome; *Prov* **when in Rome, (do as the Romans do)** = il faut adopter les usages de l'endroit où l'on se trouve; **Rome wasn't built in a day** Rome ne s'est pas faite *ou* Paris ne s'est pas fait en un jour; **all roads lead to Rome** tous les chemins mènent à Rome (**b**) *Rel* **(the Church of) Rome** l'Église *f* de Rome; **to go over to Rome** passer au catholicisme

Romeo ['rəʊmɪəʊ] **1** *pr n* Roméo

2 *n Hum* **he's a bit of a Romeo** c'est un Roméo

'Romeo and Juliet' *Shakespeare, Zeffirelli, Luhrmann* 'Roméo et Juliette'

Romish ['rəʊmɪʃ] *adj Pej* papiste

romp [rɒmp] **1** *vi* s'ébattre (bruyamment), gambader; **the children were romping gleefully in the garden** les enfants s'ébattaient joyeusement dans le jardin; **to romp away with a race** gagner une course haut la main; **to romp home** *(candidate, horse, runner)* arriver dans un fauteuil; **the favourite romped home ten lengths ahead** le favori est arrivé avec dix bonnes longueurs d'avance

2 *n* (**a**) *(frolic)* ébats *mpl*, gambades *fpl*; **sex romps** ébats *mpl* amoureux; *Fig* **the book is a romp through two centuries of French history** le livre nous promène à travers deux siècles d'histoire de France

(**b**) *(film, play)* farce *f*, comédie *f*

(**c**) *Br Fam (easy win)* **it was a romp** c'était du gâteau

►**romp through** *vt insep* **to romp through one's work** expédier son travail sans difficulté; **she romped through the test** elle a réussi le test haut la main

rompers ['rɒmpəz] *npl* barboteuse *f*

romper suit ['rɒmpə-] *n* barboteuse *f*

Romulus ['rɒmjʊləs] *pr n Myth* **Romulus and Remus** Romulus et Rémus

RON ['rəʊn] *n Petr (abbr* **Research Octane Number**) IOR *m*

rondeau ['rɒndəʊ] *(pl* **rondeaux** [-dəʊz]) *n Literature* rondeau *m*

rondel ['rɒndəl] *n Literature* rondel *m*

rondo ['rɒndəʊ] *(pl* **rondos**) *n Mus* rondo *m*

rone [rəʊn] *n Scot (roof-gutter)* gouttière *f*

Roneo® ['rəʊnɪəʊ] **1** *n* Ronéo® *f*

2 *vt* ronéotyper, ronéoter

röntgen, röntgenotherapy = **roentgen, roentgenotherapy**

roo [ru:] *n Austr Fam* kangourou ❑ *m*

►► *Aut* ***roo bars*** pare-buffles *m inv*

rood [ru:d] *n* (**a**) *(cross)* crucifix *m* (**b**) *Br (square measure)* ≃ 1000 m²

►► ***rood arch*** arche *f* du jubé; ***rood beam*** poutre *f* du jubé; ***rood loft*** (galerie *f* du) jubé *m*; ***rood screen*** jubé *m*

roof [ru:f] *(pl* **roofs** *or* **rooves** [ru:vz]) **1** *n* (**a**) *(of building)* toit *m*; *(of cave, tunnel, mine)* plafond *m*; *(of branches, trees)* voûte *f*; *(of car)* toit *m*, pavillon *m*; *(of furnace)* dôme *m*; **to live under the same roof** vivre sous le même toit; **shops and sports facilities under one** *or* **the same roof** des boutiques et des aménagements sportifs dans un même endroit; **I won't have this sort of behaviour under my roof** je ne tolérerai pas ce genre de comportement sous mon toit *ou* chez moi; **to be without a roof over one's head** être à la rue; **at least you have a roof over your head** au moins, tu as un endroit pour vivre; *Fig* **the roof of the world** le toit du monde; *Fig* **the Celestial roof** la voûte céleste; *Fam* **to go through** *or* **to hit the roof** *(person)* piquer une crise, sortir de ses gonds; *(prices)* flamber; *Fam* **to raise the roof** *(make noise)* faire le diable à quatre; *(cause fuss)* protester à grands cris

(**b**) *(roof covering)* toiture *f*

(**c**) *Anat* **roof of the mouth** voûte *f* du palais

2 *vt* couvrir d'un toit; **roofed with corrugated iron** avec un toit en tôle ondulée

►► ***roof garden*** jardin *m* sur le toit; ***roof light*** *(of vehicle)* plafonnier *m*; *(window)* lucarne *f*; ***roof rack*** *(on car)* galerie *f*; ***roof support*** solive *f*

►**roof over** *vt sep* recouvrir

-roofed [ru:ft] *suff* **flat-roofed warehouses** des entrepôts *mpl* à toits plats *ou* en terrasse

roofer ['ru:fə(r)] *n* (**a**) *Constr* couvreur *m* (**b**) *Fam (letter of thanks)* lettre *m* de remerciement ❑ *(écrite à un hôte)*

roofing ['ru:fɪŋ] *n (operation)* pose *f* de la toiture; *(material)* toiture *f*

►► ***roofing felt*** carton *m* bitumé *ou* goudronné, *Belg* roofing *m*; ***roofing materials*** matériaux *mpl* pour toitures

roofless ['ru:flɪs] *adj* sans toit, à ciel ouvert

roofscape ['ru:fskeɪp] *n Art* paysage *m* de toits

rooftop ['ru:ftɒp] *n* toit *m*; **a chase over the rooftops** une poursuite sur les toits; *Fig* **to shout** *or* **to proclaim sth from the rooftops** crier qch sur les toits; **police marksmen have taken up rooftop positions** des tireurs d'élite ont pris position sur le toit

rooftree ['ru:ftri:] *n Constr* poutre *f* de faîte, faîtage *m*

rooinek ['rɔɪnek] *n SAfr Fam Pej* = Sud-Africain d'origine britannique

rook [rʊk] **1** *n* (**a**) *Orn* freux *m*, corbeau *m* (**b**) *(in chess)* tour *f* (**c**) *Old-fashioned (swindler)* escroc *m*, filou *m*

2 *vt Fam* rouler, escroquer

rooked [rʊkt] *adj Scot Fam (having no money)* fauché, à sec

rookery ['rʊkərɪ] *(pl* **rookeries**) *n (of rooks)* colonie *f* de freux; **a rookery of seals/penguins** une colonie de phoques/manchots

rookie ['rʊkɪ] *n Am Fam (recruit)* bleu *m*; *(inexperienced person)* novice ❑ *mf*; *(addition to a team)* nouveau membre ❑ *m*; **rookie cop** flic *m* débutant, bleu *m*

room [ru:m, rʊm] **1** *n* (**a**) *(in building, public place)* salle *f*; *(in house)* pièce *f*; *(bedroom, in hotel)* chambre *f*; **the house has ten rooms** la maison comporte dix pièces; **room to let** *or* **to rent** *(sign)* chambre à louer; **his rooms are in Bayswater** il habite à Bayswater; **to live in rooms** vivre dans un meublé; **(furnished) rooms to let** *(sign)* chambres (meublées) à louer; **room and board** chambre *f* avec pension; **room 22 wants some coffee** *(in hotel)* du café pour la chambre 22; *Fam Euph* **the smallest room in the house** *(toilet)* le petit coin; **the room fell silent** le silence s'est fait dans la pièce *ou* dans la salle; **the whole room burst out laughing** toute la salle a éclaté de rire

(**b**) *(space)* place *f*; **is there enough room for everybody?** y a-t-il assez de place pour tout le monde?; **there's plenty of room** il y a beaucoup de place; **it takes up too much room** ça prend trop de place; *Fam* **there isn't (enough) room to swing a cat in here** c'est grand comme un placard ici; **to make room for sb** faire une place *ou* de la place pour qn; *Fig* laisser la place à qn; *Fig* **it's time to make room for young people with fresh ideas** il est temps de laisser la place à des gens jeunes avec des idées neuves; **is there room for one more?** *(person)* est-ce qu'il y a encore de la place pour une personne?; **room for one more inside!** *(on bus)* il y a encore de la place pour une personne; **room to** *or* **for manoeuvre** place *f* pour manœuvrer; *Fig* marge *f* de manœuvre; **the new legislation leaves little room for manoeuvre** la nouvelle loi laisse une faible marge de manœuvre; **there's room for improvement** il y a des progrès à faire; **there's still room for discussion/hope** on peut encore discuter/espérer; **there's no room for doubt** il n'y a plus aucun doute possible; **there's no room for slackers in this company** les fainéants n'ont pas leur place dans cette société

2 *vi Am* loger; **to room with sb** *(share apartment)* partager un appartement avec qn; *(in hotel)* partager une chambre avec qn; **to room together** vivre ensemble dans le même appartement

►► *Am* ***room clerk*** réceptionniste *mf*; ***room divider*** cloison *f*, écran *m*; ***room key*** clé *f* de la chambre; **your room key** la clé de votre chambre; ***room number*** *(in hotel)* numéro *m* de chambre; ***room service*** service *m* dans les chambres; **to provide room service** servir dans les chambres; **to call room service** appeler le service en chambre *ou* le garçon d'étage; ***room temperature*** température *f* ambiante; **to keep sth at room temperature** garder qch à la température ambiante *ou* de la pièce; **this plant must be kept at room temperature** cette plante doit être placée dans une pièce chauffée; **serve at room temperature** *(on packaging)* servir chambré

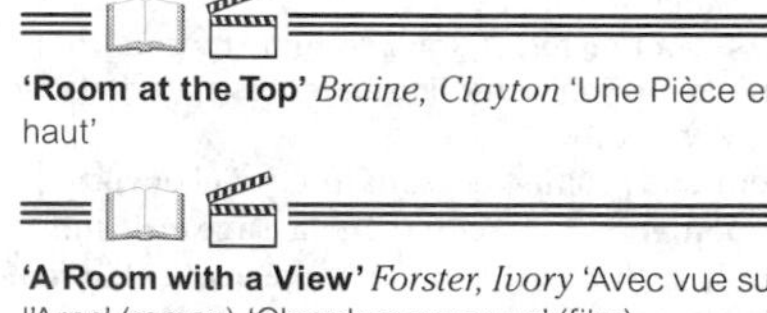

'Room at the Top' *Braine, Clayton* 'Une Pièce en haut'

'A Room with a View' *Forster, Ivory* 'Avec vue sur l'Arno' (roman), 'Chambre avec vue' (film)

'A Room of One's Own' *Woolf* 'Une Chambre à soi'

> **No room at the inn**
> Cette phrase provient de la nativité lorsque Joseph et Marie se virent refuser l'accès à l'auberge de Bethléem et trouvèrent refuge dans une étable. On utilise cette formule ("il n'y a aucune chambre de libre dans l'auberge") de façon allusive lorsqu'un hôtel est complet ou lorsqu'un hôpital ne peut accueillir de nouveaux patients, par exemple.

-roomed [ruːmd] *suff* **a five-roomed flat** un appartement de cinq pièces, un cinq-pièces

roomer [ˈruːmə(r)] *n Am* pensionnaire *mf*

roomette [ruːˈmet] *n Am* = petit wagon-lit à une place

roomful [ˈruːmfʊl] *n* pleine salle *f ou* pièce *f*; **a roomful of furniture** une pièce pleine de meubles; **a roomful of people** une salle pleine de monde

roomie [ˈruːmɪ] *n Am Fam (room-mate)* colocataire *mf*, coloc *mf*

roominess [ˈruːmɪnɪs] *n (of house etc)* dimensions *fpl* spacieuses *ou* généreuses; *(of clothes)* coupe *f* confortable *ou* ample; *(of car)* dimensions *fpl* spacieuses

rooming house [ˈruːmɪŋ-] *n Am* immeuble *m (avec chambres à louer)*

room-mate *n (in boarding school, college)* camarade *mf* de chambre; *Am (in apartment)* colocataire *mf*

roomy [ˈruːmɪ] *(compar* **roomier**, *superl* **roomiest**) *adj (house, office, car)* spacieux; *(suitcase, bag)* grand; *(clothes)* ample

roorback [ˈrʊəbæk] *n Am Pol* pamphlet *m* diffamatoire

roost [ruːst] **1** *n* perchoir *m*; *(for domestic fowl)* juchoir *m*; *Fig (for person)* logement *m*, gîte *m*

2 *vi (bird)* se percher; *(domestic fowl)* (se) jucher; *Fig* **to come home to roost** *(crime, mistake)* se retourner contre son auteur; *Fig* **your chickens have come home to roost** ça s'est retourné contre toi, ça a fait boomerang

rooster [ˈruːstə(r)] *n Am* coq *m*

root [ruːt] **1** *n* **(a)** *(of plant) & Fig* racine *f*; **to pull up a plant by its roots** déraciner une plante; **to take root** *(plant) & Fig* prendre racine; **to put down roots** *(plant) & Fig* prendre racine, s'enraciner

(b) *Anat (of tooth, hair etc)* racine *f*; **to touch up one's roots** *(person with dyed hair)* refaire ses racines; **to get one's roots done** se faire refaire les racines

(c) *(source)* source *f*; *(cause)* cause *f*; *(bottom)* fond *m*; **to have its roots in sth** *(of crisis etc)* avoir ses origines dans qch; **the root of all evil** la source de tout les maux; **to get at** *or* **to the root of the problem** aller au fond du problème; **poor housing is at the root of much delinquency** la mauvaise qualité des logements est souvent à l'origine de la délinquance

(d) *Ling (in etymology)* racine *f*; *(base form)* radical *m*, base *f*

(e) *Comput (directory)* racine *f*, répertoire *m* principal

(f) *Math* racine *f*

(g) *Mus* fondamentale *f*

(h) *(idiom)* **corruption must be eliminated root and branch** il faut éradiquer la corruption

2 *comp (cause, problem)* fondamental, de base

3 *vt* **(a)** *(fix)* enraciner; *Fig* **he stood rooted to the spot** il est resté cloué sur place; **her political convictions are rooted in her upbringing** c'est dans son éducation qu'il faut chercher les racines de ses convictions politiques

(b) *Austr very Fam (have sex with)* s'envoyer en l'air avec

4 *vi* **(a)** *(plant)* s'enraciner, prendre racine

(b) *(animal)* fouiller *(avec le museau)*; **to root for truffles** chercher des truffes

(c) *Austr very Fam (have sex)* s'envoyer en l'air

5 roots *npl (of person → origin)* racines *fpl*, origines *fpl*; **he has no real roots** il n'a pas de véritables racines; **she is in search of her roots** elle est à la recherche de ses origines; **to get back to one's roots** retrouver ses racines; **their actual roots are in Virginia** en fait ils sont originaires de Virginie

►► *Am* ***root beer*** = boisson gazeuse à base d'extraits végétaux; *Anat* ***root canal*** canal *m* dentaire; ***root canal treatment, root canal work*** traitement *m* canalaire; *Am* ***root cellar*** cave *f* potagère; *Bot* ***root climber*** plante *f* grimpante à racines crampons; ***root crop*** racine *f* comestible; *Comput* ***root directory*** racine *f*, répertoire *m* principal; *Bot* ***root hair*** poil *m* radiculaire; *Math* ***root mean square*** moyenne *f* quadratique; ***roots music*** musique *f* "roots" *(influencée par la musique traditionelle)*; *Bot* ***root rot*** piétin *m*; ***root vegetable*** légume *m* à racine comestible

►**root about, root around** *vi (animal)* fouiller *(avec le museau)*; *(person)* fouiller; **to root about for sth** fouiller pour trouver qch; **to root about in a drawer** fouiller dans un tiroir

►**root for** *vt insep (team)* encourager, soutenir; **to root for a candidate** appuyer un candidat; **we're all rooting for you** nous sommes de votre côté

►**root out** *vt sep* **(a)** *(from earth)* déterrer; *(from hiding place)* dénicher

(b) *(suppress)* supprimer, extirper

►**root through** *vt insep (search through)* fouiller dans

►**root up** *vt sep (plant)* déraciner; *(of pig)* déterrer

root-and-branch *adj (reform)* complet(ète)

rootbound [ˈruːtbaʊnd] *adj Hort* **this shrub is rootbound** les racines de cet arbuste sont trop à l'étroit

root-eating *adj Zool* radicivore

rooted [ˈruːtɪd] *adj* **(a)** *(plant, prejudice, belief, habits)* enraciné; **deeply rooted superstitions** des superstitions *fpl* bien enracinées *ou* profondément ancrées **(b)** *Austr very Fam (exhausted)* naze, lessivé

rootedness [ˈruːtɪdnɪs] *n* enracinement *m*

rooting [ˈruːtɪŋ] *n* enracinement *m*

►► *Hort* ***rooting compost*** compost *m* spécial pour boutures; ***rooting out*** *(of abuse, malpractice)* extirpation *f*, éradication *f*

rootle [ˈruːtəl] *vi Br (pig)* fouiller *(avec le groin)*

rootless [ˈruːtlɪs] *adj* sans racine *ou* racines

rootlet [ˈruːtlɪt] *n Bot* radicelle *f*

rootstock [ˈruːtstɒk] *n Bot* **(a)** *(rhizome)* rhizome *m* **(b)** *(stem receiving graft)* porte-greffe *m*, sujet *m*; *(plant from which graft is taken)* plante *f* mère *(sur laquelle on prélève un greffon)*

rootsy [ˈruːtsɪ] *adj (music)* roots *(influencé par la musique traditionnelle)*

ropable = **ropeable**

rope [rəʊp] **1** *n* **(a)** *(gen)* corde *f*; *(collectively)* cordage *m*; *(of steel, wire)* filin *m*; *(cable)* câble *m*; *(for bell, curtains)* cordon *m*; **a piece** *or* **length of rope** un bout de corde, une corde; **the rope** *(death by hanging)* la pendaison; **to bring back the rope** remettre la pendaison en vigueur; *Fig* **to come to the end of one's rope** être au bout du rouleau; *Fig* **to give sb more rope** laisser à qn une plus grande liberté d'action, lâcher la bride à qn; *Fig* **she gave him plenty of rope** elle lui a donné une grande liberté d'action *ou* marge de manœuvre; *Fig* **give him enough rope and he'll hang himself** si on le laisse faire, il creusera sa propre tombe

(b) *(in mountaineering)* cordée *f*

(c) *(of pearls)* collier *m*; *(long)* sautoir *m*; *(of onions)* chapelet *m*

2 *vt* **(a)** *(package)* attacher avec une corde, corder; **the climbers were roped together** les alpinistes étaient encordés; **he was roped to a post** il a été attaché à un poteau

(b) *Am (cattle, horses)* prendre au lasso

3 ropes *npl* **(a)** *Boxing* cordes *fpl*; **to be on the ropes** *(boxer)* se retrouver dans les cordes; *Fig (company, economy etc)* battre de l'aile; *Fig* **to be up against the ropes** être le dos au mur; **to have sb on the ropes** *Boxing* mettre qn dans les cordes; *Fig* acculer qn, mettre qn dans une position difficile

(b) *(know-how)* **to know the ropes** connaître les ficelles *ou* son affaire; **to show** *or* **to teach sb the ropes** montrer les ficelles du métier à qn; **to learn the ropes** se mettre au courant, apprendre à se débrouiller

►► ***rope bridge*** pont *m* de corde; ***rope ladder*** échelle *f* de corde; ***rope maker*** cordier(ère) *m,f*; ***rope sandals*** espadrilles *fpl*; ***rope trick*** = tour de prestidigitation réalisé avec une cordelette; ***rope yarn*** fil *m* de caret

►**rope in** *vt sep* **(a)** *(land)* entourer de cordes, délimiter par des cordes **(b)** *(cattle)* mettre dans un enclos **(c)** *Fig* **to rope sb in to do sth** enrôler qn pour faire qch; **he got himself roped in as chairman** il a été forcé d'accepter la présidence

►**rope off** *vt sep (part of hall, of church)* délimiter par une corde; *(street, building)* interdire l'accès de

►**rope up 1** *vi (climbers)* s'encorder

2 *vt sep* **(a)** *(parcel)* attacher avec une corde, corder **(b)** *(climbers)* encorder

ropeable [ˈrəʊpəbəl] *adj Austr & NZ Fam* **(a)** *(cattle, horse)* rebelle ❑ **(b)** *(person)* furibond ❑

ropedancer [ˈrəʊpˌdɑːnsə(r)] *n* funambule *mf*, danseur(euse) *m,f* de corde

ropedancing [ˈrəʊpˌdɑːnsɪŋ] *n* funambulie *f*, danse *f* sur la corde

rope's-end 1 *n* **(a)** *Naut* garcette *f* **(b)** *(of hangman)* corde *f* (de potence)

2 *vt Naut* passer à la garcette

rope-soled [-səʊld] *adj (sandals)* à semelles de corde

ropewalk [ˈrəʊpwɔːk] *n* corderie *f*

ropewalker [ˈrəʊpˌwɔːkə(r)] *n* funambule *mf*

ropeway [ˈrəʊpweɪ] *n* **(a)** *(cable railway)* funiculaire *m* **(b)** *(rope bridge)* pont *m* de corde

ropey [ˈrəʊpɪ] *(compar* **ropier**, *superl* **ropiest**) *adj Br* **(a)** *(substance)* visqueux **(b)** *Fam (mediocre)* médiocre ❑, pas fameux; *(ill)* mal fichu, patraque; **to feel a bit ropey** se sentir patraque, ne pas être dans son assiette

ropiness [ˈrəʊpɪnɪs] *n* **(a)** *(of substance)* viscosité *f*; *(in beer, wine)* graisse *f*, pousse *f* **(b)** *Fam (poor quality)* mauvaise qualité ❑ *f*

ropy = **ropey**

roquet [ˈrəʊkeɪ] **1** *n (in croquet)* touche *f (de la balle de l'adversaire avec la sienne)*

2 *vt (in croquet)* toucher *(une autre balle avec la sienne)*

ro-ro ['rəʊ,rəʊ] **1** *n (ship)* (navire *m*) transbordeur *m*, ferry-boat *m*; *(system)* roll on-roll off *m inv*, manutention *f* par roulage
2 *adj (ferry)* transbordeur, ro-ro *(inv)*; *(port)* à roulage direct

rorqual ['rɔːkwəl] *n Zool* rorqual *m*, balénoptère *m*

Rorschach test ['rɔːʃæk-] *n Psy* test *m* de Rorschach

rort [rɔːt] *Austr Fam* **1** *n* (**a**) *(trick, fraud)* arnaque *f* (**b**) *(party)* fiesta *f*, nouba *f*
2 *vi* (**a**) *(protest)* gueuler (**b**) *Horseracing* annoncer la cote [a] (**c**) *(commit fraud)* faire une arnaque

ROS [,ɑːrəʊ'es] *n Fin* (*abbr* **return on sales**) retour *m* sur ventes

rosace [rəʊ'zeɪs] *n Archit* rosace *f*

rosacea [rəʊ'zeɪʃɪə] *n Med* rosacée *f*

rosaceous [rəʊ'zeɪʃəs] *adj Bot* rosacé

rosaniline [rəʊ'zænɪlaɪn] *n Chem* rosaniline *f*

rosarian [rəʊ'zeərɪən] *n* rosiériste *mf*

rosarium [rəʊ'zeərɪəm] *n* roseraie *f*

rosary ['rəʊzərɪ] (*pl* **rosaries**) *n* (**a**) *Rel (beads)* chapelet *m*, rosaire *m*; *(prayers)* rosaire *m*; **to tell** *or* **to say the rosary** dire son rosaire (**b**) *(rose garden)* roseraie *f*

Roscommon [,rɒs'kɒmən] *n* (**a**) *(town)* Roscommon (**b**) *(county)* le comté de Roscommon, = comté dans le centre de la République d'Irlande; **in Roscommon** dans le comté de Roscommon

rose [rəʊz] **1** *pt of* **rise**
2 *n* (**a**) *(flower)* rose *f*; *(bush)* rosier *m*; **life's not all roses** tout n'est pas rose dans la vie; **there's no rose without a thorn** il n'y a pas de roses sans épines, chaque médaille a son revers; *Fig* **to always come up smelling of roses** s'en sortir toujours très bien; **to come up roses** *(enterprise)* marcher comme sur des roulettes; *(person)* réussir, avoir le vent en poupe; *Literary* **under the rose** en cachette, en confidence; **that'll put the roses back into your cheeks** ça va te redonner des couleurs
(**b**) *(rose shape → on hat, dress)* rosette *f*; *(→ on ceiling)* rosace *f*
(**c**) *(colour)* rose *m*
(**d**) *(on hosepipe, watering can)* pomme *f*
3 *adj* rose, de couleur rose
►► *Entom* ***rose beetle*** cétoine *f* dorée, hanneton *m* vert; ***the Rose Bowl*** = match de football universitaire organisé le jour de l'an à Pasadena, en Californie; *Entom* ***rose chafer*** cétoine *f* dorée, hanneton *m* vert; *Tech* ***rose engine*** machine *f ou* tour *m* à guillocher; ***rose garden*** roseraie *f*; ***rose grower*** rosiériste *mf*; *Bot* ***rose of Jericho*** rose *f* de Jéricho; *Bot* ***rose madder*** rose *f* garance; *Bot* ***rose mallow*** primerose *f*; ***the Rose Parade*** = défilé annuel de chars fleuris du jour de l'an à Pasadena, en Californie; ***rose pink*** rose *m*; *Miner* ***rose quartz*** quartz *m* rose; ***rose red*** vermillon *m*; *Bot* ***rose of Sharon*** rose *f* de Saron; ***Rose of Tralee*** = reine de beauté irlandaise (ou d'origine irlandaise) élue chaque année dans la ville de Tralee; *Bot* ***rose tree*** rosier *m*; *Archit* ***rose window*** rosace *f*

rosé ['rəʊzeɪ] *n* (vin *m*) rosé *m*

roseate [illegible] *adj Literary* rose; **to take a roseate view of things** voir la vie en rose
►► *Orn* ***roseate tern*** sterne *f* de Dougall

rosebay ['rəʊzbeɪ] *n Bot* laurier-rose *m*
►► ***rosebay willowherb*** épilobe *m* à épi(s)

rosebed ['rəʊzbed] *n* parterre *m ou* massif *m* de roses

rosebud ['rəʊzbʌd] *n* bouton *m* de rose
►► ***rosebud mouth*** bouche *f* en cerise

rosebush ['rəʊzbʊʃ] *n* rosier *m*

rose-coloured *adj* rose, rosé; **to see life through rose-coloured spectacles** voir la vie en rose

rose-cut *adj (diamond etc)* (taillé) en rose

rosefinch ['rəʊzfɪntʃ] *n Orn* roselin *m* rose

rosehip ['rəʊzhɪp] *n Bot* gratte-cul *m inv*, *Spec* cynorhodon *m*
►► ***rosehip syrup*** sirop *m* d'églantine

rosella [rəʊ'zelə] *n Orn* platycerque *m*

rosemary ['rəʊzmərɪ] (*pl* **rosemaries**) *n Bot* romarin *m*
►► ***rosemary bush*** buisson *m* de romarin

Rosenberg ['rəʊzənbɜːg] *pr n* Rosenberg
►► *Am Hist* ***the Rosenberg case*** l'affaire *f* Rosenberg

THE ROSENBERG CASE

Ce procès aboutit à l'exécution, en 1953, des époux Rosenberg, scientifiques américains accusés d'avoir livré à l'URSS des informations sur la bombe atomique. Premiers civils à être condamnés à mort pour espionnage, leur exécution souleva des protestations dans le monde entier de la part de ceux qui y voyaient l'œuvre du maccarthysme.

roseola [rəʊ'ziːələ] *n (UNCOUNT) Med* roséole *f*

rose-pink *adj* (couleur de) rose

rose-red *adj* vermeil

rose-scented *adj* parfumé à la rose, au parfum de rose

rose-tinted *adj* teinté en rose; **to see life through rose-tinted glasses** *or* **spectacles** voir la vie en rose

Rosetta [rə'zetə] *pr n* Rosette
►► ***the Rosetta stone*** la pierre de Rosette

rosette [rəʊ'zet] *n* (**a**) *(made of ribbons)* rosette *f*; *Sport* cocarde *f* (**b**) *Archit (carving)* rosette *f*; *(window)* rosace *f* (**c**) *Bot* rosette *f*

rosewater ['rəʊz,wɔːtə(r)] *n* eau *f* de rose

rosewood ['rəʊzwʊd] *Bot* **1** *n* bois *m* de rose
2 *comp* en bois de rose

Rosh Hashanah [,rɒʃhə'ʃɑːnə] *n Rel* Roch hashana *m inv*

Rosicrucian [,rəʊzɪ'kruːʃən] **1** *n* rosicrucien(enne) *m,f*, rose-croix *m inv*
2 *adj* rosicrucien

Rosicrucianism [,rəʊzɪ'kruːʃənɪzəm] *n* philosophie *f* de l'ordre de la Rose-Croix

rosie ['rəʊzɪ] *n SEng Fam (rhyming slang* **rosie lee** *=* **tea**) thé [a] *m*

rosin ['rɒzɪn] **1** *n* colophane *f*, arcanson *m*
2 *vt* traiter à la colophane, enduire de colophane

rosiness ['rəʊzɪnɪs] *n* couleur *f* rose, rose *m*; *Literary* roseur *f*; **the rosiness of her cheeks** le rose de ses joues

RoSPA ['rɒspə] *n Br* (*abbr* **Royal Society for the Prevention of Accidents**) = association britannique pour la prévention des accidents

Ross's goose ['rɒsəs-] *n Orn* oie *f* de Ross

roster ['rɒstə(r)] **1** *n (list)* liste *f*; *(for duty)* tableau *m* de service; **by roster** à tour de rôle; **promotion roster** tableau *m* d'avancement
2 *vt* inscrire au tableau de service *ou* au planning; **I'm rostered on Sunday** je suis de service dimanche

Rostov ['rɒstɒv] *n* Rostov-sur-le-Don

rostrum ['rɒstrəm] (*pl* **rostrums** *or* **rostra** [-trə]) *n* (**a**) *(platform → for speaker)* estrade *f*, tribune *f*; *(→ for conductor)* estrade *f*; *Sport* podium *m*; **to take the rostrum** monter sur l'estrade *ou* à la tribune (**b**) *Antiq (of ship)* rostre *m*; *(platform in forum)* rostres *mpl* (**c**) *Zool* rostre *m*
►► *Cin & TV* ***rostrum camera*** banc-titre *m*

rosulate ['rɒsjʊleɪt] *adj Bot* en rosette

rosy ['rəʊzɪ] (*compar* **rosier,** *superl* **rosiest**) *adj (in colour)* rose, rosé; *Fig (future, situation)* prometteur, qui se présente bien; **to have rosy cheeks** avoir les joues roses; *Fig* **to paint a rosy picture of sth** dépeindre qch sous un jour optimiste; **to have a rosy view of life** voir la vie en rose
►► ***rosy cross*** = la croix et la rose rouge, symbole de la Rose-Croix

rosy-fingered *adj Literary* **the rosy-fingered dawn** l'aurore *f* aux doigts de rose

rot [rɒt] (*pt & pp* **rotted,** *cont* **rotting**) **1** *vi* (**a**) *(gen)* pourrir; *(meat, body)* se putréfier; *(compost matter)* se décomposer; *(teeth)* se carier
(**b**) *Fig (person)* pourrir; **to rot in prison** pourrir *ou* croupir en prison; *Fam* **let them rot!** qu'ils crèvent!
2 *vt (vegetable, fibres)* (faire) pourrir; *(tooth)* carier, gâter; **sugar rots your teeth** le sucre gâte les dents *ou* donne des caries
3 *n* (**a**) *(of fruit, vegetable, wood)* pourriture *f*; *(of tooth)* carie *f*
(**b**) *Fig (in society)* pourriture *f*; **the rot has set in** ça commence à se gâter; **to stop the rot** empêcher les choses de se dégrader, remonter la pente; **we've stopped the rot** on remonte la pente
(**c**) *(UNCOUNT) Fam* foutaises *fpl*; **don't talk rot!** arrête de raconter n'importe quoi!; **that's utter rot!, what rot!** c'est vraiment n'importe quoi!

►**rot away** *vi & vt sep* = **rot** *vi & vt*

►**rot down** *vi (compost material)* se décomposer

rota ['rəʊtə] **1** *n Br (system)* roulement *m*; *(for duty → list)* tableau *m* de service, planning *m*; **we have a rota for the housework** nous faisons le ménage (chacun) à tour de rôle; **on a rota basis** à tour de rôle, par roulement
2 Rota *n Rel* rote *f*

Rotarian [rəʊ'teərɪən] **1** *adj* rotarien
2 *n* rotarien(enne) *m,f*

rotary ['rəʊtərɪ] (*pl* **rotaries**) **1** *adj* rotatif
2 *n Am* rond-point *m*
►► ***the Rotary Club*** le Rotary Club; ***Rotary Club member*** rotarien(enne) *m,f*; ***rotary cultivator*** motoculteur *m*; ***rotary engine*** moteur *m* rotatif; *Typ* ***rotary press*** rotative *f*; *Typ* ***rotary printer*** *(person)* rotativiste *mf*; *Am* ***rotary tiller*** pulvériseur *m*

rotate 1 *vt* [rəʊ'teɪt] (**a**) *(turn)* faire tourner; *(on pivot)* faire pivoter
(**b**) *Agr (crops)* alterner
(**c**) *(staff)* faire un roulement de; *(jobs)* faire à tour de rôle *ou* par roulement
2 *vi* [rəʊ'teɪt] (**a**) *(turn)* tourner; *(on pivot)* pivoter
(**b**) *(staff)* changer de poste par roulement; **the presidency rotates every two years among the members** les membres assument la présidence à tour de rôle tous les deux ans
3 *adj* ['rəʊteɪt] *Bot* rotacé

rotating [rəʊ'teɪtɪŋ] **1** *adj* (**a**) *(turning)* tournant, rotatif; **rotating body** corps *m* en rotation (**b**) **on a rotating basis** *(in turns)* à tour de rôle
2 *n* (**a**) *(turning)* rotation *f* (**b**) *Agr (of crops)* alternance *f*
►► *Agr* ***rotating crops*** cultures *fpl* alternantes *ou* en rotation

rotation [rəʊ'teɪʃən] *n* (**a**) *(of machinery, planets)* rotation *f*; **rotations per minute** tours *mpl* par minute (**b**) *(of staff, jobs)* roulement *m*; **in** *or* **by rotation** par roulement, à tour de rôle (**c**) *Agr (of crops)* alternance *f*

rotational [rəʊ'teɪʃənəl] *adj* rotatif, de rotation
►► *Phys* ***rotational inertia*** inertie *f* de rotation

rotator [rəʊ'teɪtə(r)] *n* (**a**) *(spindle)* axe *m* rotatif; *(machine)* appareil *m* rotateur; *(propeller)* hélice *f* (**b**) *Anat* (muscle *m*) rotateur *m*

rotatory ['rəʊtətərɪ] *adj* rotatoire

rotavate = **rotovate**

Rotavator® = **Rotovator**®

ROTC [,ɑːrəʊ,tiː'siː, 'rɒtsɪ] *n Mil* (*abbr* **Reserve Officer Training Corps**) = préparation militaire proposée par l'armée de terre américaine aux étudiants désireux de se faire payer leurs études, en échange de quoi ces derniers s'engagent à passer quatre ans dans l'armée

rote [rəʊt] *n* routine *f*; **to learn sth by rote** apprendre qch par cœur
►► ***rote learning*** apprentissage *m* par cœur

rotenone ['rəʊtɪnəʊn] *n Chem* roténone *f*

rotgut ['rɒtgʌt] *n (UNCOUNT) Fam (spirits)* tord-boyaux *m inv*, gnôle *f*; *(wine)* piquette *f*

rotifer ['rəʊtɪfə(r)] *n Zool* rotifère *m*

rotisserie [rəʊ'tɪːsərɪ] *n (spit)* rôtissoire *f*

rotogravure [,rəʊtəgrə'vjʊə(r)] *n* rotogravure *f*

rotor ['rəʊtə(r)] *n* rotor *m*
►► ***rotor arm*** *(of helicopter)* rotor *m*; *(of engine)* rotor *m*, balai *m*; ***rotor blade*** pale *f* de rotor

Rotorooter® ['rəʊtə,ruːtə(r)] *n* = appareil pour déboucher les canalisations

Rototiller® ['rəʊtə,tɪlə(r)] *n Am* motoculteur *m*

rotovate ['rəʊtəveɪt] *vt Br* labourer avec un motoculteur

Rotovator® ['rəʊtəveɪtə(r)] *n Br* motoculteur *m*

rotproof ['rɒtpruːf] *adj (wood)* imputrescible; *(fabric)* qui résiste à l'humidité *ou* à la chaleur

rotten ['rɒtən] *adj* (**a**) *(fruit, egg, wood)* pourri; *(tooth)* carié, gâté; **to smell rotten** sentir le pourri; **to go rotten** pourrir
(**b**) *(corrupt)* pourri, corrompu; **rotten through and through** *or* **to the core** complètement pourri, corrompu jusqu'à la moelle

(**c**) *Fam (person → unkind)* vache, dégueulasse; **to be rotten to sb** être vache *ou* dégueulasse avec qn; **don't be rotten!** ne sois pas vache!; **that was a rotten thing to do** c'était un sale tour, c'est vraiment vache *ou* dégueulasse d'avoir fait ça; **what a rotten thing to say!** c'est moche de dire des choses pareilles!; **what a rotten trick!** quel sale tour!; *Fam* **you rotten so-and-so!** espèce de salaud!

(**d**) *Fam (guilty)* **to feel rotten** se sentir coupable □; **I felt rotten about it** j'en étais malade; **I feel rotten about this, but...** *(sorry)* ça me rend malade mais...

(**e**) *Fam (ill)* **to feel rotten** se sentir patraque; **you look rotten** vous n'avez pas l'air en forme

(**f**) *Fam (worthless)* nul, pourri; *(weather)* pourri; **the weather was rotten** il a fait un temps de chien, le temps était vraiment pourri; **he's a rotten goalkeeper** il est nul *ou* il ne vaut rien comme gardien de but; **he's a rotten cook** il est complètement nul comme cuisinier; **what rotten luck!** quelle poisse!; **I always get the rotten jobs!** on me refile toujours les sales besognes!; **I've had a rotten time recently** j'ai traversé une sale période récemment; **we had a rotten time at the party** on s'est vraiment embêtés à la soirée

(**g**) *Fam (in indignation)* fichu; **keep your rotten (old) sweets!** tes bonbons pourris, tu peux te les garder!

►► *Hist* ***rotten borough*** = circonscription électorale britannique dont les électeurs, bien que peu nombreux, pouvaient élire un député (avant 1832)

rottenly ['rɒtənlɪ] *adv* abominablement; **to behave rottenly to sb** se conduire d'une manière inqualifiable avec qn

rottenness ['rɒtənnɪs] *n* (**a**) *(of wood, fruit, vegetable)* pourriture *f* (**b**) *Fam (poor quality)* caractère *m* lamentable □, nullité □ *f*

rottenstone ['rɒtən,stəʊn] *n Geol* diatomite *f*, tripoli *m*

rotter ['rɒtə(r)] *n Br Fam Old-fashioned* crapule *f*, sale type *m*

Rotterdam ['rɒtədæm] *n* Rotterdam

rotting ['rɒtɪŋ] *adj* qui pourrit, pourri

rottweiler ['rɒt,vaɪlə(r)] *n* (**a**) *(dog)* rottweiler *m (race de chiens réputés dangereux)* (**b**) *Fig Hum (fierce person)* **to be a rottweiler** avoir la dent dure

rotund [rəʊ'tʌnd] *adj* (**a**) *(shape)* rond, arrondi; *(person)* rondelet; **his rotund figure** ses formes arrondies (**b**) *(style, speech)* grandiloquent

rotunda [rəʊ'tʌndə] *n Archit* rotonde *f*

rotundity [rəʊ'tʌndətɪ] *n* (**a**) *(of person)* embonpoint *m*, rotondité *f* (**b**) *(of style, speech)* grandiloquence *f*

rouble ['ru:bəl] *n* rouble *m*

roué ['ru:eɪ] *n Arch or Hum* roué *m*, débauché *m*

rouge [ru:ʒ] **1** *n* rouge *m* (à joues)

2 *vt* **she had rouged cheeks** elle s'était mis du rouge aux joues

ROUGH [rʌf]

rêche	►**1 (a)**
rugueux	►**1 (a)**
brutal	►**1 (b)**
rude	►**1 (c), (d)**
agité	►**1 (e)**
rauque	►**1 (f)**
approximatif	►**1 (g)**
brouillon	►**2 (b)**
avec rudesse	►**3**

1 *adj* (**a**) *(uneven → skin, cloth, paper)* rêche; *(→ surface)* rugueux; *(→ road)* accidenté, rocailleux; *(→ coast)* accidenté; *(→ edge)* rugueux

(**b**) *(violent → behaviour, person, treatment)* brutal; *(→ neighbourhood)* dur, mal fréquenté; **they came in for some rough treatment** ils ont été malmenés; **the parcels got some rough handling** les paquets ont été traités sans ménagement *ou* malmenés; **he received some rough handling from the press** la presse l'a présenté de façon défavorable; **they were rough with** *or* **on the new recruits** ils n'ont pas été tendres avec les nouvelles recrues; **she's terribly rough with the children** elle est très brutale avec les enfants; **they're rough kids** ce sont des petites brutes *ou* des petits voyous; **he's a rough customer** c'est un dur; **rugby can be a rough game** le rugby peut être un jeu brutal; **you see some rough behaviour at football matches** on voit des violences *ou* des brutalités aux matchs de foot; **he has a rough tongue** il ne mâche pas ses mots; **to give sb the rough edge of one's tongue** réprimander qn, ne pas ménager ses reproches à qn

(**c**) *(unrefined → person, manners)* rude, fruste; *(→ speech, accent)* rude, grossier; **to knock the rough edges off sb/sth** dégrossir qn/qch

(**d**) *(unpleasant, hard)* rude, dur; **to have a rough life** avoir une vie dure; **she's had a rough time of it** elle en a vu des dures *ou* de toutes les couleurs; **they gave him a rough time** *or* **ride** ils lui ont mené la vie dure; **he's had a rough deal** ça a été très dur pour lui; **to make things rough for sb** mener la vie dure à qn; **it's rough on her** *(unlucky)* c'est dur pour elle; *(unjust)* c'est injuste pour elle; **it's rough on the skin** c'est mauvais pour la peau; **divorce is rough on children** le divorce est dur pour les enfants; **you were too rough on them** tu as été trop sévère avec eux; **it's rough having to work on Saturdays** c'est dur de devoir travailler le samedi; *Br* **rough luck!** pas de veine!

(**e**) *(sea)* agité, houleux; *(climate)* rude; **we had a rough crossing** on a eu une traversée agitée; **rough weather** gros temps *m*

(**f**) *(harsh → sound, voice)* rauque; *(→ tone)* brusque; *(→ taste)* âpre; *(→ wine)* rêche

(**g**) *(approximate → calculation, estimate, translation)* approximatif; *(rudimentary → equipment)* rudimentaire, grossier; **at a rough guess** grosso modo, approximativement; **I only need a rough estimate** je n'ai pas besoin d'une réponse précise; **to have a rough idea of sth** avoir une idée approximative de qch; **it gives you a rough guide** cela vous donne une indication approximative; **in a** *or* **its rough state** à l'état brut; **they built a rough canoe from a log** ils ont construit un canoë de fortune avec un tronc d'arbre

(**h**) *Br Fam (ill)* patraque; **I'm feeling a bit rough** je ne suis pas dans mon assiette; **to look rough** ne pas par avoir l'air dans son assiette

2 *n* (**a**) *(ground)* terrain *m* rocailleux; *Golf* rough *m*; **to take the rough with the smooth** prendre les choses comme elles viennent

(**b**) *(draft)* brouillon *m*; *(of design)* crayonné *m*, esquisse *f*; *(of drawing)* ébauche *f*; **in rough** à l'état de brouillon *ou* d'ébauche; **he drafted the proposal in rough** il rédigea un brouillon de la proposition

(**c**) *Fam (hoodlum)* dur *m*, voyou *m*

(**d**) *Fam* **she likes a bit of rough** *(person)* elle aime s'envoyer un prolo de temps en temps; *(sexual activity)* elle aime qu'on la malmène un peu pendant l'amour

3 *adv (speak)* avec rudesse; **to play rough** *(children etc)* jouer brutalement; *(in business, relationship)* ne pas faire de cadeaux; **to treat sb rough** malmener qn; **to live rough** vivre à la dure; **to sleep rough** coucher à la dure *ou* dans la rue

4 *vt Br Fam* **to rough it** vivre à la dure; **we'll just have to rough it** il faudra qu'on fasse avec les moyens du bord □

►► ***rough book*** brouillard *m*; ***rough copy*** brouillon *m*; *TV & Cin* ***rough cut*** premier montage *m*; ***rough diamond*** diamant *m* brut; *Br Fig* **he's a rough diamond** il est bourru mais il a un cœur d'or; ***rough draft*** brouillon *m*; *TV & Cin* ***rough edit*** montage *m* bout à bout; *TV & Cin* ***rough focus*** première mise *f* au point; ***rough ground*** *(bumpy)* terrain *m* rocailleux *ou* raboteux; *(waste)* terrain *m* vague; *Bot* ***rough hawkbit*** liondent *m* hispide; ***rough justice*** justice *f* sommaire; ***rough linen*** gros lin *m*; ***rough paper*** papier *m* brouillon; ***rough passage*** traversée *f* difficile; *Fig* **the bill had a rough passage through the House** le projet de loi a eu des difficultés à passer à la Chambre; *Sport* ***rough play*** jeu *m* brutal; ***rough sketch*** croquis *m*, ébauche *f*; **just give me a rough sketch** *or* **outline of your plans** donnez-moi juste un aperçu de vos projets; ***rough sleeper*** *(homeless person)* SDF *mf*; *Fam* ***rough stuff*** brutalités □ *fpl*; *Fam* ***rough trade*** *(male prostitute)* = jeune prostitué homosexuel à tendances violentes; *(working-class male homosexual)* homosexuel *m* prolo; ***rough work*** brouillon *m*

►**rough out** *vt sep Br (drawing, plan)* ébaucher, esquisser

►**rough up** *vt sep* (**a**) *(hair)* ébouriffer; *(clothes)* mettre en désordre

(**b**) *Fam (person)* tabasser, passer à tabac

roughage ['rʌfɪdʒ] *n (UNCOUNT)* fibres *fpl* (alimentaires)

rough-and-ready *adj* (**a**) *(makeshift → equipment, apparatus)* rudimentaire, de fortune; *(careless → work)* grossier, fait à la hâte; *(→ methods)* grossier, expéditif (**b**) *(unrefined → person)* fruste, rustre; *(→ living conditions)* dur

rough-and-tumble 1 *adj (life → hectic)* mouvementé; *(→ disorderly)* désordonné

2 *n (fight)* bagarre *f*; *(hurly-burly)* tohu-bohu *m inv*; **the rough-and-tumble of politics** le bouillonnement de la politique; **the rough-and-tumble world of publishing** la jungle de l'édition; **I enjoyed the rough-and-tumble of circus life** la vie mouvementée du cirque me plaisait

roughcast ['rʌfkɑ:st] **1** *adj* crépi

2 *n* crépi *m*

3 *vt* crépir

rough-dry *(pt & pp* **rough-dried***)* **1** *vt* sécher sans repasser *ou* repassage

2 *adj* séché sans repassage

roughen ['rʌfən] **1** *vt (surface)* rendre rugueux; *(hands)* rendre rugueux *ou* rêche

2 *vi* (**a**) *(surface)* devenir rugueux (**b**) *(sea)* grossir, devenir houleux

rough-hewn *adj* taillé grossièrement; *Fig* **his rough-hewn features** son visage taillé à coups de serpe

rough-house *Am Fam* **1** *n* bagarre □ *f*; **there was a bit of a rough-house in the bar last night** il y a eu de la bagarre au bar hier soir

2 *vt* bousculer □

3 *vi (children)* faire du chahut

roughly ['rʌflɪ] *adv* (**a**) *(brutally)* avec brutalité, brutalement; **they treated us very roughly** ils nous ont traités avec brutalité; **he answered her very roughly** il lui a répondu sur un ton très sec

(**b**) *(sketchily → draw)* grossièrement; *(crudely → make)* grossièrement, sans soin; **to sketch sth roughly** faire un croquis sommaire de qch; **the dress is roughly stitched** la robe est grossièrement cousue

(**c**) *(approximately)* approximativement, à peu près; **roughly 500** à peu près *ou* environ 500; **it was roughly five o'clock** il était environ cinq heures; **roughly speaking** en gros, approximativement; **she told me roughly how to get there** elle m'a expliqué en gros comment y aller; **they live in roughly the same area** ils habitent plus ou moins le même quartier

roughneck ['rʌfnek] *n* (**a**) *Fam (thug)* voyou *m*, dur *m* (**b**) *(oil-rig worker)* = ouvrier travaillant sur une plate-forme pétrolière

roughness ['rʌfnɪs] *n* (**a**) *(of surface)* caractère *m* rugueux; *(of skin, cloth, paper)* caractère *m* rêche; *(of road, ground)* inégalités *fpl* (**b**) *(of manner)* rudesse *f*; *(of reply, speech)* brusquerie *f*, *(of person)* rudesse *f*, brutalité *f*, *(of living conditions)* rudesse *f*, dureté *f* (**c**) *(turbulence)* **because of the roughness of the sea** parce que la mer était agitée

roughrider ['rʌf,raɪdə(r)] *n* dresseur(euse) *m,f* de chevaux

roughshod ['rʌfʃɒd] **1** *adj Br (horse)* ferré à glace

2 *adv (idiom)* **to ride roughshod over** *(person)* traiter cavalièrement, fouler aux pieds; *(objections)* fouler aux pieds

rough-spoken *adj (vulgar)* au langage grossier

roulade [ru:'lɑ:d] *n Mus & Culin* roulade *f*

roulette [ru:'let] *n* roulette *f*; **to play roulette** jouer à la roulette

►► ***roulette table*** table *f* de roulette; ***roulette wheel*** roulette *f*

Roumania, Roumanian = **Romania, Romanian**

ROUND [raʊnd]

rond	► **1 (a) – (c); 4 (a)**
autour (de)	► **2 (a), (c), (e); 3 (a)**
environ	► **2 (g); 6**
série	► **4 (c)**
tournée	► **4 (d), (h)**
tour	► **4 (f)**
partie	► **4 (g)**

1 *adj* (**a**) *(circular)* rond, circulaire; *(spherical)* rond, sphérique; **to become round** s'arrondir; **the earth is round** la terre est ronde; **to have a round face** avoir la figure ronde; **she looked up, her eyes round with surprise** elle leva des yeux écarquillés de surprise; **round hand** *or* **handwriting** écriture *f* ronde

(**b**) *(curved → belly, cheeks)* rond; **to have round shoulders** avoir le dos rond *ou* voûté

(**c**) *(figures)* rond; **in round figures** en chiffres ronds; **that's 500, in round figures** ça fait 500 tout rond; **a round dozen** une douzaine tout rond

(**d**) *(considerable)* **a round sum** une somme rondelette

(**e**) *Literary (candid)* net, franc (franche); **they gave a round denial** ils ont nié tout net

(**f**) *(rich, sonorous → tone, voice)* sonore

(**g**) *Ling (vowel)* arrondi

2 *prep* (**a**) *(on all sides of)* autour de; **sitting round the fire/table** assis autour du feu/de la table; **the village is built round a green** le village est construit autour d'un jardin public; **they were all grouped round the teacher** ils étaient tous rassemblés autour du professeur; **the story centres round one particular family** l'histoire est surtout centrée autour d'une famille

(**b**) *(measuring the circumference of)* **the pillar is three feet round the base** la base du pilier fait trois pieds de circonférence; **he's 95 cm round the chest** il fait 95 cm de tour de poitrine

(**c**) *(in the vicinity of, near)* autour de; **the countryside round Bath is lovely** la campagne autour de Bath est très belle; **they live somewhere round here** ils habitent quelque part par ici

(**d**) *(to the other side of)* **the nearest garage is just round the corner** le garage le plus proche est juste au coin de la rue; **the grocer round the corner** l'épicier du coin; **she disappeared round the back of the house** elle a disparu derrière la maison; **the orchard is round the back** le verger est derrière; **to go round the corner** passer le coin, tourner au coin; **to go round an obstacle** contourner un obstacle; **there must be a way round the problem** il doit y avoir un moyen de contourner ce problème

(**e**) *(so as to encircle)* autour de; **he put his arm round her shoulders/waist** il a passé son bras autour de ses épaules/de sa taille; **she wears a scarf round her neck** elle porte une écharpe autour du cou; **he put a blanket round her legs** il lui enveloppa les jambes d'une couverture; **the shark swam round the boat** le requin faisait des cercles autour du bateau; **Drake sailed round the world** Drake a fait le tour du monde en bateau; **the earth goes** *or* **moves round the sun** la terre tourne autour du soleil; **they were dancing round a fire** ils dansaient autour d'un feu

(**f**) *(all over, everywhere in)* **all round the world** dans le monde entier, partout dans le monde; **to travel round the world/country** faire le tour du monde/du pays; **she looked round the room** elle a promené son regard autour de la pièce; **to walk round the town** faire le tour de la ville (à pied); **we went for a stroll round the garden** nous avons fait une balade dans le jardin; **there's a rumour going round the school** une rumeur circule dans l'école

(**g**) *(approximately)* environ, aux environs de; **round six o'clock** aux environs de *ou* vers les six heures; **round Christmas** aux environs de Noël

(**h**) *(idiom)* **round the clock** 24 heures sur 24; **we worked round the clock** nous avons travaillé 24 heures d'affilée; **he slept round the clock** il a fait le tour du cadran

3 *adv* (**a**) *(on all sides)* autour; **there's a fence all round** il y a une clôture tout autour; **there are trees all the way round** il y a des arbres tout autour; **taking things all round, taken all round** à tout prendre, tout compte fait; **all round, it was a good result** dans l'ensemble, c'était un bon résultat

(**b**) *(to other side)* **you'll have to go round, the door's locked** il faudra faire le tour, la porte est fermée à clé; **we drove round to the back** nous avons fait le tour (par derrière)

(**c**) *(in a circle or cycle)* **turn the wheel right round** *or* **all the way round** faites faire un tour complet à la roue; **the shark swam round in circles** le requin tournait en rond; **all year round** tout au long de *ou* toute l'année; **summer will soon be** *or* **come round again** l'été reviendra vite

(**d**) *(in the opposite direction)* **turn round and look at me** retournez-vous et regardez-moi; **she looked round at us** elle se retourna pour nous regarder; **we'll have to turn the car round** on va devoir faire demi-tour; **to have one's hat/jumper on the wrong way round** avoir son chapeau/son pull à l'envers; **to do sth the wrong way round** faire qch à l'envers; **it's the other way round** *(quite the opposite)* c'est (tout) le contraire; **try the key the other way round** essaie la clef dans l'autre sens

(**e**) *(to various parts)* **we spent the summer just travelling round** on a passé l'été à voyager; **can I have a look round?** je peux jeter un coup d'œil?

(**f**) *(from one person to another)* **hand the sweets round, hand round the sweets** faites passer les bonbons; **there's a rumour going round** il y a une rumeur qui court; **there wasn't enough to go round** il n'y en avait pas assez pour tout le monde

(**g**) *(to a particular place)* **she came round to see me** elle est passée me voir; **let's invite some friends round** et si on invitait des amis?; **come round for dinner some time** viens dîner un soir; **take these cakes round to her house** apportez-lui ces gâteaux; **he'll be round** il passera; **to order the car round** demander qu'on amène la voiture

(**h**) *(to a different place, position)* **she's always moving the furniture round** elle passe son temps à changer les meubles de place; **try shifting the aerial round a bit** essaie de bouger un peu l'antenne

(**i**) *(by indirect route)* **we had to take the long way round** on a dû faire le grand tour *ou* un grand détour; **she went round by the stream** elle fit un détour par le ruisseau

(**j**) *(in circumference)* **the tree is 5 metres round** l'arbre fait 5 mètres de circonférence

4 *n* (**a**) *(circle)* rond *m*, cercle *m*

(**b**) *Br (slice → of ham, cheese, bread, toast)* tranche *f*; **a round of sandwiches** = un sandwich au pain de mie coupé en deux ou en quatre

(**c**) *(one in a series → of discussions, negotiations)* série *f*; *(→ of elections)* tour *m*; *(→ of increases)* série *f*, train *m*; **the next round of talks will be held in Moscow** les prochains pourparlers auront lieu à Moscou

(**d**) *(regular route → for delivery)* tournée *f*; *(→ of sentry, patrol)* ronde *f*; **to do a paper/milk round** distribuer les journaux/le lait à domicile; **to do a hospital round** faire sa visite à l'hôpital, visiter ses malades; **to go on** *or* **do one's rounds** *(paperboy, milkman)* faire sa tournée; *(doctor)* faire ses visites; *(guard, policeman)* faire sa ronde; **to go** *or* **do** *or* **make the rounds** *(story, rumour, cold)* circuler; **there are several theories going the rounds at the moment** il y a plusieurs théories qui circulent en ce moment; **there's a joke/rumour/virus going the rounds in the office** il y a une blague/une rumeur/un virus qui circule au bureau; **she's doing** *or* **making the rounds of literary agents/travel agents** elle fait le tour des agents littéraires/des agences de voyages

(**e**) *(routine)* **the daily round** le train-train quotidien, la routine quotidienne; **the daily round of cooking and cleaning** les travaux quotidiens de cuisine et de ménage; **his life is one long round of parties** il passe sa vie à faire la fête

(**f**) *(stage of competition)* tour *m*, manche *f*; **to be/get through to the next round** se qualifier/s'être qualifié pour la manche suivante; **she's through to the final round** elle participera à la finale

(**g**) *(of golf, cards)* partie *f*; *(in boxing, wrestling)* round *m*, reprise *f*; *Horseriding* **there were six clear rounds** six chevaux avaient fait un sans-faute; *Boxing* **he only went three rounds** il n'a fait que trois rounds; **to play a round of golf** faire une partie de golf; **he had the best round of the day** c'est lui qui a fait le meilleur parcours *ou* round

(**h**) *(of drinks)* tournée *f*; **to buy** *or* **stand a round of drinks** payer une tournée (générale); **it's my round** c'est ma tournée; **let's have another round** prenons encore un verre

(**i**) *(of cheering)* salve *f*

(**j**) *(of ammunition)* cartouche *f*; **how many rounds have we got left?** combien de cartouches nous reste-t-il?

(**k**) *(song)* canon *m*

(**l**) *Theat* **theatre in the round** théâtre *m* en rond

(**m**) *Art* **sculpture in the round** ronde-bosse *f*

5 *vt* (**a**) *(lips, vowel)* arrondir

(**b**) *(corner)* tourner; *Naut (cape)* doubler, franchir

6 round about 1 *prep* environ; **we need round about 6,000 posters** il nous faut environ 6000 affiches; **she's round about forty** elle a la quarantaine; **round about midnight** vers minuit **2** *adv* alentour, des alentours; **the villages round about** les villages alentour *ou* des alentours

7 round and round 1 *adv* **to go round and round** tourner; **we drove round and round for hours** on a tourné en rond pendant des heures; **my head was spinning round and round** j'avais la tête qui tournait **2** *prep* **we drove round and round the field** on a fait plusieurs tours dans le champ; **the helicopter flew round and round the lighthouse** l'hélicoptère a tourné plusieurs fois autour du phare

►► ***round of applause*** des applaudissements *mpl*; **give her a round of applause!** on peut l'applaudir!; **they got a round of applause** ils se sont fait applaudir; *Archit* ***round arch*** arc *m* en plein cintre; *Culin* ***round of beef*** gîte *m* à la noix; *Typ* ***round brackets*** parenthèses *fpl*; ***round dance*** ronde *f*; ***round figure*** chiffre *m* rond; **in round figures** en chiffres *mpl* ronds; ***round robin*** *(letter)* pétition *f (où les signatures sont disposées en rond)*; *esp Am (contest)* poule *f*; ***the Round Table*** la Table ronde; ***round table*** table *f* ronde; ***round trip*** (voyage *m*) aller et retour *m*; **I did the round trip in six hours** j'ai fait l'aller-retour en six heures; *Anat* ***round window*** fenêtre *f* ronde

►**round down** *vt sep* arrondir au chiffre inférieur; **their prices were rounded down to the nearest £10** ils ont arrondi leurs prix aux 10 livres inférieures

►**round off** *vt sep* (**a**) *(finish, complete)* terminer, clore; **he rounded off his meal with a glass of brandy** il a terminé son repas par un verre de cognac; **to round things off...** pour finir...

(**b**) *(figures → round down)* arrondir au chiffre inférieur; *(→ round up)* arrondir au chiffre supérieur

►**round on** *vt insep* attaquer, s'en prendre à

►**round out 1** *vt sep (complete)* compléter; *(deepen)* approfondir

2 *vi* prendre des rondeurs

►**round up** *vt sep* (**a**) *(cattle, people)* rassembler; *(criminals)* ramasser

(**b**) *(figures)* arrondir au chiffre supérieur

roundabout ['raʊndəbaʊt] **1** *n Br* (**a**) *(at fairground, playground)* manège *m* (**b**) *Aut* rond-point *m*, *Suisse* giratoire *m*

2 *adj* détourné, indirect; **to take a roundabout route** prendre un chemin détourné; **to hear of sth in a roundabout way** apprendre qch indirectement; **to lead up to a question in a roundabout way** aborder une question de biais; **he has a roundabout way of doing things** il a une façon détournée de faire les choses; **by roundabout means** par des moyens détournés

round-arm *adj (blow, punch)* latéral

rounded ['raʊndɪd] *adj* (**a**) *(shape)* arrondi;

(cheeks) rond, rebondi; *(breasts)* plein; *(vowel)* arrondi (**b**) *(number)* arrondi (**c**) *(style)* harmonieux

roundel ['raʊndəl] *n* (**a**) *Literature* rondeau *m* (**b**) *Aviat* cocarde *f* (**c**) *(window)* œil-de-bœuf *m*; *(panel, medal)* médaillon *m*

roundelay ['raʊndɪleɪ] *n (dance)* ronde *f*; *(song)* rondeau *m*

rounders ['raʊndəz] *n (UNCOUNT) Br* = sport proche du baseball

round-eyed *adj* aux yeux ronds; *Fig (surprised)* avec des yeux ronds

round-faced *adj* au visage rond

roundhand ['raʊndhænd] *n* ronde *f*

Roundhead ['raʊndhed] *n Hist* **the Roundheads** les Têtes rondes *(partisans du Parlement pendant la guerre civile anglaise, de 1642 à 1646)*

▸▸ ***Roundhead army*** armée *f* des Têtes rondes; ***Roundhead victory*** victoire *f* des Têtes rondes

roundhouse ['raʊndhaʊs, *pl* -haʊzɪz] *n* rotonde *f*

rounding ['raʊndɪŋ] *n Comput & Math* arrondi *m*, arrondissage *m*

▸▸ ***rounding error*** erreur *f* d'arrondi

roundish ['raʊndɪʃ] *adj* plutôt rond; **she has a roundish figure** elle est plutôt rondelette

roundly ['raʊndlɪ] *adv* (**a**) *(severely)* vivement, sévèrement; **the film was roundly attacked for its racist content** le film fut vivement critiqué pour son caractère raciste; **roundly beaten** battu à plate(s) couture(s) (**b**) *Br (plainly)* carrément; **he told her roundly what he thought** il lui a dit carrément ce qu'il pensait

roundness ['raʊndnɪs] *n* (**a**) *(shape)* rondeur *f* (**b**) *(frankness)* franchise *f* (**c**) *(of sound, voice)* richesse *f*, ampleur *f*

round-shouldered [-'ʃəʊldəd] *adj* **to be round-shouldered** avoir le dos rond, être voûté

roundsman ['raʊndzmən] (*pl* **roundsmen** [-mən]) *n Br* livreur *m*; *Am* **night roundsman** gardien *m* de nuit

round-table *adj*

▸▸ ***round-table discussions, round-table talks*** table *f* ronde

round-the-clock *adj* 24 heures sur 24; **a round-the-clock vigil** une permanence nuit et jour

round-trip ticket *n Am* (billet *m*) aller-retour *m*

round-up *n* (**a**) *(of cattle, people)* rassemblement *m*; *(of criminals)* rafle *f* (**b**) *(of news)* résumé *m* de l'actualité

roundworm ['raʊndwɜːm] *n Zool* ascaride *m*

rouse [raʊz] *vt* (**a**) *(wake → person)* réveiller; **the burglar roused them (from their sleep)** le cambrioleur les a réveillés *ou* les a tirés de leur sommeil; **he was roused from his thoughts by the doorbell** la sonnette l'a arraché à ses pensées; **to rouse oneself** se secouer; **to rouse oneself to do sth** s'efforcer de faire qch; **to rouse sb to action** pousser qn à agir; **to rouse sb from his/her apathy** faire sortir qn de son apathie; **to rouse the camp** donner l'alerte au camp

(**b**) *(provoke → interest, passion)* éveiller, exciter; *(→ hope)* éveiller; *(→ suspicion)* éveiller, susciter; *(→ admiration, anger, indignation)* susciter, provoquer; **to rouse a crowd** exciter une foule; **to rouse sb to action** pousser *ou* inciter qn à agir; **to rouse sb to anger, to rouse sb's anger** susciter la colère de qn, mettre qn en colère; **to be roused to anger** se mettre en colère; **now she's roused, sparks will fly** maintenant qu'elle s'est mise en colère, ça va barder

(**c**) *Hunt (game)* lever

rouseabout ['raʊzə,baʊt] *n Austr & NZ* = ouvrier agricole dans un élevage ovin

roused [raʊzd] *adj (angry)* en colère

rousing ['raʊzɪŋ] *adj (speech)* vibrant, passionné; *(march, music)* entraînant; *(applause, welcome)* enthousiaste

roust [raʊst] *vt* **to roust sb (out) from bed** faire sortir qn du lit

roustabout ['raʊstə,baʊt] *n* ouvrier *m*, manœuvre *m*; *(on farm)* ouvrier *m* agricole; *Austr & NZ* = ouvrier agricole dans un élevage ovin

rout [raʊt] **1** *n* (**a**) *Mil* déroute *f*, débâcle *f*; **to put an enemy/army to rout** mettre un ennemi/une armée en déroute; *Fig* **the election was a rout fou the government** l'élection a été une débâcle pour le gouvernement

(**b**) *Law* attroupement *m* illégal

2 *vt Mil* mettre en déroute *ou* en fuite; *Fig (team, opponent)* battre à plate couture, écraser

3 *vi* fouiller; **the pigs were routing in the soil for worms** les porcs fouillaient le sol pour y trouver des vers

▸**rout about** *vi* fouiller

▸**rout out** *vt sep* (**a**) *(find)* dénicher

(**b**) *(remove, force out)* déloger, expulser; **they routed us out of our hiding-place** ils nous ont délogés de notre cachette

route [*Br* ruːt, *Am* raʊt] **1** *n* (**a**) *(way → gen)* route *f*, itinéraire *m*; *(→ of plane, ship)* route *f*, voie *f*; *(→ of procession, demonstration)* parcours *m*; **what is the best route to Manchester?** quel est le meilleur itinéraire pour aller à Manchester?; **the climbers took the easy route up the south face** les alpinistes ont emprunté l'itinéraire *ou* la voie la plus facile, par la face sud; **a large crowd lined the route** il y avait une foule nombreuse sur tout le parcours; **all routes** *(road sign)* toutes directions; *Fig* **the route to success** le chemin de la réussite; *Fig* **giving up one's studies is hardly the best route to success** le meilleur moyen de réussir ce n'est pas d'abandonner ses études; **sea/air route** voie *f ou* route *f* maritime/aérienne

(**b**) *(for buses)* trajet *m*, parcours *m*; **we need a map of the bus routes** il nous faut un plan des lignes d'autobus; **are they on a bus route?** sont-ils desservis par les autobus?

(**c**) *Med* voie *f*; **by oral route** par voie orale

(**d**) *Am (for deliveries)* tournée *f*; **he's got a paper route** il livre des journaux à domicile

(**e**) *Am (highway)* ≃ route *f* (nationale), ≃ nationale *f*; **Route 66** ≃ la nationale 66

2 *vt* (**a**) *(procession, motorist)* fixer l'itinéraire de, diriger; *(train, bus)* fixer l'itinéraire de; **the police routed the marchers via Post Street** la police a fait passer les manifestants par Post Street; **during the building work, the buses are routed along the sidestreets** pendant les travaux, les bus passent par les petites rues

(**b**) *(luggage, parcel)* expédier, acheminer; **our bags have been routed to Hong Kong** nos bagages ont été expédiés sur *ou* à Hongkong; **the flight was routed via Turkey** notre itinéraire passait par la Turquie

3 en route *adv* en route; **we were en route for the park when it started to hail** nous nous dirigions vers le parc quand il a commencé à grêler; **we stopped en route for a meal** nous nous sommes arrêtés en route pour manger; *Fig* **he's en route for success** il est sur la voie du succès

▸▸ ***route map*** *(for roads)* carte *f* routière; *(for buses)* plan *m* du réseau; *(for trains)* carte *f* du réseau; *Mil* ***route march*** marche *f* d'entraînement

router[1] ['raʊtə(r)] *n Carp (tool)* détoureuse *f*

router[2] ['ruːtə(r)] *n Comput* routeur *m*

routine [ruː'tiːn] **1** *n* (**a**) *(habit)* routine *f*, habitude *f*; **our Sunday morning walk has become a regular routine** notre promenade du dimanche matin est devenue une habitude

(**b**) *Pej (dull habit)* routine *f*; **the daily routine** la routine quotidienne, le train-train quotidien

(**c**) *(formality)* formalité *f*; **it's just routine** c'est une simple formalité

(**d**) *(performance)* numéro *m*, séquence *f*; *(of dancer)* enchaînement *m*; **they taught us some new dance routines** ils nous ont appris de nouveaux enchaînements de danse

(**e**) *(insincere act)* **don't give me that old routine!** toujours la même chose *ou* le même refrain, change de disque!

(**f**) *Comput* sous-programme *m*, routine *f*

2 *adj* (**a**) *(ordinary)* de routine; *(investigation, examination)* de routine, d'usage; **can I ask you some routine questions?** puis-je vous poser quelques questions de routine?; **routine enquiries** *(of police)* constatations *fpl* d'usage; **it's just a routine enquiry** c'est simplement pour les constatations d'usage; **she comes in once a year for a routine check-up** elle vient une fois par an pour un examen de routine; **it was a routine flight** c'était un vol sans histoire

(**b**) *(everyday)* de routine

(**c**) *(monotonous)* routinier, monotone

routinely [ruː'tiːnlɪ] *adv* systématiquement

routing ['ruːtɪŋ] *n (action)* routage *m*; *(route)* itinéraire *m*; *(of parcel, goods)* acheminement *m*

roux [ruː] (*pl* **inv** [ruːz]) *n Culin* roux *m*

rove [rəʊv] **1** *pt & pp of* **reeve**

2 *vi* (**a**) *(person)* errer, vagabonder (**b**) *(eyes)* errer; **her eyes roved over the page/the crowd** son regard errait sur la page/parmi la foule; *Literary* **his mind roved back to his youth** sa pensée vagabonde revint sur sa jeunesse

3 *vt (country)* parcourir, errer dans; *(streets)* errer dans; *(the seas)* écumer

▸▸ *Entom* ***rove beetle*** staphylin *m*

rover ['rəʊvə(r)] **1** *n* vagabond(e) *m,f*

2 Rover *n* = nom typique pour un chien, ≃ Médor

roving ['rəʊvɪŋ] **1** *adj* vagabond, nomade; **he has a roving commission** il a toute liberté de manœuvre; *Fig* **he has a roving eye** il aime bien lorgner les filles; **roving life** vie *f* de nomade; **to lead a roving life** mener une vie de nomade

2 *n* vagabondage *m*

▸▸ ***roving reporter*** reporter *m (qui va sur le terrain)*

row[1] [rəʊ] **1** *n* (**a**) *(of chairs, trees, houses)* rangée *f*; *(of vegetables, seeds)* rang *m*; *(of people → next to one another)* rangée *f*; *(→ behind one another)* file *f*, queue *f*; *(of cars)* file *f*; *(in knitting)* rang *m*; **for the third time in a row** pour la troisième fois de suite; **she put the boxes in a row** elle aligna les boîtes; **they sat/stood in a row** ils étaient assis/debout en rang; **in rows** par rangs; **in two rows** sur deux rangs

(**b**) *(in cinema, hall)* rang *m*; **in the third row** au troisième rang

(**c**) *Sport (in rugby)* ligne *f*; **the front/second/back row** la première/deuxième/troisième ligne; **a front/second/back row forward** une première/deuxième/troisième ligne

(**d**) *Br (in street names)* rue *f*; **56 Charrington Row** 56 rue Charrington

(**e**) *Comput (in spreadsheet)* ligne *f*

(**f**) *(in boat)* promenade *f* (en bateau à rames); **to go for a row** faire une promenade en canot à rames; **to have a row round the island** faire le tour de l'île à la rame; **it was a hard row** il a fallu ramer dur; **a great row from the British team** un très bel effort de l'équipage britannique

2 *vi (in boat)* ramer; *Sport* faire de l'aviron; **to row across a lake** traverser un lac à la rame; **to row hard** ramer de toutes ses forces, faire force de rames; **the Cambridge team rowed round the canal bend in the lead** l'équipe d'aviron de Cambridge arriva en tête au virage du canal

3 *vt (boat)* faire avancer à la rame *ou* à l'aviron; *(passengers)* transporter en canot; **he rowed the boat across the lake** il traversa le lac à la rame; **he rowed the tourists across the lake** il fit traverser le lac aux touristes dans un bateau à rames; **to row a race** faire une course d'aviron; **Redgrave rowed a great/poor race** Redgrave a fait une belle/mauvaise course

▸▸ *Am* ***row house*** = maison attenante aux maisons voisines

row[2] [raʊ] **1** *n Br* (**a**) *(quarrel)* dispute *f*, querelle *f*; **to have a row with sb** se disputer avec qn; **to get into a row with sb** *(into quarrel)* se disputer avec qn; **I got into a row with the bus driver** je me suis disputé avec le chauffeur du bus; *Scot* **the boss gave me a row for being late** le patron m'a enguirlandé parce que j'étais en retard; **a row broke out as a result of the new legislation** la nouvelle loi a fait beaucoup de raffut

(**b**) *(noise)* tapage *m*, vacarme *m*; **to make a row** *(be noisy)* faire du tapage *ou* du vacarme; *(protest)* faire toute une histoire; **stop that row!** arrêtez ce boucan!; **what's all the row about?** qu'est-ce que c'est que tout ce raffut?; *Fam* **shut your row!** la ferme!

2 *vi* se disputer; **to row with sb** se disputer avec qn

rowan ['raʊən, 'rəʊən] *n Bot (tree)* sorbier *m* des oiseleurs *ou* des oiseaux; *(fruit)* sorbe *f*

rowboat ['rəʊbəʊt] *n Am* bateau *m* à rames

rowdiness ['raʊdɪnɪs] *n* tapage *m*, chahut *m*

rowdy ['raʊdɪ] (*compar* **rowdier**, *superl* **rowdiest**, *pl* **rowdies**) **1** *adj (person)* chahuteur, bagarreur; *(behaviour)* chahuteur; **to be rowdy** chahuter; **what a rowdy bunch!** quelle bande de chahuteurs!

2 *n* bagarreur(euse) *m,f*, voyou *m*

rowdyism ['raʊdɪɪzəm] *n Br* tapage *m*, chahut *m*

rowel ['raʊəl] *n (on spur)* molette *f*

rower ['rəʊə(r)] *n* rameur(euse) *m,f*; **he's a good rower** c'est un bon rameur

rowing ['rəʊɪŋ] *n* canotage *m*; *Sport* aviron *m*; **to go rowing** faire du canotage/de l'aviron

▸▸ *Br* ***rowing boat*** bateau *m* à rames; ***rowing club*** club *m* d'aviron; ***rowing machine*** rameur *m*

rowlock ['rɒlək] *n (U-shaped)* dame *f* de nage; *(pin)* tolet *m*

royal ['rɔɪəl] **1** *adj* (**a**) *(seal, residence, visit)* royal; *(horse, household, vehicle)* royal, du roi, de la reine; **by royal charter** par acte du souverain; **the royal "we"** le "nous" de majesté

(**b**) *Fig Formal (splendid)* royal, princier; **they gave us a (right) royal welcome** ils nous ont accueillis comme des rois; **to be in royal spirits** être d'excellente humeur

(**c**) *Fam (for emphasis)* sombre, de première; **that guy is a right royal pain in the neck** ce type est un véritable emmerdeur; **her whining gives me a royal pain** elle me fait vraiment chier avec ses jérémiades; **he's a royal idiot** c'est un sombre crétin *ou* un crétin de première

(**d**) *(paper)* (format *m*) grand raisin *m*; **royal octavo/quarto** in-huit *m*/in-quarto *m* raisin

2 *n Fam* = membre de la famille royale; **the Royals** la famille royale ❑

▸▸ ***the Royal Academy (of Arts)*** Académie *f* royale britannique des beaux-arts; ***the Royal Academy of Dramatic Art*** = Conservatoire national d'art dramatique, à Londres; ***the Royal Academy of Music*** = conservatoire national de musique, à Londres; ***the Royal Air Force*** armée *f* de l'air britannique; ***Royal Ascot*** = événement hippique annuel, étalé sur plusieurs jours, qui entre dans le calendrier mondain de la haute société anglaise; ***royal assent*** = signature royale qui officialise une loi; ***the Royal Ballet*** = compagnie nationale de ballet qui a son siège à Covent Garden à Londres; ***royal blue*** bleu *m* roi; ***the Royal British Legion*** = association britannique d'anciens militaires; ***royal burgh*** ville *f* établie par charte royale; ***the Royal Canadian Mounted Police*** la Gendarmerie royale du Canada; ***the Royal College of Music*** Collège *m* royal de musique *(école de musique située à Londres)*; ***the Royal College of Physicans*** Collège *m* royal de médecine *(organisation de médecins)*; ***the Royal College of Surgeons*** Collège *m* royal de chirurgie *(organisation de chirurgiens)*; ***the Royal College of Veterinary Surgeons*** Collège *m* royal de médecine vétérinaire *(organisation de vétérinaires)*; ***the Royal Commission*** = commission nommée par le monarque sur recommandation du premier ministre; ***the Royal Court*** = théâtre à Londres; ***Royal Doulton*** = porcelaine fine anglaise; ***the Royal Enclosure*** = tribune de la famille royale à Royal Ascot; ***the Royal Engineers*** le génie militaire britannique; ***the Royal Family*** la famille royale; *Bot* ***royal fern*** osmonde *f* royale; *Cards* ***royal flush*** quinte *f* royale; *(in poker)* flush *m* royal; ***Royal Highland Show*** = grande foire agricole annuelle qui a lieu à Ingleston, près d'Édimbourg; ***Your Royal Highness*** Votre Altesse Royale; **His Royal Highness, the Prince of Wales** Son Altesse Royale, le prince de Galles; ***Their Royal Highnesses*** Leurs Altesses Royales; ***the Royal Horse Guards*** = la garde à cheval qui assure la garde du palais et du souverain; *Br Culin* ***royal icing*** = glaçage à base de sucre glace et de blancs d'œufs (utilisé pour les cakes); ***the Royal Institute of British Architects*** = institut d'architectes, à Londres; ***the Royal Institution*** l'Académie *f* des sciences britannique; ***royal jelly*** gelée *f* royale; ***the Royal Mail*** = la Poste britannique; ***the Royal Marines*** les Marines *mpl* (britanniques); *Naut* ***royal mast*** mât *m* de cacatois; ***the Royal Mile*** = rue d'Édimbourg qui relie le château au palais de Holyrood; ***the Royal Mint*** = la Monnaie britannique, ≃ (l'hôtel *m* de) la Monnaie; ***the Royal Navy*** la marine *f* nationale britannique; ***the Royal Opera House*** l'opéra *m* de Covent Garden; *Bot* ***royal palm*** palmier *m* royal; ***royal prerogative*** prérogative *f* du souverain; **to exercise the royal prerogative** faire acte de souverain; ***the Royal School of Music*** École *f* royale de musique; ***Royal Scottish Academy*** Académie *f* royale écossaise des beaux-arts; ***the Royal Shakespeare Company*** = célèbre troupe de théâtre basée à Stratford-on-Avon et à Londres; ***the Royal Show*** = le salon annuel de l'agriculture en Grande-Bretagne; ***the Royal Society*** l'Académie *f* des sciences britannique; ***Royal Society of Medicine*** Fondation *f* britannique de médecine; ***the Royal Society for the Prevention of Cruelty to Animals*** = société britannique protectrice des animaux, ≃ SPA *f*; *Br* ***the Royal Society for the Prevention of Cruelty to Children*** ≃ Fondation *f* pour l'enfance; ***the Royal Society for the Protection of Birds*** = ligue britannique pour la protection des oiseaux; ***royal standard*** = drapeau représentant les armoiries de la couronne britannique, hissé lorsque le monarque est au château; ***the Royal Tournament*** = meeting annuel destiné au public organisé par les forces armées, avec entre autres choses des démonstrations de gymnastique; ***the Royal Ulster Constabulary*** = corps de police d'Irlande du Nord; ***the Royal Variety Show*** = spectacle de variétés organisé à Londres en faveur de la Fédération des artistes de variétés; ***royal warrant*** brevet *m* de fournisseur du souverain; ***Royal Worcester*** = porcelaine fine anglaise

> **THE ROYAL SOCIETY**
>
> Cette société à vocation scientifique, fondée par Charles II en 1660, contribua à renforcer la crédibilité des hommes de science, qui jouirent également d'une plus grande liberté. En firent notamment partie Isaac Newton et Robert Boyle.

royal-blue *adj* bleu roi *(inv)*

royalism ['rɔɪəlɪzəm] *n* royalisme *m*

royalist ['rɔɪəlɪst] **1** *adj* royaliste

2 *n* royaliste *mf*

royally ['rɔɪəlɪ] *adv* (**a**) *also Fig (regally)* royalement; *(like a king)* en roi; *(like a queen)* en reine (**b**) *Fam (for emphasis)* dans les grandes largeurs; **they messed up royally** ils se sont plantés dans les grandes largeurs, ils se sont plantés, et pas qu'un peu

royalty ['rɔɪəltɪ] **1** *n* (**a**) *(royal family)* famille *f* royale; **a hotel patronized by royalty** un hôtel fréquenté par les membres de la famille royale; **is he royalty?** est-ce qu'il fait partie de la famille royale?; **we were treated like royalty** nous avons été traités comme des princes

(**b**) *(rank)* royauté *f*

(**c**) *(for writer, musician)* droits *mpl* d'auteur; *(for patent)* royalties *fpl*, redevance *f*

2 royalties *npl (for writer, musician)* droits *mpl* d'auteur; *(for patent)* royalties *fpl*, redevance *f*

▸▸ ***royalty payments*** *(for writer)* (paiement *m* des) droits *mpl* d'auteur; *(for patent)* (paiement *m* des) royalties *fpl*

Roy Rogers [,rɔɪ'rɒdʒəz] *n Am (drink)* ≃ diabolo *m* grenadine

rozzer ['rɒzə(r)] *n Br Fam Old-fashioned* flic *m*, poulet *m*

RP [,ɑː'piː] *n Ling* (*abbr* **received pronunciation**) = prononciation de l'anglais britannique considérée comme la norme

RPB [,ɑːpiː'biː] *n* (*abbr* **recognized professional body**) = organisme professionnel agréé

RPI [,ɑːpiː'aɪ] *n Br Fin* (*abbr* **Retail Price Index**) indice *m* des prix de détail

RPM [,ɑːpiː'em] *n* (*abbr* **retail price maintenance**) prix *m* imposé

rpm [,ɑːpiː'em] *n Tech* (*abbr* **revolutions per minute**) tr/min

RPO [,ɑːpiː'əʊ] *n* (*abbr* **Royal Philharmonic Orchestra**) = orchestre philharmonique basé à Londres

RPV [,ɑːpiː'viː] *n Mil* (*abbr* **remotely piloted vehicle**) véhicule *m* télécommandé *ou* téléguidé

RR [,ɑː'rɑː(r)] (**a**) *Am* (*written abbr* **railroad**) chemin *m* de fer (**b**) *Am* (*written abbr* **rural route**) = route de campagne desservie par le facteur (**c**) (*written abbr* **Right Reverend**) **RR James Brown** le très révérend James Brown

RRP [,ɑːrɑː'piː] *n Br* (*abbr* **recommended retail price**) prix *m* recommandé, prix *m* conseillé

RS [,ɑː'res] *n Br* (*abbr* **Royal Society**) Académie *f* des sciences britannique

RSA [,ɑːres'eɪ] *n* (**a**) *Br* (*abbr* **Royal Society of Arts**) Société *f* royale des arts (**b**) (*abbr* **Republic of South Africa**) Afrique *f* du Sud (**c**) (*abbr* **Royal Scottish Academy**) Académie *f* écossaise des beaux-arts

RSC [,ɑːres'siː] *n Br* (*abbr* **Royal Shakespeare Company**) = célèbre troupe de théâtre basée à Stratford-on-Avon et à Londres

RSFSR [,ɑːres,efes'ɑː(r)] *n* (*abbr* **Russian Soviet Federal Socialist Republic**) RSFSR *f*; **in the RSFSR** en RSFSR

RSI [,ɑːres'aɪ] *n (UNCOUNT) Med* (*abbr* **repetitive strain** *or* **stress injury**) lésions *fpl* attribuables au travail répétitif

RSJ [,ɑːres'dʒeɪ] *n Constr* (*abbr* **rolled steel joist**) solive *f* en I

RSM [,ɑːres'em] *n* (**a**) *Mil* (*abbr* **regimental sergeant major**) ≃ adjudant-chef *m* (**b**) *Br* (*abbr* **Royal School of Music**) École *f* royale de musique (**c**) *Br* (*abbr* **Royal Society of Medicine**) Fondation *f* de médecine britannique

RSNO [,ɑːres,en'əʊ] *n* (*abbr* **Royal Scottish National Orchestra**) = orchestre national d'Écosse

RSPB [,ɑːres,piː'biː] *n* (*abbr* **Royal Society for the Protection of Birds**) = ligue britannique pour la protection des oiseaux

RSPCA [,ɑːres,piːsiː'eɪ] *n* (*abbr* **Royal Society for the Prevention of Cruelty to Animals**) = société britannique protectrice des animaux, ≃ SPA *f*

RSPCC [,ɑːres,piːsiː'siː] *n Br* (*abbr* **Royal Society for the Prevention of Cruelty to Children**) ≃ Fondation *f* pour l'enfance

RSV [,ɑːres'viː] *n Bible* (*abbr* **Revised Standard Version**) = traduction américaine de la Bible établie en 1952

RSVP [,ɑːres,viː'piː] (*abbr* **répondez s'il vous plaît**) RSVP

RT [,ɑː'tiː] *n Biol* (*abbr* **reverse transcriptase**) transcriptase *f* inverse

RTA [,ɑːtiː'eɪ] *n* (*abbr* **road traffic accident**) accident *m* de la route

RTE [,ɑːtiː'iː] *n* (*abbr* **Radio Telefis Éireann**) = office de radio et de télévision irlandais

RTGS [,ɑːtiː,dʒiː'es] *n Fin* (*abbr* **Real-Time Gross Settlement**) RTGS *m*

▸▸ ***RTGS system*** système *m* RTGS

Rt Hon *Br* (*written abbr* **Right Honourable**) = titre utilisé pour s'adresser à certains hauts fonctionnaires ou à quelqu'un ayant un titre de noblesse

RTM [,ɑːtiː'em] *n* (*abbr* **registered trademark**) marque *f* déposée

Rt Rev (*written abbr* **Right Reverend**) **the Rt Rev James Brown** le très révérend James Brown

RTW [,ɑːtiː'dʌbəljuː] *n* (*abbr* **round the world**) tour *m* du monde

RU [,ɑː'juː] *n* (*abbr* **Rugby Union**) *(sport)* rugby *m* (à quinze); *(authority)* fédération *f* de rugby

rub [rʌb] (*pt & pp* **rubbed**, *cont* **rubbing**) **1** *n* (**a**) *(rubbing)* frottement *m*; *(massage)* friction *f*, massage *m*; *(with rag, duster)* coup *m* de chiffon; *(with brush)* coup *m* de brosse; *(with tea towel)* coup *m* de torchon; **to give sth a rub** frotter qch; *(massage)* frictionner qch; *(with tea towel)* donner un coup de torchon à qch; **can you give my back a rub?** pouvez-vous me frotter le dos?; **give it a rub!** *(after injury)* frotte!; **give the table/glasses a rub** passez un coup de chiffon sur la table/les verres; **give your shoes a rub** *(with cloth)* donne un coup de chiffon à tes chaussures; *(with brush)* donne un coup de brosse à tes chaussures

(**b**) *Sport (unevenness)* inégalité *f* (du terrain)

(**c**) *(difficulty)* **there's the rub!** voilà le nœud du problème!, c'est là que le bât blesse!; **what's the rub?** où est le problème?

2 *vt* (**a**) *(gen)* frotter; *(massage)* frictionner; **to rub sth with a pad/cloth** frotter qch avec un tampon/chiffon; **she was rubbing her leg against the chair** elle se frottait la jambe contre la chaise; **the cat rubbed itself against my leg** le chat s'est frotté contre ma jambe; **to rub one's eyes/chin** se frotter les yeux/le menton; **to rub one's hands (in delight)** se frotter les mains (de joie); **to rub sb's hands** frictionner les mains à qn; **we rubbed ourselves dry with a towel** nous nous sommes séchés *ou* essuyés avec une serviette; **rub it clean with meths** nettoyez-le en le frottant avec de l'alcool à brûler; **rub it better!** *(to child)* frotte!; **rub the ointment into the skin** faire pénétrer la pommade; **rub your chest with the ointment** frottez-vous la poitrine avec la pommade; **these shoes rub my heels** ces chaussures me blessent aux talons; *Fig* **to rub shoulders with millionaires/movie stars** côtoyer des millionaires/des stars du cinéma

(**b**) *(polish)* astiquer, frotter

3 *vi* frotter; **the cat rubbed against my leg** le chat s'est frotté contre ma jambe; **her leg rubbed against mine** sa jambe a effleuré la mienne; **my shoe is rubbing** ma chaussure me fait mal

▸**rub along** *vi Br Fam* (**a**) *(manage)* se débrouiller❑; **she rubs along in tennis** elle se débrouille au tennis; **we don't have much money, but we rub along** on n'a pas beaucoup d'argent mais on se débrouille

(**b**) *(get on → people)* s'entendre❑; **they rub along (together)** ils s'entendent tant bien que mal

▸**rub away** **1** *vt sep* (**a**) *(stain, writing)* faire disparaître en frottant; **the inscription has been rubbed away** l'inscription a été effacée

(**b**) *(wipe → tears, sweat)* essuyer; **she rubbed away the sweat with a towel** elle s'épongea avec une serviette

2 *vi* disparaître en frottant; **these stains won't rub away** on a beau frotter, ces taches ne partent pas

▸**rub down** *vt sep* (**a**) *(horse)* bouchonner; *(dog)* frotter *(pour sécher)*; *(person)* frictionner; **to rub oneself down** se sécher

(**b**) *(clean → wall)* frotter, nettoyer en frottant; *(with sandpaper)* frotter, poncer

▸**rub in** *vt sep (lotion, oil)* faire pénétrer (en frottant); *Culin (butter)* incorporer; **rub the ointment in** faites bien pénétrer la pommade; **put some polish on the cloth and rub it in** mettez un peu de cirage sur le chiffon et frottez bien; **to rub a hole in sth** faire un trou dans qch à force de frotter; *Culin* **rub the butter into the mixture** travailler la pâte (du bout des doigts) pour incorporer le beurre; *Fig* **to rub it in** remuer le couteau dans la plaie, insister lourdement; **there's no need to rub it in** inutile de remuer le couteau dans la plaie; **he is always rubbing it in that he was right all along** il ne manque jamais de rappeler qu'il avait raison depuis le début; *Fam Fig* **to rub sb's nose in it** mettre le nez de qn dans son caca; *Fig* **she really rubbed his nose in it** elle a retourné le couteau dans la plaie

▸**rub off** **1** *vt sep (erase → writing)* effacer; *(→ mark, dirt)* enlever en frottant

2 *vi* (**a**) *(mark)* s'en aller, partir; **the red dye has rubbed off on my shirt/hands** la teinture rouge a déteint sur ma chemise/m'a déteint sur les mains; **the newspaper ink rubbed off on the cushions** l'encre du journal a noirci les coussins

(**b**) *Fig* **to rub off on sb** *(manners, enthusiasm etc)* déteindre sur qn; **with a bit of luck, her common sense will rub off on him** avec un peu de chance, son bon sens déteindra sur lui; **some of it is bound to rub off** il y aura forcément des influences

▸**rub on** *vt sep (spread)* étaler (en frottant); *(apply)* appliquer (en frottant)

▸**rub out** **1** *vt sep* (**a**) *(erase → stain, writing)* effacer

(**b**) *Am Fam (kill)* liquider, descendre

2 *vi (mark, stain)* partir, s'en aller (en frottant)

▸**rub together** *vt sep* frotter l'un contre l'autre; **I rubbed my hands together to try to keep warm** je me suis frotté les mains pour essayer de me réchauffer

▸**rub up** **1** *vt sep* (**a**) *(polish)* frotter, astiquer; **to rub oneself up against sb/sth** se frotter contre qn/qch; *Fig* **to rub sb up the wrong way** prendre qn à rebrousse-poil

(**b**) *Fam (revise)* potasser; **it's time you rubbed up your Greek** il est temps que tu potasses ton grec

2 *vi* (**a**) *(animal)* se frotter; **the cat rubbed up against my leg** le chat s'est frotté contre ma jambe; *Fig* **to rub up against sb** côtoyer qn, coudoyer qn

(**b**) *Fam (revise)* **to rub up on sth** potasser qch

rubato [rʊ'bɑːtəʊ] *(pl* **rubatos***) Mus* **1** *n* rubato *m*

2 *adj* rubato

3 *adv* rubato

rubber ['rʌbə(r)] **1** *adj (ball, gloves, hose)* en *ou* de caoutchouc; *(bullet)* en caoutchouc; *Am Fam Pol* **the rubber chicken circuit** = série de visites dans de petites villes au cours d'une campagne électorale

2 *n* (**a**) *(material)* caoutchouc *m*; *Fig* **my legs feel like rubber** j'ai les jambes en coton; *Am Fam Aut* **to lay rubber** démarrer en trombe *ou* sur les chapeaux de roue

(**b**) *Br (eraser → for pencil)* gomme *f*; **(board) rubber** *(with wooden back)* tampon *m (pour essuyer le tableau)*; *(rag)* chiffon *m*

(**c**) *Am Fam (condom)* préservatif❑ *m*, capote *f* (anglaise)

(**d**) *(in bridge, whist)* robre *m*, rob *m*; **to play a rubber** faire un robre

3 rubbers *npl Am (boots)* caoutchoucs *mpl*, bottes *fpl* en caoutchouc

▸▸ ***rubber band*** élastique *m*; *Am* ***rubber boots*** bottes *fpl* en caoutchouc; ***rubber cement*** dissolution *f* de caoutchouc; *Fam Br* ***rubber cheque,*** *Am* ***rubber check*** chèque *m* sans provision❑, chèque *m* en bois; ***rubber dinghy*** canot *m* pneumatique; *Bot* ***rubber plant*** caoutchouc *m*, ficus *m*; ***rubber plantation*** plantation *f* d'hévéas; ***rubber planter*** planteur(euse) *m,f* d'hévéas; ***rubber ring*** bouée *f (de natation)*; ***rubber stamp*** tampon *m ou* timbre *m* en caoutchouc; *Fam* ***rubber stamp parliament*** = parlement qui ne fait qu'entériner les lois; *Bot* ***rubber tree*** hévéa *m*

rubberize, -ise ['rʌbəraɪz] *vt* caoutchouter

rubberneck ['rʌbənek] *Fam* **1** *n* (**a**) *(onlooker)* badaud(e)❑ *m,f*; *(at scene of accident)* curieux(euse)❑ *m,f (qui s'attarde sur le lieu d'un accident)* (**b**) *(tourist)* touriste❑ *mf (qui assiste à des visites guidées)*

2 *vi* (**a**) *(look on)* faire le badaud❑; *(at accident)* = faire le curieux sur le lieu d'un accident (**b**) *(tourist)* faire le touriste❑ *(en assistant à des visites guidées)*

rubber-stamp *vt* tamponner; *Fig (decision)* approuver sans discussion

rubbery ['rʌbərɪ] *adj* caoutchouteux

rubbing ['rʌbɪŋ] *n* (**a**) *(gen)* frottement *m* (**b**) *Art* frottis *m*; **to take a rubbing of an inscription** décalquer une inscription *(en frottant)*

▸▸ ***rubbing alcohol*** alcool *m* à 90 (degrés); *Naut* ***rubbing strake*** liston *m*

rubbish ['rʌbɪʃ] **1** *n (UNCOUNT)* (**a**) *(from household)* ordures *fpl* (ménagères); *(from garden)* détritus *mpl*; *(from factory)* déchets *mpl*; *(from building site)* gravats *mpl*

(**b**) *Fam (worthless goods)* camelote *f*, pacotille *f*; **shall I keep this? – no, it's just rubbish** je garde ça? – non, c'est bon à jeter; **it's amazing how much rubbish one accumulates** c'est incroyable toutes les cochonneries qu'on peut accumuler

(**c**) *Fam (nonsense)* foutaises *fpl*, sottises *fpl*; **don't talk rubbish!** ne dis pas de bêtises!, arrete de raconter n'importe quoi!; **(what) rubbish!, what a load of (old) rubbish!** quelles foutaises!; **her latest book is a load of rubbish** son dernier livre est vraiment nul

2 *adj Fam* nul, pourri; **that was a rubbish film/meal** ce film/repas était nul

3 *vt Fam* éreinter; **he always rubbishes my ideas** il faut toujours qu'il débine mes idées

4 *exclam Fam* n'importe quoi!

▸▸ *Br* ***rubbish bin*** poubelle *f*; *Br* ***rubbish chute*** *(in building)* vide-ordures *m inv*; *(at building site)* gaine *f* d'évacuation des gravats; ***rubbish collection*** ramassage *m* des ordures; *Br* ***rubbish dump*** décharge *f* (publique), dépotoir *m*; *Br* ***rubbish heap*** *(household)* tas *m* d'ordures; *(garden)* tas *m* de détritus; *(public)* décharge *f*, dépotoir *m*; *Fig* **to throw sb/sth on the rubbish heap** se débarrasser de qn/qch; *Br* ***rubbish tip*** décharge *f* (publique), dépotoir *m*; *Br* ***rubbish van*** camion *m* d'éboueurs

rubbishy ['rʌbɪʃɪ] *adj Br Fam (worthless)* sans valeur❑; *(poor quality)* de mauvaise qualité❑; *(book, play)* nul

rubble ['rʌbəl] *n (UNCOUNT)* (**a**) *(ruins)* décombres *mpl*; *(debris)* débris *mpl*; *(stones)* gravats *mpl*; **the building was reduced to (a heap of) rubble** l'immeuble n'était plus qu'un amas de décombres; *Fig* **they built a new democratic society on the rubble of the old regime** ils ont construit une nouvelle société démocratique sur les ruines du régime précédent (**b**) *(for roadmaking, building)* blocage *m*, blocaille *f*

rubblework ['rʌbəlwɜːk] *n* maçonnerie *f* en moellons bruts

rubdown ['rʌbdaʊn] *n* friction *f*; **to give sb a rubdown** frictionner qn; **to give a horse a rubdown** bouchonner un cheval

rube [ruːb] *n Am Fam* plouc *m*, péquenot *m*

rubefacient [ˌruːbɪ'feɪʃənt] *Med* **1** *n* rubéfiant *m*

2 *adj* rubéfiant

rubefaction [ˌruːbɪ'fækʃən] *n Med* rubéfaction *f*

Rube Goldberg [ˌruːb'gəʊldbɜːg] *adj Am (device)* de bric et de broc; *(plan, idea)* tarabiscoté

rubella [ruː'belə] **1** *n (UNCOUNT) Med* rubéole *f*

2 *comp (injection, vaccine)* contre la rubéole

rubellite ['ruːbɪlaɪt] *n Miner* rubellite *f*

Rubenesque [ˌruːbe'nesk] *adj* aux formes plantureuses

rubeola [rʊ'bɪələ] *n Med* rougeole *f*

rubescent [ruː'besənt] *adj* rubescent

Rubicon ['ruːbɪkən] *n* Rubicon *m*; *Fig* **to cross** *or* **to pass the Rubicon** franchir le Rubicon

rubicund ['ruːbɪkənd] *adj Literary* rubicond

rubidium [ruː'bɪdɪəm] *n Chem* rubidium *m*

rubiginous [rʊ'bɪdʒɪnəs] *adj Literary* (**a**) *(rusty)* rubigineux (**b**) *(rust-coloured)* couleur de rouille

rubious ['ruːbɪəs] *adj Literary (ruby-coloured)* vermeil, rubis *(inv)*

ruble = **rouble**

rub-out *n Am Fam* assassinat❑ *m*

rubric ['ruːbrɪk] *n* rubrique *f*

rubricate ['ruːbrɪkeɪt] *vt* (**a**) *(mark in red)* traiter en rouge (**b**) *(put rubrics in)* rubriquer

ruby[1] ['ruːbɪ] *(pl* **rubies***)* **1** *n* (**a**) *(jewel)* rubis *m*; *Bible or Literary* **her price is far above rubies** elle a bien plus de prix que les perles *ou* le corail (**b**) *(colour)* couleur *f* (de) rubis, couleur *f* vermeille

2 *adj* (**a**) *(in colour)* vermeil, rubis *(inv)*; **ruby (red) lips** des lèvres *fpl* vermeilles (**b**) *(made of rubies)* de rubis; **ruby earrings/necklace** boucles *fpl* d'oreille/collier *m* en rubis

▸▸ ***ruby port*** porto *m* rouge; ***ruby wedding (anniversary)*** noces *fpl* de vermeil

ruby[2] *n Br Fam (rhyming slang* **Ruby Murray** = **curry***)* curry❑ *m*

ruby-throated hummingbird *n Orn* petit rubis *m* de la Caroline

RUC [ˌɑːjuː'siː] *n (abbr* **Royal Ulster Constabulary***)* = corps de police d'Irlande du Nord

ruche [ruːʃ] **1** *n* ruché *m*

2 *vt* garnir d'un ruché

ruched [ruːʃt] *adj* à ruchés

ruck [rʌk] **1** *n* (**a**) *(in rugby)* mêlée *f* ouverte

(**b**) *Br Fam (fight)* bagarre❑ *f*, baston *m ou f*; **there was a bit of a ruck last night** il y a eu de la bagarre hier soir

(**c**) *(crease)* faux pli *m*, godet *m*

(**d**) *(masses)* **the (common) ruck** les masses *fpl*, la foule

2 *vi* (**a**) *(in rugby)* former une mêlée ouverte; **the Welsh forwards rucked well** les avants gallois étaient bons dans les mêlées ouvertes

(**b**) *(crease)* se froisser, se chiffonner

3 *vt (crease)* froisser, chiffonner

▸**ruck up** *vi* se froisser

rucksack ['rʌksæk] *n esp Br* sac *m* à dos

ruckus ['rʌkəs] *n esp Am Fam (argument, controversy)* bagarre❑ *f*; *(noise)* chahut *m*, vacarme❑ *m*; **to make a ruckus** faire du chahut *ou* du vacarme; *(complain noisily)* faire un scandale; **to cause a ruckus** *(of news etc)* faire du foin

ructions ['rʌkʃənz] *npl Fam* grabuge *m*; **there'll be ructions if they find out** il va y avoir du grabuge *ou* ça va barder s'ils l'apprennent

rudd [rʌd] *n Ich* rotengle *m*

rudder ['rʌdə(r)] *n (of boat)* gouvernail *m*; *(plane)* gouverne *f*

rudderless ['rʌdəlɪs] *adj (boat)* sans gouvernail; *Fig* à la dérive

ruddiness ['rʌdɪnɪs] *n* teint *m* rouge

ruddle ['rʌdəl] **1** *n* ocre *m* rouge

2 *vt* teindre à l'ocre rouge

ruddy ['rʌdɪ] *(compar* **ruddier**, *superl* **ruddiest***)* **1**

adj (**a**) *(red → gen)* rougeâtre, rougeoyant; *(→ face)* rougeaud, rubicond; **to have a ruddy complexion** avoir le teint rouge, être rougeaud; **a ruddy glow** *(of fire)* une lueur rouge

(**b**) *Br Fam (as intensifier)* fichu, sacré; **he's eaten the ruddy lot!** il a tout mangé, ce sale goinfre!; **ruddy hell!** nom de dieu!; **you ruddy idiot!** espèce d'andouille!; **he's a ruddy liar!** c'est un sacré menteur!

2 *adv Br Fam (as intensifier)* sacrément, vachement; **he was ruddy marvellous!** il a été super chouette!; **it's ruddy cold** il fait rudement froid; **you look ruddy ridiculous** t'as l'air vraiment ridicule

►► *Orn* ***ruddy duck*** érismature *m* roux

rude [ruːd] *adj* (**a**) *(ill-mannered)* impoli, mal élevé; *(stronger)* grossier; *(insolent)* insolent; **rude words** gros mots *mpl*; **to be rude to sb** être impoli envers qn; **it's rude to talk with your mouth full** c'est mal élevé de parler la bouche pleine; **he was very rude about my new hairstyle** il a fait des commentaires très désagréables sur ma nouvelle coiffure

(**b**) *Br (indecent)* indécent, obscène, grossier; **to make a rude gesture** faire un geste obscène; **a rude joke** une histoire grivoise *ou* scabreuse

(**c**) *(sudden)* rude, violent, brutal; **a rude shock** un choc brutal; **to receive a rude awakening** recevoir un choc; **it was a bit of a rude awakening** le réveil a été brutal

(**d**) *Literary (rudimentary → tool, hut)* rudimentaire, grossier; *(→ drawing)* primitif

(**e**) *Literary (primitive → tribesman, lifestyle)* primitif, rude

(**f**) *Literary (vigorous)* vigoureux; **to be in rude health** être en pleine santé

rudely ['ruːdlɪ] *adv* (**a**) *(impolitely)* impoliment, de façon mal élevée; *(stronger)* grossièrement; *(insolently)* insolemment; **as I was saying, before you so rudely interrupted me,...** comme je le disais, avant que vous ne m'interrompiez très impoliment,...

(**b**) *(indecently)* indécemment, d'une manière obscène; **to gesture rudely** faire un geste obscène

(**c**) *(suddenly)* violemment, brutalement; **to be rudely awakened** être réveillé brusquement; *Fig* sortir brusquement de sa torpeur; **they were rudely awakened to the difficulties which such an operation entails** ils se rendirent soudain compte des difficultés qu'une telle opération implique

(**d**) *(in a rudimentary way → made, drawn)* grossièrement; **rudely made tools** des outils *mpl* rudimentaires

rudeness ['ruːdnɪs] *n* (**a**) *(impoliteness)* impolitesse *f*; *(stronger)* grossièreté *f*; *(insolence)* insolence *f* (**b**) *Br (indecency)* indécence *f*, obscénité *f* (**c**) *(suddenness)* violence *f*, brutalité *f* (**d**) *(rudimentary nature)* caractère *m* rudimentaire; *(primitive nature)* caractère *m* primitif

ruderal ['ruːdərəl] *Bot* **1** *n* plante *f* rudérale

2 *adj* rudéral

rudiment ['ruːdɪmənt] **1** *n Anat* rudiment *m*

2 rudiments *npl (of a language, a skill)* rudiments *mpl*, notions *fpl* élémentaires

rudimentary [ˌruːdɪ'mentərɪ] *adj (gen) & Anat* rudimentaire; **to have a rudimentary grasp of sth** comprendre les rudiments de qch; **I speak rudimentary Chinese** j'ai des rudiments de chinois

Rudolph ['ruːdɒlf] *pr n Hist* Rodolphe; **Rudolph I** Rodolphe Ier

rue [ruː] **1** *vt Literary or Hum* regretter; **I lived to rue my words** toute ma vie, j'ai regretté mes propos; **I rue the day I met him** je maudis le jour où je l'ai rencontré; **you'll rue the day** *(that you did this)* tu vas le regretter

2 *n Bot & Culin* rue *f*

rueful ['ruːfʊl] *adj (sad)* triste; *(regretful)* plein de regret

ruefully ['ruːfʊlɪ] *adv (sadly)* tristement; *(regretfully)* avec regret

ruefulness ['ruːfʊlnɪs] *n (sadness)* tristesse *f*; **the ruefulness of his voice** son ton emprunt de regret

rue-leaved saxifrage *n Bot* saxifrage *f* à trois doigts

RUF [ˌɑːjuː'ef] *n Fin (abbr* **revolving underwriting facility***)* facilité *f* renouvelable de prise ferme

rufescent [rʊ'fesənt] *adj Bot* roussâtre

ruff [rʌf] **1** *n* (**a**) *(collar)* collerette *f*; *Hist* fraise *f* (**b**) *Zool (on bird, animal)* collier *m* (**c**) *Orn* (chevalier *m*) combattant *m* (**d**) *(in cards)* action *f* de couper; **I was expecting a ruff** je m'attendais à ce que la carte soit coupée

2 *vt (in cards)* couper

ruffed [rʌft] *adj* (**a**) *Hist (person)* portant une fraise (**b**) *Zool (animal, bird)* à collier

ruffian ['rʌfɪən] *n* voyou *m*; *Hum (naughty child)* petit(e) vaurien(enne) *m,f*

ruffianly ['rʌfɪənlɪ] *adj (person)* brutal; *(appearance, behaviour)* de voyou

ruffle ['rʌfəl] **1** *vt* (**a**) *(hair, fur, feathers)* ébouriffer; *(clothes)* friper, froisser, chiffonner; **the wind ruffled her hair** le vent ébouriffait ses cheveux; **the parrot ruffled its feathers** le perroquet hérissa ses plumes; *Fig* **to ruffle sb's feathers** froisser qn; **to ruffle sb's composure** faire perdre contenance à qn

(**b**) *(surface of water)* troubler, rider; *(grass)* agiter

(**c**) *(upset → person)* troubler, décontenancer

2 *n* (**a**) *(frill → at wrist)* manchette *f* (en dentelle); *(→ at throat)* jabot *m* plissé

(**b**) *(of bird)* collier *m*, cravate *f*

(**c**) *(ripple → on lake, sea)* ride *f*

ruffled ['rʌfəld] *adj* (**a**) *(flustered)* décontenancé; *(annoyed, irritated)* irrité; **to get ruffled** perdre contenance; *(get annoyed)* s'irriter (**b**) *(rumpled → sheets)* froissé; *(→ hair)* ébouriffé (**c**) *(decorated with frill)* ruché, plissé

rufous ['ruːfəs] *adj* roussâtre

►► *Orn* ***rufous hummingbird*** colibri *m* sasin

rug [rʌg] *n* (**a**) *(for floor)* carpette *f*, (petit) tapis *m*; *Fig* **to pull the rug from under sb's feet** couper l'herbe sous le pied à qn; *Am Fig* **to sweep sth under the rug** enterrer qch (**b**) *Br (blanket)* couverture *f*; **tartan rug** plaid *m* (**c**) *Fam (hairpiece)* moumoute *f*

rugby ['rʌgbɪ] **1** *n* rugby *m*

2 *comp (ball, match, team)* de rugby

►► ***rugby football*** rugby *m*; ***rugby league*** rugby *m ou* jeu *m* à treize; ***rugby player*** joueur(euse) *m,f* de rugby, rugbyman *m*; ***rugby shirt*** maillot *m* de rugby; ***rugby tackle*** plaquage *m*; ***rugby union*** rugby *m* à quinze

rugby-tackle *vt* plaquer; **the policeman rugby-tackled him** le policier l'a plaqué

rugged ['rʌgɪd] *adj* (**a**) *(countryside, region)* accidenté; *(road, path → bumpy)* cahoteux, défoncé; *(→ rocky)* rocailleux; *(coastline)* échancré, découpé

(**b**) *(face, features)* rude; **he had rugged good looks** il était d'une beauté virile

(**c**) *(unrefined → person, character, manners)* rude, mal dégrossi; *(→ lifestyle)* rude, fruste; *(determined → resistance)* acharné; **rugged individualist** individualiste *mf* farouche *ou* forcené(e)

(**d**) *(clothing, equipment, vehicle)* solide, robuste

ruggedness ['rʌgɪdnɪs] *n (UNCOUNT)* (**a**) *(of countryside, region)* caractère *m* accidenté; *(of road, path)* inégalités *fpl*; *(of coastline)* échancrures *fpl*; **the ruggedness of the terrain** les inégalités *fpl* du terrain (**b**) *(of face, features)* irrégularité *f* (**c**) *(of person, manners, lifestyle)* rudesse *f* (**d**) *(of clothing, equipment, vehicle)* solidité *f*, robustesse *f*

rugger ['rʌgə(r)] *n Br Fam* rugby □ *m*

►► *Pej* ***rugger bugger*** amateur *m* de rugby

rugose ['ruːgəʊs] *adj Bot, Zool & Anat* rugueux

rugosity [ruː'gɒsɪtɪ] *n Bot, Zool & Anat* rugosité *f*

rugrat ['rʌgræt] *n Fam* môme *mf*, chiard *m*

ruin ['ruːɪn] **1** *n* (**a**) *(usu pl) (remains)* ruine *f*; **the monastery is now a ruin** le monastère n'est plus qu'une ruine; **the ruins of an old castle** les ruines *fpl* d'un vieux château; **to be in ruins** *(building, economy)* être en ruine(s); *(career)* être fini; *(hopes)* être anéanti

(**b**) *(destruction)* ruine *f*; **this spelt the ruin of our hopes** c'était la fin de nos espoirs; **to fall into ruin** tomber en ruine(s); **to go to ruin** *(economy, country)* tomber en ruine(s); *(person)* sombrer; **he's on the road to ruin** il va *ou* court à la ruine *ou* à sa perte; **to be the ruin of sb** être la perte de qn; **it will be the ruin of him** ça le perdra; **gambling has led to his ruin** le jeu l'a perdu *ou* l'a mené à sa perte

(**c**) *(bankruptcy)* ruine *f*; **the business was on the brink of (financial) ruin** l'affaire était au bord de la ruine

2 *vt* (**a**) *(destroy → health, economy, country)* ruiner; *(→ person, career)* détruire; *(damage → clothes)* abîmer; *(spoil → event, meal, holiday)* gâcher; **that's ruined our chances** ça nous a fait perdre toutes nos chances; **you're ruining your eyesight** tu es en train de t'abîmer la vue *ou* les yeux; **to ruin one's health** se ruiner la santé; **the rain ruined our trip** la pluie a gâché notre voyage; **you've ruined my best dress** tu as abîmé ma plus jolie robe; **to ruin sb's plans** faire échouer les projets de qn; **the injury ruined his chances of playing in the World Cup** sa blessure l'a empêché de participer à la Coupe du monde; **the small villages along the coast have been ruined by mass tourism** les petits villages de la côte ont perdu tout leur charme à cause du tourisme de masse

(**b**) *(bankrupt)* ruiner

ruination [ˌruːɪ'neɪʃən] *n* ruine *f*, perte *f*; **you'll be the ruination of me!** tu me perdras!; **the ruination of the countryside** la destruction de la campagne

ruined ['ruːɪnd] *adj* (**a**) *(house, reputation, health)* en ruine(s), ruiné; *(clothes)* abîmé; **the meal is ruined** le repas est gâché (**b**) *(financially)* ruiné; **we're ruined** nous sommes ruinés

ruinous ['ruːɪnəs] *adj* (**a**) *(expensive)* ruineux; **maintaining such a large house proved ruinous** l'entretien d'une aussi grande maison s'est avéré ruineux (**b**) *(disastrous)* désastreux; **tobacco and alcohol are ruinous to the health** le tabac et l'alcool ruinent la santé

ruinously ['ruːɪnəslɪ] *adv* de façon ruineuse; **ruinously expensive** ruineux

RULE [ruːl]

règle	► 1 (a), (b), (d), (e)
règlement	► 1 (a)
gouvernement	► 1 (c)
gouverner	► 2 (a)
dominer	► 2 (b)
juger	► 2 (c)
régner	► 3 (a), (b)
statuer	► 3 (c)

1 *n* (**a**) *(principle)* règle *f*; *(regulation)* règlement *m*; **the rules of chess/grammar** les règles *fpl* du jeu d'échecs/de la grammaire; **to break the rules** ne pas respecter les règles; **to play according to the rules** *or* **by the rules (of the game)** jouer suivant les règles (du jeu); **the rules and regulations** le règlement; **the club rules are very strict on this point** le règlement du club est très strict sur ce point; **smoking is against the rules, it's against the rules to smoke** le règlement interdit de fumer; **that contravenes rule 5b** c'est contraire à la règle 5b; **to stretch** *or* **to bend the rules (for sb)** faire une entorse au règlement (pour qn); *Math* **rule of three** règle *f* de trois; **rule of thumb** point *m* de repère; **as a rule of thumb, allow one pound of meat for four people** en règle générale, compter une livre de viande pour quatre personnes

(**b**) *(usual practice, custom)* règle *f*; **as a (general) rule** en règle générale; **rules of conduct** règles *fpl* de conduite; **he makes it a rule not to trust anyone** il a comme *ou* pour règle de ne faire confiance à personne; **we must make it a rule that everyone contributes equally** nous devons poser comme principe que chacun contribue à part égale; **tipping is the rule here** les pourboires sont de règle ici; **long hair was the rule in those days** tout le monde avait les cheveux longs à cette époque; **it's often the case, but there's no hard and fast rule** c'est souvent le cas, mais il n'y a pas de règle absolue; **politeness seems to be the exception rather than the rule** on dirait que la politesse est l'exception plutôt que la règle; **the exception proves the rule** l'exception confirme la règle

(**c**) *(government)* gouvernement *m*, autorité *f*; *(reign)* règne *m*; **a return to majority/mob rule**

un retour à la démocratie/à l'anarchie; **the territories under French rule** les territoires *mpl* sous autorité française; **in the days of British rule** à l'époque de la domination britannique; **majority rule, the rule of the majority** règle *f* majoritaire; **the rule of law** (l'autorité *f* de) la loi
(**d**) *(for measuring)* règle *f*; **folding rule** mètre *m* pliant; **metre rule** mètre *m*; **pocket rule** règle *f* *ou* mètre *m* de poche
(**e**) *(of religious order)* règle *f*
2 *vt* (**a**) *(govern → country, people)* gouverner; **if I ruled the world** si j'étais maître du monde
(**b**) *(dominate → person)* dominer; *(→ emotion)* maîtriser; **their lives are ruled by fear** leur vie est dominée par la peur; **don't let him rule your life** ne le laisse pas mener ta vie; **don't be ruled by what he says** ce n'est pas à lui de vous dire ce que vous avez à faire; **don't let your heart rule your head** ne laisse pas tes émotions l'emporter sur la raison; **to rule the roost** faire la loi; **to rule the waves** tenir la mer, être maître *ou* maîtresse des mers
(**c**) *(judge, decide)* juger, décider; **the referee ruled the ball out** *or* **that the ball was out** l'arbitre a déclaré *ou* jugé que la balle était hors jeu; **the strike was ruled illegal** la grève a été jugée illégale; **the court ruled that he should have custody of the children** c'est à lui que la cour a accordé la garde des enfants; **the chairperson ruled her** *or* **her remark out of order** le président a déclaré que sa remarque n'était pas valable
(**d**) *(draw → line, margin)* tirer à la règle; *(draw lines on → paper)* régler
3 *vi* (**a**) *(govern → monarch, dictator)* régner; *(→ elected government)* gouverner; **he ruled over a vast kingdom** il régna sur un vaste royaume; *Fam* **Chelsea rule OK!** vive Chelsea!❑; **Rule Britannia** = chant patriotique britannique
(**b**) *(prevail)* régner; **chaos ruled** le désordre régnait; **the philosophy currently ruling in the party** la philosophie actuellement en vigueur au parti
(**c**) *Law (decide)* statuer (**on sth** sur qch); **to rule on a dispute** statuer sur un litige; **to rule against/in favour of sb** décider *ou* prononcer contre/en faveur de qn
▸**rule off** *vt sep* tirer une ligne sous; *Fin (account)* clore, arrêter
▸**rule out** *vt sep (possibility, suggestion, suspect)* exclure, écarter; **we cannot rule out that possibility** on ne saurait exclure cette éventualité; **she cannot be ruled out of the inquiry** elle n'a pas encore été mise hors de cause; **the police have ruled out murder** la police exclut la possibilité d'un meurtre; **the presence of hostages ruled out an attack** la présence d'otages rendait toute attaque impossible; **the injury rules him out of Saturday's game** sa blessure ne lui permettra pas de jouer samedi

---

rulebook ['ru:lbʊk] *n* règlement *m*; **the rulebook** le règlement, les règles *fpl*; **to do sth by the rulebook** faire qch strictement selon les règles; **to go by the rulebook** suivre scrupuleusement le règlement; **to throw away the rule book** faire fi des règles

ruled [ru:ld] *adj (paper, block)* réglé

rule-governed [-gʌvənd] *adj* qui suit des règles

ruler ['ru:lə(r)] *n* (**a**) *(sovereign)* souverain(e) *m,f*; *(president, prime minister etc)* chef *m* d'État, dirigeant(e) *m,f* (**b**) *(for measuring)* règle *f*; *Comput (in word processor, in DTP)* règle *f*
▸▸ *Comput* ***ruler line*** règle *f*

ruling ['ru:lɪŋ] **1** *adj* (**a**) *(monarch)* régnant; *(party)* au pouvoir; *(class)* dirigeant (**b**) *(passion, factor)* dominant
2 *n (of judge, umpire)* décision *f*; **to give** *or* **hand down a ruling in favour of sb** décider en faveur de qn
▸▸ ***ruling body*** instances *fpl* (dirigeantes)

rum [rʌm] *(compar* **rummer**, *superl* **rummest**) **1** *n (drink)* rhum *m*
2 *comp (ice cream, toddy)* au rhum
3 *adj Br Fam Old-fashioned (odd)* bizarre❑; **he's a rum old chap** c'est un drôle de bonhomme; **I was feeling a bit rum** je n'étais pas dans mon assiette; **it was a bit of a rum do** c'était un peu louche
▸▸ *Br Culin* ***rum baba*** baba *m* au rhum; ***rum runner*** trafiquant(e) *m,f* d'alcool

Rumania, Rumanian = **Romania, Romanian**

rumba ['rʌmbə] **1** *n* rumba *f*
2 *vi* danser la rumba

rumble ['rʌmbəl] **1** *n* (**a**) *(of thunder, traffic, cannons)* grondement *m*; *(of conversation)* bourdonnement *m*, bruit *m* confus; *(of cart)* roulement *m*; *(in stomach)* borborygme *m*, gargouillis *m*, gargouillement *m*; **there were rumbles of discontent in the hall** il y avait des murmures de protestation dans la salle; **this caused rumbles of discontent in the press/party** cela a soulevé des vagues dans la presse/au sein du parti
(**b**) *Fam (fight)* baston *m ou f*
2 *vi* (**a**) *(thunder, traffic, cannons)* gronder; *(stomach)* gargouiller; **trucks were rumbling past all night** toute la nuit, on entendait le grondement des camions
(**b**) *Fam (fight)* se bagarrer❑, se friter
3 *vt* (**a**) *Br Fam (see through → scheme, plot)* flairer❑; *(→ person)* voir venir❑; **we've been rumbled** on a deviné notre jeu; **I soon rumbled their little game** j'ai tout de suite pigé leur petit jeu
(**b**) *(comment, remark)* grommeler, bougonner
▸▸ *Am* ***rumble seat*** strapontin *m*; *Aut* ***rumble strip*** bande *f* rugueuse
▸**rumble on** *vi (person)* palabrer; *(conversation, debate)* ne pas en finir; **he rumbled on about India for a good hour** il a palabré sur l'Inde pendant une bonne heure; **the dispute's been rumbling on for weeks now** le conflit dure depuis des semaines

rumbling ['rʌmbəlɪŋ] **1** *n (of thunder, traffic, cannons)* grondement *m*; *(of stomach)* borborygmes *mpl*, gargouillis *mpl*, gargouillements *mpl*
2 *adj* **a rumbling noise** un grondement
3 rumblings *npl (of discontent)* grondement *m*, grondements *mpl*; *(omens)* présages *mpl*; **I've heard rumblings to that effect** j'ai entendu des bruits qui semblent le confirmer

rumbustious [rʌm'bʌstʃəs] *adj Br Fam (boisterous)* exubérant❑; *(unruly)* turbulent❑, indiscipliné❑; *Theat (farce)* joyeux❑

rum-dum [-dʌm] *n Am Fam* (**a**) *(idiot)* abruti(e) *m,f*, crétin(e) *m,f* (**b**) *(drunken tramp)* **he's a rum-dum** c'est un clodo et un poivrot

rumen ['ru:men] *(pl* **rumens** *or* **rumina** [-mɪnə]) *n Zool* panse *f (de ruminant)*, rumen *m*

ruminant ['ru:mɪnənt] **1** *adj* (**a**) *Zool* ruminant (**b**) *Literary (person)* pensif, méditatif; *(look, mood)* pensif
2 *n Zool* ruminant *m*

ruminate ['ru:mɪneɪt] **1** *vi* (**a**) *Zool* ruminer (**b**) *Formal (person)* ruminer; **to ruminate over** *or* **about** *or* **on sth** ruminer qch, réfléchir longuement à qch
2 *vt* (**a**) *Zool* ruminer (**b**) *Formal (of person)* ruminer

rumination [,ru:mɪ'neɪʃən] *n* (**a**) *Zool* rumination *f* (**b**) *Formal (of person)* rumination *f*; **after much rumination** après avoir longuement réfléchi *ou* ruminé

ruminative ['ru:mɪnətɪv] *adj (person)* pensif, méditatif; *(look, mood)* pensif

ruminatively ['ru:mɪnətɪvlɪ] *adv* pensivement

rummage ['rʌmɪdʒ] **1** *n* (**a**) *(search)* **to have a rummage through** *or* **around in sth** fouiller (dans) qch; **I had a quick rummage in his suitcase** j'ai rapidement fouillé sa valise (**b**) *Am (jumble)* bric-à-brac *m inv*
2 *vi* fouiller; **he rummaged in** *or* **through his pockets** il fouilla dans ses poches
▸▸ *Am* ***rummage sale*** vente *f* de charité
▸**rummage about, rummage around** *vi* fouiller; **what are you rummaging around in here for?** qu'est-ce que tu farfouilles?
▸**rummage out, rummage up** *vt sep* dénicher

rummer ['rʌmə(r)] *n* grand verre *m* à pied

rummy ['rʌmɪ] *(pl* **rummies**, *compar* **rummier**, *superl* **rummiest**) **1** *n* (**a**) *(card game)* rami *m*; **to play rummy** jouer au rami (**b**) *Am Fam (drunk)* alcolo *mf*, poivrot(e) *m,f*
2 *adj (taste)* de rhum

rumour, *Am* **rumor** ['ru:mə(r)] **1** *n* (**a**) *(information)* rumeur *f*, bruit *m* (qui court); **there's a rumour going round that..., rumour has it that...** le bruit court que...; **the rumour that she's left the country is untrue** la rumeur selon laquelle elle aurait quitté le pays n'est pas fondée; **so rumour has it** c'est ce qu'on dit; **to hear a rumour that...** entendre dire que...; **there are rumours of a takeover** on parle de *ou* d'un rachat; **have you heard any rumours about what's going to happen?** est-ce que vous avez entendu parler de ce qui va se passer?; **it's only a rumour** ce n'est qu'une rumeur *ou* qu'un bruit qui court *ou* qu'un on-dit
(**b**) *Arch or Literary (sound)* **the rumour of the sea/wind** la rumeur des flots/du vent
2 *vt* **it is rumoured that...** le bruit court que...; **she is rumoured to be extremely rich** on la dit extrêmement riche; **he is rumoured to have killed a man** on dit *ou* le bruit court qu'il a tué un homme; **he was rumoured to be in hiding** le bruit courait qu'il se cachait; **so it was rumoured** c'est ce qu'on a dit
▸▸ *Fig* ***the rumour mill*** la rumeur publique; **the rumour mill has been working overtime** la rumeur a pris beaucoup d'ampleur

> **Rumours of my death have been greatly exaggerated**
> Cette phrase ("les rumeurs concernant ma mort sont très exagérées") aurait été prononcée par Mark Twain après qu'un journal avait annoncé son décès par erreur.
> Aujourd'hui on utilise cette phrase lorsque l'on veut démentir une rumeur ou une idée reçue. On pourra dire par exemple **rumours of the death of vinyl records have been greatly exaggerated** ("les rumeurs concernant la fin des disques vinyle sont très exagérées").

rumoured, *Am* **rumored** ['ru:məd] *adj* **the rumoured takeover of the company/cancellation of the project** la rumeur selon laquelle l'entreprise serait rachetée/le projet serait annulé; **the table was sold for a rumoured £2m** selon la rumeur, la table aurait été vendue 2 millions de livres

rumourmonger, *Am* **rumormonger** ['ru:mə-,mʌŋgə(r)] *n* commère *f*

rump [rʌmp] *n* (**a**) *(of mammal)* croupe *f*; *Culin* culotte *f*; *(of bird)* croupion *m*; *Hum (of person)* croupe *f*
(**b**) *(of army, political party)* restant *m*; **the rump Yugoslavia** ce qui reste de la Yougoslavie; **the organization was reduced to a rump** il ne restait pas grand-chose de l'organisation
▸▸ *Br Hist* ***Rump Parliament*** le Parlement croupion *(nom du Parlement anglais pendant la période du Protectorat de Cromwell, de 1649 à 1660)*; ***rump state*** état *m* croupion; ***rump steak*** romsteck *m*, rumsteck *m*

rumple ['rʌmpəl] *vt (clothes)* friper, froisser, chiffonner; *(banknote, letter)* froisser; *(hair, fur)* ébouriffer; **the wind had rumpled my hair** le vent m'avait décoiffé; **pages rumpled at the edges** des pages cornées

rumpled ['rʌmpəld] *adj (clothes)* fripé, froissé, chiffonné; *(hair, fur)* ébouriffé; **to look rumpled** *(person)* avoir l'air ébouriffé

rumpus ['rʌmpəs] *n Fam (noise)* chahut *m*, vacarme❑ *m*; *(argument, protest)* bagarre❑ *f*; **to kick up** *or* **make** *or* **raise** *or* **cause a rumpus** *(be noisy)* faire un chahut à tout casser; *(protest)* faire du raffut; **there's been a bit of a rumpus about her appointment** il y a eu toute une histoire à propos de sa nomination
▸▸ *esp Am* ***rumpus room*** salle *f* de jeu *(souvent située au sous-sol et également utilisée pour des fêtes)*

rumpy-pumpy [,rʌmpɪ'pʌmpɪ] *n Br Fam Hum (sex)* zig-zig *m*, crac-crac *m*; **to have a bit of rumpy-pumpy** faire une partie de jambes en l'air, faire zig-zig *ou* crac-crac

---

RUN [rʌn]

course	▸ **1 (a), (b)**
excursion	▸ **1 (c)**
trajet	▸ **1 (e)**
vol	▸ **1 (f)**
série	▸ **1 (i), (k)**
tendance	▸ **1 (l)**

ruée	►1 (m)
diriger	►2 (a)
organiser	►2 (b)
(faire) marcher	►2 (c); 3 (k)
courir	►2 (e); 3 (a), (b)
transporter	►2 (i)
conduire	►2 (k)
(faire) passer	►2 (l), (m); 3 (d)
se sauver	►3 (c)
couler	►3 (h), (i)
fondre	►3 (i)
circuler	►3 (l)
durer	►3 (m)
être à l'affiche	►3 (n)
(se) présenter	►2 (q); 3 (r)

(*pt* **ran** [ræn], *pp* **run**, *cont* **running**) **1** *n* (**a**) *(action)* course *f*; **he took a short run and cleared the gate** après un court élan il a franchi la barrière; **at a run** en courant; **to go for a run** aller faire du jogging; **to go for a 5-mile run** ≃ courir 8 kilomètres; **I took the dog for a run in the park** j'ai emmené le chien courir dans le parc; **two policemen arrived at a run** deux policiers sont arrivés au pas de course; **to break into a run** se mettre à courir; **to make a run for it** prendre la fuite, se sauver; **the murderer is on the run** le meurtrier est en cavale; **she was on the run from her creditors/the police** elle essayait d'échapper à ses créanciers/à la police; **we've got them on the run!** nous les avons mis en déroute!; *Fig* **we have the run of the house while the owners are away** nous disposons de toute la maison pendant l'absence des propriétaires; **we give the au pair the run of the place** nous laissons à la jeune fille au pair la libre disposition de la maison; **you've had a good run (for your money), it's time to step down** tu en as bien profité, maintenant il faut laisser la place à un autre; **they gave the Russian team a good run for their money** ils ont donné du fil à retordre à l'équipe soviétique; *Fam* **to have the runs** *(diarrhoea)* avoir la courante

(**b**) *(race)* course *f*; **a charity run** une course de charité

(**c**) *(drive)* excursion *f*, promenade *f*; **we went for a run down to the coast** nous sommes allés nous promener au bord de la mer; **she took me for a run in her new car** elle m'a emmené faire un tour dans sa nouvelle voiture; *Hum* **shall I make** *or* **do a beer run?** je vais chercher de la bière?; **I do the school run in the morning** c'est moi qui emmène les enfants à l'école tous les matins

(**d**) *(for smuggling)* passage *m*; **the gang used to make runs across the border** le gang passait régulièrement la frontière

(**e**) *(route, itinerary)* trajet *m*, parcours *m*; **the buses on the London to Glasgow run** les cars qui font le trajet *ou* qui assurent le service Londres-Glasgow; **he used to do the London (to) Glasgow run** *(pilot, bus or train driver)* il faisait la ligne Londres–Glasgow; **it's only a short run into town** le trajet jusqu'au centre-ville n'est pas long; **there was very little traffic on the run down** nous avons rencontré très peu de circulation

(**f**) *Aviat (flight)* vol *m*, mission *f*; **bombing run** mission *f* de bombardement

(**g**) *Sport (in cricket, baseball)* point *m*; **to make 10 runs** marquer 10 points

(**h**) *(track → for skiing, bobsleighing)* piste *f*

(**i**) *(series, sequence)* série *f*, succession *f*, suite *f*; **they've had a run of ten defeats** ils ont connu dix défaites consécutives; **the recent run of events** la récente série d'événements; **a run of bad luck** une série *ou* suite de malheurs; **you seem to be having a run of good/bad luck** on dirait que la chance est/n'est pas de ton côté en ce moment; **the play had a triumphant run on Broadway** la pièce a connu un succès triomphal à Broadway; **the play had a run of nearly two years** la pièce a tenu l'affiche (pendant) presque deux ans; **to have a long run** *(of fashion, person in power)* tenir longtemps; *(of play)* tenir longtemps l'affiche; **in the long/short run** à long/court terme

(**j**) *(in card games)* suite *f*

(**k**) *(of product)* lot *m*, série *f*; *(of book)* tirage *m*; **a run of fewer than 500 would be uneconomical** fabriquer une série de moins de 500 unités ne serait pas rentable

(**l**) *(general tendency, trend)* tendance *f*; **to score against the run of play** marquer contre le jeu; **I was lucky and got the run of the cards** j'avais de la chance, les cartes m'étaient favorables; **the usual run of colds and upset stomachs** les rhumes et les maux de ventre habituels; **she's well above the average** *or* **ordinary run of students** elle est bien au-dessus de la moyenne des étudiants; **the ordinary run of mankind** le commun des mortels; **in the ordinary run of things** normalement, en temps normal; **out of the common run** hors du commun

(**m**) *(great demand → on product, currency, Stock Exchange)* ruée *f* (**on** sur); **the heatwave caused a run on suntan cream** la vague de chaleur provoqua une ruée sur les crèmes solaires; **a run on the banks** un retrait massif des dépôts bancaires; *St Exch* **there was a run on the dollar** il y a eu une ruée sur le dollar

(**n**) *(operation → of machine)* opération *f*; **computer run** passage *m* machine

(**o**) *(bid → in election)* candidature *f*; **his run for the presidency** sa candidature à la présidence

(**p**) *(ladder → in stocking, tights)* échelle *f*, maille *f* filée; **I've got a run in my tights** mon collant est filé

(**q**) *(enclosure → for animals)* enclos *m*; **chicken run** poulailler *m*

(**r**) *(of salmon)* remontée *f*

(**s**) *Mus* roulade *f*

2 *vt* (**a**) *(manage → company, office)* diriger, gérer; *(→ shop, restaurant, club)* tenir; *(→ theatre)* diriger; *(→ farm)* exploiter; *(→ newspaper, magazine)* rédiger; *(→ house)* tenir; *(→ country)* gouverner, diriger; **she runs the bar while her parents are away** elle tient le bar pendant l'absence de ses parents; **a badly run organization** une organisation mal gérée; **the library is run by volunteer workers** la bibliothèque est tenue par des bénévoles; **the farm was too big for him to run alone** la ferme était trop grande pour qu'il puisse s'en occuper seul; **who's running this outfit?** qui est le patron ici?; **I wish she'd stop trying to run my life!** j'aimerais bien qu'elle arrête de me dire comment vivre ma vie!

(**b**) *(organize, lay on → service, course, contest)* organiser; *(→ train, bus)* mettre en service; **to run a bridge tournament/a raffle** organiser un tournoi de bridge/une tombola; **they run evening classes in computing** ils organisent des cours du soir en informatique; **they run extra trains in the summer** l'été ils mettent (en service) des trains supplémentaires; **several private companies run buses to the airport** plusieurs sociétés privées assurent un service d'autobus pour l'aéroport

(**c**) *(operate → piece of equipment)* faire marcher, faire fonctionner; *Comput (program)* exécuter, faire tourner; **you can run it off solar energy/the mains** vous pouvez le faire fonctionner à l'énergie solaire/sur secteur; **this computer runs most software** on peut utiliser la plupart des logiciels sur cet ordinateur; *Aviat* **to run the engines** *(for checking)* faire le point fixe; **I can't afford to run a car any more** je n'ai plus les moyens d'avoir une voiture; **she runs a Porsche** elle roule en Porsche

(**d**) *(conduct → experiment, test)* effectuer

(**e**) *(do or cover at a run → race, distance)* courir; **to run the marathon** courir le marathon; **I can still run 2 km in under 7 minutes** j'arrive encore à courir *ou* à couvrir 2 km en moins de 7 minutes; **the children were running races** les enfants faisaient la course; **the race will be run in Paris next year** la course aura lieu à Paris l'année prochaine; **to run messages** *or* **errands** faire des commissions *ou* des courses; **he'd run a mile if he saw it** il prendrait ses jambes à son cou s'il voyait ça; **it looks as if his race is run** on dirait qu'il a fait son temps

(**f**) *(cause to run)* **to be run off one's feet** être débordé; **you're running the poor boy off his feet!** le pauvre, tu es en train de l'épuiser!; **to run oneself to a standstill** courir jusqu'à l'épuisement

(**g**) *(enter for race → horse, greyhound)* faire courir

(**h**) *(hunt, chase)* chasser; **to run deer** chasser le cerf; **the outlaws were run out of town** les hors-la-loi furent chassés de la ville

(**i**) *(transport → goods)* transporter; *(give lift to → person)* conduire, emmener; **I'll run you to the bus stop** je vais te conduire à l'arrêt de bus; **to run sb back home** reconduire qn chez lui; **I've got to run these boxes over to my new house** je dois emporter ces boîtes dans ma nouvelle maison

(**j**) *(smuggle)* faire le trafic de; **he's suspected of running drugs/guns** il est soupçonné de trafic de drogue/d'armes

(**k**) *(drive → vehicle)* conduire; **I ran the car into the driveway** j'ai mis la voiture dans l'allée; **could you run your car back a bit?** pourriez-vous reculer un peu votre voiture?; **I ran my car into a lamppost** je suis rentré dans un réverbère (avec ma voiture); **he tried to run me off the road!** il a essayé de me faire sortir de la route!

(**l**) *(pass, quickly or lightly)* passer; **he ran his hand through his hair** il se passa la main dans les cheveux; **he ran a comb through his hair** il se donna un coup de peigne; **I'll run a duster over the furniture** je passerai un coup de chiffon sur les meubles; **she ran her hands over the controls** elle promena ses mains sur les boutons de commande; **she ran her finger down the list/her eye over the text** elle parcourut la liste du doigt/le texte des yeux

(**m**) *(send via specified route)* faire passer; **it would be better to run the wires under the floorboards** ce serait mieux de faire passer les fils sous le plancher; **we could run a cable from the house** nous pourrions amener un câble de la maison; **run the other end of the rope through the loop** passez l'autre bout de la corde dans la boucle

(**n**) *(go through or past → blockade)* forcer; *(→ rapids)* franchir; *Am (→ red light)* brûler

(**o**) *(cause to flow)* faire couler; **run the water into the basin** faites couler l'eau dans la cuvette; **to run a bath** faire couler un bain

(**p**) *(publish)* publier; **the local paper is running a series of articles on the scandal** le journal local publie une série d'articles sur le scandale; **to run an ad (in the newspaper)** passer *ou* faire passer une annonce (dans le journal)

(**q**) *(enter for election)* présenter; **they're running a candidate in every constituency** ils présentent un candidat dans chaque circonscription

(**r**) *Med* **to run a temperature** *or* **fever** avoir de la fièvre

(**s**) *(expose oneself to)* **to run the danger** *or* **risk of doing sth** courir le risque de faire qch; **you run the risk of a heavy fine** vous risquez une grosse amende; **do you realize the risks you're running?** est-ce que vous réalisez les risques que vous prenez?

3 *vi* (**a**) *(gen)* courir; **I run every morning in the park** je cours tous les matins dans le parc; **to come running towards sb** accourir vers qn; **they ran out of the house** ils sont sortis de la maison en courant; **to run upstairs/downstairs** monter/descendre l'escalier en courant; **I had to run for the train** j'ai dû courir pour attraper le train; **she ran for the police** elle a couru chercher la police; **run and fetch me a glass of water** cours me chercher un verre d'eau; **I'll just run across** *or* **round** *or* **over to the shop** je fais un saut à l'épicerie; **to run to meet sb** courir *ou* se précipiter à la rencontre de qn; **I've been running all over the place looking for you** j'ai couru partout à ta recherche; *Fig* **I didn't expect her to go running to the press with the story** je ne m'attendais pas à ce qu'elle coure raconter l'histoire à la presse; **don't come running to me with your problems** ne viens pas m'embêter avec tes problèmes

(**b**) *(compete in race)* courir; *(score in cricket, baseball)* marquer; **to run in a race** *(horse, person)* participer à une course; **there are twenty horses running in the race** vingt chevaux participent à la course; **she ran for her country in the Olympics** elle a couru pour son pays aux jeux Olympiques

(**c**) *(flee)* se sauver, fuir; **run for your lives!**

sauve qui peut!; *Fam* **if the night watchman sees you, run for it!** si le veilleur de nuit te voit, tire-toi *ou* file!; *Fig* **you can't just keep running from your past** vous ne pouvez pas continuer à fuir votre passé

(**d**) *(pass → road, railway, boundary)* passer; **a tunnel runs under the mountain** un tunnel passe sous la montagne; **the railway line runs through a valley/over a viaduct** le chemin de fer passe dans une vallée/sur un viaduc; **the pipes run under the road** les tuyaux passent sous la route; **the road runs alongside the river/parallel to the coast** la route longe la rivière/la côte; **hedgerows run between the fields** des haies séparent les champs; **the road runs due north** la route va droit vers le nord; **to run north and south** être orienté nord-sud; **a canal running from London to Birmingham** un canal qui va de Londres à Birmingham; **a high fence runs around the building** une grande barrière fait le tour du bâtiment; **the lizard has red markings running down its back** le dos du lézard est zébré de rouge; **the line of print ran off the page** la ligne a débordé de la feuille; *Fig* **our lives seem to be running in different directions** il semble que nos vies prennent des chemins différents

(**e**) *(move, go → ball, vehicle)* rouler; *(slip, slide → rope, cable)* filer; **the pram ran down the hill out of control** le landau a dévalé la côte; **the tram runs on special tracks** le tramway roule sur des rails spéciaux; **the crane runs on rails** la grue se déplace sur des rails; **the piano runs on casters** le piano est monté sur (des) roulettes; **the truck ran off the road** le camion a quitté la route; **let the cord run through your hands** laissez la corde filer entre vos mains; **his fingers ran over the controls** ses doigts se promenèrent sur les boutons de commande; **her eyes ran down the list** elle parcourut la liste des yeux; **a shiver ran down my spine** un frisson me parcourut le dos; **his thoughts ran to that hot August day in Paris** cette chaude journée d'août à Paris lui revint à l'esprit

(**f**) *(words, text)* **how does that last verse run?** c'est quoi la dernière strophe?; **their argument** *or* **reasoning runs something like this** voici plus ou moins leur raisonnement; **the conversation ran something like this** voilà en gros ce qui s'est dit

(**g**) *(spread → rumour, news)* se répandre

(**h**) *(flow → river, water, tap, nose)* couler; **let the water run until it's hot** laisse couler l'eau jusqu'à ce qu'elle soit chaude; **the water's run cold** l'eau est froide au robinet; **you've let the water run cold** tu as laissé couler l'eau trop longtemps, elle est devenue froide; **your bath is running** ton bain est en train de couler; **your nose is running** tu as le nez qui coule; **the cold made our eyes run** le froid nous piquait les yeux; **the hot water runs along/down this pipe** l'eau chaude passe/descend dans ce tuyau; **their faces were running with sweat** leurs visages ruisselaient de transpiration; **tears ran down her face** des larmes coulaient sur son visage; **the streets were running with blood** le sang coulait dans les rues; **the river ran red with blood** les eaux de la rivière étaient rouges de sang; **the Jari runs into the Amazon** le Jari se jette dans l'Amazone

(**i**) *(butter, ice cream, wax)* fondre; *(cheese)* couler; *(paint)* goutter; **her mascara had run** son mascara avait coulé

(**j**) *(in wash → colour, fabric)* déteindre; **wash that dress separately, the colour might run** lave cette robe à part, elle pourrait déteindre

(**k**) *(operate → engine, machine, business)* marcher, fonctionner; **to run on** *or* **off electricity/gas/diesel** fonctionner à l'électricité/au gaz/au diesel; **this machine runs off the mains** cet appareil se branche sur (le) secteur; **the tape recorder was still running** le magnétophone était encore en marche; **leave the engine running** laissez tourner le moteur; **the engine is running smoothly** le moteur tourne rond; **the new assembly line is up and running** la nouvelle chaîne de montage est en service; *Comput* **do not interrupt the program while it is running** ne pas interrompre le programme en cours d'exécution; *Comput* **this software runs on DOS** ce logiciel tourne sous DOS; *Comput* **running at...** cadencé à...; *Fig* **everything is running smoothly** tout marche très bien

(**l**) *(public transport)* circuler; **this train doesn't run/only runs on Sundays** ce train ne circule pas/ne circule que le dimanche; **some bus lines run all night** certaines lignes d'autobus sont en service toute la nuit; **the buses stop running at midnight** après minuit il n'y a plus de bus; **trains running between London and Manchester** trains qui circulent entre Londres et Manchester; **trains running to Calais are cancelled** les trains à destination de Calais sont annulés; **he took the tube that runs through Clapham** il prit la ligne de métro qui passe par Clapham

(**m**) *(last)* durer; *(be valid → contract)* être *ou* rester valide; *(→ agreement)* être *ou* rester en vigueur; *Fin (→ interest)* courir; **the sales run from the beginning to the end of January** les soldes durent du début à la fin janvier; **the sales have only another two days to run** il ne reste que deux jours de soldes; **the meeting ran for an hour longer than expected** la réunion a duré une heure de plus que prévu; **I'd like the ad to run for a week** je voudrais que l'annonce passe pendant une semaine; **the lease has another year to run** le bail n'expire pas avant un an; **your subscription will run for two years** votre abonnement sera valable deux ans; **interest runs from 1 January** les intérêts courent à partir du 1 janvier

(**n**) *Cin & Theat (be performed → play, film)* être à l'affiche; **the play has been running for a year** la pièce est à l'affiche depuis un an; **the film is currently running in Hull** le film est actuellement sur les écrans à Hull; **his new musical should run and run!** sa nouvelle comédie musicale devrait tenir l'affiche pendant des mois!; *TV* **this soap opera has been running for twenty years** ça fait vingt ans que ce feuilleton est diffusé; **America's longest-running TV series** la plus longue série télévisée américaine

(**o**) *(occur → inherited trait, illness)* **twins run in our family** les jumeaux sont courants dans la famille; **heart disease runs in the family** les maladies cardiaques sont fréquentes dans notre famille

(**p**) *(range)* aller; **the colours run from dark blue to bright green** les couleurs vont du bleu foncé au vert vif

(**q**) *(indicating current state or condition)* **to run high** *(sea)* être grosse *ou* houleuse; **feelings** *or* **tempers were running high** les esprits étaient échauffés; **their ammunition was running low** ils commençaient à manquer de munitions; **our stores are running low** nos provisions s'épuisent *ou* tirent à leur fin; **he's running scared** il a la frousse; **to be running late** être en retard, avoir du retard; **programmes are running ten minutes late** les émissions ont toutes dix minutes de retard; **sorry I can't stop, I'm running a bit late** désolé, je ne peux pas rester, je suis un peu en retard; **events are running in our favour** les événements tournent en notre faveur; **inflation was running at 18 percent** le taux d'inflation était de 18 pour cent

(**r**) *(be candidate, stand)* se présenter; **to run for president** *or* **the presidency** se présenter aux élections présidentielles, être candidat aux élections présidentielles *ou* à la présidence; **to run for office** se porter candidat; **she's running on a law-and-order ticket** elle se présente aux élections avec un programme basé sur la lutte contre l'insécurité; **he ran against Reagan in 1984** il s'est présenté contre Reagan en 1984

(**s**) *(drive)* faire un tour *ou* une promenade; **why don't we run down to the coast/up to London?** si on faisait un tour jusqu'à la mer/jusqu'à Londres?

(**t**) *Naut (boat)* **to run (before the wind)** filer vent arrière; **to run aground** échouer; *Fig (project, plan)* capoter

(**u**) *(ladder → stocking, tights)* filer

(**v**) *(salmon)* remonter les rivières

(**w**) *(tide)* monter

►**run about** *vi Br* courir (çà et là); **I've been running about all day looking for you!** j'ai passé ma journée à te chercher partout!

►**run across 1** *vt insep (meet → acquaintance)* rencontrer par hasard, tomber sur; *(find → book, reference)* trouver par hasard, tomber sur

2 *vi* traverser en courant

►**run after** *vt insep also Fig* courir après; **it's not like her to run after a man** ce n'est pas son genre de courir après un homme; **she spends half her life running after her kids** elle passe son temps à être derrière les enfants; **he's got all these assistants running after him the whole time** il a tout un tas d'assistants qui passent sans arrêt derrière ce qu'il fait

►**run along** *vi (go away)* s'en aller, partir; **it's getting late, I must be running along** il se fait tard, il faut que j'y aille; **run along to bed now, children!** allez les enfants, au lit maintenant!

►**run around** *vi Fam* (**a**) *(from place to place)* courir (çà et là)❑; **I've been running around all day looking for you!** j'ai passé ma journée à te chercher partout!❑

(**b**) *(be unfaithful → husband)* courir après les femmes; *(→ wife)* courir après les hommes; **he was sure his wife was running around** il était sûr que sa femme le trompait❑

►**run around with** *vt insep Fam (be friendly with)* fréquenter❑; *(have affair with)* sortir avec❑; **he's always running around with other women** il est toujours en train de courir après d'autres femmes

►**run away** *vi* (**a**) *(flee)* se sauver, s'enfuir; **their son has run away from home** leur fils a fait une fugue; **I'll be with you in a minute, don't run away** je serai à toi dans un instant, ne te sauve pas; **run away and play now, children** allez jouer ailleurs, les enfants; *Fig* **to run away from one's responsibilities** fuir ses responsabilités; **to run away from the facts** se refuser à l'évidence

(**b**) *(elope)* partir

►**run away with** *vt insep* (**a**) *(secretly or illegally)* partir avec; **he ran away with his best friend's wife** il est parti avec la femme de son meilleur ami; **he ran away with the takings** il est parti avec la caisse

(**b**) *(overwhelm)* **don't let your excitement run away with you** gardez votre calme; **she tends to let her imagination run away with her** elle a tendance à se laisser emporter par son imagination

(**c**) *(get → idea)* **don't go running away with the idea** *or* **the notion that it will be easy** n'allez pas vous imaginer que ce sera facile

(**d**) *(win → race, match)* emporter haut la main; *(→ prize)* remporter; **they ran away with nearly all the medals** ils ont remporté presque toutes les médailles

►**run back 1** *vt sep* (**a**) *(drive back)* raccompagner (en voiture); **she ran me back home** elle m'a ramené *ou* raccompagné chez moi en voiture; **he ran me back on his motorbike** il m'a raccompagné en moto

(**b**) *(rewind → tape, film)* rembobiner

2 *vi* (**a**) *(return)* retourner *ou* revenir en courant; *Fam* **to come running back** *(errant husband etc)* revenir❑

(**b**) *(review)* **to run back over sth** passer qch en revue

►**run by** *vt sep* **to run sth by sb** *(submit)* soumettre qch à qn; **you'd better run that by the committee** vous feriez mieux de demander l'avis du comité; **run that by me again** répétez-moi ça

►**run down 1** *vt sep* (**a**) *(reduce, diminish → gen)* réduire; *(→ number of employees)* diminuer; *(→ stocks)* laisser s'épuiser; *(→ industry, factory)* fermer progressivement; **they are running down their military presence in Africa** ils réduisent leur présence militaire en Afrique; **the government was accused of running down the steel industry** le gouvernement a été accusé de laisser dépérir la sidérurgie; **you've run the battery down** vous avez déchargé la pile; *(of car)* vous avez vidé *ou* déchargé la batterie, vous avez mis la batterie à plat

(**b**) *Fam (criticize, denigrate)* rabaisser❑; **they're always running her friends down** ils passent leur temps à dire du mal de *ou* à dénigrer ses amis❑; **stop running yourself down all the time** cesse de te rabaisser constamment (**c**) *(in car → pedestrian, animal)* renverser, écraser; **he was run down by a bus** il s'est fait renverser par un bus

(**d**) *(track down → animal, criminal)* (traquer et) capturer; *(→ person, object)* dénicher; **I finally ran down the reference in the library** j'ai fini par dénicher la référence à la bibliothèque

2 *vi* (**a**) *(person)* descendre en courant

(**b**) *(clock, machine)* s'arrêter; *(battery → through use)* s'user; *(→ through a fault)* se décharger; **the batteries in the radio are beginning to run down** les piles de la radio commencent à être usées

▶**run in 1** *vt sep* (**a**) *Br (car, engine)* roder

(**b**) *Fam (arrest)* pincer

2 *vi* (**a**) *(person)* entrer en courant

(**b**) *Br (car, engine)* **running in** en rodage

▶**run into** *vt insep* (**a**) *(encounter → problem, difficulty)* rencontrer

(**b**) *(meet → acquaintance)* rencontrer (par hasard), tomber sur; **to run into debt** faire des dettes, s'endetter

(**c**) *(collide with → of car, driver)* percuter, rentrer dans; **I ran into a lamppost** je suis rentrée dans un réverbère; **you should be more careful, you nearly ran into me!** tu devrais faire attention, tu as failli me rentrer dedans!

(**d**) *(amount to)* s'élever à; **debts running into millions of dollars** des dettes qui s'élèvent à des millions de dollars; **takings run into five figures** la recette atteint les cinq chiffres

(**e**) *(merge into)* se fondre dans, se confondre avec; **the red runs into orange** le rouge devient orange; **the words began to run into each other before my eyes** les mots commençaient à se confondre devant mes yeux

▶**run off 1** *vt sep* (**a**) *(print)* tirer, imprimer; *(photocopy)* photocopier; **run me off five copies of this report** faites-moi cinq copies de ce rapport

(**b**) *(write quickly) (article)* pondre

(**c**) *Sport (race)* disputer; **the heats will be run off tomorrow** les éliminatoires se disputeront demain

(**d**) *(lose → excess weight, fat)* perdre en courant

(**e**) *(liquid)* laisser s'écouler

2 *vi* (**a**) *(flee)* se sauver, s'enfuir; **I'll be with you in a minute, don't run off** je serai à toi dans un instant, ne te sauve pas

(**b**) *(liquid)* s'écouler

▶**run on 1** *vt sep (lines of writing)* ne pas découper en paragraphes; *(letters, words)* ne pas séparer, lier

2 *vi* (**a**) *(continue)* continuer, durer; *(drag on)* s'éterniser; **the play ran on for hours** la pièce a duré des heures; **the discussion ran on for an extra hour** la discussion a duré une heure de plus que prévu

(**b**) *Fam (talk non-stop)* parler sans cesse ❑; **he does run on rather** quand il est parti celui-là, il ne s'arrête plus; **he can run on for hours if you let him** si tu le laisses faire il peut tenir le crachoir pendant des heures

(**c**) *(line of text)* suivre sans alinéa; *(verse)* enjamber

▶**run out 1** *vt sep* (**a**) *(cable, rope)* laisser filer

(**b**) *(in cricket)* **to run a batsman out** mettre un batteur hors jeu

2 *vi* (**a**) *(person, animal)* sortir en courant; *(liquid)* s'écouler

(**b**) *(be used up → supplies, money etc)* s'épuiser, (venir à) manquer; *(→ time)* filer; **hurry up, time is running out!** dépêchez-vous, il ne reste plus beaucoup de temps!; **their luck finally ran out** la chance a fini par tourner, leur chance n'a pas duré

(**c**) *(expire → contract, passport, agreement)* expirer, venir à expiration

▶**run out of** *vt insep* manquer de; **we're running out of ammunition** nous commençons à manquer de munitions; **we're running out of sugar** nous allons nous trouver à court de sucre; **he's run out of money** il n'a plus d'argent; **to run out of patience** être à bout de patience; **to run out of petrol** tomber en panne d'essence

▶**run out on** *vt insep (spouse, colleague)* laisser tomber, abandonner; **she ran out on her husband** elle a quitté son mari; **his assistants all ran out on him** ses assistants l'ont tous abandonné *ou* laissé tomber

▶**run over 1** *vt sep (pedestrian, animal)* écraser; **I nearly got run over** j'ai failli me faire écraser; **he's been run over** il s'est fait écraser; **the car ran over his legs** la voiture lui est passé sur les jambes

2 *vt insep* (**a**) *(review)* revoir; *(rehearse)* répéter; *(recap)* récapituler; **let's run over the arguments one more time before the meeting** reprenons les arguments une dernière fois avant la réunion; **could you run over the main points for us?** pourriez-vous nous récapituler les principaux points?

(**b**) *(exceed)* **to run over the allotted time** excéder le temps imparti

3 *vi* (**a**) *(overflow)* déborder; *Literary* **my cup runneth over** je nage dans le bonheur; **to run over with energy/enthusiasm** déborder d'énergie/d'enthousiasme

(**b**) *(run late)* dépasser l'heure; *Rad & TV* dépasser le temps d'antenne, déborder sur le temps d'antenne; **the programme ran over by twenty minutes** l'émission a dépassé son temps d'antenne de vingt minutes

▶**run past 1** *vt sep* = **run by**

2 *vi* passer en courant

▶**run through 1** *vt insep* (**a**) *(cross → of person)* traverser en courant; *Fig* **money runs through his fingers like water** l'argent lui brûle les doigts

(**b**) *(pervade → of thought, feeling)* **a strange idea ran through my mind** une idée étrange m'a traversé l'esprit; **a thrill of excitement ran through her** un frisson d'émotion la parcourut; **an angry murmur ran through the crowd** des murmures de colère parcoururent la foule; **his words kept running through my head** ses paroles ne cessaient de retentir dans ma tête; **an air of melancholy runs through the whole film** une atmosphère de mélancolie imprègne tout le film

(**c**) *(review)* revoir; *(rehearse)* répéter; *(recap)* récapituler; **she ran through the arguments in her mind** elle repassa les arguments dans sa tête; **let's just run through the procedure one more time** reprenons une dernière fois la marche à suivre; **I'll run through your speech with you** je vous ferai répéter votre discours

(**d**) *(read quickly)* parcourir (des yeux), jeter un coup d'œil sur

(**e**) *(use up → money)* dépenser; *(→ case of wine, coffee)* consommer; *(squander → fortune)* gaspiller; **he runs through a dozen shirts a week** il lui faut une douzaine de chemises par semaine

2 *vt sep* **to run sb through (with a sword)** transpercer qn (d'un coup d'épée)

▶**run to** *vt insep* (**a**) *(amount to)* se chiffrer à; **her essay ran to twenty pages** sa dissertation faisait vingt pages

(**b**) *Br (afford, be enough for)* **your salary should run to a new computer** ton salaire devrait te permettre d'acheter un nouvel ordinateur; **the budget won't run to champagne** le budget ne nous permet pas d'acheter du champagne

▶**run up 1** *vt sep* (**a**) *(debt, bill)* laisser s'accumuler; **I've run up a huge overdraft** j'ai un découvert énorme

(**b**) *(flag)* hisser

(**c**) *(sew quickly)* coudre rapidement *ou* à la hâte

2 *vi (climb rapidly)* monter en courant; *(approach)* approcher en courant; **a young man ran up to me** un jeune homme s'approcha de moi en courant

▶**run up against** *vt insep (encounter)* se heurter à; **we've run up against some problems** nous nous sommes heurtés à quelques problèmes

runabout ['rʌnəbaʊt] *n Fam (car)* petite voiture ❑ *f*, voiture *f* de ville ❑; *(boat)* runabout ❑ *m*; *(plane)* petit avion ❑ *m*

runaround ['rʌnəraʊnd] *n Fam* **to give sb the runaround** raconter des salades à qn; *(lover, husband, wife)* tromper qn ❑

runaway ['rʌnəweɪ] **1** *n (gen)* fugitif(ive) *m,f*; *(child, teenager)* fugueur(euse) *m,f*; *(horse)* cheval *m* emballé *ou* échappé

2 *adj* (**a**) *(convict)* fugitif; *(child, teenager)* fugueur; *(horse)* emballé, échappé; *(train, car)* fou (folle); **a runaway marriage** un mariage clandestin

(**b**) *(inflation)* galopant; *(success)* fou (folle); **her book was this year's runaway bestseller** son livre a été le best-seller de l'année; **a runaway victory** une victoire remportée haut la main

rundown ['rʌndaʊn] *n* (**a**) *(reduction)* réduction *f*, déclin *m*; **the rundown of the coal industry** le déclin de l'industrie houillère (**b**) *Fam (report)* compte rendu ❑ *m*; **to give sb a rundown of** *or* **on sth** mettre qn au courant de qch ❑

run-down *adj* (**a**) *(tired)* vanné, crevé; **I think you're just a bit run-down** je pense que c'est juste un peu de surmenage; **I'm feeling very run-down** je me sens complètement à plat (**b**) *(building)* délabré (**c**) *(battery)* à plat

rune [ru:n] *n* rune *f*; **to read the runes** déchiffrer les runes; *Fig* **if I'm reading the runes correctly, I think that...** si je ne me trompe pas, il me semble que...

run-flat *adj (tyre)* anti-crevaison

rung [rʌŋ] **1** *pp of* **ring**

2 *n (of ladder)* barreau *m*, échelon *m*; *(of chair)* barreau *m*; *Fig (in hierarchy)* échelon *m*; **he's on the top rung of his profession** il a atteint l'échelon le plus élevé dans sa profession; **it's the first rung on the ladder to becoming a qualified vet** c'est la première étape pour devenir vétérinaire

runic ['ru:nɪk] *adj* runique

run-in *n* (**a**) *Fam (quarrel)* engueulade *f*, prise *f* de bec; **I had a bit of a run-in with the police last week** j'ai eu un petit accrochage avec la police la semaine dernière (**b**) *Sport* élan *m*; **she only takes a short run-in** elle ne prend pas beaucoup d'élan (**c**) *(period before)* période *f* préparatoire; **the run-in to the elections** la période qui précède les élections *ou* pré-électorale

runnel ['rʌnəl] *n Literary* ruisselet *m*, ru *m*

runner ['rʌnə(r)] *n* (**a**) *(in race → person)* coureur(euse) *m,f*; *(→ horse)* partant *m*; **he's a good/fast runner** il court bien/vite; **the runners and riders for the 3.00 race** les partants pour la course de 15 heures; *Fig* **the runners and riders** *(in election)* les candidats *mpl*; *(in competition)* les concurrents *mpl*

(**b**) *(messenger)* coursier(ère) *m,f*; *(for film crew)* stagiaire *mf*, grouillot *m*

(**c**) *(usu in cpds) (smuggler)* contrebandier(ère) *m,f*, trafiquant(e) *m,f*; **drug runner** trafiquant(e) *m,f* de drogue

(**d**) *(for door, car seat)* glissière *f*; *(for drawer)* coulisseau *m*; *(of sledge)* patin *m*; *(of skate)* lame *f*

(**e**) *Bot* coulant *m*, stolon *m*; *(on strawberry)* marcotte *f*

(**f**) *(for table)* chemin *m* de table; *(carpet → for stairs)* chemin *m* d'escalier; *(→ for passage)* chemin *m* de couloir

(**g**) *(for desk)* rallonge *f*

(**h**) *Br Fam (idiom)* **to do a runner** *(run away)* décaniller, se débiner; *(leave without paying)* partir sans payer

▶▶ *Br* ***runner bean*** haricot *m* d'Espagne

runner-up (*pl* **runners-up**) *n* second(e) *m,f*; **her novel was runner-up for the Prix Goncourt** son roman était le second favori pour le prix Goncourt; **there will be fifty consolation prizes for the runners-up** il y aura cinquante lots de consolation pour les autres gagnants

running ['rʌnɪŋ] **1** *n* (**a**) *(on foot)* course *f* (à pied); **I like running** j'aime courir; **I go running every weekend** je vais courir tous les week-ends; **running is forbidden in the corridors** il est interdit de courir dans les couloirs; **no running** *(sign)* défense de courir; **to make the running** *Sport* mener le train; *Fig* prendre l'initiative; **to make all the running** *(in contest)* être en tête; *(in relationship)* toujours prendre les devants; **to be in the running for sth** être sur les rangs pour qch, être dans la course pour qch; **he may not win but he's in the running** il ne gagnera peut-être pas, mais il est dans la course; **he's in the running to get the job** il a des chances d'obtenir le poste; **to be out of the running** ne plus être dans la course

(**b**) *(management)* gestion *f*, direction *f*; *(organization)* organisation *f*; **she leaves the day-to-day running of the department to her assistant** elle laisse son assistant s'occuper de la gestion quotidienne du service

(**c**) *(working, functioning)* marche *f*, fonctionnement *m*; **we apologize for the late running of this train** nous vous prions d'excuser le retard de ce train

(**d**) *(operating)* conduite *f*, maniement *m*

(**e**) *(usu in cpds) (smuggling)* contrebande *f*; **drug running** trafic *m* de drogue

(**f**) *(of water)* écoulement *m*, ruissellement *m*

(**g**) *Comput (of program)* exécution *f*

2 *comp (shorts, vest)* de course (à pied)

3 *adj* (**a**) *(at a run → person, animal)* courant, qui court; **to take a running kick at sth** prendre son élan pour donner un coup de pied dans qch

(**b**) *(after n) (consecutive)* de suite; **three times/weeks/years running** trois fois/semaines/années de suite

(**c**) *(continuous)* continu, ininterrompu

(**d**) *(flowing)* **the sound of running water** *(stream)* le bruit de l'eau qui coule; **to wash sth under running water** laver qch à l'eau courante; **all the rooms have running water** toutes les chambres ont l'eau courante; **a running tap** un robinet qui coule; **a running sore** *Med* une plaie suppurante; *Fig* une source de problèmes

(**e**) *(working, operating)* **in running order** en état de marche; **to be up and running** être opérationnel

(**f**) *(handwriting)* cursif

►► *Fin* ***running account*** compte *m* courant; *Am* ***running back*** *(in American football)* demi *m* à l'attaque; ***running battle*** lutte *f* continuelle; **they have a running battle about housework** ils se bagarrent continuellement à propos des travaux ménagers; ***running board*** marchepied *m*; *Rad & TV* ***running commentary*** commentaire *m* en direct; *Fig* **she gave us a running commentary on what the neighbours were doing** elle nous a expliqué en détail ce que les voisins étaient en train de faire; ***running costs*** frais *mpl* d'exploitation; *(of car)* frais *mpl* d'entretien; ***running down*** *(criticism → of person, play)* dénigrement *m*; *(reduction → of staff)* réduction *f*, diminution *f*; *(→ of industry, factory)* réduction *f* *ou* diminution *f* de la production; *Typ* ***running head*** titre *m* courant; ***running jump*** saut *m* avec élan; *Fam* **(go) take a running jump** *or Am* **a running jump at the moon!** va te faire voir (ailleurs)!, va voir ailleurs si j'y suis; ***running knot*** nœud *m* coulant; *Naut* ***running lights*** feux *mpl* de position; *Am Pol* ***running mate*** candidat(e) *m,f* à la vice-présidence; *TV* ***running order*** ordre *m* de passage; ***running repairs*** réparations *fpl* courantes; ***running shoe*** chaussure *f* de course; *Sewing* ***running stitch*** point *m* droit; *Typ* ***running title*** titre *m* courant; ***running total*** total *m* cumulé; **to keep a running total of sth** calculer qch au fur et à mesure; **the running total of the number of casualties is 32** on dénombre jusqu'à présent 32 victimes; ***running track*** piste *f*

runny [ˈrʌnɪ] *(compar* **runnier**, *superl* **runniest**) *adj* (**a**) *(sauce, honey)* liquide; *(liquid)* (très) fluide; *(omelette)* baveux; **a runny egg** un œuf dont le jaune coule (**b**) *(nose)* qui coule; *(eye)* qui pleure; **I've got a runny nose** j'ai le nez qui coule

run-off *n* (**a**) *Sport (final)* finale *f*; *(after tie)* belle *f*; *Pol* élection *f* pour départager deux candidats (**b**) *(water)* trop-plein *m*

►► *Pol* ***run-off election*** élection *f* pour départager deux candidats

run-of-the-mill *adj* ordinaire, banal

run-on *n* (**a**) *Typ (text)* texte *m* composé à la suite *(sans alinéa)* (**b**) *Typ (extra quantity of books)* exemplaires *mpl* supplémentaires (**c**) *(in dictionary)* sous-entrée *f*

run-out *n* (**a**) *Ski* zone *f* d'arrivée (**b**) *(of film, tape)* amorce *f* de fin de bobine

run-proof, run-resist *adj (tights)* indémaillable

runt [rʌnt] *n* (**a**) *(animal)* avorton *m* (**b**) *Fam (person)* avorton *m*

run-through *n (review)* révision *f*; *(rehearsal)* répétition *f*; *(recap)* récapitulation *f*; **to have a run-through** *(rehearse)* répéter

runtime [ˈrʌntaɪm] *n Comput*

►► ***runtime system*** système *m* en phase d'exécution; ***runtime version*** version *f* exécutable

run-up *n* (**a**) *Sport* élan *m*; **she only takes a short run-up** elle ne prend pas beaucoup d'élan (**b**) *(period before)* période *f* préparatoire; **the run-up to the elections** la période qui précède les élections *ou* pré-électorale (**c**) *Am (increase)* augmentation *f*, hausse *f*

runway [ˈrʌnˌweɪ] *n* (**a**) *Aviat* piste *f* (d'atterrissage *ou* d'envol) (**b**) *Sport* piste *f* d'élan (**c**) *Am (catwalk)* passerelle *f* (de défilé de mode)

►► *Aviat* ***runway lights*** feux *mpl* de piste

rupee [ruːˈpiː] *n* roupie *f*

rupiah [ruːˈpɪə] *n Med* rupiah *f*

rupture [ˈrʌptʃə(r)] **1** *n* (**a**) *(split → gen)* rupture *f*; *Med (→ of artery)* éclatement *m*, rupture *f* (**b**) *Med (hernia)* hernie *f*

2 *vt* (**a**) *(split)* rompre; *Med (blood vessel, appendix)* se rompre; *(spleen)* se faire éclater (**b**) *Med* **to rupture oneself** se faire une hernie

3 *vi (split)* éclater, se rompre; *Med (blood vessel, appendix)* se rompre; *(spleen)* éclater

ruptured [ˈrʌptʃəd] *adj Med (organ)* hernié; *(blood vessel, appendix)* rompu; *(spleen)* éclaté

rural [ˈrʊərəl] *adj (life, economy, community, area)* rural; *(landscape, scene, atmosphere)* champêtre

►► *Br Rel* ***rural dean*** doyen *m* rural; *Br* ***rural district*** ≃ canton *m*; *Br* ***rural district council*** conseil *m* municipal rural; ***rural planning*** aménagement *m* rural; *Am* ***rural route*** = route de campagne desservie par le facteur

rurally [ˈrʊərəlɪ] *adv* à la campagne

Ruritania [ˌrʊərɪˈteɪnɪə] *n* = nom d'un petit pays imaginaire d'Europe centrale, théâtre par excellence d'intrigues et d'aventures romanesques

rusa [ˈruːsə] *n Zool* sambar *m*

ruse [ruːz] *n* ruse *f*; **it's just a ruse to get us to agree** ce n'est qu'une ruse pour obtenir notre accord

RUSH [rʌʃ]

précipitation	► **1 (a)**
ruée	► **1 (b), (c)**
heure de pointe	► **1 (d)**
attaque	► **1 (e)**
expédier	► **3 (a)**
faire à la hâte	► **3 (a)**
bousculer	► **3 (b)**
presser	► **3 (b)**
attaquer	► **3 (c)**
transporter d'urgence	► **3 (d)**
se précipiter	► **4 (a)**
se ruer	► **4 (a)**
s'engouffrer	► **4 (b)**

1 *n* (**a**) *(hurry)* précipitation *f*, hâte *f*; **to do sth in a rush** faire qch à la hâte; **to be in a rush** être (très) pressé; **what's the rush?** pourquoi tant de précipitation?; **there's no (great) rush** rien ne presse; **it'll be a bit of a rush, but we should make it** il faudra se dépêcher mais on devrait y arriver; **in the rush to finish the article, he forgot to check the spelling** dans sa hâte de terminer l'article, il a oublié de vérifier l'orthographe; **we left in such a rush that...** nous sommes partis avec une telle précipitation que...; **your essay was written in too much of a rush** vous avez fait votre dissertation à la va-vite

(**b**) *(dash, stampede)* ruée *f*, bousculade *f*; **there was a rush for the door** tout le monde s'est rué *ou* précipité vers la porte; **he made a rush for the exit** il s'est rué *ou* précipité vers la sortie; **I lost a shoe in the rush** j'ai perdu une chaussure dans la bousculade; **let's leave before the rush starts** partons avant la bousculade

(**c**) *(great demand)* ruée *f* (**on** sur); **there was a rush for the papers** on s'arrachait les journaux; **there's been a rush on** *or* **for tickets** les gens se sont rués sur les billets; **there's a rush on that particular model** ce modèle est très demandé

(**d**) *(busy period)* heure *f* de pointe *ou* d'affluence; **the six o'clock rush** la foule de dix-huit heures; **I try to avoid the lunchtime rush** j'essaie d'éviter la foule de l'heure du déjeuner; **we had a rush (of customers) in the afternoon** les clients sont arrivés en masse l'après-midi; **the holiday rush** *(leaving)* les grands départs *mpl* en vacances; *(returning)* les embouteillages *mpl* des retours de vacances

(**e**) *(attack)* attaque *f*, assaut *m*; **to make a rush at** *or* **for sb** se jeter sur qn

(**f**) *(surge → of water)* jaillissement *m*; *(→ of air)* bouffée *f*; *(→ of emotion, nausea)* accès *m*, montée *f*; **I could hear nothing above the rush of water** le bruit de l'eau (qui bouillonnait) m'empêchait d'entendre quoi que ce soit; **she had a rush of blood to the head** le sang lui est monté à la tête

(**g**) *Bot* jonc *m*; *(for chair)* jonc *m*, paille *f*; **the floor is covered with rush matting** des nattes (de jonc) recouvrent le sol

(**h**) *Fam Drugs slang (from drugs)* flash *m*; *Fam* **I got a real rush from that coffee** ce café m'a donné un coup de fouet; **to get a head rush** avoir la tête qui tourne

2 *adj* (**a**) *(urgent)* urgent; **it's a rush job for Japan** c'est un travail urgent pour le Japon

(**b**) *(hurried)* **I'm afraid it's a bit of a rush job** je suis désolé, le travail a été fait un peu vite *ou* a été un peu bâclé

(**c**) *(busy → period)* de pointe, d'affluence

3 *vt* (**a**) *(do quickly)* expédier; *(do overhastily)* faire à la hâte *ou* à la va-vite; **I don't like having to rush my work** je n'aime pas devoir expédier mon travail; **they had obviously rushed the work** à l'évidence, ils avaient travaillé trop vite; **I'll rush it off on the computer** l'ordinateur me fera ça en deux minutes; **don't rush your food** ne mange pas trop vite; **a horse that rushes its fences** un cheval qui se précipite sur les obstacles avec trop d'impétuosité; *Fig* **don't rush your fences!** réfléchissez donc!

(**b**) *(cause to hurry)* bousculer, presser; *(pressurize)* faire pression sur, forcer la main à; **don't rush me!** ne me bouscule pas!; **to rush sb into sth** *or* **doing sth** forcer qn à faire qch à la hâte; **don't be rushed into signing** ne signez pas sous la pression; **let's not rush things** ne nous précipitons pas

(**c**) *(attack → person)* attaquer, agresser; *(→ place)* attaquer, prendre d'assaut; **a group of prisoners rushed the guards** un groupe de prisonniers s'attaqua aux gardiens

(**d**) *(transport quickly)* transporter d'urgence; *(send quickly)* envoyer *ou* expédier d'urgence; **the injured were rushed to hospital** les blessés ont été transportés d'urgence à l'hôpital; **they rushed a first aid team to the site** ils ont envoyé en toute hâte une équipe de premiers secours sur les lieux; **please rush me your new catalogue** veuillez me faire parvenir au plus vite votre nouveau catalogue

(**e**) *Am Fam (court)* courtiser ❑

(**f**) *Br Fam (charge a lot)* **how much did they rush you for that?** combien est-ce qu'ils t'ont fait cracher pour ça?

4 *vi* (**a**) *(hurry, dash → individual)* se précipiter; *(→ crowd)* se ruer, se précipiter; *(→ vehicle)* foncer; **I rushed home after work** je me suis précipité chez moi après le travail; **people rushed out of the blazing house** les gens se ruèrent hors de la maison en flammes; **there's no need to rush** pas besoin de se presser; **passers-by rushed to help the injured man** des passants se sont précipités au secours du blessé; **he came rushing down the stairs** il a dégringolé l'escalier; **I must rush** il faut que je me dépêche; **the dog rushed at me** le chien s'est précipité *ou* jeté sur moi; **a group of demonstrators rushed at the speaker** un groupe de manifestants se rua sur l'orateur; **to rush forward** se précipiter (en avant); **he rushed past** il est passé à toute allure; *Prov* **fools rush in (where angels fear to tread)** = agir sans réfléchir peut avoir des conséquences fâcheuses

(**b**) *(surge → air)* s'engouffrer; *(→ liquid)* jaillir; **the cold water rushed over her bare feet** l'eau froide déferla sur ses pieds nus; **I could hear the wind rushing through the trees** j'entendais le vent s'engouffrer dans les branches; **the blood rushed to her head** le sang lui est monté à la tête; **I felt the blood rush to my face** j'ai senti le sang me monter au visage (**c**) *(in American football)* **he rushed for 137 yards** il a fait une course de 137 yards avec le ballon

5 rushes *npl Cin* rushes *mpl*, épreuves *fpl* de tournage

►► ***rush candle*** chandelle *f* à mèche de jonc; *Br Fam* ***rush goalie*** gardien *m* de but volant ❑; ***rush hour*** heure *f* de pointe *ou* d'affluence; **I never travel at rush hour** je ne me déplace jamais aux heures de pointe; ***rush job*** travail *m* de première urgence; ***rush light*** chandelle *f* à mèche de jonc; ***rush mat*** natte *f* (de jonc); ***rush order*** commande *f* urgente; *Am Univ* ***rush week*** = semaine pendant laquelle les associations d'étudiants américains essaient de recruter de nouveaux membres

►**rush about, rush around** *vi* courir çà et là; **stop rushing about!** arrête de courir dans tous les sens!

►**rush away 1** *vt sep (person)* emmener d'urgence

2 *vi* partir précipitamment; **do you have to rush away?** est-ce qu'il faut vraiment que vous partiez aussi vite?

►**rush in** *vi* entrer précipitamment *ou* à toute allure; *Fig* **you always rush in without thinking first** tu fonces toujours tête baissée sans réfléchir

►**rush into 1** *vt insep* **to rush into a room** entrer précipitamment *ou* faire irruption dans une pièce; *Fig* **to rush into things** agir sans réfléchir; **now don't rush into anything** ne va pas foncer tête baissée; **to rush into a decision** prendre une décision à la hâte; **to rush into marriage/divorce** se marier/divorcer trop vite

2 *vt sep* **to rush sb into sth** forcer qn à faire qch trop vite; **to be rushed into doing sth** être obligé *ou* contraint à faire qch précipitamment; **to be rushed into a decision/answer** être contraint à *ou* obligé de prendre une décision/donner une réponse à la hâte; **don't let yourself be rushed into anything** ne te sens pas obligé de faire quoi que ce soit à la hâte

►**rush off** *vi & vt sep* = **rush away**

►**rush out 1** *vt sep (book, new product, advertisement)* sortir rapidement; *(troops)* envoyer d'urgence

2 *vi* sortir précipitamment *ou* à toute allure

►**rush through** *vt sep (job)* expédier; *(goods ordered)* envoyer d'urgence; *(order, application)* traiter d'urgence; *(bill, legislation)* faire voter à la hâte

►**rush up 1** *vt sep* envoyer d'urgence; **troops were rushed up as reinforcements** on envoya d'urgence des troupes en renfort

2 *vi* accourir

---

rushed [rʌʃt] *adj (person)* bousculé; *(work)* fait à la hâte *ou* à la va-vite, bâclé; **she was too rushed to stay and talk** elle était trop pressée pour rester bavarder; **he doesn't like to be rushed** il n'aime pas qu'on le bouscule; **the meal was a bit rushed** on a dû se dépêcher pour manger

rushee [rʌ'ʃiː] *n Am* bizut *m*

rush-hour *adj (crowds, traffic)* des heures de pointe *ou* d'affluence

rushing ['rʌʃɪŋ] *adj (wind, river)* déchaîné, *Literary* impétueux

rusk [rʌsk] *n* = biscuit pour bébés

russet ['rʌsɪt] **1** *n* (**a**) *(colour)* brun *m* roux *inv* (**b**) *(apple)* reinette *f*

2 *adj (colour)* brun roux *(inv)*

Russia ['rʌʃə] *n* Russie *f*; **in Russia** en Russie

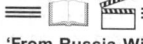

'From Russia With Love' *Fleming, Young* 'Bons baisers de Russie'

Russian ['rʌʃən] **1** *n* (**a**) *(person)* Russe *mf* (**b**) *(language)* russe *m*

2 *adj* russe

3 *comp (embassy)* de Russie; *(history)* de la Russie; *(teacher)* de russe

►► ***Russian dolls*** poupées *fpl* russes, poupées *fpl* gigognes; *Culin* ***Russian dressing*** sauce *f* (de salade) relevée au piment; ***the Russian Federation*** la Fédération de Russie; *Rel* ***the Russian Orthodox Church*** l'Église *f* orthodoxe russe; *Hist* ***the Russian Revolution*** la révolution russe; ***Russian roulette*** roulette *f* russe; *Culin* ***Russian salad*** salade *f* russe; ***Russian service*** *(from silver salver onto plate)* service *m* à la russe; ***the Russian steppes*** les steppes russes; ***Russian tea*** thé *m* russe; *Zool* ***Russian wolfhound*** lévrier *m* russe

Russianization [ˌrʌʃənaɪ'zeɪʃən] *n* russification *f*

Russianize, -ise ['rʌʃənaɪz] *vt* russifier

Russian-speaking *adj* russophone

Russification [ˌrʌsɪfɪ'keɪʃən] *n* russification *f*

Russify ['rʌsɪfaɪ] *vt* russifier

Russky ['rʌskɪ] (*pl* **Russkies**) *n Fam* Ruskof *m*, Ruski *mf*

Russo- ['rʌsəʊ] *pref* russo-

Russophil, Russophile ['rʌsəʊfaɪl] **1** *n* russophile *mf*

2 *adj* russophile

Russophobe ['rʌsəʊfəʊb] **1** *n* russophobe *mf*

2 *adj* russophobe

russula ['rʌsjʊlə] *n Bot* russule *f*

rust [rʌst] **1** *n* (**a**) *(on metal)* & *Bot* rouille *f* (**b**) *(colour)* couleur *f* rouille

2 *adj* **rust (coloured)** rouille *(inv)*

3 *vi* rouiller, se rouiller; **it's completely rusted through** il est complètement mangé par la rouille; **the car was left to rust away** la voiture fut abandonnée à la rouille

4 *vt* rouiller; **badly rusted** très rouillé

►► ***Rust Belt*** = États du Nord des États-Unis (principalement le Michigan et l'Illinois) dont l'industrie (sidérurgie et automobile) a périclité; *Br Fam* ***rust bucket, rust heap*** *(car)* poubelle *f*, tas *m* de feraille; ***rust inhibitor, rust preventer*** antirouille *m*; ***rust red*** rouille *(inv)*

►**rust up** *vi* rouiller, se rouiller; **the hinges have rusted up** les gonds sont bloqués par la rouille

rusted ['rʌstɪd] *adj esp Am* rouillé

rustic ['rʌstɪk] **1** *adj* rustique

2 *n* paysan(anne) *m,f*, campagnard(e) *m,f*

rustically ['rʌstɪkəlɪ] *adv* rustiquement

rusticate ['rʌstɪkeɪt] *Formal* **1** *vt Br Univ (student)* renvoyer *ou* expulser temporairement

2 *vi (retire to country)* se retirer à la campagne; *(live in country)* vivre à la campagne

rustication [ˌrʌstɪ'keɪʃən] *n Br Formal Univ (of student)* renvoi *m* temporaire

rusticity [rʌ'stɪsɪtɪ] *n* rusticité *f*

rustiness ['rʌstɪnɪs] *n* rouille *f*; *Fig* **because of the rustiness of my French** parce que mon français est un peu rouillé

rustle ['rʌsəl] **1** *vi* (**a**) *(leaves)* bruire, frémir; *(silk, dress)* faire frou-frou, froufrouter; *(paper)* froisser; **to hear papers rustling** entendre des froissements de papier; **something was rustling against the window** quelque chose frottait contre la fenêtre; **the leaves rustled in the wind** les feuilles bruissaient dans le vent

(**b**) *(steal cattle)* voler du bétail

2 *vt* (**a**) *(leaves)* faire bruire; *(silk, dress)* faire froufrouter; *(paper)* froisser

(**b**) *(cattle)* voler

3 *n (of leaves)* bruissement *m*, frémissement *m*; *(of silk, dress)* frou-frou *m*; *(of paper)* froissement *m*

►**rustle up** *vt sep Fam (meal)* faire en vitesse ❑; **I could rustle up an omelette for you** je pourrais te faire une omelette en vitesse; **to rustle up some coffee** faire du café ❑; **to rustle up support** rassembler des partisans ❑

rustler ['rʌsələ(r)] *n* (**a**) *(of cattle)* voleur(euse) *m,f* (de bétail); **horse rustler** voleur(euse) *m,f* de chevaux (**b**) *Am Fam (dynamic person)* homme *m*/femme *f* dynamique ❑

rustling ['rʌsəlɪŋ] *n* (**a**) *(of leaves)* bruissement *m*, frémissement *m*; *(of silk, dress)* frou-frou *m*; *(of paper)* froissement *m* (**b**) *(of cattle)* vol *m* (de bétail); **horse rustling** vol *m* de chevaux

rustproof ['rʌstpruːf] **1** *adj (metal, blade)* inoxydable; *(paint)* antirouille *(inv)*

2 *vt* traiter contre la rouille

rustproofing ['rʌstˌpruːfɪŋ] *n (product)* (produit *m*) antirouille *m*; *(process)* traitement *m* antirouille

rust-resistant *adj (metal, blade)* inoxydable; *(paint)* antirouille *(inv)*

rusty ['rʌstɪ] (*compar* **rustier**, *superl* **rustiest**) *adj* (**a**) *(metal)* rouillé; **to get rusty** se rouiller; *Fig* **my French is a bit rusty** mon français est un peu rouillé; **my playing is very/a bit rusty** je suis très/un peu rouillé; **the pianist sounded/the batsman looked a bit rusty** le pianiste était/le batteur semblait un peu rouillé

(**b**) *(colour)* rouille *(inv)*; **a rusty red** un marron rouille

►► ***rusty nail*** *(cocktail)* rusty nail *m (cocktail à base de whisky et de Drambuie®)*

rut [rʌt] (*pt & pp* **rutted**, *cont* **rutting**) **1** *n* (**a**) *(in ground)* ornière *f*

(**b**) *Fig* routine *f*; **to get into a rut** s'encroûter; **to be (stuck) in a rut** être prisonnier d'une routine; *Fig* **to get out of the rut** sortir de l'ornière

(**c**) *(of stag)* rut *m*; **in rut** en rut

2 *vt (ground)* sillonner; **the track had been deeply rutted by tractors** des tracteurs avaient creusé de profondes ornières dans le chemin

3 *vi (stag)* être en rut

rutabaga [ˌruːtə'beɪgə] *n Am* rutabaga *m*, chou-navet *m*

Ruth [ruːθ] *pr n Bible* Ruth

ruth [ruːθ] *n Arch* pitié *f*, compassion *f*

Ruthenia [ruː'θiːnɪə] *n* Ruthénie *f*; **in Ruthenia** en Ruthénie

Ruthenian [ruː'θiːnɪən] **1** *n* Ruthène *mf*

2 *adj* ruthène

ruthenium [ruː'θiːnɪəm] *n Chem* ruthénium *m*

rutherford ['rʌðəfəd] *n Phys* rutherford *m*

rutherfordium [ˌrʌðə'fɔːdɪəm] *n Chem* rutherfordium *m*

ruthless ['ruːθlɪs] *adj (person)* impitoyable, sans pitié; *(act)* brutal; *(determination, schedule, pace)* impitoyable; **to be ruthless in enforcing the law** être impitoyable dans l'application de la loi; **he was ruthless in shortening the text** il n'a pas fait de sentiments quand il s'est agi d'abréger le texte; **I'm going to have to be ruthless** il faut que j'y aille carrément

ruthlessly ['ruːθlɪslɪ] *adv (pitilessly)* impitoyablement, sans pitié

ruthlessness ['ruːθlɪsnɪs] *n (of person, behaviour)* caractère *m* impitoyable, dureté *f*

rutilant ['ruːtɪlənt] *adj Literary* rutilant

rutile ['ruːtaɪl] *n Miner* rutile *m*, schorl *m* rouge

rutin ['ruːtɪn] *n Chem* rutine *f*, rutoside *m*

rutted ['rʌtɪd] *adj* sillonné; **a badly rutted road** une route complètement défoncée

rutting ['rʌtɪŋ] *n (of stag)* rut *m*

►► ***rutting season*** saison *f* du rut

ruttish ['rʌtɪʃ] *adj* (**a**) *(stag)* en rut (**b**) *Pej (person)* libidineux, salace

rutty ['rʌtɪ] *adj* (**a**) *(path, road)* coupé d'ornières (**b**) *Tech* strié de grippures

RV [ˌɑː'viː] *n* (**a**) *Bible* (*abbr* **Revised Version**) = traduction anglaise de la Bible faite en 1885 (**b**) *Am* (*abbr* **recreational vehicle**) camping-car *m*

Rwanda [rʊ'ændə] *n* (**a**) *(country)* Rwanda *m*; **in Rwanda** au Rwanda (**b**) *(language)* rwanda *m*

Rwandan [rʊ'ændən] **1** *n* Rwandais(e) *m,f*

2 *adj* rwandais

3 *comp (embassy, history)* du Rwanda; *(teacher)* de rwanda

rye [raɪ] *n* (**a**) *(cereal)* seigle *m* (**b**) *(bread)* pain *m* de seigle (**c**) *(drink)* whisky *m* (de seigle)

►► ***rye bread*** pain *m* de seigle; ***rye whiskey*** whisky *m* (de seigle)

ryot ['raɪət] *n (in India)* ryot *m*, paysan(anne) *m,f*

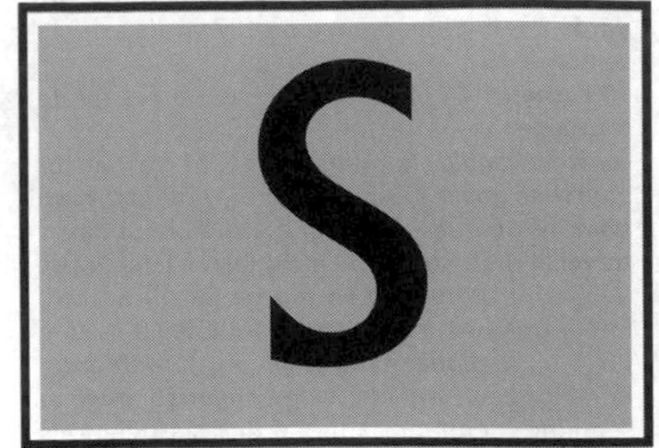

S¹, s [es] *n* S, s *m inv*; **two s's** deux s; **S for Susan** ≃ S comme Sutane

S² (**a**) (*written abbr* **south**) S (**b**) (*written abbr* **small**) (*on clothes label*) S

SA¹ [ˌes'eɪ] *n* (*abbr* **Salvation Army**) Armée *f* du salut

SA² (**a**) (*written abbr* **South Africa**) Afrique *f* du Sud (**b**) (*written abbr* **South America**) Amérique *f* du Sud

Saami ['sɑːmɪ] **1** *n* Saami *mf inv*, Same *mf inv*
2 *npl (race)* **the Saami** les Saami *mpl ou* Sames *mpl*
3 *adj* saami *(inv)*, same *(inv)*

Saar [sɑː(r)] *n* **the Saar** la Sarre

Saarbrücken [ˌsɑː'brʊkən] *n* Sarrebruck

Saarburg ['sɑːbɜːg] *n* Sarrebourg

Saarland ['sɑːlænd] *n* Sarre *f*; **in Saarland** dans la Sarre

Saarlander ['sɑːlændə(r)] *n* Sarrois(e) *m,f*

sabadilla [ˌsæbə'dɪlə] *n Bot* cévadille *f*

Sabah [sə'bɑː] *n* Sabah *m*

Sabahan [sə'bɑːhən] **1** *n* habitant(e) *m,f* de Sabah
2 *adj* de Sabah

Sabbatarian [ˌsæbə'teərɪən] *n* (**a**) *(Christian)* observateur(trice) *m,f* du dimanche; *(Jew)* observateur(trice) *m,f* du sabbat (**b**) *Rel & Hist* sabbataire *mf*

Sabbath ['sæbəθ] *n Rel* (**a**) *(Christian)* dimanche *m*, jour *m* du Seigneur; *(Jewish)* sabbat *m*; **to observe/to break the Sabbath** *(Christian)* observer/violer le repos du dimanche; *(Jew)* observer/violer le sabbat (**b**) **witches' Sabbath** sabbat *m* (de sorcières)

sabbatical [sə'bætɪkəl] **1** *adj (gen) & Rel* sabbatique; **to take a sabbatical year** prendre une année sabbatique
2 *n* congé *m* sabbatique; **to be on sabbatical** être en congé sabbatique

saber *Am* = **sabre**

sabin ['seɪbɪn] *n Phys* sabin *m*

Sabine ['sæbaɪn] *Antiq & Hist* **1** *n* Sabin(e) *m,f*; **the rape of the Sabines** l'enlèvement *m* des Sabines
2 *adj* sabin

sable ['seɪbəl] **1** *n* (**a**) *(animal, fur)* zibeline *f* (**b**) *(colour)* noir *m*
2 *comp (coat)* de *ou* en zibeline; *(paintbrush)* en poil de martre
3 *adj (colour)* noir; *Her* sable *(inv)*
►► *Zool* ***sable antelope*** hippotrague *m* noir; ***sable fur*** zibeline *f*

sabot ['sæbəʊ] *n* (**a**) *(shoe)* sabot *m* (**b**) *Mil* sabot *m*

sabotage ['sæbətɑːʒ] **1** *n* sabotage *m*
2 *vt* saboter

saboteur [ˌsæbə'tɜː(r)] *n* saboteur(euse) *m,f*

sabra ['sæbrə] *n Am Fam* sabra *mf*

sabre, *Am* **saber** ['seɪbə(r)] *n* sabre *m*

sabre-rattling **1** *n (UNCOUNT)* attitude *f* menaçante
2 *adj* menaçant

sabre-toothed tiger *n* machairodonte *m*

sabulous ['sæbjʊləs] *adj* (**a**) *(sandy)* sablonneux (**b**) *Med (urine)* graveleux

sac [sæk] *n Anat & Bot* sac *m*; **yolk sac** membrane *f* vitelline; **ink sac** *(of squid, sepia etc)* poche *f* d'encre

saccade [sæ'kɑːd] *n* (**a**) *(of eye)* tressautement *m* (**b**) *(jerky movement, of horse's reins)* saccade *f*

saccharide ['sækəraɪd] *n Chem* saccharide *m*, glucide *m*

saccharification [ˌsækərɪfɪ'keɪʃən] *n Chem* saccharification *f*; **saccharification of starch** amylolyse *f*

saccharify [sə'kærɪfaɪ] *vt Chem* saccharifier

saccharimeter [ˌsækə'rɪmɪtə(r)] *n* saccharimètre *m*

saccharin ['sækərɪn] *n Chem* saccharine *f*

saccharine ['sækərɪn] **1** *adj* (**a**) *Chem* saccharin (**b**) *Fig Pej (exaggeratedly sweet → smile)* mielleux; *(→ politeness)* onctueux; *(→ sentimentality)* écœurant; *(→ story, film etc)* édulcoré
2 *n* saccharine *f*

saccharization [ˌsækəraɪ'zeɪʃən] *n Chem* saccharification *f*; **saccharization of starch** amylolyse *f*

saccharoid ['sækərɔɪd] *adj Geol* saccharoïde

saccharose ['sækərəʊz] *n Chem* saccharose *m*

saccule ['sækjʊl] *n Anat* saccule *m*

sacerdotal [ˌsæsə'dəʊtəl] *adj* sacerdotal

sacerdotalism [ˌsæsə'dəʊtəlɪzəm] *n* sacerdotalisme *m*

sachem ['seɪtʃəm] *n* (**a**) *Am Fam (leader)* grosse huile *f*, grand manitou *m* (**b**) *(tribal chief)* sachem *m*

sachet ['sæʃeɪ] *n* sachet *m*

sack [sæk] **1** *n* (**a**) *(bag)* (grand) sac *m*; **two sacks of potatoes** deux sacs *mpl* de pommes de terre; *Am* **grocery sack** sac *m* à provisions
(**b**) *Br Fam (dismissal)* licenciement❑ *m*; **to give sb the sack** virer qn; **to get the sack** se faire virer; **you'll get me the sack** tu vas me faire perdre mon boulot
(**c**) *(pillage)* sac *m*, pillage *m*
(**d**) *Fam (bed)* pieu *m*, plumard *m*; **to hit the sack** se pieuter; *very Fam* **to be good/no good in the sack** être/ne pas être une affaire au pieu
(**e**) *Arch (wine)* vin *m* blanc sec *(d'Espagne ou du Portugal)*
2 *vt* (**a**) *Fam (dismiss)* virer, mettre à la porte❑
(**b**) *(pillage)* mettre à sac, piller
(**c**) *(put in sacks) (coal etc)* ensacher, mettre en sac
▸**sack out** *vi Am Fam* se pieuter, se bâcher, se pager

sackbut ['sækbʌt] *n Mus* saqueboute *f*

sackcloth ['sækklɒθ] *n* toile *f* à sac *ou* d'emballage; *Rel* **to wear sackcloth and ashes** faire pénitence avec le sac et la cendre; *Fig* **to be in sackcloth and ashes** être contrit

sackful ['sækfʊl] *n* sac *m*; **(whole) sackfuls of flour** des sacs *mpl* entiers de farine; **we've been getting letters by the sackful** nous avons reçu des sacs entiers de lettres

sacking ['sækɪŋ] *n* (**a**) *Tex* toile *f* à sac *ou* d'emballage (**b**) *Fam (dismissal)* licenciement❑ *m* (**c**) *(pillaging)* sac *m*, pillage *m*

sackload ['sækləʊd] = **sackful**

sack race *n* course *f* en sac

sacral¹ ['seɪkrəl] *adj Anat* sacré, du sacrum

sacral² *adj (rite)* sacral

sacrament ['sækrəmənt] **1** *n* sacrement *m*; **to take** *or* **receive the sacraments** communier
2 Sacrament *n* **the Blessed** *or* **Holy Sacrament** le saint sacrement

sacramental [ˌsækrə'mentəl] **1** *adj (rite)* sacramentel; *(theology)* sacramentaire
2 *n* sacramental *m*

sacramentally [ˌsækrə'mentəlɪ] *adv* sacramentellement, sacramentalement

sacramentarian [ˌsækrəmen'teərɪən] *n Rel & Hist* sacramentaire *m*

sacrarium [sæ'kreərɪəm] (*pl* **-ia** [-ɪə]) *n* (**a**) *Antiq* sacrarium *m* (**b**) *Rel (sanctuary)* sanctuaire *m*; *(piscina)* piscine *f*

sacred ['seɪkrɪd] **1** *adj* (**a**) *(holy)* sacré, saint; **a sacred place** un lieu saint; **sacred to their gods** consacré à leurs dieux; **sacred to his memory** voué *ou* dédié à sa mémoire; **sacred to the memory of…** *(on tombstone)* à la mémoire de…
(**b**) *(solemn, important → task, duty)* sacré, solennel; *(→ promise, right)* inviolable, sacré; *(revered, respected)* sacré; **nothing was sacred in his eyes** il n'y avait rien de sacré pour lui; **is nothing sacred any more?** on ne respecte donc plus rien aujourd'hui?
2 *n* **the sacred and the profane** le sacré et le profane
►► *Fig* ***sacred cow*** vache *f* sacrée; *Rel* ***Sacred Heart*** Sacré-Cœur *m*; *Orn* ***sacred ibis*** ibis *m* sacré; ***sacred music*** musique *f* sacrée *ou* religieuse; ***sacred writings*** livres *mpl* sacrés

sacredly ['seɪkrɪdlɪ] *adv* (**a**) *(in a religious manner)* religieusement, pieusement (**b**) *(inviolably)* inviolablement

sacredness ['seɪkrɪdnɪs] *n* (**a**) *(holiness)* caractère *m* sacré (**b**) *(solemness, importance)* inviolabilité *f*

sacrifice ['sækrɪfaɪs] **1** *n Rel & Fig* sacrifice *m*; **to offer sth (up) as a sacrifice to the gods** offrir qch en sacrifice aux dieux; **I've made a lot of sacrifices for you** j'ai fait beaucoup de sacrifices pour vous; **to make the supreme sacrifice** faire le sacrifice suprême; **human sacrifice** sacrifice *m* humain
2 *vt Rel & Fig* sacrifier; **to sacrifice sth to God** sacrifier qch à Dieu; **she sacrificed herself for her children** elle s'est sacrifiée pour ses enfants; **to sacrifice one's career/independence** sacrifier sa carrière/son indépendance

sacrificer ['sækrɪfaɪsə(r)] *n* sacrificateur(trice) *m,f*

sacrificial [ˌsækrɪ'fɪʃəl] *adj (rite, dagger)* sacrificiel; *(victim)* du sacrifice
►► ***sacrificial lamb*** agneau *m* du sacrifice; *Fig* victime *f* expiatoire

sacrilege ['sækrɪlɪdʒ] *n also Fig* sacrilège *m*; **to commit sacrilege** commettre un sacrilège

sacrilegious [ˌsækrɪ'lɪdʒəs] *adj also Fig* sacrilège

sacrilegiously [ˌsækrɪ'lɪdʒəslɪ] *adv* d'une manière sacrilège

sacristan ['sækrɪstən] *n* sacristain *m*

sacristy ['sækrɪstɪ] (*pl* **sacristies**) *n* sacristie *f*

sacroiliac [ˌsækrəʊ'ɪlɪæk] *Anat* **1** *n* articulation *f* sacroiliaque
2 *adj* sacroiliaque

sacrosanct ['sækrəʊˌsæŋkt] *adj also Fig* sacrosaint

sacrum ['seɪkrəm] (*pl* **sacra** [-krə]) *n Anat* sacrum *m*

SAD [ˌeseɪ'diː] *n* (*abbr* **seasonal affective disorder**) dépression *f* saisonnière

sad [sæd] (*compar* **sadder**, *superl* **saddest**) *adj* (**a**) *(unhappy, melancholy)* triste; *(stronger)* affligé; **it makes me sad to see what's become of them** ça me rend triste *ou* m'attriste de voir ce qu'ils sont devenus; **I shall be sad to see you leave** je serai désolé de vous voir partir; **to be sad at heart** avoir le cœur gros; **the flowers look** *or* **are a bit sad** les fleurs ont triste mine; **he came through the experience a sadder and a wiser man** l'expérience a été dure mais profitable
(**b**) *(depressing → news, day, story)* triste; *(→ sight, occasion)* triste, attristant; *(→ painting, music etc)* lugubre, triste; *(→ loss)* cruel, douloureux; **but sad to say it didn't last long** mais, malheureusement, cela n'a pas duré; **that's very sad news** c'est bien triste; **she came to a sad end** elle a eu une triste fin; **the sad fact is**

that he's incompetent c'est malheureux à dire, mais c'est un incapable

(**c**) *(regrettable)* triste, regrettable; **it's a sad state of affairs when this sort of thing can go unpunished** il est vraiment regrettable que de tels actes restent impunis; **it's a sad reflection on modern society** malheureusement, cela en dit long sur la société moderne; **it's a sad day for trade unionism/Scottish football** c'est un jour bien sombre pour le syndicalisme/le foot écossais; **it's a sad day when you can't walk the streets at night in safety** c'est quand même triste de ne pas pouvoir se sentir en sécurité dans les rues la nuit

(**d**) *Fam (pathetic)* minable; **to be a sad case** être minable; **he's still living with his parents, how sad can you get?** il habite toujours chez ses parents, il est grave *ou* il craint!; *very Fam* **what a sad bastard!** quel gros nullard!; **they've got really sad taste in music** ils écoutent de la musique vraiment craignos

▸▸ *Am Fam* ***sad sack*** *(person)* raté(e) *m,f*

sadden ['sædən] *vt* rendre triste, attrister; *(stronger)* affliger

saddle ['sædəl] **1** *n* (**a**) *(on horse, bicycle)* selle *f*; *also Fig* **to be in the saddle** être en selle; **you'll soon be back in the saddle again** vous allez bientôt pouvoir vous remettre en selle

(**b**) *Culin (of lamb, mutton)* selle *f*; *(of hare)* râble *m*

(**c**) *Geog* col *m*

2 *vt* (**a**) *(horse)* seller

(**b**) *Fam (lumber)* **to saddle sb with sth** refiler qch à qn; **I always get saddled with doing the nasty jobs** c'est toujours moi qui fais le sale boulot; **she was saddled with the children** elle s'est retrouvée avec les enfants sur les bras; **I don't want to saddle myself with any more work** je ne veux pas me taper du travail supplémentaire; **saddled with debts** grevé de dettes ▫

▸▸ *Am* ***saddle blanket*** tapis *m* de selle; ***saddle horse*** cheval *m* de selle; ***saddle post*** *(of bicycle)* tube *m* de selle; ***saddle room*** sellerie *f*; *Am* ***saddle shoes*** chaussures *fpl* basses bicolores; ***saddle soap*** cirage *m* pour selles; ***saddle sore*** *(on rider)* = meurtrissures provoquées par de longues heures en selle; *(on horse)* écorchure *f* *ou* excoriation *f* sous la selle; ***saddle stitch*** *(in needlework)* point *m* sellier; *(in bookbinding)* piqûre *f* à cheval

▸**saddle up** **1** *vi (rider)* seller sa monture

2 *vt sep (horse)* seller

saddleback ['sædəlbæk] *n* (**a**) *Archit* toit *m* en bâtière (**b**) *(of hill)* ensellement *m* (**c**) *(pig)* = cochon noir avec une ceinture blanche

saddlebacked ['sædəlbækt] *adj (horse)* ensellé

saddlebag ['sædəlbæg] *n (for bicycle, motorcycle)* sacoche *f*; *(for horse)* sacoche *f* de selle

saddlebill ['sædəlbɪl] *n Orn* jabiru *m*

saddlebow ['sædəlbəʊ] *n (pommel)* pommeau *m* (de selle); *(front)* arçon *m*

saddlecloth ['sædəlklɒθ] *n* tapis *m* de selle

saddler ['sædlə(r)] *n* sellier *m*

saddlery ['sædlərɪ] (*pl* **saddleries**) *n (trade, shop, goods)* sellerie *f*

saddle-sore *adj* **he was saddle-sore** il avait les fesses meurtries par de longues heures à cheval/à vélo

saddle-stitch *vt* coudre au point sellier

saddletree ['sædəltri:] *n* (**a**) *(frame of saddle)* bois *m* de selle (**b**) *Am Bot* tulipier *m*

saddling ['sædəlɪŋ] *n (of horse)* sellage *m*

Sadducee ['sædjʊsi:] *n Rel* Saducéen(enne) *m,f*, Sadducéen(enne) *m,f*

sadhu ['sɑ:du:] *n Rel* sadhu *m*

Sadie Hawkins Day [,seɪdɪ'hɔ:kɪnz-] *n* = aux États-Unis, jour où les femmes invitent les hommes à une soirée dansante

sadiron ['sædaɪən] *n* fer *m* à repasser

sadism ['seɪdɪzəm] *n* sadisme *m*

sadist ['seɪdɪst] *n* sadique *mf*

sadistic [sə'dɪstɪk] *adj* sadique

sadistically [sə'dɪstɪkəlɪ] *adv* sadiquement, avec sadisme

Sadler's Wells [,sædləz'welz] *n* = théâtre londonien

sadly ['sædlɪ] *adv* (**a**) *(unhappily)* tristement; **she looked at me sadly** elle m'a regardé tristement *ou* d'un air triste; **he is sadly missed** il nous/leur manque beaucoup; **my aunt, who sadly died two years ago** ma tante qui, hélas *ou* malheureusement, est morte il y a deux ans

(**b**) *(unfortunately)* malheureusement; **sadly, I won't be able to come** malheureusement, je ne pourrai pas venir; **compassion is sadly lacking in our society** la compassion fait tristement défaut dans notre société

(**c**) *(regrettably)* déplorablement; **you are sadly mistaken** vous vous trompez lourdement; **the house had been sadly neglected** la maison était dans un état déplorable

sadness ['sædnɪs] *n* tristesse *f*

sadomasochism [,seɪdəʊ'mæsəkɪzəm] *n* sadomasochisme *m*

sadomasochist [,seɪdəʊ'mæsəkɪst] *n* sadomasochiste *mf*

sadomasochistic ['seɪdəʊ,mæsə'kɪstɪk] *adj* sadomasochiste

Saducee = **Sadducee**

s.a.e., sae, SAE [,eseɪ'i:] *n* (*abbr* **stamped addressed envelope**) enveloppe *f* timbrée *(portant l'adresse à laquelle elle doit être renvoyée)*; **please return the form with an s.a.e.** veuillez renvoyer le formulaire ainsi qu'une enveloppe timbrée à votre adresse

safari [sə'fɑ:rɪ] *n* safari *m*; **they've gone on** *or* **they're on safari** ils font un safari

▸▸ ***safari jacket*** saharienne *f*; ***safari park*** réserve *f* d'animaux sauvages; ***safari suit*** ensemble *m* avec saharienne

Safavid [sɑ:'fɑ:wɪd] *Hist* **1** *n* Séfévide *mf*

2 *adj* séfévide

SAFE [seɪf]

sûr	▸ **1 (a), (d) – (f)**
solide	▸ **1 (a)**
pas dangereux	▸ **1 (a)**
sans danger	▸ **1 (a), (e)**
en sécurité	▸ **1 (b)**
hors de danger	▸ **1 (b)**
sain et sauf	▸ **1 (c)**
sans risques	▸ **1 (e)**
coffre-fort	▸ **2 (a)**

1 *adj* (**a**) *(not dangerous → car, machine, area)* sûr; *(→ structure, building, fastening)* solide; *(→ beach)* pas dangereux; *(→ chemical, water)* sans danger; **this part of town is/isn't safe at night** ce quartier est/n'est pas sûr la nuit; **the staircase doesn't look very safe** l'escalier n'a pas l'air très sûr; **they claim nuclear power is perfectly safe** ils prétendent que l'énergie nucléaire n'est pas du tout dangereuse; **this medicine is/isn't safe for young children** ce médicament convient/ne convient pas aux enfants en bas âge; **she assured me the water was perfectly safe to drink** elle m'a assuré qu'on pouvait boire l'eau sans danger *ou* sans risque; **is it safe to come out now?** est-ce qu'on peut sortir (sans danger *ou* sans crainte) maintenant?; **is it safe to swim here?** est-ce qu'on peut nager ici?, est-ce dangereux de nager ici?; **it isn't safe to play in the street** il est dangereux de jouer dans la rue; **the bomb has been made safe** la bombe a été désamorcée; **the police kept the crowd at a safe distance** les policiers ont empêché la foule d'approcher de trop près; **the safe period** = période du cycle pendant laquelle la femme est censée ne pas être féconde

(**b**) *(protected, not in danger)* en sécurité; *(no longer in danger)* hors de danger; **I don't feel safe alone at night** je ne me sens pas en sécurité tout seul la nuit; **the money's safe in the bank** l'argent est en sécurité à la banque; *Am* **keep safe!** prends bien soin de toi!; **the secret will be safe with her** elle ne risque pas d'ébruiter le secret; **safe from attack/from suspicion** à l'abri d'une attaque/des soupçons; **you don't look very safe standing on that chair** tu as l'air d'être en équilibre instable debout sur cette chaise; **(have a) safe journey!** bon voyage!; *Hum* **no woman is safe with him** c'est un coureur invétéré

(**c**) *(unharmed, undamaged → person)* sain et sauf; **to come home safe** rentrer sain et sauf; **safe and sound** sain et sauf; **I'm glad to hear you're safe** je suis content d'apprendre qu'il ne t'est rien arrivé; **we shall pay upon safe delivery of the goods** nous payerons après réception des marchandises

(**d**) *(secure → place)* sûr; **keep it in a safe place** gardez-le en lieu sûr; **is there anywhere safe to leave my handbag?** y a-t-il un lieu sûr où je puisse laisser mon sac à main?; **in safe custody** *(child)* sous bonne garde; *(securities, assets etc)* en dépôt; **in safe hands** en mains sûres; **in safe keeping** en lieu sûr, en sûreté; **to give sth to sb for safe keeping** confier qch à qn; **it's in his safe keeping** c'est sous sa garde

(**e**) *(not risky, certain → course of action)* sans risque *ou* risques, sans danger; *(→ investment)* sûr; *(→ estimate)* raisonnable; **I played it safe and arrived an hour early** pour ne pas prendre de risques, je suis arrivé une heure en avance; **you're always safe ordering a steak** on ne prend jamais de risques en commandant un steak; **a safe winner** un (une) gagnant(e) certain(e); **the steak's a safe bet** on ne prend jamais de risques en commandant le steak; **it's a safe bet that he'll be late** on peut être sûr qu'il arrivera en retard; **it's a safe guess that...** on ne prend pas beaucoup de risques en disant que...; **the safest option** l'option la moins risquée; **I think it's safe to say that everybody enjoyed themselves** je pense que l'on peut dire avec certitude que ça a plu à tout le monde; **it is a safe assumption that...** on peut présumer sans risque que...; **take an umbrella (just) to be on the safe side** prends un parapluie, c'est plus sûr *ou* au cas où; **it's as safe as houses** cela ne présente pas le moindre risque; *Prov* **better safe than sorry** deux précautions valent mieux qu'une

(**f**) *(reliable → driver)* sûr, prudent; **is he safe with the money/the children?** est-ce qu'on peut lui confier l'argent/les enfants (sans crainte)?; **she's a very safe driver** c'est une conductrice très sûre *ou* très prudente; **he's a safe pair of hands** *(goalkeeper)* il a les mains très sûres; *(manager, minister etc)* il est très fiable

2 *n* (**a**) *(for money, valuables etc)* coffre-fort *m*; **night** *or* **deposit safe** coffre *m* de nuit

(**b**) *(for food)* garde-manger *m inv*

▸▸ ***safe area*** zone *f* de sécurité; ***safe deposit*** dépôt *m* en coffre-fort; ***safe haven*** *(gen)* refuge *m*; *Mil* zone *f* de sécurité; ***safe house*** *(for spies, wanted man)* refuge *m*; ***safe load*** *(for lorry)* charge *f* admissible; *(for lift)* charge *f* maximum; *Elec* charge *f* de sécurité; *Br Pol* ***safe seat*** = siège de député qui traditionnellement va toujours au même parti; ***safe sex*** rapports *mpl* sexuels protégés

safeblower ['seɪf,bləʊə(r)] *n* perceur(euse) *m,f* de coffres-forts *(qui emploie des explosifs)*

safebreaker ['seɪf,breɪkə(r)] *n* perceur(euse) *m,f* de coffres-forts

safe-conduct [-'kɒndʌkt] *n* sauf-conduit *m*

safecracker ['seɪf,krækə(r)] *Am* = **safebreaker**

safe-deposit box *n* coffre *m (dans une banque)*

safeguard ['seɪfgɑ:d] **1** *vt* sauvegarder; **to safeguard sb/sth against sth** protéger qn/qch contre qch

2 *vi* **to safeguard against sth** se protéger contre qch; **the government must take measures to safeguard against a recurrence of such incidents** le gouvernement doit prendre des mesures pour éviter que de tels incidents (ne) se reproduisent

3 *n* sauvegarde *f*; **as a safeguard against theft** comme précaution contre le vol

safeguarding ['seɪfgɑ:dɪŋ] *n* sauvegarde *f*, protection *f*

safekeeping [,seɪf'ki:pɪŋ] *n* (bonne) garde *f*; **she was given the documents for safekeeping** on lui a confié les documents; **the money is in your safekeeping** je vous confie l'argent

safelight ['seɪflaɪt] *n Phot* lampe *f* inactinique

safely ['seɪflɪ] *adv* (**a**) *(without danger)* en toute sécurité; **drive safely!** soyez prudent sur la route!; **an area where women can safely go out at night** un quartier où les femmes peuvent sortir la nuit en toute sécurité; **you can safely invest with them** vous pouvez investir chez eux en toute tranquillité

(**b**) *(without incident)* **to arrive safely** *(person →*

gen) bien arriver; *(→ after dangerous journey)* arriver sain et sauf; *(parcel etc)* arriver sans dommage; *(ship etc)* arriver à bon port; **I'm just phoning to say I've arrived safely** je téléphone juste pour dire que je suis bien arrivé; **the bill was seen safely through Parliament** le projet de loi fut voté sans problème par le Parlement

(**c**) *(securely)* en sécurité, à l'abri; **I've put the money away safely** j'ai mis l'argent en sécurité; **all the doors and windows are safely locked** toutes les portes et les fenêtres sont bien fermées; **the kids are safely tucked up in bed** les enfants sont bien bordés dans leur lit

(**d**) *(confidently, certainly)* avec confiance *ou* certitude; **we can safely predict that...** nous pouvons prédire avec certitude que...

safeness ['seɪfnɪs] *n* (**a**) *(absence of danger)* sécurité *f*; **a feeling of safeness** un sentiment de sécurité *ou* de sûreté (**b**) *(of structure, building)* solidité *f*; *(of nuclear power, electrical appliances)* sûreté *f* (**c**) *(certainty → of deal, investment, choice)* sûreté *f*

safety ['seɪftɪ] **1** *n (absence of danger)* sécurité *f*; **the injured were helped to safety** on a aidé les blessés à se mettre à l'abri; **there are fears for the safety of the hostages** on craint pour la vie des otages; **we are concerned about the safety of imported toys** nous craignons que les jouets importés présentent certains dangers; **to seek safety in flight** chercher son salut dans la fuite; **he ran for safety** il a couru se mettre à l'abri; **he reached safety** il arriva en lieu sûr; **in a place of safety** en lieu sûr; **there's safety in numbers** plus on est nombreux, plus on est en sécurité; **safety in the home/workplace** la sécurité à la maison/au travail; **road safety** sécurité *f* routière; **to guarantee sb's safety** *(of police etc)* assurer la protection de qn; **safety first!** ne prenez pas de risques!

2 *comp (device, mechanism, measures etc)* de sécurité

▸▸ ***safety belt*** ceinture *f* de sécurité; *Am* ***safety car*** pace car *m or f*; ***safety catch*** *(on gun)* cran *m* de sécurité; *(on window, door)* cran *m* de sûreté; *(on bonnet)* crochet *m* de sécurité; ***safety cell*** cellule *f* de sécurité; ***safety chain*** *(on door)* chaîne *f* de sûreté; *(on bracelet)* chaînette *f* de sûreté; *Theat* ***safety curtain*** rideau *m* de fer; ***safety drill*** exercice *m* d'évacuation; *Tech* ***safety factor*** facteur *m* de sécurité; ***safety feature*** *(device)* dispositif *m* de sécurité; *Phot* ***safety film*** film *m* de protection; ***safety glass*** verre *m* de sécurité; ***safety helmet*** casque *m* (de protection); *Am* ***safety island*** refuge *m (sur une route)*; ***safety lamp*** lampe *f* de mineur; ***safety margin*** marge *f* de sécurité; ***safety match*** allumette *f* de sûreté; ***safety net*** filet *m*; *Fig* filet *m* de sécurité; **without a safety net** sans filet; ***safety officer*** responsable *mf* de la sécurité; ***safety pin*** *(fastener)* épingle *f* de nourrice *ou* de sûreté; *(of grenade, bomb)* goupille *f* de sûreté; ***safety razor*** rasoir *m* de sûreté; ***safety regulations*** consignes *fpl* de sécurité; ***safety standards*** normes *fpl* de sécurité; *also Fig* ***safety valve*** soupape *f* de sûreté

safety-conscious *adj* **she's very safety-conscious** elle se préoccupe beaucoup de tout ce qui a trait à la sécurité

safety-deposit box = **safe-deposit box**

safety-first *adj (campaign, measures)* de sécurité; *(investment, shares)* de toute sécurité

safflower ['sæflaʊə(r)] *n Bot* carthame *m*

▸▸ ***safflower oil*** huile *f* de carthame

saffron ['sæfrən] **1** *n* (**a**) *Bot & Culin* safran *m* (**b**) *(colour)* jaune *m* safran

2 *adj* (jaune) safran *(inv)*

▸▸ ***saffron rice*** riz *m* au safran

safranine ['sæfrəniːn] *n* safranine *f*

SAG [sæg] *n Am (abbr* **Screen Actors' Guild**) = syndicat américain des acteurs

sag [sæg] *(pt & pp* **sagged**, *cont* **sagging**) **1** *vi* (**a**) *(roof, beam, shelf, bridge)* s'affaisser; *(branch)* ployer; *(cable, rope → state)* être détendu, pendre; *(→ action)* se détendre; *(jowls, cheeks, hemline)* pendre; *(breasts)* tomber; **the bed sags in the middle** le lit s'affaisse au milieu

(**b**) *(prices, stocks, demand)* fléchir, baisser; *(conversation)* traîner; **the novel sags a bit in the middle** le roman perd un peu de son intérêt au milieu; **their spirits sagged** ils perdirent courage

2 *n* (**a**) *(in rope)* relâchement *m*; *(of structure)* affaissement *m*

(**b**) *(in prices, stocks, demand)* fléchissement *m*, baisse *f*

saga ['sɑːgə] *n* (**a**) *(legend, film)* saga *f*; *(novel)* saga *f*, roman-fleuve *m*

(**b**) *(complicated story)* **I heard the whole saga of her trip to France** elle m'a raconté son voyage en France en long et en large; **it's a saga of bad management and wrong decisions** c'est une longue histoire de mauvaise gestion et de mauvaises décisions; **the continuing saga of the minister's resignation still dominates the headlines** le feuilleton de la démission du ministre domine toujours l'actualité; *Hum* **do you want to hear the latest in the continuing saga of our washing machine?** tu sais ce qui m'est encore arrivé avec ma machine à laver?

sagacious [sə'geɪʃəs] *adj Literary (person)* sagace, perspicace, avisé; *(remark)* judicieux

sagaciously [sə'geɪʃəslɪ] *adv Literary* avec sagacité, judicieusement

sagaciousness [sə'geɪʃəsnɪs], **sagacity** [sə'gæsətɪ] *n Literary* sagacité *f*

sagamore ['sægəmɔː(r)] *n* sachem *m*

sage [seɪdʒ] **1** *n* (**a**) *Literary (wise person)* sage *m* (**b**) *Bot & Culin* sauge *f*; **sage and onion stuffing** farce *f* à la sauge et à l'oignon

2 *adj Literary (wise)* sage, judicieux

▸▸ ***sage green*** vert *m* cendré

sagebrush ['seɪdʒbrʌʃ] *n Bot* armoise *f*

▸▸ ***the Sagebrush State*** = surnom donné au Nevada

sage-green *adj* vert cendré *(inv)*

sagely ['seɪdʒlɪ] *adv* avec sagesse, avec sagacité

saggar ['sægə(r)] *n Cer* casette *f*; *Metal* caisse *f* de cémentation

sagging ['sægɪŋ], **saggy** ['sægɪ] *adj* (**a**) *(bed, roof, bridge)* affaissé; *(shelf, beam)* qui ploie; *(rope)* détendu; *(hemline)* qui pend; *(jowls, cheeks)* pendant; *(breasts)* tombant (**b**) *(prices, demand)* en baisse; *(spirits)* abattu, découragé; *(enthusiasm)* fléchissant, faiblissant

Sagitta [sə'dʒɪtə] *n Astron* la Flèche

sagittal ['sædʒɪtəl] *adj* sagittal

▸▸ *Anat* ***sagittal suture*** suture *f* sagittale

Sagittarian [ˌsædʒɪ'teərɪən] *Astrol* **1** *n* **to be a Sagittarian** être (du signe du) Sagittaire

2 *adj* du Sagittaire; **the Sagittarian male** les hommes *mpl* du Sagittaire

Sagittarius [ˌsædʒɪ'teərɪəs] **1** *n* (**a**) *Astron* Sagittaire *m* (**b**) *Astrol* Sagittaire *m*; **he's a Sagittarius** il est (du signe du) Sagittaire

2 *adj Astrol* du Sagittaire; **he's Sagittarius** il est (du signe du) Sagittaire

sago ['seɪgəʊ] *n* sagou *m*

▸▸ *Bot* ***sago palm*** sagoutier *m*; ***sago pudding*** sagou *m* au lait

saguaro [sə'gwɑːrəʊ] *(pl* **saguaros**) *n Bot* saguaro *m*

Sahara [sə'hɑːrə] *n* le (désert du) Sahara

▸▸ ***the Sahara Desert*** le désert du Sahara

Saharan [sə'hɑːrən] **1** *n Ling* saharien *m*

2 *adj* saharien; **sub-Saharan Africa** Afrique *f* subsaharienne

sahib ['sɑːɪb] *n* sahib *m*

said [sed] **1** *pt & pp of* **say**

2 *adj* **the said Howard Riley** le dit *ou* dénommé Howard Riley; **the said Anne Smith** la dite *ou* dénommée Anne Smith; **the said articles** les dits articles *mpl*

Saida ['saɪdə] *n Geog* Saïda, Sayda

saiga ['saɪgə] *n Zool* saïga *m*

Saigon [saɪ'gɒn] *n Geog* Saïgon *m*

sail [seɪl] **1** *n* (**a**) *(on boat)* voile *f*; **to set sail** prendre la mer, appareiller; **to set sail for...** partir pour..., appareiller pour...; **to make sail** *(hoist sails)* hisser les voiles; *(leave)* prendre la mer, appareiller; **in full sail, with all sails set** toutes voiles dehors; **the boat was under sail** le bateau était sous voiles; **they rounded the cape under sail** ils doublèrent le cap à la voile; **under 300 m² of sail** avec une voilure de 300 m²

(**b**) *(journey)* voyage *m* en bateau; *(pleasure trip)* promenade *f* en bateau; **to go for a sail** faire un tour en bateau; **it's a few hours' sail from here** c'est à quelques heures d'ici en bateau

(**c**) *(of windmill)* aile *f*

2 *vi* (**a**) *(move over water → boat, ship)* naviguer; **the trawler was sailing north** le chalutier se dirigeait *ou* cinglait vers le nord; **the boat sailed up/down the river** le bateau remonta/descendit le fleuve; **the ferry sailed into Dover** le ferry-boat entra dans le port de Douvres; **they sailed around the Mediterranean** ils ont fait le tour de la Méditerranée; **to sail round a cape** contourner un promontoire; **to sail close to the wind** naviguer au (plus) près; *Fig* jouer un jeu dangereux

(**b**) *(set off → boat, passenger)* partir, prendre la mer, appareiller; **the Britannica sails at noon** le Britannica appareille à midi

(**c**) *(travel by boat)* voyager (en bateau); **are you flying or sailing?** est-ce que vous y allez en avion ou en bateau?; **they sailed from Liverpool to Boston** ils ont fait le voyage de Liverpool à Boston en bateau

(**d**) *(as sport or hobby)* **to sail, to go sailing** faire de la voile

(**e**) *Fig* **swans sailed by on the lake** des cygnes glissaient sur le lac; **there were clouds sailing by** des nuages voguaient dans le ciel; **birds sailed across the sky** des oiseaux passaient dans le ciel; **a sports car sailed past me** une voiture de sport m'a doublé à toute vitesse; **the balloons sailed into the air** les ballons se sont envolés; **the ball sailed over the wall** la balle est passée par-dessus le mur; **my hat sailed off my head and into the water** un coup de vent a fait voler mon chapeau dans l'eau; **to sail into a room** entrer majestueusement dans une pièce; **she sailed across the room to greet me** elle traversa la pièce d'un pas majestueux pour venir à ma rencontre

3 *vt* (**a**) *(boat → of captain)* commander; *(→ of helmsman, yachtsman)* barrer; **have you ever sailed a catamaran before?** est-ce que vous avez déjà barré un catamaran?; **to sail a boat through a channel** manœuvrer un bateau dans un chenal; **she sailed the boat into port** elle a manœuvré *ou* piloté le bateau jusque dans le port

(**b**) *(cross → sea, lake)* traverser; **to sail the Atlantic single-handed** traverser l'Atlantique en solitaire; **to sail the seas** parcourir les mers

▸**sail into** *vt insep Fam (attack)* tomber à bras raccourcis sur

▸**sail through** *Fig* **1** *vt insep (succeed in)* réussir haut la main; **he sailed through the exam** il a réussi l'examen haut la main

2 *vi (succeed)* réussir haut la main

sailboard ['seɪlbɔːd] **1** *n* planche *f* à voile

2 *vi Sport* faire de la planche à voile *ou* du véliplanche

sailboarder ['seɪlˌbɔːdə(r)] *n* véliplanchiste *mf*

sailboarding ['seɪlˌbɔːdɪŋ] *n* planche *f* à voile *(activité)*

sailboat ['seɪlbəʊt] *n Am* voilier *m*, bateau *m* à voile

sailcloth ['seɪlklɒθ] *n* toile *f* à voile *ou* à voiles

sailfish ['seɪlfɪʃ] *n Ich* voilier *m*

sailing ['seɪlɪŋ] *n* (**a**) *(activity)* navigation *f*; *(hobby)* voile *f*, navigation *f* de plaisance; *(sport)* voile *f*; **to go sailing** faire de la voile (**b**) *(departure)* départ *m*; **there are three sailings a day for Cherbourg** il y a trois départs par jour pour Cherbourg; **the 12 o'clock sailing** le bateau de midi

▸▸ ***sailing boat*** voilier *m*, bateau *m* (à voiles); ***sailing dinghy*** canot *m* à voile; ***sailing ship*** (grand) voilier *m*, navire *m* à voile *ou* à voiles

sailmaker ['seɪlˌmeɪkə(r)] *n* voilier *m (personne)*

sailmaking ['seɪlˌmeɪkɪŋ] *n* voilerie *f*

sailor ['seɪlə(r)] *n* (**a**) *(gen)* marin *m*, navigateur(trice) *m,f*; **I'm a good/bad sailor** j'ai/je n'ai pas le pied marin (**b**) *(as rank)* matelot *m*

▸▸ ***sailor collar*** col *m* marin; ***sailor hat*** *(for boys)* béret *m* de marin; *(for women)* canotier *m*; ***sailor suit*** costume *m* marin

sailplane ['seɪlpleɪn] *n* planeur *m*

sain [seɪn] *vt Arch or Literary* bénir (d'un signe de croix); **to sain oneself** se signer

sainfoin ['sænfɔɪn] *n Bot* sainfoin *m*

saint [seɪnt] *n* saint(e) *m,f*; *Fig* **he's no saint** ce n'est pas un petit saint; *Fam* **it would try the patience of a saint** cela ferait s'impatienter le plus patient de hommes

►► ***Saint Andrew*** saint André *(saint patron de l'Écosse)*; ***Saint Andrew's cross*** croix *f* de Saint-André, = croix en X blanche sur fond bleu figurant sur le drapeau écossais; ***Saint Andrew's Day*** la Saint-André *(fête nationale de l'Écosse, le 30 novembre)*; ***Saint Anthony*** saint Antoine; ***Saint Anthony's cross*** croix *f* de Saint-Antoine; ***Saint Augustine*** saint Augustin; ***Saint Bartholomew*** saint Barthélemy; ***the Saint Bartholomew's Day Massacre, the Massacre of Saint Bartholomew*** le massacre de la Saint-Barthélemy; ***Saint Benedict*** saint Benoît; ***Saint Bernard*** *(dog)* saint-bernard *m inv*; ***Saint Catherine*** sainte Catherine; ***Saint Catherine's Day*** la Sainte-Catherine; ***Saint Cecilia*** sainte Cécile; ***Saint Christopher*** saint Christophe; ***Saint Clement*** saint Clément; ***Saint David*** saint David *(saint patron du pays de Galles)*; ***Saint David's Day*** la Saint-David *(fête nationale du pays de Galles, le 1 mars)*; ***Saint David's (Church)*** (l'église *f*) Saint-David; ***saint's day*** fête *f (d'un saint)*; ***Saint Dominic*** saint Dominique; ***Saint Elizabeth*** sainte Élisabeth; ***Saint Elmo's fire*** feu *m* Saint-Elme; ***Saint Francis (of Assisi)*** saint François (d'Assise); ***Saint George*** saint Georges *(saint patron de l'Angleterre)*; ***Saint George's Cross*** croix *f* de Saint-Georges, = croix rouge sur fond blanc figurant sur le drapeau anglais; ***Saint George's Day*** la Saint-Georges *(fête nationale de l'Angleterre, le 23 avril)*; ***the Saint Gotthard Pass*** le col du Saint-Gothard; ***Saint Gregory*** saint Grégoire; ***Saint Helena*** *(island)* Sainte-Hélène; **on Saint Helena** à Sainte-Hélène; ***Saint James*** saint Jacques; ***Saint Jerome*** saint Jérôme; ***Saint John*** saint Jean; ***Saint John the Baptist*** Saint Jean-Baptiste; *Bot* ***Saint John's wort*** millepertuis *m*; ***the Saint Lawrence (River)*** le Saint-Laurent; ***the Saint Lawrence Seaway*** la voie maritime du Saint-Laurent ***Saint Louis*** saint Louis; ***Saint Lucia*** Sainte-Lucie; ***Saint Luke*** saint Luc; ***Saint Mark*** saint Marc; ***Saint Mark's Square*** la place Saint-Marc; ***Saint Michael*** saint Michel; ***Saint Nicholas*** saint Nicolas; ***Saint Nicholas' Day*** la Saint-Nicolas; ***Saint Patrick*** saint Patrick *(saint patron de l'Irlande)*; ***Saint Patrick's Day*** la Saint-Patrick *(fête nationale de l'Irlande, le 17 mars)*; ***Saint Paul*** saint Paul; ***Saint Peter*** saint Pierre; ***Saint Peter's Basilica*** la basilique Saint-Pierre; *Ich* ***Saint Peter's fish*** saint-pierre *m inv*; ***Saint Petersburg*** Saint-Pétersbourg; ***Saint Pierre and Miquelon*** Saint-Pierre-et-Miquelon; **in Saint Pierre and Miquelon** à Saint-Pierre-et-Miquelon; ***Saint Sebastian*** saint Sébastien; ***Saint Stephen*** saint Étienne; *Ir* ***Saint Stephen's Day*** = le 26 decembre; ***Saint Swithin's day*** = le 15 juillet (un ancien dicton veut que, s'il pleut ce jour-là, il pleuvra ensuite pendant quarante jours mais, si le temps est sec, il restera sec pendant quarante jours); ***Saint Sylvester*** saint Sylvestre; ***Saint Theodore*** saint Théodore; ***Saint Thomas Aquinas*** saint Thomas d'Aquin; ***Saint Valentine's Day*** la Saint-Valentin; *Geog* ***Saint Vincent*** Saint-Vincent-et-les Grenadines; *Med* ***Saint Vitus' dance*** danse *f* de Saint-Guy, chorée *f*; ***Saint Walpurgis*** Sainte Walpurgis, Sainte Walburge

SAINT PATRICK'S DAY

Patrick, le saint patron de l'Irlande, est célébré le 17 mars, qui est le jour de sa mort, en l'an 461. Saint Patrick convertit les Irlandais au christianisme et établit monastères, églises et écoles dans tout le pays. Selon la légende, il aurait également réussi à chasser tous les serpents d'Irlande. Chômée en Irlande, la St Patrick est également fêtée dans certaines villes américaines comptant une forte proportion de personnes d'origine irlandaise.

sainted ['seɪntɪd] *adj (person)* sanctifié; *(place)* sacré, consacré; *Fam Old-fashioned* **my sainted aunt!** vingt dieux!

sainthood ['seɪnthʊd] *n* sainteté *f*

saintlike ['seɪntlaɪk] = **saintly**

saintliness ['seɪntlɪnɪs] *n* sainteté *f*

saintly ['seɪntlɪ] *(compar* **saintlier,** *superl* **saintliest**) *adj (life, behaviour, humility, virtue)* de saint; **she was a saintly woman** c'était une vraie sainte; **to put on a saintly air** prendre un air de petit saint

saintpaulia [sənt'pɔːlɪə] *n Bot* saintpaulia *m*

saith [seθ] *Arch & Bible 3rd pers sing of* **say**

saithe [seɪθ] *n Br Ich* colin *m*, lieu *m* noir

sake[1] [seɪk] *n* **for sb's sake** *(for their good)* pour (le bien de) qn; *(out of respect for)* par égard pour qn; *(out of love for)* pour l'amour de qn; **do it for my sake/for your own sake** fais-le pour moi/pour toi; **I only came for your sake** je ne suis venu qu'à cause de toi *ou* que pour toi; **please come, for both our sakes** viens s'il te plaît, fais-le pour nous deux; **for all our sakes, tell no one** ne le dis à personne dans notre intérêt à tous; **they decided not to divorce for the sake of the children** ils ont décidé de ne pas divorcer à cause des enfants; **I walk to work for its own sake, not to save money** je vais travailler à pied pour le plaisir, pas par esprit d'économie; **they're just talking for the sake of talking** *or* **of it** ils parlent pour ne rien dire; **art for art's sake** l'art pour l'art; **for the sake of higher profits** pour réaliser de plus gros bénéfices; **all that for the sake of a few dollars** tout ça pour quelques malheureux dollars; **for old times' sake** en souvenir du passé; **for the sake of argument, let's assume it costs £100** (pour les besoins de la discussion,) admettons que ça coûte 100 livres; **for goodness** *or* **God's** *or* **Christ's** *or* **pity's** *or* **heaven's sake!** pour l'amour du ciel *ou* de Dieu!

sake[2] ['sɑːkɪ] *n (drink)* saké *m*

saker ['seɪkə(r)] *n Orn* faucon *m* sacre

Sakhalin ['sækəliːn] *n* Sakhaline

saki[1] ['sɑːkɪ] *n Zool* saki *m*

saki[2] *n (drink)* saké *m*

sal [sæl] *n Chem* sel *m*

►► ***sal ammoniac*** sel *m* ammoniac; ***sal volatile*** sel *m* volatile, sels *mpl* (anglais)

salaam [sə'lɑːm] **1** *n* salutation *f* à l'orientale

2 *vt* saluer à l'orientale

3 *vi* saluer à l'orientale

4 *exclam* salam!

salable ['seɪləbəl] *adj* vendable

salacious [sə'leɪʃəs] *adj Formal (joke, book, look)* salace, grivois, obscène

salaciousness [sə'leɪʃəsnɪs], **salacity** [sə'læsɪtɪ] *n Formal* salacité *f*, grivoiserie *f*, obscénité *f*

salad ['sæləd] *n* salade *f*; **green salad** salade *f* (verte); **chicken salad** salade *f* au poulet; **cheese/ham salad** salade *f* au fromage/jambon; **tomato/fruit/mixed salad** salade *f* de tomates/de fruits/mixte

►► ***salad bar*** *(restaurant)* = restaurant où l'on mange des salades, *(area)* salad bar *m*; ***salad bowl*** saladier *m*; *Bot* ***salad burnet*** pimprenelle *f*; *Br* ***salad cream*** = sorte de mayonnaise (vendue en bouteille); ***salad days*** années *fpl* de jeunesse; ***salad dressing*** *(gen)* sauce *f (pour salade)*; *(French dressing)* vinaigrette *f*; ***salad oil*** huile *f* pour assaisonnement; ***salad servers*** couverts *mpl* à salade; ***salad spinner*** essoreuse *f* à salade

Salamanca [,sælə'mæŋkə] *n* Salamanque

salamander ['sælə,mændə(r)] *n Zool* salamandre *f*

salami [sə'lɑːmɪ] *n* salami *m*, saucisson *m* sec; *very Fam Hum* **to play hide the salami** *(have sex)* faire crac-crac, s'envoyer en l'air

►► ***salami tactics*** travaux *mpl* de sape graduels

salaried ['sælərɪd] *adj* salarié

►► ***salaried employee*** salarié(e) *m,f*; ***salaried job*** *(gen)* emploi *m* salarié; *(as opposed to wage-earning)* = emploi dont le salaire est mensuel et non hebdomadaire

salary ['sælərɪ] *(pl* **salaries**) **1** *n* salaire *m*; **I have to bring up a family on a teacher's salary** je dois faire vivre ma famille avec un salaire d'enseignant

2 *comp (bracket, level)* des salaires

►► ***salary cap*** plafond *m* de salaires; ***salary earner*** salarié(e) *m,f*; ***salary increase, salary increment*** augmentation *f* de salaire; ***salary scale*** échelle *f* de salaires; ***salary structure*** structure *f* des salaires

salchow ['sælkəʊ] *n (in ice skating)* salchow *m*

sale [seɪl] **1** *n* **(a)** *(gen)* vente *f*; **to make a sale** conclure une vente; **the sale of alcohol is forbidden** la vente d'alcool est interdite; **sales of satellite TV dishes are growing** les ventes d'antennes paraboliques sont en hausse; **the branch with the highest sales** la succursale dont le chiffre d'affaires est le plus élevé; **for sale** *(sign)* à vendre; **I'm afraid that article is not for sale** je regrette, cet article n'est pas à vendre; **to put sth up for sale** mettre qch en vente; **our house is up for sale** nous avons mis notre maison en vente; **on sale** en vente; **on sale at a supermarket near you** en vente dans tous les supermarchés; **we bought the goods on a sale or return basis** nous avons acheté la marchandise à condition; **sale by private agreement** vente *f* à l'amiable; **sale by sealed tender** vente *f* par soumission cachetée; **sale with option of repurchase** vente *f* avec faculté de rachat; **sale by auction** vente *f* aux enchères

(b) *(event)* soldes *mpl*; **the January sales attract huge crowds** les soldes de janvier attirent les foules; **the sales are on in London** les soldes ont commencé à Londres; **I got it in a sale** je l'ai acheté en solde; **closing-down sale** liquidation *f*

(c) *(auction)* vente *f* (aux enchères)

2 *comp (goods)* soldé

3 sales *comp (campaign, force, team)* de vente; *(promotion, forecasts)* des ventes

►► ***sales account*** compte *m* des ventes; ***sales acumen*** sens *m* du commerce; ***sales agent*** agent *m* commercial; ***sales area*** *(in store)* surface *f ou* espace *m* de vente; *(district)* région *f* desservie; ***sales assistant*** vendeur(euse) *m,f*; ***sales budget*** budget *m* commercial, budget *m* des ventes; *Am* ***sales clerk*** vendeur(euse) *m,f*; ***sales conference*** conférence *f* du personnel des ventes; ***sales consultant*** conseiller(ère) *m,f* commercial(e); ***sales counter*** comptoir *m* de vente; ***sales department*** service *m* commercial, service *m* des ventes; ***sales director*** directeur(trice) *m,f* des ventes; ***sales drive*** campagne *f* de vente; ***sales engineer*** ingénieur *m* technico-commercial, ingénieur *m* commercial, ingénieur *m* des ventes; ***sales executive*** cadre *m* commercial; ***sales figures*** chiffre *m* de vente; ***sales literature*** brochures *fpl* publicitaires; ***sales manager*** directeur(trice) *m,f* commercial(e); ***sales and marketing*** vente-marketing *f*; ***sales and marketing director*** directeur(trice) *m,f* des ventes et du marketing; ***sales network*** réseau *m* de vente; ***sales objective*** objectif *m* de vente; ***sales outlet*** point *m* de vente; ***sales pitch*** arguments *mpl* de vente; *(verbal)* boniment *m*, argumentation *f*; ***sales policy*** politique *f* de vente; ***sales potential*** potentiel *m* de vente; ***sale price*** *(selling price)* prix *m* de vente; *(reduced price)* prix *m* soldé; ***sales projection*** prévision *f* des ventes; ***sales rep, sales representative*** représentant(e) *m,f* (de commerce); ***sales resistance*** réticence *f* de la part du consommateur; **our product met with some initial sales resistance** le public n'a pas accepté notre produit tout de suite; *Am* ***sales slip*** ticket *m* de caisse; ***sales staff*** personnel *m* de vente; ***sales support*** soutien *m* commercial; ***sales talk*** boniment *m*; ***sales target*** objectif *m* de vente; *Am* ***sales tax*** TVA *f*; ***sales technique*** technique *f* de vente; ***sales tool*** instrument *m* de vente; ***sale of work*** vente *f* de charité

saleability [,seɪlə'bɪlɪtɪ] *n Com* facilité *f* d'écoulement

saleable = **salable**

Salem ['seɪləm] *n* Salem

►► *Am Hist* ***the Salem witch trials*** la chasse aux sorcières de Salem

THE SALEM WITCH TRIALS

Il s'agit d'une série de procès qui se déroulèrent dans une atmosphère d'hystérie collective et aboutirent à la pendaison d'une vingtaine de personnes accusées de sorcellerie, dans la ville américaine de Salem (Massachusetts) en 1692.

saleratus [,sælə'reɪtəs] *n Am Culin* bicarbonate *m* de soude

Salerno [sə'lɜːnəʊ] *n* Salerne

saleroom ['seɪlrʊm], *Am* **salesroom** ['seɪlzrʊm] *n* salle *f* des ventes

salesclerk ['seɪlzklɜːrk] *n Am* vendeur(euse) *m,f*

sai–sal

salesgirl ['seɪlzgɜːl] *n* vendeuse *f*

salesman ['seɪlzmən] (*pl* **salesmen** [-mən]) *n* *(in shop)* vendeur *m*; *(rep)* représentant *m* (de commerce); **an insurance salesman** un représentant en assurances

salesmanship ['seɪlzmənʃɪp] *n* art *m* de la vente, technique *f* de vente; **high-pressure** *or* **aggressive salesmanship** techniques *fpl* de vente agressives

salesperson ['seɪlz,pɜːsən] (*pl* **salespeople** [-,piːpəl]) *n* *(in shop)* vendeur(euse) *m,f*; *(rep)* représentant(e) *m,f* (de commerce)

salesroom *Am* = **saleroom**

saleswoman ['seɪlz,wʊmən] (*pl* **saleswomen** [-,wɪmɪn]) *n* *(in shop)* vendeuse *f*; *(rep)* représentante *f* (de commerce)

Salian ['seɪlɪən] *Hist* **1** *n* Salien(enne) *m,f*
2 *adj* salien, salique

salicin, salicine ['sælɪsɪn] *n Pharm* salicine *f*

Salic law ['sælɪk-] *n Hist* loi *f* salique

salicylate [sə'lɪsɪleɪt] *n Chem* salicylate *m*

salicylic [,sælɪ'sɪlɪk] *adj Chem* salicylique
►► ***salicylic acid*** acide *m* salicylique; ***salicylic aldehyde*** aldéhyde *m* salicylique

salience ['seɪlɪəns], **saliency** ['seɪlɪənsɪ] *n Formal* **(a)** *(salient nature)* nature *f* saillante, caractère *m* saillant **(b)** *(salient feature)* saillant *m*, saillie *f*

salient ['seɪlɪənt] **1** *adj Formal* saillant, principal
2 *n Archit & Mil* saillant *m*

Salientia [,seɪlɪ'enʃə] *n Zool* anoures *mpl*

salientian [,seɪlɪ'enʃən] *adj Zool* anoure

saliferous [sæ'lɪfərəs] *adj Geol (of rock)* salifère, salicole
►► ***saliferous system*** système *m* salifèrien

salification [,sælɪfɪ'keɪʃən] *n Chem* salification *f*

salify ['sælɪfaɪ] (*pt & pp* **salified**) *vt Chem* salifier

salina [sə'laɪnə] *n* *(marsh)* marais *m* salant; *(spring)* source *f* saline; *(lake)* lac *m* salé

saline ['seɪlaɪn] **1** *adj* salin
2 *n Med (salt solution)* sérum *m* physiologique
►► *Med* ***saline drip*** perfusion *f* saline; ***saline solution*** solution *f* saline

salinity [sə'lɪnɪtɪ] *n* salinité *f*

salinometer [,sælɪ'nɒmɪtə(r)] *n* salinomètre *m*

Salisbury steak ['sɔːlzbərɪ-] *n Am Culin* = steak tranché fin, en sauce

saliva [sə'laɪvə] *n* salive *f*

salivary gland ['sælɪvərɪ-] *n* glande *f* salivaire

salivate ['sælɪveɪt] *vi also Fig* saliver

salivation [,sælɪ'veɪʃən] *n* salivation *f*

Salk vaccine [sɔːlk-] *n Med* vaccin *m* de Salk

sallow ['sæləʊ] **1** *adj (gen)* jaunâtre; *(face, complexion)* jaunâtre, cireux
2 *n Bot* saule *m*

sallowness ['sæləʊnɪs] *n* *(of person, complexion)* teint *m* cireux

Sally ['sælɪ] *pr n*
►► *Br Fam* ***the Sally Army*** l'Armée *f* du salut[□]; *Br Culin* ***Sally Lunn*** = petit pain au lait qui se mange rôti et beurré

sally ['sælɪ] (*pl* **sallies**, *pt & pp* **sallied**) *n* **(a)** *Mil* sortie *f*; *(excursion)* excursion *f*, sortie *f*; **his first sally into travel writing** sa première tentative de récit de voyage **(b)** *Formal (quip)* boutade *f*, saillie *f*

►**sally forth, sally out** *vi Literary* sortir; **we all sallied forth** *or* **out into the snow** nous sommes tous partis gaillardement sous la neige

salmagundi [,sælmə'gʌndɪ] *n* **(a)** *Culin* = ragoût de viande hachée, d'œufs, d'anchois et de vinaigre **(b)** *(medley)* mélange *m*

salmon ['sæmən] (*pl* **inv** *or* **salmons**) *n Ich* saumon *m*; **young salmon** tacon *m*
►► ***salmon farm*** élevage *m* de saumons; ***salmon fillet*** filet *m* de saumon; ***salmon ladder, salmon leap*** échelle *f* à saumon(s); ***salmon pink*** (rose *m*) saumon *m*; ***salmon steak*** darne *f* de saumon; *Ich* ***salmon trout*** truite *f* saumonée

salmonella [,sælmə'nelə] (*pl* **salmonellae** [-liː]) *n Biol* salmonella *f inv*, salmonelle *f*
►► *Med* ***salmonella poisoning*** salmonellose *f*

salmonellosis [,sælmone'ləʊsɪs] *n Med* salmonellose *f*

salmon-pink *adj* (rose) saumon *(inv)*

Salome [sə'ləʊmɪ] *pr n Bible* Salomé

salon ['sælɒn] *n* salon *m*

Salonica, Salonika [sə'lɒnɪkə] *n* Salonique, Thessalonique

saloon [sə'luːn] *n* **(a)** *Br Aut* berline *f*
(b) *(public room)* salle *f*, salon *m*; *(on ship)* salon *m*
(c) *Am (bar)* bar *m*; *(in Wild West)* saloon *m*
(d) *Br (in pub)* salle *f* de pub *(plus confortable que le bar principal)*
►► *Br* ***saloon bar*** salle *f* de pub *(plus confortable que le bar principal)*; *Br* ***saloon car*** *Aut* berline *f*; *Rail* voiture-salon *f*; *Am Hist* ***saloon girl*** entraîneuse *f* de saloon

salopettes [,sælə'pets] *npl Br* combinaison *f* de ski

salpa ['sælpə] *n Zool* salpe *f*

salpiglossis [,sælpɪ'glɒsɪs] *n Bot* salpiglossis *m*

salpingectomy [,sælpɪn'dʒektəmɪ] *n Med* salpingectomie *f*

salpingian [sæl'pɪndʒɪən] *adj Anat* salpingien

salpingitis [,sælpɪn'dʒaɪtɪs] *n Med* salpingite *f*

salpinx ['sælpɪŋks] *n* **(a)** *Antiq* salpinx *m* **(b)** *Anat (Eustachian tube)* trompe *f* d'Eustache; *(Fallopian tube)* trompe *f* de Fallope

salsa ['sælsə] **1** *n* **(a)** *(music, dance)* salsa *f* **(b)** *(sauce)* salsa *f* mexicaine
2 *vi* danser la salsa

salsify ['sælsɪfɪ] (*pl* **salsifies**) *n Bot* salsifis *m*

SALT [sɔːlt, sɒlt] *n* (*abbr* **Strategic Arms Limitation Talks** *or* **Treaty**) SALT *m*
►► ***SALT talks*** négociations *fpl* SALT

salt [sɔːlt, sɒlt] **1** *n* **(a)** *Chem & Culin* sel *m*; **kitchen salt** gros sel *m*; **there's too much salt in the soup** la soupe est trop salée; *Bible* **the salt of the earth** le sel de la terre; **she's the salt of the earth, that woman!** cette femme est la bonté incarnée!; *Fig* **to rub salt into the wound** remuer le couteau dans la plaie; *Fig* **to take sth with a pinch** *or* **grain of salt** ne pas prendre qch au pied de la lettre; **you must take what he says with a pinch of salt** il ne faut pas prendre ce qu'il dit pour argent comptant; **any athlete worth his/her salt** n'importe quel(le) athlète digne de ce nom, n'importe quel(le) athlète qui se respecte; *Literary* **to eat salt with sb** partager le pain et le sel avec qn
(b) *Fam (sailor)* **old salt** (vieux) loup *m* de mer
2 *vt* **(a)** *(food)* saler
(b) *(roads)* saler, répandre du sel sur
3 *adj* salé; *Literary* **to weep salt tears** pleurer amèrement
4 salts *npl Pharm* sels *mpl*; *Fam* **like a dose of salts** rapidement[□]; **to get through sth like a dose of salts** faire qch en deux temps trois mouvements *ou* en deux coups de cuillère à pot; **that curry went through me like a dose of salts** sitôt avalé, le curry m'a donné la courante
►► ***salt beef*** bœuf *m* salé; ***salt box*** *(object)* salière *f*; *Am Archit* = maison à toit mansardé ayant deux étages à l'avant et un étage à l'arrière; ***salt cellar*** salière *f*; ***salt cod*** morue *f* salée; ***salt flat*** salant *m*; ***salt lake*** lac *m* salé; ***Salt Lake City*** Salt Lake City; ***salt marsh*** marais *m* salant; ***salt mine*** mine *f* de sel; ***salt pork*** porc *m* salé, petit salé *m*; *Am* ***salt shaker*** salière *f*; *Hist* ***salt tax*** gabelle *f*; ***salt water*** eau *f* salée

►**salt away** *vt sep Fam Fig (money)* mettre de côté[□]

►**salt down** *vt sep* saler, conserver dans du sel

saltant ['sæltənt] *adj Her* sautant, saillant

saltation [sæl'teɪʃən] *n* **(a)** *(leaping)* saut *m* **(b)** *Biol* mutation *f* **(c)** *Geol* saltation *f*

saltationism [sæl'teɪʃənɪzəm] *n Biol* mutationnisme *m*

saltationist [sæl'teɪʃənɪst] *n Biol* mutationniste *mf*

saltatorial [,sæltə'tɔːrɪəl], **saltatorious** [,sæltə'tɔːrɪəs], **saltatory** ['sæltətərɪ] *adj Zool* saltatoire

saltbush ['sɔːltbʊʃ] *n Bot* atriplex *m*

salted ['sɔːltɪd] *adj* salé

salter ['sɔːltə(r)] *n* **(a)** *(producer of salt)* salinier(ère) *m,f*, fabricant(e) *m,f* de sel; *(worker in salt production)* salinier(ère) *m,f*, saunier *m* **(b)** *(person preserving foods in salt)* saleur(euse) *m,f*

saltern ['sɔːltɜːn] *n* *(saltworks)* saline *f*; *(area of land)* marais *m* salant

salt-free *adj* sans sel

saltigrade ['sæltɪgreɪd] *Zool* **1** *n* araignée *f* sauteuse
2 *adj* sauteur

saltine® ['sɔːltiːn] *n* cracker *m*

saltiness ['sɔːltɪnɪs] *n* *(quality of salt)* salinité *f*; *(taste)* goût *m* salé

salting ['sɔːltɪŋ] *n* **(a)** *(of food → for preserving)* salaison *f*; *(→ for flavouring)* salage *m* **(b)** *Geog* **saltings** marais *m* salant

saltire ['sɔːltaɪə(r)] *n Her* sautoir *m*; **saltire couped** flanchis *m*, flanquis *m*; **a saltire or** au sautoir d'or

saltlick ['sɔːltlɪk] *n* **(a)** *(block)* pain *m* de sel **(b)** *(place)* salant *m*

saltmill ['sɔːltmɪl] *n* moulin *m* à sel

saltpan ['sɔːltpæn] *n* marais *m* salant

saltpetre, *Am* **saltpeter** [,sɔːlt'piːtə(r)] *n* salpêtre *m*

saltspoon ['sɔːltspuːn] *n* cuillère *f* à sel

saltwater ['sɔːltwɔːtə(r)] *adj* *(fish, plant)* de mer

saltweed ['sɔːltwiːd] *n Am Bot* hédéoma *m* faux-pouliot

saltworks ['sɔːltwɜːks] (*pl* **inv**) *n* saline *f*

saltwort ['sɔːltwɜːt] *n Bot* **(a)** *(plant of genus Salsola)* soude *f*; **prickly saltwort** kali *m* **(b)** *(salicornia)* salicorne *f*

salty ['sɔːltɪ] (*compar* **saltier**, *superl* **saltiest**) *adj* **(a)** *(food, taste)* salé; *(deposit)* saumâtre **(b)** *Fam (anecdote, book)* piquant[□]; *Old-fashioned (licentious)* salé, corsé

salubrious [sə'luːbrɪəs] *adj* **(a)** *(respectable)* respectable, bien; **it's not the most salubrious of bars** c'est un bar plutôt mal famé **(b)** *(healthy)* salubre, sain

salubriously [sə'luːbrɪəslɪ] *adv* salubrement

salubriousness [sə'luːbrɪəsnɪs] *n* salubrité *f*

salubrity [sə'luːbrɪtɪ] *n* salubrité *f*

saluki [sə'luːkɪ] *n* *(dog)* sloughi *m*

salutary ['sæljʊtərɪ] *adj* salutaire; **a salutary lesson** une leçon salutaire

salutation [,sæljʊ'teɪʃən] *n* **(a)** *(greeting)* salut *m*, salutation *f* **(b)** *(on letter)* formule *f* de début de lettre

salutatory [,sæljʊ'teɪtrɪ] *adj* de salutation
►► *Am Sch & Univ* ***salutatory oration*** allocution *f* de bienvenue

salute [sə'luːt] **1** *n* **(a)** *Mil (with hand)* salut *m*; *(with guns)* salve *f*; **to give (sb) a salute** faire un salut (à qn); **the lieutenant returned his salute** le lieutenant lui a rendu son salut; **to stand at salute** garder le salut; **to take the salute** passer les troupes en revue; **to fire a salute** tirer une salve; **a twenty-one gun salute** une salve de vingt et un coups de canon
(b) *(greeting)* salut *m*, salutation *f*
(c) *(tribute)* hommage *m*; **a salute to British artists** un hommage aux artistes britanniques
2 *vt* **(a)** *Mil (with hand)* saluer; *(with guns)* tirer une salve en l'honneur de; **to salute the flag** saluer le drapeau
(b) *(greet)* saluer; **she saluted me with a wave** elle m'a salué d'un geste de la main
(c) *(acknowledge, praise)* saluer, acclamer; **the press today salutes a new world champion** la presse salue aujourd'hui un nouveau champion du monde
3 *vi Mil* faire un salut

Salvador ['sælvədɔː(r)] *n* Salvador *(port)*

Salvadorean, Salvadorian [,sælvə'dɔːrɪən] **1** *n* Salvadorien(enne) *m,f*
2 *adj* salvadorien

salvage ['sælvɪdʒ] **1** *vt* **(a)** *(vessel, cargo, belongings)* sauver; *(old newspapers, scrap metal)* récupérer; **they managed to salvage some furniture from the fire** ils ont réussi à sauver quelques meubles de l'incendie; **a counter salvaged from an old butcher's shop** un comptoir récupéré dans une ancienne boucherie
(b) *Fig (mistake, meal)* rattraper; *(situation)* rattraper, sauver; **to salvage one's reputation** sauver sa réputation
2 *n* **(a)** *(recovery → of vessel, cargo, belongings, furniture)* sauvetage *m*; *(→ of old newspapers, scrap metal)* récupération *f*
(b) *(UNCOUNT) (things recovered → from shipwreck, disaster)* objets *mpl* sauvés; *(→ for re-use, recycling)* objets *mpl* récupérés
(c) *(payment)* indemnité *f* ou prime *f* de sauvetage; *(paid to salvage tug)* indemnité *f* de remorquage
3 *comp (operation)* de sauvetage
►► ***salvage company*** = compagnie spécialisée dans le remorquage et le renflouage de navires;

salvaged goods matériel *m* récupéré; ***salvage money*** prime *f* de sauvetage; ***salvage tug*** remorqueur *m (pour les sauvetages)*; ***salvage value*** récupérabilité *f*; ***salvage vessel*** navire *m* de relevage

salvageable ['sælvɪdʒəbəl] *adj* récupérable

salvager ['sælvɪdʒə(r)] *n* sauveteur *m*

salvation [sæl'veɪʃən] *n* (**a**) *Rel* salut *m* (**b**) *Fig* salut *m*; **writing has always been my salvation** écrire m'a toujours sauvé; **the country's salvation does not lie in rearmament** le pays ne va pas trouver son salut dans le réarmement, ce n'est pas le réarmement qui va sauver le pays

►► ***the Salvation Army*** l'Armée *f* du salut

salvationist [sæl'veɪʃənɪst] *n* (**a**) *(member of evangelical sect)* salutiste *mf* (**b**) *(member of Salvation Army)* salutiste *mf*

salve [sælv] **1** *n* (**a**) *(ointment)* baume *m*, pommade *f* (**b**) *Fig (relief)* baume *m*, apaisement *m*

2 *vt* (**a**) *(relieve)* calmer, soulager; **I did it to salve my conscience** je l'ai fait par acquit de conscience (**b**) *(salvage)* sauver

salver ['sælvə(r)] *n* plateau *m* (de service); **a silver salver** un plateau en argent

salvia ['sælvɪə] *n Bot* salvia *f*, sauge *f*

Salvo ['sælvəʊ] *(pl* **Salvos** *or* **Salvoes**) *n Austr Fam (member of Salvation Army)* = membre de l'Armée du salut; **the Salvos** *(Salvation Army)* l'Armée *f* du salut ❑

salvo ['sælvəʊ] *(pl* **salvos** *or* **salvoes**) *n* (**a**) *Mil* salve *f* (**b**) *Fig (of applause)* salve *f*; *(of laughter)* éclat *m*; *(of insults)* torrent *m*

salvor ['sælvə(r)] *n* sauveteur *m* (en mer)

Salyut [sæl'ju:t] *n Astron* Saliout *f*

Salzburg ['sæltsbɜ:g] *n* Salzbourg

SAM [sæm] *n (abbr* **surface-to-air missile**) missile *m* sol-air

samara [sə'mɑ:rə] *n Bot* samare *f*

Samaria [sə'meərɪə] *n* Samarie *f*; **in Samaria** en Samarie

Samaritan [sə'mærɪtən] **1** *n Rel* Samaritain(e) *m,f*

2 *adj* samaritain

3 Samaritans *npl* **the Samaritans** = association proposant un soutien moral par téléphone aux personnes déprimées, ≃ SOS Amitié

samarium [sə'meərɪəm] *n Chem* samarium *m*

samba ['sæmbə] **1** *n* samba *f*

2 *vi* danser la samba

sambar ['sæmbə(r)] *n Zool* sambar *m*

sambo ['sæmbəʊ] *(pl* **sambos**) *n Br very Fam Old-fashioned* nègre ❑ *m*, négresse ❑ *f*, bamboula *m*, = terme raciste désignant un Noir

Sam Browne [sæm'braʊn] *n (belt)* ceinture *f* avec baudrier

►► ***Sam Browne belt*** ceinture *f* avec baudrier

sambuca [sæm'bju:kə] *n Antiq & Mus* sambuque *f*

SAME [seɪm]

même	► **1; 2 (a)**
identique	► **2 (b)**
la même chose	► **2 (c)**
de la même façon	► **3**

1 *adj* même; **she's wearing the same glasses as you** elle porte les mêmes lunettes que toi; **you saw the same movie I did** tu as vu le même film que moi; **their son is the same age as ours** leur fils a le même âge que le nôtre; **are you still at the same address?** êtes-vous toujours à la même adresse?; **the two suitcases are exactly the same colour/shape** les deux valises sont exactement de la même couleur/ont exactement la même forme; **it always seems to be the same people who suffer** on dirait que ce sont toujours les mêmes qui souffrent; **we are going the same way** nous allons dans la même direction; **do you still feel the same way?** est-ce que vos sentiments sont toujours les mêmes?; **they are one and the same person** ils ne font qu'un; **they are one and the same thing** c'est une seule et même chose; **it all boils down to the same thing** cela revient au même; **it is always the same thing** c'est toujours la même chose; **see you same time, same place** je te retrouve à la même heure, au même endroit; **she's still the same (old) Sarah** c'est toujours notre bonne vieille Sarah; *Fam* **same difference!** c'est du pareil au même!

2 *pron* (**a**) **the same** *(unchanged → singular)* le même, la même; *(→ plural)* les mêmes *mfpl*; **it's the same as before** c'est comme avant; **life's just not the same now they're gone** les choses ont changé depuis qu'ils sont partis; **the house isn't the same without her** la maison n'est pas pareille sans elle; **the city centre is still the same** le centre-ville n'a pas changé; **she is exactly the same** elle n'a pas changé du tout; **he had an accident and he's never been the same since** il a eu un accident et il n'est plus le même depuis

(**b**) *(identical)* identique; **the two vases are exactly the same** les deux vases sont identiques

(**c**) *(used in comparisons)* **the same** la même chose; **it's the same in Italy** c'est la même chose *ou* c'est pareil en Italie; **it's always the same** c'est toujours la même chose *ou* toujours pareil; **it's not a bit the same** ce n'est pas du tout la même chose *ou* pas du tout pareil; **it's the same here as in France** c'est la même chose ici qu'en France; **aren't you Freddie Fortescue? – the very same** vous n'êtes pas Freddie Fortescue? – lui-même; **(the) same again, please** la même chose (, s'il vous plaît); **if it's all the same to you, I'll go now** si cela ne vous fait rien, je vais partir maintenant; **it's all** *or* **just the same to me what you do** tu peux faire ce que tu veux, ça m'est bien égal; **the same is true of, the same holds for** il en va de même pour; *Fam* **I was really cross – same here!** j'étais vraiment fâché – et moi donc!; **Happy Christmas – (and the) same to you!** Joyeux Noël – à vous aussi *ou* de même!; *Fam* **stupid idiot – and the same to you!** espèce d'imbécile! – imbécile toi-même!

(**d**) *Law* **the same** *(aforementioned)* le (la) susdit(e)

(**e**) *Com* **and for delivery of same** et pour livraison de ces (mêmes) articles

3 *adv* **the same** de la même façon; **it's not spelt the same** ça ne s'écrit pas de la même façon; **to think/feel/act the same** penser/sentir/agir de même; **they all taste the same** ils ont tous le même goût; **all these houses look the same to me** je trouve que ces maisons se ressemblent toutes; **all her songs sound the same** toutes ses chansons se ressemblent

4 all the same, just the same *adv* quand même; **all** *or* **just the same, I would like to know what happened** quand même, j'aimerais bien savoir ce qui s'est passé; **all the same, I still like her** je l'aime bien quand même; **thanks all the same** merci quand même

---

same-day *adj Com (processing, delivery)* dans la journée

►► *Com* ***same-day delivery*** livraison *f* le jour même; *Banking* ***same-day value*** valeur *f* jour

sameness ['seɪmnɪs] *n* (**a**) *(similarity)* similitude *f*, ressemblance *f* (**b**) *(tedium)* monotonie *f*, uniformité *f*

same-sex *adj* entre personnes du même sexe

same-sexer [-'seksə(r)] *n* homosexuel(elle) *m,f*

samey ['seɪmɪ] *adj Br Fam Pej* monotone ❑, ennuyeux ❑

Samian ['seɪmɪən] *Geog* **1** *n* Samien(ne) *m,f*

2 *adj* samien

►► *Archeol* ***Samian ware*** poteries *fpl* arétines *ou* d'Arezzo

samisen ['sæmɪsen] *n Mus* shamisen *m*

samizdat ['sæmɪzdæt] *n* samizdat *m*

Samoa [sə'məʊə] *n* Samoa *m*; **in Samoa** à Samoa

Samoan [sə'məʊən] **1** *n* (**a**) *(person)* Samoan(e) *m,f* (**b**) *Ling* samoan *m*

2 *adj* samoan

samosa [sə'məʊsə] *(pl* **inv** *or* **samosas**) *n* samosa *m (petit pâté indien à la viande ou aux légumes)*

samovar ['sæmə,vɑ:(r)] *n* samovar *m*

Samoyed [sə'mɔɪəd] *(pl* **inv** *or* **Samoyeds**) **1** *npl (people)* **the Samoyed** les Samoyèdes *mpl*

2 *n* (**a**) *Ling* samoyède *m* (**b**) *(dog)* samoyède *m*

sampan ['sæmpæn] *n* sampan *m*, sampang *m*

samphire ['sæmfaɪə(r)] *n Bot* **(rock) samphire** criste-marine *f*

sample ['sɑ:mpəl] **1** *n* (**a**) *(gen) & Com* échantillon *m*; **a free sample** un échantillon gratuit; **a representative sample of the population** un échantillon représentatif de la population; **please bring a sample of your work** veuillez apporter un échantillon de votre travail; *Com* **up to sample** conforme à l'échantillon; **to buy sth from sample** acheter qch d'après échantillon

(**b**) *Geol, Med & (science)* échantillon *m*, prélèvement *m*; *(of blood)* prélèvement *m*; *(of urine)* échantillon *m*; **water/rock samples** prélèvements *mpl* d'eau/de roche; **to take a sample** prélever un échantillon, faire un prélèvement; **to take a blood sample** faire une prise de sang

(**c**) *Mus* sample *m*; **he uses a lot of samples** il utilise beaucoup de samples

2 *comp* **a sample bottle/pack** un échantillon; **we'll send you a sample bottle of our shampoo** nous vous enverrons un échantillon de notre shampooing; **do the sample exercise first** faites d'abord l'exercice donné à titre d'exemple; **a sample question from last year's exam paper** un exemple de question tiré de l'examen de l'année dernière

3 *vt* (**a**) *(food, drink)* goûter (à), déguster; *(experience)* goûter à

(**b**) *Mus* échantillonner

(**c**) *(public opinion)* sonder

4 *vi Mus* échantillonner

►► *Com* ***sample book*** catalogue *m* d'échantillons, livre *m* d'échantillons; ***sample prices*** prix *mpl* donnés à titre d'exemple; *Mktg* ***sample survey*** enquête *f* par sondage

sampler ['sɑ:mplə(r)] *n* (**a**) *Sewing* modèle *m* de broderie (**b**) *(collection of samples)* échantillonnage *m*, sélection *f* (**c**) *Mus* échantillonneur *m* (**d**) *(person)* échantillonneur(euse) *m,f*

sampling ['sɑ:mplɪŋ] *n* (**a**) *(gen) & Com* échantillonnage *m* (**b**) *Mus* sampling *m*

►► ***sampling error*** erreur *f* d'échantillonnage; ***sampling method*** méthode *f* d'échantillonnage; ***sampling quota*** quota *m* d'échantillonnage

Samson ['sæmsən] *pr n Bible* **Samson and Delilah** Samson et Dalila; **he's a real Samson** il est fort comme un Turc

Samuel ['sæmjʊəl] *pr n Bible* Samuel; **the Books of Samuel** les livres *mpl* de Samuel

samurai ['sæmʊraɪ] *(pl* **inv**) *n* samouraï *m*, samourai *m inv*

►► *Fin* ***samurai bond*** obligation *f* samouraï

Sana'a [sɑ:'nɑ:] *n Geog* San'a, Sanaa

San Andreas Fault [,sænæn'dreɪəs-] *n* **the San Andreas Fault** la faille de San Andreas *(faille géologique à l'origine de nombreux tremblements de terre en Californie)*

sanative ['sænətɪv] **1** *n* remède *m*

2 *adj* curatif

sanatorium [,sænə'tɔ:rɪəm] *(pl* **sanatoriums** *or* **sanatoria** [-rɪə]), *Am* **sanitarium** [,sænɪ'teərɪəm] *(pl* **sanitariums** *or* **sanitaria** [-rɪə]) *n (nursing home)* sanatorium *m*; *(sick bay)* infirmerie *f*

sanatory ['sænətərɪ] *adj Literary* curatif, guérisseur

sancta ['sæŋktə] *pl of* **sanctum**

sanctification [,sæŋktɪfɪ'keɪʃən] *n* sanctification *f*

sanctified ['sæŋktɪfaɪd] *adj* sanctifié

sanctify ['sæŋktɪfaɪ] *(pt & pp* **sanctified**) *vt* sanctifier

sanctimonious [,sæŋktɪ'məʊnɪəs] *adj* moralisateur; **I hate his sanctimonious manner** je ne supporte pas ses airs de petit saint

sanctimoniously [,sæŋktɪ'məʊnɪəslɪ] *adv (look)* d'un air de petit saint; *(speak)* d'un ton bigot *ou* moralisateur

sanctimoniousness [,sæŋktɪ'məʊnɪəsnɪs], **sanctimony** ['sæŋktɪmənɪ] *n* airs *mpl* de petit saint, pharisaïsme *m*

sanction ['sæŋkʃən] **1** *n* (**a**) *(approval)* sanction *f*, accord *m*, consentement *m*; **with the sanction of the government** avec l'accord du gouvernement; **it hasn't yet been given official sanction** ceci n'a pas encore été officiellement approuvé *ou* sanctionné, ceci n'a pas encore eu l'approbation *ou* sanction officielle; **it has the sanction of long usage** c'est consacré par l'usage

(**b**) *(punitive measure)* sanction *f*; **to impose (economic) sanctions on a country** prendre des sanctions (économiques) à l'encontre d'un pays

2 *vt (authorize)* sanctionner, entériner; *(approve → behaviour)* approuver; **to sanction a plan** donner son accord *or* son aval à un plan; **tradition has long sanctioned this error** la tradition a entériné *ou* consacré cette erreur depuis longtemps

▸▸ ***sanctions busting*** violation *f* des sanctions; **the firm was accused of sanctions busting** la société a été accusée d'avoir violé les sanctions

sanctity ['sæŋktɪtɪ] *n (of person, life)* sainteté *f*; *(of marriage, property, place → holiness)* caractère *m* sacré; *(→ inviolability)* inviolabilité *f*

sanctuary ['sæŋktʃʊərɪ] *(pl* **sanctuaries***) n* **(a)** *(holy place)* sanctuaire *m*; *Literary* **the sanctuary of the heart** le sanctuaire du cœur **(b)** *(refuge)* refuge *m*, asile *m*; **to seek sanctuary** chercher asile *ou* refuge; **to take sanctuary** trouver asile **(c)** *(for animals)* réserve *f*

sanctum ['sæŋktəm] *(pl* **sanctums** *or* **sancta** [-tə]*) n* **(a)** *(holy place)* sanctuaire *m* **(b)** *Hum (private place)* refuge *m*, retraite *f*, tanière *f*; **he's in his inner sanctum** il s'est retiré dans sa tanière

Sanctus ['sæŋktəs] *n Rel & Mus* sanctus *m*

▸▸ ***sanctus bell*** = cloche qui sonne le sanctus

sand [sænd] **1** *n* **(a)** *(gen)* sable *m*; **miles of golden sands** des kilomètres *mpl* de sable doré; **shifting sand** sables *mpl* mouvants; **the sands of time** le temps qui passe; **the sands of time are running out for us** nous n'aurons bientôt plus le temps, le temps qui nous est imparti sera bientôt écoulé; *Fig* **to build on sand** bâtir sur le sable; *Fig* **to draw a line in the sand** fixer une limite à ne pas dépasser

(b) *Am Fam (courage)* cran *m*

2 *comp (dune)* de sable

3 *vt* **(a)** *(with sandpaper)* poncer au papier de verre

(b) *(spread sand on)* sabler

▸▸ *Constr* ***sand bed*** couchis *m*; *Bot* ***sand crocus*** , romulée *f* de Colonna; *Zool* ***sand dollar*** clypéastéroïde *m*; ***sand dune*** dune *f*; *Zool* ***sand eel*** lançon *m*, équille *f*; *Zool* ***sand flea*** *(sandhopper)* puce *f* de mer, talitre *m*; *(chigoe)* chique *f*; *Entom* ***sand fly*** phlébotome *m*, mouche *f* des sables; *Zool* ***sand lance*** lançon *m*, équille *f*; *Zool* ***sand lizard*** lézard *m* agile; *Am* ***sand lot*** terrain *m* vague; *Br Orn* ***sand martin*** hirondelle *f* de rivage; ***sand painting*** peinture *f* au sable; *Bot* ***sand spurrey*** spergulaire *f* rouge; *Bot* ***sand toadflax*** linaire *f* de sables; *Am Golf* ***sand trap*** bunker *m* (de sable); *Golf* ***sand wedge*** sandwedge *m*; ***sand yacht*** char *m* à voile

▸**sand down** *vt sep (wood, metal)* poncer au papier de verre, décaper

sandal ['sændəl] *n* **(a)** *(footwear)* sandale *f* **(b)** = **sandalwood**

sandalwood ['sændəlwʊd] *n* bois *m* de santal

▸▸ ***sandalwood oil*** essence *f* de bois de santal

sandarac, sandarach ['sændəræk] *n* **(a)** *(tree)* thuya *m* de Berbérie **(b)** *(resin)* sandaraque *f*

sandbag ['sændbæg] *(pt & pp* **sandbagged***)* **1** *n* **(a)** sac *m* de sable *ou* de terre **(b)** *Fin (in takeover bid)* = tactique de temporisation utilisée par une entreprise faisant l'objet d'une OPA

2 *vt* **(a)** *(shore up)* renforcer avec des sacs de sable; *(protect)* protéger avec des sacs de sable **(b)** *Fam (hit)* assommer ❑ *(d'un coup de gourdin sur la nuque)* **(c)** *Am Fam (coerce)* **to sandbag sb into doing sth** forcer qn à faire qch ❑

sandbank ['sændbæŋk] *n* banc *m* de sable

sandbar ['sændbɑː(r)] *n* barre *f (dans la mer, dans un estuaire)*

sandbath ['sændbɑːθ, *pl* -bɑːðz] *n Chem* bain *m* de sable

sandblast ['sændblɑːst] **1** *vt* décaper à la sableuse, sabler

2 *n* jet *m* de sable

sandblaster ['sænd,blɑːstə(r)] *n* sableuse *f*

sandblasting ['sænd,blɑːstɪŋ] *n* décapage *m* à la sableuse, sablage *m*

sand-blind *adj* mal voyant

sandbox ['sændbɒks] *n* **(a)** *Rail* sablière *f* **(b)** *(for children)* bac *m* à sable

sandboy ['sændbɔɪ] *n see* **happy**

sand-cast *vt* couler en sable

sandcastle ['sænd,kɑːsəl] *n* château *m* de sable

sander ['sændə(r)] *n (tool)* ponceuse *f*

sanderling ['sændəlɪŋ] *n Orn* bécasseau *m* sanderling

sandglass ['sændglɑːs] *n* sablier *m*

sandgrouse ['sændgraʊs] *n Orn* ganga *m*

sandhill crane ['sændhɪl] *n Orn* grue *f* du Canada

sandhog ['sændhɒg] *n Am Fam* = ouvrier travaillant dans l'air comprimé

sandhopper ['sænd,hɒpə(r)] *n Zool* puce *f* de mer

Sandhurst ['sændhɜːst] *n* = centre de formation militaire britannique établi à Sandhurst, dans le Berkshire

sandiness ['sændɪnɪs] *n* qualité *f* sablonneuse

sanding ['sændɪŋ] *n* **(a)** *(of wood, plaster)* ponçage *m* **(b)** *(of roads)* sablage *m*

Sandinista [,sændɪ'niːstə] **1** *adj* sandiniste

2 *n* sandiniste *mf*

S&L [,esə'nel] *n Am (abbr* **savings and loan association***)* ≃ société *f* de crédit immobilier

S&M [,esən'dem] *n Fam* **(a)** *(abbr* **sadomasochism***)* sadomasochisme ❑ *m* **(b)** *(abbr* **sales & marketing***)* ventes *fpl* et marketing ❑

sandman ['sændmæn] *n Fig* marchand *m* de sable; **the sandman is coming** le marchand de sable va passer

Sandown Park ['sændaʊn-] *n* = champ de courses dans le Surrey (Angleterre)

sandpail ['sændpeɪl] *n Am* seau *m (pour faire des châteaux de sable)*

sandpaper ['sænd,peɪpə(r)] **1** *n* papier *m* de verre

2 *vt* poncer (au papier de verre)

sandpapering ['sænd,peɪpərɪŋ] *n* ponçage *m* (au papier de verre)

sandpie ['sændpaɪ] *n* pâté *m* de sable

sandpiper ['sænd,paɪpə(r)] *n Orn* bécasseau *m*, chevalier *m*

sandpit ['sændpɪt] *n Br* **(a)** *(for children)* bac *m* à sable **(b)** *(quarry)* sablière *f*, sablonnière *f*

Sandringham ['sændrɪŋəm] *n* = village du Norfolk où la famille royale possède une résidence de campagne

sandshoe ['sændʃuː] *n Br* tennis *m* en toile

sandsoap ['sændsəʊp] *n* savon *m* minéral

sandstone ['sændstəʊn] *n* grès *m*; **red/grey sandstone** grès *m* rouge/gris

sandstorm ['sændstɔːm] *n* tempête *f* de sable

sandtiger shark ['sændtaɪgə-] *n Ich* requintaureau *m*

sandwich ['sænwɪdʒ] **1** *n* **(a)** *(bread)* sandwich *m*; **a ham sandwich** un sandwich au jambon; *Br Fam Hum* **to be one sandwich short of a picnic** ne pas être net

(b) *Br (cake)* gâteau *m* fourré

2 *vt* **(a)** *Fam (place)* intercaler ❑; **I'll try to sandwich you (in) between appointments** j'essaierai de vous caser entre deux rendez-vous

(b) *Fam (trap)* prendre en sandwich, coincer; **I was sandwiched (in) between two people** j'étais coincé *ou* pris en sandwich entre deux personnes

(c) *(join → gen)* joindre; *(→ with glue)* coller; **we sandwiched the boards together with glue** nous avons collé les planches

▸▸ *Br* ***sandwich bar*** ≃ snack *m (où on vend des sandwichs)*; ***sandwich board*** panneau *m* publicitaire *(porté par un homme-sandwich)*; *Br* ***sandwich cake*** gâteau *m* fourré; *Br* ***sandwich course*** = stage de formation professionnelle en alternance; ***Sandwich Islands*** îles *fpl* Sandwich; ***sandwich loaf*** ≃ pain *m* de mie; ***sandwich man*** homme-sandwich *m*; *Orn* ***Sandwich tern*** sterne *f* caugek; ***sandwich toaster*** appareil *m* à croque-monsieur

sandworm ['sændwɜːm] *n Zool* arénicole *f* des pêcheurs

sandwort ['sændwɜːt] *n Bot* sabline *f*, *Spec* arénaire *f*

sandy ['sændɪ] *(compar* **sandier**, *superl* **sandiest***) adj* **(a)** *(beach, desert)* de sable; *(soil, road)* sablonneux; *(water, alluvium)* sableux; *(floor, clothes)* couvert de sable **(b)** *(in colour)* (couleur) sable *(inv)*; **sandy bottom** *(of sea, river)* fond de sable; **he has sandy** *or* **sandy-coloured hair** il a les cheveux blond roux

sand-yachting *n* char *m* à voile; **to go sand-yachting** faire du char à voile

sane [seɪn] *adj* **(a)** *(person)* sain d'esprit; **to be of sane mind** être sain d'esprit; **how do you manage to stay sane in this environment?** comment fais-tu pour ne pas devenir fou dans une ambiance pareille? **(b)** *(action)* sensé; *(attitude, approach, policy)* raisonnable, sensé

sanely ['seɪnlɪ] *adv* raisonnablement

Sanfilippo's syndrome [,sænfɪ'lɪpəʊz-] *n Med* maladie *f* de Sanfilippo, oligophrénie *f* polydystrophique

Sanforize® ['sænfəraɪz] *vt* sanforiser

San Franciscan [,sænfrən'sɪskən] **1** *n* habitant(e) *m,f* de San Francisco

2 *adj* de San Francisco

San Francisco [,sænfrən'sɪskəʊ] *n* San Francisco

▸▸ ***the San Francisco earthquake*** le tremblement de terre de San Francisco

THE SAN FRANCISCO EARTHQUAKE

C'est la plus importante catastrophe naturelle qu'aient connue les États-Unis (avril 1906). L'incendie provoqué par le séisme dura trois jours et détruisit les trois quarts de la ville, jetant 225 000 personnes à la rue et faisant 400 millions de dollars de dégâts. La ville fut reconstruite très rapidement avec l'aide du pays tout entier.

sang [sæŋ] *pt of* **sing**

sangfroid [,sɒŋ'frwɑː] *n* sang-froid *m inv*

Sangrail [sæn'greɪl], **Sangreal** [sæn'grɪəl] *n* **the Sangrail** le Saint-Graal

sangria [sæŋ'grɪə] *n* sangria *f*

sanguinary ['sæŋgwɪnərɪ] *adj Literary (murderer, tyrant)* sanguinaire; *(battle)* sanglant

sanguine ['sæŋgwɪn] **1** *adj* **(a)** *(optimistic → person, temperament)* optimiste, confiant; *(→ attitude, prospect)* **he was sanguine about the company's prospects** il voyait l'avenir de l'entreprise avec optimisme **(b)** *Literary (ruddy → complexion)* sanguin, rubicond

2 *n Art* sanguine *f*

sanguinely ['sæŋgwɪnlɪ] *adv* avec optimisme *ou* confiance

sanguineness ['sæŋgwɪnnɪs] *n* confiance *f*, optimisme *m*

sanguineous [sæŋ'gwɪnɪəs] = **sanguine** *adj*

Sanhedrim [sæn'hedrɪm], **Sanhedrin** [sæn'hedrɪn] *n Hist* Sanhédrin *m*

sanicle ['sænɪkəl] *nf Bot* sanicle *f*

sanies ['seɪniːz] *n* pus *m*

sanitarium [,sænɪ'teərɪəm] *Am* = **sanatorium**

sanitary ['sænɪtərɪ] *adj* **(a)** *(hygienic)* hygiénique; **the kitchen didn't look very sanitary** la cuisine n'avait pas l'air très propre **(b)** *(conditions, measures, equipment)* sanitaire; **sanitary arrangements/facilities** dispositions *fpl*/installations *fpl* sanitaires

▸▸ ***sanitary arrangements*** dispositions *fpl* sanitaires; ***sanitary disposal bag*** sachet *m* pour garniture périodique; ***sanitary engineer*** technicien(enne) *m,f* du service sanitaire; ***sanitary engineering*** génie *m* sanitaire; ***sanitary facilities*** installations *fpl* sanitaires; ***sanitary inspector*** inspecteur(trice) *m,f* de la santé publique; *Br* ***sanitary towel,*** *Am* ***sanitary napkin*** serviette *f* hygiénique; ***sanitary ware*** appareils *mpl* sanitaires

sanitation [,sænɪ'teɪʃən] *n (public health)* hygiène *f* publique; *(sewers)* système *m* sanitaire; *(toilets, showers)* sanitaires *mpl*; **the shanty towns have no sanitation whatsoever** les bidonvilles n'ont absolument aucun système sanitaire

▸▸ *Am* ***sanitation worker*** éboueur *m*

sanitize, -ise ['sænɪtaɪz] *vt* **(a)** *(disinfect)* désinfecter; *Fig (area of town)* assainir; **this is the sanitized image he would like to project** c'est l'image aseptisée qu'il voudrait présenter **(b)** *Fig (expurgate → document, novel)* expurger; **the original tapes had been sanitized** les bandes originales avaient été expurgées

sanitorium [,sænɪ'tɔːrɪəm]= **sanatorium**

sanity ['sænɪtɪ] *n* **(a)** *(mental health)* santé *f* mentale; **to lose one's sanity** perdre la raison **(b)** *(reasonableness)* bon sens *m*, rationalité *f*

sank [sæŋk] *pt of* **sink**

San Marino [,sænmə'riːnəʊ] *n* Saint-Marin; **in San Marino** à Saint-Marin

San Quentin [,sæn'kwentɪn] *n* = prison en Californie

sans [sænz] *prep Arch* sans
San Salvador [ˌsæn'sælvədɔː(r)] *n* San Salvador
sansculotte [sænzkjʊ'lɒt, sænzkʊ'lɒt] *n* (**a**) *Hist* sans-culotte *m* (**b**) *(revolutionary, extremist)* révolutionnaire *mf*
San Sebastian [ˌsænsə'bæstɪən] *n* Saint-Sébastien
sanserif, sans serif [sæn'serɪf] *Typ* **1** *n* caractères *mpl* sans empattement
2 *adj* sans empattement
Sanskrit ['sænskrɪt] **1** *adj* sanskrit
2 *n* sanskrit *m*
Santa ['sæntə] *pr n Fam* le père Noël ❑
▶▶ ***Santa Claus*** le père Noël ❑; ***Santa Fe*** Santa Fe; ***the Santa Fe Trail*** = route empruntée par les colons américains au XIXème siècle entre le Missouri et Santa Fe
Santiago [ˌsæntɪ'ɑːgəʊ] *n* Santiago
▶▶ ***Santiago de Compostela*** Saint-Jacques-de-Compostelle
santonica [ˌsæn'tɒnɪkə] *n Bot* santonine *f*
santonin ['sæntənɪn] *n Chem* santonine *f*
Santorini [ˌsæntə'riːnɪ] *n* Santorin
Sao Paulo [ˌsaʊ'paʊləʊ] *n* (**a**) *(city)* São Paulo (**b**) *(state)* São Paulo *m*, l'État *m* de São Paulo; **in Sao Paulo** dans le São Paulo
▶▶ ***Sao Paulo State*** São Paulo *m*, l'État *m* de São Paulo
sap [sæp] *(pt & pp* **sapped**, *cont* **sapping)** **1** *n* (**a**) *Bot* sève *f*; **the sap is rising** la sève monte; *Fig* **to feel the sap rising** être tout ragaillardi
(**b**) *Am Fam (fool)* bêta(asse) *m,f*, andouille *f*; *(gullible person)* nigaud(e) *m,f*, poire *f*
(**c**) *Am Fam (cosh)* matraque ❑ *f*, gourdin ❑ *m*
(**d**) *Mil (trench)* sape *f*
2 *vt* (**a**) *Fig (strength, courage)* saper, miner; **the fever has sapped (him of) his strength** la fièvre l'a miné
(**b**) *Am Fam (cosh)* assommer (d'un coup de gourdin) ❑
(**c**) *Mil* saper
sapele [sə'piːlɪ] *n Bot (tree, wood)* sapelli *m*, sapelly *m*
saphead ['sæphed] *n* (**a**) *Am Fam* bêta(asse) *m,f*, andouille *f* (**b**) *Mil* tête *f* de sape
sapid ['sæpɪd] *adj Formal* (**a**) *(food)* sapide, savoureux (**b**) *(conversation, writing)* intéressant
sapidity [sæ'pɪdɪtɪ] *n Formal* sapidité *f*
sapience ['seɪpɪəns] *n Formal* sagesse *f*
sapient ['seɪpɪənt] *adj Formal* sage
sapless ['sæplɪs] *adj (plant, wood)* sans sève, desséché
sapling ['sæplɪŋ] *n* (**a**) *Bot* jeune arbre *m* (**b**) *Literary (youth)* jouvenceau *m*
sapodilla [ˌsæpə'dɪlə] *n Bot (tree)* sapotillier *m*; *(fruit)* sapotille *f*
saponaceous [ˌsæpə'neɪʃəs] *adj* saponacé
saponification [sæˌpɒnɪfɪ'keɪʃən] *n Chem* saponification *f*
saponify [sæ'pɒnɪfaɪ] *vt Chem* saponifier
saponin ['sæpənɪn] *n Chem* saponine *f*
sapor ['seɪpɔː(r)] *n Literary* saveur *f*
sapper ['sæpə(r)] *n Br Mil (engineer)* soldat *m* du génie; *(who makes saps)* sapeur *m*
Sapphic ['sæfɪk] **1** *adj* (**a**) *(relating to Sappho)* saphique (**b**) *Old-fashioned (lesbian)* saphique
2 *n Literature* saphique *m*
▶▶ *Literature* ***Sapphic metre*** vers *m* saphique
sapphire ['sæfaɪə(r)] **1** *n (gem, colour)* saphir *m*
2 *comp (ring, pendant)* de saphir
3 *adj (in colour)* (bleu) saphir *(inv)*
▶▶ ***sapphire blue*** (bleu *m*) saphir *m (inv)*
sapphire-blue *adj* (bleu) saphir *(inv)*
sapphism ['sæfɪzəm] *n* saphisme *m*
Sappho ['sæfəʊ] *pr n Antiq* Sapho, Sappho; *Euph* **daughter of Sappho** lesbienne *f*
sappiness ['sæpɪnɪs] *n (of tree etc)* abondance *f* de sève, teneur *f* en sève
sappy ['sæpɪ] *(compar* **sappier**, *superl* **sappiest)** *adj* (**a**) *(tree, leaves)* plein de sève; *(wood)* vert (**b**) *Am Fam (stupid)* cloche (**c**) *Am Fam (corny)* nunuche
saprogenic [ˌsæprəʊ'dʒenɪk] *adj Biol & Med* saprogène
saprolite ['sæprəʊlaɪt] *n Geol* saprolite *f*
saprophyte ['sæprəfaɪt] *n Biol* saprophyte *m*
saprophytic [ˌsæprə'fɪtɪk] *adj Biol* saprophyte
saprozoic [ˌsæprəʊ'zəʊɪk] *adj Biol* saprozoïte
sapsucker ['sæpsʌkə(r)] *n Orn* pic *m*
sapwood ['sæpwʊd] *n Bot* aubier *m*
saraband(e) ['særəbænd] *n Mus* sarabande *f*
Saracen ['særəsən] **1** *n* Sarrasin(e) *m,f*
2 *adj* sarrasin
Saragossa [ˌsærə'gɒsə] *n* Saragosse
Sarah ['seərə] *pr n Bible* Sarah, Sara
Sarajevo [ˌsærə'jeɪvəʊ] *n* Sarajevo
Saran wrap® [sə'ræn-] *n Am* film *m* alimentaire transparent
Saratoga [ˌsærə'təʊgə] *n* Saratoga; **the battle of Saratoga** la bataille de Saratoga

THE BATTLE OF SARATOGA 

C'est à l'issue de cette bataille décisive de la guerre de l'Indépendance américaine que les Anglais durent se rendre, en 1777. Cette victoire décida la France à apporter son aide aux États-Unis.

Sarawak [sə'rɑːwɑk] *n* Sarawak; **in Sarawak** à Sarawak
sarcasm ['sɑːkæzəm] *n (UNCOUNT)* sarcasme *m*; **his constant sarcasm** ses sarcasmes *mpl* continuels; **enough of your sarcasm!** ça suffit, les sarcasmes!
sarcastic [sɑː'kæstɪk] *adj* sarcastique
sarcastically [sɑː'kæstɪkəlɪ] *adv* d'un ton sarcastique
sarcocarp ['sɑːkəʊkɑːp] *n Bot* sarcocarpe *m*
sarcoma [sɑː'kəʊmə] *(pl* **sarcomas** *or* **sarcomata** [-mətə]) *n Med* sarcome *m*
sarcomatosis [sɑːˌkəʊmə'təʊsɪs] *n Med* sarcomatose *f*
sarcomere ['sɑːkəʊmɪə(r)] *n Anat* sarcomère *m*
sarcophagus [sɑː'kɒfəgəs] *(pl* **sarcophaguses** *or* **sarcophagi** [-gaɪ]) *n* sarcophage *m*
sarcoplasm ['sɑːkəʊˌplæzəm] *n Anat* sarcoplasme *m*
sard [sɑːd] *n Miner* sardoine *f*
sardine [sɑː'diːn] **1** *n* sardine *f*; **we were packed in like sardines** nous étions serrés comme des sardines
2 **sardines** *n Br (game)* = jeu de cache-cache dans lequel les participants cherchent une seule personne, et doivent rejoindre cette dernière dans sa cachette lorsqu'ils la découvrent
Sardinia [sɑː'dɪnɪə] *n* Sardaigne *f*; **in Sardinia** en Sardaigne
Sardinian [sɑː'dɪnɪən] **1** *n* (**a**) *(person)* Sarde *mf* (**b**) *Ling* sarde *m*
2 *adj* sarde
sardius ['sɑːdɪəs] *n Miner* sardoine *f*
sardonic [sɑː'dɒnɪk] *adj* sardonique
sardonically [sɑː'dɒnɪkəlɪ] *adv* sardoniquement
sardonyx ['sɑːdənɪks] *n Geol* sardonyx *f*
sargasso [sɑː'gæsəʊ] *(pl* **sargassos)** *n Bot* sargasse *f*
▶▶ ***the Sargasso Sea*** la mer des Sargasses
sarge [sɑːdʒ] *n Fam (abbr* **sergeant)** sergent ❑ *m*
sari ['sɑːrɪ] *n* sari *m*
Sark [sɑːk] *n* Sercq; **on Sark** à Sercq
sarky ['sɑːkɪ] *(compar* **sarkier**, *superl* **sarkiest)** *adj Br Fam* sarcastique ❑; **don't you get sarky with me!** ne sois pas sarcastique avec moi!
Sarmatia [sɑː'meɪʃə] *n Geog* Sarmatie *f*
Sarmatian [sɑː'meɪʃən] **1** *n* (**a**) *(person)* Sarmate *mf* (**b**) *(language)* sarmate *m*
2 *adj* sarmatique, sarmate
sarmentose [sɑː'mentəʊs], **sarmentous** [sɑː'mentəs] *adj Bot* sarmenteux
sarnie ['sɑːnɪ] *n Br Fam (abbr* **sandwich)** sandwich ❑ *m*, casse-dalle *m*
sarod [sæ'rəʊd] *n Mus* sarod(e) *m*
sarong [sə'rɒŋ] *n* sarong *m*
saros ['seərɒs, 'sɑːrɒs] *n Astron* saros *m*
sarrusophone [sə'rʌsəfəʊn] *n Mus* sarrusophone *m*
sarsaparilla [ˌsɑːspə'rɪlə] *n (plant)* salsepareille *f*; *(drink)* boisson *f* à la salsepareille
sarsenet ['sɑːsnɪt] *n Tex* = sorte de taffetas léger
sartorial [sɑː'tɔːrɪəl] *adj* vestimentaire; **his sartorial elegance** son élégance vestimentaire, l'élégance *f* de sa mise
sartorially [sɑː'tɔːrɪəlɪ] *adv* **sartorially elegant** très bien mis, très élégant; *Hum* **he's sartorially challenged** il ne sait vraiment pas s'habiller
sartorius [sɑː'tɔːrɪəs] *n Anat* sartorius *m*
Sartrean, Sartrian ['sɑːtrɪən] *adj* sartrien
Sarum use ['seərəm-] *n Rel* = rituel pratiqué à la cathédrale de Salisbury à la fin du Moyen Âge
Sarus crane ['seərəs-] *n Orn* grue *f* antigone
SAS [ˌeseɪ'es] *n Br Mil (abbr* **Special Air Service)** = commando d'intervention spéciale de l'armée britannique
SASE [ˌeseɪˌes'iː] *n Am (abbr* **self-addressed stamped envelope)** enveloppe *f* timbrée *(portant l'adresse à laquelle elle doit être renvoyée)*
sash [sæʃ] *n* (**a**) *(belt)* ceinture *f* (en étoffe); *(sign of office)* écharpe *f* (**b**) *(frame of window)* châssis *m* à guillotine
▶▶ ***sash cord*** corde *f (d'une fenêtre à guillotine)*; ***sash window*** fenêtre *f* à guillotine
sashay ['sæʃeɪ] *vi* (**a**) *(walk indolently)* marcher d'un pas nonchalant; *(walk with swaying motion)* marcher en se déhanchant (**b**) *Am Fam* **I'll just sashay down to Joe's place** *(go)* je vais juste faire un tour chez Joe
sashimi ['sæʃɪmɪ] *n Culin* sashimi *m*
sasine ['seɪsɪn] *n Scot Law* saisine *f*
Sask *(written abbr* **Saskatchewan)** Saskatchewan *m*
Saskatchewan [sæs'kætʃɪwən] *n* le Saskatchewan; **in Saskatchewan** dans le Saskatchewan
sasquatch ['sæskwætʃ] *n* = animal légendaire (sorte de yéti) du Canada et du nord des États-Unis
sass [sæs] *Am Fam* **1** *n* culot *m*, toupet *m*
2 *vt* répondre (avec impertinence) à ❑; **don't you sass me!** ne me réponds pas sur ce ton! ❑
sassaby ['sæsəbɪ] *(pl* **sassabies)** *n Zool* damalisque *m*
sassafras ['sæsəfræs] *n Bot* sassafras *m*
▶▶ ***sassafras oil*** essence *f* de sassafras
Sassenach ['sæsənæk] *n Scot Fam Pej* = terme péjoratif par lequel les Écossais désignent les Anglais
sassy ['sæsɪ] *(compar* **sassier**, *superl* **sassiest)** *adj Fam* (**a**) *(streetwise)* cool *(inv)* et branché; **she looks sassy in that dress** elle en jette dans cette robe (**b**) *Am (stylish)* chic *(inv)* (**c**) *Am (cheeky)* culotté, gonflé (**d**) *Am (vigorous)* plein de pêche
SAT [sæt, ˌeseɪ'tiː] *n* (**a**) *Am (abbr* **Scholastic Aptitude Test)** = examen d'entrée à l'université aux États-Unis (**b**) *Br (abbr* **Standard Assessment Task)** = dans le cadre du "National Curriculum", contrôle des connaissances auquel doivent se soumettre les élèves de 7, 11 et 14 ans
Sat. *(written abbr* **Saturday)** sam
sat [sæt] *pt & pp of* **sit**
Satan ['seɪtən] *pr n* Satan; *Hum* **get thee behind me, Satan!** n'essaie pas de me tenter!
satanic [sə'tænɪk] *adj* satanique

'The Satanic Verses' *Rushdie* 'Les Versets sataniques'

satanically [sə'tænɪkəlɪ] *adv* sataniquement, d'une manière satanique
satanism ['seɪtənɪzəm] *n* satanisme *m*
satanist ['seɪtənɪst] **1** *adj* sataniste
2 *n* sataniste *mf*
satay ['sæteɪ] *n Culin* satay *m*
▶▶ ***satay sauce*** sauce *f* satay
satchel ['sætʃəl] *n* cartable *m*
sate [seɪt] *vt (satisfy → person)* rassasier; *(→ hunger)* assouvir; *(→ thirst)* étancher
sated ['seɪtɪd] *adj (person)* rassasié; *(hunger)* assouvi; *(thirst)* étanché
sateen [sæ'tiːn] *n* satinette *f*
satellite ['sætəlaɪt] **1** *n* (**a**) *Astron & Tel* satellite *m*; **(tele)communications satellite** satellite *m* de télécommunications; **meteorological** *or* **weather satellite** satellite *m* météorologique; **broadcast live by satellite** transmis en direct par satellite
(**b**) *(country)* pays *m* satellite; **the country is a satellite of the United States** c'est un pays satellite des États-Unis
(**c**) *(in airport)* satellite *m*
2 *comp* (**a**) *(broadcast, broadcasting, network,*

relay) par satellite; **ten satellite channels** dix chaînes *fpl* (de télévision) par satellite
(**b**) *(country)* satellite
►► ***satellite dish*** antenne *f* parabolique; ***satellite link*** liaison *f* par satellite; ***satellite picture*** *Phot* photo *f* satellite; *Met* animation *f* satellite; ***satellite state*** état *m* satellite; ***satellite station*** station *f* satellite; ***satellite television*** télévision *f* par satellite; ***satellite town*** ville *f* satellite

satiable [ˈseɪʃəbəl] *adj Literary (hunger, desire)* qui peut être assouvi; *(thirst)* qui peut être étanché

satiate [ˈseɪʃɪeɪt] *vt Literary* (**a**) *(satisfy → hunger, desire)* assouvir; *(→ thirst)* étancher (**b**) *(gorge)* rassasier

satiated [ˈseɪʃɪeɪtɪd] *adj Formal (with food)* rassasié; *(with pleasure)* comblé

satiating [ˈseɪʃɪeɪtɪŋ] *adj* rassasiant, affadissant

satiation [ˌseɪʃɪˈeɪʃən] *n* satiété *f*; **to the point of satiation** à satiété, jusqu'à satiété

satiety [səˈtaɪətɪ] *n* satiété *f*

satin [ˈsætɪn] **1** *n* satin *m*
2 *comp (dress, shirt, sheets)* en *ou* de satin
►► ***satin finish*** *(of paper etc)* apprêt *m* satiné; **to have a satin finish** être satiné; *Sewing* ***satin stitch*** passé *m* plat; ***satin weave*** armure *f* satin

satinet, satinette [ˌsætɪˈnet] *n* satinette *f*

satinwood [ˈsætɪnwʊd] *n Bot* citronnier *m* de Ceylan

satiny [ˈsætɪnɪ] *adj* satiné

satire [ˈsætaɪə(r)] *n* satire *f*; **it's a satire on the English** c'est une satire contre les Anglais; **her novels are full of satire** ses romans sont pleins d'observations satiriques

satirical [səˈtɪrɪkəl] *adj* satirique

satirically [səˈtɪrɪkəlɪ] *adv* satiriquement

satirist [ˈsætərɪst] *n (writer)* satiriste *mf*; *(comedian)* chansonnier(ère) *m,f*, comédien(enne) *m,f* satirique

satirize, -ise [ˈsætəraɪz] *vt* faire la satire de; **in her book, she satirizes English manners** son livre est une satire *ou* fait la satire des mœurs anglaises

satisfaction [ˌsætɪsˈfækʃən] *n* (**a**) *(fulfilment → of curiosity, hunger, demand, conditions)* satisfaction *f*; *(→ of contract)* exécution *f*, réalisation *f*; *(→ of debt)* acquittement *m*, remboursement *m*; **the satisfaction of the union's demands** la satisfaction des revendications syndicales
(**b**) *(pleasure)* satisfaction *f*, contentement *m*; **to have the satisfaction of doing sth** avoir la satisfaction de faire qch; **they get great satisfaction from their grandchildren** ce sont des grands-parents comblés; **it was a source of satisfaction to him** c'était pour lui un sujet de satisfaction; **to our (great) satisfaction, they left early** à notre (grande) satisfaction, ils sont partis tôt; **is everything to your satisfaction?** est-ce que tout est à votre convenance?; **the plan was agreed to everyone's satisfaction** le projet fut accepté à la satisfaction générale; **to the satisfaction of the court** d'une manière qui a convaincu le tribunal; **I don't get much job satisfaction** je ne tire pas beaucoup de satisfaction de mon travail; *Com* **satisfaction guaranteed** satisfaction *f* garantie
(**c**) *(pleasing thing)* satisfaction *f*; **life's little satisfactions** les petites satisfactions *fpl* de la vie
(**d**) *(redress → of a wrong)* réparation *f*; *(→ of damage)* dédommagement *m*; *(→ of an insult)* réparation *f*; **to demand satisfaction** *(gen)* exiger réparation; *(in a duel)* demander satisfaction

satisfactorily [ˌsætɪsˈfæktərəlɪ] *adv* de façon satisfaisante; **the trip went off most satisfactorily** le voyage s'est déroulé de manière tout à fait satisfaisante

satisfactoriness [ˌsætɪsˈfæktərɪnɪs] *n* caractère *m* satisfaisant

satisfactory [ˌsætɪsˈfæktərɪ] *adj* satisfaisant; **the result is not very satisfactory** le résultat n'est pas très satisfaisant *ou* laisse à désirer; **we're looking for a solution satisfactory to both sides** nous recherchons une solution satisfaisante pour les deux parties; **their progress is only satisfactory** leurs progrès sont satisfaisants, sans plus; **I hope she has a satisfactory excuse** j'espère qu'elle a une excuse valable; **the patient's condition is satisfactory** l'état du malade est satisfaisant

satisfiable [ˌsætɪsˈfaɪəbəl] *adj* que l'on peut satisfaire *ou* contenter

satisfied [ˈsætɪsfaɪd] *adj* (**a**) *(happy)* satisfait, content; **a satisfied customer** un client satisfait; **a satisfied sigh** un soupir de satisfaction; **the teacher isn't satisfied with their work** le professeur n'est pas satisfait de leur travail; **are you satisfied now you've made her cry?** tu es content de l'avoir fait pleurer?; **they'll have to be satisfied with what they've got** ils devront se contenter de ce qu'ils ont; *Ironic* **not satisfied with that she then broke the other chair** comme ça ne lui suffisait pas, elle a cassé l'autre chaise
(**b**) *(convinced)* convaincu, persuadé; **I'm not entirely satisfied with the truth of his story** je ne suis pas tout à fait convaincu que son histoire soit vraie

satisfy [ˈsætɪsfaɪ] *(pt & pp* **satisfied***)* **1** *vt* (**a**) *(please)* satisfaire, contenter; **nothing satisfies him** il n'est jamais content; *Sch* **to satisfy the examiners** *(of examinee)* être reçu à l'examen
(**b**) *(fulfil → curiosity, desire, hunger)* satisfaire; *(→ thirst)* étancher; *(→ demand, need, requirements)* satisfaire à, répondre à; *(→ conditions, terms of contract)* remplir; *(→ debt)* s'acquitter de
(**c**) *(prove to → gen)* persuader, convaincre; *(→ authorities)* prouver à; **I am satisfied that he was telling the truth** je suis convaincu *ou* persuadé *ou* sûr qu'il disait la vérité; **you have to satisfy the authorities that you have been resident here for three years** vous devez prouver aux autorités que vous résidez ici depuis trois ans; **I satisfied myself that all the windows were closed** je me suis assuré que toutes les fenêtres étaient fermées
2 *vi* donner satisfaction; **the drink that satisfies** la boisson qui étanche la soif

satisfying [ˈsætɪsˌfaɪɪŋ] *adj (job, outcome, evening)* satisfaisant; *(meal)* substantiel

satisfyingly [ˈsætɪsˌfaɪɪŋlɪ] *adv* de façon satisfaisante

satrap [ˈsætrəp] *n* satrape *m*

satrapy [ˈsætrəpɪ] *(pl* **satrapies***) n* satrapie *f*

satsuma [ˌsætˈsuːmə] *n Br* mandarine *f*

saturable [ˈsætʃərəbəl] *adj Chem* saturable

saturant [ˈsætʃərənt] *Chem* **1** *n* substance *f* saturante
2 *adj* saturant

saturate [ˈsætʃəreɪt] *vt* (**a**) *Fig (swamp)* saturer; **to saturate sb with sth** saturer qn de qch; **the market is saturated** le marché est saturé (**b**) *(drench)* tremper; **my clothes were saturated** mes vêtements étaient complètement trempés (**c**) *Chem* saturer

saturated [ˈsætʃəreɪtɪd] *adj* (**a**) *Chem* saturé (**b**) *(very wet → person, cloth)* trempé; *(→ ground)* détrempé (**c**) *(colour)* saturé
►► ***saturated fats*** graisses *fpl* saturées; *Chem* ***saturated solution*** solution *f* saturée; *Phys* ***saturated vapour pressure*** pression *f* de vapeur saturante

saturation [ˌsætʃəˈreɪʃən] *n* saturation *f*
►► *Mktg* ***saturation advertising*** publicité *f* intensive; ***saturation bombing*** bombardement *m* intensif; *Mktg* ***saturation campaign*** campagne *f* intensive, campagne *f* de saturation; *TV* ***saturation coverage*** couverture *f* maximum; *Pej* couverture *f* outrancière; *also Fig* ***saturation point*** point *m* de saturation; **we've reached saturation point** nous sommes arrivés à saturation; **the market is at** *or* **has reached saturation point** le marché est saturé

Saturday [ˈsætədɪ] *n* samedi *m*; *see also* **Friday**
►► ***Saturday girl*** vendeuse *f (travaillant le samedi)*; ***Saturday job*** = petit boulot que l'on fait le samedi; *Am Fam* ***Saturday night special*** *(gun)* flingue *m*, feu *m (bon marché et de qualité médiocre, que l'on peut se procurer facilement)*

'Saturday Night Fever' *Badham* 'La Fièvre du samedi soir'

'Saturday Night and Sunday Morning' *Sillitoe, Reisz* 'Samedi soir, dimanche matin'

Saturn [ˈsætən] **1** *pr n Myth* Saturne
2 *n Astron* Saturne *f*

saturnalia [ˌsætəˈneɪlɪə] *n* saturnales *fpl*

saturnalian [ˌsætəˈneɪlɪən] *adj* des saturnales

Saturnian [sæˈtɜːnɪən] *adj Myth & Astron* saturnien, de Saturne
►► ***the Saturnian age*** l'âge *m* d'or; ***Saturnian verse*** vers *mpl* saturniens

saturnine [ˈsætənaɪn] *adj* saturnien

saturnism [ˈsætənɪzəm] *n Med* saturnisme *m*, intoxication *f* par le plomb

satyr [ˈsætə(r)] *n* satyre *m*

satyriasis [ˌsætəˈraɪəsɪs] *n* satyriasis *m*

satyric [səˈtɪrɪk] *adj* satyrique
►► ***satyric drama*** drame *m* satyrique, satyre *f*

satyrid [səˈtɪrɪd] *n Entom* satyride *m*, satyridé *m*

sauce [sɔːs] *n* (**a**) *Culin (with savoury dishes)* sauce *f*; *(with desserts)* coulis *m*; **tomato sauce** sauce *f* tomate; **raspberry sauce** coulis *m* de framboises; **chocolate sauce** sauce *f* au chocolat; *Prov* **what's sauce for the goose is sauce for the gander** = ce qui est bon pour l'un est bon pour l'autre; *Arch or Literary* **the sauce of danger** le sel du danger
(**b**) *Br Fam Old-fashioned (insolence)* culot *m*, toupet *m*; **that's enough of your sauce!** arrête de faire l'insolent! ❑
(**c**) *Fam (alcohol)* alcool ❑ *m*, bibine *f*; **to hit the sauce** se mettre à picoler; **to be on the sauce** s'être remis à picoler; **to be off the sauce** être au régime sec
►► ***sauce boat*** saucière *f*

saucebox [ˈsɔːsbɒks] *n Fam* petit(e) effronté(e) ❑ *m,f*

sauced [sɔːst] *adj Fam (drunk)* beurré, bourré, pété

saucepan [ˈsɔːspən] *n* casserole *f*

saucepanful [ˈsɔːspənfʊl] *n* casserolée *f*

saucer [ˈsɔːsə(r)] *n* soucoupe *f*, *Belg & Suisse* sous-tasse *f*

saucerful [ˈsɔːsəfʊl] *n* (pleine) soucoupe *f*

saucily [ˈsɔːsɪlɪ] *adv Fam* (**a**) *(cheekily)* avec effronterie ❑ (**b**) *(suggestively)* d'un air coquin ❑

sauciness [ˈsɔːsɪnɪs] *n Fam* (**a**) *(cheekiness)* effronterie ❑ *f* (**b**) *(suggestiveness → of joke, clothes)* côté *m* coquin ❑

saucy [ˈsɔːsɪ] *(compar* **saucier**, *superl* **sauciest***)* *adj Fam* (**a**) *(cheeky, pert)* effronté ❑; **saucy little hat** petit chapeau *m* coquet ❑ (**b**) *(suggestive → postcard, joke, clothes)* coquin ❑

Saudi [ˈsaʊdɪ] **1** *adj* saoudien
2 *n Fam* (**a**) *(person)* Saoudien(enne) ❑ *m,f* (**b**) *(country)* Arabie *f* Saoudite ❑
►► ***Saudi Arabia*** Arabie *f* Saoudite; **in Saudi Arabia** en Arabie Saoudite; ***Saudi Arabian*** **1** *n* Saoudien(enne) *m,f* **2** *adj* saoudien

sauerkraut [ˈsaʊəkraʊt] *n* choucroute *f*

Saul [sɔːl] *pr n Bible* Saül

sauna [ˈsɔːnə] *n* sauna *m*

saunter [ˈsɔːntə(r)] **1** *vi* se promener d'un pas nonchalant, flâner; **to saunter in/out/across** entrer/sortir/traverser d'un pas nonchalant; **to saunter down the street** descendre la rue d'un pas nonchalant; **I think I'll saunter down to the library** je pense que je vais aller faire un petit tour jusqu'à la bibliothèque; **to saunter up to sb** s'approcher de qn d'un pas nonchalant; **she sauntered in, half an hour late** elle est arrivée tranquillement, une demi-heure en retard
2 *n* petit tour *m*; **to go for a saunter** (aller) faire un petit tour

sauntering [ˈsɔːntərɪŋ] *n* flânerie *f*

saurian [ˈsɔːrɪən] **1** *adj* saurien
2 *n* saurien *m*

saury [ˈsɔːrɪ] *(pl* **sauries***) n Ich* scombrésoce *m*

sausage [ˈsɒsɪdʒ] *n* (**a**) *(food)* saucisse *f*; *(of precooked meats)* saucisson *m*; **she rolled her napkin into a sausage** elle a fait un boudin de sa serviette; **pork sausages** saucisses *fpl* de porc; *Br Fam* **not a sausage!** que dalle!, des clous!; *Br Fam* **you silly sausage!** espèce de nouille! (**b**) *Br Fam Hum (penis)* chipolata *f*
►► *Br Fam* ***sausage dog*** saucisse *f* à pattes, teckel ❑ *m*; ***sausage machine*** machine *f* à saucisses; ***sausage meat*** chair *f* à saucisse; ***sausage roll*** = sorte de friand à la saucisse; ***sausage skin*** boyau *m*

Saussurian [səʊ'sjʊərɪən] *Ling* **1** *adj* saussurien
2 *n* saussurien(enne) *m,f*

sauté [*Br* 'səʊteɪ, *Am* səʊ'teɪ] (*pt & pp* **sautéed**, *cont* **sautéing**) **1** *vt* faire sauter; **sauté the potatoes in a little butter** faire sauter les pommes de terre dans un peu de beurre
2 *n* sauté *m*
▶▶ ***sauté potatoes*** pommes *fpl* de terre sautées

sautéed ['səʊteɪd] *adj* sauté

savage ['sævɪdʒ] **1** *adj* (**a**) *(ferocious → person)* féroce, brutal; *(→ dog)* méchant; *(→ fighting, tiger)* féroce; *(→ reply, attack)* violent, féroce; **he came in for some savage criticism from the press** il a été violemment critiqué dans la presse; **the new policy deals a savage blow to the country's farmers** la nouvelle politique porte un coup très dur *ou* fatal aux agriculteurs
(**b**) *(primitive → tribe)* primitif; *(→ customs)* barbare, primitif
2 *n* sauvage *mf*; **they behaved like savages** ils se sont comportés comme des sauvages; **they're little better than savages** ce sont de vrais sauvages
3 *vt* (**a**) *(of animal)* attaquer; **she was savaged by a tiger** elle a été attaquée par un tigre
(**b**) *(of critics, press)* éreinter; **the opposition leader savaged the government's latest proposals** le chef de l'opposition a violemment attaqué les dernières propositions du gouvernement

savagely ['sævɪdʒlɪ] *adv* sauvagement, brutalement

savageness ['sævɪdʒnɪs] = **savagery** (**a**)

savagery ['sævɪdʒrɪ] *n* (**a**) *(brutality)* sauvagerie *f*, férocité *f*, brutalité *f*; **the savagery of the assault** la brutalité de l'agression (**b**) *(primitive state)* **the tribe still lives in savagery** la tribu vit toujours à l'état sauvage

savanna, savannah [sə'vænə] *n* savane *f*

savant ['savɑ̃, 'sævənt] *n* savant(e) *m,f*

SAVE [seɪv]

arrêt	▶ **1 (a)**
sauvegarde	▶ **1 (b)**
sauver	▶ **2 (a), (g)**
économiser	▶ **2 (b), (c); 3 (a)**
epargner	▶ **2 (b), (d); 3 (b)**
mettre de côté	▶ **2 (b)**
éviter	▶ **2 (d)**
arrêter	▶ **2 (f)**
sauvegarder	▶ **2 (h); 3 (c)**
faire des économies (de)	▶ **2 (c); 3 (a), (b)**

1 *n* (**a**) *Ftbl* arrêt *m*; **great save!** superbe arrêt!
(**b**) *Comput* sauvegarde *f*; **save command** commande *f* de sauvegarde
2 *vt* (**a**) *(rescue)* sauver; **she saved my life** elle m'a sauvé la vie; **the doctors managed to save her eyesight** les médecins ont pu lui sauver la vue; **to save sb from a fire/from drowning** sauver qn d'un incendie/de la noyade; **he saved me from making a terrible mistake** il m'a empêché de faire une erreur monstrueuse; **they had only the belongings they had saved from the flood** ils n'avaient que les affaires qu'ils avaient sauvées de l'inondation; **nothing can save their marriage now** rien ne peut plus sauver leur mariage; **to save a species from extinction** sauver une espèce en voie de disparition; **saved by the bell!** sauvé par le gong!; *Fam* **to save one's neck** *or* **skin** *or* **hide** *or* **bacon** sauver sa peau; *Fam* **I couldn't climb up there to save my life** je serais incapable de grimper là-haut❑; *Fam* **he can't sing/play tennis to save his life** il chante/joue au tennis comme un pied; **to save face** sauver la face; **to save the day** sauver la mise
(**b**) *(put by, keep → money)* économiser, épargner, mettre de côté; *(→ food, papers, old jars etc)* garder, mettre de côté; *(collect → stamps, cards)* collectionner; **I save £100 a month in a special account** j'économise 100 livres par mois sur un compte spécial; **how much money have you got saved?** à combien se montent vos économies?, combien d'argent avez-vous mis de côté?; **I'm saving money to buy a car** je fais des économies pour acheter une voiture; **I'll save you a place** je te garderai une place; **I always save the best part till last** je garde toujours le meilleur pour la fin; **to save oneself for sth** se réserver pour qch; **save a dance for me** réservez-moi une danse; **do you still save stamps?** est-ce que tu collectionnes toujours les timbres?
(**c**) *(economize on → fuel, electricity)* économiser, faire des économies de; *(→ money)* économiser; *(→ time, space)* gagner; *(→ strength)* ménager, économiser; **buy now and save £15!** achetez dès maintenant et économisez 15 livres!; **their advice saved me a fortune** leurs conseils m'ont fait économiser une fortune; **you'd save a lot of time if you used a computer** vous gagneriez beaucoup de temps si vous utilisiez un ordinateur; **a computer would save you a lot of time** un ordinateur vous ferait gagner beaucoup de temps; **I might as well have saved my breath** j'aurais mieux fait d'économiser ma salive
(**d**) *(spare → trouble, effort)* éviter, épargner; *(→ expense)* éviter; **it'll save you getting up early/going into town** ça t'évitera de te lever tôt/d'aller en ville; **thanks, you've saved me a trip/having to go myself** merci, vous m'avez évité un trajet/d'y aller moi-même; **this has saved him a great deal of expense/trouble** cela lui a évité *ou* épargné beaucoup de dépense/peine
(**e**) *(protect → eyes, shoes)* ménager; **God save the King/the Queen!** vive le Roi/la Reine!
(**f**) *Ftbl (shot, penalty)* arrêter; **to save a goal** arrêter *ou* bloquer un tir
(**g**) *Rel (sinner, mankind)* sauver, délivrer; *(soul)* sauver
(**h**) *Comput (document)* sauvegarder, enregistrer; **to save sth to disk** sauvegarder qch sur disquette; **do you want to save changes?** voulez-vous enregistrer les modifications?; **save as…** enregistrer sous…
3 *vi* (**a**) *(spend less)* faire des économies, économiser; **you save if you buy in bulk** on fait des économies en achetant en gros; **to save on fuel** économiser sur le carburant
(**b**) *(put money aside)* faire des économies, épargner; **I'm saving for a new car** je fais des économies pour acheter une nouvelle voiture
(**c**) *Comput* sauvegarder, enregistrer
4 *prep Formal* sauf, hormis; **we'd thought of every possibility save one** nous avions pensé à tout sauf à ça
5 save for *prep* à part; **save for the fact that we lost, it was a great match** à part le fait qu'on a perdu, c'était un très bon match; **she was utterly alone, save for one good friend** à part une seule amie, elle n'avait personne
▶▶ ***Save the Children Fund*** = organisme international d'assistance à l'enfance

▶**save up 1** *vt sep (put by, keep → money)* économiser, épargner, mettre de côté; *(→ food, papers, old jars etc)* garder, mettre de côté; *(collect → stamps, cards)* collectionner; **I'm saving up money to buy a car** je fais des économies pour acheter une voiture
2 *vi* faire des économies, épargner; **I'm saving up for a new car** je fais des économies pour acheter une nouvelle voiture

'Saving Private Ryan' *Spielberg* 'Il faut sauver le soldat Ryan'

save-all *n* (**a**) *Tech* appareil *m* économiseur (**b**) *Hist (for burning candle ends)* brûle-bout(s) *m inv*, brûle-tout *m inv* (**c**) *Naut & Hist* = petite voile supplémentaire établie au-dessous d'une autre voile

save-as-you-earn *n*
▶▶ *Br Fin* ***save-as-you-earn-scheme*** = plan d'épargne à contributions mensuelles produisant des intérêts exonérés d'impôts

saveloy ['sævəlɔɪ] *n* cervelas *m*

saver ['seɪvə(r)] *n* (**a**) *(person)* épargnant(e) *m,f*; **small savers** les petits épargnants (**b**) *(product)* bonne affaire *f*; **super saver (ticket)** billet *m* à tarif réduit

-saver ['seɪvə(r)] *suff* **it's a real money-saver** ça permet d'économiser de l'argent *ou* de faire des économies

Savile Row [,sævɪl'rəʊ] *n* = rue de Londres célèbre pour ses tailleurs de luxe

savin, savine ['sævɪn] *n Bot & Pharm* sabine *f*

saving ['seɪvɪŋ] **1** *n* (**a**) *(thrift)* épargne *f*; **measures to encourage saving** des mesures pour encourager l'épargne
(**b**) *(money saved)* économie *f*; **savings** économies *fpl*; *Econ* dépôts *mpl* d'épargne; **to make a saving** faire une économie; **we made a saving of £20 on the usual price** nous avons fait une économie de 20 livres sur le prix habituel; **he drew all his savings out of the bank** il a retiré toutes ses économies de la banque
(**c**) *(rescue → of lives etc)* sauvetage *m*; *(→ of person, souls)* salut *m*; **this was the saving of him** cela a été son salut
2 *prep Formal* sauf, hormis; *Formal* **saving Your Grace** sauf le respect que je dois à Votre Excellence
▶▶ ***savings account*** compte *m* (de caisse) d'épargne; ***savings bank*** caisse *f* d'épargne; *Am* ***savings bond*** bon *m* d'épargne; *Br* ***savings book*** livret *m* (de caisse) d'épargne; *Br* ***savings certificate*** bon *m* d'épargne; ***savings club*** club *m* d'épargne; ***saving grace*** = bon côté qui rachète des défauts; **her sense of humour is her saving grace** on lui pardonne tout parce qu'elle a de l'humour; **the movie has one saving grace** une seule chose sauve le film; *Am* ***savings and loan association*** caisse *f* d'épargne logement; ***savings plan, savings scheme*** plan *m* d'épargne; *Br* ***savings stamp*** timbre-épargne *m*

-saving ['seɪvɪŋ] *suff* **energy-saving** *(device)* d'économie, d'énergie; **time-saving** qui fait gagner du temps

saviour, *Am* **savior** ['seɪvjə(r)] *n* sauveur *m*; *Rel* **the Saviour** le Sauveur

savoir-faire [,sævwɑː'feə(r)] *n (know-how)* savoir-faire *m inv*; *(social skills)* savoir-vivre *m inv*

savoir-vivre [,sævwɑː'viːvrə] *n* savoir-vivre *m inv*

savor, savoriness *etc Am* = **savour, savouriness** *etc*

savory ['seɪvərɪ] (*pl* **savories**) *n Bot* sarriette *f*

savour, *Am* **savor** ['seɪvə(r)] **1** *n* (**a**) *(taste)* goût *m*, saveur *f*; **it has a savour of garlic** il y a un petit goût d'ail
(**b**) *(interest, charm)* saveur *f*; **life had lost its savour for him** il avait perdu toute joie de vivre
2 *vt (taste)* goûter (à), déguster; *(enjoy → food, experience, one's freedom)* savourer; **he savoured the memory of his triumph** il savourait le souvenir de son succès triomphal
3 *vi* **to savour of sth** sentir qch; **it savours of heresy** cela sent l'hérésie

savouriness, *Am* **savoriness** ['seɪvərɪnɪs] *n* saveur *f*

savourless, *Am* **savorless** ['seɪvəlɪs] *adj* fade, insipide, sans saveur

savoury (*pl* **savouries**), *Am* **savory** (*pl* **savories**) ['seɪvərɪ] **1** *adj* (**a**) *(salty)* salé; *(spicy)* épicé; **savoury biscuits** biscuits *mpl* salés
(**b**) *(appetizing)* savoureux, appétissant; **a savoury meal** un repas savoureux
(**c**) *Formal (wholesome)* **it's not a very savoury subject** c'est un sujet peu ragoûtant; **he's not a very savoury individual** c'est un individu peu recommandable; **one of the less savoury aspects of the affair** l'un des aspects les moins reluisants de l'affaire
2 *n* = petit plat salé servi soit comme hors d'œuvre, soit en fin de repas après le dessert

Savoy [sə'vɔɪ] **1** *n Géog* Savoie *f*; **in Savoy** en Savoie
2 *adj* savoyard
▶▶ *Culin* ***savoy cabbage*** chou *m* frisé de Milan

savvy ['sævɪ] *Fam* **1** *n (know-how)* savoir-faire❑ *m inv*; *(shrewdness)* jugeote *f*, perspicacité❑ *f*; **to have no technical/computer savvy** être nul pour tout ce qui est technique/en informatique
2 *vi Old-fashioned* **no savvy** j'sais pas
3 *adj (well-informed)* calé, bien informé❑; *(shrewd)* perspicace❑, astucieux❑; **to be computer savvy** être calé en informatique

saw [sɔː] (*Br pt* **sawed**, *pp* **sawed** *or* **sawn** [sɔːn], *Am pt & pp* **sawed**) **1** *pt of* **see**
2 *n* (**a**) *(tool)* scie *f*; **to cut sth up with a saw** couper *ou* débiter qch à la scie; **metal saw** scie *f* à métaux
(**b**) *(saying)* dicton *m*

3 *vt* scier; **to saw a tree into logs** débiter un arbre en rondins; **he sawed the table in half** il a scié la table en deux; *Fig* **his arms sawed the air** il battait l'air de ses bras; *Am Fam Hum* **to saw wood** *(snore)* ronfler❑

4 *vi* scier; **she sawed through the branch** elle a scié la branche; *Fig* **he was sawing away at the cello** il raclait le violoncelle

▸▸ ***saw set*** tourne-à-gauche *m inv*

▸**saw down** *vt sep (tree)* abattre

▸**saw off** *vt sep* scier, enlever à la scie

▸**saw up** *vt sep* scier en morceaux, débiter à la scie

sawbill ['sɔːbɪl] *n Orn* merganser *m*

sawbones ['sɔːbəʊnz] *n Fam* chirurgien❑ *m*

sawbuck ['sɔːbʌk] *n Am* (**a**) = **sawhorse** (**b**) *($10)* (billet *m* de) dix dollars *mpl*

sawdust ['sɔːdʌst] *n* sciure *f* (de bois)

sawed-off ['sɔːd-] *Am* = **sawn-off**

sawfish ['sɔːfɪʃ] *n Ich* poisson-scie *m*

sawfly ['sɔːflaɪ] (*pl* **sawflies**) *n Entom* mouche *f* à scie, tenthrède *f*

sawhorse ['sɔːhɔːs, *pl* -hɔːsɪz] *n* chevalet *m (pour scier du bois)*, chèvre *f*

sawing ['sɔːɪŋ] *n (of wood)* sciage *m*; **sawing up** débitage *m*

sawmill ['sɔːmɪl] *n* scierie *f*

sawn [sɔːn] *pp of* **saw**

sawn-off *adj* (**a**) *(truncated)* scié, coupé (à la scie) (**b**) *Br Fam (short → person)* court sur pattes

▸▸ ***sawn-off shotgun*** carabine *f* à canon scié

sawpit ['sɔːpɪt] *n* fosse *f* de scieur de long

▸▸ ***sawpit frame, sawpit horse*** baudet *m*

sawtooth ['sɔːtuːθ] 1 *n* dent *f* de scie

2 *adj* en dents de scie

sawtoothed ['sɔːtuːθt] *adj* en dents de scie

sawyer ['sɔːjə(r)] *n* scieur *m*

sax [sæks] *n Fam (abbr* **saxophone**) saxo *m*

saxboard ['sæksbɔːd] *n (in rowing)* plat-bord *m*

saxhorn ['sækshɔːn] *n Mus* saxhorn *m*

saxicolous [sæk'sɪkələs] *adj Bot* saxicole, saxatile

saxifrage ['sæksɪfreɪdʒ] *n* saxifrage *f*

Saxon ['sæksən] 1 *n* (**a**) *(person)* Saxon(onne) *m,f* (**b**) *Ling* saxon *m*

2 *adj* saxon

Saxony ['sæksənɪ] *n* Saxe *f*; **in Saxony** en Saxe; **Lower Saxony** Basse-Saxe *f*

saxophone ['sæksəfəʊn] *n* saxophone *m*

saxophonist [*Br* ˌsæk'sɒfənɪst, *Am* 'sæksəˌfəʊnɪst] *n* saxophoniste *mf*

SAY [seɪ]

dire	▸**1 (a) – (f); 2**
penser	▸**1 (e)**
indiquer	▸**1 (g)**
marquer	▸**1 (g), (h)**
exprimer	▸**1 (h)**

(*pt & pp* **said** [sed], *3rd pers sing* **says** [sez]) **1** *vt* (**a**) *(put into words)* dire; **to say sth (to sb)** dire qch (à qn); **to say hello/goodbye to sb** dire bonjour/au revoir à qn; **say hello to them for me** dites-leur bonjour de ma part; *Fig* **I think you can say goodbye to your money** je crois que vous pouvez dire adieu à votre argent; **as I said yesterday/in my letter** comme je l'ai dit hier/dans ma lettre; **to say yes/no** dire oui/non; **did you say yes or no to his offer?** tu as répondu oui ou non à sa proposition?, tu as accepté ou refusé sa proposition?; **I wouldn't say no!** je ne dis pas non!, ce n'est pas de refus!; **I wouldn't say no to a cold drink** je prendrais volontiers *ou* bien une boisson fraîche; **to say please/thank you** dire s'il vous plaît/merci; **to say a prayer (for)** dire une prière (pour); **to say one's prayers** faire sa prière; **I can't say Russian names properly** je n'arrive pas à bien prononcer les noms russes; **I said to myself "let's wait a bit"** je me suis dit "attendons un peu"; **what did he say about his plans?** qu'a-t-il dit de ses projets?; **have you said anything about it to him?** est-ce que vous lui en avez parlé?; **don't say too much about our visit** ne parlez pas trop de notre visite; **the less said the better** moins nous parlerons, mieux cela vaudra; **what did you say?** *(repeat what you said)* pardon?, qu'avez-vous dit?; *(in reply)* qu'avez-vous répondu?; **well, say something then!** eh bien, dites quelque chose!; **I can't think of anything to say** je ne trouve rien à dire; **I have nothing to say** *(gen)* je n'ai rien à dire; *(no comment)* je n'ai aucune déclaration à faire; **I have nothing more to say on the matter** je n'ai rien à ajouter là-dessus; **nothing was said about going to Moscow** on n'a pas parlé d'aller *ou* il n'a pas été question d'aller à Moscou; **let's say no more about it** n'en parlons plus; **can you say that again?** pouvez-vous répéter ce que vous venez de dire?; **you can say that again!** c'est le cas de le dire!, je ne vous le fais pas dire!; *Tel* **who shall I say is calling?** c'est de la part de qui?; **say what you think** dites ce que vous pensez; **say what you mean** dites ce que vous avez à dire; **the chairman would like to say a few words** le président voudrait dire quelques mots; **he didn't have a good word to say about the plan** il n'a dit que du mal du projet; **he doesn't have a good word to say about anybody** il n'a jamais rien de positif à dire sur personne; **what have you got to say for yourself?** eh bien, expliquez-vous!; **he didn't have much to say for himself** *(spoke little)* il n'avait pas grand-chose à dire; *(no excuses)* il n'avait pas de véritable excuse à donner; **he certainly has a lot to say for himself** il n'a pas la langue dans la poche; **as you might say** pour ainsi dire; **so saying, he walked out** sur ces mots, il est parti; **to say nothing of the overheads** sans parler des frais; *Br* **just say the word, you only have to say (the word)** vous n'avez qu'un mot à dire; **having said that** ceci (étant) dit; **to say one's piece** dire ce qu'on a à dire; **it goes without saying that we shall travel together** il va sans dire *ou* il va de soi que nous voyagerons ensemble; *Fam* **you said it!** tu l'as dit!, comme tu dis!; *Fam* **don't say you've forgotten!** ne me dis pas que tu as oublié!; **say no more** n'en dis pas plus; **enough said** *(I understand)* je vois; **well said!** bien dit!; **say when** dis-moi stop; *Am* **say what?** quoi?; **when all's said and done** tout compte fait, au bout du compte

(**b**) *(with direct or indirect speech)* dire; **"not at all", she said** "pas du tout", dit-elle; **she says (that) the water's too cold** elle dit que l'eau est trop froide; **she said (we were) to come** elle a dit qu'on devait venir; **she said to get back early** elle a dit qu'on devait rentrer tôt; **they said on the news that...** on a dit *ou* annoncé aux informations que...; **they said it was going to rain** ils ont annoncé de la pluie

(**c**) *(claim, allege)* dire; **they say ghosts really do exist** ils disent que les fantômes existent vraiment; **you know what they say, no smoke without fire** tu sais ce qu'on dit, il n'y a pas de fumée sans feu; **as they say** comme ils disent *ou* on dit; **it is said that no one will ever know the real story** on dit que personne ne saura jamais ce qui s'est vraiment passé; **I've heard it said that...** j'ai entendu dire que... + *indicative*; **these fans are said to be very efficient** ces ventilateurs sont très efficaces, d'après ce qu'on dit; **he is said to be rich, they say he is rich** on le dit riche, on dit qu'il est riche; **he is said to have emigrated** on dit qu'il a émigré

(**d**) *(expressing personal opinion)* dire; **as you say, he is the best candidate** comme tu dis, c'est lui le meilleur candidat; **so he says, that's what he says** c'est ce qu'il dit; **I can't say how long it will last** je ne peux pas dire combien de temps cela va durer; **who can say?** qui sait?; **who can say when he'll come?** qui peut dire quand il viendra?; **(you can) say what you like, but I'm going** vous pouvez dire ce que vous voulez, moi je m'en vais; **I must say she's been very helpful** je dois dire *ou* j'avoue qu'elle nous a beaucoup aidés; **well this is a fine time to arrive, I must say!** en voilà une heure pour arriver!; **I'll say this much for them, they don't give up easily** au moins, on peut dire qu'ils n'abandonnent pas facilement; **I'll say this for him, he certainly tries hard** je dois reconnaître qu'il fait tout son possible; **you might as well say we're all mad!** autant dire qu'on est tous fous!; **you don't mean to say he's eighty-six** vous n'allez pas me dire qu'il a quatre-vingt-six ans; **is he stupid? – I wouldn't say that** est-ce qu'il est bête? – je n'irais pas jusque-là; **I should say so** bien sûr que oui, je pense bien; **I should say not!** bien sûr que non!; **if you say so** si *ou* puisque tu le dis; **and so say all of us** et nous sommes tous d'accord *ou* de cet avis; **there's no saying what will happen** impossible de prédire ce qui va arriver; **to say the least** c'est le moins qu'on puisse dire; **it's rather dangerous, to say the least** c'est plutôt dangereux, c'est le moins qu'on puisse dire; **I was surprised, not to say astounded** j'étais surpris, pour ne pas dire stupéfait; **there's something to be said for the idea** l'idée a du bon; **there's not much to be said for the idea** l'idée ne vaut pas grand-chose; **there's a lot to be said for doing sport** il y a beaucoup d'avantages à faire du sport; **there is little to be said for beginning now** on n'a pas intérêt à commencer dès maintenant; **that's not saying much** ça ne veut pas dire grand-chose; **it doesn't say much for his powers of observation** cela en dit long sur son sens de l'observation; **you're honest, I'll say that for you** je dirais en votre faveur que vous êtes honnête; **that isn't saying much for him** ce n'est pas à son honneur; **it says a lot for his courage/about his real motives** cela en dit long sur son courage/ses intentions réelles; **the way you dress says something about you as a person** la manière dont les gens s'habillent est révélatrice de leur personnalité

(**e**) *(think)* dire, penser; **I say you should leave** je pense que vous devriez partir; **what do you say?** qu'en dites-vous?, qu'en pensez-vous?; **what will people say?** que vont dire les gens?; **what did they say to your offer?** qu'ont-ils dit de votre proposition?; **what do you say we drive over** *or* **to driving over to see them?** que diriez-vous de prendre la voiture et d'aller les voir?; **what would you say to a picnic?** que diriez-vous d'un pique-nique?, ça vous dit de faire un pique-nique?; **when would you say would be the best time for us to leave?** quel serait le meilleur moment pour partir, à votre avis?; **to look at them, you wouldn't say they were a day over forty** à les voir, on ne leur donnerait pas plus de quarante ans

(**f**) *(suppose, assume)* **(let's) say your plan doesn't work, what then?** admettons *ou* supposons que votre plan ne marche pas, qu'est-ce qui se passe?; **say he doesn't arrive, who will take his place?** si jamais il n'arrive pas, qui prendra sa place?; **look at, say, Jane Austen or George Eliot...** prends Jane Austen ou George Eliot, par exemple...; **if I had, say, £100,000 to spend** si j'avais, mettons *ou* disons, 100 000 livres à dépenser; **come tomorrow, say after lunch** venez demain, disons *ou* mettons après le déjeuner; **shall we say Sunday?** disons dimanche, d'accord?

(**g**) *(indicate, register)* indiquer, marquer; **the clock says 10.40** la pendule indique 10 heures 40; **what does your watch say?** quelle heure est-il à ta montre?; **the sign says 50 km** le panneau indique 50 km; **the gauge says 3.4** la jauge indique *ou* marque 3,4; **it says "shake well"** c'est marqué "bien agiter"; **the instructions say (to) open it out of doors** dans le mode d'emploi, on dit qu'il faut l'ouvrir dehors; **it says in the newspaper that...** on dit dans le journal que... + *indicative*; **the Bible says** *or* **it says in the Bible that...** comme il est écrit dans la Bible...

(**h**) *(express → of intonation, eyes)* exprimer, marquer; **his expression said everything** son expression était très éloquente *ou* en disait long; **that look says a lot** ce regard en dit long

(**i**) *(mean)* **that is to say** c'est-à-dire; **it's short, that's to say, about twenty pages** c'est court, ça fait dans les vingt pages; **that's not to say I don't like it** cela ne veut pas dire que je ne l'aime pas

2 *vi (tell)* dire; **he won't say** il ne veut pas le dire; **I'd rather not say** je préfère ne rien dire; **I can't say exactly** je ne sais pas au juste; **it's not for me to say** *(speak)* ce n'est pas à moi de le dire; *(decide)* ce n'est pas à moi de décider; **I can't say fairer than that** je ne peux pas mieux dire; **so to say** pour ainsi dire; **I say!** *(expressing surprise)* eh bien!; *(expressing indignation)* dites donc!; *(to attract attention)* dites!; *Am* **say!**

dites donc!; **I mean to say!** tout de même!, quand même!; **I'll say!** et comment donc!; **you don't say!** sans blague!, ça alors!

3 *n* **to have a say in sth** avoir son mot à dire dans qch; **I had no say in choosing the wallpaper** on ne m'a pas demandé mon avis pour le choix du papier peint; **I have no say in the matter** je n'ai pas voix au chapitre; **we had little say in the matter** on ne nous a pas vraiment demandé notre avis; **to have one's say** dire ce qu'on a à dire; **now you've had your say, let me have mine** maintenant que vous avez dit ce que vous aviez à dire, laissez-moi parler

---

SAYE [ˌeseɪˌwaɪ'iː] *n Br Fin (abbr* **save-as-you-earn**) = plan d'épargne à contributions mensuelles produisant des intérêts exonérés d'impôts

saying ['seɪɪŋ] *n* dicton *m*, proverbe *m*; **as the saying goes** *(proverb)* comme dit le proverbe; *(as we way)* comme on dit

say-so *n Br* (**a**) *(authorization)* **I'm not going without her say-so** je n'irai pas sans qu'elle m'y autorise *ou* sans son accord; **he refused to do it without the boss's say-so** il a refusé de le faire sans avoir l'aval du patron; **you may open the box only on my say-so** n'ouvrez *ou* vous ne pourrez ouvrir la boîte que lorsque je vous le dirai, n'ouvrez pas la boîte avant que je vous le dise

(**b**) *(assertion)* **I won't believe it just on his say-so** ce n'est pas parce qu'il l'a dit que j'y crois

SBA [ˌesbiː'eɪ] *n Am (abbr* **Small Business Administration**) = organisme fédéral américain d'aide aux petites entreprises

S-bend *n Br* double virage *m*, virage *m* en S

SBS [ˌesbiː'es] *n (abbr* **sick building syndrome**) = syndrome comprenant des maux de tête etc qu'on retrouve chez des personnes résidant ou travaillant dans des bâtiments équipés de la climatisation, *Can* ≃ syndrome *m* des bâtiments malsains

SBU [ˌesbiː'juː] *n (abbr* **strategic business unit**) DAS *m*, UAS *f*

SC[1] [ˌes'siː] *n Law (abbr* **Supreme Court**) Cour *f* suprême *(des États-Unis)*

SC[2] *(written abbr* **South Carolina**) Caroline *f* du Sud

S/C *(written abbr* **self-contained**) *(flat)* indépendant

scab [skæb] *(pt & pp* **scabbed**, *cont* **scabbing**) **1** *n* (**a**) *Med (from cut, blister)* croûte *f* (**b**) *Bot & Vet* gale *f* (**c**) *Fam Pej (strikebreaker)* jaune *mf* (**d**) *Fam (cad)* crapule *f*, sale type *m*

2 *vi* (**a**) *Med* former une croûte (**b**) *Fam Pej (strikebreaker)* briser une grève❑, refuser de faire grève❑

▸**scab over** *vi* former une croûte

scabbard ['skæbəd] *n (for sword)* fourreau *m*; *(for dagger, knife)* gaine *f*, étui *m*

scabbard-fish *n* sabre *m*

scabbiness ['skæbɪnɪs] *n* (**a**) *Med (of wound, skin)* état *m* croûteux (**b**) *Vet (of animal)* état *m* galeux (**c**) *Fam Pej (meanness)* mesquinerie❑ *f*

scabbing ['skæbɪŋ] *n Med* formation *f* d'une croûte

scabby ['skæbɪ] *(compar* **scabbier**, *superl* **scabbiest**) *adj* (**a**) *Med (skin)* croûteux, recouvert d'une croûte (**b**) *Vet (sheep etc)* galeux (**c**) *Fam Pej (mean → person)* mesquin❑; *(→ attitude)* moche (**d**) *Br Fam (worthless)* merdique; **you can keep your scabby car!** tu peux te la garder, ta caisse de merde! (**e**) *Br Fam (shabby)* merdique, craignos; *(dirty)* cradingue, crado

scabies ['skeɪbiːz] *n (UNCOUNT) Med* gale *f*

scabious ['skeɪbɪəs] **1** *adj Med* scabieux

2 *n Bot* scabieuse *f*

scabrous ['skeɪbrəs] *adj Literary* (**a**) *(joke, story)* scabreux, osé; *(subject)* scabreux, risqué (**b**) *(skin, surface)* rugueux, rêche

scabrousness ['skeɪbrəsnɪs] *n* (**a**) *(of joke, story)* scabreux *m*, caractère *m* scabreux (**b**) *(of skin, surface)* rugosité *f*

scad [skæd] *(pl sense* (**a**) **inv** *or* **scads**) *n* (**a**) *(fish)* carangue *f*, chinchard *m* (**b**) *Fam (usu pl) (lots)* **scads (of)** un paquet (de), des tas (de), une tapée (de); **scads of money** un paquet de pognon

scaffie ['skæfɪ] *n Scot Fam* (**a**) *(refuse collector)* éboueur❑ *m* (**b**) *(street sweeper)* balayeur(euse)❑ *m,f*

scaffold ['skæfəʊld] *n* (**a**) *Constr* échafaudage *m* (**b**) *(for execution)* échafaud *m*; **to go to the scaffold** monter à l'échafaud

scaffolder ['skæfəldə(r)] *n* monteur *m* d'échafaudages

scaffolding ['skæfəldɪŋ] *n (framework)* échafaudage *m*

scag [skæg] *n Fam* (**a**) *Drugs slang (heroin)* héro *f*, blanche *f* (**b**) *Am (ugly woman)* boudin *m*, cageot *m*

scalable font ['skeɪləbl-] *n Comput* police *f* de taille variable

scalar ['skeɪlə(r)] **1** *adj* scalaire

2 *n* scalaire *m*

scalare [skə'lɑːrɪ] *n Ich* scalaire *m*, ange *m* noir du Brésil

scalawag ['skæləwæg] *Am* = **scallywag**

scald [skɔːld] **1** *vt* (**a**) *(hands, skin)* ébouillanter; **I scalded myself with the milk** je me suis ébouillanté avec le lait; **the hot tea scalded my tongue** le thé bouillant m'a brûlé la langue

(**b**) *Culin (tomatoes)* ébouillanter; *(milk)* porter presque à ébullition; *(pot, container)* échauder, ébouillanter

(**c**) *(sterilize)* stériliser

2 *vi* brûler

3 *n* brûlure *f (causée par un liquide, de la vapeur)*; **I got a nasty scald** je me suis bien ébouillanté

scaldfish ['skɔːldfɪʃ] *n Ich* fausse limande *f*

scalding ['skɔːldɪŋ] **1** *adj* (**a**) *(water)* bouillant; *(metal, tea, soup, tears)* brûlant (**b**) *(sun)* brûlant; *(heat)* suffocant, torride; *(weather)* très chaud, torride (**c**) *(criticism)* cinglant, acerbe

2 *adv* **scalding hot** *(coffee)* brûlant; *(weather)* torride

scale [skeɪl] **1** *n* (**a**) *(of model, drawing)* échelle *f*; **the sketch was drawn to scale** l'esquisse était à l'échelle; **the map is on a scale of 1 cm to 1 km** l'échelle de la carte est de 1 cm pour 1 km; **the scale of the map is 1 to 50,000** la carte est au 50 millième; **the drawing is out of scale** *or* **is not to scale** le croquis n'est pas à l'échelle

(**b**) *(for measurement, evaluation)* échelle *f*; *(of thermometer)* échelle *f* (graduée), graduation *f*; *(of salaries, taxes)* échelle *f*, barème *m*; *(of values)* échelle *f*; **the social scale** l'échelle *f* sociale; **at the top of the scale** en haut de l'échelle; **it all depends on your scale of values** tout dépend de votre échelle de valeurs; **to judge sth on a scale of one to ten** noter qch sur dix

(**c**) *(extent)* ampleur *f*, étendue *f*; *(size)* importance *f*; **the scale of the devastation** l'étendue *f* des dégâts; **the sheer scale of the problem/task** l'énormité *f* du problème/de la tâche; **to do sth on a large scale** faire qch sur une grande échelle; **on an industrial scale** à l'échelle industrielle; **economies of scale** économies *fpl* d'échelle

(**d**) *Mus* gamme *f*; **to practise** *or* **to do one's scales** faire ses gammes; **the scale of D major** la gamme de ré majeur

(**e**) *(of fish, reptile)* écaille *f*; *(of epidermis)* squame *f*; *Fig* **the scales fell from her eyes** les écailles lui sont tombées des yeux

(**f**) *(in kettle, pipes)* tartre *m*, (dépôt *m*) calcaire *m*; *(on teeth)* tartre *m*

(**g**) *(of paint, plaster, rust)* écaille *f*, écaillure *f*

(**h**) *(scale pan)* plateau *m* (de balance)

(**i**) *Am (for weighing)* pèse-personne *m*, balance *f*

2 *vt* (**a**) *(climb over → wall, fence)* escalader

(**b**) *(drawing)* dessiner à l'échelle

(**c**) *(test)* graduer, pondérer

(**d**) *(fish, paint)* écailler; *(teeth, pipes)* détartrer

3 *vi (paint, rust)* s'écailler; *(skin)* peler, se desquamer

4 scales *npl (for food)* balance *f*; *(for letters)* pèse-lettre *m*; *(in bathroom etc)* pèse-personne *m*; *(for babies)* pèse-bébé *m*; *(public)* bascule *f*; **pair of scales** balance *f* à plateaux; **(a pair of) kitchen scales** une balance de cuisine

▸▸ ***scale drawing*** dessin *m* à l'échelle; *Entom* ***scale insect*** coccidé *m*; ***scale model*** *(of car, plane)* modèle *m* réduit; *(of building, town centre)* maquette *f*

▸**scale down** *vt sep* (**a**) *(drawing)* réduire l'échelle de; *Typ (font)* réduire (la taille de) (**b**) *(figures, demands)* réduire, baisser, diminuer; **production is being scaled down** on a entrepris de réduire la production

▸**scale off** **1** *vi (paint, rust)* s'écailler

2 *vt sep* écailler

▸**scale up** *vt sep* (**a**) *(drawing)* augmenter l'échelle de; *Typ (font)* agrandir (**b**) *(figures, demands)* réviser à la hausse, augmenter; **allowances were scaled up by 10 percent** les allocations ont été augmentées de 10 pour cent

scaleboard ['skeɪlbɔːd] *n* lame *f* mince (de bois)

scaled [skeɪld] *adj (pipe, kettle, tooth)* entartré

scalene ['skeɪliːn] *adj Geom & Anat* scalène

scalenus [ˌskeɪ'liːnəs] *n Anat* scalène *m*

▸▸ ***scalenus muscle*** scalène *m*

scalepan ['skeɪlpæn] *n* plateau *m* de balance

scaler ['skeɪlə(r)] *n* (**a**) *(of fish)* écailleur(euse) *m,f* (**b**) *(in dentistry)* détartreur *m*

scaling ['skeɪlɪŋ] *n* (**a**) *(removal of incrustation → of teeth)* détartrage *m*; *(→ of boiler, pipes)* détartrage *m*, désincrustation *f* (**b**) *(deposit inside pipe, boiler, kettle)* tartre *m*, calcaire *m*; *(process of incrustation)* formation *f* du tartre, entartrage *m*

▸▸ ***scaling down*** réduction *f*, diminution *f*; *(proportionately)* réduction *f* proportionnelle; ***scaling ladder*** échelle *f* d'escalade; ***scaling up*** augmentation *f*

scallion ['skælɪən] *n Am & Ir (spring onion)* oignon *m* blanc; *Am (leek)* poireau *m*; *Am & Ir (shallot)* échalote *f*

scallop ['skɒləp] **1** *vt* (**a**) *Culin (fish, vegetable)* gratiner (**b**) *Sewing (edge, hem)* festonner

2 *n* (**a**) *Ich* coquille *f* Saint-Jacques (**b**) *Austr Culin* = croquette de pommes de terre frite

3 scallops *npl Sewing* festons *mpl*

scalloped ['skɒləpt] *adj Sewing (edge, hem)* festonné

▸▸ *Culin* ***scalloped potatoes*** = fines tranches de pommes de terre sautées ou cuites au four

scallywag ['skælɪwæg], *Am* **scalawag** ['skæləwæg] *n* (**a**) *Fam (rascal)* voyou *m*, coquin(e)❑ *m,f*; **little scallywag** *(child)* petit(e) coquin(e) *m,f* (**b**) *Am Hist* = sudiste favorable à l'émancipation des Noirs (et par conséquent considéré comme un traître par les siens)

scalp [skælp] **1** *n* (**a**) *(top of head)* cuir *m* chevelu

(**b**) *(Indian trophy)* scalp *m*

(**c**) *Fig (trophy)* trophée *m*; *Hunt* trophée *m* de chasse

(**d**) *Am Fam (profit)* petit profit❑ *m*

2 *vt* (**a**) *(person, animal)* scalper; *Hum (of hairdresser)* ratiboiser

(**b**) *Am Fam (tickets)* = acheter pour revendre au noir; **to scalp shares** *or* **securities** boursicoter

(**c**) *Fam (cheat)* arnaquer; **to get scalped** se faire avoir *ou* arnaquer

(**d**) *Am Fam (defeat)* battre à plate couture

scalpel ['skælpəl] *n* scalpel *m*

scalper ['skælpə(r)] *n Fam* (**a**) *Am (ticket tout)* revendeur(euse) *m,f* de tickets à la sauvette❑ *(pour un concert, un match etc)* (**b**) *St Exch* spéculateur(trice) *m,f* à la journée❑

scalping ['skælpɪŋ] *n* (**a**) *(removal of scalp)* scalp *m* (**b**) *Am Fam (of tickets)* trafic *m* (**c**) *Fam St Exch* boursicotage *m*

▸▸ *Med* ***scalping iron*** rugine *f*

scaly ['skeɪlɪ] *(compar* **scalier**, *superl* **scaliest**) *adj (creature)* écailleux; *(paint)* écaillé; *(skin)* squameux; *(pipe)* entartré

scam [skæm] *n Fam* arnaque *f*, escroquerie❑ *f*

scammony ['skæmənɪ] *(pl* **scammonies**) *n Bot & Pharm* scammonée *f*

scamp [skæmp] *n Fam (child)* garnement❑ *m*, coquin(e)❑ *m,f*; *(rogue)* fripouille❑ *f*

scamper ['skæmpə(r)] **1** *vi* (**a**) *(mice)* trottiner; *(children)* gambader, galoper; **the kids scampered into the house/up the stairs** les gosses sont entrés dans la maison/ont monté l'escalier en courant; **the squirrel scampered up the tree** l'écureuil a grimpé à l'arbre en un clin d'œil (**b**) *Fam (work quickly)* **I positively scampered through the book** j'ai lu le livre à toute vitesse❑

2 *n* trottinement *m*

▸**scamper about** *vi (animal)* courir *ou* trottiner çà et là; *(children)* gambader
▸**scamper away, scamper off** *vi* détaler, se sauver

scampi ['skæmpɪ] *n (UNCOUNT)* scampi *mpl*

scan [skæn] *(pt & pp* **scanned**, *cont* **scanning**) **1** *vt* (**a**) *(look carefully at)* scruter, fouiller du regard; *(read carefully)* lire attentivement; **we scanned the horizon** nous avons scruté l'horizon; **the troops scanned the sky for enemy planes** les soldats scrutaient *ou* observaient le ciel à la recherche d'avions ennemis; **I scanned her face for some reaction** j'ai scruté son visage pour y déceler quelque réaction
(**b**) *(consult quickly → report, notes)* lire en diagonale, parcourir rapidement; *(→ magazine)* feuilleter; *(→ screen, image)* balayer; *(→ tape, memory)* lire; **he scans the local papers for bargains** il parcourt le journal local à la recherche de bonnes affaires
(**c**) *Phys (spectrum)* balayer, parcourir; *(of radar, searchlight)* balayer
(**d**) *Med* examiner au scanner *ou Offic* au scanographe, faire une scanographie de; *(using ultrasound)* faire une échographie à
(**e**) *Electron & TV* balayer
(**f**) *Literature* scander
(**g**) *Comput* passer au scanner *ou* au scanneur
2 *vi Literature* se scander; **this line doesn't scan** ce vers est faux
3 *n* (**a**) *(look)* regard *m* appuyé; **after a quick scan around the room they left** ils examinèrent rapidement la pièce et s'en allèrent
(**b**) *Med (examination → by tomography)* examen *m* au scanner *ou Offic* au scanographe; *(→ by ultrasound)* échographie *f*; **to have a scan** se faire faire un examen au scanner *ou Offic* au scanographe; *(ultrasound)* se faire faire une échographie
(**c**) *Literature* scansion *f*
(**d**) *Electron & TV* balayage *m*
(**e**) *Comput* lecture *f* au scanner *ou* au scanneur
▸**scan in** *vt sep Comput (graphics)* insérer par scanner *ou* scanneur, capturer au scanner *ou* au scanneur

scandal ['skændəl] *n* (**a**) *(disgrace)* scandale *m*; **the whole business is an absolute scandal!** toute cette affaire est absolument scandaleuse *ou* est un véritable scandale!; **to cause** *or* **create a scandal** provoquer un scandale; **it would cause a dreadful scandal if the newspapers found out** cela provoquerait un horrible scandale si les journaux en entendaient parler; **it's a scandal that people like them should be let free** c'est scandaleux de laisser des gens pareils en liberté; **it's a national scandal** c'est une honte nationale *ou* un scandale public
(**b**) *(UNCOUNT) (gossip)* ragots *mpl*; *(evil)* médisance *f*, médisances *fpl*, calomnie *f*; **to spread scandal about sb** répandre des ragots sur le compte de qn; **this newspaper specializes in scandal** c'est un journal à scandale; **the latest society scandal** les derniers potins *mpl* mondains; **a juicy bit of scandal** des ragots *mpl* savoureux *ou* croustillants
▸▸ *Press* ***scandal sheet*** journal *m* à scandale

scandalize, -ise ['skændəlaɪz] *vt* scandaliser, choquer; **he was scandalized by what she said** il a été scandalisé par ses propos; **she's easily scandalized** elle se scandalise *ou* s'indigne vite

scandalmonger ['skændəl,mʌŋgə(r)] *n* mauvaise langue *f*, colporteur(euse) *m,f* de ragots

scandalmongering ['skændəl,mʌŋgərɪŋ] **1** *n (UNCOUNT)* commérage *m*, médisance *f*
2 *adj (journalist etc)* qui cherche le scandale

scandalous ['skændələs] *adj* (**a**) *(conduct)* scandaleux, choquant; *(news, price)* scandaleux; **it's absolutely scandalous!** c'est un véritable scandale! (**b**) *(gossip)* calomnieux

scandalously ['skændələslɪ] *adv* (**a**) *(act)* scandaleusement (**b**) *(speak, write)* de manière diffamatoire; **she gave a scandalously explicit account of their affair** elle a raconté leur liaison en termes si explicites que c'en était choquant

scandalousness ['skændələsnɪs] *n* caractère *m* scandaleux

scandent ['skændənt] *adj Bot* grimpant

Scandinavia [,skændɪ'neɪvɪə] *n* Scandinavie *f*; **in Scandinavia** en Scandinavie

Scandinavian [,skændɪ'neɪvɪən] **1** *n* (**a**) *(person)* Scandinave *mf* (**b**) *Ling* scandinave *m*
2 *adj* scandinave

scandium ['skændɪəm] *n Chem* scandium *m*

scank = **skank**

scanky = **skanky**

scanner ['skænə(r)] *n* (**a**) *Med* scanner *m*, *Offic* scanographe *m*; *(ultrasound)* échographe *m*
(**b**) *Electron* scanner *m*
(**c**) *(for radar)* antenne *f*
(**d**) *Comput* scanner *m*, scanneur *m*

scanning ['skænɪŋ] *n* (**a**) *(in prosody → of verse)* scansion *f*
(**b**) *(close examination)* examen *m* minutieux
(**c**) *Electron & Rad* balayage *m*; *Med* examen *m* au scanner *ou Offic* au scanographe; *(with ultrasound)* échographie *f*; **radar scanning** balayage *m* radar
(**d**) *Comput* passage *m* au scanne(u)r, scannérisation *f*
(**e**) *Mktg* veille *f* technologique
▸▸ ***scanning electron microscope*** microscope *m* électronique à balayage

scansion ['skænʃən] *n Literature* scansion *f*

scansorial [,skæn'sɔːrɪəl] *Zool* **1** *n* grimpeur *m*
2 *adj* grimpeur

scant [skænt] **1** *adj* maigre; **to pay scant attention to sb/sth** ne prêter que peu d'attention à qn/qch; **she received scant praise** elle n'a reçu que de maigres louanges; **they showed scant regard for our feelings** ils ne se sont pas beaucoup souciés *ou* ils se sont peu souciés de ce que nous pouvions ressentir; **a scant teaspoonful** une cuillerée à café rase
2 *vt* (**a**) *(skimp on)* lésiner sur; *(restrict)* restreindre
(**b**) *(treat superficially)* traiter de manière superficielle

scantily ['skæntɪlɪ] *adv (furnished)* pauvrement, chichement; *(dressed)* légèrement; **scantily clad bathing beauties** de belles baigneuses *fpl* légèrement vêtues *ou* en tenue légère

scantiness ['skæntɪnɪs] *n (of meal)* frugalité *f*; *(of crops)* maigreur *f*; *(of knowledge)* insuffisance *f*; *(of dress)* légèreté *f*

scanty ['skæntɪ] *(compar* **scantier**, *superl* **scantiest**) *adj* (**a**) *(small in number, quantity → meal, crops)* maigre, peu abondant; *(→ income, payment)* maigre, modeste; *(→ information, knowledge)* maigre, limité; *(→ applause)* maigre, peu fourni; *(→ audience)* clairsemé; *(→ praise, aid)* limité
(**b**) *(brief → clothing)* léger; **she was wearing only a scanty negligee** elle ne portait qu'un négligé qui ne cachait pas grand-chose

Scapa Flow [,skæpə-] *n* Scapa Flow *(base navale britannique dans les îles Orcades où de nombreux bâtiments de guerre allemands furent rassemblés et coulés à l'issue de la Première Guerre mondiale)*

scape [skeɪp] *n* (**a**) *Bot* hampe *f*, scape *m* (**b**) *Orn (of feather)* tuyau *m*; *Entom (of antenna)* scape *m*
(**c**) *Arch or Literary (escape)* fuite *f*, évasion *f*
▸▸ ***scape wheel*** *(in clockmaking)* roue *f* de rencontre

scapegoat ['skeɪpgəʊt] *n* bouc *m* émissaire

scapegrace ['skeɪpgreɪs] *n Br* voyou *m*, vaurien(enne) *m,f*

scaphoid ['skæfɔɪd] *adj Anat* scaphoïde
▸▸ ***scaphoid bone*** os *m* scaphoïde, scaphoïde *m*

scapolite ['skæpə,laɪt] *n Miner* scapolite *f*, wernérite *f*

scapula ['skæpjʊlə] *(pl* **scapulas** *or* **scapulae** [-liː]) *n Anat* omoplate *f*

scapular ['skæpjʊlə(r)] **1** *adj* scapulaire
2 *n* scapulaire *m*

scapulary ['skæpjʊlərɪ] *(pl* **scapularies**) *n Rel* scapulaire *m*

scapulectomy [,skæpjʊ'lektəmɪ] *(pl* **scapulectomies**) *n Med* scapulectomie *f*

scar [skɑː(r)] *(pt & pp* **scarred**, *cont* **scarring**) **1** *n* (**a**) *(from wound, surgery)* cicatrice *f*; *(from deep cut on face)* balafre *f*; **to have acne scars** avoir des traces d'acné
(**b**) *Fig (on land, painted surface, tree)* cicatrice *f*, marque *f*; *(emotional, psychological)* cicatrice *f*; **the scars of battle** les traces *fpl* de la bataille; **the mine was like an ugly scar on the landscape** la mine déparait terriblement le paysage; **the city still bears the scars of its divided past/the bombing** la ville porte encore les cicatrices d'un passé de divisions/du bombardement; **he carried the (mental) scars for the rest of his life** il est resté marqué à vie
(**c**) *(rock)* rocher *m* escarpé; *(in river)* écueil *m*
2 *vt* (**a**) *(skin, face)* laisser une cicatrice sur; *(with knife etc)* balafrer; **his hands were badly scarred** il avait sur les mains de profondes cicatrices; **smallpox had scarred his face** il avait le visage grêlé par la variole
(**b**) *Fig* marquer; **the paintwork was badly scarred** la peinture était tout éraflée; **to be scarred for life** *(person → by experience etc)* être marqué à vie; **war-scarred** *(country etc)* dévasté par la guerre
3 *vi (form scar)* se cicatriser; *(leave scar)* laisser une cicatrice
▸▸ ***scar tissue*** tissu *m* cicatriciel
▸**scar over** *vi (form scar)* former une cicatrice; *(close up)* se cicatriser

scarab ['skærəb] *n* (**a**) *Entom* **scarab (beetle)** scarabée *m* (**b**) *(precious stone)* scarabée *m*

scarabaeid [,skærə'biːɪd] *n Entom* scarabéidé *m*

Scaramouche [,skærə'muːʃ] *pr n* Scaramouche

scarce ['skeəs] **1** *adj (rare)* rare; *(infrequent)* peu fréquent; *(in short supply)* peu abondant; **sugar is scarce at the moment** il y a une pénurie de sucre en ce moment; **to become scarce** se faire rare; **water is becoming scarce** l'eau commence à manquer; **rain is scarce in this region** il ne pleut pas souvent dans cette région; *Fam* **to make oneself scarce** *(run away)* se sauver, décamper; *(get out)* débarrasser le plancher; **can you make yourself scarce for half an hour?** peux-tu disparaître pendant une demi-heure?
2 *adv Literary* à peine; **I could scarce believe my eyes** j'en croyais à peine mes yeux
▸▸ *Fin* ***scarce currency*** devise *f* forte

scarcely ['skeəslɪ] *adv* (**a**) *(no sooner)* à peine; **we had scarcely begun** *or* **scarcely had we begun when the bell rang** nous avions tout juste commencé quand *ou* à peine avions-nous commencé que la cloche a sonné
(**b**) *(barely)* à peine, guère; **we scarcely saw her** nous l'avons à peine vue, nous ne l'avons guère vue; **he scarcely spoke to me** c'est tout juste s'il m'a adressé la parole; **she's scarcely more than a child** elle n'est encore qu'une enfant; **scarcely any** presque pas de; **scarcely anybody** presque personne; **scarcely anything** presque rien; **I know scarcely any of those people** je ne connais pratiquement personne parmi ces gens *ou* pratiquement aucune de ces personnes; **he has scarcely any hair left** il n'a presque plus de cheveux; **they were scarcely ever together** ils n'étaient presque jamais ensemble
(**c**) *(indicating difficulty)* à peine, tout juste; **I could scarcely tell his mother, now could I!** je ne pouvais quand même pas le dire à sa mère, non?; **I scarcely know where to begin** je ne sais pas trop par où commencer; **I can scarcely wait** je bous d'impatience; **I can scarcely wait to meet her** j'ai hâte de la rencontrer; **I can scarcely believe what you're saying** j'ai du mal à croire ce que vous dites; **it is scarcely likely that...** il est peu vraisemblable que...

scarceness ['skeəsnɪs] = **scarcity**

scarcity ['skeəsɪtɪ] *(pl* **scarcities**) *n (rarity)* rareté *f*; *(lack)* manque *m*; *(shortage)* manque *m*, pénurie *f*; **there is a scarcity of new talent today** les nouveaux talents se font rares; **the scarcity of food** le manque de vivres, la disette
▸▸ ***scarcity value*** valeur *f* de rareté; **the book has a high scarcity value** ce livre vaut cher parce qu'il est pratiquement introuvable *ou* parce qu'il n'en existe que très peu d'exemplaires

scare [skeə(r)] **1** *vt* effrayer, faire peur à; **thunder really scares me** le tonnerre me fait vraiment très peur; **you'll scare her** vous allez lui faire peur *ou* l'effrayer; **the high costs scared them off the idea** les coûts élevés leur en ont fait abandonner l'idée; *Fam* **the movie scared me stiff!** le film m'a flanqué une de ces frousses!; *Fam* **to scare the wits** *or* **the living daylights** *or* **the life out of sb** flanquer une peur bleue *ou* une trouille pas possible à qn; *Fam* **he scared**

the hell *or Vulg* **the shit out of me** il m'a foutu les jetons

2 *vi* s'effrayer, prendre peur; **he scares easily** il a peur de tout, un rien l'effraie; **I don't scare easily** je ne suis pas peureux

3 *n* (**a**) *(fright)* peur *f*, frayeur *f*; **to give sb a scare** effrayer qn, faire peur à qn

(**b**) *(alert)* alerte *f*; *(rumour)* bruit *m* alarmiste, rumeur *f*; **health scare** = vague de panique concernant la santé publique; **the revelations about the contaminated meat have resulted in a food scare** les révélations sur la viande contaminée ont provoqué une vague de panique chez les consommateurs; **a takeover scare** des rumeurs *fpl* concernant une possible OPA; **a bomb/fire scare** une alerte à la bombe/au feu

4 *comp (sensational)* alarmiste; *(frightening)* effrayant, qui fait peur

►► ***scare story*** histoire *f* pour faire peur; ***scare tactics*** manœuvres *fpl* d'intimidation

►**scare away, scare off** *vt sep (bird, customer)* faire fuir

►**scare up** *vt sep Am Fam* dénicher

scarecrow ['skeəkrəʊ] *n (for birds)* épouvantail *m*; *Fig (person → thin)* squelette *m*; *(→ badly dressed)* épouvantail *m*

scared ['skeəd] *adj (frightened)* effrayé; *(nervous)* craintif, peureux; **to be scared (of sth)** avoir peur (de qch); **he was scared to ask** il avait peur de demander; **he's scared of being told off/that she might tell him off** il craint de se faire gronder/qu'elle ne le gronde; *Fam* **to be scared stiff** *or* **to death** avoir une peur bleue; *Fam* **I was scared out of my wits!** j'étais mort de peur!; **to run like a scared rabbit** courir comme un dératé

scaredy cat ['skeədɪ-] *n Fam (in children's language)* froussard(e) *m,f*, poule *f* mouillée

scaremonger ['skeəˌmʌŋgə(r)] *n* alarmiste *mf*

scaremongering ['skeəˌmʌŋgərɪŋ] *n* alarmisme *m*

scarey = **scary**

scarf [skɑːf] *(pl sense* (**a**) **scarfs** *or* **scarves** [skɑːvz], *pl sense* (**b**) **scarfs**) **1** *n* (**a**) *(long)* écharpe *f*; *(headscarf, cravat)* foulard *m* (**b**) *Constr* enture *f*, assemblage *m* à mi-bois (**c**) *(cut)* entaille *f*

2 *vt* (**a**) *Constr (join)* joindre par enture (**b**) *(cut)* entailler (**c**) *Am Fam (eat)* bouffer, boulotter

►► *Constr* ***scarf joint*** enture *f*, assemblage *m* à mi-bois

►**scarf down** *vt sep Am Fam (eat)* bouffer, boulotter

Scarface ['skɑːfeɪs] *pr n* le Balafré

scarfskin ['skɑːfskɪn] *n Anat* épiderme *m*, cuticule *f*

scarification [ˌskærɪfɪ'keɪʃən] *n Agr & Med* scarification *f*

scarificator ['skærɪfɪˌkeɪtə(r)] *n Agr & Med* scarificateur *m*

scarifier ['skærɪfaɪə(r)] *n* (**a**) *Constr* **(road) scarifier** scarificateur *m*, piocheuse *f* scarificatrice (**b**) *Agr* scarificateur *m*

scarify ['skeərɪfaɪ] *(pt & pp* **scarified**) *vt* (**a**) *Agr & Med* scarifier (**b**) *(frighten)* donner la frousse à

scarily ['skeərɪlɪ] *adv* à faire peur; **we came scarily close to being killed** on est passé à deux doigts de la mort

scarlatina [ˌskɑːlə'tiːnə] *n (UNCOUNT) Med* scarlatine *f*

scarlet ['skɑːlət] **1** *adj (gen)* écarlate; *(face → from illness, effort)* cramoisi; *(→ from shame)* écarlate, cramoisi

2 *n* écarlate *f*

►► *Med* ***scarlet fever*** *(UNCOUNT)* scarlatine *f*; *Orn* ***scarlet ibis*** ibis *m* rouge; *Bot* ***scarlet pimpernel*** mouron *m* rouge; *Br Bot* ***scarlet runner*** haricot *m* (à rames); *Orn* ***scarlet tanager*** tangara *m* rouge; *Br Hum* ***scarlet woman*** femme *f* de mauvaise vie

'The Scarlet Letter' *Hawthorne* 'La Lettre écarlate'

'Scarlet and Black' *Stendhal* 'Le Rouge et le noir'

The Scarlet Pimpernel

Le Mouron rouge est le titre français du roman de la Baronne Orczy *The Scarlet Pimpernel* (1905), ainsi que le surnom de Sir Percy Blakeney, qui en est le personnage principal. L'histoire se déroule pendant la Révolution française et Blakeney, qui est passé maître dans l'art du déguisement, aide des membres de l'aristocratie française à s'enfuir en Angleterre. Il parvient toujours à échapper à ses poursuivants, comme en témoigne le passage suivant: **They seek him here, they seek him there, Those Frenchies seek him everywhere, Is he in Heaven or is he in Hell?, That damned elusive pimpernel** ("les Français le cherchent partout mais jamais ne l'attrapent, est-il au ciel ou en enfer, ce sacré mouron rouge?").

Aujourd'hui on utilise cette citation (ou simplement le terme **Scarlet Pimpernel**) sur le ton de la plaisanterie à propos de quelqu'un d'introuvable ou avec qui il est particulièrement difficile d'entrer en contact.

scarp [skɑːp] *n* (**a**) *Geog (of hill)* escarpement *m* (**b**) *Mil (in fortifications)* escarpe *f*

scarped [skɑːpt] *adj* escarpé, abrupt

scarper ['skɑːpə(r)] *vi Br Fam* déguerpir, se barrer, se tirer; **scarper!** fichez le camp!

SCART [skɑːt] *n Elec (abbr* **Syndicat des Constructeurs d'Appareils Radiorécepteurs et Téléviseurs**)

►► ***SCART cable*** câble *m* péritel®; ***SCART plug*** prise *f* péritel®

scarves [skɑːvz] *pl of* **scarf** (**a**)

scary ['skeərɪ] *(compar* **scarier**, *superl* **scariest**) *adj Fam* (**a**) *(frightening → place, person)* effrayant ❑; *(→ story)* qui donne le frisson (**b**) *(fearful)* peureux ❑

scat [skæt] *(pt & pp* **scatted**, *cont* **scatting**) **1** *vi Fam (go away)* se sauver, ficher le camp, se casser; **scat!** allez, ouste!, casse-toi!, dégage!

2 *n Mus* scat *m*

scathe [skeɪð] *Arch or Literary* **1** *n (harm, injury)* dommage *m*, blessure *f*; **without scathe** indemne

2 *vt* (**a**) *(injure)* nuire, causer du dommage à (**b**) *(criticize)* cingler

scathing ['skeɪðɪŋ] *adj (criticism, remark)* caustique, cinglant; **to give sb a scathing look** foudroyer qn du regard; **he can be very scathing** il sait se montrer acerbe *ou* cinglant; **the critics were scathing about his new movie** les critiques ont été féroces à propos de son dernier film

scathingly ['skeɪðɪŋlɪ] *adv (retort, criticize)* de manière cinglante; **she refers to him scathingly as "the toad"** elle l'appelle méchamment "le crapaud"

scatological [ˌskætə'lɒdʒɪkəl] *adj* scatologique

scatology [skæ'tɒlədʒɪ] *n* scatologie *f*

scatter ['skætə(r)] **1** *vt* (**a**) *(strew)* éparpiller, disperser; **don't scatter your toys all over the room** n'éparpille pas tes jouets partout dans la pièce; **papers had been scattered all over the desk** le bureau était jonché *ou* couvert de papiers

(**b**) *(spread)* répandre; *(sprinkle)* saupoudrer; **she scattered crumbs for the birds** elle a jeté des miettes de pain aux oiseaux; **to scatter seeds** semer des graines à la volée

(**c**) *(disperse → crowd, mob)* disperser; *(→ enemy)* mettre en fuite; *(→ clouds)* dissiper, disperser; **my friends are scattered all over the world** mes amis sont dispersés aux quatre vents *ou* un peu partout dans le monde

(**d**) *Phys (light)* disperser

2 *vi* (**a**) *(people, clouds)* se disperser; **they told us to scatter** ils nous ont dit de partir

(**b**) *(beads, papers)* s'éparpiller

3 *n* (**a**) *(of rice, bullets)* pluie *f*; **a scatter of farms on the hillside** quelques fermes *fpl* éparpillées à flanc de coteau

(**b**) *(in statistics)* dispersion *f*

►► ***scatter bomb*** obus *m* à mitraille, shrapnel *m*, shrapnell *m*; ***scatter cushion*** petit coussin *m*; *Math* ***scatter diagram*** diagramme *m* de dispersion; ***scatter rug*** petit tapis *m*, carpette *f*

►**scatter about, scatter around** *vt sep* éparpiller

scatterbrain ['skætəbreɪn] *n* tête *f* de linotte, étourdi(e) *m,f*

scatterbrained ['skætəbreɪnd] *adj* écervelé, étourdi

scattered ['skætəd] *adj* (**a**) *(strewn)* éparpillé; **papers/toys lying scattered all over the floor** des papiers/des jouets éparpillés par terre; **the table was scattered with empty cups** il y avait des tasses vides éparpillées sur la table

(**b**) *(sprinkled)* parsemé; **the tablecloth was scattered with crumbs** la nappe était parsemée de miettes

(**c**) *(dispersed → population)* dispersé, disséminé; *(→ clouds)* épars; *(→ villages, houses)* épars; *(→ light)* diffus; *(→ fortune)* dissipé; **she tried to collect her scattered thoughts** elle essaya de mettre de l'ordre dans ses idées

(**d**) *Am (scatterbrained)* écervelé, étourdi

►► *Met* ***scattered showers*** averses *fpl* éparses

scatter-gun *n* fusil *m* de chasse

scattering ['skætərɪŋ] *n* (**a**) *(small number)* **a scattering of followers** une poignée d'adeptes; **there was a scattering of farms** il y avait quelques fermes çà et là (**b**) *(dispersion)* dispersion *f*

scattily ['skætɪlɪ] *adv Br Fam* étourdiment ❑

scattiness ['skætɪnɪs] *n Br Fam* étourderie ❑ *f*

scatty ['skætɪ] *(compar* **scattier**, *superl* **scattiest**) *adj Br Fam* étourdi ❑, écervelé ❑

scaup [skɔːp] *n Orn* **scaup (duck)** fuligule *m* milouinan

scavenge ['skævɪndʒ] **1** *vi* (**a**) *(bird, animal)* **to scavenge (for food)** chercher sa nourriture

(**b**) *(person)* fouiller; **to scavenge in the dustbins** fouiller *ou* faire les poubelles; **if you haven't got any tools, you'll have to scavenge** si vous n'avez pas d'outils, il va falloir en récupérer à droite et à gauche

2 *vt* (**a**) *(material, metals)* récupérer; **he managed to scavenge a meal** il a finalement trouvé quelque chose à se mettre sous la dent

(**b**) *(streets)* nettoyer

(**c**) *Tech (combustion engine)* balayer

scavenger ['skævɪndʒə(r)] *n* (**a**) *Zool (eating flesh)* charognard *m*; *(eating refuse)* animal *m* qui se nourrit d'ordures (**b**) *(salvager)* ramasseur(euse) *m,f* d'épaves; *(in rubbish)* pilleur(euse) *m,f* de poubelles (**c**) *Br (street cleaner)* éboueur *m*

►► ***scavenger hunt*** ≃ chasse *f* au trésor

scavenging ['skævɪndʒɪŋ] *n* (**a**) *(searching for food etc)* **scavenging seems to be this dog's main occupation** ce chien est toujours à fouiller dans les poubelles (**b**) *(cleaning streets)* ébouage *m*, enlèvement *m* des ordures (**c**) *Tech (of combustion engine)* balayage *m*

►► *Tech* ***scavenging valve*** soupape *f* de balayage

SCE [ˌesiː'iː] *n Sch (abbr* **Scottish Certificate of Education**) – examen de fin d'études secondaires en Écosse

scenario [sɪ'nɑːrɪəʊ] *(pl* **scenarios**) *n Cin & Fig* scénario *m*

scenarist [*Br* 'siːnərɪst, *Am* sɪ'nɑːrɪst] *n* scénariste *mf*

scene [siːn] *n* (**a**) *Cin & Theat (in film)* scène *f*, séquence *f*; *(in play)* scène *f*; **the murder/love/balcony scene** la scène du meurtre/d'amour/du balcon; **Act IV scene 2** Acte IV scène 2; **to set the scene** planter le décor; **the scene is set** *or* **takes place in Bombay** la scène se passe *ou* l'action se déroule à Bombay; *Fig* **this set the scene for more riots** ceci a marqué le début d'une série d'émeutes; **this set the scene for a major confrontation** ceci a jeté les bases d'une vaste confrontation; **the scene was set for the arms negotiations** tout était prêt pour les négociations sur les armements

(**b**) *Theat (scenery)* décor *m*; **scenes painted by...** décors *mpl* par...; *also Fig* **behind the scenes** dans la *ou* les coulisse(s)

(**c**) *(sphere of activity, milieu)* scène *f*, situation *f*; **the world political scene** la scène politique internationale; **she's a newcomer on** *or* **to the sports scene** c'est une nouvelle venue sur la scène sportive *ou* dans le monde du sport; **the drug scene** le monde de la drogue; **she came on the scene just when we needed her** elle est arrivée juste au moment où nous avions besoin d'elle; **he disappeared from the scene for a few years** il a disparu de la circulation *ou* de la scène pendant quelques années; **a change of**

scene will do you good un changement d'air *ou* de décor vous fera du bien; *Fam* **hip-hop isn't really my scene** le hip-hop, ça n'est pas vraiment mon truc

(**d**) *(place, spot)* lieu *m*, lieux *mpl*, endroit *m*; **the scene of the disaster** l'endroit *m* où s'est produit la catastrophe; **the scene of the crime** le lieu du crime; **to arrive** *or* **come on the scene** arriver sur les lieux *ou* sur place; **the police were soon on the scene** la police est rapidement arrivée sur les lieux *ou* sur place; **I was first on the scene** j'étais le premier présent *ou* le premier sur les lieux; **to arrive on the scene** arriver sur place; *Mil* **scene of operations** théâtre *m* des opérations

(**e**) *(image)* scène *f*, spectacle *m*; *(incident)* scène *f*, incident *m*; *(view)* spectacle *m*, perspective *f*, vue *f*; **scenes of horror/violence** scènes d'horreur/de violence; **scenes from** *or* **of village life** scènes de la vie villageoise; **just picture the scene** essayez de vous représenter la scène; **there were some nasty scenes at the match** il y a eu des incidents violents lors du match; **a scene of married bliss** une scène de bonheur conjugal; **a scene of calm beauty lay before us** nous avions devant nous un paysage d'une beauté paisible

(**f**) *Art* tableau *m*, scène *f*; **country/city scenes** scènes champêtres/de ville

(**g**) *(fuss, row)* scène *f*; **to make a scene** faire une scène; **to have a scene with sb** se disputer avec qn; **he made an awful scene about it** il en a fait toute une histoire

►► *Theat* ***scene change*** changement *m* de décors; *Theat* ***scene designer*** décorateur(trice) *m,f* de théâtre; *Theat* ***scene dock*** case *f* à décor *ou* décors; *Theat* ***scene painter*** décorateur(trice) *m,f* de théâtre

scene-of-crime officer *n* = agent responsable de l'enquête sur le lieu du crime

scenery ['si:nərɪ] *n* (**a**) *(natural setting)* paysage *m*; **mountain scenery** paysages *mpl* de montagne; **I was admiring the scenery** j'admirais le paysage; **the scenery round here is lovely** les paysages sont très beaux par ici; **we drove through picturesque scenery** nous avons traversé des paysages très pittoresques; *Fig* **she needs a change of scenery** elle a besoin de changer de décor *ou* d'air (**b**) *Theat* décor *m*, décors *mpl*

scene-set *n TV & Cin* mise *f* en place

sceneshifter ['si:n,ʃɪftə(r)] *n Theat* machiniste *mf*

sceneshifting ['si:n,ʃɪftɪŋ] *n Theat* changement *m* de décors

scenic ['si:nɪk] *adj* (**a**) *(surroundings)* pittoresque; **let's take the scenic route** prenons la route touristique; *Fig Hum* prenons le chemin des écoliers; **an area of great scenic beauty** une région qui offre de très beaux panoramas (**b**) *Art & Theat* scénique

►► *Theat* ***scenic cloth*** rideau *m* de fond scénique; *Theat* ***scenic design*** décoration *f* de théâtre, scénographie *f*; *Theat* ***scenic designer*** décorateur(trice) *m,f* de théâtre, scénographe *mf*; ***scenic railway*** *(for tourists)* petit train *m* (touristique); *(in fairground)* montagnes *fpl* russes; *Theat* ***scenic workshop*** atelier *m* de décors

scenographer [si:'nɒgrəfə(r)] *n* scénographe *mf*

scenographic [,si:nə'græfɪk], **scenographical** [,si:nə'græfɪkəl] *adj* scénographique

►► ***scenographic scale*** échelle *f* perspective

scenography [si:'nɒgrəfɪ] *n* (**a**) *Theat* scénographie *f* (**b**) *Art* dessin *m* en perspective

scent [sent] **1** *n* (**a**) *(smell)* parfum *m*, odeur *f*; **the scent of new-mown hay** l'odeur *f* du foin fraîchement fauché; **the scent of polished wood** le parfum *ou* l'odeur *f* de bois ciré

(**b**) *Hunt (of animal)* fumet *m*; *(of person)* odeur *f*; *(track)* trace *f*, piste *f*; **the hounds are on the scent** *or* **have picked up the scent of a fox** les chiens sont sur la trace d'un renard *ou* ont dépisté un renard; **they've lost the scent** ils ont perdu la piste; **to put** *or* **to throw sb off the scent** semer qn; **we're on the scent of a major scandal** nous flairons un gros scandale

(**c**) *Br (perfume)* parfum *m*

(**d**) *(sense of smell → of dog)* odorat *m*, flair *m*

2 *vt* (**a**) *(smell → prey)* flairer; *(detect → danger, treachery)* flairer, subodorer; *Fig* **to scent blood** sentir que sa victime est affaiblie

(**b**) *(perfume)* parfumer, embaumer

►► ***scent gland*** glande *f* à sécrétion odoriférante

scented ['sentɪd] *adj (soap etc)* parfumé

►► ***scented notepaper*** papier *m* à lettres parfumé

scentless ['sentlɪs] *adj (odourless → substance)* inodore; *(→ flower)* sans parfum

►► *Bot* ***scentless mayweed*** camomille *f* inodore

scepter *Am* = **sceptre**

sceptic, *Am* **skeptic** ['skeptɪk] **1** *adj* sceptique

2 *n* sceptique *mf*

sceptical, *Am* **skeptical** ['skeptɪkəl] *adj* sceptique

sceptically, *Am* **skeptically** ['skeptɪkəlɪ] *adv* avec scepticisme

scepticism, *Am* **skepticism** ['skeptɪsɪzəm] *n* scepticisme *m*

sceptre, *Am* **scepter** ['septə(r)] *n* sceptre *m*

sceptred ['septəd] *adj Br Literary* **this sceptred isle** = expression tirée de 'Richard III', de Shakespeare, et servant aujourd'hui à désigner la Grande-Bretagne sur un ton lyrique, parfois nationaliste

SCF [,essi:'ef] *n (abbr* **Save the Children Fund**) = organisme international d'assistance à l'enfance

SCG [,essi:'dʒi:] *n (abbr* **Sydney Cricket Ground**) = célèbre terrain de cricket de Sydney où se jouent des matches internationaux

schadenfreude ['ʃɑ:dən,frɔɪdə] *n* = joie maligne qu'on éprouve en face du malheur d'autrui

schedule [*Br* 'ʃedju:l, *Am* 'skedʒʊl] **1** *n* (**a**) *(programme)* programme *m*; *(calendar)* programme *m*, calendrier *m*; *(timetable)* programme *m*, emploi *m* du temps; *(plan)* prévisions *fpl*, plan *m*; **I have a busy schedule** *(for visit)* j'ai un programme chargé; *(in general)* j'ai un emploi du temps chargé; *(over period)* j'ai un calendrier chargé; **everything went according to schedule** tout s'est déroulé comme prévu; **I work to a very tight schedule** mon emploi du temps est très chargé; **the work was carried out according to schedule** le travail a été effectué selon les prévisions; **we are on schedule** *or* **up to schedule** nous sommes dans les temps; **our work is ahead of/behind schedule** nous sommes en avance/en retard dans notre travail; **the bridge was opened on/ahead of schedule** le pont a été ouvert à la date prévue/en avance sur la date prévue; **the doors opened on schedule** les portes se sont ouvertes à l'heure prévue; **a schedule was agreed for the work** on s'est mis d'accord sur un programme de travail *ou* un planning pour le travail; **to fall behind schedule** prendre du retard sur les prévisions de travail

(**b**) *(timetable → for transport)* horaire *m*; **the train is on/is running behind schedule** le train est à l'heure/a du retard

(**c**) *(list → of prices)* barème *m*; *(→ of contents)* inventaire *m*; *(→ of items)* nomenclature *f*; *(→ of payments)* échéancier *m*

(**d**) *Law (to law, articles of association etc)* annexe *f*, avenant *m*

2 *vt* (**a**) *(plan → event)* prévoir, programmer; *(→ appointment)* fixer; **the meeting was scheduled for three o'clock/Wednesday** la réunion était prévue pour trois heures/mercredi; **the plane was scheduled to touch down at 18.45** il était prévu que l'avion arrive *ou* l'arrivée de l'avion était prévue à 18 heures 45; **the building is scheduled for demolition** il est prévu que le bâtiment soit démoli; **she wasn't scheduled to arrive until Sunday** elle ne devait pas arriver *ou* il n'était pas prévu qu'elle arrive avant dimanche; **which day is the film scheduled for?** quel jour a été retenu pour le film?; **it's scheduled for Saturday** il est programmé pour samedi; **you aren't scheduled to sing until later** d'après le programme, vous devez chanter plus tard (dans la soirée)

(**b**) *(period, work, series)* organiser; **to schedule one's time** aménager *ou* organiser son temps; **to schedule a morning** établir l'emploi du temps d'une matinée; **our whole week is scheduled** notre programme *ou* emploi du temps pour cette semaine est déjà établi; **that lunch hour is already scheduled** ce déjeuner est déjà réservé; **to schedule one's reading** se faire un plan de lecture

(**c**) *(topic, item)* inscrire; **it's scheduled as a topic for the next meeting** c'est inscrit à l'ordre du jour de la prochaine réunion

(**d**) *Br Admin (monument)* classer

(**e**) *Law (add as appendix)* ajouter en annexe

scheduled [*Br* 'ʃedju:ld, *Am* 'skedʒʊld] *adj* (**a**) *(planned)* prévu; **at the scheduled time** à l'heure prévue; **he didn't make his scheduled speech** il n'a pas prononcé le discours qu'il avait prévu; *TV* **we announce a change to our scheduled programmes** nous annonçons une modification de nos programmes

(**b**) *(regular → flight)* régulier; *(→ stop, change)* habituel

(**c**) *(official → prices)* tarifé

(**d**) *Br Admin* **the scheduled territories** la zone sterling

►► *Br Admin* ***scheduled building*** bâtiment *m* classé monument historique; ***scheduled castes*** = castes en Inde qui ont droit à certains privilèges; ***schedule of charges*** tarifs *mpl*

scheduler [*Br* 'ʃedju:lə(r), *Am* 'skedʒu:lə(r)] *n Comput (package)* logiciel *m* de planification (de projets)

scheduling [*Br* 'ʃedju:lɪŋ, *Am* 'skedʒu:lɪŋ] *n TV & Rad* programmation *f*

►► *TV & Rad* ***scheduling director*** directeur(-trice) *m,f* des programmes

scheelite ['ʃi:laɪt] *n Miner* scheelite *f*

Scheherazade [ʃə,herə'zɑ:d] *pr n* Shéhérazade, Schéhérazade

schema ['ski:mə] *(pl* **schemata** [-mətə]) *n* (**a**) *(diagram)* schéma *m* (**b**) *Phil & Psy* schème *m*

schematic [skɪ'mætɪk] **1** *adj* schématique

2 *n* schéma *m*

schematically [skɪ'mætɪkəlɪ] *adv* schématiquement

schematism ['ski:mətɪzəm] *n* schématisme *m*

schematization [,ski:mətaɪ'zeɪʃən] *n* schématisation *f*

schematize, -ise ['ski:mətaɪz] *vt* schématiser

scheme [ski:m] **1** *n* (**a**) *(plan)* plan *m*, projet *m*; **a scheme for helping the homeless** un projet pour aider les sans-abri; **a scheme for new investment** un plan *ou* projet pour de nouveaux investissements; **a scheme to get rich quick** un procédé pour s'enrichir rapidement; **he's always dreaming up mad schemes for entertaining the children** il a toujours des idées lumineuses pour distraire les enfants; **the scheme of things** l'ordre *m* des choses; **where does he fit into the scheme of things?** quel rôle joue-t-il dans cette affaire?; **it just doesn't fit into her scheme of things** cela n'entre pas dans sa conception des choses; **where does mankind fit into the great** *or* **cosmic scheme of things?** quelle est la place de l'humanité dans l'univers?

(**b**) *(plot)* intrigue *f*, complot *m*; *(unscrupulous)* procédé *m* malhonnête; **their little scheme didn't work** leur petit complot a échoué

(**c**) *Br Admin* plan *m*, système *m*; **the firm has a profit-sharing/a pension scheme** l'entreprise a un système de participation aux bénéfices/un régime de retraites complémentaires; **the unions would not agree to the new productivity scheme** les syndicats ont refusé d'accepter *ou* ont rejeté le nouveau plan de productivité; **government unemployment schemes** plans *mpl* antichômage du gouvernement; **National Savings Scheme** ≃ Caisse *f* nationale d'épargne

(**d**) *(arrangement)* disposition *f*, schéma *m*

2 *vi* intriguer, *Fam* magouiller; **to scheme to do sth** projeter de faire qch; **they schemed against the general** ils ont comploté contre le général

3 *vt* combiner, manigancer

schemer ['ski:mə(r)] *n* intrigant(e) *m,f*; *(in conspiracy)* conspirateur(trice) *m,f*

scheming ['ski:mɪŋ] **1** *n (UNCOUNT)* intrigues *fpl*, machinations *fpl*

2 *adj* intrigant, conspirateur

scherzando [,skeət'sændəʊ] *(pl* **scherzandos** *or* **scherzandi** [-di:]) *Mus* **1** *n* scherzo *m*

2 *adv* scherzando

scherzo ['skeətsəʊ] *(pl* **scherzos** *or* **scherzi** [-tsi:]) *n Mus* scherzo *m*
schilling ['ʃɪlɪŋ] *n* schilling *m*
schism ['sɪzəm, 'skɪzəm] *n* schisme *m*; *Hist* **the Great Schism** *(between the Eastern and Western churches)* le schisme d'Orient; *(within the Roman Catholic Church)* le grand schisme d'Occident
schismatic [sɪz'mætɪk, skɪz'mætɪk] **1** *adj* schismatique
2 *n* schismatique *mf*
schismatical [sɪz'mætɪkəl, skɪz'mætɪkəl] *adj* schismatique
schist [ʃɪst] *n Geol* schiste *m*
►► ***schist oil*** huile *f* de schiste
schistosomiasis [ˌʃɪstəsəʊ'maɪəsɪs] *n Med* schistosomiase *f*
schitz, schiz [skɪts] *Am* = **schizo**
schizo ['skɪtsəʊ] *Fam (abbr* **schizophrenic**) *(pl* **schizos**) **1** *adj* schizo; *Fig (mad)* cinglé
2 *n* schizo *mf*; *Fig (mad person)* cinglé(e) *m,f*
schizocarp ['skɪtsəʊkɑ:p] *n Bot* fruit *m* schizocarpique
schizoid ['skɪtsɔɪd] **1** *adj* schizoïde
2 *n* schizoïde *mf*
schizomycete [ˌskɪtsəʊmaɪ'si:t] *n Biol* schizomycète *m*
schizophrenia [ˌskɪtsə'fri:nɪə] *n* schizophrénie *f*; **to suffer from schizophrenia** être atteint de schizophrénie, être schizophrène
schizophrenic [ˌskɪtsə'frenɪk] **1** *adj* schizophrène
2 *n* schizophrène *mf*
schizothymia [ˌskɪtsəʊ'θaɪmɪə] *n Psy* schizothymie *f*
schlemiel, schlemihl [ʃlə'mi:l] *n esp Am very Fam* minable *mf*
schlep, schlepp [ʃlep] *(pt & pp* **schlepped,** *cont* **schlepping**) *esp Am Fam* **1** *vt* trimbaler, trimballer; **I've got to schlep(p) all this stuff over to the office** il faut que je trimbal(l)e *ou* transbahute tous ces trucs au bureau
2 *vi (walk)* crapahuter; **to schlep home** rentrer chez soi à pinces; **I had to schlep to the grocery store** il a fallu que je crapahute jusqu'à l'épicerie
3 *n* (**a**) *(person)* crétin(e) *m,f*, lourdaud(e)❑ *m,f*
(**b**) *esp Am Fam (journey)* trotte *f*; **it's a bit of a schlep to the supermarket** ça fait une trotte jusqu'au supermarché
►**schlep(p) about, schlep(p) around** *Am* **1** *vt insep* **to schlep around the town** crapahuter en ville
2 *vi* crapahuter
Schleswig-Holstein [ˌʃlezvɪg'hɒlstaɪn] *n* Schleswig-Holstein *m*; **in Schleswig-Holstein** dans le Schleswig-Holstein
schlock [ʃlɒk] *esp Am Fam* **1** *n* (**a**) *(junk)* camelote *f* (**b**) *(lazy person)* flemmard(e) *m,f*
2 *adj (worthless)* qui ne vaut pas un clou, nul; *(jewellery)* en toc
schlong [ʃlɒŋ] *n Am Vulg* queue *f*, bite *f*
schmaltz [ʃmɔ:lts] *n Fam* guimauve❑ *f*
schmaltzy ['ʃmɔ:ltsɪ] *adj Fam* à l'eau de rose❑, à la guimauve❑
schmalz, schmalzy = **schmaltz, schmaltzy**
schmo [ʃməʊ] *(pl* **schmoes**) *n Am Fam (unlucky person)* guignard(e) *m,f*; *(stupid person)* nul (nulle) *m,f*
schmooze [ʃmu:z] *vi Fam (chat)* bavarder❑, jaspiner, jacasser❑; *(at social gathering)* faire des mondanités❑
schmuck [ʃmʌk] *n Am Fam* andouille *f*, courge *f*
schnaps, schnapps [ʃnæps] *(pl* **inv**) *n* schnaps *m*
schnauzer ['ʃnaʊtsə(r)] *n (dog)* schnauzer *m*
schnitzel ['ʃnɪtsəl] *n* côtelette *f* de veau
schnook [ʃnʊk] *n Am Fam* poire *f*, pigeon *m*
schnorkel *Br* = **snorkel**
schnozz [ʃnɒz], **schnozzle** ['ʃnɒzəl] *n Fam* pif *m*, tarin *m*, blair *m*
scholar ['skɒlə(r)] *n* (**a**) *(academic)* érudit(e) *m,f*, savant(e) *m,f*; *(specialist)* spécialiste *mf*; *(intellectual)* intellectuel(elle) *m,f*; **an Egyptian scholar** un spécialiste de l'Égypte; **Latin scholar** latiniste *mf*; **I'm not much of a scholar** je ne suis pas très savant
(**b**) *(holder of grant)* boursier(ère) *m,f*
(**c**) *Old-fashioned (pupil)* élève *mf*; **she's a poor/good scholar** c'est une mauvaise/bonne élève
scholarly ['skɒləlɪ] *adj* (**a**) *(person)* érudit, cultivé (**b**) *(article, work)* savant (**c**) *(approach)* rigoureux, scientifique (**d**) *(circle)* universitaire
scholarship ['skɒləʃɪp] *n* (**a**) *Sch & Univ (grant)* bourse *f*; **to win a scholarship to Stanford** obtenir une bourse pour Stanford *(sur concours)* (**b**) *(knowledge)* savoir *m*, érudition *f*
►► ***scholarship holder, scholarship student*** boursier(ère) *m,f*
scholastic [skə'læstɪk] **1** *adj* (**a**) *(ability, record, supplier)* scolaire; *(profession)* d'enseignant; *(competition)* inter-écoles *(inv)* (**b**) *(philosophy, approach, argument)* scolastique
2 *n* scolastique *m*
►► ***scholastic agency*** agence *f* de placement (pour enseignants)
scholasticism [skə'læstɪsɪzəm] *n* scolastique *f*
scholiast ['skəʊlɪæst] *n* scoliaste *m*, scholiaste *m*
school [sku:l] **1** *n* (**a**) *(educational establishment)* école *f*, établissement *m* scolaire; *(secondary school → to age 15)* collège *m*; *(→ 15 to 18)* lycée *m*; *(classes)* école *f*, classe *f*, classes *fpl*, cours *mpl*; **to go to school** aller à l'école *ou* au collège *ou* au lycée; **to be at** *or* **in school** être à l'école *ou* en classe; **to go back to school** *(after illness)* reprendre l'école; *(after holidays)* rentrer; **to send one's children to school** envoyer ses enfants à l'école; **parents have a duty to send their children to school** les parents ont le devoir d'envoyer leurs enfants à l'école *ou* de scolariser leurs enfants; **what are you going to do when you leave school?** qu'est-ce que tu comptes faire quand tu auras quitté l'école *ou* fini ta scolarité?; **I was at school with him** j'étais en classe avec lui, c'était un de mes camarades de classe; **he's still at school** il va encore à l'école; **to go skiing/sailing with the school** ≃ aller en classe de neige/de mer; **television for schools** télévision *f* scolaire; **there's no school today** il n'y a pas (d')école *ou* il n'y a pas classe aujourd'hui; **school starts at nine** *(primary)* l'école *ou* la classe commence à neuf heures; *(secondary)* les cours commencent à neuf heures; **school starts back next week** c'est la rentrée (scolaire *ou* des classes) la semaine prochaine; **see you after school** on se voit après l'école *ou* la classe; **the whole school is** *or* **are invited** toute l'école est invitée; *Fig* **the school of life** l'école *f* de la vie; **I went to the school of hard knocks** j'ai été à rude école
(**b**) *(institute)* école *f*, académie *f*
(**c**) *Univ (department)* département *m*, institut *m*; *(faculty)* faculté *f*; *(college)* collège *m*; *Am (university)* université *f*; **London School of Economics** = institut d'études économiques de l'université de Londres; **she's at law school** elle fait des études de droit, elle fait son droit
(**d**) *(of art, literature)* école *f*; *Fig* **a doctor of the old school** un médecin de la vieille école *ou* de la vieille garde; **the Florentine/classical school** l'école florentine/classique
(**e**) *(training session)* stage *m*; **a two-day school for doctors** un stage de deux jours pour les médecins
(**f**) *(in Oxford and Cambridge)* **schools** *(examination hall)* salle *f* d'examen; *(examinations)* examens *mpl* de la licence
(**g**) *Hist* **the Schools** l'École *f*, la scolastique
(**h**) *(of fish, porpoises)* banc *m*
2 *comp (trip, doctor)* scolaire; **I'm not allowed to stay up late on school nights** je n'ai pas le droit de me coucher tard quand il y a école le lendemain; *Br* **to do the school run** emmener les enfants à l'école *(à tour de rôle)*
3 *vt* (**a**) *(train → person)* entraîner; *(→ animal)* dresser; **to be schooled in monetary/military matters** être rompu aux questions monétaires/militaires; **she schooled herself to listen to what others said** elle a appris à écouter (ce que disent) les autres; **she is well schooled in diplomacy** elle a une bonne formation diplomatique
(**b**) *(send to school)* envoyer à l'école, scolariser
►► ***school age*** âge *m* scolaire; ***school attendance*** *(going to school)* scolarisation *f*; *(not being absent)* présence *f* à l'école; ***school board*** conseil *m* d'établissement; *Rad & TV* ***schools broadcasting*** émissions *fpl* scolaires; ***school buildings*** bâtiments *mpl* scolaires; ***school bus*** car *m* de ramassage scolaire; ***school of dance, dancing school*** académie *f ou* école *f* de danse; ***school day*** journée *f* scolaire *ou* d'école; ***school dinners*** repas *mpl* servis à la cantine (de l'école); ***school district*** = aux États-Unis, autorité locale décisionnaire dans le domaine de l'enseignement primaire et secondaire; ***school fees*** frais *mpl* de scolarité; ***school friend*** camarade *mf* de classe *ou* d'école, *Fam* copain (copine) *m,f* de classe *ou* d'école; *Br* ***school governor*** membre *m* du conseil de gestion de l'école; ***school holiday*** jour *m* de congé scolaire; **tomorrow is a school holiday** il n'y a pas école *ou* classe *ou* cours demain; **during the school holidays** pendant les vacances *ou* congés scolaires; ***school hours*** heures *fpl* de classe *ou* d'école; **in school hours** pendant les heures de classe; **out of school hours** en dehors des heures de classe; ***school magazine*** journal *m* de l'école; ***school of medicine*** faculté *f* de médecine; ***school milk*** = lait offert aux élèves dans le primaire; ***school of motoring*** auto-école *f*, école *f* de conduite; ***school of music*** *(gen)* école *f* de musique; *(superior level)* conservatoire *m*; ***school report*** bulletin *m* scolaire; ***school of thought*** école *f* de pensée; *Fig* théorie *f*; **one school of thought argues that this is due to genetic factors** il existe une théorie selon laquelle ceci a une origine génétique; ***school tie*** = cravate propre à une école et faisant partie de l'uniforme; ***school uniform*** uniforme *m* scolaire; ***school year*** année *f* scolaire; **my school years** ma scolarité, mes années *fpl* d'école; **the school year runs from September to July** l'année scolaire dure de septembre à juillet

'The School for Scandal' *Sheridan* 'L'École de la médisance'

school-age *adj* d'âge scolaire
schoolbag ['sku:lbæg] *n* cartable *m*
schoolbook ['sku:lbʊk] *n* livre *m ou* manuel *m* scolaire
schoolboy ['sku:lbɔɪ] *n* écolier *m*; *(11 to 15)* collégien *m*; *(15 to 18)* lycéen *m*
►► ***schoolboy humour*** humour *m* de potache; ***schoolboy slang*** argot *m* scolaire
schoolchild ['sku:ltʃaɪld] *(pl* **schoolchildren** [-tʃɪldrən]) *n* écolier(ère) *m,f*
schooldays ['sku:ldeɪz] *npl* années *fpl* d'école; **in my schooldays** quand j'étais à l'école
schoolfellow ['sku:lˌfeləʊ] *n Old-fashioned* camarade *m ou* copain *m* de classe
schoolgirl ['sku:lgɜ:l] *n* écolière *f*; *(11 to 15)* collégienne *f*; *(15 to 18)* lycéenne *f*; **she had the usual schoolgirl crush on the gym teacher** comme toutes les filles de son âge, elle était tombée amoureuse de son prof de gym
►► ***schoolgirl complexion*** teint *m* de jeune fille
schoolhouse ['sku:lhaʊs, *pl* -haʊzɪz] *n* école *f* (du village)
schooling ['sku:lɪŋ] *n* (**a**) *(education)* instruction *f*, éducation *f*; *(enrolment at school)* scolarité *f*; **I haven't had much schooling** je ne suis pas allé longtemps à l'école, je ne suis pas très instruit; **schooling is compulsory** la scolarité est obligatoire (**b**) *(of horse)* dressage *m*
schoolkid ['sku:lkɪd] *n Fam* écolier(ère)❑ *m,f*; **he's only a schoolkid** ce n'est qu'un gosse
school-leaver [-ˌli:və(r)] *n Br* = jeune qui entre dans la vie active à la fin de sa scolarité
school-leaving age [-'li:vɪŋ-] *n* fin *f* de la scolarité obligatoire; **the school-leaving age was raised to sixteen** l'âge légal de fin de scolarité a été porté à seize ans
schoolma'am, schoolmarm ['sku:lmɑ:m] *n Fam* (**a**) *Hum (teacher)* maîtresse *f* d'école❑ (**b**) *Br Pej (prim woman)* bégueule *f*
schoolman ['sku:lmən] *(pl* **schoolmen** [-mən]) *n Hist & Phil* scolastique *m*
schoolmarmish ['sku:lmɑ:mɪʃ] *adj Br Fam Pej* **she's very schoolmarmish** elle fait très maîtresse d'école❑
schoolmaster ['sku:lˌmɑ:stə(r)] *n Br (at primary*

sch–sh

school) maître *m*, instituteur *m*; *(at secondary school)* professeur *m*

schoolmate ['sku:lmeɪt] *n* camarade *mf* d'école

schoolmistress ['sku:lˌmɪstrɪs] *n Br (primary school)* maîtresse *f*, institutrice *f*; *(secondary school)* professeur *m*

schoolroom ['sku:lrʊm] *n* (salle *f* de) classe *f*; *(in private house)* salle *f* d'étude

schoolteacher ['sku:lˌti:tʃə(r)] *n (at any level)* enseignant(e) *m,f*; *(at primary school)* instituteur(trice) *m,f*; *(at secondary school)* professeur *m*

schoolteaching ['sku:lˌti:tʃɪŋ] *n* enseignement *m*

schooltime ['sku:ltaɪm] *n (school hours)* heures *fpl* d'école; *(outside holidays)* année *f* scolaire

schoolwork ['sku:lwɜ:k] *n (UNCOUNT)* travail *m* scolaire; *(at home)* devoirs *mpl*, travail *m* à la maison

schooner ['sku:nə(r)] *n* (**a**) *Naut* schooner *m*, goélette *f* (**b**) *Br & Austr (for sherry, beer)* grand verre *m*; **a schooner of sherry** un verre de xérès

schottische [ʃɒ'ti:ʃ] *n Mus* scottisch *f*, scottich *f*

schtuk [ʃtʊk] *n Br Fam* **to be in schtuk** être dans le pétrin, être dans la panade

schtum [ʃtʊm] *adj Br Fam* **to keep schtum** ne pas piper mot

Schubert ['ʃu:bət] *pr n* Schubert

schuss [ʃʊs] *Ski* **1** *n* schuss *m*

2 *vi* descendre tout schuss

schwa [ʃwɑ:] *n Ling* schwa *m*

.sci *Comput (written abbr* **science**) *(in Internet newsgroups)* = abréviation désignant les forums de discussion scientifiques

sciatic [saɪ'ætɪk] *adj Anat* sciatique

▸▸ ***sciatic nerve*** nerf *m* sciatique

sciatica [saɪ'ætɪkə] *n (UNCOUNT) Med* sciatique *f*

SCID [skɪd] *n Med (abbr* **severe combined immunodeficiency**) syndrome *m* de déficience immune combinée sévère, déficit *m* immunitaire combiné sévère

science ['saɪəns] **1** *n (UNCOUNT)* science *f*; **modern science** la science moderne; **she studied science** elle a fait des études de science *ou* scientifiques; **I've always been interested in science** j'ai toujours été intéressé par les sciences; **farming is becoming more and more of a science** l'agriculture devient de plus en plus scientifique

2 *comp (exam)* de science; *(teacher)* de science, de sciences; *(student)* en sciences; *(lab, subject)* scientifique

▸▸ ***science fiction*** science-fiction *f*; ***science park*** parc *m* scientifique; ***Science Research Council*** = Conseil de la recherche scientifique

scientific [ˌsaɪən'tɪfɪk] *adj* (**a**) *(research, expedition)* scientifique; **on scientific principles** selon des principes scientifiques (**b**) *(precise, strict)* scientifique, rigoureux

scientifically [ˌsaɪən'tɪfɪkəlɪ] *adv* scientifiquement, de manière scientifique; **scientifically speaking** d'un *ou* du point de vue scientifique

scientism ['saɪəntɪzəm] *n Phil* scientisme *m*

scientist ['saɪəntɪst] *n (worker)* scientifique *mf*; *(academic)* scientifique *mf*, savant(e) *m,f*

scientistic [ˌsaɪən'tɪstɪk] *adj Pej* prétendument scientifique

Scientologist [ˌsaɪən'tɒlədʒɪst] *n* scientologiste *mf*

Scientology® [ˌsaɪən'tɒlədʒɪ] *n Rel* scientologie *f*

sci-fi ['saɪfaɪ] *Fam (abbr* **science fiction**) **1** *n* SF *f*

2 *adj* de SF

scilicet ['saɪlɪset] *adv Formal* à savoir, c'est-à-dire

scilla ['sɪlə] *n Bot* scille *f*

Scillies ['sɪliz] = **Scilly Isles**

Scillonian [sɪ'ləʊnɪən] **1** *n (resident)* habitant(e) *m,f* des îles Sorlingues; *(native)* natif(ive) *m,f* des îles Sorlingues

2 *adj* des îles Sorlingues

Scilly Isles ['sɪlɪ-] *npl* **the Scilly Isles** les îles *fpl* Sorlingues; **in the Scilly Isles** aux îles Sorlingues

scimitar ['sɪmɪtə(r)] *n* cimeterre *m*

scintigram ['sɪntɪgræm] *n Med* scinti(llo)gramme *m*

scintigraphy [sɪn'tɪgrəfɪ] *n Med* scinti(llo)graphie *f*

scintilla [sɪn'tɪlə] *n* **there is not a scintilla of doubt that...** il n'y a pas le moindre doute *ou* il ne fait pas l'ombre d'un doute que...

scintillate ['sɪntɪleɪt] *vi (stars)* scintiller, briller; *Fig (person → in conversation)* briller, être brillant; **to scintillate with wit** briller par son esprit, pétiller d'esprit

scintillating ['sɪntɪleɪtɪŋ] *adj (conversation, wit)* brillant, pétillant, étincelant; *(person, personality)* brillant

scintillation [ˌsɪntɪ'leɪʃən] *n* scintillation *f*

▸▸ *Phys* ***scintillation counter*** compteur *m* à scintillations, scintillateur *m*

sciolism ['saɪəlɪzəm] *n Literary* prétention *f* à la culture

sciolist ['saɪəlɪst] *n Literary* personne *f* qui prétend être cultivée

scion ['saɪən] *n* (**a**) *Literary (descendant)* descendant(e) *m,f* (**b**) *Bot* scion *m*

Scipio ['skɪpɪəʊ] *pr n* Scipion

scirrhus ['sɪrəs] *n Med* squirre *m*

scissel ['sɪsəl] *n* cisaille *f*, rognures *fpl*

scissile ['sɪsaɪl] *adj Miner* scissile, fissile

scission ['sɪʃən] *n* scission *f*

scissor ['sɪzə(r)] **1** *vt* couper avec des ciseaux

2 scissors *npl* **(a pair of) scissors** (une paire de) ciseaux *mpl*

▸▸ *Orn* ***scissor bill*** bec-en-ciseaux *m*; *Sport* ***scissors hold*** ciseau *m*; *Sport* ***scissors jump*** saut *m* en ciseaux, ciseau *m*; *Sport* ***scissors kick*** ciseau *m*

scissors-and-paste *adj* **it's just a scissors-and-paste job** c'est du montage

sciurine ['saɪʊraɪn] *adj Zool* de l'écureuil, des sciuridés

sclera ['sklɪərə] *n Anat* sclérotique *f*, cornée *f* opaque

scleral ['sklɪərəl] *adj Anat* scléral

scleroderma [ˌsklɪərə'dɜ:mə], **sclerodermia** [ˌsklɪərə'dɜ:mɪə] *n Med* sclérodermie *f*

scleroma [ˌsklɪə'rəʊmə] *(pl* **scleromas** *or* **scleromata** [-mətə]) *n Med* rhinosclérome *m*, scléríase *f*

scleroprotein [ˌsklɪərəʊ'prəʊti:n] *n Biol & Chem* scléroprotéine *f*

sclerosis [sklə'rəʊsɪs] *n (UNCOUNT) Bot, Med & Fig* sclérose *f*

sclerotic [sklə'rɒtɪk] *adj* (**a**) *Med* sclérosé (**b**) *Bot* scléreux, sclérosé

sclerous ['sklɪərəs] *adj Med* scléreux

scoff [skɒf] **1** *vi* (**a**) *(mock)* se moquer, être méprisant; **they scoffed at my efforts/ideas** ils se sont moqués de mes efforts/idées; **don't scoff, I'm serious** ne te moque pas de moi, je parle sérieusement

(**b**) *Fam (eat)* s'empiffrer

2 *vt Fam (eat)* bouffer, boulotter; **he scoffed the whole packet** il s'est enfilé tout le paquet; **don't scoff your food like that** ne t'empiffre pas comme ça

3 *n* (**a**) *(expression of mockery)* **we had a good scoff at his expense** nous nous sommes bien moqués de lui

(**b**) *Br Fam (food)* bouffe *f*, graille *f*

scoffer ['skɒfə(r)] *n* railleur(euse) *m,f*

scoffing ['skɒfɪŋ] **1** *n* moquerie *f*, sarcasme *m*

2 *adj* railleur, sarcastique

scoffingly ['skɒfɪŋlɪ] *adv* en dérision, en raillant, par moquerie

scofflaw ['skɒflɔ:] *n Am* grugeur(euse) *m,f*, filou *m*

scold [skəʊld] **1** *vt* gronder, réprimander; **we were scolded** *or* **we got scolded for giggling in class** on s'est fait gronder pour avoir pouffé de rire *ou* parce qu'on avait pouffé de rire en classe; **she scolded him for being late** elle l'a grondé à cause de son retard

2 *vi* rouspéter

3 *n Old-fashioned* chipie *f*, mégère *f*

scolding ['skəʊldɪŋ] **1** *n* gronderie *f*, gronderies *fpl*, réprimande *f*, réprimandes *fpl*; **to give sb a scolding for doing sth** gronder qn pour avoir fait qch; **he got a good scolding from his mother for lying** il s'est fait attraper par sa mère pour avoir menti

2 *adj (tone)* de réprimande

scoliosis [ˌskəʊlɪ'əʊsɪs] *n* scoliose *f*

scoliotic [ˌskɒlɪ'ɒtɪk] *adj Med* scoliotique

scollop ['skɒləp] = **scallop**

sconce [skɒns] *n* (**a**) *(with handle)* bougeoir *m* (**b**) *(on wall)* applique *f*

scone [skɒn] *n* scone *m (petit pain rond)*; **cheese scone** scone *m* au fromage

scooby ['sku:bɪ] *n Br Fam (rhyming slang* **Scooby Doo** = **clue**) **he hasn't got a scooby** *(is incompetent)* il est vraiment nul; *(doesn't suspect)* il se doute de rien □; *(doesn't know)* il en a pas la moindre idée □

scoop [sku:p] **1** *n* (**a**) *Press* scoop *m*, exclusivité *f*; **to get** *or* **to make a scoop** faire un scoop; **the paper got a scoop on the story** le journal a publié la nouvelle en exclusivité

(**b**) *(utensil, ladle → for ice-cream, mashed potatoes)* cuillère *f* à boule; *(→ for flour, grain)* pelle *f*; *(→ for water)* écope *f*; *(on crane, dredger)* pelle *f*; *(on bulldozer)* lame *f*

(**c**) *(amount scooped → of ice-cream, potatoes)* boule *f*; *(→ of flour, grain)* pelletée *f*; *(→ of earth, rocks)* pelletée *f*

(**d**) *Naut (bailer)* épuisette *f*, écope *f*; *(of dredger)* godet *m*

(**e**) *Br Fam (profit)* bénéfice *m* (important) □; **to make a scoop** faire un gros bénéfice

2 *vt* (**a**) *(take, measure, put)* prendre (avec une mesure); *(serve)* servir (avec une cuillère); **to scoop flour/grain from a bin** prendre de la farine/du grain dans un tonneau; **the ice-cream was scooped into a dish** on a mis la glace dans un plat (à l'aide d'une cuillère); **she scooped the papers into her case** elle a ramassé les journaux dans sa mallette; **we had to scoop the water out of the barrel** nous avons dû vider le tonneau avec un récipient; **she scooped the grain out of the bucket** elle a pris le grain dans le seau à l'aide d'une mesure; **he scooped the potatoes onto my plate** il m'a servi des pommes de terre

(**b**) *Fin (market)* s'emparer de; *(competitor)* devancer; **they scooped a big profit** ils ont ramassé un gros bénéfice; *Fig* **to scoop the field** *or* **the pool** tout rafler

(**c**) *Press (story)* publier en exclusivité; *(competitor)* publier avant, devancer

▸▸ ***scoop neck*** décolleté *m* rond; *Fishing* ***scoop net*** drague *f*

▸**scoop out** *vt sep* (**a**) *(take → with scoop)* prendre (avec une cuillère); *(→ with hands)* prendre (avec les mains) (**b**) *(hollow → wood, earth)* creuser; *(empty, remove)* vider; **scoop out the tomatoes** épépinez *ou* égrenez les tomates; **scoop out the flesh from the grapefruit** évidez le pamplemousse

▸**scoop up** *vt sep* (**a**) *(take, pick up → in scoop)* prendre *ou* ramasser à l'aide d'une pelle *ou* d'un récipient; *(→ in hands)* prendre *ou* ramasser dans les mains; **she scooped up the last of her soup** elle finit son assiette d'un coup de cuillère; **the gangsters scooped the money up and jumped into the car** les gangsters ont ramassé l'argent et ont sauté dans la voiture; **she scooped the papers up in her arms** elle a ramassé une brassée de journaux; **the helicopter scooped him up** l'hélicoptère le repêcha

(**b**) *(gather together)* entasser; **can you scoop up the spilt beans?** pouvez-vous faire un tas avec les haricots qui ont été renversés?

scoopful ['sku:pfʊl] *n* pelletée *f*

scoot [sku:t] *Fam* **1** *vi* se sauver, filer; **the children scooted across the fields/up the stairs** les enfants ont filé à travers champs/ont monté les escaliers à toute vitesse □; **to scoot over** *(move over)* se pousser, se décaler; **scoot!** fichez le camp!, allez, ouste!

2 *n Br* **to make a scoot for it** prendre ses jambes à son cou

▸**scoot away, scoot off** *vi Fam* se sauver, filer

scooter ['sku:tə(r)] *n* (**a**) *(child's)* trottinette *f* (**b**) *(moped)* **(motor) scooter** scooter *m* (**c**) *Am (ice yacht)* yacht *m* à glace

scope [skəʊp] **1** *n* (**a**) *(range)* étendue *f*, portée *f*; *(limits)* limites *fpl*; **what is the scope of the enquiry?** jusqu'où portent *ou* vont les ramifications de l'enquête?; **does the matter fall within the scope of the law?** est-ce que l'affaire tombe sous le coup de la loi?; **it is beyond the scope of this study/of my powers** cela dépasse le cadre de cette étude/de mes compétences; **to extend the scope of one's activities/of an enquiry** élargir le champ de ses activités/le cadre d'une enquête; **the book is too narrow in scope** le livre est d'une portée trop limitée

(**b**) *(size, extent → of change)* étendue *f*; *(→ of*

undertaking) étendue *f*, envergure *f*; **it's a venture of unusual scope** c'est une entreprise d'une envergure exceptionnelle

(**c**) *(opportunity, room)* occasion *f*, possibilité *f*; **the guidelines leave a lot of scope for interpretation** les instructions laissent une grande place à l'interprétation; **there's plenty of scope for development/for improvement** les possibilités de développement/d'amélioration ne manquent pas; **the job gave him full/little scope to demonstrate his talents** son travail lui fournissait de nombreuses/peu d'occasions de montrer ses talents; **I'd like a job with more scope** j'aimerais un poste qui me donne plus de perspectives d'évolution; **there's little scope for people with your qualifications** il y a peu de possibilités pour des gens avec des qualifications telles que les vôtres

(**d**) *Fam (telescope)* télescope ❑ *m*; *(microscope)* microscope ❑ *m*; *(periscope)* périscope ❑ *m*

2 *vt* (**a**) *Med (examine)* examiner par endoscopie

(**b**) *Am Fam (look at)* mater, reluquer; **he's at the beach scoping the babes** il est à la plage en train de mater les nanas

(**c**) *Am Fam (see)* voir ❑; **did you scope that ring he was wearing?** t'as vu un peu la bague qu'il avait au doigt?

►**scope out** *vt sep Am (look at)* mater, reluquer; **I'm going to scope out the neighborhood and find a good restaurant** je vais repérer un peu le quartier pour essayer de trouver un bon restaurant

scopolamine [skə'pɒləmi:n] *n Pharm* scopolamine *f*

scops owl [skɒps-] *n Orn* scops *m*, hibou *m* petit-duc

scorbutic [skɔ:'bju:tɪk] *adj* scorbutique

scorch [skɔ:tʃ] **1** *vt* (**a**) *(with iron → clothing, linen)* roussir, brûler légèrement; *(with heat → skin)* brûler; *(→ meat)* brûler, carboniser; *(→ woodwork)* brûler, marquer

(**b**) *(grass, vegetation → with sun)* roussir, dessécher; *(→ with fire)* brûler

(**c**) *Fam (criticize)* éreinter ❑

2 *vi* (**a**) *(linen)* roussir

(**b**) *Br Fam (in car)* filer à toute allure; *(on bike)* pédaler comme un fou (folle) *ou* à fond de train; **we were soon scorching along at over 100 mph** nous filions bientôt à plus de 160 à l'heure; **he scorched after her** il courut après elle ❑

3 *n (on linen)* marque *f* de roussi; *(on hand, furniture)* brûlure *f*; **there's a scorch (mark) on my shirt** ma chemise a été roussie; **the cigarette has left a scorch (mark) on the table** la cigarette a fait une marque de brûlure sur la table

scorched-earth policy ['skɔ:tʃt-] *n Mil & Fig* politique *f* de la terre brûlée

scorcher ['skɔ:tʃə(r)] *n Fam* (**a**) *(hot day)* journée *f* de forte chaleur ❑; **yesterday was a real scorcher** hier c'était une vrai fournaise (**b**) *(something exciting, fast etc)* **this film is a scorcher** ce film est absolument génial; **she's a real scorcher** c'est une fille superbe ❑

scorching ['skɔ:tʃɪŋ] **1** *adj* (**a**) *(weather, tea, surface)* brûlant; **the sun is scorching** il fait un **soleil de plomb** (**b**) *(criticism)* cinglant (**c**) *Fam (speed)* **the car does a scorching 120 mph** la voiture file à 190 à l'heure

2 *adv* **scorching hot** *(water, drink, saucepan etc)* brûlant; *(day)* torride

scorchingly ['skɔ:tʃɪŋlɪ] *adv* **it's scorchingly hot** il fait une chaleur torride

SCORE [skɔ:(r)]

score	► 1 (a)
points	► 1 (a), (b)
note	► 1 (a)
avantage	► 1 (b)
titre	► 1 (c)
partition	► 1 (d)
entaille	► 1 (e)
rayure	► 1 (e)
vingtaine	► 1 (f)
marquer	► 2 (a); 3 (a), (b)
obtenir	► 2 (a)
érafler	► 2 (b)

1 *n* (**a**) *Sport* score *m*; *Cards* points *mpl*; *(in exam, test → mark)* note *f*; *(→ result)* résultat *m*; **the score was five-nil** le score était de cinq à zéro; **after 20 minutes there was still no score** après 20 minutes le score était toujours zéro à zéro; **to get a high score** *Sport, Cards & (in games)* faire beaucoup de points; *(in test)* obtenir une bonne note; **to keep the score** *Sport* tenir le score; *Cards & (in games)* compter *ou* marquer les points; *(on scorecard)* tenir la marque; **the final score** *(gen)* le résultat final; *Sport* le score final; **what's the score?** *Sport* quel est le score?; *Cards & (in games)* on a marqué combien de points?; *(in tennis)* où en est le jeu?; *Fam Fig* qu'est-ce qui se passe? ❑; *Fam Fig* **to know the score** connaître le topo, savoir à quoi s'en tenir ❑

(**b**) *Fig (advantage → in debate etc)* avantage *m*, points *mpl*; **to make a score off an opponent** marquer des points sur son adversaire

(**c**) *(reason, motive)* sujet *m*, titre *m*; **don't worry on that score** ne vous inquiétez pas à ce sujet; **he deserved to be rejected on more than one score** il méritait d'être refusé à plus d'un titre; **on what score was I turned down?** à quel titre *ou* sous quel prétexte ai-je été refusé?

(**d**) *Mus* partition *f*; *Cin & Theat* musique *f*; **piano/vocal score** partition *f* pour piano/vocale; **to follow the score** suivre (sur) la partition; **Cleo wrote the (film) score** Cleo est l'auteur de la musique (du film)

(**e**) *(notch, deep cut)* entaille *f*; *(scratch)* rayure *f*; *Geol (in rock)* strie *f*

(**f**) *(twenty)* vingtaine *f*; *Arch* **three score and ten** soixante-dix

(**g**) **scores** *(many)* beaucoup; **scores of people** beaucoup de gens; **I've told you scores of times** je vous l'ai dit des centaines de fois; **motorbikes by the score** un nombre incroyable de motos

(**h**) *(debt, account)* compte *m*; *Fig* **to have an old score to settle with sb** avoir un vieux compte à régler avec qn; **I prefer to forget old scores** je préfère oublier les vieilles histoires

2 *vt* (**a**) *Sport (goal, point, try)* marquer; *(in test, exam → marks)* obtenir; **to score 5 goals/50 points for one's team** marquer 5 buts/50 points pour son équipe; **she scored the highest mark** elle a obtenu *ou* eu la note la plus élevée; **to score a hit** *(with bullet, arrow, bomb)* atteindre la cible; *(in fencing)* toucher; *Fig (of idea etc)* faire un tabac; *(of person)* faire des ravages; **the bomber scored a direct hit** le bombardier a visé en plein sur la cible; *Fig* **to score a success** remporter un succès; *Fig* **he scored a point off me right at the start of the debate** il a marqué un point dès le début du débat qui nous opposait; **he's always trying to score points off me** il essaie toujours d'avoir le dessus avec moi

(**b**) *(scratch)* érafler; *(cut a line in → paper)* couper; *(→ wood)* entailler; *(→ ground)* tracer une raie sur; *(→ pastry, meat)* inciser, faire des incisions dans; *Geol (→ rock)* strier; **she scored her name on the bench** elle grava son nom sur le banc; **mountainside scored by torrents** flanc *m* de montagne creusé *ou* raviné par les torrents; **water had scored grooves into the rock** l'eau avait creusé des rainures dans le rocher

(**c**) *Mus (symphony, opera)* orchestrer; *Cin & Theat* composer la musique de; **the piece is scored for six trombones/treble voices** le morceau est écrit pour six trombones/pour soprano

(**d**) *Am (grade, mark → test)* noter

(**e**) *Fam Drugs slang (drugs)* acheter ❑

3 *vi* (**a**) *Sport (team, player)* marquer un point/des points; *Ftbl* marquer un but/des buts; *(in rugby)* marquer un essai/des essais; *(in basketball)* marquer un panier/des paniers; **the team didn't score** l'équipe n'a pas marqué; **to score high/low** *(in test)* obtenir un bon/mauvais score

(**b**) *(keep the score)* marquer les points; **would you mind scoring for us?** vous voulez bien marquer les points pour nous?

(**c**) *Fam (succeed)* avoir du succès ❑, réussir ❑; **he certainly scores with the girls** il a du succès auprès des filles, c'est sûr; **that's where we score** c'est là que nous l'emportons ❑, c'est là que nous avons l'avantage ❑; **this is where the new Renault really scores** c'est là que la nouvelle Renault est vraiment super; **he scores on looks but not much else** il est mignon mais ça s'arrête là

(**d**) *Fam (sexually)* lever quelqu'un, emballer quelqu'un; **did you score?** tu as réussi à lever une nana/un mec?

(**e**) *Fam Drugs slang (get drugs)* acheter de la came

►► *Ftbl* ***score draw*** match *m* nul *(où chaque équipe a marqué)*

►**score off 1** *vt insep (win point in argument etc)* prendre l'avantage sur, marquer des points sur

2 *vt sep (delete)* rayer, barrer; **score his name off the list** rayez son nom de la liste

►**score out, score through** *vt sep Br* biffer, barrer

►**score over** *vt insep* (**a**) = **score off** *vt insep* (**b**) *(be more successful than)* avoir l'avantage sur

►**score up** *vt sep* (**a**) *(points)* marquer (**b**) *(debt)* marquer, noter

scoreboard ['skɔ:bɔ:d] *n* tableau *m* d'affichage *(du score)*

scorecard ['skɔ:kɑ:d] *n* (**a**) *(for score → in game)* fiche *f* de marques *ou* de score; *(→ in golf)* carte *f* de parcours; *(→ at shooting range)* carton *m* (**b**) *(list of players)* liste *f* des joueurs

scorekeeper ['skɔ:,ki:pə(r)] *n* marqueur(euse) *m,f*

scoreline ['skɔ:laɪn] *n* score *m*

scorer ['skɔ:rə(r)] *n* (**a**) *Ftbl (regularly)* buteur(euse) *m,f*; *(of goal)* marqueur(euse) *m,f*; **Beckham was the scorer** c'est Beckham qui a marqué le but; **the team's top scorer** le meilleur buteur de l'équipe (**b**) *(scorekeeper)* marqueur(euse) *m,f* (**c**) *(in test, exam)* **the highest scorer** le candidat qui obtient le meilleur score

scoresheet ['skɔ:ʃi:t] *n* feuille *f* de match

scoria ['skɔ:rɪə] *(pl* **scoriae** [-rɪi:]) *n Geol & Metal* scorie *f*

scoring ['skɔ:rɪŋ] *n (UNCOUNT)* (**a**) *(of goals)* marquage *m* d'un but; *(number scored)* buts *mpl* (marqués); **to open the scoring** ouvrir la marque; **the scoring was fairly slow** *(in cricket)* l'attente était assez longue entre chaque point

(**b**) *Cards & (in games → scorekeeping)* marquage *m* des points, marque *f*; *(→ points scored)* points *mpl* marqués; **I'm not sure about the scoring** je ne suis pas sûr de la manière dont on marque les points

(**c**) *(scratching)* rayures *fpl*, éraflures *fpl*; *(notching)* entaille *f*, entailles *fpl*; *Geol* striage *m*

(**d**) *Mus (orchestration)* orchestration *f*; *(arrangement)* arrangement *m*; *(composition)* écriture *f*

scorn [skɔ:n] **1** *n* (**a**) *(contempt)* mépris *m*, dédain *m*; **I feel nothing but scorn for them** ils ne m'inspirent que du mépris; **to pour scorn on sth** rejeter qch avec mépris

(**b**) *(object of derision)* (objet *m* de) risée *f*; **she was the scorn of the whole school** elle était la risée de toute l'école

2 *vt* (**a**) *(be contemptuous of)* mépriser

(**b**) *(reject → advice, warning)* rejeter, refuser d'écouter; *(→ idea)* rejeter; *(→ help)* refuser, dédaigner; *Literary* **she scorned to answer** elle n'a pas daigné répondre

scornful ['skɔ:nfʊl] *adj* dédaigneux, méprisant; **she's rather scornful about** *or* **of my ideas** elle manifeste un certain mépris envers mes idées

scornfully ['skɔ:nfʊlɪ] *adv* avec mépris, dédaigneusement; **they looked at us scornfully** ils nous ont regardés avec dédain *ou* d'un air méprisant; **"of course not", he said scornfully** "bien sûr que non", dit-il d'un ton méprisant

scornfulness ['skɔ:nfʊlnɪs] *n (of person)* dédain *m*, mépris *m*; *(of look)* air *m* dédaigneux; *(of words)* ton *m* dédaigneux

scorper ['skɔ:pə(r)] *n (for wood engraving)* gouge *f*

Scorpio ['skɔ:pɪəʊ] **1** *n* (**a**) *Astron* Scorpion *m* (**b**) *Astrol* Scorpion *m*; **he's a Scorpio** il est (du signe du) Scorpion

2 *adj Astrol* du Scorpion; **he's Scorpio** il est (du signe du) Scorpion

scorpion ['skɔ:pɪən] *n Entom* scorpion *m*

►► *Ich* ***scorpion fish*** rascasse *f*, *Spec* scorpène *f*

Scot [skɒt] *n* Écossais(e) *m,f*; **the Scots** les Écossais

SCO–SCO

Scotch [skɒtʃ] **1** *n (whisky)* scotch *m*; **a glass of Scotch** un verre de scotch

2 *npl esp Am (people)* **the Scotch** les Écossais *mpl*

3 *adj* écossais

►► *Culin* ***Scotch bonnet*** piment *m* Scotch Bonnet; *Culin* ***Scotch broth*** = soupe écossaise à base de légumes et d'orge perlée; *Culin* ***Scotch egg*** = œuf dur entouré de chair à saucisse et enrobé de chapelure; ***Scotch mist*** bruine *f*; *Fam* **what do you think that is then, Scotch mist?** si tu allais à la mer, tu n'y trouverais pas d'eau; *Culin* ***Scotch pancake*** = crêpe épaisse; ***Scotch pine*** pin *m* sylvestre; *Am* ***Scotch tape***® Scotch® *m*; ***Scotch terrier*** scottish-terrier *m*, Scotch-terrier *m*; ***Scotch whisky*** scotch *m*, whisky *m* écossais

scotch [skɒtʃ] *vt* (**a**) *(suppress → revolt, strike)* mettre fin à, réprimer, étouffer; *(→ rumour)* étouffer; **we'll have to scotch that idea** il faudra abandonner cette idée (**b**) *(hamper → plans)* entraver, contrecarrer (**c**) *(block → wheel)* caler

Scotch-Irish *esp Am* **1** *npl* **the Scotch-Irish** = américains dont les ancêtres étaient des Écossais protestants installés dans le nord de l'Irlande; *Hist* = Écossais protestants installés dans le nord de l'Irlande

2 *adj* irlando-écossais

Scotchman ['skɒtʃmən] *(pl* **Scotchmen** [-men]*)* *n* Écossais *m*

Scotch-tape® *vt* scotcher

Scotchwoman ['skɒtʃwʊmən] *(pl* **Scotchwomen** [-wɪmɪn]*)* *n* Écossaise *f*

scoter ['skəʊtə(r)] *n Orn* macreuse *f*

scot-free *adj* impuni; **they were let off scot-free** on les a relâchés sans les punir

Scotia ['skəʊʃə] *n Hist* Scotie *f*; *Literary* Écosse *f*

Scotic ['skɒtɪk] *adj Hist* des Scots, de la Scotie

Scoticism ['skɒtɪsɪzəm] *n* expression *f* propre à l'anglais d'Écosse

Scotism ['skəʊtɪzəm] *n Phil & Rel* scotisme *m*

Scotist ['skəʊtɪst] *Phil & Rel* **1** *n* scotiste *mf*

2 *adj* scotiste

Scotland ['skɒtlənd] *n* Écosse *f*; **in Scotland** en Écosse

►► ***Scotland Yard*** = ancien nom du siège de la police à Londres (aujourd'hui "New Scotland Yard"), ≃ Quai *m* des Orfèvres

scotoma [skɒ'təʊmə] *(pl* **scotomas** *or* **scotomata** [-mətə]*)* *n Med* scotome *m*

scotopic [skɒ'tɒpɪk] *adj Med* scotopique

Scots [skɒts] **1** *n (language → Gaelic)* gaélique *m* d'Écosse, erse *m*; *(→ Lallans)* anglais *m* d'Écosse

2 *adj (accent, law etc)* écossais; **do you know the Scots language?** connaissez-vous l'écossais?

►► ***the Scots Greys*** = régiment écossais de l'armée britannique; ***the Scots Guards*** la Garde écossaise *(régiment de l'armée britannique)*; ***Scots pine*** pin *m* sylvestre

Scots-Irish **1** *npl* **the Scots-Irish** = américains dont les ancêtres étaient des Écossais protestants installés dans le nord de l'Irlande; *Hist* = Écossais protestants installés dans le nord de l'Irlande

2 *adj* irlando-écossais

Scotsman ['skɒtsmən] *(pl* **Scotsmen** [-mən]*)* *n* Écossais *m*; *Press* **The Scotsman** = un des grands quotidiens écossais

Scotswoman ['skɒtswʊmən] *(pl* **Scotswomen** [-,wɪmɪn]*)* *n* Écossaise *f*

Scott [skɒt] *exclam Old-fashioned* **Great Scott!** Grand Dieu!

Scotticism ['skɒtɪsɪzəm] *n* expression *f* propre à l'anglais d'Écosse

Scottie ['skɒtɪ] *n Fam* **Scottie (dog)** scottish-terrier ❑ *m*, Scotch-terrier ❑ *m*

Scottish ['skɒtɪʃ] **1** *npl* **the Scottish** les Écossais *mpl*

2 *adj* écossais; *Theat* **the Scottish play** *('Macbeth')* = expression utilisée pour éviter de désigner la pièce de Shakespeare par son nom, le mot Macbeth étant censé porter malheur

►► *Archit* ***Scottish Baronial*** = style architectural de l'époque victorienne inspiré d'une vision romanesque des châteaux écossais; *Sch* ***Scottish Certificate of Education*** = examen de fin d'études secondaires en Écosse; *Ling* ***Scottish Gaelic*** gaélique *m* d'Écosse, erse *m*; ***the Scottish Highlands*** les Highlands *mpl*; *Pol* ***the Scottish National Party*** = parti indépendantiste écossais fondé en 1934; ***the Scottish Office*** = ministère des Affaires écossaises, basé à Édimbourg; ***the Scottish Parliament*** le parlement écossais; ***Scottish Rugby Union*** = association écossaise de rugby à quinze; ***Scottish terrier*** scottish-terrier *m*, Scotch-terrier *m*

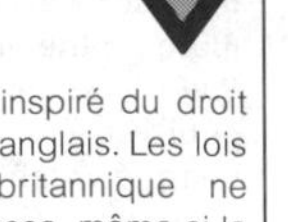

SCOTTISH LAW

Le système juridique écossais, inspiré du droit romain, est différent du système anglais. Les lois édictées par le Parlement britannique ne s'appliquent pas toujours en Écosse, même si la plus haute instance judiciaire reste, comme en Angleterre, la Chambre des lords.

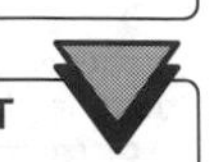

THE SCOTTISH PARLIAMENT

Le parlement écossais fut établi dans le cadre du projet de décentralisation du gouvernement travailliste et fut inauguré à Édimbourg en mai 1999. Les 129 membres du parlement écossais ("MSP") siègent sous la houlette du "First Minister". Le parlement est pourvu d'une grande autonomie en matière de fiscalité mais ses pouvoirs législatifs sont néanmoins limités. Ainsi, il n'est pas habilité à légiférer dans certains domaines qui restent le privilège du parlement de Westminster, tels que la politique extérieure et la défense. Voir aussi l'encadré sur **Devolution**.

scotty ['skɒtɪ] *(pl* **scotties***)* = **Scottie**

scoundrel ['skaʊndrəl] *n* bandit *m*, vaurien(enne) *m,f*; *(child)* vilain(e) *m,f*, coquin(e) *m,f*; **come here, you little scoundrel!** viens ici, petit coquin *ou* vaurien!

scour ['skaʊə(r)] **1** *vt* (**a**) *(clean → pan)* récurer; *(→ metal surface)* décaper; *(→ floor)* lessiver, frotter; *(→ tank)* vidanger, purger

(**b**) *(scratch)* rayer

(**c**) *(of water, erosion)* creuser; **the rainwater had scoured a deep channel in the hillside** l'eau de pluie avait creusé une profonde rigole sur le flanc de la colline

(**d**) *(search → area)* ratisser, fouiller; **the surrounding countryside was scoured for the missing girl** on a ratissé *ou* fouillé la campagne environnante pour retrouver la jeune fille disparue; **the police spent the weekend scouring the woods** la police a passé le week-end à battre les bois; **I've scoured the whole library looking for her** j'ai fouillé toute la bibliothèque pour la trouver

2 *n* **give the pans a good scour** récurez bien les casseroles; **the sink could do with a scour** l'évier aurait bien besoin d'être récuré

►**scour about** *vi Br* battre la campagne; **they scoured about after** *or* **for a red car** ils ont parcouru toute la région à la recherche d'une voiture rouge

►**scour away** *vt sep* éroder, emporter par érosion

►**scour off** *vt sep* enlever (à l'aide d'un tampon à récurer)

scourer ['skaʊrə(r)] *n (metal)* tampon *m* à récurer; *(sponge)* éponge *f* à récurer

scourge [skɜːdʒ] **1** *n* (**a**) *(bane)* fléau *m*; **the scourge of war/of disease** le fléau de la guerre/de la maladie; **pollution is the scourge of the century** la pollution est le fléau de ce siècle (**b**) *(person)* peste *f* (**c**) *(whip)* fouet *m*

2 *vt* (**a**) *(afflict)* ravager (**b**) *(whip)* fouetter, flageller

scourger ['skɜːdʒə(r)] *n* flagellateur *m*, fouetteur *m*

scouring ['skaʊərɪŋ] **1** *n (scrubbing)* récurage *m*; *(metal surface)* décapage *m*

2 scourings *npl* résidu *m* (de récurage)

►► ***scouring pad*** *(metal)* tampon *m* à récurer; *(sponge)* éponge *f* à récurer; ***scouring powder*** poudre *f* à récurer; *Bot* ***scouring rush*** prêle *f*

Scouse [skaʊs] *Br Fam* **1** *n* (**a**) *(person)* = personne originaire de Liverpool (**b**) *(dialect)* = dialecte de la région de Liverpool (**c**) *(in Liverpool dialect)* ragoût ❑ *m (souvent à base de restes de viande)*

2 *adj* de Liverpool ❑

Scouser ['skaʊsə(r)] *n Br Fam* = personne originaire de Liverpool

scout [skaʊt] **1** *n* (**a**) *(boy)* scout *m*; *(girl)* scoute *f*; *Am* **he's a good scout** c'est un chouette *ou* brave type; **scout's honour** parole *f* de scout

(**b**) *Mil (searcher)* éclaireur *m*; *(watchman)* sentinelle *f*, guetteur *m*; *(ship)* vedette *f*; *(aircraft)* avion *m* de reconnaissance

(**c**) *(for players, models, dancers)* dénicheur(euse) *m,f* de vedettes

(**d**) *(search)* tour *m* de reconnaissance; **to have** *or* **to take a scout around** (aller) reconnaître le terrain; **to have a scout around for sth** chercher qch

(**e**) *Br Aut (patrolman)* dépanneur *m*

(**f**) *Br Univ (servant)* garçon *m* de service *(à Oxford)*

2 *comp (knife, uniform)* (de) scout, d'éclaireur; **the scout movement** le mouvement scout, le scoutisme

3 *vt (area)* explorer; *Mil* reconnaître; **to scout (out) a trail** reconnaître une piste

4 *vi* partir en reconnaissance; **he used to scout for the cavalry** il était éclaireur dans *ou* il effectuait des missions de reconnaissance pour la cavalerie

►► ***the Scout Association*** l'association britannique de scoutisme; ***scout camp*** camp *m* scout; *Mil* ***scout car*** scout-car *m*

►**scout about, scout around** *vi* explorer les lieux; *Mil* partir en reconnaissance; **to scout about for an excuse** chercher un prétexte

scouter ['skaʊtə(r)] *n (in the Scouts)* chef *m* de troupe

scouting ['skaʊtɪŋ] *n* (**a**) *(movement)* **scouting, Scouting** scoutisme *m* (**b**) *Mil* reconnaissance *f*

scoutmaster ['skaʊt,mɑːstə(r)] *n* chef *m* scout

Scoville ['skəʊvɪl] *n*

►► ***Scoville scale*** échelle *f* de Scoville; ***Scoville unit*** unité *f* de force Scoville

scow [skaʊ] *n Naut* chaland *m*

scowl [skaʊl] **1** *n (angry)* mine *f* renfrognée *ou* hargneuse, air *m* renfrogné; *(threatening)* air *m* menaçant; **judging from his scowl, I gathered he had lost** à (en juger par) son air renfrogné, j'ai compris qu'il avait perdu; **she had an angry scowl on her face** la colère se lisait sur son visage; **"of course not", she said with a scowl** "bien sûr que non", dit-elle d'un air renfrogné

2 *vi (angrily)* se renfrogner, faire la grimace; *(threateningly)* prendre un air menaçant; **to scowl at sb** jeter un regard mauvais à qn

scowling ['skaʊlɪŋ] *adj (face)* renfrogné, hargneux; **he fell silent, a scowling look on his face** il s'est tu, l'air renfrogné

scowlingly ['skaʊlɪŋlɪ] *adv* d'un air renfrogné

SCR [,essiː'ɑː(r)] *n Br (abbr* **senior common room***)* = salle des étudiants de troisième cycle

Scrabble® ['skræbəl] *n* Scrabble® *m*; **do you fancy a game of Scrabble®?** tu veux faire un Scrabble®?

scrabble ['skræbəl] **1** *vi* (**a**) *(search)* **she was scrabbling in the grass for the keys** elle cherchait les clés à tâtons dans l'herbe; **the man was scrabbling for a handhold on the cliff face** l'homme cherchait désespérément une prise sur la paroi de la falaise

(**b**) *(scrape)* gratter

(**c**) *(scuffle)* **to scrabble with sb for sth** lutter avec qn pour s'emparer de qch

2 *n (scramble)* **there was a wild scrabble for the food** les gens se ruèrent sur la nourriture

►**scrabble about, scrabble around** *vi (grope)* fouiller, tâtonner; **I had to scrabble about in the drawer for a bit of string** j'ai dû fouiller dans le tiroir pour trouver un bout de ficelle; **she was scrabbling about on all fours looking for her contact lens** à quatre pattes, elle cherchait à tâtons son verre de contact; **beggars were scrabbling about in the dirt for coins** des mendiants grattaient dans la saleté pour trouver des pièces

scrag [skræg] *(pt & pp* **scragged,** *cont* **scragging***)* **1** *n* (**a**) *(person)* personne *f* très maigre; *(horse)* haridelle *f* (**b**) *Fam (neck)* cou ❑ *m* (**c**) *Br Culin* collet *m (de mouton ou de veau)*

2 *vt* (**a**) *(wring the neck of)* tordre le cou à (**b**) *Fam Old-fashioned (tease, rag)* asticoter (**c**)

Fam (attack) sauter sur; *(beat up)* casser la figure à

▸▸ *Br Culin* ***scrag end*** collet *m (de mouton ou de veau)*

scragginess ['skrægɪnɪs] *n* (**a**) *(of person, neck, animal)* maigreur *f* (**b**) *(jaggedness)* aspect *m* déchiqueté; *(of rock)* rugosité *f*; *(of branch)* état *m* noueux; *(of tree)* rabougrissement *m*

scraggy ['skrægɪ] *(compar* **scraggier,** *superl* **scraggiest**) *adj* (**a**) *(thin → neck, person)* efflanqué, maigre, décharné; *(→ horse, cat)* efflanqué (**b**) *(jagged)* déchiqueté; *(rock)* rugueux; *(branch)* noueux; *(tree)* rabougri

scram [skræm] *(pt & pp* **scrammed,** *cont* **scramming**) **1** *vi* (**a**) *Fam (get out)* déguerpir, ficher le camp, se casser; **scram!** du vent!, file!; **scram, all of you!** fichez-moi tous le camp! (**b**) *(reactor)* être arrêté d'urgence

2 *vt (reactor)* arrêter d'urgence

3 *n (of reactor)* arrêt *m* d'urgence

scramble ['skræmbəl] **1** *vi* (**a**) *(move hurriedly or with difficulty)* **they scrambled for shelter** ils se sont précipités pour se mettre à l'abri; **he scrambled into a diving suit** il a enfilé à la hâte une combinaison de plongée; **he scrambled to his feet** il s'est levé précipitamment; **to scramble away** s'enfuir à toutes jambes; **to scramble down** dégringoler; **to scramble up** grimper avec difficulté; **she scrambled out of the path of the bus** elle a tout juste eu le temps de s'écarter pour ne pas être renversée par le bus; **I had to scramble over three rows of seats** j'ai dû escalader trois rangées de sièges; **to scramble over rocks** escalader des rochers en s'aidant des mains; **the soldiers scrambled up the hill** les soldats ont escaladé la colline tant bien que mal

(**b**) *(scrabble, fight)* **to scramble for seats** se bousculer pour trouver une place assise, se ruer sur les places assises; **everyone was scrambling to get to the telephones** tout le monde se ruait vers les téléphones; **young people are having to scramble for jobs** les jeunes doivent se battre *ou* se démener pour trouver un boulot

(**c**) *Aviat & Mil* décoller sur-le-champ

(**d**) *Sport* **to go scrambling** faire du trial

(**e**) *(in rock climbing)* grimper à quatre pattes

2 *vt* (**a**) *Rad & Tel (message)* brouiller; *(encode)* crypter

(**b**) *(jumble)* mélanger

(**c**) *Aviat & Mil (aircraft)* ordonner le décollage immédiat de

(**d**) *Culin (eggs)* brouiller; **I'll scramble some eggs** je vais faire des œufs brouillés

3 *n* (**a**) *(rush)* bousculade *f*, ruée *f*; **my glasses were broken in the scramble to get out** mes lunettes ont été cassées dans la ruée vers la sortie; **there was a scramble for seats** on s'est bousculé pour avoir une place assise, on s'est rué sur les places assises; *(for tickets)* on s'est arraché les places; **there was a scramble for the door** tout le monde s'est rué vers la porte; **a scramble for profits/for jobs** une course effrénée au profit/à l'emploi; *Hist* **the scramble for Africa** = la lutte des puissances coloniales pour se répartir l'Afrique

(**b**) *Sport (on motorbikes)* course *f* de trial

(**c**) *Aviat & Mil* décollage *m* immédiat

(**d**) *(in rock climbing)* grimpée *f* à quatre pattes

▸▸ ***scrambled egg(s)*** *(food)* œufs *mpl* brouillés; *Fam Mil* = insigne d'officier porté sur la casquette ou l'épaulette; *Mktg* ***scrambled merchandising, scrambled retailing*** présentation *f* d'articles variés

scrambler ['skræmbələ(r)] *n Rad & Tel* brouilleur *m*

scrambling ['skræmbəlɪŋ] *n* (**a**) *Br Sport* trial *m* (**b**) *(in rock climbing)* grimpée *f* à quatre pattes

▸▸ *Rad & Electron* ***scrambling circuit*** circuit *m* de cryptage

scramjet ['skræmdʒet] *n Aviat* statoréacteur *m* à combustion supersonique

scran [skræn] *n Fam* (**a**) *Br (food)* bouffe *f*, graille *f* (**b**) *Ir* **bad scran to you!** que le diable vous emporte!

scrap [skræp] *(pt & pp* **scrapped,** *cont* **scrapping**) **1** *n* (**a**) *(small piece → of paper, cloth)* bout *m*; *(→ of bread, cheese)* petit bout *m*; *(→ of conversation)* bribe *f*; *(→ for scrapbook)* image *f*; **he left a few scraps of poetry** il a laissé quelques vers; **scraps of news/of information** des bribes de nouvelles/d'informations; **there isn't a scrap of truth in the story** il n'y a pas une parcelle de vérité *ou* il n'y a absolument rien de vrai dans cette histoire; **it didn't do me a scrap of good** *(action)* cela ne m'a servi absolument à rien; *(medicine)* cela ne m'a fait aucun bien; **what I say won't make a scrap of difference** ce que je dirai ne changera rien du tout

(**b**) *(metal)* ferraille *f*; **we sold the car for scrap** on a vendu la voiture à la ferraille *ou* à la casse; **it has no value even as scrap** même à la casse, ça ne vaut rien

(**c**) *Fam (fight)* bagarre *f*, baston *m ou f*; **to get into** *or* **to have a scrap with sb** se bagarrer avec qn, se castagner avec qn

2 *vt* (**a**) *(discard → shoes, furniture)* jeter; *(→ idea, plans)* renoncer à, abandonner; *(→ system)* abandonner, mettre au rancart; *(→ machinery)* mettre au rebut *ou* au rancart; **you can scrap the whole idea** vous pouvez laisser tomber *ou* abandonner cette idée

(**b**) *(send for scrap → car, ship)* envoyer *ou* mettre à la ferraille *ou* à la casse

3 *vi Fam (fight)* se bagarrer, se castagner

4 **scraps** *npl (food)* restes *mpl*; *(fragments)* débris *mpl*

▸▸ ***scrap lead*** plomb *m* de récupération; ***scrap iron*** ferraille *f*; *Br* ***scrap merchant*** ferrailleur *m*; ***scrap metal*** ferraille *f*; ***scrap (metal) dealer*** ferrailleur *m*; ***scrap paper*** (papier *m*) brouillon *m*; ***scrap value*** valeur *f* à la casse

scrapbook ['skræpbʊk] *n* (**a**) *(for photos, press cuttings etc)* album *m* (**b**) *Comput (on Macintosh®)* album *m*

scrape [skreɪp] **1** *n* (**a**) *(action)* coup *m* de grattoir *ou* de racloir; *(wound on skin)* éraflure *f*; **just give the saucepan a quick scrape** frotte *ou* gratte un peu la casserole; **he had a nasty scrape on his knee** il avait une méchante éraflure au genou, il s'était bien éraflé le genou; **she had given the car a nasty scrape on the side** elle avait fait une belle éraflure sur le côté de la voiture

(**b**) *Fam (dilemma, trouble)* pétrin *m*; **to get into a scrape** se mettre dans le pétrin; **now you've really got yourself into a scrape!** vous voilà dans de beaux draps *ou* dans un sacré pétrin!; **to get (oneself) out of a scrape** se tirer d'affaire *ou* d'embarras; **you got me into this scrape, now get me out of it!** c'est vous qui m'avez mis dans ce pétrin, maintenant il faut me tirer de là!

(**c**) *(sound)* grattement *m*, grincement *m*

(**d**) *(thin layer)* mince couche *f*; **toast with a scrape of butter** du pain grillé recouvert d'une mince couche de beurre

2 *vt* (**a**) *(clean → boots, saucepan, earth)* gratter, racler; *(→ tools)* gratter, décaper; *(→ vegetables, windows)* gratter; **scrape the mud off your shoes** enlève *ou* gratte la boue de tes chaussures; **I spent the afternoon scraping the paint off the door** j'ai passé l'après-midi à gratter la peinture de la porte; **to scrape sth clean/smooth** gratter qch pour qu'il soit propre/lisse; **I scraped the ground with a stick** j'ai gratté le sol avec un bâton; *Fig* **to scrape (the bottom of) the barrel** *(looking for money)* racler les fonds de tiroir; *(be reduced to extremes)* être tombé bien bas; **you took him on? you must really be scraping the bottom of the barrel!** tu as embauché ce type-là? tu devais vraiment être coincé!

(**b**) *(scratch → paint, table, wood)* rayer; *(→ skin, knee)* érafler; *(touch lightly)* effleurer, frôler; **I scraped my knee** je me suis éraflé le genou; **I just scraped the garage door as I drove in** j'ai seulement frôlé *ou* effleuré la porte du garage en rentrant la voiture; **the plane just scraped the surface of the water** l'avion frôla *ou* rasa la surface de l'eau; **to scrape the bottom** *(ship)* sillonner *ou* talonner le fond

(**c**) *(drag)* traîner; **don't scrape the chair across the floor like that** ne traîne pas la chaise par terre comme ça

(**d**) *(achieve with difficulty)* **to scrape a living** arriver tout juste à survivre, vivoter; **to scrape a pass** *(in exam)* réussir de justesse; *Br* **to scrape acquaintance with sb** se débrouiller pour faire la connaissance de qn

3 *vi* (**a**) *(rub)* frotter; *(rasp)* gratter; **the branches scrape against the shutters** les branches frottent contre les volets; **the door scraped shut** la porte s'est refermée en grinçant; **the gardener scraped at the ground with a stick** le jardinier grattait la terre avec un bâton; **I heard the noise of his pen scraping across the paper** j'entendais le grattement de son stylo sur le papier

(**b**) *(manage with difficulty)* **to scrape home** *(win game, race)* gagner de justesse; **she just scraped clear of the bus in time** elle a évité le bus de justesse; **the ambulance just scraped past** l'ambulance est passée de justesse

(**c**) *(economize)* faire des petites économies

(**d**) *(be humble)* faire des courbettes *ou* des ronds de jambes

▸**scrape along** *vi (financially)* se débrouiller, vivre tant bien que mal; **she had to scrape along on a small pension** elle devait se débrouiller avec une petite retraite; **we'll scrape along somehow** on va se débrouiller avec ce qu'on a

▸**scrape away** **1** *vt sep* enlever en grattant

2 *vi* gratter; **the gardener was scraping away at the dry earth** le jardinier grattait la terre sèche; **to scrape away at a violin** racler du violon

▸**scrape back** *vt sep (hair)* tirer en arrière; **with her hair scraped back** les cheveux tirés en arrière

▸**scrape by** *vi (financially)* se débrouiller; **I have just enough to scrape by (on)** j'ai juste assez d'argent pour me débrouiller

▸**scrape down** *vt sep (paintwork)* décaper; *(woodwork, door)* gratter

▸**scrape in** *vi (in election)* être élu de justesse; *(in entering university)* entrer de justesse; *Sport (in qualifying)* se qualifier de justesse; **I just scraped in as the doors were closing** j'ai réussi à entrer juste au moment où les portes se fermaient

▸**scrape into** *vt insep* **he just scraped into university/parliament** il est entré à l'université/au parlement d'extrême justesse

▸**scrape off** **1** *vt sep (mud, paint)* enlever au grattoir *ou* en grattant; *(skin)* érafler; *Hum* **we had to scrape him off the ground** il a fallu le ramasser à la petite cuillère

2 *vi* s'enlever au grattoir; **this paint scrapes off easily** pour enlever cette peinture, il suffit de la gratter

▸**scrape out** *vt sep* (**a**) *(saucepan)* récurer, racler; *(residue)* enlever en grattant *ou* raclant; **to scrape out a mixing bowl** *(with spatula)* racler un bol avec une spatule; *(with finger)* racler un bol avec le doigt

(**b**) *(hollow)* creuser

▸**scrape through** **1** *vt insep (exam)* réussir de justesse; *(doorway, gap)* passer (de justesse); **the government will probably just scrape through the next election** le gouvernement va probablement l'emporter de justesse aux prochaines élections

2 *vi (in exam)* réussir de justesse; *(in election)* être élu *ou* l'emporter de justesse; *(gap)* passer de justesse; *(financially)* se débrouiller tout juste

▸**scrape together** *vt sep* (**a**) *(two objects)* frotter l'un contre l'autre

(**b**) *(into pile)* mettre en tas

(**c**) *(collect → supporters, signatures)* réunir *ou* rassembler à grand-peine; *(→ money for oneself)* réunir en raclant les fonds de tiroirs; *(→ money for event)* réunir avec beaucoup de mal

▸**scrape up** *vt sep* (**a**) *(into pile → leaves, stones)* mettre en tas

(**b**) *(collect → supporters, signatures)* réunir *ou* rassembler à grand-peine; *(→ money for oneself)* réunir en raclant les fonds de tiroirs; *(→ money for event)* réunir avec beaucoup de mal

(**c**) *Hum* **he scraped himself up off the floor** il a fini par se relever

scraper ['skreɪpə(r)] *n* grattoir *m*; *(for muddy shoes)* décrottoir *m*

scraperboard ['skreɪpəbɔːd] *n* carte *f* à gratter

scrapheap ['skræphiːp] *n* (**a**) décharge *f*; **to throw sth on the scrapheap** mettre qch à la ferraille *ou* au rebut (**b**) *Fig* rebut *m*; **to be**

thrown on *or* **consigned to the scrapheap** être mis au rebut; **he ended up on the scrapheap** on l'a mis au rebut

scrapie ['skreɪpɪ] *n Vet* maladie *f* tremblante des moutons, tremblante *f*

scraping ['skreɪpɪŋ] **1** *adj (sound)* de grattement
2 *n* (**a**) *(sound)* grattement *m*; **I could hear the sound of scraping** j'ai entendu un grattement *ou* un bruit de grattement; **the scraping of chalk on the blackboard** le crissement *ou* le grincement de la craie sur le tableau
(**b**) *(thin layer)* mince couche *f*; **toast with a scraping of butter** du pain grillé recouvert d'une mince couche de beurre
3 scrapings *npl (food)* déchets *mpl*, restes *mpl*; *(from paint, wood)* raclures *fpl*; **give the scrapings to the dogs** donnez les restes aux chiens

scrapman ['skræpmən] (*pl* **scrapmen** [-men]) *n* ferrailleur *m*, casseur *m*

scrapper ['skræpə(r)] *n Br Fam* bagarreur(euse) *m,f*

scrappily ['skræpɪlɪ] *adv* de façon décousue

scrapping ['skræpɪŋ] *n* (**a**) *(discarding → of machinery, equipment)* mise *f* au rebut; *(→ of system, theory)* mise *f* au rancart (**b**) *(sending for scrap → of car, ship)* mise *f* à la ferraille *ou* à la casse

scrapple ['skræpəl] *n Am Culin* = plat de viande et de Maïzena®

scrappy ['skræpɪ] (*compar* **scrappier**, *superl* **scrappiest**) *adj* (**a**) *(disconnected → speech, film, novel)* décousu; *(→ work, performance)* inégal; **I had rather a scrappy education** je n'ai pas bénéficié d'une instruction très suivie; **it was a rather scrappy second half** la deuxième mi-temps a été assez inégale (**b**) *Am Fam (quarrelsome)* bagarreur, chamailleur

scrapyard ['skræpjɑːd] *n* chantier *m* de ferraille, casse *f*; **I found it in a scrapyard** je l'ai trouvé à la ferraille *ou* à la casse

scratch [skrætʃ] **1** *n* (**a**) *(action → to relieve itch)* grattement *m*; *(wound → with fingernail)* coup *m* d'ongle; *(→ with claw)* coup *m* de griffe; **to have a scratch** se gratter; **could you give my back a scratch?** tu peux me gratter le dos?; **the dog was having a good scratch** le chien se grattait un bon coup
(**b**) *(wound → from thorns, nail)* égratignure *f*, écorchure *f*; *(→ made by claw)* griffure *f*; *(mark → on furniture)* rayure *f*, éraflure *f*; *(→ on glass, record)* rayure *f*; **how did you get that scratch?** comment est-ce que tu t'es égratigné?; **I've got a scratch on my hand** je me suis égratigné la main; **her hands were covered in scratches** elle avait les mains tout écorchées *ou* couvertes d'égratignures; **it's only a scratch** ce n'est qu'une égratignure; **we escaped without a scratch** on s'en est sorti sans une égratignure
(**c**) *Golf* **to play off scratch** être scratch
(**d**) *(sound → of pen on paper)* grincement *m*
(**e**) *Am Fam (money)* fric *m*, pognon *m*, flouze *m*
(**f**) *(idioms)* **to start from scratch** partir de rien *ou* de zéro; *(restart)* repartir à zéro; **to build a house from scratch** construire une maison de bout en bout; **she built the business up from scratch** elle a monté l'affaire à partir de rien; **I learnt Italian from scratch in six months** j'ai appris l'italien en six mois en partant de zéro; **to be up to scratch** être à la hauteur; **her work still isn't up to scratch** son travail n'est toujours pas satisfaisant *ou* à la hauteur; **their performance wasn't up to** *or* **didn't come up to scratch** leur performance n'était pas suffisante *ou* à la hauteur; **we must get the team up to scratch before April** il faut mettre l'équipe à niveau avant avril
2 *adj* (**a**) *(team, meal)* improvisé
(**b**) *Golf (player)* scratch *(inv)*, sans handicap
3 *vt* (**a**) *(rub → itch, rash)* gratter; **to scratch one's head** se gratter la tête; *Fig* **you scratch my back, and I'll scratch yours** donnant donnant
(**b**) *(wound → of cat, person)* griffer; *(→ of thorn, nail)* égratigner, écorcher; **the cat scratched my hand** le chat m'a griffé la main; **she scratched her hand on the brambles** elle s'est écorché *ou* égratigné la main dans les ronces; **he was badly scratched** il était tout écorché
(**c**) *(mark → woodwork, marble)* rayer, érafler; *(→ glass, record)* rayer; **the car's hardly scratched** la voiture n'a presque rien *ou* n'a pratiquement aucune éraflure; **the paintwork's badly scratched** la peinture est sérieusement éraflée; **someone has scratched their initials on the tree** quelqu'un a gravé ses initiales sur l'arbre; **she quickly scratched a few notes on her pad** elle griffonna rapidement quelques notes sur son calepin; *Fig* **you've barely scratched the surface** vous avez fait un travail très superficiel, vous avez seulement effleuré la question; *Fig* **scratch any patriot and you will invariably find a bigot** si l'on gratte un peu, on trouve un fanatique derrière chaque patriote; *Br Fig* **they scratch a living selling secondhand books** ils gagnent péniblement leur vie en vendant des livres d'occasion
(**d**) *(of bird, animal → ground)* gratter
(**e**) *(irritate)* gratter; **this wool scratches my skin** cette laine me gratte la peau
(**f**) *(cancel → meeting, match)* annuler; *(withdraw)* **to scratch sb off** *or* **from a list** rayer *ou* biffer qn d'une liste; **to scratch sb from a team** exclure qn d'une équipe; *Horseracing* **to scratch a horse** déclarer forfait pour un cheval; *(stewards)* scratcher un cheval
(**g**) *Am Pol (candidate)* rayer de la liste
4 *vi* (**a**) *(person, animal → to relieve itch)* se gratter; **stop scratching** arrête de te gratter
(**b**) *(bird → in ground)* gratter; **I could hear something scratching at the door** j'entendais quelque chose gratter à la porte, j'entendais un grattement à la porte
(**c**) *(cat)* griffer; *(brambles, nail)* griffer, écorcher; *(wool, new clothes)* gratter
(**d**) *(pen etc)* grincer, gratter
(**e**) *Sport (competitor)* déclarer forfait
►► ***scratch mark*** *(on hand)* égratignure *f*; *(on leather, furniture)* rayure *f*, éraflure *f*; *Am* ***scratch paper*** (papier *m*) brouillon *m*; *Am* ***scratch sheet*** *(for horse races)* journal *m* des courses; *Med* ***scratch test*** test *m* cutané; ***scratch video*** scratch vidéo *m*

►**scratch off** *vt sep* enlever en grattant

►**scratch out** *vt sep (word)* raturer; **to scratch sb's eyes out** arracher les yeux à qn

►**scratch together** *vt sep Br (team)* réunir (difficilement); *(sum of money)* réunir *ou* rassembler (en raclant les fonds de tiroir)

►**scratch up** *vt sep* (**a**) *(dig up → bone, plant)* déterrer (**b**) *Br (money)* réunir (en raclant les fonds de tiroir)

scratchboard ['skrætʃbɔːd] *n* papier *m* procédé

scratchcard ['skrætʃkɑːd] *n (lottery card)* carte *f* à gratter

scratching ['skrætʃɪŋ] *n* (**a**) *(with fingernail)* coups *mpl* d'ongle; *(to relieve itch)* grattement *m* (**b**) *(damaging → action)* rayage *m*; *(→ result)* rayures *fpl* (**c**) *(sound)* grattement *m*; *(of pen nib)* grincement *m*; *(of record)* craquement(s) *m(pl)*
►► ***scratching post*** *(for cat)* grattoir *m*

scratchpad ['skrætʃpæd] *n Am* bloc-notes *m*
►► *Comput* ***scratchpad memory*** mémoire *f* bloc-notes

scratchproof ['skrætʃpruːf] *adj* inrayable

scratchy ['skrætʃɪ] (*compar* **scratchier**, *superl* **scratchiest**) *adj* (**a**) *(prickly → jumper, blanket)* rêche, qui gratte; *(→ bush)* piquant (**b**) *(pen → messy)* qui gratte; *(→ noisy)* qui grince *(sur le papier)* (**c**) *(drawing, writing)* griffonné (**d**) *(record)* qui craque

scrawl [skrɔːl] **1** *n* griffonnage *m*, gribouillage *m*; **I can't read this scrawl** je ne peux pas déchiffrer ce gribouillage; **I thought I recognized his scrawl** je pensais bien avoir reconnu ses gribouillis; **her signature is just a scrawl** sa signature est totalement illisible
2 *vt* griffonner, gribouiller; **she left me a scrawled note** elle m'a laissé quelques mots griffonnés; **he scrawled her a note** il lui a griffonné un mot; **someone has scrawled anti-war slogans on the walls** quelqu'un a gribouillé des slogans pacifistes sur le mur
3 *vi* gribouiller

scrawly ['skrɔːlɪ] *adj* **scrawly writing** pattes *fpl* d'araignée, pattes *fpl* de mouche

scrawny ['skrɔːnɪ] (*compar* **scrawnier**, *superl* **scrawniest**) *adj* (**a**) *(person, neck)* efflanqué, décharné; *(cat, chicken)* efflanqué (**b**) *(vegetation)* maigre

scream [skriːm] **1** *vi* (**a**) *(shout → once)* pousser un cri perçant *ou* aigu, hurler; *(→ repeatedly)* pousser des cris aigus, hurler; *(baby)* crier, hurler; *(birds, animals)* crier; **to scream at sb** crier après qn; **to scream in anger/with pain** hurler de colère/de douleur; **to scream in delight** crier *ou* hurler de plaisir; **she screamed for help** elle cria à l'aide *ou* au secours; **they were screaming with laughter** ils se tordaient de rire, ils riaient aux éclats
(**b**) *(tyres)* crisser; *(engine, siren)* hurler; **bombers screamed over the rooftops** les bombardiers hurlèrent en survolant les toits
2 *vt* (**a**) *(shout)* hurler; **she just stood there screaming insults at me** elle est restée plantée là à me couvrir d'insultes; *Literary* **she screamed her anger** elle hurlait sa colère; **she screamed herself hoarse** elle cria jusqu'à en perdre la voix
(**b**) *(order, answer)* hurler; **"come here at once!" she screamed** "viens ici tout de suite!" hurla-t-elle
(**c**) *(newspaper)* étaler; **headlines screamed the news of his defeat** la nouvelle de sa défaite s'étalait en gros titres
3 *n* (**a**) *(cry)* cri *m* perçant, hurlement *m*; **she gave a loud scream** elle a poussé un hurlement; **I heard terrible screams coming from next door** j'ai entendu des hurlements atroces qui venaient d'à côté; **screams of laughter** des éclats *mpl* de rire
(**b**) *(of tyres)* crissement *m*; *(of sirens, engines)* hurlement *m*
(**c**) *Fam (person)* **he's an absolute scream** il est vraiment tordant; **you look a scream in that hat!** vous êtes tordant avec ce chapeau!; **it was a scream** *(situation, event)* c'était tordant, c'était à se tordre de rire; **the party was a scream** on s'est amusés comme des fous à la soirée; **it's a scream the way they clamber up the bars** c'est vraiment tordant de les voir grimper aux barreaux

►**scream out 1** *vi* pousser de grands cris; **to scream out in pain** hurler de douleur; **she screamed out in her sleep** elle a poussé un grand cri pendant qu'elle dormait; *Fig* **to be screaming out for sth** avoir sacrément besoin de qch
2 *vt sep* hurler

'The Scream' *Munch* 'Le Cri'

screamer ['skriːmə(r)] *n* (**a**) *(shouter)* = personne qui crie (beaucoup) (**b**) *Fam Typ* point *m* d'exclamation (**c**) *Br Fam (powerful shot)* fusée *f* (**d**) *Orn* kamichi *m*

screaming ['skriːmɪŋ] **1** *n (of person)* cris *mpl*, hurlements *mpl*; *(of birds, animals)* cris *mpl* perçants
2 *adj (fans)* qui crie, qui hurle; *(tyres)* qui crisse; *(sirens, jets)* qui hurle; *(need)* criant; **he tends to dress in screaming reds and greens** il s'habille souvent de rouges et de verts criards
►► ***screaming headlines*** grandes manchettes *fpl*; *Fam* ***screaming queen*** grande folle *f*

screamingly ['skriːmɪŋlɪ] *adv Fam* **screamingly funny** on ne peut plus drôle, à se tordre *ou* à mourir de rire

scree [skriː] *n (UNCOUNT)* éboulis *m*, pierraille *f*

screech [skriːtʃ] **1** *vi* (**a**) *(owl)* ululer, hululer, huer; *(gull)* crier, piailler; *(parrot)* crier; *(monkey)* hurler
(**b**) *(person → in high voice)* pousser des cris stridents *ou* perçants; *(→ loudly)* hurler; *(singer)* crier, chanter d'une voie stridente
(**c**) *(tyres)* crisser; *(brakes, machinery)* grincer (bruyamment); *(siren, jets)* hurler; **the car screeched to a halt** la voiture s'est arrêtée dans un crissement de pneus; **the machine screeched to a stop** la machine s'est arrêtée en grinçant; **the car came screeching round the corner** la voiture a pris le virage dans un crissement de pneus
2 *vt (order)* hurler, crier à tue-tête; **"never", she screeched** "jamais", dit-elle d'une voix stridente
3 *n* (**a**) *(of owl)* ululement *m*, hululement *m*; *(of gull)* cri *m*, piaillement *m*; *(of parrot)* cri *m*; *(of monkey)* hurlement *m*; **the parrot gave a**

loud screech le perroquet a poussé un grand cri

(**b**) *(of person)* cri *m* strident *ou* perçant; *(with pain, rage)* hurlement *m*; **we heard screeches of laughter coming from next door** on entendait des rires perçants qui venaient d'à côté; **"never", she said with a screech** "jamais", dit-elle d'une voix stridente

(**c**) *(of tyres)* crissement *m*; *(of brakes)* grincement *m*; *(of sirens, jets)* hurlement *m*; **we stopped with a screech of brakes/tyres** on s'arrêta dans un grincement de freins/dans un crissement de pneus

►► *Orn* ***screech owl*** chat-huant *m*, hulotte *f*

screeching ['skri:tʃɪŋ] **1** *adj (laugh)* perçant, aigu; *(tyres)* qui crissent

2 *n (cries)* cris *mpl* perçants *ou* aigus; *(of tyres)* crissement *m*

screed [skri:d] *n* (**a**) *(essay, story)* longue dissertation *f*; *(letter)* longue lettre *f*; *(speech)* laïus *m*; **he wrote screeds and screeds on the French Revolution** il écrivit des pages et des pages *ou* des volumes sur la Révolution française (**b**) *Constr (level)* règle *f* à araser le béton; *(depth guide)* guide *m*; *(plaster)* plâtre *m* de ragrément *ou* de ragréage

screen [skri:n] **1** *n* (**a**) *Cin, Phot & TV* écran *m*; **stars of stage and screen** des vedettes de théâtre et de cinéma; **the book was adapted for the screen** le livre a été porté à l'écran; **the big screen** *(cinema)* le grand écran; **the small screen** *(television)* le petit écran

(**b**) *(for protection → in front of fire)* pare-étincelles *m inv*; *(→ over window)* moustiquaire *f*; *(→ against draught)* paravent *m*

(**c**) *(for privacy)* paravent *m*; **the girls formed a screen round her while she changed** les filles ont fait écran autour d'elle pendant qu'elle se changeait; **a screen of trees** un rideau d'arbres; **the rooms are divided by sliding screens** les pièces sont séparées par des cloisons coulissantes

(**d**) *Fig (mask)* écran *m*, masque *m*; **it's only a screen to hide his embarrassment** ce n'est qu'un masque pour cacher sa gêne; **the shop was just a screen for her criminal activities** le magasin n'était qu'une couverture pour ses activités criminelles

(**e**) *(sieve)* tamis *m*, crible *m*; *Am (ventilation grill in door)* grille *f* de ventilation

(**f**) *(filter → for employees, candidates)* filtre *m*, crible *m*

(**g**) *(in basketball)* écran *m*

(**h**) *Comput* écran *m*; **to work on screen** travailler sur écran; **to bring up the next screen** amener l'écran suivant

2 *comp (star)* de cinéma

3 *vt* (**a**) *Cin & TV (film)* projeter, passer; *(show on television)* passer à l'écran

(**b**) *(shelter, protect)* protéger; **he screened his eyes from the sun with his hand** il a mis sa main devant ses yeux pour se protéger du soleil; **they've tried to screen her from the harsh realities of life** ils ont essayé de la protéger des dures réalités de la vie

(**c**) *(hide)* cacher, masquer; **to screen sth from sight** cacher *ou* masquer qch aux regards; **a line of trees screened the entrance** une rangée d'arbres cachait l'entrée

(**d**) *(filter, check → employees, applications, suspects)* passer au crible; **we screen all our security staff** nous faisons une enquête préalable sur tous les candidats aux postes d'agent de sécurité; **all airlines now screen passengers systematically** les compagnies aériennes font maintenant passer systématiquement tous les passagers par un détecteur; *Med* **the hospital screens thousands of women a year for breast cancer** l'hôpital fait passer un test de dépistage du cancer du sein à des milliers de femmes tous les ans

(**e**) *(sieve → coal, dirt, grain)* cribler, passer au crible

►► *Cin* ***screen actor*** acteur *m* de cinéma; *Cin & TV* ***Screen Actors' Guild*** = syndicat américain des acteurs; *Cin* ***screen actress*** actrice *f* de cinéma; *Cin & TV* ***screen adaptation*** adaptation *f* à l'écran; *Comput* ***screen capture*** capture *f* d'écran; *Comput* ***screen controller*** contrôleur *m* d'écran; *Comput* ***screen display*** affichage *m*; *Am* ***screen door*** porte *f* avec moustiquaire; *Comput* ***screen dump*** capture *f* d'écran; *Comput* ***screen font*** fonte *f* écran; ***screen generation*** génération *f* d'écrans; *Electron* ***screen grid*** grille-écran *f*; *Cin & TV* ***screen image*** image *f* à l'écran; ***screen line*** ligne-écran *f*; *Psy* ***screen memory*** souvenir-écran *m*; ***screen print*** sérigraphie *f*; ***screen printing*** sérigraphie *f*; ***screen process*** sérigraphie *f*; *Comput* ***screen refresh*** actualisation *f ou* régénération *f* de l'écran; *Cin* ***screen rights*** droits *mpl* d'adaptation à l'écran; *Comput* ***screen saver*** économiseur *m* d'écran; *Comput* ***screen shot*** capture *f* d'écran; *Cin* ***screen test*** bout *m* d'essai; *St Exch* ***screen trader*** opérateur(trice) *m,f* sur écran; *St Exch* ***screen trading*** opérations *fpl* sur écran; *Aut* ***screen wash*** lave-glace *m*; *TV & Cin* ***screen writing*** écriture *f* de scénarios

►**screen off** *vt sep* (**a**) *(put screens round → patient)* abriter derrière un paravent; *(→ bed)* entourer de paravents; **the police had screened off the garden** la police avait mis des bâches autour du jardin

(**b**) *(divide, separate → with partition)* séparer par une cloison; *(→ with curtain)* séparer par un rideau; *(→ with folding screen)* séparer par un paravent; **the manager's office is screened off by a glass partition** le bureau du directeur est séparé par une cloison vitrée

(**c**) *(hide → with folding screen)* cacher derrière un paravent; *(→ with curtain)* cacher derrière un rideau; *(→ behind trees, wall)* cacher; **the house was screened off from the road by tall trees** de grands arbres empêchaient de voir la maison depuis la route

►**screen out** *vt sep* filtrer, éliminer; **this cream screens out UV rays** cette crème protège des UV, cette crème absorbe *ou* filtre les UV; **unsuitable blood donors are screened out** les donneurs dont le sang est inutilisable sont exclus *ou* éliminés

screener ['skri:nə(r)] *n* cribleur(euse) *m,f*

screening ['skri:nɪŋ] *n* (**a**) *Cin* projection *f* (en salle); *TV* passage *m* (à l'écran), diffusion *f*; **when the movie had its first screening** quand le film est passé pour la première fois à l'écran

(**b**) *(of applications, candidates)* tri *m*, sélection *f*; *(for security)* contrôle *m*; *Med (for disease)* test *m ou* tests *mpl* de dépistage; **she went for cancer screening** elle est allée passer un test de dépistage du cancer

(**c**) *(mesh)* grillage *m*

(**d**) *(of coal, dirt, grain)* criblage *m*; **coal screenings** *(waste)* déchets *mpl* de charbon

►► *Cin & TV* ***screening room*** salle *f* de projection

screen-oriented *adj Comput* orienté écran

screenplay ['skri:npleɪ] *n* scénario *m*

screenporch ['skri:npɔ:tʃ] *n Am* véranda *f (entourée d'une moustiquaire)*

screen-test *vt* faire faire un bout d'essai à; **she was screen-tested for the part** on lui a fait faire un bout d'essai pour le rôle

screenwriter ['skri:nˌraɪtə(r)] *n* scénariste *mf*

screw [skru:] **1** *n* (**a**) *(for wood)* vis *f*; *(bolt)* boulon *m*; *(in vice)* vis *f*; *Fig* **to turn the screw** *or* **screws** serrer la vis; *Fam* **to put the screws on sb** faire pression sur qn; **the Mafia put the screws on him** la Mafia lui a forcé la main; *Fam* **to have a screw loose** avoir la tête fêlée, avoir une case de vide

(**b**) *(turn)* tour *m* de vis; **give it a couple more screws** donnez-lui encore un ou deux tours de vis

(**c**) *(thread)* pas *m* de vis

(**d**) *(propeller)* hélice *f*

(**e**) *Br (of salt, tobacco)* cornet *m*; **a screw of paper** un cornet en papier

(**f**) *Br Fam Crime slang (prison guard)* maton(onne) *m,f*

(**g**) *Br Fam (salary)* salaire ❑ *m*, paye ❑ *f*; **he's on a good screw** il gagne plein de fric

(**h**) *Vulg (sexual intercourse)* **to have a screw** baiser, s'envoyer en l'air; **to be a good screw** être un bon coup; **she's a good screw** elle baise bien

(**i**) *(in snooker, pool)* effet *m*

2 *vt* (**a**) *(bolt, screw)* visser; *(handle, parts)* fixer avec des vis; *(lid on bottle)* visser; **to screw sth shut** fermer qch (en vissant); **to screw the lid on a bottle** visser le bouchon d'une bouteille; **screw it tight** vissez-le bien

(**b**) *(crumple)* froisser, chiffonner; **I screwed the letter/my handkerchief into a ball** j'ai fait une boule de la lettre/de mon mouchoir

(**c**) *(wrinkle → face)* **he screwed his face into a grimace** une grimace lui tordit le visage; **he screwed his face into a forced smile** il grimaça un sourire

(**d**) *Tech (cut thread in → screw, bolt)* fileter

(**e**) *Fam (obtain)* arracher ❑; **to screw a promise/an agreement out of sb** arracher une promesse/un accord à qn; **he managed to screw the money/the answer out of her** il a réussi à lui soutirer l'argent/la réponse ❑

(**f**) *very Fam (con)* arnaquer, baiser; **we've been screwed!** on s'est fait arnaquer *ou* baiser!; **they're out to screw you for every penny you've got** ils essayent de vous extorquer tout l'argent que vous avez ❑

(**g**) *Vulg (have sex with → of man)* baiser, troncher; *(→ of woman)* baiser avec, s'envoyer

(**h**) *very Fam (as invective)* **screw the expense!** et merde, je peux bien m'offrir ça!; **screw you!** va te faire foutre!

(**i**) *Am Fam* **to screw the pooch** *(blunder)* faire une gaffe *ou* une boulette

3 *vi* (**a**) *(bolt, lid)* se visser

(**b**) *(in snooker, pool → ball)* revenir en arrière

(**c**) *Vulg (have sex)* baiser, s'envoyer en l'air

►► ***screw eye*** vis *f* à œil; ***screw jack*** cric *m* à vis; *Naut* ***screw propeller*** hélice *f*; ***screw shot*** = coup avec effet; ***screw thread*** pas *m ou* filet *m* de vis; ***screw top*** couvercle *m* qui se visse; **the jar has a screw top** le couvercle du pot se visse

►**screw around 1** *vi* (**a**) *Am very Fam (waste time)* glander, glandouiller; *(fool about)* déconner (**b**) *Vulg (sleep around)* baiser avec n'importe qui, coucher à droite à gauche

2 *vt sep very Fam* **to screw sb around** *(treat badly)* se foutre de la gueule de qn; *(waste time of)* faire perdre son temps à qn ❑

►**screw back** *vi (in snooker, pool → player)* faire de l'effet rétrograde, faire un rétro; *(→ ball)* revenir en arrière

►**screw down 1** *vt sep* visser

2 *vi* se visser

►**screw off 1** *vt sep* dévisser

2 *vi* se dévisser

►**screw on 1** *vt sep* visser; **the cupboard was screwed on to the wall** le placard était vissé au mur

2 *vi* se visser; **it screws on to the wall** ça se visse dans le mur

►**screw over** *vt sep Fam (cheat)* **to screw sb over** arnaquer qn, refaire qn

►**screw round** *vt sep Br* visser, tourner; **he screwed his head round to see** il a brusquement tourné la tête pour voir

►**screw up** *vt sep* **1** (**a**) *(tighten, fasten)* visser

(**b**) *(crumple → handkerchief, paper)* chiffonner, faire une boule de

(**c**) *Br (eyes)* plisser; **she screwed up her eyes** elle plissa les yeux; **he screwed up his face in concentration** la concentration fit se plisser les traits de son visage; **to screw up one's courage** prendre son courage à deux mains

(**d**) *Fam (mess up → plans, chances)* bousiller, foutre en l'air, faire foirer; **you've screwed everything up** tu as tout foutu en l'air; **he's screwed up any chance of promotion** il a foutu en l'air toute chance de promotion

(**e**) *Fam (person)* mettre dans tous ses états, rendre cinglé; **the divorce really screwed her up** le divorce l'a complètement perturbée ❑ *ou* déboussolée

2 *vi* (**a**) *(lid, nut etc)* se visser

(**b**) *(eyes)* plisser; **her face screwed up in distaste** *or* **disgust** elle fit une grimace de dégoût

(**c**) *Fam (make a mess of something)* foirer, merder

screwball ['skru:bɔ:l] *Am Fam* **1** *n* (**a**) *(person)* cinglé(e) *m,f*, dingue *mf* (**b**) *(in baseball)* = balle qui dévie de sa trajectoire

2 *adj* cinglé, dingue

screwdriver ['skru:ˌdraɪvə(r)] *n* (**a**) *(tool)* tournevis *m* (**b**) *(drink)* vodka-orange *f*

►► ***screwdriver blade*** lame *f* de tournevis; ***screwdriver handle*** poignée *f* de tournevis

screwed [skru:d] *adj very Fam* **to be screwed** *(in trouble)* être foutu

screwed-up *adj* (**a**) *(crumpled)* froissé, chiffonné (**b**) *Fam (anxious, psychologically disturbed)* perturbé❑, angoissé❑, mal dans ses baskets; **I just feel very screwed-up about the whole thing** tout ça me fait vraiment flipper; **he's very screwed-up** il est vraiment pas bien dans ses baskets

screwing ['skru:ɪŋ] *n* (**a**) *(tightening → of bolt, screw)* vissage *m*; **screwing up** *or* **down** *or* **on** vissage *m*; **screwing off** dévissage *m* (**b**) *Tech (cutting thread)* filetage *m* (**c**) *Vulg (sex)* baise *f*

►► *Tech* ***screwing die*** filière *f*

screw-loose *adj Am Fam* loufoque, loufedingue

screw-on *adj (earrings)* à vis; *Phot (lens)* détachable, mobile

screw-top *adj* dont le couvercle se visse

screw-up *n Am Fam (bungler)* manche *m*; *(misfit)* paumé(e) *m,f*

screwy ['skru:ɪ] *(compar* **screwier**, *superl* **screwiest**) *adj Fam (person)* cinglé, dingue; *(situation)* bizarre❑

scribble ['skrɪbəl] **1** *vt* (**a**) *(note, drawing)* gribouiller, griffonner; **she left me a hastily scribbled note** elle m'a laissé un mot gribouillé à la hâte; **she scribbled a few lines to her sister** elle griffonna quelques lignes à l'intention de sa sœur

(**b**) *(wool)* carder

2 *vi* gribouiller

3 *n* (**a**) *(act of scribbling)* gribouillis *m*, gribouillage *m*, griffonnage *m*; **the last word was an illegible scribble** le dernier mot n'était qu'un illisible gribouillis; **I can't read this scribble** je n'arrive pas à déchiffrer ce gribouillage; **what are all these scribbles?** qu'est-ce que c'est que tous ces gribouillis?

(**b**) *(bad handwriting)* écriture *f* illisible, pattes *fpl* de mouche; **his handwriting is nothing but a scribble** son écriture est illisible

►**scribble down** *vt sep (address, number)* griffonner, noter (rapidement)

►**scribble out** *vt sep* (**a**) *(cross out)* biffer, raturer (**b**) *(write)* griffonner

scribbler ['skrɪbələ(r)] *n Br Pej (author)* écrivaillon *m*

scribbling ['skrɪbəlɪŋ] *n* gribouillis *m*, gribouillage *m*; *Fam* **scribblings** *(inferior writings)* écrits *mpl* de deuxième zone

►► ***scribbling pad*** bloc-notes *m*; ***scribbling paper*** (papier *m*) brouillon *m*

scribe [skraɪb] **1** *n* scribe *m*

2 *vt* graver

scriber ['skraɪbə(r)] *n* traçoir *m*, traceret *m*

scrim [skrɪm] *n Tex* canevas *m* léger

scrimmage ['skrɪmɪdʒ] **1** *n* (**a**) *(in American football)* mêlée *f*; **line of scrimmage** ligne *f* de mêlée (**b**) *(brawl)* mêlée *f*, bagarre *f*

2 *vi Sport* faire une mêlée

3 *vt Sport (ball)* mettre dans la mêlée

scrimp [skrɪmp] **1** *vi* lésiner; **she scrimps on food** elle lésine sur la nourriture; **to scrimp and save** économiser sur tout, se serrer la ceinture

2 *vt (children, family)* se montrer pingre avec; *(food)* lésiner sur

scrimpy ['skrɪmpɪ] = **skimpy**

scrimshank ['skrɪmʃæŋk] *vi Br Fam* tirer au flanc

scrimshanker ['skrɪm,ʃæŋkə(r)] *n Br Fam* tire-au-flanc *m inv*

scrimshaw ['skrɪmʃɔ:] *n* = objet de coquillage ou d'os de baleine que les marins gravaient à leurs heures perdues

scrip [skrɪp] *n* (**a**) *St Exch* titre *m* provisoire (**b**) *(of paper)* morceau *m* (**c**) *Fam (prescription)* ordonnance❑ *f*

►► *St Exch* ***scrip certificate*** certificat *m* d'actions provisoire; *Am St Exch* ***scrip dividend*** certificat *m* de dividende provisoire; *St Exch* ***scrip issue*** émission *f* d'actions gratuites

scripholder ['skrɪp,həʊldə(r)] *n Fin & St Exch* détenteur(trice) *m,f* de titres

script [skrɪpt] **1** *n* (**a**) *(text)* script *m*, texte *m*; *Cin* script *m*

(**b**) *(UNCOUNT) (handwriting)* script *m*, écriture *f* script; **the letter is written in beautiful script** la lettre est superbement calligraphiée; **to write in script** écrire en script

(**c**) *(lettering, characters)* écriture *f*, caractères *mpl*, lettres *fpl*; **Arabic script** caractères *mpl* arabes, écriture *f* arabe; **in italic script** en italique

(**d**) *(copy) & Law* original *m*; *Univ (answer paper)* copie *f* (d'examen)

2 *vt Cin* écrire le script de

►► ***script editor*** scénariste *mf* (de réécriture); ***script girl*** scripte *mf*, script girl *f*

scripted ['skrɪptɪd] *adj (speech, interview etc)* (dont le texte a été) écrit d'avance

scriptorium [,skrɪp'tɔ:rɪəm] *(pl* **scriptoriums** *or* **scriptoria** [-rɪə]) *n (in monastery)* écriture *f (de monastère)*

scriptural ['skrɪptʃərəl] *adj* biblique

Scripture ['skrɪptʃə(r)] *n* (**a**) *(Christian)* Écriture *f* (sainte); **a reading from the Scriptures** une lecture biblique *ou* de la Bible; **a Scripture lesson** une leçon d'études bibliques (**b**) *(non-Christian)* **the Scriptures** les textes *mpl* sacrés

scriptwriter ['skrɪpt,raɪtə(r)] *n* scénariste *mf*

scriptwriting ['skrɪpt,raɪtɪŋ] *n* écriture *f* de scénarios

scrivener ['skrɪvənə(r)] *n Hist* écrivain *m* public

scrod [skrɒd] *n Am Culin* moruette *f*

scrofula ['skrɒfjʊlə] *n (UNCOUNT)* scrofule *f*

scrofulous ['skrɒfjʊləs] *adj* scrofuleux

scroll [skrəʊl] **1** *n* (**a**) *(of paper, parchment)* rouleau *m*

(**b**) *(manuscript)* manuscrit *m* (ancien)

(**c**) *(on column, violin, woodwork)* volute *f*; *(in writing)* enjolivement *m*, arabesque *f*; *(in engraving etc)* cartouche *m (encadrant un titre)*

(**d**) *Comput* défilement *m*

2 *vt Comput* faire défiler

3 *vi Comput* défiler

►► *Comput* ***scroll bar*** barre *f* de défilement; *Comput* ***scroll box*** ascenseur *m*; *Comput* ***scroll button*** bouton *m* de défilement; *Comput* ***scroll lock (key)*** touche *f* arrêt défil; ***scroll saw*** scie *f* à chantourner

►**scroll down** *Comput* **1** *vt insep* faire défiler un document vers le bas; **to scroll down a page** passer à la page suivante

2 *vi (person)* faire défiler de haut en bas; *(text)* défiler de haut en bas

►**scroll through** *vt insep Comput* faire défiler d'un bout à l'autre, parcourir

►**scroll up** *Comput* **1** *vt insep* **to scroll up a document** faire défiler un document vers le haut; **to scroll up a page** passer à la page précédente

2 *vi (person)* faire défiler de bas en haut; *(text)* défiler de bas en haut

scrolling ['skrəʊlɪŋ] *n Comput* défilement *m*

scrollwork ['skrəʊlwɜ:k] *n Archit* ornementation *f* en volute

scrooge [skru:dʒ] **1** *n* grippe-sou *m*, harpagon *m*

2 Scrooge *pr n* = personnage de Dickens incarnant l'avarice

scrotal ['skrəʊtəl] *adj Anat* scrotal

scrotum ['skrəʊtəm] *(pl* **scrotums** *or* **scrota** [-tə]) *n Anat* scrotum *m*

scrounge [skraʊndʒ] *Fam* **1** *vt (sugar, pencil)* piquer, emprunter❑; *(meal)* se faire offrir❑; *(money)* se faire prêter❑; **he tried to scrounge $10 off me** il a essayé de me taper de 10 dollars; **can I scrounge a cigarette off you?** je peux te taper *ou* te taxer une cigarette?; **could I scrounge a lift from someone?** est-ce que quelqu'un peut m'emmener?❑

2 *vi* **he came scrounging** *Br* **round** *or Am* **around to see what he could find** il est venu faire un tour pour voir s'il n'y avait pas quelque chose à récolter; **to scrounge on** *or* **off sb** *(habitually)* vivre aux crochets de qn; **he's always scrounging off his friends** *(gen)* il tape toujours ses amis; *(for food, meals)* il fait toujours le pique-assiette chez ses amis; **I'm sorry to be always scrounging** je suis désolé d'être toujours à quémander

3 *n* **to be on the scrounge** *(for food)* venir quémander de quoi manger; *(for cigarette)* venir quémander une cigarette; **she's on the scrounge for a meal** elle veut se faire inviter à manger; **he's always on the scrounge** il vit toujours aux crochets des autres

scrounger ['skraʊndʒə(r)] *n Fam* pique-assiette *mf*, parasite❑ *m*; *(living off state benefits)* parasite❑ *m*

scrub [skrʌb] *(pt & pp* **scrubbed**, *cont* **scrubbing**) **1** *vt* (**a**) *(clean, wash → floor, carpet)* nettoyer à la brosse, frotter avec une brosse; *(→ saucepan, sink)* frotter, récurer; *(→ clothes, face, back)* frotter; *(→ fingernails)* brosser; **to scrub sth clean** nettoyer qch à fond, récurer qch; **scrub yourself all over** frotte-toi bien partout; **have you scrubbed your hands clean?** est-ce que tu t'es bien nettoyé les mains?

(**b**) *Fam (cancel → order)* annuler❑; *(→ plans, holiday)* annuler❑, laisser tomber❑; *(recording, tape)* effacer❑; **we'll have to scrub dinner** il faudra qu'on se passe de dîner❑; **I'd prefer to scrub that remark** j'aimerais mieux que cette remarque soit effacée; **she's been scrubbed from the team** on l'a virée de l'équipe

(**c**) *Tech (gas)* laver

2 *vi* **I spent the morning scrubbing** j'ai passé la matinée à frotter les planchers *ou* les sols

3 *n* (**a**) *(with brush)* coup *m* de brosse; **give the floor a good scrub** frotte bien le plancher; **can you give my back a scrub?** peux-tu me frotter le dos?

(**b**) *(vegetation)* broussailles *fpl*

(**c**) *Am Sport (team)* équipe *f* de seconde zone; *(player)* joueur(euse) *m,f* de second ordre

(**d**) *Austr Fam (wilderness)* cambrousse *f*

►► *Am* ***scrub brush*** brosse *f* à récurer

►**scrub away** **1** *vt sep (mark, mud)* faire partir en brossant

2 *vi* partir à la brosse

►**scrub down** *vt sep (wall, paintwork)* lessiver; *(horse)* bouchonner

►**scrub out** **1** *vt sep* (**a**) *(dirt, stain)* faire partir à la brosse; *(bucket, tub)* nettoyer à la brosse; *(pan)* récurer; *(ears)* nettoyer, bien laver

(**b**) *(erase → graffiti, comment)* effacer; *(→ name)* barrer, biffer

2 *vi* partir à la brosse

►**scrub up** *vi Med (before operation)* se laver les mains

scrubbable ['skrʌbəbəl] *adj* lavable, nettoyable

scrubber ['skrʌbə(r)] *n* (**a**) *(for saucepans)* tampon *m* à récurer (**b**) *Br very Fam Pej (woman)* pute *f*, salope *f*

scrubbing ['skrʌbɪŋ] *n (cleaning → of saucepan)* récurage *m*; *(→ with brush)* nettoyage *m* avec une brosse dure

►► *Br* ***scrubbing brush*** brosse *f* à récurer

scrubby ['skrʌbɪ] *(compar* **scrubbier**, *superl* **scrubbiest**) *adj* (**a**) *(land)* broussailleux (**b**) *(tree, vegetation)* rabougri (**c**) *Br Fam (messy)* en désordre❑

scrubland ['skrʌblænd] *n* maquis *m*, garrigue *f*

scrubwoman ['skrʌb,wʊmən] *(pl* **scrubwomen** [-,wɪmɪn]) *n Am* femme *f* de ménage

scruff [skrʌf] *n* (**a**) *Br Fam (untidy person)* individu *m* débraillé *ou* dépenaillé *ou* peu soigné; *(ruffian)* voyou *m*; **you look a real scruff** tu es ficelé comme l'as de pique; **a scruff like you** quelqu'un d'aussi peu soigné que toi (**b**) *(idiom)* **by the scruff of the neck** par la peau du cou

scruffily ['skrʌfɪlɪ] *adv* **scruffily dressed** dépenaillé, mal habillé

scruffiness ['skrʌfɪnɪs] *n (in dress, appearance)* négligence *f*; *(of district)* état *m* de délabrement

scruffy ['skrʌfɪ] *(compar* **scruffier**, *superl* **scruffiest**) *adj (appearance)* négligé; *(clothes)* dépenaillé; *(hair)* ébouriffé; *(person)* débraillé, dépenaillé, peu soigné; *(building, area)* délabré, miteux; **he's a scruffy dresser** il s'habille mal

scrum [skrʌm] *(pt & pp* **scrummed**, *cont* **scrumming**) **1** *n* (**a**) *(in rugby)* mêlée *f* (**b**) *(brawl)* mêlée *f*, bousculade *f*; **there was a scrum for tickets** les gens se sont bousculés pour obtenir des billets

2 *vi* former une mêlée

►**scrum down** *vi (in rugby)* former une mêlée; **scrum down!** *(as instruction)* mêlée!

scrum-cap *n* casquette *f (de joueur de rugby)*

scrum-half *n (in rugby)* demi *m* de mêlée

scrummage ['skrʌmɪdʒ] **1** *n* (**a**) *(in rugby)* mêlée *f* (**b**) *(brawl)* mêlée *f*, bousculade *f*; **there was a scrummage for the best bargains** les gens se sont arrachés les soldes les plus intéressants

2 *vi (in rugby)* former une mêlée

scrummy [,skrʌmɪ] *adj Br Fam* délicieux❑, super bon

scrump [skrʌmp] *Br Fam* **1** *vi* **to go scrumping (for apples)** aller chaparder (des pommes)
2 *vt (apples)* chaparder

scrumptious ['skrʌmpʃəs] *adj Fam* délicieux❑, succulent❑

scrumpy ['skrʌmpɪ] *n* = cidre brut et sec fabriqué dans le sud-ouest de l'Angleterre

scrunch [skrʌntʃ] **1** *vt (biscuit, apple)* croquer; *(snow, gravel)* faire craquer *ou* crisser; *(paper → noisily)* froisser (bruyamment)
2 *vi (footsteps → on gravel, snow)* craquer, faire un bruit de craquement; *(gravel, snow → underfoot)* craquer crisser
3 *n (of gravel, snow, paper)* craquement *m*, bruit *m* de craquement

►**scrunch up** *vt sep* (**a**) *(crumple → paper)* froisser; **he scrunched up his face in disgust** il a fait une grimace de dégoût (**b**) *Am (hunch)* **she was sitting with her shoulders scrunched up** elle était assise, les épaules rentrées

scrunch-dry *vt (hair)* sécher en froissant; **to scrunch-dry one's hair** se sécher les cheveux en les froissant

scrunchie, scrunchy ['skrʌntʃɪ] *n* chouchou *m* *(pour tenir les cheveux)*

scruple ['skru:pəl] **1** *n* scrupule *m*; **he has no scruples** il n'a aucun scrupule; **he had scruples about accepting payment** il avait des scrupules à accepter qu'on le paie; **to act without scruple** agir sans scrupule
2 *vi* **they don't scruple to cheat** ils n'ont aucun scrupule *ou* ils n'hésitent pas à tricher; **I would scruple to steal even if I was starving** j'aurais scrupule à voler même si je mourais de faim

scrupulous ['skru:pjʊləs] *adj* (**a**) *(meticulous)* scrupuleux, méticuleux; **she's very scrupulous about her dress** elle prête une attention scrupuleuse à la façon dont elle s'habille; **they're rather scrupulous about punctuality** ils tiennent beaucoup à la ponctualité; **the papers were all in scrupulous order** les papiers avaient été rangés avec un soin méticuleux; **he acted with scrupulous honesty** il a agi avec une honnêteté irréprochable
(**b**) *(conscientious)* scrupuleux

scrupulously ['skru:pjʊləslɪ] *adv (meticulously)* scrupuleusement, parfaitement; *(honestly)* scrupuleusement, avec scrupule; **scrupulously clean** d'une propreté impeccable; **scrupulously honest** d'une honnêteté irréprochable; **scrupulously punctual** parfaitement à l'heure

scrupulousness ['skru:pjʊləsnɪs] *n (quality)* esprit *m* scrupuleux; **his scrupulousness in noting down all his expenses** les scrupules qu'il avait à relever toutes les dépenses

scrutator [,skru:'teɪtə(r)] *n* (**a**) *(investigator)* investigateur(trice) *m,f* (**b**) *(scrutineer)* scrutateur(trice) *m,f*

scrutineer [,skru:tɪ'nɪə(r)] *n Br Pol* scrutateur(trice) *m,f*

scrutinize, -ise ['skru:tɪnaɪz] *vt* scruter, examiner attentivement

scrutinizer ['skru:tɪnaɪzə(r)] *n* (**a**) *(investigator)* investigateur(trice) *m,f* (**b**) *(scrutineer)* scrutateur(trice) *m,f*

scrutinizing ['skru:tɪnaɪzɪŋ] **1** *n (UNCOUNT)* examen *m* minutieux *ou* approfondi
2 *adj* inquisiteur; **scrutinizing look** regard *m* pénétrant

scrutiny ['skru:tɪnɪ] (*pl* **scrutinies**) *n* (**a**) *(examination)* examen *m* minutieux *ou* approfondi; *(watch)* surveillance *f*; *(gaze)* regard *m* insistant; **to be under scrutiny** *(prisoners)* être sous surveillance; *(accounts, staff)* faire l'objet d'un contrôle; **to come under scrutiny** être contrôlé; **everything we do is under close scrutiny** tous nos actes sont surveillés de près; **her work does not stand up to close scrutiny** son travail ne résiste pas à un examen minutieux
(**b**) *Br Pol* deuxième pointage *m* (des suffrages)

SCSI ['skʌzɪ] *n Comput* (*abbr* **small computer systems interface**) SCSI *f*
►► ***SCSI card*** carte *f* SCSI

scuba ['sku:bə] *n* scaphandre *m* autonome
►► ***scuba dive*** plongée *f* sous-marine; ***scuba diver*** plongeur(euse) *m,f* sous-marin(e); ***scuba diving*** plongée *f* sous-marine; **to go scuba diving** faire de la plongée sous-marine

scuba-dive *vi* faire de la plongée sous-marine

scud [skʌd] (*pt & pp* **scudded**, *cont* **scudding**) *vi* glisser, filer; **clouds scudded across the sky** des nuages filaient dans le ciel; **two boats scudded across the lake** deux voiliers filaient sur le lac; **she sent the pebble scudding over the waves** elle envoya le galet voler au-dessus des vagues

scuff [skʌf] **1** *vt* (**a**) *(shoe, leather)* érafler, râper; **her shoes were all scuffed (up)** ses chaussures étaient toutes éraflées *ou* râpées (**b**) *(drag)* **to scuff one's feet** marcher en traînant les pieds, traîner les pieds
2 *vi* marcher en traînant les pieds
3 *n (mark)* éraflure *f*; *(on floor)* rayure *f*
►► ***scuff mark*** éraflure *f*; *(on floor)* rayure *f*

scuffed [skʌft] *adj (shoe)* éraflé; *(floor)* rayé

scuffing ['skʌfɪŋ] *n (UNCOUNT) (on piston)* rayures *fpl* (d'usure)

scuffle ['skʌfəl] **1** *n* (**a**) *(fight)* bagarre *f*, échauffourée *f*; **after a brief scuffle, he was marched away by the police** après une courte bagarre, il fut emmené par les policiers
(**b**) *(of feet)* piétinement *m*
2 *vi* (**a**) *(fight)* se bagarrer, se battre; **demonstrators scuffled with the police** des manifestants se sont battus avec la police, il y a eu des bagarres entre manifestants et policiers
(**b**) *(with feet)* marcher en traînant les pieds; **they scuffled along the corridor** ils avançaient dans le couloir en traînant les pieds

scuffling ['skʌfəlɪŋ] *n* bruit *m* étouffé

scull [skʌl] **1** *n* (**a**) *(double paddle)* godille *f*; *(single oar)* aviron *m*; **double sculls** rameurs *mpl* en couple (**b**) *(boat)* yole *f*
2 *vt (with double paddle)* godiller; *(with oars)* ramer
3 *vi* ramer en couple; **to go sculling** faire de l'aviron

sculler ['skʌlə(r)] *n* (**a**) *(person → gen)* rameur(euse) *m,f* de couple; *(→ using double paddle)* godilleur(euse) *m,f* (**b**) *(boat)* yole *f*; **double sculler** outrigger *m* à deux rameurs de couple, double-scull *m*

scullery ['skʌlərɪ] (*pl* **sculleries**) *n Br* arrière-cuisine *f*
►► *Br* ***scullery maid*** fille *f* de cuisine

sculling ['skʌlɪŋ] *n (UNCOUNT) (with double paddle)* nage *f* à la godille; *(with oars)* nage *f* à couple

sculpin ['skʌlpɪn] *n Ich* callionyme *m*

sculpt [skʌlpt] **1** *vt* sculpter
2 *vi* faire de la sculpture

sculptor ['skʌlptə(r)] *n* sculpteur *m*

sculptress ['skʌlptrɪs] *n* (femme *f*) sculpteur *mf*, sculptrice *f*

sculptural ['skʌlptʃərəl] *adj* sculptural

sculpturally ['skʌlptʃərəlɪ] *adv* conformément aux règles de la sculpture; **sculpturally beautiful** plastiquement belle

sculpture ['skʌlptʃə(r)] **1** *n* (**a**) *(art)* sculpture *f* (**b**) *(object)* sculpture *f*; **it's a beautiful (piece of) sculpture** c'est une très belle sculpture
2 *vt* sculpter; **she has finely sculptured features** elle a le visage très fin
3 *vi* faire de la sculpture; **to sculpture in bronze** sculpter dans le bronze

sculpturesque [,skʌlptʃə'resk] *adj (gen)* sculptural; *(beauty)* plastique

scum [skʌm] *n* (**a**) *(on liquid, sea)* écume *f*; *(in bath)* (traînées *fpl* de) crasse *f*; *Metal* écume *f*, scories *fpl*; **to take the scum off** *(liquid)* écumer; *(bath)* nettoyer (**b**) *Fam (people)* rebut❑ *m*, ordures *fpl*; **he's scum** c'est une ordure; **he's the scum of the earth** c'est le dernier des derniers; **they're just scum** ce sont des minables; **they treated us like scum** on nous a traités comme des moins que rien *ou* des chiens (**c**) *Am Vulg (semen)* foutre *m*

scumbag ['skʌmbæg] *n* (**a**) *Fam (person)* salaud *m*, ordure *f* (**b**) *Am Vulg (condom)* capote *f* (anglaise)

scumble ['skʌmbəl] *Art* **1** *n* glacis *m*, frottis *m*, frotté *m*
2 *vt* (**a**) *(sky, background)* glacer, frotter; **background scumbled with blue** fond *m* frotté de bleu (**b**) *(line)* estomper

scummy ['skʌmɪ] (*compar* **scummier**, *superl* **scummiest**) *adj* (**a**) *(liquid)* écumeux (**b**) *very Fam (person)* salaud; *(object)* crade

scuncheon ['skʌntʃən] *n Archit* battée *f*

scunner ['skʌnə(r)] *Scot* **1** *n (dislike)* **to take a scunner to sb/sth** prendre qn/qch en grippe
2 *vt* détester, avoir horreur de

scunnered ['skʌnəd] *adj Scot* **to be scunnered (with)** en avoir marre (de)

scupper ['skʌpə(r)] **1** *vt Br* (**a**) *(ship)* saborder (**b**) *Fam (plans, attempt)* saborder❑, faire capoter; **we're completely scuppered unless we can find the cash** on est finis si on ne trouve pas l'argent
2 *n Naut* dalot *m*

scurf [skɜ:f] *n (UNCOUNT) (dandruff)* pellicules *fpl*; *(on skin)* squames *fpl*; *(on plant)* lamelles *fpl*

scurfy ['skɜ:fɪ] (*compar* **scurfier**, *superl* **scurfiest**) *adj (scalp)* couvert de pellicules; *(skin)* squameux

scurrility [skʌ'rɪlɪtɪ] (*pl* **scurrilities**) *n* (**a**) *(of remarks)* caractère *m* calomnieux *ou* outrageant; *(of action)* bassesse *f* (**b**) *(vulgarity)* grossièreté *f*

scurrilous ['skʌrɪləs] *adj (lying)* calomnieux, mensonger; *(insulting)* outrageant, ignoble; *(bitter)* fielleux; *(vulgar)* grossier, vulgaire

scurrilously ['skʌrɪləslɪ] *adv (insultingly)* injurieusement; *(coarsely)* grossièrement

scurrilousness ['skʌrɪləsnɪs] = **scurrility**

scurry ['skʌrɪ] (*pt & pp* **scurried**, *pl* **scurries**) **1** *vi* se précipiter, courir; **all the animals were scurrying for shelter** tous les animaux couraient pour se mettre à l'abri; **they scurried for the trees** ils se précipitèrent vers les arbres; **the sound of scurrying feet** le bruit de pas précipités
2 *n* (**a**) *(rush)* course *f* (précipitée), débandade *f*; **there was a scurry for the door** tout le monde s'est rué vers la porte
(**b**) *(sound → of feet)* bruit *m* de pas précipités

►**scurry away, scurry off** *vi (animal)* détaler; *(person)* décamper, prendre ses jambes à son cou

►**scurry out** *vi (animal)* détaler; *(person)* sortir à toute vitesse

S-curve *n Am* double virage *m*, virage *m* en S

scurvy ['skɜ:vɪ] (*compar* **scurvier**, *superl* **scurviest**) **1** *n (UNCOUNT) Med* scorbut *m*
2 *adj (trick)* honteux, ignoble; *Arch or Hum* **you scurvy knave!** (espèce de) misérable fripon!
►► *Bot* ***scurvy grass*** cochléaria *m*

scut [skʌt] *n (of rabbit, hare)* couette *f*

scutate ['skju:teɪt] *adj* (**a**) *Zool* pourvu d'un scutum (**b**) *Bot* scutiforme

scutcheon ['skʌtʃən] = **escutcheon**

scute [skju:t] *n Zool* scutum *m*

scutellum [,skju:'teləm] *n* (**a**) *Bot* scutellum *m* (**b**) *Zool* scutelle *f*

scuttle ['skʌtəl] **1** *vi (run)* courir à pas précipités, se précipiter
2 *vt* (**a**) *(ship)* saborder; **the whole fleet was scuttled** tout la flotte a été sabordée (**b**) *(hopes)* ruiner; *(plans)* saborder, faire échouer
3 *n* (**a**) *(run)* course *f* précipitée, débandade *f* (**b**) **(coal) scuttle** seau *m* à charbon (**c**) *Naut* écoutille *f* (**d**) *Am (in ceiling, floor)* trappe *f*

►**scuttle away, scuttle off** *vi (animal)* détaler; *(person)* déguerpir, se sauver

►**scuttle out** *vi* sortir précipitamment

scuttlebutt ['skʌtəlbʌt] *n* (**a**) *(for drinking)* fontaine *f*; *Naut* tonneau *m* d'eau douce (**b**) *Am Fig (gossip)* ragots *mpl*

scuttling ['skʌtəlɪŋ] *n (of ship)* sabordage *m*

scutum ['skju:təm] *n* (**a**) *Zool & Entom* scutum *m* (**b**) *Hist (Roman shield)* scutum *m*

scuzzy ['skʌzɪ] *adj Fam* dégueulasse, cradingue

Scylla ['sɪlə] *see* **Charybdis**

scythe [saɪð] **1** *n* faux *f*
2 *vt* faucher

►**scythe through** *vt insep (with a weapon)* faucher; **her stick scythed through the air** son bâton fendit l'air

SD (*written abbr* **South Dakota**) Dakota *m* du Sud

SDI [,esdi:'aɪ] *n Mil* (*abbr* **strategic defence initiative**) initiative *f* de défense stratégique

SDLP [,esdi:,el'pi:] *n* (*abbr* **Social Democratic and Labour Party**) = parti politique d'Irlande du Nord

SDP [,esdi:'pi:] *n* (*abbr* **Social Democratic Party**) Parti *m* social démocrate

SDRAM [ˌesdiː'ræm] *n Comput* (*abbr* **synchronous dynamic random access memory**) SDRAM *f*

SDRs [ˌesdiː'ɑːz] *npl Econ* (*abbr* **special drawing rights**) DTS *mpl*

SE (*written abbr* **south-east**) S-E

SEA [ˌesiː'eɪ] *n EU* (*abbr* **Single European Act**) AUE *m*

sea [siː] *n* (**a**) *(gen)* mer *f*; **by land and sea** par terre et par mer; **to travel by sea** voyager par mer *ou* par bateau; **the goods were sent by sea** les marchandises ont été expédiées par bateau; **he's spent all his life on the sea** il a passé toute sa vie en mer; **at sea** *(boat, storm)* en mer; *(as sailor)* de *ou* comme marin; **we spent six months at sea** on a passé six mois en mer; **life at sea** la vie en mer *ou* de marin; **to swim in the sea** nager *ou* se baigner dans la mer; **to put (out) to sea** prendre la mer; **to go to sea** *(boat)* prendre la mer; *(sailor)* se faire marin; **to run away to sea** partir se faire marin; **to look out to sea** regarder vers le large; **the little boat was swept** *or* **washed out to sea** le petit bateau a été emporté vers le large; **across** *or* **over the sea** *or* **seas** outre-mer; **a heavy sea, heavy seas** une grosse mer; **the Sea of Tranquillity** la mer de la Tranquillité; **sea and air search** recherches *fpl* maritimes et aériennes; *Br Fam* **to be at sea** *(be lost)* nager (complètement); *(be mixed-up)* être déboussolé *ou* désorienté ❑; **when it comes to computers, I'm all at sea** je ne connais strictement rien aux ordinateurs ❑; **he's been all at sea since his wife left him** il est complètement déboussolé *ou* il a complètement perdu le nord depuis que sa femme l'a quitté; **the resignation of our secretary has left the reference department all at sea** la démission de notre secrétaire a totalement perturbé notre service des archives ❑; *Fam* **to find** *or* **to get one's sea legs** s'amariner ❑, s'habituer à la mer ❑

(**b**) *(seaside)* bord *m* de la mer; **they live by** *or* **beside the sea** ils habitent au bord de la mer; **the town is by the sea** la ville est au bord de la mer

(**c**) *(large quantity → of blood, mud)* mer *f*; *(→ of problems, faces)* multitude *f*

▸▸ ***sea air*** air *m* marin *ou* de la mer; ***sea anchor*** ancre *f* flottante; *Zool* ***sea anemone*** anémone *f* de mer; *Bot* ***sea aster*** aster *m* maritime; *Ich* ***sea bass*** bar *m*, loup *m*; ***sea bathing*** bains *mpl* de mer; ***sea battle*** bataille *f* navale; *Bot* ***sea bindweed*** liseron *m* du mer; *Ich* ***sea bream*** daurade *f*, dorade *f*; ***sea breeze*** *(wind)* brise *f* marine; *(cocktail)* sea breeze *m*; *Zool* ***sea calf*** veau *m* marin, phoque *m*; *Bot* ***sea campion*** silène *m* maritime; ***sea captain*** capitaine *m* de la marine marchande; ***sea change*** changement *m* radical, profond changement *m*; *Naut* ***sea chest*** coffre *m* de marin *ou* de bord; *Zool* ***sea cow*** vache *f* marine, sirénien *m*; ***sea crossing*** traversée *f*; *Ich* ***sea cucumber*** concombre *m* de mer, holothurie *f*; ***sea dog*** (**a**) *Ich* roussette *f*, chien *m* de mer; *Zool (seal)* phoque *m* (**b**) *Literary or Hum (sailor)* (vieux) loup *m* de mer (**c**) *(in fog)* arc-en-ciel *m (aperçu dans le brouillard)*; *Orn* ***sea eagle*** aigle *m* des mers; *Zool* ***sea elephant*** éléphant *m* de mer; ***sea fight*** combat *m* naval; ***sea fish*** poisson *m* de mer; ***sea fishery*** pêche *f* maritime; ***sea fishing*** pêche *f* maritime; ***sea floor*** fond *m* de la mer; ***sea fog*** brouillard *m (en mer)*; ***sea freight*** fret *m* maritime; ***sea freight services*** messageries *fpl* maritimes; ***sea god*** dieu *m* marin *ou* de la mer; ***sea green*** vert *m* glauque; *Zool* ***sea hare*** lièvre *m* marin, *Spec* aplysie *f*; *Bot* ***sea holly*** panicaut *m* maritime; *Bot* ***sea island cotton*** coton *m* longues soies; *Bot* ***sea kale*** chou *m* marin, crambe *m*; ***sea kayak*** kayak *m* de mer; ***sea kayaking*** kayak *m* de mer; **to go sea kayaking** faire du kayak de mer; ***sea lane*** couloir *m* de navigation; *Bot* ***sea lavender*** lavande *f* de mer; ***sea level*** niveau *m* de la mer; **above/below sea level** au-dessus/au-dessous du niveau de la mer; *Zool* ***sea lily*** crinoïde *m*, lis *m* de mer; *Zool* ***sea lion*** otarie *f*; *Scot* ***sea loch*** bras *m* de mer; *Br Mil* ***Sea Lord*** lord *m* de l'Amirauté; *Zool* ***sea louse*** pou *m* de saumon; ***sea mile*** mille *m* marin; ***sea mist*** brume *f* de mer; *Zool* ***sea otter*** loutre *f* de mer; *Zool* ***sea pen*** plume *f* de mer; *Bot* ***sea rocket*** roquette *f* maritime; ***sea salt*** sel *m* marin *ou* de mer; *Ich* ***sea scorpion*** chabot *m*, scorpion *m* de mer; ***sea scout*** scout *m* marin; *Zool* ***sea serpent*** serpent *m* de mer; ***sea shanty*** chanson *f* de marins; *Zool* ***sea slater*** ligie *f*; *Zool* ***sea slug*** nudibranche *m*; *Zool* ***sea snail*** lipars *m*, *Can* limace *f*; *Zool* ***sea snake*** serpent *m* de mer; *Zool* ***sea spider*** araignée *f* de mer; *Zool* ***sea squirt*** ascidie *f*, outre *f* de mer; ***sea traffic*** navigation *f ou* trafic *m* maritime; *Ich* ***sea trout*** truite *f* de mer; *Zool* ***sea urchin*** oursin *m*; ***sea view*** vue *f* sur la mer; ***sea wall*** digue *f*; *Austr* ***sea wasp*** cuboméduse *f*

seabed ['siːbed] *n* fond *m* de la mer *ou* marin

seabird ['siːbɜːd] *n* oiseau *m* de mer

seaboard ['siːbɔːd] *n (coastline)* littoral *m*, côte *f*; *(coastal region)* bord *m* de la mer, région *f* côtière; **on the Atlantic seaboard** sur la côte atlantique

seaboots ['siːbuːts] *npl* bottes *fpl* de marin *ou* de mer

seaborgium [siː'bɔːgɪʌm] *n Chem* seaborgium *m*

seaborne ['siːbɔːn] *adj (trade)* maritime; *(goods, troops)* transporté par mer *ou* par bateau

seacoast [ˌsiː'kəʊst] *n* côte *f*, littoral *m*

Sea-Doo® [ˌsiː'duː] *n* scooter *m* des mers, *Can* motomarine *f*

seafarer ['siːˌfeərə(r)] *n* marin *m*

seafaring ['siːˌfeərɪŋ] **1** *adj (nation)* maritime, de marins; *(life)* de marin

2 *n* vie *f* de marin

seafloor ['siːflɔː(r)] *n* fond *m* de (la) mer *ou* marin

seafood ['siːfuːd] *n (UNCOUNT)* (poissons *mpl* et) fruits *mpl* de mer

seafront ['siːfrʌnt] *n* bord *m* de mer, front *m* de mer

seagirt ['siːgɜːt] *adj Literary* entouré *ou* ceint par la mer; **a seagirt island** une île ceinturée par les flots

seagoing ['siːˌgəʊɪŋ] *adj (trade, nation)* maritime; *(life)* de marin; **a seagoing man** un marin, un homme de mer; **a seagoing ship** un navire de haute mer, un (navire) long-courrier

seagrass ['siːgrɑːs] *n Bot* jonc *m* de mer

sea-green *adj* vert glauque *(inv)*

seagull ['siːgʌl] *n* mouette *f*

'The Seagull' *Chekhov* 'La Mouette'

seahorse ['siːhɔːs, *pl* -hɔːsɪz] *n Zool* hippocampe *m*

seal [siːl] **1** *n* (**a**) *Zool* phoque *m*

(**b**) *(on document, letter)* sceau *m*; *(on bottle of wine)* cachet *m*; *(on crate)* plombage *m*; *(on battery, gas cylinder)* bande *f* de garantie; *(on meter)* plomb *m*; *Br Admin & Law* **given under my hand and seal** signé et scellé par moi; **to put one's seal to a document** apposer son sceau à un document; **does the project have her seal of approval?** est-ce qu'elle a approuvé le projet?; **to put** *or* **to set the seal on sth** *(confirm)* sceller qch; *(bring to end)* mettre fin à qch

(**c**) *(UNCOUNT) Law (on door)* scellé *m*, scellés *mpl*; **under seal** sous scellés; *Fig* **under (the) seal of secrecy/of silence** ≃ sous le sceau du secret/du silence; *Rel* **under the seal of confession** *or* **of the confessional** dans le secret de la confession

(**d**) *(tool)* sceau *m*, cachet *m*; *Admin* **the Great Seal** le Grand Sceau *(employé pour les actes publics)*

(**e**) *Com* label *m*

(**f**) *(joint → for engine, jar, sink)* joint *m* d'étanchéité; *(putty)* mastic *m*

(**g**) *(stamp)* **Christmas seal** timbre *m* de Noël

2 *vt* (**a**) *(document)* apposer son sceau à, sceller; **sealed with a kiss** scellé d'un baiser; **sealed orders** des ordres scellés sous pli; *Fig* **her fate is sealed** son sort est réglé; *Fig* **they finally sealed the deal** ils ont enfin conclu l'affaire

(**b**) *(close → envelope, package)* cacheter, fermer; *(→ with sticky tape)* coller, fermer; *(→ jar)* sceller, fermer hermétiquement; *(→ can)* souder; *(→ tube, mineshaft)* sceller; *(window, door → for insulation)* isoler; *Fig* **my lips are sealed** mes lèvres sont scellées

(**c**) *Law (door)* apposer des scellés sur; *(evidence)* mettre sous scellés; *(at customs → goods)* (faire) sceller

(**d**) *Culin (meat)* saisir

▸▸ *Com* ***seal of quality*** label *m* de qualité; ***seal ring*** chevalière *f*

▸**seal in** *vt sep* enfermer hermétiquement; **the flavour is sealed in by freeze-drying** le produit garde toute sa saveur grâce à la lyophilisation; **fry the meat at a high temperature to seal in the flavour** faites revenir la viande à feu vif afin de lui conserver toute sa saveur

▸**seal off** *vt sep (passage, road)* interdire l'accès de; *(entrance)* condamner; **the street had been sealed off** la rue avait été fermée (à la circulation)

▸**seal up** *vt sep (close → envelope)* cacheter, fermer; *(→ with sticky tape)* coller, fermer; *(→ jar)* sceller, fermer hermétiquement; *(→ can)* souder; *(→ tube, mineshaft)* sceller; *(window, door → for insulation)* isoler

sealant ['siːlənt] *n* (**a**) *(paste, putty)* produit *m* d'étanchéité; *(paint)* enduit *m* étanche; *(for radiator)* anti-fuite *m* (**b**) *(joint)* joint *m* d'étanchéité

sealark ['siːlɑːk] *n Orn* alouette *f* de mer

sealed [siːld] *adj (document)* scellé; *(envelope)* cacheté; *(orders)* scellé sous pli; *(jar)* fermé hermétiquement; *(mineshaft)* obturé, bouché; *(joint)* étanche

▸▸ *Com* ***sealed bid*** soumission *f* cachetée; *Aut* ***sealed cooling system*** circuit *m* de refroidissement pressurisé; *Austr* ***sealed road*** route *f* avec revêtement; *Com* ***sealed tender*** soumission *f* cachetée

sealed-beam *adj*

▸▸ *Aut* ***sealed-beam headlight*** phare *m* scellé

sealed-bid *adj*

▸▸ *Com* ***sealed-bid pricing*** fixation *f* d'un prix de soumission

sealer ['siːlə(r)] *n* (**a**) *(hunter)* chasseur(euse) *m,f* de phoques; *(ship)* navire *m* équipé pour la chasse aux phoques (**b**) *(paint, varnish)* enduit *m*, première couche *f*

sealery ['siːlərɪ] (*pl* **sealeries**) *n* (**a**) *(hunting grounds)* pêcherie *f* de phoques (**b**) *(seal colony)* colonie *f ou* rookerie *f* de phoques

sealine ['siːlaɪn] *n* (**a**) *(at sea)* horizon *m*, ligne *f* d'horizon (**b**) *Petr* conduite *f* marine

sealing ['siːlɪŋ] *n* (**a**) *(hunting)* chasse *f* aux phoques; **to go sealing** aller à la chasse aux phoques (**b**) *(of document)* cachetage *m*; *(of crate)* plombage *m*; *(of door)* scellage *m*; *(of shaft, mine)* fermeture *f*, obturation *f*

▸▸ ***sealing wax*** cire *f* à cacheter

seal-point *n* seal-point *m*

sealskin ['siːlskɪn] **1** *n* peau *f* de phoque

2 *adj* en peau de phoque

Sealyham ['siːlɪəm] *n* sealyham terrier *m*

▸▸ ***Sealyham terrier*** sealyham terrier *m*

seam [siːm] **1** *n* (**a**) *(on garment, stocking)* couture *f*; *(in airbed, bag)* couture *f*, joint *m*; *(weld)* soudure *f*; *(between planks)* joint *m*; **your coat is coming** *or* **falling apart at the seams** votre manteau se découd; **my suitcase was bulging** *or* **bursting at the seams** ma valise était pleine à craquer; *Fig* **the building was bursting at the seams** le bâtiment était plein à craquer; *Fig* **their marriage is coming** *or* **falling apart at the seams** leur mariage craque

(**b**) *(of coal, ore)* filon *m*, veine *f*; *(in rocks)* couche *f*

2 *vt (garment)* faire une couture dans, coudre; *(plastic, metal, wood)* faire un joint à

▸▸ ***seam bowler*** *(in cricket)* = lanceur qui utilise les coutures de la balle pour la faire dévier

seaman ['siːmən] (*pl* **seamen** [-mən]) *n* (**a**) *(sailor)* marin *m* (**b**) *(in US Navy)* quartier-maître *m* de 2ème classe

▸▸ ***seaman apprentice*** matelot *m* en formation; ***seaman recruit*** matelot *m*

seamanlike ['siːmənlaɪk] **1** *adj* de marin, d'un bon marin

2 *adv* en bon marin

seamanship ['siːmənʃɪp] *n (UNCOUNT)* qualités *fpl* de marin

seamark ['siːmɑːk] *n Naut* amer *m*, repère *m*

seamed [siːmd] *adj (furrowed)* ridé, sillonné; **the rock was seamed with quartz** la roche était veinée de quartz; **his face was seamed by deep wrinkles** son visage était marqué de profondes rides

seamen ['siːmən] *pl of* **seaman**

seamew ['siːmjuː] *n Orn* mouette *f*

seamless ['siːmlɪs] *adj* (**a**) *(stocking)* sans couture; *(made from single piece of metal)* sans soudure (**b**) *Fig (changeover, whole)* continu; **a seamless transition** une transition en douceur

seamlessly ['siːmlɪslɪ] *adv* d'une façon cohérente *ou* homogène

seamstress ['semstrɪs] *n* couturière *f*

seamy ['siːmɪ] *(compar* **seamier**, *superl* **seamiest)** *adj* sordide, louche; **the seamy side of life** le côté sordide de la vie

séance, seance ['seɪɑːns] *n* (**a**) *(for raising spirits)* séance *f* de spiritisme (**b**) *(meeting)* séance *f*, réunion *f*

seaplane ['siːpleɪn] *n* hydravion *m*

seaport ['siːpɔːt] *n* port *m* maritime

SEAQ [ˌesiːˌeɪ'kjuː] *n (abbr* **Stock Exchange Automated Quotations System**) système *m* de cotation automatisé

sear [sɪə(r)] **1** *vt* (**a**) *(burn)* brûler; *(brand)* marquer au fer rouge; *Med* cautériser; **the scene seared itself on my memory** la scène est restée gravée *ou* marquée dans ma mémoire (**b**) *Culin (meat etc)* saisir (**c**) *(wither)* dessécher, flétrir (**d**) *Arch (harden → heart, feelings)* endurcir

2 *n (burn)* (marque *f* de) brûlure *f*

3 *adj Literary* desséché, flétri

▸**sear through** *vt insep (metal, wall)* traverser, percer; **the pain seared through me** la douleur me transperça

search [sɜːtʃ] **1** *vt* (**a**) *(look in → room)* chercher (partout) dans; *(→ pockets, drawers)* fouiller (dans), chercher dans; **we've searched the whole house for the keys** nous avons cherché dans toute la maison pour retrouver les clés; **she searched her bag for a comb** elle fouilla dans son sac à la recherche d'un peigne

(**b**) *(of police, customs)* fouiller; *(with warrant)* perquisitionner, faire une perquisition dans; **the flat was searched for drugs** on a fouillé l'appartement pour trouver de la drogue; **the spectators were searched before they were let in** les spectateurs ont été fouillés à l'entrée; **they searched the undergrowth for the murder weapon** on a fouillé le sous-bois *ou* on a passé le sous-bois au peigne fin pour retrouver l'arme du crime; **customs searched our luggage/our car** les douaniers ont fouillé nos bagages/notre voiture; *Fam* **search me!** je n'en ai pas la moindre idée ❑!

(**c**) *(examine, consult → records)* chercher dans; *(→ memory)* chercher dans, fouiller; *(→ conscience)* sonder; *Comput (→ file, directory)* rechercher dans; **I searched her face for some sign of emotion** j'ai cherché sur son visage des signes d'émotion; *Comput* **to search and replace sth** rechercher et remplacer qch

2 *vi* chercher; **to search for sth** chercher qch, rechercher qch; **to search after the truth** rechercher la vérité; *Comput* **to search for a file** rechercher un fichier; **searching** *(on computer screen)* recherche

3 *n* (**a**) *(gen)* recherche *f*, recherches *fpl*; **in the search for** *or* **in my search for ancestors, I had to travel to Canada** au cours des recherches ou de mes recherches pour retrouver mes ancêtres, j'ai dû me rendre au Canada; **the search for the missing climbers has been resumed** les recherches ont repris pour retrouver les alpinistes disparus; **helicopters made a search for survivors** des hélicoptères ont fait *ou* effectué des recherches pour retrouver des survivants; **to make a search through one's pockets/the drawers** fouiller (dans) ses poches/les tiroirs; **search and rescue operation** opération *f* de recherche et secours

(**b**) *(by police, customs → of house, person, bags)* fouille *f*; *(→ with warrant)* perquisition *f*; **the police made a thorough search of the premises** la police a fouillé les locaux de fond en comble; **customs carried out a search of the van** les douaniers ont procédé à la fouille de la camionnette; **the search unearthed a stockpile of arms** la fouille a permis de mettre à jour une cache d'armes

(**c**) *Comput* recherche *f*; **to do a search** faire une recherche; **to do a search for sth** rechercher qch; **search and replace** recherche et remplacement *m*

4 in search of *prep* à la recherche de; **in search of the truth** à la recherche de la vérité; **I went in search of a restaurant** je suis parti à la recherche d'un restaurant

▸▸ *Comput* ***search engine*** moteur *m* de recherche; ***search party*** équipe *f* de secours; ***search warrant*** mandat *m* de perquisition

▸**search out** *vt sep (look for)* rechercher; *(find)* trouver, dénicher

▸**search through** *vt insep (drawer, pockets)* fouiller (dans); *(case, documents)* fouiller; *(records)* consulter, faire des recherches dans; *(memory)* fouiller, chercher dans

searchable ['sɜːtʃəbəl] interrogeable; **searchable database** base *f* de données interrogeable

searcher ['sɜːtʃə(r)] *n* chercheur(euse) *m,f*; **300 searchers combed the woods** 300 personnes ont passé les bois au peigne fin; **searchers after the truth** ceux qui sont à la recherche de la vérité

searching ['sɜːtʃɪŋ] **1** *n (of suspect, house, ship etc)* fouille *f*; *(at customs)* visite *f*; *Law* perquisition *f*

2 *adj* (**a**) *(look, eyes)* pénétrant; **he gave me a searching look** il m'a lancé un regard pénétrant (**b**) *(examination)* rigoureux, minutieux; **he asked me some searching questions** il m'a posé des questions inquisitrices

searchingly ['sɜːtʃɪŋlɪ] *adv (look)* de façon pénétrante; *(examine)* rigoureusement; *(question)* minutieusement

searchlight ['sɜːtʃlaɪt] *n* projecteur *m*; **to turn a searchlight on sth** braquer un projecteur sur qch; **in the searchlight** à la lumière des projecteurs

searing ['sɪərɪŋ] *adj* (**a**) *(pain)* fulgurant; *(light)* éclatant, fulgurant (**b**) *(attack, criticism)* sévère, impitoyable

Sears Roebuck® [ˌsɪəz'rəʊbʌk] *n* = grande chaîne de magasins américains

seascape ['siːskeɪp] *n* (**a**) *(view)* paysage *m* marin (**b**) *Art* marine *f*

seashell ['siːʃel] *n* coquillage *m*

seashore ['siːʃɔː(r)] *n (edge of sea)* rivage *m*, bord *m* de (la) mer; *(beach)* plage *f*

seasick ['siːsɪk] *adj* **to be seasick** avoir le mal de mer

seasickness ['siːsɪknɪs] *n* mal *m* de mer

seaside ['siːsaɪd] **1** *n* bord *m* de (la) mer; **we spent the afternoon at the seaside** nous avons passé l'après-midi au bord de la mer *ou* à la mer; **we live by** *or* **at the seaside** nous habitons au bord de la mer

2 *comp (holiday, vacation)* au bord de la mer, à la mer; *(town, hotel)* au bord de la mer, de bord de mer

▸▸ *Bot* ***seaside arrow grass*** triglochin *m* maritime; *Br* ***seaside landlady*** = propriétaire d'une pension de famille au bord de la mer

season ['siːzən] **1** *n* (**a**) *(summer, winter etc)* saison *f*

(**b**) *(for trade)* saison *f*; **the start of the tourist/of the holiday season** le début de la saison touristique/des vacances; **at the height of the Christmas season** en pleine période de Noël; **it's a busy season for tour operators** c'est une époque très chargée pour les voyagistes; **the low/high season** la basse/haute saison; **in season** en saison; **off season** hors saison

(**c**) *(for fruit, vegetables)* saison *f*; **strawberries are in/out of season** les fraises sont/ne sont pas de saison, c'est/ce n'est pas la saison des fraises

(**d**) *(for breeding)* époque *f*, période *f*; **to be in season** *(animal)* être en chaleur

(**e**) *(for sport, entertainment)* saison *f*; **the football season** la saison de football; **next season, he's playing for Liverpool** la saison prochaine, il joue dans l'équipe de Liverpool

(**f**) *(for show, actor)* saison *f*; **the summer season** la saison d'été; **he did a season at Brighton** il a fait la saison de Brighton; *Rad & TV* **a new season of French drama** un nouveau cycle de pièces de théâtre français

(**g**) *(for hunting)* saison *f*, période *f*; **the hunting/fishing season** la saison de la chasse/de la pêche; **the grouse season** la saison de (la chasse à) la grouse; **the start of the season** *Hunt* l'ouverture *f* de la chasse; *Fishing* l'ouverture *f* de la pêche

(**h**) *(for socializing)* saison *f*; **the social season** la saison mondaine; **the London/New York season** la saison londonienne/new-yorkaise

(**i**) *(Christmas)* **Season's Greetings** *(on card)* Joyeux Noël et Bonne Année

(**j**) *Literary (suitable moment)* moment *m* opportun; **in due season** en temps voulu, au moment opportun

2 *vt* (**a**) *(food → with seasoning)* assaisonner; *(→ with spice)* épicer; *Fig* **his speech was seasoned with witty remarks** son discours était parsemé *ou* agrémenté de remarques spirituelles

(**b**) *(timber)* (faire) sécher, laisser sécher; *(cask)* abreuver; *(wine)* mûrir

(**c**) *Formal (moderate)* modérer, tempérer

▸▸ ***season ticket*** (carte *f* d')abonnement *m*; **to take out a season ticket** prendre un abonnement; ***season ticket holder*** abonné(e) *m,f*

seasonable ['siːzənəbəl] *adj* (**a**) *(weather)* de saison (**b**) *(opportune)* à propos, opportun

seasonably ['siːzənəblɪ] *adv (opportunely)* opportunément, à propos

seasonal ['siːzənəl] *adj* saisonnier

▸▸ *Econ* ***seasonal adjustment*** ajustement *m* saisonnier; ***seasonal affective disorder*** dépression *f* saisonnière; ***seasonal employment*** emploi *m* saisonnier; ***seasonal fluctuation*** fluctuation *f* saisonnière; ***seasonal worker*** saisonnier(ère) *m,f*

seasonally ['siːzənəlɪ] *adv* de façon saisonnière

▸▸ *Econ* ***seasonally adjusted statistics*** statistiques *fpl* corrigées des variations saisonnières, statistiques *fpl* désaisonnalisées

seasoned ['siːzənd] *adj* (**a**) *(food)* assaisonné, épicé; **highly seasoned** bien épicé *ou* relevé (**b**) *(wood)* desséché, séché; *(wine)* mûr (**c**) *(experienced)* expérimenté, chevronné, éprouvé; **a seasoned political campaigner** un (une) militant(e) politique chevronné(e); **a seasoned traveller** un (une) voyageur(euse) expérimenté(e)

seasoning ['siːzənɪŋ] *n* (**a**) *(process → of food)* assaisonnement *m* (**b**) *(process → of wood)* séchage *m*; *(→ of wine)* maturation *f*; *(→ of cask)* abreuvage *m* (**c**) *(condiment)* assaisonnement *m*, condiment *m*

seat [siːt] **1** *n* (**a**) *(chair, stool)* siège *m*; *(on bicycle)* selle *f*; *(in car → single)* siège *m*; *(→ bench)* banquette *f*; *(on train, at table)* place *f*; *(of toilet)* lunette *f*, siège *m*; **take a seat** asseyez-vous, prenez un siège; **please stay in your seats** restez assis s'il vous plaît; **keep a seat for me** gardez-moi une place

(**b**) *(accommodation, place → in theatre, cinema, train)* place *f*; *(space to sit)* place *f* (assise); **I'd like to book two seats for tomorrow** je voudrais réserver deux places pour demain; **please take your seats** veuillez prendre *ou* gagner vos places; **there were no seats left** il n'y avait plus de places; **I couldn't find a seat on the train** je n'ai pas pu trouver de place (assise) dans le train

(**c**) *(of trousers)* fond *m*; *(of chair)* siège *m*; *(buttocks)* derrière *m*; **they grabbed him by the seat of his pants** ils l'ont attrapé par le fond du pantalon; *Fam* **by the seat of one's pants** de justesse ❑

(**d**) *Pol* siège *m*; **he kept/lost his seat** il a été/il n'a pas été réélu; **she has a seat in Parliament** elle est députée; **he was elected to a seat on the council** *(municipal)* il a été élu conseiller municipal; *(commercial)* il a été élu au conseil; **the government has a thirty-seat majority** le gouvernement a une majorité de trente sièges

(**e**) *(centre → of commerce)* centre *m*; *Admin* siège *m*; *Med (of disease, infection)* foyer *m*; **the seat of government/of learning** le siège du gouvernement/du savoir

(**f**) *(manor)* **(country) seat** manoir *m*

(**g**) *Horseriding* **to have a good seat** se tenir bien en selle, avoir une bonne assiette; **to lose one's seat** être désarçonné

(**h**) *Tech (of valve)* siège *m*; *(of machine)* embase *f*, surface *f* d'appui

2 *vt* (**a**) *(passengers, children)* faire asseoir;

(guests → at table) placer; **please be seated** veuillez vous asseoir; **please remain seated** restez *ou* veuillez rester assis

(**b**) *(accommodate)* avoir des places assises pour; **the plane can seat four hundred** l'avion a une capacité de quatre cents personnes; **how many does the bus seat?** combien y a-t-il de places assises dans le bus?; **how many does the table seat?** combien de personnes peut-on asseoir autour de la table?; **we can only seat forty people** nous n'avons de place que pour quarante personnes

(**c**) *(chair)* mettre un fond à; *(with straw)* rempailler; *(with cane)* canner

(**d**) *Tech (valve)* ajuster le siège de

3 *vi (skirt, trousers)* se déformer (à l'arrière)

►► ***seat belt*** ceinture *f* de sécurité

seatback ['siːtbæk] *n* dossier *m*

-seater ['siːtə(r)] *suff* **two/four-seater (car)** voiture *f* à deux/quatre places

seating ['siːtɪŋ] *n (UNCOUNT)* (**a**) *(seats)* sièges *mpl*; *(benches, pews)* bancs *mpl*; **the seating isn't very comfortable** les sièges ne sont pas très confortables

(**b**) *(sitting accommodation)* places *fpl* (assises); **there's additional seating at the back** il y a des places (assises) supplémentaires au fond; **there's seating for three hundred in the hall** il y a trois cents places dans la salle; **there's seating for eight round this table** on peut asseoir huit personnes autour de cette table

(**c**) *(plan)* affectation *f* des places; **who's in charge of the seating?** qui est chargé de placer les gens?

(**d**) *(material → cloth, canvas)* (tissu *m* du) siège *m*; *(→ wicker)* cannage *m*

(**e**) *Tech (of bearing)* logement *m*; *(of valve)* siège *m*

►► ***seating accommodation*** nombre *m* de places assises; **the hall has seating accommodation for eight hundred people** la salle a une capacité de huit cents places (assises); ***seating arrangements*** le placement *ou* la disposition des gens; ***seating capacity*** nombre *m* de places assises; **the theatre has a seating capacity of five hundred** il y a cinq cents places dans le théâtre; ***the seating plan*** *(in theatre)* plan *m* de la disposition des places; *(at table)* plan *m* de table

SEATO ['siːtəʊ] *n Formerly (abbr* **Southeast Asia Treaty Organization**) OTASE *f*

seat-of-the-pants *adj Fam* **the project has been a bit of a seat-of-the-pants operation** le projet a été mené au pif

seatwork ['siːtwɜːk] *n Am (UNCOUNT)* travail *m* sur table

seaward ['siːwəd] **1** *adj* de (la) mer; **on the seaward side** du côté de la mer

2 *adv* vers la mer *ou* le large

►► ***seaward breeze*** brise *f* de mer

seawards ['siːwədz] *adv* vers la mer *ou* le large; **to sail seawards** mettre le cap au large

seawater ['siːˌwɔːtə(r)] *n* eau *f* de mer

►► ***seawater therapy*** thalassothérapie *f*

seaway ['siːweɪ] *n* route *f* maritime

seaweed ['siːwiːd] *n (UNCOUNT)* algues *fpl*; **a piece of seaweed** une algue

seaworthiness ['siːˌwɜːðɪnɪs] *n* navigabilité *f*

seaworthy ['siːˌwɜːðɪ] *adj (boat)* en état de naviguer

sebaceous [sɪ'beɪʃəs] *adj Anat* sébacé

sebacic [sɪ'bæsɪk] *adj Chem* sébacique

Sebastopol [sɪ'bæstəpəl] *n* Sébastopol

sebiferous [se'bɪfərəs], **sebific** [se'bɪfɪk] *adj Anat & Bot* sébifère

seborrhoea, *Am* **seborrhea** [ˌsebə'riːə] *n Med* séborrhée *f*

seborrhoeic, *Am* **seborrheic** [ˌsebə'riːɪk] *adj Med* séborrhéique

sebum ['siːbəm] *n Anat* sébum *m*

SEC [ˌesiː'siː] *n (abbr* **Securities and Exchange Commission**) = commission américaine des opérations de Bourse, ≃ COB *f*

sec [sek] *n Fam (abbr* **second**) seconde ❑ *f*, instant ❑ *m*; **in a sec!** une seconde!; **I'll only be a sec** j'en ai pour une seconde

SECAM ['siːkæm] *n TV (abbr* **séquentiel couleur à mémoire**) Secam *m*

secant ['siːkənt] *Math* **1** *adj* sécant

2 *n* sécante *f*

secateurs [ˌsekə'tɜːz] *npl Br* **(pair of) secateurs** sécateur *m*

secede [sɪ'siːd] *vi* faire sécession, se séparer; **they voted to secede from the federation** ils ont voté en faveur de leur sécession de la fédération

seceder [sɪ'siːdə(r)] *n Pol* sécessionniste *mf*, séparatiste *mf*; *Rel* dissident(e) *m,f*

seceding [sɪ'siːdɪŋ] *adj Pol* sécessionniste; *Rel* dissident

secession [sɪ'seʃən] *n* sécession *f*, scission *f*

secessionism [sɪ'seʃənɪzəm] *n* sécessionnisme *m*

secessionist [sɪ'seʃənɪst] **1** *adj* sécessionniste

2 *n* sécessionniste *mf*, séparatiste *mf*

sech [sek, sek'eɪtʃ] *n Math* sécante *f* hyperbolique

seclude [sɪ'kluːd] *vt* éloigner du monde, isoler; **they are secluded from the world** ils sont retirés du monde; **she secludes herself from contact with society** elle se coupe de tout contact avec autrui

secluded [sɪ'kluːdɪd] *adj (village)* retiré, à l'écart; *(garden)* tranquille; **to live a secluded life** mener une vie solitaire, vivre en reclus; **I tried to find a secluded corner to read** j'ai essayé de trouver un coin tranquille pour lire

seclusion [sɪ'kluːʒən] *n (isolation → chosen)* solitude *f*, isolement *m*; *(→ imposed)* isolement *m*; **he lives a life of total seclusion** il vit en solitaire *ou* retiré du monde; **the seclusion of women** l'isolement *m* des femmes

SECOND [1] ['sekənd]

seconde	► 1 (a) – (c), (f), (h)
second	► 1 (d); 2 (a), (b)
deuxième	► 1 (d); 2 (a), (b)
en seconde place	► 3 (a)
deuxièmement	► 3 (c)

1 *n* (**a**) *(unit of time)* seconde *f*; **the ambulance arrived within seconds** l'ambulance est arrivée en quelques secondes

(**b**) *(instant)* seconde *f*, instant *m*; **I'll be with you in a second** je serai à vous dans un instant; **I'll only be a second** j'en ai seulement pour deux secondes; **just a** *or* **half a second!** une seconde!

(**c**) *Math & Astron* seconde *f*

(**d**) *(in order)* second(e) *m,f*, deuxième *mf*; **I was the second to arrive** je suis arrivé deuxième *ou* le deuxième; **to come a close second** *(in race)* être battu de justesse

(**e**) *(in duel)* témoin *m*, second *m*; *(in boxing)* soigneur *m*; **seconds out!** soigneurs hors du ring!

(**f**) *Aut* seconde *f*; **in second** en seconde

(**g**) *Br Univ* **an upper/lower second** une licence avec mention bien/assez bien

(**h**) *Mus* seconde *f*; **major/minor second** seconde *f* majeure/mineure

2 *adj* (**a**) *(in series)* deuxième; *(of two)* second; **every second person** une personne sur deux; **Charles the Second** Charles Deux *ou* II; **the second of March** le deux mars; **for the second time** pour la deuxième fois; **to be second in command** *(in hierarchy)* être deuxième dans la hiérarchie; *Mil* commander en second; **he's second in line for promotion** il sera le second à bénéficier d'une promotion; **he's second in line for the throne** c'est le deuxième dans l'ordre de succession au trône; *Gram* **in the second person singular/plural** à la deuxième personne du singulier/pluriel; **to take second place** *(in race)* prendre la deuxième place; *(in exam)* être deuxième; **his wife took second place to his career** sa femme venait après sa carrière; **and in the second place...** *(in demonstration, argument)* et en deuxième lieu...; **it's second nature to her** c'est une seconde nature chez elle; **he's second only to his teacher as a violinist** en tant que violoniste, il n'y a que son professeur qui le surpasse *ou* qui lui soit supérieur; **as a goalkeeper, he's second to none** comme gardien de but, il n'a pas son pareil; **her short stories are second to none** ses nouvelles sont inégalées *ou* sans pareil

(**b**) *(another, additional)* deuxième, second, autre; **a second Camus/Churchill** un nouveau Camus/Churchill; **he was given a second chance (in life)** on lui a accordé une seconde chance (dans la vie); **you are unlikely to get a second chance to join the team** il est peu probable que l'on vous propose à nouveau de faire partie de l'équipe; **to take a second helping** se resservir; **would you like a second helping/a second cup?** en reprendrez-vous (un peu/une goutte)?; **can I have a second helping of meat?** est-ce que je peux reprendre de la viande?; **they have a second home in France** ils ont une résidence secondaire en France; **France is my second home** la France est ma seconde patrie; **I'd like a second opinion** *(said by doctor)* je voudrais prendre l'avis d'un confrère; *(said by patient)* je voudrais consulter un autre médecin; **I need a second opinion on these results** j'aimerais avoir l'avis d'un tiers sur ces résultats; **to have second thoughts** avoir des doutes, hésiter; **are you having second thoughts?** est-ce que vous hésitez?; **he left his family without a second thought** il a quitté sa famille sans réfléchir *ou* sans se poser de questions; **on second** *Br* **thoughts** *or Am* **thought I'd better go myself** réflexion faite, il vaut mieux que j'y aille moi-même

3 *adv* (**a**) *(in order)* en seconde place; **to come second** *(in race)* arriver en seconde position; **she arrived second** *(at party, meeting)* elle est arrivée la deuxième; **the horse came second to Juniper's Lad** le cheval s'est classé deuxième derrière Juniper's Lad

(**b**) *(with superlative adj)* **he's the second oldest player in the team** après le doyen de l'équipe c'est lui le plus vieux; **the second largest/second richest** le second par la taille/second par le revenu; **the second largest city in the world/in Portugal** la deuxième ville du monde/du Portugal

(**c**) *(secondly)* en second lieu, deuxièmement

4 *vt (motion)* appuyer; *(speaker)* appuyer la motion de; **I'll second that!** je suis d'accord!

5 *npl* **seconds** (**a**) *Com (goods)* articles *mpl* de second choix; *(crockery)* vaisselle *f* de second choix

(**b**) *Fam (of food)* rab *m*; **are there any seconds?** il y a du rab?

►► ***second ballot*** deuxième tour *m*; ***second base*** *(in baseball)* deuxième base *f*; ***second best*** **1** *n* pis-aller *m inv*; **I refuse to make do with second best** je refuse de me contenter d'un pis-aller; **she knew she would never be more than second best** *(in person's affection)* elle savait qu'elle ne serait jamais plus qu'un second choix; *(athlete)* elle savait qu'elle serait toujours deuxième **2** *adv* **to come off second best** être battu, se faire battre; *Pol* ***second chamber*** *(gen)* deuxième chambre *f*; *(in UK)* Chambre *f* des lords; *(in US)* Sénat *m*; ***second childhood*** gâtisme *m*, seconde enfance *f*; **he's in his second childhood** il est retombé en enfance; *Rail* ***second class*** seconde *f* (classe *f*); *Rel* ***the Second Coming*** le second avènement du Messie; ***second cousin*** cousin(e) *m,f* issu(e) de germains; *Br* ***second eleven*** *(in soccer, cricket)* équipe *f* de réserve *(dans le cadre scolaire ou amateur)*; ***second floor*** *(in UK)* deuxième étage *m*; *(in US)* premier étage *m*; *Aut* ***second gear*** seconde *f*; *Am Sch* ***second grade*** = classe de primaire pour les 6–7 ans; *Sport* ***second half*** deuxième mi-temps *f inv*; ***second hand*** *(of watch, clock)* aiguille *f* des secondes, trotteuse *f*; ***second language*** deuxième langue *f*; *Journ* ***second lead*** gros titre *m* de deuxième ordre; ***second lieutenant*** *(in army)* ≃ sous-lieutenant *m*; *Belg & Suisse* ≃ lieutenant *m*; *(in air force)* ≃ sous-lieutenant *m*; ***second name*** nom *m* de famille; *Naut* ***second officer*** (officier *m* en) second *m*; ***second row*** *(in rugby)* deuxième ligne *f*; ***second showing*** deuxième représentation *f*; ***second sight*** seconde *ou* double vue *f*; **to have second sight** avoir un don de double vue; *Mil* ***second strike*** seconde frappe *f*, deuxième frappe *f*; *Sport* ***second team*** équipe *f* de réserve; ***second teeth*** deuxième dentition *f*, dentition *f* définitive; *Mus* ***second violin*** deuxième violon *m*

second² [sɪ'kɒnd] *vt Br (employee)* détacher, envoyer en détachement; *Mil* détacher; **she**

was seconded to the UN elle a été détachée à l'ONU; **Peter was seconded for service abroad** Peter a été envoyé en détachement à l'étranger

secondary ['sekəndərɪ] (*pl* **secondaries**) **1** *adj* (**a**) *(gen) & Med* secondaire; *(minor)* secondaire, de peu d'importance; **the word has a secondary meaning** le mot a un sens secondaire; **this issue is of secondary importance** cette question est d'une importance secondaire; **it's only a secondary problem** c'est un problème secondaire *ou* qui a peu d'importance; **any other considerations are secondary to her wellbeing** son bien-être prime sur toute autre considération

(**b**) *Sch* secondaire

2 *n* (**a**) *(deputy)* subordonné(e) *m,f*, adjoint(e) *m,f*

(**b**) *Astron* satellite *m*

(**c**) *Med (tumour)* tumeur *f* secondaire, métastase *f*

▸▸ *Ling* ***secondary accent*** accent *m* secondaire; *Phil* ***secondary cause*** cause *f* seconde; *Elec* ***secondary cell*** accumulateur *m*; ***secondary colour*** couleur *f* secondaire *ou* binaire; ***secondary data*** informations *fpl ou* données *fpl* secondaires; ***secondary education*** enseignement *m* secondaire *ou* du second degré; *Phys* ***secondary emission*** émission *f* secondaire; *Geol* ***secondary era*** (ère *f*) secondaire *m*; *Br* ***secondary modern (school)*** = établissement secondaire d'enseignement général et technique, aujourd'hui remplacé par la "comprehensive school"; *Br Ind* ***secondary picketing*** *(UNCOUNT)* piquets *mpl* de grève de solidarité; ***secondary product*** sous-produit *m*; ***secondary production*** production *f* manufacturée; *Transp* ***secondary road*** route *f* secondaire *ou* départementale; ***secondary school*** = établissement secondaire, *Can & Suisse* école *f* secondaire; ***secondary school teacher*** professeur *m* du secondaire; *Econ* ***secondary sector*** secteur *m* secondaire; *Ling* ***secondary stress*** accent *m* secondaire

second-best *adj (clothes, objects)* de tous les jours

second-class 1 *adj* (**a**) *Rail* de seconde (classe); **two second-class returns to Glasgow** deux allers (et) retours pour Glasgow en seconde (classe); **a second-class season ticket** un abonnement de seconde

(**b**) *(hotel)* de seconde catégorie

(**c**) *(mail)* à tarif réduit *ou* lent

(**d**) *(inferior)* de qualité inférieure

2 *adv* (**a**) *Rail* en seconde (classe); **to travel second-class** voyager en seconde

(**b**) *(for mail)* **to send a parcel second-class** expédier un paquet en tarif réduit

▸▸ ***second-class citizen*** citoyen(enne) *m,f* de seconde zone; **to be treated like a second-class citizen** être traité comme un citoyen de seconde zone; *Br Univ* ***second-class honours degree*** ≃ licence *f* avec mention (assez) bien

SECOND-CLASS MAIL

Le tarif postal réduit est utilisé en Grande-Bretagne pour les lettres et les paquets non urgents. Aux États-Unis, il est réservé aux magazines et aux journaux.

second-degree *adj*

▸▸ ***second-degree burn*** brûlure *f* au deuxième degré; *Am Law* ***second-degree murder*** meurtre *m* sans préméditation

seconder ['sekəndə(r)] *n* (**a**) *(in debate → of motion)* personne *f* qui appuie une motion (**b**) *(of candidate)* deuxième parrain *m*

second-generation *adj (immigrant, computer)* de la seconde génération

second-guess *vt Fam* (**a**) *(after event)* comprendre après coup ❑ (**b**) *(before event)* essayer de prévoir *ou* d'anticiper ❑

second-hand 1 *adj* (**a**) *(car, clothes, books)* d'occasion; **the second-hand market** le marché de l'occasion (**b**) *(information)* de seconde main

2 *adv* (**a**) *(buy)* d'occasion (**b**) *(indirectly)* **I heard the news second-hand** j'ai appris la nouvelle indirectement

▸▸ ***second-hand dealer*** *(gen)* marchand(e) *m,f* d'articles d'occasion; *(in clothes)* fripier(ère) *m,f*; *(in books)* bouquiniste *mf*; ***second-hand market*** marché *m* de revente; ***second-hand shop*** magasin *m* d'articles d'occasion

second-in-command *n Mil* commandant *m* en second; *Naut* second *m*, officier *m* en second; *(in hierarchy)* second *m*, adjoint *m*

secondly ['sekəndlɪ] *adv* deuxièmement, en deuxième lieu

secondment [sɪ'kɒndmənt] *n Br Formal* détachement *m*, affectation *f* provisoire; **to be on secondment** *(teacher)* être en détachement; *(diplomat)* être en mission

second-rate *adj (goods, equipment)* de qualité inférieure; *(movie, book)* médiocre; *(politician, player)* médiocre, de second ordre

second-row forward *n (in rugby)* (avant *m* de) deuxième ligne *f*

second-strike *adj Mil (weapons)* de seconde *ou* deuxième frappe

second-string *adj Am Sport* remplaçant

secrecy ['si:krəsɪ] *n (UNCOUNT)* secret *m*; **why all the secrecy?** pourquoi tous ces secrets?; **the negotiations were carried out in the strictest secrecy** les négociations ont été menées dans le plus grand secret; **absolute secrecy is vital to the success of the mission** le secret absolu est essentiel pour le succès de la mission; **there's no secrecy about their financial dealings** ils ne font aucun mystère de leurs affaires financières

secret ['si:krɪt] **1** *n* (**a**) *(information kept hidden)* secret *m*; **it's a secret between you and me** c'est un secret entre nous; **I have no secrets from her** je ne lui cache rien; **can you keep a secret?** pouvez-vous garder un secret?; **it can be our little secret** ça sera notre petit secret à nous; **shall we let them into the secret?** est-ce qu'on va les mettre dans le secret *ou* dans la confidence?; **I'll tell you** *or* **I'll let you into a secret** je vais vous dire *ou* révéler un secret; **not many people were in on the secret** il n'y avait pas beaucoup de gens qui étaient dans la confidence *ou* au courant; **I make no secret of** *or* **about my humble origins** je ne cache pas mes origines modestes

(**b**) *(explanation)* secret *m*; **the secret of his success** le secret de sa réussite; **the secret is to warm the dish first** le secret consiste à chauffer le plat d'abord; **the secret of making pastry** le secret pour réussir une pâte

(**c**) *(mystery)* secret *m*, mystère *m*; **the secrets of nature** les secrets *mpl ou* les mystères *mpl* de la nature; **these locks have** *or* **hold no secret for me** ces serrures n'ont pas de secret pour moi

2 *adj* (**a**) *(meeting, plan)* secret(ète); **the news was kept secret** la nouvelle a été gardée *ou* tenue secrète, on n'a pas révélé la nouvelle; **to keep sth secret** tenir qch secret

(**b**) *(personal)* secret(ète); **it's my secret belief that he doesn't really love her** je crois secrètement *ou* en mon for intérieur qu'il ne l'aime pas vraiment

(**c**) *(hidden → door)* caché, dérobé; *(→ compartment, safe)* caché; **a secret hiding place** une cachette secrète; *Literary* **the secret places of the heart** les plis et les replis du cœur

(**d**) *(identity)* inconnu; **the flowers were from a secret admirer of hers** les fleurs venaient d'un admirateur inconnu

(**e**) *(secluded → beach, garden)* retiré, secret(ète)

3 in secret *adv* en secret, secrètement

▸▸ ***secret agent*** agent *m* secret; ***secret ballot*** vote *m* à bulletin secret; ***secret funds*** caisse *f* noire, fonds *mpl* secrets; ***secret police*** police *f* secrète; ***secret service*** *(government organization)* services *mpl* secrets; ***the Secret Service*** = service de protection des hauts fonctionnaires américains et de leurs familles; *Literature* ***the Secret Seven*** le Clan des Sept

secretaire [,sekrɪ'teə(r)] *n* secrétaire *m (meuble)*

secretarial [,sekrə'teərɪəl] *adj (tasks)* de secrétaire, de secrétariat; **I have a part-time secretarial job** j'ai un travail de secrétaire à mi-temps; **I followed a secretarial course** j'ai pris des cours de secrétariat

▸▸ ***secretarial college, secretarial school*** école *f* de secrétariat; ***secretarial skills*** notions *fpl* de secrétariat; ***the secretarial staff*** le secrétariat; ***secretarial work*** travail *m* de secrétaire; **she does secretarial work** elle fait un travail de secrétariat *ou* de secrétaire

secretariat [,sekrə'teərɪət] *n* secrétariat *m*

secretary [*Br* 'sekrətərɪ, *Am* 'sekrə,terɪ] (*pl* **secretaries**) *n* (**a**) *(gen) & Com* secrétaire *mf* (**b**) *Pol (in UK → minister)* ministre *m*; *(→ non-elected official)* secrétaire *mf* d'État; *(in US)* secrétaire *mf* d'État (**c**) *(diplomat)* secrétaire *mf* d'ambassade

▸▸ *Orn* ***secretary bird*** serpentaire *m*, secrétaire *m*; ***secretary of state*** *(in UK)* ministre *m*; *(in US)* secrétaire *mf* d'État, ministre *m* des Affaires étrangères

secretary-general *n* secrétaire *mf* général(e)

secretaryship ['sekrətərɪʃɪp] *n* secrétariat *m*

secrete [sɪ'kri:t] *vt* (**a**) *Anat & Med* sécréter (**b**) *Formal (hide)* cacher

secretion [sɪ'kri:ʃən] *n* (**a**) *Anat & Med* sécrétion *f* (**b**) *Formal (act of hiding)* action *f* de cacher

secretive ['si:krətɪv] *adj (nature)* secret(ète); *(behaviour)* cachottier; **she's very secretive about her new job** elle ne dit pas grand-chose de son nouveau travail; **she's quite a secretive person** c'est une personne assez secrète; **why are you being so secretive about it?** pourquoi fais-tu tant de cachotteries là-dessus?

secretively ['si:krətɪvlɪ] *adv* en cachette, secrètement

secretiveness ['si:krətɪvnɪs] *n (UNCOUNT) (of character)* réserve *f*; *(keeping secrets)* cachotteries *fpl*

secretly ['si:krɪtlɪ] *adv (do, act)* en secret, secrètement; *(believe, think)* en son for intérieur, secrètement

secretory [sɪ'kri:tərɪ] *Biol* **1** *adj (duct)* sécréteur; *(process)* sécrétoire

2 *n* organe *m* sécréteur

sect [sekt] *n* secte *f*

sectarian [sek'teərɪən] **1** *n* sectaire *mf*

2 *adj* sectaire

▸▸ ***sectarian killing*** assassinat *m* sectaire; ***sectarian violence*** violence *f* d'origine religieuse

sectarianism [sek'teərɪənɪzəm] *n* sectarisme *m*

sectary ['sektərɪ] (*pl* **sectaries**) *n (member of sect)* membre *m* d'une secte

sectile ['sektaɪl] *adj* sécable

section ['sekʃən] **1** *n* (**a**) *(sector)* section *f*, partie *f*; **the business section of the community** les commerçants et les hommes d'affaires de notre communauté; **there has been snow over large sections of Southern England** il a neigé sur une grande partie du sud de l'Angleterre; **the residential section of the town** les quartiers résidentiels de la ville

(**b**) *(division → of company, staff, services)* section *f*; *(→ in army)* groupe *m* de combat; *(→ in orchestra)* section *f*

(**c**) *(component part → of furniture)* élément *m*; *(→ of tube)* section *f*; *(→ of track, road)* section *f*, tronçon *m*; *Rail* section *f*; **the kitchen units/the shelves come in easy-to-assemble sections** les éléments de cuisine/les étagères se vendent en kit

(**d**) *(subdivision → of law)* article *m*; *(→ of book, exam, text)* section *f*, partie *f*; *(of newspaper → page)* page *f*; *(→ pages)* pages *fpl*; *(→ of library)* section *f*; **the children's section** la section pour enfants; **the sports/women's section** les pages *fpl* des sports/réservées aux femmes

(**e**) *(in department store)* rayon *m*; **furniture/children's section** rayon *m* meubles/enfants

(**f**) *Am Rail (train)* train *m* supplémentaire; *(sleeper)* compartiment-lits *m*

(**g**) *(cut, cross-section → drawing)* coupe *f*, section *f*; *Geom* section *f*; *(→ for microscope)* coupe *f*, lamelle *f*; *(→ in metal)* profilé *m*

(**h**) *Med* sectionnement *m*

(**i**) *Am (land)* = division (administrative) d'un mille carré

2 *vt* (**a**) *(divide into sections)* sectionner

(**b**) *Br (send to psychiatric hospital)* interner

▸▸ *Am* ***Section Eight*** = disposition réglementant la réforme militaire pour raisons psychiatriques; *Am Rail* ***section gang*** (équipe *f* de) terrassiers *mpl*; *Am Rail* ***section hand*** terrassier *m*; *Typ* ***section mark*** signe *m* de paragraphe

▸**section off** *vt sep* séparer; **part of the church was sectioned off** l'accès à une partie de l'église était interdit

SECTION 28

Introduite par le gouvernement de Margaret Thatcher, la "Section 28" (ainsi nommée car il s'agit de l'article 28 du "Local Government Act" de 1986) avait pour but d'empêcher les enseignants d'aborder le thème de l'homosexualité dans les écoles et les collèges. Le gouvernement travailliste, élu en 1997, affirma sa volonté de révoquer cette clause. En Angleterre et au pays de Galles, la Chambre des lords s'oppose toujours à sa révocation. En Écosse, le parlement décida de ne pas tenir compte de l'opposition des lords et révoqua la clause en l'an 2000 malgré une campagne d'opposition de grande envergure menée par l'Église et renforcée par un référendum dont le financement privé donna lieu à une vive polémique.

sectional ['sekʃənəl] **1** *adj* (**a**) *(furniture)* en kit (**b**) *(interests)* d'un groupe (**c**) *(drawing)* en coupe
2 *n Am (sofa)* canapé *m* d'angle

sectionalism ['sekʃənəlɪzəm] *n* défense *f* des intérêts régionaux *ou* d'un groupe

sectionalize, -ise ['sekʃənəlaɪz] *vt* sectionner

sector ['sektə(r)] **1** *n* (**a**) *(area, realm)* secteur *m*, domaine *m*; *Econ* secteur *m*; *(part, subdivision)* secteur *m*, partie *f*; *Comput (of screen, disk)* secteur *m*; **the banking sector** le secteur bancaire; **whole sectors of society live below the poverty line** des catégories sociales entières vivent en dessous du seuil de pauvreté
(**b**) *Mil* secteur *m*, zone *f*
(**c**) *Geom* secteur *m*
(**d**) *(for measuring)* compas *m* de proportion
2 *vt (gen)* diviser en secteurs; *Admin & Geog* sectoriser

sectoral ['sektərəl] *adj* sectoriel

sectorial [sek'tɔːrɪəl] *adj* (**a**) *(sectoral)* sectoriel (**b**) *Zool (tooth)* incisif

secular ['sekjʊlə(r)] *adj* (**a**) *(life, clergy)* séculier (**b**) *(education, school)* laïque (**c**) *(music, art)* profane (**d**) *(ancient)* séculaire (**e**) *Astron* séculaire

secularism ['sekjʊlərɪzəm] *n* laïcisme *m*

secularist ['sekjʊlərɪst] **1** *n* laïciste *mf*
2 *adj* laïciste

secularity [ˌsekjʊ'lærɪtɪ] *n* (**a**) *(of clergy)* sécularité *f*; *(of education)* laïcité *f* (**b**) *Astron* caractère *m* séculaire

secularization [ˌsekjʊləraɪ'zeɪʃən] *n* sécularisation *f*; *(of education)* laïcisation *f*

secularize, -ise ['sekjʊləraɪz] *vt* séculariser; *(education)* laïciser

secure [sɪ'kjʊə(r)] **1** *adj* (**a**) *(protected)* sûr, en sécurité, en sûreté; **put the papers in a secure place** mettez les papiers en lieu sûr; **to be put in secure accommodation** être placé sous bonne garde; **I feel secure from** *or* **against attack** je me sens à l'abri des attaques
(**b**) *(guaranteed → job)* sûr; *(→ victory, future)* assuré; **a country must ensure its borders are secure** un pays doit assurer ses frontières *ou* faire en sorte que ses frontières soient sûres
(**c**) *(calm, confident)* tranquille, sécurisé; **now she's married, she feels more secure** maintenant qu'elle est mariée, elle se sent plus sécurisée; **I was secure in the belief that all danger was past** j'étais intimement persuadé que tout danger était écarté
(**d**) *(solid → investment, base)* sûr; *(→ foothold, grasp)* sûr, ferme; *(solidly fastened → bolt, window)* bien fermé; *(→ scaffolding, aerial)* solide, qui tient bien; *(→ knot)* solide; **can you make the door/the rope secure?** pouvez-vous vous assurer que la porte est bien fermée/la corde est bien attachée?
2 *vt* (**a**) *Formal (obtain)* se procurer, obtenir; *(agreement)* obtenir; *(loan)* obtenir, se voir accorder; **to secure a majority** *(gen)* obtenir une majorité; *Pol* emporter la majorité; **to secure the release of sb** obtenir la libération de qn; **will it be possible to secure a hall for the debate?** serait-il possible de réserver une salle pour le débat?
(**b**) *(fasten, fix → rope)* attacher; *(→ parcel)* ficeler; *(→ ladder, aerial)* bien fixer; *(→ window, lock)* bien fermer; *(→ cargo)* arrimer; **the rope was secured around a rock** la corde était solidement attachée à un rocher; **secure the ladder against the wall first** assurez-vous d'abord que l'échelle est bien appuyée contre le mur; **doors and windows should be properly secured** les portes et les fenêtres doivent être bien fermées
(**c**) *(guarantee → future)* assurer; *(→ debt)* garantir; *(→ borrower)* garantir; **that secured his future with the company** cela a assuré son avenir dans l'entreprise
(**d**) *(from danger)* préserver, protéger; **to secure a pass** *(in mountains)* garder un défilé; **we did everything we could to secure the boat against** *or* **from the storm** nous avons tout fait pour protéger le bateau contre la tempête
▸▸ *Comput* ***secure electronic transaction*** protocole *m* SET; *Comput* ***secure HTTP*** protocole *m* HTTP sécurisé; *Comput* ***secure server*** serveur *m* sécurisé; *Comput* ***secure sockets layer*** protocole *m* SSL; ***secure tenancy*** location *f* assurée *ou* garantie; ***secure unit*** *(in psychiatric hospital)* quartier *m* de haute sécurité; *(in children's home)* section *f* surveillée; *Comput* ***secure Web site*** site *m* sécurisé

secured [sɪ'kjʊəd] *adj Fin (debt, loan)* garanti
▸▸ *Fin* ***secured bond*** obligation *f* cautionnée; ***secured creditor*** créancier(ère) *m,f* privilégié(e); ***secured debenture*** obligation *f* cautionnée; ***secured debt*** créance *f* garantie; ***secured loan*** prêt *m* garanti

securely [sɪ'kjʊəlɪ] *adv* (**a**) *(firmly)* fermement, solidement; **the door was securely fastened** la porte était bien fermée *ou* verrouillée (**b**) *(safely)* en sécurité, en sûreté; **put the jewels securely away** mettez les bijoux en lieu sûr; **he is securely behind bars** il est hors d'état de nuire

securitization [sɪˌkjʊərɪtaɪ'zeɪʃən] *n St Exch* titrisation *f*

securitize, -ise [sɪ'kjʊərɪtaɪz] *vt St Exch* titriser

security [sɪ'kjʊərətɪ] (*pl* **securities**) **1** *n* (**a**) *(safety)* sécurité *f*; **terrorism is a threat to national security** le terrorisme menace la sécurité nationale; **the President's national security advisers** les conseillers du président en matière de sécurité nationale; **she's considered to be a security risk** on considère qu'elle représente un risque pour la sécurité; **they slipped through the security net** ils sont passés au travers des mailles du filet des services de sécurité
(**b**) *(police measures, protection etc)* sécurité *f*; **for reasons of security** par mesure de *ou* pour des raisons de sécurité; **there was maximum security for the President's visit** des mesures de sécurité exceptionnelles ont été prises pour la visite du président; **maximum security wing** *(in prison)* quartier *m* de haute surveillance
(**c**) *(UNCOUNT) (assurance)* sécurité *f*; **job security** sécurité *f* de l'emploi; **to have security of tenure** *(in job)* être titulaire, avoir la sécurité de l'emploi; *(as tenant)* avoir un bail qui ne peut être résilié; **what she really needs is emotional security** ce qu'il lui faut vraiment c'est une sécurité affective; **financial security** sécurité *f* matérielle *ou* financière
(**d**) *(guarantee)* garantie *f*, caution *f*; **what security do you have for the loan?** quelle garantie avez-vous pour couvrir ce prêt?; **to give sth as security** donner qch en cautionnement; **to lend money on security** prêter de l'argent sur nantissement *ou* sur garantie; **have you anything to put up as security?** qu'est-ce que vous pouvez fournir comme garantie?; **she gave her diamonds as security for the loan** elle a donné ses diamants comme garantie pour le prêt; **loans without security** prêts *mpl* sans garantie
(**e**) *(guarantor)* garant(e) *m,f*; *Br* **to stand security for sb** se porter garant de qn; **to stand security for a loan** avaliser un prêt
(**f**) *(department)* sécurité *f*; **please call security** appelez la sécurité s'il vous plaît
(**g**) *Comput* sécurité *f*
2 securities *npl Fin* titres *mpl*, actions *fpl*, valeurs *fpl*; **government securities** titres *mpl* d'État; **the securities market** le marché des valeurs
▸▸ ***security alert*** alerte *f* au danger; ***security blanket*** doudou *m*; *Psy* objet *m* transitionnel; ***security booth*** guichet *m* (du gardien); *Comput* ***security certificate*** certificat *m* de sécurité; *Admin & Mil* ***security clearance*** habilitation *f*; *(document)* laissez-passer *m inv*; ***security code*** code *m* confidentiel; ***Security Council*** Conseil *m* de sécurité; *Fin* ***securities department*** service *m* des titres; *Fin* ***security deposit*** dépôt *m* de garantie; ***security device*** sécurité *f*; *Am* ***Securities and Exchange Commission*** = commission américaine des opérations de Bourse, ≃ COB *f*; ***security firm*** société *f* de gardiennage; ***security forces*** forces *fpl* de sécurité; ***security guard*** garde *m* (chargé de la sécurité); *(for armoured van)* convoyeur(euse) *m,f* de fonds; ***securities house*** société *f* de Bourse; *Br* ***Securities and Investment Board*** = commission britannique des opérations de Bourse, ≃ COB *f*; ***security leak*** = fuite de documents ou d'informations concernant la sécurité; *Comput* ***security level*** niveau *m* de sécurité; *Fin* ***securities market*** marché *m* des titres, marché *m* des valeurs (mobilières); ***security measures*** mesures *fpl* de sécurité; ***security officer*** *(on ship)* officier *m* chargé de la sécurité; *(in firm)* employé(e) *m,f* chargé(e) de la sécurité; *(inspector)* inspecteur(trice) *m,f* de la sécurité; *Comput* ***security password*** mot *m* de passe sécuritaire; ***security patrol*** patrouille *f* de sûreté *ou* de protection; ***security personnel*** personnel *m* de sécurité; ***security police*** (services *mpl* de la) sûreté *f*; *Fin* ***securities portfolio*** portefeuille *m* de titres; ***security tag*** agrafe *f* antivol

security-coded *adj (radio)* codé, à code de sécurité
▸▸ *Aut* ***security-coded immobilizer*** antidémarrage *m* codé

secy (*written abbr* **secretary**) secr

sedan [sɪ'dæn] *n* (**a**) *Am (car)* berline *f* (**b**) *Hist (chair)* chaise *f* à porteurs
▸▸ *Hist* ***sedan chair*** chaise *f* à porteurs

sedate [sɪ'deɪt] **1** *adj (person, manner)* calme, posé; *(behaviour)* calme, pondéré; **we strolled home at a sedate pace** nous sommes rentrés chez nous sans hâte *ou* en flânant; **we live a very sedate existence** nous menons une existence très calme
2 *vt* donner des sédatifs à; **he's heavily sedated** on lui a donné de fortes doses de calmants

sedately [sɪ'deɪtlɪ] *adv* posément, calmement; **she walked sedately back to her house** elle est revenue chez elle d'un pas lent *ou* tranquille

sedateness [sɪ'deɪtnɪs] *n* manière *f* posée, maintien *m* calme

sedation [sɪ'deɪʃən] *n* sédation *f*; **under sedation** sous calmants

sedative ['sedətɪv] **1** *adj* calmant
2 *n* calmant *m*

sedentarily ['sedəntərɪlɪ] *adv* sédentairement

sedentariness ['sedəntərɪnɪs] *n* (**a**) *(sedentary life)* vie *f* sédentaire; *(sedentary habits)* habitudes *fpl* sédentaires (**b**) *Zool* sédentarité *f*

sedentary ['sedəntərɪ] *adj* sédentaire

sederunt [se'dɪərənt] *n Scot Law* séance *f*

sedge [sedʒ] *n Bot* laîche *f*, carex *m*
▸▸ *Orn* ***sedge warbler*** phragmite *m* des joncs

sedilia [se'dɪlɪə] *npl* stalles *fpl*

sediment ['sedɪmənt] **1** *n* (**a**) *Geol* sédiment *m* (**b**) *(in liquid)* sédiment *m*, dépôt *m*; *(in wine)* dépôt *m*, lie *f*
2 *vt* déposer
3 *vi* se déposer

sedimental [ˌsedɪ'mentəl] *adj* sédimentaire

sedimentary [ˌsedɪ'mentərɪ] *adj* sédimentaire
▸▸ *Geol* ***sedimentary rock*** roche *f* sédimentaire

sedimentate ['sedɪmenteɪt] *vt* **to sedimentate sewage** traiter les eaux d'égout pour les faire déposer

sedimentation [ˌsedɪmen'teɪʃən] *n* sédimentation *f*

sedimentology [ˌsedɪmen'tɒlədʒɪ] *n Geol* sédimentologie *f*

sedition [sɪ'dɪʃən] *n* sédition *f*

seditionary [sɪ'dɪʃənərɪ] **1** *n* séditieux(euse) *mf*
2 *adj* séditieux

seditionist [sɪ'dɪʃənɪst] *n* séditieux(euse) *mf*

seditious [sɪ'dɪʃəs] *adj* séditieux

seditiously [sɪ'dɪʃəslɪ] *adv* séditieusement; **to speak seditiously** tenir des propos séditieux

seduce [sɪ'dju:s] *vt* (**a**) *(sexually)* séduire (**b**) *(attract)* séduire, attirer; *(draw)* entraîner; **she was seduced away from the company** on l'a persuadée de *ou* incitée à quitter la société

seducer [sɪ'dju:sə(r)] *n* séducteur(trice) *m,f*

seduction [sɪ'dʌkʃən] *n* séduction *f*

seductive [sɪ'dʌktɪv] *adj (person)* séduisant; *(personality)* séduisant, attrayant; *(voice, smile)* aguichant, séducteur; *(offer)* séduisant, alléchant; **she was wearing a rather seductive dress** elle était plutôt séduisante dans cette robe

seductively [sɪ'dʌktɪvlɪ] *adv (dress)* d'une manière séduisante; *(smile)* d'une manière enjôleuse

seductiveness [sɪ'dʌktɪvnɪs] *n (of person)* séduction *f*, charme *m*; *(of personality)* caractère *m* séduisant *ou* attrayant; *(of voice, smile)* caractère *m* aguichant *ou* séducteur; *(of offer)* caractère *m* séduisant *ou* alléchant

sedulous ['sedjʊləs] *adj Formal* diligent, persévérant

sedulously ['sedjʊləslɪ] *adv Formal* assidûment, avec persévérance

sedum ['si:dəm] *n Bot* sédum *m*

SEE [si:]

voir	▸ **1 (a) – (h), (j) – (o), (q) – (s), (u); 2 (a) – (e)**
consulter	▸ **1 (d)**
rencontrer	▸ **1 (e)**
recevoir	▸ **1 (g)**
comprendre	▸ **1 (j)**
s'imaginer	▸ **1 (l)**
s'assurer	▸ **1 (p)**
connaître	▸ **1 (r)**
accompagner	▸ **1 (t)**
comprendre	▸ **2 (d)**

(*pt* **saw** [sɔ:], *pp* **seen** [si:n]) **1** *vt* (**a**) *(perceive with eyes)* voir; **can you see me?** est-ce que tu me vois?; **I can't see a thing** je ne vois rien; **she could see a light in the distance** elle voyait une lumière au loin; **I could see she'd been crying** je voyais qu'elle avait pleuré; **he saw her talk** *or* **talking to the policeman** il l'a vue parler *ou* qui parlait au policier; **did anyone see you take it?** est-ce que quelqu'un t'a vu le prendre?; **did you see what happened?** avez-vous vu ce qui s'est passé?; **let me see your hands** fais-moi voir *ou* montre-moi tes mains; **now see what you've done!** regarde ce que tu as fait!; **can I see your newspaper a minute?** puis-je voir votre journal *ou* jeter un coup d'œil sur votre journal un instant?; **I see her around a lot** je la croise assez souvent; **I don't want to be seen with him** je ne veux pas être vu *ou* qu'on me voie avec lui; **there wasn't a car to be seen** il n'y avait pas une seule voiture en vue; **the cathedral can be seen from a long way off** on voit la cathédrale de très loin; **nothing more was ever seen of her** on ne l'a plus jamais revue; **it has to be seen to be believed** il faut le voir pour le croire; **she began to see spies everywhere** elle s'est mise à voir des espions partout; **there's nothing there, you're seeing things!** il n'y a rien, tu as des hallucinations!; **I could see what was going to happen (a mile off)** je le voyais venir (gros comme une maison); *Fam* **they saw you coming (a mile off)** ils t'ont vu arriver de loin; **could you see your way (clear) to lending me £20?** est-ce que vous pourriez me prêter 20 livres?; **to see the back** *or* **last of sth** en avoir fini avec qch; **I'll be glad to see the back** *or* **last of her** je serai content d'être débarrassé d'elle

(**b**) *(watch → movie, play, programme)* voir; **I saw it on the news** je l'ai vu au journal télévisé; **did you see the match last night?** as-tu vu le match hier soir?

(**c**) *(refer to → page, chapter)* voir; **see page 317** voir page 317; **see above** voir plus haut; **see (on) the back** voir au verso

(**d**) *(consult → doctor, lawyer)* consulter, voir; **you should see a doctor** tu devrais voir *ou* consulter un médecin; **I'll be seeing my lawyer about this** je vais consulter mon avocat à ce sujet; **I'll be seeing the candidates next week** je verrai les candidats la semaine prochaine; **I want to see the manager** je veux voir le directeur; **can I see you for a minute in my office?** je peux vous voir un instant dans mon bureau?; **I'd like to see you on business** je voudrais vous parler affaires

(**e**) *(meet by chance)* voir, rencontrer; **guess who I saw at the supermarket!** devine qui j'ai vu *ou* qui j'ai rencontré au supermarché!

(**f**) *(visit → person, place)* voir; **come round and see me some time** passe me voir un de ces jours; **they came to see me in hospital** ils sont venus me voir à l'hôpital; **I've always wanted to see China** j'ai toujours voulu voir la Chine

(**g**) *(receive a visit from)* recevoir, voir; **he's too ill to see anyone** il est trop malade pour voir qui que ce soit; **she can't see you right now, she's busy** elle ne peut pas vous recevoir *ou* voir maintenant, elle est trop occupée

(**h**) *(spend time with socially)* voir; **do you still see the Browns?** est-ce que vous voyez toujours les Brown?; **we've seen quite a lot of them recently** nous les avons beaucoup vus dernièrement; **we see less of them these days** nous les voyons moins en ce moment; **is he seeing anyone at the moment?** *(going out with)* est-ce qu'il a quelqu'un en ce moment?

(**i**) *Fam (saying goodbye)* **see you!, (I'll) be seeing you!** salut!; **see you later!** à tout à l'heure!; **see you around!** à un de ces jours!; **see you tomorrow!** à demain!; **see you in London!** on se verra à Londres!

(**j**) *(understand)* voir, comprendre; **I see what you mean** je vois *ou* comprends ce que vous voulez dire; **I don't see what's so funny!** je ne vois pas ce qu'il y a de si drôle!; **he can't see the joke** il ne comprend pas la plaisanterie; **I could see his point** je voyais ce qu'il voulait dire; **I don't see any point in going back now** je ne vois pas du tout l'intérêt qu'il y aurait à y retourner maintenant; **I can see why you were worried** je vois pourquoi vous étiez inquiet; **I can't see that it matters** je ne vois pas quelle importance ça a

(**k**) *(consider, view)* voir; **try to see things from my point of view** essayez de voir les choses de mon point de vue; **we see things differently** nous ne voyons pas les choses de la même façon; **you'll see things differently in the morning** demain tu verras les choses d'un autre œil; **that's how I see it** c'est comme ça que je vois les choses; **he doesn't see his drinking as a problem** il ne se considère pas comme un alcoolique; **how do you see the current situation?** que pensez-vous de la situation actuelle?; **as I see it, it's the parents who are to blame** à mon avis, ce sont les parents qui sont responsables

(**l**) *(envisage, picture)* voir, s'imaginer; **I can't see him getting married** je ne le vois pas *ou* je ne me l'imagine pas se mariant; **I can't see them accepting this** je ne peux pas croire qu'ils vont accepter cela; **I can't see you as a boxer** je ne te vois pas en boxeur; **she just couldn't see herself as a wife and mother** elle ne s'imaginait pas se mariant et ayant des enfants; **I can't see it myself** je n'y crois pas trop; **they say this will be more efficient but I don't see it** ils disent que cela sera plus efficace, mais je n'y crois pas; **I don't see any chance of that** à mon avis c'est peu probable; **can I borrow the car? – I don't see why not** est-ce que je peux prendre la voiture? – je n'y vois pas d'inconvénients; **will you finish in time? – I don't see why not** vous aurez fini à temps? – il n'y a pas de raison; **what do you see happening next?** d'après vous, qu'est-ce qui va se passer ensuite?; **how do you see things developing?** comment est-ce que vous envisagez l'avenir?

(**m**) *(try to find out)* voir; **I'll see if I can fix it** je vais voir si je peux le réparer; **I'll see what I can do** je vais voir ce que je peux faire; **go and see if he's still asleep** va voir s'il dort encore; **she called by to see what had happened** elle est venue pour savoir ce qui s'était passé

(**n**) *(perceive)* voir; **I can't see any improvement** je ne vois pas d'amélioration; **to see oneself in one's children** se reconnaître dans ses enfants; **what can she possibly see in him?** qu'est-qu'elle peut bien lui trouver?; **they must have seen how worried I was** ils ont dû voir combien j'étais inquiet

(**o**) *(discover, learn)* voir; **I'm pleased to see you're enjoying life** je suis heureux de voir que tu profites de la vie; **I'll be interested to see how he gets on** je serais curieux de voir comment il se débrouillera; **I see (that) he's getting married** j'ai appris qu'il allait se marier; **I saw it in the paper this morning** je l'ai vu *ou* lu ce matin dans le journal; **as we shall see in a later chapter** comme nous le verrons dans un chapitre ultérieur; **I see she's in the new Scorsese movie** je vois qu'elle est dans le nouveau film de Scorsese

(**p**) *(make sure)* s'assurer, veiller à; **see that all the lights are out before you leave** assurez-vous que *ou* veillez à ce que toutes les lumières soient éteintes avant de partir; **see that everything's ready for when they arrive** veillez à ce que tout soit prêt pour leur arrivée; **I shall see that he comes** je me charge de le faire venir; *Fam* **she'll see you right** elle veillera à ce que tu ne manques de rien ❑, elle prendra bien soin de toi ❑

(**q**) *(inspect → file, passport, ticket)* voir; **can I see your ticket, sir?** puis-je voir votre ticket, Monsieur?

(**r**) *(experience)* voir, connaître; **he thinks he's seen it all** il croit tout savoir; **most recruits never see active service** la plupart des recrues ne voient jamais la guerre de près; **our car has seen better days** notre voiture a connu des jours meilleurs; **the city hasn't seen such crowds in decades** la ville n'a pas connu une foule pareille depuis des dizaines d'années; **the country saw many changes** le pays a connu de grands changements

(**s**) *(witness)* voir; **they have seen their purchasing power halved** ils ont vu leur pouvoir d'achat diminuer de moitié; **last year saw an increase in profits** l'année dernière a vu une augmentation des bénéfices; **the next decade will see enormous changes** la prochaine décennie verra se produire des changements considérables; **I never thought I'd see the day when he'd admit he was wrong** je n'aurais jamais cru qu'un jour il admettrait avoir tort; **you don't see athletes like her any more!** il n'y a plus beaucoup d'athlètes comme elle!

(**t**) *(accompany)* accompagner; **I'll see you to the bus stop** je t'accompagne à *ou* jusqu'à l'arrêt du bus; **I'll see you home** je te raccompagne chez toi; **see Mr Smith to the door, please** veuillez raccompagner M. Smith jusqu'à la porte; **he saw her into a taxi/onto the train** il l'a mise dans un taxi/le train; **to see sb across the road** aider qn à traverser la rue

(**u**) *(in poker)* voir; **I'll see you** je vous vois; **I'll see your $10 and raise you 20** je vous suis à 10 dollars et je relance de 20

2 *vi* (**a**) *(perceive with eyes)* voir; **I can't see without (my) glasses** je ne vois rien sans mes lunettes; **he may never see again** il se peut qu'il ne voie plus jamais; **on a clear day you can see as far as the coast** par temps clair on voit jusqu'à la mer; **you can see for miles around** la vue s'étend sur des kilomètres; **cats can see in the dark** les chats voient dans l'obscurité; **I haven't quite finished – so I see** je n'ai pas tout à fait terminé – c'est ce que je vois; **to see into the future** voir *ou* lire dans l'avenir; **she can't see any further than the end of her nose** elle ne voit pas plus loin que le bout de son nez; **for all to see** au vu et au su de tous

(**b**) *(look)* voir; **can I see?** je peux voir?; **let me see!, let's see!** fais voir!; **see for yourself** voyez par vous-même; *Fam* **see! I told you he wouldn't let us down** tu vois! je t'avais dit qu'il ne nous laisserait pas tomber

(**c**) *(find out)* voir; **is that the baby crying? – I'll go and see** c'est le bébé qu'on entend pleurer? – je vais voir; **you'll see!** tu verras!; **we shall see** nous verrons (bien); **we'll soon see** on le saura vite; **we'll soon see if...** on saura vite si...

(**d**) *(understand)* voir, comprendre; **it makes no difference as far as I can see** autant que je puisse en juger, ça ne change rien; **you see, there's something else you should know** tu vois, il y a quelque chose d'autre que tu devrais savoir; **I was tired, you see, and...** j'étais fatigué, voyez-vous, et...; **I see** je vois; *Fam* **I don't want any trouble, see?** je ne veux pas d'histoires, OK?; *Fam Old-fashioned* **now see here, young man!** écoutez-moi, jeune homme!

(**e**) *(consider)* **let me** *or* **let's see** voyons voir; **it was, let me see, in 1938** c'était, voyons (voir), en 1938; **Mum said you'd take us to the fair – we'll see** Maman a dit que tu nous amènerais à la foire – on verra (ça)

3 *n Rel (of bishop)* siège *m* épiscopal, évêché *m*; *(of archbishop)* archevêché *m*

▸**see about** *vt insep* (**a**) *(deal with)* s'occuper de; **I'll see about making the reservations** je m'occuperai des réservations; **they're sending someone to see about the gas** ils envoient quelqu'un pour vérifier le gaz

(**b**) *(consider)* voir; **I'll see about it** je verrai ça; **we'll have to see about getting a new car** il va falloir songer à acheter une nouvelle voiture; *Fam* **they won't let us in – we'll (soon) see about that!** ils ne veulent pas nous laisser entrer – c'est ce qu'on va voir!

▸**see around** *vt insep* = **see round**

▸**see in 1** *vt sep* (**a**) *(escort)* faire entrer

(**b**) *(celebrate)* **to see in the New Year** fêter le Nouvel An

2 *vi* voir à l'intérieur; **the curtains were drawn, so we couldn't see in** les rideaux étaient tirés, nous ne pouvions pas voir à l'intérieur

▸**see off** *vt sep* (**a**) *(say goodbye to)* dire au revoir à; **she came to see me off at the station** elle est venue à la gare me dire au revoir

(**b**) *(chase away)* chasser; **see him off!** *(to dog)* chasse-le!

(**c**) *(repel → attack)* repousser

▸**see out** *vt sep* (**a**) *(accompany to the door)* reconduire *ou* raccompagner à la porte; **can you see yourself out?** pouvez-vous trouver la sortie tout seul?; **goodbye, I'll see myself out** au revoir, ce n'est pas la peine de me raccompagner

(**b**) *(stay or last until end of)* **I'll see another year out here then go home** je vais passer une autre année ici puis je rentrerai; **we've got enough food to see the week out** nous avons assez à manger pour tenir jusqu'à la fin de la semaine; **I don't think these boots will see the winter out** je ne crois pas que ces bottes feront l'hiver; **he isn't expected to see out the week** il y a peu de chances qu'il survive jusqu'à la fin de la semaine; **he'll see us all out!** *(will survive us)* il nous enterrera tous!

(**c**) *(celebrate)* **to see out the Old Year** fêter le Nouvel An

▸**see over** *vt insep* = **see round**

▸**see round** *vt insep* visiter; **they came to see round the house** ils sont venus pour visiter la maison

▸**see through 1** *vt insep* (**a**) *(window, fabric)* voir à travers

(**b**) *(be wise to → person)* percer à jour, voir dans le jeu de; *(→ trick, scheme, behaviour)* ne pas se laisser tromper par; **I saw through him** je l'ai percé à jour, j'ai vu dans son jeu; **she saw through his apparent cheerfulness** elle ne s'est pas laissée tromper par *ou* elle n'a pas été dupe de son apparente bonne humeur; **I saw through their little game** j'ai vite compris leur petit jeu

2 *vt sep* (**a**) *(bring to a successful end)* mener à bonne fin; **we can count on her to see the job through** on peut compter sur elle pour mener l'affaire à bien

(**b**) *(stay until end of)* **to see a show/film through** assister à un spectacle/regarder un film jusqu'au bout

(**c**) *(support, sustain)* **I've got enough money to see me through the week** j'ai assez d'argent pour tenir jusqu'à la fin de la semaine; **£20 should see me through (to Monday)** 20 livres devraient me suffire (jusqu'à lundi); **their love has seen them through many a crisis** leur amour les a aidés à surmonter de nombreuses crises; **her good humour will always see her through any difficulties** sa bonne humeur lui permettra toujours de traverser les moments difficiles

▸**see to** *vt insep* (**a**) *(look after)* s'occuper de; **I'll see to the dinner** je m'occuperai du dîner; **I'll see to it** je vais m'en occuper, je m'en charge; **see to it that everything's ready by 5 p.m.** veillez à ce que tout soit prêt pour 17 heures; **she saw to it that our picnic was ruined** elle a fait en sorte de gâcher notre pique-nique

(**b**) *(repair)* réparer; **you should get the brakes seen to** tu devrais faire réparer les freins

---

seed [si:d] **1** *n* (**a**) *Bot & Hort* graine *f*; *(UNCOUNT)* graines *fpl*, semence *f*; **grass seed** semence *f* pour gazon; **to go** *or* **to run to seed** *Hort* monter en graine; *Fig (physically)* se laisser aller, se décatir; *(mentally)* perdre ses facultés; **his mother has really gone to seed during the past year** sa mère a bien baissé *ou* s'est bien décatie au cours de l'année passée

(**b**) *(in fruit, tomatoes)* pépin *m*

(**c**) *(source)* germe *m*; **the seeds of doubt/of suspicion** les germes *mpl* du doute/de la suspicion

(**d**) *Bible & Literary (offspring)* progéniture *f*; *(sperm)* semence *f*

(**e**) *Sport* tête *f* de série; **the top seeds** les meilleurs joueurs *mpl* classés

2 *vt* (**a**) *Bot & Hort (garden, field)* ensemencer; *(plants)* planter; **seeded borders** bordures *fpl* ensemencées

(**b**) *Met* **to seed clouds** ensemencer les nuages

(**c**) *(take seeds from → melon, grapes)* épépiner

(**d**) *Sport* **he's seeded number 5** il est tête de série numéro 5; **seeded player** tête *f* de série

3 *vi (lettuce)* monter en graine; *(corn)* grener, grainer

▸▸ *Fin* ***seed capital*** capital *m* initial *ou* de départ, mise *f* de fonds initiale; *Agr* ***seed drill*** semoir *m*; *Br* ***seed merchant*** grainetier(ère) *m,f*; *Fin* ***seed money*** capital *m* initial *ou* de départ, mise *f* de fonds initiale; ***seed pearl*** perle *f* minuscule; ***seed pearls*** semence *f* de perles; ***seed potato*** pomme *f* de terre de semence; *Hort* ***seed tray*** terrine *f* à semis; *Bot* ***seed vessel*** péricarpe *m*

seedbed ['si:dbed] *n Hort* semis *m*, couche *f* à semis; *Fig* **a seedbed of revolution** les germes *mpl* d'une révolution

seedbox ['si:dbɒks] *n Hort* germoir *m*

seedcake ['si:dkeɪk] *n* gâteau *m* aux graines de carvi

seedcorn ['si:dkɔ:n] *n* blé *m* de semence

▸▸ *Fin* ***seedcorn investments*** investissements *mpl* pour l'avenir

seeder ['si:də(r)] *n* (**a**) *Agr* semoir *m* (**b**) *(fish)* poisson *m* qui fraye

seedily ['si:dɪlɪ] *adv* minablement, de façon miteuse

seediness ['si:dɪnɪs] *n* (**a**) *(appearance)* aspect *m* miteux *ou* minable (**b**) *Fam Old-fashioned (ill health)* mauvais état ❑ *m*

seeding machine ['si:dɪŋ-] *n* semoir *m*

seedless ['si:dlɪs] *adj* sans pépins

seedling ['si:dlɪŋ] *n (plant)* semis *m*, jeune plant *m*; *(tree)* jeune plant *m*

seedpod ['si:dpɒd] *n Bot* cosse *f*

seedsman ['si:dzmən] *(pl* **seedsmen** [-mən]) *n* grainetier *m*

seedsnipe ['si:dsnaɪp] *n Orn* thinocore *m*, attagis *m*

seedy ['si:dɪ] *(compar* **seedier**, *superl* **seediest**) *adj* (**a**) *(person, hotel, clothes)* miteux, minable; *(area)* délabré; **a seedy-looking drunk approached her** un ivrogne d'aspect minable *ou* miteux s'avança vers elle; **the hotel was in the seediest part of town** l'hôtel était dans le quartier le plus délabré de la ville (**b**) *Fam (unwell)* patraque, mal fichu (**c**) *(fruit)* plein de pépins

seeing ['si:ɪŋ] **1** *n (vision)* vue *f*, vision *f*; *Prov* **seeing is believing** = il faut le voir pour le croire

2 *conj* vu que + *indicative*; *Fam* **seeing (that** *or* **as how) no one came, we left** vu que *ou* étant donné que personne n'est venu, nous sommes partis ❑; *Fam* **I decided not to encourage him, seeing as how he was married** je décidai de ne pas l'encourager, puisqu'il était *ou* vu qu'il était marié ❑

▸▸ *Am* ***seeing eye (dog)*** chien *m* d'aveugle

seeing-to *n Br Fam* **to give sb a good seeing-to** *(beat up)* tabasser qn; *(have sex with)* faire passer qn à la casserole

seek [si:k] *(pt & pp* **sought** [sɔ:t]) **1** *vt* (**a**) *(search for → job, person, solution)* chercher, rechercher; **he constantly sought her approval** il cherchait constamment à obtenir son approbation; **he sought revenge on them** il a cherché à se venger d'eux; **they sought an answer to their problems** ils ont cherché une réponse à leurs problèmes; **we'd better seek help** il vaut mieux aller chercher de l'aide; **they sought shelter from the rain** ils ont cherché à se mettre à l'abri de la pluie; **we sought shelter in a shop doorway** nous avons cherché refuge *ou* à nous réfugier dans l'entrée d'un magasin; **to seek one's fortune** chercher fortune; **to seek re-election** chercher à se faire réélire; **gentleman, 50s, seeks mature woman…** *(in personal column)* homme, la cinquantaine, recherche femme mûre…

(**b**) *(ask for → advice, help)* demander, chercher; **I sought professional advice** j'ai demandé conseil à un professionnel, j'ai cherché conseil auprès d'un professionnel; **he sought my help** il m'a demandé de l'aide *ou* de l'aider

(**c**) *(attempt)* **to seek to do sth** chercher à faire qch, tenter de faire qch; **we are seeking to improve housing conditions** nous nous efforçons d'améliorer *ou* nous cherchons à améliorer les conditions de logement

(**d**) *(move towards)* chercher; **water seeks its own level** l'eau atteint spontanément son niveau

2 *vi* chercher; **to seek after sth** rechercher qch; *Bible* **seek and ye shall find** cherchez et vous trouverez

▸▸ *Comput* ***seek time*** temps *m* d'accès

▸**seek after** *vt insep* rechercher

▸**seek out** *vt sep* (**a**) *(go to see)* aller voir (**b**) *(search for)* chercher, rechercher; *(dig out)* dénicher

seeker ['si:kə(r)] *n* chercheur(euse) *m,f*; **a seeker after truth** une personne qui recherche la vérité

-seeker ['si:kə(r)] *suff* **peace-seeker** personne *f* qui recherche la paix

---

SEEM [si:m]

sembler	▸ (**a**), (**d**), (**e**)
avoir l'air	▸ (**a**)
paraître	▸ (**d**), (**f**)

vi (**a**) *(with adjective)* sembler, avoir l'air; **he seems very nice** il a l'air très gentil; **you don't seem very pleased with the result** vous n'avez pas l'air ravi du résultat; **you seem (to be) lost** vous semblez (être) *ou* vous avez l'air (d'être) perdu; **things aren't always what they seem (to be)** les apparences sont parfois trompeuses; **just do whatever seems right** fais ce que tu jugeras bon de faire; **the wind makes it seem colder than it is** on dirait qu'il fait plus froid à cause du vent; **her behaviour seemed perfectly normal to me** son comportement m'a semblé tout à fait normal; **how does the situation seem to you? – it seems hopeless** que pensez-vous de la situation? – elle me semble désespérée; **how did grandfather seem to you? – he seemed much older** comment as-tu trouvé grand-père? – j'ai trouvé qu'il avait beaucoup vieilli

(**b**) *(with infinitive)* sembler, avoir l'air; **the door seemed to open by itself** la porte sembla s'ouvrir toute seule; **she seems to have recovered completely** elle a l'air d'être tout à fait remise; **she seemed to be trying to say something** elle semblait essayer de dire quelque chose; **he didn't seem to know, he seemed not to know** il n'avait pas l'air de savoir; **you seem to think you can do as you like here** vous avez l'air de croire que vous pouvez faire ce que vous voulez ici; **I seem to have heard his name somewhere** il me semble avoir entendu son nom quelque part; **I seem to sleep better with the window open** je crois que je dors mieux avec la fenêtre ouverte; **I seem to remember (that)…** je crois bien me souvenir que… + *indicative*; **I'm sorry, I seem to have forgotten your name** excusez-moi, je crois que j'ai oublié votre nom; **I seemed to be floating on a cloud** j'avais l'impression de flotter sur un nuage; **now, what seems to be the problem?** alors, quel est le problème d'après vous?

(**c**) *(with "can't", "couldn't")* **I can't seem to do it** je n'y arrive pas; **I can't seem to remember** je n'arrive pas à me souvenir; **I couldn't seem to get any answer** impossible d'obtenir une réponse

(**d**) *(with noun, often with "like")* sembler, paraître; **he seems (like) a nice boy** il a l'air très sympathique *ou* d'un garçon charmant; **it seems (like) an excellent idea** cela me semble (être) une excellente idée; **after what seemed (like) ages, the doctor arrived** après une attente qui parut interminable, le médecin arriva; **it all seems (like) a long time ago now** ça me paraît loin maintenant; **it seems like only yesterday** il me semble que c'était hier; **it seems like a dream** on croit rêver

(**e**) *(impersonal use)* sembler; **it seemed that** *or* **as if nothing could make her change her mind** il semblait que rien ne pourrait la faire changer d'avis; **it seemed as though I'd known her for years** j'avais l'impression de la connaître depuis des années; **it seems to be raining** on dirait qu'il pleut; **it seemed best to leave** il semblait préférable de partir; **it seems like only yesterday** c'est comme si c'était hier; **it seems likely that this will happen soon** cela risque d'arriver bientôt; **it seems to me that...** il me semble que... + *indicative*, j'ai l'impression que... + *indicative*; **it seems to me there's no solution** j'ai l'impression qu'il n'y a pas de solution; **there seems to be some mistake** on dirait qu'il y a une erreur, il semble y avoir une erreur; **there seem to be many opponents of the bill** il semble y avoir *ou* qu'il y ait beaucoup de gens qui s'opposent au projet de loi; **there doesn't seem (to be) much point in going on** je ne crois pas qu'il y ait *ou* j'ai l'impression qu'il n'y a pas grand intérêt à continuer; **we've been having a spot of bother – so it seems** *or* **would seem!** nous avons eu un petit problème – on dirait bien!

(**f**) *(indicating that information is hearsay or second-hand)* paraître; **it seems over two hundred people were killed** il paraît que plus de deux cents personnes ont été tuées; **it would seem so** il paraît que oui; **it would seem not** il paraît que non, apparemment pas; **he doesn't seem to have known about the operation** apparemment, il n'était pas au courant de l'opération; **it seems** *or* **it would seem (that) he already knew** il semble *ou* il semblerait qu'il était déjà au courant

---

seeming ['siːmɪŋ] *adj* apparent; **I don't trust him, for all his seeming concern over our welfare** je n'ai aucune confiance en lui bien qu'il semble se préoccuper de notre bien-être; **her explanation soon resolved any seeming contradictions in her story** ses précisions ne tardèrent pas à lever les apparentes contradictions de son récit

seemingly ['siːmɪŋlɪ] *adv* (**a**) *(judging by appearances)* apparemment, en apparence; **she has seemingly limitless amounts of money** les sommes d'argent dont elle dispose semblent être illimitées (**b**) *(from reports)* à ce qu'il paraît; **seemingly so/not** il paraît que oui/non; **he seemingly never received the letter** à ce qu'il paraît, il n'a jamais reçu la lettre

seemliness ['siːmlɪnɪs] *n* (**a**) *(of behaviour)* bienséance *f* (**b**) *(of dress)* décence *f*

seemly ['siːmlɪ] *(compar* **seemlier**, *superl* **seemliest**) *adj* (**a**) *(behaviour)* convenable, bienséant; **it is not seemly to ask personal questions** cela ne se fait pas de poser des questions personnelles (**b**) *(dress)* décent; **it was hardly the most seemly attire for a supper party** ce n'était certainement pas la tenue la plus indiquée pour un dîner

seen [siːn] **1** *pp of* **see**

2 *adj Sch* **a seen translation** une traduction préparée

seep [siːp] *vi* filtrer, s'infiltrer; **water was seeping through the cracks in the floor** l'eau s'infiltrait par *ou* filtrait à travers les fissures du sol

►**seep away** *vi* s'écouler goutte à goutte

►**seep in** *vi* (**a**) *(liquid)* s'infiltrer (**b**) *Fig* faire son effet

►**seep out** *vi* (**a**) *(blood, liquid)* suinter; *(gas, smoke)* se répandre (**b**) *(information, secret)* filtrer

seepage ['siːpɪdʒ] *n (gradual → process)* suintement *m*, infiltration *f*; *(→ leak)* fuite *f*

seer ['sɪə(r)] *n Literary* prophète *m*, prophétesse *f*

seersucker ['sɪə,sʌkə(r)] *n Tex* coton *m* gaufré, seersucker *m*

seesaw ['siːsɔː] **1** *n* bascule *f*, tape-cul *m*

2 *comp (motion)* de bascule

3 *vi* (**a**) *(play on a seesaw)* jouer à la bascule, faire du tape-cul (**b**) *(machine part etc)* basculer; *Fig (oscillate)* osciller

►► *Fin* ***seesaw effect*** effet *m* balançoire

seethe [siːð] *vi* (**a**) *(liquid, lava)* bouillir, bouillonner; *(sea)* bouillonner (**b**) *(with anger, indignation)* bouillir; **he was seething (with anger)** il bouillait de rage; **the country is currently seething with unrest** le mécontentement gronde en ce moment dans le pays (**c**) *(teem)* grouiller; **the streets seethed with shoppers** les rues grouillaient de gens qui faisaient leurs courses

seething ['siːðɪŋ] *adj* (**a**) *(liquid, lava, sea)* bouillonnant (**b**) *(furious)* furieux (**c**) *(teeming)* grouillant; **a seething mass of people** une masse fourmillante de gens

see-through, *Am* **see-thru** *adj* transparent

segment 1 *n* ['segmənt] (**a**) *(piece → gen) & Anat & Geom* segment *m*; *(→ of fruit)* quartier *m*; **in segments** par segments (**b**) *(part → of book, film, programme)* partie *f* (**c**) *Ling* segment *m* (**d**) *Mktg (of market, population)* segment *m*

2 *vt* [seg'ment] segmenter, diviser *ou* partager en segments

3 *vi* [seg'ment] se segmenter

►► *Acct* ***segment margin*** marge *f* sectorielle; ***segment reporting*** analyse *f* par secteur d'activité

segmental [seg'mentəl] *adj* segmentaire

►► *Archit* ***segmental arch*** arc *m* surbaissé, voûte *f* surbaissée; *(of bridge)* arche *f* surbaissée; *(pointed)* ogive *f* surbaissée

segmentation [,segmen'teɪʃən] *n* segmentation *f*

segmented [seg'mentɪd] *adj* segmentaire

Segovia [sɪ'gəʊvɪə] *n* Ségovie

segregate ['segrɪgeɪt] **1** *vt (separate)* séparer; *(isolate)* isoler; **he went to a school where the sexes were segregated** l'école qu'il a fréquentée n'était pas mixte; **the children were segregated into racial groups** les enfants ont été regroupés en fonction de leur race; **the sick were segregated from the other villagers** les malades étaient tenus à l'écart des autres habitants du village

2 *vi (in genetics)* se diviser

segregated ['segrɪgeɪtɪd] *adj Pol* où l'on pratique la ségrégation

segregation [,segrɪ'geɪʃən] *n* (**a**) *Pol* ségrégation *f* (**b**) *(separation → of sexes, patients)* séparation *f* (**c**) *(in genetics)* division *f*

segregationist [,segrɪ'geɪʃənɪst] **1** *adj* ségrégationniste

2 *n* ségrégationniste *mf*

segregative ['segrɪgeɪtɪv] *adj* ségrégatif

segue ['segweɪ] **1** *n Mus* enchaînement *m*; *Fig* transition *f*

2 *vi* **one track neatly segued into the other** les morceaux s'enchaînaient parfaitement; *Fig* **summer segued into autumn** peu à peu, l'été fit place à l'automne

sei [seɪ] *adj*

►► *Zool* ***sei whale*** rorqual *m* boréal

seiche [seɪʃ] *n Geog* seiche *f*, oscillation *f* du niveau

seigneur [seɪn'jɜː(r)] *n* seigneur *m*

seigneurial [seɪn'jɜːrɪəl] *adj* seigneurial

Seine [seɪn] *n* **the (River) Seine** la Seine

seine [seɪn] *n Fishing* senne *f*

►► ***seine net*** senne *f*

seise [siːz] *vt Law* mettre en possession de; **to be** *or* **to stand seised of a property** posséder une propriété de droit

seism ['saɪzəm] *n* séisme *m*, tremblement *m* de terre

seismal ['saɪzməl] *adj* sismal, séismal

seismic ['saɪzmɪk] *adj* sismique, séismique; *Fig (changes)* gigantesque; **an increase/change of seismic proportions** une augmentation/un changement aux proportions gigantesques

seismograph ['saɪzməgrɑːf] *n* sismographe *m*, séismographe *m*

seismographer [saɪz'mɒgrəfə(r)] *n* sismologue *mf*, séismologue *mf*

seismographic [,saɪzmə'græfɪk], **seismographical** [,saɪzmə'græfɪkəl] *adj* sismographique, séismographique

seismography [saɪz'mɒgrəfɪ] *n* sismographie *f*, séismographie *f*

seismological [,saɪzmə'lɒdʒɪkəl] *adj* sismologique, séismologique

seismologist [saɪz'mɒlədʒɪst] *n* sismologue *mf*, séismologue *mf*

seismology [saɪz'mɒlədʒɪ] *n* sismologie *f*, séismologie *f*

seizable ['siːzəbəl] *adj (goods, property)* saisissable

seize [siːz] **1** *vt* (**a**) *(grasp)* attraper, saisir; *(in fist)* saisir, empoigner; **my mother seized me by the arm/the collar** ma mère m'a attrapé par le bras/le col; **she seized the rail to steady herself** elle s'agrippa à la rampe pour ne pas tomber; **he seized a knife and held it to my throat** il s'empara d'un couteau *ou* il saisit un couteau et l'appuya sur ma gorge; **to seize hold of sth** saisir *ou* attraper qch; **someone seized hold of my arm** quelqu'un m'a empoigné par le bras

(**b**) *(by force)* s'emparer de, saisir; **to seize power** s'emparer du pouvoir; **the rebels have seized control of the radio station** les rebelles se sont emparés de la station de radio; **pirates seized the ship** des pirates se sont rendus maîtres du navire; **five hostages were seized during the hold-up** les auteurs du hold-up ont pris cinq otages

(**c**) *(arrest → terrorist, smuggler)* se saisir de, appréhender, capturer; *(capture, confiscate → contraband, arms)* se saisir de, saisir; *Law (property)* saisir; **all copies of the book were seized** tous les exemplaires du livre ont été saisis

(**d**) *(opportunity)* saisir, sauter sur; **seize any opportunity that comes your way** saute sur la moindre occasion qui se présentera

(**e**) *(understand → meaning)* saisir; **he is quick to seize the implications** il saisit vite les implications

(**f**) *(overcome)* saisir; **to be seized with fright** être saisi d'effroi; **to be seized with rage** avoir un accès de rage; **she was seized with a desire to travel** elle fut prise d'une envie irrésistible de voyager; **the story never really seizes your imagination** l'histoire ne parvient jamais à vraiment frapper l'imagination

(**g**) *Am* = **seise**

2 *vi (mechanism)* se gripper

►**seize on** *vt insep (opportunity)* saisir, sauter sur; *(excuse)* saisir; *(idea)* saisir, adopter

►**seize up** *vi* (**a**) *(machinery)* se gripper; **the brakes seized up** les freins se sont grippés *ou* bloqués

(**b**) *(system)* se bloquer; **traffic in the centre has seized up completely** la circulation dans le centre est complètement bloquée

(**c**) *(leg)* s'ankyloser; *(back)* se bloquer; *(heart)* s'arrêter

►**seize upon** = **seize on**

seizure ['siːʒə(r)] *n* (**a**) *(UNCOUNT) (of goods, property)* saisie *f*; *(of city, fortress)* prise *f*; *(of ship)* capture *f*; *(arrest)* arrestation *f*; **seizure of power** prise *f* de pouvoir; **the police made a big arms seizure** la police a saisi un important stock d'armes

(**b**) *Med* crise *f*, attaque *f*; *also Fig* **to have a seizure** avoir une attaque; *Fam* **he just about had a seizure when he found out!** il a failli faire une crise quand il a su!; **heart seizure** crise *f* cardiaque

selachian [sɪ'leɪkɪən] *n Ich* sélacien *m*

seldom ['seldəm] *adv* rarement; **I seldom see her** je la vois rarement, je la vois peu; **he seldom comes** il ne vient que *ou* il vient rarement; **he seldom, if ever, visits his mother** il rend rarement, pour ne pas dire jamais, visite à sa mère; **seldom have I heard such nonsense** j'ai rarement entendu des bêtises pareilles

select [sɪ'lekt] **1** *vt* (**a**) *(gen)* choisir; *(team)* sélectionner; **you have been selected from among our many customers** vous avez été choisi parmi nos nombreux clients; **she hopes to be selected to play for Ireland** elle espère faire partie de la sélection qui jouera pour l'Irlande (**b**) *Comput* **select enter** tapez entrée; **to select an option** activer une option

2 *adj* (**a**) *(elite → restaurant, neighbourhood)* chic *(inv)*, sélect; *(→ club)* fermé, sélect; **the membership is very select** les membres appartiennent à la haute société; **she invited a few select friends** elle a invité quelques amis choisis; **only a select few were informed** seuls quelques privilégiés furent informés

(**b**) *(in quality → goods)* de (premier) choix

►► *Pol* ***select committee*** commission *f* d'enquête parlementaire

selectable [sɪ'lektəbəl] *adj Comput* qui peut être sélectionné

selected [sɪ'lektɪd] *adj (friends, poems)* choisi; *(customers)* privilégié; *(fruit, cuts of meat)* de (premier) choix; **before a selected audience** devant un public choisi

selection [sɪ'lekʃən] **1** *n* (**a**) *(act of choosing)* choix *m*, sélection *f*; *(of team)* sélection *f*; **to make a selection** faire un choix; **no one thought he stood a chance of selection** personne ne pensait qu'il serait sélectionné; **make your selection from among the books on the bottom shelf** faites votre choix parmi les livres de l'étagère du bas

(**b**) *(range)* choix *m*; **a wide selection** un grand choix; **a narrow selection** un choix limité; **the restaurant offers an excellent selection of wines** ce restaurant propose un excellent choix de vins *ou* dispose d'une excellente carte des vins; **they don't have a very good selection** ils n'ont pas beaucoup de choix

(**c**) *(of stories, music)* choix *m*, sélection *f*; **a selection of poems** *(in book)* poèmes *mpl* choisis; *(for recital)* un choix de poèmes; **selections from Balzac** morceaux *mpl* choisis de Balzac

2 *comp (committee, criteria)* de sélection

►► ***selection box*** (**a**) *(of chocolates)* assortiment *m* de barres chocolatées (**b**) *Comput* rectangle *m* de sélection; *Mktg* ***selection error*** erreur *f* d'echantillonnage; *Mktg* ***selection method*** méthode *f* de sélection

selective [sɪ'lektɪv] *adj* (**a**) *(gen)* sélectif; **we can't take them all, we have to be selective** on ne peut pas les emmener tous, il faut faire un choix; **you should be more selective in your choice of friends/in your reading** vous devriez choisir vos amis/vos lectures avec plus de discernement; **there was a wave of selective strikes** il y eut une série de grèves tournantes (**b**) *Electron* sélectif

►► ***selective breeding*** élevage *m* sélectif; *Sch* ***selective entry*** sélection *f*; ***selective marketing*** marketing *m* sélectif; ***selective selling*** distribution *f* sélective; *Am Mil* ***selective service*** service *m* militaire obligatoire, conscription *f*; ***selective weedkiller*** herbicide *m* sélectif; ***selective welfare*** allocations *fpl* sociales sélectives

selectively [sɪ'lektɪvlɪ] *adv* sélectivement, de manière sélective

selectivity [ˌsɪlek'tɪvətɪ] *n* (**a**) *(choice)* discernement *m* (**b**) *Electron* sélectivité *f*

selectman [sɪ'lektmən] (*pl* **selectmen** [-men]) *n Am (in New England)* ≃ conseiller *m* municipal

selector [sɪ'lektə(r)] *n* (**a**) *(gen) & Sport* sélectionneur(euse) *m,f* (**b**) *Tel & TV* sélecteur *m*

Selene [sɪ'li:nɪ] *pr n Myth* Séléné

selenite ['selənaɪt] *n Geol* sélénite *f*

selenium [sɪ'li:nɪəm] *n Chem* sélénium *m*

selenography [ˌsi:lə'nɒgrəfɪ] *n* sélénographie *f*

selenology [ˌsi:lə'nɒlədʒɪ] *n* sélénologie *f*

self [self] (*pl* **selves** [selvz]) **1** *n* (**a**) *(individual)* **she's back to her old** *or* **usual self** elle est redevenue elle-même *ou* comme avant; **she's only a shadow of her former self** elle n'est plus que l'ombre d'elle-même; **he was his usual tactless self** il a fait preuve de son manque de tact habituel; **they began to reveal their true selves** ils ont commencé à se montrer sous leur véritable jour

(**b**) *Psy* moi *m*; **the conscious self** le moi conscient

(**c**) *(self-interest)* **all she thinks of is self, self, self** elle ne pense qu'à sa petite personne

(**d**) *(on cheque)* **pay self** = mention portée sur un chèque libellé à son propre nom

2 *adj (matching)* assorti

self- [self] *pref* (**a**) *(of oneself)* de soi-même, auto-; *Psy* **self-actualization** épanouissement *m* de la personnalité; **self-accusation** autoaccusation *f*; **self-admiration** narcissisme *m* (**b**) *(by oneself)* auto-, par soi-même; **self-financing** qui s'autofinance (**c**) *(automatic)* auto-, automatique; **self-checking** à contrôle automatique; **self-lubricating** autolubrifiant; **self-opening** à ouverture automatique

self-abandonment *n* abnégation *f*, renoncement *m* de soi-même

self-abasement *n* humiliation *f* de soi-même; *Rel* anéantissement *m*

self-abnegation *n* abnégation *f*, sacrifice *m* de soi

self-absorbed [-əb'sɔ:bd] *adj* égocentrique

self-absorption *n* égocentrisme *m*

self-abuse *n Pej* onanisme *m*, masturbation *f*

self-acting *adj* automatique

self-addressed [-ə'drest] *adj* **send three self-addressed (stamped) envelopes** envoyez trois enveloppes (timbrées) à votre adresse

self-adhesive *adj* autocollant, autoadhésif

self-adjusting *adj* à autoréglage, à réglage automatique

►► ***self-adjusting tappet*** poussoir *m* autorégleur

self-advertisement *n* = publicité qu'on se fait à soi-même; **to indulge in self-advertisement** aimer se faire de la publicité

self-advocacy *n esp Am Admin (of mentally handicapped person)* affirmation *f* de soi

self-aggrandizement *n* autoglorification *f*

self-analysis *n* autoanalyse *f*

self-apparent *adj* évident

self-appointed *adj* qui s'est nommé *ou* proclamé lui-même, autoproclamé; **she is our self-appointed guide** elle a assumé d'elle-même le rôle de guide au sein de notre groupe

self-appraisal *n* auto-évaluation *f*

►► ***self-appraisal scheme*** système *m* d'auto-évaluation

self-approving *adj* suffisant

self-assembly 1 *n* **the furniture is flat-packed for easy self-assembly** les meubles sont emballés sous forme de kit pour faciliter le montage

2 *adj (furniture)* en kit

self-assertion *n* affirmation *f* de soi

self-assertive *adj* sûr de soi

self-assertiveness *n* affirmation *f* de soi

self-assessment *n* (**a**) *(gen)* auto-évaluation *f* (**b**) *Br (for taxes)* = système de déclaration des revenus pour le paiement des impôts, par opposition au prélèvement à la source

self-assurance *n* confiance *f* en soi, aplomb *m*; **she has plenty of self-assurance** elle ne manque pas de confiance en elle

self-assured *adj* sûr de soi, plein d'assurance; **he's very self-assured** il est très sûr de lui

self-aware *adj* conscient de soi-même

self-awareness *n* conscience *f* de soi

self-belief *n* confiance *f* en soi; **to have self-belief** croire en soi-même

self-betterment *n (material)* amélioration *f* de sa condition; *(spiritual)* progrès *mpl* spirituels

self-catering 1 *adj Br (flat, accommodation)* indépendant *(avec cuisine)*; *(holiday)* dans un appartement *ou* un logement indépendant

2 *adv* **to go self-catering** louer un meublé pour ses vacances

self-censorship *n* autocensure *f*; **to practise self-censorship** s'autocensurer

self-centred, *Am* **self-centered** *adj* égocentrique

self-centredness, *Am* **self-centeredness** [-'sentədnɪs] *n* égocentrisme *m*

self-certification *n* = système dans lequel les employés n'ont pas besoin de certificat médical pour justifier d'une absence

self-check routine *n Comput* routine *f* d'autotest

self-cleaning *adj* autonettoyant

self-closing *adj* à fermeture automatique

self-cocking [-ˌkɒkɪŋ] *adj Mil* à armement automatique

self-collected *adj* calme, serein, plein de sang-froid

self-coloured, *Am* **self-colored** *adj* uni

self-command *n* maîtrise *f* de soi

self-complacent *adj* satisfait de soi, suffisant

self-composed *adj* posé, calme

self-composure *n* calme *m*, sang-froid *m inv*; **to keep/to lose one's self-composure** garder/perdre son sang-froid

self-conceited *adj* vaniteux, suffisant

self-concept *n* image *f* de soi

self-confessed *adj (murderer, rapist)* qui reconnaît sa culpabilité; **he's a self-confessed drug addict** il avoue lui-même qu'il se drogue

self-confidence *n* confiance *f* en soi, assurance *f*; **she is full of/she lacks self-confidence** elle a une grande/elle manque de confiance en elle

self-confident *adj* sûr de soi, plein d'assurance

self-confidently *adv* avec assurance *ou* aplomb

self-congratulation *n* autosatisfaction *f*

self-congratulatory *adj* satisfait de soi

self-conscious *adj* (**a**) *(embarrassed)* timide, gêné; **to make sb feel self-conscious** intimider qn; **he's very self-conscious about his red hair** il fait un complexe de ses cheveux roux; **I feel very self-conscious in front of all these people** je me sens très mal à l'aise devant tous ces gens (**b**) *(style)* appuyé; **I find her writing too self-conscious** je trouve son style un peu trop appuyé

self-consciously *adv* timidement

self-consciousness *n* timidité *f*, gêne *f*

self-contained *adj* (**a**) *(device)* autonome (**b**) *(flat)* indépendant (**c**) *(person)* réservé

self-contempt *n* mépris *m* de soi-même; **to be full of self-contempt** se mépriser

self-content *n* contentement *m* de soi

self-contented *adj* content de soi

self-contentment *n* contentement *m* de soi

self-contradictory *adj* qui se contredit; **your arguments are self-contradictory** vos arguments se contredisent

self-control *n* sang-froid *m inv*, maîtrise *f* de soi; **to lose one's self-control** perdre son sang-froid; **to have no self-control** ne pas savoir se maîtriser; **to regain one's self-control** se ressaisir

self-controlled *adj* maître de soi

self-correcting [-kə'rektɪŋ] *adj* à correction automatique, autocorrecteur

self-critical *adj* qui fait son autocritique; **to be self-critical** être critique envers soi-même; **you're too self-critical** tu es trop sévère avec toi-même

self-criticism *n* autocritique *f*

self-deceit, self-deception *n* aveuglement *m*; **it's pure self-deceit on his part** il se fait des illusions

self-defeating [-dɪ'fi:tɪŋ] *adj* contraire au but recherché

self-defence, *Am* **self-defense** *n* (**a**) *(physical)* autodéfense *f*; **the art of self-defence** l'art de l'autodéfense; **a course in self-defence** un cours d'autodéfense *ou* de self-défense (**b**) *Law* légitime défense *f*; **it was self-defence** j'étais/il était/*etc* en état de légitime défense; **to plead self-defence** plaider la légitime défense; **to act in self-defence** agir en état de légitime défense; **I shot him in self-defence** j'ai tiré sur lui en état de légitime défense

self-delusion *n* illusion *f*; **it is nothing but self-delusion on her part** elle se fait des illusions

self-denial *n* abnégation *f*, sacrifice *m* de soi

self-denying [-dɪ'naɪɪŋ] *adj* qui fait preuve d'abnégation; **a self-denying life** une vie de sacrifice

self-deprecating *adj (person → ironically)* qui pratique l'autodérision; *(→ due to sense of inferiority)* qui se dénigre; **her self-deprecating humour** son humour caractérisé par l'autodérision

self-deprecation *n (ironic)* autodérision *f*; *(from sense of inferiority)* dénigrement *m* de soi-même

self-deprecatory = **self-deprecating**

self-destruct 1 *vi* s'autodétruire

2 *adj (mechanism)* autodestructeur

self-destruction *n* (**a**) *(of spacecraft, missile)* autodestruction *f* (**b**) *Psy (of personality)* autodestruction *f* (**c**) *(suicide)* suicide *m*

self-destructive *adj* autodestructeur

self-determination *n Pol* autodétermination *f*

self-determined *adj Pol* autodéterminé

self-discipline *n (self-control)* maîtrise *f* de soi; *(good behaviour)* autodiscipline *f*

self-disciplined *adj (self-controlled)* maître de soi; *(well-behaved)* qui fait preuve d'autodiscipline
self-doubt *n* doute *m* de soi-même
self-drive *adj Br*
►► ***self-drive car*** voiture *f* sans chauffeur; ***self-drive car hire*** location *f* de voitures sans chauffeur
self-educated *adj* autodidacte
self-effacing *adj* modeste, effacé
self-elected *adj* élu *ou* nommé par soi-même
self-employed 1 *adj* indépendant, qui travaille à son compte
2 *npl* **the self-employed** les travailleurs *mpl* indépendants
self-employment *n* travail *m* en indépendant, travail *m* à son propre compte
self-esteem *n* respect *m* de soi, amour-propre *m*; **to suffer from low self-esteem** avoir peu d'estime de soi
self-evident *adj* évident, qui va de soi, qui saute aux yeux; **the truth is self-evident** la vérité saute aux yeux; **it's self-evident that neither side can win** il est évident qu'aucune des deux parties ne peut gagner
self-evidently *adv* bien évidemment
self-examination *n (of conscience)* examen *m* de conscience; *(of breast, testicles)* autopalpation *f*
self-explanatory *adj* qui se passe d'explications, évident
self-expression *n* expression *f* libre
self-extracting archive [-iks'trӕktɪŋ-] *n Comput* archive *f* autodécompactable
self-feeder *n* appareil *m* d'alimentation automatique
self-fertilization *n Biol* autofécondation *f*
self-fertilizing [-'fɜːtɪlaɪzɪŋ] *adj Biol* autofécondant
self-financing 1 *n* autofinancement *m*
2 *adj* autofinancé
self-focusing *adj Phot* autofocus *(inv)*, à mise au point automatique
self-fulfilling *adj*
►► ***self-fulfilling prophecy*** = prophétie défaitiste qui se réalise
self-fulfilment, *Am* **self-fulfillment** *n* épanouissement *m*
self-funding *adj* qui s'autofinance
self-governing *adj Pol* autonome
self-government *n Pol* autonomie *f*
self-harm 1 *n* automutilation *f*
2 *vi* s'automutiler
self-hatred *n* haine *f* de soi
self-heal *n Bot* brunelle *f*
self-help *n* autonomie *f*; *(in welfare)* entraide *f*
►► ***self-help group*** groupe *m* d'entraide; ***self-help guide*** = guide pour apprendre à résoudre ses problèmes par soi-même
selfhood ['selfhʊd] *n Psy* le soi
self-hypnosis *n* autohypnose *f*
self-ignition *n Aut* autoallumage *m*
self-image *n* image *f* de soi-même
self-importance *n* suffisance *f*
self-important *adj* vaniteux, suffisant
self-imposed [-ɪm'pəʊzd] *adj* que l'on s'impose à soi-même
►► ***self-imposed exile*** exil *m* volontaire
self-improvement *n* perfectionnement *m* des connaissances personnelles
self-induced *adj* que l'on provoque soi-même
self-induction *n Elec* self-induction *f*, auto-induction *f*
►► ***self-induction coil*** bobine *f* de self-induction
self-indulgence *n* complaisance *f* envers soi-même, habitude *f* de ne rien se refuser
self-indulgent *adj (person)* qui ne se refuse rien; *(book, film)* complaisant
self-inflicted [-ɪn'flɪktɪd] *adj* **his wounds were self-inflicted** il s'était auto-infligé ses blessures
self-interest *n* intérêt *m* personnel; **to act out of self-interest** agir par intérêt personnel
self-interested *adj* intéressé, qui agit par intérêt personnel
selfish ['selfɪʃ] *adj* égoïste; **you're acting out of purely selfish motives** vous agissez par pur égoïsme
selfishly ['selfɪʃlɪ] *adv* égoïstement
selfishness ['selfɪʃnɪs] *n* égoïsme *m*
self-justification *n* autojustification *f*
self-knowledge *n* connaissance *f* de soi
selfless ['selflɪs] *adj* altruiste, désintéressé
selflessly ['selflɪslɪ] *adv* de façon désintéressée, avec désintéressement
selflessness ['selflɪsnɪs] *n* altruisme *m*, désintéressement *m*
self-liquidating [-'lɪkwɪdeɪtɪŋ] *adj Fin* auto-amortissable
►► ***self-liquidating premium*** prime *f* autopayante
self-loading *adj (gun)* automatique
self-loathing *n* dégoût *m* de soi-même
self-locking *adj* à verrouillage automatique
self-love *n* narcissisme *m*, amour *m* de soi-même
self-made *adj* qui a réussi tout seul *ou* par ses propres moyens; **a self-made man** un self-made-man
self-mailer *n Mktg* carte *f* de publicité directe *(qui est mise à la poste sans enveloppe)*
self-mockery *n* autodérision *f*
self-mocking *adj (tone)* d'autodérision; *(remarks)* empreint d'autodérision
self-motivated *adj* capable de prendre des initiatives
self-motivation *n* motivation *f*
self-mutilation *n* mutilation *f* volontaire
self-obsessed *adj* obsédé par soi-même
self-opinionated *adj* sûr de soi
self-perpetuating [-pə'petʃʊeɪtɪŋ] *adj* qui se perpétue
self-pity *n* apitoiement *m* sur son sort; **she's full of self-pity** elle s'apitoie beaucoup sur son sort; **to wallow in self-pity** s'apitoyer sur son sort
self-pitying *adj* qui s'apitoie sur son (propre) sort; **don't be so self-pitying** cesse de t'apitoyer sur ton sort
self-pollination *n Bot* autopollinisation *f*, pollinisation *f* directe
self-portrait *n (in painting)* autoportrait *m*; *(in book)* portrait *m* de l'auteur par lui-même
self-possessed *adj* maître de soi, qui garde son sang-froid
self-possession *n* sang-froid *m inv*
self-praise *n* éloge *m* de soi-même; **I'm not saying that in self-praise** ce n'est pas laudatif à mon égard
self-preservation *n* instinct *m* de conservation
self-proclaimed [-prə'kleɪmd] *adj* **he is the self-proclaimed king of the ring** il s'est proclamé lui-même roi du ring; **she's a self-proclaimed art critic** elle se proclame critique d'art
self-propelled [-prə'peld], **self-propelling** [-prə'pelɪŋ] *adj* autopropulsé
self-propulsion *n* autopropulsion *f*
self-protection *n* autoprotection *f*
self-publicist *n* **he is an accomplished self-publicist** il sait soigner sa publicité
self-raising [-'reɪzɪŋ] *adj Br*
►► ***self-raising flour*** farine *f* avec levure incorporée
self-realization *n* prise *f* de conscience de soi-même
self-referential *adj* autoréférentiel
self-regard *n* égoïsme *m*
self-regarding *adj* qui ne considère que soi-même; **from self-regarding motives** par intérêt
self-regulating *adj* autorégulateur
self-regulation *n* autorégulation *f*
self-regulatory organization *n Br St Exch* organisme *m* autoréglementé *ou* autonome
self-reliance *n* indépendance *f*
self-reliant *adj* indépendant; **you must learn to be more self-reliant** tu dois apprendre à moins compter sur les autres
self-replicate *vi* s'autoreproduire
self-replicating [-'replɪkeɪtɪŋ] *adj* autoreproducteur
self-replication *n* autoreproduction *f*
self-respect *n* respect *m* de soi, amour-propre *m*
self-respecting *adj* qui se respecte; **no self-respecting girl would be seen dead going out with him** une fille qui se respecte ne sortirait pour rien au monde avec lui
self-restrained *adj* retenu, qui sait se contenir
self-restraint *n* retenue *f*; **to exercise self-restraint** se retenir; **with great self-restraint** avec beaucoup de retenue
self-righteous *adj* suffisant
self-righteousness *n* suffisance *f*, *Formal* pharisaïsme *m*
self-righting [-'raɪtɪŋ] *adj (boat)* inchavirable
self-rising *Am* = **self-raising**
self-rule *n Pol* autonomie *f*
self-sacrifice *n* abnégation *f*; **there's no need for self-sacrifice** vous n'avez pas besoin de vous sacrifier
self-sacrificing [-'sӕkrɪfaɪsɪŋ] *adj* qui se sacrifie, qui a l'esprit de sacrifice
self-same *adj* même, identique; *Fam* **the self-same day I got the sack** le jour même j'ai été viré
self-satisfaction *n* suffisance *f*, contentement *m* de soi, fatuité *f*
self-satisfied *adj (person)* suffisant, content de soi; *(look, smile, attitude)* suffisant, satisfait; **she gave a self-satisfied smile** elle esquissa un sourire empreint de suffisance
self-sealing *adj (envelope)* autocollant, autoadhésif; *(tank)* à obturation automatique
self-seeking [-'siːkɪŋ] *adj* égoïste
self-serve *Am* = **self-service** *adj*
self-service 1 *adj* en self-service, en libre service
2 *n (restaurant)* self-service *m*; *(garage, shop)* libre-service *m*
►► ***self-service restaurant*** self-service *m*; ***self-service shop*** libre-service *m*
self-serving *adj* intéressé
self-starter *n* (**a**) *Aut* starter *m* automatique (**b**) *(person)* personne *f* pleine d'initiative; **to be a self-starter** être autonome
self-styled [-'staɪld] *adj* prétendu, soi-disant; **he's a self-styled expert on the matter** il se prétend *ou* c'est un soi-disant expert en la matière
self-sufficiency *n* (**a**) *(of person → independence)* indépendance *f*; *(→ self-assurance)* suffisance *f* (**b**) *Econ (of nation, resources)* autosuffisance *f*; *Pol* **(economic) self-sufficiency** autarcie *f*
self-sufficient *adj* (**a**) *(person → independent)* indépendant; *(→ self-assured)* plein de confiance en soi, suffisant (**b**) *(nation) Econ* autosuffisant; *Pol* autarcique; **self-sufficient in copper** autosuffisant en cuivre
self-supporting *adj* (**a**) *(financially)* indépendant (**b**) *(framework)* autoporteur, autoportant
self-tapping *adj*
►► ***self-tapping screw*** vis *f* autotaraudeuse
self-taught *adj* autodidacte
self-test *Comput* **1** *n* autotest *m*
2 *vi* s'autotester
►► ***self-test button*** bouton *m* d'autotest; ***self-test program*** programme *m* d'autotest
self-watering planter *n* bac *m* à réserve d'eau
self-willed *adj* têtu, obstiné
self-winding [-'waɪndɪŋ] *adj (watch)* qui n'a pas besoin d'être remonté, (à remontage) automatique

SELL [sel]

vendre	► **2 (a); 3 (b)**
faire vendre	► **2 (b)**
faire accepter	► **2 (c)**
se vendre	► **3 (a)**

(pt & pp **sold** [səʊld]) **1** *n* (**a**) *Com* vente *f*
(**b**) *Fam (disappointment)* déception▫ *f*; *(hoax)* attrape-nigaud▫ *m*
2 *vt* (**a**) *(goods)* vendre; **to sell sb sth** *or* **sth to sb** vendre qch à qn; **he sold me his car for $1,000** il m'a vendu sa voiture (pour) 1000 dollars; **stamps are now also sold in some shops** les timbres sont maintenant vendus aussi dans certains magasins; **he sells computers for a living** il gagne sa vie en vendant des ordinateurs; **a shop that sells clothes/furniture** un magasin de vêtements/meubles; **the book sold 50,000 copies, 50,000 copies of the book were sold** le livre s'est vendu à 50 000 exemplaires; **to sell sth for cash** vendre qch au comptant; **to sell sth on credit** vendre qch à crédit; **to sell sth cheap** vendre qch à bas prix; **to sell sth at a loss** vendre qch à perte; **they sell**

sel–s

the cassettes at £3 each ils vendent les cassettes 3 livres pièce; **she was sold into slavery/prostitution** on l'a vendue comme esclave/prostituée; **she sold her body** *or* **herself to buy food** elle s'est prostituée pour acheter à manger; **they sold classified information to our competitors** ils ont vendu des renseignements confidentiels à nos concurrents; **he sold state secrets to the enemy** il a vendu des secrets d'État à l'ennemi; **he'd sell his own grandmother for a pint of beer** il vendrait son âme pour une bière; **to sell one's soul to the devil** vendre son âme au diable; *Hum* **I'd sell my soul for a holiday in the Caribbean** je ferais *ou* donnerais n'importe quoi pour passer des vacances aux Caraïbes; **to sell sb short** *(cheat)* rouler qn; *(belittle)* ne pas rendre justice à qn; **to sell oneself short** ne pas se montrer à sa juste valeur; **don't sell yourself short** il faut vous mettre en valeur; **I'm often accused of selling the country short** on m'accuse souvent de donner une mauvaise image du pays; *Fam* **we were sold a pup** *or* **a dud** *(cheated)* on nous a roulés; *(sold rubbish)* on nous a vendu de la camelote; **to sell sb down the river** trahir qn

(**b**) *(cause to be sold)* faire vendre; **what really sells newspapers is scandal** ce sont les scandales qui font vraiment vendre les journaux; **you need a star to sell the movie** *(to backers)* il faut une star dans la distribution du film pour intéresser les investisseurs potentiels; *(to the public)* il faut une star dans la distribution du film pour attirer le public

(**c**) *(promote → idea, image, policy)* faire accepter; **she sold the idea to the whole council** elle a fait accepter l'idée à tout le conseil; **to sell an idea to the electorate** faire passer une idée auprès des électeurs; **a campaign to sell the new party** une campagne de publicité pour le nouveau parti; **as a politician, it is important to be able to sell yourself** les hommes politiques doivent savoir se mettre en valeur

(**d**) *Fam (make believe → story, excuse)* faire avaler; **she tried to sell me some story** *or* **line about running out of petrol** elle a essayé de me faire avaler une histoire de panne d'essence

(**e**) *Fam (cheat, deceive)* rouler; **we've been sold!** on s'est fait avoir *ou* posséder!

3 *vi* (**a**) *(goods)* se vendre; **the record is selling well** le disque se vend bien; **the cakes sell for** *or* **at 70 pence each** les gâteaux se vendent (à) *ou* valent 70 pence pièce; **shares in the company are selling at 109 pence** les actions de cette compagnie s'échangent à 109 pence; **to sell like hot cakes** se vendre comme des petits pains

(**b**) *(person, shop)* vendre; **sorry, I'm not interested in selling** désolé, je ne cherche pas à vendre; *St Exch* **to sell short** vendre à découvert

►► *Am* ***sell date*** date *f* limite de vente; *St Exch* ***sell order*** injonction *f* à la vente; *St Exch* ***sell price*** prix *m* (du) comptant

►**sell back** *vt sep* revendre

►**sell forward** *Fin* **1** *vi* vendre à terme

2 *vt sep* **to sell sth forward** vendre qch à terme

►**sell off** *vt sep (at reduced price)* solder; *(clear)* liquider; *(get cash)* vendre; *(privatize)* privatiser; **the house was sold off to pay debts** la maison a été vendue pour régler des créances; **they're selling the plates off at bargain prices** ils liquident les assiettes à des prix défiant toute concurrence

►**sell on** *vt sep* revendre *(en faisant du bénéfice)*

►**sell out 1** *vt sep* (**a**) *(usu passive) (concert, match)* **the match was sold out** le match s'est joué à guichets fermés; **the tickets are sold out** tous les billets ont été vendus

(**b**) *(betray → person, principles)* trahir

(**c**) *St Exch* vendre, réaliser

2 *vi* (**a**) *Com (sell business)* vendre son commerce; *(sell stock)* liquider (son stock); *(run out)* vendre *ou* écouler tout le stock; **my father sold out and retired** mon père a vendu son affaire et a pris sa retraite; **he sold out to some Japanese investors** il a vendu à des investisseurs japonais; **we've sold out of sugar** nous n'avons plus de sucre, nous avons vendu *ou* écoulé tout notre stock de sucre

(**b**) *Fin (sell shares)* vendre ses parts; **to sell out to sb** vendre ses parts à qn

(**c**) *(betray one's principles)* renier ses principes; **to sell out to the enemy** passer à l'ennemi; **the government were accused of selling out to terrorism** le gouvernement fut accusé d'avoir traité avec les terroristes; **critics accused the writer of selling out** les critiques ont accusé l'écrivain d'avoir renié ses principes pour plaire au plus grand nombre

►**sell up** *Br* **1** *vt sep* (**a**) *Fin & Law (goods)* opérer la vente forcée de, procéder à la liquidation de (**b**) *Com (business)* vendre, liquider

2 *vi (shopkeeper)* vendre son fonds de commerce *ou* son affaire; *(businessman)* vendre son affaire; **he sold up and went to Canada** il a tout vendu et est parti au Canada

---

sellable ['seləbəl] *adj* vendable

Sellafield ['seləfi:ld] *n* = usine de retraitement des déchets radioactifs dans le nord de l'Angleterre

sell-by date *n Br* date *f* limite de vente; *Fig* **the TV programme/minister is past its/his sell-by date** l'émission de télévision/le ministre a fait son temps; **she knew she would soon be past her sell-by date** *(unmarried woman)* elle avait conscience qu'elle serait bientôt trop vieille pour plaire

seller ['selə(r)] *n* (**a**) *(person → gen)* vendeur(euse) *m,f*; *(→ merchant)* vendeur(euse) *m,f*, marchand(e) *m,f*; *St Exch (of stocks, shares)* réalisateur(trice) *m,f* (**b**) *(goods)* **these shoes are good/poor sellers** ces chaussures se vendent bien/mal; **it's one of our biggest sellers** c'est un des articles qui se vend le mieux

►► ***seller's market*** *(for property)* c'est un marché vendeur *ou* favorable aux vendeurs; *St Exch (for stocks, shares)* marché *m* à la hausse; *St Exch* ***seller's option*** prime *f* vendeur

selling ['selɪŋ] *n (UNCOUNT)* vente *f*

►► ***selling costs*** frais *mpl* commerciaux; ***selling licence*** licence *f* de vente; ***selling off, selling out*** *(of stock)* liquidation *f*; *St Exch (of stocks, shares)* (re)vente *f*; ***selling point*** avantage *m*, atout *m*, point *m* fort; ***selling power*** puissance *f* de vente; ***selling price*** prix *m* de vente; ***selling rate*** *(of currency)* taux *m* de vente

sell-off *n (gen)* vente *f*; *St Exch (of stocks, shares)* (re)vente *f*

Sellotape® ['seləteɪp] *n Br* Scotch® *m*, ruban *m* adhésif

sellotape ['seləteɪp] *vt* scotcher, coller avec du ruban adhésif

sell-out *n* (**a**) *Com* liquidation *f* (**b**) *(betrayal)* trahison *f*; *(capitulation)* capitulation *f* (**c**) *(play, concert etc)* **it was a sell-out** on a vendu tous les billets; **the match was a sell-out** le match s'est joué à guichets fermés

seltzer ['seltsə(r)] *n* eau *f* de Seltz

►► ***seltzer water*** eau *f* de Seltz

selvage, selvedge ['selvɪdʒ] *n Tex* lisière *f (d'un tissu)*

selves [selvz] *pl of* **self**

semanteme [sɪ'mænti:m] *n Ling* sémantème *m*

semantic [sɪ'mæntɪk] *adj* sémantique

semantically [sɪ'mæntɪkəlɪ] *adv* du point de vue sémantique

semantician [,sɪmæn'tɪʃən] *n* sémanticien(enne) *m,f*

semanticist [sɪ'mæntɪsɪst] *n* sémanticien(enne) *m,f*

semantics [sɪ'mæntɪks] *n (UNCOUNT)* sémantique *f*; **it's all a question of semantics** tout dépend du sens que l'on donne aux mots

semaphore ['seməfɔ:(r)] **1** *n* (**a**) *(UNCOUNT) (signals)* signaux *mpl* à bras; **in** *or* **by semaphore** par signaux à bras (**b**) *Rail & Naut* sémaphore *m*

2 *vt* transmettre par signaux à bras

semaphorist ['seməfɔ:rɪst] *n* sémaphoriste *mf*

sematic [sə'mætɪk] *adj Biol* sématique

semblance ['sembləns] *n* semblant *m*, apparence *f*; **a semblance of order** un semblant d'ordre; **we need to show at least some semblance of unity** nous devons au moins montrer un semblant d'unité

semeiology = **semiology**

sememe ['si:mi:m] *n Ling* sémème *m*

semen ['si:mən] *n (UNCOUNT)* sperme *m*, semence *f*

semester [sɪ'mestə(r)] *n* semestre *m*

semi ['semɪ] *n Fam* (**a**) *Br (abbr* **semi-detached house**) maison *f* jumelée ☐ (**b**) *(abbr* **semifinal**) demi-finale ☐ *f* (**c**) *Am, Austr & NZ (abbr* **semi-trailer**) semi *m*

semi- ['semɪ] *pref* (**a**) *(partly)* semi-, demi-; **in semi-darkness** dans la pénombre *ou* la semi-obscurité; **he's in semi-retirement** il est en semi-retraite (**b**) *(twice)* **semi-yearly** semestriel

semi-annual *adj* semestriel; *Bot* semi-annuel

semi-annually *adv* semestriellement, deux fois par an

semi-arid *adj* semi-aride

semi-automatic 1 *adj* semi-automatique

2 *n* arme *f* semi-automatique

semibreve ['semɪbri:v] *n Br Mus* ronde *f*

►► ***semibreve rest*** pause *f*

semi-centennial *adj* qui revient tous les cinquante ans

semicircle ['semɪ,sɜ:kəl] *n* demi-cercle *m*

semicircular [,semɪ'sɜ:kjʊlə(r)] *adj* demi-circulaire, semi-circulaire

►► *Anat* ***semicircular canal*** canal *m* semi-circulaire

semicolon [,semɪ'kəʊlən] *n* point-virgule *m*

semiconduction [,semɪkən'dʌkʃən] *n Phys* semi-conduction *f*

semiconductor [,semɪkən'dʌktə(r)] *n Phys* semi-conducteur *m*

semiconscious [,semɪ'kɒnʃəs] *adj* à demi *ou* moitié conscient; **she was only semiconscious** *(losing consciousness)* elle avait pratiquement perdu connaissance; *(regaining consciousness)* elle n'avait pas encore tout à fait repris connaissance

semiconsciousness [,semɪ'kɒnʃəsnɪs] *n* **in a state of semiconsciousness** à demi conscient

semiconsonant [,semɪ'kɒnsənənt] *n Ling* semi-consonne *f*

semi-darkness *n* pénombre *f*, semi-obscurité *f*

semi-detached *n* maison *f* jumelée

►► ***semidetached house*** maison *f* jumelée

semi-documentary *n* film *m* semi-documentaire

semifinal [,semɪ'faɪnəl] *n* demi-finale *f*; **she lost in the semifinals** elle a perdu en demi-finale

semifinalist [,semɪ'faɪnəlɪst] *n* demi-finaliste *mf*

semi-finished goods *npl Ind* produits *mpl* semi-finis

semifluid [,semɪ'flu:ɪd] **1** *adj* semi-liquide, semi-fluide

2 *n* semi-fluide *m*

semi-graphics *n Comput* semi-graphisme *m*

semi-invalid *n* **he is a semi-invalid** il n'est pas très valide

semiliterate [,semɪ'lɪtərət] *adj* quasi analphabète

semilunar [,semɪ'lu:nə(r)] *adj* semi-lunaire

semi-manufactured product [-,mænjʊ'fæktʃəd-] *n* demi-produit *m*

seminal ['semɪnəl] *adj* (**a**) *Anat & Bot* séminal (**b**) *(important)* majeur, qui fait école; **she was a seminal influence on his art** elle eut une influence majeure sur son art

►► *Anat & Bot* ***seminal duct*** voie *f* séminale; *Anat & Bot* ***seminal fluid*** liquide *m* séminal

seminar ['semɪnɑ:(r)] *n* (**a**) *(conference)* séminaire *m*, colloque *m* (**b**) *Univ (class)* séminaire *m*, travaux *mpl* dirigés

seminarian [,semɪ'neərɪən] *n* séminariste *mf*

seminarist ['semɪnərɪst] *n Rel* séminariste *m*

seminary ['semɪnərɪ] *(pl* **seminaries**) *n Rel & Sch (for boys, priests)* séminaire *m*; *(for girls)* pensionnat *m* de jeunes filles

seminiferous [,semɪ'nɪfərəs] *adj Anat & Bot* séminifère

semi-nude *adj* à moitié nu, à demi nu

semi-obscurity *n (darkness)* pénombre *f*, *Fig* quasi-obscurité *f*

semi-official *adj* semi-officiel

semi-officially *adv* d'une manière semi-officielle, officieusement

semiologist [,semɪ'ɒlədʒɪst] *n* sémioticien(enne) *m,f*, sémiologue *mf*

semiology [,semɪ'ɒlədʒɪ] *n* sémiologie *f*

semiotic [,semɪ'ɒtɪk] *adj* sémiotique

semiotician [,semɪə'tɪʃən] *n* sémioticien(enne) *m,f*

semiotics [ˌsemɪˈɒtɪks] *n (UNCOUNT)* sémiotique *f*

semipermeable [ˌsemɪˈpɜːmɪəbəl] *adj* semi-perméable

semiprecious [ˈsemɪˌpreʃəs] *adj* semi-précieux

semiprofessional [ˌsemɪprəˈfeʃənəl] **1** *adj* semi-professionnel

2 *n* semi-professionnel(elle) *m,f*

semi-profile *adj (portrait)* de trois quarts

semiquaver [ˈsemɪˌkweɪvə(r)] *n Br Mus* double croche *f*

semi-retired *adj* en préretraite progressive

semi-retirement *n* préretraite *f* progressive

semi-rigid *adj* semi-rigide

semi-skilled *adj (worker)* spécialisé

semi-skimmed *adj (milk)* demi-écrémé

semi-solid *adj* semi-solide

semisubmersible [ˌsemɪsəbˈmɜːsəbəl] **1** *adj* semi-submersible

2 *n* plateforme *f* semi-submersible

Semite [ˈsiːmaɪt] *n* Sémite *mf*

Semitic [sɪˈmɪtɪk] **1** *n Ling* langue *f* sémitique, sémitique *m*

2 *adj* sémite, sémitique

semitone [ˈsemɪtəʊn] *n Mus* demi-ton *m*

semitonic [ˌsemɪˈtɒnɪk] *adj Mus* d'un demi-ton

▸▸ *Mus* ***semitonic scale*** gamme *f* chromatique

semitrailer [ˌsemɪˈtreɪlə(r)] *n* semi-remorque *m*

semi-transparency *n* demi-transparence *f*, semi-transparence *f*

semi-transparent *adj* demi-transparent, semi-transparent

semitropical [ˌsemɪˈtrɒpɪkəl] *adj* semi-tropical

semivowel [ˈsemɪˌvaʊəl] *n Ling* semi-voyelle *f*

semolina [ˌseməˈliːnə] *n* semoule *f*

▸▸ *Culin* ***semolina pudding*** gâteau *m* de semoule

sempiternal [ˌsempɪˈtɜːnəl] *adj Literary* sempiternel, éternel

sempstress [ˈsempstrɪs] *n* couturière *f*

SEN [ˌesiːˈen] *n* (*abbr* **State Enrolled Nurse**) aide-soignant(e) *m,f* diplômé(e)

sen [sen] *n NEng Fam* soi; **get tha sen down here this minute** amène-toi, et plus vite que ça

Sen. (*written abbr* **Senator**) sénateur *m*

sen. (*written abbr* **senior**) *(in rank)* (de grade) supérieur; **John Brown sen.** John Brown père

senate [ˈsenɪt] *n* (**a**) *Hist & Pol* sénat *m*; **the United States Senate** le Sénat américain (**b**) *Univ* conseil *m* d'université

SENATE

Le Sénat constitue, avec la Chambre des représentants, l'organe législatif américain; composé de 100 membres (deux par État), il détient l'exclusivité du droit d'impeachment.

senator [ˈsenətə(r)] *n* sénateur *m*

senatorial [ˌsenəˈtɔːrɪəl] *adj* sénatorial

SEND [send] (*pt & pp* **sent** [sent]) **1** *vt* (**a**) *(dispatch → gen)* envoyer; *(→ by post)* envoyer, expédier; **to send sb a letter, to send a letter to sb** envoyer une lettre à qn; **he sent (us) word that he would be delayed** il (nous) a fait savoir qu'il aurait du retard; **he sent word to say he would be late** il a fait dire *ou* savoir qu'il serait en retard; **she sends her love** *or* **regards** elle vous envoie ses amitiés; **send them our love** embrassez-les pour nous; **send them our best wishes** faites-leur nos amitiés; **I sent my luggage by train** j'ai fait expédier *ou* envoyer mes bagages par le train; **to send clothes to the laundry** donner du linge à blanchir; **images sent by satellite** images transmises par satellite; **to send a message over the radio** envoyer un message radio; **it's like manna sent from heaven** c'est une véritable aubaine; **what will the future send us?** que nous réserve l'avenir?; **we sent help to the refugees** nous avons envoyé des secours aux réfugiés; **they sent a car to fetch us** ils ont envoyé une voiture nous chercher

(**b**) *(cause to go → person)* envoyer; **the government sent an ambassador to Mexico** le gouvernement envoya un ambassadeur au Mexique; **I was sent to bed/to my room** on m'a envoyé me coucher/dans ma chambre; **to send sb home** *(from school)* renvoyer qn chez lui; *(from abroad)* rapatrier qn; *Ind (lay off)* mettre qn en chômage technique; **to send sb to prison** envoyer qn en prison; **to send sb to school** envoyer qn à l'école; **send the children indoors** faites rentrer les enfants; **send him to me** envoyez-le moi; **send him to my office** dites-lui de venir dans mon bureau, envoyez-le moi; **she sent her daughter for the meat** *or* **to get the meat** elle a envoyé sa fille chercher la viande; **she sent her brother on an errand/with a message** elle a envoyé son frère faire une course/porter un message; **the children were sent to say goodnight** on envoya les enfants dire bonsoir; **the dogs were sent after him** on lança les chiens à sa poursuite *ou* à ses trousses; **heavy smoking sent him to an early grave** il est mort prématurément parce qu'il fumait trop; *Fam* **to send sb packing** *or* **about his business** envoyer promener qn, envoyer qn sur les roses; *Fig* **don't send a boy to do a man's job** il faut que la personne soit à la mesure de la tâche

(**c**) *(propel, cause to move)* envoyer; **he sent the ball over the heads of the spectators** il envoya le ballon par-dessus la tête des spectateurs; **the collision sent showers of sparks/clouds of smoke into the sky** la collision fit jaillir une gerbe d'étincelles/provoqua des nuages de fumée; **it sends a current down the wire** il fait passer un courant dans le fil; **the sound sent shivers down my spine** le bruit m'a fait froid dans le dos; **I sent the cup flying** j'ai envoyé voler la tasse; **the blow sent me flying** le coup m'a envoyé rouler par terre; **a gust of wind sent the papers flying across the table** un coup de vent balaya les papiers qui se trouvaient sur la table; **a sudden storm sent us all running for shelter** un orage soudain nous força à courir nous mettre à l'abri; **the boy sent the marbles rolling across the floor** le garçon envoya les billes rouler par terre; **to send profits tumbling** faire chuter les bénéfices; **to send prices sky-high** faire flamber les prix; **the news sent a murmur of excitement through the hall** la nouvelle provoqua un murmure d'agitation dans la salle

(**d**) *(into a specific state)* rendre; **the noise is sending me mad** *or* **out of my mind** le bruit me rend fou; **that sent him into fits of laughter** cela l'a fait éclater de rire; **the news sent them into a panic** les nouvelles les ont fait paniquer; **to send sb into a rage** enrager qn; **to send sb to sleep** endormir qn

(**e**) *Fam Old-fashioned (thrill)* emballer; **his voice really sends me** sa voix me fait vraiment craquer

2 *vi* (**a**) *(send word)* **he sent to say he couldn't come** il nous a fait savoir qu'il ne pouvait pas venir

(**b**) *(for information, equipment)* **we sent to Paris for a copy** nous avons demandé une copie à Paris

▸**send along** *vt sep* envoyer; **send him along!** envoyez-le-moi

▸**send away** **1** *vt sep* (**a**) *(letter, parcel)* expédier, mettre à la poste; **to send a radio away to be repaired** expédier une radio chez le réparateur

(**b**) *(dismiss → person)* renvoyer, faire partir; **the children were sent away to school** les enfants furent mis en pension

2 *vi* **to send away for sth** *(by post)* se faire envoyer qch; *(by catalogue)* commander qch; **send away for your free copy now** demandez maintenant votre exemplaire gratuit

▸**send back** *vt sep (return → books, goods, food in restaurant)* renvoyer; **send the chocolates back to the shop** renvoyez les chocolats au magasin; **we sent her back to fetch a coat** *or* **for a coat** nous l'avons renvoyée prendre un manteau

▸**send down** **1** *vt sep* (**a**) *(person, lift)* faire descendre, envoyer en bas; **they sent me down to the cellar** ils m'ont fait descendre à la cave; **she was sent down to ask if they wanted coffee** on l'a envoyée en bas pour demander s'ils voulaient du café

(**b**) *(cause to fall → prices, temperature)* faire baisser, provoquer la baisse de

(**c**) *Br Univ (student)* expulser, renvoyer

(**d**) *Br Fam (to prison)* coffrer; **he was sent down for twenty years** il a écopé de vingt ans (de prison), il en a pris pour vingt ans

2 *vi (by message or messenger)* **to send down for sth** (se) faire monter qch

▸**send for** *vt insep* (**a**) *(doctor, taxi)* faire venir, appeler; *(mother, luggage)* faire venir; *(police)* appeler; *(help)* envoyer chercher; **we sent for another bottle** *(in hotel, restaurant)* on a demandé une autre bouteille; **we sent for a couple of pizzas** *(home delivery)* nous nous sommes fait livrer deux pizzas

(**b**) *(by post)* se faire envoyer; *(by catalogue)* commander; *(catalogue, price list)* demander

▸**send forth** *vt insep Literary* (**a**) *(army, messenger)* envoyer

(**b**) *(produce → leaves)* produire; *(→ light)* produire, émettre; *(→ smell)* répandre; *(→ cry)* pousser

(**c**) *Am Pol* **the Senate has sent forth the bill to the president** le Sénat a transmis le projet de loi au président

▸**send in** *vt sep* (**a**) *(visitor)* faire entrer; *(troops, police)* envoyer

(**b**) *(submit → bill, report, form)* envoyer; *(→ suggestions, resignation)* envoyer, soumettre; **why don't you send your name in for the competition?** pourquoi ne pas vous inscrire au concours?; **to send in a request** faire une demande; **please send in a written application** veuillez envoyer une demande écrite; *(for job)* veuillez poser votre candidature par écrit

▸**send off** **1** *vt sep* (**a**) *(by post)* expédier, mettre à la poste

(**b**) *(person)* envoyer; **I sent him off home/upstairs** je l'ai envoyé chez lui/en haut; **they sent us off to bed/to get washed** ils nous ont envoyés nous coucher/nous laver; **they are sent off to school every morning** on les envoie à l'école tous les matins

(**c**) *Sport* expulser

(**d**) *also Fig* **to send sb off (to sleep)** endormir qn

2 *vi* **to send off for sth** *(by post)* se faire envoyer qch; *(by catalogue)* commander qch

▸**send on** *vt sep* (**a**) *(mail)* faire suivre; *(luggage)* expédier; **to send a message on to sb** faire suivre un message à qn; **my luggage was sent on to New York** *(in advance)* on a expédié mes bagages à New York; *(by mistake)* mes bagages ont été expédiés à New York par erreur; **if you've forgotten anything, we'll send it on** si vous avez oublié quelque chose, nous vous le renverrons

(**b**) *(person)* **they sent us on ahead** *or* **in front** ils nous ont envoyés en éclaireurs; **we sent them on to find a hotel** nous les avons envoyés en éclaireurs pour trouver un hôtel; **they sent me on to Dundee** *(further)* ils m'ont envoyé jusqu'à Dundee

(**c**) *Sport (player)* faire entrer (sur le terrain)

▸**send out** **1** *vt sep* (**a**) *(by post → invitations)* expédier, poster

(**b**) *(messengers, search party)* envoyer, dépêcher; *(patrol)* envoyer; *(outside)* envoyer dehors; **we sent her out for coffee** nous l'avons envoyée chercher du café; **they sent me out to Burma** ils m'ont envoyé en Birmanie; **they sent out a car for us** ils ont envoyé une voiture nous chercher; **we sent them all out into the garden** on les a tous envoyés dans le jardin; **send the children out to play** envoyez les enfants jouer dehors

(**c**) *(transmit → message, signal)* envoyer; **a call was sent out for Dr Bramley** on a fait appeler le Dr Bramley

(**d**) *(produce, give out → leaves)* produire; *(→ light, heat)* émettre, répandre, diffuser; *(→ fumes, smoke)* répandre; **the chimney/engine sent out billows of smoke** la cheminée/le moteur crachait des tourbillons de fumée

2 *vi* **to send out for coffee/sandwiches** envoyer quelqu'un chercher du café/des sandwiches

▸**send round** *vt sep* (**a**) *(circulate → petition)* faire circuler; *Fig* **to send the hat round** faire la quête

(**b**) *(dispatch → messenger, repairman)* envoyer; *(→ message)* faire parvenir; **they sent a car round** ils ont envoyé une voiture; **her**

mother sent her round to our house for some sugar sa mère l'a envoyée chez nous demander du sucre

►**send up** *vt sep* (**a**) *(messenger, luggage, drinks)* faire monter; *(rocket, flare)* lancer; *(plane)* faire décoller; *(smoke)* répandre

(**b**) *(raise → price, pressure, temperature)* faire monter

(**c**) *Br Fam (ridicule)* mettre en boîte, se moquer de❑; *(parody)* parodier❑

(**d**) *Am Fam (to prison)* coffrer

---

sender ['sendə(r)] *n* expéditeur(trice) *m,f*; **return to sender** retour à l'expéditeur

sending ['sendɪŋ] *n* envoi *m*; **sending by rail** expédition *f* par chemin de fer

►► ***sending depot*** dépôt *m* d'expédition

sending-off *n Br Sport* expulsion *f*

send-off *n* **to give sb a send-off** dire au revoir à qn, souhaiter bon voyage à qn; **to give sb a big send-off** venir nombreux pour dire au revoir à qn; **he was given a warm send-off by all his colleagues** tous ses collègues sont venus lui faire des adieux chaleureux; **to give sb a good send-off** *(funeral)* faire à qn de belles funérailles

send-up *n Br Fam* parodie❑ *f*

Seneca[1] ['senɪkə] *pr n Antiq* Sénèque

Seneca[2] *n* (**a**) *(tribe)* Indiens *mpl* Seneca, Seneca *mpl* (**b**) *(member of tribe)* Indien(enne) *m,f* Seneca, Seneca *mf inv* (**c**) *(language)* Seneca *m*

Senegal [ˌsenɪ'gɔːl] *n* Sénégal *m*; **in Senegal** au Sénégal

Senegalese [ˌsenɪgə'liːz] *(pl* **inv**) **1** *npl* **the Senegalese** les Sénégalais *mpl*

2 *n* Sénégalais(e) *m,f*

3 *adj* sénégalais

Senegambia [ˌsenɪ'gæmbɪə] *n* Sénégambie *f*

Senegambian [ˌsenɪ'gæmbɪən] **1** *n* Sénégambien(enne) *m,f*

2 *adj* sénégambien

senescence [sɪ'nesəns] *n* sénescence *f*

senescent [sɪ'nesənt] *adj* sénescent

seneschal ['senɪʃəl] *n Hist* sénéchal *m*

senile ['siːnaɪl] *adj* sénile

►► ***senile decay*** dégénérescence *f* sénile; ***senile dementia*** démence *f* sénile

senility [sɪ'nɪlətɪ] *n* sénilité *f*

senior ['siːnjə(r)] **1** *adj* (**a**) *(in age)* plus âgé, aîné; *(in rank)* (de grade) supérieur; *(longer-serving)* plus ancien; **he's two years senior to me** il est mon aîné de deux ans; **I am senior to them** *(have higher position)* je suis leur supérieur; *(have served longer)* j'ai plus d'ancienneté qu'eux; **she holds a senior position in the company** elle est haut placée dans la société; **George is the senior partner in our firm** George est l'associé principal de notre société

(**b**) *Sch* **the senior boys/girls of a school** les garçons *mpl*/filles *fpl* des grandes classes

2 *n* (**a**) *(older person)* aîné(e) *m,f*; **he is my senior by six months, he is six months my senior** il a six mois de plus que moi, il est de six mois mon aîné

(**b**) *Am (senior citizen)* personne *f* âgée *ou* du troisième âge

(**c**) *Am Sch* élève *mf* de terminale; *Univ* étudiant(e) *m,f* de licence

(**d**) *Br Sch* **the seniors** ≃ les grands (grandes) *mpl, fpl*

(**e**) *(in hierarchy)* supérieur(e) *m,f*

3 Senior *adj (in age)* **John Brown Senior** John Brown père

►► *Br* ***senior aircraftman*** ≃ caporal *m*; *Am* ***senior airman*** ≃ caporal-chef *m*; ***senior airport officials*** la direction de l'aéroport; ***senior citizen*** personne *f* âgée *ou* du troisième âge; ***senior citizen's club*** club *m* du troisième âge; ***senior citizen's rail pass*** ≃ Carte *f* Vermeil; ***senior clerk*** commis *m* principal, chef *m* de bureau; *Br Univ* ***Senior Common Room*** salle *f* des professeurs; ***senior executive*** cadre *m* supérieur; ***senior government official*** haut(e) fonctionnaire *mf*; *Am* ***senior high school*** lycée *m*; *Br Med* ***senior house officer*** ≃ interne *mf (de rang supérieur au "house officer")*; ***(the) senior management*** la direction; *Br Sch* ***senior master*** professeur *m* principal; ***senior officer*** officier *m* supérieur; *Br* ***Senior Service*** marine *f*; ***senior partner*** associé(e) *m,f* principal(e); *Sch* ***senior year*** terminale *f*, dernière année *f* d'études secondaires

seniority [ˌsiːnɪ'ɒrətɪ] *n* (**a**) *(in age)* priorité *f* d'âge; **he became chairman by virtue of seniority** il est devenu président parce qu'il était le plus âgé *ou* le doyen (**b**) *(in rank)* supériorité *f*; *(in length of service)* ancienneté *f*; **to have seniority over sb** être le supérieur de qn; **according to** *or* **by seniority** en fonction de *ou* à l'ancienneté

senna ['senə] *n Bot* séné *m*

►► *Pharm* ***senna pods*** follicules *mpl* de séné; ***senna tea*** infusion *f ou* tisane *f* de séné

sensate ['senseɪt] *adj* perçu par les sens

sensation [sen'seɪʃən] *n* (**a**) *(UNCOUNT) (sensitivity)* sensation *f*; **the cold made me lose all sensation in my hands** le froid m'a complètement engourdi les mains

(**b**) *(impression)* impression *f*, sensation *f*; **I had a strange sensation in my leg** j'avais une drôle de sensation dans la jambe; **I had the sensation of falling** j'avais la sensation *ou* l'impression de tomber

(**c**) *(excitement, success)* sensation *f*; **to cause** *or* **to be a sensation** faire sensation; **the film was a sensation** le film a fait sensation

sensational [sen'seɪʃənəl] *adj* (**a**) *(causing a sensation)* sensationnel, qui fait sensation; **a sensational story** une histoire sensationnelle; **a sensational crime/trial** un crime/procès qui fait sensation; **it was the most sensational event of the year** ce fut l'événement le plus sensationnel de l'année

(**b**) *(press, newspaper, novel, film)* à sensation

(**c**) *(wonderful)* formidable, sensationnel; **you look sensational** tu es superbe; **that's sensational news** c'est une nouvelle formidable *ou* sensationnelle

sensationalism [sen'seɪʃənəlɪzəm] *n* (**a**) *(in press, novels etc)* sensationnalisme *m* (**b**) *Phil* sensationnisme *m* (**c**) *Psy* sensualisme *m*

sensationalist [sen'seɪʃənəlɪst] **1** *n (writer)* auteur *m* à sensation; *(journalist)* journaliste *mf* qui fait du sensationnel

2 *adj (article, style, journalism)* à sensation; **to be sensationalist** *(tabloids, reporting)* faire du sensationnel

sensationalize, -ise [sen'seɪʃənəlaɪz] *vt (event)* faire du sensationnel sur; **it's been so sensationalized that...** on a fait tant de sensationnel là-dessus que...

sensationally [sen'seɪʃənəlɪ] *adv* (**a**) *(describe, write)* d'une manière sensationnelle; **the incident was sensationally reported in the tabloids** l'incident a été couvert dans la presse populaire à grand renfort de sensationnalisme (**b**) *(as intensifier → beautiful, successful, popular)* extraordinairement; **we found this sensationally good restaurant** on a découvert un restaurant vraiment génial

---

SENSE [sens]

sens	► **1 (a), (c), (e), (f)**
sensation	► **1 (b)**
sentiment	► **1 (b)**
notion	► **1 (c)**
bon sens	► **1 (d)**
sentir	► **2 (a)**
raison	► **3**

1 *n* (**a**) *(faculty)* sens *m*; **the five senses** les cinq sens *mpl*; **to have a keen sense of smell/hearing** avoir l'odorat fin/l'ouïe fine; **she seemed to have a sixth sense** elle semblait posséder un sixième sens; **to be in possession of all one's senses** jouir de toutes ses facultés; **to excite the senses** exciter les sens

(**b**) *(sensation)* sensation *f*; *(feeling)* sentiment *m*; **a sense of pleasure/warmth** une sensation de plaisir/chaleur; **I felt a certain sense of pleasure** j'ai ressenti un certain plaisir; **a sense of achievement/injustice** un sentiment d'accomplissement/d'injustice; **to have a sense of belonging** avoir le sentiment d'être intégré; **I felt a sense of shame** je me suis senti honteux; **children need a sense of security** les enfants ont besoin de se sentir en sécurité; **there's a new sense of foreboding in her writing** ses écrits sont maintenant empreints d'un sentiment d'angoisse devant l'avenir

(**c**) *(notion)* sens *m*, notion *f*; **she seems to have lost all sense of reality** elle semble avoir perdu le sens des réalités; **I lost all sense of time** j'ai perdu toute notion de l'heure; **to have a (good) sense of direction** avoir le sens de l'orientation; *Fig* **she lost her sense of direction when her husband died** elle s'est sentie complètement désorientée après la mort de son mari; **he has a good sense of humour** il a le sens de l'humour; **I try to teach them a sense of right and wrong** j'essaie de leur inculquer la notion du bien et du mal; **she acted out of a sense of duty/of responsibility** elle a agi par sens du devoir/des responsabilités; **they have no business sense at all** ils n'ont aucun sens des affaires; **he has an overdeveloped sense of his own importance** il est trop imbu de lui-même

(**d**) *(practical wisdom)* bon sens *m*; **to show good sense** faire preuve de bon sens; **there's a lot of sense in what she says** il y beaucoup de bon sens dans ce qu'elle dit, ce qu'elle dit est tout à fait sensé; **to have the (good) sense to do sth** avoir l'intelligence *ou* le bon sens de faire qch; **to have more sense than to do sth** avoir assez de bon sens pour ne pas faire qch; **they didn't even have enough sense to telephone** ils n'ont même pas eu l'idée de téléphoner

(**e**) *(reason, rational quality)* sens *m*; **there's no sense in all of us going** cela ne rime à rien d'y aller tous; **I can't see any sense** *or* **the sense in continuing this discussion** je ne vois pas l'intérêt de continuer cette discussion; **to see sense** entendre raison; **to talk sense** dire des choses sensées; **oh, come on, talk sense!** voyons, ne dis pas n'importe quoi!; **to make sense** *(words)* avoir un sens; *(be logical)* tenir debout, être sensé; **can you make (any) sense of this message?** est-ce que vous arrivez à comprendre ce message?; **it makes no sense** ça n'a pas de sens; **it makes/doesn't make sense to wait** c'est une bonne idée/idiot d'attendre; **it makes more sense to do this first** c'est plus logique de commencer par cela; **that makes good sense** c'est logique, c'est une bonne idée; **it makes good political/business sense to...** il est bon sur le plan politique/commercial de...

(**f**) *(meaning → of word, expression)* sens *m*, signification *f*; *(→ of text)* sens *m*; **don't take what I say in its literal sense** ne prenez pas ce que je dis au sens propre *ou* au pied de la lettre; **in every sense of the word** dans tous les sens du terme; **in the normal sense (of the word)** à proprement parler; **I got the general sense** j'ai saisi le sens général; **I think we have, in a very real sense, grasped the problem** je crois que nous avons parfaitement saisi le problème; **this is not in any real sense a change of policy** ça ne représente pas du tout un changement de politique; **in a sense** dans un sens; **in no sense** en aucune manière; **in more senses than one** dans tous les sens; **in the sense that...** en ce sens que..., dans le sens où...

2 *vt* (**a**) *(feel → presence)* sentir; *(→ danger, catastrophe)* pressentir; **I sensed something was wrong** j'ai senti que quelque chose n'allait pas; **I sensed as much** c'est bien l'impression *ou* le sentiment que j'avais; **I sensed her meaning** j'ai compris ce qu'elle voulait dire

(**b**) *Electron* détecter; *Comput* lire

3 senses *npl (sanity, reason)* raison *f*; **to come to one's senses** *(become conscious)* reprendre connaissance; *(be reasonable)* revenir à la raison; **to take leave of one's senses** perdre la raison *ou* la tête; **to bring sb to his/her senses** ramener qn à la raison

►► ***sense organ*** organe *m* sensoriel *ou* des sens

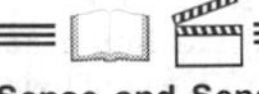

'Sense and Sensibility' *Austen, Lee* 'Raison et sentiments'

---

senseless ['senslɪs] *adj* (**a**) *(pointless, futile)* insensé, absurde; **it's senseless trying to persuade her** inutile d'essayer *ou* on perd son temps à essayer de la persuader; **a senseless killing** un meurtre gratuit; **what a senseless**

waste of time! quelle perte de temps stupide!; **what a senseless waste of human life** *(one person)* voilà une vie humaine absurdement gâchée; *(more than one person)* que de vies humaines gâchées

(**b**) *(unconscious)* sans connaissance; **to knock sb senseless** assommer qn; **he fell senseless to the floor** il est tombé par terre sans connaissance

senselessly ['senslɪslɪ] *adv* stupidement, de façon absurde

senselessness ['senslɪsnɪs] *n (silliness)* manque *m* de bon sens, stupidité *f*; *(absurdity)* absurdité *f*

sensibility [,sensɪ'bɪlətɪ] *(pl* **sensibilities**) **1** *n (physical or emotional)* sensibilité *f*; **he's a man of great sensibility** c'est un homme d'une grande sensibilité; **sensibility to pain** sensibilité à la douleur

2 sensibilities *npl* sensibilité *f*; **we must avoid offending our viewers' sensibilities** nous devons éviter de heurter la sensibilité de nos spectateurs

sensible ['sensɪbəl] *adj* (**a**) *(reasonable → choice)* judicieux, sensé; *(→ reaction, person)* sensé, raisonnable; **it's a very sensible idea** c'est une très bonne idée; **the most sensible thing to do is to phone** la meilleure chose à faire, c'est de téléphoner; **it would be more sensible to...** il serait plus raisonnable de...; **be sensible** soyez raisonnable

(**b**) *(practical → clothes, shoes)* pratique; **you need sensible walking shoes** il vous faut de bonnes chaussures de marche; **it's not a very sensible swimsuit** ce maillot de bain n'est pas très pratique

(**c**) *Formal (notable → change, quantity, difference)* sensible, appréciable

(**d**) *Formal or Literary (aware)* **I am sensible of the fact that things have changed between us** j'ai conscience du fait que les choses ont changé entre nous

sensibly ['sensɪblɪ] *adv* (**a**) *(reasonably)* raisonnablement; **they very sensibly decided to give up before someone got hurt** ils se sont montrés très raisonnables et ont décidé de renoncer avant que quelqu'un ne soit blessé; **to be sensibly dressed** porter des vêtements pratiques (**b**) *Formal (perceptibly)* sensiblement, perceptiblement

sensing ['sensɪŋ] *n (UNCOUNT) Electron* exploration *f*, sondage *m*

sensitive ['sensɪtɪv] *adj* (**a**) *(eyes, skin)* sensible; **my eyes are very sensitive to bright light** j'ai les yeux très sensibles à la lumière vive; **special soaps for sensitive skin** savons spéciaux pour peaux sensibles *ou* délicates; **to be sensitive to the cold** *(person)* être frileux

(**b**) *(emotionally)* sensible; **she's very sensitive** elle est très sensible; **to be sensitive to sth** être sensible à qch; **we are all sensitive to kindness** nous sommes tous sensibles à la gentillesse

(**c**) *(aware)* sensibilisé; **the seminar made us more sensitive to the problem** le séminaire nous a sensibilisés au problème

(**d**) *(touchy → person)* susceptible; *(→ age)* où l'on est susceptible; *(→ public opinion)* sensible; **she's very sensitive about her height** elle n'aime pas qu'on lui parle de sa taille

(**e**) *(issue, topic)* délicat, épineux; *(information)* confidentiel; **you're touching on a sensitive area** vous abordez un sujet délicat *ou* épineux; **avoid such politically sensitive issues** évitez des questions politiques aussi délicates

(**f**) *(instrument)* sensible; *Phot (film)* sensible; *(paper)* sensibilisé

(**g**) *St Exch (market)* instable

►► *Bot* ***sensitive plant*** sensitive *f*

-sensitive ['sensɪtɪv] *suff* sensible; **heat-sensitive** sensible à la chaleur, thermosensible; **price-sensitive** sensible aux fluctuations des prix; **voice-sensitive** sensible à la voix

sensitively ['sensɪtɪvlɪ] *adv* avec sensibilité

sensitiveness ['sensɪtɪvnɪs], **sensitivity** [,sensɪ'tɪvɪtɪ] *n (of person, skin, machine, instrument)* sensibilité *f*; *Phot* impressionnabilité *f*, rapidité *f*; *(of question, issue)* caractère *m* délicat; *(of document, information)* caractère *m* confidentiel; *St Exch* instabilité *f*

sensitization [,sensɪtaɪ'zeɪʃən] *n Med & Phot* sensibilisation *f*

sensitize, -ise ['sensɪtaɪz] *vt* sensibiliser, rendre sensible

sensitized ['sensɪtaɪzd] *adj Phot (paper)* sensibilisé

sensitizer ['sensɪtaɪzə(r)] *n Phot* sensibilisateur *m*

sensitometer [,sensɪ'tɒmɪtə(r)] *n Phot* sensitomètre *m*

sensor ['sensə(r)] *n* détecteur *m*, capteur *m*

sensorium [sen'sɔːrɪəm] *(pl* **sensoriums** *or* **sensoria** [-rɪə]) *n Anat* sensorium *m*

sensory ['sensərɪ] *adj (nerve, system)* sensoriel
►► ***sensory deprivation*** isolation *f* sensorielle; ***sensory organs*** organes *mpl* des sens; ***sensory perception*** perception *f* sensorielle

sensual ['sensjʊəl] *adj* sensuel

sensualism ['sensjʊəlɪzəm] *n (gen)* sensualité *f*; *Phil* sensualisme *m*

sensualist ['sensjʊəlɪst] *n (gen)* personne *f* sensuelle; *Phil* sensualiste *mf*

sensuality [,sensjʊ'ælətɪ] *n* sensualité *f*

sensually ['sensjʊəlɪ] *adv* avec sensualité, sensuellement

sensuous ['sensjʊəs] *adj (language, poetry)* très imagé; *(lips, person)* sensuel

sensuously ['sensjʊəslɪ] *adv* voluptueusement, sensuellement

sensuousness ['sensjʊəsnɪs] *n* volupté *f*

sent [sent] *pt & pp of* **send**

sentence ['sentəns] **1** *n* (**a**) *Gram* phrase *f*

(**b**) *Law (conviction)* condamnation *f*, sentence *f*; *(period in prison)* peine *f*; **to pass sentence on sb** prononcer une condamnation contre qn; **to pronounce sentence** prononcer la sentence *ou* condamnation; **under sentence of death** condamné à mort; **he got a five-year sentence for burglary** il a été condamné à cinq ans de prison *ou* à une peine de cinq ans pour cambriolage; **while he was serving his sentence** pendant qu'il purgeait sa peine

2 *vt Law* condamner; **to sentence sb to life imprisonment** condamner qn à la prison à perpétuité

►► *Gram* ***sentence structure*** structure *f* de phrase

sententious [sen'tenʃəs] *adj* sententieux, pompeux

sententiously [sen'tenʃəslɪ] *adv* sententieusement

sententiousness [sen'tenʃəsnɪs] *n (personality)* caractère *m* sententieux; *(in speech)* ton *m* sententieux

sentient ['sentɪənt] *adj Formal* doué de sensation

sentiment ['sentɪmənt] *n* (**a**) *(feeling)* sentiment *m*; **your sentiments towards my sister** vos sentiments envers ma sœur, les sentiments que vous éprouvez pour ma sœur

(**b**) *(opinion)* sentiment *m*, avis *m*, opinion *f*; **these are my sentiments** voilà mon sentiment *ou* mon opinion; **my sentiments exactly** je partage entièrement votre avis

(**c**) *(sentimentality)* sentimentalité *f*; *(mawkish)* sensiblerie *f*; **there's no place for sentiment in business matters** il n'y a pas de place pour les sentiments en affaires

sentimental [,sentɪ'mentəl] *adj also Pej* sentimental; **the photos have sentimental value** ces photos ont une valeur sentimentale; **to have a sentimental attachment to sth** être attaché à qch pour des raisons sentimentales; **to be sentimental about animals/children** se laisser attendrir par les animaux/les enfants

sentimentalism [,sentɪ'mentəlɪzəm] *n* (**a**) *(of film, novel, image, attitude etc)* sentimentalisme *m*; *Pej* sensiblerie *f* (**b**) *Literature* sentimentalisme *m*

sentimentalist [,sentɪ'mentəlɪst] *n* sentimental(e) *m,f*

sentimentality [,sentɪmen'tælətɪ] *(pl* **sentimentalities**) *n* sentimentalité *f*; *Pej* sensiblerie *f*

sentimentalize, -ise [,sentɪ'mentəlaɪz] **1** *vt (to others)* présenter de façon sentimentale; *(to oneself)* percevoir de façon sentimentale

2 *vi* faire du sentiment

sentimentally [,sentɪ'mentəlɪ] *adv also Pej* sentimentalement, de manière sentimentale; **he spoke sentimentally about his past** il a évoqué son passé avec émotion

sentinel ['sentɪnəl] *n* sentinelle *f*, factionnaire *m*; *also Fig* **to stand sentinel over sth** monter la garde devant qch

sentry ['sentrɪ] *(pl* **sentries**) *n* sentinelle *f*, factionnaire *m*; *also Fig* **to stand sentry (over sth)** monter la garde (devant qch)
►► ***sentry box*** guérite *f*; *Mil* ***sentry duty*** faction *f*; **to be on sentry duty** être en *ou* de faction

Seoul [səʊl] *n* Séoul *m*

sepal ['sepəl] *n Bot* sépale *m*

separability [,sepərə'bɪlɪtɪ] *n* séparabilité *f*

separable ['sepərəbəl] *adj* séparable

separate 1 *adj* ['sepərət] (**a**) *(different, distinct → category, meaning, issue)* distinct, à part; *(→ incident, times, episodes)* différent; **that's quite a separate matter** ça, c'est une toute autre affaire; **the two issues are quite separate** les deux problèmes sont distincts; **they sleep in separate rooms** *(children)* ils ont chacun leur chambre; *(couple)* ils font chambre à part; **administration and finance are in separate departments** l'administration et les finances relèvent de services différents; **the canteen is separate from the main building** la cantine se trouve à l'extérieur du bâtiment principal; **begin each chapter on a separate page** commencez chaque chapitre sur une nouvelle page; **use a separate piece of paper** utilisez une feuille séparée; **I'd prefer them to come on separate days** je préférerais qu'ils viennent à des jours différents; **it happened on four separate occasions** cela s'est produit à quatre reprises; **she likes to keep her home life separate from the office** elle tient à ce que son travail n'empiète pas sur sa vie privée; **the peaches must be kept separate from the lemons** les pêches et les citrons ne doivent pas être mélangés; **he was kept separate from the other children** on le tenait à l'écart *ou* on l'isolait des autres enfants; **separate but equal** = doctrine en vigueur aux États-Unis de 1896 à 1954, selon laquelle la séparation entre Noirs et Blancs était licite du moment qu'ils bénéficiaient de services (éducation, transports etc) équivalents

(**b**) *(independent → entrance, living quarters)* indépendant, particulier; *(→ existence, organization)* indépendant; **they lead very separate lives** ils mènent chacun leur vie; **they went their separate ways** *(after meeting)* ils sont partis chacun de leur côté; *Fig (in life)* chacun a suivi sa route

2 *n* ['sepərət] (**a**) *(in stereo)* élément *m* séparé (**b**) *Am (offprint)* tiré *m* à part

3 *vt* ['sepəreɪt] (**a**) *(divide, set apart)* séparer; *(detach → parts, pieces)* séparer, détacher; **he stepped in to separate the fighting dogs** il est intervenu pour séparer les chiens qui se battaient; **the last three coaches will be separated from the rest of the train** les trois derniers wagons seront détachés du reste du train; **the Bosphorus separates Europe from Asia** le Bosphore sépare l'Europe de l'Asie; **the seriously ill were separated from the other patients** les malades gravement atteints étaient isolés des autres patients; **the records can be separated into four categories** les disques peuvent être divisés *ou* classés en quatre catégories

(**b**) *(keep distinct)* séparer, distinguer; **to separate reality from myth** distinguer le mythe de la réalité, faire la distinction entre le mythe et la réalité

(**c**) *Culin (milk)* écrémer; *(egg)* séparer; **separate the whites from the yolks** séparez les blancs des jaunes

4 *vi* ['sepəreɪt] (**a**) *(go different ways)* se quitter, se séparer; **they separated after the meeting** ils se sont quittés après la réunion

(**b**) *(split up → couple)* se séparer, rompre; *(→ in boxing, duel)* rompre; *Pol (→ party)* se scinder; **they separated on good terms** ils se sont séparés à l'amiable; **the party separated into various factions** le parti s'est scindé en diverses factions

(**c**) *(come apart, divide → liquid)* se séparer; *(→ parts)* se séparer, se détacher, se diviser; **the boosters separate from the shuttle** les propulseurs auxiliaires se détachent de la navette; **the**

model separates into four parts la maquette se divise en quatre parties

5 separates *npl* ['sepərəts] *(clothes)* coordonnés *mpl*

▸▸ *Can* **separate school** ≃ école *f* libre

▸**separate out 1** *vt sep* séparer, trier

2 *vi* se séparer

▸**separate up** *vt sep* séparer, diviser; **to separate sth up into equal shares** diviser *ou* partager qch en parts égales

separated ['sepəreɪtɪd] *adj (not living together)* séparé; **her parents are separated** ses parents sont séparés

separately ['sepərətlɪ] *adv* (**a**) *(apart)* séparément, à part; **woollens must be washed separately** les lainages doivent être lavés séparément (**b**) *(individually)* séparément; **can we pay separately?** pouvons-nous payer séparément *ou* avoir des additions séparées?; **they don't sell yogurts separately** ils ne vendent pas les yaourts à l'unité

separateness ['sepərətnɪs] *n* séparation *f*

separation [,sepə'reɪʃən] *n* (**a**) *(division)* séparation *f*; **the separation of Church and State** la séparation de l'Église et de l'État; **her separation from her family caused her great heartache** sa séparation d'avec sa famille l'a beaucoup chagrinée

(**b**) *(of couple)* séparation *f*

▸▸ ***separation allowance*** *Mil* allocation *f* mensuelle *(versée par l'armée à la femme d'un soldat)*; *(alimony)* pension *f* alimentaire; *Psy* ***separation anxiety*** peur *f* de l'abandon; *Pol* ***separation of powers*** séparation *f* des pouvoirs

separatism ['sepərətɪzəm] *n* séparatisme *m*

separatist ['sepərətɪst] **1** *adj* séparatiste

2 *n* séparatiste *mf*

separative ['sepərətɪv] *adj* séparatif, séparateur

separator ['sepəreɪtə(r)] *n (gen)* séparateur *m*; *Culin (for milk)* écrémeuse *f*

Sephardi [se'fɑːdiː] (*pl* **Sephardim** [-dɪm]) *n Rel* Séfarade *mf*

Sephardic [se'fɑːdɪk] *adj Rel* séfarade

sepia ['siːpjə] **1** *n* (**a**) *(pigment, print)* sépia *f* (**b**) *(fish)* seiche *f*

2 *adj* sépia *(inv)*

sepoy ['siːpɔɪ] *n* cipaye *m*

sepsis ['sepsɪs] *n Med* septicité *f*

Sept. (*written abbr* **September**) sept

septal ['septəl] *adj Anat* septal, du septum, des septums

septarium [sep'teərɪəm] (*pl* **septaria** [-ɪə]) *n Geol* nodule *m* de calcaire argileux

September [sep'tembə(r)] *n* septembre *m*; *see also* **February**

Septembrist [sep'tembrɪst] *n Hist* septembriseur *m*

septenary ['septɪnərɪ] *adj* septénaire

septennial [sep'tenɪəl] *adj* septennal

septennially [sep'tenɪəlɪ] *adv* tous les sept ans

septennium [sep'tenɪəm] *n* septennat *m*

septet [sep'tet] *n Mus* septuor *m*

septic ['septɪk] *adj* septique; *(wound)* infecté; **to go** *or* **to become septic** s'infecter; **I have a septic finger** j'ai une blessure infectée au doigt

▸▸ ***septic poisoning*** septicémie *f*; ***septic tank*** fosse *f* septique

septicaemia, *Am* **septicemia** [,septɪ'siːmɪə] *n (UNCOUNT) Med* septicémie *f*

septicaemic, *Am* **septicemic** [,septɪ'siːmɪk] *adj Med* septicémique

septillion [sep'tɪlɪən] *n* (**a**) *(10^{42})* septillion *m* (**b**) *(10^{24})* quatrillion *m*

septuagenarian [,septjʊədʒɪ'neərɪən] **1** *adj* septuagénaire

2 *n* septuagénaire *mf*

Septuagesima [,septjʊə'dʒesɪmə] *n Rel* septuagésime *f*

Septuagint ['septjʊədʒɪnt] *n Rel* **the Septuagint** la version des Septante

septum ['septəm] *n Anat* septum *m*

septuple ['septjuːpəl] **1** *n* septuple *m*

2 *adj* septuple

septuplet [sep'tjuːplɪt] *n* (**a**) *(baby)* septuplé(e) *m,f*; **septuplets** des septuplés *mpl* (**b**) *Mus* septolet *m*

sepulcher *Am* = **sepulchre**

sepulchral [sɪ'pʌlkrəl] *adj (figure, voice)* sépulcral; *(atmosphere)* funèbre, lugubre; *(silence)* de mort

sepulchre, *Am* **sepulcher** ['sepəlkə(r)] *n* sépulcre *m*

sepulture ['sepəltʃʊə(r)] *n Rel* sépulture *f*

sequacious [sɪ'kweɪʃəs] *adj Literary* (**a**) *(person → unoriginal)* qui manque d'originalité; *(→ imitator)* servile (**b**) *(argument)* cohérent

sequel ['siːkwəl] *n* (**a**) *(result, aftermath)* conséquence *f*; *(to illness, war)* séquelles *fpl*; **as a sequel to this event** à la suite de cet événement; **it was a decision that had an unfortunate sequel** c'est une décision qui a eu des répercussions fâcheuses (**b**) *(to novel, movie etc)* suite *f*

sequela [sɪ'kwiːlə] *n Med* séquelle *f*

sequelize, -ise ['siːkwəlaɪz] *vt esp Am (movie)* donner une suite à

sequence ['siːkwəns] **1** *n* (**a**) *(order)* suite *f*, ordre *m*; **in sequence** *(in order)* par ordre, en série; *(one after another)* l'un après l'autre; **numbered in sequence** numérotés dans l'ordre; **in historical sequence** par ordre chronologique; **the pages were out of sequence** les pages n'étaient pas dans l'ordre; **he saw the episodes of the TV series out of sequence** il a vu le feuilleton dans le désordre; **logical sequence** ordre *m* logique

(**b**) *(series)* série *f*; *(in cards)* séquence *f*; **the sequence of events** le déroulement *ou* l'enchaînement *m* des événements

(**c**) *Cin & Mus* séquence *f*; **dance sequence** numéro *m* de danse

(**d**) *Ling & Math* séquence *f*

(**e**) *Biol & Chem* séquençage *m*

(**f**) *Comput* séquence *f*

2 *vt* (**a**) *(order)* classer, ordonner

(**b**) *Biol & Chem* faire le séquençage de

(**c**) *Comput* mettre en séquence

▸▸ *Gram* ***sequence of tenses*** concordance *f* des temps

sequencer ['siːkwənsə(r)] *n* séquenceur *m*

sequencing ['siːkwənsɪŋ] *n* (**a**) *Biol & Chem* séquençage *m* (**b**) *Comput* mise *f* en séquence

sequent ['siːkwənt] *adj Literary* conséquent, qui s'ensuit, résultant; **sequent to** consécutif à

sequential [sɪ'kwenʃəl] *adj* (**a**) *Comput* séquentiel (**b**) *Formal (following)* subséquent; **a lower income is sequential upon retirement** la retraite entraîne une baisse de revenus

▸▸ *Comput* ***sequential access*** accès *m* séquentiel; *Comput* ***sequential processing*** traitement *m* séquentiel

sequentially [sɪ'kwenʃəlɪ] *adv (follow, happen)* séquentiellement

sequester [sɪ'kwestə(r)] *vt* (**a**) *Formal (set apart)* isoler, mettre à part (**b**) *Formal (shut away)* séquestrer; **he was sequestered in his office** il était/a été séquestré dans son bureau; **to sequester oneself (from the world)** se retirer (du monde) (**c**) *Law (goods, property)* séquestrer, placer sous séquestre

sequestered [sɪ'kwestəd] *adj Literary (place)* retiré, isolé; **to lead a sequestered life** vivre à l'écart, mener une vie de reclus

sequestrate [sɪ'kwestreɪt] *vt* (**a**) *Law* séquestrer, placer sous séquestre (**b**) *Formal (confiscate)* saisir

sequestration [,siːkwe'streɪʃən] *n* (**a**) *Law* mise *f* sous séquestre (**b**) *Formal (confiscation)* saisie *f* (**c**) *Literary* retraite *f*, éloignement *m* du monde

▸▸ *Law* ***sequestration order*** ordonnance *f* de mise sous séquestre

sequestrator ['siːkwe,streɪtə(r)] *n Law* séquestre *m (personne)*

sequin ['siːkwɪn] *n* paillette *f*

sequined ['siːkwɪnd] *adj* pailleté, à paillettes

sequoia [sɪ'kwɔɪə] *n Bot* séquoia *m*

serac ['seræk] *n Geol* sérac *m*

seraglio [se'rɑːlɪəʊ] (*pl* **seraglios**) *n* sérail *m*

serape [sə'rɑːpɪ] *n* serape *m*, = couverture colorée portée par les cavaliers dans certains pays d'Amérique latine

seraph ['serəf] (*pl* **seraphs** *or* **seraphim** [-fɪm]) *n Rel* séraphin *m*

seraphic [se'ræfɪk] *adj Literary* séraphique

seraphically [se'ræfɪkəlɪ] *adv Literary* d'une manière *ou* d'un air séraphique

seraphim ['serəfɪm] *pl of* **seraph**

Serb [sɜːb] **1** *n* Serbe *mf*

2 *adj* serbe

Serbia ['sɜːbɪə] *n* Serbie *f*; **in Serbia** en Serbie

Serbian ['sɜːbɪən] **1** *n* (**a**) *(person)* Serbe *mf* (**b**) *Ling* serbe *m*

2 *adj* serbe

Serbo-Croat [,sɜːbəʊ'krəʊæt], **Serbo-Croatian** [,sɜːbəʊkrəʊ'eɪʃən] **1** *n* (**a**) *(person)* Serbo-croate *mf* (**b**) *Ling* serbo-croate *m*

2 *adj* serbo-croate

sere [sɪə(r)] *adj Literary* flétri, desséché

serenade [,serə'neɪd] **1** *n* sérénade *f*

2 *vt (sing)* chanter une sérénade à; *(play)* jouer une sérénade à; **she serenaded me to sleep** elle m'a chanté une sérénade pour m'endormir

serenata [,serə'nɑːtə] *n Mus* sérénade *f*

serendipitous [,serən'dɪpɪtəs] *adj Literary* fortuit

serendipity [,serən'dɪpɪtɪ] *n Literary* = don de faire des trouvailles; **you don't find such things by serendipity** ces choses-là ne tombent pas du ciel

serene [sɪ'riːn] *adj (person, existence, sky, expression)* serein; *(sea, lake)* calme; *Formal* **His/Her Serene Highness** Son Altesse Sérénissime

serenely [sɪ'riːnlɪ] *adv* sereinement, avec sérénité; **she was serenely unaware of what was going on** elle vivait dans la douce inconscience de ce qui se passait autour d'elle; **"of course not", she answered serenely** "bien sûr que non", répondit-elle tranquillement

serenity [sɪ'renətɪ] *n* sérénité *f*

serf [sɜːf] *n (male)* serf *m*; *(female)* serve *f*

serfdom ['sɜːfdəm] *n* servage *m*

serge [sɜːdʒ] *Tex* **1** *n* serge *f*

2 *comp (cloth, trousers)* de *ou* en serge; **a blue serge suit** un costume de *ou* en serge bleue

sergeant ['sɑːdʒənt] *n* (**a**) *(in infantry, air force)* ≃ sergent *m*; *(in artillery, armoured corps, cavalry)* ≃ maréchal *m* des logis (**b**) *(in police)* brigadier *m*

▸▸ ***sergeant major*** sergent-chef *m*

sergeant-at-arms *n* huissier *m* d'armes

serial ['sɪərɪəl] **1** *n* (**a**) *Rad & TV* feuilleton *m*; *(in magazine)* feuilleton *m*, roman-feuilleton *m*; **TV serial** feuilleton *m* télévisé; **published in serial form** publié sous forme de feuilleton

(**b**) *(periodical)* périodique *m*

2 *adj* (**a**) *(arranged in series)* en série; *(from series)* d'une série; *(forming series)* formant une série; **in serial order** en ordre sériel

(**b**) *(music)* sériel

(**c**) *Comput (processing, transmission, data)* série *(inv)*

▸▸ *Comput* ***serial access*** accès *m* séquentiel; *Comput* ***serial cable*** câble *m* série; *Comput* ***serial interface*** interface *f* série; ***serial killer*** tueur(euse) *m,f* en série; ***serial killings*** meurtres *mpl* en série; ***serial monogamist*** = personne qui a une succession de relations monogamiques; ***serial monogamy*** = succession de relations monogamiques; ***serial murderer*** tueur(euse) *m,f* en série; ***serial murders*** meurtres *mpl* en série; ***serial number*** *(of product, publication)* numéro *m* de série; *(of cheque, voucher)* numéro *m*; *(of soldier)* (numéro *m*) matricule *m*; *Comput* ***serial port*** port *m* série; ***serial printer*** imprimante *f* série; ***serial rights*** droits *mpl* de reproduction en feuilleton; ***serial writer*** feuilletoniste *mf*

serialism ['sɪərɪəlɪzəm] *n Mus* sérialisme *m*

serialization [,sɪərɪəlaɪ'zeɪʃən] *n (of book)* publication *f* en feuilleton; *(of play, film)* adaptation *f* en feuilleton

serialize, -ise ['sɪərɪəlaɪz] *vt (book)* publier en feuilleton; *(play, film)* adapter en feuilleton; *(in newspaper)* publier *ou* faire paraître en feuilleton; **serialized in six parts** *(novel etc)* publié en six épisodes; *TV & Rad* diffusé en six parties; **it's being serialized in the Observer** ça sort en feuilleton dans l'Observer

serially ['sɪərɪəlɪ] *adv* (**a**) *Math* en série (**b**) *Press (as series)* en feuilleton, sous forme de feuilleton; *(periodically)* périodiquement, sous forme de périodique

seriate ['sɪərɪeɪt] **1** *adj* sérié, disposé par séries, en série

2 *vt* sérier

seriated ['sɪərɪeɪtɪd] *adj* sérié, disposé par séries, en série

seriatim [,sɪərɪ'eɪtɪm] *adv Formal* successivement, l'un après l'autre; **to examine the questions seriatim** examiner successivement les questions, examiner les questions l'une après l'autre

sericeous [sə'rɪʃəs] *adj* soyeux

sericulture ['sɪərɪˌkʌltʃə(r)] *n* sériciculture *f*

sericulturist [ˌsɪərɪ'kʌltʃərɪst] *n* sériciculteur(-trice) *m,f*

series ['sɪəri:z] (*pl* **inv**) *n* (**a**) *(set, group → gen)* & *Chem & Geol* série *f*; *(sequence → gen)* & *Math* séquence *f*, suite *f*; *Ling & Mus* série *f*, séquence *f*; **we drove through a series of mining villages** on a traversé en voiture une série de villages miniers; **a whole series of catastrophes** toute une série de catastrophes

(**b**) *(of cars, clothes)* série *f*; **a series IV computer** un ordinateur série IV

(**c**) *Rad & TV* série *f*; *(in magazine, newspaper)* série *f* d'articles; **an American detective series** une série policière américaine; **TV series** série *f* télévisée; **there's a series on** *or* **about the life of the stars** il y a une série d'articles sur la vie des stars

(**d**) *(collection → of stamps, coins, books)* collection *f*, série *f*; **a new detective series** une nouvelle série *ou* collection de romans policiers

(**e**) *Elec* série *f*; **wired in series** branché en série

(**f**) *Sport* série *f* de matches; **a Test series between the West Indies and Australia** une série de matches entre les Antilles et l'Australie

▸▸ *Elec* ***series connection*** montage *m* en série

series-connected *adj Elec* monté en série

series-wound motor *n Elec* moteur *m* à enroulements série

serif ['serɪf] *n Typ* empattement *m*

serigraph ['serɪgrɑ:f] *n* sérigraphie *f*

serigraphy [sə'rɪgrəfɪ] *n* sérigraphie *f*

serin ['serɪn] *n Orn* serin *m*

serine ['seri:n] *n Biol & Chem* sérine *f*

seriocomic [ˌsɪərɪəʊ'kɒmɪk] *adj* tragicomique

serious ['sɪərɪəs] *adj* (**a**) *(not frivolous → suggestion, subject, writer, publication)* sérieux; *(→ occasion)* solennel; **is that a serious offer?** c'est une offre sérieuse?; **she's not really a serious novelist** *(doesn't write real literature)* ce n'est pas un écrivain majeur; **she's a serious actress** *(cinema)* elle fait des films sérieux; *(theatre)* elle joue dans des pièces sérieuses; **the serious cinemagoer** le cinéphile averti; **the book is meant for the serious student of astronomy** le livre est destiné aux personnes qui possèdent déjà de solides connaissances en astronomie; **life is a serious business** la vie est une affaire sérieuse; **can I have a serious conversation with you?** est-ce qu'on peut parler sérieusement?

(**b**) *(in speech, behaviour)* sérieux; **you can't be serious!** vous n'êtes pas sérieux!, vous plaisantez!; **I'm quite serious** je suis tout à fait sérieux, je ne plaisante absolument pas; **is he serious about emigrating?** est-ce qu'il envisage sérieusement d'émigrer?; **is she serious about Peter?** est-ce qu'elle tient vraiment à Peter?

(**c**) *(thoughtful → person, expression)* sérieux, plein de sérieux; *(→ voice, tone)* sérieux, grave; *(careful → examination)* sérieux, approfondi; *(→ consideration)* sérieux, sincère; **don't look so serious** ne prends pas cet air sérieux; **to give serious thought** *or* **consideration to sth** songer sérieusement à qch

(**d**) *(grave → mistake, problem, illness, injury)* grave; *(→ loss)* lourd; *(→ doubt)* sérieux; **the situation is serious** la situation est préoccupante; **serious crime** délit *m* grave; **those are serious allegations** ce sont de graves accusations; **it poses a serious threat to airport security** cela constitue une menace sérieuse pour la sécurité des aéroports; **there have been several serious border clashes** il y a eu plusieurs affrontements graves à la frontière; *Med* **his condition is described as serious** son état est jugé préoccupant; **the fire caused serious damage to the hotel** l'incendie a causé d'importants dégâts à l'hôtel

(**e**) *Fam (as intensifier)* **we're talking serious money here** il s'agit de grosses sommes d'argent □; **she makes serious money** elle gagne un fric fou; **they go in for some really serious drinking at the weekends** le week-end, qu'est-ce qu'ils descendent!; **that is one serious computer** c'est pas de la gnognotte, cet ordinateur

▸▸ *Br* ***serious crime squad*** brigade *f* criminelle; *Br* ***Serious Fraud Office*** ≃ Service *m* de la répression des fraudes

seriously ['sɪərɪəslɪ] *adv* (**a**) *(earnestly)* sérieusement, avec sérieux; **to take sb/sth seriously** prendre qn/qch au sérieux; **he takes himself too seriously** il se prend trop au sérieux; **are you seriously suggesting we sell it?** pensez-vous sérieusement que nous devrions vendre?; **she is seriously thinking of leaving him** elle pense *ou* songe sérieusement à le quitter; **think about it seriously before you do anything** réfléchissez-y bien avant de faire quoi que ce soit; **seriously though, what are you going to do?** sérieusement, qu'est-ce que vous allez faire?; **you can't seriously expect me to believe that!** vous plaisantez, j'espère?

(**b**) *(severely → damage)* sérieusement, gravement; *(→ ill)* gravement; *(→ injured, wounded)* grièvement; *Mil* **the seriously wounded** les grands blessés *mpl*; **she is seriously worried about him** elle se fait énormément de souci à son sujet

(**c**) *Fam (very)* **he's seriously rich** il est méchamment riche, il est riche et pas qu'un peu; **she's getting seriously fat** elle devient énorme □; **he was seriously drunk** il était complètement soûl; **her boyfriend is seriously gorgeous** son petit ami est super canon

serious-minded *adj* sérieux

seriousness ['sɪərɪəsnɪs] *n* (**a**) *(of person, expression)* sérieux *m*; *(of voice, manner)* (air *m*) sérieux *m*; *(of intentions, occasion, writing)* sérieux *m*; **in all seriousness** sérieusement, en toute sincérité

(**b**) *(of illness, situation, loss)* gravité *f*; *(of allegation)* sérieux *m*; *(of damage)* importance *f*, étendue *f*; **it is a matter of some seriousness** c'est une affaire assez sérieuse; **it will take some weeks to assess the seriousness of the damage** on ne pourra pas évaluer l'étendue *ou* l'ampleur des dégâts avant plusieurs semaines; **you don't seem aware of the seriousness of the problem** vous ne semblez pas avoir conscience de la gravité du problème

serjeant = **sergeant**

Serliana [sɜ:lɪ'ɑ:nə] *n Archit* (fenêtre *f*) serlienne *f*

sermon ['sɜ:mən] *n* (**a**) *Rel* sermon *m*; **to give** *or* **to preach a sermon** faire un sermon; *Bible* **the Sermon on the Mount** le Sermon sur la Montagne (**b**) *Fig Pej* sermon *m*, laïus *m*; **he gave me a sermon on the evils of drink** il m'a fait un sermon sur les effets néfastes de l'alcool

sermonize, -ise ['sɜ:mənaɪz] **1** *vt* sermonner

2 *vi* faire des sermons, prêcher

sermonizer ['sɜ:mənaɪzə(r)] *n Pej* sermonneur(-euse) *m,f*

sermonizing ['sɜ:mənaɪzɪŋ] *n (UNCOUNT) Pej* prêchi-prêcha *m inv*

seroconversion [ˌsɪərəʊkən'vɜ:ʃən] *n Med* séroconversion *f*

serologist [sɪə'rɒlədʒɪst] *n* sérologiste *mf*

serology [sɪə'rɒlədʒɪ] *n* sérologie *f*

seronegative [ˌsɪərəʊ'negətɪv] *adj Med* séronégatif

seronegativity [ˌsɪərəʊnegə'tɪvɪtɪ] *n Med* séronégativité *f*

seropositive [ˌsɪərəʊ'pɒzɪtɪv] *adj Med* séropositif

seropositivity [ˌsɪərəʊpɒzɪ'tɪvɪtɪ] *n Med* séropositivité *f*

serotonin [ˌserə'təʊnɪn] *n Physiol* sérotonine *f*

serous ['sɪərəs] *adj* séreux

serow [sə'rəʊ] *n Zool* capricorne *m*

serpent ['sɜ:pənt] *n* serpent *m*

▸▸ *Bot* ***serpent grass*** renouée *f* vivipare

serpentine ['sɜ:pəntaɪn] **1** *adj Literary (winding)* sinueux, qui serpente

2 *n Miner* serpentine *f*

serpigo [sɜ:'paɪgəʊ] *n Med* serpigo *m*

SERPS [sɜ:ps] *n Br* (*abbr* **State Earnings-Related Pension Scheme**) = régime de retraite minimal en Grande-Bretagne

serrated [sɪ'reɪtɪd] *adj (edge)* en dents de scie, dentelé; *(knife, scissors, instrument)* cranté, en dents de scie

serration [sɪ'reɪʃən] *n* dentelure *f*

serried ['serɪd] *adj* serré; **in serried ranks** en rangs serrés

serriform ['serɪfɔ:m] *adj* serriforme, denté en scie

serrulate ['serʊleɪt], **serrulated** ['serʊleɪtɪd] *adj* serrulé, denticulé

serrulation [ˌserʊ'leɪʃən] *n* dentelure *f* fine

serum ['sɪərəm] (*pl* **serums** *or* **sera** [-rə]) *n* sérum *m*

▸▸ *Med* ***serum hepatitis*** hépatite *f* B

serval ['sɜ:vəl] *n Zool* serval *m*

▸▸ ***serval cat*** serval *m*

servant ['sɜ:vənt] *n* (**a**) *(in household)* domestique *mf*; *(maid)* bonne *f*, servante *f*; **I'm not your servant!** je ne suis pas ta bonne!; **a large staff of servants** une nombreuse domesticité

(**b**) *(of God, of people)* serviteur *m*; **politicians are the servants of the community** les hommes politiques sont au service de la communauté

(**c**) *Formal or Old-fashioned (in correspondence)* **your most obedient servant** votre très humble *ou* dévoué serviteur

▸▸ ***servant girl*** servante *f*, bonne *f*; ***servants' hall*** office *m*; ***servants' quarters*** appartements *mpl* des domestiques

serve [sɜ:v] **1** *vt* (**a**) *(employer, monarch, country, God)* servir; **to have served one's country well** avoir bien servi sa patrie, *Literary* bien mériter de la patrie; **she has served the company well over the years** elle a bien servi la société pendant des années; *Prov* **you cannot serve two masters** nul ne peut servir deux maîtres

(**b**) *(in shop, restaurant → customer)* servir; **to serve sb with sth** servir qch à qn; **are you being served?** est-ce qu'on s'occupe de vous?

(**c**) *(provide → with electricity, gas, water)* alimenter; *(→ with transport service)* desservir; **the village is served with water from the local reservoir** le village est alimenté en eau depuis le réservoir voisin; **the town is well served with transport facilities** la ville est bien desservie par les transports en commun; **this train serves all stations south of Queensferry** ce train dessert toutes les gares au sud de Queensferry

(**d**) *(food, drink)* servir; **dinner is served** le dîner est servi; **coffee is now being served in the lounge** le café est servi au salon; **they served me (with) some soup** ils m'ont servi de la soupe; **melon is often served with port** on sert souvent le melon avec du porto; **the wine should be served at room temperature** le vin doit être servi chambré; **this recipe serves four** cette recette est prévue pour quatre personnes; *Rel* **to serve mass** servir la messe

(**e**) *(be suitable for)* servir; **the plank served him as a rudimentary desk** la planche lui servait de bureau rudimentaire; **this box will serve my purpose** cette boîte fera l'affaire; **when the box had served its purpose, he threw it away** quand il n'eut plus besoin de la boîte, il la jeta; **it must serve some purpose** cela doit bien servir à quelque chose; **it serves no useful purpose** cela ne sert à rien de spécial

(**f**) *(term, apprenticeship)* faire; **he has served two terms (of office) as president** il a rempli deux mandats présidentiels; **to serve one's apprenticeship as an electrician** faire son apprentissage d'électricien; **to serve one's time** *Mil* faire son service; *(prison sentence)* purger sa peine; **to serve time** faire de la prison; **he has served his time** il a purgé sa peine; **she served four years for armed robbery** elle a fait quatre ans (de prison) pour vol à main armée

(**g**) *Law (summons, warrant, writ)* notifier, remettre; **to serve sb with a summons, to serve a summons on sb** remettre une assignation à qn; **to serve sb with a writ, to serve a writ on sb** assigner qn en justice

(**h**) *Sport* servir; **she served the ball into the net** son service a échoué dans le filet

(**i**) *Agr* servir

(**j**) *(idioms)* **it serves you right** c'est bien fait pour toi; **it serves them right for being so selfish!** ça leur apprendra à être si égoïstes!; *Am Fam* **a 3 p.m. meeting? – it serves my turn** une réunion à 15 heures? – ça me va

2 *vi* (**a**) *(in shop or restaurant, at table)* servir; *(be in service → maid, servant)* servir; **to serve at table** servir à table; **could you serve, please?** pourriez-vous faire le service, s'il vous plaît?;

she served as Lady Greenmount's maid elle était au service de Lady Greenmount

(**b**) *(as soldier)* servir; **to serve in the army** servir dans l'armée; **he served as a corporal during the war** il a servi comme caporal pendant la guerre; **her grandfather served under General Adams** son grand-père a servi sous les ordres du général Adams

(**c**) *(in profession)* **he served as treasurer for several years** il a exercé les fonctions de trésorier pendant plusieurs années

(**d**) *(on committee)* **she serves on the housing committee** elle est membre de la commission au logement

(**e**) *(function, act → as example, warning)* servir; **let that serve as a lesson to you!** que cela vous serve de leçon!; **it only serves to show that you shouldn't listen to gossip** cela prouve qu'il ne faut pas écouter les commérages; **the tragedy should serve as a reminder of the threat posed by nuclear power** cette tragédie devrait rappeler à tous la menace que représente l'énergie nucléaire; **this stone will serve to keep the door open** cette pierre servira à maintenir la porte ouverte; **their bedroom had to serve as a cloakroom for their guests** leur chambre a dû servir *ou* faire office de vestiaire pour leurs invités

(**f**) *Sport* servir, être au service; **whose turn is it to serve?** c'est à qui de servir?; **Simmons to serve** au service, Simmons; **he served into the net** son service a échoué dans le filet

(**g**) *Rel* servir la messe

(**h**) *Literary* **when occasion serves** lorsque l'occasion est favorable

3 *n Sport* service *m*; **it's your serve** c'est à vous de servir; **to have a good serve** avoir un bon service

►**serve out 1** *vt sep* (**a**) *(food)* servir; *(provisions)* distribuer

(**b**) *(period of time)* faire; **the president retired before he had served his term out** le président a pris sa retraite avant d'arriver à *ou* d'atteindre la fin de son mandat; **to serve out a prison sentence** purger une peine (de prison)

2 *vi Sport* sortir son service

►**serve up** *vt sep (meal, food)* servir; *Fig (facts, information)* servir, débiter; **she serves up the same old excuse every time** elle ressort chaque fois la même excuse

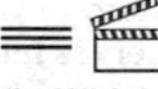

'In Which We Serve' *Lean* 'Ceux qui servent sur mer'

server ['sɜːvə(r)] *n* (**a**) *(at table)* serveur(euse) *m,f* (**b**) *Sport* serveur(euse) *m,f* (**c**) *Rel* servant *m* (d'autel) (**d**) *(utensil)* couvert *m* de service; **(set of) salad/fish servers** service *m* à salade/à poisson (**e**) *Comput* serveur *m*

►► *Comput* ***server administrator*** administrateur *m* de serveur

servery ['sɜːvərɪ] *(pl* **serveries***)* *n (hatch)* guichet *m*, passe-plat *m*; *(counter)* comptoir *m*

SERVICE ['sɜːvɪs] **1** *n* (**a**) *(to friend, community, country, God)* service *m*; **in the service of God/one's country** au service de Dieu/sa patrie; **he was rewarded for services rendered to industry/to his country** il a été récompensé pour services rendus à l'industrie/à son pays; **to require the services of a priest/of a doctor** avoir recours aux services d'un prêtre/d'un médecin; **many people gave their services free** beaucoup de gens donnaient des prestations bénévoles; **to offer one's services** proposer ses services; **for services rendered** pour services rendus; **at your service** à votre service, à votre disposition; **to be of service to sb** rendre service à qn, être utile à qn; **can I be of service (to you)?** puis-je vous aider *ou* vous être utile?; *(in shop)* qu'y a-t-il pour votre service?; **she's always ready to be of service** elle est très serviable, elle est toujours prête à rendre service; **the jug had to do service as a teapot** le pichet a dû faire office de *ou* servir de théière; **to do sb a service** rendre (un) service à qn; **he did me a great service by not telling them** il m'a rendu un grand service en ne leur disant rien; **the car has given us/has seen good service** la voiture nous a bien servi/a fait long usage

(**b**) *(working order → of machine)* service *m*; **to bring** *or* **put a machine into service** mettre une machine en service; **to come into service** *(system, bridge)* entrer en service; **the cash dispenser isn't in service at the moment** le distributeur automatique de billets est hors service *ou* n'est pas en service en ce moment

(**c**) *(employment → in firm)* service *m*; **twenty years' service with the same company** vingt ans de service dans la même entreprise; **bonuses depend on length of service** les primes sont versées en fonction de l'ancienneté

(**d**) *Old-fashioned (as domestic servant)* service; **to be in service** être domestique; **to go into** *or* **to enter sb's service** entrer au service de qn

(**e**) *(in shop, hotel, restaurant)* service *m*; **the food was good but the service was poor** on a bien mangé mais le service n'était pas à la hauteur; **you get fast service in a supermarket** on est servi rapidement dans un supermarché; **10 percent service included/not included** *(on bill, menu)* service 10 pour cent compris/non compris; **10 percent is added for service** *(on bill, menu)* service 10 pour cent non compris; **service with a smile** *(slogan)* servi avec le sourire

(**f**) *Mil* service *m*; **he saw active service in Korea** il a servi en Corée, il a fait la campagne de Corée; **fit/unfit for service** apte/inapte au service; *Naut* **service afloat/ashore** service *m* à bord/à terre; **the services** les (différentes branches des) forces *fpl* armées; **their son is in the services** leur fils est dans les forces armées

(**g**) *(department, scheme)* service *m*; **bus/train service** service *m* d'autobus/de trains; **postal/telephone services** services *mpl* postaux/téléphoniques; **a new 24-hour banking service** un nouveau service bancaire fonctionnant 24 heures sur 24; **a bus provides a service between the two stations** un autobus assure la navette entre les deux gares

(**h**) *Rel (Catholic)* service *m*, office *m*; *(Protestant)* service *m*, culte *m*; **to attend (a) service** assister à l'office *ou* au culte

(**i**) *(of car, machine → upkeep)* entretien *m*; *(→ overhaul)* révision *f*; **the car is due for its 20,000 mile service** la voiture arrive à la révision des 32 000 km

(**j**) *(set of tableware)* service *m*

(**k**) *Sport* service *m*; **Smith broke his opponent's service** Smith a pris le service de son adversaire *ou* a fait le break

(**l**) *Law (of summons, writ)* signification *f*, notification *f*; **service of documents** signification *f* d'actes

(**m**) *(tree)* alisier *m*, sorbier *m*

2 *comp* (**a**) *(entrance, hatch, stairs)* de service

(**b**) *Aut & Tech (manual, history, record)* d'entretien

(**c**) *Mil (family, pay)* de militaire; *(conditions)* dans les forces armées

3 *vt* (**a**) *(overhaul → central heating, car)* réviser; **to have one's car serviced** faire réviser sa voiture; **the car has been regularly serviced** la voiture a été régulièrement entretenue

(**b**) *Fin (debt)* assurer le service de

(**c**) *(supply needs of)* pourvoir aux besoins de

(**d**) *Agr (of bull, stallion)* couvrir, servir

4 services *npl* (**a**) *Br (on motorway)* aire *f* de service

(**b**) *Com & Econ* services *mpl*; **goods and services** biens *mpl* et services *mpl*; **more and more people will be working in services** de plus en plus de gens travailleront dans le tertiaire

►► *Am* ***service academy*** école *f* militaire; ***service agreement*** contrat *m* de service; ***service area*** *Aut (on motorway)* aire *f* de service; *TV & Rad* zone *f* desservie *ou* de réception; *Aut* ***service bay*** *(in garage)* zone *f* de travail; ***service bell*** *(in hotel)* sonnette *f (pour appeler un employé de l'hôtel)*; *Comput* ***service bureau*** société *f* de traitement à façon; *Austr & NZ* ***service bus*** autocar *m*; *Austr & NZ* ***service car*** autocar *m*; *Aviat* ***service ceiling*** plafond *m* de fonctionnement normal; *Am Aut* ***service center*** aire *f* de services *(au bord d'une autoroute)*; ***service charge*** service *m*; **they've forgotten to include the service charge on the bill** ils ont oublié de facturer le service; *Am* ***service club*** club *m* à vocation caritative; ***service company*** entreprise *f* prestataire de services; ***service court*** *(in tennis)* rectangle *m* de service; ***service engineer*** technicien(enne) *m,f* de maintenance; ***service fault*** *(in tennis)* faute *f* de service; ***service fee*** prestation *f* de service; *Br* ***service flat*** = appartement avec services ménagers et de restauration; ***service game*** *(in tennis)* jeu *m* de service; ***service hatch*** passe-plat *m*; ***service industry*** industrie *f* de services; ***service life*** durée *f* de vie; *Br* ***service lift*** monte-charge *m*; ***service line*** *(in tennis)* ligne *f* de service; *Astron* ***service module*** module *m* de service; *Mil* ***service personnel*** personnel *m* militaire; *Am* ***service plaza*** relais *m*; ***service provider*** *(person, company)* prestataire *m* de service(s); *Comput (for Internet)* fournisseur *m* d'accès; *Mil* ***service rifle*** fusil *m* réglementaire *ou* de l'armée; ***service road*** *(behind shops, factory)* = voie d'accès réservée aux livreurs; *(on motorway)* = voie d'accès réservée à l'entretien et aux services d'urgence; *Com & Econ* ***service sector*** secteur *m* tertiaire, tertiaire *m*; ***service station*** station-service *f*; *Bot* ***service tree*** alisier *m*, sorbier *m*; *Mil* ***service vehicle*** véhicule *m* militaire *ou* de l'armée

serviceability [ˌsɜːvɪsə'bɪlɪtɪ] *n* (**a**) *(durability)* solidité *f*, durabilité *f* (**b**) *(usefulness)* commodité *f*

serviceable ['sɜːvɪsəbəl] *adj* (**a**) *(durable → clothes, material)* qui fait de l'usage, qui résiste à l'usure; *(→ machine, construction)* durable, solide (**b**) *(useful → clothing, tool)* commode, pratique (**c**) *(usable)* utilisable, qui peut servir; **this coat is still serviceable** ce manteau peut encore servir (**d**) *(ready for use)* prêt à servir

serviceableness ['sɜːvɪsəbəlnɪs] *n (usefulness)* utilité *f*

serviceberry ['sɜːvɪsˌberɪ] *(pl* **serviceberries***)* *n Bot* sorbe *f*, corme *f*

serviced ['sɜːvɪst] *adj* avec service d'entretien

►► ***serviced accommodation*** résidence *f* hôtelière; ***serviced apartment*** appartement *m* dans une résidence hôtelière

serviceman ['sɜːvɪsmən] *(pl* **servicemen** [-mən]*)* *n* (**a**) *Mil* militaire *m* (**b**) *Am (mechanic)* dépanneur *m*

servicewoman ['sɜːvɪsˌwʊmən] *(pl* **servicewomen** [-ˌwɪmɪn]*)* *n Mil* femme *f* soldat

servicing ['sɜːvɪsɪŋ] *n* (**a**) *(of heating, car)* entretien *m* (**b**) *(by transport)* desserte *f*; **the servicing of an area by rail** la desserte d'une région par chemin de fer

serviette [ˌsɜːvɪ'et] *n Br* serviette *f* (de table)

►► ***serviette ring*** rond *m* de serviette

servile ['sɜːvaɪl] *adj* (**a**) *(person, behaviour)* servile, obséquieux; *(admiration, praise)* servile; *(condition, task)* servile, d'esclave (**b**) *(imitation, translation)* servile

servilely ['sɜːvaɪllɪ] *adv* (**a**) *(behave)* servilement, avec servilité (**b**) *(imitate, translate)* servilement

servility [sɜː'vɪlətɪ] *n* servilité *f*

serving ['sɜːvɪŋ] **1** *n* (**a**) *(of drinks, meal)* service *m* (**b**) *(helping)* portion *f*, part *f*

2 *adj Admin (member, chairman)* actuel, en exercice; **the longest-serving employee** l'employé ayant le plus d'ancienneté; **the longest-serving monarch/prime minister** le monarque/premier ministre qui est resté le plus longtemps au pouvoir

►► ***serving dish*** plat *m*, assiette *f* de service; *Br* ***serving hatch***, *Am* ***serving window*** passe-plat *m*

servitor ['sɜːvɪtɔː(r)] *n Literary* serviteur *m*

servitude ['sɜːvɪtjuːd] *n* servitude *f*; **in a state of servitude** en esclavage

servo ['sɜːvəʊ] *(pl* **servos***)* *Tech* **1** *adj* servo-

2 *n (mechanism)* servomécanisme *m*; *(motor)* servomoteur *m*

►► *Aut* ***servo brake*** servofrein *m*

servo-assistance *n Tech* servo-assistance *f*

servo-assisted [-ə'sɪstɪd] *adj Tech* assisté

►► *Aut* ***servo-assisted brakes*** freinage *m* assisté, servofreins *mpl*

servocontrol [ˌsɜːvəʊkən'trəʊl] *n Tech* servocommande *f*

ser–ser

servomechanism ['sɜːvəʊˌmekənɪzəm] *n Tech* servomécanisme *m*

servomotor ['sɜːvəʊˌməʊtə(r)] *n Tech* servomoteur *m*

servo-unit *n Tech* servomoteur *m*

sesame ['sesəmɪ] *n* sésame *m*; **open sesame!** sésame, ouvre-toi!

►► *Culin* **sesame oil** huile *f* de sésame; *Culin* **sesame seed** graine *f* de sésame

sesamoid ['sesəmɔɪd] **1** *n Anat (bone)* sésamoïde *m*

2 *adj* en forme de graine de sésame

►► *Anat* **sesamoid bone** os *m* sésamoïde

sesh [seʃ] *n Br Fam (abbr* **session**) **to have a drinking sesh** se pinter; **we had a bit of a sesh last night** on s'en est donné hier soir

sesquicentennial [ˌseskwɪsen'tiːnɪəl] *n* cent cinquantième anniversaire *m*

sesquipedalian [ˌseskwɪpə'deɪlɪən] *adj* (**a**) *(word)* polysyllabique (**b**) *Pej (person)* qui utilise des mots compliqués

sessile ['sesaɪl] *adj* sessile

session ['seʃən] *n* (**a**) *Admin, Law & Pol* séance *f*, session *f*; **this court is now in session** l'audience est ouverte; **the House is not in session during the summer months** la Chambre ne siège pas pendant les mois d'été; **to go into secret session** siéger à huis clos

(**b**) *(interview, meeting, sitting)* séance *f*; *(for painter, photographer)* séance *f* de pose; **morning/evening session** *(at swimming pool etc)* séance *f* du matin/soir; **he had a long session with his psychiatrist** il a eu un long entretien avec son psychiatre; **we're having another session tomorrow** *(working)* nous avons encore une séance de travail *ou* nous allons retravailler demain; *(negotiation, discussion)* nous avons encore une séance (de négociations *ou* d'entretiens) demain; **a drinking session** une beuverie

(**c**) *Sch (classes)* cours *mpl*

(**d**) *Am & Scot Univ (term)* trimestre *m*; *(year)* année *f* universitaire; *Am* **school is in session** on est en période scolaire

(**e**) *Rel* conseil *m* presbytéral

►► **session musician** musicien(enne) *m,f* de studio

sessional ['seʃənəl] *adj* de séance

sesterce ['sestɜːs], **sestertius** [ses'tɜːʃəs] *n Hist* sesterce *m*

sestet [ses'tet] *n Mus* sizain *m*

sestina [ses'tiːnə] *n Literature* sextine *f*

SET[1] [ˌesiː'tiː] *n Tel (abbr* **satellite experimental terminal**) SET *m*

SET[2]® *n Comput (written abbr* **secure electronic transaction**) SET *f*

SET [set]

jeu	▶ 1 (a)
série	▶ 1 (a)
ensemble	▶ 1 (a), (c)
cercle	▶ 1 (b)
appareil	▶ 1 (d)
poste	▶ 1 (d)
set	▶ 1 (e)
fixe	▶ 2 (a)
arrêté	▶ 2 (b)
figé	▶ 2 (b)
résolu	▶ 2 (c)
prêt	▶ 2 (d)
mettre	▶ 3 (a), (c), (d)
poser	▶ 3 (a), (c), (e), (i)
situer	▶ 3 (b)
régler	▶ 3 (c)
fixer	▶ 3 (f), (i)
établir	▶ 3 (f)
faire prendre	▶ 3 (h)
se coucher	▶ 4 (a)
prendre	▶ 4 (b)

(*pt & pp* **set**, *cont* **setting**) **1** *n* (**a**) *(of tools, keys, golf clubs, sails)* jeu *m*; *(of numbers, names, instructions, stamps, weights)* série *f*; *(of books)* collection *f*; *(of furniture)* ensemble *m*; *(of cutlery, dishes, glasses)* service *m*; *(of lingerie)* parure *f*; *(of wheels)* train *m*; *(of facts, conditions, characteristics, data)* ensemble *m*; *(of events, decisions, questions)* série *f*, suite *f*; *Typ (of proofs, characters)* jeu *m*; *Comput (of characters, instructions)* jeu *m*, ensemble *m*; **a set of matching luggage** un ensemble de valises assorties; **a set of table/bed linen** une parure de table/de lit; **a set of sheets** une parure de lit; **badminton/chess set** jeu *m* de badminton/d'échecs; **they're playing with Damian's train set** ils jouent avec le train électrique de Damian; **the cups/the chairs are sold in sets of six** les tasses/les chaises sont vendues par six; **I can't break up the set** je ne peux pas les dépareiller; **they make a set** ils vont ensemble; **to collect the (whole) set** rassembler toute la collection, faire la collection; **he made me a duplicate set** *(of keys)* il m'a fait un double des clés; *(of contact lenses)* il m'en a fait une autre paire; **a full set of the encyclopedia** une encyclopédie complète; **a full set of Tolstoy's works** les œuvres complètes de Tolstoï; **they've detected two sets of fingerprints** ils ont relevé deux séries d'empreintes digitales *ou* les empreintes digitales de deux personnes; **given another set of circumstances, things might have turned out differently** dans d'autres circonstances, les choses auraient pu se passer différemment; **the first set of reforms** la première série *ou* le premier train de réformes; **they ran a whole set of tests on me** ils m'ont fait subir toute une série d'examens

(**b**) *(social group)* cercle *m*, milieu *m*; **he's not in our set** il n'appartient pas à notre cercle; **we don't go around in the same set** nous ne fréquentons pas le même milieu *ou* monde; **the riding/yachting set** le monde *ou* milieu de l'équitation/du yachting; **the literary set** les milieux *mpl* littéraires; **the Markham set** Markham et ses amis

(**c**) *Math* ensemble *m*

(**d**) *(electrical device)* appareil *m*; *(radio, TV)* poste *m*; **a colour TV set** un poste de télévision *ou* un téléviseur couleur

(**e**) *Sport* set *m*, manche *f*; **first set to Miss Williams** set Williams

(**f**) *Cin & TV* plateau *m*; *Theat (stage)* scène *f*; *(scenery)* décor *m*; **on (the) set** *Cin & TV* sur le plateau; *Theat* sur scène

(**g**) *(part of performance → by singer, group)* **he'll be playing two sets tonight** il va jouer à deux reprises ce soir; **her second set was livelier** la deuxième partie de son spectacle a été plus animée

(**h**) *Br Sch* groupe *m* de niveau

(**i**) *(for hair)* mise *f* en plis; **to have a set** se faire faire une mise en plis

(**j**) *(posture → of shoulders, body)* position *f*, attitude *f*; *(→ of head)* port *m*; **I could tell he was angry by the set of his jaw** rien qu'à la façon dont il serrait les mâchoires, j'ai compris qu'il était en colère

(**k**) *(direction → of wind, current)* direction *f*; **suddenly the set of the wind changed** le vent a tourné soudainement

(**l**) *Psy (tendency)* tendance *f*

(**m**) *Hort (seedling)* semis *m*; *(cutting)* bouture *f*; **tomato/tulip sets** tomates *fpl*/tulipes *fpl* à repiquer

(**n**) *(clutch of eggs)* couvée *f*

(**o**) *Hunt (of hound)* arrêt *m*

(**p**) *Constr (paving stone)* pavé *m*

(**q**) *(of badger)* terrier *m*

2 *adj* (**a**) *(specified, prescribed → rule, price, quantity, sum, wage)* fixe; **meals are at set times** les repas sont servis à heures fixes; **there are no set rules for raising children** il n'y a pas de règles toutes faites pour l'éducation des enfants; **the tasks must be done in the set order** les tâches doivent être accomplies dans l'ordre prescrit; **with no set purpose** sans but précis

(**b**) *(fixed, rigid → ideas, views)* arrêté; *(→ smile, frown)* figé; **her day followed a set routine** sa journée se déroulait selon un rituel immuable; **he has a set way of doing it** il a sa méthode pour le faire; **to be set in one's ways** avoir ses (petites) habitudes; **to become set in one's views** devenir rigide dans ses opinions

(**c**) *(intent, resolute)* résolu, déterminé; **to be set on** *or* **upon sth** vouloir qch à tout prix; **I'm (dead) set on finishing it tonight** je suis (absolument) déterminé à le finir ce soir; **he's dead set against it** il s'y oppose formellement

(**d**) *(ready, in position)* prêt; **are you (all) set to go?** êtes-vous prêt à partir?

(**e**) *(likely)* probablement; **he seems well set to win** il semble être sur la bonne voie *ou* être bien parti pour gagner; **house prices are set to rise steeply** les prix de l'immobilier vont vraisemblablement monter en flèche

(**f**) *Br Sch (book, subject)* au programme; **one of our set books is 'Oliver Twist'** un des ouvrages au programme est 'Oliver Twist'

3 *vt* (**a**) *(put in specified place or position)* mettre, poser; **he set his cases down on the platform** il posa ses valises sur le quai; **to set sth before sb** *(dish, glass)* placer qch devant qn; *(proposal, plan)* présenter qch à qn; **she set the steaming bowl before him** elle plaça le bol fumant devant lui; **to set a proposal before the board** présenter un projet au conseil d'administration; **to set sb on his/her feet again** remettre qn sur pied; **to set a match to sth** mettre le feu à qch; **to set sb ashore** débarquer qn

(**b**) *(usu passive) (locate, situate → building, story)* situer; **the house is set in large grounds** la maison est située dans un grand parc; **his eyes are set too close together** ses yeux sont trop rapprochés; **the story is set in Tokyo** l'histoire se passe *ou* se déroule à Tokyo; **her novels are set in the 18th century** ses romans se passent au XVIIIème siècle

(**c**) *(adjust → clock, mechanism)* régler; *(→ alarm)* mettre; *Comput (→ tabs, format)* poser; **I set my watch to New York time** j'ai réglé ma montre à l'heure de New York; **set your watches an hour ahead** avancez vos montres d'une heure; **he's so punctual you can set your watch by him!** il est si ponctuel qu'on peut régler sa montre sur lui!; **I've set the alarm for six** j'ai mis le réveil à (sonner pour) six heures; **how do I set the margins?** comment est-ce que je fais pour placer les marges?; **set the timer for one hour** mettez le minuteur sur une heure; **first set the control knob to the desired temperature** mettez tout d'abord le bouton de réglage sur la température voulue; **the lever was set in the off position** le levier était sur "arrêt"

(**d**) *(fix into position)* mettre, fixer; *(jewel, diamond)* sertir, monter; **the handles are set into the drawers** les poignées sont encastrées dans les tiroirs; **there was a peephole set in the door** il y avait un judas dans la porte; **to set a stake in the ground** enfoncer *ou* planter un pieu dans la terre; **metal bars had been set in the concrete** des barres en métal avaient été fixées dans le béton; **the brooch was set with pearls** la broche était sertie de perles; **the ruby was set in a simple ring** le rubis était monté sur un simple anneau; *Med* **to set a bone** réduire une fracture; *Fig* **his face was set in a frown** son visage était figé dans une grimace renfrognée; **she set her jaw and refused to budge** elle serra les dents et refusa de bouger; **we had set ourselves to resist** nous étions déterminés à résister

(**e**) *(lay, prepare in advance → trap)* poser, tendre; **to set the table** mettre le couvert *ou* la table; **to set the table for two** mettre deux couverts; **set an extra place at table** rajoutez un couvert

(**f**) *(establish → date, price, schedule, terms)* fixer, déterminer; *(→ rule, guideline, objective, target)* établir; *(→ mood, precedent)* créer; **they still haven't set a date for the party** ils n'ont toujours pas fixé de date pour la réception; **you've set yourself a tough deadline** *or* **a tough deadline for yourself** vous vous êtes fixé un délai très court; **it's up to them to set their own production targets** c'est à eux d'établir *ou* de fixer leurs propres objectifs de production; **a deficit ceiling has been set** un plafonnement du déficit a été imposé *ou* fixé *ou* décidé; **to set a value on sth** décider de la valeur de qch; *Fig* **they set a high value on creativity** ils accordent une grande valeur à la créativité; **the price was set at £500** le prix a été fixé à 500 livres; **the judge set bail at $1,000** le juge a fixé la caution à 1000 dollars; **how are exchange rates set?** comment les taux de change sont-ils déterminés?; **to set an age limit at...** fixer une limite d'âge à...; **to set a new fashion** *or* **trend** lancer une nouvelle mode; **to set a new world record** établir un nouveau record mondial; **to set the tone for** *or* **of sth** donner le ton de qch

(**g**) *(indicating change of state or activity)* **to set sth alight** *or* **on fire** mettre le feu à qch; **it sets my nerves on edge** ça me crispe; *also Fig* **she set me in the right direction** elle m'a mis sur la bonne voie; **to set sb against sb** monter qn contre qn; **he/the incident set the taxman on my trail** il/l'incident a mis le fisc sur ma piste; **to set the dogs on sb** lâcher les chiens sur qn; **the incident set the family against him** l'incident a monté la famille contre lui; **it will set the country on the road to economic recovery** cela va mettre le pays sur la voie de la reprise économique; **his failure set him thinking** son échec lui a donné à réfléchir; **the scandal will set the whole town talking** le scandale va faire jaser toute la ville; **to set the dog barking** faire aboyer le chien; **the wind set the leaves dancing** le vent a fait frissonner les feuilles; **to set a machine going** mettre une machine en marche

(**h**) *(solidify → yoghurt, jelly, concrete)* faire prendre; **pectin will help to set the jam** la pectine aidera à épaissir la confiture

(**i**) *(pose → problem)* poser; *(assign → task)* fixer; **the strikers' demands set the management a difficult problem** les exigences des grévistes posent un problème difficile à la direction; **I set them to work tidying the garden** je les ai mis au désherbage du jardin; **I've set myself the task of writing to them regularly** je me suis fixé la tâche de leur écrire régulièrement

(**j**) *Br Sch (exam)* composer, choisir les questions de; *(books, texts)* mettre au programme; **she set the class a maths exercise, she set a maths exercise for the class** elle a donné un exercice de maths à la classe; **who sets the test questions?** qui choisit les questions de l'épreuve?

(**k**) *(hair)* **to set sb's hair** faire une mise en plis à qn; **and I've just had my hair set!** et je viens de me faire faire une mise en plis!; **I set my own hair** je me fais moi-même mes mises en plis

(**l**) *Hort (plant)* planter

(**m**) *Typ (text, page)* composer; **to set type** composer

(**n**) *Mus (poem, words)* **to set sth to music** mettre qch en musique

4 *vi* (**a**) *(sun, moon, stars)* se coucher; **we saw the sun setting** nous avons vu le coucher du soleil

(**b**) *(become firm → glue, cement, plaster, jelly, yoghurt)* prendre; **her features had set in an expression of determination** ses traits s'étaient durcis en une expression de très forte détermination

(**c**) *(bone)* se ressouder

(**d**) *(start)* se mettre; **he set to work** il s'est mis au travail

(**e**) *(plant, tree)* prendre racine

(**f**) *(hen)* couver

(**g**) *(wind, tide)* **the wind looks set fair to the east** on dirait un vent d'ouest

(**h**) *Hunt (hound)* tomber en arrêt

▸▸ *Theat, Cin & TV* ***set designer*** décorateur(-trice) *m,f*; *Gram* ***set expression*** expression *f* figée; ***set figures*** *(in skating)* figures *fpl* imposées; ***set meal, set menu meal*** menu *m*; *Gram* ***set phrase*** expression *f* figée; ***set piece*** (**a**) *Art, Literature & Mus* morceau *m* de bravoure (**b**) *(fireworks)* pièce *f* (de feu) d'artifice (**c**) *(of scenery)* élément *m* de décor (**d**) *Sport* combinaison *f* préparée *ou* calculée; *Sport* ***set point*** *(in tennis)* balle *f* de set; *Tech* ***set screw*** vis *f* de réglage; *Sport* ***set scrum*** *(in rugby)* mêlée *f* fermée; ***set square*** équerre *f (à dessiner)*; ***set task*** tâche *f* assignée; **to give sb a set task to do** assigner à qn une tâche bien précise; *Math* ***set theory*** théorie *f* des ensembles

►**set about** *vt insep* (**a**) *(start → task)* se mettre à; **she set about changing the tyre** elle s'est mise à changer le pneu; **I didn't know how to set about it** je ne savais pas comment m'y prendre; **how does one set about getting a visa?** comment fait-on pour obtenir un visa?

(**b**) *(attack)* attaquer, s'en prendre à; **he set about the mugger with his umbrella** il s'en est pris à son agresseur à coups de parapluie

►**set against** *vt sep* (**a**) *(compare)* **to set sth against sth** comparer qch à qch; **to set the benefits against the costs** évaluer les bénéfices par rapport aux coûts; **we must set the government's promises against its achievements** nous devons examiner les promesses du gouvernement à la lumière de ses actions

(**b**) *Fin (offset)* **some of these expenses can be set against tax** certaines de ces dépenses peuvent être déduites des impôts

(**c**) *(friends, family)* monter contre; **religious differences have set family against family** les différences religieuses ont monté les familles les unes contre les autres; **to set oneself** *or* **one's face against sth** s'opposer résolument à qch

►**set ahead** *vt sep Am* **to set the clock ahead** avancer l'horloge; **we're setting the clocks ahead tonight** on change d'heure cette nuit

►**set apart** *vt sep* (**a**) *(place separately → object)* mettre à part *ou* de côté; **there was one deck chair set slightly apart from the others** il y avait une chaise longue un peu à l'écart des autres; **they set themselves apart** ils faisaient bande à part

(**b**) *(distinguish)* distinguer (**from** de); **her talent sets her apart from the other students** son talent la distingue des autres étudiants

►**set aside** *vt sep* (**a**) *(put down → knitting, book)* poser; **could you set aside what you're working on for a while?** pouvez-vous laisser ce que vous êtes en train de faire un moment?

(**b**) *(reserve, keep → time, place)* réserver; *(→ money)* mettre de côté; *(→ arable land)* mettre en friche; **I've set tomorrow aside for house hunting** j'ai réservé la journée de demain pour chercher une maison; **the room is set aside for meetings** la pièce est réservée aux réunions; **can you set the book aside for me?** pourriez-vous me mettre ce livre de côté?; **chop the onions and set them aside** coupez les oignons et réservez-les

(**c**) *(overlook, disregard)* mettre de côté, oublier, passer sur; **they set their differences aside in order to work together** ils ont mis de côté leurs différences pour travailler ensemble

(**d**) *(reject → dogma, proposal, offer)* rejeter

(**e**) *Law (annul → contract, will)* annuler; *(→ verdict, judgment)* casser

►**set back** *vt sep* (**a**) *(situate towards the rear)* **the building is set back slightly from the road** l'immeuble est un peu en retrait par rapport à la route

(**b**) *(delay → plans, progress)* retarder; **his illness set him back a month in his work** sa maladie l'a retardé d'un mois dans son travail; **the news may set him** *or* **his recovery back** la nouvelle risque de retarder sa guérison; **this decision will set the economy back ten years** cette décision va faire revenir l'économie dix ans en arrière

(**c**) *Fam (cost)* coûter à[□]; **the trip will set her back a bit** le voyage va lui coûter cher

►**set down** *vt sep* (**a**) *(tray, bag etc)* poser

(**b**) *Br (passenger)* déposer; **the bus sets you down in front of the station** le bus vous dépose devant la gare

(**c**) *(note, record)* noter, inscrire; **try and set your thoughts down on paper** essayez de mettre vos pensées par écrit

(**d**) *(establish → rule, condition)* établir, fixer; **the government has set down a margin for pay increases** le gouvernement a fixé une fourchette pour les augmentations de salaire; **permissible levels of pollution are set down in the regulations** les taux de pollution tolérés sont fixés dans les réglementations; **to set sth down in writing** coucher qch par écrit; **it is clearly set down that drivers must be insured** il est clairement signalé *ou* indiqué que tout conducteur doit être assuré

►**set forth 1** *vt insep Formal (expound → plan, objections)* exposer, présenter; **the recommendations are set forth in the last chapter** les recommandations sont détaillées *ou* énumérées dans le dernier chapitre

2 *vi Literary* partir, se mettre en route

►**set in 1** *vi (problems)* survenir, surgir; *(disease)* se déclarer; *(winter)* commencer; *(night)* tomber; **if infection sets in** si la plaie s'infecte; **the bad weather has set in for the winter** le mauvais temps s'est installé pour tout l'hiver; **panic set in** *(began)* la panique éclata; *(lasted)* la panique s'installa

2 *vt sep Sewing (sleeve)* monter

►**set off 1** *vt sep* (**a**) *(alarm)* déclencher; *(bomb)* faire exploser; *(fireworks)* faire partir

(**b**) *(reaction, process, war)* déclencher, provoquer; **their offer set off another round of talks** leur proposition a déclenché une autre série de négociations; **it set her off on a long tirade against bureaucracy** cela eut pour effet de la lancer dans une longue tirade contre la bureaucratie; **to set sb off laughing** faire rire qn; **this answer set them off (laughing)** cette réponse a déclenché les rires; **one look at his face set me off again** en le voyant, mon fou rire a repris de plus belle; **if you say anything it'll only set him off (crying) again** si tu dis quoi que ce soit, il va se remettre à pleurer; **the smallest amount of pollen will set her off** la moindre dose de pollen lui déclenche une réaction allergique; **don't mention Maradona or you'll set him off again** surtout ne prononce pas le nom de Maradona sinon il va recommencer; **someone mentioned the war and of course that set Uncle Arthur off** quelqu'un prononça le mot guerre, et évidemment, oncle Arthur embraya aussitôt sur le sujet; *Fig* **to set sb off on the wrong track** mettre qn sur une fausse piste

(**c**) *(enhance)* mettre en valeur; **the vase sets off the flowers beautifully** le vase met vraiment les fleurs en valeur

(**d**) *Fin (offset)* **some of these expenses can be set off against tax** certaines de ces dépenses peuvent être déduites des impôts

2 *vi* partir, se mettre en route; **he set off at a run** il est parti en courant; **I set off to explore the town** je suis parti explorer la ville; **after lunch, we set off again** après le déjeuner, nous avons repris la route

►**set on 1** *vt insep (attack)* attaquer, s'en prendre à

2 *vt sep* (**a**) *(cause to follow)* **to set the police on the tracks of a thief** mettre la police aux trousses d'un voleur; **to set sb on his/her way** mettre qn sur les rails

(**b**) *(cause to attack)* **to set a dog on sb** lâcher un chien sur qn

►**set out 1** *vt sep* (**a**) *(arrange → chairs, game pieces)* disposer; *(→ merchandise)* étaler; **the shopping centre is very well set out** le centre commercial est très bien conçu

(**b**) *(present → ideas)* exposer, présenter; **the information is set out in the table below** ces données sont présentées dans le tableau ci-dessous

2 *vi* (**a**) *(leave)* se mettre en route, partir; **just as he was setting out** au moment de son départ; **to set out for school** partir pour l'école; **to set out again** repartir; **to set out in pursuit/in search of sb** se mettre à la poursuite/à la recherche de qn

(**b**) *(undertake course of action)* entreprendre; **he has trouble finishing what he sets out to do** il a du mal à terminer ce qu'il entreprend; **I can't remember now what I set out to do** je ne me souviens plus de ce que je voulais faire à l'origine; **they all set out with the intention of changing the world** au début, ils veulent tous changer le monde; **she didn't deliberately set out to annoy you** il n'était pas dans ses intentions de vous froisser; **his theory sets out to prove that...** sa théorie a pour objet de prouver que...

►**set to** *vi* (**a**) *(begin work)* commencer, s'y mettre; **we set to with a will** nous nous y sommes mis avec ardeur

(**b**) *Fam (two people → start arguing)* avoir une prise de bec; *(→ start fighting)* en venir aux mains

►**set up 1** *vt sep* (**a**) *(install → equipment, computer)* installer; *(→ roadblock)* installer, disposer; *(→ experiment)* préparer; **everything's set up for the show** tout est préparé *ou* prêt pour le spectacle; **set the chairs up in a circle** mettez *ou* disposez les chaises en cercle; **he set the chessboard up** il a disposé les pièces sur l'échiquier; **the equation sets up a relation**

between the two variables l'équation établit un rapport entre les deux variables; **the system wasn't set up to handle so many users** le système n'était pas conçu pour gérer autant d'usagers; **he set the situation up so she couldn't refuse** il a arrangé la situation de telle manière qu'elle ne pouvait pas refuser

(**b**) *(erect, build → tent, furniture kit, crane, flagpole)* monter; *(→ shed, shelter)* construire; *(→ monument, statue)* ériger; **to set up camp** installer *ou* dresser le camp

(**c**) *(start up, institute → business, scholarship)* créer; *(→ hospital, school)* fonder; *(→ committee, task force)* constituer; *(→ system of government, republic)* instaurer; *(→ programme, review process, system)* mettre en place; *(→ inquiry)* ouvrir; *(→ dinner, meeting, appointment)* organiser; **to set up house** *or* **home** s'installer; **they set up house together** ils se sont mis en ménage; **to set up a dialogue** entamer le dialogue; **you'll be in charge of setting up training programmes** vous serez responsable de la mise en place des programmes de formation; **the medical system set up after the war** le système médical mis en place après la guerre

(**d**) *(financially, in business → person)* installer, établir; **he set his son up in a dry-cleaning business** il a acheté à son fils une entreprise de nettoyage à sec; **she could finally set herself up as an accountant** elle pourrait enfin s'installer comme comptable; **the money would set him up for life** l'argent le mettrait à l'abri du besoin pour le restant de ses jours; **the army set him up as a dictator** l'armée l'installa comme dictateur

(**e**) *(provide)* **we're well set up with supplies** nous sommes bien approvisionnés; **she can set you up with a guide/the necessary papers** elle peut vous procurer un guide/les papiers qu'il vous faut; **I can set you up with a girlfriend of mine** je peux te présenter à *ou* te faire rencontrer une de mes copines

(**f**) *(restore energy to)* remonter, remettre sur pied; **have a brandy, that'll set you up** prends un cognac, ça va te remonter

(**g**) *Fam (frame)* monter un coup contre; **she claims she was set up** elle prétend qu'elle est victime d'un coup monté; **he was set up as the fall guy** on a fait de lui le bouc émissaire ❑, il a joué le rôle de bouc émissaire ❑

(**h**) *Typ (text)* composer

2 *vi* s'installer, s'établir; **he's setting up in the fast-food business** il se lance dans la restauration rapide; **to set up on one's own** *(business)* s'installer à son compte; *(home)* prendre son propre appartement

►**set upon** *vt insep (physically or verbally)* attaquer, s'en prendre à

seta ['si:tə] *n Bot & Zool* sétule *m*

setaside ['setəsaɪd] *n Agr* gel *m* des terres

setback ['setbæk] *n* revers *m*, échec *m*; *(minor)* contretemps *m*; *Fin & St Exch* tassement *m*, repli *m*; *Med* rechute *f*; **to suffer a setback** essuyer un revers; **the government has suffered a setback in its plans to change the legislation** le gouvernement a vu son projet de réforme compromis; **this has been a severe setback for the government** cela a constitué un grave revers *ou* échec pour le gouvernement

set-in *adj (sleeve)* rapporté

sett [set] *n* (**a**) *(for paving)* pavé *m* (**b**) *(of badger)* terrier *m* (de blaireau)

settee [se'ti:] *n* canapé *m*

setter ['setə(r)] *n* (**a**) *(dog)* setter *m* (**b**) *(of jewels)* sertisseur(euse) *m,f* (**c**) *Typ* compositeur(trice) *m,f*

setting ['setɪŋ] *n* (**a**) *(of sun, moon)* coucher *m*

(**b**) *(situation, surroundings)* cadre *m*, décor *m*; *Theat* décor *m*; **the house is in a lovely country setting** la maison est située dans un très beau cadre campagnard; **they photographed the foxes in their natural setting** ils ont photographié les renards dans leur milieu naturel; **the film has Connemara as its setting** le film a pour cadre le Connemara

(**c**) *(position, level → of machine, instrument)* réglage *m*; **try a higher setting** *(of oven, iron, microwave etc)* augmentez la température; **what setting was it on?** sur quoi était-elle réglée?

(**d**) *Comput* **settings** paramètres *mpl*

(**e**) *(for jewels)* monture *f*; *(of jewels)* sertissage *m*

(**f**) *(at table)* set *m* de table

(**g**) *Mus (of poem, play)* mise *f* en musique; *(for instruments)* arrangement *m*, adaptation *f*; **setting for male voice** arrangement *m* pour voix d'homme

(**h**) *(of fracture)* réduction *f*; *(in plaster)* plâtrage *m*

(**i**) *(of jam)* prise *f*; *(of cement)* prise *f*, durcissement *m*

(**j**) *Typ* composition *f*

►► ***setting lotion*** lotion *f* pour mise en plis

setting-up *n* (**a**) *(of company, organization)* lancement *m*, création *f*; *(of enquiry)* ouverture *f* (**b**) *Typ* composition *f*

SETTLE ['setəl]

régler	► **1 (a), (c)**
fixer	► **1 (b)**
installer	► **1 (d)**
coloniser	► **1 (e)**
calmer	► **1 (f)**
s'installer	► **2 (a), (b)**
s'établir	► **2 (a)**
se calmer	► **2 (c)**
tenir	► **2 (d)**
se poser	► **2 (d)**
se tasser	► **2 (e)**

1 *vt* (**a**) *(solve → question, issue)* régler; *(→ dispute, quarrel, differences)* régler, trancher; **to settle a matter** régler une question; **the case was settled out of court** l'affaire a été réglée à l'amiable; **questions not yet settled** questions *fpl* en suspens; **to settle one's affairs** mettre ses affaires en ordre, régler ses affaires; **to settle an old score** *or* **old scores** régler des comptes

(**b**) *(determine, agree on → date, price)* fixer; **have you settled where to go for the picnic?** avez-vous décidé d'un endroit pour le pique-nique?; **it was settled that I would go to boarding school** il fut convenu *ou* décidé que j'irais en pension; **you must settle that among yourselves** il va falloir que vous arrangiez cela entre vous; **nothing is settled yet** rien n'est encore décidé *ou* arrêté; **that's one point settled** voilà déjà un point d'acquis; **that's that settled then!** voilà une affaire réglée!; **that's settled then, I'll meet you at 8 o'clock** alors c'est entendu *ou* convenu, on se retrouve à 8 heures; **that settles it, the party's tomorrow!** c'est décidé, la fête aura lieu demain!; **that settles it, he's fired** trop c'est trop, il est renvoyé!

(**c**) *(pay → debt, account, bill)* régler; **to settle a claim** *(insurance)* régler un litige

(**d**) *(install)* installer; *(arrange, place → on table, surface)* installer, poser (soigneusement); **when I'm settled, I'll write to you** quand je serai installé, je vous écrirai; **to settle oneself comfortably in an armchair** s'installer confortablement dans un fauteuil; **he settled the children for the night** il a mis les enfants au lit, il est allé coucher les enfants; **to get settled** s'installer (confortablement); **to settle one's feet in the stirrups** bien installer ses pieds dans les étriers; **she settled the rug over her knees** elle enroula la couverture autour de ses genoux

(**e**) *(colonize)* coloniser; **Peru was settled by the Spanish** le Pérou a été colonisé par les Espagnols, les Espagnols se sont établis au Pérou

(**f**) *(calm → nerves, stomach)* calmer, apaiser; **this brandy will settle your nerves** ce cognac te calmera les nerfs; **give me something to settle my stomach** donnez-moi quelque chose pour l'estomac; **to settle sb's doubts** dissiper les doutes de qn; **the rain settled the dust** la pluie a fait retomber la poussière

(**g**) *Law (money, allowance, estate)* constituer; **to settle an annuity on sb** constituer une rente à qn; **she settled all her money on her nephew** elle a légué toute sa fortune à son neveu; *Fig* **how are you settled for money at the moment?** est-ce que tu as suffisamment d'argent en ce moment?

2 *vi* (**a**) *(go to live → gen)* s'installer, s'établir; *(→ colonist)* s'établir; **she finally settled abroad** elle s'est finalement installée à l'étranger

(**b**) *(install oneself → in new flat, bed)* s'installer; *(adapt → to circumstances)* s'habituer; **she lived here a few years, but didn't settle** *(didn't stay)* elle a vécu ici quelques années, mais ne s'est pas installée définitivement; *(didn't adapt)* elle a vécu ici quelques années, mais ne s'est jamais habituée; **to settle in an armchair/for the night** s'installer dans un fauteuil/pour la nuit; **I couldn't settle** *(in bed)* je n'arrivais pas à m'endormir; **to settle to work/to do sth** se mettre sérieusement au travail/à faire qch; **he can't settle to anything** il n'arrive pas à se concentrer sur quoi que ce soit

(**c**) *(become calm → nerves, stomach, storm)* s'apaiser, se calmer; *(→ situation)* s'arranger; **wait for things to settle before you do anything** attends que les choses se calment *ou* s'arrangent avant de faire quoi que ce soit; **the weather is settling** le temps se calme

(**d**) *(come to rest → snow)* tenir; *(→ dust, sediment)* se déposer; *(→ liquid, beer)* reposer; *(→ bird, insect, eyes)* se poser; **the snow began to settle (on the ground)** la neige commençait à tenir; **a fly settled on the butter** une mouche s'est posée sur le beurre; **let your dinner settle before you go out** prends le temps de digérer avant de sortir; **let the dregs settle** laissez se déposer la lie; **allow the mixture to settle** laissez reposer le mélange; **her gaze settled on the book** son regard se posa sur le livre; **a look of despair/utter contentment settled on his face** son visage prit une expression de désespoir/profonde satisfaction; **an eerie calm settled over the village** un calme inquiétant retomba sur le village; **the cold settled on his chest** le rhume lui est tombé sur la poitrine

(**e**) *(road, wall, foundations)* se tasser; **cracks appeared in the walls as the house settled** des fissures apparaissaient dans les murs au fur et à mesure que la maison s'affaissait; *Com* **contents may settle during transport** *(on packaging)* le contenu risque de se tasser pendant le transport

(**f**) *(financially)* **to settle with sb for sth** régler le prix de qch à qn; **can I settle with you tomorrow?** est-ce que je peux vous régler demain?

(**g**) *Law* **to settle out of court** régler une affaire à l'amiable

3 *n (seat)* banquette *f* à haut dossier

►**settle down 1** *vi* (**a**) *(in armchair, at desk)* s'installer; *(in new home)* s'installer, se fixer; *(at school, in job)* s'habituer, s'adapter; *(adopt steady lifestyle)* se ranger, s'assagir; **they settled down by the fire for the evening** ils se sont installés près du feu pour la soirée; **to settle down to watch television** s'installer (confortablement) devant la télévision; **it took the children some weeks to settle down in their new school** il a fallu plusieurs semaines aux enfants pour s'habituer à leur nouvelle école; **Susan is finding it hard to settle down to life in Paris** Susan a du mal à s'habituer *ou* à s'adapter à la vie parisienne; **they never settle down anywhere for long** ils ne se fixent jamais nulle part bien longtemps; **it's about time Tom got married and settled down** il est temps que Tom se marie et qu'il se range; **he's not someone you could imagine settling down with** ce n'est pas le genre de personne avec qui on peut imaginer se marier

(**b**) *(concentrate, apply oneself)* **to settle down to do sth** se mettre à faire qch; **to settle down to work** se mettre au travail; **I can't seem to settle down to anything these days** je n'arrive pas à me concentrer sur quoi que ce soit ces jours-ci

(**c**) *(become calm → excitement)* s'apaiser; *(→ situation)* s'arranger; **things are settling down** *(calming down)* les choses sont en train de se calmer; *(becoming more definite)* les choses commencent à prendre tournure; **as soon as the market settles down** aussitôt que le marché se sera stabilisé; **settle down, children!** calmez-vous, les enfants!, du calme, les enfants!

2 *vt sep (person)* installer; **to settle oneself down in an armchair** s'installer (confortablement) dans un fauteuil; **she settled the patient/**

the baby down for the night elle a installé le malade/le bébé pour la nuit

►**settle for** *vt insep* accepter, se contenter de; **I settled for £100** j'ai accepté 100 livres; **I won't settle for less than £200** 200 livres, c'est mon dernier prix, je ne descendrai pas au-dessous de 200 livres; **I insist on the best quality, I never settle for (anything) less** j'exige ce qu'il y a de mieux, je n'accepte jamais rien en dessous; **there was no wine left so they had to settle for beer** comme il ne restait plus de vin, ils durent se contenter de bière

►**settle in** *vi (at new house)* s'installer; *(at new school, job)* s'habituer, s'adapter; **once we're settled in, we'll invite you round** une fois que nous serons installés, nous t'inviterons; **it took him a while to settle in at his new school** il a mis un certain temps à s'habituer à sa nouvelle école

►**settle into 1** *vt insep (job, routine)* s'habituer à, s'adapter à; **she soon settled into her new post** elle s'est vite adaptée à son nouveau poste; **life soon settled into the usual dull routine** la vie reprit bientôt son rythme monotone
2 *vt sep* installer dans; **she's busy settling her daughter into her new flat** elle est occupée à installer sa fille dans son nouvel appartement

►**settle on** *vt insep (decide on)* décider de; **they've settled on Rome for their honeymoon** ils ont décidé d'aller passer leur lune de miel à Rome; **they've settled on a Volkswagen** ils se sont décidés pour une Volkswagen; **they couldn't settle on a price** ils n'ont pas réussi à se mettre d'accord sur un prix; **they settled on a compromise solution** ils ont finalement choisi le compromis

►**settle up 1** *vi* régler (la note); **I must settle up with the plumber** il faut que je règle le plombier; **can we settle up?** est-ce qu'on peut faire les comptes?
2 *vt sep* régler

settled ['setəld] *adj* (**a**) *(stable, unchanging → person)* rangé, établi; *(→ life)* stable, régulier; *(→ habits)* régulier; **he's very settled in his ways** il est très routinier, il a ses petites habitudes; **she is settled in her job** elle est habituée à son emploi (**b**) *Met (calm)* beau (belle); **the weather will remain settled** le temps demeurera au beau fixe (**c**) *(inhabited)* peuplé; *(colonized)* colonisé (**d**) *(fixed → population)* fixe, établi (**e**) *(account, bill)* réglé

settlement ['setəlmənt] *n* (**a**) *(resolution → of question, dispute)* règlement *m*, solution *f*; *(→ of problem)* solution *f*
(**b**) *(payment)* règlement *m*; **I enclose a cheque in settlement of your account** veuillez trouver ci-joint un chèque en règlement de votre facture; **out-of-court settlement** règlement *m* à l'amiable
(**c**) *(agreement)* accord *m*; **to reach a settlement** parvenir à *ou* conclure un accord; **wage settlement** accord *m* salarial; **marriage settlement** contrat *m* de mariage
(**d**) *(decision → on details, date)* décision *f*; **settlement of the final details will take some time** il faudra un certain temps pour régler les derniers détails
(**e**) *Law (financial)* donation *f*; *(dowry)* dot *f*; *(of annuity)* constitution *f*; **to make a settlement on sb** faire une donation à *ou* en faveur de qn
(**f**) *(colony)* colonie *f*; *(village)* village *m*; *(dwellings)* habitations *fpl*
(**g**) *(of people in a country)* établissement *m*, installation *f*; *(colonization)* colonisation *f*, peuplement *m*; **there were signs of human settlement** il y avait des traces de présence humaine
(**h**) *(of contents, road)* tassement *m*; *(of sediment)* dépôt *m*
►► *St Exch* ***settlement day*** jour *m* de (la) liquidation; *Com* ***settlement discount*** remise *f* pour règlement rapide; *Com* ***settlement period*** délai *m* de règlement; *St Exch* ***settlement price*** cours *m* de résiliation; *St Exch* ***settlement value*** valeur *f* liquidative

settler ['setələ(r)] *n* colonisateur(trice) *m,f*, colon *m*

settling ['setlɪŋ] **1** *n* (**a**) *(of question, problem, dispute)* règlement *m* (**b**) *(of account, debt)* règlement *m* (**c**) *(of contents)* tassement *m* (**d**) *(of country)* colonisation *f*
2 settlings *npl (sediment)* dépôt *m*, sédiment *m*

set-to (*pl* **set-tos**) *n Br Fam (fight)* bagarre *f*, baston *m ou f*; *(argument)* prise *f* de bec

set-top box *n TV* décodeur *m* numérique

set-up *n* (**a**) *(arrangement, system)* organisation *f*, système *m*; **the project manager explained the set-up to me** le chef de projet m'a expliqué comment les choses fonctionnaient *ou* étaient organisées; **this is the set-up** voici comment ça se passe; **what's the economic set-up in these countries?** quel est le système économique de ces pays?; **you've got a nice set-up here** vous êtes bien installé ici; **it's an odd set-up** *(company)* c'est une drôle de boîte; *(marriage, relationship)* c'est un drôle de ménage; *(collection of people)* c'est une drôle d'équipe
(**b**) *Fam (trap, trick)* coup *m* monté, machination □ *f*
(**c**) *Comput* configuration *f*
►► *Comput* ***set-up CD-ROM*** CD-ROM *m inv ou* cédérom *m* d'installation; ***set-up charge*** frais *mpl* d'inscription; *Acct* ***set-up costs*** frais *mpl* de lancement; ***set-up fee*** frais *mpl* d'inscription; *Comput* ***set-up program*** programme *m* d'installation

seven ['sevən] **1** *n (number, numeral)* sept *m inv*
2 *pron* sept
3 *adj* sept; **the seven deadly sins** les sept péchés *mpl* capitaux; *see also* **five**
►► ***seven seas*** toutes les mers *fpl* (du monde); **to sail the seven seas** parcourir les mers; *Hist* ***the Seven Years' War*** la guerre de Sept Ans

'The Seven Pillars of Wisdom' *T E Lawrence* 'Les Sept piliers de la sagesse'

seven-bit character *n Comput* caractère *m* à sept bits

seven-bit data *n Comput* données *fpl* à sept bits

sevenfold ['sevənfəʊld] **1** *adj* septuple
2 *adv* au septuple; **profits have increased sevenfold** les bénéfices ont été multipliés par sept

seven-inch *n (record)* quarante-cinq-tours *m inv*
►► ***seven-inch single*** quarante-cinq-tours *m inv*

seven-league boots *npl* bottes *fpl* de sept lieues

seventeen [ˌsevən'tiːn] **1** *n* dix-sept *m inv*
2 *pron* dix-sept
3 *adj* dix-sept; *see also* **five**

seventeenth [ˌsevən'tiːnθ] **1** *n* (**a**) *(fraction)* dix-septième *m* (**b**) *(in series)* dix-septième *mf* (**c**) *(of month)* dix-sept *m inv*
2 *adj* dix-septième
3 *adv* dix-septièmement; *(in contest)* en dix-septième position, à la dix-septième place; *see also* **fifth**

seventh ['sevənθ] **1** *n* (**a**) *(fraction)* septième *m* (**b**) *(in series)* septième *mf* (**c**) *(of month)* sept *m inv* (**d**) *Mus* septième *f*
2 *adj* septième
3 *adv* septièmement; *(in contest)* en septième position, à la septième place; *see also* **fifth**
►► *Rel* ***Seventh Day Adventist*** adventiste *mf* du septième jour; *Am Sch* ***seventh grade*** = classe de lycée pour les 11–12 ans; ***seventh heaven*** le septième ciel; **to be in (one's) seventh heaven** être au septième ciel

'The Seventh Seal' *Bergman* 'Le Septième sceau'

seventhly ['sevənθlɪ] *adv* septièmement, en septième lieu

seventieth ['sevəntjəθ] **1** *n* (**a**) *(fraction)* soixante-dixième *m* (**b**) *(in series)* soixante-dixième *mf*
2 *adj* soixante-dixième
3 *adv* soixante-dixièmement; *(in contest)* en soixante-dixième position, à la soixante-dixième place; *see also* **fifth**

seventy ['sevəntɪ] **1** *n* (*pl* **seventies**) soixante-dix *m inv*, *Belg & Suisse* septante *m inv*
2 *pron* soixante-dix, *Belg & Suisse* septante
3 *adj* soixante-dix, *Belg & Suisse* septante
4 *comp* **seventy-one** soixante-onze; **seventy-two** soixante-douze; **seventy-nine** soixante-dix-neuf; **seventy-first** soixante-onzième; **seventy-second** soixante-douzième; *see also* **fifty**

seventy-eight *n (record)* 78 tours *m inv*; **a collection of old 78s** une collection de vieux 78 tours

seven-year itch *n Hum* tentation *f* d'infidélité *(après sept ans de mariage)*

'The Seven Year Itch' *Wilder* 'Sept ans de réflexion'

sever ['sevə(r)] **1** *vt* (**a**) *(cut off → rope, limb)* couper, trancher; **his hand was severed (at the wrist)** il a eu la main coupée (au poignet); **a severed head** une tête coupée; **the roadworks severed a watermain** les travaux ont crevé une canalisation d'eau; **communications with outlying villages have been severed** les communications avec les villages isolés ont été rompues
(**b**) *(cease → relationship, contact)* cesser, rompre; **they severed all connections with the organization** ils ont cessé toute relation avec l'organisation; **she severed all ties with her family** elle a rompu tous les liens avec sa famille
2 *vi* se rompre, casser, céder; **the rope severed under the strain** la corde a cédé sous la tension

'A Severed Head' *Murdoch* 'Une Tête coupée'

several ['sevərəl] **1** *adj* plusieurs; **on several occasions** à plusieurs occasions *ou* reprises; **several thousand dollars** plusieurs milliers *mpl* de dollars
2 *pron* plusieurs; **several of my colleagues have left** plusieurs de mes collègues sont partis; **several of us** plusieurs d'entre nous; **there are several of them** ils sont plusieurs; **several of us got together to organize a party** nous nous sommes mis à plusieurs pour organiser une soirée
3 *adj Law (separate)* distinct; **they went their several ways** ils s'en allèrent, chacun de son côté

severally ['sevərəlɪ] *adv Formal* séparément, individuellement

severance ['sevərəns] *n (of relations)* rupture *f*, cessation *f*; *(of communications, contact)* interruption *f*, rupture *f*
►► ***severance pay*** *(UNCOUNT)* indemnité *f ou* indemnités *fpl* de licenciement

severe [sɪ'vɪə(r)] *adj* (**a**) *(harsh → criticism, punishment, regulations)* sévère, dur; *(→ conditions)* difficile, rigoureux; *(→ storm)* violent; *(→ winter, climate)* rude, rigoureux; *(→ frost)* intense; *(→ competition)* rude, serré; *(strict → tone, person)* sévère; **severe weather conditions** conditions *fpl* météorologiques très rudes; **she's too severe with her children** elle est trop dure avec ses enfants; **I gave them a severe telling-off** je les ai sévèrement grondés
(**b**) *(serious → illness, handicap)* grave, sérieux; *(→ defeat)* grave; *(→ pain)* vif, aigu(uë); **I've got severe backache/toothache** j'ai très mal au dos/une rage de dents; **to suffer severe losses** subir de lourdes pertes; **his death was a severe blow to them/to their chances** sa mort les a sérieusement ébranlés/a sérieusement compromis leurs chances; **it will be a severe test of our capabilities** cela mettra nos aptitudes à rude épreuve
(**c**) *(austere → style, dress, haircut)* sévère, strict; **the building has a certain severe beauty** l'édifice a une certaine beauté austère
(**d**) *Br Fam (for emphasis)* sacré, vache (de); **he is a severe nuisance** c'est un sacré emmerdeur
►► *Med* ***severe combined immunodeficiency syndrome*** syndrome *m* de déficience immune combinée sévère, déficit *m* immunitaire combiné sévère

severely [sɪ'vɪəlɪ] *adv* (**a**) *(harshly → punish, treat, criticize)* sévèrement, durement; *(strictly)* strictement, sévèrement; **don't judge them too severely** ne les jugez pas trop sévèrement *ou* avec trop de sévérité; **he spoke severely to them** il leur parla d'un ton sec
(**b**) *(seriously → ill, injured, disabled)* gravement, sérieusement; **to be severely handicapped** être gravement handicapé; **her**

patience was severely tried by his behaviour sa patience a été durement éprouvée par son comportement

(**c**) *(austerely)* d'une manière austère, sévèrement; **she dresses very severely** elle s'habille de manière très austère

(**d**) *Br Fam (for emphasis)* sérieusement ❑, vachement; **we were severely drunk last night** on était sérieusement déchirés hier soir; **you are severely annoying me!** tu me cours sérieusement sur le haricot!

severity [sɪ'verɪtɪ] *n* (**a**) *(harshness → of judgement, treatment, punishment, criticism)* sévérité *f*, dureté *f*; *(→ of climate)* rigueur *f*, dureté *f*; *(→ of frost, cold)* intensité *f* (**b**) *(seriousness → of illness, injury, handicap)* gravité *f*, sévérité *f* (**c**) *(austerity)* austérité *f*, sévérité *f*

Severn ['sevən] *n* **the Severn** la Severn

►► ***the Severn Bridge*** le pont sur la Severn *(pont suspendu reliant le sud-ouest de l'Angleterre au sud du pays de Galles)*

Seville [sə'vɪl] *n* Séville

►► ***Seville orange*** orange *f* amère, bigarade *f*

sew [səʊ] (*pt* **sewed,** *pp* **sewn** [səʊn] *or* **sewed**) **1** *vt* coudre; **to sew a button on(to) a shirt** coudre *ou* recoudre un bouton sur une chemise; **she can't even sew a button on** elle ne sait même pas coudre un bouton; **could you sew this armband on for me?** pouvez-vous me coudre ce brassard?; **he sewed the money into the lining** il a cousu l'argent dans la doublure; **you'll have to sew the pieces together again** il va falloir recoudre les pièces ensemble

2 *vi* coudre, faire de la couture

►**sew up** *vt sep* (**a**) *(tear, slit)* coudre, recoudre; *(seam)* faire; *Med (wound)* coudre, recoudre, suturer; *(hole)* raccomoder (**b**) *Fam Fig (arrange, settle → contract)* régler ❑; *(→ details)* régler ❑, mettre au point ❑; **the deal is all sewn up** l'affaire est dans le sac; **multinationals have sewn up the economy** les multinationales contrôlent l'économie ❑; **they've got the election all sewn up** l'élection est gagnée d'avance ❑

sewage ['suːɪdʒ] *n (UNCOUNT)* vidanges *fpl*, eaux *fpl* d'égout, eaux-vannes *fpl*

►► ***sewage disposal*** évacuation *f* des eaux usées; ***sewage farm*** champ *m* d'épandage; ***sewage outlet*** émissaire *m* d'évacuation; ***sewage plant*** station *f* d'épuration; ***sewage system*** égouts *mpl*; ***sewage tanker*** camion-citerne *m*; ***sewage treatment plant*** station *f* d'épuration; ***sewage works*** champ *m* d'épandage

sewer[1] ['səʊə(r)] *n (person who sews)* couseur(euse) *m,f*; **to be a good/bad sewer** être bon(onne)/mauvais(e) couturier(ère)

sewer[2] ['sʊə(r)] *n (drain)* égout *m*; **open sewer** égout *m* à ciel ouvert; *Fig* **sewer of vice** cloaque *m* de vice; **he's got a mind like a sewer** il a l'esprit mal placé

►► ***sewer rat*** rat *m* d'égout

sewerage ['sʊərɪdʒ] *n (UNCOUNT)* (**a**) *(disposal)* évacuation *f* des eaux usées (**b**) *(system)* égouts *mpl*, réseau *m* d'égouts (**c**) *(sewage)* eaux *fpl* d'égout

sewerman ['sʊəmən] (*pl* **sewermen** [-men]) *n* égoutier *m*

sewermouth ['sʊəmaʊθ] *n Am Fam* **to be a sewermouth** jurer comme un charretier

sewing ['səʊɪŋ] **1** *n* (**a**) *(activity)* couture *f*; **she likes sewing** elle aime coudre *ou* la couture (**b**) *(piece of work)* couture *f*, ouvrage *m*; **what have I done with my sewing?** où ai-je posé ma couture?

2 *comp (kit)* à couture; *(cotton, thread)* à coudre; *(class)* de couture

►► ***sewing basket*** boîte *f* à couture; *Am* ***sewing bee*** = réunion entre femmes où l'on fait de la couture en bavardant; ***sewing machine*** machine *f* à coudre; ***sewing needle*** aiguille *f* à coudre

sewn [səʊn] *pp of* **sew**

sex [seks] **1** *n* (**a**) *(gender)* sexe *m*; **the club is open to both sexes** le club est ouvert aux personnes des deux sexes; **single sex school** établissement *m* scolaire non mixte

(**b**) *(UNCOUNT) (sexual intercourse)* relations *fpl* sexuelles, rapports *mpl* (sexuels); **to have sex with sb** avoir des rapports (sexuels) *ou* faire l'amour avec qn

(**c**) *(sexual activity)* sexe *m*; **that film is just full of sex** il n'y a que du sexe dans ce film; **all he ever thinks about is sex** c'est un obsédé (sexuel); **there is too much sex and violence on TV** il y a trop de sexe et de violence à la télévision

2 *comp* sexuel

3 *vt (animal)* déterminer le sexe de

►► ***sex addict*** dépendant(e) *m,f* sexuel(elle); ***sex addiction*** dépendance *f* sexuelle; ***sex aid*** gadget *m* érotique; ***sex appeal*** sex-appeal *m*; *Fam Pej* ***sex beast*** pervers(e) *m,f* (sexuel(elle)) ❑; ***sex bomb*** bombe *f* sexuelle; ***sex change (operation)*** (opération *f* de) changement *m* de sexe; **to have a sex change (operation)** changer de sexe; ***sex chromosome*** chromosome *m* sexuel; ***sex crime*** crime *m* sexuel; ***sex discrimination*** discrimination *f* sexuelle; ***the Sex Discrimination Act*** = loi britannique de 1975 interdisant la discrimination sexuelle, notamment dans les domaines de l'emploi et de l'enseignement; ***sex drive*** pulsion *f* sexuelle, pulsions *fpl* sexuelles, libido *f*; **to have a low/high sex drive** avoir un appétit sexuel faible/élevé; ***sex education*** éducation *f* sexuelle; ***sex fiend*** maniaque *mf* sexuel(elle); *Fam* **sex god** apollon ❑ *m*; *Fam* **sex goddess** bombe *f* sexuelle; ***sex hormone*** hormone *f* sexuelle; ***the sex industry*** l'industrie *f* du sexe; *Fam* **sex kitten** bombe *f* sexuelle; ***sex life*** vie *f* sexuelle; *Hum* **how's your sex life?** et ta vie amoureuse, comment ça va?; *Biol* ***sex linkage*** hérédité *f* liée au sexe; ***sex maniac*** obsédé(e) *m,f* sexuel(elle); ***sex object*** objet *m* sexuel; ***sex offender*** auteur *m* d'un délit sexuel; ***sex organ*** organe *m* sexuel; ***sex partner*** partenaire *mf* sexuel(elle); *Fam* **sex pest** obsédé *m (qui harcèle les femmes)*; ***sex scandal*** affaire *f* de mœurs, scandale *m* sexuel; ***sex scene*** scène *f* érotique; ***sex shop*** sex-shop *m*; ***sex symbol*** sex-symbol *m*; ***sex therapist*** sexologue *mf*; ***sex therapy*** sexothérapie *f*; ***sex toy*** gadget *m* érotique; ***sex tourism*** tourisme *m* sexuel; ***sex urge*** pulsion *f* sexuelle; ***sex worker*** = personne qui gagne de l'argent grâce à l'industrie du sexe; *(prostitute)* prostitué(e) *m,f*

sexadecimal [,seksə'desɪməl] *adj* sexadécimal

sexagenarian [,seksədʒɪ'neərɪən] **1** *adj* sexagénaire

2 *n* sexagénaire *mf*

Sexagesima [,seksə'dʒesɪmə] *n Rel* sexagésime *f*

sexagesimal [,seksə'dʒesɪməl] *Math* **1** *n* fraction *f* sexagésimale

2 *adj* sexagésimal

sexed [sekst] *adj Biol & Zool* sexué; **to be highly sexed** *(person)* avoir une forte libido

sexennial [sek'senɪəl] *adj* sexennal

sexily ['seksɪlɪ] *adv* de façon sexy; **he dances very sexily** il danse de façon très sensuelle

sexiness ['seksɪnɪs] *n* caractère *m* sexy; **the sexiness of her appearance** son air sexy; **they are all agreed on his sexiness** ils sont tous d'accord pour dire qu'il est sexy; **the sexiness of the way she walks** sa démarche sexy

sexism ['seksɪzəm] *n* sexisme *m*

sexist ['seksɪst] **1** *adj* sexiste

2 *n* sexiste *mf*

sexless ['sekslɪs] *adj* (**a**) *Biol* asexué (**b**) *(person → asexual)* asexué; *(→ frigid)* frigide; **theirs is a sexless marriage** ils sont mariés mais n'ont pas de rapports sexuels

sex-linked *adj Biol* lié au sexe

sex-mad *adj Fam* **he's/she's sex-mad** il/elle ne pense qu'à ça

sexological [,seksə'lɒdʒɪkəl] *adj* sexologique

sexologist [sek'sɒlədʒɪst] *n* sexologue *mf*

sexology [sek'sɒlədʒɪ] *n* sexologie *f*

sexploitation [,seksplɔɪ'teɪʃən] *n* exploitation *f* du sexe; **a sexploitation movie** un film dont le propos se résume au sexe

sexploits ['seksplɔɪts] *npl Fam Hum* aventures *fpl* sexuelles ❑

sexpot ['sekspɒt] *n Fam (woman)* femme *f* très sexy, bombe *f* sexuelle; *(man)* homme *m* très sexy

sex-starved *adj Hum* (sexuellement) frustré

sext [sekst] *n Rel* sexte *f*

sextant ['sekstənt] *n* sextant *m*

sextet [seks'tet] *n* sextuor *m*

sextillion [seks'tɪlɪən] *n* (**a**) *(10^{36})* sextillion *m* (**b**) *(10^{21})* mille trillions *mpl*

sexto ['sekstəʊ] (*pl* **sextos**) *n Typ* in-six *m inv*

sextodecimo [,sekstəʊ'desɪməʊ] (*pl* **sextodecimos**) *n Typ* in-seize *m inv*

sexton ['sekstən] *n* sacristain *m*, bedeau *m*

sextuple ['sekstjʊpəl] **1** *adj* sextuple

2 *n* sextuple *m*

3 *vi* sextupler

4 *vt* sextupler

sextuplet ['sekstjʊplɪt] *n* (**a**) *(child)* sextuplé(e) *m,f* (**b**) *Mus* sextolet *m*

sextuplicate [seks'tjuːplɪkət] **1** *n* sextuple *m*; **in sextuplicate** en six exemplaires

2 *adj* sextuple

Sextus ['sekstəs] *pr n* Sextus

sexual ['sekʃʊəl] *adj* sexuel

►► ***sexual abuse*** *(UNCOUNT)* sévices *mpl* sexuels; ***sexual assault*** agression *f* sexuelle; *Fam* ***sexual athlete*** bête *f* de sexe; ***sexual attraction*** attirance *f* sexuelle; ***sexual discrimination*** discrimination *f* sexuelle, sexisme *m*; ***sexual equality*** égalité *f* entre les sexes; ***sexual harassment*** harcèlement *m* sexuel; ***sexual intercourse*** *(UNCOUNT)* rapports *mpl* sexuels; ***sexual liberation*** libération *f* sexuelle; ***sexual orientation*** tendances *fpl* sexuelles; ***sexual politics*** = (étude du) rôle respectif des hommes et des femmes dans la société; ***sexual reproduction*** reproduction *f* sexuelle; ***the sexual revolution*** la révolution sexuelle

sexuality [,sekʃʊ'ælɪtɪ] *n* sexualité *f*

sexualize, -ise ['sekʃʊəlaɪz] *vt* sexualiser

sexually ['sekʃʊəlɪ] *adv* sexuellement; **sexually active** qui a une activité sexuelle; **to be sexually assaulted** être victime d'une agression sexuelle

►► *Med* ***sexually transmitted disease*** maladie *f* sexuellement transmissible, *Can* maladie *f* transmise sexuellement

sexy ['seksɪ] (*compar* **sexier,** *superl* **sexiest**) *adj Fam* (**a**) *(person)* sexy *(inv)*; *(book, film)* érotique; **hi there sexy!** *(to man)* salut, beau gosse!; *(to woman)* salut, beauté! (**b**) *(product, idea, car)* branché

Seychelles [seɪ'ʃelz] *npl* **the Seychelles** les Seychelles *fpl*; **in the Seychelles** aux Seychelles

sez [sez] *Fam* = **says**

SF [,es'ef] (*abbr* **science fiction**) **1** *n* SF *f*

2 *adj* de SF

SFA [,esef'eɪ] *n* (*abbr* **Scottish Football Association**) Fédération *f* écossaise de football

SFO [,esef'əʊ] *n* (*abbr* **Serious Fraud Office**) = service britannique de la répression des fraudes

sforzando [sfɔːt'sændəʊ] *Mus* **1** *adj* sforzando

2 *adv* sforzando

sfumato [sfuː'mɑːtəʊ] *n* (*pl* **sfumatos**) *Art* sfumato *m*

sfx [,esef'eks] *n Cin* (*abbr* **special effects**) effets *mpl* spéciaux

SG [,es'dʒiː] *n* (*abbr* **Surgeon General**) (**a**) *Mil* médecin-général *m* (**b**) *Am Admin* chef *m* des services de santé

SGML [,esdʒiː,em'el] *n Comput* (*abbr* **Standard Generated Mark-up Language**) SGML *m*

sgraffito [,sgræ'fiːtəʊ] (*pl* **sgraffiti** [-tiː]) *n Art* sgraffite *m*

Sgt (*written abbr* **sergeant**) Sgt

sh [ʃ] *exclam* chut!

shabbily ['ʃæbɪlɪ] *adv* (**a**) *(dressed, furnished)* pauvrement (**b**) *(behave, treat)* mesquinement, petitement; **I think she's been very shabbily treated** je trouve qu'on l'a traitée de manière très mesquine

shabbiness ['ʃæbɪnɪs] *n* (**a**) *(poor condition → of dress, person)* aspect *m* misérable; *(→ of house, street)* délabrement *m*; *(→ of carpet, furniture, clothes)* mauvais état *m* (**b**) *(meanness → of behaviour, treatment, trick)* mesquinerie *f*, petitesse *f* (**c**) *(mediocrity → of excuse, reasoning)* médiocrité *f*

shabby ['ʃæbɪ] (*compar* **shabbier,** *superl* **shabbiest**) *adj* (**a**) *(clothes)* râpé, élimé; *(carpet, curtains)* usé, élimé; *(person)* pauvrement vêtu; *(hotel, house, furniture)* miteux, minable; *(street, area)* misérable, miteux (**b**) *(mean → behaviour, treatment)* mesquin, vil, bas; **that was a shabby trick** c'était vraiment mesquin (**c**) *(mediocre → excuse)* piètre; *(→ reasoning)* médiocre

shabby-genteel *adj* désargenté mais digne

shack [ʃæk] *n* cabane *f*, case *f*, hutte *f*

▸**shack up** *vi Fam* **to shack up with sb** se mettre à la colle avec qn, s'installer avec qn □; **they've shacked up together** ils se sont mis à la colle

shackle [ˈʃækəl] **1** *vt* enchaîner, mettre aux fers; **he was shackled to the post** on l'a enchaîné au poteau; *Fig* **shackled by convention** entravé par les conventions

2 shackles *npl* chaînes *fpl*, fers *mpl*; *Fig* chaînes *fpl*, entraves *fpl*; *Fig* **the shackles of convention** le carcan des conventions sociales

shacktown [ˈʃæktaʊn] *n Am Fam* bidonville □ *m*

shad [ʃæd] *n Ich* alose *f*

shadbush [ˈʃædbʊʃ] *n Bot* amélanchier *m*

shaddock [ˈʃædɒk] *n* = sorte de pamplemousse

shade [ʃeɪd] **1** *n* (**a**) *(shadow)* ombre *f*; *Art* ombre *f*, ombres *fpl*; **to sit in the shade** s'asseoir à l'ombre; **45 degrees in the shade** 45 degrés à l'ombre; **in the shade of a tree** à l'ombre d'un arbre; **these trees give plenty of shade** ces arbres font beaucoup d'ombre; **the use of light and shade in the painting** l'utilisation *f* des ombres et des lumières *ou* du clair-obscur dans le tableau; *Fig* **to put sb in the shade** éclipser qn; **his achievements really put mine in the shade** ses réalisations éclipsent vraiment les miennes

(**b**) *(nuance → of colour)* nuance *f*, ton *m*; *(→ of meaning, opinion)* nuance *f*; **a different shade of green** un ton de vert différent, une autre nuance de vert; **an attractive shade of blue** un joli bleu; **all shades of political opinion were represented** toutes les nuances politiques étaient représentées, tous les courants politiques étaient représentés; *Comput* **shades of grey** niveaux *mpl ou* tons *mpl* de gris

(**c**) *(for lamp)* abat-jour *m inv*; *(for eyes)* visière *f*; *Am (blind → on window)* store *m*; **to pull the shades (down)** baisser les stores

(**d**) *Literary (spirit)* ombre *f*, fantôme *m*; *Myth* **the Shades** les Enfers *mpl*, le royaume des ombres

2 *vt* (**a**) *(screen → eyes, face)* abriter; *(→ place)* ombrager, donner de l'ombre à; *(of hat → face)* obscurcir; **to shade one's eyes with one's hand** s'abriter les yeux de la main; **to shade sth from the sun** protéger qch du soleil

(**b**) *(cover → light, lightbulb)* masquer, voiler

(**c**) *Art (painting)* ombrer; *(by hatching)* hachurer; **I've shaded the background green** j'ai coloré l'arrière-plan en vert

(**d**) *Am Com* **to shade prices** établir des prix dégressifs; **prices shaded for quantities** tarif *m* dégressif pour le gros

3 *vi (merge)* se dégrader, se fondre; **the blue shades into purple** le bleu se fond en violet; **these categories shade into one another** ces catégories se confondent; **questions of right and wrong tend to shade into each other** les questions du bien et du mal ont tendance à se rejoindre

4 a shade *adv* **she's a shade better today** elle va un tout petit peu mieux aujourd'hui; **his books are just a shade too sentimental for me** ses livres sont un peu trop sentimentaux pour moi

5 shades *npl* (**a**) *Literary (growing darkness)* **the shades of evening** les ombres *fpl* du soir

(**b**) *Fam (sunglasses)* lunettes *fpl* de soleil □, lunettes *fpl* noires □

(**c**) *(reminder, echo)* échos *mpl*; **shades of Proust** des échos *mpl* proustiens; **there are shades of 1968** ça rappelle 1968

▸**shade in** *vt sep (background)* hachurer, tramer; *(with colour)* colorer

▸**shade off 1** *vt sep (change by degrees → colours)* dégrader

2 *vi* **red shading off into pink** du rouge qui se fond en rose

shadeband [ˈʃeɪdbænd] *n Aut* bande *f* pare-soleil

shaded [ˈʃeɪdɪd] *adj* (**a**) *(path, corner)* ombragé; *(lamp)* à abat-jour (**b**) *Art (drawing)* ombré; *(area on diagram, map)* hachuré

shadeless [ˈʃeɪdlɪs] *adj* sans ombre

shade-loving *adj Bot* sciaphile

shadiness [ˈʃeɪdɪnɪs] *n* (**a**) *(of place)* ombre *f*, ombrage *m* (**b**) *Fam (of behaviour, dealings)* caractère *m* louche *ou* suspect □

shading [ˈʃeɪdɪŋ] *n (UNCOUNT) Art (in painting)* ombres *fpl*; *(hatching)* hachure *f*, tramage *m*, hachures *fpl*; *Fig (difference)* nuance *f*

shadoof [ʃɑːˈduːf] *n* shadouf *m*, chadouf *m*

shadow [ˈʃædəʊ] **1** *n* (**a**) *(of figure, building)* ombre *f*; **to see a shadow on a wall** voir une ombre sur un mur; **the shadow of suspicion fell on them** on a commencé à les soupçonner; **she's a shadow of her former self** elle n'est plus que l'ombre d'elle-même; *Fig* **he's afraid of his own shadow** il a peur de son ombre; *Fig* **to live in sb's shadow** vivre dans l'ombre de qn; **to cast a shadow on** *or* **over sth** projeter une ombre sur qch; *Fig* jeter une ombre sur qch

(**b**) *(under eyes)* cerne *m*

(**c**) *(shade)* ombre *f*, ombrage *m*; **in the shadow of the trees/the mountain** à l'ombre des arbres/de la montagne; **in the shadow of the doorway** dans l'ombre de la porte; **she was standing in (the) shadow** elle se tenait dans l'ombre; **the gardens lie in shadow now** les jardins sont maintenant à l'ombre

(**d**) *(slightest bit)* ombre *f*; **without** *or* **beyond a** *or* **the shadow of a doubt** sans l'ombre d'un doute

(**e**) *(detective)* **I want a shadow put on him** je veux qu'on le fasse suivre; **he managed to lose his shadow** il a réussi à semer la personne qui l'avait pris en filature

(**f**) *(companion)* ombre *f*; **he follows me everywhere like a shadow** il me suit comme mon ombre, il ne me lâche pas d'une semelle

(**g**) *Med (on lung)* voile *m*

2 *vt* (**a**) *(follow secretly)* filer, prendre en filature; **our job was to shadow enemy submarines** nous étions chargés de suivre les sous-marins ennemis

(**b**) *Literary (screen from light)* ombrager; **tall trees shadowed the pathway** de grands arbres ombrageaient le chemin

3 *adj Br* **the Shadow Education Secretary/Defence Secretary** le porte-parole de l'opposition pour l'éducation/pour la défense nationale

4 shadows *npl Literary (darkness)* ombre *f*, ombres *fpl*, obscurité *f*; **the shadows of the evening** les ombres *fpl* du soir

▸▸ *Br Pol* ***shadow cabinet*** cabinet *m* fantôme; *Br Pol* ***shadow minister*** ministre *mf* fantôme; *Comput* ***shadow printing*** impression *f* ombrée; ***shadow puppet*** = silhouette découpée utilisée dans les spectacles d'ombres chinoises

SHADOW CABINET

En Grande-Bretagne, le "shadow cabinet" est composé de parlementaires de l'opposition qui deviendraient ministres si l'opposition accédait au pouvoir. Chaque ministre du gouvernement dispose de son homologue "fantôme" dans l'opposition (on parle de "shadow minister"), qui étudie les mêmes dossiers et se spécialise ainsi dans un domaine donné. Les ministres fantômes occupent les "frontbenches" de l'opposition à la Chambre des communes.

shadow-box *vi Sport* faire de la boxe à vide

shadow-boxing *n Sport* boxe *f* à vide; *Fig* attaque *f* de pure forme; **the negotiations were largely a display of shadow-boxing** c'étaient des négociations de pure forme; **let's stop all this shadow-boxing and get down to business** arrêtons de tourner autour du pot et parlons sérieusement

shadowgraph [ˈʃædəʊgrɑːf] *n* (**a**) *(shadow picture)* silhouette *f*, ombre *f (faite avec les mains)*; *(show)* ombres *fpl* chinoises (**b**) *Med* radiographie *f*

shadowing [ˈʃædəʊɪŋ] *n (tailing)* filature *f*

shadow-mask tube *n TV* tube-image *m* trichrome

shadowy [ˈʃædəʊɪ] *adj* (**a**) *(shady → woods, path)* ombragé; **he looked into the shadowy depths** il scruta les profondeurs insondables (**b**) *(vague → figure, outline)* vague, indistinct; *(→ plan)* vague, imprécis

shady [ˈʃeɪdɪ] *(compar* **shadier,** *superl* **shadiest)** *adj* (**a**) *(place)* ombragé (**b**) *Fam (person, behaviour)* louche, suspect □; *(dealings)* louche; **a shady character** un individu louche

Shaef [ʃeɪf] *n (abbr* **Supreme Headquarters, Allied Expeditionary Force, World War II)** SHAEF *m*, Commandement *m* suprême des forces expéditionnaires alliées

shaft [ʃɑːft] **1** *n* (**a**) *(of spear)* hampe *f*; *(of feather)* tuyau *m*; *Archit (of column)* fût *m*; *Anat (of bone)* diaphyse *f*

(**b**) *(of axe, tool, golf club)* manche *m*

(**c**) *(of cart, carriage)* brancard *m*, limon *m*; **to put a horse between the shafts** atteler un cheval

(**d**) *Tech (for propeller, in machine)* arbre *m*, axe *m*

(**e**) *(in mine)* puits *m*; *(of ventilator)* puits *m*, cheminée *f*; *(of lift)* cage *f*; **air** *or* **ventilation shaft** puits *m* d'aérage, conduit *m* d'air

(**f**) *(of light)* rayon *m*; *(of lightning)* éclair *m*; *Fig* **a shaft of wit** un trait d'esprit

(**g**) *Literary (arrow)* flèche *f*

(**h**) *Vulg (penis)* chibre *m*, queue *f*

(**i**) *Am very Fam (idiom)* **he got the shaft** *(got shouted at)* qu'est-ce qu'il s'est pris!; *(got fired)* il s'est fait virer; *(got cheated)* il s'est fait arnaquer

2 *vt* (**a**) *very Fam (cheat)* baiser, entuber; **to get shafted** se faire baiser *ou* entuber

(**b**) *Br Vulg (have sex with)* baiser, tringler

Shaftesbury Avenue [ˈʃɑːftsbərɪ-] *n* = rue de Londres célèbre pour ses théâtres

shag [ʃæg] *(pt & pp* **shagged)** **1** *n* (**a**) *(of hair, wool)* toison *f*

(**b**) *(tobacco)* tabac *m* (très fort)

(**c**) *Orn* cormoran *m* huppé

(**d**) *Br very Fam (sex)* baise *f*; **to have a shag** baiser, tirer un coup, s'envoyer en l'air; **to be a good shag** *(person)* être un bon coup

(**e**) *Am (dance)* shag *m (danse traditionnelle américaine)*

(**f**) *Am (ballboy)* ramasseur *m* de balles

(**g**) *Br very Fam (boring task)* plaie *f*; **it's a real shag having to get up so early every morning** c'est vraiment chiant de devoir se lever si tôt tous les matins

2 *vt* (**a**) *Br very Fam (have sex with → of man)* baiser, troncher; *(→ of woman)* baiser avec, s'envoyer

(**b**) *Am (follow)* poursuivre

(**c**) *Am (fetch)* aller chercher

(**d**) *Am Fam* **to shag ass** mettre les voiles, mettre les bouts

3 *vi* (**a**) *Br very Fam (have sex)* baiser, s'envoyer en l'air

(**b**) *Am (dance)* danser le shag

▸▸ ***shag (pile) carpet*** moquette *f* à poils longs; ***shag tobacco*** tabac *m* (très fort)

▸**shag out** *vt sep Br Fam (exhaust)* crever; **I'm shagged out** je suis crevé

shaggable [ˈʃægəbəl] *adj Br very Fam* baisable

shagged [ʃægd] *adj Br Fam (exhausted)* crevé

shagger [ˈʃægə(r)] *n Br very Fam* baiseur *m*

shagginess [ˈʃægɪnɪs] *n (of dog, pony, rug)* longueur *f* de poil; **the shagginess of his beard** sa barbe hirsute

shaggy [ˈʃægɪ] *(compar* **shaggier,** *superl* **shaggiest)** *adj (hair, beard)* hirsute, touffu; *(eyebrows)* hérissé, broussailleux; *(dog, pony)* à longs poils (rudes); *(carpet, rug)* à longs poils; **a shaggy-looking man** un homme hirsute

shaggy-dog story *n* histoire *f* sans queue ni tête

shagreen [ʃæˈgriːn] *n* chagrin *m (cuir)*

shah [ʃɑː] *n* chah *m*, shah *m*; **the Shah of Persia** le chah de Perse

shake [ʃeɪk] *(pt* **shook** [ʃʊk], *pp* **shaken** [ˈʃeɪkən]) **1** *n* (**a**) *(movement)* secousse *f*, ébranlement *m*; *(trembling → of hand, voice etc)* tremblement *m*; **to give sb/sth a shake** secouer qn/qch; **she gave the thermometer a few shakes** elle secoua un peu le thermomètre; **to give oneself a shake** se secouer; **with a shake of his head** *(in refusal, in resignation, sympathy)* avec un hochement de tête; **with a shake in his voice** d'une voix tremblotante; **give him a shake** *(to waken)* secouez-le; **I feel like giving him a good shake** *(to stimulate)* j'ai une furieuse envie de le secouer; *Br Fam* **to be all of a shake** être tout tremblant❑; *Fam* **to have the shakes** avoir la tremblote

(**b**) *Fam (moment)* instant❑ *m*; **you go, I'll be there in a shake** *or* **a couple of shakes** vas-y, j'arrive dans un instant *ou* dans une seconde❑; **in two shakes (of a lamb's tail)** en un clin d'œil❑, en moins de deux

(**c**) *Am Fam (earthquake)* tremblement *m* de terre❑

(**d**) *(drink)* milk-shake *m*; **a banana shake** un milk-shake à la banane

(**e**) *Am Fam (deal)* **he'll give you a fair shake** il ne te roulera pas

(**f**) *Fam (idiom)* **it's/he's no great shakes** ça/il casse pas des briques, ça/il casse pas trois pattes à un canard; **he's no great shakes at painting** *or* **as a painter** il ne casse rien *ou* il casse pas des briques comme peintre

(**g**) *Mus* trille *m*

2 *vt* (**a**) *(rug, tablecloth, person)* secouer; *(bottle, cocktail, dice)* agiter; *(of earthquake, explosion)* ébranler, faire trembler; **he had to be shaken awake** on a dû le secouer pour le réveiller; **she shook me by the shoulders** elle m'a secoué par les épaules; **the wind shook the branches** le vent agitait les branches; **they shook the apples from the tree** ils secouèrent l'arbre pour (en) faire tomber les pommes; **to shake the snow from one's head** secouer sa tête pour se débarrasser de la neige; **he shook the gravel into the bag** il secouait le gravier pour le faire tomber dans le sac; **to shake sugar onto sth** saupoudrer qch de sucre; **to shake vinegar onto sth** asperger qch de vinaigre; **to shake salt/pepper onto sth** saler/poivrer qch; **shake well before use** *(on packaging)* bien agiter avant l'emploi; **the dog shook itself (dry)** le chien s'est ébroué (pour se sécher); **they shook themselves free** ils se sont libérés d'une secousse; **I can't seem to shake him out of his apathy** je n'arrive pas à le tirer de son apathie; **he shook his head** *(in refusal)* il a dit *ou* fait non de la tête; *(in resignation, sympathy)* il a hoché la tête; *Fam* **shake a leg!** secoue-toi!, remue-toi!; *Fig* **to shake the dust from one's feet** partir le cœur léger

(**b**) *(brandish)* brandir; **to shake one's finger at sb** *(in warning)* avertir qn en lui faisant signe du doigt; *(threateningly)* menacer qn du doigt; **he shook his fist at him** il l'a menacé du poing; **the farmer shook his stick at the boys** le fermier menaçait les garçons de son bâton; *Br Fam* **he's won more awards than you can shake a stick at** on lui a décerné une flopée de prix

(**c**) *(hand)* serrer; **to shake hands with sb, to shake sb's hand** serrer la main à qn; **they shook hands** ils se sont serré la main; **let me shake you by the hand** permettez-moi de vous serrer la main; **let's shake hands on the deal** serrons-nous la main pour sceller cet accord

(**d**) *(upset → faith, confidence, reputation)* ébranler; *(→ person)* secouer, bouleverser; **that has shaken my faith in him** cela a ébranlé la confiance que j'avais en lui; **his beliefs would not be that easily shaken** ses convictions ne sauraient être ébranlées pour si peu; **the whole world was shaken by the news** le monde entier a été ébranlé par la nouvelle; **she shook everyone with her revelations** tout le monde a été bouleversé par ses révélations; **they were rather shaken by the news** ils ont été plutôt secoués par la nouvelle; **to feel shaken after a fall** se ressentir d'une chute; **I bet that shook him!** voilà qui a dû le secouer!

(**e**) *Austr Fam (steal)* piquer

3 *vi* (**a**) *(ground, floor, house)* trembler, être ébranlé; *(leaves, branches)* trembler, être agité; **the whole house shook with the sound** la maison entière a été ébranlée par le bruit; **the whole building shook** *(after explosion etc)* tout le bâtiment a tremblé; **the door shakes whenever a bus passes** à chaque fois qu'un bus passe, ça fait trembler la porte; **the child shook free of his captor** l'enfant a échappé à son ravisseur

(**b**) *(with emotion → voice)* trembler, frémir; *(→ body, knees)* trembler; **her whole frame shook** elle tremblait de tous ses membres; **in a voice shaking with emotion** d'une voix émue *ou* tremblotante; **to shake with laughter** se tordre de rire; **to shake with fear** trembler de peur; **to shake with cold** trembler de froid, grelotter; **to shake like a jelly** *or* **leaf** trembler comme une feuille; **to shake in one's shoes** avoir une peur bleue, être mort de peur; **his hands were shaking uncontrollably** il ne pouvait empêcher ses mains de trembler

(**c**) *(in agreement)* **let's shake on it!** tope-là!; **they shook on the deal** ils ont scellé leur accord par une poignée de main

►**shake down 1** *vt sep* (**a**) *(from tree)* faire tomber en secouant; **to shake cherries down from a tree** secouer un arbre pour en faire tomber les cerises

(**b**) *(after fall)* **to shake oneself down** s'ébrouer, se secouer

(**c**) *Am Fam* **to shake sb down** *(rob)* racketter qn❑; *(blackmail)* faire chanter qn❑

(**d**) *Am Fam (search)* fouiller❑, palper❑

(**e**) *Am Fam (test)* essayer❑, tester❑

2 *vi* (**a**) *Fam (go to bed)* coucher❑; **they had to shake down on the floor for the night** ils ont dû dormir *ou* coucher par terre

(**b**) *Fam (adapt → to new situation, job)* s'habituer❑; **she's new to the job but she'll shake down soon enough** elle débute dans le métier mais elle s'y fera rapidement

(**c**) *(contents of packet, bottle)* se tasser

►**shake off** *vt sep* (**a**) *(physically)* secouer; **to shake the sand/water off sth** secouer le sable/l'eau de qch

(**b**) *(get rid of → cold, pursuer, depression)* se débarrasser de; *(→ habit)* se défaire de, se débarrasser de; **I can't shake him off** il ne me lâche pas d'une semelle; **she's always phoning me up, I can't shake her off** elle me téléphone sans cesse, je n'arrive pas à m'en débarrasser

►**shake out 1** *vt sep (tablecloth, rug)* (bien) secouer; *(sail, flag)* déferler, déployer; *(bag)* vider en secouant; **he shook the coins out of the bag** il a fait tomber les pièces en secouant le sac; **he picked up his shoes and shook the sand out** il a ramassé ses chaussures et en a secoué le sable

2 *vi Mil* se disperser, se disséminer

►**shake up** *vt sep* (**a**) *(physically → pillow)* secouer, taper; *(→ bottle)* agiter

(**b**) *Fig (upset → person)* secouer, bouleverser; **they were badly shaken up after the accident** ils ont été très secoués après l'accident

(**c**) *(rouse → person)* secouer; **he needs shaking up a bit** il a besoin qu'on le secoue un peu

(**d**) *Fam (overhaul → organization, company)* remanier❑, réorganiser de fond en comble❑

shakedown [ˈʃeɪkdaʊn] **1** *n* (**a**) *(bed)* lit *m* improvisé *ou* de fortune

(**b**) *Fam (of ship, plane → test)* essai❑ *m*; *(→ flight, voyage)* voyage *m ou* vol *m* d'essai❑

(**c**) *Am Fam (search)* fouille❑ *f*

(**d**) *Am Fam (extortion)* racket❑ *m*, chantage❑ *m*

2 *adj (test, flight, voyage)* d'essai

shaken [ˈʃeɪkən] **1** *pp of* **shake**

2 *adj (upset)* secoué; *(stronger)* bouleversé, ébranlé

shake-out *n Econ* dégraissage *m*

shaker [ˈʃeɪkə(r)] *n (for cocktails)* shaker *m*; *(for salad)* panier *m* à salade; *(for dice)* cornet *m*

Shakers [ˈʃeɪkəz] *npl Rel* **the Shakers** les Shakers *mpl (secte protestante du XVIIIème siècle, aujourd'hui presque disparue, qui prêchait le célibat)*

Shakespearean [ʃeɪkˈspɪərɪən] *adj* shakespearien

Shakespeareana [ˈʃeɪkˌspɪərɪˈɑːnə] *npl (by Shakespeare)* écrits *mpl* de Shakespeare; *(about Shakespeare)* articles *mpl* et livres *mpl* sur Shakespeare

Shakespearian = **Shakespearean**

shake-up *n Fam* (**a**) *(of company, organization)* remaniement❑ *m*, restructuration❑ *f* (**b**) *(emotional)* bouleversement❑ *m*

shakily [ˈʃeɪkɪlɪ] *adv* (**a**) *(unsteadily → walk)* d'un pas chancelant *ou* mal assuré; *(→ write)* d'une main tremblante; *(→ speak)* d'une voix tremblante *ou* chevrotante (**b**) *(uncertainly)* d'une manière hésitante *ou* peu assurée; **she started shakily then went on to win the game** au début, elle n'était pas très sûre d'elle, mais elle a fini par gagner la partie

shakiness [ˈʃeɪkɪnɪs] *n* (**a**) *(unsteadiness → of chair, table)* manque *m* de stabilité; *(→ of foundations, building)* manque *m* de solidité; *(→ of hand)* tremblement *m*; *(→ of voice)* chevrotement *m*, tremblement *m* (**b**) *(weakness, uncertainty → of health, memory, argument, faith)* faiblesse *f*; *(→ of knowledge)* insuffisance *f*; *(→ of position, authority)* fragilité *f*, précarité *f*; *(→ of future)* incertitude *f*

shaking [ˈʃeɪkɪŋ] *n Med* tremblement *m*

shako [ˈʃækəʊ] (*pl* **shakos** *or* **shakoes**) *n Mil (headgear)* shako *m*, schako *m*

shaky [ˈʃeɪkɪ] (*compar* **shakier**, *superl* **shakiest**) *adj* (**a**) *(unsteady → chair, table)* branlant, peu solide; *(→ ladder)* branlant, peu stable; *(→ hand)* tremblant, tremblotant; *(→ writing)* tremblé; *(→ voice)* tremblotant, chevrotant; *(→ steps)* chancelant; **he's a bit shaky on his legs** il ne tient pas bien *ou* il n'est pas très solide sur ses jambes; **I'm still shaky after my accident** je ne me suis pas encore complètement remis de mon accident; **to be based** *or* **built on shaky foundations** avoir des bases chancelantes

(**b**) *(uncertain, weak → health, faith)* précaire, vacillant; *(→ authority, regime)* incertain, chancelant; *(→ future, finances)* incertain, précaire; *(→ business)* incertain; **her memory is a bit shaky** sa mémoire n'est pas très sûre; **my memories of the war are rather shaky** mes souvenirs de la guerre sont assez vagues; **things got off to a shaky start** les choses ont plutôt mal commencé; **my knowledge of German is a bit shaky** mes notions d'allemand sont plutôt vagues; **he came up with some very shaky arguments** ses arguments étaient très peu convaincants

shale [ʃeɪl] *n Geol* argile *f* schisteuse, schiste *m* argileux

►► ***shale oil*** huile *f* de schiste

shall [ʃəl, *stressed* ʃæl]

> On trouve généralement **I/you/he**/*etc* **shall** sous leurs formes contractées **I'll/you'll/he'll/** *etc.* La forme négative correspondante est **shan't** que l'on écrira **shall not** dans des contextes formels.

modal aux v (**a**) *(as future auxiliary)* **I shall** *or* **I'll come tomorrow** je viendrai demain; **I shall not** *or* **I shan't be able to come** je ne pourrai pas venir; **we shall have finished by tomorrow** nous aurons fini demain; **I shall now attempt a triple somersault** je vais à présent essayer d'exécuter un triple saut périlleux; **as we shall see** comme nous le verrons, comme nous allons le voir

(**b**) *(in suggestions, questions)* **shall I open the window?** voulez-vous que j'ouvre la fenêtre?; **shall we go for a drive?** on va faire un tour en voiture?; **I'll shut that window, shall I?** je peux fermer cette fenêtre, si vous voulez; **we'll all go then, shall we?** dans ce cas, pourquoi n'y allons-nous pas tous?; **what shall we buy?** qu'est-ce qu'on va acheter?; **where shall we go?** où est-ce qu'on va aller?

(**c**) *Formal (emphatic use)* **you shall go to the ball!** vous irez au bal!; **it shall be done** ce sera fait; *Bible* **thou shalt not kill** tu ne tueras point

shallop [ˈʃæləp] *n Naut* chaloupe *f*, péniche *f*, pinache *f*

shallot [ʃəˈlɒt] *n* échalote *f*

shallow [ˈʃæləʊ] **1** *adj* (**a**) *(water, soil, dish, grave)* peu profond; **the shallow end** *(of swimming pool)* le petit bain, *Can* la partie peu profonde (**b**) *(superficial → person, mind, character)* superficiel, qui manque de profondeur; *(→ conversation)* superficiel, futile; *(→ argument)* superficiel (**c**) *(breathing)* superficiel

2 *vi Formal* devenir moins profond

3 shallows *npl* bas-fond *m*, bas-fonds *mpl*, haut-fond *m*, hauts-fonds *mpl*

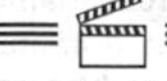

'Shallow Grave' *Boyle* 'Petits meurtres entre amis'

shallow-minded *adj* **to be shallow-minded** être superficiel *ou* futile

shallowness [ˈʃæləʊnɪs] *n* (**a**) *(of water, soil,*

dish) faible profondeur *f* (**b**) *(of mind, character, sentiments)* manque *m* de profondeur; *(of person)* esprit *m* superficiel, manque *m* de profondeur; *(of talk, ideas)* futilité *f* (**c**) *(of breathing)* **the shallowness of his breathing** sa respiration *f* superficielle

shallow-rooted *adj (tree)* à enracinement superficiel

shalt [ʃælt] *Arch 2nd pers sing of* **shall**

shaly [ˈʃeɪlɪ] *adj* schisteux

sham [ʃæm] *(pt & pp* **shammed**, *cont* **shamming***)*
1 *n* (**a**) *(pretence → of sentiment, behaviour)* comédie *f*, farce *f*, faux-semblant *m*; **what he says is all sham** il n'y a rien de vrai dans ce qu'il dit; **her illness/grief is a sham** sa maladie/son chagrin n'est qu'une mascarade; **their marriage is a complete sham** leur mariage est une véritable farce; **the elections were a sham** les élections ont été une véritable farce
(**b**) *(impostor → person)* imposteur *m*; *(→ organization)* imposture *f*
2 *adj* (**a**) *(pretended → sentiment, illness)* faux (fausse), feint, simulé; *(→ battle)* simulé
(**b**) *(mock → jewellery)* fantaisie, faux (fausse); **a sham election** un simulacre d'élections; **a sham peace** une paix de pacotille
3 *vt* feindre, simuler; **to sham illness** faire semblant d'être malade
4 *vi* faire semblant, jouer la comédie; **he's not really ill, he's only shamming** il n'est pas vraiment malade, il fait semblant

shaman [ˈʃɑːmən] *n* chaman *m*

shamanism [ˈʃɑːmənɪzəm] *n* chamanisme *m*

shamanist [ˈʃɑːmənɪst] **1** *n* chamaniste *mf*
2 *adj* chamaniste

shamanistic [ˌʃɑːməˈnɪstɪk] *adj* chamanistique

shamateur [ˈʃæmətɜː(r)] *Fam Sport* **1** *n* = sportif prétendument amateur
2 *adj (competition, game, race)* = auquel participent des sportifs prétendument amateurs

shamateurism [ˈʃæmətərɪzəm] *n Fam Sport* amateurisme *m* bidon

shamble [ˈʃæmbəl] *vi* **to shamble (along)** marcher en traînant les pieds; **to shamble in/out/past** entrer/sortir/passer en traînant les pieds; **he shambled up to them** il s'approcha d'eux d'un pas traînant; **a shambling gait** une démarche traînante

shambles [ˈʃæmbəlz] *n Fam* (**a**) *(place)* désordre❑ *m*, foutoir *m*; **your room is a total shambles!** quelle pagaille dans ta chambre!, ta chambre est un vrai foutoir!; **the house was in a shambles** la maison était sens dessus dessous; **what a shambles!** quelle pagaille!
(**b**) *(department, company, accounts)* foutoir *m*; *(situation, event)* désastre❑ *m*; **his life is (in) a real shambles** sa vie est un véritable désastre; **the evening was a shambles** la soirée fut un vrai désastre; **to make a shambles of a job** saboter un travail❑; **what a shambles!** quelle pagaille!, quel foutoir!

shambolic [ʃæmˈbɒlɪk] *adj Br Fam* désordonné❑

shame [ʃeɪm] **1** *n* (**a**) *(feeling)* honte *f*, confusion *f*; **to my great shame** à ma grande honte; **he has no sense of shame** il n'a aucune honte; **to lose all sense of shame** perdre toute honte; **to have no shame** *(no scruples)* n'avoir aucune honte; **have you no shame?** vous n'avez pas honte?
(**b**) *(disgrace, dishonour)* honte *f*; **to bring shame on one's family/country** déshonorer sa famille/sa patrie, couvrir sa famille/sa patrie de honte; **to put sb to shame** faire honte à qn; **she works so hard, she puts you to shame** elle vous ferait honte, tellement elle travaille; **the shame of it!** quelle honte!; **shame on him!** c'est honteux!, quelle honte; *Literary or Hum* **for shame!** c'est une honte!; **her speech brought cries of "shame!"** *(in Parliament)* son discours provoqua des huées
(**c**) *(pity)* dommage *m*; **it's a shame!** c'est dommage!; **what a shame!** quel dommage!; **it's a shame he can't come** c'est dommage qu'il ne puisse pas venir; **it would be a great shame if she missed it** ce serait vraiment dommage qu'elle ne le voie pas; **what a shame he forgot to tell you!** quel dommage qu'il ait oublié de vous le dire!
2 *vt (disgrace → family, country)* être la honte de, faire honte à, déshonorer; *(put to shame)* faire honte à; **their record on staff training shames other firms** ce qu'ils réalisent en matière de formation du personnel devrait faire honte aux autres entreprises; **it shames me to admit it** j'ai honte de l'avouer; **to shame sb into doing sth** obliger qn à faire qch en lui faisant honte; **she was shamed into admitting the truth** elle avait tellement honte qu'elle a dû avouer la vérité

shamefaced [ˌʃeɪmˈfeɪst] *adj* (**a**) *(ashamed)* honteux, penaud; **he was a bit shamefaced about it** il en avait un peu honte (**b**) *(bashful)* timide, pudique; *(modest)* modeste

shamefacedly [ˌʃeɪmˈfeɪsɪdlɪ] *adv* (**a**) *(looking ashamed)* d'un air honteux *ou* penaud; **he admitted, rather shamefacedly, that it was his fault** il a reconnu, d'un air plutôt penaud, que c'était (de) sa faute (**b**) *(bashfully)* timidement, avec pudeur; *(modestly)* modestement, avec modestie

shamefacedness [ˌʃeɪmˈfeɪsɪdnɪs] *n* (**a**) *(shame)* air *m* honteux *ou* penaud (**b**) *(bashfulness)* timidité *f* pudique; *(modesty)* modestie *f*

shameful [ˈʃeɪmfʊl] *adj* honteux, indigne; **it's shameful to spread such rumours!** c'est honteux *ou* une honte de faire courir de telles rumeurs!; **it's a shameful waste of talent** c'est un gaspillage de talent honteux *ou* scandaleux

shamefully [ˈʃeɪmfʊlɪ] *adv* honteusement, indignement; **she has been treated shamefully** elle a été traitée de façon honteuse; **they've been shamefully neglected** ils ont été honteusement négligés; **he was shamefully ignorant about the issue** son ignorance sur la question était honteuse

shamefulness [ˈʃeɪmfʊlnɪs] *n* honte *f*, infamie *f*

shameless [ˈʃeɪmlɪs] *adj* (**a**) *(without shame → conduct)* effronté; *(→ person)* effronté, sans vergogne; **that's a shameless lie!** c'est un mensonge éhonté!; **they are quite shameless about it!** ils ne s'en cachent pas! (**b**) *(immodest → person)* sans pudeur, dévergondé; *(→ conduct)* impudique; *Hum or Old-fashioned* **a shameless (little) hussy** une dévergondée

shamelessly [ˈʃeɪmlɪslɪ] *adv* (**a**) *(without shame → abuse, exploit)* sans honte, sans vergogne; **to lie shamelessly** mentir effrontément (**b**) *(immodestly)* avec impudeur; **they were walking about quite shamelessly with nothing on** ils se promenaient tout nus sans la moindre gêne *ou* sans que ça ait l'air de les gêner

shamelessness [ˈʃeɪmlɪsnɪs] *n* (**a**) *(lack of shame)* effronterie *f*, impudence *f* (**b**) *(sexual immodesty)* impudeur *f*; *(of conduct)* impudicité *f*

shaming [ˈʃeɪmɪŋ] *adj* mortifiant, humiliant; **how shaming!** quelle humiliation!

shammy [ˈʃæmɪ] *n (leather)* peau *f* de chamois
▸▸ ***shammy leather*** peau *f* de chamois

shampoo [ʃæmˈpuː] **1** *n* shampooing *m*, shampoing *m*; **shampoo and set** shampooing *m* (et) mise *f* en plis
2 *vt (person, animal)* faire un shampooing à; *(carpet)* shampouiner; **to shampoo one's hair** se faire un shampooing, se laver les cheveux; **to have one's hair shampooed** se faire faire un shampooing
▸▸ ***shampoo basin*** lave-tête *m inv*

shampooer [ʃæmˈpuːə(r)] *n* (**a**) *(person)* shampouineur(euse) *m,f* (**b**) *(machine)* **(carpet) shampooer** shampouineur *m*, shampouineuse *f*

shampooing [ʃæmˈpuːɪŋ] *n* shampooing *m*
▸▸ ***shampooing machine*** *(for carpets)* shampouineur *m*, shampouineuse *f*

shamrock [ˈʃæmrɒk] *n Bot* trèfle *m (en tant qu'emblème de l'Irlande)*

> **SHAMROCK**
>
> Le "shamrock" est l'emblème de l'Irlande. Selon la légende, saint Patrick se serait servi d'un trèfle à trois feuilles pour expliquer le concept de la sainte Trinité à la population. Les Irlandais portent un trèfle à la boutonnière le jour de la Saint-Patrick, ce qui est censé porter chance.

shamus [ˈʃeɪməs] *n Am Fam Old-fashioned (policeman)* flic *m*, poulet *m*; *(detective)* (détective *m*) privé *m*

shandy [ˈʃændɪ] *(pl* **shandies***) n Br* panaché *m*

shandygaff [ˈʃændɪgæf] *n Am* panaché *m*

Shanghai [ˌʃæŋˈhaɪ] *n* Shanghai

shanghai [ˌʃæŋˈhaɪ] *vt* (**a**) *Naut* embarquer de force *(comme matelot)* (**b**) *Fam Fig* **to shanghai sb into doing sth** forcer qn à faire qch❑; **I was shanghaied into it** on m'a forcé la main

Shangri-la [ˌʃæŋgrɪˈlɑː] *n* paradis *m* terrestre

shank [ʃæŋk] **1** *n* (**a**) *Anat* jambe *f*; *(of horse)* canon *m*; *Culin (of beef)* jarret *m* (**b**) *(stem → of screw)* manche *m*; *(→ of anchor)* verge *f*; *(→ of glass)* pied *m*; *(→ of key, rivet)* tige *f*; *Typ (→ of letter)* corps *m*, tige *f* (**c**) *Am Fam (knife)* surin *m*, lame❑ *f*
2 *vt Am Fam (stab)* planter

shanks's pony, shanks's mare [ˈʃæŋksɪz-] *n Fam Hum* **to go on shanks's pony** aller pedibus *ou* à pattes

shanny [ˈʃænɪ] *(pl* **shannies***) n Ich* blennie *f*

shan't [ʃɑːnt] = **shall not**

shantung [ˌʃænˈtʌŋ] *n Tex* shantung *m*, chantoung *m*

shanty [ˈʃæntɪ] *(pl* **shanties***) n* (**a**) *(shack)* baraque *f*, cabane *f* (**b**) *(song)* chanson *f* de marins

shantytown [ˈʃæntɪtaʊn] *n* bidonville *m*

SHAPE [ʃeɪp] *n (abbr* **Supreme Headquarters Allied Powers Europe***)* SHAPE *m*

SHAPE [ʃeɪp]

forme	▸ **1 (a) – (f)**
silhouette	▸ **1 (b)**
façonner	▸ **2 (a)**
influencer	▸ **2 (b)**
prendre forme	▸ **3**

1 *n* (**a**) *(outer form)* forme *f*; **what shape is it?** de quelle forme est-ce?; **the room was triangular in shape** la pièce était de forme triangulaire *ou* avait la forme d'un triangle; **a sweet in the shape of a heart** un bonbon en forme de cœur; **the house/garden is an odd shape** la maison/le jardin a une drôle de forme; **they were the same shape** ils étaient de la même forme, ils avaient la même forme; **each pebble is a different shape** chaque caillou a une forme différente; **they come in all shapes and sizes** il y en a de toutes les formes et de toutes les tailles; **to change shape** changer de forme; **she moulded the clay into shape** elle façonna l'argile; **he bent/beat the copper into shape** il plia/martela le cuivre; **my hat was knocked out of shape** mon chapeau a été déformé; **my pullover has lost its shape** *or* **is out of shape** mon pull s'est déformé
(**b**) *(figure, silhouette)* forme *f*, silhouette *f*; **vague shapes could be seen in the mist** on distinguait des formes vagues dans la brume
(**c**) *(abstract form or structure)* forme *f*; **the shape of our society** la structure de notre société; **she plans to change the whole shape of the company** elle a l'intention de modifier complètement la structure de l'entreprise; **the new technologies have changed the shape of our lives** les nouvelles technologies ont changé la façon dont nous vivons; **the shape of things to come** ce qui nous attend, ce que l'avenir nous réserve; **to take shape** prendre forme *ou* tournure; **her plan was beginning to take shape** son projet commençait à se concrétiser *ou* à prendre forme; **to give shape to sth** donner forme à qch
(**d**) *(guise)* forme *f*; **help eventually arrived in the shape of her parents** ce sont ses parents qui finirent par arriver pour lui prêter secours; **progress, in the shape of motorways/supermarkets** le progrès que représentent les autoroutes/les supermarchés; **wealth in the shape of a large house** la richesse symbolisée par la possession d'une grande maison; **he can't take alcohol in any shape or form** il ne supporte l'alcool sous aucune forme
(**e**) *(condition)* forme *f*; **to be in good shape** *(person)* être en forme; *(business, economy)* marcher bien; **to be in bad shape** *(person)* ne pas être en forme; *(business, economy)* être mal en point; **I'm rather out of shape** je ne suis pas très en forme; **I need to get (back) into shape** j'ai besoin de me remettre en forme; **the economy is in poor shape at the moment**

l'économie est mal en point actuellement; **to keep oneself** *or* **to stay in shape** garder la forme, rester en forme; **what sort of shape was he in?** dans quel état était-il?, comment allait-il?; **she was in pretty bad shape** *(very ill, badly injured)* elle était mal en point *ou* dans un sale état; **he's in no shape to be doing this kind of work!** il n'est pas en état de faire ce genre de travail!; *Fam* **to knock** *or* **to lick sth into shape** mettre qch au point❏; *Fam* **I'll soon knock** *or* **lick them into shape!** *(soldiers)* j'aurai vite fait de les dresser, moi!; *(team)* j'aurai vite fait de les remettre en forme, moi!

(**f**) *(mould → gen)* moule *m*; *(→ for hats)* forme *f*

2 *vt* (**a**) *(mould → clay)* façonner, modeler; *(→ wood, stone)* façonner, tailler; **she shaped the clay into rectangular blocks** elle a façonné l'argile en blocs rectangulaires; **he shaped a pot from the wet clay** il a façonné un pot dans l'argile; **the paper had been shaped into a cone** le papier avait été plié en forme de cône

(**b**) *(influence → events, life, future)* influencer, déterminer; **to shape sb's character** former *ou* façonner le caractère de qn; **the war shaped her perception of the army** la guerre a influencé sa perception de l'armée

(**c**) *(plan → essay)* faire le plan de; *(→ excuse, explanation, statement)* formuler

(**d**) *Sewing* ajuster; **the jacket is shaped at the waist** la veste est ajustée à la taille

3 *vi (develop → plan)* prendre forme *ou* tournure; **things are shaping well** les choses se présentent bien *ou* prennent une bonne tournure; **how is he shaping as a teacher?** comment se débrouille-t-il dans l'enseignement?

►**shape up** *vi* (**a**) *(improve)* se secouer; **you'd better shape up, young man!** il est temps que tu te secoues, jeune homme!; *Fam* **shape up or ship out!** secouez-vous sinon c'est la porte!; *Fam* **shape up and look smart!** grouille-toi!

(**b**) *Am (get fit again)* retrouver la forme

(**c**) *(progress, develop → plans, situation)* prendre (une bonne) tournure; **the business is beginning to shape up** les affaires commencent à bien marcher; **our plans are shaping up nicely** nos projets prennent une bonne tournure; **the new team is shaping up well** la nouvelle équipe commence à bien fonctionner; **they are shaping up into a good orchestra** ils commencent à former un bon orchestre; **how is she shaping up as a translator?** comment se débrouille-t-elle *ou* comment s'en sort-elle en tant que traductrice?; **she isn't shaping up too badly** elle ne se débrouille *ou* ne s'en sort pas trop mal

shaped [ʃeɪpt] *adj* (**a**) *(garment)* ajusté; *(wooden object)* façonné; *(metal object)* profilé (**b**) *(in descriptions)* **shaped like a triangle** en forme de triangle; **a rock shaped like a man's head** un rocher qui a la forme d'une tête d'homme

-shaped [ʃeɪpt] *suff* en forme de; **egg-/crescent-/heart-shaped** en forme d'œuf/de croissant/de cœur; **pear-shaped** en forme de poire, *Spec* piriforme

shapeless [ˈʃeɪplɪs] *adj (mass, garment, heap)* informe; **to become shapeless** se déformer

shapelessness [ˈʃeɪplɪsnɪs] *n* absence *f* de forme, aspect *m* informe

shapeliness [ˈʃeɪplɪnɪs] *n (of legs)* galbe *m*; *(of figure)* beauté *f*, belles proportions *fpl*

shapely [ˈʃeɪplɪ] (*compar* **shapelier,** *superl* **shapeliest**) *adj (legs)* bien galbé, bien tourné; *(figure, woman)* bien fait; **a shapely pair of legs** une belle paire de jambes

shaper [ˈʃeɪpə(r)] *n* (**a**) *(person → gen)* façonneur(euse) *m,f*; *Metal* emboutisseur *m*, estampeur(euse) *m,f*; *Carp* toupilleur *m*; **the shaper of our destinies** celui qui dirige notre destin; **the shaper of the plan** l'auteur *m* du projet (**b**) *(machine → gen)* machine *f* à façonner; *Metal* emboutissoir *m*; *Carp* toupie *f*; *Am (filing machine)* étau-limeur *m*

shaping [ˈʃeɪpɪŋ] *n (of block of stone)* façonnement *m*, façonnage *m*; *(of boiler)* emboutissage *m*; **the shaping of his character** le développement *ou* la formation de son caractère; **the shaping of a policy** la conception d'une politique

shard [ʃɑːd] *n* (**a**) *(of glass)* éclat *m*; *(of pottery)* tesson *m* (**b**) *Zool* élytre *m*

SHARE [ʃeə(r)]

part	►1 (a), (b)
action	►1 (c)
partager	►2 (a) – (d); 3
avoir en commun	►2 (c)

1 *n* (**a**) *(portion → of property, cost, food, credit, blame)* part *f*; **divided into equal shares** divisé en parts égales; **there's your share** voici votre part *ou* ce qui vous revient; **to pay one's share** payer sa part *ou* quote-part *ou* son écot; **they went shares in the cost of the present** ils ont tous participé à l'achat du cadeau; **I went half shares with her** on a payé la moitié chacun; **he got his (fair) share of the profits** il a eu sa part des bénéfices; **to have a share in the profits** *(of employees)* participer aux bénéfices; **to have a share in a business** être l'un des associés dans une affaire; **they've had their share of misfortune** ils ont eu leur part de malheurs; **he's come in for his full share of criticism** il a été beaucoup critiqué; **they have their share of responsibility in this matter** ils ont leur part de responsabilité dans cette affaire; **we've had more than our (fair) share of rain this summer** nous avons eu plus que notre compte de pluie cet été; *Law* **legal share** *(of inheritance)* réserve *f* légale

(**b**) *(part, role → in activity, work)* part *f*; **what was his share in the robbery?** quelle part a-t-il prise au vol?; **what was her share in it all?** quel rôle a-t-elle joué dans tout cela?; **to do one's share (of the work)** faire sa part (du travail); **he hasn't done his share** il n'a pas fait sa part du travail; **to have a share in doing sth** contribuer à faire qch; **she must have had a share in his downfall** elle doit être pour quelque chose dans sa chute; **you had a share in this** *(you are partly responsible)* vous y êtes pour quelque chose; *(you contributed)* votre participation a été importante

(**c**) *Fin* action *f*; **to allot shares** attribuer des actions; **to issue shares** émettre des actions; **to have shares in a company** détenir des actions dans une société; **to own 51 percent of the shares** détenir 51 pour cent du capital; **share prices have fallen** le prix des actions est tombé

(**d**) *Agr* soc *m* (de charrue)

2 *vt* (**a**) *(divide → money, property, food, chores)* partager; **he shared the chocolate with his sister/among the children** il a partagé le chocolat avec sa sœur/entre les enfants; **responsibility is shared between the manager and his assistant** la responsabilité est partagée entre le directeur et son assistant; **they must share the blame for the accident** ils doivent se partager la responsabilité de l'accident; **they shared the work between them** ils se sont partagé le travail

(**b**) *(use jointly → tools, flat, bed)* partager; **we shared a taxi home** nous avons partagé un taxi pour rentrer; **a shared bathroom** une salle de bain commune; *Tel* **shared line** ligne *f* partagée, raccordement *m* collectif

(**c**) *(have in common → interest, opinion)* partager; *(→ characteristic)* avoir en commun; *(→ worry, sorrow)* partager, prendre part à, compatir à; **I share your hope that war may be avoided** j'espère comme vous qu'on pourra éviter la guerre; **we share the same name** nous avons le même nom; **we share a common heritage** nous avons un patrimoine commun; **shared experience** expérience *f* partagée

(**d**) *(tell)* partager; **to share one's ideas/impressions with sb** partager des idées/impressions avec qn; **he shares all his secrets with me** il me fait part de tous ses secrets; *Ironic* **thank you very much for sharing that with me!** c'est vachement intéressant ce que tu dis là!; **a problem shared is a problem halved** cela soulage de parler de ses problèmes

3 *vi* partager; **he doesn't like sharing** il n'aime pas partager; **some children will have to share** certains enfants devront partager; **to share in** *(cost, work)* participer à, partager; *(profits)* participer *ou* être intéressé à; *(credit, responsibility)* partager; *(joy, sorrow)* partager, prendre part à; *(grief)* compatir à; **share and share alike** = à chacun sa part

►► *Fin* ***share account*** compte-titres *m*; *Fin* ***share capital*** capital-actions *m*; *Fin* ***share certificate*** certificat *m ou* titre *m* d'actions; *St Exch* ***share dealing*** opérations *fpl* de Bourse, négoce *m* de titres; *St Exch* ***share fluctuation*** mouvement *m* des valeurs; *St Exch* ***share index*** indice *m* boursier; ***share issue*** émission *f* d'actions; *Fin* ***share ledger*** registre *m* des actionnaires; ***share market*** marché *m* des valeurs mobilières; ***share option*** possibilité *f* d'acheter des actions; *Fin* ***share option scheme*** plan *m* de participation par achat d'actions; ***share owner*** détenteur(-trice) *m,f* d'actions; ***share ownership*** actionnariat *m*; ***share point*** point *m* de part de marché; ***share portfolio*** portefeuille *m* d'actions; ***share premium*** prime *f* d'émission; *St Exch* ***share price index*** indice *m* des cours d'actions

►**share out** *vt sep* partager, répartir; **the profits were shared out among them** ils se sont partagé les bénéfices

sharecrop [ˈʃeəkrɒp] (*pt & pp* **sharecropped**) **1** *vt Am* cultiver (en tant que métayer)

2 *vi* travailler comme métayer, avoir une ferme en métayage

sharecropper [ˈʃeəˌkrɒpə(r)] *n* métayer(ère) *m,f*

sharecropping [ˈʃeəˌkrɒpɪŋ] *n Am* = système de métayage en usage dans le sud des États-Unis après la guerre de Sécession

sharefarmer [ˈʃeəˌfɑːmə(r)] *n Austr* = fermier qui partage ses bénéfices avec ses ouvriers

shareholder [ˈʃeəˌhəʊldə(r)] *n* actionnaire *mf*; **the shareholders** l'actionnariat *m*, les actionnaires *mfpl*

►► *Fin* ***shareholders' equity*** fonds *mpl* propres, avoir *m* des actionnaires; ***shareholders' meeting*** réunion *f* d'actionnaires; *Fin* ***shareholder's register*** registre *m* des actionnaires

shareholding [ˈʃeəˌhəʊldɪŋ] *n (shares)* participation *f*; *(share ownership)* actionnariat *m*

share-out *n* partage *m*, répartition *f*

shareware [ˈʃeəweə(r)] *n Comput* shareware *m*, partagiciel *m*, logiciel *m* contributif

sharia [ʃəˈrɪə] *n Rel* charia *f*

►► ***sharia law*** charia *f*

sharing [ˈʃeərɪŋ] *n (of money, power)* partage *m*

shark [ʃɑːk] *n* (**a**) *Ich* requin *m* (**b**) *Fam Fig (swindler)* escroc *m*, filou *m*; *(predator → in business)* requin *m*; **he's a real shark** c'est un véritable escroc; **the sharks are out** les requins ont flairé un bon coup (**c**) *Am Fam (genius)* génie❏ *m*; **to be a shark at sth** être calé en qch (**d**) *Am (at match)* revendeur(euse) *m,f* de billets à la sauvette

sharkskin [ˈʃɑːkskɪn] **1** *n* peau *f* de requin

2 *comp* en peau de requin

sharon fruit [ˈʃærən-] *n Bot* kaki *m*, plaquemine *f*

sharp [ʃɑːp] **1** *adj* (**a**) *(blade, scissors, razor)* affûté, bien aiguisé; *(knife, edge)* tranchant, affilé; *(edge)* tranchant, coupant; *(point)* aigu(uë), acéré; *(teeth, thorn)* pointu; *(claw)* acéré; *(needle, pin → for sewing)* pointu; *(→ for pricking)* qui pique; *(pencil)* pointu, bien taillé; **these scissors are sharp** ces ciseaux coupent bien; **give me a sharp knife** donnez-moi un couteau qui coupe; **the sharp end** la première ligne; **the men and women at the sharp end** les hommes et les femmes en première ligne

(**b**) *(features)* anguleux, tiré; *(nose)* pointu; **she has sharp features** elle a des traits anguleux

(**c**) *(clear → photo, line, TV picture)* net; *(→ contrast, distinction)* net, marqué

(**d**) *(abrupt, sudden → blow, bend, turn)* brusque; *(→ rise, fall, change)* brusque, soudain; **the car made a sharp turn** la voiture a tourné brusquement; **a sharp rise/fall in prices** une forte hausse/baisse des prix

(**e**) *(piercing → wind, cold)* vif, pénétrant; **a sharp frost** une forte gelée

(**f**) *(intense → pain, disappointment)* vif

(**g**) *(sour, bitter → taste, food)* âpre, piquant; *(apple)* acide; *(wine)* vert

(**h**) *(harsh → words, criticism)* mordant, cinglant; *(→ reprimand)* sévère; *(→ voice, tone)* âpre, acerbe; *(→ temper)* vif; **some sharp words were exchanged** on échangea quelques propos acerbes; **he can be very sharp with customers** il lui arrive d'être très brusque avec les clients; **she has a sharp tongue** elle a la langue bien affilée

(i) *(keen → eyesight)* perçant; *(→ hearing, senses)* fin; *(in intellect, wit → person)* vif; *(→ child)* vif, éveillé; *(→ judgment)* vif; **she is sharp of hearing** elle a l'oreille *ou* l'ouïe fine; **he has a sharp eye** il a le coup d'œil; **to have a sharp eye for a bargain** savoir repérer une bonne affaire; **to keep a sharp lookout for sb** guetter qn; **keep a sharp lookout!** restez à l'affût!; **she has a very sharp mind** elle a l'esprit très vif; **she was too sharp for them** elle était trop maligne pour eux; **he's as sharp as a needle** *(intelligent)* il est malin comme un singe; *(shrewd)* il est très perspicace, rien ne lui échappe

(j) *(quick, brisk → reflex, pace)* **be sharp (about it)!** dépêche-toi!; **that was a sharp piece of work!** ça a été vite fait!, ça n'a pas traîné!

(k) *(shrill → sound, cry)* aigu(uë), perçant

(l) *Mus* **C sharp minor** do *m inv* dièse mineur; **to be sharp** *(singer)* chanter trop haut; *(violinist)* jouer trop haut

(m) *Pej (unscrupulous → trading, lawyer)* peu scrupuleux, malhonnête; **accused of sharp practice** accusé de procédés indélicats *ou* malhonnêtes

(n) *Fam (smart)* chicos, classe *(inv)*; **he's always been a sharp dresser** il s'est toujours habillé très classe

2 *adv* (a) *(precisely)* **at 6 o'clock sharp** à 6 heures pile *ou* précises

(b) *(in direction)* **turn sharp left** tournez tout de suite à gauche; **the road turns sharp left** la route tourne brusquement à gauche

(c) *Mus (sing, play)* trop haut, faux

(d) *Br Fam (idiom)* **look sharp (about it)!** grouille-toi!, dépêche-toi! ❑

3 *n* (a) *Mus* dièse *m*

(b) *Am Fam (expert)* expert(e) ❑ *m,f*

4 *vt Am Mus (sharpen)* diéser

sharpen ['ʃɑːpən] **1** *vt* (a) *(blade, knife, razor)* affiler, aiguiser, affûter; *(pencil)* tailler, *Can* affiler; *(stick)* tailler en pointe; **the cat sharpened its claws on the wood** le chat aiguisait ses griffes *ou* se faisait les griffes sur le bois

(b) *(appetite, pain)* aviver, aiguiser; *(intelligence)* affiner; **the events sharpened my desire to travel** les événements ont accru mon désir de voyager; **you'll need to sharpen your wits** il va falloir te dégourdir

(c) *(outline, image)* mettre au point, rendre plus net; *(contrast)* accentuer, rendre plus marqué

(d) *Culin (sauce)* donner du piquant à

(e) *Br Mus* diéser

2 *vi (tone, voice)* devenir plus vif *ou* âpre; *(pain)* s'aviver, devenir plus vif; *(appetite)* s'aiguiser; *(wind, cold)* devenir plus vif

sharpener ['ʃɑːpənə(r)] *n (for knife → machine)* aiguisoir *m* (à couteaux); *(→ manual)* fusil *m* (à aiguiser); *(for pencil)* taille-crayon *m inv*

sharpening ['ʃɑːpənɪŋ] *n* affilage *m*, aiguisage *m*, affûtage *m*

►► ***sharpening stone*** pierre *f* à affûter

sharper ['ʃɑːpə(r)] *n* escroc *m*; *Cards* tricheur(euse) *m,f* professionnel(elle)

sharp-eyed *adj (with good eyes)* qui a l'œil vif; *(with insight)* à qui rien n'échappe

sharp-featured [-'fiːtʃəd] *adj* aux traits anguleux

sharpish ['ʃɑːpɪʃ] *adv Br Fam (quickly)* illico presto, vite fait; **you'd better do it sharpish** t'as intérêt à le faire illico presto, t'as intérêt à faire fissa; **you'd better get over there sharpish!** tu ferais mieux d'y aller en vitesse!; **look sharpish!** grouille-toi!

sharply ['ʃɑːplɪ] *adv* (a) **sharply pointed** *(knife)* pointu; *(pencil)* à pointe fine, taillé fin; *(nose, chin, shoes)* pointu

(b) *(contrast, stand out)* nettement; *(differ)* nettement, clairement; **the bare trees stood out sharply against the snow** les arbres dénudés se détachaient nettement sur la neige; **this contrasts sharply with her usual behaviour** voilà qui change beaucoup de son comportement habituel; **to bring sth sharply home, to bring sth sharply into focus** faire apparaître qch de façon évidente

(c) *(abruptly, suddenly → curve, turn)* brusquement, soudainement; **the car took the bend too sharply** la voiture a pris le virage trop vite; **the road rises/drops sharply** la route monte/descend en pente raide; **inflation has risen sharply since May** l'inflation est montée en flèche depuis mai

(d) *(harshly → speak)* vivement, sèchement, de façon brusque; *(→ criticize)* vivement, sévèrement; *(→ reply, retort)* vertement, vivement; **she reprimanded him sharply for being late** elle lui a fait de vifs reproches pour son retard; **I had to speak to her sharply about her persistent lateness** j'ai dû lui faire des observations sévères au sujet de ses retards répétés

(e) *(alertly → listen)* attentivement

sharpness ['ʃɑːpnɪs] *n* (a) *(of blade, scissors, razor, knife)* tranchant *m*; *(of needle, pencil, thorn)* pointe *f* aiguë

(b) *(of features)* aspect *m* anguleux

(c) *(of outline, image, contrast)* netteté *f*

(d) *(of bend, turn)* angle *m* brusque; *(of rise, fall, change)* soudaineté *f*

(e) *(of wind, cold, frost)* âpreté *f*

(f) *(of taste, smell)* piquant *m*, aigreur *f*; *(of pain)* vivacité *f*

(g) *(of word, criticism, reprimand)* sévérité *f*; *(of tone, voice)* brusquerie *f*, âpreté *f*; **there was a certain sharpness in the way he spoke to me** il m'a parlé sur un ton plutôt sec

(h) *(of eyesight, hearing, senses)* finesse *f*, acuité *f*; *(of appetite, pain)* acuité *f*; *(of mind, intelligence)* finesse *f*, vivacité *f*; *(of irony, wit)* mordant *m*; **sharpness of vision** acuité *f* visuelle

sharp-set *adj* (a) *(hungry)* **to be sharp-set** avoir l'estomac creux, se sentir un creux dans l'estomac (b) *(keen)* **to be sharp-set on sth** avoir un vif désir de qch (c) *(tool)* bien aiguisé *ou* affilé

sharpshooter ['ʃɑːpˌʃuːtə(r)] *n* tireur(euse) *m,f* d'élite

sharp-sighted *adj (with good eyes)* qui a l'œil vif; *(perspicacious)* perspicace; *(observant)* observateur, à qui rien n'échappe

sharpster ['ʃɑːpstə(r)] *n Fam* escroc ❑ *m*, tricheur(euse) ❑ *m,f*

sharp-tempered *adj* coléreux, soupe au lait *(inv)*

sharp-tongued [-'tʌŋd] *adj* caustique

sharp-witted [-'wɪtɪd] *adj* à l'esprit vif *ou* fin

shat [ʃæt] *pt & pp of* **shit**

shatter ['ʃætə(r)] **1** *vt* (a) *(break → glass, window, door)* fracasser; **a stone shattered the windscreen** un caillou a fait éclater le pare-brise; **the noise shattered my eardrums** le bruit m'a assourdi

(b) *Fig (destroy → career, health)* briser, ruiner; *(→ nerves)* démolir, détraquer; *(→ confidence, faith, hope)* démolir, détruire; **they were shattered by the news, the news shattered them** ils ont été complètement bouleversés par la nouvelle, la nouvelle les a complètement bouleversés

2 *vi (glass, vase, windscreen)* voler en éclats; **her whole world shattered** son univers tout entier s'est écroulé *ou* a été anéanti

shattered ['ʃætəd] *adj* (a) *(broken → window, door)* fracassé; **shattered dreams** des rêves *mpl* brisés (b) *(upset)* bouleversé (c) *Br Fam (exhausted)* crevé, naze (d) *Am very Fam (drunk)* bourré

shattering ['ʃætərɪŋ] *adj* (a) *(emotionally → news, experience)* bouleversant; *(→ revelation)* choquant; *(→ disappointment)* fort, cruel (b) *(extreme → defeat)* écrasant; **a shattering blow** un coup violent; *Fig* un coup terrible (c) *Br Fam (exhausting)* crevant

-shattering ['ʃætərɪŋ] *suff* **an ear-shattering noise** un bruit à vous déchirer les tympans

shatterproof ['ʃætəpruːf] *adj*

►► ***shatterproof glass*** verre *m* sans éclats *ou* Securit®

shave [ʃeɪv] **1** *vt* (a) *(face, legs etc)* raser; **the barber shaved him** *or* **his face** le barbier l'a rasé *ou* lui a fait la barbe; **to shave one's legs/one's head** se raser les jambes/la tête

(b) *(wood)* raboter; **can you shave a few millimetres off the bottom of the door?** pouvez-vous raboter le bas de la porte de quelques millimètres?

(c) *(graze)* raser, frôler; **the car just shaved the garage door** la voiture n'a fait que frôler la porte du garage

2 *vi* se raser

3 *n* **to have a shave** se raser; **you need a shave** tu as besoin de te raser; **to give sb a shave** raser qn; *(of barber)* faire la barbe à qn

►**shave off** *vt sep* **to shave off one's beard/moustache/hair** se raser la barbe/la moustache/la tête; *Fig* **to shave a few pence off the price** faire un rabais de quelques centimes; **this has shaved a few points off the government's lead in the polls** cela a légèrement rogné l'avance du gouvernement dans les sondages

shaven ['ʃeɪvən] *adj (face, head)* rasé

shaver ['ʃeɪvə(r)] *n* (a) *(razor)* rasoir *m* (électrique) (b) *Fam Old-fashioned (youngster)* gosse *m*, gamin *m*

►► *Am* ***shaver outlet***, *Br* ***shaver point*** prise *f* pour rasoir électrique

Shavian ['ʃeɪvɪən] **1** *adj (writings)* de George Bernard Shaw; *(style)* à la Shaw; *(society)* consacré à Shaw

2 *n* partisan *m ou* disciple *mf* de George Bernard Shaw

shaving ['ʃeɪvɪŋ] **1** *n (act)* rasage *m*

2 *comp (cream, foam)* à raser

3 **shavings** *npl (of wood)* copeaux *mpl*; *(of metal)* copeaux *mpl*, rognures *fpl*; *(of paper)* rognures *fpl*

►► ***shaving brush*** blaireau *m*; ***shaving mirror*** miroir *m* à raser; ***shaving soap*** savon *m* à barbe; ***shaving stick*** (bâton *m* de) savon *m* à barbe

shaw [ʃɔː] *n Arch or Literary* taillis *m*, fourré *m*

shawl [ʃɔːl] *n* châle *m*

►► ***shawl collar*** col *m* châle

shawm [ʃɔːm] *n Mus* chalumeau *m*

Shawnee [ˌʃɔː'niː] *n* (a) *(tribe)* Shawnee *mpl* (b) *(member)* Shawnee *mf inv*

she [ʃiː] **1** *pron* (a) *(referring to woman, girl)* elle; **she's tall** elle est grande; **she's a teacher/an engineer** elle est enseignante/ingénieur; **she's a very interesting woman** c'est une femme très intéressante; **SHE can't do it** elle? elle ne peut pas le faire; *Formal* **if I were she** si j'étais elle, si j'étais à sa place; *Formal* **she who** *or* **whom he loves** celle qu'il aime

(b) *(referring to boat, car, country)* **she's a fine ship** c'est un bateau magnifique; **she can do over 120 mph** elle fait plus de 150 km à l'heure

(c) *(referring to female animal)* **she's a lovely dog** c'est une chienne adorable

2 *n (referring to animal, baby)* **it's a she** *(animal)* c'est une femelle; *(baby)* c'est une fille

> **She who must be obeyed**
>
> Il s'agit d'une expression tirée de *She* (*Elle*), un roman d'aventures publié en 1887 par l'auteur anglais Henry Rider Haggard. Cette expression ("celle à qui l'on doit obéir") y désignait la reine Ayesha, qui régnait sur le royaume de Kôr.
>
> Aujourd'hui, on utilise cette phrase sur le mode humoristique à propos de toute femme qui inspire le respect et une certaine crainte, qu'elle soit supérieure hiérarchique, mère ou épouse. On pourra dire par exemple **I've got to go into work early tomorrow. She who must be obeyed has called a meeting for 8.30** ("il faut que je sois au travail plus tôt que d'habitude demain, j'ai une réunion avec la patronne à 8h30"). Cette allusion a été popularisée par l'auteur anglais John Mortimer et sa série de romans *Rumpole of the Bailey*, dans lesquels le héros éponyme utilise cette expression à propos de sa femme.

she- [ʃiː] *pref* **she-elephant** éléphant *m* femelle; **she-bear** ourse *f*, **she-dog** chienne *f*, **she-wolf** louve *f*

s/he *(written abbr* **she/he**) il ou elle

shea [ʃiː, ʃɪə] *n Bot* karité *m*

►► *Bot* ***shea tree*** karité *m*

sheading ['ʃiːdɪŋ] *n* = subdivision administrative de l'île de Man

sheaf [ʃiːf] *(pl* **sheaves** [ʃiːvz]) **1** *n* (a) *(of papers, letters)* liasse *f* (b) *(of barley, corn)* gerbe *f*; *(of arrows)* faisceau *m*

2 *vt* gerber, engerber

shear [ʃɪə(r)] *(pt* **sheared,** *pp* **sheared** *or* **shorn** [ʃɔːn]) **1** *vt* (a) *(sheep, wool)* tondre; **her blonde**

locks had been shorn on avait tondu ses boucles blondes; *Fig* **to be shorn of sth** être dépouillé de qch; **he was shorn of all real power** il s'est vu dépouiller de tout pouvoir véritable

(**b**) *(metal)* couper (net), cisailler; **the girder had been shorn in two** la poutre métallique avait été coupée en deux

2 *vi* céder

3 shears *npl (for gardening)* cisaille *f*; *(for sewing)* grands ciseaux *mpl*; *(for sheep)* tondeuse *f*; **a pair of shears** *(for gardening)* une paire de cisailles; *(for sewing)* une paire de grands ciseaux

►► *Tech* ***shear pin*** goupille *f* de cisaillement

►**shear off 1** *vt sep (wool, hair)* tondre; *(branch)* couper, élaguer; *(something projecting)* couper, enlever; **the tail section of the car had been sheared off on impact** la partie arrière de la voiture avait été arrachée par le choc

2 *vi (part, branch)* se détacher; **the wing sheared right off** l'aile a été complètement arrachée

shearer ['ʃɪərə(r)] *n (machine)* tondeuse *f* (à moutons); *(person)* tondeur(euse) *m,f* (de moutons)

shearing ['ʃɪərɪŋ] **1** *n (process)* tonte *f*

2 shearings *npl* **shearings (of wool)** laine *f* tondue

shearling ['ʃɪəlɪŋ] *n Agr* = agneau ou mouton qui a été tondu une fois

shearwater ['ʃɪəˌwɔːtə(r)] *n Orn* puffin *m*

sheatfish ['ʃiːtfɪʃ] *n Ich* silure *m*

sheath [ʃiːθ] (*pl* **sheaths** [ʃiːðz]) *n* (**a**) *(scabbard, case → for sword)* fourreau *m*; *(→ for dagger)* gaine *f*; *(→ for scissors, tool)* étui *m* (**b**) *(covering → for cable)* gaine *f*; *(→ for water pipe)* gaine *f*, manchon *m*; *Bot, Anat & Zool* gaine *f* (**c**) *Br (condom)* préservatif *m* (**d**) *(dress)* (robe *f*) fourreau *m*

►► ***sheath dress*** (robe *f*) fourreau *m*; ***sheath knife*** couteau *m* à gaine

sheathbill ['ʃiːθbɪl] *n Orn* chionis *m*, bec-en-fourreau *m*

sheathe [ʃiːð] *vt* (**a**) *(sword, dagger)* rengainer; **the cat sheathed her claws** la chatte a rentré ses griffes; *Literary* **to sheathe the sword** cesser les hostilités, faire la paix (**b**) *(cable)* gainer; *(water pipe)* gainer, mettre dans un manchon protecteur; *Fig* **she was sheathed from head to foot in black satin** elle était moulée dans du satin noir de la tête aux pieds

sheathing ['ʃiːðɪŋ] *n (gen)* revêtement *m*; *(of cable)* gaine *f*

sheave [ʃiːv] *vt* gerber, engerber

sheaves [ʃiːvz] *pl of* **sheaf**

Sheba ['ʃiːbə] *n* Saba; **the Queen of Sheba** la reine de Saba; *Ironic* **yes, and I'm the Queen of Sheba!** à d'autres!; *Ironic* **who do you think you are, the Queen of Sheba?** mais pour qui te prends-tu?

shebang [ʃɪ'bæŋ] *n Fam* **the whole shebang** et tout le tremblement, et tout le bataclan

shebeen [ʃɪ'biːn] *n Ir, Scot & SAfr* débit *m* de boissons clandestin

she-cat *n* chatte *f*; *Fig* furie *f*

shechita [ʃɪ'xiːtə] *n Rel* shechitah *f*

shed [ʃed] (*pt & pp* **shed,** *cont* **shedding**) **1** *n* (**a**) *(in garden)* abri *m*, remise *f*, resserre *f*; *(lean-to)* appentis *m*

(**b**) *(barn)* grange *f*, hangar *m*; *(for trains, aircraft, vehicles)* hangar *m*; **bicycle shed** *(big)* hangar *m* à vélos; *(small)* remise *f* à vélos

(**c**) *(in factory)* atelier *m*

2 *vt* (**a**) *(cast off → leaves, petals)* perdre; *(→ skin, shell)* se dépouiller de; *(take off → garments)* enlever; **the snake regularly sheds its skin** le serpent mue; **the dog has shed her hairs all over the carpet** la chienne a laissé des poils partout sur la moquette; **the trees are beginning to shed their leaves** les arbres commencent à perdre leurs feuilles; **with the heat, he shed first his tie, then his jacket** avec la chaleur, il a enlevé d'abord sa cravate, puis sa veste; **to shed one's clothes** se dépouiller de ses vêtements

(**b**) *(get rid of → inhibitions, beliefs)* se débarrasser de, se défaire de; *(→ staff)* congédier; **to shed jobs** supprimer des emplois

(**c**) *(tears, blood)* verser, répandre; *(weight)* perdre; **to shed bitter tears over sth** verser des larmes amères sur qch; **they came to power without shedding civilian blood** ils ont pris le pouvoir sans faire couler le sang des civils; **before more blood is shed** avant que davantage de sang ne soit versé; **too much blood has been shed in the name of this cause** trop de sang a été versé au nom de cette cause

(**d**) *Br (eject, lose)* déverser; *Astron* larguer; **the truck shed its load on the by-pass** le camion a perdu son chargement sur la rocade; **the plane needs to shed 10 tons of fuel** l'avion doit larguer 10 tonnes de carburant

(**e**) *(idiom)* **to shed light on** éclairer; *Fig* éclairer, éclaircir; **perhaps this will shed some new light on the situation** ça éclairera peut-être la situation d'un jour nouveau

she'd [ʃɪd, *stressed* ʃiːd] (**a**) = **she had** (**b**) **she would**

shedder ['ʃedə(r)] *n Zool* (**a**) *(female salmon)* = saumon femelle après la fraieson (**b**) *(crab)* = crabe qui vient de jeter sa carapace

shedding ['ʃedɪŋ] *n* (**a**) *(of leaves, petals, hair)* perte *f*, chute *f*; *Elec* **load shedding** délestage *m* (**b**) *(of blood)* effusion *f*

she-devil *n* furie *f*

sheen [ʃiːn] *n (on satin, wood, hair, silk)* lustre *m*; *(on apple)* poli *m*; **his fur has lost its sheen** son poil a perdu son lustre; **the cello had a beautiful red sheen** le violoncelle avait de magnifiques reflets rouges

sheeny ['ʃiːnɪ] (*pl* **sheenies**) *n very Fam* youpin(e) *m,f*, youtre *mf*, = terme injurieux désignant un Juif

sheep [ʃiːp] (*pl* **inv**) **1** *n* mouton *m*; *(ewe)* brebis *f*; *Pej* **they're just a load of sheep** ils se comportent comme des moutons (de Panurge) *ou* un troupeau de moutons; *Fig* **to separate** *or* **to sort out the sheep from the goats** séparer le bon grain de l'ivraie; *Fam Old-fashioned* **to cast** *or* **to make sheep's eyes at sb** faire les yeux doux à qn

2 *comp (farm, farming)* de moutons

►► *Bot* ***sheep's bit*** jasione *f* des montagnes; ***sheep farmer*** éleveur(euse) *m,f* de moutons; *Entom* ***sheep ked*** mélophage *m*; ***sheep pen*** parc *m* à moutons; *Bot* ***sheep's sorrel*** oxalide *f* blanche; ***sheep station*** grand élevage *m* de moutons; *Entom* ***sheep tick*** mélophage *m*

sheepcote ['ʃiːpkəʊt] *n* bergerie *f*

sheep-dip *n* bain *m* parasiticide (pour moutons)

sheepdog ['ʃiːpdɒg] *n* chien *m* de berger

►► ***sheepdog trials*** concours *m* de chiens de berger

sheepfold ['ʃiːpfəʊld] *n* parc *m* à moutons, bergerie *f*

sheepish ['ʃiːpɪʃ] *adj* penaud

sheepishly ['ʃiːpɪʃlɪ] *adv* d'un air penaud

sheepishness ['ʃiːpɪʃnɪs] *n* air *m* penaud

sheeplike ['ʃiːplaɪk] *adj Pej* **they're completely sheeplike** ce sont de vrais moutons (de Panurge)

sheepman ['ʃiːpmən] (*pl* **sheepmen** [-men]) *n Am* éleveur *m* de moutons

sheepshank ['ʃiːpʃænk] *n Naut* (nœud *m* de) jambe *f* de chien

sheepshearer ['ʃiːpˌʃɪərə(r)] *n (person)* tondeur(euse) *m,f* (de moutons); *(machine)* tondeuse *f* (à moutons)

sheepshearing ['ʃiːpˌʃɪərɪŋ] *n* tonte *f* (des moutons)

sheepskin ['ʃiːpskɪn] **1** *n* (**a**) *Tex* peau *f* de mouton (**b**) *Am Fam (diploma)* parchemin *m*

2 *comp (coat, rug)* en peau de mouton

►► ***sheepskin jacket*** canadienne *f*, veste *f* en peau lainée

sheepwalk ['ʃiːpwɔːk] *n* pâturage *m* à moutons

sheer [ʃɪə(r)] **1** *adj* (**a**) *(as intensifier)* pur; **it was sheer coincidence** c'était une pure coïncidence; **the sheer scale of the project was intimidating** l'envergure même du projet était impressionnante; **the sheer boredom of her job drove her mad** elle s'ennuyait tellement dans son travail que ça la rendait folle; **by sheer accident** *or* **chance** tout à fait par hasard, par pur hasard; **out of** *or* **in sheer boredom** par pur ennui; **in sheer desperation** en désespoir de cause; **it was sheer stupidity** c'était franchement stupide; **that's sheer nonsense!** c'est complètement absurde!; **it's sheer folly!** c'est de la folie pure!

(**b**) *(steep → cliff)* à pic, abrupt; **it's a sheer 50-metre drop** cela descend à pic sur 50 mètres; **a sheer drop to the sea** un à-pic jusqu'à la mer; **we came up against a sheer wall of water** nous nous sommes trouvés devant un véritable mur d'eau

(**c**) *Tex (stockings)* extra fin

2 *adv* à pic, abruptement

3 *vi Naut (ship)* faire une embardée

4 sheers *npl Am (curtains)* voilages *mpl*

►► *Naut* ***sheer deck*** livet *m* (de pont); *Naut* ***sheer rail*** liston *m*

►**sheer away** *vi* (**a**) *(ship)* larguer les amarres, prendre le large

(**b**) *(animal, shy person)* filer, détaler; **to sheer away from** éviter

►**sheer off** *vi* (**a**) *(ship)* faire une embardée

(**b**) *Fig (person)* changer de chemin *ou* de direction; **when he saw us, he sheered off in the opposite direction** il a fait demi-tour en nous apercevant

sheerly ['ʃɪəlɪ] *adv* (**a**) *(completely)* complètement (**b**) *(steeply)* à pic, abruptement

sheet [ʃiːt] **1** *n* (**a**) *(for bed)* drap *m*; *(for furniture)* housse *f*; *(shroud)* linceul *m*; *(tarpaulin)* bâche *f*; **to change the sheets (on a bed)** changer les draps (d'un lit); **to get between the sheets** se mettre au lit; *Fam* **what's he like between the sheets?** comment est-il au lit?

(**b**) *(of paper)* feuille *f*; *(of glass, metal)* feuille *f*, plaque *f*; *(of cardboard, plastic)* feuille *f*; *(of iron, steel)* tôle *f*, plaque *f*; **loose sheet** feuille *f* volante; **a sheet of newspaper** une feuille de journal; **the book is still in sheets** le livre n'a pas encore été relié; **order sheet** bulletin *m* de commande

(**c**) *(newspaper)* feuille *f*, journal *m*; **it's a weekly union sheet** c'est une feuille syndicale hebdomadaire

(**d**) *(of water, snow)* nappe *f*, étendue *f*; *(of rain)* rideau *m*, torrent *m*; *(of flames)* rideau *m*; **a sheet of ice** une plaque de glace; *(on road)* une plaque de verglas; **the rain came down in sheets** il pleuvait des hallebardes *ou* à torrents

(**e**) *Culin* **baking sheet** plaque *f* de four *ou* à gâteaux

(**f**) *Naut* écoute *f*; *Fam Fig* **to be three sheets to the wind** avoir du vent dans les voiles

2 *vt (figure, face)* draper, couvrir d'un drap; *(furniture)* couvrir de housses; *Fig* **sheeted (over) in snow** couvert de neige

►► ***sheet anchor*** *Naut* ancre *f* de veille; *Fig* ancre *f* de salut; *Naut* ***sheet bend*** nœud *m* d'écoute; *Comput* ***sheet feed*** avancement *m* du papier; *Comput* ***sheet feeder*** bac *m* d'alimentation papier; ***sheet ice*** plaque *f* de glace; *(on road)* (plaque *f* de) verglas *m*; ***sheet lightning*** éclair *m* en nappe *ou* en nappes; ***sheet metal*** tôle *f*; ***sheet music*** *(UNCOUNT)* partitions *fpl*; ***sheet steel*** tôle *f* d'acier

►**sheet down** *vi (rain, snow)* tomber à torrents

sheet-fed *adj (printer)* feuille à feuille

sheeting ['ʃiːtɪŋ] *n* (**a**) *(cloth)* toile *f* pour draps (**b**) *(plastic, polythene)* feuillet *m*; *(metal)* feuille *f*, plaque *f*

Sheffield ['ʃefiːld] *n* Sheffield

►► ***the Sheffield Shield*** = principale compétition de cricket en Australie

sheik [ʃeɪk] *n* cheikh *m*

sheikdom ['ʃeɪkdəm] *n* territoire *m* sous l'autorité d'un cheikh

sheikh = **sheik**

sheikhdom = **sheikdom**

sheila ['ʃiːlə] *n Austr & NZ Fam* nana *f*

shekel ['ʃekəl] **1** *n (Israeli currency)* shekel *m*; *Bible* sicle *m*

2 shekels *npl esp Am Fam (money)* fric *m*, sous *mpl*

sheldrake ['ʃeldreɪk] *n Orn* tadorne *m*

shelduck ['ʃeldʌk] *n Orn* tadorne *m* de Belon

shelf [ʃelf] (*pl* **shelves** [ʃelvz]) *n* (**a**) *(individual)* planche *f*, étagère *f*; *(as part of set, in fridge)* étagère *f*; *(short)* tablette *f*; *(in oven)* plaque *f*; *(in shop)* étagère *f*, rayon *m*; **(set of) shelves** étagère *f*; **to put up shelves/a shelf** monter des étagères/une étagère; **to buy sth off the shelf** acheter qch tout fait; **I bought the cakes off the**

shelf j'ai acheté les gâteaux tout faits; **you can't buy alcohol off the shelf in that shop** l'alcool n'est pas en vente libre dans ce magasin; **to stay on the shelves** *(goods)* se vendre difficilement; **to be left on the shelf** *(woman)* rester vieille fille; *(man)* rester vieux garçon

(**b**) *Geol* banc *m*, rebord *m*, saillie *f*; *(under sea)* écueil *m*, plate-forme *f*

▸▸ *Mktg* ***shelf facing*** facing *m*, frontale *f*; ***shelf filler*** *(person in supermarket)* réassortisseur(euse) *m,f*; *Mktg* ***shelf impact*** impact *m* en linéaire; *Com* ***shelf life*** durée *f* de conservation avant vente; **bread has a short shelf life** le pain ne se conserve pas très longtemps; *Fig* **to have a short shelf life** *(idea, pop group etc)* avoir une durée de vie courte; ***shelf mark*** *(of book)* cote *f*; *Com* ***shelf space*** linéaire *m*, rayonnage *m*; ***shelf stacker*** *(person in supermarket)* réassortisseur(euse) *m,f*; *Com* ***shelf yield*** vente *f* par mètre linéaire

shell [ʃel] **1** *n* (**a**) *Biol (gen → of egg, mollusc, nut)* coquille *f*; *(→ of peas)* cosse *f*; *(→ of crab, lobster, tortoise)* carapace *f*; *(empty → on seashore)* coquillage *m*; *also Fig* **to come out of one's shell** sortir de sa coquille; *also Fig* **to go back** *or* **to retire into one's shell** rentrer dans sa coquille; **to bring sb out of his/her shell** faire sortir qn de sa coquille; **defeated, he crawled back into his shell** vaincu, il rentra dans sa coquille

(**b**) *(of building)* carcasse *f*; *(of car, ship, machine)* coque *f*; **he's just an empty shell** il n'est plus que l'ombre de lui-même

(**c**) *Culin* fond *m* (de tarte)

(**d**) *Mil* obus *m*; *Am (cartridge)* cartouche *f*

(**e**) *(in rowing → boat)* outrigger *m*

2 *comp (ornament, jewellery)* de *ou* en coquillages

3 *vt* (**a**) *(peas)* écosser, égrener; *(nut)* décortiquer, écaler; *(oyster)* ouvrir; *(prawn, crab)* décortiquer

(**b**) *Mil* bombarder (d'obus)

▸▸ *Com* ***shell company*** société *f* fictive; *Am* ***shell game*** *(game)* bonneteau *m* avec des gobelets; *(swindle)* escroquerie *f*; *Bot* ***shell ginger*** zérumbet *m*; *Comput* ***shell program*** logiciel *m* shell; ***shell shock*** *(UNCOUNT)* syndrome *m* commotionnel; ***shell suit*** survêtement *m (en polyamide froissé et doublé)*

▸**shell out** *Fam* **1** *vi* casquer; **to shell out for sth** casquer pour qch, payer qch; **I'm always shelling out** je suis toujours en train de casquer; **she had to shell out for new school uniforms** elle a dû casquer pour acheter de nouveaux uniformes scolaires

2 *vt insep* raquer; **I had to shell out £500** j'ai dû raquer 500 livres

she'll [ʃiːl] = **she will**

shellac [ʃə'læk] *(pt & pp* **shellacked**) **1** *n* gomme-laque *f*

2 *vt* (**a**) *(varnish)* laquer (**b**) *Am Fam (defeat)* battre à plate(s) couture(s), écrabouiller; **to get shellacked** être battu à plates coutures, se faire écrabouiller

shellacking [ʃə'lækɪŋ] *n Am Fam* (**a**) *(defeat)* raclée *f*, déculottée *f*; **to give sb a shellacking** battre qn à plate(s) couture(s), écrabouiller qn; **to take a shellacking** être battu à plates coutures, se faire écrabouiller (**b**) *(beating)* **to give sb a shellacking** tabasser qn, passer qn à tabac; **to take a shellacking** se faire tabasser, se faire passer à tabac

shellback ['ʃelbæk] *n* (**a**) *Zool* tortue *f* aquatique (**b**) *Fam (experienced sailor)* vieux marsouin *m*, vieux loup *m* de mer

shellbark ['ʃelbɑːk] *n Bot* hickory *m*

▸▸ *Bot* ***shellbark hickory*** hickory *m*

shelled [ʃeld] *adj (peas)* écossé, égrené; *(nut, shellfish)* décortiqué

shellfire ['ʃelfaɪə(r)] *n (UNCOUNT)* tirs *mpl* d'obus; **we heard a lot of shellfire** on a entendu beaucoup de tirs d'obus; **to be under shellfire** subir des tirs d'obus; **we came under heavy shellfire** nous avons subi un pilonnage intensif

shellfish ['ʃelfɪʃ] *(pl* **inv**) *n* (**a**) *Zool (crab, lobster, shrimp)* crustacé *m*; *(mollusc)* coquillage *m* (**b**) *(UNCOUNT) Culin* fruits *mpl* de mer

shelling ['ʃelɪŋ] *n Mil* pilonnage *m*

shell-like *n Br Fam (ear)* **can I have a word in your shell-like?** je peux te causer deux minutes❑?

shellproof ['ʃelpruːf] *adj Mil* blindé, à l'épreuve des obus

shell-shaped *adj* en forme de coquillage, conchoïde

shell-shocked [-,ʃɒkt] *adj* commotionné *(après une explosion)*; **a shell-shocked soldier** un commotionné (de guerre); *Fig* **I'm still feeling pretty shell-shocked by it all** je suis encore sous le choc après toute cette histoire

Shelta ['ʃeltə] *n Ling* = patois des Romanichels d'Irlande

shelter ['ʃeltə(r)] **1** *n* (**a**) *(cover, protection)* abri *m*; **to take** *or* **to get under shelter** se mettre à l'abri *ou* à couvert; **they took** *or* **sought shelter from the rain under a tree** ils se sont abrités de la pluie *ou* mis à l'abri de la pluie sous un arbre; **where can we find shelter?** où peut-on trouver un abri?; **we ran for shelter** nous avons couru nous mettre à l'abri; **under the shelter of the mountain** à l'abri de la montagne

(**b**) *(accommodation)* asile *m*, abri *m*; **to give shelter to sb** *(hide)* donner asile à *ou* cacher qn; *(accommodate)* héberger qn; **they gave us food and shelter** il nous ont offert le gîte et le couvert

(**c**) *(enclosure → gen)* abri *m*; *(→ for sentry)* guérite *f*; **(bus) shelter** Abribus® *m*

(**d**) *(for homeless people, battered wives etc)* refuge *m*

2 *vt* (**a**) *(protect → from rain, sun, bombs)* abriter; *(→ from blame, suspicion)* protéger; **to shelter sb from sth** protéger qn de qch; **the trees sheltered us from the wind** les arbres nous abritaient du vent; **her reputation sheltered her from any scandal** sa réputation lui évita le scandale; **we were sheltered from the rain/from danger** nous étions à l'abri de la pluie/du danger

(**b**) *(give asylum to → fugitive, refugee)* donner asile à, abriter; **the police suspected them of sheltering a murderer** la police les soupçonnait d'abriter un assassin

3 *vi* s'abriter, se mettre à l'abri; *(from bullets)* se mettre à couvert; **he sheltered from the rain in a shop doorway** il s'est abrité de la pluie *ou* il s'est mis à l'abri de la pluie dans l'entrée d'un magasin

4 **Shelter** *n* = association britannique d'aide aux sans-abris

shelterbelt ['ʃeltəbelt] *n* ceinture *f* de protection

sheltered ['ʃeltəd] *adj* (**a**) *(position, garden, cove, waters)* abrité (**b**) *(upbringing, life)* protégé; **she had a very sheltered upbringing** elle a eu une enfance très protégée; **to lead a sheltered life** vivre à l'abri des soucis (**c**) *(protected → industry)* protégé *(de la concurrence)*; *(→ work)* dans un centre pour handicapés

▸▸ ***sheltered accommodation, sheltered housing*** = logement dans une résidence pour personnes âgées ou handicapées; *Am* ***sheltered workshop*** = atelier pour personnes handicapées

shelterless ['ʃeltəlɪs] *adj* sans abri

sheltie, shelty ['ʃeltɪ] *n Scot* (**a**) *(pony)* poney *m* de Shetland (**b**) *(dog)* chien *m* de berger de Shetland

shelve [ʃelv] **1** *vt* (**a**) *(put aside, suspend)* laisser en suspens; **the project was shelved for two years** le projet a été mis en veilleuse pendant deux ans; **the problem has been shelved** le problème reste en suspens; **all discussion on the question has been shelved** toute discussion sur la question a été ajournée *ou* suspendue

(**b**) *(books → in shop)* mettre sur les rayons; *(→ at home)* mettre sur les étagères

(**c**) *(wall, room → in shop)* garnir de rayons; *(→ at home)* garnir d'étagères

2 *vi (ground)* être en pente douce; **the land shelves down to the sea** le terrain descend en pente douce jusqu'à la mer; **the beach shelves steeply** la plage descend en pente raide

shelves [ʃelvz] *pl of* **shelf**

shelving ['ʃelvɪŋ] *n (UNCOUNT)* (**a**) *(in shop)* rayonnage *m*, rayonnages *mpl*, étagères *fpl*; *(at home)* étagères *fpl* (**b**) *(suspension → of plan, question etc)* mise *f* en attente *ou* en suspens (**c**) *Geol* plateau *m*

Shem [ʃem] *pr n Bible* Sem

shemozzle [ʃɪ'mɒzəl] *esp Am Fam* **1** *n* (**a**) *(confusion)* bazar *m*, pagaille *f*, merdier *f* (**b**) *(fight)* chamaillerie *f*, bagarre *f*

2 *vi* décamper, filer

shenanigans [ʃɪ'nænɪgənz] *npl Fam* (**a**) *(mischief)* malice❑ *f*, espièglerie❑ *f* (**b**) *(scheming, tricks)* manigances❑ *fpl*, combines *fpl*; **there have been some shenanigans going on here** il s'est passé des choses pas très claires ici❑

shepherd ['ʃepəd] **1** *n* (**a**) berger *m*, *Literary* pâtre *m*

(**b**) *Rel & Literary* pasteur *m*, berger *m*; **the Good Shepherd** le bon Pasteur *ou* Berger; *Bible* **the Lord is my Shepherd** l'Éternel est mon berger

2 *vt* (**a**) *(tourists, children)* guider, conduire; **the boys were shepherded onto the coach** on a fait entrer les garçons dans le car; **to shepherd sb out of a room** escorter qn jusqu'à la porte; **to shepherd sb into a room** faire entrer *ou* introduire qn dans une pièce

(**b**) *(sheep)* garder, surveiller; **he shepherded all the ewes into the fold** il a conduit toutes les brebis à la bergerie

▸▸ ***shepherd boy*** jeune berger *m ou Literary* pâtre *m*; ***shepherd's crook*** bâton *m* de berger, houlette *f*; ***shepherd dog*** (chien *m* de) berger *m*; *Culin* ***shepherd's pie*** hachis *m* Parmentier, *Can* pâté *m* chinois; *Bot* ***shepherd's purse*** bourse-à-pasteur *f*

'The Shepherd's Calendar' *Spenser* 'Le Calendrier du berger'

shepherdess [,ʃepə'des] *n* bergère *f*

Sheraton ['ʃerətən] *n (furniture)* = style de mobilier aux lignes élégantes créé par l'ébéniste Thomas Sheraton vers 1800

sherbet ['ʃɜːbət] *n* (**a**) *Br (powder → sweet)* poudre *f* acidulée; *(→ for drink)* = poudre servant à préparer une boisson gazeuse (**b**) *Am (water ice)* sorbet *m*

sherd [ʃɜːd] *n Archeol (of pottery)* tesson *m*

sheriff ['ʃerɪf] *n* (**a**) *Am (in Wild West and today)* shérif *m* (**b**) *Eng Law (crown officer)* shérif *m*, officier *m* de la Couronne (**c**) *Scot Law* ≃ juge *m* au tribunal de grande instance

▸▸ *Scot Law* ***sheriff court*** ≃ tribunal *m* de grande instance; *Scot Law* ***sheriff officer*** = fonctionnaire du tribunal de grande instance chargé notamment des actions contre les débiteurs et des sommations à comparaître

sheriffdom ['ʃerɪfdəm] *n* (**a**) *Am* fonction *f* de shérif (**b**) *Eng Law* fonction *f* de shérif, fonction *f* d'officier de la Couronne

Sherlock ['ʃɜːlɒk] *pr n Fam Ironic* **well done, Sherlock!** dis donc, tu es un vrai Sherlock Holmes, toi!

Sherman tank ['ʃɜːmən-] *n Mil* tank *m* Sherman, Sherman *m*

Sherpa ['ʃɜːpə] *n* Sherpa *m*

sherry ['ʃerɪ] *(pl* **sherries**) *n* sherry *m*, xérès *m*, vin *m* de Xérès

▸▸ ***sherry glass*** verre *m* à madère

Sherwood forest ['ʃɜːwʊd-] *n* = ancienne région de forêts au centre de l'Angleterre où Robin des Bois aurait vécu

she's [ʃiːz] (**a**) = **she has** (**b**) = **she is**

Shetland ['ʃetlənd] **1** *n* **the Shetlands** les (îles *fpl*) Shetland *fpl*; **in the Shetlands** *or* **the Shetland Isles** *or* **the Shetland Islands** dans les Shetland

2 *adj* (**a**) *Geog* shetlandais (**b**) *Tex (pullover)* en shetland

▸▸ ***the Shetland Isles, the Shetland Islands*** les (îles *fpl*) Shetland *fpl*; ***Shetland pony*** poney *m* des Shetland; ***Shetland sheepdog*** berger *m* des Shetland; ***Shetland wool*** laine *f* d'Écosse *ou* de Shetland

Shetlander ['ʃetləndə(r)] *n* Shetlandais(e) *m,f*

shew [ʃəʊ] *(pt* **shewed,** *pp* **shewn** [ʃəʊn] *or* **shewed**) *Arch* = **show** *vt & vi*

shh [ʃ] *exclam* chut!

Shia(h) ['ʃiːə] **1** *n* (**a**) *(religion)* chiisme *m* (**b**) *(Shiite)* **Shia(h) (Muslim)** chiite *mf*

2 *adj* chiite

shiatsu, shiatzu [ʃɪ'ætsuː] *n Med* shiatsu *m*

shibboleth ['ʃɪbə,leθ] *n Bible* schibboleth *m*; *Fig*

(custom, tradition) coutume *f*/tradition *f* dépassée; *(idea)* idée *f* dépassée; *(catchword → of party etc)* mot *m* d'ordre

shield [ʃiːld] **1** *n* (**a**) *(carried by soldier, warrior)* bouclier *m*; *Her* écu *m*, écusson *m*

(**b**) *Fig* bouclier *m*, paravent *m*; **to provide a shield against sth** protéger contre qch; **to use sb/sth as a shield** se servir de qn/qch comme bouclier

(**c**) *Tech (on machine)* écran *m* de protection *ou* de sécurité; *(on nuclear reactor, spacecraft)* bouclier *m*; **nuclear shield** bouclier *m* atomique; **sun shield** pare-soleil *m inv*

(**d**) *(trophy)* trophée *m*

(**e**) *(police badge)* plaque *f* de policier

(**f**) *(in spray painting)* masque *m*, cache *m*

2 *vt* (**a**) protéger; **to shield sb from sth** protéger qn de *ou* contre qch; **to shield one's eyes** se protéger les yeux; **we need a shelter to shield us from the wind/sun** il nous faut un abri contre le vent/soleil; **the police think he's trying to shield somebody** la police pense qu'il essaie de protéger quelqu'un; **she shielded him with her own body** elle lui a fait un bouclier *ou* rempart de son corps

(**b**) *(in spray painting → surfaces)* masquer

shieling ['ʃiːlɪŋ] *n Scot* (**a**) *(pasture)* pâturage *m* (d'été) (**b**) *(hut)* abri *m ou* cabane *f* (de berger)

shift [ʃɪft] **1** *n* (**a**) *(change)* changement *m*; **a shift in position/opinion** un changement de position/d'avis; **there was a sudden shift in public opinion/the situation** il y a eu un revirement d'opinion/de situation; **there was a light shift in the wind** le vent a légèrement tourné; *Pol* **a shift to the right/left** un glissement à droite/gauche; *Ling* **a shift in meaning** un glissement de sens; *Ling* **consonant/vowel shift** mutation *f* consonantique/vocalique; *Astron* **blue/red shift** décalage *m* vers le bleu/rouge

(**b**) *(move)* déplacement *m*; **there's been a shift of population towards the towns** on a assisté à un déplacement de la population vers les villes; *Br Fam* **get a shift on!** grouille-toi!, magne-toi!

(**c**) *Ind (work period)* poste *m*; *(group of workers)* équipe *f*, brigade *f*; **what shift are you on this week?** à quel poste avez-vous été affecté cette semaine?; **I'm on the night/morning shift** je suis dans l'équipe de nuit/du matin; **she works long shifts** elle fait de longues heures; **he's on eight-hour shifts** il fait les trois-huit; **to work shifts, to be on shifts** travailler en équipe, faire les trois-huit; **when does** *or* **do the morning shift arrive?** à quelle heure arrive l'équipe du matin?

(**d**) *(turn, relay)* relais *m*; **to do sth in shifts** se relayer; **there was a lot of work so they did it in shifts** comme il y avait beaucoup de travail, ils se sont relayés (pour le faire); **I'm exhausted, can you take a shift at the wheel?** je suis épuisé, peux-tu me relayer au volant?

(**e**) *Am Aut* **(gear) shift** *(lever)* levier *m* de (changement de) vitesse; *(action)* changement *m* de vitesse

(**f**) *Old-fashioned (expedient)* expédient *m*; **to make shift with sth** se contenter de qch

(**g**) *(dress)* (robe *f*) fourreau *m*; *Old-fashioned (woman's slip)* combinaison *f*

(**h**) *Comput (in word processing, telegraphy etc)* touche *f* majuscule; *(in arithmetical operation)* décalage *m*; **press shift** appuyer sur la touche majuscule; **an asterisk is shift 8** pour l'astérisque, il faut appuyer simultanément sur la touche majuscule et la touche 8

2 *vt* (**a**) *(move → object)* déplacer, bouger; *(→ part of body)* bouger, remuer; *Theat (scenery)* changer; **it took three strong men to shift the wardrobe** il a fallu trois hommes forts pour déplacer l'armoire; **help me shift the bed nearer the window** aide-moi à rapprocher le lit de *ou* pousser le lit vers la fenêtre; **the drawer's stuck, I can't shift it** le tiroir est coincé, je ne peux le faire bouger; *Fam* **shift yourself!** *(move)* pousse-toi!, bouge-toi!; *(hurry)* remue-toi!, grouille-toi!; **he's got a job shifting scenery** il a trouvé du travail comme machiniste

(**b**) *(transfer → employee) (to new job, place of work)* muter; *(to new department)* affecter; *(→ blame, responsibility)* rejeter; **they've shifted offices again** ils ont déménagé de nouveau; **he keeps getting shifted to a different job** on n'arrête pas de le muter; **they're trying to shift the blame onto me** ils essaient de rejeter la responsabilité sur moi; **we're trying to shift the balance towards exports** nous essayons de mettre l'accent sur les exportations; **the latest developments have shifted attention away from this area** les événements récents ont détourné l'attention de cette région; **they won't be shifted from their opinion** impossible de les faire changer d'avis; **to shift ground** *or* **one's position** changer de position

(**c**) *(remove → stain)* enlever, faire partir

(**d**) *Am* **to shift gears** changer de vitesse

(**e**) *Fam (sell)* écouler□, fourguer; **how can we shift this old stock?** comment écouler *ou* nous débarrasser de ces vieilles marchandises?

(**f**) *Fam (eat, drink)* s'envoyer; **hurry up and shift that pint!** dépêche-toi d'écluser ta pinte!

3 *vi* (**a**) *(move)* se déplacer, bouger; **the cargo has shifted in the hold** la cargaison s'est déplacée dans la cale; **the table won't shift, it's bolted to the floor** on ne peut pas bouger la table, elle est fixée au sol; **the anticyclone is expected to shift eastwards** l'anticyclone devrait se déplacer vers l'est; **she kept shifting from one foot to the other** elle n'arrêtait pas de se balancer d'un pied sur l'autre; **could you shift?** *(out of the way)* pouvez-vous dégager?

(**b**) *(change, switch → gen)* changer; *(→ wind)* tourner; **their policy has shifted over the last week** leur politique a changé *ou* s'est modifiée au cours de la semaine; *Theat* **the scene shifts** la scène change; **in the second act the scene shifts to Venice** dans le deuxième acte, l'action se déroule à Venise; **he wouldn't shift** *(in negotiations etc)* il est resté ferme sur ses positions; *Am Aut* **to shift into fourth (gear)** passer en quatrième (vitesse)

(**c**) *Br Fam (move quickly)* foncer; **he was really shifting** il fonçait carrément; **this car can really shift!** cette voiture est un vrai bolide!

(**d**) *(manage)* **to shift for oneself** se débrouiller tout seul; **he's had to learn to shift for himself since his wife left** il a dû apprendre à se débrouiller tout seul depuis le départ de sa femme; **she can** *or* **knows how to shift for herself** elle est débrouillarde

(**e**) *(stain)* partir, s'enlever; **this stain won't shift** cette tache ne veut pas partir

(**f**) *Br Fam (sell)* se vendre□; **those TVs just aren't shifting at all** ces télévisions ne se vendent pas du tout

►► *Comput* ***shift key*** touche *f* majuscule; *Comput* ***shift lock*** touche *f* de blocage des majuscules; *Am Aut* ***shift stick*** levier *m* de (changement de) vitesse, *Can* bras *m* de vitesse; ***shift work*** travail *m* en équipe; **she does shift work** elle fait les trois-huit; ***shift worker*** = personne qui fait les trois-huit

►**shift over, shift up** *vi Fam* se pousser□, se déplacer□; **can you shift over** *or* **up a bit?** tu peux te pousser un peu?

shift-click *Comput* **1** *n* majuscule-clic *m*

2 *vi* faire un majuscule-clic

shifter ['ʃɪftə(r)] *Am* = **shift stick**

shiftily ['ʃɪftɪlɪ] *adv* sournoisement

shiftiness ['ʃɪftɪnɪs] *n* sournoiserie *f*

shifting ['ʃɪftɪŋ] *adj (ideas, opinions)* changeant; *(alliances)* instable; *(ground)* mouvant

►► ***shifting sands*** sables *mpl* mouvants; *Fig* terrain *m* mouvant

shiftless ['ʃɪftlɪs] *adj (lazy)* paresseux, fainéant; *(apathetic)* apathique, mou (molle); *(lacking initiative)* qui manque de ressource, peu débrouillard

shiftlessly ['ʃɪftlɪslɪ] *adv (inefficiently)* d'une manière inefficace, futile; *(without initiative)* sans initiative

shiftlessness ['ʃɪftlɪsnɪs] *n (laziness)* paresse *f*, fainéantise *f*; *(apathy)* apathie *f*, mollesse *f*; *(lack of initiative)* manque *m* de ressource *ou* d'initiative

shifty ['ʃɪftɪ] (*compar* **shiftier**, *superl* **shiftiest**) *adj Fam (person)* louche□; *(look)* fuyant□; **shifty eyes** regard *m* fuyant; **he looks a shifty customer** il a l'air louche

shigella [ʃɪ'gelə] *n Biol* shigelle *f*

Shiism ['ʃiːɪzəm] *n Rel* chiisme *m*

Shiite ['ʃiːaɪt] *Rel* **1** *n* **Shiite (Muslim)** chiite *mf*

2 *adj* chiite

Shikoku ['ʃiːkəʊkuː] *n Geog* Shikoku *f*

shiksa ['ʃɪksə] *n very Fam* non-juive□*f*, goyette *f*, = terme injurieux désignant une non-juive

shill [ʃɪl] *n esp Am Fam (encouraging buyers)* baron *m*, = complice d'un camelot qui attire les clients par achats simulés; *(of gambler)* compère *m (d'un joueur professionnel)*; **half the players there are shills** *(in gaming house)* la moitié des joueurs sont (des employés) de la maison

shillelagh [ʃɪ'leɪlɪ] *n* gourdin *m*

shilling ['ʃɪlɪŋ] *n* (**a**) *(in Britain)* shilling *m (ancienne pièce britannique valant 12 pence, soit un vingtième de livre)*; *Old-fashioned* **to take the (King's** *or* **Queen's) shilling** s'engager dans l'armée (**b**) *(in Kenya, Tanzania etc)* shilling *m*

shilly-shally ['ʃɪlɪ,ʃælɪ] (*pt & pp* **shilly-shallied**) *vi Fam Pej* hésiter□, tergiverser□; **stop shilly-shallying (around)!** décide-toi enfin!□

shilly-shallying ['ʃɪlɪ,ʃælɪɪŋ] *n (UNCOUNT) Fam Pej* hésitations□ *fpl*, valse-hésitation *f*; **after a lot of shilly-shallying they eventually came to an agreement** après de longues hésitations *ou* une longue valse-hésitation, ils ont fini par se mettre d'accord

shim [ʃɪm] *n Tech* rondelle *f* de calage, cale *f*

shimmer ['ʃɪmə(r)] **1** *vi (sequins, jewellery, silk)* chatoyer, scintiller; *(water)* miroiter; **the sea shimmered in the moonlight, the moonlight shimmered on the sea** la mer miroitait au clair de lune; **the pavements shimmered in the heat** l'air tremblait au-dessus des trottoirs brûlants

2 *n (of sequins, jewellery, silk)* chatoiement *m*, scintillement *m*; *(of water)* miroitement *m*; **the shimmer of the moon on the lake** les reflets *mpl* de la lune sur le lac

shimmering ['ʃɪmərɪŋ] *adj (light)* scintillant; *(jewellery, silk)* chatoyant; *(water)* miroitant

shimmy ['ʃɪmɪ] (*pl* **shimmies**, *pt & pp* **shimmied**) **1** *n* (**a**) *(dance)* shimmy *m*; **to do the shimmy** danser le shimmy (**b**) *Am Aut* shimmy *m*, flottement *m* des roues directrices

2 *vi* (**a**) *(dance)* danser le shimmy (**b**) *Am Aut* avoir du shimmy; **at speed it tends to shimmy** la direction a tendance à flotter à grande vitesse

►**shimmy up** *vt insep* grimper

shin [ʃɪn] (*pt & pp* **shinned**) **1** *n* (**a**) *Anat* tibia *m*; **she kicked him in the shins** elle lui a donné un coup de pied dans les tibias (**b**) *Culin (of beef)* gîte *m ou* gîte-gîte *m* (de bœuf); *(of veal)* jarret *m* (de veau)

2 *vi* grimper; **to shin (up) a lamp post** grimper à un réverbère; **he shinned to the top of the mast** il a grimpé au sommet du mât; **I shinned down the drainpipe** je suis descendu le long de la gouttière

shinbone ['ʃɪnbəʊn] *n* tibia *m*

shindig ['ʃɪndɪg] *n Fam* (**a**) *(party)* (grande) fête□*f*; **to have a shindig** faire la fiesta; **we had a real shindig last night** on a fait une sacrée java hier soir (**b**) *(fuss)* tapage *m*, raffut *m*; **he kicked up a real shindig** il a fait un sacré tapage

shindy ['ʃɪndɪ] (*pl* **shindies**) *n Fam* (**a**) *Br (din)* raffut *m*, ramdam *m*; **to kick up a shindy** *(make a din)* faire du raffut *ou* du ramdam; **to kick up a shindy about sth** *(protest loudly)* faire du raffut pour protester contre qch (**b**) *Am* = **shindig** (**a**)

shine [ʃaɪn] (*pt & pp vt* (**a**) *& vi* **shone** [ʃɒn], *vt sense* (**b**) **shined**) **1** *vi* (**a**) *(sun, moon, lamp, candle)* briller; *(surface, glass, hair)* briller, luire; **the sun was shining** le soleil brillait, il y avait du soleil; **the moon shone down** la lune brillait; **the sun was shining in my eyes** j'avais le soleil dans les yeux, le soleil m'éblouissait; **there was a light shining in the window** une lumière brillait à la fenêtre; **bright light shone from the window** une lumière vive brillait à la fenêtre; **a small desk lamp shone on the table** une petite lampe de bureau éclairait la table; **his eyes shone with excitement** ses yeux brillaient *ou* son regard brillait d'émotion; **her face shone with joy** son visage rayonnait de joie; *very Fam* **stick it where the sun don't shine!** tu peux te le mettre où je pense!

(**b**) *(excel)* briller; **John shines at sports** John

est très bon en sport; **he doesn't shine in company** il ne brille pas en société

2 *vt* (**a**) *(focus)* braquer, diriger; **the guard shone his torch on the prisoner** le gardien a braqué sa lampe sur le prisonnier; **don't shine that lamp in my eyes** ne m'éblouis pas avec cette lampe

(**b**) *(polish)* faire briller, faire reluire, astiquer

3 *n* (**a**) *(polished appearance)* éclat *m*, brillant *m*, lustre *m*; **to put a shine on sth, to give sth a shine** faire reluire *ou* briller qch; **to take the shine off sth** délustrer qch, ternir qch; *Fig* faire perdre de son éclat à qch; *Fam* **to take a shine to sb** *(take a liking to)* se prendre d'amitié pour qn ❑; *(get a crush on)* s'enticher de qn

(**b**) *(polish)* polissage *m*; **your shoes need a shine** tes chaussures ont besoin d'un coup de brosse *ou* chiffon

▸**shine down** *vi* briller; **the hot sun shone down on us** le soleil tapait dur

▸**shine out** *vi (light)* jaillir; *Fig (courage, skill, generosity)* rayonner, briller; **she shines out from the others in the class** elle dépasse tous ses camarades de classe de la tête et des épaules

▸**shine through** *vi (light)* jaillir; *Fig (courage, skill, generosity)* rayonner, briller

▸**shine up to** *vt insep Am Fam* faire de la lèche à

shiner [ˈʃaɪnə(r)] *n Fam (black eye)* coquard *m*, œil *m* au beurre noir

shingle [ˈʃɪŋgəl] **1** *n* (**a**) *(UNCOUNT) (pebbles)* galets *mpl* (**b**) *Constr (for roofing)* bardeau *m*, aisseau *m* (**c**) *Am (nameplate → of doctor, lawyer etc)* plaque *f* (**d**) *(haircut)* coupe *f* à la garçonne

2 *vt* (**a**) *(roof)* couvrir de bardeaux *ou* d'aisseaux (**b**) *(hair)* couper à la garçonne

▸▸ ***shingle beach*** plage *f* de galets; ***shingle roof*** toit *m* en bardeaux

shingles [ˈʃɪŋgəlz] *n (UNCOUNT) Med* zona *m*

shingly [ˈʃɪŋgəlɪ] *adj (ground)* couvert de galets; *(beach)* de galets

shinguard [ˈʃɪngɑːd] *n* jambière *f*

shininess [ˈʃaɪnɪnɪs] *n* éclat *m*, brillant *m*

shining [ˈʃaɪnɪŋ] *adj* (**a**) *(gleaming → glass, metal, shoes)* luisant, reluisant; *(→ eyes)* brillant; *(→ face)* rayonnant (**b**) *(outstanding)* éclatant, remarquable; **a shining example of bravery** un modèle de courage; **John is a shining example to us all** John est un modèle pour nous tous

▸▸ *Bot* ***shining crane's bill*** géranium *m* luisant

Shinner [ˈʃɪnə(r)] *n Ir Fam* partisan *m* de Sinn Féin ❑

shinny [ˈʃɪnɪ] *(pt & pp* **shinnied***) Am* = **shin** *vi*

shin-pad *n* protège-tibia *m*

Shinto [ˈʃɪntəʊ] *Rel* **1** *n* shinto *m*

2 *adj* shintoïste

Shintoism [ˈʃɪntəʊɪzəm] *n Rel* shintoïsme *m*

Shintoist [ˈʃɪntəʊɪst] *Rel* **1** *adj* shintoïste

2 *n* shintoïste *mf*

shinty [ˈʃɪntɪ] *n Br* = sorte de hockey sur gazon d'origine écossaise

shiny [ˈʃaɪnɪ] *(compar* **shinier**, *superl* **shiniest***) adj* (**a**) *(gleaming → glass, metal, shoes)* luisant, reluisant; **my nose is shiny** j'ai le nez qui brille (**b**) *(clothing → with wear)* lustré; **shiny at the elbows** lustré aux coudes

ship [ʃɪp] *(pt & pp* **shipped***)* **1** *n* (**a**) *Naut* navire *m*; *(smaller)* bateau *m*; *(esp warship)* bâtiment *m*; **on board** *or* **aboard ship** à bord; *Literary* **the good ship Calypso** la Calypso; **sailing ship** bateau *m* à voiles, voilier *m*; *Old-fashioned* **to take ship for France** prendre le bateau pour la France; *Fam* **when my ship comes in** *or* **home** *(money)* quand je serai riche ❑, quand j'aurai fait fortune ❑; *(success)* quand j'aurai réussi dans la vie ❑; **the ship of the desert** le vaisseau du désert; **the ship of State** le char de l'État; *Fig* **to be like ships that pass in the night** *(lovers)* être des amants de passage; **these days we are like ships that pass in the night** ces temps-ci on ne fait que se croiser

(**b**) *(airship)* dirigeable *m*; *(spaceship)* vaisseau *m* (spatial)

2 *vt* (**a**) *(send by ship)* expédier (par bateau *ou* par mer); *(carry by ship)* transporter (par bateau *ou* par mer); **we're having most of our luggage shipped** nous expédions la plupart de nos bagages par bateau

(**b**) *(send by any means)* expédier; *(carry by any means)* transporter; **the goods will be shipped by train** *(sent)* les marchandises seront expédiées par le train; *(transported)* les marchandises seront transportées par chemin de fer

(**c**) *(embark → passengers, cargo)* embarquer

(**d**) *(take into boat → gangplank, oars)* rentrer; *(→ water)* embarquer

3 *vi* (**a**) *(passengers, crew)* embarquer, s'embarquer

(**b**) *Com (product)* sortir de l'usine

▸▸ ***ship's biscuit*** biscuit *m* de mer; ***ship's boy*** mousse *m*; ***ship canal*** canal *m* maritime; ***ship's chandler*** shipchandler *m*, marchand(e) *m,f* d'articles de marine; ***ship's company*** équipage *m*; ***ship's papers*** papiers *mpl* de bord

▸**ship off** *vt sep Fam* expédier ❑; **we've shipped the kids off to their grandparents'** nous avons expédié les gosses chez leurs grands-parents

▸**ship out 1** *vt sep (send → goods)* expédier; *(→ troops etc)* envoyer

2 *vi esp Am Fam (leave)* mettre les voiles

> **I see no ships**
>
> Il s'agit d'une phrase qu'aurait prononcée l'amiral Nelson lors de la bataille de Copenhague en 1801. Nelson était borgne et lorsque ses officiers l'informèrent que des navires de guerre danois approchaient, il aurait levé sa lunette vers son mauvais œil et aurait déclaré **I see no ships** ("je ne vois aucun navire"), donnant ainsi l'occasion à la flotte anglaise d'engager le combat, et de le gagner.
>
> Aujourd'hui, on utilise cette expression en allusion à Nelson lorsque quelqu'un fait exprès de ne pas remarquer quelque chose.

shipboard [ˈʃɪpbɔːd] **1** *n* **on shipboard** à bord (d'un navire)

2 *adj (romance, drama)* qui a lieu à bord d'un navire

shipbroker [ˈʃɪpˌbrəʊkə(r)] *n* courtier *m* maritime

shipbrokerage [ˈʃɪpˌbrəʊkərɪdʒ] *n* courtage *m* maritime

shipbuilder [ˈʃɪpˌbɪldə(r)] *n* constructeur *m* de navires

shipbuilding [ˈʃɪpˌbɪldɪŋ] *n* construction *f* navale; **the shipbuilding industry** (l'industrie *f* de) la construction navale

shipload [ˈʃɪpləʊd] *n* cargaison *f*, fret *m*

shipmaster [ˈʃɪpˌmɑːstə(r)] *n* capitaine *m*, commandant *m*

shipmate [ˈʃɪpmeɪt] *n* compagnon *m* de bord

shipment [ˈʃɪpmənt] *n* (**a**) *(goods sent)* cargaison *f*; **arms shipment** cargaison *f* d'armes (**b**) *(sending of goods)* expédition *f*; **the containers awaiting shipment** les conteneurs prêts pour l'expédition

shipowner [ˈʃɪpˌəʊnə(r)] *n* armateur *m*

shipped [ʃɪpt] *adj* embarqué

▸▸ *Com* ***shipped bill*** connaissement *m* embarqué; *Com* ***shipped weight*** poids *m* embarqué

shipper [ˈʃɪpə(r)] *n (charterer)* affréteur *m*, chargeur *m*; *(transporter)* transporteur *m*; *(sender)* expéditeur(trice) *m,f*

shipping [ˈʃɪpɪŋ] **1** *n (UNCOUNT)* (**a**) *(ships)* navires *mpl*; *(traffic)* navigation *f*; **dangerous to shipping** dangereux pour la navigation; **all shipping has been warned to steer clear of the area** on a prévenu les navires qu'il fallait éviter le secteur; **the decline of British merchant shipping** le déclin de la marine marchande britannique; *Rad* **attention all shipping** = formule utilisée dans les bulletins de la météo marine pour attirer l'attention des bateaux, notamment avant un avis de mauvais temps

(**b**) *(transport → gen)* transport *m*; *(→ by sea)* transport *m* maritime; **cost includes shipping** le coût du transport est compris

(**c**) *(loading)* chargement *m*, embarquement *m*

2 *comp (line)* maritime, de navigation; *(sport, trade, intelligence)* maritime

▸▸ ***shipping agent*** agent *m* maritime; ***shipping charges*** frais *mpl* d'expédition; ***shipping clerk*** expéditionnaire *mf*; ***shipping company*** entreprise *f* de transport routier; ***shipping forecast*** météo *f ou* météorologie *f* marine; ***shipping lane*** couloir *m* de navigation; ***shipping office*** bureau *m* d'expédition

shipshape [ˈʃɪpʃeɪp] *adj* en ordre, rangé; **let's try to get this place shipshape** essayons de mettre un peu d'ordre ici; *Fam Old-fashioned Hum* **all shipshape and Bristol fashion!** tout est impeccable! ❑

ship-to-shore radio *n* liaison *f* radio navire-terre *ou* navire-sol

shipway [ˈʃɪpweɪ] *n* (**a**) *(for launching ship)* couettes *fpl* dormantes *ou* de lancement (**b**) *(ship canal)* canal *m* maritime

shipworm [ˈʃɪpwɜːm] *n Zool* taret *m*

shipwreck [ˈʃɪprek] **1** *n* (**a**) *(disaster at sea)* naufrage *m*; **they died in a shipwreck** ils ont péri dans un naufrage (**b**) *(wrecked ship)* épave *f*

2 *vt* (**a**) **they were shipwrecked on a desert island** ils ont échoué sur une île déserte (**b**) *Fig (ruin, spoil)* ruiner

shipwrecked [ˈʃɪprekt] *adj* **to be shipwrecked** *(boat)* faire naufrage; *(crew, passenger)* être naufragé; **a shipwrecked sailor** un marin naufragé

shipwright [ˈʃɪpraɪt] *n (company)* constructeur *m* de navires; *(worker)* ouvrier(ère) *m,f* de chantier naval

shipyard [ˈʃɪpjɑːd] *n* chantier *m* naval; **hundreds of shipyard workers were sacked** des centaines d'ouvriers des chantiers navals ont été licenciés

Shiraz [ˈʃɪræz] *n* Chiraz *m*

shire [ˈʃaɪə(r)] **1** *n Br* (**a**) *(county)* comté *m* (**b**) (horse) shire *m*

2 Shires *npl* **the Shires** = les comtés (ruraux) du centre de l'Angleterre

▸▸ ***shire horse*** shire *m*

shirk [ʃɜːk] **1** *vt (work, job, task)* éviter de faire, échapper à; *(duty)* se dérober à; *(problem, difficulty, question)* esquiver, éviter; **he always shirks doing the washing-up** il s'arrange toujours pour éviter de *ou* pour ne pas faire la vaisselle; **she doesn't shirk her responsibilities** elle n'essaie pas de se dérober à ses responsabilités

2 *vi* tirer au flanc

shirker [ˈʃɜːkə(r)] *n* tire-au-flanc *mf inv*

Shirley Temple [ˌʃɜːlɪˈtempəl] *n Am (drink)* ≃ diabolo *m* grenadine

shirr [ʃɜː(r)] *vt Sewing* froncer

▸▸ *Am Culin* ***shirred eggs*** œufs *mpl* en ramequin

shirring [ˈʃɜːrɪŋ] *n Sewing* fronces *fpl*

shirt [ʃɜːt] *n (gen)* chemise *f*; *(footballer's, cyclist's etc)* maillot *m*; **shirt collar/cuff** col *m*/manchette *f* de chemise; *Fam Fig* **keep your shirt on!** ne vous énervez pas! ❑, du calme! ❑; *Br Fam Fig* **to put one's shirt on sth** miser toute sa fortune sur qch ❑, miser jusqu'à son dernier centime sur qch ❑; *Fam Fig* **to lose one's shirt** *(lose everything)* y laisser sa chemise, perdre tout ce qu'on a ❑; *Am (lose one's temper)* s'emporter ❑, prendre la mouche; *Fam Fig* **to take the shirt off sb's back** faire cracher jusqu'à son dernier centime à qn; *Fam Fig* **he'd give you the shirt off his back** il donnerait jusqu'à sa chemise

shirtfront [ˈʃɜːtfrʌnt] *n* plastron *m*

shirting [ˈʃɜːtɪŋ] *n* shirting *m*, tissu *m* pour chemises

shirtless [ˈʃɜːtlɪs] *adj* sans chemise

shirtlifter [ˈʃɜːtˌlɪftə(r)] *n Br very Fam* tantouze *f*, tapette *f*, = terme injurieux désignant un homosexual

shirtmaker [ˈʃɜːtˌmeɪkə(r)] *n* chemisier *m (magasin)*

shirt-sleeved *adj* en manches *ou* bras de chemise

shirtsleeves [ˈʃɜːtsliːvz] *npl* **to be in (one's) shirtsleeves** être en manches *ou* bras de chemise

shirt-tail *n* pan *m* de chemise

shirtwaister [ˈʃɜːtˌweɪstə(r)], *Am* **shirtwaist** [ˈʃɜːtweɪst] *n* robe *f* chemisier

shirty [ˈʃɜːtɪ] *(compar* **shirtier**, *superl* **shirtiest***) adj Br Fam* désagréable ❑; **don't get shirty with me** ne te mets pas en rogne contre moi

shish kebab [ˈʃɪʃ-] *n Culin* chiche-kebab *m*

shit [ʃɪt] *(pt & pp* **shat** [ʃæt], *cont* **shitting***) very*

Fam **1** *n* **(a)** *(excrement)* merde *f*; **to** *Br* **have** *or Am* **take a shit** (aller) chier; **to have the shits** avoir la chiasse; **dog shit** merde *f* de chien; **tough shit!** tant pis pour ma/ta/sa/*etc* gueule!; **she thinks she's hot shit** elle ne se prend pas pour de la merde; **to kick** *or* **to beat** *or* **to knock the shit out of sb** casser la gueule à qn, défoncer la gueule à qn; **to scare the shit out of sb** foutre une trouille bleue à qn; **to bore the shit out of sb** faire crever qn d'ennui; **I don't give a shit** je m'en fous, j'en ai rien à foutre; **who gives a shit?** qu'est-ce que ça peut foutre?; **to treat sb like shit** traiter qn comme de la merde; **to be in the shit** être dans la merde; **to drop sb in the shit** foutre qn dans la merde; **when the shit hits the fan** quand nous serons dans la merde (jusqu'au cou); **to get one's shit together** se ressaisir❑; **to be up shit creek (without a paddle)** être dans une merde noire; *Vulg* **he thinks his shit doesn't stink** il se prend pas pour de la merde; *Vulg* **eat shit (and die)!** va te faire foutre!; **shit happens** ce sont des choses qui arrivent❑

(b) *(UNCOUNT) (nonsense, rubbish)* conneries *fpl*; **I hate it when he starts on his anarchy shit** je déteste quand il se met à débiter ses conneries sur l'anarchie; **that's a load of shit!** c'est des conneries, tout ça!; **don't give me that shit!** arrête tes conneries!; **to talk shit** raconter des conneries; **he's full of shit** il dit que des conneries, il sait pas ce qu'il dit; **no shit!** sans déconner!, sans dec!

(c) *(person)* ordure *f*, bâton *m* merdeux; **he's been a real shit to her** il s'est vraiment conduit en salaud avec elle

(d) *Drugs slang (hashish)* shit *m*, hasch *m*, chichon *m*; *(heroin)* héro *f*, blanche *f*

(e) *(anything)* **I can't see shit** j'y vois que dalle, j'y vois goutte; **that doesn't mean shit** ça veut rien dire; **he doesn't do shit** il en rame pas une, il en fout pas une rame

(f) *(worthless things)* **to be a load of shit,** *Am* **to be the shits** être de la merde

(g) *(useless things)* bordel *m*, foutoir *m*; **clear all that shit off your desk** vire-moi ce bordel de ton bureau

(h) *(disgusting substance)* merde *f*, saloperie *f*; **I can't eat this shit** je peux pas bouffer cette merde

(i) *(unfair treatment)* **to give sb shit** faire chier qn; **I don't need this shit!** j'ai pas envie de m'emmerder avec ce genre de conneries!

(j) to feel/look like shit *(ill)* se sentir/avoir l'air patraque

2 *vi* **(a)** *(defecate)* chier; *Fig* **shit or get off the pot!** alors, tu te décides?❑

(b) to shit on sb *(treat badly)* traiter qn comme de la merde; *Br* **to shit on sb from a great height** *(treat badly)* traiter qn comme de la merde; *(defeat)* battre qn à plates coutures, écrabouiller qn; *Am* **shit on that!** et puis merde!

(c) *Am (react with anger)* piquer une crise; *(react with surprise)* ne pas en revenir; **your parents will shit when they see what you've done!** tes parents vont piquer une crise quand ils se rendront compte de ce que t'as fait!

3 *vt* **(a) to shit oneself** *(defecate, be scared)* chier dans son froc; *(react with anger)* piquer une crise; *(react with surprise)* ne pas en revenir; **to shit a brick** *or* **bricks** chier dans son froc, *Can* chier dans ses culottes

(b) *Am* **to shit sb** *(lie to)* raconter des craques à qn; *(deceive)* se foutre de la gueule de qn

4 *adj (worthless)* merdique; **to feel shit** *(ill)* se sentir patraque; *(guilty)* se sentir coupable❑, avoir les boules *ou* les glandes; **I had a really shit time** j'en ai bavé; **he's a shit driver** il conduit comme un pied

5 *adv* **to be shit out of luck** ne pas avoir de bol *ou* de pot

6 *exclam* merde!

shitake [ʃɪ'tækɪ] *n*

▸▸ ***shitake mushrooms*** champignons *mpl* shitake

shit-can *vt Am very Fam (discard)* balancer, foutre en l'air; *(disregard, abandon)* passer aux oubliettes

shite [ʃaɪt] *Br very Fam* **1** *n* **(a)** *(excrement)* merde *f*

(b) *(nonsense)* conneries *fpl*; **he's full of shite** il raconte que des conneries, il sait pas ce qu'il dit; **to talk shite** raconter des conneries, déconner; **that's shite!** n'importe quoi!❑; **don't believe that shite!** n'écoute pas ces conneries!

2 *adj (bad)* merdique; **to feel shite** *(ill)* se sentir patraque; *(guilty)* se sentir coupable❑, avoir les boules *ou* les glandes; **I had a really shite time** j'ai passé un moment dégueulasse; **he's a shite singer** il chante comme un pied

3 *exclam* merde!

shit-faced *adj very Fam (drunk)* bourré, pété, beurré; *(on drugs)* défoncé, raide

shitfit ['ʃɪtfɪt] *n Am very Fam* **to have a shitfit** piquer une crise

shit-for-brains *n very Fam* abruti(e) *m,f*, tache *f*, gogol *mf*

shithead ['ʃɪthed] *n very Fam (unpleasant person)* enfoiré(e) *m,f*

shit-heel *n Am very Fam (person)* pécore *mf*, bouseux(euse) *m,f*

shithole ['ʃɪthəʊl] *n very Fam (dirty place)* porcherie *f*, taudis❑ *m*; **this town's a complete shithole** *(boring, ugly)* cette ville est un vrai trou

shit-hot *adj very Fam* vachement bon; **he's shit-hot as an actor** il est vachement bon comme acteur

shithouse ['ʃɪthaʊs, *pl* -haʊzɪz] *n very Fam* chiottes *fpl*, gogues *mpl*; **built like a brick shithouse** bâti comme une armoire à glace❑

shit-kicker *n Am very Fam (farmhand)* garçon *m* de ferme❑; *(rustic)* pedzouille *mf*, pécore *mf*

shitless ['ʃɪtlɪs] *adj very Fam* **to be scared shitless** avoir une trouille bleu, être mort de trouille; **to be bored shitless** se faire chier à mort

shitload ['ʃɪtləʊd] *n very Fam* **a shitload (of)** une chiée (de)

shit-scared *adj very Fam* **to be shit-scared** avoir une trouille bleu, être mort de trouille

shit-stirrer *n Br very Fam* fouteur(euse) *m,f* de merde

shitty ['ʃɪtɪ] (*compar* **shittier**, *superl* **shittiest**) *adj very Fam* **(a)** *(worthless)* merdique; **we stayed in a really shitty hotel** nous sommes descendus dans un hôtel vraiment merdique **(b)** *(mean)* dégueulasse; **what a shitty thing to do!** c'est dégueulasse de faire ça!; **to feel shitty** *(ill)* se sentir patraque; *(guilty)* se sentir coupable❑, avoir les boules *ou* les glandes

shiv [ʃɪv] *Am Fam Crime slang* **1** *n (knife)* surin *m*, lame❑ *f*

2 *vt (stab)* planter

Shiva ['ʃiːvə] *pr n Rel* Shiva

shiver ['ʃɪvə(r)] **1** *vi* **(a)** *(gen)* frissonner, trembler; *(with excitement)* frissonner, trembler; *(with cold, fever)* grelotter, trembler; **she shivered at the mention of his name** elle eut un frisson quand elle entendit son nom

(b) *Naut (sail)* faseyer

(c) *(splinter)* se fracasser, voler en éclats

2 *vt (break)* casser en morceaux; **shiver me timbers!** = expression stéréotypée de marin, ≃ mille sabords!

3 *n* **(a)** *(from cold, fever, fear)* frisson *m*, tremblement *m*; *(from excitement)* frisson *m*; *Fam* **it gives me the shivers** ça me donne le frisson *ou* des frissons❑; **it sent cold shivers down my back** cela m'a fait froid dans le dos

(b) *(fragment)* éclat *m*

shivering ['ʃɪvərɪŋ] **1** *adj* frissonnant; *(with cold, fever)* grelottant

2 *n (UNCOUNT) (gen)* frissonnement *m*; *(with cold, fever)* grelottement *m*; **to have a shivering fit** être pris de frissons

shivery ['ʃɪvərɪ] *adj (from cold)* grelottant; *(frightened)* frissonnant, tremblant; *(feverish)* grelottant de fièvre; **to feel shivery** avoir des frissons; **it gives you a shivery feeling** cela donne le frisson

SHO [,esertʃ'əʊ] *n Br Med (abbr* **Senior House Officer**) ≃ interne *mf (de rang supérieur au "house officer")*

shoal [ʃəʊl] **1** *n* **(a)** *(of fish)* banc *m* **(b)** *Fig (large numbers)* foule *f*; **shoals of tourists** une foule de touristes **(c)** *(shallows)* haut-fond *m* **(d)** *(sandbar)* barre *f*; *(sandbank)* banc *m* de sable

2 *vi (fish)* se mettre *ou* se rassembler en bancs

shoat [ʃəʊt] *n Am (piglet)* goret *m*

shock [ʃɒk] **1** *n* **(a)** *(surprise)* choc *m*, surprise *f*; **she got a shock when she saw me again** ça lui a fait un choc de me revoir; **what a shock you gave me!** qu'est-ce que tu m'as fait peur!

(b) *(upset)* choc *m*, coup *m*; **that comes as no shock to me** ça ne m'étonne pas; **it's all been a bit of a shock for us** tous ces événements nous ont bouleversés; **the shock killed him, he died of the shock** le choc l'a tué; **the news of his death came as a terrible shock to me** la nouvelle de sa mort a été un grand choc pour moi; **it came as a shock to the system to see her ex again after ten years** ça lui a fait un choc de revoir son ex au bout de dix ans; **getting up at 6 a.m. every morning/moving to Poland came as a shock to the system** ça m'a fait un sacré changement de me lever à six heures tous les matins/de partir vivre en Pologne; *Fam Hum & Ironic* **shock horror!** l'horreur!

(c) *Elec* décharge *f* (électrique); **to get a shock** recevoir *ou* prendre une décharge (électrique); **I got a nasty shock from the toaster** j'ai pris une sacrée décharge en touchant le grille-pain

(d) *(impact → of armies, vehicles)* choc *m*, heurt *m*; *(vibration → from explosion, earthquake)* secousse *f*

(e) *Med* choc *m*; **to be in (a state of) shock, to be suffering from shock** être en état de choc; **postoperative shock** choc *m* post-opératoire

(f) *Fam (shock absorber)* amortisseur❑ *m*

(g) *(mass)* **a shock of hair** une tignasse

2 *comp (measures, argument, headline)* choc *(inv)*; *(attack)* surprise *(inv)*; *(tactics)* de choc; *(result, defeat, decision)* inattendu; **to use shock tactics** employer la manière forte

3 *vt* **(a)** *(surprise greatly)* stupéfier; *(upset)* bouleverser; **I was shocked to hear that she had left** j'ai été stupéfait d'apprendre qu'elle était partie; **she was deeply shocked by her daughter's death** elle a été profondément bouleversée par la mort de sa fille

(b) *(offend, scandalize)* choquer, scandaliser; **his behaviour shocked them** son comportement les a choqués *ou* scandalisés; **a book that shocked the public** un livre qui a fait scandale; **she is easily shocked** elle se choque facilement; **I'm not easily shocked, but that book…** il en faut beaucoup pour me choquer, mais ce livre…

(c) *(force)* **to shock sb into action** secouer qn pour qu'il/elle agisse; **to shock sb into doing sth** secouer qn jusqu'à ce qu'il/elle fasse qch; **the news reports shocked them out of their apathy** les bulletins d'information les ont fait sortir de leur torpeur

(d) *Elec* donner une secousse *ou* un choc électrique à

▸▸ ***shock absorber*** amortisseur *m*; *Am Fam* ***shock jock*** = animateur ou animatrice de radio au ton irrévérencieux et provocateur; ***shock therapy, shock treatment*** *Med* (traitement *m* par) électrochoc *m*, sismothérapie *f*; *Fig* traitement *m* de choc; *Mil* ***shock troops*** troupes *fpl* de choc

shockable ['ʃɒkəbəl] *adj* **he's easily/not easily shockable** il se choque facilement/ne se choque pas facilement

shocked [ʃɒkt] *adj* **(a)** *(upset, distressed)* bouleversé; *(stunned)* stupéfait; **a shocked meeting was told of the takeover** c'est avec stupéfaction que l'assemblée a appris le rachat de l'entreprise; **there was a shocked silence when…** il y eut un silence atterré lorsque…; **they all listened in shocked silence** ils ont tous écouté, muets de stupéfaction

(b) *(offended, scandalized)* choqué, scandalisé; **I tried to look suitably shocked** je me suis efforcée de prendre un air scandalisé; **she spoke in shocked tones** elle parlait d'un ton scandalisé

shocker ['ʃɒkə(r)] *n Fam* **(a)** *(book)* livre *m* à sensation❑; *(film)* film *m* à sensation❑; *(news)* nouvelle *f* sensationnelle❑; *(play)* pièce *f* à sensation❑; *(story)* histoire *f* sensationnelle❑; **that's a real shocker of a story** cette histoire est vraiment choquante **(b)** *Hum (atrocious person)* **you little shocker!** petit monstre!

shock-headed *adj* hirsute

shock-horror *adj Fam (story, headline)* à sensation❑

shocking [ˈʃɒkɪŋ] **1** *adj* (**a**) *(scandalous)* scandaleux, choquant; **a shocking price** un prix scandaleux; **it's shocking the way he behaves** son comportement est scandaleux, sa conduite est scandaleuse; **a shocking new film** un nouveau film scandaleux
(**b**) *(horrifying)* atroce, épouvantable; **a shocking crime** un crime odieux *ou* atroce; **the shocking truth about conditions in our prisons** la terrible vérité sur les conditions de vie dans nos prisons
(**c**) *Fam (very bad)* affreux ❑, épouvantable ❑; **you look shocking today** tu as une mine affreuse aujourd'hui; **his room is in a shocking state** sa chambre est dans un état épouvantable; **shocking weather, isn't it?** quel temps affreux *ou* épouvantable!; **he's a shocking actor** il est nul comme acteur; **I'm shocking at football** je suis nul au football
2 *adv Fam* **it was raining something shocking!** il fallait voir ce qu'il *ou* comme ça tombait!
►► ***shocking pink*** rose *m* bonbon

shockingly [ˈʃɒkɪŋlɪ] *adv* (**a**) *(as intensifier)* affreusement, atrocement; **this whisky is shockingly expensive** ce whisky est affreusement cher; **the weather has been shockingly bad lately** la météo est vraiment affreuse depuis quelque temps; **in shockingly bad taste** du dernier mauvais goût
(**b**) *(extremely badly)* très mal, lamentablement; **he played shockingly on Saturday** il a très mal joué samedi
(**c**) *(scandalously → to behave)* scandaleusement; *(→ to treat)* abominablement

shocking-pink *adj* rose bonbon *(inv)*

shockproof [ˈʃɒkpruːf] *adj* résistant aux chocs

shockwave [ˈʃɒkweɪv] *n* onde *f* de choc; *Fig* remous *mpl*; *Fig* **the news sent shockwaves through the financial world** la nouvelle a provoqué des remous dans le monde de la finance

shod [ʃɒd] *pt & pp of* **shoe**

shoddily [ˈʃɒdɪlɪ] *adv* (**a**) *(built, made)* mal (**b**) *(meanly, pettily)* de façon mesquine; **they've treated you shoddily** ils ont été mesquins avec vous

shoddiness [ˈʃɒdɪnɪs] *n* (**a**) *(poor quality)* mauvaise qualité *f* (**b**) *(meanness, pettiness)* mesquinerie *f*

shoddy [ˈʃɒdɪ] *(compar* **shoddier**, *superl* **shoddiest**, *pl* **shoddies**) **1** *adj* (**a**) *(of inferior quality)* de mauvaise qualité; **shoddy workmanship** du travail *m* mal fait; **a shoddy imitation** une piètre *ou* médiocre imitation (**b**) *(mean, petty)* sale; **that's a shoddy trick to play on her!** on lui a joué un sale tour!; **I want no part in that shoddy affair** je ne veux pas être mêlé à cette sale affaire
2 *n Tex* tissu *m* shoddy *ou* de renaissance

shoe [ʃuː] *(pt & pp* **shod** [ʃɒd]) **1** *n* (**a**) *(gen)* chaussure *f*; **a pair of shoes** une paire de chaussures; **a man's/woman's shoe** une chaussure d'homme/de femme; **to take off one's shoes** enlever ses chaussures, se déchausser; **to put on one's shoes** mettre ses chaussures, se chausser; **he wasn't wearing any shoes, he didn't have any shoes on** il ne portait pas de chaussures; *Fig* **I wouldn't like to be in his shoes** je n'aimerais pas être à sa place; *Fig* **put yourself in my shoes** mettez-vous à ma place; *Fig* **to step into** *or* **to fill sb's shoes** prendre la place de qn, succéder à qn; *Am Fig* **if the shoe fits, wear it** qui se sent morveux (qu'il) se mouche
(**b**) **(horse) shoe** fer *m* (à cheval)
(**c**) *(in casino → for baccarat etc)* sabot *m*
(**d**) *(on electric train)* frotteur *m*
2 *vt* (**a**) *(horse)* ferrer
(**b**) *(usu passive) Literary (person)* chausser; **John was shod in sandals** John était chaussé de *ou* portait des sandales; **to be well shod** être bien chaussé
►► ***shoe box*** boîte *f* à chaussures; ***shoe cleaner*** produit *m* pour chaussures; ***shoe cream*** cirage *m* en crème; ***shoe leather*** cuir *m* pour chaussures; **save your shoe leather and take the bus** prenez l'autobus au lieu d'user vos souliers; ***shoe polish*** cirage *m*; ***shoe repairer*** cordonnier(ère) *m,f*; ***shoe repairs*** cordonnerie *f*; ***shoe scraper*** gratte-pieds *m inv*; ***shoe shop*** magasin *m* de chaussures; **I was in the shoe shop** j'étais chez le marchand de chaussures; ***shoe size*** pointure *f*

shoebill [ˈʃuːbɪl] *n Orn* bec-en-sabot *m*

shoeblack [ˈʃuːblæk] *n Old-fashioned* cireur(euse) *m,f* (de chaussures)

shoebrush [ˈʃuːbrʌʃ] *n* brosse *f* à chaussures

shoehorn [ˈʃuːhɔːn] **1** *n* chausse-pied *m*
2 *vt Fig* **we can shoehorn a few more in** on peut en faire tenir encore quelques-uns

shoeing [ˈʃuːɪŋ] *n (of horse)* ferrage *m*, ferrure *f*

shoelace [ˈʃuːleɪs] *n* lacet *m* (de chaussures); **your shoelace is undone** ton lacet est défait; *Fig* **he's not fit to tie your shoelaces** il n'est pas digne de cirer vos chaussures

shoemaker [ˈʃuːˌmeɪkə(r)] *n (manufacturer)* fabricant(e) *m,f* de chaussures; *(who makes and sells shoes)* chausseur *m*; *(cobbler)* cordonnier(ère) *m,f*; *(craftsman)* bottier *m*; *Prov* **the shoemaker's children are always the worst shod** les cordonniers sont toujours les plus mal chaussés

'The Shoemaker's Holiday' *Dekker* 'La Fête du cordonnier'

shoemaking [ˈʃuːˌmeɪkɪŋ] *n* fabrication *f* de chaussures; **the shoemaking industry** (l'industrie *f* de) la chaussure

shoemender [ˈʃuːˌmendə(r)] *n* cordonnier(ère) *m,f*

shoe-polishing machine *n* machine *f* à cirer les chaussures

shoeshine [ˈʃuːʃaɪn] *n* (**a**) *(action)* cirage *m*; **to get a shoeshine** se faire cirer les chaussures (**b**) *Fam (boy)* (petit) cireur *m* (de chaussures) ❑
►► ***shoeshine boy*** (petit) cireur *m* (de chaussures)

shoestring [ˈʃuːstrɪŋ] *n* (**a**) *Am (shoelace)* lacet *m* (de chaussure) (**b**) *Fam (idiom)* **on a shoestring** avec trois fois rien; **the film was made on a shoestring** c'est un film à très petit budget ❑; **cookery on a shoestring** la cuisine économique *ou* bon marché ❑; **a shoestring budget** un petit budget

shoetree [ˈʃuːtriː] *n* embauchoir *m*

shone [ʃɒn] *pt & pp of* **shine**

shonky [ˈʃɒŋkɪ] *adj Austr Fam* (**a**) *(risky, dangerous → plan, idea)* risqué ❑ (**b**) *(untrustworthy → person, scheme)* louche ❑ (**c**) *(not working properly, unstable)* douteux ❑

shoo [ʃuː] *(pt & pp* **shooed**) **1** *exclam (to animal, children)* allez!, ouste!
2 *vt* chasser
►**shoo away, shoo off** *vt sep* chasser

shoo-fly pie *n Am Culin* tarte *f* à la mélasse

shoogle [ˈʃʊgəl] *Scot* **1** *n* **to give sth a shoogle** secouer *ou* agiter qch
2 *vt* secouer, agiter

shoo-in *n esp Am Fam* **he's/she's a shoo-in** il/elle gagnera à coup sûr; **it's a shoo-in** c'est couru d'avance

shook [ʃʊk] **1** *pt of* **shake**
2 *n Agr* gerbe *f*, botte *f*

shook-up *adj Fam* bouleversé ❑

shoot [ʃuːt] *(pt & pp* **shot** [ʃɒt]) **1** *n* (**a**) *Bot (young plant)* pousse *f*; *(offshoot)* rejet *m*, scion *m*; *(of vine)* sarment *m*
(**b**) *Br Hunt (party)* partie *f* de chasse; *(land)* (terrain *m* de) chasse *f*; **he went on a pheasant shoot** il est allé chasser le faisan; **to rent a shoot** louer une chasse; **private shoot** *(sign)* chasse gardée
(**c**) *Am (chute → for coal, rubbish etc)* glissière *f*
(**d**) *Cin* tournage *m*
(**e**) *Phot* séance *f* photo, prise *f* de vues
(**f**) *Am (rapids)* rapide *m*
(**g**) *(shooting contest)* concours *m* de tir
(**h**) *Mil* tir *m*
(**i**) *Am Astron* tir *m*, lancement *m*
(**j**) *Fam (idiom)* **the whole (bang) shoot** tout le tremblement
2 *vt* (**a**) *(hit)* atteindre d'une balle; *(injure)* blesser par balle; *(kill)* tuer par balle; *(execute by firing squad)* fusiller; **he's been badly shot** il a été grièvement blessé par balle; **she was shot in the arm/leg** elle a reçu une balle dans le bras/la jambe; **to shoot sb through the head** tirer une balle dans la tête de qn; **she was shot through the heart** elle a été tuée d'une balle en plein cœur; **a man was shot (and killed) yesterday** un homme a été tué par balle hier; **they shot him (dead)** ils l'ont tué *ou* abattu; **to shoot oneself** se tuer, se tirer une balle; *Fam* **to shoot oneself in the foot** se desservir ❑; *Fig* **don't shoot the pianist** ne tirez pas sur le pianiste; **spies will be shot** les espions seront fusillés; *Fam Hum* **you'll get me shot** je vais me faire incendier à cause de toi
(**b**) *(fire → gun)* tirer un coup de; *(→ bullet)* tirer; *(→ arrow)* tirer, lancer, décocher; *(→ rocket, dart, missile)* lancer; **they were shooting their rifles in the air** ils tiraient des coups de feu en l'air; **to shoot holes in sb's argument/case** démonter les arguments/la théorie de qn; **to shoot questions at sb** bombarder *ou* mitrailler qn de questions; **to shoot a glance at sb** lancer *ou* décocher un regard à qn; **she shot a shy smile at him** elle lui jeta un petit sourire timide
(**c**) *(hunt)* chasser, tirer; **to shoot grouse** chasser la grouse
(**d**) *Cin* tourner; *Phot* prendre (en photo); **the movie was shot in Rome** le film a été tourné à Rome; **the photos were all shot on location in Paris** les photos ont toutes été prises à Paris; *TV & Cin* **to shoot sound** effectuer une prise de son
(**e**) *Sport & (games → play)* jouer; *(→ score)* marquer; **to shoot pool** jouer au billard américain; **to shoot dice** jouer aux dés; **to shoot a goal/basket** marquer un but/panier; *Golf* **he shot (a) 71 in the first round** il a fait 71 au premier tour
(**f**) *(send)* envoyer; **the explosion shot debris high into the air** l'explosion a projeté des débris dans les airs; **to shoot the ball into the net** envoyer le ballon dans les filets
(**g**) *(go through → rapids)* franchir; *Br (→ traffic lights)* brûler; **the car shot the lights** la voiture a brûlé le feu rouge
(**h**) *(bolt → close)* fermer; *(→ open)* ouvrir, tirer
(**i**) *Fam (drugs)* se shooter à; **to shoot heroin** se shooter à l'héroïne
(**j**) *(idioms) Am* **to shoot** *Fam* **the breeze** *or* **(the) bull** *or very Fam* **the shit** tailler une bavette, discuter le bout de gras; *Am* **to shoot (for) the moon** demander la lune; *Vulg* **to shoot one's load** *or* **wad** *(ejaculate)* tirer son coup, décharger
3 *vi* (**a**) *(with gun)* tirer; **shoot!** tirez!, feu!; **don't shoot!** ne tirez pas!; **shoot first and ask questions later** tirez d'abord et posez des questions ensuite; **to shoot at sb/sth** tirer sur qn/qch; **to shoot on sight** tirer à vue; **to shoot to kill** tirer pour tuer; **to shoot into the air** tirer en l'air; *Fig* **to shoot from the hip** parler franchement
(**b**) *(hunt)* chasser; **to go shooting** aller à la chasse; **do you shoot?** est-ce que vous chassez?
(**c**) *(go fast)* **to shoot in/past** entrer/passer en trombe; **she shot across the road** elle a traversé la rue comme une flèche; **he shot ahead of the other runners** il a rapidement distancé les autres coureurs; **she shot along the corridor** elle a couru à toutes jambes le long du couloir; **the bus was shooting along** le bus filait à toute vitesse; **shoot along to the baker's and get a loaf, will you?** est-ce que tu peux filer à la boulangerie acheter du pain?; **the rabbit shot into its burrow** le lapin s'est précipité dans son terrier; **debris shot into the air** des débris ont été projetés en l'air; **Paul has shot ahead at school recently** Paul a fait d'énormes progrès à l'école ces derniers temps; **a violent pain shot up my leg** j'ai senti une violente douleur dans la jambe; **I've got pains shooting through my shoulder** j'ai des élancements dans l'épaule
(**d**) *Cin* tourner; **shoot!** moteur!, on tourne!; **we'll begin shooting next week** nous commencerons à tourner la semaine prochaine
(**e**) *Sport* tirer, shooter
(**f**) *Bot (sprout)* pousser; *(bud)* bourgeonner
(**g**) *Fam (go ahead, speak)* **can I ask you something? – shoot!** je peux te poser une question? – vas-y! ❑
(**h**) *Am* **to shoot for** *or* **at** *(aim for)* viser
4 *exclam Am Fam* zut!, mince!
►**shoot back** **1** *vi* (**a**) *(fire back)* riposter; **a sniper shot at them and they shot back at him** un

tireur isolé leur a tiré dessus et ils ont riposté (**b**) *(return quickly)* revenir à toute vitesse

2 *vt sep (retort)* répliquer, riposter; **the candidate shot back his answers** le candidat répondait du tac au tac

▸**shoot down** *vt sep (person, plane, helicopter)* abattre; *also Fig* **to shoot sb/sth down in flames** descendre qn/qch en flammes; *Fam* **my proposal was shot down by the chairman** ma proposition a été démolie par le président; *Am Fam* **well, shoot me down! if it isn't Willy Power!** ça alors! mais c'est Willy Power!

▸**shoot off 1** *vt sep* (**a**) *(weapon)* tirer, décharger; **they shot off their rifles to celebrate their victory** ils ont tiré des coups de feu en l'air pour fêter la victoire; **she shot off a few rounds into the darkness** elle a tiré dans le noir; **he shot off an entire magazine** il a vidé son chargeur

(**b**) *(limb)* emporter, arracher

(**c**) *very Fam (idiom)* **to shoot one's mouth off** parler à tort et à travers; **I'd told him not to tell anyone but he had to go and shoot his mouth off** je lui avais dit de n'en parler à personne mais il a fallu qu'il ouvre sa grande gueule; **don't go shooting your mouth off about it** ne va pas le gueuler sur les toits; **they killed him to stop him shooting his mouth off to the police** ils l'ont tué pour l'empêcher d'aller cafter à la police

2 *vi* (**a**) *(leave quickly)* s'enfuir à toutes jambes; **he shot off down the alley** il s'est enfui à toutes jambes dans la ruelle

(**b**) *Vulg (ejaculate)* décharger

▸**shoot out 1** *vt sep* (**a**) *(extend quickly → sparks etc)* lancer; **the snake shot out its tongue** le serpent a dardé sa langue; **she shot out a hand** elle a étendu le bras d'un geste vif; **we were shot out of the car** nous avons été éjectés de la voiture

(**b**) *(use gun, destroy with gunshots → light, window)* tirer dans; **his right eye had been shot out** il avait perdu l'œil droit dans une fusillade; **the robbers tried to shoot their way out** les voleurs tentèrent de se sauver en tirant des coups de feu; *Fam* **to shoot it out (with sb)** s'expliquer (avec qn) à coups de revolver *ou* de fusil

2 *vi (emerge quickly → water, flames)* jaillir; **the water shot out of the hose** l'eau a jailli du tuyau d'arrosage; **I shot out after her** j'ai couru après elle; **the car shot out in front of us** *(changed lanes)* la voiture a déboîté tout d'un coup devant nous; *(from another street)* la voiture a débouché devant nous

▸**shoot through** *vi Br Fam* se tirer, mettre les bouts

▸**shoot up 1** *vi* (**a**) *(move skywards → flame, geyser, lava)* jaillir; *(→ rocket)* monter en flèche

(**b**) *(increase → inflation, price)* monter en flèche

(**c**) *(grow → plant)* pousser rapidement *ou* vite; *(→ person)* grandir; **you've really shot up since I last saw you!** qu'est-ce que tu as grandi depuis que je t'ai vu la dernière fois!

(**d**) *Fam (take drugs)* se shooter, se piquer

2 *vt sep* (**a**) *Fam (with weapon)* **they shot up the saloon/town** ils ont terrorisé tout le monde dans le saloon/la ville en tirant plein de coups de feu; **they shot the bar up** ils ont mitraillé le bar; **he was badly shot up in the war** il a été sérieusement blessé à la guerre❑; **he's been shot up** il a reçu des balles (dans la peau)

(**b**) *Fam (drug)* se faire un shoot de; *(habitually)* se shooter à, se piquer à

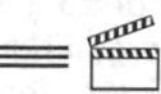

'They Shoot Horses, Don't They?' *Pollack* 'On achève bien les chevaux'

shoot-'em-up *n Fam* = film ou jeu vidéo ultra-violent

shooter ['ʃuːtə(r)] *n* (**a**) *Fam (gun)* flingue *m*, feu *m* (**b**) *(drink)* cocktail *m* servi dans un petit verre

shooting ['ʃuːtɪŋ] **1** *n* (**a**) *(UNCOUNT) (firing)* coups *mpl* de feu, fusillade *f*; **we heard a lot of shooting in the night** nous avons entendu de nombreux coups de feu dans la nuit

(**b**) *(incident)* fusillade *f*; *(killing)* meurtre *m*; **four people died in the shooting** quatre personnes ont trouvé la mort au cours de la fusillade; **there have been several shootings in the area** plusieurs personnes ont été tuées *ou* abattues dans le secteur

(**c**) *(ability to shoot)* tir *m*; **he's useless at shooting** il tire mal

(**d**) *(sport → at targets)* tir *m*; *Br (→ at birds, animals)* chasse *f*; **I've done a lot of shooting** j'ai beaucoup chassé

(**e**) *Cin* tournage; **shooting starts next week on her new movie** le tournage de son nouveau film commence la semaine prochaine

2 *comp* (**a**) *(with weapon)* **shooting incident** fusillade *f*; **shooting practice** entraînement *m* au tir

(**b**) *Hunt* de chasse; **the shooting season** la saison de la chasse; **he's not a shooting man** ce n'est pas un chasseur

3 *adj (pain)* lancinant

▸▸ *Br Aut* ***shooting brake*** break *m*; ***shooting gallery*** (**a**) *(at fairground)* stand *m* de tir (**b**) *Am Fam Drugs slang (for buying drugs)* = lieu où l'on achète, vend et consomme de la drogue; *Am Fam* ***shooting iron*** *(gun)* flingue *m*, feu *m*; *Hunt* ***shooting lodge*** pavillon *m* de chasse; ***shooting match*** concours *m* de tir; *Fam Fig* **the whole shooting match** *(things)* tout le bazar; *(people)* le ban et l'arrière-ban; *Hunt* ***shooting party*** partie *f* de chasse; ***shooting range*** champ *m* de tir; *Cin* ***shooting script*** découpage *m*; ***shooting star*** étoile *f* filante; ***shooting stick*** canne-siège *f*; ***shooting war*** guerre *f* chaude

shootist ['ʃuːtɪst] *n Am (person who shoots)* tireur(euse) *m,f*; *(marksman)* bon (bonne) tireur(euse) *m,f*

shoot-out *n Fam* fusillade❑ *f*; **there was a shoot-out at the saloon** il y a eu une fusillade *ou* un règlement de comptes au bar

shop [ʃɒp] *(pt & pp* **shopped**, *cont* **shopping**) **1** *n* (**a**) *Br (store)* magasin *m*; *(smaller)* boutique *f*; **she's gone out to the shops** elle est sortie faire des courses; **to have** *or* **to keep a shop** être propriétaire d'un magasin, tenir un magasin; **you can't get these in the shops** on ne les trouve pas en magasin; **would you mind the shop for me for a few hours?** est-ce que vous voulez bien me tenir le magasin pendant quelques heures?; **at the chemist's shop** chez le pharmacien, à la pharmacie; **at the fruit shop** chez le marchand de fruits, chez le fruitier, à la fruiterie; **the new book should reach the shops in July** le nouveau livre devrait être en vente en juillet; **to set up shop** ouvrir un magasin; *Fig* s'établir, s'installer; **he's set up shop as a freelance translator** il s'est installé comme traducteur indépendant; *also Fig* **to shut up shop** fermer boutique; *Fam* **all over the shop** *(everywhere)* partout❑; *(in disorder)* en pagaille; *Fam* **my notes are all over the shop** c'est la pagaille dans mes notes; *Fam* **they're all over the shop on defence policy** leur politique de défense n'est absolument pas cohérente❑; *Fam Fig* **you've come to the wrong shop** vous vous trompez de porte; **to talk shop** parler boutique

(**b**) *(shopping trip)* **to do one's weekly shop** faire les courses *ou* les achats de la semaine

(**c**) *Br (workshop)* atelier *m*; **the repair/paint/assembly shop** l'atelier de réparations/de peinture/de montage

2 *vi (for food, necessities)* faire les *ou* ses courses; *(for clothes, gifts etc)* faire les magasins, faire du shopping, *Can* magasiner; **he usually shops on Mondays** d'habitude, il fait ses courses le lundi; **I always shop at the local supermarket** je fais toujours mes courses *ou* mes achats au supermarché du coin; **to go shopping** faire des courses, courir les magasins; **I went shopping for a new dress** je suis allée faire les magasins pour m'acheter une nouvelle robe

3 *vt Br Fam (inform on)* dénoncer❑, balancer

▸▸ *Br* ***shop assistant*** vendeur(euse) *m,f* (de magasin), employé(e) *m,f* de magasin; ***shop floor*** *(place)* atelier *m*; ***the shop floor*** *(workers)* les ouvriers *mpl*; **he was on the shop floor for twenty-two years** il a travaillé vingt-deux ans comme ouvrier; ***shop foreman*** chef *m* d'atelier; *Br* ***shop front*** devanture *f*; ***shop steward*** porte-parole *mf inv* des ouvriers, délégué(e) *m,f* syndical(e); ***shop window*** vitrine *f* (de magasin); *Fig* **a shop window for British exports** une vitrine pour les exportations britanniques

▸**shop around** *vi* comparer les prix; **prices vary a lot, so shop around** les prix varient énormément, il vaut mieux faire plusieurs magasins avant d'acheter; **I shopped around before opening a bank account** j'ai comparé plusieurs banques *ou* je me suis renseigné auprès de plusieurs banques avant d'ouvrir un compte; **our company is shopping around for new premises** notre société est à la recherche de nouveaux locaux

shopaholic [ˌʃɒpə'hɒlɪk] *n* **he's a real shopaholic** il adore faire les boutiques

shopfitter ['ʃɒpˌfɪtə(r)] *n Br* décorateur(trice) *m,f* de magasins

shopfitting ['ʃɒpˌfɪtɪŋ] *n Br* décoration *f* de magasins

shop-floor *adj* **the decision was taken at shop-floor level** la décision a été prise par la base

▸▸ ***shop-floor worker*** ouvrier(ère) *m,f*

shopfront ['ʃɒpfrʌnt] *n Br* devanture *f* (de magasin)

shopgirl ['ʃɒpgɜːl] *n Br Old-fashioned* vendeuse *f*

shop-in-shop *n Com* boutiquage *m*, magasin *m* à l'intérieur d'une grande surface

shopkeeper ['ʃɒpˌkiːpə(r)] *n Br* commerçant(e) *m,f*; **small shopkeeper** petit(e) commerçant(e) *m,f*

shoplift ['ʃɒplɪft] *vt* voler à l'étalage

shoplifter ['ʃɒpˌlɪftə(r)] *n* voleur(euse) *m,f* à l'étalage

shoplifting ['ʃɒpˌlɪftɪŋ] *n* vol *m* à l'étalage

shopman ['ʃɒpmən] *(pl* **shopmen** [-men]) *n Am* mécanicien *m (dans un atelier de réparations)*

shopper ['ʃɒpə(r)] *n* (**a**) *(person)* personne *f* qui fait ses courses; **the streets were crowded with Christmas shoppers** les rues étaient bondées de gens qui faisaient leurs courses pour Noël; **for the convenience of shoppers** *(sign in shop)* pour mieux servir nos clients (**b**) *(shopping bag)* cabas *m*, sac *m* à provisions

shopping ['ʃɒpɪŋ] **1** *n (UNCOUNT)* (**a**) *(for food, necessities)* courses *fpl*; *(for clothes, gifts etc)* courses *fpl*, shopping *m*, *Can* magasinage *m*; **I do all the shopping** c'est moi qui fais toutes les courses; **we're going into town to do some shopping** nous allons en ville pour faire des courses *ou* pour faire le tour des magasins; **this area is good for shopping** ce quartier est bon pour faire les courses; **to do a bit of shopping** faire quelques (petites) courses *ou* emplettes; **to do one's Christmas shopping** faire ses achats de Noël; **there is late-night shopping on Thursdays** les magasins restent ouverts tard le jeudi

(**b**) *(goods bought)* achats *mpl*, courses *fpl*, emplettes *fpl*; **there were bags of shopping everywhere** il y avait des cabas remplis de provisions partout

2 *comp (street, area)* commerçant; **my weekly shopping trip** mes courses *fpl* hebdomadaires; **only three shopping days to Christmas** il ne reste plus que trois jours pour faire les courses avant Noël

▸▸ ***shopping arcade*** galerie *f* marchande; ***shopping bag*** sac *m ou* filet *m* à provisions, cabas *m*; ***shopping basket*** panier *m* (à provisions); *Econ* panier *m* de la ménagère; *Comput (for Internet shopping)* caddie *m*; *Am* ***shopping cart*** chariot *m*, Caddie® *m*; *Comput (for Internet shopping)* caddie *m*; ***shopping centre*** centre *m* commercial; *TV* ***shopping channel*** chaîne *f* de télé-achat; ***shopping list*** liste *f* des courses; *Am* ***shopping mall*** galerie *f* marchande; ***shopping plaza*** centre *m* commercial; *Br* ***shopping precinct*** centre *m* commercial; *Br* ***shopping trolley*** chariot *m*, Caddie® *m*

shopsoiled ['ʃɒpsɔɪld] *adj Br also Fig* défraîchi

shoptalk ['ʃɒptɔːk] *n* **all I ever hear from you is shoptalk** tu ne fais que parler boutique *ou* travail

shopwalker ['ʃɒpˌwɔːkə(r)] *n Br* = dans un grand magasin, personne chargée de renseigner les clients et de surveiller le travail des vendeurs

shopworn ['ʃɒpwɔːn] *adj Am also Fig* défraîchi

shoran ['ʃɔːræn] *n Tel* système *m* de navigation à courte portée *ou* de radionavigation shoran

shore [ʃɔː(r)] **1** *n* (**a**) *(edge, side → of sea)* rivage *m*, bord *m*; (→ *of lake, river*) rive *f*, rivage *m*, bord *m*; (*coast*) côte *f*, littoral *m*; **the shores of the Mediterranean** les rivages *mpl* de la Méditerranée; **can you see the houses on the other shore?** vois-tu les maisons sur l'autre rive?

(**b**) (*dry land*) terre *f*; **all the crew members are on shore** tous les membres de l'équipage sont à terre; **to go on shore** débarquer

(**c**) (*prop*) étai *m*, étançon *m*

2 *vt* étayer, étançonner

3 shores *npl Literary* (*country*) rives *fpl*; **he was one of the first Europeans to set foot on these shores** il fut l'un des premiers Européens à poser le pied sur ces rives; **this bird is a rare visitor to these shores** on observe rarement cet oiseau dans nos contrées

►► *Zool* ***shore crab*** crabe *m* vert *ou* enragé; *Am Culin* ***shore dinner*** repas *m* de poissons et de fruits de mer; ***shore excursion*** excursion *f* (*lors d'une escale*); *Orn* ***shore lark*** alouette *f* hausse-col, alouette *f* oreillarde; ***shore leave*** permission *f* à terre; *Am* ***shore patrol*** police *f* militaire (de la Marine)

►**shore up** *vt sep Br* (**a**) (*prop up*) étayer, étançonner (**b**) *Fig* soutenir; **the army shored up the crumbling dictatorship** l'armée a maintenu au pouvoir la dictature qui s'effondrait; **the government must act to shore up the pound** le gouvernement doit prendre des mesures visant à soutenir la livre

shorebird ['ʃɔːbɜːd] *n* oiseau *m* des rivages

shoreless ['ʃɔːlɪs] *adj Literary* (*ocean*) sans bornes

shoreline ['ʃɔːlaɪn] *n* littoral *m*

shoreward ['ʃɔːwəd] **1** *adj* (*near the shore*) près du rivage *ou* de la côte; (*facing the shore*) face au rivage *ou* à la côte

2 *adv* vers le rivage *ou* la côte

shorewards ['ʃɔːwədz] *adv* vers le rivage *ou* la côte

shorn [ʃɔːn] **1** *pp of* **shear**

2 *adj* (**a**) (*head, hair*) tondu (**b**) *Fig* **shorn of** dépouillé de

SHORT [ʃɔːt]

court-métrage	► **1 (a)**
court	► **2 (a), (c), (d)**
petit	► **2 (b)**
brusque	► **2 (f), (g)**
short	► **9 (a)**

1 *n* (**a**) *Cin* court-métrage *m*

(**b**) *Br* (*drink*) alcool *m* fort

(**c**) *Fam Elec* court-circuit❑ *m*

(**d**) (*in prosody* → *syllable*) brève *f*; *Ling* (→ *vowel*) voyelle *f* brève

(**e**) *St Exch* (*sale*) vente *f* à découvert; (*person*) vendeur(euse) *m,f* à découvert

2 *adj* (**a**) (*in length*) court; **her dress is too short/shorter than yours** sa robe est trop courte/plus courte que la tienne; **to have short hair** avoir les cheveux courts; *Fam Fig* **to have sb by the short hairs** *or Br* **by the short and curlies** avoir qn à sa merci❑, pouvoir faire ce qu'on veut de qn❑; **to be short in the leg** (*trousers*) être court; **it's short in the arms** (*jacket*) les manches sont trop courtes; **skirts are getting shorter and shorter** les jupes raccourcissent de plus en plus *ou* sont de plus en plus courtes; **the editor made the article shorter by a few hundred words** le rédacteur a raccourci l'article de quelques centaines de mots; **a short history of France** un précis d'histoire de France; **short and to the point** bref et précis; **to be in short trousers** être en culottes courtes; **short back and sides** (*haircut*) coupe *f* dégagée sur la nuque et les oreilles

(**b**) (*in height* → *person*) petit, de petite taille; **he's short and stocky** il est petit et râblé

(**c**) (*in distance* → *gen*) court; (→ *walk*) petit, court; **a straight line is the shortest distance between two points** la ligne droite est le plus court chemin entre deux points; **what's the shortest way home?** quel est le chemin le plus court pour rentrer?; **it's shorter this way** c'est plus court par ici; **we took the shortest route** nous avons pris le chemin le plus court; **to go for a short walk** faire une petite promenade; **a few short miles away** à quelques kilomètres de là à peine; **at short range** à courte portée; **how could he have missed at such short range?** comment a-t-il pu rater de si près?; **it's only a short distance from here** ce n'est pas très loin (d'ici); **she lives a short distance from the church** elle n'habite pas très loin de l'église; **they continued for a short distance** ils ont poursuivi un peu leur chemin; *Sport* **to win/to lose by a short head** gagner/perdre d'une courte tête

(**d**) (*not lasting long* → *period, interval*) court, bref; **a short stay** un court séjour; **you should take a short holiday** vous devriez prendre quelques jours de vacances; **we've just got time for a short game** nous avons juste le temps de faire une petite partie; **at short intervals** à intervalles rapprochés; **after a short time** après un court intervalle *ou* un petit moment; **to have a short memory** avoir la mémoire courte; **for a short time I thought of becoming an actress** pendant quelque temps, j'ai pensé devenir actrice; **she was in London for a short time** elle a passé quelque temps à Londres; **I met him a short time** *or* **while later** je l'ai rencontré peu (de temps) après; **it's rather short notice to invite them for tonight** c'est un peu juste pour les inviter ce soir; **time's getting short** il ne reste plus beaucoup de temps; **a few short hours/years ago** il y a à peine quelques heures/années; **the days are getting shorter** les jours raccourcissent; **to demand shorter hours/a shorter working week** exiger une réduction des heures de travail/une réduction du temps de travail hebdomadaire; **to be on short time** faire des journées réduites; **she made a short speech** elle a fait un court *ou* petit discours; **he read out a short statement** il a lu une courte *ou* brève déclaration; **I'd just like to say a few short words** j'aimerais dire quelques mots très brefs; **the short answer is "no"** en deux mots, la réponse est "non"; **in short order** en vitesse; **he dealt with the naughty children in short order** il a eu vite fait de s'occuper de ces enfants désobéissants; **to be short and sweet** être bref; **I'll keep it short and sweet** je serai bref; *Ironic* **her stay with us was short and sweet** heureusement, son séjour chez nous fut de courte durée; **in the short run** à court terme

(**e**) (*abbreviated*) **HF is short for high frequency** HF est l'abréviation de haute fréquence; **Bill is short for William** Bill est un diminutif de William

(**f**) (*gruff*) brusque, sec (sèche); **she tends to be a bit short with people** elle a tendance à être un peu brusque avec les gens; **Mary was very short with me on the telephone** Mary a été très sèche avec moi au téléphone; **to have a short temper** être irascible, s'emporter facilement

(**g**) (*sudden* → *sound, action*) brusque; **her breath came in short gasps** elle avait le souffle court; **he gave a short laugh** il eut un rire bref; **short, sharp shock** = punition sévère mais de courte durée; **short, sharp shock treatment** = régime pénal des années 80–90 où les jeunes délinquants étaient détenus pour une courte période dans des conditions très sévères destinées à décourager la récidive

(**h**) (*lacking, insufficient*) **to give sb short weight** ne pas donner le bon poids à qn; **money is short** on manque d'argent, l'argent manque; **whisky is in short supply** on manque *ou* on est à court de whisky; **it is 2 francs short** il manque 2 francs; **I am 20 francs short** il me manque 20 francs; **to be short of breath** (*in general*) avoir le souffle court; (*at the moment*) être hors d'haleine; **to be short of staff** manquer de personnel; **to be short of sleep** n'avoir pas assez dormi; **I'm a bit short (of money) at the moment** je suis un peu à court (d'argent) en ce moment; **he's a bit short on imagination** il manque un peu d'imagination; *Fam Hum* **he's one sandwich short of a picnic** il a une case vide

(**i**) *Br* (*drink*) **a short drink** un petit verre

(**j**) *Ling* bref

(**k**) *Fin & St Exch* (*sale, seller*) à découvert; **bills at short date** billets *mpl ou* traites *fpl* à courte échéance

(**l**) *Culin* (*pastry*) brisé

(**m**) (*in betting* → *odds*) faible

3 *adv* (**a**) (*abruptly*) **to stop short** s'arrêter net; **the driver stopped short just in front of the child** le conducteur s'arrêta net juste devant l'enfant; **to stop short of doing sth** se retenir de faire qch; **she stopped short of actually calling him a liar** pour un peu, elle le traitait de menteur; **to pull** *or* **to bring sb up short** couper qn dans son élan

(**b**) (*idioms*) **to fall short of** (*objective, target*) ne pas atteindre; (*expectations*) ne pas répondre à; **his winnings fell far short of what he had expected** ses gains ont été bien moindres que ce à quoi il s'attendait; **to go short of sth** manquer de qch; **my children never went short (of anything)** mes enfants n'ont jamais manqué de rien; **I don't want you to go short** je ne veux pas que tu manques de quoi que ce soit; **to run short (of sth)** être à court (de qch); **we're running short of fuel/money/sugar** nous sommes presque à court de carburant/d'argent/de sucre; **supplies are running short** les provisions sont presque épuisées; **time is running short** le temps commence à manquer; *Br Fam* **to be taken** *or* **caught short** être pris d'un besoin pressant❑

(**c**) *St Exch* **to buy short** acheter à court terme; **to sell short** vendre à découvert

4 *vt Elec* court-circuiter

5 *vi Elec* se mettre en court-circuit

6 for short *adv* **they call him Ben for short** on l'appelle Ben pour faire plus court; **trinitrotoluene, or TNT for short** le trinitrotoluène ou TNT en abrégé

7 in short *adv* (en) bref

8 short of *prep* (**a**) (*except*) sauf; **he would do anything short of stealing** il ferait tout sauf voler; **nothing short of a miracle can save him now** seul un miracle pourrait le sauver maintenant; **short of resigning, what can I do?** à part démissionner, que puis-je faire?

(**b**) (*less than*) **they were £50 short of their target** il leur manquait 50 livres pour atteindre la somme qu'ils s'étaient fixée; **he is not far short of thirty** il frise la trentaine; **it is little short of folly** c'est de la folie (pure); **it was nothing short of a masterpiece** ce n'était rien moins qu'un chef-d'œuvre

9 shorts *npl* (**a**) (*short trousers*) short *m*; (*underpants*) caleçon *m*; **a pair of khaki shorts** un short kaki; *Am Fam* **eat my shorts!** tu me gonfles!

(**b**) *St Exch* valeurs *fpl* à courte échéance

(**c**) *Fam* **to have the shorts** (*have little money*) être fauché, être raide

►► *Fin & St Exch* ***short bills*** billets *mpl ou* traites *fpl* à courte échéance; *Austr* ***short black*** café *m* express, express *m*; ***short break*** (*holiday*) mini-séjour *m*; *Elec* ***short circuit*** court-circuit *m*; *St Exch* ***short covering*** couverture *f* de position; *Math* ***short division*** division *f* à un ou deux chiffres; ***short game*** (*in golf*) petit jeu *m*; *Fin & St Exch* ***short investment*** investissement *m* à court terme; *Fin & St Exch* ***short loan*** prêt *m* à court terme; *Culin* ***short pastry*** pâte *f* brisée; *Fin* ***short payment*** moins-perçu *m*; *Fin & St Exch* ***short position*** position *f* vendeur, position *f* à découvert; *Literature* ***short story*** nouvelle *f*; *Ling* ***short syllable*** syllabe *f* brève; ***short tennis*** tennis *m* pour enfants; ***short ton*** tonne *f* (américaine), short ton *f*; *Ling* ***short vowel*** voyelle *f* brève; *Rad* ***short wave*** onde *f* courte; **on short wave** sur ondes courtes

shortage ['ʃɔːtɪdʒ] *n* (*of labour, resources, materials*) manque *m*, pénurie *f*; (*of money*) manque *m*; **a petrol shortage, a shortage of petrol** une pénurie d'essence; **the housing/energy shortage** la crise du logement/de l'énergie; **food shortage** disette *f*, pénurie *f* de vivres; **there's no shortage of good restaurants in this part of town** les bons restaurants ne manquent pas dans ce quartier

short-arse *n Br very Fam* rase-bitume *mf*, bas-du-cul *mf*

shortbread ['ʃɔːtbred] *n Culin* sablé *m*

►► *Br* ***shortbread biscuit*** sablé *m*

shortcake ['ʃɔːtkeɪk] *n* (**a**) *Br Culin* (*biscuit*) sablé *m* (**b**) (*cake*) tarte *f* sablée

short-change *vt* (**a**) **to short-change sb** ne pas rendre assez (de monnaie) à qn (**b**) *Fam* (*swindle*) rouler, escroquer❑

short-circuit 1 *vt Elec & Fig* court-circuiter
2 *vi Elec* se mettre en court-circuit

shortcoming ['ʃɔːt,kʌmɪŋ] *n* défaut *m*

shortcrust pastry ['ʃɔːtkrʌst-] *n Culin* pâte *f* brisée

shortcut ['ʃɔːtkʌt] *n* raccourci *m*; **to take a shortcut** prendre un raccourci; *Fig* **there are no shortcuts** il n'y a pas moyen d'aller plus vite
►► *Comput* ***shortcut key*** touche *f* de raccourci

short-cycle *adj Sch* à cycle court (sans obtention d'un diplôme)

short-dated *adj Fin (bill)* à courte échéance; *(paper)* court

short-eared owl *n Orn* hibou *m* des marais

shorten ['ʃɔːtən] **1** *vt* (**a**) *(in length → garment, string)* raccourcir; *(→ text, article, speech)* raccourcir, abréger; **the name James is often shortened to Jim** Jim est un diminutif courant de James
(**b**) *(in time)* écourter; **we had to shorten our trip** nous avons dû écourter notre voyage; **the new railway line will shorten the journey time to London** la nouvelle ligne de chemin de fer réduira le temps de trajet jusqu'à Londres
(**c**) *Culin* **to shorten pastry** travailler la pâte avec une matière grasse
2 *vi* (**a**) *(gen)* (se) raccourcir
(**b**) *(in betting → odds)* devenir moins favorable

shortening ['ʃɔːtənɪŋ] *n* (**a**) *Culin* matière *f* grasse (**b**) *(of garment, string)* raccourcissement *m*; *(of text, speech)* raccourcissement *m*, abrègement *m*; *(of time, distance)* réduction *f*

shortfall ['ʃɔːtfɔːl] *n* insuffisance *f*, manque *m*; **there's a shortfall of $100** il manque 100 dollars; **a shortfall in coal supplies was expected** on prévoyait que les réserves de charbon seraient insuffisantes

short-focus lens *n Phot* objectif *m* à courte focale

short-haired *adj (person)* aux cheveux courts; *(animal)* à poil ras

shorthand ['ʃɔːthænd] *n* sténographie *f*, sténo *f*; **to take notes in shorthand** prendre des notes en sténo; *Fig* **this term has become shorthand for corruption** ce terme est devenu synonyme de corruption
►► ***shorthand typing*** sténodactylographie *f*; ***shorthand typist*** sténodactylo *mf*

shorthanded [,ʃɔːt'hændɪd] *adj* à court de personnel; **we're very shorthanded at the moment** nous sommes vraiment à court *ou* nous manquons vraiment de personnel en ce moment

short-haul *adj (flight, route, aircraft)* court-courrier
►► ***short-haul aircraft*** court-courrier *m*

shorthorn ['ʃɔːthɔːn] *n Zool* shorthorn *m (race de bovins)*

shortie ['ʃɔːtɪ] *n* (**a**) *Fam* = **shorty** (**b**) *(nightdress)* chemise *f* de nuit courte, nuisette *f*

shortish ['ʃɔːtɪʃ] *adj (in length)* plutôt court; *(in height)* plutôt petit; *(in time)* plutôt court *ou* bref

short-legged *adj* aux jambes courtes

shortlist ['ʃɔːtlɪst] *Br* **1** *n* liste *f* de candidats présélectionnés
2 *vt* présélectionner; **five candidates have been shortlisted** cinq candidats ont été présélectionnés; **you've been shortlisted** on a retenu votre candidature

short-lived [-'lɪvd] *adj (gen)* de courte durée, éphémère, bref; *(animal, species)* éphémère

shortly ['ʃɔːtlɪ] *adv* (**a**) *(soon)* bientôt; *(in a couple of minutes)* sous peu; **I'll join you shortly** je vous rejoindrai bientôt; **shortly afterwards** peu (de temps) après; **President Smith who was shortly to be** *or* **would shortly be re-elected** le président Smith qui allait bientôt être réélu (**b**) *(gruffly)* sèchement, brusquement (**c**) *(briefly → answer)* brièvement, en peu de mots

shortness ['ʃɔːtnɪs] *n* (**a**) *(in length)* manque *m* de longueur; *(in height)* petite taille *f* (**b**) *(in time)* brièveté *f*; *(of speech, essay)* brièveté (**c**) *(abruptness)* brusquerie *f*

short-order cook *n* = cuisinier qui prépare les plats au fur et à mesure des commandes

short-range *adj* (**a**) *(weapon)* de courte portée; *(vehicle, aircraft)* à rayon d'action limité (**b**) *(prediction, outlook)* à court terme

shortsheet ['ʃɔːtʃiːt] *vt Am (bed)* = refaire de façon à ce que le drap de dessus ne couvre pas les pieds

shortsighted [,ʃɔːt'saɪtɪd] *adj* (**a**) *(myopic)* myope (**b**) *Fig (person)* qui manque de perspicacité *ou* de prévoyance; *(plan, policy)* à courte vue; **I find their attitude extremely shortsighted** je trouve qu'ils font preuve d'un manque total de prévoyance

shortsightedly [,ʃɔːt'saɪtɪdlɪ] *adv* (**a**) **he peered shortsightedly at the book** il scruta le livre de ses yeux myopes (**b**) *Fig* **to act shortsightedly** agir sans prévoyance

shortsightedness [,ʃɔːt'saɪtɪdnɪs] *n* (**a**) *(myopia)* myopie *f* (**b**) *Fig* myopie *f*, manque *m* de perspicacité *ou* de prévoyance

short-sleeved *adj* à manches courtes

short-staffed [-'stɑːft] *adj* à court de personnel; **we're a bit short-staffed** nous sommes un peu à court de *ou* nous manquons un peu de personnel

short-stay *adj*
►► ***short-stay car park*** parking *m* courte durée; ***short-stay patient*** patient(e) *m,f* hospitalisé(e) pour une courte durée

short-stemmed *adj Bot* brévicaule

short-tail *n Orn* brève *f*, grive *f* superbe

short-tailed [-teɪld] *adj Zool* brévicaude

short-tempered *adj* irascible, irritable

short-term *adj (solution, memory)* à court terme; *(contract)* de courte durée; *(prisoner)* qui purge une peine de prison de courte durée
►► ***short-term borrowings*** emprunts *mpl* à court terme; ***short-term contract*** contrat *m* à courte durée; ***short-term credit*** crédit *m* (à) court terme; ***short-term debt*** dette *f* à court terme; ***short-term financing*** financement *m* à court terme; ***short-term loan*** prêt *m* à court terme; ***short-term maturity*** échéance *f* à court terme

short-termism [-'tɜːmɪzəm] *n Br* politique *f* du court terme

short-time 1 *n* **to be on short-time** être en chômage partiel
2 *adj* **to be on short-time working** être en chômage partiel

short-toed treecreeper *n Orn* grimpereau *m* des jardins

short-track speed skating *n Sport* patinage *m* de vitesse sur courte piste, short-track *m*

short-waisted *adj (person)* court de poitrine, qui a le buste court; *(dress, jacket)* à taille haute

short-wave *adj (radio)* à ondes courtes; *(programme, broadcasting)* sur ondes courtes

short-winded [-'wɪndɪd] *adj* au souffle court; **to be short-winded** manquer de souffle

shorty ['ʃɔːtɪ] *(pl* **shorties***)* *n Fam* rase-bitume *mf*, bas-du-cul *mf*; **hey, shorty!** hé, rase-bitume!

Shostakovich [,ʃɒstə'kəʊvɪtʃ] *pr n* Chostakovitch

shot [ʃɒt] **1** *pt & pp of* **shoot**
2 *n* (**a**) *(instance of firing)* coup *m* (de feu); **he fired four shots** il a tiré quatre coups de feu; **to have** *or* **to fire** *or* **to take a shot at sth** tirer sur qch; **he hit it with his first shot** il l'a atteint du premier coup; *also Fig* **a shot across the bows** un coup de semonce; *Fig* **it was a shot in the dark** j'ai/il a/*etc* dit ça au hasard; *Fam* **to do sth like a shot** *(speedily)* faire qch à tout berzingue, *(with no hesitation)* faire qch sans hésiter❑; *Fam* **the dog was off like a shot** le chien est parti comme une flèche; *Fam* **would you marry him? – like a shot!** est-ce que tu l'épouserais? – sans hésiter❑ *ou* et comment!; *Fam* **I'd accept the offer like a shot** j'accepterais l'offre sans la moindre hésitation❑; *Hist* **the shot heard around the world** = expression évoquant le début de la guerre de l'Indépendance américaine
(**b**) *(sound of gun)* coup *m* de feu; **I was woken by a shot** j'ai été réveillé par un coup de feu
(**c**) *(UNCOUNT) (shotgun pellets)* plomb *m*, plombs *mpl*
(**d**) *(marksman)* tireur(euse) *m,f*, fusil *m*; **she's a good shot** c'est une excellente tireuse, elle tire bien; **she's a poor shot** elle tire mal
(**e**) *Sport (at goal → in football, hockey etc)* tir *m*; *(stroke → in tennis, cricket, billiards etc)* coup *m*; *(throw → in darts)* lancer *m*; **his first shot at goal hit the post** son premier tir a touché le poteau; **each player has three shots** chaque joueur joue trois fois; **good shot!** bien joué!; **to call the shots** mener le jeu; *Am Fam* **to call one's shot** annoncer la couleur
(**f**) *Sport* **to put the shot** lancer le poids
(**g**) *Astron (launch)* tir *m*
(**h**) *Phot* photo *f*; *Cin* plan *m*, prise *f* de vue; **you can get a good shot of the castle from here** d'ici vous prendrez bien le château; **the opening shots of the movie** les premières images *fpl* du film
(**i**) *Fam (try)* tentative❑ *f*, essai❑ *m*; **I'd like to have a shot at it** j'aimerais tenter le coup; **it's worth having a shot at** ça vaut le coup; **give it your best shot** fais pour le mieux; **I gave it my best shot** j'ai fait ce que j'ai pu
(**j**) *Fam (injection)* piqûre❑ *f*; **tetanus shot** piqûre *f* antitétanique; *Fig* **a shot in the arm** un coup de fouet
(**k**) *(drink)* (petit) verre *m*; **have a shot of vodka** prenez un petit verre de vodka
(**l**) *Am Fam* **the whole shot** tout le tremblement
3 *adj* (**a**) *Br (rid) Fam* **to get shot of sb/sth** se débarrasser de qn/qch❑; **I'll be glad to be shot of them** je serai content d'en être débarrassé; **I can't wait to be shot of this house** j'ai hâte de me débarrasser de cette maison
(**b**) *(streaked)* strié; **her dress was of a deep red shot through with gold** sa robe était rouge foncé avec des stries dorées; *Fig* **the book is shot through with subtle irony** le livre est plein d'une ironie subtile
(**c**) *esp Am Fam (exhausted)* épuisé❑, crevé; *(broken, spoilt)* fichu, bousillé; **my nerves are shot** je suis à bout de nerfs; **that's another day shot!** une autre journée de foutue (en l'air)!
►► ***shot glass*** petit verre *m*; *Sport* ***shot put*** lancer *m* du poids; *Sport* ***shot putter*** lanceur(euse) *m,f* de poids; *Sport* ***shot putting*** (lancer *m* du) poids *m*; *Tex* ***shot silk*** soie *f* changeante

> **THE SHOT HEARD AROUND THE WORLD**
> 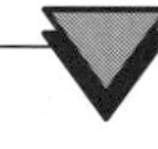
>
> C'est le titre d'un poème de Ralph Waldo Emerson, en hommage au premier coup de feu échangé entre les "Minutemen" américains et les forces anglaises, en avril 1775, à Lexington. L'écrivain y loue la détermination des colons et salue l'avènement d'une nouvelle nation.

shotblasting ['ʃɒt,blɑːstɪŋ] *n Tech* grenaillage *m*, décapage *m* au jet d'abrasif

shote = **shoat**

shotgun ['ʃɒtgʌn] **1** *n (weapon)* fusil *m* de chasse
2 *adj (forced)* forcé; **a shotgun merger** une fusion imposée
3 *adv Am* **to ride shotgun** voyager comme passager
►► *Am* ***shotgun house*** = maison sur un seul étage, traversée par un couloir sur toute la longueur; ***shotgun wedding*** mariage *m* forcé *(lorsque la future mariée est enceinte)*

SHOULD [ʃʊd]

> La forme négative **should not** s'écrit **shouldn't** en forme contractée

modal aux v (**a**) *(indicating duty, necessity)* **I should be working, not talking to you** je devrais être en train de travailler au lieu de parler avec vous; **papers should not exceed ten pages** les devoirs ne devront pas dépasser dix pages; **you really should call her, you know** tu devrais l'appeler, tu sais; **they should be severely punished** ils devraient être sévèrement punis
(**b**) *(indicating likelihood)* **they should have arrived by now** ils devraient être arrivés maintenant; **I should have finished the work yesterday** j'aurais dû finir ce travail hier; **the election results should be out soon** on devrait bientôt connaître les résultats des élections
(**c**) *(indicating what is acceptable, desirable etc)* **I should never have married him** je n'aurais jamais dû l'épouser; **you shouldn't have done that!** tu n'aurais pas dû faire ça!; **a present?, oh you shouldn't have!** un cadeau?, vous n'auriez pas dû! *ou* il ne fallait pas!; **you shouldn't laugh at him** vous avez tort de vous moquer de lui;

you should have seen the state of the house! si tu avais vu dans quel état était la maison!; **you should hear the way he talks!** il faut voir comment il s'exprime!; **should he tell her? – yes he should** est-ce qu'il devrait le lui dire? – oui, sans aucun doute; **I'm very sorry – and so you should be!** je suis vraiment désolé – il y a de quoi!; **why shouldn't I enjoy myself now and then?** pourquoi est-ce que je n'aurais pas le droit de m'amuser de temps en temps?; **I don't remember – well you should** je ne m'en souviens pas – eh bien tu devrais; **I didn't want to, but he told me I should** je ne voulais pas, mais il m'a dit que je devais le faire; **I should perhaps say, at this point, that…** à ce stade, je devrais peut-être dire que… + *indicative*

(**d**) *(forming conditional tense) (would)* **I should like to meet your parents** j'aimerais rencontrer vos parents; **if I were you I should apologize** si j'étais à votre place, je présenterais mes excuses; **had you written to me I should have answered you** si vous m'aviez écrit, je vous aurais répondu; **I shouldn't be surprised if they got married** cela ne m'étonnerait pas qu'ils se marient; **I should say** *or* **think it costs about £50** je dirais que ça coûte dans les 50 livres; **I should have thought the answer was obvious** j'aurais pensé que la réponse était évidente; **should you be interested, I know a good hotel there** si cela vous intéresse, je connais un bon hôtel là-bas; **how should I know?** comment voulez-vous que je le sache?; **I should think so/not!** j'espère bien/bien que non!

(**e**) *(were to → indicating hypothesis, speculation)* **if I should forget, should I forget** si (jamais) j'oublie; **I'll be upstairs should you need me** je serai en haut si (jamais) vous avez besoin de moi; **suppose nobody should come?** et si personne ne venait?; **should the occasion arise** le cas échéant; *Literary* **lest it should rain** de crainte *ou* de peur qu'il ne pleuve

(**f**) *(after "that" and in expressions of feeling, opinion etc)* **it's strange (that) she should do that** c'est bizarre qu'elle fasse cela; **I'm anxious that she should come** je tiens à ce qu'elle vienne; **we decided we should meet at the station** nous avons décidé de nous retrouver à la gare

(**g**) *(after "who" or "what") (expressing surprise)* **and who should I meet but Betty!** et sur qui je tombe? Betty!

(**h**) *Fam Ironic (needn't)* **he should worry (about money), he owns half of Manhattan!** tu parles qu'il a des soucis d'argent, la moitié de Manhattan lui appartient!; **I should worry!** ce n'est pas mon affaire!

---

shoulda [ˈʃʊdə] *Fam* = **should have**

shoulder [ˈʃəʊldə(r)] **1** *n* (**a**) *(part of body, of garment)* épaule *f*; **he's got broad shoulders** il est large d'épaules; **round shoulders** dos *m* rond *ou* voûté; **it's a bit big on the shoulders** c'est un peu large aux épaules *ou* de carrure; **she put an arm around my shoulder** elle mit son bras autour de mon épaule; **slung across** *or* **over the shoulder** *(bag, rifle etc)* en bandoulière; **you can carry it over your shoulder** tu peux le porter en bandoulière; **put a jacket over your shoulders** mets une veste sur tes épaules; **I looked over my shoulder** j'ai jeté un coup d'œil derrière moi; **it's a heavy burden to place on his shoulders** c'est une lourde charge à mettre sur ses épaules; *Fig* **to cry on sb's shoulder** pleurer sur l'épaule de qn; **we all need a shoulder to cry on** nous avons tous besoin d'une épaule pour pleurer; **to have a good head on one's shoulders** avoir la tête sur les épaules; *Fig* **to put one's shoulder to the wheel** s'atteler à la tâche; **to stand shoulder to shoulder** être coude à coude

(**b**) *Culin* épaule *f*; **shoulder of lamb** épaule *f* d'agneau

(**c**) *(along road)* accotement *m*, bas-côté *m*

(**d**) *(of hill, mountain)* replat *m*; *(of bottle)* renflement *m*

2 *vt* (**a**) *(pick up)* charger sur son épaule; **she shouldered the heavy load** elle chargea le lourd fardeau sur son épaule; **to shoulder one's gun** mettre son fusil sur l'épaule; *Mil* **to shoulder arms** se mettre au port d'armes; *Mil* **shoulder arms!** portez armes!

(**b**) *Fig (take on → blame)* assumer; *(→ responsibility)* endosser, assumer; *(→ cost)* faire face à

(**c**) *(push)* pousser (de l'épaule); **he shouldered me aside** il m'écarta d'un coup d'épaule; **I shouldered my way through the crowd** je me suis frayé un chemin à travers la foule (en jouant des épaules)

▸▸ ***shoulder bag*** sac *m* à bandoulière; ***shoulder belt*** ceinture *f* épaulière; ***shoulder blade*** omoplate *f*; *(of horse etc)* paleron *m*; *Mil* ***shoulder braid*** fourragère *f*; ***shoulder charge*** charge *f* épaule contre épaule; ***shoulder holster*** holster *m*; *Am Mil* ***shoulder loop*** patte *f* d'épaule, épaulette *f*; ***shoulder pad*** *(in garment)* épaulette *f* *(coussinet de rembourrage)*; *Sport* protège-épaule *m*; ***shoulder rate*** *(in tourism)* tarif *m* moyenne saison; ***shoulder season*** *(in tourism)* moyenne saison *f*; ***shoulder strap*** *(on dress, bra, accordion)* bretelle *f*; *(on bag)* bandoulière *f*; *Mil* patte *f* d'épaule, épaulette *f*

shoulder-charge *vt* charger épaule contre épaule

shoulder-high 1 *adj* qui arrive (jusqu') à l'épaule; **we pushed through the shoulder-high grass** nous nous frayâmes un chemin dans l'herbe qui nous arrivait (jusqu') à l'épaule

2 *adv* **to carry sb shoulder-high** porter qn en triomphe

shoulder-length *adj (hair)* mi-long, qui arrive (jusqu')aux épaules

shouldn't [ˈʃʊdənt] = **should not**

should've [ˈʃʊdəv] = **should have**

shout [ʃaʊt] **1** *n* (**a**) *(cry)* cri *m*, hurlement *m*; **I heard a shout of joy** j'ai entendu un cri de joie; *Fam* **give me a shout if you need a hand** appelle-moi si tu as besoin d'un coup de main; *Fam* **give me a shout over the weekend** *(phone me)* appelle-moi ce week-end

(**b**) *Br & Austr Fam (round of drinks)* tournée ❑ *f*; **whose shout is it?** c'est à qui de payer la tournée?; **it's my shout** c'est ma tournée

2 *vi* (**a**) *(cry out)* crier, hurler; **there's no need to shout, I can hear you** pas besoin de crier comme ça, je ne suis pas sourd; **to shout at the top of one's voice** crier à tue-tête; **to shout (out) for help** appeler au secours; **he shouted (out) to her to be careful** il lui a crié de faire attention; **he shouted at me for being late** il a crié parce que j'étais en retard; **don't shout at me!** baisse le ton!; *Fig* **it's nothing to shout about** *(to boast about)* il n'y a pas de quoi se vanter; *Fam* **my new job is nothing to shout about** mon nouveau travail n'a rien de bien passionnant ❑

(**b**) *Austr Fam (pay for drinks)* **I'll shout** c'est ma tournée ❑

3 *vt* (**a**) *(cry out)* crier; **the sergeant shouted (out) an order** le sergent hurla un ordre; **they shouted themselves hoarse** ils crièrent jusqu'à en perdre la voix

(**b**) *Br & Austr Fam (treat)* **to shout sb a meal** inviter qn ❑

▸**shout down** *vt sep (speaker)* empêcher de parler en criant; *(speech)* couvrir par des cris; **she was shouted down** les gens ont hurlé tellement fort qu'elle n'a pas pu parler

shouter [ˈʃaʊtə(r)] *n* crieur(euse) *m,f*

shouting [ˈʃaʊtɪŋ] *n (UNCOUNT)* cris *mpl*, vociférations *fpl*; **within shouting distance** à deux pas, tout près; *Fig* **it's all over bar the shouting** l'affaire est dans le sac

shove [ʃʌv] **1** *vt* (**a**) *(push)* pousser; *(push roughly)* pousser sans ménagement; *(insert, stick)* enfoncer; **we shoved all the furniture up against the walls** nous avons poussé tous les meubles contre les murs; **he shoved me out of the way** il m'a écarté sans ménagement; **she shoved him down the stairs** elle l'a poussé dans les escaliers; **he shoved an elbow into my ribs** il m'enfonça son coude dans les côtes

(**b**) *Fam (put hurriedly or carelessly)* mettre ❑, flanquer, ficher; **shove it in the drawer** fiche-le dans le tiroir; **shove a few good quotes in and it'll be fine** tu y ajoutes quelques citations bien choisies et ce sera parfait

2 *vi* (**a**) *(push)* pousser; *(jostle)* se bousculer; **people kept pushing and shoving** les gens n'arrêtaient pas de se bousculer; **stop shoving!** arrêtez de pousser!; **she shoved past me** elle m'a bousculé en passant

(**b**) *Br Fam (move up)* se pousser ❑; **shove up** *or* **over** *or* **along a bit** pousse-toi un peu

3 *n* (**a**) *(push)* poussée *f*; **to give sb/sth a shove** pousser qn/qch; *Fig* **he's lazy, he just needs a little shove** il est paresseux, il a juste besoin qu'on le pousse un peu

(**b**) *Fam (idioms)* **to give sb the shove** sacquer qn; **to get the shove** se faire sacquer

▸**shove about, shove around** *vt sep (jostle)* bousculer; *(mistreat)* malmener; **don't let him shove you about!** ne le laisse pas te marcher sur les pieds!

▸**shove off 1** *vi* (**a**) *Fam (go away)* se casser, se tirer; **shove off, I'm busy!** casse-toi, je suis occupé! (**b**) *(boat)* pousser au large

2 *vt sep (boat)* pousser au large, déborder

shove-halfpenny *n* jeu *m* de palet de table

shovel [ˈʃʌvəl] *(Br pt & pp* **shovelled,** *cont* **shovelling,** *Am pt & pp* **shoveled,** *cont* **shoveling) 1** *n* pelle *f*; *(on excavating machine)* pelle *f*, godet *m*; **coal shovel** pelle *f* mécanique

2 *vt (coal, earth, sand)* pelleter; *(snow)* déblayer (à la pelle); **they shovelled the gravel onto the drive** avec une pelle, ils ont répandu les gravillons sur l'allée; **shovel all that rubble into a corner** prenez une pelle et mettez tous ces gravats dans un coin; *Fam* **to shovel food into one's mouth** enfourner de la nourriture; *Fam* **he shovelled his meal down** il a englouti son repas

▸**shovel up** *vt sep* ramasser *ou* entasser à la pelle

shoveler [ˈʃʌvələ(r)] *n Orn* souchet *m*

shovelful [ˈʃʌvəlfʊl] *n* pelletée *f*

shovelling [ˈʃʌvəlɪŋ] *n* pellage *m*, pelletage *m*; **shovelling up** ramassage *m* à la pelle; **shovelling (away)** *(of snow)* déblaiement *m*

SHOW [ʃəʊ]

démonstration	▸ **1 (a)**
semblant	▸ **1 (a)**
ostentation	▸ **1 (a)**
spectacle	▸ **1 (b)**
émission	▸ **1 (b)**
exposition	▸ **1 (c)**
foire	▸ **1 (c)**
montrer	▸ **2 (a) – (c), (e), (f)**
présenter	▸ **2 (a)**
exposer	▸ **2 (a)**
faire preuve de	▸ **2 (b)**
marquer	▸ **2 (d)**
indiquer	▸ **2 (d), (f)**
enregistrer	▸ **2 (h)**
passer	▸ **2 (i); 3 (b)**
se voir	▸ **3 (a)**

(pt **showed,** *pp* **shown** [ʃəʊn]) **1** *n* (**a**) *(demonstration, display)* démonstration *f*, manifestation *f*; *(pretence)* semblant *m*, simulacre *m*; *(ostentation)* ostentation *f*, parade *f*; **a show of strength/unity** une démonstration de force/d'unité; **a show of hands** un vote à main levée; **she put on a show of indifference** elle a fait semblant d'être indifférente; **to make a show of being angry** faire semblant *ou* faire mine d'être fâché; **to make a great show of friendship** faire de grandes démonstrations d'amitié; **show of generosity** affectation *f* de générosité; **it's all a show** ce n'est qu'une façade; **he always makes such a show of his knowledge** il faut toujours qu'il fasse étalage de ses connaissances; **the metal strips are just for show** les bandes métalliques ont une fonction purement décorative

(**b**) *Theat* spectacle *m*; *TV & Rad* émission *f*; **to go to a show** aller au spectacle; **we went to a restaurant after the show** nous sommes allés au restaurant après le spectacle; **variety show** émission *f* de variétés; **the show must go on** le spectacle continue; *Fig* il faut continuer; *Fig* **let's get this show on the road!** allez, c'est parti *ou* on y va!; **to make a show of oneself** se donner en spectacle

(**c**) *(exhibition)* exposition *f*; *(trade fair)* foire *f*, salon *m*; **have you been to the Picasso show?** avez-vous visité l'exposition Picasso?; **to be on**

show être exposé; **I dislike most of the paintings on show** je n'aime pas la plupart des tableaux exposés; **the agricultural/motor show** le salon de l'agriculture/de l'auto

(**d**) *Fam (business, affair)* affaire❑ *f*; **she planned and ran the whole show** c'est elle qui a tout organisé et qui s'est occupée de tout❑; **it's up to you, it's your show** c'est à toi de décider❑, c'est toi le chef

(**e**) *(performance)* performance *f*, prestation *f*; **the team put up a good show** l'équipe s'est bien défendue; **it's a pretty poor show when your own mother forgets your birthday** c'est un peu triste que ta propre mère oublie ton anniversaire; *Old-fashioned* **(jolly) good show, Henry!** bravo, Henry!

2 *vt* (**a**) *(display, present → gen)* montrer, faire voir; *(→ passport, ticket)* présenter; *(exhibit → work of art, prize, produce)* exposer; **to show sth to sb, to show sb sth** montrer qch à qn; **show me your presents** fais-moi voir *ou* montre-moi tes cadeaux; **you have to show your pass/your ticket on the way in** il faut présenter son laissez-passer/son billet à l'entrée; **you're showing a lot of leg this evening!** tu es habillée bien court ce soir!; **that dress shows everything she's got** cette robe ne cache pas grand-chose; **a TV screen shows what's happening in the next room** un écran de télévision permet de voir ce qui se passe dans la pièce d'à côté; **some of the drawings have never been shown in Europe before** quelques-uns des dessins n'ont jamais été exposés en Europe auparavant; **to show one's wares** étaler ses marchandises; **this jacket/colour really shows the dirt** cette veste/couleur est vraiment salissante; **come out from behind there and show yourself!** sortez de là-derrière et montrez-vous!; **if he ever shows himself** *or* **his face round here again, I'll kill him!** si jamais il se montre encore par ici, je le tue!; **to have sth to show for one's money** en avoir pour son argent; **I had very little to show for my efforts** mes efforts n'avaient donné que peu de résultats; **three months' work, and what have we got to show for it?** trois mois de travail, et qu'est-ce que cela nous a rapporté?

(**b**) *(reveal → talent, affection, readiness, reluctance)* montrer, faire preuve de; **she never shows any emotion** elle ne laisse jamais paraître *ou* ne montre jamais ses sentiments; **to show itself** *(emotion, tendency)* se manifester; **she showed herself more than willing to join in** elle s'est montrée plus que prête à participer; **she showed herself to be a hard worker** elle s'est révélée *ou* avérée dure à la tâche; **to show a preference for sth** manifester une préférence pour qch; **to show a taste for sth** témoigner d'un goût pour qch; **they will be shown no mercy** ils seront traités sans merci; **the audience began to show signs of restlessness** le public a commencé à s'agiter; **the situation is showing signs of improvement** la situation semble être en voie d'amélioration; **to show one's age** faire son âge

(**c**) *(prove)* montrer, démontrer, prouver; **first I shall show that Greenham's theory cannot be proved** je démontrerai d'abord que la théorie de Greenham ne peut être juste; **it just shows the strength of public opposition to the plan** cela montre à quel point le public est opposé à ce projet; **it just goes to show that nothing's impossible** c'est la preuve que rien n'est impossible; **it just goes to show what you can do if you work hard** cela montre *ou* c'est la preuve de ce que l'on peut faire en travaillant dur; **which only** *or* **all goes to show that...** ce qui prouve que... + *indicative*

(**d**) *(register → of instrument, dial, clock)* marquer, indiquer; **the thermometer shows a temperature of 20°C** le thermomètre indique 20°C

(**e**) *(represent, depict)* montrer, représenter; **this photo shows him at the age of seventeen** cette photo le montre à l'âge de dix-sept ans; **the picture shows three figures** le tableau représente trois personnes

(**f**) *(point out, demonstrate)* montrer, indiquer; **show me how to do it** montrez-moi comment faire; **to show (sb) the way** montrer le chemin (à qn); *Fig* **to show the way** donner l'exemple; **the government has very much shown the way with its green policies** le gouvernement a bien donné l'exemple avec sa politique écologique; *Fam* **I'll show you!** tu vas voir!

(**g**) *(escort, accompany)* **let me show you to your room** je vais vous montrer votre chambre; **will you show this gentleman to the door?** veuillez reconduire Monsieur à la porte; **an usherette showed us to our seats** une ouvreuse nous a conduits à nos places; **to show sb into a room** introduire *ou* faire entrer qn dans une pièce

(**h**) *(profit, loss)* enregistrer; **prices show a 10 percent increase on last year** les prix sont en hausse *ou* ont augmenté de 10 pour cent par rapport à l'an dernier

(**i**) *(put on → film, TV programme)* passer; **the film has never been shown on television** le film n'est jamais passé à la télévision; **as shown on TV** *(on packaging, sign)* vu à la télé

(**j**) *Comput (files, records)* afficher

3 *vi* (**a**) *(be visible → gen)* se voir; *(→ petticoat)* dépasser; **she doesn't like him, and it shows** elle ne l'aime pas, et ça se voit; **a patch of sky showed through a hole in the roof** on voyait un pan de ciel à travers un trou dans le toit; **she lets her feelings show too much** elle laisse trop voir ses sentiments; **it shows in your face** cela se voit *ou* se lit sur votre visage; **fear showed in his eyes** la peur se lisait dans ses yeux; **their tiredness is beginning to show** ils commencent à donner des signes de fatigue; **it doesn't show** ça ne se voit pas, on ne dirait pas; **ah well, it just** *or* **all goes to show!** eh oui, c'est la vie!

(**b**) *(be on → film, TV programme)* passer

(**c**) *Br (in a vote)* lever la main; **all those in favour please show** que tous ceux qui sont pour lèvent la main

(**d**) *Fam (turn up)* arriver❑, se pointer; *Br* **he didn't show** il n'est pas venu❑

►► ***show house*** maison *f* témoin; ***show jumper*** *(rider)* cavalier(ère) *m,f (participant à des concours de saut d'obstacle)*; *(horse)* sauteur *m*; ***show jumping*** jumping *m*, concours *m* de saut d'obstacles; *Law* ***show trial*** procès *m* à grand spectacle

►**show around** *vt sep* faire visiter; **to show sb around the town** faire visiter *ou* faire voir la ville à qn; **my secretary will show you around (the factory)** ma secrétaire va vous faire visiter (l'usine); **we were shown around the house** on nous a fait visiter la maison

►**show in** *vt sep* faire entrer

►**show off 1** *vt sep* (**a**) *(parade)* faire étalage de; **to show off one's skill/culture** faire étalage de son savoir-faire/sa culture; **he only came to show off his new girlfriend/car** il n'est venu que pour exhiber sa nouvelle petite amie/voiture; **she came in to show off her new baby** elle est venue faire admirer son nouveau-né

(**b**) *(set off)* mettre en valeur; **wearing white shows off a tan** porter du blanc met le bronzage en valeur; **the black background shows off the colours nicely** le fond noir fait bien ressortir les couleurs; **coat that shows off the figure well** manteau *m* qui marque *ou* dessine bien la taille

2 *vi* faire l'intéressant(e), frimer; **to show off in front of sb** chercher à épater qn; **stop showing off!** arrête de faire l'intéressant!, **you don't have to drive that fast, you're just showing off** tu n'as pas besoin de conduire aussi vite, tu fais juste l'intéressant

►**show out** *vt sep* reconduire *ou* raccompagner (à la porte); **it's okay, I'll show myself out** inutile de vous déranger, je saurai retrouver le chemin (tout seul)

►**show over** *Br* = **show around**

►**show round** = **show around**

►**show through 1** *vt insep* se voir à travers; **her knickers showed through her trousers** sa culotte se voyait à travers son pantalon

2 *vi* se voir (à travers), transparaître; **the old paint still shows through** l'ancienne peinture se voit encore à travers; **her knickers showed through under her dress** on voyait ses sous-vêtements au travers de sa robe

►**show up 1** *vt sep* (**a**) *(unmask → impostor)* démasquer; **the investigation showed him up for the coward he is** l'enquête a révélé sa lâcheté

(**b**) *(draw attention to → deficiency, defect)* faire apparaître, faire ressortir; **the poor results show up the deficiencies in the training programme** les mauvais résultats font apparaître les défauts du programme de formation

(**c**) *(embarrass)* faire honte à; *(deliberately humiliate)* humilier; **you're always showing me up in public** il faut toujours que tu me fasses honte en public

(**d**) *(escort upstairs)* accompagner en haut

2 *vi* (**a**) *Fam (turn up, arrive)* arriver❑; **only two of our guests have shown up** seuls deux de nos invités sont arrivés; **to fail to show up** ne pas se présenter❑; **you're the boss, you really ought to show up** tu es le patron, tu devrais vraiment y aller *ou* te montrer❑

(**b**) *(be visible)* se voir, ressortir; **the dirt really shows up on a white carpet** la saleté ressort *ou* se voit vraiment sur une moquette blanche; **the difference is so slight it hardly shows up at all** la différence est tellement minime qu'elle se remarque à peine

---

show-and-tell *n Am Sch* = exposé sur un objet que l'on a apporté en classe

showbiz ['ʃəʊbɪz] *n Fam* show-biz *m inv*, monde *m* du spectacle❑; **she wants to get into showbiz** elle veut entrer dans le show-biz

►► ***showbiz personality*** personnalité *f* du show-biz *ou* du monde du spectacle❑

showboat ['ʃəʊbəʊt] **1** *n* (**a**) *(boat)* bateau-théâtre *m* (**b**) *Fam (person)* crâneur(euse) *m,f*, frimeur(euse) *m,f*

2 *vi Fam (show off)* crâner, frimer

showboating ['ʃəʊbəʊtɪŋ] *n Fam (showing off)* frime *f*

showbusiness ['ʃəʊbɪznɪs] *n* show-business *m inv*, monde *m* du spectacle

►► ***showbusiness personality*** personnalité *f* du monde du spectacle

showcard ['ʃəʊkɑːd] *n (in shop)* pancarte *f*; *(of samples)* carte *f* d'échantillons

showcase ['ʃəʊkeɪs] **1** *n* vitrine *f*; *Fig* **a showcase for British exports** une vitrine pour les exportations britanniques

2 *adj (role)* prestigieux; *(operation)* de prestige

3 *vt Com* exposer, présenter; *Fig* servir de vitrine à; **the exhibition will showcase our new product range** nous présenterons notre nouvelle gamme de produits dans le cadre de l'exposition

showdown ['ʃəʊdaʊn] *n* (**a**) *(confrontation)* confrontation *f*, épreuve *f* de force (**b**) *(in poker)* étalement *m* du jeu

shower ['ʃaʊə(r)] **1** *n* (**a**) *(for washing)* douche *f*; **to have** *or* **to take a shower** prendre une douche; **he was in the shower for half an hour** il est resté une demi-heure sous la douche

(**b**) *Met* averse *f*; **scattered showers** averses *fpl* intermittentes; **a snow shower** une chute de neige

(**c**) *(stream → of confetti, gravel)* pluie *f*; *(→ of sparks)* gerbe *f*; *(→ of praise, abuse)* avalanche *f*; *(→ of blows)* pluie *f*, volée *f*, grêle *f*

(**d**) *Am (party)* = fête au cours de laquelle les invités offrent des cadeaux; **they're having a baby shower** ils font une fête où les invités apporteront des cadeaux pour leur bébé

(**e**) *Br Fam Pej (group)* bande❑ *f*; **what a shower!** quelle bande de nuls!; **you lazy shower!** bande de flemmards!

2 *vi* (**a**) *(have a shower)* prendre une douche, se doucher

(**b**) *(rain)* pleuvoir par averses; **it's started to shower** il a commencé à pleuvoir

(**c**) *Fig (rain down)* pleuvoir

3 *vt* **passers-by were showered with broken glass** des passants ont été atteints par des éclats de verre; **they showered him with gifts, they showered gifts on him** ils l'ont comblé de cadeaux; **to shower sb with kisses** couvrir qn de baisers; **to shower sb with praise** encenser qn

►► *Old-fashioned* ***shower bath*** bain-douche *m*; ***shower cabinet*** cabine *f* de douche; ***shower cap*** bonnet *m* de douche; ***shower curtain*** rideau *m* de douche; ***shower gel*** gel *m* de douche; ***shower head*** pomme *f* de douche; ***shower unit*** bloc-douche *m*

▸**shower down** *vi (rocks)* tomber; *Fig (compliments, insults)* pleuvoir; **rocks showered down on us** des pierres s'abattirent sur nous

showerproof [ˈʃaʊə,pruːf] *adj* imperméable

showery [ˈʃaʊərɪ] *adj* **the weather was showery** il pleuvait de façon intermittente; **it will be rather a showery day tomorrow** il y aura des averses demain

showgirl [ˈʃəʊgɜːl] *n* girl *f*

showground [ˈʃəʊgraʊnd] *n* parc *m* d'expositions

showily [ˈʃəʊɪlɪ] *adv* de façon voyante *ou* ostentatoire

showiness [ˈʃəʊɪnɪs] *n* ostentation *f*; *(of jewellery)* clinquant *m*; *(of dress, decoration)* aspect *m* tapageur

showing [ˈʃəʊɪŋ] *n* (**a**) *(of paintings, sculpture)* exposition *f*; *(of film)* projection *f*, séance *f*; **a private showing of her new film** une projection privée de son nouveau film; **a special midnight showing** une séance spéciale à minuit (**b**) *(performance)* performance *f*, prestation *f*; **on its present showing our party should win hands down** à en juger par ses performances actuelles, notre parti devrait gagner haut la main

showing off *n* **I've had enough of his showing off** j'en ai assez de sa vantardise

showman [ˈʃəʊmən] (*pl* **showmen** [-mən]) *n Theat* metteur *m* en scène; *(in fairground)* forain *m*; *(circus manager)* propriétaire *m* de cirque; *Fig* **he's a real showman** il a vraiment le sens de la mise en scène

showmanship [ˈʃəʊmənʃɪp] *n* sens *m* de la mise en scène

show-me *adj Am Fam (attitude)* incrédule ❑; **we cannot discuss this with the boss, he has a show-me attitude** nous ne pouvons pas discuter de ça avec le chef, il ne croit que ce qu'il voit

▸▸ ***the Show-Me State*** = surnom donné au Missouri

shown [ʃəʊn] *pp of* **show**

show-off *n Fam* frimeur(euse) *m,f*; **stop being such a show-off!** arrête de frimer!

showpiece [ˈʃəʊpiːs] *n* **that carpet is a real showpiece** ce tapis est une pièce remarquable; **the showpiece of his collection** le joyau de sa collection; **the school had become a showpiece of educational excellence** l'école est devenue un modèle quant à la qualité de l'enseignement

showplace [ˈʃəʊpleɪs] *n* endroit *m* pittoresque, site *m* touristique

showring [ˈʃəʊrɪŋ] *n (at auction → for horses, cattle)* arène *f* de vente; *(at equestrian event)* arène *f* de concours hippique

showroom [ˈʃəʊrʊm] *n* salle *f ou* salon *m* d'exposition; **the new model will be in the showrooms soon** le nouveau modèle sera bientôt chez votre concessionnaire; **a car in showroom condition** une voiture à l'état neuf

show-stopper *n* numéro *m* sensationnel; **her song was a real show-stopper** sa chanson a eu *ou* remporté un succès fou

show-stopping *adj* sensationnel

showy [ˈʃəʊɪ] (*compar* **showier**, *superl* **showiest**) *adj* voyant; *(jewellery)* clinquant; **he's a bit showy in the way he dresses** la façon dont il s'habille est un peu voyante

shrank [ʃræŋk] *pt of* **shrink**

shrapnel [ˈʃræpnəl] *n* (**a**) *(UNCOUNT) (fragments)* éclats *mpl* d'obus; **a piece of shrapnel** un éclat d'obus (**b**) *(shell)* shrapnel *m*

▸▸ ***shrapnel wound*** blessure *f* provoquée par des éclats d'obus

shred [ʃred] **1** *n* (**a**) *(of paper, fabric)* lambeau *m*; **in shreds** en lambeaux; *Fig* **his reputation was in shreds** sa réputation était ruinée; **to tear sth to shreds** déchirer qch en petits morceaux; *Fig* démolir qch; *Fig* **to tear sb to shreds** démolir qn

(**b**) *(of truth, evidence)* parcelle *f*; **anyone with a shred of decency would have refused** n'importe qui ayant un minimum de décence aurait refusé

2 *vt* (**a**) *(tear up → paper, fabric)* déchiqueter; **shred this document as soon as you have read it** détruisez ce document dès que vous l'aurez lu

(**b**) *Culin* couper en lamelles; **shredded cabbage** chou *m* coupé en lamelles *ou* haché

shredder [ˈʃredə(r)] *n (for documents)* destructeur *m* de documents

shredding [ˈʃredɪŋ] *n (of paper, fabric)* déchiquetage *m*; *(of confidential documents)* destruction *f*

▸▸ ***shredding machine*** déchiqueteuse *f*, broyeuse *f*

shrew [ʃruː] *n* (**a**) *Zool* musaraigne *f* (**b**) *Pej (woman)* mégère *f*, harpie *f*

shrewd [ʃruːd] *adj (person → astute)* perspicace; *(→ crafty)* astucieux, rusé, habile; *(judgment)* perspicace; **I had a shrewd suspicion that they were up to something** je les soupçonnais fortement de manigancer quelque chose; **that was a shrewd move** c'était bien joué; **to make a shrewd guess** deviner juste; **a shrewd investment** un placement judicieux

shrewdly [ˈʃruːdlɪ] *adv (act)* avec perspicacité *ou* sagacité; *(answer, guess)* astucieusement

shrewdness [ˈʃruːdnɪs] *n (astuteness)* perspicacité *f*; *(craftiness)* habileté *f*, ruse *f*

shrewish [ˈʃruːɪʃ] *adj (woman, character)* acariâtre, hargneux

shrewishly [ˈʃruːɪʃlɪ] *adv* d'une façon acariâtre *ou* hargneuse

shrewishness [ˈʃruːɪʃnɪs] *n* humeur *f* acariâtre *ou* hargneuse

shriek [ʃriːk] **1** *vi* hurler, crier; **to shriek with pain** pousser un cri de douleur; **to shriek with laughter** hurler de rire

2 *vt* hurler, crier; **"stop!" he shrieked** "arrêtez!" hurla-t-il

3 *n (of person, animal)* cri *m* aigu *ou* perçant; **shrieks of joy** cris *mpl* joyeux; **shrieks of laughter** grands éclats *mpl* de rire; **to give a shriek** pousser un cri perçant

shrieking [ˈʃriːkɪŋ] *n* cris *mpl* aigus *ou* perçants

shrieval [ˈʃriːvəl] *adj* qui a rapport au shérif

shrievalty [ˈʃriːvəltɪ] (*pl* **shrievalties**) *n (jurisdiction)* juridiction *f* du shérif; *(period of office)* période *f* d'exercice des fonctions de shérif; *(office)* fonction *f* de shérif

shrift [ʃrɪft] *n* (**a**) *Arch (confession)* confession *f*; *(absolution)* absolution *f* (**b**) *(idiom)* **to give sb short shrift** envoyer promener qn; **I got short shrift from him** il m'a envoyé promener

shrike [ʃraɪk] *n Orn* pie-grièche *f*

shrill [ʃrɪl] **1** *adj* perçant, aigu(uë), strident

2 *vi (siren, whistle)* retentir

3 *vt* crier d'une voix perçante; **"cooee!" she shrilled** "coucou!" cria-t-elle d'une voix perçante

shrillness [ˈʃrɪlnɪs] *n (of voice)* ton *m* perçant *ou* aigu; *(of note, whistle)* stridence *f*

shrilly [ˈʃrɪllɪ] *adv (say, sing)* d'une voix perçante *ou* aiguë; *(whistle)* d'une manière stridente

shrimp [ʃrɪmp] (*pl sense* (**a**) *Am* **inv**) **1** *n* (**a**) *Zool* crevette *f* (**b**) *Fam Pej (small person)* minus *m*, avorton *m*

2 *vi* **to go shrimping** aller aux crevettes

▸▸ ***shrimp boat*** crevettier *m*; *Am* ***shrimp cocktail*** cocktail *m* de crevettes; ***shrimp net*** haveneau *m*

shrimper [ˈʃrɪmpə(r)] *n* (**a**) *(person)* pêcheur(euse) *m,f* de crevettes (**b**) *(boat)* crevettier *m*

shrimping net [ˈʃrɪmpɪŋ-] *n* crevettier *m (filet)*

shrine [ʃraɪn] *n* (**a**) *(place of worship)* lieu *m* saint (**b**) *(container for relics)* reliquaire *m* (**c**) *(tomb)* tombe *f*, mausolée *m* (**d**) *Fig* haut lieu *m*; **a shrine of learning** un haut lieu du savoir

Shriner [ˈʃraɪnə(r)] *n* = membre d'une association à but caritatif composée de personnes haut placées dans la hiérarchie franc-maçonne

shrink [ʃrɪŋk] (*pt* **shrank** [ʃræŋk], *pp* **shrunk** [ʃrʌŋk]) **1** *vi* (**a**) *(garment, cloth)* rétrécir; *(timber)* se contracter; **to shrink in the wash** rétrécir au lavage

(**b**) *(grow smaller → gen)* rétrécir, rapetisser; *(→ economy)* se ralentir; *(→ meat)* réduire; *(→ person)* rapetisser; *(→ numbers, profits, savings)* diminuer, baisser; *(→ business, trade)* se réduire; **the wood has shrunk** le bois a dégonflé; **the village seems to have shrunk** le village semble plus petit; **the number of candidates has shrunk alarmingly** le nombre de candidats a diminué de façon inquiétante; **the size of computers has shrunk dramatically** les ordinateurs sont devenus nettement plus compacts; **my savings have shrunk (away) to nothing** mes économies ont complètement fondu

(**c**) *(move backwards)* reculer; **they shrank (away** *or* **back) in horror** ils reculèrent, horrifiés; **to shrink into oneself** se refermer *ou* se replier sur soi-même

(**d**) *(shy away)* se dérober; *(hesitate)* répugner; **he shrinks from any responsibility** il se dérobe devant n'importe quelle responsabilité; **she shrank from the thought of meeting him again** l'idée de le revoir lui faisait peur

2 *vt* (faire) rétrécir; **old age had shrunk him** il s'était tassé avec l'âge

3 *n Fam Pej (psychiatrist, psychoanalyst)* psy *mf*

shrinkable [ˈʃrɪŋkəbəl] *adj* rétrécissable

shrinkage [ˈʃrɪŋkɪdʒ] *n (UNCOUNT)* (**a**) *(of garment, cloth)* rétrécissement *m*; *(of timber)* retrait *m* (**b**) *(of economy)* ralentissement *m*; *(of numbers, profits, savings)* diminution *f*, réduction *f*; **allow for shrinkage** tenir compte du rétrécissement; **they forecast a further shrinkage in output** ils prévoient une nouvelle diminution de la production (**c**) *Com (of goods in transit)* pertes *fpl*; *(through pilferage)* coulage *m*; *(through damage)* casse *f*

shrinking [ˈʃrɪŋkɪŋ] *adj (fearful)* craintif; *(shy)* timide

▸▸ ***shrinking violet*** = personne sensible et timide; **she's no shrinking violet** elle est loin d'être timide

shrink-wrap (*pt & pp* **shrink-wrapped,** *cont* **shrink-wrapping**) *vt* emballer sous film plastique

shrink-wrapped *adj* emballé sous film plastique

shrink-wrapping *n* (**a**) *(process)* emballage *m* sous film plastique (**b**) *(material)* film *m* plastique

shrive [ʃraɪv] (*pt* **shrived** *or* **shrove** [ʃrəʊv], *pp* **shrived** *or* **shriven** [ˈʃrɪvən]) *Arch* **1** *vt* confesser, absoudre

2 *vi* se confesser

shrivel [ˈʃrɪvəl] (*Br pt & pp* **shrivelled,** *cont* **shrivelling,** *Am pt & pp* **shriveled,** *cont* **shriveling**) **1** *vi (fruit, vegetable)* se dessécher, se ratatiner; *(leaf)* se recroqueviller; *(flower, crops)* se flétrir; *(face, skin)* se flétrir; *(meat, leather)* se racornir; **I almost shrivelled up with shame** j'ai failli mourir de honte

2 *vt (fruit, vegetable)* dessécher, ratatiner; *(leaf)* dessécher; *(flower, crops)* flétrir; *(face, skin)* flétrir, rider, parcheminer; *(meat, leather)* racornir

▸**shrivel up** *vi & vt sep* = **shrivel**

shrivelled [ˈʃrɪvəld] *adj* ratatiné; **a shrivelled old woman** une vieille femme toute ratatinée

shrivelling [ˈʃrɪvəlɪŋ] *n* **shrivelling (up)** *(of fruit)* dessèchement *m*; *(of skin)* flétrissement; *(of meat, leather)* racornissement *m*

shriven [ˈʃrɪvən] *pp of* **shrive**

Shropshire [ˈʃrɒp,ʃɪə(r)] *n* le Shropshire, = comté dans l'ouest de l'Angleterre; **in Shropshire** dans le Shropshire

shroud [ʃraʊd] **1** *n* (**a**) *(burial sheet)* linceul *m*, suaire *m*

(**b**) *Fig (covering)* voile *m*, linceul *m*; **a shroud of mist/mystery** un voile de brume/mystère; *Literary* **under a shroud of darkness** sous les voiles de la nuit

(**c**) *(shield → for spacecraft)* coiffe *f*

(**d**) *(rope, cord → for aerial, mast etc)* hauban *m*; *(→ on parachute)* suspente *f*

2 *vt* (**a**) *(body)* ensevelir, envelopper dans un linceul *ou* suaire; **she always shrouds herself in voluminous black clothes** elle se drape toujours dans de grands vêtements noirs

(**b**) *(obscure)* voiler, envelopper; **the town was shrouded in mist/darkness** la ville était noyée dans la brume/plongée dans l'obscurité; **its origins are shrouded in mystery** ses origines sont entourées de mystère

shrouding [ˈʃraʊdɪŋ] *n* (**a**) *(of body)* ensevelissement *m*, enveloppement *m* dans un linceul *ou* suaire (**b**) *(covering)* enveloppement *m* (**c**) *(of waterwheel)* bandage *m*

shrove [ʃrəʊv] *pt of* **shrive**

Shrovetide [ˈʃrəʊvtaɪd] *n* les jours *mpl* gras *(précédant le Carême)*

Shrove Tuesday [ʃrəʊv-] *n* Mardi *m* gras

shrub¹ [ʃrʌb] *n* arbrisseau *m*, arbuste *m*

shrub² *n* (**a**) *(alcoholic)* = boisson à base de jus de fruit et d'alcool (rhum notamment) (**b**) *Am (non-alcoholic)* = boisson à base de jus de framboise, de sucre et de vinaigre

shrubbery ['ʃrʌbərɪ] *(pl* **shrubberies***) n (shrub garden)* jardin *m* d'arbustes; *(scrubland)* maquis *m*

shrubby ['ʃrʌbɪ] *(compar* **shrubbier**, *superl* **shrubbiest***) adj* arbustif

shrug [ʃrʌg] *(pt & pp* **shrugged**, *cont* **shrugging***)* **1** *vt* **to shrug one's shoulders** hausser les épaules

2 *vi* hausser les épaules

3 *n* (**a**) *(of shoulders)* haussement *m* d'épaules (**b**) *(garment)* boléro *m*

►**shrug off** *vt sep (disregard)* dédaigner; **to shrug off an illness** se débarrasser d'une maladie; **to shrug off one's problems** faire abstraction de ses problèmes; **she just shrugged off her failure** elle ne s'est pas laissé abattre par son échec; **it's not a problem you can simply shrug off** on ne peut pas faire simplement comme si le problème n'existait pas

shrunk [ʃrʌŋk] *pp of* **shrink**

shrunken ['ʃrʌŋkən] *adj (garment, fabric)* rétréci; *(person, body)* ratatiné, rapetissé; *(head)* réduit; **shrunken with age** *(person)* tassé par l'âge

shtick [ʃtɪk] *n Am Fam (of comedian)* numéro ❑ *m*

shtuk = **schtuk**

shtum = **schtum**

shuck [ʃʌk] *Am* **1** *n* (**a**) *(pod)* cosse *f*; *(of nut)* écale *f*; *(of chestnut)* bogue *f*; *(of maize)* spathe *f*; *(of oyster, clam)* coquille *f*

(**b**) *Fam (trick)* arnaque *f*

2 *vt* (**a**) *(beans, peas)* écosser; *(nuts)* écaler; *(chestnuts, maize)* éplucher; *(oysters, clams)* écailler

(**b**) *Fam (discard)* se débarrasser de ❑; **to shuck (off) one's clothes** se déshabiller ❑

(**c**) *Fam (tease)* faire marcher, mener en bateau; *(trick)* arnaquer

3 *vi Fam* **to shuck (and jive)** *(act foolishly)* faire l'andouille; *(speak misleadingly, bluff)* baratiner

►**shuck off** *vt sep Am (rid oneself of → bad habit)* se défaire de ❑

shucks [ʃʌks] *exclam Am Fam* mince!, punaise!

shudder ['ʃʌdə(r)] **1** *n (of person)* frisson *m*, frémissement *m*; *(of engine)* vibration *f*; *Fam* **it gives me the shudders** j'en ai des frissons

2 *vi* (**a**) *(person)* frissonner, frémir, trembler; **I shudder to think how much it must have cost!** je frémis rien que de penser au prix que ça a dû coûter!; **I shudder to think what went into this soup** je frémis à l'idée de ce qu'il peut y avoir dans cette soupe; **I wonder what they're doing now? – I shudder to think!** je me demande ce qu'ils sont en train de faire – je n'ose même pas y penser!

(**b**) *(vehicle, machine)* vibrer; *(stronger)* trépider; **the train shuddered to a halt** le train s'arrêta dans une secousse

shuddering ['ʃʌdərɪŋ] *n (of person)* frisson *m*, frémissement *m*, frissonnement *m*; *(of vehicle, engine)* vibration *f*, secousse *f*

shuffle ['ʃʌfəl] **1** *vi* (**a**) *(walk)* traîner les pieds; **don't shuffle!** ne traîne pas les pieds!; **she shuffles round the house in her slippers** elle traîne dans la maison en pantoufles; **he shuffled shamefacedly into the room** il est entré tout penaud dans la pièce

(**b**) *(fidget)* remuer, s'agiter; **the children were shuffling in their seats** les enfants s'agitaient sur leur chaise

(**c**) *(in card games)* battre les cartes

2 *vt* (**a**) *(drag, walk)* **to shuffle one's feet** *(when walking)* traîner les pieds; **he stood there shuffling his feet** il était là debout dansant d'un pied sur l'autre; *Fig* **he'll have trouble shuffling his way out of this one!** cette fois-ci, il ne va pas s'en tirer comme ça!

(**b**) *(move round → belongings, papers)* remuer; **she was shuffling the papers on her desk** elle déplaçait les papiers qui se trouvaient sur son bureau

(**c**) *(cards)* battre, brasser, mélanger; *(dominoes)* mélanger, brasser

3 *n* (**a**) *(in walking)* pas *m* traînant; *(in dancing)* pas *mpl* glissés

(**b**) *(of cards)* battage *m*; **let's give the cards a shuffle** on va battre *ou* mélanger les cartes; **it's your shuffle** c'est à toi de battre *ou* mélanger (les cartes)

►**shuffle off 1** *vi sep* partir en traînant les pieds; **the badger shuffled off into the bushes** le blaireau disparut dans les buissons en trottinant

2 *vt sep (responsibility)* se dérober à; **he shuffled the responsibility off on to me** il s'est déchargé de la responsabilité sur moi

3 *vt insep Literary or Hum* **to shuffle off this mortal coil** quitter cette vie

shuffleboard ['ʃʌfəlbɔːd] *n* jeu *m* de palet

shuffler ['ʃʌflə(r)] *n Fam* = personne qui use de faux-fuyants ou de détours

shuffling ['ʃʌflɪŋ] *adj (gait)* traînant

shufti, shufty ['ʃʊftɪ] *n Br Fam* coup *m* d'œil ❑; **to have a shufty at sth** jeter un coup d'œil à qch; **have a quick shufty at this!** regarde un peu ça!

shun [ʃʌn] *(pt & pp* **shunned**, *cont* **shunning***) vt* fuir, éviter; **she shuns all publicity** elle fuit toute publicité

'shun [ʃʌn] *exclam Mil* garde-à-vous!

shunt [ʃʌnt] **1** *vt* (**a**) *(move)* déplacer; **the neighbours upstairs were shunting furniture around** les voisins du dessus déplaçaient des meubles; **they shunted him off to the Fresno office** ils l'ont muté à Fresno; **he just shunted me out of his way** il m'a poussé hors de son chemin

(**b**) *Br Rail (move about)* manœuvrer; *(direct)* aiguiller; *(marshal)* trier; **the carriages had been shunted into a siding** les wagons avaient été mis sur une voie de garage

(**c**) *Elec (circuit)* shunter, monter en dérivation; *(current)* dériver

2 *vi* (**a**) *Rail* manœuvrer

(**b**) *(travel back and forth)* faire la navette; **I spent the day shunting back and forth between the two offices** j'ai passé ma journée à faire la navette entre les deux bureaux

3 *n* (**a**) *Rail* manœuvre *f* (de triage)

(**b**) *Elec* shunt *m*, dérivation *f*

(**c**) *Med* shunt *m*

(**d**) *Br Fam (car crash)* collision ❑ *f*

shunter ['ʃʌntə(r)] *n Rail* locomotive *f* de manœuvre

shunting ['ʃʌntɪŋ] **1** *n* (**a**) *Rail* manœuvres *fpl* (de triage) (**b**) *Elec* shuntage *m*, dérivation *f*

2 *comp Rail (engine, track)* de manœuvre

►► *Rail* ***shunting yard*** gare *f* de triage

shush [ʃʊʃ] **1** *exclam* chut!

2 *vt* **he kept shushing us** il n'arrêtait pas de nous dire de nous taire

shut [ʃʌt] *(pt & pp* **shut**, *cont* **shutting***)* **1** *vt* (**a**) *(close)* fermer; **shut your eyes!** fermez les yeux!; *Fig* **you shouldn't shut your eyes to the problem** vous ne devriez pas fermer les yeux sur le problème; **shut your books** refermez *ou* fermez vos livres; **please shut the door after you** veuillez fermer *ou* refermer la porte derrière vous; *Fam* **shut your mouth** *or* **face, shut it!** ferme ton clapet!, la ferme!

(**b**) *(trap)* **her skirt got shut in the door** sa robe est restée coincée dans la porte; **I shut my finger in the door** je me suis pris le doigt dans la porte

2 *vi* (**a**) *(door, window, container etc)* (se) fermer; **the door won't shut** la porte ne ferme pas; **the lid shuts very tightly** le couvercle ferme hermétiquement

(**b**) *(shop, gallery etc)* fermer; **the post office shuts at 6 p.m.** la poste ferme à 18 heures

3 *adj* fermé; *Fam* **keep your mouth** *or* **trap shut!** ferme-la!, boucle-la!

►**shut away** *vt sep (criminal, animal)* enfermer; *(precious objects)* mettre sous clé; **I shut myself away for two months to finish my novel** je me suis enfermé pendant deux mois pour terminer d'écrire mon roman

►**shut down 1** *vt sep* (**a**) *(store, factory, cinema)* fermer

(**b**) *(machine, engine)* arrêter; *(computer)* éteindre

(**c**) *Sport (mark closely)* marquer de près

2 *vi* (**a**) *(store, factory, cinema)* fermer

(**b**) *Comput (system)* s'arrêter

►**shut in** *vt sep* enfermer; **he went to the bathroom and shut himself in** il est allé à la salle de bains et s'y est enfermé; **to feel shut in** avoir un sentiment d'étouffement; **we're shut in by hills** nous sommes entourés de collines

►**shut off 1** *vt sep* (**a**) *(cut off → supplies, water, electricity)* couper; *(→ radio, machine)* éteindre, arrêter; *(→ light)* éteindre

(**b**) *(isolate)* couper, isoler; **the village was shut off from the rest of the world** le village a été coupé du reste du monde; **she shut herself off from other people** elle s'isolait du reste des gens

(**c**) *(block)* boucher; **that new building shuts off all our sunlight** ce nouvel immeuble nous cache la lumière du jour

2 *vi* se couper, s'arrêter; **it shuts off automatically** ça s'arrête automatiquement

►**shut out** *vt sep* (**a**) *(out of building, room)* **she shut us out** elle nous a enfermés dehors; **we got shut out** nous ne pouvions plus rentrer

(**b**) *(exclude)* exclure; **he drew the curtains to shut out the light** il tira les rideaux pour empêcher la lumière d'entrer; **she felt shut out from all decision-making** elle avait l'impression que toutes les décisions étaient prises sans qu'elle soit consultée

(**c**) *(block out → thought, feeling)* chasser (de son esprit)

(**d**) *(turn off → light)* éteindre

(**e**) *Sport (opponent)* empêcher de marquer

►**shut up 1** *vi* (**a**) *Fam (be quiet)* la fermer, la boucler; **shut up!** la ferme!, boucle-la!; **shut up and do your work** ferme-la et fais ton travail; **he never knows when to shut up** il ne sait pas se taire ❑ *ou* la fermer quand il faut; **she hasn't shut up about her holiday since she got back** elle n'a pas arrêté de parler de ses vacances depuis qu'elle est rentrée ❑

(**b**) *(close)* fermer; **we decided to shut up early** nous avons décidé de fermer tôt

2 *vt sep* (**a**) *(close → shop, factory)* fermer; **to shut up shop** *(close shop at end of day)* fermer le magasin; *(close shop permanently)* fermer boutique; *(of theatre, factory)* fermer ses portes

(**b**) *(lock up)* enfermer; **to shut oneself up** s'enfermer chez soi

(**c**) *Fam (silence)* **to shut sb up** clouer le bec à qn; **that shut him up!** ça lui a cloué le bec!; **will somebody shut those kids up!** faites taire ces gosses!

shutdown ['ʃʌtdaʊn] *n* (**a**) *(of shop, factory)* fermeture *f* définitive (**b**) *Comput* fermeture *f*, arrêt *m* de fin de session

shut-eye *n Fam* **to get some shut-eye** piquer un roupillon, roupiller; **I need a bit of shut-eye** il faut que je roupille un peu

shut-in 1 *adj* confiné, enfermé

2 *n Am* malade *mf* qui reste confiné(e)

shutoff ['ʃʌtɒf] *n* (**a**) *(device)* **the automatic shutoff didn't work** le dispositif d'arrêt automatique n'a pas fonctionné (**b**) *(action)* arrêt *m*

shutout ['ʃʌtaʊt] *n* (**a**) *Ind* lock-out *m inv* (**b**) *Sport* = match où l'on n'a laissé passer aucun but

►► *Cards* ***shutout bid*** ouverture *f* préventive

shutter ['ʃʌtə(r)] *n* (**a**) *(on window)* volet *m*; *(slatted)* persienne *f*; **to put up the shutters** *(gen)* mettre les volets; *(on shop)* fermer boutique (**b**) *Phot* obturateur *m*; **to release the shutter** actionner l'obturateur

►► *Phot* ***shutter priority*** priorité *f* à la vitesse; ***shutter release*** déclencheur *m* d'obturateur; ***shutter speed*** vitesse *f* d'obturation

shuttered ['ʃʌtəd] *adj (with shutters fitted)* à volets; *(with shutters closed)* aux volets fermés; **all the windows were tightly shuttered** les volets de toutes les fenêtres étaient bien fermés

shuttering ['ʃʌtərɪŋ] *n (for concrete)* coffrage *m*

shutting ['ʃʌtɪŋ] *n* fermeture *f*

►► ***shutting down*** (**a**) *(of shop, factory)* fermeture *f* définitive (**b**) *(of computer)* fermeture *f*, arrêt *m* de fin de session

shuttle ['ʃʌtəl] **1** *n* (**a**) *(vehicle, service)* navette *f*; **there is a shuttle bus service from the station to the stadium** il y a une navette d'autobus entre la gare et le stade; **the 8 o'clock shuttle to Glasgow** la navette de 8 heures pour Glasgow

(**b**) *(on weaving loom, sewing machine)* navette *f*
(**c**) *(shuttlecock)* volant *m (au badminton)*
2 *vi* faire la navette; **he shuttles between New York and Chicago** il fait la navette entre New York et Chicago
3 *vt* **a helicopter shuttled the injured to hospital** un hélicoptère a fait la navette pour transporter les blessés à l'hôpital; **passengers are shuttled to the airport by bus** les passagers sont transportés en bus à l'aéroport
►► ***shuttle diplomacy*** navette *f* diplomatique

shuttlecock [ˈʃʌtəlkɒk] *n* volant *m (au badminton)*

shuttling [ˈʃʌtlɪŋ] *n* va-et-vient *m inv*, navette *f*

shwa = **schwa**

shy [ʃaɪ] *(compar* **shyer,** *superl* **shyest,** *pl* **shies,** *pt & pp* **shied) 1** *adj* (**a**) *(person → timid)* timide; *(→ ill at ease)* gêné, mal à l'aise; *(→ unsociable)* sauvage; **she gave a shy smile** elle sourit timidement; **he's shy of adults** il est timide avec les adultes; **he's always been shy and retiring** il a toujours été timide; **she's camera shy** elle n'aime pas être prise en photo; **to make sb shy** intimider qn; **most people are shy of speaking in public** la plupart des gens ont peur de parler en public; **don't be shy of asking for more** n'hésitez pas à en redemander; **he fought shy of admitting his interest** il a fait tout ce qu'il a pu pour ne pas avoir à admettre qu'il était intéressé
(**b**) *(animal, bird)* peureux
(**c**) *Am (short, lacking)* **to be shy of** manquer de, être à court de; **we're $600 shy of making our goal** il nous manque 600 dollars pour atteindre notre objectif
2 *n Br* (**a**) *(throw)* lancer *m*, jet *m*; **he took a shy at the pigeon with a stone** il a lancé une pierre sur le pigeon
(**b**) *Old-fashioned (attempt)* essai *m*, tentative *f*; **she decided to have** *or* **to take a shy at skiing** elle a décidé d'essayer le ski
3 *vi (horse)* broncher; **his horse shied at the last fence** son cheval a bronché devant le dernier obstacle
4 *vt* lancer, jeter
▸**shy away from** *vt insep* **to shy away from sth/doing sth** éviter qch/de faire qch; **she shied away from talking to him** elle a évité de lui parler

Shylock [ˈʃaɪlɒk] *n Pej* usurier(ère) *m,f*

shyly [ˈʃaɪlɪ] *adv* timidement

shyness [ˈʃaɪnɪs] *n* timidité *f*

shyster [ˈʃaɪstə(r)] *esp Am Fam* **1** *n (crook)* escroc ❑ *m*, filou *m*; *(corrupt lawyer)* avocat *m* marron; *(businessman)* homme *m* d'affaires véreux ❑; *(politician)* politicien *m* véreux ❑
2 *adj* malhonnête ❑, véreux ❑

SI [ˌesˈaɪ] *n* (**a**) *(abbr* **Système International**) SI *m* (**b**) *(in golf) (abbr* **stroke index**) stroke index *m*, coefficient *m* de difficulté
►► ***SI unit*** unité *f* SI

si [siː] *n Mus* si *m inv*

sial [ˈsaɪəl] *n Geol* sial *m*

sialic [saɪˈælɪk] *adj*
►► *Biol & Chem* ***sialic acid*** acide *m* sialique

Siam [ˌsaɪˈæm] *n* Siam *m*; **in Siam** au Siam

siamang [ˈsaɪəmæŋ] *n Zool* siamang *m*

Siamese [ˌsaɪəˈmiːz] *(pl* **inv**) **1** *n* (**a**) *(person)* Siamois(e) *m,f* (**b**) *Ling* siamois *m* (**c**) *(cat)* siamois *m*
2 *adj* siamois
►► ***Siamese cat*** chat *m* siamois; ***Siamese twins*** *(male)* frères *mpl* siamois; *(female)* sœurs *fpl* siamoises; *Fam Fig* **they're like Siamese twins, those two!** c'est des vrais siamois, ces deux-là!

SIB [ˌesaɪˈbiː] *n (abbr* **Securities and Investments Board**) = commission britannique des opérations de Bourse, ≃ COB *f*

sib [sɪb] *Fam* = **sibling**

Siberia [saɪˈbɪərɪə] *n* Sibérie *f*; **in Siberia** en Sibérie

Siberian [saɪˈbɪərɪən] **1** *n* Sibérien(enne) *m,f*
2 *adj* sibérien
►► *Orn* ***Siberian jay*** mésangeai *m* imitateur *ou* de malheur

sibilance [ˈsɪbɪləns] *n Ling* sifflement *m*

sibilant [ˈsɪbɪlənt] *Ling* **1** *adj* sifflant
2 *n* sifflante *f*

sibilate [ˈsɪbɪleɪt] **1** *vt* prononcer en sifflant
2 *vi* siffler

sibilation [ˌsɪbɪˈleɪʃən] *n* sifflement *m*

sibling [ˈsɪblɪŋ] *n (brother)* frère *m*; *(sister)* sœur *f*; **all his siblings** tous ses frères et sœurs, *Spec* sa fratrie; **Tom and Sue are siblings** Tom et Sue sont frère et sœur
►► ***sibling rivalry*** rivalité *f* entre frères et sœurs

sibyl [ˈsɪbəl] *n* sibylle *f*

sibylline [ˈsɪbəlaɪn] *adj* sibyllin
►► *Hist* ***the Sibylline Books*** les Livres *mpl* sibyllins

sic [sɪk] *adv* sic

siccative [ˈsɪkətɪv] *n* siccatif *m*

Sicilian [sɪˈsɪlɪən] **1** *n* (**a**) *(person)* Sicilien(enne) *m,f* (**b**) *Ling* sicilien *m*
2 *adj* sicilien

Sicily [ˈsɪsɪlɪ] *n* Sicile *f*; **in Sicily** en Sicile

sick [sɪk] **1** *adj* (**a**) *(unwell → person, plant, animal)* malade; *(→ state)* maladif; **to fall sick,** *Am* **to take sick,** *Am & Ir* **to get sick** tomber malade; *Am* **to look sick** avoir l'air malade; **my secretary is off sick** ma secrétaire est en congé de maladie; **they care for sick people** ils soignent les malades; *Mil* **to report** *or Fam* **to go sick** se faire porter malade ❑ *ou* pâle; *Fam* **are you sick in the head or something?** ça va pas la tête?; **to be sick with fear/worry** être malade de peur/d'inquiétude; *Am Fam* **you're so good at it you make me look sick!** tu le fais si bien que j'ai l'air complètement nul!
(**b**) *(nauseous)* **to be sick** vomir; **to feel sick** avoir envie de vomir *ou* mal au cœur; **I get sick at the sight of blood** la vue du sang me rend malade *ou* me soulève le cœur; **oysters make me sick** les huîtres me rendent malade; **you'll make yourself sick if you eat too fast** tu vas te rendre malade si tu manges trop vite; **the very idea gives me a sick feeling in my stomach** rien que d'y penser j'ai mal au cœur; **I felt sick to my stomach** j'avais mal au cœur; *Fam* **to be sick as a dog** être malade comme un chien; *Hist* **the Sick Man of Europe** l'homme *m* malade de l'Europe
(**c**) *(fed up, disgusted)* écœuré, dégoûté; *Fam* **to be sick (and tired) of sb/sth** en avoir marre *ou* ras le bol de qn/qch; **I'm sick (and tired) of telling you!** j'en ai assez de te le répéter!; **it made him sick to think of all that waste** ça l'écœurait de penser à tout ce gâchis; **you make me sick!** tu m'écœures *ou* me dégoûtes!; **he was sick of living alone** il en avait assez de vivre seul; *Fam* **to be sick to death** *or* **sick of the sight of sb/sth** en avoir sa claque de qn/qch; *Br Fam* **I was as sick as a parrot!** j'en étais malade!; *Literary* **to be sick at heart** avoir la mort dans l'âme
(**d**) *Fam (unwholesome)* malsain ❑, pervers ❑; *(morbid → humour)* malsain ❑; *(→ joke)* macabre ❑; **I find their relationship really sick** je trouve leurs rapports vraiment malsains; **that's the sickest thing I ever heard!** je n'ai jamais entendu quelque chose d'aussi écœurant! ❑
(**e**) *Literary (longing)* **to be sick for sb/sth** languir après qn/qch
2 *npl* **the sick** les malades *mpl*
3 *n Br Fam (vomit)* vomi ❑ *m*
4 *exclam Am (to a dog)* attaque!
►► ***sick benefit*** prestations *fpl* de l'assurance maladie; ***sick building syndrome*** syndrome *m* des bâtiments malsains, = syndrome comprenant des maux de tête, qu'on retrouve chez des personnes résidant ou travaillant dans des bâtiments équipés de la climatisation; ***sick call*** (**a**) *(visit → by doctor)* visite *f* à domicile; *(→ by priest)* visite *f* aux malades (**b**) *Am Mil (soldiers)* = ensemble des soldats se rendant à la consultation; *(time)* = heure à laquelle les soldats se rendent à la consultation; *Br* ***sick headache*** migraine *f*; ***sick leave*** congé *m* (de) maladie; **to be (away) on sick leave** être en congé (de) maladie; ***sick list*** liste *f* des malades; **to be on the sick list** se faire porter malade; *Br* ***sick note*** mot d'absence *(pour cause de maladie)*; *Br Mil* ***sick parade*** *(soldiers)* = ensemble des soldats se rendant à la consultation; *(time)* = heure à laquelle les soldats se rendent à la consultation; **to go on sick parade** se faire porter malade; ***sick pay*** indemnité *f* de maladie *(versée par l'employeur)*

▸**sick up** *vt sep Br Fam* dégueuler, vomir ❑

sickbag [ˈsɪkbæg] *n Br* = sachet mis à la disposition des passagers malades dans les avions et les bateaux; *Fam Fig* **pass the sickbag!** ça me fout la nausée!

sickbay [ˈsɪkbeɪ] *n* infirmerie *f*

sickbed [ˈsɪkbed] *n* lit *m* de malade

sicken [ˈsɪkən] **1** *vt* (**a**) *(disgust, distress)* écœurer, dégoûter; **it sickened him to see them together** ça l'écœurait de les voir ensemble
(**b**) *(make nauseous)* donner mal au cœur à, écœurer; *(make vomit)* faire vomir; **the smell sickens me** cette odeur me soulève le cœur *ou* me donne des hauts-le-cœur
2 *vi* (**a**) *(fall ill → person, animal)* tomber malade; *(→ plant)* dépérir; *Br* **he's sickening for something** il couve quelque chose
(**b**) *Literary (become weary)* se lasser; **she sickened of her idle life** elle se lassa de mener une vie désœuvrée

sickener [ˈsɪkənə(r)] *n Fam (experience)* aventure *f* écœurante ❑; *(sight)* spectacle *m* écœurant ❑

sickening [ˈsɪkənɪŋ] *adj* (**a**) *(nauseating → smell, mess)* nauséabond, écœurant; *(→ sight)* écœurant (**b**) *Fig (disgusting, distressing)* écœurant, répugnant; **it's sickening the way the refugees are treated** c'est écœurant, la façon dont on traite les réfugiés; **he fell with a sickening thud** il est tombé avec un bruit qui laissait présager le pire; *Hum* **she's so talented it's sickening!** elle est si douée que c'en est écœurant!

sickeningly [ˈsɪkənɪŋlɪ] *adv* **he's sickeningly pious** il est d'une piété écœurante; *Hum* **she's sickeningly successful** elle réussit si bien que c'en est écœurant

sickie [ˈsɪkɪ] *n Br, Austr & NZ Fam* **to take a sickie** se faire porter pâle *(lorsqu'on est bien portant)*

sickle [ˈsɪkəl] *n* faucille *f*; **a sickle moon** un mince croissant de lune

sickle-cell anaemia *n Med* drépanocytose *f*, anémie *f* à hématies falciformes

sickliness [ˈsɪklɪnɪs] *n* (**a**) *(of person)* faiblesse *f*, fragilité *f*; *(of complexion)* pâleur *f* maladive (**b**) *(of food)* goût *m* écœurant

sickly [ˈsɪklɪ] *(compar* **sicklier,** *superl* **sickliest)** *adj* (**a**) *(person)* chétif, maladif; *(complexion, pallor)* maladif; *(plant)* chétif; *(dawn, light, glare)* blafard; *(smile)* pâle (**b**) *(nauseating)* écœurant; *(sentimentality)* mièvre; **sickly sweet** écœurant, douceâtre (**c**) *Arch (unwholesome → vapour, climate)* insalubre, malsain

sick-making *adj Fam* dégueulasse

sickness [ˈsɪknɪs] *n* (**a**) *(nausea)* nausée *f* (**b**) *(illness)* maladie *f*; **in sickness and in health** ≃ pour le meilleur et pour le pire
►► *Br* ***sickness benefit*** prestations *fpl* de l'assurance maladie

sicko [ˈsɪkəʊ] *(pl* **sickos**) *Fam* **1** *adj* dérangé, malade
2 *n* malade *mf*, tordu(e) *m,f*

sick-out *n Am* = grève où tous les employés prétendent être malades le même jour

sickroom [ˈsɪkrʊm] *n (sickbay)* infirmerie *f*; *(in home)* chambre *f* de malade

sidalcea [sɪˈdælsɪə] *n Bot* sidalcea *m*

SIDE [saɪd]

côté	▸ **1 (a) – (d), (f) – (h)**
flanc	▸ **1 (a), (e)**
face	▸ **1 (c)**
paroi	▸ **1 (c)**
bord	▸ **1 (d)**
part	▸ **1 (f)**
camp, équipe, parti	▸ **1 (h)**
page	▸ **1 (k)**
chaîne	▸ **1 (l)**
latéral	▸ **2 (a), (b)**
de côté	▸ **2 (b)**
prendre parti	▸ **3**

1 *n* (**a**) *(part of body → of person)* côté *m*; *(→ of animal)* flanc *m*; **lie on your side** couchez-vous sur le côté; **I've got a pain in my right/left side** j'ai mal au côté droit/gauche; **her fists were clenched at her sides** ses poings étaient serrés le long de son corps; **I sat down/stood at** *or* **by his side** je me suis assis/j'étais debout à ses

shu–sid

côtés *ou* à côté de lui; **the child remained at her mother's side** l'enfant restait à côté de sa mère; **she was called to the president's side** elle a été appelée auprès du président; *Fig* **to get on sb's good/bad side** s'attirer la sympathie/l'antipathie de qn

(**b**) *(as opposed to top, bottom, front, back)* côté *m*; **lay the barrel on its side** mettez le fût sur le côté; **her hair is cut short at the sides** ses cheveux sont coupés court sur les côtés; **there's a door at the side** il y a une porte sur le côté; **the bottle was on its side** la bouteille était couchée; **the car was hit from the side** la voiture a subi un choc latéral

(**c**) *(outer surface → of cube, pyramid)* côté *m*, face *f*; *(inner surface → of bathtub, cave, stomach)* paroi *f*; *(of flat object → of biscuit, sheet of paper, cloth)* côté *m*; *(→ of coin, record, tape)* côté *m*, face *f*; **the sides of the crate are lined with newspaper** l'intérieur de la caisse est recouvert de papier journal; **printed on one side only** imprimé d'un seul côté; **write on both sides of the paper** écrivez recto verso; **grill for three minutes on each side** passez au grill trois minutes de chaque côté; **this side up** *(on packaging)* haut; **the right/wrong side of the cloth** l'endroit *m* /l'envers *m* du tissu; **the under/upper side of sth** le dessous/le dessus de qch; **the other side of the tape is blank** l'autre face de la cassette est vierge; *Fig* **the other side of the coin** *or* **picture** le revers de la médaille; **to know which side one's bread is buttered on** savoir où est son intérêt

(**d**) *(edge → of triangle, lawn)* côté *m*; *(→ of road, pond, river, bed)* bord *m*; **there's a wall on three sides of the property** il y a un mur sur trois côtés du terrain; **she held on to the side of the pool** elle s'accrochait au rebord de la piscine; **a wave washed him over the side (of the ship)** une vague l'emporta par-dessus bord; **I sat on the side of the bed** je me suis assis sur le bord du lit; **I sat on** *or* **at the side of the road** je me suis assis au bord de la route; **she was kneeling by the side of the bed** elle était agenouillée à côté du lit

(**e**) *(slope → of mountain, hill, valley)* flanc *m*, versant *m*; **the village is set on the side of a mountain** le village est situé sur le flanc d'une montagne

(**f**) *(opposing part, away from centre)* côté *m*; **on the other side of the room/wall** de l'autre côté de la pièce/du mur; **on** *or* **to one side of the door** d'un côté de la porte; **you're driving on the wrong side!** vous conduisez du mauvais côté!; **on the left/right hand side** à (main) gauche/droite; **on the south side** du côté sud; **which side of the bed do you sleep on?** de quel côté du lit dors-tu?; **she got in on the driver's side** elle est montée côté conducteur; **the sunny side of the stadium** le côté ensoleillé du stade; **the dark side of the moon** la face cachée de la lune; **the Mexican side of the border** le côté mexicain de la frontière; **the lamppost leaned to one side** le réverbère penchait d'un côté; **he wore his hat on one side** il portait son chapeau de côté; **move the bags to one side** écartez *ou* poussez les sacs; **to jump to one side** faire un bond de côté; **to put sth on** *or* **to one side** mettre qch de côté; **to take sb on** *or* **to one side** prendre qn à part; **to stand on** *or* **to one side** se tenir à l'écart *ou* à part; **leaving that on one side for the moment...** en laissant cela de côté pour l'instant...; **Manhattan's Lower East Side** le quartier sud-est de Manhattan; **it's way on the other side of town** c'est à l'autre bout de la ville; **on both sides** des deux côtés, de part et d'autre; **on every side, on all sides** de tous côtés, de toutes parts; **they were attacked on** *or* **from all sides** ils ont été attaqués de tous côtés *ou* de toutes parts; **there were flames on every side** il y avait des flammes de tous (les) côtés; **from side to side** d'un côté à l'autre; **the ship rolled from side to side** le bateau roulait; **he's on the right/wrong side of forty** il n'a pas encore/il a dépassé la quarantaine; **stay on the right side of the law** restez dans la légalité; **he operates on the wrong side of the law** il fait des affaires en marge de la loi; **to get on the wrong side of sb** prendre qn à rebrousse-poil; **to get/keep on the right side of sb** se mettre/rester bien avec qn; *esp Am* **to live on the right/wrong side of the tracks** habiter un bon/mauvais quartier; *esp Am* **to come from the wrong side of the tracks** être issu d'un milieu défavorisé; **there's no other hotel this side of Reno** il n'y a pas d'autre hôtel entre ici et Reno; **these are the best beaches this side of Hawaii** ce sont les meilleures plages après celles de Hawaii; **I can't see myself finishing the work this side of Easter** je ne me vois pas finir ce travail d'ici Pâques; **it's a bit on the pricey/small side** c'est un peu cher/petit

(**g**) *(facet, aspect → of problem, situation)* aspect *m*, côté *m*; *(→ of person)* côté *m*; **to examine all sides of an issue** examiner un problème sous tous ses aspects; **there are many sides to this issue** c'est une question complexe; **there are many sides to her character** elle a bien des facettes à son caractère; **there are two sides to every argument** dans toute discussion il y a deux points de vue; **he's told me his side of the story** il m'a donné sa version de l'affaire; **I could see the funny side of the situation** je voyais le côté drôle de la situation; **I can't see the funny side of that** je ne vois pas ce qu'il y a de drôle là-dedans; **he stressed the positive/humanitarian side** il a souligné le côté positif/humanitaire; **he always looks on the gloomy side of things** il voit tout en noir; **I've kept my side of the deal** j'ai tenu mes engagements dans cette affaire; **she's very good at the practical side of things** elle est excellente sur le plan pratique; **she has her good side** elle a ses bons côtés; **I've seen his cruel side** je sais qu'il peut être cruel; **to have a jealous side** avoir un côté jaloux; **she showed an unexpected side of herself** elle a révélé une facette inattendue de sa personnalité

(**h**) *(group, faction)* côté *m*, camp *m*; *(team)* équipe *f*; *Pol (party)* parti *m*; **the winning side** le camp des vainqueurs; **to pick sides** faire les équipes; **whose side is he on?** de quel côté est-il?, dans quel camp est-il?; **he's on our side** il est avec nous *ou* de notre côté; **they fought on our side** ils se sont battus à nos côtés; **which side won the war?** qui a gagné la guerre?; **the rebel side** les rebelles *mpl*; **there is mistrust on both sides** il y a de la méfiance dans les deux camps; **there's still no concrete proposal on** *or* **from their side** il n'y a toujours pas de proposition concrète de leur part; **to go over to the other side, to change sides** changer de camp; **luck is on our side** la chance est avec nous; **time is on their side** le temps joue en leur faveur; **he has youth on his side** il a l'avantage de la jeunesse; **he really let the side down** il nous/leur/*etc* a fait faux bond; **don't let the side down!** nous comptons sur vous!; **she tried to get the committee on her side** elle a essayé de mettre le comité de son côté; **to take sides** prendre parti; **he took Tom's side against me** il a pris le parti de Tom contre moi; **to be on the side of peace** être pour la paix

(**i**) *(line of descent)* **she's a Smith on her mother's side** c'est une Smith par sa mère; **he's Polish on both sides** ses parents sont tous les deux polonais; **my grandmother on my mother's/father's side** ma grand-mère maternelle/paternelle; **she gets her love for music from her mother's side of the family** elle tient son goût pour la musique du côté maternel de sa famille; **they are all blond on her father's side of the family** ils sont tous blonds du côté de *ou* dans la famille de son père

(**j**) *Culin* **side of pork** demi-porc *m*; **side of bacon** flèche *f* de lard; **side of beef/lamb** quartier *m* de bœuf/d'agneau

(**k**) *Br (page of text)* page *f*; **I wrote ten sides** j'ai écrit dix pages

(**l**) *Br Fam (TV channel)* chaîne ❑ *f*; **what's on the other side?** qu'est-ce qu'il y a sur l'autre chaîne?

(**m**) *Br (in snooker, billiards etc)* effet *m*

(**n**) *Br Fam (cheek)* culot *m*; *(arrogance)* fierté ❑ *f*; **to put on side** se donner des airs ❑; **there's no side to him** c'est quelqu'un de très simple ❑

(**o**) *Am (side order)* **a pork chop with a side of fries** une côte de porc avec des frites *(servies à part)*

2 *adj* (**a**) *(situated on one side → chapel, window)* latéral

(**b**) *(directional → view)* de côté, de profil; *(→ elevation, kick)* latéral; **to do a side split** *(in dance)* faire un grand écart latéral; *Sport* **to put side spin on a ball** donner de l'effet à une balle

(**c**) *(additional)* en plus; **would anyone like any side orders?** *(in restaurant)* désirez-vous un plat d'accompagnement?; **I'd like a side order of fries** je voudrais aussi des frites

3 *vi* **to side with sb** se ranger *ou* se mettre du côté de qn, prendre parti pour qn; **it's in our interest to side with the majority** nous avons intérêt à nous ranger du côté de la majorité; **they all sided against her** ils se sont tous mis contre elle

4 on the side *adv* **to make a bit of money on the side** *(gen)* se faire un peu d'argent en plus *ou* supplémentaire; *(dishonestly)* se remplir les poches; **she's an artist but works as a taxi driver on the side** elle est artiste mais elle fait le chauffeur de taxi pour arrondir ses fins de mois; **a hamburger with salad on the side** un hamburger avec une salade; *Am* **anything on the side, sir?** *(in restaurant)* et avec cela, Monsieur?

5 side by side *adv* côte à côte; **they were walking side by side** ils marchaient côte à côte; **to put two boxes side by side** mettre deux boîtes l'une à côté de l'autre; **the road and the river run side by side** la route longe la rivière; **the tribes lived peacefully side by side** les tribus vivaient paisiblement côte à côte; **we'll be working side by side with the Swiss on this project** nous travaillerons en étroite collaboration avec les Suisses sur ce projet

►► ***side aisle*** *(in church)* bas-côté *m*; *Theat* allée *f* latérale; *Chem* ***side chain*** chaîne *f* latérale; ***side chair*** chaise *f (de salle à manger etc)*; ***side chapel*** chapelle *f* latérale; ***side dish*** plat *m* d'accompagnement; *(of vegetables)* garniture *f*; **with a side dish of spinach** avec une garniture d'épinards; ***side door*** porte *f* latérale; *Fig* **to enter a profession by the side door** entrer dans une profession par la petite porte; ***side drum*** tambour *m*; ***side effect*** effet *m* secondaire; **the drug was found to have harmful side effects** on a découvert que le médicament avait des effets secondaires nocifs *ou* indésirables; **consumers suffered the side effects of inflation** les consommateurs ont subi les répercussions de l'inflation; ***side entrance*** entrée *f* latérale; ***side face*** profil *m*; ***side glance*** regard *m* oblique *ou* de côté; *Fig (allusion)* allusion *f*; ***side impact*** *(between vehicles)* choc *m* latéral; ***side issue*** question *f* secondaire; **the side issues of a question** les à-côtés *mpl* d'une question; *Am Fam* ***side meat*** poitrine *f* fumée ❑; ***the side netting*** *(of goal)* le côté du filet; ***side panel*** *(of vehicle)* ridelle *f*; ***side plate*** petite assiette *f (que l'on met à gauche de chaque convive)*; ***side pocket*** poche *f* extérieure; ***side rail*** *(on bridge)* garde-fou *m*; *Naut* rambarde *f*; ***side road*** *(minor road → in country)* route *f* secondaire; *(→ in town)* petite rue *f*; *(road at right angles)* rue *f* transversale; **the car was coming out of a side road** la voiture débouchait d'une route transversale; ***side salad*** salade *f (pour accompagner un plat)*; ***side street*** *(minor street)* petite rue *f*; *(at right angles)* rue *f* transversale; ***side table*** petite table *f*; *(for dishes)* desserte *f*; *(beside bed)* table *f* de chevet

---

sidearm ['saɪdɑːm] *n* arme *f* de poing

sideband ['saɪdbænd] *n Rad* bande *f* latérale

sidebar ['saɪdbɑː(r)] *n* (**a**) *(of saddle)* aube *f (de selle)* (**b**) *Comput* menu *m* latéral

sideboard ['saɪdbɔːd] *n* (**a**) *(for dishes)* buffet *m* bas (**b**) *Br* **sideboards** *(whiskers)* pattes *fpl*

sideburns ['saɪdbɜːnz] *npl* pattes *fpl*

sidecar ['saɪdkɑː(r)] *n* (**a**) *(of motorbike)* side-car *m* (**b**) *(drink)* side-car *m (cocktail composé de cognac, de cointreau et de jus de citron)*

-sided ['saɪdɪd] *suff* **three/five-sided** à trois/cinq côtés; **a many-sided figure** une figure polygonale; **a glass-sided box** une boîte à parois de verre; **a steep-sided valley** une vallée encaissée

side-impact bar *n Aut* renfort *m* anti-impact latéral

sidekick ['saɪdkɪk] *n Fam* acolyte[a] *m*

sidelight ['saɪdlaɪt] *n* (**a**) *Br Aut* feu *m* de position (**b**) *Naut* feu *m* de position (**c**) *Constr (window)* fenêtre *f* latérale (**d**) *(information)* **to give sb a sidelight on sth** donner à qn un aperçu de qch

sideline ['saɪdlaɪn] **1** *n* (**a**) *Sport (gen)* ligne *f* de côté; *(touchline)* (ligne *f* de) touche *f*, ligne *f* de jeu; **to wait on the sidelines** *Sport* attendre sur la touche; *Fig* attendre dans les coulisses; **to watch from the sidelines** *Sport* regarder de la ligne de touche; *Fig* être là en spectateur; **her injury kept her on the sidelines all season** sa blessure l'a laissée sur la touche pendant toute la saison; *Fig* **I prefer to stand on the sidelines** je préfère ne pas m'en mêler

(**b**) *(job)* activité *f ou* occupation *f* secondaire; **he takes wedding photos as a sideline** il fait des photos de mariage pour arrondir ses fins de mois

(**c**) *Com (product line)* ligne *f* de produits secondaires; **they've made recycling a profitable sideline** ils ont fait du recyclage une activité secondaire rentable; **it's only a sideline for us** ce n'est pas notre spécialité

2 *vt Sport & Fig* mettre sur la touche; *Fig* **to be feeling sidelined** avoir l'impression d'avoir été laissé sur la touche

sidelong ['saɪdlɒŋ] **1** *adj* oblique, de côté; **they exchanged sidelong glances** ils ont échangé un regard complice

2 *adv* en oblique, de côté

sideman ['saɪdmən] (*pl* **sidemen** [-mən]) *n Mus* membre *m* de l'orchestre; **he was one of Count Basie's sidemen in Chicago** il a joué avec Count Basie à Chicago

side-on 1 *adv* de profil; **side-on, she looks very like you** de profil, elle te ressemble beaucoup; **the car was hit side-on** la voiture a subi un choc latéral

2 *adj (photo)* de profil; *(collision)* latéral

sidereal [saɪ'dɪərɪəl] *adj Astron* sidéral

siderite ['saɪdəraɪt] *n Miner* sidérite *f*

siderosis [,sɪdə'rəʊsɪs] *n Med* sidérose *f*

siderostat ['sɪdərəʊstæt] *n Astron* sidérostat *m*

siderous ['sɪdərəs] *adj Miner* sidéré

sidesaddle ['saɪd,sædəl] **1** *n* selle *f* de femme

2 *adv* **to ride sidesaddle** monter en amazone

sideshow ['saɪdʃəʊ] *n* (**a**) *(in fair → booth)* stand *m*, baraque *f* foraine; *(→ show)* attraction *f* (**b**) *(minor event)* détail *m*

sideslip ['saɪdslɪp] (*pt & pp* **sideslipped**, *cont* **sideslipping**) **1** *n* (**a**) *Aviat* glissade *f* sur l'aile (**b**) *Aut & Ski* dérapage *m*; **to go into sideslip** déraper

2 *vi* (**a**) *Aviat* glisser sur l'aile (**b**) *Aut & Ski* déraper

sidesman ['saɪdzmən] (*pl* **sidesmen** [-mən]) *n Br Rel* adjoint *m* du bedeau

sidesplitting ['saɪd,splɪtɪŋ] *adj Fam (story, joke)* tordant, bidonnant

sidesplittingly ['saɪd,splɪtɪŋlɪ] *adv Fam* **sidesplittingly funny** drôle à se tordre de rire

sidestep ['saɪdstep] (*pt & pp* **sidestepped**, *cont* **sidestepping**) **1** *n* crochet *m*; *Sport* esquive *f*

2 *vt* (**a**) *(in football, rugby → opponent, tackle)* crocheter; *(in boxing → punch)* esquiver

(**b**) *(issue, question)* éluder, éviter; *(difficulty)* esquiver; **he'll sidestep making any decision** il évitera de prendre quelque décision que ce soit; **they'll sidestep the regulations/the law** ils contourneront le règlement/la loi

3 *vi* (**a**) *(dodge)* esquiver

(**b**) *(in skiing)* **to sidestep up a slope** monter une pente en escalier

(**c**) *(be evasive)* rester évasif

sidestroke ['saɪdstrəʊk] *n* nage *f* indienne; **to swim sidestroke** nager à l'indienne

sideswipe ['saɪdswaɪp] **1** *n* (**a**) *(blow → glancing)* coup *m* oblique; *(→ severe)* choc *m* latéral (**b**) *(remark)* allusion *f* désobligeante; **he took a few sideswipes at the project** il a fait quelques allusions désobligeantes sur le projet

2 *vt Am* faucher

sidetrack ['saɪdtræk] **1** *vt* (**a**) *(person → in talk)* faire dévier de son sujet; *(→ in activity)* distraire; *(enquiry, investigation)* détourner; **the speaker kept getting sidetracked** le conférencier s'écartait sans cesse de son sujet; **sorry, I got sidetracked for a moment** pardon, je m'égare; **he's easily sidetracked** il se laisse facilement distraire

(**b**) *Am Rail (in yard)* garer; *(off main line)* dévier

2 *n* (**a**) *(digression)* digression *f*; **he went off on a sidetrack** *(topic)* il s'est écarté de son sujet; *(activity)* il s'est laissé distraire

(**b**) *Am Rail (in yard)* voie *f* de garage; *(off main line)* voie *f* d'évitement

sidetracking ['saɪd,trækɪŋ] *n Am Rail (in yard)* mise *f* en garage; *(off main line)* déviation *f*

sidewalk ['saɪdwɔːk] *n Am* trottoir *m*; *Fam* **to hit the sidewalks** chercher du boulot

►► *Am* ***sidewalk artist*** artiste *mf* de rue *(qui dessine à la craie sur le trottoir)*; *Am* ***sidewalk café*** café *m* avec terrasse; *Am* ***sidewalk furniture*** mobilier *m* urbain

sidewall ['saɪdwɔːl] *n* (**a**) *(of tunnel)* paroi *f* latérale (**b**) *(of lock)* bajoyer *m* (**c**) *(of tyre)* flanc *m*

sideward ['saɪdwəd] **1** *adj (movement, view)* de côté

2 *adv* de côté

sidewards ['saɪdwədz] *adv* de côté

sideways ['saɪdweɪz] **1** *adv (lean)* d'un côté; *(glance)* obliquement, de côté; *(walk)* en crabe; **to step sideways** faire un pas de côté; **I was thrown sideways** j'ai été projeté sur le côté; **the cup slid sideways** la tasse glissa de côté; **now turn sideways** maintenant mettez-vous de profil; **the pieces can move only sideways** les pièces ne peuvent se déplacer que latéralement; *Fam* **the news really knocked him sideways** *(astounded him)* la nouvelle l'a vraiment époustouflé; *(upset him)* la nouvelle l'a vraiment mis dans tous ses états

2 *adj (step)* de côté; *(look)* oblique, de côté; **the job is a sideways move** c'est une mutation et non pas une promotion

side-wheeler *n Am* bateau *m* à aubes

side-whiskers *npl* favoris *mpl*

sidewinder ['saɪd,waɪndə(r)] *n* (**a**) *Am (blow)* grand coup *m* de poing (**b**) *Zool* crotale *m* cornu

►► *Mil* ***Sidewinder missile*** missile *m* Sidewinder *(missile air-air tactique américain)*

sideyard ['saɪdjɑːd] *n Am* cour *f (à côté d'une maison)*

siding ['saɪdɪŋ] *n* (**a**) *Rail (in yard)* voie *f* de garage; *(off main track)* voie *f* d'évitement (**b**) *Am Constr (of wall)* parement *m* (extérieur), bardage *m*

sidle ['saɪdəl] *vi* se faufiler; **to sidle up** *or* **over to sb** se glisser vers *ou* jusqu'à qn; **to sidle in/out** entrer/sortir furtivement; **to sidle along** marcher de côté, avancer de biais

Sidon ['saɪdən] *n* Sidon

SIDS [sɪdz] *n Med* (*abbr* **sudden infant death syndrome**) mort *f* subite du nourrisson

siege [siːdʒ] **1** *n Mil & Fig* siège *m*; **to lay siege to sth** assiéger qch; **to be under siege** être assiégé; **to raise a siege** lever le siège; **a state of siege has been declared** l'état de siège a été déclaré

2 *comp (machine, warfare)* de siège; **to have a siege mentality** être toujours sur la défensive

►► ***siege economy*** économie *f* protectionniste

Siegfried ['siːgfriːd] *pr n Myth* Siegfried

siemens ['siːmənz] (*pl* **inv**) *n* siemens *m*

Siena [sɪ'enə] *n* Sienne

sienna [sɪ'enə] **1** *n* (**a**) *(earth)* terre *f* de Sienne; **raw/burnt sienna** terre *f* de Sienne naturelle/brûlée (**b**) *(colour)* ocre *m* brun

2 *adj* ocre brun *(inv)*

sierra [sɪ'erə] *n* sierra *f*

►► ***Sierra Club*** = groupe écologique américain qui promeut les activités de plein air; ***Sierra Leone*** Sierra Leone *f*; **in Sierra Leone** en Sierra Leone; ***Sierra Leonean* 1** *n* Sierra-Léonais(e) *m,f* **2** *adj* de la Sierra Leone; ***Sierra Madre*** la Sierra Madre; ***Sierra Nevada*** la Sierra Nevada

siesta [sɪ'estə] *n* sieste *f*; **to have** *or* **to take a siesta** faire la sieste

sieve [sɪv] **1** *n (gen)* tamis *m*; *(kitchen utensil)* passoire *f*; *(for gravel, seed, ore)* crible *m*; **I've got a memory** *or* **mind like a sieve!** ma mémoire est une vraie passoire!

2 *vt (flour, sand, powder)* tamiser, passer au tamis; *(purée, soup)* passer; *(gravel, seed, ore)* cribler, passer au crible

►► *Bot* ***sieve tube*** crible *m*

sievert ['siːvət] *n* sievert *m*

sift [sɪft] **1** *vt* (**a**) *(ingredients, soil)* tamiser, passer au tamis; *(gravel, seed, ore)* cribler, passer au crible; **sift a little sugar onto the cakes** saupoudrez un peu de sucre sur les gâteaux

(**b**) *(scrutinize → evidence, proposal)* passer au crible; **the experts are sifting the facts** les experts passent les faits au crible

(**c**) = **sift out**

2 *vi* (**a**) *(search)* fouiller; **they sifted through the garbage/the ruins** ils fouillaient (dans) les ordures/les ruines; **he was sifting through some old correspondence** il était en train de fouiller dans une vieille correspondance

(**b**) *(pass, filter)* filtrer; **dust had sifted in through the cracks** la poussière s'était infiltrée par les fentes; **I let the sand sift through my fingers** j'ai laissé le sable couler entre mes doigts

►**sift out** *vt sep* (**a**) *(remove → lumps, debris)* enlever (à l'aide d'un tamis *ou* d'un crible); **he sifted out the lumps from the flour** il a tamisé la farine pour enlever les grumeaux (**b**) *Fig (distinguish)* dégager, distinguer; **they sifted out the relevant information** ils n'ont retenu que les éléments intéressants

sifter ['sɪftə(r)] *n (sieve → for flour, powder, soil)* tamis *m*; *(→ for gravel, seed, ore)* crible *m*; *(shaker)* saupoudreuse *f*

sifting ['sɪftɪŋ] **1** *n (of flour, powder, soil)* tamisage *m*; *(of gravel, seed, ore)* criblage *m*

2 siftings *npl (residue)* résidu *m*; *Agr* criblure *f*

SIG [,esaɪ'dʒiː] *n Am* (*abbr* **special interest group**) groupe *m* d'intérêt

sigh [saɪ] **1** *vi* (**a**) *(gen)* soupirer, pousser un soupir; **to sigh with relief** pousser un soupir de soulagement

(**b**) *Literary (lament)* se lamenter; **to sigh over sth** se lamenter sur qch

(**c**) *Literary (grieve)* soupirer; **to sigh for** *or* **over sb/sth** soupirer pour qn/qch

(**d**) *(wind)* murmurer; *(tree, reed)* bruire

2 *vt* **"it's so lovely here", she sighed** "c'est tellement joli ici", soupira-t-elle

3 *n* soupir *m*; **to give** *or* **to heave a sigh of relief** pousser un soupir de soulagement

sighing ['saɪɪŋ] *n (UNCOUNT) (of person)* soupirs *mpl*; *(of wind)* murmure *m*; *(of trees)* bruissement *m*

SIGHT [saɪt]

vue	► **1 (a) – (c)**
spectacle	► **1 (d)**
curiosité	► **1 (e)**
avis	► **1 (f)**
pagaille	► **1 (g)**
viseur	► **1 (h)**
voir	► **2 (a)**
repérer	► **2 (a)**
viser	► **1 (h); 2 (b)**
beaucoup	► **3**

1 *n* (**a**) *(faculty, sense)* vue *f*; **to have good/bad sight** avoir une bonne/mauvaise vue; **her sight is failing** sa vue baisse; **to lose/to recover one's sight** perdre/recouvrer la vue

(**b**) *(act, instance of seeing)* vue *f*; **he fainted at the sight of the blood** il s'est évanoui à la vue du sang; **it was my first sight of the Pacific** c'était la première fois que je voyais le Pacifique; **at first sight the place seemed abandoned** à première vue, l'endroit avait l'air abandonné; **it was love at first sight** ce fut le coup de foudre; **do you believe in love at first sight?** est-ce que tu crois au coup de foudre?; **to catch sight of sb/sth** apercevoir *ou* entrevoir qn/qch; **to lose sight of sb/sth** perdre qn/qch de vue; *Fig* **we mustn't lose sight of the fact that...** il ne faut pas perdre de vue (le fait) que... + *indicative*; **I can't stand** *or* **bear the sight of him!** je ne le supporte pas!; **I can't stand the sight of blood** je ne supporte pas la vue du sang; **to know sb by sight** connaître qn de vue; **to buy sth sight unseen** acheter qch sans l'avoir vu; *Com* **we need to have sight of it first** il faut le voir d'abord; **he can play music at** *or* *Am* **by sight** il sait déchiffrer une partition; **to shoot at** *or* **on sight** tirer à vue; **payable at** *or* *Am* **on sight** payable à vue (**c**) *(range of vision)* (portée *f* de) vue *f*; **the plane was still in sight** l'avion était encore en vue; **there wasn't a taxi in sight** il n'y avait pas un (seul) taxi en vue; **I heard her voice but she was nowhere in sight** j'entendais sa voix mais je ne la voyais nulle part; **is the end in sight?** est-ce que tu en vois la fin?; **there's still no end in sight** je n'en vois pas la fin; **keep that car/your goal in sight** ne perdez pas cette voiture/votre but de vue; **the mountains came into sight** les montagnes sont apparues; **the runners came into sight** les coureurs sont apparus; **out of sight** *(invisible)* hors de vue; *Fam Old-fashioned (excellent)* sensas; **I watched her until she was out of sight** je l'ai regardée jusqu'à ce qu'elle disparaisse de ma vue; **keep out of sight!** ne vous montrez pas!, cachez-vous!; **keep it out of sight** ne le montrez pas, cachez-le; **she never lets him out of her sight** elle ne le perd jamais de vue; **(get) out of my sight!** hors de ma vue!; **get that dog out of my sight!** faites disparaître ce chien!; **a peace settlement now seems within sight** un accord de paix semble maintenant possible; **it was impossible to get within sight of the accident** il était impossible de s'approcher du lieu de l'accident pour voir ce qui se passait; **he had to give up within sight of the summit** il a dû renoncer à quelques mètres du sommet; *Prov* **out of sight, out of mind** loin des yeux, loin du cœur

(**d**) *(spectacle)* spectacle *m*; **the cliffs were an impressive sight** les falaises étaient impressionnantes à voir; **beggars are a common sight on the streets** on voit beaucoup de mendiants dans les rues; **it was not a pretty sight** ça n'était pas beau à voir; **the waterfalls are a sight worth seeing** les cascades valent la peine d'être vues; **it was a sight for sore eyes** c'était un soulagement de voir ça; **you're a sight for sore eyes!** *(you're a welcome sight)* Dieu merci te voilà!; *(you look awful)* tu fais vraiment peine à voir!

(**e**) *(tourist attraction)* curiosité *f*; **one of the sights of Rome** une des choses à voir à Rome; **I'll show you** *or* **take you round the sights tomorrow** je vous ferai visiter *ou* voir la ville demain; **to see the sights of the town** visiter la ville

(**f**) *Literary (opinion, judgment)* avis *m*, opinion *f*; **in my father's sight she could do no wrong** aux yeux de mon père, elle était incapable de faire du mal; **we are all equal in the sight of God** nous sommes tous égaux devant Dieu

(**g**) *Fam (mess)* pagaille *f*; *(ridiculously dressed person)* tableau *m*; **the kitchen was a sight!** quelle pagaille dans la cuisine!; **your hair is a sight!** tu as vu tes cheveux?; **what a sight you are!, you look a sight!** *(wet, dirty)* te voilà dans un drôle d'état!; *(ridiculous)* de quoi tu as l'air comme ça!; **you're** *or* **you look a sight in that outfit!** tu as vu de quoi tu as l'air dans cette tenue?; **I must look a sight!** je ne dois pas être beau à voir!; **what a sight!** quel tableau!

(**h**) *(aiming device)* viseur *m*; *(on mortar)* appareil *m* de pointage; **to take a sight on sth** viser qch; **front sight** guidon *m*; **notch sight** cran *m* de mire; **angle of sight** angle *m* de visée *ou* de site, site *m*; **to have sth in one's sights** avoir qch dans sa ligne de tir; *Fig* avoir qch en vue; *Fig* **to lower one's sights** viser moins haut; **to set one's sights on sth** viser qch; **to set one's sights on doing sth** avoir pour ambition de faire qch; **he's set his sights on becoming a doctor** son ambition est de devenir médecin; **she has her sights set on the presidency/a diplomatic career** elle vise la présidence/une carrière de diplomate

2 *vt* (**a**) *(see)* voir, apercevoir; *(spot)* repérer; **the clouds parted and we sighted the summit** les nuages se déchirèrent et nous aperçûmes le sommet; **a submarine was sighted** un sous-marin a été repéré

(**b**) **to sight one's gun** *(aim)* viser; *(adjust sights of)* régler le viseur de son fusil; **he carefully sighted his pistol at the target** il visa soigneusement la cible avec son pistolet

3 a sight *adv Br Fam* beaucoup ❑; **you'd earn a (damn) sight more money working in industry** votre salaire serait beaucoup plus important si vous travailliez dans l'industrie; **it's a (far) sight worse than before** c'est bien pire qu'avant ❑; **he's a sight too modest** il est bien *ou* beaucoup trop modeste; **not by a long sight** loin de là ❑, bien au contraire ❑

►► *Fin* ***sight bill*** effet *m* à vue; *Tech* ***sight check*** contrôle *m* à vue, contrôle *m* visuel; *Fin* ***sight deposit*** dépôt *m* à vue; *Fin* ***sight draft*** traite *f* à vue; ***sight gag*** gag *m* visuel; *Fin* ***sight letter of credit*** crédit *m* utilisable à vue; *St Exch* ***sight quotation*** cotation *f* à vue

---

sighted ['saɪtɪd] *adj* voyant; **the school also accepts sighted students** l'école reçoit aussi des élèves voyants; **partially sighted** mal voyant

sighter ['saɪtə(r)] *n (in rifle competition)* balle *f* d'essai; *Mil* coup *m* de réglage

sighting ['saɪtɪŋ] *n* (**a**) *(act of seeing)* **UFO sightings have increased** un nombre croissant de personnes déclarent avoir vu des ovnis; **several sightings of teal have been reported** on a vu des sarcelles à plusieurs reprises (**b**) *Fin (of bill)* présentation *f*

►► ***sighting shot*** *(in rifle competition)* balle *f* d'essai; *Mil* coup *m* de réglage

sightless ['saɪtlɪs] *adj (blind)* aveugle

sightlessness ['saɪtlɪsnɪs] *n* cécité *f*

sightline ['saɪtlaɪn] *n* champ *m* de vision; **to block sb's sightline** boucher la vue de qn; **drivers need an unobstructed sightline at intersections** les conducteurs doivent avoir un champ de vision dégagé aux croisements

sightly ['saɪtlɪ] (*compar* **sightlier**, *superl* **sightliest**) *adj* agréable à regarder

sight-read [-riːd] (*pt & pp* **sight-read** [-red]) *Mus* **1** *vi* déchiffrer

2 *vt* déchiffrer

sight-reading *n Mus* déchiffrage *m*

sightscreen ['saɪtskriːn] *n (in cricket)* = grand panneau blanc mobile placé derrière le lanceur, destiné à offrir au batteur un champ visuel uniforme

sightsee ['saɪtsiː] *vi* **to go sightseeing** faire du tourisme; *(in town)* visiter la ville

sightseeing ['saɪtˌsiːɪŋ] **1** *n* tourisme *m*; **to do some sightseeing** faire du tourisme; *(in town)* visiter la ville

2 *comp* **I went on a sightseeing tour of Rome** j'ai fait une visite guidée de Rome

►► ***sightseeing bus*** car *m* de touristes

sightseer ['saɪtˌsiːə(r)] *n* touriste *mf*

sigillographer [ˌsɪdʒɪ'lɒgrəfə(r)] *n* sigillographe *mf*

sigillography [ˌsɪdʒɪ'lɒgrəfɪ] *n* sigillographie *f*

sigma ['sɪgmə] *n* sigma *m*

SIGN [saɪn]

signe	► **1 (a), (b), (e) – (g)**
symbole	► **1 (a)**
geste	► **1 (b)**
signal	► **1 (c)**
panneau	► **1 (d)**
écriteau	► **1 (d)**
enseigne	► **1 (d)**
signer	► **2 (a); 3 (a)**
engager	► **2 (b)**
signer un contrat	► **3 (b)**

1 *n* (**a**) *(symbol → gen)* signe *m*, symbole *m*; *Math, Mus & Ling* signe *m*; **this sign means "real leather"** ce symbole signifie "cuir véritable"; **plus/minus sign** signe *m* plus/moins

(**b**) *(gesture, motion)* signe *m*; **to make a sign to sb** faire signe à qn; **to make a rude sign** faire un geste grossier; **she made a sign for me to enter** elle m'a fait signe d'entrer; **the chief made signs for me to follow him** le chef m'a fait signe de le suivre; **to make the sign of the cross** faire le signe de croix; **wait until the policeman gives the sign to cross** attendez que le policier vous fasse signe de traverser; **the victory sign** le signe de la victoire

(**c**) *(arranged signal)* signal *m*; **a lighted lamp in the window is the sign that it's safe** une lampe allumée à la fenêtre signifie qu'il n'y a pas de danger; **when I give the sign, run** à mon signal, courez

(**d**) *(written notice → gen)* panneau *m*; *(→ smaller)* écriteau *m*; *(→ on shop, bar, cinema etc)* enseigne *f*; **the signs are all in Arabic** tous les panneaux sont en arabe; **follow the signs for Manchester** suivre les panneaux indiquant Manchester; **I didn't see the stop sign** je n'ai pas vu le stop; **traffic signs** panneaux *mpl* de signalisation; **a 'for sale' sign** un écriteau 'à vendre'

(**e**) *(evidence, indication)* signe *m*, indice *m*; *Med* signe *m*; **his speech was interpreted as a sign of goodwill** on a interprété son discours comme un signe de bonne volonté; **as a sign of respect** en témoignage *ou* en signe de respect; **they wear red as a sign of mourning** ils portent le rouge en signe de deuil; **a distended belly is a sign of malnutrition** un ventre dilaté est un signe de sous-alimentation; **a red sunset is a sign of fair weather** un coucher de soleil rouge est signe qu'il fera beau; **it's a sign of the times** c'est un signe des temps; **it's a good sign if he's making jokes** c'est bon signe s'il fait des plaisanteries; **at the first sign of trouble, he goes to pieces** au premier petit problème, il craque; **it's a sure sign that...** à n'en pas douter, c'est le signe que...+ *indicative*; **were there any signs of a struggle?** y avait-il des traces de lutte?; **all the signs are that the economy is improving** tout laisse à penser que l'économie s'améliore; **the room showed signs of having been recently occupied** il était clair que la pièce avait récemment été occupée; **there's no sign of her changing her mind** rien n'indique qu'elle va changer d'avis; **there's no sign of the file anywhere** on ne trouve trace du dossier nulle part; **he gave no sign of having heard me** il n'a pas eu l'air de m'avoir entendu; **is there any sign of Amy yet? – not a sign** est-ce qu'on a eu des nouvelles de Amy? – pas la moindre nouvelle; **is there any sign of the missing child?** est-ce qu'il y a une trace de l'enfant disparu?; **since then, he's given no sign of life** depuis lors, il n'a pas donné signe de vie; **there is little sign of progress in the negotiations** les négociations ne semblent pas avancer

(**f**) *Astrol* signe *m*; **what sign are you?** de quel signe êtes-vous?

(**g**) *Rel (manifestation)* signe *m*; **a sign from God** un signe de Dieu

2 *vt* (**a**) *(document, book)* signer; **sign your name here** signez ici; **here are the letters to be signed** voici les lettres à signer; **a signed Picasso lithograph** une lithographie signée par Picasso; **he gave me a signed photo of himself** il m'a donné une photo dédicacée; *Am* **do you want to sign this to your room?** je le mets sur votre note?; **she signs herself A.M. Hall** elle signe A.M. Hall; **to sign a deal** passer un marché; **the deal will be signed and sealed tomorrow** l'affaire sera définitivement conclue demain; *Law* **signed, sealed and delivered in the presence of...** fait et signé en présence de...; *Fig* **you're signing your own death warrant** vous signez votre arrêt de mort

(**b**) *(footballer, musician, band)* engager; **he's been signed for next season** il a été engagé pour la saison prochaine

(**c**) *(provide with signs)* signaliser; **the museum is not very well signed** la signalisation du musée n'est pas très bonne

(**d**) *(signal)* **to sign assent** faire signe que oui; **to sign sb to do sth** faire signe à qn de faire qch

3 *vi* (**a**) *(write name)* signer; **he signed with an X** il a signé d'une croix; **to sign on the dotted line** signer à l'endroit indiqué; *Fig* s'engager

(**b**) *(footballer, musician, band)* signer un contrat; **he signed for United** il a signé avec United

(**c**) *(signal)* **to sign to sb to do sth** faire signe à qn de faire qch

(**d**) *(know sign language)* connaître la langue des signes; *(use sign language)* communiquer en langue des signes *ou* par signes; **they were signing to each other** ils se parlaient par signes

►► ***sign language*** *(UNCOUNT)* langue *f* des signes; **to speak in sign language** parler par signes; **using sign language, he managed to ask for food** (en s'exprimant) par signes, il s'est débrouillé pour demander à manger; ***sign painter*** *(of lettering)* peintre *m* en lettres; *(of pub signs etc)* peintre *m* d'enseignes

►**sign away** *vt sep (right, land, inheritance)* se désister de; *(independence)* renoncer à; *(power, control)* abandonner; **I felt I was signing away my freedom** j'avais l'impression qu'en signant je renonçais à ma liberté; **you're signing your life away** c'est comme si tu signais ton arrêt de mort

▸**sign for** *vt insep* (**a**) *(acknowledge receipt of)* **to sign for a delivery/a registered letter** signer un bon de livraison/le récépissé d'une lettre recommandée; **the files have to be signed for** il faut signer pour retirer les dossiers

(**b**) *(undertake work on)* **she's signed for another series** elle s'est engagée à faire un autre feuilleton

▸**sign in 1** *vi* (**a**) *(at hotel)* remplir sa fiche (d'hôtel); *(in club)* signer le registre

(**b**) *(worker)* pointer (en arrivant)

2 *vt sep* (**a**) *(guest)* inscrire *(en faisant signer le registre)*; **I'm a member, so I can sign you in** je suis membre, donc je peux vous faire entrer; **guests must be signed in** les visiteurs doivent se faire inscrire dès leur arrivée

(**b**) *(file, book)* rendre, retourner

▸**sign off** *vi* (**a**) *Rad & TV* terminer l'émission; **it's time to sign off for today** il est l'heure de nous quitter pour aujourd'hui

(**b**) *(in letter)* **I'll sign off now** je vais conclure ici

▸**sign on 1** *vi Br* (**a**) *(register as unemployed)* s'inscrire au chômage; **you have to sign on every two weeks** il faut pointer (au chômage) toutes les deux semaines

(**b**) *(enrol)* s'inscrire; **she signed on for an evening class** elle s'est inscrite à des cours du soir

(**c**) *Comput* ouvrir une session

2 *vt sep* (**a**) *Br (enrol → student, participant)* inscrire

(**b**) *esp Am (recruit → employee, staff)* embaucher

▸**sign out 1** *vt sep* (**a**) *(file, car)* retirer (contre décharge); *(library book)* emprunter; **the keys are signed out to Mr Hill** c'est M. Hill qui a signé pour retirer les clés

(**b**) *(hospital patient)* autoriser le départ de; **he signed himself out** il est parti sous sa propre responsabilité

2 *vi (guest)* signer le registre (en partant); *(worker)* pointer (en partant)

▸**sign over** *vt sep* transférer; **she signed the property over to her son** elle a transféré la propriété au nom de son fils; **the house is being signed over to its new owners tomorrow** les nouveaux propriétaires entrent en possession de la maison demain

▸**sign up 1** *vt sep* (**a**) *(employee)* embaucher; *Mil (recruit)* engager; *(player, musician)* engager

(**b**) *(student, participant)* inscrire

2 *vi* (**a**) *(for job)* se faire embaucher; **he signed up as a crew member** il s'est fait embaucher comme membre d'équipage

(**b**) *Mil (enlist)* s'engager; **to sign up for the Marines** s'engager dans les marines

(**c**) *(enrol)* s'inscrire; **she signed up for an evening class** elle s'est inscrite à des cours du soir

---

signal ['sɪgnəl] (*Br pt & pp* **signalled,** *cont* **signalling**, *Am pt & pp* **signaled,** *cont* **signaling**) **1** *n* (**a**) *(indication)* signal *m*; **to give sb the signal to do sth** donner à qn le signal de faire qch; **he'll give the signal to attack** il donnera le signal de l'attaque; **she gave the signal for us to leave** elle nous a donné le signal de départ; **you're sending all the wrong signals if you want her to realize you're attracted to her** si tu veux qu'elle comprenne que tu es attiré par elle, il faut que ton attitude le montre; **he's putting out a lot of confusing signals** son attitude n'est pas claire; **it was the first signal (that) the regime was weakening** c'était le premier signe de l'affaiblissement du régime; **the demonstration is a clear signal to the government to change its policy** la manifestation signifie clairement que le gouvernement doit changer de politique; **to send smoke signals** envoyer des signaux de fumée

(**b**) *Rail* sémaphore *m*

(**c**) *Rad, Tel & TV* signal *m*; **radio signal** signal *m* radio; *Rad* **station signal** indicatif *m* (de l'émetteur)

2 *comp Rad & Tel (strength, frequency)* de signal

3 *adj Formal* insigne; **you showed a signal lack of tact** vous avez fait preuve d'une maladresse insigne

4 *vt* (**a**) *(send signal to)* envoyer un signal à; **to signal sb** faire signe à qn; **he signalled the plane forward** il a fait signe au pilote d'avancer; **the brain signals the muscles to contract** le cerveau envoie aux muscles le signal de se contracter

(**b**) *(indicate → refusal)* indiquer, signaler; *(→ malfunction)* signaler, avertir de; **the parachutist signalled his readiness to jump** le parachutiste fit signe qu'il était prêt à sauter; **the linesman signalled the ball out** le juge de ligne a signalé que le ballon était sorti; **the cyclist signalled a left turn** le cycliste a indiqué qu'il tournait à gauche

(**c**) *(announce, mark → beginning, end, change)* marquer; **the speech signalled a radical change in policy** le discours a marqué une réorientation politique radicale; **this signals the start of the rainy season** cela indique le début *ou* c'est le signe du début de la saison des pluies; **her resignation signalled the beginning of the end** sa démission a marqué le début de la fin

5 *vi* (**a**) *(gesture)* faire des signes; **to signal to sb to do sth** faire signe à qn de faire qch; **he signalled for the bill** il a fait signe qu'il voulait l'addition; **she was signalling for us to stop** elle nous faisait signe de nous arrêter

(**b**) *(send signal)* envoyer un signal; **the satellite is still signalling** le satellite émet *ou* envoie toujours des signaux

(**c**) *Aut (with indicator)* mettre son clignotant; *(with arm)* indiquer de la main un changement de direction

▸▸ *Aviat & Naut* ***signal beacon*** balise *f*; *Naut* ***signal book*** code *m* international des signaux; *Rail* ***signal box*** poste *m* de signalisation; ***signal communications*** télécommunications *fpl*, transmissions *fpl*; ***signal flag*** *Mil* fanion *m* de signalisation; *Naut* pavillon *m* pour signaux; ***signal flare*** *(rocket)* fusée *f* éclairante; *(stationary)* feu *m* de Bengale; ***signal lamp*** *(for making signals)* lampe *f ou* projecteur *m* de signalisation; *(serving as a signal)* (lampe *f*) témoin *m*; ***signal light*** *Naut* fanal *m*; *Mil* voyant *m* (lumineux); *Br Mil* ***signals officer*** officier *m* des transmissions; *Am* ***signal red*** vermillon *m* chinois; ***signal rocket*** fusée *f* de signalisation; *Am* ***signal tower*** poste *m* d'aiguillage

signaling *Am* = **signalling**

signalization [ˌsɪgnəlaɪ'zeɪʃən] *n* signalisation *f*

signalize, -ise ['sɪgnəlaɪz] *vt* (**a**) *Am (call attention to)* signaler, faire remarquer (**b**) *Formal (distinguish, mark)* marquer; **his term of office was signalized by numerous scandals** son mandat a été marqué par de nombreux scandales

signaller ['sɪgnələ(r)] *n* signaleur *m*

signalling, *Am* **signaling** ['sɪgnəlɪŋ] **1** *n* (**a**) *Aviat, Aut, Naut & Rail* signalisation *f*

(**b**) *(warning)* avertissement *m*; **the signalling of any malfunction is automatic** toute défaillance est signalée par un dispositif automatique

(**c**) *(of electronic message)* transmission *f*; **the satellite signalling was interrupted** le satellite a cessé d'émettre des signaux

2 *comp (error, equipment)* de signalisation

▸▸ ***signalling flag*** *Naut* pavillon *m* de signalisation; *Mil* drapeau *m* de signalisation

signally ['sɪgnəlɪ] *adv Formal* **they have signally failed to achieve their goal** ils n'ont manifestement pas pu atteindre leur but

signalman ['sɪgnəlmən] (*pl* **signalmen** [-mən]) *n Rail* aiguilleur *m*; *Mil & Naut* signaleur *m*

signal-to-noise ratio *n* rapport *m* signal-bruit

signatory ['sɪgnətrɪ] (*pl* **signatories**) **1** *n* signataire *mf*; **Namibia is a signatory to** *or* **of the treaty** la Namibie a ratifié le traité

2 *adj* signataire; **the signatory nations** les nations *fpl* signataires

signature ['sɪgnətʃə(r)] **1** *n* (**a**) *(name)* signature *f*; **to put one's signature to sth** apposer sa signature sur qch; **his signature was on the letter** la lettre portait sa signature

(**b**) *(signing)* signature *f*; **to witness a signature** signer comme témoin; *Am Pol* **the bill is awaiting signature** le projet de loi attend la signature du président

(**c**) *Am Pharm (instructions)* posologie *f*

(**d**) *Typ (section of book)* cahier *m*; *(mark)* signature *f*

2 *comp* **Chanel and her signature two-piece suit** Chanel et son fameux tailleur

▸▸ ***signature book*** parapheur *m*; ***signature stamp*** griffe *f*; *Br Rad & TV* ***signature tune*** indicatif *m* (musical); *Fig* **the song became their signature tune** cette chanson est devenue leur indicatif

signboard ['saɪnbɔːd] *n (gen)* panneau *m*; *(for notices)* panneau *m* d'affichage; *(for ads)* panneau *m* publicitaire; *(on shop, bar, cinema etc)* enseigne *f*

signer ['saɪnə(r)] *n* signataire *mf*

signet ['sɪgnɪt] *n* sceau *m*, cachet *m*

▸▸ ***signet ring*** chevalière *f*; *Hist (for sealing)* anneau *m* sigillaire

significance [sɪg'nɪfɪkəns] *n* (**a**) *(importance, impact)* importance *f*, portée *f*; **what happened? – nothing of any significance** qu'est-ce qui s'est passé? – rien d'important *ou* de spécial; **his decision is of no significance to our plans** sa décision n'aura aucune incidence sur nos projets

(**b**) *(meaning)* signification *f*, sens *m*; **sounds take on a new significance at night** la nuit, les bruits se chargent d'un autre sens *ou* acquièrent une autre signification; **the significance of her words escaped me at the time** la signification de ses paroles m'a échappé sur le coup; **the stones have religious significance for the tribe** les pierres ont une signification religieuse pour la tribu

(**c**) *(in statistics)* signification *f*

▸▸ ***significance test*** test *m* de signification

significant [sɪg'nɪfɪkənt] *adj* (**a**) *(notable → change, amount, damage)* important, considérable; *(→ discovery, idea, event)* de grande portée; **no significant progress has been made** aucun progrès notable n'a été réalisé; **was anything significant decided at the meeting?** s'est-il décidé quelque chose d'important à la réunion?

(**b**) *(meaningful, indicative → look, pause)* significatif; **the government has made a small but significant gesture** le gouvernement a fait un geste petit mais significatif

(**c**) *(in statistics)* significatif

▸▸ *Math* ***significant digits, significant figures*** chiffres *mpl* significatifs; ***significant other*** partenaire *mf (dans une relation affective)*; *Psy* = personne dont on se sent très proche

significantly [sɪg'nɪfɪkəntlɪ] *adv* (**a**) *(differ, change, increase)* considérablement, sensiblement; **his health has improved significantly** sa santé s'est considérablement améliorée; **taxes have been significantly reduced** les impôts ont été considérablement réduits; **unemployment figures are not significantly lower** le nombre de chômeurs n'a pas considérablement baissé; **there have been significantly fewer problems** on a eu nettement moins de problèmes

(**b**) *(nod, frown, wink)* de façon significative; **she smiled significantly** elle a eu un sourire lourd de signification *ou* qui en disait long; **significantly, she arrived early** fait révélateur, elle est arrivée en avance

(**c**) *(in statistics)* de manière significative

signification [ˌsɪgnɪfɪ'keɪʃən] *n* signification *f*

significative [sɪg'nɪfɪkətɪv] *adj* significatif

signified ['sɪgnɪfaɪd] *n Ling* signifié *m*

signifier ['sɪgnɪfaɪə(r)] *n Ling* signifiant *m*

signify ['sɪgnɪfaɪ] (*pt & pp* **signified**) **1** *vt* (**a**) *(indicate, show)* signifier, indiquer; **she stood up, signifying that the interview was over** elle se leva, signifiant ainsi que l'entrevue était terminée; **the riots signify an urgent need for reform** les émeutes indiquent un besoin pressant de réforme

(**b**) *(mean)* signifier, vouloir dire; **for him, socialism signified chaos** pour lui, le socialisme était synonyme de chaos

2 *vi Fam* (**a**) *(be important)* être important ▫; **it doesn't signify!** c'est sans importance! ▫

(**b**) *Am (exchange banter)* = se livrer à des joutes verbales entre amis

signing ['saɪnɪŋ] *n* (**a**) *(of document etc)* signature *f*; *(of deed)* passation *f*; *Com (of bill)* acceptation *f*; **a manager with signing authority** un fondé de pouvoir
(**b**) *(sign language)* = traduction simultanée en langage des signes; **her signing is excellent** elle connaît très bien le langage des signes
(**c**) *Ftbl (transfer)* transfert *m*; *(player)* recrue *f*; **Arsenal's newest signing will make his debut this Saturday** la nouvelle recrue d'Arsenal fera ses débuts samedi

signing-in *n (of employees)* pointage *m*

sign-off *n TV* annonce *f* de la fin des émissions

signpost ['saɪnpəʊst] **1** *n* (**a**) *(giving directions)* poteau *m* indicateur (**b**) *Fig (guide)* repère *m*; *(omen)* présage *m*
2 *vt (provide with signs)* signaliser, baliser; *also Fig (indicate)* indiquer; **the village is clearly signposted** le chemin du village est bien indiqué

signposting ['saɪn,pəʊstɪŋ] *n* signalisation *f*, balisage *m*; *Fig* indications *fpl*

signwriter ['saɪn,raɪtə(r)] *n* peintre *m* en lettres

Sikh [si:k] *Rel* **1** *n* Sikh *mf*
2 *adj* sikh

Sikhism ['si:kɪzəm] *n Rel* sikhisme *m*

silage ['saɪlɪdʒ] *n Agr* ensilage *m*

silence ['saɪləns] **1** *n* silence *m*; **silence** *(sign)* défense de parler; **an embarrassed/a shocked silence** un silence gêné/scandalisé; **an explosion shattered the silence of the night** une explosion déchira le silence de la nuit; **there was a sudden silence** soudain, il y a eu un silence; **a silence fell between them** un silence s'installa entre eux; **to suffer in silence** souffrir en silence; **to pass sth over in silence** passer qch sous silence; **his silence on the issue/about his past intrigues me** le silence qu'il garde à ce sujet/sur son passé m'intrigue; **there's been complete silence from head office** le siège est resté totalement silencieux; **what's my silence worth to you?** combien êtes-vous disposé à payer pour acheter mon silence?; **to observe a minute's silence** observer une minute de silence; *Prov* **silence is golden** le silence est d'or
2 *vt* (**a**) *(person)* réduire au silence, faire taire; *(sound)* étouffer; *(guns)* faire taire; **she silenced the child with a look** d'un regard elle fit taire l'enfant; **dissidents cannot be silenced forever** on ne peut pas réduire les dissidents au silence *ou* faire taire les dissidents très longtemps
(**b**) *(stifle → opposition)* réduire au silence; *(→ conscience, rumours, complaints)* faire taire

'The Silence of the Lambs' *Harris, Demme* 'Le Silence des agneaux'

silencer ['saɪlənsə(r)] *n* (**a**) *(on gun)* silencieux *m* (**b**) *Aut* pot *m* d'échappement, silencieux *m*

silencing ['saɪlənsɪŋ] *n* (**a**) *(of gun)* amortissement *m* du son (**b**) *(of engine)* réduction *f* du bruit (**c**) *Fig (of dissent, opposition)* muselage *m*; *(of dissidents)* réduction *f* au silence

silene [saɪ'li:nɪ] *n Bot* silène *m*

silent ['saɪlənt] **1** *adj* (**a**) *(saying nothing)* silencieux; **he was silent for a moment** il resta silencieux un moment; **to fall silent** se taire; **to keep** *or* **to be silent** garder le silence, rester silencieux; **history remains** *or* **is silent on this point** l'histoire ne dit rien sur ce point; *Fam* **to give sb the silent treatment** ne pas adresser la parole à qn ❑
(**b**) *(taciturn)* silencieux, taciturne; **he's the strong, silent type** il est du genre fort et taciturne
(**c**) *(unspoken → prayer, emotion, reproach)* muet; **his mouth twisted in silent agony** sa bouche se tordit dans un cri de douleur muette
(**d**) *(soundless → room, forest)* silencieux, tranquille; *(→ tread)* silencieux; *(→ film)* muet; **the machines/the wind fell silent** le bruit des machines/du vent cessa; **as silent as the grave** muet comme la tombe
(**e**) *Ling* muet; **the g is silent** le g est muet
2 *n Cin* film *m* muet; **the silents** le (cinéma) muet
▸▸ ***silent majority*** majorité *f* silencieuse; *Rel* ***silent order*** ordre *m* silencieux; *Am Com* ***silent partner*** (associé *m*) commanditaire *m*, bailleur *m* de fonds

silently ['saɪləntlɪ] *adv* silencieusement

Silenus [saɪ'li:nəs] *pr n Myth* Silène

Silesia [saɪ'li:zjə] *n* Silésie *f*; **in Silesia** en Silésie; **Lower Silesia** la basse Silésie; **Upper Silesia** la haute Silésie

silex ['saɪleks] *n* silex *m*

silhouette [,sɪlu:'et] **1** *n* silhouette *f*; **I saw her silhouette at the window** j'ai aperçu sa silhouette à la fenêtre; **he could just see the church in silhouette against the sky** il ne voyait que la silhouette de l'église qui se découpait contre le ciel
2 *vt (usu passive)* **to be silhouetted against sth** se découper contre qch; **the tower was silhouetted against the sky** la tour se découpait sur le ciel; **she stood at the window, silhouetted against the light** elle se tenait à la fenêtre, sa silhouette se détachant à contre-jour

silhouettist [,sɪlu:'etɪst] *n* faiseur(euse) *m,f* de silhouettes

silica ['sɪlɪkə] *n* silice *f*
▸▸ ***silica gel*** gel *m* de silice; ***silica glass*** verre *m* de silice

silicate ['sɪlɪkɪt] *n Chem* silicate *m*

siliceous [sɪ'lɪʃəs] *adj Chem* siliceux

silicic [sɪ'lɪsɪk] *adj Chem* silicique

silicide ['sɪlɪsaɪd] *n Chem* siliciure *m*

siliciferous [,sɪlɪ'sɪfərəs] *adj* silicifère

silicify [sɪ'lɪsɪfaɪ] **1** *vt* (**a**) *(of natural agency → wood, stone)* silicifier (**b**) *Ind (convert into silica)* silicatiser; *(impregnate with silica)* imprégner de silicate
2 *vi* se silicifier

silicious = **siliceous**

silicon ['sɪlɪkən] *n Chem* silicium *m*
▸▸ ***silicon carbide*** carbure *m* de silicium; ***silicon chip*** puce *f*; ***Silicon Glen*** = appellation, formée sur le modèle de Silicon Valley ("glen" signifie "vallée" en écossais), d'une région du centre de l'Écosse où sont concentrées un grand nombre de sociétés informatiques; ***Silicon Valley*** Silicon Valley *f (centre de l'industrie électronique américaine, situé en Californie)*; ***silicon wafer*** tranche *f* de silicium

silicone ['sɪlɪkəʊn] *n Chem* silicone *f*
▸▸ ***silicone implant*** implant *m* mammaire en silicone

silicosis [,sɪlɪ'kəʊsɪs] *n (UNCOUNT) Med* silicose *f*

silk [sɪlk] **1** *n* (**a**) *(fabric)* soie *f*; *(thread)* fil *m* de soie; **fine ladies in their silks and satins** de belles dames dans leurs plus beaux atours
(**b**) *(filament → from insect, on maize)* soie *f*
(**c**) *Br Law (King's, Queen's Counsel)* conseiller *m* du roi/de la reine; *(collectively)* conseillers *mpl* du roi/de la reine; **to take silk** être nommé avocat de la couronne
(**d**) *Am Fam* **to hit the silk** sauter en parachute ❑
2 *comp (scarf, blouse etc)* de *ou* en soie; *Prov* **you can't make a silk purse out of a sow's ear** = on ne fait pas du bon avec du mauvais
3 silks *npl (jockey's jacket)* casaque *f*; **Jo Burns, in the Graham (Stable) silks** Jo Burns, portant les couleurs (de l'Écurie) Graham
▸▸ ***silk cotton*** kapok *m*; ***silk cotton tree*** fromager *m*; ***silk finish paint*** peinture *f* satinée; ***silk hat*** haut-de-forme *m*, chapeau *m* haut-de-forme; ***the silk industry*** l'industrie *f* de la soie; ***silk merchant*** marchand(e) *m,f* de soierie, soyeux *m*; ***silk moth*** bombyx *m* du mûrier; ***the Silk Road*** la route de la soie; ***silk screen (printing*** *or* ***process)*** sérigraphie *f*; *Am Fam* ***silk stocking*** *(aristocratic person)* aristocrate ❑ *mf*; *(wealthy person)* riche ❑ *mf*; ***silk trader*** marchand(e) *m,f* de soierie, soyeux *m*

silken ['sɪlkən] *adj Literary* (**a**) *(made of silk)* de *ou* en soie (**b**) *(like silk → hair, cheek etc)* soyeux; *(→ voice, tone)* doux (douce)

silkiness ['sɪlkɪnɪs] *n* (**a**) *(of fabric, hair, skin)* toucher *m* soyeux (**b**) *(of voice, tone)* douceur *f*

silk-screen *vt* sérigraphier, imprimer en sérigraphie

silkweed ['sɪlkwi:d] *n Bot* asclépias *m*, plante *f* à soie

silkworm ['sɪlkwɜ:m] *n* ver *m* à soie
▸▸ ***silkworm breeder*** sériciculteur(trice) *m,f*; ***silkworm breeding*** sériciculture *f*; ***silkworm farm*** magnanerie *f*; ***silkworm moth*** bombyx *m* du mûrier; ***silkworm nursery*** magnanerie *f*

silky ['sɪlkɪ] *(compar* **silkier**, *superl* **silkiest**) *adj* (**a**) *(like silk → fabric, hair, cheek)* soyeux (**b**) *(suave → tone, manner)* doux (douce) (**c**) *(made of silk)* de *ou* en soie

sill [sɪl] *n* (**a**) *(ledge → gen)* rebord *m*; *(→ of window)* rebord *m*, appui *m*; *(→ of door)* seuil *m* (**b**) *Aut* marchepied *m* (**c**) *Mining (deposit)* filon *m*, gisement *m*

sillabub = **syllabub**

silliness ['sɪlɪnɪs] *n* bêtise *f*, stupidité *f*; **I want no more silliness from you!** arrête de faire l'idiot!

silly ['sɪlɪ] *(compar* **sillier**, *superl* **silliest**) **1** *adj* (**a**) *(foolish → person)* bête, stupide; *(→ quarrel, book, grin, question)* bête, stupide, idiot; *(infantile)* bébête; **I'm sorry, it was a silly thing to say** excusez-moi, c'était bête de dire ça; **I'll pay – don't be silly!** je vais payer – ah ça, pas question!; **don't do anything silly** ne fais pas de bêtises; **how silly of me!** que je suis bête!; **it's silly to worry** c'est idiot de s'inquiéter; **it was silly of me to ask** c'était idiot de ma part de demander ça; **you silly idiot!** espèce d'idiot *ou* d'imbécile!; **you look silly in that tie** tu as l'air ridicule avec cette cravate; **but that's silly, she was here half an hour ago** mais c'est ridicule, elle était ici il y a une demi-heure; **there was a new manager every week, it was** *or* **things were getting silly** il y avait un nouveau gérant chaque semaine, ça en devenait ridicule; *Fam* **I couldn't get the silly door open** je n'arrivais pas à ouvrir cette fichue *ou* satanée porte; *Br Press* **the silly season** la période creuse *(pour les journalistes)*
(**b**) *(comical → mask, costume, voice)* comique, drôle; **we all wore silly hats** nous portions tous des chapeaux marrants
2 *adv Fam (senseless)* **the blow knocked me silly** le coup m'a étourdi ❑; **to laugh oneself silly** mourir de rire; **I was bored silly** je m'ennuyais à mourir; **I was scared silly** j'avais une peur bleue; **he drank himself silly** il s'est complètement soûlé; **she's been worrying herself silly** elle est morte d'inquiétude
3 *n Fam* idiot(e) ❑ *m,f*; **don't be such a silly!** que tu es bête!

silly-billy *(pl* **silly-billies**), *Am* **silly-willy** *(pl* **silly-willies**) *n Fam* gros bêta *m*, grosse bêtasse *f*

silo ['saɪləʊ] *(pl* **silos**) *n Agr & Mil* silo *m*

siloxane [sɪ'lɒkseɪn] *n Chem* siloxane *m*

silt [sɪlt] *n Geol* limon *m*; *(mud)* vase *f*

▸**silt up** **1** *vi (with mud)* s'envaser; *(with sand)* s'ensabler
2 *vt sep (of mud)* envaser; *(of sand)* ensabler; **the old harbour is now completely silted up** le vieux port est maintenant complètement ensablé

siltation [sɪl'teɪʃən] *n (with mud)* envasement *m*; *(with sand)* ensablement *m*

silting ['sɪltɪŋ] *n* **silting (up)** *(with mud)* envasement *m*; *(with sand)* ensablement *m*

silty ['sɪltɪ] *adj* limoneux

Silurian [saɪ'lʊərɪən] *Geol* **1** *adj* silurien
2 *n* silurien *m*

Silvanus [sɪl'vɑ:nəs] *pr n Myth* Sylvain

silver ['sɪlvə(r)] **1** *n* (**a**) *(metal)* argent *m*
(**b**) *(UNCOUNT) Br (coins)* pièces *fpl* (d'argent); **I'd like two £10 notes and the rest in silver** je voudrais deux billets de 10 livres et le reste en pièces (de monnaie); **a pound in silver** une livre en argent, une livre en pièces *ou* en monnaie d'argent
(**c**) *(UNCOUNT) (dishes)* argenterie *f*; *(cutlery → gen)* couverts *mpl*; *(→ made of silver)* argenterie *f*, couverts *mpl* en argent; **to clean the silver** nettoyer *ou* faire l'argenterie
(**d**) *(colour)* (couleur *f*) argent *m*
(**e**) *Sport (medal)* médaille *f* d'argent; **he's hoping to win the silver** il espère remporter la médaille d'argent
2 *adj* (**a**) *(of silver)* d'argent, en argent; **is your ring silver?** est-ce que votre bague est en argent?; **he was born with a silver spoon in his mouth** il est né coiffé

(**b**) *(in colour)* argenté, argent *(inv)*; **silver hair** des cheveux argentés
(**c**) *(sound)* argentin; **she has a silver tongue** elle sait parler
3 *adv* **to go silver** *(record)* devenir disque d'argent
4 *vt* (**a**) *(gen) & Fig* argenter; **the moon silvered the lake** la lune donnait au lac des reflets d'argent
(**b**) *(mirror)* étamer
►► ***silver birch*** bouleau *m* blanc; ***silver bromide*** bromure *m* d'argent; ***silver certificate*** papier-monnaie *m (garanti par les réserves métalliques en argent)*; ***silver chloride*** chlorure *m* d'argent; ***silver collection*** quête *f*; ***silver disc*** disque *m* d'argent; ***silver fir*** *(gen)* sapin *m* blanc *ou* pectiné; *(ornamental)* sapin *m* argenté; ***silver foil*** papier *m* d'aluminium; ***silver fox*** renard *m* argenté; ***silver grey*** gris *m* argenté; ***silver iodide*** iodure *m* d'argent; ***silver jubilee*** (fête *f* du) vingt-cinquième anniversaire *m*; **the Queen's silver jubilee** le vingt-cinquième anniversaire de l'accession au trône de la reine; ***silver maple*** érable *m* à sucre *ou* du Canada; *Sport* ***silver medal*** médaille *f* d'argent; ***silver mine*** mine *f* d'argent; ***silver nitrate*** nitrate *m* d'argent; ***silver ore*** minerai *m* argentifère; ***silver paper*** papier *m* d'argent; ***silver plate*** (**a**) *(coating)* plaquage *m* d'argent; **the cutlery is silver plate** les couverts sont en plaqué argent (**b**) *(tableware)* argenterie *f*; ***silver plating*** argentage *m*; *(layer)* argenture *f*; ***the silver screen*** le grand écran, le cinéma; **stars of the silver screen** stars *fpl* du grand écran; ***silver service*** *(in restaurant)* service *m* de grande classe; *esp Br* ***silver service waiter*** serveur *m* pour service au guéridon; *esp Br* ***silver service waitress*** serveuse *f* pour service au guéridon; ***silver standard*** étalon *m* argent; ***the Silver State*** = surnom donné au Nevada; ***silver wedding (anniversary)*** noces *fpl* d'argent

silvered ['sɪlvəd] *adj Literary* argenté

silverfish ['sɪlvəfɪʃ] (*pl* **inv** *or* **silverfishes**) *n Entom* poisson *m* d'argent, lépisme *m*

silver-gilt 1 *n* vermeil *m*
2 *comp* en vermeil

silver-grey *adj* gris argenté *(inv)*

silver-haired *adj* aux cheveux argentés

silvering ['sɪlvərɪŋ] *n* (**a**) *(action → of metal)* argenture *f*, argentage *m*, argentation *f*; *(of mirror)* étamage *m* (**b**) *(layer → on metal)* argenture *f*; *(→ on mirror)* tain *m*

silvern ['sɪlvɜːn] *adj Literary* argenté

silver-plate *vt* argenter

silver-plated [-'pleɪtɪd] *adj* argenté, plaqué argent; **silver-plated tableware** argenterie *f*

silverside ['sɪlvəsaɪd] *n Br Culin* ≃ gîte *m* à la noix

silversides ['sɪlvəsaɪdz] (*pl* **inv**) *n Ich* prêtre *m*

silverskin ['sɪlvəskɪn] *n Culin* = petit oignon blanc confit au vinaigre

silversmith ['sɪlvəsmɪθ] *n* orfèvre *m*

Silverstone ['sɪlvəstən] *n* = circuit de courses automobiles en Angleterre

silvertail ['sɪlvəˌteɪl] *n Austr Fam* rupin(e) *m,f*

silverware ['sɪlvəweə(r)] *n* (**a**) *(gen)* argenterie *f* (**b**) *Am (cutlery)* couverts *mpl*

silverweed ['sɪlvəwiːd] *n Bot* argentine *f*, patte-d'oie *f*

silverwork ['sɪlvəwɜːk] *n* orfèvrerie *f*

silvery ['sɪlvərɪ] *adj (hair, fabric, cloud, water)* argenté; *(voice, sound)* argentin

silviculture ['sɪlvɪˌkʌltʃə(r)] *n* sylviculture *f*

SIM [sɪm] *n (abbr* **subscriber identity module**)
►► ***SIM card*** *(in mobile phone)* carte *f* SIM

sim [sɪm] *n (in computer games)* sim *f*

sima ['saɪmə] *n Geol* sima *m*

Simeon ['sɪmɪən] *pr n Bible* Siméon

simian ['sɪmɪən] **1** *adj* simien; *(resembling ape)* simiesque
2 *n* simien *m*

similar ['sɪmɪlə(r)] *adj* (**a**) *(showing resemblance)* similaire, semblable; **they're very similar** ils se ressemblent beaucoup; **other customers have had similar problems** d'autres clients ont eu des problèmes similaires *ou* analogues *ou* du même ordre; **they are very similar in content** leurs contenus sont pratiquement identiques; **your case is similar to mine** votre cas est semblable au mien; **the print is similar in quality to that of a typewriter** la qualité de l'impression est proche de celle d'une machine à écrire; **it's an assembly similar to the US Senate** c'est une assemblée comparable au Sénat américain; **something similar happened to me** il m'est arrivé quelque chose de semblable; **a fruit similar to the orange** un fruit voisin de l'orange
(**b**) *Geom (triangles)* semblable

similarity [ˌsɪmɪ'lærətɪ] (*pl* **similarities**) **1** *n (resemblance)* ressemblance *f*, similarité *f*; **there is a certain similarity to her last novel** ça ressemble un peu à son dernier roman; **there are points of similarity in their strategies** leurs stratégies ont des points communs *ou* présentent des similitudes; **there the similarity ends** c'est là que s'arrête la comparaison
2 similarities *npl (features in common)* ressemblances *fpl*, points *mpl* communs; **the molecules show similarities in structure** les molécules présentent des analogies de structure; **our similarities are more important than our differences** nos points communs sont plus importants que nos différends

similarly ['sɪmɪləlɪ] *adv* (**a**) *(in a similar way)* d'une façon similaire; **the houses are similarly constructed** les maisons sont construites sur le même modèle; **other people were similarly treated** d'autres personnes ont été traitées de la même manière (**b**) *(likewise)* de même; **similarly, it is obvious that...** de même, il est évident que... *+ indicative*

simile ['sɪmɪlɪ] *n Literature* comparaison *f*

similitude [sɪ'mɪlɪtjuːd] *n* similitude *f*

SIMM [sɪm] *n Comput (abbr* **single in-line memory module**) SIMM *m*

simmer ['sɪmə(r)] **1** *vi* (**a**) *(water, milk, sauce)* frémir; *(soup, stew, vegetables)* mijoter
(**b**) *(smoulder → violence, quarrel, discontent)* couver, fermenter; *(seethe → with anger, excitement)* être en ébullition; **unrest is simmering in the big cities** des troubles couvent dans les grandes villes; **the audience simmered with excitement** les spectateurs étaient en ébullition; **tempers are simmering** les passions s'échauffent; **his anger simmered just below the surface** il bouillait de colère
(**c**) *(be hot)* rôtir; *(when humid)* mijoter; **the city simmered in the heat** la ville était accablée par la canicule
2 *vt (water, milk, sauce)* laisser frémir; *(soup, stew, vegetables)* faire mijoter
3 *n* faible ébullition *f*

►**simmer down** *vi Fam (person)* se calmer[❑]; **simmer down!** calme-toi!, du calme!

simmering ['sɪmərɪŋ] **1** *adj (water, milk, sauce)* qui frémit; *(soup, stew)* qui mijote
2 *n* (**a**) *(of water, milk, sauce)* frémissement *m*; *(of soup, stew)* cuisson *f* à petits bouillons *ou* à feu doux (**b**) *(of rebellion)* ferment *m*

simnel cake ['sɪmnəl-] *n Br* = gâteau aux fruits confits, recouvert de pâte d'amandes ou fourré à la pâte d'amandes (mangé traditionnellement à Pâques)

simoleon [sɪ'məʊlɪən] *n Am Fam (dollar)* dollar[❑] *m*

Simon ['saɪmən] *pr n* Simon
►► ***Simon says*** *(game)* Jacques a dit *m*

simon crane ['saɪmən-] *n TV & Cin* grue *f* hydraulique

simony ['saɪmənɪ] *n* simonie *f*

simoom [sɪ'muːm], **simoon** [sɪ'muːn] *n* simoun *m*

simp [sɪmp] *n Am Fam Pej (abbr* **simpleton**) andouille *f*, crétin(e) *m,f*

simper ['sɪmpə(r)] **1** *vi* minauder
2 *vt* **"of course, madam", he simpered** "bien sûr, chère Madame", dit-il en minaudant
3 *n* sourire *m* affecté; **"may I help you?" she said with a simper** "vous désirez?", dit-elle en minaudant

simperer ['sɪmpərə(r)] *n* minaudier(ère) *m,f*

simpering ['sɪmpərɪŋ] *n (UNCOUNT)* minauderies *fpl*

simperingly ['sɪmpərɪŋlɪ] *adv* en minaudant

simple ['sɪmpəl] *adj* (**a**) *(easy)* simple, facile; *(uncomplicated)* simple; **his reasons are never simple** ses raisons ne sont jamais simples; **it's a simple operation** c'est une opération simple; **getting there was the simple part** ce n'est pas d'y aller qui était difficile; **it's a simple meal to prepare** c'est un repas facile à préparer; **it would be simpler to do it myself** ce serait plus simple que je le fasse *ou* si je le faisais moi-même; **it should be a simple matter to change your ticket** tu ne devrais avoir aucun mal à changer ton billet; **to yearn for the simple life** aspirer au retour à la nature; **let's hear your story, then, but keep it simple** bon, racontez votre histoire, mais passez-moi les détails; **it's as simple as that** c'est aussi simple que ça
(**b**) *(plain → tastes, ceremony, life, style)* simple; **she wore a simple black dress** elle portait une robe noire toute simple; **I want a simple "yes" or "no"** répondez-moi simplement par "oui" ou par "non"; **let me explain in simple terms** *or* **language** laissez-moi vous expliquer ça en termes simples; **I did it for the simple reason that I had no choice** je l'ai fait pour la simple raison que je n'avais pas le choix
(**c**) *(unassuming)* simple, sans façons; **despite her success, she remains simple and unaffected** malgré sa réussite, elle est restée simple et naturelle
(**d**) *(naive)* simple, naïf; *(feeble-minded)* simple, niais; **he's a bit simple** il est un peu simplet
(**e**) *(basic → substance, fracture, sentence)* simple
(**f**) *Biol (eye)* simple
►► *Law* ***simple contract*** convention *f* verbale, acte *m* sous seing privé; *Math* ***simple equation*** équation *f* du premier degré; *Math* ***simple fraction*** fraction *f* ordinaire; *Med* ***simple fracture*** fracture *f* simple; *Phys* ***simple harmonic motion*** mouvement *m* harmonique simple; *Fin* ***simple interest*** *(UNCOUNT)* intérêts *mpl* simples; ***simple machine*** pièce *f* (d'un mécanisme); ***Simple Simon*** naïf *m*, nigaud *m*; *Gram* ***simple tense*** temps *m* simple

simple-hearted *adj (person)* candide, ouvert; *(wisdom, gesture)* simple, naturel

simple-minded *adj (naive)* naïf, simplet; *(feeble-minded)* simple d'esprit; **it's a very simple-minded view of society** c'est une vision très simpliste de la société

simple-mindedness [-'maɪndɪdnɪs] *n (naivety)* naïveté *f*; *(feeble-mindedness)* simplicité *f* d'esprit

simpleness ['sɪmpəlnɪs] = **simplicity**

simpleton ['sɪmpəltən] *n Old-fashioned* nigaud(e) *m,f*

simplex ['sɪmpleks] **1** *adj Comput & Tel* simplex *(inv)*, unidirectionnel
2 *n Comput & Tel* simplex *m*, transmission *f* unidirectionnelle; *Geom* simplexe *m*; *Ling (sentence)* unité *f* proportionnelle; *(word)* mot *m* simple

simplicity [sɪm'plɪsətɪ] *n* (**a**) *(UNCOUNT) (candour)* candeur *f*, simplicité *f*; *(foolishness)* bêtise *f*, sottise *f* (**b**) *(UNCOUNT) (easiness)* simplicité *f*; **the instructions are simplicity itself** les instructions sont simples comme bonjour *ou* tout ce qu'il y a de plus simple (**c**) (*pl* **simplicities**) *(simplistic idea)* idée *f* simpliste; *(simplistic attitude)* attitude *f* simpliste; *Literary* **the simplicities of childhood** les choses *fpl* simples de l'enfance

simplification [ˌsɪmplɪfɪ'keɪʃən] *n* simplification *f*

simplifier ['sɪmplɪfaɪə(r)] *n* simplificateur(trice) *m,f*

simplify ['sɪmplɪfaɪ] (*pt & pp* **simplified**) *vt* simplifier

simplifying ['sɪmplɪfaɪɪŋ] **1** *adj* simplificateur
2 *n* simplification *f*

simplism ['sɪmplɪzəm] *n* simplisme *m*

simplistic [sɪm'plɪstɪk] *adj* simpliste

simplistically [sɪm'plɪstɪklɪ] *adv* de manière simpliste

simply ['sɪmplɪ] *adv* (**a**) *(in a simple way)* simplement, avec simplicité; **put quite simply, it's a disaster** c'est tout simplement une catastrophe
(**b**) *(just, only)* simplement, seulement; **it's not simply a matter of money** ce n'est pas une simple question d'argent; **I simply told her the truth** je lui ai tout simplement dit la vérité
(**c**) *(as intensifier)* absolument; **it's simply perfect!** c'est absolument parfait!; **I simply don't understand you** je ne vous comprends

vraiment pas; **we simply must go now** il faut absolument que nous partions maintenant

simulacrum [ˌsɪmjʊˈleɪkrəm] *(pl* **simulacra** [-krə]) *n Formal or Literary* simulacre *m*, semblant *m*

simulate [ˈsɪmjʊleɪt] *vt* (**a**) *(imitate → blood, battle, sound)* simuler, imiter; **the insect simulates a piece of bark** l'insecte prend l'apparence d'un morceau d'écorce (**b**) *(feign → pain, pleasure)* simuler, feindre (**c**) *Comput & Tech* simuler

simulated [ˈsɪmjʊleɪtɪd] *adj* simulé; **a simulated nuclear disaster** une catastrophe nucléaire simulée

►► ***simulated fur*** fausse fourrure *f*; ***simulated leather*** similicuir *m*; ***simulated marble*** marbre *m* artificiel; *(painted)* faux marbre *m*

simulation [ˌsɪmjʊˈleɪʃən] *n* simulation *f*

►► *Comput* ***simulation model*** modèle *m* de simulation

simulator [ˈsɪmjʊleɪtə(r)] *n* simulateur *m*

simulcast [ˈsaɪməlkæst] *Am* **1** *vt* diffuser simultanément à la télévision et à la radio

2 *adj* radiotélévisé

3 *n* émission *f* radiotélévisée

simultaneity [*Br* ˌsɪməltəˈniːətɪ, *Am* ˌsaɪməltəˈniːətɪ] *n* simultanéité *f*

simultaneous [*Br* ˌsɪməlˈteɪnɪəs, *Am* ˌsaɪməlˈteɪnɪəs] *adj* simultané

►► ***simultaneous broadcast*** émission *f* diffusée simultanément, retransmission *f* simultanée; *Math* ***simultaneous equations*** système *m* d'équations simultanées; ***simultaneous translation*** traduction *f* simultanée

simultaneously [*Br* ˌsɪməlˈteɪnɪəslɪ, *Am* ˌsaɪməlˈteɪnɪəslɪ] *adv* simultanément, en même temps

simultaneousness [*Br* ˌsɪməlˈteɪnɪəsnɪs, *Am* ˌsaɪməlˈteɪnɪəsnɪs] *n* simultanéité *f*

sin [sɪn] *(pt & pp* **sinned**, *cont* **sinning**) **1** *n* péché *m*; **to commit a sin** pécher, commettre un péché; **sins of omission/commission** péchés *mpl* par omission/action; **the sin of pride** le péché d'orgueil; **it's a sin to tell a lie** mentir *ou* le mensonge est un péché; **it would be a sin to sell it** ce serait un crime de le vendre; *Hum* **for my sins, I'm the person in charge of all this** malheureusement pour moi, c'est moi le responsable de tout ça; *Rel or Hum* **to live in sin** vivre dans le péché

2 *vi* pécher; **to sin against sth** pécher contre qch; **to be more sinned against than sinning** être plus victime que coupable

►► *Fam* ***sin bin*** (**a**) *Am (brothel)* bordel *m*, lupanar◻ *m* (**b**) *Sport* banc *m* des pénalités◻, prison *f*

Sinai [ˈsaɪnaɪ] *n (region)* Sinaï *m*; **the Sinai (Desert)** le (désert du) Sinaï; **(Mount) Sinai** le (mont) Sinaï

►► ***the Sinai Peninsula*** la presqu'île de Sinaï

Sinbad [ˈsɪnbæd] *pr n* **Sinbad the Sailor** Sinbad le marin

sin-bin *vt Fam Sport* envoyer sur le banc des pénalités◻, envoyer en prison

since [sɪns] **1** *prep* depuis; **he has been talking about it since yesterday/since before Christmas** il en parle depuis hier/depuis avant Noël; **the fair has been held annually (ever) since 1950** la foire a lieu chaque année depuis 1950; **she's the best soul singer since Aretha Franklin** c'est la meilleure chanteuse de soul depuis Aretha Franklin; **how long is it since their divorce?** ça fait combien de temps qu'ils ont divorcé?; **since then** depuis lors; **that was in 1966, since when the law has been altered** c'était en 1966 – depuis, la loi a été modifiée; **since when have you been married?** depuis quand êtes-vous marié?; *Fam Ironic* **they really have changed – oh yes, since when?** ils ont vraiment changé – ah oui, depuis quand?

2 *conj* (**a**) *(in time)* depuis que; **I've worn glasses since I was six** je porte des lunettes depuis que j'ai six ans *ou* depuis l'âge de six ans; **how long has it been since you last saw Hal?** ça fait combien de temps que tu n'as pas vu Hal?; **it's been ages since we've gone to a play** ça fait une éternité que nous ne sommes pas allés au théâtre; **since leaving New York, I...** depuis que j'ai quitté New York, je...; **it had been ten years since I had seen him** cela faisait dix ans que je ne l'avais pas revu

(**b**) *(expressing cause)* puisque, comme; **since you don't want to go, I'll go by myself** puisque *ou* comme tu ne veux pas y aller, j'irai tout seul; **I'll do it since it's you that's asking** je le ferai puisque c'est vous qui me le demandez

3 *adv* depuis; **she used to be his assistant, but she's since been promoted** elle était son assistante, mais depuis elle a été promue; **I've never seen it/her since** je ne l'ai jamais revu/revue depuis

4 ever since 1 *conj* depuis que; **ever since she resigned, things have been getting worse** depuis qu'elle a démissionné *ou* depuis sa démission, les choses ont empiré **2** *prep* depuis; **ever since that day he's been afraid of dogs** depuis ce jour-là, il a peur des chiens **3** *adv* depuis; **he arrived at 9 o'clock and he's been sitting there ever since** il est arrivé à 9 heures et il est assis là depuis

5 long since *adv* **I've long since forgotten why** il y a longtemps que j'ai oublié pourquoi; **I've long since got used to it** il y a longtemps que j'y suis habitué

sincere [sɪnˈsɪə(r)] *adj* sincère; **please accept my sincere apologies** veuillez accepter mes sincères excuses; **it is my sincere belief that war can be avoided** je crois sincèrement qu'on peut éviter la guerre

sincerely [sɪnˈsɪəlɪ] *adv* sincèrement; **sincerely held views** des opinions *fpl* auxquelles on croit sincèrement; **I sincerely hope we can be friends** j'espère sincèrement que nous serons amis; *Br* **Yours sincerely,** *Am* **Sincerely yours** je vous prie d'agréer, Monsieur/Madame, mes sentiments les meilleurs

sincerity [sɪnˈserətɪ] *n* sincérité *f*; **to doubt sb's sincerity** douter de la sincérité *ou* bonne foi de qn; **in all sincerity, I must admit that...** en toute sincérité, je dois admettre que... + *indicative*

sincipital [sɪnˈsɪpɪtəl] *adj Anat* sincipital

sinciput [ˈsɪnsɪpʊt] *n Anat* sinciput *m*

sine [saɪn] *n Math* sinus *m*

►► ***sine wave*** onde *f* sinusoïdale

sinecure [ˈsaɪnɪˌkjʊə(r)] *n* sinécure *f*

sinecurism [ˈsaɪnɪˌkjʊrɪzəm] *n* sinécurisme *m*

sinecurist [ˈsaɪnɪˌkjʊrɪst] *n* sinécuriste *mf*

sine die [ˌsaɪnɪˈdaɪiː] *adv* sine die

sine qua non [ˌsaɪnɪkweɪˈnɒn] *n* condition *f* sine qua non

sinew [ˈsɪnjuː] **1** *n (tendon)* tendon *m*; *(muscle)* muscle *m*; *Literary (strength)* force *f*, forces *fpl*; **I will resist with every sinew of my body** je résisterai de toutes mes forces

2 sinews *npl Literary (source of strength)* nerf *m*, vigueur *f*; **coal and steel were the sinews of our economy** le charbon et la sidérurgie étaient le nerf de notre économie

sinewy [ˈsɪnjuːɪ] *adj* (**a**) *(muscular → person, body, arm)* musclé; *(→ neck, hands)* nerveux (**b**) *(with tendons → tissue)* tendineux; **sinewy meat** viande *f* nerveuse *ou* tendineuse (**c**) *Literary (forceful → style)* vigoureux, nerveux

sinfonia [sɪnˈfəʊnɪə] *n Mus* symphonie *f*

sinfonietta [ˌsɪnfəʊnɪˈetə] *n Mus* sinfonietta *f*

sinful [ˈsɪnfʊl] *adj (deed, urge, thought)* coupable, honteux; *(world)* plein de péchés, souillé par le péché; **his sinful ways** sa vie de péché; **sinful man** pécheur *m*; **sinful woman** pécheresse *f*; **how could such pleasure be sinful?** comment un tel plaisir pourrait-il être coupable?; **she thought alcohol was sinful** pour elle, boire de l'alcool était un péché; **it's downright sinful!** c'est un vrai scandale!

sinfully [ˈsɪnfʊlɪ] *adv* d'une façon coupable *ou* scandaleuse

sinfulness [ˈsɪnfʊlnɪs] *n (of deed, thought)* caractère *m* honteux; **his/her sinfulness** son état de pécheur/pécheresse; **a life of sinfulness** une vie de péché

sing [sɪŋ] *(pt* **sang** [sæŋ], *pp* **sung** [sʌŋ]) **1** *vi* (**a**) *(person)* chanter; **to sing like a lark** *or* **a nightingale** chanter comme un rossignol

(**b**) *(bird, kettle)* chanter; *(wind, arrow)* siffler; *(ears)* bourdonner, siffler; **bullets sang past his ears** des balles sifflaient à ses oreilles; **the noise made my ears sing** ce bruit m'a fait bourdonner les oreilles

(**c**) *Am Fam (confess, inform)* cracher, lâcher le morceau, se mettre à table; **he sang like a songbird at the trial** il s'est mis à table au procès; **somebody's been singing to our competitors** quelqu'un a vendu la mèche à *ou* tuyauté nos concurrents

2 *vt* (**a**) *(song, note, mass)* chanter; **to sing opera/jazz** chanter de l'opéra/du jazz; **who sings tenor?** qui est ténor?; **to sing sb to sleep** chanter pour endormir qn; *Fig* **now they're singing another** *or* **a different tune** ils ont changé de ton

(**b**) *(laud)* célébrer, chanter; **to sing the praises of sb/sth** chanter *ou* célébrer les louanges de qn/qch; **to sing one's own praises** chanter ses propres louanges, faire son propre éloge

►**sing along** *vi* chanter (tous) ensemble *ou* en chœur; **they sang along with her in the chorus** ils ont repris le refrain avec elle; **to sing along to** *or* **with the radio** chanter en même temps que la radio

►**sing out** *vi* (**a**) *(sing loudly)* chanter fort

(**b**) *Fam (shout)* crier◻; **when you're ready, sing out** quand tu seras prêt, fais-moi signe◻

►**sing up** *vi* chanter plus fort; **sing up!** plus fort!

singable [ˈsɪŋəbəl] *adj* chantable

sing-along *n* chants *mpl* en chœur; **let's have a sing-along** chantons tous en chœur *ou* tous ensemble

Singapore [ˌsɪŋəˈpɔː(r)] *n* Singapour

►► ***Singapore dollar*** dollar *m* de Singapour

Singaporean [ˌsɪŋəˈpɔːrɪən] **1** *n* Singapourien(enne) *m,f*

2 *adj* singapourien

singe [sɪndʒ] *(cont* **singeing**) **1** *vt* (**a**) *(gen)* brûler légèrement; *(shirt, fabric, paper)* roussir; **the lighter singed his moustache** il s'est brûlé la moustache avec le briquet (**b**) *Culin (carcass, chicken)* flamber, passer à la flamme

2 *vi (fabric)* roussir

3 *n (burn)* brûlure *f* (légère); *(mark)* marque *f* de brûlure

singeing [ˈsɪndʒɪŋ] *n (gen)* brûlage *m*; *(of shirt, fabric, paper)* roussissement *m*; *Hist* **the singeing of the King of Spain's beard** = l'attaque de Cadix par Francis Drake, en 1587

singer [ˈsɪŋə(r)] *n* (**a**) *(of songs)* chanteur(euse) *m,f*; **she's a jazz singer** elle est chanteuse de jazz; **I'm a terrible singer** je chante affreusement mal; **singer songwriter** auteur-compositeur-interprète *mf* (**b**) *Br Fam (informer)* indic *mf*

Singhalese = **Sinhalese**

singing [ˈsɪŋɪŋ] **1** *n* (**a**) *(of person, bird)* chant *m*; *(of kettle, wind)* sifflement *m*; *(in ears)* bourdonnement *m*, sifflement *m*; **the singing went on until dawn** on a chanté *ou* les chants ont continué jusqu'à l'aube; **we left after the singing of the national anthem** nous sommes partis après l'hymne national

(**b**) *(art)* chant *m*; **to study singing** étudier le chant; **her singing has improved** elle chante mieux

2 *adj (lesson, teacher, contest)* de chant; **she's got a fine singing voice** elle a une belle voix; **it's a singing role** c'est un rôle qui comporte des passages chantés

►► ***singing telegram*** = vœux présentés sous forme chantée, généralement à l'occasion d'un anniversaire

'Singin' in the Rain' *Donen & Kelly* 'Chantons sous la pluie'

SINGLE [ˈsɪŋgəl]

single	► **1 (a)**
aller simple	► **1 (b); 2 (f)**
chambre	► **1 (c)**
seul	► **2 (a), (b)**
unique	► **2 (a)**
simple	► **2 (c)**
singulier	► **2 (c)**
pour une personne	► **2 (d)**
célibataire	► **2 (e)**

1 *n* (**a**) *(record)* 45 tours *m inv*, single *m*; *(CD, cassette)* single *m*

(**b**) *Br (ticket → for journey)* aller *m* simple; *Theat* **we only have singles left** il ne nous reste que des places séparées (**c**) *(hotel room)* chambre *f* pour une personne *ou* individuelle; **I've reserved a single with bath** j'ai réservé une chambre pour une personne avec bain

(**d**) *(usu pl) (money) Br* pièce *f* d'une livre; *Am* billet *m* d'un dollar; **she gave me the change in singles** *(in pounds)* elle m'a rendu la monnaie en pièces d'une livre; *(in dollars)* elle m'a rendu la monnaie en billets d'un dollar

(**e**) *(in cricket)* point *m*

2 *adj* (**a**) *(sole)* seul, unique; **the room was lit by a single lamp** la pièce était éclairée par une seule lampe; **the report comes in a single volume** le rapport est publié en un (seul) volume; **he gave her a single red rose** il lui a donné une rose rouge; **I can't think of one single reason why I should do it** je n'ai aucune raison de le faire; **there wasn't a single person in the street** il n'y avait pas un chat dans la rue; **not a single one of her friends came** pas un seul de ses amis *ou* aucun de ses amis n'est venu; **I couldn't think of a single thing to say** je ne trouvais absolument rien à dire; **don't say a single word** ne dites pas un (seul) mot

(**b**) *(individual, considered separately)* **our single most important resource is oil** notre principale ressource est le pétrole; **what would my single best investment be?** quel serait le meilleur placement?; **we sell single items at a higher price per unit** le prix unitaire est plus élevé; **single copies cost more** un exemplaire seul coûte plus cher; **in any single year, average sales are ten million** sur une seule année, les ventes sont en moyenne de dix millions; **every single day** tous les jours; **every single apple** *or* **every single one of the apples was rotten** toutes les pommes sans exception étaient pourries; **every single time I take the plane, there's some problem** chaque fois que je prends l'avion, il y a un problème

(**c**) *(not double → flower, thickness)* simple; *(→ combat)* singulier; **five years ago we had single figure inflation** il y a cinq ans nous avions un taux d'inflation inférieur à 10 pour cent; **the score is still in single figures** le score est toujours inférieur à dix

(**d**) *(for one person → bed)* à une place, pour une personne; *Naut (→ cabin)* individuel; **a single sheet** un drap pour un lit d'une personne

(**e**) *(unmarried)* célibataire; **a single man/woman** un/une célibataire; **the single life seems to agree with you** la vie de célibataire a l'air de te convenir

(**f**) *Br (one way)* **a single ticket to Oxford** un aller (simple) pour Oxford; **the single fare is £12** un aller simple coûte 12 livres

►► *Br* ***single cream*** crème *f* (fraîche) liquide; ***single currency*** monnaie *f* unique; ***the Single European Act*** l'Acte *m* unique européen; ***the Single (European) Market*** le Marché unique (européen); ***single file*** file *f* indienne; **to walk in single file** marcher en file indienne *ou* à la queue leu leu; *Br Univ* ***single honours*** = licence portant sur une seule matière; ***single occupancy*** *(of hotel room)* occupation *f* par une seule personne; ***single parent*** *(gen)* père *m*/mère *f* célibataire; *Admin* parent *m* isolé; **he's a single parent** c'est un père célibataire; *Ins* ***single premium*** prime *f* unique; ***single price*** prix *m* unique; ***single quotes*** guillemets *mpl*; ***single room*** chambre *f* pour une personne *ou* individuelle; ***single (room) supplement*** supplément *m* chambre individuelle; ***single scull*** *(in rowing)* skiff *m*; *Comput* ***single sheet feed*** alimentation *f* feuille à feuille; *Typ* ***single spacing*** interlignage *m* simple; *Rail* ***single track*** voie *f* unique; *Pol* ***single transferable vote*** scrutin *m* uninominal préférentiel avec report de voix; *Comput* ***single user licence*** licence *f* individuelle d'utilisation; ***single yellow line*** = ligne jaune indiquant que le stationnement est autorisé à certaines heures

►**single out** *vt sep (for attention, honour)* sélectionner, distinguer; **a few candidates were singled out for special praise** quelques candidats ont eu droit à des félicitations supplémentaires; **they were all guilty, so why single anyone out?** ils étaient tous coupables, alors pourquoi accuser quelqu'un en particulier?

single-action *adj (firearm)* = que l'on doit réarmer avant chaque coup

single-breasted [-'brestɪd] *adj (jacket, coat)* droit

single-celled [-seld] *adj Biol* unicellulaire

single-column *adj Typ* à une colonne

single-cylinder *adj*

►► *Aut* ***single-cylinder engine*** moteur *m* monocylindrique

single-decker [-'dekə(r)] *n* autobus *m* sans impériale

►► ***single-decker bus*** autobus *m* sans impériale

single-density *adj*

►► *Comput* ***single-density disk*** disquette *f* simple densité

single-drive *adj (computer)* à un seul lecteur de disquettes

single-engined [-,endʒɪnd] *adj (plane)* monomoteur

single-entry bookkeeping *n* comptabilité *f* en partie simple

single-handed [-'hændɪd] **1** *adv (on one's own)* tout seul, sans aucune aide; **she's tripled our sales single-handed** elle a triplé nos ventes à elle toute seule

2 *adj* (**a**) *(unaided → voyage)* en solitaire; **to be single-handed** être tout seul, n'avoir aucune aide

(**b**) *(using one hand)* à une main

►► ***single-handed backhand shot*** *(in tennis, squash etc)* revers *m* à une main; ***single-handed saw*** (scie *f*) égoïne *f*

single-handedly [-'hændɪdlɪ] *adv* (**a**) *(on one's own)* tout seul, sans l'aide de personne; **she was single-handedly responsible for the firm's success** c'est grâce à elle seule que l'entreprise a réussi (**b**) *(with one hand)* d'une seule main

single-income *adj (family, couple)* à salaire unique

single-lane *adj (traffic)* à voie unique

single-lens *adj*

►► *Phot* ***single-lens camera*** appareil-photo *m* monoculaire; *Phot* ***single-lens reflex*** reflex *m* (mono-objectif)

single-masted [-'mɑːstɪd] *adj* à un (seul) mât

single-minded *adj* résolu, acharné; **the single-minded pursuit of money** la poursuite acharnée de l'argent; **to be single-minded about sth** s'acharner sur qch; **he is single-minded in his efforts to block the project** il fait tout ce qu'il peut pour bloquer le projet

single-mindedly [-'maɪndɪdlɪ] *adv* avec acharnement

single-mindedness [-'maɪndɪdnɪs] *n* résolution *f*, acharnement *m*

singleness ['sɪŋgəlnɪs] *n* **with singleness of purpose** avec un seul but en vue; **his singleness of purpose** sa détermination

single-parent family *n* famille *f* monoparentale

single-party *adj* à parti unique

single-phase *adj (current)* monophasé

singles ['sɪŋgəlz] *(pl* **inv***)* **1** *n* (**a**) *Sport* simple *m*; **the men's/women's singles champion** le champion du simple messieurs/dames (**b**) *(unmarried people)* célibataires *mpl*; **a package holiday for singles** des vacances organisées pour célibataires

2 *comp (bar, club, magazine)* pour célibataires; **Tuesday is singles night** mardi, c'est la soirée pour célibataires

single-seater *n Aviat* (avion *m*) monoplace *m*

single-sex *adj Sch* non mixte

single-sided *adj Comput (disk)* à une seule face

single-space *vt (on typewriter)* taper avec un interligne simple; *(on printer)* imprimer avec un interligne simple; **the typescript should be single-spaced** le texte dactylographié devra être en interligne simple

single-spaced [-speɪst] *adj Typ* à interligne simple

single-span *adj Archit (bridge)* à travée unique

single-spoke *adj (steering wheel)* monobranche

singlet ['sɪŋglɪt] *n Br (undergarment)* maillot *m* de corps; *Sport* maillot *m*

singletasking [,sɪŋgəl'tɑːskɪŋ] *Comput* **1** *n* monotâche *m*

2 *adj* monotâche

singleton ['sɪŋgəltən] *n* (**a**) *Cards & Math* singleton *m*

(**b**) *Br Fam (single person)* célibataire ▫ *mf*

single-track *adj* à voie unique

singly ['sɪŋglɪ] *adv* (**a**) *(one at a time)* séparément; **I'd rather see them singly** je préférerais les voir séparément (**b**) *(alone)* seul; **they arrived either in couples or singly** ils sont arrivés en couples ou seuls (**c**) *(individually → packaged)* individuellement; **you can't buy them singly** vous ne pouvez pas les acheter à la pièce

Sing Sing ['sɪŋsɪŋ] *n* = prison new-yorkaise de haute sécurité

singsong ['sɪŋsɒŋ] **1** *n* (**a**) *(melodious voice, tone)* **to speak in a singsong** parler d'une voix chantante (**b**) *Br (singing)* chants *mpl* (en chœur); **let's have a singsong** chantons tous ensemble *ou* en chœur

2 *adj (voice, accent)* chantant; **in a singsong voice** d'une voix chantante

singular ['sɪŋgjʊlə(r)] **1** *adj* (**a**) *(remarkable)* singulier; *(odd)* singulier, bizarre (**b**) *Gram* singulier

2 *n Gram* singulier *m*; **in the third person singular** à la troisième personne du singulier

singularity [,sɪŋgjʊ'lærətɪ] *(pl* **singularities***)* *n* singularité *f*

singularize, -ise ['sɪŋgjʊləraɪz] *vt* (**a**) *(distinguish)* singulariser (**b**) *Gram* mettre au singulier

singularly ['sɪŋgjʊləlɪ] *adv* singulièrement; **I was singularly unimpressed** cela ne m'a vraiment pas impressionné

Sinhalese [,sɪnhə'liːz] **1** *n* (**a**) *(person)* Cinghalais(e) *m,f* (**b**) *Ling* cinghalais *m*

2 *adj* cinghalais

sinister ['sɪnɪstə(r)] *adj* (**a**) *(ominous, evil)* sinistre; **he looks very sinister in black** le noir lui donne un air sinistre (**b**) *Her* senestre, sénestre

sinistral ['sɪnɪstrəl] *adj* senestre, sénestre

►► ***sinistral shell*** coquille *f* senestre *ou* sénestre

sinistrally ['sɪnɪstrəlɪ] *adv* sinistrorsum

sinistrorse [,sɪnɪ'strɔːs] *adj* sinistrorse

Sinitic [sɪ'nɪtɪk] *Ling* **1** *n* langues *fpl* chinoises

2 *adj* chinois

SINK [sɪŋk]

évier	► **1 (a)**
lavabo	► **1 (a)**
couler	► **2 (a); 3 (a)**
faire échouer	► **2 (b)**
oublier	► **2 (c)**
enfoncer	► **2 (d)**
creuser	► **2 (e)**
investir	► **2 (f)**
sombrer	► **3 (a), (f)**
s'enfoncer	► **3 (b), (f), (g)**
baisser	► **3 (c), (e)**
s'affaiser	► **3 (c)**
s'écrouler	► **3 (d)**
plonger	► **2 (a); 3 (e)**

(pt **sank** [sæŋk], *pp* **sunk** [sʌŋk]) **1** *n* (**a**) *(in kitchen)* évier *m*; *(in bathroom)* lavabo *m*; **double sink** évier *m* à deux bacs

(**b**) *(cesspool)* puisard *m*; *Fig* **a sink of sin and corruption** un cloaque du vice

(**c**) *Geol* doline *f*

2 *vt* (**a**) *(boat, submarine)* couler, envoyer par le fond; *Fig* **to be sunk in thought** être plongé dans ses pensées

(**b**) *(ruin → plans)* faire échouer; **their bid has sunk any chance of us getting the contract** leur offre a réduit à néant nos chances de décrocher le contrat; **this latest scandal looks certain to sink him** ce dernier scandale va sûrement le couler; *Fam* **if they don't come we're sunk!** s'ils ne viennent pas, nous sommes fichus!

(**c**) *(forget)* oublier; **he sank his troubles in drink** il noya ses soucis dans l'alcool; **they'll have to learn to sink their differences** il faudra qu'ils apprennent à oublier leurs différends

(**d**) *(plunge, drive → knife, spear, stake)* enfoncer; **they're sinking the piles for the jetty** ils sont en train de mettre en place les pilotis de la jetée; **the fishpond was a metal basin sunk in the ground** l'étang à poissons était un bassin en métal enfoncé dans le sol; **I sank my teeth into the peach** j'ai mordu dans la pêche; **the dog sank its teeth into my leg** le chien m'enfonça *ou* me planta ses crocs dans la jambe

(**e**) *(dig, bore → well, mine shaft)* creuser, forer

(**f**) *(invest → money)* mettre, investir; *(→ extravagantly)* engloutir; **we sank a fortune into this company** nous avons englouti une fortune dans cette société

(**g**) *Sport (score → basket)* marquer; *(→ putt)* réussir; **to sink the ball** *(in snooker)* couler la bille; *(in basketball)* réussir le tir *ou* le panier; *(in golf)* envoyer la balle dans le trou

(**h**) *Fin (debt)* amortir

(**i**) *Br Fam (drink down)* s'envoyer, siffler; **to sink a pint** s'envoyer une pinte de bière

3 *vi* (**a**) *(below surface → boat)* couler, sombrer; *(→ person, stone, log)* couler; **to sink like a stone** couler à pic; **the bottle sank slowly to the bottom of the pool** la bouteille a coulé lentement jusqu'au fond de la piscine; **the prow had not yet sunk beneath the surface** la proue n'était pas encore submergée; **Atlantis sank beneath the seas** l'Atlantide a été engloutie par les mers; **to sink without (a) trace** disparaître sans laisser de trace; *Fig* tomber dans l'oubli; *Fig* **it was a case of sink or swim** il a bien fallu se débrouiller; **now it's up to them to sink or swim by themselves** à eux maintenant de se débrouiller comme ils peuvent

(**b**) *(in mud, snow etc)* s'enfoncer; **at each step, I sank up to my knees in water** à chaque pas, je m'enfonçais dans l'eau jusqu'aux genoux; **the wheels sank into the mud** les roues s'enfonçaient dans la boue; **to sink into quicksand** s'enliser dans des sables mouvants

(**c**) *(subside → level, water, flames)* baisser; *(→ building, ground)* s'affaisser; **Venice is sinking** Venise est en train de s'affaisser; **the sun/moon is sinking** le soleil/la lune disparaît à l'horizon; **the moon sank behind the mountains** la lune a disparu derrière les montagnes; **as I climbed, the valley sank out of sight** au fur et à mesure que je grimpais, la vallée disparaissait

(**d**) *(sag, slump → person)* s'affaler, s'écrouler; *(→ hopes)* s'écrouler; **I sank back in my seat** je me suis enfoncé dans mon fauteuil; **her head sank back on the pillow** sa tête retomba sur l'oreiller; **he sank onto the bed** il s'est affalé *ou* il s'est laissé tomber sur le lit; **to sink to the ground** s'effondrer; **to sink to one's knees** tomber à genoux; **she sank down on her knees** elle tomba à genoux; **my heart** *or* **spirits sank when I saw I was too late** j'ai perdu courage en voyant que j'arrivais trop tard; **his heart sinks every time he gets a letter from her** il a un serrement de cœur chaque fois qu'il reçoit une lettre d'elle

(**e**) *(decrease, diminish → wages, rates, temperature)* baisser; *(more dramatically)* plonger, chuter; *(→ voice)* se faire plus bas; **you have sunk in my estimation** tu as baissé dans mon estime; **the dollar has sunk to half its former value** le dollar a perdu la moitié de sa valeur; **profits have sunk to an all-time low** les bénéfices sont au plus bas; **her voice had sunk to a whisper** *(purposefully)* elle s'était mise à chuchoter; *(weakly)* sa voix n'était plus qu'un murmure

(**f**) *(slip, decline)* sombrer, s'enfoncer; **to sink into apathy/depression** sombrer dans l'apathie/dans la dépression; **he sank deeper into crime** il s'enfonça dans la délinquance; **the house sank into decay and ruin** la maison est tombée en ruines; **how could you sink so low?** comment as-tu pu tomber si bas?; **to sink to new depths** tomber plus bas; **the patient is sinking fast** le malade décline rapidement; **he has sunk into a coma** il est tombé dans le coma; **I sank into a deep sleep** j'ai sombré dans un sommeil profond

(**g**) *(penetrate → blade, arrow)* s'enfoncer; **I felt the dog's teeth sink into my arm** j'ai senti les crocs du chien s'enfoncer dans mon bras

▸▸ *Am* ***sink board*** égouttoir *m*; *Br* ***sink estate*** cité *f* dépotoir; ***sink tidy*** = rangement pour ustensiles sur un évier; ***sink unit*** bloc-évier *m*

▸**sink in** *vi* (**a**) *(nail, blade)* s'enfoncer

(**b**) *(soak → varnish, cream)* pénétrer

(**c**) *(register → news)* être compris *ou* assimilé; *(→ allusion)* faire son effet; **I heard what you said, but it didn't sink in at the time** je vous ai entendu, mais je n'ai pas vraiment saisi sur le moment; **the implications of the epidemic have not yet sunk in** on ne se rend pas encore vraiment compte *ou* on ne réalise pas encore quelles seront les conséquences de cette épidémie; **I paused to let my words sink in** j'ai marqué une pause pour que mes paroles fassent leur effet; **it was beginning to sink in that things had changed** je commençais/il commençait/*etc* à comprendre que les choses avaient changé

sinkable ['sɪŋkəbəl] *adj* submersible

sinker ['sɪŋkə(r)] *n* (**a**) *(weight)* plomb *m (pour la pêche)* (**b**) *Am Fam (doughnut)* beignet❑ *m*; **sinkers and suds** des beignets et du café❑

sinkhole ['sɪŋkhəʊl] *n Geol* entonnoir *m*

sinking ['sɪŋkɪŋ] **1** *n* (**a**) *(of ship → accidental)* naufrage *m*; *(→ deliberate)* torpillage *m*

(**b**) *(of building, ground)* affaissement *m*

(**c**) *(of well)* creusage *m*, forage *m*

(**d**) *Fin (of debt)* amortissement *m*

2 *adj* **I experienced that sinking feeling you get when you've forgotten something** j'ai eu cette angoisse que l'on ressent quand on sait que l'on a oublié quelque chose; **I get that sinking feeling every time I think about what happened** à chaque fois que je pense à ce qui s'est passé, j'ai l'estomac qui se serre

▸▸ *Fin* ***sinking fund*** caisse *f ou* fonds *mpl* d'amortissement

sinless ['sɪnlɪs] *adj* sans péché; *(pure)* innocent, pur

sinlessly ['sɪnlɪslɪ] *adv* sans péché; *(purely)* purement

sinlessness ['sɪnlɪsnɪs] *n* innocence *f*, pureté *f*

sinner ['sɪnə(r)] *n* pécheur(eresse) *m,f*

Sinn Féin [,ʃɪn'feɪn] *n* le Sinn Féin *(faction politique de l'IRA)*

SINN FÉIN

Il s'agit d'un mouvement nationaliste irlandais fondé en 1902, qui se consacrait à l'origine à la lutte pour l'indépendance de l'Irlande et à la renaissance de la culture gaélique. Force politique vitale en Irlande à partir de 1916, il devient après la Seconde Guerre mondiale la branche politique de l'IRA (Irish Republican Army) qui œuvre pour la réunification du pays, coupé en deux après l'accès à l'indépendance du sud de l'île en 1921 (l'Irlande du Nord restant attachée au Royaume-Uni). Tourné vers le socialisme, il remporte cinq sièges en Irlande du Nord aux élections britanniques de 1982. Après 1994, le Sinn Féin participe au processus de paix en Irlande du Nord, qui aboutit en 1998 à l'établissement d'une assemblée semi-autonome à Belfast, dont le Sinn Féin fait partie.

sinning ['sɪnɪŋ] *n* péché *m*

Sino- ['saɪnəʊ] *pref* sino-; *Hist* **the Sino-Japanese War** la guerre sino-japonaise

sinological [,saɪnə'lɒdʒɪkəl] *adj* sinologique

sinologist [saɪ'nɒlədʒɪst], **sinologue** ['saɪnəlɒg] *n* sinologue *mf*

sinology [saɪ'nɒlədʒɪ] *n* sinologie *f*

sinophile ['saɪnəfaɪl] *n* sinophile *mf*

Sino-Tibetan *Ling* **1** *n* langues *fpl* sino-tibétaines

2 *adj* sino-tibétain

sinter ['sɪntə(r)] **1** *n* tuf *m* siliceux

2 *vt* fritter

sinuosity [,sɪnjʊ'ɒsətɪ] *n* sinuosité *f*

sinuous ['sɪnjʊəs] *adj (road, neck, movement, reasoning)* sinueux; **he danced with sinuous grace** lorsqu'il dansait, son corps ondulait avec grâce

sinus ['saɪnəs] *n* sinus *m*; **for fast sinus relief** pour dégager rapidement les sinus

sinusitis [,saɪnə'saɪtɪs] *n (UNCOUNT) Med* sinusite *f*

sinusoid ['saɪnəsɔɪd] *n* (**a**) *Math* sinusoïde *f*, onde *f* sinusoïdale (**b**) *Anat* sinusoïde *m*

sinusoidal [,saɪnə'sɔɪdəl] *adj Anat & Math* sinusoïdal

Siouan ['suːən] *adj* sioux *(inv)*

Sioux [suː] *(pl* **inv** [suː, suːz]) **1** *n* (**a**) *(person)* Sioux *mf inv* (**b**) *Ling* sioux *m*

2 *adj* sioux *(inv)*; **the Sioux Indians** les Sioux *mpl*

sip [sɪp] *(pt & pp* **sipped**, *cont* **sipping**) **1** *vt (drink slowly)* boire à petites gorgées *ou* à petits coups; *(savour)* siroter

2 *vi* **to sip at sth** boire qch à petites gorgées; **he was at the bar, sipping at a cognac** il était au comptoir, sirotant un cognac

3 *n* petite gorgée *f*; **can I have a sip?** je peux goûter *ou* en boire un peu?; **she took a sip of wine** elle a bu une petite gorgée de vin

siphon ['saɪfən] **1** *n* siphon *m*

2 *vt* (**a**) *(liquid, petrol)* siphonner

(**b**) *(money, resources)* transférer; *(illicitly)* détourner; **the money is siphoned from one account into another** l'argent est transféré d'un compte à un autre; **huge sums were siphoned into public housing** des sommes énormes ont été injectées dans les logements sociaux

▸**siphon off** *vt sep* (**a**) *(liquid, petrol)* siphonner

(**b**) *(remove → money)* absorber, éponger; *(divert illegally)* détourner; **the private sector is siphoning off the best graduates** le secteur privé absorbe les meilleurs diplômés; **the road will siphon traffic off from the city centre** la route va détourner une bonne partie de la circulation du centre-ville

siphonage ['saɪfənɪdʒ] *n* siphonnement *m*; *Med* siphon(n)age *m*

siphonal ['saɪfənəl] *adj Zool* siphoïde

siphonic [saɪ'fɒnɪk] *adj* siphonal, siphoïde

siphoning ['saɪfənɪŋ] *n* siphonnement *m*

sir [sɜː(r)] *n* (**a**) *(term of address)* monsieur *m*; **no, sir** non, Monsieur; *Mil (to officer)* non, mon général/mon colonel/*etc*; **Dear Sir** *(in letter)* (Cher) Monsieur; **Dear Sirs** Messieurs; *Fam* **not for me, no sir** *(emphatic)* pas pour moi, ça non *ou* pas question! (**b**) *(title of knight, baronet)* **Sir Ian Hall** sir Ian Hall; **to be made a sir** être anobli (**c**) *Br Fam (male teacher)* **Sir's coming!** le maître arrive!❑

sirdar ['sɜːdɑː(r)] *n Mil* sirdar *m*

sire ['saɪə(r)] **1** *n* (**a**) *(animal)* père *m* (**b**) *Arch (father)* père *m* (**c**) *(term of address)* **no, sire** *(to king)* non, sire; *(to lord)* non, seigneur

2 *vt* engendrer; **Buttons, sired by Goldfly** Buttons, issu de Goldfly

siree = **sirree**

siren ['saɪərən] *n* (**a**) *(device)* sirène *f*; **ambulance/police siren** sirène *f* d'ambulance/de voiture de police (**b**) *Myth* sirène *f*; *Fig (temptress)* sirène *f*, femme *f* fatale

▸▸ ***siren call, siren song*** chant *m* des sirènes; *Fig* attrait *m*, appât *m*; **who can resist the siren call of fame and wealth?** qui peut résister à l'attrait de la gloire et de la fortune?

Sirius ['sɪrɪəs] *n Astron* Sirius *m*

sirloin ['sɜːlɔɪn] *n* aloyau *m*; **a sirloin steak** un bifteck dans l'aloyau

sirocco [sɪ'rɒkəʊ] *(pl* **siroccos**) *n* sirocco *m*, siroco *m*

sirree [sɜː'riː] *exclam Am Fam* **yes/no sirree!** ça oui/non!

sirup *Am* = **syrup**

sis [sɪs] *n Fam (abbr* **sister**) frangine *f*, sœurette *f*

sisal ['saɪsəl] **1** *n* sisal *m*

2 *adj* en *ou* de sisal

siskin ['sɪskɪn] *n Orn* tarin *m* (des aulnes)

sissy ['sɪsɪ] *(pl* **sissies**) *Fam* **1** *n* (**a**) *(coward)* poule *f* mouillée, peureux(euse)❑ *m,f* (**b**) *(effeminate person)* **he's a real sissy** c'est une vraie mauviette; **that's a game for sissies!** c'est un jeu de fillettes!

2 *adj* (**a**) *(cowardly)* peureux❑ (**b**) *(effeminate)* **don't be so sissy** t'es une mauviette, ou quoi?

sister ['sɪstə(r)] **1** *n* (**a**) *(member of family)* sœur *f*; **they're sisters** elles sont sœurs; **my big/little sister** ma grande/petite sœur

(**b**) *(nun)* religieuse *f*, (bonne) sœur *f*; **no, Sister** non, ma sœur; **Sister Pauline** sœur Pauline; **Sister of Mercy** sœur *f* de la Charité; **the Little Sisters of the Poor** les Petites Sœurs *fpl* des pauvres

(**c**) *Br (nurse)* infirmière *f* en chef; **I'll have to ask Sister** il faudra que je demande à l'infirmière en chef

(**d**) *(fellow woman, feminist)* sœur *f*; *(term of address)* ma fille; **our sisters in Africa** nos sœurs d'Afrique

(**e**) *Am Fam (black woman)* = nom donné par les Noirs américains à une femme noire; *(term of address)* ma fille; **you don't treat your sisters like that!** c'est pas des façons de traiter d'autre Noires!

2 *adj (publication, hotel)* qui appartient au même groupe; **sister state/party** pays *m*/parti *m* frère; **sister company** société *f* sœur

▸▸ *Am* ***sister cities*** villes *fpl* jumelées; **to be a sister city with** être jumelé avec; ***sister ship*** *(belonging to same company)* navire *m* de la même ligne; *(identical)* navire-jumeau *m*, sister-ship *m*

sisterhood [ˈsɪstəhʊd] *n* (**a**) *(group of women)* communauté *f* de femmes; *Rel* communauté *f* religieuse (**b**) *(solidarity)* solidarité *f* entre femmes

sister-in-law *(pl* **sisters-in-law***)* *n* belle-sœur *f*

sisterliness [ˈsɪstəlɪnɪs] *n* affection *f ou* sympathie *f* de soeur

sisterly [ˈsɪstəlɪ] *adj (advice)* de sœur; **sisterly devotion** dévouement *m* de sœur

Sistine Chapel [ˈsɪstiːn-] *n* **the Sistine Chapel** la chapelle Sixtine

Sisyphus [ˈsɪsɪfəs] *pr n Myth* Sisyphe; **the myth of Sisyphus** le mythe de Sisyphe

SIT [sɪt]

asseoir	▸ **1 (a)**
faire asseoir	▸ **1 (b)**
passer	▸ **1 (c); 2 (f)**
s'asseoir	▸ **2 (a)**
être assis	▸ **2 (a)**
poser	▸ **2 (b)**
être en séance	▸ **2 (d)**
garder les enfants	▸ **2 (e)**
être	▸ **2 (g)**
se trouver	▸ **2 (g)**
rester	▸ **2 (a), (h)**

(pt & pp **sat** [sæt], *cont* **sitting***)* **1** *vt* (**a**) *(place)* asseoir, installer; **he sat the child in the pram/on his knee** il a assis l'enfant dans le landau/sur ses genoux

(**b**) *(invite to be seated)* faire asseoir; **she sat me in the waiting room** elle m'a fait asseoir dans la salle d'attente

(**c**) *Br (examination)* se présenter à, passer

(**d**) *Horseriding* **to sit a horse badly/well** monter (un cheval) mal/bien, avoir une mauvaise/bonne assiette

(**e**) *Literary (suit)* **with an impudent air that sat him ill** d'un air effronté qui lui seyait mal

2 *vi* (**a**) *(take a seat)* s'asseoir; *(be seated)* être assis; **she came and sat next to me** elle est venue s'asseoir à côté de moi; **she sat by me all evening** elle était assise à côté de moi toute la soirée; **sit in the back of the car** mettez-vous à l'arrière (de la voiture); **she was sitting reading** elle était assise à lire *ou* en train de lire; **where would you like me to sit?, where shall I sit?** où est-ce que je me mets?; **they were sitting at (the) table** ils étaient à table, ils étaient attablés; **we usually sit in the living room** nous sommes d'ordinaire dans le salon; **sit still!** tiens-toi *ou* reste tranquille!; **sit!** *(to dog)* assis!; **they sat over the meal for hours** ils sont restés à table pendant des heures; **to sit at home,** *Am* **to sit home** rester à la maison; **don't think I'm just going to sit and wait for you!** ne t'imagine pas que je vais rester là à t'attendre!; **he sits in front of the television all day** il passe toute la journée devant la télévision; *Fam* **sit tight, I'll be back in a moment** ne bouge pas, je reviens tout de suite; **we just have to sit tight and wait for things to get better** on ne peut qu'attendre patiemment que les choses s'arrangent

(**b**) *Art & Phot (pose)* poser; **she sat for Modigliani** elle a posé pour Modigliani

(**c**) *(be a member)* **to sit on a board** faire partie *ou* être membre d'un conseil d'administration; *Br Pol* **to sit in Parliament** = être député; **he sat for Swansea** il était député de Swansea

(**d**) *(be in session)* être en séance, siéger; **the council was still sitting at midnight** à minuit, le conseil siégeait toujours *ou* était toujours en séance; **the House sits for another two months** la session de la Chambre doit durer encore deux mois

(**e**) *Fam (baby-sit)* **I'll ask Amy to sit for us** je demanderai à Amy de garder les enfants ☐; **she's sitting for the neighbours** elle garde les enfants des voisins ☐

(**f**) *Br Sch & Univ (be a candidate)* **to sit for an exam** se présenter à *ou* passer un examen

(**g**) *(be situated → building)* être, se trouver; *(→ vase)* être posé; **the houses sit nestled in a beautiful valley** les maisons sont nichées *ou* blotties dans une belle vallée; **a clock sat on the mantelpiece** une horloge était posée sur la cheminée; **your keys are sitting right in front of you** tes clés sont là, devant ton nez; **her mail sat in a pile on her desk** son courrier était empilé sur son bureau; **a tank sat in the middle of the road** un char d'assaut était planté au milieu de la route; *Literary* **joy sat on every countenance** la joie régnait sur tous les visages; *Literary* **the wind sits in the east** le vent vient de l'est

(**h**) *(remain inactive or unused)* rester; **the plane sat waiting on the runway** l'avion attendait sur la piste; **the letter sat unopened** la lettre n'avait pas été ouverte

(**i**) *(fit → coat, dress)* tomber; **the jacket sits well on you** la veste vous va parfaitement; **the collar should sit flat** le col devrait rester à plat; *Fig* **age sits well on him** la maturité lui va bien; **the thought sat uneasily on my conscience** cette pensée me pesait sur la conscience

(**j**) *(bird → perch)* se percher, se poser; *(→ brood)* couver; **they take turns sitting on the eggs** ils couvent les œufs à tour de rôle

▸**sit about, sit around** *vi* rester à ne rien faire, traîner; **she just sits around (the house) all day** elle reste toute la journée à la maison à ne rien faire; **I'm not going to sit around waiting for you** je ne vais pas passer mon temps à t'attendre

▸**sit back** *vi* (**a**) *(relax)* s'installer confortablement; **to sit back (in an armchair)** se caler *ou* s'installer confortablement dans un fauteuil; **I sat back against the cushions** je me suis calé contre les coussins; **just sit back and close your eyes** installe-toi bien et ferme les yeux; **sit back and enjoy it** détends-toi et profites-en

(**b**) *(refrain from intervening)* **I can't just sit back and watch!** je ne peux pas rester là à regarder sans rien faire!; **he just sits back and lets the others do the work** il regarde les autres travailler sans lever le petit doigt; **we can't just sit back and ignore the danger** nous ne pouvons tout de même pas faire comme s'il n'y avait pas de danger

▸**sit by** *vi* rester sans rien faire; **how can you sit by while others suffer?** comment peux-tu rester sans rien faire quand d'autres souffrent?

▸**sit down 1** *vt sep (place → person)* asseoir, installer; **he sat himself down beside me** il s'est assis à côté de moi; **sit yourself down and have a drink** asseyez-vous et prenez un verre

2 *vi* s'asseoir; **please sit down** asseyez-vous, je vous en prie; **to be sitting down** être assis; **I was just sitting down to work when the phone rang** j'étais sur le point de me mettre au travail quand le téléphone a sonné; **to sit down to table** se mettre à table, s'attabler; **to sit down to a game of bridge** s'installer pour faire une partie de bridge; **I think we should sit down and talk about it** je crois qu'il faut qu'on en discute *ou* parle; **the two sides have decided to sit down together at the negotiating table** les deux camps ont décidé de s'asseoir à la table des négociations

▸**sit in** *vi* (**a**) *(attend)* assister (sans participer); **do you mind if I sit in for a while?** cela vous ennuie-t-il si je reste à écouter un moment?; **to sit in on a meeting/a class** assister à une réunion/un cours

(**b**) *(replace)* **to sit in for sb** remplacer qn

(**c**) *(hold a demonstration)* faire un sit-in

▸**sit on** *vt insep Fam* (**a**) *(suppress, quash → file, report)* garder le silence sur ☐; *(→ suggestion, proposal)* repousser ☐, rejeter ☐; **any new initiative is promptly sat on** on décourage rapidement toute nouvelle initiative ☐

(**b**) *(take no action on)* ne pas s'occuper de ☐; **his office has been sitting on those recommendations for months now** ça fait des mois que son bureau a ces recommandations sous le coude; **they mustn't sit on their one-goal lead** il ne faut pas qu'ils s'endorment sur leurs lauriers maintenant qu'ils ont un but d'avance

(**c**) *(silence → person)* faire taire ☐; *(rebuff)* rabrouer ☐

▸**sit out 1** *vt sep* (**a**) *(endure)* attendre la fin de; **it was very boring but I sat it out** c'était très ennuyeux, mais je suis restée jusqu'au bout

(**b**) *(not take part in)* **I think I'll sit the next one out** *(dance)* je crois que je ne vais pas danser la prochaine danse; *(in cards)* je crois que je ne jouerai pas la prochaine main

2 *vi (sit outside)* s'asseoir *ou* se mettre dehors; *(be seated outside)* être assis dehors

▸**sit through** *vt insep* attendre la fin de; **he sat through the whole play** il est resté jusqu'à la fin de la pièce; **I can't bear to sit through another of his speeches** je ne supporterai pas un autre de ses discours; **we had to sit through two hours of Wagner** nous avons dû nous payer deux heures de Wagner; **we sat through dinner in silence** nous avons passé tout le dîner sans rien dire

▸**sit up 1** *vi* (**a**) *(raise oneself to sitting position)* s'asseoir; *(sit straight)* se redresser; **she was sitting up in bed reading** elle lisait, assise dans son lit; **the baby can sit up now** le bébé peut se tenir assis maintenant; **sit up straight!** redresse-toi!, tiens-toi droit!; *Fig* **to make sb sit up** secouer qn, secouer les puces à qn; **the public began to sit up and take notice** le public a commencé à montrer un certain intérêt; **her competitors are beginning to sit up and take notice** ses concurrents commencent à prendre conscience de son existence

(**b**) *(not go to bed)* rester debout, ne pas se coucher; **don't bother sitting up for me** ne m'attendez pas; **I sat up watching TV until 3 a.m.** j'ai regardé la télé jusqu'à 3 heures du matin; **I'll sit up with her until the fever passes** je vais rester avec elle jusqu'à ce que sa fièvre tombe

2 *vt sep (child, patient)* asseoir, redresser; **to sit sb up against a wall** adosser qn contre un mur

Are you sitting comfortably? (Then I'll begin)

Cette expression ("Êtes-vous assis confortablement? Je peux donc commencer") est la formule d'introduction classique que l'on prononce avant de raconter une histoire à des enfants. Le narrateur de l'émission de radio britannique *Listen with Mother* l'employait systématiquement avant chaque récit.

Aujourd'hui, cette expression témoigne d'une attitude quelque peu condescendante de la part de celui qui l'emploie. On l'utilise lorsqu'on veut capter l'attention de personnes inattentives ou bien sur le mode humoristique avant un discours.

sitar [sɪˈtɑː(r)] *n* sitar *m*

sitcom [ˈsɪtkɒm] *n* comédie *f* de situation, sitcom *m*

sit-down 1 *n Fam (rest)* **I could do with a bit of a sit-down** j'aimerais bien m'asseoir un peu ☐; **come and have a sit-down** viens t'asseoir ☐

2 *adj* **there are too many guests for a sit-down meal** il y a trop d'invités pour que tout le monde puisse s'asseoir à table

▸▸ ***sit-down dinner*** dîner *m* pris à table; *Br* ***sit-down strike*** grève *f* sur le tas

site [saɪt] **1** *n* (**a**) *(piece of land)* terrain *m*; **the development project includes sites for small businesses** le projet immobilier prévoit des terrains pour de petites entreprises

(**b**) *(place, location)* emplacement *m*, site *m*; **there's been a church on this site for centuries** cela fait des siècles qu'il y a une église à cet endroit *ou* ici; **this forest has been the site of several battles** cette forêt a été le théâtre de plusieurs batailles

(**c**) *Constr* **(building) site** chantier *m*; **helmets must be worn on (the) site** le port du casque est obligatoire sur le chantier; **demolition site** chantier *m* de démolition

(**d**) *Archeol* site *m*

(**e**) *Med (of pain)* siège *m*

(**f**) *Comput (on Internet)* site *m*

2 *comp Constr (office, inspection, visit)* de chantier

3 *vt* placer, situer; **the argument continues over where the new airport should be sited** les discussions continuent pour décider de l'emplacement du nouvel aéroport

4 on site *adv* sur place

▸▸ ***site manager*** chef *m* de chantier; ***Site of Special Scientific Interest*** = site protégé présentant un intérêt particulier du point de vue de la faune, de la flore ou de la géologie

sit-in *n* (**a**) *(demonstration)* sit-in *m inv*; **to stage** *or* **to hold a sit-in** faire un sit-in (**b**) *(strike)* grève *f* sur le tas

siting ['saɪtɪŋ] *n* **the siting of the nuclear plant is highly controversial** le choix de l'emplacement de la centrale nucléaire provoque une vive controverse; **access is important in the siting of the stadium** l'accessibilité est un facteur important dans le choix du site pour le stade

sitter ['sɪtə(r)] *n* (**a**) *(for children)* baby-sitter *mf*; **I couldn't find a sitter for the dog/house** je n'ai trouvé personne pour garder le chien/la maison
(**b**) *Art (model)* modèle *m*
(**c**) *(hen)* couveuse *f*
(**d**) *Br Fam (easy chance)* coup *m* facile; **to miss a sitter** rater un coup facile
(**e**) *Br Fam Horseracing (certain winner)* cheval *m* donné gagnant ❑; **I backed a sitter in the 3:30** j'ai parié sur un cheval donné gagnant dans la course de trois heures et demie
(**f**) *(at seance)* = personne qui participe à une séance de spiritisme

sitting ['sɪtɪŋ] **1** *n* (**a**) *(for meal)* service *m*; **first/second sitting** premier/deuxième service *m*; **to serve 500 people in** *or* **at one sitting** servir 500 personnes à la fois
(**b**) *Art (for portrait)* séance *f* de pose; **to paint a portrait in three sittings** faire un portrait en trois séances
(**c**) *(of assembly, committee, court)* séance *f*; **I read the book at** *or* **in one sitting** j'ai lu le livre d'une traite
2 *adj* (**a**) *(seated)* assis; **he propped up the body in a sitting position** il a calé le corps en position assise
(**b**) *(in office)* en exercice; **the sitting member for Leeds** le député actuel de Leeds
(**c**) *(hen)* en train de couver
▸▸ ***sitting duck*** *Fam (target)* cible *m* facile ❑; *(victim)* proie *f* facile ❑, pigeon *m*; **old people are sitting ducks for all sorts of confidence tricksters** les personnes âgées sont des proies faciles pour les escrocs en tous genres; *Br* ***sitting room*** salon *m*, salle *f* de séjour; *Br* ***sitting target*** cible *f* facile; *Br* ***sitting tenant*** locataire *mf* en place; *Horseriding* ***sitting trot*** trot *m* assis

situate ['sɪtjʊeɪt] *vt Formal (in place)* situer, implanter; *(in context)* resituer; **they plan to situate the new hospital near the town centre** ils envisagent d'implanter le nouvel hôpital près du centre-ville

situated ['sɪtjʊeɪtɪd] *adj* (**a**) *(physically)* situé; **the house is conveniently situated for shops and public transport** la maison est située à proximité des commerces et des transports en commun; **the town is well/badly situated for tourist development** la situation de la ville est/n'est pas favorable à son développement touristique; **the island is strategically situated** l'île occupe une position stratégique
(**b**) *(circumstantially)* **how are we situated as regards the competition?** quelle est notre position par rapport à la concurrence?; **he's well situated to know what's going on** il est bien placé pour savoir ce qui se passe

situation [ˌsɪtjʊ'eɪʃən] *n* (**a**) *(state of affairs)* situation *f*; **the situation at work/in China is getting worse** la situation au travail/en Chine ne s'arrange pas; **I've got myself into a ridiculous situation** je me suis mis dans une situation ridicule; **what would you do in my situation?** qu'est-ce que tu ferais à ma place *ou* dans ma situation?; **can't you do something about the situation?** ne pouvez-vous pas faire quelque chose?; **the firm's financial situation isn't good** la situation financière de la société n'est pas bonne; *Fam* **what's** *or* **how's the coffee situation?** combien nous reste-t-il de café? ❑; **a crisis situation** une situation de crise; **it won't work in a classroom situation** ça ne marchera pas dans une salle de classe; **the skills needed in an interview situation** les compétences dont on a besoin pour faire face à un entretien
(**b**) *(job)* situation *f*, emploi *m*; **situations vacant/wanted** offres *fpl*/demandes *fpl* d'emploi
(**c**) *(location)* situation *f*, emplacement *m*
▸▸ *TV & Rad* ***situation comedy*** sitcom *m*; *Phil* ***situation ethics*** éthique *f* de situation

situational [ˌsɪtjʊ'eɪʃənəl] *adj* situationnel

situationism [ˌsɪtjʊ'eɪʃənɪzəm] *n* situationnisme *m*

situationist [ˌsɪtjʊ'eɪʃənɪst] **1** *adj* situationniste
2 *n* situationniste *mf*

sit-up *n Sport* redressement *m* assis; **to do sit-ups** faire des abdominaux; **I do fifty sit-ups every morning** je fais une série de cinquante abdominaux tous les matins

sit-upon *n Fam Old-fashioned* derrière *m*, postérieur *m*

six [sɪks] **1** *n* (**a**) *(number, numeral)* six *m inv*; *Br* **to be at sixes and sevens** être sens dessus dessous; **I'm at sixes and sevens as to what to do** je ne sais absolument pas quoi faire; *Fam* **it's six of one and half a dozen of the other, it's six and half a dozen** c'est blanc bonnet et bonnet blanc, c'est kif-kif; *Br Fam Old-fashioned Sch* **to get six of the best** se faire fouetter ❑
(**b**) *(ice hockey team)* équipe *f*; *(cub or brownie patrol)* patrouille *f*
(**c**) *(in cricket)* six points *mpl*; **he scored five sixes** il a marqué cinq fois six points; *Br Fam Fig* **to knock for six** *(person → knock down)* étendre ❑; *(→ flabbergast)* abasourdir ❑; *(enemy, opponent)* battre à plate(s) couture(s)
2 *pron* six
3 *adj* six; *Fam* **to be six feet under** être six pieds sous terre, manger les pissenlits par la racine
4 Six *npl* **the Six** *(Common Market pre-1973)* les Six *mpl*; *see also* **five**
▸▸ ***the Six Counties*** (les six comtés *mpl* de) l'Irlande *f* du Nord; *Hist* ***the Six Day War*** la guerre des Six-Jours; *Sport* ***the Six Nations (Tournament)*** le Tournoi des Six Nations

sixain ['sɪkseɪn] *n Literature* sizain *m*, sixain *m*

sixer ['sɪksə(r)] *n (in cubs, brownies)* chef *m* de patrouille

six-fingered [-'fɪŋgəd] *adj (hand)* sexdigital; *(person)* sexdigitaire

sixfold ['sɪksfəʊld] **1** *adj* sextuple
2 *adv* au sextuple; **the population has increased sixfold** la population a sextuplé *ou* s'est multipliée par six; **profits are up sixfold on last year** les bénéfices sont six fois plus importants que *ou* se sont multipliés par six depuis l'année dernière

six-foot *adj (beam)* de six pieds; **a six-foot bodyguard** un garde du corps d'un mètre quatre-vingts

six-footer [-'fʊtə(r)] *n Fam* **both her sons are six-footers** ses deux fils mesurent plus d'un mètre quatre-vingts ❑

six-gun = **six-shooter**

six-pack *n* (**a**) *(of beer)* pack *m* de six; **he polishes off a couple of six-packs every night** il s'envoie une bonne douzaine de bières chaque soir; *Br Fam Hum* **he's one can short of a six-pack** il n'est pas très net (**b**) *Fam Hum (stomach muscles)* abdos *mpl*; **he's got a great six-pack** il a des supers abdos

sixpence ['sɪkspəns] *n* (**a**) *(sum)* six pence *mpl* (**b**) *(coin)* pièce *f* de six pence

sixpenny ['sɪkspənɪ] *adj Old-fashioned (costing six pence)* qui coûte six pence; *(stamp)* de six pence
▸▸ ***sixpenny piece*** pièce *f* de six pence

sixpennyworth [sɪks'penɪwəθ] *n Old-fashioned* **to buy sixpennyworth of chocolate** acheter pour six pence de chocolat

six-shooter *n Am Fam* pistolet *m* à six coups ❑, six-coups *m inv*

six-sided *adj* qui a six côtés, hexagonal

sixteen [sɪks'tiːn] **1** *n* seize *m inv*; **she was sweet sixteen** c'était une jolie jeune fille de seize ans
2 *pron* seize
3 *adj* seize; *see also* **five**

sixteenmo [sɪks'tiːnməʊ] (*pl* **sixteenmos**) *Typ* **1** *adj* in-seize *(inv)*
2 *n* in-seize *m inv*

sixteenth [sɪks'tiːnθ] **1** *n* (**a**) *(fraction)* seizième *m* (**b**) *(in series)* seizième *mf* (**c**) *(of month)* seize *m inv*
2 *adj* seizième
3 *adv* seizièmement; *(in contest)* en seizième position, à la seizième place; *see also* **fifth**
▸▸ *Am Mus* ***sixteenth note*** double croche *f*

sixteenthly [sɪks'tiːnθlɪ] *adv* seizièmement

sixth [sɪksθ] **1** *n* (**a**) *(fraction)* sixième *m*
(**b**) *(in series)* sixième *mf*
(**c**) *(of month)* six *m inv*
(**d**) *Mus* sixte *f*
(**e**) *Br Sch* **to be in the lower/upper sixth** ≃ être en première/en terminale
2 *adj* sixième
3 *adv* sixièmement; *(in contest)* en sixième position, à la sixième place; *see also* **fifth**
▸▸ *Br Sch* ***sixth form*** = classe terminale de l'enseignement secondaire en Angleterre et au pays de Galles, préparant aux "A-levels", ≃ classes *fpl* de première et de terminale; *Br Sch* ***sixth form college*** = établissement préparant aux "A-levels"; *Br Sch* ***sixth former*** = élève de première ou de terminale; **all the sixth formers** tous les élèves de première et de terminale; *Am Sch* ***sixth grade*** = classe du primaire pour les 10–11 ans; ***sixth sense*** sixième sens *m*; **some sixth sense told me she wouldn't come** j'avais l'intuition qu'elle ne viendrait pas

sixth-form *adj Br (student, teacher)* = de première ou de terminale

sixthly ['sɪksθlɪ] *adv* sixièmement, en sixième lieu

sixtieth ['sɪkstɪəθ] **1** *n* (**a**) *(fraction)* soixantième *m* (**b**) *(in series)* soixantième *mf*
2 *adj* soixantième
3 *adv* soixantièmement; *(in contest)* en soixantième position, à la soixantième place; *see also* **fifth**

six-toed [-təʊd] *adj (foot)* sexdigital; *(person)* sexdigitaire

Sixtus ['sɪkstəs] *pr n* Sixte

sixty ['sɪkstɪ] **1** *n* (*pl* **sixties**) soixante *m inv*; **sixties pop music** la musique pop des années soixante
2 *pron* soixante; **about sixty** une soixantaine
3 *adj* soixante; *see also* **fifty**

sixty-four **1** *adj* soixante-quatre; *Fam* **the sixty-four (thousand) dollar question** la question cruciale ❑
2 *n* soixante-quatre *m*

sixty-fourmo [-'fɔːməʊ] (*pl* **sixty-fourmos**) *Typ* **1** *adj (book, format)* in-soixante-quatre *(inv)*
2 *n* in-soixante-quatre *m inv*

sixty-nine *n Fam (sexual position)* soixante-neuf *m*

six-yard box *n Ftbl* zone *f* de la surface de but

sizable = **sizeable**

sizar ['saɪzə(r)] *n* étudiant(e) *m,f* boursier(ère) *(à l'université de Cambridge et à Trinity College, Dublin)*

size [saɪz] **1** *n* (**a**) *(gen)* taille *f*; *(of ball, tumour)* taille *f*, grosseur *f*; *(of region, desert, forest)* étendue *f*, superficie *f*; *(of carpet, machine, car)* dimensions *fpl*, taille *f*; *(of difficulty, operation, problem)* importance *f*, ampleur *f*; *(of debt, bill, sum)* montant *m*, importance *f*; *Comput (of file)* taille *f*; *(of font)* corps *m*, taille *f*; **to buy a house of comparable size in London would be impossible** on ne pourrait pas acheter une maison de cette taille à Londres; **the two rooms are the same size** les deux pièces sont de la même taille *ou* ont les mêmes dimensions; **it's about the size of a dinner plate** c'est à peu près de la taille d'une assiette; **the kitchen is the size of a cupboard** la cuisine est grande comme un placard; **my garden is half the size of hers** mon jardin fait la moitié du sien; **average family size is four persons** la famille moyenne est composée de quatre personnes; **you should have seen the size of the truck!** si tu avais vu la taille du camion!; **it's a city of some size** c'est une ville assez importante; **the town has no hotels of any size** la ville n'a pas d'hôtel important; **I was surprised by the size of the bill** j'ai été étonné par le montant de la note; **we weren't expecting a crowd of this size** nous ne nous attendions pas à une foule aussi nombreuse; **the crowd was steadily growing in size** la foule grossissait à vue d'œil; **the tumour is increasing in size** la tumeur grossit; **the budget will have to double in size** le budget devra être multiplié par deux; **the army has doubled in size** les effectifs de

sit–siz

l'armée ont doublé; **a block of marble one cubic metre in size** un bloc de marbre d'un mètre cube; **the cupboards can be built to size** les placards peuvent être construits sur mesure; *Fam* **that's about the size of it!** en gros, c'est ça!

(**b**) *(of clothes → gen)* taille *f*; *(of shoes, gloves, hat)* pointure *f*, taille *f*; **what size are you?, what size do you take?** *(for clothes)* quelle taille faites-vous?; *(for shoes)* quelle est votre pointure?, vous chaussez du combien?; **I take (a) size 40** je fais du 40; **I take a size 5 shoe** ≃ je chausse du 38; **I need a size larger/smaller** *(clothes)* il me faut la taille au-dessus/au-dessous; *(shoes)* il me faut la pointure au-dessus/au-dessous; **we've nothing in your size** nous n'avons rien dans votre taille; **try this jacket on for size** essayez cette veste pour voir si c'est votre taille; *Fam* **try this one for size!** prends ça!

(**c**) *(for paper, textiles, leather)* apprêt *m*; *(for plaster)* enduit *m*

2 *vt* (**a**) *(sort)* trier selon la taille

(**b**) *(make)* fabriquer aux dimensions voulues; **the clothing is sized for the American market** les vêtements sont faits pour le marché américain

(**c**) *(paper, textiles, leather)* apprêter; *(plaster)* enduire

(**d**) *Comput* dimensionner

▸▸ *Comput* ***size box*** case *f* de dimensionnement

▸**size up** *vt sep (stranger, rival)* jauger; *(problem, chances)* mesurer; **we all waited outside, sizing each other up** nous attendions tous dehors, nous observant les uns les autres; **she sized up the situation immediately** elle a tout de suite compris ce qui se passait

-size = **-sized**

sizeable ['saɪzəbəl] *adj (piece, box, car)* assez grand; *(apple, egg, tumour)* assez gros (grosse); *(sum, income, quantity, crowd)* important; *(town)* assez important; *(error)* de taille; **they were elected by a sizeable majority** ils ont été élus à une assez large majorité

sizeably ['saɪzəblɪ] *adv* considérablement

-sized [saɪzd] *suff* **medium-sized** de taille moyenne; **small and medium-sized businesses** petites et moyennes entreprises *fpl*, PME *fpl*; **a fair-sized crowd** une foule assez nombreuse; **a man-sized portion** une grosse portion

sizer ['saɪzə(r)] *n* (**a**) *(person who sorts)* trieur(euse) *m,f* (**b**) *(machine)* calibreur *m* (**c**) *Tex (person)* encolleur(euse) *m,f*

Sizewell ['saɪzwel] *n* = centrale nucléaire dans le Suffolk (Angleterre)

sizing ['saɪzɪŋ] *n Tech* (**a**) *(process)* apprêtage *m*; *(of wallpaper)* collage *m*, encollage *m* (**b**) *(substance)* colle *f*; *(in painting)* apprêt *m*

sizzle ['sɪzəl] **1** *vi* (**a**) *(sputter)* grésiller (**b**) *Fam (be hot)* **the city sizzled in the heat** la ville étouffait sous la chaleur ❏

2 *n* grésillement *m*

sizzler ['sɪzlə(r)] *n Fam* journée *f* torride ❏; **it's going to be a sizzler!** il va faire une chaleur torride aujourd'hui!

sizzling ['sɪzlɪŋ] **1** *adj* (**a**) *(sputtering)* grésillant (**b**) *Fam (hot)* brûlant ❏

2 *adv Fam* **sizzling hot** brûlant ❏

3 *n* grésillement *m*

sjambok ['ʃæmbɒk] *n SAfr* = gros fouet en cuir de rhinocéros

SK *Can (written abbr* **Saskatchewan**) Saskatchewan *m*

ska [skɑː] *n Mus* ska *m*

skag = **scag**

skank [skæŋk] *n Am Fam (ugly woman)* cageot *m*, boudin *m*

skanky [ˌskæŋkɪ] *adj Am Fam (ugly)* hyper moche

skat [skæt] *n* = jeu de cartes nécessitant trois joueurs et un jeu de 32 cartes

skate [skeɪt] *(pl sense* (**b**) **inv** *or* **skates**) **1** *n* (**a**) *(ice skate)* patin *m* à glace; *(roller skate)* patin *m* à roulettes; *Br Fam* **to get** *or* **to put one's skates on** se magner, se grouiller; **get your skates on!** magne-toi!, grouille-toi!

(**b**) *Ich* raie *f*

2 *vi* (**a**) *(gen)* patiner; **to go skating** *(ice-skating)* faire du patin *ou* du patinage; *(roller-skating)* faire du patin à roulettes; **we used to skate to school** nous allions à l'école en patins à roulettes; **couples skated around the rink** des couples patinaient autour de la piste; *Fig* **to be skating on thin ice** être sur un terrain dangereux, avancer en terrain miné

(**b**) *(slide → person, pen, plate)* glisser; **his legs skated out from under him** ses jambes se sont dérobées sous lui

▸**skate around, skate over** *vt insep (problem, issue)* esquiver, éviter; **the book skates around** *or* **over his two divorces** le livre passe sous silence ses deux divorces

skateboard ['skeɪtbɔːd] **1** *n* skateboard *m*, planche *f* à roulettes

2 *vi* faire du skate *ou* de la planche à roulettes

skateboarder ['skeɪtbɔːdə(r)] *n* = personne qui fait du skate; **a champion skateboarder** un champion du skate

skateboarding ['skeɪtbɔːdɪŋ] *n* le skate; **to go skateboarding** faire du skate

skater ['skeɪtə(r)] *n (on ice)* patineur(euse) *m,f*; *(on roller skates)* patineur(euse) *m,f* à roulettes

skating ['skeɪtɪŋ] **1** *n (on ice)* patin *m* (à glace); *(on roller skates)* patin *m* (à roulettes)

2 *adj* de patinage

▸▸ ***skating rink*** *(for ice-skating)* patinoire *f*; *(for roller-skating)* piste *f* pour patin à roulettes

skean dhu [ˌskiːən'duː] *n Scot* = dague décorative que l'on porte dans la chaussette

skedaddle [skɪ'dædəl] *vi Fam* décamper, se tailler; **I'd better skedaddle** il faut que je me sauve *ou* que je file

skeeter ['skiːtə(r)] *n Am Fam (mosquito)* moustique ❏ *m*

skeet shooting [skiːt-] *n* (tir *m* au) skeet *m*

skeezer [ˌskiːzə(r)] *n Am very Fam* (**a**) *(ugly woman)* cageot *m*, boudin *m* (**b**) *(promiscuous woman)* pouffiasse *f*, traînée *f*

skeg [skeg] *n (on yacht)* talon *m* de quille; *(on surfboard, rowing boat)* aileron *m*, dérive *f*

skein [skeɪn] *n* (**a**) *(of wool, silk)* écheveau *m* (**b**) *(flight → of geese)* vol *m*

skeletal ['skelɪtəl] *adj* squelettique; *Fig (presentation, report)* sommaire

skeleton ['skelɪtən] **1** *n* (**a**) *Anat* squelette *m*; **he was little more than a skeleton** il n'avait plus que la peau sur les os; *Fig* **to have a skeleton in the** *Br* **cupboard** *or Am* **closet** avoir un squelette dans le placard

(**b**) *Constr & Chem (structure)* squelette *m*

(**c**) *(outline → of book, report)* ébauche *f*, esquisse *f*; *(→ of project, strategy, speech)* schéma *m*, grandes lignes *fpl*

2 *comp (team)* (réduit au) minimum; **a skeleton** *Br* **staff** *or Am* **crew** des effectifs *mpl* réduits au minimum; **they're running a skeleton train service** ils assurent un service minimum de trains

▸▸ ***skeleton contract*** contrat-type *m*; ***skeleton key*** passe-partout *m inv*, passe *m*; ***skeleton organization*** organisation *f* squelettique

skeletonize, -ise ['skelɪtənaɪz] *vt* (**a**) *(reduce to a skeleton → leaf, bird)* squelettiser (**b**) *(outline → book, play)* ébaucher (**c**) *(cut → staff)* réduire au minimum

skelp [skelp] *Scot* **1** *n (smack → on face)* taloche *f*, gifle *f*; *(→ on bottom)* fessée *f*

2 *vt (smack → on face)* donner une taloche *ou* une gifle à, talocher; *(→ on bottom)* donner une fessée à

skelping ['skelpɪŋ] *n Scot (on face)* taloche *f*, gifle *f*; *(on bottom)* fessée *f*

skeptic, skeptical *etc Am* = **sceptic, sceptical** *etc*

skerry ['skerɪ] *(pl* **skerries**) *n (reef)* récif *m*; *(rock)* rocher *m* isolé

sketch [sketʃ] **1** *n* (**a**) *(drawing)* croquis *m*, esquisse *f*; **the map is only a sketch** la carte n'est qu'un croquis

(**b**) *(brief description)* résumé *m*; **historical sketch** résumé *m* historique; **a biographical sketch of the author** une biographie succincte de l'auteur; *(on book jacket)* une notice biographique sur l'auteur

(**c**) *(preliminary outline → of book)* ébauche *f*; *(→ of proposal, speech, campaign)* grandes lignes *fpl*; **give us a rough sketch of your plan** donnez-nous un aperçu de ce que vous proposez

(**d**) *Theat* sketch *m*

2 *vt* (**a**) *(person, scene)* faire un croquis *ou* une esquisse de, croquer, esquisser; *(line, composition, form)* esquisser, croquer; *(portrait, illustration)* faire (rapidement); **he began by sketching the foreground** il a commencé par esquisser *ou* croquer le premier plan

(**b**) *(book)* ébaucher, esquisser; *(proposal, speech)* ébaucher, préparer dans les grandes lignes

▸**sketch in** *vt sep* (**a**) *(provide → background, main points)* indiquer; **Harry will sketch a few more details in for you** Harry va vous donner encore quelques précisions

(**b**) *(draw)* ajouter, dessiner

▸**sketch out** *vt sep* (**a**) *(book)* ébaucher, esquisser; *(plan, speech)* ébaucher, préparer dans les grandes lignes; *(details, main points)* indiquer

(**b**) *(draw)* ébaucher

sketchblock ['sketʃblɒk] *n* bloc *m* à croquis *ou* à dessins

sketchbook ['sketʃbʊk] *n* carnet *m* à dessins; **Picasso's sketchbooks** les carnets *mpl* (de dessins) de Picasso

sketcher ['sketʃə(r)] *n* dessinateur(trice) *m,f* de croquis

sketchily ['sketʃɪlɪ] *adv (describe, report)* sommairement; **his article is very sketchily researched** son article repose sur des recherches très superficielles

sketchiness ['sketʃɪnɪs] *n* manque *m* de précision *ou* de détails

sketching ['sketʃɪŋ] *n (action)* action *f* de croquer *ou* d'esquisser; *(picture)* croquis *m*, esquisse *f*

▸▸ ***sketching block*** bloc *m* à croquis *ou* à dessins; ***sketching pad*** carnet *m* à dessins

sketchpad ['sketʃpæd] *n* carnet *m* à dessins

sketchy ['sketʃɪ] *(compar* **sketchier**, *superl* **sketchiest**) *adj (description, account)* sommaire; *(research, work, knowledge)* superficiel; *(idea, notion)* vague; *(plan)* peu détaillé; **my memory of that day is very sketchy** mes souvenirs de cette journée sont très flous

skew [skjuː] **1** *vt (distort → facts, results)* fausser; *(→ idea, truth)* dénaturer; **it will skew the sample** *(in statistics)* ça va fausser l'échantillonnage; **this reform is skewed toward higher earners** cette réforme avantage ceux qui ont de gros revenus

2 *vi* obliquer, dévier de sa trajectoire; **the truck skewed across the intersection** le camion a traversé le carrefour en biais; **he skewed off the road** il a quitté la route

3 *adj (crooked → picture)* de travers; *(→ pole)* penché

4 *n Br* **to be on the skew** être de travers

▸▸ ***skew distribution*** *(in statistics)* distribution *f* asymétrique

skewbald ['skjuːbɔːld] **1** *adj* pie *(inv)*

2 *n* cheval *m* pie

skewed [skjuːd] *adj* (**a**) *(crooked → picture)* de travers; *(→ pole)* penché (**b**) *(distorted → notion, view, data, results)* faussé (**by** par) (**c**) *(angled, slanting)* oblique, en biais

skewer ['skjʊə(r)] **1** *n Culin* brochette *f*; *(larger)* broche *f*

2 *vt Culin (roast, duck)* embrocher; *(meat, mushrooms, tomatoes)* mettre en brochette; *Fig (person)* transpercer

skew-whiff *Br Fam* **1** *adj* de traviole, de travers ❏

2 *adv* de traviole, de travers ❏

skewy ['skjuːɪ] *(compar* **skewier**, *superl* **skewiest**) *adj Fam* (**a**) *(crooked → picture, hat)* de traviole, de travers ❏; **the shelf is skewy** l'étagère est de traviole *ou* de travers; **the steering is skewy** la direction est faussée ❏, il y a du jeu dans la direction ❏ (**b**) *(weird, odd)* farfelu

ski [skiː] **1** *n* (**a**) *Sport (equipment)* ski *m*; **a pair of skis** une paire de skis

(**b**) *Aviat* patin *m*, ski *m*

2 *vi* faire du ski, skier; **to go skiing** *(activity)* faire du ski; *(on holiday)* partir aux sports d'hiver *ou* faire du ski; **they skied down the slope** ils descendirent la pente à ski

3 *comp (clothes, boots, lessons)* de ski

4 *vt* **I've never skied the red run** je n'ai jamais descendu la piste rouge

▸▸ ***ski instructor*** moniteur(trice) *m,f* de ski; ***ski***

jump *(ramp)* tremplin *m* de ski; ***ski jumping*** saut *m* à skis; ***ski lift*** *(gen)* remontée *f* mécanique; *(chair lift)* télésiège *m*; ***ski pants*** fuseau *m*, pantalon *m* de ski; ***ski pass*** forfait *m* de remonte-pente; ***ski plane*** avion *m* à skis; ***ski pole*** bâton *m* de ski; ***ski resort*** station *f* de ski; ***ski run, ski slope*** piste *f* de ski; *Am* ***ski stick*** bâton *m* de ski; ***ski suit*** combinaison *f* de ski; ***ski tow*** téléski *m*; ***ski trail*** piste *f* de ski; ***ski wax*** fart *m* (pour skis)

skiascopy [skaɪ'æskəpɪ] *n Med & Opt* skiascopie *f*, pupilloscopie *f*

skibob ['skiːbɒb] *n* ski-bob *m*, véloski *m*

skid [skɪd] (*pt & pp* **skidded**, *cont* **skidding**) **1** *vi* (**a**) *(on road → driver, car, tyre)* déraper; *(wheel)* patiner; **the car skidded across the junction** la voiture a traversé le carrefour en dérapant; **I skidded into the truck** j'ai dérapé et percuté le camion; **to skid to a halt** s'arrêter en dérapant; **his glasses went skidding across the table** ses lunettes ont glissé jusqu'à l'autre bout de la table

(**b**) *(slide → person, object)* déraper, glisser; **I skidded on the wet floor** j'ai dérapé *ou* glissé sur le sol mouillé; **the plates skidded off the tray** les assiettes ont glissé du plateau

(**c**) *Aviat* glisser (sur l'aile)

2 *vt (vehicle)* **he skidded the truck into the ditch** il a perdu le contrôle du camion qui est parti dans le fossé

3 *n* (**a**) *(action) Aut* dérapage *m*; *Aviat* glissade *f*; *Aut* **to go into a skid** partir en dérapage, déraper; *Aut* **to get out of** *or* **to correct a skid** redresser *ou* contrôler un dérapage

(**b**) *(wedge)* cale *f*

(**c**) *Aviat (runner for landing)* béquille *f*

(**d**) *Am (log)* rondin *m*; *(dragging platform)* traîneau *m*, ≃ schlitte *f*

(**e**) *Fam Fig* **to put the skids on** *or* **under sb** mettre des bâtons dans les roues à qn; **to hit the skids** *(company, sales, prices)* dégringoler; **to be on the skids** *(company, marriage)* battre de l'aile

►► ***skid mark*** *(on road)* trace *f* de pneus *(après un dérapage)*; *Fam Hum (on underpants, nappy)* trace *f*; *Am* ***skid road*** (**a**) *(for logs)* voie *f* faite de troncs d'arbres, ≃ chemin *m* de schlitte (**b**) *Fam (vagrant area)* bas-fonds *mpl*, quartier *m* mal famé; *Am Fam* ***skid row*** bas-fonds *mpl*, quartier *m* mal famé; **you'll end up on skid row!** tu es sur une mauvaise pente!; **a skid-row bum** un clochard

skidding ['skɪdɪŋ] *n* (**a**) *(of car, tyre)* dérapage *m*; *(of wheel)* patinage *m* (**b**) *Aviat* glissement *m* (sur l'aile)

skiddoo [skɪ'duː] *vi Am Fam Old-fashioned* mettre les voiles, déguerpir; **twenty-two skiddoo!** *(get out)* foutez-le camp, et plus vite que ça!; *(let's go)* barrons-nous!, tirons-nous!

skid-lid *n Br Fam* casque *m* (de moto)❑

skidoo [skɪ'duː] **1** *n* scooter *m* des neiges, motoski *m*, *Can* motoneige *m*

2 *vi* = **skiddoo**

skidpan ['skɪdpæn] *n Br* piste *f* d'entraînement au dérapage

skidproof ['skɪdpruːf] *adj* antidérapant

skidway ['skɪdweɪ] *n Am* (**a**) *(road made from logs)* voie *f* faite de troncs d'arbres (**b**) *(for transporting logs)* voie *f* de glissement

skier ['skiːə(r)] *n* skieur(euse) *m,f*

skiff [skɪf] *n* skiff *m*, yole *f*

skiffle ['skɪfəl] *n* skiffle *m (type de musique pop des années 50 jouée avec des guitares et des instruments à percussion improvisés)*

skiing ['skiːɪŋ] **1** *n* ski *m (activité)*

2 *comp (lessons, accident, clothes)* de ski; **to go on a skiing holiday** partir aux sports d'hiver

►► ***skiing instructor*** moniteur(trice) *m,f* de ski

ski-jump *vi* faire du saut à skis

skilful, *Am* **skillful** ['skɪlfʊl] *adj* habile, adroit; **a skilful carpenter** un menuisier habile; **a skilful pianist** un pianiste accompli; **she's very skilful with the scissors** elle sait se servir d'une paire de ciseaux; **a skilful move** une démarche habile

skilfully, *Am* **skillfully** ['skɪlfʊlɪ] *adv* habilement, avec habileté, adroitement

skilfulness, *Am* **skillfulness** ['skɪlfʊlnɪs] *n* habileté *f*, adresse *f*

skill [skɪl] *n* (**a**) *(ability)* compétence *f*, aptitude *f*; *(dexterity)* habileté *f*, adresse *f*; *(expertise)* savoir-faire *m inv*; **you don't need any special skill** ça ne demande aucune compétence précise; **it involves a lot of skill** ça demande beaucoup d'habileté; **with great skill** *(in manoeuvre)* avec une grande habileté; *(diplomacy)* avec un grand savoir-faire; *(dexterity)* avec beaucoup d'adresse; **his work shows skill and imagination** son travail est plein de talent et d'imagination

(**b**) *(learned technique)* aptitude *f*, technique *f*; *(knowledge)* connaissances *fpl*; **management skills** techniques *fpl* de gestion; **poor reading skills** de faibles aptitudes *fpl* pour la lecture; **language skills** aptitudes *fpl* linguistiques; **computer technology requires us to learn new skills** l'informatique nous oblige à acquérir de nouvelles compétences

Skillcentre ['skɪl,sentə(r)] *n* = centre de formation professionnelle relevant du ministère de l'Emploi en Grande-Bretagne

skilled [skɪld] *adj* (**a**) *Ind (engineer, worker)* qualifié; *(task)* de spécialiste; **skilled labour** main-d'œuvre *f* qualifiée (**b**) *(experienced → driver, negotiator)* habile, expérimenté; *(expert)* habile, expert; *(manually)* adroit; *(clever → gesture)* habile, adroit; **skilled in the art of public speaking** versé dans l'art oratoire, rompu aux techniques oratoires; **to be skilled at doing sth** être doué pour faire qch

skillet ['skɪlɪt] *n Am* poêle *f* (à frire)

skillful, skillfully *etc Am* = **skilful, skilfully** *etc*

skim [skɪm] (*pt & pp* **skimmed**, *cont* **skimming**) **1** *vt* (**a**) *(milk)* écrémer; *(jam)* écumer; *(floating matter → with skimmer)* écumer, enlever avec une écumoire; *(→ with spatula)* enlever avec une spatule; **to skim the froth from** *or* **off a glass of beer** enlever la mousse d'un verre de bière; **to skim the fat from the gravy** dégraisser la sauce; **to skim the cream from the milk** écrémer le lait

(**b**) *(glide over → surface)* effleurer, frôler; **the seagull skimmed the waves** la mouette volait au ras de l'eau *ou* rasait les vagues; **the glider skimmed the tops of the trees** le planeur frôlait *ou* rasait la cime des arbres; **the stone skimmed the lake** la pierre a ricoché à la surface du lac; *Fig* **the book only skims the surface** le livre ne fait qu'effleurer *ou* que survoler la question

(**c**) *(stone)* faire ricocher; **the children were skimming stones over the lake** les enfants faisaient des ricochets sur le lac

(**d**) *(read quickly → letter, book)* parcourir, lire en diagonale; *(→ magazine)* parcourir, feuilleter

(**e**) *Com (market)* écrémer

2 *vi* **to skim over the ground/across the waves** *(bird)* raser le sol/les vagues; **to skim over** *or* **across the lake** *(stone)* faire des ricochets sur le lac

►► *Am* ***skim milk*** lait *m* écrémé

►**skim off** *vt sep* (**a**) *(cream, froth)* enlever (avec une écumoire); *Fig* **the book dealers skimmed off the best bargains** les marchands de livres ont fait les meilleures affaires; **the accounts department skims off the best recruits** la comptabilité récupère les meilleures recrues

(**b**) *(steal → money)* **he skimmed a little off the top for himself** il s'est un peu servi au passage

►**skim over** *vt insep (letter, report)* parcourir, lire en diagonale; *(difficult passage)* lire superficiellement, parcourir rapidement

►**skim through** *vt insep (letter, page)* parcourir, lire en diagonale; *(magazine)* feuilleter; **I only had time to skim through the report** je n'ai eu que le temps de lire le rapport en vitesse

skimmed milk [skɪmd-] *n* lait *m* écrémé

skimmer ['skɪmə(r)] *n* (**a**) *Orn* bec-en-ciseaux *m* (**b**) *Culin* écumoire *f*

skimmia ['skɪmɪə] *n Bot* skimmia *m*

skimming ['skɪmɪŋ] *n* (**a**) *Am Fam (tax fraud)* fraude *f* fiscale❑ (**b**) *Com (of market)* écrémage *m*

►► *Com* ***skimming price*** prix *m* d'écrémage

skimp [skɪmp] **1** *vi* lésiner; **to skimp on sth** lésiner sur qch; **the builders skimped on materials** les constructeurs ont lésiné sur les matériaux

2 *vt (resources, food)* économiser sur, lésiner sur; *(job)* faire à la va-vite

skimpily ['skɪmpɪlɪ] *adv (furnished)* parcimonieusement; **skimpily made** *(garment)* étriqué; **skimpily dressed** légèrement vêtu

skimpiness ['skɪmpɪnɪs] *n* insuffisance *f*; *(of garment)* aspect *m* étriqué

skimpy ['skɪmpɪ] (*compar* **skimpier**, *superl* **skimpiest**) *adj* (**a**) *(mean → meal, offering, praise, thanks)* maigre, chiche (**b**) *(clothes, dress → too small)* trop juste; *(→ light)* léger; **a skimpy skirt** une jupe étriquée

skin [skɪn] (*pt & pp* **skinned**, *cont* **skinning**) **1** *n* (**a**) *(of person)* peau *f*; **to have dark/fair skin** avoir la peau brune/claire; **to have bad/good skin** avoir une vilaine/jolie peau; **I always wear cotton next to my skin** je porte toujours du coton sur la peau; **you're nothing but skin and bone** tu n'as que la peau et les os; **we're all human under the skin** au fond, nous sommes tous humains; **she escaped by the skin of her teeth** elle l'a échappé belle, elle s'en est tirée de justesse; **he got into office by the skin of his teeth** il a été élu de justesse; **she nearly jumped out of her skin** elle a sauté au plafond; *Fam* **it's no skin off my nose** ça m'est égal, ce n'est pas mon problème; *Fam* **he really gets under my skin** il me tape sur les nerfs, celui-là; *Fam* **I've got her under my skin** je l'ai dans la peau; **to save one's skin** sauver sa peau; **to be soaked to the skin** être trempé jusqu'aux os; *Am Fam* **gimme some skin!** tape-moi dans la main!

(**b**) *(of animal)* peau *f*; **to cast** *or* **shed its skin** *(snake)* muer; **a crocodile-skin handbag** un sac en crocodile

(**c**) *(on fruit, vegetable, sausage)* peau *f*; *(on onion)* pelure *f*; **potatoes cooked in their skins** des pommes de terre en robe de chambre *ou* des champs

(**d**) *(on milk, sauce, pudding)* peau *f*; **take the skin off the custard** enlevez la peau de la crème anglaise

(**e**) *(of plane)* revêtement *m*; *(of building)* revêtement *m* extérieur; *(of drum)* peau *f*

(**f**) *(for wine)* outre *f*

(**g**) *Fam (abbr* **skinhead***)* skinhead❑ *mf*, skin *mf*

(**h**) *Br Fam (cigarette paper)* papier *m* à cigarette❑

2 *comp (cancer, disease, tone)* de la peau

3 *vt* (**a**) *(animal)* dépouiller, écorcher; *(vegetable)* éplucher; *Fig* **if I find him I'll skin him alive** si je le trouve, je l'écorche vif; *Prov* **there's more than one way to skin a cat** = il y a bien des moyens d'arriver à ses fins

(**b**) *(graze → limb)* écorcher; **I skinned my knee** je me suis écorché le genou

(**c**) *Fam (swindle)* arnaquer; *(rob)* plumer; **he got skinned at cards** il s'est laissé plumer aux cartes; **you've been skinned** tu t'es fait avoir *ou* arnaquer

(**d**) *Am Fam* **skin me!** tape-moi dans la main!

4 skins *npl very Fam (drums)* batterie❑ *f*

►► ***skin cream*** crème *f* pour la peau; ***skin diver*** plongeur(euse) *m,f*; ***skin diving*** plongée *f* sous-marine; *Fam* ***skin flick*** film *m* porno; ***skin food*** *(UNCOUNT)* crème *f* nourrissante (pour la peau); *Fam* ***skin game*** arnaque *f*; ***skin graft*** greffe *f* de la peau; **to have a skin graft** subir une greffe de la peau; ***skin grafting*** greffage *m* de la peau; *Fam* ***skin mag*** revue *f* porno; ***skin patch*** timbre *m* transdermique; *Med* ***skin test*** cuti-réaction *f*

►**skin up** *vi Br Fam Drugs slang* rouler un joint

skincare ['skɪnkeə(r)] *n* soins *mpl* de la peau

►► ***skincare product*** produit *m* (de soin) pour la peau

skin-deep **1** *adj* superficiel; **beauty is only skin-deep** la beauté n'est pas tout

2 *adv* superficiellement

skinflint ['skɪnflɪnt] *n Fam* radin(e) *m,f*

skinful ['skɪnfʊl] *n Br Fam* **to have had a skinful** tenir une bonne cuite

skinhead ['skɪnhed] *n* skinhead *mf*

skink [skɪŋk] *n Zool* scinque *m*

skinless ['skɪnlɪs] *adj (sausages)* sans peau

skinned [skɪnd] *adj (rabbit)* à qui on a enlevé la peau; **to keep one's eyes skinned** ouvrir l'œil; **keep your eyes skinned** ouvre l'œil (et le bon); **to keep one's eyes skinned for sb/sth** guetter

ski–ski

qn/qch; **I'll keep my eyes skinned for one** j'en guette un

-skinned [skɪnd] *suff* à la peau...; **she's dark-skinned** elle a la peau foncée

skinniness ['skɪnɪnɪs] *n* maigreur *f*; *(no negative overtones)* minceur *f*

skinny ['skɪnɪ] *(compar* **skinnier,** *superl* **skinniest) 1** *n Am Fam (inside information)* renseignements ❑ *mpl*; **what's the skinny on the situation?** est-ce qu'il y a du nouveau? ❑

2 *adj* **(a)** *(person → too thin)* maigre; *(without negative overtones)* mince; **the skinny look is in fashion** c'est à la mode d'être très mince; **she's a skinny little thing** elle est petite et menue; *Am* **as skinny as a rail** mince comme un fil

(b) *(sweater, T-shirt etc)* collant

skinny-dip *(pt & pp* **skinny-dipped,** *cont* **skinny-dipping)** *vi Fam* se baigner à poil

skinny-dipping *n Fam* baignade *f* à poil; **to go skinny-dipping** se baigner à poil

skinny-malinky [-mə'lɪŋkɪ] *n Fam* asperge *f*

skin-pop *Fam Drugs slang* **1** *vt (drugs)* se piquer *ou* se shooter à

2 *vi (inject drugs)* se piquer, se shooter

skint [skɪnt] *adj Br Fam* fauché, raide

skin-tight *adj* moulant

skip [skɪp] *(pt & pp* **skipped,** *cont* **skipping) 1** *vi* **(a)** *(with skipping rope)* sauter à la corde

(b) *(jump)* sautiller; **he skipped out of the way** il s'est écarté d'un bond; **the children were skipping around in the garden** les enfants gambadaient dans le jardin; *Fig* **the book keeps skipping from one subject to another** le livre passe sans arrêt d'un sujet à l'autre

(c) *Fam (go)* faire un saut, aller ❑; **we skipped across to Paris for the weekend** on a fait un saut à Paris pour le week-end; **he's just skipped out to the shops** il vient d'aller faire des courses ❑

2 *vt* **(a)** *(omit)* sauter, passer; **skip the details** passez les détails, épargnez-nous les détails; **let's skip the next chapter** sautons le chapitre suivant

(b) *(miss → meeting, meal)* sauter; *Sch (class)* sécher; **we decided to skip lunch** nous avons décidé de sauter le déjeuner *ou* de ne pas déjeuner; *Fam* **to skip bail** se dérober à la justice ❑ *(alors qu'on jouit de la liberté provisoire)*; *Fig* **my heart skipped a beat** mon cœur s'est arrêté de battre pendant une seconde; *Fam* **skip it!** laisse tomber!

(c) *Fam (leave)* fuir ❑, quitter ❑; **the thieves have probably skipped the country by now** à l'heure qu'il est, les voleurs ont probablement quitté le pays

(d) *Comput (command)* sauter

3 *n* **(a)** *Fam Naut (gen)* capitaine ❑ *m*; *(of yacht)* skipper ❑ *m*

(b) *(jump)* (petit) saut *m*; **with a little skip, she jumped over the rope** d'un bond léger, elle sauta par-dessus la corde

(c) *Br (on lorry, for rubbish)* benne *f*

►**skip off** *vi Fam* **(a)** *(disappear)* décamper; **they skipped off without doing the washing up** ils ont décampé sans faire la vaisselle

(b) *(go)* faire un saut; **we skipped off to Greece for a holiday** on est allés passer quelques jours de vacances en Grèce ❑

►**skip over** *vt insep (omit)* sauter, passer

skipjack ['skɪpdʒæk] *n* **(a)** *Hist* = jouet d'enfant en forme d'animal sauteur fabriqué avec la lunette d'une volaille **(b)** *Ich* bonite *f* à ventre rayé **(c)** *Entom* taupin *m*

►► ***skipjack tuna*** bonite *f* à ventre rayé

skipper ['skɪpə(r)] **1** *n* **(a)** *(of ship, plane)* capitaine *m*; *(of yacht)* skipper *m* **(b)** *Sport* capitaine *m*, chef *m* d'équipe **(c)** *Fam (boss)* patron ❑ *m* **(d)** *Entom* **skipper (butterfly)** hespéride *f*, hespérie *f*

2 *vt* **(a)** *(ship, plane)* commander, être le capitaine de; *(yacht)* skipper **(b)** *Sport (team)* être le capitaine de

skipping ['skɪpɪŋ] *n* saut *m* à la corde

►► ***skipping rope*** corde *f* à sauter

skirl [skɜːl] **1** *vi (emit a sound)* sonner; *(player)* jouer de la cornemuse

2 *n* son *m* (de la cornemuse)

skirmish ['skɜːmɪʃ] **1** *n Mil* escarmouche *f*, échauffourée *f*; *Fig* escarmouche *f*, accrochage *m*; **I had a bit of a skirmish with the authorities** j'ai eu un différend avec les autorités

2 *vi Mil* s'engager dans une escarmouche; *Fig* **to skirmish with sb (over sth)** avoir un accrochage *ou* s'accrocher avec qn (au sujet de qch)

skirmisher ['skɜːmɪʃə(r)] *n Mil* tirailleur *m*

skirmishing ['skɜːmɪʃɪŋ] *n Mil* escarmouches *fpl*; **in skirmishing order** en tirailleurs

skirt [skɜːt] **1** *n* **(a)** *(garment)* jupe *f*; *(part of coat)* pan *m*, basque *f*

(b) *Tech* jupe *f*

(c) *Br (cut of meat)* ≃ flanchet *m*

(d) **(saddle) skirt** petit quartier *m* (de la selle)

(e) *(of hovercraft)* jupe *f*

(f) *(UNCOUNT) Br Fam (women)* nanas *fpl*, gonzesses *fpl*; **they've gone out looking for skirt** ils sont allés draguer; **a bit of skirt** une nana, une gonzesse

2 *vt* **(a)** *(go around)* contourner; **the road skirts the mountain** la route contourne la montagne

(b) *(avoid → issue, problem)* éluder, esquiver

►► ***skirt clearance*** jeu *m* à la jupe

►**skirt around,** *Br* **skirt round** *vt insep* = **skirt** *vt*

skirting (board) ['skɜːtɪŋ-] *n Br* plinthe *f*

skit [skɪt] *n* parodie *f*, satire *f*; **to do a skit on sth** parodier qch; **it's a skit on football commentators** c'est une parodie des commentateurs de football

skite [skaɪt] **1** *n* **(a)** *Scot (slip)* glissade *f* **(b)** *Scot (blow)* coup *m* **(c)** *Austr & NZ Fam (boastful person)* vantard(e) ❑ *m,f* **(d)** *Austr & NZ Fam (boasting)* vantardise ❑ *f*

2 *vi* **(a)** *Scot (slip)* glisser **(b)** *Scot (strike)* frapper **(c)** *Austr & NZ Fam (boast)* se vanter ❑

skitter ['skɪtə(r)] *vi* **(a)** *(small animal)* trottiner; *(bird)* voleter; **the bird skittered over the ground** l'oiseau volait en rase-mottes **(b)** *(ricochet)* faire des ricochets; **the stone skittered across the lake** la pierre a fait des ricochets sur le lac

skittish ['skɪtɪʃ] *adj* **(a)** *(person → playful)* espiègle; *(→ frivolous)* frivole **(b)** *(horse)* ombrageux, difficile

skittishly ['skɪtɪʃlɪ] *adv* **(a)** *(of person → playfully)* avec espièglerie; *(→ frivolously)* avec frivolité **(b)** *(of horse)* d'une manière ombrageuse

skittishness ['skɪtɪʃnɪs] *n* **(a)** *(of person → playfulness)* espièglerie *f*; *(→ frivolousness)* frivolité *f* **(b)** *(of horse)* caractère *m* ombrageux

skittle ['skɪtəl] **1** *n* quille *f*

2 skittles *n* (jeu *m* de) quilles *fpl*; **to play skittles** jouer aux quilles, faire une partie de quilles

►► ***skittle alley*** piste *f* de jeu de quilles

skive [skaɪv] *Br Fam* **1** *vi (avoid work)* tirer au flanc, tirer au cul; *Sch* sécher les cours

2 *n (easy job)* planque *f*; **she's taking PE because it's such a skive** elle a choisi éducation physique parce que c'est pépère

►**skive off** *Br Fam* **1** *vi* se défiler, tirer au flanc, tirer au cul; *Sch* sécher les cours

2 *vt insep* **to skive off school** sécher les cours; **to skive off work** ne pas aller bosser

skiver ['skaɪvə(r)] *n Br Fam* tire-au-flanc *mf inv*, tire-au-cul *mf inv*

skiving ['skaɪvɪŋ] *n Br Fam* **there's too much skiving round here** il y a trop de tire-au-flanc ici

skivvy ['skɪvɪ] *(pl* **skivvies) 1** *vi Br Fam* faire la boniche; **I won't skivvy for you** je ne vais pas vous servir de boniche

2 *n* **(a)** *Br Fam Pej* bonne *f* à tout faire ❑; **I'm not your skivvy** je ne suis pas ta boniche **(b)** *Austr (garment)* polo *m*

3 skivvies *npl Am Fam (for women)* dessous ❑ *mpl*; *(for men → underwear)* sous-vêtements ❑ *mpl*; *(→ underpants)* calbute *m*, calcif *m*

skrimshank = **scrimshank**

skua ['skjuːə] *n Orn* skua *m*, labbe *m*

skulduggery [skʌl'dʌgərɪ] *n (UNCOUNT)* combines *fpl ou* manœuvres *fpl* douteuses

skulk [skʌlk] *vi* rôder; **there's somebody skulking (about) in the garden/bushes** il y a quelqu'un qui rôde dans le jardin/qui se cache dans les buissons; **to skulk away** *or* **off** s'éclipser

skull [skʌl] *n* crâne *m*; *Fam Fig* **can't you get it into your thick skull that she doesn't like you!** tu n'as toujours pas compris qu'elle ne t'aime pas! ❑; *Fam* **to be out of one's skull** *(drunk)* être plein comme une barrique, être rond comme une queue de pelle; *Fam* **I was bored out of my skull** je crevais d'ennui

►► ***skull and crossbones*** *(motif)* tête *f* de mort; *(flag)* pavillon *m* à tête de mort

skullcap ['skʌlkæp] *n* **(a)** *(headgear)* calotte *f* **(b)** *Bot* scutellaire *f*

skullduggery = **skulduggery**

skunk [skʌŋk] *(pl sense* **(a)** **inv** *or* **skunks,** *pl sense* **(b) skunks) 1** *n* **(a)** *Zool* moufette *f*, mouffette *f*, sconse *m*, *Can* bête *f* puante; *(fur)* sconse *m* **(b)** *Fam (person)* canaille *f*, ordure *f* **(c)** *(UNCOUNT) Fam Drugs slang (type of cannabis)* skunk *m*

2 *vt Am Fam (opponent)* battre à plate couture, flanquer une déculottée à

sky [skaɪ] *(pl* **skies,** *pt & pp* **skied** *or* **skyed) 1** *n (gen)* ciel *m*; **the sky went dark** le ciel s'est assombri; **smoke rose into the sky** de la fumée s'élevait dans le ciel; **the sky at night** le ciel nocturne; *Fam* **the sky's the limit** tout est possible ❑

2 *vt* **(a)** *Sport (ball)* envoyer au ciel

(b) *(in rowing)* **to sky the oars** lever les avirons trop haut

3 skies *npl (climate)* cieux *mpl*; *(descriptive)* ciels *mpl*; **we spend the winter under sunnier skies** nous passons l'hiver sous des cieux plus cléments; **Turner is famous for his skies** Turner est renommé pour ses ciels

►► ***sky blue*** bleu ciel *m*; *TV* ***sky cloth*** rideau *m* de fond; *Old-fashioned Mil slang* ***sky pilot*** aumônier ❑ *m (dans l'armée)*

sky-blue *adj* bleu ciel *(inv)*

skyboarding ['skaɪbɔːdɪŋ] *n* sky surf *m*

skycap ['skaɪkæp] *n Am* porteur *m (dans un aéroport)*

skydiver ['skaɪˌdaɪvə(r)] *n* parachutiste *mf* (en chute libre)

skydiving ['skaɪˌdaɪvɪŋ] *n* saut *m* en chute libre

Skye [skaɪ] *n* (l'île *f* de) Skye *f*

►► ***Skye terrier*** skye-terrier *m*

sky-high 1 *adj* très haut dans le ciel; *Fig (prices)* inabordable, exorbitant

2 *adv* **(a)** *(high into the air)* très haut dans le ciel **(b)** *Fig (very high)* **prices soared** *or* **went sky-high** les prix ont grimpé en flèche; **the explosion blew the building sky-high** l'explosion a complètement soufflé le bâtiment; **our plans were blown sky-high** nos projets sont complètement tombés à l'eau

skyjack ['skaɪdʒæk] *vt Fam (plane)* détourner ❑

skyjacker ['skaɪˌdʒækə(r)] *n Fam* pirate *m* de l'air ❑

skyjacking ['skaɪˌdʒækɪŋ] *n Fam* piraterie *f* aérienne ❑

skylark ['skaɪlɑːk] **1** *n Orn* alouette *f* des champs

2 *vi Fam Old-fashioned* faire le fou (folle), chahuter

skylarker ['skaɪˌlɑːkə(r)] *n Fam Old-fashioned* chahuteur(euse) *m,f*

skylarking ['skaɪˌlɑːkɪŋ] *n Fam Old-fashioned* chahut *m*

skylight ['skaɪlaɪt] *n* lucarne *f*

skyline ['skaɪlaɪn] *n (horizon)* (ligne *f* d')horizon *m*; *(of city)* silhouette *f*; **it radically alters the skyline** ça change radicalement le profil de la ville

skyrocket ['skaɪˌrɒkɪt] **1** *n* fusée *f*

2 *vi Fam (prices)* grimper en flèche

skysail ['skaɪseɪl] *n Naut* contre-cacatois *m inv*

skyscape ['skaɪskeɪp] *n Art & Phot* ciel *m*

skyscraper ['skaɪˌskreɪpə(r)] *n* gratte-ciel *m inv*

skyward ['skaɪwəd] **1** *adv* vers le ciel

2 *adj* vers le ciel

skywards ['skaɪwədz] *adv* vers le ciel

skyway ['skaɪweɪ] *n* **(a)** *Aviat* couloir *m* aérien **(b)** *Am Aut* route *f* surélevée

skywriting ['skaɪˌraɪtɪŋ] *n* publicité *f* aérienne *(tracée dans le ciel par un avion)*

slab [slæb] *(pt & pp* **slabbed,** *cont* **slabbing) 1** *n* **(a)** *(block → of stone, wood)* bloc *m*; *(flat)* plaque *f*, dalle *f*; *(for path)* pavé *m*; **the path was made of stone slabs** le chemin était pavé de pierres; **a wooden slab** un bloc de bois; **a concrete slab** une dalle de béton

(b) *(piece → of cake)* grosse tranche *f*; *(→ of chocolate)* tablette *f*; *(→ of meat)* pavé *m*

(c) *(table, bench → of butcher)* étal *m*; **on the**

slab *(in mortuary)* sur la table d'autopsie; *(for operation)* sur la table d'opération

2 *vt (cut → stone)* tailler en blocs; *(→ log)* débiter

slack [slæk] **1** *adj* (**a**) *(loose → rope, wire)* lâche, insuffisamment tendu; *(→ knot)* mal serré, desserré; *(→ chain)* lâche; *(→ grip)* faible; *(→ handshake)* mou (molle); **the rope is very slack** la corde a du mou; **the chain is very slack** la chaîne n'est pas assez tendue

(**b**) *(careless → work)* négligé; *(→ worker, student)* peu sérieux, peu consciencieux; **he's becoming very slack about his appearance/ his work** il commence à négliger son apparence/son travail; **her work has become rather slack lately** il y a eu un certain laisser-aller dans son travail dernièrement; **she's very slack about** *or* **at getting orders ready on time** elle n'est pas très sérieuse pour ce qui est de préparer les commandes en temps voulu

(**c**) *(slow, weak → demand)* faible; *(→ business)* calme; **the slack season for tourists** la période creuse pour le tourisme; **after lunch is my slack period** après le déjeuner, c'est mon heure creuse; **business is slack at the moment** les affaires marchent au ralenti en ce moment

(**d**) *(lax → discipline, laws, control)* mou (molle), relâché; *(→ parents)* négligent; **they're rather slack about discipline** ils sont plutôt laxistes

(**e**) *Naut* **slack water, slack tide** mer *f* étale

2 *n* (**a**) *(in rope)* mou *m*; *(in cable joint)* jeu *m*; *Naut (in cable)* battant *m*; **to take up the slack in a rope** tendre une corde; **leave a bit of slack** laissez un peu de mou; *Am Fam Fig* **cut me some slack!** fiche-moi la paix!

(**b**) *Fig (in economy)* secteurs *mpl* affaiblis; **to take up the slack in the economy** relancer les secteurs faibles de l'économie

(**c**) *(still water)* eau *f* morte; *(tide)* mer *f* étale

(**d**) *(coal)* poussier *m*

3 *vi (person → become negligent)* se laisser aller; *(→ in one's work, efforts)* se relâcher

▸**slack off, slack up** *vi Fam (slow down)* se laisser aller

slacken ['slækən] **1** *vt* (**a**) *(loosen → cable, rope)* détendre, relâcher; *(→ reins)* relâcher; *(→ grip, hold)* desserrer

(**b**) *(reduce → pressure, speed)* réduire, diminuer; *(→ pace)* ralentir; **the train slackened speed** le train a ralenti

2 *vi* (**a**) *(rope, cable)* se relâcher; *(grip, hold)* se desserrer

(**b**) *(lessen → speed, demand, interest)* diminuer; *(→ business)* ralentir; *(→ wind)* diminuer de force; *(→ standards)* baisser

▸**slacken off 1** *vt sep* (**a**) *(rope)* relâcher, donner du mou à

(**b**) *(speed, pressure)* diminuer; *(efforts)* relâcher

2 *vi* (**a**) *(rope)* se relâcher

(**b**) *(speed, demand)* diminuer

▸**slacken up** *vi (speed)* diminuer; *(person)* se relâcher

slackening ['slækənɪŋ] *n (in speed)* diminution *f*, réduction *f*; *(in interest)* diminution *f*; *(in demand)* affaiblissement *m*; *(in knot)* desserrement *m*; *(in rope)* relâchement *m*; *(in standards)* abaissement *m*; **a slackening of speed** un ralentissement

slacker ['slækə(r)] *n Fam* fainéant(e) *m,f*, raté(e) *m,f*; **she's no slacker** elle n'est pas fainéante

slackly ['slæklɪ] *adv (work)* négligemment, sans soin; *(hang)* mollement

slackness ['slæknɪs] *n* (**a**) *(of rope, wire)* mou *m* (**b**) *(in business)* ralentissement *m* (**c**) *(negligence)* négligence *f*, paresse *f*

slacks [slæks] *npl Old-fashioned* **(pair of) slacks** pantalon *m*

slacksuit ['slæksu:t] *n Am* tailleur-pantalon *m*

slag [slæg] *(pt & pp* **slagged,** *cont* **slagging) 1** *n* (**a**) *(UNCOUNT) (waste → from mine)* stériles *mpl*; *(→ from foundry)* scories *fpl*, crasses *fpl*; *(→ from volcano)* scories *fpl* volcaniques

(**b**) *Br very Fam Pej (person)* enfoiré(e) *m,f*

(**c**) *Br very Fam (promiscuous woman)* pouffiasse *f*, traînée *f*

2 *vt Br very Fam* (**a**) *(criticize)* débiner, éreinter, descendre en flammes

(**b**) *(make fun of)* se foutre de

▸**slag off** *vt sep Br very Fam* (**a**) *(criticize)* débiner, éreinter, descendre en flammes

(**b**) *(make fun of)* se foutre de

slagging ['slægɪŋ] *n Br very Fam* **to give sb a slagging** *(criticize)* débiner *ou* éreinter qn, descendre qn en flammes; *(make fun of)* se foutre de qn

slaggy ['slægɪ] *adj Metal* scoriacé

▸▸ ***slaggy cobalt*** cobalt *m* oxydé noir; *Geol* ***slaggy lava*** laves *fpl* scoriacées, scories *fpl* volcaniques

slagheap ['slæghi:p] *n* terril *m*, crassier *m*

slain [sleɪn] **1** *pp of* **slay**

2 *npl Literary* **the slain** les soldats *mpl* tombés au champ d'honneur

slake [sleɪk] *vt* (**a**) *Literary (thirst)* étancher; *(desire)* assouvir (**b**) *Chem (lime)* éteindre

slaked lime [sleɪkt-] *n Chem* chaux *f* éteinte

slakeless ['sleɪklɪs] *adj Literary (thirst)* inextinguible; *(desire)* insatiable

slaking ['sleɪkɪŋ] *n* (**a**) *Literary (of thirst)* étanchement *m*; *(of desire)* assouvissement *m* (**b**) *Chem (of lime)* extinction *f*

slalom ['slɑ:ləm] **1** *n* slalom *m*

2 *vi* slalomer, faire du slalom

slam [slæm] *(pt & pp* **slammed,** *cont* **slamming) 1** *vt* (**a**) *(close → window, door)* claquer; *(→ drawer)* fermer violemment; **to slam the door shut** claquer la porte; **I tried to explain but she slammed the door in my face** j'ai essayé de lui expliquer mais elle m'a claqué la porte au nez

(**b**) *(bang)* **he slammed the books on the desk** il a posé bruyamment les livres sur le bureau; **he slammed the ball into the net** il a envoyé le ballon dans le filet d'un grand coup de pied

(**c**) *Fam (defeat)* écraser; **our team got slammed** notre équipe a été battue à plate couture

(**d**) *Fam (criticize)* éreinter, descendre en flammes; **to get slammed** se faire éreinter, se faire descendre en flammes

2 *vi (door, window)* claquer; **the door slammed shut** la porte a claqué

3 *n* (**a**) *(of door, window)* claquement *m*; **the door swung shut with a slam** la porte s'est refermée en claquant; **give the door a good slam** claque la porte un bon coup; **I heard a loud slam** j'ai entendu un grand claquement

(**b**) *Cards* chelem *m*; **to make a slam** faire (le) chelem

▸▸ *Am Sport* ***slam dunk*** smash *m* au panier

▸**slam down** *vt sep (lid)* refermer en claquant; *(books, keys)* poser bruyamment; **she slammed the money down on the table** elle a jeté l'argent sur la table; **he slammed the phone down** il raccrocha d'un geste furieux

▸**slam on** *vt sep* **to slam on the brakes** freiner brutalement; **he slammed on a hat and stormed out** il enfonça un chapeau sur sa tête et sortit comme un ouragan

▸**slam to** *vt sep* refermer en claquant; **she slammed the gate to** elle a refermé la porte en la claquant

slam-bang *adv Am Fam* (**a**) *(directly)* **she ran slam-bang into me** elle m'est rentrée (en plein) dedans (**b**) *(recklessly)* sans faire attention ❑, n'importe comment ❑

slammer ['slæmə(r)] *n Fam (jail)* taule *f*, cabane *f*; **in the slammer** en taule, en cabane

slamming ['slæmɪŋ] *n (of door, window)* claquement *m*

slander ['slɑ:ndə(r)] **1** *vt (gen)* calomnier, dire du mal de; *Law* diffamer

2 *n (gen)* calomnie *f*; *Law* diffamation *f*

slanderer ['slɑ:ndərə(r)] *n (gen)* calomniateur(-trice) *m,f*; *Law* diffamateur(trice) *m,f*

slandering ['slɑ:ndərɪŋ] *n (gen)* calomnie *f*; *Law* diffamation *f*

slanderous ['slɑ:ndərəs] *adj (gen)* calomniateur; *Law* diffamatoire

▸▸ ***slanderous gossip*** calomnies *fpl*

slanderously ['slɑ:ndərəslɪ] *adv (gen)* calomnieusement; *Law* de façon diffamatoire

slang [slæŋ] **1** *n* argot *m*; **he uses a lot of slang** il emploie beaucoup de mots d'argot; **prison slang** argot *m* carcéral *ou* de prison

2 *adj* argotique, d'argot

3 *vt Br Fam* traiter de tous les noms ❑; **they started slanging each other in the street** ils commencèrent à se traiter de tous les noms dans la rue

slangily ['slæŋɪlɪ] *adv (speak, express oneself)* en argot

slanginess ['slæŋɪnɪs] *n (of conversation, style)* caractère *m* argotique

slanging match ['slæŋɪŋ-] *n Br Fam* prise *f* de bec, engueulade *f*; **to have a slanging match (with sb)** avoir une prise de bec (avec qn), s'engueuler (avec qn)

slangy ['slæŋɪ] *(compar* **slangier,** *superl* **slangiest)** *adj* argotique

slant [slɑ:nt] **1** *n* (**a**) *(line)* ligne *f* oblique; *(slope)* inclinaison *f*; **the table has a slant** *or* **is on a slant** la table penche *ou* n'est pas d'aplomb

(**b**) *(point of view)* perspective *f*, point *m* de vue; **his articles usually have an anti-government slant** il a tendance à critiquer le gouvernement dans ses articles; **to put a different slant on things** apporter une perspective différente sur les choses; **the book gives a different slant on the whole business** le livre offre un point de vue différent sur toute cette affaire *ou* présente toute l'affaire sous un jour différent

(**c**) *Fam (Oriental)* bridé(e) *m,f*, = terme injurieux désignant un Asiatique

2 *vt* (**a**) *(news, evidence)* présenter avec parti pris *ou* de manière peu objective; **the article was slanted** l'article était orienté

(**b**) *(line, perspective)* incliner, faire pencher

3 *vi (line, handwriting)* pencher; *(ray of light)* passer obliquement

slant-eyed *adj* aux yeux bridés, qui a les yeux bridés

slanting ['slɑ:ntɪŋ] *adj (floor, table, roof)* en pente, incliné; *(writing)* penché; *(line)* oblique, penché

slantingly ['slɑ:ntɪŋlɪ] *adv* obliquement, de *ou* en biais

slantways ['slɑ:ntweɪz] *adv* en *ou* de biais

slantwise ['slɑ:ntwaɪz] *adv (hang, fall)* en oblique, obliquement; *(write)* d'une écriture penchée

slap [slæp] *(pt & pp* **slapped,** *cont* **slapping) 1** *vt* (**a**) *(hit)* donner une claque à; **she slapped his face, she slapped him across the face** elle l'a giflé, elle lui a donné une gifle; **to slap sb on the back** *(for hiccups, in greeting)* donner à qn une tape dans le dos; *(in praise)* féliciter qn en lui donnant une tape dans le dos; **to slap sb's wrist** *or* **wrists, to slap sb on the wrist** *or* **wrists** taper sur les doigts de qn

(**b**) *(put)* **just slap some paint over it** passe un coup de pinceau dessus; **slap some Sellotape® across it** mets juste un bout de Scotch® dessus

2 *vi* **the waves slapped against the harbour wall** les vagues battaient contre la digue; **the flag was slapping against the mast** le drapeau claquait contre le mât

3 *n* (**a**) *(smack)* claque *f*; *(on face)* gifle *f*; *(on back)* tape *f* dans le dos; *(on wrist)* tape *f*; **they gave him a slap on the back** *(in praise)* ils lui ont donné une tape dans le dos pour le féliciter; **I got a slap in the face** j'ai reçu une gifle; *Fig* **it was a real slap in the face** ça m'a fait l'effet d'une gifle; **I got away with just a slap on the wrist** j'en ai été quitte pour une tape sur les doigts

(**b**) *(noise)* **the slap of bare feet on the floor** le bruit de pieds nus sur le plancher; **the slap of the waves against the side of the boat** le clapotis des vagues contre la coque

(**c**) *Br Fam (make-up)* maquillage ❑ *m*

4 *adv Fam* en plein; **she rode slap into me** elle m'est rentrée en plein dedans; **I ran slap into a tree** je suis rentré en plein *ou* tout droit dans un arbre; **slap in the middle of the meeting** en plein *ou* au beau milieu de la réunion

▸▸ ***slap shot*** *(in ice-hockey)* lancer *m* frappé, tir *m* frappé

▸**slap around** *vt sep* battre

▸**slap down** *vt sep* (**a**) *(book, money)* poser bruyamment; **she slapped £1,000 down on the table** elle a jeté une liasse de 1000 livres sur la table

(**b**) *Fam (suggestion)* rejeter ❑; *(person)* rembarrer

▸**slap on** *vt sep* (**a**) *(paint)* appliquer n'importe comment *ou* à la va-vite; *(jam, butter)* étaler généreusement; **slap some paint on the door** donne un coup de pinceau sur la porte; **the whitewash only needs to be slapped on** le blanc de chaux n'a pas besoin d'être étalé soigneusement; **hang on, I'll just slap some make-up on** attends, je vais juste me maquiller vite fait

(**b**) *(tax, increase)* **they slapped on a 3 percent surcharge** ils ont mis une surtaxe de 3 pour cent; **10 percent was slapped on the price** ils ont augmenté le prix de 10 pour cent

slap and tickle *n Br Fam* pelotage *m*; **a bit of slap and tickle** une partie de pelotage

slap-bang *adv Fam* en plein, tout droit; **she went slap-bang(-wallop) into a tree** elle est rentrée en plein *ou* tout droit dans un arbre; *Fig* **he walked slap-bang into his boss** il s'est trouvé nez à nez avec son patron

slapdash ['slæpdæʃ] **1** *adv* à la va-vite, sans soin, n'importe comment

2 *adj (work)* fait n'importe comment *ou* à la va-vite; *(person)* négligent; **he's very slapdash in everything he does** il fait tout un peu n'importe comment *ou* à la va-vite

slaphappy ['slæp,hæpɪ] *adj Fam* relax

slaphead ['slæphed] *n Br Fam* chauve □ *m*, crâne *m* d'œuf; **he's a slaphead** il n'a pas un poil sur le caillou, il a une casquette en peau de fesse

slapjack ['slæpdʒæk] *n Am Culin* crêpe *f*

SLAPP [slæp] *n Am* (*abbr* **strategic lawsuit against public participation**) = procès intenté par une société à des activistes, visant à intimider ces derniers et stopper leur action

slapper ['slæpə(r)] *n Br Fam* (**a**) *(promiscuous woman)* pouffiasse *f*, traînée *f*, salope *f* (**b**) *Pej (any woman)* gonzesse *f*, grognasse *f*

slapping ['slæpɪŋ] *n (blows)* claques *fpl*, gifles *fpl*

slapstick ['slæpstɪk] **1** *n* grosse farce *f*, bouffonnerie *f*

2 *adj (humour)* bouffon

►► ***slapstick comedy*** comédie *f* bouffonne

slap-up *adj Br Fam* **a slap-up meal** un repas de derrière les fagots □; **he invited me out for a slap-up lunch** il m'a invité à déjeuner dans un restaurant chic □

slash [slæʃ] **1** *vt* (**a**) *(cut → gen)* taillader; *(→ face)* balafrer; **he slashed my arm with a knife** il m'a tailladé le bras avec un couteau; **the bus seats had been slashed by vandals** les sièges du bus avaient été lacérés par des vandales; **he slashed his way through the jungle** il s'est taillé *ou* frayé un chemin à travers la jungle à coups de couteau

(**b**) *(hit → with whip)* frapper, cingler; *(→ with stick)* battre; **the rider slashed the horse with his whip** le cavalier frappait *ou* cinglait le cheval de son fouet; **she slashed the bushes with a stick** elle donnait des coups de bâton dans les buissons

(**c**) *Am (verbally)* critiquer violemment; **she slashed the government in her speech** elle a violemment critiqué le gouvernement dans son discours

(**d**) *(prices)* casser; *(cost, taxes, unemployment)* réduire considérablement; **prices slashed!** *(sign)* prix cassés!; **prices have been slashed by 40 percent** les prix ont été réduits de 40 pour cent

(**e**) *Sewing* **a green jacket slashed with blue** une veste verte avec des crevés laissant apercevoir du bleu

2 *vi* **to slash at sb with a knife** donner des coups de couteau en direction de qn; **he slashed at the bushes with a stick** il donna des coups de bâton dans les buissons; **they slashed through the undergrowth** ils se sont taillés un chemin dans les sous-bois

3 *n* (**a**) *(with knife)* coup *m* de couteau; *(with sword)* coup *m* d'épée; *(with whip)* coup *m* de fouet; *(with stick)* coup *m* de bâton

(**b**) *(cut)* entaille *f*; *(on face)* balafre *f*

(**c**) *Sewing* crevé *m*

(**d**) *Typ & Comput* (barre *f*) oblique *f*

(**e**) *(UNCOUNT) Am (wood chips)* copeaux *mpl*

(**f**) *Br Fam (idioms)* **to have a slash** pisser; **to go for a slash** aller pisser un coup

slash-and-burn *adj Agr* sur brûlis

slasher ['slæʃə(r)] *n* (**a**) *Fam (fighter)* batailleur(euse) *m,f* (**b**) *(saw)* fauchard *m* (**c**) *Tex* machine *f* à encoller

►► *Fam* ***slasher film*** = film d'horreur particulièrement sanglant

slashing ['slæʃɪŋ] **1** *adj (attack, criticism)* cinglant

2 *n (severe criticism)* critique *f* acerbe

slat [slæt] *n (in blinds, louvre)* lamelle *f*; *(wooden)* latte *f*; *Aviat* aileron *m*

slate [sleɪt] **1** *n* (**a**) *Constr & Sch* ardoise *f*; *Br Fam Fig* **put it on the slate** mettez-le sur mon compte □; *Br Fam* **to have a slate loose** *(person)* avoir une case de vide, avoir une araignée au plafond

(**b**) *Am Pol* liste *f* provisoire de candidats; **the Republicans have a full slate** les Républicains présentent des candidats dans toutes les circonscriptions

(**c**) *(colour)* gris ardoise *m inv*

2 *comp (mine)* d'ardoise; *(roof)* en ardoise *ou* ardoises, d'ardoise; *(industry)* ardoisier; **slate pencil** crayon *m* d'ardoise; **slate quarry** carrière *f* d'ardoise, ardoisière *f*

3 *adj (in colour)* gris ardoise *(inv)*

4 *vt* (**a**) *(cover → roof)* couvrir d'ardoises

(**b**) *Am Pol* proposer *(un candidat)*; **Magee is slated for President** Magee a été choisi comme candidat aux élections présidentielles

(**c**) *Am (expect)* prévoir; **we're slating a full house** nous comptons faire salle comble; **she was slated for a gold medal/for victory** *(destined)* elle devait remporter une médaille d'or/la victoire

(**d**) *Br Fam (criticize)* éreinter, descendre en flammes; **his latest novel was slated by the critics** les critiques ont descendu son dernier roman

►► ***slate blue*** bleu ardoise *m inv*

slate-blue *adj* bleu ardoise *(inv)*

slate-coloured *adj* ardoise *(inv)*

slate-grey *adj* gris ardoise *(inv)*

slateman ['sleɪtmən] (*pl* **slatemen** [-men]) *n* ardoisier *m*, perrier *m*, perrayeur *m*

slater ['sleɪtə(r)] *n* (**a**) *(roofer)* couvreur *m* (**b**) *Ir, Scot, Austr & NZ (woodlouse)* cloporte *m*

slateworks ['sleɪtwɜːks] *n* ardoiserie *f*

slather ['slæðə(r)] **1** *n Br Fam* **slathers of cream** des masses *fpl ou* des tonnes *fpl* de crème

2 *vt Am Fam* (**a**) *(waste)* gaspiller □ (**b**) *(spread → butter)* étaler généreusement □

slating ['sleɪtɪŋ] *n* (**a**) *(UNCOUNT) Constr (of roof)* couverture *f*; *(material)* ardoises *fpl* (**b**) *Br Fam (reprimand)* savon *m*; *(severe criticism)* critique *f* acerbe □; **he got a slating from the PM** il s'est fait passer un savon par le Premier ministre; **the play got a slating in the press** la pièce a été éreintée par la presse

slatted ['slætɪd] *adj* à lattes

slattern ['slætən] *n* souillon *f*

slatternliness ['slætənlɪnɪs] *n* manque *m* d'ordre *ou* de propreté

slatternly ['slætənlɪ] *adj (woman)* mal soigné; *(habit, dress)* négligé

slaty ['sleɪtɪ] *adj (in colour)* ardoise *(inv)*; *(in appearance, texture)* qui ressemble à l'ardoise

slaughter ['slɔːtə(r)] **1** *vt* (**a**) *(kill → animal)* abattre, tuer; *(→ people)* massacrer, tuer (sauvagement) (**b**) *Fam Fig (defeat → team, opponent)* écrabouiller, battre à plates coutures

2 *n (of animal)* abattage *m*; *(of people)* massacre *m*, tuerie *f*

slaughtered [,slɔːtəd] *adj Br Fam (drunk)* bourré, beurré, pété

slaughterer ['slɔːtərə(r)] *n (in abattoir)* abatteur *m*, tueur *m (dans un abattoir)*; *(murderer)* meurtrier(ère) *m,f*; *(in massacre)* massacreur(euse) *m,f*

slaughterhouse ['slɔːtəhaʊs, *pl* -haʊzɪz] *n* abattoir *m*

'Slaughterhouse Five' *Vonnegut* 'Abattoir Cinq'

slaughtering ['slɔːtərɪŋ] *n* (**a**) *(of animals)* abattage *m* (**b**) *(of people)* carnage *m*, massacre *m*, boucherie *f*

slaughterman ['slɔːtəmən] (*pl* **slaughtermen** [-men]) *n* abatteur *m*, tueur *m (dans un abattoir)*

slaughterous ['slɔːtərəs] *adj Literary* meurtrier

Slav [slɑːv] **1** *adj* slave

2 *n* Slave *mf*

slave [sleɪv] **1** *n also Fig* esclave *mf*; **to be a slave to fashion/habit** être esclave de la mode/de ses habitudes; **he's a slave to drink** il est prisonnier de l'alcool; *Fam Hum* **what did your last slave die of?** je ne suis pas ta bonne!

2 *vi* travailler comme un esclave *ou* un forçat, trimer; **I've been slaving over a hot stove all morning** j'ai travaillé comme un forçat à la cuisine toute la matinée; **he slaved over his books all day long** il était plongé dans ses livres à longueur de journée; **they slaved to get their house finished in time** ils ont travaillé comme des forçats pour terminer leur maison à temps

►► ***slave camera*** caméra *f* asservie *ou* esclave; ***slave cylinder*** cylindre *m* récepteur; ***slave driver*** meneur *m* d'esclaves; *Fig* négrier *m*; ***slave labour*** *(work)* travail *m* fait par des esclaves; *Fig* travail *m* de forçat; **the Great Wall was built by slave labour** la Grande Muraille a été construite par des esclaves; **I'm not working there any more, it's slave labour** je ne travaillerai plus pour eux, c'est le *ou* un vrai bagne; ***slave ship*** négrier *m (bateau)*; *Am Hist* ***Slave State*** État *m* esclavagiste; ***slave trade*** commerce *m* des esclaves; *(of Africans)* traite *f* des Noirs; ***slave trader*** marchand *m* d'esclaves, négrier *m*

►**slave away** *vi (work hard)* trimer (**over** *or* **at** sur)

slaveholder ['sleɪv,həʊldə(r)] *n* propriétaire *mf* d'esclaves

slaver¹ ['sleɪvə(r)] *n* (**a**) *(trader)* marchand *m* d'esclaves (**b**) *(ship)* (vaisseau *m*) négrier *m*

slaver² ['slævə(r)] **1** *vi (dribble)* baver; **the dog was slavering at the mouth** le chien bavait

2 *n* (**a**) *(saliva)* bave *f* (**b**) *Literary (flattery)* flatterie *f* grossière, flagornerie *f*

►**slaver over** *vt insep (person)* s'extasier devant; *(possession)* convoiter; *(event)* se délecter de

slavering ['slævərɪŋ] **1** *adj* baveur

2 *n* émission *f* de bave

slavery ['sleɪvərɪ] *n* esclavage *m*; **to be sold into slavery** être vendu comme esclave; **to reduce to slavery** *(person)* réduire en esclavage; *(a people)* asservir; **this work is sheer slavery** ce travail est un véritable esclavage

slavey ['sleɪvɪ] *n Br Fam* boniche *f*

Slavic ['slɑːvɪk] = **Slavonic**

slavish ['sleɪvɪʃ] *adj (mentality, habits)* d'esclave; *(devotion)* servile; *(imitation)* sans aucune originalité, servile

slavishly ['sleɪvɪʃlɪ] *adv (work)* comme un forçat; *(copy, worship)* servilement

slavishness ['sleɪvɪʃnɪs] *n* servilité *f*

Slavonia [slə'vəʊnɪə] *n* Slavonie *f*

Slavonian [slə'vəʊnɪən] **1** *adj* slavon

2 *n* Slavon(onne) *m,f*

►► *Orn* ***Slavonian grebe*** grèbe *m* esclavon, grèbe *m* oreillard

Slavonic [slə'vɒnɪk] **1** *n Ling* slave *m*; *Hist* slavon *m*

2 *adj* slave

slaw [slɔː] *n Am* salade *f* de chou cru

slay [sleɪ] (*pt* **slew** [sluː], *pp* **slain** [sleɪn]) *vt* (**a**) *(kill)* tuer (**b**) *Br Fam (impress)* impressionner □; *(amuse)* faire mourir de rire; *Fam* **this one will really slay you** *(joke, story)* celle-là va vous faire mourir de rire; *Ironic* **you slay me!** tu es impayable!

slayer ['sleɪə(r)] *n Literary* tueur(euse) *m,f*

slaying ['sleɪɪŋ] *n Literary (killing → of dragon)* destruction *f*; *(→ of person)* meurtre *m*; *esp Am Journ (murder)* assassinat *m*, meurtre *m*

sleaze [sliːz] *Fam* **1** *n* (**a**) *(squalidness)* aspect *m* miteux □, caractère *m* sordide □

(**b**) *(pornography)* porno *m*

(**c**) *(corruption)* corruption □ *f*; **it's the sleaze factor that led to the government's downfall** ce sont les affaires de corruption dans lesquelles le gouvernement a été impliqué qui en ont provoqué la chute

2 *vi* (**a**) *(live immoral life)* mener une vie dissolue □

(**b**) *(move or act sleazily)* **he sleazed up to the bar** il s'approcha du bar en roulant des mécaniques

sleazebag ['sliːzbæg], **sleazeball** ['sliːzbɔːl] *n Fam* (**a**) *(despicable person)* ordure *f*, raclure *f* (**b**) *(repulsive man)* gros dégueulasse *m*

sleaziness ['sliːzɪnɪs] *n Fam* sordide □ *m*

sleazo ['sli:zəʊ] (*pl* **sleazos**) *n Fam* personne *f* louche ᵅ; **he's a sleazo** c'est un type louche

sleazy ['sli:zɪ] (*compar* **sleazier**, *superl* **sleaziest**) *adj Fam (squalid)* miteux ᵅ, sordide ᵅ; *(disreputable)* mal famé ᵅ; *(person)* louche ᵅ; **a sleazy bar** un bar miteux *ou* mal famé

sled [sled] *n Am* (**a**) *(for fun or sport)* luge *f* (**b**) *(pulled by animals)* traîneau *m*

►► ***sled dog*** chien *m* de traîneau; ***sled race*** course *f* de traîneaux

sledding ['sledɪŋ] *n Am (travelling)* promenades *fpl* en traîneau; *(conveying)* transport *m* en traîneau; *Fig* **easy** *or* **smooth sledding** travail *m* facile, travail *m* qui va comme sur des roulettes; *Fig* **tough** *or* **hard sledding** travail *m* pénible *ou* tuant

sledge [sledʒ] **1** *n* (**a**) *(for fun or sport)* luge *f* (**b**) *(pulled by animals)* traîneau *m*

2 *vi* (**a**) *Br (for fun or sport)* faire de la luge; **to go sledging** faire de la luge; **children were sledging down the slope** des enfants descendaient la pente sur une *ou* en luge (**b**) *(pulled by animals)* faire du traîneau

3 *vt* transporter en traîneau

sledgehammer ['sledʒ,hæmə(r)] *n (tool)* masse *f*; *Fig* **a sledgehammer blow** un coup très violent; *Fam* **he's as subtle as a sledgehammer!** il est d'un lourd!; *Fig* **to use a sledgehammer to crack a walnut** employer les grands moyens (pour régler un problème mineur)

sledging ['sledʒɪŋ] *n* (**a**) *(travelling)* promenades *fpl* en traîneau; *(conveying)* transport *m* en traîneau (**b**) *Sport (intimidation)* intimidation *f* de l'opposant

sleek [sli:k] *adj* (**a**) *(fur, hair)* luisant, lustré, lisse; *(feathers)* brillant, luisant; *(bird)* aux plumes luisantes; *(cat)* au poil soyeux *ou* brillant

(**b**) *(person → in appearance)* soigné, tiré à quatre épingles; *(→ in manner)* onctueux, doucereux

(**c**) *(vehicle, plane)* aux lignes pures; **the car has very sleek lines** cette voiture a une très belle ligne; **a sleek black limousine** une limousine d'un noir brillant

►**sleek back, sleek down** *vt sep* **to sleek one's hair back** *or* **down** se lisser les cheveux

sleekly ['sli:klɪ] *adv* (**a**) *(glossily)* **its fur shone sleekly** il/elle avait le poil luisant (**b**) *(elegantly → dress)* élégamment, avec chic (**c**) *(unctuously → behave)* onctueusement, doucereusement

sleekness ['sli:knɪs] *n* (**a**) *(of fur, hair, feathers)* brillant *m*, luisant *m*; **the sleekness of the bird** les plumes *fpl* luisantes de l'oiseau (**b**) *(of person → in appearance)* chic *m*, élégance *f*; *(→ in manner)* onctuosité *f* (**c**) *(of vehicle, plane)* pureté *f* de lignes, ligne *f* aérodynamique

SLEEP [sli:p]

sommeil	► **1 (a)**
dormir	► **1 (a); 3 (a)**
s'endormir	► **1 (a)**
endormir	► **1 (a)**
faire une somme	► **1 (b)**
coucher	► **3 (b)**
passer la nuit	► **3 (b)**
rêvasser	► **3 (c)**
chassie	► **1 (c)**

(*pt & pp* **slept** [slept]) **1** *n* (**a**) *(rest)* sommeil *m*; **to turn over in one's sleep** se retourner dans son sommeil; **to talk in one's sleep** parler en dormant *ou* dans son sommeil; **to walk in one's sleep** être somnambule; **she walked in her sleep last night** elle a fait une crise de somnambulisme *ou* a marché en dormant la nuit dernière; **to be in a deep sleep** dormir profondément; **to have a good (night's) sleep** bien dormir; **you need (to get) a good night's sleep** il te faut une bonne nuit de sommeil; **I only had two hours' sleep** je n'ai dormi que deux heures; **I need my sleep** j'ai besoin de beaucoup de sommeil; **I couldn't get to sleep** je n'arrivais pas à m'endormir; **to go to sleep** s'endormir; **to go** *or* **get back to sleep** se rendormir; **my legs have gone to sleep** *(numb)* j'ai les jambes engourdies; *(tingling)* j'ai des fourmis dans les jambes; **to read oneself to sleep** lire pour s'endormir; **to sing a child to sleep** chanter une berceuse à un enfant; **you're not going to lose sleep over it!** tu ne vas pas en perdre le sommeil!; **I won't lose any sleep over it** cela ne va pas m'empêcher de dormir; **to put to sleep** endormir; *Euph (horse, dog)* piquer; **I was put to sleep before the operation** on m'a endormi avant l'opération; **the horse had to be put to sleep** on a dû faire piquer le cheval; **to send sb to sleep** endormir qn; *Fig (bore)* endormir qn, assommer qn

(**b**) *(nap)* **to have a sleep** faire un somme; **the children usually have a sleep in the afternoon** en général les enfants font la sieste l'après-midi; **I could do with a sleep** je ferais bien un petit somme

(**c**) *(substance in eyes)* chassie *f*; **to rub the sleep out of one's eyes** se frotter les yeux *(au réveil)*

(**d**) *Literary (death)* la mort

2 *vt* (**a**) *(accommodate)* **the sofa bed sleeps two** deux personnes peuvent coucher dans le canapé-lit; **the house sleeps four** on peut coucher à quatre dans cette maison

(**b**) *Literary* **to sleep the sleep of the just** dormir du sommeil du juste

3 *vi* (**a**) *(rest)* dormir; **sleep well** *or* **tight!** bonne nuit!; **did you sleep well?** avez-vous bien dormi?; **I'm not sleeping well at the moment** je ne dors pas bien en ce moment; **to sleep (for) six hours** dormir six heures; **he can't sleep for thinking about it** il n'en dort pas; **to sleep late** faire la grasse matinée; **to sleep soundly** dormir profondément *ou* à poings fermés; **to sleep like a log** dormir comme une souche *ou* comme un loir, dormir à poings fermés

(**b**) *(spend night)* coucher, passer la nuit; **can I sleep at your place?** est-ce que je peux coucher *ou* dormir chez vous?; **to sleep on the floor** coucher *ou* dormir par terre; **the bed had not been slept in** le lit n'avait pas été défait; **where did you sleep last night?** où est-ce que tu as passé la nuit?; **to sleep rough** coucher sur la dure

(**c**) *(daydream)* rêvasser, rêver; **Walsh is sleeping at the back of the class as usual** Walsh rêvasse au fond de la classe, comme d'habitude

(**d**) *Euph or Literary (be dead)* dormir du dernier sommeil

(**e**) *Comput* être en veille; **to put a notebook to sleep** mettre un portable en veille

►► *Med* ***sleep apnoea*** *or Am* ***apnea*** apnée *f* du sommeil; *Med* ***sleep apnoea*** *or Am* ***apnea syndrome*** syndrome *m* d'apnée du sommeil; *Comput* ***sleep mode*** veille *f*

►**sleep around** *vi Fam* coucher à droite et à gauche

►**sleep away** *vt sep* **he slept the night away** il a dormi toute la nuit; **he sleeps the day away** il passe toute la journée à dormir

►**sleep in** *vi* (**a**) *(lie in → voluntarily)* faire la grasse matinée; *(→ involuntarily)* se lever en retard, ne pas se réveiller (à l'heure)

(**b**) *(sleep at home)* coucher à la maison; *(staff)* être logé sur place

►**sleep off** *vt sep (hangover, fatigue)* dormir pour faire passer *ou* se remettre de; **he's sleeping off the effects of the journey** il dort pour se remettre de la fatigue du voyage; *Fam* **he's sleeping it off** il cuve son vin

►**sleep on 1** *vi* continuer à dormir; **let her sleep on a bit** laisse-la dormir encore un peu; **she slept on until lunchtime** elle a dormi jusqu'à l'heure du déjeuner

2 *vt insep* **I'll sleep on it** la nuit porte conseil; **sleep on it** la nuit porte conseil

►**sleep out** *vi (away from home)* découcher; *(in the open air)* coucher à la belle étoile; *(in tent)* coucher sous la tente; **some of the nurses sleep out** les infirmières ne sont pas toutes logées sur place

►**sleep over** *vi Am* **can I sleep over?** est-ce que je peux rester la nuit?

►**sleep through 1** *vi* **he slept through till five o'clock** il a dormi jusqu'à cinq heures

2 *vt insep* **I slept through the last act** j'ai dormi pendant tout le dernier acte; **she slept through her alarm** elle n'a pas entendu son réveil; **she slept through the storm** la tempête ne l'a pas réveillée; **they slept through my speech** ils ont dormi pendant mon discours

►**sleep together** *vi* coucher ensemble

►**sleep with** *vt insep* coucher avec

sleeper ['sli:pə(r)] *n* (**a**) *(sleeping person)* dormeur(euse) *m,f*; **to be a light/heavy sleeper** avoir le sommeil léger/lourd; **a late sleeper** un (une) couche-tard

(**b**) *(train)* train-couchettes *m*; *(sleeping car)* wagon-lit *m*, voiture-lit *f*; *(berth)* couchette *f*; **I took the sleeper to Rome** je suis allé à Rome en train-couchettes

(**c**) *Am (sofa bed)* canapé-lit *m*

(**d**) *Br Rail (track support)* traverse *f*, *Can* dormant *m*

(**e**) *(spy)* agent *m* dormant *ou* en sommeil

(**f**) *(earring)* dormeuse *f*

(**g**) *Fam (unexpected success)* révélation ᵅ *f*

sleepily ['sli:pɪlɪ] *adv (look)* d'un air endormi; *(speak)* d'un ton endormi; **she wandered sleepily into the kitchen** elle est arrivée à moitié endormie dans la cuisine; **a village nestled sleepily in the hills** un village blotti tranquillement contre les collines

sleepiness ['sli:pɪnɪs] *n (of person)* envie *f* de dormir; *(of town)* torpeur *f*

sleeping ['sli:pɪŋ] **1** *adj* dormant, endormi; *Prov* **let sleeping dogs lie** ne réveillez pas le chat qui dort

2 *n* sommeil *m*; **the house has sleeping accommodation for ten** c'est une maison où dix personnes peuvent dormir; **there's no sleeping accommodation here** il n'y a rien pour dormir; **what are the sleeping arrangements?** et pour dormir, comment on fait?; **she was a bit vague about the sleeping arrangements** elle est restée vague concernant les lits

►► ***sleeping bag*** sac *m* de couchage; *Rail & Naut* ***sleeping berth*** couchette *f*; *Rail* ***sleeping car, sleeping carriage*** wagon-lit *m*; *Br* ***sleeping draught*** soporifique *m*; *Fig* ***sleeping giant*** = pays ou organisation dont le très fort potentiel reste inexploité; *Br Com* ***sleeping partner*** (associé *m*) commanditaire *m*, bailleur *m* de fonds; ***sleeping pill*** somnifère *m*; *Br* ***sleeping policeman*** casse-vitesse *m inv*, ralentisseur *m*; ***sleeping quarters*** chambres *fpl* à coucher; *Mil* chambrées *fpl*; *Sch* dortoir *m*; ***sleeping sickness*** maladie *f* du sommeil; *Am* ***sleeping suit*** grenouillère *f*, ***sleeping tablet*** somnifère *m*

'Sleeping Beauty' *Perrault, Tchaikovsky, Disney* 'La Belle au bois dormant'

sleep-learning *n* apprentissage *m* en dormant, hypnopédie *f*

sleepless ['sli:plɪs] *adj* (**a**) *(without sleep)* sans sommeil; **I had** *or* **spent a sleepless night** j'ai passé une nuit blanche, je n'ai pas fermé l'œil de la nuit (**b**) *Literary (person)* qui ne peut trouver le sommeil; **sleepless vigilance** vigilance *f* sans faille (**c**) *Literary (mind)* sans cesse en éveil; *(sea)* agité

'Sleepless in Seattle' *Ephron* 'Nuits blanches à Seattle'

sleeplessly ['sli:plɪslɪ] *adv* sans pouvoir dormir

sleeplessness ['sli:plɪsnɪs] *n (UNCOUNT)* insomnie *f*, insomnies *fpl*

sleepover ['sli:pəʊvə(r)] *n* = nuit passée chez un copain, le plus souvent à plusieurs

sleepsuit ['sli:psu:t] *n* grenouillère *f*

sleepwalk ['sli:pwɔ:k] *vi* être somnambule; **he's sleepwalking** il marche en dormant; **I sleepwalked last night** j'ai eu une crise de somnambulisme la nuit dernière; *Fig* **we are sleepwalking into disaster** nous allons tout droit à la catastrophe sans nous en rendre compte

sleepwalker ['sli:p,wɔ:kə(r)] *n* somnambule *mf*

sleepwalking ['sli:p,wɔ:kɪŋ] *n* somnambulisme *m*

sleepwear ['sli:pweə(r)] *n (UNCOUNT)* vêtements *mpl* de nuit

sleepy ['sli:pɪ] (*compar* **sleepier**, *superl* **sleepiest**) *adj* (**a**) *(person)* qui a envie de dormir, somnolent; **I'm** *or* **I feel sleepy** j'ai sommeil, j'ai envie de dormir; **to make sb (feel) sleepy** endormir qn; **sleepy look** air *m* endormi (**b**) *(town)* plongé dans la torpeur

sleepyhead ['sli:pɪhed] *n Fam* **come on, sleepyhead, it's time for bed!** allez, va au lit, tu dors debout!□; **wake up, sleepyhead!** debout, paresseux/paresseuse!

sleet [sliːt] **1** *n* **(a)** *(icy rain)* neige *f* fondue *(tombant du ciel)* **(b)** *Am (ice)* verglas *m*

2 *vi* **it's sleeting** il tombe de la neige fondue

sleety ['sliːtɪ] *adj* **(a)** *(wind)* chargé de pluie mêlée de neige **(b)** *(weather, day)* de pluie et de neige, où il tombe de la neige fondue

sleeve [sliːv] *n* **(a)** *(of garment)* manche *f*; **short sleeve** manche *f* courte; *Fig* **to have** *or* **to keep something up one's sleeve** avoir plus d'un tour dans son sac; **he's got a surprise up his sleeve** il nous/leur/*etc* réserve une surprise; **I wonder what else she's got up her sleeve** je me demande ce qu'elle nous réserve encore comme surprise; **I've still got a few ideas up my sleeve** j'ai encore quelques idées en réserve

(b) *Tech (tube)* manchon *m*; *(lining)* chemise *f*, fourreau *m*

(c) *Br (for record)* pochette *f*

►► ***sleeve board*** jeannette *f*; ***sleeve hole*** *(in clothing)* emmanchure *f*; *Br* ***sleeve notes*** = texte figurant au dos des pochettes de disques

-sleeved [sliːvd] *suff* à manches...; **short-sleeved** à manches courtes

sleeveless ['sliːvlɪs] *adj* sans manches

sleeving ['sliːvɪŋ] *n Br Elec* gaine *f* isolante

sleigh [sleɪ] **1** *n* traîneau *m*

2 *vi* se promener en traîneau, aller en traîneau

►► ***sleigh bell*** grelot *m* (de traîneau); ***sleigh ride*** promenade *f* en traîneau

sleigher ['sleɪə(r)] *n* voyageur(euse) *m,f ou* promeneur(euse) *m,f* en traîneau

sleighing ['sleɪɪŋ] *n* promenades *fpl* en traîneau

sleight of hand [ˌslaɪt-] *n* *(skill)* dextérité *f*; *(trick)* tour *m* de passe-passe; **by sleight of hand** par un tour de passe-passe

slender ['slendə(r)] *adj* **(a)** *(slim → figure)* mince, svelte; *(→ fingers, waist, neck, stem)* fin; **Peter is tall and slender** Peter est grand et élancé

(b) *(limited → resources)* faible, maigre, limité; *(→ majority, margin)* étroit, faible; *(→ hope, chance)* maigre, faible; *(→ knowledge)* faible, limité; **the slenderest of margins** une marge des plus étroites; **there is a very slender chance that...** il y a une chance très faible que... + *subjunctive*; *Euph* **he's a person of slender means** il ne roule pas sur l'or

slenderize ['slendəraɪz] *Am Fam* **1** *vi* maigrir□, mincir□

2 *vt* mincir□, amincir□

slenderizing ['slendəraɪzɪŋ] *Am Fam* **1** *n* amaigrissement□ *m*

2 *adj* *(diet)* amaigrissant□; *(cream, product)* amincissant□; *(exercises)* pour maigrir□; *(lunch)* qui ne fait pas grossir□

slenderly ['slendəlɪ] *adv* **slenderly built** svelte, mince

slenderness ['slendənɪs] *n* **(a)** *(of figure)* minceur *f*, sveltesse *f*; *(of neck, waist, fingers)* finesse *f* **(b)** *(of resources)* insuffisance *f*; *(of hope, majority, margin)* faiblesse *f*

slept [slept] *pt & pp of* **sleep**

sleuth [sluːθ] *Fam Hum* **1** *n* (fin) limier *m*, détective□ *m*

2 *vi* enquêter□

3 *vt* enquêter sur□

'Sleuth' *Shaffer, Mankiewicz* 'Le Limier'

sleuthhound ['sluːθhaʊnd] *n* **(a)** *Fam Hum (detective)* (fin) limier *m*, détective□ *m* **(b)** *(dog)* limier *m*

sleuthing ['sluːθɪŋ], **sleuthwork** ['sluːθwɜːk] *n Fam Hum* travail *m* de détective□; **I decided to do a bit of sleuthing of my own** j'ai décidé de mener ma propre petite enquête□; **a good bit of sleuthing** un travail de fin limier

S-level *n Br* = examen de niveau supérieur au "A-level" que passent les élèves les plus doués, généralement en même temps que ce dernier

slew [sluː] **1** *pt of* **slay**

2 *vi* **(a)** *(pivot)* pivoter, se retourner; **he slewed round in his chair** il a pivoté sur sa chaise

(b) *(vehicle → skid)* déraper; *(→ turn)* virer; *(→ turn right round)* faire un tête-à-queue; **the car slewed into the ditch** la voiture a dérapé et a fini dans le fossé

3 *vt* **(a)** *(twist)* faire tourner *ou* pivoter; *Naut (mast)* virer, déviRer

(b) *(vehicle)* faire déraper; **he slewed the car around** il a fait un tête-à-queue

4 *n* **(a)** *Fam (large number)* **a slew of, slews of** un tas de; **a whole slew of photographers** un tas de photographes; **slews of people** des *ou* un tas de gens

(b) *(of vehicle → turn)* virage *m*; *(→ 180 degree turn)* tête-à-queue *m inv*

slewed [sluːd] *adj Br Fam (drunk)* rond, ivre□; **to get slewed** prendre une cuite

slewing ['sluːɪŋ] *n* **(a)** *(pivoting)* pivotement *m*, virage *m* **(b)** *Electron* balayage *m*; **slewing rate** vitesse *f* de balayage

slice [slaɪs] **1** *n* **(a)** *(of bread, meat, cake, cheese)* tranche *f*; *(of pizza)* part *f*; *(round → of lemon, sausage, carrot, onion, banana etc)* rondelle *f*; **to cut sth into slices** *(bread, meat, cake, cheese)* couper qch (en tranches); *(pizza)* couper qch (en parts); *(lemon, sausage, carrot, onion, banana etc)* couper qch (en rondelles); **he cut himself a large slice of bread** il s'est coupé une grande tranche de pain

(b) *Fig (share, percentage)* part *f*, partie *f*; **a large slice of my income goes on rent** une bonne partie de mes revenus est absorbée par le loyer; **to take a large slice of the credit for sth** s'attribuer une large part du mérite de qch; **a slice of the profits** une part des bénéfices; *Fam* **they were all very keen to get a slice of the action** tout le monde voulait participer□

(c) *(utensil)* pelle *f*, spatule *f*; **cake slice** pelle *f* à gâteau

(d) *(in golf)* slice *m*; *(in tennis)* balle *f* coupée; **she puts a lot of slice on her serve** elle slice beaucoup ses balles au service

(e) *Culin* **apple slice** tartelette *f* aux pommes

2 *vt* **(a)** *(cut into pieces → cake, bread, ham)* couper (en tranches); *(→ pizza)* couper (en parts); *(→ sausage, carrot, courgette, banana)* couper (en rondelles); *Am Fam* **any way you slice it** il n'y a pas à tortiller

(b) *(cut)* couper, trancher; **to slice sth in two** *or* **in half** couper qch en deux; **to slice sth open** ouvrir qch en le coupant

(c) *(in golf)* slicer; *(in tennis)* couper

3 *vi* *(knife)* couper; *(bread)* se couper; **this bread doesn't slice very easily** ce pain n'est pas très facile à couper; **the knife sliced into the flesh** le couteau a pénétré dans la chair

►► ***slice of life*** *Theat* tranche *f* de vie; *(novel)* description *f* réaliste; *TV* **a slice of life documentary** un documentaire très réaliste

►**slice away** *vt sep (branch)* couper

►**slice off** *vt sep (branch)* couper; **to slice off the tip of one's finger** se trancher le bout du doigt; **slice me off some ham/cheese** coupe-moi une tranche de jambon/fromage

►**slice through** *vt insep* **(a)** *(cut → rope, cable)* couper (net), trancher; **he sliced through the red tape** il a éliminé toute la paperasserie d'un seul coup

(b) *(go, move)* traverser (rapidement), fendre; **the boat sliced through the water** le bateau fendait l'eau; **the arrow sliced through the air** la flèche fendit l'air; **the river slices through the city** la rivière coupe la ville en deux; **to slice through the enemy lines** transpercer les lignes adverses

►**slice up** *vt sep (cake, ham, bread)* couper (en tranches); *(pizza)* couper (en parts); *(banana, sausage, carrot, courgette)* couper (en rondelles)

sliced [slaɪst] *adj (cake, ham, bread)* en tranches; *(pizza)* découpée en parts; *(banana, sausage, carrot, courgette)* en rondelles

►► ***sliced bread*** pain *m* (coupé) en tranches; *Fam* **it's the best thing since sliced bread** c'est ce qu'on a fait de mieux depuis l'invention du fil à couper le beurre□; *Fam* **he thinks she's the best thing since sliced bread** il la trouve formidable

slicer ['slaɪsə(r)] *n (gen)* machine *f* à trancher; *(for bread)* machine *f* à couper le pain; *(for meat)* machine *f* à couper la viande; *(for salami, ham)* coupe-jambon *m inv*

slicing ['slaɪsɪŋ] *n* coupe *f*

slick [slɪk] **1** *adj* **(a)** *Pej (glib)* qui a du bagout; *(in manner)* doucereux; *(in content)* superficiel; **she always has a slick excuse** elle a toujours une bonne excuse; **he always has a slick answer** il a toujours réponse à tout; **the explanation was rather too slick** l'explication était trop bonne (pour être vraie)

(b) *(smoothly efficient)* habile; **she made a slick gear change** elle effectua un changement de vitesse en souplesse; **a slick campaign** une campagne astucieuse; **a slick sale** une vente rondement menée; **a slick take-over** un rachat rondement mené

(c) *(smart)* chic, tiré à quatre épingles; *(style, magazine)* beau (belle); **you're looking very slick** tu fais très chic

(d) *(hair)* lisse, lissé, luisant; *(tyre)* lisse

(e) *Am (slippery)* glissant; **the pavement was slick with rain** la pluie avait rendu le trottoir glissant; **the road was slick with ice/mud** le verglas/la boue avait rendu la chaussée glissante

(f) *Am (cunning)* malin(igne), rusé

2 *n* **(a)** *(oil spill → on sea)* nappe *f* de pétrole; *(→ on beach)* marée *f* noire

(b) *(tyre)* pneu *m* lisse

(c) *Am (glossy magazine)* = magazine en papier glacé contenant surtout des articles et des photos sur la vie privée des stars

►**slick back** *vt sep* **to slick back one's hair** se lisser les cheveux en arrière

►**slick down** *vt sep* **to slick one's hair down** se lisser les cheveux

►**slick up** *Am Fam* **1** *vt sep (appearance)* mettre en valeur□; *(house, room)* astiquer□, faire reluire□; **to slick oneself up** se pomponner□

2 *vi (dress smartly)* se pomponner□

slickenside ['slɪkənsaɪd] *n Geol* surface *f* de glissement, strie *f* de froissement

slicker ['slɪkə(r)] *n* **(a)** *(person)* **(city) slicker** homme *m* de finance habile, *Pej* requin *m* **(b)** *Am (raincoat)* imperméable *m*; *(oilskin)* ciré *m*

slickly ['slɪklɪ] *adv* **(a)** *(skilfully)* habilement; *(perform)* brillamment; **the deal went through slickly enough** l'affaire fut assez rondement menée **(b)** *Pej (say, reply)* doucereusement **(c)** **his hair shone slickly** il avait les cheveux luisants

slickness ['slɪknɪs] *n* **(a)** *(of hair)* brillant *m*, luisant *m* **(b)** *Pej (in speech)* bagout *m*; *(in manner)* caractère *m* doucereux; *(in style)* brillance *f* (apparente) **(c)** *(skill)* habileté *f*, adresse *f*

slide [slaɪd] (*pt & pp* **slid** [slɪd]) **1** *vi* **(a)** *(on ice, slippery surface)* glisser; **he slid on the ice** il a glissé sur la glace; **he slid down the banisters** il a descendu l'escalier en glissant sur la rampe; **the dish slid off the table/onto the floor** le plat a glissé de la table/sur le sol; **tears slid down her face** des larmes roulèrent sur son visage

(b) *(move quietly)* se glisser; **she slid into/out of the room** elle s'est glissée dans la pièce/hors de la pièce; **the pilot slid into the cockpit** le pilote s'est glissé dans le cockpit; **the car slid away into the dark** la voiture s'enfonça dans l'obscurité; **the door slid open/shut** la porte s'est ouverte/fermée en glissant; **her eyes slid over the familiar objects in the room** elle promena son regard sur les objets familiers de la pièce

(c) *(go gradually)* glisser; **the sheet music slid (down) behind the piano** la partition a glissé derrière le piano; **she slid slowly into debt** elle a fini par s'endetter; **the country was sliding into anarchy** le pays glissait vers l'anarchie; **he's sliding into bad habits** il est en train de prendre de mauvaises habitudes; **to let things slide** laisser les choses aller à la dérive

(d) *Tech (between runners etc)* coulisser

(e) *(prices, value)* baisser

2 *vt* faire glisser, glisser; **I slid the book into my pocket** j'ai glissé le livre dans ma poche; **he slid the door open/shut** il a ouvert/fermé la porte en la faisant coulisser; **slide the lid into place** faites glisser le couvercle à sa place; **she slid the money across the table** elle fit glisser l'argent sur la table

3 *n* **(a)** *(in playground)* toboggan *m*; *(on ice, snow)* glissoire *f*; *(for logs)* glissoire *f*; **(escape) slide** *(of plane)* toboggan *m* d'évacuation (**b**) *(act of sliding)* glissade *f*; **to go into a slide** faire une glissade

(**c**) *(landslide)* glissement *m* de terrain; **a mud slide** une coulée de boue; **a rock slide** un éboulement

(**d**) *(fall → in prices)* baisse *f*, chute *f*; **the stock exchange is on a downward slide** la Bourse est en baisse; **the slide in standards** la dégradation des valeurs; **the alarming slide of the economy** le dérapage alarmant de l'économie; **a slide in popularity** une baisse de popularité; **this began his slide into despair** c'est alors qu'il commença à sombrer dans le désespoir

(**e**) *Phot* diapositive *f*, diapo *f*

(**f**) *(for microscope)* porte-objet *m*; *(what is on the slide)* préparation *f*; **I illustrated my lecture with slides** j'ai illustré mon cours avec des diapositives

(**g**) *Br (for hair)* barrette *f*

(**h**) *(of machine, trombone)* coulisse *f*; *(of slide guitar)* slide *m*; *(of slide rule)* coulisseau *m*, réglette *f*; *(in rowing)* glissière *f*

(**i**) *Mus (between notes)* coulé *m*; *(in violin etc playing)* glissade *f*

▸▸ *Am **slide fastener*** fermeture *f* à glissière, fermeture *f* Éclair®; ***slide guitar*** slide guitar *f*; *TV **slide matter*** cache *m* latéral; ***slide projector*** projecteur *m* de diapositives; ***slide rule*** règle *f* à calcul; ***slide show*** diaporama *m*; *Comput* diaporama *m*, projection *f* de diapositives; ***slide trombone*** trombone *m* à coulisse; ***slide valve*** (soupape *f* à) clapet *m*

▸**slide down** 1 *vi (go down by sliding)* descendre en glissant

2 *vt insep (go down by sliding)* descendre en glissant; **to slide down a rope** se laisser couler *ou* glisser le long d'une corde; **to slide down the banisters** glisser le long de la rampe; **it's sliding down the charts** il perd des places au hit-parade

▸**slide off** *vi* (**a**) *(lid)* s'enlever en glissant; **this part slides off easily** il suffit de faire coulisser cette pièce pour l'enlever

(**b**) *(fall)* glisser; **the book keeps sliding off** le livre n'arrête pas de glisser

(**c**) *(sneak away)* s'en aller discrètement, s'éclipser; **where are you sliding off to?** où est-ce que tu te sauves comme ça?; **she slid off to the bar in the interval** elle s'est éclipsée à l'entracte pour aller au bar

▸**slide out** 1 *vi* (**a**) *(come out by sliding)* sortir (en glissant)

(**b**) *(sneak outside)* se glisser dehors

2 *vt sep (drawers, battery)* enlever en faisant glisser

▸**slide out of** *vt insep (evade)* se sortir de; **to slide out of doing the housework** échapper aux tâches ménagères; **I'd like to see him slide out of that one** j'aimerais bien voir comment il va se tirer d'affaire

▸**slide over** 1 *vt insep (evade → issue)* passer sur

2 *vi* se glisser; **she slid over to me in the interval** elle m'a rejoint pendant l'entracte; **slide over and let me drive** pousse-toi et laisse-moi le volant

slider ['slaɪdə(r)] *n* (**a**) *(person)* glisseur(euse) *m,f* (**b**) *Zool* tortue *f* aquatique (**c**) *Electron* curseur *m* (**d**) *Naut* chariot *m* de gouvernail (**e**) *Comput* languette *f*

sliding ['slaɪdɪŋ] 1 *adj (part)* qui glisse; *(movement)* glissant; *(door)* coulissant; *(panel)* mobile

2 *n* glissement *m*

▸▸ *Aut **sliding roof*** toit *m* ouvrant; ***sliding scale*** *(for salaries)* échelle *f* mobile; *(for prices)* barème *m* des prix; *(for tax)* barème *m* des impôts; ***sliding seat*** *(in rowing boat)* banc *m* à coulisses *ou* à glissières; *(in car)* siège *m* réglable *ou* mobile

sliding-scale *adj*

▸▸ ***sliding-scale taxation*** impôt *m* dégressif

slight [slaɪt] 1 *adj* (**a**) *(minor → error, movement)* petit; *(→ increase, improvement)* léger; *(→ difference)* petit, léger; *(→ cut, graze)* léger; **a slight accident** un petit incident; **there's a slight drizzle/wind** il y a un peu de crachin/de vent; **the difference is only very slight, there's only a very slight difference** la différence est minime, il n'y a qu'une très légère différence; **he has a slight accent** il a un léger accent; **she has a slight temperature** elle a un peu de température; **she has a slight cold** elle est un peu enrhumée; **there's a slight chance of some sunshine tomorrow** il y a une petite chance qu'il fasse beau demain; **a slight piece of work** un ouvrage insignifiant

(**b**) *(in superlative)* **it makes not the slightest bit of difference** ça ne change absolument rien; **I haven't the slightest idea** je n'en ai pas la moindre idée; **he gets angry at the slightest thing** il se fâche pour un rien; **they haven't the slightest chance of winning** ils n'ont pas la moindre chance *ou* la plus petite chance de l'emporter; **not in the slightest** pas le moins du monde, pas du tout; **they weren't (in) the slightest bit interested, they weren't interested in the slightest** ils n'étaient pas le moins du monde intéressés

(**c**) *(person → slender)* menu, mince; *(→ frail)* frêle; *(structure)* fragile, frêle; **she is of slight build** elle est fluette

2 *vt (snub)* manquer d'égards envers; *(insult)* insulter; *(offend)* froisser, blesser; **she felt slighted** elle a été blessée *ou* froissée; **to slight sb's memory** faire affront à la mémoire de qn

3 *n (snub)* manque *m* d'égards; *(insult)* insulte *f*; *(offence)* affront *m*; **it's a slight on her reputation** c'est un affront à sa réputation

slighting ['slaɪtɪŋ] *adj* offensant, désobligeant

slightingly ['slaɪtɪŋlɪ] *adv (behave)* d'une manière désobligeante; **to speak slightingly of sb** faire des remarques désobligeantes sur qn

slightly ['slaɪtlɪ] *adv* (**a**) *(a little)* un peu, légèrement; **I know him only slightly** je le connais très peu; **slightly better** légèrement mieux, un peu mieux; **a slightly higher number** un chiffre un peu plus élevé; *Br* **I felt ever so slightly ridiculous** je me suis senti légèrement ridicule (**b**) *(slenderly)* **slightly built** menu, mince

slightness ['slaɪtnɪs] *n* (**a**) *(of number, increase)* caractère *m* insignifiant *ou* négligeable; *(of difference)* petitesse *f*; *(of damage)* insignifiance *f* (**b**) *(of build)* minceur *f*; *(frailty)* minceur *f*

Sligo ['slaɪgəʊ] *n* (**a**) *(town)* Sligo (**b**) *(county)* le comté de Sligo, = comté dans le nord-ouest de la république d'Irlande; **in Sligo** dans le comté de Sligo

slily = slyly

slim [slɪm] *(compar* **slimmer**, *superl* **slimmest**, *pt & pp* **slimmed**, *cont* **slimming**) 1 *adj* (**a**) *(person, waist, figure)* mince, svelte; *(wrist)* fin, délicat; **tall and slim** élancé; **a slim-hipped young man** un jeune homme aux hanches étroites; **to keep slim** rester mince

(**b**) *(book, wallet)* mince

(**c**) *(faint, feeble → hope, chance)* faible, minime; *(→ pretext)* mince, piètre, dérisoire; **they have only a slim chance of winning the next election** ils n'ont que de faibles chances de gagner les prochaines élections

2 *vi (get thin)* maigrir, mincir; *(diet)* faire *ou* suivre un régime

3 *vt (of diet, exercise)* faire maigrir

▸**slim down** 1 *vt sep* (**a**) *(of diet)* faire maigrir; *(of clothes)* amincir

(**b**) *Fig (industry)* dégraisser; *(workforce)* réduire; *(ambitions, plans)* limiter, réduire; *(design, car)* épurer, alléger; **the company is slimming down its electronics operation** la société réduit ses activités dans le domaine de l'électronique; **a slimmed-down version of the old model** une version épurée de l'ancien modèle

2 *vi* (**a**) *(person → get thin)* maigrir; *(→ diet)* suivre un régime

(**b**) *(company, army etc)* diminuer de taille

slime [slaɪm] *n* (**a**) *(sticky substance)* substance *f* gluante *ou* poisseuse; *(from snail, slug)* bave *f*; *(mud)* vase *f* (**b**) *Fam (person)* ordure *f*

▸▸ *Biol **slime mould*** myxomycète *m*

slimebag ['slaɪmbæg], **slimeball** ['slaɪmbɔːl] *n Fam (despicable person)* ordure *f*, raclure *f*; *(repulsive man)* gros dégueulasse *m*

sliminess ['slaɪmɪnɪs] *n* (**a**) *(muddiness)* état *m* vaseux (**b**) *Fam (servility)* servilité ◻ *f*, obséquiosité ◻ *f*

slimline ['slɪmlaɪn] *adj* (**a**) *(butter)* allégé; *(milk, cheese)* sans matière grasse, minceur *(inv)*; *(soft drink)* light *(inv)* (**b**) *(slim)* **clothes for the new slimline you** des vêtements pour votre nouvelle silhouette allégée; **the slimline version of the 1998 model** la version épurée du modèle 98

slimly ['slɪmlɪ] *adv* **slimly built** svelte

slimmer ['slɪmə(r)] *n* = personne qui suit un régime (amaigrissant); **good news for slimmers** une bonne nouvelle pour ceux qui veulent maigrir *ou* perdre du poids; **ideal for slimmers** l'idéal pour maigrir

slimming ['slɪmɪŋ] 1 *n* amaigrissement *m*; **slimming can be bad for you** les régimes amaigrissants ne sont pas toujours bons pour la santé

2 *adj* (**a**) *(diet)* amaigrissant; *(cream, product)* amincissant; *(exercises)* pour maigrir; *(meal)* à faible teneur en calories (**b**) *(flattering → dress, suit, colour)* amincissant

▸▸ ***slimming club*** centre *m* d'amaigrissement

slimness ['slɪmnɪs] *n* (**a**) *(of person, waist, figure)* minceur *f*, sveltesse *f*; *(of wrist, ankle)* minceur *f*, finesse *f*, délicatesse *f*; *(of book)* minceur *f* (**b**) *(of chances, hopes)* faiblesse *f*

slimy ['slaɪmɪ] *(compar* **slimier**, *superl* **slimiest**) *adj* (**a**) *(with mud)* vaseux, boueux; *(with oil, secretion)* gluant, visqueux; *(wall)* suintant; **slimy stones** des pierres *fpl* glissantes; **the frog felt all slimy** la grenouille était toute visqueuse; **the slug left a slimy trail** la limace laissa une traînée visqueuse

(**b**) *Br Fam (person)* mielleux ◻; *(manners)* doucereux ◻, obséquieux ◻; **I can't stand him, he's so slimy** je ne le supporte pas, il est tellement mielleux

sling [slɪŋ] *(pt & pp* **slung** [slʌŋ]) 1 *vt* (**a**) *(fling)* jeter, lancer; **the children were slinging stones at the statue** les enfants lançaient des pierres sur la statue; **sling the ball back to me!** relance-moi le ballon!; **she slung the case into the back of the car** elle a jeté la valise à l'arrière de la voiture; *Br Fam* **can you sling me (over) the salt?** tu peux me balancer le sel?; *Br Fam* **if he's not careful, he'll get slung off the course** s'il ne fait pas attention, il se fera virer du cours; *Fig* **to sling mud at sb** couvrir qn de boue; **they were slinging insults at each other** ils se lançaient des insultes; *Fam* **to sling one's hook** mettre les bouts, ficher le camp

(**b**) *(lift, hang → load)* hisser; *Naut* élinguer; **the hammock was slung between two trees** le hamac était suspendu *ou* accroché entre deux arbres; **the soldiers wore rifles slung across** *or* **over their shoulders** les soldats portaient des fusils en bandoulière; **the jacket was slung over the back of the chair** la veste était négligemment jetée sur le dossier de la chaise; **he slung his jacket over his shoulder** il a jeté sa veste par-dessus son épaule; **I slung the towel over the washing line** j'ai jeté la serviette par-dessus la corde à linge

2 *n* (**a**) *Br (for broken arm)* écharpe *f*; **she had her arm in a sling** elle avait le bras en écharpe

(**b**) *(for baby)* porte-bébé *m*

(**c**) *(for loads) & Naut* élingue *f*; *(belt)* courroie *f*; *(rope)* corde *f*, cordage *m*; *(for removal men)* corde *f*, courroie *f*; *(for rifle)* bretelle *f*; *(for mast)* cravate *f*

(**d**) *(weapon)* fronde *f*; *(toy)* lance-pierres *m inv*

(**e**) *(for climber)* baudrier *m*

(**f**) *(cocktail)* sling *m (cocktail à base de spiritueux et de jus de citron, allongé d'eau plate ou gazeuse)*

▸**sling away** *vt sep Br Fam* bazarder, balancer, ficher en l'air

▸**sling out** *vt sep Br Fam (person)* flanquer *ou* ficher à la porte; *(rubbish, magazines etc)* bazarder, balancer; **he was slung out on his ear** il a été fichu à la porte, on l'a fichu dehors

▸**sling over** *vt sep Br Fam* lancer ◻, envoyer ◻; **can you sling the paper over?** tu peux me lancer le journal?

▸**sling up** *vt sep Fam* suspendre ◻, accrocher ◻

slingback ['slɪŋbæk] *n Br* chaussure *f* à talon découvert

slinger ['slɪŋə(r)] *n* (**a**) *Hist & Mil* frondeur *m* (**b**) *Fam (thrower)* lanceur(euse) ◻ *m,f*, jeteur(euse) ◻ *m,f* (**c**) *Naut* élingueur *m* (**d**) *Tech* bague *f* d'étanchéité; **sand slinger** machine *f* à projeter du sable

►► *Aviat* ***slinger ring*** anneau *m* distributeur, bague *f* distributrice

slinging ['slɪŋɪŋ] *n Naut (of load)* élingage *m*

slingshot ['slɪŋʃɒt] *n Am* lance-pierres *m inv*

slink [slɪŋk] *(pt & pp* **slunk** [slʌŋk]) **1** *vi* **to slink in/out** entrer/sortir furtivement; **she slunk into the room** elle s'est glissée discrètement dans la pièce; **to slink off** *or* **away** s'éclipser

2 *vt (animal)* mettre bas avant terme

slinkily ['slɪŋkɪlɪ] *adv Fam (walk)* d'une démarche ondoyante❑; *(dress)* d'une manière sexy; **she sidled slinkily up to him** elle s'est dirigée vers lui en roulant des hanches

slinking ['slɪŋkɪŋ] **1** *adj (look)* furtif

2 *n* (**a**) **slinking off** *or* **away** départ *m* furtif; **slinking in** entrée *f* furtive (**b**) *(of animal)* mise *f* bas avant terme

Slinky® ['slɪŋkɪ] *n (toy)* = long ressort dont on se sert comme jouet

slinky ['slɪŋkɪ] *(compar* **slinkier,** *superl* **slinkiest**) *adj Fam (figure)* svelte❑, mince❑; *(manner)* aguichant❑; *(dress)* moulant❑; *(walk)* ondoyant❑, chaloupé❑; *(voice)* sexy *(inv)*

SLIP [slɪp] *n Comput (abbr* **serial line Internet protocol**) protocole *m* SLIP

SLIP [slɪp]

bout de papier	►**1 (a)**
bon	►**1 (a)**
fiche	►**1 (a)**
glissade	►**1 (b)**
erreur	►**1 (c)**
bévue	►**1 (c)**
étourderie	►**1 (c)**
écart	►**1 (c)**
éboulis	►**1 (d)**
combinaison	►**1 (e)**
glisser	►**2 (a); 3 (a), (b)**
échapper à	►**2 (b); 3 (a)**
s'ébouler	►**3 (a)**
se glisser	►**3 (c)**
baisser	►**3 (d)**

(pt & pp **slipped,** *cont* **slipping**) **1** *n* (**a**) *(piece of paper)* bout *m* de papier; *(coupon)* bon *m*; *(docket)* fiche *f*; **slip of paper** bout *m* de papier; **withdrawal slip** *(in bank)* bordereau *m* de retrait; *Com* **delivery slip** bordereau *m* de livraison

(**b**) *(on ice, banana skin)* glissade *f*

(**c**) *(mistake)* erreur *f*; *(blunder)* bévue *f*; *(careless oversight)* étourderie *f*; *(moral)* écart *m*, faute *f* légère; **slip of the tongue/pen** lapsus *m*; *Br Prov* **there's many a slip 'twixt cup and lip** il y a loin de la coupe aux lèvres

(**d**) *(landslide)* éboulis *m*, éboulement *m*

(**e**) *(petticoat → full length)* combinaison *f*, fond *m* de robe; *(→ skirt)* jupon *m*

(**f**) *Bot* bouture *f*

(**g**) *(usu pl) Naut* cale *f*; **the Queen Helen is still on the slips** le Queen Helen est toujours en cale sèche

(**h**) *(in pottery)* engobe *m*

(**i**) *Aviat* glissade *f* sur l'aile

(**j**) *(idioms) Br* **a (mere) slip of a girl** une petite jeune, une gamine; **to give sb the slip** fausser compagnie à qn

2 *vt* (**a**) *(give or put discreetly)* glisser; **to slip sb a note** glisser un mot à qn; **to slip a letter into sb's hand/pocket** glisser une lettre dans la main/la poche de qn; **I slipped the pen into my pocket** j'ai glissé le stylo dans ma poche; **slip the car into gear** mettez la voiture en prise; **she slipped the jigsaw piece into place** elle a fait glisser le morceau de puzzle à sa place; **I slipped my arm round her waist** j'ai glissé mon bras autour de sa taille; **to slip sth into the conversation** glisser qch dans la conversation; **to slip the bolt (home)** pousser le verrou à fond

(**b**) *(escape)* **it slipped my mind** ça m'est sorti de la tête; **her name has completely slipped my memory** j'ai complètement oublié son nom; **to slip sb's attention** échapper à qn

(**c**) *(release) Br* **he slipped the dog's lead** il a lâché la laisse du chien; *Br* **the dog slipped its lead** le chien s'est dégagé de sa laisse; *Naut* **to slip anchor/a cable** filer l'ancre/un câble

(**d**) *Knitting* **to slip a stitch** glisser une maille

(**e**) *Med* **to have slipped a disc, to have a slipped disc** avoir une hernie discale

(**f**) *Aut (clutch)* faire patiner

3 *vi* (**a**) *(slide → gen)* glisser; *(→ knot)* couler, courir; *(→ earth)* s'ébouler; **I slipped on the ice** j'ai glissé sur une plaque de verglas; **he slipped and fell** il glissa et tomba; **the knife slipped and cut my finger** le couteau a glissé et je me suis coupé le doigt; **my hand slipped** ma main a glissé; **the cup slipped out of my hands** la tasse m'a glissé des mains; **she let the sand slip through her fingers** elle laissa le sable glisser entre ses doigts; *Fig* **the prize slipped from her grasp** *or* **from her fingers** le prix lui a échappé; **somehow, the kidnappers slipped through our fingers** je ne sais comment les ravisseurs nous ont filé entre les doigts; **money just slips through his fingers** l'argent lui file entre les doigts

(**b**) *(go gradually)* glisser; **the patient slipped into a coma** le patient a glissé *ou* s'est enfoncé peu à peu dans le coma; **she slipped into the habit of visiting him every day** petit à petit elle a pris l'habitude d'aller le voir tous les jours; **to slip into bad habits** prendre de mauvaises habitudes

(**c**) *(go quickly, smoothly etc)* se glisser; **to slip into bed** se glisser dans son lit; **she slipped quietly into the room** elle s'est glissée discrètement dans la pièce; **some misprints have slipped into the text** des coquilles se sont glissées dans le texte; **the back should just slip into place** l'arrière devrait glisser à sa place; **the thieves managed to slip through the road blocks** les voleurs ont réussi à passer à travers les barrages routiers; **why don't you slip through the kitchen/round the back?** pourquoi ne passez-vous pas par la cuisine/par derrière?; **we slipped through the rush hour traffic** on s'est faufilés dans les embouteillages des heures de pointe; **he slipped into a dressing gown** il a passé *ou* mis une robe de chambre; **I'll slip into something cooler** je vais enfiler *ou* mettre quelque chose de plus léger

(**d**) *(go down → prices)* baisser; **prices have slipped (by) 10 percent** les prix ont baissé de 10 pour cent

(**e**) *Fam (be less efficient)* **you're slipping!** dis donc, tu baisses!; **I must be slipping!** je crois que je perds mes capacités!

(**f**) *Aut (clutch)* patiner

(**g**) *TV (picture)* descendre

(**h**) *(idiom)* **to let slip** *(opportunity)* laisser passer *ou* échapper; *(word)* lâcher, laisser échapper; **she let (it) slip that she was selling her house** elle a laissé échapper qu'elle vendait sa maison; **he let his guard slip** il a baissé sa garde; **don't let your concentration slip** ne relâche pas ta concentration

4 *npl* **slips** (**a**) *Theat* coulisses *fpl*

(**b**) *Sport (in cricket)* = partie du terrain ou joueurs situés à gauche du guichet, du point de vue du lanceur, si le batteur est droitier (et vice versa)

►► *Br* ***slip road*** bretelle *f* d'accès; *Typ* ***slip sheet*** feuille *f* intercalaire; *Sewing* ***slip stitch*** point *m* perdu; *Rail* ***slip switch*** traversée-jonction *f*; ***single/double slip switch*** traversée-jonction *f* simple/double

►**slip along** *vi (go quickly)* faire un saut; **I'll just slip along to the chemist's** je fais juste un saut à la pharmacie

►**slip away** *vi (person)* s'éclipser, partir discrètement; *(moment)* passer; *(boat)* s'éloigner doucement; **I felt my life slipping away** j'avais l'impression que ma vie me glissait entre les doigts; **control of the party was slipping away from her** elle perdait peu à peu son emprise sur le parti; **the patient was slipping away** le malade s'éteignait doucement; **you're slipping away from me** *(in relationship)* tu t'éloignes de moi

►**slip back** *vi (car)* glisser (en arrière); *(person)* revenir discrètement; **she slipped back for a sweater** elle est retournée chercher un pullover; **he slipped back into a coma** il est retombé dans le coma; **he slipped back into his old habits** il est retombé dans ses vieilles habitudes

►**slip by** *vi (time)* passer; *(person)* se faufiler; **I slipped by without being noticed** je me suis faufilé sans qu'on me remarque; *Fig* **you shouldn't let this chance slip by** tu ne devrais pas laisser passer cette chance

►**slip down** *vi (fall → picture, car, socks, skirt)* glisser; **this whisky slips down very nicely** ce whisky descend tout seul

►**slip in 1** *vt sep (moving part)* faire glisser à sa place; *(quotation, word)* glisser, placer; **she slipped in several references to...** elle a placé plusieurs allusions à...; *Aut* **to slip the clutch in** embrayer

2 *vi (person)* entrer discrètement *ou* sans se faire remarquer; *(boat)* entrer lentement; **I just slipped in for five minutes** je n'ai fait qu'entrer *ou* je suis juste passé cinq minutes; **a blank page has slipped in by mistake** une page blanche s'y est glissée par erreur; **some misprints have slipped in** des fautes de frappe se sont glissées dans le texte

►**slip off 1** *vt sep (remove → coat, hat)* enlever, ôter; *(→ shoe, ring, sock)* enlever; *(→ top, lid)* faire glisser pour ouvrir

2 *vi* (**a**) *(go away)* s'éclipser

(**b**) *(fall → bottle, hat, book)* glisser (et tomber)

►**slip on** *vt sep (dress, ring, coat)* mettre, enfiler; *(lid)* mettre *ou* remettre (en faisant glisser)

►**slip out** *vi* (**a**) *(leave unseen → person)* sortir discrètement, s'esquiver

(**b**) *(escape → animal, child)* s'échapper; **the soap slipped out of my hands** le savon m'a glissé des mains; **the word slipped out before he could stop himself** le mot lui a échappé; **it just slipped out!** ça m'a échappé!; **the story slipped out** l'affaire s'est ébruitée

(**c**) *(go out)* sortir (un instant); **I'm just slipping out for a few minutes** je m'éclipse quelques minutes, je reviens dans une minute; **I'll slip out and buy some milk** je sors juste acheter du lait

►**slip over 1** *vi* aller; **we slipped over to Blackpool to see them** nous avons fait un saut à Blackpool pour les voir

2 *vt sep Fam* **to slip one over on sb** rouler qn

►**slip past** *vi (time)* passer; *(person)* se faufiler; **I managed to slip past unseen** j'ai réussi à passer discrètement

►**slip round** *vi* (**a**) *Br (go)* passer; **can you slip round after supper?** peux-tu passer (chez moi) après souper?

(**b**) *(saddle)* se retourner; *(skirt)* tourner

►**slip through** *vi (person)* passer sans se faire remarquer; *(mistake)* passer inaperçu

►**slip up** *vi Fam* faire une gaffe; **you've slipped up badly here** tu as fait une sacrée gaffe, tu t'es bien planté

Do you mind if I slip into something more comfortable?

Cette formule ("Est-ce que ça vous dérange si j'enfile quelque chose de plus confortable?") a pour origine *Hell's Angels* ("Les Anges de l'Enfer"), un film américain de 1930 avec Jean Harlow. La phrase exacte que prononce l'actrice est **would you be shocked if I changed into something more comfortable?** ("est-ce que ça vous choquerait si j'enfilais quelque chose de plus confortable?") Cette formule évoque les vedettes féminines du cinéma américain des années 30 et 40 et notamment les scènes dans lesquelles celles-ci font des numéros de charme en revêtant des tenues sexy.

Aujourd'hui on utilise cette phrase en allusion à l'air séducteur de Jean Harlow, le plus souvent sur le mode humoristique.

slipcase ['slɪpkeɪs] *n (for single volume)* étui *m*; *(for several volumes, for records)* coffret *m*

slipcover ['slɪpkʌvə(r)] *n Am* (**a**) *(for furniture)* housse *f* (**b**) = **slipcase**

slipknot ['slɪpnɒt] *n* nœud *m* coulant

slip-on 1 *adj (shoe)* sans lacets

2 *n* (**a**) *(shoe)* chaussure *f* sans lacets (**b**) *Am (sweater)* pull-over *m*

slipover ['slɪp,əʊvə(r)] **1** *adj (garment)* qui s'enfile par la tête

2 *n* débardeur *m (vêtement)*

slippage ['slɪpɪdʒ] *n* (**a**) *Tech* patinage *m* (**b**) *(in targeting)* retard *m (par rapport aux prévisions)*;

(in standards) baisse *f*; **there's too much slippage** *(loss of time)* on perd de plus en plus de temps

slipped disc [ˌslɪpt-] *n Med* hernie *f* discale

slipper [ˈslɪpə(r)] **1** *n* chausson *m*, pantoufle *f*; *(with no back)* mule *f*; *(for dancing)* escarpin *m*

2 *vt Br (hit)* **to slipper sb** donner une fessée à qn *(avec une pantoufle)*

▸▸ ***slipper bath*** **1** *n (in bathroom)* (baignoire *f*) sabot *m* **2 slipper baths** *npl Old-fashioned (public)* bains *mpl* publics

slipperiness [ˈslɪpərɪnɪs] *n* (**a**) *(of surface, soap)* caractère *m* glissant; **the slipperiness of the road/floor** l'état *m* glissant de la route/du sol (**b**) *(of person → evasiveness)* caractère *m* insaisissable *ou* fuyant; *(→ unreliability)* nature *f* peu fiable

slipperwort [ˈslɪpəwɜːt] *n Bot* calcéolaire *f*

slippery [ˈslɪpərɪ] *adj* (**a**) *(surface, soap)* glissant; **the path is slippery** le chemin est glissant; **it's slippery (underfoot)** ça glisse; *Fig* **to be on slippery ground** être sur un terrain glissant; *Fig* **we're on the slippery slope to bankruptcy** nous allons droit à la faillite

(**b**) *Fam (person → evasive)* fuyant ❑; *(→ unreliable)* sur qui on ne peut pas compter ❑; **he's a slippery customer** c'est le genre de type à qui on ne peut pas se fier; **he's as slippery as an eel** il glisse comme une *ou* est aussi insaisissable qu'une anguille

slippy [ˈslɪpɪ] *(compar* **slippier,** *superl* **slippiest)** *adj Fam* (**a**) *(slippery)* glissant ❑ (**b**) *Br (fast)* **you'll have to be pretty slippy about it** il va falloir que tu fasses ficelle; **look slippy!** grouille-toi!

slipshod [ˈslɪpʃɒd] *adj (appearance)* négligé, débraillé; *(habits, behaviour)* négligent; *(style)* peu soigné, négligé; *(work)* négligé, mal fait

slipshodness [ˈslɪpʃɒdnɪs] *n* négligence *f*

slipstream [ˈslɪpstriːm] **1** *n (of car, boat)* sillage *m*; *(of plane)* souffle *m ou* vent *m* de l'hélice; *Fig* **to be dragged along in sb's slipstream** se laisser entraîner par qn

2 *vt (driver, cyclist)* rester dans le sillage de

3 *vi (in cycling, motor racing)* = courir dans le sillage d'autres concurrents pour diminuer la résistance à l'air

slip-up *n Fam* bévue ❑ *f*, gaffe *f*; **there's been a slip-up** quelqu'un a fait une gaffe; **to make a slip-up** faire une gaffe; **there mustn't be any slip-ups** pas de gaffe

slipware [ˈslɪpweə(r)] *n Cer* faïence *f* engobée

slipway [ˈslɪpweɪ] *n Naut (for repairs)* cale *f* de construction; *(for launching)* cale *f* de lancement

slit [slɪt] *(pt & pp* **slit,** *cont* **slitting)** **1** *n (narrow opening)* fente *f*; *(cut)* incision *f*; *(for shooting through)* meurtrière *f*; **the skirt has a slit at the back** la jupe a une fente *ou* est fendue dans le dos; **make a slit in the surface** faire une incision superficielle

2 *vt (split)* fendre; *(cut)* inciser, couper; **the skirt was slit up the side** la jupe était fendue sur le côté; **the mattress had been slit open** le matelas avait été éventré; **she slit the packet open with a knife** elle a ouvert le paquet avec un couteau; **to slit sb's throat** égorger qn; **she slit her wrists** elle s'est ouvert les veines

3 *adj (skirt)* fendu; *(eyes)* bridé

▸▸ ***slit pocket*** poche *f* fendue; *Mil* ***slit trench*** tranchée *f* étroite

slit-eyed *adj* aux yeux bridés; **to be slit-eyed** avoir les yeux bridés

slither [ˈslɪðə(r)] *vi* (**a**) *(snake, worm)* ramper, onduler (**b**) *(car, person → slide)* glisser, patiner; *(→ skid)* déraper; **the car slithered on a patch of oil** la voiture a dérapé sur une flaque d'huile; **I slithered down the tree/drainpipe** je me suis laissé glisser le long de l'arbre/de la gouttière; **the dog was slithering about on the ice** le chien dérapait sur la glace

slithering [ˈslɪðərɪŋ] *n (of snake, worm)* reptation *f*; *(of person)* glissade *f*; *(of car)* dérapage *m*

slithery [ˈslɪðərɪ] *adj (surface)* glissant; *(snake)* ondulant

sliver [ˈslɪvə(r)] *n* (**a**) *(of glass, wood)* éclat *m* (**b**) *(small slice)* tranche *f* fine

slivovitz [ˈslɪvəvɪts] *n* slivovitz *m*

Sloane [sləʊn] *n Br Fam* jeune femme *f* BCBG

▸▸ ***Sloane Ranger*** jeune femme *f* BCBG

Sloaney [ˈsləʊnɪ] *adj Br Fam* ≃ BCBG *(inv)*

slob [slɒb] *n Fam (dirty)* souillon *mf*; *(uncouth)* plouc *m*; *(lazy)* flemmard(e) *m,f*; **big fat slob** gros lard *m*

▸**slob about, slob around** *Fam* **1** *vi* traînasser

2 *vt insep* traînasser dans; **he just slobs about the house all day** il passe ses journées à traînasser dans la maison

slobber [ˈslɒbə(r)] **1** *vi* (**a**) *(dribble)* baver; **to slobber over** baver sur; **the baby has slobbered all over the book** le bébé a bavé partout sur le livre; **the dog came and slobbered all over me** le chien est venu baver sur moi (**b**) *Fam Fig* **to slobber over** *(person, possession, pet)* baver d'admiration devant

2 *n* (**a**) *(dribble)* bave *f* (**b**) *Pej (behaviour)* sensiblerie *f*

slobberer [ˈslɒbərə(r)] *n* baveur(euse) *m,f*

slobbering [ˈslɒbərɪŋ] *adj* baveux

slobbery [ˈslɒbərɪ] *adj* baveux

sloe [sləʊ] *n (berry)* prunelle *f*; *(tree)* prunellier *m*

▸▸ ***sloe gin*** gin *m* à la prunelle

sloe-eyed *adj* aux yeux de biche

slog [slɒg] *(pt & pp* **slogged,** *cont* **slogging)** *Fam* **1** *n* (**a**) *(hard task)* boulot *m* pénible; *(effort)* (gros) effort ❑ *m*; **it was a real slog to finish in time** on a dû bosser comme des malades pour finir à temps; **what a slog!** quelle corvée! ❑; **it was a slog teaching them history** leur enseigner l'histoire n'était pas une mince affaire ❑; **this book is a hard slog** ce livre est vraiment dur à lire ❑; **it's been a long hard slog for her to get where she is** elle en a bavé pour arriver là où elle est; **it was quite a slog getting up that hill** on en a bavé pour monter cette côte

(**b**) *Br (hit)* grand coup ❑ *m*; **he gave the ball an almighty slog** il a frappé la balle de toutes ses forces ❑

2 *vi* (**a**) *(work hard)* trimer, bosser; **she slogged on until ten o'clock** elle est restée bosser jusqu'à dix heures; **do we really have to slog through all this paperwork?** est-ce qu'il est indispensable de se farcir toute cette paperasse?

(**b**) *(walk, go)* avancer péniblement ❑; **he slogged (along) through the snow** il avançait péniblement dans la neige; **we slogged slowly up the hill** nous avons gravi la côte à pas lents ❑

3 *vt* (**a**) *(move)* **we slogged our way through the snow** nous nous sommes péniblement frayé un chemin dans la neige ❑; **he slogged his way through the text** il a déchiffré le texte avec grande difficulté ❑

(**b**) *Br (hit → ball)* donner un grand coup dans ❑; *(→ person)* cogner sur ❑; **to slog it out** *(fight)* se tabasser; *(argue)* s'engueuler

▸**slog along** *vi Fam (keep walking)* marcher d'un pas lourd *ou* péniblement ❑

▸**slog away** *vi Fam (keep working, trying)* trimer

▸**slog away at** *vt insep Fam* (**a**) *(work hard at)* **to slog away (at sth)** travailler comme un dingue (à qch); **she spent all weekend slogging away at that report** elle a passé tout le week-end à trimer sur ce rapport

(**b**) *(keep hitting)* continuer à frapper ❑

▸**slog on** *vi Fam* (**a**) = **slog along**

(**b**) *(keep working)* continuer à trimer; **I think I'll slog on a little longer** je pense que je vais continuer à bosser encore un peu

slogan [ˈsləʊgən] *n* slogan *m*

slogger [ˈslɒgə(r)] *n Br Fam* (**a**) *(in boxing, cricket)* cogneur ❑ *m* (**b**) *(hard worker)* bûcheur(euse) *m,f*

slo-mo [ˈsləʊməʊ] *adj Fam (abbr* **slow-motion)** au ralenti ❑

sloop [sluːp] *n Naut* sloop *m*

slop [slɒp] *(pt & pp* **slopped,** *cont* **slopping)** **1** *vi (spill)* renverser; *(overflow)* déborder; **the tea slopped into the saucer/onto the tablecloth** le thé s'est renversé dans la soucoupe/sur la nappe; **the soup slopped onto the cooker** la soupe a débordé sur la cuisinière

2 *vt* renverser; **he slopped soup onto the tablecloth** il a renversé *ou* répandu de la soupe sur la nappe; **don't slop water all over the floor** ne renverse pas d'eau par terre

3 *n* (**a**) **slop(s)** *(liquid waste → for pigs)* pâtée *f*; *(→ from tea, coffee)* fond *m* de tasse; *Pej (tasteless food)* mixture *f*

(**b**) *(UNCOUNT) Fam (sentimentality)* bêtises *fpl* à l'eau de rose

▸▸ *Br* ***slop basin*** vide-tasses *m inv*; ***slop bucket, slop pail*** *(gen)* seau *m* (à ordures); *(in prison)* seau *m* hygiénique; *(for pigs)* seau *m* à pâtée

▸**slop about, slop around** **1** *vi* (**a**) *(liquid)* clapoter

(**b**) *(paddle)* patauger; **the children were slopping about in the puddles** les enfants pataugeaient dans les flaques d'eau

(**c**) *Fam (be lazy)* traînasser; **I just slopped around all morning** j'ai traînassé *ou* flemmardé toute la matinée

2 *vt sep (paint)* éclabousser; *(tea)* renverser

3 *vt insep Fam* **he slops about the house doing nothing** il traîne à la maison à ne rien faire ❑

▸**slop out** *vi (prisoner)* vider les seaux hygiéniques

▸**slop over** **1** *vi (spill)* se renverser; *(overflow)* déborder; **the water slopped over onto the floor** l'eau s'est renversée *ou* a débordé sur le sol

2 *vt sep* renverser, répandre

slope [sləʊp] **1** *n (incline → of roof)* inclinaison *f*, pente *f*; *(→ of ground)* pente *f*; **a steep/gentle slope** une pente raide/douce; **the house is built on a slope** la maison a été construite sur une pente; *Mil* **rifle at the slope** fusil sur l'épaule

(**b**) *(hill → up)* côte *f*, montée *f*; *(→ down)* pente *f*, descente *f*; *(mountainside)* versant *m*, flanc *m*; **tea is grown on the higher slopes** on cultive le thé plus haut sur les versants de la montagne; **on the slopes of Mount Fuji** sur les versants du mont Fuji; **halfway down/up the slope** à mi-pente

(**c**) *(for skiing)* piste *f*

(**d**) *Am very Fam (Oriental)* Jaune *mf*, = terme injurieux désignant un Asiatique

2 *vi (roof)* être en pente *ou* incliné; *(writing, picture)* pencher; **to slope forward/backward** *(writing)* pencher à droite/à gauche; **the beach sloped gently to the sea** la plage descendait en pente douce vers la mer; **the football pitch slopes from left to right** le terrain de foot descend vers la droite; **the ground slopes up to the house** le terrain monte en pente vers la maison; **the table slopes** la table penche *ou* n'est pas droite

3 *vt* incliner; *Mil* **to slope arms** mettre l'arme sur l'épaule; **slope arms!** arme sur l'épaule!

▸**slope off** *vi Fam* filer

sloping [ˈsləʊpɪŋ] *adj (table, roof)* en pente, incliné; *(writing)* penché; *(shoulders)* tombant

sloppily [ˈslɒpɪlɪ] *adv* (**a**) *(work)* sans soin; *(dress)* de façon négligée (**b**) *Br Fam (sentimentally)* avec sensiblerie ❑

sloppiness [ˈslɒpɪnɪs] *n* (**a**) *(of work)* manque *m* de soin *ou* de sérieux; *(in dress)* négligence *f*, manque *m* de soin; *(of thought)* flou *m*, manque *m* de précision (**b**) *Fam (sentimentality)* sensiblerie ❑ *f*, mièvrerie ❑ *f*

slopping out [ˈslɒpɪŋ-] *n (in prison)* vidange *f* des seaux hygiéniques

sloppy [ˈslɒpɪ] *(compar* **sloppier,** *superl* **sloppiest)** *adj* (**a**) *(untidy → appearance)* négligé, débraillé; *(careless → work)* bâclé, négligé; *(→ worker)* négligent; *(→ writing)* peu soigné; *(→ thinking)* flou, vague, imprécis; **he has a very sloppy way of speaking** il s'exprime d'une manière peu élégante

(**b**) *Fam (loose → garment)* large ❑, lâche ❑

(**c**) *Fam (sentimental → person, letter)* sentimental ❑; *(→ book, film)* à l'eau de rose ❑; **stop all that sloppy talk!** arrête de faire du sentiment! ❑

▸▸ *Fam* ***sloppy joe*** (**a**) *Br (sweater)* gros pull *m* (**b**) *Am (hamburger)* hamburger ❑ *m*

slosh [slɒʃ] **1** *vt* (**a**) *(spill)* renverser, répandre

(**b**) *Fam (pour → onto floor)* répandre ❑; *(→ into glass, bucket)* verser ❑; *(apply → paint, glue)* flanquer; **she sloshed some bleach into the bucket** elle a versé de l'eau de Javel dans le seau; **she sloshed whitewash on** *or* **over the wall** elle a barbouillé le mur de blanc de chaux ❑

(**c**) *Br Fam (hit)* flanquer un coup de poing à

2 *vi* (**a**) *(liquid → spill)* se répandre; *(→ move*

sli–slo

around) clapoter; **the juice sloshed all over the tablecloth** le jus s'est renversé partout sur la nappe; **water sloshed over the edge** l'eau a débordé

(**b**) *(move → in liquid, mud)* patauger; **we sloshed through the mud** on a pataugé dans la boue

3 *onomat* plouf

►**slosh about, slosh around** *vi (liquid)* clapoter; *(person)* patauger; **the water sloshed about in the bucket** l'eau clapotait dans le seau; **the children were sloshing about in puddles** les enfants pataugeaient dans des flaques d'eau

sloshed [slɒʃt] *adj Fam* bourré, pété, beurré; **to get sloshed** prendre une cuite

sloshing ['slɒʃɪŋ] *n* (**a**) *(spilling)* éclaboussement *m*; *(moving around)* clapotement *m* (**b**) *Br Fam (beating)* rossée *f*, pile *f*

sloshy ['slɒʃɪ] *adj* (**a**) *(muddy)* boueux, bourbeux; *(snow)* fondu; *(ground)* détrempé (**b**) *Fam (sentimental)* excessivement sentimental ❑

slot [slɒt] (*pt & pp* **slotted**, *cont* **slotting**) **1** *n* (**a**) *(opening → for coins, papers)* fente *f*; *(groove, in screw head)* rainure *f*; **put the coin in the slot** mettez la pièce dans la fente; **there's a slot in the door for letters** il y a une fente dans la porte pour le courrier

(**b**) *(in schedule, timetable)* créneau *m*; *Rad & TV* créneau *m*, tranche *f ou* plage *f* horaire; **we could put the new series in the 7:30 slot** on pourrait caser *ou* placer le nouveau feuilleton dans le créneau de 19h30; **what shall we put in the slot before the news?** qu'est-ce qu'on va mettre dans la tranche *ou* le créneau qui précède les informations?; **we've missed our slot for take-off** nous avons raté notre créneau de décollage

(**c**) *(job opening)* créneau *m*; **there's a slot for someone with marketing skills** il y a un créneau pour quelqu'un qui s'y connaît en marketing

(**d**) *Aviat (in aerofoil)* fente *f*

(**e**) *Comput* emplacement *m*

2 *vt* (**a**) *(insert)* emboîter; **slot this bit in here** *(in machine, model)* introduisez cette pièce ici; *(in jigsaw)* posez *ou* mettez cette pièce ici

(**b**) *(find time for, fit)* insérer, faire rentrer; **she managed to slot me into her timetable** elle a réussi à me réserver un moment *ou* à me caser dans son emploi du temps

3 *vi* (**a**) *(fit → part)* rentrer, s'encastrer, s'emboîter; **the tape slots into the recorder here** c'est ici qu'on introduit la cassette dans le magnétophone; **the blade slots into the handle** la lame rentre dans le manche

(**b**) *(in timetable, schedule)* rentrer, s'insérer; **our programme slots into the space after the news** notre émission s'insère dans le créneau qui suit les informations; **where do we slot into the scheme?** où intervenons-nous dans le projet?

►► ***slot machine*** *(for vending)* distributeur *m* (automatique); *(for gambling)* machine *f* à sous; *Br* ***slot meter*** compteur *m* à pièces

►**slot in 1** *vt sep (into schedule)* faire rentrer; *(patient, customer etc)* caser; **she just slots me in when it suits her** elle n'est disponible pour moi que quand ça l'arrange; **when can you slot me in?** quand pouvez-vous me caser *ou* trouver un moment pour moi?

2 *vi (part)* s'emboîter, s'encastrer; *(programme)* s'insérer; **she slotted into the department well** elle s'est bien intégrée au service

►**slot together 1** *vt sep* emboîter, encastrer; **slot these two parts together** emboîtez ces deux pièces l'une dans l'autre

2 *vi* s'emboîter, s'encastrer; **the two parts slot together** les deux pièces s'emboîtent l'une dans l'autre

sloth [sləʊθ] *n* (**a**) *(laziness)* paresse *f* (**b**) *Zool* paresseux *m*

►► ***sloth bear*** ours *m* lippu

slothful ['sləʊθfʊl] *adj* paresseux

slothfully ['sləʊθfʊlɪ] *adv* paresseusement, avec indolence

slothfulness ['sləʊθfʊlnɪs] *n* paresse *f*

slot-in card *n Comput* carte *f* enfichable

slotted ['slɒtɪd-] *adj*

►► *Am* ***slotted spatula*** pelle *f* à poisson; ***slotted spoon*** écumoire *f*

slouch [slaʊtʃ] **1** *vi (hold oneself badly)* être avachi; *(walk badly)* avoir une démarche mollasse; **she was slouching against the wall** elle était nonchalamment adossée au mur; **stop slouching!** redresse-toi!; **to slouch in/out** entrer/sortir en traînant les pieds

2 *vt* **to slouch one's shoulders** rentrer les épaules

3 *n* (**a**) *(way of walking)* démarche *f* mollasse; *(deportment)* allure *f* avachie *ou* molle; **slouch of the shoulders** épaules *fpl* tombantes; **to have a slouch** avoir le dos voûté

(**b**) *Fam (person)* **he's no slouch** ce n'est pas un empoté

►► ***slouch hat*** chapeau *m* à larges bords

►**slouch about, slouch around** *vi* se traîner; *(at home, in front of television)* traînasser

sloucher ['slaʊtʃə(r)] *n* (**a**) *(person who walks with a slouch)* lourdaud(e) *m,f* (**b**) *(lazy person)* fainéant(e) *m,f*

slouching ['slaʊtʃɪŋ] *adj* (**a**) *(person → gen)* qui a une allure molle, qui traîne le pas; *(→ with stooped shoulders)* aux épaules arrondies (**b**) *(walk, gait)* mollasse

slough[1] [slaʊ] *n (mud pool)* bourbier *m*; *(swamp)* marécage *m*; *Literary* **to sink into a slough of gloom/despair** sombrer dans la mélancolie/le désespoir; *Literary* **the Slough of Despond** le plus profond désespoir

> **Slough of Despond**
>
> Il s'agit d'une allusion à l'œuvre allégorique de l'écrivain puritain anglais John Bunyan, *The Pilgrim's Progress* ("Le Voyage du pèlerin"). L'histoire raconte les tribulations du héros, qui entreprend un pèlerinage en quête du paradis céleste. En chemin, il rencontre toutes sortes d'obstacles, parmi lesquels figure un marécage profond et redoutable, le **Slough of Despond**, symbolisant l'abîme du désespoir mais que le héros arrive néanmoins à traverser.
>
> L'expression est couramment utilisée pour évoquer de façon facétieuse un état d'abattement et de découragement, généralement passager. Par exemple, **it took him several weeks to emerge from this slough of despond** ("il lui a fallu plusieurs semaines pour sortir de son abattement").

slough[2] [slʌf] **1** *n* (**a**) *(skin → of snake)* dépouille *f*, mue *f*; *Med* escarre *f*

(**b**) *Cards* carte *f* défaussée

2 *vt* **to slough its skin** *(reptile, insect)* muer; *Literary* **to slough a bad habit** se débarrasser d'une mauvaise habitude

►**slough off 1** *vt sep* **to slough off its skin** *(reptile, insect)* muer; *Fig* **to slough off one's worries** chasser ses idées noires; *Literary* **to slough off a bad habit** se débarrasser d'une mauvaise habitude

2 *vi (scab)* se détacher, tomber

sloughing ['slʌfɪŋ] *n* (**a**) *(of snake)* mue *f*; *Vet* **sloughing of the hoof** avalure *f* du sabot (**b**) *Med* formation *f* d'une escarre, escarrification *f*

Slovak ['sləʊvæk] **1** *n* (**a**) *(person)* Slovaque *mf* (**b**) *Ling* slovaque *m*

2 *adj* slovaque

Slovakia [slə'vækɪə] *n* Slovaquie *f*; **in Slovakia** en Slovaquie

Slovakian [slə'vækɪən] **1** *n* Slovaque *mf*

2 *adj* slovaque

sloven ['slʌvən] *n* (**a**) *(untidy person)* mal soigné(e) *m,f*; *(woman)* souillon *f* (**b**) *Old-fashioned (careless worker)* saboteur(euse) *m,f*

Slovene ['sləʊviːn] **1** *n* (**a**) *(person)* Slovène *mf* (**b**) *Ling* slovène *m*

2 *adj* slovène

Slovenia [slə'viːnɪə] *n* Slovénie *f*; **in Slovenia** en Slovénie

Slovenian [slə'viːnɪən] **1** *n* Slovène *mf*

2 *adj* slovène

slovenliness ['slʌvənlɪnɪs] *n (of dress)* négligé *m*, débraillé *m*; *(of habits)* laisser-aller *m inv*; *(of work)* manque *m* de soin

slovenly ['slʌvənlɪ] *adj (appearance)* négligé, débraillé; *(habits)* relâché; *(work)* peu soigné; *(style, expression)* relâché, négligé; **he's often slovenly in appearance** il fait souvent négligé; **done in a slovenly way** fait sans soin

SLOW [sləʊ]

lent	► **1 (a), (c)**
calme	► **1 (b)**
ennuyeux	► **1 (d)**
qui retarde	► **1 (e)**
lentement	► **2**
ralentir	► **3**

1 *adj* (**a**) *(not fast → movements, runner, speed, service, traffic)* lent; **he's a slow worker** il travaille lentement; **it's slow work** c'est un travail qui n'avance pas vite *ou* de longue haleine; **to make slow progress** *(in work, on foot)* avancer lentement; **it was slow going, the going was slow** ça n'avançait pas; **a slow dance** un slow; **with slow steps** d'un pas lent; **we had a painfully slow journey** le voyage a duré un temps fou; **the pace of life is slow** on vit au ralenti; **you're very slow today** tu es très lent aujourd'hui; **you were a bit slow there** là, tu t'es laissé prendre de vitesse; **the fog was slow to clear** le brouillard a mis longtemps à se dissiper; **he was rather slow to make up** *or* **in making up his mind** il a mis assez longtemps à se décider; **she wasn't slow to offer her help/in accepting the cheque** elle ne se fit pas prier pour proposer son aide/pour accepter le chèque; **I was rather slow to understand** *or* **in understanding** il m'a fallu assez longtemps pour comprendre; **she's very slow to anger** il lui en faut beaucoup pour se mettre en colère; **the company was slow to get off the ground** la société a été lente à démarrer; *Br* **to be slow off the mark** *(to start)* être lent à démarrer; *(to understand)* être dur à la détente; *Fam* **to be as slow as** *Br* **treacle** *or Am* **molasses (in winter)** être lent comme un escargot *ou* une tortue ❑; *Prov* **slow and steady wins the race** rien ne sert de courir, il faut partir à point

(**b**) *(slack → business, market)* calme; **business is slow** les affaires ne marchent pas fort; **slow economic growth** une faible croissance économique

(**c**) *(intellectually)* lent; **he's a slow learner/reader** il apprend/lit lentement; **they're rather slow in that class** les élèves de cette classe sont assez lents

(**d**) *(dull → evening, film, party)* ennuyeux

(**e**) *(clock)* qui retarde; **your watch is (half an hour) slow** ta montre retarde (d'une demi-heure)

(**f**) *Culin* **bake in a slow oven** faire cuire à four doux

(**g**) *Sport (green, court, surface)* lourd

(**h**) *Am Fam* **to do a slow burn** sentir la colère monter ❑

2 *adv* lentement; **go a bit slower** ralentissez un peu; **the clock is going** *or* **running slow** l'horloge prend du retard; *Ind* **to go slow** faire une grève perlée; **slow** *(road marking)* ralentir; *Naut* **slow ahead/astern!** en avant/arrière doucement!

3 *vt* ralentir; **these drugs slow the heart rate** ces médicaments ralentissent le rythme cardiaque; **the mud slowed our progress** la boue nous a ralentis; **I slowed the horse to a trot** j'ai mis le cheval au trot

►► *Culin* ***slow burner*** feu *m* doux; ***slow cooker*** mijoteuse *f*; *Anat & Bot* ***slow growth*** croissance *f* lente; *Br* ***slow handclap*** applaudissements *mpl* rythmés *(pour montrer sa désapprobation)*; **they gave him the slow handclap** ≃ ils l'ont sifflé; ***the slow lane*** *(when driving on left)* la file de gauche; *(when driving on right)* la file de droite; ***slow match*** mèche *f* à combustion lente; *Cin & TV* ***slow motion*** ralenti *m*; **in slow motion** au ralenti; *Mus* ***slow movement*** mouvement *m* lent; *Phys* ***slow neutron*** neutron *m* lent; *Sport* ***slow pitch*** slow pitch *m (sport proche du softball)*; *Tech* ***slow running*** ralenti *m*; ***slow train*** omnibus *m*; *Med* ***slow virus*** virus *m* lent

►**slow down, slow up 1** *vt sep* ralentir; **the roadworks slowed us down considerably** les travaux nous ont considérablement ralentis; **having to write the addresses by hand slowed the work down** le fait de devoir écrire les adresses à la main a ralenti le travail; **production is slowed down during the winter** pendant l'hiver, la production tourne au ralenti; **I'll only slow you down** je vais vous retarder

2 *vi (driver, train, speed)* ralentir; *Fig (person)* ralentir (le rythme); **if he doesn't slow down he'll have a heart attack** s'il ne ralentit pas le rythme il va faire une crise cardiaque; **slow down!** moins vite!; **growth slowed down in the second quarter** il y a eu une diminution *ou* un ralentissement de la croissance au cours du deuxième trimestre

---

slow-acting *adj* à action lente

slow-burning *adj (fuse, fuel)* à combustion lente; *Fig* **slow-burning anger** colère *f* froide; **he's got a slow-burning temper** il refoule sa colère jusqu'au moment où il explose

slowcoach ['sləʊkəʊtʃ] *n Br Fam (in moving)* lambin(e) *m,f*, traînard(e) *m,f*; *(in thought)* balourd(e) *m,f*, lourdaud(e) *m,f*; **come on, slowcoach!** allez, du nerf!

slow-cook *vt* mitonner, mijoter

slowdown ['sləʊdaʊn] *n* (**a**) *Am (go-slow)* grève *f* perlée (**b**) *(slackening)* ralentissement *m*

slowing ['sləʊɪŋ] *n* **slowing (down** *or* **up)** ralentissement *m*

slowly ['sləʊlɪ] *adv* (**a**) *(not fast)* lentement; **the bus came slowly down the hill** le bus a descendu la côte lentement; **could you walk/speak more slowly?** pouvez-vous marcher/parler moins vite?; **the time/morning has gone very slowly** le temps/la matinée a passé très lentement; **to cook sth slowly** faire cuire qch à feu doux; **slowly but surely** lentement mais sûrement

(**b**) *(gradually)* peu à peu; **he's slowly realizing that...** il se rend compte peu à peu que... *+ indicative*

slow-motion *adj* (tourné) au ralenti

▸▸ *TV* ***slow-motion replay*** ralenti *m*

slow-moving *adj (person, car, queue, river)* lent; *(film, play, plot)* dont l'action est lente; *(market)* stagnant

▸▸ ***slow-moving target*** cible *f* qui bouge lentement

slowness ['sləʊnɪs] *n* (**a**) *(of progress, reaction, service, traffic)* lenteur *f*; *(of plot, play, film)* lenteur *f*, manque *m* d'action (**b**) *(of intellect)* lenteur *f* (d'esprit) (**c**) *(of trading, market)* stagnation *f* (**d**) *(of watch, clock)* retard *m*

slowpoke ['sləʊpəʊk] *Am Fam* = **slowcoach**

slow-release *adj Med (medicine)* à libération prolongée; *Agr (fertilizer)* à action lente

slow-running jet *n Aut* gicleur *m* de ralenti

slow-witted [-'wɪtɪd] *adj* lent

slowworm ['sləʊwɜ:m] *n* orvet *m*

SLR [,esel'ɑ:(r)] *n Phot (abbr* **single-lens reflex**) reflex *m* à un objectif

slub [slʌb] *(pt & pp* **slubbed,** *cont* **slubbing**) *Tex* **1** *n* (**a**) *(lump)* bouton *m* floche (**b**) *(roll of yarn)* mèche *f* (de laine cardée)

2 *vt (yarn)* boudiner

▸▸ ***slub yarn*** fil *m* flammé

sludge [slʌdʒ] *n (UNCOUNT)* (**a**) *(mud)* boue *f*, vase *f*; *(snow)* neige *f* fondue (**b**) *(sediment)* dépôt *m*, boue *f*; *(in engine)* cambouis *m* (**c**) *(sewage)* **(sewage) sludge** vidanges *fpl*

sludgy ['slʌdʒɪ] *adj* (**a**) *(muddy)* vaseux (**b**) *(sediment)* boueux (**c**) *(sea)* plein de glaçons

slue *Am* = **slew** *vi & vt*

sluff = **slough**[2] *n* (**b**)

slug [slʌg] *(pt & pp* **slugged,** *cont* **slugging**) **1** *n* (**a**) *Zool* limace *f*

(**b**) *Fam Fig (lazy person)* mollusque *m*

(**c**) *Typ (of metal)* lingot *m*

(**d**) *Am (token)* jeton *m*

(**e**) *Fam (blow)* beigne *f*

(**f**) *Fam (of drink)* coup *m*; *(mouthful)* goulée *f*, lampée *f*; **to take a slug of whisky** boire une lampée de whisky

(**g**) *Fam (bullet)* pruneau *m*, bastos *f*

2 *vt Fam* (**a**) *(hit)* frapper (fort) ❑, cogner ❑; **he was slugged over the head with a rubber cosh** il a reçu un coup de matraque en caoutchouc sur la tête ❑

(**b**) *(idiom)* **to slug it out** *(fight)* se bastonner, se castagner; *(argue)* s'enguirlander; **I left them to slug it out** *(fight)* je les ai laissés régler leurs comptes à coups de poing ❑

▸▸ ***slug pellet*** pastille *f* anti-limace

slugabed ['slʌgəbed] *n Fam Arch* paresseux(euse) ❑ *m,f (qui fait la grasse matinée)*

slugfest ['slʌgfest] *n Am Fam* (**a**) *Boxing* combat ❑ *m* (**b**) *(fight)* baston *m ou f*, castagne *f*

sluggard ['slʌgəd] *n Literary* paresseux(euse) *m,f*, fainéant(e) *m,f*

slugger ['slʌgə(r)] *n Fam (boxer)* cogneur ❑ *m*, puncheur ❑ *m*; *(in ball games)* joueur(euse) *m,f* qui frappe très fort ❑

sluggish ['slʌgɪʃ] *adj* (**a**) *(person, day → lazy)* paresseux, *Fam* flemmard; *(→ not energetic)* léthargique

(**b**) *(mind)* lent, engourdi; *(response, attempt, engine)* mou (molle); *(river, pulse)* lent, paresseux; *(market)* stagnant; *(sales)* médiocre; *(organization, bureaucracy)* lourd; **at a sluggish pace** au ralenti; **trading is always rather sluggish on Mondays** les affaires ne marchent jamais très bien *ou* très fort le lundi; **the engine is very sluggish in the mornings** le moteur est très lent à démarrer le matin

sluggishly ['slʌgɪʃlɪ] *adv* (**a**) *(lazily)* paresseusement; *(lethargically)* mollement (**b**) *(slowly)* lentement; **trading began sluggishly** les affaires ont démarré lentement; **the market reacted sluggishly** la bourse a réagi faiblement; **the car started sluggishly** la voiture a démarré avec difficulté

sluggishness ['slʌgɪʃnɪs] *n* (**a**) *(of person → laziness)* paresse *f*, *Fam* flemme *f*; *(→ lethargy)* mollesse *f* (**b**) *(of mind, reaction, pulse, market)* lenteur *f*; *(of growth)* faiblesse *f*, lenteur *f*; *(of engine)* mollesse *f*; *(of organization, bureaucracy)* lourdeur *f*

sluice [slu:s] **1** *n* (**a**) *(lock)* écluse *f*; *(gate)* porte *f ou* vanne *f* d'écluse; *(channel)* canal *m* à vannes; *(UNCOUNT) (lock water)* eaux *fpl* retenues par la vanne

(**b**) *(in hospital)* égout *m*

(**c**) *(wash)* **to give sth a sluice (down)** laver qch à grande eau; **to give sb a sluice (down)** asperger qn d'eau

2 *vt* (**a**) *(drain)* drainer; *(irrigate)* irriguer

(**b**) *(wash)* laver à grande eau; *Mining (ore)* laver

▸▸ ***sluice gate, sluice valve*** porte *f ou* vanne *f* d'écluse

▸**sluice down** *vt sep (wash down)* laver à grande eau; **to sluice oneself down with cold water** s'asperger d'eau fraîche; **we sluiced down the meal with cheap red wine** on a arrosé le repas d'un petit vin rouge

▸**sluice out 1** *vt sep* (**a**) *Tech (release → water from reservoir)* laisser échapper (par les vannes)

(**b**) *(rinse → cup, pot etc)* rincer; **to sluice out one's mouth** se rincer la bouche; **they sluiced out the stable** ils ont lavé l'écurie à grande eau

2 *vi (water → flow out in great quantity)* couler à flots

sluiceway ['slu:sweɪ] *n* canal *m* à vannes

sluicing ['slu:sɪŋ] *n* (**a**) *Tech* **sluicing out** vidange *f* par les écluses (**b**) *(washing)* lavage *m* à grande eau (**c**) *Mining* **ground sluicing** exploitation *f* des alluvions par canaux

▸▸ ***sluicing water*** éclusée *f*

slum [slʌm] *(pt & pp* **slummed,** *cont* **slumming**) **1** *n also Fig (house)* taudis *m*; *(district)* quartier *m* pauvre, bas quartiers *mpl*

2 *vt Fam Hum* **to slum it** *(live in substandard conditions)* renoncer au luxe auquel on est habitué ❑; *(when socializing)* s'encanailler

3 *vi Fam Hum* **we're slumming tonight** on va s'encanailler ce soir

▸▸ *Br* ***slum clearance*** rénovation *f ou* aménagement *m* des quartiers insalubres; ***slum dwelling*** taudis *m*; ***slum landlord*** marchand *m* de sommeil

slumber ['slʌmbə(r)] *Literary* **1** *n* sommeil *m* (profond); **deep in slumber** plongé dans un sommeil profond; **her slumber was** *or* **her slumbers were interrupted by...** son sommeil a été interrompu par...; *Fig* **the country had finally awoken from its slumbers** le pays était enfin sorti de sa torpeur; *Fig* **he awoke from his intellectual slumbers** il est sorti de ses hibernations intellectuelles

2 *vi* sommeiller

▸▸ *Am* ***slumber party*** soirée *f* entre copines *(au cours de laquelle on regarde des films, on discute et on dort dans la même pièce)*

slumberer ['slʌmbərə(r)] *n Literary* dormeur(euse) *m,f*

slumbering ['slʌmbərɪŋ] *adj Literary* qui dort, endormi

slumberous ['slʌmbərəs] *adj Literary* somnolent, assoupi

slumberwear ['slʌmbəweə(r)] *n (UNCOUNT)* vêtements *mpl* de nuit

slumlord ['slʌmlɔ:d] *n* marchand *m* de sommeil

slummy ['slʌmɪ] *(compar* **slummier,** *superl* **slummiest**) *adj (area, house, lifestyle)* sordide, misérable; **the slummy area of town** les bas quartiers *mpl*

slump [slʌmp] **1** *n* (**a**) *(in attendance, figures, popularity)* chute *f*, forte baisse *f*, baisse *f* soudaine; **there has been a slump in investment** les investissements sont en forte baisse; **a slump in prices/demand** une forte baisse des prix/de la demande

(**b**) *Econ (depression)* crise *f* économique; *(recession)* récession *f*; *St Exch* effondrement *m* (des cours), krach *m* (boursier)

(**c**) *Am Sport* passage *m* à vide

2 *vi* (**a**) *(person)* s'écrouler, s'effondrer; **she slumped into an armchair** elle s'est effondrée dans un fauteuil

(**b**) *(shoulders)* **her shoulders slump** elle a les épaules tombantes; **her shoulders slumped when she heard the bad news** elle eut l'air complètement abattue quand elle entendit la nouvelle

(**c**) *(business, prices, market)* s'effondrer; *(morale, attendance)* baisser soudainement

3 *vt (usu passive)* **to be slumped in an armchair** être affalé *ou* affaissé dans un fauteuil; **he was slumped over the wheel** *(in car)* il était affaissé sur le volant

▸**slump back** *vi* retomber en arrière

slumping ['slʌmpɪŋ] *n (of prices, market)* effondrement *m*

slung [slʌŋ] *pt & pp of* **sling**

slunk [slʌŋk] *pt & pp of* **slink**

slur [slɜ:(r)] *(pt & pp* **slurred,** *cont* **slurring**) **1** *n* (**a**) *(insult)* insulte *f*, affront *m*; *(on reputation)* tache *f*; **a racial slur** une insulte raciste; **it's a slur on his character** c'est une tache à sa réputation; **to cast a slur on sb** porter atteinte à la réputation de qn

(**b**) *(in speech)* mauvaise articulation *f*; **in a drunken slur** de la voix traînante d'un ivrogne; **to speak with a slur** mal articuler; *(as result of stroke etc)* parler d'une voix traînante

(**c**) *Mus (sign)* liaison *f*; *(passage)* coulé *m*

2 *vt* (**a**) *(speech, words)* mal articuler

(**b**) *(denigrate)* dénigrer

(**c**) *Mus (two notes)* lier; *(passage)* couler

3 *vi (speak indistinctly)* mal articuler ses mots, manger la moitié de ses mots; **his speech slurred** ses paroles étaient indistinctes

slurp [slɜ:p] **1** *vi (when drinking)* faire du bruit en buvant; *(when eating)* faire du bruit en mangeant

2 *vt* **to slurp sth** boire/manger qch en faisant du bruit

3 *n* **a loud slurp** un lapement bruyant; *Fam* **can I have a quick slurp of your tea?** je peux boire une gorgée de ton thé? ❑

Slurpee® ['slɜ:pi] *n* granité *m*

slurred [slɜ:d] *adj* mal articulé; **his speech was slurred** il articulait mal; *(because of stroke etc)* il avait des troubles de l'élocution; *Mus* **slurred notes** notes *fpl* liées coulant

slurry ['slʌrɪ] *(pl* **slurries**) *n* (**a**) *(cement, clay)* barbotine *f* (**b**) *(manure)* purin *m*

slush [slʌʃ] *n* (**a**) *(snow)* neige *f* fondue; *(mud)* gadoue *f* (**b**) *Fam (sentimentality)* sensiblerie ❑ *f*

▸▸ ***slush fund*** caisse *f* noire *(servant généralement au paiment des pots-de-vin)*; *Fam* ***slush money*** dessous-de-table ❑ *mpl*

slushy ['slʌʃɪ] *(compar* **slushier,** *superl* **slushiest**) *adj* (**a**) *(snow)* fondu; *(ground)* détrempé; *(path)* couvert de neige fondue (**b**) *Fam (film, book)* à l'eau de rose; *(person)* fleur bleue *(inv)*

slut [slʌt] *n Pej* (**a**) *(slovenly woman)* souillon *f* (**b**) *(promiscuous woman)* salope *f*, pouffiasse *f*, traînée *f*; *(prostitute)* pute *f*

sluttish ['slʌtɪʃ] *adj Pej* (**a**) *(dirty)* sale; **to lead a sluttish existence** vivre salement (**b**) *(morals)* dépravé; *(behaviour)* débauché, dépravé; **a sluttish woman** une débauchée

sluttishly ['slʌtɪʃlɪ] *adv Pej* (**a**) *(dirtily)* malproprement, salement (**b**) *(promiscuously)* comme une débauchée

sluttishness ['slʌtɪʃnɪs] *n Pej* (**a**) *(dirtiness)* saleté *f* (**b**) *(promiscuity)* conduite *f* débauchée *ou* dépravée

sly [slaɪ] (*compar* **slyer** *or* **slier,** *superl* **slyest** *or* **sliest**) **1** *adj* (**a**) *(cunning, knowing)* rusé; **he's a sly (old) devil** *or* **dog** c'est un fin renard; **he gave me a sly look/smile** il m'a regardé/souri d'un air rusé

(**b**) *(deceitful → person)* sournois; *(→ behaviour)* déloyal; *(→ trick)* malhonnête

(**c**) *(mischievous)* malin(igne), espiègle

(**d**) *(secretive)* dissimulé; **he's a sly one!** c'est un petit cachottier!

2 *n Fam* **on the sly** en douce

slyboots ['slaɪbu:ts] *n Br Fam* (petit) malin ❑ *m*, (petite) maligne ❑ *f*

slyly ['slaɪlɪ] *adv* (**a**) *(cunningly)* de façon rusée, avec ruse (**b**) *(deceitfully)* sournoisement (**c**) *(mischievously)* avec espièglerie, de façon espiègle (**d**) *(secretly)* discrètement

slyness ['slaɪnɪs] *n* (**a**) *(cunning)* ruse *f* (**b**) *(deceitfulness)* sournoiserie *f* (**c**) *(mischief)* espièglerie *f* (**d**) *(secrecy)* dissimulation *f*

slype [slaɪp] *n Rel & Archit* corridor *m*

SM [ˌes'em] *n Mil* (*abbr* **sergeant major**) sergent-chef *m*

s/m [ˌes'em] *n* (*abbr* **sadomasochism**) sadomasochisme *m*

smack [smæk] **1** *n* (**a**) *(slap → gen)* grande tape *f*, claque *f*; *(→ on face)* gifle *f*; *(→ on bottom)* fessée *f*; **to give sb a smack in the face** gifler qn; **to give sb a smack on the bottom** donner une claque sur les fesses à qn; *Fig* **a smack in the face** *or* **eye** une gifle, une rebuffade; **give the ball a good smack** donne un grand coup dans le ballon

(**b**) *(sound)* bruit *m* sec; *(of whip)* claquement *m*; **with a smack of his lips** avec un claquement de langue; **the smack of the waves** le fouettement des vagues; **there was a resounding smack as the bat hit the ball** la batte heurta la balle avec un claquement sonore

(**c**) *(slight taste)* léger *ou* petit goût *m*; *Culin* soupçon *m*; *Fig* **the smack of hypocrisy** une nuance d'hypocrisie

(**d**) *(boat)* smack *m*, sémaque *m*

(**e**) *Fam (kiss)* gros baiser ❑ *m*; **to give sb a smack on the lips** embrasser qn bruyamment sur les lèvres ❑

(**f**) *Br Fam (try)* **to have a smack at doing sth** essayer de faire qch ❑; **I'll have a smack at it** je vais essayer

(**g**) *Fam Drugs slang (heroin)* héro *f*, blanche *f*

2 *vt (person → gen)* donner une grande tape à, donner une claque à; *(→ in face)* donner une gifle à, gifler; *(→ on bottom)* donner une claque sur les fesses à; **to smack sb's face** *or* **sb in the face** gifler qn, donner une gifle à qn; **to smack sb's bottom** *(in punishment)* donner la fessée à qn; *(in play)* donner une tape sur les fesses à qn; **she smacked the book down on the table** elle posa le livre sur la table avec un claquement sonore; **to smack one's lips** se lécher les babines

3 *vi also Fig* **to smack of sth** sentir qch; **the whole thing smacks of corruption** tout ça, ça sent la corruption

4 *adv* (**a**) *(forcefully)* en plein; **she went smack into a wall** elle est rentrée en plein dans un mur; **he caught him smack on the chin** il l'a frappé en plein sur le menton; **she kissed him smack on the lips** elle l'a embrassé en plein sur la bouche

(**b**) *(exactly)* en plein; **smack** *or Am Fam* **smack dab in the middle** en plein milieu ❑, au beau milieu ❑; **we arrived smack** *or Am Fam* **smack dab in the middle of the meeting** nous sommes arrivés au beau milieu de la réunion

smacker ['smækə(r)] **1** *Fam* (**a**) *(kiss)* gros baiser ❑ *m* (**b**) *(pound)* livre ❑ *f*; *(dollar)* dollar ❑ *m*; **fifty smackers** cinquante livres *fpl* /dollars *mpl*

2 smackers *npl Fam (lips)* lèvres ❑ *fpl*

smackeroo [ˌsmækə'ru:] *n Am Fam (dollar)* dollar ❑ *m*

smacking ['smækɪŋ] **1** *n* fessée *f*; **to give sb a smacking** donner une fessée à qn

2 *adj Br Fam* **at a smacking pace** à vive allure ❑, à toute vitesse ❑

s-mail ['esmeɪl] *n esp Am Fam* courrier *m* escargot, = courrier postal

small [smɔ:l] **1** *adj* (**a**) *(in size)* petit; **small children** les jeunes enfants *mpl*; **small child** *(young)* enfant *mf* en bas âge, petit(e) enfant *mf*; *(small in size)* enfant *mf* de petite taille; **a small coffee** une petite tasse (de café); *Euph* **the smallest room** le petit coin; **the small screen** le petit écran; **small sizes** les petites tailles *fpl*; **to get** *or* **to grow smaller** devenir plus petit, diminuer; **to make smaller** *(hole)* réduire; **the new wallpaper makes the room look smaller** le nouveau papier peint rapetisse la pièce; **to make oneself small** se faire tout petit

(**b**) *(in number → crowd, family, population)* peu nombreux; *(in quantity → dose, amount, percentage)* petit, faible; *(→ resources)* faible; *(→ supply)* petit; *(→ salary, sum)* petit, modeste; *(→ helping)* petit, peu copieux; *(→ meal)* léger; **the audience was very small** l'assistance était très peu nombreuse, il y avait très peu de monde; **the smallest possible number of guests** le moins d'invités possible; **in small numbers** en petit nombre; **to get** *or* **to grow smaller** diminuer, décroître; **the problems don't get any smaller** les problèmes ne vont pas (en) s'amenuisant; **to make smaller** *(income)* diminuer; *(staff)* réduire

(**c**) *(in scale, range)* petit; *(minor)* petit, mineur; **down to the smallest details** jusqu'aux moindres détails; **a small voice** une petite voix; **it's no small achievement** c'est une réussite non négligeable; **it makes not the smallest difference** ça ne fait pas la moindre différence; **there's the small matter of the £150 you still owe me** il reste ce petit problème des 150 livres que tu me dois; **it's small wonder that they lost** ce n'est guère étonnant qu'ils aient perdu; **I like to be able to help in a small way** j'aime me sentir utile; **I do some acting, in a small way** je fais un peu de théâtre; **he felt responsible in his own small way** il se sentait responsable à sa façon; **in her own small way she had made a worthwhile contribution** dans la limite de ses moyens, elle avait apporté une pierre à l'édifice; *Fam* **it's** *Br* **small beer** *or Am* **small potatoes** c'est de la petite bière; *Fam* **we're very** *Br* **small beer** *or Am* **small potatoes in the advertising world** nous ne représentons pas grand-chose dans le monde de la publicité ❑

(**d**) *(petty)* petit, mesquin; **I felt very small** *(ashamed)* je n'étais pas fier; *(humiliated)* je me suis senti très humilié; **to make sb look** *or* **feel small** humilier qn, rabaisser qn; **they've got small minds** ce sont des esprits mesquins

2 *adv (chop)* menu, fin; *(write)* petit; **to cut sth up small** couper qch en tout petits morceaux; **to roll sth up small** *(lengthways)* rouler qch bien serré; *(in a ball)* rouler qch en petite boule; **the cat curled itself up small** le chat s'est roulé en boule; **to think small** voir petit

3 *n* (**a**) *(small part)* **small of the back** creux *m ou* chute *f* des reins; **I have a pain in the small of my back** j'ai mal aux reins *ou* au creux des reins; **he took her by the small of the waist** il l'a prise par la taille

(**b**) *(size)* petite taille *f*; **this T-shirt's a small** ce tee-shirt est une petite taille

4 smalls *npl Fam Hum* sous-vêtements ❑ *mpl*; **to wash one's smalls** faire sa petite lessive

►► ***small ad*** petite annonce *f*; ***small arms*** armes *fpl* portatives; **the sound of small arms fire** des tirs *mpl* d'arme portative; ***small business*** *(firm)* petite entreprise *f*, PME *f*; *(shop)* petit commerce *m*; ***small businessman*** petit entrepreneur *m ou* patron *m*; *Typ & Comput* ***small capitals, small caps*** petites capitales *fpl*; ***small change*** petite monnaie *f*; *Aut* ***small end*** *(of connecting rod)* pied *m*; ***small fry*** menu fretin *m*; **he's** *Br* **small fry** *or Am* **a small fry** il ne compte pas; ***small hours*** petit matin *m*; **in the small hours** au petit matin; *Anat* ***small intestine*** intestin *m* grêle; *Fin* ***small investor*** petit porteur *m*; ***small letter*** (lettre *f*) minuscule *f*; **in small letters** en (lettres) minuscules; ***small print*** petits caractères *mpl*; **make sure you read the small print before you sign** lisez bien ce qui est écrit en petits caractères avant de signer; ***small scale*** petite échelle *f*; **on a small scale** sur une petite échelle; ***small talk*** *(UNCOUNT)* banalités *fpl*; **to make small talk** échanger des banalités; **to make small talk with sb** faire la conversation à qn; **I'm no good at small talk** je ne sais pas faire la conversation; *Typ* ***small type*** petits corps *mpl*

'Small World' *Lodge* 'Un Tout petit monde'

small-bore *adj* de petit calibre

small-claims court *n Law* tribunal *m* d'instance

small-flowered *adj*

►► *Bot* ***small-flowered crane's bill*** géranium *m* fluet

smallholder ['smɔ:lˌhəʊldə(r)] *n Br* petit exploitant *m*

smallholding ['smɔ:lˌhəʊldɪŋ] *n Br* petite exploitation *f*

smallish ['smɔ:lɪʃ] *adj (gen)* assez petit; *(income)* assez modeste; *(family)* assez peu nombreux

small-minded *adj (attitude, person)* mesquin

small-mindedness [-'maɪndɪdnɪs] *n* mesquinerie *f*, petitesse *f*

smallness ['smɔ:lnɪs] *n* (**a**) *(of child)* petite taille *f*; *(of hand, room)* petitesse *f*; *(of salary, fee)* modicité *f*; *(of extent)* caractère *m* limité (**b**) *(pettiness)* **the smallness of his mind** sa mesquinerie

smallpox ['smɔ:lpɒks] *n* variole *f*; **a smallpox case** un cas de variole

small-scale *adj (replica, model)* à taille réduite, réduit; *(map, operation)* à petite échelle; **a small-scale event** un événement de peu d'importance

►► *Comput* ***small-scale integration*** intégration *f* à petite échelle

small-time *adj* peu important, de petite envergure; **a small-time thief/crook** un petit voleur/escroc

small-timer *n Fam* minable *mf*

small-town *adj* provincial; **a small-town attitude** une mentalité provinciale

►► ***small-town America*** l'Amérique *f* profonde; ***small-town gossip*** commérages *mpl* de quartier; ***small-town rivalries*** rivalités *fpl* de clocher

smalt [smɔ:lt] *n* smalt *m*

smarm [smɑ:m] *Br Fam Pej* **1** *vt* faire du plat *ou* lécher les bottes à; **you won't smarm your way out of this one!** tu ne t'en tireras pas avec des flatteries, cette fois-ci! ❑

2 *vi* **to smarm up to sb** passer de la pommade à *ou* lécher les bottes à qn

3 *n* obséquiosité ❑ *f*; **full of smarm** très obséquieux ❑

►**smarm down** *vt sep Br Fam* **to smarm down one's hair** se brillantiner les cheveux ❑

smarmily ['smɑ:mɪlɪ] *adv Br Fam Pej* avec onctuosité ❑, mielleusement ❑

smarminess ['smɑ:mɪnɪs] *n Br Fam Pej* caractère *m* doucereux ❑ *ou* mielleux ❑; **his smarminess gets on my nerves** son côté mielleux me tape sur les nerfs

smarmy ['smɑ:mɪ] (*compar* **smarmier,** *superl* **smarmiest**) *adj Br Fam Pej (toadying)* lèche-bottes *(inv)*; *(obsequious)* doucereux ❑, mielleux ❑

smart [smɑ:t] **1** *adj* (**a**) *Br (elegant → person, clothes, hotel)* chic, élégant; *(attractive)* coquet, pimpant; **she's a smart dresser** elle s'habille avec beaucoup de chic; **to make oneself look smart** se faire beau (belle); *(for interview etc)* bien s'habiller; **you look very smart in your new suit** vous avez beaucoup d'allure avec votre nouveau costume; **the smart set** les gens *mpl* chics, le beau monde

(**b**) *(clever)* habile, intelligent; *(shrewd, resourceful)* malin(igne); *(quick-thinking)* à l'esprit vif; **he's a smart lad** il n'est pas bête; **it isn't smart to break the law** ce n'est pas malin de ne pas respecter la loi; **it was smart of her to think of it** c'était futé de sa part d'y penser; **she was too smart for them** elle était trop maligne *ou* futée pour eux; **trying to be smart, eh?** tu essaies de faire le malin, hein?; **don't try to be smart with me** n'essaie pas de faire le malin avec moi; **that wasn't very smart, was it?** ce n'était pas très malin, tu ne trouves pas?; **smart businesswoman** femme *f* d'affaires habile; **a smart move** une sage décision; *Fam* **he's a smart one** c'est un malin ❑; *Fam* **all the smart money is on him to win the presidency** tous les spécialistes le donnent comme favori aux élections présidentielles ❑; **the smart money is on Jenkins for chairman** les gens au parfum prédisent Jenkins comme P-DG

(**c**) *(cheeky)* impertinent, audacieux; **don't get smart with me!** n'essaie pas de jouer au plus malin avec moi!

(**d**) *(quick)* vif, prompt; **a smart pace** une allure vive; **that was smart work!** voilà du travail rapide!, voilà qui a été vite fait!; **look smart!** grouille-toi!; **smart reprimand** réprimande *f* assez sèche; **a smart slap across the face** une bonne gifle; **give the top a smart tap** donnez une bonne tape sur le dessus; **give the top a smart pull** tirez fort sur le dessus

(**e**) *Comput* intelligent

(**f**) *(bomb, weapon)* intelligent

2 *vi* (**a**) *(eyes, wound)* picoter, brûler; **her eyes were smarting** elle avait les yeux qui piquaient; **the onion made her eyes smart** les oignons lui piquaient les yeux *ou* la faisaient pleurer; **my face was still smarting from the blow** le visage me cuisait encore du coup que j'avais reçu

(**b**) *(person)* être piqué au vif; **he's still smarting from the insult** il n'a toujours pas digéré l'insulte

3 *adv (quickly → walk)* vivement, à vive allure; *(→ act)* vivement, promptement

4 *n* (**a**) *(pain)* douleur *f* cuisante; *Fig* effet *m* cinglant

(**b**) *Am Fam (useful hint)* tuyau *m*, combine *f*

5 smarts *npl Am Fam (intelligence)* intelligence ❑ *f*; **to have smarts** en avoir dans le ciboulot; **he's pretty low on smarts** c'est pas une lumière

►► *Fam* ***smart alec, smart aleck*** petit(e) malin(-igne) ❑ *m,f*; ***smart card*** carte *f* à puce; ***smart card reader*** lecteur *m* de cartes à puce *ou* de cartes à mémoire; ***smart drug*** psychotrope *m*; *Comput* ***smart quotes*** = conversion automatique des guillemets saisis au clavier en guillemets typographiques

smart-alec, smart-aleck *adj Fam (reply, comment)* gonflé

smartarse ['smɑːtɑːs], *Am* **smartass** ['smɑːtæs] *very Fam* **1** *n* petit(e) malin(igne) ❑ *m,f*

2 *adj (reply, comment)* sarcastique ❑

smarten ['smɑːtən] *vt* (**a**) *(improve appearance)* **to smarten (the appearance of) sth** arranger qch; **to smarten oneself** se faire beau (belle)

(**b**) *Br (speed up)* **to smarten one's pace** accélérer l'allure

►**smarten up 1** *vi* (**a**) *(improve appearance → person)* se faire beau (belle); *(→ restaurant)* devenir plus chic, être retapé; *(→ town, street)* devenir plus pimpant; **I went upstairs to smarten up** je suis monté me faire beau

(**b**) *Br (output, speed)* s'accélérer

(**c**) *Fam (improve)* se reprendre ❑

2 *vt sep* (**a**) *(person)* pomponner; *(room, house, town)* arranger, rendre plus élégant; **a coat of paint would help smarten the restaurant/the car up** une couche de peinture et le restaurant/la voiture aurait déjà meilleure allure; **to smarten oneself up** se faire beau (belle), soigner son apparence

(**b**) *(production)* accélérer

(**c**) *Fam (improve)* **you'd better smarten up your ideas** *or* **your act!** tu ferais bien de te reprendre ❑; *(to lazy person)* tu ferais bien de te secouer

(**d**) *Am Fam (realize what is happening)* **smarten up!** ouvre les yeux!, cesse de faire l'imbécile!

smarting ['smɑːtɪŋ] **1** *adj (pain, eyes)* brûlant

2 *n* douleur *f* cuisante

smartish ['smɑːtɪʃ] *adv Br Fam* vite fait, en vitesse ❑; **you'd better get ready pretty smartish** tu ferais mieux de te préparer vite fait

smartly ['smɑːtlɪ] *adv* (**a**) *Br (elegantly)* avec beaucoup d'allure *ou* de chic, élégamment (**b**) *(cleverly)* habilement, adroitement (**c**) *(quickly → move)* vivement; *(→ act, work)* rapidement, promptement (**d**) *(sharply → reprimand)* vertement; *(→ reply)* du tac au tac, sèchement

smartness ['smɑːtnɪs] *n* (**a**) *Br (elegance → of appearance, dress, style)* allure *f*, chic *m*, élégance *f* (**b**) *(cleverness)* intelligence *f*, habileté *f*; *(shrewdness)* astuce *f*, vivacité *f* (d'esprit); *(ingenuity)* débrouillardise *f* (**c**) *(impertinence)* impertinence *f* (**d**) *(quickness → of pace)* rapidité *f*; *(→ of reply, behaviour)* promptitude *f*, rapidité *f*

smarty ['smɑːtɪ] *(pl* **smarties**), **smarty-pants** *(pl* **inv**) *n Fam* (Monsieur/Madame/Mademoiselle) je-sais-tout *mf inv*, petit(e) malin(igne) ❑ *m,f*; **OK, smarty-pants, show me how to do it** allez, vas-y, montre-moi comment faire puisque tu es si malin

smash [smæʃ] **1** *n* (**a**) *(noise → of breaking)* fracas *m*; **with a loud smash** avec un grand fracas; **the vase fell with a smash** le vase s'est fracassé en tombant; **there was a tremendous smash as the two cars collided** il y eut un très violent fracas quand les deux voitures entrèrent en collision

(**b**) *(blow)* coup *m ou* choc *m* violent; **forearm smash** manchette *f*; **a smash on the head** un coup violent sur la tête

(**c**) *Fam (collision)* collision ❑ *f*; *(accident)* accident ❑ *m*; *(pile-up)* carambolage ❑ *m*, télescopage ❑ *m*; **a five-car smash** un carambolage de cinq voitures

(**d**) *(collapse → of business, market)* débâcle *f* (financière), effondrement *m* (financier); *St Exch* krach *m*, effondrement *m* des cours; *(bankruptcy)* faillite *f*

(**e**) *(in tennis, badminton, table-tennis)* smash *m*

(**f**) *Fam (success)* succès *m* bœuf; **it was a smash** ça a fait un tabac

(**g**) *Am (drink)* = boisson composée d'une liqueur, de menthe, de sucre et d'eau gazeuse

2 *onomat* patatras

3 *adv* **to go** *or* **to run smash into a wall** heurter un mur avec violence, rentrer en plein dans un mur

4 *vt* (**a**) *(break → cup, window)* casser, briser; **to smash sth to pieces** briser qch en morceaux; **I've smashed my glasses** j'ai cassé mes lunettes; **to smash sth open** *(box, crate)* ouvrir qch d'un grand coup; **to smash the door open** enfoncer la porte; **he smashed his head open on a rock** il s'est ouvert la tête en heurtant un rocher

(**b**) *(crash, hit)* écraser; **he smashed his fist (down) on the table** il écrasa son poing sur la table; **she smashed him over the head with a chair** elle lui a cassé une chaise sur la tête; **they smashed their way in** ils sont entrés par effraction *(en enfonçant la porte ou la fenêtre)*; **the raft was smashed against the rocks** le radeau s'est fracassé contre *ou* sur les rochers; **he smashed the ball into the back of the net** *(in football)* d'un tir terrible, il a envoyé le ballon au fond des filets

(**c**) *(in tennis, badminton, table-tennis)* **to smash the ball** faire un smash, smasher; **he smashed the ball into the net** il a envoyé son smash dans le filet

(**d**) *(destroy → gen)* briser; *(→ resistance, opposition)* briser, écraser; *(→ opponent, record)* pulvériser; **to smash a drugs ring** démanteler un réseau de trafiquants de drogue

(**e**) *Phys (atom)* désintégrer

5 *vi (break, crash)* se briser, se casser; **to smash into bits** se briser en mille morceaux; **the car smashed into the lamppost** la voiture s'est écrasée contre le réverbère

►► ***smash hit*** *(song, record)* gros succès *m*; **this record is a smash hit in America** ce disque fait fureur *ou* connaît un succès fou en Amérique

►**smash down** *vt sep (door)* défoncer

►**smash in** *vt sep (door, window)* enfoncer, défoncer; *(safe)* forcer; *Fam* **to smash sb's face in** casser la figure *ou très Fam* la gueule à qn; **I'll smash your face in** je te casse la gueule

►**smash up** *vt sep (furniture)* casser, démolir; *(room, shop)* tout casser *ou* démolir dans; *(car)* démolir; **they smashed the place up in revenge** ils ont tout démoli pour se venger

smash-and-grab (raid) *n Br* pillage *m* de vitrine; **the jewels were stolen in a smash-and-grab (raid)** des cambrioleurs ont brisé la vitrine et se sont enfuis avec les bijoux

smashed [smæʃt] *adj Fam (drunk)* bourré, pété, beurré; *(on drugs)* raide, défoncé; **to get smashed** *(drunk)* se bourrer; *(on drugs)* se défoncer

smasher ['smæʃə(r)] *n Br Fam* (**a**) *(person)* **she's a real smasher** *(in appearance)* c'est un vrai canon; *(in character)* elle est vraiment sensass (**b**) *(object)* **it's a real smasher!** c'est sensass!

smashing ['smæʃɪŋ] *adj Br Fam* super *(inv)*, génial, géant; **it was a smashing party!** ça a été une soirée du tonnerre!; **we had a smashing time!** on s'est super bien amusés!; **she's a smashing girl** c'est une fille super

smash-up *n (accident)* accident *m*; *(collision)* carambolage *m*, télescopage *m*; **five cars were involved in the smash-up** cinq voitures se sont télescopées

smattering ['smætərɪŋ] *n (UNCOUNT) (of knowledge)* notions *fpl* vagues; *(of people, things)* poignée *f*, petit nombre *m*; **they only have a smattering of grammar** ils n'ont que quelques vagues notions de grammaire; **she has a smattering of Italian** elle a quelques notions d'italien, elle sait un peu d'italien; **there was the usual smattering of artists at the party** comme toujours, il y avait un petit groupe d'artistes à la réception

smaze [smeɪz] *n Am Fam* brume ❑ *f*, smog ❑ *m*

SME [ˌesem'iː] *n (abbr* **small and medium-sized enterprise**) PME *f*

smear [smɪə(r)] **1** *n* (**a**) *(mark → on glass, mirror, wall)* trace *f*, tache *f*; *(longer)* traînée *f*; *(of ink)* pâté *m*, bavure *f*; **smears of blood/paint** des traînées *fpl* de sang/de peinture

(**b**) *(defamation)* diffamation *f*; *(spoken)* calomnie *f*; **a smear on sb's integrity/reputation** une atteinte à l'honneur/à la réputation de qn; **to use smear tactics** avoir recours à la calomnie

(**c**) *Med* frottis *m*, prélèvement *m*

2 *vt* (**a**) *(spread → butter, oil)* étaler; *(coat)* barbouiller; **to smear sth with grease, to smear grease on sth** étaler de la graisse sur qch; **she smeared the dish with butter** elle a beurré le plat; **to smear paint/chocolate on one's face** se barbouiller le visage de peinture/de chocolat; **they smeared red paint everywhere** ils ont tout barbouillé de peinture rouge; *Culin* **chicken breasts smeared with garlic butter** des blancs *mpl* de poulet cuits dans du beurre à l'ail

(**b**) *(smudge)* **the ink on the page was smeared** l'encre a coulé sur la page; **the rain has smeared the address** la pluie a en partie effacé l'adresse; **don't smear the wet paint/varnish** ne faites pas de taches de peinture/de vernis; **the walls were smeared with blood** les murs étaient tout maculés de sang; **the mirror was smeared with fingermarks** il y avait des traces de doigts sur la glace

(**c**) *(defame → person)* diffamer; *(verbally)* calomnier; *(→ person's reputation)* salir; **an attempt to smear the prime minister** une tentative de diffamation du premier ministre

(**d**) *Am Fam (defeat easily)* battre à plates coutures

3 *vi (paint)* couler; *(ink)* baver

►► ***smear campaign*** campagne *f* de diffamation ou dénigrement; *Med* ***smear test*** frottis *m* (vaginal), *Can* test *m* de Papanicolaou

smeary ['smɪərɪ] *adj (stained)* taché, barbouillé; *(windows, mirror)* sale

smectic ['smektɪk] *adj Chem* smectique

smeg [smeg] *n Br very Fam* saloperies *fpl*

smeggy ['smegɪ] *adj Br very Fam* dégueulasse, cradingue

smegma ['smegmə] *n Physiol* smegma *m*

smell [smel] *(Br pt & pp* **smelled** *or* **smelt** [smelt], *Am pt & pp* **smelled**) **1** *vt* (**a**) *(notice an odour of)* sentir; **to smell gas** sentir le gaz, *Am* sentir le gaz *ou* l'essence; **I can smell (something) burning** (je trouve que) ça sent le brûlé; **she smelt** *or* **she could smell alcohol on his breath** elle s'aperçut que son haleine sentait l'alcool

(**b**) *Fig (sense → trouble, danger)* flairer, pressentir; **to smell a rat** flairer quelque chose de louche

(**c**) *(sniff at → food)* sentir, renifler; *(→ flower)* sentir, humer; *(of dog)* flairer, renifler; **she smelt the cream to see if it was fresh** elle a senti la crème pour voir si elle était fraîche

2 *vi* (**a**) *(have odour)* sentir; **to smell good** *or* **sweet** sentir bon; **to smell bad** sentir mauvais; **it smells musty** ça sent le renfermé; **that soup smells delicious!** cette soupe sent délicieusement bon!; **what does it smell of** *or* **like?** qu'est-ce que ça sent?; **it smells of lavender** ça sent la lavande; **it smells like lavender** on dirait de la lavande; *Fig* **to smell of treachery/hypocrisy** sentir la trahison/l'hypocrisie; *Fam* **to smell fishy** sembler louche ❑

(**b**) *(have bad odour)* sentir (mauvais); **it smells (awful) in here!** ça pue ici!; **his breath smells** il a mauvaise haleine; **the dog smells** le chien sent mauvais *ou* pue

(**c**) *(perceive odour)* **he can't smell** il n'a pas d'odorat; **you smell with your nose** le nez sert à sentir

3 *n* (**a**) *(sense → of person)* odorat *m*; *(→ of animal)* odorat *m*, flair *m*; **he has no sense of smell** il n'a pas d'odorat; **I've lost my sense of smell** j'ai perdu l'odorat; **to have a keen sense of smell** avoir le nez fin; *(dog etc)* avoir beaucoup de flair

(**b**) *(odour)* odeur *f*; *(of flowers, fruit)* parfum *m*; *(bad odour)* mauvaise odeur *f*; *(stench)* puanteur *f*; **there's a bad smell** ça sent mauvais; **what's that smell?** quelle est cette odeur?; **there's a strong smell of gas in here** il y a une forte odeur de gaz ici; **there was a smell of burning in the kitchen** il y avait une odeur de brûlé dans la cuisine; **the smell of onions cooking** l'odeur *f* d'oignons qui cuisent; **there was a lovely smell of lavender** ça sentait bon la lavande; **it has no smell** ça n'a pas d'odeur; **natural gas has no smell** le gaz naturel n'a pas d'odeur *ou* est inodore; **what an awful smell!** qu'est-ce que ça sent mauvais!; *Fig* **the smell of defeat/fear** l'odeur *f* de la défaite/de la peur; *Fig* **I don't like the smell of this at all** ça ne me plaît pas du tout, c'est louche

(**c**) *(sniff)* **to have** *or* **take a smell of sth** sentir qch, renifler qch; **have a smell of this** sentez-moi ça

►**smell out** *vt sep* (**a**) *(of dog)* dénicher en flairant; *Fig (of person)* découvrir, dépister; *(secret, conspiracy)* découvrir

(**b**) **his cigarettes are smelling the office out** ses cigarettes empestent *ou* empuantissent le bureau

►**smell up** *vt insep Am* = **smell out** (**b**)

smelliness ['smelɪnɪs] *n* mauvaise odeur *f*; *(stench)* puanteur *f*

smelling salts ['smelɪŋ-] *npl* sels *mpl*

smelly ['smelɪ] (*compar* **smellier**, *superl* **smelliest**) *adj* (**a**) *(person, socks etc)* qui sent mauvais, qui pue; **it's awfully smelly in here** ça sent horriblement mauvais *ou* ça pue ici; **to have smelly feet** sentir des pieds (**b**) *Fam Pej (unpleasant)* dégueulasse; **you can stuff your smelly homework!** tes devoirs, tu peux te les mettre où je pense; **I hate my smelly sister** je déteste ma cruche de sœur

smelt [smelt] (*pl* **inv** *or* **smelts**) **1** *pt & pp of* **smell**

2 *n Ich* éperlan *m*

3 *vt Metal (ore)* fondre; *(metal)* extraire par fusion

smelter ['smeltə(r)] *n Metal* haut-fourneau *m*

smeltery ['smeltərɪ] *n Metal* fonderie *f*

smelting ['smeltɪŋ] *n (of ore)* fonte *f*, fusion *f*; *(of metal)* extraction *f* par fusion

►► ***smelting works*** fonderie *f*

smew [smjuː] *n Orn* (**a**) harle *m* piette (**b**) *Am* harle *m* couronné

smidgen, smidgin ['smɪdʒɪn] *n Fam* **just a smidgen** juste un petit peu ❑; **a smidgen of** un tout petit peu de; **there isn't a smidgen of truth in what he says** il n'y a pas une ombre de vérité dans ce qu'il dit ❑

smilax ['smaɪlæks] *n Bot* (**a**) *(of lily family)* smilax *m*, salepareille *f* (**b**) *(of asparagus family)* asparagus *m*

smile [smaɪl] **1** *n* sourire *m*; **with a smile on her lips** (avec) le sourire aux lèvres; **"of course", he said with a smile** "bien sûr", dit-il en souriant; **he has a nice smile** il a un joli sourire; **come on, give us a smile!** allez, fais-nous un sourire!; **she gave me a friendly little smile** elle m'a adressé un petit sourire amical; **to have a smile on one's face** avoir le sourire; **take that smile off your face!** arrête de sourire comme ça!; **that'll take** *or* **wipe the smile off his face!** cela va lui faire passer l'envie de sourire!; **to be all smiles** être tout souriant *ou* tout sourire; *(as a pretence)* elle était tout sucre tout miel

2 *vi* sourire; **to smile at sb** sourire à qn; **smile (please)!** *(for photograph)* souriez!; **to smile to oneself** sourire pour soi; **she smiled at his awkwardness** sa maladresse l'a fait sourire; **he smiled to think of it** il a souri en y pensant, y penser le faisait sourire; **keep smiling!** gardez le sourire!; **he always comes up smiling** il garde toujours le sourire; **she smiled back (at him)** elle lui rendit son sourire; *Fig* **fortune smiled on him** la fortune lui sourit; *Literary* **to smile in the face of adversity** faire contre mauvaise fortune bon cœur

3 *vt* **to smile one's approval** exprimer son approbation par un sourire; **to smile one's thanks** remercier d'un sourire; **to smile a welcome to sb** accueillir qn avec *ou* par un sourire; **she smiled a sad smile** elle eut un sourire triste

smiley ['smaɪliː] *n Comput* souriant *m*, émoticon *m*, *Can* binette *f*

smiling ['smaɪlɪŋ] *adj* souriant

smilingly ['smaɪlɪŋlɪ] *adv* en souriant, avec un sourire

smirch [smɜːtʃ] *Literary* **1** *vt* (**a**) *(stain)* salir, souiller (**b**) *Fig (name, reputation)* salir, ternir

2 *n* tache *f*, salissure *f*, souillure *f*

smirk [smɜːk] **1** *vi (smugly)* sourire d'un air suffisant *ou* avec suffisance; *(foolishly)* sourire bêtement

2 *n (smug)* petit sourire *m* satisfait *ou* suffisant; *(foolish)* sourire *m* bête

smirking ['smɜːkɪŋ] **1** *adj* suffisant

2 *n (smug)* petits sourires *mpl* satisfaits *ou* suffisants; *(foolish)* sourires *mpl* bêtes

smirr [smɜː(r)] *n Scot* bruine *f*

smite [smaɪt] *vt* (*pt* **smote** [sməʊt], *pp* **smitten** ['smɪtən]) (**a**) *Arch or Literary (strike → object)* frapper; *(→ enemy)* abattre (**b**) **to be smitten with blindness** être frappé de cécité; **to be smitten with remorse** être pris de remords; **to be smitten with a desire to do sth** être pris d'un *ou* du désir de faire qch (**c**) *Bible (punish)* châtier

►**smite down** *vt sep Arch or Literary* abattre

smiter ['smaɪtə(r)] *n Arch or Literary* frappeur(euse) *m,f*

smith [smɪθ] *n* forgeron *m*; *(who shoes horses)* maréchal-ferrant *m*

Smith and Wesson® ['smɪθənd'wesən] *n* = marque d'armes à feu

smithereens [ˌsmɪðə'riːnz] *npl* morceaux *mpl*; **to smash sth to smithereens** briser qch en mille morceaux; **he was blown to smithereens in the explosion** il a été déchiqueté dans l'explosion; **the house was blown to smithereens in the explosion** la maison a été complètement soufflée par l'explosion

smithery ['smɪθərɪ] (*pl* **smitheries**) *n* (**a**) *(work → gen)* travaux *mpl* de forge; *(→ of blacksmith)* travaux *mpl* de maréchalerie (**b**) *(forge)* forge *f*; *(blacksmith's workshop)* (atelier *m* de) maréchalerie *f*

Smithfield Market ['smɪθfiːld-] *n* = marché de gros de la viande à Londres

Smithsonian Institution [smɪθ'səʊnɪən-] *n* = complexe culturel à Washington

smithsonite ['smɪθsənaɪt] *n Miner* smithsonite *f*

Smith Square *n* = place à Londres où se trouve le siège du parti conservateur

smithy ['smɪðɪ] (*pl* **smithies**) *n* forge *f*; *(blacksmith's workshop)* (atelier *m* de) maréchalerie *f*

smitten ['smɪtən] **1** *pp of* **smite**

2 *adj* **he was smitten with** *or* **by her beauty** il a été ébloui par sa beauté; **he's really smitten (with that girl)** il est vraiment très épris (de cette fille)

smock [smɒk] **1** *n (loose garment)* blouse *f*, sarrau *m*; *(maternity wear → blouse)* tunique *f* de grossesse; *(→ dress)* robe *f* de grossesse

2 *vt Sewing* faire des smocks à

►► ***smock mill*** moulin *m* à toit tournant

smocking ['smɒkɪŋ] *n (UNCOUNT)* smocks *mpl*

smog [smɒg] *n* smog *m*

smoggy ['smɒgɪ] (*compar* **smoggier**, *superl* **smoggiest**) *adj* **a smoggy day** une journée de smog; **it's smoggy** il y a du smog

smokable ['sməʊkəbəl] **1** *adj* que l'on peut fumer, fumable; **quite a smokable cigar** un cigare qui se laisse fumer

2 *Am* **smokables** *npl* tabac *m*

smoke [sməʊk] **1** *n* (**a**) *(from fire, cigarette)* fumée *f*; **to go up in smoke** *(building)* brûler; *Fig (plans)* partir *ou* s'en aller en fumée; *Fam* **he had smoke coming out of his ears** *(was angry)* ses yeux lançaient des éclairs ❑; *Prov* **there's no smoke without fire** il n'y a pas de fumée sans feu

(**b**) *(act of smoking)* **to have a smoke** fumer; **I went outside for a smoke** je suis sorti fumer une cigarette

(**c**) *Fam (cigarette)* clope *f*; *(cigar)* cigare ❑ *m*; **have you got any smokes?** t'as des clopes?

(**d**) *Fam Drugs slang (cannabis cigarette)* joint *m*; *(cannabis)* chichon *m*, shit *m*

(**e**) *Br Fam* **the (Big) Smoke** *(any big city)* la grande ville ❑; *(London)* Londres ❑

2 *vi* (**a**) *(fireplace, chimney, lamp)* fumer; **the horses' flanks were smoking** les chevaux étaient tout fumants

(**b**) *(person)* fumer; **do you smoke?** (est-ce que) vous fumez?; **do you mind if I smoke?** ça vous gêne si je fume?; *Fam* **to smoke like a chimney** fumer comme un pompier *ou* un sapeur

3 *vt* (**a**) *(cigarette, pipe, opium etc)* fumer; **to smoke a pipe** fumer la pipe; **to smoke twenty a day** fumer vingt cigarettes par jour

(**b**) *Culin (fish, meat)* fumer

(**c**) *(glass)* fumer

(**d**) *(fumigate → plants, greenhouse, room)* soumettre à des fumigations

►► ***smoke alarm*** détecteur *m* de fumée; ***smoke bomb*** bombe *f* fumigène; ***smoke detector*** détecteur *m* de fumée; ***smoke hood*** hotte *f* (aspirante); *Am* ***smoke shop*** tabac *m*; ***smoke signal*** signal *m* de fumée

►**smoke out** *vt sep* (**a**) *(fugitive, animal)* enfumer; *Fig (traitor, bandits)* débusquer; *(conspiracy, plot)* découvrir

(**b**) *(room)* enfumer

(**c**) *(finish)* **my pipe is smoked out** j'ai fini ma pipe

►**smoke up** *vt sep Am (room)* enfumer

smoked [sməʊkt] *adj* fumé

►► ***smoked glass*** verre *m* fumé; ***smoked salmon*** saumon *m* fumé

smoke-dried *adj* fumé

smoke-filled [-fɪld] *adj* enfumé; *Fig* **in smoke-filled rooms** dans les salles du pouvoir

smokehouse ['sməʊkhaʊs, *pl* -haʊzɪz] *n* fumoir *m (pour aliments)*

smokeless fuel ['sməʊklɪs-] *n* combustible *m* non polluant

smokeless zone *n* = zone dans laquelle seul l'usage de combustibles non polluants est autorisé

smoker ['sməʊkə(r)] *n* (**a**) *(person)* fumeur(euse) *m,f*; **cigarette/pipe smoker** fumeur(euse) *m,f* de cigarettes/pipe; **heavy smoker** gros (grosse) fumeur(euse) *m,f*; **to have a smoker's cough** avoir une toux de fumeur (**b**) *(train compartment)* compartiment *m* fumeurs

smokescreen ['sməʊkskriːn] *n Mil* écran *m ou* rideau *m* de fumée; *Fig* paravent *m*, couverture *f*

smokestack ['sməʊkstæk] *n* cheminée *f*

►► ***smokestack industry*** industrie *f* lourde

smokewood ['sməʊkwʊd] *n Bot* fustet *m*

Smokey the Bear ['sməʊkɪ-] *n* = mascotte du service américain de protection des forêts

smokiness ['sməʊkɪnɪs] *n* (**a**) *(of place)* atmosphère *f* enfumée (**b**) *(of taste)* goût *m* de fumée

smoking ['sməʊkɪŋ] **1** *adj* fumant, qui fume; **smoking or non-smoking?** fumeurs ou non-fumeurs?

2 *n* (**a**) *(of tobacco → habit)* tabagisme *m*; **the effects of smoking on the foetus** les effets *mpl* du tabagisme sur le fœtus; **smoking can damage your health** fumer nuit à votre santé; **I've given up smoking** j'ai arrêté de fumer; **no smoking** *(sign)* défense de fumer; **smoking can cause cancer** le tabac peut provoquer le cancer

(**b**) *Culin (of meat, fish)* fumage *m*

►► ***smoking area*** zone *f* fumeurs; ***smoking carriage*** voiture *f* fumeurs; ***smoking compartment*** compartiment *m* fumeurs; *Fig* ***smoking gun*** *(clue)* indice *m* flagrant; ***smoking jacket*** veste *f* d'intérieur; ***smoking room*** fumoir *m (pour fumeurs)*

smoky ['sməʊkɪ] *(compar* **smokier,** *superl* **smokiest)** *adj* (**a**) *(atmosphere, room)* enfumé (**b**) *(chimney, lamp, fire)* qui fume (**c**) *(ceiling, wall)* noirci par la fumée (**d**) *(taste)* de fumée; *(food)* qui sent le fumé, qui a un goût de fumé (**e**) *(in colour)* **smoky blue** gris bleu *(inv)*

►► ***smoky grey*** gris fumée *m inv*; *Geol* ***smoky quartz*** quartz *m* fumé

smolder, smoldering *Am* = **smoulder, smouldering**

smolt [sməʊlt] *n Ich* tacon *m*

smooch [smuːtʃ] *Fam* **1** *n* (**a**) **to have a smooch** *(kiss)* se bécoter; *(cuddle)* se peloter (**b**) *Br* **to have a smooch** *(dance)* danser joue contre joue[❑]

2 *vi* (**a**) *(kiss)* se bécoter; *(cuddle)* se peloter (**b**) *Br (dance)* danser joue contre joue[❑]

smoochy [-smuːtʃɪ] *(compar* **smoochier,** *superl* **smoochiest)** *adj Fam (music)* sentimental[❑], tendre[❑]

smooth [smuːð] **1** *adj* (**a**) *(surface)* lisse; *(pebble, stone)* lisse, poli; *(skin)* lisse, doux (douce); *(chin → close-shaven)* rasé de près; *(→ beardless)* glabre, lisse; *(hair, fabric, road)* lisse; *(sea, water)* calme; **this razor gives a smooth shave** ce rasoir vous rase de près; **the steps were worn smooth** les marches étaient devenues lisses; **the stone had been washed** *or* **worn smooth by the sea** la pierre avait été polie par la mer; *Br Fam* **as smooth as a baby's bottom** *(skin, face)* doux comme une peau de bébé

(**b**) *(comfortable → ride, flight)* confortable; *(→ take-off, landing)* en douceur; **they had a smooth crossing** la traversée a été calme

(**c**) *(trouble-free → life, course of events)* paisible, calme; *(→ journey)* sans anicroches; *(→ organization)* qui marche bien; *(→ rhythm, style)* fluide; **to get off to a smooth start** bien démarrer; **to make things smooth for sb** faciliter les choses pour qn; **the smooth running of the department** le bon fonctionnement du service; **the way is now smooth for further reforms** il n'y a plus d'obstacles maintenant aux nouvelles réformes; **the bill had a smooth passage through Parliament** le projet de loi a été voté sans problèmes au Parlement

(**d**) *Culin (in texture)* onctueux, homogène; *(in taste)* moelleux

(**e**) *Pej (slick, suave)* doucereux, onctueux, suave; *Fam* **he's a smooth operator** il sait y faire; **to be a smooth talker, to have a smooth tongue** être beau parleur

2 *vt* (**a**) *(tablecloth, skirt)* défroisser; *(hair, feathers)* lisser; *(wood)* rendre lisse, planer; **to smooth one's brow** dérider son front; **to smooth the way for sb, to smooth sb's path** aplanir les difficultés pour qn

(**b**) *(rub → oil, cream)* masser; **to smooth oil into one's skin** mettre de l'huile sur sa peau *(en massant doucement)*

(**c**) *(polish)* lisser, polir

(**d**) [illegible]

3 *n* (**a**) **to give one's hair a smooth** lisser ses cheveux, se lisser les cheveux; **to give sth a smooth down with sandpaper** égaliser qch avec du papier de verre

(**b**) *(smooth part)* partie *f* lisse; *(smooth surface)* surface *f* unie

►► *Anat* ***smooth muscle*** muscle *m* lisse, muscle *m* viscéral; *Zool* ***smooth snake*** coronelle *f*

►**smooth away** *vt sep (problems, fears)* faire oublier

►**smooth back** *vt sep (hair)* lisser en arrière; *(sheet)* rabattre en lissant

►**smooth down** *vt sep (hair, feathers)* lisser; *(sheets, dress)* lisser, défroisser; *(wood)* planer, aplanir; *Fig (person)* apaiser, calmer

►**smooth out** *vt sep (clothes, sheet, map, piece of paper)* lisser, défroisser; *(crease, pleat, wrinkle)* faire disparaître (en lissant); *Fig (difficulties, obstacles)* aplanir, faire disparaître

►**smooth over** *vt sep* (**a**) *(gravel, sand)* rendre lisse (en ratissant); *(soil)* aplanir, égaliser

(**b**) *Fig (difficulties, obstacles)* aplanir; **to smooth things over** *(embarrassing situation)* arranger les choses

smoothbore ['smuːðbɔː(r)] *Mil* **1** *adj* à canon lisse

2 *n* fusil *m* non rayé

smoothbored ['smuːðbɔːd] *adj* à canon lisse

smooth-faced *adj* au visage lisse; *(after shaving)* rasé de près; *Fig Pej* trop suave *ou* poli, onctueux

smoothie ['smuːðɪ] *n* (**a**) *Fam (smooth talker)* individu *m* mielleux[❑]; **he's a real smoothie** *(in manner)* il roule les mécaniques; *(in speech)* c'est vraiment un beau parleur[❑] (**b**) *(drink)* = boisson à base de jus de fruit mélangé à du yaourt ou à du lait

smoothing ['smuːðɪŋ] *n* lissage *m*

►► ***smoothing iron*** fer *m* à repasser *(non électrique)*; *Carp* ***smoothing plane*** rabot *m* à repasser; ***smoothing stick*** formoir *m*

smoothly ['smuːðlɪ] *adv* (**a**) *(easily, steadily → operate, drive, move)* sans à-coups, en douceur; **to run smoothly** *(engine)* tourner bien; *(operation, meeting)* marcher comme sur des roulettes; **things are not going very smoothly between them** ça ne va pas très bien entre eux; **the meeting went off quite smoothly** la réunion s'est déroulée sans heurt *ou* accroc; **the journey went smoothly** le voyage s'est déroulé sans anicroches; **the interview went quite smoothly until I...** l'entretien s'est bien passé jusqu'à ce que je...

(**b**) *(gently → rise, fall)* doucement, en douceur; **the plane took off smoothly** l'avion a décollé en douceur

(**c**) *Pej (talk)* doucereusement; *(behave)* (trop) suavement

smoothness ['smuːðnɪs] *n* (**a**) *(of surface)* égalité *f*, aspect *m* uni *ou* lisse; *(of fabric, skin, hair)* douceur *f*; *(of road)* surface *f* lisse; *(of sea)* calme *m*; *(of stone)* aspect *m* lisse *ou* poli; *(of tyre)* aspect *m* lisse; **she has a wonderful smoothness of touch on the piano** elle a un merveilleux doigté au piano

(**b**) *(of flow, breathing, pace, supply)* régularité *f*; *(of engine, machine)* bon fonctionnement *m*; *(of life, course of events)* caractère *m* paisible *ou* serein; *Fig (of temperament)* calme *m*, sérénité *f*; **the operation was carried out with great smoothness** l'opération s'est déroulée sans accroc *ou* heurt

(**c**) *Culin (of texture)* onctuosité *f*; *(of taste)* moelleux *m*

(**d**) *(of voice)* douceur *f*

(**e**) *Pej (suaveness)* caractère *m* doucereux *ou* mielleux, onctuosité *f*

smooth-running *adj (machine)* qui fonctionne bien *ou* sans à-coups; *(engine)* qui tourne bien; *(business, organization)* qui marche bien; *(plan, operation)* qui se déroule bien

smooth-shaven *adj* rasé de près

smooth-spoken *adj* doucereux, mielleux

smooth-talk *vt* **don't let him smooth-talk you** ne te laisse pas enjôler par lui; **she was smooth-talked into accepting the job** ils l'ont convaincue d'accepter le travail à force de belles paroles; **let's see if he can smooth-talk his way out of this one** voyons s'il est assez beau [illegible]

smooth-talking *adj* doucereux, mielleux

smooth-tongued *adj* doucereux, mielleux

smoothy = **smoothie**

smorgasbord ['smɔːgəsbɔːd] *n Culin* smorgasbord *m*, buffet *m* scandinave; *Fig* grande variété *f*, grande diversité *f*

smorzando [smɔː'zændəʊ] *Mus* **1** *adv* smorzando

2 *adj* smorzando

smote [sməʊt] *pt of* **smite**

smother ['smʌðə(r)] **1** *vt* (**a**) *(suppress → fire, flames)* étouffer; *(→ sound)* étouffer, amortir; *(→ cry)* étouffer, retenir; *(→ emotions, laughter, yawn)* réprimer; *(→ scandal, criticism, opposition)* étouffer

(**b**) *(suffocate → person)* étouffer; **she felt smothered by her mother** elle se sentait étouffée par sa mère

(**c**) *(cover)* couvrir, recouvrir; **strawberries smothered in** *or* **with cream** des fraises *fpl* couvertes de crème; **she was smothered in furs** elle était emmitouflée dans des fourrures

(**d**) *(overwhelm → with kindness, love)* combler; **to smother sb with kisses** couvrir *ou* dévorer qn de baisers; **to smother sb with attention** être aux petits soins pour qn

2 *vi (person)* étouffer

smothered ['smʌðəd] *adj (cry)* sourd, étouffé; *(sound)* étouffé

smothering ['smʌðərɪŋ] *n* étouffement *m*

smother-love *n Fam* amour *m* étouffant d'une mère[❑]

smoulder, *Am* **smolder** ['sməʊldə(r)] *vi* (**a**) *(fire → before flames)* couver; *(→ after burning)* fumer (**b**) *(feeling, rebellion)* couver; **her eyes smouldered with passion** son regard brûlait de désir

smouldering, *Am* **smoldering** ['sməʊldərɪŋ] *adj (fire, anger, passion, jealousy)* qui couve; *(embers, ruins)* fumant; *(eyes)* de braise

SMS [ˌesem'es] *n Tel (abbr* **short message service)** service *m* SMS

SMSA [ˌesemˌes'eɪ] *n Am (abbr* **Standard Metropolitan Statistical Area)** = zone urbaine utilisée comme base d'études statistiques

SMTP [ˌesemˌtiː'piː] *n Comput (abbr* **Simple Mail Transfer Protocol)** protocole *m* SMTP

smudge [smʌdʒ] **1** *n* (**a**) *(on face, clothes, surface)* (petite) tache *f*; *(of make-up)* traînée *f*; *(on page of print)* bavure *f*; **you've got a smudge on your chin** tu as du noir sur le menton; **the ship was just a smudge on the horizon** le navire n'était plus qu'une tache à l'horizon

(**b**) *Am (fire)* feu *m* (de jardin)

2 *vt (face, hands)* salir; *(clothes, surface)* tacher, salir; *(ink)* répandre; *(writing)* etaler; *(eye make-up)* faire couler; **you've made me smudge my lipstick** à cause de toi je me suis mis du rouge à lèvres partout

3 *vi (ink, make-up)* faire des taches; *(print)* être maculé; *(wet paint)* s'étaler

smudgy ['smʌdʒɪ] *(compar* **smudgier,** *superl* **smudgiest)** *adj (make-up, ink)* étalé; *(print, page)* maculé; *(writing)* à demi effacé; *(face)* sali, taché; *(outline)* estompé, brouillé

smug [smʌg] *(compar* **smugger,** *superl* **smuggest)** *adj Pej (person)* content de soi, suffisant; *(attitude, manner, voice)* suffisant; **he has a smug look** il a un air suffisant, il a l'air content de lui; **stop looking so smug** arrête de te croire supérieur; **he's so smug!** ce qu'il peut être suffisant! *ou* content de sa petite personne!; **you sound awfully smug about the whole thing** tu as l'air content *ou* fier de toi

smuggle ['smʌgəl] **1** *vt (contraband)* passer en contrebande; *(into prison → mail, arms)* introduire clandestinement; **to smuggle sth through customs** passer qch en fraude à la douane; **to smuggle sb into a country** faire entrer qn clandestinement dans un pays; **to smuggle sb out of a country** faire sortir qn clandestinement d'un pays; **the terrorists were smuggled over the border** les terroristes ont passé la frontière clandestinement; **he managed to smuggle a knife into the prison** il a réussi à faire entrer *ou* passer clandestinement un couteau dans la prison; **they are suspected of smuggling arms/heroin** on les soupçonne de trafic d'armes/d'héroïne; *Fig* **to smuggle sth into a room** [illegible] une pièce

2 *vi* faire de la contrebande

►**smuggle in** *vt sep (on a large scale → drugs, arms)* faire entrer *ou* passer en contrebande; *(as tourist → cigarettes, alcohol)* introduire en fraude; *(into prison, classroom)* introduire clandestinement

►**smuggle out** *vt sep (arms, drugs)* faire sortir en contrebande; *(when coming through customs)* faire sortir en fraude; *(from prison, classroom)* faire sortir clandestinement

smuggled ['smʌgəld] *adj (arms, drugs)* passé en contrebande; *(excised goods)* de contrebande; **smuggled goods** contrebande *f*

smuggler ['smʌglə(r)] *n* contrebandier(ère) *m,f*

smuggling ['smʌglɪŋ] *n (of drugs, arms etc)* trafic *m*, contrebande *f*; *(when coming through customs)* fraude *f*

►► ***smuggling operation*** opération *f* de contrebande

smugly ['smʌglɪ] *adv (say)* d'un ton suffisant,

S–Sms

avec suffisance; *(look, smile)* d'un air suffisant, avec suffisance

smugness ['smʌgnɪs] *n* suffisance *f*

Smurf [smɜːf] *n* Schtroumpf *m*

smut [smʌt] *(pt & pp* **smutted,** *cont* **smutting)** **1** *n* **(a)** *(UNCOUNT) (obscenity)* cochonneries *fpl*; *(pornography)* porno *m*; **that bookshop sells nothing but smut** cette librairie ne vend que du porno; **to talk smut** dire des cochonneries; **that book's/film's just smut** il n'y a que des cochonneries dans ce livre/film
(b) *Br (speck of dirt)* poussière *f*; *(smudge of soot)* tache *f* de suie; **you've got a smut on your cheek** tu as de la suie sur la joue; **I've got a smut in my eye** j'ai une poussière dans l'œil
(c) *Agr* charbon *m ou* nielle *f* du blé
2 *vt (smudge, stain)* salir, noircir

smutch [smʌtʃ] = **smudge**

smuttily ['smʌtɪlɪ] *adv* indécemment, grossièrement

smuttiness ['smʌtɪnɪs] *n* obscénité *f*

smutty ['smʌtɪ] *(compar* **smuttier,** *superl* **smuttiest)** *adj* **(a)** *(obscene)* cochon; *(pornographic)* porno; **a book full of smutty stories** un livre plein d'histoires cochonnes **(b)** *(dirty → hands, face, surface)* sali, noirci

Smyrna ['smɜːnə] *n* Smyrne

snack [snæk] **1** *n* **(a)** *(light meal)* casse-croûte *m inv*, en-cas *m inv*; **to have a snack** casser la croûte, manger un morceau; **if you eat too many snacks between meals...** si vous grignotez (trop) entre les repas...; **to have a snack lunch** déjeuner sur le pouce
(b) *(usu pl) (appetizer → crisps, peanuts etc)* amuse-gueule *m*
2 *vi* manger entre les repas; **I've been snacking on chocolates all day** j'ai passé la journée à grignoter des chocolats; **a panda snacking on some bamboo** un panda qui mange des pousses de bambou
▸▸ ***snack bar*** snack *m*, snack-bar *m*; ***snack food*** *(UNCOUNT)* amuse-gueules *mpl*

snaffle ['snæfəl] **1** *vt* **(a)** *Br Fam (get)* rafler; *(steal)* piquer, faucher; **who's snaffled my pen?** qui est-ce qui m'a piqué mon stylo?; **they snaffled all the prizes** ils ont raflé tous les prix
(b) *Horseriding* mettre un bridon à
2 *n Horseriding* mors *m* brisé, bridon *m*
▸▸ *Horseriding* ***snaffle bit*** mors *m* brisé, bridon *m*

►**snaffle up** *vt sep Br Fam (bargains, cakes etc)* rafler; **they snaffled up all the prizes** ils ont raflé tous les prix

snafu [snæ'fuː] *Fam* **1** *adj* en pagaille, bordélique
2 *vt Am* mettre la pagaille *ou* le bordel dans
3 *n (confused situation)* pagaille *f*, bordel *m*; *(blunder)* grosse gaffe *f*

snag [snæg] *(pt & pp* **snagged,** *cont* **snagging)** **1** *n* **(a)** *(problem)* problème *m*, hic *m*; **to come across** *or* **to run into a snag** tomber sur un hic *ou* sur un os; **there are several snags in your plan** il y a plusieurs choses qui clochent dans ton projet; **that's the snag!** voilà le hic!; **the only snag is that you have to pay first** le seul problème, c'est qu'il faut payer d'abord
(b) *(tear → in garment)* accroc *m*; *(→ in stocking)* fil *m* tiré
(c) *(sharp protuberance)* aspérité *f*; *(tree stump)* chicot *m*; **I caught my dress on a snag** j'ai fait un accroc à ma robe
(d) *Austr Fam (sausage)* saucisse ❑ *f*
2 *vt* **(a)** *(tear → cloth, garment)* faire un accroc à, déchirer; **she snagged her stocking on the brambles** elle a accroché son bas *ou* fait un accroc à son bas dans les ronces
(b) *Am Fam (obtain)* dégoter
3 *vi* s'accrocher; **the rope snagged on the ledge** la corde s'est trouvée coincée sur le rebord

snaggletooth ['snægəltuːθ] *n* dent *f* saillante

snaggle-toothed ['snægəl-] *adj Am* aux dents mal rangées

snail [sneɪl] *n* escargot *m*; **at a snail's pace** *(move)* comme un escargot; *(change, progress)* très lentement
▸▸ *Aut* ***snail cam*** came *f* en colimaçon; *Fam Hum* ***snail mail*** courrier *m* escargot, = courrier postal

snailfish ['sneɪlfɪʃ] *n Ich* limace *f* de mer

snake [sneɪk] **1** *n* **(a)** *(reptile)* serpent *m*; *Fam Old-fashioned* **snakes alive!** ciel!
(b) *(person)* vipère *f*; **he's a real snake** c'est un faux jeton; **a snake in the grass** un faux jeton
(c) *Econ* serpent *m* (monétaire)
2 *vi* serpenter, *Literary* sinuer; **the smoke snaked upwards** une volute de fumée s'élevait vers le ciel; **the path snaked between the trees** le chemin serpentait entre les arbres
3 *vt* **the river/road snakes its way down to the sea** le fleuve serpente/la route descend en lacets jusqu'à la mer
▸▸ ***snake charmer*** charmeur(euse) *m,f* de serpent; ***snake oil*** remède *m* de charlatan; *Am Fig* ***snake pit*** fosse *f* aux serpents, nid *m* de vipères

snakebird ['sneɪkbɜːd] *n Orn* oiseau-serpent *m*

snakebite ['sneɪkbaɪt] *n* **(a)** *(wound)* morsure *f* de serpent **(b)** *Fam (drink)* = boisson comprenant une mesure de bière et une mesure de cidre

snake-like *adj* anguiforme, ophidien

snakes and ladders *n (UNCOUNT) Br* = jeu d'enfants ressemblant au jeu de l'oie

snakeskin ['sneɪkskɪn] **1** *n* peau *f* de serpent
2 *comp (shoes, handbag)* en (peau de) serpent

snaky ['sneɪkɪ] *(compar* **snakier,** *superl* **snakiest)** *adj* **(a)** *(sinuous → river, road, movement)* sinueux **(b)** *(treacherous → person)* insidieux, perfide; *(→ cunning, acts)* perfide

snap [snæp] *(pt & pp* **snapped,** *cont* **snapping)** **1** *n* **(a)** *(of whip)* claquement *m*; *(of something breaking, opening, closing)* bruit *m* sec; **with a snap of his fingers** en claquant des doigts; **to open/to close sth with a snap** ouvrir/refermer qch d'un coup sec; **the branch broke with a snap** la branche a cassé avec un bruit sec
(b) *(of jaws)* **to make a snap at sb/sth** essayer de mordre qn/qch; **the dog made a snap at the bone** le chien a essayé de happer l'os
(c) *Fam (photo)* photo ❑ *f*, instantané ❑ *m*; **to take a snap of sb** prendre qn en photo; **holiday snaps** photos *fpl* de vacances
(d) *Br Cards* ≃ bataille *f*; **to play snap** ≃ jouer à la bataille
(e) *Met* **a cold snap, a snap of cold weather** une vague de froid
(f) *Fam (effort)* effort ❑ *m*; *(energy)* énergie ❑ *f*; **put some snap into it!** allez, mettez-y un peu de nerf!
(g) *Am Fam (easy task)* **it's a snap!** c'est simple comme bonjour!
(h) *Culin* biscuit *m*, petit gâteau *m* sec
(i) *(clasp, fastener)* fermoir *m*; *(press stud)* bouton-pression *m*
(j) *NEng Fam (food)* bouffe *f*
(k) *(in American football)* remise *f* directe
2 *adj* **(a)** *(vote)* éclair; *(reaction)* immédiat; *(judgment)* irréfléchi, hâtif; **she made a snap decision to go to Paris** elle décida tout à coup d'aller à Paris; **the President made a snap decision to send troops** le Président décida immédiatement d'envoyer des troupes; **to call a snap election** procéder à une élection surprise
(b) *Am Fam (easy)* facile ❑
3 *vt* **(a)** *(break)* casser net; **to snap sth in two** *or* **in half** casser qch en deux d'un coup sec
(b) *(crack → whip, fingers, rubber band)* faire claquer; **she snapped her case shut** elle ferma sa valise d'un coup sec; **she only needs to snap her fingers and he comes running** il lui suffit de claquer des doigts pour qu'il arrive en courant; **to snap one's fingers at sb** *(to gain attention)* faire claquer ses doigts pour attirer l'attention de qn; *(mockingly)* faire la nique à qn; **they snapped their fingers at the idea** ils ont rejeté l'idée avec mépris
(c) *(say brusquely)* dire d'un ton sec *ou* brusque; **"no", he snapped** "non", dit-il d'un ton sec; **to snap an order at sb** lancer un ordre à qn d'un ton sec
(d) *(seize → gen)* saisir; *(→ of dog)* happer; **she snapped the letter out of my hand** elle m'a arraché la lettre des mains
(e) *Fam (photograph)* prendre une photo de ❑
4 *vi* **(a)** *(break → branch)* se casser net *ou* avec un bruit sec, craquer; *(→ elastic band)* claquer; *(→ rope)* se casser, rompre; **to snap in two** se casser net
(b) *(make cracking sound → whip, fingers, jaw)* claquer; **to snap open/shut** s'ouvrir/se fermer avec un bruit sec *ou* avec un claquement; *Fam* **snap to it!** grouille-toi!, magne-toi!
(c) *Fig (person, nerves)* craquer; **after his divorce he just snapped** après son divorce, il a craqué
(d) *(speak brusquely)* **to snap at sb** parler à qn d'un ton sec; **there's no need to snap!** tu n'as pas besoin de me/lui/*etc* parler sur ce ton-là!
(e) *(try to bite)* **to snap at** chercher à *ou* essayer de mordre; **the dog snapped at his ankles** le chien essayait de lui mordre les chevilles; **the fish snapped at the bait** les poissons cherchaient à happer l'appât; *Fig* **the taxmen were beginning to snap at his heels** les impôts commençaient à le talonner
(f) *Fam (take photos)* **tourists snapping away with their cameras** des touristes qui n'arrêtent pas de prendre des photos
5 *exclam Br* **(a)** *Cards* **snap!** ≃ bataille!
(b) *Fam (in identical situation)* **snap!** tiens! ❑, quelle coïncidence! ❑; **my mother's a teacher – snap, so's mine!** ma mère est prof – tiens! la mienne aussi!
6 *adv* **to go snap** casser net
▸▸ *Am* ***snap bean*** haricot *m* vert; ***snap fastener*** *(press stud)* bouton-pression *m*, pression *f*; *(clasp → on handbag, necklace)* fermoir *m* (à pression)

►**snap back** *vi* **(a)** *(trigger, elastic)* revenir brusquement
(b) *(reply brusquely)* répondre d'un ton sec

►**snap off 1** *vt sep* casser; **he snapped off a piece of chocolate** il a cassé un morceau de chocolat; *Fam* **to snap sb's head off** envoyer promener qn
2 *vi* (se) casser net

►**snap on** *vt sep Am* **to snap a light on** allumer une lampe

►**snap out 1** *vt sep (question)* poser d'un ton sec; *(order, warning)* lancer brutalement; **"stop!", he snapped out** "arrête!", lança-t-il brutalement
2 *vi* **to snap out of** *(depression, mood, trance)* se sortir de, se tirer de; *(temper)* dominer, maîtriser; **snap out of it!** *(out of depression)* secoue-toi!; *(out of bad temper)* arrête de t'énerver comme ça!; **he can't seem to snap out of this mood he's in** il n'a pas l'air de vouloir changer d'humeur

►**snap up** *vt sep* **(a)** *(of dog, fish)* happer, attraper
(b) *(bargain, offer, opportunity)* sauter sur, se jeter sur; **the records were snapped up in no time** les disques sont partis *ou* se sont vendus en un rien de temps; **the cakes/the best bargains were soon snapped up** les gâteaux sont partis/les meilleures affaires sont parties très vite
(c) *Am Fam (idiom)* **snap it up!** dépêchons!

snapback ['snæpbæk] *n Am (recovery → of prices)* redressement *m*; **our team made a snapback to win in the last minutes** notre équipe s'est ressaisie et a remporté le match dans les dernières minutes

snapdragon ['snæp,drægən] *n Bot* muflier *m*, gueule-de-loup *f*

snap-on *adj (collar, cuffs, hood)* détachable, amovible (à pressions)

snapper ['snæpə(r)] *(pl* **inv** *or* **snappers)** *n Ich* vivaneau *m*

snappily ['snæpɪlɪ] *adv* **(a)** *(dress)* avec chic **(b)** *(act, converse)* vivement; *(work)* vite, sans traîner; *(reply)* d'un ton brusque

snapping ['snæpɪŋ] *adj*
▸▸ *Zool* ***snapping turtle*** tortue *f* happante

snappish ['snæpɪʃ] *adj (dog)* hargneux, toujours prêt à mordre; *(person)* hargneux; *(voice)* mordant, cassant; *(reply)* brusque, cassant, sec (sèche); **she's in a very snappish mood today** elle n'est pas à prendre avec des pincettes aujourd'hui

snappishly ['snæpɪʃlɪ] *adv (reply)* d'un ton hargneux

snappishness ['snæpɪʃnɪs] *n* hargne *f*

snappy ['snæpɪ] *(compar* **snappier,** *superl* **snappiest)** *adj* **(a)** *(fashionable)* **she's a snappy dresser** elle sait s'habiller
(b) *(lively → pace, rhythm)* vif, entraînant; *(→ dialogue, debate)* plein d'entrain, vivant; *(→ style, slogan)* qui a du punch; *(→ reply)* bien

envoyé; *Fam* **look snappy!** grouille-toi!, active!; *Fam* **make it snappy!** grouille-toi!, et que ça saute!

(**c**) *(unfriendly → person)* hargneux; *(→ answer)* brusque; *(→ voice)* cassant; **you're a bit snappy today!** tu es de mauvais poil aujourd'hui!; **a snappy little dog** un petit roquet

snapshot ['snæpʃɒt] *n* instantané *m*

snare [sneə(r)] **1** *n* (**a**) *(in hunting)* lacet *m*, collet *m*; *Fig* piège *m*, traquenard *m*; **to lay** *or* **set a snare** *(for animal)* poser un collet; *Fig* tendre un piège; **to be caught in a snare** *(animal)* être pris au lacet; *Fig (person)* être pris au piège; *Literary* **the snares of love** les pièges *mpl* de l'amour

(**b**) *Mus* caisse *f* claire

2 *vt (bird)* prendre au filet; *(animal)* prendre au collet *ou* au lacet; *Fig (person)* prendre au piège

►► *Mus* ***snare drum*** caisse *f* claire

snarf [snɑːf] *vt Am Fam* descendre, bâfrer

snarl [snɑːl] **1** *vi* (**a**) *(dog)* gronder, grogner; *(tiger)* feuler; *(person)* gronder; **the dog snarled at me as I walked past** le chien a grogné quand je suis passé; **the lions snarled at their tamer** les lions rugissaient contre leur dompteur; **there's no need to snarl at me!** tu n'as pas besoin de prendre ce ton hargneux pour me parler!

(**b**) *(thread, rope, hair)* s'emmêler; *(traffic)* se bloquer; *(plan, programme)* cafouiller

2 *vt* (**a**) *(of person)* lancer d'une voix rageuse, rugir; **to snarl a reply** répondre d'une voix rageuse; **"go away!", he snarled** "va-t-en!", gronda-t-il

(**b**) *(thread, rope, hair)* enchevêtrer, emmêler; **you hair is all snarled** tu as les cheveux tout emmêlés; **the wool is all snarled** la laine est tout enchevêtrée

(**c**) *Metal* repousser

3 *n* (**a**) *(sound)* grognement *m*, grondement *m*; *(of tiger)* feulement *m*; **to give a snarl** *(dog)* pousser un grognement; *(tiger)* feuler; *(person)* gronder; **she answered him with a snarl** elle lui a répondu d'un ton hargneux

(**b**) *(tangle → in thread, wool, hair)* nœud *m*, nœuds *mpl*; **caught in a snarl of traffic** pris dans un embouteillage *ou* un bouchon

►**snarl up** **1** *vi (thread, rope, hair)* s'emmêler; *Br (traffic)* se bloquer; *(plan, programme)* cafouiller

2 *vt sep (usu passive)* (**a**) *(thread, rope, hair)* emmêler, enchevêtrer; **to get snarled up** s'emmêler, s'enchevêtrer

(**b**) *Br (traffic)* bloquer, coincer; *(plans)* faire cafouiller; **the traffic gets snarled up at the traffic lights** la circulation bouchonne aux feux; **the postal service is completely snarled up** le service des postes est complètement bloqué

snarler ['snɑːlə(r)] *n* (**a**) *(ill-tempered person)* grognon *mf* (**b**) *Metal (person)* travailleur *m* au repoussé; *(snarling iron)* repoussoir *m*

snarling ['snɑːlɪŋ] **1** *adj* grondant, grognant

2 *n (sound)* grondement *m*, grognement *m*

►► *Metal* ***snarling iron*** repoussoir *m*

snarl-up *n Br (of traffic)* bouchon *m*, embouteillage *m*; *(of plans)* cafouillage *m*

snarly ['snɑːlɪ] *adj* hargneux, grognon

snatch [snætʃ] **1** *vt* (**a**) *(seize → bag, money)* saisir; *(→ opportunity)* saisir, sauter sur; **to snatch sth from sb** arracher qch à qn; **to snatch sth from sb's hands** arracher qch des mains de qn; **a boy on a motorbike snatched her bag** un garçon en moto lui a arraché son sac; **his mother snatched him out of the path of the bus** sa mère l'a attrapé par le bras pour l'empêcher d'être renversé par le bus

(**b**) *(manage to get → meal, drink)* avaler à la hâte; *(→ holiday, rest)* réussir à avoir; **to snatch some sleep** réussir à dormir un peu; **I snatched three hours' sleep** j'ai fait un petit somme de trois heures; **I was only able to snatch a sandwich** j'ai juste eu le temps d'avaler un sandwich; **to snatch a glance at sb** lancer un coup d'œil furtif à qn

(**c**) *(steal → gen)* voler; *(→ kiss)* voler, dérober; *(→ victory)* décrocher; **she had her bag snatched** on lui a volé son sac

(**d**) *(kidnap)* kidnapper

(**e**) *(in weightlifting)* arracher

2 *vi* **don't snatch!** *(to child → from hand)* prends-le doucement!; *(→ from plate)* prends ton temps!

3 *n* (**a**) *(grab)* geste *m* vif de la main *(pour attraper qch)*; **to make a snatch at sth** essayer de saisir *ou* d'attraper qch; *Fig* **to make a snatch at victory** essayer de s'emparer de la victoire

(**b**) *Br Fam (robbery)* vol *m* à l'arraché ❑; **bag snatch** vol *m* (de sac) à l'arraché; **to carry out a wages/jewellery snatch** voler la paye/des bijoux ❑

(**c**) *(kidnapping)* kidnapping *m*

(**d**) *(fragment → of conversation)* fragment *m*, bribes *fpl*; *(→ of song, music)* fragment *m*, mesure *f*; *(→ of poetry)* fragment *m*, vers *m*; **she could only catch a few snatches of their conversation/the song** elle ne put saisir que quelques bribes de leur conversation/quelques mesures de la chanson

(**e**) *(short period)* courte période *f*; **to sleep in snatches** dormir par intervalles *ou* de façon intermittente; **to work in snatches** travailler par à-coups

(**f**) *(in weightlifting)* arraché *m*

(**g**) *Vulg (woman's genitals)* cramouille *f*, chatte *f*

►► *Br* ***snatch squad*** = groupe de policiers chargé d'arrêter les meneurs (lors d'une manifestation)

►**snatch at** *vt insep (try to grab)* essayer de saisir *ou* d'attraper qch; *Fig* **to snatch at an opportunity** saisir une occasion (au vol); *Fig* **she snatches at the slightest hope/opportunity** elle s'accroche au moindre espoir/saute sur la moindre occasion

►**snatch away** *vt sep (letter, plate etc)* arracher, enlever d'un geste vif; *(hope)* ôter, enlever; **to snatch sth away from sb** arracher qch à qn; **she snatched her hand away from the hot stove** elle a vite enlevé sa main du fourneau brûlant; **victory was snatched away from them in the last minute** la victoire leur a été soufflée à la dernière minute

►**snatch up** *vt sep* ramasser vite *ou* vivement *ou* d'un seul coup; **she snatched up her child** elle a saisi *ou* empoigné son enfant

-snatcher ['snætʃə(r)] *suff* **bag-snatcher** voleur(euse) *m,f* (de sac) à l'arraché

snatchy ['snætʃɪ] (*compar* **snatchier,** *superl* **snatchiest**) *adj Fam (sleep)* intermittent ❑; *(work)* fait par à-coups *ou* de façon intermittente ❑, *(conversation)* à bâtons rompus ❑

snazzily ['snæzɪlɪ] *adv Fam (dress)* avec chic ❑

snazzy ['snæzɪ] (*compar* **snazzier,** *superl* **snazziest**) *adj Fam* chicos *(inv)*, classe *(inv)*; **she's a snazzy dresser** elle s'habille avec chic ❑, elle est toujours bien sapée; **he's got a snazzy new suit** il s'est acheté un nouveau costume drôlement chic

sneak [sniːk] (*Br pt & pp* **sneaked**, *Am pt & pp* **sneaked** *or* **snuck** [snʌk]) **1** *vi* (**a**) *(verb of movement)* se glisser, se faufiler; *(furtively)* se glisser furtivement; *(quietly)* se glisser à pas feutrés *ou* sans faire de bruit; *(secretly)* se glisser sans se faire remarquer; **to sneak up/down the stairs** monter/descendre l'escalier furtivement; **to sneak into/out of a room** entrer dans une pièce/sortir d'une pièce à pas feutrés; **he sneaked into her bedroom** il s'est glissé *ou* faufilé dans sa chambre; **we sneaked in at the back** nous nous sommes glissés dans le fond discrètement *ou* sans nous faire remarquer; **they sneaked into the cinema without paying** ils se sont introduits dans le cinéma sans payer; **we managed to sneak past the guards/window** nous avons réussi à passer devant les gardes/la fenêtre sans nous faire remarquer; **I sneaked round to the back door** je me suis glissé sans bruit jusqu'à la porte de derrière

(**b**) *Fam (tell tales)* cafter, cafarder; **to sneak on sb** cafter qn, cafarder qn

2 *vt* (**a**) *(give → letter, message)* glisser en douce *ou* sans se faire remarquer; **they sneaked the money to her** ils lui ont glissé l'argent en douce; **the visitor managed to sneak him a knife** le visiteur réussit à lui glisser un couteau sans se faire remarquer; **she sneaked her boyfriend into her bedroom** elle fit entrer son petit ami en douce dans sa chambre

(**b**) *(take)* enlever, prendre; **he sneaked the keys from her pocket** il a pris les clés dans sa poche sans qu'elle s'en aperçoive; **to sneak a look at sth** lancer *ou* jeter un coup d'œil furtif à qch

(**c**) *Fam (steal)* chiper, piquer, faucher

3 *n* (**a**) *Fam (devious person)* faux jeton *m*

(**b**) *Br Fam (tell-tale)* cafardeur(euse) *m,f*, mouchard(e) *m,f*

(**c**) *Am Fam* **sneaks** *(sneakers)* baskets ❑ *fpl*

4 *adj (attack)* furtif

►► ***sneak preview*** avant-première *f* privée; **I was given a sneak preview of the new film** j'ai pu voir le nouveau film en avant-première; *Br* ***sneak thief*** chapardeur(euse) *m,f*

►**sneak about, sneak around** *vi (move furtively)* rôder

►**sneak away, sneak off** *vi* se défiler, s'esquiver

►**sneak up** *vi* s'approcher à pas feutrés *ou* furtivement; **to sneak up on** *or* **behind sb** s'approcher de qn à pas feutrés

sneaker ['sniːkə(r)] *n Am* (chaussure *f* de) tennis *m or f*, basket *f*

sneakily ['sniːkɪlɪ] *adv (slyly)* sournoisement; *(furtively)* en cachette

sneaking ['sniːkɪŋ] *adj (feeling, respect)* inavoué, secret(ète); **she had a sneaking suspicion that he was guilty** quelque chose lui disait qu'il était coupable; **she felt a sneaking admiration for him** elle ne pouvait (pas) s'empêcher de l'admirer; **I had a sneaking feeling that he was right** quelque chose me disait qu'il avait raison

sneakingly ['sniːkɪŋlɪ] *adv (furtively)* furtivement, en cachette

sneaky ['sniːkɪ] (*compar* **sneakier,** *superl* **sneakiest**) *adj (person)* sournois; *(action)* fait en cachette, fait à la dérobée; **I caught him having a sneaky cigarette** je l'ai surpris en train de fumer une cigarette en cachette

sneer [snɪə(r)] **1** *vi* ricaner, sourire avec mépris *ou* d'un air méprisant; **don't sneer** ne sois pas si méprisant; **to sneer at sb/sth** se moquer de qn/qch

2 *n (facial expression)* ricanement *m*, rictus *m*; *(remark)* raillerie *f*, sarcasme *m*; **"who do you think you are?", he said with a sneer** "pour qui est-ce que tu te prends?", dit-il en ricanant *ou* ricana-t-il

sneerer ['snɪərə(r)] *n* ricaneur(euse) *m,f*, moqueur(euse) *m,f*

sneering ['snɪərɪŋ] **1** *adj* ricaneur, méprisant

2 *n (UNCOUNT)* ricanement *m*, ricanements *mpl*

sneeringly ['snɪərɪŋlɪ] *adv (look)* d'un air ricaneur, en ricanant; *(say)* d'un ton ricaneur, en ricanant

sneeze [sniːz] **1** *n* éternuement *m*

2 *vi* éternuer; *Fam Fig* **an offer not to be sneezed at** une proposition qui n'est pas à dédaigner ❑ *ou* sur laquelle il ne faut pas cracher; **when America sneezes Britain/Asia catches a cold** les problèmes des États-Unis se répercutent toujours sur la Grande-Bretagne/l'Asie

sneezer ['sniːzə(r)] *n* éternueur(euse) *m,f*

sneezewort ['sniːzwɜːt] *n Bot* achillée *f* sternutatoire

sneezing ['sniːzɪŋ] *n* éternuement *m*; **his sneezing irritates me** ses éternuements m'agacent

►► ***sneezing fit*** crise *f* d'éternuements; ***sneezing powder*** poudre *f* à éternuer

snell [snel] *n Fishing* empile *f*

snib [snɪb] *Scot* **1** *n (latch)* loquet *m*

2 *vt (door, window)* fermer au loquet

snick [snɪk] **1** *n* (**a**) *(notch)* petite entaille *f*, encoche *f*; **to make a snick in sth** faire une entaille *ou* une encoche à qch (**b**) *(in cricket)* = coup (de batte) qui fait dévier la balle

2 *vt* (**a**) *(cloth, wood)* faire une petite entaille *ou* une encoche dans (**b**) *(in cricket → ball)* couper

snicker ['snɪkə(r)] **1** *n* (**a**) *(snigger)* ricanement *m* (**b**) *(of horse)* (petit) hennissement *m*

2 *vi* (**a**) *(snigger)* ricaner; **to snicker at sb** se moquer de qn (**b**) *(horse)* hennir doucement

snide [snaɪd] *adj (sarcastic)* narquois, railleur; *(unfriendly)* inamical; **I've had enough of your snide remarks!** j'en ai assez de tes sarcasmes!; **a**

snide dig at his colleagues une remarque désobligeante sur ses collègues

snidely ['snaɪdlɪ] *adv (sarcastically)* railleusement; *(in an unfriendly manner)* insidieusement

sniff [snɪf] **1** *vi* (**a**) *(from cold, crying etc)* renifler
(**b**) *(disdainfully)* faire la grimace *ou* la moue
2 *vt* (**a**) *(smell → food, soap)* renifler, sentir l'odeur de; *(→ rose, perfume)* humer, sentir l'odeur de; *(of dog)* renifler, flairer
(**b**) *(inhale → air)* humer, respirer; *(→ smelling salts)* respirer; *(→ cocaine)* sniffer, priser; *(→ snuff)* priser; *(→ glue)* respirer, sniffer
(**c**) *(say disdainfully)* dire d'un air méprisant *ou* dédaigneux; **"it's not my cup", she sniffed** "ce n'est pas ma tasse", fit-elle d'un air méprisant
3 *n (gen)* reniflement *m*; **to give a sniff** renifler; *(scornfully)* faire la grimace *ou* la moue; **"I've no idea", she said with a scornful sniff** "je n'en ai aucune idée", dit-elle d'un air dédaigneux; **to have** *or* **to take a sniff of sth** renifler *ou* flairer qch; **take a sniff of this meat/this perfume** renifle-moi cette viande/ce parfum; *Fam* **one sniff of that stuff is enough to knock you out** une bouffée de ce truc et tu tombes raide; *Fig* **I didn't even get a sniff of a cup of coffee** ils ne m'ont même pas offert une tasse de café

▸**sniff at** *vt insep* (**a**) **to sniff at sth** *(of person)* renifler qch; *(of dog)* renifler *ou* flairer qch
(**b**) *Fig* faire la grimace *ou* la moue devant; **to sniff at an idea/a suggestion** faire la grimace devant une idée/suggestion; **their offer is not to be sniffed at** leur offre n'est pas à dédaigner

▸**sniff out** *vt sep (of dog)* découvrir en reniflant *ou* en flairant; *(of person → criminal)* découvrir, dépister; *(→ secret)* découvrir

sniffer ['snɪfə(r)] *n (person → gen)* renifleur(euse) *m,f*; **cocaine sniffer** = personne qui sniffe de la cocaïne
▸▸ ***sniffer dog*** chien *m* policier *(dressé pour le dépistage de la drogue ou des explosifs)*

sniffing ['snɪfɪŋ] **1** *adj* qui renifle
2 *n* reniflement *m*

sniffle ['snɪfəl] **1** *vi (sniff)* renifler; *(have runny nose)* avoir le nez qui coule
2 *n (sniff)* (léger) reniflement *m*; *(cold)* petit rhume *m* de cerveau; *Fam* **to have the sniffles** avoir le nez qui coule ❑

sniffling ['snɪflɪŋ] **1** *adj* qui renifle
2 *n* reniflement *m*

sniffy ['snɪfɪ] *(compar* **sniffier,** *superl* **sniffiest)** *adj Fam* méprisant ❑, dédaigneux ❑; **to be sniffy about sth** faire le dédaigneux devant qch

snifter ['snɪftə(r)] *n* (**a**) *Br Fam (drink)* petit verre *m* (d'alcool) ❑; **fancy a snifter?** tu prends un petit verre? (**b**) *Am (glass)* verre *m* à dégustation

snigger ['snɪgə(r)] **1** *vi* ricaner, rire dans sa barbe; **to snigger at** *(appearance)* se moquer de, ricaner à la vue de; **he sniggered at this suggestion** il a ricané en entendant cette suggestion
2 *n* ricanement *m*; **to give a snigger** ricaner

sniggerer ['snɪgərə(r)] *n* ricaneur(euse) *m,f*

sniggering ['snɪgərɪŋ] **1** *n (UNCOUNT)* ricanements *mpl*
2 *adj* ricaneur

snip [snɪp] *(pt & pp* **snipped,** *cont* **snipping) 1** *n* (**a**) *(cut)* petit coup *m (de ciseaux etc)*, petite entaille *f ou* incision *f*; *Br Fam* **to have the snip** *(vasectomy)* se faire faire une vasectomie ❑
(**b**) *(sound)* clic *m*; **he could hear the snip of scissors** il entendait le clic-clac de ciseaux
(**c**) *(small piece → of cloth, paper)* petit bout *m*; *(→ of hair)* mèche *f* (coupée)
(**d**) *Br Fam (bargain)* affaire ❑ *f*, occase *f*; *(horse)* tuyau *m* sûr
(**e**) *Br Fam (cinch)* **it's a snip!** c'est du gâteau!, c'est simple comme bonjour!
2 *vt* couper *(en donnant de petits coups de ciseaux)*
3 *vi* **he was snipping at the hedge** il coupait la haie

▸**snip off** *vt sep* couper *ou* enlever (à petits coups de ciseaux); **the rose heads had been snipped off** les roses avaient été décapitées

snipe [snaɪp] *(pl* **inv) 1** *n Orn* bécassine *f*
2 *vi* (**a**) *(shoot)* tirer (d'une position cachée); **to snipe at sb** tirer sur qn; *Fig (criticize)* critiquer qn par en-dessous; **sniping criticism** critiques *fpl* insidieuses (**b**) *Hunt* aller à la chasse aux bécassines

sniper ['snaɪpə(r)] *n* tireur *m* embusqué *ou* isolé; **killed by a sniper's bullet** abattu par un tireur (embusqué)

sniping ['snaɪpɪŋ] **1** *n Mil* tir *m* d'embuscade; *Fig* critique *f* sournoise (**at sb** de qn)
2 *adj (criticism, remarks)* sournois

snippet ['snɪpɪt] *n (of material, paper)* petit bout *m*; *(of conversation, information)* bribe *f*; **a snippet of news** une petite nouvelle

snipping ['snɪpɪŋ] *n (piece cut off)* morceau *m* coupé; *(of material)* petit coupon *m*

snippy ['snɪpɪ] *(compar* **snippier,** *superl* **snippiest)** *adj Fam (curt)* sec (sèche) ❑

snit [snɪt] *n Am Fam* **to be in a snit** être fumasse *ou* furibard

snitch [snɪtʃ] *Fam* **1** *n* (**a**) *(telltale)* cafard(e) *m,f*, cafteur(euse) *m,f* (**b**) *Br (nose)* blaire *m*, tarin *m* (**c**) *Br (idiom)* **it's a snitch** *(easy)* c'est simple comme bonjour; *(bargain)* c'est une (bonne) occase
2 *vi (tell tales)* cafter, cafarder; **to snitch on sb** cafter qn, cafarder qn
3 *vt (steal)* chiper, piquer, faucher

snitcher ['snɪtʃə(r)] *n Fam* cafard(e) *m,f*, cafteur(euse) *m,f*

snivel ['snɪvəl] *(Br pt & pp* **snivelled,** *cont* **snivelling,** *Am pt & pp* **sniveled,** *cont* **sniveling) 1** *vi (whine)* pleurnicher; *(sniff because of cold)* renifler (continuellement); *(have runny nose)* avoir le nez qui coule; **stop snivelling!** *(crying)* arrête de pleurnicher comme ça!; *(sniffing)* arrête de renifler comme ça!
2 *vt* **"it wasn't my fault", he snivelled** "ce n'était pas de ma faute", fit-il en pleurnichant
3 *n (sniffing)* reniflement *m*, reniflements *mpl*; *(tears)* pleurnichements *mpl*; **to have a snivel** pleurnicher

sniveller, *Am* **sniveler** ['snɪvələ(r)] *n* pleurnicheur(euse) *m,f*, pleurnichard(e) *m,f*

snivelling, *Am* **sniveling** ['snɪvəlɪŋ] **1** *adj* pleurnicheur, larmoyant; **shut up, you snivelling little wretch!** tais-toi, espèce de pleurnicheur!
2 *n (UNCOUNT) (crying)* pleurnicheries *fpl*; *(sniffing because of cold)* reniflements *mpl*; **stop your snivelling!** *(tears)* arrête de pleurnicher comme ça!; *(sniffing)* arrête de renifler comme ça!

SNO [ˌesen'əʊ] *n* (**a**) *Formerly (abbr* **Scottish National Orchestra)** = ancien nom de l'orchestre national d'Écosse (**b**) *(abbr* **Scottish National Opera)** = compagnie nationale écossaise d'opéra

snob [snɒb] *n* snob *mf*; **she's an awful snob/a bit of a snob** elle est terriblement/un peu snob; **to be an intellectual/a literary snob** être un snob intellectuel/en matière de littérature; **reverse** *or Br* **inverted snob** = personne d'origine modeste qui affiche un mépris pour les valeurs bourgeoises

snobbery ['snɒbərɪ] *n* snobisme *m*; **reverse** *or Br* **inverted snobbery** snobisme *m* à rebours; **intellectual snobbery** snobisme *m* intellectuel

snobbish ['snɒbɪʃ] *adj* snob

snobbishly ['snɒbɪʃlɪ] *adv* en snob

snobbishness ['snɒbɪʃnɪs] *n* snobisme *m*

snobby ['snɒbɪ] *(compar* **snobbier,** *superl* **snobbiest)** *adj Fam* snobinard

Sno-Cat® = **snowcat**

snog [snɒg] *(pt & pp* **snogged,** *cont* **snogging)** *Br Fam* **1** *vi* se bécoter, se rouler des pelles *ou* des patins
2 *vt* bécoter, rouler des pelles *ou* des patins à
3 *n* **to have a snog** se bécoter, se rouler des pelles *ou* des patins

snogging ['snɒgɪŋ] *n Br Fam* **there was a lot of snogging going on** ça se bécotait dans tous les coins

snood [snu:d] *n* (**a**) *(for hair)* résille *f* (**b**) *(hood)* cagoule *f* (**c**) *Fishing* empile *f* (**d**) *Scot Hist (headband)* = bandeau porté autrefois dans les cheveux par les jeunes femmes célibataires

snook [snu:k] *n* (**a**) *Ich* brochet *m* de mer (**b**) *(gesture)* pied *m* de nez; *Fam also Fig* **to cock a snook at sb** faire un pied de nez à qn

snooker ['snu:kə(r)] **1** *n* (**a**) *(game)* = billard qui se joue avec 22 boules
(**b**) *(shot)* snooker *m*
2 *vt* (**a**) *Br Fam (thwart)* mettre dans de beaux draps *ou* dans le pétrin, mettre dans l'embarras ❑; **if that doesn't work, we're snookered!** si ça marche pas, on est dans de beaux draps *ou* dans le pétrin!
(**b**) *Am Fam (trick)* arnaquer, avoir; **they've got us snookered!** ils nous ont eus!; **don't get snookered into anything!** te laisse pas arnaquer!
(**c**) *(in game of snooker)* = mettre dans une position difficile en faisant un snooker

snoop [snu:p] *Fam* **1** *vi* fourrer son nez dans les affaires des autres; **someone has been snooping about in my room** quelqu'un est venu fouiner dans ma chambre; **to snoop on sb** espionner qn ❑; **he's always snooping around** il est toujours à se mêler des affaires des autres ❑ *ou* de ce qui ne le regarde pas ❑
2 *n* (**a**) *(search)* **to have a snoop around** fouiller, fouiner; **she had a good snoop around the house** elle a fouillé *ou* fureté partout dans la maison; **I'll have a snoop around** je vais jeter un petit coup d'œil ❑
(**b**) *(nosy person)* fouineur(euse) *m,f*

snooper ['snu:pə(r)] *n Pej* fouineur(euse) *m,f*; **she's a born snooper** c'est une vraie fouineuse

snooperscope ['snu:pəskəʊp] *n Am* caméra *f* infrarouge

snoopy ['snu:pɪ] *adj Fam* curieux ❑, fouineur, fureteur

snoot [snu:t] *n Fam (nose)* blaire *m*, tarin *m*, pif *m*

snootiness ['snu:tɪnɪs] *n Fam* snobisme ❑ *m*

snooty ['snu:tɪ] *(compar* **snootier,** *superl* **snootiest)** *adj Fam (person)* bêcheur; *(restaurant)* snob; **she's very snooty** c'est une bêcheuse

snooze [snu:z] **1** *n* (**a**) *Fam (nap)* petit somme ❑ *m*, roupillon *m*; **to have a snooze** faire un petit somme ❑, piquer un roupillon; *(in afternoon)* faire la sieste ❑
(**b**) *(on alarm clock)* (position *f*) sommeil *m*
2 *vi Fam* sommeiller ❑, piquer un roupillon; *(in afternoon)* faire la sieste ❑
▸▸ ***snooze button*** bouton *m* de veille; ***snooze position*** *(on alarm clock)* (position *f*) sommeil *m*

snore [snɔ:(r)] **1** *vi* ronfler
2 *n* ronflement *m*

snorer ['snɔ:rə(r)] *n* ronfleur(euse) *m,f*

snoring ['snɔ:rɪŋ] *n (UNCOUNT)* ronflement *m*, ronflements *mpl*

snorkel ['snɔ:kəl] *(Br pt & pp* **snorkelled,** *cont* **snorkelling,** *Am pt & pp* **snorkeled,** *cont* **snorkeling) 1** *n (of swimmer)* tuba *m*; *(on submarine)* schnorchel *m*, schnorkel *m*
2 *vi* nager sous l'eau *(avec un tuba)*

snorkelling, *Am* **snorkeling** ['snɔ:klɪŋ] *n* **to go snorkelling** faire de la plongée avec un tuba

snort [snɔ:t] **1** *vi* (**a**) *(horse)* s'ébrouer; *(pig)* grogner; *(bull)* renâcler
(**b**) *(person → in anger)* grogner, ronchonner; **to snort with laughter** s'étouffer *ou* pouffer de rire; **he snorted in disbelief** il eut un petit grognement incrédule
2 *vt* (**a**) *(angrily)* grogner; *(laughingly)* dire en pouffant de rire; **"nonsense!", he snorted** "c'est absurde!", grommela-t-il
(**b**) *Fam Drugs slang (cocaine)* sniffer
3 *n* (**a**) *(of bull, horse)* ébrouement *m*; *(of person)* grognement *m*; **the horse gave a loud snort** le cheval s'ébroua bruyamment; **he gave a snort of contempt** il poussa un grognement de mépris; **he gave a snort of laughter** il pouffa de rire
(**b**) *Fam (drink)* petit verre *m* (d'alcool) ❑
(**c**) *Fam Drugs slang (of drug)* **to have a snort** se faire une ligne

snorter ['snɔ:tə(r)] *n Br Fam* (**a**) *(as intensifier)* **her second serve was a snorter** son deuxième service a été terrible; **a snorter of a performance** une interprétation époustouflante; **a snorter of a problem** un vrai casse-tête, un sacré problème; **he wrote them a real snorter of a letter** il leur a écrit une vraie lettre d'engueulade (**b**) *(drink)* petit verre *m* (d'alcool) ❑; **to have a snorter** prendre un petit verre

snorting ['snɔ:tɪŋ] **1** *adj (horse)* qui s'ébroue; *(pig)* qui grogne; *(bull)* qui renâcle
2 *n (of animal)* ébrouement *m*; *(of person)* grognement *m*

snot [snɒt] *n Fam* (**a**) *(mucus)* morve❑ *f*; (**b**) *(person)* morveux(euse) *m,f*; **you pathetic little snot!** pauvre petit morveux!
►► ***snot rag*** tire-jus *m*, tire-moelle *m*

snotty ['snɒtɪ] *(compar* **snottier,** *superl* **snottiest,** *pl* **snotties)** *Fam* **1** *adj* (**a**) *(nose, handkerchief)* morveux❑, plein de morve❑; *(face, child)* morveux❑ (**b**) *(haughty)* bêcheur, prétentiard; *(insolent)* insolent❑; **one of those incredibly snotty officials** un de ces officiels qui pètent plus haut que leur cul
2 *n Naut* aspi *m*

snotty-faced *adj Fam* morveux❑, qui a le nez qui coule❑

snotty-nosed *adj Fam also Fig* morveux

snout [snaʊt] *n* (**a**) *(of pig)* groin *m*, museau *m*; *(of other animal)* museau *m*; *Fam Fig* **to have/get one's snout in the trough** avoir/prendre sa part du gâteau❑ (**b**) *(projection)* saillie *f*; *(of gun)* canon *m* (**c**) *Fam Hum (nose)* pif *m* (**d**) *Br very Fam (cigarette)* sèche *f*, clope *f*; *(tobacco)* tabac❑ *m*, foin *m* (**e**) *Br Fam (informer)* mouchard(e) *m,f*, indic *m*

snow [snəʊ] **1** *n* (**a**) *(gen)* neige *f*; **heavy snow is forecast** la météo prévoit d'abondantes chutes de neige; **the snows of yesteryear** les neiges *fpl* d'antan; **the roads are covered with snow** les routes sont enneigées
(**b**) *Fig (on screen)* neige *f*
(**c**) *Fam Drugs slang (cocaine)* coco *f*, neige *f*; *(heroin crystals)* cristaux *mpl* d'héroïne❑
2 *vi* neiger; **it's snowing** il neige
3 *vt Am Fam (persuade)* **to snow sb into doing sth** baratiner qn pour qu'il fasse qch; **she snowed him into giving her the money** elle l'a embobiné pour qu'il lui donne l'argent; **the president is just snowing people into believing in his tax program** le président essaie d'embobiner le monde avec son programme fiscal
►► ***snow blindness*** cécité *f* des neiges; ***snow blower*** chasse-neige *m* à soufflerie; *Am Fam* ***snow bunny*** = jeune femme séduisante qui fréquente les stations de ski; *Orn* ***snow bunting*** bruant *m* des neiges; *Aut* ***snow chains*** chaînes *fpl* (à neige); ***snow fence*** pare-neige *m inv*; *Orn* ***snow finch*** niverolle *f* des Alpes; *Orn* ***snow goose*** oie *f* des neiges; ***snow hole*** *(in mountaineering)* trou *m* de neige; *Am Fam* ***snow job*** baratin *m*; **to give sb a snow job** baratiner qn, rouler qn dans la farine; ***snow leopard*** léopard *m* des neiges, once *f*; *Am* ***snow pea*** mange-tout *m inv*; ***snow route*** = artère sur laquelle il est interdit de stationner par temps de neige; ***snow scooter*** scooter *m* des neiges, motoski *m*, *Can* motoneige *m*; ***snow tyre*** pneu *m* neige

►**snow in** *vt sep* **to be snowed in** être bloqué par la neige

►**snow under** *vt sep Fig* **to be snowed under with work** être débordé *ou* complètement submergé de travail; **they're snowed under with applications/offers** ils ont reçu une avalanche de demandes/d'offres

►**snow up** *vt sep* **to be snowed up** *(house, village, family)* être bloqué par la neige; *(road)* être complètement enneigé

'Snow White and the Seven Dwarfs' *Grimm, Disney* 'Blanche-Neige et les sept nains'

'The Snow Maiden' *Rimsky-Korsakov* 'Fleur de neige'

snowball ['snəʊbɔːl] **1** *n* (**a**) *(made of snow)* boule *f* de neige, *Can* balle *f* de neige; *Fam* **he hasn't a snowball's chance in hell** il n'a pas l'ombre d'une chance❑
(**b**) *(cocktail)* snowball *m (advokaat allongé de limonade)*
2 *vt* bombarder de boules de neige, lancer des boules de neige à
3 *vi Fig* faire boule de neige
►► ***snowball effect*** effet *m* boule de neige; ***snowball fight*** bataille *f* de boules de neige; **they had a snowball fight** ils ont fait une bataille de boules de neige

snowbank ['snəʊbæŋk] *n* congère *f*

snowberry ['snəʊbərɪ] *(pl* **snowberries)** *n Bot* boule-de-neige *f*, symphorine *f*

snowbike ['snəʊbaɪk] *n* motoski *m*

snowbird ['snəʊbɜːd] *n Fam Drugs slang* cocaïnomane❑ *mf*

snow-blind *adj* **to be snow-blind** être atteint de *ou* souffrir de la cécité des neiges

snowblink ['snəʊblɪŋk] *n* reflet *m ou* clarté *f* des glaces (sur l'horizon)

snowboard ['snəʊbɔːd] *n* planche *f* de snowboard

snowboarder ['snəʊbɔːdə(r)] *n* snowboarder *m*, surfeur(euse) *m,f* des neiges

snowboarding ['snəʊbɔːdɪŋ] *n* snowboard *m*; **to go snowboarding** faire du snowboard

snow-boot *n* après-ski *m*

snowbound ['snəʊbaʊnd] *adj (person, house, village)* bloqué par la neige; *(road)* enneigé

snowcap ['snəʊkæp] *n* sommet *m* couronné de neige

snow-capped [-kæpt] *adj* couronné de neige

snowcat ['snəʊkæt] *n* scooter *m* des neiges, motoski *m*, *Can* motoneige *m*

snow-clad *adj* couvert de neige, enneigé

Snowdon ['snəʊdən] *n (mountain)* Snowdon *m*

Snowdonia [snəʊ'dəʊnɪə] *n* le parc national de Snowdonia

snowdrift ['snəʊdrɪft] *n* congère *f*

snowdrop ['snəʊdrɒp] *n Bot* perce-neige *m or f inv*

snowfall ['snəʊfɔːl] *n* (**a**) *(snow shower)* chute *f* de neige (**b**) *(amount)* enneigement *m*

snowfield ['snəʊfiːld] *n* champ *m* de neige

snowflake ['snəʊfleɪk] *n* (**a**) *(of snow)* flocon *m* de neige (**b**) *Bot* nivéole *f*

snowiness ['snəʊɪnɪs] *n* nivosité *f*

snowline ['snəʊlaɪn] *n* limite *f* des neiges éternelles

snowman ['snəʊmæn] *(pl* **snowmen** [-men]) *n* bonhomme *m* de neige

snowmobile ['snəʊməbiːl] *n* scooter *m* des neiges, motoski *m*, *Can* motoneige *m*

snowplough, *Am* **snowplow** ['snəʊplaʊ] **1** *n* (**a**) *(vehicle, implement)* chasse-neige *m inv* (**b**) *(in skiing)* chasse-neige *m inv*
2 *vi (in skiing)* faire du chasse-neige

snowscape ['snəʊskeɪp] *n Art* paysage *m* de neige

snowshoe ['snəʊʃuː] *n* raquette *f (pour marcher sur la neige)*

snowslide ['snəʊslaɪd], **snowslip** ['snəʊslɪp] *n* avalanche *f*

snowstorm ['snəʊstɔːm] *n* tempête *f* de neige

snowsuit ['snəʊsuːt] *n* combinaison *f* de ski

snow-white *adj* (**a**) *(in colour)* blanc (blanche) comme neige (**b**) *Fig* pur, innocent

snowy ['snəʊɪ] *(compar* **snowier,** *superl* **snowiest)** *adj* (**a**) *(weather, region etc)* neigeux; *(countryside, roads etc)* enneigé, couvert *ou* recouvert de neige; *(day)* de neige; **a snowy Christmas** un Noël enneigé (**b**) *Fig (hair, beard)* de neige; *(sheets, tablecloth)* blanc (blanche) comme neige
►► *Orn* ***snowy owl*** chouette *f* blanche, harfang *m*

SNP [ˌesen'piː] *n (abbr* **Scottish National Party)** = parti indépendantiste écossais fondé en 1934

Snr *(written abbr* **Senior)** **Ralph Todd Snr** Ralph Todd père

snub [snʌb] *(pt & pp* **snubbed,** *cont* **snubbing)** **1** *n* rebuffade *f*
2 *vt (person)* snober; *(offer, suggestion)* repousser (dédaigneusement); **to be snubbed** essuyer une rebuffade
3 *adj (nose)* retroussé

snub-nosed *adj* au nez retroussé
►► ***snub-nosed revolver*** revolver *m* au canon court

snuck [snʌk] *Am pt & pp of* **sneak**

snuff [snʌf] **1** *n* tabac *m* à priser; **to take snuff** priser; **a pinch of snuff** une prise (de tabac); *Fam Old-fashioned* **to be up to snuff** *(in good health)* être en forme❑; *(of sufficient quality)* être à la hauteur❑
2 *vi (sniff)* priser
3 *vt* (**a**) *(candle)* moucher
(**b**) *Am Fam (murder)* buter, refroidir, zigouiller
(**c**) *(sniff)* renifler, flairer
(**d**) *Fam (idiom)* **to snuff it** *(die)* calancher, passer l'arme à gauche
►► *Fam* ***snuff movie*** = film pornographique au cours duquel un participant est réellement assassiné

►**snuff out** *vt sep (candle)* éteindre, moucher; *Fig (hope)* ôter, supprimer; *(rebellion)* étouffer; *(enthusiasm)* briser

snuffbox ['snʌfbɒks] *n* tabatière *f (pour tabac à priser)*

snuffer ['snʌfə(r)] **1** *n* **(candle) snuffer** éteignoir *m*
2 snuffers *npl* mouchettes *fpl*

snuffle ['snʌfəl] **1** *vi* (**a**) *(sniffle)* renifler (**b**) *(in speech)* parler du nez, nasiller
2 *vt* dire *ou* prononcer d'une voix nasillarde
3 *n* (**a**) *(sniffle)* reniflement *m*; **to have the snuffles** être un peu enrhumé (**b**) *(in speech)* voix *f* nasillarde; **to speak in a snuffle** parler d'une voix nasillarde

snuffling ['snʌflɪŋ] **1** *adj* (**a**) *(sniffling)* qui renifle (**b**) *(nasal → accent, voice)* nasillard
2 *n* (**a**) *(sniffling)* reniflement *m* (**b**) *(in speech)* nasillement *m*

snug [snʌg] **1** *adj* (**a**) *(warm and cosy → bed, room)* douillet, (bien) confortable; *(→ sleeping bag, jacket)* douillet, bien chaud; **a snug little house** une petite maison confortable; **it's very snug in this room** on est bien *ou* il fait bon dans cette pièce; **I wish I was home and snug in bed** j'aimerais être bien au chaud dans mon lit; *Fam* **to be (as) snug as a bug in a rug** être bien au chaud❑
(**b**) *(clothing)* bien ajusté; **it's a snug fit** *(clothing)* c'est bien ajusté; *(machine part etc)* ça s'emboîte parfaitement; **it's a bit of a snug fit, it's a bit too snug** *(too tight → clothing)* c'est un peu trop serré
(**c**) *(harbour)* bien abrité; *(hideout)* sûr
2 *n Br (in pub)* petite arrière-salle *f*

snuggery ['snʌgərɪ] *(pl* **snuggeries)** *n Br* petite pièce *f* douillette; *(in pub)* petite arrière-salle *f*

snuggle ['snʌgəl] **1** *vi* se blottir, se pelotonner; **to snuggle into a corner** se blottir *ou* se pelotonner dans un coin; **village snuggling in the valley** village *m* niché dans la vallée
2 *vt (child, kitten)* serrer contre soi, câliner
3 *n* câlin *m*; **to have a snuggle** (se) faire un câlin

►**snuggle down** *vi* se blottir, se pelotonner; **to snuggle down under the blankets** s'enfouir sous les couvertures; **she snuggled down to sleep** elle se pelotonna pour dormir; **she snuggled down beside her mum** elle s'est blottie contre sa maman

►**snuggle up** *vi* **to snuggle up to sb** se blottir *ou* se serrer contre qn; **to snuggle up with a good book** s'installer bien confortablement avec un bon livre

snugly ['snʌglɪ] *adv* (**a**) *(cosily)* douillettement, confortablement; *(warmly)* bien au chaud; **soon they were settled snugly by the fire** ils se retrouvèrent bientôt réunis autour d'un bon feu (**b**) *(in fit)* **the skirt fits snugly** la jupe est très ajustée; **the two parts fit together snugly** les deux pièces s'emboîtent parfaitement

snugness ['snʌgnɪs] *n* confort *m*, bien-être *m inv (associé à la chaleur)*

SO *(written abbr* **standing order)** prélèvement *m* (bancaire) automatique

So. (**a**) *(written abbr* **South)** S (**b**) *(written abbr* **Southern)** S

SO¹ [səʊ]

si	► **1 (a), (b)**
tellement	► **1 (a)**
tant	► **1 (a)**
aussi	► **1 (b), (e)**
ainsi	► **1 (f)**
donc	► **2 (a)**
alors	► **2 (a), (d) – (f)**
pour que	► **2 (b); 4**
de même	► **2 (c)**
environ	► **3**
pour	► **5**

1 *adv* (**a**) *(to such an extent → before adjective or adverb)* si, tellement; *(→ with verb)* tellement; **it's so easy** c'est si *ou* tellement facile; **I'm so glad to see you** ça me fait tellement plaisir *ou* je suis si content de te voir; **he can be so irritating at times** il est tellement énervant par moments; **she makes me so angry** elle a le don de me mettre en colère; **I've never been so surprised in all my life** jamais de ma vie je n'avais eu une surprise pareille *ou* une telle surprise; **I have never seen so beautiful a sight** je n'ai jamais rien vu d'aussi beau; **she was so shocked (that) she couldn't speak** elle était tellement choquée qu'elle ne pouvait pas parler; **the problem was so complex (that) it baffled even the experts** le problème était si *ou* tellement complexe que même les experts ne comprenaient pas; **his handwriting's so bad (that) it's illegible** il écrit si mal que c'est impossible à lire; **he's so rich that he doesn't know what he's worth** il est riche au point d'ignorer le montant de sa fortune; **she so detests him** *or* **she detests him so that she won't even speak to him** elle le hait au point de refuser *ou* elle le déteste tellement qu'elle refuse de lui parler; **he was upset, so much so that he cried** il était bouleversé, à tel point qu'il en a pleuré; **would you be so kind as to carry my case?** auriez-vous l'amabilité *ou* la gentillesse de porter ma valise?; **is it so very hard to say you're sorry?** est-ce si difficile de demander pardon?; **you mustn't worry so** il ne faut pas te faire du souci comme ça; **I loved her so (much)** je l'aimais tant; **you do exaggerate so!** tu exagères tellement!; **we so enjoyed ourselves** nous nous sommes tellement amusés; **I wish he wouldn't go on so** j'aimerais qu'il arrête de radoter

(**b**) *(in negative comparisons)* si, aussi; **I'm not so sure** je n'en suis pas si sûr; **it's not so bad, there's only a small stain** ça n'est pas si grave que ça, il n'y a qu'une petite tache; **the young and the not so young** les jeunes et les moins jeunes; **he's not so handsome as his father/as all that** il n'est pas aussi beau que son père/si beau que ça; **he was not so ill (that) he couldn't go out** il n'était pas malade au point de ne pas pouvoir sortir; **she wouldn't be so stupid as to do that** elle ne serait pas bête au point de faire cela, elle ne serait pas assez bête pour faire cela

(**c**) *(indicating an unspecified size, amount)* **the table is about so high/wide** la table est haute/large comme ça à peu près; **a little girl so high** une petite fille grande comme ça

(**d**) *(referring to previous statement, question, word etc)* **I believe/think/suppose so** je crois/pense/suppose (que oui); **I don't believe/think so** je ne crois/pense pas; **I don't suppose so** je suppose que non; **he's clever – do you think so?** il est intelligent – vous trouvez?; **I hope so** *(answering question)* j'espère que oui; *(agreeing)* j'espère bien, je l'espère; **I'm afraid so** j'en ai bien peur, je le crains; **who says so?** qui dit ça?; **I told you so!** je vous l'avais bien dit!; **if so** si oui; **how/why so?** comment/pourquoi cela?; **perhaps so** peut-être bien; **quite so** tout à fait, exactement; **so I believe/see** c'est ce que je crois/vois; **so I've been told/he said** c'est ce qu'on m'a dit/qu'il a dit; **is she really ill? – so it seems** elle est donc vraiment malade? – à ce qu'il paraît; **I'm not very organized – so I see!** je ne suis pas très organisé – c'est ce que je vois!; **is that so?** vraiment?; **that is so** c'est vrai, c'est exact; **if that is so** si c'est le cas, s'il en est ainsi; **that being so** *(as this is the case)* puisqu'il en est ainsi; *(should this prove the case)* dans ces conditions; **isn't that Jane over there? – why, so it is!** ce ne serait pas Jane là-bas? – mais si (c'est elle)!; **he was told to leave the room and did so immediately** on lui a ordonné de quitter la pièce et il l'a fait immédiatement; **she was furious and understandably/and justifiably so** elle était furieuse et ça se comprend/et c'est normal; **the same only more so** tout autant sinon plus; **he's very sorry – so he should be!** il est désolé – c'est la moindre des choses *ou* j'espère bien!; **he thinks he can do it – so he can** il pense qu'il peut le faire – en effet il le peut; **so help me God!** que Dieu me vienne en aide!; *Arch or Hum* **so be it!** soit!, qu'il en soit ainsi!; *Fam* **I can so!** si, je peux!❑; *Fam* **I didn't say that! – you did so!** je n'ai pas dit ça! – si, tu l'as dit!❑

(**e**) *(likewise)* aussi; **I had brought food, and so had they** j'avais apporté de quoi manger et eux aussi; **we arrived early and so did he** nous sommes arrivés tôt et lui aussi; **if he can do it, then so can I** s'il peut le faire, alors moi aussi; **my shoes are Italian and so is my shirt** mes chaussures sont italiennes et ma chemise aussi

(**f**) *(like this, in such a way)* ainsi; **hold the pen (like) so** tenez le stylo ainsi *ou* comme ceci; **any product so labelled is guaranteed lead-free** tous les produits portant cette étiquette sont garantis sans plomb; **the laptop computer is so called because...** l'ordinateur lap-top tient son nom de...; **the helmet is so constructed as to absorb most of the impact** le casque est conçu de façon à amortir le choc; **it (just) so happens that...** il se trouve (justement) que... + *indicative*; **she likes everything (to be) just so** elle aime que tout soit parfait; **it has to be positioned just so or it won't go in** il faut le mettre comme ça sinon ça n'entre pas

2 *conj* (**a**) *(therefore)* donc, alors; **the door was open, so I went in** la porte était ouverte, alors je suis entré; **she has a bad temper, so be careful** elle a mauvais caractère, donc faites attention

(**b**) *(indicating purpose)* pour que + *subjunctive*, afin que + *subjunctive*; **give me some money so I can buy some sweets** donne-moi de l'argent pour que je puisse acheter des bonbons

(**c**) *(in the same way)* de même; **as 3 is to 6, so 6 is to 12** le rapport entre 6 et 12 est le même qu'entre 3 et 6; **as he has lived so will he die** il mourra comme il a vécu

(**d**) *(introductory remark)* **so then she left** alors elle est partie; **and so to bed!** et maintenant au lit!; **and so we come to the next question** et maintenant nous en venons à la question suivante; **so what's the problem?** alors, qu'est-ce qui ne va pas?; **so we can't go after all** donc nous ne pouvons plus y aller; **so, what do we do?** eh bien, qu'est-ce qu'on fait?

(**e**) *(in exclamations)* alors; **so you're Anna's brother!** alors (comme ça) vous êtes le frère d'Anna?; **so that's why she didn't phone!** alors c'est pour ça qu'elle n'a pas téléphoné!; **so there you are!** vous voilà donc!; **so publish it!** eh bien *ou* alors allez-y, publiez-le!; *esp Am* **so long!** au revoir!

(**f**) *(introducing a concession)* et alors; **so I'm late, who cares?** je suis en retard, et alors, qu'est-ce que ça peut faire?; **so it costs a lot of money, we can afford it** ça coûte cher, et alors? on peut se le permettre; **so?** et alors?, et après?; **he'll be angry – so what?** il va se fâcher! – qu'est-ce que ça peut (me) faire *ou* et alors?; **so what if she does find out?** qu'est-ce que ça peut faire si elle s'en rend compte?

3 **or so** *adv* environ, à peu près; **it costs £5 or so** ça coûte environ 5 livres; **there were thirty or so people** il y avait trente personnes environ *ou* à peu près, il y avait une trentaine de personnes

4 **so as** *conj Fam* pour que❑ + *subjunctive*, afin que❑ + *subjunctive*; **give me some money so as I can buy some sweets** donne-moi de l'argent pour que je puisse acheter des bonbons

5 **so as to** *conj* pour, afin de; **she went to bed early so as not to be tired next day** elle s'est couchée tôt afin de *ou* pour ne pas être fatiguée le lendemain

6 **so that** *conj* (**a**) *(in order that)* pour que + *subjunctive*, afin que + *subjunctive*; **they tied him up so that he couldn't escape** ils l'ont attaché afin qu'il *ou* pour qu'il ne s'échappe pas; **I took a taxi so that I wouldn't be late** j'ai pris un taxi pour *ou* afin de ne pas être en retard

(**b**) *(with the result that)* si bien que + *indicative*, de façon à ce que + *subjunctive*; **she didn't eat enough, so that in the end she fell ill** elle ne mangeait pas assez, de telle sorte *ou* si bien qu'elle a fini par tomber malade; **the crates had fallen over so that we couldn't get past** comme les caisses étaient tombées, nous n'avons pas pu passer

7 **so to speak, so to say** *adv* pour ainsi dire

so² *n Mus* sol *m inv*

soak [səʊk] 1 *vt* (**a**) *(washing, food)* faire *ou* laisser tremper; **he soaked the shirts in warm water** il a fait tremper les chemises dans de l'eau chaude; **soak the prunes overnight** laisser tremper les pruneaux toute la nuit; **to soak oneself (in the bath)** faire trempette dans la baignoire

(**b**) *(drench → person, dog etc)* tremper; **I got soaked waiting in the rain** je me suis fait tremper en attendant sous la pluie

(**c**) *Fig (immerse)* imprégner; **to soak oneself in the history of a period** se plonger dans *ou* s'imprégner de l'histoire d'une époque

(**d**) *Fam (exploit → by swindling)* rouler, arnaquer; *(→ through taxation)* faire casquer; **to soak the rich** faire casquer les riches

2 *vi (washing)* tremper; **he put the washing (in) to soak** il a mis le linge à tremper; **to soak in the bath** faire trempette dans la baignoire

3 *n* (**a**) *(in water)* trempage *m*; **the shirts are having a soak** les chemises sont en train de tremper; **these shirts need a good soak** il faut laisser *ou* bien faire tremper ces chemises; **I had a nice long soak in the bath** je suis resté longtemps plongé dans un bon bain

(**b**) *Fam (heavy drinker)* **(old) soak** soûlard(e) *m,f*, pochard(e) *m,f*

(**c**) *Br Fam (rain shower)* saucée *f*, rincée *f*

▶**soak in** *vi* (**a**) *(water)* pénétrer, s'infiltrer

(**b**) *Fam Fig (comment, news)* faire son effet❑; **she told me what happened, but it hasn't soaked in yet** elle m'a dit ce qui s'est passé, mais je n'ai pas encore vraiment bien compris❑

▶**soak out** 1 *vi (dirt, stains)* partir (au trempage)

2 *vt sep (dirt, stains)* faire disparaître *ou* partir (en faisant tremper)

▶**soak through** *vi (liquid)* filtrer au travers, s'infiltrer

▶**soak up** *vt sep* (**a**) *(absorb)* absorber; **we spent a week soaking up the sun** nous avons passé une semaine à lézarder *ou* à nous faire dorer au soleil; **to soak up the atmosphere** s'imprégner de l'atmosphère; **they come to Europe to soak up the culture** ils viennent en Europe pour s'imbiber de culture

(**b**) *Fam Hum (drink)* **he can really soak it up** il peut vraiment boire comme un trou

soakage ['səʊkɪdʒ] *n* (**a**) *(water)* eau *f* d'infiltration *ou* d'imbibition (**b**) *(action)* infiltration *f*

soakaway ['səʊkəweɪ] *n Tech* puisard *m*

soaked [səʊkt] *adj* trempé; *(ground)* détrempé; *Fig (immersed)* imprégné; **to be soaked through** *or* **to the skin** être trempé jusqu'aux os; **his shirt was soaked with** *or* **in blood/sweat** sa chemise était maculée de sang/trempée de sueur; **the place is soaked in history** l'endroit est imprégné d'histoire

soaker ['səʊkə(r)] *n Fam* (**a**) *(drunkard)* soûlard(e) *m,f*, pochard(e) *m,f* (**b**) *(heavy rainfall)* pluie *f* battante❑, déluge *m* de pluie❑

soaking ['səʊkɪŋ] 1 *adj* trempé; **take off your shirt, it's soaking** enlève ta chemise, elle est trempée; **I'm soaking (wet)!** je suis trempé jusqu'aux os!

2 *n* (**a**) *(gen)* trempage *m*; **these clothes need a good soaking** il faut laisser tremper ces vêtements

(**b**) *Fam (in rain)* **to get a soaking** se faire tremper❑ *ou* saucer

(**c**) *Fam (financial loss)* perte *f* financière❑; **we got a real soaking on the stock market** on a vraiment beaucoup perdu à la Bourse❑

▶▶ ***soaking solution*** *(for contact lenses)* solution *f* de trempage

so-and-so (*pl* **so-and-sos**) *n Fam* (**a**) *(referring to stranger)* untel *m*, unetelle *f*; **Mr so-and-so** Monsieur Untel; **Mrs so-and-so** Madame Unetelle (**b**) *(annoying person)* **you little so-and-so!** espèce de petit minable!; **the old so-and-so!** *(angry)* le salaud!; *(admiring, surprised)* le bougre!; **you greedy old so-and-so** espèce de gourmand!; **don't cry, you silly old so-and-so!** faut pas pleurer, espèce d'idiot!

soap [səʊp] 1 *n (UNCOUNT)* (**a**) *(gen)* savon *m*; **a bar of soap** un savon, une savonnette

(**b**) *Fam (flattery)* flagornerie❑ *f*, flatterie(s)❑ *f(pl)*

(**c**) *Fam Rad & TV* soap opera❑ *m*, feuilleton *m* (populaire)❑

(**d**) *Am Fam (idiom)* **no soap!** des clous!, des nèfles!

2 *vt* savonner

▶▶ ***soap bubble*** bulle *f* de savon; *Rad & TV* ***soap opera*** feuilleton *m* (populaire), soap opera *m*; ***soap powder*** lessive *f* (en poudre), poudre *f* à laver

▶**soap down** *vt sep* savonner; **to soap oneself down** se savonner

▶**soap up 1** *vt sep Fam* (**a**) *(flatter)* passer de la pommade à

(**b**) *Am (bribe)* soudoyer❑

2 *vi (while washing)* se savonner

SOAP OPERA

Le soap opera est un genre radiophonique et télévisé très populaire en Grande-Bretagne, aux États-Unis et en Australie. Il s'agit de feuilletons diffusés à raison de trois ou quatre épisodes par semaine sur une très longue période. Ainsi le feuilleton radiophonique 'The Archers' débuta en 1951 sur la BBC, et 'Coronation Street' est diffusé à la télévision britannique depuis 1960. Les soap operas sont ainsi nommés car les premiers d'entre eux étaient financés par des marques de détergents, aux États-Unis. Il n'est pas rare que les soap operas alimentent les conversations de tous les jours, ou soient le sujet d'articles de journaux. Les soap operas britanniques ('Eastenders' et 'Coronation Street' par exemple) ont souvent pour cadre le milieu ouvrier et diffèrent en cela de leurs équivalents américains et australiens dont le ton est beaucoup moins réaliste et dont l'action se déroule le plus souvent dans des milieux privilégiés.

soapbark ['səʊpbɑːk] *n Bot* bois *m* de Panama

▶▶ ***soapbark tree*** quillaja *m* savonneaux

soapberry ['səʊpberɪ] (*pl* **soapberries**) *n Bot* (**a**) *(fruit)* pomme *f* de savon (**b**) *(tree)* savonnier *m*

soapbox ['səʊpbɒks] **1** *n* (**a**) *(container)* caisse *f* à savon; *Fig (for speaker)* tribune *f* improvisée *ou* de fortune; **to get up on a soapbox** faire un discours improvisé, haranguer les foules; **get off your soapbox!** ne monte pas sur tes grands chevaux! (**b**) *(go-kart)* chariot *m*, ≃ kart *m (sans moteur)*

2 *comp Pej (oratory)* de démagogue; **he's just a soapbox orator** ce n'est qu'un harangueur

soapdish ['səʊpdɪʃ] *n* porte-savon *m*

soapflakes ['səʊpfleɪks] *npl* paillettes *fpl* de savon, savon *m* en paillettes

soapiness ['səʊpɪnɪs] *n* caractère *m* savonneux

soapstone ['səʊpstəʊn] *n* stéatite *f*

soapsuds ['səʊpsʌdz] *npl (foam)* mousse *f* de savon; *(soapy water)* eau *f* savonneuse

soapwort ['səʊpwɜːt] *n Bot* saponaire *f*

soapy ['səʊpɪ] (*compar* **soapier,** *superl* **soapiest**) *adj* (**a**) *(water, hands, surface)* savonneux; *(taste)* de savon (**b**) *Fam Fig (person, manner, voice)* onctueux❑, mielleux❑

soar [sɔː(r)] *vi* (**a**) *(bird, plane → rise)* monter en flèche; *(→ glide)* planer *(en utilisant les courants ascendants)*; *(flames)* jaillir; **to soar into the sky** *or* **the air** *(bird, balloon etc)* s'élever dans les airs; **the ball soared over the fence/our heads** le ballon s'est envolé au-dessus de la clôture/de nos têtes; **the jet soared above us** l'avion est monté en flèche au-dessus de nous

(**b**) *(spire)* s'elancer vers le ciel; *(mountain)* s'élever vers le ciel; **the mountain seemed to soar into the clouds** la montagne paraissait s'élancer dans les nuages

(**c**) *(temperature, profits, prices)* grimper en flèche; *(suddenly)* faire un bond; **sales have soared since the TV adverts** les ventes ont grimpé en flèche depuis les publicités à la télé; **rents have soared** les loyers ont grimpé en flèche *ou* augmenté de façon vertigineuse

(**d**) *(spirits)* remonter en flèche; *(hopes)* grandir démesurément; *(reputation)* monter en flèche

(**e**) *(sound, music)* s'élever

soaring ['sɔːrɪŋ] **1** *adj* (**a**) *(bird, glider)* qui s'élève dans le ciel; *(spire, tower)* qui s'élance vers le ciel; *(mountain)* qui s'élève vers le ciel; **the soaring spire of the cathedral** la flèche de la cathédrale qui s'élance vers le ciel; **the soaring flight of the eagle** le vol majestueux de l'aigle

(**b**) *(prices, inflation)* qui monte *ou* qui grimpe en flèche; *(hopes, reputation)* grandissant

2 *n (of bird)* essor *m*, élan *m*; *(of plane)* envol *m*; *(of prices)* envolée *f*, explosion *f*

SOAS ['səʊæs] *n* (*abbr* **School of Oriental and African Studies**) = école des études orientales et africaines de Londres

sob[1], **SOB** [ˌesəʊ'biː] *n Am very Fam* (*abbr* **son of a bitch**) salaud *m*, fils *m* de pute

sob[2] [sɒb] (*pt & pp* **sobbed,** *cont* **sobbing**) **1** *n* sanglot *m*; **she answered him with a sob** elle lui répondit dans un sanglot; **"it wasn't me", he said with a sob** "ce n'est pas moi", dit-il en sanglotant; **with a sob in her voice** la voix étouffée par un sanglot

2 *vi* sangloter

3 *vt* **to sob oneself to sleep** s'endormir à force de sangloter *ou* en sanglotant; **"I can't remember", he sobbed** "je ne me rappelle pas", dit-il en sanglotant

▶▶ *Am Fam* ***sob sister*** journaliste *f* qui fait le courrier du cœur❑; *Fam Pej* ***sob story*** histoire *f* larmoyante❑, histoire *f* à vous fendre le cœur❑; **she's always full of sob stories** elle cherche toujours à vous apitoyer *ou* à vous fendre le cœur avec ses histoires❑; **he told us some sob story about his deprived childhood** il nous a cherché à nous apitoyer en nous parlant de son enfance malheureuse❑; *Fam Pej* ***sob stuff*** sensiblerie❑ *f*, mélo *m*

▶**sob out** *vt sep* raconter en sanglotant; **she sobbed out her grief** son chagrin se traduisait par des sanglots; **to sob one's heart out** sangloter de tout son corps, pleurer à gros sanglots

sobbing ['sɒbɪŋ] **1** *n (UNCOUNT)* sanglots *mpl*; **stop your sobbing** arrête de sangloter

2 *adj* sanglotant

sober ['səʊbə(r)] **1** *adj* (**a**) *(not drunk)* **are you sure he was sober?** tu es sûr qu'il n'avait pas bu?; **he's never sober** il est toujours ivre; **to be as sober as a judge** *(serious)* être sérieux comme un pape; *(temperate)* être sobre comme un chameau

(**b**) *(sobered up)* dessoûlé; **wait until he's sober again** attends qu'il dessoûle

(**c**) *(moderate → person)* sérieux, posé, sensé; *(→ attitude, account, opinion)* modéré, mesuré; *(→ manner)* sérieux, posé

(**d**) *(serious, solemn → atmosphere, occasion)* solennel, plein de solennité; *(→ expression)* grave, plein de gravité; *(→ voice)* grave, empreint de gravité; *(→ reminder)* solennel; **you're in (a) sober mood** vous êtes d'humeur bien solennelle

(**e**) *(subdued → colour, clothing)* discret(ète), sobre; **he was wearing a sober blue tie** il portait une cravate d'un bleu sobre; **of sober appearance** d'aspect sobre

(**f**) *(plain → fact, reality)* (tout) simple; *(→ truth)* simple, tout nu; *(→ tastes)* simple, sobre; **the sober fact is...** le fait est que... + *indicative*

2 *vt (calm)* calmer, assagir

▶**sober down 1** *vi (calm down)* se calmer, s'assagir

2 *vt sep (calm)* calmer, assagir

▶**sober up 1** *vi* dessoûler

2 *vt sep* dessoûler

sobering ['səʊbərɪŋ] *adj* **it's a sobering thought** cela donne à réfléchir; **what she said had a sobering effect on everyone** ce qu'elle a dit donnait à réfléchir à tous

soberly ['səʊbəlɪ] *adv (act, speak)* avec sobriété *ou* modération *ou* mesure; *(dress)* sobrement, discrètement; **he said soberly** *(calmly)* dit-il d'un ton posé *ou* mesuré; *(solemnly)* dit-il d'un ton grave; **the soldiers filed soberly past** les soldats défilèrent solennellement

sober-minded *adj (serious)* sérieux, réfléchi

soberness ['səʊbənɪs] *n* (**a**) *(non-drunkenness)* sobriété *f* (**b**) *(of style, dress, character)* sobriété *f*; *(seriousness)* sérieux *m*

sobersides ['səʊbəsaɪdz] *n Br Fam* **he's a real sobersides** c'est un vrai bonnet de nuit

sobriety [səʊ'braɪətɪ] *n* (**a**) *(non-drunkenness)* sobriété *f*; **his sobriety cannot be guaranteed** rien ne garantit qu'il ne sera pas ivre (**b**) *(moderation → of person)* sobriété *f*, sérieux *m*; *(→ of opinion, judgement)* mesure *f*, modération *f*; *(→ of manner, style, tastes)* sobriété *f* (**c**) *(solemnity → of occasion)* solennité *f*; *(→ of voice)* ton *m* solennel *ou* grave; *(→ of mood)* sobriété *f* (**d**) *(of colour, dress)* sobriété *f*

sobriquet ['səʊbrɪkeɪ] *n Literary* sobriquet *m*

Soc [sɒk] *n* (*abbr* **Society**) ≃ club *m (abréviation utilisée dans la langue parlée notamment par les étudiants pour désigner les différents clubs universitaires)*

.soc *Comput* (*written abbr* **social**) *(in newsgroups)* = abréviation désignant les forums de discussion qui ont pour thème les faits de société

soca ['səʊkə] *n Mus* soca *f*

socage ['sɒkɪdʒ] *n Hist* socage *m*

so-called [-kɔːld] *adj* (**a**) *(supposed)* soi-disant *(inv)*, prétendu; **his so-called aunt** sa soi-disant tante; **so-called social workers** des soi-disant assistants *mpl* sociaux; **her so-called boudoir** son boudoir, comme elle l'appelle; **so-called progress** de prétendus progrès *mpl* (**b**) *(so named)* appelé ainsi, ainsi nommé; **the so-called temperate zone** la zone dite tempérée

soccage = **socage**

soccer ['sɒkə(r)] **1** *n* football *m*, foot *m*

2 *comp (pitch, match, team)* de football, de foot; *(supporter)* d'une équipe de foot

▶▶ ***soccer hooligans*** hooligans *mpl (lors de matchs de football)*; *Am* ***soccer mom*** = femme de milieu bourgeois qui accompagne et encourage ses enfants lors de leurs séances d'entraînement de foot; ***soccer player*** footballeur(euse) *m,f*

sociability [ˌsəʊʃə'bɪlətɪ] *n* sociabilité *f*

sociable ['səʊʃəbəl] **1** *adj* (**a**) *(enjoying company)* sociable, qui aime la compagnie (des gens); *(friendly)* sociable, amical; *(evening)* amical, convivial; **try to be more sociable** *(go out more)* essaie de sortir un peu et de rencontrer des gens; *(mix more)* essaie d'être un peu plus sociable; **I had a drink with them to be sociable** j'ai pris un verre avec eux pour me montrer sociable; **I'm not in a sociable mood** je ne suis pas d'humeur sociable, je n'ai pas envie de voir du monde

(**b**) *(in sociology) & Zool* sociable

2 *n Am* fête *f*

▶▶ *Orn* ***sociable weaver*** républicain *m*

sociably ['səʊʃəblɪ] *adv (behave)* de manière sociable, amicalement; *(say)* amicalement

social ['səʊʃəl] **1** *adj* (**a**) *(background, behaviour, conditions, reform, tradition)* social; *(phenomenon)* social, de société; **to bow to social pressures** se plier aux pressions sociales; **they are our social equals** ils sont de même condition sociale que nous; *Hum* **it's social death to wear such clothes there** plus personne ne te connaît si tu t'habilles comme ça pour y aller; **they move in high** *or* **the best social circles** ils évoluent dans les hautes sphères de la société

(**b**) *(in society → activities)* mondain; *(leisure)* de loisir *ou* loisirs; **his life is one mad social whirl** il mène une vie mondaine insensée

(**c**) *(evening, function)* amical; **it was the social event of the year** c'était l'événement mondain de l'année; **to pay someone a social call** faire à quelqu'un une visite amicale; **I'm afraid this isn't just a social call** je crains que ceci ne soit pas qu'une visite amicale

(**d**) *Zool* social; **ants are social insects** la fourmi est un insecte social; **man is a social animal** l'homme est un animal social

2 *n* soirée *f* (dansante)

▶▶ ***social accounting*** comptabilité *f* nationale; ***social anthropologist*** spécialiste *mf* d'anthropologie sociale; ***social anthropology*** anthropologie *f* sociale; ***social behaviourism*** behaviorisme *m* social; ***social benefits*** prestations *fpl* sociales; *EU* ***the Social Chapter*** le volet social *(du traité de Maastricht)*; ***social charges*** *(levied on employers)* charges *fpl* sociales; *EU* ***Social Charter*** Charte *f* sociale; ***social class*** classe *f* sociale; ***social cleansing*** = élimination ou expulsion des éléments indésirables de la société; ***social climber*** arriviste *mf*; ***social climbing*** arrivisme *m*; ***social club*** club *m*; ***social conscience*** conscience *f* sociale; **to have a social conscience** avoir conscience des problèmes sociaux; ***social contract*** contrat *m* social; *Can*

soa–s

Econ & Hist ***social credit*** = doctrine populiste canadienne selon laquelle le gouvernement doit exercer un contrôle sur les prix afin de remédier aux inégalités de pouvoir d'achat; ***social Darwinism*** darwinisme *m* social; ***social democracy*** (**a**) *(system)* social-démocratie *f* (**b**) *(country)* démocratie *f* socialiste; **we live in a social democracy** nous vivons dans une démocratie socialiste; ***social democrat*** social-démocrate *mf*; ***social democratic*** social-démocrate *mf*; ***Social Democratic and Labour Party*** = parti travailliste d'Irlande du Nord; ***Social Democratic Party*** Parti *m* social-démocrate; ***social disease*** *(gen)* maladie *f* provoquée par des facteurs socio-économiques; *Euph (venereal)* maladie *f* vénérienne; ***social drinker*** = personne qui ne boit d'alcool qu'en société; **he's purely a social drinker** il ne boit pas seul, il boit seulement en société *ou* en compagnie; ***social drinking*** = consommation d'alcool lors de réunions entre amis; ***social dumping*** dumping *m* social; ***social engineering*** manipulation *f* des structures sociales; ***social fund*** = caisse d'aide sociale; ***social graces*** bonnes manières *fpl*; ***social historian*** spécialiste *mf* d'histoire sociale; ***social history*** histoire *f* sociale; ***social housing*** logements *mpl* sociaux; ***social insurance*** *(UNCOUNT)* prestations *fpl* sociales; ***social life*** vie *f* mondaine; **to have a busy social life** sortir beaucoup; **he doesn't have much of a social life** il ne sort pas beaucoup; **work is getting in the way of my social life** j'ai trop de travail pour pouvoir sortir; **there isn't much of a social life in this town** les gens ne sortent pas beaucoup dans cette ville, il ne se passe rien dans cette ville; **what's the social life like here?** est-ce que vous sortez beaucoup ici?; ***social mobility*** mobilité *f* sociale; ***social order*** ordre *m* social; ***social outcast*** paria *m*; ***social position*** rang *m* dans la société; ***social psychology*** psychologie *f* sociale, psychosociologie *f*; ***social realism*** réalisme *m* social; *Am* ***Social Register*** Bottin *m* mondain; ***social science*** sciences *fpl* humaines; ***social scientist*** spécialiste *mf* des sciences humaines; ***social secretary*** *(of organization)* = secrétaire chargé d'organiser les événements mondains; *(personal secretary)* secrétaire *mf* particulier(ère); ***social security*** (**a**) *(gen)* prestations *fpl* sociales; **to be on social security** toucher une aide sociale (**b**) *Br (money paid to unemployed)* ≃ allocations *fpl* de chômage; *Am* ***Social Security Administration*** ≃ Sécurité *f* sociale; ***social security contribution*** prélèvement *m* social; *Am* **social security number** numéro *m* de Sécurité sociale; ***social services*** services *mpl* sociaux; ***social skills*** = manière de se comporter en société; **to have good/poor social skills** être à l'aise/ne pas être à l'aise en société; **he has no social skills** il ne sait pas comment se comporter en société; ***social spending*** dépenses *fpl* sociales; ***social structure*** structure *f* sociale; ***social studies*** sciences *fpl* sociales; ***social work*** assistance *f* sociale, travail *m* social; ***social worker*** assistant(e) *m,f* social(e), travailleur(euse) *m,f* social(e)

socialism ['səʊʃəlɪzəm] *n* socialisme *m*

socialist ['səʊʃəlɪst] **1** *adj* socialiste

2 *n* socialiste *mf*

▸▸ *Art & Literature* ***Socialist Realism*** réalisme *m* socialiste

socialistic [ˌsəʊʃə'lɪstɪk] *adj* socialiste, de nature socialiste

socialite ['səʊʃəlaɪt] *n* mondain(e) *m,f*, personne *f* qui fréquente la haute société; **she's a famous socialite** elle est connue pour fréquenter beaucoup la haute société

sociality [ˌsəʊʃɪ'ælətɪ] *n* socialité *f*

socialization [ˌsəʊʃəlaɪ'zeɪʃən] *n Pol & Psy* socialisation *f*

socialize, -ise ['səʊʃəlaɪz] **1** *vi (go out)* sortir, fréquenter des gens; *(make friends)* se faire des amis; **to socialize with sb** fréquenter qn; **she used to socialize a lot when she was at college** elle sortait beaucoup quand elle était étudiante; **he finds it difficult to socialize** il a du mal à lier connaissance, il est très peu sociable

2 *vt Pol & Psy* socialiser

▸▸ *Am* ***socialized medicine*** médecine *f* socialisée

socializing ['səʊʃəlaɪzɪŋ] *n* fait *m* de fréquenter des gens; **they do a lot of socializing** ils voient beaucoup de gens; **socializing between teachers and pupils is discouraged** les relations entre élèves et professeurs ne sont pas encouragées

socially ['səʊʃəlɪ] *adv* socialement; **socially acceptable behaviour** comportement *m* socialement acceptable; **we've never met socially** on ne s'est jamais rencontrés en société; **I saw her socially for a while, but nothing beyond that** je l'ai vaguement fréquentée pendant un temps, mais rien de plus; **to be socially inadequate** ne pas être doué pour les relations avec les gens; **socially inferior** socialement inférieur; **socially disadvantaged** défavorisé

societal [sə'saɪətəl] *adj* sociétal

society [sə'saɪətɪ] *(pl* **societies**) **1** *n* (**a**) *(social community)* société *f*; **it is a danger to society** cela constitue un danger pour la société; **for the good of society** dans l'intérêt de la société; **woman's place in society** la place de la femme dans la société

(**b**) *(nation, group)* société *f*; **primitive/industrial societies** des sociétés *fpl* primitives/industrielles; **Western society** la société occidentale

(**c**) *(fashionable circles)* **(high) society** la haute société, le (beau *ou* grand) monde; **to make one's debut in society** faire ses débuts dans le monde

(**d**) *Literary (company)* société *f*, compagnie *f*; **to avoid the society of sb** éviter la société de qn; **I do not care for their society** je ne me plais pas en leur compagnie *ou* en leur société; **in polite society** dans la bonne société *ou* le (beau) monde

(**e**) *(association, club)* société *f*, association *f*; *(for sports)* club *m*, association *f*; *Sch & Univ (for debating, study etc)* société *f*; **charitable society** œuvre *f* de charité, association *f* caritative

2 *comp (gossip, news, wedding)* mondain; *(hostess)* de soirées mondaines; **a society man/woman** un homme/une femme du monde, un mondain/une mondaine; *Press* **the society column** la chronique mondaine

▸▸ ***the Society of Friends*** la Société des Amis *(les Quakers)*; ***the Society of Jesus*** la Compagnie de Jésus; ***the Society for the Prevention of Cruelty to Animals*** = société américaine protectrice des animaux, ≃ la SPA; ***the Society for the Prevention of Cruelty to Children*** = société américaine pour la protection de l'enfance; ***the Society for the Protection of the Unborn Child*** = ligue américaine contre l'avortement

sociobiology [ˌsəʊsɪəʊbaɪ'ɒlədʒɪ] *n* sociobiologie *f*

sociocultural [ˌsəʊsɪəʊ'kʌltʃərəl] *adj* socioculturel

sociodemographic ['səʊsɪəʊˌdemə'græfɪk] *adj* sociodémographique

▸▸ *Mktg* ***sociodemographic data*** données *fpl* sociodémographiques; *Mktg* ***sociodemographic profile*** profil *m* démographique; *Mktg* ***sociodemographic segment*** segment *m* démographique

socioeconomic ['səʊsɪəʊˌiːkə'nɒmɪk] *adj* socio-économique

▸▸ *Mktg* ***socioeconomic classification*** classification *f* socioprofessionnelle

sociogram ['səʊsɪəʊgræm] *n* sociogramme *m*

sociohistorical ['səʊsɪəʊˌhɪ'stɒrɪkəl] *adj* sociohistorique

sociolect ['səʊsɪəʊlekt] *n Ling* sociolecte *m*

sociolinguistic [ˌsəʊsɪəʊlɪŋ'gwɪstɪk] *adj* sociolinguistique

sociolinguistics [ˌsəʊsɪəʊlɪŋ'gwɪstɪks] *n* sociolinguistique *f*

sociological [ˌsəʊsɪə'lɒdʒɪkəl] *adj* sociologique

sociologist [ˌsəʊsɪ'ɒlədʒɪst] *n* sociologue *mf*

sociology [ˌsəʊsɪ'ɒlədʒɪ] *n* sociologie *f*

sociometric [ˌsəʊsɪəʊ'metrɪk] *adj* sociométrique

sociometrist [ˌsəʊsɪ'ɒmɪtrɪst] *n* sociométriste *mf*

sociometry [ˌsəʊsɪ'ɒmɪtrɪ] *n* sociométrie *f*

sociopath [ˌsəʊsɪəʊ'pæθ] *n* sociopathe *mf*

sociopathic [ˌsəʊsɪəʊ'pæθɪk] *adj* sociopathe, sociopathique

sociopathy [ˌsəʊsɪ'ɒpəθɪ] *n* sociopathie *f*

sociopolitical [ˌsəʊsɪəʊpə'lɪtɪkəl] *adj* sociopolitique

socioprofessional [ˌsəʊsɪəʊprə'feʃənəl] *adj* socioprofessionnel

▸▸ ***socioprofessional group*** catégorie *f* socioprofessionnelle, CSP *f*

sock [sɒk] **1** *n* (**a**) *(garment)* chaussette *f*; *Fam* **it'll knock your socks off!** tu vas tomber à la renverse!; *Fam* **to pull one's socks up** se secouer (les puces); *Br Fam* **to put a sock in it** la fermer, la boucler

(**b**) *(insole)* semelle *f* (intérieure)

(**c**) *(of horse)* paturon *m*

(**d**) *Aviat & Met* **(wind) sock** manche *f* à air

(**e**) *Fam (blow)* beigne *f*, châtaigne *f*; **she gave him a sock in the face** elle lui a filé une beigne; **I got a sock on the jaw** j'ai pris une beigne

(**f**) *Antiq* **the sock and buskin** le socque et la cothurne; *Literary* **to put on the sock** chausser le brodequin, jouer la comédie

2 *adv Fam* **the blow caught him sock in the face** il a pris le coup en pleine poire

3 *vt Fam (hit)* filer une beigne *ou* une châtaigne à; **she socked him in the face** elle lui a filé une beigne dans la tronche; **they socked me over the head with a cosh** ils m'ont flanqué un coup de matraque sur la tête; **sock it to him!, sock him one!** fous-lui une beigne!, cogne-le!; *Fig* **to sock it to sb** montrer à qn ce que l'on sait faire; **sock it to them!** vas-y, montre-leur ce que tu sais faire!, vas-y, donne le maximum!; **sock it to me then!** allez, accouche!

►**sock away** *vt sep Am Fam (money)* mettre de côté ☐, économiser ☐; **to sock it away** remplir son bas de laine

►**sock in** *vt sep Am Fam (airport)* fermer *(à cause de mauvaises conditions météorologiques)*

sockdolager, sockdologer [sɒk'dɒlədʒə(r)] *n Am Fam* (**a**) *(decisive blow)* coup *m* décisif ☐ (**b**) *(remarkable person)* personne *f* extraordinaire ☐; *(phenomenon)* chose *f* extraordinaire ☐; **that was a sockdolager of a thunderstorm/movie!** quel orage incroyable/film génial!

socket ['sɒkɪt] *n* (**a**) *Elec (for bulb)* douille *f*; *Br (in wall)* prise *f* (de courant)

(**b**) *Tech* cavité *f*; *(in carpentry)* mortaise *f*; **it fits into a socket** ça s'emboîte dans un support prévu à cet effet

(**c**) *Comput (slot)* prise *f* (femelle); *(on Internet)* socket *f*, port *m*

(**d**) *Anat (of arm, hipbone)* cavité *f* articulaire; *(of tooth)* alvéole *f*; *(of eye)* orbite *f*; **her arm was pulled out of its socket** elle a eu l'épaule luxée; *Fig* **her eyes almost popped** *or* **jumped out of their sockets** les yeux lui en sont presque sortis de la tête

▸▸ ***socket joint*** (**a**) *(in carpentry)* joint *m* à rotule (**b**) *Anat* énarthrose *f*; ***socket set*** coffret *m* de douilles; ***socket wrench*** clef *f* à douille

sockeye ['sɒkaɪ] *n Ich* saumon *m* rouge

socking ['sɒkɪŋ] *adv Br Fam (as intensifier)* vachement; **he had a socking great bruise!** il avait un de ces bleus!

socle ['səʊkəl] *n Archit* socle *m*

Socrates ['sɒkrətiːz] *pr n* Socrate

Socratic [sɒ'krætɪk] *adj* socratique

▸▸ ***Socratic irony*** ironie *f* socratique

sod [sɒd] *(pt & pp* **sodded**, *cont* **sodding**) **1** *n* (**a**) *Br very Fam (obnoxious person)* enfoiré(e) *m,f*, con (conne) *m,f*; **the stupid sod!** tu parles d'un enfoiré!; **you (rotten) sod!** espèce de saligaud!; **he's a real sod!** c'est un salopard!

(**b**) *Br very Fam (fellow)* bougre *m*, con *m*; **poor sod** le pauvre con; **he's not such a bad old sod** ce n'est pas un mauvais bougre

(**c**) *Br very Fam (difficult or unpleasant thing)* saloperie *f*; **it's a sod of a job** c'est un boulot vraiment chiant; **these screws are real sods to get out** ces vis sont vraiment emmerdantes *ou* chiantes à enlever

(**d**) *Br very Fam* **sod all** que dalle; **they do sod all all day** ils n'en fichent pas une rame de la journée; **sod all money** pas d'argent du tout; **there's sod all to eat** il y a que dalle à bouffer; **they've got sod all hope of winning** ils n'ont pas une putain de chance de gagner

(**e**) *(of turf)* motte *f* (de gazon); *(earth and grass)* terre *f*; *(lawn)* gazon *m*; **to cut** *or* **turn the first sod** donner le premier coup de bêche; **under the sod** *(buried)* enterré; **the sod of old Ireland** la bonne vieille terre d'Irlande

2 *vt Br very Fam* **sod it!** merde!; **sod him!** qu'il aille se faire foutre!; **sod the expense, let's just go!** tant pis si ça coûte cher, allons-y!

►► *Br Fam* ***Sod's law*** la loi de l'emmerdement maximum; **that's Sod's law!** c'est la poisse!

►**sod off** *vi Br very Fam* foutre le camp, dégager; **sod off!** fous le camp!, dégage!

soda ['səʊdə] *n* (**a**) *Chem* soude *f*

(**b**) *(fizzy water)* eau *f* de Seltz; **a whisky and soda** un whisky soda

(**c**) *Am (soft drink)* soda *m*

►► ***soda ash*** soude *f* du commerce; *Br* ***soda biscuit*** = biscuit sec à la levure chimique; ***soda bread*** pain *m* à la levure chimique; *Am* ***soda cracker*** = biscuit sec à la levure chimique; *Am* ***soda fountain*** (**a**) *(café)* ≃ café *m*; *(counter)* buvette *f (où sont servis des sodas)* (**b**) *(device)* siphon *m* (d'eau de Seltz); *Am Fam* ***soda jerk*** serveur(euse)❑ *m,f (de soda)*; ***soda lime*** chaux *f* sodée; *Am* ***soda pop*** boisson *f* gazeuse; ***soda siphon*** siphon *m* (d'eau de Seltz); ***soda water*** eau *f* de Seltz

sodalite ['səʊdəlaɪt] *n Miner* sodalite *f*

sodality [səʊ'dælətɪ] (*pl* **sodalities**) *n* (**a**) *Formal (fellowship)* fraternité *f*, camaraderie *f* (**b**) *Rel (association)* confrérie *f*

sodden ['sɒdən] *adj (ground)* détrempé; *(clothes)* trempé; *Fig* **to be sodden with drink** être abruti par l'alcool

sodding ['sɒdɪŋ] *Br very Fam* **1** *adj (for emphasis)* sacré, foutu; **get that sodding dog out of here!** fous-moi cette saleté de clébard dehors!; **sodding hell!** merde alors!; **I lost my sodding umbrella** j'ai perdu ce foutu parapluie

2 *adv (for emphasis)* vachement; **you can sodding well do it yourself!** démerde-toi tout seul pour le faire!; **don't be so sodding lazy!** ce que tu peux être flemmard!

sodium ['səʊdɪəm] *n* sodium *m*

►► ***sodium bicarbonate*** bicarbonate *m* de soude; ***sodium borate*** borate *m* de sodium; ***sodium carbonate*** carbonate *m* de sodium, soude *f*; ***sodium chloride*** chlorure *m* de sodium; ***sodium hydroxide*** hydroxyde *m* de sodium; ***sodium lamp*** lampe *f* à vapeur de sodium; ***sodium nitrate*** nitrate *m* de sodium; ***sodium sulphate*** sulfate *m* de sodium

sodium-vapour lamp *n* lampe *f* à vapeur de sodium

Sodom ['sɒdəm] *n* Sodome; **Sodom and Gomorrah** Sodome et Gomorrhe

sodomite ['sɒdəmaɪt] *n* sodomite *m*

sodomize, -ise ['sɒdəmaɪz] *vt* sodomiser

sodomy ['sɒdəmɪ] *n* sodomie *f*

soever [səʊ'evə(r)] *adv Literary* **in any way soever** n'importe comment; **how great soever it may be** quelque grand que ce soit

sofa ['səʊfə] *n* sofa *m*, canapé *m*

►► ***sofa bed*** canapé-lit *m*

SOFFEX ['sɒfeks] *n St Exch* (*abbr* **Swiss Options and Financial Futures Exchange**) SOFFEX *f* *(Bourse suisse pour le négoce des options et des contrats à terme)*

soffit ['sɒfɪt] *n Archit* soffite *m*, intrados *m*

Sofia ['səʊfɪə] *n* Sofia

SOFT [sɒft]

doux	► **1 (a), (d), (e), (g), (h), (m), (p) – (r)**
mou	► **1 (b), (j)**
souple	► **1 (a)**
moelleux	► **1 (b)**
ramolli	► **1 (b)**
tendre	► **1 (c), (h)**
gras	► **1 (c)**
léger	► **1 (d)**
estompé	► **1 (f)**
indulgent	► **1 (i)**
facile	► **1 (m)**
modéré	► **1 (n)**
faible	► **1 (o)**

1 *adj* (**a**) *(to touch → skin, hands, wool, fur)* doux (douce); *(→ leather)* souple; *(→ material, hair)* doux (douce), soyeux; **as soft as velvet/as a baby's bottom** doux comme du velours/comme une peau de bébé; **soft to the touch** doux au toucher; **to become soft** *or* **softer, to get soft** *or* **softer** *(skin)* s'adoucir; *(leather)* s'assouplir; **the cream will make your hands/the leather soft** la crème t'adoucira les mains/assouplira le cuir

(**b**) *(yielding, not firm → bed, mattress, pillow)* moelleux; *(→ collar, ground, snow)* mou (molle); *(→ butter)* mou (molle), ramolli; *(→ muscles, body)* ramolli, avachi, flasque; *(too yielding → bed, mattress)* mou (molle); **a nice soft bed** un lit moelleux; **this bed is too soft** ce lit est trop mou; **the butter has gone soft** le beurre s'est ramolli; **mix to a soft paste** mélanger jusqu'à obtention d'une pâte molle; **these chocolates have soft centres** ces chocolats sont mous à l'intérieur; *Horseracing* **the going is soft** le terrain est mou; **the brakes are soft** il y a du mou dans les freins

(**c**) *(malleable → metal, wood, stone)* tendre; *(→ pencil)* gras (grasse), tendre

(**d**) *(quiet, not harsh → voice, music)* doux (douce); *(→ sound, accent)* doux (douce), léger; *(→ tap, cough)* petit, léger; *(→ step)* feutré; **"yes", he said in a soft whisper/voice** "oui", murmura-t-il doucement/dit-il d'une voix douce; **she gave a soft laugh** elle rit doucement

(**e**) *(muted → colour, glow)* doux (douce); *(→ shade)* doux (douce), pastel *(inv)*; *(→ light, lighting)* doux (douce), tamisé

(**f**) *(blurred → outline)* estompé, flou

(**g**) *(gentle, mild → breeze, rain, words)* doux (douce); *(→ expression, eyes)* doux (douce), tendre; *(→ curve, shadow)* doux (douce); *(→ climate, weather)* doux (douce), clément; **she suits a softer hairstyle** ce qui lui va bien, c'est une coiffure plus souple; *Br* **it's a soft day** il bruine aujourd'hui

(**h**) *(kind → person)* doux (douce), tendre; **to have a soft heart** avoir le cœur tendre; **to have a soft nature** être doux de nature

(**i**) *(lenient)* indulgent; **you're too soft with the boy** vous êtes trop indulgent avec le garçon; **to be soft on sb** se montrer indulgent envers qn, faire preuve d'indulgence envers qn; **to be soft on terrorism** faire preuve de laxisme envers le terrorisme

(**j**) *(weak → physically)* mou (molle); **the boy's too soft** ce garçon n'a pas de caractère; **you're getting soft** tu te ramollis; **city life has made you soft** la vie citadine t'a ramolli

(**k**) *Fam (stupid)* **he's going soft in his old age** il devient gâteux en vieillissant; **you must be soft in the head!** ça va pas, non?; **don't be soft** arrête de dire des bêtises

(**l**) *(fond) Fam* **to be soft on sb** avoir le béguin pour qn; **to have a soft spot for sb** avoir un faible pour qn

(**m**) *(easy → life)* doux (douce), tranquille, facile; *(→ job)* facile; *Fam* **to have a soft time of it** se la couler douce; **it's the soft option** c'est la solution de facilité; **to take the soft option** opter pour la solution de facilité

(**n**) *(moderate)* modéré; *Pol* **the soft left** la gauche modérée; **to take a soft line on sth** adopter une ligne modérée sur qch; *(compromise)* adopter une politique de compromis sur qch

(**o**) *Econ & Fin (currency)* faible; *(market)* faible, lourd

(**p**) [illegible] doux (douce)

(**q**) *Ling (consonant)* doux (douce)

(**r**) *(drug)* doux (douce)

2 *adv* (**a**) *Literary (softly)* doucement

(**b**) *Fam* **don't talk soft!** ne sois pas idiot!

3 softs *npl Com* biens *mpl* non durables

►► ***soft cheese*** fromage *m* à pâte molle; ***soft coal*** houille *f* grasse; *Com* ***soft commodities*** biens *mpl* non durables; ***soft contact lenses*** lentilles *fpl* souples; *Comput* ***soft copy*** visualisation *f* sur écran; *Fin* ***soft currency*** devise *f* faible; ***soft drink*** boisson *f* non alcoolisée; *Phot* ***soft focus*** flou *m* artistique, point *m* diffus; *Fig* **to see things in soft focus** avoir une vision idéalisée du monde; ***soft fruit*** *(UNCOUNT)* ≃ fruits *mpl* rouges; *Br* ***soft furnishings*** tissus *mpl* d'ameublement; *Br* ***soft goods*** tissus *mpl*, textiles *mpl*; *Comput* ***soft hyphen*** césure *f* automatique, tiret *m* conditionnel; *Chem* ***soft iron*** fer *m* doux; *Comput* ***soft key*** touche *f* programmable; *also Fig* ***soft landing*** atterrissage *m* en douceur; *Am Pol* ***soft line*** ligne *f* de conduite modérée; *Econ & Fin* ***soft loan*** prêt *m* avantageux *ou* à des conditions avantageuses; ***soft margarine*** margarine *f*; *Am Pol* ***soft money*** = sommes employées pour le financement d'une campagne électorale en employant divers stratagèmes afin de rester dans la légalité; *Anat* ***soft palate*** voile *m* du palais; ***soft pedal*** *(on piano)* pédale *f* douce, sourdine *f*; ***soft porn*** pornographie *f* peu explicite, *Fam* soft *m*; ***soft-porn film*** film *m* érotique; ***soft-porn magazine*** revue *f* de charme; ***soft-porn magazines*** presse *f* de charme; *Comput* ***soft return*** saut *m* de ligne automatique; ***the soft sciences*** ≃ les sciences *fpl* humaines; *Comput* ***soft sectoring*** formatage *m* logiciel; *Com* ***soft sell*** = méthodes de vente non agressives; **she has a flair for the soft sell** elle a le don de *ou* pour circonvenir ses clients; ***soft shoulder*** *(on road)* accotement *m* non stabilisé; ***soft soap*** (**a**) *Med* savon *m* vert (**b**) *(UNCOUNT) Fam (flattery)* flagornerie❑ *f*, flatterie❑ *f*, flatteries❑ *fpl*; ***soft target*** cible *f* facile; *Econ & Fin* ***soft terms*** conditions *fpl* favorables; *Anat* ***soft tissue*** parties *fpl* charnues; *Fam* ***soft top*** (voiture *f*) décapotable❑ *f*; *Br Fam* ***soft touch*** bonne poire *f*; **he's a real soft touch** *(easily fooled)* il est vraiment bonne poire; *(for money)* il se laisse facilement taper; ***soft toy*** (jouet *m* en) peluche *f*; ***soft verge*** *(on road)* accotement *m* non stabilisé

softback ['sɒftbæk] *n* (livre *m* de) poche *m*

►► ***softback version*** version *f* poche

softball ['sɒftbɔːl] *n* (**a**) *(game)* = sorte de base-ball joué sur un terrain plus petit et avec une balle moins dure, *Can* balle *f* molle (**b**) *(ball)* = balle utilisée au "softball" (plus grande et plus molle qu'une balle de base-ball)

soft-boiled *adj*

►► ***soft-boiled egg*** œuf *m* (à la) coque

softbound ['sɒftbaʊnd] = **soft-cover**

soft-centre *n (chocolate)* chocolat *m* fourré

soft-centred *adj (chocolate)* fourré; *(sweet)* mou (molle); *(person)* au cœur tendre; *(film)* à l'eau de rose

soft-core *adj (pornography)* soft *(inv)*

soft-cover *adj* broché

soften ['sɒfən] **1** *vt* (**a**) *(butter, ground, wax)* ramollir; *(skin, water)* adoucir; *(fabric, wool, leather)* assouplir; **a cream to soften chapped skin** une crème pour adoucir les peaux gercées; **soften the paste by kneading it between your fingers** ramollir la pâte en la malaxant avec les doigts; **centuries of erosion had softened the stone** des siècles d'érosion avaient rendu la pierre tendre

(**b**) *(voice, tone)* adoucir, radoucir; *(colour, light, sound)* adoucir, atténuer; **to soften one's voice** *(make less strident)* parler d'une voix plus douce; *(make quieter)* parler moins fort

(**c**) *(make less strict)* assouplir; **he has softened his stance on vegetarianism** son attitude envers le végétarisme est plus modérée qu'avant

(**d**) *(lessen → pain, emotion)* soulager, adoucir, atténuer; *(→ shock, effect, impact)* adoucir, amoindrir; *(→ opposition, resistance)* réduire, amoindrir; *also Fig* **to soften the blow** amortir le choc

2 *vi* (**a**) *(butter, ground, wax)* se ramollir; *(skin)* s'adoucir; *(cloth, wool, leather)* s'assouplir

(**b**) *(become gentler → eyes, expression, voice)* s'adoucir; *(→ breeze, rain)* s'atténuer; *(→ lighting, colour)* s'atténuer, s'adoucir; *(→ angle, outline)* s'adoucir, s'estomper

(**c**) *(become friendlier, more receptive)* **to soften towards sb** se montrer plus indulgent envers qn; **their attitude towards immigration has softened noticeably** leur position par rapport à l'immigration est nettement plus tolérante; **his face softened** son expression se radoucit; **her heart softened at the sound of his voice** elle s'attendrit en entendant sa voix

►**soften up 1** *vt sep* (**a**) *Fam (make amenable → gen)* attendrir❑, rendre plus souple❑; *(→ by persuasion)* amadouer❑; *(→ aggressively)* intimider❑; **they tried to soften us up with champagne lunches** ils ont essayé de nous amadouer à coups de déjeuners au champagne; **they sent in bully boys to soften the shopkeepers up** ils ont envoyé des gros bras pour intimider les commerçants

(**b**) *Mil* affaiblir

sod–s

(**c**) *(make softer → butter, ground, wax)* ramollir; *(→ skin)* adoucir; *(→ cloth, wool, leather)* assouplir

2 *vi* (**a**) *(ground)* devenir mou (molle), se ramollir; *(butter, wax)* se ramollir; *(leather)* s'assouplir; *(skin)* s'adoucir

(**b**) *(become gentler → person, voice)* s'adoucir; **to soften up on sb** faire preuve de plus d'indulgence envers qn

softener ['sɒfənə(r)] *n* (**a**) *(for water)* adoucisseur *m* (d'eau); *(for fabric)* assouplissant *m* (textile) (**b**) *Fam (bribe)* pot-de-vin ❑ *m*

softening ['sɒfənɪŋ] *n (of substance, ground)* ramollissement *m*; *(of cloth, wool, leather)* assouplissement *m*, adoucissement *m*; *(of attitude, expression, voice)* adoucissement *m*; *(of colours, contrasts)* atténuation *f*; **there has been no softening of attitude on the part of the management** la direction n'a pas modéré son attitude; *Med* **softening of the brain** ramollissement *m* cérébral

soft-eyed [-aɪd] *adj* aux yeux doux

soft-faced hammer [-feɪst-] *n* maillet *m*

soft-focus *adj*

►► ***soft-focus lens*** objectif *m* pour créer des effets de flou

soft-headed *adj Fam (weak-minded)* faible d'esprit ❑; *(silly)* bête, idiot ❑

softhearted [,sɒft'hɑːtɪd] *adj* (au cœur) tendre; **he's too softhearted** il a trop de cœur

softheartedness [,sɒft'hɑːtɪdnɪs] *n (kindness)* bonté *f* de coeur; *(indulgence)* indulgence *f*

softie ['sɒftɪ] *n Fam* (**a**) *(weak person)* mauviette *f*, mollasson(onne) *m,f*; *(coward)* poule *f* mouillée, dégonflé(e) *m,f* (**b**) *(gentle person)* bonne pâte *f*; **he's just a big softie really** au fond, c'est un grand sentimental

softly ['sɒftlɪ] *adv* (**a**) *(quietly → breathe, say)* doucement; *(→ move, walk)* à pas feutrés, (tout) doucement (**b**) *(gently → blow, touch)* doucement, légèrement (**c**) *(fondly → smile, look)* tendrement, avec tendresse

softly-softly *Br* **1** *adv* tout doucement, avec prudence

2 *adj* prudent; **try a softly-softly approach** allez-y doucement

softness ['sɒftnɪs] *n* (**a**) *(to touch → of skin, hands, hair)* douceur *f*; *(→ of fabric, wool, fur, pillow)* douceur *f*, moelleux *m*; *(→ of leather)* souplesse *f*

(**b**) *(to pressure → of bed, ground, snow, butter)* mollesse *f*; *(→ of collar)* souplesse *f*; *(→ of wood)* tendreté *f*

(**c**) *(gentleness → of breeze, weather, voice, music)* douceur *f*; *(→ of expression, manner)* douceur *f*, gentillesse *f*; *(→ of eyes, light, colour)* douceur *f*; *(→ of outline, curve)* flou *m*, douceur *f*

(**d**) *(kindness → of person)* douceur *f*; *(→ of heart)* tendresse *f*; *(indulgence)* indulgence *f*

(**e**) *(weakness → of character, person)* mollesse *f*

(**f**) *(easiness → of life)* douceur *f*; *(→ of job)* facilité *f*

(**g**) *Fam (silliness)* niaiserie ❑ *f*, stupidité ❑ *f*

soft-pedal **1** *vi* (**a**) *Mus* mettre la sourdine (**b**) *Fig* **to soft-pedal on reforms** ralentir le rythme des réformes

2 *vt Fig* glisser sur, atténuer

soft-sectored [-'sektəd] *adj Comput (disk)* formaté par programme, à secteurs logiciels

soft-shell, soft-shelled *adj (nut, mollusc)* à coquille molle; *(egg)* hardé; *(tortoise, lobster)* à carapace molle

►► ***soft-shell crab*** crabe *m* à carapace molle; ***soft-shell turtle*** tortue *f* à carapace molle

soft-shoe shuffle *n* = danse de music-hall ressemblant aux claquettes mais exécutée en chaussures à semelle souple

soft-skinned *adj* à (la) peau douce

►► *Mil* ***soft-skinned vehicles*** véhicules *mpl* non blindés

soft-soap *vt Fam* passer de la pommade à

soft-solder *vt* souder à la soudure tendre *ou* à l'étain

soft-spoken *adj* à la voix douce; **to be soft-spoken** avoir la voix douce

soft-top *adj* décapotable

software ['sɒftweə(r)] *n Comput* logiciel *m*, software *m*; **a piece of software** un logiciel

►► ***software company*** éditeur *m* de logiciels; ***software developer*** développeur(euse) *m,f*; ***software error*** erreur *f* de logiciel; ***software house*** éditeur *m* de logiciels; ***software package*** logiciel *m*; ***software piracy*** piratage *m* de logiciels; ***software platform*** plate-forme *f* logicielle; ***software problem*** problème *m* de logiciel; ***software tool*** outil *m* logiciel; ***software writer*** concepteur *m* de logiciel

software-compatible *adj* compatible du point de vue logiciel

softwood ['sɒftwʊd] **1** *n* bois *m* tendre, *Can* bois *m* mou

2 *comp* en bois tendre, *Can* en bois mou

softy *(pl* **softies***)* = **softie**

SOGAT ['səʊgæt] *n Br (abbr* **Society of Graphical and Allied Trades***)* = syndicat britannique des métiers du graphisme

soggy ['sɒgɪ] *(compar* **soggier**, *superl* **soggiest***) adj (ground)* détrempé, imbibé d'eau; *(clothes)* trempé; *(bread, cake)* mou (molle); *(rice)* trop cuit, collant; **the ground is soggy underfoot** on s'enfonce dans le sol détrempé; **my shoes are all soggy** mes chaussures sont trempées

soh [səʊ] *n Mus* sol *m*

SoHo ['səʊhəʊ] *n* = quartier chic de Manhattan

Soho ['səʊhəʊ] *n* = quartier chaud de Londres connu pour ses restaurants

soigné ['swæŋeɪ] *adj* soigné, élégant

soil [sɔɪl] **1** *n* (**a**) *(earth)* terre *f*; **to work the soil** travailler la terre

(**b**) *(type of earth)* terre *f*, sol *m*; **good farming soil** de la bonne terre agricole; **sandy/clay soils** sols *mpl* sablonneux/argileux, terres *fpl* sablonneuses/argileuses

(**c**) *Fig (land)* terre *f*, sol *m*; **his native soil** sa terre natale; **on Irish soil** sur le sol irlandais

(**d**) *(UNCOUNT) (excrement)* excréments *mpl*, ordures *fpl*; *(sewage)* vidange *f*

2 *vt* (**a**) *(dirty → clothes, linen, paper)* salir, souiller; **she refused to soil her hands with such work** elle a refusé de se salir les mains avec ce genre de travail

(**b**) *Fig (reputation)* salir, souiller, entacher

3 *vi (clothes, material)* se salir; **these covers soil easily** ces housses sont salissantes

►► ***the Soil Association*** = organisation britannique de normalisation des produits issus de l'agriculture biologique; ***soil erosion*** érosion *f* du sol; *Geog* ***soil horizon*** horizon *m*; ***soil pipe*** tuyau *m* de chute unique; *Geog* ***soil profile*** profil *m* de sol, profil *m* pédologique; ***soil science*** science *f* du sol

soiled [sɔɪld] *adj (dressings)* usagé; *(bedlinen)* souillé; *(goods)* défraîchi; **if it's soiled the shop won't exchange it** si c'est sale la boutique ne fera pas l'échange; **some slightly soiled items at reduced prices** des articles *mpl* légèrement salis à prix réduits

soirée ['swɑːreɪ] *n* soirée *f*

sojourn ['sɒdʒɜːn] *Literary* **1** *n* séjour *m*

2 *vi* séjourner

sojourner ['sɒdʒənə(r)] *n Literary* **I was a sojourner in a strange land** j'étais de passage dans un pays étranger

soke [səʊk] *n Law & Hist* (**a**) *(right of jurisdiction)* droit *m* de juridiction (**b**) *(jurisdiction)* juridiction *f*, ressort *m*

sol¹ [sɒl] *n Mus* sol *m inv*

sol² *n Chem* sol *m*

solace ['sɒləs] *Literary* **1** *n* consolation *f*, réconfort *m*; **he found solace in religion** il a trouvé un réconfort dans la religion

2 *vt (person)* consoler, réconforter; *(pain, suffering)* soulager

solan ['səʊlən] *n Orn* fou *m* (de Bassan)

►► ***solan goose*** fou *m* (de Bassan)

sola of exchange ['səʊlə-] *n Fin* seule *f* de change

solar ['səʊlə(r)] *adj* (**a**) *(of, concerning the sun → heat, radiation)* solaire, du soleil; *(→ cycle, year)* solaire

(**b**) *(using the sun's power → energy, heating)* solaire

►► ***solar battery*** batterie *f* solaire; ***solar cell*** pile *f* solaire, photopile *f*; ***solar eclipse*** éclipse *f* solaire; ***solar flare*** éruption *f* solaire; ***solar furnace*** four *m* solaire; ***solar panel*** panneau *m* solaire; *Anat* ***solar plexus*** plexus *m* solaire; ***solar power*** énergie *f* solaire; ***solar system*** système *m* solaire; ***solar wind*** vent *m* solaire

solarium [sə'leərɪəm] *(pl* **solariums** *or* **solaria** [-rɪə]*) n* solarium *m*

solarization [,səʊləraɪ'zeɪʃən] *n Phot* solarisation *f*

solarize, -ise ['səʊləraɪz] *Phot* **1** *vt* solariser

2 *vi* se solariser

►► ***solarized image*** image *f* de solarisation

solar-powered [-'paʊəd] *adj* à énergie solaire

solatium [səʊ'leɪʃɪəm] *n* (**a**) *(compensation)* compensation *f* (**b**) *Law* = dommages-intérêts payés à titre de réparation morale (en sus des dommages-intérêts matériels)

sold [səʊld] **1** *pt & pp of* **sell**

2 *adj* (**a**) *Com* vendu

(**b**) *Fam Fig* **to be sold on sb/sth** être emballé par qn/qch; **he's really sold on her** il est vraiment entiché *ou* toqué d'elle; **she's sold on the new plan** elle est complètement emballée par le nouveau projet

3 sold out *adj* (**a**) *(goods)* épuisé; **sold out** *(for play, concert)* complet; **the concert was completely sold out** tous les billets pour le concert ont été vendus

(**b**) *(stockist)* **we're sold out of bread** nous avons vendu tout le pain, il ne reste plus de pain

solder ['səʊldə(r)] **1** *vt* souder; **to solder a wire to a contact** souder un fil à un plot

2 *n* soudure *f*, métal *m* d'apport; **brazing solder** soudure *f* au laiton, brasure *f*; **soft solder** soudure *f* à l'étain, brasure *f* tendre

solderer ['səʊldərə(r)] *n* soudeur(euse) *m,f*

soldering ['səʊldərɪŋ] *n* soudure *f*

►► ***soldering iron*** fer *m* à souder

soldier ['səʊldʒə(r)] **1** *n* (**a**) *(gen)* soldat *m*, militaire *m*; **to become a soldier** se faire soldat, entrer dans l'armée; **to play (at) soldiers** *(children)* jouer aux soldats *ou* à la guerre; *Pej (country, adults)* jouer à la guerre *ou* à la guéguerre; *Mil* **old soldier** vétéran *m*; *Fam* **don't come** *or* **play the old soldier with me** ne prenez pas de grands airs avec moi ❑

(**b**) *Entom* soldat *m*

(**c**) *(strip of bread)* mouillette *f*

2 *vi* être soldat, servir dans l'armée

►► ***soldier ant*** (fourmi *f*) soldat *m*; ***soldier of Christ*** soldat *m* du Christ; *Ich* ***soldier fish*** poisson-soldat *m*; ***soldier of fortune*** soldat *m* de fortune

►**soldier on** *vi Br* continuer *ou* persévérer (malgré tout); **despite the freezing conditions they soldiered on** ils ont persévéré en dépit d'un froid glacial; **I'll soldier on with this for another half hour** je vais encore m'escrimer là-dessus pendant une demi-heure

'The Soldier's Tale' *Stravinsky* 'L'Histoire du soldat'

soldiering ['səʊldʒərɪŋ] *n* carrière *f ou* vie *f* (de) militaire; **to go soldiering** partir à l'armée *ou* à la guerre; **their love of soldiering** leur amour de la vie militaire; **after many years' soldiering** après avoir servi pendant de nombreuses années dans l'armée

soldierlike ['səʊldʒəlaɪk], **soldierly** ['səʊldʒəlɪ] *adj (act, behaviour)* de soldat; *(appearance, manner, bearing)* militaire

soldiery ['səʊldʒərɪ] *n Old-fashioned* (**a**) *(soldiers collectively)* soldats *mpl*, militaires *mpl* (**b**) *(profession)* métier *m* de soldat

sole [səʊl] *(pl sense* (**c**) **inv** *or* **soles***)* **1** *adj* (**a**) *(only)* seul, unique; **the sole survivor** le seul survivant

(**b**) *(exclusive)* exclusif; **to have sole rights on sth** avoir l'exclusivité des droits sur qch; **to have sole responsibility for sth** être entièrement responsable de qch

2 *n* (**a**) *(of foot)* plante *f*

(**b**) *(of shoe, sock)* semelle *f*

(**c**) *Ich* sole *f*

3 *vt* ressemeler; **to have one's shoes soled** faire ressemeler ses chaussures

►► ***sole agency*** représentation *f* exclusive; ***sole agency contract*** contrat *m* de représentation exclusive; ***sole agent*** agent *m* exclusif; **to be sole agent for Rover** avoir la représentation exclusive de Rover; *Com* ***sole dealer*** concessionnaire *mf* exclusif(ive); *Law* ***sole legatee*** légataire *mf* universel(elle); ***sole owner*** propriétaire *mf* unique; ***sole right*** droit *m* exclusif; *Br Com* ***sole trader*** entreprise *f* individuelle *ou* unipersonnelle

solecism ['sɒlɪsɪzəm] *n* (**a**) *Gram* solécisme *m* (**b**) *Formal (social error)* manque *m* de savoir-vivre

solecistic [ˌsɒlɪ'sɪstɪk] *adj Gram* **solecistic construction** solécisme *m*

solecize, -ise ['sɒlɪsaɪz] *vi Gram* faire un solécisme, *Formal* solécise r

-soled [səʊld] *suff* à semelle de; **rubber-soled shoes** chaussures *fpl* à semelles de caoutchouc

solely ['səʊllɪ] *adv* (**a**) *(only)* seulement, uniquement (**b**) *(entirely)* entièrement; **to be solely responsible for sth** être entièrement responsable de qch

solemn ['sɒləm] *adj* (**a**) *(grave, serious)* sérieux, grave, solennel; **a solemn face** un visage grave *ou* solennel (**b**) *(sombre)* sobre; **a solemn grey suit** un costume gris sobre (**c**) *(formal → agreement, promise)* solennel; **a solemn oath** un serment solennel (**d**) *(grand → occasion, music)* solennel

►► ***solemn mass*** grand-messe *f*, messe *f* solennelle

solemness ['sɒləmnɪs] *n* sérieux *m*, gravité *f*

solemnify [sə'lemnɪfaɪ] *(pt & pp* **solemnified***) vt* rendre solennel *ou* sérieux

solemnity [sə'lemnətɪ] *(pl* **solemnities***) n* (**a**) *(serious nature)* sérieux *m*, gravité *f* (**b**) *(formality)* solennité *f*; **she was received with great solemnity** elle fut accueillie très solennellement (**c**) *(usu pl) Literary (solemn event)* solennité *f*; **the Easter solemnities** les solennités *fpl* de Pâques

solemnization [ˌsɒləmnaɪ'zeɪʃən] *n Literary (gen)* solennisation *f*; *(of marriage)* célébration *f*

solemnize, -ise ['sɒləmnaɪz] *vt Literary (gen)* solenniser; *(marriage)* célébrer

solemnizing ['sɒləmnaɪzɪŋ] *n Literary (gen)* solennisation *f*; *(of marriage)* célébration *f*

solemnly ['sɒləmlɪ] *adv* (**a**) *(seriously, gravely)* gravement, solennellement; **"it's time I left", he said solemnly** "il est temps que je parte", dit-il d'un ton grave; **she solemnly believes that what she did was right** elle croit fermement que ce qu'elle a fait était juste

(**b**) *(formally)* solennellement; **they solemnly swore to avenge their brother's death** ils jurèrent solennellement de venger la mort de leur frère

(**c**) *(grandly)* solennellement, avec solennité

solemnness = **solemness**

solenoid ['səʊlɪnɔɪd] *n Elec* solénoïde *m*

►► ***solenoid switch*** contacteur *m* à solénoïde

Solent ['səʊlənt] *n* **the Solent** = chenal entre l'île de Wight et l'Angleterre

sol-fa [ˌsɒl'fɑː] *n Mus* solfège *m*

solfatara [ˌsɒlfə'tɑːrə] *n Geol* solfatare *f*, soufrière *f*

solfeggio [sɒl'fedʒɪəʊ] *(pl* **solfeggios** *or* **solfeggi** [-dʒɪ]*) n Mus* solfège *m*

solicit [sə'lɪsɪt] **1** *vt* (**a**) *(business, support, information)* solliciter; *(opinion)* demander (**b**) *(of prostitute)* racoler

2 *vi (prostitute)* racoler

solicitation [səˌlɪsɪ'teɪʃən] *n* sollicitation *f*

soliciting [sə'lɪsɪtɪŋ] *n (by prostitute)* racolage *m*

solicitor [sə'lɪsɪtə(r)] *n* (**a**) *Br Law (for drawing up documents, conveyancing)* ≃ notaire *m*; *(for court work, divorce cases)* avocat(e) *m,f*

(**b**) *Am Admin* conseil *m* juridique d'une municipalité

(**c**) *(person who solicits)* solliciteur(euse) *m,f*; *Am* **caution, unofficial solicitors** *(sign)* attention aux démarcheurs non autorisés

►► ***solicitor general*** (**a**) *(in UK)* conseil *m* juridique de la Couronne (**b**) *(in US)* représentant(e) *m,f* du gouvernement *(auprès de la Cour suprême)*

solicitor-advocate *n Scot Law* = avocat autorisé à plaider à la "High Court" ou à la "Court of Session"

solicitous [sə'lɪsɪtəs] *adj (showing consideration, concern)* plein de sollicitude; *(eager, attentive)* empressé; *(anxious)* soucieux; **he was most solicitous about your future happiness** il était extrêmement soucieux de votre avenir et de votre bonheur

solicitously [sə'lɪsɪtəslɪ] *adv (with consideration, concern)* avec sollicitude; *(eagerly, attentively)* avec empressement; *(anxiously)* avec inquiétude

solicitousness [sə'lɪsɪtəsnɪs], **solicitude** [sə'lɪsɪtjuːd] *n (consideration, concern)* sollicitude *f*; *(eagerness, attentiveness)* empressement *m*; *(anxiety)* souci *m*, préoccupation *f*

solid ['sɒlɪd] **1** *adj* (**a**) *(not liquid or gas)* solide; **a solid body** un corps solide; **frozen solid** complètement gelé; **the fat had set solid** la graisse était complètement figée; **she can't eat solid food** elle ne peut pas absorber d'aliments solides

(**b**) *(of one substance)* massif; **her necklace is solid gold** son collier est en or massif; **solid oak furniture** meubles *mpl* en chêne massif; **they dug until they reached solid rock** ils ont creusé jusqu'à ce qu'ils atteignent la roche compacte; **caves hollowed out of solid rock** des grottes *fpl* creusées à même la roche

(**c**) *(not hollow)* plein; **solid tyres** pneus *mpl* pleins

(**d**) *(unbroken, continuous)* continu; **a solid yellow line** une ligne jaune continue; **I worked for eight solid hours** *or* **eight hours solid** j'ai travaillé sans arrêt pendant huit heures, j'ai travaillé huit heures d'affilée; **we had two solid weeks of rain** nous avons eu deux semaines de pluie ininterrompue

(**e**) *Am (of one colour)* uni; **the walls were painted a solid green** les murs étaient peints en vert uni

(**f**) *(dense, compact)* dense, compact; **knead it until it forms a solid mass** travailler jusqu'à ce que cela forme une masse compacte; **the streets were a solid mass of people** les rues étaient noires de monde; **the concert hall was packed solid** la salle de concert était bondée

(**g**) *(powerful → blow)* puissant; **I gave him a solid punch to the jaw** je lui ai asséné un violent coup de poing sur la mâchoire

(**h**) *(sturdy, sound → structure, understanding, relationship)* solide; *(→ evidence, argument)* solide, irréfutable; *(→ advice)* valable, sûr; **a man of solid build** un homme bien charpenté; **their marriage was never solid** leur mariage n'a jamais été très solide; **I have very solid reasons for believing the opposite** j'ai de solides raisons de croire le contraire; **we need somebody with some solid experience in the field** nous avons besoin de quelqu'un qui possède une solide expérience de travail sur le terrain; **he's a good solid worker** c'est un bon travailleur; **to be on solid ground** être sur la terre ferme; *Fig* être en terrain sûr

(**i**) *(respectable, worthy)* respectable, honorable; **the solid citizens of this town** les respectables citoyens *mpl* de cette ville

(**j**) *Pol (firm)* massif; *(unanimous)* unanime; **we have the solid support of the electorate** nous avons le soutien massif des électeurs; **the south is solid for the Christian Democrats** le sud soutient massivement les démocrates-chrétiens; **the strike was 100 percent solid** la grève était totale; **the committee was solid against the proposal** le comité a rejeté la proposition à l'unanimité

(**k**) *Am Fam (excellent)* génial, super *(inv)*

2 *n Geom & Phys* solide *m*

3 *adv Am Fam (absolutely)* absolument □; **I solid gotta do it!** il faut absolument que je le fasse!

4 solids *npl* (**a**) *(solid food)* aliments *mpl* solides; **I can't eat solids** je ne peux pas absorber d'aliments solides

(**b**) *Chem* particules *fpl* solides; **milk solids** extrait *m* du lait

►► *Math* ***solid angle*** angle *m* solide; *Gram* ***solid compound*** composé *m* écrit en un seul mot; *Math* ***solid figure*** solide *m*; ***solid fuel*** combustible *m* solide; *Math* ***solid geometry*** géométrie *f* des solides

solidarist ['sɒlɪdərɪst] *n* solidariste *mf*

solidaristic [ˌsɒlɪdə'rɪstɪk] *adj* solidariste

solidarity [ˌsɒlɪ'dærətɪ] **1** *n* solidarité *f*; **they went on strike in solidarity with the miners** ils ont fait grève par solidarité avec les mineurs

2 *comp (strike)* de solidarité

solid-fuel *adj* à combustible solide; **a solid-fuel heating system** un chauffage à combustibles solides

solidifiable [ˌsəlɪdɪ'faɪəbəl] *adj* qui peut se solidifier

solidification [səˌlɪdɪfɪ'keɪʃən] *n* solidification *f*

solidify [sə'lɪdɪfaɪ] *(pt & pp* **solidified***)* **1** *vi* (**a**) *(liquid, gas)* se solidifier (**b**) *(system, opinion)* se consolider

2 *vt* (**a**) *(liquid, gas)* solidifier (**b**) *(system, opinion)* consolider

solidifying [sə'lɪdɪfaɪɪŋ] *n* solidification *f*

solidity [sə'lɪdətɪ] *n* solidité *f*

solidly ['sɒlɪdlɪ] *adv* (**a**) *(sturdily)* solidement; **the town hall stands solidly in the middle of the square** la mairie est solidement plantée au milieu de la place; **to be solidly built** *(person)* avoir une forte carrure

(**b**) *(thoroughly)* très, tout à fait; **a solidly established reputation** une réputation solidement établie

(**c**) *(massively)* massivement, en masse; **Massachusetts voted solidly for the Democrats** l'État du Massachussetts a voté massivement *ou* en masse pour les démocrates

(**d**) *(continuously)* sans arrêt; **I worked solidly for five hours** j'ai travaillé sans interruption pendant cinq heures

solidness ['sɒlɪdnɪs] *n* solidité *f*

solid-state *adj* (**a**) *Phys* des solides (**b**) *Electron* à semi-conducteurs

solidus ['sɒlɪdəs] *(pl* **solidi** [-daɪ]*) n Typ* barre *f* oblique

solifluction, solifluxion [ˌsɒlɪ'flʌkʃən] *n Geol* solifluction *f*

soliloquist [sə'lɪləkwɪst] *n* monologueur *m*

soliloquize, -ise [sə'lɪləkwaɪz] *vi* soliloquer, monologuer

soliloquizer [sə'lɪləkwaɪzə(r)] = **soliloquist**

soliloquy [sə'lɪləkwɪ] *(pl* **soliloquies***) n* soliloque *m*, monologue *m*

solipsism ['sɒlɪpsɪzəm] *n* solipsisme *m*

solipsist ['sɒlɪpsɪst] **1** *n* solipsiste *mf*

2 *adj* solipsiste

solipsistic [ˌsɒlɪp'sɪstɪk] *adj* solipsiste

solitaire [ˌsɒlɪ'teə(r)] *n* (**a**) *(pegboard)* solitaire *m* (**b**) *Am (card game)* réussite *f*, patience *f*; **to play solitaire** faire des réussites *ou* des patiences (**c**) *(gem)* solitaire *m*

solitarily ['sɒlɪtərəlɪ] *adv* solitairement, tout seul

solitariness ['sɒlɪtərɪnɪs] *n* solitude *f*

solitary ['sɒlɪtərɪ] *(pl* **solitaries***)* **1** *adj* (**a**) *(alone → person, life, activity)* solitaire; **she had a solitary childhood** elle a eu une enfance solitaire

(**b**) *(single)* seul, unique; **a solitary tree on the horizon** un seul arbre à l'horizon; **can you give me one solitary reason why I should go?** peux-tu me donner une seule raison d'y aller?

(**c**) *(remote → place)* retiré, isolé

(**d**) *(empty of people)* vide, désert; **the solitary streets of the suburbs** les rues *fpl* désertes de la banlieue

2 *n* (**a**) *Fam (solitary confinement)* isolement *m* cellulaire □

(**b**) *(person)* solitaire *mf*

►► ***solitary confinement*** isolement *m* cellulaire □

solitude ['sɒlɪtjuːd] *n* (**a**) *(feeling)* solitude *f*; **to live in solitude** vivre dans la solitude (**b**) *Literary (place)* lieu *m* solitaire

solo ['səʊləʊ] *(pl* **solos***)* **1** *n* (**a**) *Mus* solo *m*; **he played a violin/drum solo** il a joué un solo de violon/de batterie

(**b**) *(flight)* vol *m* solo

(**c**) *(card game)* solo *m (variante du whist)*

2 *adj* (**a**) *Mus* solo; **she plays solo violin** elle est soliste de violon, elle est violon solo

(**b**) *(unaided)* en solitaire; **a solo act** un one-man-show; **the first solo attempt on the north face** la première tentative d'escalade de la face nord en solitaire; **her first solo flight** son premier vol en solo

3 *adv* (**a**) *Mus* en solo; **to play/to sing solo** jouer/chanter en solo

(**b**) *(unaided)* seul, en solitaire, en solo; **to fly solo** voler en solo

►► ***solo album*** album *m* solo; ***solo whist*** solo *m (variante du whist)*

soloist ['səʊləʊɪst] *n* soliste *mf*

Solomon [ˈsɒləmən] *pr n Bible* Salomon
▸▸ ***Solomon Islander*** Salomonien(enne) *m,f*; ***the Solomon Islands*** les îles *fpl* Salomon; **in the Solomon Islands** dans les îles Salomon; *Bot* ***Solomon's seal*** sceau-de-Salomon *m*

Solothurn [ˈsɒlə,θɜːn] *n* Soleure; **in Solothurn** en Soleure

solstice [ˈsɒlstɪs] *n* solstice *m*; **the winter/summer solstice** le solstice d'hiver/d'été

solubility [,sɒljʊˈbɪlətɪ] *n* solubilité *f*

solubilize, -ise [ˈsɒljʊbɪlaɪz] *vt* solubiliser

soluble [ˈsɒljʊbəl] *adj* (**a**) *(substance)* soluble (**b**) *(problem)* soluble

solus [ˈsəʊləs] *adj* (**a**) *Theat* seul (**b**) *Mktg* isolé
▸▸ *Mktg* ***solus advertisement*** publicité *f* isolée; *Mktg* ***solus position*** emplacement *m* isolé; *Mktg* ***solus site*** emplacement *m* isolé

solute [ˈsɒljuːt] *n Chem & Pharm* soluté *m*, corps *m* dissous

solution [səˈluːʃən] *n* (**a**) *(answer → to problem, equation, mystery)* solution *f*; **a political solution to the conflict** une solution politique au conflit; **there is no real solution to this** il n'y a aucune solution dans ce cas
(**b**) *(act of solving → of problem, equation, mystery)* résolution *f*; **our main aim should be the rapid solution of the problem** notre principal objectif devrait être de résoudre rapidement le problème
(**c**) *Chem & Pharm* solution *f*; **salt in solution** sel *m* en solution

solvable [ˈsɒlvəbəl] *adj* soluble

solvate [ˈsɒlveɪt] *n Chem* solvate *m*

solvated [sɒlˈveɪtɪd] *adj Chem* solvatisé

solvation [sɒlˈveɪʃən] *n Chem* solvatisation *f*

solve [sɒlv] *vt (equation)* résoudre; *(problem)* résoudre, trouver la solution de; *(crime, mystery)* élucider; **I couldn't solve a single clue in the Times crossword** je n'ai pas réussi à trouver une seule définition dans les mots croisés du 'Times'

solvency [ˈsɒlvənsɪ] *n* solvabilité *f*

solvent [ˈsɒlvənt] **1** *adj* (**a**) *(financially)* solvable (**b**) *(substance, liquid)* dissolvant
2 *n* solvant *m*, dissolvant *m*
▸▸ ***solvent abuse*** usage *m* de solvants hallucinogènes; ***solvent abuser*** toxicomane *mf* utilisant des solvants hallucinogènes

solver [ˈsɒlvə(r)] *n* **there will be a prize for the solver of the riddle** celui qui trouvera la solution à l'énigme recevra un prix; **he's an excellent problem solver** il est très doué pour résoudre les problèmes

Solzhenitsyn [sɒlʒəˈnɪtsɪn] *pr n* Soljenitsyne

Som. *(written abbr* **Somerset**) Somerset *m*

soma [ˈsəʊmə] *(pl* **somas** *or* **somata** [-mətə]) *n Biol* soma *m*

Somali [səˈmɑːlɪ] **1** *n* (**a**) *(person)* Somalien(enne) *m,f* (**b**) *Ling* somali *m*
2 *adj* somalien
▸▸ ***the Somali Democratic Republic*** la République démocratique de Somalie

Somalia [səˈmɑːlɪə] *n* Somalie *f*; **in Somalia** en Somalie

Somalian [səˈmɑːlɪən] = **Somali**

Somaliland [səˈmɑːlɪlænd] *n* Somalie *f*; **British/Italian Somaliland** Somalie *f* britannique/italienne

somatic [səˈmætɪk] *adj* somatique

somatogenic [,səʊmətəʊˈdʒenɪk] *adj Biol* somatogène

somatology [,səʊməˈtɒlədʒɪ] *n* somatologie *f*

somatotrophin [,səʊmətəʊˈtrəʊfɪn] *n Physiol* somatotrophine *f*, somatotropine *f*

somatotype [ˈsəʊmətəʊtaɪp] *n Physiol* type *m* somatique

sombre, *Am* **somber** [ˈsɒmbə(r)] *adj* (**a**) *(dark → colour, place)* sombre (**b**) *(grave, grim → outlook, person, day)* sombre, morne; **what are you looking so sombre about?** pourquoi cet air si sombre?; **a sombre episode in the history of Europe** un épisode sombre dans l'histoire de l'Europe

sombrely, *Am* **somberly** [ˈsɒmbəlɪ] *adv* sombrement

sombreness, *Am* **somberness** [ˈsɒmbənɪs] *n* (**a**) *(darkness)* obscurité *f*; **the sombreness of the colours** les couleurs *fpl* sombres (**b**) *(gravity, grimness)* gravité *f*, caractère *m* sombre; **the news was announced with great sombreness** on annonça la nouvelle avec beaucoup de gravité

sombrero [sɒmˈbreərəʊ] *(pl* **sombreros**) *n* sombrero *m*

SOME [sʌm]

du, de la, de l', des	▸ 1 (a)
certains	▸ 1 (b); 2 (b)
un certain	▸ 1 (c)
quelques	▸ 1 (c)
quelques-uns	▸ 2 (a), (b)
en	▸ 2 (a)
quelque	▸ 3 (a)
environ	▸ 3 (a)
un peu	▸ 3 (b)

1 *adj* (**a**) *(a quantity of)* du, de la, de l'; *(a number of)* des; **don't forget to buy some cheese/beer/garlic** n'oublie pas d'acheter du fromage/de la bière/de l'ail; **I ate some fruit** j'ai mangé des fruits; **let me give you some advice** laissez-moi vous donner un conseil; **we've invited some friends round** nous avons invité des amis à la maison; **some red flowers** des fleurs *fpl* rouges; **some pretty flowers** de *ou* des jolies fleurs *fpl*; **I met some old friends last night** j'ai rencontré de *ou* des vieux amis hier soir
(**b**) *(not all, certain)* certains *mpl*, certaines *fpl*; **some wine/software is very expensive** certains vins/logiciels coûtent très cher; **some petrol still contains lead** il existe encore de l'essence avec plomb; **some English people like frogs' legs** certains Anglais aiment les cuisses de grenouille; **some employees like the new system, others don't** certains employés aiment le nouveau système, d'autres pas; **some people say...** certains disent..., il y en a *ou* il y a des gens qui disent...; **some cars shouldn't be allowed on the road** il y a des voitures qu'on ne devrait pas laisser circuler
(**c**) *(a considerable amount of)* un certain, une certaine; *(a considerable number of)* quelques *mfpl*; **I haven't been abroad for some time** ça fait un certain temps que je ne suis pas allé à l'étranger; **it happened (quite) some time ago** ça s'est passé il y a (bien) longtemps; **it will be some time before it's finished** ça va prendre un certain temps *ou* un moment avant que ça soit fini; **it's some distance from here** c'est assez loin d'ici; **the money should go some way towards compensating them** l'argent devrait les dédommager dans une certaine mesure; **at some length** assez longuement; **not without some opposition** non sans rencontrer une certaine opposition; **it happened some years/months ago** ça s'est passé il y a quelques années/mois
(**d**) *(a small amount or number of)* **you might have shown some gratitude!** tu aurais pu faire preuve d'un peu de gratitude(, quand même)!; **I felt some uneasiness** je ressentais quelque inquiétude; **you must have some idea of how much it will cost** vous devez avoir une petite idée de combien ça va coûter; **I hope I've been of some help to you** j'espère que je vous ai un peu aidé; **in some measure, to some degree** jusqu'à un certain point, dans une certaine mesure; **I'm glad some people understand me!** je suis content qu'il y ait quand même des gens qui me comprennent!
(**e**) *(unknown, unspecified)* **we must find some alternative** il faut que nous trouvions une autre solution; **he's gone to some town in the north** il est parti dans une ville quelque part dans le nord; **she works for some publishing company** elle travaille pour je ne sais quelle maison d'édition; **some fool left the door open** un imbécile a laissé la porte ouverte; **some book or other** un livre quelconque; **I'll get even with them some day!** je me vengerai d'eux un de ces jours *ou* un jour ou l'autre!; **come back some other time** revenez un autre jour
(**f**) *Fam (expressing scorn, irritation)* **did you go to the party? – some party!** est-ce que tu es allé à la fête? – tu parles d'une fête!; **some hope we've got of winning!** comme si on avait la moindre chance de gagner! ❑; **some people!** il y a des gens, je vous assure!
(**g**) *Fam (expressing admiration, approval)* **that was some party!** ça c'était une fête!; **(that was) some storm!** quelle tempête! ❑; **that was some meal!** ce que nous avons bien mangé!; **she's some girl!** c'est une fille formidable!; **he's some tennis player!** c'est un sacré tennisman!
2 *pron* (**a**) *(an unspecified number or amount → as subject)* quelques-uns *mpl*, quelques-unes *fpl*, certains *mpl*, certaines *fpl*; *(→ as object)* en; **some are plain and some are patterned** certains sont unis et certains ont des motifs; **they went off, some one way, some another** ils se sont dispersés, les uns d'un côté, les autres de l'autre; **some say it wasn't an accident** certains disent *ou* il y a des gens qui disent que ce n'était pas un accident; **I've got too much cake, do you want some?** j'ai trop de gâteau, en voulez-vous un peu?; **can I have some more?** est-ce que je peux en reprendre?; **I have some more** *(I have some left)* j'en ai encore; *(I have some others)* j'en ai d'autres; **where are the envelopes? – there are some in my drawer** où sont les enveloppes? – il y en a dans mon tiroir; **he wants the lot and then some** il veut tout et puis le reste
(**b**) *(not all)* **some of the snow had melted** une partie de la neige avait fondu; **some of the time** une partie du temps; **I only believe some of what I read in the papers** je ne crois pas tout ce que je lis dans les journaux; **some of the most beautiful scenery in the world is in Australia** certains des plus beaux paysages du monde se trouvent en Australie; **I've seen some of her films** j'ai vu quelques-uns *ou* certains de ses films; **if you need pencils, take some of these/mine** si vous avez besoin de crayons à papier, prenez quelques-uns de ceux-ci/des miens; **do you want some or all of them?** en voulez-vous quelques-uns ou les voulez-vous tous?; **some of us/them** certains d'entre nous/eux; **some of my friends** certains de mes amis; **some of the guests had already left** quelques invités étaient déjà partis
3 *adv* (**a**) *(approximately)* quelque, environ; **it's some fifty kilometres from London** c'est à environ cinquante kilomètres *ou* c'est à une cinquantaine de kilomètres de Londres; **some 500 people** quelque 500 personnes; **some thirty pounds** une trentaine de livres, quelque trente livres; **some fifteen minutes** un bon quart d'heure; **some few minutes ago** il y a quelques minutes
(**b**) *Am Fam (a little)* un peu ❑; *(a lot)* beaucoup ❑, pas mal; **I need to rest up some** j'ai besoin de me reposer un peu; **admit it, you like her some!** avoue-le, tu l'aimes bien! ❑

somebody [ˈsʌmbədɪ] *pron* (**a**) *(an unspecified person)* quelqu'un; **somebody else** quelqu'un d'autre; **somebody big/small** quelqu'un de grand/de petit; **they're looking for somebody with a lot of experience** ils cherchent quelqu'un qui ait beaucoup d'expérience; **he's not somebody you can trust** ce n'est pas quelqu'un en qui on peut avoir confiance; **there's somebody on the phone for you** on vous demande au téléphone; **somebody's at the door, there's somebody at the door** on a frappé; **somebody in the crowd/from head office** quelqu'un dans la foule/à la direction; **we need somebody a bit taller/who speaks Russian** il nous faut quelqu'un d'un peu plus grand/qui parle russe; **somebody has left their/his/her umbrella behind** quelqu'un a oublié son parapluie; **is this somebody's wallet?** est-ce que ce portefeuille est à quelqu'un?; **somebody or other** quelqu'un, je ne sais qui
(**b**) *(an important person)* **he's (a) somebody** c'est un personnage, ce n'est pas le premier venu; **you really think you're somebody, don't you?** tu te crois vraiment quelqu'un, n'est-ce pas?

someday [ˈsʌmdeɪ] *adv* un jour (ou l'autre), un de ces jours; **someday we'll go to the Bahamas** un jour (ou l'autre), nous irons aux Bahamas

somehow [ˈsʌmhaʊ] *adv* (**a**) *(in some way)* d'une manière ou d'une autre, d'une façon ou d'une autre; **don't worry, we'll manage somehow (or other)** ne t'inquiète pas, nous nous débrouillerons d'une façon ou d'une autre; **she'd**

sol–som

somehow (or other) managed to lock herself in elle avait trouvé moyen de s'enfermer

(**b**) *(for some reason)* pour une raison ou pour une autre, je ne sais pas trop pourquoi; **somehow I'm not surprised he didn't come** je ne sais pas trop pourquoi, mais cela ne m'étonne pas qu'il ne soit pas venu; **it somehow doesn't look right** je ne sais pas pourquoi, mais il me semble qu'il y a quelque chose qui ne va pas

someone ['sʌmwʌn] = **somebody** (**a**)

someplace ['sʌmpleɪs] *Am* = **somewhere** (**a**)

somersault ['sʌməsɔːlt] **1** *n* (**a**) *(on ground or accidentally)* culbute *f*; *(in air)* saut *m* périlleux; *(by car)* tonneau *m*; **to turn** *or* **do a somersault** *(on ground or accidentally)* faire la culbute; *(in air)* faire un saut périlleux; *(car)* faire un tonneau

(**b**) *esp Am (of opinion)* volte-face *f*

2 *vi (on ground or accidentally)* faire la culbute; *(in air)* faire un saut périlleux/des sauts périlleux; *(car)* faire un tonneau/des tonneaux; **the car somersaulted twice** la voiture a fait deux tonneaux

Somerset ['sʌməset] *n* le Somerset, = comté du sud-ouest de l'Angleterre; **in Somerset** dans le Somerset

►► ***Somerset House*** = édifice situé dans le centre de Londres, où se trouvaient autrefois l'état civil, les impôts et d'autres administrations

SOMETHING ['sʌmθɪŋ] **1** *pron* (**a**) *(an unspecified object, event, action etc)* quelque chose; **there must be something going on** il doit se passer quelque chose; **I've got something in my eye** j'ai quelque chose dans l'œil; **I've thought of something** j'ai eu une idée; **don't just stand there, do something!** ne reste pas là, fais quelque chose!; **something else** quelque chose d'autre, autre chose; **something or other** quelque chose; **something big/small** quelque chose de grand/de petit; **I've done/said something stupid** j'ai fait/dit une bêtise; **was it something I said?** est-ce que j'ai dit quelque chose (qu'il ne fallait pas)?; **I've got a feeling there's something wrong** j'ai le sentiment que quelque chose ne va pas; **there's something wrong with the ship's computer** l'ordinateur de bord ne marche pas bien; **take something to read on the train** prenez quelque chose à lire *ou* prenez de quoi lire dans le train; **he gave them something to eat/drink** il leur a donné à manger/boire; **would you like something to eat?** voulez-vous manger quelque chose?; **something to live for** une raison de vivre; **to have something to cry/be annoyed about** avoir une bonne raison de pleurer/se fâcher; **a film with something for everybody** un film qui peut plaire à tout le monde; **they all want something for nothing** ils veulent tous avoir tout pour rien; **you can't get something for nothing** on n'a rien pour rien; **there's something about him/in the way he talks that reminds me of Gary** il y a quelque chose chez lui/dans sa façon de parler qui me rappelle Gary; **she's something in the City/in insurance** elle travaille dans la finance/dans les assurances; **would you like a little something to drink?** voulez-vous un petit quelque chose à boire?; **she slipped the head waiter a little something** elle a glissé un petit pourboire au maître d'hôtel; **I've brought you a little something** je vous ai apporté un petit quelque chose *ou* une bricole; **I'm sure she's got something going with him** je suis sûr qu'il y a quelque chose entre elle et lui; **to be** *or* **have something to do with sth** avoir un rapport avec qch; **her job is** *or* **has something to do with the Stock Exchange** son travail a un rapport avec la Bourse; **I don't know what it means, I think it's got something to do with nuclear physics** je ne sais pas ce que ça veut dire, je crois que ça a (quelque chose) à voir avec la physique nucléaire; **I'm sure the weather has something to do with it** je suis sûre que le temps y est pour quelque chose *ou* que ça a un rapport avec le temps

(**b**) *(thing of significance, value etc)* **to make something of oneself** *or* **one's life** faire quelque chose de sa vie; **at least they've replied to my letter, that's something** au moins ils ont répondu à ma lettre, c'est toujours *ou* déjà ça; **there must be something in** *ou* **to all these rumours** il doit y avoir quelque chose de vrai dans toutes ces rumeurs; **there's something in her plan** son projet mérite considération; **there's something in what you say** il y a du vrai dans ce que vous dites; **I think you've got something there** ce n'est pas bête ce que vous dites là; **that new singer has got something** ce nouveau chanteur n'est pas mal; **he's got a certain something** il a un petit quelque chose; *Fam* **that was quite something!, that was something else!** c'était vraiment quelque chose!; *Fam* **that meal was something else!** c'était quelque chose, ce repas!; *Fam* **he really is something else!** *(wonderful)* il est vraiment génial!; *(exasperating)* il est pas possible!; *Fam* **well, isn't that something?** et bien, ça alors!; *Fam* **it was really something to see those kids dancing!** c'était quelque chose de voir ces gosses danser!; *Fam* **the new model is really something** le nouveau modèle est sensationnel

(**c**) *(replacing forgotten amount, word, name etc)* **the battle took place in 1840 something** la bataille a eu lieu dans les années 1840; **he's forty something** il a dans les quarante ans; **it cost £7 something** ça a coûté 7 livres et quelques; **her friend, Maisie something (or other)** son amie, Maisie quelque chose

2 *adv* (**a**) *(a little)* un peu; **something over a month's salary** un peu plus d'un mois de salaire; **temperatures were something under what we expected** les températures étaient un peu en-dessous de ce que nous attendions; **something in the region of $10,000** quelque chose comme 10 000 dollars; **an increase of something between 10 and 15 percent** une augmentation de 10 à 15 pour cent

(**b**) *Fam (as intensifier)* **something rotten** *or* **awful** *or* **terrible** vachement; **it hurts something awful** ça fait vachement mal; **he was screaming something terrible** il gueulait comme un putois; **he fancies her something rotten** il est dingue d'elle

3 something like *prep* (**a**) *(rather similar to)* **it looks something like a grapefruit** ça ressemble un peu à un pamplemousse; **now that's something like it!** c'est déjà mieux!

(**b**) *(roughly)* environ; **it's something like 5 metres long/wide** ça fait quelque chose comme 5 mètres de long/large; **it costs something like £500** ça coûte quelque chose comme *ou* dans les 500 livres

4 something of *adv (rather)* **he's something of an expert in the field** c'est en quelque sorte un expert dans ce domaine; **she became something of a legend** elle est devenue une sorte de légende; **she's something of a miser** elle est un peu *ou* quelque peu avare; **how they do it remains something of a mystery** comment ils s'y prennent, ça c'est un mystère

5 or something *adv* **would you like a cup of tea or something?** veux-tu une tasse de thé, ou autre chose?; **she must be ill or something** elle doit être malade ou quelque chose dans ce genre-là; **I thought they were engaged or something** je croyais qu'ils étaient fiancés ou quelque chose comme ça; **are you deaf or something?** tu es sourd ou quoi?

sometime ['sʌmtaɪm] **1** *adv* (**a**) *(in future)* un jour (ou l'autre), un de ces jours; **you must come and see us sometime** il faut que vous veniez nous voir un de ces jours; **I hope we'll meet again sometime soon** j'espère que nous nous reverrons bientôt; **you'll have to face up to it sometime or other** un jour ou l'autre il faudra bien voir les choses en face; **her baby is due sometime in May** elle attend son bébé pour le mois de mai; **sometime after/before next April** après le mois/d'ici au mois d'avril; **sometime next year** dans le courant de l'année prochaine

(**b**) *(in past)* **she phoned sometime last week** elle a téléphoné (dans le courant de) la semaine dernière; **the last time I saw him was sometime in August** la dernière fois que je l'ai vu, c'était en août; **it happened sometime before/after the Second World War** ça s'est passé avant/après la Seconde Guerre mondiale; **sometime around 1920** vers 1920; **sometime between 1927 and 1931** entre 1927 et 1931

2 *adj* (**a**) *(former)* ancien; **Mrs Evans, the club's sometime president** l'ancienne présidente du club, Mme Evans

(**b**) *Am (occasional)* intermittent; **he was a baseball player and sometime golfer** il jouait au base-ball et parfois au golf; *Fam* **it's very much a sometime thing** c'est très épisodique ❑

sometimes ['sʌmtaɪmz] *adv* quelquefois, parfois; **I sometimes think that it's a waste of time** parfois je me dis que c'est une perte de temps; **you can be so irritating sometimes!** qu'est-ce que tu peux être agaçant quelquefois!; **sometimes they're friendly, sometimes (they're) not** tantôt ils sont aimables, tantôt (ils ne le sont) pas

someway ['sʌmweɪ] *Am Fam* = **somehow** (**a**)

somewhat ['sʌmwɒt] *adv* quelque peu, un peu; **I was somewhat disappointed** j'ai été quelque peu déçu; **everybody came, somewhat to my surprise** tout le monde est venu, ce qui n'a pas été sans me surprendre; **I was in somewhat of a hurry to get home** j'étais quelque peu pressé de rentrer chez moi; **it was somewhat of a failure** c'était plutôt un échec

somewhere ['sʌmweə(r)] *adv* (**a**) *(indicating an unspecified place)* quelque part; **somewhere in the drawer/on the desk** quelque part dans le tiroir/sur le bureau; **somewhere in the world** quelque part (dans le monde); **somewhere in France** quelque part en France; **somewhere near us** pas bien loin de nous; **she's somewhere around** elle est quelque part par là, elle n'est pas loin; **let's go somewhere else** allons ailleurs *ou* autre part; **but it's got to be somewhere or other!** mais il doit bien être quelque part!; **I read somewhere that it can be fatal** j'ai lu quelque part que ça peut être mortel; **I'm looking for somewhere to stay** je cherche un endroit où loger; **I need somewhere quiet to work** j'ai besoin d'un endroit calme pour travailler; **she's found somewhere more comfortable to sit** elle a trouvé un siège plus confortable; **now we're getting somewhere!** nous arrivons enfin à quelque chose!

(**b**) *(approximately)* environ; **she earns somewhere around $2,000 a month** elle gagne quelque chose comme 2000 dollars par mois; **somewhere between five and six hundred people were there** il y avait entre cinq et six cents personnes; **he must be somewhere in his forties** il doit avoir entre quarante et cinquante ans

somite ['səʊmaɪt] *n Zool* somite *m*

somnambulant [sɒm'næmbjʊlənt] **1** *n* somnambule *mf*

2 *adj* somnambule

somnambulate [sɒm'næmbjʊleɪt] *vi* marcher dans son sommeil

somnambulism [sɒm'næmbjʊlɪzəm] *n* somnambulisme *m*

somnambulist [sɒm'næmbjʊlɪst] *n* somnambule *mf*

somnambulistic [sɒmˌnæmbjʊ'lɪstɪk] *adj* somnambule, somnambulique

somniferous [sɒm'nɪfərəs] *adj* soporifique, somnifère

somnolence ['sɒmnələns] *n* somnolence *f*

somnolent ['sɒmnələnt] *adj* somnolent

son[1] [sʌn] **1** *n* (**a**) *(family member)* fils *m*; **she's got two sons** elle a deux fils *ou* garçons; *Fig* **the sons of Ireland** les fils *mpl* de l'Irlande; **son and heir** héritier *m* (**b**) *Fam (term of address)* fiston *m*

2 Son *n Rel* Fils *m*; **the Son of God** le Fils de Dieu; **the Son of Man** le Fils de l'Homme

►► *Am Hist **Sons of Liberty*** = groupes clandestins formés avant la Révolution américaine luttant pour l'indépendance des colonies

'Dombey and Son' *Dickens* '(Dossier de la maison de) Dombey et fils'

'Sons and Lovers' Lawrence 'Amants et fils' *ou* 'Fils et amants'

son² [səʊn] *n Mus* son *m*

sonant ['səʊnənt] *Ling* **1** *adj* sonore
2 *n* sonore *f*

sonar ['səʊnɑː(r)] *n* sonar *m*

sonata [sə'nɑːtə] *n* sonate *f*; **piano/violin sonata** sonate *f* pour piano/violon

sonatina [ˌsɒnə'tiːnə] *n* sonatine *f*

sonde [sɒnd] *n Astron & Met* sonde *f*

sone [səʊn] *n* sone *m*

son et lumière [ˌsɒneɪ'luːmjeə(r)] *n* spectacle *m* son et lumière, son et lumière *m*

song [sɒŋ] *n* (**a**) *(piece of music with words)* chanson *f*; **I'll sing you a song** je vais vous chanter une chanson; **give us a song** chantenous quelque chose; **a song and dance act** un numéro de comédie musicale; **it was going for a song** ça se vendait pour une bouchée de pain *ou* trois fois rien; *Literary* **with a song in one's heart** la joie au cœur, le cœur léger; *Br Fam* **to make a song and dance about sth** faire toute une histoire pour qch; *Fam* **she gave me that old song and dance about being broke** elle m'a ressorti son couplet habituel, comme quoi elle était fauchée; *Br Fam* **to be on song** être en super forme
(**b**) *(songs collectively, act of singing)* chanson *f*; **an anthology of British song** une anthologie de la chanson britannique; **they all burst into song** ils se sont tous mis à chanter; **we raised our voice in song** nous avons entonné une chanson à pleins poumons
(**c**) *(of birds, insects)* chant *m*
▸▸ ***song cycle*** cycle *m* de chansons; *Bible* ***the Song of Songs, the Song of Solomon*** le Cantique des cantiques; ***song thrush*** grive *f* musicienne

'Songs of Innocence' *Blake* 'Les Chants d'innocence'

songbird ['sɒŋbɜːd] *n* oiseau *m* chanteur

songbook ['sɒŋbʊk] *n* recueil *m* de chansons

songfest ['sɒŋfest] *n Am* festival *m* de chant

songless ['sɒŋlɪs] *adj Orn* qui ne chante pas

songsmith ['sɒŋsmɪθ] *n (songwriter)* auteur *m* de chansons; *(performer)* auteur-compositeur *m* interprète

songster ['sɒŋstə(r)] *n* (**a**) *(person)* chanteur(euse) *m,f* (**b**) *Literary (bird)* oiseau *m* chanteur

songstress ['sɒŋstrɪs] *n Literary* chanteuse *f*

songwriter ['sɒŋˌraɪtə(r)] *n (of lyrics)* parolier(ère) *m,f*; *(of music)* compositeur(trice) *m,f*; *(of lyrics and music)* auteur-compositeur *m*

sonic ['sɒnɪk] **1** *adj* (**a**) *(involving, producing sound)* acoustique (**b**) *(concerning speed of sound)* sonique
2 sonics *n* acoustique *f*
▸▸ ***sonic bang*** bang *m*; ***sonic barrier*** mur *m* du son; ***sonic boom*** bang *m*; ***sonic frequency*** fréquence *f* acoustique

sonically ['sɒnɪkəlɪ] *adv* (**a**) *(involving sound)* acoustiquement (**b**) *(concerning speed of sound)* soniquement

soniferous [sɒ'nɪfərəs] *adj* (**a**) *(sound-bearing)* qui propage le son (**b**) *(sonorous)* sonore, résonnant

son-in-law (*pl* **sons-in-law**) *n* gendre *m*, beau-fils *m*

sonnet ['sɒnɪt] *n* sonnet *m*

sonny ['sʌnɪ] *n Fam* fiston *m*; **come here, sonny (boy** *or* **Jim)** viens-là, fiston

sonobuoy ['səʊnəˌbɔɪ] *n* bouée *f* acoustique

son-of-a-bitch (*pl* **sons-of-bitches**) *n Am very Fam* **1** *n* (**a**) *(man)* fils *m* de pute; **you old son-of-a-bitch, how are you doing?** comment ça va, enfoiré? (**b**) *(object)* saloperie *f*; **this son-of-a-bitch is too heavy to carry** cette saloperie est trop lourde à porter
2 *exclam* putain!

son-of-a-gun (*pl* **sons-of-guns**) **1** *n Am Fam* salaud *m*; **hi, you old son-of-a-gun!** salut, vieux bandit!
2 *exclam* putain!

sonogram ['səʊnəgræm] *n Phys* sonagramme *m*

sonograph ['səʊnəgrɑːf] *n Phys* sonagraphe *m*

sonometer [sɒ'nɒmɪtə(r)] *n Phys* sonomètre *m*

sonorific [ˌsɒnə'rɪfɪk] *adj* sonore, résonnant

sonority [sə'nɒrətɪ] *n* sonorité *f*

sonorous ['sɒnərəs] *adj* (**a**) *(resonant)* sonore (**b**) *(grandiloquent → tone, language)* grandiloquent

sonorously ['sɒnərəslɪ] *adv* (**a**) *(speak, sing)* d'une voix sonore; *(echo, crash)* avec un bruit retentissant (**b**) *Pej (declare, announce)* de manière grandiloquente

sonorousness ['sɒnərəsnɪs] *n* sonorité *f*; *Pej (of tone, language)* grandiloquence *f*

sook [sʊk] *n Fam Pej* (**a**) *Austr (weak person)* mauviette *f*, poule *f* mouillée (**b**) *Scot (grovelling person)* lèche-bottes *mf inv*

soon [suːn] **1** *adv* (**a**) *(in a short time)* bientôt, sous peu; **(I'll) see you/speak to you soon!** à bientôt!; **write soon!** écris-moi vite!; **I'll be back soon** je serai vite de retour; **a burglar can soon open a lock like that** un cambrioleur a vite fait d'ouvrir une serrure comme celle-ci; **she phoned soon after you'd left** elle a téléphoné peu après ton départ; **soon after** peu après; **soon after four** (un) peu après quatre heures; **it will soon be three years since...** voici bientôt trois ans que... + *indicative*, cela fera bientôt trois ans que... + *indicative*; **they were soon making friends** ils se sont bien vite fait des amis
(**b**) *(early)* tôt; **oh dear, I spoke too soon!** mince, j'ai parlé trop tôt!; **it's too soon to make any predictions** il est trop tôt pour se prononcer; **how soon can you finish it?** pour quand pouvez-vous le terminer?; **the police have arrived, and not a moment too soon** les policiers sont arrivés, et ce n'est pas trop tôt
2 as soon as *conj* dès que + *indicative*, aussitôt que + *indicative*; **I'll see him as soon as he comes** je le verrai aussitôt *ou* dès qu'il arrivera; **as soon as possible** dès *ou* aussitôt que possible; **phone me as soon as you hear anything** téléphonez-moi dès que vous aurez des nouvelles; **he came as soon as he could** il est venu dès *ou* aussitôt qu'il a pu
3 (just) as soon *adv* **I'd (just) as soon go by boat as by plane** j'aimerais autant *ou* mieux y aller en bateau qu'en avion; **do you want to come with us? – I'd just as soon not, if you don't mind** veux-tu venir avec nous? – j'aimerais autant *ou* mieux pas, si ça ne t'ennuie pas; **I'd just as soon he came tomorrow** j'aimerais autant *ou* mieux qu'il vienne demain; **I'd as soon die as do that!** plutôt mourir que de faire ça!

Sooner ['suːnə(r)] *n* = habitant ou natif de l'Oklahoma
▸▸ ***the Sooner State*** = surnom donné à l'Oklahoma

sooner ['suːnə(r)] **1** *adv* (*compar of* **soon**) (**a**) *(earlier)* plus tôt; **the sooner the better** le plus tôt sera le mieux; **the sooner it's over the sooner we can leave** plus tôt ce sera fini, plus tôt nous pourrons partir; **no sooner said than done!** aussitôt dit, aussitôt fait!; **no sooner had I sat down than the phone rang again** je venais juste de m'asseoir quand le téléphone a de nouveau sonné; **it was bound to happen sooner or later** cela devait arriver tôt ou tard; **the problem should be dealt with sooner rather than later** il faut faire face au problème le plus tôt possible
(**b**) *(indicating preference)* **would you sooner I called back tomorrow?** préférez-vous que je rappelle demain?; **shall we go out tonight? – I'd sooner not** si on sortait ce soir? – j'aimerais mieux pas; **I'd sooner die than go through that again!** plutôt mourir que de revivre ça!; **someone will have to do it – sooner you than me!** quelqu'un devra le faire – il vaudrait mieux que ce soit vous, plutôt que moi!
2 *n Am (pioneer)* pionnier(ère) *m,f* du Far West *(se dit surtout de ceux qui s'installaient sans posséder de titre légal de propriété)*

soonish ['suːnɪʃ] *adv* assez rapidement

soot [sʊt] *n* suie *f*

▸**soot up** *vt sep (dirty)* couvrir *ou* recouvrir de suie; *(clog)* encrasser

sooth [suːθ] *n Arch* **in sooth** en vérité

soothe [suːð] *vt* (**a**) *(calm, placate)* calmer, apaiser (**b**) *(relieve → pain)* calmer, soulager; **this will soothe your sore throat** ça va soulager votre mal de gorge

soothe [suːð] *vt (pain, burn etc)* calmer, apaiser; *(the mind)* tranquilliser; *(person)* apaiser; **to soothe sb's anger** apaiser la colère de qn

▸**soothe down** *vt sep (make less angry, worried → person)* calmer

soothing ['suːðɪŋ] *adj* (**a**) *(music, words, voice)* apaisant; *(atmosphere, presence)* rassurant; **the music had a soothing effect on them** la musique les a calmés; **the chairman made the usual soothing noises** le président a fait son laïus habituel pour calmer les esprits (**b**) *(lotion, ointment)* apaisant, calmant

soothingly ['suːðɪŋlɪ] *adv (gen)* d'une manière apaisante *ou* rassurante; *(say, speak)* d'un ton apaisant *ou* tranquillisant

soothsayer ['suːθˌseɪə(r)] *n* devin *m*, devineresse *f*

soothsaying ['suːθˌseɪɪŋ] *n* divination *f*

sootiness ['sʊtɪnɪs] *n* (**a**) *(gen)* noirceur *f* (**b**) *(of engine)* encrassement *m*

sooty ['sʊtɪ] (*compar* **sootier**, *superl* **sootiest**) *adj* (**a**) *(dirty)* couvert de suie, noir de suie (**b**) *(dark)* **sooty (black)** noir comme de la suie (**c**) *(deposit)* de suie

SOP [ˌesəʊ'piː] *n* (*abbr* **standard operating procedure**) = marche à suivre normale

sop [sɒp] **1** *n* (**a**) *(concession)* **as a sop to his conscience** pour soulager sa conscience; **they threw in the measure as a sop to the ecologists** ils ont ajouté cette mesure pour amadouer les écologistes; **she said it as a sop to their pride/feelings** elle l'a dit pour flatter leur amour-propre/pour ménager leur sensibilité
(**b**) *Fam (weak person)* mauviette *f*
2 sops *npl Culin* pain *m* trempé

▸**sop up** *vt sep (absorb)* absorber; *(mop up)* éponger; **he sopped up the sauce in his plate with a piece of bread** il a essuyé la sauce qu'il y avait dans son assiette avec un morceau de pain

soph [sɒf] *n Am Fam* (*abbr* **sophomore**) étudiant(e) *m,f* de deuxième année ❑

sophism ['sɒfɪzəm] *n* sophisme *m*

sophist ['sɒfɪst] **1** *n (false reasoner)* sophiste *mf*
2 Sophist *n Phil* sophiste *m*

sophistic [sə'fɪstɪk], **sophistical** [sə'fɪstɪkəl] *adj* sophistique, captieux

sophistically [sə'fɪstɪkəlɪ] *adv* sophistiquement

sophisticate [sə'fɪstɪkeɪt] *n* personne *f* raffinée; **New York sophisticates** la bonne société new-yorkaise; **he thinks he's a sophisticate** il se croit raffiné

sophisticated [sə'fɪstɪkeɪtɪd] *adj* (**a**) *(person, manner, tastes → refined)* raffiné; *(→ chic)* chic, élégant; *(→ well-informed)* bien informé; *(→ mature)* mûr; *(style)* recherché; **they used to think it was sophisticated to smoke** ils croyaient que ça faisait chic de fumer; **a sophisticated restaurant** un restaurant chic; **our more sophisticated readers** nos lecteurs les plus avertis; **the electorate has become too sophisticated to believe that promise** l'électorat est désormais trop bien informé *ou* trop averti pour croire à cette promesse
(**b**) *(argument, novel, film → subtle)* subtil; *(→ complicated)* complexe
(**c**) *(machine, system, technology → advanced)* sophistiqué, perfectionné

sophistication [səˌfɪstɪ'keɪʃən] *n* (**a**) *(of person, manners, tastes → refinement)* raffinement *m*; *(→ chic)* chic *m*, élégance *f*; *(→ maturity)* maturité *f*; **lack of sophistication** *(unworldliness)* simplicité *f*; *(lack of polish)* manque *m* de raffinement; **the growing sophistication of cinema audiences** le fait que le public de cinéma est de plus en plus averti
(**b**) *(of argument, novel, film → subtlety)* subtilité *f*; *(→ complexity)* complexité *f*
(**c**) *(of system, technology)* sophistication *f*, degré *m* de perfectionnement *m*

sophistry ['sɒfɪstrɪ] (*pl* **sophistries**) *n* (**a**) *(argumentation)* sophistique *f* (**b**) *(argument)* sophisme *m*

Sophocles ['sɒfəkliːz] *pr n* Sophocle

sophomore ['sɒfəmɔː(r)] *n Am* étudiant(e) *m,f* de seconde année; **in my sophomore year** lorsque j'étais en seconde année

sophomoric [ˌsɒfə'mɔːrɪk] *adj Am* prétentieux, suffisant

sopor ['səʊpɔː(r)] *n Med* sopor *m*

soporific [ˌsɒpəˈrɪfɪk] **1** *adj* soporifique
2 *n* soporifique *m*, somnifère *m*

soppiness [ˈsɒpɪnɪs] *n Br Fam (sentimentality)* sentimentalisme❑ *m*, sensiblerie❑ *f*

sopping [ˈsɒpɪŋ] *adj & adv Fam* **sopping (wet)** *(person)* trempé (jusqu'aux os)❑; *(shirt, cloth)* détrempé❑

soppy [ˈsɒpɪ] (*compar* **soppier**, *superl* **soppiest**) *adj Br Fam* (**a**) *(sentimental → person)* sentimental❑, fleur bleue❑ *(inv)*; *(→ story, picture)* sentimental❑, à l'eau de rose❑ (**b**) *(silly)* nigaud, bébête (**c**) *(in love)* **to be soppy about sb** avoir le béguin pour qn

sopranino [ˌsɒprəˈniːnəʊ] (*pl* **sopraninos**) *n Mus* sopranino *m*

soprano [səˈprɑːnəʊ] (*pl* **sopranos** *or* **soprani** [-niː]) **1** *n (singer)* soprano *mf*; *(voice, part, instrument)* soprano *m*; **to sing soprano** avoir une voix de soprano
2 *adj (voice, part)* de soprano; *(music)* pour soprano
►► ***soprano saxophone*** saxophone *m* soprano

SOR (*written abbr* **sale or return**) **to buy sth on an SOR basis** acheter qch à condition

sora rail [ˈsɔːrə-] *n Orn* marouette *f* de la Caroline

sorb [sɔːb] *n (fruit)* sorbe *f*; *(tree)* sorbier *m*

sorbet [ˈsɔːbeɪ] *n Br* sorbet *m*

sorbic [ˈsɔːbɪk] *adj Chem* sorbique
►► ***sorbic acid*** acide *m* sorbique

sorbitol [ˈsɔːbɪtɒl] *n* sorbitol *m*

sorcerer [ˈsɔːsərə(r)] *n* sorcier *m*

'The Sorcerer's Apprentice' *Dukas* 'L'Apprenti sorcier'

sorceress [ˈsɔːsərɪs] *n* sorcière *f*

sorcery [ˈsɔːsərɪ] (*pl* **sorceries**) *n* sorcellerie *f*

sordid [ˈsɔːdɪd] *adj* (**a**) *(dirty, wretched)* sordide, misérable; **they live in extremely sordid conditions** ils vivent dans des conditions vraiment sordides (**b**) *(base, loathsome)* sordide, infâme, vil; **they've got sordid little minds** ce sont des esprits mesquins et sordides; **a sordid affair** une affaire sordide; **I'll spare you the sordid details** je vous épargnerai les détails sordides

sordidly [ˈsɔːdɪdlɪ] *adv* sordidement

sordidness [ˈsɔːdɪdnɪs] *n (gen)* sordidité *f*; *(of business, motives)* bassesse *f*

sordino [sɔːˈdiːnəʊ] (*pl* **sordini** [-niː]) *n Mus* sourdine *f*

sore [sɔː(r)] **1** *adj* (**a**) *(aching → gen)* douloureux, endolori; *(→ eyes, gums)* irrité; **we stopped to rest our sore feet** nous nous sommes arrêtés pour reposer nos pieds endoloris; **I'm sore all over** j'ai mal partout; **I've a sore throat** j'ai mal à la gorge; **my arms/legs are sore** j'ai mal aux bras/jambes, mes bras/jambes me font mal; **don't touch me there, it's sore** ne me touche pas là, ça fait mal; **where is it sore?** où as-tu mal?; *Fig* **it's a sore point with her** elle est très sensible sur ce point *ou* là-dessus
(**b**) *Am Fam (angry)* en boule; *(resentful)* vexé❑, amer❑; **are you still sore at me?** est-ce que tu es toujours en boule contre moi?; **he got sore** il s'est mis en boule; **he's sore because they left him out of the team** il est vexé parce qu'ils l'ont laissé en dehors de l'équipe
(**c**) *Literary (great)* grand; **in sore distress** dans une grande détresse; **to be in sore need of sth** avoir grand besoin de qch
2 *n* plaie *f*; **open sores** des plaies *fpl* ouvertes
3 *adv Arch* grandement; **they were sore afraid** ils éprouvèrent une grande frayeur

sorehead [ˈsɔːhed] *n Am Fam* ronchon(onne) *m,f*, grincheux(euse) *m,f*; **don't be such a sorehead!** ne râle pas comme ça!, quel râleur (râleuse) tu fais!

sorely [ˈsɔːlɪ] *adv* (**a**) *(as intensifier)* grandement; **the house is sorely in need of a new coat of paint** la maison a grandement *ou* bien besoin d'être repeinte; **we are sorely pressed for time** nous manquons cruellement de temps; **she will be sorely missed** elle nous manquera cruellement; **I was sorely tempted to accept her offer** j'ai été très tenté d'accepter sa proposition
(**b**) *Literary (painfully)* **sorely wounded** grièvement blessé

soreness [ˈsɔːnɪs] *n* douleur *f*

sorghum [ˈsɔːgəm] *n Bot* sorgho *m*

soroptimist [sɒˈrɒptɪmɪst] *n* = membre d'un cercle féminin professionnel

sororal [səˈrɔːrəl], **sororial** [səˈrɔːrɪəl] *adj* sororal

sorority [səˈrɒrətɪ] (*pl* **sororities**) *n Am Univ (association)* club *m* d'étudiantes; *(residence)* résidence *f* (universitaire) pour jeunes femmes

sorosis [səˈrəʊsɪs] *n Bot* sorose *f*

sorrel [ˈsɒrəl] **1** *n* (**a**) *Bot & Culin* oseille *f* (**b**) *(colour)* roux *m*, brun rouge *m* (**c**) *(horse)* alezan *m* clair
2 *adj (gen)* roux (rousse); *(horse)* alezan clair *(inv)*

Sorrento [səˈrentəʊ] *n* Sorrente

sorrow [ˈsɒrəʊ] **1** *n* chagrin *m*, peine *f*, tristesse *f*; *(stronger)* affliction *f*, douleur *f*; **I am writing to express my sorrow at your sad loss** je vous écris pour vous faire part de la tristesse que j'ai éprouvée en apprenant votre deuil; **her sorrow at** *or* **over losing the match was short-lived** le chagrin qu'elle a éprouvé *ou* la tristesse qu'elle a éprouvée d'avoir perdu le match n'a pas duré; **to our great sorrow** à notre grand regret; **more in sorrow than in anger** avec plus de tristesse que de colère; **his son's failure was a great sorrow to him** l'échec de son fils lui a fait *ou* causé beaucoup de peine; **life is full of joys and sorrows** la vie est faite de joies et de peines; **one for sorrow, two for joy** = maxime que l'on prononce par supersitition lorsqu'on voit une pie, une pie seule étant censée porter malheur tandis que deux pies sont censées porter bonheur
2 *vi Literary* éprouver du chagrin *ou* de la peine; **he is still sorrowing over his son's death** il pleure encore la mort de son fils

'The Sorrows of Young Werther' *Goethe* 'Les Souffrances du jeune Werther'

sorrowful [ˈsɒrəfʊl] *adj (person)* triste; *(look, smile)* affligé

sorrowfully [ˈsɒrəfəlɪ] *adv* tristement

sorrowing [ˈsɒrəʊɪŋ] *adj* attristé, affligé

SORRY [ˈsɒrɪ]

désolé	► (a), (c)
excusez-moi	► (a)
pardon	► (a)
regretter	► (b)
navré	► (c)
plaindre	► (d)
triste	► (e)

(*compar* **sorrier**, *superl* **sorriest**) *adj* (**a**) *(in apologies)* désolé; **I'm sorry we won't be able to fetch you** je regrette que *ou* je suis désolé que nous ne puissions venir vous chercher; **(I'm) sorry to have bothered you** (je suis) désolé *ou* excusez-moi de vous avoir dérangé; **I'm sorry to have kept you waiting** je suis désolé *ou* excusez-moi de vous avoir fait attendre; **I'm so** *or* **very** *or* **terribly sorry** je suis vraiment navré; **ouch, that's my foot! – (I'm) sorry!** aïe! mon pied! – je suis désolé *ou* excusez-moi!; **(I'm) sorry about the mess** excusez le désordre; **I'm sorry about the mix-up** excusez-moi pour la confusion; **I'm sorry, but that's absolute rubbish!** désolé, mais c'est vraiment n'importe quoi!; **sorry to interrupt you but you're wanted on the phone** excusez-moi de vous interrompre mais on vous demande au téléphone; **sorry about forgetting your birthday** désolé d'avoir oublié ton anniversaire; **he said he was sorry** il a présenté ses excuses; **say (you're) sorry to the lady** demande pardon à la dame; **what's the time? – sorry?** quelle heure est-il? – pardon? *ou* comment?; **they're coming on Tuesday, sorry, Thursday** ils viennent mardi, pardon, jeudi
(**b**) *(regretful)* **to be sorry** regretter; **I'm sorry I ever came here!** je regrette d'être venu ici!; **I'm only sorry we couldn't have stayed longer** je regrette que nous n'ayons pas pu rester plus longtemps; **I'm sorry to say there's little we can do** malheureusement, nous ne pouvons pas faire grand-chose; **we are sorry to inform you that...** nous avons le regret *ou* nous sommes au regret de vous informer que... + *indicative*; **you'll be sorry for this** tu le regretteras; **you won't be sorry** tu ne le regretteras pas; **I'll make him sorry** je le lui ferai regretter; **I'll make him sorry (that) he ever came here** je lui ferai regretter d'être venu ici
(**c**) *(expressing sympathy)* désolé, navré, peiné; **I was sorry to hear about your father's death** j'ai été désolé *ou* peiné *ou* navré d'apprendre la mort de votre père
(**d**) *(expressing pity)* **to be** *or* **to feel sorry for sb** plaindre qn; **it's the children I feel sorry for** ce sont les enfants que je plains; **there's no need to feel sorry for them** ils ne sont pas à plaindre; **she felt sorry for him and gave him a pound** elle eut pitié de lui et lui donna une livre; **to be** *or* **to feel sorry for oneself** s'apitoyer sur soi-même *ou* sur son propre sort; **stop feeling sorry for yourself!** arrête un peu de t'apitoyer sur ton propre sort!; **he's just feeling a bit sorry for himself** il est juste un peu déprimé; **to look sorry for oneself** faire grise mine
(**e**) *(pitiful, wretched)* triste, piteux; **to cut a sorry figure** faire triste *ou* piètre figure; **they were a sorry sight after the match** ils étaient dans un triste état après le match; **to be in a sorry plight** être dans une mauvaise passe; **the garden was in a sorry state** le jardin était en piteux état *ou* dans un triste état; **it's a sorry state of affairs** c'est bien triste; **the whole sorry tale** toute cette malheureuse affaire
►► ***Sorry Day*** = journée annuelle de réconciliation entre Aborigènes et Australiens d'origine européenne au cours de laquelle sont organisées des activités sur les spoliations dont les Aborigènes ont été victimes

sorry-ass, sorry-assed *adj Am very Fam (inferior, contemptible)* à la con

SORT [sɔːt]

sorte	► 1 (a)
espèce	► 1 (a)
genre	► 1 (a)
tri	► 1 (c)
classer	► 2 (a)
trier	► 2 (a)

1 *n* (**a**) *(kind, type)* sorte *f*, espèce *f*, genre *m*; *(brand)* marque *f*; **a hat with a sort of veil** un chapeau avec une sorte *ou* une espèce *ou* un genre de voile; **it's a strange sort of film** c'est un drôle de film; **it's a different sort of problem** c'est un autre type de problème; **the trees formed a sort of arch** les arbres formaient comme une arche; **I've got a sort of feeling about what the result will be** j'ai comme un pressentiment sur ce que sera le résultat; **I think that he's some sort of specialist** *or* **that he's a specialist of some sort** je crois que c'est un genre de spécialiste; **she's not the sort (of woman) to let you down** elle n'est pas du genre à vous laisser tomber; **this** *or Fam* **these sort of people** les gens de cette espèce, ces gens-là; **they're not our sort (of people)** nous ne sommes pas du même monde; **I know your sort!** les gens de ton espèce, je les connais!; **there's too much of this sort of thing going on** il se passe trop de choses de ce genre; **good luck, and all that sort of thing!** bonne chance, et tout et tout!; **what sort of fish are we having?** qu'est-ce qu'on mange comme poisson?; **what sort of washing machine have you got?** qu'est-ce que vous avez comme (marque de) machine à laver?; **what sort of dog is that?** qu'est-ce que c'est comme chien *ou* comme race de chien?; **what sort of woman is she?** quel genre de femme est-ce?; **what sort of girl do you take me for?** pour qui me prenez-vous?; **what sort of way is that to speak to your grandmother?** en voilà une façon de parler à ta grand-mère!; **what sort of day did you have?** comment s'est passée ta journée?; **that's my sort of holiday** voilà des vacances comme je les aime; **all sorts of people** des gens de toutes sortes; **you get all sorts at these parties** on rencontre toutes sortes de gens dans ces soirées; **there are all sorts of materials to choose from** on peut choisir parmi toutes sortes de matériaux; **I've heard all sorts of good things about you** j'ai entendu dire beaucoup de bien de vous; **to be out of**

sorts *(a little unwell)* ne pas être dans son assiette; *(in a bad mood)* être de mauvaise humeur; **something of the sort** *or* **of that sort** quelque chose de pareil *ou* de semblable *ou* dans ce genre-là; **I said nothing of the sort!** je n'ai rien dit de pareil *ou* de tel!; **you were drunk last night – I was nothing of the sort!** tu étais ivre hier soir – absolument pas! *ou* mais pas du tout!; *Prov* **it takes all sorts (to make a world)** il faut de tout pour faire un monde

(**b**) *Fam (person)* **she's a good** *or* **decent sort** *(young woman)* c'est une brave fille; *(older woman)* c'est une brave femme; **he's not a bad sort** ce n'est pas le mauvais cheval

(**c**) *(gen) & Comput (→ putting in order)* tri *m*; **the program will do an alphabetical sort** le programme exécutera un tri alphabétique; **sort routine** routine *f* de tri; *Fam* **I've had a sort through all the winter clothes** j'ai trié tous les vêtements d'hiver ❑

2 *vt* (**a**) *(classify)* classer, trier; *(divide up)* répartir; *(separate)* séparer; *Comput* trier; **to sort mail** trier le courrier; **I've sorted the index cards into alphabetical order** j'ai classé *ou* trié les fiches par ordre alphabétique; **they were sorting the shirts according to colour** ils triaient les chemises selon leur couleur; **sort the cards into two piles** répartissez les cartes en deux piles; **sort the letters into urgent and less urgent** répartissez les lettres entre celles qui sont urgentes et celles qui le sont moins; **help me sort the good fruit from the bad** aidez-moi à séparer les bons fruits des mauvais; *Comput* **to sort sth in ascending/descending order** trier qch par ordre croissant/décroissant

(**b**) *(organize)* = **sort out** (**b**)

3 *vi Comput (arrange in list)* trier; *(file, data)* se trier

4 of sorts, of a sort *adv* **they served us champagne of sorts** *or* **of a sort** ils nous ont servi une espèce de champagne; **a peace/solution of sorts** un semblant de paix/de solution; **they live in a home of sorts** ils habitent dans une maison, si on peut appeler ça une maison

5 sort of *adv Fam* **I sort of expected it to rain** je m'attendais un peu à ce qu'il pleuve ❑; **I'm sort of glad that I missed them** je suis plutôt content de les avoir ratés; **it's sort of big and round** c'est du genre grand et rond; **it's sort of heavy** c'est un peu lourd, c'est plutôt lourd ❑; **he sort of apologized** d'une certaine façon, il s'est excusé ❑; **did you hit him? – well, sort of** tu l'as frappé? – en quelque sorte, oui ❑

►**sort out** *vt sep* (**a**) *(separate)* séparer; **to sort out the foreign stamps from the British ones** séparer les timbres étrangers des timbres britanniques

(**b**) *(select and set aside)* trier; **I've been sorting out some books for you to take** j'ai trié quelques livres pour que tu les emportes; **we've already sorted out the likely candidates from the rest** nous avons déjà trié les candidats intéressants (et les autres)

(**c**) *(tidy up, put in order → papers, clothes, room, cupboard)* ranger; *(→ finances, ideas)* mettre en ordre; **give me a few minutes to get (myself) sorted out** *or* **to sort myself out** donnez-moi quelques minutes pour m'organiser; **she needs to get her personal life sorted out** il faut qu'elle règle ses problèmes personnels

(**d**) *(settle, resolve → problem, dispute)* régler, résoudre; **I'm glad that bit of bother has been sorted out** je suis content que ce petit problème ait été réglé; **they still haven't sorted out the mistake in my tax demand** ils n'ont toujours pas réglé cette erreur dans ma feuille d'impôts; **everything's sorted out now** tout est arrangé *ou* réglé maintenant; **once the initial confusion had sorted itself out** une fois que la confusion du début se fut dissipée; **things will sort themselves out in the end** les choses finiront par s'arranger; *Fam* **two aspirins ought to sort out that headache** deux aspirines devraient avoir raison de ce mal de tête ❑

(**e**) *(establish, clarify)* **have you sorted out how to do it?** est-ce que tu as trouvé le moyen de le faire?; **she couldn't sort out what they wanted** elle n'arrivait pas à savoir au juste ce qu'ils voulaient; **I'm trying to sort out what's been going on** j'essaie de savoir *ou* de comprendre ce qui s'est passé; **you've got to sort out your priorities** il faut que tu définisses ce qui prime pour toi

(**f**) *(arrange)* arranger, fixer; **we still have to sort out a date for the next meeting** il nous faut encore arranger *ou* choisir une date pour la prochaine réunion; **I'll go and sort the tickets out** je vais m'occuper des billets; **to sort out the details** faire le nécessaire; **to sort out a room for sb** préparer une chambre pour qn

(**g**) *Br Fam (solve the problems of → person)* **he's very depressed, you should try to sort him out** il est très déprimé, tu devrais essayer de l'aider à s'en sortir ❑; **she needs time to sort herself out** il lui faut du temps pour régler ses problèmes ❑

(**h**) *Br Fam (punish)* régler son compte à ❑; **just wait till he gets home, I'll sort him out!** attends un peu qu'il rentre à la maison, je vais lui régler son compte!

►► *Banking* ***sort code*** code *m* guichet

►**sort through** *vt insep* trier; **I've been sorting through the old magazines** j'ai trié les vieux magazines

---

sorta ['sɔːtə] *Fam* = **sort of**

sorted ['sɔːtɪd] *Br Fam* **1** *adj* **to be sorted** *(psychologically)* être équilibré ❑, être bien dans ses baskets *ou* dans sa peau; *(have everything one needs)* être paré ❑; **to be sorted for sth** disposer de qch ❑

2 *exclam* super!, génial!

sorter ['sɔːtə(r)] *n* (**a**) *(person)* trieur(euse) *m,f*; **letter sorter** employé(e) *m,f* au tri postal (**b**) *(machine → gen)* trieur *m*; *(→ for punched cards)* trieuse *f*

sortie ['sɔːtiː] *n Mil* sortie *f*; **thirty sorties were flown today** il y a eu trente sorties aujourd'hui; *Hum* **I sometimes make the odd sortie to the pub/shops** de temps en temps je fais un petit tour dans les pubs/magasins

sortilege ['sɔːtɪlɪdʒ] *n* divination *f* par le tirage au sort

sorting ['sɔːtɪŋ] *n* tri *m*

►► *Banking* ***sorting code*** code *m* guichet; ***sorting office*** centre *m* de tri; *Comput* ***sorting routine*** routine *f* de tri

sort-out *n Br Fam (tidying)* rangement ❑ *m*; **the attic needs a good sort-out** il faudrait ranger le grenier ❑

sorus ['sɔːrəs] *n Bot* sore *m*

SOS [ˌesəʊ'es] *n* (*abbr* **save our souls**) SOS *m*; **to send out an SOS** lancer un SOS; **we received an SOS call** *or* **message** nous avons reçu un SOS; *Fig* **relief organizations are sending out an SOS for food and clothing** les organisations d'aide demandent d'urgence de la nourriture et des vêtements

so-so *adj Fam* pas fameux; *(in health)* comme ci comme ça, couci-couça; **the film was only so-so** le film n'était pas fameux

sostenuto [ˌsɒstə'nuːtəʊ] *Mus* **1** *adj* sostenuto

2 *adv* sostenuto

sot [sɒt] *n Literary* ivrogne(esse) *m,f*

soteriology [sɒˌtɪərɪ'ɒlədʒɪ] *n Rel* sotériologie *f*

Sotheby's ['sʌðəbiːz] *n* = société londonienne de vente aux enchères

sottish ['sɒtɪʃ] *adj Literary* sot (sotte), stupide, abruti

sotto voce [ˌsɒtəʊ'vəʊtʃɪ] *adv* (**a**) *(gen)* à voix basse (**b**) *Mus* sotto voce

sou [suː] *n* sou *m*

soubrette [suː'bret] *n Theat* soubrette *f*

souffle ['suːfəl] *n Med* souffle *m*

soufflé ['suːfleɪ] *n* soufflé *m*; **cheese/chocolate soufflé** soufflé *m* au fromage/au chocolat

►► ***soufflé dish*** moule *m* à soufflé

sough [saʊ] *Literary* **1** *vi* murmurer, susurrer

2 *n* murmure *m*, susurrement *m (du vent)*

sought [sɔːt] *pt & pp of* **seek**

sought-after *adj* recherché; **furniture of this period is much sought-after** les meubles de cette époque sont très recherchés (actuellement)

souk [suːk] *n* souk *m*

soukous ['suːkʊs] *n Mus* soukous *m*

soul [səʊl] **1** *n* (**a**) *Rel* âme *f*; **God rest his soul!** que Dieu ait son âme!; **to pray for sb's soul** prier pour l'âme de qn; *Old-fashioned* **upon my soul!** grands dieux!; *Fig* **I can't call my soul my own these days** je ne m'appartiens plus ces jours-ci; *Fig* **it's good for the soul** *(character-forming)* ça forme le caractère; *(makes a person feel better)* c'est bon pour le moral

(**b**) *(emotional depth)* profondeur *f*; **it was a polished performance, but it lacked soul** c'était une prestation impeccable, mais sans âme; **you've got no soul!** tu n'as pas de cœur!

(**c**) *(leading figure)* âme *f*; **she was the soul of the early feminist movement** elle était l'âme du mouvement féministe à ses débuts

(**d**) *(perfect example)* modèle *m*; **the soul of discretion** la discrétion même *ou* personnifiée

(**e**) *(person)* personne *f*, âme *f*; **poor old soul!** le (la) pauvre! *m,f*; **without meeting a (living) soul** sans rencontrer âme qui vive; **there wasn't a soul in the streets** il n'y avait pas âme qui vive dans les rues; **I didn't know a soul at the party** je ne connaissais personne à la réception; **I won't tell a soul** je ne le dirai à personne; **she's a happy soul** elle a un tempérament heureux *ou* optimiste; **he's a gentle soul** c'est quelqu'un de très doux; *Literary* **a town of 20,000 souls** une ville de 20 000 âmes; **the ship went down with all souls** le navire a sombré corps et biens

(**f**) *(music)* (musique *f*) soul *f*, soul music *f*; **a soul singer** un(e) chanteur(euse) *m,f* de soul

2 *adj Am Old-fashioned* = caractéristique de la culture des Noirs américains

►► *Am Fam* ***soul brother*** = nom que les Noirs américains donnent aux hommes noirs; *Fam* ***soul food*** cuisine *f* afroaméricaine ❑; ***soul music*** musique *f* soul, soul music *f*; *Am Fam* ***soul sister*** = nom que les Noirs américains donnent aux femmes noires

soul-destroying [-dɪˌstrɔɪɪŋ] *adj (job)* abrutissant; *(situation, place)* déprimant

soulful ['səʊlfʊl] *adj (song, performance, sigh)* émouvant, attendrissant; *(look, eyes)* mélancolique

soulfully ['səʊlfəlɪ] *adv (sing, perform, sigh)* de façon émouvante *ou* attendrissante; *(look)* d'un air mélancolique

soulless ['səʊllɪs] *adj* (**a**) *(inhuman → place)* inhumain, sans âme; *(→ work)* abrutissant (**b**) *(heartless)* sans cœur, insensible

soullessly ['səʊllɪslɪ] *adv* sans émotion; **the house had been soullessly renovated** on avait rénové la maison sans aucune sensibilité

soullessness ['səʊllɪsnɪs] *n* (**a**) *(of building)* côté *m* inhumain; **the soullessness of my surroundings** le cadre inhumain qui m'entoure (**b**) *(of person)* manque *m* de sensibilité

soulmate ['səʊlmeɪt] *n* âme *f* sœur

soul-searching *n* introspection *f*; **after much soul-searching she decided to leave** après mûre réflexion *ou* après avoir mûrement réfléchi, elle décida de partir

soul-stirring *adj* (profondément) émouvant

SOUND [saʊnd]

bruit	► **1 (a)**
son	► **1 (a) – (d)**
musique	► **1 (e)**
sonde	► **1 (g), (h)**
solide	► **3 (a), (c)**
en bon état	► **3 (a)**
sain	► **3 (a), (b)**
en bonne santé	► **3 (b)**
sensé	► **3 (c)**
valable	► **3 (c)**
bon	► **3 (c), (d)**
profond	► **3 (e)**
sonore	► **4**
sonner	► **6 (a); 7 (a)**
prononcer	► **6 (b)**
ausculter	► **6 (c)**
sonder	► **6 (c) – (e)**
résonner	► **7 (a)**
retentir	► **7 (a)**
sembler	► **7 (c)**

1 *n* (**a**) *(noise → of footsteps, thunder, conversation)* bruit *m*; *(→ of voice, musical instrument)* son *m*; **I was woken by the sound of voices/laughter** j'ai été réveillé par un bruit de voix/par des éclats de rires; **the sound of a dog barking/a door closing** le bruit d'un chien qui aboie/d'une porte qui se ferme; **a scratching sound** un grattement; **a grating sound** un grincement; **don't make a sound!** surtout ne faites pas de bruit!; **they tiptoed out without (making) a sound** ils sont sortis sur la pointe des pieds sans faire de bruit; **there was not a sound to be heard** on n'entendait pas le moindre bruit; **I love the sound of her voice** j'adore le son de sa voix; **the plaintive sound of the bagpipes** le son plaintif de la cornemuse; **within (the) sound of the church bells** à portée du son des cloches de l'église

(**b**) *Phys* son *m*; **light travels faster than sound** la lumière se déplace plus vite que le son; **the speed of sound** la vitesse du son

(**c**) *Ling* son *m*; **it's a similar sound to the Scots "ch"** c'est un son qui ressemble au "ch" écossais; **the English vowel sounds** les sons *mpl* vocaliques de l'anglais

(**d**) *Rad & TV* son *m*; **the sound is very poor** le son est mauvais; **to turn the sound up/down** monter/baisser le son *ou* volume

(**e**) *(type of music)* style *m* de musique, musique *f*; **the Liverpool sound** la musique de Liverpool; **a brand new sound has hit the charts** un son complètement nouveau a fait son entrée au hit-parade

(**f**) *(impression, idea)* **I don't like the sound of these new measures** ces nouvelles mesures ne me disent rien qui vaille; **it's pretty easy by the sound of it** ça a l'air assez facile; **he's angry by the sound of it** on dirait bien qu'il est fâché

(**g**) *Med (probe)* sonde *f*

(**h**) *Naut (sounding line)* (ligne *f* de) sonde *f*

(**i**) *Geog (channel)* détroit *m*, bras *m* de mer

(**j**) *Ich (air bladder)* vessie *f* natatoire

2 sounds *npl Fam (music)* zizique *f*, zicmu *f*

3 *adj* (**a**) *(structure, building, wall → sturdy)* solide; *(→ in good condition)* en bon état, sain; **built on sound foundations** construit sur des fondations solides

(**b**) *(healthy → person)* en bonne santé; *(→ body, mind, limbs)* sain; **to be of sound mind** être sain d'esprit; **sound in body and mind** sain de corps et d'esprit; **to be as sound as a bell** être en parfaite santé; **to be sound of wind and limb** avoir bon pied bon œil

(**c**) *(solid, well-founded → advice, idea, strategy)* sensé, judicieux; *(→ argument, claim)* valable, fondé, solide; *(→ reason)* valable; *(→ basis, knowledge)* solide; *(→ manager, musician, lawyer etc)* compétent, fiable; *(→ investment)* sûr; *(→ company, business)* solide; **to show sound judgment** faire preuve de jugement; **do you think that was a sound move?** croyez-vous que c'était une décision judicieuse; **a sound piece of advice** un bon conseil; **we need somebody with a sound grasp of the subject** il nous faut quelqu'un ayant de solides connaissances en la matière; **my knowledge of German history isn't too sound** mes connaissances en ce qui concerne l'histoire de l'Allemagne laissent à désirer; **his grammar's pretty sound** il a de bonnes bases en grammaire; **it makes good sound sense** c'est tout à fait raisonnable; **Crawford seems a sound enough chap** Crawford semble être quelqu'un en qui on peut avoir confiance; **is she politically sound?** ses convictions politiques sont-elles solides?; **ecologically sound legislation** législation *f* juste du point de vue écologique; **sound financial position** situation *f* financière saine; *Br Fam* **sound (as a pound)!** super!, génial!

(**d**) *(severe → defeat)* total; *(→ hiding)* bon; **he needs a sound thrashing** il a besoin d'une bonne correction

(**e**) *(deep → sleep)* profond; **I'm a very sound sleeper** j'ai le sommeil profond

4 *comp (level, recording)* sonore; *(broadcasting)* radiophonique; *Ling (change)* phonologique

5 *adv* **to be sound asleep** dormir profondément *ou* à poings fermés

6 *vt* (**a**) *(bell)* sonner; *(wind instrument)* sonner de; **the huntsman sounded his horn** le chasseur sonna du cor; **to sound the horn** klaxonner; **the driver behind me sounded his horn** le conducteur derrière moi a klaxonné; *also Fig* **to sound the alarm** sonner *ou* donner l'alarme; **they sounded the church bells** ils sonnèrent les cloches; **the bugler sounded the reveille** le clairon sonna le réveil; **to sound a warning** lancer un avertissement

(**b**) *(pronounce)* prononcer; **the "p" isn't sounded** le "p" ne se prononce pas; **he doesn't sound his aitches** il ne prononce pas ses "h"

(**c**) *Med (chest, lungs)* ausculter; *(cavity, passage)* sonder

(**d**) *Naut* sonder

(**e**) *(person)* sonder; **to sound public opinion** sonder l'opinion publique; **I'll try to sound their feelings on the matter** j'essaierai de connaître leur sentiment à cet égard

7 *vi* (**a**) *(make a sound)* sonner, résonner, retentir; **it sounds hollow if you tap it** ça sonne creux lorsqu'on tape dessus; **their voices sounded very loud in the empty house** leurs voix résonnaient bruyamment dans la maison vide; **sirens sounded in the streets** des sirènes retentissaient dans les rues; **if the alarm sounds, run** si vous entendez l'alarme, enfuyez-vous

(**b**) *Br (be pronounced)* se prononcer; **in English words are rarely spelt as they sound** en anglais, les mots s'écrivent rarement comme ils se prononcent

(**c**) *(seem)* sembler, paraître; **he sounded sad** il semblait triste; **he sounded bored** il semblait s'ennuyer; **the name sounded French** le nom avait l'air d'être *ou* sonnait français; **she sounds French** elle a l'air d'être française; **the translation still sounds a bit French** la traduction sonne toujours un peu français; **it doesn't sound very interesting to me** ça ne m'a pas l'air très intéressant; **"attractive four-bedroomed house", how does that sound?** "belle maison avec quatre chambres à coucher", qu'est-ce que tu en penses?; **(that) sounds like a good idea** ça semble être une bonne idée; **two weeks in Crete, that sounds nice!** deux semaines en Crète, pas mal du tout!; **that sounds like trouble!** voilà les ennuis!; **it sounds like Mozart** on dirait du Mozart; **you sound as though** *or* **as if** *or* **like you've got a cold** on dirait que tu es enrhumé; **it sounds to me as though they don't want to do it** j'ai l'impression qu'ils ne veulent pas le faire; **It doesn't sound to me as though they want to do it** je n'ai pas l'impression qu'ils veuillent le faire; **you sound just like your brother on the phone** tu as la même voix que ton frère *ou* on dirait vraiment ton frère au téléphone; **it's an instrument which sounds rather like a flute** c'est un instrument dont le son ressemble assez à *ou* est assez proche de la flûte; **that sounds like the postman now** je crois entendre le facteur

►► ***sound archives*** phonothèque *f*; **a recording from the BBC sound archives** un enregistrement qui vient des archives de la BBC; ***sound barrier*** mur *m* du son; **to break the sound barrier** franchir le mur du son; *Mus* ***sound box*** caisse *f* de résonance; *Comput* ***sound card*** carte *f* son; ***sound check*** soundcheck *m*; *Cin, TV & Rad* ***sound crew*** équipe *f* du son; ***sound effects*** bruitage *m*; *Rad* ***sound effects person*** bruiteur(euse) *m,f*; ***sound engineer*** ingénieur *m* du son; ***sound hole*** *(of violin, viola etc)* ouïe *f*, esse *f*; *(of guitar, lute etc)* rosace *f*, rose *f*; ***sound mixer*** [illegible] bande *f* son; *Ling* ***sound shift*** mutation *f* phonologique; ***sound studio*** auditorium *m ou* studio *m* d'enregistrement; ***sound system*** *(hi-fi)* chaîne *f* hifi; *(PA system)* sonorisation *f*; ***sound wave*** onde *f* sonore

►**sound off** *vi Fam* (**a**) *(declare one's opinions)* crier son opinion sur tous les toits; *(complain)* râler; **he's always sounding off about the management** il est toujours à râler contre la direction; **to sound off at sb** *(angrily)* passer un savon à qn

(**b**) *(boast)* se vanter ❑

►**sound out** *vt sep (person, public opinion)* sonder; **the company is sounding out potential buyers** la compagnie sonde les acheteurs potentiels

'The Sound and the Fury' *Faulkner* 'Le Bruit et la fureur'

'The Sound of Music' *Wise* 'La Mélodie du bonheur'

soundbite ['saʊndbaɪt] *n* petite phrase *f (prononcée par un homme politique à la radio ou à la télévision pour frapper les esprits)*

soundboard ['saʊndbɔːd] *n* (**a**) *(over pulpit, rostrum)* abat-voix *m inv* (**b**) *Mus* table *f* d'harmonie

sounder ['saʊndə(r)] *n Naut* sondeur *m*

sounding ['saʊndɪŋ] **1** *n* (**a**) *Aviat, Met & Naut (measuring)* sondage *m*

(**b**) *(of bell, horn)* son *m*; **wait for the sounding of the alarm** attendez le signal d'alarme *ou* que le signal d'alarme retentisse; *Mil* **the sounding of the retreat** le signal de la retraite

2 soundings *npl (investigations)* sondages *mpl*; **to take soundings** faire des sondages

►► ***sounding board*** (**a**) *(over pulpit, rostrum)* abat-voix *m inv* (**b**) *Fig (person)* **she uses her assistants as a sounding board for any new ideas** elle essaie toutes ses nouvelles idées sur ses assistants (**c**) *(of piano, violin)* table *f* d'harmonie; *(of organ)* tamis *m*; ***sounding lead*** (plomb *m* de) sonde *f*; ***sounding line*** sonde *f*

-sounding ['saʊndɪŋ] *suff* **a foreign-sounding name** un nom à consonance étrangère; **high-sounding phrases** des phrases *fpl* ronflantes *ou* grandiloquentes

soundless ['saʊndlɪs] *adj* (**a**) *(silent)* silencieux

(**b**) *Literary (deep)* insondable

soundlessly ['saʊndlɪslɪ] *adv (silently)* silencieusement, sans bruit

soundly ['saʊndlɪ] *adv* (**a**) *(deeply → sleep)* profondément, à poings fermés; **we can all sleep soundly in our beds now that we know that the murderer has been caught** nous pouvons tous dormir sur nos deux oreilles maintenant que nous savons que le meurtrier a été arrêté

(**b**) *(sensibly → advise, argue)* judicieusement, avec bon sens

(**c**) *(safely → invest)* de façon sûre, sans risque *ou* risques

(**d**) *(competently → work, run)* avec compétence

(**e**) *(thoroughly)* **to be soundly beaten** *(defeated)* être battu à plates coutures; **he deserves to be soundly thrashed** il mérite une bonne correction

soundness ['saʊndnɪs] *n* (**a**) *(of body, mind)* santé *f*, équilibre *m*; *(of health)* robustesse *f* (**b**) *(of building, structure)* solidité *f*; *(of business, financial situation)* solvabilité *f*; *(of decision, advice)* sagesse *f*; *(of argument, reasoning)* justesse *f* (**c**) *(of sleep)* profondeur *f*

soundproof ['saʊndpruːf] **1** *adj* insonorisé

2 *vt* insonoriser

soundproofing ['saʊndpruːfɪŋ] *n (act, process)* insonorisation *f*; *(material)* matériau *m* isolant *ou* insonore

soundtrack ['saʊndtræk] *n* bande *f* sonore; **soundtrack (album)** bande *f* originale

soup [suːp] *n* (**a**) *Culin* soupe *f*; *(thin or blended)* soupe *f*, potage *m*; *(smooth and creamy)* velouté *m*; **onion/fish/leek soup** soupe *f* à l'oignon/de poisson/aux poireaux; **cream of mushroom soup** velouté *m* de champignons; *Fam* **to be in the soup** être dans le pétrin *ou* dans la panade; *Am Fam* **from soup to nuts** du début à la fin ❑

(**b**) *very Fam (nitroglycerine)* nitroglycérine ❑ *f*, nitro *f*

►► ***soup kitchen*** soupe *f* populaire; ***soup ladle*** louche *f*; ***soup plate*** assiette *f* creuse *ou* à soupe; ***soup spoon*** cuillère *f ou* cuiller *f* à soupe; ***soup tureen*** soupière *f*

►**soup up** *vt sep Fam (engine)* gonfler; *(car)* gonfler le moteur de; *(machine, computer program)* perfectionner ❑

soupçon ['suːpsɒn] *n Formal or Hum* soupçon *m*, pointe *f*

souped-up [suːpt-] *adj Fam (engine)* gonflé, poussé; *(car)* au moteur gonflé *ou* poussé; *(machine, computer program)* perfectionné ❑; **a souped-up version of the previous model** une version plus performante du modèle précédent ❑; **the movie is a souped-up version of the original TV drama series** le film reprend l'histoire de la série télévisée avec beaucoup plus de moyens ❑

soup-strainer *n Am Fam Hum (large moustache)* grosses bacchantes *fpl*

soupy ['suːpɪ] *(compar* **soupier,** *superl* **soupiest)** *adj* (**a**) *(thick)* épais(aisse), dense (**b**) *Am Fam (sentimental)* à l'eau de rose ❑

sour ['saʊə(r)] **1** *adj* (**a**) *(flavour, taste)* aigre; *(wine)* suret, verjuté

(**b**) *(rancid → milk)* tourné, aigre; *(→ breath)* fétide; **the milk has gone** *or* **turned sour** le lait a tourné

(**c**) *(disagreeable → person, character, mood)* aigre, revêche, hargneux; *(→ look)* hargneux; *(→ comment, tone)* aigre, acerbe

(**d**) *(wrong, awry)* **to go** *or* **to turn sour** mal tourner; **everything suddenly went sour on us** tout a soudainement mal tourné pour nous; **their marriage went sour** leur mariage a tourné au vinaigre

(**e**) *(too acidic → soil)* trop acide

2 *vi* (**a**) *(wine)* surir, s'aigrir; *(milk)* tourner, aigrir

(**b**) *(person, character)* s'aigrir; *(relationship)* se dégrader, tourner au vinaigre; *(situation)* mal tourner; **her temper has soured** son caractère s'est aigri

3 *vt* (**a**) *(milk, wine)* aigrir

(**b**) *(person, character)* aigrir; *(relationship)* gâter, empoisonner; *(situation)* gâter; **the experience soured his view of life** cette expérience l'a aigri

4 *n* whisky *m* sour

▸▸ ***sour cream*** crème *f* aigre; ***sour grapes*** dépit *m*; **it's a simple case of sour grapes** c'est tout simplement du dépit; **it was just sour grapes that made her say that** elle a simplement dit ça par rancœur *ou* dépit; ***sour mash*** = pâte spéciale utilisée dans la fabrication de certains whiskies américains

sourball ['saʊə,bɔːl] *n Am* bonbon *m* acidulé

source [sɔːs] **1** *n* (**a**) *(gen)* source *f*; **a good source of vitamin C** une bonne source de vitamine C; **they have traced the source of the power cut** ils ont découvert l'origine de la panne de courant; **energy sources** sources *fpl* d'énergie; **at source** à la source; *Med* **source of infection** foyer *m* d'infection

(**b**) *(of information)* source *f*; **I have it from a good source** je le sais *ou* tiens de source sûre; **the journalist refused to name his sources** le journaliste a refusé de nommer ses sources; **according to reliable sources war is imminent** selon des sources sûres *ou* bien informées, la guerre est imminente

(**c**) *(of river)* source *f*

2 *vt* (**a**) *Com (products)* s'approvisionner en, se fournir en; **to be sourced from** provenir de

(**b**) *(give source of)* **the quotations are sourced in footnotes** la source des citations figure dans les notes en bas de page

▸▸ *Acct* ***source and application of funds*** état *m* de flux de trésorie; *Comput* ***source disk*** disque *m* source; *(floppy)* disquette *f* source; *Comput* ***source document*** document *m* de base, document *m* source; *Comput* ***source file*** fichier *m* source; ***source language*** (**a**) *Ling* langue *f* source (**b**) *Comput* langage *m* source; ***source material*** *or* ***materials*** *(documents)* documentation *f*; *Comput* ***source program*** programme *m* source; *Comput* ***source text*** texte *m* de départ

sourdough ['saʊədəʊ] *n* (**a**) *Am* levain *m* (**b**) *(pioneer)* pionnier(ère) *m,f (de l'Alaska ou de l'ouest du Canada)*

▸▸ *Culin* ***sourdough bread*** pain *m* au levain

soured ['saʊəd] *adj* (**a**) *(food)* aigri (**b**) *(person)* aigri, revêche

▸▸ *Br* ***soured cream*** crème *f* aigre

sourface ['saʊəfeɪs] *n Fam (ill-tempered person)* grincheux(euse) ❑ *m,f*; *(kill-joy)* rabat-joie ❑ *m inv*

sour-faced *adj* à la mine revêche; **what are you looking so sour-faced about?** pourquoi cet air maussade *ou* cette mine revêche?

souring ['saʊərɪŋ] *n* aigrissement *m*; *Fig* détérioration *f*

sourish ['saʊərɪʃ] *adj* aigrelet, suret

sourly ['saʊəlɪ] *adj* aigrement, avec aigreur

sourness ['saʊənɪs] *n* (**a**) *(of flavour, taste)* aigreur *f*, acidité *f*; *(of milk)* aigreur *f* (**b**) *(of person, character, mood)* aigreur *f*; *(of speech, comment)* ton *m* aigre

sourpuss ['saʊəpʊs] *n Fam (ill-tempered person)* grincheux(euse) ❑ *m,f*; *(kill-joy)* rabat-joie ❑ *m inv*

soursop ['saʊəsɒp] *n (fruit)* corossol *m*, cachiman *m* épineux

sousaphone ['suːzəfəʊn] *n Mus* sousaphone *m*

sous chef ['suːʃef] *n* second *m*, assistant *m* du chef de cuisine

souse [saʊs] **1** *vt* (**a**) *Culin (in vinegar)* (faire) mariner dans du vinaigre; *(in brine)* (faire) mariner dans de la saumure

(**b**) *(immerse)* immerger, plonger; *(drench)* tremper; **he soused himself with cold water** il s'aspergea abondamment d'eau froide

(**c**) *Fam (make drunk)* soûler

2 *n* (**a**) *Culin (vinegar)* marinade *f* de vinaigre; *(brine)* saumure *f*

(**b**) *Am Fam (person)* alcoolo *mf*, poivrot(e) *m,f*

soused [saʊst] *adj* (**a**) *Culin* mariné (**b**) *very Fam (drunk)* bourré, pété; **to get soused** se soûler; **he comes home soused every night** il rentre soûl tous les soirs

▸▸ *Culin* ***soused herrings*** harengs *mpl* marinés

souslik ['sʌslɪk] *n Zool* souslik *m*

soutache ['suːtæʃ] *n* soutache *f*

soutane [suː'tɑːn] *n* soutane *f*

souter ['suːtə(r)] *n Scot & NEng* cordonnier *m*

souterrain ['suːtəreɪn] *n Archeol* souterrain *m*

south [saʊθ] **1** *n* (**a**) *Geog* sud *m*; **in the south** au sud, dans le sud; **the region to the south of Edinburgh** la région au sud d'Édimbourg; **two miles to the south** trois kilomètres au sud; **look towards the south** regardez vers le sud; **I was born in the south** je suis né dans le Sud; **in the south of India** dans le sud de l'Inde; **in the South of France** dans le Midi (de la France); **the wind is in the south** le vent est au sud; **the wind is coming from the south** le vent vient *ou* souffle du sud; *Hist* **the South** *(of United States)* le Sud, les États *mpl* du Sud

(**b**) *Cards* sud *m*

2 *adj* (**a**) *Geog* sud *(inv)*, du sud, méridional; *(country, state)* du Sud; *(wall)* exposé au sud; **the south coast** la côte sud; **in south London** dans le sud de Londres; **in South India** en Inde du Sud; **the South Atlantic/Pacific** l'Atlantique *m*/le Pacifique Sud; **the South Seas** les mers *fpl* du Sud; **the South Bank** = complexe sur la rive sud de la Tamise réunissant des salles de concert, des théâtres et des musées; **the South Circular** = voie rapide périphérique au sud de Londres

(**b**) *(wind)* de sud, du sud

3 *adv* au sud; *(travel)* vers le sud, en direction du sud; **the village lies south of York** le village est situé au sud de York; **the living room faces south** la salle de séjour est exposée au sud; **the path heads (due) south** le chemin va *ou* mène (droit) vers le sud; **walk south until you come to a main road** marchez vers le sud jusqu'à ce que vous arriviez à une route principale; **I drove south for two hours** j'ai roulé pendant deux heures en direction du sud; **we're going south for our holidays** nous allons passer nos vacances dans le Sud; **I travelled south** je suis allée vers le sud; **to sail south** naviguer cap sur le sud; **it's 20 miles south of Birmingham** c'est à 32 kilomètres au sud de Birmingham; **they live down south** ils habitent dans le Sud; **south by east/west** sud-quart-sud-est/-ouest; **further south** plus au sud

▸▸ ***South Africa*** l'Afrique *f* du Sud; **in South Africa** en Afrique du Sud; **the Republic of South Africa** la République d'Afrique du Sud; ***South African*** **1** *n* Sud-Africain(e) *m,f* **2** *adj* sud-africain, d'Afrique du Sud; ***South America*** l'Amérique *f* du Sud; **in South America** en Amérique du Sud; ***South American*** **1** *n* Sud-Américain(e) *m,f* **2** *adj* sud-américain, d'Amérique du Sud; ***South Australia*** l'Australie-Méridionale *f*; **in South Australia** en Australie-Méridionale; ***South Carolina*** la Caroline du Sud; **in South Carolina** en Caroline du Sud; ***South Dakota*** le Dakota du Sud; **in South Dakota** dans le Dakota du Sud; ***South Georgia*** la Géorgie du Sud; ***South Glamorgan*** le South Glamorgan, = comté du sud du pays de Galles; **in South Glamorgan** dans le South Glamorgan; ***South Island*** l'île *f* du Sud; ***South Korea*** la Corée du Sud; **in South Korea** en Corée du Sud; ***South Korean*** **1** *n* Sud-Coréen(enne) *m,f*, Coréen(enne) *m,f* du Sud **2** *adj* sud-coréen; ***South Pole*** le pôle Sud; **at the South Pole** au pôle Sud; ***South Sea Bubble*** = krach financier de 1720 en Angleterre; ***South Sea Islands*** l'Océanie *f*; ***South Vietnam*** le Viêt-nam du Sud; **in South Vietnam** au Viêt-nam du Sud; ***South Vietnamese*** **1** *n* Sud-Vietnamien(enne) *m,f*; ***the South Vietnamese*** les Sud-Vietnamiens *mpl* **2** *adj* sud-vietnamien; ***South Wales*** le sud du pays de Galles; ***South Yemen*** le Yémen du Sud; **in South Yemen** au Yémen du Sud; ***South Yorkshire*** le South Yorkshire, = comté du nord de l'Angleterre; **in South Yorkshire** dans le South Yorkshire

> **THE SOUTH SEA BUBBLE**
>
> Ce krach financier eut lieu en 1720, après que la "South Sea Company" eut repris à son compte la dette nationale britannique en échange du monopole du commerce sur les mers du sud. Cette nouvelle provoqua une ruée sur les actions de la compagnie et une spéculation avide, entraînant la chute des cours et la ruine de nombreux investisseurs.

southbound ['saʊθbaʊnd] *adj (traffic)* en direction du sud; *(lane)* du sud; *(road)* vers le sud; **southbound traffic is subject to delays** la circulation est ralentie dans le sens sud; *Br* **the southbound carriageway of the motorway is closed** l'axe sud de l'autoroute est fermé (à la circulation); **there are roadworks on the southbound carriageway of the motorway** il y a des travaux sur l'autoroute en direction du sud; **there's a jam on the southbound carriageway** il y a un bouchon en direction du sud

south-east **1** *n* sud-est *m*; **in the south-east of England** dans le sud-est de l'Angleterre

2 *adj* (**a**) *Geog* sud-est *(inv)*, du sud-est; **in south-east England** dans le sud-est de l'Angleterre

(**b**) *(wind)* de sud-est, du sud-est

3 *adv* au sud-est; *(travel)* vers le sud-est, en direction du sud-est; **it's 50 miles south-east of Liverpool** c'est à 80 kilomètres au sud-est de Liverpool

▸▸ ***South-east Asia*** Asie *f* du Sud-Est; **in South-east Asia** en Asie du Sud-Est; ***South-east Asia Treaty Organization*** Organisation *f* du traité de l'Asie du Sud-Est

south-easter [-'iːstə(r)] *n* vent *m* de *ou* du sud-est; *Naut* suet *m*

south-easterly *(pl* **south-easterlies)** **1** *adj* (**a**) *Geog* sud-est *(inv)*, du sud-est; **to travel in a south-easterly direction** aller vers le sud-est; *Naut* **to steer a south-easterly course** faire route vers le sud-est; *(when setting out)* mettre le cap au sud-est (**b**) *(wind)* de sud-est, du sud-est

2 *adv* vers le sud-est, en direction du sud-est

3 *n* vent *m* de *ou* du sud-est; *Naut* suet *m*

south-eastern *adj* sud-est *(inv)*, du sud-est; *(wind)* de sud-est, du sud-est; **the south-eastern suburbs** la banlieue sud-est

south-eastward **1** *adj* vers le sud-est, en direction du sud-est

2 *adv* vers le sud-est, en direction du sud-est; **to sail south-eastward** naviguer cap sur le sud-est

3 *n* sud-est *m*

south-eastwardly **1** *adj* du sud-est

2 *adv* vers le sud-est, en direction du sud-est

south-eastwards *adv* vers le sud-est, en direction du sud-est; **to sail south-eastwards** naviguer cap sur le sud-est

souther ['saʊðə(r)] *n Naut* fort vent *m* de *ou* du sud

southerly ['sʌðəlɪ] *(pl* **southerlies)** **1** *adj* (**a**) *Geog* sud *(inv)*, du sud; **in a southerly direction** vers le sud; **southerly point** point *m* situé au sud *ou* vers le sud; **the most southerly point of the United States** le point situé le plus au sud des États-Unis; **a room with a southerly aspect** une pièce exposée au sud *ou* au midi; *Naut* **to steer**

a southerly course faire route vers le sud; *(when setting out)* mettre le cap au sud

(**b**) *(wind)* de sud, du sud

2 *adv* vers le sud, en direction du sud

3 *n* vent *m* de *ou* du sud

▸▸ *Austr Fam* ***southerly buster*** = vent du sud-est qui souffle dans le sud-est de l'Australie

southern ['sʌðən] *adj* (**a**) *Geog* sud *(inv)*, du sud, méridional; **he has a southern accent** il a un accent du sud; *(in France)* il a l'accent méridional; **the southern wing of the castle** l'aile *f* sud du château; **in southern India** dans le sud de l'Inde; **the southern hemisphere** l'hémisphère *m* sud *ou* austral

(**b**) *(wind)* de sud, du sud

(**c**) *Hist (in American Civil War)* sudiste

▸▸ ***southern Africa*** l'Afrique *f* australe; ***Southern belle*** = belle jeune femme de bonne famille du sud des États-Unis; *Astron* ***the Southern Cross*** la Croix du Sud; ***southern Europe*** l'Europe *f* méridionale; *Literature* ***Southern Gothic*** = genre littéraire originaire du sud des États-Unis, caractérisé par le caractère excentrique des personnages et une atmosphère insolite, parfois à la limite du fantastique; ***Southern Ireland*** l'Irlande *f* du Sud; **in Southern Ireland** en Irlande du Sud; ***southern lights*** aurore *f* australe; *Formerly* ***Southern Rhodesia*** la Rhodésie du Sud; ***the Southern States*** = les États du sud-est des États-Unis, au sud de la ligne Mason-Dixie

Southerner, southerner ['sʌðənə(r)] *n* (**a**) *(gen)* habitant(e) *m,f* du sud; *(in continental Europe)* méridional(e) *m,f*; **she's a southerner** elle vient du sud (**b**) *Hist (in American Civil War)* sudiste *mf*

southernmost ['sʌðənməʊst] *adj* le plus au sud; **the southernmost town in Chile** la ville la plus au sud du Chili; **the southernmost limits of the Sahara** les limites méridionales du Sahara

southernwood ['sʌðənwʊd] *n Bot* auronne *f*, aurone *f*

south-facing *adj (house, wall)* (exposé) au sud *ou* au midi

southing ['saʊðɪŋ] *n Naut* chemin *m* sud

southmost ['saʊθməʊst] *adj* le plus au sud

southpaw ['saʊθpɔː] *Am Fam* **1** *n* gaucher(ère)❑ *m,f*

2 *adj* gaucher❑

south-south-east 1 *n* sud-sud-est *m*

2 *adj* (**a**) *Geog* sud-sud-est *(inv)*, du sud-sud-est (**b**) *(wind)* de *ou* du sud-sud-est

3 *adv* au sud-sud-est; *(travel)* vers le sud-sud-est, en direction du sud-sud-est

south-south-west 1 *n* sud-sud-ouest *m*

2 *adj* (**a**) *Geog* sud-sud-ouest *(inv)*, du sud-sud-ouest (**b**) *(wind)* de *ou* du sud-sud-ouest

3 *adv* au sud-sud-ouest; *(travel)* vers le sud-sud-ouest, en direction du sud-sud-ouest

southward ['saʊθwəd] **1** *adj* vers le sud, en direction du sud

2 *adv* vers le sud, en direction du sud; **to sail southward** naviguer cap sur le sud

3 *n* sud *m*

southwardly ['saʊθwədlɪ] **1** *adj* du sud

2 *adv* vers le sud, en direction du sud

southwards ['saʊθwədz] *adv* vers le sud, en direction du sud; **to sail southwards** naviguer cap sur le sud

south-west 1 *n* sud-ouest *m*; **in the south-west of the United States** dans le sud-ouest des États-Unis

2 *adj* (**a**) *Geog* sud-ouest *(inv)*, du sud-ouest; **in south-west Scotland** dans le sud-ouest de l'Écosse (**b**) *(wind)* de sud-ouest, du sud-ouest

3 *adv* au sud-ouest; *(travel)* vers le sud-ouest, en direction du sud-ouest; **it's south-west of London** c'est au sud-ouest de Londres

south-wester [-'westə(r)] *n* vent *m* de *ou* du sud-ouest; *Naut* suroît *m*

south-westerly *(pl* **south-westerlies***)* **1** *adj* (**a**) *Geog* sud-ouest *(inv)*, du sud-ouest; **in a south-westerly direction** vers le sud-ouest; *Naut* **to steer a south-westerly course** faire route vers le sud-ouest; *(when setting out)* mettre le cap au sud-ouest

(**b**) *(wind)* de sud-ouest, du sud-ouest

2 *adv* vers le sud-ouest, en direction du sud-ouest

3 *n* vent *m* de *ou* du sud-ouest; *Naut* suroît *m*

south-western *adj* sud-ouest *(inv)*, du sud-ouest; **the south-western States** *(of USA)* les États *mpl* du sud-ouest; **the south-western frontier** la frontière sud-ouest

south-westward 1 *adj* vers le sud-ouest, en direction du sud-ouest

2 *adv* vers le sud-ouest, en direction du sud-ouest; **to sail south-westward** naviguer cap sur le sud-ouest

3 *n* sud-ouest *m*

south-westwardly 1 *adj* du sud-ouest

2 *adv* vers le sud-ouest, en direction du sud-ouest

south-westwards *adv* vers le sud-ouest, en direction du sud-ouest; **to sail south-westwards** naviguer cap sur le sud-ouest

souvenir [ˌsuːvə'nɪə(r)] *n* souvenir *m (objet)*

▸▸ ***souvenir shop*** boutique *f* de souvenirs

sou'wester, sou'-wester [saʊ'westə(r)] *n* (**a**) *(headgear)* suroît *m* (**b**) *(wind)* vent *m* de *ou* du sud-ouest; *Naut* suroît *m*

sovereign ['sɒvrɪn] **1** *n* (**a**) *(monarch)* souverain(e) *m,f*

(**b**) *(coin)* souverain *m (pièce d'or de la valeur d'une livre)*

2 *adj* (**a**) *Pol (state, territory)* souverain; *(powers)* souverain, suprême; *(rights)* de souveraineté; **the sovereign good** le bien souverain; **Parliament remains sovereign** le Parlement reste souverain

(**b**) *Literary (excellent → remedy)* souverain *(utmost → scorn, indifference)* souverain, absolu

sovereignty ['sɒvrɪntɪ] *(pl* **sovereignties***)* *n* souveraineté *f*; **with no loss of sovereignty** sans perte de souveraineté

soviet ['səʊvɪət] **1** *n (council)* soviet *m*

2 Soviet 1 *n (inhabitant)* Soviétique *mf* **2** *adj* soviétique; *Formerly* **the Union of Soviet Socialist Republics** l'Union *f* des républiques socialistes soviétiques

▸▸ *Hist* ***the Soviet Bloc*** le bloc soviétique; *Formerly* ***Soviet Russia*** la Russie soviétique; *Formerly* ***the Soviet Union*** l'Union *f* soviétique; **in the Soviet Union** en Union soviétique

sovietism ['səʊvɪətɪzəm] *n* soviétisme *m*

sovietization [ˌsəʊvɪətaɪ'zeɪʃən] *n* soviétisation *f*

sovietize, -ise ['səʊvɪətaɪz] *vt* soviétiser

sovietologist [ˌsəʊvɪə'tɒlədʒɪst] *n* soviétologue *mf*

sow^1 [səʊ] *(pt* **sowed,** *pp* **sowed** *or* **sown** [səʊn], *cont* **sowing***)* **1** *vt* (**a**) *(seed, crop)* semer; *(field)* ensemencer

(**b**) *Fig* semer; **to sow discord/terror** semer la discorde/la terreur; **he sowed (the seeds of) doubt in their minds** il a semé le doute dans leur esprit; **it was at this time that the seeds of the Industrial Revolution were sown** c'est à cette époque que remontent les origines de la révolution industrielle; *Prov* **sow the wind and reap the whirlwind** qui sème le vent récolte la tempête

2 *vi* semer; *Bible* **as you sow so shall you reap** comme tu auras semé tu moissonneras

sow^2 [saʊ] *n (pig)* truie *f*; *(wild pig)* laie *f*

▸▸ *Am* ***sow bug*** cloporte *m*; *Bot* ***sow thistle*** laiteron *m* (potager)

sower ['səʊə(r)] *n (person)* semeur(euse) *m,f*; *(farm tool)* semoir *m*

sowing ['səʊɪŋ] *n* (**a**) *(act)* ensemencement *m* (**b**) *(UNCOUNT) (work, period, seed)* semailles *fpl*

sown [səʊn] *pp of* **sow**

sox [sɒks] *npl Am Fam* chaussettes❑ *fpl*

soy [sɔɪ] *n (sauce)* sauce *f* de soja

▸▸ ***soy sauce*** sauce *f* de soja

soya ['sɔɪə] *n* soja *m*

▸▸ *Br* ***soya bean*** graine *f* de soja; ***soya flour*** farine *f* de soja; ***soya milk*** lait *m* de soja

soybean ['sɔɪbiːn] *n Am* graine *f* de soja

sozzled ['sɒzəld] *adj Br Fam* bourré, beurré

SP [ˌes'piː] *n (abbr* **starting price***)* *Horseracing* cote *f* au départ; *Br Fam Fig* **to give sb the SP (on)** mettre qn au parfum (à propos de *ou* concernant)

spa [spɑː] *n* (**a**) *(resort)* station *f* thermale (**b**) *(spring)* source *f* minérale (**c**) *(whirlpool bath)* bain *m* à remous (**d**) *(health club)* centre *m* de fitness (**e**) *Ir very Fam Pej (idiot)* crétin(e) *m,f*, idiot(e)❑ *m,f*

▸▸ ***spa town*** ville *f* d'eau, station *f* thermale

space [speɪs] **1** *n* (**a**) *Astron & Phys* espace *m*; **the first man in space** le premier homme dans l'espace; **a particular point in space and time** un point particulier dans l'espace et le temps; **she sat staring into space** elle était assise, le regard perdu dans le vide

(**b**) *(room)* espace *m*, place *f*; **there's too much wasted space in this kitchen** il y a trop de place perdue *ou* d'espace inutilisé dans cette cuisine; **to take up a lot of space** prendre *ou* occuper beaucoup de place; **the large windows give an impression of space** les grandes fenêtres donnent une impression d'espace; **he cleared a** *or* **some space on his desk for the tray** il a fait un peu de place sur son bureau pour le plateau; **can you make space for one more?** pouvez-vous faire de la place pour une personne de plus?; **the author devotes a lot of space to philosophical speculations** l'auteur fait une large part aux spéculations philosophiques; *Fig* **I need some space** j'ai besoin de liberté; **to invade sb's personal space** empiéter sur l'espace vital de qn

(**c**) *(volume, area, distance)* espace *m*; **open spaces** *(green)* espaces *mpl* verts; *(not built on)* étendues *fpl* non bâties; **wide open spaces** grands espaces *mpl*; **an enclosed space** un espace clos; **there are at least five pubs in the space of a few hundred yards** il y a au moins cinq pubs sur quelques centaines de mètres; **advertising space** espace *m* publicitaire

(**d**) *(gap)* espace *m*, place *f*; *(on page, official form)* espace *m*, case *f*; *Typ (gap between words)* espace *m*, blanc *m*; *(blank type)* espace *m*; **there's barely any space between the houses** il n'y a pratiquement pas d'espace entre les maisons; **leave a space for the teacher's comments** laissez un espace pour les remarques du professeur; **please add any further details in the space provided** veuillez ajouter tout détail supplémentaire dans la case prévue à cet effet

(**e**) *(period of time, interval)* intervalle *m*, espace *m* (de temps), période *f*; **in** *or* **within the space of six months** en (l'espace de) six mois; **over a space of several years** sur une période de plusieurs années; **it'll all be over in a very short space of time** tout sera fini dans très peu de temps *ou* d'ici peu

(**f**) *(seat, place)* place *f*

2 *comp (programme, research, travel, flight)* spatial; **the space age** l'ère *f* spatiale

3 *vt* = **space out**

▸▸ ***space bar*** *(on keyboard)* barre *f* d'espacement; ***space blanket*** couverture *f* de survie; *Fam* ***space cadet*** allumé(e) *m,f*; **he's a bit of a space cadet** il est toujours en train de planer; ***space capsule*** capsule *f* spatiale; *Am Fam* ***space case*** allumé(e) *m,f*; ***space flight*** vol *m ou* voyage *m* spatial; ***space heater*** radiateur *m*; ***space helmet*** casque *m* d'astronaute; ***the Space Needle*** la Space Needle *(tour de 185m, emblématique de la ville de Seattle)*; ***space opera*** space opera *m*; ***space platform*** station *f* spatiale *ou* orbitale; ***space probe*** sonde *f* spatiale; ***space race*** course *f* pour la suprématie dans l'espace; ***space rescue vehicle*** véhicule *m* spatial de sauvetage; ***space rocket*** fusée *f* spatiale *ou* interplanétaire; *Typ* ***space rule*** filet *m* maigre; ***space shot*** lancement *m* spatial; ***space shuttle*** navette *f* spatiale; ***space sickness*** mal *m* de l'espace; ***space station*** station *f* spatiale *ou* orbitale; ***space travel*** voyages *mpl* dans l'espace, *Spec* astronautique *f*

▸**space out** *vt sep* (**a**) *(in space)* espacer; **evenly spaced out** régulièrement espacés; **the buoys are well spaced out** les bouées sont largement espacées; **space yourselves out a bit more** écartez-vous un peu plus les uns des autres

(**b**) *(in time)* échelonner, espacer; **spaced out over a period of ten years** échelonné sur une période de dix ans

'2001: A Space Odyssey' *Clarke, Kubrick* '2001: l'odyssée de l'espace'

space-age *adj* (**a**) *(of the period of space exploration)* de l'ère spatiale (**b**) *(futuristic)* futuriste

spacecraft ['speɪskrɑːft] *n* vaisseau *m* spatial

-spaced [speɪst] *suff* (**a**) *(gen)* **the buildings are**

sou–spa

closely/widely-spaced les bâtiments sont proches les uns des autres/largement espacés; **widely-spaced eyes** des yeux *mpl* très écartés (**b**) *Typ* **single/double-spaced** à interligne simple/double

spaced out *adj Fam* **to be** *or* **feel spaced out** *(dazed)* être dans le coaltar; *(after taking drugs)* être raide, planer

spacelab ['speɪslæb] *n* laboratoire *m* spatial

spaceless ['speɪslɪs] *adj* sans bornes, illimité

spaceman ['speɪsmæn] (*pl* **spacemen** [-men]) *n (gen)* spationaute *m*, astronaute *m*; *(Russian)* cosmonaute *m*

spaceport ['speɪspɔːt] *n* base *f* de lancement

spacer ['speɪsə(r)] *n Tech* pièce *f* d'écartement

space-saving *adj* qui fait gagner de la place

spaceship ['speɪsʃɪp] *n* vaisseau *m* spatial habité

space-sick *adj* **to be space-sick** avoir le mal de l'espace

spacesuit ['speɪssuːt] *n* combinaison *f* spatiale

space-time *n Phys* espace-temps *m*

▸▸ ***space-time continuum*** continuum *m* espace-temps *ou* spatio-temporel

spacewalk ['speɪswɔːk] **1** *n* marche *f* dans l'espace

2 *vi* marcher dans l'espace

spacewoman ['speɪsˌwʊmən] (*pl* **spacewomen** [-ˌwɪmɪn]) *n (gen)* spationaute *f*, astronaute *f*; *(Russian)* cosmonaute *f*

spacey ['speɪsɪ] (*compar* **spacier**, *superl* **spaciest**) *adj Fam* (**a**) *(music)* planant (**b**) *(person)* **to feel spacey** être dans les vapes

spacial = **spatial**

spacing ['speɪsɪŋ] *n* (**a**) *(of text on page → horizontal)* espacement *m*; *(→ vertical)* interligne *m*; **typed in single/double spacing** tapé avec interligne simple/double (**b**) *(between trees, columns, buildings etc)* espacement *m*, écart *m*

spacious ['speɪʃəs] *adj (house, room, office)* spacieux, grand; *(park, property)* étendu, grand

spaciousness ['speɪʃəsnɪs] *n* grandeur *f*, dimensions *fpl* spacieuses

Spackle® ['spækəl] *n Am* enduit *m*

spade [speɪd] *n* (**a**) *(tool)* bêche *f*; **to call a spade a spade** appeler un chat un chat; *Fam* **to have sth in spades** avoir des tonnes de qch; **and you've got it in spades** et tu en as à revendre

(**b**) *(in cards)* pique *m*; **my partner played a spade** mon partenaire a joué pique; **the ace/ten of spades** l'as *m*/le dix de pique

(**c**) *Fam (black man)* nègre *m*, bamboula *m*, = terme injurieux désignant un Noir; *(black woman)* négresse *f*, = terme injurieux désignant une Noire

spadefish ['speɪdfɪʃ] *n Ich* éphippe *m*

spadeful ['speɪdfʊl] *n* pelletée *f*

spadework ['speɪdwɜːk] *n* travail *m* de préparation *ou* de déblayage

spadger ['spædʒə(r)] *n Orn* moineau *m*, piaf *m*

spadix ['speɪdɪks] *n Bot* spadice *m*, massue *f*

spag bol [ˌspæg'bɒl] *n Br Fam* (*abbr* **spaghetti bolognese**) spaghettis *mpl* (à la) bolognaise ❑

spaghetti [spə'getɪ] *n (UNCOUNT)* (**a**) *Culin* spaghetti *mpl*, spaghettis *mpl* (**b**) *Fam Fig (cables, wires)* enchevêtrement ❑ *m (de fils, de câbles)*

▸▸ ***spaghetti bolognese*** spaghettis *mpl* (à la) bolognaise; ***Spaghetti Junction*** = surnom d'un échangeur sur l'autoroute M6 au nord de Birmingham; *Fig* **it's like Spaghetti Junction around here!** tous ces échangeurs, c'est compliqué!; ***spaghetti western*** western-spaghetti *m*

spahi ['spɑːhɪ] *n Hist* spahi *m*

Spain [speɪn] *n* Espagne *f*; **in Spain** en Espagne

spake [speɪk] *Arch pt of* **speak**

spall [spɔːl] **1** *n (splinter of rock, ore)* éclat *m*

2 *vt Constr* smiller; *Mining* broyer

3 *vi (splinter)* s'effriter

spallation [spɔː'leɪʃən] *n Phys* spallation *f*

spalled [spɔːld] *adj Constr* smillé; **spalled rubble** appareil *m* en moellons smillés

spalling ['spɔːlɪŋ] *n* (**a**) *Constr* smillage *m*; *Mining* broyage *m* (**b**) *(splintering)* effritement *m*

▸▸ ***spalling hammer*** smille *f*

spalpeen ['spælpiːn] *n Ir* (**a**) *(migratory labourer)* ouvrier *m* agricole itinérant (**b**) *(worthless person)* coquin *m*, fripon *m* (**c**) *(young boy)* gamin *m*

Spam® [spæm] *n* = pâté de jambon en conserve

spam [spæm] *Comput* **1** *n* messages *mpl* publicitaires

2 *vi* envoyer des messages publicitaires en masse

spammer ['spæmə(r)] *n Comput* = personne qui envoie des messages publicitaires en masse

spamming ['spæmɪŋ] *n Comput* envoi *m* de messages publicitaires en masse

span [spæn] (*pt & pp* **spanned**, *cont* **spanning**) **1** *n* (**a**) *(duration)* durée *f*, laps *m* de temps; **a short attention span** une capacité d'attention limitée; **man's span on earth** le séjour terrestre de l'homme; **his work covers a span of twenty-odd years** son œuvre s'étend sur une vingtaine d'années

(**b**) *(range)* gamme *f*; **we cover only a limited span of subjects** nous ne couvrons qu'un nombre restreint de sujets

(**c**) *(of hands, arms, wings)* envergure *f*

(**d**) *(of bridge)* travée *f*; *(of arch, dome, girder)* portée *f*

(**e**) *(unit of measurement)* empan *m*

(**f**) *(matched pair → of horses, oxen)* paire *f*

2 *vt* (**a**) *(encompass, stretch over → in time, extent)* couvrir, embrasser; **her career spanned more than 50 years** sa carrière s'étend sur plus de 50 ans; **her knowledge spans a wide range of subjects** ses connaissances couvrent une grande variété de sujets

(**b**) *(cross → river, ditch etc)* enjamber, traverser; **a modern bridge now spans the valley** un pont moderne enjambe maintenant la vallée

(**c**) *(build bridge over)* jeter un pont sur; **once the river had been spanned** une fois qu'on a eu construit un pont pour traverser la rivière

3 *Arch pt of* **spin**

spandex ['spændeks] *n* = textile proche du Lycra®

spandrel ['spændrəl] *n Archit* écoinçon *m*; *(of arch)* tympan *m*

▸▸ ***spandrel wall*** = mur qui remplit le tympan

spang [spæŋ] *adv Am Fam* directement ❑, pile; **spang on target** en plein dans le mille

spangle ['spæŋgəl] **1** *n* paillette *f*

2 *vt* pailleter, décorer de paillettes; **spangled with gold** pailleté d'or; **stars spangled the night sky** le ciel était semé d'étoiles

spangly ['spæŋglɪ] *adj* pailleté

Spaniard ['spænjəd] *n* Espagnol(e) *m,f*

spaniel ['spænjəl] *n* épagneul *m*

Spanish ['spænɪʃ] **1** *adj* espagnol

2 *n Ling* espagnol *m*

3 *npl* **the Spanish** les Espagnols *mpl*

▸▸ ***Spanish America*** Amérique *f* hispanophone; ***the Spanish Armada*** l'Invincible Armada *f*; ***the Spanish Civil War*** la guerre (civile) d'Espagne; ***Spanish fly*** (**a**) *(insect)* cantharide *f*, mouche *f* d'Espagne (**b**) *(product)* poudre *f* de cantharide; ***Spanish guitar*** guitare *f* classique; ***the Spanish Inquisition*** l'Inquisition *f* espagnole; ***the Spanish Main*** la mer des Caraïbes; *Bot* ***Spanish moss*** tillandsie *f*; ***Spanish omelette*** omelette *f* à l'espagnole; ***Spanish onion*** oignon *m* d'Espagne

> **THE SPANISH ARMADA**
>
> Cette flotte fut envoyée par Philippe II d'Espagne en 1588 dans le but d'envahir l'Angleterre et d'y rétablir le catholicisme. Malgré une supériorité numérique et une longue préparation, une série de contretemps et la maniabilité de la flotte britannique firent échouer le projet.

Spanish-American **1** *n* (**a**) *(in the US)* Hispanique *mf* (**b**) *(in Latin America)* Hispano-Américain(e) *m,f*

2 *adj* (**a**) *(in the US)* hispanique (**b**) *(in Latin America)* hispano-américain

▸▸ *Am Hist* ***the Spanish-American War*** la guerre hispano-américaine

> **THE SPANISH-AMERICAN WAR**
>
> Ce conflit opposa, en 1898, les États-Unis à l'Espagne dans les Caraïbes. Se posant en défenseurs des Cubains opprimés par les Espagnols, les Américains eurent la victoire facile. Elle leur permit d'étendre leur influence sur le Pacifique et les Caraïbes tout en conférant à leur pays le statut de puissance mondiale.

Spanish-speaking *adj* hispanophone

spank [spæŋk] **1** *vt* donner une fessée à, fesser

2 *vi (go at a lively pace)* **to be** *or* **to go spanking along** aller bon train *ou* à bonne allure

3 *n* tape *f* sur les fesses; **to give a child a spank** donner une tape sur les fesses à un enfant

spanker ['spæŋkə(r)] *n Naut* brigantine *f*

spanking ['spæŋkɪŋ] **1** *n* fessée *f*; **to give sb a spanking** donner une fessée à qn

2 *adj* (**a**) *Fam (excellent)* épatant; **in spanking condition** en excellent état ❑ (**b**) *(brisk)* vif; **a spanking breeze** une bonne brise; **to go at a spanking pace** aller bon train *ou* à bonne allure

3 *adv Fam* **spanking new** flambant neuf; **spanking clean** propre comme un sou neuf

spanner ['spænə(r)] *n* clé *f*, clef *f (outil)*; **to throw** *or* **to put a spanner in the works** poser des problèmes; **if they both arrived together that would really put a spanner in the works** s'ils arrivaient tous les deux ensemble ça poserait vraiment des problèmes; **that's put a spanner in the works** ça a tout chamboulé

spar [spɑː(r)] (*pt & pp* **sparred**, *cont* **sparring**) **1** *vi* (**a**) *Sport (in boxing → train)* s'entraîner (avec un sparring-partner); *(→ test out opponent)* faire des feintes *(pour tester son adversaire)*; **they sparred with each other for a few rounds** ils boxèrent amicalement durant quelques rounds (**b**) *(argue)* se disputer

2 *n* (**a**) *(pole → gen)* poteau *m*, mât *m*; *Naut* espar *m* (**b**) *Aviat* longeron *m* (**c**) *Miner* spath *m*

sparaxis [spə'ræksɪs] *n Bot* sparaxis *f*

spar-deck *n Naut* spardeck *m*

SPARE [speə(r)]

pièce de rechange	▸ **1 (a)**
roue de secours	▸ **1 (a)**
disponible	▸ **2 (a)**
libre	▸ **2 (a)**
de réserve	▸ **2 (a)**
de rechange	▸ **2 (a)**
en plus	▸ **2 (a)**
maigre	▸ **2 (b)**
austère	▸ **2 (c)**
accorder	▸ **3 (a)**
se passer de	▸ **3 (a)**
épargner	▸ **3 (b), (c)**
ménager	▸ **3 (d)**

1 *n* (**a**) *(spare part)* pièce *f* de rechange; *(wheel)* roue *f* de secours; *(tyre)* pneu *m* de rechange; **I've lost my pencil, have you got a spare?** j'ai perdu mon crayon, en as-tu un à me prêter?

(**b**) *(in ten-pin bowling)* honneur *m* simple; **to get** *or* **to score a spare** réussir un honneur simple

2 *adj* (**a**) *(free, not in use)* disponible, libre; *(kept in reserve)* de réserve, de rechange; *(extra, surplus)* en plus, de trop, en trop; **take a spare pullover** prenez un pull de rechange; **have you got a spare piece of paper?** est-ce que tu as une feuille de papier à me prêter?; **have you got any spare cash on you?** est-ce que tu peux me prêter de l'argent?; **we had no spare cash left to buy souvenirs** nous n'avions plus assez d'argent pour acheter des souvenirs; **with the spare cash they bought a table** avec l'argent qui leur restait ils ont acheté une table; **I've got two spare tickets for the match** j'ai deux billets en plus *ou* en trop pour le match; **you can stay here if you want, we have a spare bed** tu peux rester ici si tu veux, nous avons un lit pour toi; **there are plenty of spare seats at the back** il y a de nombreuses places libres au fond; **call in next time you have a spare moment** passez la prochaine fois que vous aurez un moment de libre; *Fam* **I'll have some more cake if there's any going spare** je vais reprendre du gâteau s'il en reste ❑

(**b**) *(lean)* maigre, sec (sèche)

(**c**) *(austere → style, decor)* austère; *(frugal → meal)* frugal

(**d**) *Br Fam (mad)* **to go spare** péter les plombs, péter une durite; **to drive sb spare** rendre qn chèvre, faire tourner qn en bourrique

3 *vt* (**a**) *(make available, give)* accorder, consacrer; *(do without)* se passer de; **Mr Austen**

can spare you a few minutes this afternoon M. Austen peut vous consacrer quelques minutes cet après-midi; **come and see us if you can spare the time** venez nous voir si vous avez le temps; **I can't spare the time to finish it** je n'ai pas le temps de le finir; **spare a thought for their poor parents!** pensez un peu à leurs pauvres parents!; **less money can be spared for research these days** on ne peut plus consacrer autant d'argent à la recherche aujourd'hui; **can you spare (me) a few pounds?** vous n'auriez pas quelques livres (à me passer)?; **I need £50, if you think you can spare it** j'aurais besoin de 50 livres si c'est possible; **I'm afraid we can't spare anyone at the moment** je regrette mais nous ne pouvons nous passer de personne *ou* nous avons besoin de tout le monde en ce moment; **young people with money to spare** des jeunes qui ont de l'argent à dépenser; **to have nothing to spare** n'avoir que le strict nécessaire, ne rien avoir de superflu; **he's got enough money and to spare** il a plus d'argent qu'il ne lui en faut; **there is room to spare** la place ne manque pas; **I've got no time to spare** je n'ai pas le temps; **there's no time to spare!** il n'y a de temps *ou* pas une minute à perdre!; **to have no time to spare for sb/sth** ne pas avoir de temps à consacrer à qn/qch; **do you have a few minutes to spare?** avez-vous quelques minutes de libres *ou* devant vous?; **we got to the airport with over an hour to spare** nous sommes arrivés à l'aéroport avec plus d'une heure d'avance; **I caught the train with just a few seconds to spare** à quelques secondes près je ratais le train

(**b**) *(refrain from harming, punishing, destroying)* épargner; **a few villages were miraculously spared** par miracle, quelques villages furent épargnés; **the flood spared nothing** l'inondation n'a rien épargné; **the report spared no one** le rapport ne ménageait personne; **to spare sb's life** épargner la vie de qn; **spare me!** *(don't kill me)* de grâce!, épargnez-moi!; *(don't expose me to that etc)* par pitié, pas ça!; **to spare sb's feelings** ménager les sentiments de qn; **to spare sb's blushes** épargner qn; **spare my blushes!** ne me faites pas rougir!

(**c**) *(save → trouble, suffering)* épargner, éviter; **I could have spared myself the bother** j'aurais pu m'épargner le dérangement; **to spare sb the trouble of doing sth** éviter à qn la peine de faire qch; **you could have spared yourself/us the trouble** vous auriez pu vous/nous éviter cette peine; **she was spared further distress by the judge's intervention** l'intervention du juge mit fin à ses tortures; **he was spared the shame of a public trial** la honte d'un procès public lui a été épargnée; **spare me the details!** épargne-moi les détails!; **I'll spare you the rest** je vous fais grâce du reste

(**d**) *(economize)* ménager; **they spared no expense on the celebrations** ils n'ont reculé devant aucune dépense pour les fêtes; **the first prize is a real luxury trip, with no expense spared** le premier prix est un voyage de rêve pour lequel on n'a pas regardé à la dépense; **we shall spare no effort to push the plan through** nous ne ménagerons pas nos efforts pour faire [illegible] beaucoup de mal; *Prov* **spare the rod and spoil the child** qui aime bien châtie bien

►► ***spare part*** pièce *f* de rechange, pièce *f* détachée; ***spare rib*** travers *m* de porc; **barbecue spare ribs** travers *mpl* de porc grillés sauce barbecue; ***spare room*** chambre *f* d'amis; ***spare time*** temps *m* libre; **what do you do in your spare time?** que faites-vous pendant votre temps libre *ou* pendant vos moments de loisirs?; *Br* ***spare tyre***, *Am* ***spare tire*** (**a**) *Aut* pneu *m* de secours *ou* de rechange (**b**) *Fam Hum (roll of fat)* pneu *m* de secours, bourrelet *m* de graisse; **to get a spare tyre** prendre de l'embonpoint; *Br* ***spare wheel*** roue *f* de secours

---

spare-part surgery *n Fam* chirurgie *f* des greffes ❑

spare-time *adj*

►► ***spare-time activities*** loisirs *mpl*

sparge [spɑːdʒ] *vt (in brewing)* arroser

sparing ['speərɪŋ] *adj* (**a**) *(economical → person)* économe; **she's very sparing with her compliments/praise** elle est très avare de compliments/louanges; **they were sparing in their efforts to help us** ils ne se sont pas donnés beaucoup de mal pour nous aider

(**b**) *(meagre → quantity)* limité, modéré; *(→ use)* modéré, économe; **to make sparing use of sth** utiliser qch avec parcimonie *ou* modération; **the author makes sparing use of metaphors** l'auteur utilise la métaphore avec parcimonie *ou* modération

sparingly ['speərɪŋlɪ] *adv (eat)* frugalement; *(drink, use)* avec modération; *(praise)* chichement, avec parcimonie; **they should be watered often but sparingly** il faudrait les arroser souvent mais avec modération; **use your strength sparingly** ménagez vos forces

spark [spɑːk] **1** *vi* (**a**) *(produce sparks → gen)* jeter des étincelles

(**b**) *Aut (spark plug, ignition system)* allumer *(par étincelle)*

2 *vt* = **spark off**

3 *n* (**a**) *(from flame, electricity)* étincelle *f*; *Fig* **whenever they meet the sparks fly** chaque fois qu'ils se rencontrent, ça fait des étincelles; **they strike sparks off each other** ils se stimulent mutuellement

(**b**) *(flash, trace → of excitement, wit)* étincelle *f*, lueur *f*; *(→ of interest, enthusiasm)* lueur *f*; **she hasn't a spark of common sense** elle n'a pas le moindre bon sens; **his eyes retained a spark of life** il restait une lueur de vie dans ses yeux

4 sparks *n Br Fam (electrician)* électricien(enne) ❑ *m,f*; *Fam Old-fashioned Naut & Aviat (radio operator)* radio ❑ *m*

►► *Phys* ***spark chamber*** chambre *f* à étincelles; *Elec* ***spark coil*** bobine *f* d'allumage; *Aut* ***spark gap*** écartement *m* des électrodes; *Aut* ***spark plug*** bougie *f*; ***spark plug spanner*** clé *f* à bougie

►**spark off** *vt sep (trigger → interest, argument)* susciter, provoquer; **the incident was the catalyst that sparked the revolution** c'est l'incident qui a déclenché la révolution; **the news sparked off an intense debate** la nouvelle déclencha un débat animé

sparking plug ['spɑːkɪŋ-] *n Br Aut* bougie *f*

sparkle ['spɑːkəl] **1** *vi* (**a**) *(jewel, frost, glass, star)* étinceler, scintiller; *(sea, lake)* étinceler, miroiter; *(eyes)* étinceler, pétiller

(**b**) *(person)* briller; *(conversation)* être brillant

(**c**) *(wine, cider, mineral water)* pétiller

2 *n* (**a**) *(of jewel, frost, glass, star)* scintillement *m*; *(of sea, lake)* étincellement *m*, miroitement *m*; *(of eyes)* éclat *m*; **she has a sparkle in her eye** elle a des yeux pétillants

(**b**) *(of person, conversation, wit, performance)* éclat *m*; **he's lost his sparkle** il a perdu sa joie de vivre; **to add sparkle to sth** *(glamour)* donner de l'éclat à qch; *(liven up)* égayer qch; **if the sparkle has gone out of your marriage...** si la magie a disparu de votre mariage...

sparkler ['spɑːklə(r)] *n* (**a**) *(firework)* cierge *m* magique (**b**) *Fam (diamond)* diam *m*

sparkling ['spɑːklɪŋ] **1** *adj* (**a**) *(jewel, frost, glass, star)* étincelant, scintillant; *(sea, lake)* étincelant, miroitant; *(eyes)* étincelant, pétillant (**b**) *(person, conversation, wit, performance)* brillant (**c**) *(soft drink, mineral water)* gazeux, pétillant

2 *adv* **sparkling clean/white** d'une propreté/blancheur éclatante

►► ***sparkling wine*** vin *m* mousseux

sparklingly ['spɑːklɪŋlɪ] *adv* (**a**) *(shine, glint)* d'une manière étincelante (**b**) *(vivaciously)* vivement, avec vivacité

sparling ['spɑːlɪŋ] *n Ich* éperlan *m*

sparring ['spɑːrɪŋ] *n Boxing* entraînement *m*; *(arguing)* échanges *mpl* verbaux; **it was just a little good-natured sparring** *(verbal)* ce n'était qu'une petite bagarre amicale

►► ***sparring match*** (**a**) *(in boxing)* combat *m* d'entraînement (**b**) *(argument)* discussion *f* animée; ***sparring partner*** (**a**) *(in boxing)* sparring-partner *m* (**b**) *Fig* adversaire *m*

sparrow ['spærəʊ] *n* moineau *m*

sparrowgrass ['spærəʊgrɑːs] *n Fam* asperges ❑ *fpl*

sparrowhawk ['spærəʊhɔːk] *n Orn* **(Eurasian) sparrowhawk** épervier *m*; **American sparrowhawk** faucon *m* des moineaux

sparse [spɑːs] *adj (trees, vegetation, population)* clairsemé, épars; *(crowd, audience)* clairsemé; **sparse hair** cheveux *mpl* rares *ou* clairsemés; **the sparse furnishings in the room** le peu de meubles qu'il y avait dans la pièce

sparsely ['spɑːslɪ] *adv (wooded, populated)* peu; **the room was sparsely furnished** la pièce contenait peu de meubles; **it grows only sparsely in the north** ça ne pousse pas beaucoup dans le nord

sparseness ['spɑːsnɪs] *n (of population)* faible densité *f*; *(of hair, vegetation)* manque *m*

Sparta ['spɑːtə] *n* Sparte

Spartacist ['spɑːtəsɪst] **1** *adj* spartakiste

2 *n* spartakiste *mf*

Spartacus ['spɑːtəkəs] *pr n* Spartacus

spartan ['spɑːtən] **1** *adj Fig (lifestyle)* spartiate; *(meal)* frugal; **spartan living conditions** des conditions *fpl* de vie spartiates; **a spartan room** une chambre austère *ou* sans aucun confort

2 Spartan *Hist* **1** *n* Spartiate *mf* **2** *adj* spartiate

spasm ['spæzəm] *n* (**a**) *(muscular contraction)* spasme *m* (**b**) *(fit)* accès *m*; **a spasm of anger/pain** un accès de colère/de douleur; **he had a spasm of coughing** il a eu une quinte de toux; **she went into spasms of laughter** elle a été prise d'une crise de fou rire; *Br* **I tend to work in spasms** j'ai tendance à travailler de façon irrégulière

spasmodic [spæz'mɒdɪk] *adj* (**a**) *(intermittent)* intermittent, irrégulier (**b**) *Med (pain, contraction)* spasmodique

spasmodically [spæz'mɒdɪklɪ] *adv* de façon intermittente, par à-coups

spastic ['spæstɪk] **1** *n* (**a**) *Med (gen)* handicapé(e) *m,f* (moteur); *(person affected by spasms)* spasmophile *mf* (**b**) *very Fam (clumsy person)* gol *mf*, gogol *mf*

2 *adj* (**a**) *Med (gen)* handicapé (moteur); *(affected by spasms)* spasmophile (**b**) *very Fam (clumsy)* empoté, gourde

►► ***spastic paralysis*** tétanie *f*

spasticity [spæs'tɪsɪtɪ] *n Med* spasmodicité *f*

spat [spæt] **1** *pt & pp of* **spit**

2 *n* (**a**) *(on shoe)* guêtre *f* (**b**) *Fam (quarrel)* prise *f* de bec (**c**) *(shellfish)* naissain *m*

spatchcock ['spætʃkɒk] *n Culin* poulet *m* à la crapaudine

spate [speɪt] *n* (**a**) *(of letters, visitors)* avalanche *f*; *(of abuse, insults)* torrent *m*; **a spate of murders/burglaries** une série de meurtres/cambriolages (**b**) *Br (flood)* crue *f*; **the river was in spate** le fleuve était en crue; *Fig* **to interrupt sb in full spate** interrompre qn en plein discours

spathe [speɪð] *n Bot* spathe *f*

spathic ['spæθɪk] *adj Miner* spathique

spathose ['spæθəʊs] *adj* (**a**) *Miner* spathique (**b**) *Bot* spathé, spathiforme

spatial ['speɪʃəl] *adj* spatial

►► ***spatial awareness, spatial intelligence*** perception *f* de l'espace

spatiality [ˌspeɪʃɪ'ælɪtɪ] *n* spatialité *f*

spatialization [ˌspeɪʃəlaɪ'zeɪʃən] *n* spatialisation *f*

spatially ['speɪʃəlɪ] *adv* dans l'espace

spatiotemporal [ˌspeɪʃɪəʊ'tempərəl] *adj* spatio-temporel

spatter ['spætə(r)] **1** *vt (splash)* éclabousser; **he spattered ink on** *or* **over the table** il a fait des éclaboussures d'encre sur la table; **the car spattered me with mud, the car spattered mud over me** l'auto m'a éclaboussé *ou* aspergé de boue; **the wall was spattered with grease** le mur était couvert d'éclaboussures *ou* tout éclaboussé de graisse

2 *vi (liquid)* gicler; *(oil)* crépiter; **rain spattered on the windowpane** la pluie crépitait sur la vitre

3 *n (on garment)* éclaboussure *f*, éclaboussures *fpl*; *(sound → of rain, oil, applause)* crépitement *m*

spatterdash ['spætədæʃ] *n Am* (**a**) *(roughcast)* crépi *m* (**b**) *(gaiter)* **spatterdashes** guêtres *fpl*

-spattered ['spætəd] *suff* **blood/mud/oil-spattered** couvert d'éclaboussures de sang/de boue/d'huile

spatula ['spætjʊlə] *n* (**a**) *Culin* spatule *f* (**b**) *Med* abaisse-langue *m inv*, spatule *f*

spatular ['spætjʊlə(r)] *adj* spatulé
spatulate ['spætjʊleɪt] *adj Zool* spatulé
►► ***spatulate fingers*** doigts *mpl* en spatule
spavin ['spævɪn] *n Vet* éparvin *m*, épervin *m*
spavined ['spævɪnd] *adj Vet* atteint d'éparvin
spawn [spɔːn] **1** *n (UNCOUNT)* (**a**) *Zool (of frogs, fish)* œufs *mpl*, frai *m* (**b**) *Bot (of mushrooms)* mycélium *m* (**c**) *Fig Pej (offspring)* progéniture *f*
2 *vt* (**a**) *Zool* pondre (**b**) *Fig (produce)* engendrer, donner naissance à; **the organization/movement spawned various offshoots** l'organisation/le mouvement a donné naissance à plusieurs ramifications
3 *vi Zool* frayer
spawner ['spɔːnə(r)] *n Zool* poisson *m* qui fraye
spawning ['spɔːnɪŋ] *n Zool* frai *m*
►► ***spawning ground*** frayère *f*; ***spawning season*** frai *m*
spay [speɪ] *vt Vet* castrer
spaying ['speɪɪŋ] *n Vet* castration *f*
spaz, spazz [spæz] *n Fam* (**a**) *(spastic)* infirme❑ *mf*, = terme injurieux désignant un handicapé moteur (**b**) *(idiot)* crétin(e) *m,f*, idiot(e)❑ *m,f*
►**spaz out** *vi Fam* faire le con
spazzy ['spæzɪ] = **spaz**
SPCA [ˌespiːˌsiː'eɪ] *n Am (abbr* **Society for the Prevention of Cruelty to Animals**) = société américaine protectrice des animaux, ≃ SPA *f*
SPCC [ˌespiːˌsiː'siː] *n Am (abbr* **Society for the Prevention of Cruelty to Children**) = société américaine pour la protection de l'enfance

SPEAK [spiːk] *(pt* **spoke** [spəʊk], *pp* **spoken** ['spəʊkən]) **1** *vt* (**a**) *(say, pronounce)* dire, prononcer; **the baby spoke his first words** le bébé a dit ses premiers mots; **I only had three lines to speak in the play** je n'avais que trois lignes à dire dans la pièce; **to speak one's mind** dire ce qu'on pense; **she spoke my name in her sleep** elle a prononcé mon nom dans son sommeil; **he didn't speak a word** il n'a pas dit un mot; **without a word being spoken** sans qu'un mot ne soit prononcé; **to speak the truth** dire la vérité; **their behaviour speaks volumes for their generosity** leur comportement en dit long sur leur générosité *ou* montre à quel point ils sont généreux; **his silence speaks volumes** son silence en dit long
(**b**) *(language)* parler; **he doesn't speak a word of Greek** il ne parle pas un mot de grec; **English spoken** *(sign)* ici on parle anglais; *Fig* **we just don't speak the same language** nous ne parlons pas le même langage, c'est tout
2 *vi* (**a**) *(talk)* parler; **to speak to** *or esp Am* **with sb** parler à *ou* avec qn; **to speak about** *or* **of sth** parler de qch; **to speak to sb about sth** parler à qn de qch; **I'll speak to her about it** je lui en parlerai; **to speak in a whisper** chuchoter; **speak to me!** dites(-moi) quelque chose!; **don't speak to your mother like that!** ne parle pas à ta mère sur ce ton!; **speak when you're spoken to!** ne parlez que lorsque l'on s'adresse à vous!; **don't speak with your mouth full** ne parle pas la bouche pleine; **it seems I spoke too soon** on dirait que j'ai parlé un peu vite; **speak now or forever hold your peace** parlez maintenant ou gardez le silence pour toujours; **she isn't speaking to me** elle ne me parle plus; **she hasn't spoken to me since** elle ne m'a pas adressé la parole depuis; **they're not speaking (to each other)** ils ne s'adressent pas *ou* plus la parole; **isn't it about time you two started speaking again?** est-ce que vous ne devriez pas faire la paix?; **I know them by sight but not to speak to** je ne les connais que de vue; **are you on speaking terms with them?** *(do you know them?)* tu les connais?; *(are you reconciled with them?)* vous vous parlez?; **we're no longer on speaking terms** nous ne nous parlons plus; **speaking of which** justement, à ce propos; **generally speaking** en général; **personally speaking** en ce qui me concerne, quant à moi; **financially/legally speaking** financièrement/légalement parlant, du point de vue financier/légal; **speaking as a politician** en tant qu'homme politique; **you shouldn't speak ill of the dead** tu ne devrais pas dire du mal des morts; **he always speaks well/highly of you** il dit toujours du bien/beaucoup de bien de vous
(**b**) *(on telephone)* parler; **who's speaking?** *(gen)* qui est à l'appareil?; *(on switchboard)* c'est de la part de qui?; **Kate Smith speaking** Kate Smith à l'appareil, c'est Kate Smith; **may I speak to Kate? – speaking** puis-je parler à Kate? – c'est moi; **I'm speaking from Australia** j'appelle d'Australie
(**c**) *(in debate, meeting etc → make a speech)* faire un discours, parler; *(→ intervene)* prendre la parole, parler; **he began to speak** il a pris la parole; **she got up to speak** elle s'est levée pour parler; **the chair called upon Mrs Fox to speak** le président a demandé à Mme Fox de prendre la parole; **he was invited to speak to us on** *or* **about Chile** il a été invité à venir nous parler du Chili; **she spoke for an hour on imperialism** elle a parlé de l'impérialisme pendant une heure; **to speak to** *or* **on a motion** soutenir une motion; **to speak from the floor** intervenir dans un débat
(**d**) *Fig (give an impression)* **everything he saw seemed to speak to him of Greece** tout ce qu'il voyait lui semblait évoquer la Grèce; **his paintings speak of terrible loneliness** ses peintures expriment une immense solitude; **the gift speaks well of her concern for old people** son don témoigne de l'intérêt qu'elle porte aux personnes âgées; **this speaks of large-scale corruption** c'est le signe d'une corruption à grande échelle
(**e**) *Literary (sound → trumpet)* sonner, retentir; *(→ organ pipe)* parler; *(→ gun)* retentir
3 not to speak of *prep* sans parler de; **his plays are hugely popular, not to speak of his many novels** ses pièces sont extrêmement populaires, sans parler de ses nombreux romans
4 so to speak *adv* pour ainsi dire
5 to speak of *adv* **there's no wind/mail to speak of** il n'y a presque pas de vent/de courrier
►**speak against** *vt insep (motion, bill, proposal)* se prononcer contre; **she spoke passionately against the practice** elle a condamné cette pratique avec virulence
►**speak for** *vt insep* (**a**) *(speak on behalf of)* parler au nom de, parler pour; *(speak in support of)* parler en faveur de, plaider pour; **I'm sure I speak for everyone when I say...** je suis sûr que j'exprime la pensée générale lorsque je dis...; **speaking for myself** pour ma part, en ce qui me concerne; **let her speak for herself!** laisse-la s'exprimer!; **I'll tell him when to leave, I can speak for myself!** c'est moi qui lui dirai de partir, je suis parfaitement capable de le faire moi-même!; **he is old enough to speak for himself** *(ask for something)* il est assez grand pour le demander tout seul; *(say something)* il est assez grand pour le dire lui-même; *Fam* **speak for yourself!** parle pour toi!; *Fig* **the facts speak for themselves** les faits parlent d'eux-mêmes; **the title speaks for itself** le titre se passe de commentaire
(**b**) **to be spoken for** *(to be reserved)* être réservé; *(of person → gen)* ne pas être libre; *(→ at dance)* être accompagné; *(→ have girlfriend, boyfriend)* avoir un(e) petit(e) ami(e); *(→ have wife, husband)* être marié; **these goods are already spoken for** ces articles sont déjà réservés *ou* retenus; **she's already spoken for** elle est déjà prise
►**speak out** *vi* parler franchement, ne pas mâcher ses mots; **don't be afraid to speak out** n'aie pas peur de parler franchement *ou* de dire ce que tu penses; **to speak out for sth** parler en faveur de qch; **to speak out against sth** s'élever contre qch; **she spoke out strongly against the scheme** elle a condamné le projet avec véhémence
►**speak up** *vi* (**a**) *(louder)* parler plus fort; *(more clearly)* parler plus clairement (**b**) *(be frank)* parler franchement; **to speak up for sb** parler en faveur de qn, défendre les intérêts de qn; **why didn't you speak up?** pourquoi n'avez-vous rien dit?

-speak [spiːk] *suff Pej* **psycho-speak** jargon *m* psychologique *ou* des psychologues; **computer-speak** langage *m ou* jargon *m* de l'informatique
speakeasy ['spiːkˌiːzɪ] *(pl* **speakeasies**) *n Am* bar *m* clandestin *(pendant la prohibition)*
speaker ['spiːkə(r)] *n* (**a**) *(gen)* celui *m* /celle *f* qui parle; *(in discussion)* interlocuteur(trice) *m,f*; *(in public)* orateur(trice) *m,f*; *(during debate, at conference)* intervenant(e) *m,f*; **she's a good speaker** elle sait parler *ou* s'exprimer en public; **the chairman called the next speaker** le président a appelé l'orateur(trice) *m,f* suivant(e)
(**b**) *Ling* locuteur(trice) *m,f*; **native speakers of English** ceux dont la langue maternelle est l'anglais; **Spanish speaker** hispanophone *mf*; **as a speaker of Italian** *or* **an Italian speaker myself...** moi qui parle italien...; **my parents are Welsh speakers** mes parents sont galloisants *ou* parlent (le) gallois; **there are very few surviving speakers of the language** il reste très peu de personnes qui parlent cette langue
(**c**) *Pol* speaker *m*, président(e) *m,f* de l'assemblée **the Speaker (of the House of Commons)** = le président de la Chambre des communes; **the Speaker of the House** = le président de la Chambre des représentants américaine
(**d**) *(loudspeaker)* haut-parleur *m*; *(in stereo system)* enceinte *f*, baffle *m*
►► ***Speakers' Corner*** = angle nord-est de Hyde Park, à Londres, où chacun peut venir le week-end haranguer la foule sur des tribunes improvisées; ***speaker phone*** téléphone *m* avec haut-parleur

SPEAKER OF THE HOUSE 

Le président de la Chambre des représentants est l'une des personnalités politiques les plus influentes à la Maison Blanche, et vient en deuxième position pour remplacer le président des États-Unis en cas de force majeure.

speaking ['spiːkɪŋ] **1** *adj* (**a**) *(involving speech)* **do you have a speaking part in the play?** est-ce que vous avez du texte?; **she has a good speaking voice** elle a une belle voix (**b**) *(which speaks → robot, machine, doll)* parlant
2 *n* art *m* de parler
►► *Br* ***speaking clock*** horloge *f* parlante; ***speaking tube*** tuyau *m* acoustique
-speaking ['spiːkɪŋ] *suff* (**a**) *(person)* **they're both German/Spanish-speaking** ils sont tous deux germanophones/hispanophones; **a child of Polish-speaking parents** un enfant dont les parents sont de langue *ou* d'origine polonaise (**b**) *(country)* **French/English-speaking countries** les pays *mpl* francophones/anglophones; **the Arab-speaking world** le monde arabophone
spear [spɪə(r)] **1** *n* (**a**) *(weapon)* lance *f*; *(harpoon)* harpon *m*
(**b**) *(of asparagus, broccoli etc)* pointe *f*
2 *vt* (**a**) *(enemy)* transpercer d'un coup de lance; *(fish)* harponner
(**b**) *(food)* piquer; **he speared a piece of meat with his fork/on a skewer** il a piqué un morceau de viande avec sa fourchette/enfilé un morceau de viande sur une brochette
►► ***spear fishing*** pêche *f ou* chasse *f* (sous-marine) au harpon; *Bot* ***spear grass*** pâturin *m*
spear-carrier *n Hist* soldat *m (armé d'une lance)*; **to be a spear-carrier** *Theat* être figurant, jouer les hallebardiers; *Fig* avoir un rôle mineur
spearfish ['spɪəfɪʃ] *(pl* **inv** *or* **spearfishes**) **1** *n* marlin *m*
2 *vi Am* pratiquer la pêche sous-marine *(au harpon)*
speargun ['spɪəgʌn] *n* fusil *m* sous-marin *ou* à harpon
spearhead ['spɪəhed] **1** *n also Fig* fer *m* de lance
2 *vt (attack)* être le fer de lance de; *(campaign, movement)* mener, être à la tête de
spearman ['spɪəmən] *(pl* **spearmen** [-men]) *n Hist* soldat *m (armé d'une lance)*
spearmint ['spɪəmɪnt] **1** *n* (**a**) *(plant)* menthe *f* verte; *(flavour)* menthe *f* (**b**) *(sweet)* bonbon *m* à la menthe
2 *adj (flavour)* de menthe; *(toothpaste, chewing gum)* à la menthe
spearwort ['spɪəwɜːt] *n Bot* douve *f*
spec [spek] *n* (**a**) *(abbr* **specification**) spécifications *fpl* (**b**) *Br Fam (idiom)* **on spec** au hasard❑; **I called by on spec** je suis passé au hasard; **he**

bought the car on spec il a risqué le coup en achetant la voiture; **he bought the books on spec** il a acheté les livres dans l'espoir de faire une affaire ❑

speccy ['spekɪ] *Br Fam* **1** *n* binoclard(e) *m,f*
2 *adj* binoclard

special ['speʃəl] **1** *adj* (**a**) *(exceptional, particular → offer, friend, occasion, ability)* spécial; *(→ reason, effort, pleasure)* particulier; **pay special attention to the details** faites particulièrement attention aux détails; **this is a very special moment for me** c'est un moment particulièrement important pour moi; **as a special treat** *(present)* comme cadeau; *(outing)* pour vous faire plaisir; **can you do me a special favour?** pouvez-vous me rendre un grand service?; **I'll do it as a special favour to you** je le ferai, mais c'est bien pour toi *ou* parce que c'est toi; **it's a special case** c'est un cas particulier *ou* à part; **a special feature of the church is its Gothic belltower** le clocher gothique de l'église est l'un de ses traits distinctifs; **a special feature** *(in newspaper)* un article spécial; *(on TV)* une émission spéciale; **they put on a special train for the match** ils ont prévu un train supplémentaire pour le match; **what did you do last night? – nothing special** qu'as-tu fait hier soir? – rien de spécial; **the food was OK but nothing special** la nourriture était assez bonne mais elle n'avait rien d'exceptionnel; **I'm going to cook something special for dinner tonight** ce soir, je vais cuisiner quelque chose qui sorte de l'ordinaire; **what's so special about this car?** qu'est-ce que cette voiture a de si extraordinaire?; **to get special treatment** bénéficier d'un traitement de faveur
(**b**) *(specific → need, problem)* spécial, particulier; *(→ equipment)* spécial; *(→ adviser)* particulier; **special characteristic** particularité *f*; **you need special permission** il vous faut une autorisation spéciale; **by special permission of the Lyme museum** avec l'aimable autorisation du musée Lyme; **she has a special interest in Italian art** elle s'intéresse beaucoup à *ou* porte un intérêt tout particulier à l'art italien; **minister with special responsibility for economic development** ministre chargé du développement économique; **children with special needs** enfants ayant des difficultés d'apprentissage
(**c**) *(valued)* cher; **this house is very special to me** cette maison m'est très chère; **you're very special to me** je tiens beaucoup à toi; **a special relationship** des rapports *mpl* privilégiés; *Pol* **the special relationship** = relations d'amitié entre les USA et la Grande-Bretagne; **a present for a special person** un cadeau pour un être cher; **for someone special** *(on card)* pour quelqu'un qui m'est cher
2 *n* (**a**) *(train)* train *m* supplémentaire; *(bus)* car *m* supplémentaire; **they put on a football/holiday special** ils ont mis un train/car supplémentaire pour le match de football/les départs en vacances
(**b**) *(in restaurant)* spécialité *f*; **the chef's/the house special** la spécialité du chef/de la maison; **today's special** le plat du jour
(**c**) *TV* émission *f* spéciale; *Journ (issue)* numéro *m* spécial; *(feature)* article *m* spécial; **they brought out a special on the war** ils ont sorti un numéro spécial sur la guerre
(**d**) *Br (police officer)* auxiliaire *mf* de police
(**e**) *Am Com* offre *f* spéciale; **sugar is on special today** le sucre est en promotion aujourd'hui
▸▸ ***special agent*** *(spy etc)* agent *m* secret; ***Special Air Service*** = commando d'intervention spéciale de l'armée britannique; ***Special Branch*** = service de police britannique chargé des crimes contre la sûreté de l'État, ≃ Renseignements *mpl* généraux; *Br* ***special constable*** auxiliaire *mf* de police; *Journ* ***special correspondent*** envoyé(e) *m,f* spécial(e); ***special delivery*** = service postal britannique garantissant la distribution du courrier sous 24 heures; **to send sth special delivery** envoyer qch en exprès; *Fin* ***special drawing rights*** droits *mpl* de tirage spéciaux; ***special education*** enseignement *m* spécialisé; *Cin & TV* ***special effects*** effets *mpl* spéciaux; *Comput* ***special interest group*** groupe *m* d'intérêt; ***special interest holidays*** vacances *fpl* à thème; *Br* ***special licence*** dispense *f* de bans; **to be married by special licence** se marier avec dispense de bans; ***special offer*** promotion *f*; **to be on special offer** être en promotion; ***special pleading*** *(gen)* argument *m* spécieux; *Law* plaidoyer *m* partial; *Pol* ***special powers*** pouvoirs *mpl* extraordinaires; *Br* ***special school*** établissement *m* d'enseignement spécialisé *(pour enfants handicapés ou inadaptés)*; *Typ* ***special sort*** caractère *m* spécial

SPECIAL RELATIONSHIP

Les liens étroits qu'entretiennent la Grande-Bretagne et les États-Unis depuis l'époque coloniale, tant sur le plan culturel que sur le plan diplomatique, sont souvent désignés par l'expression "the special relationship" ("la relation privilégiée"). Par ailleurs, les liens forgés entre les deux pays à l'occasion des deux guerres mondiales et durant toute la guerre froide ont fait de la Grande-Bretagne l'allié privilégié de la superpuissance américaine. La "special relationship" connut son apogée durant les années 80, qui virent Margaret Thatcher adopter une politique résolument pro-américaine, au détriment des liens avec les partenaires européens de la Grande-Bretagne. Aujourd'hui, certains critiques reprochent au personnel politique britannique de s'aligner systématiquement sur Washington en matière de politique extérieure au nom de la "special relationship".

specialism ['speʃəlɪzəm] *n* spécialisation *f*; **my specialism is maths** je me spécialise dans les maths

specialist ['speʃəlɪst] **1** *n* (**a**) *(gen) & Med* spécialiste *mf*; **she's a heart specialist** elle est cardiologue; **he's a specialist in rare books** c'est un spécialiste en livres rares
(**b**) *Am Mil* officier *m* technicien
2 *adj (skills, vocabulary, knowledge)* spécialisé, de spécialiste; *(writing, publication)* pour spécialistes; *(bookshop, TV channel, dictionary)* spécialisé; **it's a specialist job** c'est un travail de spécialiste; **to seek specialist advice** demander conseil à *ou* consulter un spécialiste
▸▸ *Com* ***specialist retailer*** détaillant(e) *m,f* spécialisé(e); ***specialist teacher*** professeur *m* spécialisé; **she's a specialist maths teacher** elle n'enseigne que *ou* enseigne uniquement les maths

speciality [ˌspeʃɪ'ælətɪ] *(pl* **specialities**), *Am* **specialty** ['speʃəltɪ] *(pl* **specialties**) *n* (**a**) *(service, product)* spécialité *f*; **a local speciality** une spécialité de la région; **he made a speciality of croissants** il s'est spécialisé dans les croissants; **our speciality is electronic components** nous nous spécialisons *ou* nous sommes spécialisés dans les composants électroniques
(**b**) *(of academic)* domaine *m* de spécialité; **her speciality is Chinese history** c'est une spécialiste de l'histoire chinoise; **what's his speciality?** dans quel domaine est-ce qu'il s'est spécialisé?

specialization [ˌspeʃəlaɪ'zeɪʃən] *n* spécialisation *f*; **his specialization is computers** il est spécialisé en informatique

specialize, -ise ['speʃəlaɪz] *vi (company, restaurant, student)* se spécialiser; **to specialize in sth** se spécialiser en *ou* dans qch

specialized ['speʃəlaɪzd] *adj* spécialisé; **highly specialized equipment** un matériel hautement spécialisé; **we need somebody with specialized knowledge** il nous faut un spécialiste

specially ['speʃəlɪ] *adv* (**a**) *(particularly)* spécialement, particulièrement, surtout; **she was specially interested in old cars** elle s'intéressait (tout) particulièrement *ou* surtout aux vieilles voitures; **I would specially like to hear that song** j'aimerais beaucoup écouter cette chanson; **the chocolate mousse is specially good here** la mousse au chocolat est particulièrement bonne ici; **do you want to come? – not specially** (est-ce que) tu veux venir? – pas spécialement; **she specially requested a non-smoking seat** elle a bien spécifié qu'elle voulait un siège non-fumeurs
(**b**) *(on purpose, specifically)* exprès, spécialement; **I made your favourite meal specially** j'ai fait exprès ton repas préféré; **the coat was specially made for him** le manteau a été fait tout spécialement pour lui; **we've driven 500 miles specially to see you** nous avons fait 800 kilomètres spécialement pour venir te voir

specialty ['speʃltɪ] *(pl* **specialties**) *n* (**a**) *Am* = **speciality** (**b**) *Law* contrat *m* sous seing privé

speciate ['spiːsɪeɪt] *vi Biol* subir la spéciation

speciation [ˌspiːsɪ'eɪʃən] *n Biol* spéciation *f*

specie ['spiːʃiː] *n (UNCOUNT) (coins)* espèces *fpl*, numéraire *m*; **in specie** en espèces, en numéraire; *Fig* de manière identique

species ['spiːʃiːz] *(pl inv) n* (**a**) *Biol* espèce *f*; **the human species** l'espèce *f* humaine; **a rare species of butterfly** une espèce rare de papillon (**b**) *Fig* espèce *f*; **an unusual species of politician** un homme politique d'une espèce rare

speciesism ['spiːʃiːzɪzəm] *n* = théorie selon laquelle l'homme est supérieur aux animaux et peut donc les exploiter à ses propres fins

specifiable [ˌspesɪ'faɪəbəl] *adj* qu'on peut préciser *ou* spécifier

specific [spə'sɪfɪk] **1** *adj* (**a**) *(precise)* précis; **I gave him specific instructions** je lui ai donné des instructions précises; **could you please be a little** *or* **a bit more specific?** pourriez-vous être un peu plus précis?; **she was quite specific about it** elle s'est montrée très claire *ou* précise à ce sujet, elle a été très explicite sur ce point
(**b**) *(particular → gen)* particulier, précis; *(→ role, problem, conditions, needs)* spécifique, particulier; **in this specific case** dans ce cas précis *ou* particulier; **give me a specific example** donnez-moi un exemple précis; **what did he say? – nothing specific** qu'a-t-il dit? – rien de précis *ou* de particulier; **specific to** spécifique à, propre à
2 *n Med* (remède *m*) spécifique *m*; **insulin is a specific for diabetes** l'insuline est le médicament spécifique pour le diabète
3 specifics *npl* détails *mpl*; **let's not bother with the specifics of the case** inutile d'entrer dans les détails de l'affaire
▸▸ *Phys* ***specific gravity*** densité *f*; *Phys* ***specific heat*** chaleur *f* spécifique; *Biol & Bot* ***specific name*** nom *m* spécifique *ou* d'espèce

specifically [spə'sɪfɪklɪ] *adv* (**a**) *(precisely)* précisément, de façon précise; *(clearly)* clairement, expressément; *(explicitly)* explicitement; **your name was mentioned specifically** votre nom a été mentionné explicitement; **his book does not specifically say what happened** son livre ne dit pas clairement *ou* ne précise pas ce qui s'est passé; **I specifically asked to speak to Mr Myers** j'avais bien spécifié *ou* précisé que je voulais parler à M. Myers; **I specifically told you to telephone** je t'avais bien dit de téléphoner
(**b**) *(particularly)* particulièrement; *(specially)* spécialement; *(purposely)* exprès, expressément; **our kitchens are specifically designed for the modern family** nos cuisines sont (tout) spécialement conçues pour la famille moderne; **it's not a specifically British problem** ce n'est pas un problème spécifiquement britannique; **we were specifically forbidden to...** il nous était expressément défendu de...

specification [ˌspesɪfɪ'keɪʃən] *n* (**a**) *(often pl) (in contract → of machine, building materials etc)* spécifications *fpl*; *(→ for technical project, including work schedule)* cahier *m* des charges; **made (according) to specification** construit en fonction de spécifications techniques; **the builder didn't follow the architect's specifications** le constructeur n'a pas respecté le cahier des charges rédigé par l'architecte; **standard specifications** normes *fpl* de qualité
(**b**) *(stipulation)* spécification *f*, précision *f*; **there was no specification as to age** l'âge n'était pas précisé
(**c**) *Comput* spécifications *fpl*
▸▸ *Com* ***specification buying*** achats *mpl* spécifiés

specificity [ˌspesɪ'fɪsətɪ] *(pl* **specificities**) *n* spécificité *f*

specify ['spesɪfaɪ] *(pt & pp* **specified**) *vt* spécifier, préciser; **the rules specify a five-minute break** le règlement spécifie une pause de cinq minutes; **unless otherwise specified** sauf indication contraire; **the person previously specified** la personne précitée *ou* déjà nommée; **on a specified date** à une date précise

specimen ['spesɪmən] **1** *n* (**a**) *(sample → of work, handwriting)* spécimen *m*; *(→ of blood)* prélèvement *m*; *(→ of urine)* échantillon *m*

(**b**) *(single example)* spécimen *m*; **this butterfly is a superb specimen** ce papillon est un superbe spécimen; **a fine specimen of Gothic architecture** un bel exemple d'architecture gothique; **the finest specimens in his collection** les plus belles pièces de sa collection

(**c**) *Fam Pej (person)* spécimen *m*; **he's a peculiar specimen** c'est un drôle de spécimen; **that pathetic specimen is her husband** ce triste spécimen est son mari

2 *comp (page, letter, reply)* spécimen; **they will ask you for a specimen signature** ils vous demanderont un exemplaire de votre signature

►► ***specimen bottle*** flacon-échantillon *m*; ***specimen copy*** spécimen *m (livre, magazine)*

speciosity [ˌspiːʃɪ'ɒsɪtɪ] *n* caractère *m* spécieux

specious ['spiːʃəs] *adj (argument, reasoning)* spécieux; *(appearance)* trompeur

speciously ['spiːʃəslɪ] *adv* spécieusement

speciousness ['spiːʃəsnɪs] *n* caractère *m* spécieux

speck [spek] **1** *n* (**a**) *(of dust, dirt)* grain *m*; *(in eye)* poussière *f*; **there wasn't a speck of dust anywhere** il n'y avait pas le moindre grain de poussière

(**b**) *(stain, mark → gen)* petite tache *f*; *(→ on skin, fruit)* tache *f*, tavelure *f*; *(→ of blood)* petite tache *f*; **I keep seeing black specks in front of my eyes** j'ai souvent des taches noires devant les yeux

(**c**) *(dot → on horizon, from height)* point *m* noir; **from the top of the tower, the people looked like mere specks** vus du haut de la tour, les gens avaient l'air de minuscules points noirs

(**d**) *(tiny amount)* tout petit peu *m*; **there isn't a speck of truth in the rumour** il n'y a pas la moindre vérité *ou* un atome de vérité dans cette rumeur

2 *vt (usu passive)* tacheter

speckle ['spekəl] **1** *n* moucheture *f*

2 *vt* tacheter, moucheter; **speckled with yellow** tacheté *ou* moucheté de jaune

speckled ['spekəld] *adj (egg)* tacheté, moucheté; *(plumage)* grivelé; *(hen)* tacheté

specs [speks] *npl Fam (abbr* **spectacles***)* carreaux *mpl*, hublots *mpl*

spectacle ['spektəkəl] *n* (**a**) *(sight)* spectacle *m*; **he was a sorry** *or* **sad spectacle** il était triste à voir; **to make a spectacle of oneself** se donner en spectacle (**b**) *Cin, Theat & TV* superproduction *f*

spectacled ['spektəkəld] *adj (gen) & Zool* à lunettes

►► *Zool* ***spectacled bear*** ours *m* à lunettes

spectacles ['spektəkəlz] *npl* lunettes *fpl*; **a pair of spectacles** une paire de lunettes

spectacular [spek'tækjʊlə(r)] **1** *adj (event, defeat, result, view)* spectaculaire; **it was the most spectacular success of the decade** ce fut la réussite la plus spectaculaire de la décennie; **there has been a spectacular rise in house prices** le prix des maisons a fait un bond spectaculaire

2 *n Cin, Theat & TV* superproduction *f*

spectacularly [spek'tækjʊləlɪ] *adv (big, beautiful)* extraordinairement; **it went spectacularly wrong** ça s'est vraiment très mal passé; **the movie was spectacularly successful** le film a eu un succès monstre; **the government has failed spectacularly in its effort to combat unemployment** le gouvernement a échoué lamentablement dans sa tentative de lutte contre le chômage

spectate [spek'teɪt] *vi* = être présent en tant que spectateur

spectator [spek'teɪtə(r)] *n* spectateur(trice) *m,f*; **we don't want any spectators** nous ne voulons pas qu'on nous regarde

►► *Am* ***spectator pumps*** escarpins *mpl* bicolores; ***spectator sport*** sport *m* grand public; **swimming is not a very good spectator sport** la natation n'est pas un sport très intéressant à regarder; *Fig* **television has turned war into a spectator sport** la télévision a transformé la guerre en spectacle

specter *Am* = **spectre**

spectra ['spektrə] *pl of* **spectrum**

spectral ['spektrəl] *adj* (**a**) *Phys (analysis, band, colour, density)* spectral (**b**) *(ghostly)* fantomatique, spectral

►► *Phys* ***spectral line*** raie *f* spectrale; *Phys* ***spectral range*** domaine *m* spectral

spectre, *Am* **specter** ['spektə(r)] *n* spectre *m*; *Fig* **the spectre of war/famine** *(threat)* le spectre de la guerre/la famine; **to be the spectre at the feast** jeter une ombre au tableau

> **Spectre at the feast**
> Cette formule est tirée de l'acte III du *Macbeth* de Shakespeare. Au cours d'un banquet, Macbeth est pris de délire lorsqu'apparaît le fantôme de Banquo, l'ancien camarade qu'il vient de faire assassiner, et dévoile ainsi sa culpabilité; la fête est gâchée et les invités s'enfuient.
> On emploie l'expression lorsque la présence indésirable de quelqu'un à une réunion fait l'effet d'une douche froide. Par exemple, **his first wife turned up at the wedding like the spectre at the feast** ("en venant au mariage, sa première épouse a véritablement joué les trouble-fête").

spectrochemistry [ˌspektrəʊ'kemɪstrɪ] *n* spectrochimie *f*

spectrogram ['spektrəgræm] *n* spectrogramme *m*

spectrograph ['spektrəgrɑːf] *n* spectrographe *m*

spectrographer [spek'trɒgrəfə(r)] *n* spectroscopiste *mf*

spectrographic [ˌspektrəʊ'græfɪk] *adj* spectrographique

spectrography [spek'trɒgrəfɪ] *n* spectrographie *f*

spectrology [spek'trɒlədʒɪ] *n* étude *f* des fantômes

spectrometer [spek'trɒmɪtə(r)] *n* spectromètre *m*

spectrometry [spek'trɒmɪtrɪ] *n* spectrométrie *f*

spectrophotography [ˌspektrəʊfə'tɒgrəfɪ] *n* spectrophotographie *f*

spectrophotometry [ˌspektrəʊfə'tɒmɪtrɪ] *n* spectrophotométrie *f*, photométrie *f* spectrale

spectroradiometry ['spektrəʊˌreɪdɪ'ɒmɪtrɪ] *n* spectroradiométrie *f*

spectroscope ['spektrəskəʊp] *n* spectroscope *m*

spectroscopic [ˌspektrəʊ'skɒpɪk], **spectroscopical** [ˌspektrəʊ'skɒpɪkəl] *adj* spectroscopique

►► ***spectroscopic analysis*** analyse *f* spectroscopique, analyse *f* spectrale; ***spectroscopic notation*** notation *f* spectroscopique; *Astron* ***spectroscopic parallax*** parallaxe *f* spectroscopique

spectroscopist [spek'trɒskəpɪst] *n* spectroscopiste *mf*

spectroscopy [spek'trɒskəpɪ] *n* spectroscopie *f*

spectrum ['spektrəm] *(pl* **spectrums** *or* **spectra** [-trə]*)* *n* (**a**) *Phys* spectre *m*; **the colours of the spectrum** les couleurs *fpl* spectrales *ou* du spectre

(**b**) *Fig (range)* gamme *f*; **right across the spectrum** sur toute la gamme; **we've covered the whole spectrum of opinion** nous avons couvert tous les secteurs d'opinion; **the political spectrum** l'éventail *m* politique; **people across the political spectrum** des représentants de toutes les tendances politiques

►► ***spectrum analysis*** analyse *f* spectrale

specular ['spekjʊlə(r)] *adj (ore)* spéculaire

►► *Opt & Phot* ***specular density*** densité *f* par réflexion; ***specular iron ore*** fer *m* spéculaire; ***specular pig(-iron)*** fonte *f* miroitante

speculate ['spekjʊleɪt] *vi* (**a**) *(wonder)* s'interroger, se poser des questions; *(make suppositions)* faire des suppositions; *Phil* spéculer; **we can only speculate** nous ne pouvons que faire des suppositions; **the press is speculating about the future of the present government** la presse s'interroge sur l'avenir du gouvernement actuel; **it is widely speculated that...** nombreux sont ceux qui supposent que... + *indicative*

(**b**) *Com & Fin* spéculer; **to speculate on the stock market** spéculer *ou* jouer en Bourse

speculation [ˌspekjʊ'leɪʃən] *n* (**a**) *(UNCOUNT) (supposition, conjecture)* conjecture *f*, conjectures *fpl*, supposition *f*, suppositions *fpl*; *Phil* spéculation *f*; **it's pure speculation** ce n'est qu'une conjecture *ou* supposition; **there's been a lot of speculation about her motives** tout le monde s'est demandé quels étaient ses motifs; **the affair has been the subject of intense speculation in the press** l'affaire a donné lieu à toutes sortes de conjectures dans la presse

(**b**) *(guess)* supposition *f*, conjecture *f*

(**c**) *Com & Fin* spéculation *f*; **speculation in oil** spéculation *f* sur le pétrole

speculative ['spekjʊlətɪv] *adj* spéculatif

►► *Fin & St Exch* ***speculative buying*** achats *mpl* spéculatifs; ***speculative selling*** vente *f* spéculative; ***speculative shares*** valeurs *fpl* spéculatives

speculatively ['spekjʊlətɪvlɪ] *adv (to suggest, argue)* à titre d'hypothèse; *(to invest)* spéculativement

speculator ['spekjʊleɪtə(r)] *n Com & Fin* spéculateur(trice) *m,f*

speculum ['spekjʊləm] *(pl* **speculums** *or* **specula** [-lə]*)* *n Med* spéculum *m*; *Opt* miroir *m*, réflecteur *m*

sped [sped] *pt & pp of* **speed**

speech [spiːtʃ] *n* (**a**) *(faculty)* parole *f*; *(spoken language)* parole *f*, langage *m* parlé; **their poetry is based on speech rather than writing** leur poésie relève de la tradition orale plus que de l'écriture; **to express oneself in speech** s'exprimer oralement *ou* par la parole; **things which people say in everyday speech** des choses que les gens disent dans la langue de tous les jours; *Prov* **speech is silver but silence is golden** la parole est d'argent, mais le silence est d'or

(**b**) *(manner of speaking)* façon *f* de parler, langage *m*; *(elocution)* élocution *f*, articulation *f*; **his speech was slurred** il bafouillait; **her speech grew hesitant** son élocution devenait hésitante

(**c**) *(dialect, language)* parler *m*, langage *m*; **the speech of the islanders/local fishermen** le parler des habitants de l'île/des pêcheurs du coin

(**d**) *(talk)* discours *m*, *Formal* allocution *f*; *(shorter, more informal)* speech *m*; **to make a speech on** *or* **about sth** faire *ou* prononcer un discours sur qch; **speech! speech!** un discours! un discours!; **the Queen's Speech** le discours du Trône

(**e**) *Theat* tirade *f*

►► *Ling* ***speech act*** acte *m* de parole; ***speech bubble*** bulle *f*; *Ling* ***speech community*** communauté *f* linguistique; *Br Sch* ***speech day*** distribution *f* des prix; **on speech day** le jour de la distribution des prix; ***speech defect*** défaut *m* de prononciation, *Spec* trouble *f* du langage; ***speech impediment*** défaut *m* d'élocution *ou* de prononciation; ***speech pattern*** schéma *m* linguistique; ***speech processing*** compréhension *f* du langage parlé; *Comput* ***speech recognition*** reconnaissance *f* de la parole; *Ling* ***speech sound*** phone *m*, son *m* linguistique; ***speech synthesizer*** synthétiseur *m* de parole; ***speech therapist*** orthophoniste *mf*, *Belg & Suisse* logopède *mf*; ***speech therapy*** orthophonie *f*

> **SPEECH DAY**
> À la fin de l'année scolaire en Grande-Bretagne, certaines écoles invitent une personnalité à prononcer un discours et à distribuer des prix.

speechifier ['spiːtʃɪfaɪə(r)] *n Pej* discoureur(euse) *m,f*, faiseur(euse) *m,f* de discours

speechify ['spiːtʃɪfaɪ] *(pt & pp* **speechified***)* *vi Pej* discourir, faire de beaux discours

speechifying ['spiːtʃɪfaɪɪŋ] *n Pej* beaux discours *mpl*, laïus *m*

speechless ['spiːtʃlɪs] *adj* (**a**) *(with amazement, disbelief)* muet, interloqué; *(with rage, joy)* muet; **she was speechless with admiration** elle était muette d'admiration; **to leave sb speechless** laisser qn sans voix; *Fam* **I'm speechless!** je ne sais pas quoi dire![❑], les bras m'en tombent! (**b**) *(inexpressible → rage, fear)* muet

speechlessly ['spiːtʃlɪslɪ] *adv* d'un air interdit *ou* interloqué

speechlessness ['spiːtʃlɪsnɪs] *n* mutisme *m*; **it reduced him to speechlessness** il en est resté sans voix

speechmaker ['spiːtʃˌmeɪkə(r)] *n* orateur(trice) *m,f*

speechmaking ['spiːtʃˌmeɪkɪŋ] *n (UNCOUNT)* discours *mpl*; *Pej* beaux discours *mpl*

speechwriter ['spiːtʃˌraɪtə(r)] *n* = personne qui écrit des discours; **she's the mayor's speechwriter** c'est elle qui écrit les discours du maire

speed [spiːd] *(pt & pp vi sense* (**a**) **sped** [sped], *vi sense* (**b**) **speeded**, *vt* **sped** [sped] or **speeded**) **1** *n* (**a**) *(rate, pace → of car, progress, reaction, work)* vitesse *f*; **I was driving** *or* **going at a speed of 65 mph** je roulais à 100 km/h; **to do a speed of 100 km/h** faire du 100 km/h; **at (a) great** *or* **high speed** à toute vitesse, à grande vitesse; **at top** *or* **full speed** *(drive)* à toute vitesse *ou* allure; *(work)* très vite, en quatrième vitesse; **at the speed of light/sound** à la vitesse de la lumière/du son; **reading speed** vitesse *f* de lecture; **typing/shorthand speed** nombre *m* de mots-minute en dactylo/en sténo; *Literary* **to make all speed** faire diligence, se hâter; *Fam* **to be up to speed on sth** être au courant de qch❑; *Fam* **to bring sb up to speed on sth** mettre qn au courant de qch❑

(**b**) *(rapid rate)* vitesse *f*, rapidité *f*; **the speed with which she learnt/the building was completed** la vitesse à laquelle elle a appris/le bâtiment a été terminé; **he replied with speed** *(quickly)* il a répondu rapidement; *(promptly)* il a répondu avec promptitude; *Br* **I hate having to work at speed** j'ai horreur de devoir travailler vite; *Br* **the actress delivered her lines at speed** l'actrice a débité son texte à toute allure; **to pick up/to lose speed** prendre/perdre de la vitesse

(**c**) *(gear → of car, bicycle)* vitesse *f*; **a 10-speed racer** un vélo de course à 10 vitesses

(**d**) *Phot (of film)* rapidité *f*, sensibilité *f*; *(of shutter)* vitesse *f*; *(of lens)* luminosité *f*

(**e**) *Fam Drugs slang (amphetamines)* amphets *fpl*, speed *m*

(**f**) *Comput* vitesse *f*; **32 speed CD-ROM drive** lecteur *m* de CD-ROM 32 x

2 *vi* (**a**) *(go fast)* aller à toute allure; **we sped across the field** nous avons traversé le champ à toute allure; **I saw her speeding down the street** je l'ai vue descendre la rue à toute allure; **he sped away** il est parti à toute vitesse, il a pris ses jambes à son cou; **time seems to speed by** le temps passe comme un éclair; **the jet sped through the sky** le jet traversa le ciel comme un éclair; **the torpedo sped through the water** la torpille se déplaçait dans l'eau à toute vitesse

(**b**) *Aut (exceed speed limit)* faire des excès de vitesse, rouler trop vite

(**c**) *Fam Drugs slang* **to be speeding** *(have taken amphetamines)* être sous amphets, speeder

3 *vt (person)* **to speed sb on his way** souhaiter bon voyage à qn; **I gave him a drink to speed him on his way** je lui ai offert quelque chose pour la route; *Arch* **God speed (you)!** (que) Dieu vous garde!

▸▸ ***speed bump*** casse-vitesse *m*, ralentisseur *m*; ***speed camera*** radar *m*; ***speed chase*** [illegible] rapides; *Am Fam* ***speed cop*** motard *m* (de la police); *Am Fam* ***speed demon*** mordu(e) *m,f* de vitesse; *Tel* ***speed dial*** numérotation *f* abrégée; *Am Fam* ***speed freak*** *(drug addict)* drogué(e) *m,f* aux amphétamines❑; ***speed gun*** radar *m* à main; ***speed limit*** limitation *f* de vitesse; **the speed limit is 60** la vitesse est limitée à 60; *Br, Austr & NZ Fam* ***speed merchant*** mordu(e) *m,f* de vitesse; *Sport* ***speed skating*** patinage *m* de vitesse; ***speed trap*** contrôle *m* de vitesse

▸**speed along 1** *vi (in car, on bike)* rouler vite, *Fam* foncer; *(walk)* marcher vite; *(run)* courir vite; **the work is speeding along** le travail avance à bonne allure

2 *vt sep (work)* faire avancer *ou* progresser en vitesse

▸**speed off 1** *vi (on foot, in car)* partir à toute allure

2 *vt sep* **they sped him off to hospital** ils l'ont transporté à l'hôpital à toute vitesse

▸**speed up 1** *vi (gen)* aller plus vite; *(driver)* rouler plus vite; *(worker)* travailler plus vite; *(machine, film)* accélérer; **can't you get him to speed up?** *(work harder)* vous ne pouvez pas le faire travailler plus vite?; *(hurry)* vous ne pouvez pas le faire se dépêcher?

2 *vt sep (worker)* faire travailler plus vite; *(person)* faire aller plus vite; *(work)* activer, accélérer; *(pace)* presser; *(production)* accélérer, augmenter; *(reaction, film)* accélérer

speedball ['spiːdbɔːl] *n Fam Drugs slang* speedball *m (mélange d'héroïne et de cocaïne)*

speedboat ['spiːdbəʊt] *n* vedette *f* (rapide); *(with outboard engine)* hors-bord *m inv*

speeder ['spiːdə(r)] *n (fast driver)* = personne qui conduit vite; *(convicted driver)* = automobiliste condamné pour excès de vitesse

speedily ['spiːdɪlɪ] *adv (quickly)* vite, rapidement; *(promptly)* promptement, sans tarder; *(soon)* bientôt

speediness ['spiːdɪnɪs] *n* rapidité *f*

speeding ['spiːdɪŋ] *n Aut* excès *m* de vitesse; **I was stopped for speeding** j'ai été arrêté pour excès de vitesse

▸▸ ***speeding conviction*** condamnation *f* pour excès de vitesse; ***speeding fine*** contravention *f* pour excès de vitesse; ***speeding ticket*** P-V *m* pour excès de vitesse; ***speeding up*** accélération *f*

speedo ['spiːdəʊ] *(pl* **speedos**) *n Br Fam* compteur *m* de vitesse❑

speedometer [spɪ'dɒmɪtə(r)] *n* compteur *m* de vitesse

speed-read *vi & vt* lire selon la méthode de lecture rapide

speed-reading *n* lecture *f* rapide

speedster ['spiːdstə(r)] *n (car)* bolide *m*; *(driver)* fou (folle) *m,f* du volant, *Pej* chauffard *m*

speed-up *n* accélération *f*

speedway ['spiːdweɪ] *n* (**a**) *(racing)* speedway *m* (**b**) *Am (track)* piste *f* de vitesse pour motos (**c**) *Am (expressway)* voie *f* express *ou* rapide

speedwell ['spiːdwel] *n Bot* véronique *f*

Speedwriting® ['spiːdˌraɪtɪŋ] *n* sténo *f* alphabétique

speedy ['spiːdɪ] *(compar* **speedier**, *superl* **speediest**) *adj* (**a**) *(rapid)* rapide; *(prompt)* prompt; **her help brought a speedy end to the dispute** son aide a permis de mettre rapidement fin au différend; **to wish sb a speedy recovery** souhaiter à qn un prompt rétablissement (**b**) *(car)* rapide, nerveux

speiss [spaɪs] *n Metal* speiss *m*

spelaean, spelean [spe'liːən] *adj* des cavernes, qui habite les cavernes

speleologist [ˌspiːlɪ'ɒlədʒɪst] *n* spéléologue *mf*

speleology [ˌspiːlɪ'ɒlədʒɪ] *n* spéléologie *f*

spell [spel] *(Br pt & pp* **spelt** [spelt] *or* **spelled**, *Am pt & pp* **spelled**) **1** *vt* (**a**) *(write)* écrire, orthographier; *(aloud)* épeler; **they've spelt my name wrong** ils ont mal écrit mon nom; **his name is spelt J-O-N** son nom s'écrit J-O-N; **how do you spell it?** comment est-ce que ça s'écrit?; **she spells Maud with an "e"** elle écrit Maud avec un "e"; **shall I spell my name for you?** voulez-vous que j'épelle mon nom?

(**b**) *(of letters)* former, donner; **C-O-U-G-H spells "cough"** C-O-U-G-H donnent "cough"

(**e**) *Fig (mean)* signifier; **the floods spell disaster for our region** les inondations signifient le désastre pour notre région; **her discovery could spell success for our business** sa découverte pourrait être très profitable à notre entreprise

(**d**) *Am (worker, colleague)* relayer; **can I spell you at the wheel?** est-ce que je peux vous relayer au volant?

2 *vi* **to learn to spell** apprendre l'orthographe; **she can't spell very well** elle n'est pas très bonne en orthographe

3 *n* (**a**) *(period)* (courte) période *f*; **a spell of cold weather** une vague de froid; **during the cold spell** pendant la vague de froid; **we're in for a spell of wet weather** le temps se met à la pluie; **scattered showers and sunny spells** des averses locales et des éclaircies; **she did** *or* **had a spell as a reporter** elle a été journaliste pendant un certain temps; **it's his second spell in prison** c'est son deuxième séjour en prison; **he had a dizzy spell** il a été pris de vertige

(**b**) *(of duty etc)* tour *m*; **do you want me to take** *or* **to do a spell at the wheel?** voulez-vous que je vous relaie au volant *ou* que je conduise un peu?

(**c**) *(magic words)* formule *f* magique, incantation *f*; **she muttered a spell** elle marmonna une incantation

(**d**) *(enchantment)* charme *m*, sort *m*, sortilège *m*; **to cast** *or* **to put a spell on sb** jeter un sort *ou* un charme à qn, ensorceler *ou* envoûter qn; **she was put under an evil spell** on lui a jeté un maléfice *ou* mauvais sort; **to break the spell** rompre le charme; *also Fig* **to be under sb's spell** être sous le charme de qn

▸**spell out** *vt sep* (**a**) *(read out letter by letter)* épeler; *(decipher)* déchiffrer

(**b**) *(make explicit)* expliquer bien clairement; **let me spell out the implications of his study** laissez-moi expliquer en détail la portée de son étude; **she spelt out in detail what the scheme would cost** elle a expliqué en détail quel serait le coût du projet; **do I have to spell it out for you?** est-ce qu'il faut que je mette les points sur les i?

spellbinder ['spelˌbaɪndə(r)] *n* (**a**) *(speaker)* orateur(trice) *m,f* fascinant(e) (**b**) *(fascinating thing)* **her latest novel is a spellbinder** son dernier roman est un enchantement; **the match was a spellbinder** le match a tenu tout le monde en haleine

spellbinding ['spelˌbaɪndɪŋ] *adj* ensorcelant, envoûtant

spellbound ['spelbaʊnd] *adj (spectator, audience)* captivé, envoûté; **the children listened spellbound** les enfants écoutaient, captivés; **the movie held me spellbound from start to finish** le film m'a tenu en haleine *ou* m'a captivé du début jusqu'à la fin

spellcheck ['speltʃek] *Comput* **1** *n* correction *f* orthographique; **to do** *or* **run a spellcheck on a document** effectuer la correction orthographique sur un document

2 *vt* faire la vérification orthographique de

spellchecker ['spelˌtʃekə(r)] *n Comput* correcteur *m* orthographique *ou* d'orthographe

speller ['spelə(r)] *n* (**a**) *(person)* **he is a good/bad speller** il est bon/mauvais en orthographe (**b**) *(book)* livre *m* d'orthographe

spelling ['spelɪŋ] **1** *n* (**a**) *(word formation)* orthographe *f*; **what is the spelling of this word?** quelle est l'orthographe de *ou* comment s'écrit ce mot?

(**b**) *(ability to spell)* orthographe *f*; **his spelling is awful** il est nul en orthographe; **he is good at spelling** il est fort en orthographe

2 *comp (error, test, book)* d'orthographe; *(pronunciation)* orthographique

▸▸ *Am* ***spelling bee*** concours *m* d'orthographe; *Comput* ***spelling checker*** correcteur *m* orthographique *ou* d'orthographe; ***spelling mistake*** faute *f* d'orthographe

spelt [spelt] **1** *Br pt & pp of* **spell**

2 *n Bot* épeautre *m*

spelter ['speltə(r)] *n* zinc *m*

▸▸ ***spelter solder*** zinc *m* à souder

spelunker [spɪ'lʌŋkə(r)] *n Am* spéléologue *mf*

spelunking [spɪ'lʌŋkɪŋ] *n Am* spéléologie *f*

spencer ['spensə(r)] *n (jacket)* spencer *m*

spend [spend] *(pt & pp* **spent** [spent]) **1** *vt* (**a**) *(money, fortune)* dépenser; **to spend money on** *(food, clothes)* dépenser de l'argent en; *(house, car)* dépenser de l'argent pour, consacrer de l'argent à; **how much do you spend on the children's clothes?** combien (d'argent) dépensez-vous pour habiller vos enfants?; **he spends all his money (on) gambling** il dépense tout son argent au jeu; **he spends most of his pocket money on (buying) records** la plus grande partie de son argent de poche passe dans l'achat de disques; **I consider it money well spent** je considère que c'est un bon investissement; **without spending a penny** sans dépenser un centime, sans bourse délier; *Br Fam Euph* **to spend a penny** aller au petit coin

(**b**) *(time → pass)* passer; *(→ devote)* consacrer; **to spend time on sth/on doing sth** passer du temps sur qch/à faire qch; **she spent the whole afternoon reading** elle a passé tout l'après-midi à lire; **I spent three hours on the job** le travail

m'a pris *ou* demandé trois heures; **what a way to spend Easter!** quelle façon de passer les vacances de Pâques!; **how do you spend your weekends?** qu'est-ce que tu fais le week-end?; **I spent a lot of time and effort on this** j'y ai consacré beaucoup de temps et d'efforts; **she spent her life helping the underprivileged** elle a consacré sa vie à aider les défavorisés
(**c**) *(exhaust, use up → one's strength, ammunition)* épuiser; **the gale had spent itself** le vent avait fini par tomber; **she has at last spent her indignation** son indignation s'est enfin calmée
2 *vi* dépenser, faire des dépenses
3 *n Br (allocated money)* allocation *f*, dépenses *fpl*; **we must increase our marketing spend** nous devons augmenter le budget marketing

spendable ['spendəbəl] *adj*
▸▸ ***spendable income*** revenu *m* dépensable

spendaholic [ˌspendə'hɒlɪk] *n Fam* grand(e) dépensier(ère) ❑ *m,f*

spender ['spendə(r)] *n* dépensier(ère) *m,f*; **she's a big spender** elle est très dépensière

spending ['spendɪŋ] *n (UNCOUNT)* dépenses *fpl*; **public** *or* **government spending** dépenses *fpl* publiques; **a cut in defence spending** une réduction du budget de la défense; **we went on a spending spree** nous avons fait des folies, nous avons dépensé des sommes folles
▸▸ ***spending cuts*** réductions *fpl* des dépenses; ***spending money*** argent *m* de poche; ***spending power*** pouvoir *m* d'achat

spendthrift ['spendθrɪft] **1** *n* dépensier(ère) *m,f*; **she's a terrible spendthrift** elle est terriblement dépensière, elle jette l'argent par les fenêtres
2 *adj* dépensier

Spenserian [spen'sɪərɪən] *adj (in style)* à la manière de Spenser; *(of Spenser)* de Spenser

spent [spent] **1** *pt & pp of* **spend**
2 *adj* (**a**) *(used up → fuel, bullet, match)* utilisé; *(→ cartridge)* brûlé; **he's a spent force in the firm** il n'a plus rien à apporter à l'entreprise; **the party is a spent force in politics** le parti n'a plus l'influence qu'il avait en politique; **her courage was spent** elle n'avait plus de courage; **her strength/energy was all but spent** elle n'avait presque plus de forces/d'énergie
(**b**) *(tired out)* épuisé; **he was completely spent** il était épuisé *ou* à bout

sperm [spɜːm] *(pl* **inv** *or* **sperms**) *n* (**a**) *(cell)* spermatozoïde *m* (**b**) *(liquid)* sperme *m*
▸▸ ***sperm bank*** banque *f* de sperme; ***sperm count*** nombre *m* de spermatozoïdes; **to have a low sperm count** avoir un nombre de spermatozoïdes peu élevé; ***sperm oil*** blanc *m* de baleine, spermaceti *m*; *Zool* ***sperm whale*** cachalot *m*

spermaceti [ˌspɜːmə'setɪ] *n* blanc *m* de baleine, spermaceti *m*

spermatic [spɜː'mætɪk] *adj* spermatique
▸▸ ***spermatic cord*** cordon *m* spermatique; ***spermatic fluid*** sperme *m*

spermatid ['spɜːmətɪd] *n Zool* spermatide *f*

spermatium [spɜː'mætɪəm] *n Bot* spermatie *f*

spermatocyte ['spɜːmətəʊsaɪt] *n Bot & Zool* spermatocyte *m*

spermatogenesis [ˌspɜːmətəʊ'dʒenɪsɪs] *n* spermatogénèse *f*

spermatogonium [ˌspɜːmətə'gəʊnɪəm] *n Zool* spermatogonie *f*

spermatophore ['spɜːmətəfɔː(r)] *n Zool* spermatophore *m*

spermatophyte [spɜː'mætəfaɪt] *n Bot* spermatophyte *m*, spermophyte *m*

spermatozoid [ˌspɜːmətəʊ'zəʊɪd] *n Bot* spermatozoïde *m*

spermatozoon [ˌspɜːmətəʊ'zəʊɒn] *(pl* **spermatozoa** [-'zəʊə]) *n* spermatozoïde *m*

spermicidal [ˌspɜːmɪ'saɪdəl] *adj* spermicide
▸▸ ***spermicidal cream*** crème *f* spermicide; ***spermicidal jelly*** gelée *f* spermicide

spermicide ['spɜːmɪsaɪd] *n* spermicide *m*

spermiogenesis [ˌspɜːmɪəʊ'dʒenɪsɪs] *n* spermiogénèse *f*

spermophyte ['spɜːməfaɪt] *n Bot* spermatophyte *m*, spermophyte *m*

spew [spjuː] **1** *vt Fam* dégueuler, gerber; **to spew one's guts up** rendre tripes et boyaux
2 *vi* (**a**) *Fam (vomit)* dégueuler, gerber (**b**) *Fig (pour out)* gicler; **the acid spewed everywhere** l'acide a giclé partout
3 *n Fam* vomi ❑ *m*, dégueulis *m*
▸**spew forth, spew out** *Literary* **1** *vi* vomir
2 *vt sep* vomir
▸**spew up** *Fam* **1** *vi* dégueuler, gerber
2 *vt sep* dégueuler, gerber

SPF [ˌespiː'ef] *n (abbr* **sun protection factor**) indice *m* de protection solaire

sphagnum ['sfægnəm] *n Bot* sphaigne *f*
▸▸ ***sphagnum moss*** sphaigne *f*

sphalerite ['sfæləraɪt] *n Miner* sphalérite *f*, blende *f*

sphene [sfiːn] *n Miner* sphène *m*

sphenoid ['sfiːnɔɪd] *Anat* **1** *adj* sphénoïde
2 *n* sphénoïde *m*

sphenoidal [sfɪː'nɔɪdəl] *adj Anat* sphénoïdal
▸▸ ***sphenoidal bone*** (os *m*) sphénoïde *m*; ***sphenoidal fissure*** fente *f* sphénoïdale; ***sphenoidal sinus*** sinus *m* sphénoïdal

sphere [sfɪə(r)] *n* (**a**) *(globe)* sphère *f*; *Literary (sky)* cieux *mpl*; **the heavenly sphere** la sphère céleste
(**b**) *Fig (of interest, activity)* sphère *f*, domaine *m*; **her sphere of activity** *(professional)* son domaine d'activité; *(personal)* sa sphère d'activité; **it's not my sphere** ce n'est pas de mon domaine, cela ne relève pas de mes compétences; **the question is outside the committee's sphere** la question ne relève pas des compétences du comité; **the guests came from various social and professional spheres** les invités venaient de divers horizons sociaux et professionnels; **sphere of influence** sphère *f* d'influence; **in the public sphere** *(in industry)* dans le domaine public; *(in politics)* dans la vie politique

spherical ['sferɪkəl], **spheric** ['sferɪk] *adj* sphérique
▸▸ ***spherical geometry*** géométrie *f* sphérique; ***spherical triangle*** triangle *m* sphérique; ***spherical trigonometry*** trigonométrie *f* sphérique

spherically ['sferɪklɪ] *adv* sphériquement

sphericity [sfe'rɪsɪtɪ] *n* sphéricité *f*

spheroid ['sfɪərɔɪd] *n* sphéroïde *m*

spheroidal [ˌsfɪə'rɔɪdəl] *adj* sphéroïdal

spherometer [ˌsfe'rɒmɪtə(r)] *n Phys* sphéromètre *m*

spherule ['sferuːl] *n* sphérule *f*

sphincter ['sfɪŋktə(r)] *n* sphincter *m*

Sphinx [sfɪŋks] *n Myth* **the Sphinx** le Sphinx

sphinx-like *adj* de sphinx; *(smile)* énigmatique

sphragistics [sfrə'dʒɪstɪks] *n (UNCOUNT)* sphragistique *f*, sigillographie *f*

sphyg [sfɪg] *n Fam Med* sphygmomanomètre ❑ *m*

sphygmogram ['sfɪgməʊgræm] *n Med* sphygmogramme *m*

sphygmograph ['sfɪgməʊgrɑːf] *n Med* sphygmographe *m*

sphygmomanometer [ˌsfɪgməʊmə'nɒmɪtə(r)] *n Med* sphygmomanomètre *m*

spic [spɪk] *n Am very Fam* métèque *mf*, = terme injurieux désignant une personne d'origine latino-américaine

spica ['spaɪkə] *n* (**a**) *Bot* epi *m* (**b**) *Med (bandage)* spica *m*, spic *m*

spiccato [spɪ'kɑːtəʊ] *Mus* **1** *adj* spiccato
2 *adv* spiccato

spice [spaɪs] **1** *n* (**a**) *Culin* épice *f*; **it needs more spice** ce n'est pas assez épicé *ou* relevé; **mixed spice** *(UNCOUNT)* épices *fpl* mélangées
(**b**) *Fig* piquant *m*, sel *m*; **the story lacks spice** l'histoire manque de sel *ou* de piquant; **it added a bit of spice to our routine** ça a ajouté un peu de piquant à *ou* ça a pimenté notre train-train quotidien
2 *vt* (**a**) *Culin* épicer, parfumer; **spiced with nutmeg** parfumé à la muscade
(**b**) *Fig* pimenter, corser; **the story is spiced with political anecdotes** l'histoire est pimentée d'anecdotes politiques
▸▸ ***spice cake*** gâteau *m* aux épices; *Hist* ***the Spice Islands*** les Moluques *fpl*; ***spice rack*** étagère *f ou* présentoir *m* à épices
▸**spice up** *vt sep* = **spice** *vt*

spicebush ['spaɪsbʊʃ] *n Bot* benjoin *m* odoriférant

spiciness ['spaɪsɪnɪs] *n* (**a**) *(of food)* goût *m* épicé *ou* relevé (**b**) *Fig (of story, adventure)* piquant *m*

spick = **spic**

spick-and-span *adj Fam (room)* nickel, impeccable ❑; *(appearance)* tiré à quatre épingles ❑

spicule ['spɪkjuːl] *n* (**a**) *(crystal)* cristal *m* spiculaire *ou* apiciforme (**b**) *Zool (of sponge)* spicule *m* (**c**) *Bot* épillet *m*, aiguillon *m* (**d**) *Med (splinter of bone)* esquille *f* (**e**) *Astron* spicule *m*

spicy ['spaɪsɪ] *(compar* **spicier**, *superl* **spiciest**) *adj* (**a**) *(food)* épicé (**b**) *Fig (book, story)* piquant, corsé

spider ['spaɪdə(r)] *n* (**a**) *Entom* araignée *f* (**b**) *Br (for luggage)* araignée *f* (à bagages) (**c**) *Am Culin* poêle *f* (à trépied) (**d**) *(snooker rest)* râteau *m*
▸▸ ***spider crab*** araignée *f* (de mer); ***spider monkey*** singe *m* araignée; ***spider plant*** chlorophytum *m*; ***spider's web*** toile *f* d'araignée

spiderman ['spaɪdəmæn] *(pl* **spidermen** [-men]) *n Br Fam* = ouvrier travaillant sur de hautes constructions

spiderweb ['spaɪdəweb] *n Am* toile *f* d'araignée

spidery ['spaɪdərɪ] *adj (in shape)* en forme d'araignée; *(finger)* long (longue) et mince; **spidery handwriting** pattes *fpl* de mouches

spiegeleisen ['spiːgəlˌaɪzən] *n Metal* spiegel *m*

spiel [ʃpiːl, spiːl] *Fam* **1** *n* baratin *m*, speech *m*; *(of salesperson)* boniment *m*; **he gave me some spiel about having been held up at the airport** il m'a servi tout un baratin comme quoi il avait été bloqué à l'aéroport
2 *vi* baratiner
▸**spiel off** *vt sep Am Fam (recite)* débiter ❑

spieler ['spiːlə(r)] *n Fam* (**a**) *(smooth talker)* baratineur(euse) *m,f*; *(salesperson)* bonimenteur(euse) *m,f* (**b**) *Austr & NZ (gen)* escroc ❑ *m*; *(card-sharp)* tricheur(euse) *m,f* aux cartes

spiffing ['spɪfɪŋ] *adj Br Fam Old-fashioned* épatant

spifflicate ['spɪflɪkeɪt] *vt Br Fam Old-fashioned* écrabouiller

spiffy ['spɪfɪ] *(compar* **spiffier**, *superl* **spiffiest**) *adj Am* chic

spigot ['spɪgət] *n* (**a**) *(in cask)* fausset *m* (**b**) *(part of tap)* clé *f* (**c**) *Am (tap)* robinet *m* (extérieur)

spike [spaɪk] **1** *vt* (**a**) *(shoes, railings)* garnir de pointes
(**b**) *(impale)* transpercer
(**c**) *Fam (drink)* corser ❑; **my coffee was spiked with brandy** mon café était arrosé de cognac ❑
(**d**) *(thwart → affair)* faire avorter; *(→ plan)* contrecarrer, entraver; *Mil & Hist (canon, guns)* enclouer; *Fig* **to spike sb's guns** priver qn de ses moyens d'action, mettre qn hors d'action
(**e**) *Press (story)* rejeter
2 *vi (in volleyball)* smasher
3 *n* (**a**) *(on railings, shoe, helmet)* pointe *f*; *(on barbed wire)* piquant *m*; *(on cactus)* épine *f*; *(on tyre)* clou *m*; *(for paper)* pique-notes *m inv*; *Press* **the story was put on the spike** l'article a été rejeté
(**b**) *(peak → on graph)* pointe *f*
(**c**) *(nail)* gros clou *m*
(**d**) *(antler)* dague *f*
(**e**) *(in volleyball)* smash *m*
(**f**) *Bot* épi *m*
(**g**) *Fam Drugs slang (hypodermic needle)* shooteuse *f*, pompe *f*
4 spikes *npl Fam (shoes)* chaussures *fpl* à pointes ❑
▸▸ ***spike heels*** (chaussures *fpl* à) talons *mpl* aiguilles; ***spike lavender*** lavande *f* aspic *m*, spic *m*

spiked [spaɪkt] *adj (railings)* garni *ou* hérissé de pointes; *(shoes)* à pointes; *(tyre)* clouté, à clous
▸▸ *Bot* ***spiked speedwell*** véronique *f* en épi

spikenard ['spaɪknɑːd] *n Bot* nard *m* (indien)

spiky ['spaɪkɪ] *(compar* **spikier**, *superl* **spikiest**) *adj* (**a**) *(branch, railings)* garni *ou* hérissé de pointes; *(writing)* pointu; **spiky hair** *(sticking up, tousled)* cheveux *mpl* en épis; *(as hairstyle)* cheveux *mpl* hérissés (**b**) *Br Fam (bad-tempered)* chatouilleux ❑, ombrageux ❑

spile [spaɪl] **1** *n* (**a**) *(of cask)* fausset *m* (**b**) *(pile)* pilot *m*, pieu *m*
2 *vt* (**a**) *(stop up → hole)* boucher avec un fausset (**b**) *Am (broach → cask)* pratiquer un trou de fausset dans

spill [spɪl] *(Br pt & pp* **spilt** [spɪlt] *or* **spilled**, *Am pt & pp* **spilled**) **1** *vt* (**a**) *(liquid, salt etc)* renverser,

spe–spi

répandre; **she spilt coffee down** *or* **over her dress** elle a renversé du café sur sa robe; **try to carry the bucket upstairs without spilling any water** essaie de monter le seau sans renverser d'eau; **she spilt the contents of her handbag onto the bed** elle vida (le contenu de) son sac à main sur le lit
(**b**) *Fam Fig (secret)* dévoiler ❑; **to spill the beans** vendre la mèche
(**c**) *(blood)* verser, faire couler; **not a drop of blood was spilled** pas une goutte de sang n'a été versée
(**d**) *(person)* **he was spilled from his motorbike** il est tombé de sa moto; **the rider was spilled into the stream** le cavalier a été projeté dans le ruisseau
(**e**) *Naut* **to spill (wind from) a sail** étouffer une voile *ou* la toile
2 *vi* (**a**) *(liquid, salt etc)* se renverser, se répandre
(**b**) *(crowd)* se déverser; **the huge crowd spilled into the square** l'immense foule se répandit *ou* se déversa sur la place
(**c**) *Fam (reveal information)* vendre la mèche; *(under interrogation)* cracher *ou* lâcher le morceau; **come on, spill!** allez, accouche!
3 *n* (**a**) *(spillage → of liquid)* renversement *m*
(**b**) *(fall → from horse, bike)* chute *f*, culbute *f*; *Old-fashioned (accident)* accident *m*; **to take a spill** faire la culbute
(**c**) *(channel)* déversoir *m*
(**d**) *Austr Pol* remaniement *m*
(**e**) *(for fire)* allume-feu *m*
►► *TV* ***spill light*** lumière *f* parasite, mouche *f*
►**spill out 1** *vt sep* (**a**) *(contents, liquid)* renverser, répandre
(**b**) *Fig (secret)* dévoiler, révéler; **he got drunk and spilled out all his problems** il a bu et s'est mis à parler de tous ses problèmes
2 *vi* (**a**) *(contents, liquid)* se renverser, se répandre; **the water spilt out onto the floor** l'eau s'est renversée par terre
(**b**) *Fig (crowd)* se déverser, s'échapper; **the commuters spilled out of the train** un flot de banlieusards s'est échappé du train
►**spill over** *vi* (**a**) *(liquid)* déborder, se répandre; **the tea spilled over into the saucer** le thé a débordé dans la soucoupe
(**b**) *Fig (overflow)* se déverser, déborder; **the city's population has spilled over into the surrounding villages** les habitants de la ville ont envahi les villages environnants; **the conflict could spill over into neighbouring countries** le conflit risquerait de s'étendre aux pays voisins; **her work spills over into her family life** son travail empiète sur sa vie familiale
spillage ['spɪlɪdʒ] *n (act of spilling)* renversement *m*, fait *m* de renverser; *(liquid spilt)* liquide *m* renversé; **we managed to avoid too much spillage** nous avons réussi à ne pas trop en renverser; **there's been a diesel spillage on the M25** un chargement de gasoil s'est renversé sur la M25
spillikin ['spɪlɪkɪn] *n* jonchet *m*; **to play spillikins** jouer aux jonchets
spillover ['spɪlˌəʊvə(r)] *n* (**a**) *(act of spilling)* renversement *m*; *(quantity spilt)* quantité *f* renversée (**b**) *(excess)* excédent *m* (**c**) *Econ* retombées *fpl* (économiques)
spillway ['spɪlweɪ] *n* déversoir *m*
spilt [spɪlt] *Br pt & pp of* **spill**
spin [spɪn] *(pt & pp* **spun** [spʌn], *cont* **spinning**) **1** *n* (**a**) *(rotation)* tournoiement *m*; *Aviat* vrille *f*; **give the wheel a spin** faites tourner la roue; **give the top a spin** lancez la toupie; **the plane went into a spin** *(accidentally)* l'avion a fait une chute en vrille; *(in aerobatics)* l'avion a effectué une descente en vrille; **the car went into a spin** la voiture a fait un tête-à-queue
(**b**) *(in spin-dryer)* essorage *m*; **long/short spin** essorage *m* complet/court; **to give sth a spin** essorer qch; **give the washing a quick spin** donne un petit coup d'essorage au linge
(**c**) *Fam (panic)* **to be in a (flat) spin** être dans tous ses états; **the news sent him into a spin** la nouvelle l'a complètement paniqué ❑; **the office was thrown into a (flat) spin by the arrival of the boss** les employés se sont affolés en voyant arriver le patron ❑
(**d**) *Sport (on ball)* effet *m*; **to put spin on a ball** donner de l'effet à une balle; **there was a lot of spin on that ball** il y avait beaucoup d'effet dans cette balle
(**e**) *Fam (on information)* **to put the right spin on a story** présenter une affaire sous un angle favorable ❑; **the government put its own spin on the situation** le gouvernement a présenté la situation sous un angle qui lui convenait ❑; **the government has been criticized for indulging in too much spin** on a reproché au gouvernement de trop manipuler les informations fournies au public ❑; **this government is all spin and no substance** ce gouvernement est très fort pour le bavardage mais n'a aucun programme réel ❑
(**f**) *Fam (ride → in car)* tour ❑ *m*, balade ❑ *f*; **to go for a spin** faire une (petite) balade en voiture
(**g**) *Fam (try)* **to give sth a spin** essayer *ou* tenter qch ❑; **would you like to give the car a spin?** voulez-vous essayer la voiture?
(**h**) *Austr Fam (luck)* coup *m* de chance; *(bad luck)* malchance ❑ *f*
2 *vt* (**a**) *(cause to rotate → wheel, chair)* faire tourner; *(→ top)* lancer, faire tournoyer; *Sport (→ ball)* donner de l'effet à; **to spin the wheel** *(in casino)* faire tourner la roue; *(in car)* braquer; **to spin a coin** jouer à pile ou face
(**b**) *(yarn, glass)* filer; *(thread)* fabriquer; **he spun the glass into the shape of a swan** il a filé le verre en forme de cygne
(**c**) *(of spider, silkworm)* tisser
(**d**) *(invent → tale)* inventer, débiter; **she spun some yarn about the buses being on strike** elle a prétexté que les bus étaient en grève; **he spins a good yarn** il raconte bien les histoires
(**e**) *(in spin-dryer)* essorer
(**f**) *Fam (present in a good light → image, information, event)* présenter sous un angle favorable ❑; **to spin sb/sth as** présenter qn/qch comme ❑
3 *vi* (**a**) *(rotate → planet, wheel)* tourner (sur soi-même); *(→ skater, top)* tournoyer, tourner; *Sport (→ ball)* tournoyer; **it spins on its axis** il tourne sur son axe *ou* sur lui-même; **the skater/ballerina spun on one foot** le patineur/la ballerine virevolta sur un pied; **the room seemed to be spinning (around me)** la pièce semblait tourner autour de moi; **a strange shape was spinning across the sky** une forme étrange traversait le ciel en tournoyant sur elle-même; **the wheels were spinning in the mud** les roues patinaient dans la boue; **to spin out of control** *(plane)* tomber en vrille; *(car)* faire un tête-à-queue
(**b**) *Fig (grow dizzy)* tourner; **my head's spinning** j'ai la tête qui (me) tourne; **these figures make your head spin** ces chiffres vous donnent le tournis *ou* le vertige; **his mind was spinning from the recent events** les derniers événements lui donnaient le vertige
(**c**) *(spinner)* filer; *(spider)* tisser sa toile
(**d**) *(in spin-dryer)* essorer; **put the clothes in to spin** mets le linge à essorer
(**e**) *(travel fast)* **we were spinning along at a hundred** on filait à cent à l'heure
(**f**) *Fishing* **to spin for pike** pêcher le brochet à la cuiller *ou* cuillère
(**g**) *Fam (spin doctor)* présenter les choses sous un angle favorable ❑
►► *Sport* ***spin bowler*** = lanceur qui donne de l'effet à la balle; *Fam Pej Pol* ***spin doctor*** = chargé des relations publiques d'un parti politique
►**spin around** = **spin round**
►**spin off 1** *vt sep (product)* **they're going to spin off some toys from the cartoon** ils vont commercialiser des jouets tirés des personnages du dessin animé; **products that have been spun off from popular films** des produits dérivés *ou* tirés de films à succès
2 *vi (product)* **to spin off from** être dérivé de
►**spin out** *vt sep (story, idea)* délayer; *(discussion)* faire durer; *(supplies, money)* faire durer, économiser
►**spin round** *Br* **1** *vi* (**a**) *(planet, wheel)* tourner (sur soi-même); *(skater, top)* tournoyer, tourner
(**b**) *(face in opposite direction)* se retourner; **he suddenly spun round** il pivota sur ses talons *ou* se retourna brusquement; **she spun round and faced me** elle se retourna vivement vers moi
2 *vt sep (wheel)* faire tourner; *(dancer, top)* faire tourner *ou* tournoyer
spina bifida [ˌspaɪnə'bɪfɪdə] *n Med* spina-bifida *m inv*
spinach ['spɪnɪdʒ] *n (UNCOUNT)* épinards *mpl*
spinal ['spaɪnəl] *adj (nerve, muscle)* spinal; *(ligament, disc)* vertébral; **a spinal injury** une blessure à la colonne vertébrale
►► ***spinal anaesthesia*** anesthésie *f* rachidienne, rachianesthésie *f*; ***spinal canal*** canal *m* vertébral; ***spinal column*** colonne *f* vertébrale; ***spinal cord*** moelle *f* épinière; ***spinal curvature*** déviation *f* de la colonne vertébrale; ***spinal fluid*** liquide *m* céphalo-rachidien; ***spinal tap*** ponction *f* lombaire
spindle ['spɪndəl] *n* (**a**) *(for spinning → by hand)* fuseau *m*; *(→ by machine)* broche *f* (**b**) *Tech* broche *f*, axe *m*; *(in motor, lathe)* arbre *m*; *(of valve)* tige *f*
►► ***spindle tree*** fusain *m*
spindleshanks ['spɪndəlˌʃæŋks] *n (man)* grand gringalet *m*
spindling ['spɪndlɪŋ] *adj* filiforme
spindly ['spɪndlɪ] *(compar* **spindlier**, *superl* **spindliest**) *adj (legs)* grêle; *(body)* chétif, maigrichon; *(tree)* grêle; *(plant)* étiolé
spin-drier *n* essoreuse *f*
spindrift ['spɪndrɪft] *n (UNCOUNT)* embruns *mpl*
spin-dry 1 *vi* essorer
2 *vt* essorer
spin-dryer *n* essoreuse *f*
spin-drying *n* essorage *m*
spine [spaɪn] *n* (**a**) *Anat* colonne *f* vertébrale; *Zool* épine *f* dorsale (**b**) *(prickle → of hedgehog)* piquant *m*; *(→ of plant, rose)* épine *f* (**c**) *(of book)* dos *m* (**d**) *(of hill)* crête *f* (**e**) *Am (courage)* résolution *f*, volonté *f*
spine-chiller *n (book)* livre *m* d'horreur; *(film)* film *m* d'épouvante; **that story is a real spine-chiller** c'est une histoire à vous glacer le sang
spine-chilling *adj* à vous glacer le sang, terrifiant
spined [spaɪnd] *adj* (**a**) *Anat* vertébré (**b**) *(spiny) Bot* à épines, épineux; *Zool* à piquants
spinel [spɪ'nel] *n Miner* spinelle *m*
spineless ['spaɪnlɪs] *adj* (**a**) *(weak)* mou (molle); *(cowardly)* lâche (**b**) *Zool* invertébré (**c**) *Bot* sans épines
spinelessly ['spaɪnlɪslɪ] *adv* lâchement
spinelessness ['spaɪnlɪsnɪs] *n* lâcheté *f*
spinet [spɪ'net] *n Mus* épinette *f*
spinnaker ['spɪnəkə(r)] *n Naut* spinnaker *m*, spi *m*
spinner ['spɪnə(r)] *n* (**a**) *Tex (person)* fileur(euse) *m,f* (**b**) *(in fishing)* cuiller *f*, cuillère *f* (**c**) *(spin-dryer)* essoreuse *f* (**d**) *Br Sport (bowler in cricket)* = lanceur qui donne de l'effet à une balle; *(ball)* = balle qui a de l'effet; **to bowl a spinner** lancer une balle avec de l'effet (**e**) *Fam Pej Pol (spin doctor)* = chargé des relations publiques d'un parti politique (**f**) *Mktg (for displaying goods)* tourniquet *m*
spinneret ['spɪnəret] *n Entom & Tex* filière *f*
spinnery ['spɪnərɪ] *(pl* **spinneries**) *n* filature *f*
spinney ['spɪnɪ] *n Br* bosquet *m*, boqueteau *m*, petit bois *m*
spinning ['spɪnɪŋ] **1** *n* (**a**) *Tex (by hand)* filage *m*; *(by machine)* filature *f* (**b**) *(in fishing)* pêche *f* à la cuiller *ou* cuillère
2 *adj (rotating)* tournant, qui tourne
►► ***spinning factory*** filature *f*; ***spinning jenny*** jenny *f*; ***spinning mill*** filature *f*; ***spinning top*** toupie *f*; ***spinning wheel*** rouet *m*
spin-off *n* (**a**) *(by-product)* retombée *f*, produit *m* dérivé; **the spin-offs from research into nuclear physics** les retombées des recherches en physique nucléaire (**b**) *(work derived from another)* **the book is a spin-off from the TV series** le roman est tiré de la série télévisée; **the TV series gave rise to a number of spin-offs** la série télévisée a donné lieu à plusieurs produits dérivés
►► *Mktg* ***spin-off product*** produit *m* dérivé
spinose [spaɪ'nəʊs], **spinous** ['spaɪnəs] *adj Biol* épineux
spinster ['spɪnstə(r)] *n Admin & Law* célibataire *f*; *Pej* vieille fille *f*
spinsterhood ['spɪnstəhʊd] *n* célibat *m (pour une femme)*

spinsterish ['spɪnstərɪʃ] *adj Pej* de vieille fille

spin-the-bottle *n* = jeu consistant à faire pivoter chacun à son tour une bouteille au centre du groupe et à embrasser la personne désignée par la bouteille lorsque celle-ci s'arrête de tourner

spinule ['spaɪnju:l] *n Biol* spinule *f*

spiny ['spaɪnɪ] (*compar* **spinier**, *superl* **spiniest**) *adj* épineux, couvert d'épines

▸▸ *Zool* ***spiny anteater*** échidné *m*; *Zool* ***spiny lobster*** langouste *f*

spiracle ['spaɪrəkəl] *n* (**a**) *Zool (in insect)* stigmate *m*; *(in whale)* évent *m*, spiracle *m*; *(in fish)* ouïe *f* (**b**) *Geol* fissure *f*

spiraea, *Am* **spirea** [spaɪ'rɪə] *n Bot* spirée *f*

spiral ['spaɪərəl] (*Br pt & pp* **spiralled**, *cont* **spiralling**, *Am pt & pp* **spiraled**, *cont* **spiraling**) **1** *n* (**a**) *(gen) & Econ & Geom* spirale *f*; **in a spiral** en spirale; **a spiral of smoke rose into the sky** une volute de fumée s'éleva dans le ciel; **inflationary spiral** spirale *f* inflationniste; **the wage-price spiral** la spirale des prix et des salaires

(**b**) *Aviat* vrille *f*

2 *adj (motif, shell, curve)* en (forme de) spirale; *(descent, spring)* en spirale; **the plane went into a spiral descent** l'avion amorça une descente en vrille

3 *vi* (**a**) *(in flight → plane)* vriller; *(→ bird)* voler en spirale; *(in shape → smoke, stairs)* monter en spirale

(**b**) *(prices, inflation)* s'envoler, monter en flèche; **to spiral downwards** chuter

▸▸ ***spiral binding*** reliure *f* à spirale; *Astron* ***spiral galaxy*** galaxie *f* spirale; ***spiral staircase*** escalier *m* en colimaçon

▸**spiral down** *vi (plane)* descendre en vrille; *(leaf, feather)* tomber en tourbillonnant

▸**spiral up** *vi (plane, smoke)* monter en spirale; *(prices)* monter en flèche

spiral-bound *adj (notebook)* à spirale

spirally ['spaɪərəlɪ] *adv (gen)* en spirale; *Aviat* en vrille

spirant ['spaɪərənt] *Ling* **1** *adj* spirant

2 *n* spirante *f*

▸▸ ***spirant consonant*** consonne *f* spirante, spirante *f*

spire ['spaɪə(r)] *n* (**a**) *Archit* flèche *f* (**b**) *(of blade of grass)* tige *f*; *(of mountain, tree)* cime *f*

spirea *Am* = **spiraea**

spirit ['spɪrɪt] **1** *n* (**a**) *(non-physical part of being, soul)* esprit *m*; **the poor in spirit** les pauvres d'esprit; **the spirit is willing but the flesh is weak** l'esprit est prompt mais la chair est faible; **he is with us in spirit** il est avec nous en pensée *ou* par la pensée

(**b**) *(supernatural being)* esprit *m*; **I don't believe in ghosts or spirits** je ne crois ni aux fantômes ni aux esprits; **she is possessed by spirits** elle est possédée par des esprits; **to call up the spirits of the dead** évoquer les âmes des morts; **evil spirits** esprits *mpl* malins; **the spirit world** le monde des esprits

(**c**) *(person)* esprit *m*, âme *f*; **he is a generous spirit** il a une âme généreuse, c'est une bonne âme; **he is a courageous spirit** il est courageux; **he is a leading spirit in the movement** il est l'un de ceux qui donnent son impulsion au mouvement; **he is one of the great spirits of modern philosophy** c'est un des grands esprits de la philosophie moderne

(**d**) *(attitude, mood)* esprit *m*; **the spirit of the age** l'esprit *m ou* le génie de l'époque; **to do sth in a spirit of fun** faire qch pour s'amuser; **you mustn't do it in a spirit of vengeance** il ne faut pas le faire par esprit de vengeance; **to take sth in the right/wrong spirit** prendre qch bien/mal; **she took my remarks in the wrong spirit** elle a mal pris mes remarques; **he went about the job entirely in the wrong spirit** il n'a pas compris dans quel esprit il devait travailler; **he took it in the spirit in which it was intended** il l'a pris comme il fallait; **to have the party spirit** avoir envie de s'amuser; **to enter into the spirit of things** *(at party)* se mettre au diapason; *(in work)* participer de bon cœur; *Fam* **that's the spirit!** voilà comment il faut réagir!❑, à la bonne heure!

(**e**) *(deep meaning)* esprit *m*, génie *m*; **the spirit of the law** l'esprit *m* de la loi; **you haven't understood the spirit of the poem** vous n'avez pas saisi l'esprit du poème

(**f**) *(energy)* énergie *f*, entrain *m*; *(courage)* courage *m*; *(character)* caractère *m*; **to do sth with spirit** faire quelque chose avec entrain; **he replied with spirit** il a répondu énergiquement; **they sang with spirit** ils ont chanté avec entrain; **a man of spirit** un homme de caractère; **he is entirely lacking in spirit** il est complètement amorphe; **to show spirit** montrer du caractère *ou* du courage; **to have spirit** avoir de l'allant; **his spirit was broken** il avait perdu courage

(**g**) *Br (alcoholic drink)* alcool *m*, spiritueux *m*; **wines and spirits** vins *mpl* et spiritueux *mpl*; **I prefer beer to spirits** je préfère la bière aux spiritueux; **brandy is my favourite spirit** le cognac est mon alcool préféré; **taxes on spirits have increased** les taxes sur les spiritueux ont augmenté

(**h**) *Chem* essence *f*, sel *m*

2 *vt (move secretly)* **they spirited her in/out by a side door** ils l'ont fait entrer/sortir discrètement par une porte dérobée; **he seems to have been spirited into thin air** il semble avoir disparu comme par enchantement; **to spirit sth in/out** introduire/sortir discrètement qch

3 spirits *npl (mood, mental state)* humeur *f*, état *m* d'esprit; *(morale)* moral *m*; **to be in good spirits** être de bonne humeur, avoir le moral; **to feel out of spirits** avoir le cafard; **to be in high spirits** être de très bonne humeur, avoir le moral au beau fixe; **to be in low spirits** être déprimé; **you must keep your spirits up** il faut garder le moral, il ne faut pas vous laisser abattre; **my spirits rose at the thought** mon moral est remonté rien que d'y penser; **to raise sb's spirits** remonter le moral à qn

▸▸ ***spirit*** *or* ***spirits of ammonia*** ammoniaque *m* liquide; ***spirit gum*** colle *f* gomme; *Br* ***spirit lamp*** lampe *f* à alcool; ***spirit level*** niveau *m* à bulle; ***Spirit of Saint Louis*** = avion spécialement conçu pour l'aviateur américain Charles Lindbergh, avec lequel il effectua, en 1927, la première traversée de l'Atlantique sans escale, de New York à Paris; ***spirit stove*** réchaud *m* à alcool; ***spirit of turpentine*** (essence *f* de) térébenthine *f*; ***spirit varnish*** vernis *m* à alcool

▸**spirit away, spirit off** *vt sep (carry off secretly)* faire disparaître (comme par enchantement); *(steal)* escamoter, subtiliser

spirited ['spɪrɪtɪd] *adj* (**a**) *(lively → person)* vif, plein d'entrain; *(→ horse)* fougueux; *(→ manner, reply, argument)* vif; *(→ music, rhythm, dance)* entraînant; **to give a spirited performance** *(musician)* jouer avec brio *ou* avec verve; *(team, player)* jouer avec brio

(**b**) *(courageous → person, action, decision, defence)* courageux; **spirited attack** attaque *f* pleine de fougue; **to put up a spirited resistance** résister courageusement, opposer une résistance courageuse; **he's a spirited young fellow** il ne manque pas de courage, ce petit

spiritedly ['spɪrɪtɪdlɪ] *adv* (**a**) *(in a lively manner)* avec entrain; *(reply)* vivement; *(play → musician)* avec brio *ou* verve; *(→ team, player)* avec brio (**b**) *(courageously)* courageusement

spiritedness ['spɪrɪtɪdnɪs] *n* (**a**) *(liveliness)* entrain *m*, verve *f*; *(of horse)* fougue *f* (**b**) *(courage)* courage *m*

spiritless ['spɪrɪtlɪs] *adj (lifeless)* sans vie, sans entrain, apathique; *(depressed)* démoralisé, déprimé; *(cowardly)* lâche

spiritlessly ['spɪrɪtlɪslɪ] *adv (lifelessly)* sans vie, sans entrain; *(in a depressed manner)* tristement; *(in a cowardly manner)* sans courage

spiritlessness ['spɪrɪtlɪsnɪs] *n (lifelessness)* manque *m* d'entrain; *(lack of courage)* manque *m* de courage

spiritual ['spɪrɪtʃʊəl] **1** *adj* (**a**) *(relating to the spirit)* spirituel; **a very spiritual man** un homme d'une grande spiritualité; **a spiritual heir** un successeur spirituel; **China is her spiritual home** elle se sent chez elle en Chine; **his spiritual home is probably 18th century Holland** c'est probablement dans la Hollande du XVIIIème siècle qu'il se sentirait le plus à l'aise

(**b**) *(religious, sacred)* religieux, sacré

2 *n (song)* (negro) spiritual *m*

▸▸ ***spiritual adviser*** conseiller(ère) *m,f* spirituel(elle); ***spiritual life*** vie *f* spirituelle

spiritualism ['spɪrɪtʃʊəlɪzəm] *n Rel* spiritisme *m*; *Phil* spiritualisme *m*

spiritualist ['spɪrɪtʃʊəlɪst] **1** *adj Rel* spirite; *Phil* spiritualiste

2 *n Rel* spirite *mf*; *Phil* spiritualiste *mf*

spiritualistic [,spɪrɪtʃʊə'lɪstɪk] *adj Rel* spirite; *Phil* spiritualiste

spirituality [,spɪrɪtʃʊ'ælətɪ] (*pl* **spiritualities**) **1** *n* spiritualité *f*

2 spiritualities *npl (Church property)* biens *mpl* ecclésiastiques

spiritualization [,spɪrɪtʃʊəlaɪ'zeɪʃən] *n* spiritualisation *f*

spiritualize, -ise ['spɪrɪtʃʊəlaɪz] *vt* spiritualiser

spiritually ['spɪrɪtʃʊəlɪ] *adv* spirituellement

spirituous ['spɪrɪtʃʊəs] *adj Formal* spiritueux, alcoolique

▸▸ ***spirituous liquor*** alcool *m* fort, spiritueux *m*

spirochaete, *Am* **spirochete** ['spaɪrəʊki:t] *n Biol* spirochète *m*

spirograph ['spaɪrəgrɑ:f] *n Med* spirographe *m*

spirogyra [,spaɪrə'dʒaɪrə] *n Biol* spirogyre *f*

spirometer [,spaɪ'rɒmɪtə(r)] *n Med* spiromètre *m*, pnéomètre *m*

spirt = **spurt**

spit [spɪt] (*pt & pp* **spit** *or* **spat** [spæt], *cont* **spitting**) **1** *vi* (**a**) *(in anger, contempt)* cracher; **to spit at sb** cracher sur qn; **to spit in sb's face** cracher à la figure de qn; **she spat at him** elle lui a craché dessus

(**b**) *(while talking)* postillonner, envoyer des postillons

(**c**) *(fire)* crépiter; *(hot fat)* sauter, grésiller; **the oil spat onto my hand** l'huile m'a éclaboussé la main

(**d**) *(idiom)* **it's spitting (with rain)** il bruine, il pleut légèrement

2 *vt* (**a**) *also Fig (blood, flames, venom, words)* cracher

(**b**) *Culin (put on a spit)* embrocher, mettre à la broche

3 *n* (**a**) *(UNCOUNT) (spittle → in mouth)* salive *f*; *(→ spat out)* crachat *m*; *(→ ejected while speaking)* postillon *m*; *(act of spitting)* crachement *m*; *Mil* **spit and polish** astiquage *m*; *Br Fam* **it's a bit of a spit and sawdust pub** c'est un pub sans prétentions❑

(**b**) *Br Fam (likeness)* **to be the (very) spit of sb** être le portrait craché de qn; **he's the spit of his dad** c'est son père tout craché

(**c**) *(of insects)* écume *f* printanière, crachat *m* de coucou

(**d**) *Culin* broche *f*

(**e**) *Geog* pointe *f*, langue *f* de terre

(**f**) *Hort (spade's depth)* **to dig the ground three spits deep** creuser la terre à une profondeur de trois fers de bêche

(**g**) *(idiom)* **there was just a spit of rain** il n'est tombé que quelques gouttes de pluie

▸▸ *Am* ***spit curl*** accroche-cœur *m*; ***spit roast*** rôti *m* à la broche

▸**spit out** *vt sep (food, medicine)* cracher, recracher; *(words, invective)* cracher; **"you're fired!", he spat out** "vous êtes viré!", lança-t-il; *Fam* **come on, spit it out!** allez, accouche!

▸**spit up** *vt sep (blood, food)* cracher

spitball ['spɪtbɔ:l] *n* (**a**) *(paper)* boulette *f* (de papier mâché) (**b**) *(baseball)* = balle de baseball humectée de salive, ayant de ce fait une trajectoire inhabituelle

spitchcock ['spɪtʃkɒk] *n Culin* = anguille coupée en deux puis frite ou grillée

spite [spaɪt] **1** *n (pique)* dépit *m*; *(malice)* méchanceté *f*, malveillance *f*; **to do sth out of spite** *(out of pique)* faire qch par dépit; *(maliciously)* faire qch par pure méchanceté; **he broke her toy out of pure** *or* **sheer spite** il a cassé son jouet par pure méchanceté envers elle; **she didn't go to the party out of spite** elle n'est pas allée à la soirée par dépit

2 *vt* contrarier, vexer

3 in spite of *prep* en dépit de, malgré; **he went out in spite of my advice** il est sorti en dépit de mes conseils; **in spite of myself** malgré moi; **in spite of the fact that we have every chance of winning** bien que nous ayons toutes les chances de gagner

spi–spi

spiteful ['spaɪtfʊl] *adj (person, remark, character)* malveillant; *(because of a grudge)* rancunier, vindicatif; **that was a spiteful thing to say** c'était méchant de dire ça; **to have a spiteful tongue** avoir une langue de vipère

spitefully ['spaɪtfʊlɪ] *adv* par dépit, par méchanceté, méchamment

spitefulness ['spaɪtfʊlnɪs] *n* méchanceté *f*, malveillance *f*; *(because of grudge)* rancœur *f*

spitfire ['spɪtfaɪə(r)] *n (person)* furie *f*; **she's a real spitfire** elle est très soupe au lait

spit-roast *vt* faire rôtir à la broche

Spitsbergen ['spɪts,bɜːgən] *n* Spitsberg, Spitzberg

spitting ['spɪtɪŋ] *n* **no spitting** *(sign)* défense de cracher; *Fam* **he was within spitting distance of me** il était à deux pas de moi❑; *Fam* **he's the spitting image of his father** c'est son père tout craché

spittle ['spɪtəl] *n (saliva → of person)* salive *f*; *(→ on floor)* crachat *m*; *(→ of dog)* bave *f*

spittoon [spɪ'tuːn] *n* crachoir *m*

spitz [spɪts] *n (dog)* loulou *m*

Spitzbergen = **Spitsbergen**

spiv [spɪv] *n Br Fam* filou *m*

spivvy ['spɪvɪ] *adj Br Fam (appearance, clothes)* tape-à-l'œil *(inv)*, tapageur❑; **do I look a bit spivvy in this?** n'ai-je pas l'air un peu filou avec ça?

splanchnic ['splæŋknɪk] *adj Anat* splanchnique

splash [splæʃ] **1** *vt* (**a**) *(with water, mud)* éclabousser; **the bus splashed us with mud** *or* **splashed mud over us** le bus nous a éclaboussés de boue; **to splash water at one another** se jeter de l'eau; **she splashed wine on** *or* **over her dress** elle a éclaboussé sa robe de vin; **I splashed my face with cold water** *or* **cold water onto my face** je me suis aspergé le visage d'eau froide *ou* avec de l'eau froide; **he splashed his way across the river** il a traversé la rivière en pataugeant

(**b**) *(pour carelessly)* répandre; **he splashed bleach on the tiles** il a répandu de l'eau de Javel sur le carrelage; **I splashed disinfectant round the sink** j'ai aspergé le tour de l'évier de désinfectant

(**c**) *(daub)* barbouiller; **he splashed whitewash on the wall** il a barbouillé le mur au blanc de chaux

(**d**) *Press* étaler; **the story was splashed across the front page** l'affaire était étalée à la une des journaux

2 *vi* (**a**) *(rain, liquid)* faire des éclaboussures; *(waves → gen)* clapoter; *(→ more violently)* se briser; **the tea splashed onto the floor/over the book** le thé éclaboussa le sol/le livre; **the paint splashed on my trousers** la peinture a éclaboussé mon pantalon; **heavy drops of rain splashed on the ground** de grosses gouttes de pluie s'écrasaient sur le sol

(**b**) *(walk, run etc)* patauger, barboter; **we splashed across the stream** nous avons traversé le ruisseau en pataugeant; **he splashed through the mud/puddles** il a traversé la boue/les flaques d'eau en pataugeant

3 *n* (**a**) *(noise)* plouf *m*; **the ball made a loud splash** le ballon a fait un grand plouf; **he fell/jumped in with a splash** il est tombé/il a sauté dedans avec un grand plouf

(**b**) *(of mud, paint)* éclaboussure *f*; *(of colour, light)* tache *f*; **to give sth a splash of colour** donner une touche de couleur à qch; **splashes of white** des taches blanches; **there was a bright splash of light on the wall** il y avait une tache de lumière vive sur le mur

(**c**) *(small quantity → of liquid)* goutte *f*; **would you like a splash of soda in your whisky?** voulez-vous un peu de soda dans votre whisky?; **just a splash of lemonade, please** juste une goutte de limonade, s'il vous plaît

(**d**) *Fam Fig (sensation)* sensation❑ *f*; **to make a splash** faire sensation; **his arrival caused a bit of a splash** son arrivée n'est pas passée inaperçue❑

4 *adv* **to go/to fall splash into the water** entrer/tomber dans l'eau en faisant plouf

►► ***splash headline*** manchette *f*; *Comput* ***splash screen*** splash screen *m*

►**splash about, splash around 1** *vi (duck, swimmer)* barboter; **he was splashing about in the bath/swimming pool** il barbotait dans son bain/la piscine

2 *vt sep (liquid)* faire jaillir, faire gicler; *(money)* dépenser sans compter

►**splash down** *vi (spaceship)* amerrir

►**splash out** *Fam* **1** *vi (spend)* faire des folies; **to splash out on sth** se payer qch

2 *vt insep (money)* claquer; **she splashed out a lot of money on a camera** elle a claqué un argent fou pour s'acheter un appareil photo

►**splash up 1** *vi (be thrown up → liquid, mud etc)* gicler

2 *vt sep (liquid, mud etc)* faire gicler

splashback ['splæʃbæk] *n* panneau *m* de protection *(derrière un évier, un lavabo)*

splashboard ['splæʃbɔːd] *n (on car)* garde-boue *m inv*

splashdown ['splæʃdaʊn] *n (of spaceship)* amerrissage *m*

splashguard ['splæʃgɑːd] *n Am* garde-boue *m inv*

splashing ['splæʃɪŋ] **1** *adj (water)* qui jaillit en éclaboussures; *(wave)* qui clapote

2 *n* (**a**) *(noise)* plouf *m* (**b**) *(patch → of mud, paint)* éclaboussure *f*; *(→ of colour, light)* tache *f*

splashproof ['splæʃpruːf] *adj* étanche aux projections d'eau

splashy ['splæʃɪ] *adj Am Fam* tape-à-l'œil

splat [splæt] **1** *n* floc *m*

2 *adv* **to go splat** faire floc

splatter ['splætə(r)] **1** *vt* éclabousser; **splattered with mud/blood** éclaboussé de boue/sang

2 *vi (rain)* crépiter; *(mud)* éclabousser; **the tomato splattered against the wall** la tomate a giclé sur le mur

3 *n* (**a**) *(mark → of mud, ink)* éclaboussure *f* (**b**) *(sound → of rain)* crépitement *m*

►► *Fam* ***splatter movie*** = film violent et sanglant

splay [spleɪ] **1** *vt (fingers, legs)* écarter; *(feet)* tourner en dehors

2 *vi (fingers, legs)* s'écarter; *(feet)* se tourner en dehors

►**splay out** = **splay**

splayfoot ['spleɪfʊt] *n* pied *m* plat (tourné en dehors)

splayfooted [,spleɪ'fʊtɪd] *adj (person)* aux pieds plats; *(horse)* panard

spleen [spliːn] *n* (**a**) *Anat* rate *f* (**b**) *(bad temper)* humeur *f* noire, mauvaise humeur *f*; **to vent one's spleen on sb/sth** décharger sa mauvaise humeur *ou* sa bile sur qn/qch (**c**) *Arch or Literary (melancholy)* spleen *m*

splendent ['splendənt] *adj* (**a**) *(mineral, insect etc)* luisant (**b**) *Literary (person)* éminent, illustre

splendid ['splendɪd] **1** *adj* (**a**) *(beautiful, imposing → dress, setting, decor)* splendide, superbe, magnifique

(**b**) *(very good → idea, meal)* excellent, magnifique; *(→ work)* excellent, superbe; **I think he's a splendid cook** je trouve que c'est un excellent cuisinier; **splendid isolation** splendide isolement *m*; **a policy of splendid isolation** une politique isolationniste; *Fig* **the statue stands in splendid isolation looking down on the park** la statue domine le parc, solitaire et majestueuse; **we had a splendid time on holiday** nous avons passé d'excellentes vacances; **how splendid for you!** mais c'est formidable pour vous!

2 *exclam* excellent!, parfait!

splendidly ['splendɪdlɪ] *adv* (**a**) *(dress, decorate, furnish)* magnifiquement, superbement; *(entertain)* somptueusement; **he was splendidly turned out in military uniform** il était vraiment superbe en uniforme militaire (**b**) *(perform)* superbement; **you acted splendidly!** tu as été merveilleux!; **the children behaved splendidly** les enfants ont été des anges; **my work is going splendidly** mon travail avance à merveille

splendiferous [,splen'dɪfərəs] *adj Fam Hum* épatant, mirobolant

splendour, *Am* **splendor** ['splendə(r)] *n* splendeur *f*; **the mountains in all their splendour** les montagnes dans toute leur splendeur; **to live in splendour** mener grand train; **the splendours of the Scottish Highlands/India** les beautés *fpl* des Highlands/de l'Inde

splenectomy [splɪ'nektəmɪ] *(pl* **splenectomies***) n Med* splénectomie *f*

splenetic [splɪ'netɪk] *adj Literary (ill-humoured)* atrabilaire

splenic ['splenɪk] *adj Anat* splénique

►► *Vet* ***splenic fever*** (maladie *f* du) charbon *m*

splenitis [splɪ'naɪtɪs] *n Med* splénite *f*

splenius ['spliːnɪəs] *n Anat* splénius *m*

splice [splaɪs] **1** *vt* (**a**) *(join)* **to splice (together)** *(film, tape)* coller; *Naut (rope, cable)* épisser; *Carp (pieces of wood)* enter; **to splice one piece of tape onto another** coller un morceau de bande sur un autre; **to splice the mainbrace** *Naut* border l'artimon; *Fam Fig* boire un coup; **splice the mainbrace!** à border l'artimon!

(**b**) *Br Fam (marry)* **to get spliced** se maquer

2 *n (in tape, film)* collure *f*; *Naut (in rope)* épissure *f*; *Carp (in wood)* enture *f*

splicer ['splaɪsə(r)] *n* colleuse *f*

splicing ['splaɪsɪŋ] *n (of film, magnetic tape)* collage *m*; *Naut (of rope, cable)* épissage *m*; *Carp (of two pieces of wood)* enture *f*

►► ***splicing table*** table *f* de montage (de films); ***splicing tape*** ruban *m* de collage; ***splicing unit*** presse *f* à coller

spliff [splɪf] *n Fam Drugs slang* pétard *m*, joint *m*

spline [splaɪn] *n Tech (in wheel)* clavette *f* linguiforme

splint [splɪnt] **1** *n Med* éclisse *f*, attelle *f*; **to put a limb in splints** éclisser un membre; **her arm was in a splint** *or* **in splints** elle avait le bras dans une attelle

2 *vt* éclisser, mettre dans une attelle

►► ***splint coal*** houille *f* flambante

splinter ['splɪntə(r)] **1** *n (of glass, wood)* éclat *m*; *(of bone)* esquille *f*; *(in foot, finger)* écharde *f*

2 *vt (glass, windscreen, bone)* briser *(en formant des éclats)*; *(wood)* fendre en éclats

3 *vi (glass, windscreen, bone)* se briser *(en formant des éclats)*; *(marble, wood)* se fendre *(en formant des éclats)*; *(political party)* se scinder, se fractionner

►► ***splinter group*** groupe *m* dissident *ou* scissionniste

splinterproof ['splɪntəpruːf] *adj (glass)* se brisant sans éclats

split [splɪt] *(pt & pp* **split,** *cont* **splitting) 1** *n* (**a**) *(in wood)* fissure *f*, fente *f*; *(in rock → gen)* fissure *f*; *(→ deeper)* crevasse *f*; *(in skin)* gerçure *f*; *(in garment → on purpose)* fente *f*; *(→ tear)* déchirure *f*; **there is a long split in the wood** le bois est fendu sur une bonne longueur

(**b**) *(division)* division *f*; *(separation)* séparation *f*; *(quarrel)* rupture *f*; *Pol* scission *f*, schisme *m*; *Rel* schisme *m*; *(gap)* fossé *m*, écart *m*; **a split in the ranks** une division dans les rangs; **there was a three-way split in the voting** les votes étaient répartis en trois groupes; **a deep split within the party** un schisme profond au sein du parti; **the split between rich and poor nations** l'écart entre les pays riches et les pays pauvres

(**c**) *(share)* part *f*; **he asked to be given his split of the booty** il a demandé qu'on lui donne sa part du butin; **they suggested a two-way split of the profits** ils ont proposé de partager les bénéfices en deux parts égales

(**d**) *Culin* coupe *f* glacée

(**e**) *(half bottle → of soft drink)* petite bouteille *f*; *(→ of champagne)* demi-bouteille *f*; *(half glass → of spirits)* petit verre *m*

2 *adj (lip, skirt)* fendu; **in a split second** en une fraction de seconde; **it only took a split second** cela n'a demandé qu'une fraction de seconde; **he works a split shift** sa journée de travail est divisée en deux tranches horaires

3 *vt* (**a**) *(cleave → wood, stone)* fendre; *(→ slate)* cliver; **he was splitting wood for the fire** il fendait du bois pour faire du feu; **the lightning split the oak right down the middle** la foudre a fendu le chêne en plein milieu; **karate experts can split bricks with their bare hands** les karatékas sont capables de casser des briques à main nue; **to split sth in two** *or* **in half** casser *ou* fendre qch en deux; **to split sth open** ouvrir qch *(en le coupant en deux ou en le fendant)*; **the customs split the boxes open** les douaniers ont ouvert les cartons d'un coup de canif; **he split his head open on the concrete** il s'est fendu le crâne sur le béton; **they split open the**

mattress in their search for drugs ils ont éventré le matelas à la recherche de stupéfiants; *Phys* **to split the atom** fissionner l'atome; *Fam* **to split one's sides (laughing)** se tenir les côtes (de rire)

(**b**) *(tear)* déchirer; **the plastic sheet had been split right down the middle** la bâche en plastique avait été fendue en plein milieu; **I've split my trousers** j'ai déchiré mon pantalon

(**c**) *(separate into groups → family)* diviser; *Pol (→ party)* diviser, créer *ou* provoquer une scission dans; **we were split into two groups** on nous a divisés en deux groupes; **the committee is split on this issue** le comité est divisé sur cette question; **this split the party three ways** ceci a divisé *ou* scindé le parti en trois; **to split the vote** disperser les voix; **the vote was split down the middle** les deux camps avaient obtenu exactement le même nombre de voix; **we were split 30-70** on était 30 pour cent d'un côté et 70 pour cent de l'autre; *Am Pol* **to split one's ticket** panacher son bulletin de vote

(**d**) *(divide and share → profits)* (se) partager, (se) répartir; *(→ bill)* (se) partager; *Fin (→ stocks)* faire une redistribution de; **they decided to split the work between them** ils ont décidé de se partager le travail; **to split the profits four ways** diviser les bénéfices en quatre; **you can't split it in three** on ne peut pas le diviser en trois; **to split a bottle** partager une bouteille; **to split the difference** *(share out)* partager la différence; *(compromise)* couper la poire en deux

(**e**) *Gram* **to split an infinitive** = intercaler un adverbe ou une expression adverbiale entre "to" et le verbe

(**f**) *Comput (file, image)* découper

(**g**) *Fam (leave)* quitter❑; **we split town** nous avons quitté la ville; **I'm going to split this scene** je me tire *ou* barre

4 *vi* (**a**) *(break → wood, slate)* se fendre, éclater; **the ship split in two** le navire s'est brisé (en deux); *Fig* **my head is splitting** j'ai un mal de tête atroce

(**b**) *(tear → fabric)* se déchirer; *(→ seam)* craquer; **the bag split open** le sac s'est déchiré; **her dress split right down the back** le dos de sa robe s'est déchiré de haut en bas

(**c**) *(divide → gen)* se diviser; *(→ political party)* se scinder; *(→ road, railway)* se diviser, bifurquer; **the hikers split into three groups** les randonneurs se sont divisés en trois groupes; **the party split over the question of pollution** le parti s'est scindé *ou* divisé sur la question de la pollution; **the committee split down the middle on the issue** le comité s'est divisé en deux clans sur la question

(**d**) *(separate → couple)* se séparer; *(→ family, group)* s'éparpiller, se disperser; **she has split with her old school friends** elle ne voit plus ses anciennes camarades de classe

(**e**) *Fam (leave)* se casser, mettre les bouts; **let's split!** on se casse!; **they split for San Francisco** ils sont partis à San Fransisco❑

5 splits *npl Br* **to do the splits,** *Am* **to do splits** faire le grand écart

►► ***split cane*** osier *m*; *Sport* ***split decision*** *(in boxing)* victoire *f*, décision *f* aux points; ***split end*** fourche *f*; **I tend to get split ends** j'ai des cheveux qui ont tendance à fourcher; *Gram* ***split infinitive*** = infinitif où un adverbe ou une expression adverbiale est intercalé entre "to" et le verbe; ***split pea*** pois *m* cassé; ***split personality*** double personnalité *f*, dédoublement *m* de la personnalité; **he has a split personality** il souffre d'un dédoublement de personnalité; *Br* ***split pin*** goupille *f* fendue; ***split ring*** bague *f* à fente; *Cin & Comput* ***split screen*** écran *m* divisé; ***split second*** fraction *f* de seconde; *Am Pol* ***split ticket*** panachage *m*; *Sport* ***split time*** *(in cycling, athletics, motor racing)* temps *m* de passage

►**split off 1** *vt sep* (**a**) *(break, cut → branch, piece)* enlever (en fendant)

(**b**) *(person, group)* séparer; **our branch was split off from the parent company** notre succursale a été séparée de la maison mère

2 *vi* (**a**) *(branch, splinter)* se détacher; **a large rock split off from the cliff** un gros rocher s'est détaché de la falaise

(**b**) *(separate → person, group)* se séparer; **we split off (from the others) to visit the museum** nous avons quitté les autres pour visiter le musée; **a radical movement split off from the main party** un mouvement radical s'est détaché du gros du parti

►**split on** *vt insep Br Fam (inform on)* vendre, moucharder; **he split on his friend to the police** il a donné son ami à la police; **don't split on him!** ne le vends pas!

►**split up 1** *vt sep* (**a**) *(wood)* fendre; *(cake)* couper en morceaux; **he split the wood up into small pieces** il a fendu le bois en petits morceaux

(**b**) *(divide → loot, profits)* partager; *(→ work)* répartir; **let's split the work up between us** répartissons-nous le travail; **the teaching syllabus is split up into several chapters** le programme d'enseignement est divisé en plusieurs chapitres; *Chem* **to split up a compound into its elements** dédoubler un composé en ses éléments

(**c**) *(couple, people fighting)* séparer; *(disperse)* disperser; **the teacher split the boys up** le professeur a séparé les garçons; **the police split up the meeting/crowd** la police a mis fin à la réunion/dispersé la foule

2 *vi* (**a**) *(wood, marble)* se fendre; *(ship)* se briser

(**b**) *(couple)* se séparer, rompre; *(friends)* rompre, se brouiller; *(meeting, members)* se disperser; *Pol* se diviser, se scinder; **to split up with sb** rompre avec qn; **the band split up in 1992** le groupe s'est séparé en 1992; **the search party split up into three groups** l'équipe de secours s'est divisée en trois groupes

split-cane *adj* en osier

split-level *adj (house, flat)* à deux niveaux

►► ***split-level cooker*** cuisinière *f* à éléments de cuisson séparés

split-second *adj (timing, reaction)* au quart de seconde

splitter (box) ['splɪtə(r)] *n Aut* doubleur *m* de gamme

splitting ['splɪtɪŋ] **1** *n* (**a**) *(of wood, marble)* fendage *m*; *Phys* **the splitting of the atom** la fission de l'atome (**b**) *(of fabric, seams)* déchirure *f* (**c**) *(division)* division *f* (**d**) *(sharing)* partage *m*

2 *adj* **I have a splitting headache** j'ai un mal de tête atroce

►► ***splitting up*** (**a**) *(of wood)* fendage *m* (**b**) *(division)* division *f* (**c**) *(of two people)* séparation *f*; *(of political party)* scission *f*

split-up *n (gen)* rupture *f*, séparation *f*; *Pol* scission *f*

split-view mirror *n Aut* rétroviseur *m* à double miroir

splodge ['splɒdʒ] *Br Fam* **1** *n* (**a**) *(splash → of paint, ink)* éclaboussure❑ *f*, tache❑ *f*; *(→ of colour)* tache❑ *f* (**b**) *(dollop → of cream, of jam)* grosse cuillerée❑ *f*

2 *vt (stain)* éclabousser❑, barbouiller❑ (**with** de); **he splodged a great lump of cream on top** il balança une grosse cuillerée de chantilly pardessus

3 *vi* s'étaler❑, faire des pâtés❑

splodgy ['splɒdʒɪ] *adj Br Fam* taché❑, barbouillé❑

splosh [splɒʃ] *Fam* **1** *vi* (**a**) *(splash → liquid)* faire des éclaboussures❑; **the water sploshed on the floor** l'eau a éclaboussé le sol❑ (**b**) *(as verb of movement)* **we sploshed through the mud/puddles** nous avons traversé la boue/les flaques d'eau en pataugeant❑

2 *vt (pour → water, disinfectant)* verser❑; *(daub → paint)* barbouiller❑

3 *n* éclaboussure❑ *f*

splotch [splɒtʃ] = **splodge**

splotchy ['splɒtʃɪ] *adj Fam* taché❑, barbouillé❑

splurge [splɜːdʒ] *Fam* **1** *n* (**a**) *(spending spree)* folie❑ *f*, folles dépenses❑ *fpl*; **I went on** *or* **I had a splurge and bought a fur coat** j'ai fait une folie, je me suis acheté un manteau de fourrure

(**b**) *(display)* fla-fla *m*, tralala *m*; **the book came out in a splurge of publicity** la sortie du livre a été accompagnée d'un grand battage publicitaire; **a great splurge of colour** une débauche de couleur❑

2 *vt (spend)* dépenser❑; *(waste)* dissiper❑; **she splurged her savings on a set of encyclopedias** toutes ses économies ont été englouties par l'achat d'une encyclopédie❑

►**splurge out** *vi* faire une folie *ou* des folies; **to splurge out on sth** se payer qch

splutter ['splʌtə(r)] **1** *vi* (**a**) *(spit → speaker)* postillonner; *(→ flames, fat)* crépiter, grésiller; *(→ pen, ink)* cracher

(**b**) *(stutter → speaker)* bredouiller; *(→ engine)* tousser, avoir des ratés; **she was spluttering with rage** elle bredouillait de rage; **the engine spluttered and died** le moteur toussa et s'arrêta

2 *vt (protest, apology, thanks)* bredouiller, balbutier, bafouiller

3 *n* (**a**) *(spitting → in speech)* crachotement *m*; *(→ of fat, flames)* crépitement *m*, grésillement *m*

(**b**) *(stutter → in speech)* bredouillement *m*, balbutiement *m*; *(→ of engine)* toussotement *m*

splutterer ['splʌtərə(r)] *n* (**a**) *(person who spits)* lanceur(euse) *m,f* de postillons (**b**) *(person who stutters)* bredouilleur(euse) *m,f*

spluttering ['splʌtərɪŋ] *n* (**a**) *(spitting → in speech)* crachotement *m*; *(→ of fat, flames)* crépitement *m*, grésillement *m*; *(→ of pen)* crachotement *m* (**b**) *(stutter → in speech)* bredouillement *m*, balbutiement *m*; *(→ of engine)* toussotement *m*

Spode [spəʊd] *n* **Spode (china)** = porcelaine fabriquée par la manufacture Spode

spoil [spɔɪl] (*pt & pp* **spoilt** [spɔɪlt] *or* **spoiled**) **1** *vt* (**a**) *(make less attractive or enjoyable)* gâter, gâcher; **the tall chimneys spoil the view** les hautes cheminées gâchent *ou* gâtent la vue; **our holiday was spoilt by the wet weather** le temps pluvieux a gâché nos vacances; **you've spoilt everything by your foolish behaviour** tu as tout gâché avec ton comportement stupide; **the ending spoilt the movie for me** la fin m'a gâché le film; **don't spoil the ending for me** ne me raconte pas la fin, ça va tout gâcher; **the dinner was spoilt because they were late** le dîner a été gâché par leur retard; **to spoil sb's appetite** couper l'appétit *ou* la faim à qn; **if you eat those chocolates, you'll spoil your appetite for dinner** si tu manges ces chocolats, tu n'auras plus faim *ou* plus d'appétit à l'heure du dîner

(**b**) *(damage → goods, objects)* abîmer, endommager; **to get spoilt** *or* **spoiled** s'abîmer; **I spoilt my eyesight by reading in the dark** je me suis abîmé la vue *ou* les yeux en lisant dans la pénombre; *Prov* **to spoil the ship for a hap'orth of tar** faire des économies de bouts de chandelle

(**c**) *(pamper)* gâter; *Fam* **she's spoilt rotten** elle est super gâtée; **we like to spoil our clients** nous aimons gâter nos clients; **to spoil oneself** s'offrir une petite folie

(**d**) *Pol (ballot paper)* rendre nul

2 *vi (fruit, food)* se gâter, s'abîmer; *(in store, hold of ship)* s'avarier, devenir avarié

3 *n (UNCOUNT)* (**a**) = **spoils** (**a**) (**b**) *(earth, diggings)* déblai *m*, déblais *mpl*

4 spoils *npl* (**a**) *(loot)* butin *m*, dépouilles *fpl*; *(profit)* bénéfices *mpl*, profits *mpl*; *(prize)* prix *m*; **he made off with the spoils** il s'est enfui avec le butin; *Fig* **to claim one's share of the spoils** demander sa part du gâteau; **the spoils of war** les dépouilles *fpl* de la guerre

(**b**) *Am Pol Pej* assiette *f* au beurre

►► *Am Pol Pej* ***spoils system*** système *m* des dépouilles, assiette *f* au beurre

►**spoil for** *vt insep* **to be spoiling for a fight/an argument** chercher la bagarre/la dispute

spoilage ['spɔɪlɪdʒ] *n (UNCOUNT) (damage)* détérioration *f*; *(spoilt matter)* déchets *mpl*

spoiled [spɔɪld] = **spoilt**

spoiler ['spɔɪlə(r)] *n* (**a**) *Aut* becquet *m*; *Aviat* aérofrein *m*

(**b**) *(person)* empêcheur(euse) *m,f* de tourner en rond; *(candidate)* = candidat qui se présente dans le seul but de compromettre les chances d'un autre candidat

(**c**) *Journ* = tactique utilisée pour s'approprier le scoop d'un journal rival

►► *Mktg* ***spoiler campaign*** = campagne lancée par une entreprise pour minimiser l'impact d'une campagne publicitaire menée par une société concurrente

spoilsman ['spɔɪlsmən] (*pl* **spoilsmen** [-mən]) *n*

Am Pol Pej = personne qui bénéficie d'un piston politique

spoilsport ['spɔɪlspɔːt] *n* trouble-fête *mf inv*, rabat-joie *mf inv;* **don't be a spoilsport!** ne joue pas les trouble-fête *ou* les rabat-joie!

spoilt [spɔɪlt] **1** *pt & pp of* **spoil**
2 *adj* (**a**) *(child)* gâté; *(behaviour)* d'enfant gâté; **we're spoilt here, not many cities have twenty theatres** nous sommes gâtés ici, peu de villes comptent vingt théâtres; **to be spoilt for choice** avoir l'embarras du choix, n'avoir que l'embarras du choix (**b**) *(harvest)* abîmé; *(food, dinner)* gâché, gâté (**c**) *Pol (ballot paper)* nul

spoke [spəʊk] **1** *pt of* **speak**
2 *n (in wheel)* rayon *m*; *(in ladder)* barreau *m*, échelon *m*; *(on ship's wheel)* manette *f*; *Br Fig* **to put a spoke in sb's wheel** mettre des bâtons dans les roues à qn

spoken ['spəʊkən] **1** *pp of* **speak**
2 *adj (dialogue)* parlé, oral; **the spoken word** la parole; **spoken language** langue *f* parlée; **she's better at the spoken language** elle est meilleure à l'oral

-spoken ['spəʊkən] *suff* **soft-spoken** à la voix douce; **well-spoken** qui s'exprime bien

spoken-voice *adj (record)* parlé

spokeshave ['spəʊkʃeɪv] *n* vastringue *f*

spokesman ['spəʊksmən] (*pl* **spokesmen** [-mən]) *n* porte-parole *m inv*; **a government spokesman, a spokesman for the government** un porte-parole du gouvernement

spokesperson ['spəʊks,pɜːsən] (*pl* **spokespersons** *or* **spokespeople** [-,piːpəl]) *n* porte-parole *m inv*

spokeswoman ['spəʊks,wʊmən] (*pl* **spokeswomen** [-,wɪmɪn]) *n* porte-parole *m inv (femme)*

spoliate ['spəʊlɪeɪt] *vt* spolier

spoliation [,spəʊlɪ'eɪʃən] *n* (**a**) *(plundering)* spoliation *f*, pillage *m* (**b**) *Law (of document)* altération *f*

spondaic [spɒn'deɪɪk] *adj (in prosody)* spondaïque

spondee ['spɒndiː] *n (in prosody)* spondée *m*

spondulicks, spondulix [spɒn'djuːlɪks] *npl Fam* fric *m*, pognon *m*, flouze *m*

spondylitis [,spɒndɪ'laɪtɪs] *n Med* spondylite *f*; **rheumatoid** *or* **ankylosing spondylitis** spondylarthrite *f* ankylosante; **spondylitis deformans** spondylose *f* rhizomélique

sponge [spʌndʒ] **1** *n* (**a**) *Zool* éponge *f*
(**b**) *(for cleaning, washing)* éponge *f*; **I gave the table a sponge** j'ai passé un coup d'éponge sur la table; *Fig* **to throw in the sponge** jeter l'éponge
(**c**) *Fam Pej (scrounger)* parasite ❑ *m*
(**d**) *Br (cake)* gâteau *m* de Savoie; **jam/cream sponge** gâteau *m* de Savoie fourré à la confiture/à la crème
2 *vt* (**a**) *(wipe → table, window)* donner un coup d'éponge à; *(→ wound, body, spilt liquid)* éponger; **she sponged his face** elle lui a épongé le visage; **can you sponge the milk off the table?** peux-tu éponger le lait renversé sur la table?
(**b**) *Fam (cadge → food, money)* taper; **I sponged £20 off** *or* **from him** je l'ai tapé de 20 livres; **can I sponge a cigarette off you?** est-ce que je peux te taper une cigarette?; **she sponged a meal off her friends** elle s'est fait inviter à manger par ses amis ❑
3 *vi Fam (cadge)* jouer au parasite ❑; **to sponge on** *or* **from sb** vivre aux crochets de qn ❑; **she's always sponging** c'est un vrai parasite; **too many people sponge off the state** trop de gens vivent aux crochets de l'État
►► *Br* ***sponge bag*** trousse *f ou* sac *m* de toilette; ***sponge bath*** toilette *f* à l'éponge; ***sponge cake*** biscuit *m* de Savoie, génoise *f*; *Br* ***sponge finger*** boudoir *m (biscuit)*; ***sponge pudding*** = dessert chaud fait avec une pâte de gâteau de Savoie; ***sponge rubber*** mousse *f*, caoutchouc *m* Mousse®

►**sponge down** *vt sep* éponger, laver à l'éponge; **he sponged himself down** il s'est lavé avec une éponge

►**sponge up** *vt sep (liquid)* éponger

sponge-down *n* coup *m* d'éponge

sponger ['spʌndʒə(r)] *n Fam Pej (gén)* parasite ❑ *m*, *(for meals)* pique-assiette *mf*

spongiform ['spʌndʒɪfɔːm] *adj* spongiforme

sponginess ['spʌndʒɪnɪs] *n (gen)* spongiosité *f*; *(of cake, pastry)* moelleux *m*; *(of road surface)* caractère *m* mou; *(of soles)* souplesse *f*

spongy ['spʌndʒɪ] (*compar* **spongier**, *superl* **spongiest**) *adj (gen)* spongieux; *(cake, pastry)* moelleux; *(road surface)* mou; *(soles)* souple

sponsion ['spɒnʃɪən] *n Law* garantie *f*, caution *f*

sponson ['spɒnsən] *n Naut* encorbellement *m*

sponsor ['spɒnsə(r)] **1** *n* (**a**) *Com & Sport (of sportsman, team, tournament)* sponsor *m*; *(of film, TV programme)* sponsor *m*, commanditaire *m*; *(of artist, musician)* commanditaire *m*, mécène *m*; *(of student, studies)* parrain *m*; *(for charity)* donateur(trice) *m,f*; **he's looking for sponsors for his Channel swim** *(financial backers)* il cherche des sponsors pour financer sa traversée de la Manche à la nage; *(charitable donations)* il cherche des gens qui accepteront de faire une donation aux bonnes œuvres s'il réussit sa traversée de la Manche à la nage; **to act as sponsor for sb** sponsoriser qn
(**b**) *(of would-be club member)* parrain *m*, marraine *f*; *(guarantor → for loan)* répondant(e) *m,f*, garant(e) *m,f*; *(backer → for business)* parrain *m*, bailleur *m* de fonds; **he was the sponsor of the proposal** c'est lui qui a lancé la proposition; **her uncle stood (as) sponsor to her** *(for loan)* son oncle a été son répondant; *(for business)* son oncle l'a parrainée
(**c**) *Am (of godchild)* parrain *m*, marraine *f*; **to stand sponsor to a child** *(at baptism)* tenir un enfant sur les fonts (baptismaux)
2 *vt* (**a**) *Com & Sport* sponsoriser; *Rad & TV (programme)* sponsoriser, parrainer; *(concert, exhibition)* parrainer, commanditer; *(studies, student)* parrainer; **the rally is sponsored by the milk industry** le rallye est sponsorisé par l'industrie laitière; **our firm sponsored her to the tune of £10,000** notre firme l'a sponsorisée pour un montant de 10 000 livres
(**b**) *(for charity)* **I sponsored him to swim 10 miles** je me suis engagé à lui donner de l'argent (pour des œuvres charitables) s'il faisait *ou* parcourait 10 milles à la nage
(**c**) *(appeal, proposal)* présenter; *(would-be club member)* parrainer; *(loan, borrower)* se porter garant de; *(firm)* patronner; *Pol* **to sponsor a bill** présenter un projet de loi
(**d**) *(godchild)* être le parrain/la marraine de
►► ***sponsored walk*** = marche parrainée

SPONSORED EVENT

La Grande-Bretagne compte de très nombreuses organisations caritatives ("charities") œuvrant pour des causes aussi diverses que la recherche médicale, l'aide à l'enfance défavorisée ou l'établissement de centres pour animaux abandonnés. L'un des moyens employés pour rassembler des fonds est de s'engager auprès d'autres gens (généralement des amis, voisins et collègues de travail) à accomplir une épreuve en échange d'une somme d'argent déterminée. Il peut s'agir d'épreuves physiques ("sponsored walk", "sponsored swim") ou de défis saugrenus, tels que se rendre au bureau en pyjama ou bien encore garder le silence pendant toute une journée ("sponsored silence"). Des "sponsored events" sont également organisés par des écoles et des clubs sportifs afin d'obtenir de l'argent pour acheter du matériel.

sponsoring ['spɒnsərɪŋ] *n* (**a**) *Com & Sport* sponsoring *m*, parrainage *m* (**b**) *(of appeal, proposal)* présentation *f*; *(of would-be club member, godchild)* parrainage *m*; *(of loan, borrower)* cautionnement *m*

sponsorship ['spɒnsəʃɪp] *n* (**a**) *Com & Sport* sponsoring *m*, parrainage *m*; **under the sponsorship of** sous le parrainage de
(**b**) *(of appeal, proposal)* présentation *f*; *Pol (of bill)* proposition *f*, présentation *f*; *(of would-be club member, godchild)* parrainage *m*; *(of loan, borrower)* cautionnement *m*
►► ***sponsorship agreement*** contrat *m* de sponsoring; ***sponsorship budget*** budget *m* alloué au sponsoring; ***sponsorship deal*** contrat *m* de sponsoring

spontaneity [,spɒntə'neɪətɪ] *n* spontanéité *f*

spontaneous [spɒn'teɪnɪəs] *adj* spontané
►► ***spontaneous combustion*** combustion *f* spontanée; *Biol* ***spontaneous generation*** génération *f* spontanée

spontaneously [spɒn'teɪnɪəslɪ] *adv* spontanément

spoof [spuːf] *Fam* **1** *n* (**a**) *(mockery)* satire ❑ *f*, parodie ❑ *f*; **it's a spoof on horror films** c'est une parodie des films d'horreur
(**b**) *(trick)* blague ❑ *f*, canular ❑ *m*; **the whole thing was just a spoof** c'était un simple canular du début à la fin
2 *adj* faux ❑, fait par plaisanterie ❑; **a spoof horror movie/documentary** une parodie de film d'horreur/de documentaire ❑; **a spoof phone call** un canular téléphonique ❑; **he sent around a spoof memo about redundancies** il a fait passer une circulaire bidon *ou* une fausse circulaire parlant de licenciements
3 *vi* raconter des blagues ❑
4 *vt (book, style)* parodier ❑; *(person)* faire marcher

spook [spuːk] **1** *n* (**a**) *(ghost)* fantôme *m* (**b**) *Am Fam (spy)* barbouze *mf* (**c**) *Am very Fam (black man)* nègre *m*, bamboula *m*, = terme injurieux désignant un Noir; *(black woman)* négresse *f*, = terme injurieux désignant une Noire
2 *vt Fam* (**a**) *(startle)* foutre la trouille à; *(frighten, disturb)* donner la chair de poule à ❑ (**b**) *(haunt)* hanter ❑

spooky ['spuːkɪ] (*compar* **spookier**, *superl* **spookiest**) *adj Fam* (**a**) *(atmosphere)* qui donne la chair de poule ❑, qui fait froid dans le dos ❑; *(person)* sinistre ❑; **it's spooky here at night** c'est sinistre ici le soir (**b**) *Am (skittish)* peureux ❑ (**c**) *(odd)* bizarre ❑

spool [spuːl] **1** *n (of film, tape, thread)* bobine *f*; *(for fishing)* tambour *m*; *(of wire)* rouleau *m*; *(of sewing machine, weaving machine)* cannette *f*; **(ribbon) spool** *(for typewriter)* bobine *f* du ruban
2 *vt (gen)* bobiner; *Comput* spouler

►**spool off** *vt sep* débobiner, dévider

spooler ['spuːlə(r)] *n Comput* spouleur *m*, pilote *m* de mise en file d'attente

spooling ['spuːlɪŋ] *n* bobinage *m*
►► ***spooling machine*** bobineuse *f*, bobinoir *m*; ***spooling off*** débobinage *m*, dévidage *m*

spoon [spuːn] **1** *n* (**a**) *(utensil)* cuiller *f*, cuillère *f*
(**b**) *(quantity)* cuillerée *f*; **add two spoons of sugar** ajoutez deux cuillerées de sucre
(**c**) *Fishing* cuiller *f*, cuillère *f*
(**d**) *(in golf)* spoon *m*
2 *vt (food → serve)* servir à l'aide d'une cuiller; *(→ transfer)* verser à l'aide d'une cuiller; **to spoon the cream from** *or* **off the milk** enlever la crème du lait avec une cuiller; **to spoon the fat from** *or* **off the gravy** dégraisser la sauce à l'aide d'une cuiller; **he spooned the ice cream into a bowl** il a servi la glace dans un bol (avec une cuiller); **she spooned the porridge into his mouth** elle lui a fait manger la bouillie avec une cuiller
3 *vi Fam Old-fashioned* se faire des mamours

►**spoon out** *vt sep (serve)* servir à l'aide d'une cuiller *ou* cuillère; *(transfer)* verser à l'aide d'une cuiller *ou* cuillère

►**spoon up** *vt sep (eat)* manger avec une cuiller *ou* cuillère; [illegible] *ou* cuillère

spoonbill ['spuːnbɪl] *n Orn* spatule *f*

spoonbread ['spuːnbred] *n Am Culin* = pain de maïs très tendre

spoonerism ['spuːnərɪzəm] *n* contrepèterie *f*

spoon-feed *vt* (**a**) *(child, sick person)* nourrir à la cuiller *ou* cuillère (**b**) *Fig* **to spoon-feed sb** mâcher le travail à qn

spoonful ['spuːnfʊl] *n* cuillerée *f*

spoor [spɔː(r)] *n* trace *f*, traces *fpl*, empreintes *fpl*

Sporades ['spɒrədiːz] *npl* **the Sporades** les Sporades *fpl*; **in the Sporades** aux Sporades

sporadic [spə'rædɪk] *adj* sporadique; **sporadic fighting** des combats *mpl* sporadiques; **sporadic outbreaks of gunfire** des coups *mpl* de feu isolés *ou* sporadiques; **sporadic violence** des accès *mpl* de violence sporadiques; **sporadic showers** des averses *fpl* éparses

sporadically [spə'rædɪklɪ] *adv* sporadiquement; **to work sporadically** travailler par à-coups

sporangium [spɒ'rændʒɪəm] *n Bot* sporange *m*

spore [spɔ:(r)] *n Biol* spore *f*

sporophyl, sporophyll ['spɒrəfɪl] *n Bot* sporophylle *m*

sporophyte ['spɒrəfaɪt] *n Bot* sporophyte *m*

sporran ['spɒrən] *n* = aumônière en cuir parfois agrémentée de fourrure, portée sur le devant du kilt

sport [spɔ:t] **1** *n* (**a**) *(physical exercise)* sport *m*; **she does a lot of sport** elle fait beaucoup de sport, elle est très sportive; **you shouldn't mix sport and politics** tu ne devrais pas mélanger sport et politique; **minority sports** les sports *mpl* minoritaires; **I hated sport** *or* **sports at school** je détestais le sport *ou* les sports à l'école; **the sport of kings** *(horse racing)* les courses *fpl* de chevaux

(**b**) *Literary (hunting)* chasse *f*; *(fishing)* pêche *f*; **to have good sport** *(in hunting)* faire bonne chasse; *(in fishing)* faire bonne pêche *ou* bonne prise

(**c**) *Literary (fun)* amusement *m*, divertissement *m*; **to say sth in sport** dire qch pour rire *ou* en plaisantant; **it's great sport flying these remote-controlled planes** c'est très amusant de faire voler ces avions radio-guidés; **to make sport of sb/sth** se moquer de qn/qch, tourner qn/qch en ridicule

(**d**) *Fam (friendly person)* chic type *m*, chic fille *f*; **he's a real sport** c'est vraiment un chic type; **go on, be a sport!** allez, sois sympa!

(**e**) *(good loser)* **to be a (good) sport** être beau joueur; **they're not very good sports** ils sont plutôt mauvais joueurs

(**f**) *(gambler)* joueur(euse) *m,f*; *(high flyer)* bon vivant *m*

(**g**) *Austr & NZ Fam (fellow)* pote *m*, vieux *m*

(**h**) *Old-fashioned (term of address)* **hallo, old sport!** bonjour, mon vieux!

(**i**) *Biol* variété *f* anormale

(**j**) *Literary* **to be the sport of fortune/of circumstances** être le jouet *ou* le jeu de la fortune/des circonstances

2 *vt (wear)* porter, arborer; **he was sporting a tartan jacket/a yellow carnation** il portait une veste tartan/arborait un œillet jaune

3 *vi* (**a**) *Literary (amuse oneself)* batifoler, s'ébattre

(**b**) *Biol (plants, animals)* produire une variété anormale

4 sports 1 *npl (athletics meeting)* meeting *m* d'athlétisme; *(competition)* compétition *f* sportive; **this weekend is the inter-regional sports** ce week-end ont lieu les compétitions sportives inter-régionales; **the school sports** la compétition sportive scolaire **2** *comp (equipment, programme, reporter)* sportif; *(fan)* de sport

►► ***sports bag*** sac *m* de sport; ***sports bar*** = bar où l'on passe des cassettes vidéo d'événements sportifs, où l'on suit certains matches en direct à la télévision etc; ***sports bra*** soutien-gorge *m* de sport; ***sports car*** voiture *f* de sport; ***sports centre*** complexe *m ou* centre *m* sportif, *Suisse* halle *f* de gymnase; ***sports club*** club *m* de sport; *Am* ***sports coat*** veste *f* sport; ***sports commentator*** commentateur(trice) *m,f* sportif(ive); *Br Sch* ***sports day*** = réunion sportive annuelle où les parents sont invités; ***sports desk*** service *m* des sports; ***sports editor*** rédacteur *m* en chef sportif; ***sports facilities*** installations *fpl* sportives; ***sports ground*** terrain *m* de sport *ou* de jeux; ***sports hall*** salle *f* de sport, gymnase *m*, *Suisse* halle *f* de gymnase; ***sports jacket***, *Am* ***sport jacket*** veste *f* sport; ***sports page*** *(of newspaper)* page *f* des sports; ***sports reporter*** journaliste *mf* sportif(ive); *TV etc* ***sports results*** résultats *mpl* sportifs; *Aut* ***sports saloon*** berline *f* sport; *Am* ***sports scholarship*** = bourse pour les élèves qui sont bons en sport; ***sports science*** sciences *fpl* du sport; ***sports shoe*** training *m*; ***sports shop*** magasin *m* de sport

sporting ['spɔ:tɪŋ] *adj* (**a**) *Sport (fixtures, interests)* sportif

(**b**) *(friendly, generous → behaviour)* chic *(inv)*; **it's very sporting of you** c'est très chic de votre part

(**c**) *(fairly good → chance)* assez bon; **we're in with a sporting chance (of winning)** on a une assez bonne chance de gagner; **there's a sporting chance he'll come** il y a de fortes chances (pour) qu'il vienne

►► ***sporting event*** manifestation *f* sportive; ***sporting man/woman*** *(horseracing enthusiast)* turfiste *mf*

'This Sporting Life' *Storey, Anderson* 'Le Prix d'un homme'

sportingly ['spɔ:tɪŋlɪ] *adv* (très) sportivement

sportive ['spɔ:tɪv] *adj Literary* folâtre, badin

sportscast ['spɔ:tskɑ:st] *n Am* émission *f* sportive

sportscaster ['spɔ:ts,kɑ:stə(r)] *n Am* reporter *m* sportif

sportsman ['spɔ:tsmən] *(pl* **sportsmen** [-mən]) *n* (**a**) *(player of sport)* sportif *m* (**b**) *(in attitude, approach)* **he's a real sportsman** *(plays fair)* il a l'esprit sportif; *(good loser)* il est beau joueur

sportsmanlike ['spɔ:tsmənlaɪk] *adj* sportif; **in a sportsmanlike way** sportivement

sportsmanship ['spɔ:tsmənʃɪp] *n* sportivité *f*, esprit *m* sportif

sportsperson ['spɔ:ts,pɜ:sən] *(pl* **sportspeople** [-,pi:pəl]) *n* sportif(ive) *m,f*

sportswear ['spɔ:tsweə(r)] *n (UNCOUNT)* vêtements *mpl* de sport

sportswoman ['spɔ:ts,wʊmən] *(pl* **sportswomen** [-,wɪmɪn]) *n* (**a**) *(player)* sportive *f* (**b**) *(in attitude, approach)* **she's a real sportswoman** *(plays fair)* elle a l'esprit sportif; *(good loser)* elle est belle joueuse

sport-utility vehicle *n Am* 4 x 4 *m*

sporty ['spɔ:tɪ] *(compar* **sportier**, *superl* **sportiest**) *adj* (**a**) *(person)* sportif; *(garment)* de sport; **he's got a very sporty image** il a un look très sport (**b**) *(car)* de sport

sporule ['spɒru:l] *n Biol* petit spore *m*

SPOT [spɒt]

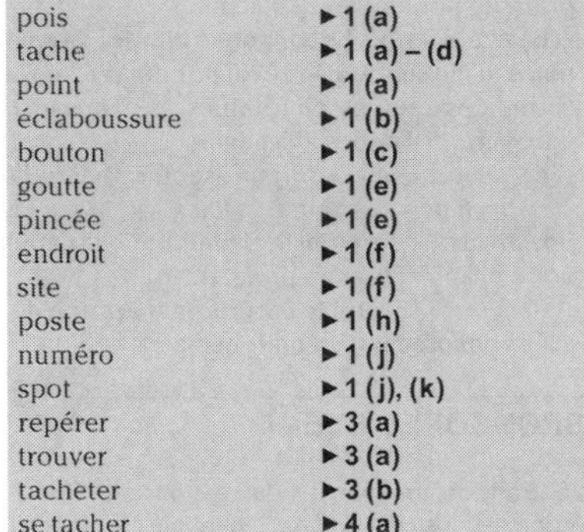

pois	► **1 (a)**
tache	► **1 (a) – (d)**
point	► **1 (a)**
éclaboussure	► **1 (b)**
bouton	► **1 (c)**
goutte	► **1 (e)**
pincée	► **1 (e)**
endroit	► **1 (f)**
site	► **1 (f)**
poste	► **1 (h)**
numéro	► **1 (j)**
spot	► **1 (j), (k)**
repérer	► **3 (a)**
trouver	► **3 (a)**
tacheter	► **3 (b)**
se tacher	► **4 (a)**

(pt & pp **spotted**, *cont* **spotting**) **1** *n* (**a**) *(dot → on material, clothes)* pois *m*; *(→ on leopard, giraffe)* tache *f*, moucheture *f*; *(→ on dice, playing card)* point *m*; **a tie with red spots** une cravate à pois rouges; **a leopard's spots** les taches *ou* les mouchetures d'un léopard; **I've got spots before my eyes** j'ai des points lumineux *ou* des taches devant les yeux; **the carnations brought a spot of colour into the church** les œillets apportaient une tache de couleur dans l'église

(**b**) *(stain, unwanted mark)* tache *f*; *(on fruit)* tache *f*, tavelure *f*; *(splash)* éclaboussure *f*; **a dirty spot** une tache, une salissure; **there are some spots of mould on the jam** il y a des taches de moisissure sur la confiture; **how did you get these spots of blood on your shirt?** d'où viennent ces taches de sang sur ta chemise?

(**c**) *(pimple)* bouton *m*; *(freckle)* tache *f* de son *ou* de rousseur; **I've got a spot on my chin** j'ai un bouton sur le menton; **to come out in spots** avoir une éruption de boutons; **to suffer from spots** souffrir d'acné

(**d**) *(blemish → on character)* tache *f*, souillure *f*; **there isn't a spot on his reputation** sa réputation est sans tache

(**e**) *Fam (small amount → of liquid)* goutte □ *f*; *(→ of salt)* pincée □ *f*; *(→ of irony, humour)* pointe □ *f*, soupçon □ *m*; **would you like cream in your coffee? – just a spot** voulez-vous de la crème dans votre café? – juste un soupçon; **a spot of whisky** une larme de whisky; **there were a few spots of rain** il est tombé quelques gouttes (de pluie); **I've got a spot of bad news** j'ai une mauvaise nouvelle □; **to do a spot of work** faire un peu de travail □; **she hardly did a spot of work** elle n'a quasiment rien fait □; **I'm having a spot of bother with the neighbours** j'ai quelques ennuis *ou* problèmes avec les voisins □; **I could do with a spot of sleep** un petit somme me ferait du bien □; **do you want a spot of supper?** veux-tu manger un morceau?

(**f**) *(place)* endroit *m*, coin *m*; *(site)* site *m*; *(on body)* endroit *m*, point *m*; **this is a peaceful spot** c'est un endroit très tranquille; **this is the exact spot where the market cross was situated** c'est l'endroit exact où se trouvait la croix du marché; **X marks the spot** *(of crime etc)* la croix indique le lieu; **a tender** *or* **sore spot** un point sensible; **to find sb's weak spot** trouver le défaut dans la cuirasse de qn, trouver le point faible de qn; **that hits the spot!** ça fait du bien!

(**g**) *(aspect, feature, moment)* **the only bright spot of the week** le seul bon moment de la semaine

(**h**) *(position, job)* poste *m*, position *f*

(**i**) *(difficult situation) Fam* **to be in a spot** être dans le pétrin; *Fam* **we're in a bit of a (tight) spot** nous sommes dans le pétrin *ou* dans de beaux draps; *Fam* **you're putting us in a spot** tu nous mets dans le pétrin; **to put sb on the spot** *(put in difficult position)* mettre qn dans une situation difficile; *(force to answer difficult questions)* mettre qn en mauvaise posture *(en posant des questions difficiles)*

(**j**) *Rad & TV (for artist, interviewee)* numéro *m*; *(news item)* brève *f*; *(advertisement)* spot *m* publicitaire; **he got a spot on the Margie Warner show** *(as singer, comedian)* il a fait un numéro dans le show de Margie Warner; *(interview)* il s'est fait interviewer *ou* il est passé dans le show de Margie Warner; **advertising spot** message *m ou* spot *m* publicitaire

(**k**) *(spotlight → in home etc)* spot *m*; *Theat & Cin* projecteur *m*

(**l**) *(in billiards, snooker)* mouche *f*

2 *comp (random → count, test)* fait à l'improviste

3 *vt* (**a**) *(notice → friend, object)* repérer, apercevoir; *(→ talent, mistake)* trouver, déceler; *Horseracing etc (winner)* prédire, repérer; *Mil* repérer, observer; **I could spot him a mile off** je pourrais le repérer à des kilomètres; **I spotted her in the crowd** je l'ai repérée au milieu de la foule; **she was spotted in the pub** on l'a vue au pub; **I spotted him as a potential troublemaker** j'ai très vite repéré qu'il était un agitateur; **to spot sb doing sth** apercevoir qn en train de faire qch; **to spot an opportunity** repérer une occasion; **I'd never have spotted it** je ne l'aurais jamais remarqué; **well spotted!** bien vu!

(**b**) *(mark with spots)* tacheter; *(stain)* tacher; **the wall is spotted with mildew** le mur est taché *ou* piqué d'humidité; **the rain spotted the pavement** des gouttes de pluie formaient des taches sur le trottoir

(**c**) *Am (opponent)* accorder un avantage à; **he spotted his opponent ten points** il a cédé *ou* concédé dix points à son adversaire

(**d**) *Am (remove → stain)* enlever; **a chemical for spotting clothes** un produit pour détacher les vêtements

(**e**) *Am Fam (lend)* prêter □; **can somebody spot me ten dollars?** est-ce que quelqu'un peut me prêter dix dollars?

4 *vi* (**a**) *(garment, carpet)* se tacher, se salir

(**b**) *(rain)* **it's spotting (with rain)** il tombe quelques gouttes de pluie

(**c**) *Mil* servir d'observateur

(**d**) *Med* **to be spotting** *(woman)* avoir des pertes (de sang)

5 on the spot *adv (at once)* sur-le-champ; *(at the scene)* sur les lieux, sur place; **the police are on the spot** la police est sur les lieux; **he was killed on the spot** il a été tué sur le coup; **to be fined on the spot** recevoir une amende sur-le-champ; **to have sb on the spot** *(reporter, representative, agent)* avoir qn sur place; **our reporter on the spot, Mary Smith** notre correspondante sur place, Mary Smith; **the doctor arrived on the spot in five minutes** le docteur est arrivé sur les lieux en cinq minutes; **to run on the spot** courir sur place

►► *TV* ***spot advertisement*** spot *m* publicitaire; ***spot announcement*** flash *m*; *Fin* ***spot buying*** achat *m* au comptant; *Br* ***spot cash*** argent *m* liquide; ***spot check*** *(investigation)* contrôle *m* surprise; *(for quality)* contrôle *m* par sondage; *(by customs)* fouille *f* au hasard; *Comput & Typ* ***spot colour*** couleur *f* (du nuancier) Pantone®; *St Exch* ***spot deal*** opération *f ou* transaction *f* au comptant; *Geog* ***spot height*** altitude *f*; *Fin* ***spot market*** marché *m* au comptant; ***spot news*** brève *f*; *Fin* ***spot price*** cours *m* spot; *Fin* ***spot rate*** cours *m* à vue, cours *m* spot; *Fin* ***spot trading*** négociations *fpl* au comptant; *St Exch* ***spot transaction*** opération *f ou* transaction *f* au comptant

---

spot-check *vt* contrôler au hasard; *(for quality)* contrôler par sondage; *(without notice)* faire des contrôles surprises de; **athletes are regularly spot-checked for anabolic steroids** on effectue souvent des contrôles surprises sur les athlètes pour détecter les anabolisants

spotless ['spɒtlɪs] *adj (gen)* impeccable; *(character)* sans tache

spotlessly ['spɒtlɪslɪ] *adv* **spotlessly clean** reluisant de propreté, d'une propreté impeccable

spotlessness ['spɒtlɪsnɪs] *n* propreté *f*

spotlight ['spɒtlaɪt] *(pt & pp* **spotlit** [-lɪt]) **1** *n* (**a**) *(in theatre → device)* spot *m*, projecteur *m*; *(→ beam)* lumière *f* de projecteur; *also Fig* **in the spotlight** sous le feu *ou* la lumière des projecteurs; **to turn the spotlight on sb** braquer les projecteurs sur qn; *Fig* mettre qn en vedette; **the spotlight was on her** les projecteurs étaient braqués sur elle, *Fig (she was in the limelight)* elle était en vedette; *(she was the focus of unwelcome media attention)* elle était sur la sellette; **the political spotlight was on Mrs Warner this week** les feux de l'actualité étaient braqués sur Mme Warner cette semaine

(**b**) *(lamp → in home, on car)* spot *m*

2 *vt* (**a**) *Theat* diriger les projecteurs sur

(**b**) *Fig (personality, talent)* mettre en vedette; *(pinpoint → flaws, changes)* mettre en lumière, mettre le doigt sur

spotlighting ['spɒtlaɪtɪŋ] *n* éclairage *m* à effet

spotlit ['spɒtlɪt] *adj* éclairé par des projecteurs

spot-on *Br Fam* **1** *adj* (**a**) *(correct → measurement)* pile, très précis❑; *(→ guess)* en plein dans le mille; **his answer was spot-on** sa réponse était parfaitement exacte *ou* correcte❑; **his remark was spot-on** sa remarque était vachement bien vue❑ (**b**) *(perfect)* parfait❑

2 *adv (guess)* en plein dans le mille; **he timed it spot-on** il a calculé son coup à la seconde près❑

spotted ['spɒtɪd] **1** *pt & pp of* **spot**

2 *adj* (**a**) *(leopard, bird)* tacheté, moucheté; *(apple, pear)* tavelé

(**b**) *(tie, dress)* à pois

(**c**) *(stained → carpet, wall)* taché

►► *Orn* ***spotted crake*** marouette *f* ponctuée, râle *m* ponctué; *Br* ***spotted dick*** = pudding aux raisins secs consommé chaud; ***spotted fever*** fièvre *f* éruptive; *Orn* ***spotted flycatcher*** gobe-mouches *m inv* gris; *Bot* ***spotted medick*** luzerne *f* d'Arabie; *Orn* ***spotted sandpiper*** chevalier *m* grivelé

[illegible] teur(trice) *m,f*; *(lookout)* dénicheur(euse) *m,f* (**b**) *Br (enthusiast)* **train/plane spotter** passionné(e) *m,f* de trains/d'avions (**c**) *Am Fam (checking on colleagues)* surveillant(e) *m,f* du personnel❑

2 *comp (plane)* d'observation

spotting ['spɒtɪŋ] *n* **train/plane spotting** repérage *m* de trains/d'avions

spotty ['spɒtɪ] *(compar* **spottier**, *superl* **spottiest**) *adj* (**a**) *(pimply → face, person)* couvert de boutons, boutonneux; **a spotty adolescent** un adolescent boutonneux (**b**) *(covered with spots → wallpaper)* piqué *ou* taché d'humidité; *(→ mirror)* piqueté, piqué; *(stained)* taché (**c**) *(patterned → fabric, tie)* à pois (**d**) *(patchy)* irrégulier; **a spotty performance** une représentation inégale

spot-weld 1 *vt* souder par points

2 *n* soudure *f* par points

spot-welding *n* soudure *f* par points

spousals ['spaʊzəlz] *npl Formal* mariage *m*

spouse [spaʊs] *n Formal* époux *m*, épouse *f*; *Admin & Law* conjoint(e) *m,f*

spout [spaʊt] **1** *n* (**a**) *(of teapot, kettle, carton)* bec *m* verseur; *(of watering can)* tuyau *m*; *(of tap)* brise-jet *m inv*; *(of pump)* dégorgeoir *m*; *(of gutter)* gargouille *f*; *(of pipe)* embout *m*

(**b**) *(of water → from fountain, geyser)* jet *m*; *(→ from whale)* jet *m*, souffle *m* d'eau; *(of flame)* colonne *f*; *(of lava)* jet *m*; **a spout of boiling water** un jet d'eau bouillante

(**c**) *Br Fam (idiom)* **to be up the spout** *(ruined)* être fichu *ou* foutu; *(pregnant)* être en cloque; **our plans are up the spout** nos projets sont tombés à l'eau; **now we're really up the spout** maintenant nous sommes vraiment dans de beaux draps *ou* dans le pétrin; **that's our holidays up the spout** on peut faire une croix sur nos vacances❑

2 *vi* (**a**) *(water, oil)* jaillir; *(whale)* souffler; **water spouted out of the pipe** de l'eau jaillit du tuyau

(**b**) *Fam Pej (talk)* dégoiser; **he's always spouting (on) about politics** il est toujours à dégoiser sur la politique

3 *vt* (**a**) *(water, oil)* faire jaillir un jet de; *(fire, smoke)* vomir, émettre un jet de

(**b**) *Fam Pej (words, poetry)* débiter, sortir❑; **she's always spouting Latin quotations** elle est toujours en train de débiter *ou* sortir des citations latines

►**spout out 1** *vi (water, lava)* jaillir, sortir en giclant; **the liquid was spouting out of the barrel** le liquide sortait du tonneau en giclant, le liquide jaillissait du tonneau

2 *vt sep* (**a**) *(liquid)* faire jaillir un jet de; *(lava)* cracher; **the pipe spouted out water** de l'eau jaillissait du tuyau

(**b**) *Fam Fig (utter → statistics, poetry, quotations)* débiter

sprain [spreɪn] **1** *vt (joint → gen)* se fouler; *(→ more seriously)* se faire une entorse à; *(muscle)* s'étirer; **she has sprained her ankle** *or* **has a sprained ankle** elle s'est foulé la cheville; *(more serious)* elle s'est fait une entorse à la cheville

2 *n* foulure *f*; *(more serious)* entorse *f*

sprang [spræŋ] *pt of* **spring**

sprat [spræt] *n Ich* sprat *m*; *Fig* **It's a sprat to catch a mackerel** c'est un bien petit sacrifice pour un grand gain

sprauncy ['sprɔːnsɪ] *adj Br Fam* (**a**) *(lively)* plein de peps (**b**) *(stylish)* chic❑

sprawl [sprɔːl] **1** *vi* (**a**) *(be sitting, lying)* être affalé *ou* vautré; *(sit down, lie down)* s'affaler, se laisser tomber; **she was sprawling in the armchair/on the bed** elle était avachie dans le fauteuil/vautrée sur le lit; **the blow sent him sprawling** le coup l'a fait tomber de tout son long

(**b**) *(spread → gen)* s'étaler, s'étendre; *(→ plant)* s'étendre, se déployer; **the new industrial estate is beginning to sprawl into the countryside** la nouvelle zone industrielle commence à grignoter *ou* envahir la campagne; **her signature sprawled across half the page** sa signature s'étalait sur la moitié de la page

2 *vt (usu passive)* **she was sprawled in the armchair/on the pavement** elle était vautrée dans le fauteuil/étendue de tout son long sur [illegible]

3 *n* (**a**) *(position)* position *f* affalée; **he lay in an ungainly sprawl** il était étendu de tout son long de façon peu élégante

(**b**) *(of city)* étendue *f*; **suburban sprawl** *(suburb)* banlieue *f* tentaculaire; **an urban sprawl** une agglomération; **the problem of urban sprawl** le problème de l'expansion urbaine

sprawling ['sprɔːlɪŋ] *adj (body)* affalé; *(suburbs, metropolis)* tentaculaire; **sprawling handwriting** écriture *f* irrégulière et étalée

spray [spreɪ] **1** *vt* (**a**) *(treat → crops, garden, tree)* faire des pulvérisations sur, traiter; *(→ field)* pulvériser; *(→ house plant)* arroser au vaporisateur; *(sprinkle → road)* asperger; **to spray one's hair** se laquer les cheveux; **to spray a plant with insecticide** pulvériser de l'insecticide sur une plante; **I got sprayed with cold water** je me suis fait arroser *ou* asperger d'eau froide; *Fig* **they sprayed the bar with bullets/with machine-gun fire** ils arrosèrent le bar de balles/de rafales de mitrailleuses

(**b**) *(apply → water, perfume)* vaporiser; *(→ paint, insecticide)* pulvériser; *(→ coat of paint, fixer)* mettre, appliquer; *(→ graffiti, slogan)* écrire, tracer (à la bombe); **to spray insecticide on a plant** pulvériser de l'insecticide sur une plante; **she sprayed perfume behind her ears** elle se vaporisa du parfum derrière les oreilles; **she sprayed her hairstyle in place** elle s'est mis de la laque pour faire tenir sa coiffure; **they sprayed water on the flames** ils vaporisèrent de l'eau sur les flammes; **she sprayed air freshener around the room** elle vaporisa du désodorisant dans la pièce; **three layers of paint are sprayed onto the metal** on passe trois couches de peinture au pistolet sur le métal; **slogan sprayed on a wall** slogan écrit à la bombe sur un mur

2 *vi* (**a**) *(liquid)* jaillir; **the water sprayed (out) over** *or* **onto the road** l'eau a jailli sur la route; **water sprayed up in our faces** de l'eau éclaboussait nos visages

(**b**) *(against crop disease)* pulvériser, faire des pulvérisations

3 *n* (**a**) *(droplets)* fines gouttelettes *fpl*; *(from sea)* embruns *mpl*; **the wind blew a fine spray of rain against her face** de fines gouttelettes de pluie portées par le vent lui mouillaient le visage; **the liquid comes out in a fine spray** le liquide est pulvérisé

(**b**) *(container → for aerosol)* bombe *f*, aérosol *m*; *(→ for perfume)* atomiseur *m*; *(→ for cleaning fluids, water, lotion)* vaporisateur *m*; **this deodorant is a spray** ce déodorant est un aérosol; **throat spray** vaporisateur *m* pour la gorge

(**c**) *(act of spraying → of crops)* pulvérisation *f*; *(→ against infestation)* traitement *m* (par pulvérisation); *(→ of aerosol product)* coup *m* de bombe; **to give sth a spray** *(fields, roses etc)* pulvériser qch; *(walls etc)* peindre qch au pistolet; *(hair)* mettre du spray *ou* de la laque sur qch

(**d**) *Fig (of bullets)* grêle *f*; **the welding sent up sprays** *or* **a spray of bright sparks** la soudure faisait voler des gerbes d'étincelles

(**e**) *(cut branch)* branche *f*; **forsythia sprays** branches *fpl* de forsythia; **a single spray of orchids in a vase** une simple branche d'orchidées dans un vase

(**f**) *(bouquet)* (petit) bouquet *m*

(**g**) *(brooch)* aigrette *f*

4 *comp (insecticide, deodorant)* en aérosol; *Br Fam* **he took the car in for a spray job** il a amené la voiture au garage pour la faire repeindre❑

►► ***spray can*** *(for aerosol)* bombe *f*, aérosol *m*; *(refillable)* vaporisateur *m*; ***spray gun*** *(for paint)* pistolet *m* (à peinture); ***spray paint*** peinture *f* en bombe; **a can of spray paint** une bombe de peinture

►**spray on 1** *vt sep* appliquer (à la bombe); **he sprayed on some deodorant** il s'est mis un peu de déodorant; **spray the paint on evenly** vaporisez la peinture de façon uniforme

2 *vi (paint, polish, cleaner)* s'appliquer (par pulvérisation); **the product sprays on** le produit est présenté sous forme d'aérosol

sprayer ['spreɪə(r)] *n* (**a**) *(container → for perfume)* atomiseur *m*; *(spray gun)* pistolet *m* (à pein- [illegible] risateur *m*; *(plane)* avion-pulvérisateur *m* (**c**) *(person)* arroseur(euse) *m,f*

spraying ['spreɪɪŋ] *n* (**a**) *(of crops)* pulvérisation *f*; *(against infestation)* traitement *m* (par pulvérisation) (**b**) *(of liquid)* arrosage *m*, arrosement *m*

►► ***spraying mixture*** bouillie *f*

spray-on *adj (lotion, conditioner, lacquer, product)* en bombe, en aérosol; *Fam Hum (jeans)* = qui colle comme une deuxième peau

►► ***spray-on deodorant*** déodorant *m* en bombe *ou* en spray

spray-paint *vt (with can)* peindre à la bombe; *(with spray gun)* peindre au pistolet

spread [spred] *(pt & pp* **spread**) **1** *n* (**a**) *(diffusion, growth → of epidemic, fire)* propagation *f*, progression *f*; *(→ of technology, idea)* diffusion *f*, dissémination *f*; *(→ of religion)* propagation *f*; **they are trying to prevent the spread of unrest to other cities** ils essaient d'empêcher les troubles d'atteindre *ou* de gagner d'autres villes (**b**) *(range → of ages, interests)* gamme *f*, éventail *m*; **spread in interest rates** différentiel *m* de taux d'intérêt; **the commission represented a broad spread of opinion** la commission représentait un large éventail d'opinions; **maximum May temperatures show a ten-point spread** les températures maximales du mois de mai montrent une variation de dix degrés

(**c**) *(of wings)* envergure *f*

(**d**) *(of land)* étendue *f*

(**e**) *(period)* période *f*; **growth occurred over a spread of several years** la croissance s'étala sur une période de plusieurs années

(**f**) *(cover → for bed)* couvre-lit *m* *(tablecloth)* nappe *f*; *(dustcover)* housse *f*

(**g**) *Culin (paste)* pâte *f* à tartiner; *(jam)* confiture *f*; *(butter substitute)* ≃ margarine *f*; **salmon spread** beurre *m* de saumon; **chocolate spread** chocolat *m* à tartiner

(**h**) *Press & Typ (two pages)* double page *f*; *(two-page advertisement)* double page *f* publicitaire; **the event was given a good spread** l'événement a été largement couvert par la presse

(**i**) *Fam (meal)* festin ❑ *m*; **the hotel lays on a decent spread** l'hôtel propose des repas tout à fait convenables ❑; **cold spread** repas *m* froid ❑

(**j**) *Am Fam (farm)* ferme ❑ *f*; *(ranch)* ranch ❑ *m*; **nice spread you've got here!** belle propriété que vous avez là!

(**k**) *St Exch* spread *m*

2 *adj* (**a**) *(arms, fingers, legs)* écarté

(**b**) *Ling (vowel)* non arrondi

3 *vt* (**a**) *(apply → paint, jam, icing, plaster, glue)* étaler; *(→ asphalt)* répandre; *(→ manure)* épandre; **I spread mustard on the ham, I spread the ham with mustard** j'ai étalé de la moutarde sur le jambon; **he spread butter on a slice of toast** *or* **a slice of toast with butter** il a tartiné de beurre une tranche de pain grillé; **to spread ointment on a burn** appliquer *ou* mettre de la pommade sur une brûlure; **to spread the paint evenly** étendre *ou* étaler la peinture en couches égales

(**b**) *(open out, unfold → wings, sails)* étendre, déployer; *(→ arms, legs, fingers)* écarter; *(→ map, napkin, blanket)* étaler; *(→ rug)* étendre; *(→ fan)* ouvrir; **he spread his handkerchief over his face** il étala son mouchoir sur son visage; **she lay on her back, her arms spread** elle était allongée sur le dos, les bras écartés; **a bird with its wings spread** un oiseau aux ailes déployées; *Fig* **it's time you spread your wings** il est temps que vous voliez de vos propres ailes

(**c**) *(disseminate → disease, fire)* propager, répandre; *(→ news, idea, faith)* propager; *(→ rumour)* répandre, faire courir; *(→ lies)* colporter; *(→ terror, panic)* répandre; **the disease is spread by rats** la maladie est propagée par les rats; **the wind will spread the fire to the fields** le vent va propager l'incendie jusque dans les champs; **trade helped to spread the new technology to Asia** le commerce a facilité la diffusion *ou* la dissémination de cette nouvelle technologie en Asie; **the attack is at noon, spread the word!** l'attaque est pour midi, faites passer *ou* passez le mot!; **to spread the gospel** prêcher *ou* répandre l'Évangile; *Fig* répandre la bonne parole

(**d**) *(distribute over an area → photos, cards, possessions)* étaler; *(sand, straw)* répandre; **he spread his papers on the desk** il étala ses papiers sur le bureau; **her hair was spread over the pillow** ses cheveux s'étalaient sur l'oreiller; **we spread the contents of the bag over the floor** nous étalâmes le contenu du sac sur le sol; **the floor was spread with straw** le sol était recouvert de paille; **take your shoes off, you're spreading dirt everywhere!** enlève tes chaussures, tu salis tout!; **the explosion had spread debris over a large area** l'explosion avait dispersé des débris sur une grande superficie; **their troops are spread too thinly to be effective** leurs troupes sont trop dispersées pour être efficaces; *Fig* **to spread oneself too thinly** se disperser

(**e**) *(space out over a period of time)* échelonner, étaler; **the tourist season is now spread over six months** la saison touristique s'étale maintenant sur six mois; **the payments are spread over several months** les paiements sont échelonnés *ou* étalés *ou* répartis sur plusieurs mois; **to spread the losses over five years** répartir les pertes sur cinq ans

(**f**) *(divide up → tax burden, work load)* répartir; **a policy designed to spread wealth more evenly** une mesure qui vise à distribuer plus équitablement les richesses

(**g**) *Mus (chord)* arpéger

4 *vi* (**a**) *(stain)* s'élargir; *(disease, fame, suburb)* s'étendre; *(fire, desert, flood)* gagner du terrain, s'étendre; *(rumour, ideas, faith, terror, crime, suspicion)* se répandre; **panic spread through the crowd** la panique a envahi *ou* gagné la foule; **the epidemic is spreading to other regions** l'épidémie gagne de nouvelles régions; **the cancer had spread through her whole body** le cancer s'était généralisé; **the suburbs are spreading further everyday** les banlieues s'étendent chaque jour un peu plus; **the flood waters have spread across** *or* **over the whole plain** l'inondation a gagné toute la plaine; **the species spread throughout Africa** l'espèce s'est répandue à travers toute l'Afrique

(**b**) *(extend → over a period of time, a range of subjects)* s'étendre; **their correspondence spreads over twenty years** leur correspondance s'étend sur vingt ans

(**c**) *(butter, glue)* s'étaler; **the icing should spread easily** le glaçage devrait s'étaler facilement

(**d**) *St Exch* spéculer sur les différentiels de cours

▸▸ ***spread betting*** = système de paris portant sur le résultat d'un événement sportif ou autre, où les gains sont proportionnels à la justesse des prédictions, selon une fourchette de résultats préétablie; ***spread eagle*** (**a**) *Her* aigle *f* éployée (**b**) *(in skating)* grand aigle *m*; **to do a spread eagle** faire un grand aigle

▸**spread about, spread around** *vt sep (rumour)* répandre; **have you been spreading it about that I...?** est-ce que tu as été raconter partout que je...?

▸**spread out 1** *vt sep* (**a**) *(disperse)* disperser, éparpiller; **the buildings are spread out among the trees** les bâtiments sont dispersés parmi les arbres; **the runners are now spread out (along the course)** les coureurs sont maintenant éparpillés le long du parcours; **the population is very spread out** la population est très dispersée; **in a city as spread out as Los Angeles** dans une ville aussi étendue que Los Angeles

(**b**) *(space out in time → deliveries, payments)* échelonner; **to spread out over several financial years** étaler sur plusieurs exercices; **to spread out the losses over five years** répartir les pertes sur cinq ans

(**c**) *(open out, unfold → wings)* étendre, déployer; *(→ arms, legs, fingers)* écarter; *(→ map, napkin, blanket)* étaler; *(→ rug)* étendre; *(→ fan)* ouvrir; *(lay out → photos, cards, possessions)* étaler; **she lay on her back, her arms spread out** elle était allongée sur le dos, les bras écartés; **a bird with its wings spread out** un oiseau aux ailes déployées; **to spread oneself out** *(on sofa etc)* s'étendre, s'allonger; **the plain lay spread out in front of us** la plaine s'étalait *ou* se déployait devant nous; **he spread his papers out on the desk** il étala ses papiers sur le bureau; **their troops are spread out too thinly to be effective** leurs troupes sont trop dispersées pour être efficaces

2 *vi* (**a**) *(town, forest)* s'étendre

(**b**) *(disperse)* se disperser; *(in formation)* se déployer; **the search party had spread out through the woods** l'équipe de secours s'était déployée à travers les bois

(**c**) *(open out → sail)* se déployer, se gonfler

(**d**) *(make oneself at ease)* s'installer confortablement; **I need an office where I can spread out** j'ai besoin d'un bureau où je puisse étaler mes affaires

spread-eagle 1 *vt* (**a**) *(lay flat)* **he spread-eagled himself against the wall** il se plaqua contre le mur, bras et jambes écartés (**b**) *(knock flat)* envoyer par terre; **he was spread-eagled by the blow** le coup l'a fait tomber à la renverse

2 *adj* (**a**) *(lying flat)* bras et jambes écartés (**b**) *Am Fam (chauvinistic)* chauvin ❑

spread-eagled [-ˌiːgəld] *adj* bras et jambes écartés; **the police had him spread-eagled against the wall** les policiers l'ont plaqué contre le mur, bras et jambes écartés; **sunbathers lay spread-eagled on the sand** des baigneurs étaient étalés sur le sable

spreader [ˈspredə(r)] *n* (**a**) *Agr & Tech (for fertilizer, manure, asphalt)* épandeur *m*, épandeuse *f*; *(for putty, plaster etc)* spatule *f* (**b**) *(person) (of idea)* propagateur(trice) *m,f*; *(of news)* rapporteur(euse) *m,f*; *(of rumour)* colporteur(euse) *m,f*, propagateur(trice) *m,f*

spreading [ˈspredɪŋ] **1** *adj* **a spreading waistline** une taille qui s'épaissit; **under a spreading chestnut tree** sous un châtaignier à la belle ramure

2 *n* (**a**) *(of paint, jam, glue)* étalement *m*; *(of asphalt)* répandage *m*; *(of manure)* épandage *m*; *(of ointment)* application *f*

(**b**) *(of wings, sails)* déploiement *m*

(**c**) *(of disease, fire, news, rumours, ideas)* propagation *f*; *(of lies)* colportage *m*

(**d**) *(over time → of payments)* échelonnement *m*

(**e**) *(division → of burden, work load)* répartition *f*

(**f**) *Mus* arpègement *m*

▸▸ *Entom* ***spreading board*** planche *f* à épingler; *Tex* ***spreading machine*** élargisseuse *f*

spreadsheet [ˈspredʃiːt] *n Comput (document)* feuille *f* de calcul; *(software)* tableur *m*

spree [spriː] *n* fête *f*; **to go/to be on a spree** faire la fête; **her drinking/gambling sprees** les périodes où elle boit/joue; **to go on a shopping spree** faire des folies dans les magasins; **killing spree** accès *m* de folie meurtrière

sprig [sprɪg] *n* brin *m*

sprightliness [ˈspraɪtlɪnɪs] *n (of person)* vivacité *f*, vitalité *f*; *(of tune)* gaieté *f*

sprightly [ˈspraɪtlɪ] (*compar* **sprightlier**, *superl* **sprightliest**) *adj (person)* alerte, fringant; *(step)* vif; *(tune, whistle)* gai; **he's a sprightly 80-year-old** c'est un alerte octogénaire

spring [sprɪŋ] (*pt* **sprang** [spræŋ] *or* **sprung** [sprʌŋ], *pp* **sprung**) **1** *n* (**a**) *(season)* printemps *m*; **in (the) spring** au printemps; **spring is here!** c'est le printemps!

(**b**) *(device, coil)* ressort *m*; *Aut* **the springs** la suspension

(**c**) *(natural source)* source *f*; **hot** *or* **thermal spring** source *f* thermale; **volcanic springs** sources *fpl* volcaniques

(**d**) *(leap)* bond *m*, saut *m*; **he made a sudden spring for the knife** tout à coup, il bondit pour s'emparer du couteau

(**e**) *(resilience)* élasticité *f*; **the diving board has plenty of spring** le plongeoir est très élastique; **the mattress has no spring left** le matelas n'a plus de ressort; **the news put a spring in her step** la nouvelle l'a rendue toute guillerette; **he set out with a spring in his step** il est parti d'un pas alerte

2 *comp* (**a**) *(flowers, weather, colours)* printanier, de printemps; **his new spring collection** sa nouvelle collection de printemps

(**b**) *(mattress)* à ressorts

(**c**) *(water)* de source

3 *vi* (**a**) *(leap)* bondir, sauter; **to spring to one's feet** se lever vivement *ou* d'un bond; **to spring at** bondir *ou* se jeter sur; **the cat sprang at the bird** le chat bondit sur l'oiseau; **he saw the blow coming and sprang away in time** il a vu le coup arriver et l'a esquivé de justesse; **she sprang back in horror** elle recula d'un bond, horrifiée; **the couple sprang apart** le couple se sépara hâtivement; **the bus stopped and she sprang off** le bus s'arrêta et elle descendit d'un bond; **he sprang ashore** il sauta à terre; **the car sprang forward** la voiture fit un bond en avant; **springing out of the armchair** bondissant du fauteuil; **to spring to attention** bondir au garde-à-vous

(**b**) *(be released)* **to spring shut/open** se fermer/s'ouvrir brusquement; **the branch sprang back** la branche s'est redressée d'un coup

(**c**) *Fig* **the police sprang into action** les forces de l'ordre passèrent rapidement à l'action; **the engine sprang to** *or* **into life** le moteur s'est mis soudain en marche *ou* a brusquement démarré; **she sprang to his defence** elle a vivement pris sa défense; **the issue has made the town spring to life** l'affaire a galvanisé la ville; **new towns/companies have sprung into existence** des villes nouvelles/de nouvelles sociétés ont surgi d'on ne sait où *ou* sont soudain apparues; **to spring to the rescue** se précipiter pour porter secours; **tears sprang to his eyes** les larmes lui sont montées *ou* venues aux yeux; **a protest sprang to her lips** elle eut envie de protester; **just say the first thing which springs to mind** dites simplement la première chose qui vous vient à l'esprit; **you didn't notice anything strange? – nothing that springs to mind** vous n'avez rien remarqué d'anormal? – rien qui me frappe particulièrement; **he sprang to fame overnight** il est devenu célèbre du jour au lendemain; *Fam* **where did you spring from?** d'où est-ce que tu sors?; *Literary* **to spring to arms** voler aux armes

(**d**) *(originate)* **to spring from** venir de, provenir de; **the problem springs from a misunderstanding** le problème provient *ou* vient d'un malentendu; **their conservatism springs from fear** leur conservatisme vient de ce qu'ils ont peur

(**e**) *(plank → warp)* gauchir, se gondoler; *(→ crack)* se fendre

(**f**) *Am Fam (pay)* **to spring for sth** casquer pour qch

4 *vt* (**a**) *(trap)* déclencher; *(mine)* faire sauter; *(bolt)* fermer; **the mousetrap had been sprung but it was empty** la souricière avait fonctionné, mais elle était vide

(**b**) *(car)* munir de ressorts; **sprung carriage** voiture *f* suspendue

(**c**) *(make known → decision, news)* annoncer de but en blanc *ou* à brûle-pourpoint; **I hate to have to spring it on you like this** cela m'embête d'avoir à vous l'annoncer de but en blanc comme ça; **he doesn't like people springing surprises on him** il n'aime pas les surprises *ou* qu'on lui réserve des surprises; **to spring a question on sb** poser une question à qn de but en blanc

(**d**) *(develop)* **to spring a leak** *(boat)* commencer à prendre l'eau; *(tank, pipe)* commencer à fuir; **the radiator has sprung a leak** il y a une fuite dans le radiateur

(**e**) *(jump over → hedge, brook)* sauter

(**f**) *(plank → warp)* gauchir, gondoler; *(→ crack)* fendre

(**g**) *Hunt (game)* lever

(**h**) *Fam (prisoner)* faire évader❑; **the gang sprung him from prison with a helicopter** le gang l'a fait évader de prison en hélicoptère

►► *Br* ***spring balance*** peson *m* à ressort; ***the Spring Bank Holiday*** = le dernier lundi de mai, jour férié en Grande-Bretagne; ***spring binding*** reliure *f* à ressort; ***spring chicken*** (**a**) *Am Culin* poulet *m (à rôtir)* (**b**) *(young person)* **he's no spring chicken** il n'est plus tout jeune, il n'est plus de la première jeunesse; ***spring fever*** excitation *f*; **to have spring fever** *(gen)* être tout excité; *(be in love)* être amoureux; *Bot* ***spring gentian*** gentiane *f* printanière; ***spring greens*** choux *mpl* précoces; *Vet* ***spring halt*** éparvin *m* sec, épervin *m* sec; ***spring lock*** serrure *f* à fermeture automatique; *Br* ***spring onion*** petit oignon *m*; ***spring roll*** rouleau *m* de printemps; ***spring snow*** neige *f* de printemps; *Sch & Univ* ***spring term*** ≃ dernier trimestre *m*; ***spring tide*** grande marée *f*; *(at equinox)* marée *f* d'équinoxe (de printemps); ***spring water*** eau *f* de source

►**spring up** *vi* (**a**) *(get up)* se lever d'un bond

(**b**) *(move upwards)* bondir, rebondir; **the lid sprang up** le couvercle s'est ouvert brusquement; **several hands sprang up** plusieurs mains se sont levées

(**c**) *(grow in size, height)* pousser; **hasn't Lisa sprung up this year!** comme Lisa a grandi cette année!

(**d**) *(appear → towns, factories)* surgir, pousser comme des champignons; *(→ doubt, suspicion, rumour, friendship)* naître; *(→ difficulty, threat)* surgir; *(→ breeze)* se lever brusquement; **new companies are springing up every day** de nouvelles entreprises apparaissent chaque jour; **an argument/friendship sprang up between them** une querelle éclata/une amitié naquit entre eux

springboard ['sprɪŋbɔːd] *n Sport & Fig* tremplin *m*; **the job is a springboard for ministerial office** ce poste est un tremplin pour un portefeuille ministériel

springbok ['sprɪŋbɒk] *(pl* **inv** *or* **springboks***)* **1** *n Zool* springbok *m*

2 Springboks *npl* **the Springboks** *(rugby team)* les Springboks *mpl*

spring-clean 1 *vi* faire un nettoyage de printemps

2 *vt* nettoyer de fond en comble

3 *n Br* nettoyage *m* de printemps; **to give the house a spring-clean** nettoyer la maison de fond en comble; *Fig* **the accounting department needs a spring-clean** le service comptabilité a besoin d'un bon coup de balai

spring-cleaning *n* nettoyage *m* de printemps

springe [sprɪndʒ] *n (snare)* collet *m*

springer ['sprɪŋə(r)] *n* (**a**) *(dog)* springer *m* (**b**) *Archit (stone)* sommier *m*; *(impost)* imposte *f*

►► ***springer spaniel*** springer *m*

springhead ['sprɪŋhed] *n* source *f*, fontaine *f*

springiness ['sprɪŋɪnɪs] *n (of spring)* effet *m* de ressort; *(of hair)* gonflant *m*; *(of mattress)* élasticité *f*; *(of turf, ground)* souplesse *f*

springing ['sprɪŋɪŋ] *adj* (**a**) *Literary* **springing corn** blé *m* qui lève (**b**) **a springing step** un pas dansant (**c**) *Her* élancé

springless ['sprɪŋlɪs] *adj Tech* sans ressort(s)

springlike ['sprɪŋlaɪk] *adj (gen)* de printemps; *(dress)* printanier

spring-loaded *adj* à ressort

springtail ['sprɪŋteɪl] *n Entom* podure *f*

springtide ['sprɪŋtaɪd] *n Literary* printemps *m*

springtime ['sprɪŋtaɪm] *n* printemps *m*; *Literary* **she died in the springtime of life** elle est morte dans le printemps de sa vie

springwood ['sprɪŋwʊd] *n* bois *m* de printemps

springy ['sprɪŋɪ] *(compar* **springier**, *superl* **springiest***)* *adj (mattress, diving board)* élastique; *(step)* souple, élastique; *(floor)* souple; *(moss, carpet)* moelleux; *(hair)* dru

sprinkle ['sprɪŋkəl] **1** *vt* (**a**) *(with salt, sugar, spices, breadcrumbs, talc)* saupoudrer (**with** de); *(with parsley, raisins)* parsemer (**with** de); *(with liquid)* arroser légèrement (**with** de); **I sprinkled sugar on** *or* **over my cereal, I sprinkled my cereal with sugar** j'ai saupoudré mes céréales de sucre; **sprinkle with grated cheese** recouvrez de fromage râpé; **he sprinkled sawdust on the floor** il a répandu de la sciure par terre; **to sprinkle water on sth** *or* **sth with water** asperger qch d'eau; **he sprinkled vinegar on** *or* **over his chips** il mit un peu de vinaigre sur ses frites

(**b**) *(usu passive) (strew, dot)* parsemer, semer; **the sky was sprinkled with stars** le ciel était parsemé d'étoiles; **the fields were sprinkled with snow** les champs étaient tachetés de neige; **his hair was sprinkled with grey** ses cheveux étaient légèrement grisonnants; **a speech sprinkled with metaphors** un discours émaillé de métaphores; **a few policemen were sprinkled among the crowd** quelques policiers étaient disséminés dans la foule

2 *vi (rain)* tomber des gouttes

3 *n* (**a**) *(rain)* petite pluie *f*; **I felt a sprinkle (of rain)** j'ai senti quelques gouttes (de pluie)

(**b**) = **sprinkling**

sprinkler ['sprɪŋklə(r)] *n* (**a**) *Agr & Hort* arroseur *m* (automatique) (**b**) *(fire-extinguishing device)* sprinkler *m* (**c**) *(for sugar)* saupoudreuse *f* (**d**) *(for holy water)* goupillon *m*, aspersoir *m*

►► ***sprinkler head*** *(of shower)* pommeau *m*; *(of watering can)* pomme *f*; *(buried in ground)* arroseur *m*; ***sprinkler system*** installation *f* d'extinction automatique d'incendie, installation *f* sprinkler; ***sprinkler truck*** arroseuse *f*

sprinkling ['sprɪŋklɪŋ] *n* (**a**) *(action → with sugar etc)* saupoudrage *m*; *(→ with water)* arrosage *m* léger; *Rel* **sprinkling of holy water** aspergès *m*, aspersion *f*

(**b**) *(small quantity)* petite quantité *f*; *(pinch)* pincée *f*; **a sprinkling of paprika makes all the difference** une pincée de paprika fait toute la différence; **it was a male audience with a sprinkling of women** c'était une assistance masculine avec quelques rares femmes; **a sprinkling of new faces in the congregation** quelques nouvelles têtes ici et là dans la congrégation; **with a liberal sprinkling of literary references** avec moult références littéraires données ici et là; **a sprinkling of freckles gave his face a youthful look** quelques taches de rousseur donnaient à son visage un air de jeunesse; **there was a sprinkling of grey in her hair** elle avait quelques cheveux gris

sprint [sprɪnt] **1** *n Sport (dash)* sprint *m*; *(race)* course *f* de vitesse, sprint *m*; **he was beaten in the finishing sprint** il a été battu au sprint final; **the 60 metre sprint** le 60 mètres; **to break into** *or* **to put on a sprint** piquer un sprint

2 *vi* sprinter; **I was good at sprinting** j'étais bon dans les courses de vitesse; **the little boy sprinted off** le petit garçon s'élança à toutes jambes; **he sprinted upstairs** il est monté en courant; **he sprinted after her** il a couru derrière elle à toute vitesse; **I had to sprint for the bus** j'ai dû courir *ou Fam* piquer un sprint pour attraper le bus

►► ***sprint finish*** sprint *m*; **there was a sprint finish** il y a eu un sprint à l'arrivée; **he has a good sprint finish** il est très rapide dans les sprints (de fin de course)

sprinter ['sprɪntə(r)] **1** *n* sprinter *m*

2 Sprinter *n Br Transp* = train de banlieue express

sprit [sprɪt] *n* livarde *f*, balestron *m*

sprite [spraɪt] *n Myth (male)* lutin *m*, farfadet *m* ; *(female)* nymphe *f*; **water sprite** naïade *f*

spritzer ['sprɪtsə(r)] *n* = mélange de vin blanc et de soda

sprocket ['sprɒkɪt] *n* (**a**) *(wheel)* pignon *m*; *Phot* **film transport sprocket** pignon *m* d'entraînement de la pellicule (**b**) *(cog)* dent *f* (de pignon)

►► ***sprocket hole*** *(for film)* perforation *f*

sprog [sprɒg] *n Br Fam* (**a**) *(child)* gosse *mf*, môme *mf* (**b**) *Mil (novice)* bleu *m*

sprout [spraʊt] **1** *n* (**a**) *(on plant, from ground)* pousse *f*; *(from bean, potato)* germe *m*, *Belg* jet *m*; **alfalfa sprouts** germes de luzerne

(**b**) **(Brussels) sprouts** choux *mpl* de Bruxelles

(**c**) *Am Fam (child)* gosse *mf*, môme *mf*

2 *vi* (**a**) *(germinate → bean, seed, onion)* germer, *Belg* jeter

(**b**) *(grow → plant, leaves, hair)* pousser; **he had hair sprouting from his ears** des touffes de poils lui sortaient des oreilles

(**c**) *(appear)* apparaître, surgir; **satellite TV receivers have sprouted on all the rooftops** des antennes paraboliques ont surgi sur tous les toits

3 *vt* (**a**) *(grow → leaves)* pousser, produire; *(→ beard)* se laisser pousser; **some lizards can sprout new tails** la queue de certains lézards repousse; *Fam* **to sprout a moustache** se laisser pousser la moustache❑

(**b**) *(germinate → seeds, beans, lentils)* faire germer

►**sprout up** *vi* (**a**) *(grow → grass, wheat, plant)* pousser, pointer; *(→ person)* pousser; **hasn't she sprouted up!** comme elle a poussé!

(**b**) *(appear → towns, factories)* pousser comme des champignons, surgir; *(→ new community, sect)* surgir, naître; **a tented city had sprouted up overnight** une ville de toile avait poussé *ou* surgi pendant la nuit

spruce [spruːs] *(pl* **inv***)* **1** *n Bot* épicéa *m*; *(timber)* épinette *f*

2 *adj (person, car, building, town)* pimpant; *(haircut)* net; *(garment)* impeccable; **spruce white curtains** des rideaux blancs impeccables; **she looked very spruce in her uniform** elle était toute pimpante dans son uniforme

►**spruce up** *vt sep (car, building, town)* donner un coup de neuf à; *(paintwork)* refaire; *(child)* faire beau (belle); **a coat of paint will spruce the room up** une couche de peinture rafraîchira la pièce; **his image needs sprucing up** son image de marque a besoin d'être rafraîchie; **to spruce oneself up, to get spruced up** se faire beau; **he was all spruced up** il était tiré à quatre épingles, il était sur son trente et un

sprucely ['spru:slɪ] *adv (painted, polished, starched)* impeccablement; **sprucely dressed** tiré à quatre épingles

spruceness ['spru:snɪs] *n (of person)* mise *f* soignée; *(of house, room)* propreté *f*

sprue¹ [spru:] *n Tech* (**a**) *(channel of mould)* trou *m* de coulée (**b**) *(solidifed metal or plastic)* carotte *f*, queue *f* de coulée

sprue² *n Med* sprue *f*, psilosis *m*

spruik ['spru:ɪk] *vi Austr Fam (salesperson)* faire l'article

spruiker ['spru:ɪkə(r)] *n Austr Fam (salesperson)* = personne qui fait l'article

sprung [sprʌŋ] **1** *pt & pp of* **spring**

2 *adj (mattress)* à ressorts

►► *Literature* ***sprung rhythm*** = mètre heurté proche du rythme naturel de la parole

spry [spraɪ] *(compar* **sprier** *or* **spryer,** *superl* **spriest** *or* **spryest**) *adj (person)* alerte, leste

spryly ['spraɪlɪ] *adv* agilement, lestement; **she leapt spryly out of bed** elle sauta lestement hors du lit

SPUC [spʌk] *n (abbr* **Society for the Protection of the Unborn Child**) = ligue américaine contre l'avortement

spud [spʌd] **1** *n* (**a**) *Fam (potato)* patate *f* (**b**) *(gardening tool)* sarcloir *m*

2 *vt Petr* **to spud a well (in)** amorcer un puits

spud-bashing *n Br Fam* corvée *f* de patates

spumaretrovirus ['spju:məretrəʊˌvaɪrəs] *n Med* rétrovirus *m* spumeux

spume [spju:m] *n Literary* écume *f*

spumescence [spju:'mesəns] *n* spumosité *f*

spumescent [spju:'mesənt] *adj* spumescent

spun [spʌn] **1** *pt & pp of* **spin**

2 *adj* filé; **her hair was like spun gold** elle avait des cheveux d'or

►► ***spun glass*** verre *m* filé; ***spun silk*** schappe *f*; *Culin* ***spun sugar*** sucre *m* filé; ***spun yarn*** bitord *m*

spunk [spʌŋk] *n* (**a**) *Fam (pluck)* cran *m*, nerf *m*; **show some spunk!** un peu de nerf, voyons! (**b**) *Br Vulg (semen)* foutre *m* (**c**) *Austr Fam (attractive woman)* canon *m*; *(attractive man)* beau mec *m*

spunky ['spʌŋkɪ] *(compar* **spunkier,** *superl* **spunkiest**) *adj Fam* (**a**) *(courageous → person)* plein de cran, qui a du cran; *(→ retort, fight)* courageux (**b**) *Br & Austr (attractive)* canon

spur [spɜ:(r)] *(pt & pp* **spurred,** *cont* **spurring**) **1** *n* (**a**) *Horseriding* éperon *m*; **to dig in one's spurs** piquer des éperons; *Hist* **to win one's spurs** gagner son épée de chevalier; *Fig* faire ses preuves

(**b**) *Fig (stimulation)* aiguillon *m*; **the spur of competition** l'aiguillon de la concurrence; **easy credit is a spur to consumption** le crédit facile pousse *ou* incite à la consommation; **on the spur of the moment** sans réfléchir

(**c**) *Geog (ridge)* éperon *m*, saillie *f*

(**d**) *Rail (siding)* voie *f* latérale *ou* de garage; *(branch line)* embranchement *m*; **the warehouse is served by a spur line** l'entrepôt est desservi par un embranchement

(**e**) *(on motorway)* bretelle *f*

(**f**) *(breakwater)* brise-lames *m inv*, digue *f*

(**g**) *Bot & Zool* éperon *m*; *(on gamecock)* ergot *m*

2 *vt* (**a**) *(horse)* éperonner

(**b**) *Fig* inciter; **her words spurred me into action** ses paroles m'ont incité à agir

►**spur on** *vt sep* (**a**) *(horse)* éperonner

(**b**) *Fig* éperonner, aiguillonner; **their shouts spurred us on** leurs cris nous aiguillonnaient *ou* encourageaient; **to spur sb on to do sth** inciter *ou* pousser qn à faire qch; **these developments in business have been spurred on by the information technology revolution** cette évolution commerciale a été favorisée par la révolution des technologies de l'information

spurge [spɜ:dʒ] *n Bot* euphorbe *f*

►► ***spurge laurel*** daphné *m*

spurious ['spʊərɪəs] *adj* (**a**) *(false → gen)* faux (fausse); *(→ comparison, argument, reason, objection, distinction)* spécieux; **your claim is a spurious one** votre revendication est sans fondement (**b**) *(pretended → enthusiasm, sympathy)* simulé; *(→ flattery, compliment)* hypocrite (**c**) *(of doubtful origin → text)* apocryphe

spuriously ['spjʊərɪəslɪ] *adv* faussement

spuriousness ['spjʊərɪəsnɪs] *n* (**a**) *(gen)* fausseté *f*; *(of comparison, argument, reason, distinction)* non-validité *f* (**b**) *(of enthusiasm, sympathy)* fausseté *f* (**c**) *(of text)* caractère *m* apocryphe

spurn [spɜ:n] *vt (gen)* dédaigner, mépriser; *(suitor)* éconduire, rejeter; **those who spurn tradition** ceux qui dédaignent les traditions; **a spurned lover** un amoureux éconduit

spur-of-the-moment *adj (purchase, phone call)* fait sur le coup *ou* sans réfléchir; *(excuse, tactics, invitation)* improvisé; **I made a spur-of-the-moment decision** je me suis décidé sur le moment

spurred [spɜ:d] *adj (boots)* à éperons

spurrey ['spʌrɪ] *(pl* **spurries**) *n Bot* spergule *f*

Spurs [spɜ:z] *n* = surnom donné à l'équipe de football Tottenham Hotspur

spurt [spɜ:t] **1** *vi* (**a**) *(water, blood)* jaillir, gicler; *(flames, steam)* jaillir; **beer spurted (out) from the can** la bière a giclé de la boîte; **the milk spurted into the pail** le lait gicla dans le seau; **some lemon juice spurted into my eye** j'ai reçu une giclée de jus de citron dans l'œil

(**b**) *(dash → runner, cyclist)* sprinter, piquer un sprint; **he spurted past us** il nous a dépassés comme une flèche; **the car spurted through the maze of streets** la voiture fila à travers le dédale de rues

2 *vt (gush → of pierced container)* laisser jaillir; *(spit → of gun, chimney)* cracher; **his wound spurted blood** le sang gicla *ou* jaillit de sa blessure; **we spurted each other with water** nous nous sommes mutuellement aspergés d'eau; **the pipe spurted water everywhere** de l'eau jaillissait du tuyau; **the pen spurted ink onto the carpet** l'encre jaillit du stylo et tacha la moquette

3 *n* (**a**) *(of steam, water, flame)* jaillissement *m*; *(of blood, juice)* giclée *f*; **the water came out of the tap in spurts** l'eau jaillit du robinet par à-coups; **a spurt of machine gun fire** une rafale de mitrailleuse

(**b**) *(dash)* accélération *f*; *(at work)* coup *m* de collier; *(revival)* regain *m*; *(flash → of temper, jealousy, sympathy)* sursaut *m*; **to put on a spurt** *(while running, cycling)* piquer un sprint; *(while working)* donner un coup de collier; **after a brief spurt of economic growth** après un bref regain de croissance économique; **a spurt in prices** une poussée *ou* flambée des prix; **her inspiration came in spurts** l'inspiration lui venait par à-coups

►**spurt out** *vi* = **spurt** *vi* (**a**)

spurtle ['spɜ:təl] *n Scot* = bâton en bois servant à remuer le porridge, la soupe etc

Sputnik ['spʊtnɪk] *n* Spoutnik *m*

sputter ['spʌtə(r)] **1** *vi* (**a**) *(motor)* toussoter, crachoter; *(fire, candle)* crépiter; *(meat on grill)* grésiller; **the engine sputtered to a halt** le moteur s'arrêta dans un toussotement

(**b**) *(stutter)* bredouiller, bafouiller; **he sputtered angrily** il bredouillait de colère

(**c**) *(spit → gen)* crachoter; *(→ when talking)* postillonner

2 *vt (apology, curses)* bredouiller, bafouiller

3 *n* (**a**) *(of motor)* toussotement *m*, hoquet *m*; *(of fire, candle)* crépitement *m*; **the engine gave a final sputter** le moteur toussa une dernière fois

(**b**) *(stuttering)* bredouillement *m*; **"go away!" he said with a sputter** "va-t'en!", bredouilla-t-il

►**sputter out** *vi (candle, enthusiasm, anger)* s'éteindre

sputum ['spju:təm] *(pl* **sputa** [-tə]) *n Med* crachat *m*, expectoration *f*

spy [spaɪ] *(pl* **spies,** *pt & pp* **spied**) **1** *n* espion(onne) *m,f*

2 *comp (novel, film, scandal)* d'espionnage; *(network)* d'espions

3 *vi (engage in espionage)* faire de l'espionnage; **accused of spying for the enemy** accusé d'espionnage au profit de l'ennemi

4 *vt Literary (notice)* apercevoir; *(make out)* discerner; **he spied someone running away** il a aperçu quelqu'un qui se sauvait

►► ***spy plane*** avion-espion *m*; ***spy ring*** réseau *m* d'espions; ***spy satellite*** satellite *m* espion

►**spy on** *vt insep* espionner; **they now spy on each other using satellites** maintenant ils s'espionnent à l'aide de satellites; **you've been spying on me!** tu m'as espionné!

►**spy out** *vt sep (sb's methods, designs)* chercher à découvrir (subrepticement); *(landing sites)* repérer; *also Fig* **to spy out the land** reconnaître le terrain

'The Spy Who Came in From the Cold' *Le Carré*
'L'Espion qui venait du froid'

spycatcher ['spaɪˌkætʃə(r)] *n* chasseur *m* d'espions

spyglass ['spaɪglɑ:s] *n* longue-vue *f*

spyhole ['spaɪhəʊl] *n* judas *m*

spying ['spaɪɪŋ] *n (gen) & Ind* espionnage *m*

spymaster ['spaɪˌmɑ:stə(r)] *n* chef *m* des services secrets

Sq. *(written abbr* **Square**) *(in addresses)* ≃ Place

sq. ft. *(written abbr* **square foot/feet**) pied(s) carré(s)

SQL [ˌeskju:'el] *n Comput (abbr* **structured query language**) SQL *m*

►► ***SQL engine*** processeur *m* SQL

Sqn. Ldr. *Br Mil (written abbr* **Squadron Leader**) ≃ commandant *m*, *Belg & Can* ≃ major *m*

squab [skwɒb] *(pl* **inv** *or* **squabs,** *compar* **squabber,** *superl* **squabbest**) **1** *n* (**a**) *Orn* pigeonneau *m* (**b**) *(person)* homme *m* rond *ou* rondelet, femme *f* ronde *ou* rondelette (**c**) *(cushion)* coussin *m* bien rembourré; *(sofa)* sofa *m*; *Aut (of car seat)* dossier *m*

2 *adj* (**a**) *(tubby)* rond, enrobé (**b**) *Orn* sans plumes

squabble ['skwɒbəl] **1** *vi* se disputer, se quereller

2 *n* dispute *f*, querelle *f*

squabbler ['skwɒbələ(r)] *n* querelleur(euse) *m,f*, chamailleur(euse) *m,f*

squabbling ['skwɒbəlɪŋ] *n (UNCOUNT)* chamailleries *fpl*, disputes *fpl*

squacco heron ['skwækəʊ-] *n Orn* héron *m* crabier

squad [skwɒd] *n* (**a**) *(group → gen)* équipe *f*, escouade *f*; *Sport* **the England football squad** l'équipe anglaise de football (**b**) *Mil* escouade *f*, section *f* (**c**) *(of police detachment)* brigade *f*

►► ***squad car*** voiture *f* de patrouille de police

squaddie, squaddy ['skwɒdɪ] *(pl* **squaddies**) *n Br Fam* bidasse *m*, troufion *m*

squadron ['skwɒdrən] *n (in air force)* escadron *m*; *(in navy → small)* escadrille *f*; *(→ large)* escadre *f*; *(in armoured regiment, cavalry)* escadron *m*

►► *Br* ***squadron leader*** *(in air force)* ≃ commandant *m*, *Belg & Can* ≃ major *m*

squalid ['skwɒlɪd] *adj* sordide

squalidity [skwɒ'lɪdɪtɪ] *n (sordid conditions)* conditions *fpl* sordides; *(filth)* saleté *f* repoussante

squalidly ['skwɒlɪdlɪ] *adv* de façon sordide

squalidness ['skwɒlɪdnɪs] *n (sordid conditions)* conditions *fpl* sordides; *(filth)* saleté *f* repoussante

squall [skwɔ:l] **1** *n* (**a**) *Met (storm)* bourrasque *f*, rafale *f*; *Naut* grain *m*; *(rain shower)* grain *m*; **snow squalls** bourrasques *fpl* de neige (**b**) *(argument)* dispute *f*; **the treaty ratification caused a squall in Parliament** la ratification du traité a soulevé une tempête au Parlement (**c**) *(bawling)* braillement *m*

2 *vi* (**a**) *(bawl)* brailler; **he could hear squalling children** il entendait brailler des enfants (**b**) *Naut* **it was squalling** on a pris un grain

3 *vt* **"no!" he squalled** "non!", brailla-t-il

squaller ['skwɔ:lə(r)] *n* braillard(arde) *m,f*, brailleur(euse) *m,f*

squalling ['skwɔ:lɪŋ] **1** *adj* braillard

2 *n* braillements *mpl*

squally ['skwɔ:lɪ] *(compar* **squallier,** *superl* **squalliest**) *adj (wind)* qui souffle par *ou* en rafales; *(rain)* qui tombe en rafales; **there will be squally showers in the morning** il y aura des averses en rafales dans la matinée

squalor ['skwɒlə(r)] *n (UNCOUNT) (sordid conditions)* conditions *fpl* sordides; *(filth)* saleté *f* repoussante; **to live in squalor** vivre dans des conditions sordides *ou* dans une misère noire;

the squalor of *or* **in the stairwell** la saleté repoussante de la cage d'escalier

squama ['skweɪmə] *n* (**a**) *Zool & Med* squame *f* (**b**) *Bot* écaille *f*

squamate ['skweɪmeɪt] *adj (reptile)* squamifère

squamous ['skweɪməs] *adj (scaly)* écailleux; *(flaky)* squameux

▸▸ *Biol* ***squamous cell*** cellule *f* épithéliale; ***squamous epithelium*** épithélium *m* simple

squander ['skwɒndə(r)] *vt (resources, time, money)* gaspiller; *(fortune, inheritance)* dissiper; *(opportunity)* gâcher, passer à côté de; **huge sums were squandered on unworkable schemes** des sommes énormes ont été dépensées en pure perte pour des projets irréalisables

squanderer ['skwɒndərə(r)] *n (of resources, time, money)* gaspilleur(euse) *m,f*; *(of fortune, inheritance)* dissipateur(trice) *m,f*

squandering ['skwɒndərɪŋ] *n (of resources, time, money)* gaspillage *m*; *(of fortune, inheritance)* dissipation *f*; *(of opportunity)* fait *m* de gâcher *or* de passer à côté de

SQUARE [skweə(r)]

carré	▸ 1 (a), (b), (e); 2 (a), (b)
case	▸ 1 (c)
place	▸ 1 (d)
square	▸ 1 (d)
équerre	▸ 1 (f)
ringard	▸ 1 (g); 2 (g)
à angle droit	▸ 2 (c)
honnête	▸ 2 (d)
net	▸ 2 (e)
équilibré	▸ 2 (f)
quitte	▸ 2 (f)
mettre droit	▸ 4 (a)
carrer	▸ 4 (a), (b)
concilier	▸ 4 (c)
régler	▸ 4 (d)
arranger	▸ 4 (f)

1 *n* (**a**) *(shape → gen) & Geom* carré *m*; **she arranged the pebbles in a square** elle a disposé les cailloux en carré; **he folded the napkin into a neat square** il a plié la serviette en un carré bien net; **cut the cake into squares** coupez le gâteau en carrés; *Fam* **to be on the square** être réglo; *Fam* **I'm telling you this on the square** je vous le dis carrément

(**b**) *(square object → gen)* carré *m*; *(→ tile)* carreau *m*; **a silk square** un carré de soie; **a square of chocolate** un carré *ou* morceau de chocolat; **a bathroom in grey and white squares** une salle de bains avec un carrelage gris et blanc

(**c**) *(square space → in matrix, crossword, board game)* case *f*; **to divide a map into squares** quadriller une carte; **locate square D4 on the map** trouvez la case D4 sur la carte; *Fig* **we're back at** *or* **to square one** nous voilà revenus à la case départ; **I had to start from square one again** j'ai dû repartir à zéro

(**d**) *(in town, village → with streets)* place *f*; *(→ with gardens)* square *m*; *Mil (parade ground)* place *f* d'armes; **barrack square** cour *f* de caserne; **the town square** la place, la grand-place

(**e**) *Math (of number)* carré *m*; **nine is the square of three** neuf est le carré de trois

(**f**) *Math & Tech (instrument)* équerre *f*; **to cut sth on the square** couper qch à angles droits; **out of square** qui n'est pas d'équerre

(**g**) *Fam Pej (person)* ringard(e) *m,f*; **he's such a square!** qu'est-ce qu'il est ringard!

2 *adj* (**a**) *(in shape → field, box, building, face)* carré; **a tall man with square shoulders** un homme grand aux épaules carrées; *Fig* **to be a square peg in a round hole** ne pas être à sa place; *Hum* **you'll get square eyes if you keep watching TV all day** tu vas t'abîmer les yeux à force de regarder la télé

(**b**) *(metre, mile, inch etc)* carré; **10 square kilometres** 10 kilomètres carrés; **the room is 5 metres square** la pièce fait 5 mètres sur 5

(**c**) *(right-angled)* à angle droit; **a square corner** un angle droit; **the shelves aren't square** les étagères ne sont pas droites; **square with** *or* **to** *(at right angles)* à angle droit avec; *(parallel)* parallèle à

(**d**) *(fair, honest)* honnête, correct; **to be square with sb** être honnête *ou* correct avec qn; **to give sb a square deal** agir correctement avec qn; **I got a square deal on the car rental** je n'ai rien à redire au prix de location de la voiture; **the farmers aren't getting a square deal** les perdants dans l'affaire, ce sont les agriculteurs

(**e**) *(blunt → denial, refusal)* net, catégorique; **he won't give me a square answer** il refuse de me donner une réponse claire et nette

(**f**) *(even, balanced → accounts, books)* équilibré; **to be square with sb** être quitte envers qn; **they are (all) square** *(financially)* ils sont quittes; *(in competition)* ils sont à égalité; **they were (all) square at two games each** ils étaient à égalité deux parties chacun; **to get square with sb** *(get revenge)* régler son compte à qn; *(settle debts)* être quitte envers qn; **did you get things square with Julia?** est-ce que tu as pu arranger les choses avec Julia?

(**g**) *Fam (old-fashioned)* ringard

(**h**) *(proper)* **I haven't had a square meal in days** ça fait plusieurs jours que je n'ai pas fait de vrai repas;

3 *adv* (**a**) *(at right angles)* **she set the box square with** *or* **to the edge of the paper** elle a aligné la boîte sur les bords de la feuille de papier

(**b**) *(parallel)* **the house stands square to the street** la maison est parallèle à la rue

(**c**) *(directly)* **square in the middle** en plein milieu; **he hit the ball square in the middle of the racket** il frappa la balle avec le milieu de sa raquette; **she looked him square in the face/eyes** elle le regarda bien en face/droit dans les yeux; **the blow landed square on his nose** il a reçu le coup en plein sur le nez

(**d**) *(honestly)* honnêtement

4 *vt* (**a**) *(make square → pile of paper)* mettre droit, aligner; *(→ stone)* carrer; *(→ log)* équarrir; *(→ shoulders)* redresser; **it's like trying to square the circle** c'est la quadrature du cercle

(**b**) *Math* carrer, élever au carré; **three squared is nine** trois au carré égale neuf

(**c**) *(reconcile)* concilier; **how do you square your wealth with being a socialist?** comment arrivez-vous à concilier votre richesse avec vos idées socialistes?; **I couldn't square the story with the image I had of him** je n'arrivais pas à faire coïncider cette histoire avec l'image que j'avais de lui

(**d**) *(settle → account, bill)* régler; *(→ debt)* acquitter; *(→ books)* balancer, mettre en ordre; **to square accounts with sb** *(pay money owed)* régler (ses comptes avec) qn; *(get revenge)* régler son compte à qn

(**e**) *Sport* **his goal squared the match** son but a mis les équipes à égalité

(**f**) *(arrange)* arranger; **can you square it with the committee?** pourriez-vous arranger cela avec le comité?; **how do you square it with your conscience?** comment arrangez-vous cela avec votre conscience?; **we shouldn't do it unless we square it with them first** nous ne devrions pas le faire avant d'avoir arrangé ça avec eux

(**g**) *Fam (bribe)* soudoyer ❑

5 *vi* cadrer, concorder; **his story doesn't square with the facts** son histoire ne cadre *ou* ne coïncide pas avec les faits; **her figures/results don't square with mine** ses chiffres/résultats ne cadrent pas avec les miens; **does their offer square with your asking price?** leur offre correspond-elle au prix que vous demandez?

▸▸ *Sport* ***square ball*** passe *f* latérale; ***square bracket*** crochet *m*; **in square brackets** entre crochets; ***square dance*** quadrille *m*, *Can* danse *f* carrée; ***square dancing*** quadrille *m* américain, *Can* danse *f* carrée; **there'll be square dancing at the saloon tonight** on va danser au saloon ce soir; *Am* ***square knot*** nœud *m* plat; ***square leg*** *(in cricket)* = chasseur situé derrière le batteur; ***square measure*** mesure *f* de surface *ou* de superficie; ***the Square Mile*** = la City de Londres *(dont la superficie fait environ un mile carré)*; ***square number*** carré *m*; ***square pass*** passe *f* latérale; *Naut* ***square rigger*** navire *m* gréé en carré; ***square root*** racine *f* carrée; *Am Fam* ***square shooter*** personne *f* franche ❑; *Electron* ***square wave*** onde *f* carrée *ou* rectangulaire

▸**square away** *vt sep Am Fam* régler ❑, mettre en ordre ❑; **did you get everything squared away?** est-ce que tu as pu tout régler?

▸**square off 1** *vt sep* (**a**) *(piece of paper, terrain)* quadriller

(**b**) *(stick, log)* mettre d'équerre, équarrir

2 *vi (opponents, boxers)* se mettre en garde

▸**square up 1** *vt sep (make square → end of plank)* mettre d'équerre, équarrir

2 *vi* (**a**) *(settle debt)* faire les comptes; **to square up with sb** régler ses comptes avec qn; **I'll square up with you when you have finished all the work** je réglerai mes comptes avec toi dès que tu auras fini tout le travail

(**b**) *(opponents, boxers)* se mettre en garde

(**c**) *Am Fam (criminal)* raccrocher, se ranger des voitures; *(drug addict)* décrocher

▸**square up to** *vt insep (confront → difficulties, situation, criticism)* faire face *ou* front à; *(→ opponent, boxer)* se mettre en position de combat contre; **he squared up to me** il se mit en garde devant moi; **the unions are squaring up to the management** les syndicats cherchent la confrontation avec la direction

---

square-bashing *n (UNCOUNT) Br Fam Mil slang* exercice ❑ *m*

square-built *adj (person)* aux épaules carrées; *(short and sturdy)* trapu; *(building)* carré

square-cut *adj (gem, rock)* coupé à angle droit *ou* d'équerre; *(log)* équarri; *Fig (jaw)* carré

squared [skweəd] *adj (paper)* quadrillé

square-dance *vi* danser le quadrille, *Can* faire une danse carrée

square-eyed *adj Fam Hum* qui passe sa vie devant la télévision

square-headed *adj* à tête carrée

squarely ['skweəlɪ] *adv* (**a**) *(firmly)* fermement, carrément; *(directly)* en plein; **squarely opposed to** fermement opposé à; **we must confront the dilemma squarely** nous devons affronter ce dilemme avec fermeté; **to look sb squarely in the eye** regarder qn droit dans les yeux; **squarely in the middle** en plein milieu; **the blow landed squarely on his nose** il a reçu le coup en plein sur le nez (**b**) *(honestly)* honnêtement; **to deal squarely with sb** agir avec qn de façon honnête

squareness ['skweənɪs] *n* (**a**) *(shape)* forme *f* carrée (**b**) *Fam (of person, views)* conservatisme ❑ *m*

square-rigged *adj Naut (boat)* gréé en carré

square-shouldered [-'ʃəʊldəd] *adj* aux épaules carrées

square-toed *adj (shoes)* à bout carré

squarial ['skweərɪəl] *n Br* = antenne carrée permettant de recevoir la télévision par satellite

squaring ['skweərɪŋ] *n* (**a**) *(of account)* règlement *m* (**b**) **the squaring of the circle** la quadrature du cercle

squarish ['skweərɪʃ] *adj (shape)* plutôt carré; *(person)* trapu

squarrose [skwæ'rəʊs] *adj Biol* squarreux

squash [skwɒʃ] **1** *vt* (**a**) *(crush)* écraser; **he sat on my hat and squashed it** en s'asseyant il a écrasé mon chapeau; **you're squashing me!** tu m'écrases!; **I was squashed between two large ladies** j'étais serré *ou* coincé entre deux grosses dames; **we were squashed in like sardines** nous étions serrés comme des sardines

(**b**) *(cram, stuff)* fourrer; **she squashed the laundry down in the bag** elle a tassé le linge dans le sac; **I squashed another sweater into my rucksack** j'ai pu faire entrer un pull supplémentaire dans mon sac à dos

(**c**) *(silence, repress → person)* remettre à sa place; *(→ objection)* écarter; *(→ suggestion)* repousser; *(→ argument)* réfuter; *(→ hopes)* réduire à néant; *(→ rumour)* mettre fin à; *(→ rebellion)* réprimer; **she squashed him with a look** elle l'a foudroyé du regard

2 *vi* (**a**) *(push → people)* s'entasser; **all seven of us managed to squash into her car** on a réussi à s'entasser à sept dans sa voiture

(**b**) *(fruit, package)* s'écraser; **be careful, the fruit squashes easily** faites attention, ces fruits s'écrasent facilement

3 *n* (**a**) *(crush of people)* cohue *f*; **with five of us it'll be a bit of a squash** à cinq, nous serons un peu serrés

(**b**) *Sport* squash *m*

(**c**) *Br (drink)* **lemon/orange squash** sirop *m* de citron/d'orange

(**d**) *(vegetable)* courge *f*

4 *comp (ball, court, champion, racket)* de squash

►► ***squash court*** court *m* de squash; *Old-fashioned* ***squash hat*** chapeau *m* mou; *Br* ***squash rackets*** *(game)* squash *m*

►**squash in** *vi (people)* s'entasser; **the lift arrived and everybody squashed in** l'ascenseur arriva et tout le monde s'entassa dedans; **I squashed in between two very fat men** je me suis fait une petite place entre deux hommes énormes

►**squash together 1** *vi (people)* se serrer (les uns contre les autres), s'entasser

2 *vt sep* serrer, tasser

►**squash up 1** *vi (people)* se serrer (les uns contre les autres), s'entasser

2 *vt sep* écraser

squashy ['skwɒʃɪ] *(compar* **squashier,** *superl* **squashiest)** *adj (fruit, package)* mou (molle); *(cushion, sofa)* moelleux; *(ground)* spongieux

squat [skwɒt] *(pt & pp* **squatted,** *cont* **squatting,** *compar* **squatter,** *superl* **squattest) 1** *vi* (**a**) *(crouch → person)* s'accroupir; *(→ animal)* se tapir; **we ate squatting (down) on our haunches** nous avons mangé accroupis

(**b**) *(occupy building)* vivre dans un squat; **they're allowed to squat in abandoned buildings** on leur permet de squatter dans des immeubles abandonnés

2 *vt (building)* squatter, squattériser

3 *n* (**a**) *(building)* squat *m*; *(action)* squat *m*, occupation *f* de logements vides; **the squat held out for two years** le squat a duré deux ans

(**b**) *(crouch)* accroupissement *m*

(**c**) *Am very Fam (nothing)* que dalle

4 *adj (person, figure)* trapu; *(building)* trapu, massif; **he had short, squat legs** il avait des petites jambes trapues

►► *Zool* ***squat lobster*** galathée *f*; ***squat thrust*** = exercice de musculation des jambes effectué accroupi

squatter ['skwɒtə(r)] *n* (**a**) *(unlawful occupier)* squatter *m*; **there are squatter settlements all round the town** il y a des communautés de squatters un peu partout autour de la ville (**b**) *Austr (rancher)* squatter *m*, éleveur *m*

squattocracy [ˌskwɒ'tɒkrəsɪ] *n Austr Fam Pej* gros propriétaires *mpl* terriens *(en Australie)*

squaw [skwɔː] *n* (**a**) *(American Indian)* squaw *f* (**b**) *Fam Pej or Hum (woman)* femme ❑ *f*, gonzesse *f*; *(wife)* épouse ❑ *f*; **my squaw** la patronne, ma bourgeoise

squawk [skwɔːk] **1** *vi* (**a**) *(bird)* criailler; *(person)* brailler

(**b**) *Fam (complain)* criailler ❑, râler

(**c**) *Fam (inform)* moucharder, vendre la mèche

2 *vt* **"let go of me!" she squawked** "lâchez-moi!", brailla-t-elle

3 *n* (**a**) *(of bird)* criaillement *m*, cri *m*; *(of person)* cri *m* rauque; **to let out** *or* **to give a squawk** pousser un cri rauque; *Fig* **the measure raised squawks of protest from the oil industry** cette mesure a suscité de vives protestations au sein de l'industrie pétrolière

(**b**) *Am Fam (complaint)* plainte ❑ *f*; **what's your squawk?** c'est quoi ton problème?

►► *Am Fam* ***squawk box*** *(loudspeaker)* haut-parleur ❑ *m*; *(intercom)* interphone ❑ *m*; *(telephone)* bigophone *m*

squawker ['skwɔːkə(r)] *n* (**a**) *(loudspeaker)* haut-parleur *m* (**b**) *Am Fam (complainer)* rouspéteur(euse) *m,f*

squawman ['skwɔːmən] *n Am Pej* = mari ou ami d'une femme indienne d'Amérique qui n'est pas lui-même indien

squeak [skwiːk] **1** *vi* (**a**) *(floorboard, chalk, wheel, machine part)* grincer; *(animal)* piauler, piailler; *(person)* glapir; *(shoes)* crisser; *(toy)* couiner; **she squeaked with delight** elle poussa un cri de joie

(**b**) *Fam (succeed narrowly)* **the team squeaked into the finals** l'équipe s'est qualifiée de justesse pour la finale ❑; **they squeaked past Canada to become the biggest wheat producer** ils ont dépassé le Canada de justesse pour devenir le plus grand producteur de blé ❑

(**c**) *Fam (inform)* moucharder; **to squeal on sb** balancer *ou* moucharder qn

2 *vt* **"who, me?" he squeaked** "qui? moi?", glapit-il

3 *n* (**a**) *(of floorboard, chalk, wheel, machine part)* grincement *m*; *(of animal)* piaillement *m*; *(of person)* petit cri *m* aigu, glapissement *m*; *(of shoes)* crissement *m*; *(of toy)* couinement *m*; **to let out** *or* **to give a squeak of pleasure** pousser un petit cri de plaisir; **don't let me hear one more squeak out of you!** et que je ne t'entende plus!

(**b**) *(idiom)* **that was a narrow squeak!** on l'a échappé belle!

►**squeak by, squeak through** *vi Fam* (**a**) *(pass through)* se faufiler ❑; **there was just enough room to squeak by** il y avait juste assez de place pour se faufiler

(**b**) *(succeed narrowly)* réussir de justesse ❑; *(in exam)* être reçu de justesse ❑; *(in election)* l'emporter de justesse ❑

squeaker ['skwiːkə(r)] *n* (**a**) *Fam (informant)* mouchard(arde) *m,f*, indic *mf* (**b**) *(young bird)* jeune oiseau *m* (**c**) *(squeaky toy)* jouet *m* qui couine

squeaking ['skwiːkɪŋ] *n (of floorboard, chalk, wheel, machine part)* grincement *m*; *(of animal)* piaillement *m*, piaillements *mpl*; *(of person)* petits cris *mpl* aigus, glapissements *mpl*; *(of shoes)* crissement *m*; *(of toy)* couinement *m*

squeaky ['skwiːkɪ] *(compar* **squeakier,** *superl* **squeakiest)** *adj (floorboard, bed, hinge)* grinçant; *(voice)* aigu(uë); *(toy)* qui couine; *Am Hum* **it's the squeaky wheel that gets the grease** *or* **oil** il n'y a que les rouspéteurs qui obtiennent satisfaction

►► ***squeaky clean*** *Fam* (**a**) *(hands, hair)* extrêmement propre ❑; **a shampoo that leaves your hair squeaky clean** un shampooing qui donne à vos cheveux une propreté impeccable ❑ (**b**) *(image, reputation)* sans tache ❑

squeal [skwiːl] **1** *vi* (**a**) *(person, animal)* pousser un cri perçant; *(tyres, brakes)* crisser; *(pig)* couiner; **to squeal with pain** pousser un cri de douleur; **to squeal with laughter** hurler de rire; **the car squealed around the corner** la voiture prit le virage dans un crissement de pneus; **he was squealing like a stuck pig** il criait comme un cochon qu'on égorge

(**b**) *very Fam (inform)* moucharder; **to squeal on sb** balancer *ou* moucharder qn

(**c**) *Fam (complain)* protester ❑, jeter les hauts cris ❑

2 *vt* **"ouch!" she squealed** "aïe!", cria-t-elle

3 *n (of person, animal)* cri *m* perçant; *(of tyres, brakes)* crissement *m*; **he gave a squeal of delight** il poussa un cri de joie

squealer ['skwiːlə(r)] *n very Fam (informer)* mouchard(e) *m,f*, indic *mf*

squealing ['skwiːlɪŋ] *n (of person)* cris *mpl* aigus; *(of tyres, brakes)* crissement *m*

squeamish ['skwiːmɪʃ] **1** *adj* (**a**) *(oversensitive)* trop émotif, impressionnable; **it makes me feel squeamish** ça me donne mal au cœur; **I'm very squeamish about the sight of blood** je ne supporte pas la vue du sang; **she's squeamish about physical violence** elle ne supporte pas les scènes de violence; **he was too squeamish even to taste it** il n'a même pas eu le courage d'y goûter; **don't be so squeamish** ne fais pas le délicat; **he wasn't squeamish about evicting them in the middle of winter** il n'a eu aucun scrupule à les expulser en plein hiver

(**b**) *(prudish)* prude

2 *npl* **the squeamish** les âmes *fpl* sensibles, les petites natures *fpl*; **this film is not for the squeamish** ce film n'est pas conseillé aux âmes sensibles

squeamishness ['skwiːmɪʃnɪs] *n* (**a**) *(oversensitivity)* trop grande émotivité *f*; **her squeamishness about mice/spiders** sa peur des souris/araignées; **because of his squeamishness about violence** du fait qu'il ne supportait pas la violence; **because of his squeamishness about seafood** parce qu'il a horreur des fruits de mer (**b**) *(prudishness)* pruderie *f*

squeegee ['skwiːdʒiː] **1** *n* (**a**) *(with rubber blade)* raclette *f*; *(sponge mop)* balai-éponge *m*; *Phot (roller)* rouleau *m (en caoutchouc)* (**b**) *(person)* = personne qui lave les pare-brises

2 *vt (window)* passer une raclette sur, laver avec une raclette

squeezable ['skwiːzəbəl] *adj* (**a**) *(that can be compressed)* comprimable, compressible (**b**) *(person)* à qui l'on peut arracher *ou* extorquer de l'argent

squeeze [skwiːz] **1** *n* (**a**) *(pressure, grip)* pression *f*; *(handshake)* poignée *f* de main; *(hug)* étreinte *f*; **to give sth a squeeze** *(toothpaste, lemon)* presser qch; *(cloth)* essorer qch; **he gave my hand a reassuring squeeze** il a serré ma main pour me rassurer; **to give sb a squeeze** serrer qn dans ses bras; *Fam* **to put the squeeze on sb** faire pression sur qn ❑

(**b**) *(crush of people)* cohue *f*; **it was a tight squeeze** *(in vehicle, room)* on était très serré; *(through opening)* on est passé de justesse

(**c**) *(small amount → of liquid)* quelques gouttes *fpl*; **a squeeze of lemon** quelques gouttes de citron; **a squeeze of toothpaste** un peu de dentifrice

(**d**) *Fam (difficult situation)* situation *f* difficile ❑; **in a squeeze you can always borrow my car** en cas de problème, tu peux toujours emprunter ma voiture

(**e**) *Econ & Fin (on profits, wages)* baisse *f* (**on** de); **(credit) squeeze** resserrement *m* du crédit; **a squeeze on jobs** des suppressions *fpl* d'emploi; **since her husband lost his job, they've really been feeling the squeeze** depuis que son mari a perdu son emploi, ils ont de sérieux problèmes d'argent

(**f**) *(in bridge)* squeeze *m*

(**g**) *Fam* **(main) squeeze** *(boyfriend)* mec *m*, Jules *m*; *(girlfriend)* nana *f*, gonzesse *f*

2 *vt* (**a**) *(press → tube, sponge, pimple)* presser; *(→ cloth)* essorer; *(→ trigger)* presser sur, appuyer sur; *(→ package)* palper; *(→ hand, shoulder)* serrer; **I squeezed as hard as I could** j'ai serré aussi fort que j'ai pu; **she squeezed her knees together** elle serra les genoux; **I kept my eyes squeezed tight shut** j'ai gardé les yeux bien fermés; **to squeeze the life out of sb** étouffer qn

(**b**) *(extract, press out → liquid)* exprimer; *(→ paste, glue)* faire sortir; *Fig (money, information)* soutirer; **I squeezed a dab of cream onto my nose** je me suis mis un peu de crème sur le nez; **a glass of freshly squeezed orange juice** une orange pressée; **to squeeze the juice out of a lemon** extraire le jus d'un citron; **to squeeze the water out of a sponge** essorer une éponge; **to squeeze the air out of** *or* **from sth** faire sortir l'air de qch en appuyant dessus; **it won't be easy to squeeze the results out of him** il ne sera pas facile de lui soutirer les résultats; **you won't squeeze another penny out of me!** tu n'auras pas un sou de plus!; **they want to squeeze more concessions from the EC** ils veulent forcer la Communauté européenne à faire de nouvelles concessions; **she's squeezing a lot of publicity out of the issue** elle exploite le sujet au maximum pour se faire de la publicité

(**c**) *(cram, force)* faire entrer (avec difficulté); **I can't squeeze another thing into my suitcase** je ne peux plus rien faire entrer dans ma valise; **they're squeezing more and more circuits onto microchips** ils réussissent à mettre de plus en plus de circuits sur les puces; **she squeezed the ring onto her finger** elle enfila la bague avec difficulté; **he squeezed his way under the fence** il s'est glissé *ou* faufilé sous le grillage; **he squeezed his huge bulk behind the steering wheel** il parvint à glisser son corps volumineux derrière le volant; **20 men were squeezed into one small cell** 20 hommes étaient entassés dans une petite cellule; **the airport is squeezed between the sea and the mountains** l'aéroport est coincé entre la mer et les montagnes

(**d**) *(constrain → profits, budget)* réduire; *(→ taxpayer, workers)* pressurer; **universities are being squeezed by the cuts** les réductions (de budget) mettent les universités en difficulté; **the British car industry has been squeezed by foreign competition** l'industrie automobile britannique subit la pression de la concurrence étrangère; *Fam* **I'm a bit squeezed for time/money** question temps/argent, je suis un peu juste

(**e**) *(in bridge)* squeezer

3 *vi* **the lorry managed to squeeze between the posts** le camion a réussi à passer de justesse entre les poteaux; **I squeezed into the crowded room** j'ai réussi à me glisser dans la salle bondée; **they all squeezed onto the bus** ils se sont tous entassés dans le bus; **can you squeeze into that parking space?** y a-t-il assez de place pour te garer là?; **try and squeeze into these trousers** essayez de rentrer dans ce pantalon; **it was possible just to squeeze under the wire** il était tout juste possible de se glisser sous le fil de fer

►**squeeze in 1** *vi (get in)* se faire une petite place; **I had to squeeze in past six people to reach my seat** j'ai dû me glisser devant six personnes pour atteindre mon siège

2 *vt sep (in schedule)* réussir à faire entrer; **she's hoping to squeeze in a trip to Rome too** elle espère avoir aussi le temps de faire un saut à Rome; **the dentist says he can squeeze you in** le dentiste dit qu'il peut vous prendre entre deux rendez-vous; **can you squeeze in a lunch with me next week?** vous n'auriez pas une petite heure disponible pour déjeuner avec moi la semaine prochaine?

►**squeeze out** *vt sep* (**a**) *(sponge, wet clothes)* essorer

(**b**) *(liquid)* exprimer; *Tech (plastic)* extruder; **I squeezed out the last of the glue** j'ai fini le tube de colle; **she gently squeezed the splinter out** en pressant doucement, elle a fait sortir l'écharde

(**c**) *(get rid of → candidate, competitor)* évincer; **they're trying to squeeze me out** ils essaient de se débarrasser de moi; **we were squeezed out by a German firm** une société allemande nous a devancés d'une courte tête; **the Japanese are squeezing them out of the market** ils sont en train de se faire évincer du marché par les Japonais

►**squeeze up** *vi* se serrer, se pousser; **squeeze up a bit so Jane can sit down** serrez-vous un peu pour que Jane puisse s'asseoir

squeezebox ['skwi:zbɒks] *n Fam (accordion)* accordéon□ *m*, piano *m* à bretelles; *(concertina)* concertina□ *m*

squeezer ['skwi:zə(r)] *n Culin* presse-agrumes *m inv*

squelch [skweltʃ] **1** *vi* (**a**) *(walk → in wet terrain)* patauger; *(→ with wet shoes)* marcher les pieds trempés; **I squelched across the field** j'ai traversé le champ en pataugeant; **he squelched into the kitchen** il entra dans la cuisine avec les pieds trempés

(**b**) *(make noise → mud)* clapoter; **I heard something soft squelch beneath my foot** j'ai entendu quelque chose de mou s'écraser sous mon pied; **the water squelched in his shoes** l'eau gargouillait dans ses chaussures

2 *vt* (**a**) *(crush)* écraser

(**b**) *Fam (rumour)* étouffer□; *(person)* clouer le bec à

3 *n (noise)* clapotement *m*; **I heard the squelch of tyres in mud** j'ai entendu le bruit des pneus dans la boue

squib [skwɪb] *n* (**a**) *(firecracker)* pétard *m* (**b**) *(piece of satire)* pamphlet *m*

squid [skwɪd] (*pl* **inv** *or* **squids**) *n Zool* cal(a)mar *m*, encornet *m*

squidgy ['skwɪdʒɪ] (*compar* **squidgier**, *superl* **squidgiest**) *adj Br Fam* mou (molle)□, spongieux□

squiffy ['skwɪfɪ] (*compar* **squiffier**, *superl* **squiffiest**) *adj Br Fam Old-fashioned* éméché, pompette

squiggle ['skwɪgəl] **1** *n* (**a**) *(scrawl, doodle)* gribouillis *m* (**b**) *(wavy line, mark)* ligne *f* ondulée; **something had left squiggles in the sand** quelque chose avait laissé des traces sinueuses sur le sable

2 *vi* (**a**) *(scrawl, doodle)* gribouiller, faire des gribouillages (**b**) *(twist → road, lines)* sinuer, serpenter; *(→ worm)* se tortiller

squiggly ['skwɪglɪ] *adj* pas droit, ondulé

squilla ['skwɪlə] *n Ich* squille *f*

squillion ['skwɪlɪən] *n Br Fam Hum* **squillions (of)** une foultitude (de), une ribambelle (de)

squinancy [skwɪ'nænsɪ] *n Arch Med* esquinancie *f*

squinancywort [skwɪ'nænsɪ,wɔ:t] *n Bot* aspérule *f* à l'esquinancie

squinch [skwɪntʃ] **1** *n Archit* trompe *f*

2 *vt Am Fam* **to squinch one's eyes** plisser les yeux□; **to squinch one's face up** faire une grimace□

squint [skwɪnt] **1** *n* (**a**) *Med* strabisme *m*; **to have a squint** loucher

(**b**) *Fam (glimpse)* coup *m* d'œil□; **have** *or* **take a squint at this!** vise-moi un peu ça!

2 *adj* (**a**) *(eyes)* louche

(**b**) *Fam (crooked)* de traviole

3 *vi* (**a**) *Med* loucher

(**b**) *(half-close eyes)* plisser les yeux; **they're all squinting because of the sun** ils font tous la grimace à cause du soleil; **he squinted at the photo** *(with difficulty)* il regarda la photo en plissant les yeux; *(quickly)* il jeta un coup d'œil à la photo; *(sidelong)* il regarda la photo du coin de l'œil

squint-eyed *adj* (**a**) *Fam (cross-eyed)* qui louche□, bigleux (**b**) *(sidelong)* de côté

squinting ['skwɪntɪŋ] *n* strabisme *m*

squinty-eyed ['skwɪntɪ-] *adj Fam (cross-eyed)* qui louche□, bigleux; **to be squinty-eyed** loucher

squirarchy = **squirearchy**

squire ['skwaɪə(r)] **1** *n* (**a**) *Br (landowner)* propriétaire *m* terrien, ≃ châtelain *m*; **he's the village squire** c'est le propriétaire du plus grand domaine du coin; **Squire Greaves** le squire Greaves (**b**) *(for knight)* écuyer *m* (**c**) *Old-fashioned (escort)* cavalier *m*; **her squire for the evening** son cavalier pour la soirée (**d**) *Br Fam (term of address)* **evening, squire!** bonsoir, chef!

2 *vt Old-fashioned (woman)* escorter, accompagner

squirearchy ['skwaɪərɑ:kɪ] (*pl* **squirearchies**) *n* propriétaires *mpl* terriens, ≃ châtelains *mpl*; **the island's planters form a squirearchy** les planteurs de l'île forment une petite noblesse terrienne

squirm [skwɜ:m] **1** *vi* (**a**) *(wriggle)* se tortiller; **he squirmed out of my grasp** il a échappé à mon étreinte en se tortillant; **she squirmed with impatience** elle était tellement impatiente qu'elle ne tenait plus en place

(**b**) *(be ill-at-ease)* être gêné, être très mal à l'aise; *(be ashamed)* avoir honte; **to squirm with embarrassment** être mort de honte; **the reporters are going to make him squirm!** devant la presse, il ne saura pas où se mettre!; **I still squirm when I remember how I treated her** j'ai encore honte quand je pense à la manière dont je l'ai traitée; **his speech was so bad it made me squirm** son discours était si mauvais que j'en ai eu honte pour lui

2 *vt* **to squirm one's way out of a situation** se sortir d'une situation; **to squirm one's way out of one's commitments** se défiler de ses obligations

squirrel [*Br* 'skwɪrəl, *Am* 'skwɜ:rəl] (*Br pt & pp* **squirrelled**, *cont* **squirrelling**, *Am pt & pp* **squirroled**, *cont* **squirreling**) **1** *n* (**a**) *(rodent)* écureuil *m* (**b**) *Fig (hoarder)* **she's a real squirrel** c'est une vraie fourmi

►► *Zool* ***squirrel monkey*** saïmiri *m*

►**squirrel away** *vt sep (hoard, store)* engranger; *(hide)* cacher; **he's got a fortune squirrelled away in various Swiss banks** il a amassé une fortune dans plusieurs banques suisses

squirrelfish ['skwɪrəlfɪʃ] *n Ich* holocentridé *m*

squirrelly ['skwɪrəlɪ] *adj Am Fam (eccentric)* loufedingue

squirt [skwɜ:t] **1** *vt (liquid)* faire gicler; *(mustard, ketchup, washing-up liquid)* faire jaillir; **squirt some oil on the hinges** mettez quelques gouttes d'huile sur les gonds; **they were squirting each other with water, they were squirting water at each other** ils s'aspergeaient d'eau mutuellement; **he squirted some soda water into his whisky** il versa une rasade d'eau de Seltz dans son whisky; **she squirted perfume on her wrists** elle se vaporisa du parfum sur les poignets

2 *vi (juice, blood, ink)* gicler; *(water)* jaillir; **juice squirted onto my shirt** le jus a giclé sur ma chemise; **the milk squirted (out) into the pail** le lait giclait dans le seau

3 *n* (**a**) *(of juice, ink)* giclée *f*; *(of water)* jet *m*; *(of mustard, ketchup, washing-up liquid)* dose *f*; *(of oil, perfume)* quelques gouttes *fpl*

(**b**) *Fam Pej (person)* minus *m*; *(short person)* avorton *m*, demi-portion *f*; *(child)* mioche *mf*; **get lost, you little squirt!** va donc, eh minus!

(**c**) *Fam Crime slang (ammonia)* = ammoniaque versée dans une bouteille de liquide vaisselle pour être ensuite projetée dans les yeux de la victime

►► *Am* ***squirt gun*** pistolet *m* à eau

squish [skwɪʃ] *Fam* **1** *vt (crush)* écrabouiller; **he squished his nose against the glass** il a écrasé son nez contre la vitre□; **the cake got all squished** le gâteau était complètement écrabouillé

2 *vi* (**a**) *Am (squash → insect, fruit)* s'écrabouiller (**b**) *(squelch)* clapoter□; **the mud squished between my toes** la boue s'infiltrait entre mes orteils□

squishy ['skwɪʃɪ] (*compar* **squishier**, *superl* **squishiest**) *adj Fam (fruit, wax)* mou (molle)□; *(chocolate)* ramolli□; *(ground)* boueux□; **a squishy blob of dough** un petit tas de pâte molle□

squit [skwɪt] *Br Fam* **1** *n* (**a**) *(person)* minus *m* (**b**) *(UNCOUNT) (nonsense)* bêtises□ *fpl*, conneries *fpl*

2 *npl* **the squits** *(diarrhoea)* la courante

Sr (**a**) (*written abbr* **senior**) **Ralph Todd Sr** Ralph Todd père (**b**) (*written abbr* **sister**) sœur *f*

SRAM ['esræm] *n Comput* (*abbr* **static random access memory**) mémoire *f* vive statique

SRC [,esɑ:'si:] *n* (**a**) *Br* (*abbr* **students' representative council**) = comité étudiant (**b**) (*abbr* **Science Research Council**) = conseil de la recherche scientifique

Sri Lanka [,sri:'læŋkə] *n* Sri Lanka *m*; **in Sri Lanka** au Sri Lanka

Sri Lankan [,sri:'læŋkən] **1** *n* Sri Lankais(e) *m,f*

2 *adj* sri lankais

SRN [,esɑ:'ren] *n Br* (*abbr* **State Registered Nurse**) infirmier(ère) *m,f* diplômé(e) *(remplacé en 1992 par "Registered Nurse")*

SRO[1] [,esɑ:'rəʊ] *Br St Exch* (*abbr* **self-regulatory organization**) organisme *m* auto-réglementé *ou* autonome

SRO[2] *Am* (*written abbr* **single room occupancy**) = tarif pour une seule personne *(d'une chambre d'hôtel)*

SRU [,esɑ:'ju:] *n* (*abbr* **Scottish Rugby Union**) = association écossaise de rugby à quinze

SRV [,esɑ:'vi:] *n* (*abbr* **space rescue vehicle**) véhicule *m* spatial de sauvetage

SS [,es'es] *n* (**a**) *Naut* (*abbr* **steamship**) = initiales précédant le nom des navires de la marine marchande; **the SS Norfolk** le Norfolk (**b**) (*abbr* **Schutzstaffel**) **the SS** les SS; **an SS officer** un officier SS

SSA [,eses'eɪ] *n Am* (*abbr* **Social Security Administration**) ≃ Sécurité *f* sociale

SSAE [,eses,eɪ'i:] *n Am* (*abbr* **stamped self-addressed envelope**) enveloppe *f* timbrée *(portant l'adresse à laquelle elle doit être renvoyée)*; **please return the form with an SSAE** veuillez renvoyer le formulaire ainsi qu'une enveloppe timbrée à votre adresse

SSE (*written abbr* **south-south-east**) S-SE

ssh [ʃ] *exclam* chut!

SSL [,eses'el] *n Comput* (*abbr* **secure sockets layer**) protocole *m* SSL

SSN [,eses'en] *n Am* (*abbr* **social security number**) numéro *m* de Sécurité sociale

SSP [,eses'pi:] *n* (*abbr* **statutory sick pay**) = indemnité de maladie versée par l'employeur

SSRI [,eses,ɑ:'raɪ] *n Pharm* (*abbr* **Selective Serotonin Re-uptake Inhibitor**) ISRS *m*, inhibiteur *m* sélectif de recapture de la sérotonine

SSSI [,eses,es'aɪ, ,trɪpəles'aɪ] *n Br* (*abbr* **Site of Special Scientific Interest**) = en Grande-Bretagne, site déclaré d'intérêt scientifique

SST [,eses'ti:] *n* (*abbr* **supersonic transport**) transport *m* supersonique

SSW (*written abbr* **South Southwest**) S-SO, S-SW

ST (*written abbr* **Standard Time**) heure *f* légale

St (**a**) (*written abbr* **saint**) St, Ste (**b**) (*written abbr* **street**) rue *f*

st (*written abbr* **stone**) (*unit of weight*) ≃ 6 kg

stab [stæb] (*pt & pp* **stabbed,** *cont* **stabbing**) **1** *vt* (**a**) (*injure → with knife*) donner un coup de couteau à, poignarder; (*→ with bayonet*) blesser d'un coup de baïonnette; (*→ with spear*) blesser avec une lance; **he stabbed me in the arm** il me donna un coup de couteau dans le bras; **they were stabbed to death** ils ont été tués à coups de couteau; **he was stabbed to death with a kitchen knife** il a été tué avec un couteau de cuisine; **to stab sb in the back** poignarder qn dans le dos; *Fig* trahir qn

(**b**) (*thrust, jab*) planter; **she stabbed the needle into my arm** elle planta l'aiguille dans mon bras; **I stabbed myself in the thumb with a pin** je me suis enfoncé une épingle dans le pouce; **I stabbed my finger in his eye** je lui ai enfoncé mon doigt dans l'œil; **I stabbed a turnip with my fork** j'ai piqué un navet avec ma fourchette

2 *vi* **he stabbed at the map with his finger** il frappa la carte du doigt; **she stabbed frantically at the different control buttons** elle poussa frénétiquement les différents boutons de contrôle; **he stabbed at the leaves with his walking stick** il piquait les feuilles de la pointe de sa canne

3 *n* (**a**) (*with dagger*) coup *m* de poignard; (*with knife*) coup *m* de couteau; **he made a vicious stab at me with the broken bottle** il fit un mouvement agressif vers moi avec la bouteille cassée; **she felt the stab of the needle in her finger** elle a senti la piqûre de l'aiguille dans son doigt; **stab wound** blessure *f* par arme blanche; **a man was rushed to hospital with stab wounds** un homme blessé à coups de couteau a été transporté d'urgence à l'hôpital; **it was a stab in the back** c'était un véritable coup de poignard dans le dos

(**b**) *Literary* (*of neon, colour*) éclat *m*; **a stab of lightning** un éclair

(**c**) (*sensation*) **stab of pain** élancement *m*; **I felt a stab of doubt** l'espace d'un instant je fus saisi par le doute; **I felt a stab of envy** je sentis un pincement de jalousie

(**d**) *Fam* (*try*) **to have** *or* **to make** *or* **to take a stab at (doing) sth** s'essayer à (faire) qch ❑; **why don't you have a stab at it?** pourquoi n'essayez-vous pas?; **I'll have a stab** je vais essayer

stabber ['stæbə(r)] *n* (*person who stabs*) poignardeur(euse) *m,f*

stabbing ['stæbɪŋ] **1** *n* (*knife attack*) agression *f* (à l'arme blanche); **there was a stabbing in the pub last night** quelqu'un s'est fait poignarder au pub hier soir; **there were two fatal stabbings at the football match** deux personnes ont été tuées à coups de couteau au match de football; **the number of stabbings has increased** le nombre d'attaques à l'arme blanche est en hausse

2 *adj* (*pain*) lancinant

stability [stə'bɪlətɪ] *n* stabilité *f*; **a period of political stability** une période de stabilité politique; **it will undermine the stability of their marriage** cela va ébranler leur mariage; **his mental stability** son équilibre mental

stabilization [ˌsteɪbəlaɪ'zeɪʃən] *n* stabilisation *f*

stabilize, -ise ['steɪbəlaɪz] **1** *vt* stabiliser

2 *vi* se stabiliser; **the political situation has stabilized** la situation politique s'est stabilisée

stabilizer ['steɪbəlaɪzə(r)] *n* (**a**) *Aviat, Aut & Elec* (*device*) stabilisateur *m*; *Naut* stabilisateur *m*; (*on bicycle*) stabilisateur *m*; *Fig* **the measure is intended to act as an economic stabilizer** cette mesure a pour but de stabiliser l'économie (**b**) *Chem* (*in food*) stabilisateur *m*, stabilisant *m*

stabilizing ['steɪbəlaɪzɪŋ] *adj* stabilisateur; **to have** *or* **to exert a stabilizing effect on prices** exercer une action stabilisatrice sur les prix; **her new job had a stabilizing effect on her** son nouvel emploi a eu un effet stabilisateur *ou* équilibrant sur elle

▸▸ ***stabilizing agent*** (*in foodstuffs*) agent *m* stabilisant

stable ['steɪbəl] **1** *adj* (**a**) (*steady, permanent → gen*) stable; (*→ marriage*) solide; **the patient's condition is stable** l'état du malade est stationnaire; **he never had a stable family life** il n'a jamais eu de vie de famille stable

(**b**) (*person, personality*) stable, équilibré; **he's not stable** il n'est pas équilibré, il est instable

(**c**) *Chem & Phys* stable

2 *n* (**a**) (*building*) écurie *f*; **riding stable** *or* **stables** centre *m* d'équitation

(**b**) (*group → of racehorses, sportspeople*) écurie *f*; (*→ of authors, actors*) équipe *f*; (*→ of companies, businesses*) groupe *m*

3 *vt* (*take to stable*) mettre à l'écurie; **her horse is stabled at Dixon's** son cheval est en pension chez Dixon; **we can stable three horses** nous avons de la place pour trois chevaux

▸▸ ***stable boy*** valet *m* d'écurie, lad *m*; ***stable door*** porte *f* d'écurie, porte *f* à deux vantaux *ou* battants; *Fig* **to shut** *or* **to lock the stable door after the horse has bolted** réagir trop tard, arriver après la bataille; ***stable girl*** valet *m* d'écurie (*fille*); ***stable lad*** lad *m*

stableford ['steɪbəlfəd] *n Golf* **stableford (competition)** partie *f* par points

stablemate ['steɪbəlmeɪt] *n* (**a**) (*horse*) compagnon *m* d'écurie (**b**) *Fig* (*person → at work*) collègue *mf* de travail; (*→ from same school*) camarade *mf* d'études; (*→ in sport, film*) membre *m* de la même équipe

stabling ['steɪbəlɪŋ] *n* (*UNCOUNT*) (**a**) (*of horses*) logement *m* dans une écurie (**b**) (*space in stables*) **we have plenty of stabling** nous ne manquons pas de place aux écuries; **we supply stabling for 40 horses** nous pouvons accueillir 40 chevaux

stably ['steɪbəlɪ] *adv* stablement, d'une manière stable

staccato [stə'kɑːtəʊ] (*pl* **staccatos**) **1** *adj* (**a**) *Mus* (*note*) piqué; (*passage*) joué en staccato (**b**) (*noise, rhythm*) saccadé; **in a staccato voice** d'une voix saccadée

2 *adv Mus* staccato

3 *n Mus* staccato *m*; **she replied in a rapid staccato** elle répondit d'un ton rapide et saccadé

▸▸ *Mus* ***staccato mark*** trait *m* vertical

stache [stæʃ] *n Am Fam* (*abbr* **mustache**) bacchantes *fpl*, moustagache *f*

stack [stæk] **1** *n* (**a**) (*pile*) tas *m*, pile *f*; **a huge stack of books** une pile énorme de livres

(**b**) *Fam* (*large quantity*) tas *m*; **stacks of...** des tas de...; **I've written a stack of** *or* **stacks of postcards** j'ai écrit un tas de cartes postales; **we've got stacks of time** on a largement le temps; **she has stacks of money** elle est bourrée de fric

(**c**) *Agr* (*of hay, straw*) meule *f*

(**d**) (*chimney*) cheminée *f*; (*of locomotive*) cheminée *f*

(**e**) *Aviat* avions *mpl* en attente, empilage *m*; **the stack is twenty planes high** il y a vingt avions qui attendent le feu vert de la tour de contrôle pour atterrir

(**f**) *Comput* (*file*) pile *f*

(**g**) *Mil* (*of rifles*) faisceau *m*

(**h**) (*in library*) **the stack** *or* **stacks** les rayons *mpl*

(**i**) *Br* (*measure of firewood*) ≃ 3 stères *mpl* (3,06 mètres cubes)

(**j**) (*idiom*) *Am Fam* **to blow one's stack** exploser, piquer une crise

2 *vt* (**a**) (*pile → chairs, boxes etc*) empiler; **stack the glasses in the cupboard** empilez les verres dans l'armoire; **oil cans were stacked in pyramids** des bidons d'huile étaient empilés en pyramide

(**b**) *Agr* (*hay*) mettre en meule *ou* meules

(**c**) (*fill → room, shelf*) remplir; **his desk was stacked high with files** des piles de dossiers s'entassaient sur son bureau

(**d**) *Comput* empiler

(**e**) *Aviat* (*planes*) mettre en attente (à altitudes échelonnées)

(**f**) (*fix, rig → committee*) remplir de ses partisans; **to stack the cards** *or* **the deck** truquer les cartes; *Fig* **he's playing with a stacked deck** (*in his favour*) les dés sont pipés en sa faveur; (*against him*) les dés sont pipés contre lui; *Fig* **the cards** *or* **the odds are stacked against us** nous sommes dans une mauvaise situation; **a woman in this profession starts with the cards stacked against her** dans ce métier les femmes partent avec un handicap; **the election system is heavily stacked against the smaller parties** ce mode de scrutin défavorise fortement les petits partis

3 *vi* s'empiler

4 stacks *adv Br Fam* vachement; **it's stacks easier** c'est vachement plus facile

▸**stack up 1** *vt sep* (*pile up*) empiler

2 *vi* (**a**) *Am Fam* (*add up, work out*) **I don't like the way things are stacking up** je n'aime pas la tournure que prennent les événements ❑; **I wanted someone honest and dynamic and that's how Jan stacks up** je voulais quelqu'un d'honnête et de dynamique et Jan fait parfaitement l'affaire ❑

(**b**) (*compare*) se comparer; **our product stacks up well against theirs** notre produit soutient bien la comparaison avec le leur; **how does he stack up against** *or* **with the other candidates?** que vaut-il comparé aux autres candidats?

stackable ['stækəbəl] *adj* empilable

stacked [stækt] *adj very Fam* (*woman*) **she's (well) stacked** il y a du monde au balcon

▸▸ ***stacked heel*** talon *m* compensé

stacker ['stækə(r)] *n* (*worker*) manutentionnaire *mf*; (*pallet truck*) transpalette *m*

stacker-retriever *n* **stacker-retriever (crane)** transstockeur *m*

stacking chairs ['stækɪŋ-] *npl* chaises *fpl* superposables

stadium ['steɪdjəm] (*pl* **stadiums** *or* **stadia** [-djə]) *n* stade *m*

▸▸ ***stadium Australia*** = stade construit à Sydney pour les jeux Olympiques de l'an 2000 et où ont lieu également des matchs de rugby, des concerts etc

staff [stɑːf] (*pl senses* (**c**) & (**d**) **staffs** *or* **staves** [steɪvz]) **1** *n* (**a**) (*work force*) personnel *m*; (*teachers*) professeurs *mpl*, personnel *m* enseignant; **the company has a staff of fifty** l'effectif de la société est de cinquante personnes; **we have ten lawyers on the staff** notre personnel comprend dix avocats; **reductions in the clerical staff** une réduction du personnel administratif; **is he staff** *or* **a member of staff?** est-ce qu'il fait partie du personnel?; **staff only** (*sign*) réservé au personnel; **staff/student ratio** taux *m* d'encadrement, rapport *m* entre le nombre de professeurs et le nombre d'étudiants

(**b**) *Mil & Pol* état-major *m*; **she was asked to join the President's campaign staff** on lui a demandé de faire partie de l'état-major de campagne du Président

(**c**) (*rod*) bâton *m*; (*flagpole*) mât *m*; (*of banner, lance*) hampe *f*; (*for shepherd*) houlette *f*; (*for bishop*) crosse *f*, bâton *m* pastoral; *Br* (*in surveying*) jalon *m*; *Fig* (*support*) soutien *m*; **the staff of life** (*bread*) l'aliment de base; *Fig* le pain et le sel de la vie

(**d**) *Mus* portée *f*; **treble staff** portée en clé de sol

2 *comp* (*canteen, outing etc*) du personnel

3 *vt* (*usu passive*) pourvoir en personnel; **the branch is staffed by** *or* **with competent people** le personnel de la succursale est compétent; **the office is only staffed between the hours of 2 and 4 pm** il y a quelqu'un au bureau de 14h à 16h seulement; **the committee is completely staffed by volunteers** le comité est entièrement composé de bénévoles

▸▸ ***staff association*** ≃ comité *m* d'entreprise; *Mil* ***staff college*** école *f* supérieure de guerre; *Mil* ***staff corporal*** ≃ sergent-major *m*; ***staff manager*** chef *m* du personnel; *Br* ***staff nurse*** infirmier(ère) *m,f* diplômé(e); *Mil* ***staff officer*** officier *m* d'état-major; *Mil* ***staff sergeant*** *Br* ≃ sergent-chef *m*; *Am* ≃ sergent *m*; ***staff training*** formation *f* du personnel; ***staff turnover*** roulement *m* du personnel

staffer ['stɑːfə(r)] *n* (**a**) *Journ* rédacteur(trice) *m,f*, membre *m* de la rédaction (**b**) *Am* (*staff member*) membre *m* du personnel

staffing ['stɑːfɪŋ] *n* (*recruiting*) recrutement *m*; **the delay is due to staffing difficulties** le retard est dû à des problèmes de recrutement

▸▸ ***staffing arrangements*** organisation *f* du personnel; ***staffing levels*** effectifs *mpl*; ***staffing policy*** politique *f* de recrutement du personnel

staffman ['stɑːfmən] (*pl* **staffmen** [-mən]) *n Br* (*in surveying*) jalonneur *m*

Staffordshire ['stæfədʃɪə(r)] *n* le Staffordshire, = comté du centre de l'Angleterre; **in Staffordshire** dans le Staffordshire
►► ***Staffordshire bull terrier*** bull-terrier *m* du Staffordshire, Staffordshire bull-terrier *m*

staffroom ['stɑːfrʊm] *n Br Sch* salle *f* des enseignants *ou* des professeurs

Staffs (*written abbr* **Staffordshire**) Staffordshire *m*

Staffy ['stæfɪ] *n Br Fam* bull-terrier *m* du Staffordshire ❑, Staffordshire bull-terrier ❑ *m*

stag [stæg] (*pl* **inv** *or* **stags**) **1** *n* (**a**) *(animal)* cerf *m* (**b**) *Br St Exch* loup *m*
2 *adj (event → for men)* entre hommes
3 *adv Am Fam* **to go stag** sortir en célibataire ❑
►► *Entom* ***stag beetle*** cerf-volant *m*, *Spec* lucane *m*; *Fam* ***stag film*** film *m* porno; ***stag night, stag party*** *(gen)* soirée *f* entre hommes; **we're having** *or* **holding a stag night for Bob** *(before wedding day)* nous enterrons la vie de garçon de Bob

STAGE [steɪdʒ]

stade	► **1 (a)**
phase	► **1 (a)**
étape	► **1 (a)**
scène	► **1 (b)**
théâtre	► **1 (b); 2**
plate-forme	► **1 (c)**
étage	► **1 (d), (f)**
diligence	► **1 (e)**
monter	► **3 (a) (b)**
mettre en scène	► **3 (a)**
organiser	► **3 (b)**

1 *n* (**a**) *(period, phase → of development, career etc)* stade *m*; *(→ of illness, negotiations, project, process)* stade *m*, phase *f*; *(→ of journey, life)* étape *f*; **larval stage** stade *m* larvaire; **the first/final stage of the project** la première/dernière phase du projet; **the next stage in computer technology** le stade suivant *ou* l'étape suivante du développement de l'informatique; **at this stage** à ce stade; **at this stage of the negotiations, I won't venture to comment** à ce stade des négociations, je m'interdirai tout commentaire; **at one stage it looked like he was going to win** à un moment donné il avait l'air parti pour gagner; **the bill is at the committee stage** le projet de loi va maintenant être examiné par un comité; **we'll deal with that at a later stage** nous nous en occuperons plus tard; **at a later stage in his life** plus tard dans la vie; **the conflict is still in its early stages** le conflit n'en est encore qu'à ses débuts; **stage by stage** étape par étape; **to do sth one stage at a time** faire qch étape par étape; **to do sth by** *or* **in stages** faire qch par étapes; **the changes were instituted in stages** les changements ont été introduits progressivement; **we travelled to Lisbon in (easy) stages** nous avons voyagé jusqu'à Lisbonne par (petites) étapes
(**b**) *Theat (place)* scène *f*; **the stage** *(profession, activity)* le théâtre; **on stage** sur scène; **stage right/left** côté jardin/cour; **to go on stage** monter sur (la) scène; **to go on the stage** *(as career)* monter sur les planches, faire du théâtre; **he first appeared on the stage in 1920** il a commencé à faire du théâtre en 1920; **to write for the stage** écrire pour la scène; **she was the first to bring the play to the London stage** elle a été la première à monter cette pièce sur la scène londonienne; *Fig* **the political stage** la scène politique; **on the stage of world events** sur la scène internationale; **his concerns always take centre stage** ses soucis à lui doivent toujours passer avant tout; **to set the stage for sth** préparer le terrain pour qch; **now the stage was set for...** maintenant tout était prêt pour...
(**c**) *(platform → gen)* plate-forme *f*; *(→ for speaker, presenter)* estrade *f*; *(→ on microscope)* platine *f*; *(scaffolding)* échafaudage *m*
(**d**) *Astron* étage *m*; **a three-stage satellite launcher** un lanceur spatial à trois étages
(**e**) *(stagecoach)* diligence *f*
(**f**) *Electron (circuit part)* étage *m*
2 *comp (version)* pour le théâtre; **a stage Irishman** une caricature d'Irlandais; **she has great stage presence** elle a énormément de présence sur scène
3 *vt* (**a**) *Theat (put on → play)* monter, mettre en scène; **it's the first time the play has been staged** c'est la première fois qu'on monte cette pièce; **Macbeth was very well staged** la mise en scène de Macbeth était très réussie; **the company is staging plays in parks this summer** la troupe joue dans les parcs cet été
(**b**) *(organize, hold → ceremony, demonstration, festival, robbery)* organiser; *(→ coup)* monter; *(fake → accident)* monter, manigancer; **to stage a hijacking** détourner un avion; **to stage a diversion** créer une *ou* faire diversion; **she staged her entrance for maximum effect** elle prépara son entrée de façon à faire le plus d'effet possible; **the handshake was staged for the TV cameras** la poignée de main était une mise en scène destinée aux caméras de télévision; **they staged an argument for your benefit** ils ont fait semblant de se disputer parce que vous étiez là; **the murder was staged to look like a suicide** le meurtre a été maquillé en suicide
►► ***stage design*** décoration *f* de théâtre, scénographie *f*; ***stage designer*** décorateur(trice) *m,f* de théâtre, scénographe *mf*; ***stage direction*** indication *f* scénique; ***stage door*** entrée *f* des artistes; ***stage effect*** effet *m* scénique; ***stage fright*** trac *m*; **to have stage fright** avoir le trac, être pris de trac; ***stage manager*** régisseur *m*; ***stage name*** nom *m* de scène; ***stage play*** pièce *f* de théâtre; ***stage school*** cours *m* de théâtre; ***stage set*** décor *m*; ***stage show*** pièce *f* de théâtre; ***stage whisper*** aparté *m*; **"it's midnight", he announced in a loud stage whisper** "il est minuit", chuchota-t-il, suffisamment fort pour que tout le monde l'entende

stagecoach ['steɪdʒkəʊtʃ] *n* diligence *f*

'Stagecoach' *Ford* 'La Chevauchée fantastique'

stagecraft ['steɪdʒkrɑːft] *n (of playwright)* maîtrise *f* de l'écriture théâtrale; *(of director)* maîtrise *f* de la mise en scène; *(of actor)* maîtrise *f* du jeu

staged ['steɪdʒd] *adj* (**a**) *(gradual → withdrawal, introduction, process)* graduel, progressif (**b**) *(event, trial, revolt)* monté de toutes pièces (**c**) *Constr* bâti en étages

stage-diving *n* = fait de se jeter dans la foule depuis la scène

stagehand ['steɪdʒhænd] *n Theat* machiniste *mf*

stage-manage *vt* (**a**) *Theat (play, production)* s'occuper de la régie sur
(**b**) *(press conference, appearance)* orchestrer, mettre en scène; **her arrival at the airport was stage-managed to generate publicity** son arrivée à l'aéroport a été une vraie mise en scène publicitaire; **the unrest was stage-managed to coincide with the summit meeting** les troubles ont été orchestrés de manière à coïncider avec le sommet

stager ['steɪdʒə(r)] *n* (**a**) *(veteran)* **old stager** vieux *m* de la vieille (**b**) *Arch (actor)* acteur *m*

stagestruck ['steɪdʒstrʌk] *adj* possédé par le démon du théâtre, qui rêve de faire du théâtre

stagey *Am* = **stagy**

stagflation [stæg'fleɪʃən] *n* stagflation *f*

stagger ['stægə(r)] **1** *vi (totter → person, horse)* chanceler, tituber; **to stagger with tiredness** chanceler de fatigue; **to stagger out** sortir en chancelant *ou* titubant; **I staggered over to the chair** je me suis dirigé vers la chaise d'un pas chancelant; **I staggered under the weight** je titubais sous le poids; **we staggered into bed at 3 o'clock in the morning** nous nous sommes écroulés sur nos lits à 3 heures du matin
2 *vt* (**a**) *(usu passive) (payments)* échelonner; *(holidays)* étaler; **they plan to bring in staggered working hours** ils ont l'intention de mettre en place un système d'échelonnement des heures de travail; **employees' vacation times are staggered over the summer months** les vacances du personnel sont étalées sur tout l'été; **lampposts were staggered along the street** la rue était jalonnée de réverbères
(**b**) *(usu passive) (astound)* **to be staggered** être atterré, être stupéfait; **I was staggered to learn of his decision** j'ai été stupéfait d'apprendre sa décision
3 *n (totter)* pas *m* chancelant; **he got up with a stagger** il s'est levé en chancelant
4 staggers *n (in diver)* ivresse *f* des profondeurs; **(blind) staggers** *(in sheep)* tournis *m*, cœnurose *f*; *(in horses)* vertigo *m*

staggered ['stægəd] *adj (amazed)* atterré, stupéfait
►► *Fin* ***staggered instalment*** versement *m* échelonné; ***staggered junction*** carrefour *m* décalé; ***staggered payments*** paiements *mpl* échelonnés; *Sport* ***staggered start*** *(on oval track)* départ *m* décalé; *Aviat* ***staggered wings*** ailes *fpl* décalées

staggering ['stægərɪŋ] **1** *adj (news, amount)* stupéfiant, ahurissant; *(problems)* énorme; *Fig* **it was a staggering blow** ce fut un sacré coup; **the price tag is a staggering $500,000** ça vaut la somme astronomique de 500 000 dollars
2 *n* (**a**) *(of vacations)* étalement *m*; *(of payments)* échelonnement *m* (**b**) *(unsteady gait)* démarche *f* chancelante

staghorn ['stæghɔːn] *n* bois *mpl* de cerf

staghound ['stæghaʊnd] *n* chien *m* d'équipage

staghunt ['stæghʌnt], **staghunting** ['stæg,hʌntɪŋ] *n* chasse *f* au cerf

staginess ['steɪdʒɪnɪs] *n* caractère *m* théâtral

staging ['steɪdʒɪŋ] *n* (**a**) *Theat (of play)* mise *f* en scène (**b**) *(scaffolding)* échafaudage *m*; *(shelving)* rayonnage *f* (**c**) *Astron* largage *m (d'un étage de fusée)*
►► *Mil* ***staging area, staging point*** lieu *m* de rassemblement; *Br* ***staging post*** lieu *m ou* point *m* de ravitaillement; *Aviat* escale *f* aérienne; *Hist (for coaches)* relais *m* (de diligences)

stagnancy ['stægnənsɪ] *n* stagnation *f*

stagnant ['stægnənt] *adj* (**a**) *(water, pond → still)* stagnant; *(→ stale)* croupissant; *(air → still)* confiné; *(→ stale)* qui sent le renfermé (**b**) *(economy, trade, career)* stagnant; *(society)* statique, en stagnation

stagnate [stæg'neɪt] *vi* (**a**) *(water → be still)* stagner; *(→ be stale)* croupir (**b**) *(economy, trade, career)* stagner; *(person)* croupir; **he stagnated in the same job for years** il a croupi dans le même emploi pendant des années

stagnation [stæg'neɪʃən] *n* stagnation *f*

stagy, *Am* **stagey** ['steɪdʒɪ] (*compar* **stagier**, *superl* **stagiest**) *adj* théâtral; **she's very stagy** elle a des manières très théâtrales

staid [steɪd] *adj (person)* rangé; *(colours)* sobre, discret(ète); *(job)* très ordinaire; **a man of staid habits** un homme rangé; **a staid and simple life** une vie simple et rangée; **the party was all very staid** la soirée fut sans surprises *ou* très banale

staidly ['steɪdlɪ] *adv (sit, watch)* calmement; *(walk, dance)* dignement; *(dress)* sobrement

staidness ['steɪdnɪs] *n* sobriété *f*

stain [steɪn] **1** *n* (**a**) *(mark, spot)* tache *f*; **coffee/ink stains** taches *fpl* de café/d'encre; **to leave a stain** laisser une tache; **I couldn't get the stain out** je n'ai pas réussi à enlever *ou* faire disparaître la tache
(**b**) *Fig (on character)* tache *f*; **it was a stain on his reputation** cela a entaché sa réputation
(**c**) *(colour, dye)* teinte *f*, teinture *f*; **a wood stain** une teinture pour bois; **oak/mahogany stain** teinte chêne/acajou
2 *vt* (**a**) *(soil, mark)* tacher; **the sink was stained with rust** l'évier était taché de rouille; **smoking stains your teeth** le tabac jaunit les dents; *also Fig* **his hands are stained with blood** il a du sang sur les mains
(**b**) *(character, reputation)* tacher, entacher, ternir
(**c**) *(colour, dye → wood)* teindre; *(→ glass, cell specimen)* colorer; **the lake was stained pink by the dawn** la lumière rosée de l'aube se reflétait dans le lac
3 *vi* (**a**) *(mark → wine, oil etc)* tacher; **white wine doesn't stain** le vin blanc ne tache pas
(**b**) *(become marked → cloth)* se tacher; **silk stains easily** la soie se tache facilement *ou* est salissante
►► ***stain remover*** détachant *m*

stained [steɪnd] *adj* (**a**) *(soiled → collar, sheet)*

taché; *(→ teeth)* jauni (**b**) *(coloured → gen)* coloré; *(→ wood)* teint
▸▸ ***stained glass*** vitrail *m*; **she works in stained glass** elle fabrique des vitraux

-stained [steɪnd] *suff* taché; **rust/ink-stained** taché de rouille/d'encre; **his sweat-stained shirt** sa chemise tachée de transpiration; **nicotine-stained** jauni par la nicotine

stained-glass *adj*
▸▸ ***stained-glass window*** vitrail *m*

staining ['steɪnɪŋ] *n (of wood)* teinture *f*

stainless ['steɪnlɪs] *adj* (**a**) *(rust-resistant)* inoxydable (**b**) *Fig* sans tache, pur; **a stainless reputation** une réputation sans tache
▸▸ ***stainless steel*** **1** *n* acier *m* inoxydable, Inox® *m* **2** *comp* en acier inoxydable, en Inox®

stair [steə(r)] **1** *n* (**a**) *(step)* marche *f*; **the bottom stair** la première marche
(**b**) *(staircase)* escalier *m*
2 stairs *npl (stairway)* escalier *m*, escaliers *mpl*; **I slipped on the stairs** j'ai glissé dans l'escalier; **to run up/down the stairs** monter/descendre les escaliers en courant; **at the top of the stairs** en haut de l'escalier; **at the bottom** *or* **the foot of the stairs** en bas *ou* au pied de l'escalier; **we passed on the stairs** on s'est croisés dans les escaliers; *Br* **above/below stairs** chez les patrons/les domestiques
▸▸ ***stair carpet*** tapis *m* d'escalier; *Constr* ***stair stringer*** limon *m*

staircase ['steəkeɪs] *n* escalier *m*

stairhead ['steəhed] *n* haut *m* de l'escalier, palier *m*

stair-rod *n* tringle *f* d'escalier; **it's raining stair-rods** il pleut des cordes *ou* des hallebardes

stairway ['steəweɪ] *n* escalier *m*

stairwell ['steəwel] *n* cage *f* d'escalier

stake [steɪk] **1** *n* (**a**) *(post, pole)* pieu *m*; *(in surveying)* piquet *m*, jalon *m*; *(for plant)* tuteur *m*; *(for vine)* échalas *m*; *(for tethering animal)* piquet *m*; *(for tent)* piquet *m*; *(for execution)* poteau *m*; **to die** *or* **to be burned at the stake** mourir sur le bûcher; **she went to the stake for her beliefs** ses convictions l'ont menée au bûcher; *Fig* **it's an important principle but I'm not about to go to the stake for it** c'est un principe important mais je ne me sacrifierais pas *ou* je ne mourrais pas pour le défendre; *Am* **to (pull) up stakes** *(leave place, job)* faire ses valises; *(leave one's home)* déménager
(**b**) *(in gambling)* enjeu *m*, mise *f*; **to lose one's stake** perdre sa mise; **the stakes are too high for me** l'enjeu est trop important pour moi; *also Fig* **to play for high stakes** jouer gros jeu; **to raise the stakes** augmenter la mise; *Fig* faire monter les enchères
(**c**) *(interest, share)* intérêt *m*, part *f*; *(investment)* investissement *m*, investissements *mpl*; *(shareholding)* participation *f*; **she has a 10% stake in the company** elle a une participation de 10% dans la société, elle détient 10% du capital de la société; **the company has a big stake in nuclear energy** la société a misé gros sur *ou* a fait de gros investissements dans le nucléaire; **we all have a stake in the education of the young** l'éducation des jeunes nous concerne tous
(**d**) *Am (savings)* (petit) pécule *m*, bas *m* de laine
(**e**) *(idioms)* **to be at stake** être en jeu; **what** *or* **how much is at stake?** quels sont les enjeux?, qu'est-ce qui est en jeu?; **our honour is at stake** il y va de notre honneur, notre honneur est en jeu; **basic issues of public health are at stake** les bases mêmes de la santé publique sont en jeu; **there are lives at stake!** il y a des vies en jeu!; **she has a lot at stake** elle joue gros jeu, elle risque gros
2 *vt* (**a**) *(bet → sum of money, valuables)* jouer, miser; *Fig (→ reputation)* jouer, risquer; **he staked $10 on Birdy** il a joué *ou* misé *ou* mis 10 dollars sur Birdy; **she had staked her reputation on the outcome of the negotiations** elle avait risqué *ou* joué sa réputation sur le résultat des négociations; **he had staked everything** *or* **his all on getting the job** il avait tout misé sur l'acceptation de sa candidature; **I'd stake my all** *or* **my life on it** j'en mettrais ma main au feu
(**b**) *Am (aid financially)* financer; **he is staking the newspaper for half a million dollars** il investit un demi-million de dollars dans le journal; *Fam* **can you stake me for a new suit?** est-ce que tu peux m'avancer de quoi m'acheter un nouveau costume?
(**c**) *(fasten → boat, animal)* attacher à un piquet; *(→ tent)* attacher avec des piquets; *(→ plant)* tuteurer; *(→ vine)* échalasser
(**d**) *(mark out → piece of land)* jalonner, piqueter; *(in surveying → line, road)* jalonner; **to stake one's claim to a territory** revendiquer un territoire *(en le délimitant avec des piquets)*; **each gang has staked its claim to a piece of the territory** chaque gang a délimité sa part de territoire; **she has staked her claim to a place in the history of our country** elle mérite une place d'honneur dans l'histoire de notre pays
3 stakes *npl (horse race)* course *f* de chevaux; *(prize)* prix *m*; *Horseracing* **the Bingham Stakes** le Prix de Bingham; *Fig* **the promotion stakes** la course à l'avancement; **she hasn't got much going for her in the beauty/personality stakes** elle n'est pas particulièrement gâtée physiquement/côté caractère
▸▸ ***stake boat*** bateau *m* de ligne de départ

▸**stake off** *vt sep* = **stake out** (**a**)

▸**stake out** *vt sep* (**a**) *(delimit → area, piece of land)* délimiter (avec des piquets); *(→ boundary, line)* marquer, jalonner; *Fig (→ sphere of influence)* définir; *(→ market)* se tailler; *(→ job, research field)* s'approprier
(**b**) *(keep watch on)* mettre sous surveillance, surveiller; **they've got the house staked out** ils surveillent la maison

stakeholder ['steɪk,həʊldə(r)] *n (for bets)* dépositaire *mf* des enjeux; *(for property)* dépositaire *mf* d'enjeux; *(in enterprise, business)* personne *f* participant à une affaire, partie *f* prenante
▸▸ ***stakeholder pension*** = système de retraite accessible aux salariés (notamment ceux qui ont de faibles revenus) ne bénéficiant pas d'une retraite complémentaire; ***stakeholder society*** = terme popularisé par Tony Blair, qui désigne un type de société où chaque citoyen a un rôle à jouer car il y va de son propre intérêt

stakeout ['steɪkaʊt] *n Am (activity)* surveillance *f*; *(place)* locaux *mpl* sous surveillance; **to be on stakeout** effectuer une surveillance

Stakhanovism [stə'kænəvɪzəm] *n* stakhanovisme *m*

Stakhanovite [stə'kænəvaɪt] *n* stakhanoviste *mf*

staking ['steɪkɪŋ] *n* (**a**) *(marking off → of piece of land)* jalonnement *m*, piquetage *m* (**b**) *(support → of plants)* tuteurage *m*; *(→ of vine)* échalassage *m*

stalactite ['stæləktaɪt] *n* stalactite *f*

stalag ['stælæg] *n* stalag *m*

stalagmite ['stæləgmaɪt] *n* stalagmite *f*

stale [steɪl] **1** *adj* (**a**) *(bread, cake)* rassis, sec (sèche); *(chocolate, cigarette)* vieux (vieille); *(cheese → hard)* desséché; *(→ mouldy)* moisi; *(fizzy drink)* éventé, plat; *(air → foul)* vicié; *(→ confined)* confiné; **the car smelt of stale cigarette smoke** la voiture sentait le tabac froid; **stale breath** haleine *f* fétide; **to go stale** *(bread)* (se) rassir; *(chocolate, cigarette)* perdre son goût; *(cheese)* se dessécher; *(beer)* s'éventer
(**b**) *(idea, plot, joke)* éculé, rebattu; *(discovery, news)* éventé, dépassé; *(pleasure)* émoussé, qui n'a plus de goût; *(beauty)* fané, défraîchi; *Fin (market)* lourd, plat; **his arguments were stale and unconvincing** ses arguments étaient éculés et peu convaincants
(**c**) *(person, relationship)* **he's getting stale in that job** il s'encroûte dans ce poste; **to go stale** *(athlete etc)* se surentraîner; *(actor, musician etc)* perdre son inspiration; **her marriage had gone stale** son bonheur conjugal s'était fané
(**d**) *Law (warrant)* périmé; *(debt)* impayable
2 *vi Literary (novelty, place, activity)* perdre son charme
▸▸ *Fin* ***stale cheque*** chèque *m* prescrit

stalemate ['steɪlmeɪt] **1** *n* (**a**) *(in chess)* pat *m*; **the game ended in stalemate** la partie s'est terminée par un pat
(**b**) *(deadlock)* impasse *f*; **the nuclear arms stalemate** l'impasse de la course aux armements nucléaires; **the argument ended in (a) stalemate** la discussion s'est terminée dans une impasse; **the announcement broke the stalemate in the negotiations** l'annonce a fait sortir les négociations de l'impasse
2 *vt (usu passive) (in chess → opponent)* faire pat à; **Black is stalemated** les Noirs sont pat; *Fig* **the negotiations were stalemated** les négociations étaient dans l'impasse

staleness ['steɪlnɪs] *n (of food, air)* manque *m* de fraîcheur; *(of information, joke etc)* manque *m* de nouveauté; **a feeling of staleness** un sentiment de lassitude

Stalin ['stɑːlɪn] *pr n* Staline

Stalingrad ['stɑːlɪngræd] *n* Stalingrad

Stalinism ['stɑːlɪnɪzəm] *n* stalinisme *m*

Stalinist ['stɑːlɪnɪst] **1** *adj* stalinien
2 *n* stalinien(enne) *m,f*

stalk [stɔːk] **1** *n* (**a**) *Bot (of flower, plant)* tige *f*; *(of cabbage, cauliflower)* trognon *m*; *(of fruit)* queue *f*; *(of wheat, corn)* chaume *m*; *(of bunch of grapes)* rafle *f*, râpe *f*
(**b**) *Zool* pédoncule *m*; *Fam* **his eyes stood out on stalks** il avait les yeux qui lui sortaient de la tête
(**c**) *(gen → long object)* tige *f*
2 *vt* (**a**) *(game, fugitive etc)* traquer; *(of private detective)* filer; *(of obsessive fan etc)* suivre en permanence *(de façon obsessionnelle)*
(**b**) *(prowl about in)* rôder dans; **to stalk the woods/the bush on foot** *(gen)* battre les bois/la brousse à pied; *Hunt* faire une battue dans les bois/la brousse; **enemy patrols stalked the hills** des patrouilles ennemies rôdaient dans les collines
(**c**) *Literary (of disease, terror)* régner dans, rôder dans; **hunger stalked the countryside** la faim régnait dans les campagnes; **evil stalks the night** les forces du mal rôdent dans la nuit
3 *vi* (**a**) *(person)* **she stalked out angrily/in disgust** elle sortit d'un air furieux/dégoûté; **he was stalking up and down the deck** il arpentait le pont
(**b**) *(prowl → tiger, animal)* rôder; *(hunt)* chasser; **a stalking lion** un lion en chasse; *Literary* **famine stalked through the land** la famine régnait dans le pays

stalked jellyfish [stɔːkt-] *n Zool* lucernaire *f*

stalker ['stɔːkə(r)] *n* (**a**) *(criminal)* = criminel suivant sa victime à la trace; *(obsessive fan etc)* = admirateur obsessionnel qui suit une personne en permanence (**b**) *(hunter)* chasseur *m* à l'approche

stalking ['stɔːkɪŋ] *n* (**a**) *(in hunting)* chasse *f* à l'approche (**b**) *(form of harassment)* = forme de harcèlement qui consiste à suivre quelqu'un en permanence
▸▸ ***stalking horse*** *Hunt* cheval *m* d'abri; *Fig (pretext)* prétexte *m*; *Pol* **we'll use him as a stalking horse** on va s'en servir comme d'un candidat bidon

stall [stɔːl] **1** *n* (**a**) *(at market)* étal *m*, éventaire *m*; *(at fair, exhibition)* stand *m*; **I bought some peaches at a fruit stall** j'ai acheté des pêches chez un marchand de fruits; *Br* **flower stall** *(on street)* kiosque *m* de fleuriste
(**b**) *(for animal)* stalle *f*; *Horseracing* **(starting) stalls** stalles *fpl* de départ
(**c**) *(cubicle)* cabine *f*
(**d**) *(in church)* stalle *f*
(**e**) *Br Cin & Theat* orchestre *m*, fauteuil *m* d'orchestre; **the stalls** l'orchestre *m*; **a seat in the stalls** un fauteuil d'orchestre
(**f**) *Am (in parking lot)* emplacement *m (de parking)*
(**g**) *(for finger)* doigtier *m*
(**h**) *Aviat* décrochage *m*; *Aut* calage *m (du moteur)*; **the aircraft went into a stall** l'avion a décroché
(**i**) *(delaying tactic)* manœuvre *f* dilatoire; *(pretext)* prétexte *m*
2 *vi* (**a**) *(motor, vehicle, driver)* caler; *(plane)* décrocher; *(pilot)* faire décrocher son avion
(**b**) *(delay)* **to stall for time** essayer de gagner du temps; **I can stall for another month** je peux essayer de gagner du temps pendant encore un mois; **I think they're stalling on the loan until we make more concessions** je crois qu'ils vont retarder le prêt jusqu'à ce que nous leur fassions davantage de concessions
3 *vt* (**a**) *(motor, vehicle)* caler; *(plane)* faire décrocher

(**b**) *(delay → sale, decision)* retarder; *(→ person)* faire attendre; **try to stall him (off)!** essayez de gagner du temps!; **I'll stall her in the lobby while you grab a taxi** je la retiendrai dans le hall le temps que tu sautes dans un taxi; **I can't stall them (off) for much longer** je ne peux guère les faire attendre plus longtemps; **the project/his career is stalled** le projet/sa carrière est au point mort; **we managed to stall the enemy's advance** nous avons réussi à retarder la progression de l'ennemi

(**c**) *(animal)* mettre à l'étable

stall-fed *adj (cattle)* engraissé à l'étable

stall-feed *vt (pt & pp* **stall-fed** [-fed]) *(cattle)* engraisser à l'étable

stallholder ['stɔːl,həʊldə(r)] *n Br (in market)* marchand(e) *m,f* de *ou* des quatre-saisons; *(in fair)* forain(e) *m,f*; *(in exhibition)* exposant(e) *m,f*

stalling ['stɔːlɪŋ] *n (UNCOUNT)* atermoiements *mpl*, manœuvres *fpl* dilatoires

►► ***stalling tactic*** manœuvre *f* dilatoire

stallion ['stælɪən] *n* (**a**) *(horse)* étalon *m* (**b**) *Fam (man)* étalon *m* (**c**) *Am Fam (woman)* canon *m*

stalwart ['stɔːlwət] **1** *adj (person)* robuste; *(citizen, fighter)* vaillant, brave; *(work, worker)* exemplaire; **he was a stalwart supporter of the England team** c'était un supporter inconditionnel de l'équipe d'Angleterre; **they put up a stalwart defence** ils se sont défendus d'arrache-pied

2 *n* fidèle *mf*; **the party stalwarts** les fidèles du parti

stamen ['steɪmən] *(pl* **stamens** *or* **stamina** ['stæmɪnə]) *n Bot* étamine *f*

stamina ['stæmɪnə] *n (physical)* résistance *f*, endurance *f*; *(mental)* force *f* intérieure, résistance *f*; *Sport* **to build up one's stamina** développer son endurance; **she has more stamina than he does** elle est plus résistante que lui

staminate ['stæmɪneɪt] *adj Bot* staminé

stammer ['stæmə(r)] **1** *vi (through fear, excitement)* balbutier, bégayer; *(through speech defect)* bégayer, être bègue

2 *vt* bredouiller, bégayer; **I managed to stammer (out) an apology** j'ai réussi à bredouiller des excuses

3 *n (through fear, excitement)* balbutiement *m*, bégaiement *m*; *(through speech defect)* bégaiement *m*; **to have a stammer** bégayer, être bègue; **he has a bad stammer** il est affligé d'un bégaiement prononcé

stammerer ['stæmərə(r)] *n* bègue *mf*

stammering ['stæmərɪŋ] *n (through fear, excitement)* bégaiement *m*, balbutiement *m*; *(speech defect)* bégaiement *m*

stammeringly ['stæmərɪŋlɪ] *adv* en bégayant, en bredouillant

stamp [stæmp] **1** *n* (**a**) *(on letter, document)* timbre *m*; **(postage) stamp** timbre *m*, timbre-poste *m*; **fiscal** *or* **revenue stamp** timbre *m* fiscal; **UNESCO stamps** timbres *mpl* de l'Unesco; **television (licence) stamp** timbre *m* pour la redevance; *Br* **(national insurance) stamp** cotisation *f* de sécurité sociale

(**b**) *(device for marking → rubber)* tampon *m*, timbre *m*; *(→ for metal)* poinçon *m*; *(→ for leather)* fer *m*; **signature stamp** griffe *f*

(**c**) *(mark, impression → in passport, library book etc)* cachet *m*, tampon *m*; *(→ on metal)* poinçon *m*; *(→ on leather)* motif *m*; *(→ on antique)* estampille *f*; *(postmark)* cachet *m* (d'oblitération de la poste); **he has an Israeli stamp in his passport** il a un tampon de la douane israélienne sur son passeport; **silversmith's stamp** poinçon *m* d'orfèvre; *Fig* **stamp of approval** approbation *f*, aval *m*

(**d**) *(distinctive trait)* marque *f*, empreinte *f*; **a work which bears the stamp of genius** une œuvre qui porte l'empreinte du génie; **his story had the stamp of authenticity** son histoire semblait authentique; **poverty has left its stamp on him** la pauvreté a laissé son empreinte sur lui *ou* l'a marqué de son sceau; **their faces bore the stamp of despair** le désespoir se lisait sur leur visage

(**e**) *(type, ilk, class)* genre *m*, *Pej* acabit *m*; *(calibre)* trempe *f*; **we need more teachers of his stamp** nous avons besoin de plus d'enseignants de sa trempe; **of the old stamp** *(servant, worker)* comme on n'en fait plus; *(doctor, disciplinarian)* de la vieille école

(**f**) *(noise → of boots)* bruit *m* (de bottes); *(→ of audience)* trépignement *m*; **"no!" he cried with an angry stamp of his foot** "non!", cria-t-il en tapant rageusement du pied

2 *comp (collection)* de timbres, de timbres-poste

3 *vt* (**a**) *(envelope, letter)* timbrer, affranchir

(**b**) *(mark → document)* tamponner; **he stamped the firm's name on each document** il a tamponné le nom de la société sur chaque document; **incoming mail is stamped with the date received** la date de réception est tamponnée sur le courrier qui arrive; **the machine stamps the time on your ticket** la machine marque *ou* poinçonne l'heure sur votre ticket; **it's stamped "fragile"** c'est marqué "fragile"

(**c**) *(imprint → leather, metal)* estamper; **the belt has a stamped design** la ceinture porte un motif estampé; **a design is stamped on the butter** un dessin est imprimé dans le beurre

(**d**) *(affect, mark → society, person)* marquer; **as editor she stamped her personality on the magazine** comme rédactrice en chef, elle a marqué la revue du sceau de sa personnalité

(**e**) *(characterise, brand)* étiqueter; **recent events have stamped the president as indecisive** le président a été taxé d'indécision au vu des derniers événements; **her actions stamped her as a pacifist in the eyes of the public** son comportement lui a valu une réputation de pacifiste

(**f**) *(foot)* **she stamped her foot in anger** furieuse, elle tapa du pied; **the audience were stamping their feet and booing** la salle trépignait et sifflait; **they were stamping their feet to keep warm** ils sautillaient sur place pour se réchauffer; **he stamped the snow off his boots** il a tapé du pied pour enlever la neige de ses bottes

4 *vi* (**a**) *(in one place → person)* taper du pied; *(→ audience)* trépigner; *(→ horse)* piaffer

(**b**) *(walk)* **to stamp in/out** *(noisily)* entrer/sortir bruyamment; *(angrily)* entrer/sortir en colère; **he stamped up the stairs** il monta l'escalier d'un pas lourd; **they were stamping about** *or* **around to keep warm** ils sautillaient sur place pour se réchauffer

►► *Am Hist* ***the Stamp Act*** le Stamp Act; ***stamp album*** album *m* de timbres-poste; ***stamp book*** *(of postage stamps)* carnet *m* de timbres *ou* de timbres-poste; *(for trading stamps)* carnet *m* pour coller les vignettes-épargne; **I got the toaster for ten stamp books** j'ai eu le grille-pain avec dix carnets de vignettes; ***stamp collecting*** philatélie *f*; ***stamp collector*** collectionneur(euse) *m,f* de timbres *ou* de timbres-poste, philatéliste *mf*; *Law* ***stamp duty*** droit *m* de timbre, timbre *m* fiscal; ***stamp hinge*** charnière *f*; ***stamp machine*** distributeur *m* automatique de timbres-poste

►**stamp down** *vt sep (loose earth, snow)* tasser avec les pieds; *(peg)* enfoncer du pied

►**stamp on** *vt insep* (**a**) *(step on → cockroach, worm)* ecraser (avec le talon); **I stamped on his fingers** je lui ai marché sur les doigts; **he stamped on the rotten plank and it broke** il a tapé du pied sur la planche pourrie et elle s'est cassée

(**b**) *Fig (rebellion)* écraser; *(dissent, protest)* étouffer; *(proposal)* repousser

►**stamp out** *vt sep* (**a**) *(fire)* éteindre avec les pieds *ou* en piétinant

(**b**) *(end → disease, crime, corruption, abuse)* éradiquer; *(→ strike, movement, rebellion)* réprimer; *(→ dissent, protest)* étouffer

(**c**) *(hole)* découper (à l'emporte-pièce); *(medal)* frapper; *(pattern)* estamper

THE STAMP ACT

Il s'agit de l'impôt britannique auquel furent soumises les colonies américaines à partir de 1765. Portant sur un certain nombre de publications, dont les actes juridiques et les journaux, il doit son nom au timbre justifiant de son acquittement. Premier impôt direct levé par la Couronne, il souleva une violente opposition chez les colons, qui obtinrent sa suppression un an plus tard.

stamped [stæmpt] *adj (letter, envelope)* timbré; **send a stamped addressed envelope** envoyez une enveloppe timbrée à votre adresse

stampede [stæm'piːd] **1** *n* (**a**) *(of animals)* fuite *f*, débandade *f*; **what started the stampede?** qu'est-ce qui a provoqué cette débandade?

(**b**) *(of people → flight)* sauve-qui-peut *m inv*, débandade *f*; *(→ rush)* ruée *f*; **several people were injured in the stampede** plusieurs personnes ont été blessées dans la panique; **there was a stampede for seats** il y a eu une ruée vers *ou* sur les sièges; **there's been a stampede to buy up the share issue** les acheteurs se sont précipités *ou* se sont jetés sur la souscription

2 *vi (flee)* s'enfuir (pris d'affolement); *(rush)* se ruer, se précipiter; **the cattle stampeded across the river** pris d'affolement, le bétail a traversé la rivière; **shoppers stampeded for the sales counters** les clients se sont rués *ou* se sont précipités vers les rayons des soldes; **the children came stampeding along the corridor** les enfants se sont rués dans le couloir

3 *vt* (**a**) *(animals)* faire fuir; *(crowd)* semer la panique dans

(**b**) *(pressurize)* forcer la main à; **to stampede a nation into war** précipiter un peuple dans la guerre; **to stampede sb into doing sth** presser qn de faire qch, bousculer qn pour qu'il fasse qch; **I don't want to stampede you into (making) a decision** je ne veux pas te bousculer dans ta décision; **don't let yourself be stampeded into anything** ne vous laissez pas forcer la main

stamping ['stæmpɪŋ] *n* (**a**) *(of letters, parcels)* affranchissement *m*, timbrage *m* (**b**) *(in metalwork)* estampage *m*, étampage *m*; *(item)* pièce *f* estampée (**c**) *(with feet)* piétinement *m*, trépignement *m*

►► *Fam* ***stamping ground*** lieu *m* favori; **this was one of my old stamping grounds** j'y allais tout le temps; ***stamping out*** *(of disease, crime, corruption, abuse)* éradication *f*; *(of strike, movement, rebellion)* répression *f*; *(of dissent, protest)* étouffement *m*; ***stamping press*** estampeuse *f*

stance [stæns] *n* (**a**) *(physical posture)* posture *f*; **she altered her stance slightly** elle changea légèrement de position; **he took up a boxer's stance** il adopta la position d'un boxeur; **he took up his usual stance in front of the fire** il s'est planté devant le feu à sa place habituelle; *Sport* **widen your stance** écartez les jambes (**b**) *(attitude)* position *f*; **to adopt** *or* **to take a tough stance on sth** adopter *ou* prendre une position ferme sur qch

stanch [stɑːntʃ] *Am* = **staunch** *vt*

stanchion ['stænʃən] *n* (**a**) *(post)* étai *m*, étançon *m*; *(in window)* montant *m* (**b**) *(for cow)* attache *f*

STAND [stænd]

stand	► **1 (a)**
étal	► **1 (a)**
support	► **1 (b)**
plate-forme	► **1 (c)**
tribune	► **1 (c), (d)**
barre	► **1 (f)**
position	► **1 (g)**
mettre	► **2 (a)**
poser	► **2 (a)**
supporter	► **2 (b) – (d)**
se lever	► **3 (a)**
être debout	► **3 (b), (c)**
être	► **3 (b), (e), (f)**
se tenir	► **3 (b)**
reposer	► **3 (d), (g)**
se trouver	► **3 (e)**
rester	► **3 (g)**
rester valable	► **3 (h)**
se classer	► **3 (j)**

(pt & pp **stood** [stʊd]) **1** *n* (**a**) *(stall, booth → at exhibition, trade fair)* stand *m*; *(→ in market)* étal *m*, éventaire *m*; *(kiosk)* kiosque *m*; **a shooting**

stand un stand de tir; **newspaper stand** kiosque *m* (à journaux)

(**b**) *(frame, support → gen)* support *m*; *(→ for lamp, sink)* pied *m*; *(→ on bicycle, motorbike)* béquille *f*; *(→ for pipes, guns)* râtelier *m*; *Com (→ for magazines, sunglasses)* présentoir *m*; *(lectern)* lutrin *m*; **bicycle stand** *(in street)* râtelier *m* à bicyclettes; **plant stand** sellette *f*; **plate stand** support *m* à assiette, présentoir *m*; *Com* **revolving stand** tourniquet *m*, présentoir *m* rotatif

(**c**) *(platform → gen)* plate-forme *f*; *(→ for speaker)* tribune *f*; *(pulpit)* chaire *f*

(**d**) *(in sports ground)* tribune *f*; **the stands roared** un rugissement s'éleva des tribunes *ou* des gradins

(**e**) *(for taxis)* **(taxi) stand** station *f* de taxis

(**f**) *(in courtroom)* barre *f*; **the first witness took the stand** le premier témoin est venu à la barre

(**g**) *(position, stance)* position *f*; **to take a stand on sth** prendre position sur qch; **what's your stand on the issue?** quelle est votre position sur la question?; **he refuses to take a stand** il refuse de prendre position

(**h**) *Mil & Fig (defensive effort)* résistance *f*, opposition *f*; **to make a stand** résister; **they made a stand at the foot of the hill** ils ont résisté au pied de la colline; **to make a stand against an abuse** s'opposer résolument à un abus; *Hist* **Custer's last stand** la dernière bataille de Custer

(**i**) *(of trees)* bosquet *m*, futaie *f*; *(of crop)* récolte *f* sur pied; **a fine stand of corn** un beau champ de blé; **a stand of bamboo** un massif de bambous

2 *vt* (**a**) *(set, place)* mettre, poser; **he stood the boy on a chair** il a mis le garçon debout sur une chaise; **she stood her umbrella in the corner** elle a mis son parapluie dans le coin; **to stand sth on (its) end** mettre qch debout; **help me stand the bedstead against the wall** aide-moi à dresser le sommier *ou* mettre le sommier debout contre le mur

(**b**) *(endure, withstand)* supporter; **his heart couldn't stand the shock** son cœur n'a pas résisté au *ou* n'a pas supporté le choc; **it will stand high temperatures without cracking** cela peut résister à *ou* supporter des températures élevées sans se fissurer; **how much weight can the bridge stand?** quel poids le pont peut-il supporter?; **the motor wasn't built to stand intensive use** le moteur n'a pas été conçu pour supporter un usage intensif; **wool carpeting can stand a lot of hard wear** les moquettes en laine sont très résistantes; **she's not strong enough to stand another operation** elle n'est pas assez forte pour supporter une nouvelle opération; **he certainly doesn't stand comparison with Bogart** il n'est absolument pas possible de le comparer avec Bogart; **their figures don't stand close inspection** leurs chiffres ne résistent pas à un examen sérieux

(**c**) *(put up with, bear → toothache, cold)* supporter; *(→ behaviour)* supporter, tolérer; **I can't stand it any longer!** je n'en peux plus!; **how can you stand working with him?** comment est-ce que vous faites pour *ou* comment arrivez-vous à travailler avec lui?; **I've had as much as I can stand of your griping!** j'en ai assez de tes jérémiades!; **if there's one thing I can't stand, it's hypocrisy** s'il y a quelque chose que je ne supporte pas, c'est bien l'hypocrisie; **I can't stand (the sight of) him!** je ne peux pas le supporter!, je ne peux pas le voir en peinture!; **she can't stand Wagner/smokers** elle ne peut pas supporter Wagner/les fumeurs; **he can't stand flying** il déteste prendre l'avion

(**d**) *Fam (do with, need)* supporter ❑, avoir besoin de ❑; **oil company profits could certainly stand a cut** une diminution de leurs bénéfices ne ferait aucun mal aux compagnies pétrolières; **he could stand a bath!** un bain ne lui ferait pas de mal!; *Am* **could I stand a drink!** je prendrais bien un petit verre!

(**e**) *(perform duty of)* remplir la fonction de; **to stand witness for sb** *(at marriage)* être le témoin de qn

(**f**) *Fam (treat to)* **to stand sb a meal** payer un repas à qn; *Br* **I'll stand you a drink,** *Am* **I'll stand you to a drink** je t'offre un verre

(**g**) *(idiom)* **to stand a chance (of doing sth)** avoir de bonnes chances (de faire qch); **you don't stand a chance!** vous n'avez pas la moindre chance!; **the plans stand little chance of being approved** les projets ont peu de chances d'être approuvés

3 *vi* (**a**) *(rise to one's feet)* se lever, se mettre debout; **he refused to stand for the national anthem** il a refusé de se lever pendant l'hymne national

(**b**) *(be on one's feet)* être debout, se tenir debout; *(in a specified location, posture)* être, se tenir; **I've been standing all day** je suis resté debout toute la journée; **I had to stand all the way** j'ai dû voyager debout pendant tout le trajet; **she was so tired she could hardly stand** elle était si fatiguée qu'elle avait du mal à tenir debout *ou* sur ses jambes; **wear flat shoes if you have to stand a lot** portez des chaussures à talons plats si vous devez rester debout pendant des heures; **I don't mind standing** ça ne me gêne pas de rester debout; **don't stand near the edge** ne restez pas près du bord; **don't just stand there, do something!** ne restez pas là à ne rien faire!; **stand clear!** écartez-vous!; **I saw her standing at the window** je l'ai vue (debout) à la fenêtre; **a man stood in the doorway** un homme se tenait à la porte; **do you see that man standing over there?** vous voyez cet homme là-bas?; **where should I stand? – beside Yvonne** où dois-je me mettre? – à côté d'Yvonne; **I'll be standing outside the theatre** j'attendrai devant le théâtre; **small groups of men stood talking at street corners** des hommes discutaient par petits groupes au coin des rues; **he was standing at the bar** il était debout au comptoir; **is there a chair I can stand on?** y a-t-il une chaise sur laquelle je puisse monter?; **they were standing a little way off** ils se tenaient un peu à l'écart; **excuse me, you're standing on my foot** excusez-moi, vous me marchez sur le pied; *Am* **to stand in line** faire la queue; *Sch* **stand in the corner!** au coin!; **to stand upright** *or* **erect** se tenir droit; **he was so nervous he couldn't stand still** il était si nerveux qu'il ne tenait pas en place; **I stood perfectly still, hoping they wouldn't see me** je me suis figé sur place en espérant qu'ils ne me verraient pas; **stand still!** ne bougez pas!, ne bougez plus!; **stand with your feet apart** écartez les pieds; **the heron was standing on one leg** le héron se tenait debout sur une patte; **to stand on tiptoe** se tenir sur la pointe des pieds; **stand and deliver!** la bourse ou la vie!; *Fig* **to stand on one's own two feet** se débrouiller tout seul; *Fig* **he left the others standing** *(gen)* il était de loin le meilleur; *(in race)* il a laissé les autres sur place

(**c**) *(be upright → post, target etc)* être debout; **not a stone (of the building) was left standing** le bâtiment était complètement détruit; **the house is still standing** la maison tient toujours debout; **the aqueduct has stood for centuries** l'aqueduc est là depuis des siècles; **the wheat stood high** les blés étaient hauts

(**d**) *(be supported, be mounted)* reposer; **the coffin stood on trestles** le cercueil reposait sur des tréteaux; **the house stands on solid foundations** la maison repose *ou* est bâtie sur des fondations solides; *Fig* **this argument stands on three simple facts** ce raisonnement repose sur trois simples faits

(**e**) *(be located → building, tree, statue)* se trouver; *(→ clock, vase, lamp)* être, être posé; **the fort stands on a hill** la forteresse se trouve en haut d'une colline; **this is where the city gates once stood** c'est ici qu'autrefois se dressaient les portes de la ville; **the piano stood in the centre of the room** le piano était au centre *ou* occupait le centre de la pièce; **the bottles stood in rows of five** les bouteilles étaient disposées en rangées de cinq; **do you see the lorry standing next to my car?** vous voyez le camion qui est à côté de ma voiture?; **a wardrobe stood against one wall** il y avait une armoire contre un mur

(**f**) *(indicating current state of affairs, situation)* être; **how do things stand?** où en est la situation?; **how do we stand?** *(in work etc)* où en sommes-nous?; *(financially)* où en sont nos comptes?; **I'd like to know where I stand with you** j'aimerais savoir où en sont les choses entre nous; **I don't know where I stand** j'ignore quelle est ma situation *ou* ma position; **you never know how** *or* **where you stand with her** on ne sait jamais sur quel pied danser avec elle; **as things stand, as matters stand** telles que les choses se présentent; **he's dissatisfied with the contract as it stands** il n'est pas satisfait du contrat tel qu'il a été rédigé; **just print the text as it stands** imprimez le texte tel quel; **he stands accused of rape** il est accusé de viol; **she stands alone in advocating this approach** elle est la seule à préconiser cette approche; **I stand corrected** je reconnais m'être trompé *ou* mon erreur; **the doors stood wide open** les portes étaient grandes ouvertes; **I've got a taxi standing ready** j'ai un taxi qui attend; **the police are standing ready to intervene** la police se tient prête à intervenir; **the party stands united behind him** le parti est uni derrière lui; **no-one stands above the law** personne n'est au-dessus des lois; **to stand at** *(gauge, barometer)* indiquer; *(score)* être de; *(unemployment)* avoir atteint; **their turnover now stands at three million pounds** leur chiffre d'affaires atteint désormais les trois millions de livres; **the exchange rate stands at 5 francs to the dollar** le taux de change est de 5 francs pour un dollar; **we're standing right behind you** nous sommes avec vous; **with the union standing behind him** avec le soutien du syndicat; **nothing stood between her and victory** rien ne pouvait désormais l'empêcher de gagner; **it's the only thing standing between us and financial disaster** c'est la seule chose qui nous empêche de sombrer dans un désastre financier; **to stand in need of...** avoir besoin de...; **he stands in danger of losing his job** il risque de perdre son emploi; **I stood lost in admiration** j'en suis resté béat d'admiration; **to stand in sb's way** bloquer le passage à qn; *Fig* **don't stand in my way!** n'essaie pas de m'en empêcher!; **nothing stands in our way now** maintenant, la voie est libre; **if you want to leave school I'm not going to stand in your way** si tu veux quitter l'école, je ne m'y opposerai pas; **it's his lack of experience that stands in his way** c'est son manque d'expérience qui le handicape; **their foreign debt stands in the way of economic recovery** leur dette extérieure constitue un obstacle à la reprise économique; **her pride is the only thing standing in the way of their reconciliation** son orgueil est le seul obstacle à leur réconciliation

(**g**) *(remain)* rester; *(be left undisturbed → marinade, dough)* reposer; *(→ tea)* infuser; **the machines stood idle** les machines étaient arrêtées; **the houses stood empty awaiting demolition** les maisons, vidées de leurs occupants, attendaient d'être démolies; **time stood still** le temps semblait s'être arrêté; **the car has been standing in the garage for a year** ça fait un an que la voiture n'a pas bougé du garage; **I've decided to let my flight reservation stand** j'ai décidé de ne pas changer ma réservation d'avion; **let the mixture stand until the liquid is clear** laissez reposer le mélange jusqu'à ce que le liquide se clarifie; **the champion stands unbeaten** le champion reste invaincu; **his theory stood unchallenged for a decade** pendant dix ans, personne n'a remis en cause sa théorie; **the government will stand or fall on the outcome of this vote** le maintien ou la chute du gouvernement dépend du résultat de ce vote; **united we stand, divided we fall** l'union fait la force

(**h**) *(be valid, effective → offer, law)* rester valable; *(→ decision)* rester inchangé; **my invitation still stands** vous êtes toujours invité; **the verdict stands unless there's an appeal** le jugement reste valable à moins que l'on ne fasse appel; **even with this new plan, our objection still stands** ce nouveau projet ne remet pas en cause notre objection première; **the bet stands** le pari tient; **what you said last week, does that still stand?** et ce que tu as dit la semaine dernière, ça tient toujours?

(**i**) *(measure → person, tree)* mesurer; **she stands 5 feet in her stocking feet** elle mesure moins de 1,50 m pieds nus; **the building stands ten storeys high** l'immeuble compte dix étages

(**j**) *(rank)* se classer, compter; **this hotel stands among the best in the world** cet hôtel figure parmi les meilleurs du monde; *Am* **she stands first/last in her class** elle est la première/la dernière de sa classe; **I know she stands high in your opinion** je sais que tu as une très bonne opinion d'elle; **for price and quality, it stands high on my list** en ce qui concerne le prix et la qualité, je le range *ou* le compte parmi les meilleurs

(**k**) *(on issue)* **how** *or* **where does he stand on the nuclear issue?** quelle est sa position *ou* son point de vue sur la question du nucléaire?; **you ought to tell them where you stand** vous devriez leur faire part de votre position

(**l**) *(be likely)* **to stand to lose** risquer de perdre; **to stand to win** avoir des chances de gagner; **they stand to make a huge profit on the deal** ils ont des chances de faire un bénéfice énorme dans cette affaire; **no one stands to gain from a quarrel like this** personne n'a rien à gagner d'une telle querelle

(**m**) *Br (run in election)* se présenter, être candidat; **she stood for Waltham** elle a été candidate à la circonscription de Waltham; **will he stand for re-election?** va-t-il se représenter aux élections?; **she's standing as an independent** elle se présente en tant que candidate indépendante

(**n**) *Am (stop)* s'arrêter *(pour un court instant)*; **no standing** *(sign)* arrêt interdit

(**o**) *Am (pay)* payer la tournée; **you're standing** c'est ta tournée

▸**stand about, stand around** *vi* rester là; **we stood about** *or* **around waiting for the flight announcement** nous restions là à attendre que le vol soit annoncé; **the prisoners stood about** *or* **around in small groups** les prisonniers se tenaient par petits groupes; **after Mass, the men stand about** *or* **around in the square** après la messe, les hommes s'attardent sur la place; **I can't afford to pay people to stand around all day doing nothing** je n'ai pas les moyens de payer les gens à ne rien faire; **I'm not just going to stand about waiting for you to make up your mind!** je n'ai pas l'intention de rester là à attendre que tu te décides!

▸**stand aside** *vi (move aside)* s'écarter; **stand aside, someone's fainted!** écartez-vous, quelqu'un s'est évanoui!; **he politely stood aside to let us pass** il s'écarta *ou* s'effaça poliment pour nous laisser passer; *Fig* **to stand aside in favour of sb** *(gen)* laisser la voie libre à qn; *Pol* se désister en faveur de qn

▸**stand back** *vi* (**a**) *(move back)* reculer, s'écarter; **stand back from the doors!** écartez-vous des portes!; **she stood back to look at herself in the mirror** elle recula pour se regarder dans la glace; **the painting is better if you stand back from it** le tableau est mieux si vous prenez du recul

(**b**) *(be set back)* être en retrait *ou* à l'écart; **the house stands back from the road** la maison est en retrait (de la route)

(**c**) *(take mental distance)* prendre du recul; **I need to stand back and take stock** j'ai besoin de prendre du recul et de faire le point

▸**stand by** **1** *vt insep* (**a**) *(support → person)* soutenir; **I'll stand by you through thick and thin** je te soutiendrai *ou* je resterai à tes côtés quoi qu'il arrive

(**b**) *(adhere to → promise, word)* tenir; *(→ decision, offer)* s'en tenir à; **to stand by an agreement** respecter un accord; **I stand by what I said/my original analysis of the situation** je m'en tiens à ce que j'ai dit/ma première analyse de la situation

2 *vi* (**a**) *(not intervene)* rester là (sans rien faire *ou* sans intervenir); **how could you just stand by and watch them mistreat that poor dog?** comment as-tu pu rester là à les regarder maltraiter ce pauvre chien (sans intervenir)?; **I stood by helplessly while they searched the room** je restais là, impuissant, pendant qu'ils fouillaient la pièce

(**b**) *(be ready → person)* être *ou* se tenir prêt; *(→ vehicle)* être prêt; *(→ army, embassy)* être en état d'alerte; **the police were standing by to disperse the crowd** la police se tenait prête à disperser la foule; **we have an oxygen machine standing by** nous avons une machine à oxygène prête en cas d'urgence; **stand by!** attention!; *Naut* paré!, attention!; *Aviat* **stand by for takeoff** préparez-vous pour le décollage; *Rad* **stand by to receive** prenez l'écoute; *Mil* **standing by for orders!** à vos ordres!

▸**stand down** **1** *vi* (**a**) *Br Pol (withdraw)* se désister; *(resign)* démissionner; **will he stand down in favour of a younger candidate?** va-t-il se désister en faveur d'un candidat plus jeune?

(**b**) *(leave witness box)* quitter la barre; **you may stand down, Mr Simms** vous pouvez quitter la barre, M. Simms

(**c**) *Mil (troops)* être déconsigné *(en fin d'alerte)*; **stand down!** *(after drill)* rompez (les rangs)!

2 *vt sep (workers)* licencier

▸**stand for** *vt insep* (**a**) *(represent)* représenter; **what does DNA stand for?** que veut dire l'abréviation ADN?; **the R stands for Ryan** le R signifie Ryan; **the dove stands for peace** la colombe symbolise la paix; **we want our name to stand for quality and efficiency** nous voulons que notre nom soit synonyme de qualité et d'efficacité; **she supports the values and ideas the party once stood for** elle soutient les valeurs et les idées qui furent autrefois celles du parti; **I detest everything that they stand for!** je déteste tout ce qu'ils représentent!

(**b**) *(tolerate)* tolérer, supporter; *(allow)* permettre; **I'm not going to stand for it!** je ne le tolérerai *ou* permettrai pas!

▸**stand in** *vi* assurer le remplacement; **to stand in for sb** remplacer qn; *Cin* doubler qn

▸**stand off** **1** *vt sep Br (workers)* mettre en chômage technique

2 *vt insep Naut (coast, island)* croiser au large de; **they have an aircraft carrier standing off Aden** ils ont un porte-avions qui croise au large d'Aden

3 *vi* (**a**) *(move away)* s'écarter

(**b**) *Naut (take up position)* croiser; *(sail away)* mettre le cap au large

▸**stand out** *vi* (**a**) *(protrude → vein)* saillir; *(→ ledge)* faire saillie, avancer; **the veins in his neck stood out** les veines de son cou saillaient *ou* étaient gonflées

(**b**) *(be clearly visible → colour, typeface)* ressortir, se détacher; *(→ in silhouette)* se découper; **the pink stands out against the green background** le rose ressort *ou* se détache sur le fond vert; **the masts stood out against the sky** les mâts se découpaient *ou* se dessinaient contre le ciel; **the name on the truck stood out clearly** le nom sur le camion était bien visible; **she stands out in a crowd** on la remarque dans la foule; *Fig* **I don't like to stand out in a crowd** je n'aime pas me singulariser; **this one book stands out from all his others** ce livre-ci surclasse tous ses autres livres; **there is no one issue which stands out as being more important than the others** il n'y a pas une question qui soit plus importante que les autres; **the qualities that stand out in his work** les qualités marquantes de son œuvre; **she stands out above all the rest** elle surpasse *ou* surclasse tous les autres; **the day stands out in my memory** cette journée est marquée d'une pierre blanche dans ma mémoire; *Fam* **that stands out a mile!** *(is very obvious)* ça se voit comme le nez au milieu de la figure!; **it really stands out that he's not a local** ça se voit *ou* se remarque vraiment qu'il n'est pas d'ici

(**c**) *(resist, hold out)* tenir bon, tenir, résister; **they won't be able to stand out for long** ils ne pourront pas tenir *ou* résister longtemps; **to stand out against** *(attack, enemy)* résister à; *(change, tax increase)* s'opposer avec détermination à; **to stand out for sth** revendiquer qch; **they are standing out for a pay increase** ils revendiquent *ou* réclament une augmentation de salaire

▸**stand over** **1** *vt insep (watch over)* surveiller; **I can't work with someone standing over me** je ne peux pas travailler quand quelqu'un regarde par-dessus mon épaule; **she stood over him until he'd eaten every last bit** elle ne l'a pas lâché avant qu'il ait mangé la dernière miette

2 *vt sep Br (postpone)* remettre (à plus tard); **I'd prefer to stand this discussion over until we have more information** je préférerais remettre cette discussion jusqu'à ce que nous disposions de plus amples renseignements

3 *vi Br* être remis (à plus tard); **we have two items standing over from the last meeting** il nous reste deux points à régler depuis la dernière réunion

▸**stand to** **1** *vt sep Mil* mettre en état d'alerte

2 *vi Mil* se mettre en état d'alerte; **stand to!** à vos postes!

▸**stand together** *vi* être *ou* rester solidaire

▸**stand up** **1** *vt sep* (**a**) *(set upright → chair, bottle)* mettre debout; **they stood the prisoner up against a tree** ils ont adossé le prisonnier à un arbre; **stand the ladder up against the wall** mettez *ou* appuyez l'échelle contre le mur; **to stand a child up (again)** (re)mettre un enfant sur ses pieds

(**b**) *Fam (fail to meet)* poser un lapin à; **I was stood up twice in a row** on m'a posé un lapin deux fois de suite

2 *vi* (**a**) *(rise to one's feet)* se lever, se mettre debout; **she stood up to offer me her seat** elle se leva pour m'offrir sa place; **stand up!** levez-vous!, debout!; *Fig* **to stand up and be counted** avoir le courage de ses opinions

(**b**) *(be upright)* être debout; **I can't get the candle to stand up straight** je n'arrive pas à faire tenir la bougie droite

(**c**) *(last)* tenir, résister; **how is that repair job standing up?** est-ce que cette réparation tient toujours?

(**d**) *(be valid → argument, claim)* être valable, tenir debout; **his evidence won't stand up in court** son témoignage ne sera pas valable en justice

▸**stand up for** *vt insep* défendre; **to stand up for oneself** se défendre

▸**stand up to** *vt insep* **to stand up to sth** résister à qch; **to stand up to sb** tenir tête à *ou* faire face à qn; **he's too weak to stand up to her** il est trop faible pour lui tenir tête; **she had a hard time standing up to their criticism** ça ne lui a pas été facile de faire face à leurs critiques; **it won't stand up to that sort of treatment** ça ne résistera pas à ce genre de traitement; **her hypothesis doesn't stand up to empirical testing** son hypothèse ne résiste pas à la vérification expérimentale

---

stand-alone *Comput* **1** *adj (system)* autonome; **it has stand-alone capability** ça peut fonctionner de façon autonome

2 *n* poste *m* autonome

▸▸ ***stand-alone computer*** ordinateur *m* autonome

standard ['stændəd] **1** *n* (**a**) *(level of quality)* niveau *m*; *(criterion)* critère *m*; **to have high/low standards** *(of person)* être exigeant/ne pas être exigeant; *(of school)* exiger un bon niveau/ne pas exiger un bon niveau; **he sets high standards for himself** il est très exigeant avec lui-même; **a high standard of playing/academic achievement** un niveau de jeu/de réussite scolaire élevé; **your work isn't up to standard** *or* **is below standard** votre travail laisse à désirer; **to be up to/below standard** être au/en dessous du niveau requis; **most of the goods are** *or* **come up to standard** la plupart des marchandises sont de qualité satisfaisante; **she's an Olympic standard swimmer** c'est une nageuse de niveau olympique; **it's a difficult task by any standard** *or* **by anybody's standards** c'est indiscutablement une tâche difficile; **we apply the same standards to all candidates** nous jugeons tous les candidats selon les mêmes critères; **their only standard of success is money** leur unique critère de réussite, c'est l'argent; **we don't have the same aesthetic standards** nous n'avons pas les mêmes valeurs esthétiques; **standard of living** niveau *m* de vie

(**b**) *(official specification, norm)* norme *f*; **to set quality standards for a product** fixer des normes de qualité pour un produit; **to comply with** *or* **to meet government standards** être conforme aux normes établies par le gouvernement; **their salaries are low by European standards** leurs salaires sont bas par rapport aux salaires européens; **high safety standards** des règles de sécurité très strictes; **standards and practices** normes et usages

(**c**) *(moral principle)* principe *m*; **I won't do it! I have my standards!** je ne le ferai pas! j'ai des principes!; **to have high moral standards** avoir de grands principes moraux

(**d**) *(for measures, currency → model)* étalon *m*; *(in coins → proportion)* titre *m*

(**e**) *(tune)* classique *m*; **a jazz standard** un classique du jazz, un standard

(**f**) *Am (car)* **I can't drive a standard** je ne sais conduire que les voitures à boîte de vitesse automatique

(**g**) *(flag)* étendard *m*; *(of sovereign, noble)* bannière *f*; *Naut* pavillon *m*; *Fig* **under the standard of Liberty** sous l'étendard de la liberté

(**h**) *(support → pole)* poteau *m*; *(→ for flag)* mât *m*; *(→ for lamp)* pied *m*; *(→ for power-line)* pylône *m*

(**i**) *Br (lamp)* lampadaire *m* (de salon)

(**j**) *Agr & Hort (fruit tree)* haute-tige *f*

(**k**) *Bot (petal)* étendard *m*

(**l**) *Br Old-fashioned (class)* classe *f*

2 *adj* (**a**) *(ordinary, regular → gen)* normal; *(→ model, size)* standard; **they come in three standard sizes** ils existent en trois tailles standard; **catalytic converters are now standard features** les pots catalytiques sont désormais la norme; **headrests are standard** *or* **are fitted as standard** les appuis-têtes sont montés en série; **the standard return fare is $500** l'aller-retour au tarif normal coûte 500 dollars; **what's the standard tip?** que laisse-t-on normalement comme pourboire?; **there's a standard procedure for reporting accidents** il y a une procédure bien établie pour signaler les accidents; **any standard detergent will do** n'importe quel détergent usuel fera l'affaire; **it was just a standard hotel room** c'était une chambre d'hôtel ordinaire; **the cooking is fairly standard** la cuisine n'a rien de sensationnel; **she has a standard speech for such occasions** elle a un discours tout prêt pour ce genre d'occasions; **one of his standard jokes** une de ses plaisanteries habituelles

(**b**) *(measure → metre, kilogramme etc)* étalon *(inv)*

(**c**) *(text, work)* classique, de base; **the standard works in English poetry** les ouvrages classiques de la poésie anglaise; **it's the standard work on the Reformation** c'est l'ouvrage de base sur la Réforme

(**d**) *Ling (pronunciation, spelling etc)* standard

(**e**) *Agr & Hort (fruit tree, shrub)* à haute tige

►► ***standard bearer*** *(of cause)* porte-drapeau *m*; *(of political party)* chef *m* de file; *(of flag)* porte-étendard *m*; ***standards catalogue*** catalogue *m* de normes; ***standards committee*** organisme *m* de normalisation; ***standards conversion*** *(in broadcasting)* transcodage *m*; ***standards converter*** *(in broadcasting)* transcodeur *m*; ***standard deviation*** *(in statistics)* écart-type *m*; ***standard document*** document *m* type; ***standard English*** l'anglais *m* standard; ***standard error*** *(in statistics)* écart-type *m*; *Rail* ***standard gauge*** voie *f* normale, écartement *m* normal; *Am Aut* ***standard gear shift*** changement *m* de vitesse manuel; *Scot Sch* ***Standard grade*** = premier examen de fin de scolarité en Écosse, équivalent du GCSE anglais; *Br* ***standard lamp*** lampadaire *m* (de salon); ***standard operating procedure*** = marche à suivre normale; ***standard practice*** pratique *f* courante; ***standard rate*** *(of tax)* taux *m* standard; *Bot* ***standard rose*** rose *f* tige; *Mktg* ***standard sample*** échantillon *m* modèle; ***standard time*** heure *f* légale

standard-gauge *adj (line)* à voie normale; *(carriage, engine)* pour voie normale

standardization [ˌstændədaɪˈzeɪʃən] *n* (**a**) *(gen)* standardisation *f*; *(of dimensions, terms etc)* normalisation *f* (**b**) *Tech (verification)* étalonnage *m*

standardize, -ise [ˈstændədaɪz] *vt* (**a**) *(gen)* standardiser; *(dimensions, products, terms)* normaliser (**b**) *Tech (verify)* étalonner

►► ***standardized parts*** pièces *fpl* standardisées *ou* standard

standard-winged nightjar *n Orn* engoulevent *m* porte-étendards

standaway [ˈstændəweɪ] *adj (skirt, sleeve)* bouffant

►► ***standaway collar*** = col qui dégage le cou ou les épaules

standby [ˈstændbaɪ] *(pl* **standbys***)* **1** *adj* (**a**) *(equipment, provisions etc)* de réserve; *(generator)* de secours; **to be on standby duty** *(doctor)* être de garde *ou* d'astreinte; *(flight personnel, emergency repairman)* être d'astreinte; *(troops, police, firemen)* être prêt à intervenir; **the standby team can take over operations within an hour** l'équipe de secours est prête à prendre le contrôle des opérations en moins d'une heure; **the shortages meant some factories were put on a standby basis** à cause de la pénurie, certaines usines ont dû ralentir leur rythme de production; *Rad* **in standby position** en écoute

(**b**) *Aviat (ticket, fare)* stand-by *(inv)*; *(passenger)* stand-by *(inv)*, en attente

2 *n* (**a**) *(substitute → person)* remplaçant(e) *m,f*; *Theat (understudy)* doublure *f*; **to be on standby** *(doctor)* être de garde *ou* d'astreinte; *(flight personnel, emergency repairman)* être d'astreinte; *(troops, police, firemen)* être prêt à intervenir; **we have a repair crew on standby** nous avons une équipe de dépannage prête à intervenir en cas de besoin; **make sure you have a standby** *(equipment)* vérifiez que vous en avez un/une de secours; *(person)* assurez-vous que vous pouvez vous faire remplacer; **I'll keep the old typewriter as a standby** je garderai la vieille machine à écrire en cas de besoin *ou* au cas où; **eggs are a great standby in the kitchen** il est toujours bon d'avoir des œufs dans une cuisine; **that story is an old standby of his** cette histoire lui a beaucoup servi

(**b**) *Aviat (system)* stand-by *m inv*; *(passenger)* (passager(ère) *m,f*) stand-by *m inv*; **to be on standby** *(passenger)* être en stand-by *ou* sur la liste d'attente

3 *adv (travel)* en stand-by

►► *Fin* ***standby agreement*** accord *m* d'aide en réserve; *Fin* ***standby credit*** crédit *m* stand-by *ou* de soutien; *Aviat* ***standby list*** liste *f* d'attente; *Fin* ***standby loan*** prêt *m* conditionnel; *Comput* ***standby mode*** veille *f*; **in standby mode** en veille

standee [stænˈdiː] *n Am (in theatre)* = spectateur qui n'a pas de place assise; *(in public transport)* passager(ère) *m,f* debout

stand-in **1** *n (gen)* remplaçant(e) *m,f*; *Cin (for lighting check)* doublure *f*; *(stunt person)* cascadeur(euse) *m,f*; *Theat (understudy)* doublure *f*; **she asked him to go as her stand-in** elle lui a demandé de la remplacer

2 *adj (gen)* remplaçant; *(office worker)* intérimaire; *(teacher)* suppléant, qui fait des remplacements; **we'll need stand-in staff during the summer** nous aurons besoin d'intérimaires pendant l'été; **I can't find a stand-in speaker for tomorrow's session** je ne trouve personne qui puisse remplacer le conférencier prévu pour demain

standing [ˈstændɪŋ] **1** *adj* (**a**) *(upright → position, person, object)* debout *(inv)*

(**b**) *(grain, timber)* sur pied

(**c**) *(stagnant → water)* stagnant

(**d**) *(permanent → army, offer etc)* permanent; *(→ claim)* de longue date; **it's a standing joke with us** c'est une vieille plaisanterie entre nous; **you have a standing invitation** tu peux venir chez moi/nous quand tu veux

2 *n* (**a**) *(reputation)* réputation *f*; *(status)* standing *m*; **a man of your standing needs to be more careful** un homme de votre standing se doit d'être plus prudent; **an economist of considerable standing** un économiste de grand renom *ou* très réputé; **people of lower/higher social standing** des gens d'une position sociale moins/plus élevée; **they are a family of some standing in the community** c'est une famille qui jouit d'une certaine position dans la communauté; **enquiries were made into his financial standing** on a enquêté sur sa situation financière; **Mr Pym is a client in good standing with our bank** M. Pym est un client très estimé de notre banque; **the scandal has damaged the company's standing in the eyes of the public** le scandale a nui à la réputation de la société auprès du public

(**b**) *(ranking)* rang *m*, place *f*; *Sch & Sport (ordered list)* classement *m*; **her standing in the opinion polls is at its lowest yet** sa cote de popularité dans les sondages est au plus bas; **the standings in the Senate are Liberals 62 seats and Conservatives 30** la répartition des sièges au Sénat est de 62 sièges pour les libéraux et 30 pour les conservateurs; **what's their standing in the league table?** quel est leur classement dans le championnat?

(**c**) *(duration)* durée *f*; **of long standing** de longue date; **of 15 years' standing** *(collaboration, feud)* qui dure depuis 15 ans; *(treaty, account)* qui existe depuis 15 ans; *(friend, member)* depuis 15 ans; **an employee of 10 years' standing** un salarié qui a 10 ans d'ancienneté dans l'entreprise

(**d**) *Am Aut* **no standing** *(sign)* arrêt interdit

(**e**) *Am Law* position *f* en droit; **homosexuals have no standing to collect alimony payments** aucune disposition légale n'autorise les homosexuels à toucher une pension alimentaire

►► ***standing charges*** *(on bill)* frais *mpl* d'abonnement; ***standing committee*** comité *m* permanent; *Agr* ***standing crop*** récolte *f* sur pied; *Biol (of plankton)* biomasse *f*; *Sport* ***standing jump*** saut *m* à pieds joints; *Am* ***standing lamp*** lampadaire *m* (de salon); *Br Banking* ***standing order*** virement *m* automatique; **to pay by standing order** payer par prélèvement (bancaire) automatique; **I get paid by standing order** je reçois mon salaire par virement bancaire; *Br Pol* ***standing orders*** règlement *m* intérieur *(d'une assemblée délibérative)*; ***standing ovation*** ovation *f*; **to get a standing ovation** se faire ovationner; ***standing places*** places *fpl* debout; ***standing room*** places *fpl* debout; **it was standing room only on the train** il n'y avait plus de places assises dans le train; **it was standing room only at the meeting** la salle était pleine à craquer lors de la réunion; *Sport* ***standing start*** départ *m* debout; *Aut* départ *m* arrêté; **it reaches 100 mph in 40 seconds from a standing start** elle atteint les 160 km/h en 40 secondes départ arrêté; ***standing stone*** pierre *f* levée; *Phys* ***standing wave*** onde *f* stationnaire

standoff [ˈstændɒf] *n* (**a**) *Pol (inconclusive clash)* affrontement *m* indécis; *(deadlock)* impasse *f*; **their debate ended in a standoff** leur débat n'a rien donné; **the standoff over the budget is making Wall Street nervous** l'impasse dans laquelle se trouve le budget inquiète Wall Street

(**b**) *Am Sport (tie)* match *m* nul

(**c**) *Br (in rugby)* demi *m* d'ouverture

►► *Br* ***standoff half*** *(in rugby)* demi *m* d'ouverture; ***standoff missile*** missile *m* tiré à distance de sécurité

standoffish [ˌstændˈɒfɪʃ] *adj* distant, froid; **there's no need to be standoffish** ce n'est pas la peine de prendre cet air supérieur

standoffishness [ˌstændˈɒfɪʃnɪs] *n* raideur *f*, réserve *f*

standout [ˈstændaʊt] *n* **his article was a real standout** son article sortait vraiment du lot; **the second book in the series is the standout** le deuxième tome de la série est celui qui ressort (par rapport aux autres)

standpipe [ˈstændpaɪp] *n* (**a**) *(in street → for fire brigade)* bouche *f* d'incendie; *(→ for public)* point *m* d'alimentation en eau de secours (**b**) *(in pumping system)* tuyau *m* ascendant, colonne *f* d'alimentation

standpoint [ˈstændpɔɪnt] *n* point *m* de vue; **try to see the situation from her standpoint** essayez de voir la situation de son point de vue à elle; **from a late 20th-century standpoint** dans une perspective de fin de XXème siècle

standstill [ˈstændstɪl] *n* arrêt *m*; **to come to a standstill** *(vehicle, person)* s'immobiliser; *(talks, work etc)* piétiner; **to bring to a standstill** *(vehicle, person)* arrêter; *(talks, traffic)* paralyser; **to be at a standstill** *(talks, career)* être au point mort; *(traffic)* être paralysé; *(economy)* piétiner, stagner

►► *Fin* ***standstill agreement*** moratoire *m*

stand-up **1** *n (comedy)* spectacle *m* comique; **to do stand-up** faire des spectacles comiques

2 *adj* (**a**) *(collar)* droit; *(meal)* (pris) debout; **a stand-up fight** *(physical)* une bagarre en règle;

(verbal) une discussion violente (**b**) *Am Fam (decent)* bien

►► ***stand-up comic*** *or* ***comedian*** comique *mf (qui se produit seul en scène)*; ***stand-up comedy*** spectacles *mpl* comiques; *Am* ***stand-up counter, stand-up diner*** buvette *f*

Stanford ['stænfəd] *n* = prestigieuse université près de San Francisco

stanhope ['stænhəʊp] *n* cabriolet *m* découvert

stank [stæŋk] *pt of* **stink**

Stanley knife® ['stænlɪ-] *n* cutter *m*

stannary ['stænərɪ] (*pl* **stannaries**) *n* mine *f* d'étain

stannic ['stænɪk] *adj Chem* stannique

stannite ['stænaɪt] *n Miner* stannine *f*, stannite *f*

stannous ['stænəs] *adj Chem* stanneux

stanza ['stænzə] *n* (**a**) *(in poetry)* strophe *f* (**b**) *Am Sport* période *f*

stapes ['steɪpi:z] *n Anat* étrier *m*

staphylococcus [ˌstæfɪləʊ'kɒkəs] (*pl* **staphylococci** [-'kɒksaɪ]) *n* staphylocoque *m*

staple ['steɪpəl] **1** *n* (**a**) *(for paper)* agrafe *f*

(**b**) *(for wire)* cavalier *m*, crampillon *m*

(**c**) *(foodstuff)* aliment *m ou* denrée *f* de base; **kitchen** *or* **household staples** provisions *fpl* de base; **staples are being rationed** en ce moment, les produits de première nécessité sont rationnés

(**d**) *Com & Econ (item)* article *m* de base; *(raw material)* matière *f* première

(**e**) *(constituent)* partie *f* intégrante; **divorce cases are a staple of his law practice** son cabinet s'occupe essentiellement de divorces; **sex scandals are a staple of the tabloid press** la presse à sensation se nourrit des scandales sexuels; **such accusations are a staple of the annual conference** ces accusations reviennent régulièrement à chaque conférence annuelle

(**f**) *Tex* fibre *f* artificielle à filer

2 *vt (paper, upholstery etc)* agrafer; **staple the sheets together** agrafez les feuilles; **posters were stapled on** *or* **onto** *or* **to the walls** des posters étaient agrafés aux murs

3 *adj (food, products)* de base; *(export, crop)* principal; **a staple diet of rice and beans** un régime à base de riz et de haricots; **for young children, milk is the staple diet** pour les jeunes enfants, le lait est l'aliment de base; *Fig* **the staple diet of these TV channels consists of soap operas** les programmes de ces chaînes de télévision sont essentiellement constitués de feuilletons; **their staple commodity is cotton** le coton est leur produit de base; **tanks are a staple feature of conventional warfare** les tanks sont un des éléments de base de la guerre conventionnelle

►► *Tex* ***staple fibre*** fibre *f* artificielle à filer; ***staple gun*** agrafeuse *f* (professionnelle); ***staple remover*** arrache-agrafes *m inv*

stapler ['steɪplə(r)] *n* agrafeuse *f* (de bureau)

stapling ['steɪpəlɪŋ] *n (of paper, upholstery)* fixation *f* à l'aide d'agrafes, agrafage *m*

star [stɑ:(r)] (*pt & pp* **starred,** *cont* **starring**) **1** *n* (**a**) *(in sky)* étoile *f*; **to sleep (out) under the stars** dormir *ou* coucher à la belle étoile; **the morning/evening star** l'étoile du matin/du soir; **to have stars in one's eyes** être sur un petit nuage; *Fig* **to see stars** voir trente-six chandelles; *Fig* **to reach for the stars** essayer d'atteindre les sommets

(**b**) *(symbol of fate, luck)* étoile *f*; *Astrol* astre *m*, étoile *f*; **his star is rising** son étoile brille chaque jour davantage; **his star is on the wane** son étoile pâlit; **to be born under a lucky star** être né sous une bonne étoile; **I thanked my (lucky) stars I wasn't chosen** j'ai remercié le ciel de ne pas avoir été choisi; **the influence of the stars** l'influence des astres; *Fam* **what do my stars say today?** que dit mon horoscope aujourd'hui ▫?; **it's written in the stars** c'est le destin

(**c**) *(figure, emblem)* étoile *f*; *Sch* bon point *m*; **the restaurant has gained another star** le restaurant s'est vu décerner une étoile supplémentaire; **the Star of David** l'étoile de David; **the Stars and Bars** le drapeau des États Confédérés; **the Stars and Stripes** la bannière étoilée *(le drapeau américain)*

(**d**) *(asterisk)* astérisque *m*

(**e**) *(celebrity)* vedette *f*, star *f*; **one movie won't make him a star** il ne deviendra pas une star en un seul film; **she was an up-and-coming rock star** elle était en train de devenir une grande star du rock; **he's a rising star in the Labour party** il est en train de devenir un personnage important du parti travailliste; **to be the star of the class** être la vedette de la classe

(**f**) *(blaze → on animal)* étoile *f*

(**g**) *Mktg (successful product)* vedette *f*

2 *comp* (**a**) *Cin & Theat* **the star attraction of tonight's show** la principale attraction du spectacle de ce soir; **the star turn** la vedette; **to get star billing** être en tête d'affiche; **to give sb star billing** mettre qn en tête d'affiche; **the hotel gives all its clients star treatment** cet hôtel offre à sa clientèle un service de première classe

(**b**) *(salesman, pupil etc)* meilleur; **he's our star witness** c'est notre témoin-vedette *ou* notre témoin principal

(**c**) *Comput* **in a star configuration** connecté en étoile

3 *vt* (**a**) *Cin & Theat* avoir comme *ou* pour vedette; **the play starred David Caffrey** la pièce avait pour vedette David Caffrey; **"Casablanca", starring Humphrey Bogart and Ingrid Bergman** "Casablanca", avec Humphrey Bogart et Ingrid Bergman (dans les rôles principaux)

(**b**) *(mark with asterisk)* marquer d'un astérisque

(**c**) *Literary (adorn with stars)* étoiler; **candles starred the darkness** des bougies étoilaient l'obscurité; **the bay was starred with sail boats** la baie était parsemée de voiliers

4 *vi Cin & Theat* être la vedette; **who starred with Redford in "The Sting"?** qui jouait avec Redford dans "L'Arnaque"?; **"Othello", with Laurence Olivier starring in the title role** "Othello", avec Laurence Olivier dans le rôle principal; **he's starring in a new TV serial** il est la vedette d'un nouveau feuilleton télévisé; **he starred as a gangster** il avait un rôle de gangster

►► ***star anise*** anis *m* étoilé; ***star apple*** pomme *f* étoilée; *Br Hist* ***Star Chamber*** tribunal *m* correctionnel; *Fig Pej* tribunal *m* arbitraire *ou* inquisitorial; **Court of Star Chamber** = tribunal anglais de 1487; *Elec* ***star connection*** couplage *m* en étoile; ***star fruit*** carambole *f*; ***star jump*** *(exercise)* = saut avec extension latérale des membres; *Comput* ***star network*** réseau *m* en étoile; *Comput* ***star point*** point *m* neutre; ***star ruby*** rubis *m* étoilé; ***star sapphire*** saphir *m* étoilé; *Mil* ***star shell*** obus *m* éclairant; ***star sign*** signe *m* (du zodiaque); *Comput* ***star structure*** structure *f* en étoile; ***star system*** (**a**) *Cin & Theat* star-system *m* (**b**) *Astron* système *m* stellaire; ***star turn*** numéro *m* de premier ordre; *Fam (of performance, conference, evening)* clou *m*; ***Star Wars*** la guerre des étoiles *(nom donné à l'Initiative de défense stratégique, programme militaire spatial mis en place dans les années 80 par le président américain Reagan)*; ***Star Wars research*** la recherche sur la défense stratégique

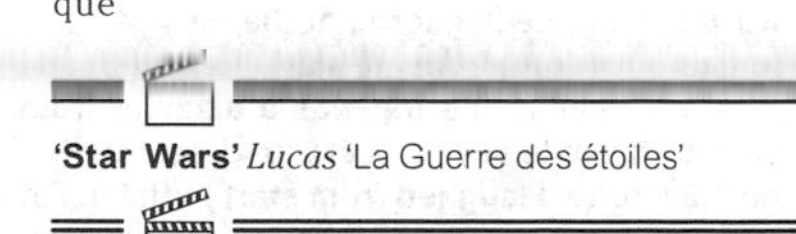

'Star Wars' *Lucas* 'La Guerre des étoiles'

'A Star Is Born' *Wellman, Cukor* 'Une étoile est née'

COURT OF STAR CHAMBER

En 1487, Henri VII mit en place cet organe judiciaire dans le but de renforcer l'autorité de son gouvernement. Ce tribunal jouissait d'une grande popularité de par son impartialité et le fait qu'il échappait à la corruption des nobles, les obligeant à se plier à la justice royale.

-star [stɑ:(r)] *suff* **a two-star hotel** un hôtel deux étoiles; **a four-star general** un général à quatre étoiles; *Br* **two-star petrol** (essence *f*) ordinaire *m*; *Br* **four-star petrol** super *m*

starboard ['stɑ:bəd] **1** *n Naut* tribord *m*; *Aviat* tribord *m*, droite *f*; **on the starboard side, to starboard** à tribord; **vessel to starboard!** navire par tribord!

2 *adj Naut (rail, lights)* de tribord; *Aviat (door, wing)* droit, de tribord

3 *vt Naut* **to starboard the helm** *or* **rudder** mettre la barre à tribord

starch [stɑ:tʃ] **1** *n* (**a**) *(for laundry)* amidon *m*, empois *m* (**b**) *(in cereals)* amidon *m*; *(in root vegetables)* fécule *f*; **try and avoid starch** *or* **starches** essayez d'éviter les féculents (**c**) *(UNCOUNT) Fam (formality)* manières *fpl* guindées ▫ (**d**) *Am (idiom)* **to take the starch out of sb** *(critic, bully)* rabattre le caquet à qn

2 *vt* empeser, amidonner

star-chamber *adj Pej (decision)* arbitraire; *(trial, procedure)* arbitraire, inquisitorial; **star-chamber sessions of the town council** des réunions secrètes *ou* à huis clos du conseil municipal

starched [stɑ:tʃt] *adj* amidonné

starchily ['stɑ:tʃɪlɪ] *adv Pej (stiffly → gen)* d'un air guindé; *(reply, say)* d'un ton guindé

starchiness ['stɑ:tʃɪnɪs] *n Pej* manières *fpl* guindées *ou* compassées

starch-reduced *adj (bread)* de régime; *(diet)* pauvre en féculents

starchy ['stɑ:tʃɪ] (*compar* **starchier,** *superl* **starchiest**) *adj* (**a**) *(diet)* riche en féculents; *(taste)* farineux (**b**) *Pej (person)* guindé, compassé; **he's so starchy!** on dirait qu'il a avalé son parapluie!

►► ***starchy foods*** féculents *mpl*

star-crossed *adj Literary* maudit par le sort

stardom ['stɑ:dəm] *n* célébrité *f*, vedettariat *m*; **to rise to stardom** devenir célèbre, devenir une vedette; **he never actively sought stardom** il n'a jamais vraiment couru après la célébrité; **she has been groomed for stardom** on l'a façonnée pour en faire une vedette

stardust ['stɑ:dʌst] *n (UNCOUNT) (illusions)* chimères *fpl*, illusions *fpl*; *(sentimentality)* sentimentalité *f*; **to have stardust in one's eyes** *(be deluded)* être en proie aux chimères; *(be a romantic)* être très fleur bleue

stare [steə(r)] **1** *vi* regarder (fixement); **to stare at sb/sth** regarder qn/qch fixement; **it's rude to stare!** ça ne se fait pas de regarder les gens comme ça!; **stop it, people are staring!** arrête, les gens nous regardent!; **I stared into his eyes** je l'ai regardé dans le blanc des yeux; **she stared at me in disbelief** elle m'a regardé avec des yeux incrédules; **to stare in amazement** regarder d'un air ébahi; **he stared straight ahead** il regardait fixement devant lui; **she sat staring into the distance** elle était assise, le regard perdu (au loin); **I stared out of the train window** j'ai regardé longuement par la fenêtre du train; **doesn't being stared at in the street bother you?** ça ne vous gêne pas d'attirer les regards des gens dans la rue?

2 *vt* (**a**) *(intimidate)* **to stare sb into silence** faire taire qn en le fixant du regard; **her steely eyes stared him into submission** son regard d'acier l'a réduit à l'obéissance

(**b**) *(idioms)* **the answer is staring you in the face!** mais la réponse saute aux yeux!; **I'd looked everywhere for my keys and there they were staring me in the face** j'avais cherché mes clefs partout alors qu'elles étaient là sous mon nez; **failure was staring us in the face** nous courions à l'échec

3 *n* regard *m* (fixe); **to give sb a hostile/an incredulous stare** fixer qn d'un regard hostile/incrédule

►**stare out,** *Am* **stare down** *vt sep* faire baisser les yeux à

'Staring at the Sun' *Barnes* 'Le Soleil en face'

starfish ['stɑ:fɪʃ] (*pl* **inv** *or* **starfishes**) *n Zool* étoile *f* de mer

starflower ['stɑ:flaʊə(r)] *n Bot* dame-d'onze-heures *f*, *Spec* ornithogale *m*

stargaze ['stɑ:geɪz] *vi* (**a**) *(watch)* observer les étoiles (**b**) *(daydream)* rêvasser

stargazer ['stɑ:ˌgeɪzə(r)] *n* (**a**) *(astronomer)* astronome *mf*; *(astrologer)* astrologue *mf* (**b**) *(daydreamer)* rêveur(euse) *m,f*, rêvasseur(euse) *m,f* (**c**) *Ich* uranoscope *m*

stargazing ['stɑː,geɪzɪŋ] *n* (**a**) *(astronomy)* observation *f* des étoiles; *(astrology)* astrologie *f*; *Fig* **economists are often accused of indulging in stargazing** on accuse souvent les économistes de tirer des plans sur la comète (**b**) *(UNCOUNT) (daydreaming)* rêveries *fpl*, rêvasseries *fpl*

staring ['steərɪŋ] **1** *adj (bystanders)* curieux; **to have staring eyes** *(fixed)* avoir les yeux fixes; *(wide-open)* avoir les yeux écarquillés; *(blank)* avoir les yeux vides; **he looked at her with staring eyes** il la fixa du regard

2 *adv see* **stark** *adv*

stark [stɑːk] **1** *adj* (**a**) *(bare, grim → landscape)* désolé; *(→ branches, hills, crag)* nu; *(→ room, façade)* austère; *(→ silhouette)* net; **in the stark light of day** à la lumière crue du jour; **the chimneys rose in stark relief against the sky** les cheminées se découpaient nettement contre le ciel; **the stark simplicity of the shapes** l'austère dépouillement des formes; **the stark beauty of the landscape** la beauté âpre du paysage

(**b**) *(blunt → description, statement)* cru, sans ambages; *(→ refusal, denial)* catégorique; *(harsh → words)* dur; **the stark realities of war** les dures réalités de la guerre; **those are the stark facts** ce sont les faits tels qu'ils sont; **the stark realism of her book** le réalisme cru de son livre

(**c**) *(utter → brutality, terror)* absolu; *(→ madness)* pur; **in stark poverty** dans la misère absolue *ou* la plus noire; **in stark violation of the ceasefire** en violation flagrante du cessez-le-feu; **their foreign policy success is in stark contrast to the failure of their domestic policies** la réussite de leur politique étrangère contraste nettement avec l'échec de leur politique intérieure

2 *adv* complètement; *Fam* **stark raving** *or* **staring mad** complètement dingue; **stark naked** tout nu

starkers ['stɑːkəz] *Br Fam* **1** *adj* à poil

2 *adv* à poil

starkly ['stɑːklɪ] *adv (describe)* crûment; *(tell)* carrément, sans ambages; *(stand out)* nettement; **the room was starkly lit** la pièce était éclairée par une lumière crue; **in starkly realistic terms** en termes d'un réalisme cru

starkness ['stɑːknɪs] *n (of landscape, scene)* désolation *f*; *(of room, façade)* austérité *f*; *(of branches)* nudité *f*; *(of light)* crudité *f*; *(of life, reality)* dureté *f*; **the starkness of the author's style** le style dépouillé de l'auteur; **a mirror offset the starkness of the bare walls** une glace adoucissait l'austérité des murs nus

starless ['stɑːlɪs] *adj (sky, night)* sans étoiles

starlet ['stɑːlɪt] *n* starlette *f*

starlight ['stɑːlaɪt] *n* lumière *f* des étoiles; **by starlight** à *ou* sous la lumière des étoiles

starling ['stɑːlɪŋ] *n Orn* étourneau *m*, sansonnet *m*

starlit ['stɑːlɪt] *adj (night)* étoilé; *(landscape, beach, sea)* illuminé par les étoiles, baigné par la lumière des étoiles

star-nosed mole *n Zool* taupe *f* à nez étoilé

star-of-Bethlehem *n Bot* étoile *f* de Bethléem

starred [stɑːd] *adj Typ (asterisked)* marqué d'un astérisque

▸▸ *Univ* ***starred first*** *(degree)* = mention spéciale décernée aux étudiants particulièrement brillants

starry ['stɑːrɪ] *(compar* **starrier**, *superl* **starriest***)* *adj* (**a**) *(adorned with stars)* étoilé; **a starry night** une nuit étoilée; **the starry light** la lumière des étoiles (**b**) *(sparkling)* étincelant, brillant; **a starry diadem** un diadème étincelant (**c**) *Literary Fig (lofty)* élevé; **the starry heights of Mount Olympus** les hauteurs infinies de l'Olympe

starry-eyed *adj (idealistic)* idéaliste; *(naive)* naïf, ingénu; *(dreamy)* rêveur, dans la lune; **the children stood starry-eyed in front of the Christmas tree** les enfants se tenaient devant le sapin de Noël, émerveillés; **there's nothing starry-eyed about her** elle a vraiment les pieds sur terre

starship ['stɑːʃɪp] *n* vaisseau *m* spatial

star-spangled [-'spæŋgld] *adj (flag)* étoilé; *(sky)* semé *ou* parsemé d'étoiles

▸▸ ***the Star-Spangled Banner*** *(flag)* la bannière étoilée; *(national anthem)* l'hymne *m* national des États-Unis

star-studded *adj* (**a**) *(show, film)* à vedettes; **a star-studded cast** une distribution où figurent de nombreuses vedettes *ou* qui réunit une brochette de stars (**b**) = **star-spangled**

START [stɑːt] *n (abbr* **Strategic Arms Reduction Talks***)* négociations *fpl* START

START [stɑːt]

commencement	▸ 1 (a)
début	▸ 1 (a)
départ	▸ 1 (a), (b)
avance	▸ 1 (c)
sursaut	▸ 1 (d)
commencer	▸ 2 (a); 3 (a), (c)
amorcer	▸ 2 (a)
déclencher	▸ 2 (b)
démarrer	▸ 2 (d); 3 (d), (f)
se mettre en marche	▸ 3 (d)
créer	▸ 2 (f)
installer	▸ 2 (g)
débuter	▸ 3 (b)
partir	▸ 3 (e)
sursauter	▸ 3 (g)

1 *n* (**a**) *(beginning → gen)* commencement *m*, début *m*; *(→ of inquiry)* ouverture *f*; *(of journey, race)* départ *m*; **it's the start of a new era** c'est le début *ou* le commencement d'une ère nouvelle; **the start of the school year** la rentrée scolaire; **the start of the footpath is marked by an arrow** le début du sentier est signalé par une flèche; **£5 isn't much, but it's a start** 5 livres ce n'est pas grand-chose, mais c'est un début; **I've cleaned the kitchen – well, it's a start** j'ai nettoyé la cuisine – eh bien, c'est déjà ça; **things are off to a bad/good start** ça commence mal/bien, c'est mal/bien parti; **my new boss and I didn't get off to a very good start** dès le début, mes rapports avec mon nouveau patron ont été un peu difficiles; **it was a good/bad start to the day** la journée commençait bien/mal; **it was an inauspicious start to his presidency** c'était un début peu prometteur pour sa présidence; **to get a good start in life** prendre un bon départ dans la vie *ou* l'existence; **we want an education that will give our children a good start** nous voulons une éducation qui donne à nos enfants des bases solides; **a second honeymoon will give us a fresh start** une deuxième lune de miel nous fera repartir d'un bon pied; **the programme will give ex-prisoners a fresh** *or* **new start (in life)** le programme va donner aux anciens détenus une seconde chance (dans la vie); **to make a start** *(gen)* commencer; *(begin journey)* se mettre en route; **to make** *or* **to get an early start** *(gen)* commencer de bonne heure; *(on journey)* partir de bonne heure; **to make a start on sth** commencer qch; **I've made a good start on my Christmas shopping** j'ai déjà fait une bonne partie de mes achats de Noël; **I was lonely at the start** au début je me sentais seule; **at the start of the war** au début de la guerre; **at the very start** au tout début; **(right) from the start** dès le début *ou* commencement; **the trip was a disaster from start to finish** le voyage a été un désastre d'un bout à l'autre; **I laughed from start to finish** j'ai ri du début à la fin; **the project was ill-conceived from start to finish** le projet était mal conçu de bout en bout

(**b**) *Sport (departure line)* (ligne *f* de) départ *m*; *(signal)* signal *m* de départ; **they are lined up for** *or* **at the start** ils sont sur la ligne de départ; **where's the start of the rally?** où est le départ du rallye?; **wait for the start** attendez le signal de départ

(**c**) *(lead, advance)* avance *f*; **she has two hours' start** *or* **a two-hour start on us** elle a une avance de deux heures sur nous; **he gave him 20 metres' start** *or* **a 20-metre start** il lui a accordé une avance de 20 mètres; **our research gives us a start over our competitors** nos recherches nous donnent de l'avance sur nos concurrents; **to have a start on sb** être en avance sur qn

(**d**) *(jump)* sursaut *m*; **she woke up with a start** elle s'est réveillée en sursaut; **with a start, I recognized my own handwriting** j'ai eu un sursaut quand j'ai reconnu ma propre écriture; **he gave a start** il a tressailli, il a sursauté; **to give sb a start** faire sursauter *ou* tressaillir qn; **you gave me such a start!** tu m'as fait une de ces peurs!

2 *vt* (**a**) *(begin → gen)* commencer; *(→ climb, descent)* amorcer; **I've started the first chapter** *(write)* j'ai commencé (à écrire) le premier chapitre; *(read)* j'ai commencé (à lire) le premier chapitre; **to start doing** *or* **to do sth** commencer à *ou* se mettre à faire qch; **it's starting to rain** il commence à pleuvoir; **it had just started raining** *or* **to rain when I left** il venait juste de commencer à pleuvoir quand je suis parti; **she started driving** *or* **to drive again a month after her accident** elle a recommencé à conduire *ou* elle s'est remise à conduire un mois après son accident; **to start school** *(for the first time)* commencer l'école; *(after holidays)* rentrer à *ou* reprendre l'école; **she started her speech with a quotation from the Bible** elle a commencé son discours par une citation de la Bible; **I started my investigation with a visit to Carl** j'ai commencé mon enquête par une visite chez Carl; **they started the year with a deficit** ils ont commencé l'année avec un déficit; **he started work at sixteen** il a commencé à travailler à seize ans; **when do you start your new job?** quand commencez-vous votre nouveau travail?; **he started life as a delivery boy** il débuta dans la vie comme garçon livreur; **frogs start life as tadpoles** les grenouilles commencent par être des têtards; **go ahead and start lunch without me** allez-y, vous pouvez commencer (à déjeuner) sans moi; **I like to finish anything I start** j'aime aller au bout de tout ce que j'entreprends; **I think I'm starting a cold** je crois que j'attrapé un rhume; **to get started** *(person → on task)* commencer, s'y mettre; *(→ on journey)* partir, se mettre en route; *(→ in career)* débuter, démarrer; **I got started on the dishes** j'ai commencé la vaisselle; **shall we get started on the washing-up?** si on attaquait la vaisselle?; **to help sb get started in life** aider qn à démarrer dans la vie; **let's get started!** allons-y!; **once he gets started there's no stopping him** une fois lancé, il n'y a pas moyen de l'arrêter; **I need a coffee to get me started in the morning** j'ai besoin d'un café pour commencer la journée

(**b**) *(initiate, instigate → reaction, revolution, process)* déclencher; *(→ fashion)* lancer; *(→ violence)* déclencher, provoquer; *(→ conversation, discussion)* engager, amorcer; *(→ rumour)* faire naître; **her article started the controversy** son article a été à l'origine de la controverse; **to start legal proceedings** engager une action en justice; **which side started the war?** quel camp a déclenché la guerre?; **you started it** c'est toi qui as commencé; **it wasn't me who started the quarrel/the fight!** ce n'est pas moi qui ai commencé la dispute/la bagarre!; **the breakup of the empire started the process of decline** le démantèlement de l'empire a déclenché le processus de déclin; **to start a fire** *(in fireplace)* allumer le feu; *(campfire)* faire du feu; *(by accident, bomb)* mettre le feu; **the fire was started by arsonists** l'incendie a été allumé par des pyromanes; *Fam* **are you trying to start something?** tu cherches la bagarre, ou quoi?

(**c**) *(cause to do → person)* faire; **it started her (off) crying/laughing** cela l'a fait pleurer/rire; **the news is going to start tongues wagging** la nouvelle va faire jaser; **I'll start a team (working) on it right away** je vais mettre une équipe là-dessus tout de suite; **if you start him on this subject he will never stop** si vous le lancez sur ce sujet il ne tarira pas

(**d**) *(set in motion → motor, car)* (faire) démarrer, mettre en marche; *(→ machine, device)* mettre en marche; *(→ meal)* mettre en route; **how do I start the tape (going)?** comment est-ce que je dois faire pour mettre le magnétophone en marche?; **I couldn't get the car started** je n'ai pas réussi à faire démarrer la voiture; **to start the printer again, press this key** pour remettre en marche l'imprimante, appuyez sur cette touche

(**e**) *(begin using → bottle, pack)* entamer

(**f**) *(establish, found → business, school, political party)* créer, fonder; *(→ restaurant, shop)* ouvrir; *(→ social programme)* créer, instaurer; **to start a newspaper** créer *ou* fonder un journal; **to start a family** fonder un foyer

(**g**) *(person → in business, work)* installer, établir; **he started his son in the family business** il a fait entrer son fils dans l'entreprise familiale; **his election success started him on his political career** son succès aux élections l'a lancé dans sa carrière d'homme politique; **they start new pilots on domestic flights** ils font débuter les nouveaux pilotes sur les vols intérieurs

(**h**) *Sport* **to start the race** donner le signal du départ; **the referee blew his whistle to start the match** l'arbitre siffla pour signaler le début du match

(**i**) *Hunt (flush out → hare, stag)* lever

3 *vi* (**a**) *(begin)* commencer; **the movie starts at 8 o'clock** le film commence à 20 heures; **when did the contractions start?** quand les contractions ont-elles commencé?; **school starts on September 5th** la rentrée a lieu *ou* les cours reprennent le 5 septembre; **our problems are just starting** nos ennuis ne font que commencer; **before the New Year/the rainy season starts** avant le début de l'année prochaine/de la saison des pluies; **before the cold weather starts** avant qu'il ne commence à faire froid; **starting (from) next week** à partir de la semaine prochaine; **to start again** *or* **afresh** recommencer; **to start all over again, to start again from scratch** recommencer à zéro; **calm down and start at the beginning** calmez-vous et commencez par le commencement; **I didn't know where to start** je ne savais pas par quel bout commencer; **she started with a joke/by introducing everyone** elle a commencé par une plaisanterie/par faire les présentations; **I'd like to start by saying how pleased I am to be here tonight** j'aimerais commencer par vous dire à quel point je suis heureux d'être parmi vous ce soir; **the book starts with a quotation** le livre commence par une citation; **I'll have the soup to start (with)** pour commencer, je prendrai du potage; **to start as one means to go on** donner la mesure dès le début; **isn't it time you got a job? – don't YOU start!** il serait peut-être temps que tu trouves du travail – tu ne vas pas t'y mettre, toi aussi!

(**b**) *(in career, job)* débuter; **she started in personnel/as an assistant** elle a débuté au service du personnel/comme assistante; **have you been working here long? – no, I've just started** vous travaillez ici depuis longtemps? – non, je viens de commencer; **I start on $500 a week** je débute à 500 dollars par semaine; **gymnasts have to start young** les gymnastes doivent commencer jeunes

(**c**) *(in space → desert, fields, slope, street)* commencer; *(→ river)* prendre sa source; **the neutral zone starts at the river** la zone neutre commence à la rivière; **there's an arrow where the path starts** il y a une flèche qui indique le début du sentier; **the bus route starts at the station** la ligne de bus commence à la gare; **where does the tunnel start?** où est l'entrée du tunnel?

(**d**) *(car, motor)* démarrer, se mettre en marche; **the engines started with a roar** les moteurs ont démarré en vrombissant; **why won't the car start?** pourquoi la voiture ne veut-elle pas démarrer?

(**e**) *(set off → person, convoy)* partir, se mettre en route; *(→ train)* s'ébranler; **the tour starts at** *or* **from the town hall** la visite part de la mairie; **I'll have to start for the airport soon** il va bientôt falloir que je parte pour l'aéroport; **we start tomorrow** nous partons demain; **the train was starting across** *or* **over the bridge** le train commençait à traverser le pont *ou* s'engageait sur le pont; **she started along the path** elle s'engagea sur le sentier; *Sport* **only four horses started** quatre chevaux seulement ont pris le départ

(**f**) *(prices)* démarrer; **houses here start at $100,000** ici, le prix des maisons démarre à 100 000 dollars; **return fares start from £299** on trouve des billets aller retour à partir de 299 livres

(**g**) *(jump involuntarily → person)* sursauter; *(→ horse)* tressaillir, faire un soubresaut; *(jump up)* bondir; **he started in surprise** il a tressailli de surprise; **she started from her chair** elle bondit de sa chaise; **to start out of one's sleep** se réveiller en sursaut

(**h**) *(gush)* jaillir, gicler; **tears started to his eyes** les larmes lui sont montées aux yeux

4 for a start *adv* pour commencer, d'abord

5 for starts *adv Am Fam* pour commencer, d'abord

6 to start with *adv* (**a**) *(firstly)* pour commencer, d'abord; **to start with, my name isn't Jo** pour commencer *ou* d'abord, je ne m'appelle pas Jo

(**b**) *(in the beginning)* au début; **there were only six members to start with** il n'y avait que six membres au début; **she was an architect to start with, then a journalist** elle a d'abord été architecte, puis journaliste

►► *Comput* ***start bit*** bit *m* de départ; *Comput* ***start button*** *(in Windows)* bouton *m* Démarrer; *Comput* ***start code*** code *m* de départ

►**start back** *vi* (**a**) *(turn back)* rebrousser chemin

(**b**) *(start again)* recommencer; **the children start back at school tomorrow** c'est la rentrée scolaire demain

►**start in on** *vt insep* s'attaquer à; **I started in on the pile of mail** je me suis attaqué à la pile de courrier; **once he starts in on liberty and democracy, there's no stopping him** une fois qu'il est lancé sur le sujet de la liberté et de la démocratie, il n'y a plus moyen de l'arrêter; *Fam* **to start in on sb** s'en prendre à qn❑, tomber à bras raccourcis sur qn

►**start off 1** *vt sep* (**a**) *(begin → book, meeting, show)* commencer; **she started the meeting off with introductions** elle a commencé la réunion en faisant les présentations

(**b**) *(person → on task, in business)* **here's some wool to start you off** voici de la laine pour commencer; **he lent us a couple of thousand pounds to start us off** il nous a prêté quelques milliers de livres pour nous aider à démarrer; **the pianist played a few bars to start them off** le pianiste a joué quelques mesures d'introduction

(**c**) *(set off)* déclencher; **what started the alarm off?** qu'est-ce qui a déclenché l'alarme?; **if you mention it it'll only start her off again** n'en parle pas, sinon elle va recommencer; **to start sb off laughing/crying** faire rire/pleurer qn; **the baby's crying again, what started him off this time?** le bébé s'est remis à pleurer, qu'est-ce qu'il a cette fois?; **dad's finally calmed down, don't you start him off again** papa s'est enfin calmé, ne va pas l'énerver

2 *vi* (**a**) *(leave)* partir, se mettre en route; **he started off at a run** il est parti en courant; **when do you start off on your trip?** quand est-ce que vous partez en voyage?

(**b**) *(begin → speech, film)* commencer; **it starts off with a description of the town** ça commence par une description de la ville; **start off with a summary of the problem** commencez par un résumé du problème; **she started off by talking about...** elle commença en parlant de...; **the interview started off badly/well** l'entretien a mal/bien commencé; **I started off agreeing with him** au début, j'étais d'accord avec lui

(**c**) *(in life, career)* débuter; **he started off as a cashier** il a débuté comme caissier; **she started off as a Catholic** elle était catholique à l'origine; **you're starting off with all the advantages** vous partez avec tous les avantages

►**start on** *vt insep* (**a**) *(begin → essay, meal)* commencer; *(→ task, dishes)* se mettre à; *(→ new bottle, pack)* entamer; **they had already started on their dessert** ils avaient déjà commencé à manger *ou* entamé leur dessert; **after they'd searched the car they started on the luggage** après avoir fouillé la voiture, ils sont passés aux bagages

(**b**) *(attack, berate)* s'en prendre à; **don't start on me, I'm not to blame!** ne t'en prends pas à moi, ce n'est pas de ma faute!

►**start out** *vi* (**a**) *(begin journey)* partir, se mettre en route

(**b**) *(begin career)* débuter; **he started out as a cashier** il a débuté comme caissier; **she started out as a Catholic** elle était catholique à l'origine; **he started out in business with his wife's money** il s'est lancé dans les affaires avec l'argent de sa femme; **when she started out there were only a few women lawyers** quand elle a commencé sa carrière, il y avait très peu de femmes avocats

(**c**) *(intend)* **he started out to write a novel** au départ il voulait écrire un roman

►**start over** *Am* **1** *vi* recommencer (depuis le début)

2 *vt sep* recommencer (depuis le début)

►**start up 1** *vt sep* (**a**) *(establish, found → business, school, political party)* créer, fonder; *(→ restaurant, shop)* ouvrir

(**b**) *(set in motion → car, motor)* faire démarrer; *(→ machine)* mettre en marche; *(→ computer)* mettre en route; *(→ program)* lancer, démarrer

2 *vi* (**a**) *(guns, music, noise, band)* commencer; *(wind)* se lever; **the applause started up again** les applaudissements ont repris

(**b**) *(car, motor)* démarrer, se mettre en marche; *(machine)* se mettre en marche; *(computer, program)* se mettre en route

(**c**) *(set up business)* se lancer, s'installer, s'établir; **he decided to start up by himself** il a décidé de se mettre à son compte

---

> **I've started so I'll finish**
>
> Le jeu télévisé britannique *Mastermind* fut diffusé de 1972 à 1997. Les concurrents de ce jeu portant sur la culture générale devaient répondre au plus grand nombre de questions possible en l'espace de deux minutes. Si l'animateur était en train de poser une question lorsque retentissait la sonnerie qui annonçait la fin du temps imparti, il prononçait rituellement ces mots ("j'ai commencé, je vais donc finir") avant de finir de lire la question au concurrent.
>
> Aujourd'hui, on utilise cette phrase par allusion au jeu télévisé lorsqu'on est interrompu.

starter ['stɑːtə(r)] *n* (**a**) *Aut (motor, button)* démarreur *m*; *(on motorbike)* kick *m*, démarreur *m* au pied

(**b**) *(runner, horse)* partant *m*; *(in relay race)* premier coureur *m*, première coureuse *f*; **to be a slow starter** *(gen)* & *Sport* être lent à démarrer

(**c**) *Sport (official)* starter *m*, juge *m* de départ; **to be under starter's orders** *(in horseracing)* attendre le signal du starter

(**d**) *(fermenting agent)* ferment *m*; **yoghurt starter** ferment *m* lactique pour yaourt

(**e**) *Br (first course of meal)* hors-d'œuvre *m inv*; **for starters** *(in meal)* comme hors-d'œuvre; *Fig* pour commencer; **that was just for starters** ce n'était qu'un hors-d'œuvre

(**f**) *Am Fam (house)* première maison❑ *f (achetée par un individu ou un couple)*

►► *Br* ***starter flat*** = appartement convenant à ceux qui achètent pour la première fois; ***starter's gun*** pistolet *m* du starter; *Am Aut* ***starter handle*** manivelle *f*; ***starter home*** première maison *f (achetée par un individu ou un couple)*; ***starter motor*** démarreur *m*; ***starter pack*** kit *m* de base; *Comput (for Internet)* kit *m* de connexion; ***starter's pistol*** pistolet *m* du starter; *Am* ***starter*** [illegible] ***switch*** bouton *m* de démarrage

> **Starter for ten**
>
> *University Challenge* est un jeu télévisé britannique qui fait s'opposer deux équipes composées d'étudiants de deux universités britanniques. L'animateur pose des questions valant 10 points aux deux équipes. L'équipe qui appuie la première sur le bouton et donne la bonne réponse a le droit de répondre à trois autres questions, valant cinq points chacune. La première question donnant droit aux trois suivantes s'appelle **starter for ten** (première question pour 10 points).
>
> On utilise cette formule sur le mode humoristique par allusion au jeu lorsqu'on pose une question difficile à quelqu'un, comme dans l'exemple suivant: **OK, clever-clogs, here's your starter for ten: why do...** ("puisque tu es si malin que ça, essaie de répondre à cette question: pourquoi est-ce que...").

sta–sta

starting [ˈstɑːtɪŋ] **1** *n* (**a**) *(beginning)* commencement *m*; **who wants to be responsible for the starting of a nuclear war?** qui veut assumer la responsabilité du déclenchement d'une guerre nucléaire?

(**b**) *(of business etc)* mise *f* en route *ou* en train (**c**) *(of engine etc)* mise *f* en marche, démarrage *m*; *(of machine)* lancement *m*

2 *adj* initial; **the starting line-up** la composition initiale de l'équipe

►► ***starting block*** *(in athletics)* starting-block *m*; *(for swimmers)* plot *m* de départ; ***starting gate*** *Sport (for horse)* starting-gate *f*; *(for skier)* porte *f* de départ; ***starting grid*** *(in motor racing)* grille *f* de départ; *Br Aut* ***starting handle*** manivelle *f*; *Sport* ***starting line*** ligne *f* de départ; *Tech* ***starting motor*** moteur *m* de démarrage; ***starting pistol*** pistolet *m* du starter; ***starting point*** point *m* de départ; *Sport* ***starting post*** ligne *f* de départ; ***starting price*** *(gen)* prix *m* initial; *(in horseracing)* cote *f* au départ; *(at auction)* mise *f* à prix, prix *m* d'appel; ***starting salary*** salaire *m* d'embauche; ***starting signal*** signal *m* de *ou* du départ; *Horseracing* ***starting stalls*** stalles *fpl* de départ; ***starting up*** *(of business etc)* mise *f* en route *ou* en train; *(of engine)* mise *f* en marche, démarrage *m*; *(of machine)* lancement *m*

startle [ˈstɑːtəl] **1** *vt (person → surprise)* surprendre, étonner; *(→ frighten, alarm)* faire peur à, alarmer; *(→ cause to jump)* faire sursauter; *(animal, bird, fish)* effaroucher; **I didn't mean to startle you** je ne voulais pas vous faire peur; **it startled me** *or* **I was startled to see how much he had aged** j'ai été surpris *ou* ç'a été un choc pour moi de voir à quel point il avait vieilli; **the noise startled him out of his reverie** le bruit l'a brusquement tiré de ses rêveries

2 *vi* s'effaroucher

startled [ˈstɑːtld] *adj (person)* étonné; *(expression, shout, glance)* de surprise; *(animal)* effarouché; **there was a startled silence** il y a eu un silence étonné; **the startled waiter dropped the tray** le serveur, surpris, a laissé tomber son plateau; **the startled guests didn't move** les invités, ahuris, restaient sans bouger

startling [ˈstɑːtlɪŋ] *adj* étonnant, surprenant; *(contrast, resemblance)* saisissant; **startling green eyes** des yeux d'un vert saisissant

start-up *n* (**a**) *Comput* démarrage *m* (**b**) *(of new business)* ouverture *f*, lancement *m*; **there have been 500 start-ups this year** il y a eu 500 créations d'entreprises cette année (**c**) *(Internet company)* start-up *f*, jeune pousse *f*

►► *Fin* ***start-up capital*** capital *m* initial, capital *m* de départ; *Fin* ***start-up costs*** frais *mpl* d'établissement; *Comput* ***start-up disk*** disquette *f* de démarrage; ***start-up loan*** prêt *m* initial; *Comput* ***start-up screen*** écran *m* d'accueil

starvation [stɑːˈveɪʃən] *n* famine *f*; **to die of** *or* **from starvation** mourir de faim; **starvation had decimated the troops** la famine avait décimé les troupes

►► ***starvation diet*** ration *f* de famine; *Fig* régime *m* draconien; **the prisoners subsisted on a starvation diet of rice and water** les prisonniers devaient se contenter de riz et d'eau; ***starvation wages*** salaire *m* de famine *ou* de misère; **they pay starvation wages** ce sont des affameurs

starve [stɑːv] **1** *vi (suffer)* souffrir de la faim, être affamé; **to starve (to death)** *(die)* mourir de faim; *Fam* **I'm starving!** je meurs de faim!

2 *vt* (**a**) *(cause to suffer)* affamer; **he starved himself to feed his child** il s'est privé de nourriture pour donner à manger à son enfant; *Fam* **I'm starved!** je meurs de faim!; **the garrison was starved into surrender** la garnison affamée a fini par se rendre

(**b**) *(cause to die)* laisser mourir de faim; **they were prepared to starve themselves to death rather than give in** ils étaient prêts à se laisser mourir de faim plutôt que de capituler

(**c**) *(deprive)* priver; **the libraries have been starved of funds** les bibliothèques manquent cruellement de subventions; **to be starved of affection** être privé d'affection; **the inhabitants were starved of news** les habitants étaient privés d'informations

►**starve out** *vt sep (rebels, inmates)* affamer, réduire par la faim; *(animal)* obliger à sortir en l'affamant

starveling [ˈstɑːvlɪŋ] *n Literary (person)* crève-la-faim *m inv*; *(animal)* animal *m* famélique

starving [ˈstɑːvɪŋ] *adj* affamé; *Fam* **I've got four starving kids to feed!** j'ai quatre gosses affamés à nourrir!; **think of all the starving people in the world** pense à tous ces gens qui meurent de faim dans le monde

stash [stæʃ] *Fam* **1** *vt* (**a**) *(hide)* planquer; **it was stashed under the bed** c'était planqué sous le lit; **he's probably got it stashed (away) here somewhere** il l'a certainement planqué quelque part par ici; **he's got a lot of money stashed (away) somewhere** il a plein de fric planqué quelque part

(**b**) *(put away)* ranger □; **let me stash my things** attends que je ramasse mon bazar

2 *n* (**a**) *(reserve)* réserve □ *f*; **a stash of money** un magot; **the police found a big stash of guns/of cocaine** la police a découvert une importante cache d'armes □/un important stock de cocaïne □

(**b**) *(hiding place)* planque *f*; *(hidden supply)* provision □ *f*; **the police found his stash under the floorboards** la police a trouvé sa réserve de drogue planquée sous le plancher

►**stash away** *vt sep* = **stash** *vt*

stasis [ˈsteɪsɪs] *(pl* **stases** [-siːz]*)* *n* (**a**) *Med* stase *f* (**b**) *(equilibrium)* équilibre *m*, repos *m*; *(stagnation)* stagnation *f*

STATE [steɪt]

état	►**1 (a)**
État	►**1 (b), (c)**
d'État, de l'État	►**2 (a), (b)**
officiel	►**2 (c)**
déclarer	►**3**
formuler	►**3**

1 *n* (**a**) *(condition)* état *m*; **the country is in a state of war/shock** le pays est en état de guerre/choc; **a state of confusion prevailed** la confusion régnait; **he was in a state of confusion** il ne savait plus où il en était; **he was in a state of panic** il a été pris de panique; **she was in a state of terror** elle était terrifiée; **the married state** le mariage; **the single state** le célibat; **chlorine in its gaseous/liquid state** le chlore à l'état gazeux/liquide; **to be in a good/bad state** *(road, carpet, car)* être en bon/mauvais état; *(person, economy, friendship)* aller bien/mal; **the house was in a good/poor state of repair** la maison était en bon/mauvais état; **to be in a terrible state** *(person → emotionally)* être dans tous ses états; *(→ physically)* être dans un état lamentable; *(room, papers)* être sens dessus dessous; **she was in no (fit) state to make a decision** elle était hors d'état de *ou* elle n'était pas en état de prendre une décision; **the car's not in a state to be driven** la voiture n'est pas en état de rouler; **what's the current state of play?** où en sont-ils?; **what's the current state of play on the project?** où en est le projet?; *Fam* **to get into a state** se mettre dans tous ses états; **he gets into an awful state if I don't phone** si je ne lui téléphone pas, il se met dans tous ses états; **there's no need to get into such a state about it** ce n'est pas la peine de te mettre dans un état pareil

(**b**) *Pol (nation, body politic)* État *m*; **a state within a state** un État dans l'État; **the member states** les États membres; **the head of state** le chef de l'État; **heads of state** chefs *mpl* d'État; **the separation of (the) Church and (the) State** la séparation de l'Église et de l'État

(**c**) *(in US, Australia, India etc → political division)* État *m*; *Fam* **the States** les États-Unis □, les US; **the State of Ohio** l'État de l'Ohio

(**d**) *(pomp)* apparat *m*, pompe *f*; **he was in his robes of state** il était en costume d'apparat

(**e**) *Arch (social position, estate)* état *m*

2 *adj* (**a**) *(government → secret)* d'État; *(→ subsidy, intervention, pension)* de l'État; *Econ (→ sector)* public; *(→ airline, funeral)* national

(**b**) *Am (not federal → legislature, policy, law)* de l'État; **the state capital** la capitale de l'État; **a state university** une université d'État *ou* publique; **the Michigan State team** l'équipe de l'État du Michigan; **a state park** un parc régional; *Am* **to turn state's evidence** *or* **state's witness** = témoigner contre ses complices en échange d'une remise de peine

(**c**) *(official, ceremonious → ball, dinner, visit)* officiel; *(→ coach, carriage)* d'apparat; **state occasion** cérémonie *f* officielle; **the State Opening of Parliament** = l'ouverture officielle du Parlement britannique en présence du souverain

3 *vt (utter, say)* déclarer; *(express, formulate → intentions)* déclarer; *(→ demands)* formuler; *(→ proposition, problem, conclusions, views)* énoncer, formuler; *(→ conditions)* poser; **the president stated emphatically that the rumours were untrue** le président a démenti catégoriquement les rumeurs; **I have already stated my position on that issue** j'ai déjà fait connaître ma position à ce sujet; **I have stated my opinion** j'ai donné mon opinion; **we state the current figures on page five** les chiffres actuels sont donnés en page cinq; **the regulations clearly state that daily checks must be made** le règlement dit *ou* indique clairement que des vérifications quotidiennes doivent être effectuées; **please state salary expectations** veuillez indiquer le salaire souhaité; **state your name and address** donnez vos nom, prénoms et adresse; **the man refused to state his business** l'homme a refusé d'expliquer ce qu'il voulait; **as stated above** comme indiqué plus haut; **state the figure as a percentage** exprimez *ou* indiquez le chiffre en pourcentage; **to state one's case** présenter ses arguments; *Law* **to state the case for the defence/the prosecution** présenter le dossier de la défense/de l'accusation

4 State *n Am (department)* le Département d'État

5 in state *adv* en grand apparat, en grande pompe; **to travel in state** voyager en grand apparat; **to dine in state** dîner en grande pompe; **to lie in state** être exposé solennellement; **to live in state** mener grand train

►► ***state of affairs*** circonstances *fpl* actuelles; **nothing can be done in the present state of affairs** vu les circonstances actuelles, on ne peut rien faire; **this is an appalling state of affairs** c'est une situation épouvantable; *Ironic* **this is a fine state of affairs!** c'est du propre!; ***state apartments*** appartements *mpl* de parade; ***state of the art*** *(of procedures, systems)* ce qui se fait de mieux; **the state of the art in linguistics** l'état actuel des connaissances en linguistique; ***state attorney*** procureur *m*; *Am* ***state bank*** banque *f* de dépôt *(agréée par un État)*; ***state buildings*** bâtiments *mpl* publics; ***state capitalism*** capitalisme *m* d'État; ***state church*** église *f* d'État; ***state control*** contrôle *m* étatique; *(doctrine)* étatisme *m*; **to be put** *or* **placed under state control** être nationalisé; **state control of the means of communication** nationalisation *f* des moyens de communication; *Am* ***State Department*** ministère *m* des Affaires étrangères; ***state of emergency*** état *m* d'urgence; **a state of emergency has been declared** l'état d'urgence a été déclaré; *Br* ***State Enrolled Nurse*** aide-soignant *m* diplômé, aide-soignante *f* diplômée; *Hist* ***States General*** États généraux *mpl*; *Am* ***state line*** frontière *f* entre États; *Am* ***state lottery*** loterie *f* d'État; ***state of mind*** état *m* d'esprit; **in your present state of mind** dans l'état d'esprit qui est le vôtre; **success is just a state of mind** la réussite n'est qu'un état d'esprit; **is he in a better state of mind?** est-ce qu'il est dans de meilleures dispositions?; ***state pension*** pension *f* de l'État; ***state police*** police *f* de l'État; *Am* ***state prison*** prison *f* d'État *(pour les longues peines)*; *Br* ***State Registered Nurse*** infirmier *m* diplômé, infirmière *f* diplômée *(remplacé en 1992 par "Registered Nurse")*; *Am* ***states' rights*** = principe selon lequel, si la constitution des États-Unis n'octroie ni ne refuse un pouvoir à un État particulier, ce pouvoir appartient de fait à l'État et non au gouvernement fédéral; *Br* ***state school*** école *f* publique; *Br* ***state sector*** secteur *m* public; ***state socialism*** socialisme *m* d'État; ***State Supreme Court*** = instance judiciaire suprême dans chaque État américain; ***the state system*** *(education)* le public, l'enseignement *m* public; *Am* ***state trooper*** ≃ gendarme *m*; ***State of the Union address*** discours *m* sur l'état de l'Union; *Pol* ***state visit*** visite *f* officielle; **he's on a state visit to Japan** il est en visite officielle *ou* voyage officiel au Japon

STATE OF THE UNION ADDRESS

Ce discours radiotélévisé, dans lequel le président des États-Unis dresse le bilan de son programme et en définit les orientations, est prononcé devant le Congrès. L'allocution présidentielle a lieu tous les ans en janvier.

state-aided [-eɪdɪd] *adj* subventionné par l'État

state-controlled *adj (industry)* nationalisé; *(economy)* étatisé; *(activities)* soumis au contrôle de l'État; **the oil company is 51 per cent state-controlled** l'État détient 51 pour cent des actions de la compagnie pétrolière

statecraft ['steɪtkrɑːft] *n (skill → in politics)* habileté *f* politique; *(→ in diplomacy)* (art *m* de la) diplomatie *f*; **he is a master of statecraft** c'est un maître confirmé de la diplomatie

stated ['steɪtɪd] *adj (amount, date)* indiqué; *(limit)* prescrit; *(aim)* déclaré; **it will be finished within the stated time** cela va être terminé dans les délais prescrits *ou* prévus; **at the stated times** aux heures indiquées; **on the stated dates** aux jours indiqués; **at the stated price** au prix indiqué; **do not exceed the stated dose** ne pas dépasser la dose prescrite

statehood ['steɪthʊd] *n* **the struggle for statehood** la lutte pour l'indépendance; **to achieve statehood** devenir un État

Statehouse ['steɪthaʊs] *n* = siège de l'assemblée législative d'un État aux États-Unis

stateless ['steɪtlɪs] *adj* apatride
 ▸▸ ***stateless person*** apatride *mf*

statelessness ['steɪtlɪsnɪs] *n* apatridie *f*

statelet ['steɪtlət] *n Pol* micro-État *m*

stateliness ['steɪtlɪnɪs] *n (of ceremony, building, monument)* majesté *f*, grandeur *f*; *(of person, bearing)* dignité *f*

stately ['steɪtlɪ] (*compar* **statelier**, *superl* **stateliest**) *adj (ceremony, building)* majestueux, imposant; *(person, bearing)* noble, plein de dignité
 ▸▸ ***stately home*** = château ou manoir à la campagne, généralement ouvert au public

statement ['steɪtmənt] *n* (**a**) *(declaration → gen)* déclaration *f*; *(→ to the press)* communiqué *m*; **a written/policy statement** une déclaration écrite/de principe; **can you back that statement up?** pouvez-vous confirmer cette déclaration?; **to put out** *or* **to issue** *or* **to make a statement about sth** émettre un communiqué concernant qch; **the chairman was asked to withdraw his statement** le président a été prié de retirer sa déclaration; **a statement to the effect that...** une déclaration selon laquelle...; *Fig* **the film is making a statement** il y a un message dans ce film; *Fig* **someone who wears jeans to a wedding reception is making a statement** quelqu'un qui va à un mariage en jeans veut faire comprendre quelque chose
 (**b**) *(act of stating → of theory, opinions, policy, aims)* exposition *f*; *(→ of problem)* exposé *m*, formulation *f*; *(→ of facts, identity)* exposé *m*, compte-rendu *m*; **to call him a thief is nothing more than a statement of fact** le traiter de voleur est une simple constatation
 (**c**) *Law* déposition *f*; **to make a statement to the police** faire une déposition dans un commissariat de police; **to take sb's statement** prendre la déposition de qn; **a sworn statement** une déposition faite sous serment
 (**d**) *Com, Fin & Banking* relevé *m*; *(of expenses, sales figures)* état *m*
 (**e**) *Ling* affirmation *f*
 (**f**) *Comput* instruction *f*
 ▸▸ *Acct* ***statement of account*** état *m ou* relevé de compte; *Com, Fin & Banking* ***statement of affairs*** *(in bankruptcy)* bilan *m* de liquidation; ***statement of assets and liabilities*** relevé *m* des dettes actives et passives; *Law* ***statement of claim*** demande *f* introductive d'instance; ***statement of expenses*** état *m ou* relevé *m* des dépenses; *Ins* ***statement of loss*** certificat *m* d'avarie

Staten Island ['stætən-] *n* Staten Island *(quartier de New York)*

state-of-the-art *adj (design, device)* de pointe; **the method incorporates state-of-the-art technology** la méthode utilise des techniques de pointe; *Fam* **it's state-of-the-art** c'est ce qui se fait de mieux ▫, c'est du dernier cri ▫

state-owned [-'əʊnd] *adj* nationalisé
 ▸▸ ***state-owned company*** société *f* d'État, entreprise *f* publique

stateroom ['steɪtrʊm] *n* (**a**) *(in ship)* cabine *f* de grand luxe; *Am (in railway coach)* compartiment *m* privé (**b**) *(in public building)* salon *m* (de réception)

stateside ['steɪtsaɪd] *Am Fam* **1** *adj* (**a**) *(in the United States)* aux États-Unis ▫ (**b**) *(of the United States)* des États-Unis ▫
 2 *adv* aux États-Unis ▫, ≃ au pays; **he has a wife stateside** il a une épouse au pays

statesman ['steɪtsmən] (*pl* **statesmen** [-mən]) *n* homme *m* d'État

statesmanlike ['steɪtsmənlaɪk] *adj (protest, reply)* diplomatique; *(solution)* de grande envergure; *(caution)* pondéré

statesmanship ['steɪtsmənʃɪp] *n* qualités *fpl* d'homme d'État; **he showed great statesmanship in dealing with the problem** il a traité ce problème avec toute l'habileté d'un grand chef d'État

stateswoman ['steɪts,wʊmən] (*pl* **stateswomen** [-,wɪmɪn]) *n* femme *f* politique

state-wide **1** *adj Am (support, protest, celebration)* dans tout l'État; **the epidemic/our distribution is state-wide** l'épidémie/notre réseau de distribution s'étend à tout l'État
 2 *adv* dans tout l'État; **better schools are needed state-wide** on a besoin de meilleures écoles dans tout l'État

static ['stætɪk] **1** *adj* (**a**) *(stationary, unchanging)* stationnaire, stable; **prices are fairly static just now** les prix sont relativement stables en ce moment; **the situation remains static** la situation reste inchangée
 (**b**) *Elec* statique
 2 *n (UNCOUNT)* (**a**) *Rad & Tel* parasites *mpl*
 (**b**) *Elec* électricité *f* statique; **you get a lot of static from nylon carpets** les moquettes en nylon produisent beaucoup d'électricité statique
 (**c**) *Am Fam (aggravation, criticism)* **to give sb static about** *or* **over sth** passer un savon à qn à propos de qch; **to get a lot of static (about** *or* **over) sth** se faire enguirlander (pour qch)
 ▸▸ *Elec* ***static electricity*** électricité *f* statique; ***static lap belt*** ceinture *f* ventrale statique; *Comput* ***static RAM*** mémoire *f* vive statique; *TV & Cin* ***static shot*** plan *m* fixe

statically ['stætɪkəlɪ] *adv* statiquement; **statically balanced** équilibré statiquement; **statically determinate system** système *m* isostatique

statics ['stætɪks] *n (UNCOUNT) Phys* statique *f*

station ['steɪʃən] **1** *n* (**a**) *Transp* gare *f*; *(underground)* station *f* (de métro); **I'll meet you at Brighton station** je vous retrouverai à la gare de Brighton
 (**b**) *(establishment, building)* station *f*, poste *m*; **I must ask you to accompany me to the station** je dois vous demander de m'accompagner au commissariat
 (**c**) *Mil (gen → position)* poste *m*; **to take up one's station** prendre position; **action** *or* **battle stations!** à vos postes!
 (**d**) *Mil (base)* poste *m*, base *f*; *Br* **airforce station** base *f* aérienne
 (**e**) *Rad & TV (broadcasting organization)* station *f*; *(channel)* chaîne *f*; **commercial radio station** station *f* de radio commerciale, radio *f* commerciale; *Rad* **to change stations** changer de fréquence *ou* de station
 (**f**) *(social rank)* rang *m*, condition *f*, situation *f*; **they tend to forget their true station in life** ils ont tendance à oublier leur véritable position sociale; **to marry below one's station** faire une mésalliance; **to marry above one's station** se marier au-dessus de sa condition sociale
 (**g**) *Comput* station *f*
 (**h**) *Rel* **the Stations of the Cross** le chemin de Croix
 (**i**) *Austr & NZ (farm)* = ferme (et ses dépendances)
 2 *comp (buffet, platform etc)* de gare
 3 *vt* (**a**) *(position)* placer, poster; **police were stationed at all the exits** des policiers étaient postés à toutes les issues
 (**b**) *Mil (garrison)* **British troops stationed in Germany** les troupes britanniques stationnées en Allemagne
 ▸▸ *Am* ***station break*** pause *f* publicitaire, page *f* de publicité; *Am* ***station house*** *(police station)* poste *m* de police, commissariat *m*; *(fire station)* caserne *f* de pompiers; *Rail* ***station manager*** chef *m* de gare; *Am Aut* ***station wagon*** break *m*

stationary ['steɪʃnərɪ] *adj* (**a**) *(not moving)* stationnaire; **he hit a stationary vehicle** il a heurté un véhicule à l'arrêt *ou* en stationnement (**b**) *(fixed)* fixe
 ▸▸ *Tech* ***stationary engine*** moteur *m* fixe; *Met* ***stationary front*** front *m* stationnaire; *Tech* ***stationary shaft*** arbre *m* fixe; *Mil* ***stationary target*** cible *f* fixe; *Phys* ***stationary wave*** onde *f* stationnaire

stationer ['steɪʃnə(r)] *n Br* papetier(ère) *m,f*; **stationer's (shop)** papeterie *f*; **at the stationer's** à la papeterie

stationery ['steɪʃnərɪ] *n (in general)* papeterie *f*; *(writing paper)* papier *m* à lettres; **a letter written on hotel stationery** une lettre écrite sur le papier à en-tête d'un hôtel; **school/office stationery** fournitures *fpl* scolaires/de bureau
 ▸▸ *Br Admin* ***the Stationery Office*** = maison d'édition britannique publiant les documents approuvés par le Parlement, les ministères et autres organismes officiels, ≃ l'Imprimerie *f* nationale

stationmaster ['steɪʃn,mɑːstə(r)] *n* chef *m* de gare

statism ['steɪtɪzəm] *n* étatisme *m*

statist ['steɪtɪst] *adj* étatiste

statistic [stə'tɪstɪk] *n* chiffre *m*, statistique *f*; **that particular statistic is certain to embarrass the government** ces chiffres *ou* statistiques vont sûrement embarrasser le gouvernement; **he may be just another statistic to the police, but he was my brother** ce n'est peut-être qu'une statistique de plus pour la police, mais il s'agissait de mon frère

statistical [stə'tɪstɪkəl] *adj (analysis, data, technique)* statistique; *(error)* de statistique; **it's a statistical certainty** c'est statistiquement certain; **statistical mechanism** mécanique *f* statistique

statistically [stə'tɪstɪklɪ] *adv* statistiquement

statistician [,stætɪ'stɪʃən] *n* statisticien(enne) *m,f*

statistics [stə'tɪstɪks] **1** *n (UNCOUNT) (science)* statistique *f*
 2 *npl* (**a**) *(figures)* statistiques *fpl*, chiffres *mpl*
 (**b**) *Fam (of woman)* mensurations ▫ *fpl*

stative ['steɪtɪv] *adj*
 ▸▸ ***stative verb*** verbe *m* d'état

stator ['steɪtə(r)] *n* stator *m*

statoscope ['stætəskəʊp] *n Met* statoscope *m*

stats [stæts] *Fam (statistics)* stats *fpl*

statuary ['stætʃʊərɪ] **1** *n (UNCOUNT) Formal (statues collectively)* statues *fpl*; *(art)* statuaire *f*
 2 *adj* statuaire
 ▸▸ ***statuary marble*** marbre *m* statuaire

statue ['stætʃuː] *n* statue *f*; **the Statue of Liberty** la statue de la Liberté

statuesque [,stætjʊ'esk] *adj* sculptural; **a statuesque woman** une femme d'une beauté sculpturale

statuette [,stætjʊ'et] *n* statuette *f*

stature ['stætʃə(r)] *n* (**a**) *(height)* stature *f*, taille *f*; **he is rather short in** *or* **of stature** il est plutôt petit (**b**) *(greatness)* envergure *f*, calibre *m*; **he doesn't have the stature to be prime minister** il n'a pas l'envergure d'un premier ministre; **a mathematician of considerable stature** un mathématicien d'une très grande envergure

status [*Br* 'steɪtəs, *Am* 'stætəs] **1** *n* (**a**) *(position → in society, hierarchy etc)* rang *m*, position *f*, situation *f*; **what's your status in the company?** quelle est votre position dans l'entreprise?; **she quickly achieved celebrity status** elle est vite devenue une célébrité
 (**b**) *(prestige)* prestige *m*, standing *m*; **living here definitely confers a certain status** le fait de vivre ici confère indéniablement un certain standing *ou* prestige

(**c**) *(legal or official standing)* statut *m*; **legal status** statut *m* légal

(**d**) *(general state or situation)* état *m*, situation *f*, condition *f*; **to make a status report on sth** faire le point sur qch; **their financial status is under investigation** on enquête sur leur situation financière

(**e**) *Med* **HIV-positive status** séropositivité *f*

2 *comp (car, club)* de prestige, prestigieux

►► *Comput* ***status bar*** barre *f* d'état; *Comput* ***status box*** zone *f* d'état; ***status enquiry*** *(about creditworthiness)* prise *f* de renseignements sur la solvabilité; ***status enquiry department*** service *m* des renseignements commerciaux; *Comput* ***status line*** ligne *f* d'état; ***status meeting*** réunion *f* de bilan; *Comput* ***status printout*** *(of printer)* impression *f* des paramètres de l'imprimante; ***status quo*** statu quo *m*; **to maintain** *or* **to preserve the status quo** maintenir le statu quo; *Comput* ***status report*** état *m* du projet; ***status symbol*** marque *f* de prestige

statute ['stætju:t] *n* (**a**) *Law* loi *f*; *Br Pol (act)* acte *m* du Parlement (**b**) *(of club, company, university)* règle *f*; **the statutes** le règlement, les statuts *mpl*

►► *Br* ***statute book*** code *m* (des lois), recueil *m* de lois; **the new law is not yet on the statute book** la nouvelle loi n'est pas encore entrée en vigueur; ***statute law*** droit *m* écrit; ***statute of limitations*** loi *f* de prescription, prescription *f* légale; **the statute of limitations in this country is ten years** dans ce pays, il y a prescription de dix ans

statutorily ['stætjʊtərɪlɪ] *adv* statutairement

statutory ['stætjʊtrɪ] *adj* (**a**) *(regulations)* statutaire; *(duties, penalty)* statutaire, juridique; *(holiday)* légal; *(offence)* prévu par la loi; *(price controls, income policy)* obligatoire

(**b**) *Br (token)* **the statutory woman** la femme-alibi *(présente pour que soit respectée la réglementation sur l'égalité des sexes)*

►► ***statutory company*** entreprise *f* de service public; *Am* ***statutory rape*** détournement *m* de mineur; ***statutory report*** = rapport annuel sur l'état de l'entreprise *(obligatoire dans le cadre de la loi sur les sociétés)*; ***statutory reserve*** réserve *f* statutaire; ***statutory rights*** droits *mpl* statutaires; ***statutory sick pay*** = indemnité de maladie versée par l'employeur; ***statutory tenant*** locataire *mf* en place

staunch [stɔ:ntʃ] **1** *adj (loyal)* loyal, dévoué; *(unswerving)* constant, inébranlable; **he's my staunchest ally** c'est mon allié le plus sûr; **a staunch Catholic** un(e) catholique à tout crin; **a staunch socialist** un(e) socialiste convaincu(e)

2 *vt (liquid, blood)* étancher; *(flow)* arrêter, endiguer

staunchly ['stɔ:ntʃlɪ] *adv (loyally)* loyalement, avec dévouement; *(unswervingly)* avec constance, fermement; **their house is in a staunchly Republican area** ils habitent un quartier résolument républicain

staunchness ['stɔ:ntʃnɪs] *n (loyalty)* loyauté *f*, dévouement *m*; *(firmness)* constance *f*, fermeté *f*

stave [steɪv] *(pt & pp* **staved** *or* **stove** [stəʊv]) **1** *n* (**a**) *Mus* portée *f* (**b**) *(stanza)* strophe *f* (**c**) *(part of barrel)* douve *f*, douelle *f*

2 *vt Scot (finger, toe)* se faire une entorse à

►**stave in** *vt sep* enfoncer, défoncer

►**stave off** *vt sep (defeat)* retarder; *(worry, danger)* écarter; *(disaster, threat)* conjurer; *(misery, hunger, thirst)* tromper; *(questions)* éluder; **to stave off a cold** éviter un rhume; **his lawyer tried to stave off any awkward questions** son avocat a essayé d'éluder toute question gênante

staves [steɪvz] *pl of* **staff, stave**

STAY [steɪ]

séjour	► 1 (a)
étai	► 1 (c), (d)
aller jusqu'au bout de	► 2 (a)
arrêter	► 2 (b)
retarder	► 2 (b)
étayer	► 2 (c)
rester	► 3 (a), (b)
loger	► 3 (b)

1 *n* (**a**) *(sojourn)* séjour *m*; **enjoy your stay!** bon séjour!; **an overnight stay in hospital** une nuit d'hospitalisation

(**b**) *Law (suspension)* suspension *f*

(**c**) *(support, prop)* étai *m*, support *m*, soutien *m*

(**d**) *(cable, wire → for mast, flagpole etc)* étai *m*, hauban *m*

(**e**) *(in corset)* baleine *f*

(**f**) *Literary (delay)* retard *m*; **he will endure no stay** il ne supportera aucun retard

2 *vt* (**a**) *(last out)* aller jusqu'au bout de, tenir jusqu'à la fin de; *Sport & Fig* **to stay the distance** tenir la distance; **to stay the course** *Sport* finir la course; *Fig* tenir jusqu'au bout

(**b**) *(stop)* arrêter, enrayer; *(delay)* retarder; **to stay sb's hand** retenir qn; **to stay one's hand** se retenir; *Law* **to stay judgement/proceedings** surseoir au jugement/aux poursuites

(**c**) *(prop up → wall)* étayer; *(secure with cables → mast)* haubaner

3 *vi* (**a**) *(remain)* rester; **to stay still** rester tranquille; **to stay at home** rester à la maison *ou* chez soi; **to stay in bed** rester au lit; *(when ill)* garder le lit; **stay here** *or Fam* **stay put until I come back** restez ici *ou* ne bougez pas jusqu'à ce que je revienne; *Fam* **I'll stay put, I'm staying put** j'y suis, j'y reste; **stay!** *(to dog)* pas bouger!; **I can't stay long, I've got a train to catch** je ne peux pas rester longtemps, j'ai un train à prendre; **would you like to stay for** *or* **to dinner?** voulez-vous rester dîner?; **I don't want to stay in the same job all my life** je ne veux pas faire le même travail toute ma vie; **to stay awake all night** rester éveillé toute la nuit, ne pas dormir de la nuit; **it stays dark here until at least 10 o'clock in the morning** ici, il ne fait pas jour avant 10 heures du matin; **the weather stayed fine/wet all week** le temps est resté au beau/à la pluie toute la semaine; **if the weather stays like this** si le temps se maintient; **let's try and stay calm** essayons de rester calmes; **she managed to stay ahead of the others** elle a réussi à conserver son avance sur les autres; **stay tuned for the news** restez à l'écoute pour les informations; **personal computers have come to stay** *or* **are here to stay** l'ordinateur personnel fait désormais partie de notre quotidien; **it looks like the mobile phone is here to stay** il semblerait que les téléphones portables fassent désormais partie de notre quotidien

(**b**) *(reside temporarily → in hotel, with friends)* loger; *(→ in a city)* rester; **how long are you staying in New York?** combien de temps restez-vous à New York?; **we decided to stay an extra week** nous avons décidé de rester une semaine de plus *ou* de prolonger notre séjour d'une semaine; **I always stay at the same hotel** je descends toujours au *ou* je loge toujours dans le même hôtel; **we met a couple staying at the same hotel as us** nous avons rencontré un couple qui logeait dans le même hôtel que nous; **to look for a place to stay** chercher un endroit où loger; **she's staying with friends** elle loge chez des amis; **he has come to stay (for a few days/weeks)** il est venu passer quelques jours/semaines chez nous; **I like having people to stay** j'aime bien avoir des gens chez moi; **you can stay here for the night, you can stay the night here** tu peux coucher ici cette nuit *ou* passer la nuit ici

(**c**) *Literary (stop, pause)* s'arrêter

(**d**) *Scot (live)* habiter, demeurer

4 stays *npl* corset *m*

►► *Law* ***stay of execution*** ordonnance *f* à surseoir (à un jugement), sursis *m*; *Fig* sursis; ***stays list*** *(at hotel)* liste *f* des clients en recouche; *Law* ***stay of proceedings*** suspension *f* d'instances; ***stay stitch*** point *m* d'arrêt

►**stay away** *vi (not go)* ne pas aller; *(not come)* ne pas venir; *(not approach)* ne pas approcher; **she stayed away from school last week** elle n'est pas allée à l'école la semaine dernière; **people are staying away from the beaches** les plages sont désertées en ce moment; **to stay away from danger** se tenir à l'écart du danger; **you can play outside but stay away from the road** tu peux jouer dehors mais ne va pas sur la route; **stay away from my sister!** ne t'approche pas de ma sœur!

►**stay behind** *vi* rester; **I'll stay behind to clear up** je vais rester pour ranger; **a few pupils stayed behind to talk to the teacher** quelques élèves sont restés (après le cours) pour parler au professeur

►**stay down** *vi* (**a**) *(gen)* rester en bas; *(remain crouched)* rester accroupi; *(remain lying)* rester couché; *(remain under water)* rester sous l'eau

(**b**) *(hair, lid)* tenir en place

(**c**) *Br Sch* redoubler; **she had to stay down a year** elle a dû redoubler

(**d**) *(food)* **I do eat, but nothing will stay down** je mange, mais je ne peux rien garder

►**stay in** *vi* (**a**) *(stay at home)* rester à la maison, ne pas sortir; *(stay indoors)* rester à l'intérieur, ne pas sortir

(**b**) *(be kept in after school)* être consigné, être en retenue

(**c**) *(not fall out)* rester en place, tenir; **I can't get this nail to stay in** je n'arrive pas à faire tenir ce clou

►**stay off 1** *vt insep* (**a**) *(keep away from → main roads, private property)* éviter, ne pas passer par; *(→ alcohol, drugs)* ne pas prendre, éviter; **stay off the whisky!** pas de whisky!

(**b**) *(not attend → school, work)* ne pas aller à

2 *vi (bad weather)* ne pas arriver; **we're hoping the rain will stay off a little longer** nous espérons que la pluie attendra encore un peu

►**stay on** *vi* (**a**) *(not leave)* rester; **more pupils are staying on at school after the age of 16** de plus en plus d'élèves poursuivent leur scolarité au-delà de l'âge de 16 ans; **he's staying on in the firm as product manager** il va rester dans l'entreprise en tant que chef de produit

(**b**) *(remain in place → hat, wig)* tenir *ou* rester en place; *(sticker, handle)* tenir

►**stay out** *vi* (**a**) *(not come home)* ne pas rentrer; *(remain outside)* rester dehors; **she stayed out all night** elle n'est pas rentrée de la nuit; **to stay out late** rentrer tard; **don't stay out there in the rain!** ne reste pas dehors sous la pluie!; **get out and stay out!** sors d'ici et ne t'avise pas de revenir!

(**b**) *(remain on strike)* rester en grève; **the miners stayed out for nearly a year** la grève des mineurs a duré près d'un an

(**c**) *(not get involved)* ne pas se mêler (**of** de); **stay out of this!** ne te mêle pas de ça!

►**stay over** *vi* (**a**) *(not leave)* prolonger son séjour, rester plus longtemps; **we decided to stay over until the weekend** nous avons décidé de prolonger notre séjour jusqu'au week-end

(**b**) *(stay the night)* passer la nuit; **do you want to stay over?** veux-tu passer la nuit ici?

►**stay up** *vi* (**a**) *(not go to bed)* veiller, ne pas se coucher; **don't stay up too late** ne veillez pas *ou* ne vous couchez pas trop tard; **we stayed up all night talking** nous sommes restés à parler toute la nuit; **my parents always stay up until I get home** mes parents attendent toujours que je sois rentré pour aller se coucher

(**b**) *(remain in place → building, mast)* rester debout; *(→ shelf, socks, trousers)* tenir; *(→ pictures, decorations)* rester en place

►**stay with** *vt insep Fam* **just stay with it, you can do it** accroche-toi, tu vas y arriver

---

stay-at-home *Fam Pej* **1** *n* pantouflard(e) *m,f*

2 *adj* pantouflard, popote *(inv)*

stayer ['steɪə(r)] *n* (**a**) *Sport (runner)* coureur *m* de fond; *(cyclist)* stayer *m*; *(horse)* stayer, cheval *m* qui a du fond (**b**) *(person who perseveres)* personne *f* persévérante; **she's a real stayer** elle va jusqu'au bout de ce qu'elle entreprend; **gifted but not a stayer** doué mais manque de suivi *ou* de persévérance

staying power ['steɪɪŋ-] *n* résistance *f*, endurance *f*

staysail ['steɪseɪl] *n* voile *f* d'étai

stay-ups *npl (tights)* bas *mpl* autofixants, Dim-ups® *mpl*

STD [,esti:'di:] *n* (**a**) *Br Tel (abbr* **subscriber trunk dialling**) automatique *m* (interurbain) (**b**) *(abbr* **sexually transmitted disease**) MST *f*

►► ***STD code*** indicatif *m* de zone

stead [sted] *n Br Formal* **in sb's stead** à la place de qn; **he asked me to go in his stead** il m'a demandé d'y aller à sa place; **to stand sb in**

sta–ste

good stead rendre grand service *ou* être très utile à qn

steadfast ['stedfɑːst] *adj* (**a**) *(unswerving)* constant, inébranlable; *(loyal)* loyal, dévoué; **to be steadfast in one's support of sb** apporter un soutien inconditionnel à qn (**b**) *(steady → stare, gaze)* fixe

steadfastly ['stedfɑːstlɪ] *adv* avec constance, fermement; **she has steadfastly refused to identify her sources** elle a toujours refusé de désigner ses sources

steadfastness ['stedfɑːstnɪs] *n* constance *f*, fermeté *f*; **they showed great steadfastness of purpose** ils ont fait preuve d'une grande ténacité *ou* persévérance

Steadicam® ['stedɪkæm] *n TV & Cin* Steadicam® *m*

►► ***Steadicam operator*** opérateur *m* steadicam

steadily ['stedɪlɪ] *adv* (**a**) *(at regular rate → increase, decline)* régulièrement, progressivement; *(→ breathe)* régulièrement; **to work steadily at sth** travailler assidûment à qch

(**b**) *(non-stop → rain)* sans interruption, sans cesse; **her health grew steadily worse** sa santé s'est progressivement détériorée

(**c**) *(firmly → stand)* planté *ou* campé sur ses jambes; *(→ walk)* d'un pas ferme; *(→ gaze)* fixement, sans détourner les yeux; **she looked at him steadily** elle l'a fixé du regard, elle l'a regardé fixement

steadiness ['stedɪnɪs] *n* (**a**) *(regularity → of growth, increase, decline, speed, pace, pulse)* régularité *f* (**b**) *(firmness, stability → of ladder, boat, relationship, market)* stabilité *f*; *(→ of structure, desk, chair)* stabilité *f*, solidité *f*; *(→ of hand)* sûreté *f* (**c**) *(firmness → of voice)* fermeté *f*; *(→ of gaze)* fixité *f*; *(→ of nerves)* solidité *f* (**d**) *(reliability → of person)* sérieux *m*

steady ['stedɪ] *(compar* **steadier**, *superl* **steadiest**, *pl* **steadies**, *pt & pp* **steadied**) **1** *adj* (**a**) *(regular, constant → growth, increase, decline)* régulier, progressif; *(→ speed, pace)* régulier, constant; *(→ demand)* suivi; *(→ pulse)* régulier, égal; *(→ work)* stable; *(→ income)* régulier; **inflation remains at a steady 5 percent** l'inflation s'est stabilisée à 5 pour cent; **to drive at a steady 90** rouler constamment à 90; **he's never been able to hold down a steady job** il n'a jamais pu garder un emploi stable; **I've got several boyfriends but no one steady** j'ai des flirts, mais pas de petit ami attitré

(**b**) *(firm, stable → ladder, boat, relationship, market)* stable; *(→ structure, desk, chair)* solide, stable; **hold the ladder steady for me** tiens-moi l'échelle; **to have a steady hand** avoir la main sûre; **to be steady on one's feet** *or* **legs** être d'aplomb sur ses jambes

(**c**) *(calm → voice)* ferme; *(→ gaze)* fixe; *(→ nerves)* solide

(**d**) *(reliable → person)* sérieux

2 *adv* **to go steady with sb** sortir avec qn; **are Diana and Paul going steady?** c'est sérieux entre Diana et Paul?

3 *n Fam* petit ami *m*, petite amie *f*

4 *exclam Br* **steady (on)!** *(be careful)* attention!; *(calm down)* du calme!; **steady! you almost knocked me over!** eh! doucement! tu as failli me faire tomber!

5 *vt* (**a**) *(stabilize)* stabiliser; *(hold in place)* maintenir, retenir; **I reached out to steady the vase** j'ai tendu le bras pour retenir le vase; **he almost fell off, but he managed to steady himself** il a failli tomber, mais il a réussi à se rattraper; **she rested her elbows on the wall to steady the camera** elle appuya ses coudes sur le mur pour que l'appareil photo ne bouge pas; **we were trying to steady the boat** nous essayions de stabiliser le bateau

(**b**) *(calm)* calmer; **drink this, it'll steady your nerves** bois ça, ça te calmera (les nerfs); **marriage has steadied him** le mariage lui a donné un certain équilibre

6 *vi (boat, prices, stock market)* se stabiliser; *(pulse, breathing)* devenir régulier; *(person → regain balance)* retrouver son équilibre; *(→ calm down)* se calmer

►► ***steady boyfriend*** petit *m* ami attitré; **she has a steady boyfriend** elle sort avec le même copain depuis longtemps; ***steady girlfriend*** petite amie *f* attitrée; **he has a steady girlfriend** il sort avec la même copine depuis longtemps; ***steady rain*** pluie *f* persistante; *Phys* ***steady state theory*** théorie *f* de l'état *ou* de l'univers stationnaire

steadying ['stedɪɪŋ] *adj* **to take a steadying breath** inspirer un bon coup pour se calmer; **to be a steadying influence on sb** avoir une influence apaisante sur qn; **living with Jennifer has had a steadying influence on him** il s'est assagi *ou* calmé depuis qu'il vit avec Jennifer

steak [steɪk] *n* (**a**) *(beefsteak → for frying, grilling)* steak *m*, bifteck *m*; **steak and chips** steak frites *m*

(**b**) *(beef → for stews, casseroles)* bœuf *m* à braiser; *Br* **steak and kidney pie** = tourte à la viande et aux rognons cuite au four; *Br* **steak and kidney pudding** = tourte à la viande et aux rognons cuite à la vapeur

(**c**) *(cut → of veal, turkey)* escalope *f*; *(→ of other meat)* tranche *f*; *(→ of fish)* tranche *f*, darne *f*

►► ***steak knife*** couteau *m* à steak *ou* à viande; ***steak tartare*** steak *m* tartare

steakhouse ['steɪkhaʊs, *pl* -haʊzɪz] *n* grill *m*, grill-room *m*

steal [stiːl] *(pt* **stole** [stəʊl], *pp* **stolen** ['stəʊlən]) **1** *vt* (**a**) *(money, property)* voler; **to steal sth from sb** voler qch à qn; **he stole money from her purse** il a volé de l'argent dans son porte-monnaie; **I've had my purse stolen** on m'a volé mon porte-monnaie; **several paintings have been stolen from the museum** plusieurs tableaux ont été volés au musée; **they've stolen my idea!** ils ont volé mon idée!

(**b**) *Fig (time)* voler, prendre; *(attention, affection)* détourner; **to steal sb's heart** séduire qn; **to steal a kiss** voler un baiser; **to steal all the credit for sth** s'attribuer tout le mérite de qch; **may I steal a few moments of your precious time?** pouvez-vous m'accorder quelques instants de votre temps si précieux?; **to steal a glance at sb** jeter un regard furtif à qn; *Br* **to steal a march on sb** prendre qn de vitesse, couper l'herbe sous le pied à qn; **to steal the show from sb** ravir la vedette à qn; **he really stole the show with that act of his!** son numéro a été le clou du spectacle!; **to steal sb's thunder** éclipser qn

2 *vi* (**a**) *(commit theft)* voler; **he was caught stealing** il a été pris en train de voler; *Bible* **thou shalt not steal** tu ne voleras point

(**b**) *(move secretively)* **to steal in/out** entrer/sortir à pas furtifs *ou* feutrés; **to steal into a room** se glisser *ou* se faufiler dans une pièce; **she stole up on me from behind** elle s'est approchée de moi par derrière sans faire de bruit; *Fig Literary* **shadows began to steal across the courtyard** des ombres commencèrent à envahir la cour; *Literary* **a strange sadness stole over me** une étrange tristesse m'envahit

3 *n* (**a**) *Fam (bargain)* affaire *f*; **it was a steal** c'était une bonne affaire

(**b**) *Sport (in basketball)* récupération *f* du ballon

►**steal away** *vi* partir furtivement, s'esquiver

stealer ['stiːlə(r)] *n* voleur(euse) *m,f*; **sheep stealer** voleur *m* de moutons

stealing ['stiːlɪŋ] *n* vol *m*

stealth [stelθ] *n* (**a**) *(of animal)* ruse *f* (**b**) *(UNCOUNT) (underhandedness)* moyens *mpl* détournés; **the documents were obtained by stealth** nous nous sommes procuré les documents en cachette *ou* par des moyens détournés

►► ***stealth bomber, stealth plane*** avion *m* furtif

stealthily ['stelθɪlɪ] *adv* furtivement, subrepticement, en catimini

stealthiness ['stelθɪnɪs] *n (of action etc)* caractère *m* furtif; *(of person)* manières *fpl* furtives; **his stealthiness in defaming his rivals** la ruse avec laquelle il parvenait à diffamer ses rivaux

stealthy ['stelθɪ] *(compar* **stealthier**, *superl* **stealthiest**) *adj* furtif

steam [stiːm] **1** *n* (**a**) *(vapour)* vapeur *f*; *(condensation)* buée *f*; **she wiped the steam from the mirror** elle essuya la buée sur la glace

(**b**) *Tech & Rail (as power)* vapeur *f*; **to run on** *or* **to work by steam** marcher à la vapeur; **at full steam** à toute vapeur, à pleine vitesse; **full steam ahead!** en avant toute!; **to do sth under one's own steam** faire qch par ses propres moyens; **to get up** *or* **to pick up steam** *(vehicle)* prendre de la vitesse; *(campaign)* être lancé; **the battle against drugs is finally picking up steam** la lutte contre la drogue est enfin bien lancée; *Fam* **to let off steam** se défouler; *Fam* **to run out of steam** s'essouffler❑, s'épuiser❑

2 *comp (boiler, locomotive etc)* à vapeur

3 *vt* (**a**) *(unstick with steam)* **steam the stamps off the envelope** passez l'enveloppe à la vapeur pour décoller les timbres; **to steam open an envelope** décacheter une enveloppe à la vapeur

(**b**) *Culin* (faire) cuire à la vapeur; **steamed vegetables** légumes *mpl* (cuits) à la vapeur

4 *vi* (**a**) *(give off steam → soup, kettle, wet clothes)* fumer

(**b**) *(cook in steam)* cuire à la vapeur

(**c**) *(go → train, ship)* **the train steamed into/out of the station** le train entra en gare/quitta la gare; **the liner steamed into the harbour** le paquebot entra dans le port; **cargo boats regularly steamed across the Atlantic** des cargos à vapeur traversaient régulièrement l'Atlantique; *Fig* **my brother steamed on ahead** mon frère filait devant; *Fig* **she steamed into/out of the room** elle est entrée dans/sortie de la pièce comme une furie

►► ***steam bath*** bain *m* de vapeur; ***steam coal*** charbon *m* à vapeur, houille *f* de chaudière; ***steam cooking*** cuisson *f* à la vapeur; ***steam engine*** *Tech* moteur *m* à vapeur; *Rail* locomotive *f* à vapeur; ***steam heat*** chaleur *f* fournie par la vapeur; ***steam iron*** fer *m* (à repasser) à vapeur; *Tech* ***steam jacket*** enveloppe *f* de cylindre, chemise *f* de vapeur; ***steam point*** point *m* d'ébullition; ***steam power*** vapeur *f*; *Br Fam Old-fashioned* ***steam radio*** *(broadcasting)* ≃ la bonne vieille radio *(par opposition à la télévision)*; *(set)* poste *m* de radio antédiluvien; *Am* ***steam shovel*** bulldozer *m*; ***steam turbine*** turbine *f* à vapeur; ***steam whistle*** sifflet *m* à vapeur

►**steam up** **1** *vi (window, glasses)* s'embuer, se couvrir de buée

2 *vt sep* (**a**) *(window, glasses)* embuer

(**b**) *Am Fam (infuriate)* **to steam sb up** mettre qn en pétard *ou* en boule

steamboat ['stiːmbəʊt] *n* bateau *m* à vapeur, vapeur *m*

steam-driven *adj* à vapeur

steamed [stiːmd] *adj (fish, vegetables etc)* à la vapeur

►► ***steamed pudding*** = pudding cuit au bain-marie

steamed-up *adj Fam (angry)* énervé❑, dans tous ses états❑; **what's he all steamed-up about?** pourquoi est-il dans tous ses états *ou* dans un état pareil?; **she got very steamed-up about the whole business** (toute) cette histoire l'a mise dans tous ses états *ou* l'a beaucoup énervée

steamer ['stiːmə(r)] *n* (**a**) *Naut* bateau *m* à vapeur, vapeur *m* (**b**) *Culin (pan)* marmite *f* à vapeur; *(basket inside pan)* panier *m* de cuisson à la vapeur

steamie ['stiːmɪ] *n Scot Hist* lavoir *m*

steaming ['stiːmɪŋ] **1** *adj* (**a**) *(very hot)* fumant (**b**) *Am Fam (angry)* en pétard, en boule (**c**) *Br Fam (drunk)* complètement bourré *ou* pété

2 *adv* **steaming hot** fumant; *Br Fam* **steaming drunk** complètement bourré *ou* pété

3 *n* (**a**) *Culin* cuisson *f* à la vapeur (**b**) *Fam Crime slang* = vol de sacs à main pratiqué en bande, dans les endroits publics aux heures de grande affluence

steamroll ['stiːmrəʊl] *vt (road)* cylindrer

steamroller ['stiːmˌrəʊlə(r)] **1** *n* rouleau *m* compresseur; *Fig* **to use steamroller tactics** employer la technique du rouleau compresseur

2 *vt* (**a**) *(road)* cylindrer (**b**) *Fig (crush → opposition, obstacle)* écraser (**c**) *Fig (force)* **to steamroller a bill through Parliament** = faire passer une loi à la Chambre sans tenir compte de l'opposition; **to steamroller sb into doing sth** forcer qn à faire qch

steamroom ['stiːmruːm] *n* hammam *m*

steamship ['stiːmʃɪp] *n* navire *m* à vapeur, vapeur *m*

steamy ['sti:mɪ] *(compar* **steamier,** *superl* **steamiest)** *adj* **(a)** *(room)* plein de vapeur; *(window, mirror)* embué **(b)** *Fam (erotic)* chaud, sexy

stearate ['stɪəreɪt] *n Chem* stéarate *m*

stearic [stɪ'ærɪk] *adj* stéarique

▸▸ ***stearic acid*** acide *m* stéarique

stearin ['stɪərɪn] *n* stéarine *f*

steatite ['stɪə,taɪt] *n* stéatite *f*

steatopygia [,stɪətəʊ'pɪdʒɪə] *n* stéatopygie *f*

steed [sti:d] *n Literary* coursier *m*

steel [sti:l] **1** *n* **(a)** *(iron alloy)* acier *m*; **to have nerves of steel** avoir des nerfs d'acier; **a grip/a will of steel** une poigne/une volonté de fer

(b) *(steel industry)* industrie *f* sidérurgique, sidérurgie *f*; **the nationalization of steel** la nationalisation de l'industrie sidérurgique

(c) *(for sharpening knives)* aiguisoir *m*

(d) *Literary (sword)* fer *m*

2 *comp (industry, plant)* sidérurgique; *(strike)* des sidérurgistes

3 *adj (helmet, cutlery etc)* en acier

4 *vt* **(a)** *Br (harden)* **to steel oneself against sth** se cuirasser contre qch; **he steeled himself against any further hurt** il s'est cuirassé contre toute nouvelle blessure sentimentale; **steel yourself for a terrible ordeal** préparez-vous à affronter une rude épreuve; **I had steeled myself for the worst** je m'étais préparé au pire

(b) *Metal* aciérer

▸▸ *Mus* ***steel band*** steel band *m*; ***steel blue*** bleu *m* acier; ***steel grey*** gris *m* acier; ***steel guitar*** steel guitar *f*; ***the steel industry*** la sidérurgie; ***steel manufacturer*** sidérurgiste *mf*; ***steel mill*** aciérie *f*; ***steel wool*** paille *f* de fer

steel-blue *adj* bleu acier *(inv)*

steelclad ['sti:lklæd] *adj (gen)* couvert *ou* revêtu d'acier; *Literary (knight)* bardé de fer

steel-grey *adj* gris acier *(inv)*

steeliness ['sti:lɪnɪs] *n (determination)* inflexibilité *f*

steel-plated *adj* cuirassé

steelwork ['sti:lwɜ:k] *n (UNCOUNT) Tech* tôleries *fpl*; **constructional steelwork** profilés *mpl* pour constructions

steelworker ['sti:l,wɜ:kə(r)] *n* sidérurgiste *mf*

steelworks ['sti:lwɜ:ks] *(pl* **inv)** *n* aciérie *f*, usine *f* sidérurgique

steely ['sti:lɪ] *adj* **(a)** *(in colour)* d'acier, gris acier *(inv)* **(b)** *(strong → determination, will)* de fer; *(→ look)* d'acier

▸▸ ***steely blue*** bleu *m* acier

steelyard ['sti:ljɑ:d] *n* balance *f* romaine

steely-blue *adj* bleu acier *(inv)*

steenbok ['sti:nbɒk] *n* steinbock *m*

steep [sti:p] **1** *adj* **(a)** *(hill)* raide, abrupt, escarpé; *(slope)* fort, raide; *(cliff)* abrupt; *(road, path)* raide, escarpé; *(staircase)* raide; **it's a steep climb to the village** la montée est raide pour arriver au village; **the plane went into a steep dive** l'avion se mit à piquer du nez

(b) *(increase, fall)* fort; **a steep drop in share prices** une forte chute du prix des actions

(c) *Fam (fee, price)* excessif[❑], élevé[❑]; **the prices are a bit steep** l'addition est plutôt salée

(d) *Fam (unreasonable)* **it's a bit steep asking us to do all that work by Friday** c'est un peu fort *ou* un peu raide de nous demander de faire tout ce travail pour vendredi

2 *vt (soak)* (faire) tremper; *Culin* (faire) macérer, (faire) mariner; **steep the onions in vinegar** faites macérer les oignons dans du vinaigre; *Fig* **I want to steep myself in the atmosphere of the place** je veux m'imprégner de l'atmosphère de l'endroit

3 *vi (gen)* tremper; *Culin* macérer, mariner

steeped [sti:pt] *adj* **steeped in tradition/mystery/history** imprégné de tradition/mystère/d'histoire; **steeped in prejudice** plein *ou* pétri de préjugés

steepen ['sti:pən] *vi* **(a)** *(slope, road, path)* devenir plus raide *ou* escarpé; **the climb steepened as we neared the top** la pente devenait de plus en plus raide à mesure que nous approchions du sommet **(b)** *(increase → inflation, rate)* croître

steepening ['sti:pənɪŋ] *adj* **steepening prices** prix en hausse *ou* à la hausse; **steepening path** sentier qui devient plus raide

steepish ['sti:pɪʃ] *adj (gradient)* assez raide; *(price)* plutôt raide

steeple ['sti:pəl] *n (bell tower)* clocher *m*; *(spire)* flèche *f* (de clocher)

steeplechase ['sti:pəltʃeɪs] *n (in horse racing, athletics)* steeple *m*, steeple-chase *m*

steeplechaser ['sti:pəl,tʃeɪsə(r)] *n* **(a)** *(jockey)* jockey *m* de steeple *ou* steeple-chase **(b)** *(runner)* coureur(euse) *m,f* de steeple *ou* steeple-chase

steeplechasing ['sti:pəl,tʃeɪsɪŋ] *n (in horse racing, athletics)* steeple-chases *mpl*

steeplejack ['sti:pəldʒæk] *n Br* = réparateur de clochers et de cheminées

steeply ['sti:plɪ] *adv* en pente raide, à pic; **the path climbs steeply** le chemin monte en pente raide; **a steeply sloping field leads down to the lake** un champ descend en pente raide jusqu'au lac; **costs are rising steeply** les coûts montent en flèche

steepness ['sti:pnɪs] *n* **(a)** *(of climb, road, staircase)* raideur *f* **(b)** *(of price rise)* importance *f*

steer ['stɪə(r)] **1** *vt* **(a)** *(car)* conduire; **the lorry was surprisingly easy to steer** le camion était étonnamment facile à conduire; **she steered the car into the garage/out onto the main road** elle a rentré la voiture au garage/conduit jusqu'à la route principale

(b) *Naut (boat)* gouverner, barrer; **to steer a course for** mettre le cap sur; *Fig* **to steer a middle course** trouver un compromis; *Fig* **the management has decided to steer a radically different course** la direction a décidé de changer radicalement de cap; *Fig* **it's a dangerous course you're steering** vous vous engagez sur un terrain dangereux; **steered course** route *f* au compas *ou* apparente

(c) *(person)* guider, diriger; **she steered me over to a sofa** elle m'a guidé vers un canapé; **try to steer him away from the bar** essayez de l'éloigner du bar

(d) *(conversation, project etc)* diriger; **I tried to steer the conversation round to/away from the subject** j'ai essayé d'amener la conversation sur le sujet/de détourner la conversation du sujet; **she successfully steered the company through the crisis** elle a réussi à sortir la société de la crise; **to steer a bill through Parliament** réussir à faire voter un projet de loi par le Parlement

2 *vi* **(a)** *(driver)* conduire; **I'd feel safer if you steered with both hands!** je me sentirais mieux si tu conduisais des deux mains!; **I steered carefully into the garage** j'ai manœuvré avec soin pour entrer dans le garage; **she steered smoothly round the bend** elle prit le virage en douceur

(b) *Naut (helmsman)* gouverner, barrer; *(boat)* se diriger; **the ferry was steering for Dover** le ferry se dirigeait vers Douvres; **steer for that buoy** mettez le cap sur cette bouée; **to steer clear of sb/sth** éviter qn/qch; **steer clear of her husband, he's a real bore** évite son mari, c'est un vrai raseur

(c) *(car)* **this car steers very well/badly** cette voiture a une excellente/très mauvaise direction; **a taxi steered out of a side street** un taxi a débouché d'une rue latérale

3 *n* **(a)** *Agr* bœuf *m*

(b) *Am Fam (piece of advice)* conseil[❑] *m*; *(tip)* tuyau *m*

steerage ['stɪərɪdʒ] *n Naut* **(a)** *Old-fashioned (accommodation)* entrepont *m* **(b)** *(steering)* conduite *f*, pilotage *m*

▸▸ ***steerage passengers*** passagers *mpl* d'entrepont

steerageway ['stɪərɪdʒ,weɪ] *n Naut* vitesse *f* acquise, *Spec* erre *f*; **to get up/to lose steerageway** augmenter/diminuer l'erre

steering ['stɪərɪŋ] **1** *n* **(a)** *Aut (apparatus, mechanism)* direction *f*; *(manner of driving)* conduite *f*

(b) *Naut* conduite *f*, pilotage *m*

2 *comp Aut (arm, lever)* de direction

▸▸ *Aut* ***steering box*** boîtier *m* de direction; ***steering column*** colonne *f* de direction; *Br* ***steering committee*** comité *m* directeur; *Aviat & Aut* ***steering gear*** mécanisme *m* de direction; *Naut* appareil *m* à gouverner; *Aut* ***steering geometry*** géométrie *f* du train avant; *Aut* ***steering lock*** *(turning circle)* rayon *m* de braquage; *(antitheft device)* antivol *m* de direction; ***steering play*** jeu *m* à la direction; ***steering rod*** bielle *f* de direction; ***steering wheel*** *Aut* volant *m*; *Naut* roue *f* du gouvernail, barre *f*; *Aut* ***steering wheel cover*** housse *f* de volant

steersman ['stɪəzmən] *(pl* **steersmen** [-mən]) *n* timonier *m*, barreur *m*

steeve [sti:v] *Naut* **1** *n* apiquage *m*

2 *vt* apiquer

3 *vi* être apiqué

stegosaurus [,stegə'sɔ:rəs] *n* stégosaure *m*

stein ['staɪn] *n* chope *f*

steinbok = **steenbok**

stele *n* **(a)** *Antiq* ['sti:lɪ] *(pl* **stelae** [-i:]) stèle *f* **(b)** *Bot* ['sti:lɪ, sti:l] *(pl* **steles** *or* **stelae** [-i:]) stèle *f*

stellar ['stelə(r)] *adj* **(a)** *Astron* stellaire **(b)** *Fam Theat* **the play boasts a stellar cast** cette pièce a une distribution éblouissante[❑]

stellarator ['stelәreɪtə(r)] *n Phys* stellarator *m*

stellate ['steleɪt], **stellated** [ste'leɪtɪd] *adj* étoilé, en étoile

stelliform ['stelɪfɔ:m] *adj* stelliforme

stellular ['steljʊlə(r)], **stellulate** ['steljʊleɪt] *adj* stellulé

stem [stem] *(pt & pp* **stemmed,** *cont* **stemming) 1** *n* **(a)** *Bot (of plant, tree)* tige *f*; *(of fruit, leaf)* queue *f*

(b) *(of glass)* pied *m*

(c) *(of tobacco pipe)* tuyau *m*

(d) *Ling (of word)* radical *m*

(e) *Tech (in lock, watch, valve)* tige *f*; **winding stem** tige *f* de remontoir

(f) *(vertical stroke → of letter)* hampe *f*; *(→ of musical note)* queue *f*

(g) *Naut (timber, structure)* étrave *f*; *(forward section)* proue *f*; **from stem to stern** de l'étrave à l'étambot; *Fig* **the party is split from stem to stern on this issue** le parti est totalement divisé sur cette question

(h) *Bible (family, stock)* souche *f*

(i) *Sport (in skiing)* stem(m) *m*; **stem Christie/parallel** stem(m) *m* christie/parallèle

(j) *Am Fam* **stems** *(legs)* quilles *fpl*, gambettes *fpl*

2 *vt* **(a)** *(check, stop → flow, spread, bleeding)* arrêter, endiguer; *(→ blood)* étancher; *(→ river, flood)* endiguer, contenir; **the government has taken new measures to stem the flow of capital abroad** le gouvernement a pris de nouvelles mesures pour arrêter la fuite des capitaux à l'étranger; **to stem the rise in unemployment/crime** enrayer la montée du chômage/de la criminalité; **they are trying to stem the tide of protest** ils essaient d'endiguer le nombre croissant de protestations

(b) *Sport* **to stem one's skis** faire un stem *ou* stemm

3 *vi* **(a)** *(derive)* **to stem from** avoir pour cause, être le résultat de; **all her difficulties stem from her insecure childhood** tous ses problèmes ont pour cause une enfance difficile

(b) *Sport (in skiing)* faire du stem *ou* stemm

▸▸ *Biol* ***stem cell*** cellule *f* souche; ***stem ginger*** gingembre *m* confit; ***stem glass*** verre *m* à pied; ***stem turn*** *(in skiing)* stem(m) *m*

stemless ['stemlɪs] *adj* **(a)** *Bot* sans tige(s) **(b)** *Literary (flow)* qu'on ne peut pas arrêter

stemmed [stemd] *adj (glass)* à pied

-stemmed [stemd] *suff* **(a)** *Bot* à tige...; **a long/short/thin-stemmed plant** une plante à tige longue/courte/mince **(b)** *(gen)* **a long/short-stemmed glass** un verre à pied haut/bas; **a long/short-stemmed pipe** une pipe à tuyau long/court

stemson ['stemsən] *n Naut* marsouin *m* (de l'avant)

stemware ['stemweə(r)] *n Am (glasses)* verres *mpl*

stem-winder *n* montre *f* à remontoir

Sten [sten] *pr n*

▸▸ ***Sten gun*** mitraillette *f* légère

stench [stentʃ] *n* puanteur *f*, odeur *f* nauséabonde; *Fig* **the stench of decay** l'odeur nauséabonde de la putréfaction

stencil ['stensəl] *(Br pt & pp* **stencilled,** *cont* **stencilling,** *Am pt & pp* **stenciled,** *cont* **stenciling) 1** *n* **(a)** *(for typing)* stencil *m* **(b)** *(template)* pochoir *m* **(c)** *(pattern → drawn)* dessin *m* au pochoir; *(→ painted)* peinture *f* au pochoir

2 *vt (draw)* dessiner au pochoir; *(paint)* peindre au pochoir

stencilling ['stensəlɪŋ] *n (drawn)* dessin *m* au pochoir; *(painted)* peinture *f* au pochoir

steno ['stenəʊ] *(pl* **stenos***)* *n Am Fam* (**a**) *(stenographer)* sténo *mf* (**b**) *(stenography)* sténo *f*

stenograph ['stenəgrɑːf] *n* sténotype *f*

stenographer [stə'nɒgrəfə(r)] *n Am* sténographe *mf*

stenography [stə'nɒgrəfɪ] *n* sténographie *f*

stenohaline [ˌstenəʊ'heɪliːn] *adj Ecol* sténohalin

Stenotype® ['stenəʊtaɪp] *n* sténotype *f*

stenotypist ['stenəʊˌtaɪpɪst] *n* sténotypiste *mf*

stenotypy ['stenətaɪpɪ] *n* sténotypie *f*

Stentor ['stentɔː(r)] *pr n Myth* Stentor

stentorian [sten'tɔːrɪən] *adj Literary (voice)* de stentor

STEP [step]

pas	▸ **1 (a), (b), (d)**
mesure	▸ **1 (b)**
étape	▸ **1 (c)**
marche	▸ **1 (e)**
seconde	▸ **1 (f)**
faire un pas	▸ **3 (a)**
marcher	▸ **3 (a), (b)**

(pt & pp **stepped**, *cont* **stepping***)* **1** *n* (**a**) *(pace)* pas *m*; **with quick steps** d'un pas rapide; **to take two steps forwards/backwards** faire deux pas en avant/en arrière; **I grew wearier with every step I took** je m'épuisais un peu plus à chaque pas (que je faisais); **I heard her step** *or* **steps on the stairs** j'ai entendu (le bruit de) ses pas dans l'escalier; **that's certainly put a spring in her step** ça lui a donné un peu de ressort, c'est sûr; **he was following a few steps behind me** il me suivait à quelques pas; **it's only a (short) step to the shops** les magasins sont à deux pas d'ici; **within a few steps of the house** à quelques pas de la maison; **watch** *or* **mind your step!** faites attention où vous mettez les pieds!; *Fig* faites attention!

(**b**) *(move, action)* pas *m*; *(measure)* mesure *f*, disposition *f*; **it's a great step forward for mankind** c'est un grand pas en avant pour l'humanité; **our first step will be to cut costs** notre première mesure sera de réduire les coûts; **to take steps to do sth** prendre des mesures pour faire qch; **the government should take steps to ban the book** le gouvernement devrait prendre des mesures pour interdire le livre; **what steps have you taken?** quelles mesures avez-vous prises?; **it's only a short step from what you are suggesting to an outright ban** entre ce que vous suggérez et une interdiction absolue, il n'y a qu'un pas; **it's a step in the right direction** c'est un pas dans la bonne direction; **this promotion is a big step up for me** cette promotion est un grand pas en avant pour moi; **we are still one step ahead of our competitors** nous conservons une petite avance sur nos concurrents

(**c**) *(stage)* étape *f*; **the different steps in the manufacturing process** les différentes étapes du processus de fabrication; **the next step is to ...** l'étape suivante consiste à ...; **if I may take your argument one step further** si je peux pousser votre raisonnement un peu plus loin; **we'll support you every step of the way** nous vous soutiendrons à fond *ou* sur toute la ligne; **they fought us every step of the way** ils nous ont combattus sans répit *ou* sur chaque point; **one step at a time** petit à petit; **step by step** petit à petit

(**d**) *(in marching, dancing)* pas *m*; **a minuet step** un pas de menuet; **in step** au pas; **to march in step** marcher au pas; **out of step** désynchronisé; **to be out of step** ne pas être en cadence; **they were walking out of step** ils ne marchaient pas en cadence; **to break step** rompre le pas; **to change step** changer de pas; **to fall into step with sb** s'aligner sur le pas de qn; *Fig* se ranger à l'avis de qn; **he fell into step beside me** arrivé à ma hauteur, il régla son pas sur le mien; **to keep (in) step** marcher au pas; **do try and keep step!** *(in dancing)* essaie donc de danser en mesure!; **to be in step with the times/with public opinion** être au diapason de son temps/de l'opinion publique; **to be out of step with the times/with public opinion** être déphasé par rapport à son époque/à l'opinion publique; **supply has got out of step with demand** l'offre ne correspond plus à la demande

(**e**) *(stair → gen)* marche *f*; *(→ into bus, train etc)* marche-pied *m*; **a flight of steps** *(indoors)* un escalier; *(outdoors)* un perron; **the church steps** le perron de l'église; **mind the step** *(sign)* attention à la marche; **to cut steps** *(in mountaineering)* tailler des marches

(**f**) *Am Mus (interval)* seconde *f*

(**g**) *(aerobics)* step *m*; **I go to step twice a week** je vais à un cours de step deux fois par semaine

2 *vt* (**a**) *(measure out)* mesurer

(**b**) *(space out)* échelonner

3 *vi* (**a**) *(take a single step)* faire un pas; *(walk, go)* marcher, aller; **step this way, please** par ici, je vous prie; **step inside!** entrez!; **he carefully stepped round the sleeping dog** il contourna précautionneusement le chien endormi; **I stepped onto/off the train** je suis monté dans le/descendu du train; **she stepped lightly over the ditch** elle enjamba le fossé lestement; *Fig* **to step out of line** s'écarter du droit chemin

(**b**) *(put one's foot down, tread)* marcher; **to step on sb's foot** marcher sur le pied de qn; **I stepped on a banana skin/in a puddle** j'ai marché sur une peau de banane/dans une flaque d'eau; *Fam* **step on it!** appuie sur le champignon!

4 steps *npl Br (stepladder)* **(pair of) steps** escabeau *m*

▸▸ ***step aerobics*** step *m*

▸**step aside** *vi* (**a**) *(move to one side)* s'écarter, s'effacer

(**b**) *(quit position, job)* se retirer, se désister; **he stepped aside in favour of a younger person** il a cédé la place à quelqu'un de plus jeune

▸**step back** *vi* (**a**) reculer, faire un pas en arrière

(**b**) *Fig* prendre du recul; **we don't have time to step back and figure out what it all means** nous n'avons pas le temps de prendre du recul pour essayer de comprendre tout cela

▸**step down 1** *vt sep Elec (voltage)* abaisser

2 *vi* (**a**) *(descend)* descendre (**from** de)

(**b**) *(quit position, job)* se retirer, se désister; **he stepped down in favour of a younger person** il a cédé la place à quelqu'un de plus jeune; **he has stepped down as managing director** il a démissionné de son poste de directeur général

▸**step forward** *vi* faire un pas en avant; *Fig (make oneself known)* se manifester; *(volunteer)* se porter volontaire

▸**step in** *vi* (**a**) *(enter)* entrer

(**b**) *(intervene)* intervenir

▸**step out** *vi* (**a**) *(go out of doors)* sortir

(**b**) *(walk faster)* presser le pas

(**c**) *Am Old-fashioned* **to be stepping out with sb** sortir avec qn; **to step out on sb** laisser tomber qn

▸**step up 1** *vt sep* (**a**) *(increase → output, pace)* augmenter, accroître; *(→ activity, efforts)* intensifier

(**b**) *Elec (voltage)* augmenter

[illegible] **to step up to sb/sth** s'approcher de qn/qch; **step up!, step up!, come and see...** approchez! approchez! venez voir...; **he stepped up onto the platform** il est monté sur le podium

stepbrother ['stepˌbrʌðə(r)] *n* demi-frère *m (fils du beau-père ou de la belle-mère)*

step-by-step 1 *adv (gradually)* pas à pas, petit à petit

2 *adj (point by point)* **a step-by-step guide to buying your own house** *(title)* acheter une maison: guide détaillé

stepchild ['stepˌtʃaɪld] *(pl* **stepchildren** [-ˌtʃɪldrən]*)* *n* beau-fils *m*, belle-fille *f (fils ou fille du conjoint)*

stepdaughter ['stepˌdɔːtə(r)] *n* belle-fille *f (fille du conjoint)*

step-down transformer *n* abaisseur *m* de tension

stepfather ['stepˌfɑːðə(r)] *n* beau-père *m (conjoint de la mère)*

> **The Stepford wives**
>
> Il s'agit du titre original d'un film américain de 1974 tiré du roman éponyme de Ira Levin (en français *Les Femmes de Stepford*). Stepford est une petite ville américaine où toutes les femmes semblent trouver l'épanouissement complet dans leur rôle de ménagères et de femmes au foyer; il s'avère par la suite que les hommes se sont débarrassés de leurs épouses et les ont remplacées par des androïdes.
>
> On utilise l'expression **Stepford wife** à propos d'une femme qui semble obsédée par les tâches ménagères ou bien qui a le regard vide.

stephanotis [ˌstefə'nəʊtɪs] *n Bot* jasmin *m* de Madagascar

Stephen ['stiːvən] *pr n Hist* **King Stephen** le roi Étienne

step-in *adj (skirt)* à enfiler *(sans boutons ni fermeture Éclair®)*

stepladder ['stepˌlædə(r)] *n* escabeau *m*

stepless transmission ['steplɪs-] *n Aut* transmission *f* à variation continue

stepmother ['stepˌmʌðə(r)] *n* belle-mère *f (conjointe du père)*

stepparent ['stepˌpeərənt] *n* beau-parent *m*; *(stepfather)* beau-père *m (conjoint de la mère)*; *(stepmother)* belle-mère *f (conjointe du père)*; **relations between children and their stepparents are often difficult** les rapports entre un enfant et son beau-père ou sa belle-mère sont souvent difficiles

steppe [step] *n* steppe *f*

▸▸ *Orn* ***steppe eagle*** aigle *m* des steppes

stepped-up [stept-] *adj (output)* accru, augmenté; *(pace)* plus rapide; *(activity, efforts, war)* intensifié

stepper ['stepə(r)] *n*

▸▸ *Elec* ***stepper motor*** moteur *m* pas-à-pas

stepping-stone ['stepɪŋ-] *n* pierre *f* de gué; *Fig* tremplin *m*; **a stepping-stone to a new career** un tremplin pour (se lancer dans) une nouvelle carrière

stepping up *n* (**a**) *(of output, pace)* augmentation *f*; *(of activity, efforts)* intensification *f* (**b**) *Elec (of voltage)* augmentation *f*

stepsister ['stepˌsɪstə(r)] *n* demi-soeur *f (fille du beau-père ou de la belle-mère)*

stepson ['stepsʌn] *n* beau-fils *m (fils du conjoint)*

step-up transformer *n* transformateur *m* (élévateur)

steradian [stə'reɪdɪən] *n Geom* stéradian *m*

stercoraceous [ˌstɜːkə'reɪʃəs] *adj* stercoraire

stere [stɪə(r)] *n* stère *m*

stereo ['sterɪəʊ] *(pl* **stereos***)* **1** *n* (**a**) *(stereo sound)* stéréo *f*; **broadcast in stereo** retransmis en stéréo (**b**) *(hi-fi system)* chaîne *f* (stéréo); **I need a new stereo** il me faudrait une nouvelle chaîne

2 *adj (cassette, record, record player)* stéréo *(inv)*; *(recording, broadcast)* en stéréo

▸▸ ***stereo signal*** signal *m* stéréo; ***stereo system*** chaîne *f* stéréo; ***stereo transmitter*** émetteur *m* stéréo

stereochemistry [ˌsterɪəʊ'kemɪstrɪ] *n Chem* stéréochimie *f*

stereogram ['sterɪəgræm] *n* (**a**) *(image)* stéréo- [illegible]

stereograph ['sterɪəgrɑːf] *n* stéréogramme *m*

stereographic [ˌstɪərɪəʊ'græfɪk] *adj* stéréographique

stereographically [ˌstɪərɪəʊ'græfɪkəlɪ] *adv* stéréographiquement

stereography [ˌsterɪ'ɒgrəfɪ] *n* stéréographie *f*

stereoisomer [ˌsterɪəʊ'aɪsəmə(r)] *n Chem* stéréoisomère *m*

stereometer [ˌsterɪ'ɒmɪtə(r)] *n* stéréomètre *m*

stereometry [ˌsterɪ'ɒmɪtrɪ] *n* stéréométrie *f*

stereophonic [ˌsterɪə'fɒnɪk] *adj* stéréophonique

stereoscope ['sterɪəʊskəʊp] *n* stéréoscope *m*

stereoscopic [ˌsterɪə'skɒpɪk] *adj* stéréoscopique

stereoscopy [ˌsterɪ'ɒskəpɪ] *n* stéréoscopie *f*

stereotype ['sterɪətaɪp] **1** *n* (**a**) *(idea, trait, convention)* stéréotype *m*; **they don't really conform to our stereotype of what Americans are like** ils ne correspondent pas vraiment au stéréotype que nous avons des Américains (**b**) *Typ* cliché *m*

2 *vt* (**a**) *(person, role)* stéréotyper (**b**) *Typ* clicher

stereotyped ['sterɪəʊtaɪpt] *adj* stéréotypé; **the film is full of very stereotyped images of women** dans ce film, les personnages de femmes sont très stéréotypés *ou* les femmes ont des rôles très stéréotypés

stereotypical [ˌsterɪəʊ'tɪpɪkəl] *adj* stéréotypé

stereotyping ['sterɪəʊˌtaɪpɪŋ] *n* **we want to avoid sexual stereotyping** nous voulons éviter les stéréotypes sexuels

steric ['stɪərɪk] *adj Chem* stérique

sterile ['steraɪl] *adj* stérile

sterility [ste'rɪlətɪ] *n* stérilité *f*

sterilization [ˌsterəlaɪ'zeɪʃən] *n* stérilisation *f*

sterilize, -ise ['sterəlaɪz] *vt* stériliser

sterilized ['sterəlaɪzd] *adj* stérilisé

sterilizer ['sterəlaɪzə(r)] *n* stérilisateur *m*

sterilizing ['sterəlaɪzɪŋ] *n* stérilisation *f*

►► ***sterilizing tablets*** comprimés *mpl* purificateurs d'eau

Steristrip® ['sterɪstrɪp] *n Med* Stéristrip® *m*

sterling ['stɜːlɪŋ] **1** *n* (**a**) *(currency)* sterling *m inv*; **to pay in sterling** payer en livres sterling; **twenty thousand pounds sterling** vingt mille livres sterling

(**b**) *(standard)* titre *m*

(**c**) *(silverware)* argenterie *f*

2 *comp (reserves, balances)* en sterling; *(traveller's cheques)* en livres sterling

3 *adj* (**a**) *(metal)* fin

(**b**) *Formal (first-class)* excellent, de premier ordre; **a sterling fighter** un combattant inlassable

►► ***sterling area*** zone *f* sterling; ***sterling qualities*** qualités *fpl* solides; ***sterling silver*** argent *m* fin; **a sterling silver spoon** une cuillère en argent

stern [stɜːn] **1** *adj* (**a**) *(strict, harsh → person, measure)* sévère, strict; *(→ appearance)* sévère, austère; *(→ discipline, punishment)* sévère, rigoureux; *(→ look, rebuke)* sévère, dur; *(→ warning)* solennel, grave

(**b**) *(robust)* solide, robuste; **his wife is made of sterner stuff** sa femme est d'une autre trempe

2 *n* (**a**) *Naut* arrière *m*, poupe *f*

(**b**) *(of horse)* croupe *f*

►► *Naut* ***stern post*** étambot *m*; ***stern sheets*** chambre *f* (d'embarcation)

sterna ['stɜːnə] *pl of* **sternum**

sternforemost [stɜːn'fɔːməʊst] *adv Naut* par l'arrière

sternly ['stɜːnlɪ] *adv* sévèrement

sternness ['stɜːnnɪs] *n* sévérité *f*

Sterno can® ['stɜːnəʊ-] *n Am* = boîte contenant une substance inflammable qui sert à cuisiner en camping

sternpost ['stɜːnpəʊst] *n Naut* étambot *m*

sternum ['stɜːnəm] (*pl* **sternums** *or* **sterna** [-nə]) *n Anat* sternum *m*

sternutation [ˌstɜːnjʊ'teɪʃən] *n Formal* sternutation *f*

sternutator [ˌstɜːnjʊ'teɪtə(r)] *n Formal* substance *f* sternutatoire

sternward(s) ['stɜːnwəd(z)] *adv Naut* vers l'arrière

sternway ['stɜːnweɪ] *n Naut* aculée *f*

steroid ['stɪərɔɪd] *n* stéroïde *m*; **the doctor put him on a course of steroids** le médecin lui a prescrit *ou* donné un traitement stéroïdien

sterol ['stɪərɒl] *n* stérol *m*

stertorous ['stɜːtərəs] *adj Literary* stertoreux, ronflant

stet [stet] *Typ* **1** *n (on proof)* bon, à maintenir

2 *vt* maintenir

stethoscope ['steθəskəʊp] *n* stéthoscope *m*

Stetson® ['stetsən] *n* Stetson® *m*, chapeau *m* de cow-boy

stevedore ['stiːvədɔː(r)] **1** *n Am* docker *m*, débardeur *m*

2 *vi* travailler comme docker *ou* débardeur

stew¹ [stjuː] **1** *n Culin* ragoût *m*; **lamb/vegetable stew** ragoût d'agneau/de légumes; *Br Fam* **to be in a stew** *(bothered)* être dans tous ses états; *(in a mess)* être dans de beaux draps *ou* dans le pétrin

2 *vt (meat)* préparer en ragoût, cuire (en ragoût); *(fruit)* (faire) cuire en compote

3 *vi* (**a**) *Culin (meat)* cuire en ragoût, mijoter; *(fruit)* cuire; **leave the meat to stew for at least two hours** laissez mijoter la viande pendant deux bonnes heures; *Br Fam* **to let sb stew (in his/her own juice)** laisser cuire *ou* mijoter qn dans son jus

(**b**) *(tea)* infuser trop longtemps

(**c**) *(worry)* **to stew over sth** ruminer qch; **don't just sit there and stew** ne reste pas là assis à ruminer

(**d**) *Br Fam (person)* **to be stewing** crever de chaleur; **it's stewing in here** il fait une chaleur à crever ici

stew² *n Am Fam (abbr* **stewardess**) hôtesse *f* de l'air ❑

steward ['stjʊəd] *n* (**a**) *(on aeroplane, ship)* steward *m* (**b**) *(at race, sports event)* commissaire *m* (**c**) *(at dance, social event)* organisateur(trice) *m,f*; *(at meeting, demonstration)* membre *m* du service d'ordre (**d**) *(of property)* intendant(e) *m,f*; *(of estate, finances)* régisseur(euse) *m,f*; *(in college)* économe *mf*

►► *Br* ***steward's enquiry*** enquête *f* des commissaires

stewardess ['stjʊədɪs] *n* hôtesse *f*

stewardship ['stjʊədʃɪp] *n* intendance *f*, économat *m*; *Fig* **under his stewardship the situation improved markedly** quand il était responsable, les choses s'étaient nettement améliorées

stewbeef ['stjuːbiːf] *Am* = **stewing steak**

stewed [stjuːd] *adj* (**a**) *Culin* **we had stewed lamb for supper** au dîner, nous avons mangé un ragoût d'agneau (**b**) *(tea)* trop infusé (**c**) *Fam (drunk)* bourré, cuité; **to get stewed** se cuiter; **stewed to the gills** rond comme une queue de pelle, pété à mort

►► ***stewed fruit*** compote *f* de fruits; ***stewed meat*** ragoût *m*

stewing ['stjuːɪŋ] *n (of meat)* préparation *f* en ragoût, cuisson *f* (en ragoût); *(of fruit)* cuisson *f* en compote

►► ***stewing beef*** bœuf *m* à braiser; ***stewing pan*** (grande) casserole *f*; ***stewing pears*** poires *fpl* à cuire; *Br* ***stewing steak*** bœuf *m* à braiser

stewpan ['stjuːpæn] *n* (grande) casserole *f*

stewpot ['stjuːpɒt] *n* cocotte *f*, fait-tout *m inv*

St. Ex. *(written abbr* **stock exchange**) Bourse *f*

stg *(written abbr* **sterling**) sterling *inv*

sthenic ['sθenɪk] *adj Med* sthénique

stibine ['stɪbaɪn] *n* stibine *f*

stich [stɪk] *n Literature* vers *m*

stichomythia [ˌstɪkəʊ'mɪθɪə] *n* stichomythie *f*

STICK [stɪk]

bâton	► **1 (a) – (c)**
canne	► **1 (a)**
baguette	► **1 (a)**
morceau	► **1 (b)**
crosse	► **1 (c)**
critiques	► **1 (e)**
planter	► **2 (a)**
enfoncer	► **2 (a)**
mettre	► **2 (b)**
fixer	► **2 (c)**
coller	► **2 (d); 3 (b)**
supporter	► **2 (f)**
se planter	► **3 (a)**
se coincer	► **3 (c)**
rester	► **3 (d)**

(pt & pp **stuck** [stʌk]) **1** *n* (**a**) *(piece of wood)* bâton *m*; *(for kindling)* bout *m* de bois; *(twig)* petite branche *f*, brindille *f*; *(walking stick)* canne *f*, bâton *m*; *(for plants)* rame *f*, tuteur *m*; *(drumstick)* baguette *f*; *(for lollipop)* bâton *m*; **gather some sticks, we'll make a fire** ramassez du bois, on fera du feu; **she had legs like sticks** elle avait des jambes comme des allumettes; **I'm going to take a stick to that boy one day!** un jour je vais donner une bonne correction à ce garçon!; *Fig* **the threat of redundancy has become a stick with which industry beats the unions** pour le patronat, la menace du licenciement est devenue une arme contre les syndicats; **his behaviour became a stick to beat him with** son comportement s'est retourné contre lui; **to get (hold of) the wrong end of the stick** mal comprendre, comprendre de travers; **you've got (hold of) the wrong end of the stick about this business** vous avez tout compris de travers dans cette histoire; **to get the short** *or* **dirty end of the stick** être mal loti; **she got the short** *or* **dirty end of the stick as usual** c'est tombé sur elle comme d'habitude; *Prov* **sticks and stones may break my bones (but words will never hurt me)** la bave du crapaud n'atteint pas la blanche colombe

(**b**) *(piece → of chalk)* bâton *m*, morceau *m*; *(→ of cinnamon, incense, liquorice, dynamite)* bâton *m*; *(→ of charcoal)* morceau *m*; *(→ of chewing gum)* tablette *f*; *(→ of glue, deodorant)* bâton *m*, stick *m*; *(→ of celery)* branche *f*; *(→ of rhubarb)* tige *f*

(**c**) *Sport (in lacrosse)* crosse *f*; *(in hockey)* crosse *f*, stick *m*; *(ski pole)* bâton *m* (de ski); *(baseball bat)* batte *f*; *(billiard cue)* queue *f* de billard; *(in pick-up-sticks)* bâton *m*, bâtonnet *m*, jonchet *m*

(**d**) *Br Fam (furniture)* meuble ❑ *m*; **a few sticks (of furniture)** quelques vagues meubles; **we don't have one stick of decent furniture** nous n'avons pas un seul meuble convenable

(**e**) *(UNCOUNT) Br Fam (criticism)* critiques *fpl* ❑; **to take a lot of stick** *(to be criticized)* se faire éreinter *ou* démolir; *(to be mocked)* se faire chambrer *ou* charrier; **to give sb stick (for sth)** *(criticize)* éreinter *ou* démolir qn (à cause de qch); *(laugh at)* chambrer *ou* charrier qn (à cause de qch); **the police got a lot of stick from the press** la police s'est fait éreinter *ou* démolir par la presse; **he got a lot of stick from his friends about his new hairstyle** ses amis l'ont bien chambré *ou* charrié avec sa nouvelle coupe

(**f**) *esp Am Fam (joystick)* manche *m* à balai ❑; *(gear lever)* levier *m* de vitesse ❑

(**g**) *Mil (cluster → of bombs)* chapelet *m*; *(→ of parachutists)* stick *m*

(**h**) *Br Fam Old-fashioned (person)* type *m*; **a dry old stick** un pince-sans-rire; **she's a funny old stick** c'est un drôle de personnage; **she's not a bad old stick, she's a nice old stick** elle est plutôt sympa

(**i**) *Fam (glue)* colle ❑ *f*; *(stickiness)* pouvoir *m* adhésif ❑

(**j**) *Am Fam (cannabis cigarette)* stick *m*

(**k**) *Br very Fam* **to be up the stick** *(pregnant)* être en cloque

2 *vt* (**a**) *(jab, stab → spear, nail, knife)* planter, enfoncer; *(→ needle)* piquer, planter; *(→ pole, shovel)* planter; *(→ elbow, gun)* enfoncer; **he stuck his fork into a potato** il a planté sa fourchette dans une pomme de terre; **she stuck the spade into the ground** elle a planté la bêche dans le sol; **don't stick drawing pins in the wall** ne plantez pas de punaises dans le mur; **there were maps with coloured pins stuck in them** il y avait des cartes avec des épingles de couleur; **I've got a splinter stuck in my finger** je me suis planté une écharde dans le doigt; **a ham stuck with cloves** un jambon piqué de clous de girofle; **watch out! you almost stuck your umbrella in my eye!** fais attention! tu as failli m'enfoncer ton parapluie dans l'œil!; **he stuck his elbow in my ribs** il m'a enfoncé son coude dans les côtes; **she stuck the revolver in his back** elle lui a enfoncé le revolver dans le dos; **stick the skewer through the chicken** enfilez le poulet sur la broche, embrochez le poulet

(**b**) *(put)* mettre; *(insert)* insérer, mettre; *Fam (put casually)* mettre ❑, coller; **stick the candles in the holders** mettez les bougies dans les bougeoirs; **he stuck a rose in his lapel** il s'est mis une rose à la boutonnière; **she stuck the cork in the bottle** elle a enfoncé le bouchon dans le goulot de la bouteille; **to stick a flower in one's hair** piquer une fleur dans ses cheveux; **here, stick this under the chair leg** tenez, calez la chaise avec ça; **he stuck his foot in the door** il glissa son pied dans l'entrebâillement de la porte; **he stood there with a cigar stuck in his mouth/with his hands stuck in his pockets** il était planté là, un cigare entre les dents/les mains enfoncées dans les poches; **he stuck the card back in the pack** il a remis la carte dans le jeu; **she stuck her head into the office/out of the window** elle a passé la tête dans le bureau/par la fenêtre; **I had to stick my fingers**

down my throat il a fallu que je me mette les doigts dans la bouche; *Fam* **mix it all together and stick it in the oven** mélange bien et mets-le au four❑; *Fam* **stick it in your pocket** colle ça dans ta poche; *Fam* **can you stick my name on the list?** tu peux ajouter mon nom sur la liste?❑; *Fam* **he pulled out his gun and stuck it in my face** il a sorti son revolver et me l'a collé sous le nez; *very Fam* **you can stick your job/money!** ton boulot/fric, tu peux te le mettre où je pense!; *very Fam* **stick it!** va te faire voir!

(**c**) *(fasten)* fixer; *(pin up)* punaiser; **she stuck the broom head on the handle** elle a fixé la brosse à balai au manche; **it was stuck on the notice-board with tacks** c'était punaisé au tableau d'affichage

(**d**) *(with adhesive)* coller; **to stick a stamp on an envelope** coller un timbre sur une enveloppe; **help me stick this vase together** aide-moi à recoller le vase; **he had posters stuck to the walls with Sellotape®** il avait scotché des posters aux murs; **stick no bills** *(sign)* défense d'afficher

(**e**) *(kill → pig)* égorger

(**f**) *Br Fam (tolerate)* supporter❑; **I can't stick him** je peux pas l'encadrer; **I don't know how you've stuck it for so long** je ne sais pas comment tu as fait pour supporter ça si longtemps; **what I can't stick is her telling me how to run my life** ce que je ne peux pas encaisser c'est qu'elle me dise comment je dois mener ma vie; **I'm amazed she stuck a term, let alone three years** je suis étonné qu'elle ait tenu (le coup) un trimestre, et à plus forte raison trois ans

(**g**) *Fam (with chore, burden)* **to stick sb with a fine/the blame** coller une amende/faire endosser la responsabilité❑ à qn

(**h**) *Am Fam (give injection to)* faire une piqûre à❑, piquer❑

3 *vi* (**a**) *(be embedded → arrow, dart, spear)* se planter; **you'll find some tacks already sticking in the notice-board** vous trouverez quelques punaises déjà plantées dans le tableau d'affichage; **the point was sticking through the lining** la pointe avait percé la doublure; **don't leave the spade sticking in the ground** ne laisse pas la pelle plantée dans le sol; **they had straw sticking in their hair** ils avaient des brins de paille dans les cheveux

(**b**) *(attach, adhere → wet clothes, bandage, chewing gum)* coller; *(→ gummed label, stamp)* tenir, coller; *(→ burr)* s'accrocher; **the dough stuck to my fingers** la pâte collait à mes doigts; **the damp has made the stamps stick together** l'humidité a collé les timbres les uns aux autres; **the dust will stick to the wet varnish** la poussière va coller sur le vernis frais; **her shirt stuck to her back** elle avait la chemise collée au dos; **a butterfly had stuck to the flypaper** un papillon était venu se coller au papier tue-mouches; **these badges stick to any surface** ces autocollants adhèrent sur toutes les surfaces; **food won't stick to these pans** ces casseroles n'attachent pas; **the noodles had got all stuck together** les nouilles avaient collé *ou* étaient toutes collées; *Br Fam* **have some porridge! that'll stick to your ribs!** prends du porridge, ça tient au corps!

(**c**) *(become jammed, wedged → mechanism, drawer, key)* se coincer, se bloquer; **the lorry stuck fast in the mud** le camion s'est complètement enlisé dans la boue; **this drawer keeps sticking** ce tiroir n'arrête pas de se coincer *ou* de se bloquer; **a fishbone stuck in my throat** j'avais une arête (de poisson) coincée dans la gorge; *Fig* **it stuck in my throat** ça m'est resté en travers de la gorge; **having to ask him for a loan really sticks in my throat** ça me coûte vraiment d'avoir à lui demander de me prêter de l'argent; **the words stuck in his throat** les mots lui restèrent dans la gorge

(**d**) *(remain, keep)* rester; **they called him Boney as a child and the name stuck** quand il était petit, on le surnommait Boney et le nom lui est resté; **she has the kind of face that sticks in your memory** elle a un visage qu'on n'oublie pas *ou* dont on se souvient; **dates just never stick in my head** je n'ai vraiment pas la mémoire des dates

(**e**) *Fam (be upheld)* **we know he's guilty, but will the charge stick?** nous savons qu'il est coupable, mais est-ce qu'un tribunal le condamnera❑?; **to make the charge** *or* **charges stick** prouver la culpabilité de qn❑; **the important thing now is to make the agreement stick** ce qui compte maintenant, c'est de faire respecter l'accord❑

(**f**) *(in card games)* (**I**) **stick** j'arrête, je ne veux pas d'autre carte; **the dealer must stick on** *or* **with seventeen** le donneur doit s'arrêter à dix-sept

4 sticks *npl Fam* **the sticks** la cambrousse; **they live out in the sticks** ils habitent en pleine cambrousse

►► ***stick bean*** haricot *m* à rames; ***stick deodorant*** déodorant *m* en stick; ***stick figure*** personnage *m* stylisé; ***stick insect*** phasme *m*; *Am Aut* ***stick shift*** levier *m* de vitesse; **I don't know how to drive a stick shift** je ne sais pas conduire une voiture à vitesses manuelles

►**stick around** *vi Fam (stay)* rester (dans les parages); *(wait)* attendre❑; **stick around if you want, she'll be back in a little while** tu peux rester si tu veux, elle ne va pas tarder à rentrer; **I'm not sticking around a moment longer!** je n'attendrai pas une minute de plus!

►**stick at** *vt insep* (**a**) *Br (persevere)* **to stick at it** persévérer

(**b**) *(stop)* **to stick at nothing** ne reculer *ou* n'hésiter devant rien; **she'll stick at nothing to get her way** elle ne reculera devant rien pour parvenir à ses fins

►**stick away** *vt sep Fam (put away)* ranger❑; *(hide)* planquer

►**stick by** *vt insep* (**a**) *(person)* soutenir; **don't worry, I'll always stick by you** sois tranquille, je serai toujours là pour te soutenir

(**b**) *(one's decision)* s'en tenir à; **I stick by what I said** je maintiens ce que j'ai dit

►**stick down 1** *vt sep* (**a**) *(flap, envelope)* coller

(**b**) *Br Fam (note down)* noter❑; *(scribble)* griffonner❑

(**c**) *Fam (place)* coller; **stick the box down in the corner** colle le carton dans le coin; **he stuck the plate down in front of me** il a collé l'assiette devant moi

2 *vi (flap, envelope)* (se) coller

►**stick in 1** *vt sep* (**a**) *(nail, knife, spear)* planter, enfoncer; *(needle)* piquer, enfoncer; *(pole, shovel)* enfoncer, planter; **he stuck the knife all the way in** il a enfoncé le couteau jusqu'au bout *ou* jusqu'à la garde; **she stuck the knife in again and again** elle donna plusieurs coups de couteau

(**b**) *(insert → coin, bank card)* insérer; *(→ electric plug)* brancher; *(→ cork, sink plug)* enfoncer; *(→ word, sentence)* ajouter; **it's simple, just stick the key in and turn** c'est très simple, il suffit d'insérer la clé et de tourner; **I stuck my hand in to test the water temperature** j'ai plongé la main pour vérifier la température de l'eau; **he stuck his head in through the door** il passa la tête par la porte; **she's stuck in a lot of footnotes to give weight to her thesis** elle a ajouté un tas de notes pour donner du poids à sa thèse

(**c**) *(glue in)* coller; **there's not enough space to stick in all these stamps/photos** il ne reste pas assez de place pour coller tous ces timbres/toutes ces photos

2 *vi* (**a**) *(dart, arrow, spear)* se planter; **if the javelin doesn't stick in the throw doesn't count** si le javelot ne se plante pas, le jet ne compte pas; **the last dart failed to stick in** la dernière fléchette n'est pas restée plantée

(**b**) *Fam (persevere)* **stick in there!** tenez bon!

►**stick on 1** *vt sep* (**a**) *(fasten on → gummed badge, label, stamp)* coller; *(→ china handle)* recoller; *(→ broom head)* fixer

(**b**) *Fam (jacket, boots)* enfiler❑; **he hurriedly stuck a hat on** il s'est collé en vitesse un chapeau sur la tête

2 *vi* coller, se coller; **the stamp won't stick on** le timbre ne colle pas; **the patch sticks on when ironed** la pièce se colle au tissu quand on la repasse

►**stick out 1** *vt sep* (**a**) *(extend → hand, leg)* tendre, allonger; *(→ feelers, head)* sortir; **to stick one's tongue out (at sb)** tirer la langue (à qn); **he stuck his foot out to trip me up** il a allongé la jambe pour me faire un croche-pied; **I opened the window and stuck my head out** j'ai ouvert la fenêtre et j'ai passé la tête au dehors; **to stick one's chest out** bomber le torse; **to stick out one's lower lip** faire la moue

(**b**) *Fam (persevere)* **to stick it out** tenir le coup jusqu'au bout

2 *vi* (**a**) *(protrude → nail, splinter)* sortir; *(→ teeth)* avancer; *(→ plant, shoot)* pointer; *(→ ledge, balcony)* être en saillie; **his belly stuck out over his belt** son ventre débordait au-dessus de sa ceinture; **her ears stick out** elle a les oreilles décollées; **her teeth stick out** elle a les dents qui avancent; **my feet stuck out over the end of the bed** mes pieds dépassaient du lit; **the front of the car stuck out of the garage** l'avant de la voiture dépassait du garage; **his ticket was sticking out of his pocket** son billet sortait *ou* dépassait de sa poche; **one leg was sticking out of the sheets** une jambe dépassait de sous les draps; **only her head was sticking out of the water** seule sa tête sortait *ou* émergeait de l'eau

(**b**) *(be noticeable → colour)* ressortir; **the red Mercedes really sticks out** on ne voit que la Mercedes rouge; **I don't like to stick out in a crowd** je n'aime pas me singulariser *ou* me faire remarquer; **it's her accent that makes her stick out** c'est à cause de son accent qu'on la remarque; **it sticks out a mile** c'est clair comme le jour

►**stick out for** *vt insep* s'obstiner à vouloir, exiger; **the union is sticking out for a five per cent rise** le syndicat continue à revendiquer une augmentation de cinq pour cent; **after sticking out for higher quotas, they had to settle for last year's levels** après s'être battus pour obtenir une augmentation des quotas, ils ont dû se contenter de ceux de l'année dernière

►**stick to** *vt insep* (**a**) *(keep to → schedule)* tenir, respecter; *(→ plan)* tenir; **I can never stick to diets** je n'arrive jamais à suivre un régime longtemps; **we must stick to our plan** nous devons continuer à suivre notre plan; **once I make a decision I stick to it** une fois que j'ai pris une décision, je m'y tiens *ou* je n'en démords pas; **to stick to one's word** *or* **promises** tenir (sa) parole; **to stick to one's principles** rester fidèle à ses principes; **stick as close to the truth as possible** restez aussi près que possible de la vérité

(**b**) *(continue to affirm)* maintenir; **I stick to what I said** je maintiens ce que j'ai dit; **she's still sticking to her story** elle maintient ce qu'elle a dit; **that's my story and I'm sticking to it** c'est ma version et je m'y tiens

(**c**) *(restrict oneself to)* s'en tenir à; **stick to the point!** ne vous éloignez pas du sujet!, tenez-vous en au sujet!; **stick to the facts!** tenez-vous-en aux faits!; **can we stick to the business in hand?** peut-être pourrions-nous revenir au sujet qui nous occupe?; **to stick to the text** serrer le texte de près; **the author would be better off sticking to journalism** l'auteur ferait mieux de se cantonner au journalisme

(**d**) *(not leave)* **to stick to one's post** rester à son poste; **he sticks to his room** il ne sort pas de sa chambre; **stick to the main road** suivez la route principale

(**e**) *(stay near)* **stick close to the house** restez près de la maison; **his bodyguards stick close to him at all times** ses gardes du corps l'accompagnent partout *ou* ne le quittent jamais d'une semelle; **to stick to sb like glue** se cramponner *ou* s'accrocher à qn, coller qn

►**stick together 1** *vt sep* coller (ensemble)

2 *vi* (**a**) *(pages etc)* être collé (ensemble)

(**b**) *(stay together → people)* rester ensemble; *Fig* se serrer les coudes; **we'd better stick together** il vaut mieux que nous restions ensemble, il vaut mieux ne pas nous séparer; *Fig* **we'll get through this bad patch if we stick together** on sortira de cette mauvaise passe si on se serre les coudes

►**stick up 1** *vt sep* (**a**) *(sign, notice, poster)* afficher; *(postcard)* coller; *(with drawing pins)* punaiser

(**b**) *(raise → pole)* dresser; **stick the target back up** redressez la cible; **to stick one's hand up** lever la main; *Fam* **stick 'em up!** haut les mains!

(**c**) *Fam (rob → person, bank, supermarket)* braquer

2 *vi (point upwards → tower, antenna)* se dresser; *(→ plant shoots)* pointer; **I saw a chimney sticking up in the distance** j'ai vu une cheminée qui se dressait au loin; **the antenna was sticking straight up** l'antenne se dressait toute droite; **a branch was sticking up out of the water** une branche sortait de l'eau; **his hair's sticking up** il est ébouriffé

▸**stick up for** *vt insep* **to stick up for sb** prendre la défense *ou* le parti de qn; **stick up for yourself!** ne te laisse pas faire!; **she can stick up for herself** elle peut se défendre toute seule; **he has trouble sticking up for himself/his rights** il a du mal à défendre ses intérêts/à faire valoir ses droits

▸**stick with** *vt insep* (**a**) *(activity, subject)* s'en tenir à, persister dans; **now I've started the job, I'm going to stick with it** maintenant que j'ai commencé ce travail, je ne le lâche pas; **I'm sticking with my old car for now** je garde ma vieille voiture pour le moment

(**b**) *Fam (person)* **stick with me, kid, and you'll be all right** reste avec moi, petit, et tout ira bien

stickball ['stɪkbɔːl] *n Am* base-ball *m* (joué dans la rue)

sticker ['stɪkə(r)] *n* (**a**) *(adhesive label)* autocollant *m* (**b**) *Fam (determined person)* **she's a sticker** elle est persévérante ❑, elle va au bout de ce qu'elle entreprend ❑

▸▸ *Mktg* ***sticker price*** prix *m* affiché, prix *m* à la vente

stickiness ['stɪkɪnɪs] *n* (**a**) *(of substance, surface, jamjar)* caractère *m* gluant *ou* poisseux; **the stickiness of his hands** ses mains poisseuses (**b**) *(of weather, climate)* moiteur *f*, humidité *f*

sticking ['stɪkɪŋ] *adj*

▸▸ *Br* ***sticking plaster*** pansement *m* adhésif, sparadrap *m*; *Fig* ***sticking point*** point *m* de désaccord, point *m* de friction

stick-in-the-mud *n Fam (fogey)* vieux croûton *m*; *(killjoy)* rabat-joie *m inv*; **don't be such a stick-in-the-mud!** ne sois pas rabat-joie!

stickleback ['stɪklbæk] *n Ich* épinoche *f (de rivière)*

stickler ['stɪklə(r)] *n* **to be a stickler for** *(regulations, discipline, good manners)* être à cheval sur; *(tradition, routine)* insister sur

stickman ['stɪkmæn] (*pl* **stickmen** [-men]) *n Am* (**a**) *(croupier)* croupier *m* (**b**) *Sport (hockey player)* hockeyeur *m*, joueur *m* de hockey; *(lacrosse player)* joueur *m* de lacrosse; *(billiard player)* joueur *m* de billard (**c**) *(drawn figure)* personnage *m* stylisé

stick-on *adj* autocollant

stickpin ['stɪkpɪn] *n Am* épingle *f* de cravate

stick-to-it-iveness [stɪk'tʊɪtɪvnɪs] *n Am Fam* ténacité ❑ *f*

stick-up *n Fam* braquage *m*, hold-up *m*; **this is a stick-up!** c'est un hold-up!

stickweed ['stɪkwiːd] *n Bot* jacobée *f*

sticky ['stɪkɪ] (*compar* **stickier**, *superl* **stickiest**) *adj* (**a**) *(adhesive)* adhésif, gommé

(**b**) *(tacky, gluey → hands, fingers)* collant, poisseux; *(→ substance, surface, jamjar)* gluant, poisseux; **his mouth was all sticky with jam** il avait la bouche poisseuse de confiture; **to have sticky fingers** avoir les doigts collants *ou* poisseux; *Fig* être porté sur la fauche

(**c**) *(sweaty)* moite

(**d**) *(humid → weather)* moite, humide; **it was a hot, sticky afternoon** c'était un après-midi chaud et moite

(**e**) *Fam (awkward → situation)* difficile ❑, délicat ❑; *Br* **to be (batting) on a sticky wicket** être dans une situation difficile ❑; *Br* **to come to a sticky end** mal finir ❑

(**f**) *Fam Comput (site, advert)* qui attire de nombreux utilisateurs ❑

▸▸ *Fam* ***sticky bun*** petit pain *m* sucré; ***sticky label*** étiquette *f* autocollante, étiquette *f* gommée; ***sticky tape*** ruban *m* adhésif; ***sticky toffee pudding*** = pudding au caramel cuit à la vapeur

stickybeak ['stɪkɪbiːk] *Austr & NZ Fam* **1** *n* fouineur(euse) *m,f*, fouinard(arde) *m,f*

2 *vi* fouiner, fureter

sticky-fingered *adj Fam* **to be sticky-fingered** être porté sur la fauche

stiff [stɪf] **1** *adj* (**a**) *(rigid)* raide, rigide; **stiff paper/cardboard** papier/carton rigide; **a stiff brush** une brosse à poils durs; **to be stiff with terror** être glacé de terreur **as stiff as a poker** raide comme un piquet; **to keep a stiff upper lip** garder son flegme

(**b**) *(thick, difficult to stir)* ferme, consistant; **beat the mixture until it is stiff** battez jusqu'à obtention d'une pâte consistante; **beat the eggwhites until stiff** battre les blancs en neige jusqu'à ce qu'ils soient (bien) fermes

(**c**) *(difficult to move)* dur; **this door handle is very stiff** cette poignée de porte est très dure; **the drawers have got a bit stiff** les tiroirs sont devenus un peu durs à ouvrir

(**d**) *(aching)* courbaturé, raide; **I'm still stiff after playing squash the other day** j'ai encore des courbatures d'avoir joué au squash l'autre jour; **to have a stiff back** avoir mal au dos; **to have a stiff neck** avoir un *ou* le torticolis

(**e**) *(over-formal → smile, welcome)* froid; *(→ person, manners, behaviour)* froid, guindé; *(→ style)* guindé

(**f**) *(difficult)* dur, ardu; **to face stiff competition** avoir affaire à forte concurrence; **it will be a stiff match** la partie sera dure; **competition for university places is getting stiffer** la compétition pour les places à l'université devient de plus en plus acharnée

(**g**) *(severe)* sévère; **a stiff sentence** une condamnation sévère, une lourde condamnation; **I sent them a stiff letter** je leur ai envoyé une lettre bien sentie

(**h**) *(strong → breeze, drink)* fort; **you need a stiff drink** tu as besoin d'un remontant; **she poured herself a stiff whisky** elle s'est versé un whisky bien tassé

(**i**) *(high → price, bill)* élevé

(**j**) *(determined → resistance, opposition)* tenace, acharné; *(→ resolve)* ferme, inébranlable

(**k**) *Br Fam (full)* plein (à craquer); **the place was stiff with men in suits** l'endroit était plein de mecs en costume

(**l**) *Am Fam (drunk)* bourré, rond, beurré

2 *adv Fam* **to be bored stiff** mourir d'ennui ❑; **to be worried/scared stiff** être mort d'inquiétude/de peur; **I was frozen stiff** j'étais frigorifié

3 *n* (**a**) *Fam (corpse)* macchabée *m*

(**b**) *very Fam (erection)* **to have a stiff** bander

(**c**) *Br Fam (failure)* bide *m*

(**d**) *Am Fam (tramp)* clodo *mf*

(**e**) *Am Fam (stupid person)* nul (nulle) *m,f*

4 *vt Fam (kill)* buter

stiffen ['stɪfən] **1** *vt* (**a**) *(paper, fabric)* raidir, renforcer

(**b**) *(thicken → batter, paste, concrete)* donner de la consistance à; *(→ sauce)* lier

(**c**) *(make painful → arm, leg, muscle)* courbaturer; **his joints had become stiffened by arthritis** ses articulations s'étaient raidies à cause de l'arthrite

(**d**) *(strengthen → resistance, resolve)* renforcer

2 *vi* (**a**) *(harden → paper, fabric)* devenir raide *ou* rigide

(**b**) *(tense, stop moving)* se raidir; **everybody in the room suddenly stiffened** tout à coup, tout le monde dans la pièce retint son souffle *ou* s'immobilisa

(**c**) *(thicken → batter, paste, concrete)* épaissir, devenir ferme; *(→ sauce)* se lier

(**d**) *(become hard to move → hinge, handle, door)* se coincer

(**e**) *(start to ache)* s'ankyloser

(**f**) *(strengthen → resistance, resolve)* se renforcer; *(→ breeze)* forcir

stiffener ['stɪfənə(r)] *n* (**a**) *(in collar)* baleine *f* (**b**) *Br Fam (drink)* remontant ❑ *m*

stiffening ['stɪfənɪŋ] *n* renforcement *m*

stiffie = **stiffy**

stiffish ['stɪfɪʃ] *adj* (**a**) *(inflexible)* assez raide, plutôt raide (**b**) *(difficult)* assez difficile

stiffly ['stɪflɪ] *adv* (**a**) *(rigidly)* **stiffly starched** très empesé *ou* amidonné; **he stood stiffly to attention** il se tenait au garde-à-vous, très raide (**b**) *(painfully → walk, bend)* avec raideur (**c**) *(coldly → smile, greet)* froidement, d'un air distant

stiff-necked *adj* qui a le torticolis; *Fig* opiniâtre, entêté, intraitable

stiffness ['stɪfnɪs] *n* (**a**) *(of paper, fabric)* raideur *f*, rigidité *f*

(**b**) *(of batter, paste, concrete)* consistance *f*, fermeté *f*

(**c**) *(of hinge, handle, door)* dureté *f*

(**d**) *(of joints, limbs)* raideur *f*, courbatures *fpl*

(**e**) *(of manners, smile, welcome)* froideur *f*, distance *f*; *(of style)* caractère *m* guindé

(**f**) *(difficulty → of exam, competition)* difficulté *f*, dureté *f*

(**g**) *(severity → of sentence, warning)* sévérité *f*

(**h**) *(determination → of resistance)* ténacité *f*, acharnement *m*; *(→ of resolve)* fermeté *f*

stiffy ['stɪfɪ] (*pl* **stiffies**) *n Br very Fam (erection)* **to have a stiffy** bander; **to get a stiffy** se mettre à bander

stifle ['staɪfəl] **1** *vt* (**a**) *(suppress → resistance, creativity, progress)* réprimer, étouffer; *(→ tears, anger, emotion)* réprimer; **to stifle a cough** réprimer une envie de tousser; **I tried to stifle my laughter/a yawn** j'ai essayé de ne pas rire/bâiller (**b**) *(suffocate)* étouffer, suffoquer

2 *vi* étouffer, suffoquer

stifled ['staɪfəld] *adj (cry)* étouffé; **with a stifled voice** d'une voix éteinte

stifling ['staɪflɪŋ] *adj* suffocant, étouffant; **open the window, it's stifling in here!** ouvre la fenêtre, on étouffe ici!; **it was a stifling hot day** il faisait une chaleur étouffante

stigma ['stɪgmə] *n* (**a**) *(social disgrace)* honte *f*; **the stigma attached to having been in prison** l'opprobe qui ne quitte pas ceux qui ont fait de la prison; **there is no longer any stigma in being a single mother** il n'y a plus de honte à être mère célibataire (**b**) *Bot, Med & Zool* stigmate *m*

stigmata [stɪg'mɑːtə] *npl Rel* stigmates *mpl*

stigmatic [stɪg'mætɪk] **1** *adj* (**a**) *Opt (lens)* stigmatique, anastigmate, anastigmatique (**b**) *Bot* stigmatique (**c**) *Rel* stigmatisé

2 *n Rel* stigmatisé(e) *m,f*

stigmatism ['stɪgmətɪzəm] *n Opt* stigmatisme *m*

stigmatist ['stɪgmətɪst] *n Rel* stigmatisé(e) *m,f*

stigmatization [ˌstɪgmətaɪ'zeɪʃən] *n* stigmatisation *f*

stigmatize, -ise ['stɪgmətaɪz] *vt* stigmatiser

stilb [stɪlb] *n Phys* stilb *m*

stilbene ['stɪlbiːn] *n Chem* stilbène *m*

stilboestrol, *Am* **stilbestrol** [stɪl'biːstrəl] *n Biol & Chem* stilbœstrol *m*

stile [staɪl] *n* (**a**) *(over fence)* échalier *m* (**b**) *(turnstile)* tourniquet *m* (**c**) *Constr (upright)* montant *m*

stiletto [stɪ'letəʊ] (*pl* **stilettos**) **1** *n* (**a**) *(heel)* talon *m* aiguille (**b**) *(knife)* stylet *m* (**c**) *(for sewing, leatherwork)* poinçon *m*

2 stilettos *npl* (chaussures *fpl* à) talons *mpl* aiguilles

▸▸ ***stiletto heel*** talon *m* aiguille

still[1] [stɪl] *adv* (**a**) *(as of this moment)* encore, toujours; **he's still here** il est encore *ou* toujours ici; **he's still not here** il n'est toujours pas là; **is it still raining?** est-ce qu'il pleut encore *ou* toujours?; **we're still waiting for the repairman to come** nous attendons toujours que le réparateur vienne; **there's still a bit of cake left** il reste encore un morceau de gâteau; **the worst was still to come** le pire n'était pas encore arrivé; **it's stuck still?** c'est coincé encore?; **I still have 500 francs** il me reste 500 francs, j'ai encore 500 francs; **I still can't see what was wrong with my suggestion** je ne vois toujours pas en quoi ma suggestion était mauvaise

(**b**) *(all the same)* quand même; **it's certainly difficult, but it's still better than my last job** c'est difficile, c'est sûr, mais c'est quand même mieux que mon dernier emploi; **whatever she's done, she's still your mother** quoi qu'elle ait fait, c'est quand même ta mère; **it's a shame we lost – still, it was a good game** (c'est) dommage que nous ayons perdu – quand même, c'était un bon match; *Fam* **still and all** quand même ❑

(**c**) *(with comparatives) (even)* encore; **still more/less** encore plus/moins; **still further, further still** encore plus loin; **the sea was getting still rougher** la mer était de plus en plus agitée

still[2] **1** *adj* (**a**) *(motionless → person, air, surface)*

sti–sti

immobile; **her eyes were never still** ses yeux ne restaient jamais immobiles; **be still!** arrête de remuer!; *Prov* **still waters run deep** méfie-toi de l'eau qui dort

(**b**) *(calm)* calme, tranquille; *(quiet)* silencieux; **a still night** une nuit calme; *Literary or Ironic* **be still my beating heart** je ne me tiens plus d'impatience!

(**c**) *(not fizzy)* plat

2 *adv* sans bouger; **stand still!** ne bougez pas!; **my heart stood still** mon cœur a cessé de battre; **they're so excited they can't sit still** ils sont tellement excités qu'ils ne peuvent pas rester en place; **try to hold the camera still** essaie de ne pas bouger l'appareil photo

3 *vt Literary* (**a**) *(silence)* faire taire; **the voices of protest had been stilled** on avait fait taire les contestataires; **that mighty pen is stilled for ever** cet écrivain génial s'est tu à jamais

(**b**) *(allay → doubts, fears)* apaiser, calmer

4 *vi Literary* se calmer; **the storm had stilled** la tempête s'était apaisée

5 *n* (**a**) *Literary (silence)* silence *m*; **in the still of the night** dans le silence de la nuit

(**b**) *Cin* photo *f* (de plateau)

(**c**) *(apparatus)* alambic *m*

▸▸ ***still life*** nature *f* morte; ***still mineral water*** eau *f* minérale non gazeuse *ou* plate; ***still photographer*** photographe *mf* de plateau

stillage [ˈstɪlɪdʒ] *n* palette *f*

stillbirth [ˈstɪlbɜːθ] *n (birth)* mort *f* à la naissance; *(fœtus)* enfant *m* mort-né, enfant *f* mort-née; **the number of stillbirths** la mortinatalité

stillborn [ˈstɪlbɔːn] *adj* (**a**) *Med* mort-né (**b**) *Fig (idea, plan)* avorté

stillness [ˈstɪlnɪs] *n* (**a**) *(motionlessness)* immobilité *f* (**b**) *(calm)* tranquillité *f*, paix *f*

stillroom [ˈstɪlruːm] *n* (**a**) *Hist* laboratoire *m* de distillerie (**b**) *(pantry)* office *m*

Still's disease [stɪlz-] *n Med* maladie *f* de Still, polyarthrite *f* rhumatoïde de l'enfant

stilt [stɪlt] *n* (**a**) *(for walking)* échasse *f*; **to walk on stilts** marcher sur des échasses (**b**) *Archit* pilotis *m* (**c**) *Orn* échasse *f*

stilted [ˈstɪltɪd] *adj* (**a**) *(speech, writing, person)* guindé, emprunté; *(discussion)* qui manque de naturel (**b**) *Archit (arch)* surhaussé, surélevé

stiltedness [ˈstɪltɪdnɪs] *n (of person)* manière *f* guindée; *(of speech)* ton *m* guindé; *(writing)* style *m* guindé

Stilton® [ˈstɪltən] *n* stilton *m*, fromage *m* de Stilton

stimulant [ˈstɪmjʊlənt] **1** *n* stimulant *m*; **devaluation acts as a stimulant to exports** la dévaluation stimule les exportations

2 *adj* stimulant

stimulate [ˈstɪmjʊleɪt] *vt* (**a**) *(person, enthusiasm)* stimuler; *(mind, appetite etc)* aiguiser; *Ind (production)* encourager, activer; **the bracing sea air stimulated me** l'air de la mer m'a revigoré; **to stimulate sb to do sth** inciter *ou* encourager qn à faire qch; **sexually stimulated** excité (sexuellement) (**b**) *Med (organ)* stimuler

stimulating [ˈstɪmjʊleɪtɪŋ] *adj* (**a**) *(medicine, drug)* stimulant (**b**) *(work, conversation, experience)* stimulant, enrichissant; **intellectually stimulating** intellectuellement stimulant

stimulation [ˌstɪmjʊˈleɪʃən] *n* (**a**) *(of person)* stimulation *f* (**b**) *(stimulus)* stimulant *m*

▸▸ ***stimulation marketing*** marketing *m* de stimulation

stimulative [ˈstɪmjʊlətɪv] **1** *adj* stimulant

2 *n* stimulant *m*

stimulus [ˈstɪmjʊləs] (*pl* **stimuli** [-laɪ, -liː]) *n* (**a**) *(incentive)* stimulant *m*, incitation *f*; **her example will be a powerful stimulus to others** son exemple sera un stimulant extrêmement efficace pour d'autres (**b**) *Physiol* stimulus *m*

▸▸ ***stimulus response*** réponse *f stimulée*

sting [stɪŋ] (*pt & pp* **stung** [stʌŋ]) **1** *vt* (**a**) *(of insect, nettle, scorpion)* piquer; *(of smoke)* piquer, brûler; *(of vinegar, acid, disinfectant)* brûler; *(of whip, rain)* cingler; **the smoke stung my eyes** la fumée me brûlait *ou* me piquait les yeux; **a bee stung her finger** *or* **stung her on the finger** une abeille lui a piqué le doigt

(**b**) *(of remark, joke, criticism)* piquer (au vif), blesser; **she was stung by their sharp criticisms** leurs critiques acérées l'ont piquée au vif; **to sting sb into action** inciter *ou* pousser qn à agir; **our comments might sting them into doing something** nos remarques les inciteront peut-être à faire quelque chose

(**c**) *Fam (swindle)* arnaquer, refaire; **to get stung** se faire arnaquer, se faire refaire; **they stung him for a hundred quid** ils l'ont arnaqué *ou* refait de cent livres

2 *vi* (**a**) *(insect, nettle, scorpion)* piquer; *(vinegar, acid, disinfectant)* brûler, piquer; *(whip, rain)* cingler; **this is going to sting a bit** ça va faire un peu mal

(**b**) *(eyes, skin)* piquer, brûler; **my eyes are stinging** j'ai les yeux qui piquent

3 *n* (**a**) *(organ → of bee, wasp, scorpion)* aiguillon *m*, dard *m*; *(→ of nettle)* poil *m* (urticant); *Br* **there's a sting in the tail** il y a une mauvaise surprise à la fin; **his remarks often have a sting in the tail** ses remarques sont rarement innocentes; **to take the sting out of sth** rendre qch moins douloureux, adoucir qch

(**b**) *(wound, pain, mark → from insect, nettle, scorpion)* piqûre *f*; *(→ from vinegar, acid, disinfectant)* brûlure *f*; *(→ from whip)* douleur *f* cinglante

(**c**) *Fam (swindle)* arnaque *f*

(**d**) *Am Fam (police operation)* coup *m* monté *(dans le cadre d'une opération de police)*

'The Sting' *Hill* 'L'Arnaque'

stingaree [ˈstɪŋəriː] *n Am & Austr Ich* pastenague *f*

stinger [ˈstɪŋə(r)] *n* (**a**) *Fam (stinging nettle)* ortie *f*❑ (**b**) *(police device)* = pointes que la police dispose sur la route afin de crever les pneus d'une voiture qu'elle veut arrêter (**c**) *Mil* (missile *m*) Stinger *m* (**d**) *Fam (blow)* beigne *f* (**e**) *Austr Fam (box jellyfish)* cuboméduse *f*❑

stingily [ˈstɪndʒɪlɪ] *adv (give, serve out, behave)* chichement

stinginess [ˈstɪndʒɪnɪs] *n (of person, behaviour)* avarice *f*, pingrerie *f*; *(of amount, helping)* insuffisance *f*

stinging [ˈstɪŋɪŋ] *adj* (**a**) *(wound, pain)* cuisant; *(bite, eyes)* qui pique; *(lash, rain)* cinglant (**b**) *(remark, joke, criticism)* cinglant, mordant

▸▸ ***stinging nettle*** ortie *f*

stingless [ˈstɪŋlɪs] *adj* sans aiguillon *ou* dard

▸▸ ***stingless bees*** mélipones *fpl*

stingray [ˈstɪŋreɪ] *n Ich* pastenague *f*

stingy [ˈstɪndʒɪ] *adj Fam (person)* radin; *(amount, helping)* misérable❑; **he's too stingy with his money** il est trop radin; **they're never stingy about food** ils ne lésinent jamais sur la nourriture❑

stink [stɪŋk] (*pt* **stank** [stæŋk], *pp* **stunk** [stʌŋk]) **1** *vi* (**a**) *(smell)* puer, empester; **the room stank of cigarette smoke** la pièce puait *ou* empestait la fumée de cigarette; **it stinks in here** ça pue ici; *Fam Fig* **to stink of money** puer le fric; **the whole business stinks of corruption** tout ça sent la corruption à plein nez

(**b**) *Fam (be bad)* être nul, craindre; **don't bother going to the concert, it stinks!** ne va pas au concert, c'est nul!; **what do you think of my plan? – it stinks!** qu'est-ce que tu penses de mon projet? – il est nul!; **this town stinks!** cette ville est pourrie!

2 *n* (**a**) *(stench)* puanteur *f*, odeur *f* nauséabonde; *Fam* **what a stink!** qu'est-ce que ça pue!

(**b**) *Fam (fuss)* foin *m*; **to raise** *or* **to make** *or Br* **to kick up a stink (about sth)** faire toute un foin (de qch)

▸**stink out** *vt sep Fam (room, place)* empester❑; **your cigar's stinking the whole house out!** ton cigare empeste toute la maison!

stink-bomb *n* boule *f* puante

stinker [ˈstɪŋkə(r)] *n Fam* (**a**) *(person)* peau *f* de vache, ordure *f*

(**b**) *(unpleasant, difficult thing)* **to be a stinker** être vachement dur, être coton; **the German exam was a real stinker** l'examen d'allemand était vraiment coton; **today's crossword's a stinker** les mots croisés d'aujourd'hui sont vachement durs; **I've got a stinker of a cold** j'ai un rhume carabiné

(**c**) *(worthless thing)* **to be a stinker** être nul, être merdique; **his new movie's a total stinker** son nouveau film est complètement nul

stinkhorn [ˈstɪŋkhɔːn] *n Bot* phallus *m* impudique, satyre *m* puant

stinking [ˈstɪŋkɪŋ] **1** *adj* (**a**) *(smelly)* puant, nauséabond

(**b**) *Fam (as intensifier)* **I'm tired of seeing this stinking mess all the time!** j'en ai assez de voir tout le temps cette pagaille *ou* ce bazar!; **I've got a stinking cold** j'ai un rhume carabiné

(**c**) *Fam (worthless)* merdique, nul

2 *adv Fam* vachement; **to be stinking drunk** être soûl comme un cochon; **to be stinking rich** être plein aux as, *Pej* puer le fric

▸▸ *Bot* ***stinking camomile*** camomille *f* puante, maroute *f*; *Bot* ***stinking iris*** iris *m* fétide

stinko [ˈstɪŋkəʊ] *adj Am Fam (drunk)* pété, bourré, fait

stinkpot [ˈstɪŋkpɒt] *n Fam Old-fashioned (unpleasant person)* salaud *m*, salope *f*; **what a stinkpot!** *(smelly)* qu'est-ce qu'il pue!

stinkweed [ˈstɪŋkwiːd] *n Bot (gen)* diplotaxis *m*; *(thorn-apple)* stramoine *f*

stinkwood [ˈstɪŋkwʊd] *n Bot* ocotea *m* bullata

stinky [ˈstɪŋkɪ] *adj* (**a**) *(smelly)* puant, nauséabond (**b**) *Fam (worthless)* merdique, nul

stint [stɪnt] **1** *n* (**a**) *(period of work)* période *f* de travail; *(share of work)* part *f* de travail; **she did a stint in Africa/as a teacher** elle a travaillé pendant un certain temps en Afrique/comme professeur; **she had a two-year stint in the army** elle a fait deux ans dans l'armée; **we expect everybody to do their stint** nous attendons de chacun qu'il fournisse sa part du travail; **I'll take** *or* **I'll do another stint at the wheel** je vais reprendre le volant

(**b**) *Formal (limitation)* **without stint** *(spend)* sans compter; *(give)* généreusement; *(work)* inlassablement

2 *vt Br* (**a**) *(skimp on)* lésiner sur; **don't stint the cream** ne lésine pas sur la crème (**b**) *(deprive)* priver; **he's incapable of stinting himself of anything** il est incapable de se priver de quoi que ce soit

3 *vi Br* **to stint on sth** lésiner sur qch

stipend [ˈstaɪpend] *n* traitement *m*, appointements *mpl*

stipendiary [staɪˈpendjərɪ] (*pl* **stipendiaries**) **1** *adj* *(work, person)* rémunéré; *Law* **stipendiary magistrate** magistrat *m* professionnel *(rémunéré)*

2 *n* *(clergyman)* = prêtre percevant un traitement; *Law (magistrate)* magistrat *m* professionnel *(rémunéré)*

stipple [ˈstɪpəl] *vt* (**a**) *(apply → paint)* appliquer par petites touches (**b**) *(mark → cement, wet paint)* granuler

stippled [ˈstɪpld] *adj* tacheté, moucheté; **stippled with yellow** tacheté *ou* moucheté de jaune

stipulate [ˈstɪpjʊleɪt] **1** *vt* stipuler; **please stipulate the quantity on your order form** veuillez stipuler la quantité sur votre commande; **the contract stipulates that the work must be finished by March** le contrat stipule que le travail doit être terminé d'ici le mois de mars

2 *vi Formal* **to stipulate for sth** stipuler qch; **the sum of money stipulated for** la somme stipulée

stipulation [ˌstɪpjʊˈleɪʃən] *n* stipulation *f*; **they accepted, but with the stipulation that the time limit be extended** ils ont accepté sous réserve que les délais soient prolongés

stir [stɜː(r)] (*pt & pp* **stirred,** *cont* **stirring**) **1** *vt* (**a**) *(mix)* remuer, tourner; **your tea is sugared but not stirred** ton thé est sucré mais il faut le remuer; **stir the flour into the sauce** incorporez la farine à la sauce en remuant

(**b**) *(move)* agiter, remuer; **a light breeze stirred the leaves** une brise légère agitait les feuilles; *Br Fam* **stir yourself** *or* **your stumps, it's time to go!** grouille-toi, il est l'heure de partir!

(**c**) *(touch)* émouvoir; **his story has stirred us deeply** son histoire nous a profondément émus

(**d**) *(rouse, excite)* éveiller, exciter; **to stir sb's curiosity/sympathy** éveiller la curiosité/sympathie de qn; **to stir sb to do sth** inciter *ou* pousser qn à faire qch; **to stir sb into action** pousser qn à agir

(**e**) *Br Fam* **to stir it** *(cause trouble)* semer la zizanie

2 *vi* (**a**) *(move → person)* bouger, remuer; *(→*

leaves) remuer; **I shan't stir from my bed until midday** je ne bougerai pas de mon lit avant midi; **to stir in one's sleep** remuer dans son sommeil; **the audience were stirring in their seats** les spectateurs s'agitaient dans leur fauteuil

(**b**) *(awaken, be roused → feeling, anger)* s'éveiller; **a mood of nationalism was stirring in the country** un sentiment nationaliste s'éveillait dans le pays

(**c**) *Fam (cause trouble)* semer la zizanie

3 *n* (**a**) *(act of mixing)* **to give sth a stir** remuer qch; **the sauce needs a stir** il faudrait remuer la sauce

(**b**) *(commotion)* émoi *m*, agitation *f*; **to cause** *or* **to create** *or* **to make quite a stir** soulever un vif émoi, faire grand bruit; **there was a big stir about** *or* **over the unemployment figures** les chiffres du chômage ont soulevé un vif émoi

(**c**) *(movement)* mouvement *m*; **a stir of excitement** un frisson d'excitation

(**d**) *Fam (prison)* taule *f*, placard *m*, cabane *f*; **in stir** en taule, en cabane, à l'ombre; **stir crazy** cinglé *(à force d'être en prison)*

►**stir in** *vt sep Culin* ajouter *ou* incorporer en remuant

►**stir up** *vt sep* (**a**) *(disturb → dust, mud)* soulever

(**b**) *(incite, provoke → trouble)* provoquer; *(→ emotions)* exciter, attiser; *(→ dissent)* fomenter; *(→ memories)* réveiller; *(→ crowd, followers)* ameuter; **he likes stirring it** *or* **things up** il aime provoquer

(**c**) *Literary (fire)* attiser, tisonner

stir-fry 1 *vt* faire sauter à feu vif *(tout en remuant)*

2 *adj* sauté; **stir-fry pork** porc sauté

3 *n* sauté *m*

stirrer ['stɜːrə(r)] *n* (**a**) *Fam (troublemaker)* fouteur(euse) *m,f* de merde (**b**) *Culin (implement)* fouet *m*

stirring ['stɜːrɪŋ] **1** *adj (music, song)* entraînant; *(story)* excitant, passionnant; *(speech)* vibrant; **it's stirring stuff** c'est passionnant

2 *n* **he felt vague stirrings of guilt** il éprouva un vague sentiment de culpabilité; **the first stirrings of what was to become the Romantic movement** les premières manifestations de ce qui allait devenir le mouvement romantique

stirringly ['stɜːrɪŋlɪ] *adv* d'une façon entraînante

stirrup ['stɪrəp] **1** *n* (**a**) *Horseriding* étrier *m*; **to put one's feet in the stirrups** chausser les étriers

(**b**) *Anat (in ear)* étrier *m*

2 stirrups *npl Med* étriers *mpl*

►► ***stirrup cup*** coup *m* de l'étrier; ***stirrup leather*** étrivière *f*; ***stirrup pump*** seau-pompe *m*

stitch [stɪtʃ] **1** *n* (**a**) *(in sewing)* point *m*; *(in knitting, crochet)* maille *f*; **to make a stitch** faire une maille; **to drop a stitch** sauter une maille; **to pick up a stitch** reprendre une maille; *Fam* **I didn't have a stitch (of clothing) on** j'étais nu comme un ver, *Hum* j'étais dans le plus simple appareil❑; *Prov* **a stitch in time saves nine** un point à temps en vaut cent

(**b**) *Med* point *m* de suture; **she had to have ten stitches in her face** il a fallu lui faire dix points de suture au visage; **I'm having my stitches (taken) out tomorrow** on m'ôte les points demain

(**c**) *(pain)* point *m* de côté; **to get a stitch** attraper un point de côté

(**d**) *Am Fam (amusing person, thing)* **to be a stitch** être tordant *ou* crevant

(**e**) *Fam (idioms)* **to be in stitches** se tenir les côtes (de rire), être plié de rire; **to have sb in stitches** faire rire qn aux larmes❑

2 *vt* (**a**) *(material, shirt, hem)* coudre; **he stitched the button back on his shirt** il a recousu son bouton de chemise

(**b**) *Med* suturer

(**c**) *(in bookbinding)* brocher

►► *Tech* ***stitch welding*** soudure *f* par points

►**stitch down** *vt sep* rabattre

►**stitch up** *vt sep* (**a**) *(material, shirt, hem)* coudre

(**b**) *Med* suturer

(**c**) *Fam (deal)* conclure❑

(**d**) *Br Fam (frame)* **to stitch sb up** monter un coup contre qn; **he reckons the police stitched him up** il pense que la police a monté un coup contre lui

stitching ['stɪtʃɪŋ] *n* (**a**) *(in sewing)* couture *f*; *(ornamental)* broderie *f*; **the stitching's coming undone** la couture se défait (**b**) *Med* suture *f* (**c**) *(in bookbinding)* brochage *m*

St John Ambulance, St John's Ambulance *n* = organisme bénévole de secours d'urgence en Grande-Bretagne

St Leger [-'ledʒə(r)] *n* = course pour chevaux de trois ans qui se tient chaque année à Doncaster (Angleterre)

stoa ['stəʊə] *n Archit* portique *m*

stoat [stəʊt] *n Zool* hermine *f (brune)*

stoater ['stəʊtə(r)] *n Scot Fam* (**a**) *(excellent thing)* **what a stoater of a goal!** quel but d'enfer!; **we had a stoater of an idea** on a eu une idée géniale (**b**) *(beautiful person)* canon *m*; **his new girlfriend's a wee stoater!** sa nouvelle copine est canon!

stochastic [stɒ'kæstɪk] *adj* stochastique

stocious ['stəʊʃəs] *adj Br Fam* bourré, beurré

stock [stɒk] **1** *n* (**a**) *(supply)* réserve *f*, provision *f*, stock *m*; *Com & Ind* stock *m*; **we got in a stock of food** nous avons fait tout un stock de nourriture; **huge stocks of nuclear weapons** d'énormes stocks d'armes nucléaires; **she always has a wonderful stock of funny stories** elle a toujours un tas d'histoires drôles en réserve; **in stock** en stock, en magasin; **to keep sth in stock** stocker qch; **out of stock** épuisé; **while stocks last** jusqu'à épuisement des stocks; **I'm afraid we're out of stock** je regrette, nous n'en avons plus en stock; **to take stock** faire l'inventaire, *Fig* faire le point; **we took stock of the situation** nous avons fait le point de la situation

(**b**) *(total amount)* parc *m*; **the housing stock** le parc de logements

(**c**) *(usu pl) St Exch (gen)* valeur *f* mobilière; *(share)* action *f*; *(bond)* obligation *f*; **mining stocks are falling** les actions minières sont en baisse; **to invest in stocks and shares** investir dans des actions et obligations *ou* en portefeuille; **government stocks** obligations *fpl ou* titres *mpl* d'État

(**d**) *Fin (equity)* capital *m*; **he already owns 27% of the company's stock** il possède déjà 27 % du capital de la société

(**e**) *Fig (value, credit)* cote *f*; **the Prime Minister's stock is rising/falling** la cote du Premier ministre est en hausse/en baisse; **to put stock in sth** faire (grand) cas de qch; **I don't put much stock in this new system** je ne suis pas très convaincu par ce nouveau système

(**f**) *(descent, ancestry)* souche *f*, lignée *f*; **of peasant/noble stock** de souche paysanne/noble

(**g**) *Agr (animals)* cheptel *m*

(**h**) *Culin* bouillon *m*; **beef/chicken/vegetable stock** bouillon *m* de bœuf/poulet/légumes

(**i**) *(handle, butt → of gun, plough)* fût *m*; *(→ of whip)* manche *m*; *(→ of fishing rod)* gaule *f*

(**j**) *Bot* giroflée *f*

(**k**) *(tree trunk)* tronc *m*; *(tree stump)* souche *f*

(**l**) *Hort (stem receiving graft)* porte-greffe *m*, sujet *m*; *(plant from which graft is taken)* plante *f* mère *(sur laquelle on prélève un greffon)*

(**m**) *(in card games, dominoes)* talon *m*, pioche *f*

(**n**) *Theat* répertoire *m*

(**o**) *(neckcloth)* lavallière *f*, foulard *m*; **riding stock** col-cravate *m*

(**p**) *Naut (of anchor)* jas *m*

2 *vt* (**a**) *Com (have in stock)* avoir (en stock), vendre; **I'm afraid we don't stock that item any more** je regrette, mais nous ne vendons plus *ou* nous ne faisons plus cet article; **we stock all leading makes of furniture** nous faisons toutes les grandes marques de meubles

(**b**) *(supply)* approvisionner; *(fill)* remplir; **they have a well stocked cellar** ils ont une cave bien approvisionnée; **we stocked the fridge with food** nous avons rempli le frigo de nourriture

(**c**) *(stream, lake)* empoissonner; *(farm)* monter en bétail

3 *adj* (**a**) *(common, typical → phrase, expression)* tout fait; *(→ question, answer, excuse)* classique; **he has three stock speeches** il a, en tout et pour tout, trois discours qu'il ressort périodiquement

(**b**) *Com (kept in stock)* en stock; *(widely available)* courant; **the sale of stock goods** la liquidation du stock; **available in all stock sizes** disponible dans toutes les tailles courantes

(**c**) *Agr (for breeding)* destiné à la reproduction

(**d**) *Theat (play)* du répertoire

4 stocks *npl* (**a**) *(instrument of punishment)* pilori *m*; **sentenced to the stocks** condamné au pilori

(**b**) *Naut (frame)* cale *f*; **on the stocks** en chantier

►► ***stock car*** (**a**) *Aut* stock-car *m*; ***stock car racing*** (courses *fpl* de) stock-car *m* (**b**) *Am Rail* wagon *m* à bestiaux; *Am* ***stock certificate*** titre *m*; *Fin* ***stock check*** contrôle *m* des stocks; ***stock clearance*** liquidation *f* de stock; *Am* ***stock company*** (**a**) *Fin* société *f* anonyme par actions (**b**) *Theat* troupe *f* à demeure *(dans une ville)*; ***stock control*** contrôle *m* des stocks; *Culin* ***stock cube*** bouillon *m* Kub®; *Orn* ***stock dove*** petit ramier *m*, colombin *m*; ***stock exchange*** Bourse *f*; **he lost a fortune on the stock exchange** il a perdu une fortune à la Bourse; ***Stock Exchange Daily Official List*** cours *mpl* de clôture quotidiens; ***stock exchange dealer*** opérateur(trice) *m,f* boursier(ère); ***stock farm*** élevage *m* (de bétail); ***stock farmer*** éleveur *m*; ***stock farming*** élevage *m* (de bétail) *(activité)*; *Cin & TV* ***stock footage*** séquences *fpl* d'archives; ***stock index*** indice *m* de la Bourse; ***stock in hand*** marchandises *fpl* en stock, marchandises *fpl* en magasin; ***stock market*** Bourse *f* (des valeurs), marché *m* financier; **he lost a fortune on the stock market** il a perdu une fortune à la Bourse; **the London stock market is rising** la Bourse de Londres est en hausse; ***stock market price*** cours *m* de la Bourse; ***stock market report*** bulletin *m* des cours de la Bourse; ***stock market value*** valeur en Bourse; ***stock option*** option *f* de titres; *Austr* ***stock rider*** cow-boy *m*; *Am* ***stock saddle*** selle *f* de cow-boy; *TV* ***stock shot*** image *f ou* document *m* d'archives; *Com* ***stock take*** inventaire *m* des stocks; *Com* ***stock turnover*** rotation *f* des stocks; *Com* ***stock valuation*** évaluation *f* des stocks

►**stock up 1** *vi* s'approvisionner; **to stock up on** *or* **with sth** s'approvisionner en qch

2 *vt sep* approvisionner, garnir

stockade [stɒ'keɪd] **1** *n* (**a**) *(enclosure)* palissade *f* (**b**) *Am Mil (prison)* prison *f* (militaire)

2 *vt* palissader

stockboy ['stɒkbɔɪ] *n* magasinier *m*

stockbreeder ['stɒk,briːdə(r)] *n* éleveur(euse) *m,f* de bétail

stockbreeding ['stɒk,briːdɪŋ] *n* élevage *m* de bétail

stockbroker ['stɒk,brəʊkə(r)] *n* agent *m* de change

►► *Br Fam* ***the stockbroker belt*** la banlieue aisée❑; *Br* ***Stockbroker Tudor*** = architecture néo-Tudor en vogue dans les années 20 et 30 dans les banlieues résidentielles

stockbroking ['stɒk,brəʊkɪŋ] *n* commerce *m* des valeurs en Bourse

►► ***stockbroking firm*** société *f* de Bourse

stockbuild ['stɒkbɪld] *vi* **CWX have been stockbuilding in Gomez for several months** cela fait plusieurs mois que CWX accumule des actions de Gomez

stockbuilding ['stɒk,bɪldɪŋ] *n* achat *m* d'actions

stock-exchange *adj* boursier, de la Bourse

►► ***stock-exchange prices*** cours *m* des actions

stockfish ['stɒkfɪʃ] *n* stockfisch *m*, poisson *m* séché

stockgirl ['stɒkgɜːl] *n* magasinière *f*

stockholder ['stɒk,həʊldə(r)] *n* actionnaire *mf*

Stockholm ['stɒkhəʊm] *n* Stockholm

stockily ['stɒkɪlɪ] *adv* **stockily built** trapu, râblé

stockiness ['stɒkɪnɪs] *n* aspect *m* trapu *ou* râblé; **he inherited his stockiness from his father** il a hérité de la silhouette trapue *ou* râblée de son père

stockinet, stockinette [,stɒkɪ'net] *n (fabric)* jersey *m*; *(stitch)* point *m* de jersey

stocking ['stɒkɪŋ] *n* (**a**) *(for women)* bas *m*; **silk stockings** bas *mpl* de soie (**b**) *Old-fashioned (sock)* bas *m* de laine; **in one's stocking feet** sans chaussures, en chaussettes, *Can* en pied de bas

►► ***stocking filler*** = petit cadeau destiné à remplir le "Christmas stocking" à Noël;

stocking mask bas *m (utilisé par un bandit masqué)*; ***stocking stitch*** point *m* de jersey

stockinged ['stɒkɪŋd] *adj* **in one's stockinged feet** sans chaussures, en chaussettes, *Can* en pied de bas

stock-in-trade *n* (**a**) *Com* marchandises *fpl* en stock *ou* en magasin (**b**) *Fig* **charm is part of an actor's stock-in-trade** le charme est l'un des atouts indispensables du comédien; **the kind of scandalmongering that is the stock-in-trade of tabloid newspapers** le type de scandales dont se nourrissent les journaux à sensation

stockist ['stɒkɪst] *n* stockiste *mf*

stockjobber ['stɒk,dʒɒbə(r)] *n St Exch* (**a**) *Br Formerly* = intermédiaire en Bourse qui traite directement avec les agents de change et non avec le public (cette fonction n'existe plus depuis 1987) (**b**) *Am Pej* agent *m* de change

stockkeeper ['stɒk,kiːpə(r)] *n* (**a**) *(cowherd)* vacher(ère) *m,f*, bouvier(ère) *m,f* (**b**) *Am (storekeeper)* magasinier(ère) *m,f*

stockless purchase plan ['stɒklɪs-] *n Com* plan *m* d'achat sans stock

stocklist ['stɒklɪst] *n Br* inventaire *m*

stockman ['stɒkmən] (*pl* **stockmen** [-mən]) *n* (**a**) *(cowherd)* vacher *m*, bouvier *m*; *(breeder)* éleveur *m* (de bétail) (**b**) *Am (warehouseman)* magasinier *m*

stock-market *adj* boursier, de la Bourse

►► ***stock-market crash*** krach *m* boursier; ***stock-market prices*** cours *m* des actions

stockpile ['stɒkpaɪl] **1** *n* stock *m*, réserve *f*

2 *vt (goods)* stocker, constituer un stock de; *(weapons)* amasser, accumuler

3 *vi* faire des stocks

stockpiling ['stɒkpaɪlɪŋ] *n* stockage *m (de nourriture, d'armes etc)*; **to accuse sb of stockpiling** *(food)* accuser qn de faire des réserves de nourriture; *(weapon)* accuser qn de faire des réserves d'armes

stockpot ['stɒkpɒt] *n* marmite *f (pour le bouillon)*

stockroom ['stɒkrʊm] *n* magasin *m*, réserve *f*

stock-still *adv* (complètement) immobile; **she was standing stock-still in the middle of the road** elle se tenait complètement immobile au milieu de la route

stocktake ['stɒk,teɪk] *vi Br* faire *ou* dresser un inventaire

stocktaking ['stɒk,teɪkɪŋ] *n* (**a**) *Com* inventaire *m*; **closed for stocktaking** *(sign)* fermé pour inventaire (**b**) *Fig* **to do some stocktaking** faire le point; **the time has come for some long overdue stocktaking** assez attendu! le moment est venu de faire le point

stocky ['stɒkɪ] (*compar* **stockier,** *superl* **stockiest**) *adj* trapu, râblé

stockyard ['stɒkjɑːd] *n* parc *m* à bestiaux

stodge [stɒdʒ] *n (UNCOUNT) Br Fam* (**a**) *(food)* trucs *mpl* bourratifs, étouffe-chrétien *m inv*; **the canteen food is pure stodge** ce qu'on mange à la cantine est vraiment bourratif (**b**) *(writing)* littérature *f* indigeste ❑

stodgy ['stɒdʒɪ] (*compar* **stodgier,** *superl* **stodgiest**) *adj Fam* (**a**) *(food, meal)* bourratif (**b**) *(style)* lourd ❑, indigeste ❑ (**c**) *(person, manners, ideas)* guindé ❑

stogie, stogy ['stəʊgɪ] (*pl* **stogies**) *n Am Fam* cigare *m* bon marché

stoic ['stəʊɪk] **1** *adj* stoïque

2 *n* stoïque *mf*

3 Stoic *n Phil* stoïcien(enne) *m,f*

stoical ['stəʊɪkəl] *adj* stoïque

stoically ['stəʊɪklɪ] *adv* stoïquement, avec stoïcisme

stoichiometry [,stɔɪkaɪ'ɒmɪtrɪ] *n Chem* stœchiométrie *f*

stoicism ['stəʊɪsɪzəm] **1** *n* stoïcisme *m*

2 Stoicism *n Phil* stoïcisme *m*

stoke [stəʊk] *vt* (**a**) *(fire, furnace)* alimenter, entretenir; *(locomotive, boiler)* chauffer (**b**) *Fig (emotions, feelings, anger)* entretenir, alimenter

►**stoke up 1** *vi* (**a**) *(put fuel on → fire)* alimenter le feu; *(→ furnace)* alimenter la chaudière (**b**) *Br Fam (fill one's stomach)* s'empiffrer

2 *vt sep* = **stoke**

stoked [stəʊkd] *adj Am Fam* **to be stoked (about sth/on sb)** *(excited)* être emballé (par qch/qn)

stokehold ['stəʊkhəʊld] *n Naut* chambre *f* de chauffe, chaufferie *f*

stokehole ['stəʊkhəʊl] *n* (**a**) *(in boiler, furnace)* porte *f* de chauffe (**b**) *Naut* chambre *f* de chauffe, chaufferie *f*

Stoke Mandeville [stəʊk'mændəvɪl] *n* = hôpital britannique spécialisé dans les traitements du dos

stoker ['stəʊkə(r)] *n* chauffeur *m ou* chargeur *m (d'un four, d'une chaudière etc)*

STOL [stɒl] *n* (*abbr* **short takeoff and landing**) *(system)* décollage *m* et atterrissage *m* courts; *(aircraft)* ADAC *m*

stole [stəʊl] **1** *pt of* **steal**

2 *n* (**a**) *(shawl)* étole *f*, écharpe *f*; **mink stole** étole *f* de *ou* en vison (**b**) *Rel* étole *f*

stolen ['stəʊlən] **1** *pp of* **steal**

2 *adj (goods, car)* volé; **a stolen kiss** un baiser volé

stolid ['stɒlɪd] *adj* flegmatique, impassible

stolidity [stɒ'lɪdətɪ] *n* flegme *m*, impassibilité *f*

stolidly ['stɒlɪdlɪ] *adv* flegmatiquement, avec flegme, de manière impassible

stolidness ['stɒlɪdnɪs] *n* flegme *m*

stolon ['stəʊlən] *n Bot & Zool* stolon *m*

stoma ['stəʊmə] (*pl* **stomata** [-mətə]) *n* stomate *m*

stomach ['stʌmək] **1** *n* (**a**) *(organ)* estomac *m*; **to have an upset stomach** avoir l'estomac barbouillé; **I can't work on an empty stomach** je ne peux pas travailler l'estomac vide; **he has a cast-iron stomach** il a l'estomac solide; **to have a pain in one's stomach** avoir mal à l'estomac; *(lower)* avoir mal au ventre; **the sight was enough to turn your stomach** le spectacle avait de quoi vous soulever le cœur; **an army marches on its stomach** une armée ne peut pas se battre l'estomac vide

(**b**) *(region of body)* ventre *m*; **he has a fat stomach** il a du ventre; **lie on your stomach** couchez-vous sur le ventre

(**c**)*(usu neg) (desire, appetite)* envie *f*, goût *m*; **she has no stomach for spicy food** elle supporte mal la cuisine épicée; **I've no stomach for his vulgar jokes this evening** je n'ai aucune envie d'écouter ses plaisanteries vulgaires ce soir

2 *comp (infection)* de l'estomac, gastrique; *(ulcer, operation)* à l'estomac; *(pain)* à l'estomac, au ventre

3 *vt Fam* (**a**) *(tolerate → person)* blairer, encaisser; *(→ thing)* encaisser; **I like him but I can't stomach his brother** lui, je l'aime bien, mais je peux pas blairer son frère; **I can't stomach the way he looks at me** il a une façon de me regarder qui me débecte; **I just can't stomach the thought of him being my boss** je ne peux vraiment pas encaisser l'idée qu'il soit mon patron

(**b**) *(digest)* digérer; **I can't stomach too much rich food** je ne digère pas bien la cuisine riche

►► ***stomach pump*** pompe *f* stomacale

stomach-ache *n* mal *m* de ventre; **to have (a) stomach-ache** avoir mal au ventre; **don't eat so much, you'll get (a) stomach-ache** ne mange pas tant, ça va te donner mal au ventre

stomacher ['stʌməkə(r)] *n Hist* pièce *f* d'estomac *(d'un corsage de femme)*

stomachic [stə'mækɪk] *adj* stomachique, stomacal

stomatitis [,stəʊmə'taɪtɪs] *n (UNCOUNT)* stomatite *f*

stomato- ['stəʊmətəʊ] *pref* stomato-

stomatologist [,stəʊmə'tɒlədʒɪst] *n* stomatologiste *mf*, stomatologue *mf*

stomatology [,stəʊmə'tɒlədʒɪ] *n* stomatologie *f*

stomatoplasty [,stəʊmətəʊ'plæstɪ] *n* stomatoplastie *f*

stomp [stɒmp] *Fam* **1** *vi* marcher d'un pas lourd ❑; **he stomped out of the room** il est sorti de la pièce d'un pas lourd

2 *n* (**a**) *(tread)* pas *m* lourd ❑ (**b**) *(dance)* = jazz que l'on danse en frappant du pied pour marquer le rythme

3 *vt Am Fam (defeat)* flanquer une peignée *ou* une déculottée à

stomping ground ['stɒmpɪŋ-] *n* lieu *m* favori; **this was one of my old stomping grounds** j'y allais tout le temps

stone [stəʊn] (*pl senses* (**a**) *to* (**f**) **stones,** *pl sense* (**g**) **inv** *or* **stones**) **1** *n* (**a**) *(material)* pierre *f*; **the houses are built of stone** les maisons sont en pierre; *Fig* **are you made of stone?** n'as-tu donc pas de cœur?; *Fig* **a heart of stone** un cœur de pierre

(**b**) *(piece of rock)* pierre *f*, caillou *m*; *(on beach)* galet *m*; **they threw stones at me** ils m'ont lancé des pierres; **to fall like a stone** tomber comme une pierre; **to leave no stone unturned** remuer ciel et terre; **we will leave no stone unturned to find the culprits** nous remuerons ciel et terre pour retrouver les coupables; **it's within a stone's throw of the countryside** c'est à deux pas de la campagne

(**c**) *(memorial)* stèle *f*, pierre *f*

(**d**) *(gem)* pierre *f*

(**e**) *Med* calcul *m*; **he has a stone in his kidney** il a un calcul rénal

(**f**) *(in fruit)* noyau *m*

(**g**) *(unit of weight)* ≃ 6 kg; **she weighs about 8 stone** *or* **stones** elle pèse dans les 50 kilos

(**h**) *(colour)* gris *m* mastic

2 *adj* (**a**) *(made of stone)* de *ou* en pierre; **a stone jar** un pot de grès

(**b**) *(in colour)* mastic *(inv)*

(**c**) *Am Fam (absolute, real)* vrai ❑, total ❑; **this is turning into a stone drag!** ça devient vraiment galère!

3 *vt* (**a**) *(fruit, olive)* dénoyauter

(**b**) *(person, car)* jeter des pierres sur, bombarder de pierres; *(as punishment)* lapider

(**c**) *Br Fam (idiom)* **stone the crows!, stone me!** mince alors!

►► ***Stone Age*** âge *m* de (la) pierre; ***stone axe*** hache *f* de pierre; *Ich* ***stone bass*** cernier *m*; ***stone circle*** cromlech *m*; *Orn* ***stone curlew*** œdicnème *m* (criard), courlis *m* de terre; ***the Stone of Destiny, the Stone of Scone*** = pierre qui, selon la tradition, servait de trône aux rois et aux reines d'Écosse lors de leur couronnement; *Br* ***stone fruit*** fruit *m* à noyau; *Zool* ***stone marten*** fouine *f*; ***stone saw*** scie *f* à pierre *ou* de carrier; *Journ* ***stone sub*** correcteur *m* de mise en page

Stone-Age *adj (man, dwelling, weapon)* de l'âge de (la) pierre

stone-blind *adj* complètement aveugle

stonebreaker ['stəʊn,breɪkə(r)] *n (person)* casseur *m* de pierres; *(machine)* concasseur *m*

stone-broke = **stony-broke**

stonechat ['stəʊntʃæt] *n Orn* traquet *m* (pâtre)

stone-cold 1 *adj* (**a**) complètement froid (**b**) *Am Fam (absolute, real)* vrai ❑, total ❑

2 *adv Fam* **stone-cold sober** pas du tout soûl

stonecrop ['stəʊnkrɒp] *n* orpin *m*

stonecutter ['stəʊn,kʌtə(r)] *n* (**a**) *(person → of stone)* tailleur *m* de pierre; *(→ of precious stones)* lapidaire *m* (**b**) *(machine)* lapidaire *m*

stoned [stəʊnd] *adj* (**a**) *Fam (on drugs)* raide, défoncé; **to get stoned** se défoncer (**b**) *Fam Old-fashioned (drunk)* bourré, schlass (**c**) *(fruit)* dénoyauté

stone-dead 1 *adj* raide mort

2 *adv* raide mort; **the blow killed him stone-dead** le coup l'a tué instantanément; *Fig* **to kill a proposal stone-dead** sonner le glas d'une proposition

stone-deaf *adj* complètement sourd

stonefish ['stəʊnfɪʃ] *n Ich* poisson-pierre *m*

stonefly ['stəʊnflaɪ] (*pl* **stoneflies**) *n Entom* plécoptère *m*

stone-ground *adj* moulu à la pierre

Stonehenge ['stəʊnhendʒ] *n* = monument mégalithique dans le sud de l'Angleterre

stonemason ['stəʊn,meɪsən] *n* tailleur *m* de pierre

stoner ['stəʊnə(r)] *adj Fam Drugs slang* adepte *mf* de la fumette

stone-still *adj* **to stay stone-still** rester cloué sur place

Stonewall [,stəʊn'wɔːl] *n* (**a**) *Am Hist* Stonewall (**b**) *(gay rights group)* = association britannique de défense des droits des homosexuels

STONEWALL

Ce terme fait référence à un bar new-yorkais fréquenté par des homosexuels où, en 1969, les incessantes descentes de police provoquèrent des émeutes. Celles-ci préludèrent à la naissance du mouvement pour l'égalité des droits des homosexuels puis à celle de l'association britannique du même nom.

stonewall [ˌstəʊn'wɔːl] **1** *vi* (**a**) *(obstruct discussion)* monopoliser la parole *(pour empêcher les autres de parler)*; *(avoid questions)* donner des réponses évasives (**b**) *Sport (in cricket)* jouer très prudemment, bétonner
2 *vt Parl* bloquer, faire barrage à

stonewaller [ˌstəʊn'wɔːlə(r)] *n* (**a**) *Sport* = joueur prudent qui ne risque rien (**b**) *Parl* obstructionniste *mf*

stonewalling [ˌstəʊn'wɔːlɪŋ] *n* (**a**) *Sport (in cricket)* jeu *m* défensif (**b**) *Parl* obstructionnisme *m*

stoneware ['stəʊnweə(r)] *n* (poterie *f* en) grès *m*

stonewashed ['stəʊnwɒʃt] *adj (jeans, denim)* délavé *(avant l'achat)*

stonework ['stəʊnwɜːk] *n* maçonnerie *f*, ouvrage *m* en pierre

stonily ['stəʊnɪlɪ] *adv* froidement; **to look at sb stonily** regarder qn froidement

stoniness ['stəʊnɪnɪs] *n* (**a**) *(of soil, land)* nature *f* pierreuse (**b**) *(of heart)* dureté *f*; *(of look)* froideur *f*

stoning ['stəʊnɪŋ] *n (of person)* lapidation *f*

stonker ['stɒŋkə(r)] *n Br Fam* **what a stonker of a goal!** quel but d'enfer!; **their latest album's a complete stonker!** leur dernier album est absolument génial!

stonking ['stɒŋkɪŋ] *adj Br Fam* super, génial, d'enfer; **he scored a stonking goal** il a marqué un but d'enfer

stony ['stəʊnɪ] (*compar* **stonier**, *superl* **stoniest**) *adj* (**a**) *(covered with stones → ground, soil, road, land)* pierreux, caillouteux, rocailleux; *(→ beach)* de galets; *Fig* **his requests fell on stony ground** ses revendications n'ont rien donné (**b**) *(stone-like → texture, feel)* pierreux (**c**) *(unfeeling → gen)* insensible; *(→ reception)* froid; *(→ look, silence)* glacial; **a stony heart** un cœur de pierre

stony-broke *adj Br Fam* fauché (comme les blés), raide

stony-faced *adj* au visage impassible

stony-hearted *adj* au cœur de pierre; **he's stony-hearted** il a un cœur de pierre

stood [stʊd] *pt & pp of* **stand**

stooge [stuːdʒ] **1** *n* (**a**) *Fam Pej (lackey)* larbin *m* (**b**) *Theat (straight man)* faire-valoir *m inv* (**c**) *Fam (dupe)* pigeon *m*, poire *f* (**d**) *Fam (idiot)* andouille *f*, crétin(e) *m,f*
2 *vi Theat* **to stooge for a comedian** servir de faire-valoir à un comique

stook [stʊk] **1** *n* moyette *f*
2 *vt* moyetter

stookie ['stʊkɪ] *n Scot* (**a**) *(plaster of Paris)* plâtre *m* de Paris, plâtre *m* à mouler; *(on limb)* plâtre *m* (**b**) *Fam (person)* cruche *f*, nouille *f*; **don't just stand there like a stookie!** ne reste pas planté là comme un piquet!

stool [stuːl] *n* (**a**) *(seat)* tabouret *m*; *Br* **to fall between two stools** être assis entre deux chaises (**b**) *Med* selle *f* (**c**) *Hort (tree stump)* souche *f*; *(shoot)* rejet *m* de souche; *(base of plant)* pied *m* de plante (**d**) *Am (windowsill)* rebord *m* de fenêtre (**e**) *Fam (informer)* indic *mf*, mouchard(e) *m,f*
▶▶ *Fam* ***stool pigeon*** indic *mf*, mouchard(e) *m,f*

stoolie ['stuːlɪ] *n Am Fam* indic *mf*, mouchard(e) *m,f*

stoop [stuːp] **1** *vi* (**a**) *(bend down)* se baisser, se pencher; **she stooped to pick up her pen** elle se baissa *ou* se pencha pour ramasser son stylo
(**b**) *(stand, walk with a stoop)* avoir le dos voûté; **he was beginning to stoop** il commençait à se voûter
(**c**) *(abase oneself)* s'abaisser; **I can't believe he stooped to lying** je n'arrive pas à croire qu'il se soit abaissé à mentir; **she would stoop to anything** elle est prête à toutes les bassesses
(**d**) *(condescend)* daigner; **she wouldn't stoop to doing the dirty work herself** elle ne s'abaisserait pas à faire elle-même le sale travail
(**e**) *(bird of prey)* fondre, plonger
2 *vt* baisser, pencher, incliner; **he stooped his head to go through the door** il a baissé la tête pour passer la porte
3 *n* (**a**) *(of person)* **to walk with** *or* **to have a stoop** avoir le dos voûté
(**b**) *(by bird of prey)* attaque *f* en piqué
(**c**) *Am (veranda)* véranda *f*, porche *m*

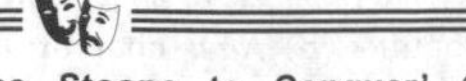

'She Stoops to Conquer' *Goldsmith* 'Elle s'abaisse pour triompher'

stooping ['stuːpɪŋ] *adj (back, shoulders, figure)* voûté

STOP [stɒp]

arrêt	▶ 1 (a) – (c), (f)
gare	▶ 1 (a)
station	▶ 1 (a)
pause	▶ 1 (b)
arrêter	▶ 3 (a), (c), (d), (f)
cesser	▶ 3 (a); 4 (b)
empêcher	▶ 3 (b)
interrompre	▶ 3 (d)
couper	▶ 3 (d)
mettre fin à	▶ 1 (d); 3 (e)
retenir	▶ 3 (g)
s'arrêter	▶ 4 (a), (b)

(*pt & pp* **stopped**, *cont* **stopping**) **1** *n* (**a**) *(stopping place → for buses)* arrêt *m*; *(→ for trains)* gare *f*; *(→ for underground)* station *f*; **we get off at the next stop** nous descendons au prochain arrêt
(**b**) *(break → in journey, process)* arrêt *m*, halte *f*; *(→ in work)* pause *f*; *Aviat & Naut* escale *f*; **ten minutes' stop, a ten-minute stop** dix minutes d'arrêt; **to make a stop** *(gen)* s'arrêter; *(of plane, boat)* faire escale; **we made several stops to pick up passengers** nous nous sommes arrêtés à plusieurs reprises pour prendre des passagers; **we travelled/worked all day without a stop** nous avons voyagé/travaillé toute la journée sans nous arrêter; **our first stop was Brussels** nous avons fait une première halte à Bruxelles; **let's have a stop for lunch** faisons une pause pour le déjeuner; **my whole career has been full of stops and starts** ma carrière entière est faite de hauts et de bas
(**c**) *(standstill)* arrêt *m*; **to come to a stop** s'arrêter; **to bring sth to a stop** arrêter qch; **to be at a stop** être arrêté
(**d**) *(end)* **to put a stop to sth** mettre fin *ou* un terme à qch
(**e**) *Br (full stop)* point *m*; *(in telegrams)* stop *m*
(**f**) *Sport (save)* arrêt *m*
(**g**) *(on organ → pipes)* jeu *m* (d'orgue); *(→ knob)* registre *m* (d'orgue); *Fig* **to pull out all the stops (to do sth)** remuer ciel et terre (pour faire qch)
(**h**) *(plug, stopper)* bouchon *m*
(**i**) *(blocking device → gen)* butoir *m*; *(→ for drawer)* butée *f*; *(→ on typewriter)* taquet *m*
(**j**) *Phot* diaphragme *m*
(**k**) *Ling* occlusive *f*
(**l**) *(in bridge)* contrôle *m*; **to have a stop in hearts** avoir un contrôle à cœur
2 *comp (button, mechanism, signal)* d'arrêt
3 *vt* (**a**) *(cease, finish)* arrêter, cesser; **to stop doing** arrêter *ou* cesser de faire; **it hasn't stopped raining all day** il n'a pas arrêté *ou* cessé de pleuvoir toute la journée; **you should stop smoking** tu devrais arrêter de fumer; **he never stops talking** il n'arrête pas de parler, il parle sans cesse; **I wish they'd stop that noise!** j'aimerais qu'ils arrêtent ce bruit!; **she stopped work when she got married** elle a arrêté de travailler quand elle s'est mariée; **stop it!** *(to naughty child)* ça suffit!, assez!; **stop it, that hurts!** arrête, ça fait mal!
(**b**) *(prevent)* empêcher; **to stop sb (from) doing sth** empêcher qn de faire qch; **it's too late to stop the meeting from taking place** il est trop tard pour empêcher la réunion d'avoir lieu; **she's made up her mind and there's nothing we can do to stop her** elle a pris sa décision et nous ne pouvons rien faire pour l'arrêter; **what's stopping you?** qu'est-ce qui vous retient?, qu'est-ce qui vous en empêche?; **I couldn't stop myself** je n'ai pas pu m'en empêcher
(**c**) *(cause to halt → person, car, machine)* arrêter; **this lever stops the motor** ce levier arrête le moteur; **I managed to stop the car** j'ai réussi à arrêter la voiture; **a policeman stopped the traffic** un agent arrêta la circulation; **we could do nothing to stop the bleeding** nous ne pouvions rien faire pour arrêter l'hémorragie; **a woman stopped me to ask the way to the station** une femme m'a arrêté pour me demander le chemin de la gare; **the sound of voices stopped him short** *or* **stopped him in his tracks** un bruit de voix le fit s'arrêter net; *Fam* **to stop a bullet** se prendre une balle; **stop thief!** au voleur!
(**d**) *(interrupt → activity, production)* interrompre, arrêter; *(cut off → electricity, gas, water)* couper; *(suspend → grant, payment, subscription)* suspendre; **once he starts talking about the war there's no stopping him** une fois qu'il commence à parler de la guerre, on ne peut plus l'arrêter; **the referee stopped the fight in the third round** l'arbitre a arrêté le combat à la troisième reprise; **I forgot to stop the newspaper** j'ai oublié de faire suspendre mon abonnement au journal; **his father threatened to stop his allowance** son père menaça de lui couper les vivres; *Mil* **all leave is stopped** toutes les troupes sont consignées, toutes les permissions sont suspendues; **to stop a cheque** faire opposition à un chèque
(**e**) *(put an end to → abuse, rumours)* mettre fin à, faire cesser; **dumping nuclear waste should be stopped** il faut qu'on arrête de jeter n'importe où les déchets nucléaires; **it ought to be stopped** il faut que cela cesse
(**f**) *(arrest)* arrêter
(**g**) *Br (withhold → sum of money, salary)* retenir; **the money will be stopped out of your wages** la somme sera retenue sur votre salaire; **he had £10 a week stopped out of his wages** on lui retenait 10 livres par semaine sur son salaire; **taxes are stopped at source** les impôts sont retenus à la source
(**h**) *Sport (check → blow)* parer; *Boxing (defeat → opponent)* mettre un adversaire K.O.
(**i**) *(block, fill → hole)* boucher; **to stop one's ears** se boucher les oreilles; **to stop a gap** *(around door etc)* boucher un espace; *Fig* combler une lacune
(**j**) *(fill → tooth)* plomber
(**k**) *Hort* pincer
(**l**) *Mus (string)* presser; *(wind instrument)* boucher les trous de
4 *vi* (**a**) *(halt, pause → person, vehicle, machine)* s'arrêter; **to stop to do** s'arrêter pour faire; **go on, don't stop** continue, ne t'arrête pas; **my watch has stopped** ma montre s'est *ou* est arrêtée; **does the bus stop near the church?** le bus s'arrête-t-il près de l'église?; **we can stop for tea on the way** nous pouvons nous arrêter en chemin pour prendre le thé; **we drove from London to Edinburgh without stopping** nous avons roulé de Londres à Édimbourg d'une traite; **the bus kept stopping and starting** le bus a fait beaucoup d'arrêts en cours de route; *Naut* **to stop at a port** faire escale à *ou* dans un port; **I used to play football but I stopped last year** je jouais au football mais j'ai arrêté l'année dernière; **she doesn't know where** *or* **when to stop** elle ne sait pas s'arrêter; **she did not stop at that** elle ne s'en tint pas là; **they'll stop at nothing to get what they want** ils ne reculeront devant rien pour obtenir ce qu'ils veulent; **we don't have time to stop and think** nous n'avons pas le temps de nous arrêter pour réfléchir; **if you stopped to consider, you'd never do anything** si on prenait le temps de réfléchir, on ne ferait jamais rien; **to stop dead in one's tracks, to stop short** s'arrêter net; **she began talking then stopped short** elle commença à parler puis s'arrêta net *ou* brusquement; **they stopped short of actually harming him** ils ne lui ont pas fait de mal, mais il s'en est fallu de peu
(**b**) *(come to an end)* cesser, s'arrêter, se terminer; **the rain has stopped** la pluie s'est arrêtée; **wait for the music to stop** attendez que la musique s'arrête; **the road stops a few miles east of Alice Springs** la route se termine à quelques kilomètres à l'est d'Alice Springs; **the matter will not stop there** l'affaire n'en restera *ou* demeurera pas là
(**c**) *Br Fam (stay)* rester ❑; *(reside)* loger ❑; **I'm late, I can't stop** je suis en retard, je ne peux pas rester; **we've got friends stopping with us** nous avons des amis chez nous en ce moment; **which**

hotel did you stop at? dans quel hôtel êtes-vous descendus ❑?

►► *Aut* **stopping distance** distance *f* d'arrêt; *Br* **stopping train** omnibus *m*

stopwatch ['stɒpwɒtʃ] *n* chronomètre *m*

storable ['stɔːrəbəl] *adj* (**a**) *(foodstuff)* que l'on peut conserver (**b**) *Comput (of data)* enregistrable

storage ['stɔːrɪdʒ] **1** *n* (**a**) *(putting into store)* entreposage *m*, emmagasinage *m*, stockage *m*; *(keeping, conservation)* stockage *m*; **careful packing should prevent the goods being damaged in storage** un bon emballage devrait empêcher la détérioration des marchandises pendant le stockage; **our furniture is in storage** nos meubles sont au garde-meubles

(**b**) *Comput* (mise *f* en) mémoire *f*

(**c**) *(costs)* frais *mpl* de stockage *ou* d'emmagasinage, (frais *mpl* de) magasinage *m*

(**d**) *(available space → in store, for storing)* espace *m* disponible; *(→ of business)* entrepôts *mpl*, magasins *mpl*

2 *comp* (**a**) *(charges)* de stockage, d'emmagasinage, de magasinage

(**b**) *Comput* de mémoire

►► **storage battery** accumulateur *m*, batterie *f* secondaire; *Comput* **storage capacity** capacité *f* de stockage; **storage card** carte *f* à mémoire; **storage cell** accumulateur *m*, batterie *f* secondaire; *Comput* **storage device** dispositif *m* de stockage; *Br* **storage heater** radiateur *m* à accumulation; *Br* **storage heating** chauffage *m* par accumulation; *Comput* **storage medium** support *m* de stockage; **storage room** *(small)* cagibi *m*; *(larger)* débarras *m*; **storage space** espace *m* de rangement; **there is additional storage space for luggage in the rack above your head** vous pouvez également déposer vos bagages dans les casiers au-dessus de vos têtes; *Br* **storage radiator** radiateur *m* à accumulation; **storage tank** *(for fuel)* réservoir *m* (de stockage); *(for rainwater)* citerne *f*; **storage tray** *(in car)* vide-poche *m*; **storage unit** meuble *m* de rangement

storax ['stɔːræks] *n (tree, resin)* styrax *m*, storax *m*

store [stɔː(r)] **1** *n* (**a**) *(large shop)* grand magasin *m*; *Am (shop)* magasin *m*; *Am* **candy store** confiserie *f*

(**b**) *(stock → of goods)* stock *m*, réserve *f*, provision *f*; *(→ of food)* provision *f*; *(→ of facts, jokes, patience, knowledge)* réserve *f*; *(→ of wisdom)* fonds *m*; **we should get in** *or* **lay in a store of coal** nous devrions faire provision de charbon; **I have my own private store of tea** j'ai ma provision personnelle de thé

(**c**) *(place → warehouse)* entrepôt *m*, dépôt *m*; *(→ in office, home, shop)* réserve *f*; *(→ in factory)* magasin *m*, réserve *f*; *Br* **goods in store** marchandises *fpl* en entrepôt; **furniture store** garde-meubles *m inv*

(**d**) *Comput (memory)* mémoire *f*

(**e**) *(value)* **to lay** *or* **to put** *or* **to set great store by sth** faire grand cas de qch; **I don't set much store by his advice** je ne fais pas grand cas de ses conseils

2 *comp Am (store-bought → gen)* de commerce; *(→ clothes)* de confection; **a store cake** un gâteau acheté dans une pâtisserie

3 *vt* (**a**) *(put away, put in store → goods, food)* emmagasiner, entreposer; *(→ grain, crop)* engranger; *(→ heat)* accumuler, emmagasiner; *(→ electricity)* accumuler; *(→ files, documents)* classer; *(→ facts, ideas)* engranger, enregistrer dans sa mémoire; **we stored our furniture at my mother's house** nous avons laissé *ou* mis nos meubles chez ma mère; **they stored the ship with provisions for the voyage** ils ont rempli le bateau de provisions pour le voyage

(**b**) *(keep)* conserver, stocker; **store in a cool place** *(on packaging)* à conserver au frais

(**c**) *(fill with provisions)* approvisionner; **he stored the larder with enough tinned goods to last the winter** il a rempli le placard avec assez de boîtes de conserve pour passer l'hiver

(**d**) *Comput* stocker

4 *vi (goods)* **these goods don't store well** ces produits ne se conservent pas bien

5 stores *npl (provisions)* provisions *fpl*; **the expedition's stores are running low** l'expédition commence à manquer de provisions

6 in store *adv* **they had a surprise in store for her** ils lui avaient réservé une surprise; **who knows what the future has in store?** qui sait ce que l'avenir nous réserve?; **if only we'd realised all the problems that were in store for us** si seulement nous nous étions rendu compte de tous les problèmes qui nous attendaient

►► *Mktg* **store audit** contrôle *m* des points de vente; *Mktg* **store brand** marque *f* de magasin; **store card** carte *f* de crédit *(d'un grand magasin)*; **store cupboard** placard *m* de rangement; **store detective** vigile *m (dans un magasin)*; **store manager** chef *m* de magasin; *Am* **store window** vitrine *f*, devanture *f*

►**store away** *vt sep* garder en réserve; **he stored away the joke for future use** il a noté la blague en se disant qu'il la replacerait

►**store up** *vt sep (goods, food)* emmagasiner; *(heat, electricity)* accumuler; *(memories, emotions)* accumuler; **he's just storing up trouble for himself by keeping silent** en ne disant rien, il ne fait que se préparer des ennuis

store-bought *adj (gen)* de commerce; *(clothes)* de confection; **a store-bought cake** un gâteau de pâtisserie

storefront ['stɔːfrʌnt] *n Am* devanture *f* de magasin

►► **storefront church** = lieu de culte, généralement évangélique, possédant une vitrine sur la rue

storehouse ['stɔːhaʊs, *pl* -haʊzɪz] *n* (**a**) *(warehouse)* magasin *m*, entrepôt *m*, dépôt *m* (**b**) *Fig (of information, memories)* mine *f*

storekeeper ['stɔːˌkiːpə(r)] *n* (**a**) *(in warehouse)* magasinier(ère) *m,f* (**b**) *Am (shopkeeper)* commerçant(e) *m,f*

storeman ['stɔːmən] (*pl* **storemen** [-mən]) *n Br* manutentionnaire *m*

storeroom ['stɔːrʊm] *n* (**a**) *(in office, shop)* réserve *f*; *(in factory)* magasin *m*, réserve *f*; *(in home)* débarras *m* (**b**) *Naut* soute *f*, magasin *m*

storey (*pl* **storeys**), *Am* **story** (*pl* **stories**) ['stɔːrɪ] *n* étage *m*; **a four-storey building** un immeuble de quatre étages

-storey, -storeyed ['stɔːrɪd] *suff* **a single-storey/five-storey building** un bâtiment à un étage/à cinq étages

storied ['stɔːrɪd] *adj* (**a**) *Art* historié (**b**) *Arch or Literary (place)* célébré dans la légende

-storied *Am* = **-storey**

storing ['stɔːrɪŋ] *n* (**a**) *(of goods, food)* emmagasinage *m*, entreposage *m*; *(of grain, crop)* engrangement *m*; *(of heat)* accumulation *f*, emmagasinage *m*; *(of electricity)* accumulation *f*; *(of files, documents)* archivage *m* (**b**) *(keeping)* conservation *f*, stockage *m* (**c**) *(filling with provisions)* approvisionnement *m* (**d**) *Comput* stockage *m*

stork [stɔːk] *n Orn* cigogne *f*; **young stork** cigogneau *m*

storm [stɔːm] **1** *n* (**a**) *Met* tempête *f*; *(thunderstorm)* orage *m*; *(on Beaufort scale)* tempête *f*; *Br* **it was a storm in a teacup** ce fut une tempête dans un verre d'eau

(**b**) *Fig (furore)* tempête *f*, ouragan *m*; *(roar)* tempête *f*; **the arms deal caused a political storm** la vente d'armes a déclenché un véritable scandale politique; **a storm of protest** une tempête de protestations; **a storm of criticism** une marée de condamnations; **a storm of applause** une tempête d'applaudissements; **a storm of abuse** une tornade d'injures

(**c**) *Mil* **to take by storm** prendre d'assaut; *Fig* **the show took Broadway by storm** le spectacle a connu un succès foudroyant à Broadway

2 *vi* (**a**) *(go angrily)* **to storm in/out** entrer/sortir comme un ouragan; **she stormed off without saying a word** elle est partie furieuse, sans dire un mot; **she was storming about the place like a madwoman** elle se démenait dans la pièce comme une folle

(**b**) *(be angry)* tempêter, fulminer

(**c**) *(rain)* tomber à verse; *(wind)* souffler violemment; *(blizzard)* faire rage; **it stormed all night** il y a eu de l'orage toute la nuit

(**d**) *Mil* donner *ou* livrer l'assaut; **the enemy stormed through our defences** l'ennemi donna l'assaut et franchit nos lignes de défense

3 *vt* prendre d'assaut; **the troops stormed the ramparts** les troupes ont pris d'assaut les remparts

stop-and-go *Am* = **stop-go**

stop-and-search *n* fouilles *fpl* dans la rue

stopcock ['stɒpkɒk] *n Br* robinet *m* d'arrêt

stope [stəʊp] *n* gradin *m*

stopgap ['stɒpgæp] **1** *n Br* bouche-trou *m*

2 *adj* de remplacement; **a stopgap measure** un palliatif

stop-go *adj*

►► *Br Econ* **stop-go policy** politique *f* économique en dents de scie *(alternant arrêt de la croissance et mesures de relance)*, politique *f* du stop-and-go

stoplight ['stɒplaɪt] *n* (**a**) *(traffic light)* feu *m* rouge (**b**) *Br (brake-light)* stop *m*

stop-limit order *n St Exch* ordre *m* stop à cours limité

stop-list *n Banking (for lost cheques)* liste *f* de chèques volés ou perdus

stop-off *n* halte *f*, courte halte *f*

stopover ['stɒpˌəʊvə(r)] *n (gen)* halte *f*; *(on flight)* escale *f*

stoppage ['stɒpɪdʒ] *n* (**a**) *(strike)* grève *f*, arrêt *m* de travail (**b**) *Br (sum deducted)* retenue *f*; **my wages are a lot less after stoppages** après les retenues, il ne reste plus grand-chose de mon salaire (**c**) *(halting, stopping)* arrêt *m*, interruption *f*; *Ftbl* arrêt *m* de jeu (**d**) *(blockage)* obstruction *f*; *Med* occlusion *f*

►► *Sport* **stoppage time** arrêts *mpl* de jeu

stopper ['stɒpə(r)] **1** *n* (**a**) *(for bottle, jar)* bouchon *m*; *(for sink)* bouchon *m*, bonde *f*; *(for pipe)* obturateur *m*; *(on syringe)* embout *m* de piston; **I can't get the stopper out of the jar/back on the jar** je n'arrive pas à déboucher/à reboucher le bocal (**b**) *Ftbl* stoppeur *m* (**c**) *(in bridge)* arrêt *m*; **to have a stopper in clubs** avoir un arrêt à trèfle

2 *vt* boucher, fermer

stopping ['stɒpɪŋ] **1** *n* (**a**) *(coming or bringing to a halt)* arrêt *m* (**b**) *(blocking)* obturation *f*; **the stopping (up) of a leak** le colmatage d'une fuite (**c**) *(cancellation → of payment, leave etc)* suspension *f*; *(→ of service)* suppression *f*; *(→ of cheque)* opposition *f*

2 *adj (place)* où l'on s'arrête

►► *Am* ***storm cellar*** abri *m* contre les cyclones; ***storm centre*** *Met* œil *m* de la tempête *ou* du cyclone; *Fig* centre *m* de l'agitation, point *m* névralgique; ***storm cloud*** *Met* nuage *m* d'orage; *Fig* nuage *m* menaçant; **the storm clouds of war were gathering** le danger *ou* la menace d'une guerre grandissait; ***storm cock*** draine *f*, grive *f* de gui; ***storm cone*** cône *m* de tempête; ***storm damage*** dommages *mpl ou* dégâts *mpl* causés par l'orage *ou* la tempête; *Am* ***storm door*** porte *f* extérieure *(qui double la porte de la maison pour éviter les courants d'air)*; ***storm drain*** égout *m* pluvial; ***storm lantern*** lampe *f* tempête; *Orn* ***storm petrel*** pétrel-tempête *m*; ***storm sewer*** égout *m* pluvial; ***storm trooper*** membre *m* des troupes d'assaut; ***storm troops*** troupes *fpl* d'assaut; ***storm warning*** avis *m* de tempête; ***storm window*** contre-fenêtre *f*

stormbound ['stɔːmbaʊnd] *adj* bloqué par l'orage *ou* la tempête

stormily ['stɔːmɪlɪ] *adv* orageusement

storminess ['stɔːmɪnɪs] *n* caractère *m* orageux

storming ['stɔːmɪŋ] *n (attack)* assaut *m*; *(capture)* prise *f* (d'assaut); *Hist* **the storming of the Bastille** la prise de la Bastille

Stormont ['stɔːmənt] *n* = château de la banlieue de Belfast, siège de l'Assemblée d'Irlande du Nord

stormproof ['stɔːmpruːf] *adj* à l'épreuve de la tempête

stormtrooper ['stɔːm,truːpə(r)] *adj (tactics)* brutal, impitoyable

stormwater ['stɔːm,wɔːtə(r)] *n* eau *f* pluviale

stormy ['stɔːmɪ] (*compar* **stormier**, *superl* **stormiest**) *adj* (**a**) *(weather)* orageux, d'orage; *(sea)* houleux, démonté; **it was a stormy day** il faisait un temps orageux (**b**) *Fig (relationship)* orageux; *(debate)* houleux; *(look)* furieux; *(career, life)* tumultueux, mouvementé

►► *Orn* ***stormy petrel*** pétrel-tempête *m*

story ['stɔːrɪ] (*pl* **stories**) *n* (**a**) *(tale, work of fiction* → *spoken)* histoire *f*; *(*→ *written)* histoire *f*, conte *m*; *Literature (short story)* nouvelle *f*; **to tell sb a story** raconter une histoire à qn; **ghost/murder story** histoire *f* de fantômes/de meurtre; **fairy story** conte *m* de fées; **he stopped halfway through his story** il s'interrompit en plein milieu de son récit; **this is a true story** c'est une histoire vraie; **a collection of her poems and stories** un recueil de ses poèmes et nouvelles; **there is a story that..., the story goes that...** on raconte que...; *Fig* **the stories this old castle could tell!** les murs de ce château en ont vu de belles!; **there's a story behind** *or* **attached to every exhibit in the museum** chacune des pièces du musée a sa propre histoire

(**b**) *(plot)* intrigue *f*, scénario *m*; **the story of the film is very complicated** l'intrigue du film est très compliquée; **I like a play with a good story to it** j'aime les pièces qui ont une bonne intrigue; **the story is set in wartime London** l'histoire se passe à Londres, pendant la guerre

(**c**) *(account)* histoire *f*; **I got the inside story from his wife** j'ai appris la vérité sur cette histoire par sa femme; **let me tell you my side of the story** laisse-moi te donner ma version de l'histoire; *Hum* **well, that's my story and I'm sticking to it** c'est la version officielle; **the witness changed his story** le témoin est revenu sur sa version des faits; **but that's another story** mais ça, c'est une autre histoire; **that's not the whole story, that's only part of the story** mais ce n'est pas tout; **we'll probably never know the whole** *or* **full story** nous ne saurons peut-être jamais le fin mot de l'histoire; **it's always the same old story, it's the old, old story** c'est toujours la même histoire *ou* chanson; **these bruises tell their own story** ces meurtrissures en disent long; **each photo tells its** *or* **a story** toutes les photos racontent une histoire; **it's a long story** c'est toute une histoire, c'est une longue histoire; **to** *Br* **cut** *or Am* **make a long story short** enfin bref

(**d**) *(history)* histoire *f*; **his life story** l'histoire de sa vie; *Hum* **that's the story of my life!** ça m'arrive tout le temps!

(**e**) *Euph (lie)* histoire *f*; **are you telling stories again?** est-ce que tu racontes encore des histoires?

(**f**) *(rumour)* rumeur *f*, bruit *m*; **there's a story going about that they're getting divorced** le bruit court qu'ils vont divorcer; **or so the story goes** c'est du moins ce que l'on raconte

(**g**) *Press (article)* article *m*; *(event, affair)* affaire *f*; **there's a front-page story about** *or* **on the riots** il y a un article en première page sur les émeutes; **the editor refused to run her story** le rédacteur en chef a refusé de publier son article; **all the papers ran** *or* **carried the story** tous les journaux en ont parlé; **have you been following this corruption story?** est-ce que vous avez suivi cette affaire de corruption?; **what's the story?** quelle nouvelle?; **the story broke just after the morning papers had gone to press** on a appris la nouvelle juste après la mise sous presse des journaux du matin

(**h**) *Am* = **storey**

storyboard ['stɔːrɪbɔːd] *n* story-board *m*, *Offic* scénarimage *m*

storybook ['stɔːrɪbʊk] **1** *n* livre *m* de contes

2 *adj* **a storybook ending** une fin digne d'un conte de fées; **a storybook romance** une idylle de conte de fées; **a storybook castle** un château de conte de fées

storyline ['stɔːrɪlaɪn] *n (of book)* intrigue *f*; *(of film)* intrigue *f*, scénario *m*; **it was quite hard to follow the storyline** j'ai/il a/*etc* eu du mal à suivre le fil de l'histoire; **his novels always have a strong storyline** l'intrigue de ses romans est toujours passionnante

storyteller ['stɔːrɪ,telə(r)] *n* (**a**) *(narrator)* conteur(euse) *m,f*; **to be a good/bad storyteller** être bon/mauvais conteur (**b**) *Euph (liar)* menteur(euse) *m,f*

storytelling ['stɔːrɪ,telɪŋ] *n* (**a**) *(art)* art *m* de conter; **to be good at storytelling** avoir l'art de raconter des histoires (**b**) *Euph (telling lies)* mensonges *mpl*

stotinka [stɒ'tɪŋkə] (*pl* **stotinki** [-kɪ]) *n* stotinka *m*

stoup [stuːp] *n Rel* bénitier *m*

stout [staʊt] **1** *adj* (**a**) *(corpulent)* corpulent, fort; **to grow stout** prendre de l'embonpoint (**b**) *(strong* → *stick)* solide; *(*→ *structure, material)* solide, robuste; *(sturdy)* costaud *m*; **a pair of stout walking shoes** une paire de chaussures de marche solides *ou* robustes (**c**) *(firm, resolute* → *resistance, opposition, enemy)* acharné; *(*→ *support, supporter)* fidèle, loyal (**d**) *(brave)* vaillant, courageux; **a stout heart** un cœur vaillant

2 *n* stout *m*, bière *f* brune forte

stouthearted [,staʊt'hɑːtɪd] *adj* vaillant, courageux

stoutheartedly [,staʊt'hɑːtɪdlɪ] *adv* vaillamment, courageusement

stoutheartedness [,staʊt'hɑːtɪdnɪs] *n* courage *m*, vaillance *f*

stoutish ['staʊtɪʃ] *adj* (**a**) *(corpulent)* assez gros, assez corpulent (**b**) *(door, box)* assez solide

stoutly ['staʊtlɪ] *adv* (**a**) *(firmly, resolutely* → *resist, defend, oppose)* avec acharnement; *(*→ *support)* fidèlement, loyalement; **she still stoutly maintains she was in the right** elle continue à prétendre dur comme fer qu'elle avait raison (**b**) *(bravely)* vaillamment, courageusement (**c**) *(solidly)* solidement, robustement; **stoutly built houses** des maisons solides

stoutness ['staʊtnɪs] *n* (**a**) *(corpulence)* corpulence *f*, embonpoint *m* (**b**) *(solidity, strength* → *of structure, materials)* solidité *f*, robustesse *f* (**c**) *(firmness, resolution* → *of resistance, defence, opposition)* acharnement *m*; *(*→ *of support, supporter)* fidélité *f*, loyauté *f* (**d**) *(bravery)* vaillance *f*, courage *m*; **stoutness of heart** vaillance *f*, courage *m*

stove [stəʊv] **1** *pt & pp of* **stave**

2 *n* (**a**) *(for heating)* poêle *m* (**b**) *(cooker* → *gen)* cuisinière *f*; *(*→ *portable)* réchaud *m*; *(kitchen range)* fourneau *m* (**c**) *Ind (kiln)* four *m*, étuve *f*

►► ***stove enamel*** laque *f ou* vernis *m* à cuire

stove-in *adj Am* défoncé, enfoncé

stovepipe ['stəʊvpaɪp] **1** *n* (**a**) tuyau *m* de poêle (**b**) *Fam* **stovepipe (hat)** tuyau *m* de poêle

2 stovepipes *npl Br (trousers)* pantalon-cigarette *m*

stovies ['stəʊvɪz] *npl Culin* = ragoût écossais de pommes de terre et d'oignons

stow [stəʊ] *vt* (**a**) *(store)* ranger, stocker; *(in warehouse)* emmagasiner; *Naut (cargo)* arrimer; *(equipment, sails)* ranger; **where do you stow the coffee?** où rangez-vous le café?; **he stowed the keys behind the clock** *(hid)* il a caché les clés derrière la pendule; *(hurriedly)* il a fait disparaître les clés derrière la pendule

(**b**) *(pack, fill)* remplir

(**c**) *Br very Fam (idiom)* **stow it!** *(stop)* ça suffit!; *(shut up)* la ferme!

►**stow away 1** *vi (on ship, plane)* s'embarquer clandestinement, être passager clandestin; **I stowed away to Brazil** je me suis embarqué clandestinement pour le Brésil

2 *vt sep* (**a**) = **stow** (**a**)

(**b**) *Br Fam (food)* enfourner; **he can certainly stow it away!** qu'est-ce qu'il descend!

stowage ['stəʊɪdʒ] *n* (**a**) *(of goods* → *in warehouse)* emmagasinage *m*; *Naut (*→ *on ship)* arrimage *m*; *(cost)* frais *mpl* d'arrimage (**b**) *(capacity* → *gen)* espace *m* utile *ou* de rangement; *(*→ *in warehouse)* espace *m* d'emmagasinage; *(*→ *on ship)* espace *m* d'arrimage

stowaway ['stəʊəweɪ] *n* passager *m* clandestin, passagère *f* clandestine

strabismal [strə'bɪzməl], **strabismic** [strə'bɪzmɪk] *adj Med* strabique

strabismus [strə'bɪzməs] *n Med* strabisme *m*

Strad [stræd] *n Fam* stradivarius❑ *m*

straddle ['strædəl] **1** *vt* (**a**) *(sit astride of* → *horse, bicycle)* chevaucher; *(*→ *wall, chair)* se mettre à califourchon sur; *(mount* → *horse, bicycle)* enfourcher; *(step over* → *ditch, obstacle)* enjamber

(**b**) *(span, spread over)* enjamber; **the bridge straddles the river** le pont enjambe la rivière; **the park straddles the state line** le parc est à cheval sur la frontière entre les États; **their empire straddled the Mediterranean** leur empire englobait la Méditerranée; **a company that straddles two continents** une entreprise qui a des intérêts dans deux continents

(**c**) *Mil (target)* encadrer

(**d**) *Am Fam* **to straddle the fence** *(be noncommittal)* ne pas prendre position❑; **you can't straddle the fence** vous devez prendre position

2 *vi Am Fam Fig (sit on the fence)* ne pas prendre position❑

3 *n St Exch* ordre *m* lié, opération *f* à cheval; **to take a straddle position** = jumeler simultanément un achat sur une époque avec une vente sur une autre

Stradivarius [,strædɪ'veərɪəs] *n* stradivarius *m*

strafe [strɑːf] *vt (with machine guns)* mitrailler en rase-mottes; *(with bombs)* bombarder (à faible altitude)

straggle ['strægəl] **1** *vi* (**a**) *(spread in long line* → *roots, creeper, branches)* pousser de façon désordonnée; *(be scattered* → *trees, houses)* être disséminé; *(hang untidily* → *hair)* pendre lamentablement; **vines straggled over the fence** la vigne envahissait la clôture; **the suburbs straggled on for miles along the railway line** la banlieue s'étendait sur des kilomètres le long de la voie ferrée; **the excavations straggled down the hillside** les fouilles s'étendaient jusqu'en bas de la colline; **her hair straggled over her forehead** des mèches pendaient lamentablement sur son front

(**b**) *(linger)* traîner, traînasser; **she was straggling behind all the others** elle traînassait derrière tous les autres; **stop straggling! do try and keep up!** ne traînez pas! essayez de rester groupés!; **to straggle in/out** entrer/sortir de manière dispersée *ou* par petits groupes; **the crowd began to straggle away from the scene** la foule commença à se disperser petit à petit

2 *n* **there was a constant straggle of visitors** il y a eu un défilé ininterrompu de visiteurs; **all I saw was a straggle of houses/trees on the hillside** je n'ai aperçu que quelques maisons disséminées/quelques arbres disséminés sur la colline; **a straggle of islands** un long chapelet d'îles

straggler ['stræglə(r)] *n* (**a**) *(lingerer)* traînard(e) *m,f*; *(in race)* retardataire *mf* (**b**) *Bot* gourmand *m*

straggling ['stræglɪŋ] *adj (vine, plant)* maigre, (qui pousse) tout en longueur; *(houses, trees)* épars, éparpillé; *(village, street)* tout en longueur; *(beard)* épars; **to have straggling hair** avoir les cheveux fins et ternes

straggly ['strægli] *adj (hair)* fins et ternes; *(beard)* épars; *(roots)* long (longue) et mince; **a straggly line of refugees** une file désordonnée de réfugiés

STRAIGHT [streɪt]

ligne droite	► **1 (a)**
droit	► **2 (a) – (c), (g); 3 (a) – (c)**
raide	► **2 (a)**
honnête	► **2 (c)**
franc	► **2 (c)**
clair	► **2 (d)**
en ordre	► **2 (e)**
quitte	► **2 (f)**
pur	► **2 (h)**
consécutif	► **2 (i)**
directement	► **3 (c), (d)**
franchement	► **3 (e)**

1 *n* (**a**) *(on racetrack, railway track)* ligne *f* droite; **the final** *or* **home straight** la dernière ligne droite; *Fig* **we're on the home straight now** nous sommes dans la dernière ligne droite; **to keep to the straight and narrow** rester dans le droit chemin

(**b**) *(level)* **to be out of straight** être de biais *ou* de travers; **to cut a material on the straight** couper une étoffe de droit fil

(**c**) *(in poker)* quinte *f*

(**d**) *Fam (heterosexual)* hétéro *mf*

(**e**) *Fam (conventional person)* personne *f* conventionnelle *ou* sérieuse ❑; **don't be such a straight!** sois pas si sérieux!

(**f**) *Fam Drugs slang (cigarette)* clope *f (par opposition à une cigarette de haschisch)*

2 *adj* (**a**) *(not curved → line, road, nose)* droit; *(→ hair)* raide; *Math* **a straight line** une (ligne) droite; **in a straight line** en ligne droite; **to have a straight back** avoir le dos bien droit, se tenir bien droit; **keep your back straight** tiens-toi droit, redresse-toi; *Fig* **to play with** *or* **to keep a straight bat** se conduire honorablement

(**b**) *(level, upright)* droit; **the picture isn't straight** le tableau n'est pas droit *ou* est de travers; **is my tie straight?** est-ce que ma cravate est droite?; **to put** *or* **to set straight** *(picture)* remettre d'aplomb, redresser; *(hat, tie)* ajuster; **hold** *or* **keep the tray straight** tenez le plateau bien droit

(**c**) *(honest → person)* honnête, droit; *(frank → person, answer)* franc (franche); **straight as a die** d'une droiture *ou* honnêteté absolue; **he's always been straight in his dealings with me** il a toujours été honnête avec moi; **to be straight with sb** être franc avec qn; **are you being straight with me?** est-ce que tu joues franc jeu avec moi?; **to play a straight game** jouer franc jeu; **to give sb a straight answer** répondre franchement à qn; **to have a straight talk about sth** parler franchement de qch; **to do some straight talking** parler franchement; **at the meeting he did some straight talking** il n'a pas mâché ses mots à la réunion; **it's time we did some straight talking** il faut qu'on parle, tous les deux; *Am Fam* **a straight shooter** une personne franche ❑; *Am Fam* **a straight arrow** *(man)* un brave type; *(woman)* une brave femme; **he's a straight arrow** *(person of integrity)* on peut compter sur lui ❑; *(too conventional)* il est un peu coincé

(**d**) *(correct, clear)* clair; **to put** *or* **to set the record straight** mettre les choses au clair; **just to set the record straight** pour que ce soit bien clair; **I'd like to get things straight before I leave** je voudrais mettre les choses au clair avant de partir; **let's get this straight** entendons-nous bien là-dessus; **let's get this straight, he left at two o'clock?** mettons les choses au clair, il est parti à deux heures?; **have you put her straight?** as-tu mis les choses au point avec elle?; **you ought to put her straight about what he's (really) like** tu devrais lui dire comment il est vraiment; **now just you get this straight!** mets-toi bien ceci dans la tête!, qu'on se mette bien d'accord sur ce point!

(**e**) *(tidy, in order → room, desk, accounts)* en ordre; **to put** *or* **to set straight** *(room, house)* mettre en ordre, mettre de l'ordre dans; *(affairs, accounts)* mettre de l'ordre dans; **put your desk straight** rangez votre bureau; **put your things straight on the desk** mettez un peu d'ordre sur le bureau

(**f**) *(quits)* quitte; **here's the £5 I owe you, now we're straight** voilà les 5 livres que je te dois, maintenant nous sommes quittes; **I need five hundred pounds to get myself straight** il me faut cinq cents livres pour me remettre d'aplomb *ou* me refaire

(**g**) *(direct)* droit, direct; *Boxing* **he hit him a straight left/right** il lui a porté un direct du gauche/du droit; *Am* **to vote a straight ticket** voter pour une liste sans panachage

(**h**) *(pure, utter)* pur; **it's just straight prejudice** ce sont des préjugés, tout simplement; **it's just straight propaganda** c'est de la propagande pure et simple

(**i**) *(consecutive)* consécutif, de suite; **to have three straight wins** gagner trois fois de suite *ou* d'affilée; *Sport* **to win in three straight sets** *(in tennis)* gagner en trois sets; **he won in straight sets** *(best of three sets)* il a gagné en deux sets; *(best of five sets)* il a gagné en trois sets; **we worked for three straight days** nous avons travaillé trois jours d'affilée; **he got straight As all term** il n'a eu que de très bonnes notes tout le semestre; **a straight A student** un étudiant brillant; **a straight flush** *(in poker)* une quinte flush

(**j**) *(neat → whisky, vodka)* sec (sèche)

(**k**) *(serious)* sérieux; **to keep a straight face** garder son sérieux; **it's the first straight role she's played in years** c'est son premier rôle sérieux depuis des années

(**l**) *Fam (conventional)* conventionnel ❑, sérieux ❑

(**m**) *Fam (heterosexual)* hétéro

(**n**) *Fam* **to be straight** *(not criminal)* être rangé des voitures; *(not on drugs)* être clean

(**o**) *Aut (cylinders)* en ligne; **a straight eight engine** un moteur huit cylindres en ligne

(**p**) *Geom (angle)* plat

(**q**) *Am Fam (true)* vrai ❑; **this is the straight story of what happened** voici comment ça s'est vraiment passé

3 *adv* (**a**) *(in a straight line)* droit, en ligne droite; **try and walk straight!** essaie de marcher droit!; **the rocket shot straight up** la fusée est montée à la verticale *ou* en ligne droite; **to shoot straight** viser juste; *Fam* **to go straight** *(criminal)* se ranger des voitures

(**b**) *(upright → walk, sit, stand)* (bien) droit; **sit up straight!** tiens-toi droit *ou* redresse-toi (sur ta chaise)!

(**c**) *(directly)* (tout) droit, directement; **he looked me straight in the face/in the eye** il me regarda bien en face/droit dans les yeux; **to drink straight from the bottle** boire à (même) la bouteille; **it's straight across the road** c'est juste en face; **the car came straight at me** la voiture a foncé droit sur moi; **the ball went straight through the window** la balle est passée par la fenêtre; **the knife went straight through my arm** le couteau m'a transpercé le bras; **we drove straight through Nantes** nous avons traversé Nantes sans nous arrêter; **to read a book straight through** *(from beginning to end)* lire un livre d'un bout à l'autre; *(without stopping)* lire un livre d'une traite; **he looked straight through me** il m'a regardé sans me voir; **it went straight to his heart** cela lui est allé droit au cœur; **straight ahead** tout droit; **where's the crossroads? – it's straight ahead** où se trouve le carrefour? – c'est tout droit devant vous; **he looked straight ahead** il regarda droit devant lui; **straight on** tout droit; **go straight on till you come to a roundabout** continuez tout droit jusqu'à ce que vous arriviez à un rond-point; **at the roundabout go straight over** au rond-point allez tout droit; *Fam* **to let sb have it straight** dire son fait à qn ❑; **to come straight out with sth** dire qch tout net; **she gave it me straight from the shoulder** elle me l'a dit sans ambages *ou* sans prendre de gants

(**d**) *(without delay)* directement; **come straight home after the concert!** rentre à la maison tout de suite après le concert!; **go straight to bed!** va tout de suite te coucher!; **I'll be straight back** je reviens directement; **they mostly go straight from school to university** pour la plupart, ils passent directement du lycée à l'université; **to come straight to the point** aller droit au fait; **to get straight on with one's work** se mettre directement au travail; **straight away** immédiatement, aussitôt, tout de suite; *Fam* **straight off** tout de suite ❑

(**e**) *(frankly, honestly)* franchement, carrément; **I told him straight (out) what I thought of him** je lui ai dit franchement ce que je pensais de lui; **to play straight** jouer franc jeu; *Fam* **I'm giving it to you straight** je vous le dis tout net ❑; *Br Fam* **straight up?** sans blague?; **straight up!** sans blague!, je t'assure!

(**f**) *(clearly)* **I can't see straight** je ne vois pas bien; **I can't think straight** je n'ai pas les idées claires

(**g**) *(neat, unmixed)* **to drink whisky straight** boire son whisky sec

(**h**) *(conventionally)* **to play (it) straight** *Theat* jouer de façon classique; *Mus* suivre la partition

►► *Theat* ***straight actor*** acteur(trice) *m,f* sérieux(euse); ***straight four*** *(in rowing)* quatre *m* de pointe sans barreur; *Theat* ***straight man*** *(of comedian)* faire-valoir *m inv*; *Theat* ***straight part*** rôle *m* sérieux; *Am* ***straight razor*** rasoir *m* à main; ***straight theatre*** le théâtre traditionnel; *Am Pol* ***straight ticket*** liste *f* non panachée

straight-arm **1** *vt* raffûter

2 *adj*

►► ***straight-arm tackle*** *(in American football)* raffût *m*

straightaway [,streɪtə'weɪ] **1** *adv* tout de suite, sur-le-champ

2 *adj Am* droit

3 *n Am* ligne *f* droite

straight-cut *adj (tobacco)* = en tranches coupées dans le sens de la longueur des feuilles

straightedge ['streɪtedʒ] *n (gen)* règle *f*; *(in carpentry)* limande *f*

straight-edge *adj Am Fam (person)* sérieux ❑, rangé ❑

straight-edged *adj (blade)* à tranchant droit

straighten ['streɪtən] **1** *vt* (**a**) *(remove bend or twist from → line, wire)* redresser; *(→ nail)* redresser, défausser; *(→ wheel)* redresser, dévoiler; *(→ hair)* défriser

(**b**) *(adjust → picture)* redresser, remettre d'aplomb; *(→ tie, hat)* redresser, ajuster; *(→ hem)* arrondir, rectifier; **she straightened her back** *or* **shoulders** elle se redressa; **he had his nose straightened** il s'est fait redresser le nez

(**c**) *(tidy → room, papers)* ranger, mettre de l'ordre dans; *(organize → affairs, accounts)* mettre en ordre, mettre de l'ordre dans; **straighten your desk before you leave** rangez votre bureau avant de partir

2 *vi (person)* se dresser, se redresser; *(plant)* pousser droit; *(hair)* devenir raide; *(road)* devenir droit

►**straighten out 1** *vt sep* (**a**) *(nail, wire)* redresser; **he straightened out the crumpled bedclothes** il a remis les draps en place

(**b**) *(situation)* débrouiller, arranger; *(problem)* résoudre; *(mess, confusion)* mettre de l'ordre dans, débrouiller; **don't worry, things will straighten themselves out** ne t'en fais pas, les choses vont s'arranger

(**c**) *Fam* **to straighten sb out** *(help)* remettre qn dans la bonne voie ❑; *(punish)* remettre qn à sa place ❑; **I'll soon straighten her out!** je vais lui apprendre!

2 *vi (road)* devenir droit; *(plant)* pousser droit; *(hair)* devenir raide

►**straighten up 1** *vi (person)* se dresser, se redresser; *(plant)* pousser droit

2 *vt sep (room, papers)* ranger, mettre de l'ordre dans; *(affairs)* mettre de l'ordre dans, mettre en ordre

straightener ['streɪtənə(r)] *n* (**a**) *(person)* redresseur(euse) *m,f* (**b**) *(machine)* machine *f* à équerrer *ou* redresser (**c**) *Aviat (of wind tunnel)* grille *f*

straightening ['streɪtənɪŋ] *n* redressement *m*, redressage *m*

►► *Metal* ***straightening press*** presse *f* à dresser

straight-faced *adj* qui garde son sérieux, impassible

straightforward [ˌstreɪtˈfɔːwəd] *adj* (**a**) *(direct → person)* direct, franc (franche); *(→ explanation)* franc (franche); *(→ account)* très clair; **to give a straightforward answer to a question** répondre franchement *ou* sans détours à une question; **it's impossible to get a straightforward answer out of her** il est impossible d'obtenir d'elle une réponse nette et précise

(**b**) *(easy, simple → task, problem)* simple, facile; *(→ instructions)* clair; **it was all quite straightforward** ce n'était pas compliqué du tout

(**c**) *(pure, utter)* pur; **it's straightforward elitism** c'est de l'élitisme pur et simple

straightforwardly [ˌstreɪtˈfɔːwədlɪ] *adv* (**a**) *(honestly → act, behave)* avec franchise; *(→ answer)* franchement, sans détour (**b**) *(without complications)* simplement; **it can be assembled straightforwardly enough** le montage est assez facile; **the meeting did not go off quite as straightforwardly as hoped** la réunion ne s'est pas passée aussi bien qu'on l'avait espéré

straightforwardness [ˌstreɪtˈfɔːwədnɪs] *n* (**a**) *(directness → of person)* franchise *f* (**b**) *(simplicity → of matter, question)* simplicité *f*

straightjacket = **straitjacket**

straightlaced = **straitlaced**

straight-line *adj Econ & Fin* constant

▸▸ *Acct* ***straight-line depreciation*** amortissement *m* linéaire

straightness [ˈstreɪtnɪs] *n* (**a**) *(of line)* rectitude *f* (**b**) *(of conduct)* droiture *f*, rectitude *f*

straight-out *adj Am Fam* (**a**) *(forthright → answer)* franc (franche)❑; *(→ refusal)* catégorique❑; **he gave a straight-out answer** il a répondu franchement❑ (**b**) *(utter → liar, hypocrite)* sacré; *(→ lie, dishonesty)* pur❑; *(→ opponent, supporter)* inconditionnel❑

straight-to-video *adj (movie)* sorti directement sur cassette vidéo

straightway [ˈstreɪtweɪ] *adv Arch* tout de suite, sur-le-champ

strain [streɪn] **1** *n* (**a**) *Tech (pressure)* pression *f*; *(tension)* tension *f*; *(pull)* traction *f*; *(weight)* poids *m*; **the rope snapped under the strain** la corde a rompu sous la tension; **the weight put too much strain on the rope** le poids a exercé une trop forte tension sur la corde; **to collapse under the strain** *(bridge, animal)* s'effondrer sous le poids; **I took most of the strain** c'est moi qui ai fourni le plus gros effort; **the buttress takes the strain off the wall** le contrefort réduit la pression qui s'exerce sur le mur; **the girder can't take the strain** la poutre ne peut pas supporter cette pression; *Fig* **the war is putting a great strain on the country's resources** la guerre grève sérieusement les ressources du pays; **the new taxes take the strain off the budget** les nouveaux impôts renflouent le budget

(**b**) *(mental or physical effort)* (grand) effort *m*; *(overwork)* surmenage *m*; *(tiredness)* (grande) fatigue *f*; *(stress)* stress *m*, tension *f ou* fatigue *f* nerveuse; **he's beginning to feel/show the strain** il commence à sentir la fatigue/à donner des signes de fatigue; **I've been under great physical strain** je me suis surmené; **it was quite a strain for me to have to stand** j'ai trouvé très fatigant de devoir rester debout; **the strain of making polite conversation** l'effort que ça demande de faire la conversation à quelqu'un; **the situation has put our family under a great deal of strain** la situation a mis notre famille à rude épreuve; **recent events have placed considerable strain on their relationship** les événements récents ont mis leur relation à rude épreuve; **he can't take the strain anymore** il ne peut plus supporter cette situation stressante; **it's a terrible strain on her nerves** ses nerfs sont mis à rude épreuve; **they've been under a lot of strain recently** leurs nerfs ont été mis à rude épreuve ces derniers temps; **the arrival of a new secretary took the immediate strain off me** avec l'arrivée d'une nouvelle secrétaire, j'ai été immédiatement soulagée d'une partie de mon travail; **I couldn't stand the strain of commuting** je trouvais trop épuisant de prendre les transports en commun tous les matins

(**c**) *Med (of muscle)* froissement *m*; *(sprain → of ankle, wrist)* entorse *f*; **to give one's back a strain** se donner un tour de reins

(**d**) *(breed, variety → of animal, insect)* race *f*; *(→ of virus, bacteria)* souche *f*; *(→ of plant, grain)* variété *f*

(**e**) *(style)* genre *m*, style *m*; **his other books are all very much in the same strain** ses autres livres sont tout à fait dans le même genre *ou* dans le même style *ou* dans le même esprit

(**f**) *(streak, tendency)* fond *m*, tendance *f*; **there is a strain of madness in the family** il y a une prédisposition à la folie dans la famille; **there's a strong strain of fantasy in his novels** il y a une grande part de rêve dans ses romans

2 *vt* (**a**) *(rope, cable, girder)* tendre (fortement); *Fig (resources, economy, budget)* grever; *(patience)* mettre à l'épreuve, abuser de; *(friendship, relationship)* mettre à l'épreuve, mettre à rude épreuve; **he strained the canvas over the frame** il a tendu la toile sur le cadre; **to be strained to breaking point** être tendu au point de se rompre; **this new expense is straining our income to the limit** nos revenus nous permettent tout juste cette dépense supplémentaire

(**b**) *(force → voice)* forcer; **he strained his ears to hear what they were saying** il tendit l'oreille pour entendre ce qu'ils disaient; **to strain one's eyes to see sth** plisser les yeux pour mieux voir qch; **to strain every nerve** *or* **sinew to do sth** s'efforcer de faire qch

(**c**) *(hurt, damage → eyes)* fatiguer; **reading small print strains your eyes** ça fatigue les yeux de lire des petits caractères; **you'll strain your eyes** tu vas te fatiguer les yeux; **to strain a muscle** se froisser un muscle; **I have to be careful not to strain my heart** il faut que je veille à ménager mon cœur; **to strain one's back** se donner un tour de reins; **I've strained my arm** je me suis froissé un muscle du bras; **to strain oneself** *(by gymnastics, lifting)* se froisser un muscle; *(by overwork)* se surmener; **mind you don't strain yourself lifting that typewriter** attention de ne pas te faire mal en soulevant cette machine à écrire; *Ironic* **don't strain yourself!** surtout ne te fatigue pas!; **she lent a hand, but she didn't exactly strain herself** elle a mis la main à la pâte, mais elle ne s'est pas vraiment fatiguée

(**d**) *(distort → meaning)* forcer; *(→ word)* forcer le sens de; **it would be straining the truth to call the play a masterpiece** dire que cette pièce est un chef-d'œuvre serait exagéré

(**e**) *Culin (soup, milk)* passer; *(vegetables)* (faire) égoutter

(**f**) *Tech (deform → part)* déformer

(**g**) *Literary (press → child, lover)* serrer; **she strained the child to her breast** elle serra l'enfant contre sa poitrine

3 *vi* (**a**) *(pull)* tirer fort; *(push)* pousser fort; **she was straining at the door** *(pulling)* elle tirait sur la porte de toutes ses forces; *(pushing)* elle poussait (sur) la porte de toutes ses forces; **to strain at a rope/at the oars** tirer sur une corde/sur les rames; **the dog strained at the leash** le chien tirait sur sa laisse; *Fig* **to be straining at the leash** piaffer d'impatience; **I had to strain against the wind** j'ai dû lutter contre le vent; **she strained under the weight** elle ployait sous la charge

(**b**) *(strive)* s'efforcer, faire beaucoup d'efforts; **to strain to do sth** s'efforcer de faire qch; **I strained to understand/hear what they were saying** je me suis efforcé de comprendre/d'entendre ce qu'ils disaient; **he tends to strain after effect** il a tendance à vouloir se faire remarquer

(**c**) *(be under tension → rope, cable)* se tendre; *(→ beam)* fatiguer, travailler; *(become deformed)* gauchir, se fausser

(**d**) *(liquid)* filtrer (**through** à travers)

(**e**) *Literary* **to strain at sth** *(be unwilling)* se faire un scrupule de qch; **to strain at doing sth** avoir des scrupules à faire qch

4 strains *npl (of music)* accents *mpl*, accords *mpl*; **the crowd rose to the strains of the national anthem** le public s'est levé aux accents de l'hymne national

▸**strain off** *vt sep (liquid)* vider, égoutter

strained [streɪnd] *adj* (**a**) *(forced → manner, laugh)* forcé, contraint; *(→ voice)* forcé; *(→ language, style, interpretation)* forcé, exagéré; **she gave me a strained smile** elle m'adressa un sourire contraint *ou* forcé

(**b**) *(tense → atmosphere, relations, person)* tendu

(**c**) *(sprained → ankle, limb)* foulé; *(→ muscle)* froissé; **to have a strained shoulder** s'être froissé un muscle à l'épaule; **to have a strained neck** avoir un torticolis

(**d**) *(tired → eyes)* fatigué; **his eyes looked strained** il avait l'air d'avoir les yeux fatigués

(**e**) *Culin (liquid)* filtré; *(soup)* passé; *(vegetables)* égoutté; *(baby food)* en purée

strainer [ˈstreɪnə(r)] *n* passoire *f*

strait [streɪt] **1** *n Geog* **strait, straits** détroit *m*

2 *adj Arch* étroit

3 straits *npl (difficulties)* gêne *f*, situation *f* fâcheuse; **to be in financial straits** avoir des ennuis financiers *ou* des problèmes d'argent

▸▸ ***the Straits of Dover*** le pas de Calais; ***the Strait of Gibraltar*** le détroit de Gibraltar; ***the Strait of Hormuz*** *or* ***of Ormuz*** le détroit d'Hormuz *ou* d'Ormuz; ***the Strait of Magellan*** le détroit de Magellan; ***the Strait of Malacca*** le détroit de Malacca

straitened [ˈstreɪtənd] *adj* **in straitened circumstances** dans le besoin *ou* la gêne

straitjacket [ˈstreɪtˌdʒækɪt] **1** *n* camisole *f* de force; *Fig* **a financial straitjacket** un carcan financier

2 *vt Fig* gêner, entraver; **to be straitjacketed by a lack of investment/by censorship** être bloqué par le manque d'investissement/par la censure

straitlaced [ˌstreɪtˈleɪst] *adj* collet monté *(inv)*; **he was always very proper and straitlaced** il était toujours très correct et très collet monté

strake [streɪk] *n* (**a**) *Tech (on wheel)* sabot *m* antidérapant, crampon *m* (d'adhérence) (**b**) *Naut* virure *f*

stramonium [strəˈməʊnɪəm] *n* (**a**) *Bot* stramoine *f*, stramonium *m* (**b**) *Pharm* stramonine *f*

strand [strænd] **1** *n* (**a**) *(of thread, string, wire)* brin *m*, toron *m*; *(of cotton)* brin *m*; **a strand of hair** une mèche de cheveux

(**b**) *(in argument, plot, sequence)* fil *m*; **the main strand of the narrative** le fil conducteur (du récit)

(**c**) *Ir or Literary (beach)* plage *f*; *(shore)* grève *f*, rivage *m*

2 *vt* (**a**) *(ship, whale)* échouer; **the ship was stranded on a mudbank** le bateau s'est échoué sur un banc de vase

(**b**) *(usu passive)* **to be stranded** *(person, vehicle)* rester en plan *ou* coincé; **she was stranded in Seville with no money** elle s'est retrouvée coincée à Séville sans un sou vaillant; **we were left stranded with no way of getting home** on est restés en plan sans aucun moyen de rentrer chez nous

3 Strand *n* **the Strand** = quartier du centre de Londres célèbre pour ses théâtres

stranded [ˈstrændɪd] *adj* (**a**) *(person, car)* bloqué; **the stranded holidaymakers camped out in the airport** les vacanciers, ne pouvant pas partir, campèrent à l'aéroport (**b**) *Biol & Chem (molecule, sequence)* torsadé

strange [streɪndʒ] *adj* (**a**) *(odd)* étrange, bizarre; *(peculiar)* singulier, insolite; **it's strange that he should be so late** c'est bizarre *ou* étrange qu'il ait tant de retard; **she has some strange ideas** elle a des idées bizarres *ou* de drôles d'idées; **strange beasts** bêtes *fpl* fantastiques; **it was strange to see her in a dress** ça faisait bizarre *ou* drôle de la voir en robe; **it feels strange to be back in Scotland again** cela me fait bizarre d'être de retour en Écosse; **it's bound to feel a little strange at first** c'est forcé que ça te fasse bizarre au début; **strange to say, I've never been there** chose curieuse *ou* étrange, je n'y suis jamais allé; **strange as it may seem** aussi étrange que cela paraisse *ou* puisse paraître; **truth is stranger than fiction** la vérité dépasse la fiction

(**b**) *(unfamiliar)* inconnu; **to find oneself in strange surroundings** se trouver dans un endroit inconnu; **strange faces** des visages inconnus; **I woke up to find a strange man in my room** lorsque je me suis réveillé il y avait un

str–str

inconnu dans ma chambre; **she awoke in a strange bed** elle s'est réveillée dans un lit qui n'était pas le sien; **I can never sleep in a strange bed** je n'arrive pas à dormir quand je ne suis pas dans mon lit; **a strange car was seen in the neighbourhood earlier in the week** en début de semaine on avait remarqué la présence dans le voisinage d'une voiture qu'on ne connaissait pas

(**c**) *(unaccustomed)* **he is still strange to city life** il n'est pas encore accoutumé à *ou* il n'a pas encore l'habitude de la vie citadine

(**d**) *(unwell)* bizarre; **to look/to feel strange** avoir l'air/se sentir bizarre

(**e**) *Phys (matter, particle)* étrange

strangely ['streɪndʒlɪ] *adv* étrangement, bizarrement; **strangely enough, I never saw him again** chose curieuse *ou* chose étrange, je ne l'ai jamais revu; **her face was strangely familiar to him** son visage lui était singulièrement familier; **he spoke in a strangely calm voice** il parla d'une voix étonnamment calme

strangeness ['streɪndʒnɪs] *n* (**a**) *(of person, situation)* étrangeté *f*, bizarrerie *f*, singularité *f* (**b**) *Phys* étrangeté *f*

stranger ['streɪndʒə(r)] *n* (**a**) *(unknown person)* inconnu(e) *m,f*; **never talk to strangers** ne parle jamais à des inconnus; **we are complete strangers** nous ne nous sommes jamais rencontrés; **we were strangers until yesterday** nous ne nous connaissons que depuis hier; **a perfect stranger** un parfait inconnu; **they greeted each other for all the world like perfect strangers** ils se sont salués comme de parfaits étrangers; **she has become a stranger to her own family** elle est devenue une étrangère pour sa propre famille; **you've become quite a stranger round here** on ne vous voit plus beaucoup par ici *ou* dans les parages; **don't be a stranger!** donne des nouvelles!; *Hum* **hello stranger!** tiens, un revenant!

(**b**) *(person from elsewhere)* étranger(ère) *m,f*; **strangers to the town often get lost** les étrangers se perdent souvent dans cette ville; **I'm a stranger here myself** je ne suis pas d'ici non plus; **little stranger** *(newborn baby)* nouveau-né(e) *m,f*; **I spy strangers!** *(in House of Commons)* je demande le huis clos!

(**c**) *(novice)* novice *mf*; **I am not exactly a stranger to jazz** je ne suis pas complètement ignorant en matière de jazz; **he is no stranger to loneliness/misfortune** il sait ce qu'est la solitude/le malheur; **no stranger to controversy, he...** étant habitué aux polémiques, il...

▸▸ ***Strangers' Gallery*** = la tribune du public à la Chambre des communes et à la Chambre des lords

'Strangers on a Train' *Hitchcock, Highsmith*
'L'Inconnu du Nord-Express'

Strangeways ['streɪndʒweɪz] *n* = prison à Manchester

strangle ['stræŋgəl] *vt* (**a**) étrangler; **I could cheerfully have strangled that child** ce n'est pas l'envie qui me manquait d'étrangler cet enfant (**b**) *Fig (opposition, growth, originality)* étrangler, étouffer

strangled ['stræŋgəld] *adj (cry, sob)* étranglé, étouffé; *(voice)* étranglé

stranglehold ['stræŋgəlhəʊld] *n (grip around throat)* étranglement *m*, étouffement *m*, strangulation *f*; *(in wrestling)* étranglement *m*; *also Fig* **to have a stranglehold on sb** tenir qn à la gorge; *Fig* **to have a stranglehold on sth** avoir la mainmise sur qch; **they have a stranglehold on the government** ils tiennent le gouvernement à leur merci; **superstition still retains a stranglehold on the country** l'emprise des superstitions sur le pays est toujours très forte; **to have a stranglehold on the market/economy** jouir d'un monopole sur le marché/l'économie

strangler ['stræŋglə(r)] *n* étrangleur(euse) *m,f*

strangles ['stræŋgəlz] *n Vet* gourme *f*

strangling ['stræŋglɪŋ] *n* (**a**) *(killing)* étranglement *m*, strangulation *f*; *Fig (of opposition, protest, originality)* étranglement *m*, étouffement *m* (**b**) *(case)* **there has been yet another strangling** une nouvelle victime a été étranglée; **that brings to five the number of stranglings** cela porte à cinq le nombre de personnes étranglées

strangulate ['stræŋgjʊleɪt] *vt* (**a**) *Med* étrangler (**b**) = **strangle**

strangulated ['stræŋgjʊleɪtɪd] *adj* étranglé

▸▸ *Med* ***strangulated hernia*** hernie *f* étranglée

strangulation [ˌstræŋgjʊ'leɪʃən] *n* strangulation *f*; **the victim died of strangulation** la victime est morte étranglée; *Fig* **economic strangulation** asphyxie *f* économique

strangury ['stræŋgjʊrɪ] *n Med* strangurie *f*

strap [stræp] *(pt & pp* **strapped,** *cont* **strapping**) **1** *n* (**a**) *(belt → of leather)* courroie *f*, sangle *f*, lanière *f*; *(→ of cloth, metal)* sangle *f*, bande *f*

(**b**) *(for carrying → of bag, harness)* sangle *f*; *(→ of shoulder bag or camera)* bandoulière *f*; *(fastening → for dress, bra)* bretelle *f*; *(→ for hat, bonnet)* bride *f*; *(→ for helmet)* attache *f*; *(→ for sandal)* lanière *f*; *(→ under trouser leg)* sous-pied *m*; *(→ for watch)* bracelet *m*

(**c**) *(as punishment)* **to give sb the strap** administrer à qn une correction (à coups de ceinture); **to get the strap** recevoir une correction (à coups de ceinture)

(**d**) *(on bus, underground)* poignée *f*

(**e**) *(for razor)* cuir *m* (à rasoir)

(**f**) *Tech* lien *m*

2 *vt* attacher *(avec une sangle)*; **she had a knife strapped to her leg** elle portait un couteau attaché à sa jambe

▸**strap down** *vt sep* sangler, attacher avec une sangle *ou* une courroie

▸**strap in** *vt sep (in car)* attacher la ceinture (de sécurité) de; *(child → in high chair, pram)* attacher avec un harnais *ou* avec une ceinture; **let me strap you in** laisse-moi attacher ta ceinture; **he strapped himself into the driving seat** il s'est installé au volant et a attaché sa ceinture de sécurité; **are you strapped in?** as-tu mis ta ceinture?

▸**strap on** *vt sep (bag, watch)* attacher; **the diver strapped his aqualung on** le plongeur mit son scaphandre

▸**strap up** *vt sep (suitcase, parcel)* sangler; *Br (limbs, ribs)* mettre un bandage à, bander

straphang ['stræphæŋ] *vi Br Fam* voyager debout ☐ *(en se tenant à la courroie ou à la poignée, dans les transports en commun)*

straphanger ['stræphæŋə(r)] *n Br Fam* voyageur(euse) *m,f* debout ☐ *(qui se tient à la courroie ou à la poignée, dans les transports en commun)*

strapless ['stræplɪs] *adj (dress, bra etc)* sans bretelles

▸▸ ***strapless top*** bustier *m*

strapline ['stræplaɪn] *n* (**a**) *Press* sous-titre *m* (**b**) *Mktg* signature *f*

strappado [strə'pɑːdəʊ] *(pl* **strappadoes**) *n Hist* estrapade *f*

strapped [stræpt] *adj Fam* (**a**) *(lacking money)* **to be strapped (for cash)** être fauché, ne pas avoir un rond (**b**) *Am (armed)* armé ☐, chargé

strapper ['stræpə(r)] *n Fam* costaud(e) *m,f*

strapping ['stræpɪŋ] *adj Fam* costaud; **strapping fellow** grand gaillard; **a fine strapping girl** un beau brin de fille

strappy ['stræpɪ] *adj (shoes)* à lanières; *(dress, top)* à bretelles

strap-work *n Archit* entrelacs *m*, tresse *f*

Strasbourg ['stræzbɜːg] *n* Strasbourg

strass [stræs] *n* strass *m*

strata ['strɑːtə] *pl of* **stratum**

stratagem ['strætədʒəm] *n* stratagème *m*

strategic [strə'tiːdʒɪk] *adj* stratégique; **we decided on a strategic withdrawal of our troops** nous avons décidé d'opérer un repli stratégique de nos troupes; **a strategic position** une position stratégique

▸▸ ***strategic business unit*** domaine *m* d'activité stratégique; *Mil* ***Strategic Defense Initiative*** initiative *f* de défense stratégique; ***strategic marketing*** marketing *m* stratégique; ***strategic management*** gestion *f* stratégique; ***strategic planning*** planification *f* stratégique; *Mktg* ***strategic targeting*** ciblage *m* stratégique; *Mktg* ***strategic withdrawal*** *(of product, campaign)* repli *m* stratégique

strategically [strə'tiːdʒɪklɪ] *adv* stratégiquement, du point de vue de la stratégie; **strategically placed** *(country, town)* situé à un endroit stratégique; *Hum (object)* placé à un endroit stratégique

strategics [strə'tiːdʒɪks] *n (UNCOUNT) Mil* (l'art *m* de la) stratégie *f*

strategist ['strætɪdʒɪst] *n* stratège *m*

strategy ['strætɪdʒɪ] *(pl* **strategies**) *n (gen) & Mil* stratégie *f*; **marketing strategies** stratégies *fpl* de marketing

strath [stræθ] *n Scot* vallée *f*

Strathclyde [ˌstræθ'klaɪd] *n* le Strathclyde, = région de l'ouest de l'Écosse; **in Strathclyde** dans le Strathclyde

strathspey [ˌstræθ'speɪ] *n Mus* branle *m* écossais

strati ['streɪtaɪ] *pl of* **stratus**

straticulate [strə'tɪkjʊleɪt] *adj Geol* en couches minces et régulières

stratification [ˌstrætɪfɪ'keɪʃən] *n* stratification *f*

stratificational [ˌstrætɪfɪ'keɪʃənəl] *adj Ling* stratificationnel

stratified ['strætɪfaɪd] *adj* stratifié

▸▸ ***stratified sample*** échantillon *m* stratifié; ***stratified sampling*** échantillonnage *m* stratifié

stratiform ['strætɪfɔːm] *adj* stratiforme

stratify ['strætɪfaɪ] *(pt & pp* **stratified**) **1** *vt* stratifier

2 *vi* se stratifier

stratigrapher [strə'tɪgrəfə(r)] *n Geol* stratigraphe *mf*

stratigraphic [ˌstrætɪ'græfɪk], **stratigraphical** [ˌstrætɪ'græfɪkəl] *adj Geol* stratigraphique

stratigraphy [strə'tɪgrəfɪ] *n Geol* stratigraphie *f*

stratocirrus [ˌstrætəʊ'sɪrəs] *n Met* cirrostratus *m*

stratocumulus [ˌstrætəʊ'kjuːmjʊləs] *(pl* **stratocumuli** [-laɪ]) *n Met* strato-cumulus *m inv*

stratopause ['strætəʊpɔːz] *n Met* stratopause *f*

stratosphere ['strætəˌsfɪə(r)] *n* stratosphère *f*

stratospheric [ˌstrætə'sferɪk] *adj* stratosphérique

stratum ['strɑːtəm] *(pl* **strata** [-tə]) *n* (**a**) *Geol* strate *f*, couche *f* (**b**) *Fig* couche *f*; **the various strata of society** les différentes couches de la société

stratus ['streɪtəs] *(pl* **strati** [-taɪ]) *n Met* stratus *m*

Stravinsky [strə'vɪnskɪ] *pr n* Stravinski, Stravinsky

straw [strɔː] **1** *n* (**a**) *Agr* paille *f*; *Br Fig* **man of straw** homme *m* de paille

(**b**) *(for drinking)* paille *f*; **to drink sth through a straw** boire qch avec une paille

(**c**) *(idioms)* **to catch** *or* **to clutch at a straw** *or* **at straws** se raccrocher désespérément à la moindre lueur d'espoir; **you're just grasping at straws** vous vous raccrochez à de faux espoirs; **to draw** *or* **to get the short straw** être tiré au sort, être de corvée; **a straw in the wind** un aperçu (de ce que l'avenir nous réserve); **that's the last straw** *or* **the straw that breaks the camel's back** c'est la goutte d'eau qui fait déborder le vase; **it's the last straw!** ça c'est le comble *ou* le bouquet!; *Br Fam* **I don't care a straw** *or* **two straws!** je m'en fiche!; *Fam* **it's not worth a straw** ça ne vaut pas un clou

2 *comp (gen)* de *ou* en paille; *(roof)* en paille, en chaume

▸▸ *Am* ***straw boss*** homme *m* de terrain; ***straw hat*** chapeau *m* de paille; *Am Fig* ***straw man*** homme *m* de paille; ***straw mat*** paillasson *m*; ***straw mattress*** paillasse *f*; *Am* ***straw poll, straw vote*** *(vote)* vote *m* blanc; *(opinion poll)* sondage *m* d'opinion

strawberry ['strɔːbərɪ] *(pl* **strawberries**) **1** *n (fruit)* fraise *f*; *(plant)* fraisier *m*; **wild strawberry,** *Am* **field strawberry** fraise des bois

2 *comp (jam)* de fraises; *(tart)* aux fraises; *(ice cream)* à la fraise

▸▸ ***strawberry bed*** planche *f ou* plant *m* de fraisiers; ***strawberry blonde*** **1** *adj* blond vénitien *(inv)* **2** *n* blonde *f* qui tire sur le roux; ***strawberry field*** fraiseraie *f*; ***strawberry mark*** tache *f* de vin, envie *f*

STRAWBERRIES AND CREAM

En Grande-Bretagne, les fraises à la crème sont traditionnellement consommées lors de certaines manifestations en plein air, notamment au tournoi de tennis de Wimbledon.

strawboard ['strɔːbɔːd] *n* carton-paille *m*

straw-coloured *adj* (couleur) paille *(inv)*

stray [streɪ] **1** *vi* (**a**) *(child, animal)* s'égarer; **some sheep had strayed onto the railway line** des moutons s'étaient aventurés sur la ligne de chemin de fer; **the children strayed (away) from the rest of the group** les enfants se sont écartés du groupe; **the plane had strayed off course** l'avion s'était écarté de sa route; **we strayed into what must have been the red light area** nous nous sommes retrouvés dans ce qui devait être le quartier des prostituées; *also Fig* **to stray from the fold** s'écarter du troupeau; **to stray (away) from the right path** faire fausse route; *Fig* s'écarter du droit chemin

(**b**) *(speaker, writer)* s'éloigner du sujet; **but I am straying from the point** mais je m'écarte du sujet

(**c**) *(thoughts)* errer, vagabonder; **her thoughts strayed (back) to her days in Japan** elle se mit à penser à sa vie au Japon

2 *n (dog)* chien *m* errant *ou* perdu; *(cat)* chat *m* errant *ou* perdu; *(cow, sheep)* animal *m* égaré; *(child)* enfant *m* perdu *ou* abandonné; **she set up a home for strays** elle a ouvert un centre pour recueillir les chiens et les chats perdus

3 *adj* (**a**) *(lost → dog, cat)* perdu, errant; *(→ cow, sheep)* égaré; *(→ child)* perdu, abandonné

(**b**) *(random → bullet)* perdu; *(→ thought)* vagabond; *(→ memory)* fugitif; **she pushed back a few stray curls** elle repoussa quelques mèches folles *ou* rebelles

(**c**) *(occasional → car, boat)* isolé, rare; **a few stray cars drove by** quelques rares voitures passaient par là

4 strays *npl Rad & Tel* parasites *mpl*, friture *f*

streak [stri:k] **1** *n* (**a**) *(smear → of blood)* filet *m*; *(→ of dirt, ink, paint)* traînée *f*; *(line, stripe → of light)* trait *m*, rai *m*; *(→ of ore)* filon *m*, veine *f*; *(→ in marble)* veine *f*; **there were streaks of green ink across the page** il y avait des traînées d'encre verte sur la page; **there were a few streaks of cloud in an otherwise blue sky** il y avait quelques traînées nuageuses dans le ciel bleu; **the first streaks of dawn** les premières lueurs de l'aube; **the tears had left grubby streaks down her face** les larmes avaient laissé des traînées sales sur ses joues; **black wings with white streaks** des ailes noires avec des traînées blanches; **the carpet has green streaks** la moquette est striée de vert; **her hair has grey streaks in it** elle a des cheveux gris; **to have blond streaks put in one's hair** se faire faire des mèches blondes; **streaks of lightning lit up the sky** des éclairs zébraient le ciel; **they drove past like a streak of lightning** leur voiture est passée comme un éclair

(**b**) *(of luck)* période *f*; **I've had a streak of (good) luck** j'ai eu de la chance; **he's hit a winning streak, he's on a winning streak** *(in gambling)* la chance lui sourit; *(good deal)* il tient un bon filon; **to be on a losing streak** *(in gambling) & Fig* être dans une mauvaise passe; **he's just had a streak of bad luck lately** il vient d'essuyer toute une série de revers

(**c**) *(tendency, trace)* côté *m*; **he has a mean streak** *or* **a streak of meanness in him** il a un côté mesquin; **there was a streak of cowardice in him** il avait un côté lâche; **there has always been a streak of madness in the family** il y a toujours eu une prédisposition à la folie dans la famille; **there's a streak of Indian blood in the family** il y a un peu de sang indien dans la famille

(**d**) *Fam (naked dash)* **to do a streak** = traverser un lieu public nu en courant

(**e**) *Br very Fam* **he's a long streak of piss** *(tall and thin)* c'est une grande perche; *(insipid in character)* c'est une lavette

2 *vt (smear)* tacher; *(stripe)* strier, zébrer; **the wall was streaked with paint** il y avait des traînées de peinture sur le mur; **her hands were streaked with blue ink** elle avait des taches d'encre bleue sur les mains; **the mirror was streaked with finger marks** il y avait des traces de doigts sur le miroir; **the sink was streaked with coffee stains** il y avait des taches de café partout dans l'évier; **their cheeks were streaked with tears** leurs joues étaient couvertes de larmes; **the carpet is streaked with green** la moquette est striée de vert; **marble streaked with red** du marbre strié de rouge; **fur streaked with black** pelage rayé de noir; **her hair is streaked with grey** *(natural)* elle a des cheveux gris; *(artificial)* elle s'est fait des mèches grises; **she's had her hair streaked** elle s'est fait faire des mèches

3 *vi* (**a**) *(go quickly)* **to streak in/out** entrer/sortir comme un éclair; **to streak off** partir à toute allure; **to streak past** passer en trombe

(**b**) *(run naked)* = traverser un lieu public nu en courant; **he was arrested for streaking** ≃ il a été arrêté pour exhibitionnisme

streaked [stri:kt] *adj* (**a**) *(pattern, surface)* rayé, strié (**b**) *(meat)* entrelardé, persillé (**c**) *Am (person)* agité, énervé

streaker ['stri:kə(r)] *n* = personne nue qui traverse un lieu public en courant

streaking ['stri:kɪŋ] *n* (**a**) *(streaks)* raies *fpl*, rayures *fpl*, bandes *fpl*; *(in hairdressing)* effet *m* de mèches (**b**) *Fam* = pratique consistant à traverser un lieu public nu en courant

streaky ['stri:kɪ] *(compar* **streakier**, *superl* **streakiest**) *adj* (**a**) *(colour, surface)* marbré, zébré, jaspé; *(rock, marble)* veiné; *(glass, window)* couvert de traînées; **streaky pattern** stries *fpl*, zébrures *fpl*; **streaky clouds** de longues traînées nuageuses; **her make-up had gone streaky** son maquillage avait dégouliné

(**b**) *Culin (meat)* entrelardé, persillé

(**c**) *Am (person)* agité, énervé

►► *Br Culin* ***streaky bacon*** bacon *m* entrelardé

stream [stri:m] **1** *n* (**a**) *(brook)* ruisseau *m*; **mountain stream** torrent *m*

(**b**) *(current)* courant *m*; **to go with the stream** aller au fil de l'eau; *Fig* suivre le courant *ou* le mouvement; *also Fig* **to go against the stream** aller à contre-courant

(**c**) *(flow → of liquid)* flot *m*, jet *m*; *(→ of air)* courant *m*; *(→ of blood, lava)* ruisseau *m*, flot *m*, cascade *f*, torrent *m*; *(→ of people, traffic)* flot *m*, défilé *m* (continu); *(→ of tears)* ruisseau *m*, torrent *m*; **the vent sent out a stream of hot air** du conduit s'échappait un courant d'air chaud; **a stream of water shot out of the tap** l'eau jaillit à flot du robinet; **a red hot stream of lava flowed down the mountain** une coulée de lave incandescente descendait le flanc de la montagne; **there was a continuous stream of visitors** il y avait un défilé continu *ou* ininterrompu de visiteurs; **streams of wellwishers have been arriving all day** des flots de sympathisants sont arrivés tout au long de la journée; **we've received a steady stream of applications** nous avons reçu un flot incessant de candidatures; **she unleashed a stream of insults** elle lâcha un torrent d'injures

(**d**) *Ind & Tech* **to be on/off stream** être en service/hors service; **to come on stream** être mis en service

(**e**) *Br Sch* classe *f* de niveau; **we're in the top stream** nous sommes dans la section forte

2 *vi* (**a**) *(flow → water, tears)* ruisseler, couler à flots; *(→ blood)* ruisseler; **the wall was streaming with condensation, condensation streamed down the wall** la condensation ruisselait le long du mur; **tears streamed down her face** des larmes ruisselaient sur son visage; **the onions made her eyes stream** les oignons l'ont fait pleurer; **sunlight streamed into the room** le soleil entra à flots dans la pièce

(**b**) *(flutter)* flotter, voleter; **flags were streaming in the wind** des drapeaux flottaient au vent; **her long hair streamed (out) behind her** ses longs cheveux flottaient derrière elle

(**c**) *(people, traffic)* **to stream in/out** entrer/sortir à flots; **cars streamed out of the city in their thousands** des milliers de voitures sortaient de la ville en un flot ininterrompu; **I watched as the demonstrators streamed past** je regardai passer les flots de manifestants

3 *vt* (**a**) *(flow with)* **to stream blood/tears** ruisseler de sang/de larmes

(**b**) *Br Sch* répartir en groupes de niveau

►► *Literature* ***stream of consciousness*** monologue *m* intérieur; **a stream of consciousness novel** un roman qui utilise la technique du monologue intérieur

streamer ['stri:mə(r)] *n* (**a**) *(decoration)* serpentin *m* (**b**) *(banner)* banderole *f*; *(pennant)* flamme *f* (**c**) *Astron* flèche *f* lumineuse (**d**) *Journ* manchette *f*

streamertail ['stri:mɔteɪl] *n Orn* colibri *m* à tête noire

streaming ['stri:mɪŋ] **1** *n Br Sch* répartition *f* en classes de niveau

2 *adj (surface, window, windscreen)* ruisselant; *Br* **I've got a streaming cold** j'ai attrapé un gros rhume

streamline ['stri:mlaɪn] **1** *vt* (**a**) *Aut & Aviat* donner un profil aérodynamique à, caréner (**b**) *Econ & Ind (company, production)* rationaliser; *(industry)* dégraisser, restructurer

2 *n* (**a**) *Aut & Aviat* ligne *f* aérodynamique (**b**) *Phys* écoulement *m* non perturbé

streamlined ['stri:mlaɪnd] *adj* (**a**) *Aut & Aviat* aérodynamique; *Naut (ship)* hydrodynamique; *Zool (fish, animal)* à la forme hydrodynamique (**b**) *Fig (building)* aux contours harmonieux; *(kitchen, bathroom)* aux lignes épurées; *(figure)* svelte (**c**) *Econ & Ind (company, production)* rationalisé; *(industry)* dégraissé, restructuré

streamlining ['stri:mlaɪnɪŋ] *n* (**a**) *Aut & Aviat* carénage *m* (**b**) *Econ & Ind (of business, organization)* rationalisation *f*; *(of industry)* dégraissage *m*, restructuration *f*

street [stri:t] **1** *n* rue *f*; *Br* **in** *or Am* **on a street** dans une rue; **a street of houses** une rue résidentielle; **the whole street knows about it** toute la rue est au courant; **to put** *or* **to turn sb out into the street** mettre qn à la rue; **to be on the street** *or* **streets** *(as prostitute)* faire le trottoir; *(homeless person)* être à la rue; **to take to the streets** *(protestors)* descendre dans la rue; **to walk the streets** *(as prostitute)* faire le trottoir *ou Fam* le tapin; *(from idleness)* battre le pavé, flâner dans les rues; *(in search)* faire les rues; **they walked the streets looking for her** ils ont parcouru la ville à pied à sa recherche; *Hum* **that'll keep him off the streets!** ça l'empêchera de faire des bêtises!; **that's right up his street!** *(competence)* c'est tout à fait son rayon *ou* dans ses cordes!; *(interest)* c'est tout à fait son truc!

2 *comp (noises)* de la rue; *(musician)* des rues

3 streets *adv Fam* **to be streets ahead of sb** dépasser qn de loin[❑]; **she's streets ahead of the rest of the class** elle dépasse largement *ou* de loin le reste de la classe, elle est largement en tête de la classe; **they're streets apart in the way they think** ils ne partagent pas du tout les mêmes opinions

►► *Br Old-fashioned* ***street Arab*** gamin(e) *m,f ou* gosse *mf* des rues; ***street art*** peintures *fpl* murales *(dans la rue)*; ***street atlas*** plan *m* de la ville; *Br* ***street café*** café *m* avec terrasse; **we had breakfast at a street café** nous avons pris le petit déjeuner à la terrasse d'un café; ***street cleaner*** *(person)* balayeur(euse) *m,f*; *(machine)* balayeuse *f*; *Fam* ***street cred, street credibility*** image *f* cool *ou* branchée; **she thinks that the leather jacket gives her more street cred** elle trouve que son blouson en cuir fait très branché *ou* lui donne l'air encore plus cool; **this won't do much for my street cred** ça va craindre pour mon image de marque; ***street cry*** cri *m* de colporteur; **the street cries of old Paris** le cri des colporteurs du vieux Paris; *St Exch* ***street dealing*** transactions *fpl* hors Bourse; ***street directory*** plan *m* de la ville; ***street door*** porte *f* (qui donne) sur la rue, porte *f* d'entrée; ***street fighting*** combats *mpl* de rue; ***street furniture*** mobilier *m* urbain; ***street guide*** plan *m* de la ville; ***street hawker*** colporteur(euse) *m,f*; *Am Sport* ***street hockey*** hockey *m* sur roulettes; ***street level*** rez-de-chaussée *m inv*; **below street level** au sous-sol; ***street lighting*** éclairage *m* public; **the street lighting comes on at sunset** on allume la lumière dans les rues au coucher du soleil; ***street map*** plan *m* de la ville; ***street market*** marché *m* en plein air *ou* à ciel ouvert; *St Exch* marché *m* hors Bourse; ***street musician*** musicien(enne) *m,f* des rues; ***street organ*** orgue *m* de Barbarie; ***street party*** = fête de rue organisée pour célébrer un événement; ***street person*** SDF *mf*; ***street photographer*** photostoppeur(euse) *m,f*; ***street plan*** plan *m* de la ville; *St Exch* ***street price*** cours *m* hors Bourse; *(of drugs)* prix *m* à la revente; ***street sweeper*** *(person)* balayeur(euse) *m,f*; *(machine)* balayeuse *f*; ***street theatre*** théâtre *m* de rue *ou* de foire;

street trader marchand(e) *m,f* ambulant(e); ***street trading*** vente *f* ambulante; *Old-fashioned* ***street urchin*** gamin(e) *m,f ou* gosse *mf* des rues; ***street value*** *(of drugs)* valeur *f* marchande; *Am* ***street vendor*** marchand(e) *m,f* ambulant(e)

streetcar ['striːtkɑː(r)] *n Am* tramway *m*

'A Streetcar Named Desire' *Williams, Kazan* 'Un tramway nommé Désir'

streetlamp ['striːtlæmp], **streetlight** ['striːtlaɪt] *n* réverbère *m*

streetsmart ['striːtsmɑːt] *adj Am Fam* dégourdi

streetwalker ['striːtˌwɔːkə(r)] *n Old-fashioned* prostituée *f*; **to be a streetwalker** faire le trottoir

streetwalking ['striːtˌwɔːkɪŋ] *n Old-fashioned* racolage *m*

streetwise ['striːtˌwaɪz] *adj Fam* dégourdi

strelitzia [strə'lɪtsɪə] *n Bot* strelitzia *m*

strength [streŋθ] **1** *n* (**a**) *(UNCOUNT) (physical power → of person, animal, muscle)* force *f*, puissance *f*; *(health)* forces *fpl*; **she doesn't know her own strength** elle ne connaît pas sa force; **his strength failed him** ses forces l'ont trahi *ou* abandonné; **I haven't the strength to lift these boxes** je n'ai pas assez de force *ou* je ne suis pas assez fort pour soulever ces cartons; **he has great strength in his arms/hands** il a beaucoup de force dans les bras/les mains; **to lose strength** perdre des forces, s'affaiblir; **by sheer strength** de force; **with all my strength** de toutes mes forces; **to get one's strength back** reprendre des *ou* recouvrer ses forces; **to go from strength to strength** *(sick person)* aller de mieux en mieux; *Fig (business)* être en plein essor

(**b**) *(of faith, opinion, resolution)* force *f*, fermeté *f*; *(of emotion, feeling)* force *f*; *(of music, art)* force *f*; **strength of character** force *f* de caractère; **strength of purpose** résolution *f*; **they have no strength of purpose** ils n'ont aucune détermination; **they have great strength of purpose** ils sont très déterminés; **strength of will** volonté *f*; **I haven't the strength to start again** je n'ai pas le courage de recommencer; **give me strength!** pitié!

(**c**) *(intensity → of earthquake, wind)* force *f*, intensité *f*; *(→ of current, light)* intensité *f*; *(→ of sound, voice, lens, magnet)* force *f*, puissance *f*

(**d**) *(strong point, asset)* force *f*, point *m* fort; **her ambition is her main strength** son ambition fait l'essentiel de sa force; **the nation's strength lies in its young people** ce sont les jeunes qui font la force du pays; **it's one of their strengths** c'est un de leurs points forts

(**e**) *(solidity)* solidité *f*; *Fig (of claim, position, relationship)* solidité *f*; *(vigour → of argument, protest)* force *f*, vigueur *f*; *Fin (→ of currency, economy)* solidité *f*; **to argue from a position of strength** être en position de force; **the dollar has gained/fallen in strength** le dollar s'est consolidé/a chuté

(**f**) *(of alcohol)* teneur *f* en alcool; *(of solution)* titre *m*; *(of coffee, tobacco)* force *f*; **solution at full strength, full-strength solution** solution *f* concentrée

(**g**) [illegible] effectifs *mpl*; **the office staff is below** *or* **under strength** il nous manque du personnel de bureau; **we're at full strength** nos effectifs sont au complet; **the staff must be brought up to strength** il faut engager du personnel; **the protestors turned up in strength** les manifestants sont venus en force *ou* en grand nombre

2 on the strength of *prep* en vertu de, sur la foi de; **to do sth on the strength of what one has been told** faire qch en se fiant à *ou* en s'appuyant sur ce qu'on vous a dit; **he was accepted on the strength of his excellent record** il a été accepté grâce à ses excellents antécédents; **I was convicted on the strength of the flimsiest of evidence** j'ai été condamné sur la foi de preuves bien minces

strengthen ['streŋθən] **1** *vt* (**a**) *(physically → body, muscle)* fortifier, raffermir; *(→ person)* fortifier, tonifier; *(→ voice)* renforcer; *(improve → eyesight, hearing)* améliorer; **to strengthen one's body by exercise** fortifier son corps en faisant de l'exercice; *also Fig* **to strengthen one's grip** *or* **hold on sth** resserrer son emprise sur qch

(**b**) *(reinforce → firm, nation)* renforcer; *(→ fear, emotion, effect)* renforcer, intensifier; *(→ belief, argument)* renforcer; *(→ link, friendship)* renforcer, fortifier; *(morally → person)* fortifier; **the decision strengthened my resolve** la décision n'a fait que renforcer ma détermination; **I felt strengthened by the experience** je suis sorti plus fort de cette expérience

(**c**) *(foundation, structure)* renforcer, consolider; *(material)* renforcer

(**d**) *Fin (currency, economy)* consolider, raffermir

2 *vi* (**a**) *(physically → body)* se fortifier, se raffermir; *(→ voice)* devenir plus fort; *(→ grip)* se resserrer

(**b**) *(increase → influence, effect, desire)* augmenter, s'intensifier; *(→ wind)* forcir; *(→ current)* augmenter, se renforcer; *(→ friendship, character, resolve)* se renforcer, se fortifier

(**c**) *Fin (prices, market)* se consolider, se raffermir

strengthener ['streŋθənə(r)] *n (gen)* renfort *m*; *Med* fortifiant *m*

strengthening ['streŋθənɪŋ] **1** *n* (**a**) *(physical → of body, muscle)* raffermissement *m*; *(→ of voice)* renforcement *m*; *(→ of hold, grip)* resserrement *m*

(**b**) *(increase → of emotion, effect, desire)* renforcement *m*, augmentation *f*, intensification *f*; *(reinforcement → of character, friendship, position)* renforcement *m*; *(→ of wind, current)* renforcement *m*

(**c**) *(of structure, building)* renforcement *m*, consolidation *f*; *(of material)* renforcement *m*

(**d**) *Fin* consolidation *f*

2 *adj* fortifiant, remontant; *Med* tonifiant; **to have a strengthening effect on sb** fortifier qn

strenuous ['strenjʊəs] *adj* (**a**) *(physically → activity, exercise, sport)* ardu; **it was a long, strenuous climb** ce fut une ascension longue et ardue; **I'm not allowed to do anything strenuous** je ne dois pas me fatiguer; **avoid very strenuous games like squash** évitez les sports comme le squash qui demandent une grande dépense d'énergie; **she leads a strenuous life** elle mène une vie stressante

(**b**) *(vigorous → opposition, support)* acharné, énergique; *(→ protest)* vigoureux, énergique; *(→ opponent, supporter)* zélé, très actif; **to make strenuous efforts to do sth** faire des efforts acharnés pour faire qch; **he is a strenuous campaigner for civil rights** il milite avec acharnement pour les droits civils

strenuously ['strenjʊəslɪ] *adv* (**a**) *(play, swim, work)* en se dépensant beaucoup, en faisant de gros efforts (**b**) *(fight, oppose, resist)* avec acharnement, énergiquement

strenuousness ['strenjʊəsnɪs] *n* (**a**) *(of activity, work)* dureté *f* *(de l'effort physique exigé)* (**b**) *(of opposition)* acharnement *m*

strep [strep] *Fam* **1** *n* streptocoque ▫ *m*

2 *adj (infection)* streptococcique ▫

►► ***strep throat*** gorge *f* atteinte d'une infection streptococcique ▫

strepitous ['strepɪtəs] *adj Literary* bruyant, tumultueux

streptococcal [ˌstreptə'kɒkəl], **streptococcic** [ˌstreptə'kɒksɪk] *adj* streptococcique

streptococcus [ˌstreptə'kɒkəs] (*pl* **streptococci** [-'kɒksaɪ]) *n* streptocoque *m*

streptomycin [ˌstreptə'maɪsɪn] *n* streptomycine *f*

stress [stres] **1** *n* (**a**) *(nervous tension)* stress *m*, tension *f* nerveuse; **to suffer from stress** être stressé; **to be under stress** *(person)* être stressé; *(relationship)* être tendu; **she's been under a lot of stress lately** elle a été très stressée ces derniers temps; **how does he react under stress?** comment réagit-il sous le stress *ou* sous la pression?; **it puts our relationship under stress** ça crée des tensions dans nos relations; **the stresses and strains of city life** le stress de la vie urbaine; **the stresses and strains of being a parent** les angoisses qu'on éprouve lorsqu'on a des enfants; **she copes well in times of stress** elle sait faire face dans les moments difficiles; **I always work better under stress** je travaille toujours mieux quand je suis sous pression

(**b**) *Constr & Tech* contrainte *f*, tension *f*; **to be in stress** *(beam, girder)* être sous contrainte; **there is too much stress on the foundations** la contrainte que subissent les fondations est trop forte; **we have measured the stresses produced in the metal plates** nous avons mesuré l'effort que produisent les plaques métalliques; **can the girders take the stress?** est-ce que les poutres peuvent soutenir la charge *ou* la tension?; **earthquakes are caused by subterranean stresses** les tremblements de terre sont provoqués par des tensions souterraines

(**c**) *(emphasis)* insistance *f*; **to lay stress on sth** *(fact, point, detail)* insister sur, souligner; *(qualities, values, manners)* insister sur, mettre l'accent sur; **the stress has always been on productivity** nous avons toujours mis l'accent sur la productivité

(**d**) *Ling (gen)* accentuation *f*; *(accent on syllable)* accent *m (tonique)*; *(accented syllable)* syllabe *f* accentuée; **the rules of English sentence stress** les règles d'accentuation de la phrase anglaise; **the stress is** *or* **falls on the third syllable** l'accent tombe sur la troisième syllabe; **there are three stresses in the sentence** il y a trois syllabes accentuées dans la phrase

(**e**) *Mus* accent *m*

2 *vt* (**a**) *(emphasize → fact, point, detail)* insister sur, faire ressortir, souligner; *(→ value, qualities)* insister sur, mettre l'accent sur; **this point cannot be stressed enough** on ne saurait trop insister sur ce point; **she stressed that no decision had been taken** elle a insisté sur *ou* souligné le fait qu'aucune décision n'avait été prise

(**b**) *(in phonetics, poetry, music)* accentuer

(**c**) *Constr & Tech (structure, foundation)* mettre sous tension *ou* en charge; *(concrete, metal)* solliciter

3 *vi Fam* stresser

►► *Med* ***stress fracture*** fracture *f* de surmenage; ***stress management*** gestion *f* du stress; *Ling* ***stress mark*** marque *f* d'accent

stressed [strest] *adj* (**a**) *(person)* stressé, tendu; *(relationship)* tendu (**b**) *(syllable, word)* accentué

stressed-out *adj Fam* stressé

stressful ['stresfʊl] *adj (lifestyle, job, conditions)* stressant; *(moments)* de stress; **to lead a stressful life** mener une vie très stressante

stressor ['stresə(r)] *n Am* facteur *m* de stress

stress-related *adj* dû au stress

►► ***stress-related illnesses*** maladies *fpl* dues au stress

stress-timed *adj*

►► ***stress-timed language*** = langue dont le rythme est fonction des syllabes accentuées

stretch [stretʃ] **1** *n* (**a**) *(expanse → of land, water)* étendue *f*; **this stretch of the road is particularly dangerous in the winter** cette partie de la route est très dangereuse en hiver; **a new stretch of road/motorway** un nouveau tronçon de route/d'autoroute; **a long straight stretch** une longue route en ligne droite; **it's a lovely stretch of river/scenery** cette partie de la rivière/du paysage est magnifique; *Horseracing & Fig* **to go into the final** *or* **finishing** *or* **home stretch** entamer la dernière ligne droite

(**b**) *(period of time)* période *f*; **for a long stretch of time** pendant longtemps; **for long stretches at a time there was nothing to do** il n'y avait rien à faire pendant de longues périodes; **to do a stretch of ten years in the army** passer dix ans dans l'armée; *Fam* **he did a stretch in Dartmoor** il a fait de la taule à Dartmoor; *Fam* **he was given a five-year stretch** *(in prison)* il a écopé de cinq ans

(**c**) *(act of stretching)* étirement *m*; **he stood up, yawned and had a stretch** il se leva, bâilla et s'étira; **to give one's legs a stretch** se dégourdir les jambes; **do a couple of stretches before breakfast** faites quelques étirements avant le petit déjeuner; *Mus* **stretch of the fingers** *(at the piano)* écart *m* des doigts; **by no stretch of the imagination** même en faisant un gros effort d'imagination; **he's the better writer by a long stretch** c'est de loin le meilleur écrivain; **not by a long stretch!** loin de là!

(**d**) *(elasticity)* élasticité *f*; **there isn't much**

str–st

stretch in these gloves ces gants ne sont pas très souples; **there's a lot of stretch in these stockings** ces bas sont très élastiques *ou* s'étirent facilement; **with two-way stretch** *(of elastic fabric)* extensible dans les deux sens

2 *adj Tex (material)* élastique, Stretch® *(inv)*; *(cover)* extensible

3 *vt* **(a)** *(pull tight)* tendre; **stretch the rope tight** tendez bien la corde; **a cable was stretched across the ravine** on avait tendu un câble à travers le ravin; **they stretched a net over the pit** ils ont tendu un filet au-dessus de la fosse; *Art* **to stretch the canvas on the frame** tendre la toile sur le châssis

(b) *(pull longer or wider → elastic)* étirer; *(→ spring)* tendre; *(→ garment, shoes)* élargir; **to stretch sth out of shape** déformer qch; **don't pull your socks like that, you'll stretch them** ne tire pas sur tes chaussettes comme ça, tu vas les déformer

(c) *(extend, reach to full length)* étendre; **stretch your arms upwards** tendez les bras vers le haut; **he stretched his arm through the broken window** il allongea le bras à travers le carreau cassé; **if I stretch up my hand I can reach the ceiling** si je tends la main je peux toucher le plafond; **to stretch one's neck to see sth** tendre le cou pour voir qch; **to stretch oneself** s'étirer; **to stretch one's legs** étirer ses jambes; *Fam Fig* se dégourdir les jambes; **the bird stretched its wings** l'oiseau déploya ses ailes; *Fig* **to stretch one's wings** *(become more independent)* voler de ses propres ailes; *(seek out new challenges)* aller de l'avant

(d) *(force, bend → meaning)* forcer; *(→ rules)* tourner, contourner, faire une entorse à; *(→ principle)* faire une entorse à; *(→ imagination)* faire un gros effort de; **you're really stretching my patience** ma patience a des limites; **to stretch the truth** exagérer; **they have stretched their authority a bit too far** ils ont un peu abusé de leur autorité; **that's stretching it a bit!** il ne faut pas exagérer!; **it would be stretching a point to call him a diplomat** dire qu'il est diplomate serait exagérer *ou* aller un peu loin; **I suppose we could stretch a point and let him stay** je suppose qu'on pourrait faire une entorse au règlement et lui permettre de rester

(e) *(budget, income, resources, supplies → get the most from)* tirer le maximum de; *(→ overload)* surcharger, mettre à rude épreuve; **our resources are stretched to the limit** nos ressources sont exploitées *ou* utilisées au maximum; **I can't stretch my income that far** mon salaire ne me permet pas de faire de telles dépenses; **we should be able to stretch the food until the weekend** nous devrions pouvoir faire durer les provisions jusqu'au week-end; **our staff are really stretched today** le personnel travaille à la limite de ses possibilités aujourd'hui; **to be fully stretched** *(machine, engine)* tourner à plein régime; *(factory, economy)* fonctionner à plein régime; *(resources, services)* être sollicité à fond; *(person, staff)* faire son maximum; **the job won't stretch you enough** le travail ne sera pas assez stimulant pour vous; **she believes young people need to be stretched** elle pense qu'il faut être exigeant avec les jeunes pour qu'ils donnent le meilleur d'eux-mêmes

(f) *(ligament, muscle)* étirer

4 *vi* **(a)** *(be elastic)* s'étirer; *(become longer)* s'allonger; *(become wider)* s'élargir; **this fabric tends to stretch** ce tissu a tendance à s'étirer; **the shoes will stretch with wear** vos chaussures vont se faire *ou* s'élargir à l'usage; **my pullover has stretched out of shape** mon pull s'est déformé

(b) *(person, animal → from tiredness)* s'étirer; *(→ on ground, bed)* s'étendre, s'allonger; *(→ to reach something)* tendre la main; **she stretched lazily** elle s'étira nonchalamment; **he had to stretch to reach it** *(reach out)* il a dû tendre le bras pour l'atteindre; *(stand on tiptoe)* il a dû se mettre sur la pointe des pieds pour l'atteindre; **she stretched across me to get the salt** elle a passé le bras devant moi pour attraper le sel; **can you stretch over and get me the paper?** pouvez-vous tendre le bras et me passer le journal?; **he stretched up to touch the cupboard** il s'est mis sur la pointe des pieds pour atteindre le placard

(c) *(spread, extend → in space, time)* s'étendre; **the forest stretches as far as the eye can see** la forêt s'étend à perte de vue; **the road stretches away into the distance** la route s'étend au lointain; **the road stretched across 500 miles of desert** la route parcourait 800 km de désert; **the rope stretched across the ravine** le corde allait d'un côté à l'autre du ravin; **minutes stretched into hours** les minutes devenaient des heures; **our powers don't stretch as far as you imagine** nos pouvoirs ne sont pas aussi étendus que vous l'imaginez

(d) *(money, resources)* **my salary won't stretch to a new car** mon salaire ne me permet pas d'acheter une nouvelle voiture; **my resources won't stretch to that** mes moyens (pécuniaires) ne vont pas jusque-là

5 at a stretch *adv* **(a)** *(in a row)* d'affilée; **we worked for five hours at a stretch** nous avons travaillé cinq heures d'affilée

(b) *(with much effort)* à la limite, à la rigueur; **we could finish by Monday at a stretch** à la limite *ou* à la rigueur, on pourrait finir pour lundi; **we could fit six people in the car at a stretch** à la rigueur, on pourrait tenir à six dans la voiture

6 at full stretch *adv* **to be at full stretch** *(factory, machine)* fonctionner à plein régime *ou* à plein rendement; *(person)* se donner à fond, faire son maximum; **we were working at full stretch** nous travaillions d'arrache-pied; **even at full stretch, we can't meet the delivery date** même en tournant à plein régime, nous ne pouvons pas respecter les délais de livraison

►► ***stretch class*** cours *m* de stretching; ***stretch fabric*** Stretch® *m*; ***stretch limo*** limousine *f* à la carrosserie allongée

►**stretch out 1** *vt sep* **(a)** *(pull tight)* tendre; **the sheets had been stretched out on the line to dry** on avait étendu les draps sur le fil à linge pour qu'ils sèchent; **the plastic sheet was stretched out on the lawn** la bâche en plastique était étalée sur la pelouse

(b) *(extend, spread → arms, legs)* allonger, étendre; *(→ hand)* tendre; *(→ wings)* déployer; **she stretched out her hand towards him/for the cup** elle tendit la main vers lui/pour prendre la tasse; **she lay stretched out in front of the television** elle était allongée par terre devant la télévision

(c) *(prolong → interview, meeting)* prolonger, faire durer; *(→ account)* allonger; **she has to stretch her thesis out a bit for publication** il faut qu'elle étoffe un peu sa thèse pour la publier

(d) *(make last → supplies, income)* faire durer

2 *vi* **(a)** *(person, animal)* s'étendre, s'allonger; **they stretched out on the lawn in the sun** ils se sont allongés au soleil sur la pelouse

(b) *(forest, countryside)* s'étendre; *(prospects, season)* s'étendre, s'étaler; **a nice long holiday stretched out before them** ils avaient de longues vacances devant eux

stretcher ['stretʃə(r)] *n* **(a)** *Med* brancard *m*, civière *f*; **he was carried off on a stretcher** on l'a emmené sur une civière *ou* un brancard

(b) *(for shoes)* tendeur *m*, forme *f*; *(for gloves)* ouvre-gant *m*; *(in umbrella)* baleine *f*; *Art & Sewing (for canvas)* cadre *m*, châssis *m*

(c) *Constr (brick, stone)* panneresse *f*, carreau *m*

(d) *(crossbar → in structure)* traverse *f*, tirant *m*; *(→ on chair)* barreau *m*, bâton *m*

►► ***stretcher case*** = blessé ou malade ayant besoin d'être porté sur un brancard; *Hum* **I was practically a stretcher case by the time the parents got home** je ne tenais plus debout *ou* j'étais bon pour l'hôpital quand les parents sont rentrés; ***stretcher party*** détachement *m* de brancardiers

►**stretcher off** *vt sep Sport* **to stretcher sb off** emmener sur une civière *ou* un brancard

stretcher-bearer *n* brancardier *m*

stretching ['stretʃɪŋ] *n* **(a)** *Sport (warm-up)* étirement *m* (musculaire) **(b)** *Fig* **stretching of the rules** entorse *f* au règlement

stretchmarks ['stretʃmɑːks] *npl* vergetures *fpl*

stretchy ['stretʃɪ] *(compar* **stretchier**, *superl* **stretchiest**) *adj* élastique, extensible

stretto ['stretəʊ] *(pl* **strettos** *or* **stretti** [-tiː]) *n Mus* strette *f*

strew [struː] *(pt* **strewed**, *pp* **strewn** [struːn] *or* **strewed**) *vt Literary* **(a)** *(cover → ground, floor, path)* joncher, parsemer; *(→ table)* joncher; **the path was strewn with leaves/litter** l'allée était jonchée de feuilles/de détritus

(b) *(scatter → seeds, flowers, leaves)* répandre, éparpiller; *(throw → toys, papers)* éparpiller, jeter; *(→ debris)* éparpiller, disséminer; **they strewed sand on the floor** ils ont répandu du sable sur le sol; **the guests strewed confetti over the bride** les invités ont lancé des confettis sur la mariée; **wreckage was strewn all over the road** il y avait des débris partout sur la route; **references to classical literature are strewn throughout his work** son œuvre est émaillée de références à la littérature classique

strewth [struːθ] *exclam Br & Austr Fam* mince alors!

stria ['straɪə] *(pl* **striae** [-iː]) *n* **(a)** *Bot & Zool* strie *f*, striure *f*; **stria of light** raie *f* lumineuse **(b)** *Geol* **glacial striae** stries *fpl* glaciaires **(c)** *Archit* listel *m*, listeau *m*

striate [straɪ'eɪt] **1** *vt* strier

2 *adj* strié

striated [straɪ'eɪtɪd] *adj* strié

striation [straɪ'eɪʃən] *n* striation *f*

stricken ['strɪkən] *adj Formal* **(a)** *(ill)* malade; *(wounded)* blessé; *(damaged, troubled)* ravagé, dévasté; **to be stricken in years** être âgé et infirme; **our stricken industry** notre industrie dévastée; **the stricken vessel** le vaisseau en détresse *ou* naufragé; **the stricken city** la ville sinistrée; **the stricken army retreated** l'armée défaite battit en retraite

(b) *(afflicted → person, voice, look)* affligé; **stricken by** *or* **with blindness** frappé de cécité; **stricken by** *or* **with polio** atteint de polio; **they were stricken with grief/fear** ils étaient accablés de chagrin/transis de peur

(c) *Arch or Literary* **stricken in years** d'un âge très avancé

-stricken ['strɪkən] *suff* **grief-stricken** accablé de chagrin; **terror-stricken** saisi d'épouvante

strickle ['strɪkəl] *n* **(a)** *(for levelling)* racloir *m* **(b)** *(for sharpening scythes)* pierre *f* à aiguiser les faux

strict [strɪkt] *adj* **(a)** *(severe, stern → person, discipline)* strict, sévère; *(inflexible → principles)* strict, rigoureux; *(→ deadline)* strict; *(→ belief, code, rules)* strict, rigide; *(→ Catholic, Muslim etc)* de stricte obédience; **you must be very strict with him** il faut être très strict avec lui; **they belong to a strict religious sect** ils appartiennent à une secte religieuse très stricte; **she's a strict vegetarian** c'est une végétarienne pure et dure; **I gave strict orders not to be disturbed** j'ai formellement ordonné qu'on ne me dérange pas; **I'm on a strict diet** je suis un régime très strict

(b) *(exact, precise → meaning, interpretation)* strict; **the strict minimum** le strict minimum; **in the strict sense of the word** au sens strict du terme; **the strict truth** la stricte vérité; **it's a strict translation from the Hebrew** c'est une traduction exacte *ou* fidèle de l'hébreu

(c) *(absolute → accuracy, hygiene)* strict, absolu; **he told me in the strictest confidence** il me l'a dit à titre strictement confidentiel; **in strict secrecy** dans le plus grand secret

►► *Am Law* ***strict construction*** interprétation *f* stricte de la constitution

strictly ['strɪktlɪ] *adv* **(a)** *(severely → act, treat)* strictement, avec sévérité; **the children were very strictly brought up** les enfants ont reçu une éducation extrêmement stricte

(b) *(exactly → interpret, translate)* fidèlement, exactement; **strictly speaking** à strictement *ou* à proprement parler

(c) *(absolutely, rigorously)* strictement, absolument; **what you say is not strictly accurate** ce que vous dites n'est pas tout à fait exact; **strictly confidential** strictement confidentiel; **to adhere strictly to one's principles** adhérer rigoureusement à ses principes; **the rules must be strictly observed** le règlement doit être scrupuleusement observé; **to adhere strictly to one's**

diet suivre scrupuleusement son régime; **strictly forbidden** *or* **prohibited** formellement interdit; **smoking strictly forbidden** *(sign)* défense absolue de fumer

strictness ['strɪktnɪs] *n* (**a**) *(severity → of person, rules, diet)* sévérité *f*; **their strictness in applying the rules** la rigueur avec laquelle ils appliquent le règlement (**b**) *(exactness → of interpretation)* exactitude *f*, rigueur *f*

stricture ['strɪktʃə(r)] *n Formal* (**a**) *(criticism)* critique *f* sévère; **to pass stricture on sb/sth** critiquer qn/qch sévèrement (**b**) *(restriction)* restriction *f* (**c**) *Med* striction *f*, sténose *f*

strictured ['strɪktʃəd] *adj Med* rétréci

stride [straɪd] *(pt* **strode** [strəʊd], *pp* **stridden** ['strɪdən]) **1** *n* (**a**) *(step)* grand pas *m*, enjambée *f*; *(when running)* foulée *f*; **to take big** *or* **long strides** faire de grandes enjambées; **to shorten/lengthen one's stride** ralentir/allonger le pas; **with giant strides** à pas de géant; **he crossed the threshold in** *or* **with one stride** il a franchi le seuil d'une seule enjambée; **she recognized him by his purposeful stride** elle l'a reconnu à son pas décidé; **to get** *or Am* **hit into one's stride** trouver son rythme; *Am* **to be caught off stride** être pris au dépourvu; **to take sth in one's stride** *or Am* **in stride** *(do easily)* faire qch sans le moindre effort; *(not be disconcerted by)* ne pas se laisser troubler par qch; **he took all their criticisms in his stride** leurs critiques n'ont pas semblé le déranger; **they've always taken exams in their stride** ils ont toujours réussi leurs examens facilement; **she takes everything in her stride** elle ne se laisse jamais démonter *ou* abattre; **to put sb off their stride** faire perdre le rythme à qn

(**b**) *Fig (progress)* **to make great strides** faire de grands progrès, avancer à pas de géant; **he is making great strides in German** il fait de grands progrès en allemand; **he is making great strides with his research** sa recherche avance à grands pas

2 *vi* marcher à grands pas *ou* à grandes enjambées; **to stride away/in/out** s'éloigner/entrer/sortir à grands pas; **he came striding over** *or* **up to them** il avança vers eux à grands pas; **she strode away across the fields** elle s'éloigna à travers les champs à grands pas; **he strode up and down the street** il faisait les cent pas dans la rue; **he strode up and down the room** il arpentait la pièce

3 *vt (streets, fields, deck)* arpenter

4 strides *npl Br & Austr Fam (trousers)* bénard *m*, bène *m*

stridency ['straɪdənsɪ] *n* stridence *f*; *(of protests)* véhémence *f*

strident ['straɪdənt] *adj* strident; *(colour)* criard; *(protest)* véhément; **strident demands** des revendications véhémentes

stridently ['straɪdəntlɪ] *adv (call, cry, sing)* d'une voix stridente; *(sound, ring)* en faisant un bruit strident; *(demand, protest)* avec véhémence, à grands cris

stridor ['straɪdə(r)] *n Med* stridor *m*

stridulate ['strɪdjʊleɪt] *vi* striduler

strife [straɪf] *n (UNCOUNT) Formal (conflict)* dissensions *fpl*; *(struggles)* luttes *fpl*; *(quarrels)* querelles *fpl*; **a period of political strife** une période marquée par des dissensions politiques; **industrial strife** conflits *mpl* sociaux; **sectarian strife** luttes *fpl* sectaires

strife-torn *adj* déchiré par les conflits

striga ['straɪgə] *n* (**a**) *Bot* poil *m* raide (**b**) *Zool* strie *f*, rayure *f* transversale

strigil ['strɪdʒɪl] *n Antiq* strigile *m*

STRIKE [straɪk]

grève	▶ 1 (a)
raid	▶ 1 (b)
attaque	▶ 1 (b)
escadre	▶ 1 (c)
découverte	▶ 1 (d)
sonnerie	▶ 1 (e)
frapper	▶ 3 (a), (c) – (e), (n); 4 (a)
toucher	▶ 3 (a)
atteindre	▶ 3 (a)
heurter	▶ 3 (b)
sonner	▶ 3 (f); 4 (d)
jouer	▶ 3 (g)
conclure	▶ 3 (h)
rendre	▶ 3 (j)
découvrir	▶ 3 (l)
attaquer	▶ 3 (q); 4 (b)
faire grève	▶ 4 (c)

(pt & pp **struck** [strʌk], *cont* **striking**) **1** *n* (**a**) *Ind* grève *f*; **to go on strike** se mettre en *ou* faire grève; **to be (out) on strike** être en grève; **to threaten strike action** menacer de faire *ou* de se mettre en grève; **the Italian air strike** la grève des transports aériens en Italie; **railway strike** grève *f* des chemins de fer; **teachers' strike** grève *f* des enseignants; **coal** *or* **miners' strike** grève *f* des mineurs; **postal** *or* **post office strike** grève *f* des postes; **rent strike** grève *f* des loyers

(**b**) *Mil* raid *m*, attaque *f*; *(by bird of prey, snake)* attaque *f*; **to carry out air strikes against** *or* **on enemy bases** lancer des raids aériens contre des bases ennemies; **retaliatory strike** raid *m* de représailles; *(nuclear)* deuxième frappe *f*

(**c**) *Aviat & Mil (planes)* escadre *f (d'avions participant à un raid)*

(**d**) *Petr & Mining (discovery)* découverte *f*; **a gold strike** la découverte d'un gisement d'or; **the recent oil strikes in the North Sea** la découverte récente de gisements de pétrole en mer du Nord; **it was a lucky strike** c'était un coup de chance

(**e**) *(of clock → chime, mechanism)* sonnerie *f*; **life was regulated by the strike of the church clock** la vie était rythmée par la cloche de l'église

(**f**) *(act or instance of hitting)* coup *m*; *(sound)* bruit *m*; **the strike of iron on iron** le bruit du fer qui frappe le fer; **he adjusted the strike of the keys on the platen roll** il a réglé la frappe des caractères contre le cylindre

(**g**) *(in baseball)* strike *m*; *Am Fig (black mark)* mauvais point *m*; *Fig* **he has two strikes against him** il est mal parti; *Fig* **being too young was another strike against her** le fait d'être trop jeune constituait un handicap supplémentaire pour elle

(**h**) *(in bowling)* honneur *m* double; **to get** *or* **to score a strike** réussir un honneur double

(**i**) *Fishing (by fisherman)* ferrage *m*; *(by fish)* touche *f*

(**j**) *Arch* **at the strike of day** à la pointe *ou* au point du jour

2 *comp* (**a**) *(committee, movement)* de grève

(**b**) *Mil (mission)* d'intervention, d'attaque; *(aircraft)* d'assaut

3 *vt* (**a**) *(hit → gen)* frapper; *(→ of bullet, torpedo, bomb)* toucher, atteindre; **she raised her hand to strike him** elle leva la main pour le frapper; **he struck me with his fist** il m'a donné un coup de poing; **the chairman struck the table with his gavel** le président donna un coup de marteau sur la table; **she took the vase and struck him on** *or* **over the head** elle saisit le vase et lui donna un coup sur la tête; **she struck him across the face** elle lui a donné une gifle; **a light breeze struck the sails** une légère brise gonfla les voiles; **the phenomenon occurs when warm air strikes cold** ce phénomène se produit lorsque de l'air chaud entre en contact avec de l'air froid; **a wave struck the side of the boat** une vague a heurté le côté du bateau; **the arrow struck the target** la flèche a atteint la cible; **a hail of bullets struck the car** la voiture a été mitraillée; **he was struck by a piece of shrapnel** il a été touché par *ou* il a reçu un éclat de grenade; **to be struck by lightning** être frappé par la foudre, être foudroyé; **he went for them striking blows left and right** il s'est jeté sur eux, distribuant les coups de tous côtés; **who struck the first blow?** qui a porté le premier coup?, qui a frappé le premier?; **he struck the tree a mighty blow with the axe** il a donné un grand coup de hache dans l'arbre; **the trailer struck the post a glancing blow** la remorque a percuté le poteau en passant; *Fig* **to strike a blow for democracy/women's rights** *(law, event)* faire progresser la démocratie/les droits de la femme; *(person, group)* marquer des points en faveur de la démocratie/des droits des femmes

(**b**) *(bump into, collide with)* heurter, cogner; **his foot struck the bar on his first jump** son pied a heurté la barre lors de son premier saut; **she fell and struck her head on** *or* **against the kerb** elle s'est cogné la tête contre le bord du trottoir en tombant; **the Volvo struck the bus head on** la Volvo a heurté le bus de plein fouet; *Naut* **we've struck ground!** nous avons touché (le fond)!

(**c**) *(afflict → of drought, disease, worry, regret)* frapper; *(→ of storm, hurricane, disaster, wave of violence)* s'abattre sur, frapper; **an earthquake struck the city** un tremblement de terre a frappé la ville; **he was struck by a heart attack** il a eu une crise cardiaque; **the pain struck her as she tried to get up** la douleur l'a saisie au moment où elle essayait de se lever; **I was struck by** *or* **with doubts** j'ai été pris de doute, le doute s'est emparé de moi

(**d**) *(occur to)* frapper; **only later did it strike me as unusual** ce n'est que plus tard que j'ai trouvé ça *ou* que cela m'a paru bizarre; **it suddenly struck him how little had changed** il a soudain pris conscience du fait que peu de choses avaient changé; **did it never strike you that you weren't wanted there?** ne vous est-il jamais venu à l'esprit que vous étiez de trop?; **a terrible thought struck her** une idée affreuse lui vint à l'esprit; **it strikes me as useless/as the perfect gift** ça me semble *ou* paraît inutile/être le cadeau idéal; **he strikes me as (being) sincere** il me paraît sincère; **it doesn't strike me as being the best course of action** il ne me semble pas que ce soit la meilleure voie à suivre

(**e**) *(impress)* frapper, impressionner; **the first thing that struck me was his pallor** la première chose qui m'a frappé, c'était sa pâleur; **what strikes you is the silence** ce qui (vous) frappe, c'est le silence; **how did she strike you?** quelle impression vous a-t-elle faite?, quel effet vous a-t-elle fait?; **how did Tokyo/the film strike you?** comment avez-vous trouvé Tokyo/le film?; **we can eat here and meet them later, how does that strike you?** on peut manger ici et les retrouver plus tard, qu'en penses-tu?; **I was very struck** *Br* **with** *or Am* **by the flat** l'appartement m'a plu énormément; **I wasn't very struck** *Br* **with** *or Am* **by his colleague** son collègue ne m'a pas fait une grande impression

(**f**) *(chime)* sonner; **the church clock struck five** l'horloge de l'église a sonné cinq heures; **it was striking midnight as we left** minuit sonnait quand nous partîmes

(**g**) *(play → note, chord)* jouer; **she struck a few notes on the piano** elle a joué quelques notes sur le piano; **when he struck the opening chords the audience applauded** quand il a joué *ou* plaqué les premiers accords le public a applaudi; **to strike a false note** *Mus* faire une fausse note; *Fig (speech)* sonner faux; **his presence/his words struck a gloomy note** sa présence a/ses paroles ont mis une note de tristesse; **the report strikes an optimistic note/a note of warning for the future** le rapport est très optimiste/très alarmant pour l'avenir; **does it strike a chord?** est-ce que cela te rappelle *ou* dit quelque chose?; **to strike a chord with the audience** faire vibrer la foule; **her description of company life will strike a chord with many managers** beaucoup de cadres se reconnaîtront dans sa description de la vie en entreprise

(**h**) *(arrive at, reach → deal, treaty, agreement)* conclure; **to strike a bargain** conclure un marché; **I'll strike a bargain with you** je te propose un marché; **it's not easy to strike a balance between too much and too little freedom** il n'est pas facile de trouver un équilibre *ou* de trouver le juste milieu entre trop et pas assez de liberté

(**i**) *(cause a feeling of)* **to strike fear** *or* **terror into sb** remplir qn d'effroi

(**j**) *(cause to become)* rendre; **to strike sb blind/dumb** rendre qn aveugle/muet; **the news struck us speechless with horror** nous sommes restés muets d'horreur en apprenant la nouvelle; **I was struck dumb by the sheer cheek of the man!** je suis resté muet devant le culot de cet homme!; **a stray bullet struck him dead** il a été tué par une balle perdue; **she was struck dead by a heart attack** elle a été foudroyée par

une crise cardiaque; **God strike me dead if I lie!** je jure que c'est la vérité!
(**k**) *(ignite → match)* frotter, allumer; *(→ sparks)* faire jaillir; **he struck a match** *or* **a light** il a frotté une allumette; *Br Fam Old-fashioned* **strike a light!** nom de Dieu!
(**l**) *(discover → gold)* découvrir; *(→ oil, water)* trouver; *(path)* tomber sur, découvrir; *Fam Br* **to strike it lucky,** *Am* **to strike it rich** *(make material gain)* trouver le filon; *(be lucky)* avoir de la veine
(**m**) *(adopt → attitude)* adopter; **he struck an attitude of wounded righteousness** il a pris un air de dignité offensée
(**n**) *(mint → coin, medal)* frapper
(**o**) *(take down → tent)* démonter; *Naut (→ sail)* amener, baisser; **to strike camp** lever le camp; *Naut* **to strike the flag** *or* **the colours** amener les couleurs; *Theat* **to strike the set** démonter le décor
(**p**) *(delete → name, remark, person)* rayer; *(→ from professional register)* radier; **that remark must be struck** *or Am* **stricken from the record** cette remarque doit être retirée du procès-verbal
(**q**) *(attack)* attaquer
(**r**) *Am (go on strike at)* **the union is striking four of the company's plants** le syndicat a déclenché des grèves dans quatre des usines de la société; **students are striking their classes** les étudiants font la grève des cours; **the dockers are striking ships carrying industrial waste** les dockers refusent de s'occuper des cargos chargés de déchets industriels
(**s**) *Bot* **to strike roots** prendre racine; **the tree had struck deep roots into the ground** l'arbre avait des racines très profondes
4 *vi* (**a**) *(hit)* frapper; **she struck at me with her umbrella** elle essaya de me frapper avec son parapluie; **to strike home** *(blow)* porter; *(missile, remark)* faire mouche; *Fam* **to strike lucky** avoir de la veine; *Prov* **strike while the iron is hot** il faut battre le fer pendant qu'il est chaud
(**b**) *(attack → gen)* attaquer; *(→ snake)* mordre; *(→ wild animal)* sauter *ou* bondir sur sa proie; *(→ bird of prey)* fondre *ou* s'abattre sur sa proie; **the bombers struck at dawn** les bombardiers attaquèrent à l'aube; **the murderer has struck again** l'assassin a encore frappé; **these are measures which strike at the root/heart of the problem** voici des mesures qui attaquent le problème à la racine/qui s'attaquent au cœur du problème; **this latest incident strikes right at the heart of government policy** ce dernier incident remet complètement en cause la politique gouvernementale
(**c**) *Ind* faire grève; **they're striking for more pay** ils font grève pour obtenir une augmentation de salaire; **the nurses struck over the minister's decision to freeze wages** les infirmières ont fait grève suite à la décision du ministre de bloquer les salaires
(**d**) *(chime)* sonner; **midnight had already struck** minuit avait déjà sonné
(**e**) *(happen suddenly → illness, disaster, earthquake)* survenir, se produire, arriver; **we were travelling quietly along when disaster struck** nous roulions tranquillement lorsque la catastrophe s'est produite; **the first tremors struck at 3 a.m.** les premières secousses sont survenues à 3 heures du matin
(**f**) *(travel, head)* **to strike across country** prendre à travers champs; **they then struck west** ils sont ensuite partis vers l'ouest
(**g**) *Sport (score)* marquer
(**h**) *Fishing (fisherman)* ferrer; *(fish)* mordre (à l'hameçon)
(**i**) *(of cutting)* prendre (racine)
►► ***strike ballot*** = vote avant que les syndicats ne décident d'une grève; *Ins* ***strike clause*** clause *f* pour cas de grève; ***strike force*** *(nuclear capacity)* force *f* de frappe; *(of police, soldiers → squad)* détachement *m ou* brigade *f* d'intervention; *(→ larger force)* force *f* d'intervention; ***strike fund*** = caisse de prévoyance permettant d'aider les grévistes; ***strike pay*** salaire *m* de gréviste *(versé par le syndicat ou par un fonds de solidarité)*; *Fin* ***strike price*** *(for share)* prix *m* d'exercice

►**strike back** *vi* (**a**) *(retaliate)* se venger; *Mil* contre-attaquer; **the government struck back at its critics** le gouvernement a répondu à ceux qui le critiquaient
(**b**) *Sport (score in response)* marquer à son tour

►**strike down** *vt sep* foudroyer, terrasser; *Fig* **struck down by disease** terrassé par la maladie

►**strike off 1** *vt sep* (**a**) *(delete, remove → from list)* rayer, barrer; *(→ from professional register)* radier; **to be struck off** *(doctor, solicitor)* être radié
(**b**) *(sever)* couper
(**c**) *Typ* tirer
2 *vi (go)* **to strike off to the left** prendre à gauche; **we struck off into the forest** nous sommes entrés *ou* avons pénétré dans la forêt

►**strike on** *vt insep Br (solution, right answer)* trouver (par hasard), tomber sur; *(plan)* trouver; *(idea)* avoir

►**strike out 1** *vt sep* (**a**) *(cross out)* rayer, barrer
(**b**) *(in baseball)* éliminer
2 *vi* (**a**) *(set up on one's own)* s'établir à son compte
(**b**) *(go)* **she struck out across the fields** elle prit à travers champs; *Fig* **they decided to strike out into a new direction** ils ont décidé de prendre une nouvelle direction
(**c**) *(swim)* **we struck out for the shore** nous avons commencé à nager en direction de la côte
(**d**) *(aim a blow)* frapper; **she struck out at him** elle essaya de le frapper; *Fig* elle s'en est prise à lui; **they struck out in all directions with their truncheons** ils distribuaient des coups de matraque à droite et à gauche
(**e**) *(in baseball)* être éliminé

►**strike through** *vt sep Br (cross out)* rayer, barrer

►**strike up 1** *vt insep* (**a**) *(start)* **to strike up a conversation with sb** engager la conversation avec qn; **they immediately struck up a conversation** ils sont immédiatement entrés en conversation; **to strike up an acquaintance/a friendship with sb** lier connaissance/se lier d'amitié avec qn
(**b**) *Mus (start playing)* commencer à jouer; **the band struck up the national anthem** l'orchestre commença à jouer l'hymne national *ou* entonna les premières mesures de l'hymne national
2 *vi (musician, orchestra)* commencer à jouer; *(music)* commencer

►**strike upon** *Br* = **strike on**

---

strikebound ['straɪkbaʊnd] *adj (factory, department)* paralysé par une *ou* la grève; *(industry, country)* paralysé par des grèves

strikebreaker ['straɪk,breɪkə(r)] *n* briseur(euse) *m,f* de grève

strikebreaking ['straɪk,breɪkɪŋ] *n* refus *m* de faire grève

strike-out mode *n Comput* mode *m* barré

strikeover ['straɪk,əʊvə(r)] *n* surimpression *f*

striker ['straɪkə(r)] *n* (**a**) *Ind* gréviste *mf* (**b**) *Ftbl* buteur *m* (**c**) *(device → on clock)* marteau *m*; *(→ in gun)* percuteur *m*

strike-thru mode *n Comput* mode *m* barré

striking ['straɪkɪŋ] **1** *adj* (**a**) *(remarkable → sight, contrast, resemblance, beauty)* frappant, saisissant; **he cut a striking figure** il avait une allure impressionnante; **a striking example of Baroque architecture** un très bel exemple d'architecture baroque
(**b**) *(clock)* qui sonne les heures
(**c**) *Mil (force)* d'intervention
(**d**) *Ind* en grève
(**e**) *(idiom)* **within striking distance** à proximité; **she lives within striking distance of London** elle habite tout près de Londres; **they came within striking distance of finding a solution** ils ont failli trouvé *ou* presque trouvé une solution
2 *n* (**a**) *(of clock)* sonnerie *f* (des heures)
(**b**) *(of coins)* frappe *f*
►► ***striking mechanism*** sonnerie *f* (des heures); ***striking off*** *(of name)* suppression *f*; *(of lawyer, doctor)* radiation *f*; ***striking workers*** des travailleurs *mpl* en grève, des grévistes *mfpl*

strikingly ['straɪkɪŋlɪ] *adv* remarquablement; **a strikingly beautiful woman** une femme d'une beauté saisissante; **it was strikingly obvious to everyone but me** c'était une évidence pour tout le monde sauf pour moi

strikingness ['straɪkɪŋnɪs] *n* caractère *m* frappant *ou* saisissant

Strimmer® ['strɪmə(r)] *n* débroussailleuse *f* (à fil)

Strine [straɪn] *n Hum* l'anglais *m* australien

string [strɪŋ] *(pt & pp* **strung** [strʌŋ]) **1** *n* (**a**) *(gen → for parcel)* ficelle *f*; *(→ on apron, pyjamas)* cordon *m*; *(→ for puppet)* ficelle *f*, fil *m*; **a piece of string** un bout *ou* un morceau de ficelle; *Fam* **to have sb on a string** mener qn par le bout du nez; **to keep sb on a string** *(in uncertainty)* laisser qn dans l'incertitude; *(keep control over)* tenir qn en laisse; **he pulls the strings** c'est lui qui tire les ficelles; *Fam* **to pull strings for sb** *(obtain favours)* user de son influence *ou* faire jouer ses relations pour aider qn❑; *(get job, promotion)* pistonner qn; **she needs somebody to pull a few strings for her** elle a besoin d'être pistonnée *ou* d'un coup de piston; **somebody pulled strings to get him the job** il a eu le poste par piston; *Fam* **no strings attached** sans condition *ou* conditions❑; **there are no strings attached** cela n'engage à rien
(**b**) *(for bow, tennis racket, musical instrument)* corde *f*; *Mus* **the strings** les cordes; **to have more than one/a second string to one's bow** avoir plus d'une/une seconde corde à son arc
(**c**) *(row, chain → of pearls)* rang *m*, collier *m*; *(→ of onions, sausages)* chapelet *m*; *(→ of visitors, cars)* file *f*; **string of beads** collier *m*; *Rel* chapelet *m*; **a string of islands** un chapelet d'îles; **a string of fairy lights** une guirlande (électrique); **she owns a string of shops** elle est propriétaire d'une chaîne de magasins; **a string of race horses** une écurie de course
(**d**) *(series → of successes, defeats)* série *f*; *(→ of lies, insults)* kyrielle *f*, chapelet *m*; **he has a whole string of letters after his name** il a toute une kyrielle de diplômes
(**e**) *Comput & Ling* chaîne *f*; *Math* séquence *f*
(**f**) *Bot* fil *m*
2 *comp* (**a**) *Mus (band, instrument, orchestra)* à cordes
(**b**) *(made of string)* de *ou* en ficelle
3 *vt* (**a**) *(guitar, violin)* monter, mettre des cordes à; *(racket)* corder; *(bow)* mettre une corde à
(**b**) *(beads, pearls)* enfiler
(**c**) *(hang)* suspendre; *(stretch)* tendre; **Christmas lights had been strung across the street** des décorations de Noël avaient été suspendues en travers de la rue; **he strung the chain across the gateway** il a tendu *ou* attaché la chaîne en travers de l'entrée
(**d**) *Culin (beans)* enlever les fils de
►► ***string bag*** filet *m* à provisions; ***string band*** orchestre *m* à cordes; ***string bass*** contrebasse *f*; ***string bean*** (**a**) *(vegetable)* haricot *m* vert (**b**) *Am Fam (person)* grande perche *f*, asperge *f*; *Am Culin* ***string cheese*** = sorte de mozzarelle vendue en bâtonnets; ***string orchestra*** orchestre *m* à cordes; ***string player*** musicien(enne) *m,f* qui joue d'un instrument à cordes; ***string quartet*** quatuor *m* à cordes; ***string section*** les cordes *fpl*; ***string tie*** = cordon noué autour du cou et orné d'une boucle; *Comput* ***string variable*** variable *f* alphanumérique; ***string vest*** tricot *m* de corps à grosses mailles

►**string along** *Fam* **1** *vi* (**a**) *(tag along)* suivre (les autres)❑; **do you mind if I string along?** est-ce que ça vous gêne si je viens avec vous *ou* si je vous accompagne?❑
(**b**) *(agree)* **to string along with sb** se ranger à l'avis de qn❑; **he always strings along with everybody else** il est toujours d'accord avec tout le monde❑
2 *vt sep (person)* faire marcher

►**string out** *vt sep* (**a**) *(washing, lamps)* suspendre (sur une corde); **lights were strung out along the runway** des lumières s'échelonnaient le long de la piste; **armed guards were strung out along the route** des gardes armés avaient été postés tout le long du parcours
(**b**) *(in time)* **to string sth out** faire durer qch; **the TV series was strung out over six weeks** le feuilleton (de) télé a traîné pendant six semaines

►**string together** *vt sep* (**a**) *(beads)* enfiler; *(words, sentences)* enchaîner; **he can't string two sentences together** il est incapable d'aligner trois mots; **she can barely string two words together in French** c'est à peine si elle peut faire une phrase en français
(**b**) *(improvise → story)* monter, improviser; **we managed to string together some story about missing the last bus** on a raconté qu'on avait raté le dernier bus
►**string up** *vt sep* (**a**) *(lights)* suspendre; *(washing)* étendre
(**b**) *Fam (hang → person)* pendre ☐; *Fig* **I could string her up!** je lui tordrais bien le cou!
stringboard ['strɪŋbɔːd] *n Constr* limon *m* (d'escalier)
stringed [strɪŋd] *adj (instrument)* à cordes
-stringed [strɪŋd] *suff* **five-stringed** à cinq cordes
stringency ['strɪndʒənsɪ] *n* (**a**) *(severity)* rigueur *f*, sévérité *f* (**b**) *Econ & Fin* austérité *f*; **there is a need for financial stringency** des mesures d'austérité s'imposent
stringendo [strɪn'dʒendəʊ] *Mus* **1** *adj* stringendo
2 *adv* stringendo
stringent ['strɪndʒənt] *n* (**a**) *(rules)* rigoureux, strict, sévère; *(measures, conditions)* rigoureux, draconien (**b**) *Econ & Fin (market)* tendu
stringently ['strɪndʒəntlɪ] *adv* rigoureusement, strictement
stringer ['strɪŋə(r)] *n* (**a**) *Press* reporter *m* local (**b**) *Constr (timber)* poutre *f* de renforcement; *(metal)* serre *f* (**c**) *Miner* filet *m*, veine *f* (**d**) *(stringboard)* limon *m* (d'escalier)
stringiness ['strɪŋɪnɪs] *n* (**a**) *(of meat, vegetables)* consistance *f* fibreuse *ou* filandreuse; *(of cheese)* consistance *f* coulante; *(of liquid)* viscosité *f* (**b**) *(of limbs, build)* minceur *f*
stringing ['strɪŋɪŋ] *n (act → of violin)* montage *m*; *(→ of racket)* cordage *m*; *(→ of bow)* bandage *m*
stringpiece ['strɪŋpiːs] *n Constr* longrine *f*
string-puller [-,pʊlə(r)] *n* = personne qui fait jouer ses relations
string-pulling [-,pʊlɪŋ] *n* piston *m*; **he got the job through string-pulling** il a décroché ce poste grâce à ses relations
stringy ['strɪŋɪ] (*compar* **stringier**, *superl* **stringiest**) *adj* (**a**) *(meat, vegetable)* filandreux, fibreux; *(cooked cheese)* qui file; *(liquid)* visqueux (**b**) *(long → plant)* (qui pousse) tout en longueur; *(→ build, limbs)* filiforme
strip [strɪp] (*pt & pp* **stripped**) **1** *n* (**a**) *(of paper, material, carpet)* bande *f*; *(of metal)* bande *f*, ruban *m*; *(of land)* bande *f*, langue *f*; **there was a thin strip of light under the door** il y avait un mince rai de lumière sous la porte; **each house had a strip of grass in front of it** il y avait une bande de gazon devant chaque maison; **a narrow strip of water** *(sea)* un étroit bras de mer; *(river)* un étroit ruban de rivière; **can you cut off a strip of material?** pouvez-vous couper une bande de tissu?; **she cut the dough/material into strips** elle coupa la pâte en lamelles/le tissu en bandes; **to tear sth into strips** déchirer qch en bandes; *Fig* **to tear sb off a strip** sonner les cloches à qn
(**b**) *Am (street with businesses)* avenue *f* commerçante; **the Strip, Sunset Strip** = artère [illegible]
(**c**) *Aviat* piste *f*
(**d**) *(light)* **neon strip** néon *m*, tube *m* (au) néon
(**e**) *Sport* tenue *f*; **the Liverpool strip** la tenue *ou* les couleurs de l'équipe de Liverpool
(**f**) *(striptease)* strip-tease *m*; **to do a strip** faire un strip-tease
(**g**) *(cartoons)* bande *f* dessinée, BD *f*
2 *vt* (**a**) *(undress)* déshabiller, dévêtir; **they were stripped to the waist** ils étaient torse nu, ils étaient nus jusqu'à la ceinture; **to strip sb naked** déshabiller qn (complètement)
(**b**) *(remove everything from → tree)* dépouiller, dénuder; *(→ house, room)* vider; *(→ door, furniture)* décaper; *(→ wire)* dénuder; **to strip a tree (of its bark)** écorcer un arbre; **the walls need to be stripped first** *(of wallpaper)* il faut d'abord enlever *ou* arracher le papier peint; *(of paint)* il faut d'abord décaper les murs; **to strip a bed** défaire un lit; **to strip a room/house** vider une pièce/maison; **thieves have stripped the house bare** les cambrioleurs ont complètement vidé la maison; **the windows had been stripped of their curtains** on avait enlevé les rideaux des fenêtres; **the Christmas tree looks odd stripped of its decorations** le sapin a un drôle d'air une fois qu'on lui a enlevé ses décorations; **the liner is to be completely stripped and refitted** le paquebot doit être refait de fond en comble
(**c**) *(remove → gen)* enlever; *(→ paint)* décaper; **we stripped the wallpaper from the walls** nous avons arraché le papier peint des murs; **the birds have stripped the cherries from the trees** les oiseaux ont fait des ravages dans les cerisiers; **the storm stripped the leaves off the trees** la tempête a dépouillé les arbres de leurs feuilles; **the years of suffering had stripped away all pretence** les années de souffrance avaient effacé toute trace d'affectation
(**d**) *(deprive)* dépouiller, démunir; **to strip sb of their privileges/possessions** dépouiller qn de ses privilèges/biens; **he was stripped of his rank/title** on lui a retiré son grade/titre; **overcooking strips vegetables of all their nutritional value** une cuisson prolongée élimine tous les éléments nutritifs des légumes
(**e**) *(dismantle → engine, gun)* démonter
(**f**) *Tech (screw, bolt)* arracher le filet de; *(gear)* arracher les dents de
(**g**) *Com (sell off → assets)* revendre
3 *vi* (**a**) *(undress)* se déshabiller, se dévêtir; **to strip to the waist** se mettre torse nu
(**b**) *(do a striptease)* faire un strip-tease
►► *Br* ***strip cartoon*** bande *f* dessinée; ***strip club*** boîte *f* de strip-tease; ***strip cropping*** *(UNCOUNT)* culture *f* en bande *(pour limiter l'érosion)*; ***strip farming*** (**a**) *Hist* système *m* des openfields (**b**) *Agr* culture *f* en bande *(pour limiter l'érosion)*; *Fam* ***strip joint*** boîte *f* de strip-tease ☐; *Br* ***strip light*** néon *m*, tube *m* (au) néon; *Br* ***strip lighting*** éclairage *m* fluorescent *ou* au néon; *Am* ***strip mall*** = centre commercial qui longe une route; *Metal* ***strip mill*** démouleur *m*; *esp Am* ***strip mining*** extraction *f* à ciel ouvert; ***strip poker*** strip-poker *m*; ***strip search*** fouille *f* corporelle *(la personne fouillée devant se déshabiller)*; ***strip show*** (spectacle *m* de) strip-tease *m*
►**strip down 1** *vt sep* (**a**) *(bed)* défaire (complètement); *(wallpaper)* arracher, enlever; *(door, furniture)* décaper; **to strip the walls down** *(remove wallpaper)* arracher *ou* enlever le papier peint des murs; *(remove paint)* décaper les murs; *Fig* **the text has been stripped down to its bare essentials** le texte a été réduit à l'essentiel
(**b**) *(dismantle → engine, mechanism)* démonter
2 *vi* se déshabiller; **he stripped down to his underpants** il s'est déshabillé, ne gardant que son slip
►**strip off 1** *vt sep (gen)* enlever, arracher; *(clothes, shirt)* enlever; *(paint)* décaper; *(wallpaper)* décoller; **to strip the leaves off a tree** dépouiller un arbre de ses feuilles; **to strip the bark off a tree** écorcer un arbre
2 *vi* se déshabiller, se mettre nu
►**strip out** *vt sep (engine, mechanism)* démonter, démanteler
stripe [straɪp] **1** *n* (**a**) *(on animal)* rayure *f*, zébrure *f*; *(on material, shirt)* raie *f*, rayure *f*; *(on car)* filet *m*; **black with orange stripes** noir avec des rayures orange
(**b**) *Mil* galon *m*, chevron *m*; **to get/to lose one's stripes** gagner/perdre ses galons
(**c**) *(kind)* genre *m*; **they are of the same political stripe** ils partagent les mêmes idées politiques, ils appartiennent à la même famille politique
(**d**) *(lash)* coup *m* de fouet; *(mark)* marque *f* d'un coup de fouet
2 *vt* rayer, marquer de rayures
striped [straɪpt] *adj (animal)* tigré, zébré; *(material, shirt, pattern)* rayé, à rayures; **striped with blue** avec des rayures bleues
stripey = **stripy**
stripling ['strɪplɪŋ] *n Literary or Hum* tout jeune homme *m*
strippagram ['strɪpəgræm] *n* = message qu'on envoie par l'intermédiaire d'une personne qui fait un strip-tease
stripped [strɪpt] *adj (wood)* décapé; **stripped pine furniture** meubles *mpl* en pin naturel
►► *St Exch* ***stripped bond*** félin *m*, obligation *f* à coupon zéro
stripped-down *adj*
►► ***stripped-down version*** version *f* simplifiée
stripper ['strɪpə(r)] *n* (**a**) *(in strip club)* strip-teaseuse *f*; **(male) stripper** strip-teaseur *m* (**b**) *(for paint)* décapant *m*
stripping ['strɪpɪŋ] *n (UNCOUNT) Med* éveinage *m*
strip-search *vt* **to strip-search sb** fouiller qn après l'avoir fait se déshabiller; **he was strip-searched by prison warders** des gardiens de prison lui ont fait subir une fouille corporelle *ou* l'ont fouillé après l'avoir fait se déshabiller
striptease ['strɪptiːz] *n* strip-tease *m*
►► ***striptease artist*** strip-teaseur(euse) *m,f*
stripy ['straɪpɪ] (*compar* **stripier**, *superl* **stripiest**) *adj (material, shirt, pattern)* rayé, à rayures; *Zool* tigré, zébré
strive [straɪv] (*pt* **strove** [strəʊv], *pp* **striven** ['strɪvən]) *vt Formal or Literary* (**a**) *(attempt)* **to strive to do sth** s'évertuer à *ou* s'acharner à faire qch; **to strive after** *or* **for sth** faire tout son possible pour obtenir qch, s'efforcer d'obtenir qch; **to strive for effect** chercher à faire de l'effet
(**b**) *(struggle)* lutter, se battre; **to strive against misfortune** lutter *ou* se battre contre la malchance; **all her life she strove for success/recognition** toute sa vie, elle s'est battue pour réussir/être reconnue
strobe [strəʊb] *n* (**a**) lumière *f* stroboscopique (**b**) stroboscope *m*
►► ***strobe lighting*** lumière *f* stroboscopique
strobic ['strəʊbɪk] *adj Opt* strobique
strobilus [strəʊ'baɪləs] *n Bot* strobile *m*
stroboscope ['strəʊbəskəʊp] *n* stroboscope *m*
strode [strəʊd] *pt of* **stride**
stroganoff ['strɒgənɒf] *n Culin* plat *m* à la Stroganov *ou* à la Strogonoff; **beef stroganoff** bœuf *m* Stroganov *ou* Strogonoff
stroke [strəʊk] **1** *n* (**a**) *(blow, flick)* coup *m*; **with a stroke of the whip** d'un coup de fouet; **with a stroke of the brush** d'un coup de pinceau; **with a stroke of the pen** d'un trait de plume; **a stroke of lightning** un coup de foudre; **they were given fifty strokes** ils ont reçu cinquante coups de fouet
(**b**) *Sport (in golf, tennis, cricket, billiards)* coup *m*; *(in swimming → movement)* mouvement *m* des bras; *(→ style)* nage *f*; *(in rowing → movement)* coup *m* d'aviron; *(→ technique)* nage *f*; **she swam across the river with quick strokes** elle traversa rapidement la rivière à la nage; **the Oxford team rowed at 25 strokes to the minute** l'équipe d'Oxford ramait à une cadence de 25 coups à la minute; **to keep stroke** garder la cadence; *also Fig* **to set the stroke** donner la cadence; **to put sb off his stroke** *(in rowing)* faire perdre sa cadence *ou* son rythme à qn; *(in golf)* faire manquer son coup à; *Fig* faire perdre tous ses moyens à qn; **to be off one's stroke** ne pas être au mieux de sa forme; *Fig* **to put sb off his/her stroke** déconcerter qn
(**c**) *(mark → from pen, pencil)* trait *m*; *(→ from brush)* trait *m*, touche *f*; *(on letters, figures)* barre *f*; *Typ (oblique dash)* barre *f* oblique; **written with thick/thin strokes** écrit d'une écriture appuyée/fine; *Br* **225 stroke 62** 225 barre oblique 62
(**d**) *(piece, example → of luck)* coup *m*; *(→ of genius, wit)* trait *m*; **a stroke of luck** un coup de chance; **by a stroke of luck, she had remembered to take the key** par chance, elle avait pensé à prendre la clé; **it was a stroke of brilliance!** c'était un coup de génie!; *Br* **she didn't do a stroke (of work) all day** elle n'a rien fait de la journée
(**e**) *(of clock, bell)* coup *m*; **on the stroke of midnight** sur le coup de minuit; **on the stroke of 6** à 6 heures sonnantes *ou* tapantes; **he arrived on the stroke** il est arrivé à l'heure exacte *ou* précise; *Br Tel* **at the third stroke it will be 6.32 precisely** au troisième top, il sera exactement 6h32
(**f**) *Med* attaque *f* (d'apoplexie); **to have a stroke** avoir une attaque

str–st

(**g**) *(in rowing)* chef *m* de nage; **to row stroke** être chef de nage, donner la nage

(**h**) *Tech (of piston)* course *f*; **two-/four-stroke engine** un moteur à deux/quatre temps

(**i**) *(caress)* caresse *f*; **she gave the cat a stroke** elle a caressé le chat

(**j**) *Fam (compliment)* compliment *m* flatteur ❑

2 *vt* (**a**) *(caress)* caresser; **he stroked her hand** il lui caressait la main; **she stroked the piano keys with her fingers** elle caressait les touches du piano; **to stroke sb's ego** caresser qn dans le sens du poil

(**b**) *(in rowing)* **to stroke a boat** être chef de nage, donner la nage

(**c**) *Sport (ball)* frapper

(**d**) *Am Fam (flatter)* passer de la pommade à

3 *vi (in rowing)* être chef de nage, donner la nage

4 at a stroke, at one stroke *adv* d'un seul coup

▸▸ *Am very Fam* ***stroke magazine*** magazine *m* de cul; ***stroke play*** *(in golf)* partie *f* par coups; ***stroke rate*** *(in rowing)* cadence *f* de nage

stroll [strəʊl] **1** *vi* se balader, flâner; **to stroll in/out/past** entrer/sortir/passer sans se presser; **we strolled round the shops** nous avons fait un petit tour dans les magasins; **she strolled in an hour late and didn't even say sorry** elle est arrivée tranquillement avec une heure de retard et ne s'est même pas excusée

2 *vt* **to stroll the streets** se promener dans les rues

3 *n* petit tour *m*, petite promenade *f*; **to go for a stroll** aller faire un tour *ou* une petite promenade

stroller ['strəʊlə(r)] *n* (**a**) *(walker)* promeneur(euse) *m,f*, flâneur(euse) *m,f* (**b**) *Am & Austr (pushchair)* poussette *f*

strolling ['strəʊlɪŋ] *adj (musician, minstrel)* ambulant

▸▸ ***strolling player*** comédien *m* ambulant, comédienne *f* ambulante; **a troupe of strolling players** une troupe ambulante

stroma ['strəʊmə] *(pl* **stromata** [-ətə]*)* *n Anat & Bot* stroma *m*

STRONG [strɒŋ]

fort	▸ **1 (a) – (c), (e), (f), (j), (k)**
robuste	▸ **1 (a)**
solide	▸ **1 (a), (b), (d), (i)**
puissant	▸ **1 (b)**
ferme	▸ **1 (b), (i)**
énergique	▸ **1 (b)**
sérieux	▸ **1 (d), (f)**
grossier	▸ **1 (g)**

(compar **stronger** ['strɒŋgə(r)], *superl* **strongest** ['strɒŋgɪst]) **1** *adj* (**a**) *(sturdy → person, animal, constitution, arms)* fort, robuste; *(→ building)* solide; *(→ cloth, material)* solide, résistant; *(→ shoes, table)* solide, robuste; *(in health → person)* robuste; *(→ heart)* solide, robuste; *(→ eyesight)* bon; **he's not very strong** *(not muscular)* il n'est pas très fort; *(not healthy)* il n'est pas très robuste; *Fam* **you need a strong stomach to eat this junk** il faut avoir un estomac en béton pour manger des cochonneries pareilles; **you'd need a strong stomach to go and watch that movie** il faut avoir l'estomac bien accroché pour aller voir ce film; **he'll be able to go out once he's strong again** il pourra sortir quand il aura repris des forces; **to be as strong as a horse** *(powerful)* être fort comme un Turc *ou* un bœuf; *(in good health)* avoir une santé de fer

(**b**) *(in degree, force, intensity → sea current, wind, light, lens, voice)* fort, puissant; *(→ magnet)* puissant; *(→ current)* intense; *Mus (→ beat)* fort; *(→ conviction, belief)* ferme, fort, profond; *(→ protest, support)* énergique, vigoureux; *(→ measures)* énergique, draconien; *(→ desire, imagination, interest)* vif; *(→ colour)* vif, fort; *(→ character, personality)* fort, bien trempé; *(→ feelings)* intense, fort; *(→ nerves)* solide; **the wind is growing stronger** le vent forcit; **there is a strong element of suspense in the story** il y a beaucoup de suspense dans cette histoire; **there's strong evidence that he committed suicide** tout porte à croire qu'il s'est suicidé; **it's my strong suit** *(in cards)* c'est ma couleur forte; *Fig* c'est mon fort; *Fig* **tact isn't her strong suit** *or* **point** le tact n'est pas son (point) fort; **what are his strong points?** quels sont ses points forts?; **he is a strong believer in discipline** il est de ceux qui croient fermement à la discipline; **it is my strong opinion that the men are innocent** je suis convaincu *ou* persuadé que ces hommes sont innocents; **she is a strong supporter of the government** elle soutient le gouvernement avec ferveur; **she is a strong supporter of Sunday trading** c'est une ardente partisane de l'ouverture des commerces le dimanche; **to exert a strong influence on sb** exercer beaucoup d'influence *ou* une forte influence sur qn; **she has a strong personality, she's a strong character** elle a une forte personnalité; **I have strong feelings on** *or* **about the death penalty** *(against)* je suis absolument contre la peine de mort; *(for)* je suis tout à fait pour la peine de mort; **I have no strong feelings** *or* **views one way or the other** cela m'est égal; **if you have strong feelings about it** si c'est tellement important pour toi; **he had a strong sense of guilt** il éprouvait un fort sentiment de culpabilité; **to have a strong will** avoir de la volonté; **you'll have to be strong now** *(when consoling or encouraging)* il va falloir être courageux maintenant; **you've got to be strong and say "no"** il faut être ferme et dire "non"

(**c**) *(striking → contrast, impression)* fort, frappant, marquant; *(→ accent)* fort; **to bear a strong resemblance to sb** ressembler beaucoup *ou* fortement à qn; **his speech made a strong impression on them** son discours les a fortement impressionnés *ou* a eu un profond effet sur eux; **there is a strong chance** *or* **probability that he will win** il y a de fortes chances pour qu'il gagne

(**d**) *(solid → argument, evidence)* solide, sérieux; **we have strong reasons to believe them innocent** nous avons de bonnes *ou* sérieuses raisons de croire qu'ils sont innocents; **they have a strong case** ils ont de bons arguments; **to be in a strong position** être dans une position de force; **we're in a strong bargaining position** nous sommes bien placés *ou* en position de force pour négocier

(**e**) *(in taste, smell)* fort; **I like strong coffee** j'aime le café fort *ou* corsé; **this whisky is strong stuff** ce whisky est fort; **there's a strong smell of gas in here** il y a une forte odeur de gaz ici

(**f**) *(in ability → student, team)* fort; *(→ candidate, contender)* sérieux; **he is a strong contender for the presidency** il a de fortes chances de remporter l'élection présidentielle; **he's a strong candidate for the post** il a le profil idéal pour le poste; **she is particularly strong in science subjects** elle est particulièrement forte dans les matières scientifiques; **in very strong form** en très grande forme; **the film was strong on style but weak on content** le film était très bon du point de vue de la forme mais pas du tout du point de vue du contenu

(**g**) *(tough, harsh → words)* grossier; **to use strong language** dire des grossièretés, tenir des propos grossiers; **I wrote him a strong letter** je lui ai écrit une lettre bien sentie; **she gave us her opinion in strong terms** elle nous a dit ce qu'elle pensait sans mâcher ses mots; **his latest film is strong stuff** son dernier film est vraiment dur

(**h**) *(in number)* **an army 5,000 strong** une armée forte de 5000 hommes; **the marchers were 400 strong** les manifestants étaient au nombre de 400

(**i**) *Com & Econ (currency, price)* solide; *(market)* ferme; **the dollar has got stronger** le dollar s'est raffermi

(**j**) *Phys* **strong force, strong interaction** interaction *f* forte

(**k**) *Gram (verb, form)* fort

2 *adv Fam* **to be going strong** *(person)* être toujours solide ❑ *ou* toujours d'attaque; *(party)* battre son plein; *(machine, car)* fonctionner toujours bien ❑; *(business, economy)* être florissant ❑, prospérer ❑; **he's eighty years old and still going strong** il a quatre-vingts ans et toujours bon pied bon œil; **the favourite was going strong as they turned into the home straight** le favori marchait fort quand les chevaux ont entamé la dernière ligne droite ❑; **to come on strong** *(insist)* insister lourdement ❑; *(make a pass)* faire des avances ❑; **that's coming it a bit strong!** vous y allez un peu fort!, vous exagérez!

---

strongarm ['strɒŋɑːm] *adj Fam (methods)* brutal ❑, violent ❑; **to use strongarm tactics** employer la manière forte ❑

strong-arm *vt Fam* faire violence à ❑; **to strong-arm sb into doing sth** forcer la main à qn pour qu'il fasse qch ❑

strongbox ['strɒŋbɒks] *n* coffre-fort *m*

stronghold ['strɒŋhəʊld] *n* (**a**) *Mil* forteresse *f*, fort *m* (**b**) *Fig* bastion *m*, fief *m*; **a Conservative Party stronghold** un bastion *ou* fief du parti conservateur

strongish ['strɒŋɪʃ] *adj* assez fort

strong-limbed *adj* aux membres forts *ou* athlétiques *ou* vigoureux

strongly ['strɒŋlɪ] *adv* (**a**) *(greatly → regret)* vivement, profondément; *(→ impress, attract)* fortement, vivement; **the kitchen smelt strongly of bleach** il y avait une forte odeur de Javel dans la cuisine; **to be strongly in favour of sth** être fortement en faveur *ou* chaud partisan de qch; **I strongly advise you to accept** je vous conseille vivement d'accepter; **I am strongly tempted to say yes** j'ai très envie de dire oui; **I strongly disagree with you** je ne suis pas du tout d'accord avec vous; **the report was strongly critical of the hospital** le rapport était extrêmement critique à l'égard de l'hôpital; **he strongly resembles his mother** il ressemble beaucoup à sa mère

(**b**) *(firmly → believe, support)* fermement; *(forcefully → attack, defend, protest)* énergiquement, vigoureusement, avec force; *(→ emphasize)* fortement; **strongly worded letter** lettre dans laquelle on ne mâche pas ses mots; **a strongly worded protest** une lettre de protestation énergique; **I feel very strongly about the matter** c'est un sujet *ou* une affaire qui me tient beaucoup à cœur; **I don't feel strongly about it** je n'ai pas d'opinion particulière à ce sujet; **the importance of the elections cannot be too strongly stressed** on ne saurait trop insister sur l'importance des élections

(**c**) *(sturdily → constructed)* solidement; **strongly built** *(person)* costaud, bien bâti; *(wall, structure)* solide, bien construit

strongman ['strɒŋmæn] *(pl* **strongmen** [-men]*)* *n (in circus, fair)* hercule *m* (de foire); *Fig (powerful man)* homme *m* fort

strong-minded *adj* résolu, déterminé; **she is very strong-minded** elle sait ce qu'elle veut

strong-mindedly [-'maɪndɪdlɪ] *adv* avec décision

strong-mindedness [-'maɪndɪdnɪs] *n* force *f* de caractère, résolution *f*

strongroom ['strɒŋruːm] *n Br (in castle, house)* chambre *f* forte; *(in bank)* chambre *f* forte, salle *f* des coffres

strong-willed [-'wɪld] *adj* volontaire, résolu, tenace

strontium ['strɒntɪəm] *n Chem* strontium *m*; **strontium 90** strontium 90

strop [strɒp] *(pt & pp* **stropped,** *cont* **stropping)** **1** *n* (**a**) *(for razor)* cuir *m* (à rasoir) (**b**) *Br Fam* **to be in a strop** être mal luné, être de mauvais poil

2 *vt (razor)* repasser sur le cuir

strophe ['strəʊfɪ] *n* strophe *f*

strophic ['strɒfɪk] *adj* qui a rapport à la strophe *ou* aux strophes; *(verse, song)* (divisé *ou* composé) en strophes

stroppiness ['strɒpɪnɪs] *n Br Fam (insolence)* insolence ❑ *f*; **I'm fed up with his constant stroppiness** *(bad temper)* j'en ai marre de ses humeurs

stroppy ['strɒpɪ] *(compar* **stroppier,** *superl* **stroppiest)** *adj Br Fam (bad-tempered)* mal luné, de mauvais poil; *(insolent)* insolent ❑; **there's no need to get stroppy!** tu n'as pas besoin de monter sur tes grands chevaux!; **he can be a very stroppy individual at times** il peut être très embêtant par moments

strove [strəʊv] *pt of* **strive**

struck [strʌk] **1** *pt & pp of* **strike**

2 *adj Am (industry)* bloqué pour cause de grève; *(factory)* fermé pour cause de grève

structural ['strʌktʃərəl] *adj* (**a**) *(gen)* structural; *(change, problem)* structurel, de structure; *(unemployment)* structurel; *Ling (analysis)* structural, structurel

(**b**) *Constr (fault, steel, iron)* de construction; *(damage, alterations)* de structure

►► ***structural engineer*** ingénieur *m* civil; ***structural engineering*** génie *m* civil; *Chem* ***structural formula*** formule *f* de constitution; *Econ & Fin* ***structural fund*** fonds *m* structurel; ***structural linguistics*** linguistique *f* structurale; ***structural psychology*** psychologie *f* structurale; *Econ* ***structural unemployment*** chômage *m* structurel

structuralism ['strʌktʃərəlɪzəm] *n* structuralisme *m*

structuralist ['strʌktʃərəlɪst] **1** *n* structuraliste *mf*

2 *adj* structuraliste

structuralization [ˌstrʌktʃərəlaɪ'zeɪʃən] *n* structuration *f*

structuralize, -ise ['strʌktʃərəlaɪz] *vt* structurer

structurally ['strʌktʃərəlɪ] *adv* (**a**) *(gen)* du point de vue de la structure; **structurally similar** de structure semblable; **the book is structurally well written** le livre est bien structuré *ou* construit (**b**) *Constr* du point de vue de la construction; **the building is structurally sound** le bâtiment est de construction solide

structure ['strʌktʃə(r)] **1** *n* (**a**) *(composition, framework)* structure *f*; **the structure of the tower enables it to withstand winds of up to 150 mph** la structure de la tour lui permet de résister à des vents pouvant atteindre 249 km/h

(**b**) *(building)* construction *f*, bâtisse *f*; **the scaffolding was a flimsy-looking structure** l'échafaudage était une construction d'apparence fragile; *Fig* **the social structure** l'édifice social

2 *vt* structurer

structured ['strʌktʃəd] *adj* structuré

►► *Comput* ***structured query language*** langage *m* d'interrogation structuré

structureless ['strʌktʃəlɪs] *adj (gen &) Geol* amorphe; *Biol* homogène

strudel ['struːdəl] *n Culin* strudel *m*; **apple strudel** strudel *m* aux pommes

struggle ['strʌgəl] **1** *n (gen)* lutte *f*; *(physical fight)* bagarre *f*, lutte *f*; **armed struggle** lutte *f* armée; **power struggle** lutte *f* pour le pouvoir; **the class struggle** la lutte des classes; **he got hurt in the struggle** il a été blessé dans la bagarre; **there was evidence of a struggle** il y avait des traces de lutte; **the rebels put up a fierce struggle** les rebelles ont opposé une vive résistance; **they surrendered without a struggle** ils se sont rendus sans opposer de résistance; **I finally succeeded but not without a struggle** j'y suis finalement parvenu, non sans peine; **it was a struggle to convince him** on a eu du mal à le convaincre; **life is a struggle** la vie est un combat; **there was a bitter struggle for leadership of the party** les candidats à la direction du parti se sont livré une lutte acharnée; *Br* **bringing up the children on her own was an uphill struggle** élever ses enfants seule n'a pas été facile; **it's a bit of a struggle to manage on one income** ce n'est pas facile de s'en sortir avec un seul salaire; **it was a struggle for him to climb the ten flights of stairs** il a eu de la peine à monter les dix étages à pied; **it'll be a struggle but I think we'll make it** ce sera difficile *ou* dur, mais je crois que nous y arriverons

2 *vi* (**a**) *(fight)* lutter, se battre; **she struggled with her attacker** elle a lutté contre *ou* s'est battue avec son agresseur; **to struggle with one's conscience** se débattre avec sa conscience; **the child struggled and kicked** l'enfant se débattait des pieds et des mains; **he struggled violently when they tried to force him into the car** il s'est violemment débattu quand ils ont essayé de le pousser dans la voiture; **she was struggling with her umbrella** elle se débattait avec son parapluie

(**b**) *(try hard, strive)* lutter, s'efforcer, se démener; **I struggled to open the door** je me suis démené pour ouvrir la porte; **he struggled with the lock** il s'est battu avec la serrure; **she struggled to control her temper** elle avait du mal à garder son calme; **we're struggling to meet their deadlines** nous faisons tout notre possible pour finir dans les délais; **she had to struggle to make ends meet** elle a eu bien du mal à joindre les deux bouts; **many companies are struggling** *(financially)* beaucoup d'entreprises ont du mal *ou* sont en difficulté; **I left him struggling through a Latin translation** je l'ai laissé aux prises avec une traduction latine; **he was obviously struggling for** *or* **to find the right word** il avait visiblement de la peine à trouver le mot juste

(**c**) *(expressing movement)* **he struggled back up onto the ledge** il remonta avec peine *ou* avec difficulté sur la corniche; **he struggled into his clothes** il enfila ses habits avec peine; **the dog struggled out of the water** le chien s'est débattu pour sortir de l'eau; **she struggled through the undergrowth** elle s'est péniblement frayé un chemin à travers les broussailles; **to struggle to one's feet** *(old person)* se lever avec difficulté *ou* avec peine; *(in fight)* se relever péniblement; **to struggle up a hill** *(person)* gravir péniblement une colline; *(car)* peiner dans une côte

►**struggle along** *vi* peiner, avancer avec peine; *Fig* subsister avec difficulté; **we are struggling along** *(in life, with work etc)* nous nous débrouillons tant bien que mal; **how are you? – oh, struggling along** comment ça va? – oh, on fait aller

►**struggle on** *vi* (**a**) = **struggle along**

(**b**) *(keep trying)* continuer à se battre; **we must struggle on** nous devons continuer à nous battre

►**struggle through** *vi (in difficult situation)* s'en sortir tant bien que mal; **we'll struggle through somehow** on trouvera bien un moyen de se débrouiller

struggler ['strʌglə(r)] *n* lutteur(euse) *m,f*

struggling ['strʌglɪŋ] *adj (hard up → painter, writer etc)* qui tire le diable par la queue, qui a du mal à joindre les deux bouts

strum [strʌm] *(pt & pp* **strummed**, *cont* **strumming**) **1** *vt (guitar)* jouer de; **to strum a tune on the guitar** jouer un petit air à la guitare

2 *vi (guitarist)* jouer; **she started strumming on her guitar** elle commença à jouer sur sa guitare

3 *n (on guitar)* **he gave the guitar a strum** il a gratté les cordes de la guitare

struma ['struːmə] *(pl* **strumae** [-iː]) *n* (**a**) *Med* goitre *m*; *Old-fashioned* strume *f*, scrofules *fpl* (**b**) *Bot* goitre *m*

strumming ['strʌmɪŋ] *n (on guitar)* raclement *m*; **a gentle strumming from the guitar** les doux accords de la guitare

strumpet ['strʌmpɪt] *n Arch or Hum* catin *f*

strung [strʌŋ] **1** *pt & pp of* **string**

2 *adj* (**a**) *(guitar, piano)* muni de cordes, monté; *(tennis racket)* cordé (**b**) *Am Fam* à cran

strung-out *adj Fam* (**a**) *Drugs slang* **to be strung-out** *(addicted)* être accroché *ou* accro; *(high)* être shooté, planer; *(suffering withdrawal symptoms)* être en manque; **to get strung-out** se défoncer (**b**) *(uptight)* crispé ❑, tendu ❑

strung-up *adj Fam* tendu ❑, nerveux ❑; **she's all strung-up about her exams** elle est très tendue à la perspective de ses examens; **don't get strung-up about it!** ne te mets pas dans tous tes états!

strut [strʌt] *(pt & pp* **strutted**, *cont* **strutting**) **1** *n* (**a**) *(support → for roof, wall)* étrésillon *m*, étançon *m*, contrefiche *f*; *(→ for building)* étai *m*, support *m*; *(→ between uprights)* entretoise *f*, traverse *f*; *(→ for beam)* jambe *f* de force; *(→ in plane wing, model)* support *m*; **metal strut** support *m* métallique

(**b**) *(crossbar → of chair, ladder)* barreau *m*

(**c**) *(gait)* démarche *f* fière

2 *vi* **to strut (about** *or* **around)** plastronner, se pavaner; **he strutted about the room** il arpentait la pièce en se pavanant

3 *vt Am Fam* **to strut one's stuff** frimer

struthious ['struːθɪəs] *adj Orn* de l'autruche

strychnine ['strɪkniːn] *n* strychnine *f*

strychninism ['strɪknɪnɪzəm], **strychnism** ['strɪknɪzəm] *n Med* strychnisme *m*

St Thomas *n Geog* Saint Thomas

St Trinian's [-'trɪnɪənz] *n* = école de jeunes filles apparaissant dans des bandes dessinées et des films anglais, et dont le nom évoque des élèves indisciplinées et impertinentes

stub [stʌb] *(pt & pp* **stubbed**, *cont* **stubbing**) **1** *n* (**a**) *(stump → of tree)* chicot *m*, souche *f*; *(→ of pencil)* bout *m*; *(→ of tail)* moignon *m*; *(→ of cigarette)* mégot *m*; **she was trying to write with a tiny stub of pencil** elle essayait d'écrire avec un bout de crayon minuscule; **an ashtray full of cigarette stubs** un cendrier plein de mégots

(**b**) *(counterfoil → of cheque)* souche *f*, talon *m*; *(→ of ticket)* talon *m*

2 *vt* **to stub one's toe/foot** se cogner le doigt de pied/le pied; **he stubbed his toe against the kerb** il a buté contre le bord du trottoir

►► ***stub axle*** essieu *m* à chapes fermées

►**stub out** *vt sep (cigarette)* écraser

stubble ['stʌbəl] *n* (**a**) *Agr* chaume *m* (**b**) *(on chin)* barbe *f* de plusieurs jours

►► ***stubble burning*** action *f* de brûler le chaume

stubbly ['stʌblɪ] *(compar* **stubblier**, *superl* **stubbliest**) *adj* (**a**) *(chin, face)* mal rasé; *(beard)* de plusieurs jours; *(hair)* en brosse (**b**) *(field)* couvert de chaume

stubborn ['stʌbən] *adj* (**a**) *(determined → person)* têtu, obstiné; *(→ animal)* rétif, récalcitrant; *(→ opposition)* obstiné, acharné; *(→ refusal, insistence)* obstiné; **she maintained a stubborn silence** elle garda obstinément le silence *ou* s'obstina à ne rien dire (**b**) *(resistant → cold, cough, symptoms)* persistant, opiniâtre; *(→ stain)* récalcitrant, rebelle

stubbornly ['stʌbənlɪ] *adv* obstinément, opiniâtrement; **he stubbornly insisted on doing it himself** il s'obstina à le faire lui-même

stubbornness ['stʌbənnɪs] *n (of person)* entêtement *m*, obstination *f*, opiniâtreté *f*; *(of resistance)* acharnement *m*

stubby ['stʌbɪ] *(compar* **stubbier**, *superl* **stubbiest**) **1** *adj (finger)* boudiné, court et épais(aisse); *(tail)* très court, tronqué; *(person)* trapu; **a stubby pencil** un petit bout de crayon

2 *n Austr Fam (bottle of beer)* canette *f* (de bière)

STUC [ˌestiːjuː'siː] *n (abbr* **Scottish Trades Union Congress**) = section écossaise de la confédération des syndicats britanniques

stucco ['stʌkəʊ] *(pl* **stuccos** *or* **stuccoes**) **1** *n* stuc *m*

2 *comp (ceiling, wall, façade)* de *ou* en stuc, stuqué

3 *vt* stuquer

►► ***stucco work*** *(act, process)* stucage *m*; *(result)* stuc *m*

stuccoed ['stʌkəʊd] *adj* décoré de stuc

stuck [stʌk] **1** *pt & pp of* **stick**

2 *adj* (**a**) *(jammed → window, mechanism)* coincé, bloqué; *(→ vehicle, lift)* bloqué; **he got his hand stuck inside the jar** il s'est pris *ou* coincé la main dans le pot; **the window was stuck** la fenêtre était coincée; **the wheel is stuck fast** la roue est complètement coincée; **to get stuck in the mud** s'embourber; **to get stuck in the sand** s'enliser; **to be** *or* **to get stuck in traffic** être coincé *ou* bloqué dans les embouteillages; *(stranded)* coincé, bloqué; **they were** *or* **they got stuck at the airport overnight** ils sont restés bloqués *ou* ils ont dû passer toute la nuit à l'aéroport

(**b**) *(in difficulty)* **if you get stuck go on to the next question** si tu sèches, passe à la question suivante; **he's never stuck for an answer** il a toujours réponse à tout; **to be stuck for money** être à court d'argent

(**c**) *(in an unpleasant situation, trapped)* coincé; **to be stuck in a boring/dead-end job** avoir un boulot ennuyeux/sans avenir

(**d**) *Fam (lumbered)* **to get** *or* **to be stuck with sth** se retrouver avec qch sur les bras; **I always get stuck with the washing-up** je me retrouve toujours avec la vaisselle sur les bras, c'est toujours moi qui dois me taper la vaisselle; **he was stuck with the nickname "Teddy"** le surnom de "Teddy" lui est resté; **it's not a very good car but we're stuck with it** ce n'est pas génial comme voiture, mais on n'a pas le choix (**e**) *Fam (fond, keen)* **to be stuck on sb** en pincer pour qn; **I'm not exactly stuck on the idea** je ne peux pas dire que l'idée m'emballe vraiment

(**f**) *Br Fam (idioms)* **to get stuck into sb** *(physically, verbally)* rentrer dans le lard à qn; **to get stuck into sth** *(book, work, meal)* attaquer qch; **he got stuck into his work** il s'est mis au travail❑; **get stuck in!** attaque!

stuck-up *adj Fam* bêcheur, snob; **she's very stuck-up** elle s'y croit vraiment

stud [stʌd] (*pt & pp* **studded**, *cont* **studding**) **1** *n* (**a**) *(nail, spike)* clou *m (à grosse tête)*; *(decorative)* clou *m (décoratif)*; *(on shoe)* clou *m (à souliers)*, caboche *f*; *(on belt)* clou *m*; *Br (on football boots, track shoes)* crampon *m*; *(on tyre)* clou *m*

(**b**) *(earring)* clou *m* d'oreille

(**c**) *(on roadway)* catadioptre *m*

(**d**) *(on shirt)* bouton *m (servant à fermer un col, un plastron etc)*

(**e**) *Tech (screw)* goujon *m*; *(pin, pivot)* tourillon *m*; *(lug)* ergot *m*

(**f**) *Constr (upright timber)* latte *f*, montant *m*

(**g**) *(on chain)* étai *m*

(**h**) *(reproduction)* monte *f*; **animals kept for stud** animaux destinés à la monte; **to put a stallion (out) to stud** mener un étalon à la monte; **to be at stud** saillir

(**i**) *(stud farm)* haras *m*

(**j**) *(stallion)* étalon *m*

(**k**) *Fam (man)* étalon *m*; *(promiscuous man)* tombeur *m*

(**l**) *Am* stud-poker *m (variété de poker où certaines cartes sont exposées)*

2 *vt* (**a**) *(shoes, belt)* clouter; *(door, chest)* clouter, garnir de clous; *Fig* **stars studded the night sky** le ciel était parsemé d'étoiles

(**b**) *Constr* latter

►► ***stud earring*** clou *m* d'oreille; ***stud farm*** haras *m*; ***stud fastener*** pression *f (bouton)*; ***stud mare*** (jument *f*) poulinière *f*; *Am Fam* ***stud muffin*** super beau mec *m*; ***stud poker*** stud-poker *m (variété de poker où certaines cartes sont exposées)*

studbook ['stʌdbʊk] *n* stud-book *m*

studded ['stʌdɪd] *adj* (**a**) *(tyre, belt, jacket)* clouté (**b**) *(spangled)* **studded with** émaillé *ou* parsemé de; **a crown studded with jewels** une couronne émaillée de pierres précieuses; **the sky was studded with stars** le ciel était parsemé d'étoiles

-studded ['stʌdɪd] *suff* **diamond-studded** émaillé de diamants

studding ['stʌdɪŋ] *n* (**a**) *Constr (woodwork)* lattage *m*, lattis *m*; *(piece of wood)* latte *f* (**b**) *(height of a room)* hauteur *f* de plafond (**c**) *(of shoes, belt, box)* cloutage *m* (**d**) *Naut* mailletage *m*

►► *Naut* ***studding sail*** bonnette *f*; **lower studding sail** bonnette *f* basse; *Naut* ***studding sail boom*** bout-dehors *m* de bonnette

student ['stju:dənt] **1** *n Univ* étudiant(e) *m,f*; *Sch* élève *mf*, lycéen(enne) *m,f*; **she's a biology student** *or* **a student of biology** elle étudie la biologie *ou* est étudiante en biologie; **a good student** *Sch* un bon élève; *Univ* un bon étudiant; *Fig* **students of human nature/Middle Eastern politics will know that...** ceux qui s'intéressent à la nature humaine/à la politique au Moyen-Orient sauront que...

2 *comp (life)* d'étudiant, estudiantin; *(hall of residence, canteen)* universitaire; *(participation) Univ* étudiant; *Sch* des élèves; *(power, union)* étudiant; *(protest) Univ* d'étudiants, étudiant; *Sch* d'élèves, de lycéens; *(attitudes) Univ* des étudiants; *Sch* des élèves; **the student body** les étudiants *mpl*

►► ***student adviser*** conseiller(ère) *m,f* pédagogique; ***student body*** *Univ* étudiants *mpl* inscrits; *Sch* élèves *mpl* inscrits; ***student card*** carte *f* d'étudiant; ***student flat*** appartement *m* d'étudiants; ***student grant*** bourse *f* (d'études); ***student hostel*** résidence *f* universitaire; ***student house*** maison *f* d'étudiants; *Am* ***student lamp*** lampe *f* de bureau; ***student loan*** = prêt bancaire pour étudiants; ***student nurse*** élève *m* infirmier, élève *f* infirmière; ***students' representative council*** = comité étudiant; ***student teacher*** *(in primary school)* instituteur(trice) *m,f* stagiaire; *(in secondary school)* professeur *m* stagiaire; ***students' union*** *(trade union)* syndicat *m ou* union *f* des étudiants; *(premises)* ≃ foyer *m* des étudiants

STUDENTS' UNION

Dans les universités britanniques et américaines, on appelle "students' union" à la fois le syndicat et les locaux où il se trouve. Le syndicat est chargé de défendre les intérêts des étudiants, sert de centre d'information et de conseil en matière de logement, de santé et de financement, et organise des événements culturels et des activités.

studentship ['stju:dəntʃɪp] *n Br* bourse *f* (d'études)

studhorse ['stʌdhɔ:s, *pl* -hɔ:sɪz] *n* étalon *m*

studied ['stʌdɪd] *adj* (**a**) *(ease, politeness, indifference)* étudié; *(insult, rudeness, negligence)* délibéré; *(elegance)* recherché; *(manner, pose)* étudié, affecté; **he wore a look of studied boredom** il affichait l'ennui (**b**) *Literary (of person)* instruit, versé (**in** dans)

studio ['stju:dɪəʊ] (*pl* **studios**) *n (of artist, photographer)* atelier *m*, studio *m*; *Rad, TV* studio *m*; **recording studio** studio *m* d'enregistrement

►► *Am* ***studio apartment*** studio *m*; ***studio audience*** public *m (présent lors de la diffusion ou de l'enregistrement d'une émission)*; ***studio couch*** canapé-lit *m*, canapé *m* convertible; *Br* ***studio flat*** studio *m*; ***studio portrait*** portrait *m* photographique; *Cin* ***the studio system*** l'hégémonie *f* des grands studios (hollywoodiens)

studious ['stju:dɪəs] *adj* (**a**) *(diligent → person)* studieux, appliqué (**b**) *(painstaking → attention, effort)* soutenu (**c**) *(deliberate → indifference)* délibéré, voulu; **because of his studious avoidance of the topic** parce qu'il évitait soigneusement le sujet

studiously ['stju:dɪəslɪ] *adv* (**a**) *(diligently → prepare, work, examine)* minutieusement, soigneusement (**b**) *(deliberately)* d'une manière calculée *ou* délibérée; **studiously indifferent** d'une indifférence feinte; **she studiously ignored him** elle s'ingéniait à ignorer sa présence

studiousness ['stju:dɪəsnɪs] *n* (**a**) *(eagerness to study)* application *f* (à l'étude), assiduité *f* (**b**) *(carefulness)* empressement *m*, zèle *m* (**in doing sth** à faire qch)

studwork ['stʌdwɜ:k] *n Archit* colombage *m*

study ['stʌdɪ] (*pt & pp* **studied**, *pl* **studies**) **1** *vt* (**a**) *(gen) & Sch & Univ* étudier; **she's studying medicine/history** elle fait des études de médecine/d'histoire, elle est étudiante en médecine/histoire

(**b**) *(examine → plan, evidence, situation)* étudier, examiner; *(observe → expression, reactions)* étudier, observer attentivement; *(→ stars)* observer

2 *vi (gen)* étudier; *Sch & Univ* étudier, faire ses études; **she's studying to be an architect** elle fait des études pour devenir architecte *ou* des études d'architecture; **he's studying for a degree in history** il étudie dans le but d'obtenir un diplôme d'histoire; **to study for an examination** se préparer pour un examen, préparer un examen; **where's Brian? – he's upstairs studying** où est Brian? – il travaille en haut; **to study for an exam** préparer un examen; **I studied under her at university** je suivais ses cours à l'université

3 *n* (**a**) *(academic work, acquisition of knowledge)* étude *f*; **she devotes most evenings to study** elle passe la plupart de ses soirées à étudier; **he sets aside one day a week for study** il consacre un jour par semaine à ses études

(**b**) *(investigation)* étude *f* (**of** de); *(report)* étude *f*, rapport *m*; **the plan is under study** le projet est à l'étude *f*; **her thesis is a study of multi-racial communities** sa thèse est une étude des communautés *ou* sur les communautés multiraciales; **I've made an extensive study of animal behaviour** j'ai fait une étude approfondie du comportement animal; **scientific studies have shown that...** des études *ou* des recherches scientifiques ont montré que...

(**c**) *(room)* bureau *m*, cabinet *m* de travail

(**d**) *Art, Mus & Phot* étude *f*; **a study in black** une étude en noir; *Fig Literary* **her face was a study** il fallait voir son visage

4 *comp (hour, room)* d'étude

5 studies *npl Sch & Univ* études *fpl*; **how are your studies going?** comment vont vos études?; **the School of Oriental Studies** l'Institut des Études orientales

►► ***study group*** groupe *m* de travail *ou* d'étude; *Am* ***study hall*** *(place)* salle *f* d'étude; *(period)* heure *f* d'étude; ***study period*** heure *f* de permanence *ou* d'étude; **we have a study period on Monday mornings** nous avons une heure d'étude le lundi matin; ***study tour*** *or* ***trip*** voyage *m* d'études

STUFF [stʌf]

choses	► 1 (a)
substance	► 1 (a)
bêtises	► 1 (b)
affaires	► 1 (c)
étoffe	► 1 (d), (e)
bourrer	► 2 (a)
farcir	► 2 (a)
fourrer	► 2 (b)
boucher	► 2 (d)

1 *n (UNCOUNT)* (**a**) *Fam (indefinite sense → things)* choses❑ *fpl*, trucs *mpl*; *(→ substance)* substance❑ *f*, matière❑ *f*; **what's that sticky stuff in the sink?** qu'est-ce que c'est que ce truc gluant dans l'évier?; **here's some stuff to put on that burn** voilà de quoi soigner cette brûlure; **his pockets are always full of all kinds of stuff** il a toujours un tas de trucs dans les poches; **he writes some good stuff** il écrit de bons trucs; **there was some stuff about unions on the news** ils ont dit un truc sur les syndicats aux informations; **it's made of tomatoes and onions and stuff** il y a des tomates, des oignons et des trucs comme ça; **they go climbing and sailing and stuff like that** ils font de l'escalade, de la voile et des trucs du même genre; **this material is good stuff** c'est un bon tissu *ou* du tissu de bonne qualité❑; **I used to drink whisky but now I never touch the stuff** avant, je buvais du whisky, mais maintenant je n'y touche plus❑; **no thanks, I can't stand the stuff** non merci, j'ai horreur de ça; **this whisky is strong stuff** il arrache, ce whisky; **this mustard is strong stuff** cette moutarde est forte; **the book is strong stuff** *(sexually explicit)* ce livre n'est pas à mettre entre toutes les mains❑; *(hard-hitting)* ce livre est dur❑

(**b**) *Fam Pej (rubbish, nonsense)* bêtises❑ *fpl*, sottises❑ *fpl*; **stuff and nonsense!** balivernes!; **don't give me all that stuff about the British Empire!** passe-moi le topo débile sur l'empire britannique!; **you don't believe all that stuff about ghosts, do you?** vous ne croyez tout de même pas à toutes ces bêtises sur les fantômes?; **do you call that stuff art/music?** vous appelez ça de l'art/de la musique?❑; **it's no use trying on that sweet and innocent stuff with me!** pas la peine de jouer au plus fin avec moi!

(**c**) *Fam (possessions)* affaires❑ *fpl*; *(equipment)* affaires❑ *fpl*, matériel❑ *m*; **clear all that stuff off the table!** enlève tout ce bazar de sur la table!; **have you packed all your stuff?** est-ce que tu as fini de faire tes bagages?❑; **where's my shaving/fishing stuff?** où est mon matériel de rasage/de pêche?

(**d**) *(essence)* étoffe *f*; **he's the stuff that heroes are made of** il est de l'étoffe dont sont faits les héros; *Literary* **the very stuff of life** l'essence *f* même de la vie; **the very stuff of melodrama** ce dont on fait les mélodrames

(**e**) *(fabric)* étoffe *f* (de laine)

(**f**) *Fam (drugs)* came *f*

(**g**) *Br Fam (woman)* **she's a nice bit of stuff, she's hot stuff** elle est vraiment bien balancée, elle est canon; **he was there with his bit of stuff** il était là avec sa petite copine

(**h**) *Am Sport (spin)* effet *m*

(**i**) *Fam (idioms)* **to do one's stuff** faire ce qu'on a à faire❑; **get out there and do your stuff!** allez, fais ce que tu as à faire *ou* à toi de jouer!; **that's the stuff!** c'est ça!, allez-y!, parfait!; **good stuff!** bien!❑; **to know one's stuff** s'y connaître □, connaître son affaire □; **he certainly knows his stuff** il connaît son affaire; **I don't give a stuff!** rien à fiche!

2 *vt* (**a**) *(fill → gen)* bourrer (**with** de); *(→ cushion, armchair)* rembourrer; *Culin* farcir; **stuffed with sausage meat** farci de chair à saucisse; **stuffed with foam** rembourré de mousse; **their house is stuffed with souvenirs from India** leur maison est bourrée de souvenirs d'Inde; **her pockets are stuffed with sweets** elle a les poches bourrées de bonbons, elle a des bonbons plein les poches; **his teachers stuffed his head with a load of political nonsense** ses professeurs lui ont bourré le crâne d'un tas d'idées politiques fausses; **her head is stuffed with useless information** elle a la tête farcie de renseignements inutiles

(**b**) *(shove)* fourrer; **he stuffed the papers into his pocket** il a fourré les papiers dans sa poche; **just stuff everything under the bed** vous n'avez qu'à tout fourrer sous le lit

(**c**) *Fam (expressing anger, rejection etc)* **he told me I could stuff my report** il m'a dit qu'il se foutait pas mal de mon rapport; **I've had enough, he can stuff his job!** j'en ai marre! son boulot il peut se le mettre où je pense!; **stuff it!** et puis merde!; *very Fam* **get stuffed!, stuff you!** va te faire foutre!

(**d**) *(plug → gap)* boucher; **the hole had been stuffed with paper** le trou avait été bouché avec du papier

(**e**) *(in taxidermy → animal, bird)* empailler

(**f**) *Fam (with food)* **to stuff oneself** *or* **one's face** se goinfrer, s'empiffrer; **to stuff oneself with cake** s'empiffrer de gâteau; **stop stuffing your face with chocolate!** arrête de t'empiffrer de chocolat!; **I'm stuffed** je n'ai plus faim □

(**g**) *Am Pol (ballot box)* remplir de bulletins de vote truqués

(**h**) *Fam (defeat)* écrabouiller, ficher une déculottée à, battre à plates coutures □

▸**stuff away** *vt sep Fam (food)* enfourner, s'enfiler

▸**stuff up** *vt sep (block)* boucher; **my nose is all stuffed up, I'm all stuffed up** j'ai le nez complètement bouché

---

stuffed [stʌft] *adj* (**a**) *Culin* farci (**b**) *(chair, cushion)* rembourré (**c**) *(owl, fox, rabbit etc)* empaillé (**d**) *Br & Austr Fam (in trouble)* cuit, fichu; **if that cheque doesn't arrive soon, we're stuffed** si ce chèque n'arrive pas bientôt, on est cuits

▸▸ ***stuffed animal*** *(mounted)* animal *m* empaillé; *Am (toy)* peluche *f*; ***stuffed shirt*** prétentieux(euse) *m,f*; **he's a real stuffed shirt** il est vraiment prétentieux

stuffer ['stʌfə(r)] *n Mktg (insert)* encart *m*

stuffily ['stʌfɪlɪ] *adv (say, reply)* d'un ton désapprobateur

stuffiness ['stʌfɪnɪs] *n* (**a**) *(of room)* manque *m* d'air (**b**) *(of person → primness)* esprit *m* collet monté; *(→ old-fashionedness)* esprit *m* vieux jeu

stuffing ['stʌfɪŋ] *n* (**a**) *(for furniture, toys)* rembourrage *m*, bourre *f*; *(for clothes)* rembourrage *m*; *(in taxidermy)* paille *f*; **horsehair stuffing** matelassure *f* de crin; *Fig* **he's got no stuffing!** il n'a rien dans le ventre!; *Fam* **to knock the stuffing out of sb** *(defeat heavily)* mettre la pâtée à qn; *(of blow, attacker, illness)* mettre qn KO; **the news of his death really knocked the stuffing out of me** ça m'a fait un sacré coup d'apprendre qu'il était mort

(**b**) *Culin* farce *f*

stuffy ['stʌfɪ] *(compar* **stuffier**, *superl* **stuffiest**) *adj* (**a**) *(room)* mal aéré, mal ventilé, qui sent le renfermé; **it's a bit stuffy in here** *(stale)* ça sent le renfermé ici; *(stifling)* on manque d'air *ou* on étouffe ici

(**b**) *Pej (person → prim)* collet monté *(inv)*; *(→ old-fashioned)* vieux jeu *(inv)*; *(atmosphere, reception)* guindé; **don't be so stuffy!** *(shocked)* il n'y a pas de quoi être scandalisé!; *(prim)* ne sois pas si prude!; *(old-fashioned)* ne sois pas si vieux jeu!

(**c**) *(dull → book, subject, lecture)* ennuyeux

(**d**) *(nose)* bouché

stultification [ˌstʌltɪfɪ'keɪʃən] *n* (**a**) *(dulling)* abrutissement *m*; *(stifling)* étouffement *m* (**b**) *(ridiculing)* action *f* de ridiculiser

stultify ['stʌltɪfaɪ] *(pt & pp* **stultified**) *vt* (**a**) *(make stupid)* abrutir; *(stifle → creativity, talent)* étouffer (**b**) *(make ridiculous)* ridiculiser

stultifying ['stʌltɪfaɪɪŋ] *adj (work)* abrutissant, assommant; *(atmosphere)* abrutissant, débilitant; **their policies have had a stultifying effect on the country's economy** leur politique a paralysé *ou* étouffé l'économie du pays

stumble ['stʌmbəl] **1** *vi* (**a**) *(person)* trébucher, faire un faux pas; *(horse)* broncher, faire un faux pas; **she stumbled and fell** elle trébucha et tomba; **he stumbled against me** il a trébuché et m'a heurté; **he stumbled over the toys in the hall** il a trébuché sur les jouets dans le couloir; **to stumble along/in/out** avancer/entrer/sortir en trébuchant; **they stumbled, exhausted, over the finishing line** ils ont franchi la ligne d'arrivée en titubant de fatigue; **he was stumbling about in the dark** il avançait en trébuchant dans le noir; **they stumbled out into the bright light** ils sortirent en chancelant sous la lumière aveuglante

(**b**) *(in speech)* trébucher; **to stumble over a long word** trébucher sur un mot long; **he managed to stumble through his lecture** c'est d'une voix mal assurée qu'il a finalement prononcé son cours

2 *n* (**a**) *(in walking)* faux pas *m*

(**b**) *(in speech)* **she read the poem without a stumble** elle a lu le poème sans se tromper *ou* sans se reprendre une seule fois

▸**stumble across, stumble on, stumble upon** *vt insep* (**a**) *(meet)* rencontrer par hasard, tomber sur

(**b**) *(discover)* trouver par hasard, tomber sur

stumblebum ['stʌmbəlbʌm] *n Am Fam* (**a**) *(drunken vagrant)* clodo *mf* alcoolo (**b**) *(clumsy, incompetent person)* manche *m*

stumbling ['stʌmblɪŋ] *adj (speech)* hésitant; **she took her first stumbling steps** elle a fait ses premiers pas

▸▸ ***stumbling block*** pierre *f* d'achoppement

stumer ['stju:mə(r)] *n very Fam* (**a**) *(cheque)* chèque *m* sans provision; *(banknote)* faux billet *m* de banque (**b**) *(worthless thing)* chose *f* qui ne vaut rien; *(person → failure)* raté(e) *m,f*

stumm = **schtum**

stump [stʌmp] **1** *n* (**a**) *(of tree)* chicot *m*, souche *f*

(**b**) *(of limb, tail)* moignon *m*; *(of tooth)* chicot *m*; *(of pencil, blade, candle)* (petit) bout *m*

(**c**) *Am Pol* estrade *f (d'un orateur politique)*; **to be/go on the stump** faire une tournée électorale

(**d**) *Art* estompe *f*

(**e**) *(in cricket)* piquet *m*

2 *vt* (**a**) *Fam (bewilder)* laisser perplexe □, déconcerter □; *(with question)* coller; **I'm stumped** *(don't know answer)* je sèche; *(don't know what to do)* je ne sais pas quoi faire □; **the question had them stumped** la question les a laissés sans voix □; **she's stumped for an answer** *(in quiz)* elle ne connaît pas la réponse □; *(for solution)* elle ne trouve pas de solution □; **it stumps me how anybody could be so silly!** que quelqu'un puisse être aussi bête, ça me dépasse! □

(**b**) *Am Pol (constituency, state)* faire une tournée électorale dans

3 *vi* (**a**) *(walk heavily)* marcher d'un pas lourd; **to stump in/out** *(heavily)* entrer/sortir d'un pas lourd

(**b**) *Am Pol* faire une tournée électorale

4 stumps *npl Fam (legs)* quilles *fpl*

▸▸ *Art* ***stump drawing*** estompe *f*

▸**stump up** *Br Fam* **1** *vi* casquer, raquer (**for** pour); **come on, stump up!** allez, raque!; **I had to stump up for the taxi** c'est moi qui ai dû payer le taxi □

2 *vt sep (money)* cracher, aligner, casquer; *(deposit)* payer □

stumpage ['stʌmpɪdʒ] *n Am* valeur *f* de bois d'œuvre

stumpy ['stʌmpɪ] *(compar* **stumpier**, *superl* **stumpiest**) *adj (person)* boulot(otte), courtaud; *(arms, legs)* court et épais(aisse); *(tail)* tronqué

stun [stʌn] *(pt & pp* **stunned**, *cont* **stunning**) *vt* (**a**) *(knock out)* assommer (**b**) *Fig (astonish)* abasourdir, stupéfier

▸▸ ***stun grenade*** grenade *f* incapacitante; ***stun gun*** fusil *m* hypodermique

stung [stʌŋ] *pt & pp of* **sting**

stunk [stʌŋk] *pp of* **stink**

stunned [stʌnd] *adj* (**a**) *(knocked out)* assommé (**b**) *Fig* abasourdi, stupéfié; **she was stunned by the news** la nouvelle l'a abasourdie; **there was a stunned silence** il y a eu un silence de mort; **they watched in stunned silence** ils regardaient en silence, abasourdis; **he was stunned by the beauty of the landscape** il était muet d'admiration devant la beauté du paysage

stunner ['stʌnə(r)] *n Br Fam (man, woman)* canon *m*; *(car)* voiture *f* fantastique □

stunning ['stʌnɪŋ] *adj* (**a**) *(blow)* étourdissant; *Fig* **this has dealt a stunning blow to the party** ceci a porté un coup terrible au parti

(**b**) *(astounding → news, event)* stupéfiant, renversant, sidérant; *(beautiful → dress, car)* fantastique; *(→ woman, figure)* superbe; **she looked stunning in a black velvet dress** elle était superbe dans sa robe de velours noir; **the film wasn't exactly stunning** le film n'avait rien de bien sensationnel

stunningly ['stʌnɪŋlɪ] *adv* remarquablement, incroyablement; **stunningly beautiful** d'une beauté éblouissante

stunt [stʌnt] **1** *n* (**a**) *(feat)* tour *m* de force, exploit *m* spectaculaire; *(in plane)* acrobatie *f* (aérienne); **it was quite a stunt!** il fallait le faire!

(**b**) *(by stunt man)* cascade *f*; **to do a stunt** *(in plane)* faire des acrobaties; *(stunt man)* faire une cascade; **to do one's own stunts** *(actor, actress)* ne pas se faire doubler dans les scènes dangereuses

(**c**) *(trick)* truc *m*; *(hoax)* farce *f*, canular *m*; *(done to attract publicity)* coup *m* de pub; **to pull a stunt** faire un canular *ou* une farce; **it's just a stunt to raise money** ce n'est qu'un truc *ou* une combine pour se faire de l'argent

(**d**) *(plant)* plante *f* chétive *ou* rabougrie; *(animal)* = animal dont la croissance a été freinée

2 *vi* (**a**) *Aviat* faire des acrobaties

(**b**) *Cin & TV* faire des cascades

3 *vt (impede → growth, development)* retarder; *(→ person)* freiner *ou* retarder la croissance de; *(→ intelligence)* freiner le développement de

▸▸ ***stunt driver*** conducteur *m* cascadeur, conductrice *f* cascadeuse; ***stunt driving*** cascades *fpl* automobiles; *Aviat* ***stunt flying*** vol *m* acrobatique; ***stunt man*** cascadeur *m*; ***stunt pilot*** pilote *m* de voltige aérienne, voltigeur *m*; ***stunt woman*** cascadeuse *f*

stunted ['stʌntɪd] *adj (person)* chétif; *(plant)* chétif, rabougri; *(growth, intelligence)* retardé

stuntedness ['stʌntɪdnɪs] *n (of person)* caractère *m* chétif; *(of plant)* rabougrissement *m*

stupa ['stu:pə] *n* stupa *m*, stoupa *m*

stupe [stu:p] *n* (**a**) *Am Fam* andouille *f*, crétin(e) *m,f* (**b**) *Med* compresse *f*

stupefacient [ˌstju:pɪ'feɪʃənt] *Med* **1** *adj* stupéfiant

2 *n* stupéfiant *m*

stupefaction [ˌstju:pɪ'fækʃən] *n* stupéfaction *f*, stupeur *f*

stupefied ['stju:pɪfaɪd] *adj* stupéfait

stupefy ['stju:pɪfaɪ] *(pt & pp* **stupefied**) *vt* (**a**) *(of alcohol, drugs, tiredness)* abrutir; *(of blow)* assommer, étourdir (**b**) *(astound)* stupéfier, abasourdir

stupefying ['stju:pɪfaɪɪŋ] *adj* stupéfiant

stupendous [stju:'pendəs] *adj (amount, achievement, talent)* extraordinaire, prodigieux; *(event)* prodigieux, extraordinaire; *(book, film)* extraordinaire

stupendously [stju:'pendəslɪ] *adv* prodigieusement, formidablement

stupid ['stju:pɪd] **1** *adj* (**a**) *(foolish)* idiot; **he's always saying/doing stupid things** il dit/fait sans arrêt des bêtises; **I was stupid enough to go and apologize** j'ai eu la sottise d'aller *ou* j'ai été assez bête pour aller m'excuser; **he's stupid enough to believe you** il est assez bête pour vous croire; **stop being so stupid!** arrête de faire l'idiot *ou* l'imbécile!; **how stupid of me!** que je suis bête!; **what a stupid place to put it!** c'est idiot de l'avoir mis là!; **I'm not stupid, you know!** je ne suis pas idiot quand même!

(**b**) *Literary (from alcohol, drugs, sleep)* abruti, hébété; *(from blow)* étourdi; **he was still stupid from** *or* **with sleep** il était encore abruti de sommeil; **to drink oneself stupid** s'abrutir d'alcool

(**c**) *Fam (wretched, confounded)* maudit, fichu; **where did I put that stupid hammer?** où est-ce que j'ai mis ce maudit marteau?

2 *n Fam* bêta(asse) *m,f*, idiot(e)❑ *m,f*; **I'm only joking, stupid!** je plaisante, gros bêta!

stupidity [stjuːˈpɪdətɪ] (*pl* **stupidities**) *n* stupidité *f*, bêtise *f*, sottise *f*

stupidly [ˈstjuːpɪdlɪ] *adv* stupidement, bêtement; **I stupidly forgot to phone them** je suis bête, j'ai oublié de leur téléphoner

stupor [ˈstjuːpə(r)] *n* stupeur *f*, abrutissement *m*; **to be in a drunken stupor** être abruti par l'alcool

sturdily [ˈstɜːdɪlɪ] *adv* (**a**) *(solidly)* solidement, robustement; **to be sturdily built** *(person)* être costaud *ou* bien bâti; *(toys, furniture, equipment)* être solide; *(house)* être de construction solide, être robuste (**b**) *(firmly → deny, refuse, oppose)* énergiquement, vigoureusement

sturdiness [ˈstɜːdɪnɪs] *n* (**a**) *(solidity)* solidité *f*, robustesse *f* (**b**) *(firmness)* fermeté *f*; **with great sturdiness of purpose** avec une grande résolution

sturdy [ˈstɜːdɪ] (*compar* **sturdier**, *superl* **sturdiest**) *adj* (**a**) *(robust → person)* robuste, vigoureux; *(→ limbs)* robuste; *(→ table, tree, shoes)* robuste, solide (**b**) *(firm → denial, defence, opposition, support)* énergique, vigoureux; *(→ voice)* ferme; **with sturdy determination** avec une ferme résolution

sturgeon [ˈstɜːdʒən] (*pl* **inv**) *n Ich* esturgeon *m*

stushie [ˈstuːʃɪ] *n Scot Fam* (**a**) *(row, racket)* boucan *m* (**b**) *(state of anxiety, upset)* **to be in a stushie** être dans tous ses états

stutter [ˈstʌtə(r)] **1** *n* bégaiement *m*; **to speak with a** *or* **to have a stutter** bégayer, être bègue

2 *vi* bégayer; *Fig* **the engine stuttered into life** le moteur toussa avant de démarrer

3 *vt* **to stutter (out)** bégayer, bredouiller; **she stuttered (out) an apology** elle bredouilla une excuse

stutterer [ˈstʌtərə(r)] *n* bègue *mf*

stuttering [ˈstʌtərɪŋ] **1** *n* bégaiement *m*

2 *adj* bègue, qui bégaie

stutteringly [ˈstʌtərɪŋlɪ] *adv* en bégayant

STV [ˌestiːˈviː] *n* (**a**) *Pol* (*abbr* **single transferable vote**) scrutin *m* uninominal préférentiel avec report de voix (**b**) *Am* (*abbr* **subscription television**) chaînes *fpl* à péage

sty [staɪ] (*pl* **sties**) *n* (**a**) *(for pigs)* porcherie *f* (**b**) = **stye**

stye [staɪ] *n* orgelet *m*, compère-loriot *m*

Stygian [ˈstɪdʒɪən] *adj Literary* ténébreux, sombre

►► ***Stygian gloom*** ténèbres *fpl* impénétrables *ou* insondables

style [staɪl] **1** *n* (**a**) *(manner)* style *m*, manière *f*; *Art, Literature & Mus* style *m*; **in the style of Vermeer** dans le style de Vermeer; **style of life** mode *m* de vie; **I don't like his style of dressing** je n'aime pas sa façon de s'habiller; **written in the style of a 1940s thriller** écrit dans le style du roman policier des années 1940; **they've adopted a new management style** *(approach)* ils ont adopté un nouveau style de gestion; **they danced the charleston, 1920s style** ils ont dansé le charleston comme on le dansait dans les années vingt; **the meal was prepared in authentic Japanese style** le repas a été préparé dans la plus pure tradition japonaise; **you've got to admire his style!** *(way of doing things)* on ne peut qu'admirer la façon dont il s'y prend!

(**b**) *(fashion → in clothes)* mode *f*; *(model, design)* modèle *m*; **to be dressed in the latest style** être habillé à la dernière mode; **a new style of dress** un nouveau modèle de robe; **all the latest styles** tous les derniers modèles; **this winter's styles** les modèles de cet hiver; **the boots come in two styles** ces bottes existent en deux modèles

(**c**) *(elegance, sophistication → of person)* allure *f*, chic *m*; *(→ of dress, picture, building, film)* style *m*; **she's got real style** elle a vraiment de l'allure *ou* du chic; **she does everything with great style** elle fait tout avec beaucoup de style; **to live in style** mener grand train, vivre dans le luxe; **he likes to do things in style** il aime faire bien les choses; **they were dressed in style** ils étaient habillés avec beaucoup de chic; **they made their entrance in great style** ils ont fait une entrée très remarquée; **they drove off in style in a fleet of limousines** ils sont partis en grande pompe dans un cortège de limousines

(**d**) *(type)* genre *m*; **I wouldn't have thought cheating was your style** je n'aurais jamais pensé que c'était ton genre de tricher; **I don't like his style** je n'aime pas son genre; **that's the style!** c'est ça!, bravo!

(**e**) *(of calendar)* **February 12 old/new style** le 12 février vieux/nouveau style

(**f**) *Typ (in editing)* style *m*; **house style** style *m* de la maison

(**g**) *Br Formal (title)* titre *m*

(**h**) *Bot* style *m*

(**i**) = **stile**

2 *vt* (**a**) *(call)* appeler, désigner; **she styles herself "countess"** elle se fait appeler "comtesse"

(**b**) *(design → dress, jewel, house)* créer, dessiner; **dress styled by Dior** robe créée par Dior; **to style sb's hair** coiffer qn; **styled for comfort and elegance** conçu pour le confort et l'élégance

(**c**) *Press & Typ (manuscript)* mettre au point *(selon les précisions stylistiques de l'éditeur)*

3 *vi Am Fam (show off)* frimer, flamber; *(do well)* bien se démerder

►► *Comput* ***style bar*** barre *f* de style; *Comput* ***style sheet*** feuille *f* de style

-style [staɪl] *suff* dans le style de; **a sixties-style haircut** une coupe de cheveux (dans le style des) années soixante; **baroque-style architecture** architecture *f* de style baroque, baroque *m*

stylebook [ˈstaɪlbʊk] *n Typ* manuel *m ou* protocole *m* de style

stylet [ˈstaɪlɪt] *n* stylet *m*

styli [ˈstaɪlaɪ] *pl of* **stylus**

styling [ˈstaɪlɪŋ] *n (of dress)* forme *f*, ligne *f*; *(of hair)* coupe *f*; *(of car)* ligne *f*

►► ***styling brush*** brosse *f* coiffante; ***styling gel*** gel *m* coiffant; ***styling mousse*** mousse *f* coiffante

stylish [ˈstaɪlɪʃ] *adj (person)* élégant, chic *(inv)*; *(clothes, hotel, neighbourhood)* élégant, chic *(inv)*; *(book, film)* qui a du style

stylishly [ˈstaɪlɪʃlɪ] *adv (dress)* avec chic, avec allure, élégamment; *(live)* élégamment; *(travel)* dans le luxe; *(write)* avec style *ou* élégance

stylishness [ˈstaɪlɪʃnɪs] *n* chic *m*, élégance *f*; *(of prose)* élégance *f*

stylist [ˈstaɪlɪst] *n* (**a**) *(designer → for clothes)* styliste *mf* (de mode), modéliste *mf*; *(→ for cars, furniture)* styliste *mf*; **(hair) stylist** coiffeur(euse) *m,f* (**b**) *Art & Literature* styliste *mf*

stylistic [staɪˈlɪstɪk] *adj Art, Literature & Ling* stylistique

stylistically [staɪˈlɪstɪklɪ] *adv* d'un point de vue stylistique

stylistics [staɪˈlɪstɪks] *n (UNCOUNT)* stylistique *f*

stylization [ˌstaɪəlaɪˈzeɪʃən] *n* stylisation *f*

stylize, -ise [ˈstaɪəlaɪz] *vt* styliser

stylized [ˈstaɪəlaɪzd] *adj* stylisé

stylobate [ˈstaɪləbeɪt] *n Archit* stylobate *m*

stylograph [ˈstaɪləʊgrɑːf] *n* stylographe *m*

styloid [ˈstaɪlɔɪd] *Anat* **1** *adj* styloïde

2 *n* **the styloid** l'apophyse *f* styloïde

stylometry [staɪˈlɒmətrɪ] *n* stylométrie *f*

stylus [ˈstaɪləs] (*pl* **styluses** *or* **styli** [-laɪ]) *n (on record player)* pointe *f* de lecture; *(made of sapphire)* saphir *m*; *(made of diamond)* diamant *m*; *(tool)* style *m*, stylet *m*

stymie [ˈstaɪmɪ] **1** *vt* (**a**) *(in golf)* barrer le trou à (**b**) *Br Fam Fig (person)* coincer; *(plan)* ficher en l'air; **to be stymied** être coincé *ou* dans une impasse❑

2 *n (in golf)* trou *m* barré; *Fig* obstacle *m*, entrave *f*

styptic [ˈstɪptɪk] **1** *adj* styptique

2 *n* styptique *m*

►► ***styptic pencil*** crayon *m* hémostatique

styrene [ˈstaɪəriːn] *n Chem* styrène *m*, styrolène *m*

Styria [ˈstɪrɪə] *n* Styrie *f*

Styrofoam® [ˈstaɪrəfəʊm] *n* polystyrène *m* expansé

Styx [stɪks] *n Myth* **the (River) Styx** le Styx

suable [ˈsuːəbəl] *adj Law* poursuivable

suasion [ˈsweɪʒən] *n Formal* persuasion *f*; **to subject sb to moral suasion** agir sur la conscience de qn

suave [swɑːv] *adj* (**a**) *(polite, charming)* poli, *Literary* urbain; *Pej (smooth)* doucereux, mielleux, onctueux; **he's a bit too suave for my liking** je le trouve un peu trop doucereux (**b**) *(elegant)* élégant, chic

suavely [ˈswɑːvlɪ] *adv* (**a**) *(politely, charmingly)* poliment; *Pej (smoothly)* mielleusement (**b**) *(elegantly)* avec élégance

suaveness [ˈswɑːvnɪs], **suavity** [ˈswɑːvətɪ] *n* (**a**) *(politeness, charm)* politesse *f*; *Pej* manières *fpl* doucereuses (**b**) *(elegance)* élégance *f*

sub [sʌb] (*pt & pp* **subbed**) *Fam* **1** *n* (**a**) *(subscription → to club, union etc)* cotisation❑ *f*; **to pay one's subs** payer sa cotisation

(**b**) *Sport (substitute)* remplaçant(e)❑ *m,f*

(**c**) *Naut (submarine)* sous-marin❑ *m*

(**d**) *Br Journ (subeditor)* secrétaire *mf* de rédaction❑

(**e**) *Am & Ir (substitute teacher)* suppléant(e)❑ *m,f*

(**f**) *Br (small loan)* prêt❑ *m*; **to give sb a sub** dépanner qn; **to get a sub** se faire dépanner

(**g**) *(sandwich)* = grand sandwich mixte de forme allongée

2 *vi* (**a**) *(substitute)* **to sub for sb** remplacer qn❑

(**b**) *Br Journ (subedit)* travailler comme secrétaire de rédaction❑

3 *vt* (**a**) *Journ (article)* mettre au point❑, corriger❑

(**b**) *Br (lend)* **to sub sb sth** dépanner qn de qch❑; **can you sub me a fiver?** tu peux me dépanner de cinq livres?

sub- [sʌb] *pref* sub-, sous-; **to run a sub-four minute mile** courir le mile en moins de quatre minutes

sub-account *n Acct* sous-compte *m*

subacid [ˌsʌbˈæsɪd] *adj* (**a**) *(taste, flavour)* acidulé, légèrement acide (**b**) *(tone, reply)* aigre-doux (aigre-douce)

subacute [ˌsʌbəˈkjuːt] *adj Med* subaigu(uë)

sub-agency (*pl* **sub-agencies**) *n* sous-agence *f*

subagent [ˌsʌbˈeɪdʒənt] *n* sous-agent *m*

subalkaline [ˌsʌbˈælkəlaɪn] *adj Chem & Geol* subalcalin

subalpine [ˌsʌbˈælpaɪn] *adj* subalpin

►► *Orn* ***subalpine warbler*** fauvette *f* passerine

subaltern [ˈsʌbəltən] **1** *n* (**a**) *Br Mil* = officier de l'armée de terre d'un rang inférieur à celui de capitaine (**b**) *(subordinate → gen)* subalterne *mf*, subordonné(e) *m,f*

2 *adj* subalterne

sub-aqua [-ˈækwə] *adj* sous-marin, subaquatique

►► ***sub-aqua club*** club *m* de plongée sous-marine; ***sub-aqua diving*** plongée *f* sous-marine

subaquatic [ˌsʌbəˈkwætɪk] *adj* subaquatique

subaqueous [sʌbˈækwɪəs] *adj* subaquatique

subarachnoid [sʌbəˈræknɔɪd] *adj Anat* sous-arachnoïdien

►► *Med* ***subarachnoid haemorrhage*** hémorragie *f* sous-arachnoïdienne

subarctic [ˌsʌbˈɑːktɪk] **1** *adj* (**a**) *Geog* subarctique (**b**) *(very cold → weather)* glacial arctique

2 *n* zone *f* subarctique

sub-assembly (*pl* **sub-assemblies**) *n Tech (action)* préassemblage *m*; *(unit)* sous-ensemble *m*; *Comput* sous-ensemble *m*

subatomic [ˌsʌbəˈtɒmɪk] *adj* subatomique

►► *Phys* ***subatomic particle*** particule *f* subatomique

subatomics [ˌsʌbəˈtɒmɪks] *n (UNCOUNT)* physique *f* subatomique

subaxillary [ˌsʌbækˈsɪlərɪ] *adj* (**a**) *Zool* axillaire (**b**) *Bot* infra-axillaire, sous-axillaire

subbasement [ˈsʌbˌbeɪsmənt] *n* deuxième sous-sol *m*

subbed [sʌbd] *adj Journ* corrigé

subcategory [ˈsʌbˌkætəgərɪ] (*pl* **subcategories**) *n* sous-catégorie *f*

sub-charter **1** *n* [ˈsʌbˌtʃɑːtə(r)] sous-affrètement *m*

2 *vt* [ˌsʌbˈtʃɑːtə(r)] sous-affréter

sub-charterer [ˌsʌb'tʃɑːtərə(r)] *n* sous-affréteur *m*

sub-chartering [ˌsʌb'tʃɑːtərɪŋ] *n* sous-affrètement *m*

subclass ['sʌbklɑːs] *n* sous-classe *f*

subclause ['sʌbklɔːz] *n Law (of contract)* paragraphe *m*

subclavian [ˌsʌb'kleɪvɪən], **subclavicular** [ˌsʌbklə'vɪkjʊlə(r)] *adj Anat* sous-clavier, sous-claviculaire

subclinical [ˌsʌb'klɪnɪkəl] *adj* infraclinique

subcommittee ['sʌbkəˌmɪtɪ] *n* sous-comité *m*, sous-commission *f*

subcompact [ˌsʌbkəm'pækt] *n Am* (très) petite voiture *f*

subconscious [ˌsʌb'kɒnʃəs] **1** *adj* subconscient; **the subconscious mind** le subconscient

2 *n* subconscient *m*

subconsciously [ˌsʌb'kɒnʃəslɪ] *adv* d'une manière subconsciente, inconsciemment

subconsciousness [ˌsʌb'kɒnʃəsnɪs] *n Psy* subconscience *f*

subcontinent [ˌsʌb'kɒntɪnənt] *n* sous-continent *m*; **the (Indian) Subcontinent** le sous-continent indien

subcontinental [ˌsʌbkɒntɪ'nentəl] *Am* **1** *n* personne *f* originaire du sous-continent indien

2 *adj* du sous-continent indien

subcontract 1 *vt* [ˌsʌbkən'trækt] *(pass on)* (faire) sous-traiter; **they subcontract some of the work (out) to local firms** ils sous-traitent une partie du travail à des entreprises locales

2 *vi* [ˌsʌbkən'trækt] travailler en sous-traitance; **they have a lot of small companies who subcontract for them** beaucoup de petites sociétés travaillent pour eux en sous-traitance

3 *n* [ˌsʌb'kɒntrækt] (contrat *m* de) sous-traitance *f*

▸**subcontract out** *vt sep* = **subcontract** *vt*

subcontracting [ˌsʌbkən'træktɪŋ] *adj* sous-traitant

▸▸ ***subcontracting firm*** sous-traitant *m*

subcontractor [ˌsʌbkən'træktə(r)] *n* sous-traitant *m*

subcontrary [sʌb'kɒntrərɪ] (*pl* **subcontraries**) **1** *n* subcontraire *f*

2 *adj* subcontraire

subcortex [ˌsʌb'kɔːteks] *n* zone *f* (cérébrale) sous-corticale

subcortical [ˌsʌb'kɔːtɪkəl] *adj Bot* subcortical; *Anat* sous-cortical

subcostal [ˌsʌb'kɒstəl] *adj Anat & Zool* souscostal, subcostal

subcritical [ˌsʌb'krɪtɪkəl] *adj* sous-critique

subculture ['sʌbˌkʌltʃə(r)] *n* (**a**) *(gen & sociological)* subculture *f* (**b**) *Biol* culture *f* repiquée *ou* secondaire

subcutaneous [ˌsʌbkjuː'teɪnɪəs] *adj* sous-cutané

subcutaneously [ˌsʌbkjuː'teɪnɪəslɪ] *adv* de manière sous-cutanée; **to be injected subcutaneously** à administrer par injection sous-cutanée

subdeacon [ˌsʌb'diːkən] *n* sous-diacre *m*

subdeb [ˌsʌb'deb] *Fam* = **subdebutante**

subdebutante [ˌsʌb'debjuːtɑːnt] *n Am* préadolescente *f*

subdirectory ['sʌbˌdɪrektərɪ] (*pl* **subdirectories**) *n Comput* sous-répertoire *m*

subdistrict ['sʌbˌdɪstrɪkt] *n* subdivision *f* (d'arrondissement)

subdivide [ˌsʌbdɪ'vaɪd] **1** *vt* subdiviser

2 *vi* se subdiviser

subdivision [ˌsʌbdɪ'vɪʒən] *n* subdivision *f*

subdivisional [ˌsʌbdɪ'vɪʒənəl], **subdivisionary** [ˌsʌbdɪ'vɪʒənərɪ] *adj Admin* subdivisionnaire

subdominant [ˌsʌb'dɒmɪnənt] *n Biol & Mus* sous-dominante *f*

subdue [səb'djuː] *vt* (**a**) *(country, tribe, rebels)* soumettre; *(rebels)* soumettre; *(rebellion)* réprimer (**b**) *(feelings, passions)* refréner, réfréner, maîtriser; *(fears, anxiety)* apaiser

subdued [səb'djuːd] *adj* (**a**) *(person → gen)* silencieux; *(→ quieter than usual)* inhabituellement calme; *(mood)* sombre; *(emotion, feeling)* contenu; *(audience)* peu enthousiaste; **you're very subdued, what's the matter?** vous n'êtes pas très bavard, qu'est-ce qui ne va pas?; **it was rather a subdued gathering** ce fut un rassemblement plutôt sombre

(**b**) *(voice, sound)* bas; *(conversation)* à voix basse

(**c**) *(light, lighting)* tamisé, atténué; *(colours)* sobre

subedit [ˌsʌb'edɪt] *Br* **1** *vt* corriger, préparer pour l'impression

2 *vi* travailler comme secrétaire de rédaction

subediting [ˌsʌb'edɪtɪŋ] *n Br* mise *f* au point, correction *f*

subeditor [ˌsʌb'edɪtə(r)] *n Br* secrétaire *mf* de rédaction

subentry [ˌsʌb'entrɪ] (*pl* **subentries**) *n* sous-entrée *f*

subequatorial [sʌbekwə'tɔːrɪəl] *adj* subéquatorial

suber ['sjuːbə(r)] *n Bot* suber *m*

suberate ['sjuːbəreɪt] *n Chem* subérate *m*

suberic [sjuː'berɪk] *adj Chem* subérique

suberin ['sjuːbərɪn] *n Chem* subérine *f*

suberize, -ise ['sjuːbəraɪz] *vt Bot* subériser

subfamily ['sʌbˌfæməlɪ] (*pl* **subfamilies**) *n* sous-famille *f*

subfloor ['sʌbˌflɔː(r)] *n Constr* pré-dalle *f*

subfolder ['sʌbˌfəʊldə(r)] *n Comput* sous-dossier *m*

subframe ['sʌbˌfreɪm] *n Aut* faux-châssis *m inv*

subfusc ['sʌbˌfʌsk] **1** *n Br* tenue *f* universitaire *(en particulier à Oxford)*

2 *adj Literary (dark)* sombre; *(dusky)* bistre *(inv)*

subgenus [ˌsʌb'dʒiːnəs] (*pl* **subgenuses** *or* **subgenera** [-'dʒenərə]) *n* sous-genre *m*

subglacial [ˌsʌb'gleɪsɪəl] *adj Geog* sous-glaciaire

subgrade ['sʌbˌgreɪd] *n (of road)* hérisson *m*

subgroup ['sʌbˌgruːp] *n* sous-groupe *m*

subharmonic [ˌsʌbhɑː'mɒnɪk] *adj* sous-harmonique

subhead ['sʌbhed], **subheading** ['sʌbˌhedɪŋ] *n (title)* sous-titre *m*; *(division)* paragraphe *m*

subhuman [ˌsʌb'hjuːmən] **1** *adj (intelligence, species)* inférieur à celui/celle des humains; *(crime)* brutal, bestial; **to live in subhuman conditions** vivre dans des conditions terribles *ou* inhumaines; **people in these colonies were portrayed as subhuman** la population de ces colonies était décrite comme une race inférieure

2 *n* sous-homme *m*

subincision [ˌsʌbɪn'sɪʒən] *n* subincision *f*

subjacent [ˌsʌb'dʒeɪsənt] *adj* sous-jacent

subject 1 *n* ['sʌbdʒɪkt] (**a**) *(topic)* sujet *m*; **on the subject of** au sujet de, à propos de; **this will be the subject of my next lecture** ma prochaine conférence portera sur ce sujet; **to wander from the subject** s'écarter du sujet, faire une digression; **let's come** *or* **get back to the subject** revenons à nos moutons; **don't try and change the subject** n'essaie pas de changer de sujet *ou* de détourner la conversation; **let's drop the subject** parlons d'autre chose; **while we're on the subject** à (ce) propos; **while we're on the subject of holidays** puisque nous parlons de vacances; **that's a touchy subject** c'est un sujet délicat

(**b**) *(of legal case, contract)* objet *m*; *(in letters and memos)* **subject: recruitment of new staff** objet: recrutement de personnel

(**c**) *Art, Literature & Phot* sujet *m*; **the subject of her film/novel** le sujet de son film/roman; **he always photographs his subjects in natural light** il photographie toujours ses sujets en lumière naturelle

(**d**) *Gram & Phil* sujet *m*

(**e**) *Sch & Univ* matière *f*, discipline *f*; *(field)* domaine *m*; **she's taking exams in four subjects** elle passe des examens dans quatre matières; **I was always better at science subjects** j'ai toujours été plus fort en sciences; **it's not really my subject** ce n'est pas vraiment mon domaine; **that would be a good subject for a PhD thesis** ce serait un bon sujet pour une thèse de doctorat

(**f**) *Pol (of monarch)* sujet(ette) *m,f*; **she is a British subject** c'est une ressortissante britannique; **foreign subjects** ressortissants *mpl* étrangers

(**g**) *Med & Psy (of test)* sujet *m*; **she'd be a good subject for the new treatment** elle serait un bon sujet pour le nouveau traitement; **subjects were tested for their reactions** on a testé la réaction des sujets

(**h**) *(cause)* objet *m*; **he was the subject of much comment** il a été l'objet de nombreux commentaires

(**i**) *Comput (of e-mail message)* objet *m*

2 *adj* ['sʌbdʒɪkt] (**a**) *(subordinate → people, country)* assujetti, soumis; **they are subject to my authority** ils sont placés sous mon autorité, ils dépendent de moi; **we are all subject to the rule of law** nous sommes tous soumis à la loi; **subject states** États *mpl* dépendants

(**b**) *(liable, prone)* **subject to** sujet à; **he is subject to frequent lung infections** il est sujet à de fréquentes infections pulmonaires; **subject to attack** exposé à l'attaque; **to be subject to violent changes of mood/fits of jealousy** être sujet à de brusques sautes d'humeur/des crises de jalousie; **the terms are subject to alteration without notice** les termes peuvent être modifiés sans préavis; **subject to tax** imposable, assujetti à l'impôt; **the price is subject to a handling charge** les frais de manutention sont en sus; **all trains will be subject to delay** des retards sont à prévoir sur toutes les lignes

3 *vt* [səb'dʒekt] (**a**) *(country, people)* soumettre, assujettir

(**b**) *(expose)* **to subject to** soumettre à; **to subject sb/sth to an examination** faire subir un examen à qn/qch, soumettre qn/qch à un examen; **the material was subjected to intense heat** le matériau a été soumis *ou* exposé à une température très élevée; **I refuse to subject anyone to such indignities** je refuse de faire subir de tels affronts à qui que ce soit; **their plans were subjected to much criticism** leurs projets ont fait l'objet de nombreuses critiques

4 subject to *prep* ['sʌbdʒɪkt] *(save for)* sous réserve de, sauf; *(conditional upon)* à condition de; **these are the rules, subject to revision** voici le règlement, sous réserve de modification; **subject to your passing the exam** à condition de réussir *ou* à condition que vous réussissiez l'examen; **it's all subject to her approval** tout est subordonné à son approbation

▸▸ ***subject catalogue*** fichier *m* par matières; ***subject index*** index *m* des matières; ***subject matter*** *(topic)* sujet *m*, thème *m*; *(substance)* substance *f*, contenu *m*

subjection [səb'dʒekʃən] *n* (**a**) *(act of subjecting)* assujettissement *m* (**b**) *(state of being subjected)* sujétion *f*, assujettissement *m*, soumission *f*; **they live in (a state of) complete subjection** ils vivent dans la soumission la plus totale

subjective [səb'dʒektɪv] **1** *adj* (**a**) *(viewpoint, argument, criticism)* subjectif (**b**) *Gram (pronoun, case)* sujet; *(genitive)* subjectif (**c**) *Med (symptom)* subjectif

2 *n Gram* (cas *m*) sujet *m*, nominatif *m*

subjectively [səb'dʒektɪvlɪ] *adv* subjectivement

subjectivism [səb'dʒektɪvɪzəm] *n* subjectivisme *m*

subjectivity [ˌsʌbdʒek'tɪvətɪ] *n* subjectivité *f*

subjoin [ˌsʌb'dʒɔɪn] *vt* adjoindre

sub judice [-'dʒuːdɪsɪ] *adj Law* en instance, pendant; **I cannot comment on a case which is still sub judice** je ne peux faire aucun commentaire sur une affaire qui est encore en cours de jugement

subjugate ['sʌbdʒʊgeɪt] *vt* (**a**) *(people, tribe, country)* assujettir, soumettre; *(rebels)* soumettre (**b**) *(feelings)* dompter; *(reaction)* réprimer

subjugation [ˌsʌbdʒʊ'geɪʃən] *n* soumission *f*, assujettissement *m*

subjugator ['sʌbdʒʊgeɪtə(r)] *n* asservisseur *m*

subjunctive [səb'dʒʌŋktɪv] **1** *adj* subjonctif

2 *n* subjonctif *m*; **in the subjunctive** au subjonctif; **some verbs always take the subjunctive** certains verbes sont toujours suivis du subjonctif

▸▸ ***subjunctive mood*** mode *m* subjonctif

subkingdom [ˌsʌb'kɪŋdəm] *n Biol* embranchement *m*

sublease 1 *n* ['sʌbˌliːs] sous-location *f*

2 *vt* [ˌsʌb'liːs] sous-louer

sublessee [ˌsʌble'siː] *n* sous-locataire *mf*

sublessor [ˌsʌble'sɔː(r)] *n* sous-bailleur *m*, sous-bailleresse *f*

sub–sut

sublet (*pt & pp* **sublet,** *cont* **subletting**) **1** *n* ['sʌb,let] sous-location *f*
2 *vt* [,sʌb'let] sous-louer
subletter ['sʌb,letə(r)] *n* sous-bailleur *m*, sous-bailleresse *f*
subletting ['sʌb,letɪŋ] *n* sous-location *f*
sublieutenant [*Br* ,sʌblef'tenənt, *Am* ,sʌblu:'tenənt] *n* (*in navy*) ≃ enseigne *m* de vaisseau première/deuxième classe, *Can* ≃ sous-lieutenant *m*
sublimable [sə'blaɪməbəl] *adj Chem* sublimable
sublimate 1 *vt* ['sʌblɪmeɪt] (*gen*) & *Chem* sublimer
2 *n* ['sʌblɪmət] *Chem* sublimé *m*
sublimation [,sʌblɪ'meɪʃən] *n* sublimation *f*
sublime [sə'blaɪm] **1** *adj* (**a**) (*noble, inspiring*) sublime (**b**) *Fam* (*very good*) génial, sensationnel; **you look sublime** tu es superbe (**c**) (*utter* → *disregard, contempt, ignorance*) suprême, souverain
2 *n* **the sublime** le sublime; **from the sublime to the ridiculous** du sublime au grotesque
3 *vt Chem* sublimer
sublimely [sə'blaɪmlɪ] *adv* (**a**) (*extremely*) **sublimely beautiful** d'une beauté sublime (**b**) (*utterly*) complètement, totalement; **they were sublimely unaware of the danger** ils étaient totalement inconscients du danger
subliminal [,sʌb'lɪmɪnəl] *adj* subliminaire, subliminal
►► ***subliminal advertising*** publicité *f* subliminale *ou* invisible
sublimity [sə'blɪmətɪ] *n* sublimité *f*
sublinear [,sʌb'lɪnɪə(r)] *adj* sublinéaire
sublingual [,sʌb'lɪŋgwəl] *adj Anat & Med* sublingual
sublunary [,sʌb'lu:nərɪ] *adj* sublunaire; (*body*) terrestre
submachine gun [,sʌbmə'ʃi:n-] *n* mitraillette *f*
submarginal [,sʌb'mɑ:dʒɪnəl] *adj Zool* submarginal
submarine [,sʌbmə'ri:n] **1** *n* (**a**) *Naut* sous-marin *m* (**b**) (*sandwich*) = grand sandwich mixte de forme allongée
2 *adj* (*cable, volcano*) sous-marin
►► ***submarine sandwich*** = grand sandwich mixte de forme allongée; ***submarine pen*** abri *m* pour sous-marins
submariner [,sʌb'mærɪnə(r)] *n* sous-marinier *m*
sub-market *n* sous-marché *m*
submaxillary [,sʌbmæk'sɪlərɪ] *adj Anat* sous-maxillaire
submediant [,sʌb'mi:djənt] *n* sus-dominante *f*, sixte *f*
submental [,sʌb'mentəl] *adj Anat* submental
submenu [,sʌb'menju:] *n Comput* sous-menu *m*
submerge [səb'mɜ:dʒ] **1** *vt* (**a**) (*plunge*) submerger, immerger; *Fig* **to submerge oneself in work** se plonger dans le travail (**b**) (*flood*) submerger, inonder; **the flood waters had submerged the fields** les eaux en crue avaient inondé les champs; **the rocks were soon submerged by the tide** les rochers furent bientôt recouverts par la marée
2 *vi* (*submarine*) plonger
submerged [səb'mɜ:dʒd] *adj* (*field etc*) submergé; (*submarine*) en plongée; (*reef, volcano*) sous-marin; *Fig* **submerged in work** submergé de travail, qui croule sous le travail
submergence [səb'mɜ:dʒəns] *n* submersion *f*
submersibility [səb,mɜ:sə'bɪlɪtɪ] *n* submersibilité *f*
submersible [səb'mɜ:səbəl] **1** *adj* submersible
2 *n* submersible *m*
submersion [səb'mɜ:ʃən] *n* (**a**) (*in liquid*) immersion *f*; (*of submarine*) plongée *f* (**b**) (*flooding*) inondation *f*
subminiature [,sʌb'mɪnətʃə(r)] *adj* subminiature
submission [səb'mɪʃən] *n* (**a**) (*yielding*) soumission *f*; **to beat/starve sb into submission** réduire qn par la violence/la famine
(**b**) (*submissiveness*) soumission *f*, docilité *f*
(**c**) (*referral* → *gen*) soumission *f*; *Law* (*of case*) renvoi *m*; **after submission of the project to the coordinating committee** après soumission du projet au comité de coordination
(**d**) (*proposition, argument* → *gen*) thèse *f*; *Law* plaidoirie *f*; **her submission is that...** elle soutient que...; **in my submission, the defendant is lying** je soutiens que l'accusé ment
(**e**) (*in wrestling*) soumission *f*
submissive [səb'mɪsɪv] *adj* soumis
submissively [səb'mɪsɪvlɪ] *adv* (*behave, confess, accept*) docilement; (*yield, react*) avec résignation
submissiveness [səb'mɪsɪvnɪs] *n* soumission *f*, docilité *f*
submit [səb'mɪt] (*pt & pp* **submitted,** *cont* **submitting**) **1** *vi* (**a**) se rendre, se soumettre
(**b**) *Fig* se soumettre, se plier; **to submit to authority** se soumettre à l'autorité; **we shall never submit to such demands** nous n'accéderons jamais à de telles exigences; **to submit to one's fate** accepter son destin
2 *vt* (**a**) (*present*) soumettre; **to submit sth for sb's approval/for sb's inspection** soumettre *ou* présenter qch à l'approbation/à l'inspection de qn; **to submit proof of identity** présenter des pièces d'identité; **all proposals must be submitted to the coordinating committee** toutes les propositions doivent être soumises au comité de coordination; *Law* **I submit that...** je soutiens *ou* je maintiens que...
(**b**) (*yield*) **to submit oneself to sb/sth** se soumettre à qn/qch
submucosa [,sʌbmju:'kəʊsə] *n Anat* tissu *m* sous-muqueux
submucous [,sʌb'mju:kəs] *adj Anat* sous-muqueux
submultiple [,sʌb'mʌltɪpəl] *n* sous-multiple *m*
subnasal [,sʌb'neɪzəl] *adj Anat* sous-nasal
subnormal [,sʌb'nɔ:məl] *adj* (**a**) (*person*) arriéré; **educationally subnormal children** des enfants arriérés (*du point de vue scolaire*) (**b**) (*temperatures*) au-dessous de la normale
subnotebook [,sʌb'nəʊtbʊk] *n Comput* notebook *m* (*très petit*)
subnuclear [,sʌb'nju:klɪə(r)] *adj Nucl* subnucléaire
suborbital [,sʌb'ɔ:bɪtəl] *adj* (**a**) *Anat* sous-orbitaire (**b**) *Astron* sous-orbital
suborder ['sʌb,ɔ:də(r)] *n Biol* sous-ordre *m*
subordinate 1 *n* [sə'bɔ:dɪnət] subordonné(e) *m,f*, subalterne *mf*
2 *adj* [sə'bɔ:dɪnət] (**a**) (*in rank, hierarchy*) subalterne; **he is subordinate to the duty officer** son grade est inférieur à celui de l'officier de permanence; **of subordinate rank** de rang subalterne; **she had a very subordinate position in the company** elle occupait un poste tout à fait subalterne dans l'entreprise
(**b**) (*secondary*) subordonné, accessoire; **but that is subordinate to the main problem** mais c'est secondaire par rapport au problème principal
(**c**) *Gram* subordonné
3 *vt* [sə'bɔ:dɪneɪt] subordonner
►► *Gram* ***subordinate clause*** (proposition *f*) subordonnée *f*
subordinately [sə'bɔ:dɪnətlɪ] *adv* subordonnément
subordinating conjunction [sə'bɔ:dɪneɪtɪŋ-] *n Gram* conjonction *f* de subordination
subordination [sə,bɔ:dɪ'neɪʃən] *n* subordination *f*
suborn [sə'bɔ:n] *vt Law* suborner
suborning [sə'bɔ:nɪŋ] *n Law* subornation *f*
sub-paragraph *n* sous-alinéa *m*
subpena *Am* = **subpoena**
subplot ['sʌb,plɒt] *n* intrigue *f* secondaire
subpoena, *Am* **subpena** [sə'pi:nə] **1** *n* citation *f* (*à comparaître en qualité de témoin*), assignation *f*
2 *vt* citer (*à comparaître en qualité de témoin*)
sub-polar *adj* (**a**) (*climate, conditions*) subpolaire (**b**) *Astron* au-dessous du pôle céleste
subpopulation [,sʌbpɒpjʊ'leɪʃən] *n* sous-population *f*
sub-postmaster *n Br* receveur *m* (*dans un petit bureau de poste local*)
sub-postmistress *n Br* receveuse *f* (*dans un petit bureau de poste local*)
sub-post office *n Br* petit bureau *m* de poste local
sub-prefect *n Admin* sous-préfet *m*
subprogram ['sʌb,prəʊgræm] *n Comput* sous-programme *m*
subreption [səb'repʃən] *n Law* subreption *f*
subrogate ['sʌbrəgeɪt] *vt Law* subroger
subrogation [,sʌbrə'geɪʃən] *n Law* subrogation *f*; **act of subrogation** acte *m* subrogatoire *ou* subrogateur
sub rosa [-'rəʊzə] *adv* confidentiellement, sous le sceau du secret
subroutine ['sʌbru:,ti:n] *n Comput* sous-programme *m*
sub-Saharan Africa *n* Afrique *f* subsaharienne; **in sub-Saharan Africa** en Afrique noire
subscribe [səb'skraɪb] **1** *vi* (**a**) (*to magazine, service, telephone system, ISP*) s'abonner, être abonné; **to subscribe to a newspaper** (*become a subscriber*) s'abonner à un journal; (*be a subscriber*) être abonné à un journal
(**b**) (*to loan, fund, campaign, share issue*) souscrire; **to subscribe to a charity** faire des dons à une œuvre de charité
(**c**) **to subscribe to** (*opinion, belief*) souscrire à; **I cannot subscribe to that view of politics** il m'est impossible de souscrire à cette vision de la politique
2 *vt* (**a**) (*money*) verser; (*donate*) donner, faire don de; **she subscribed £800 to the election fund** elle a donné 800 livres à la caisse électorale
(**b**) *Formal* (*write* → *one's name, signature*) apposer; (*sign* → *document*) signer
subscriber [səb'skraɪbə(r)] *n* (**a**) (*to magazine, service, telephone system, ISP*) abonné(e) *m,f*; **telephone subscriber** abonné(e) *m,f* du *ou* au téléphone
(**b**) (*to fund, campaign, share issue*) souscripteur(trice) *m,f*; **subscribers to various charities** les personnes qui ont fait des dons à diverses œuvres de charité
(**c**) (*to opinion, belief*) partisan *m*, adepte *mf*
(**d**) (*of new company*) signataire *mf* des statuts
►► *Br* ***subscriber trunk dialling*** automatique *m*
subscript ['sʌbskrɪpt] **1** *n Comput, Math & Typ* indice *m*
2 *adj* en indice
subscription [səb'skrɪpʃən] *n* (**a**) (*to magazine, service, telephone system, ISP*) abonnement *m*; **to cancel a subscription** résilier un abonnement; **to take out a subscription to a magazine** s'abonner à un magazine
(**b**) (*to fund, campaign, share issue*) souscription *f*; *Br* (*to club, organization*) cotisation *f*
(**c**) (*to opinion, belief*) adhésion *f*
►► ***subscription charges*** tarifs *mpl* d'abonnement; ***subscription fee*** frais *mpl* d'inscription; (*for share purchase*) droit *m* de souscription; *Am, Austr & NZ* ***subscription television*** chaînes *fpl* à péage
subsea [,sʌb'si:] *Petr* **1** *adj* sous-marin
2 *adv* sous la mer
subsection ['sʌb,sekʃən] *n* (*of text, contract etc*) article *m*, paragraphe *m*
subsequence ['sʌbsɪkwəns] *n* (**a**) (*being subsequent*) postériorité *f* (**b**) (*event*) événement *m* subséquent; (*consequence*) conséquence *f*
subsequent ['sʌbsɪkwənt] *adj* (**a**) (*next*) suivant, ultérieur; **the subsequent days** les jours *mpl* suivants; **at a subsequent meeting** au cours d'une séance ultérieure; **to await subsequent events** attendre de connaître la suite des événements; **subsequent generations** les générations *fpl* suivantes; **subsequent to 1880** après 1880; **subsequent to this** par la suite (**b**) (*consequent*) conséquent, consécutif
subsequently ['sʌbsɪkwəntlɪ] *adv* par la suite, ultérieurement
subserve [səb'sɜ:v] *vt Formal* encourager, favoriser
subservience [səb'sɜ:vjəns] *n* (**a**) (*servility*) servilité *f* (**b**) (*subjugation*) asservissement *m*; **subservience to a foreign power** asservissement *m* à une puissance étrangère
subservient [səb'sɜ:vjənt] *adj* (**a**) (*servile*) servile, *Pej* obséquieux (**b**) (*subjugated*) asservi; **they are totally subservient to the town council** ils sont totalement dépendants de la municipalité (**c**) (*secondary*) secondaire, accessoire
subset ['sʌbset] *n* sous-ensemble *m*
subside [səb'saɪd] *vi* (**a**) (*abate* → *shooting, laughter*) cesser; (→ *storm, rage, pain*) se calmer; (*recede* → *water*) se retirer, baisser; (→ *danger*) s'éloigner (**b**) (*sink* → *house, land*)

s'affaisser; *(→ wall, foundations)* se tasser; *(settle → sediment)* se déposer

subsidence [səb'saɪdəns, 'sʌbsɪdəns] *n (of house, land)* affaissement *m*; *(of wall, foundations)* tassement *m*; **road liable to subsidence** *(sign)* ≃ chaussée déformée

subsidiarity [sʌb,sɪdɪ'ærɪtɪ] *n* subsidiarité *f*

subsidiary [səb'sɪdjərɪ] *(pl* **subsidiaries***)* **1** *adj (supplementary)* supplémentaire, complémentaire; *(secondary → question, reason)* subsidiaire; *(→ idea, action)* accessoire

2 *n Com* filiale *f*

►► ***subsidiary account*** sous-compte *m*; ***subsidiary company*** filiale *f*

subsidization [,sʌbsɪdaɪ'zeɪʃən] *n* fait *m* de subventionner

subsidize, -ise ['sʌbsɪdaɪz] *vt* subventionner; **to be subsidized by the State** recevoir une subvention de *ou* être subventionné par l'État; **why should I carry on subsidizing you?** je ne vois pas pourquoi je continuerais à te donner de l'argent!

subsidized ['sʌbsɪdaɪzd] *adj* subventionné

subsidy ['sʌbsɪdɪ] *(pl* **subsidies***)* *n* subvention *f*; **government subsidy** subvention *f* de l'État; **export subsidies** primes *fpl* à l'exportation

subsist [səb'sɪst] *vi* (**a**) *(remain in existence)* subsister; **custom that still subsists** coutume qui existe *ou* subsiste encore (de nos jours) (**b**) *(stay alive)* **to subsist on sth** vivre de qch; **they have just enough to subsist on** ils ont tout juste de quoi subsister; **they subsist on fish and rice** ils vivent de poisson et de riz

subsistence [səb'sɪstəns] **1** *n* subsistance *f*, existence *f*; **means of subsistence** moyens *mpl* d'existence

2 *comp (wage)* à peine suffisant pour vivre; *(economy)* de subsistance; **to live at subsistence level** avoir tout juste de quoi vivre

►► *Br* ***subsistence allowance*** acompte *m (perçu avant l'engagement définitif)*; *(expenses)* frais *mpl* (de subsistance); *Agr* ***subsistence crop*** culture *f* de subsistance; ***subsistence farming*** agriculture *f* de subsistance

subsistent [səb'sɪstənt] *adj* (**a**) *(existing)* qui existe (**b**) *(persisting)* qui existe encore, qui a persisté

subsoil ['sʌbsɔɪl] *n Geol* sous-sol *m*

subsolar [,sʌb'səʊlə(r)] *adj* subsolaire

subsonic [,sʌb'sɒnɪk] *adj* subsonique

subspecies ['sʌb,spiːʃiːz] *(pl* **inv***)* *n* sous-espèce *f*

substance ['sʌbstəns] **1** *n* (**a**) *(matter)* substance *f*; **tobacco contains harmful substances** le tabac contient des substances nocives; **illegal substances** stupéfiants *mpl*

(**b**) *(solidity)* solidité *f*; **it seemed to have as little substance as a ghost** cela semblait aussi immatériel qu'un fantôme

(**c**) *(essential part, gist)* essentiel *m*, substance *f*; *(basis)* fond *m*; **that's the substance of what he said** voilà en substance ce qu'il a dit; **the substance of the charges** l'essentiel *m* de l'inculpation; **the substance of the case** le fond de l'affaire; **I agree in substance** je suis d'accord sur le fond

(**d**) *(significance, weight)* étoffe *f*, poids *m*; **these developments add substance to our hypothesis** ces développements donnent davantage de poids à notre hypothèse; **I find his stories lack substance** je trouve que ses histoires manquent d'étoffe; **their claim lacks substance** leur revendication est sans fondement *ou* n'est pas fondée

(**e**) *(wealth)* richesses *fpl*; *(power)* pouvoir *m*; *(influence)* influence *f*; **a woman of substance** *(rich)* une femme riche *ou* aisée; *(powerful)* une femme puissante; *(influential)* une femme influente

2 in substance *adv (generally)* en gros, en substance; *(basically)* à la base, au fond; *(in brief)* en substance, en somme

►► ***substance abuse*** abus *m* de stupéfiants

substandard [,sʌb'stændəd] *adj* (**a**) *(work, output)* médiocre, en dessous des niveaux requis; *(meal, merchandise)* de qualité inférieure; **substandard housing** = logements ne respectant pas les normes requises; **they live in substandard housing** ils habitent des logements insalubres (**b**) *Ling* non conforme à la norme

substantial [səb'stænʃəl] *adj* (**a**) *(considerable)* considérable, important; *Law (damages)* élevé; **for a substantial sum** pour une somme importante; **substantial differences remain** il reste des divergences importantes; **a substantial number of teachers were there** il y avait de nombreux professeurs

(**b**) *(nourishing → food)* nourrissant; *(→ meal)* solide, copieux, substantiel

(**c**) *(convincing → argument, evidence)* solide, convaincant

(**d**) *(real, tangible)* réel, substantiel; *Phil* substantiel

(**e**) *(house → large)* grand; *(→ solidly built)* solide; **the town hall is a substantial Victorian building** la mairie est un solide bâtiment de l'époque victorienne

(**f**) *(rich)* riche, aisé; *(powerful)* puissant; *(influential)* influent; *(well-established)* solide, bien établi; **a substantial company** une société solidement implantée

substantialism [səb'stænʃəlɪzəm] *n Phil* substantialisme *m*

substantialize, -ise [səb'stænʃəlaɪz] *vt Phil* donner de la substance à

substantially [səb'stænʃəlɪ] *adv* (**a**) *(considerably)* considérablement; **taxes have been cut substantially** les impôts ont été considérablement réduits

(**b**) *(generally)* en gros, en grande partie; *(fundamentally)* fondamentalement, au fond; **it is substantially correct** c'est en grande partie correct; **the text is substantially unaltered** le texte est dans l'ensemble *ou* pour l'essentiel resté inchangé

(**c**) *(solidly)* solidement; **substantially built** solide

(**d**) *Phil (as for the substance)* substantiellement

substantiate [səb'stænʃɪeɪt] *vt* confirmer, apporter *ou* fournir des preuves à l'appui de; **he had no evidence to substantiate his accusation** il n'avait aucune preuve pour appuyer son accusation

substantiation [səb,stænʃɪ'eɪʃən] *n (UNCOUNT) (proof)* preuve *f*; *(reason)* bien-fondé *m*, justification *f*; **do you have any substantiation for your allegations?** pouvez-vous fournir des preuves de ce que vous avancez?

substantification [səb,stæntɪfɪ'keɪʃən] *n* substantification *f*

substantify [səb'stæntɪfaɪ] *vt* substantifier

substantival [,sʌbstən'taɪvəl] *adj Gram* substantif

substantive **1** *adj* [sʌb'stæntɪv] (**a**) *(real, important)* substantiel; *(permanent → rank)* permanent; *(independent → means, resources)* indépendant (**b**) *Gram* nominal

2 *n* ['sʌbstəntɪv] *Gram* substantif *m*

►► *Law* ***substantive law*** droit *m* positif

substantively [səb'stæntɪvlɪ] *adv (considerably)* substantiellement, considérablement

substantivize, -ise [səb'stæntɪvaɪz] *vt Gram* substantiver

substation ['sʌb,steɪʃən] *n* sous-station *f*

substituent [səb'stɪtjʊənt] *n Chem* substituant *m*

substitute ['sʌbstɪtjuːt] **1** *n* (**a**) *(person)* remplaçant(e) *m,f*, suppléant(e) *m,f*; *Sport* remplaçant(e) *m,f*; **each team is allowed three substitutes** chaque équipe a droit à trois remplaçants

(**b**) *(thing → gen)* produit *m* de remplacement *ou* de substitution; *(→ foodstuff, drug)* succédané *m*; **we'll have to find a substitute for it** il faut que nous trouvions quelque chose pour le remplacer; **use a low-fat substitute instead of butter** utilisez un produit à faible teneur en matière grasse à la place du beurre; **coffee substitute** ersatz *m ou* succédané *m* de café; **sugar substitute** édulcorant *m* de synthèse; **there's no substitute for real coffee** rien ne vaut le vrai café; **tapes are a poor substitute for live music** les cassettes ne valent pas la musique live

(**c**) *Gram* terme *m* suppléant

2 *adj* remplaçant; **a substitute goalkeeper** un gardien de but remplaçant; **it'll do as a substitute cork** ça fera office de bouchon

3 *vt (gen)* substituer, remplacer; *Sport* remplacer; **to substitute sth for sth** substituer qch à qch; **margarine may be substituted for butter** on peut remplacer le beurre par de la margarine, on peut utiliser de la margarine au lieu du beurre

4 *vi* **to substitute for sb/sth** remplacer qn/qch

►► *esp Am, Austr & Ir* ***substitute teacher*** suppléant(e) *m,f*

substitution [,sʌbstɪ'tjuːʃən] *n (gen)* remplacement *m*, substitution *f*; *Sport* remplacement *m*; **the substitution of man-made fibres for cotton** le fait d'avoir remplacé le coton par des fibres synthétiques

►► *Mktg* ***substitution market*** marché *m* de substitution, marché *m* environnant

substrata [,sʌb'strɑːtə] *pl of* **substratum**

substrate ['sʌbstreɪt] *n (gen) & Chem & Electron* substrat *m*

substratum [,sʌb'strɑːtəm] *(pl* **substrata** [-tə]) *n* (**a**) *(infrastructure, base)* fond *m* (**b**) *Geol (underlying formation)* substratum *m*; *(subsoil)* sous-sol *m* (**c**) *Ling* substrat *m* (**d**) *Phot* substratum *m*

substring ['sʌbstrɪŋ] *n Comput* sous-chaîne *f*

substructure ['sʌb,strʌktʃə(r)] *n Constr* infrastructure *f*; **various substructures make up the organization** l'organisation se compose de plusieurs services distincts

subsume [səb'sjuːm] *vt* subsumer

subsystem ['sʌb,sɪstəm] *n* sous-système *m*

subteen [,sʌb'tiːn] *Am* **1** *n* préadolescent(e) *m,f*

2 *adj (fashions, sizes)* pour les préadolescents

subteenage [,sʌb'tiːneɪdʒ] *adj Am (fashions, sizes)* pour les préadolescents

subteenager [,sʌb'tiːneɪdʒə(r)] *n Am* préadolescent(e) *m,f*

subtenancy [,sʌb'tenənsɪ] *(pl* **subtenancies***)* *n* sous-location *f*

subtenant [,sʌb'tenənt] *n* sous-locataire *mf*

subtend [səb'tend] *vt* sous-tendre

subterfuge ['sʌbtəfjuːdʒ] *n* subterfuge *m*

subterranean [,sʌbtə'reɪnɪən] *adj* souterrain; **subterranean forces were at work** des forces secrètes étaient à l'œuvre

subterrestrial [,sʌbte'restrɪəl] *adj* subterrestre

subtext ['sʌb,tekst] *n (of book, film, situation)* message *m* sous-jacent; **if you pay attention to the subtext of the minister's speech you will see that...** si vous lisez le discours du ministre entre les lignes, vous verrez que...

subtitle ['sʌb,taɪtəl] *Cin, Literature & Press* **1** *n* sous-titre *m*

2 *vt* sous-titrer; **a film with English subtitles** un film sous-titré en anglais

subtitled ['sʌb,taɪtəld] *adj* sous-titré, avec sous-titrage

subtitling ['sʌb,taɪtəlɪŋ] *n* sous-titrage *m*

subtle ['sʌtəl] *adj* subtil; **subtle distinction** distinction *f* ténue *ou* subtile; **subtle irony** fine ironie *f*, ironie *f* subtile; **a subtle sense of humour** un sens de l'humour subtil; **there's a very subtle difference between them** il y a une très légère différence entre eux; **subtle shades of green and blue** des nuances subtiles de vert et de bleu; **a subtle form of propaganda/blackmail** une forme insidieuse de propagande/de chantage; **you're not very subtle, are you?** la subtilité n'est vraiment pas ton fort!

subtlety ['sʌtəltɪ] *(pl* **subtleties***)* *n* (**a**) *(subtle nature → of style, mind, film, argument, flavour)* subtilité *f*; **subtlety is not one of his strong points** la subtilité n'est pas son fort (**b**) *(detail, distinction)* subtilité *f*

subtly ['sʌtlɪ] *adv* subtilement; **the atmosphere/his expression had subtly altered** l'atmosphère/son expression avait changé insensiblement; **subtly different** légèrement différent

subtonic [,sʌb'tɒnɪk] *n* sous-tonique *f*

subtotal ['sʌb,təʊtəl] *n* total *m* partiel

subtract [səb'trækt] *vt* soustraire, retrancher; **subtract 52 from 110** ôtez *ou* retranchez *ou* soustrayez 52 de 110

subtracter [səb'træktə(r)] *n* soustracteur *m*

subtraction [səb'trækʃən] *n* soustraction *f*

subtractive [səb'træktɪv] *adj Math & Phot* soustractif

subtrahend ['sʌbtrəhend] *n Math* quantité *f* à soustraire

subtropical [,sʌb'trɒpɪkəl] *adj* subtropical

subtropics [ˌsʌbˈtrɒpɪks] *npl* zones *fpl* subtropicales

subtype [ˈsʌbtaɪp] *n* sous-classe *f*

subulate [ˈsʌbjʊleɪt] *adj Bot* subulé

suburb [ˈsʌbɜːb] *n* banlieue *f*, *Old-fashioned* faubourg *m*; **the London suburb of Eltham** Eltham, dans la banlieue de Londres; **the suburbs stretch for miles** la banlieue s'étend sur des kilomètres; **in the suburbs** en banlieue; **the outer suburbs** la grande banlieue; **the inner suburbs** la banlieue proche

suburban [səˈbɜːbən] *adj* (**a**) *(house, street, railway, dweller)* de banlieue; *(population, growth)* de banlieue, suburbain (**b**) *Pej (mentality, outlook)* (de) petit-bourgeois

suburbanite [səˈbɜːbənaɪt] *n* banlieusard(e) *m,f*

suburbanization [səˌbɜːbənaɪˈzeɪʃən] *n* **the suburbanization of the Thames valley** le développement de la banlieue dans la vallée de la Tamise

suburbanize, -ise [səˈbɜːbənaɪz] *vt* **to become suburbanized** *(town)* prendre un air de banlieue; *(person)* devenir banlieusard

suburbia [səˈbɜːbɪə] *n* la banlieue; **in suburbia** en banlieue

subvariety [səbˈvəraɪətɪ] (*pl* **subvarieties**) *n Biol & Math* sous-variété *f*

subvention [səbˈvenʃən] *n* subvention *f*

subversion [səbˈvɜːʃən] *n* subversion *f*

subversive [səbˈvɜːsɪv] **1** *adj* subversif

2 *n* élément *m* subversif; **a group of subversives** un groupe subversif

subversively [səbˈvɜːsɪvlɪ] *adv* subversivement

subvert [səbˈvɜːt] *vt* (**a**) *(undermine → society, state, institution)* subvertir (**b**) *(corrupt → individual)* corrompre

subway [ˈsʌbweɪ] *n* (**a**) *Br (pedestrian underpass)* passage *m* souterrain (**b**) *Am (railway)* métro *m*; **it's quicker by subway** c'est plus rapide en métro

sub-zero *adj* au-dessous de zéro

succedaneum [sʌksɪˈdeɪnɪəm] *n Med & Pharm* succédané *m*

succeed [səkˈsiːd] **1** *vi* (**a**) *(do well)* réussir, avoir du succès; **we all want to succeed in life** nous voulons tous réussir dans la vie; **to succeed in business/in publishing** réussir dans les affaires/l'édition; **he succeeds in everything he does** il réussit tout ce qu'il entreprend, tout lui réussit; *Prov* **nothing succeeds like success** = un succès en entraîne un autre

(**b**) *(manage successfully)* réussir; **to succeed in doing sth** réussir *ou* parvenir *ou* arriver à faire qch; **he succeeded only in confusing things further** il n'a réussi qu'à compliquer davantage les choses; *Prov* **if at first you don't succeed, try again** = si vous ne réussissez pas du premier coup, recommencez

(**c**) *(work out)* réussir; **the first attack did not succeed** la première offensive a échoué

(**d**) *(follow on)* succéder; **to succeed to the throne** monter sur le trône

2 *vt (of person)* succéder à, prendre la suite de; *(of event, thing)* succéder à, suivre; **I succeeded him as editor** je lui ai succédé au poste de rédacteur; **as month succeeded month** au fur et à mesure que les mois passaient

succeeding [səkˈsiːdɪŋ] *adj* (**a**) *(subsequent)* suivant, qui suit; **we met several times during the succeeding weeks** nous nous sommes vus plusieurs fois pendant les semaines qui ont suivi; **each succeeding year** chaque année qui passe (**b**) *(future)* futur, à venir; **succeeding generations will right these wrongs** les générations à venir redresseront ces torts

success [səkˈses] **1** *n* réussite *f*, succès *m*; **her success in the elections** sa victoire aux élections; **his success in the exam** son succès à l'examen; **to meet with** *or* **to achieve success** réussir; **I wish you every success** je vous souhaite beaucoup de succès; **I had no success in trying to persuade them** je n'ai pas réussi à les convaincre; **I tried to convince them, but without success** j'ai essayé de les convaincre, mais sans succès; **to make a success of sth** mener qch à bien; **he made a success of the campaign** il a mené la campagne à bien; **she made a great success of her career** elle a bien réussi dans son métier; **I haven't had much success in finding work** mes recherches pour un emploi n'ont pas donné grand-chose; **to be a success** *(go well, work out well etc)* réussir, être réussi, être un succès; *(be popular → movie, book etc)* être un succès; *(→ party, cake)* être une réussite, être réussi; **their record was a great success** leur disque a eu un succès fou; **you were a great success at the party** tu as eu beaucoup de succès à la fête

2 *comp (rate)* de réussite, de succès

▸▸ ***success story*** réussite *f*; **one of the great success stories of the 20th century** une des grandes réussites du XXème siècle

successful [səkˈsesfʊl] *adj* (**a**) *(resulting in success → attempt, effort, plan)* qui réussit; *(→ negotiations)* fructueux; *(→ outcome)* heureux; *(→ performance, mission, partnership)* réussi; **his efforts were supremely successful** ses efforts ont été couronnés de succès; **were you successful?** avez-vous réussi?; **successful candidates will be notified officially** les candidats reçus en seront informés par voie officielle; **she was not successful in her application for the post** sa candidature à ce poste n'a pas été retenue; **I was successful in convincing them** j'ai réussi *ou* je suis arrivé *ou* je suis parvenu à les convaincre; **it's not been a very successful day for me** ma journée n'a pas été très fructueuse; **she brought the project to a successful conclusion** elle a mené le projet à bien

(**b**) *(thriving → singer, record, author, book, play)* à succès; *(→ businessman)* qui a réussi; *(→ life, career)* réussi; **their first record was very successful** leur premier disque a eu un succès fou; **she's a successful businesswoman** elle a réussi dans les affaires; **she's successful in everything she does** tout lui réussit, elle réussit tout ce qu'elle entreprend

successfully [səkˈsesfʊlɪ] *adv* avec succès; **to do sth successfully** réussir à faire qch; **we managed to tackle the problem successfully** nous avons trouvé une solution satisfaisante au problème; **he was successfully operated on for a stomach ulcer** il a été opéré avec succès d'un ulcère de l'estomac; **students who successfully complete the course are awarded a certificate** les étudiants qui parviennent au terme du stage reçoivent un certificat

succession [səkˈseʃən] *n* (**a**) *(series)* succession *f*, suite *f*; **a succession of visitors** une succession *ou* une suite de visiteurs; **we won three years in succession** nous avons gagné trois ans de suite; **for five years in succession** pendant cinq années consécutives *ou* cinq ans de suite; **she made three phone calls in succession** elle a passé trois coups de fil de suite; **they filed into the room in close succession** ils sont entrés dans la pièce les uns derrière les autres; **the fireworks went off in quick** *or* **rapid succession** les feux d'artifice sont partis les uns après les autres; **he got several promotions in rapid succession** il a eu plusieurs promotions coup sur coup; **they fired questions at him in rapid succession** ils l'ont soumis à un feu roulant de questions; **a succession of gains and losses** une succession de gains et de pertes

(**b**) *(ascension to power)* succession *f*; **his succession to the post** sa succession au poste; **she's first in succession (to the throne)** elle occupe la première place dans l'ordre de succession (au trône); **at the time of his succession to the throne** au moment de son accession au trône; **in succession to her boss** à la suite de son patron

(**c**) *Law (descendants)* descendance *f*; *(heirs)* héritiers *mpl*

successional [səkˈseʃənəl] *adj* (**a**) *Law* successoral (**b**) *(successive)* successif

successive [səkˈsesɪv] *adj (attempts, generations)* successif; *(days, years)* consécutif

successively [səkˈsesɪvlɪ] *adv (in turn)* successivement, tour à tour, l'un/l'une après l'autre

successiveness [səkˈsesɪvnɪs], **successivity** [ˌsʌkseˈsɪvɪtɪ] *n* successivité *f*

successor [səkˈsesə(r)] *n* (**a**) *(replacement)* successeur *m*; **I'm her successor to the position** je suis son successeur à ce poste; **I'm to be his successor** c'est moi qui dois lui succéder; **she's the successor to the throne** c'est l'héritière de la couronne (**b**) *(heir)* héritier(ère) *m,f*

succinct [səkˈsɪŋkt] *adj* succinct, concis

succinctly [səkˈsɪŋktlɪ] *adv* succinctement, avec concision

succinctness [səkˈsɪŋktnɪs] *n* concision *f*

succinic [səkˈsɪnɪk] *adj* succinique

▸▸ *Chem* ***succinic acid*** acide *m* succinique

succor *Am* = **succour**

succotash [ˈsʌkətæʃ] *n* = plat américain composé de maïs en grain et de haricots

succour, *Am* **succor** [ˈsʌkə(r)] **1** *n* secours *m*, aide *f*

2 *vt* secourir, aider

succubus [ˈsʌkjʊbəs] (*pl* **succubi** [-baɪ]) *n* succube *m*

succulence [ˈsʌkjʊləns] *n* succulence *f*

succulent [ˈsʌkjʊlənt] **1** *adj* (**a**) *(tasty)* succulent (**b**) *Bot* succulent

2 *n* plante *f* grasse

succumb [səˈkʌm] *vi* (**a**) *(yield)* succomber, céder; **don't succumb to temptation!** ne succombez pas à la tentation!; **he succumbed to her charm** il a succombé à son charme (**b**) *(die)* succomber, mourir; **he succumbed to cancer** il est mort d'un cancer; **he finally succumbed** il a finalement succombé

SUCH [sʌtʃ] **1** *adj & predet* (**a**) *(of the same specified kind)* tel, pareil; **such a song** une telle chanson, une chanson pareille *ou* de ce genre; **such songs** de telles chansons, des chansons pareilles *ou* de ce genre; **in such weather** par un temps pareil; **in such cases** en pareils cas; **how can you tell such lies?** comment peux-tu raconter de tels mensonges *ou* des mensonges pareils?; **no such place exists** un tel endroit n'existe pas; **on such an occasion** pour l'occasion; **on such occasions the ballroom is used** la salle de bal est utilisée pour de telles occasions; **we had such a case last year** nous avons eu un cas semblable l'année dernière; **have you ever heard such a thing?** avez-vous jamais entendu une chose pareille?; **you wouldn't have such a thing as a corkscrew, would you?** vous n'auriez pas un tire-bouchon, par hasard?; **such a thing is unheard-of** ce genre de chose est sans précédent; **I said no such thing!** je n'ai rien dit de tel *ou* de la sorte!; **you'll do no such thing!** il n'en est pas question!; **there is no such thing** cela n'existe pas; **there is no such thing as magic** la magie n'existe pas; **they called her Jane or some such thing** ils l'ont baptisée Jane ou quelque chose de ce genre *ou* dans ce style; **he said he didn't have enough money or some such excuse** son excuse était qu'il n'avait pas assez d'argent, ou quelque chose de ce genre *ou* dans ce style; **we will take such steps as are considered necessary** nous prendrons toutes les mesures nécessaires; **I'm not such a fool as to believe him!** je ne suis pas assez bête pour le croire!; **he speaks in such a way as to be incomprehensible** il parle de telle manière que personne ne le comprend; **until such time as is convenient to me** jusqu'à ce que cela me convienne; **such money as we have** le peu d'argent que nous avons; **their timetable is such that we never see them** leur emploi du temps est tel que nous ne les voyons jamais; **she works in such a way that we can't keep up** elle travaille de telle façon que nous ne pouvons pas suivre; **she arranges things in such a way that she is free on Saturdays** elle s'arrange de manière à être libre le samedi

(**b**) *(as intensifier)* tel; **my accounts are in such a mess!** mes comptes sont dans un de ces états!; **he is such a liar** il est tellement menteur, c'est un tel menteur; **she has such courage!** elle a un de ces courages!; **she has such ideas!** elle a de ces idées!; **it's such a pity you can't come!** c'est tellement dommage que vous ne puissiez pas venir!; **you gave me such a scare!** tu m'as fait une de ces peurs!; **such tall buildings** des immeubles aussi hauts; **such a handsome man** un si bel homme; **she has such a nice voice!** elle a une si jolie voix!; **we had such a good time** on s'est tellement amusés; **it's been such a long time since I've seen her** ça fait si longtemps que je ne l'ai pas vue; **I didn't realize it was such a long way** je ne me rendais pas compte que c'était si loin; **I've never read such beautiful poetry** je n'ai jamais lu de si belle poésie; **her grief was such that we feared for her sanity** son chagrin était tel que nous craignions pour sa santé mentale; **he was in such pain that he fainted** il souffrait tellement qu'il s'est évanoui

2 *pron* **such is the power of the media** voilà ce que peuvent faire les médias; **such was the result** voilà quel était le résultat; **such were my thoughts last night** voilà où j'en étais hier soir; **such is not my intention** ce n'est pas là mon intention; **such is life!** c'est la vie!

3 and such *adv* et d'autres choses de ce genre *ou* de la sorte; **he enjoys cakes, ices and such** il mange avec plaisir des gâteaux, des glaces et autres choses de ce genre; **detective stories, thrillers and such** des policiers, des romans à suspense et d'autres livres de ce genre *ou* de la sorte

4 as such *adv (strictly speaking)* en soi; *(in that capacity)* en tant que tel, à ce titre; **she doesn't get a salary as such** elle n'a pas de véritable salaire *ou* pas de salaire à proprement parler; **the text as such is fine but...** le texte en soi est bien mais...; **have they offered you more money? – well, not as such** vous ont-ils proposé plus d'argent? – pas véritablement; **they are not opposed to privatization as such** ils ne sont pas opposés à la privatisation en soi *ou* à proprement parler; **she's an adult and as such she has rights** elle est majeure et en tant que telle elle a des droits

5 such and such *predet* tel; **on such and such a date** à telle date; **on such and such a day in such and such a place** tel jour à tel endroit

6 such as *prep* tel que, comme; **a country such as Germany** un pays tel que *ou* comme l'Allemagne; **films such as Fellini's** les films tels que ceux de Fellini; **books such as these** *or* **such books as these are always useful** les livres de ce genre sont toujours utiles; **I can think of lots of reasons – such as?** je vois beaucoup de raisons – comme quoi par exemple?

7 such as it is *adv* **and this is my study, such as it is** et voici ce que j'appelle mon bureau; **the village boasts a bus, such as it is** le village a un autobus, si l'on peut dire; **I'll give you my opinion, such as it is** je vais vous donner mon avis, prenez-le pour ce qu'il vaut; **you're welcome to use my notes, such as they are** je te prêterai mes notes avec plaisir, elles valent ce qu'elles valent

---

suchlike [ˈsʌtʃlaɪk] *Fam* **1** *adj* semblable □, pareil □; **and other suchlike dishes** et d'autres plats du même genre □

2 *pron* **frogs, toads and suchlike** les grenouilles, les crapauds et autres animaux (du même genre) □

suck [sʌk] **1** *vt* (**a**) *(with mouth)* sucer; *(drink, sweets)* sucer, suçoter; *(mother's milk)* téter; *(pipe)* tirer sur; *(not smoking)* sucer; **to suck one's thumb** sucer son pouce; **he sucked the end of his pencil thoughtfully** il suçait pensivement le bout de son crayon; **she was sucking orange juice through a straw** elle sirotait du jus d'orange avec une paille; **he was sucking a sweet** il suçait un bonbon; **to suck poison out of a wound** extraire le poison d'une blessure en la suçant; **suck the poison out** aspirez le poison; **to suck sb dry** prendre jusqu'à son dernier sou à qn

(**b**) *(pull)* aspirer; **the dust is sucked into the bag** la poussière est aspirée dans le sac; **the whirlpool sucked him to the bottom** le tourbillon l'a entraîné au fond; *Fig* **we found ourselves sucked into an argument** nous nous sommes trouvés entraînés dans une dispute

(**c**) *Am Fam* **to suck face** se rouler des pelles *ou* des patins

2 *vi* (**a**) *(with mouth)* **to suck at** *or* **on sth** sucer *ou* suçoter qch; **the child was sucking at her breast** l'enfant tétait son sein

(**b**) *Fam (be bad)* craindre, être nul *ou* merdique; **this town sucks!** cette ville est dégueulasse!; **this bar/movie sucks** ce bar/film est vraiment nul; **this sucks, let's do something else** c'est nul, si on faisait autre chose?; **I've got to work all weekend – that sucks!** il faut que je travaille tout le week-end – ça craint!

(**c**) *Fam Old-fashioned (idiom)* **(ya boo) sucks to you!** va te faire voir!

3 *n* (**a**) *(act of sucking → gen)* **to have a suck at sth** sucer *ou* suçoter qch; **he took a long suck on his cigar** il tira longuement sur son cigare

(**b**) *(act of sucking → at breast)* tétée *f*; **to give suck** donner le sein, allaiter

(**c**) *(force)* aspiration *f*

▶**suck down** *vt sep (of sea, quicksand, whirlpool)* engloutir

▶**suck in** *vt sep (with mouth)* sucer; *(draw in by vacuum)* aspirer; *(of air pump)* aspirer; *(in vortex)* engloutir; *(cheeks)* creuser; *(knowledge)* absorber; **to get sucked in (to sth)** *(to conspiracy, plot etc)* se laisser entraîner (dans qch)

▶**suck off** *vt sep Vulg* **to suck sb off** sucer qn, tailler une pipe à qn

▶**suck up 1** *vt sep (of person)* aspirer, sucer; *(of vacuum cleaner, pump)* aspirer; *(of porous surface)* absorber

2 *vi Fam* **to suck up to sb** faire de la lèche à qn, cirer les pompes à qn

sucker [ˈsʌkə(r)] **1** *n* (**a**) *Fam (dupe)* pigeon *m*, gogo *m*; **he's a real sucker** c'est un vrai pigeon; **I'm a sucker for chocolate** je ne sais pas résister au chocolat, je raffole du chocolat; **to be a sucker for a pretty face** ne pas savoir résister à un joli visage; *Am* **you've been played for a sucker** vous vous êtes fait rouler *ou* pigeonner; **OK, sucker, you asked for it** OK, mec, tu l'auras voulu

(**b**) *Br (suction cup or pad)* ventouse *f*; **there are rubber suckers on the end of the arrows** il y a des ventouses au bout des flèches

(**c**) *Zool (of insect)* suçoir *m*; *(of octopus, leech)* ventouse *f*

(**d**) *Bot* drageon *m*

(**e**) *Am (lollipop)* sucette *f*

(**f**) *Am Fam (despicable man)* blaireau *m*

(**g**) *Am Fam (object)* truc *m*, machin *m*, bitoniau *m*; **what's this sucker for?** à quoi ça sert, ce truc?

2 *vt* (**a**) *Hort* enlever les drageons de

(**b**) *Am Fam (dupe)* refaire, pigeonner; **she suckered him out of $300** elle l'a refait de 300 dollars

3 *vi Bot (plant)* drageonner

sucking [ˈsʌkɪŋ] *n (of baby)* succion *f*; *(of pump)* aspiration *f*

▸▸ ***sucking pig*** cochon *m* de lait

suckle [ˈsʌkəl] **1** *vt* (**a**) *(child)* allaiter, donner le sein à; *(animal)* allaiter (**b**) *Fig (raise)* élever

2 *vi* téter

suckling [ˈsʌklɪŋ] *n* (**a**) *(child)* nourrisson *m*, enfant *m* encore au sein; *(animal)* animal *m* qui tète (**b**) *(act)* allaitement *m*

▸▸ ***suckling pig*** cochon *m* de lait

sucrose [ˈsuːkrəʊz] *n* saccharose *m*

suction [ˈsʌkʃən] *n* succion *f*, aspiration *f*; **it adheres by suction** ça fait ventouse

▸▸ ***suction cup, suction pad*** ventouse *f*; ***suction pump*** pompe *f* aspirante; ***suction valve*** clapet *m* *ou* soupape *f* d'aspiration

suctorial [sʌkˈtɔːrɪəl] *adj Zool* suceur

Sudan [suːˈdɑːn] *n* Soudan *m*; **in Sudan, in the Sudan** au Soudan

Sudanese [ˌsuːdəˈniːz] (*pl* **inv**) **1** *n* Soudanais(e) *m,f*

2 *adj* soudanais

Sudanic [suːˈdænɪk] **1** *adj* soudanais

2 *n Ling* soudanais *m*

sudarium [suːˈdeərɪəm] *n Rel* véronique *f*

sudatorium [ˌsuːdəˈtɔːrɪəm] *n Antiq* sudatorium *m*

sudatory [ˈsuːdətərɪ] *adj* sudatoire

sudden [ˈsʌdən] **1** *adj (gen)* soudain, subit; *(movement)* brusque; **a sudden twinge of remorse** un remords subit; **there was a sudden bend in the road** soudain il y a eu un virage; **she had a sudden change of heart** elle a soudainement *ou* subitement changé d'avis; **this is all very sudden!** c'est plutôt inattendu!

2 all of a sudden *adv* soudain, subitement, tout d'un coup; **I feel very cold all of a sudden** j'ai très froid tout d'un coup

▸▸ ***sudden death*** mort *f* subite; *(games) & Sport* = jeu pour partager les ex aequo (où le premier point perdu, le premier but concédé etc, entraîne l'élimination immédiate); ***sudden infant death syndrome*** mort *f* subite du nourrisson

suddenly [ˈsʌdənlɪ] *adv* soudainement, subitement; **he died suddenly in the night** il est mort subitement dans la nuit; **suddenly it started to rain** tout à coup il s'est mis à pleuvoir

suddenness [ˈsʌdənnɪs] *n* soudaineté *f*, caractère *m* subit *ou* imprévu; **the suddenness of the attack surprised us** la soudaineté de l'attaque nous a surpris

sudorific [ˌsuːdəˈrɪfɪk] **1** *adj* sudorifique

2 *n* sudorifique *m*

suds [sʌdz] *npl* (**a**) *(foam)* mousse *f*; *(soapy water)* eau *f* savonneuse (**b**) *Am Fam (beer)* bière □ *f*

sudsy [ˈsʌdzɪ] (*compar* **sudsier**, *superl* **sudsiest**) *adj (foamy)* mousseux; *(soapy)* savonneux

sue [suː] **1** *vt* poursuivre en justice, intenter un procès à; **to sue sb for** *or* **over sth** poursuivre qn en justice pour qch; **he sued the factory for damages** il a poursuivi l'usine pour obtenir des dommages et intérêts; **to be sued for damages/libel** être poursuivi en dommages-intérêts/en diffamation; **she's suing him for divorce** elle a entamé une procédure de divorce

2 *vi* (**a**) *Law* intenter un procès, engager des poursuites; **she threatened to sue for libel** elle a menacé d'intenter un procès en diffamation; **he's suing for divorce** il a entamé une procédure de divorce

(**b**) *Formal (solicit)* **to sue for** solliciter; *Pol* **to sue for peace** demander la paix

sueable [ˈsuːəbəl] *adj* poursuivable en justice

suede [sweɪd] **1** *n* daim *m*, *Spec* suède *m*

2 *comp (jacket, purse, shoes)* en *ou* de daim; *(leather)* suédé

suedehead [ˈsweɪdhed] *n Fam* crâne *m* rasé

suedette [sweɪˈdet] *n* suédine *f*

suet [ˈsʊɪt] *n* graisse *f* de rognon

▸▸ ***suet pudding*** = sorte de pudding sucré ou salé à base de farine et de graisse de bœuf

Suetonius [ˌswɪˈtəʊnɪəs] *pr n Antiq* Suétone

suety [ˈsʊɪtɪ] *adj (taste)* de graisse; *Pej (complexion)* cireux, blafard; *(face)* empâté

Suez [ˈsʊɪz] *n* Suez

▸▸ ***the Suez Canal*** le canal de Suez; ***the Suez crisis*** l'affaire *f* du canal de Suez

suffer [ˈsʌfə(r)] **1** *vi* (**a**) *(feel pain)* souffrir; **to suffer in silence** souffrir en silence; **he drank too much and suffered for it next day** il a trop bu et, le lendemain, il a payé ses excès; *Fig* **I'll make you suffer for this!** tu vas me payer ça!, je te revaudrai ça!

(**b**) *(be ill, afflicted)* **to suffer from** *(serious disease)* souffrir de; *(cold, headache)* avoir; **to suffer from rheumatism** souffrir de *ou* avoir des rhumatismes; **to suffer from diabetes** être diabétique; **he's still suffering from the effects of the anaesthetic** il ne s'est pas encore tout à fait remis des suites de l'anesthésie; **to suffer from a speech defect** avoir un défaut de prononciation; **they're still suffering from shock** ils sont encore sous le choc; **she suffers from an inferiority complex** elle fait un complexe d'infériorité

(**c**) *(be affected)* souffrir; **it's the children who suffer in a marriage break-up** ce sont les enfants qui souffrent lors d'une séparation; **there was a fall in investment and the company's profits suffered** les investissements ont baissé et les bénéfices s'en sont ressenti; **the low-paid will be the first to suffer** les petits salaires seront les premiers touchés; **the schools suffer from a lack of funding** les établissements scolaires manquent de crédits; **she became severely depressed and her work began to suffer** elle a sombré dans la dépression et son travail a commencé à s'en ressentir; **her health is suffering under all this stress** sa santé se ressent de tout ce stress; **the business really suffered when he left** l'affaire a beaucoup souffert de son départ; **in the wake of government cutbacks, safety standards are beginning to suffer** la sécurité commence à se ressentir *ou* à souffrir des réductions effectuées par le gouvernement

2 *vt* (**a**) *(experience → thirst)* souffrir de; *(→ hardship)* souffrir, subir; *(→ loss, indignity,* *consequence)* subir; **she suffered a lot of pain** elle a beaucoup souffert; *Fam* **I suffered agonies!** j'ai souffert le martyre!; **our scheme has suffered a serious setback** notre projet a subi *ou* essuyé un grave revers; **you'll have to suffer the consequences** vous devrez en subir les conséquences; **his popularity suffered a decline** sa cote de popularité a baissé

(**b**) *(stand, put up with)* tolérer, supporter; **I won't suffer him another minute** je ne le supporterai pas une minute de plus; **he doesn't suffer fools gladly** il ne supporte pas les imbéciles

(**c**) *Literary (allow)* permettre, *Literary* souffrir; **to suffer sb to do sth** souffrir que qn fasse qch; *Bible* **suffer the little children to come unto me** laissez venir à moi les petits enfants

sufferance ['sʌfərəns] *n* (**a**) *(tolerance)* tolérance *f*; **on sufferance** par tolérance; **remember you are only here on sufferance** n'oubliez pas que votre présence ici n'est que tolérée *ou* est tout juste tolérée (**b**) *(endurance)* endurance *f*, résistance *f* (**c**) *(suffering)* souffrance *f*

sufferer ['sʌfərə(r)] *n* malade *mf*, victime *f*; **sufferers from heart disease** les personnes *fpl* cardiaques; **polio sufferer** polio *mf*; **good news for arthritis sufferers** une bonne nouvelle pour les personnes sujettes à l'arthrite *ou* qui souffrent d'arthrite

suffering ['sʌfərɪŋ] **1** *n* souffrance *f*, souffrances *fpl*; **war causes great suffering** la guerre est cause de nombreuses souffrances; **all their sufferings have been unnecessary** toutes leurs souffrances ont été inutiles

2 *adj* souffrant, qui souffre

suffice [sə'faɪs] **1** *vi Formal* suffire, être suffisant; **will some bread and soup suffice?** du pain et de la soupe seront-ils suffisants?; **suffice it to say (that) she's overjoyed** inutile de dire qu'elle est ravie

2 *vt* suffire à, satisfaire; **empty promises will not suffice him** il ne se contentera pas de vaines promesses

sufficiency [sə'fɪʃənsɪ] *(pl* **sufficiencies***)* *n* quantité *f* suffisante; **the country already had a sufficiency of oil** le pays avait déjà suffisamment de pétrole *ou* du pétrole en quantité suffisante

sufficient [sə'fɪʃənt] *adj* (**a**) *(gen)* suffisant; **there's sufficient food for everyone** il y a assez *ou* suffisamment à manger pour tout le monde; **have you had sufficient to eat?** avez-vous mangé à votre faim?; **one light will be sufficient** une lampe suffira; **three will be quite sufficient for our needs** trois nous suffiront amplement; **is that sufficient time for you?** cela vous donne-t-il suffisamment de temps?; **let me know in sufficient time so that I can…** prévenez-moi suffisamment à l'avance pour que je puisse…; **we don't have sufficient evidence to convict them** nous ne disposons pas d'assez de preuves pour les inculper

(**b**) *Phil* suffisant; **a sufficient condition** une condition suffisante

sufficiently [sə'fɪʃəntlɪ] *adv* suffisamment, assez; **it's sufficiently strong to withstand your weight** c'est assez solide pour supporter votre poids; **a sufficiently large quantity** une quantité suffisante

suffix ['sʌfɪks] **1** *n* suffixe *m*

2 *vt* suffixer

suffixal ['sʌfɪksəl] *adj Gram* suffixal

suffixation [,sʌfɪk'seɪʃən] *n Gram* suffixation *f*

suffocate ['sʌfəkeɪt] **1** *vi* (**a**) *(die)* s'étouffer, s'asphyxier (**b**) *(be hot, lack fresh air)* suffoquer, étouffer; **open the window, I'm suffocating!** ouvre la fenêtre, j'étouffe! (**c**) *Fig (with anger, emotion etc)* s'étouffer, suffoquer

2 *vt* (**a**) *(kill)* suffoquer, étouffer, asphyxier (**b**) *Fig (repress, inhibit)* étouffer, suffoquer

suffocating ['sʌfəkeɪtɪŋ] *adj* (**a**) *(heat, room)* suffocant, étouffant; *(smoke, fumes)* asphyxiant, suffocant; **it's suffocating (in) here** on étouffe ici (**b**) *Fig* étouffant

suffocatingly [,sʌfə'keɪtɪŋlɪ] *adv* **it was suffocatingly hot** il faisait chaud à étouffer, on étouffait

suffocation [,sʌfə'keɪʃən] *n* suffocation *f*, étouffement *m*, asphyxie *f*; **to die from suffocation** mourir asphyxié

Suffolk ['sʌfək] *n* le Suffolk, = comté dans le sud-est de l'Angleterre; **in Suffolk** dans le Suffolk

▸▸ ***Suffolk punch*** *(horse)* Suffolk punch *m*

suffragan ['sʌfrəgən] **1** *n* **suffragan (bishop)** (évêque *m*) suffragant *m*

2 *adj* suffragant

suffrage ['sʌfrɪdʒ] *n* (**a**) *(right to vote)* droit *m* de suffrage *ou* de vote; **universal suffrage** suffrage *m* universel; **women's suffrage** le droit de vote pour les femmes (**b**) *Formal (vote)* suffrage *m*, vote *m*

suffragette [,sʌfrə'dʒet] *n* suffragette *f*

THE SUFFRAGETTES

Il s'agit des militantes britanniques réclamant le droit de vote pour les femmes au début du XXème siècle. Menées par Emmeline Pankhurst, elles mirent en œuvre des moyens (manifestations, interruptions de meetings, attentats, incendies criminels, grèves de la faim) qui eurent finalement raison du Premier ministre Asquith, lequel fit adopter par le Parlement, en 1917, un projet de loi accordant le droit de vote à certaines catégories de femmes (les femmes mariées, les femmes au foyer et les femmes diplômées âgées d'au moins 30 ans). En 1928, une nouvelle loi étendit ce droit à toutes les femmes.

suffuse [sə'fjuːz] *vt (usu passive)* se répandre sur, baigner; **suffused with light** inondé de lumière; **the sky was suffused with red** le ciel était tout empourpré

suffusion [sə'fjuːʒən] *n* (**a**) *Med* suffusion *f* (**b**) *(blush)* rougeur *f*

Sufi ['suːfɪ] *n* soufi(e) *m,f*

Sufism ['suːfɪzəm] *n* soufisme *m*

sugar ['ʃʊgə(r)] **1** *n* (**a**) *(gen)* & *Chem* sucre *m*; **how many sugars?** combien de sucres?; **I don't take sugar** je ne prends pas de sucre

(**b**) *Fam (term of address)* chéri(e) *m,f*

(**c**) *Fam* **she's found herself a sugar daddy** elle s'est trouvé un vieux friqué qui l'entretient; **I've no intention of being your sugar daddy** je n'ai pas l'intention de t'entretenir

2 *vt* sucrer; *Fig* **to sugar the pill (for sb)** dorer la pilule (à qn)

3 *exclam Fam* miel!, punaise!

▸▸ ***sugar almond*** dragée *f*; *Br* ***sugar basin*** sucrier *m*; ***sugar beet*** betterave *f* sucrière *ou* à sucre; *Orn* ***sugar bird*** promérops *m* du Cap; ***sugar bowl*** sucrier *m*; *Am Sport* ***the Sugar Bowl*** = tournoi de football américain de La Nouvelle-Orléans; ***sugar candy*** sucre *m* candi; ***sugar cane*** canne *f* à sucre; ***sugar cube*** morceau *m* de sucre; ***sugar lump*** morceau *m* de sucre; ***sugar maple*** érable *m* à sucre; ***sugar pea*** mange-tout *m inv*; ***sugar shaker*** saupoudreuse *f* (à sucre); *Br* ***sugar soap*** décapant *m* alcalin pour peintures; *Culin* ***sugar syrup*** sirop *m* de sucre; ***sugar tongs*** pince *f* à sucre

sugarcane ['ʃʊgəkeɪn] *n* canne *f* à sucre

sugar-coat *vt* enrober de sucre; *Fig (unpleasant measure)* faire passer

sugar-coated [-,kəʊtɪd] *adj* enrobé de sucre

▸▸ ***sugar-coated almonds*** dragées *fpl*; ***sugar-coated pill*** comprimé *m* dragéifié

sugared ['ʃʊgəd] *adj* (**a**) sucré (**b**) *Fig* mielleux, doucereux; **he spoke in sugared tones** il parlait d'un ton mielleux *ou* doucereux

▸▸ ***sugared almond*** dragée *f*

sugar-free *adj* sans sucre

sugarless ['ʃʊgəlɪs] *adj* sans sucre

sugarloaf ['ʃʊgələʊf] *(pl* **sugarloaves** [-ləʊvz]*)* *n* pain *m* de sucre

sugarplum ['ʃʊgəplʌm] *n (candied plum)* prune *f* confite; *(boiled sweet)* bonbon *m*

sugary ['ʃʊgərɪ] *adj* (**a**) *(drink, food)* (très) sucré; *(taste)* sucré (**b**) *(manner, tone)* mielleux, doucereux; **sugary sentimentality** mièvrerie *f*

suggest [sə'dʒest] *vt* (**a**) *(propose, put forward)* suggérer, proposer; **I suggest (that) we do nothing for the moment** je suggère *ou* je propose que nous ne fassions rien pour l'instant; **he suggested that the meeting be held next Tuesday** il a proposé de fixer la réunion à mardi prochain; **a solution suggested itself to me** une solution m'est venue à l'esprit; **this, I suggest, is how it happened** voici, à mon avis, comment c'est arrivé

(**b**) *(recommend)* suggérer, recommander; **who do you suggest for the job?** qui suggérez-vous pour cette tâche?

(**c**) *(imply, insinuate)* suggérer; **just what are you suggesting?** que voulez-vous dire par là?, qu'allez-vous insinuer là?; **are you suggesting that I might be wrong?** suggérez-vous que je pourrais avoir tort?

(**d**) *(indicate, point to)* suggérer, laisser supposer; **which suggests that it was an accident** ce qui semblerait indiquer qu'il s'agissait d'un accident; **recent studies suggest that radiation may be the cause** des études récentes semblent indiquer que le problème est dû à des radiations; **the marks in the sand suggest a person of about…** les traces sur le sable indiquent la présence d'une personne d'environ…

(**e**) *(evoke)* suggérer, évoquer; **what does this picture suggest to you?** qu'est-ce que ce tableau évoque pour vous?, à quoi ce tableau vous fait-il penser?

suggestibility [sə,dʒestə'bɪlətɪ] *n Psy* suggestibilité *f*

suggestible [sə'dʒestəbəl] *adj Psy* suggestible

suggestion [sə'dʒestʃən] *n* (**a**) *(proposal)* suggestion *f*, proposition *f*; **may I make a suggestion?** puis-je faire une suggestion?; **if nobody has any other suggestions, we'll move on** si personne n'a rien d'autre à suggérer *ou* à proposer, nous allons passer à autre chose; **we are always open to suggestions** toute suggestion est la bienvenue; **there's never been any suggestion before of the rules being changed** jusqu'à présent, il n'a jamais été question de modifier le règlement; **serving suggestion** *(on packaging)* suggestion *f* de présentation

(**b**) *(recommendation)* conseil *m*, recommandation *f*; **at her doctor's suggestion she stayed in bed** suivant le conseil de son médecin, elle est restée au lit; **their suggestion is that we stop work immediately** ils proposent que nous arrêtions le travail immédiatement

(**c**) *(indication)* indication *f*; **her expression gave no suggestion of what she was really thinking** son expression ne donnait aucune indication sur *ou* ne laissait rien paraître de ce qu'elle pensait vraiment

(**d**) *(trace, hint)* soupçon *m*, trace *f*; **with just a suggestion of irony** avec un soupçon d'ironie

(**e**) *(implication)* suggestion *f*, implication *f*; **there is no suggestion of negligence on their part** rien ne laisse penser qu'il y ait eu négligence de leur part

(**f**) *Psy* suggestion *f*; **the power of suggestion** le pouvoir de suggestion

▸▸ ***suggestion box*** boîte *f* à suggestions

suggestive [sə'dʒestɪv] *adj* (**a**) *(indicative, evocative)* suggestif; **his sculptures are suggestive of natural forms** ses sculptures rappellent *ou* évoquent des formes naturelles (**b**) *(erotic) (lyrics, dance, pose)* suggestif; *(joke)* grivois

suggestively [sə'dʒestɪvlɪ] *adv* de façon suggestive

suggestiveness [sə'dʒestɪvnɪs] *n (of picture etc)* caractère *m* suggestif

suicidal [suːɪ'saɪdəl] *adj* suicidaire; **suicidal tendencies** des tendances *fpl* suicidaires; **I was feeling suicidal** j'avais envie de me tuer; **to stop now would be suicidal** ce serait du suicide de s'arrêter maintenant

suicide ['suːɪsaɪd] **1** *n (act)* suicide *m*; *(person)* suicidé(e) *m,f*; **to commit suicide** se suicider; **mass suicide** suicide *m* collectif; **there were several attempted suicides** il y a eu plusieurs tentatives de suicide; **privatization would be financial suicide** la privatisation représenterait un véritable suicide financier

2 *comp (mission, plane, squad)* suicide; *(attempt, bid)* de suicide

▸▸ ***suicide bomber*** auteur *m* d'un attentat-suicide à la bombe; ***suicide pill*** *(defensive tactics in takeover)* clause *f* de suicide; ***suicide note*** lettre *f* (que l'on laisse quand on se suicide); ***suicide pact*** = accord de suicide collectif entre deux ou plusieurs personnes

suit [suːt] **1** *n* (**a**) *(outfit → for men)* costume *m*, complet *m*; *(→ for women)* tailleur *m*; *(→ for particular activity)* combinaison *f*; **he came in a**

suit and tie il est venu en costume-cravate; **two-piece/three-piece suit** complet deux/trois pièces; **the workers wear protective suits** les ouvriers portent des combinaisons de protection; **suit of clothes** tenue *f*; **suit of armour** armure *f* complète; *Fig Pej* **the men in grey suits** les bureaucrates *mpl*

(**b**) *(complete set)* jeu *m*; **a suit of sails** un jeu de voiles

(**c**) *(in card games)* couleur *f*; **long** *or* **strong suit** couleur *f* forte; *Fig* **generosity is not his strong suit** la générosité n'est pas vraiment son (point) fort; **to follow suit** fournir à la couleur (demandée); *Fig* en faire autant, faire de même

(**d**) *Law (lawsuit)* action *f*, procès *m*; **to bring** *or* **to file a suit against sb** intenter un procès à qn, poursuivre qn en justice; **criminal suit** action *f* au pénal

(**e**) *Formal (appeal)* requête *f*, pétition *f*; *Literary (courtship)* cour *f*; **to pay suit to sb** faire la cour à qn

(**f**) *Fam Pej (person)* employé(e) *m,f* de bureau ❑ *(en costume ou tailleur)*

2 *vt* (**a**) *(be becoming to → of clothes, colour)* aller à; **black really suits her** le noir lui va à merveille

(**b**) *(be satisfactory or convenient to)* convenir à, arranger; **Tuesday suits me best** c'est mardi qui me convient *ou* qui m'arrange le mieux; **their relaxed approach suits me fine** leur attitude décontractée me convient parfaitement *ou* tout à fait; *Fam* **suit yourself!** faites ce qui vous chante!, faites comme vous voudrez! ❑

(**c**) *(agree with)* convenir à, aller à, réussir à; **life in the country obviously suits her** de toute évidence, la vie à la campagne lui convient *ou* lui réussit

(**d**) *(be appropriate)* convenir à, aller à, être fait pour; **clothes to suit all tastes** des vêtements pour tous les goûts; **the role suits her perfectly** le rôle lui va comme un gant; **he is not suited to be a doctor** il n'est pas fait pour être médecin; **they are suited to each other, they suit each other** ils sont faits l'un pour l'autre

(**e**) *(adapt)* adapter, approprier; **he tries to suit his act to his audience** il essaie d'adapter son numéro à son public; **to suit the action to the word** joindre le geste à la parole

(**f**) *Am (dress in suit)* vêtir d'un costume; **his followers were suited in black** ses disciples étaient vêtus d'un costume noir

3 *vi (be satisfactory)* convenir, aller; **will that date suit?** cette date vous convient-elle *ou* est-elle à votre convenance?

▸**suit up** *vi (dress → diver, pilot, astronaut etc)* mettre sa combinaison

suitability [ˌsuːtəˈbɪlətɪ] *n (of clothing)* caractère *m* approprié; *(of behaviour, arrangements)* caractère *m* convenable; *(of act, remark)* à-propos *m*, pertinence *f*; *(of time, place)* opportunité *f*; **they doubt his suitability for the post** ils ne sont pas sûrs qu'il soit fait *ou* qu'il ait les qualités requises pour ce poste; **they're worried about the film's suitability for younger audiences** ils ont peur que le film ne convienne pas à un public jeune; **we need to assess the suitability of the accommodation** il nous faut vérifier si le logement convient

suitable [ˈsuːtəbəl] *adj* (**a**) *(convenient)* approprié, adéquat; **will that day be suitable for you?** cette date-là vous convient-elle?; **the most suitable date** la date qui conviendra le mieux; **afternoons aren't suitable** ça n'est pas possible l'après-midi

(**b**) *(appropriate → gen)* qui convient; *(→ clothing)* approprié, adéquat; *(→ behaviour)* convenable; *(→ act, remark, expression)* approprié, pertinent; *(→ time, place)* propice; **suitable for all occasions** qui convient dans toutes les occasions; **not suitable for children** *(on packaging)* réservé aux adultes; **this is hardly a suitable time for a heart to heart** ce n'est pas vraiment le bon moment pour se parler à cœur ouvert; **the most suitable candidate for the post** le candidat le plus apte à occuper ce poste; **the house is not suitable for a large family** la maison ne conviendrait pas à une famille nombreuse; **he's not suitable for our Christine** ce n'est pas l'homme qu'il faut à notre Christine; **the stage was not considered a suitable career for a woman** le théâtre n'était pas considéré comme un métier convenable pour une femme

suitably [ˈsuːtəblɪ] *adv (dress)* de façon appropriée; *(behave)* convenablement, comme il faut; **suitably matched** bien assortis; **he was suitably equipped for his trip** il était convenablement équipé pour son voyage; **I tried to look suitably surprised** j'ai essayé d'avoir l'air surpris, comme il se devait; **he was suitably impressed** il a été plutôt impressionné

suitcase [ˈsuːtkeɪs] *n* valise *f*; **I've been living out of a suitcase for weeks** ça fait des semaines que je n'ai pas défait mes valises; **she'd been travelling around, living out of a suitcase** elle avait voyagé un peu partout sans jamais vraiment s'installer

suitcoat [ˈsuːtkəʊt] *n Am* veston *m*

suite [swiːt] *n* (**a**) *(rooms)* suite *f*, appartement *m*; **a suite of rooms** une enfilade de pièces (**b**) *(furniture)* mobilier *m*; **bedroom suite** chambre *f* à coucher (**c**) *Mus* suite *f*; **a cello suite** une suite pour violoncelle (**d**) *(staff, followers)* suite *f* (**e**) *Comput (of software)* suite *f* logicielle, ensemble *m* logiciel

suited [ˈsuːtɪd] *adj* (**a**) *(appropriate)* approprié; **he's not suited to teaching** il n'est pas fait pour l'enseignement; **she's ideally suited for the job** ce travail lui convient tout à fait (**b**) *(matched)* assorti; **they are well suited (to each other)** ils sont faits l'un pour l'autre, ils sont bien assortis

suiting [ˈsuːtɪŋ] *n* tissu *m* de confection

suitor [ˈsuːtə(r)] *n* (**a**) *Old-fashioned (wooer)* amoureux *m*, soupirant *m* (**b**) *Law* plaignant(e) *m,f*

sukiyaki [ˌsuːkɪˈjækɪ] *n Culin* sukiyaki *m*

Sukkoth [ˈsʊkəʊt, ˈsʊkəʊθ] *n Rel* Soukkot, fête *f* des Tabernacles

Sulawesi [ˌsuːləˈweɪsɪ] *n* Sulawesi; **in Sulawesi** à Sulawesi

sulcus [ˈsʌlkəs] (*pl* **sulci** [-saɪ]) *n Anat* sillon *m*; *(in brain)* sulcature *f*

Suleiman [ˌsuːleɪˈmɑːn] *pr n* **Suleiman the Magnificent** Soliman le Magnifique

sulfa *Am* = **sulpha**

sulfate *Am* = **sulphate**

sulfide *Am* = **sulphide**

sulfite *Am* = **sulphite**

sulfonamide *Am* = **sulphonamide**

sulfone *Am* = **sulphone**

sulfur, sulfurate *etc Am* = **sulphur, sulphurate** *etc*

sulk [sʌlk] **1** *vi* bouder, faire la tête; **there's no need to sulk!** (ce n'est) pas la peine de faire la tête!

2 *n* bouderie *f*; **to have a sulk** *or* **(a fit of) the sulks** bouder, faire la tête

sulkily [ˈsʌlkɪlɪ] *adv (act)* en boudant, d'un air maussade; *(answer)* d'un ton maussade

sulkiness [ˈsʌlkɪnɪs] *n (mood)* bouderie *f*, humeur *f* maussade; *(temperament)* caractère *m* boudeur *ou* maussade

sulking [ˈsʌlkɪŋ] *n* bouderie *f*

sulky [ˈsʌlkɪ] (*compar* **sulkier,** *superl* **sulkiest,** *pl* **sulkies**) **1** *adj (person, mood)* boudeur, maussade; **now, don't go all sulky on me!** allez, pas la peine de me faire la tête!

2 *n* sulky *m*

sullage [ˈsʌlɪdʒ] [illegible]

sullen [ˈsʌlən] *adj* (**a**) *(person, behaviour, appearance, remark)* maussade, renfrogné (**b**) *(clouds)* menaçant

sullenly [ˈsʌlənlɪ] *adv (behave)* d'un air maussade *ou* renfrogné; *(answer, say, refuse)* d'un ton maussade; *(agree, obey)* de mauvaise grâce, à contrecœur

sullenness [ˈsʌlənnɪs] *n (temperament)* humeur *f* maussade; *(of appearance)* air *m* renfrogné

sullied [ˈsʌlɪd] *adj Formal (dirty)* souillé; *(reputation)* terni

sully [ˈsʌlɪ] (*pt & pp* **sullied**) *vt Formal* (**a**) *(dirty)* souiller (**b**) *Fig (reputation)* ternir

sulpha, *Am* **sulfa** [ˈsʌlfə] *n Pharm* sulfamide *m*

►► ***sulpha drug*** sulfamide *m*

sulphadiazine, *Am* **sulfadiazine** [ˌsʌlfəˈdaɪəziːn] *n Pharm* sulfadiazine *f*

sulphanilamide, *Am* **sulfanilamide** [ˌsʌlfəˈnɪləmaɪd] *n Pharm* sulfanilamide *m ou f*

sulphate, *Am* **sulfate** [ˈsʌlfeɪt] *n* sulfate *m*; **copper/zinc sulphate** sulfate *m* de cuivre/de zinc

sulphide, *Am* **sulfide** [ˈsʌlfaɪd] *n* sulfure *m*; **to treat sth with sulphide** sulfurer qch

sulphite, *Am* **sulfite** [ˈsʌlfaɪt] *n* sulfite *m*

sulphonamide, *Am* **sulfonamide** [sʌlˈfɒnəmaɪd] *n* sulfonamide *m*, sulfamide *m*

sulphone, *Am* **sulfone** [ˈsʌlfəʊn] *n Chem* sulfone *f*

sulphur, *Am* **sulfur** [ˈsʌlfə(r)] *n* soufre *m*

►► ***sulphur dioxide*** dioxyde *m* de soufre, anhydride *m* sulfureux; *Bot* ***sulphur tuft*** hypholome *m* en touffe *ou* en faisceau, agaric *m* doré

sulphurate, *Am* **sulfurate** [ˈsʌlfəreɪt] *vt (metal)* sulfurer; *(wool)* soufrer

sulphuration, *Am* **sulfuration** [ˌsʌlfəˈreɪʃən] *n (of metal)* sulfuration *f*; *(of wool)* soufrage *m*

sulphureous, *Am* **sulfureous** [sʌlˈfjʊərɪəs] *adj* sulfureux; *(coloured)* couleur de soufre *(inv)*, soufré

sulphuric, *Am* **sulfuric** [sʌlˈfjʊərɪk] *adj* sulfurique

►► ***sulphuric acid*** acide *m* sulfurique

sulphurous, *Am* **sulfurous** [ˈsʌlfərəs] *adj also Fig* sulfureux

sultan [ˈsʌltən] *n* sultan *m*

sultana [səlˈtɑːnə] *n* (**a**) *Br (raisin)* raisin *m* de Smyrne (**b**) *(woman)* sultane *f*

►► ***sultana cake*** gâteau *m* aux raisins de Smyrne

sultanate [ˈsʌltənət] *n* sultanat *m*

sultriness [ˈsʌltrɪnɪs] *n* (**a**) *(of weather)* chaleur *f* étouffante; **the sultriness of the weather** le temps lourd (**b**) *(sensuality)* sensualité *f*

sultry [ˈsʌltrɪ] (*compar* **sultrier,** *superl* **sultriest**) *adj* (**a**) *(weather)* lourd; *(heat)* étouffant, suffocant (**b**) *(person, look, smile)* sensuel; *(voice)* chaud, sensuel

Sulu [ˈsuːluː] *n* **the Sulu Islands** l'archipel *m* de Sulu, les Sulu *fpl*

sum [sʌm] (*pt & pp* **summed,** *cont* **summing**) **1** *n* (**a**) *(amount of money)* somme *f*; **it's going to cost us a considerable sum (of money)** ça va nous coûter beaucoup d'argent *ou* très cher

(**b**) *(total)* total *m*, somme *f*; **the whole is greater than the sum of its parts** l'ensemble est encore meilleur que la somme des éléments qui le compose

(**c**) *(arithmetical operation)* calcul *m*; *Br* **to do sums** faire du calcul; *Br* **he's very weak at sums** il est très faible en calcul; **I tried to do the sum in my head** j'ai essayé de faire le calcul de tête; *Fig* **they've really got their sums right** ils ont bien calculé leur coup

(**d**) *(gist)* somme *f*; **in sum** en somme, somme toute; **the sum and substance of her argument** les grandes lignes de son raisonnement

2 *vt (add)* additionner, faire le total de; *(calculate)* calculer

►► *Fin* ***sum payable*** charge *f* à payer; ***sum total*** totalité *f*, somme *f* totale; **the report contains the sum total of research in the field** ce rapport contient tous les résultats de la recherche en ce domaine; **that is the sum total of our knowledge** voilà à quoi se résume tout ce que nous savons; **is that the sum total of what you've done today?** c'est tout ce que vous avez fait aujourd'hui?

▸**sum up 1** *vt sep* (**a**) *(summarize)* résumer, récapituler; **one word sums the matter up** un mot suffit à résumer la question; *Law* **to sum up the case** *or* **the evidence** *(judge)* résumer les débats

(**b**) *(size up)* jauger; **he summed us up immediately** il nous a jaugés *ou* classés sur-le-champ; **I summed up the situation at a glance** un simple coup d'œil m'a suffi pour jauger la situation

2 *vi (gen)* récapituler, faire un résumé; *Law (judge)* résumer; **to sum up I will say that...** en résumé je dirai que...; **in summing up the judge said...** dans son résumé, le juge a dit...

sumach, *Am* **sumac** [ˈʃuːmæk] *n* sumac *m*

Sumatra [sʊˈmɑːtrə] *n* Sumatra; **in Sumatra** à Sumatra

Sumatran [sʊˈmɑːtrən] **1** *n* Sumatranais(e) *m,f*

2 *adj* sumatranais

►► *Zool* ***Sumatran rhinoceros*** rhinocéros *m* de Sumatra

Sumer [ˈsuːmə(r)] *n* Sumer

Sumerian [suːˈmɪərɪən] **1** *n* (**a**) *(person)* Sumérien(enne) *m,f* (**b**) *(language)* sumérien *m*

2 *adj* sumérien

summa cum laude ['sʌmə,kʊm'laʊdeɪ] *adv Am* avec les plus grands honneurs; **to graduate summa cum laude** obtenir un diplôme avec mention très honorable

summarily ['sʌmərəlɪ] *adv* sommairement; **they were summarily dismissed without any explanation** on les a sommairement *ou* tout simplement congédiés sans plus d'explications

summarize, -ise ['sʌməraɪz] *vt* résumer

summary ['sʌmərɪ] (*pl* **summaries**) **1** *n* (**a**) *(synopsis → of argument, situation)* résumé *m*, récapitulation *f*; *(→ of book, film)* résumé *m*; **he gave us a brief summary of the situation** il nous a fait un bref résumé de la situation; **there is a news summary every hour** il y a un court bulletin d'information toutes les heures; **here is a brief news summary** et maintenant le rappel des titres

(**b**) *(written list)* sommaire *m*, résumé *m*; *Fin (of accounts)* relevé *m*

2 *adj (gen) & Law* sommaire

►► ***summary dismissal*** renvoi *m* sommaire; ***summary offence*** infraction *f* mineure, délit *m*

summat ['sʌmət] *NEng Fam* = **something**

summation [sʌ'meɪʃən] *n* (**a**) *(addition)* addition *f*; *(sum)* somme *f*, total *m* (**b**) *(summary)* récapitulation *f*, résumé *m*; **the book is a summation of her life's work** ce livre constitue une récapitulation de l'œuvre de sa vie

summer ['sʌmə(r)] **1** *n* (**a**) *(season)* été *m*; **in (the) summer** en été; **in the summer of 1942** pendant *ou* au cours de l'été 1942; **a summer('s) day** un jour d'été; **they spend every summer at the seaside** ils passent tous leurs étés au bord de la mer; **we've had a good summer** *(good weather)* on a eu un bel été; *(profitable tourist season)* la saison était bonne

(**b**) *Literary (year of age)* **a youth of 15 summers** un jeune homme de 15 printemps

(**c**) *Fig (high point)* apogée *m*

2 *comp (clothes, residence, day)* d'été; *(heat, sports)* estival; **the summer holidays** *(gen)* les vacances *fpl* d'été; *Sch* les grandes vacances *fpl*

3 *vi* passer l'été

4 *vt (cattle, sheep)* estiver

►► *Am* ***summer camp*** colonie *f* de vacances; *Am* ***summer house*** maison *f* de campagne; *Br* ***summer pudding*** = pudding composé d'une compote de fruits rouges recouverte de pain; ***summer resort*** station *f* estivale; ***summer school*** université *f* d'été; ***summer solstice*** solstice *m* d'été; *Am* ***summer squash*** courgette *f* jaune; ***summer term*** troisième trimestre *m*; *Admin* ***summer time*** *(by clock)* heure *f* d'été

summerhouse ['sʌməhaʊs, *pl* -haʊzɪz] *n Br* pavillon *m* (de jardin)

summersault = **somersault**

summertime ['sʌmətaɪm] *n (season)* été *m*; **in the summertime** en été

summerweight ['sʌməweɪt] *adj* léger, d'été

summerwood ['sʌməwʊd] *n* bois *m* d'été

summery ['sʌmərɪ] *adj* d'été; **summery weather** un temps d'été *ou* estival; **you look very summery in that dress** cette robe te donne un petit air estival

summing-up [,sʌmɪŋ-] (*pl* **summings-up**) *n (gen)* résumé *m*, récapitulation *f*; *Law* résumé *m*

summit ['sʌmɪt] **1** *n* (**a**) *(peak → of mountain)* sommet *m*, cime *f*; *(→ of glory, happiness, power)* apogée *m*, summum *m* (**b**) *Pol (meeting)* sommet *m*

2 *comp (talks, agreement)* au sommet

3 *vt Fam (in mountaineering)* atteindre le sommet de❑

4 *vi Fam (in mountaineering)* atteindre le sommet❑

►► ***summit conference*** (conférence *f* au) sommet *m*

summiteer [,sʌmɪ'tɪə(r)] *n Pol* participant(e) *m,f* à un sommet

summon ['sʌmən] *vt* (**a**) *(send for → person)* appeler, faire venir; *(→ help)* appeler à, requérir; **they were summoned to the headmaster's office** ils ont été convoqués au bureau du directeur

(**b**) *(convene)* convoquer; **to summon a meeting** convoquer une réunion

(**c**) *Law* citer, assigner; **to summon sb to appear in court** citer qn en justice; **the court summoned her as a witness** la cour l'a citée comme témoin; **summon the next witness!** *(in courtroom)* faites entrer le témoin suivant

(**d**) *(muster → strength)* rassembler, faire appel à; **he couldn't summon enough courage to ask her out** il n'a pas trouvé le courage nécessaire pour lui demander de sortir avec lui

(**e**) *Formal (order)* sommer, ordonner à; **she summoned us in/up** elle nous a sommés *ou* ordonné d'entrer/de monter

►**summon up** *vt sep* (**a**) *(courage, strength)* rassembler, faire appel à; **she summoned up her courage to ask him** elle a pris son courage à deux mains pour lui poser la question; **I'll be there if I can summon up the energy** j'y serai si j'arrive à rassembler suffisamment d'énergie

(**b**) *(help, support)* réunir, faire appel à; **I can't summon up much interest in this plan** je n'arrive pas à m'intéresser beaucoup à ce projet

(**c**) *(memories, thoughts)* évoquer

(**d**) *(spirits)* invoquer

summons ['sʌmənz] (*pl* **summonses**) **1** *n* (**a**) *Law* citation *f*, assignation *f*; **he received** *or* **got a summons for speeding** il a reçu une citation à comparaître en justice pour excès de vitesse; **to take out a summons against sb** faire assigner qn en justice

(**b**) *(gen)* convocation *f*

(**c**) *Mil* sommation *f*; **the town received a summons to surrender** les habitants de la ville furent sommés de se rendre

2 *vt Law* citer *ou* assigner (à comparaître); **she was summonsed to testify** elle a été citée à comparaître en tant que témoin

sumo ['su:məʊ] *n* sumo *m*

►► ***sumo wrestler*** lutteur *m* de sumo; ***sumo wrestling*** sumo *m*

sump [sʌmp] *n* (**a**) *Tech* puisard *m*; *Br Aut* carter *m* (**b**) *(cesspool)* fosse *f* d'aisances

►► *Br* ***sump oil*** huile *f* de carter

sumptuary ['sʌmptjʊərɪ] *adj Formal* somptuaire

►► ***sumptuary law*** loi *f* somptuaire

sumptuosity [,sʌmptjʊ'ɒsɪtɪ] *n* somptuosité *f*

sumptuous ['sʌmptʃʊəs] *adj* somptueux

sumptuously ['sʌmptʃʊəslɪ] *adv* somptueusement

sumptuousness ['sʌmptʃʊəsnɪs] *n* somptuosité *f*

Sun. (*written abbr* **Sunday**) dim.

sun [sʌn] (*pt & pp* **sunned**, *cont* **sunning**) **1** *n* soleil *m*; **the sun is shining** le soleil brille, il y a du soleil; **the sun is rising/setting** le soleil se lève/se couche; **rising/setting sun** soleil *m* levant/couchant; **the sun is in my eyes** j'ai le soleil dans les yeux; **I can't stay in the sun for very long** je ne peux pas rester très longtemps au soleil; **let's get out of the sun** mettons-nous à l'abri du soleil; **she's caught the sun** elle a pris des couleurs; **the living room gets the sun in the afternoon** le salon est ensoleillé l'après-midi; **to take the sun** prendre le soleil; **to take a photograph into the sun** prendre une photo à contre-jour; **a place in the sun** une place au soleil; **I've tried everything under the sun** j'ai tout essayé; **she called him all the names under the sun** elle l'a traité de tous les noms; **every species/subject under the sun** toutes les espèces existantes/tous les sujets possibles; **there's nothing new under the sun** il n'y a rien de nouveau sous le soleil; *Hist* **the Sun King** le Roi-Soleil; *Press* **The Sun** = quotidien britannique populaire de droite; *Literary* **his sun is set** son étoile a pâli

2 *vt* **to sun oneself** *(person)* prendre le soleil, se faire bronzer; *(animal)* se chauffer au soleil

►► *Zool* ***sun bear*** ours *m* des cocotiers; ***sun block*** écran *m* total; ***sun cream*** crème *f* solaire; ***sun dance*** danse *f* du soleil; ***sun deck*** *(of house)* véranda *f*, terrasse *f*; *Naut* pont *m* supérieur, pont-promenade *m*; ***sun god*** dieu *m* solaire, dieu-soleil *m*; ***sun lotion*** lait *m* solaire; *Br* ***sun lounge*** solarium *m*; *Am* ***sun parlor, sun porch*** solarium *m*; ***sun protection factor*** indice *m* de protection solaire; *Br* ***Sun reader*** = lecteur du 'Sun' (typique de la droite populaire); ***sun visor*** *(on cap, for eyes)* visière *f*; *Aut* pare-soleil *m inv*

'The Sun Also Rises' *Hemingway* 'Le Soleil se lève aussi'

sun-and-planet *adj*

►► *Tech* ***sun-and-planet gear*** engrenage *m* à satellites; ***sun-and-planet motion*** mouvement *m* satellite

sunbaked ['sʌnbeɪkt] *adj* desséché par le soleil

sunbath ['sʌnbɑ:θ, *pl* -bɑ:ðz] *n* bain *m* de soleil

sunbathe ['sʌnbeɪð] **1** *vi* prendre un bain de soleil, se faire bronzer

2 *n Br* bain *m* de soleil

sunbather ['sʌnbeɪðə(r)] *n* = personne qui prend un bain de soleil; **hundreds of sunbathers converged on the beach** des centaines de gens se dirigeaient vers la plage pour aller s'étendre au soleil

sunbathing ['sʌnbeɪðɪŋ] *n (UNCOUNT)* bains *mpl* de soleil

sunbeam ['sʌnbi:m] *n* rayon *m* de soleil

sunbed ['sʌnbed] *n (in garden, on beach)* (fauteuil *m*) relax *m*; *(with tanning lamps)* lit *m* à ultraviolets

sunbelt ['sʌnbelt] *n Am* **the sunbelt** *or* **Sunbelt** les États du sud et de l'ouest des États-Unis

sunbird ['sʌnbɜ:d] *n Orn* souimanga *m*

sunbittern ['sʌnbɪtən] *n Orn* caurale *f* soleil

sunblind ['sʌnblaɪnd] *n Br* store *m*

sunbonnet ['sʌn,bɒnɪt] *n* capeline *f*

sunbow ['sʌnbəʊ] *n* arc *m* irisé *(produit par le soleil dans un jet d'eau)*

sunburn ['sʌnbɜ:n] *n* coup *m* de soleil

sunburnt ['sʌnbɜ:nt], **sunburned** ['sʌnbɜ:nd] *adj* brûlé par le soleil; **I get sunburnt easily** j'attrape facilement des coups de soleil

sunburst ['sʌnbɜ:st] *n* (**a**) *(through clouds)* éclaircie *f* (**b**) *(pattern)* soleil *m*; *(brooch)* broche *f* en forme de soleil; **a sunburst clock** une pendule soleil

sun-cured [-kjʊəd] *adj* séché au soleil

sundae ['sʌndeɪ] *n* = coupe de glace aux fruits et à la crème chantilly

Sunda Islands ['sʌndə-] *npl* **the Sunda Islands** les îles *fpl* de la Sonde; **in the Sunda Islands** dans les îles de la Sonde

Sundanese [,sʌndə'ni:z] **1** *adj* sondanais

2 *n* (**a**) *(person)* Sondanais(aise) *m,f* (**b**) *Ling* sondanais *m*

Sunday ['sʌndɪ] **1** *n* (**a**) *(day)* dimanche *m*

(**b**) *Br (newspaper)* **the Sundays** les journaux *mpl* du dimanche

2 *comp (clothes, newspaper, driver)* du dimanche; *(peace, rest, mass)* dominical; **the Sunday roast** *or* **joint** le rôti du dimanche; *see also* **Friday**

►► ***Sunday best*** vêtements *mpl* du dimanche; **to put on one's Sunday best** s'habiller en dimanche, s'endimancher; **they were dressed in their Sunday best** ils étaient tout endimanchés, ils avaient mis leurs vêtements du dimanche; ***Sunday opening*** = ouverture des magasins le dimanche; ***Sunday school*** ≃ catéchisme *m*; ***Sunday school teacher*** catéchiste *mf*, personne *f* qui fait le catéchisme; ***Sunday supplement*** = supplément joint à un journal du dimanche; ***Sunday trading*** = ouverture des magasins le dimanche; ***Sunday trading laws*** = lois réglementant l'ouverture des magasins le dimanche

'Sunday, Bloody Sunday' *Schlesinger* 'Un dimanche comme les autres'

SUNDAY PAPERS

La lecture des journaux du dimanche constitue une sorte de rituel pour de nombreux Britanniques. Les journaux du dimanche sont très volumineux; ils comprennent de nombreux suppléments sur des sujets tels que le sport, la mode, les voyages et les arts, et sont souvent accompagnés d'un magazine en couleurs. Ils coûtent plus cher que les journaux vendus en semaine. Certains journaux du dimanche sont des éditions dominicales de quotidiens paraissant en semaine (c'est le cas de 'The Sunday Times' et de 'The Independent on Sunday' par exemple) tandis que d'autres, comme 'The Observer', paraissent uniquement le dimanche.

sunder ['sʌndə(r)] *Arch* **1** *vt* séparer, briser
2 *n* **in sunder** en morceaux
sundew ['sʌndju:] *n Bot* drosera *m*, rossolis *m*
sundial ['sʌndaɪəl] *n* cadran *m* solaire
sundown ['sʌndaʊn] *n* coucher *m* du soleil; **at sundown** au coucher du soleil
sundowner ['sʌndaʊnə(r)] *n Fam (drink)* verre *m (qu'on prend le soir)*
sundrenched ['sʌndrentʃt] *adj* inondé de soleil
sundress ['sʌndres] *n* bain *m* de soleil *(robe)*
sun-dried *adj* séché au soleil
sundry ['sʌndrɪ] **1** *adj* divers, différent; **on sundry occasions** à diverses reprises
2 *pron* **all and sundry were having a good time** tout le monde s'amusait bien; **she told all and sundry about it** elle l'a raconté à qui voulait l'entendre
3 sundries *npl (items)* articles *mpl* divers; *(costs)* frais *mpl* divers
►► *Acct* **sundry expenses** frais *mpl* divers
sunfast ['sʌnfɑ:st] *adj* qui ne se décolore pas au soleil
sunfish ['sʌnfɪʃ] *(pl* **inv** *or* **sunfishes)** *n Ich (seawater)* poisson-lune *m*, môle *f*; *(freshwater)* poisson-lune *m*
sunflower ['sʌnˌflaʊə(r)] **1** *n* tournesol *m*
2 *comp (oil, seed)* de tournesol
►► **the Sunflower State** = surnom donné au Kansas
sung [sʌŋ] *pp of* **sing**
►► **sung mass** messe *f* chantée
sunglasses ['sʌnˌglɑ:sɪz] *npl* lunettes *fpl* de soleil, *Belg* lunettes *fpl* solaires
sunglow ['sʌnglәʊ] *n* = embrasement de l'horizon au moment du coucher ou du lever du soleil
sungun ['sʌngʌn] *n TV & Cin* sun-gun *m*, éclairage *m* sur batterie
sunhat ['sʌnhæt] *n* chapeau *m* de soleil
sunk [sʌŋk] **1** *pp of* **sink**
2 *adj Fam* fichu; **if she catches us, we're sunk** si elle nous surprend, on est fichus
►► **sunk fence** saut-de-loup *m*
sunken ['sʌŋkən] *adj* **(a)** *(boat, rock)* submergé; *(garden)* en contrebas; *(bathtub)* encastré (au ras du sol) **(b)** *(hollow → cheeks)* creux, affaissé; *(→ eyes)* creux
sunlamp ['sʌnlæmp] *n (ultraviolet lamp)* lampe *f* à rayons ultraviolets; *(for tanning)* lampe *f* à bronzer
sunless ['sʌnlɪs] *adj* sans soleil
sunlight ['sʌnlaɪt] *n* (lumière *f* du) soleil *m*; **in the sunlight** au soleil
sunlit ['sʌnlɪt] *adj* ensoleillé
sunlounger ['sʌnˌlaʊndʒə(r)] *n Br* chaise *f* longue *(où l'on s'allonge pour bronzer)*
Sunna ['sʌnə] *n* sunna *f*
Sunni ['sʌnɪ] *n* **(a)** *(religion)* sunnisme *m* **(b)** *(person)* sunnite *mf*
sunnily ['sʌnɪlɪ] *adv* radieusement, joyeusement; **to smile sunnily** sourire gaiement *ou* radieusement
sunniness ['sʌnɪnɪs] *n (of place)* ensoleillement *m*; *Fig* **the sunniness of her disposition** sa gaieté
Sunnite ['sʌnaɪt] **1** *adj* sunnite
2 *n* sunnite *mf*
sunny ['sʌnɪ] *(compar* **sunnier**, *superl* **sunniest)** *adj* **(a)** *(day, place etc)* ensoleillé; *(building)* qui reçoit beaucoup de soleil; *(side of street or building)* exposé au soleil; **it's a sunny day, it's sunny** il fait (du) soleil *ou* beau; *Met* **sunny intervals** *or* **periods** éclaircies *fpl*
(b) *Fig (cheerful → disposition)* joyeux, heureux; *(→ smile)* radieux, rayonnant; **to look on the sunny side (of things)** voir le bon côté des choses; *Br* **he's on the sunny side of sixty** il n'a pas encore la soixantaine
sunny-side up *adj* **eggs sunny-side up** œufs *mpl* sur le plat
sunproof ['sʌnpru:f] *adj (material)* inaltérable au soleil
sunray ['sʌnreɪ] *n* rayon *m* de soleil, rayon solaire
►► *Br* **sunray lamp** lampe *f* à rayons ultraviolets; *(for tanning)* lampe *f* à bronzer; **sunray pleats** plissé *m* soleil; *Med* **sunray treatment** héliothérapie *f*
sunrise ['sʌnraɪz] *n* lever *m* du soleil; **at sunrise** au lever du soleil; **to get up at sunrise** se lever avec le soleil; **sunrise is about 6 o'clock** le soleil se lève vers 6 h; **the sunrise was beautiful this morning** il y avait un superbe lever de soleil ce matin
►► **sunrise industry** industrie *f* de pointe
sunroof ['sʌnru:f] *n* toit *m* ouvrant
sunscreen ['sʌnskri:n] *n (suntan lotion)* écran *m ou* filtre *m* solaire
sunseeker *n* = touriste qui part dans un pays chaud à la recherche du soleil, notamment en hiver
sunset ['sʌnset] *n* coucher *m* du soleil; **at sunset** au coucher du soleil; **sunset is about 6 o'clock** le soleil se couche vers 18 h; **it was a beautiful sunset** le coucher de soleil était magnifique; *Literary* **the sunset of life/of an empire** le déclin de la vie/d'un empire
►► **Sunset Boulevard** = célèbre avenue d'Hollywood; **sunset industry** industrie *f* déclinante; *Am* **sunset law** = loi en vigueur dans la plupart des États américains, selon laquelle les programmes mis en place par le gouvernement doivent être régulièrement réévalués

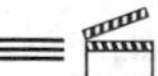

'Sunset Boulevard' *Wilder* 'Boulevard du crépuscule'

sunshade ['sʌnʃeɪd] *n (lady's parasol)* ombrelle *f*; *(for table)* parasol *m*; *(on cap)* visière *f*
sunshine ['sʌnʃaɪn] *n* **(a)** *(sunlight)* (lumière *f* du) soleil *m*; **in the sunshine** au soleil; **we generally get at least 150 hours of sunshine in July** en général, nous avons au moins 150 heures d'ensoleillement en juillet; *Fig* **his visit brought a little sunshine into our lives** sa visite a apporté un peu de soleil dans notre vie
(b) *Br Fam (term of address)* chéri(e) *m,f*; **watch it, sunshine!** fais gaffe, mon coco!
►► *Am* **sunshine law** loi *f* sur la transparence dans l'administration; **sunshine roof** toit *m* ouvrant; **the Sunshine State** = surnom donné à la Floride
sun-soaked *adj (beach)* inondé de soleil
sunspecs ['sʌnspeks] *npl Fam* lunettes *fpl* noires ❑
sunspot ['sʌnspɒt] *n* **(a)** *(on sun)* tache *f* solaire **(b)** *Fam (holiday resort)* station *f* estivale ❑; **it's our favourite winter sunspot** c'est là que nous préférons aller prendre du soleil pendant nos vacances d'hiver ❑
sunstone ['sʌnstəʊn] *n Miner* aventurine *f*
sunstroke ['sʌnstrəʊk] *n (UNCOUNT)* insolation *f*; **to have/to get sunstroke** avoir/attraper une insolation
sunsuit ['sʌnsu:t] *n* (costume *m*) bain *m* de soleil
suntan ['sʌntæn] **1** *n* bronzage *m*; **to have a suntan** être bronzé; **to get a suntan** se faire bronzer, bronzer; **where did you get that lovely suntan?** d'où est-ce que tu viens pour être bronzé comme ça?; **she's got a tremendous suntan** elle a un bronzage magnifique
2 *comp (cream, lotion, oil)* solaire, de bronzage
suntanned ['sʌntænd] *adj* bronzé
suntrap ['sʌntræp] *n* coin *m* abrité et très ensoleillé; **the garden is a real suntrap** le jardin est toujours très ensoleillé
sun-up ['sʌnʌp] *n* lever *m* du soleil; **at sun-up** au lever du soleil
sun-worship *n* culte *m* du Soleil
sun-worshipper *n* **(a)** *Rel* adorateur(trice) *m,f* du Soleil **(b)** *Fig* fanatique *mf* du bronzage
sup [sʌp] *(pt & pp* **supped**, *cont* **supping)** **1** *vi Arch (have supper)* souper; **they supped on** *or* **off some leftovers** ils ont soupé de quelques restes
2 *vt* boire à petites gorgées
3 *n* petite gorgée *f*
►**sup up** **1** *vt sep (drink up)* finir
2 *vi* finir son verre
super ['su:pə(r)] **1** *adj* **(a)** *Fam (wonderful)* super *(inv)*, formidable; **it was a super party!** c'était génial comme fête!
(b) *(superior)* supérieur, super-; **they're developing a new sort of super hydrogen bomb** ils sont en train de mettre au point une nouvelle superbombe H
2 *exclam Fam* super!, formidable!
3 *n* **(a)** *Am (petrol)* super *m*, supercarburant *m* **(b)** *Fam (police superintendent)* ≃ commissaire *m* (de police)
(c) *Am Fam (in apartment block)* concierge ❑ *mf*, gardien *m* (d'immeuble) ❑
4 *adv Fam (very)* super, hyper; **his family is super rich** sa famille est hyper riche
►► *Am* **Super Bowl** Superbowl *m (finale du championnat des États-Unis de football américain)*; **Super League** *(in rugby league)* = ligue de rugby composée des meilleures équipes britanniques; *Am* **Super Tuesday** = deuxième mardi de mars de l'année où a lieu l'élection présidentielle américaine, date à laquelle se déroulent plusieurs élections primaires importantes
superable ['su:pərəbəl] *adj* surmontable
superabundance [ˌsu:pərə'bʌndəns] *n* surabondance *f*
superabundant [ˌsu:pərə'bʌndənt] *adj* surabondant
superabundantly [ˌsu:pərə'bʌndəntlɪ] *adv* surabondamment
superaerodynamics ['su:pəˌreərəʊdaɪ'næmɪks] *n (UNCOUNT)* superaérodynamique *f*
superaltar ['su:pəˌrɔ:ltə(r)] *n Rel* **(a)** *(portable slab)* autel *m* (portatif) **(b)** *(reredos)* retable *m*
superannuate [ˌsu:pə'rænjʊeɪt] *vt* **(a)** *(person)* mettre à la retraite **(b)** *(object)* mettre au rebut
superannuated [ˌsu:pə'rænjʊeɪtɪd] *adj* **(a)** *(person)* à la retraite, retraité **(b)** *(object)* suranné, désuet(ète)
superannuation [ˌsu:pəˌrænjʊ'eɪʃən] *n Br* **(a)** *(act of retiring)* mise *f* à la retraite **(b)** *(pension)* pension *f* de retraite **(c)** *(contribution)* versement *m ou* cotisation *f* pour la retraite
►► **superannuation fund** caisse *f* de retraite
superb [su:'pɜ:b] *adj* superbe, magnifique
superblock ['su:pəblɒk] *n Am* zone *f* piétonne *ou* piétonnière
superbly [su:'pɜ:blɪ] *adv* superbement, magnifiquement; **she performed superbly** elle a merveilleusement bien joué
superbrat ['su:pəˌbræt] *n Fam* sale gosse *mf*
supercargo ['su:pəˌkɑ:gəʊ] *(pl* **supercargoes)** *n* subrécargue *m*
supercharge ['su:pətʃɑ:dʒ] *vt* **(a)** *Tech (engine)* surcomprimer, suralimenter **(b)** *Fig (atmosphere)* électriser, galvaniser, survolter
supercharged ['su:pətʃɑ:dʒd] *adj Tech (engine)* surcomprimé
supercharger ['su:pətʃɑ:dʒə(r)] *n* compresseur *m*
supercilious [ˌsu:pə'sɪlɪəs] *adj* hautain, arrogant, dédaigneux
superciliously [ˌsu:pə'sɪlɪəslɪ] *adv (act)* d'un air hautain, avec arrogance *ou* dédain; *(speak)* d'un ton hautain, avec arrogance *ou* dédain
superciliousness [ˌsu:pə'sɪlɪəsnɪs] *n* hauteur *f*, arrogance *f*, dédain *m*
superclass ['su:pəklɑ:s] *n* superclasse *f*
supercomputer [ˌsu:pəkəm'pju:tə(r)] *n Comput* superordinateur *m*
superconduction [ˌsu:pəkən'dʌkʃən] *n* supraconductivité *f*
superconductive [ˌsu:pəkən'dʌktɪv] *adj* supraconducteur
superconductivity [ˌsu:pəˌkɒndʌk'tɪvətɪ] *n* supraconductivité *f*
superconductor [ˌsu:pəkən'dʌktə(r)] *n* supraconducteur *m*
supercontinent [ˌsu:pə'kɒntɪnɪnt] *n* supercontinent *m*
supercool ['su:pəku:l] **1** *vt (liquid)* surfondre
2 *adj Fam (very trendy)* super branché; *(very relaxed)* super génial
supercooling ['su:pəˌku:lɪŋ] *n* surfusion *f*
supercritical [ˌsu:pə'krɪtɪkəl] *adj Nucl* supercritique, surcritique
super-duper [-'du:pə(r)] *adj Fam* super, superchouette
superego [ˌsu:pər'i:gəʊ] *(pl* **superegos)** *n Psy* surmoi *m*
superelevation [ˌsu:pərelɪ'veɪʃən] *n (of road)* dévers *m*
supereminence [ˌsu:pə'remɪnəns] *n* surémineence *f*, prééminence *f*
supereminent [ˌsu:pə'remɪnənt] *adj* suréminent, prééminent

supererogation [ˌsuːpəˌrerəˈgeɪʃən] *n* surérogation *f*
superfamily [ˈsuːpəˌfæməlɪ] (*pl* **superfamilies**) *n Biol* superfamille *f*
superfatted [ˈsuːpəˌfætɪd] *adj (soap)* contenant des produits insaponifiés
superfecundation [ˌsuːpəfɪkʌnˈdeɪʃən] *n* superfécondation *f*, superimprégnation *f*
superfetation [ˌsuːpəfiːˈteɪʃən] *n* superfétation *f*, superfécondation *f*
superficial [ˌsuːpəˈfɪʃəl] *adj (knowledge)* superficiel; *(differences)* superficiel, insignifiant; *(person)* superficiel, frivole, léger; *(wound)* superficiel, léger
superficiality [ˈsuːpəˌfɪʃɪˈælətɪ] *n* caractère *m* superficiel, manque *m* de profondeur
superficially [ˌsuːpəˈfɪʃəlɪ] *adv* superficiellement
superfine [ˈsuːpəfaɪn] *adj (quality, product)* extra-fin, superfin, surfin; *(analysis)* très fin; *(distinction, detail)* subtil
superfluity [ˌsuːpəˈfluːɪtɪ] *n* (**a**) *(superfluousness)* caractère *m* superflu (**b**) *(excess)* surabondance *f*; **a superfluity of details** une surabondance de détails
superfluous [suːˈpɜːflʊəs] *adj* superflu; **it is superfluous to say…** (il est) inutile de *ou* il va sans dire…; **I'm starting to feel a bit superfluous** je commence à me sentir un peu de trop ici
superfluously [suːˈpɜːflʊəslɪ] *adv* de manière superflue, inutilement
superfluousness [suːˈpɜːflʊəsnɪs] *n* superfluité *f*
super-G *n Ski* super-g *m inv*
supergiant [ˈsuːpəˌdʒaɪənt] *n Astron* supergéante *f*
super-giant *n Ski* super-géant *m*
superglue® [ˈsuːpəgluː] **1** *n* Super glue® *f*
2 *vt* coller à la Super glue®
supergrass [ˈsuːpəgrɑːs] *n Br Fam Crime slang* indic *m* de choc
supergroup [ˈsuːpəgruːp] *n* (**a**) *(successful band)* grand groupe *m* de rock (**b**) *(band formed for specific purpose)* = groupe de rock formé temporairement par des chanteurs célèbres
supergun [ˈsuːpəgʌn] *n* supercanon *m*
superheat [ˌsuːpəˈhiːt] *vt* surchauffer
▸▸ ***superheated steam*** vapeur *f* surchauffée
superhero [ˈsuːpəˌhɪərəʊ] (*pl* **superheroes**) *n* superman *m*, surhomme *m*
superhet [ˈsuːpəhet], **superheterodyne receiver** [ˌsuːpəˈhetərədaɪn-] *n* superhétérodyne *m*
superhigh frequency [ˈsuːpəhaɪ-] *n* ondes *fpl* centimétriques
superhighway [ˈsuːpəˌhaɪweɪ] *n* (**a**) *Am Aut* autoroute *f* (**b**) *Comput* autoroute *f*
superhuman [ˌsuːpəˈhjuːmən] *adj* surhumain
superhumanly [ˌsuːpəˈhjuːmənlɪ] *adv* de façon surhumaine, sur le plan surhumain
superimposable [ˌsuːpərɪmˈpəʊzəbəl] *adj* superposable
superimpose [ˌsuːpərɪmˈpəʊz] *vt* superposer; **to superimpose sth on sth** superposer qch à qch; **superimposed photos** des photos en surimpression; *Fig* **a Western culture superimposed on an indigenous one** une culture occidentale venue se superposer à une culture indigène
superimposition [ˌsuːpərɪmpəˈzɪʃən] *n* superposition *f*; *Phot & Cin* surimpression *f*
superincumbent [ˌsuːpərɪnˈkʌmbənt] *adj* superposé
superintend [ˌsuːpərɪnˈtend] *vt* (**a**) *(oversee → activity)* surveiller; *(→ person)* surveiller, avoir l'œil sur (**b**) *(run → office, institution)* diriger
superintendence [ˌsuːpərɪnˈtendəns] *n* (**a**) *(overseeing)* surveillance *f* (**b**) *(running)* direction *f*
superintendent [ˌsuːpərɪnˈtendənt] *n* (**a**) *(of institution)* directeur(trice) *m,f*; *(of department, office)* chef *m* (**b**) *(of police)* ≃ commissaire *m* (de police) (**c**) *Am (of apartment building)* gardien(enne) *m,f*, concierge *mf*
superior [suːˈpɪərɪə(r)] **1** *adj* (**a**) *(better, greater)* supérieur; **a superior wine** un vin de qualité supérieure; **superior to** supérieur à; **the book is vastly superior to the film** le livre est bien meilleur que le film; **superior in number to** supérieur en nombre à, numériquement supérieur à; **the enemy troops were superior in numbers** les troupes ennemies étaient en plus grand nombre *ou* supérieures en nombre (**b**) *(senior → officer, position)* supérieur; **superior to** supérieur à, au-dessus de; **the superior classes** les classes *fpl* dirigeantes
(**c**) *Pej (supercilious)* suffisant, hautain; **with a superior smile** avec un sourire suffisant *ou* condescendant; **in a superior voice** d'un ton suffisant *ou* supérieur; **she feels superior** elle se croit supérieure
(**d**) *(upper)* supérieur; **the superior limbs** les membres *mpl* supérieurs
(**e**) *Typ (letter, number)* supérieur, suscrit
(**f**) *Biol* supérieur; **the superior mammals** les mammifères *mpl* supérieurs
2 *n* supérieur(e) *m,f*
▸▸ *Law* ***superior court*** ≃ tribunal *m* de grande instance, *Can* Cour *f* supérieure; *Astron* ***superior planet*** planète *f* supérieure
superiority [suːˌpɪərɪˈɒrətɪ] *n* (**a**) *(higher amount, worth)* supériorité *f*; **their superiority in numbers** leur supériorité numérique; **the superiority of this brand to** *or* **over all the others** la supériorité de cette marque par rapport à toutes les autres (**b**) *Pej (arrogance)* supériorité *f*, arrogance *f*
▸▸ *Psy* ***superiority complex*** complexe *m* de supériorité
superjacent [ˌsuːpəˈdʒeɪsənt] *adj Geol* surjacent
superlative [suːˈpɜːlətɪv] **1** *adj* (**a**) *(outstanding → quality, skill, performance)* sans pareil; *(→ performer, athlete)* sans pareil, inégalé (**b**) *(overwhelming → indifference, ignorance, joy)* suprême (**c**) *Gram* superlatif
2 *n* superlatif *m*; **in the superlative** au superlatif; *Fig* **she always speaks in superlatives** elle a tendance à tout exagérer
superlatively [suːˈpɜːlətɪvlɪ] *adv* au plus haut degré, exceptionnellement; **a superlatively good candidate** un candidat exceptionnel; **she is superlatively efficient** elle est on ne peut plus efficace
superluminal [ˌsuːpəˈluːmɪnəl] *adj* plus rapide que la vitesse de la lumière
superlunar [ˌsuːpəˈluːnə(r)], **superlunary** [ˌsuːpəˈluːnərɪ] *adj (above the moon)* surlunaire; *(celestial)* supramondain
superman [ˈsuːpəmæn] (*pl* **supermen** [-men]) **1** *n Phil (gen)* surhomme *m*; *(gen)* superman *m*
2 Superman *pr n (comic book hero)* Superman
supermarket [ˈsuːpəˌmɑːkɪt] *n* supermarché *m*
▸▸ *Banking* ***supermarket bank*** = banque qui appartient à une chaîne de supermarchés; ***supermarket trolley*** caddie *m*
super-middleweight *n Boxing* poids *m* supermoyen
supermini [ˈsuːpəmɪnɪ] *n Aut* citadine *f*
supermodel [ˈsuːpəmɒdəl] *n* supermodel *m*
supermundane [ˌsuːpəmʌnˈdeɪn] *adj* supramondain
supernal [suːˈpɜːnəl] *adj Literary* céleste, divin
supernatant [ˌsuːpəˈneɪtənt] *adj* surnageant
supernatural [ˌsuːpəˈnætʃərəl] **1** *adj* surnaturel
2 *n* surnaturel *m*
supernaturality [ˌsuːpənætʃəˈrælɪtɪ] *n* surnaturalité *f*
supernaturalize, -ise [ˌsuːpəˈnætʃərəlaɪz] *vt* surnaturaliser
supernaturally [ˌsuːpəˈnætʃərəlɪ] *adv* de manière surnaturelle
supernaturalness [ˌsuːpəˈnætʃərəlnɪs] *n* surnaturalité *f*
supernormal [ˌsuːpəˈnɔːməl] *adj* (**a**) *(above average)* au-dessus de la moyenne *ou* de la normale (**b**) *(paranormal)* supranormal, paranormal
supernova [ˌsuːpəˈnəʊvə] (*pl* **supernovas** *or* **supernovae** [-viː]) *n* supernova *f*
supernumerary [ˌsuːpəˈnjuːmərərɪ] (*pl* **supernumeraries**) **1** *adj (extra)* surnuméraire; *(superfluous)* superflu
2 *n* surnuméraire *m*; *Cin & TV* figurant(e) *m,f*
superorder [ˈsuːpərˌɔːdə(r)] *n* superordre *m*
superordinate [ˌsuːpəˈrɔːdɪnət] *adj* supérieur
superphosphate [ˌsuːpəˈfɒsfeɪt] *n* superphosphate *m*
superphysical [ˌsuːpəˈfɪzɪkəl] *adj* sans cause physique connue
superpose [ˌsuːpəˈpəʊz] *vt* superposer; **to superpose sth on sth** superposer qch à qch
superposition [ˌsuːpəpəˈzɪʃən] *n* superposition *f*
superpower [ˈsuːpəˌpaʊə(r)] *n* superpuissance *f*, supergrand *m*
supersaturate [ˌsuːpəˈsætʃəreɪt] *vt* sursaturer
supersaturated [ˌsuːpəˈsætʃəreɪtɪd] *adj (liquid)* sursaturé; *(vapour)* sursaturant
superscribe [ˈsuːpəskraɪb] *vt* (**a**) *(gen)* marquer d'une inscription (**b**) *(put one's name on top of → document)* écrire son nom en tête de (**c**) *(address → letter)* mettre l'adresse sur
superscript [ˈsuːpəskrɪpt] **1** *n* exposant *m*
2 *adj* en exposant
superscription [ˌsuːpəˈskrɪpʃən] *n (gen)* inscription *f*; *(heading on document)* en-tête *m*
supersede [ˌsuːpəˈsiːd] *vt (person → get rid of)* supplanter, détrôner; *(→ replace)* succéder à, remplacer; *(object)* remplacer; **she superseded him as director** elle lui a succédé *ou* elle l'a remplacé à la direction; **this price list supersedes all previous ones** ce tarif remplace et annule les précédents; **the RWQ20 has long been superseded by smaller models** la RWQ20 a depuis longtemps été supplantée par des modèles plus petits; **superseded methods** méthodes *fpl* périmées
supersensitive [ˌsuːpəˈsensɪtɪv] *adj* hypersensible
supersonic [ˌsuːpəˈsɒnɪk] *adj* supersonique
▸▸ ***supersonic bang, supersonic boom*** bang *m* (supersonique); ***supersonic transport*** transport *m* supersonique
superstar [ˈsuːpəstɑː(r)] *n* superstar *f*
superstition [ˌsuːpəˈstɪʃən] *n* superstition *f*
superstitious [ˌsuːpəˈstɪʃəs] *adj* superstitieux; **to be superstitious about sth** être superstitieux au sujet de qch
superstitiously [ˌsuːpəˈstɪʃəslɪ] *adv* superstitieusement
superstock [ˈsuːpəstɒk] *n Am St Exch* actions *fpl* à droit de vote double
superstore [ˈsuːpəstɔː(r)] *n* hypermarché *m*, grande surface *f*
superstratum [ˌsuːpəˈstrɑːtəm] (*pl* **superstratums** *or* **superstrata** [-tə]) *n* (**a**) *Geol* couche *f* supérieure (**b**) *Ling* superstrat *m*
superstring [ˈsuːpəstrɪŋ] *n* supercorde *f*
▸▸ ***superstring theory*** théorie *f* des supercordes
superstructure [ˈsuːpəˌstrʌktʃə(r)] *n* superstructure *f*
supertanker [ˈsuːpəˌtæŋkə(r)] *n* supertanker *m*, superpétrolier *m*
supertax [ˈsuːpətæks] *n* surtaxe *f*
supertitle [ˈsuːpətaɪtəl] *n Am* surtitre *m*
supertonic [ˌsuːpəˈtɒnɪk] *n* sus-tonique *f*
superuser [ˈsuːpəjuːzə(r)] *n Comput* gros utilisateur *m*
supervene [ˌsuːpəˈviːn] *vi* survenir
supervention [ˌsuːpəˈvenʃən] *n Formal* survenue *f*
super-VGA *n Comput* Super-VGA *m*
supervise [ˈsuːpəvaɪz] **1** *vt* (**a**) *(oversee → activity, exam)* surveiller; *(→ child, staff)* surveiller, avoir l'œil sur (**b**) *(run → office, workshop)* diriger
2 *vi* surveiller
supervision [ˌsuːpəˈvɪʒən] *n* (**a**) *(of person, activity)* surveillance *f*, contrôle *m*; **the children must be under the supervision of qualified staff at all times** les enfants doivent être sous la surveillance de personnel qualifié à tout moment; **translated under the supervision of the author** traduit sous la direction de l'auteur; **her work needs supervision** elle a besoin d'être surveillée dans son travail
(**b**) *(of office)* direction *f*
▸▸ *Law* ***supervision order*** = nomination par un tribunal pour enfants d'un travailleur social chargé d'assurer la tutelle d'un enfant
supervisor [ˈsuːpəvaɪzə(r)] *n (gen)* surveillant(e) *m,f*; *Com (of department)* chef *m* de rayon; *Sch & Univ (at exam)* surveillant(e) *m,f*; *Univ (of thesis)* directeur(trice) *m,f* de thèse; *(of research)* directeur(trice) *m,f* de recherches
supervisory [ˈsuːpəvaɪzərɪ] *adj* de surveillance; **staff in supervisory posts** le personnel de surveillance; **in a supervisory role** *or* **capacity** à titre de surveillant
superwoman [ˈsuːpəˌwʊmən] (*pl* **superwomen** [-ˌwɪmɪn]) *n* superwoman *f*
supine [ˈsuːpaɪn] **1** *n Gram* supin *m*

2 *adj* (**a**) *(on one's back)* couché *ou* étendu sur le dos; **she was lying supine, she was in a supine position** elle était couchée sur le dos (**b**) *Fig (passive)* indolent, mou (molle), passif

supper ['sʌpə(r)] *n (evening meal)* dîner *m*; *(late-night snack)* souper *m*; **to have** *or* **to eat supper** dîner; *(late at night)* souper; **we had steak for supper** nous avons mangé du steak au dîner/souper; **I'll raise his salary but I intend to make him sing for his supper!** je vais lui accorder une augmentation, mais c'est donnant donnant!

►► *Am* ***supper club*** = boîte de nuit qui fait aussi restaurant

suppertime ['sʌpətaɪm] *n (in evening)* heure *f* du *ou* de dîner; *(later at night)* heure *f* du *ou* de souper; **at suppertime** à l'heure du dîner/souper

supplant [sə'plɑːnt] *vt (person)* supplanter, évincer; *(thing)* supplanter, remplacer

supplantation [səˌplɑːn'teɪʃən] *n* supplantation *f*, évincement *m*

supplanter [sə'plɑːntə(r)] *n* supplanteur(euse) *m,f*, supplantateur(trice) *m,f*

supple ['sʌpəl] *adj* souple; **to become supple** s'assouplir

supplement 1 *n* ['sʌplɪmənt] (**a**) *(additional amount → paid)* supplément *m*; *(→ received)* complément *m*; **a small supplement to my income** un petit supplément à mes revenus; **a supplement is charged for occupying a single room** il y a un supplément à payer pour les chambres à un lit; **food supplement** complément *m* alimentaire

(**b**) *Press* supplément *m*; **they have produced a supplement to the encyclopedia** ils ont sorti un supplément à l'encyclopédie

(**c**) *Br Admin (allowance)* allocation *f*

2 *vt* ['sʌplɪment] *(increase)* augmenter; *(complete)* compléter; **I work nights to supplement my income** j'augmente mes revenus en travaillant la nuit; **he supplements his diet with vitamins** il complète son régime en prenant des vitamines

supplementarily [sʌplɪ'mentərɪlɪ, *Am* sʌplɪmen'teərɪlɪ] *adv* comme supplément, en complément

supplementary [ˌsʌplɪ'mentərɪ] *adj* (**a**) *(gen)* complémentaire, additionnel; **supplementary to** en plus de; **may I ask a supplementary question?** puis-je poser encore une question? (**b**) *Geom (angle)* supplémentaire

►► *Formerly* ***supplementary benefit*** = allocation versée par l'État à ceux qui ont les plus faibles revenus; ***supplementary income*** revenus *mpl* annexes

suppleness ['sʌpəlnɪs] *n* souplesse *f*

suppletion [sə'pliːʃən] *n Ling* suppléance *f*

suppletive [sə'pliːtɪv] *adj Ling* supplétif

suppliant ['sʌplɪənt] 1 *adj* suppliant

2 *n* suppliant(e) *m,f*

supplicant ['sʌplɪkənt] *n* suppliant(e) *m,f*

supplicate ['sʌplɪkeɪt] *Literary or Formal* 1 *vt* supplier, implorer; **to supplicate sb to do sth** supplier qn de faire qch

2 *vi* **to supplicate for forgiveness/mercy** implorer le pardon/la pitié

supplicating ['sʌplɪkeɪtɪŋ] *adj* suppliant, de supplication

supplicatingly ['sʌplɪkeɪtɪŋlɪ] *adv (look)* d'un air suppliant; *(say)* d'un ton suppliant

supplication [ˌsʌplɪ'keɪʃən] *n* supplication *f*; **he knelt in supplication** il supplia à genoux

supplicatory [ˌsʌplɪ'keɪtərɪ] *adj* supplicatoire, de supplication

supplier [sə'plaɪə(r)] *n Com* fournisseur(euse) *m,f*

►► ***supplier code*** code *m* fournisseur; *Acct* ***supplier credit*** crédit-fournisseur *m*

supply[1] [sə'plaɪ] *(pt & pp* **supplied**, *pl* **supplies**) 1 *vt* (**a**) *(provide → goods, services)* fournir; **to supply sth to sb** fournir qch à qn; **to supply electricity/water to a town** alimenter une ville en électricité/eau; **they supply all the local retailers** ils fournissent tous les détaillants du coin; **cows supply milk** les vachent donnent du lait

(**b**) *(provide sth to → person, institution, city)* fournir, approvisionner; *Mil* ravitailler, approvisionner; **to supply sb with sth** fournir qch à qn, approvisionner qn en qch; **they supply all the local retailers** ils fournissent *ou* approvisionnent tous les détaillants du coin; **the farm keeps us supplied with eggs and milk** grâce à la ferme nous avons toujours des œufs et du lait; **I supplied him with the details/the information** je lui ai fourni les détails/les informations; **the arteries that supply the brain** les artères qui amènent le sang au cerveau

(**c**) *(equip)* munir; **all toys are supplied with batteries** des piles sont fournies avec tous les jouets

(**d**) *(make good → deficiency)* suppléer à; *(→ omission)* réparer, compenser; *(satisfy → need)* répondre à

2 *n* (**a**) *(stock)* provision *f*, réserve *f*; **the nation's supply of oil** les réserves *fpl* nationales de pétrole; **we're getting in** *or* **laying in a supply of coal** nous faisons des provisions de charbon, nous nous approvisionnons en charbon; **to get in a fresh supply of sth** renouveler sa provision de *ou* se réapprovisionner en qch; **water is in short supply in the southeast** on manque d'eau dans le Sud-Est

(**b**) *(provision → of goods, equipment)* fourniture *f*; *(→ of fuel)* alimentation *f*; *Mil* ravitaillement *m*, approvisionnement *m*; **the domestic hot water supply** l'alimentation *f* domestique en eau chaude; **they won a contract for the supply of 10,000 computers to schools** ils ont obtenu un contrat pour la fourniture de 10 000 ordinateurs à des établissements scolaires

(**c**) *Econ* offre *f*; **supply and demand** l'offre *f* et la demande

(**d**) *Br (clergyman, secretary, teacher)* remplaçant(e) *m,f*, suppléant(e) *m,f*; **to be on supply** faire des remplacements *ou* des suppléances

(**e**) *(usu pl) Pol (money)* crédits *mpl*

3 *comp* (**a**) *(convoy, train, truck, route)* de ravitaillement

(**b**) *(secretary)* intérimaire; *(clergyman)* suppléant

4 **supplies** *npl (gen)* provisions *fpl*; *(of food)* vivres *mpl*; *Mil* subsistances *fpl*, approvisionnements *mpl*; **our supplies are running low** nos provisions seront bientôt épuisées, nous commençons à manquer de provisions; **office supplies** fournitures *fpl* de bureau

►► *Com* ***supply curve*** courbe *f* de l'offre; *Mil* ***supply lines*** lignes *fpl* de ravitaillement; ***supply pipe*** *(for fuel)* conduite *f* d'arrivée du combustible; ***supply price*** prix *m* d'offre; ***supply ship*** ravitailleur *m*; *Br* ***supply teacher*** remplaçant(e) *m,f*; *Br* ***supply teaching*** remplacements *mpl*

supply[2] ['sʌplɪ] *adv* souplement, avec souplesse

supply-side economics [sə'plaɪ-] *n (UNCOUNT)* économie *f* de l'offre

support [sə'pɔːt] 1 *n* (**a**) *(backing)* soutien *m*, appui *m*; **support for the Socialist Party is declining** le parti socialiste est en baisse *ou* en perte de vitesse; **the rebels have little support** les rebelles bénéficient d'un soutien limité; **there is widespread support for the government/these policies** le gouvernement bénéficie/ces politiques bénéficient d'un très large soutien; **he's trying to drum up** *or* **to mobilize support for his scheme** il essaie d'obtenir du soutien pour son projet; **to give** *or* **to lend one's support to sth** appuyer *ou* soutenir qch; **she gave us her full support** elle nous a pleinement appuyés; **you have my full support on this** je vous soutiens à cent pour cent, vous pouvez compter sur mon soutien inconditionnel; **to speak in support of a motion** appuyer une motion; **they are striking in support of the miners** ils font grève par solidarité avec les mineurs; **a collection in support of the homeless** une quête au profit des sans-abri; **insufficient air for the support of life** air en quantité insuffisante pour permettre la vie

(**b**) *(assistance, encouragement)* appui *m*, aide *f*; **I couldn't have managed without the support of the neighbours** je n'aurais pas pu y arriver sans l'appui des voisins; **a mutual support scheme** un système d'entraide; **she gave me the emotional support I needed** elle m'a apporté le soutien affectif dont j'avais besoin

(**c**) *(funding)* appui *m*, soutien *m*; **they depend on the government for financial support** ils sont subventionnés par le gouvernement; **with (financial) support from the council** avec l'appui *ou* le soutien (financier) du conseil; **he has no visible means of support** ses sources de revenus sont inconnues; **what are your means of support?** quelles sont vos sources de revenus?; **she is their only means of support** ils n'ont qu'elle pour les faire vivre

(**d**) *(holding up)* soutien *m*; **the upper floors need extra support** les étages supérieurs ont besoin d'un soutien supplémentaire; **I was holding his arm for support** je m'appuyais sur son bras; **this bra gives good support** ce soutien-gorge maintient bien la poitrine

(**e**) *(person)* soutien *m*; **she's been a great support to me** elle m'a été d'un grand soutien; **she is the support of the family** *(financially)* c'est elle qui fait vivre la famille

(**f**) *(supporting structure, prop)* appui *m*; *Constr & Tech* support *m*; *Med (bandage)* bandage *m* de maintien; **the steel supports had buckled** les supports en acier s'étaient déformés

(**g**) *(substantiation, corroboration)* corroboration *f*; **in support of her theory** à l'appui de *ou* pour corroborer sa théorie; **the investigation found no support for this view** l'enquête n'a rien trouvé pour corroborer ce point de vue; **this discovery lends support to those who have argued...** cette découverte va dans le sens de ceux qui soutiennent que...

(**h**) *Am Econ (subsidy)* subvention *f*; **farm supports** subventions *fpl* agricoles

(**i**) *Cin (supporting actor)* second rôle *m*; *Mus* groupe *m* en première partie

2 *comp* (**a**) *(troops, unit)* de soutien

(**b**) *(hose, stockings)* de maintien; *(bandage)* de soutien

(**c**) *Constr & Tech (structure, device, frame)* de soutien

3 *vt* (**a**) *(back → action, campaign, person)* soutenir, appuyer; *(→ cause, idea)* être pour, soutenir; *Mil (→ troops)* soutenir; *Sport (→ team)* être pour; *(actively)* être supporter de; *(assist → person)* soutenir, aider; **she supports the Labour Party** elle est pour *ou* elle soutient le parti travailliste; **to support a candidate** appuyer *ou* soutenir un candidat; **I can't support their action** je ne peux pas approuver leur action; **we support her in her decision** nous approuvons sa décision; **the Democrats will support the bill** les Démocrates seront pour *ou* appuieront le projet de loi; **the mayor, supported by the clergy** le maire, avec le soutien du clergé; **he supports Tottenham** c'est un supporter de Tottenham; **he made it with only her love to support him** il a réussi avec son amour comme seul soutien; *Cin & Theat* **supported by a superb cast** avec une distribution superbe

(**b**) *(hold up)* supporter, soutenir; **the pillars that support the ceiling** les piliers qui soutiennent le plafond; **her legs were too weak to support her** ses jambes étaient trop faibles pour la porter; **he supported himself on a stick/my arm** il s'appuyait sur un bâton/mon bras; **will you support the shelf while I fix it to the wall?** tu peux tenir l'étagère le temps *ou* pendant que je la fixe au mur?; **she held on to the table to support herself** elle s'agrippa à la table pour ne pas tomber

(**c**) *(provide for financially → person)* subvenir aux besoins de; *(→ campaign, project)* aider financièrement; **she has three children to support** elle a trois enfants à charge; **she earns enough to support herself** elle gagne assez pour subvenir à ses propres besoins; **he supports himself by teaching** il gagne sa vie en enseignant; **his parents supported him through college** ses parents ont financé ses études; **the theatre is supported by contributions** le théâtre est financé par des contributions

(**d**) *(sustain)* faire vivre; **the land has supported four generations of tribespeople** cette terre a fait vivre la tribu pendant quatre générations; **the atmosphere on the planet could not support life** l'atmosphère de la planète ne permettrait pas le développement d'êtres vivants

(**e**) *(substantiate, give weight to)* appuyer, confirmer, donner du poids à; **there is no evidence to support his claim** il n'y a aucune preuve pour appuyer ses dires; **a theory supported by experience** une théorie confirmée par l'expérience

(**f**) *Fin (price, currency)* soutenir

(**g**) *Comput (file format, device, technology)* permettre l'utilisation de, supporter; **this package is supported by all workstations** ce progiciel peut être utilisé sur tous les postes de travail

(**h**) *(endure)* supporter, tolérer

▸▸ ***support band*** groupe *m* en première partie; **who was the support band?** qui est-ce qu'il y avait en première partie?; ***support group*** (**a**) *(for therapy)* groupe *m* de soutien (**b**) *(at concert)* groupe *m* en première partie; *Comput* ***support line*** assistance *f* technique téléphonique; ***support price*** prix *m* de soutien; *Admin* ***support services*** services *mpl* d'assistance technique; ***support staff*** personnel *m* de soutien *ou* des services généraux

supportable [sə'pɔːtəbəl] *adj Formal* supportable

supporter [sə'pɔːtə(r)] *n* (**a**) *Constr & Tech (device)* soutien *m*, support *m* (**b**) *(advocate, follower → of cause, opinion)* adepte *mf*, partisan *m*; *(→ of political party)* partisan *m*; *Sport* supporter *m*, supporteur(trice) *m,f*; **he's a Liverpool supporter** c'est un supporter de Liverpool (**c**) *Her* tenant *m*

supporting [sə'pɔːtɪŋ] *adj* (**a**) *Constr & Tech (pillar, structure)* d'appui, de soutènement; *(wall)* porteur

(**b**) *Cin & Theat (role)* secondaire, de second plan; *(actor)* qui a un rôle secondaire *ou* de second plan; **with a supporting cast of thousands** avec des milliers de figurants

(**c**) *(substantiating)* qui confirme, qui soutient; **do you have any supporting evidence?** avez-vous des preuves à l'appui?

▸▸ *Constr* ***supporting beam*** sommier *m*; ***supporting film, supporting programme*** = film qui passe en première partie de la séance

supportive [sə'pɔːtɪv] *adj (person)* qui est d'un grand soutien; *(attitude)* de soutien; **my parents have always been very supportive** mes parents m'ont toujours été d'un grand soutien; **they need supportive counselling** ils ont besoin d'être soutenus et orientés

▸▸ *Med* ***supportive therapy*** thérapie *f* de soutien

supportiveness [sə'pɔːtɪvnɪs] *n* soutien *m*, appui *m*

supposable [sə'pəʊzəbəl] *adj* supposable

suppose [sə'pəʊz] **1** *vt* (**a**) *(assume)* supposer; **I suppose it's too far to go and see them now** je suppose que c'est trop loin pour qu'on aille les voir maintenant; **if we suppose it is worth £5** si nous supposons que cela vaut 5 livres; *Math* **suppose x equals y** soit x égal à y; **I suppose you think that's funny!** je suppose que vous trouvez ça drôle!; **I suppose you can't remember THAT either!** tu ne te souviens probablement pas de ça non plus!; **let's suppose (that)...** supposons que...

(**b**) *(think, believe)* penser, croire; **do you suppose he'll do it?** pensez-vous *ou* croyez-vous qu'il le fera?; **I suppose so** *(affirmative response)* je suppose que oui; *(expressing reluctance)* oui, peut-être; **I suppose not, I don't suppose so** je ne (le) pense pas; **I don't suppose he'll agree** ça m'étonnerait qu'il soit d'accord, je ne pense pas qu'il sera d'accord; **I suppose it must be three years since I last saw her** je pense que ça doit faire trois ans que je ne l'ai pas vue; **you don't suppose anything's happened to them, do you?** tu ne penses pas qu'il leur est arrivé quelque chose?; **I don't suppose you'd have time to read this, would you?** tu n'as pas le temps de lire ceci, je suppose?; **and who do you suppose I met in the shop?** et devine qui j'ai rencontré dans le magasin!

(**c**) *(imply)* supposer; **that theory supposes a balanced budget** cette théorie suppose un budget équilibré

2 *vi* supposer, imaginer; **he's gone, I suppose?** il est parti, je suppose *ou* j'imagine?; **there were, I suppose, about fifty people there** il y avait, je dirais, une cinquantaine de personnes

3 *conj* si; **suppose they see you?** et s'ils vous voyaient?; **suppose we wait and see** et si on attendait pour voir?; **suppose I'm right and she DOES come?** mettons *ou* supposons que j'aie raison et qu'elle vienne?

supposed [sə'pəʊzd] *adj* (**a**) *(presumed)* présumé, supposé; *(alleged)* prétendu; **the supposed author of this poem** l'auteur présumé de ce poème; *Pej* **all these supposed experts** tous ces prétendus experts

(**b**) *(meant)* **to be supposed to do sth** être censé faire qch; **there is supposed to be a well in the garden** on dit qu'il y a un puits dans le jardin; **she was supposed to be at work** elle était censée être à son travail; **what's that switch supposed to do?** à quoi sert cet interrupteur?; **how am I supposed to know?** comment est-ce que je saurais *ou* suis censé savoir, moi?; **I'm not supposed to know** je ne suis pas censé savoir; **you're not supposed to do that!** tu ne devrais pas faire ça!; **the computer's not supposed to make a noise like that** l'ordinateur ne devrait pas faire un tel bruit; **how am I supposed to work in conditions like these!** comment veut-on que je travaille dans de telles conditions!; **what's that supposed to mean?** qu'est-ce que tu veux dire par là?; **we're not supposed to use dictionaries** nous n'avons pas le droit de nous servir de dictionnaires; **this restaurant is supposed to be very good** il paraît que ce restaurant est excellent; **you're supposed to be my friend!** je te croyais mon ami!

supposedly [sə'pəʊzɪdlɪ] *adv* soi-disant; **she supposedly went to get help** elle est soi-disant allée chercher de l'aide; **he's supposedly too sick to walk** il est soi-disant trop malade pour marcher

supposing [sə'pəʊzɪŋ] *conj* si, à supposer que; **supposing he still wants to go** et s'il veut encore y aller?; **even supposing she does come** même si elle vient *ou* venait; **supposing you are right** admettons *ou* mettons que vous ayez raison; **always supposing I can do it** en supposant *ou* en admettant que je puisse le faire

supposition [ˌsʌpə'zɪʃən] *n* supposition *f*, hypothèse *f*; **his theory was pure supposition** sa théorie n'était qu'une hypothèse; **on the supposition that your mother agrees** dans l'hypothèse où votre mère serait d'accord, à supposer que votre mère soit d'accord

suppositional [ˌsʌpə'zɪʃənəl] *adj* hypothétique

suppositious [ˌsʌpə'zɪʃəs], **supposititious** [səˌpɒzɪ'tɪʃəs] *adj Formal* (**a**) *(hypothetical)* hypothétique (**b**) *(fraudulent)* faux (fausse)

suppositive [sə'pɒzɪtɪv] *adj* (**a**) *(hypothetical)* hypothétique (**b**) *Gram* suppositif

suppository [sə'pɒzɪtrɪ] (*pl* **suppositories**) *n* suppositoire *m*

suppress [sə'pres] *vt* (**a**) *(put an end to)* supprimer, mettre fin à; **the new regime suppressed all forms of dissent** le nouveau régime a mis fin *ou* un terme à toute forme de dissidence

(**b**) *(withhold)* supprimer, faire disparaître; *(conceal)* supprimer, cacher; **to suppress evidence** faire disparaître des preuves; **to suppress the truth/a scandal** étouffer la vérité/un scandale

(**c**) *(withdraw from publication)* supprimer, interdire; **all opposition newspapers have been suppressed** tous les journaux d'opposition ont été interdits *ou* supprimés; **the government has suppressed the report** le gouvernement a interdit la parution du rapport

(**d**) *(delete)* supprimer, retrancher; **the judge ordered that the controversial passages should be suppressed** le juge ordonna la suppression des passages controversés

(**e**) *(inhibit → growth, weeds)* supprimer, empêcher

(**f**) *(hold back, repress → anger, yawn, smile)* réprimer; *(→ tears)* retenir, refouler; *(→ feelings, desires)* étouffer, refouler; **to suppress a cough** réprimer *ou* retenir son envie de tousser; **to suppress a sneeze** se retenir pour ne pas éternuer; **to suppress a yawn** étouffer *ou* réprimer un bâillement; **she suppressed a smile** elle réprima un sourire

(**g**) *Psy* refouler

(**h**) *Electron & Rad* antiparasiter

suppressant [sə'presənt] *n* inhibiteur *m*

suppressed [sə'prest] *adj (emotion)* étouffé, refoulé; *(anger)* refoulé; *Psy (sexuality)* refoulé; **suppressed excitement** agitation *f* contenue

suppression [sə'preʃən] *n* (**a**) *(ending → of rebellion, demonstration)* suppression *f*, répression *f*; *(→ of rights)* suppression *f*, abolition *f*; *(→ of a law, decree)* abrogation *f*

(**b**) *(concealment → of evidence, information)* suppression *f*, dissimulation *f*; *(→ of scandal)* étouffement *m*

(**c**) *(non-publication → of document, report)* suppression *f*, interdiction *f*; *(→ of part of text)* suppression *f*

(**d**) *(holding back → of feelings, thoughts)* refoulement *m*

(**e**) *Psy* refoulement *m*

(**f**) *Electron & Rad* antiparasitage *m*

suppressive [sə'presɪv] *adj* répressif

suppressor [sə'presə(r)] *n Elec* dispositif *m* antiparasite *(inv)*

▸▸ ***suppressor grid*** grille *f* d'arrêt; ***suppressor T-cell*** lymphocyte *m* T suppresseur

suppurate ['sʌpjʊreɪt] *vi* suppurer; **a suppurating wound** une plaie suppurante

suppuration [ˌsʌpjʊ'reɪʃən] *n* suppuration *f*

supra ['suːprə] *adv* supra

supracostal [ˌsuːprə'kɒstəl] *adj Anat* surcostal

supramaxillary [ˌsuːprəmæk'sɪlərɪ] *adj Anat* supramaxillaire

supramundane [ˌsuːprəmən'deɪn] *adj* supramondain

supranational [ˌsuːprə'næʃənəl] *adj* supranational

supraorbital [ˌsuːprə'ɔːbɪtəl] *adj Anat* sus-orbitaire

suprarenal [ˌsuːprə'riːnəl] *adj Anat* surrénal

▸▸ ***suprarenal gland*** glande *f* surrénale

suprasegmental [ˌsuːprəseg'mentəl] *adj* suprasegmental

suprasensible [ˌsuːprə'sensɪbəl] *adj* suprasensible

supremacist [sʊ'preməsɪst] *n* = personne qui croit en la suprématie d'un groupe; **they are white supremacists** ils croient en la suprématie de la race blanche

supremacy [sʊ'preməsɪ] *n* (**a**) *(dominance)* suprématie *f*, domination *f*; **each nation tried to gain supremacy over the other** chaque nation essayait d'avoir la suprématie sur l'autre (**b**) *(superiority)* suprématie *f*; **they believe in the supremacy of their methods over all others** ils croient leurs méthodes supérieures à *ou* meilleures que toutes les autres

suprême, supreme[1] [sʊ'priːm] *n* (**a**) *(meat)* = blanc et aile (**b**) *(sauce)* sauce *f* suprême (**c**) *(dish)* **chicken suprême** suprême *m* de poulet

supreme[2] *adj* (**a**) *(highest in rank, authority)* suprême; **the Supreme Commander of Allied Forces** le commandant suprême *ou* le commandant en chef des Forces alliées

(**b**) *(great, outstanding)* extrême; **a supreme effort** un effort suprême; **she handles politicians with supreme skill** elle sait parfaitement s'y prendre avec les hommes politiques; **it would be an act of supreme folly to do that now** ce serait de la folie pure de faire ça maintenant; **to make the supreme sacrifice** sacrifier sa vie, faire le sacrifice de sa vie

▸▸ *Rel* ***the Supreme Being*** l'Être *m* suprême; ***the Supreme Court*** la Cour suprême *(des États-Unis)*; ***Supreme Court Justice*** juge *m* à la Cour suprême; *Hist* ***the Supreme Court of Judicature*** la Cour souveraine de justice; ***Supreme Soviet*** Soviet *m* suprême

SUPREME COURT

La Cour suprême est l'organe supérieur du pouvoir judiciaire américain et est composée de membres nommés par le président des États-Unis; elle détient le pouvoir de décision final ainsi que le droit d'interpréter la Constitution.

supremely [sʊ'priːmlɪ] *adv* suprêmement, extrêmement

supremo [sʊ'priːməʊ] (*pl* **supremos**) *n Br Fam* (grand) chef *m*

Supt. (*written abbr* **superintendent**) ≃ commissaire *m* (de police)

sura, surah¹ ['sʊərə] *n (section of Koran)* surate *f*

surah² ['sʊərə] *n Tex* surah *m*

sural ['sjʊərəl] *adj Anat* sural

surbase ['sɜːbeɪs] *n Archit (on pedestal)* corniche *f*

surcease [sɜː'siːs] *n* répit *m*

surcharge ['sɜːtʃɑːdʒ] **1** *n* (**a**) *(extra duty, tax)* surtaxe *f*; **a 7 percent import surcharge** une surtaxe de 7 pour cent sur les importations

(**b**) *(extra cost)* supplément *m*; **there is a surcharge for the express train** il faut payer un supplément pour le train rapide; **some travel companies guarantee no surcharge** certains voyagistes s'engagent à ne faire payer aucun supplément

(**c**) *(overprinting → on postage stamp)* surcharge *f*

2 *vt* (**a**) *(charge extra duty or tax on)* surtaxer (**b**) *(charge a supplement to)* faire payer un supplément à

(**c**) *(overprint → postage stamp)* surcharger

surcingle ['sɜːsɪŋgəl] *n* surfaix *m*

surd [sɜːd] **1** *n* (**a**) *Ling* sourde *f* (**b**) *Math* équation *f* irrationnelle

2 *adj* (**a**) *Ling* sourd (**b**) *Math* irrationnel

SURE [ʃʊə(r)] **1** *adj* (**a**) *(convinced, positive)* sûr, certain; **are you sure of the facts?** êtes-vous sûr *ou* certain des faits?; **I'm not sure you're right** je ne suis pas sûr *ou* certain que vous ayez raison; **I'm not sure when they're coming/what he wants** je ne sais pas au juste quand ils doivent venir/ce qu'il veut; **I'm sure of it** j'en suis sûr *ou* certain; **I can't be sure, but I think it was 2 o'clock** je n'en suis pas tout à fait sûr, mais je pense qu'il était 2 heures; **are you quite sure he hasn't left yet?** êtes-vous bien sûr qu'il n'est pas encore parti?; **he's not sure whether he's going to come or not** il n'est pas sûr de venir; **she isn't sure of** *or* **about her feelings for him** elle n'est pas sûre de ses sentiments pour lui; **you seem convinced, but I'm not so sure** tu sembles convaincu, mais moi j'ai des doutes; **I wouldn't be so sure about that!** ça, ça m'étonnerait!; **he'll win, I'm sure** il gagnera, j'en suis sûr; **I'm sure I've been here before** je suis sûr d'être déjà venu ici; **she's sure she didn't receive your letter** elle est sûre de ne pas avoir reçu ta lettre; **what makes you so sure?, how can you be so sure?** qu'est-ce qui te fait dire ça?; **I don't know, I'm sure** ma foi, je ne sais pas

(**b**) *(confident, assured)* sûr; **is he someone we can be sure of?** est-ce quelqu'un de sûr?; **you can be sure of good service in this restaurant** dans ce restaurant, vous êtes sûr d'être bien servi; **to be sure of oneself** être sûr de soi, avoir confiance en soi

(**c**) *(definite, certain)* sûr, certain; **one thing is sure, he won't be back in a hurry!** une chose est sûre *ou* certaine, il ne va pas revenir de sitôt!; **we're sure to meet again** nous nous reverrons sûrement; **she's sure to be here soon** elle va sûrement arriver bientôt; **they're sure to get caught** ils vont sûrement se faire prendre; **the play is sure to be a success** la pièce va certainement avoir du succès; **it's a sure thing** c'est dans la poche; *esp Am Fam* **sure thing!** d'accord!; **be sure to be on time tomorrow** il faut que vous soyez à l'heure demain; **be sure to go to bed early** il faut que tu te couches tôt; **be sure not to lose it, be sure that you don't lose it** prenez garde de ne pas le perdre; **we made sure that no one was listening** nous nous sommes assurés *ou* nous avons vérifié que personne n'écoutait; **I'll just go and make sure** je vais vérifier; **it is his job to make sure that everyone is satisfied** c'est lui qui veille à ce que tout le monde soit satisfait; **make sure you don't lose your ticket** prends garde à ne pas perdre ton billet; **make sure you've turned off the gas** vérifie que tu as éteint le gaz

(**d**) *(firm, steady)* sûr; **with a sure hand** d'une main sûre; *Fig* **a sure grasp of the subject** des connaissances solides en la matière

(**e**) *(reliable, safe → method, remedy, judgement)* sûr; *(→ profit, success)* assuré; **there is only one sure way of doing it** il n'y a qu'un moyen sûr de le faire; **work is a sure remedy for boredom** le travail est un remède sûr contre l'ennui; **insomnia is a sure sign of depression** l'insomnie est un signe incontestable de dépression; **it's a sure bet he'll be late** il y a tout à parier qu'il sera en retard

2 *adv* (**a**) *Fam (of course)* bien sûr ❑; **can I borrow your car? – sure (you can)!** (est-ce que) je peux emprunter ta voiture? – bien sûr (que oui)!

(**b**) *esp Am Fam (really)* drôlement, rudement; **he sure is ugly** il est drôlement laid; **she sure can cook!** elle cuisine drôlement bien!; **it sure was difficult** c'était vraiment *ou* bien difficile; **are you hungry? – I sure am!** as-tu faim? – plutôt! *ou* et comment!; **I sure as hell do object!** et comment que je proteste!

(**c**) *(as intensifier)* **(as) sure as** aussi sûr que; **as sure as my name is Jones** aussi sûr que je m'appelle Jones; **as sure as I'm standing here (today), as sure as fate, as sure as eggs are** *or Fam* **is eggs** aussi sûr que deux et deux font quatre

(**d**) *Ir Fam* **sure, he's a terrible liar** c'est un grand menteur ❑; **sure, he doesn't know anything** il n'y connaît rien ❑

(**e**) *Am Fam (you're welcome)* **sure!** de rien! ❑, il n'y a pas de quoi! ❑

3 for sure *adv* **I'll give it to you tomorrow for sure** je te le donnerai demain sans faute; **one thing is for sure, I'm not staying here!** une chose est sûre, je ne reste pas ici!; **she won't come, that's for sure** elle ne viendra pas, c'est certain; **I think he's single but I can't say for sure** je crois qu'il est célibataire, mais je ne peux pas l'affirmer

4 sure enough *adv* effectivement, en effet; **she said she'd ring and sure enough she did** elle a dit qu'elle appellerait, et c'est ce qu'elle a fait; **no, it's whisky sure enough** non, c'est bien du whisky

5 to be sure *adv* **to be sure, his offer is well-intentioned** certes, son offre est bien intentionnée

---

surefire ['ʃʊəfaɪə(r)] *adj Fam* infaillible ❑, sûr ❑; **there's no surefire cure** il n'y a pas de remède infaillible

surefooted ['ʃʊə,fʊtɪd] *adj* au pied sûr; **to be surefooted** avoir le pied sûr; *Fig* **the Prime Minister gave a surefooted performance in the debate** le Premier ministre a fait une très bonne prestation

surely ['ʃʊəlɪ] *adv* (**a**) *(used to express surprise, incredulity, to contradict)* quand même, tout de même; **they surely can't have forgotten** ils n'ont pas pu oublier, quand même; **you're surely not suggesting it was my fault?** vous n'insinuez tout de même pas que c'était de ma faute?; **surely you must be joking!** vous plaisantez, j'espère?; **surely he didn't say that** il n'a pas pu dire ça; **the real figures are a lot higher, surely?** mais les chiffres sont en fait beaucoup plus élevés, non?; *Br* **surely to goodness** *or* **to God they must know by now** ce n'est pas possible qu'ils ne soient pas au courant à l'heure qu'il est; **it's all gone – surely not?** il n'y en a plus – c'est pas vrai!

(**b**) *(undoubtedly, assuredly)* sûrement, sans (aucun) doute; **they will surely succeed** ils réussiront sûrement

(**c**) *(steadily)* sûrement; **things are improving slowly but surely** les choses s'améliorent lentement mais sûrement

(**d**) *(of course)* bien sûr, certainement; **would you give me a hand? – surely!** peux-tu me donner un coup de main? – bien sûr *ou* certainement!

sureness ['ʃʊənɪs] *n* (**a**) *(certainty)* certitude *f* (**b**) *(assurance)* assurance *f* (**c**) *(steadiness)* sûreté *f*; *(accuracy)* justesse *f*, précision *f*; **he handled the problem with great sureness of touch** il a réglé le problème avec beaucoup de doigté

surety ['ʃʊərətɪ] (*pl* **sureties**) *n* (**a**) *(guarantor)* garant(e) *m,f*, caution *f*; **to act as** *or* **to stand surety (for sb)** se porter garant (de qn) (**b**) *(collateral)* caution *f*, sûreté *f*

suretyship ['ʃʊərətɪʃɪp] *n Law* cautionnement *m*, garantie *f*

surf [sɜːf] **1** *n (UNCOUNT)* (**a**) *(waves)* vagues *fpl* (déferlantes), ressac *m*; **the surf crashed against the rocks** les vagues venaient s'écraser contre les rochers; **to ride the surf** faire du surf

(**b**) *(foam)* écume *f*

(**c**) **surf and turf** *(in restaurant)* = plat à base de viande rouge et de fruits de mer

2 *vt Comput* **to surf the Net** naviguer sur l'Internet

3 *vi* (**a**) *(on surfboard)* surfer, faire du surf; **he goes surfing every weekend** il fait du surf tous les week-ends

(**b**) *Fam (on outside of train)* = s'accrocher à la paroi extérieure ou au toit d'un train

►► *Orn* **surf scoter** macreuse *f* à lunettes

surface ['sɜːfɪs] **1** *n* (**a**) *(exterior, top)* surface *f*; **the polished surface of the desk** la surface polie du bureau; **bubbles rose to the surface of the pond** des bulles montèrent à la surface de la mare; **the submarine/diver came to the surface** le sous-marin/plongeur fit surface; **the miners who work on the surface** les mineurs qui travaillent à la surface; *Fig* **all the old tensions came** *or* **rose to the surface when they met** toutes les vieilles discordes ont refait surface quand ils se sont revus

(**b**) *(flat area)* surface *f*; **roll the dough out on a smooth clean surface** étalez la pâte sur une surface lisse et propre

(**c**) *(covering layer)* revêtement *m*; **the pan has a non-stick surface** la poêle a une surface antiadhésive *ou* qui n'attache pas; **road surface** revêtement *m*

(**d**) *(outward appearance)* surface *f*, extérieur *m*, dehors *m*; **on the surface she seems nice enough** au premier abord elle paraît assez sympathique; **his politeness is only on the surface** sa politesse est toute de surface; **there was a feeling of anxiety lying beneath** *or* **below the surface** on sentait une angoisse sous-jacente; **the discussion hardly scratched the surface of the problem** le problème a à peine été abordé dans la discussion

(**e**) *Geom (area)* surface *f*, superficie *f*; **surface of revolution** surface *f* de révolution *ou* de rotation

2 *vi* (**a**) *(submarine, diver, whale)* faire surface, monter à la surface; *(return to surface)* refaire surface, remonter à la surface

(**b**) *(become manifest)* apparaître, se manifester; **he surfaced again after many years of obscurity** il a réapparu après être resté dans l'ombre pendant de nombreuses années; **rumours like this tend to surface every so often** ce type de rumeur a tendance à refaire surface de temps à autre

(**c**) *Fam (get up)* se lever ❑, émerger; **he didn't surface till 11 o'clock** il n'a pas émergé avant 11 heures

3 *vt (put a surface on → road)* revêtir; *(→ paper)* calandrer; **the track is surfaced with cement** la piste est revêtue de ciment

4 *adj* (**a**) *(superficial)* superficiel; **a surface scratch** une égratignure superficielle, une légère égratignure; *Fig* **his enthusiasm is purely surface** son enthousiasme n'est que superficiel

(**b**) *(exterior)* de surface; **surface finish** *(of metal)* état *m* de surface, finissage *m*; **surface measurements** superficie *f*

(**c**) *Mining (workers)* de surface, au jour; *(work)* à la surface, au jour; *Mil (forces)* au sol; *(fleet)* de surface

►► *Chem* ***surface activity*** tensioactivité *f*; ***surface area*** surface *f*, superficie *f*; *Ling* ***surface grammar*** grammaire *f* de surface; ***surface mail*** *(by land)* courrier *m* par voie de terre; *(by sea)* courrier *m* par voie maritime; ***surface noise*** bruit *m* de surface; ***surface speed*** *(of submarine)* vitesse *f* en surface; ***surface structure*** structure *f* superficielle *ou* de surface; ***surface tension*** tension *f* superficielle; ***surface transport*** transport *m* terrestre et/ou maritime; **by surface transport** par voie de terre et/ou maritime

surface-mounted *adj Comput (chips)* monté en surface

surface-to-air *adj* sol-air *(inv)*

surface-to-surface *adj* sol-sol *(inv)*

surfacing ['sɜːfɪsɪŋ] *n Constr* revêtement *m*

surfactant [sɜː'fæktənt] *n Chem* tensioactif *m*

surfbird [ˈsɜːfbɜːd] *n Orn* échassier *m (du littoral du Pacifique)*
surfboard [ˈsɜːfbɔːd] *n* (planche *f* de) surf *m*
surfboarder [ˈsɜːfbɔːdə(r)] *n* surfeur(euse) *m,f*
surfboarding [ˈsɜːfbɔːdɪŋ] *n* surf *m*; **to go surfboarding** faire du surf
surfboat [ˈsɜːfbəʊt] *n* pirogue *f* de barre (des Hawaïens), surf-boat *m*
surfcasting [ˈsɜːfkɑːstɪŋ] *n* = pêche à la ligne dans le ressac
surfeit [ˈsɜːfɪt] **1** *n Formal (excess)* excès *m*, surabondance *f*; **we had a surfeit of pasta when we were on holiday in Rome** nous nous sommes gavés de pâtes pendant nos vacances à Rome; **there is a surfeit of imported goods** il y a trop d'importations
2 *vt* rassasier; **to surfeit oneself with sth** se gorger de qch jusqu'à s'en dégoûter
surfer [ˈsɜːfə(r)] *n* (**a**) *(in sea)* surfeur(euse) *m,f* (**b**) *(on Internet)* internaute *mf*
surfie [ˈsɜːfɪ] *n Austr Fam* surfeur(euse) *m,f*
surfing [ˈsɜːfɪŋ] *n* (**a**) *(in sea)* surf *m*; **to go surfing** faire du surf; **surfing is forbidden on this beach** le surf est interdit sur cette plage (**b**) *(on Internet)* navigation *f*
surfride [ˈsɜːfraɪd] *vi* surfer, faire du surf
surfrider [ˈsɜːfˌraɪdə(r)] *n* surfeur(euse) *m,f*
surfriding [ˈsɜːfˌraɪdɪŋ] *n* surf *m*
surge [sɜːdʒ] **1** *n* (**a**) *(increase → of activity)* augmentation *f*, poussée *f*; *(→ of emotion)* vague *f*, accès *m*; *Elec* surtension *f*; **a big surge in demand** une forte augmentation de la demande; **a surge of pain/pity** un accès de douleur/de pitié; **he felt a surge of pride at the sight of his son** la fierté l'envahit en regardant son fils; **I felt a surge of hatred** j'ai senti la haine monter en moi
(**b**) *(rush, stampede)* ruée *f*; **there was a sudden surge for the exit** tout à coup les gens se sont rués vers la sortie; **a surge of spectators carried him forward** il fut emporté par le flot des spectateurs; **the demonstrators made a surge forward and broke through the police cordon** les manifestants se ruèrent en avant et le cordon de police céda
(**c**) *Naut* houle *f*
2 *vi* (**a**) *(well up → emotion)* monter; **I felt anger/hope/despair surge in me** j'ai senti la colère/l'espoir/le désespoir monter en moi
(**b**) *(rush → crowd)* se ruer, déferler; *(→ water)* couler à flots *ou* à torrents; *(→ waves)* déferler; **the demonstrators surged forward** les manifestants se ruèrent en avant; **the gates of the stadium opened and the fans surged in/out** les portes du stade s'ouvrirent et des flots de spectateurs s'y engouffrèrent/en sortirent; **the truck surged forward** le camion a bondi en avant; **water surged through the breach in the dam** des torrents *ou* trombes d'eau jaillirent de la brèche dans le barrage; **blood surged to her cheeks** le sang lui est monté au visage
(**c**) *Elec* subir une brusque pointe de tension
▸**surge up** *vi* = **surge** *vi* (**a**)
surgeon [ˈsɜːdʒən] *n* chirurgien(enne) *m,f*; **she hopes to become a surgeon** elle espère devenir chirurgien *ou* chirurgienne
▸▸ *Ich* ***surgeon fish*** (poisson *m*) chirurgien *m*; ***surgeon general*** *Mil* médecin-général *m*; *Am Admin* chef *m* des services de santé; ***surgeon's knot*** nœud *m* de chirurgien, nœud *m* chirurgical
surgery [ˈsɜːdʒərɪ] *(pl* **surgeries**) *n* (**a**) *(field of medicine)* chirurgie *f*; **to study surgery** étudier la chirurgie
(**b**) *(UNCOUNT) (surgical treatment)* intervention *f* chirurgicale, interventions *fpl* chirurgicales; **he'll need surgery** il faudra l'opérer; **minor/major surgery might be necessary** une intervention chirurgicale mineure/importante pourrait s'avérer nécessaire; **to perform surgery on sb** opérer qn; **to have brain/heart surgery** se faire opérer du cerveau/du cœur; **the patient is undergoing surgery** le malade est au bloc opératoire; **the surgery was successful** l'opération a réussi
(**c**) *Br (consulting room)* cabinet *m* médical *ou* de consultation; *(building)* centre *m* médical; *(consultation)* consultation *f*; **Doctor Jones doesn't take surgery on Fridays** le Dr Jones ne consulte pas le vendredi; **can I come to the surgery tomorrow?** puis-je venir au cabinet *ou* à la consultation demain?; **surgery hours** heures *fpl* de consultation
(**d**) *Br Pol* permanence *f*; **our MP holds a surgery on Saturdays** notre député tient une permanence le samedi
surgical [ˈsɜːdʒɪkəl] *adj* (**a**) *(operation, treatment)* chirurgical; *(manual, treatise)* de chirurgie; *(instrument, mask)* chirurgical, de chirurgien; *(methods, shock)* opératoire (**b**) *(appliance, boot, stocking)* orthopédique
▸▸ ***surgical collar*** minerve *f*; ***surgical cotton*** coton *m* hydrophile; ***surgical dressing*** pansement *m*; *Br* ***surgical spirit*** alcool *m* à 90 (degrés); *Mil* ***surgical strike*** attaque *f* chirurgicale
surgically [ˈsɜːdʒɪklɪ] *adv* par intervention chirurgicale; **the tumour was removed surgically** la tumeur fut enlevée par intervention chirurgicale
surging [ˈsɜːdʒɪŋ] *adj (crowd, waves)* déferlant; *(water)* qui coule à flots *ou* à torrents
suricate [ˈsʊərɪkeɪt] *n Zool* suricate *m*
Surinam [ˌsʊərɪˈnæm] *n* Surinam *m*, Suriname *m*; **in Surinam** au Surinam, au Suriname
▸▸ *Zool* ***Surinam toad*** pipa *m*
Surinamese [ˌsʊərɪnæˈmiːz] **1** *npl* **the Surinamese** les Surinamiens *mpl*
2 *n* Surinamien(enne) *m,f*
3 *adj* surinamien
surliness [ˈsɜːlɪnɪs] *n (character)* caractère *m* hargneux *ou* grincheux; *(mood)* humeur *f* hargneuse *ou* grincheuse
surly [ˈsɜːlɪ] *(compar* **surlier**, *superl* **surliest**) *adj (ill-tempered)* hargneux, grincheux
surmise [sɜːˈmaɪz] **1** *vt* conjecturer, présumer; **I can only surmise what the circumstances were** je ne puis que conjecturer quelles étaient les circonstances; **I surmised that he was lying** je me suis douté qu'il mentait
2 *n Formal* conjecture *f*, supposition *f*; **your conclusion is pure surmise** votre conclusion est entièrement hypothétique
surmount [sɜːˈmaʊnt] *vt* (**a**) *(triumph over)* surmonter, vaincre (**b**) *Formal (cap, top)* surmonter; **the building is surmounted by a large dome** le bâtiment est surmonté d'un grand dôme
surmountable [sɜːˈmaʊntəbəl] *adj* surmontable
surmullet [səˈmʌlɪt] *n Ich* surmulet *m*, rouget *m* barbet
surname [ˈsɜːneɪm] *n Br* nom *m* (de famille); **surname and Christian name** nom *m* et prénom *m*
surpass [səˈpɑːs] *vt* (**a**) *(outdo, outshine)* surpasser; *also Ironic* **you've surpassed yourselves** vous vous êtes surpassés (**b**) *(go beyond)* surpasser, dépasser; **that kind of behaviour surpasses my understanding** ce genre de comportement me dépasse; **the result surpassed all our expectations** le résultat dépassa toutes nos espérances
surpassable [səˈpɑːsəbəl] *adj* surpassable
surpassing [səˈpɑːsɪŋ] *adj Literary* sans égal; **a woman of surpassing beauty** une femme d'une beauté sans égale *ou* inégalable
surplice [ˈsɜːplɪs] *n* surplis *m*
surplus [ˈsɜːpləs] **1** *n* (**a**) *(overabundance)* surplus *m*, excédent *m*; **a labour surplus** un surplus de main-d'œuvre; **Japan's trade surplus** l'excédent *m* commercial du Japon
(**b**) *(UNCOUNT) (old military clothes)* surplus *mpl*; **an army surplus overcoat** un manteau des surplus de l'armée; **an army surplus store** un magasin de surplus de l'armée
(**c**) *Fin (in accounting)* boni *m*
2 *adj* (**a**) *(gen)* en surplus, en trop; **pour off any surplus liquid** enlevez tout excédent de liquide; **to be surplus to requirements** excéder les besoins
(**b**) *Com & Econ* en surplus, excédentaire; **they export their surplus agricultural produce** ils exportent leurs surplus agricoles
▸▸ *Com & Econ* ***surplus production*** production *f* excédentaire; *Com* ***surplus stock*** stocks *mpl* excédentaires, surplus *m*
surprise [səˈpraɪz] **1** *n* (**a**) *(unexpected event, experience etc)* surprise *f*; **it was a surprise to me** cela a été une surprise pour moi, cela m'a surpris; **it was a surprise to see her there** ce fut une surprise de la voir là; **what a lovely surprise!** quelle merveilleuse surprise!; **her death came as no surprise** sa mort n'a surpris personne; **his resignation came as a surprise to everyone** sa démission a surpris tout le monde; **the party was meant to be a surprise** la fête était censée être une surprise; **to give sb a surprise** faire une surprise à qn; **it was no surprise to learn that he had a criminal record** il n'y avait rien d'étonnant à ce qu'il ait un casier judiciaire; **you're in for (a bit of) a surprise!** tu vas être surpris!, tu vas avoir une (sacrée) surprise!
(**b**) *(astonishment)* surprise *f*, étonnement *m*; **much to my surprise, she agreed** à ma grande surprise *ou* à mon grand étonnement, elle accepta; **her announcement caused some surprise** sa déclaration a provoqué un certain étonnement; **he looked at me in surprise** il me regarda d'un air surpris *ou* étonné
(**c**) *(catching unawares)* surprise *f*; **the element of surprise is on our side** nous avons l'effet de surprise pour nous; **to take sb by surprise** surprendre qn, prendre qn au dépourvu; **their arrival took me by surprise** leur arrivée m'a pris au dépourvu; **the soldiers took the enemy by surprise** les soldats ont pris l'ennemi par surprise
2 *comp (attack, present, victory)* surprise; *(announcement)* inattendu
3 *vt* (**a**) *(amaze)* surprendre, étonner; **it surprised me that they didn't give her the job** j'ai été surpris *ou* étonné qu'ils ne l'aient pas embauchée; **shall we surprise her?** si on lui faisait une surprise?; **it wouldn't surprise me if they lost** ça ne m'étonnerait pas *ou* je ne serais pas surpris qu'ils perdent; *Ironic* **go on, surprise me!** vas-y, annonce!
(**b**) *(catch unawares)* surprendre; **the burglar was surprised by the police** le cambrioleur fut surpris par la police; **we surprised the enemy at dawn** nous avons surpris l'ennemi à l'aube
4 *exclam* **surprise(, surprise)!** coucou!
▸▸ ***surprise party*** = fête organisée pour quelqu'un sans qu'il ou elle le sache; ***surprise visit*** visite *f* surprise; **the Prime Minister made a surprise visit to Ireland** le Premier ministre a fait une visite surprise en Irlande
surprised [səˈpraɪzd] *adj* surpris, étonné; **she was surprised to learn that she had got the job** elle a été surprise d'apprendre qu'on allait l'embaucher; **don't be surprised if she doesn't come** ne vous étonnez pas si elle ne vient pas; **I wouldn't** *or* **I shoudn't be surprised if they'd forgotten** cela ne m'étonnerait pas qu'ils aient oublié; **I'm surprised by** *or* **at his reaction** sa réaction me surprend *ou* m'étonne; **I'm surprised at you!** tu m'étonnes!; **it looks easy but you'd be surprised** ça semble facile mais ne vous y fiez pas; **his lack of good manners is nothing to be surprised about** son manque de savoir-vivre n'a rien d'étonnant
surprising [səˈpraɪzɪŋ] *adj* surprenant, étonnant; **it's surprising (that) she left so early** il est surprenant *ou* étonnant qu'elle soit partie si tôt; **it's not at all** *or* **not in the least surprising** cela n'a rien d'étonnant; **that's surprising coming from him** (venant) de sa part, c'est surprenant
surprisingly [səˈpraɪzɪŋlɪ] *adv* étonnamment; **for a ten-year-old, she's surprisingly mature** elle est vraiment très mûre pour une fille de dix ans; **surprisingly, he managed to win** chose surprenante *ou* étonnante, il a quand même gagné; **he apologized, surprisingly enough** chose surprenante *ou* étonnante, il s'est excusé; **not surprisingly, the play sold out** toutes les places ont été louées, ce qui n'a rien d'étonnant
surra [ˈsʊərə, ˈsʌrə] *n Vet* surra *m*
surreal [səˈrɪəl] **1** *adj* (**a**) *(strange, dreamlike)* étrange, onirique (**b**) *Art & Literature* surréaliste
2 *n* **the surreal** le surréel
surrealism [səˈrɪəlɪzəm] *n Art & Literature* surréalisme *m*
surrealist [səˈrɪəlɪst] *Art & Literature* **1** *adj* surréaliste
2 *n* surréaliste *mf*
surrealistic [səˌrɪəlˈɪstɪk] *adj* (**a**) *Art & Literature* surréaliste (**b**) *Fig* surréel, surréaliste

surrealistically [sə,rɪə'lɪstɪkəlɪ] *adv* d'une manière *ou* dans un style surréaliste

surrender [sə'rendə(r)] **1** *vi* (**a**) *Mil (capitulate)* se rendre, capituler; **they surrendered to the enemy** ils se rendirent à *ou* ils capitulèrent devant l'ennemi

(**b**) *(give oneself up)* se livrer; **after sixteen hours the hijackers surrendered to the police** au bout de seize heures, les pirates de l'air se sont livrés à la police; *Law* **to surrender to bail** comparaître en jugement (après une libération sous caution)

(**c**) *Fig (abandon oneself)* se livrer, s'abandonner; **to surrender to temptation** se livrer *ou* s'abandonner à la tentation

2 *vt* (**a**) *(city, position)* livrer; *(relinquish → possessions, territory)* céder, rendre; *(→ one's seat)* céder, laisser; *(→ arms)* rendre, livrer; *(→ claim, authority, freedom, rights)* renoncer à; *(→ hopes)* abandonner; **to surrender oneself to sth** se livrer *ou* s'abandonner à qch

(**b**) *(hand in → ticket, coupon)* remettre

(**c**) *Ins (policy)* racheter

3 *n* (**a**) *(capitulation)* reddition *f*, capitulation *f*; **no surrender!** nous ne nous rendrons pas!; **the town was starved into surrender** la famine a obligé la ville à capituler; **the government's surrender to the unions** la capitulation du gouvernement devant les syndicats; **he laughed at the idea of surrender** l'idée de se rendre l'a fait rire

(**b**) *(relinquishing → of possessions, territory)* cession *f*; *(→ of arms)* remise *f*; *(→ of claim, authority, freedom, rights)* renonciation *f*, abdication *f*; *(→ of hopes)* abandon *m*; **it is tantamount to a surrender of all our rights** cela équivaut à l'abdication de *ou* renoncer à tous nos droits

(**c**) *Ins (of policy)* rachat *m*

▸▸ *Ins* ***surrender value*** valeur *f* de rachat

surreptitious [,sʌrəp'tɪʃəs] *adj* furtif, clandestin, *Literary* subreptice

surreptitiously [,sʌrəp'tɪʃəslɪ] *adv* furtivement, à la dérobée, *Literary* subrepticement

surreptitiousness [,sʌrəp'tɪʃəsnɪs] *n* caractère *m* furtif *ou Literary* subreptice

Surrey ['sʌrɪ] *n* le Surrey, = comté dans le sud-est de l'Angleterre; **in Surrey** dans le Surrey

surrey ['sʌrɪ] *n* = voiture hippomobile à deux places

surrogacy ['sʌrəgəsɪ] *n* maternité *f* de remplacement *ou* de substitution

surrogate ['sʌrəgeɪt] **1** *n* (**a**) *Formal (substitute → person)* remplaçant(e) *m,f*, substitut *m*; *(→ thing)* succédané *m*

(**b**) *Psy* substitut *m*

(**c**) *Am Law* magistrat *m* de droit civil *(juridiction locale)*

(**d**) *Br Rel* évêque *m* auxiliaire

2 *adj* de substitution, de remplacement; **they served as surrogate parents to her** ils ont en quelque sorte remplacé ses parents

▸▸ ***surrogate mother*** *Psy* substitut *m* maternel; *Med* mère *f* porteuse

surrogation [,sʌrə'geɪʃən] *n* substitution *f*; **surrogation of documents** = substitution de documents par d'autres dans un bureau d'information

surrosion [sə'rəʊʒən] *n Chem* augmentation *f* de poids *(due à la corrosion)*

surround [sə'raʊnd] **1** *vt* (**a**) *(gen)* entourer; **the garden is surrounded by a brick wall** le jardin est entouré d'un mur en briques; **the president surrounded himself with advisers** le président s'est entouré de conseillers; **there is a great deal of controversy surrounding the budget cuts** il y a une vive controverse autour des réductions budgétaires

(**b**) *(of troops, police, enemy)* encercler, cerner; **surrounded by enemy soldiers** encerclé *ou* cerné par des troupes ennemies

2 *n Br (border, edging)* bordure *f*

▸▸ *TV & Comput* ***surround sound*** son *m* 3D

surrounding [sə'raʊndɪŋ] **1** *adj* environnant; **there's a lovely view of the surrounding countryside** il y a une belle vue sur le paysage alentour

2 surroundings *npl* (**a**) *(of town, city)* alentours *mpl*, environs *mpl*

(**b**) *(setting)* cadre *m*, décor *m*; **it's a pleasure to be in such lovely surroundings** c'est un vrai plaisir de se trouver dans un cadre aussi joli

(**c**) *(environment)* environnement *m*, milieu *m*; **she's indifferent to her surroundings** elle est indifférente à son environnement; **to be in familiar surroundings** être en pays de connaissance

surtax ['sɜːtæks] *n* surtaxe *f*; *(on income)* = surtaxe progressive sur le revenu

surtitle ['sɜːtaɪtəl] *n* surtitre *m*

surveillance [sɜː'veɪləns] *n* surveillance *f*; **to keep sb under constant surveillance** garder qn sous surveillance continue; **the house is under police surveillance** la maison est surveillée par la police

survey 1 *vt* [sə'veɪ] (**a**) *(contemplate)* contempler; *(inspect)* inspecter, examiner; *(review)* passer en revue; **we sat surveying the view** nous étions assis à contempler le paysage; **he stepped back to survey the painting** il fit un pas en arrière pour contempler le tableau

(**b**) *(make a study of)* dresser le bilan de, étudier; **the report surveys the current state of manufacturing industry in Britain** le rapport dresse le bilan de l'industrie manufacturière en Grande-Bretagne

(**c**) *(poll)* sonder; **65 percent of women surveyed were opposed to the measure** 65 pour cent des femmes interrogées étaient contre cette mesure

(**d**) *(land)* arpenter, relever, faire un relèvement de

(**e**) *Br (house)* expertiser, faire une expertise de; **always have a house independently surveyed before buying** il faut toujours faire faire une expertise indépendante avant d'acheter une maison

2 *n* ['sɜːveɪ] (**a**) *(study, investigation)* étude *f*, enquête *f*; **they carried out a survey of retail prices** ils ont fait une enquête sur les prix au détail

(**b**) *(overview)* vue *f* d'ensemble; **the exhibition offers a comprehensive survey of contemporary British art** l'exposition présente une vision d'ensemble de l'art contemporain britannique

(**c**) *(poll)* sondage *m*

(**d**) *(of land)* relèvement *m*, levé *m*; **aerial survey** levé *m* aérien

(**e**) *Br (of house)* expertise *f*; **to have a survey done** faire faire une expertise

▸▸ *Mktg* ***survey research*** recherche *f* par sondage

surveying [sə'veɪɪŋ] *n* (**a**) *(measuring → of land)* arpentage *m*, levé *m* (**b**) *Br (examination → of buildings)* examen *m*

▸▸ ***surveying instruments*** instruments *mpl* topographiques

surveyor [sə'veɪə(r)] *n* (**a**) *(of land)* arpenteur *m*, géomètre *m* (**b**) *Br (of buildings)* géomètre-expert *m*; **the council surveyor declared the building unsafe** l'expert envoyé par la mairie déclara l'immeuble dangereux

surveyorship [sə'veɪəʃɪp] *n* (**a**) *(of land surveyor)* office *m ou* fonction *f* d'arpenteur (**b**) *Br* office *m ou* fonction *f* de géomètre-expert

survivable [sə'vaɪvəbəl] *adj* **a survivable attack** une attaque à laquelle on peut survivre; **the conditions were not survivable** il était impossible de survivre dans de telles conditions

survival [sə'vaɪvəl] **1** *n* (**a**) *(remaining alive)* survie *f*; **what are their chances of survival?** quelles sont leurs chances de survie?; *also Fig* **the survival of the fittest** la survie du plus apte

(**b**) *(relic, remnant)* survivance *f*, vestige *m*; **the custom is a survival from the Victorian era** cette coutume remonte à l'époque victorienne

2 *comp (course, kit)* de survie

▸▸ ***survival bag*** sac *m* de couchage de survie; ***survival kit*** équipement *m* de survie

survivalism [sə'vaɪvəlɪzəm] *n* = entraînement en vue de la survie en cas de catastrophe

survivalist [sə'vaɪvəlɪst] *n* = personne qui s'entraîne à la survie en cas de catastrophe

survive [sə'vaɪv] **1** *vi* (**a**) *(remain alive)* survivre; **nobody thought she'd survive** personne ne pensait qu'elle survivrait

(**b**) *(cope, pull through)* **how can they survive on such low wages?** comment font-ils pour vivre *ou* pour subsister avec des salaires si bas?; **he earned just enough to survive on** il gagnait tout juste de quoi survivre; **those toys wouldn't survive two minutes with our kids** ces jouets ne survivraient pas plus de deux minutes avec nos gamins; *Fam* **it'll be awful, I don't know how I'll survive!** ça va être horrible, je ne sais pas comment je vais m'en sortir!; *Fam* **how's things? – I'm surviving** comment ça va? – pas trop mal; *Fam* **don't worry, I'll survive!** ne t'inquiète pas, je n'en mourrai pas!

(**c**) *(remain, be left)* subsister; **only a dozen of his letters have survived** il ne subsiste *ou* reste qu'une douzaine de ses lettres

2 *vt* (**a**) *(live through)* survivre à, réchapper à *ou* de; **few of the soldiers survived the battle** peu de soldats ont survécu à la bataille; **we thought he'd never survive the shock** nous pensions qu'il ne se remettrait jamais du choc

(**b**) *(cope with, get through)* supporter; **she survived the death of her father better than expected** elle a surmonté la mort de son père mieux que prévu; **I never thought I'd survive the evening!** jamais je n'aurais cru que je tiendrais jusqu'à la fin de la soirée!

(**c**) *(outlive, outlast)* survivre à; **she survived her husband by twenty years** elle a survécu vingt ans à son mari; **she is survived by two daughters** elle laisse deux filles

(**d**) *(withstand)* survivre à, résister à; **the house didn't survive the storm** la maison n'a pas survécu *ou* résisté à la tempête; **her beauty has survived the passage of time** sa beauté a résisté au temps

surviving [sə'vaɪvɪŋ] *adj* survivant; **his only surviving son** son seul fils encore en vie; **the longest surviving whale in captivity** la baleine qui vit depuis le plus longtemps en captivité

survivor [sə'vaɪvə(r)] *n* (**a**) *(of accident, attack, earthquake)* survivant(e) *m,f*, rescapé(e) *m,f*; **the survivors of the death camps** les rescapés *mpl* des camps de la mort; **there are no reports of any survivors** aucun survivant n'a été signalé; **she'll be all right, she's a born survivor** elle s'en sortira, elle est solide (**b**) *Law* survivant(e) *m,f*

sus [sʌs] *n*

▸▸ *Br Fam* ***sus laws*** = lois abrogées en 1981, équivalant au système du contrôle d'identité et autorisant l'arrestation de personnes dont le comportement paraît suspect

susceptibility [sə,septə'bɪlətɪ] (*pl* **susceptibilities**) **1** *n* (**a**) *(predisposition → to an illness, a disease)* prédisposition *f*; **she has a susceptibility to respiratory complaints** elle a une prédisposition aux infections respiratoires

(**b**) *(vulnerability)* sensibilité *f*; **his susceptibility to flattery** sa sensibilité à la flatterie

(**c**) *Formal (sensitivity)* sensibilité *f*, émotivité *f*

(**d**) *Phys* susceptibilité *f*

2 susceptibilities *npl (feelings)* sentiments *mpl*, susceptibilité *f*; **try to spare their susceptibilities** essayez de ménager leur susceptibilité

susceptible [sə'septəbəl] *adj* (**a**) *(prone → to illness, disease)* prédisposé; **I'm very susceptible to colds** je m'enrhume très facilement; **only the more susceptible children contracted the disease** seuls les enfants les plus prédisposés ont été contaminés par la maladie

(**b**) *(responsive)* sensible; **the management is susceptible to pressure from the staff** la direction est sensible aux pressions du personnel; **susceptible to flattery** sensible à la flatterie; **the virus is not susceptible to treatment** le virus ne répond pas au traitement

(**c**) *Formal (sensitive, emotional)* sensible, émotif

(**d**) *Formal (capable)* susceptible; **her decisions are susceptible of modification** ses décisions sont susceptibles d'être modifiées

sushi ['suːʃɪ] *n* sushi *m*

▸▸ ***sushi bar*** sushi-bar *m*

suslik ['sʌslɪk] *n Zool* souslik *m*

suspect 1 *vt* [sə'spekt] (**a**) *(presume, imagine)* soupçonner, se douter de; **I suspected there would be trouble** je me doutais qu'il y aurait des problèmes; **I suspected as much!** je m'en doutais!; **what happened, I suspect, is that they had an argument** ce qui s'est passé, j'imagine, c'est qu'ils se sont disputés (**b**) *(have intuition of)* soupçonner; **to suspect foul play** soupçonner quelque chose de louche; **does your husband suspect anything?** est-ce que ton mari se doute de quelque chose?; **I never suspected it for a moment** je n'avais pas le moindre soupçon, je ne m'en suis jamais douté

(**c**) *(mistrust)* douter de, se méfier de; **to suspect sb's motives** avoir des doutes sur les intentions de qn

(**d**) *(person → of wrongdoing)* soupçonner, suspecter; **to be suspected of sth** être soupçonné de qch; **to suspect sb of sth/of doing sth** soupçonner qn de qch/d'avoir fait qch

2 *n* ['sʌspekt] (**a**) *(of crime, wrongdoing)* suspect(e) *m,f*

(**b**) *Mktg* client *m* potentiel; **suspect pool** clients *mpl* potentiels

3 *adj* ['sʌspekt] suspect; **his views on apartheid are rather suspect** ses vues sur l'apartheid sont plutôt douteuses

►► *Mktg* ***suspect pool*** clients *mpl* potentiels

suspected [sə'spektɪd] *adj* présumé; **a suspected terrorist** un terroriste présumé; **a suspected case of cholera** un cas présumé de choléra; **he's undergoing tests for a suspected tumour** on est en train de lui faire des analyses pour s'assurer qu'il ne s'agit pas d'une tumeur

suspend [sə'spend] *vt* (**a**) *(hang)* suspendre; **suspended from the ceiling/in the air** suspendu au plafond/en l'air; **particles of radioactive dust were suspended in the atmosphere** des particules radioactives étaient en suspension dans l'atmosphère

(**b**) *(discontinue)* suspendre; *(withdraw → permit, licence)* retirer (provisoirement), suspendre; **bus services have been suspended** le service des autobus a été suspendu *ou* interrompu; **the government has suspended the repayment of foreign debts** le gouvernement a suspendu le remboursement de sa dette extérieure

(**c**) *(defer)* suspendre, reporter; **to suspend judgment** suspendre son jugement; **the commission decided to suspend its decision** la commission décida de surseoir à sa décision; **to suspend one's disbelief** faire taire son incrédulité

(**d**) *(exclude temporarily → official, member, sportsman)* suspendre; *(→ worker)* suspendre, mettre à pied; *(→ pupil, student)* exclure provisoirement; **suspended for six months** suspendu pendant six mois; **two pupils have been suspended from school for smoking** deux élèves surpris à fumer font l'objet d'un renvoi provisoire; *Admin* **suspended on full pay** suspendu sans suppression de traitement; *Mil* suspendu sans suppression de solde

suspended [sə'spendɪd] *adj (gen)* suspendu; *(particles)* en suspension

►► ***suspended animation*** *(natural state)* hibernation *f*; *(induced state)* hibernation *f* artificielle; *(after accident, trauma)* syncope *f*, arrêt *m* momentané des fonctions; **to be in a state of suspended animation** *(animal)* être en hibernation; *(person)* avoir une syncope; **the scheme is in a state of suspended animation** le projet est en suspens; *Law* ***suspended sentence*** condamnation *f* avec sursis; **she got a three-month suspended sentence** elle a été condamnée à trois mois de prison avec sursis

suspender [sə'spendə(r)] **1** *n Br (for stockings)* jarretelle *f*; *(for socks)* fixe-chaussette *m*

2 suspenders *npl Am (for trousers)* bretelles *fpl*

►► *Br* ***suspender belt*** porte-jarretelles *m inv*

suspense [sə'spens] *n* (**a**) *(anticipation)* incertitude *f*; **to keep** *or* **to leave sb in suspense** laisser qn dans l'incertitude; **to break the suspense** mettre fin à l'incertitude; **to put sb out of (their) suspense** mettre fin à l'incertitude de qn; *Fam* **the suspense is killing me!** quel suspense!❑

(**b**) *(in films, literature)* suspense *m*; **she manages to maintain the suspense throughout the book** elle réussit à maintenir *ou* faire durer le suspense jusqu'à la fin du livre

(**c**) *Admin & Law* **in suspense** en suspens; **the question remains in suspense** la question reste posée *ou* en suspens

►► *Fin* ***suspense account*** compte *m* d'ordre

suspension [sə'spenʃən] *n* (**a**) *(interruption)* suspension *f*; *(withdrawal)* suspension *f*, retrait *m* (provisoire); **the suspension of hostilities/payments** la suspension des hostilités/des paiements

(**b**) *(temporary dismissal → from office, political party, club, team)* suspension *f*; *(→ from job)* suspension *f*, mise *f* à pied; *(→ from school, university)* exclusion *f* provisoire

(**c**) *Aut & Tech* suspension *f*; **independent suspension** suspension *f* à roues indépendantes

(**d**) *Chem* suspension *f*; **in suspension** en suspension

►► ***suspension bridge*** pont *m* suspendu; *Aut* ***suspension bush*** bague *f* de suspension; ***suspension cable*** câble *m* porteur; *Tech* ***suspension chain*** chaîne *f* de suspension; ***suspension file*** hamac *m*, dossier *m* suspendu; *Aut* ***suspension geometry*** géométrie *f* de la suspension; *Typ & Gram* ***suspension points*** points *mpl* de suspension

suspensor [sə'spensə(r)] *n* (**a**) *Anat (ligament)* ligament *m* suspenseur; *(muscle)* muscle *m* suspenseur (**b**) *Bot* suspenseur *m*

suspensory [sə'spensərɪ] (*pl* **suspensories**) **1** *n* (**a**) *Anat (ligament)* ligament *m* suspenseur; *(muscle)* muscle *m* suspenseur (**b**) *Med (bandage, sling)* suspensoir *m*

2 *adj* (**a**) *Anat* suspenseur (**b**) *Med (bandage, sling)* de soutien

suspicion [sə'spɪʃən] *n* (**a**) *(presumption of guilt, mistrust)* soupçon *m*, suspicion *f*; **her neighbours' strange behaviour aroused her suspicion** *or* **suspicions** le comportement étrange de ses voisins éveilla ses soupçons; **to be above** *or* **beyond suspicion** être au-dessus de tout soupçon; **I have my suspicions about this fellow** j'ai des doutes sur cet individu; **the new boss was regarded with suspicion** on considérait le nouveau patron avec méfiance; **to be under suspicion** être soupçonné; *Law* **he was arrested on suspicion of drug trafficking** il a été arrêté parce qu'on le soupçonnait de trafic de drogue

(**b**) *(notion, feeling)* soupçon *m*; **I had a growing suspicion that he wasn't telling the truth** je soupçonnais de plus en plus qu'il ne disait pas la vérité; **I had a (sneaking) suspicion you'd be here** j'avais comme un pressentiment que tu serais là

(**c**) *(trace, hint)* soupçon *m*, pointe *f*; **there was a suspicion of bitterness in her voice** il y avait un soupçon *ou* une pointe d'amertume dans sa voix

suspicious [sə'spɪʃəs] *adj* (**a**) *(distrustful)* méfiant, soupçonneux; **his strange behaviour made us suspicious** son comportement étrange a éveillé nos soupçons *ou* notre méfiance; **she became suspicious when he refused to give his name** elle a commencé à se méfier quand il a refusé de donner son nom; **I'm suspicious of his motives** je me méfie de ses intentions; **she gave him a suspicious look** elle lui jeta un regard méfiant

(**b**) *(suspect)* suspect; **the minister resigned in very suspicious circumstances** le ministre démissionna dans des circonstances très suspectes; **there are a lot of suspicious-looking characters in this pub** il y a beaucoup d'individus suspects dans ce pub; **it is suspicious that she didn't phone the police** le fait qu'elle n'a pas téléphoné à la police est suspect

suspiciously [sə'spɪʃəslɪ] *adv* (**a**) *(distrustfully)* avec méfiance, soupçonneusement

(**b**) *(strangely)* de façon suspecte; **police saw a man acting suspiciously** la police a vu un homme qui se comportait de façon suspecte; **she was suspiciously keen to leave** son empressement à partir était suspect; **they came suspiciously close to guessing the truth** il est étrange qu'ils aient failli deviner la vérité; **it looks suspiciously like malaria** ça ressemble étrangement au paludisme; **it sounded suspiciously as though she had lost it** on aurait dit qu'elle l'avait perdu

suspiciousness [sə'spɪʃəsnɪs] *n* (**a**) *(distrust)* méfiance *f* (**b**) *(suspect nature)* caractère *m* suspect

suspiration [ˌsʌspɪ'reɪʃən] *n Literary* (**a**) *(sigh)* soupir *m* (**b**) *(breath)* expiration *f (de son haleine)*

suspire [sə'spaɪə(r)] *vi Literary* (**a**) *(sigh)* soupirer (**b**) *(breathe)* expirer, souffler

suss [sʌs] **1** *vt Br Fam (work out)* découvrir❑; *(realize)* se rendre compte de❑; **I soon sussed what he was up to** j'ai vite compris son petit manège; **I haven't got her sussed yet** je l'ai pas encore vraiment cernée; **I haven't got this computer sussed yet** j'ai pas encore pigé comment fonctionne cet ordinateur; **she sussed what he was after** elle a compris où il voulait en venir❑

2 *n* = **sus**

►**suss out** *vt sep Br Fam* (**a**) **to suss sth out** *(work out)* découvrir qch❑; *(realize)* se rendre compte de qch❑; **I couldn't suss out how the modem worked** j'ai pas pigé comment le modem fonctionnait; **I haven't sussed out his motives yet** j'ai toujours pas pigé ses motivations; **we have to suss out the best places to go at night** il faut qu'on repère les endroits où sortir le soir❑

(**b**) *(person)* saisir le caractère de❑; **I've got him sussed out** je sais à qui j'ai affaire❑; **I can't quite suss her out** c'est quelqu'un que j'ai du mal à cerner❑

sussed [sʌst] *adj Fam (astute)* rusé❑, malin(-igne)❑

sustain [sə'steɪn] *vt* (**a**) *(maintain, keep up → conversation)* entretenir; *(→ effort, attack, pressure)* soutenir, maintenir; *(→ someone's interest)* maintenir; **if the present level of economic growth is sustained** si le niveau actuel de croissance économique est maintenu

(**b**) *(support physically)* soutenir, supporter; **steel girders sustain the weight of the bridge** le pont est soutenu par des poutres en acier

(**c**) *(support morally)* soutenir; **it was only their belief in God that sustained them** seule leur croyance en Dieu les a soutenus

(**d**) *Mus (note)* tenir, soutenir

(**e**) *(nourish)* nourrir; **they had only dried fruit and water to sustain them** ils n'avaient que des fruits secs et de l'eau pour subsister; **one meal a day is not enough to sustain you** l'homme a besoin pour vivre de plus d'un repas par jour; **a planet capable of sustaining life** une planète capable de maintenir la vie

(**f**) *(suffer → damage)* subir; *(→ defeat, loss)* subir, essuyer; *(→ injury)* recevoir; **to sustain an injury** recevoir une blessure, être blessé; **the man sustained a serious blow to the head** l'homme a été grièvement atteint à la tête

(**g**) *(withstand)* supporter; **her fragile condition will not sustain another shock** étant donné la fragilité de son état, elle ne supportera pas un nouveau choc

(**h**) *Law (accept as valid)* admettre; **the court refused to sustain the motion** le tribunal refusa d'admettre *ou* d'accorder la requête; **objection sustained** objection admise; **the court sustained her claim** le tribunal lui accorda gain de cause

(**i**) *(corroborate → assertion, theory, charge)* corroborer

(**j**) *Theat (role)* tenir

sustainability [səsˌteɪnə'bɪlɪtɪ] *n* **our future depends on the sustainability of our resources** notre avenir dépend des ressources renouvelables

sustainable [səs'teɪnəbəl] *adj* (**a**) *(development, agriculture, politics)* viable, durable

(**b**) *(energy, resources)* renouvelable

sustained [sə'steɪnd] *adj (effort, attack)* soutenu; *(discussion, applause)* prolongé

►► *Ecol* ***sustained yield*** rendement *m* soutenu

sustaining [sə'steɪnɪŋ] *adj* nourrissant, nutritif

►► *Mus* ***sustaining pedal*** pédale *f* forte; *Am Rad & TV* ***sustaining program*** émission *f* non sponsorisée

sustenance ['sʌstɪnəns] *n* (**a**) *(nourishment)* valeur *f* nutritive; **there is little sustenance in such foods** de tels aliments ont peu de valeur nutritive *ou* sont peu nourrissants; **stale bread provided her only form of sustenance** elle se nourrissait uniquement de pain rassis; *Fig* **his neighbours provided moral sustenance during the crisis** ses voisins l'ont soutenu moralement pendant la crise (**b**) *(means of subsistence)* subsistance *f*; **they could not derive sustenance from the land** ils ne pouvaient pas vivre de la terre

susurrant [suːˈsʌrənt] *adj Literary* susurrant, murmurant

susurrate [suːˈsʌreɪt] *vi Literary* susurrer, murmurer

susurrus [suːˈsʌrəs], **susurration** [ˌsuːsəˈreɪʃən] *n Literary* susurrement *m*

suttee [ˈsʌtiː] *n (tradition)* sati *m inv*; *(widow)* sati *f inv*

sutteeism [ˈsʌtiːɪzəm] *n* sati *m inv*

sutural [ˈsuːtʃərəl] *adj Anat & Bot* sutural

suture [ˈsuːtʃə(r)] **1** *n* (**a**) *Med* point *m* de suture (**b**) *Anat & Bot* suture *f*
2 *vt Med* suturer

suzerain [ˈsuːzəreɪn] **1** *n* (**a**) *Hist* suzerain(e) *m,f* (**b**) *Pol (state)* État *m* dominant
2 *adj* (**a**) *Hist* suzerain (**b**) *Pol (state, power)* dominant
►► ***suzerain lord*** suzerain *m*

suzeraine [ˈsuːzəreɪn] *n* suzeraine *f*

suzerainty [ˈsuːzərəntɪ] *n* (**a**) *(power)* suzeraineté *f*, dominance *f*; **under the suzerainty of** sous la suzeraineté de (**b**) *Hist (domain)* suzeraineté *f*

svelte [svelt] *adj* svelte

Svengali [ˌsveŋˈgɑːlɪ] *n* manipulateur *m*

SVGA [ˌesviːˌdʒiːˈeɪ] *n Comput (abbr* **super video graphics array***)* SVGA *m*
►► ***SVGA monitor*** moniteur *m* SVGA

SVQ [ˌesviːˈkjuː] *n (abbr* **Scottish Vocational Qualification***)* = diplôme de formation professionnelle sur le lieu de travail délivré en Écosse

SW (**a**) *(written abbr* **short wave***)* OC (**b**) *(written abbr* **south-west***)* S-O

swab [swɒb] *(pt & pp* **swabbed**, *cont* **swabbing***)* **1** *n* (**a**) *Med (cotton)* tampon *m*; *(specimen)* prélèvement *m* (**b**) *(mop)* serpillière *f* (**c**) *(brush for firearms)* écouvillon *m*
2 *vt* (**a**) *Med (clean)* nettoyer (avec un tampon) (**b**) *(mop)* laver; **to swab down the decks** laver le pont

►**swab out** *vt sep Mil (firearm)* écouvillonner; *Med (wound)* nettoyer avec un tampon

Swabia [ˈsweɪbɪə] *n* Souabe *f*; **in Swabia** en Souabe

swacked [swækt] *adj Am Fam (drunk)* bourré, fait

swaddle [ˈswɒdəl] *vt* (**a**) *(wrap)* envelopper, emmitoufler; **swaddled in blankets** enveloppé *ou* emmitouflé dans des couvertures; **her head was swaddled in bandages** elle avait la tête enveloppée de pansements (**b**) *Arch (baby)* emmailloter

swaddling clothes [ˈswɒdlɪŋ-] *npl Arch or Bible* maillot *m*, langes *mpl*; **the infant was wrapped in swaddling clothes** le nourrisson était emmailloté

swag [swæg] *Fam* **1** *n* (**a**) *Br (booty)* butin❑ *m* (**b**) *Austr & NZ (bundle)* baluchon *m*, balluchon *m*; **to go on the swag** vagabonder❑ (**c**) *Austr & NZ* **swags of** *(lots of)* un tas de, une flopée de
2 *vi Austr & NZ (roam)* vagabonder❑

swage [sweɪdʒ] *Metal* **1** *n* (**a**) *(tool, die)* emboutissoir *m* (**b**) *(moulding)* cannelure *f ou* rainure *f* circulaire
2 *vt* emboutir
►► ***swage block*** tas-étampe *m*

swagger [ˈswægə(r)] **1** *vi* (**a**) *(strut)* se pavaner; **he swaggered into/out of the room** il entra dans/sortit de la pièce en se pavanant (**b**) *(boast)* se vanter, fanfaronner, plastronner
2 *n (manner)* air *m* arrogant; *(walk)* démarche *f* arrogante; **he entered the room with a swagger** il entra dans la pièce en se pavanant
►► ***swagger cane, swagger stick*** *(gen)* badine *f*, canne *f*; *Mil* bâton *m* (d'officier)

swaggering [ˈswægərɪŋ] **1** *adj (gait, attitude)* arrogant; *(person)* fanfaron, bravache
2 *n (proud gait)* démarche *f ou* allure *f* arrogante; *(boasting)* vantardise *f*

swaggeringly [ˈswægərɪŋlɪ] *adv* d'un air arrogant

swagman [ˈswægmæn] *(pl* **swagmen** [-men]*)* *n Austr & NZ Fam* clochard❑ *m*

Swahili [swɑːˈhiːlɪ] **1** *n* (**a**) *Ling* swahili *m*, souahéli *m* (**b**) *(person)* Swahili(e) *m,f*, Souahéli(e) *m,f*
2 *adj* swahili, souahéli

swain [sweɪn] *n Arch (young man)* jeune homme *m* de la campagne; *(lover)* soupirant *m*

Swainson's thrush [ˈsweɪnsənz-] *n Orn* grive *f* de Swainson

SWALK [swɔːk] *n Fam (abbr* **sealed with a loving kiss***)* ≃ doux baisers *(écrit sur une enveloppe contenant une lettre d'amour)*

swallow [ˈswɒləʊ] **1** *vt* (**a**) *(food, drink, medicine)* avaler; **he almost swallowed his tongue** il a failli avaler sa langue
(**b**) *Fam (believe)* avaler❑, croire❑; **she swallowed the story whole** elle a avalé *ou* cru toute l'histoire; **he'll swallow anything** il avalerait n'importe quoi; **I find it hard to swallow** j'ai du mal à avaler ça
(**c**) *(accept unprotestingly)* avaler, accepter; **I find it hard to swallow** je trouve ça un peu raide; **I'm not going to swallow that sort of treatment** pas question que j'accepte d'être traité de cette façon
(**d**) *(repress)* ravaler; **to swallow one's anger/disappointment** ravaler sa colère/sa déception; **he had to swallow his pride** il a dû ravaler sa fierté
(**e**) *(retract)* **to swallow one's words** ravaler ses paroles
(**f**) *(absorb)* engloutir; **they were soon swallowed by the crowd** la foule eut tôt fait de les engloutir; **I wished the ground would open up and swallow me** j'aurais voulu être à six pieds sous terre
2 *vi* avaler, déglutir; **it hurts when I swallow** j'ai mal quand j'avale; **she swallowed hard and continued her speech** elle avala sa salive et poursuivit son discours
3 *n* (**a**) *(action)* gorgée *f*; **she took a long swallow of champagne** elle prit *ou* but une grande gorgée de champagne; **he finished his drink with one swallow** il finit sa boisson d'un trait *ou* d'un seul coup
(**b**) *Orn* hirondelle *f*; *Prov* **one swallow doesn't make a summer** une hirondelle ne fait pas le printemps
►► *Br* ***swallow dive*** saut *m* de l'ange; *Br* ***swallow hole*** gouffre *m*, aven *m*

►**swallow up** *vt sep* engloutir; **the Baltic States were swallowed up by the Soviet Union** les pays Baltes ont été engloutis par l'Union soviétique; **they were soon swallowed up in the mist** ils furent bientôt noyés dans la brume; **they were swallowed up in the crowd** ils ont disparu dans la foule

swallow-dive *vi Br* faire le saut de l'ange

swallowtail [ˈswɒləʊteɪl] *n* (**a**) *(forked tail)* queue *f* fourchue (**b**) *Fam Old-fashioned (coat)* queue-de-morue *f* (**c**) *Entom* **swallowtail (butterfly)** machaon *m*

swallow-tailed *adj* (**a**) *(bird)* à queue fourchue (**b**) *(coat)* à queue de morue

swam [swæm] *pt of* **swim**

swami [ˈswɑːmɪ] *(pl* **swamis** *or* **swamies***)* *n* swami *m*

swamp [swɒmp] **1** *n* marais *m*, marécage *m*
2 *vt* (**a**) *(flood)* inonder; *(cause to sink)* submerger
(**b**) *(overwhelm)* inonder, submerger; **she was swamped with calls** elle a été submergée d'appels; **we're swamped (with work) at the office at the moment** nous sommes débordés de travail au bureau en ce moment
►► *Am* ***swamp buggy*** *(boat)* hydroglisseur *m*; *(tractor)* tracteur *m* amphibie; *Am* ***swamp fever*** *(malaria)* paludisme *m*, malaria *f*

swampland [ˈswɒmplænd] *n (UNCOUNT)* marécages *mpl*, terrain *m* marécageux

swampy [ˈswɒmpɪ] *(compar* **swampier**, *superl* **swampiest***)* *adj* marécageux

swan [swɒn] *(pt & pp* **swanned**, *cont* **swanning***)* **1** *n* cygne *m*; **the Swan of Avon** = surnom donné à Shakespeare
2 *vi Br Fam* **they spent a year swanning round Europe** ils ont passé une année à se balader en Europe; **where's he swanning off to now?** où est-ce qu'il va encore traîner?; **they swanned off to the pub** ils sont tranquillement allés au pub❑; **he came swanning into the office at ten o' clock** il est arrivé au bureau comme si de rien n'était à dix heures❑; **he just swans around the office all day** il ne fait que musarder dans le bureau toute la journée❑; **don't think you can come swanning back just when you feel like it** ne crois pas que tu peux revenir les mains dans les poches quand tu en as envie
►► *Am* ***swan dive*** saut *m* de l'ange; ***swan neck*** col-de-cygne *m*

♫

'Swan Lake' *Tchaikovsky* 'Le Lac des cygnes'

Swanee [ˈswɒnɪ] *n Br Fam Old-fashioned* **to go down the Swanee** *(plan)* tomber à l'eau

swank [swæŋk] *Fam* **1** *n Br* (**a**) *(boasting)* frime *f*; **ignore him, it's all swank** ne fais pas attention à lui, tout ça c'est de la frime (**b**) *(boastful person)* frimeur(euse) *m,f* (**c**) *Am (luxury)* luxe❑ *m*, chic❑ *m*; **it's got lots of swank!** ça a une de ces classes!
2 *vi* se vanter❑, frimer
3 *adj* (**a**) *(chic)* classe *(inv)*, chicos (**b**) *(boastful)* frimeur

swanky [ˈswæŋkɪ] *(compar* **swankier**, *superl* **swankiest***)* *adj Fam* (**a**) *(chic)* classe *(inv)*, chicos (**b**) *(boastful)* frimeur

swan-necked *adj Br* (**a**) *(person)* au cou de cygne (**b**) *(object)* en col-de-cygne

swannery [ˈswɒnərɪ] *(pl* **swanneries***)* *n* réserve *f* de cygnes

swansdown [ˈswɒnzdaʊn] *n* (**a**) *(feathers)* duvet *m* de cygne (**b**) *Tex* molleton *m*

swansong [ˈswɒnsɒŋ] *n* chant *m* du cygne

swan-upping [ˈ-ʌpɪŋ] *n Br* = recensement et marquage annuels des cygnes de la Tamise appartenant à la Couronne

swap [swɒp] *(pt & pp* **swapped**, *cont* **swapping***)* **1** *vt* (**a**) *(possessions, places)* échanger; **to swap sth for sth** échanger qch contre qch; **I'll swap my coat for yours, I'll swap coats with you** échangeons nos manteaux; **(I'll) swap you!** je te l'échange!; **they've swapped places** ils ont échangé leurs places; **he swapped places with his sister** il a échangé sa place contre celle de sa sœur; **I wouldn't swap places with him for love nor money** je ne voudrais être à sa place pour rien au monde; **I'd swap jobs with him any day!** j'échangerais mon travail contre le sien sans hésiter!; **as soon as the music stops, everybody swap partners** dès que la musique s'arrête, tout le monde change de cavalier
(**b**) *(ideas, opinions)* échanger; **they meet to swap stories about the war** ils se rencontrent pour échanger des histoires de guerre; **they swapped insults over the garden fence** ils échangèrent des insultes par-dessus la clôture du jardin
(**c**) *St Exch* swaper
2 *vi* échanger, faire un échange *ou* un troc; **I'll swap with you** on échangera, on fera un échange
3 *n* (**a**) *(exchange)* troc *m*, échange *m*; **to do a swap** faire un troc *ou* un échange; **it's a good swap** c'est un échange avantageux; **I gave her my bicycle as a swap for hers** je lui ai donné mon vélo en échange du sien
(**b**) *(duplicate → stamp in collection etc)* double *m*
(**c**) *St Exch* swap *m*, échange *m* financier
►► *Banking* ***swap agreements*** accords *mpl* d'échanges; *Banking* ***swap facilities*** facilités *fpl* de crédits réciproques; *Am* ***swap meet*** foire *f* au troc; ***swap shop*** foire *f* au troc, magasin *m* de troc

►**swap over, swap round** **1** *vt sep* échanger, intervertir; **she swapped their glasses over** *or* **round when he left the room** elle échangea leurs verres quand il quitta la pièce
2 *vi* **do you mind swapping over** *or* **round so I can sit next to Max?** est-ce que ça te dérange qu'on échange nos places pour que je puisse m'asseoir à côté de Max?

SWAPO [ˈswɑːpəʊ] *n (abbr* **South West Africa People's Organization***)* SWAPO *f*

sward [swɔːd] *n Arch or Literary* gazon *m*, pelouse *f*

swarf [swɔːf] *n (UNCOUNT)* ébarbures *fpl*, limaille *f*

Swarfega® [swɔːˈfiːgə] *n* = gel nettoyant pour les mains

swarm [swɔːm] **1** *n* (**a**) *(of bees)* essaim *m*; *(of ants)* colonie *f*

(**b**) *Fig (of people)* essaim *m*, nuée *f*, masse *f*; **surrounded by a swarm of admirers** entouré d'une foule d'admirateurs

2 *vi* (**a**) *(bees)* essaimer

(**b**) *Fig (place)* fourmiller, grouiller; **the streets were swarming with people** les rues grouillaient de monde

(**c**) *Fig (people)* affluer; **the crowd swarmed in/out** la foule s'est engouffrée à l'intérieur/est sortie en masse; **bargain-hunters swarmed into the department store** les chercheurs d'occasions envahirent le grand magasin; **children were swarming round the ice-cream van** les enfants s'agglutinaient autour du camion du marchand de glaces

(**d**) *(climb)* grimper (lestement); **she swarmed up the tree** elle grimpa lestement à l'arbre

swarming ['swɔːmɪŋ] *n (in beekeeping)* essaimage *m*

swarthiness ['swɔːðɪnɪs] *n* teint *m* basané

swarthy ['swɔːðɪ] *(compar* **swarthier,** *superl* **swarthiest)** *adj* basané; **he has a swarthy complexion** il a le teint basané

swash [swɒʃ] **1** *n (splash)* clapotis *m*

2 *vi* clapoter

swashbuckler ['swɒʃˌbʌklə(r)] *n* (**a**) *(adventurer)* aventurier(ère) *m,f*; *(swaggerer)* fier-à-bras *m*, matamore *m* (**b**) *(film)* film *m* de cape et d'épée; *(novel)* roman *m* de cape et d'épée

swashbuckling ['swɒʃˌbʌklɪŋ] *adj (person)* fanfaron; *(film, story)* de cape et d'épée

swashplate ['swɒʃpleɪt] *n Aut* plateau *m* oscillant

swastika ['swɒstɪkə] *n Antiq* svastika *m*; *(Nazi)* croix *f* gammée

swat [swɒt] *(pt & pp* **swatted,** *cont* **swatting)** **1** *vt* (**a**) *(insect)* écraser (**b**) *Fam (slap)* frapper ❑

2 *n* (**a**) *(device)* tapette *f* (**b**) *(swipe)* **he took a swat at the mosquito** il essaya d'écraser le moustique (**c**) *Fam* = **swot**

swatch [swɒtʃ] *n* échantillon *m*

swath [swɔːθ] = **swathe** *n*

swathe [sweɪð] **1** *vt* (**a**) *(bind)* envelopper, emmailloter; **his head was swathed in bandages** sa tête était enveloppée de pansements; **she lay in bed swathed in blankets** elle était dans son lit, enveloppée *ou* emmitouflée dans des couvertures

(**b**) *(envelop)* envelopper; **swathed in mist** enveloppé de brume

2 *n* (**a**) *Agr* andain *m*

(**b**) *(strip of land)* bande *f* de terre; **the army cut a swathe through the town** l'armée a tout détruit sur son passage dans la ville; **the new motorway cuts a swathe through the countryside** la nouvelle autoroute coupe à travers la campagne; **she cut a swathe through the opposition** elle a fait des ravages dans les rangs de l'opposition

(**c**) *(strip of cloth)* lanière *f*

swatter ['swɒtə(r)] *n* tapette *f (à mouches)*

sway [sweɪ] **1** *vi* (**a**) *(pylon, bridge)* se balancer, osciller; *(tree)* s'agiter; *(bus, train)* pencher; *(boat)* rouler; *(person → deliberately)* se balancer; *(→ from tiredness, drink)* chanceler, tituber; **the poplars swayed in the wind** les peupliers étaient agités par le vent; **they were swaying to the music** ils se balançaient au rythme de la musique; **to sway from side to side** se balancer de droite à gauche; **to sway to and fro** se balancer d'avant en arrière

(**b**) *(vacillate)* vaciller, hésiter; *(incline, tend)* pencher; **to sway between two opinions** vaciller *ou* hésiter entre deux opinions; **to sway towards conservatism** pencher vers le conservatisme

2 *vt* (**a**) *(pylon)* (faire) balancer, faire osciller; *(tree)* agiter; *(hips)* rouler, balancer; **they started swaying their bodies in time to the music** ils ont commencé à se balancer au rythme de la musique

(**b**) *(influence)* influencer; **to sway sb from his/her course** détourner qn de ses projets; **to refuse to be swayed** refuser de se laisser influencer; **his plea for mercy did not sway the judge** sa demande de clémence n'a pas influencé le juge; **don't be swayed by his charm** ne te laisse pas influencer par son charme

(**c**) *Arch (rule)* régner sur

3 *n* (**a**) *(rocking → gen)* balancement *m*; *(→ of a boat)* roulis *m*

(**b**) *(influence)* influence *f*, emprise *f*, empire *m*; **under her sway** sous son empire, sous son influence; **to hold sway over sb/sth** avoir de l'influence *ou* de l'emprise sur qn/qch; **the economic theories that hold sway today** les théories économiques qui ont cours aujourd'hui

swaying ['sweɪɪŋ] **1** *adj* qui se balance de-ci de-là, qui oscille; **swaying motion** balancement *m*, mouvement *m* de va-et-vient

2 *n (motion)* balancement *m*, mouvement *m* de va-et-vient; *(of bridge, pylon)* balancement *m*, oscillation *f*; *(of boat, car)* roulis *m*; *(of person → deliberate)* balancement *m*; *(→ from tiredness, drink)* vacillement *m*

Swazi ['swɑːzɪ] *n* Swazi *mf*

Swaziland ['swɑːzɪlænd] *n* Swaziland *m*; **in Swaziland** au Swaziland

swear [sweə(r)] *(pt* **swore** [swɔː(r)], *pp* **sworn** [swɔːn]) **1** *vi* (**a**) *(curse)* jurer; **to swear at sb** injurier qn; **they started swearing at each other** ils ont commencé à se traiter de tous les noms *ou* à s'injurier; **don't swear in front of the children** ne dis pas de gros mots devant les enfants; **to swear like a trooper** jurer comme un charretier

(**b**) *(vow, take an oath)* jurer; **he swore on the Bible** il jura sur la Bible; **she swore on her honour/on her mother's grave** elle jura sur l'honneur/sur la tombe de sa mère; **I can't swear to its authenticity** je ne peux pas jurer de son authenticité; **I would swear to it** j'en jurerais; **I wouldn't swear to it, but I think it was him** je n'en jurerais pas, mais je crois que c'était lui; **I swear I'll never do it again!** je jure de ne plus jamais recommencer!; **he swears he's never seen her before** il jure qu'il ne l'a jamais vue; **did YOU break it? – no, I swear I didn't** c'est toi qui l'as cassé? – je vous jure que non *ou* que ce n'est pas moi; **it wasn't me, I swear!** ce n'était pas moi, je le jure!; **they swore to defend the family honour** ils jurèrent de défendre l'honneur de la famille

2 *vt* (**a**) *(pledge, vow)* **to swear an oath** prêter serment; **to swear allegiance to the Crown** jurer allégeance à la couronne; *Law* **to swear a charge against sb** faire une déposition sous serment contre qn

(**b**) *(make pledge)* **to swear sb to secrecy** faire jurer à qn de garder le secret

▸▸ *Br* ***swear box*** boîte *f* à gros mots *(dans laquelle on est censé mettre, en guise de punition, une pièce de monnaie à chaque fois que l'on jure)*

▸**swear by** *vt insep* (**a**) *(invoke)* jurer par; **to swear by one's honour** jurer sur l'honneur; **to swear by all that one holds sacred** jurer sur tout ce qu'on a de plus sacré

(**b**) *(have confidence in)* **she swears by that old sewing machine of hers** elle ne jure que par sa vieille machine à coudre; **you should try honey and hot milk for your cold, my mother swears by it** pour ton rhume, tu devrais essayer du miel dans du lait chaud, ma mère ne jure que par ça

▸**swear in** *vt sep (witness, president)* faire prêter serment à, *Formal* assermenter

▸**swear off** *vt insep Fam* renoncer à ❑; **he has sworn off drinking** il a renoncé à l'alcool *ou* arrêté de boire

▸**swear out** *vt sep Am Law* **he swore out a warrant for Baker's arrest** il a témoigné sous serment afin de faire arrêter Baker

swearer ['sweərə(r)] *n* = personne qui prête serment; *Law* jureur *m*

swearing ['sweərɪŋ] *n* (**a**) *(use of swearwords)* jurons *mpl*, gros mots *mpl*; **there's too much swearing on television** il y a trop de grossièretés à la télévision (**b**) *Law* **after the swearing in of the jury** après que le jury eut prêté serment

swearword ['sweəwɜːd] *n* grossièreté *f*, juron *m*, gros mot *m*

sweat [swet] *(Br pt & pp* **sweated,** *Am pt & pp* **sweat** *or* **sweated)** **1** *n* (**a**) *(perspiration)* sueur *f*, transpiration *f*; **sweat was dripping from his forehead** son front était ruisselant de sueur; **I woke up covered in sweat** je me suis réveillé en nage *ou* couvert de sueur *ou* tout en sueur; **the sweat was pouring off him** il dégoulinait de sueur; **to break out in** *or* **to come out in a cold sweat** avoir des sueurs froides; **she earned it by the sweat of her brow** elle l'a gagné à la sueur de son front

(**b**) *Fam (unpleasant task)* corvée ❑ *f*; *Br* **picking strawberries is a real sweat** la cueillette des fraises est une vraie corvée; **can you give me a hand? – no sweat!** peux-tu me donner un coup de main? – pas de problème!

(**c**) *Br Fam (anxious state)* **to work oneself (up) into a sweat (about sth)** se faire du mauvais sang (au sujet de qch); **there's no need to get into a sweat about it!** pas la peine de te mettre dans des états pareils!

(**d**) *(on wall, surface)* suintement *m*

(**e**) *Br Fam Old-fashioned* **(old) sweat** *(old soldier)* vieux soldat *m*; *(experienced worker)* vieux routier *m*

(**f**) *Am (sweatshirt)* sweat *m*

2 *vi* (**a**) *(perspire)* suer, transpirer; **the effort made him sweat** l'effort l'a mis en sueur; **she was sweating profusely** elle suait à grosses gouttes; *Fam* **to sweat like a pig** suer comme un bœuf

(**b**) *Fig (work hard, suffer)* suer; **my mother sweated over a hot stove from morning till night** ma mère suait sur ses fourneaux du matin jusqu'au soir; **I'll make them sweat for this!** ils vont me le payer!; **she's sweating over her homework** elle est en train de suer sur ses devoirs

(**c**) *Fam (worry)* se faire de la bile, se faire un sang d'encre; **I was sweating in case he found out what I'd done** j'avais la trouille qu'il découvre ce que j'avais fait; **I'm going to leave him to sweat for a while** je vais le laisser mijoter un peu

(**d**) *(ooze → walls, surface)* suer, suinter; *(→ cheese)* suer

3 *vt* (**a**) *(cause to perspire)* faire suer *ou* transpirer; **the doctor recommended sweating the patient** le médecin recommanda de faire transpirer le malade

(**b**) *(exude) Fig* **to sweat blood** suer sang et eau; **he sweated blood over this article** il a sué sang et eau sur cet article; *Fam* **to sweat buckets** suer comme un bœuf

(**c**) *Am Fam (extort)* **we sweated the information out of him** on lui a fait cracher le morceau

(**d**) *Culin* faire suer

(**e**) *Am Fam (idioms)* **don't sweat it!** pas de panique!; *Fam* **don't sweat the small stuff!** n'en fais pas tout un plat!

▸▸ *Anat* ***sweat duct*** conduit *m* sudorifère; *Am Fam Fin* ***sweat equity*** plus-value ❑ *f (acquise grâce à des améliorations, au travail fourni etc)*; ***sweat gland*** glande *f* sudoripare; ***sweat suit*** survêtement *m*, jogging *m*

▸**sweat off** *vt sep* éliminer; **you should do some exercise to sweat off those excess pounds** tu devrais faire un peu d'exercice pour éliminer ces kilos superflus

▸**sweat out** *vt sep* (**a**) *(illness)* **stay in bed and try to sweat out the cold** restez au lit et essayez de transpirer pour faire partir votre rhume

(**b**) *(idiom)* **to sweat it out** prendre son mal en patience, tenir jusqu'au bout; **leave him to sweat it out** laissez-le se débrouiller tout seul

sweatband ['swetbænd] *n* (**a**) *Sport (headband)* bandeau *m*; *(wristband)* poignet *m* (**b**) *(in a hat)* cuir *m* intérieur

sweated ['swetɪd] *adj*

▸▸ ***sweated labour*** *(staff)* main-d'œuvre *f* exploitée; *(work)* exploitation *f*

sweater ['swetə(r)] *n* pull-over *m*, pull *m*

sweatiness ['swetɪnɪs] *n* moiteur *f*

sweating ['swetɪŋ] *n* transpiration *f*, *Spec* sudation *f*; **the illness can cause heavy sweating** la maladie peut provoquer une transpiration abondante *ou* des sueurs abondantes

sweatpants ['swetpænts] *npl* pantalon *m* de survêtement

sweats [swets] *npl Am Fam* survêt *m*

sweatshirt ['swetʃɜːt] *n* sweat-shirt *m*

sweatshop ['swetʃɒp] *n* ≃ atelier *m* clandestin;

Fig Hum **it's a real sweatshop here** c'est le bagne ici

sweaty ['swetɪ] *(compar* **sweatier,** *superl* **sweatiest)** *adj* (**a**) *(person)* (tout) en sueur; *(hands)* moite; *(feet)* qui transpire; *(clothing)* trempé de sueur; **he's got sweaty feet** il transpire des pieds; **his uniform smelt sweaty** son uniforme sentait la sueur

(**b**) *(weather, place)* d'une chaleur humide *ou* moite; **she went back into the sweaty workshop** elle replongea dans la chaleur humide de l'atelier

(**c**) *(cheese)* qui sue

(**d**) *(activity)* qui fait transpirer; **it was a hard, sweaty climb** l'ascension était rude et donnait chaud

Swede [swi:d] *n* Suédois(e) *m,f*

swede [swi:d] *n Br* rutabaga *m*, chou-navet *m*

Sweden ['swi:dən] *n* Suède *f*; **in Sweden** en Suède

Swedish ['swi:dɪʃ] **1** *npl* **the Swedish** les Suédois *mpl*

2 *n Ling* suédois *m*

3 *adj* suédois

Sweeney ['swi:nɪ] *n Br Fam* **the Sweeney** = la brigade volante de Scotland Yard

sweeny ['swi:nɪ] *n Vet* atrophie *f* musculaire de l'épaule *(chez le cheval)*

sweep [swi:p] *(pt & pp* **swept** [swept]) **1** *n* (**a**) *(with a brush)* coup *m* de balai; **the room needs a good sweep** la pièce aurait besoin d'un bon coup de balai

(**b**) *(movement)* **with a sweep of her arm** d'un geste large; **with a sweep of his sword/scythe** d'un grand coup d'épée/de faux; **to make a wide sweep to take a bend** prendre du champ pour effectuer un virage; **her eyes made a sweep of the room** elle parcourut la pièce des yeux; **they jumped over the wall between two sweeps of the searchlight** ils sautèrent par-dessus le mur entre deux mouvements du projecteur; **in** *or* **at one sweep** d'un seul coup

(**c**) *(curved line, area)* (grande) courbe *f*, étendue *f*; *Archit (of arch)* courbure *f*; **a vast sweep of woodland** une vaste étendue de forêt; **from where we stood, we could see the whole sweep of the bay** de là où nous étions, nous voyions toute (l'étendue de) la baie; **the sweep of a car's lines** le galbe d'une voiture

(**d**) *(range → of gun, telescope)* champ *m*; *(→ of lighthouse)* balayage *m*, portée *f*; *(→ of wings)* envergure *f*; *(→ of knowledge)* étendue *f*; *(→ of opinion)* éventail *m*; **the members of the commission represent a broad sweep of opinion** les membres de la commission représentent un large éventail d'opinions

(**e**) *(search)* fouille *f*; *Mil (reconnaissance)* reconnaissance *f*; *Mil (attack)* attaque *f*; **police made a drugs sweep on the university** la police a ratissé l'université à la recherche de drogues; **the rescue party made a sweep of the area** l'équipe de secours a ratissé les environs *ou* passé les environs au peigne fin; **to make a sweep for mines** chercher des mines

(**f**) *(chimney sweep)* ramoneur *m*

(**g**) *Fam (sweepstake)* sweepstake ❑ *m*

(**h**) *Electron (by electron beam)* balayage *m*

(**i**) [illegible] rapide

(**j**) *Aviat* flèche *f*; **to vary the angle of sweep** varier la flèche

2 *adj (in rowing)* en pointe

3 *vt* (**a**) *(with a brush → room, street, dust, leaves)* balayer; *(→ chimney)* ramoner; **to sweep the floor** balayer le sol; **he swept the room** il a balayé la pièce; **the steps had been swept clean** quelqu'un avait balayé l'escalier; **she swept the leaves from the path into a pile** elle balaya les feuilles du chemin et les mit en tas; **I swept the broken glass into the dustpan** j'ai poussé le verre cassé dans la pelle avec le balai; *Br Fig* **to sweep sth under the carpet** *or* **the rug** tirer le rideau sur qch

(**b**) *(with hand)* **he angrily swept the papers off the desk** d'un geste furieux, il balaya les papiers de dessus le bureau; **she swept the coins off the table into her handbag** elle a fait glisser les pièces de la table dans son sac à main

(**c**) *(of wind, tide, crowd etc)* **her dress sweeps the ground** sa robe balaie le sol; **a storm swept the town** un orage ravagea la ville; **the wind swept his hat into the river** le vent a fait tomber son chapeau dans la rivière; **the small boat was swept out to sea** le petit bateau a été emporté vers le large; **three fishermen were swept overboard** un paquet de mer emporta trois pêcheurs; *Fig* **the victorious army swept all before it** l'armée victorieuse a tout balayé sur son passage; **the incident swept all other thoughts from her mind** l'incident lui fit oublier tout le reste; **he was swept to power on a wave of popular discontent** il a été porté au pouvoir par une vague de mécontentement populaire; **he swept her off to Paris for the weekend** il l'a emmenée en week-end à Paris; **to be swept off one's feet** *(fall in love)* tomber fou amoureux; *(be filled with enthusiam)* être enthousiasmé; **to sweep the board** rafler tous les prix; **the German athletes swept the board at the Olympics** les athlètes allemands ont remporté toutes les médailles aux jeux Olympiques

(**d**) *(spread through → of fire, epidemic, rumour, belief)* gagner; **a new craze is sweeping America** une nouvelle mode fait fureur aux États-Unis; **a wave of fear swept the city** une vague de peur gagna la ville; **the flu epidemic which swept Europe in 1919** l'épidémie de grippe qui sévit en Europe en 1919

(**e**) *(scan, survey)* parcourir; **her eyes swept the horizon/the room** elle parcourut l'horizon/la pièce des yeux; **to sweep the horizon with a telescope** parcourir *ou* balayer l'horizon avec un télescope; **searchlights continually sweep the open ground outside the prison camp** des projecteurs parcourent *ou* balayent sans cesse le terrain qui entoure la prison

(**f**) *(win easily)* gagner *ou* remporter haut la main; **the Popular Democratic Party swept the polls** le parti démocratique populaire a fait un raz-de-marée aux élections; *Am Sport* **she swept the tournament** elle a gagné le tournoi sans concéder une seule partie

(**g**) *Naut (mines, sea, channel)* draguer; **the port has been swept for mines** le port a été dragué

4 *vi* (**a**) *(with a brush)* balayer

(**b**) *(move quickly, powerfully)* **harsh winds swept across the bleak steppes** un vent violent balayait les mornes steppes; **the beam swept across the sea** le faisceau lumineux balaya la mer; **I watched storm clouds sweeping across the sky** je regardais des nuages orageux filer dans le ciel; **a hurricane swept through the town** un ouragan a dévasté la ville; **the Barbarians who swept into the Roman Empire** les Barbares qui déferlèrent sur l'Empire romain; **a wave of nationalism swept through the country** une vague de nationalisme a déferlé sur le pays; **the memories came sweeping back** tous ces souvenirs me/lui/*etc* sont revenus à la mémoire; **a wave of panic swept over him** une vague de panique le submergea; **the planes swept low over the town** les avions passèrent en rase-mottes au-dessus de la ville; **the fire swept through the forest** l'incendie a ravagé la forêt

(**c**) *(move confidently, proudly)* **he swept into/out of the room** il entra/sortit majestueusement de la pièce; **she swept past me without even a glance** elle passa majestueusement à côté de moi sans même m'adresser un regard

(**d**) *(stretch → land)* s'étendre; **the rolling prairies sweep away into the distance** les prairies ondoyantes se perdent dans le lointain; **the fields sweep down to the lake** les prairies descendent en pente douce jusqu'au lac; **the river sweeps round in a wide curve** le fleuve décrit une large courbe

(**e**) *Naut* **to sweep for mines** draguer, déminer

▸▸ ***sweep boat*** bateau *m* en pointe; ***sweep hand*** trotteuse *f*; ***sweep rowing*** nage *f* en pointe

▸**sweep along** *vt sep (of wind, tide, crowd)* emporter, entraîner; **we were swept along by a tide of nationalism** nous avons été balayés par une vague nationaliste

▸**sweep aside** *vt sep* (**a**) *(object, person)* écarter

(**b**) *(advice, objection)* repousser, rejeter; *(obstacle, opposition)* écarter

▸**sweep away** *vt sep* (**a**) *(dust, snow)* balayer

(**b**) *(of wind, tide, crowd)* emporter, entraîner; **three bathers were swept away by a huge wave** trois baigneurs ont été emportés par une énorme vague

▸**sweep by** *vi (car)* passer à toute vitesse; *(person → majestically)* passer majestueusement; *(→ disdainfully)* passer dédaigneusement

▸**sweep down** *vi* (**a**) *(steps)* descendre; **hills sweeping down to the sea** des collines qui descendent vers la mer

(**b**) *(attack)* **the enemy swept down on us** l'ennemi s'abattit *ou* fonça sur nous

▸**sweep out** *vt sep (clean → room)* balayer

▸**sweep past** = **sweep by**

▸**sweep up 1** *vt sep (dust, leaves)* balayer; **she swept up the pieces of glass** elle balaya les morceaux de verre; **he swept the leaves up into a pile** il fit un tas des feuilles en les balayant; **with her hair swept up into a chignon** avec ses cheveux relevés en chignon; **she swept up her two babies and...** en toute hâte, elle prit ses deux bébés dans ses bras et...

2 *vi* (**a**) *(clean up)* balayer; **can you sweep up after the meeting?** peux-tu balayer *ou* peux-tu passer un coup de balai après la réunion?

(**b**) *(approach)* **she swept up to me** *(majestically)* elle s'approcha de moi d'un pas majestueux; *(angrily)* elle s'approcha de moi d'un pas furieux; **the car swept up to the main entrance** *(quickly)* la voiture s'approcha à toute allure de l'entrée principale; *(impressively)* la voiture s'approcha à une allure majestueuse de l'entrée principale

sweepback ['swi:pbæk] *n* flèche *f* (arrière)

sweeper ['swi:pə(r)] *n* (**a**) *(person)* balayeur(euse) *m,f* (**b**) *(device → for streets)* balayeuse *f*; *(→ for carpets)* balai *m* mécanique (**c**) *Ftbl* libero *m*

▸▸ ***sweeper van*** *(in cycle race)* voiture-balai *f*

sweeping ['swi:pɪŋ] **1** *adj* (**a**) *(wide → movement, curve)* large; **with a sweeping gesture** d'un geste large, d'un grand geste; **a sweeping view** une vue panoramique

(**b**) *(indiscriminate)* **a sweeping generalization** *or* **statement** une généralisation excessive; **he makes sweeping statements about the European mentality** il fait des généralisations abusives *ou* hâtives sur la mentalité européenne; **that's rather a sweeping generalization** là, vous généralisez un peu trop

(**c**) *(significant, large → amount)* considérable; **sweeping budget cuts** des coupes *fpl* sombres dans le budget; **the opposition has made sweeping gains** l'opposition a énormément progressé

(**d**) *(far-reaching → measure, change)* de grande portée, de grande envergure; **sweeping reforms** des réformes *fpl* de grande envergure

2 sweepings *npl* balayures *fpl*

sweepingly ['swi:pɪŋlɪ] *adv (describe, criticize)* de façon trop générale *ou* hâtive

sweepstake ['swi:psteɪk] *n* sweepstake *m*

sweet [swi:t] **1** *adj* (**a**) *(in taste)* sucré; *(wine)* moelleux; **this tea is too sweet for me** ce thé est trop sucré pour moi; **to taste sweet, to have a sweet taste** être sucré, avoir un goût sucré; **to have a sweet tooth** adorer les *ou* être friand de sucreries

(**b**) *(fresh, clean → air)* doux (douce); *(→ breath)* frais (fraîche); *(→ water)* pur

(**c**) *(fragrant → smell)* agréable, suave; **the roses smell so sweet!** les roses sentent si bon!; *Fig* **the sweet smell of success** l'ivresse *f* du succès; **to enjoy the sweet smell of success** goûter à l'ivresse du succès

(**d**) *(musical → sound, voice)* mélodieux; *(→ words)* doux (douce); **the sweet song of the lark** le chant mélodieux de l'alouette; **to whisper sweet nothings (in sb's ear)** murmurer des mots d'amour (à l'oreille de qn), *Old-fashioned* conter fleurette (à qn)

(**e**) *(pleasant, satisfactory → emotion, feeling, success)* doux (douce); **revenge is sweet** la vengeance est douce

(**f**) *(kind, generous)* gentil; **a sweet old lady** une vieille dame charmante; **it was very sweet of you** c'était très gentil de votre part; **how**

sweet of her to phone! comme elle est gentille d'avoir téléphoné!; *Br* **to keep sb sweet** cultiver les bonnes grâces de qn
(**g**) *(attractive, cute)* mignon, adorable; **what a sweet little baby/hat!** quel adorable bébé/chapeau!; **a sweet little dress** une gentille petite robe, une petite robe exquise
(**h**) *Br Fam Old-fashioned* **to be sweet on sb** *(in love)* avoir le béguin pour qn
(**i**) *Fam (as intensifier)* **he'll please his own sweet self, he'll go his own sweet way** il n'en fera qu'à sa tête; **she'll come in her own sweet time** elle viendra quand ça lui chantera; **you can bet your sweet life that something funny's going on!** tu peux être sûr qu'il se passe quelque chose de louche!❑; *Br very Fam* **sweet FA** rien du tout❑, que dalle
(**j**) *Fam (excellent)* génial, super
2 *n* (**a**) *Br (piece of confectionery)* bonbon *m*; **I don't really like sweets** je n'aime pas beaucoup les sucreries
(**b**) *Br (dessert)* dessert *m*; **what's for sweet?** qu'est-ce qu'il y a comme dessert?
(**c**) *(term of address)* **my sweet** mon (ma) chéri(e)
3 *exclam Fam* cool!, génial!
►► *Bot* ***sweet alyssum*** corbeille-d'argent *f*; *Bot* ***sweet bent*** luzule *f*; *Bot* ***sweet cherry*** merisier *m*; *Bot* ***sweet chestnut*** marron *m*; *Bot* ***sweet cicely*** cerfeuil *m* musqué *ou* d'Espagne; ***sweet cider*** *Am* jus *m* de pomme *(non fermenté)*; *Br* cidre *m* doux; *Bot* ***sweet pea*** pois *m* de senteur; ***sweet pepper*** poivron *m*; ***sweet potato*** patate *f* douce; *Am* ***sweet roll*** = sorte de pâtisserie fourrée; *Br* ***sweet shop*** confiserie *f*; *Fam* ***sweet talk*** *(UNCOUNT)* flatteries❑ *fpl*, paroles *fpl* mielleuses❑; *Bot* ***sweet violet*** violette *f* odorante; *Bot* ***sweet william*** œillet *m* de poète

sweet-and-sour *adj* aigre-doux (aigre-douce)
►► ***sweet-and-sour pork*** porc *m* à la sauce aigre-douce; ***sweet-and-sour sauce*** sauce *f* aigre-douce

sweetbread ['swi:tbred] *n Culin (thymus)* ris *m*; *(pancreas)* pancréas *m*

sweetbrier [,swi:t'braɪə(r)] *n Bot* églantier *m* odorant

sweetcorn ['swi:tkɔ:n] *n* maïs *m* doux

sweeten ['swi:tən] *vt* (**a**) *(food, drink)* sucrer; **sweetened with honey** sucré avec du miel
(**b**) *(mollify, soften)* **to sweeten (up)** amadouer, enjôler; **she tried to sweeten him (up) by taking him out to dinner** elle a essayé de l'amadouer en l'emmenant dîner au restaurant; **their remarks did nothing to sweeten my temper** leurs remarques n'ont rien fait pour apaiser ma colère
(**c**) *Fam (bribe)* graisser la patte à; **how much would it cost to sweeten (up) the committee?** combien ça coûterait de graisser la patte au comité?
(**d**) *(make more attractive → task)* adoucir; *(→ offer)* améliorer
(**e**) *(improve the odour of → air)* parfumer, embaumer; *(→ breath)* purifier; **the scent of roses sweetened the air** l'odeur des roses parfumait *ou* embaumait l'atmosphère

sweetener ['swi:tənə(r)] *n* (**a**) *(for food, drink)* édulcorant *m*, sucrette *f*; **artificial sweeteners** édulcorants *mpl* artificiels (**b**) *Br Fam (present)* cadeau❑ *m*; *(bribe)* pot-de-vin❑ *m*; **they gave him a bigger office as a sweetener** ils lui ont donné un plus grand bureau pour l'amadouer❑; **the government was accused of offering the company sweeteners** on a accusé le gouvernement de donner des pots-de-vin à la compagnie

sweetening ['swi:tənɪŋ] *n (UNCOUNT)* (**a**) *(substance)* édulcorant *m*, édulcorants *mpl* (**b**) *(process → of wine)* sucrage *m*; *(→ of water)* adoucissement *m*

sweetheart ['swi:thɑ:t] *n* (**a**) *(lover)* petit(e) ami(e) *m,f*; **they're sweethearts** ils sont amoureux; **they were childhood sweethearts** ils s'aimaient *ou* ils étaient amoureux quand ils étaient enfants
(**b**) *(term of address)* (mon (ma)) chéri(e) *m,f*
►► *Ind* ***sweetheart agreement*** = accord entre un employeur et des dirigeants syndicaux dont les termes sont favorables aux deux parties mais pas aux travailleurs concernés

sweetie ['swi:tɪ] *n Fam* (**a**) *(darling)* chéri(e) *m,f*, chou *m*; **he's a real sweetie** il est vraiment adorable; **what's the matter, sweetie?** qu'est-ce qu'il y a, mon chou? (**b**) *Br (sweet)* bonbon❑ *m*

sweetie-pie *n Fam (term of address)* mon (ma) chéri(e)

sweetish ['swi:tɪʃ] *adj* sucré; *(unpleasantly)* douceâtre

sweetly ['swi:tlɪ] *adv* (**a**) *(pleasantly, kindly)* gentiment; *(cutely)* d'un air mignon; **she smiled at him sweetly** elle lui sourit gentiment; **the child smiled at them sweetly** l'enfant leur adressa un joli sourire; **he was whispering sweetly in her ear** il lui chuchotait tendrement à l'oreille
(**b**) *(smoothly)* sans à-coups; *(accurately)* avec précision; **the engine was running sweetly** le moteur ronronnait; *Br* **he's starting to hit the ball more sweetly** il commence à frapper la balle avec plus de précision
(**c**) *(musically)* harmonieusement, mélodieusement; **she sings very sweetly** elle a une voix très mélodieuse

sweetmeal ['swi:tmi:l] *adj*
►► *Br* ***sweetmeal biscuit*** sablé *m* à la farine complète

sweetmeat ['swi:tmi:t] *n Old-fashioned or Literary* friandise *f*

sweetness ['swi:tnɪs] *n* (**a**) *(in taste)* goût *m* sucré; *(of wine)* (goût *m*) moelleux *m*
(**b**) *(freshness → of air)* douceur *f*; *(→ of breath)* fraîcheur *f*; *(→ of water)* pureté *f*
(**c**) *(fragrance)* parfum *m*
(**d**) *(musicality → of sound)* son *m* mélodieux; *(→ of voice, words)* douceur *f*
(**e**) *(pleasure, satisfaction)* douceur *f*; **the sweetness of revenge** le plaisir (exquis) de la vengeance
(**f**) *(kindness, generosity)* gentillesse *f*; **she's all sweetness and light** elle est on ne peut plus gentille

sweet-scented *adj* parfumé

sweet-smelling *adj (rose)* odorant; *(perfume)* sucré

sweetsop ['swi:tsɒp] *n Bot* annone *f*, anone *f*

sweet-talk *vt Fam* embobiner; **don't try to sweet-talk me!** n'essaie pas de m'embobiner!; **she sweet-talked him into doing it** elle l'a si bien embobiné qu'il a fini par le faire

sweet-tempered *adj* doux (douce), agréable

sweet-toothed *adj* qui adore les sucreries, qui est friand de sucreries

swell [swel] (*pt* **swelled**, *pp* **swelled** *or* **swollen** ['swəʊlən]) **1** *vi* (**a**) *(distend → wood, pulses etc)* gonfler; *(→ part of body)* enfler, gonfler; **the damp has made the wood swell** l'humidité a fait gonfler le bois; **he felt his lip begin to swell** il sentit sa lèvre enfler *ou* gonfler; *Fig* **her heart swelled with joy/pride** son cœur s'est gonflé de joie/d'orgueil
(**b**) *(increase)* augmenter; **the crowd swelled to nearly two hundred** la foule grossit et il y eut bientôt près de deux cents personnes
(**c**) *(well up → emotion)* monter, surgir; **I felt anger swell in me** je sentais la colère monter en moi
(**d**) *(rise → sea, tide)* monter; *(→ river)* se gonfler, grossir
(**e**) *(grow louder)* s'enfler; **the music swelled to its climax** la musique atteignit alors son point culminant
2 *vt* (**a**) *(distend)* gonfler; **the wind swelled the sails** le vent gonfla les voiles; **her eyes were swollen with tears** ses yeux étaient pleins de larmes
(**b**) *(increase)* augmenter, grossir; **she asked her friends to come along to swell the numbers** elle a demandé à ses amis de venir pour qu'il y ait plus de monde; **to swell the ranks of the unemployed** venir grossir les rangs des chômeurs
(**c**) *(cause to rise)* gonfler, grossir; **the rivers had been swollen by torrential rains** les cours d'eau avaient été gonflés *ou* grossis par des pluies torrentielles
3 *n* (**a**) *Naut* houle *f*; **there was a deep** *or* **heavy swell** il y avait une forte houle
(**b**) *(bulge)* gonflement *m*; **the swell of the sails** le gonflement des voiles
(**c**) *(increase)* augmentation *f*; *Mus* crescendo *m*
(**d**) *Mus (device)* soufflet *m*
(**e**) *Am Fam Old-fashioned (big shot)* gros bonnet *m*; *(dandy)* dandy *m*, gandin *m*; *(rich person)* personne *f* huppée, rupin *m*
4 *adj Am Fam Old-fashioned (great)* super, chouette; **she's a swell girl** c'est une chic fille; **we had a swell time** on s'est super bien amusés
5 *exclam Am Fam Old-fashioned* super!
►► *Mus* ***swell box*** boîte *f* expressive

►**swell out** **1** *vi* (se) gonfler
2 *vt sep* gonfler

►**swell up** = **swell** *vi* (**a**)

swell-headed *adj Fam* suffisant❑, qui a la grosse tête

swelling ['swelɪŋ] **1** *n* (**a**) *Med* enflure *f*, gonflement *m*; **they gave her something to relieve the swelling** ils lui ont donné quelque chose pour que ça désenfle; **there was some swelling around the ankle** la cheville était un peu enflée (**b**) *(increase)* augmentation *f*, grossissement *m*
2 *adj (increasing)* croissant; **the swelling numbers of the unemployed** le nombre croissant des chômeurs

swelter ['sweltə(r)] *vi (feel too hot)* étouffer de chaleur; *(sweat)* suer à grosses gouttes, être en nage

sweltering ['sweltərɪŋ] *adj (day, heat)* étouffant, oppressant; **it was simply sweltering in the kitchen** il faisait une chaleur vraiment étouffante dans la cuisine

swelteringly ['sweltərɪŋlɪ] *adv* **it's swelteringly hot** il fait une chaleur étouffante; **a swelteringly hot day** une journée étouffante

swept [swept] *pt & pp of* **sweep**

sweptback ['sweptbæk] *adj Aviat (wings)* en flèche

sweptwing ['sweptwɪŋ] *Aviat* **1** *adj (aircraft)* à ailes en flèche
2 *n* avion *m* à ailes en flèche

swerve [swɜ:v] **1** *vi* (**a**) *(car, driver, ship)* faire une embardée; *(ball)* dévier; *(aeroplane, bird, runner)* virer; **I had to swerve to avoid the cyclist** j'ai dû faire une embardée *ou* j'ai dû donner un coup de volant pour éviter le cycliste; **the cyclist was swerving in and out of the traffic** le cycliste zigzaguait entre les voitures; **the car swerved to the left/towards us/round the corner/off the road** la voiture fit une embardée vers la gauche/vira pour foncer droit vers nous/prit le virage brusquement/fit une embardée et quitta la chaussée
(**b**) *Fig (budge, deviate)* dévier; **she'll never swerve from her resolve** rien ne la détournera de sa résolution
2 *vt* (**a**) *(vehicle)* faire virer; *(ball)* faire dévier; **she swerved the car to the left** elle donna un coup de volant vers la gauche
(**b**) *Fig (person)* détourner, faire dévier; **no one can swerve him from his ambition** personne ne peut le détourner de ses ambitions
3 *n (by car, driver, ship)* embardée *f*; *(by aeroplane, bird, runner, ball)* déviation *f*

swift [swɪft] **1** *adj* (**a**) *(fast)* rapide; *Literary* **swift of foot** leste, rapide à la course; *Br Fam* **let's stop here for a swift half** arrêtons-nous ici pour boire un coup en vitesse
(**b**) *(prompt)* prompt, rapide; **swift to react** prompt à réagir; **she received a swift reply** elle reçut une réponse immédiate; **he is swift in finding fault** il a la critique facile; **the government was swift to deny the rumours** le gouvernement fut prompt à démentir les rumeurs; **she took swift revenge** elle n'a pas tardé à se venger; **he has a swift temper** il est très susceptible, il se fâche facilement
(**c**) *Am Fam (clever)* malin(igne)❑; **that was a real swift move** c'était bien joué
2 *n Orn* martinet *m*; *(Apus apus)* martinet *m* noir

swift-flowing *adj (river)* au cours rapide

swift-footed *adj Literary* leste, véloce

Swiftian ['swɪftɪən] *adj (of Swift)* de (Jonathan) Swift; *(characteristic of Swift)* à la manière de (Jonathan) Swift

swiftlet ['swɪftlət] *n Orn* salangane *m*

swiftly ['swɪftlɪ] *adv* (**a**) *(quickly)* rapidement, vite; **the meeting moved swiftly to its conclusion** la réunion se termina rapidement; **moving swiftly along!** passons! (**b**) *(promptly)* promptement, rapidement; **they reacted swiftly to the threat** ils réagirent promptement à la menace

swift-moving *adj* rapide

swiftness ['swɪftnɪs] *n* (**a**) *(speed)* rapidité *f* (**b**) *(promptness)* promptitude *f*, rapidité *f*; **the ambulance arrived with remarkable swiftness** l'ambulance arriva avec une rapidité remarquable

SWIFT transfer *n Fin* virement *m* SWIFT

swig [swɪg] *(pt & pp* **swigged,** *cont* **swigging)** *Fam*
1 *vt* lamper, siffler
2 *n* lampée *f*, coup *m*; **he took a swig of whisky** il a bu une lampée *ou* gorgée ❑ de whisky; **have a swig of this** bois un coup de ça; **he took a long swig at his bottle** il porta sa bouteille à sa bouche et but un grand coup

►**swig down** *vt sep Fam* vider d'un trait ❑, siffler

swill [swɪl] **1** *vt* (**a**) *Br (wash)* laver à grande eau; **he swilled the floor (down)** il a lavé le sol à grande eau; **go and swill the glass under the tap** va passer le verre sous le robinet
(**b**) *Fam (drink)* écluser
2 *n* (**a**) *(for pigs)* pâtée *f*
(**b**) *(wash)* lavage *m* à grande eau; **to give sth a swill out** laver *ou* rincer qch à grande eau

►**swill out** *vt sep esp Br (rinse)* laver à grande eau; **to swill out a basin** rincer une cuvette à grande eau

swim [swɪm] *(pt* **swam** [swæm], *pp* **swum** [swʌm], *cont* **swimming) 1** *vi* (**a**) *(fish, animal)* nager; *(person → gen)* nager; *(→ for amusement)* nager, se baigner; *(→ for sport)* nager, faire de la natation; **to go swimming** *(gen)* (aller) se baigner; *(in swimming pool)* aller à la piscine; **to swim for one's country** faire partie de l'équipe nationale de natation; **we went swimming in the lake** nous sommes allés nous baigner dans le lac; **she's learning to swim** elle apprend à nager; **I can't swim!** je ne sais pas nager!; **the lake was too cold to swim in** le lac était trop froid pour qu'on s'y baigne; **to swim across a river** traverser une rivière à la nage; **to swim upstream/downstream** monter/descendre le courant à la nage; **she swam away from/back to the shore** elle quitta/regagna la rive à la nage; **he managed to swim to safety** il a réussi à se sauver en nageant; **the raft sank and they had to swim for it** le radeau a coulé et ils ont été obligés de nager; *also Fig* **to swim against the tide** nager à contre-courant
(**b**) *(be soaked)* nager, baigner; **the salad was swimming in oil** la salade baignait dans l'huile; **the kitchen floor was swimming with water** le sol de la cuisine était inondé
(**c**) *(spin)* **my head is swimming** j'ai la tête qui tourne; **everything swam before my eyes** tout semblait tourner autour de moi
2 *vt* (**a**) *(river, lake etc)* traverser à la nage; **she swam the (English) Channel** elle a traversé la Manche à la nage
(**b**) *(a stroke)* nager; **can you swim butterfly?** est-ce que tu sais nager le papillon?
(**c**) *(distance)* nager; **she swam ten lengths** elle a fait dix longueurs
(**d**) *(animal)* **they swam their horses across the river** ils ont fait traverser la rivière à leurs chevaux (à la nage)
3 *n* (**a**) *(for leisure)* baignade *f*; *(for exercise)* nage *f*; **to go for a swim** *(gen)* (aller) se baigner; *(in swimming pool)* aller à la piscine; **he had his morning swim** il s'est baigné comme tous les matins; **I feel like a swim** j'ai envie d'aller me baigner; **did you have a nice swim?** *(for leisure)* tu t'es bien baigné?; *(for exercise)* tu as bien nagé?; **it's a good twenty-minute swim out to the island** il faut vingt bonnes minutes pour atteindre l'île à la nage; **it was a long hard swim back to the shore** ça a été long et difficile de regagner la rive à la nage
(**b**) *Fam Fig* **to be in the swim (of things)** être dans le coup

►► ***swim bladder*** vessie *f* natatoire

swimmer ['swɪmə(r)] *n (gen)* nageur(euse) *m,f*; *(for leisure)* baigneur(euse) *m,f*; **he's an excellent swimmer** c'est un excellent nageur, il nage très bien

swimming ['swɪmɪŋ] **1** *n (gen)* nage *f*; *Sport* natation *f*; **her doctor advised her to take up swimming** son médecin lui a conseillé la natation; **no swimming** *(sign)* baignade interdite
2 *comp (lesson, classes)* de natation

►► *Br* ***swimming bath, swimming baths*** piscine *f*; ***swimming cap*** bonnet *m* de bain; *Br* ***swimming costume*** maillot *m* de bain; ***swimming crab*** étrille *f*; ***swimming instructor*** maître-nageur *m*; ***swimming pool*** piscine *f*; ***swimming trunks*** maillot *m ou* slip *m* de bain

swimmingly ['swɪmɪŋlɪ] *adv Br Fam* à merveille ❑; **your mother and I are getting on swimmingly** nous nous entendons à merveille, ta mère et moi; **everything's going swimmingly** tout marche comme sur des roulettes

swimsuit ['swɪmsuːt] *n* maillot *m* de bain

swimwear ['swɪmweə(r)] *n (UNCOUNT)* maillots *mpl* de bain

swindle ['swɪndəl] **1** *vt* escroquer; **to swindle sb out of sth** escroquer qch à qn; **they were swindled out of all their savings** on leur a escroqué toutes leurs économies
2 *n* escroquerie *f*, vol *m*; **it's a real swindle** c'est une véritable escroquerie

swindler ['swɪndlə(r)] *n* escroc *m*

swine [swaɪn] *(pl sense* (**a**) **inv,** *pl sense* (**b**) **inv** *or* **swines)** *n* (**a**) *Literary (pig)* porc *m*, pourceau *m*
(**b**) *Br Fam (unpleasant person)* salaud *m*; **he's a lazy swine!** c'est une grosse feignasse!; **you (filthy) swine!** espèce de fumier!; **it's a swine of a job** c'est un sale boulot

►► ***swine fever*** peste *f* porcine

swineherd ['swaɪnhɜːd] *n* porcher(ère) *m,f*

swing [swɪŋ] *(pt & pp* **swung** [swʌŋ]) **1** *n* (**a**) *(to-and-fro movement, sway → gen)* balancement *m*; *(→ of pendulum)* oscillation *f*; **with a swing of his arm** en balançant son bras; **the swing of her hips** le balancement de ses hanches
(**b**) *(arc described)* arc *m*, courbe *f*; **the plane came round in a wide swing** l'avion décrivit une grande courbe
(**c**) *(swipe, attempt to hit)* (grand) coup *m*; **I took a swing at him** je lui ai décoché un coup de poing; **he took a swing at the ball** il essaya de frapper la balle
(**d**) *(hanging seat)* balançoire *f*; **they're playing on the swings** ils jouent sur les balançoires; *Br* **what you lose on the swings you gain on the roundabouts** ce que l'on perd d'un côté, on le récupère de l'autre; *Br* **it's swings and roundabouts really** en fait, on perd d'un côté ce qu'on gagne de l'autre
(**e**) *(in public opinion, voting)* revirement *m*; *(in prices, market)* fluctuation *f*; **his mood swings are very unpredictable** ses sautes d'humeur sont très imprévisibles; *Econ* **seasonal swings** fluctuations *fpl* saisonnières; *St Exch* **the upward/downward swing of the market** la fluctuation du marché vers le haut/le bas; **sudden swing in public opinion** revirement inattendu de l'opinion publique; **America experienced a major swing towards conservatism** les États-Unis ont connu un important revirement vers le conservatisme; **the party needs a 10 percent swing to win the election** le parti a besoin d'un revirement d'opinion de 10 pour cent pour gagner les élections
(**f**) *(in boxing, golf)* swing *m*
(**g**) *(rhythm → gen)* rythme *m*; *Mus (style of jazz)* swing *m*; **a swing band** un orchestre de swing; **the swing era** l'époque *f* du swing
(**h**) *Am Pol (tour)* tournée *f*; **on his swing around the circle, the President visited 35 States** pendant sa tournée électorale, le Président a visité 35 États
(**i**) *Fam (idioms)* **to get into the swing of things** se mettre dans le bain; **it'll be a lot easier once you've got into the swing of things** ce sera beaucoup plus facile une fois que tu seras dans le bain; **to go with a swing** *(music)* être très rythmé *ou* entraînant ❑; *(party)* swinguer; *(business)* marcher très bien ❑
2 *vt* (**a**) *(cause to sway)* balancer; **she was swinging her umbrella as she walked** elle marchait en balançant son parapluie; **he walked along swinging his arms** il marchait en balançant les bras; **to swing one's hips** balancer les *ou* rouler des hanches; *Fig* **to swing the lead** tirer au flanc
(**b**) *(move from one place to another, in a curve)* **she swung her bag onto the back seat** elle jeta son sac sur le siège arrière; **he swung a rope over a branch** il lança une corde par-dessus une branche; **the crane swung the cargo onto the wharf** la grue pivota pour déposer la cargaison sur le quai; **he swung his son (up) onto his shoulders** il hissa son fils sur ses épaules; **I swung myself (up) into the saddle** j'ai sauté en selle; **she swung the door shut** elle ferma la porte; **he swung the axe in a wide arc** il leva la hache avec un large mouvement du bras; **she swung the bat at the ball** elle essaya de frapper la balle avec sa batte; **I swung the club at him** j'ai essayé de le frapper avec le gourdin; **to swing the ball** *(in cricket)* faire dévier la balle en l'air
(**c**) *(suspend → hammock)* suspendre, pendre, accrocher
(**d**) *(turn → steering wheel)* (faire) tourner; *(→ vehicle)* faire virer; **the helmsman swung the wheel to port** le timonier fit tourner la roue à bâbord; **I swung the lorry through 180°** j'ai pris le virage à 180° (avec le camion)
(**e**) *(cause to change)* **to swing the voters** faire changer les électeurs d'opinion; **that swung the decision our way/against us** cela a influencé la décision finale en notre faveur/en notre défaveur; **to swing the voting in favour of sb** faire pencher la balance en faveur de qn; **the accident swung public opinion against the company** l'accident a provoqué un revirement de l'opinion contre la compagnie
(**f**) *Fam (manage, pull off)* **to swing sth** réussir *ou* arriver à faire qch ❑; **I think I should be able to swing it** je crois pouvoir me débrouiller ❑; **to swing it so that...** *(arrange things)* arranger les choses de manière (à ce) que... + *subjunctive*
(**g**) *Mus (tune)* interpréter en swing; *Fam* **he can really swing it** il a vraiment le swing
3 *vi* (**a**) *(sway, move to and fro → gen)* se balancer; *(→ pendulum)* osciller; *(hang, be suspended)* pendre, être suspendu; **to swing to and fro** se balancer; **shop sign that swings (to and fro) in the wind** enseigne de magasin qui ballotte au vent; **he walked along with his arms swinging** il marchait en balançant les bras; **a basket swung from her arm** un panier se balançait à son bras; **swinging from a cord** suspendu à une corde; **a long rope swung from the ceiling** une longue corde pendait du plafond; **the door swung open/shut** la porte s'est ouverte/s'est refermée; **the gate swung back in my face** le portail s'est refermé devant moi; *Fam Fig* **to swing both ways** *(be bisexual)* marcher à voile et à vapeur
(**b**) *(move along, around)* **to swing from tree to tree** se balancer d'arbre en arbre; **to swing into the saddle** sauter à cheval *ou* en selle; **they came swinging down the street** ils ont descendu la rue d'un pas rythmé; *Fig* **to swing into action** passer à l'action
(**c**) *(make a turn)* virer; **the car swung left** la voiture vira à gauche; **the lorry swung through the gate** le camion vira pour franchir le portail; **the road swings east** la route oblique vers l'est
(**d**) *(change opinion, mood etc)* virer; **the country has swung to the left** le pays a viré à gauche; **she swings between depression and elation** elle passe de la dépression à l'exultation
(**e**) *Fam (be hanged)* être pendu ❑; **he'll swing for this!** il sera pendu pour ça!; *Fig* il le paiera!
(**f**) *(hit out, aim a blow)* essayer de frapper; **he swung at them with the hammer** il a essayé de les frapper avec le marteau; **I swung at him** je lui ai décoché un coup de poing; **he swung wildly at the ball** il essaya désespérément de frapper la balle; *Fam* **to swing for sb** essayer d'en coller une à qn
(**g**) *Fam (musician)* swinguer; *(music)* swinguer, avoir du swing; **the saxophonist really swings!** il swingue, ce saxo!
(**h**) *Fam Old-fashioned (be modern, fashionable)* être dans le vent; **he was there in the sixties, when London was really swinging** il était là dans les années soixante, quand ça bougeait à Londres
(**i**) *Fam (be lively)* chauffer; **the party was beginning to swing** la fête commençait à être très animée ❑

(**j**) *Fam (try hard)* **he's in there swinging** il fait ce qu'il peut □; **I'm in there swinging for you** je fais tout ce que je peux pour toi □

(**k**) *Fam (exchange sexual partners)* faire de l'échangisme □

4 in full swing *adj* **the party was in full swing** la fête battait son plein; **production is in full swing** on produit à plein rendement; **the town's packed when the season's in full swing** en pleine saison, il y a foule en ville; **once it's in full swing, the project will require more people** une fois lancé, il faudra plus de gens sur le projet

▸▸ ***swing bridge*** pont *m* tournant; ***swing door*** porte *f* battante; *Am* ***swing set*** balançoires *fpl*; *Am Fam* ***swing shift*** *(work period)* = poste de 16 heures à minuit; *(team)* = équipe qui travaille de 16 heures à minuit

▸**swing out** *vi (car, driver)* faire un écart; *(from side road)* déboucher; **the car in front swung out to overtake** la voiture de devant a déboîté pour doubler

▸**swing round 1** *vt sep (vehicle)* faire virer; *(person)* faire tourner; **he swung the car round the corner** il a tourné au coin; **he swung the car right round** il a fait un tête-à-queue; **he swung her round** il la fit tourner; *Fig* **to swing sb round** convaincre qn; **he managed to swing her round to his point of view** il a réussi à la convaincre qu'il avait raison

2 *vi (turn round → person)* se retourner, faire volte-face; *(→ crane)* tourner, pivoter; *Fig (public opinion, person)* faire volte-face; **he swung round to look at me** il se retourna pour me regarder; **the car swung right round** la voiture a fait un tête-à-queue

▸**swing to** *vi (door, gate)* se refermer

swingboat ['swɪŋbəʊt] *n Br* nacelle *f (balançoire de champ de foire)*

swingeing ['swɪndʒɪŋ] *adj Br (increase, drop)* énorme; *(cuts)* draconien; *(blow)* violent; *(criticism, condemnation)* sévère; *(victory, defeat)* écrasant

swinger ['swɪŋə(r)] *n Fam* (**a**) *Old-fashioned (fashionable person)* branché(e) *m,f*; *(sociable person)* fêtard(e) *m,f* (**b**) *(promiscuous person)* débauché(e) □ *m,f*; *(who swaps sexual partners)* échangiste □ *mf*

swinging ['swɪŋɪŋ] *adj* (**a**) *(swaying)* qui se balance; *(pivoting)* tournant, pivotant; **with swinging arms** les bras ballants (**b**) *(rhythmic → gen)* rythmé, entraînant; *(→ jazz)* qui swingue (**c**) *Fam Old-fashioned (fashionable)* in *(inv)*; **the swinging sixties** les folles années soixante

▸▸ *Austr* ***swinging voter*** électeur(trice) *m,f* indécis(e)

swingingly ['swɪŋɪŋlɪ] *adv* avec rythme

swingletree ['swɪŋgəltriː] *n Tech* palonnier *m*

swingometer [swɪŋ'ɒmɪtə(r)] *n Br* indicateur *m* de tendances *(lors de la diffusion télévisée des résultats d'élections législatives)*

swing-wing 1 *adj* à géométrie variable

2 *n* avion *m* à géométrie variable

swinish ['swaɪnɪʃ] *adj Fam* sale, pas sympa; **that was a swinish trick!** c'était pas sympa!

swinishly ['swaɪnɪʃlɪ] *adv* salement, bestialement; **to eat swinishly** manger comme un pourceau *ou* en goinfre; **swinishly drunk** soûl comme un cochon

swinishness ['swaɪnɪʃnɪs] *n* saleté *f*, grossièreté *f*

swipe [swaɪp] **1** *vi* **he swiped at the fly with his newspaper** il donna un grand coup de journal pour frapper la mouche; **she swiped at the ball and missed** elle donna un grand coup pour frapper la balle et la manqua

2 *vt* (**a**) *(hit)* donner un coup à; **I managed to swipe myself in the eye** j'ai réussi à me donner un coup dans l'œil

(**b**) *Fam (steal)* piquer, chouraver; **who's swiped my pen?** qui m'a piqué *ou* chouravé mon stylo?

(**c**) *(card)* passer; *(credit card)* passer (au fer à repasser)

3 *n* (grand) coup *m*; **to take a swipe at sth** donner un grand coup pour frapper qch; *Fig (criticize)* tirer à boulets rouges sur qch

▸▸ ***swipe card*** badge *m*

swirl [swɜːl] **1** *vi* tourbillonner, tournoyer; **the dead leaves swirled round our feet** les feuilles mortes tourbillonnaient *ou* tournoyaient à nos pieds; **the water swirled beneath us** l'eau tourbillonnait au-dessous de nous

2 *vt* faire tourbillonner *ou* tournoyer; **a sudden wind swirled the leaves around** une brusque bourrasque fit tournoyer *ou* tourbillonner les feuilles; **swirl a bit of water round the sink** rince un peu le lavabo; **the raft was swirled downstream** le radeau a été emporté dans le tourbillon du courant; **he swirled her round the dance floor** il la fit tournoyer autour de la piste (de danse)

3 *n* tourbillon *m*; *(of water)* remous *m*; *(of cream)* spirale *f*; **swirls of smoke rose from the fire** des tourbillons de fumée s'élevaient du feu

swirling ['swɜːlɪŋ] *adj* tourbillonnant, tournoyant

swish [swɪʃ] **1** *vi (whip)* siffler; *(leaves, wind)* chuinter, *Literary* bruire; *(fabric, skirt)* froufrouter; *(water)* murmurer; **the curtains swished open/shut** les rideaux s'ouvrirent/se refermèrent en froufroutant

2 *vt* **the horse swished its tail** le cheval donna un coup de queue

3 *n* (**a**) *(sound → of fabric, skirt)* froufroutement *m*, froissement *m*; *(→ of leaves, wind)* bruissement *m*; *(→ of water)* murmure *m*; *(of scythe)* crissement *m*

(**b**) *(movement)* **the cow flicked the flies away with a swish of its tail** la vache chassa les mouches d'un coup de queue

(**c**) *Am Fam (effeminate homosexual)* folle *f*, = terme injurieux désignant un homosexuel

4 *adj Fam* (**a**) *Br (smart)* classe *(inv)*, chicos

(**b**) *Am (effeminate)* chochotte

swishy ['swɪʃɪ] *(compar* **swishier,** *superl* **swishiest)** *Fam* (**a**) *Br (smart)* classe *(inv)*, chicos (**b**) *Am (effeminate)* chochotte

Swiss [swɪs] *(pl* **inv) 1** *npl* **the Swiss** les Suisses *mpl*

2 *n (man)* Suisse *m*; *(woman)* Suissesse *f*, Suisse *f*

3 *adj (gen)* suisse; *(confederation, government)* helvétique

▸▸ ***Swiss army knife*** couteau *m* suisse; ***Swiss bank account*** compte *m* en Suisse; ***Swiss chard*** bette *f*, blette *f*; ***Swiss cheese*** emmental *m*; ***Swiss cheese plant*** monstera *m*; ***Swiss franc*** franc *m* suisse; ***Swiss Guard*** *(papal bodyguard)* garde *f* (pontificale) suisse; *Hist (in France)* membre *m* des troupes suisses; ***the Swiss Guard*** les troupes *fpl* suisses; ***Swiss roll*** (gâteau *m*) roulé *m*; *Am* ***Swiss steak*** = bifteck fariné et braisé

Swiss-French 1 *n* (**a**) *Ling* suisse *m* romand (**b**) *(person)* Suisse *m* romand, Suisse *f* romande

2 *adj* suisse romand

Swiss-German 1 *n* (**a**) *Ling* suisse *m* allemand *ou* alémanique (**b**) *(person)* Suisse *m* allemand, Suisse *f* allemande

2 *adj* suisse allemand *ou* alémanique

Switch® [swɪtʃ] *n Br* = société de cartes de paiement britannique; **to pay by Switch**® ≃ payer par Carte bleue

▸▸ ***Switch card***® = carte de paiement utilisée en Grande-Bretagne, ≃ Carte *f* bleue

switch [swɪtʃ] **1** *n* (**a**) *Elec (for light)* interrupteur *m*; *(on radio, television)* bouton *m*; *Tech & Tel* commutateur *m*; **is the switch on/off?** est-ce que c'est allumé/éteint?; **two-way switch** (interrupteur *m*) va-et-vient *m*

(**b**) *(change → gen)* changement *m*; *(→ of opinion, attitude)* revirement *m*; **the switch to the new equipment went very smoothly** on s'est très bien adaptés au nouveau matériel; **a sudden switch in foreign policy** un subit revirement de la politique étrangère; **to make the switch from gas to electricity** passer du gaz à l'électricité

(**c**) *(swap, trade)* échange *m*

(**d**) *Am Rail* **switches** *(points)* aiguillage *m*

(**e**) *(stick)* baguette *f*, badine *f*; *(riding crop)* cravache *f*

(**f**) *(hairpiece)* postiche *m*

(**g**) *Zool (hair on tail)* fouet *m* de la queue

2 *vt* (**a**) *(change)* changer de; *(exchange)* échanger; **he switched subjects after two years at university** il a changé de filière après deux ans d'université; **the two employees asked to switch jobs** les deux employés ont demandé à échanger leurs postes; **to switch places with sb** échanger sa place avec qn; **she offered to switch jobs with me** elle a offert d'échanger son poste contre le mien; **can I switch it for another one?** puis-je l'échanger contre un autre?; **he's been switched to another department** il a été muté dans un autre service

(**b**) *(transfer → allegiance, attention)* transférer; *(divert → conversation)* orienter, détourner; **she switched her attention back to the speaker** elle reporta son attention sur le conférencier; **I tried to switch the discussion to something less controversial** j'ai essayé d'orienter la discussion vers un sujet moins épineux

(**c**) *Elec, Rad & TV (circuit)* commuter; **to switch channels/frequencies** changer de chaîne/de fréquence

(**d**) *Am Rail* aiguiller; **the freight train was switched to another track** le train de marchandises fut aiguillé sur une autre voie

(**e**) *(hit with stick)* donner un coup de baguette à; **to switch its tail** *(cow)* battre l'air de sa queue

(**f**) *St Exch* **to switch a position** reporter une position d'une échéance à une autre plus éloignée

3 *vi* changer; **she started studying medicine but switched to architecture** elle a commencé par étudier la médecine, mais elle a changé pour faire architecture; **I'd like to switch to another topic** j'aimerais changer de sujet; **can I switch to another channel?** est-ce que je peux changer de chaîne?; **the committee switched to the problem of recruitment** le comité passa au problème du recrutement; **we've switched to another brand** nous avons changé de marque; **they've switched to American equipment** ils ont adopté du matériel américain; **to switch (from gas) to electricity** passer (du gaz) à l'électricité; **he switches effortlessly from one language to another** il passe d'une langue à une autre avec une grande aisance

▸▸ *St Exch* ***switch trading*** arbitrage *m*

▸**switch around** = **switch round**

▸**switch back** *vi (revert to)* **to switch back from electricity to gas** repasser (de l'électricité) au gaz; **we switched back to gas** nous sommes revenus au gaz; **to switch back to BBC2** remettre sur BBC2

▸**switch off 1** *vt sep Br (light)* éteindre; *(electrical appliance)* éteindre, arrêter; **don't forget to switch the lights off when you leave** n'oublie pas d'éteindre la lumière en partant; **the radio switches itself off** la radio s'éteint *ou* s'arrête automatiquement; **they've switched off the power** ils ont coupé le courant; *Aut* **to switch off the ignition** *or* **engine** couper le contact, arrêter le moteur

2 *vi* (**a**) *Br (go off → light)* s'éteindre; *(→ electrical appliance)* s'éteindre, s'arrêter; **how do you get the oven to switch off?** comment tu éteins le four?

(**b**) *Br (TV viewer, radio listener)* éteindre le poste; **don't switch off!** restez à l'écoute!

(**c**) *Fam (stop paying attention)* décrocher; **he switches off whenever we talk about politics** il décroche chaque fois qu'on parle politique

▸**switch on 1** *vt sep* (**a**) *(light, heating, oven, TV, radio)* allumer; *(engine, washing machine, vacuum cleaner)* mettre en marche; **could you switch on the light?** pourrais-tu allumer (la lumière)?; **the power isn't switched on** il n'y a pas de courant; *Aut* **to switch on the ignition** mettre le contact

(**b**) *Fig* **to switch on the charm** faire du charme; **to switch on the tears** pleurer sur commande; *Fam* **they switched me on to new ideas** ils m'ont initié aux idées nouvelles

2 *vi* (**a**) *(light, heating, oven, TV, radio)* s'allumer; *(engine, washing machine, vacuum cleaner)* se mettre en marche; **the lights switch on and off automatically** les lumières s'allument et s'éteignent automatiquement

(**b**) *(TV viewer, radio listener)* allumer le poste; **don't forget to switch on at the same time tomorrow!** soyez à l'écoute demain à la même heure!

▸**switch over** *vi* (**a**) = **switch** *vi*

(**b**) *TV* changer de chaîne; *Rad* changer de station; **can we switch over at 8 o' clock?**

est-ce que nous pouvons changer de chaîne à 20 heures?

▸**switch round** **1** *vt sep* changer de place, déplacer; **why don't we switch the desks round?** et si on changeait les bureaux de place?; **he switched the glasses round when she wasn't looking** il échangea les verres pendant qu'elle ne regardait pas; **the manager has switched the team round again** l'entraîneur a encore changé la composition de l'équipe

2 *vi (two people)* changer de place; **she's switched round with her brother** elle a changé de place avec son frère

switchback ['swɪtʃbæk] **1** *n* (**a**) *(road)* route *f* en lacets (**b**) *Br (rollercoaster)* montagnes *fpl* russes

2 *adj* **a switchback road** une route accidentée et sinueuse

switchblade ['swɪtʃbleɪd] *n Am* (couteau *m* à) cran *m* d'arrêt

switchboard ['swɪtʃbɔːd] *n* (**a**) *Tel* central *m* (téléphonique); *(in hotel, office)* standard *m* (**b**) *Elec* tableau *m*

►► ***switchboard line*** ligne *f* principale; ***switchboard operator*** standardiste *mf*

switched [swɪtʃt] *adj*

►► ***switched line*** *(in datacomms)* ligne *f* commutée; *Comput* ***switched network*** réseau *m* commuté

switched-on *adj Fam* (**a**) *(fashionable)* dans le vent, in *(inv)* (**b**) *(under influence of drugs)* défoncé (**c**) *(sexually excited)* excité

switcheroo [ˌswɪtʃə'ruː] *n Am Fam* changement *m* inattendu□; **to pull a switcheroo** surprendre tout le monde□

switchgear ['swɪtʃgɪə(r)] *n* appareillage *m* de commutation

switch-hitter *n Am* (**a**) *Sport* batteur *m* ambidextre (**b**) *Fam (bisexual)* bi *mf*; **he's a switch-hitter** il marche à voile et à vapeur

switching ['swɪtʃɪŋ] *n* (**a**) *Comput, Elec & Tel* commutation *f*; *Comput* **data switching** commutation *f* de données (**b**) *St Exch* arbitrage *m* de portefeuille

switchman ['swɪtʃmən] (*pl* **switchmen** [-mən]) *n Am* aiguilleur *m*

switchover ['swɪtʃˌəʊvə(r)] *n (to another method, system)* passage *m*, conversion *f*; **there's to be a switchover from the British to the continental system** il va y avoir un passage du système britannique au système continental

switchyard ['swɪtʃjɑːd] *n Am* gare *f* de triage

swither ['swɪðə(r)] *Scot* **1** *n* (**a**) *(agitation)* agitation *f*, bouleversement *m*, émoi *m* (**b**) *(hesitation)* hésitation *f*; *(indecision)* indécision *f*

2 *vi (hesitate)* hésiter; *(be uncertain)* être indécis

Switzerland ['swɪtsələnd] *n* Suisse *f*; **in Switzerland** en Suisse; **French-/Italian-speaking Switzerland** la Suisse romande/italienne; **German-speaking Switzerland** la Suisse allemande *ou* alémanique

swivel ['swɪvəl] (*Br pt & pp* **swivelled,** *cont* **swivelling**, *Am pt & pp* **swiveled,** *cont* **swiveling**) **1** *n* (**a**) *(gen)* pivot *m*; *(for gun)* tourillon *m* (**b**) *(in rowing)* dame *f* de nage

2 *comp (lamp)* pivotant, tournant

3 *vi* pivoter, tourner; **his eyes swivelled back to the screen** ses yeux se tournèrent à nouveau vers l'écran

4 *vt* faire pivoter

►► ***swivel arm*** bras *m* pivotant; ***swivel base*** socle *m* pivotant; ***swivel chair*** chaise *f* pivotante; *(with arms)* fauteuil *m* pivotant; ***swivel joint*** (joint *m* à) rotule *f*; *Aut* ***swivel pin*** pivot *m* central

▸**swivel round** **1** *vi (turn)* pivoter, tourner; **to swivel round on one's heels** pivoter sur ses talons; **she swivelled round in her chair** elle pivota sur sa chaise

2 *vt sep* faire pivoter

swivelling, *Am* **swiveling** ['swɪvəlɪŋ] *adj* pivotant, mobile

swiz, swizz [swɪz] *n Br Fam* arnaque *f*; **what a swiz!** c'est du vol!□

swizzle ['swɪzəl] *n* (**a**) *Br Fam (swizz)* arnaque *f* (**b**) *Am (cocktail)* cocktail *m (préparé dans un verre mélangeur)*

►► ***swizzle stick*** cuillère *f* à cocktails

swollen ['swəʊlən] **1** *pp of* **swell**

2 *adj* (**a**) *(part of body)* enflé, gonflé; **her ankle was badly swollen** sa cheville était très enflée; **his face was swollen** il avait le visage enflé *ou* bouffi; **starving children with swollen abdomens** des enfants affamés au ventre ballonné; **her eyes were red and swollen with crying** elle avait les yeux rouges et gonflés à force de pleurer; *Fam Fig* **to have a swollen head** avoir la grosse tête

(**b**) *(sails)* bombé, gonflé; *(lake, river)* en crue

swollen-headed *adj Br Fam* qui a la grosse tête

swoon [swuːn] **1** *vi* (**a**) *(become ecstatic)* se pâmer, tomber en pâmoison; **he used to make all the young girls swoon** il fut un temps où toutes les jeunes filles se pâmaient devant lui

(**b**) *Old-fashioned (faint)* s'évanouir, *Literary* se pâmer

2 *n* pâmoison *f*; **to fall to the ground in a swoon** tomber par terre en pâmoison; **she was in a swoon over meeting her idol** elle était tout en émoi après avoir rencontré son idole

swoop [swuːp] **1** *vi* (**a**) *(dive → bird)* s'abattre, fondre; *(→ aircraft)* piquer, descendre en piqué; **the gulls swooped down on the rocks** les mouettes s'abattirent sur *ou* fondirent sur les rochers; **the helicopter swooped low over the battlefield** l'hélicoptère descendit en piqué au-dessus du champ de bataille

(**b**) *(make a raid → police, troops etc)* faire une descente; **the police swooped on the nightclub** la police a fait une descente dans la boîte de nuit

2 *n* (**a**) *(dive → by bird, aircraft)* descente *f* en piqué

(**b**) *(raid → by police, troops etc)* descente *f*; **a dawn swoop** une descente à l'aube; **fifteen arrested in drugs swoop** quinze personnes arrêtées dans une opération anti-drogue

(**c**) *(idiom)* **in one fell swoop** d'un seul coup

swoosh [swʊʃ] *Fam* **1** *vi (water)* bruire□; *(wind)* siffler□; **the express train swooshed past** le rapide est passé à toute vitesse□; **the car swooshed through the puddle** la voiture a fait gicler l'eau en passant dans la flaque□; **the waves swooshed over the deck** les vagues déferlaient sur le pont□; **you could hear the liquid swooshing around in the tank** on entendait le liquide clapoter dans le réservoir□

2 *n (of water)* bruissement *m*; *(of wind)* sifflement *m*

3 *vt* **he swooshed it down the loo** il l'a fait disparaître dans les toilettes; **she then swooshed it out with clean water** elle l'a ensuite rincé à grande eau; **swoosh the detergent all over the stain** répandre le détergent généreusement sur la tache

swop (*pt & pp* **swopped,** *cont* **swopping**) = **swap**

sword [sɔːd] **1** *n* épée *f*; *Mil & Naut* sabre *m*; **to draw one's sword** tirer son épée, dégainer; **they fought with swords** ils se sont battus à l'épée; **all the prisoners were put to the sword** tous les prisonniers furent passés au fil de l'épée; *Fam* **a sword and sandals movie** un péplum; **the sword of justice** le glaive de la justice; *Prov* **those that live by the sword shall die by the sword** quiconque se sert de l'épée périra par l'épée; **he lived by the sword and died by the sword** il a vécu par l'épée, il a péri par l'épée; *Fig* **to turn swords into ploughshares** faire la paix, se réconcilier

2 *comp (blow, handle, wound)* d'épée

►► ***the Sword of Damocles*** l'épée *f* de Damoclès; ***sword dance*** danse *f* du sabre; *Bot* ***sword grass*** graminée *f* ensifoliée; *Literary* ***the Sword of Justice*** le glaive de la Justice; ***sword swallower*** avaleur(euse) *m,f* de sabres

swordbearer ['sɔːdˌbeərə(r)] *n (in ceremony)* = officier qui porte le glaive

swordbelt ['sɔːdbelt] *n* ceinturon *m*

swordbill ['sɔːdbɪl] *n Orn* oiseau-mouche *m*

swordcraft ['sɔːdkrɑːft] *n (UNCOUNT)* maniement *m* de l'épée

sword-fight *n (between two people)* duel *m* (à l'épée); *(between several people)* bataille *f* à l'épée

swordfish ['sɔːdfɪʃ] (*pl* **inv** *or* **swordfishes**) *n Ich* espadon *m*, poisson-épée *m*

sword-knot *n* dragonne *f*

swordplay ['sɔːdpleɪ] *n (UNCOUNT) (skill)* maniement *m* de l'épée; *(activity)* escrime *f*; **they were taught riding and swordplay** on leur apprenait à monter à cheval et à manier l'épée; **the last scene consisted of swordplay** la dernière scène était une scène de combats à l'épée

swordsman ['sɔːdzmən] (*pl* **swordsmen** [-mən]) *n* épéiste *m*, lame *f (personne)*; **he's a fine swordsman** c'est une fine lame

swordsmanship ['sɔːdzmənʃɪp] *n* maniement *m* de l'épée; **we admired her swordsmanship** nous admirâmes sa façon de manier l'épée

swordstick ['sɔːdstɪk] *n* canne-épée *f*, canne *f* armée

swordtail ['sɔːdteɪl] *n Ich* porte-épée *m*

swore [swɔː(r)] *pt of* **swear**

sworn [swɔːn] **1** *pp of* **swear**

2 *adj* (**a**) *Law (declaration)* fait sous serment; *(evidence)* donné sous serment; **sworn affidavits** des déclarations faites sous serment; **a sworn statement** une déposition faite sous serment (**b**) *(committed → enemy)* juré; *(→ friend)* indéfectible

SWOT [swɒt] *n Mktg* (*abbr* **strengths, weaknesses, opportunities, threats**) forces, faiblesses, opportunités et menaces *fpl*

►► ***SWOT analysis*** analyse *f* des forces, faiblesses, opportunités et menaces

swot [swɒt] (*pt & pp* **swotted,** *cont* **swotting**) *Br Fam* **1** *vi* bûcher, potasser; **to swot for an exam** bûcher *ou* potasser un examen

2 *n Pej* bachoteur(euse) *m,f*

▸**swot up** *Br Fam* **1** *vi* bûcher, potasser; **to swot up on sth** bûcher *ou* potasser qch

2 *vt sep* bûcher, potasser

swotting ['swɒtɪŋ] *n Br Fam* bachotage *m*; **I'll have to do some swotting to pass my exam** il va falloir que je bûche *ou* que je potasse pour réussir mon examen

swum [swʌm] *pp of* **swim**

swung [swʌŋ] *pt & pp of* **swing**

►► *Typ* ***swung dash*** tilde *m*

sybarite ['sɪbəraɪt] *n* sybarite *mf*

sybaritic [ˌsɪbə'rɪtɪk] *adj* sybarite

sycamore ['sɪkəmɔː(r)] *n* (**a**) *Br* sycomore *m*, faux platane *m* (**b**) *Am* platane *m*

sycophancy ['sɪkəfənsɪ] *n* flagornerie *f*

sycophant ['sɪkəfænt] *n* flagorneur(euse) *m,f*

sycophantic [ˌsɪkə'fæntɪk] *adj (person)* flatteur, flagorneur; *(behaviour)* de flagorneur; *(approval, praise)* obséquieux

sycophantically [ˌsɪkə'fæntɪkəlɪ] *adv* bassement

sycosis [saɪ'kəʊsɪs] *n Med* sycosis *m*

Sydenham's chorea ['sɪdənəmz-] *n Med* chorée *f* de Sydenham, chorée *f* rhumatismale

Sydney ['sɪdnɪ] *n* Sydney

►► ***Sydney Harbour Bridge*** le pont du port de Sydney; ***the Sydney Opera House*** l'Opéra *m* de Sydney

syllabary ['sɪləbərɪ] (*pl* **syllabaries**) *n* syllabaire *m*

syllabi ['sɪləbaɪ] *pl of* **syllabus**

syllabic [sɪ'læbɪk] *adj* syllabique

syllabicate [sɪ'læbɪkeɪt] *vt* syllabiser

syllabication [sɪˌlæbɪ'keɪʃən], **syllabification** [sɪˌlæbɪfɪ'keɪʃən] *n* syllabation *f*

syllabify [sɪ'læbɪfaɪ] (*pt & pp* **syllabified**) *vt* décomposer en syllabes

syllabism ['sɪləbɪzəm] *n* syllabisme *m*

syllabize, -ise ['sɪləbaɪz] *vt* syllabiser

syllable ['sɪləbəl] *n* syllabe *f*; **I had to explain it to him in words of one syllable** j'ai dû le lui expliquer en termes simples

syllabled ['sɪləbəld] *adj* = prononcé ou écrit en syllabes

syllabub ['sɪləbʌb] *n* (**a**) *Br (dessert)* (crème *f*) sabayon *m* (**b**) *(drink)* = boisson à base de lait, alcoolisée, relevée et souvent chaude

syllabus ['sɪləbəs] (*pl* **syllabuses** *or* **syllabi** [-baɪ]) *n Sch & Univ* programme *m* (d'enseignement); **do you know what's on the syllabus?** savez-vous ce qu'il y a au programme?; **the teacher handed out copies of the syllabus** le professeur distribua des exemplaires du programme

syllepsis [sɪ'lepsɪs] (*pl* **syllepses** [-siːz]) *n Gram* syllepse *f*

sylleptic [sɪ'leptɪk] *adj* sylleptique

syllogism ['sɪlədʒɪzəm] *n* syllogisme *m*

syllogistic [ˌsɪlə'dʒɪstɪk] *adj* syllogistique
syllogistically [ˌsɪlə'dʒɪstɪkəlɪ] *adv* par syllogismes
syllogize, -ise ['sɪlədʒaɪz] *vi* raisonner par syllogismes
sylph [sɪlf] *n* (**a**) *(mythical being)* sylphe *m* (**b**) *Literary (slender woman)* sylphide *f*
sylphlike ['sɪlflaɪk] *adj Literary (figure)* gracile, de sylphe; *(woman)* gracieuse; *Hum* **you're looking positively sylphlike, my dear** tu es une vraie sylphide, ma chère
sylva ['sɪlvə] *n (trees)* forêts *fpl* (d'une région)
sylvan ['sɪlvən] *adj Literary* sylvestre
sylvanite ['sɪlvənaɪt] *n Miner* sylvanite *f* graphique
Sylvanus = **Silvanus**
sylvatic [sɪl'vætɪk] *adj* sylvestre
▸▸ *Vet* ***sylvatic diseases*** = maladies répandues par les animaux des forêts
sylviculture ['sɪlvɪˌkʌltʃə(r)] *n* sylviculture *f*
sylviculturist [ˌsɪlvɪ'kʌltʃərɪst] *n* sylviculteur(-trice) *m,f*
symbiont ['sɪmbɪɒnt] *n Biol* symbiote *m*, symbionte *m*
symbiosis [ˌsɪmbɪ'əʊsɪs] *n also Fig* symbiose *f*; **in symbiosis** en symbiose
symbiotic [ˌsɪmbɪ'ɒtɪk] *adj also Fig* symbiotique; **a symbiotic relationship** une association symbiotique
symbiotically [ˌsɪmbɪ'ɒtɪkəlɪ] *adv* en symbiose
symbol ['sɪmbəl] *n* symbole *m*
symbolic [sɪm'bɒlɪk] *adj* symbolique
▸▸ ***symbolic interactionism*** interactionnisme *m* symbolique; ***symbolic logic*** logique *f* symbolique
symbolically [sɪm'bɒlɪklɪ] *adv* symboliquement
symbolism ['sɪmbəlɪzəm] *n* symbolisme *m*
symbolist ['sɪmbəlɪst] **1** *adj* symboliste
2 *n* symboliste *mf*
symbolistic [ˌsɪmbə'lɪstɪk], **symbolistical** [ˌsɪmbə'lɪstɪkəl] *adj* symboliste
symbolization [ˌsɪmbəlaɪ'zeɪʃən] *n* symbolisation *f*
symbolize, -ise ['sɪmbəlaɪz] *vt* symboliser
symbology [sɪm'bɒlədʒɪ] *n* (**a**) *(system of symbols)* symbolique *f* (**b**) *(expression in symbols)* symbolisation *f* (**c**) *(science of symbols)* symbolisme *m*
symmetric [sɪ'metrɪk] *adj Math & (in logic)* symétrique
symmetrical [sɪ'metrɪkəl] *adj* symétrique
symmetrically [sɪ'metrɪklɪ] *adv* symétriquement
symmetrization [ˌsɪmɪtraɪ'zeɪʃən] *n* symétrisation *f*
symmetrize, -ise ['sɪmɪtraɪz] *vt* rendre symétrique, symétriser
symmetry ['sɪmətrɪ] (*pl* **symmetries**) *n* symétrie *f*
sympathetic [ˌsɪmpə'θetɪk] *adj* (**a**) *(compassionate)* compatissant; **sympathetic words** des paroles compatissantes *ou* de sympathie; **they weren't very sympathetic** ils ne se sont pas montrés très compatissants
(**b**) *(well-disposed)* bien disposé; *(understanding)* compréhensif; **the public is generally sympathetic to** *or* **towards the strikers** l'opinion publique est dans l'ensemble bien disposée envers les grévistes; **she spoke to a sympathetic audience** elle s'adressa à un auditoire bienveillant; **the town council was sympathetic to our grievances** la municipalité a accueilli nos revendications avec compréhension
(**c**) *(congenial, likeable)* sympathique, agréable; **he's not a very sympathetic character** ce n'est pas un personnage très sympathique
(**d**) *Physiol* sympathique; **the sympathetic nervous system** le système nerveux sympathique, le sympathique
(**e**) *Phys (vibration)* dû à la résonance
▸▸ ***sympathetic magic*** magie *f* sympathique; *Mus* **sympathetic string** corde *f* qui vibre par résonance
sympathetically [ˌsɪmpə'θetɪklɪ] *adv* (**a**) *(compassionately)* avec compassion; **"I understand how you feel", she said sympathetically** "je vous comprends", dit-elle avec compassion; **he patted me sympathetically on the hand** il me donna une petite tape sur la main en signe de compassion *ou* de sympathie
(**b**) *(with approval)* avec bienveillance; **she received his request sympathetically** elle reçut sa requête avec bienveillance
(**c**) *Physiol* par sympathie
(**d**) *Phys (vibrate)* par résonance
sympathize, -ise ['sɪmpəθaɪz] *vi* (**a**) *(feel compassion)* sympathiser, compatir; **we all sympathized with him when his wife left** nous avons tous compati à son malheur quand sa femme est partie; **poor Emma, I really sympathize with her!** cette pauvre Emma, je la plains vraiment!
(**b**) *(feel understanding)* **he could not sympathize with their feelings** il ne pouvait pas comprendre leurs sentiments; **we understand and sympathize with their point of view** nous comprenons et partageons leur point de vue
(**c**) *(favour, support)* sympathiser; **certain heads of state openly sympathized with the terrorists** certains chefs d'État sympathisaient ouvertement avec les terroristes; **those who sympathize with Professor Smith in his view that...** ceux qui s'associent au Professeur Smith pour dire que...
sympathizer ['sɪmpəθaɪzə(r)] *n* (**a**) *(comforter)* **she received many cards from sympathizers after her husband's death** elle a reçu de nombreuses cartes de condoléances après la mort de son mari (**b**) *(supporter)* sympathisant(e) *m,f*; **she was suspected of being a communist sympathizer** elle était soupçonnée d'être sympathisante communiste
sympathy ['sɪmpəθɪ] (*pl* **sympathies**) *n* (**a**) *(compassion)* compassion *f*; **to have** *or* **to feel sympathy for sb** éprouver de la compassion envers qn; **he showed no sympathy for the children** il n'a fait preuve d'aucune compassion envers les enfants; **her tears were only a means of gaining sympathy** elle ne pleurait que pour qu'on s'attendrisse sur elle; **you have my deepest sympathies** toutes mes condoléances; **our sympathies are with the families of the dead** nous compatissons avec les familles des victimes; **if you do catch a cold don't expect any sympathy from me!** si tu attrapes un rhume, ne compte pas sur moi pour te plaindre!
(**b**) *(approval, support)* soutien *m*; **the audience was clearly not in sympathy with the speaker** il était évident que le public ne partageait pas les sentiments de l'orateur; **she has strong left-wing sympathies** elle est très à gauche; **I have no sympathy for** *or* **with terrorism** je désapprouve tout à fait le terrorisme; **his sympathies did not lie with his own class** il ne partageait pas les valeurs de sa propre classe; **to come out in sympathy (with sb)** faire grève par solidarité (avec qn)
(**c**) *(affinity)* sympathie *f*; **there was a strong bond of sympathy between them** ils étaient liés par une forte sympathie
▸▸ ***sympathy card*** carte *f* de condoléances; ***sympathy strike*** grève *f* de solidarité
symphonic [sɪm'fɒnɪk] *adj* symphonique; **a symphonic poem** un poème symphonique
symphonically [sɪm'fɒnɪkəlɪ] *adv* symphoniquement
symphonious [sɪm'fəʊnɪəs] *adj* harmonieux
symphonist ['sɪmfənɪst] *n* symphoniste *mf*
symphony ['sɪmfənɪ] (*pl* **symphonies**) **1** *n* (**a**) *(composition)* symphonie *f*; *Fig* **the landscape was a symphony of browns and greens** le paysage était une symphonie de bruns et de verts (**b**) *Am (orchestra)* orchestre *m* symphonique
2 *comp (concert, orchestra)* symphonique
symposium [sɪm'pəʊzɪəm] (*pl* **symposiums** *or* **symposia** [-zɪə]) *n* symposium *m*, colloque *m*

'The Symposium' *Plato* 'Le Banquet'

symptom ['sɪmptəm] *n Med & Fig* symptôme *m*; **to show symptoms of fatigue** donner des signes de fatigue
symptomatic [ˌsɪmptə'mætɪk] *adj Med & Fig* symptomatique
symptomatically [ˌsɪmptə'mætɪkəlɪ] *adv* symptomatiquement
symptomatology [ˌsɪmptəmə'tɒlədʒɪ] *n* symptomatologie *f*
synaeresis (*pl* **synaereses** [-siːz]) = **syneresis**
synaesthesia, *Am* **synesthesia** [ˌsɪnɪs'θiːzɪə] *n* synesthésie *f*
synagogal [ˌsɪnə'gɒgəl], **synagogical** [ˌsɪnə'gɒgɪkəl] *adj* synagogal
synagogue ['sɪnəgɒg] *n* synagogue *f*
synalepha, synaloepha [ˌsɪnə'liːfə] *n Ling* synalèphe *f*
synapse ['saɪnæps], **synapsis** [sɪ'næpsɪs] *n* synapse *f*
synaptic [sɪ'næptɪk] *adj* synaptique
sync, synch [sɪŋk] *n Fam* (*abbr* **synchronization**) synchronisation❑ *f*; **to be in/out of sync** être/ne pas être synchro; **the engine is a bit out of sync** le moteur ne tourne pas très rond❑
▸▸ ***sync pulse*** *TV* impulsion *f* de synchronisation; *Cin* signal *m* de synchronisation
synchro ['sɪŋkrəʊ] (*pl* **synchros**) *n Fam* (**a**) *(synchromesh)* synchroniseur❑ *m* (**b**) *(synchronized swimming)* natation *f* synchronisée❑
synchroflash ['sɪŋkrəʊflæʃ] *n* flash *m* synchronisé
synchromarketing [ˌsɪŋkrəʊ'mɑːkətɪŋ] *n* synchromarketing *m*
synchromesh ['sɪŋkrəʊmeʃ] *n* synchroniseur *m*
▸▸ ***synchromesh gearbox*** boîte *f* de vitesses à synchroniseur
synchronic [sɪŋ'krɒnɪk] *adj* synchronique
synchronically [sɪŋ'krɒnɪkəlɪ] *adv* synchroniquement
synchronism ['sɪŋkrənɪzəm] *n* synchronisme *m*
synchronistic [ˌsɪŋkrə'nɪstɪk] *adj* synchronique
synchronization [ˌsɪŋkrənaɪ'zeɪʃən] *n* synchronisation *f*
synchronize, -ise ['sɪŋkrənaɪz] **1** *vt (watches, actions, movements, events)* synchroniser; *Elec (generators)* coupler en phase
2 *vi* être synchronisé; **the chimes of the clocks synchronized perfectly** les carillons des horloges étaient parfaitement synchronisés
synchronized ['sɪŋkrənaɪzd] *adj* synchronisé
▸▸ ***synchronized generators*** générateurs *mpl* synchronisés *ou* en phase; ***synchronized sound*** son *m* synchrone; ***synchronized swimming*** natation *f* synchronisée
synchronizer ['sɪŋkrənaɪzə(r)] *n* synchronisateur *m*
synchronizing generator ['sɪŋkrənaɪzɪŋ-] *n* générateur *m* de synchro
synchronoscope [ˌsɪŋ'krɒnəskəʊp] *n* synchronoscope *m*
synchronous ['sɪŋkrənəs] *adj* synchrone
synchronously ['sɪŋkrənəslɪ] *adv* synchroniquement
synchrony ['sɪŋkrənɪ] (*pl* **synchronies**) *n* (**a**) *(synchronism)* synchronisme *m* (**b**) *Ling* synchronie *f*
▸▸ *Cin* ***synchrony mark*** marque *f* *ou* signal *m* de synchronisme
synchroscope ['sɪŋkrəskəʊp] *n Elec* synchroscope *m*
synchrotron ['sɪŋkrətrɒn] *n Phys* synchrotron *m*
syncline ['sɪŋklaɪn] *n* synclinal *m*
syncopal ['sɪŋkəpəl] *adj Med* syncopal
syncopate ['sɪŋkəpeɪt] *vt Mus* syncoper
syncopated ['sɪŋkəpeɪtɪd] *adj Mus* syncopé
▸▸ ***syncopated music*** musique *f* syncopée *ou* à contre-temps; ***syncopated notes*** notes *fpl* syncopées; ***syncopated rhythm*** rythme *m* syncopé
syncopation [ˌsɪŋkə'peɪʃən] *n Mus* syncope *f*
syncope ['sɪŋkəpɪ] *n Ling & Med* syncope *f*
syncretic [sɪŋ'kretɪk] *adj* syncrétique
syncretism ['sɪŋkrɪtɪzəm] *n* syncrétisme *m*
syncretize, -ise ['sɪŋkrətaɪz] **1** *vt* rendre syncrétique
2 *vi* devenir syncrétique
syndetic [sɪn'detɪk] *adj*
▸▸ ***syndetic clause*** clause *f* reliée par syndèse
syndic ['sɪndɪk] *n* syndic *m*
syndical ['sɪndɪkəl] *adj* syndical
syndicalism ['sɪndɪkəlɪzəm] *n (doctrine)* syndicalisme *m* révolutionnaire
syndicalist ['sɪndɪkəlɪst] **1** *n* syndicaliste *mf* révolutionnaire
2 *adj* de syndicalisme révolutionnaire
syndicalistic [ˌsɪndɪkə'lɪstɪk] *adj* syndicaliste

syl–syn

syndicate 1 *n* ['sɪndɪkət] (**a**) *Com & Fin* groupement *m*, syndicat *m*; **the loan was underwritten by a syndicate of banks** le prêt était garanti par un consortium bancaire; **a syndicate of British and French companies** un groupement de sociétés françaises et britanniques
(**b**) *(of organized crime)* association *f*; **crime syndicates** associations *fpl* de grand banditisme; **the Syndicate** la Mafia
(**c**) *Journ* agence *f* de presse *(qui vend des articles, des photos etc à plusieurs journaux pour publication simultanée)*
2 *vt* ['sɪndɪkeɪt] (**a**) *Com & Fin (loan)* syndiquer
(**b**) *Journ* publier simultanément dans plusieurs journaux; *Am Rad* vendre à plusieurs stations; *Am TV* vendre à plusieurs chaînes; **she writes a syndicated column** elle écrit une chronique qui est publiée dans plusieurs journaux; **the photograph was syndicated in all the local newspapers** la photographie a été publiée dans toute la presse régionale; **a syndicated TV news programme** des informations *fpl* télévisées reprises par plusieurs chaînes
3 *vi* ['sɪndɪkeɪt] *(form a syndicate)* former un groupement *ou* syndicat
►► *Fin* ***syndicated credit*** crédit *m* consortial; ***syndicated loan*** prêt *m* en participation; *St Exch* ***syndicated shares*** actions *fpl* syndiquées

syndication [ˌsɪndɪ'keɪʃən] *n Journ (of article)* publication *f* simultanée dans plusieurs journaux
►► ***syndication agency*** agence *f* de presse

syndrome ['sɪndrəʊm] *n* syndrome *m*

synecdoche [sɪn'ekdəkɪ] *n Ling* synecdoque *f*

synecology [ˌsɪnɪ'kɒlədʒɪ] *n Biol* synécologie *f*

synectics [sɪ'nektɪks] *n (UNCOUNT)* synectique *f*

syneresis [sɪ'nɪərəsɪs] *(pl* **synereses** [-si:z]*) n* synérèse *f*

synergetic [ˌsɪnə'dʒetɪk] *adj Physiol* synergique

synergism ['sɪnədʒɪzəm] = **synergy**

synergist ['sɪnədʒɪst] *n* (**a**) *(person)* synergiste *m* (**b**) *Biol (substance)* synergiste *m*

synergistic [ˌsɪnə'dʒɪstɪk] *adj Biol & Fig* synergique

synergy ['sɪnədʒɪ] *(pl* **synergies***) n Biol & Fig* synergie *f*

synesthesia *Am* = **synaesthesia**

synod ['sɪnəd] *n* (**a**) *Rel* synode *m*; **the General Synod** le conseil d'administration de l'Église anglicane (**b**) *(council)* assemblée *f*, convention *f*

synodal ['sɪnədəl] *adj* synodal

synodic [sɪ'nɒdɪk], **synodical** [sɪ'nɒdɪkəl] *adj* (**a**) *Rel* synodique, synodal (**b**) *Astron* synodique
►► *Astron* ***synodic month*** mois *m* synodique *ou* de consécution; *(lunar month)* lunaison *f*; *Astron* ***synodic period*** période *f ou* révolution *f* synodique

synonym ['sɪnənɪm] *n* synonyme *m*

synonymic [ˌsɪnə'nɪmɪk] *adj* synonymique

synonymity [ˌsɪnə'nɪmɪtɪ] *n* synonymie *f*

synonymize, -ise [sɪ'nɒnɪmaɪz] **1** *vt (word)* donner les synonymes de
2 *vi* s'exprimer par synonymes

synonymous [sɪ'nɒnɪməs] *adj also Fig* synonyme; **success is not always synonymous with merit** le succès n'est pas toujours synonyme de mérite; **the two words are not really synonymous** les deux mots ne sont pas vraiment synonymes

synonymously [sɪ'nɒnɪməslɪ] *adv (use a word)* comme synonyme (**with** de); **these two words can be used synonymously** ces deux mots peuvent être employés comme synonymes

synonymy [sɪ'nɒnɪmɪ] *n* synonymie *f*

synopsis [sɪ'nɒpsɪs] *(pl* **synopses** [-si:z]*) n (gen)* résumé *m*; *(of a film)* synopsis *m*

synopsize, -ise [sɪ'nɒpsaɪz] *vt Am (summarize)* résumer, faire un résumé de

synoptic [sɪ'nɒptɪk] *adj* synoptique
►► ***the Synoptic Gospels*** les Évangiles *mpl* synoptiques, les synoptiques *mpl*

synovia [saɪ'nəʊvɪə] *n Anat* synovie *f*

synovial [sɪ'nəʊvɪəl] *adj Anat* synovial
►► ***synovial fluid*** liquide *m* synovial; ***synovial membrane*** membrane *f* synoviale

synovitis [ˌsaɪnəʊ'vaɪtɪs] *n Med* synovite *f*

synroc ['sɪnrɒk] *n* Synroc *m*

syntactic [sɪn'tæktɪk], **syntactical** [sɪn'tæktɪkəl] *adj* syntaxique
►► ***syntactic analysis*** analyse *f* syntaxique

syntactically [sɪn'tæktɪklɪ] *adv* du point de vue syntaxique

syntactician [ˌsɪntæk'tɪʃən] *n* syntacticien(enne) *m,f*

syntactics [sɪn'tæktɪks] *n (UNCOUNT)* syntactique *f*

syntagm ['sɪntæm] *n* syntagme *m*

syntagmatic [ˌsɪntæg'mætɪk] *adj* syntagmatique

syntax ['sɪntæks] *n* syntaxe *f*
►► *Comput* ***syntax error*** erreur *f* de syntaxe

synth [sɪnθ] *n Fam* synthétiseur❑ *m*

synthesis ['sɪnθəsɪs] *(pl* **syntheses** [-si:z]*) n* synthèse *f*; **the synthesis of vitamin D** la synthèse de la vitamine D; **his work is a synthesis of Eastern and Western philosophies** son œuvre est une synthèse des philosophies orientales et occidentales

synthesize, -ise ['sɪnθəsaɪz] *vt* (**a**) *Biol & Chem (produce by synthesis)* synthétiser; **the hormone synthesized by this gland** l'hormone synthétisée par cette glande (**b**) *(amalgamate, fuse)* synthétiser (**c**) *Mus* synthétiser

synthesizer ['sɪnθəsaɪzə(r)] *n* synthétiseur *m*; **voice synthesizer** synthétiseur *m* de voix

synthetic [sɪn'θetɪk] **1** *adj* (**a**) *(artificial, electronically produced)* synthétique; **research on synthetic speech** les recherches sur la parole synthétique
(**b**) *Fig Pej (food)* qui a un goût chimique; **the sauce tasted a bit synthetic** la sauce avait un goût un peu chimique
(**c**) *Ling* synthétique
(**d**) *Phil (reasoning, proposition)* synthétique
2 *n* produit *m* synthétique
3 synthetics *npl* fibres *fpl* synthétiques
►► ***synthetic drug*** drogue *f* de synthèse; ***synthetic fibre*** fibre *f* synthétique; ***synthetic image*** image *f* de synthèse; ***synthetic rubber*** caoutchouc *m* synthétique

synthetically [sɪn'θetɪklɪ] *adv* synthétiquement

syntonic [sɪn'tɒnɪk] *adj* syntonique

syntonin ['sɪntənɪn] *n Biol & Chem* syntonine *f*

syph [sɪf] *n Fam* syphilis❑ *f*

syphilis ['sɪfɪlɪs] *n (UNCOUNT)* syphilis *f*

syphilitic [ˌsɪfɪ'lɪtɪk] **1** *adj* syphilitique
2 *n* syphilitique *mf*

syphon = **siphon**

Syracuse ['saɪərəkju:z] *n* Syracuse *m*

Syria ['sɪrɪə] *n* Syrie *f*; **in Syria** en Syrie

Syrian ['sɪrɪən] **1** *n* Syrien(enne) *m,f*
2 *adj* syrien
►► ***the Syrian Desert*** le désert de Syrie

syringa [sɪ'rɪŋgə] *n Bot* seringa *m*, seringat *m*

syringe [sɪ'rɪndʒ] **1** *n* seringue *f*
2 *vt* seringuer; **to have one's ears syringed** se faire déboucher les oreilles (avec une seringue)

syrinx ['sɪrɪŋks] *n* (**a**) *Mus* syrinx *f* (**b**) *Orn* organe *m* phonateur, syrinx *f*

syrup, *Am* **sirup** ['sɪrəp] *n* (**a**) *(sweetened liquid)* sirop *m*; **peaches in syrup** pêches *fpl* au sirop (**b**) (*Br* **golden) syrup** mélasse *f* raffinée (**c**) *Med* sirop *m* (**d**) *Pej (sentimentality)* douceur *f* affectée (**e**) *Br Fam (rhyming slang* **syrup of figs** = **wig**) moumoute *f*
►► ***syrup of figs*** sirop *m* de figues *(utilisé comme laxatif)*

syrupy ['sɪrəpɪ] *adj* (**a**) *(viscous)* sirupeux (**b**) *Pej (sentimental)* sirupeux, à l'eau de rose

SYSOP ['sɪsɒp] *n Comput (abbr* **Systems Operator***)* sysop *m*, opérateur *m* système

syssarcosis [ˌsɪsɑ:'kəʊsɪs] *n Anat* syssarcose *f*

systaltic [sɪ'stæltɪk] *adj* systolique

system ['sɪstəm] *n* (**a**) *(organization, structure)* système *m*; **the British educational system** le système éducatif britannique; **the Social Security system** le système des prestations sociales; **they live in a democratic/totalitarian system** ils vivent dans un système démocratique/totalitaire
(**b**) *(method)* système *m*; **a new system of sorting mail** un nouveau système pour trier le courrier
(**c**) *Anat* système *m*; **the muscular system** le système musculaire
(**d**) *(orderliness)* méthode *f*; **you need some system in the way you work** vous devriez être plus systématique *ou* méthodique dans votre travail
(**e**) *(human body)* organisme *m*; **bad for the system** nuisible à l'organisme; **it's a bit of a shock to the system** ça fait un choc; *Fig* **to get sth out of one's system** se débarrasser de qch; **go on, get it out of your system!** vas-y, défoule-toi!; **she can't get him out of her system** elle n'arrive pas à l'oublier
(**f**) *(equipment, device, devices)* **the electrical system needs to be replaced** l'installation électrique a besoin d'être remplacée; **a fault in the cooling system** un défaut dans le circuit de refroidissement
(**g**) *(network)* réseau *m*; **the rail/river/road system** le réseau ferroviaire/fluvial/routier
(**h**) *Comput* système *m*
(**i**) *(established order)* **the system** le système; **they're hoping to overthrow the system** ils espèrent renverser le système (en place); *Fam* **you can't beat** *or* **buck the system** on ne peut rien contre le système❑
(**j**) *Geol* système *m*; **the Precambrian system** le système précambrien
►► *Comput* ***systems analysis*** analyse *f* des systèmes; *Comput* ***systems analyst*** analyste-programmeur(euse) *m,f*; *Comput* ***systems board*** carte *f* système; *Archit* ***system building*** préfabrication *f*; *Comput* ***system bus*** bus *m* système; *Mktg* ***systems buying*** achat *m* de système; *Mktg* ***systems contracting*** contrats *mpl* de système; *Comput* ***system crash*** panne *f* du système; ***system date*** date *f* système; *Comput* ***system disk*** disque *f* système; *Comput* ***systems engineer*** ingénieur *m* système; *Comput* ***systems engineering*** assistance *f* technico-commerciale; *Comput* ***system error*** erreur *f* système; *Comput* ***system failure*** panne *f* du système; *Comput* ***system file*** fichier *m* système; *Comput* ***system folder*** dossier *m* système; *Comput* ***systems management*** direction *f* systématisée; *Comput* ***systems operator*** sysop *m*, opérateur *m* système; ***system privilege*** privilège *m* d'accès au système; *Comput* ***system program*** programme *m* système; *Comput* ***system prompt*** invite *f* du système, message *m* d'attente du système; *Comput* ***system software*** logiciel *m* d'exploitation, logiciel *m* système

systematic [ˌsɪstə'mætɪk] *adj* systématique

systematically [ˌsɪstə'mætɪklɪ] *adv* systématiquement

systematics [ˌsɪstə'mætɪks] *n (UNCOUNT)* systématique *f*

systematization [ˌsɪstɪmətaɪ'zeɪʃən] *n* systématisation *f*

systematize, -ise ['sɪstəmətaɪz] *vt* systématiser

systemic [sɪs'temɪk] *adj* systémique

systemization [ˌsɪstəmaɪ'zeɪʃən] *n* systématisation *f*

systemize, -ise ['sɪstəmaɪz] *vt* systématiser

systolic [sɪ'stɒlɪk] *adj Physiol* systolique

T

T, t [tiː] *n* (**a**) *(letter)* T, t *m inv*; **two t's** deux t; **T for Tommy** ≃ T comme Thérèse (**b**) *(idiom)* **to a T** parfaitement, à merveille; **you've described him to a T** vous l'avez parfaitement décrit; **that's her to a T** c'est tout à fait elle; **the jacket fits/suits her to a T** la veste lui va à merveille

T4 [ˌtiːˈfɔː(r)] *n Med* (lymphocyte *m*) T4 *m*

TA [ˌtiːˈeɪ] *n* (**a**) *Br Mil* (*abbr* **Territorial Army**) armée *f* territoriale (**b**) *Am & Can Univ* (*abbr* **teaching assistant**) = étudiant de deuxième cycle qui assure quelques heures de cours en échange d'une bourse d'études

ta [tɑː] *exclam Br Fam* merci!▫

Taal [tɑːl] *n Ling* **the Taal** l'afrikaans *m*

TAB [tæb] *n Med* (*abbr* **typhoid-paratyphoid A and B**) (vaccin *m*) TAB *m*; **he's had a TAB injection** on lui a fait le TAB

tab [tæb] (*pt & pp* **tabbed**, *cont* **tabbing**) **1** *n* (**a**) *(on garment → flap)* patte *f*; *(→ loop)* attache *f*; *(over ear)* oreillette *f*; *(on shoelaces)* ferret *m*

(**b**) *(tag → on clothing, luggage)* étiquette *f*; *(→ on file, dictionary)* onglet *m*; *Fig* **to keep tabs on sb/sth** avoir qn/qch à l'œil, avoir l'œil sur qn/qch; **I'll keep tabs on how the case progresses** je vais surveiller l'évolution de cette affaire

(**c**) *(bill → gen)* note *f*; *(→ in bar, restaurant)* addition *f*; *also Fig* **to pick up the tab** payer l'addition *ou* la note

(**d**) *Br Fam (cigarette)* clope *f*, tige *f*

(**e**) *Fam Drugs slang (of LSD)* buvard *m*

(**f**) *Comput* tabulation *f*; **to set tabs (at)** régler *ou* positionner les tabulateurs (à)

(**g**) *Aviat* compensateur *m* automatique à ressort

2 *vt Comput (text)* mettre en colonnes (avec des tabulations)

▸▸ *Comput* ***tab key*** touche *f* de tabulation; ***tab stop*** taquet *m* de tabulation

tabard [ˈtæbəd] *n* tabard *m*, tabar *m*

tabaret [ˈtæbərɪt] *n Tex* satin *m* rayé

Tabasco® [təˈbæskəʊ] *n* Tabasco® *m*

tabbouleh [tæˈbuːleɪ] *n Culin* taboulé *m*

tabby [ˈtæbɪ] (*pl* **tabbies**) **1** *n* chat (chatte) *m,f* tigré(e)

2 *adj* tigré

▸▸ ***tabby cat*** chat (chatte) *m,f* tigré(e)

tab-delimited *adj Comput* délimité par des tabulations

tabernacle [ˈtæbənækəl] *n* (**a**) *Bible & Rel (tent, receptacle)* tabernacle *m* (**b**) *(place of worship)* temple *m*

tabes [ˈteɪbiːz] *n Med* tabes *m*, tabès *m*

tabla [ˈtæblə] *n Mus* tabla *m*

tablature [ˈtæblətʃə(r)] *n Mus* tablature *f*

table [ˈteɪbəl] **1** *n* (**a**) *(furniture)* table *f*; **to get round the negotiating table** s'asseoir à la table des négociations; **to set** *or Br* **lay the table** mettre *ou* dresser la table *ou* le couvert; *Formal* **to be at table** être à table; **to be (sitting) at the breakfast/dinner table** être à table pour le petit déjeuner/(le) dîner; **we sat down to table** nous nous sommes mis à table; **may I leave the table?** puis-je sortir de table *ou* quitter la table?; *Fam* **two drinks and I'm under the table** deux verres et je suis complètement paf!

(**b**) *(people seated)* table *f*, tablée *f*; **my uncle kept the whole table amused** mon oncle a diverti toute la tablée; **we were seated with a table of card players** nous étions assis à une table de joueurs de cartes

(**c**) *Formal (food)* **she keeps an excellent table** elle a une excellente table; **the restaurant has a hot and cold table** le restaurant propose des plats chauds et des plats froids

(**d**) *Tech (of machine)* table *f*; *Mus (of violin)* table *f* d'harmonie

(**e**) *(list)* liste *f*; *(chart)* table *f*, tableau *m*; *(of fares, prices)* tableau *m*, barème *m*; *Comput* tableau *m*; **the results are set out in the following table** les résultats sont donnés dans le tableau suivant

(**f**) *Sport* classement *m*; **our team came bottom in the table** notre équipe s'est classée dernière *ou* était dernière au classement

(**g**) *Sch* **(multiplication) table** table *f* (de multiplication); **we have to learn our 4 times table** il faut qu'on apprenne la table de 4

(**h**) *(slab → of stone, marble)* plaque *f*

(**i**) *Geog* plateau *m*

(**j**) *Anat (of cranium)* table *f*

(**k**) *(idioms)* **to put** *or* **to lay sth on the table** mettre qch sur la table; **we will not negotiate until they put a better offer on the table** nous ne négocierons pas tant qu'ils ne mettront pas une meilleure offre sur la table; **management has nothing new to put on the table** la direction n'a rien de nouveau à proposer; **the man offered me £100 under the table** l'homme m'a offert 100 livres en dessous-de-table

2 *comp* de table

3 *vt* (**a**) *Br Parl (submit → bill, motion)* présenter (**b**) *Am Parl (postpone → bill, motion)* ajourner, reporter; **the bill has been tabled** la discussion du projet de loi a été reportée

(**c**) *(tabulate)* présenter sous forme de tableau; *(classify)* classifier

(**d**) *(schedule)* prévoir, fixer; **the discussion is tabled for 4 o'clock** la discussion est prévue *ou* a été fixée à 4 heures

▸▸ *Geog* ***Table Bay*** la baie de la Table; ***table of contents*** table *f* des matières; ***table football*** baby-foot *m*; ***table knife*** couteau *m* de table; ***table lamp*** petite lampe *f*; *Bible* ***the Tables of the Law*** les Tables *fpl* de la Loi; ***table leg*** pied *m* de table; *Br* ***table licence*** = licence autorisant un restaurant à vendre des boissons alcoolisées uniquement avec les repas; ***table linen*** linge *m* de table; ***table manners*** manière *f* de se tenir à table; **he has terrible/excellent table manners** il se tient très mal/très bien à table; *Geog* ***Table Mountain*** la montagne de la Table; ***table napkin*** serviette *f* de table; ***table runner*** chemin *m* de table; ***table salt*** sel *m* de table, sel *m* fin; ***table top*** dessus *m* de table; ***table wine*** vin *m* de table

tableau [ˈtæbləʊ] (*pl* **tableaus** *or* **tableaux** [-bləʊz]) *n* tableau *m*

▸▸ ***tableau vivant*** tableau *m* vivant

tablecloth [ˈteɪbəlklɒθ] *n* nappe *f*

table d'hôte [ˈtɑːblˌdəʊt] *n* menu *m* à prix fixe

table-hop *vi Am* = aller de table en table dans un restaurant ou une réception, pour montrer qu'on a des relations

tableland [ˈteɪbəllænd] *n Geog* plateau *m*

tablemat [ˈteɪbəlmæt] *n* set *m* de table; *(of fabric)* napperon *m*

table-rapping *n (in spiritualism)* = coups frappés sur un guéridon, attribués à un esprit frappeur

tablespoon [ˈteɪbəlspuːn] *n (for serving)* grande cuillère *f*, cuillère *f* à soupe; *(as measure)* grande cuillerée *f*, cuillerée *f* à soupe

tablespoonful [ˈteɪbəlˌspuːnfʊl] *n* grande cuillerée *f*, cuillerée *f* à soupe

tablet [ˈtæblɪt] *n* (**a**) *(for writing → stone, wax etc)* tablette *f*; *(→ pad)* bloc-notes *m* (**b**) *(pill)* comprimé *m*, cachet *m* (**c**) *Br (of chocolate)* tablette *f*; *(of soap)* savonnette *f* (**d**) *(plaque)* plaque *f* (commémorative) (**e**) *Comput* tablette *f* (**f**) *Scot (sweet)* fondant *m* au caramel

table-tennis *n* tennis *m* de table, ping-pong *m*

▸▸ ***table-tennis ball*** balle *f* de ping-pong; *Br* ***table-tennis bat,*** *Am* ***table-tennis paddle*** raquette *f* de ping-pong; ***table-tennis player*** joueur(euse) *m,f* de ping-pong, pongiste *mf*

table-turning *n Pej (spiritualism)* spiritisme *m*

tableware [ˈteɪbəlweə(r)] *n* vaisselle *f*

tabloid [ˈtæblɔɪd] **1** *n (format)* tabloïd *m*; *(newspaper)* tabloïde *m*; **it's front-page news in all the tabloids** c'est à la une de tous les journaux à sensation

2 *adj* **in tabloid form** condensé, en résumé

▸▸ ***tabloid format*** format *m* tabloïd; ***tabloid newspaper*** tabloïde *m*; ***tabloid press*** presse *f* à sensation; ***tabloid television*** émissions *fpl* à sensation

> **TABLOIDS**
>
> Dans les pays anglo-saxons, le format tabloïde est caractéristique des journaux populaires. En Grande-Bretagne, les plus connus sont le 'Sun', le 'Daily Mirror', le 'Daily Mail' et le 'Daily Express'. Ces journaux sont très influents en Grande-Bretagne – le 'Sun' affiche ainsi les plus grands tirages de la presse britannique. Les "tabloids" privilégient tout particulièrement les histoires à scandale et à sensation, ce qui a suscité un débat sur le code de conduite de la presse et sur la législation à mettre en place pour protéger la vie privée.

tabloidese [ˌtæblɔɪˈdiːz] *n* style *m* tabloïde

taboo [təˈbuː] (*pl* **taboos**) **1** *adj (subject, word)* tabou; **to declare sth taboo** déclarer qch tabou; **these subjects are taboo** ces sujets sont tabou(s)

2 *n* tabou *m*

3 *vt* proscrire, interdire

tabor [ˈteɪbə(r)] *n Mus* tambourin *m*

Tabriz [tæˈbriːz] *n* Tabriz

tabu = **taboo**

tabular [ˈtæbjʊlə(r)] *adj* (**a**) *(statistics, figures)* tabulaire; **in tabular form** sous forme de tableau (**b**) *(crystal)* tabulaire

▸▸ ***tabular ledger*** grand livre *m* (à colonnes)

tabula rasa [ˌtæbjʊləˈrɑːzə] (*pl* **tabulae rasae** [ˌtæbjʊliːˈrɑːziː]) *n* table *f* rase

tabulate [ˈtæbjʊleɪt] *vt* (**a**) *(in table form)* mettre sous forme de table *ou* tableau; *(in columns)* mettre en colonnes (**b**) *(classify)* classifier

tabulated [ˈtæbjʊleɪtɪd] *adj* (**a**) *(in table form)* sous forme de table *ou* tableau; *(in columns)* en colonnes (**b**) *(classified)* classifié

tabulation [ˌtæbjʊˈleɪʃən] *n* (**a**) *(in tables)* présentation *f* *ou* disposition *f* en tables; *(in columns)* disposition *f* en colonnes (**b**) *(classification)* classification *f*

tabulator [ˈtæbjʊleɪtə(r)] *n Comput* tabulation *f*

▸▸ ***tabulator key*** touche *f* de tabulation

tacamahac [ˈtækəməhæk] *n* (**a**) *Bot (tree)* peuplier *m* de Giléad, peuplier *m* baumier (**b**) *Pharm (resin)* baume *m* vert

tac-au-tac [ˈtækəʊtæk] *n Fencing* touche *f* du tac au tac

tache [tæʃ] *n Fam* (*abbr* **moustache**) bacchantes *fpl*

tacheometer [ˌtækɪˈɒmɪtə(r)] *n* tachéomètre *m*

tacheometry [ˌtækɪˈɒmɪtrɪ] *n* tachéométrie *f*

tachina [ˈtækɪnə] *n Entom* tachine *m ou f*

▸▸ ***tachina fly*** tachine *m ou f*

tachism, tachisme [ˈtæʃɪzəm] *n Art* tachisme *m*

tachistoscope [tə'kɪstə,skəʊp] *n* tachistoscope *m*

tachograph ['tækəgrɑːf] *n* tachygraphe *m*

tachometer [tæ'kɒmɪtə(r)] *n* tachymètre *m*

tachometry [tæ'kɒmɪtrɪ] *n* tachymétrie *f*

tachycardia [,tækɪ'kɑːdɪə] *n Med* tachycardie *f*

tachycardiac [,tækɪ'kɑːdɪk] *adj Med* tachycardique

tachygraphy [tæ'kɪgrəfɪ] *n* tachygraphie *f*

tachymeter [tæ'kɪmɪtə(r)] *n* tachéomètre *m*

tachymetry [tæ'kɪmɪtrɪ] *n* tachéométrie *f*

tachypnoea, *Am* **tachypnea** [,tækɪp'niːə] *n Med* tachypnée *f*

tacit ['tæsɪt] *adj* tacite, implicite; **tacit approval** accord *m* tacite; **tacit knowledge** connaissances *fpl* implicites

tacitly ['tæsɪtlɪ] *adv* tacitement

taciturn ['tæsɪtɜːn] *adj* taciturne, qui parle peu; **he was a tall, taciturn gentleman** c'était un homme grand et taciturne

taciturnity [,tæsɪ'tɜːnɪtɪ] *n* taciturnité *f*

taciturnly ['tæsɪ,tɜːnlɪ] *adv* d'une manière taciturne

Tacitus ['tæsɪtəs] *pr n Antiq* Tacite

tack [tæk] **1** *n* (**a**) *(nail)* pointe *f*; *(for carpeting, upholstery)* semence *f*; *(for poster, notice etc)* punaise *f*

(**b**) *Br Sewing* point *m* de bâti; **to take out the tacks** retirer le bâti

(**c**) *Naut (course)* bordée *f*, bord *m*; **to make** *or* **to set a tack** courir *ou* tirer une bordée; **to be on a starboard/port tack** être tribord/bâbord amures; *Fig* **to be on the right tack** être sur la bonne voie; *Fig* **to be on the wrong tack** faire fausse route; *Fig* **he went off on a quite different tack** il est parti sur une toute autre piste; *Fig* **let's try another tack** essayons une autre tactique, changeons de tactique; *Fig* **she changed tack in mid-conversation** elle changea de sujet en pleine conversation

(**d**) *Fam (tacky things)* trucs *mpl* de mauvais goût; **her house is full of tack** sa maison est pleine de trucs de mauvais goût

(**e**) *Horseriding (harness)* sellerie *f*

(**f**) *Naut (ship's biscuits)* biscuits *mpl* de marin

2 *vt* (**a**) *(carpet)* clouer

(**b**) *Sewing* faufiler, bâtir

3 *vi Naut* faire *ou* courir *ou* tirer une bordée, louvoyer

►► *Horseriding* ***tack room*** sellerie *f*

►**tack down** *vt sep* (**a**) *(carpet, board)* clouer

(**b**) *Sewing* maintenir en place au point de bâti

►**tack on** *vt sep* (**a**) *(with nails)* fixer avec des clous

(**b**) *Sewing* bâtir

(**c**) *Fig* ajouter, rajouter; **the conclusion seems tacked on** la conclusion semble avoir été ajoutée après coup; **he tacked a joke on to the end of his story** il a rajouté une plaisanterie à la fin de son anecdote

►**tack up** *vt sep* (**a**) *(note, poster)* fixer au mur *(avec une punaise)*

(**b**) *Sewing* **to tack up a hem** faire le bâti d'un ourlet, faufiler un ourlet

tackily ['tækɪlɪ] *adv Fam (shoddily)* minablement; *(with bad taste)* avec mauvais goût ❑

tackiness ['tækɪnɪs] *n* (**a**) *(of paint, glue, substance)* **because of the tackiness of the paint/glue** parce que la peinture n'est pas encore sèche/la colle est encore poisseuse (**b**) *Fam (shabbiness → of shop, neighbourhood etc)* apparence *f* minable (**c**) *Fam (vulgarity → of remark, joke etc)* goût *m* douteux ❑; *(of clothes)* aspect *m* ringard; *(jewellery, decor)* kitch *m inv*; *(of person)* vulgarité ❑ *f*

tacking ['tækɪŋ] *n Sewing* bâti *m*, faufilage *m*; **you'll have to take out the tacking** il va falloir enlever le faufilage

►► ***tacking stitch*** point *m* de bâti; ***tacking thread*** fil *m* à bâtir, faufil *m*

tackle ['tækəl] **1** *vt* (**a**) *(task, problem)* s'attaquer à; *(question, subject)* s'attaquer à, aborder; **I'm going to tackle 'War and Peace' during the holidays** je vais attaquer 'Guerre et paix' pendant les vacances; **he tackled an enormous plate of chips** il attaqua une énorme assiettée de frites

(**b**) *(confront)* interroger; **I tackled him on** *or* **about his stand on abortion** je l'ai interrogé sur sa prise de position sur l'avortement; **I'll tackle her about the extra cost** je lui toucherai un mot *ou* je lui parlerai du coût supplémentaire

(**c**) *(in football, hockey)* tacler; *(in rugby, American football)* plaquer; *Fig (assailant, bank robber)* saisir, empoigner

2 *vi (in football, hockey)* faire un tacle; *(in rugby, American football)* faire un plaquage

3 *n* (**a**) *(equipment)* attirail *m*, matériel *m*; **fishing tackle** matériel *m ou* articles *mpl* de pêche

(**b**) *(ropes and pulleys)* appareil *m ou* appareils *mpl* de levage; *(hoist)* palan *m*; **under ship's tackle** sous palan

(**c**) *(challenge → in football, hockey)* tacle *m*; *(→ in rugby, American football)* plaquage *m*, placage *m*; **good tackle!** bien taclé!

(**d**) *(player → in American football)* plaqueur *m*

(**e**) *Naut (rigging)* gréement *m*

(**f**) *Br Fam Hum* **(wedding) tackle** *(man's genitals)* service *m* trois pièces, bijoux *mpl* de famille

tackler ['tæklə(r)] *n (in football, hockey)* tacleur(euse) *m,f*; *(in rugby, American football)* plaqueur(euse) *m,f*

tackling ['tæklɪŋ] *n (UNCOUNT)* (**a**) *(in football, hockey)* tacle *m*; *(in rugby, American football)* plaquage *m*, placage *m* (**b**) *(of problem, job)* manière *f* d'aborder

tacky ['tækɪ] *(compar* **tackier**, *superl* **tackiest**) *adj* (**a**) *(sticky)* collant, poisseux; *(paint)* pas encore sec (sèche); **wait until the glue is tacky** attendez que la colle ait commencé à prendre (**b**) *Fam (shoddy)* minable, moche (**c**) *Fam (vulgar → clothes)* ringard; *(→ jewellery, decor)* kitch *inv*; *(→ person)* beauf, vulgaire ❑; *(→ remark, joke)* de mauvais goût ❑

taco ['tækəʊ] *(pl* **tacos**) *n Culin* taco *m (crêpe mexicaine farcie et frite)*

tact [tækt] *n* tact *m*, diplomatie *f*, doigté *m*

tactful ['tæktfʊl] *adj (person)* plein de tact, qui fait preuve de tact; *(answer, remark, suggestion)* plein de tact; *(inquiry)* discret(ète); *(behaviour)* qui fait preuve de tact *ou* de délicatesse; **that wasn't a very tactful thing to say** ce n'était pas très diplomatique de dire ça; **try to be more tactful** essaie de faire preuve de plus de tact; **we must be tactful with her** nous devons faire preuve de tact avec elle; **they gave us a tactful hint** ils nous ont fait discrètement comprendre; **the tactful thing would have been to say nothing** il aurait mieux valu ne rien dire

tactfully ['tæktfʊlɪ] *adv* avec tact *ou* délicatesse; **I tactfully refrained from asking him** par tact *ou* délicatesse, je me suis retenu de lui poser la question

tactfulness ['tæktfʊlnɪs] = **tact**

tactic ['tæktɪk] **1** *n* tactique *f*

2 tactics *npl Mil & Sport* tactique *f*

tactical ['tæktɪkəl] *adj* (**a**) *(gen)* tactique

(**b**) *(shrewd)* adroit; **a purely tactical manoeuvre** une manœuvre purement diplomatique

►► ***tactical advantage*** avantage *m* tactique; ***tactical mistake*** erreur *f* tactique; ***tactical nuclear weapons*** armes *fpl* nucléaires tactiques; ***tactical voter*** = personne qui fait un vote utile; ***tactical voting*** vote *m* utile; **there has been a lot of tactical voting** beaucoup de gens ont voté utile

tactically ['tæktɪklɪ] *adv* du point de vue tactique; **to vote tactically** voter utile

tactician [tæk'tɪʃən] *n* tacticien(enne) *m,f*

tactile ['tæktaɪl] *adj* tactile

tactility [tæk'tɪlɪtɪ] *n* tactilité *f*

tactless ['tæktlɪs] *adj (person)* dépourvu de tact, qui manque de doigté; *(answer)* indiscret(ète), peu diplomatique; **what a tactless thing to say/to do!** il faut vraiment manquer de tact pour dire/faire une chose pareille!; **how tactless of him!** quel manque de tact de sa part!

tactlessly ['tæktlɪslɪ] *adv* sans tact; **she asked him rather tactlessly about his first wife** elle lui a posé des questions sur sa première femme, ce qui n'était pas très délicat de sa part

tactlessness ['tæktlɪsnɪs] *n* manque *m* de tact, indélicatesse *f*

tactual ['tæktjʊəl] *adj* tactile

tactually ['tæktjʊəlɪ] *adv* par le toucher

tad [tæd] *n Fam* (**a**) *(small bit)* **a tad** un peu ❑; **we only had a tad** on n'en a eu qu'un chouia; **the coat is a tad expensive** le manteau est un chouia trop cher; **I think you're exaggerating a tad** je crois que t'exagères un tantinet (**b**) *esp Am (boy)* mioche *m*, gamin *m*

tadger ['tædʒə(r)] *n Br Fam (penis)* chipolata *f*

tadpole ['tædpəʊl] *n Zool* têtard *m*

Tadzhik ['tɑːdʒɪk, tɑː'dʒiːk], **Tadzhiki** [tɑː'dʒiːkɪ] **1** *n* (**a**) *(person)* Tadjik *mf* (**b**) *(language)* tadjik *m*

2 *adj* tadjik

3 *comp (embassy, history)* du Tadjikistan; *(teacher)* de tadjik

Tadzhikistan [tɑː,dʒɪkɪ'stɑːn] *n* Tadjikistan *m*; **in Tadzhikistan** au Tadjikistan

tae kwon do [taɪkwɒn'dəʊ] *n* taekwondo *m*

taenia ['tiːnɪə] *n* (**a**) *Archit* ténie *f* (**b**) *Anat* structure *f* en ruban (**c**) *Med (tapeworm)* ténia *m* (**d**) *Hist (headband)* ténia *m*

Taff [tæf] = **Taffy**

taffeta ['tæfɪtə] **1** *n* taffetas *m*

2 *adj (dress)* en taffetas

taffrail ['tæfreɪl] *n Naut* lisse *f* de couronnement, rambarde *f* arrière

Taffy ['tæfɪ] *(pl* **Taffies**) *n Fam* = nom péjoratif ou humoristique désignant un Gallois

taffy ['tæfɪ] *(pl* **taffies**) *n Am* bonbon *m* au caramel

►► ***taffy apple*** pomme *f* d'amour

tag [tæg] *(pt & pp* **tagged**, *cont* **tagging**) **1** *n* (**a**) *(label → on clothes, suitcase)* étiquette *f*; *(→ on file)* onglet *m*; **(price) tag** étiquette *f* de prix; **(name) tag** *(gen)* étiquette *f* (où est marqué le nom); *(for dog, soldier)* plaque *f* d'identité

(**b**) *(on shoelace)* ferret *m*

(**c**) *(on jacket, coat → for hanging)* patte *f*

(**d**) *(for offender)* bracelet *m* électronique *(permettant de localiser les délinquants en liberté surveillée)*

(**e**) *(graffiti)* tag *m*

(**f**) *Am (licence plate)* plaque *f* minéralogique

(**g**) *(quotation)* citation *f*; *(cliché)* cliché *m*, lieu *m* commun; *(catchword)* slogan *m*; **a Latin tag** une citation latine

(**h**) *(epithet, nickname)* surnom *m*

(**i**) *Gram* question-tag *f*

(**j**) *(game)* chat *m*; **to play tag** jouer à chat

(**k**) *Comput (code)* balise *f*

2 *vt* (**a**) *(label → package, article, garment)* étiqueter; *(→ animal)* marquer; *(→ file)* mettre un onglet à

(**b**) *Fig (→ person)* étiqueter; **he was tagged as a trouble-maker** il a été classé parmi les agitateurs

(**c**) *(offender)* mettre un bracelet électronique à

(**d**) *Am (follow)* suivre; *(of detective)* filer

(**e**) *Am (for traffic offence → vehicle)* coller une contravention sur; *(→ person)* mettre une contravention à

(**f**) *(leave graffiti on)* faire des graffiti sur

(**g**) *(in game of tag)* toucher

(**h**) *Comput* baliser

►► *Am* ***tag day*** = journée de vente d'insignes pour une œuvre de bienfaisance; *Am* ***tag end*** *(oddment → of cloth, thread)* bout *m*; *(→ of goods)* restes *mpl*; *(end → of performance, day)* fin *f*; ***tag line*** *(in play)* mot *m* de la fin; *(in poem)* dernier vers *m*; *(of entertainer)* slogan *m*, *Journ* chute *f*; *Gram* ***tag question*** question-tag *f*

►**tag along** *vi* suivre; **to tag along with sb** *(follow)* suivre qn; *(accompany)* aller *ou* venir avec qn; **do you mind if I tag along?** ça vous gêne si je viens?; **the girl tagged along behind the others** *(followed)* la fille suivit les autres; *(lagged behind)* la fille était à la traîne derrière les autres

►**tag on 1** *vt sep* ajouter

2 *vi Fam* **to tag on to sb** suivre qn partout ❑; **to tag on behind sb** traîner derrière qn ❑

Tagalog [tə'gɑːlɒg] *n* (**a**) *(person)* Tagal *mf* (**b**) *Ling* tagalog *m*, tagal *m*

tagboard ['tægbɔːd] *n* carton *m* pour étiquettes

tagger ['tægə(r)] *n (graffitist)* taggeur(euse) *m,f*

tagine [tæ'ʒiːn] *n Culin* tagine *f*, tajine *f*

tagliatelle [,tæljə'telɪ] *n Culin* tagliatelles *fpl*

tagmeme ['tægmiːm] *n Ling* tagmème *m*

tagmemic [tæg'miːmɪk] *adj Ling* tagmémique

tagmemics [tæg'miːmɪks] *n (UNCOUNT) Ling* tagmémique *f*

Tagus ['teɪgəs] *n* **the Tagus** le Tage

tahini [tə'hi:nɪ] *n Culin* tahini *m*

Tahiti [tɑ:'hi:tɪ] *n* Tahiti; **in Tahiti** à Tahiti

Tahitian [tɑ:'hi:ʃən] **1** *n* Tahitien(enne) *m,f*
2 *adj* tahitien

tai chi [taɪ'tʃi:] *n* tai chi *m*

taiga ['taɪgə] *n Geog* taïga *f*

tail [teɪl] **1** *n* (**a**) *(of animal)* queue *f*; *Fig* **with one's tail between one's legs** la queue basse, la queue entre les jambes; **to be on sb's tail** suivre qn de près; **the detective was still on his tail** le détective le filait toujours; *Fam* **the car was right on my tail** la voiture me collait au derrière *ou* aux fesses; **to turn tail and run** prendre ses jambes à son cou; **it's a case of the tail wagging the dog** c'est le monde à l'envers; **the tail of the hostages is wagging the dog of foreign policy** le problème des otages décide de la politique étrangère
(**b**) *(of kite, comet, aircraft)* queue *f*; *(of musical note)* queue *f*
(**c**) *(of coat)* basque *f*; *(of dress)* traîne *f*; *(of shirt)* pan *m*
(**d**) *(end → of storm)* queue *f*; *(→ of procession)* fin *f*, queue *f*; *(→ of queue)* bout *m*
(**e**) *Fam (follower → police officer, detective)* = personne qui file; **to put a tail on sb** faire filer qn ❑; **we've got a tail** quelqu'un nous file ❑, nous sommes suivis ❑
(**f**) *Fam (buttocks)* fesses ❑ *fpl*; **he worked his tail off** il s'est vraiment décarcassé
(**g**) *(UNCOUNT) very Fam* **a bit of tail** *(woman)* une gonzesse; **he's looking for some tail** il cherche une femme à se mettre sur le bout
2 *vt* (**a**) *Fam (follow)* filocher, filer le train à
(**b**) *(animal)* couper la queue à
3 tails 1 *npl Fam (tailcoat)* queue *f* de pie ❑ **2** *adv (of coin)* **it's tails!** (c'est) pile!
►► *Aviat* ***tail assembly*** dérive *f*; ***tail end*** *(of storm, season, meeting, story)* fin *f*; *(of cloth)* bout *m*; *(of procession)* queue *f*, fin *f*; ***tail feather*** penne *f*; *Aut* ***tail lamp*** feu *m* arrière; *Am Aut* ***tail pipe*** tuyau *m* d'échappement; ***tail rotor*** *(of helicopter)* fenestron *m*; *Aviat* ***tail section*** arrière *m*; **a seat in the tail section** une place à l'arrière

▶**tail along** *vi* suivre; **she tailed along behind** *or* **after us** elle traînait derrière nous

▶**tail away** *vi (sound)* s'affaiblir, décroître; *(interest, enthusiasm, support)* diminuer petit à petit; *(book)* se terminer en queue de poisson; *(competitors in race)* s'espacer; **his voice tailed slowly away** peu à peu sa voix s'affaiblit

▶**tail back** *vi Br (traffic)* être arrêté, former un bouchon; *(demonstration, runners)* s'égrener, s'espacer; **the line of cars tailed back for 10 miles** la file de voitures s'étendait sur 16 km

▶**tail off** *vi (quality)* baisser; *(numbers)* diminuer, baisser; *(voice)* devenir inaudible; *(story)* se terminer en queue de poisson

tailback ['teɪlbæk] *n Br* bouchon *m* (de circulation); **a 3-mile tailback** un bouchon de 5 km

tailboard ['teɪlbɔ:d] *n* hayon *m (de camion)*

tailcoat [,teɪl'kəʊt] *n* queue *f* de pie

-tailed [teɪld] *suff* **short/long-tailed** à queue courte/longue

tailender [teɪl'endə(r)] *n (in race)* dernier(ère) *m,f*

tailfin ['teɪlfɪn] *n Zool* nageoire *f* caudale

tailgate ['teɪlgeɪt] *Aut* **1** *n* hayon *m*
2 *vt* coller au pare-chocs de
►► *Am* ***tailgate party*** pique-nique *m (où le hayon de la voiture sert de table)*

tailhopping ['teɪl,hɒpɪŋ] *n Ski* ruade *f*

tailings ['teɪlɪŋz] *npl (from mining)* déchets *mpl*

tailless ['teɪllɪs] *adj* (**a**) *(animal)* sans queue, *Spec* anoure (**b**) *Her (lion etc)* diffamé

taillight ['teɪllaɪt] *n Aut* feu *m* arrière

tailor ['teɪlə(r)] **1** *n* tailleur *m*
2 *vt* (**a**) *(garment)* faire sur mesure
(**b**) *Fig* **to tailor sth to** *(person, needs, requirements → adapt)* adapter qch à; *(→ conceptualize)* concevoir qch pour; **the car has been tailored for the American market** la voiture a été modifiée pour le marché américain; **the kitchen was tailored to our needs** la cuisine a été faite spécialement pour nous *ou* conçue en fonction de nos besoins
►► ***tailor's chalk*** craie *f* de tailleur; ***tailor's dummy*** mannequin *m*; *Fig Pej* **he looks like a tailor's dummy** il est tout endimanché; ***tailor's tack*** point *m* tailleur

tailorbird ['teɪləbɜ:d] *n Orn* fauvette *f* couturière

tailored ['teɪləd] *adj* (**a**) *(tailor-made → clothes, equipment)* (fait) sur mesure (**b**) *(fitted, well-cut → skirt)* ajusté; *(→ shirt)* cintré; **the tailored look is back** la mode des tailleurs ajustés est de retour
►► ***tailored suit*** tailleur *m*

tailoring ['teɪlərɪŋ] *n* (**a**) *(profession)* métier *m* de tailleur (**b**) *(work)* ouvrage *m* de tailleur

tailor-made *adj (specially made → clothes, equipment)* (fait) sur mesure; *(very suitable)* (comme) fait exprès; **top players have their rackets tailor-made for them** les joueurs de haut niveau ont des raquettes faites sur mesure; **the job could have been tailor-made for her** on dirait que le poste est taillé pour elle

tailpiece ['teɪlpi:s] *n* (**a**) *(addition → to speech)* ajout *m*; *(→ to document)* appendice *m*; *(→ to letter)* post-scriptum *m inv* (**b**) *Mus* cordier *m (d'un violon)* (**c**) *Typ* cul-de-lampe *m*

tailplane ['teɪlpleɪn] *n Aviat* stabilisateur *m*

tailrace ['teɪlreɪs] *n (for mill)* bief *m* d'aval

tailshaft ['teɪlʃɑ:ft] *n Aut* arbre *m* de sortie

tailskid ['teɪlskɪd] *n Aviat* béquille *f* de queue

tailspin ['teɪlspɪn] *n Aviat* vrille *f*; **to be in a tailspin** vriller; *Fig (economy, business)* être en dégringolade; *(person)* paniquer, s'affoler

tailwind ['teɪlwɪnd] *n* vent *m* arrière

taint [teɪnt] **1** *vt* (**a**) *(minds, morals)* corrompre, souiller; *(person)* salir la réputation de; *(reputation)* salir; **his personal life is tainted with scandal** sa vie privée fait beaucoup de scandale (**b**) *(food)* gâter; *(air)* polluer, vicier; *(water)* polluer, infecter
2 *n* (**a**) *(infection)* infection *f*; *(contamination)* contamination *f*; *(decay)* décomposition *f* (**b**) *Fig (of sin, corruption)* tache *f*, souillure *f*

tainted ['teɪntɪd] *adj* (**a**) *(morals)* corrompu, dépravé; *(reputation)* terni, sali; *(politician)* dont la réputation est ternie *ou* salie; *(money)* sale; **tainted motives** des raisons *fpl* malhonnêtes (**b**) *(food)* gâté; *(meat)* avarié; *(air)* vicié, pollué; *(water)* infecté, pollué; *(blood)* impur

taipan ['taɪpæn] *n Zool* taipan *m*

Taipei [taɪ'peɪ] *n* Taipei, Taibei

Taiwan [,taɪ'wɑ:n] *n* Taïwan; **in Taiwan** à Taïwan

Taiwanese [,taɪwə'ni:z] **1** *n* Taïwanais(e) *m,f*
2 *adj* taïwanais

Tajik = **Tadzhik**

Tajikistan = **Tadzhikistan**

Taj Mahal [,tɑ:dʒmə'hɑ:l] *n* **the Taj Mahal** le Tadj Mahall, le Taj Mahal

taka ['tɑ:kə] *n (currency)* taka *m*

takahe ['tækæheɪ] *n Orn* takahé *f*

TAKE [teɪk]

prendre	► **1A (a), (b); B (a), (c) – (e); C (b); D (a), (b); E (a); F (a); G (a), (b), (d); H (a), (b); I (a), (c), (d), (f), (g); 2 (a) – (c)**
porter	► **1B (a)**
mener	► **1B (b)**
conduire	► **1C (a)**
recevoir	► **1D (c)**
croire	► **1F (b)**
supporter	► **1F (d)**
supposer	► **1G (c)**
contenir	► **1I (e)**
passer	► **1I (i)**

(*pt* **took** [tʊk], *pp* **taken** ['teɪkən]) **1** *vt* **A.** (**a**) *(get hold of)* prendre; *(seize)* prendre, saisir; **let me take your coat** donnez-moi votre manteau; **she took the book from him** elle lui a pris le livre; **to take sb's hand** prendre qn par la main; **she took his arm** elle lui a pris le bras; **Peter took her in his arms** Peter l'a prise dans ses bras; **the wolf took its prey by the throat** le loup a saisi sa proie à la gorge
(**b**) *(get control of, capture → person)* prendre, capturer; *(→ fish, game)* prendre, attraper; *Mil* prendre, s'emparer de; **they took the town that night** ils prirent *ou* s'emparèrent de la ville cette nuit-là; **to take sb prisoner** faire qn prisonnier; **to take sb alive** prendre *ou* capturer qn vivant; **I took his queen with my rook** j'ai pris sa reine avec ma tour; **to take control of a situation** prendre une situation en main; **we took our courage in both hands** nous avons pris notre courage à deux mains; **you're taking your life in your hands doing that** c'est ta vie que tu risques en faisant cela; **to take the lead in sth** *(in competition)* prendre la tête de qch; *(set example)* être le premier à faire qch
B. (**a**) *(carry from one place to another)* porter, apporter; *(carry along, have in one's possession)* prendre, emporter; **she took her mother a cup of tea** elle a apporté une tasse de thé à sa mère; **he took the map with him** il a emporté la carte; **she took some towels up(stairs)/down(stairs)** elle a monté/descendu des serviettes; **don't forget to take your camera** n'oubliez pas (de prendre) votre appareil photo; *Fig* **the committee wanted to take the matter further** le comité voulait mener l'affaire plus loin; **the devil take it!** que le diable l'emporte!; **you can't take it with you** *(money when you die)* tu ne l'emporteras pas avec toi dans la tombe
(**b**) *(person → lead)* mener, emmener; *(→ accompany)* accompagner; **her father takes her to school** son père l'emmène à l'école; **could you take me home?** pourriez-vous me ramener *ou* me raccompagner?; **to take sb across the road** faire traverser la rue à qn; **may I take you to dinner?** puis-je vous inviter à dîner *ou* vous emmener dîner?; **he offered to take them to work in the car** il leur a proposé de les emmener au bureau en voiture *ou* de les conduire au bureau; **to take oneself to bed** aller se coucher; **please take me with you** emmène-moi, s'il te plaît; *Hum* **I can't take you anywhere** tu n'es pas sortable; **the estate agent took them over the house** l'agent immobilier leur a fait visiter la maison; **he took her round the museum** il lui a fait visiter le musée; **she used to take me along to meetings** (avant,) elle m'emmenait aux réunions; **this road will take you to the station** cette route vous mènera *ou* vous conduira à la gare; **I don't want to take you out of your way** je ne veux pas vous faire faire un détour; **her job took her all over Africa** son travail l'a fait voyager dans toute l'Afrique; **that's what first took me to Portugal** c'est ce qui m'a amené au Portugal; **whatever took him there?** qu'allait-il faire là-bas?; **the record took her to number one in the charts** le disque lui a permis d'être première au hit-parade
(**c**) *(obtain from specified place)* prendre, tirer; *(remove from specified place)* prendre, enlever; **she took a handkerchief from her pocket** elle a sorti un mouchoir de sa poche; **I took a chocolate from the box** j'ai pris un chocolat dans la boîte; **take a book from the shelf** prenez un livre sur l'étagère; **take your feet off the table** enlève tes pieds de la table; **he took the saucepan off the heat** il a ôté *ou* retiré la casserole du feu
(**d**) *(appropriate, steal)* prendre, voler; **to take sth from sb** prendre qch à qn; **someone's taken my wallet** on a pris mon portefeuille; **his article is taken directly from my book** le texte de son article est tiré directement de mon livre
(**e**) *(draw, derive)* prendre, tirer; **a passage taken from a book** un passage extrait d'un livre; **a phrase taken from Latin** une expression empruntée au latin; **the title is taken from the Bible** le titre vient de la Bible; **to take a print from a negative** tirer une épreuve d'un négatif
C. (**a**) *(of bus, car, train etc)* conduire, transporter; **the ambulance took him to hospital** l'ambulance l'a transporté à l'hôpital; **this bus will take you to the theatre** ce bus vous conduira au théâtre; **will this train take me to Cambridge?** est-ce que ce train va à *ou* passe par Cambridge?
(**b**) *(bus, car, plane, train)* prendre; *(road)* prendre, suivre; *Am* **take a right** prenez à droite
D. (**a**) *(have → attitude, bath, holiday)* prendre; *(make → nap, trip, walk)* faire; *(→ decision)* prendre; **she took a quick look at him** elle a jeté un rapide coup d'œil sur lui; *Am Fam* **let's take five** soufflons cinq minutes ❑; **he took a flying leap** il a bondi; *Am Vulg* **to take a shit** *or* **a dump** chier; *Arch or Literary* **to take a wife** prendre femme

(**b**) *Phot* **to take a photo** *or* **a picture** prendre une photo; **she took his picture** *or* **a picture of him** elle l'a pris en photo; **we had our picture taken** nous nous sommes fait photographier *ou* prendre en photo; *Fam* **he takes a good photo** *(is photogenic)* il est photogénique □

(**c**) *(receive, get)* recevoir; *(earn, win → prize)* remporter, obtenir; *(→ degree, diploma)* obtenir, avoir; **he took the blow on his arm** il a pris le coup sur le bras; **you can take the call in my office** vous pouvez prendre l'appel dans mon bureau; **the bookstore takes about $3,000 a day** la librairie fait à peu près 3000 dollars (de recette) par jour; **how much does he take home a month?** quel est son salaire mensuel net?; *Cards* **we took all the tricks** nous avons fait toutes les levées; **their team took the match** leur équipe a gagné *ou* remporté le match

E. (**a**) *(assume, undertake)* prendre; **to take the blame for sth** prendre la responsabilité de qch; **you'll have to take the consequences** c'est vous qui en subirez les conséquences; **she takes all the credit for our success** elle s'attribue tout le mérite de notre réussite; **I take responsibility for their safety** je me charge de leur sécurité; **to take the part of Hamlet** jouer (le rôle d')Hamlet

(**b**) *(commit oneself to)* **he took my side in the argument** il a pris parti pour moi dans la dispute; **the boy took an oath** *or* **a vow to avenge his family** le garçon a fait serment *ou* a juré de venger sa famille; *Am* **to take the Fifth (Amendment)** invoquer le Cinquième Amendement *(pour refuser de répondre)*

(**c**) *(allow oneself)* **may I take the liberty of inviting you to dinner?** puis-je me permettre de vous inviter à dîner?; **he took the opportunity to thank them** *or* **of thanking them** il a profité de l'occasion pour les remercier

F. (**a**) *(accept → job, gift, payment)* prendre, accepter; *(→ cheque, bet)* accepter; **the doctor only takes private patients** le docteur ne prend pas les patients du service public; **the owner won't take less than $100 for it** le propriétaire en veut au moins 100 dollars; **does this machine take pound coins?** cette machine accepte-t-elle les pièces d'une livre?; **to take a bribe** se laisser acheter *ou* corrompre; **you'll have to take me as I am** il faut me prendre comme je suis; **take things as they come** prenez les choses comme elles viennent; **I won't take "no" for an answer** pas question de refuser; **it's my last offer, (you can) take it or leave it** c'est ma dernière offre, c'est à prendre ou à laisser; **I'll take it from here** je prends la suite; **I'll take it from there** je verrai à ce moment-là

(**b**) *(accept as valid)* croire; **to take sb's advice** suivre les conseils de qn; **take it from me, he's a crook** croyez-moi, c'est un escroc

(**c**) *(deal with)* **let's take things one at a time** prenons les choses une par une; **the mayor took their questions calmly** le maire a entendu leurs questions avec calme; **how did she take the questioning?** comment a-t-elle réagi à *ou* pris l'interrogatoire?; **they took the news well** *or* **in their stride** ils ont plutôt bien pris la nouvelle; **to take sth badly** prendre mal qch; *Fam* **to take things easy** *or* **it easy** se la couler douce; *Fam* **take it easy!** *(don't get angry)* du calme! □

(**d**) *(bear, endure → pain, heat, pressure, criticism)* supporter; *(→ damage, loss)* subir; **don't take any nonsense!** ne te laisse pas faire!; **your father won't take any nonsense** ton père ne plaisante pas avec ce genre de choses; **she can take it** elle tiendra le coup; *esp Am* **I'm not taking any!** je ne marche pas!; **we couldn't take any more** on n'en pouvait plus; **I can't take much more of this** je commence à en avoir assez, je ne vais pas supporter cela bien longtemps; **I find his constant sarcasm rather hard to take** je trouve ses sarcasmes perpétuels difficiles à supporter; **don't expect me to take this lying down** ne comptez pas sur moi pour accepter ça sans rien dire; **those shoes have taken a lot of punishment** ces chaussures en ont vu de toutes les couleurs; **to take heavy loads** *(crane, engine etc)* supporter de lourdes charges; **it won't take your weight** ça ne supportera pas ton poids

(**e**) *(experience, feel)* **to take fright** prendre peur; **to take an interest in sb/sth** s'intéresser à qn/qch; **don't take offence** ne vous vexez pas, ne vous offensez pas; **no offence taken** il n'y a pas de mal; **we take pleasure in travelling** nous prenons plaisir à voyager; **she takes pride in her work** elle est fière de ce qu'elle fait; **to take pride in one's appearance** prendre soin de sa personne

G. (**a**) *(consider, look at)* prendre, considérer; **take Einstein (for example)** prenons (l'exemple d')Einstein; **take the case of Colombia** prenons le cas de la Colombie; **taking everything into consideration** tout bien considéré; **to take sb/sth seriously** prendre qn/qch au sérieux

(**b**) *(consider as)* **do you take me for an idiot?** vous me prenez pour un idiot?; **what do you take me for?** pour qui me prenez-vous?; **I took you for an Englishman** je vous croyais anglais; **he took me for somebody else** il m'a pris pour quelqu'un d'autre; **to take the news as** *or* **to be true** tenir la nouvelle pour vraie; **how old do you take her to be?** quel âge est-ce que tu lui donnes?

(**c**) *(suppose, presume)* supposer, présumer; **he's never been to Madrid, I take it** si je comprends bien, il n'a jamais été à Madrid; **I take it you're his mother** je suppose que vous êtes sa mère

(**d**) *(interpret, understand)* prendre, comprendre; **we never know how to take his jokes** on ne sait jamais comment prendre ses plaisanteries; **don't take that literally** ne le prenez pas au pied de la lettre; **he was slow to take my meaning** il lui a fallu un moment avant de comprendre ce que je voulais dire

H. (**a**) *(require)* prendre, demander; **how long will it take to get there?** combien de temps faudra-t-il pour y aller?; **the flight takes three hours** le vol dure trois heures; **it will take you ten minutes** vous en avez pour dix minutes; **it took him a minute to understand** il a mis une minute avant de comprendre; **it took us longer than I expected** cela nous a pris plus de temps que je ne pensais; **it takes time to learn a language** il faut du temps pour apprendre une langue; **what kind of batteries does it take?** quelle sorte de piles faut-il?; **my car takes unleaded** ma voiture roule au sans-plomb; **he took a bit of coaxing before he accepted** il a fallu le pousser un peu pour qu'il accepte; **it took four people to stop the brawl** ils ont dû se mettre à quatre pour arrêter la bagarre; **it takes a clever man to do that** bien malin *ou* habile qui peut le faire; **it takes courage to admit one's mistakes** il faut du courage pour admettre ses erreurs; **it takes patience to work with children** il faut de la patience *ou* il faut être patient pour travailler avec les enfants; **one glance was all it took** un regard a suffi; **the job took some doing** la tâche n'a pas été facile; **that will take some explaining** voilà qui va demander des explications; **her story takes some believing** son histoire n'est pas facile à croire; **to have what it takes to do/to be sth** avoir les qualités nécessaires pour faire/être qch; **we need someone with leadership qualities – she has what it takes** il nous faut quelqu'un qui ait des qualités de dirigeant – ce n'est pas ce qui lui manque; *Fam* **he's so lazy – it takes one to know one!** il est vraiment paresseux – tu peux parler!

(**b**) *Gram* **"falloir" takes the subjunctive** "falloir" est suivi du subjonctif; **noun that takes an "s" in the plural** nom qui prend un "s" au pluriel

I. (**a**) *(food, drink etc)* prendre; **do you take milk in your coffee?** prenez-vous du lait dans votre café?; **how do you take your coffee?** qu'est-ce que tu prends dans ton café?; **I invited him to take tea** je l'ai invité à prendre le thé; **she refused to take any food** elle a refusé de manger (quoi que ce soit); **to take drugs** se droguer; **how many pills has he taken?** combien de comprimés a-t-il pris *ou* absorbé?; **not to be taken internally** *(on packaging)* (à) usage externe; **to be taken twice a day** *(on packaging)* à prendre deux fois par jour; **to take the air** prendre l'air

(**b**) *(wear)* faire, porter; **she takes a size 10** elle prend du 38; **what size shoe do you take?** quelle est votre pointure?

(**c**) *(pick out, choose)* prendre, choisir; *(buy)* prendre, acheter; *(rent)* prendre, louer; **I'll take it** je le prends; **what newspaper do you take?** quel journal prenez-vous?; **take your partners** *(at dance)* invitez vos partenaires

(**d**) *(occupy → chair, seat)* prendre, s'asseoir sur; **take a seat** asseyez-vous; **take your seats!** prenez vos places!; **is this seat taken?** cette place est-elle occupée *ou* prise?

(**e**) *(hold → of container, building etc)* contenir, avoir une capacité de; **this bus takes fifty passengers** c'est un car de cinquante places

(**f**) *(ascertain, find out)* prendre; **to take sb's pulse/temperature** prendre le pouls/la température de qn; **to take a reading from a meter** lire *ou* relever un compteur

(**g**) *(write down → notes, letter)* prendre; **he took a note of her address** il a noté son adresse

(**h**) *(subtract)* soustraire, déduire; **they took 10 percent off the price** ils ont baissé le prix de 10 pour cent; **take 4 from 9 and you have 5** ôtez 4 de 9, il reste 5

(**i**) *Sch & Univ (exam)* passer, se présenter à; *(course)* prendre, suivre; **I took Latin and Greek at A level** ≃ j'ai pris latin et grec au bac; **she took her degree last year** elle a obtenu son diplôme l'an dernier; **she takes us for maths** on l'a en maths

(**j**) *(be in charge of) Rel* **to take a service** célébrer un office; **the assistant director took the rehearsals** l'assistant réalisateur s'est occupé des répétitions

(**k**) *(contract, develop)* **to take a chill, to take cold** prendre froid; **to take sick, to be taken ill** tomber malade; **I was taken with a fit of the giggles** j'ai été pris d'un fou rire; **she took an instant dislike to him** elle l'a tout de suite pris en aversion

(**l**) *(direct, aim)* **she took a swipe at him** elle a voulu le gifler; *Ftbl* **to take a penalty** tirer un penalty

(**m**) *(refer)* **she takes all her problems to her sister** elle raconte tous ses problèmes à sa sœur; **he took the matter to his boss** il a soumis la question à son patron; *Law* **they intend to take the case to the High Court** ils ont l'intention d'en appeler à la Cour suprême

(**n**) *(have recourse to)* **he took an axe to the door** il a donné des coups de hache dans la porte; **take the scissors to it** vas-y avec les ciseaux; **his father took a stick to him** son père lui a donné des coups de bâton; *Law* **they took legal proceedings against him** ils lui ont intenté un procès

(**o**) *(catch unawares)* prendre, surprendre; **to take sb by surprise** *or* **off guard** surprendre qn, prendre qn au dépourvu; **his death took us by surprise** sa mort nous a surpris

(**p**) *(negotiate → obstacle)* franchir, sauter; *(→ bend in road)* prendre, négocier

(**q**) *Fam (deceive, cheat)* avoir, rouler; **they took him for every penny (he was worth)** ils lui ont pris jusqu'à son dernier sou

(**r**) *Arch or Literary (have sex with)* prendre

2 *vi* (**a**) *(work, have desired effect)* prendre; **did the dye take?** est-ce que la teinture a pris?; **it was too cold for the seeds to take** il faisait trop froid pour que les graines germent

(**b**) *(become popular)* prendre, avoir du succès

(**c**) *(fish)* prendre, mordre

3 *n* (**a**) *(capture)* prise *f*

(**b**) *Cin, Phot & TV* prise *f* de vue; *Rad* enregistrement *m*, prise *f* de son; *(of record etc)* enregistrement *m*

(**c**) *Am (interpretation)* interprétation *f*; **what's your take on her attitude?** comment est-ce que tu interprètes son attitude?

(**d**) *Am Fam (takings)* recette □ *f*; *(share)* part □ *f*; **to be on the take** toucher des pots-de-vin □, palper

▸**take aback** *vt sep (astonish)* étonner, ébahir; *(disconcert)* déconcerter; **her question took him aback** sa question l'a déconcerté; **I was taken aback by the news** la nouvelle m'a beaucoup surpris

▸**take after** *vt insep* ressembler à, tenir de; **she takes after her mother in looks** physiquement, elle tient de sa mère

▸**take apart** *vt sep* (**a**) *(dismantle)* démonter; *Fig* **they took the room apart looking for evidence** ils ont mis la pièce sens dessus dessous pour trouver des preuves

(**b**) *(criticize)* critiquer

▸**take aside** *vt sep* prendre à part, emmener à l'écart; **the boss took her aside for a chat** le patron l'a prise à part pour discuter

▸**take away** *vt sep* (**a**) *(remove)* enlever, retirer; **take that knife away from him** enlevez-lui ce couteau; **they took away his pension** ils lui ont retiré sa pension; **they took their daughter away from the club** ils ont retiré leur fille du club; **his work took him away from his family for long periods** son travail le tenait éloigné de sa famille pendant de longues périodes; *Euph* **the police took his father away** son père a été arrêté par la police; **it takes away the fun** ça gâche tout

(**b**) *(carry away → object)* emporter; *(→ person)* emmener; *Br* **sandwiches to take away** *(sign)* sandwiches à emporter; **not to be taken away** *(in library)* à consulter sur place

(**c**) *Math* soustraire, retrancher; **nine take away six is three** neuf moins six font trois

▸**take away from** *vt insep (detract from)* **that doesn't take away from his achievements as an athlete** ça n'enlève rien à ses exploits d'athlète; **to take away from the pleasure/value of sth** diminuer le plaisir/la valeur de qch

▸**take back** *vt sep* (**a**) *(after absence, departure)* reprendre; **she took her husband back** elle a accepté que son mari revienne vivre avec elle; **the factory took back the workers** l'usine a repris les ouvriers

(**b**) *(gift, unsold goods, sale item etc)* reprendre

(**c**) *(return)* rapporter; *(accompany)* raccompagner; **take it back to the shop** rapporte-le au magasin; **he took her back home** il l'a raccompagnée *ou* ramenée chez elle

(**d**) *(retract, withdraw)* retirer, reprendre; **I take back everything I said** je retire tout ce que j'ai dit; **all right, I take it back!** d'accord, je n'ai rien dit!

(**e**) *(remind of the past)* **that takes me back to my childhood** ça me rappelle mon enfance; **that song takes me back forty years** cette chanson me ramène quarante ans en arrière; **it takes you back a bit, doesn't it?** ça ne nous rajeunit pas tout ça, hein?

(**f**) *Typ* transférer à la ligne précédente

▸**take down 1** *vt sep* (**a**) *(carry, lead downstairs → object)* descendre; *(→ person)* faire descendre; **the lift took us down to the 4th floor** l'ascenseur nous a amenés au 4ème étage

(**b**) *(lower)* descendre; **she took the book down from the shelf** elle a pris le livre sur l'étagère; **can you help me take the curtains down?** peux-tu m'aider à décrocher les rideaux?; **she took his picture down from the wall** elle a enlevé sa photo du mur; **he took his trousers down** il a baissé son pantalon

(**c**) *(note)* prendre, noter; **he took down the registration number** il a relevé le numéro d'immatriculation; **to take down a letter in shorthand** prendre une lettre en sténo

(**d**) *(dismantle → scaffolding, circus tent)* démonter

2 *vi* se démonter

▸**take in** *vt sep* (**a**) *(lead → person)* faire entrer; *(carry → washing, harvest etc)* rentrer

(**b**) *(bring into one's home → person)* héberger; *(→ boarder)* prendre; *(→ orphan, stray animal)* recueillir; **she takes in ironing** elle fait du repassage à domicile

(**c**) *(place in custody)* **the police took him in** la police l'a mis *ou* placé en garde à vue

(**d**) *(air, water, food etc)* **she can only take in food intravenously** on ne peut la nourrir que par intraveineuse; **whales take in air through their blowhole** les baleines respirent par l'évent

(**e**) *(understand, perceive)* saisir, comprendre; **he was sitting taking it all in** il était là, assis, écoutant tout ce qui se disait; **he didn't take in the real implications of her announcement** il n'a pas saisi les véritables implications de sa déclaration; **I can't take in the fact that I've won** je n'arrive pas à croire que j'ai gagné; **she took in the situation at a glance** elle a compris la situation en un clin d'œil

(**f**) *(make smaller → garment)* reprendre; *(→ in knitting)* diminuer; **you'd better take in the slack on the rope** tu ferais bien de tendre *ou* retendre la corde; *Naut* **to take in a sail** carguer *ou* serrer une voile

(**g**) *(cover → several countries etc)* comprendre, englober; *(→ questions, possibilities)* embrasser; **the tour takes in all the important towns** l'excursion passe par toutes les villes importantes

(**h**) *(attend, go to)* aller à; **to take in a show** aller au théâtre; **she took in the castle while in Blois** elle a visité le château pendant qu'elle était à Blois; **they took in the sights in Rome** ils ont fait le tour des sites touristiques à Rome

(**i**) *Fam (cheat, deceive)* tromper❑, rouler; **don't be taken in by him** ne vous laissez pas rouler par lui; **I'm not going to be taken in by your lies** je ne suis pas dupe de tes mensonges❑; **he was completely taken in** il marchait complètement

▸**take off 1** *vt sep* (**a**) *(remove → clothing, lid, make-up, tag)* enlever; **the boy took his clothes off** le garçon a enlevé ses vêtements *ou* s'est déshabillé; **she took her glasses off** elle a enlevé ses lunettes; **he often takes the phone off the hook** il laisse souvent le téléphone décroché; **to take sb off a list** rayer qn d'une liste; **the surgeon had to take her leg off** le chirurgien a dû l'amputer de la jambe; *Aut* **to take off the brake** desserrer le frein (à main); *Fig* **he didn't take his eyes off her all night** il ne l'a pas quittée des yeux de la soirée; **I tried to take her mind off her troubles** j'ai essayé de lui changer les idées *ou* de la distraire de ses ennuis; *Fam* **his retirement has taken ten years off him** sa retraite l'a rajeuni de dix ans❑; **to take sth off sb's hands** débarrasser qn de qch; **I'll take the baby off your hands for a few hours** je vais garder le bébé pendant quelques heures, ça te libérera

(**b**) *(deduct)* déduire, rabattre; **the teacher took one point off her grade** le professeur lui a retiré un point; **the manager took 10 percent off the price** le directeur a baissé le prix de 10 pour cent

(**c**) *(lead away)* emmener; **she was taken off to hospital** on l'a transportée à l'hôpital; **the murderer was taken off to jail** on a emmené l'assassin en prison; **her friend took her off to dinner** son ami l'a emmenée dîner; **she took herself off to Italy** elle est partie en Italie; **to take the passengers off** *(by boat from a ship)* débarquer les passagers; **the injured man was taken off the ship by helicopter** le blessé a été évacué du bateau par hélicoptère

(**d**) *(time)* **to take some time off** prendre un congé; **take a few days off** prenez quelques jours de vacances *ou* de congé; **she takes Thursdays off** elle ne travaille pas le jeudi

(**e**) *Fam (copy)* imiter❑; *(mimic)* imiter❑, singer

(**f**) *(discontinue → train, bus etc)* supprimer; *(→ show, programme)* annuler

2 *vi* (**a**) *(aeroplane)* décoller; **they took off for** *or* **to Heathrow** ils se sont envolés pour Heathrow

(**b**) *Fam (person → depart)* partir❑; *(hurriedly)* se barrer, se tirer; **he took off without telling us** il est parti sans nous avertir

(**c**) *Fam (become successful)* décoller

▸**take on 1** *vt sep* (**a**) *(accept, undertake)* prendre, accepter; **to take on the responsibility for sth** se charger de qch; **don't take on more than you can handle** ne vous surchargez pas; **she took it on herself to tell him** elle a pris sur elle de le lui dire; **he took the job on** *(position)* il a accepté le poste; *(task)* il s'est mis au travail; **to take on a bet** accepter un pari

(**b**) *(contend with, fight against)* lutter *ou* se battre contre; *(compete against)* jouer contre; **the unions took on the government** les syndicats se sont attaqués *ou* s'en sont pris au gouvernement; **I shouldn't like to take him on** je n'aimerais pas avoir affaire à lui; **he took us on at poker** il nous a défiés au poker

(**c**) *(acquire, assume)* prendre, revêtir; **her face took on a worried look** elle a pris un air inquiet; **the word takes on another meaning** le mot prend une autre signification

(**d**) *(load)* prendre, embarquer

(**e**) *(hire)* embaucher, engager

2 *vi Fam (fret, carry on)* s'en faire; **don't take on so!** ne t'en fais pas!

▸**take out** *vt sep* (**a**) *(remove → object)* prendre, sortir; *(→ stain)* ôter, enlever; *(extract → tooth)* arracher; **take the cheese out of the refrigerator** sors le fromage du réfrigérateur; **he took the knife out of his pocket** il a sorti le couteau de sa poche; **take your hands out of your pockets** enlève les mains de tes poches; **they took their children out of school** ils ont retiré leurs enfants de l'école; *Med* **to take out sb's appendix/tonsils** enlever l'appendice/les amygdales à qn; *Fig* **to take the food out of sb's mouth** retirer le pain de la bouche de qn

(**b**) *(carry, lead outside → object)* sortir; *(→ person)* faire sortir; *(escort)* emmener; **to take sb out to dinner/to the movies** emmener qn dîner/au cinéma; **I took her out for a bike ride** je l'ai emmenée faire un tour à vélo; **would you take the dog out?** tu veux bien sortir le chien *ou* aller promener le chien?

(**c**) *(food)* emporter; *Am* **sandwiches to take out** *(sign)* sandwiches à emporter

(**d**) *(obtain → subscription)* prendre; *(→ insurance policy)* souscrire à, prendre; *(→ licence)* se procurer; *(→ patent)* prendre; **to take out a mortgage** faire un emprunt immobilier

(**e**) *Fam (destroy → factory, town)* détruire❑; **to take sb out** *(kill)* buter qn, zigouiller qn, refroidir qn; **the planes took the factory out by bombing** les avions ont détruit l'usine (en la bombardant)

(**f**) *Cards* **to take out one's partner** changer la couleur annoncée par son partenaire

(**g**) *(idioms)* **to take sb out of himself/herself** changer les idées à qn; *Fam* **working as an interpreter takes a lot out of you** le travail d'interprète est épuisant❑; *Fam* **the operation really took it out of him** l'opération l'a mis à plat; *Fam* **it takes the fun out of it** ça gâche tout❑; *Fam* **to take it out on sb** s'en prendre à qn❑; *Fam* **he took his anger out on his wife** il a passé sa colère sur sa femme❑; *Fam* **don't take it out on me!** ne t'en prends pas à moi!❑

▸**take over 1** *vt sep* (**a**) *(assume responsibility of)* reprendre; **he wants his daughter to take over the business** il veut que sa fille reprenne l'affaire; **she took over my classes** elle a pris la suite de mes cours; **will you be taking over his job?** est-ce que vous allez le remplacer (dans ses fonctions)?

(**b**) *(gain control of, invade)* s'emparer de; **the military took over the country** l'armée a pris le pouvoir; **she takes the place over** *(by being bossy etc)* elle joue les despotes; **fast-food restaurants have taken over Paris** les fast-foods *ou Can* restaurants-minute ont envahi Paris

(**c**) *Fin (buy out)* absorber, racheter; **they were taken over by a Japanese firm** ils ont été rachetés par une entreprise japonaise

(**d**) *(carry across)* apporter; *(escort across)* emmener; **I'll take you over by car** je vais vous y conduire en voiture; **the boat took us over to Seattle** le bateau nous a emmenés jusqu'à Seattle

(**e**) *Typ* transférer à la ligne suivante

2 *vi* (**a**) *(as replacement)* **who will take over now that the mayor has stepped down?** qui va prendre la relève maintenant que le maire a donné sa démission?; **I'll take over when he leaves** je le remplacerai quand il partira; **will he allow her to take over?** va-t-il lui céder la place?; **compact discs have taken over from records** le (disque) compact a remplacé le (disque) vinyle

(**b**) *(army, dictator)* prendre le pouvoir

▸**take to** *vt insep* (**a**) *(have a liking for → person)* se prendre d'amitié *ou* de sympathie pour, prendre en amitié; *(→ activity, game)* prendre goût à; **I think he took to you** je crois que vous lui avez plu; **we took to one another at once** nous avons tout de suite sympathisé; **she didn't take to him** il ne lui a pas plu; **we've really taken to golf** nous avons vraiment pris goût au golf

(**b**) *(acquire as a habit)* se mettre à; **to take to drink** *or* **to the bottle** se mettre à boire; **to take**

to doing sth se mettre à faire qch; **she took to wearing black** elle s'est mise à s'habiller en noir

(**c**) *(make for, head for)* **he's taken to his bed with the flu** il est alité avec la grippe; **the rebels took to the hills** les insurgés se sont réfugiés dans les collines; **they took to the woods** ils se sont enfuis dans les bois; **to take to the road** prendre la route; **to take to the boats** monter dans les canots de sauvetage

►**take up 1** *vt sep* (**a**) *(carry, lead upstairs → object)* monter; *(→ person)* faire monter; **the lift took us up to the 25th floor** l'ascenseur nous a amenés au 25ème étage

(**b**) *(pick up → object)* ramasser, prendre; *(→ passenger)* prendre; *(→ paving stones, railway tracks)* enlever; **she took up the notes from the table** elle a ramassé *ou* pris les notes sur la table; **they're taking up the street** la rue est en travaux; **we finally took up the carpet** nous avons enfin enlevé la moquette

(**c**) *(absorb)* absorber

(**d**) *(shorten)* raccourcir; **you'd better take up the slack in that rope** tu ferais mieux de retendre *ou* tendre cette corde

(**e**) *(fill, occupy → space)* prendre, tenir; *(→ time)* prendre, demander; **this table takes up too much room** cette table prend trop de place *ou* est trop encombrante; **moving house took up the whole day** le déménagement a pris toute la journée; **her work takes up all her attention** son travail l'absorbe complètement

(**f**) *(begin, become interested in → activity, hobby)* se mettre à; *(→ job)* prendre; *(→ career)* commencer, embrasser; **when did you take up Greek?** quand est-ce que tu t'es mis au grec?; **I've taken up gardening** je me suis mis au jardinage

(**g**) *(continue, resume)* reprendre, continuer; **I took up the tale where Susan had left off** j'ai repris l'histoire là où Susan l'avait laissée; **she took up her knitting again** elle a repris son tricot

(**h**) *(adopt → attitude)* prendre, adopter; *(→ method)* adopter; *(→ place, position)* prendre; *(→ idea)* adopter; **they took up residence in town** ils se sont installés en ville; **to take up one's duties** entrer en fonctions

(**i**) *(accept → offer)* accepter; *(→ advice, suggestion)* suivre; *(→ challenge)* relever

(**j**) *(discuss)* discuter, parler de; *(bring up)* aborder; **take it up with the boss** parlez-en au patron

(**k**) *(shares, stock)* souscrire à

(**l**) *Fin (option)* lever, consolider; *(bill)* honorer, retirer

2 *vi* reprendre, continuer

►**take upon** *vt sep* **he took it upon himself to organize the meeting** il s'est chargé d'organiser la réunion

►**take up on** *vt sep* (**a**) *(accept offer, advice of)* **his daughter took him up on his advice** sa fille a suivi ses conseils; **he might take you up on that someday!** il risque de vous prendre au mot un jour!; **she took him up on his promise** elle a mis sa parole à l'épreuve

(**b**) *(ask to explain)* **I'd like to take you up on that point** j'aimerais revenir sur ce point avec vous

►**take up with** *vt insep* (**a**) *(befriend)* **to take up with sb** se lier d'amitié avec qn, prendre qn en amitié; **she took up with a bad crowd** elle s'est mise à fréquenter des vauriens

(**b**) *(preoccupy)* **to be taken up with doing sth** être occupé à faire qch; **she's very taken up with him** elle ne pense qu'à lui; **she's taken up with her business** elle est très prise par ses affaires; **meetings were taken up with talk about the economy** on passait les réunions à parler de l'économie

'Take the Money and Run' *Allen* 'Prends l'oseille et tire-toi'

'You Can't Take It With You' *Capra* 'Vous ne l'emporterez pas avec vous'

Take me to your leader
Il s'agit de la formule prononcée par les extra-terrestres fraîchement débarqués sur terre dans les vieux films de science-fiction et adressée au premier terrien rencontré. On emploie cette phrase ("menez-moi jusqu'à votre chef") de façon humoristique lorsque, dans une situation donnée, on désire parler au responsable.

takeaway ['teɪkəweɪ] *n Br & NZ (shop)* = boutique de plats à emporter; *(food)* plat *m* à emporter; **Chinese takeaway** *(shop)* traiteur *m* chinois; *(meal)* repas *m* chinois à emporter

►► ***takeaway food*** plats *mpl* à emporter; ***takeaway restaurant*** = restaurant qui fait des plats à emporter

take-home pay *n* salaire *m* net *(après impôts et déductions sociales)*

taken ['teɪkən] **1** *pp of* **take**

2 *adj* (**a**) *(seat)* pris, occupé (**b**) **to be taken with sb/sth** *(impressed)* être impressionné par qn/qch; *(interested)* s'intéresser à qn/qch; **they were quite taken with the performance** l'interprétation leur a beaucoup plu; **I'm rather taken with Aztec art** l'art aztèque me plaît beaucoup

take-off *n* (**a**) *Aviat* décollage *m* (**b**) *(of high-jumper, long-jumper)* appel *m* (**c**) *(imitation)* imitation *f*, caricature *f*; **he did a clever take-off of the prime minister** il a fait une très bonne imitation du premier ministre (**d**) *Econ* décollage *m* économique

►► *Sport* ***take-off board*** planche *f* d'appel; ***take-off slot*** *(for plane)* créneau *m* horaire de décollage

takeout ['teɪkaʊt] *n Am (shop)* = boutique de plats à emporter; *(food)* plat *m* à emporter

takeover ['teɪk,əʊvə(r)] *n (of power, of government)* prise *f* de pouvoir; *(of company)* prise *f* de contrôle, rachat *m*

►► *Fin* ***takeover bid*** offre *f* publique d'achat, OPA *f*; **to be the subject of a takeover bid** être l'objet d'une OPA; **to make** *or* **launch a takeover bid (for)** faire *ou* lancer une OPA (sur); *Fin* ***takeover stock*** titres *mpl* ramassés

taker ['teɪkə(r)] *n* (**a**) *(buyer)* acheteur(euse) *m,f*, preneur(euse) *m,f*; *(of suggestion, offer)* preneur(euse) *m,f*; **there were no takers** personne n'en voulait; **any takers?** y a-t-il des preneurs? (**b**) *(user)* **takers of drugs are at highest risk** ce sont les toxicomanes qui courent les plus grands risques

take-up *n (of benefits)* réclamation *f*; **there has been a 75 percent take-up rate for the new benefit** 75 pour cent des gens concernés par la nouvelle allocation l'ont effectivement demandée; **there has been a 10 percent take-up of the grants** 10 pour cent des subventions ont été attribuées; **take-up has been poor** la demande a été faible

►► ***take-up point*** *(of clutch)* point *m* de prise; *Tech* ***take-up reel*** bobine *f* enrouleuse; *Tech* ***take-up spool*** bobine *f* réceptrice

taking ['teɪkɪŋ] **1** *adj Old-fashioned (attractive)* engageant, séduisant

2 *n (of city, power)* prise *f*; *(of criminal)* arrestation *f*; *(of blood, sample)* prélèvement *m*; **the apples are there for the taking** prenez (donc) une pomme, elles sont là pour ça; **the money/job is his for the taking** il n'a qu'à accepter l'argent/le poste

3 takings *npl Br Com* recette *f*; **the day's takings** la recette de la journée; **the takings are good** la recette est bonne

takingly ['teɪkɪŋlɪ] *adv Old-fashioned* d'une manière engageante *ou* séduisante

tala ['tɑːlə] *n Mus* tala *m*, taal *m*

talc [tælk] **1** *n* talc *m*

2 *vt* talquer; **to talc oneself** se mettre du talc, se talquer

talcum powder ['tælkəm-] *n* talc *m*

tale [teɪl] *n* (**a**) *(story)* conte *m*, histoire *f*; *(legend)* histoire *f*, légende *f*; *(account)* récit *m*; **to tell a tale** raconter une histoire; **he told them the tale of his escape** il leur a raconté son évasion *ou* fait le récit de son évasion; **the astronaut lived/didn't live to tell the tale** l'astronaute a survécu/n'a pas survécu pour raconter ce qui s'est passé; **his drawn face told the tale of his sufferings** ses traits tirés en disaient long sur ses souffrances; **this painting tells its own tale** ce tableau est très parlant *ou* se passe de commentaires; **tales of romance** des histoires *fpl* romantiques; *Hum* **and thereby hangs a tale** et là-dessus il y en aurait à raconter

(**b**) *(gossip)* histoires *fpl*; **there's a tale going around that they're moving** on raconte qu'ils vont déménager; **to tell tales** *(inform)* cafter, rapporter; **to tell tales on sb** raconter des histoires sur le compte de qn; **she's been telling tales to the teacher again** elle est encore allée cafter *ou* rapporter à la maîtresse; **you shouldn't tell tales** il ne faut pas rapporter; *Fig* **to tell tales out of school** *(be indiscreet)* être indiscret, trop parler

'A Tale of Two Cities' *Dickens* 'Le Conte des deux villes'

'Tales from Shakespeare' *Lamb* 'Contes tirés de Shakespeare'

talebearer ['teɪl,beərə(r)] *n Literary* rapporteur(euse) *m,f*

talebearing ['teɪl,beərɪŋ] *n Literary* rapportage *m*

talent ['tælənt] *n* (**a**) *(gift)* talent *m*, don *m*; **she has great musical talent** elle est très douée pour la musique, elle a un grand don pour la musique; **I have quite a talent for sewing** je suis assez doué pour la *ou* en couture; **it's just one of my many hidden talents** c'est un de mes nombreux talents cachés; **you have a talent for saying the wrong thing** tu as le don pour dire ce qu'il ne faut pas

(**b**) *(talented person)* talent *m*; **she is one of our most promising young talents** c'est un de nos jeunes talents les plus prometteurs

(**c**) *Br Fam (attractive men)* beaux mecs *mpl*; *(attractive women)* belles nanas *fpl*; **he's out chatting up the local talent** il est en train de draguer les minettes du coin; **it's an OK bar, but there's not much talent** c'est pas mal comme bar, mais question mecs/nanas, ça casse pas des briques

(**d**) *Hist (coin)* talent *m*

►► ***talent scout, talent spotter*** *(for films)* dénicheur(euse) *m,f* de vedettes; *(for sport)* dénicheur(euse) *m,f* de futurs grands joueurs

talented ['tæləntɪd] *adj* talentueux, doué; **she's a talented musician** c'est une musicienne de talent; **she's really talented** elle a beaucoup de talent

talentless ['tæləntlɪs] *adj* sans talent

tales ['teɪliːz] *n Law* jurés *mpl* suppléants

tale-telling *n* rapportage *m*

Taliban ['tɑːlɪbɑːn] *n* taliban *m*

talipes ['tælɪpiːz] *n Med* pied *m* bot

talipot ['tælɪpɒt] *n Bot* talipot *m*, tallipot *m*

talisman ['tælɪzmən] (*pl* **talismans**) *n* talisman *m*

talismanic [,tælɪz'mænɪk] *adj* talismanique

TALK [tɔːk]

parler	► **1 (a), (c); 2 (a), (b)**
discuter	► **1 (a)**
s'entretenir	► **1 (a)**
causer	► **1 (b)**
conversation	► **3 (a)**
discussion	► **3 (a), (d)**
causette	► **3 (a)**
entretien	► **3 (a)**
exposé	► **3 (b)**
paroles	► **3 (c)**
racontars	► **3 (e)**
négociations	► **4**

1 *vi* (**a**) *(speak)* parler; *(discuss)* discuter; *(confer)* s'entretenir; **to talk to sb** parler à qn; **to talk with sb** parler *ou* s'entretenir avec qn; **to talk of** *or* **about sth** parler de qch; **we sat talking together** nous sommes restés à discuter *ou* à bavarder; **she didn't talk to me the whole evening** elle ne m'a pas dit un mot de la soirée; **to talk in signs/riddles** parler par signes/par énigmes; **they were talking in Chinese** ils parlaient en chinois; **I've been teaching my parakeet to talk** j'ai appris à parler à mon perroquet; **to talk**

for the sake of talking parler pour ne rien dire; **that's no way to talk!** en voilà des façons de parler!; **they no longer talk to each other** ils ne se parlent plus, ils ne s'adressent plus la parole; **who do you think you're talking to?** non, mais à qui croyez-vous parler?; **don't you talk to me like that!** je t'interdis de me parler sur ce ton!; **to talk to oneself** parler tout seul; **he likes to hear himself talk** il s'écoute parler; **I'll talk to you about it tomorrow morning** *(converse)* je vous en parlerai demain matin; *(as threat)* j'aurai deux mots à vous dire à ce sujet demain matin; **it's no use talking to him, he never listens!** on perd son temps avec lui, il n'écoute jamais!; **to talk of this and that** parler de la pluie et du beau temps *ou* de choses et d'autres; **talking of Switzerland, have you ever been skiing?** à propos de la Suisse, vous avez déjà fait du ski?; **they talked of little else** ils n'ont parlé que de cela; **he's always talking big** c'est un beau parleur; **now you're talking!** voilà, c'est beaucoup mieux!; **you can talk!, look who's talking!, you're a fine one to talk!** tu peux parler, toi!; **it's easy for you to talk, you've never had a gun in your back!** c'est facile à dire *ou* tu as beau jeu de dire ça, on ne t'a jamais braqué un pistolet dans le dos!; **talk about luck!** *(admiring)* qu'est-ce qu'il a comme chance!, quel veinard!; *(complaining)* tu parles d'une veine! **talk about lucky!** tu parles d'un coup de bol!; **talk about a waste of time!** tu parles d'une perte de temps!; **to talk through** *Fam* **one's hat** *or* **the back of one's neck** *or* **one's backside** *or Vulg* **one's arse** dire des bêtises ❑ *ou* n'importe quoi ❑

(**b**) *(chat)* causer, bavarder; *(gossip)* jaser; **you know how people talk** les gens sont tellement bavards

(**c**) *(reveal secrets)* parler; **to make sb talk** faire parler qn; **we have ways of making people talk** on a les moyens de faire parler les gens; **someone must have talked** quelqu'un a dû parler

2 *vt* (**a**) *(language)* parler; **to talk slang** parler argot; **talk sense!** ne dis pas de sottises!, ne dis pas n'importe quoi!; **now you're talking sense** vous dites enfin des choses sensées; **to talk (some) sense into sb** faire entendre raison à qn; **stop talking rubbish** *or* **nonsense!** arrête de dire des bêtises!; *Am Fam* **to talk the talk** avoir la langue bien pendue; *esp Am Fam* **he can talk the talk but can he walk the walk?** est-ce qu'il est aussi doué pour agir que pour parler? ❑

(**b**) *(discuss)* parler; **to talk business/politics** parler affaires/politique

3 *n* (**a**) *(conversation)* conversation *f*; *(discussion)* discussion *f*; *(chat)* causette *f*, causerie *f*; *(formal)* entretien *m*; **to have a talk with sb about sth** parler de qch avec qn, s'entretenir avec qn de qch; **I'll have a talk with him about it** je lui en parlerai; **we had a long talk** nous avons eu une longue discussion; **can we have a little talk?** je peux vous parler deux minutes?; **that's fighting talk!** c'est un défi!

(**b**) *(speech, lecture)* exposé *m*; **to give a talk on** *or* **about sth** faire un exposé sur qch; **there was a series of radio talks on modern Japan** il y a eu à la radio une série d'émissions où des gens venaient parler du Japon moderne

(**c**) *(UNCOUNT) (noise of talking)* paroles *fpl*, propos *mpl*; **there is a lot of talk in the background** il y a beaucoup de bruit *ou* de gens qui parlent

(**d**) *(speculative)* discussion *f*, rumeur *f*; **most of the talk was about the new road** il a surtout été question de *ou* on a surtout parlé de la nouvelle route; **there's some talk of building a concert hall** *(discussion)* il est question *ou* on parle de construire une salle de concert; *(rumour)* le bruit court qu'on va construire une salle de concert; **there has been talk of it** on en a parlé, il en a été question; **enough of this idle talk!** assez parlé!; **he's all talk** tout ce qu'il dit, c'est du vent

(**e**) *(UNCOUNT) (gossip)* racontars *mpl*, bavardages *mpl*; **it's only talk** ce sont des racontars, tout ça; **their behaviour is causing a lot of talk** leur conduite fait jaser; **it's/she's the talk of the town** on ne parle que de ça/que d'elle; **the wedding was the talk of the town** on ne parlait que du mariage

4 talks *npl (negotiations)* négociations *fpl*, pourparlers *mpl*; *(conference)* conférence *f*; **official peace talks** des pourparlers *mpl* officiels sur la paix; **so far there have only been talks about talks** jusqu'ici il n'y a eu que des négociations préliminaires

►► ***talk show*** causerie *f* (radiodiffusée/télévisée), talk-show *m*

►**talk about** *vt insep* (**a**) *(discuss)* parler de; **to talk to sb about sth** parler de qch à qn; **there's an important matter I must talk to you about** j'ai à vous parler *ou* entretenir d'une affaire importante; **the new model has been much talked about** on a beaucoup parlé du nouveau modèle; **it gives them something to talk about** ça leur fait un sujet de conversation; **this will give them something to talk about** *(gossip about)* voilà quelque chose qui va les faire jaser; **to get oneself talked about** faire parler de soi; **they were talking about going away for the weekend** ils parlaient *ou* envisageaient de partir pour le week-end

(**b**) *(mean)* **we're not talking about that!** il ne s'agit pas de cela!; **when it comes to hardship, he knows what he's talking about** pour ce qui est de souffrir, il sait de quoi il parle; **when it comes to cars, he knows what he's talking about** pour ce qui est des voitures, il connaît son affaire; **what are you talking about?** *(I don't understand)* de quoi parles-tu?; *(annoyed)* qu'est-ce que tu racontes?; **you don't know what you're talking about!** tu ne sais pas ce que tu dis!; **I don't know what you're talking about** *(in answer to accusation)* je ne sais pas ce que vous voulez dire; **it's not as if we're talking about spending millions** qui parle de dépenser des millions?; **how much are we talking about?** il faut compter combien?, ça va chercher dans les combien?; **but I'm talking about a matter of principle!** pour moi, c'est une question de principe!

►**talk at** *vt insep* **I hate people who talk at me not to me** je ne supporte pas les gens qui parlent sans se soucier de ce que j'ai à dire

►**talk away 1** *vi* passer le temps à parler, parler sans arrêt; **they were still talking away at 3 a.m.** ils étaient encore en grande conversation à 3 heures du matin

2 *vt sep* **to talk the night away** passer la nuit à parler

►**talk back** *vi (insolently)* répondre; **to talk back to sb** répondre (insolemment) à qn; **don't you talk back to me!** ne me réponds pas (comme ça)!

►**talk down 1** *vt sep* (**a**) *(silence)* **to talk sb down** réduire qn au silence (en parlant plus fort que lui/elle/*etc*)

(**b**) *(aircraft)* faire atterrir par radio-contrôle

(**c**) *(would-be suicide)* **the police managed to talk him down from the roof** la police a réussi à le convaincre de redescendre du toit

2 *vi* **to talk down to sb** parler à qn comme à un enfant

►**talk into** *vt sep* **to talk sb into doing sth** persuader qn de faire qch; **she allowed herself to be talked into going** elle s'est laissé convaincre d'y aller; **to talk oneself into a job** *(by trying to impress)* obtenir un emploi grâce à son baratin; **you've just talked yourself into a job** *(by saying that)* ce que vous avez dit là m'a convaincu et vous avez le poste

►**talk out** *vt sep* (**a**) *(problem, disagreement)* débattre de, discuter de; **they managed to talk out the problem** à force de discussions, ils sont arrivés à trouver une solution au problème

(**b**) *Pol* **to talk out a bill** = prolonger la discussion d'un projet de loi jusqu'à ce qu'il soit trop tard pour le voter avant la clôture de la séance

►**talk out of** *vt sep* **to talk sb out of doing sth** dissuader qn de faire qch; **try to talk him out of it** essayez de l'en dissuader; **to talk oneself out of trouble** se tirer d'affaire grâce à son baratin; **talk yourself out of that one!** vas-y, essaie de t'en sortir cette fois-ci!

►**talk over** *vt sep* discuter *ou* débattre de; **let's talk it over** discutons-en, parlons-en; **we'll have to talk the problem over** il va falloir que l'on parle de ce problème; **to talk things over** discuter

►**talk round 1** *vt sep (convince)* persuader, convaincre; **to talk sb round to one's way of thinking** amener qn à sa façon de penser *ou* à son point de vue; **I'm sure she can be talked round** je suis sûr qu'on peut la convaincre

2 *vt insep (problem)* tourner autour de; **I'm tired of just talking round the subject** j'en ai assez de tourner autour de la question

►**talk up** *vt sep* vanter les mérites de, faire de la publicité pour; **to talk up sb's chances** surestimer les chances de qn; **the Chancellor is trying to talk up the economy** le Chancelier s'est montré optimiste pour tenter de redynamiser l'économie

---

talkathon ['tɔːkəθɒn] *n Am Hum (in Congress, on television etc)* débat-marathon *m*

talkative ['tɔːkətɪv] *adj* bavard, loquace

talkatively ['tɔːkətɪvlɪ] *adv* loquacement

talkativeness ['tɔːkətɪvnɪs] *n* volubilité *f*, loquacité *f*

talk-back *n TV & Rad* émetteur-récepteur *m*

talker ['tɔːkə(r)] *n* (**a**) *(speaker)* causeur(euse) *m,f*, bavard(e) *m,f*; **she's a real talker** c'est une grande bavarde, c'est un vrai moulin à paroles; **my father was never much of a talker** mon père n'a jamais été très bavard; **he's a brilliant talker** c'est un beau parleur; **he's a fast talker** *(gen)* il parle vite; *Com* il a du bagout (**b**) *(talking bird)* oiseau *m* qui parle

talkie ['tɔːkɪ] *n Fam Old-fashioned* film *m* parlant ❑

talk-in *n Fam* causerie *f* suivie d'une discussion ❑

talking ['tɔːkɪŋ] **1** *n (UNCOUNT)* conversation *f*, propos *mpl*; **he did all the talking** il était le seul à parler; **let me do the talking** laisse-moi parler; **no talking, please!** pas de bavardage!

2 *adj (film)* parlant; *(bird)* qui parle

►► ***talking book*** livre *m* enregistré; *TV* ***talking head*** *(presenter)* présentateur(trice) *m,f* de télévision *(dont on ne voit que la tête et les épaules)*; *Hum or Pej (interviewee)* = expert qui s'exprime à la télévision; ***talking point*** sujet *m* de conversation *ou* de discussion; *Br* ***talking shop*** lieu *m* de palabres; **the United Nations is accused of being a talking shop** on accuse les Nations Unies de ne faire que de la parlotte

talking-to *n Fam* savon *m*; **to give sb a talking-to** passer un savon à qn; **he needs a good talking-to** il a besoin qu'on lui passe un bon savon

talky ['tɔːkɪ] *(compar* **talkier**, *superl* **talkiest**) *adj Am (film, novel)* où il y a beaucoup de dialogues, qui manque d'action

tall [tɔːl] **1** *adj* (**a**) *(person)* grand, de grande taille; **how tall are you?** combien mesurez-vous?; **I'm 6 feet tall** je mesure *ou* fais 1 mètre 80; **my sister is taller than me** ma sœur est plus grande que moi; **she's grown a lot taller in the past year** elle a beaucoup grandi depuis un an; **he's very tall and slim** il est très grand et mince

(**b**) *(building)* haut, élevé; *(tree)* grand, haut; *(grass)* haut; **how tall is that tree?** quelle est la hauteur de cet arbre?; **it's at least 80 feet tall** il fait au moins 25 mètres de haut; **it's a very tall tree** c'est un très grand arbre

(**c**) *(idioms) Hum* **he's tall, dark and handsome** c'est un beau ténébreux; **a tall** *Br* **story** *or Am* **tale** une histoire invraisemblable *ou* abracadabrante, une histoire à dormir debout; **that's a tall order** c'est beaucoup demander

2 *adv Fig* **to walk** *or* **stand tall** marcher la tête haute

►► *Bot* ***tall melilot*** mélilot *m* élevé; *Fam* ***tall poppy syndrome*** envie ❑ *f*, jalousie ❑ *f*; **he's got tall poppy syndrome** c'est un envieux *ou* un jaloux; **he's become the victim of tall poppy syndrome in the media** les journalistes s'en prennent à lui car ils sont jaloux de sa réussite; ***tall ship*** grand voilier *m*

tallboy ['tɔːlbɔɪ] *n* (**a**) *(furniture)* (grande) commode *f* (**b**) *(can of beer)* grande cannette *f* de bière

Tallin, Tallinn ['tælɪn] *n* Tallinn

tallish ['tɔːlɪʃ] *adj* assez grand

tallith ['tælɪθ] *n Rel* taleth *m*

tallness ['tɔːlnɪs] *n (of person)* (grande) taille *f*; *(of tree, building, grass)* hauteur *f*

tallow ['tæləʊ] *n* suif *m*

►► ***tallow candle*** chandelle *f*; *Austr* ***tallow wood*** grand eucalyptus *m*

tally ['tælɪ] (*pl* **tallies**, *pt & pp* **tallied**) **1** *n* (**a**) *(record)* compte *m*, enregistrement *m*; *Com* pointage *m*; *Am Sport (score)* score *m*; **to keep a tally of names** pointer des noms sur une liste; **to keep a tally of the score** compter les points; **automatic counters kept a tally of passing cars** des appareils automatiques comptaient les voitures qui passaient
(**b**) *Hist (stick)* taille *f*, baguette *f* à encoches; *(mark)* encoche *f*
(**c**) *(label)* étiquette *f*
(**d**) *(counterfoil → of cheque, ticket)* talon *m*; *(duplicate)* contrepartie *f*, double *m*
2 *vt* (**a**) *(record)* pointer
(**b**) *(count up)* compter
3 *vi* correspondre; **I couldn't make the figures tally** je ne pouvais faire concorder les chiffres; **your story must tally with mine** il faut que ta version des faits concorde avec la mienne
▸▸ ***tally clerk*** marqueur(euse) *m,f*, pointeur(euse) *m,f*; ***tally sheet*** *Com* bordereau *m*; *Sport* feuille *f* de pointage

tally-ho (*pl* **tally-hos**) **1** *exclam* taïaut!, tayaut!
2 *n* cri *m* de taïaut

tallyman ['tælɪmən] (*pl* **tallymen** [-mən]) *n* (**a**) *(recorder)* pointeur *m*, contrôleur *m* (**b**) *Br (collector)* encaisseur *m* (de traites)

Talmud ['tælmʊd] *n* Talmud *m*

Talmudic [tæl'mʊdɪk] *adj* talmudique

Talmudist ['tælmʊdɪst] *n* Talmudiste *m*

talon ['tælən] *n* (**a**) *(of hawk, eagle)* serre *f*; *(of tiger, lion)* griffe *f*; *Fig (of person)* griffe *f* (**b**) *Cards* talon *m* (**c**) *(of lock)* ergot *m* (**d**) *Archit* talon *m*, doucine *f*

taloned ['tælənd] *adj (bird)* muni de serres; *(animal)* muni de griffes

talus ['teɪləs] *n* (**a**) *Geol* talus *m* d'éboulis (**b**) *Anat* astragale *m*

tamable = **tameable**

tamale [tə'mɑːlɪ] *n Culin* tamal *m*, tamale *m* *(spécialité mexicaine à base de viande hachée et de maïs enveloppés dans une feuille de maïs)*

tamari [tæ'mɑːrɪ] *n Culin* tamari *m*

tamarillo [,tæmə'rɪləʊ] (*pl* **tamarillos**) *n Bot* tomate *f* en arbre, cyphomandra *m*

tamarin ['tæmərɪn] *n Zool* tamarin *m*

tamarind ['tæmərɪnd] *n (fruit)* tamarin *m*; *(tree)* tamarinier *m*

tamarisk ['tæmərɪsk] *n Bot* tamaris *m*, tamarix *m*

tambour ['tæm,bʊə(r)] *n* (**a**) *Sewing* tambour *m*, métier *m* à broder (**b**) *(on desk, cabinet)* rideau *m* (**c**) *Archit & Mus* tambour *m*

tambourin ['tæmbərɪn] *n Mus* tambourin *m*
▸▸ ***tambourin player*** tambourineur(euse) *m,f*

tambourine [,tæmbə'riːn] *n* tambour *m* de basque, tambourin *m*

Tamburlaine ['tæmbəleɪn] *pr n* **Tamburlaine the Great** Tamerlan le Grand

tame [teɪm] **1** *adj* (**a**) *(as pet → hamster, rabbit)* apprivoisé, domestiqué; *(normally wild → bear, hawk)* apprivoisé; *(in circus → lion, tiger)* dompté; **the deer had become very tame** les cerfs n'étaient plus du tout farouches; *Hum* **I'll ask our tame Frenchman if he knows what it means** je vais demander à notre Français de service s'il sait ce que cela veut dire
(**b**) *(insipid, weak)* fade, insipide; **the book has a very tame ending** le livre finit de manière très banale; **it was a very tame party** cette soirée n'était vraiment pas très folichonne; **the government's measures were considered rather tame** les mesures gouvernementales ont été jugées plutôt modérées
2 *vt* (**a**) *(as pet → hamster, rabbit)* apprivoiser, domestiquer; *(normally wild → bear, hawk)* apprivoiser; *(in circus → lion, tiger)* dompter
(**b**) *(person)* mater, soumettre; *(natural forces)* apprivoiser; *(passions)* dominer; *(plant, wilderness)* cultiver

tameable ['teɪməbəl] *adj (hawk, bear, rabbit)* apprivoisable; *(lion, tiger)* domptable

tamely ['teɪmlɪ] *adv (submit)* docilement, sans résistance; *(end)* platement, de manière insipide; *(write)* de manière fade, platement

tameness ['teɪmnɪs] *n* (**a**) *(of bird, hamster)* nature *f* apprivoisée; *(of lion, tiger)* nature *f* domptée (**b**) *(of person)* docilité *f*, nature *f* docile (**c**) *(of ending, style)* fadeur *f*, insipidité *f*; *(of party, film)* manque *m* d'intérêt, banalité *f*

tamer ['teɪmə(r)] *n* dompteur(euse) *m,f*

Tamil ['tæmɪl] **1** *n* (**a**) *(person)* Tamoul(e) *m,f* (**b**) *Ling* tamoul *m*
2 *adj* tamoul
▸▸ *Geog* ***Tamil Nadu*** Tamil Nadu *m*; ***the Tamil Tigers*** les Tigres *mpl* tamouls

taming ['teɪmɪŋ] *n (of hawk, bear, rabbit)* apprivoisement *m*; *(of lions, tigers)* domptage *m*, dressage *m*

'The Taming of the Shrew' *Shakespeare, Zeffirelli* 'La Mégère apprivoisée'

Tammany ['tæmənɪ] *n Am Pol* = organisation centrale du parti démocrate de New York (souvent impliquée dans des affaires de corruption)
▸▸ ***Tammany Hall*** = siège du parti démocrate new-yorkais aux 18ème et 19ème siècles

Tammanyism ['tæmənɪɪzəm] *n Am Pol* = corruption dans l'administration politique

tammy ['tæmɪ] (*pl* **tammies**) *n Fam (cap)* béret *m* écossais ❑

tam-o'-shanter [tæmə'ʃæntə(r)] *n* béret *m* écossais

tamp [tæmp] *vt (earth)* tasser, damer; *(pipe)* bourrer; *(tobacco)* tasser; *(for blasting → drill hole)* bourrer (à l'argile/au sable)

▸**tamp down** *vt sep (earth)* tasser, damer; *(gunpowder, tobacco)* tasser

tampax® ['tæmpæks] *n* tampon *m*

tamper ['tæmpə(r)] *n* (**a**) *(person)* borreur *m*
(**b**) *(tool)* dame *f* à fouler
(**c**) *Phys* réflecteur *m* de neutrons

▸**tamper with** *vt insep* (**a**) *(meddle with → brakes, machinery)* trafiquer; *(→ lock)* essayer de forcer *ou* crocheter, fausser; *(→ possessions)* toucher à; *(falsify → records, accounts, evidence)* falsifier, altérer; **someone has been tampering with my papers** on a touché à mes papiers; **stop tampering with the radio** arrête de jouer avec la radio; **the TV has been tampered with** quelqu'un a déréglé la télévision
(**b**) *Am Law (witness)* suborner; *(jury)* soudoyer

tamper-evident *adj* qui révèle toute tentative d'effraction; **tamper-evident packaging** témoin *m* d'effraction

tamperproof ['tæmpə,pruːf] *adj* scellé

tampion ['tæmpɪən] *n* bouchon *m*; *Mil* **(muzzle)** tampion tampon *m ou* tape *f* de bouche; **to put a tampion in a gun** taper un canon

tampon ['tæmpɒn] *n Med* tampon *m*; *(for menstrual use)* tampon *m* périodique *ou* hygiénique

tam-tam ['tæmtæm] *n* tam-tam *m*

tan [tæn] (*pt & pp* **tanned**, *cont* **tanning**) **1** *n* (**a**) *(from sun)* bronzage *m*; **I got a good tan in the mountains** j'ai bien bronzé à la montagne; **to have a tan** être bronzé *ou* hâlé; **to lose one's tan** perdre son bronzage
(**b**) *Math* tangente *f*
2 *vt* (**a**) *(leather, skins)* tanner; *Fam Fig* **to tan sb's hide** rosser qn
(**b**) *(of sun)* bronzer, brunir
3 *vi* bronzer; **her skin tans easily** elle a une peau qui bronze facilement; **I tan easily** je bronze facilement
4 *adj* (**a**) *(colour)* brun roux *(inv)*, brun clair *(inv)*; *(leather)* jaune
(**b**) *Am (tanned)* bronzé
▸▸ ***tan line*** marque *f* de bronzage

tanager ['tænədʒə(r)] *n Orn* tangara *m*

tandem ['tændəm] **1** *n* (**a**) *(carriage)* tandem *m*; **to harness two horses in tandem** atteler deux chevaux en tandem *ou* en flèche; *Fig* **to work in tandem** travailler en tandem *ou* en collaboration (**b**) *(bike)* tandem *m*
2 *adv* **to ride tandem** rouler en tandem
3 *adj* double
▸▸ *Tel* ***tandem exchange*** central *m* tandem

tandoori [tæn'dʊərɪ] **1** *n* cuisine *f* tandoori
2 *adj* tandoori *(inv)*
▸▸ ***tandoori chicken*** poulet *m* tandoori

tang [tæŋ] *n* (**a**) *(taste)* goût *m* (fort); **the tang of orange juice** le goût acide du jus d'orange; **the tang of mustard** le goût fort de la moutarde (**b**) *(smell)* odeur *f* forte; **the tang of the sea** l'odeur *f* forte de la mer; **the tang of the morning air** l'air *m* vif du matin (**c**) *(hint → of irony)* pointe *f* (**d**) *(of knife, sword)* soie *f*

tanga ['tæŋgə] *n* mini-slip *m*

tangelo ['tændʒələʊ] (*pl* **tangelos**) *n* tangelo *m*

tangency ['tændʒənsɪ] *n Geom* tangence *f*

tangent ['tændʒənt] *n Geom* tangente *f*; **to be at a tangent** former une tangente; *Fig* **to go off at** *or* **on a tangent** partir dans une digression

tangential [tæn'dʒenʃəl] *adj Geom* tangentiel; *Fig* **that is tangential to the main issue** étant donné le sujet, ceci est secondaire
▸▸ ***tangential line*** ligne *f* tangentielle, tangente *f*

tangentiality [tæn,dʒenʃɪ'ælətɪ] *n Geom* tangence *f*; *Fig* caractère *m* secondaire

tangentially [tæn'dʒenʃəlɪ] *adv Geom* tangentiellement; *Fig* indirectement

tangerine [,tændʒə'riːn] **1** *n* (**a**) *(fruit)* mandarine *f*; *(tree)* mandarinier *m* (**b**) *(colour)* mandarine *f*
2 *adj (in colour)* mandarine *(inv)*
▸▸ ***tangerine tree*** mandarinier *m*

tangibility [,tændʒə'bɪlətɪ] *n* tangibilité *f*

tangible ['tændʒəbəl] **1** *adj* (**a**) *(palpable)* tangible; *(real, substantial)* tangible, réel; **the tangible world** le monde sensible; **tangible proof** des preuves *fpl* tangibles; **it made no tangible difference** ça n'a pas changé grand-chose
(**b**) *Law (property)* corporel
2 *n Fin* **tangibles** actif *m* corporel, valeurs *fpl* matérielles
▸▸ *Fin* ***tangible assets*** actif *m* corporel, valeurs *fpl* matérielles; *Fin* ***tangible fixed assets*** immobilisations *fpl* corporelles

tangibly ['tændʒəblɪ] *adv* tangiblement, manifestement, de manière tangible

Tangier [tæn'dʒɪə(r)] *n* Tanger

tanginess ['tæŋɪnɪs] *n (in taste)* goût *m* fort; *(in smell)* odeur *f* forte

tangle[1] ['tæŋgəl] **1** *n* (**a**) *(of wire, string, branches, weeds)* enchevêtrement *m*; **this string is in an awful tangle** cette ficelle est tout emmêlée *ou* enchevêtrée; **to get into a tangle** *(wires, string, hair)* s'emmêler; **a tangle of hair** des cheveux *mpl* emmêlés; **a tangle of creepers** un enchevêtrement de lianes
(**b**) *(muddle)* fouillis *m*, confusion *f*; **a legal tangle** une affaire compliquée *ou* embrouillée du point de vue juridique; **to get into a tangle** *(person)* s'empêtrer, s'embrouiller; *(records, figures)* s'embrouiller; **I often get into a tangle with figures/tax returns** je m'embrouille souvent dans les chiffres/déclarations d'impôts; **she was all in a tangle** elle était toute embrouillée, elle ne savait plus où elle en était; **the accounts are in a bit of a tangle** les comptes sont un peu embrouillés; **her private life is in a terrible tangle** sa vie privée est un véritable sac de nœuds
(**c**) *(disagreement)* accrochage *m*, différend *m*; **they got into a tangle over the new salary scales** ils ont eu un différend au sujet de la nouvelle échelle des salaires; **I had a tangle with the social security officials** j'ai eu des mots *ou* maille à partir avec les employés de la sécurité sociale
2 *vt (wire, wool)* emmêler; *(figures)* embrouiller; **to get tangled** *(string)* s'emmêler; *(situation)* s'embrouiller
3 *vi* (**a**) *(wire, hair)* s'emmêler
(**b**) *Fam (disagree)* avoir un différend ❑, avoir un accrochage; **you'd better not tangle with her** il vaut mieux éviter de se frotter à elle; **they tangled over who should pay for supper** ils se sont disputés pour savoir qui allait payer le repas ❑

▸**tangle up** *vt sep* (**a**) *(make confused → threads)* emmêler, enchevêtrer; *(→ hair)* emmêler; *(→ question)* embrouiller; **to get tangled up** *(threads, wire)* s'emmêler; **to get tangled up in sth** *(of person → in ropes, net, brambles)* s'empêtrer dans qch; *(→ in barbed wire)* se prendre dans qch; *(of string)* s'emmêler *ou* s'enchevêtrer dans qch; **she had got tangled up in some barbed wire** elle était prise dans des barbelés; **the threads were all tangled up** les fils étaient emmêlés *ou* enchevêtrés
(**b**) *(involve)* **he got himself tangled up in the Smith case** il s'est retrouvé impliqué dans l'affaire Smith; **they got tangled up in**

tal–tan

something dishonest ils ont été mêlés à une affaire malhonnête

tangle² *n (seaweed)* laminaire *f*

tangled ['tæŋgəld] *adj* (**a**) *(string, wool)* emmêlé; *(creepers)* enchevêtré; *(undergrowth)* touffu; *(hair)* emmêlé (**b**) *(complex → story, excuse)* embrouillé; *(→ love life)* complexe

tangleweed ['tæŋgəlwi:d], **tanglewrack** ['tæŋgəlræk] *n (seaweed)* laminaire *f*

tango ['tæŋgəʊ] *(pl* **tangos**) **1** *n* tango *m*

2 *vi* danser le tango

tangram ['tæŋgræm] *n* casse-tête *m inv* chinois

tangy ['tæŋɪ] *(compar* **tangier**, *superl* **tangiest**) *adj (in taste)* qui a un goût fort; *(in smell)* qui a une odeur forte

tanh [tænʃ, θæn] *n Geom* tangente *f* hyperbolique

tank [tæŋk] **1** *n* (**a**) *(container → for liquid, gas)* réservoir *m*, cuve *f*, citerne *f*; *(→ for rainwater)* citerne *f*, bac *m*; *(→ for transport)* réservoir *m*, citerne *f*; *(barrel)* tonneau *m*, cuve *f*; *Aut* **(fuel** *or Br* **petrol) tank** réservoir *m* (d'essence); **(fish) tank** aquarium *m*

(**b**) *Mil* tank *m*, char *m* d'assaut; **the tanks** les blindés *mpl*; *Fam Fig* **to be built like a tank** être une armoire à glace

(**c**) *Ind (→ for processing)* cuve *f*

2 *comp Mil* de char/chars d'assaut

3 *vt* stocker *ou* mettre en réservoir

►► ***tank car*** wagon-citerne *m*; ***tank commander*** commandant *m* de char; ***tank engine*** locomotive *f* tender, machine *f* tender; ***tank regiment*** régiment *m* de chars (d'assaut); ***tank top*** débardeur *m*, pull *m* sans manches; ***tank trap*** piège *m* à chars; ***tank truck*** camion-citerne *m*; ***tank warfare*** guerre *f* combattue à l'aide de chars

►**tank along** *vi Fam (driver, vehicle)* foncer

►**tank up** *Br* **1** *vi Aut (fill fuel tank)* faire le plein d'essence

2 *vt sep Fam (usu passive)* **to get tanked up** *(drunk)* prendre une cuite; **to be tanked up** être bourré *ou* pété

tankage ['tæŋkɪdʒ] *n* (**a**) *(storing in tanks)* stockage *m ou* mise *f* en réservoir (**b**) *(storage fee)* frais *mpl* de stockage *ou* de mise en réservoir (**c**) *(capacity)* contenance *f ou* capacité *f* des réservoirs (**d**) *(system of tanks)* ensemble *m ou* série *f* de réservoirs; *Petr* **field tankage** réservoirs *mpl* de chantier (**e**) *Agr (animal residue)* déchets *mpl* de viande étuvés, farine *f* de viande d'autoclave

tankard ['tæŋkəd] *n* chope *f*

tanked *adj Fam (drunk)* bourré, pété; **to get tanked** prendre une cuite

tanker ['tæŋkə(r)] *n (lorry)* camion-citerne *m*; *(ship)* bateau-citerne *m*, navire-citerne *m*; *(plane)* avion-ravitailleur *m*; *Naut* **(oil) tanker** pétrolier *m*

►► *Br* ***tanker lorry***, *Am* ***tanker truck*** camion-citerne *m*

tankful ['tæŋkfʊl] *n (of petrol)* réservoir *m* (plein); *(of water)* citerne *f* (pleine)

tannage ['tænɪdʒ] *n* tannage *m*

tanned [tænd] *adj* (**a**) *(person)* bronzé; *(face, complexion)* bronzé, hâlé (**b**) *(leather)* tanné

tanner ['tænə(r)] *n* (**a**) *(of leather)* tanneur(euse) *m,f* (**b**) *Br Fam (coin)* = ancienne pièce de six pence

tannery ['tænərɪ] *(pl* **tanneries**) *n* tannerie *f*

tannic ['tænɪk] *adj* tannique

tannin ['tænɪn] *n* tanin *m*, tannin *m*

tanning ['tænɪŋ] *n* (**a**) *(of skin)* bronzage *m* (**b**) *(of hides)* tannage *m* (**c**) *Fam Fig (beating)* raclée *f*; **to give sb a tanning** rosser qn

►► ***tanning cream*** *(self-tanning)* crème *f* autobronzante; *(for natural tan)* crème *f* solaire; ***tanning studio*** centre *m* de bronzage

Tannoy® ['tænɔɪ] *Br* **1** *n* système *m* de haut-parleurs; **the delay was announced over the Tannoy**® le retard fut annoncé par haut-parleur

2 *vt* transmettre par haut-parleur

tansy ['tænzɪ] *(pl* **tansies**) *n Bot* tanaisie *f*, herbe *f* aux coqs

tantalic [tæn'tælɪk] *adj Chem* tantalique

►► ***tantalic acid*** acide *m* tantalique

tantalite ['tæntəlaɪt] *n Miner* tantalite *f*

tantalization [,tæntəlaɪ'zeɪʃən] *n* tourment *m*, taquinerie *f*

tantalize, -ise ['tæntəlaɪz] *vt* tourmenter, taquiner

tantalizing ['tæntə,laɪzɪŋ] *adj (woman)* provocant, aguichant; *(smell)* alléchant, appétissant; *(hint, possibility)* tentant

tantalizingly ['tæntə,laɪzɪŋlɪ] *adv* **victory was tantalizingly close** nous étions si près de la victoire que c'en était frustrant; **the cool water was tantalizingly near** cette eau fraîche à proximité était un véritable supplice; **tantalizingly slow** d'une lenteur désespérante

tantalum ['tæntələm] *n Chem* tantale *m*

Tantalus ['tæntələs] *pr n Myth* Tantale

tantalus ['tæntələs] *n* (**a**) *(for decanters)* cave *f* à liqueurs (**b**) *Orn* tantale *m*

tantamount ['tæntəmaʊnt] **tantamount to** *prep* équivalent à; **his statement was tantamount to an admission of guilt** sa déclaration équivalait à un aveu; **that's tantamount to saying I'm a liar** cela revient à dire que je mens

Tantra, tantra ['tæntrə] *n* tantra *m*

Tantric, tantric ['tæntrɪk] *adj* tantrique

►► ***Tantric sex*** sexe *m* tantrique

Tantrism ['tæntrɪzəm] *n* tantrisme *m*

tantrum ['tæntrəm] *n* crise *f* de colère *ou* de rage; **to have** *or* **to throw a tantrum** piquer une crise

Tanzania [,tænzə'nɪə] *n* Tanzanie *f*; **in Tanzania** en Tanzanie

Tanzanian [,tænzə'nɪən] **1** *n* Tanzanien(enne) *m,f*

2 *adj* tanzanien

3 *comp (embassy)* de Tanzanie; *(history)* de la Tanzanie

tanzanite ['tænzənaɪt] *n Miner* tanzanite *f*

Taoiseach ['ti:ʃəχ] *n* = titre du Premier ministre de la République d'Irlande

Taoism ['taʊɪzəm] *n* taoïsme *m*

Taoist ['taʊɪst] **1** *adj* taoïste

2 *n* taoïste *mf*

tap [tæp] *(pt & pp* **tapped**, *cont* **tapping**) **1** *vt* (**a**) *(strike)* taper légèrement, tapoter; **someone tapped me on the shoulder** quelqu'un m'a tapé sur l'épaule; **she was tapping her fingers on the table** elle pianotait *ou* tapotait sur la table; **he tapped his foot to the rhythm** il marquait le rythme en tapant du pied

(**b**) *(barrel, cask)* mettre en perce, percer; *(gas, water main)* faire un branchement sur; *(watercourse)* capter; *(tree)* inciser; *(pine tree)* gemmer; *(wine)* tirer; **the trees were tapped for their gum** on a incisé les arbres pour en recueillir la résine

(**c**) *(exploit → resources, market)* exploiter; *(→ talent, service)* faire appel à, tirer profit de; *(→ capital)* drainer; **we must tap all the resources we have** nous devons puiser dans toutes nos ressources; **to tap sb for information** soutirer des informations à qn; *Fam* **to tap sb for a loan** taper qn; *Fam* **he tapped me for £15** il m'a tapé de 15 livres

(**d**) *Tel (conversation)* écouter; **to tap sb's line** *or* **phone** mettre qn sur (table d')écoute; **the phones are tapped** les téléphones sont sur écoute

(**e**) *Tech (bolt, nut)* tarauder, fileter

(**f**) *Elec* faire une dérivation sur

(**g**) *Med* poser un drain sur

2 *vi* (**a**) *(knock)* tapoter, taper légèrement; **to tap at the door** frapper doucement à la porte; **to tap on the table** tapoter sur la table; **the boy was tapping on a drum** le garçon frappait doucement sur un tambour; **the woodpeckers are tapping on the bark** les piverts donnent des coups de bec sur l'écorce

(**b**) *(dance)* faire des claquettes

3 *n* (**a**) *(for water, gas)* robinet *m*; *(on barrel)* robinet *m*, chantepleure *f*; *(plug)* bonde *f*; **to turn a tap on/off** ouvrir/fermer un robinet; **to leave the tap running** laisser le robinet ouvert; **on tap** *(beer)* en fût; *Fam Fig (money, person, supply)* toujours disponible❑; **they seem to have funds on tap** ils semblent avoir des fonds toujours disponibles

(**b**) *(blow)* petit coup *m*, petite tape *f*; **to give sb a tap on the shoulder** donner une petite tape sur l'épaule à qn

(**c**) *(on shoe)* fer *m*

(**d**) *(dancing)* claquettes *fpl*; **to dance tap** faire des claquettes

(**e**) *Tech* **(screw) tap** taraud *m*

(**f**) *Elec* dérivation *f*, branchement *f*, prise *f*

(**g**) *Tel* **to put a tap on sb's phone** mettre (le téléphone de) qn sur écoute; **who authorized the tap?** qui a autorisé la mise sur écoute?

(**h**) *Med* drain *m*

(**i**) *Fin* = valeur du Trésor mise aux enchères; **long/medium/short tap** = valeurs émises à un prix déterminé par l'État à long/moyen/court terme

►► ***tap dance*** claquettes *fpl (danse)*; ***tap dancer*** danseur(euse) *m,f* de claquettes; ***tap dancing*** *(UNCOUNT)* claquettes *fpl (danse)*; *Fin* ***tap issue*** émission *f* des valeurs du Trésor; ***tap shoes*** claquettes *fpl (chaussures)*; *Fin* ***tap stock*** = valeur du Trésor mise aux enchères; ***tap water*** eau *f* du robinet

►**tap in** *vt sep* (**a**) *(plug)* enfoncer à petits coups

(**b**) *Comput* taper

►**tap out** *vt sep* (**a**) *(plug)* sortir à petits coups; *(pipe)* vider, débourrer

(**b**) *(code, rhythm)* taper; **to tap out a message** *(in morse code)* émettre un message

tapas ['tæpəs] *npl* tapas *fpl*; **tapas bar** bar *m* à tapas; **tapas restaurant** restaurant *m* à tapas

tap-dance *vi* faire des claquettes

tape [teɪp] **1** *n* (**a**) *(strip)* bande *f*, ruban *m*; *Sewing* ruban *m*, ganse *f*; *Med* sparadrap *m*; **to cut the tape** *(at ceremony)* couper le ruban

(**b**) *(for recording)* bande *f* (magnétique); *Comput* bande *f*; *(cassette)* cassette *f*; *(recording)* enregistrement *m*; **on tape** sur bande, enregistré; **to get** *or* **put sth on tape** enregistrer qch; **I've got it on tape** je l'ai en cassette; **she's got a really good tape collection** elle a une très bonne collection de cassettes

(**c**) *Sport* fil *m* d'arrivée; **to breast the tape** franchir la ligne d'arrivée

(**d**) *(for measuring)* mètre *m* (à ruban)

(**e**) *Horseracing* **the tapes** *(at start)* les rubans *mpl*

2 *vt* (**a**) *(record)* enregistrer

(**b**) *(fasten → package)* attacher avec du ruban adhésif; *(stick)* scotcher; **the address was taped to the suitcase** l'adresse était scotchée sur la valise

(**c**) *Am (bandage)* bander

(**d**) *Br Fam (idiom)* **she's got him taped** elle sait ce qu'il vaut❑; **we have the situation taped** on a la situation bien en main❑

►► *Comput* ***tape backup*** sauvegarde *f* sur bande; *Comput* ***tape backup system*** système *m* de sauvegarde sur bande; *Comput* ***tape backup unit*** unité *f* de sauvegarde sur bande; ***tape cleaner*** nettoyeur *m* de tête, produit *m* de nettoyage de tête; ***tape deck*** platine *f* de magnétophone; ***tape drive*** dérouleur *m* de bande (magnétique), lecteur *m* de bande (magnétique); ***tape head*** tête *f* de lecture; ***tape machine*** téléscripteur *m*, téléimprimeur *m*; ***tape measure*** mètre *m* (ruban), centimètre *m*; ***taped music*** musique *f* enregistrée; *Comput* ***tape reader*** lecteur *m* de bande; ***tape recorder*** magnétophone *m*, lecteur *m* de cassettes; ***tape recording*** enregistrement *m* (sur bande magnétique); *Comput* ***tape streamer*** streamer *m*; ***tape transport*** mécanisme *m* d'entraînement *(d'une bande magnétique)*; *Comput* ***tape unit*** unité *f* de bande

►**tape together** *vt sep (fasten)* attacher ensemble avec du ruban adhésif; *(stick)* coller (avec du ruban adhésif)

►**tape up** *vt sep* (**a**) *(fasten → parcel)* attacher avec du ruban adhésif; *(close → letterbox, hole)* fermer avec du ruban adhésif

(**b**) *Am (bandage up)* bander

tapeline ['teɪplaɪn] *n Am* mètre *m* (ruban), centimètre *m*

taper ['teɪpə(r)] **1** *vt (column, trouser leg, plane wing)* fuseler; *(stick, table leg)* effiler, tailler en pointe

2 *vi (column, trouser leg, plane wing)* être fuselé; *(stick, shape, table leg)* se terminer en pointe, s'effiler; *(finger)* être effilé; **her hair tapers in to the neck** ses cheveux sont effilés sur son cou; **it tapers to a point** c'est taillé en pointe

3 *n* (**a**) *(candle)* = longue bougie fine; *Rel* cierge *m*

(**b**) *(for lighting candle, fire)* allume-feu *m inv*

►► *Br Fin* ***taper relief*** = réduction progressive

des impôts sur les plus-values en fonction du nombre d'années pendant lequel on détient un bien avant de le vendre

▸**taper off** **1** *vt sep* effiler, tailler en pointe

2 *vi* (**a**) *(shape)* se terminer en fuseau *ou* en pointe

(**b**) *(noise)* diminuer progressivement, décroître, s'affaiblir; *(conversation)* tomber; *(level of interest, activity)* décroître progressivement; **street crime shows signs of tapering off** tout laisse à penser que les agressions sont en baisse

tape-record [-rɪˌkɔːd] *vt* enregistrer (sur bande magnétique)

tapered ['teɪpəd] *adj (trousers)* en fuseau; *(stick, candle)* en pointe, pointu; *(table leg)* fuselé; **tapered fingers** des doigts *mpl* effilés *ou* fuselés

tapering ['teɪpərɪŋ] *adj* (**a**) = **tapered** (**b**) *Fin (rate)* dégressif

tapestried ['tæpɪstrɪd] *adj* tapissé, tendu de tapisseries

tapestry ['tæpɪstrɪ] (*pl* **tapestries**) *n* tapisserie *f*; *Fig* **it's all part of life's rich tapestry** ça fait partie de la vie

tapeworm ['teɪpwɜːm] *n* ténia *m*, ver *m* solitaire

taphephobia [ˌtæfɪ'fəʊbɪə] *n Psy* taphophobie *f*, taphéphobie *f*

taphonomy [tæ'fɒnəmɪ] *n* taphonomie *f*

tapioca [ˌtæpɪ'əʊkə] *n* tapioca *m*

tapir ['teɪpə(r)] (*pl* **inv** *or* **tapirs**) *n Zool* tapir *m*

tapped [tæpt] *adj* (**a**) *Elec (coil, transformer)* à prises (**b**) *Tech (bolt, nut)* taraudé, fileté

▸▸ ***tapped resistor*** résistance *f* à prises

tappet ['tæpɪt] *n Tech* **(valve) tappet** poussoir *m* (de soupape), taquet *m*

▸▸ ***tappet clearance*** jeu *m* aux culbuteurs

tapping ['tæpɪŋ] *n* (**a**) *(knocking)* petits coups *mpl*; *(with hand)* tapotement *m*

(**b**) *Tel* **(telephone) tapping** écoutes *fpl* (de communications téléphoniques)

(**c**) *(exploitation)* exploitation *f*; **tapping of natural resources** exploitation *f* des ressources naturelles

(**d**) *(of barrel, cask)* mise *f* en perce, perçage *m*; *(of gas, water main)* branchement *m*; *(of watercourse)* captage *m*; *(of tree)* incision *f*; *(of pine tree)* gemmage *m*; *(of wine)* tirage *m*

(**e**) *Tech (of bolt, nut)* taraudage *m*

▸▸ *Tech* ***tapping attachment*** dispositif *m ou* appareillage *m* de taraudage; *Tech* ***tapping depth*** profondeur *f* de taraudage; ***tapping key*** *(in telegraphy)* manipulateur *m*, transmetteur *m*; *Tech* ***tapping machine*** machine *f* à tarauder, taraudeuse *f*

taproom ['tæprʊm] *n Br* salle *f (d'un café)*, bar *m*

taproot ['tæpruːt] *n Bot* racine *f* pivotante

taps [tæps] *n Am Mil (in evening)* = sonnerie pour l'extinction des feux; *(at funeral)* sonnerie *f* aux morts

tar [tɑː(r)] (*pt & pp* **tarred**, *cont* **tarring**) **1** *n* (**a**) *(in cigarettes)* goudron *m*; *(on road)* goudron *m*, bitume *m*; *Am Fam* **to beat the tar out of sb** flanquer une rouste à qn

(**b**) *Fam (sailor)* matelot ❑ *m*, loup *m* de mer

2 *vt (gen)* goudronner; *(road)* bitumer, goudronner; *Naut* goudronner; **to tar and feather sb** couvrir qn de goudron et de plumes; *Fig* **we're all tarred with the same brush** ou nous a tous mis dans le même panier *ou* sac

ta-ra [tə'rɑː] *exclam Br Fam* salut!, ciao!

taramasalata [ˌtærəməsə'lɑːtə] *n Culin* tarama *m*

tarantella [ˌtærən'telə] *n* tarentelle *f*

tarantism ['tærənˌtɪzəm] *n Med & Hist* tarentisme *m*, tarentulisme *m*

Taranto [tə'ræntəʊ] *n* Tarente

tarantula [tə'ræntjʊlə] (*pl* **tarantulas** *or* **tarantulae** [-liː]) *n Entom* tarentule *f*

taraxacum [tə'ræksəkəm] *n Bot* pissenlit *m*

tarboosh [tɑː'buːʃ] *n* tarbouche *m*, tarbouch *m*

tardigrade ['tɑːdɪgreɪd] *n Zool* tardigrade *m*

tardily ['tɑːdɪlɪ] *adv Formal or Literary* (**a**) *(late)* tardivement (**b**) *(slowly)* lentement

tardiness ['tɑːdɪnɪs] *n Formal or Literary* (**a**) *(lateness)* retard *m* (**b**) *(slowness)* lenteur *f*

tardy ['tɑːdɪ] (*compar* **tardier**, *superl* **tardiest**) *adj* (**a**) *Am Sch* en retard (**b**) *Formal or Literary (late)* tardif; *(slow)* lent, nonchalant

tare [teə(r)] *n* (**a**) *(weight)* tare *f*, poids *m* à vide (**b**) *Bot* vesce *f*; *Bible* **tares** ivraie *f*

TARGET ['tɑːgɪt] *n Fin* (*abbr* **Trans-European Automated Real-Time Gross Settlement Transfer System**) TARGET *m*

target ['tɑːgɪt] (*pt & pp* **targeted**, *cont* **targeting**) **1** *n* (**a**) *(for archery, shooting)* cible *f*; *Mil* cible *f*, but *m*; *(objective)* cible *f*, objectif *m*; **the target of criticism/jokes** la cible de critiques/plaisanteries; **she was an easy target for political cartoonists** elle était une cible facile pour les caricaturistes politiques; **to be on target** *(missile)* suivre la trajectoire prévue; *(plans)* se dérouler comme prévu; *(productivity)* atteindre les objectifs prévus; **to meet production/sales targets** atteindre les objectifs de production/de vente; *Mil & Fig* **moving target** cible *f* mobile

(**b**) *Electron & Phys* cible *f*

(**c**) *(in surveying)* mire *f*

(**d**) *Culin (joint)* épaule *f* de mouton

2 *comp (date, amount)* prévu; **my target weight is 10 stone** je me suis fixé le poids idéal de 63 kg, mon poids idéal est (de) 63 kg

3 *vt* (**a**) *(aim at → enemy troops, city etc)* prendre pour cible, viser; *(→ market)* cibler

(**b**) *(aim → missile)* diriger; *(of funds, resources, benefits)* viser, être destiné à; *(of advertisement, advertising campaign)* viser; **the benefits are targeted at one-parent families** les allocations visent les *ou* sont destinées aux familles monoparentales; **the programme is targeted at 18-to-25-year-olds** l'émission s'adresse aux 18 à 25 ans *ou* vise les jeunes de 18 à 25 ans

▸▸ *Mil* ***target area*** zone *f* cible; *Mktg* ***target audience*** audience *f* cible; *Mktg* ***target buyer*** acheteur(euse) *m,f* cible; *Mktg* ***target consumer*** consommateur(trice) *m,f* cible; *Mktg* ***target cost*** coût *m* ciblé; *Comput* ***target disk*** *(hard)* disque *m* cible; *(floppy)* disquette *f* cible; *Comput* ***target drive*** unité *f* de destination; ***target figures*** chiffres *mpl* prévus; *Comput* ***target file*** fichier *m* de destination; *Mktg* ***target group*** groupe *m* cible; ***target language*** langue *f* cible, langue *f* d'arrivée; *Mktg* ***target market*** marché *m* cible; *Mktg* ***target marketing*** marketing *m* ciblé; *Mktg* ***target population*** population *f* cible; *Mil* ***target practice*** *(UNCOUNT)* exercices *mpl* de tir; *Mktg* ***target price*** prix *m* d'équilibre; *Mktg* ***target pricing*** fixation *f* du prix en fonction de l'objectif; ***target readership*** lectorat *m* cible; ***target setting*** arrêt *m* des objectifs

targeted ['tɑːgɪtɪd] *adj* ciblé

targetting, targeting ['tɑːgɪtɪŋ] *n* (**a**) *(setting targets)* détermination *f* d'objectifs; **because of unrealistic targetting** en raison d'objectifs non réalistes (**b**) *Mktg* ciblage *m* (**c**) *(of funds, resources, benefits)* ciblage *m*; **we need better targetting of resources** il nous faut mieux cibler les ressources

Targum [tɑː'guːm] *n Rel* targum *m*

tarheel ['tɑːhiːl] *n Am* habitant(e) *m,f* de Caroline du Nord; **the Tarheel State** = surnom donné à la Caroline du Nord

tariff ['tærɪf] **1** *n* (**a**) *(at customs)* tarif *m* douanier (**b**) *(list of prices)* tarif *m*, tableau *m* des prix (**c**) *Br (menu)* menu *m* (**d**) *Br (rate → of gas, electricity)* tarif *m*

2 *comp* tarifaire

▸▸ ***tariff barrier*** barrière *f* douanière *ou* tarifaire; ***tariff reform*** réforme *f* des tarifs douaniers; ***tariff wall*** barrière *f* douanière *ou* tarifaire

tarlatan ['tɑːlətən] *n Tex* tarlatane *f*

tarmac® ['tɑːmæk] (*pt & pp* **tarmacked**, *cont* **tarmacking**) *Br* **1** *n* (**a**) *(on road)* tarmacadam *m*, macadam *m* (**b**) *(at airport → runway)* piste *f*; *(→ apron)* aire *f* de stationnement, piste *f* d'envol; **the plane had to wait for half an hour on the tarmac** l'avion a dû attendre une demi-heure sur l'aire de stationnement

2 *vt* macadamiser, goudronner

tarmacadam® [ˌtɑːmə'kædəm] *n* tarmacadam *m*, macadam *m*

tarn [tɑːn] *n* petit lac *m* de montagne

tarnation [tɑː'neɪʃən] *exclam Am Fam Old-fashioned* zut!, mince!

tarnish ['tɑːnɪʃ] **1** *vt* (**a**) *(metal)* ternir; *(mirror)* ternir, désargenter (**b**) *(reputation)* ternir, salir

2 *vi* se ternir

3 *n* ternissure *f*

tarnishable ['tɑːnɪʃəbəl] *adj (metal)* qui peut se ternir, qui se ternit facilement

tarnished ['tɑːnɪʃt] *adj also Fig* terni

tarnishing ['tɑːnɪʃɪŋ] *n (of metal)* ternissure *f*; **this led to the tarnishing of his reputation** cela a terni sa réputation

taro ['tɑːrəʊ] (*pl* **taros**) *n Bot* taro *m*

tarot ['tærəʊ] *n (UNCOUNT)* tarot *m*, tarots *mpl*

▸▸ ***tarot card*** carte *f* de tarot

tarp [tɑːp] *n Fam* bâche ❑ *f*

tarpaulin [tɑː'pɔːlɪn] *n* bâche *f*; *Naut* prélart *m*

tarpon ['tɑːpɒn] (*pl* **inv** *or* **tarpons**) *n Ich* tarpon *m*

tarradiddle ['tærədɪdəl] *n Br* (**a**) *(lie)* petit mensonge *m* (**b**) *(UNCOUNT) (nonsense)* bêtises *fpl*, idioties *fpl*

tarragon ['tærəgən] **1** *n* estragon *m*

2 *comp (sauce, vinegar)* à l'estragon

Tarragona [ˌtærə'gəʊnə] *n* Tarragone

tarry¹ ['tærɪ] (*pt & pp* **tarried**) *vi Literary (delay)* s'attarder, tarder; *(remain)* rester, demeurer

tarry² ['tɑːrɪ] *adj* (**a**) *(made of tar)* goudronneux, bitumineux (**b**) *(covered or stained with tar)* couvert de goudron

tarsal ['tɑːsəl] *Anat* **1** *adj* tarsien

2 *n* os *m* tarsien

tarsier ['tɑːsɪə(r)] *n Zool* tarsier *m*

tarsus ['tɑːsəs] (*pl* **tarsi** [-saɪ]) *n Anat* tarse *m*

tart [tɑːt] **1** *n* (**a**) *Culin* tarte *f*; *(small)* tartelette *f*

(**b**) *Br very Fam (prostitute)* pute *f*; *(promiscuous woman)* salope *f*, pute *f*; *(any woman)* gonzesse *f*; **you silly tart!** espèce d'andouille!

2 *adj* (**a**) *(sour → fruit)* acide; *(→ taste)* aigre, acide

(**b**) *(remark)* acerbe, caustique

▸**tart up** *vt sep Br Fam (house, room, restaurant)* retaper, rénover ❑; **to tart oneself up, to get tarted up** se pomponner; **it's just a tarted up version of the old model** ce n'est qu'une version enjolivée de l'ancien modèle ❑

tartan ['tɑːtən] **1** *n (design)* tartan *m*; *(fabric)* tartan *m*, tissu *m* écossais

2 *comp (skirt, trousers)* en tissu écossais; *(pattern)* tartan

▸▸ ***the Tartan Army*** = surnom donné aux supporters de l'équipe nationale écossaise de football

tartar ['tɑːtə(r)] **1** *n* (**a**) *(on teeth)* tartre *m* (**b**) *Br (fearsome person)* tyran *m*; **she's a real tartar** c'est un vrai tyran

2 Tartar *n* = **Tatar**

▸▸ ***tartar sauce*** sauce *f* tartare

tartare sauce ['tɑːtə-] *n* sauce *f* tartare

tartaric [tɑː'tærɪk] *adj Chem* tartrique

▸▸ ***tartaric acid*** acide *m* tartrique

Tartary = **Tatary**

tartlet ['tɑːtlɪt] *n Br* tartelette *f*

tartly ['tɑːtlɪ] *adv* avec aigreur, de manière acerbe; **"certainly not", he said tartly** "certainement pas", dit-il d'un ton acerbe

tartness ['tɑːtnɪs] *n (of fruit, wine, tone, remark)* aigreur *f*, acidité *f*

tartrate ['tɑːtreɪt] *n Chem* tartrate *m*; **ergotamine tartrate** tartrate *m* d'ergotamine

tartrazine ['tɑːtrəziːn] *n* tartrazine *f*

tarty ['tɑːtɪ] (*compar* **tartier**, *superl* **tartiest**) *adj Br very Fam (person, clothes)* qui fait pute; **to look tarty** *(person)* avoir l'air d'une pute

Tarzan ['tɑːzən] **1** *pr n* Tarzan

2 [illegible] les Tarzans

Tashkent [tæʃ'kent] *n* Tachkent

task [tɑːsk] **1** *n (chore)* tâche *f*, besogne *f*; *(job)* tâche *f*, travail *m*; *Sch* devoir *m*; *Comput* tâche *f*; **to set sb a task** imposer une tâche à qn; **convincing them will be no easy task** les convaincre ne sera pas chose facile; **to take sb to task (for sth/doing sth)** réprimander qn (pour qch/pour avoir fait qch), prendre qn à partie (pour qch/pour avoir fait qch)

2 *vt* (**a**) *(strain → patience, resources)* mettre à l'épreuve; *(→ strength, nerves)* éprouver

(**b**) *(entrust)* **to task sb with sth/with doing sth** charger qn de qch/de faire qch; **to be tasked with sth/doing sth** être chargé de qch/de faire qch

▸▸ ***task force*** *(to investigate)* commission *f*; *(to do special job)* groupe *m* de travail; *Mil* corps *m* expéditionnaire; ***task work*** travail *m* à la tâche *ou* aux pièces

taskbar ['tɑːskbɑː(r)] *n Comput* barre *f* des tâches

taskmaster ['tɑːskˌmɑːstə(r)] *n* tyran *m*; **he's a**

tap–tas

hard taskmaster il mène la vie dure à ses subordonnés, c'est un véritable négrier

Tasmania [tæz'meɪnjə] *n* Tasmanie *f*; **in Tasmania** en Tasmanie

Tasmanian [tæz'meɪnjən] **1** *n* Tasmanien(enne) *m,f*

2 *adj* tasmanien

▸▸ *Zool* ***Tasmanian devil*** diable *m* de Tasmanie; *Zool* ***Tasmanian wolf*** loup *m* de Tasmanie

Tasman Sea ['tæzmən-] *n* **the Tasman Sea** la mer de Tasman

TASS [tæs] *n Formerly (abbr* **Telegraphic Agency of the Soviet Union**) TASS *f*

tassel ['tæsəl] (*Br pt & pp* **tasselled,** *cont* **tasselling,** *Am pt & pp* **tasseled,** *cont* **tasseling**) **1** *n* (**a**) *(on clothing, furnishing)* gland *m* (**b**) *Bot* épillets *mpl* en panicule, inflorescence *f* mâle

2 *vt* garnir de glands

tasselled ['tæsəld] *adj* à glands, orné de glands

TASTE [teɪst]

goût	▸ **1 (a), (b), (d), (e)**
saveur	▸ **1 (b)**
bouchée	▸ **1 (c)**
goutte	▸ **1 (c)**
aperçu	▸ **1 (f)**
sentir	▸ **2 (a)**
goûter (à)	▸ **2 (b), (d)**
manger	▸ **2 (c)**
boire	▸ **2 (c)**

1 *n* (**a**) *(sense)* goût *m*; **to lose one's sense of taste** perdre le goût, *Spec* être atteint d'agueusie; **to be sweet/salty to the taste** avoir un goût sucré/salé

(**b**) *(flavour)* goût *m*, saveur *f*; **these apples have a lovely/strange taste** ces pommes sont délicieuses/ont un drôle de goût; **this cheese doesn't have much taste** ce fromage n'a pas beaucoup de goût *ou* est assez fade; **the cake has a taste of almonds/a burnt taste** le gâteau a un goût d'amandes/de brûlé; **add sugar to taste** ajouter du sucre à volonté; **to leave a bad taste in the mouth** *(food)* laisser un mauvais goût dans la bouche; *Fig* laisser un mauvais souvenir *ou* un goût amer

(**c**) *(small amount → of food)* bouchée *f*; *(→ of drink)* goutte *f*; **can I have a taste of the chocolate cake?** est-ce que je peux goûter au gâteau au chocolat?; **would you like (to have) a taste?** voulez-vous goûter?

(**d**) *(liking, preference)* goût *m*, penchant *m*; **to have expensive/simple tastes** avoir des goûts de luxe/simples; **to develop a taste for sth** prendre goût à qch; **to have a taste for sth** avoir un penchant *ou* un faible pour qch; **it's a matter of taste** c'est (une) affaire de goût; **musical/artistic tastes** goûts *mpl* musicaux/artistiques; **I don't share his taste in music** je ne partage pas ses goûts en (matière de) musique, nous n'avons pas les mêmes goûts en (matière de) musique; **is it to your taste?** est-ce à votre goût?, est-ce que cela vous convient?, cela vous plaît?; **did you find it to your taste?** l'avez-vous trouvé à votre goût?

(**e**) *(discernment)* goût *m*; **to have good taste** avoir du goût, avoir bon goût; **they have no taste** ils n'ont aucun goût; **she has good taste in clothes** elle s'habille avec goût; **they don't have much taste when it comes to art** en matière d'art, ils n'ont pas beaucoup de goût; **the joke was in extremely bad taste** la plaisanterie était de très mauvais goût; **it's bad taste to ask personal questions** il est de mauvais goût de poser des questions indiscrètes

(**f**) *(experience)* aperçu *m*; *(sample)* échantillon *m*; **to have a taste of freedom/happiness** avoir un aperçu de la liberté/du bonheur; **the sweet taste of success** les joies *fpl ou* les délices *fpl* de la réussite; **he's already had a taste of prison life** il a déjà tâté *ou* goûté de la prison; **the experience gave me a taste of life in the army** l'expérience m'a donné un aperçu de la vie militaire; **to give sb a taste of the whip** faire tâter du fouet à qn; **a taste of things to come** un avant-goût de l'avenir

2 *vt* (**a**) *(flavour, ingredient)* sentir (le goût de); **can you taste the brandy in it?** est-ce que vous sentez le (goût du) cognac?; **you can hardly taste the mint** on sent à peine (le goût de) la menthe

(**b**) *(sample, try)* goûter à; *(for quality)* goûter; **have you tasted the sauce?** avez-vous goûté (à) la sauce?; **to taste (the) wine** *(in restaurant)* goûter le vin; *(in vineyard)* déguster le vin

(**c**) *(eat)* manger; *(drink)* boire; **I've never tasted oysters before** je n'ai jamais mangé d'huîtres; **you don't often get a chance to taste such good wine** on n'a pas souvent l'occasion de boire un aussi bon vin

(**d**) *(experience → happiness, success)* goûter, connaître

3 *vi (food)* **to taste good/bad** avoir bon/mauvais goût; **to taste salty** avoir un goût salé; **to taste funny** avoir un drôle de goût; **it tastes fine to me** moi je trouve ça bon; **it tastes like chicken** cela a un goût de poulet; **to taste of sth** avoir le *ou* un goût de qch; **it doesn't taste of anything** cela n'a aucun goût

▸▸ ***taste bud*** papille *f* gustative

tasteful ['teɪstfʊl] *adj (decoration)* raffiné, de bon goût; *(work of art, remark, action)* de bon goût; *(clothing)* de bon goût, élégant

tastefully ['teɪstfʊlɪ] *adv* avec goût

tastefulness ['teɪstfʊlnɪs] *n (of decoration, work of art, remark, action)* bon goût *m*; *(of clothing)* chic *m*, élégance *f*

tasteless ['teɪstlɪs] *adj* (**a**) *(food)* fade, insipide, sans goût; *(medicine)* qui n'a aucun goût (**b**) *(remark)* de mauvais goût; *(decoration, outfit)* de mauvais goût, qui manque de goût

tastelessly ['teɪstlɪslɪ] *adv (decorated, dressed)* sans goût

tastelessness ['teɪstlɪsnɪs] *n* (**a**) *(of food)* fadeur *f*, manque *m* de saveur *ou* de goût; *(of medicine)* absence *f* de goût (**b**) *(of remark)* mauvais goût *m*; *(in decoration, clothes)* manque *m* de goût, mauvais goût *m*

taster ['teɪstə(r)] *n* (**a**) *(person)* dégustateur(trice) *m,f* (**b**) *(foretaste)* **this is just a taster (of what's to come)** ceci n'est qu'un avant-goût (de ce qui va suivre)

tastiness ['teɪstɪnɪs] *n* saveur *f* agréable, bon goût *m*

tasting ['teɪstɪŋ] *n* dégustation *f*

tasty ['teɪstɪ] (*compar* **tastier,** *superl* **tastiest**) *adj* (**a**) *(flavour)* savoureux, délicieux; *(dish)* qui a bon goût; **it's not very tasty** ça n'a pas beaucoup de goût; **a tasty morsel** un mets succulent (**b**) *Br Fam (attractive)* bien foutu, bien balancé; **she's a tasty piece** c'est un beau morceau

TAT [,tiːeɪ'tiː] *n Mktg (abbr* **thematic apperception test**) TAT *m*

tat [tæt] (*pt & pp* **tatted,** *cont* **tatting**) **1** *vi (make lace)* faire de la frivolité

2 *n (UNCOUNT) Br Fam Pej (clothes)* fripes *fpl*; *(goods)* camelote *f*

ta-ta [tæ'tɑː] *exclam Br Fam* au revoir!□, salut!

Tatar ['tɑːtə(r)] **1** *n* (**a**) *(person)* Tatar(e) *m,f* (**b**) *Ling* tatar *m*

2 *adj* tatar

Tatary ['tɑːtərɪ] *n* Tatarie *f*

Tate [teɪt] *n* **Tate Britain** = musée londonien consacré à l'art britannique; **Tate Modern** = musée londonien consacré à l'art moderne et contemporain; *Formerly* **the Tate (Gallery)** = musée d'art à Londres

tater ['teɪtə(r)] *n Fam (potato)* patate *f*

tattered ['tætəd] *adj (clothes)* en lambeaux, en loques; *(page, book)* en lambeaux, en morceaux, tout déchiré; *(person)* en haillons, loqueteux; *(reputation)* en miettes, ruiné; **to be (all) tattered and torn** *(clothes)* être tout en lambeaux; *(page, book)* être tout déchiré *ou* en morceaux; *(person)* être en loques et en guenilles

tatters ['tætəz] *npl* **to be in tatters** *(clothes)* être en lambeaux *ou* en loques; *Fig* **the original plan is in tatters** le projet initial est complètement à l'eau; **her reputation is in tatters** sa réputation est ruinée

tattie ['tætɪ] *n esp Scot Fam (potato)* patate *f*

tatting ['tætɪŋ] *n (UNCOUNT) (lace)* frivolité *f* *(dentelle)*

tattle ['tætəl] *Fam* **1** *vi (chatter)* jaser□, cancaner; *(tell secrets)* rapporter□

2 *n (UNCOUNT) (gossiping)* commérages *mpl*, cancans *mpl*

tattler ['tætlə(r)] *n Fam* commère *f*, bavard(e)□ *m,f*

tattle-tale = **telltale** *n* (**a**)

tattoo [tə'tuː] (*pl* **tattoos**) **1** *n* (**a**) *(on skin)* tatouage *m*; **to get a tattoo** se faire faire un tatouage; **he had tattoos across his chest** il avait la poitrine tatouée

(**b**) *Mil (signal)* retraite *f*; *(ceremony, parade)* parade *f* militaire; **to sound the tattoo** sonner la retraite

(**c**) *(on drums)* battements *mpl*; **to beat a tattoo on the drums** battre le tambour; *Fig* **he beat a furious tattoo on the door with his fists** il tambourinait violemment sur *ou* contre la porte avec ses poings

2 *vi* tatouer

3 *vt* tatouer

▸▸ ***tattoo parlour*** boutique *f* de tatouages

tattooing [tə'tuːɪŋ] *n* tatouage *m*

tattooist [tə'tuːɪst] *n* tatoueur(euse) *m,f*

tatty ['tætɪ] (*compar* **tattier,** *superl* **tattiest**) *adj Br Fam (clothes)* fatigué□, défraîchi□; *(person)* défraîchi□, miteux; *(house)* délabré□, en mauvais état□; *(book)* écorné□, en mauvais état□

tau [tɔː, taʊ] *n* tau *m*

▸▸ ***tau cross*** croix *f* en tau, croix *f* de Saint-Antoine

taught [tɔːt] *pt & pp of* **teach**

taunt [tɔːnt] **1** *vt* railler, tourner en ridicule, persifler; **to taunt sb with sth** railler qn à propos de qch

2 *n* raillerie *f*, sarcasme *m*

taunter ['tɔːntə(r)] *n* railleur(euse) *m,f*, persifleur(euse) *m,f*

taunting ['tɔːntɪŋ] **1** *n (UNCOUNT)* railleries *fpl*, sarcasmes *mpl*

2 *adj* railleur, sarcastique

tauntingly ['tɔːntɪŋlɪ] *adv* d'un ton railleur *ou* persifleur

taupe [təʊp] *adj (colour)* taupe *(inv)*

Taurean [tɔː'rɪən] *Astrol* **1** *n* **to be a Taurean** être (du signe du) Taureau

2 *adj* du Taureau

tauromachian [,tɔːrə'meɪkɪən] *adj* tauromachique

tauromachy [tɔː'rɒməkɪ] *n* tauromachie *f*

Taurus ['tɔːrəs] **1** *n* (**a**) *Astron* Taureau *m* (**b**) *Astrol* Taureau *m*; **he's a Taurus** il est (du signe du) Taureau

2 *adj Astrol* du Taureau; **he's Taurus** il est (du signe du) Taureau

taut [tɔːt] *adj (rope, cable)* tendu, raide; *(situation)* tendu

tauten ['tɔːtən] **1** *vt (rope, cable etc)* tendre, raidir

2 *vi* se tendre

tautness ['tɔːtnɪs] *n* tension *f*, raideur *f*

tautological [,tɔːtə'lɒdʒɪkəl] *adj* tautologique, pléonastique

tautologize, -ise [tɔː'tɒlədʒaɪz] *vi* faire des pléonasmes

tautology [tɔː'tɒlədʒɪ] (*pl* **tautologies**) *n* tautologie *f*, pléonasme *m*

tautomer ['tɔːtəmə(r)] *n Chem* forme *f* tautomère

tautomeric [,tɔːtə'merɪk] *adj Chem* tautomère

tautomerism [tɔː'tɒmə,rɪzəm], **tautomery** [tɔː'tɒmərɪ] *n Chem* tautomérie *f*

tautophony [tɔː'tɒfənɪ] *n Gram* tautophonie *f*, tautacisme *m*

tautosyllabic [,tɔːtəʊsɪ'læbɪk] *adj Gram* tautosyllabique

tavern ['tævən] *n* auberge *f*, taverne *f*

tawdrily ['tɔːdrɪlɪ] *adv (dressed)* de façon tapageuse *ou* voyante

tawdriness ['tɔːdrɪnɪs] *n (of clothes)* aspect *m* tapageur *ou* voyant; *(of jewellery)* clinquant *m*; *(of goods)* mauvaise qualité *f*; *(of motives, situation)* bassesse *f*, indignité *f*; **there was a tawdriness about everything in the hotel** tout dans l'hôtel était d'un luxe tapageur

tawdry ['tɔːdrɪ] (*compar* **tawdrier,** *superl* **tawdriest**) *adj (clothes)* voyant et de mauvaise qualité; *(jewellery)* clinquant; *(goods)* de mauvaise qualité; *(motives, situation)* bas, indigne

tawny ['tɔːnɪ] (*compar* **tawnier,** *superl* **tawniest**) *adj (colour)* fauve

▸▸ *Orn* ***tawny eagle*** aigle *m* ravisseur; *Orn* ***tawny owl*** chouette *f* hulotte; *Orn* ***tawny pipit*** pipit *m* rousseline; ***tawny port*** = porto qui a jauni dans le fût

tawse [tɔ:z] *n Scot Sch* martinet *m*; **to give a child the tawse** corriger un enfant avec un martinet

tax [tæks] **1** *n* (**a**) *(on income)* contributions *fpl*; *Admin & Fin* impôt *m*; **to levy** *or* **to collect taxes** lever *ou* percevoir des impôts; **most of my income goes in tax** la plus grande partie de mes revenus va aux impôts; **I don't pay much tax** je ne paie pas beaucoup d'impôts; **I paid over $5,000 in tax** j'ai payé plus de 5000 dollars d'impôts; **to be liable to tax** être assujetti à l'impôt; **after tax** net, après impôt; **before tax** avant impôt

(**b**) *(on goods, services, imports)* taxe *f*; **to levy** *or* **to put a 10 percent tax on sth** frapper qch d'une taxe de 10 pour cent, imposer *ou* taxer qch à 10 pour cent; **there is a high tax on whisky** le whisky est fortement taxé; **baby food is free of tax** les aliments pour bébés sont exempts *ou* exonérés de taxe; **a tax on books/knowledge** une taxe sur les livres/le savoir; **to be liable to tax** être assujetti à l'impôt; **before tax** hors taxe; **exclusive of tax** hors taxe

(**c**) *Fig (strain)* épreuve *f*; **it was a tax on his strength/nerves** ça l'a beaucoup éprouvé (physiquement)/(psychologiquement)

2 *vt* (**a**) *(person, company)* imposer, frapper d'un impôt; *(goods)* taxer, frapper d'une taxe; **the rich will be more heavily taxed** les riches seront plus lourdement imposés *ou* payeront plus d'impôts; **luxury goods are taxed at 28 percent** les articles de luxe sont taxés à 28 pour cent *ou* font l'objet d'une taxe de 28 pour cent; **we're being taxed out of existence** on nous accable d'impôts

(**b**) *Br* **to tax one's car** acheter la vignette (automobile)

(**c**) *Fig (strain → patience, resources)* mettre à l'épreuve; *(→ strength, nerves)* éprouver

(**d**) *Literary (accuse)* **to tax sb with sth** accuser *ou* taxer qn de qch; **to tax sb with doing sth** accuser qn d'avoir fait qch

►► ***tax adjustment*** redressement *m* fiscal *ou* d'impôt; ***tax allowance*** abattement *m* fiscal, déduction *f* fiscale; ***tax assessment*** avis *m* d'imposition, fixation *f* de l'impôt; ***tax audit*** vérification *f* fiscale; ***tax authorities*** administration *f* fiscale; ***tax avoidance*** optimisation *f* ou évasion *f* fiscale, *Can* évitement *m* fiscal; ***tax band*** tranche *f* d'imposition; ***tax base*** assiette *f* fiscale; ***tax benefit*** avantage *m* fiscal; ***tax bite*** proportion *f* du revenu pris par l'impôt; ***tax bracket*** tranche *f* d'imposition, fourchette *f* d'imposition; ***tax break*** réduction *f* d'impôt, allègement *m* fiscal; ***tax burden*** pression *f* fiscale, poids *m* de la fiscalité; ***tax ceiling*** plafond *m* fiscal, plafond *m* de l'impôt; ***tax centre*** centre *m* des impôts, CDI *m*; ***tax clearance*** quitus *m* fiscal; ***tax code*** barème *m* fiscal; ***tax collection*** recouvrement *m* d'impôts, perception *f* d'impôts; ***tax collector*** percepteur *m* d'impôt, receveur *m* des contributions; ***tax consultant*** conseiller(ère) *m,f* fiscal(e), conseil *m* fiscal; ***tax credit*** aide *f* fiscale, avoir *m* fiscal; ***tax cut*** baisse *f ou* réduction *f* des impôts; ***tax deduction*** prélèvement *m* fiscal, déduction *f* fiscale; ***tax*** [illegible] ***tax disc*** vignette *f* (automobile); *Am* ***tax dollars*** argent *m* du contribuable; ***tax domicile*** foyer *m ou* domicile *m* fiscal; ***tax evasion*** fraude *f* fiscale, évasion *f* fiscale; ***tax exemption*** exonération *f* d'impôt, exemption *f* d'impôt; ***tax exile*** = personne qui réside à l'étranger pour minimiser la responsabilité fiscale; ***tax expert*** fiscaliste *mf*; ***tax form*** feuille *f ou* déclaration *f* d'impôts; ***tax fraud*** fraude *f* fiscale; ***tax harmonization*** harmonisation *f* fiscale; ***tax haven*** paradis *m* fiscal; ***tax holiday*** période *f* de grâce *(accordée pour le paiement des impôts)*; ***tax impact*** incidence *f* fiscale; ***tax incentive*** incitation *f* fiscale, avantage *m* fiscal; ***tax inspection*** contrôle *m* fiscal; ***tax inspector*** inspecteur(trice) *m,f* des contributions directes *ou* des impôts; ***tax law*** droit *m* fiscal; ***tax liability*** *(of person)* assujetissement *m* à l'impôt; *(of goods, product)* exigibilité *f* de l'impôt; ***tax loophole*** échappatoire *f* fiscale; ***tax loss*** déficit *m* fiscal reportable; ***tax office*** centre *m* des impôts; ***tax official*** agent *m* du fisc; ***tax privilege*** privilège *m* fiscal; ***tax rate*** taux *m* d'imposition; ***tax rebate*** dégrèvement *m* fiscal; ***tax reduction*** abattement *m* fiscal; ***tax refund*** *(of income tax)* restitution *f* d'impôts; *(on goods)* détaxe *f*; ***tax relief*** *(UNCOUNT)* dégrèvement *m* fiscal; **to get tax relief on sth** obtenir un dégrèvement *ou* allégement fiscal sur qch; ***tax return*** déclaration *f* de revenu, feuille *f* d'impôt; ***tax revenue*** recettes *fpl ou* rentrées *fpl* fiscales; ***tax roll*** rôle *m* d'impôt *ou* des contributions; ***tax shelter*** avantage *m* fiscal; ***tax shield*** protection *f* fiscale; ***tax system*** régime *m* fiscal *ou* d'imposition; ***tax threshold*** minimum *m* imposable, seuil *m* d'imposition; **the government has raised tax thresholds in line with inflation** le gouvernement a relevé les tranches de l'impôt pour tenir compte de l'inflation; ***tax write-off*** *(expense)* dépense *f* déductible des impôts; *(loss)* perte *f* déductible des impôts; ***tax year*** année *f* fiscale, année *f* d'imposition *(qui commence en avril en Grande-Bretagne)*

taxable ['tæksəbəl] *adj (income, land)* imposable; *(goods)* taxable

►► ***taxable base*** base *f* d'imposition; ***taxable income*** revenu *m* imposable, assiette *f* fiscale *ou* de l'impôt; ***taxable profit*** bénéfice *m* fiscal *ou* imposable; ***taxable transaction*** opération *f* imposable

taxation [tæk'seɪʃən] **1** *n (UNCOUNT)* (**a**) *(of goods)* taxation *f*; *(of companies, people)* imposition *f*, prélèvement *m* fiscal; **taxation at source** prélèvement *m* de l'impôt à la source, imposition *f* à la source

(**b**) *(taxes)* impots *mpl*, contributions *fpl*

2 *comp (system)* fiscal

►► ***taxation authorities*** administration *f* fiscale, fisc *m*; ***taxation year*** année *f* fiscale d'imposition, exercice *m* fiscal

tax-deductible *adj* déductible des impôts, sujet à un dégrèvement d'impôts

tax-deferred *adj Am Fin* à impôt différé

taxeme ['tæksi:m] *n Ling* taxème *m*

tax-exempt *adj (goods)* exonéré de taxes, non taxé; *(income)* exonéré d'impôts

tax-free *adj (goods)* exonéré de taxes, non taxé; *(interest)* exonéré d'impôts, exempt d'impôts; *(income)* exonéré d'impôts

►► ***tax-free shop*** boutique *f* hors taxes; ***tax-free shopping*** achats *mpl* hors taxes

taxi ['tæksɪ] (*pl* **taxis** *or* **taxies**, *pt & pp* **taxied**, *cont* **taxying**) **1** *n* taxi *m*; **to take a taxi** prendre un taxi; **to hail a taxi** héler un taxi

2 *vi (aircraft)* se déplacer au sol; **the plane taxied across the tarmac** l'avion traversa lentement l'aire de stationnement

3 *vt (carry passengers)* transporter en taxi

►► *Fam* ***taxi dancer*** taxi-girl *f*; ***taxi driver*** chauffeur *m* de taxi; ***taxi fare*** *(gen)* tarif *m* de taxi; *(cost of journey)* coût *m* du taxi, prix *m* de la course (en taxi); **can you pay the taxi fare?** pouvez-vous régler *ou* payer le taxi?; ***taxi rank***, *Am* ***taxi stand*** station *f* de taxis

taxicab ['tæksɪkæb] *n* taxi *m*

taxidermal [,tæksɪ'dɜ:məl] *adj* taxidermique

taxidermist ['tæksɪ,dɜ:mɪst] *n* empailleur(euse) *m,f*, taxidermiste *mf*, naturaliste *mf*

taxidermy ['tæksɪ,dɜ:mɪ] *n* empaillage *m*, taxidermie *f*, naturalisation *f* des animaux

taxiing ['tæksɪɪŋ] *n Aviat* roulement *m*

taximan ['tæksɪmæn] (*pl* **taximen** [-men]) *n Br* chauffeur *m* de taxi

taximeter ['tæksɪ,mi:tə(r)] *n* taximètre *m*, compteur *m* (de taxi)

taxing ['tæksɪŋ] *adj (problem, time)* difficile; *(climb)* ardu

taxiplane ['tæksɪpleɪn] *n* avion-taxi *m*

taxis ['tæksɪs] *n* (**a**) *Biol* taxie *f* (**b**) *Med* taxis *m*

taxiway ['tæksɪweɪ] *n Aviat* taxiway *m*, chemin *m* de roulement

taxman ['tæksmæn] (*pl* **taxmen** [-men]) *n* (**a**) *(person)* percepteur *m* (du fisc) (**b**) *Br Fam (Inland Revenue)* **the taxman** le fisc ❑

taxonomic [,tæksə'nɒmɪk] *adj* taxinomique

taxonomist [,tæk'sɒnəmɪst] *adj* taxinomiste *mf*

taxonomy [tæk'sɒnəmɪ] (*pl* **taxonomies**) *n* taxinomie *f*

taxpayer ['tæks,peɪə(r)] *n* contribuable *mf*

Taylorism ['teɪlə,rɪzəm] *n Ind & Hist* taylorisme *m*

Tayside ['teɪsaɪd] *n* le Tayside, = région de l'est de l'Écosse; **in Tayside** dans le Tayside

TB [,ti:'bi:] *n (abbr* **tuberculosis**) tuberculose *f*

T-bar *n* (**a**) *(for skiers)* téléski *m*, remonte-pente *m* (**b**) *(wrench)* clé *f* à pipe en forme de T; *(bar)* profilé *m ou* fer *m* en T

T-bill *n Am (treasury bill)* bon *m* du trésor

T-bird *n Fam (Thunderbird)* Thunderbird ❑ *f (nom d'un modèle de Ford des années 50)*

T-bone (steak) *n* steak *m* dans l'aloyau *(sur l'os)*

tbs., tbsp. *(written abbr* **tablespoon(ful)**) cs

T-cell *n Med* lymphocyte *m* T

Tchaikovsky [tʃaɪ'kɒfskɪ] *pr n* Tchaïkovski

TCP® [,ti:si:'pi:] *n Br (abbr* **trichlorophonoxyacetic acid**) = désinfectant utilisé pour nettoyer des petites plaies ou pour se gargariser

TCP/IP [,ti:si:'pi:,aɪ'pi:] *n Comput (abbr* **transmission control protocol/Internet protocol**) TCP-IP

TD [,ti:'di:] *n* (**a**) *(abbr* **Treasury Department**) ministère *m* des Finances (**b**) *Ir Pol (abbr* **Teachta Dála**) ≃ député(e) *m,f* (**c**) *Sport (abbr* **touchdown**) essai *m*

te [ti:] *n Mus* si *m*

tea [ti:] *n* (**a**) *(drink, leaves)* thé *m*; **a cup of tea** une tasse de thé; **more tea?** encore un peu de thé?; **two teas and a coffee, please** deux thés et un café, s'il vous plaît; **all rooms have tea and coffee making facilities** toutes les chambres offrent la possibilité de préparer du thé et du café; **I wouldn't do it for all the tea in China** je ne le ferais à aucun prix *ou* pour rien au monde

(**b**) *(afternoon snack)* thé *m*; *Scot, NEng & Ir (evening meal)* repas *m* du soir; **to ask sb to tea** inviter qn à prendre le thé

(**c**) *(infusion)* infusion *f*, tisane *f*; **rosehip tea** tisane *f* d'églantine

(**d**) *(plant)* thé *m*

►► *Am* ***tea ball*** boule *f* à thé; *Br* ***tea biscuit*** gâteau *m* sec; *Br* ***tea boy*** = jeune employé chargé de préparer le thé pour ses collègues; ***tea bread*** *(UNCOUNT)* ≃ cake *m*; *Br* ***tea break*** pause *f* pour prendre le thé, pause-thé *f*; **to have** *or* **to take a tea break** s'arrêter pour prendre le thé, faire une pause-thé; ***tea caddy*** boîte *f* à thé; ***tea chest*** caisse *f* (à thé); *Br* ***tea cloth*** torchon *m* (à vaisselle); *Br* ***tea cosy***, *Am* ***tea cozy*** cosy *m*; ***tea dance*** thé *m* dansant; ***tea egg*** boule *f* à thé; ***tea garden*** *(garden)* = jardin de restaurant qui fait salon de thé; *(plantation)* plantation *f* de thé; *Old-fashioned* ***tea gown*** robe *f* d'intérieur; *Br* ***tea lady*** = dame qui prépare ou sert le thé pour les employés d'une entreprise; ***tea party*** *(for adults)* thé *m*; *(for children)* goûter *m*; **I'm having a little tea party on Sunday** j'ai invité quelques amis à prendre le thé dimanche; ***tea plant*** arbre *m* à thé, théier *m*; ***tea plantation*** plantation *f* de thé; ***tea planter*** planteur *m* de thé; *Br* ***tea plate*** petite assiette *f*, assiette *f* à dessert; ***tea rose*** rose thé *f*; ***tea service, tea set*** service *m* à thé; *Br* ***tea shop*** salon *m* de thé; ***tea strainer*** passoire *f* à thé, passe-thé *m inv*; ***tea table*** table *f* (mise) pour le thé, table *f* à thé; *Br* ***tea towel*** torchon *m* (à vaisselle); ***tea tray*** plateau *m* à thé; *Br* ***tea trolley*** table *f* roulante *(pour servir le thé)*; ***tea urn*** fontaine *f* à thé; *Am* ***tea wagon*** table *f* roulante *(pour servir le thé)*

TEA

Bien que, dans certains milieux, le thé ait été récemment supplanté par le café, le thé reste en Grande-Bretagne comme en Irlande une boisson extrêmement populaire. Si la tradition de l'"afternoon tea" a largement disparu, de même que les "tea ladies" qui servaient sur le lieu de travail le thé sur une table roulante, le rituel du thé continue cependant à jouer un rôle important dans la plupart des foyers.

teabag ['ti:bæg] *n* sachet *m* de thé

teacake ['ti:keɪk] *n* = petite brioche

teacart ['ti:kɑ:t] *n Am* table *f* roulante *(pour servir le thé)*

teach [ti:tʃ] (*pt & pp* **taught** [tɔ:t]) **1** *vt* (**a**) *(gen)* apprendre; **to teach sb sth** *or* **sth to sb** apprendre qch à qn; **she taught herself knitting/French** elle a appris à tricoter/elle a appris le français toute seule; **you can't teach them anything!** ils savent tout!, ils n'ont plus rien à

taw–tea

apprendre!; **to teach sb (how) to do sth** apprendre à qn à faire qch; **she taught them to play the piano** elle leur a appris à jouer du piano; **they taught us what to do in emergencies** ils nous ont appris *ou* montré ce qu'il fallait faire en cas d'urgence; **didn't anyone ever teach you not to interrupt people?** on ne t'a jamais dit *ou* appris qu'il ne faut pas couper la parole aux gens?; **I'll teach you to be rude to your elders!** *(as threat)* je vais t'apprendre à être insolent envers les aînés!; **that'll teach you (not) to go off on your own** ça t'apprendra à t'en aller toute seule; **that'll teach you (a lesson)!** ça t'apprendra!, c'est bien fait pour toi!; **that taught them a lesson they won't forget** cela leur a donné une leçon dont ils se souviendront; *Fam* **to teach sb a thing or two** dégourdir qn ❑; *Br Prov* **you can't teach your grandmother to suck eggs** on n'apprend pas à un vieux singe à faire la grimace

(**b**) *Sch (physics, history etc)* enseigner, être professeur de; *(pupils, class)* faire cours à; **she taught us (to speak) French** elle nous a appris *ou* enseigné le français; **she teaches geography** elle enseigne la géographie, elle est professeur de géographie; **I've been teaching 3B since Christmas** j'ai la 3B depuis Noël, je fais cours à la 3B depuis Noël; *Am* **to teach school** être enseignant; *Am* **she teaches elementary school/high school** elle est institutrice/professeur

2 *vi (as profession)* être enseignant, enseigner; *(give lessons)* faire cours; **I started teaching in 1980** j'ai commencé à enseigner *ou* je suis entré dans l'enseignement en 1980; **she spent the morning teaching** elle a fait cours toute la matinée

teachable ['ti:tʃəbəl] *adj* (**a**) *(subject)* que l'on peut enseigner, susceptible d'être enseigné; *(children)* à qui on peut apprendre quelque chose (**b**) *Am Admin* scolarisable

teacher ['ti:tʃə(r)] *n (in primary school)* instituteur(trice) *m,f*, maître *m*, maîtresse *f*; *(in secondary school)* professeur *m*, enseignant(e) *m,f*; *(in special school)* éducateur(trice) *m,f*; **French/history teacher** professeur *m* de français/d'histoire; **teachers are threatening to strike** les enseignants menacent de se mettre en grève; **teacher-pupil ratio** taux *m* d'encadrement

▸▸ *Am* ***teacher's aide*** assistant(e) *m,f* pédagogique; *Am* ***teacher certification*** diplôme *m* d'enseignement; *Am* ***teacher's college*** centre *m* de formation pédagogique, ≃ école *f* normale; *Am* ***teacher education*** formation *f* pédagogique des enseignants; *Am Univ* ***teacher evaluation*** évaluation *f* (des compétences) des enseignants; ***teacher's pet*** chouchou(oute) *m,f* du professeur; *Br* ***teacher training*** formation *f* pédagogique des enseignants; **to do one's teacher training** suivre une formation pédagogique; *Br* ***teacher training certificate*** diplôme *m* d'enseignement; *Br* ***teacher training college*** centre *m* de formation pédagogique, ≃ école *f* normale

teach-in *n* séminaire *m*

teaching ['ti:tʃɪŋ] **1** *n* (**a**) *(profession)* enseignement *m*; **to go into teaching** entrer dans l'enseignement, devenir enseignant(e)

(**b**) *(action)* enseignement *m*; **chemistry/history teaching** l'enseignement *m* de la chimie/de l'histoire; **EFL teaching** l'enseignement *m* de l'anglais (comme) langue étrangère

(**c**) *(UNCOUNT) (hours taught)* heures *fpl* d'enseignement, (heures *fpl* de) cours *mpl*; **she only does a few hours' teaching a week** elle ne donne *ou* n'a que quelques heures de cours par semaine

2 *comp (staff)* enseignant; **the teaching profession** *(teachers)* le corps enseignant

3 teachings *npl (of leader, church)* enseignements *mpl*

▸▸ ***teaching aid*** matériel *m* pédagogique; *Am & Can Univ* ***teaching assistant*** = étudiant de deuxième cycle qui assure quelques heures de cours en échange d'une bourse d'étude; ***teaching diploma*** diplôme *m* d'enseignement; *Br Univ* ***teaching fellow*** = étudiant de troisième cycle qui assure quelques heures de cours; ***teaching hospital*** centre *m* hospitalo-universitaire, CHU *m*; ***teaching machine*** = tout type d'appareil utilisant des programmes conçus à des fins pédagogiques; *Br* ***teaching practice*** *(UNCOUNT)* stage *m* pédagogique *(pour futurs enseignants)*; **to go on teaching practice** faire un stage pédagogique

teach-yourself book *n* manuel *m* d'auto-apprentissage

teacup ['ti:kʌp] *n* tasse *f* à thé

teacupful ['ti:kʌp,fʊl] *n* tasse *f* à thé *(mesure)*; **three teacupfuls of milk** trois tasses de lait

tea-drinker *n* buveur(euse) *m,f* de thé

teahouse ['ti:haʊs, *pl* -haʊzɪz] *n* maison *f* de thé *(orientale)*

teak [ti:k] **1** *n* teck *m*, tek *m*

2 *comp* en teck

teakettle ['ti:,ketəl] *n* bouilloire *f*

teal [ti:l] *(pl* **inv** *or* **teals**) *n Orn* sarcelle *f* d'hiver

tealeaf ['ti:li:f] *(pl* **tealeaves** [-li:vz]) *n* (**a**) *(of tea plant)* feuille *f* de thé; **to read the tealeaves** ≃ lire dans le marc de café (**b**) *SEng Fam (rhyming slang =* **thief**) voleur(euse) ❑ *m,f*

team [ti:m] **1** *n* (**a**) *(of players, workers)* équipe *f*; **medical/basketball team** équipe *f* médicale/de basket-ball; **he's one of the team** il fait partie de l'équipe

(**b**) *(of horses, oxen etc)* attelage *m*

2 *vt* (**a**) *(workers, players)* mettre en équipe; *(horses, oxen etc)* atteler; **I was teamed with my brother** j'ai fait équipe avec mon frère

(**b**) *(colours, garments)* assortir, harmoniser

3 *comp* **a team effort** un travail d'équipe

▸▸ ***team building*** création *f* d'un esprit d'équipe; ***team game*** jeu *m* d'équipe; ***team leader*** chef *m* d'équipe; ***team mate*** coéquipier(ère) *m,f*; ***team member*** équipier(ère) *m,f*; ***team player*** *(in sports)* = joueur qui a l'esprit d'équipe; *(employee)* = personne qui a l'esprit d'équipe; ; *Fig* **to be a (good) team player** avoir l'esprit d'équipe; **he's not much of a team player** il n'a pas l'esprit d'équipe; **must be team player** *(in job advert)* esprit d'équipe essentiel; *Cycling* ***team pursuit*** poursuite *f* par équipes; ***team spirit*** esprit *m* d'équipe; *Sport* ***team talk*** discussion *f* avec l'équipe; ***team teaching*** enseignement *m* en équipe; *Cycling* ***team time-trial*** contre-la-montre *m inv* par équipes

▸**team up** **1** *vt sep* (**a**) *(workers, players)* mettre en équipe; *(horses, oxen etc)* atteler; **we're often teamed up (together)** on fait souvent équipe (ensemble); **I got teamed up with Peter** on m'a mis en équipe avec Peter

(**b**) *(colours, clothes)* assortir, harmoniser

2 *vi* (**a**) *(workers)* faire équipe, travailler en collaboration; **to team up with sb** faire équipe avec qn; **the two villages teamed up to put on the show** les deux villages ont collaboré pour monter le spectacle

(**b**) *(colours, clothes)* être assorti, s'harmoniser

teamster ['ti:mstə(r)] *Am* **1** *n* routier *m*, camionneur *m*

2 Teamster *n* = membre du syndicat américain des camionneurs; **the Teamsters** = syndicat américain des camionneurs

teamwork ['ti:mwɜ:k] *n* travail *m* d'équipe

teapot ['ti:pɒt] *n* théière *f*

TEAR[1] [teə(r)]

déchirer	▸ **1 (a), (b), (d)**
froisser	▸ **1 (b)**
arracher	▸ **1 (c), (e)**
se déchirer	▸ **2 (a)**
se précipiter	▸ **2 (b)**
déchirure	▸ **3**

(pt **tore** [tɔ:(r)], *pp* **torn** [tɔ:n]) **1** *vt* (**a**) *(rip → page, material)* déchirer; *(→ clothes)* déchirer, faire un accroc à; *(→ flesh)* déchirer, arracher; **I tore my jacket on a nail** j'ai fait un accroc à ma veste avec un clou; **he tore a hole in the paper** il a fait un trou dans le papier; **he tore a hole in his trousers** il a fait un trou à son pantalon; **tear along the dotted line** *(on form)* détacher suivant le pointillé; **the dog was tearing the meat from a bone** le chien déchiquetait la viande d'un os; **her heart was torn by grief/remorse** elle était déchirée par la douleur/le remords; **she tore open the letter** elle ouvrit l'enveloppe en la déchirant, elle déchira l'enveloppe; **she tore open the wrapper** elle déchira l'emballage pour l'ouvrir; **to tear sth in two** *or* **in half** déchirer qch en deux; **you can tear a piece off this cloth** vous pouvez déchirer un morceau de ce tissu; *also Fig* **to tear one's hair** s'arracher les cheveux; **to tear sth to pieces** *(document, bank note etc)* déchirer qch en mille morceaux; **the fox was torn to pieces by the hounds** le renard a été déchiqueté *ou* mis en pièces par la meute; **to be torn to shreds** être en lambeaux; **to tear sth to shreds** mettre qch en lambeaux; *Fig* **the critics tore the film to shreds** *or* **pieces** les critiques ont éreinté le film; *Fig* **to tear sb to shreds** *or* **pieces** mettre qn en pièces, écharper qn

(**b**) *(muscle, ligament)* froisser, déchirer

(**c**) *(grab, snatch)* arracher; **he tore the cheque from** *or* **out of my hand** il m'a arraché le chèque des mains; **the door had been torn from its hinges by the wind** le vent avait fait sortir la porte de ses gonds

(**d**) *Fig (divide)* tirailler, déchirer; **I'm torn between going and staying** je suis tiraillé entre le désir de partir et celui de rester, j'hésite entre partir et rester; **the country had been torn by civil war for thirty years** ça faisait trente ans que le pays était déchiré par la guerre civile

(**e**) *Fig (separate)* arracher; **sorry to tear you from your reading, but I need your help** je regrette de vous arracher à votre lecture, mais j'ai besoin de votre aide; *Fam Br* **that's torn it,** *Am* **that tears it** c'est le bouquet, il ne manquait plus que cela

2 *vi* (**a**) *(paper, cloth)* se déchirer; **this cloth tears easily** ce tissu se déchire facilement

(**b**) *(as verb of movement)* **to tear after sb** se précipiter *ou* se lancer à la poursuite de qn; **to tear along** *(runner)* courir à toute allure; *(car)* filer à toute allure; **to tear up/down the stairs** monter/descendre l'escalier quatre à quatre; **the cyclists came tearing past** les cyclistes sont passés à toute allure *ou* vitesse; **the children were tearing around the playground** les enfants couraient de tous les côtés dans la cour de récréation; **she came tearing into the garden** elle a déboulé dans le jardin à toute allure, elle s'est précipitée dans le jardin

(**c**) *(hurry)* **to tear through a job** faire un travail à toute vitesse; **he tore through the book/the report** il a lu le livre/le rapport très rapidement

3 *n (in paper, cloth)* déchirure *f*; *(in clothes)* déchirure *f*, accroc *m*; **this page has a tear in it** cette page est déchirée; **who's responsible for the tears in the curtains?** qui a déchiré les rideaux?

▸**tear apart** *vt sep* (**a**) *(rip to pieces)* déchirer

(**b**) *(divide)* **no one can tear them apart** *(friends)* on ne peut pas les séparer, ils sont inséparables; *(fighters)* on n'arrive pas à les séparer; **the party was being torn apart by internal strife** le parti était déchiré *ou* divisé par des luttes intestines

▸**tear at** *vt insep* **to tear at sth** déchirer *ou* arracher qch; **the dogs tore at the meat** les chiens arrachèrent *ou* déchiquetèrent la viande; **the children tore impatiently at the wrapping paper** dans leur impatience les enfants déchirèrent le papier d'emballage

▸**tear away** *vt sep* (**a**) *(remove → wallpaper)* arracher, enlever; *Fig (→ gloss, façade)* enlever

(**b**) *(from activity)* arracher; **to tear sb away from sth** arracher qn à qch; **I just couldn't tear myself away** je ne pouvais tout simplement pas me décider à partir; **surely you can tear yourself away from your work for ten minutes?** tu ne vas pas me dire que tu ne peux pas t'éloigner de ton travail pendant dix minutes?, tu peux quand même laisser ton travail dix minutes!

▸**tear down** *vt sep* (**a**) *(remove → poster)* arracher

(**b**) *(demolish → building)* démolir; *Fig (→ argument)* démolir, mettre par terre

▸**tear into** *vt insep* (**a**) *(attack, rush at)* se précipiter sur; **the boxers tore into each other** les boxeurs se sont jetés l'un sur l'autre

(**b**) *Fam (reprimand)* enguirlander, passer un savon à; *(criticize)* taper sur, descendre (en flèche); **he really tore into me over my exam results** il m'a bien engueulé *ou* il m'a passé un bon savon au sujet de mes résultats d'examen; **the critics have really torn into his latest film** les critiques ont complètement descendu son dernier film

(**c**) *(bite into → of teeth, knife)* s'enfoncer dans; **the saw tore into the soft wood** la scie s'est enfoncée dans le bois tendre comme dans du beurre

►**tear off** *vt sep* (**a**) *(tape, wrapper)* arracher, enlever en arrachant; *(along perforations)* détacher; *(clothing)* retirer *ou* enlever rapidement; **he tore off his trousers and jumped into the water** il retira *ou* enleva son pantalon en toute hâte et sauta dans l'eau; **he had had one of his arms torn off by a machine** il avait eu le bras arraché par une machine; *Br Fam* **to tear sb off a strip, to tear a strip off sb** passer un savon à qn, enguirlander qn

(**b**) *Fam (report, essay etc → do hurriedly)* écrire à toute vitesse ❑; *(→ do badly)* bâcler, torcher

►**tear out** *vt sep (page)* arracher; *(coupon, cheque)* détacher; **to tear a page out of a book** arracher une page d'un livre; *also Fig* **to tear one's hair out** s'arracher les cheveux

►**tear up** *vt sep* (**a**) *(paper, letter)* déchirer (en morceaux); *Fig (agreement, contract)* déchirer

(**b**) *(pull up → fence, weeds, surface)* arracher; *(→ tree)* déraciner

---

tear² [tɪə(r)] *n (from eye)* larme *f*; **to be in tears** être en larmes; **to burst into tears** fondre en larmes; **to shed tears** verser des larmes; **I shed no tears over her resignation** sa démission ne m'a pas ému outre mesure *ou* ne m'a pas arraché de larmes; **to shed tears of joy** pleurer de joie, verser des larmes de joie; **he had tears** *or* **there were tears in his eyes** il avait les larmes aux yeux; **to be on the verge of tears, to be near to tears** être au bord des larmes; **to be moved to tears** être ému aux larmes; **the performance moved me to tears** *or* **brought tears to my eyes** le spectacle m'a ému aux larmes; *Fig* **to be bored to tears** s'ennuyer à mourir

►► ***tear duct*** canal *m* lacrymal; ***tear gas*** gaz *m* lacrymogène

tearaway ['teərəˌweɪ] *n Br Fam* casse-cou *mf inv*

teardrop ['tɪədrɒp] *n* larme *f*

tearful ['tɪəfʊl] *adj* (**a**) *(emotional → departure, occasion)* larmoyant; *(→ story, account)* larmoyant, à faire pleurer; **they said a tearful goodbye** ils se sont dit au revoir en pleurant (**b**) *(person)* en larmes, qui pleure; *(face)* en larmes; *(voice)* larmoyant; **I'm feeling a bit tearful** j'ai envie de pleurer; **she gave me a tearful look** elle m'a lancé un regard larmoyant

tearfully ['tɪəfʊlɪ] *adv* en pleurant, les larmes aux yeux; **"I'll be all right", she said tearfully** "ça va aller", dit-elle avec des sanglots dans la voix *ou* en pleurant

tearfulness ['tɪəfʊlnɪs] *n* larmoiement *m*

tearing ['teərɪŋ] **1** *n* déchirement *m*

2 *adj* (**a**) **a tearing sound** *(from paper)* un bruit de déchirement; *(from stitching)* un (bruit de) craquement (**b**) *Br (as intensifier)* **to be in a tearing hurry** être terriblement pressé

tearjerker ['tɪəˌdʒɜːkə(r)] *n Fam* **the film/the book is a real tearjerker** c'est un film/un livre à faire pleurer ❑

tearjerking ['tɪəˌdʒɜːkɪŋ] *adj Fam* à faire pleurer ❑

[illegible]

tear-off ['teərɒf] *adj (label)* perforé; *(reply slip)* détachable

►► ***tear-off calendar*** calendrier *m* éphéméride; *Comput* ***tear-off menu*** menu *m* flottant

tearoom ['tiːrʊm] *n* salon *m* de thé

tearproof ['teəpruːf] *adj* indéchirable

tearstained ['tɪəsteɪnd] *adj* barbouillé de larmes

tease [tiːz] **1** *vt* (**a**) *(person)* taquiner; *(sexually)* allumer; *(animal)* tourmenter; **she's always teasing her brother** elle est toujours à taquiner son frère

(**b**) *(fabric)* peigner; *(wool)* peigner, carder

(**c**) *(coax)* **he teased the wire through the slot** à force de patience, il a réussi à faire passer le fil dans la fente; **he teased the engine into life** à force de patience, il a réussi à faire démarrer le moteur

(**d**) *Am (hair)* crêper

2 *vi* faire des taquineries; **I'm only teasing** c'est pour rire

3 *n Fam* (**a**) *(person)* taquin(e) ❑ *m,f*; *(sexually)* allumeuse *f*; **don't be such a tease!** ne sois pas si taquin!

(**b**) *(behaviour)* taquinerie ❑ *f*; **it was all a tease** c'était pour rire

►**tease out** *vt sep* (**a**) *(wool, hair)* démêler

(**b**) *(information, facts)* faire ressortir; **to tease out a problem** débrouiller *ou* démêler un problème, tirer un problème au clair

teasel ['tiːzəl] *(Br pt & pp* **teaselled,** *cont* **teaselling,** *Am pt & pp* **teaseled,** *cont* **teaseling)** **1** *n* (**a**) *Bot* cardère *f* (**b**) *Tex* carde *f*

2 *vt (cloth)* peigner, démêler

teaser ['tiːzə(r)] *n Fam* (**a**) *(person)* taquin(e) ❑ *m,f* (**b**) *(problem)* problème *m* difficile ❑, colle *f* (**c**) *Mktg* aguiche ❑ *f*

►► *Mktg* ***teaser ad*** aguiche ❑ *f*; *Mktg* ***teaser campaign*** campagne *f* teasing ❑

teasing ['tiːzɪŋ] **1** *n (UNCOUNT)* (**a**) *(tormenting)* taquineries *fpl* (**b**) *Tex* peignage *m*

2 *adj* taquin

teasingly ['tiːzɪŋlɪ] *adv (in order to tease)* pour (me/te/*etc*) taquiner, par taquinerie; **..., he said teasingly** ..., dit-il d'un air taquin

Teasmaid® ['tiːzmeɪd] *n Br* = théière automatique avec horloge incorporée

teaspoon ['tiːspuːn] *n (spoon, measure)* cuiller *f ou* cuillère *f* à café

teaspoonful ['tiːspuːnˌfʊl] *adj* cuiller *f ou* cuillère *f* à café *(mesure)*

teat [tiːt] *n* (**a**) *(on breast)* mamelon *m*, bout *m* de sein; *(of animal)* tétine *f*, tette *f*; *(for milking)* trayon *m* (**b**) *Br (on bottle)* tétine *f*; *(dummy)* tétine *f*, sucette *f* (**c**) *Tech* téton *m*

teatime ['tiːtaɪm] *n* l'heure *f* du thé

teazel *(Br pt & pp* **teazelled,** *cont* **teazelling,** *Am pt & pp* **teazeled,** *cont* **teazeling)** = **teasel**

teazle = **teasel**

TEC [tek] *n (abbr* **Training and Enterprise Council)** = centre d'emploi et de formation

tech [tek] *n Br Fam Sch (abbr* **technical college)** ≃ IUT ❑ *m*

techie ['tekɪ] *n Fam* = terme péjoratif ou humoristique désignant un informaticien

technetium [tek'niːʃɪəm] *n Chem* technétium *m*

technical ['teknɪkəl] *adj* (**a**) *(gen) & Tech* technique; **don't get technical** n'emploie pas de termes trop techniques

(**b**) *(according to rules)* technique; **for technical reasons** pour des raisons d'ordre technique; *Law* **the judgment was quashed on a technical point** le jugement a été cassé pour vice de forme *ou* de procédure; *Fig* **it's a purely technical point** ce n'est qu'un point de détail

►► *Ftbl* ***technical area*** banc *m* de touche; ***technical college*** ≃ IUT *m*; *St Exch* ***technical correction*** correction *f* d'un cours en Bourse; ***technical drawing*** dessin *m* industriel; ***technical education*** enseignement *m* technique; *Sport* ***technical foul*** faute *f* technique; *Br* ***technical hitch*** incident *m* technique; *Law* ***technical irregularity*** vice *m* de forme *ou* de procédure; *Boxing* ***technical knockout*** knock-out *m inv* technique; *Law* ***technical offence*** quasi-délit *m*; ***technical school*** ≃ collège *m* technique, ≃ lycée *m* d'enseignement professionnel; *Comput* ***technical support*** support *m* technique; ***technical term*** terme *m* technique; ***technical writing*** rédaction *f* technique

technicality [ˌteknɪ'kælətɪ] *(pl* **technicalities)** *n* (**a**) *(technical nature)* technicité *f* (**b**) *(formal detail)* détail *m ou* considération *f* (d'ordre) technique; *(technical term)* terme *m* technique; **it's only a technicality** ce n'est qu'un détail technique; *Law* **to lose one's case on a technicality** perdre un procès pour vice de forme

technically ['teknɪklɪ] *adv* (**a**) *(on a technical level)* sur un plan technique; *(in technical terms)* en termes techniques; **technically, it shouldn't be able to fly** d'un point de vue technique, il ne devrait pas pouvoir voler; **technically advanced** de pointe, sophistiqué, avancé sur le plan technique; **to be technically minded** avoir l'esprit technique

(**b**) *(in theory)* en théorie, en principe; **technically, I'm in charge** théoriquement, c'est moi le responsable

technician [tek'nɪʃən] *n* technicien(enne) *m,f*

Technicolor® ['teknɪˌkʌlə(r)] **1** *n* Technicolor® *m*; **in (glorious) Technicolor**® en Technicolor

2 *adj* en technicolor; *Fam Hum* **to have a technicolor yawn** *(vomit)* gerber, dégobiller

technics ['teknɪks] *n (UNCOUNT)* technologie *f*

technique [tek'niːk] *n* technique *f*

techno ['teknəʊ] *n Mus* techno *f*

technobabble ['teknəʊˌbæbəl] *n* jargon *m* technique

technocracy [tek'nɒkrəsɪ] *(pl* **technocracies)** *n* technocratie *f*

technocrat ['teknəkræt] *n* technocrate *mf*

technocratic [ˌteknə'krætɪk] *adj* technocratique; *(person)* à la mentalité de technocrate

technographic [ˌteknə'græfɪk] *adj* technographique

technography [tek'nɒgrəfɪ] *n* technographie *f*

technological [ˌteknə'lɒdʒɪkəl] *adj* technologique

technologically [ˌteknə'lɒdʒɪklɪ] *adv* du point de vue *ou* sur le plan technologique

technologist [tek'nɒlədʒɪst] *n* technologue *mf*, technologiste *mf*

technology [tek'nɒlədʒɪ] *(pl* **technologies)** *n* technologie *f*; **the latest technology** la technologie de pointe *ou* la plus avancée

►► ***technology transfer*** transfert *m* de technologie

technophile ['teknəʊfaɪl] *n* technophile *mf*

technophobe ['teknəʊfəʊb] *n* technophobe *mf*

technophobia [ˌteknəʊ'fəʊbɪə] *n* technophobie *f*

tectonic [tek'tɒnɪk] *adj* tectonique

►► ***tectonic plates*** plaques *fpl* tectoniques

tectonics [tek'tɒnɪks] *n (UNCOUNT)* tectonique *f*

ted [ted] *(pt & pp* **tedded,** *cont* **tedding)** **1** *vt (hay)* faner

2 *n Br Fam (teddy boy)* ≃ blouson *m* noir *(personne)*

tedder ['tedə(r)] *n Agr (machine)* faneuse *f*; *(person)* faneur(euse) *m,f*

teddy ['tedɪ] *(pl* **teddies)** *n* (**a**) *(toy)* ours *m* en peluche (**b**) *(garment)* teddy *m*

►► ***teddy bear*** ours *m* en peluche; *Br* ***teddy boy*** ≃ blouson *m* noir *(personne)*

Te Deum [tiː'diːəm] *n Rel & Mus* Te Deum *m inv*

tedious ['tiːdɪəs] *adj (activity, work)* ennuyeux, fastidieux; *(time)* ennuyeux; *(journey)* fatigant, pénible; *(person)* pénible; **we spent a tedious morning typing address labels** on a passé une matinée pénible à taper des étiquettes portant noms et adresses; **it's a very tedious job** c'est un travail très fastidieux *ou* pénible; **it's a tedious business collecting signatures** recueillir des signatures est un travail fastidieux; **as he explained in tedious detail** comme il l'a expliqué en de fastidieux détails

tediously ['tiːdɪəslɪ] *adv* péniblement; *(monotonously)* de façon monotone, fastidieusement; **the journey seemed tediously long** le voyage était long et pénible

tediousness ['tiːdɪəsnɪs] *n* ennui *m*, monotonie *f*; **the sheer tediousness of the job got her down** la monotonie de son travail lui mit le moral à zéro; **an air of tediousness hung over the house** un certain ennui pesait sur la maison

tedium ['tiːdɪəm] *n* ennui *m*

[illegible] point *m* de départ; **the 17th tee** le départ du 17ème trou

2 *vt* placer sur le tee

3 *vi* placer la balle sur le tee

►► ***tee peg*** tee *m*; ***tee shirt*** tee-shirt *m*, t-shirt *m*; ***tee shot*** coup *m* de départ *(avec la balle sur le tee)*

►**tee off** **1** *vi* (**a**) *Golf* jouer sa balle *ou* partir du tee *(du tertre de départ)*; *Fig* commencer, démarrer

(**b**) *Am Fam (get angry)* se fâcher ❑, s'emporter ❑; **to tee off about sth** se fâcher au sujet de qch

2 *vt sep Am Fam (annoy)* agacer ❑, casser les pieds à; **he really tees me off with his arrogance** son arrogance m'énerve vraiment ❑; **I'm teed off** j'en ai ras le bol *ou* marre

►**tee up** **1** *vt sep* (**a**) *Golf* **to tee up the ball** placer la balle sur le tee

(**b**) *Fig* **to tee up a deal** préparer le terrain pour obtenir un contrat; **to tee up a job for sb** apporter un travail à qn sur un plateau

2 *vi Golf* placer la balle sur le tee

tea–tee

tee-hee [-'hiː] **1** *exclam* hi! hi!
2 *n* ricanement *m*
3 *vi* ricaner

teem [tiːm] *vi* (**a**) *(be crowded)* grouiller, fourmiller; **the streets were teeming (with people)** les rues grouillaient (de monde); **the river is teeming with fish** la rivière grouille de poissons; **the children came teeming through the gates** une horde d'enfants a franchi les grilles (**b**) *(rain)* **the rain was teeming down** la pluie tombait à verse; **it's absolutely teeming (with rain)** il pleut à verse *ou* à torrents

teeming ['tiːmɪŋ] *adj* (**a**) *(streets)* grouillant de monde; *(crowds, shoppers)* grouillant, fourmillant; *(ants, insects etc)* grouillant (**b**) *(rain)* battant, torrentiel

teen [tiːn] *adj (teenage → fashion, magazine)* pour adolescents *ou* jeunes; **teen idol** idole *f* des jeunes

teenage ['tiːneɪdʒ] *adj (boy, girl)* jeune, adolescent; *(habits, activities)* d'adolescents; *(fashion, magazine)* pour les jeunes *ou* adolescents; **the teenage years** l'adolescence *f*; **teenage boys and girls** les adolescents *mpl*

teenager ['tiːnˌeɪdʒə(r)] *n* jeune *mf (entre 13 et 19 ans)*, adolescent(e) *m,f*

teens [tiːnz] *npl* (**a**) *(age)* adolescence *f (entre 13 et 19 ans)*; **she's in her teens** c'est une adolescente (**b**) *(numbers)* = les chiffres entre 13 et 19; **the upper teens** = les chiffres de 17 à 19

teensy(-weensy) [ˌtiːnzɪ('wiːnzɪ)] = **teeny-weeny**

teeny ['tiːnɪ] *adj Fam* tout petit□, minuscule□

teenybopper ['tiːnɪˌbɒpə(r)] *n Fam* petite minette *f*

teeny-weeny [-'wiːnɪ], *Am* **teeny-tiny** *adj Fam* tout petit□, minuscule□

teepee = **tepee**

teeter ['tiːtə(r)] **1** *vi* (**a**) *(person)* chanceler; *(pile, object)* vaciller, être sur le point de tomber; *Fig* **to teeter on the brink of sth** être au bord de qch, friser qch (**b**) *Am (see-saw)* se balancer, basculer
2 *n Am* jeu *m* de bascule

teeter-totter *n Am* jeu *m* de bascule

teethe [tiːð] *vi* faire *ou* percer ses premières dents; **to be teething** commencer à faire ses dents

teething ['tiːðɪŋ] *n* poussée *f* dentaire, dentition *f*
▸▸ ***teething ring*** anneau *m* de dentition; ***teething troubles*** douleurs *fpl* provoquées par la poussée des dents; *Fig* difficultés *fpl* initiales *ou* de départ; **we're having teething troubles with the new computer** nous avons des problèmes de mise en route avec le nouvel ordinateur

teetotal [tiː'təʊtəl] *adj (person)* qui ne boit jamais d'alcool; *(organization)* antialcoolique

teetotalism [tiː'təʊtəlɪzəm] *n* abstention *f* de toute boisson alcoolisée; **after two weeks of enforced teetotalism** après une quinzaine de jours au régime sec

teetotaller, *Am* **teetotaler** [tiː'təʊtlə(r)] *n* = personne qui ne boit jamais d'alcool

teetotum [tiː'təʊtəm] *n Hist* toton *m*

TEFL ['tefəl] *n (abbr* **Teaching (of) English as a Foreign Language**) enseignement *m* de l'anglais langue étrangère

Teflon® ['teflɒn] *n* Téflon® *m*; **a Teflon®-coated pan** une casserole téflonisée

teg [teg] *n Agr* (agneau *m*) antennais *m*

tegmen ['tegmən] *n* (**a**) *Bot* tégument *m* (**b**) *Zool* hémélytre *m*, tegmen *m*

tegument ['tegjʊmənt] *n* tégument *m*

te-hee = **tee-hee**

Tehran, Teheran [ˌteə'rɑːn] *n* Téhéran

tektite ['tektaɪt] *n Miner* tectite *f*, tektite *f*

tel. *(written abbr* **telephone**) tél

telaesthesia, *Am* **telesthesia** [ˌtelɪs'θiːzɪə] *n* télesthésie *f*

telaesthetic, *Am* **telesthetic** [ˌtelɪs'θetɪk] *adj* télesthésique

Telautograph® [te'lɔːtəgrɑːf] *n* télautographe *m*, téléautographe *m*

telautography [ˌtelɔː'tɒgrəfɪ] *n* télautographie *f*, téléautographie *f*

Tel-Aviv [ˌtelə'viːv] *n* **Tel-Aviv(-Jaffa)** Tel-Aviv(-Jaffa)

telco ['telkəʊ] *n (abbr* **telecommunications company**) société *f* de télécommunications

telebanking ['telɪˌbæŋkɪŋ] *n* télébanque *f*

telecamera ['telɪˌkæmərə] *n* caméra *f* de télévision

telecast ['telɪkɑːst] **1** *n* émission *f* de télévision, programme *m* télédiffusé
2 *vt* diffuser, téléviser

telecaster ['telɪˌkɑːstə(r)] *n (broadcaster)* téléaste *mf*; *(broadcasting company)* société *f* de télédiffusion

telecasting ['telɪˌkɑːstɪŋ] *n* télédiffusion *f*

telecine [ˌtelɪ'sɪnɪ] *n* télécinéma *m*

telecom ['telɪkɒm] *n (UNCOUNT) (abbr* **telecommunications**) télécoms *fpl*

telecommunications ['telɪkəˌmjuːnɪ'keɪʃənz] **1** *n* télécommunications *fpl*
2 *comp (satellite)* de télécommunication
▸▸ ***telecommunications engineer*** technicien *m* des télécommunications; ***telecommunications industry*** industrie *f* des télécommunications; ***telecommunications link*** liaison *f* de télécommunications

telecommute ['telɪkəmjuːt] *vi* faire du télétravail, télétravailler

telecommuter ['telɪkəˌmjuːtə(r)] *n* télétravailleur(euse) *m,f*

telecommuting ['telɪkəˌmjuːtɪŋ] *n* télétravail *m*

telecoms ['telɪkɒmz] = **telecom**

Telecom Tower *n* = tour dans le centre de Londres, siège de British Telecom

telecon ['telɪkɒn] *n Fam* conversation *f* téléphonique□

teleconference ['telɪˌkɒnfərəns] *n* téléconférence *f*

teleconferencing ['telɪˌkɒnfərənsɪŋ] *n* téléconférence *f*

telecottage ['telɪkɒtɪdʒ] *n Br* = bâtiment équipé en matériel informatique et de télécommunications, utilisé dans les zones rurales pour le télétravail

telecottaging ['telɪkɒtɪdʒɪŋ] *n Br* télétravail *m* en zone rurale

Telefax® ['telɪfæks] *n* Téléfax® *m*

telefilm ['telɪfɪlm] *n* téléfilm *m*

telegenic [ˌtelɪ'dʒenɪk] *adj* télégénique

telegony [tɪ'legənɪ] *n* télégonie *f*

telegram ['telɪgræm] *n* télégramme *m*; *(in press, diplomacy)* dépêche *f*; **by telegram** par télégramme; **to send sb a telegram** envoyer un télégramme à qn

telegraph ['telɪgrɑːf] **1** *n* (**a**) *(system)* télégraphe *m*; *Br Press* **the Telegraph** = nom abrégé du 'Daily Telegraph' (**b**) *(telegram)* télégramme *m*
2 *comp (service, wire)* télégraphique
3 *vt* (**a**) *(news)* télégraphier; *(money)* télégraphier, envoyer par télégramme; **she telegraphed us to say she couldn't come** elle nous a télégraphié *ou* envoyé un télégramme pour dire qu'elle ne pouvait pas venir
(**b**) *Sport* **to telegraph a punch/pass** téléphoner un coup/une passe
(**c**) *Can Pol* **to telegraph votes** voter frauduleusement
4 *vi* télégraphier; **he telegraphed to say he'd be late** il a télégraphié *ou* envoyé un télégramme pour dire qu'il serait en retard
▸▸ ***telegraph pole, telegraph post*** poteau *m* télégraphique; *Br* ***Telegraph reader*** = lecteur du 'Daily Telegraph' (typiquement conservateur)

telegrapher [tɪ'legrəfə(r)] *n* télégraphiste *mf*

telegraphese [ˌtelɪgrɑː'fiːz] *n* langage *m ou* style *m* télégraphique

telegraphic [ˌtelɪ'græfɪk] *adj* télégraphique
▸▸ ***telegraphic money order*** mandat *m* télégraphique; ***telegraphic payment*** paiement *m* télégraphique; ***telegraphic transfer*** transfert *m* télégraphique

telegraphically [ˌtelɪ'græfɪklɪ] *adv (by telegram)* télégraphiquement, par télégramme; *(speak, write)* en style télégraphique

telegraphist [tɪ'legrəfɪst] *n* télégraphiste *mf*

telegraphy [tɪ'legrəfɪ] *n* télégraphie *f*

telejector ['telɪdʒektə(r)] *n TV* projecteur *m* de télévision

telekinesis [ˌtelɪkaɪ'niːsɪs] *n* télékinésie *f*

telemark ['telɪmɑːk] *n Ski* télémark *m*
▸▸ ***telemark landing*** atterrissage *m* jambes fléchies; ***telemark skiing*** télémark *m*; ***telemark skis*** skis *mpl* pour télémark

telemarket ['telɪˌmɑːkɪt] *n Mktg* télémarché *m*

telemarketing ['telɪˌmɑːkɪtɪŋ] *n Mktg* télémarketing *m*

telematics [ˌtelɪ'mætɪks] *n (UNCOUNT)* télématique *f*

Telemessage® ['telɪˌmesɪdʒ] *n Br* télégramme *m (transmis par télex ou par téléphone)*

telemeter [tɪ'lemɪtə(r)] **1** *n* télémètre *m*
2 *vt* déterminer et transmettre par télémesure

telemetric [ˌtelɪ'metrɪk], **telemetrical** [ˌtelɪ'metrɪkəl] *adj* télémétrique

telemetrist [tɪ'lemɪtrɪst] *n* télémétreur *m*

telemetry [tɪ'lemɪtrɪ] *n* télémesure *f*; **digital telemetry system** système *m* de télémesure numérique
▸▸ ***telemetry transmitter*** émetteur *m* de télémesure

teleneuron [ˌtelɪ'njʊərɒn] *n Anat* téléneurone *m*

teleological [ˌtelɪə'lɒdʒɪkəl] *adj Phil* téléologique

teleology [ˌtelɪ'ɒlədʒɪ] *n Phil* téléologie *f*

teleorder ['telɪˌɔːdə(r)] *Mktg* **1** *n* commande *f* par ordinateur
2 *vt* commander par ordinateur

telepath ['telɪpæθ] *n* télépathe *mf*

telepathic [ˌtelɪ'pæθɪk] *adj (person)* télépathe; *(message, means)* télépathique; **you must be telepathic!** tu dois avoir des dons de télépathie!; **tell me, I'm not telepathic!** dis-le moi, je ne suis pas médium!

telepathically [ˌtelɪ'pæθɪklɪ] *adv (communicate)* par télépathie

telepathist [tɪ'lepəθɪst] *n* télépathe *mf*

telepathy [tɪ'lepəθɪ] *n* télépathie *f*, transmission *f* de pensée; **by telepathy** par télépathie *ou* transmission de pensée

telepayment ['telɪˌpeɪmənt] *n* télépaiement *m*

telephone ['telɪfəʊn] **1** *n* (**a**) *(for communication)* téléphone *m*; **to be on the telephone** *(be talking)* être au téléphone, téléphoner; *(be subscriber)* avoir le téléphone, être abonné au téléphone; **she's been on the telephone for nearly an hour** ça fait presque une heure qu'elle est au téléphone *ou* qu'elle téléphone; **the boss is on the telephone for you** le patron te demande au téléphone; **you're wanted on the telephone** on vous demande au téléphone; **to answer the telephone** répondre au téléphone; **to order sth over the** *or* **by telephone** commander qch par téléphone; **I use the telephone a lot** je téléphone beaucoup
(**b**) *Am (game)* téléphone *m* arabe
2 *comp (receiver)* de téléphone; *(message)* téléphonique; *(charges)* téléphonique, de téléphone; *(service)* des télécommunications; **to have a good telephone manner** savoir bien parler au téléphone; *Am* **to play telephone tag** essayer de se joindre au téléphone sans y parvenir
3 *vt (person)* téléphoner à, appeler (au téléphone); *(place)* téléphoner à, appeler; *(news, message, invitation)* téléphoner, envoyer par téléphone; **I'll telephone him later** je lui téléphonerai *ou* je l'appellerai plus tard; **to telephone the United States/home** téléphoner aux États-Unis/chez soi; **they telephoned me (with) the good news** ils m'ont téléphoné (pour m'annoncer) la bonne nouvelle
4 *vi (call)* téléphoner, appeler; *(be on phone)* être au téléphone; **he telephoned to say he'd be late** il a téléphoné *ou* appelé pour dire qu'il serait en retard; **where are you telephoning from?** d'où appelles-tu *ou* téléphones-tu?
▸▸ ***telephone answering machine*** répondeur *m* (téléphonique); ***telephone banking*** opérations *fpl* bancaires par téléphone, banque *f* à domicile; ***telephone bill*** facture *f* de téléphone; ***telephone book*** annuaire *m* (téléphonique); ***telephone booking*** réservation *f* par téléphone; ***telephone booth,*** *Br* ***telephone box*** cabine *f* téléphonique; ***telephone call*** appel *m* téléphonique, coup *m* de téléphone; *Mktg* ***telephone canvassing*** prospection *f* téléphonique, démarchage *m* à distance, télédémarchage *m*; ***telephone conversation*** entretien *m* téléphonique; ***telephone directory*** annuaire *m* (téléphonique); ***telephone exchange*** central *m* téléphonique; *Mktg* ***telephone follow-up*** relance *f* téléphonique; ***telephone interview*** entretien *m* téléphonique, entretien *m* par téléphone; ***telephone jack*** fiche *f* téléphonique;

Br ***telephone kiosk*** cabine *f* téléphonique; ***telephone line*** ligne *f* téléphonique; ***telephone link*** liaison *f* téléphonique; ***telephone number*** numéro *m* de téléphone; ***telephone operator*** téléphoniste *mf*, standardiste *mf*; ***telephone order*** commande *f* téléphonique *ou* par téléphone; *Mktg* ***telephone prospecting*** télédémarchage *m*, démarchage *m* à distance; ***telephone sales*** ventes *fpl* par téléphone, téléventes *fpl*; ***telephone salesman*** télévendeur *m*, télé-acteur *m*; ***telephone saleswoman*** télévendeuse *f*, téléactrice *f*; ***telephone selling*** vente *f* par téléphone, télévente *f*; ***telephone subscriber*** abonné(e) *m,f* du téléphone; ***telephone survey*** enquête *f* téléphonique, enquête *f* par téléphone; ***telephone switchboard*** standard *m* téléphonique

telephone-tapping *n (system)* écoutes *fpl* de communications téléphoniques; *(act of tapping someone's phone)* mise *f* sur écoute téléphonique

telephonic [ˌtelɪ'fɒnɪk] *adj* téléphonique

telephonist [tɪ'lefənɪst] *n Br* standardiste *mf*, téléphoniste *mf*

telephony [tɪ'lefənɪ] *n* téléphonie *f*

telephotograph [ˌtelɪ'fəʊtəgrɑːf] *n* photographie *f* prise au téléobjectif, téléphotographie *f*

telephotographic [ˌtelɪˌfəʊtə'græfɪk] *adj* téléphotographique

►► ***telephotographic lens*** téléobjectif *m*

telephotography [ˌtelɪfə'tɒgrəfɪ] *n* téléphotographie *f*

telephoto lens [ˌtelɪ'fəʊtəʊ-] *n* téléobjectif *m*

teleplay ['telɪpleɪ] *n* scénario *m* de téléfilm

teleport ['telɪpɔːt] *vt* faire déplacer par télékinésie

teleportation [ˌtelɪpɔː'teɪʃən] *n* télékinésie *f*

teleprint ['telɪˌprɪnt] *vt* transmettre par téléscripteur *ou* téléimprimeur

teleprinter ['telɪˌprɪntə(r)] *n Br* téléscripteur *m*, téléimprimeur *m*

teleprinting ['telɪˌprɪntɪŋ] *n* téléimpression *f*, téléscription *f*

teleprocess ['telɪˌprəʊses] *vi Comput* faire de la télégestion

teleprocessing [ˌtelɪ'prəʊsesɪŋ] *n Comput* télégestion *f*

Teleprompter® ['telɪˌprɒmptə(r)] *n* prompteur *m*, téléprompteur *m*, *Offic* télésouffleur *m*

telerecording [ˌtelɪrɪ'kɔːdɪŋ] *n* émission *f* de télévision enregistrée

telesales ['telɪseɪlz] *n Mktg* vente *f* par téléphone, télévente *f*

telesalesperson ['telɪˌseɪlzpɜːsən] *n* vendeur(-euse) *m,f* par téléphone

telescope ['telɪskəʊp] **1** *n* télescope *m*, longue-vue *f*; *Astron* télescope *m*, lunette *f* astronomique

2 *vt* (**a**) *(make collapse → parts)* emboîter

(**b**) *Fig (shorten, condense → parts, report)* condenser, abréger

3 *vi* (**a**) *(collapse → parts)* s'emboîter

(**b**) *(railway carriages)* se télescoper; **the carriages telescoped into each other** les wagons se sont télescopés

telescopic [ˌtelɪ'skɒpɪk] *adj (aerial)* télescopique; *(umbrella)* pliant

►► ***telescopic lens*** téléobjectif *m*; ***telescopic sight*** lunette *f*

telescopy [tɪ'leskəpɪ] *n* télescopie *f*

teleselling [ˌtelɪ'selɪŋ] *n Mktg* vente *f* par téléphone

teleshopping ['telɪˌʃɒpɪŋ] *n Mktg* achats *mpl* à domicile, téléachat *m*

telesoftware [ˌtelɪ'sɒftweə(r)] *n* télélogiciel *m*, logiciel *m* de télétexte

telespectroscope [ˌtelɪ'spektrəskəʊp] *n Astron* téléspectroscope *m*

telestereoscope [ˌtelɪ'sterɪəskəʊp] *n Opt* téléstéréoscope *m*

telesthesia *Am* = **telaesthesia**

telesthetic *Am* = **telaesthetic**

telestich [tɪ'lestɪk] *n* acrostiche *m* à l'envers *(ce sont les dernières lettres de chaque vers et non les premières qui composent le mot-clé)*

teletex ['telɪteks] *n* Télétex® *m*

teletext ['telɪtekst] *n* télétexte *m*, vidéographie *f* diffusée

teletherapy [ˌtelɪ'θerəpɪ] *n Med* téléthérapie *f*

telethon ['telɪθɒn] *n* téléthon *m*

Teletype® ['telɪtaɪp] **1** *n* Télétype® *m*

2 *vt* transmettre par Télétype®

teletypewriter [ˌtelɪ'taɪpraɪtə(r)] *n Am* téléscripteur *m*, téléimprimeur *m*

teletyping ['telɪˌtaɪpɪŋ] *n* transmission *f* par Télétype®

teletypist ['telɪˌtaɪpɪst] *n* télétypiste *mf*

televangelism [ˌtelɪ'vændʒəlɪzəm] *n* = prêche évangéliste à la télévision

televangelist [ˌtelɪ'vændʒəlɪst] *n* = évangéliste qui prêche à la télévision

teleview ['telɪvjuː] *vi* regarder la télévision

televiewer ['telɪvjuːə(r)] *n* téléspectateur(trice) *m,f*

televiewing ['telɪˌvjuːɪŋ] *n (watching TV)* = action de regarder la télévision; *(programme)* programme *m* de télévision

televise ['telɪvaɪz] *vt* téléviser

television ['telɪˌvɪʒən] **1** *n* (**a**) *(system, broadcasts)* télévision *f*; **to watch television** regarder la télévision; **we don't watch much television** on ne regarde pas souvent la télévision; **to go on television** passer à la télévision; **to work in television** travailler à la télévision; **a film made for television** un téléfilm; **it makes/doesn't make good television** ça a/n'a pas un bon impact télévisuel

(**b**) *(set)* téléviseur *m*, (poste *m* de) télévision *f*; **I saw her on (the) television** je l'ai vue à la télévision; **to turn the television up/down/off/on** monter le son de/baisser le son de/éteindre/allumer la télévision; **is there anything good on television tonight?** qu'est-ce qu'il y a de bien à la télévision ce soir?; **colour/black-and-white television** télévision *f* (en) couleur/(en) noir et blanc

2 *comp (engineer, station, screen)* de télévision; *(picture)* télévisé; *(satellite)* de télédiffusion; **to make a television appearance** passer à la télévision

►► ***television advertisement*** publicité *f* télévisée; ***television advertising*** publicité *f* télévisée; ***television audience*** *(reached by advertising)* audience *f* télévisuelle; ***television broadcaster*** télédiffuseur *m*; ***television broadcasting network*** réseau *m* de télédistribution; ***television camera*** caméra *f* de télévision; **it's my first time in front of the television cameras** c'est la première fois que je suis devant les caméras; ***television campaign*** campagne *f* télévisuelle; ***television channel*** chaîne *f* de télévision; ***television commercial*** spot *m*; ***television drama*** drame *m* télévisé; ***television film*** téléfilm *m*, film *m* pour la télévision; ***television guide*** journal *m* de télévision; ***television interview*** interview *f* télévisée *ou* à la télévision; ***television journalist*** journaliste *mf* de télévision; *Br* ***television licence*** *(fee)* redevance *f*; *(document)* quittance *f* de télévision; ***television lounge*** salle *f* de télévision; ***television network*** réseau *m* télévisuel; ***television news*** journal *m* télévisé, JT *m*; ***television personality*** vedette *f* de la télévision; ***television programme*** émission *f* de télévision, programme *m* télévisé; ***television receiver*** récepteur *m* de télévision; ***television rights*** droits *mpl* de télédiffusion; ***television room*** salle *f* de télévision; ***television set*** téléviseur *m*, (poste *m* de) télévision *f*; ***television show*** spectacle *m* télévisé; ***television sponsoring*** parrainage-télévision *m*; ***television studio*** studio *m* de télévision; ***television tie-in*** (**a**) *(film)* = téléfilm tiré d'un livre ou d'un film; *(series)* = série télévisée tirée d'un livre ou d'un film (**b**) *(at conference, public event)* retransmission *f*; **there will be a television tie-in at the conference** la conférence sera retransmise à la télévision; ***television tube*** tube *m* cathodique; ***television viewer*** téléspectateur(trice) *m,f*; *Mktg* ***television viewing panel*** panel *m* de téléspectateurs

televisual [ˌtelɪ'vɪʒʊəl] *adj* télévisuel

teleworker ['telɪˌwɜːkə(r)] *n* télétravailleur(euse) *m,f*

teleworking ['telɪˌwɜːkɪŋ] *n* télétravail *m*

telewriter ['telɪˌraɪtə(r)] *n* appareil *m* de téléécriture

telewriting ['telɪˌraɪtɪŋ] *n* téléécriture *f*

telex ['teleks] **1** *n* télex *m*; **to send sth by telex** télexer qch

2 *vt* envoyer par télex, télexer

►► ***telex operator*** télexiste *mf*; ***telex transfer*** virement *m* par télex

telic ['telɪk] *adj* qui tend vers un but précis; *Gram* de but

TELL [tel]

dire (à)	► 1 (a) – (g); 2 (a)
expliquer à	► 1 (b)
raconter	► 1 (d)
annoncer	► 1 (d)
distinguer	► 1 (h)
voir	► 1 (i)
savoir	► 1 (i); 2 (b)
comprendre	► 1 (i)
se faire sentir	► 2 (c)

(pt & pp **told** [təʊld]) **1** *vt* (**a**) *(inform)* dire à; **to tell sb sth** dire qch à qn; *Fam* **to tell teacher** rapporter, cafarder; **I told him the answer/what I thought** je lui ai dit la réponse/ce que je pensais; **to tell sb about** *or Literary* **of sth** dire qch à qn, parler à qn de qch; **I told her about the new restaurant** je lui ai parlé du nouveau restaurant; **have you told them about the fire?** leur avez-vous parlé de l'incendie?; **she wrote to tell me of her father's death** elle m'a écrit pour m'annoncer la mort de son père; *Literary* **she told me of her woes** elle m'a parlé de ses malheurs; **they told me (that) they would be late** ils m'ont dit qu'ils seraient en retard; **I'm pleased to tell you you've won** j'ai le plaisir de vous informer *ou* annoncer que vous avez gagné; **are you telling me (that) you spent £50 on THAT?** tu ne vas pas me dire que tu as payé 50 livres pour ça?; **let me tell you how pleased I am** laissez-moi vous dire *ou* permettez-moi de vous dire à quel point je suis heureux; **it's not so easy, let me tell you!** ce n'est pas si facile, je t'assure *ou* je te le dis!; **we are told that there is little hope** on nous dit qu'il y a peu d'espoir; **it's just as I told you** c'est exactement ce que je t'avais dit; **I'm told he's coming tomorrow** j'ai entendu dire *ou* on m'a dit qu'il venait demain; **so I've been told** c'est ce qu'on m'a dit; **it doesn't tell us much** cela ne nous en dit pas très long, cela ne nous apprend pas grand-chose; **can you tell me the time?** pouvez-vous me dire l'heure (qu'il est)?; **can you tell me your name/age?** pouvez-vous me dire votre nom/âge?; **I know, Dennis told me** je sais, Dennis me l'a dit; **a little bird told me!** c'est mon petit doigt qui me l'a dit!

(**b**) *(explain to)* expliquer à, dire à; **this brochure tells me all I need to know** cette brochure m'explique tout ce que j'ai besoin de savoir; **I told him what to do in case of an emergency** je lui ai dit *ou* expliqué ce qu'il fallait faire en cas d'urgence; **did you tell them how to get here?** leur as-tu expliqué comment se rendre ici?; **can you tell me the way to the station/to Oxford?** pouvez-vous m'indiquer le chemin de la gare/la route d'Oxford?; **do you want me to tell you again?** voulez-vous que je vous le redise *ou* répète?; **who can tell me the best way to make omelettes?** qui peut me dire *ou* m'expliquer la meilleure façon de faire des omelettes?; **I can't tell you how pleased I am** je ne saurais vous dire combien je suis content; **if I've told you once, I've told you a thousand times!** je te l'ai dit cent fois!; **(I'll) tell you what, let's play cards** j'ai une idée, on n'a qu'à jouer aux cartes

(**c**) *(instruct, order)* **to tell sb to do sth** dire à qn de faire qch; **you can't tell me what to do!** tu n'as pas à me dire ce que je dois faire!; **do as you are told!** fais ce qu'on te dit; **tell her to wait outside** dites-lui d'attendre dehors; **I told them not to interrupt** je leur ai dit de ne pas interrompre; **I thought I told you not to run?** je croyais t'avoir interdit *ou* défendu de courir?; **I told you no!** je t'ai dit non!; **don't make me tell you twice** ne m'oblige pas à te le dire deux fois; **he didn't need to be told twice!** il ne s'est pas fait prier!, je n'ai pas eu besoin de lui dire deux fois!

(**d**) *(recount → story, joke)* raconter; *(→ news)* annoncer; *(→ secret)* dire, raconter; **to tell sb about sth** parler à qn de qch, parler de qch à qn, raconter qch à qn; **to tell sb about sb** parler à qn de qn, parler de qn à qn; **tell them about** *or* **of**

tel–tel

your life as an explorer racontez-leur votre vie d'explorateur; **tell me what you know about it** dites-moi ce que vous en savez; **I'll tell you what happened** je vais vous raconter ce qui est arrivé; **could you tell me a little about yourself?** pourriez-vous me parler un peu de vous-même?; **what does this tell us about his character?** qu'est-ce que cela nous apprend sur son caractère?; **I told myself it didn't matter** je me suis dit que cela n'avait pas d'importance; **I could tell you a thing or two about his role in it** je pourrais vous en dire long sur son rôle dans tout cela; **don't tell me you got lost!** ne me dites pas que vous vous êtes perdu!; **don't tell me, let me guess!** ne me dites rien, laissez-moi deviner!; *Fam* **tell it like it is!** n'ayez pas peur de dire la vérité!; *Fam* **tell that to the marines!, tell me another!** à d'autres!, mon œil!; **to hear tell that...** entendre dire que...+ *indicative*

(**e**) *(recite)* **to tell one's beads** dire *ou* égrener son chapelet

(**f**) *(utter → truth, lie)* dire, raconter; **to tell sb the truth** dire la vérité à qn; **to tell lies** mentir, dire des mensonges; *Fig* **I tell a lie!** je me trompe!

(**g**) *(assure)* dire à, assurer; **didn't I tell you?, I told you so!, what did I tell you!** je vous l'avais bien dit!; **let me tell you!** *(believe me)* je vous assure!, croyez-moi!; *(as threat)* tenez-vous-le pour dit!; **I can tell you!** c'est moi qui vous le dis!; *Fam* **you're telling me!, tell me about it!** à qui le dis-tu!

(**h**) *(distinguish)* distinguer; **to tell right from wrong** distinguer le bien du mal; **you can hardly tell the difference between them** on voit *ou* distingue à peine la différence entre eux; **how can you tell one from another?** comment les distinguez-vous l'un de l'autre?; **you can tell him by his voice** on le reconnaît à sa voix; **she can't tell the time** elle ne sait pas lire l'heure

(**i**) *(see)* voir; *(know)* savoir; *(understand)* comprendre; **you could tell he was disappointed** on voyait bien qu'il était déçu; **how can you tell when it's ready?** à quoi voit-on *ou* comment peut-on savoir que c'est prêt?; **no one could tell whether the good weather would last** personne ne pouvait dire si le beau temps allait durer; **I can tell it from the look in your eyes** ça se lit dans tes yeux; **there's no telling what he might do next/how he'll react** (il est) impossible de dire ce qu'il est susceptible de faire ensuite/comment il réagira

2 *vi* (**a**) *(reveal)* **that would be telling!** ce serait trahir un secret!; **I won't tell** je ne dirai rien à personne; **time will tell** qui vivra verra, le temps nous le dira; **more than words can tell** plus que les mots ne peuvent dire

(**b**) *(know)* savoir; **how can I tell?** comment le saurais-je?; **who can tell?** qui peut savoir?, qui sait?; **you never can tell** on ne sait jamais; **it's difficult** *or* **hard to tell** c'est difficile à dire; **it's too early to tell** il est trop tôt pour se prononcer

(**c**) *(have effect)* se faire sentir, avoir de l'influence; *Br Prov* **breeding tells** bon sang ne saurait mentir; **her age is beginning to tell** elle commence à accuser son âge; **the strain is beginning to tell** la tension commence à se faire sentir; **her aristocratic roots told against her** ses origines aristocratiques lui nuisaient

(**d**) *Literary (story, book)* **to tell of sth** raconter qch; **the first volume tells of the postwar period** le premier volume raconte la période d'après-guerre; **I've heard tell of phantom ships** j'ai entendu parler de navires fantômes

(**e**) *Literary (bear witness)* **to tell of** témoigner de; **the scars told of his reckless life** ses cicatrices témoignaient de sa vie mouvementée; **the stones told of battles of times past** les pierres portaient les traces de batailles des temps passés

▸**tell apart** *vt sep* distinguer (entre); **I couldn't tell the twins apart** je ne pouvais pas distinguer les jumeaux l'un de l'autre

▸**tell off** *vt sep* (**a**) *(scold)* réprimander, gronder; **to tell sb off for doing sth** gronder *ou* réprimander qn pour avoir fait qch

(**b**) *(select)* affecter, désigner

▸**tell on** *vt insep* (**a**) *(denounce)* dénoncer; **don't tell on me** ne me dénonce pas

(**b**) *(have effect on)* se faire sentir sur, produire un effet sur; **her age is telling on her** elle accuse son âge; **the strain soon began to tell on her health** la tension ne tarda pas à avoir un effet néfaste sur sa santé

'Tell me the Truth about Love' *Auden* 'Dis-moi la vérité sur l'amour'

'Go tell it on the Mountain' *Baldwin* 'Va le clamer sur la montagne'

teller ['telə(r)] *n* (**a**) *(in bank)* **(bank) teller** caissier(ère) *m,f*, guichetier(ère) *m,f* (**b**) *Pol (of votes)* scrutateur(trice) *m,f* (**c**) *(of story)* **(story) teller** conteur(euse) *m,f*, narrateur(trice) *m,f*

telling ['telɪŋ] **1** *adj* (**a**) *(effective → style)* efficace; *(→ account)* saisissant; *(→ remark, argument)* qui porte; **it was a telling blow** le coup fut bien asséné, le coup porta

(**b**) *(revealing → smile, figures, evidence)* révélateur, éloquent; **a telling look** un regard qui en dit long; **her remarks were very telling** ses remarques étaient très révélatrices

2 *n* récit *m*, narration *f*; **the story is long in the telling** l'histoire est longue à raconter

tellingly ['telɪŋlɪ] *adv* (**a**) *(effectively)* efficacement (**b**) *(revealingly)* **tellingly, he didn't invite his best friend** il n'a pas invité son meilleur ami, ce qui en dit long *ou* ce qui est révélateur

telling-off *(pl* **tellings-off**) *n* réprimande *f*; **to get a good telling-off** se faire gronder; **to give sb a telling-off** réprimander qn

telltale ['telteɪl] **1** *n* (**a**) *Br (person)* rapporteur(euse), cafteur(euse) *m,f* (**b**) *Tech* indicateur *m*

2 *adj (marks)* révélateur; *(look, blush, nod)* éloquent; **a telltale sign** un signe révélateur; **I was looking for any telltale signs of human settlement** je cherchais des traces d'habitation humaine

▸▸ ***telltale lamp*** lampe *f* témoin

tellurium [te'lʊərɪəm] *n Chem* tellure *m*

telly ['telɪ] *(pl* **tellies**) *n Br Fam* télé *f*; **on the telly** à la télé

▸▸ ***telly addict*** drogué(e) *m,f* de la télé

Telnet ['telnet] *n Comput* Telnet *m*

telomere ['teləmɪə(r)] *n Biol* télomère *m*

Telstar ['telstɑː(r)] *n* Telstar *m*

Telugu ['teləguː] *n Ling* télougou *m*

temazepam [tə'mæzəpæm] *n Pharm* témazépam *m*

temerity [tɪ'merətɪ] *n* témérité *f*, audace *f*; **he had the temerity to suggest I had lied** il a eu l'audace *ou* le front d'insinuer que j'avais menti, il a osé insinuer que j'avais menti

temp [temp] **1** *n (abbr* **temporary employee**) intérimaire *mf*

2 *adj* **to do temp work** faire de l'intérim

3 *vi* faire de l'intérim

temp. *(written abbr* **temperature**) temp

temper ['tempə(r)] **1** *n* (**a**) *(character)* caractère *m*, tempérament *m*; **to have an even temper** être d'un tempérament calme *ou* d'humeur égale; **to have a quick** *or* **hot temper** se mettre facilement en colère; **he's got a foul** *or* **an awful temper** il a mauvais caractère

(**b**) *(patience)* patience *f*; *(calm)* calme *m*, sang-froid *m inv*; **do try and keep your temper** essayez donc de garder votre calme *ou* sang-froid, essayez donc de vous maîtriser; **to lose one's temper** perdre patience, se mettre en colère; **to lose one's temper with sb** s'emporter contre qn; **don't try my temper** ne m'énerve pas

(**c**) *(mood)* humeur *f*; *(bad mood)* (crise *f* de) colère *f*, mauvaise humeur *f*; **to be in a (bad) temper** être de mauvaise humeur; **to fly into a temper** piquer une colère; **he's in a dreadful temper** il est d'une humeur massacrante

(**d**) *Metal* trempe *f*

2 *vt* (**a**) *(moderate → passions)* modérer, tempérer; *(→ pain, suffering)* atténuer; **justice tempered with mercy** la justice tempérée de pitié

(**b**) *Metal* tremper

(**c**) *(piano)* accorder par tempérament

3 *exclam Fam* **temper(, temper)!** on se calme!, du calme!

▸▸ ***temper tantrum*** crise *f* de colère; **to have** *or* **to throw a temper tantrum** piquer une colère

tempera ['tempərə] *n (paint)* tempera *f*, détrempe *f*

▸▸ ***tempera painting*** détrempe *f*

temperament ['tempərəmənt] *n (character)* tempérament *m*, nature *f*; *(moodiness)* humeur *f* changeante *ou* lunatique

temperamental [,tempərə'mentəl] *adj* (**a**) *(moody → person)* capricieux, lunatique

(**b**) *(unpredictable → animal, machine)* capricieux; **his knee has been a bit temperamental since his accident** son genou lui joue des tours depuis son accident

(**c**) *(relating to character)* du tempérament, de la personnalité; **he has a temperamental aversion to conflict/hard work** fondamentalement, il déteste les conflits/le travail

temperamentally [,tempərə'mentəlɪ] *adv* de par son caractère; **temperamentally different** d'un tempérament différent; **they were temperamentally unsuited** *(couple)* leurs caractères étaient incompatibles; **she's temperamentally unsuited to this sort of work** elle n'est pas de nature à *ou* elle n'a pas le caractère pour faire ce genre de travail

temperance ['tempərəns] **1** *n* (**a**) *(moderation)* modération *f*, sobriété *f* (**b**) *(abstinence from alcohol)* tempérance *f*

2 *comp (movement)* antialcoolique

▸▸ ***temperance hotel*** = hôtel où l'on ne sert pas de boissons alcoolisées; ***temperance society*** société *f* de tempérance, ligue *f* antialcoolique

temperate ['tempərət] *adj* (**a**) *(climate)* tempéré (**b**) *(moderate → person)* modéré, mesuré; *(→ character, appetite)* modéré; *(→ reaction, criticism)* modéré, sobre

▸▸ ***Temperate Zone*** zone *f* tempérée

temperately ['tempərətlɪ] *adv* modérément, avec modération

temperateness ['tempərətnɪs] *n* (**a**) *(moderation)* modération *f*, sobriété *f* (**b**) *(of climate)* douceur *f*

temperature ['temprətʃə(r)] **1** *n* (**a**) *Med* température *f*; **to have** *or* **to run a temperature** avoir de la température *ou* de la fièvre; **she has a temperature of 39°C** elle a 39° de fièvre; **to take sb's temperature** prendre la température de qn; *Fig* **to take the temperature of a situation** prendre le pouls d'une situation; **her contribution certainly raised the temperature of the debate** son intervention a sans aucun doute fait monter le ton du débat

(**b**) *Met & Phys* température *f*; **a drop in temperature** une baisse de température; **the temperature fell overnight** la température a baissé du jour au lendemain; **temperatures will be in the low twenties** il fera un peu plus de vingt degrés

2 *comp (change)* de température; *(control)* de la température; *(gradient)* thermique

▸▸ ***temperature chart*** feuille *f* de température; ***temperature gauge*** indicateur *m* de température

tempered ['tempəd] *adj* (**a**) *(steel)* trempé (**b**) *Mus (scale)* tempéré

-tempered ['tempəd] *suff* **good/bad-tempered** de bonne/mauvaise humeur; **an even-tempered person** une personne d'humeur égale

temperer ['tempərə(r)] *n Metal* trempeur *m* (d'acier)

tempering ['tempərɪŋ] *n* (**a**) *(moderation → of passions)* modération *f*; *(→ of pain, suffering)* atténuation *f* (**b**) *Metal* trempe *f*; **water tempering** trempe *f* à l'eau; **oil tempering** trempe *f* à l'huile

▸▸ ***tempering furnace*** four *m* à tremper; ***tempering oil*** huile *f* de trempe; ***tempering water*** eau *f* de trempe

tempest ['tempɪst] *n Literary* tempête *f*, orage *m*; *Am* **it was a tempest in a teapot** ce fut une tempête dans un verre d'eau

'The Tempest' *Shakespeare* 'La Tempête'

tempestuous [tem'pestjʊəs] *adj* (**a**) *(weather)* de tempête; *(sea)* tumultueux, *Literary* tempétueux (**b**) *(person)* impétueux, fougueux;

(meeting) agité; *(relationship)* tumultueux; *(argument)* violent; **a tempestuous love affair** une liaison orageuse *ou* tumultueuse

tempestuously [tem'pestjʊəslɪ] *adv* (**a**) *Literary* **the winds blew tempestuously outside** un vent tempétueux soufflait au dehors (**b**) *(violently → to argue etc)* violemment

tempestuousness [tem'pestjʊəsnɪs] *n* (**a**) *(of weather, sea)* violence *f* (**b**) *(of person)* impétuosité *f*, fougue *f*; *(of meeting)* caractère *m* orageux; *(of relationship)* violence *f*; *(of crowd)* turbulence *f*, agitation *f*

tempi ['tempi:] *pl of* **tempo**

temping ['tempɪŋ] *n* intérim *m*; **to do some temping** faire de l'intérim

►► ***temping agency*** société *f* d'intérim

Templar ['templə(r)] *n* (**a**) *Hist (in crusades)* **Knight Templar** chevalier *m* du Temple, templier *m* (**b**) *Br Law* avocat *m* du Temple

template ['templɪt] *n* (**a**) *Tech* gabarit *m*, calibre *m*, patron *m* (**b**) *(beam)* traverse *f* (**c**) *Comput (for keyboard)* réglette *f*; *(for program)* modèle *m*; *(for DTP document)* gabarit *m*

temple ['tempəl] *n* (**a**) *Rel* temple *m* (**b**) *Br Law* **the Temple** = édifice historique de la City de Londres abritant deux "Inns of Court" (**c**) *Anat* tempe *f*

►► ***Temple Bar*** = porte ouest de la City de Londres où le maire vient accueillir le souverain en visite

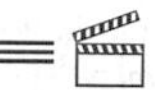

'Indiana Jones and the Temple of Doom' *Spielberg* 'Indiana Jones et le temple maudit'

templet = **template**

tempo ['tempəʊ] (*pl* **tempos** *or* **tempi** [-pi:]) *n* tempo *m*

temporal[1] ['tempərəl] *adj* (**a**) *(gen) & Gram* temporel (**b**) *(secular)* temporel, séculier

temporal[2] *adj Anat* temporal

►► ***temporal lobe*** lobe *m* temporal

temporalities [,tempə'rælɪtɪz] *npl Rel (possessions)* possessions *f* ecclésiastiques; *(revenues)* revenus *m* ecclésiastiques

temporally ['tempərəlɪ] *adv* temporellement

temporarily [*Br* 'tempərərəlɪ, *Am* ,tempə'rerəlɪ] *adv (provisionally)* provisoirement; *(for a time)* temporairement; **we were temporarily delayed** nous avons été un peu retardés

temporariness [*Br* 'tempərərɪnɪs, *Am* 'tempərerɪnɪs] *n (of accommodation, solution, powers)* caractère *m* temporaire *ou* provisoire; *(of improvement)* caractère *m* passager *ou* momentané; *(of relief)* caractère *m* passager

temporary [*Br* 'tempərərɪ, *Am* 'tempərerɪ] (*pl* **temporaries**) **1** *adj (accommodation, solution, powers)* temporaire, provisoire; *(employee, employment)* temporaire, intérimaire; *(improvement)* passager, momentané; *(relief)* passager; **on a temporary basis** à titre temporaire; **he suffered temporary hearing loss** il a eu une perte momentanée de l'ouïe; **this will at least give you temporary relief** cela vous soulagera pendant un moment; **a temporary appointment** une nomination temporaire *ou* provisoire; **a temporary job** un emploi temporaire

2 *n* intérimaire *mf*

►► ***temporary contract*** *(for employment)* contrat *m* de mission d'intérim, contrat *m* temporaire; *Comput* ***temporary file*** fichier *m* temporaire; ***temporary manager*** directeur(trice) *m,f* intérimaire; ***temporary replacement*** suppléance *f*; *Am Law* ***temporary restraining order*** injonction *f* du tribunal; ***temporary surface*** *(of road)* revêtement *m* provisoire; ***temporary tattoo*** tatouage *m* éphémère; ***temporary teacher*** professeur *m* suppléant

temporization [,tempəraɪ'zeɪʃən] *n Formal* temporisation *f*; **he advised temporization** il nous a conseillé de temporiser *ou* de chercher à gagner du temps

temporize, -ise ['tempəraɪz] *vi Formal* temporiser, chercher à gagner du temps

temporizer ['tempə,raɪzə(r)] *n Formal* temporisateur(trice) *m,f*

temporizing ['tempə,raɪzɪŋ] = **temporization**

tempt [tempt] *vt (entice)* tenter, donner envie à; *(seduce)* tenter, séduire; *(attract)* attirer, tenter; **to tempt sb to do sth** *or* **into doing sth** donner à qn l'envie de faire qch; **did you hit him? – no, but I was sorely tempted** tu l'as frappé? – non, mais ce n'est pas l'envie qui m'en manquait; **I'm tempted to accept their offer** je suis tenté d'accepter leur proposition; **and Satan tempted Christ** et Satan tenta le Christ; **a rival company tried to tempt him away** une entreprise rivale a essayé de le débaucher en lui faisant une offre alléchante; **I let myself be tempted into buying the car** je n'ai pas pu résister à la tentation d'acheter la voiture; **the mild weather tempted us into the garden** le temps doux nous a incités à aller au jardin; *Hum* **don't tempt me!** n'essayez pas de me tenter!, ne me tentez pas!; **can I tempt you to another sandwich?** je peux vous proposer encore un sandwich?, vous voulez encore un sandwich?; **to tempt fate** *or* **Providence** tenter le sort *ou* le diable

temptation [temp'teɪʃən] *n* tentation *f*; **to put temptation in sb's way** exposer qn à la tentation; **it's a great temptation** c'est très tentant; **to give in to temptation** céder *ou* succomber à la tentation; **to resist temptation** résister à la tentation; *Bible* **lead us not into temptation** ne nous soumets pas à la tentation

tempter ['temptə(r)] *n* tentateur(trice) *m,f*

tempting ['temptɪŋ] *adj (offer)* tentant, attrayant; *(smell, meal)* appétissant

temptingly ['temptɪŋlɪ] *adv* d'une manière tentante; **it looks temptingly easy** c'est tentant parce que cela a l'air facile; **the grapes glistened temptingly in their bowl** les grappes dans le plat étaient brillantes et appétissantes; **the cool water beckoned temptingly** l'eau fraîche donnait envie de se baigner

temptress ['temptrɪs] *n Literary or Hum* tentatrice *f*

tempura ['tempʊrə] *n Culin* tempura *f (beignet japonais)*

ten [ten] **1** *n (number, numeral)* dix *m inv*; **tens of thousands of refugees** des dizaines *fpl* de milliers de réfugiés; **ten to one** *(in ratio, bets)* dix contre un; **it's ten to one we won't sell anything** je te parie que nous ne vendrons rien; *Fig* **they're ten a penny** il y en a à la pelle

2 *pron* dix; **about ten** une dizaine

3 *adj* dix; **about ten people** une dizaine de personnes

4 tens *npl Math* dizaines *fpl*; *see also* **five**

►► *Bible* ***the Ten Commandments*** les dix commandements *mpl*; *Math* ***tens column*** colonne *f* des dizaines

'Ten Little Indians' *Christie* 'Dix petits nègres'

tenable ['tenəbəl] *adj* (**a**) *(argument, position)* défendable, soutenable (**b**) *(post)* que l'on occupe, auquel on est nommé; **the appointment is tenable for a five-year period** on est nommé à ce poste pour cinq ans

tenacious [tɪ'neɪʃəs] *adj* (**a**) *(persistent → person)* tenace, résolu; *(→ prejudice)* tenace; *(→ opposition)* tenace, acharné; *(→ tradition)* tenace (**b**) *(firm → grip)* ferme, solide (**c**) *(tough → stain)* tenace (**d**) *(long-lasting → memory)* excellent

tenaciously [tɪ'neɪʃəslɪ] *adv* avec ténacité, obstinément

tenaciousness [tɪ'neɪʃəsnɪs], **tenacity** [tɪ'næsətɪ] *n* (**a**) *(of person)* ténacité *f*; *(of opposition)* acharnement *m*; *(of tradition)* ténacité *f* (**b**) *(of stain)* ténacité *f*

tenaculum [tɪ'nækjʊləm] *n Med* crochet *m*

tenancy ['tenənsɪ] (*pl* **tenancies**) **1** *n* (**a**) *(of house, land)* location *f*; **to take up the tenancy on a house** prendre une maison en location

(**b**) *(period)* **(period of) tenancy** (période *f* de) location *f*; **during my tenancy of the house** quand j'étais locataire de la maison; *Fig* **during his tenancy of Government House** pendant qu'il était gouverneur

(**c**) *(property)* **a council tenancy** un logement appartenant à la municipalité, ≃ une HLM

2 *comp* de location

►► ***tenancy agreement*** contrat *m* de location

tenant ['tenənt] **1** *n* locataire *mf*

2 *comp (rights)* du locataire

3 *vt* habiter comme locataire, louer; **only half the farms were still tenanted** il n'y avait de locataires que dans la moitié des fermes

►► ***tenant farmer*** métayer(ère) *m,f*; ***tenant farming*** métayage *m*

tenantry ['tenəntrɪ] *n Agr* ensemble *m* des métayers *ou* locataires

ten-cent-store *n Am* bazar *m*

tench [tenʃ] (*pl* **inv**) *n Ich* tanche *f*

tend [tend] **1** *vi* (**a**) *(be inclined)* **to tend to** avoir tendance à, tendre à; **he does tend to take himself seriously** il a vraiment tendance à se prendre au sérieux; **we tend to think of man as being separate from nature** nous avons tendance à considérer que l'homme ne fait pas partie de la nature; **some people like that kind of film, but I tend not to** il y a des gens qui aiment ce genre de film, moi (je n'aime) pas trop; **I tend to think (that) politics is a waste of time** j'ai tendance à penser que la politique est une perte de temps; **that does tend to be the case** c'est souvent le cas

(**b**) *(colour)* **red tending to orange** rouge tirant sur l'orange

(**c**) *(go, move)* tendre; **his writings tend to** *or* **towards exoticism** ses écrits tendent vers l'exotisme; **in later life, she tended more towards a Marxist view of things** vers la fin de sa vie, elle inclina *ou* évolua vers des idées marxistes

(**d**) *(look after)* **she tended to his every wish** elle lui a passé tous ses caprices, elle a fait ses quatre volontés; **to tend to one's business/one's guests** s'occuper de ses affaires/ses invités; **to tend to sb's wounds** panser *ou* soigner les blessures de qn

2 *vt* (**a**) *(take care of → sheep)* garder; *(→ the sick, wounded)* soigner; *(→ garden)* entretenir, s'occuper de; **to tend sb's wounds** panser *ou* soigner les blessures de qn

(**b**) *Am (customer)* servir; **to tend the bar** servir au bar

tendency ['tendənsɪ] (*pl* **tendencies**) *n* (**a**) *(inclination)* tendance *f*; **he has a tendency to forget things** il a tendance à tout oublier; **she has a natural tendency to** *or* **towards laziness** elle est d'un naturel paresseux; **to have suicidal tendencies** avoir des tendances suicidaires

(**b**) *(trend)* tendance *f*; **a growing tendency towards conservatism** une tendance de plus en plus marquée vers le conservatisme; **upward/downward tendency** *(in prices)* tendance *f* à la hausse/à la baisse

(**c**) *Pol* tendance *f*, groupe *m*

tendentious [ten'denʃəs] *adj* tendancieux

tendentiously [ten'denʃəslɪ] *adv* tendancieusement

tendentiousness [ten'denʃəsnɪs] *n* caractère *m* tendancieux

tender ['tendə(r)] **1** *adj* (**a**) *(affectionate → person)* tendre, affectueux, doux (douce); *(→ heart, smile, words, look)* tendre; *(→ memories)* doux (douce); **they bade each other a tender farewell** ils se sont fait de tendres adieux; *Ironic* **I leave him to your tender mercies** je l'abandonne à vos soins

(**b**) *(sensitive → skin)* délicat, fragile; *(sore)* [illegible] **my knee is still tender** mon genou me fait encore mal; **that's rather a tender subject** c'est un sujet assez délicat; *Fig* **to touch sb on a tender spot** toucher le point sensible de qn

(**c**) *(meat, vegetables)* tendre

(**d**) *Literary (innocent → age, youth)* tendre; **she gave her first concert at the tender age of six** elle a donné son premier concert alors qu'elle n'avait que six ans; **to be of tender years** être d'âge tendre

2 *vt* (**a**) *(resignation)* donner; *(apologies)* présenter; *(thanks)* offrir; *(bid, offer)* faire

(**b**) *(money, fare)* tendre; **to tender sth to sb** tendre qch à qn

3 *vi* faire une soumission; **to tender for a contract** faire une soumission pour une adjudication, soumissionner une adjudication

4 *n* (**a**) *(statement of charges)* soumission *f*; **to make** *or* **put in a tender for sth** soumissionner *ou* faire une soumission pour qch; **to invite tenders for a job, to put a job out to tender** mettre un travail en adjudication; **by tender** par

tem–ten

voie d'adjudication; **a call for tender** un appel d'offres
(**b**) *Rail* tender *m*
(**c**) *Naut (shuttle)* navette *f*; *(supply boat)* ravitailleur *m*
(**d**) *(supply vehicle)* véhicule *m* ravitailleur; *Br* **(fire) tender** voiture *f* de pompier

'Tender is the Night' *Fitzgerald* 'Tendre est la nuit'

tenderer ['tendərə(r)] *n Com* soumissionnaire *mf*; **the successful tenderer** l'adjudicataire *mf*
tenderfoot ['tendəfʊt] (*pl* **tenderfoots** *or* **tenderfeet** [-fi:t]) *n* (**a**) *(beginner)* novice *mf*, nouveau(elle) *m,f* (**b**) *Am Fam (newcomer)* nouveau(elle) venu(e)[□] *m,f*
tenderhearted [,tendə'hɑ:tɪd] *adj* au cœur tendre, compatissant; **she's too tenderhearted** elle est trop bonne
tenderheartedly [,tendə'hɑ:tɪdlɪ] *adv* avec compassion
tenderheartedness [,tendə'hɑ:tɪdnɪs] *n* compassion *f*
tenderize, -ise ['tendəraɪz] *vt* attendrir
tenderizer ['tendəraɪzə(r)] *n* attendrisseur *m*
tenderloin ['tendəlɔɪn] *n* (**a**) *(meat)* filet *m* (**b**) *Am Fam Crime slang (district)* quartier *m* chaud *(connu pour sa corruption)*
tenderly ['tendəlɪ] *adv* tendrement, avec tendresse
tenderness ['tendənɪs] *n* (**a**) *(of person, feelings)* tendresse *f*, affection *f*; **she feels a certain tenderness for the old man** elle éprouve une certaine tendresse pour ce vieux monsieur (**b**) *(of skin)* sensibilité *f*; *(of plant)* fragilité *f*; *(soreness)* sensibilité *f* (**c**) *(of meat, vegetables)* tendreté *f*
tendinitis [,tendɪ'naɪtəs] *n Med* tendinite *f*
tendinous ['tendɪnəs] *adj* tendineux
tendon ['tendən] *n* tendon *m*
tendril ['tendrəl] *n* (**a**) *Bot* vrille *f*, cirre *m* (**b**) *(of hair)* boucle *f*
tenebrism ['tenə,brɪzəm] *n Art* ténébrisme *m*
tenebrous ['tenɪbrəs] *adj Arch* ténébreux
tenement ['tenəmənt] *n* (**a**) *Am & Scot (block of flats)* immeuble *m* (ancien) (**b**) *(slum)* taudis *m* (**c**) *(dwelling)* logement *m*
▸▸ *Am & Scot* ***tenement building*** immeuble *m* (ancien); ***tenement house*** maison *f* divisée en appartements
Tenerife [,tenə'ri:f] *n* Tenerife, Ténériffe; **in Tenerife** à Tenerife, à Ténériffe
tenesmus [tɪ'nesməs] *n Med* ténesme *m*
tenet ['tenɪt] *n (principle)* principe *m*, dogme *m*; *(belief)* croyance *f*
tenfold ['tenfəʊld] **1** *adv* dix fois autant *ou* plus, au décuple; **to increase tenfold** décupler
2 *adj* **a tenfold increase in applications** dix fois plus de demandes
ten-gallon hat *n* chapeau *m* de cowboy
tenner ['tenə(r)] *n Fam Br (ten-pound note)* billet *m* de dix livres[□]; *Am (ten-dollar note)* billet *m* de dix dollars[□]; *Br (sum)* dix livres[□] *fpl*
Tennessee [,tenə'si:] *n* le Tennessee; **in Tennessee** dans le *ou* au Tennessee
tennis ['tenɪs] *n* tennis *m*; **to play tennis** jouer au tennis; **to have** *or* **to play a game of tennis** faire une partie de tennis; **anyone for tennis?** qui veut jouer au tennis?
▸▸ ***tennis ball*** balle *f* de tennis; ***tennis club*** club *m* de tennis; ***tennis court*** court *m* de tennis; ***tennis elbow*** *(UNCOUNT)* tennis-elbow *m*, synovite *f* du coude; ***tennis player*** joueur(euse) *m,f* de tennis; ***tennis racquet, tennis racket*** raquette *f* de tennis; ***tennis shoe*** chaussure *f* de tennis, tennis *m ou f*; ***tennis whites*** tenue *f* de tennis
tenon ['tenən] *Carp* **1** *n* tenon *m*
2 *vt* tenonner
tenor ['tenə(r)] **1** *n* (**a**) *(general sense → of conversation)* sens *m* général, teneur *f*; *(→ of letter)* contenu *m*, teneur *f*
(**b**) *(general flow → of events)* cours *m*, marche *f*; **the accident interrupted the even tenor of their life** l'accident est venu interrompre le cours paisible de leur vie
(**c**) *Mus* ténor *m*
(**d**) *Fin (of bill)* (terme *m* d')échéance *f*
2 *comp Mus (part, voice)* de ténor; *(aria)* pour (voix de) ténor
3 *adv* **to sing tenor** avoir une voix de *ou* être ténor
▸▸ ***tenor clef*** clé *f* d'ut quatrième ligne; ***tenor recorder*** flûte *f* à bec; ***tenor saxophone*** saxophone *m* ténor
tenorite ['tenəraɪt] *n Miner* ténorite *f*
tenosynovitis ['tenəʊ,saɪnəʊ'vaɪtɪs] *n Med* ténosynovite *f*
tenpence ['tenpəns] *n Br (amount)* dix pence *mpl*; *(coin)* pièce *f* de dix pence
tenpenny ['tenpənɪ] *adj Br* de *ou* à dix pence
▸▸ ***tenpenny stamp*** timbre *m* de dix pence
tenpin bowling ['tenpɪn-] *n Br* bowling *m*; **to go tenpin bowling** aller faire du bowling, aller au bowling
tenpins ['tenpɪnz] *n Am* bowling *m*
tenrec ['tenrek] *n Zool* tenrec *m*, tanrec *m*
TENS machine [tens-] *n Med* appareil *m* TENS
tense [tens] **1** *adj* (**a**) *(person, situation)* tendu; *(smile)* crispé; **the audience was tense with excitement** le public contenait avec peine son enthousiasme; **her voice was tense with emotion** elle avait la voix étranglée par l'émotion; **we spent several tense hours waiting for news** nous avons passé plusieurs heures à attendre des nouvelles dans un état de tension nerveuse; **the atmosphere was very tense** l'atmosphère était très tendue; **things are getting tense in the war zone** la situation devient tendue dans la zone de combat
(**b**) *(muscles, rope, spring)* tendu; **to become tense** se tendre
(**c**) *Ling (vowel)* tendu
2 *vt (muscle)* tendre, bander; **to tense oneself** se raidir
3 *n Gram* temps *m*
▸**tense up 1** *vi (muscle)* se tendre, se raidir; *(person)* se crisper, devenir tendu; **don't tense up** détends-toi, décontracte-toi
2 *vt sep (person)* rendre nerveux; **she's all tensed up** elle est vraiment tendue
tensely ['tenslɪ] *adv (move, react)* de façon tendue; *(speak)* d'une voix tendue; **they waited tensely for the doctor to arrive** ils ont attendu le médecin dans un état de grande tension nerveuse; **we watched tensely as he approached the door** le regard tendu, nous le regardâmes s'approcher de la porte
tenseness ['tensnɪs] *n* tension *f*
tensile ['tensaɪl] *adj Tech* extensible, élastique
▸▸ ***tensile load*** charge *f* de traction; ***tensile strength*** résistance *f* à la tension, limite *f* élastique à la tension; ***tensile stress*** force *f* de tension
tensileness ['tensaɪlnɪs], **tensility** [ten'sɪlɪtɪ] *n Tech* extensibilité *f*
tension ['tenʃən] **1** *n* (**a**) *(of person, situation, voice)* tension *f*; **tension between the two countries is mounting** la tension monte entre les deux pays
(**b**) *(of muscle, rope, spring)* tension *f*; *Phys (of fluid)* tension *f*, force *f* élastique
(**c**) *Elec* tension *f*, voltage *m*
(**d**) *Tech* tension *f*, (force *f* de) traction *f*; **in tension** en traction
2 *vt* tendre
▸▸ ***tension headache*** mal *m* de tête dû à la tension nerveuse
tensional ['tenʃənəl] *adj (force)* de tension
tensioning ['tenʃənɪŋ] *n* tension *f*
tensionless ['tenʃənlɪs] *adj* sans tension
tensive ['tensɪv] *adj Med* tensif
▸▸ ***tensive pain*** douleur *f* tensive
tensor ['tensə(r)] *n Anat & Math* tenseur *m*
tensorial [ten'sɔ:rɪəl] *adj Math* tensoriel
▸▸ ***tensorial analysis*** analyse *f* tensorielle
ten-spot *n Am Fam* billet *m* de dix dollars[□]; **it'll cost you a ten-spot** ça te coûtera dix dollars
tent [tent] **1** *n (for camping)* tente *f*; **to put up** *or* **to pitch a tent** monter une tente
2 *vi* camper
▸▸ ***tent dress*** robe *f* très ample, robe *f* sac; ***tent peg*** piquet *m* de tente; ***tent pole*** mât *m* de tente
tentacle ['tentəkəl] *n* tentacule *m*
tentacled ['tentəkəld] *adj Zool* tentaculé
tentacular [ten'tækjʊlə(r)] *adj Zool* tentaculaire
tentaculate [ten'tækjʊleɪt] *adj Zool* tentaculé
tentage ['tentɪdʒ] *n (equipment)* matériel *m* de tente; *(cloth)* toile *f* de tente
tentative ['tentətɪv] *adj* (**a**) *(provisional)* provisoire; *(preliminary)* préliminaire; *(experimental)* expérimental; **a tentative offer** une offre provisoire; **our plans are only tentative** nos projets ne sont pas définitifs (**b**) *(uncertain → smile)* timide; *(→ person)* indécis, hésitant; *(→ steps)* hésitant
tentatively ['tentətɪvlɪ] *adv* (**a**) *(suggest)* provisoirement; *(act)* à titre d'essai (**b**) *(smile)* timidement; *(walk)* d'un pas hésitant
tenterhooks ['tentəhʊks] *npl Tex* clous *mpl* à crochet; *Fig* **to be on tenterhooks** être sur des charbons ardents; **to keep sb on tenterhooks** tenir qn en haleine
tenth [tenθ] **1** *n* (**a**) *(fraction)* dixième *m* (**b**) *(in series)* dixième *mf* (**c**) *(of month)* dix *m inv* (**d**) *Mus* dixième *f*
2 *adj* dixième
3 *adv* dixièmement; *(in contest)* en dixième position, à la dixième place; *see also* **fifth**
▸▸ *Am Sch* ***tenth grade*** = classe de lycée pour les 14–15 ans, *Can* 10ème année
tenthly ['tenθlɪ] *adv* dixièmement, en dixième lieu
tenting ['tentɪŋ] *n* toile *f* de tente
tenuity [te'nju:ətɪ] = **tenuousness**
tenuous ['tenjʊəs] *adj* (**a**) *(fine → distinction)* subtil, ténu; *(→ thread)* ténu; **a tenuous voice** une voix grêle *ou* fluette (**b**) *(flimsy → link, relationship)* précaire, fragile; *(→ evidence)* mince, faible; *(→ argument)* faible (**c**) *(precarious → existence)* précaire (**d**) *Phys (gas)* raréfié
tenuously ['tenjʊəslɪ] *adv* de manière ténue *ou* précaire
tenuousness ['tenjʊəsnɪs] *n* (**a**) *(of distinction)* subtilité *f*; *(of thread)* ténuité *f*; *(of voice)* faiblesse *f* (**b**) *(of link, relationship)* fragilité *f*, précarité *f*; *(of evidence)* minceur *f*, faiblesse *f*; *(of argument)* faiblesse *f* (**c**) *(of existence)* précarité *f* (**d**) *Phys* raréfaction *f*
tenure ['tenjə(r)] *n* (**a**) *Hist (of land, property)* bail *m* (**b**) *(of post)* occupation *f*; **during his tenure as chairman** pendant qu'il occupait le poste de président *ou* était président; *Am Univ* **to have tenure** être titulaire
tenured ['tenjəd] *adj (post)* titulaire
tenure-tracked *adj Am* **he's got a tenure-tracked job** son poste est en voie de titularisation
tepee ['ti:pi:] *n* tipi *m*
tephra ['tefrə] *n Am* téphra *m*
tepid ['tepɪd] *adj* (**a**) *(water)* tiède (**b**) *(welcome, thanks)* tiède, réservé
tepidity [te'pɪdɪtɪ] *n* tiédeur *f*
tepidly ['tepɪdlɪ] *adv* tièdement
tepidness ['tepidnis] *n* tiédeur *f*
tequila [tɪ'ki:lə] *n* tequila *f*
▸▸ ***tequila slammer*** tequila *f* bang bang; ***tequila sunrise*** tequila *f* sunrise
Ter. *Br (written abbr* **terrace***)* = rangée de maisons attenantes et identiques
teratoid ['terətɔɪd] *Med* **1** *adj* tératoïde
2 *n* tératome *m*
teratology [,terə'tɒlədʒɪ] *n Biol* tératologie *f*
teratoma [,terə'təʊmə] (*pl* **teratomas** *or* **teratomata** [-mətə]) *n Med* tératome *m*
terbium ['tɜ:bɪəm] *n Chem* terbium *m*
terce [tɜ:s] *n Rel* tierce *f*
tercentenary [,tɜ:sen'ti:nərɪ] (*pl* **tercentenaries**), **tercentennial** [,tɜ:sen'tenɪəl] **1** *n* tricentenaire *m*
2 *adj* du tricentenaire
tercet ['tɜ:sɪt] *n* tercet *m*
terebrate ['terɪbreɪt] *vt Arch* térébrer
teredo [te'ri:dəʊ] (*pl* **teredos** *or* **teredines** [-dɪni:z]) *n Ich* taret *m*
Teresa [tə'ri:zə] *pr n* **Teresa of Avila** sainte Thérèse d'Avila; **Mother Teresa** Mère Teresa
tergiversate ['tɜ:dʒɪvə,seɪt] *vi* tergiverser
tergiversation [,tɜ:dʒɪvə'seɪʃən] *n* tergiversation *f*
teriyaki [terɪ'jækɪ] *n Culin* teriyaki, = préparation culinaire consistant à faire mariner une viande ou un poisson puis à les griller; **beef teriyaki** bœuf *m* teriyaki

TERM [tɜːm]

terme(s)	▸ 1 (a), (e), (f); 3 (a), (d)
trimestre	▸ 1 (b)
session	▸ 1 (c)
mandat	▸ 1 (c)
peine	▸ 1 (d)
échéance	▸ 1 (g)
appeler	▸ 2
conditions	▸ 3 (a)
tarifs	▸ 3 (c)
accord	▸ 3 (e)

1 *n* (**a**) *(period, end of period)* terme *m*; *(of pregnancy)* terme *m*; **in the long/short term** à long/court terme; **to reach (full) term** *(pregnancy)* arriver *ou* être à terme; **to set** *or* **put a term to sth** mettre fin *ou* un terme à qch

(**b**) *Br Sch & Univ* trimestre *m*; **in** *or* **during term (time)** pendant le trimestre; **autumn term** trimestre *m* d'automne, premier trimestre *m*

(**c**) *Law & Pol (of court, parliament)* session *f*; *(of elected official)* mandat *m*; **the president is elected for a four-year term** le président est élu pour (une période *ou* une durée de) quatre ans; **during my term of office** *(gen)* pendant que j'étais en fonction; *Pol* pendant mon mandat

(**d**) *(in prison)* peine *f*; **term of imprisonment** peine *f* de prison; **to serve one's term** purger sa peine

(**e**) *(word, expression)* terme *m*; **medical/legal term** terme *m* médical/juridique; **she spoke of you in very flattering terms** elle a parlé de vous en (des) termes très flatteurs; **she told him what she thought in no uncertain terms** elle lui a dit carrément ce qu'elle pensait; **he condemned the invasion in the strongest possible terms** il a condamné l'invasion avec la dernière énergie

(**f**) *Math & (in logic)* terme *m*

(**g**) *Fin (of bill of exchange)* (terme *m* d')échéance *f*;

2 *vt* appeler, nommer; **I wouldn't term it a scientific book exactly** je ne dirais pas vraiment que c'est un livre scientifique; **critics termed the play a total disaster** les critiques ont qualifié la pièce d'échec complet

3 terms *npl* (**a**) *(conditions → of employment)* conditions *fpl*; *(→ of agreement, contract)* termes *mpl*; **under the terms of the agreement** selon les termes de l'accord; *Law* **terms and conditions of sale/of employment** conditions *fpl* de vente/d'emploi; **what are the inquiry's terms of reference?** quelles sont les attributions *ou* quel est le mandat de la commission d'enquête?; **what are your terms?** quelles sont vos conditions?; **to dictate terms to sb** imposer des conditions à qn; **she would only accept on her own terms** elle n'était disposée à accepter qu'après avoir posé ses conditions; **not on any terms** à aucun prix, à aucune condition

(**b**) *(perspective)* **we must think in less ambitious terms** il faut voir moins grand; **he refuses to consider the question in international terms** il refuse d'envisager la question d'un point de vue international; **in personal terms, it was a disaster** sur le plan personnel, c'était une catastrophe; **in financial terms** financièrement parlant, en matière de finance

(**c**) *(rates, tariffs)* conditions *fpl*, tarifs *mpl*; **we offer easy terms** nous proposons des facilités de paiement; **on easy terms** avec facilités de paiement; **weekly terms** *(in hotel)* tarifs *mpl* à la semaine; **special terms for families** tarifs *mpl* spéciaux pour les familles

(**d**) *(relations)* **to be on good terms with sb** être en bons termes avec qn; **we're on the best of terms** nous sommes en excellents termes; **we remained on friendly terms** nos relations sont restées amicales; **on equal terms** d'égal à égal; **they're no longer on speaking terms** ils ne se parlent plus

(**e**) *(agreement)* accord *m*; **to make terms** *or* **to come to terms with sb** arriver à *ou* conclure un accord avec qn

(**f**) *(acceptance)* **to come to terms with sth** se résigner à qch, arriver à accepter qch; **she'll have to come to terms with her problems eventually** tôt ou tard elle devra faire face à ses problèmes

4 in terms of *prep* en ce qui concerne, pour ce qui est de; **in terms of profits, we're doing well** pour ce qui est des bénéfices, tout va bien; **I was thinking more in terms of a Jaguar** je pensais plutôt à une Jaguar; **we really should be thinking more in terms of foreign competition** il nous faudrait davantage tenir compte de *ou* penser davantage à la concurrence étrangère

▸▸ *Fin* ***term bill*** effet *m* à terme; *Fin* ***terms of credit*** conditions *fpl* de crédit; *Fin* ***term day*** (jour *m* du) terme *m*; *Fin* ***term deposit*** dépôt *m* à terme; *Fin* ***term draft*** traite *f* à terme; *Fin* ***terms of exchange*** termes *mpl* d'échange; ***term insurance*** assurance *f* à terme; *Fin* ***term loan*** *(money lent)* prêt *m* à terme (fixe); *(money borrowed)* emprunt *m* à terme (fixe); ***term of notice*** période *f* de préavis; *Am Sch & Univ* ***term paper*** dissertation *f* trimestrielle; ***terms of payment*** modalités *fpl* de paiement, conditions *fpl* *ou* termes *mpl* de paiement; *Econ* ***terms of trade*** termes *mpl* de l'échange

---

termagant ['tɜːməgənt] *n* mégère *f*, harpie *f*

-termer ['tɜːmə(r)] *suff* **short/long-termer** *(prisoner)* condamné(e) *m,f* à une courte/longue peine

terminable ['tɜːmɪnəbəl] *adj (contract)* résiliable

▸▸ *Fin* ***terminable annuity*** rente *f* à terme

terminal ['tɜːmɪnəl] **1** *adj* (**a**) *(final)* terminal

(**b**) *Med (ward)* pour malades condamnés *ou* incurables; *(patient)* en phase terminale; *(disease → incurable)* incurable; *(→ in its last stages)* dans sa *ou* en phase terminale; **I'm afraid it's terminal** je crains que vous ne soyez/qu'il ne soit/*etc* condamné; **terminal cancer was diagnosed** ils ont diagnostiqué un cancer incurable; **he has terminal cancer** il a un cancer en phase terminale; *Fig* **an industry in terminal decline** une industrie irrémédiablement en déclin; *Hum* **I think I'm suffering from terminal boredom** je crois que je vais mourir d'ennui

(**c**) *(termly)* trimestriel

2 *n* (**a**) *(for bus, underground)* terminus *m*; *(at airport)* terminal *m*, aérogare *f*; **terminal B** aérogare *ou* terminal B

(**b**) *Petr (platform)* terminal *m*

(**c**) *Comput* (poste *m*) terminal *m*

(**d**) *Elec (of battery)* borne *f*

(**e**) *Ling* terminaison *f*

▸▸ *Ins* ***terminal bonus*** = bonus versé au titulaire d'une assurance-vie, au terme de celle-ci; *Fin* ***terminal charges*** charges *fpl* terminales; *Comput* ***terminal emulation*** émulation *f* de terminal; *Comput* ***terminal emulator*** émulateur *m* de terminal; *Acct* ***terminal loss*** perte *f* finale; *St Exch* ***terminal market*** marché *m* à terme; *Petr* ***terminal platform*** terminal *m*; *Fin* ***terminal price*** cours *m* du livrable; *Comput* ***terminal server*** serveur *m* de terminaux; *Rail* ***terminal station*** terminus *m*; ***terminal velocity*** vitesse *f* limite; *Elec* ***terminal voltage*** tension *f* aux bornes

terminally ['tɜːmɪnəlɪ] *adv* **to be terminally ill** être condamné; **the terminally ill** les malades *mpl* condamnés

terminate ['tɜːmɪneɪt] **1** *vt* (**a**) *(end → project, work)* terminer; *(→ employment)* mettre fin *ou* un terme à; *(→ contract)* résilier, mettre fin *ou* un terme à; *(→ pregnancy)* interrompre; **to have one's pregnancy terminated** avoir une IVG

(**b**) *Am Fam (employee)* virer

(**c**) *Fam (kill)* descendre

2 *vi* (**a**) *(end)* se terminer; **the row terminated in** *or* **with her resignation** la dispute s'est terminée par sa démission

(**b**) *Ling* se terminer

(**c**) *Rail* **this train terminates at Glasgow** ce train ne va pas plus loin que Glasgow; **this train terminates here** terminus du train!

termination [,tɜːmɪ'neɪʃən] *n* (**a**) *(end → gen)* fin *f*; *(→ of contract)* résiliation *f*; *(→ of relations, dealings etc)* cessation *f* (**b**) *(abortion)* interruption *f* (volontaire) de grossesse, IVG *f* (**c**) *Ling* terminaison *f*, désinence *f*

▸▸ ***termination of employment*** licenciement *m*

terminational [,tɜːmɪ'neɪʃənəl] *adj Gram* terminatif

terminator ['tɜːmɪneɪtə(r)] *n Comput (of chain)* terminateur *m*

▸▸ *Agr* ***terminator gene*** gène *m* terminator *ou* *Offic* terminateur

termini ['tɜːmɪnaɪ] *pl of* **terminus**

terminological [,tɜːmɪnə'lɒdʒɪkəl] *adj* terminologique

▸▸ *Euph Hum* ***terminological inexactitude*** mensonge *m*

terminologist [,tɜːmɪ'nɒlədʒɪst] *n* terminologue *mf*

terminology [,tɜːmɪ'nɒlədʒɪ] *(pl* **terminologies***)* *n* terminologie *f*

terminus ['tɜːmɪnəs] *(pl* **terminuses** *or* **termini** [-naɪ]*)* *n* terminus *m*

termitarium [,tɜːmɪ'teərɪəm] *(pl* **termitaria** [-rɪə]*)*, **termitary** ['tɜːmɪtərɪ] *(pl* **termitaries***)* *n Zool* termitière *f*

termite ['tɜːmaɪt] *n Entom* termite *m*, fourmi *f* blanche

termless ['tɜːmlɪs] *adj* (**a**) *(endless)* illimité, sans limite *ou* fin (**b**) *(unconditional)* sans condition *ou* conditions, inconditionnel

termly ['tɜːmlɪ] **1** *adj* trimestriel

2 *adv* trimestriellement, par trimestre

tern [tɜːn] *n Orn* sterne *f*

ternary ['tɜːnərɪ] *adj* ternaire

ternate ['tɜːneɪt] *adj Bot* terné, ternifolié

terpene ['tɜːpiːn] *n Chem* terpène *m*

Terpsichore ['tɜːpsɪkɔː(r)] *pr n Myth* Terpsichore

terpsichorean [,tɜːpsɪkə'rɪən] *adj* de la danse

Terr. *(written abbr* **terrace***)* = rangée de maisons attenantes et identiques

terrace ['terəs] **1** *n* (**a**) *Agr & Geol* terrasse *f*

(**b**) *(patio)* terrasse *f*

(**c**) *(embankment)* terre-plein *m*

(**d**) *Br (of houses)* = rangée de maisons attenantes et identiques; **Victorian terraces in Manchester** = des rangées de maisons victoriennes à Manchester

(**e**) *Br (house)* = maison faisant partie d'une "terrace"

2 *vt Agr* cultiver en terrasses

3 terraces *npl Sport* gradins *mpl*; **on the terraces** dans les gradins

▸▸ ***terrace cultivation*** culture *f* en terrasses

TERRACE

Ce mot désigne une rangée de maisons à un ou deux étages. À l'origine, les "terraced houses" étaient surtout des logements ouvriers (équivalents des corons) construits à proximité d'usines ou de mines de charbon.

terraced ['terəst] *adj (garden)* en terrasses; *(hillside)* cultivé en terrasses

▸▸ *Br* ***terraced house*** = maison située dans une rangée de maisons attenantes et identiques; **terraced houses** maisons *fpl* alignées

terracing ['terəsɪŋ] *n* (**a**) *Agr (action)* culture *f* en terrasses (**b**) *(terraces) Agr* terrasses *fpl*; *Sport* gradins *mpl*

terracotta [,terə'kɒtə] **1** *n* (**a**) *(earthenware)* terre *f* cuite (**b**) *(colour)* ocre *m* brun

2 *adj (colour)* ocre brun *(inv)*

3 *comp (pottery)* en terre cuite

terra firma [,terə'fɜːmə] *n Literary or Hum* terre *f* ferme; **on terra firma** sur la terre ferme

terrain [te'reɪn] *n* terrain *m*

terrapin ['terəpɪn] *n Zool* tortue *f* d'eau douce

terrarium [tə'reərɪəm] *n (for plants)* mini-serre *f*; *(for reptiles)* terrarium *m*

terrazzo [tə'rætsəʊ] *(pl* **terrazos***)* *n* granito *m*

Terrence Higgins Trust [,terəns'hɪgɪnz-] *n* **the Terrence Higgins Trust** = association britannique de lutte contre le sida

terrestrial [tə'restrɪəl] **1** *adj* terrestre

2 *n* terrien(enne) *m,f*

▸▸ ***terrestrial broadcasting*** *or* ***television*** diffusion *f* hertzienne *ou* terrestre; **the Cup Final will no longer be broadcast on terrestrial television** la finale ne sera plus diffusée sur le réseau hertzien

terrestrially [tə'restrɪəlɪ] *adv* (**a**) *TV (broadcast)* par voie hertzienne (**b**) *(as opposed to in marine environment)* sur la terre ferme

terrible ['terəbəl] *adj* (**a**) *(severe, serious → accident, shock, injury)* terrible; *(→ weather)* affreux, épouvantable; *(→ pain)* terrible, affreux, atroce; *(→ storm, heat)* terrible, épouvantable; **I**

have a terrible headache j'ai un mal de tête affreux; **it caused terrible damage** cela a provoqué d'importants dégâts; **it was a terrible blow** ce fut un coup terrible; **the heat was terrible** il faisait une chaleur terrible *ou* épouvantable

(**b**) *(very bad → experience, dream)* affreux; *(→ food, smell)* épouvantable; *(→ conditions, poverty)* épouvantable, effroyable; **to feel terrible** *(ill)* se sentir très mal; *(guilty)* s'en vouloir beaucoup, avoir des remords; **I feel terrible about the whole situation** je m'en veux beaucoup pour tout ce qui s'est passé; **I feel terrible about leaving them on their own** cela m'ennuie terriblement de les laisser seuls; **I was always terrible at French** j'ai toujours été nul en français; **the food was a terrible disappointment** on a été terriblement déçus par la nourriture; *Fam* **the terrible twos** l'âge *m* difficile chez les tout-petits❑ *(2 ans)*

(**c**) *(for emphasis)* **it's a terrible shame!** c'est vraiment dommage!; **he's a terrible gossip** *(gossips a lot)* c'est un sacré bavard

terribly ['terəblɪ] *adv* (**a**) *(as intensifier)* terriblement, extrêmement; **I'm terribly sorry** je suis vraiment désolé; **she'll be terribly disappointed** elle sera terriblement déçue; **that's terribly kind of you** c'est vraiment très gentil de votre part, vous êtes vraiment trop aimable; **the food here isn't terribly good** la nourriture ici n'est pas fameuse; **she's terribly clever** elle est drôlement *ou* rudement intelligente; **it must have hurt (you) terribly** *(physically)* cela a dû vous faire terriblement mal; *(mentally)* cela a dû vous faire énormément de peine

(**b**) *(very badly)* affreusement mal, terriblement mal; **she dresses/plays terribly (badly)** elle s'habille/joue affreusement mal; **the economy has performed terribly** les résultats économiques sont désastreux

terricolous [te'rɪkələs] *adj Zool* terricole

terrier ['terɪə(r)] **1** *n* terrier *m (chien)*; *Fig* **he's a real terrier** il n'abandonne jamais

2 Terriers *npl Br Fam* **the Terriers** la territoriale❑, l'armée *f* territoriale❑

terrific [tə'rɪfɪk] *adj* (**a**) *(extreme, intense → noise, crash)* épouvantable, effroyable; *(→ speed)* fou (folle); *(→ heat)* terrible, épouvantable; *(→ appetite)* énorme, robuste; **these trees grow to a terrific height** ces arbres atteignent une taille énorme; **it must have come as a terrific shock (to you)** cela a dû vous faire un choc terrible

(**b**) *Fam (superb)* terrible, génial, super; **you look terrific in that dress** cette robe te va super bien; **well, I think he's terrific** eh bien moi, je le trouve super *ou* génial

terrifically [tə'rɪfɪklɪ] *adv Fam* (**a**) *(extremely, enormously)* extrêmement❑, très❑; **terrifically happy** super heureux; **terrifically disappointed** terriblement déçu; **he's grown terrifically** il a énormément grandi (**b**) *(very well)* merveilleusement (bien)❑; **she sings terrifically** elle chante merveilleusement *ou* formidablement bien

terrified ['terɪfaɪd] *adj* terrifié; **to be terrified of sb/sth** avoir une peur bleue *ou* avoir très peur de qn/qch; **to be terrified (that)** être terrifié *ou* mort de peur (à l'idée que + *subjunctive*); **I was absolutely terrified** j'étais absolument mort de peur *ou* complètement terrifié *ou* complètement terrorisé

terrify ['terɪfaɪ] *(pt & pp* **terrified**) *vt* terrifier, effrayer

terrifying ['terɪfaɪɪŋ] *adj (dream)* terrifiant; *(person)* terrible, épouvantable; *(weaker use)* terrifiant, effroyable; **what a terrifying thought!** rien que d'y penser, je frémis!

terrifyingly ['terɪfaɪɪŋlɪ] *adv* de façon terrifiante *ou* effroyable

terrigenous [te'rɪdʒɪnəs] *adj* (**a**) *Arch or Literary (born from the earth)* né *ou* issu de la terre *ou* du sol (**b**) *Geol* terrigène

terrine [te'ri:n] *n* terrine *f*

territorial [,terɪ'tɔ:rɪəl] **1** *adj* (**a**) *(possessions, tax, claim etc)* territorial

(**b**) *(instinct)* territorial; **cats are very territorial (animals)** les chats sont des animaux farouchement attachés à leur territoire; *Fig* **they're very territorial about their part of the office** ils considèrent leur partie du bureau comme leur territoire exclusif

2 *n* territorial *m*; *Br Mil* **the Territorials** l'armée *f* territoriale, la territoriale

►► *Br Mil* ***Territorial Army*** (armée *f*) territoriale *f*; *Pol* ***territorial dispute*** contentieux *m* territorial; ***territorial waters*** eaux *fpl* territoriales

territorialism [,terɪ'tɔ:rɪəlɪzəm] *n* territorialisme *m*

territoriality [,terɪtɔ:rɪ'ælɪtɪ] *n* territorialité *f*

territorially [,terɪ'tɔ:rɪəlɪ] *adv* territorialement

territory ['terətrɪ] *(pl* **territories**) *n (area)* territoire *m*; *(of salesperson)* territoire *m*, région *f*; *(of knowledge)* domaine *m*; *Fig* **I'm afraid this isn't my territory** désolé, ce n'est pas mon domaine; **this will be familiar territory for his readers** le lecteur se retrouvera en terrain familier; **to be on familiar territory** être en terrain connu; **it goes with the territory** *(goes with the job)* cela fait partie du travail

terror ['terə(r)] **1** *n* (**a**) *(fear)* terreur *f*, épouvante *f*; **to be** *or* **to go in terror of one's life** craindre pour sa vie; **to be in a state of terror** être terrorisé *ou* terrifié; **there was a look of terror on her face** elle avait l'air terrorisée; **to be** *or* **to live in terror of sb** avoir une peur bleue de qn; **to have a terror of sth/of doing sth** avoir extrêmement peur *ou* la terreur de qch/de faire qch

(**b**) *(frightening event or aspect)* terreur *f*; **the terrors of the night** les terreurs *fpl* de la nuit; **to hold no terrors for sb** ne pas faire peur à qn

(**c**) *(terrorism)* terreur *f*; **campaign of terror** campagne *f* terroriste *ou* de terreur

(**d**) *Fam (person)* terreur *f*; **he was the terror of the countryside** c'était la terreur du pays; **he's a terror on his bike** c'est une terreur en vélo; **you little terror!** petite terreur, va!

2 Terror *n Hist* **the Terror** la Terreur

terrorism ['terərɪzəm] *n* terrorisme *m*; **ecological terrorism** terrorisme *m* écologique

terrorist ['terərɪst] **1** *n* terroriste *mf*

2 *adj (bomb)* de terroriste; *(campaign, attack, group)* terroriste

terrorize, -ise ['terəraɪz] *vt* terroriser

terror-stricken, terror-struck *adj* épouvanté, saisi de terreur

terry (towelling) ['terɪ-] *n* tissu-éponge *m*

►► *Br* ***terry nappy*** couche *f (en tissu-éponge)*

terse [tɜ:s] *adj (concise)* concis, succinct; *(laconic)* laconique; *(abrupt)* brusque, sec (sèche)

tersely ['tɜ:slɪ] *adv (concisely)* avec concision; *(laconically)* laconiquement; *(abruptly)* brusquement, sèchement

terseness ['tɜ:snɪs] *n (concision)* concision *f*; *(laconicism)* laconisme *m*; *(abruptness)* brusquerie *f*

tertiary ['tɜ:ʃərɪ] **1** *adj (gen) & Ind* tertiaire; *(education)* postscolaire, supérieur

2 Tertiary *Geol* **1** *adj* tertiaire **2** *n* **the Tertiary** le tertiaire

►► ***tertiary sector*** secteur *m* tertiaire

Tertullian [tɜ:'tʌlɪən] *pr n Antiq* Tertullien

Terylene® ['terəli:n] **1** *n* Térylène® *m*, ≃ Tergal®

2 *adj* en Térylène®, ≃ en Tergal®

TESL ['tesəl] *n (abbr* **Teaching (of) English as a Second Language**) enseignement *m* de l'anglais langue seconde

tesla ['teslə] *n Phys* tesla *m*

TESOL ['ti:sɒl] *n (abbr* **Teaching English to Speakers of Other Languages**) enseignement *m* de l'anglais aux étrangers *ou* comme langue étrangère

TESSA ['tesə] *n (abbr* **tax-exempt special savings account**) = en Grande-Bretagne, plan d'épargne exonéré d'impôt

tessellated ['tesɪleɪtɪd] *adj* en mosaïque

tessellation [,tesɪ'leɪʃən] *n (arrangement)* arrangement *m* en mosaïque

tessera ['tesərə] *(pl* **tesserae** [-ri:]) *n* (**a**) *(mosaic tile)* tesselle *f* (**b**) *Antiq (token)* tessère *f* (**c**) *Zool (of armadillo)* écaille *f*

tesseract ['tesərækt] *n Geom* hypercube *m*

tesseral ['tesərəl] *adj* (**a**) *(in mosaic work → relating to tesserae)* de tesselles; *(→ composed of tesserae)* en tesselles (**b**) *Math & Geol* cubique

tessitura [,tesɪ'tʊərə] *n Mus* tessiture *f*

TEST [test]

test	► 1 (a) – (e)
contrôle	► 1 (a), (c)
examen	► 1 (b)
tester	► 3 (a), (c)
analyser	► 3 (b), (f)
examiner	► 3 (b)
essayer	► 3 (c)
vérifier	► 3 (d)
contrôler	► 3 (d)
mesurer	► 3 (e)
évaluer	► 3 (e)
éprouver	► 3 (g)

1 *n* (**a**) *(examination → gen)* test *m*; *Sch* contrôle *m*, interrogation *f*; **to pass a test** réussir à un examen; **biology test** interrogation *f* de biologie; **to sit** *or* **to take a test** passer un examen; **general knowledge test** test *m* de culture générale; **I'm taking my (driving) test tomorrow** je passe mon permis (de conduire) demain; **did you pass your (driving) test?** avez-vous été reçu au permis (de conduire)?

(**b**) *Med (of blood, urine)* test *m*, analyse *f*; *(of eyes, hearing)* examen *m*; **to undergo tests** subir des tests *ou* examens; **to have a blood test** faire faire une analyse de sang; **to have an eye test** se faire examiner la vue; **the lab did a test for salmonella** le laboratoire a fait une analyse pour détecter la présence de salmonelles

(**c**) *(trial → of equipment, machine)* test *m*, essai *m*, épreuve *f*; *(→ of quality)* contrôle *m*; *Mktg (→ of reaction, popularity)* évaluation *f*; **to carry out tests on sth** effectuer des tests sur qch; **all new drugs undergo clinical tests** tous les nouveaux médicaments subissent des tests cliniques; **a test for noise levels** un contrôle des niveaux sonores; **to be on test** être testé *ou* à l'essai; **to put sth to the test** tester qch, faire l'essai de qch

(**d**) *(of character, endurance, resolve)* test *m*; **a good test of character** un bon test de personnalité, un bon moyen de tester la personnalité; **to put sb to the test** éprouver qn, mettre qn à l'épreuve; **his courage was really put to the test** son courage fut sérieusement mis à l'épreuve *ou* éprouvé; **it's the first major test for the Prime Minister** c'est la première fois que le Premier ministre est réellement mis à l'épreuve; **to stand the test** se montrer à la hauteur; *also Fig* **test of strength** épreuve *f* de force; **to stand the test of time** durer, résister à l'épreuve du temps; **her books have certainly stood the test of time** ses livres n'ont pas pris une ride

(**e**) *(measure)* test *m*; **it's a test of union solidarity** c'est un test de la solidarité syndicale; **it will be a test of popularity for the new leader** ce sera un test de popularité pour le nouveau dirigeant; **the by-election will be a good test of public opinion** l'élection partielle représentera un bon test de l'opinion publique

(**f**) *Br Sport* test-match *m*

2 *comp* d'essai

3 *vt* (**a**) *(examine → ability, knowledge, intelligence)* tester, mesurer; *Sch (→ pupils)* tester, contrôler les connaissances de; **we were tested in geography** nous avons eu un contrôle de géographie; **she was tested on her knowledge of plants** on a testé *ou* vérifié ses connaissances botaniques

(**b**) *Med (blood, urine)* analyser, faire une analyse de; *(sight, hearing)* examiner; **to have one's eyes tested** se faire examiner la vue; *Fig* **you need your eyes tested** *or Br* **testing!** il faut mettre des lunettes!; **to test sb for AIDS** faire subir le test de dépistage du sida à qn; **to test an athlete for steroids** faire subir des tests à un athlète pour détecter l'usage de stéroïdes

(**c**) *(try out → prototype, car)* essayer, faire l'essai de; *(→ product)* essayer ; *(→ weapon, procedure)* tester; *(→ drug)* tester, expérimenter; **none of our products are tested on animals** nos produits ne sont pas testés sur les animaux

(**d**) *(check → batteries, pressure, suspension)* vérifier, contrôler

(**e**) *(measure → reaction, popularity)* mesurer, évaluer; *Mktg (→ quality)* contrôler; **the day of action will test union solidarity** la journée d'action permettra de mesurer *ou* d'évaluer la solidarité syndicale

(**f**) *(analyse → soil)* analyser, faire des prélèvements dans; *(→ water)* analyser; **the water was tested for phosphates** on a analysé l'eau pour en déterminer le taux de phosphates; **to test food for starch** rechercher la présence d'amidon dans les aliments; *Fig* **to test the water** tâter le terrain

(**g**) *(tax → machinery, driver, patience)* éprouver, mettre à l'épreuve; **to test sb to the limit** pousser qn à bout *ou* à la dernière extrémité; **to test sb's patience to the limit** mettre la patience de qn à rude épreuve

4 *vi* (**a**) *(make examination)* **to test for salmonella** faire une recherche de salmonelles; **to test for AIDS** procéder à un test de dépistage du sida; **to test for the presence of gas** rechercher la présence de gaz

(**b**) *(show test result)* **she tested positive for AIDS** son test de dépistage du sida s'est révélé positif

(**c**) *Rad & Tel* **testing, testing!** un, deux, trois!

▸▸ *Law & Hist* ***the Test Act*** = loi anglaise de 1673, abrogée en 1828, interdisant aux catholiques l'accès aux postes gouvernementaux et à la fonction de député; ***test area*** région *f* test; ***test ban*** interdiction *f* des essais nucléaires; ***test ban treaty*** traité *m* de prohibition des essais nucléaires; ***test bench*** banc *m* d'essai; *Br TV* ***test card*** mire *f*; *Law* ***test case*** affaire *f* qui fait jurisprudence; **the trial has come to be regarded as a test case in environmental law** ce procès a acquis force de précédent dans le domaine de la protection de l'environnement; *Fig* **doctors regard her experiences as a test case for some of their theories** les médecins estiment que ses expériences vont leur permettre d'éprouver *ou* de mettre à l'épreuve certaines de leurs théories; ***test certificate*** certificat *m* d'essai; *TV* ***test chart*** mire *f* (de réglage); *Mktg* ***test city*** ville *f* test; ***test drive*** essai *m* sur route; **to go for a test drive** essayer une voiture; *Aviat* ***test flight*** vol *m* d'essai; ***test market*** marché-test *m*, marché *m* témoin; *Br* ***test match*** match *m* international, test-match *m*; ***test paper*** (**a**) *Chem* papier *m* réactif (**b**) *Br Sch* interrogation *f* écrite; *Am TV* ***test pattern*** mire *f* (de réglage); *Mus* ***test piece*** morceau *m* imposé *ou* de concours; ***test pilot*** pilote *m* d'essai; ***test run*** essai *m*; **to go for a test run** faire un essai; ***test shot*** lancement *m* d'essai; ***test signal*** signal *m* de mesure; ***test site*** site *m* témoin; *Aut* ***test track*** piste *f* d'essai; ***test tube*** éprouvette *f*

▸ **test out** *vt sep* (**a**) *(idea, theory)* tester

(**b**) *(prototype, product)* essayer, mettre à l'essai; **these products are tested out on animals** ces produits sont testés sur les animaux

---

testa ['testə] *(pl* **testae** [-tiː]) *n Bot* testa *m*

testaceous [tes'teɪʃəs] *adj* (**a**) *Biol* testacé (**b**) *(reddish-brown)* couleur brique *(inv)*

testament ['testəmənt] *n* (**a**) *Law* testament *m*; **to make one's (last will and) testament** tester, faire son testament (**b**) *(tribute)* preuve *f*, témoignage *m*; **the victory was a testament to her bravery** cette victoire a été le témoignage de son courage (**c**) *Bible* testament *m*; **the New Testament** le Nouveau Testament; **the Old Testament** l'Ancien Testament *m*

testamentary [ˌtestə'mentərɪ] *adj* testamentaire

testate ['testeɪt] *adj* **to die testate** mourir en ayant laissé un testament *ou* testé

testator [te'steɪtə(r)] *n Law* testateur *m*

testatrix [te'steɪtrɪks] *n Law* testatrice *f*

test-bed *n* banc *m* d'essai *ou* d'épreuve

test-drive **1** *n (of car)* essai *m* de conduite

2 *vt (car)* essayer

tester ['testə(r)] *n* (**a**) *(person)* contrôleur(euse) *m,f*, vérificateur(trice) *m,f* (**b**) *(machine)* appareil *m* de contrôle *ou* de vérification (**c**) *(sample → of make-up, perfume)* échantillon *m* (**d**) *(over bed)* baldaquin *m*, ciel *m*

testes ['testiːz] *pl of* **testis**

test-fly *vt* **to test-fly a plane** faire le vol d'essai d'un avion

testicle ['testɪkəl] *n* testicule *m*

testicular [tes'tɪkjʊlə(r)] *adj Anat* testiculaire

▸▸ ***testicular cancer*** cancer *m* du testicule; ***testicular cord*** cordon *m* testiculaire

testifier ['testɪfaɪə(r)] *n* témoin *m*

testify ['testɪfaɪ] *(pt & pp* **testified**) **1** *vt* (**a**) *(affirm, state)* déclarer, affirmer; *Law* déclarer sous serment, attester, témoigner; **I can testify that she remained at home** je peux attester qu'elle est restée à la maison

(**b**) *Literary (demonstrate, prove)* témoigner de; **this work testifies his deep knowledge of the subject** cet œuvre témoigne de sa profonde connaissance du sujet

2 *vi (be witness)* porter témoignage, témoigner; **to testify for/against sb** témoigner en faveur de/contre qn; **I can testify to her honesty** je peux attester *ou* témoigner de son honnêteté; **his behaviour testified to his guilt** son comportement témoignait de sa culpabilité

testily ['testɪlɪ] *adv* d'un ton irrité

testimonial [ˌtestɪ'məʊnɪəl] **1** *n* (**a**) *(certificate)* attestation *f*; *(reference → gen)* (lettre *f* de) recommandation *f*; *(→ given by company, manager)* références *fpl*

(**b**) *(tribute)* témoignage *m* d'estime

(**c**) *Br Sport (match)* jubilé *m*

2 *adj* qui porte témoignage; **they organized a testimonial dinner for him** ils ont organisé un dîner en son honneur

▸▸ *Mktg* ***testimonial advertising*** témoignage *m*, publicité *f* testimoniale; *Br* ***testimonial match*** jubilé *m*

testimony [*Br* 'testɪmənɪ, *Am* 'testəməʊnɪ] *(pl* **testimonies**) *n* (**a**) *(statement)* déclaration *f*; *Law* témoignage *m*, déposition *f*; **to call sb in testimony** appeler qn en témoignage (**b**) *(sign, proof)* témoignage *m*; **to bear testimony to sth** témoigner de qch; **the monument is a lasting testimony to** *or* **of his genius** ce monument est le témoignage vivant de son génie; *Law* **in testimony whereof** en foi de quoi

testiness ['testɪnɪs] *n* irritabilité *f*

testing ['testɪŋ] **1** *adj (difficult)* difficile, éprouvant; **it's been a testing time for everyone** cela a été une période éprouvante pour tout le monde

2 *n* (**a**) *(of product, machine, vehicle)* (mise *f* à l')essai *m*; *(of quality)* contrôle *m*

(**b**) *Med (of sight, hearing)* examen *m*; *(of blood, urine)* analyse *f*; *(of reaction)* mesure *f*; *(of drug, cosmetic)* expérimentation *f*

(**c**) *(of intelligence, knowledge, skills)* évaluation *f*; *(of candidate)* évaluation *f*, examen *m*

▸▸ ***testing bench*** banc *m* d'essai; ***testing ground*** terrain *m* d'essai; **Scotland was often used as a testing ground for new government policies** le gouvernement utilisait souvent l'Écosse pour tester ses nouvelles mesures politiques; ***testing laboratory*** laboratoire *m* d'essai de produits

testis ['testɪs] *(pl* **testes** [-tiːz]) *n Anat* testicule *m*

test-market *vt* tester sur le marché

testosterone [te'stɒstərəʊn] *n* testostérone *f*

test-shop *n* magasin *m* laboratoire

test-tube *adj* de laboratoire

▸▸ ***test-tube baby*** bébé-éprouvette *m*

testy ['testɪ] *(compar* **testier,** *superl* **testiest**) *adj* irritable, grincheux

tetanic [te'tænɪk] *adj Med* tétanique

▸▸ *Old-fashioned Pharm* ***tetanic drug*** médicament *m* tétanique; ***tetanic state*** tétanisme *m*

tetanize, -ise ['tetənaɪz] *vt Med* tétaniser

tetanus ['tetənəs] **1** *n* tétanos *m*

2 *comp (vaccination, injection)* antitétanique

tetany ['tetənɪ] *n Med* tétanie *f*; *Vet* **grass tetany** tétanie *f* d'herbage

tetchily ['tetʃɪlɪ] *adv* d'un ton irrité

tetchiness ['tetʃɪnɪs] *n* irritabilité *f*

tetchy ['tetʃɪ] *(compar* **tetchier,** *superl* **tetchiest**) *adj* grincheux, irascible

tête-à-tête [ˌteɪtɑː'teɪt] **1** *n* (conversation *f* en) tête-à-tête *m inv*

2 *adj* en tête-à-tête

tether ['teðə(r)] **1** *n (for horse)* longe *f*, attache *f*; **to be at the end of one's tether** *(unable to cope, depressed)* être au bout du rouleau; *(exasperated)* être à bout de patience

2 *vt (horse)* attacher

tetherball ['teðəˌbɔːl] *n* jeu *m* du ballon captif

tetra ['tetrə] *n Ich* tétra *m*

tetrachloride [ˌtetrə'klɔːraɪd] *n Chem* tétrachlorure *m*

tetrachloromethane [ˌtetrəklɔːrəʊ'miːθeɪn] *n Chem* tetrachlorométhane *m*, tétrachlorure *m* de carbone

tetracycline [ˌtetrə'saɪkliːn] *n Chem* tétracycline *f*

tetrad ['tetræd] *n* tétrade *f*

tetradactyl [ˌtetrə'dæktɪl], **tetradactylous** [ˌtetrə'dæktɪləs] *adj Zool* tétradactyle

tetragon ['tetrəgən] *n* quadrilatère *m*

tetragonal [te'trægənəl] *adj* quadrilatère

Tetragrammaton [tetrə'græmətən] *n Rel* Tetragramme *m*

tetrahedral [ˌtetrə'hiːdrəl] *adj* tétraèdre, tétraédrique

tetrahedron [ˌtetrə'hiːdrən] *(pl* **tetrahedrons** *or* **tetrahedra** [-drə]) *n* tétraèdre *m*

tetralogy [te'trælədʒɪ] *(pl* **tetralogies**) *n Literature & Mus* tétralogie *f*

▸▸ *Med* ***tetralogy of Fallot*** tétralogie *f* de Fallot

tetrameter [te'træmɪtə(r)] *n Literature* tétramètre *m*

tetraplegia [ˌtetrə'pliːdʒɪə] *n Med* tétraplégie *f*, quadriplégie *f*

tetraplegic [ˌtetrə'pliːdʒɪk] *Med* **1** *n* tétraplégique *mf*

2 *adj* tétraplégique

tetrapod ['tetrəpɒd] *n Zool* tétrapode *m*

tetrastich ['tetrəstɪk] *n Literature* poème *m* de quatre vers

tetrasyllabic [ˌtetrəsɪ'læbɪk] *adj* tétrasyllabe, tétrasyllabique

tetrasyllable ['tetrəˌsɪləbəl] *n* tétrasyllabe *m*

tetravalent [ˌtetrə'veɪlənt] *adj Chem* tétravalent, quadrivalent

tetrode ['tetrəʊd] *n Electron* tétrode *f*, tube *m* à quatre électrodes

tetter ['tetə(r)] *n Med* éruption *f* cutanée

teuchter ['tjuːχtə(r)] *n Scot Fam* = terme péjoratif utilisé par les habitants des plaines écossaises pour désigner ceux des Highlands

Teuton ['tjuːtən] *n* Teuton(onne) *m,f*

Teutonic [tjuː'tɒnɪk] *adj* teuton

Teutonism ['tjuːtəˌnɪzəm] *n* germanisme *m*

Teutonize, -ise ['tjuːtənaɪz] *vt* germaniser

Tex *(written abbr* **Texas**) Texas *m*

Texan ['teksən] **1** *n* Texan(e) *m,f*

2 *adj* texan

Texas ['teksəs] *n* le Texas; **in Texas** au Texas

Tex-Mex [ˌteks'meks] **1** *adj Culin & Mus* tex-mex *(inv)*

2 *n* (**a**) *Culin* cuisine *f* tex-mex *(cuisine mexicaine adaptée aux goûts américains)* (**b**) *(music)* tex-mex *m (musique américaine influencée par la musique mexicaine)*

text [tekst] **1** *n (gen) & Comput* texte *m*

2 *vt (send text message to)* envoyer un message texte *ou* un mini-message à

3 *vi (send text messages)* envoyer des messages texte *ou* des mini-messages

▸▸ *Comput* ***text block*** bloc *m* de texte; *Comput* ***text buffer*** mémoire *f* tampon de texte; ***text editing*** édition *f* de texte, mise *f* en forme de texte; *Comput* ***text editor*** éditeur *m* de texte; *Comput* ***text field*** champ *m* de text; *Comput* ***text file*** fichier *m* texte; *Comput* ***text layout*** disposition *f* de texte; ***text linguistics*** linguistique *f* textuelle; ***text message*** *(on mobile phone, pager)* message *m* texte, mini-message *m*; *Comput* ***text mode*** mode *m* texte; *Comput* ***text processing*** traitement *m* de texte; *Comput* ***text processor*** (unité *f* de) traitement *m* de texte; *Typ & Comput* ***text wrap*** texte *m* en habillage

textbook ['tekstbʊk] **1** *n (gen) & Sch* manuel *m*

2 *comp (typical)* typique; *(ideal)* parfait, idéal; **it's a textbook case** c'est un exemple classique *ou* typique; **they're trying too hard to be textbook parents** ils font trop d'efforts pour être des parents parfaits

▸▸ ***textbook definition*** définition *f* classique

textile ['tekstaɪl] **1** *n* textile *m*

2 *comp (industry)* textile

text-message *vt* envoyer un message texte *ou* un mini-message à

text-size *adj (newspaper)* plein format

textual ['tekstjʊəl] *adj* textuel, de texte

▸▸ ***textual analysis*** analyse *f* de texte; ***textual criticism*** critique *f* littéraire de textes; ***textual error*** erreur *f* dans le texte

textually ['tekstjʊəlɪ] *adv (in written form)* à l'écrit; *(in the text)* dans le texte; **textually interesting** intéressant au niveau du contenu

textuary ['tekstjʊərɪ] **1** *adj* textuaire

2 *n Bible* = personne bien informée sur l'Écriture sainte

texture ['tekstʃə(r)] *n* (**a**) *(of fabric)* tissage *m*; *(of leather, wood, paper, skin, stone)* grain *m*; **the paper is grainy in texture** le papier est de texture granuleuse (**b**) *(of food, soil)* texture *f*, consistance *f*; *(of writing)* structure *f*, texture *f*; **music is part of the texture of their lives** la musique fait partie intégrante de leur vie

-textured ['tekstʃəd] *suff Tex* **close-/light-textured** d'un tissage serré/léger

textured vegetable protein *n Culin* = protéine végétale ayant l'aspect et le goût de la viande

TFT [ˌtiːef'tiː] *n Electron* (*abbr* **thin film transistor**) transistor *m* en couche mince

TGIF [ˌtiːdʒiːˌaɪ'ef] *exclam Fam* (*abbr* **thank God it's Friday!**) encore une semaine de tirée!

TGWU [ˌtiːdʒiːˌdʌbəljuː'juː] *n Ind* (*abbr* **Transport and General Workers' Union**) = le plus grand syndicat interprofessionnel britannique

Thai [taɪ] (*pl* **inv** *or* **Thais**) **1** *n* (**a**) *(person)* Thaï *mf*, Thaïlandais(e) *m,f* (**b**) *(language)* thaï *m*, thaïlandais *m*

2 *adj* thaï, thaïlandais

3 *comp (embassy)* de Thaïlande; *(history)* de la Thaïlande; *(teacher)* de thaï, de thaïlandais

▸▸ ***Thai boxing*** boxe *f* thaïlandaise; ***Thai curry*** curry *m* thaïlandais

Thailand ['taɪlænd] *n* Thaïlande *f*; **in Thailand** en Thaïlande

thalamus ['θæləməs] (*pl* **thalami** [-maɪ]) *n Anat* thalamus *m*

thalassaemia, *Am* **thalassemia** [ˌθælə'siːmɪə] *n Med* thalassémie *f*

thalassic [θæ'læsɪk] *adj* thalassique

thalassotherapy [ˌθæləsəʊ'θerəpɪ] *n* thalassothérapie *f*

thaler ['tɑːlə(r)] *n* thaler *m*; **Maria Theresa thaler** thaler *m* de Marie-Thérèse

Thales ['θeɪliːz] *pr n* Thalès

thali ['tɑːlɪ] *n Culin* thali *m (repas indien composé de plusieurs petits plats servis en même temps)*

thalidomide [θə'lɪdəmaɪd] *n Pharm* thalidomide *f*

▸▸ ***thalidomide baby*** = bébé victime de la thalidomide

thallium ['θælɪəm] *n Chem* thallium *m*

thallus ['θæləs] (*pl* **thalli** [-laɪ] *or* **thalluses**) *n Bot* thalle *m*

Thames [temz] *n* **the (River) Thames** la Tamise; *Br Fam* **he'll never set the Thames on fire** il n'a pas inventé la poudre *ou* le fil à couper le beurre

▸▸ ***Thames Flood Barrier*** = digue construite à Woolwich pour protéger Londres des inondations de la Tamise; ***the Thames Valley*** la vallée de la Tamise

than [ðæn, *unstressed* ðən] **1** *conj* (**a**) *(after comparative adj, adv)* que; **he plays tennis better than I do** il joue au tennis mieux que moi; **she can walk faster than I can run** elle va plus vite en marchant que moi en courant; **it's quicker by train than by bus** ça va plus vite en train qu'en bus; **I was less/more disappointed than angry** j'étais moins/plus déçu que fâché

(**b**) *(following negative clause)* **no sooner had he finished speaking than everyone made for the door** à peine avait-il fini de parler que tout le monde s'est précipité vers la porte; **nothing is worse than to spend** *or* **spending the holidays on your own** rien n'est pire que de passer les vacances tout seul

(**c**) *(with "rather", "sooner")* **I'd do anything rather than have to see him** je ferais n'importe quoi plutôt que d'être obligé de le voir; **I'd prefer to stay here rather than go out, I'd rather** *or* **sooner stay here than go out** je préférerais rester ici que de sortir

(**d**) *(after "different")* **he is different than he used to be** il n'est plus le même

2 *prep* (**a**) *(after comparative adj, adv)* que; **he plays tennis better than me** *or* **I** il joue au tennis mieux que moi; **the cedars are older than the oaks** les cèdres sont plus vieux que les chênes

(**b**) *(indicating quantity, number)* de; **more than 15 people** plus de 15 personnes; **fewer than 15 people** moins de 15 personnes; **I've been invited more than once** j'ai été invité plus d'une fois; **there are more policemen than demonstrators** il y a plus de policiers que de manifestants

(**c**) *(after "other" in negative clauses)* **we have no sizes other than 40 or 42** nous n'avons pas d'autres tailles que 40 ou 42; **it was none other than the Prime Minister who launched the appeal** c'est le Premier ministre en personne *ou* lui-même qui a lancé l'appel

(**d**) *(after "different")* **she seems different than before** elle semble avoir changé; **she has different tastes than yours** elle a des goûts différents des vôtres

thanatology [θænə'tɒlədʒɪ] *n Med* thanatologie *f*

thane [θeɪn] *n Hist* thane *m*, ≃ baron *m*

thank [θæŋk] **1** *vt* (**a**) *(in gratitude)* remercier; **to thank sb for sth** remercier qn de *ou* pour qch; *Formal* **Madeleine Barry thanks Mr Dupont for his kind invitation** Madeleine Barry remercie M. Dupont de son invitation; **to thank sb for doing sth** remercier qn d'avoir fait qch; **she thanked us for coming** elle nous remercia d'être venus; **I can't thank you enough for what you've done** je ne sais comment vous remercier pour ce que vous avez fait pour moi; **you have your father to thank for that** tu peux dire merci à ton père pour ça, c'est à ton père que tu dois ça; *Ironic* **you have only yourself to thank for that!** c'est à toi seul qu'il faut t'en prendre!; **you won't thank me for it** vous allez m'en vouloir; **thank God** *or* **goodness!** Dieu merci!; **thank heaven** *or* **heavens you're safe!** Dieu merci vous êtes sain et sauf!

(**b**) *(as request)* **I'll thank you to keep quiet about it** je vous prierai de ne pas en parler; **I'll thank you to mind your own business!** je te prie de t'occuper de ce qui te regarde!

2 thanks 1 *npl* (**a**) *(gen)* remerciements *mpl*; **give her my thanks for the flowers** remerciez-la de ma part pour les fleurs; **(many) thanks for all your help** merci (beaucoup) pour toute votre aide; *Admin* **received with thanks** pour acquit; **that's all the thanks I get!** voilà comment on me remercie! (**b**) *Rel* louange *f*, grâce *f*; **to give thanks to God** rendre grâce à Dieu; **thanks be to God** rendons grâce à Dieu **2** *exclam* merci; **thanks a lot, thanks very much** merci beaucoup, merci bien; **thanks a million** merci mille fois; **thanks for coming** merci d'être venu; **no thanks!** (non) merci!; *Ironic* **thanks for nothing!** je te remercie!

3 thanks to *prep* grâce à; **thanks to you, we saved a lot of money** grâce à vous, nous avons économisé beaucoup d'argent; **thanks to you, we lost the contract** à cause de vous, nous avons perdu le contrat; **no thanks to you!** ce n'est sûrement pas grâce à vous!

▸▸ *Formal* ***thanks offering*** action *f* de grâce; **as a thanks offering** *(gen)* en signe de reconnaissance; *Rel* comme action de grâce

thankful ['θæŋkfʊl] *adj* reconnaissant, content; **to be thankful to sb for sth** être reconnaissant à qn de qch, *esp Formal* savoir gré à qn de qch; **I was thankful to get away** j'étais content de pouvoir partir; **I'm thankful not to have to go back** je suis content de ne pas avoir à y retourner; **she was just thankful (that) no one recognized her** elle s'estimait surtout heureuse que personne ne l'ait reconnue; **you should be thankful for what you have got/that you have your health** tu devrais t'estimer heureux de ce que tu as/d'être en bonne santé; **I'm only thankful everything went off all right** je me félicite que tout se soit bien passé

thankfully ['θæŋkfʊlɪ] *adv* (**a**) *(with gratitude)* avec reconnaissance *ou* gratitude (**b**) *(with relief)* avec soulagement (**c**) *(fortunately)* heureusement

thankfulness ['θæŋkfʊlnɪs] *n* gratitude *f*, reconnaissance *f*

thankless ['θæŋklɪs] *adj (task, person)* ingrat

thanklessly ['θæŋklɪslɪ] *adv* (**a**) *(ungratefully)* avec ingratitude (**b**) *(receiving no thanks)* sans le moindre témoignage de reconnaissance

thanklessness ['θæŋklɪsnɪs] *n* (**a**) *(of person)* ingratitude *f* (**b**) *(of task)* caractère *m* ingrat

Thanksgiving ['θæŋksˌgɪvɪŋ] *n* **Thanksgiving (Day)** *Am* = fête nationale américaine célébrée le quatrième jeudi de novembre; *Can* Action *f* de grâces *(célébrée au Canada le deuxième lundi d'octobre)*

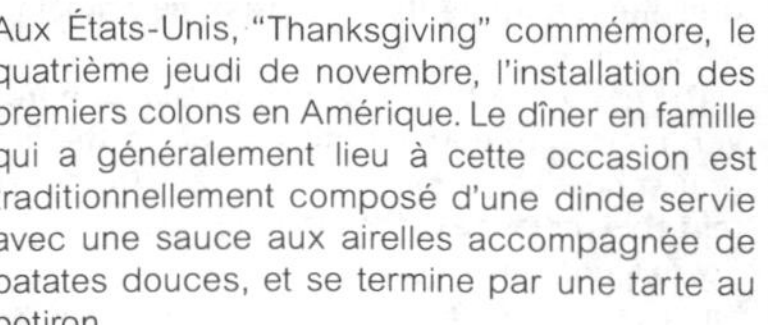

THANKSGIVING

Aux États-Unis, "Thanksgiving" commémore, le quatrième jeudi de novembre, l'installation des premiers colons en Amérique. Le dîner en famille qui a généralement lieu à cette occasion est traditionnellement composé d'une dinde servie avec une sauce aux airelles accompagnée de patates douces, et se termine par une tarte au potiron.

thanksgiving ['θæŋksˌgɪvɪŋ] *n* action *f* de grâce

thank you 1 *exclam* merci; **to say thank you** dire merci; **thank you very** *or* **so much** merci beaucoup *ou* bien; **thank you for the flowers** merci pour les fleurs; **thank you for coming** merci d'être venu; **will you have some tea? – no, thank you** veux-tu du thé? – non merci *ou* non je te remercie

2 thank-you, thank you *n* merci *m*, remerciement *m*; **without so much as a thank-you** sans même dire merci

▸▸ ***thank-you letter*** lettre *f* de remerciement

THAT

ce	▸ 1 (a); 2 (a)
cela	▸ 1 (a)
ça	▸ 1 (a)
celui-là	▸ 1 (b)
celui	▸ 1 (c)
ce…-là	▸ 2 (b)
si	▸ 3 (a), (b)
qui	▸ 4 (a)
que	▸ 4 (b); 5 (a)
lequel	▸ 4 (c)
où	▸ 4 (d)

(*pl* **those** [ðəʊz]) **1** *demonstrative pron* [ðæt] (**a**) *(thing indicated → subject)* ce, cela, ça; *(→ object)* cela, ça; **give me that** donnez-moi ça; **after/before that** après/avant cela; **what's that?** qu'est-ce que c'est que ça?; **who's that?** *(gen)* qui est-ce?; *(on phone)* qui est à l'appareil?; **what's that (that) you're holding?** qu'est-ce que tu as dans la main?; **that's Mr Thomas** c'est M. Thomas; **is that you, Susan?** c'est toi, Susan?; **is that all you've got to eat?** c'est tout ce que vous avez à manger?; **what did she mean by that?** qu'est-ce qu'elle voulait dire par là?; **those are my things** ce sont mes affaires; **those are my orders** voilà mes ordres; **those are my parents** voilà mes parents; **that is what he told me** c'est *ou* voilà ce qu'il m'a dit; **that is where I live** c'est là que j'habite; **that was three months ago** il y a trois mois de cela; **that's strange** c'est bizarre; **I've only got one coat and that's old** je n'ai qu'un manteau et encore, il est vieux; **so THAT'S how it works!** c'est donc comme ça que ça marche!; **so THAT'S settled** bon, ça c'est réglé *ou* voilà qui est réglé; **that's as may be** peut-être bien; *Fam* **it's not as hot as (all) that!** il ne fait pas si chaud que ça!; **so it's come to that** voilà donc où nous en sommes (arrivés); **if it comes to that, you can always leave** si ça en arrive là, vous pouvez toujours partir; **that's a good boy!** en voilà un gentil petit garçon!; **that's all** c'est tout, voilà tout; **that's all we need!** il ne manquait plus que ça!; **that's enough (of that)!** ça suffit!; **that's it!** *(finished)* c'est fini!; *(correct)* c'est ça!; **that's it for today!** ce sera tout pour aujourd'hui!; **that's it! you've got it!** c'est ça! tu as trouvé!; **that's life!** c'est la vie!; **that's more like it!** voilà qui est déjà mieux!; **well, that's that!** eh bien voilà!; **I said "no" and that's that!** j'ai dit "non", un point c'est tout!; **that's the government all over** *or* **for you!** c'est bien l'administration ça!; **is she intelligent? – that she is!** elle est intelligente? – ça oui *ou* pour sûr!; *Fam* **good stuff, that!** ah c'est bon ça!

(**b**) *(in contrast to "this")* celui-là (celle-là) *m,f*; **those** ceux-là (celles-là) *mpl,fpl*; **this is an ash, that is an oak** ceci est un frêne et ça, c'est un chêne; **which book do you prefer, this or**

tex–tha

that? quel livre préférez-vous, celui-ci ou celui-là?; **I'd like some flowers, but not those!** j'aimerais des fleurs, mais pas celles-là!

(**c**) *(used when giving further information)* celui (celle) *m,f*; **those** ceux (celles) *mpl,fpl*; **there are those who believe that...** il y a des gens qui croient que...; **I'm not one of those who...** je ne suis pas du genre à *ou* de ceux qui...; **a sound like that of a baby crying** un bruit comme celui que fait un bébé qui pleure; **the symptoms sound like those of malaria** les symptômes ressemblent à ceux du paludisme; **he spoke with those concerned** il a parlé à ceux qui sont concernés; **all those interested should contact the club secretary** tous ceux qui sont intéressés doivent contacter le secrétaire du club

2 *demonstrative adj* [ðæt] (**a**) *(the one indicated)* ce (cette); **those** ces; **that man** cet homme; **those questions** ces questions; **at that moment** à ce moment-là; **it was raining that day** il pleuvait ce jour-là; **in those days** en ce temps-là, à cette époque; **we all agree on that point** nous sommes tous d'accord là-dessus; **did you hear about that terrible accident on the motorway?** as-tu entendu parler de ce terrible accident sur l'autoroute?; **do you remember that play we saw last year?** tu te rappelles cette pièce que nous avons vue l'année dernière?; **how about that drink you offered me?** et ce verre que vous m'avez proposé?; **I like that idea of his** j'aime son idée; **how's that son of yours?** comment va ton fils?; *Pej* **if I get hold of that son of yours!** si je mets la main sur ton sacré fils!; **that fool of a gardener** cet imbécile de jardinier; **they rode off into the sunset, it was that kind of film** ils se sont éloignés vers le soleil couchant, c'était ce genre de film, tu vois?

(**b**) *(in contrast to "this")* ce...-là (cette...-là); **those** ces...-là; **that house over there is for sale** cette *ou* la maison là-bas est à vendre; **that one** celui-là (celle-là) *m,f*; **choose between this restaurant and that one** choisissez entre ce restaurant et l'autre; *Fam* **that there table** cette table-là❑

3 *adv* [ðæt] (**a**) *(so)* si, aussi; **can you run that fast?** pouvez-vous courir aussi vite que ça?; **he's not (all) that good-looking** il n'est pas si beau que ça; **there's a pile of papers on my desk that high!** il y a une pile de papiers haute comme ça sur mon bureau!; **I don't go there that often** *(not much)* je n'y vais pas très souvent; **I don't go there THAT often** je n'y vais pas aussi souvent que ça

(**b**) *Fam (with result clause)* si❑, tellement❑; **he was that weak he couldn't stand** il était tellement affaibli qu'il ne tenait plus debout; **I could have cried, I was that angry** j'en aurais pleuré tellement j'étais en colère

4 *relative pron* [ðət]

> On peut omettre le pronom relatif **that** sauf s'il est en position sujet.

(**a**) *(subject of verb)* qui; **the conclusions that emerge from this** les conclusions qui en ressortent; **nothing that matters** rien d'important

(**b**) *(object or complement of verb)* que; **the house that Miles built** la maison que Miles a construite; **is this the best that you can do?** est-ce que c'est ce que vous pouvez faire de mieux?; **fool that I am, I agreed** imbécile que je suis, j'ai accepté; **pessimist/optimist that he is** pessimiste/optimiste comme il est

(**c**) *(object of preposition)* lequel (laquelle) *m,f*; **the box that I put it in/on** le carton dans lequel/sur lequel je l'ai mis; **the songs that I was thinking of** *or* **about** les chansons auxquelles je pensais; **the woman/the film that we're talking about** la femme/le film dont nous parlons; **not that I know of** pas que je sache

(**d**) *(when)* où; **the week that he was sick** la semaine où il était malade; **during the months that we were in Chicago** pendant les mois que nous avons passés *ou* où nous étions à Chicago

5 *conj* [ðət]

> Sauf dans la langue soutenue, la conjonction **that** est souvent omise.

(**a**) *(gen)* que; **I said that I had read it** j'ai dit que je l'avais lu; **it's natural that you should be nervous** c'est normal que vous soyez nerveux; **it's not that she isn't friendly** ce n'est pas qu'elle ne soit pas amicale; **I'll see to it that everything is ready** je veillerai à ce que tout soit prêt; **it was so dark that I could barely see** il faisait si noir que je voyais à peine; *Formal* **that he is capable has already been proven** il a déjà prouvé qu'il était capable; *Formal* **that I should live to see the day when...** *(expressing incredulity)* je n'aurais jamais cru qu'un jour...; *Formal* **oh, that it were possible!** si seulement c'était possible!

(**b**) *Arch or Literary (in order that)* afin que, pour que; **he died that we might live** il est mort pour que nous puissions vivre

6 and (all) that *adv Fam (and so on)* et tout le bastringue; **it was a very posh do, waiters in white gloves and (all) that** c'était très classe, avec des serveurs en gants blancs et tout le bastringue; **she went on about friendship and (all) that** elle parlait d'amitié et tout ce qui s'ensuit

7 at that *adv* (**a**) *(what's more)* en plus; **it's a forgery and a pretty poor one at that** c'est une copie et une mauvaise en plus

(**b**) *Fam (indicating agreement)* en fait❑; **perhaps we're not so badly off at that** en fait, on n'est peut-être pas tellement à plaindre; **it might be worth trying at that** ça vaudrait peut-être le coup

(**c**) *(then)* à ce moment-là; **at that, he paused** à ce moment-là, il a marqué un temps d'arrêt

8 like that 1 *adj* (**a**) *(indicating character or attitude)* comme ça; **she's like that, she never says thank you** elle est comme ça, elle ne dit jamais merci; **don't be like that** ne soyez pas comme ça (**b**) *(close, intimate)* comme les deux doigts de la main; **the two of them are like that** ils sont comme les deux doigts de la main; **he's like that with the boss** il est au mieux avec le patron **2** *adv (in that way)* comme ça; **stop looking at me like that!** arrête de me regarder comme ça!

9 not that *conj* **if he refuses, not that he will, is there an alternative?** s'il refuse, même si cela est peu probable, est-ce qu'il y a une autre solution?; **he's already left, not that it matters** il est déjà parti, encore que ce soit sans importance

10 that is (to say) *adv* enfin; **I'll do anything, that's to say anything legal** je ferais n'importe quoi, enfin du moment que c'est légal; **I work at the hospital, as a receptionist that is, not as a nurse** je travaille à l'hôpital, enfin à la réception, pas comme infirmière; **I'd like to ask you something, that is, if you've got a minute** j'aimerais vous poser une question, enfin, si vous avez un instant

11 that way *adv* (**a**) *(in that manner)* de cette façon; **what makes him act that way?** qu'est-ce qui le pousse à agir comme ça?; **that way you'll only make things worse** de cette façon, tu ne feras qu'empirer les choses

(**b**) *Fam (in that respect)* **she's funny that way** c'est son côté bizarre; **I didn't know he was that way inclined** je ne connaissais pas ce côté-là de lui

12 with that *adv* là-dessus; **with that, she left** sur ce *ou* là-dessus, elle est partie

---

thatch [θætʃ] **1** *n* (**a**) *Constr* chaume *m* (**b**) *Br Fam Fig (hair)* tignasse *f*; **a thatch of blonde hair** une crinière blonde

2 *comp (roof)* de *ou* en chaume

3 *vt (roof)* couvrir de chaume

thatched [θætʃt] *adj (roof)* en *ou* de chaume; *(house)* qui a un toit en chaume

▸▸ ***thatched cottage*** chaumière *f*

thatcher ['θætʃə(r)] *n* couvreur *m* en chaume

Thatcherism ['θætʃərɪzəm] *n Pol* thatchérisme *m*

Thatcherite ['θætʃəraɪt] **1** *n* partisan *m* du thatchérisme

2 *adj (policy, view)* thatchérien

thatching ['θætʃɪŋ] *n (UNCOUNT)* couverture *f* de chaume

that's = **that is**

thaw [θɔː] **1** *vi* (**a**) *(ice, snow)* fondre; *(river, lake)* dégeler; **it's beginning to thaw** il commence à dégeler

(**b**) *(frozen food)* dégeler, se décongeler

(**c**) *(get warmer → person, hands)* se réchauffer

(**d**) *Fig (person, relations)* se dégeler, être plus détendu; **she seems at last to be thawing towards me** elle semble enfin perdre sa réserve *ou* sa froideur à mon égard

2 *vt* (**a**) *(ice, snow)* faire dégeler *ou* fondre

(**b**) *(frozen food)* dégeler, décongeler

3 *n* (**a**) *Met* dégel *m*

(**b**) *Pol* détente *f*, dégel *m*; *Fig* **a thaw in relations** un dégel *ou* une détente des relations

▸**thaw out 1** *vt sep* (**a**) *(frozen food)* décongeler, dégeler

(**b**) *(feet, hands)* réchauffer; **come and thaw yourself out in the sitting room** venez vous réchauffer au salon

(**c**) *Fig (make relaxed → person)* dégeler, mettre à l'aise

2 *vi* (**a**) *(frozen food)* se décongeler

(**b**) *(hands, feet)* se réchauffer; **I'm beginning to thaw out now** je commence à me réchauffer maintenant

(**c**) *Fig (become relaxed)* se dégeler, perdre sa froideur *ou* réserve

thawing ['θɔːɪŋ] *n (of river, lake)* dégel *m*; *(of snow, ice)* fonte *f*; *(of frozen food)* décongélation *f*; **a thawing in relations** un dégel *ou* une détente des relations

the [*before consonant sounds* ðə, *before vowel sounds* ðɪ, *stressed* ðiː] *def art* (**a**) *(singular)* le (la); *(plural)* les; **the blue dress is the prettiest** la robe bleue est la plus jolie; **the dead/poor** les morts *mpl*/pauvres *mpl*; **the French/Germans** les Français *mpl*/Allemands *mpl*; **I can't do the impossible** je ne peux pas faire l'impossible; **translated from the Latin** traduit du latin; **she's giving up her job – the woman's mad!** elle quitte son emploi – c'est une folle!

(**b**) *(with names, titles)* **the Smiths/Martins** les Smith/Martin; **Alexander the Great** Alexandre le Grand; **Elizabeth the First** Élisabeth Première

(**c**) *(with numbers, dates etc)* **Monday June the tenth** *or* **the tenth of June** le lundi 10 juin; **on the Monday he fell ill** le lundi il est tombé malade; **the 80s** *(decade)* les années 80; **the temperature was in the 80s** il faisait environ 25°C; **the 1820s** les années 1820 à 1830; **in the summer of 1946** pendant l'été 1946; **the second from the left** le second en partant de la gauche

(**d**) *(in prices, quantities)* **tomatoes are 40p the pound** les tomates sont à 40 pence la livre; **the car does 40 miles to the gallon** la voiture consomme 7 litres aux 100

(**e**) *(with comparatives)* **the more the better** plus il y en a, mieux c'est; **the less said the better** moins on en parlera, mieux cela vaudra; **the sooner the better** le plus tôt sera le mieux

(**f**) *(stressed form)* **for him Bach is THE composer** pour lui, Bach est le compositeur par excellence; **the Olympics are THE event this winter** les jeux Olympiques sont l'événement à ne pas manquer cet hiver; **do you mean THE John Irving?** vous voulez dire le célèbre John Irving?

(**g**) *(enough → singular)* le (la); *(→ plural)* les; **I haven't the time/money to do it** je n'ai pas le temps de/l'argent pour le faire

(**h**) *(instead of possessive adj)* **she took him by the hand** elle l'a pris par la main; *Fam* **how's the wife?** comment va la femme?; *Fam* **well, how's the throat then?** eh bien, et cette gorge?; **I've brought the family along** j'ai emmené la famille

thearchy ['θiːɑːkɪ] (*pl* **thearchies**) *n* théocratie *f*

theatre, *Am* **theater** ['θɪətə(r)] **1** *n* (**a**) *(building)* théâtre *m*; **to go to the theatre** aller au théâtre; **a night at the theatre** une soirée au théâtre

(**b**) *(drama)* théâtre *m*, art *m* dramatique; *(plays in general)* théâtre *m*; *(profession)* théâtre *m*; **Greek/modern theatre** le théâtre grec/moderne; **Shakespeare's theatre** le théâtre de Shakespeare; **I've been in the theatre for over thirty years** je fais du théâtre depuis plus de trente ans

(**c**) *(hall)* salle *f* de spectacle; *(for lectures)* salle *f* de conférences; *Univ* amphithéâtre *m*

(**d**) *Med* **(operating) theatre** salle *f* d'opération; **she's in (the) theatre** *(doctor)* elle est en salle d'opération; *(patient)* elle est sur la table d'opération

(**e**) *Fig (for important event)* théâtre *m*; *Mil* **the**

southern/eastern theatres les fronts *mpl* du sud/de l'est

2 *comp* (**a**) *(programme, tickets)* de théâtre; *(manager)* de théâtre

(**b**) *Med (staff, nurse)* de salle d'opération; *(routine, job)* dans la salle d'opération

►► ***theatre of the absurd*** théâtre *m* de l'absurde; ***theatre bill*** affiche *f* de théâtre; ***theatre company*** troupe *f* de théâtre, compagnie *f* théâtrale; ***theatre critic*** critique *mf* théâtral(e) *ou* de théâtre; *Mil* ***theatre of operations*** théâtre *m* d'opérations; ***theatre in the round*** théâtre *m* en rond; *Med* ***theatre sister*** infirmière *f* au bloc opératoire; *Mil* ***theatre of war*** théâtre *m* des hostilités; ***theatre workshop*** atelier *m* de théâtre

theatregoer, *Am* **theatergoer** ['θɪətə,gəʊə(r)] *n* amateur *m* de théâtre; **they're regular theatregoers** ils vont régulièrement au théâtre

theatregoing, *Am* **theatergoing** ['θɪətə,gəʊɪŋ] **1** *adj* **the theatregoing public** ceux qui vont au théâtre

2 *n* fréquentation *f* des théâtres

theatreland ['θɪətəlænd] *n Br* quartier *m* des théâtres; **in theatreland** dans le quartier des théâtres

theatrical [θɪ'ætrɪkəl] **1** *adj* (**a**) *Theat (performance, season)* théâtral

(**b**) *Fig (exaggerated* → *gesture, behaviour)* théâtral, affecté; **there's no need to resort to such theatrical behaviour** c'est inutile de faire toute cette comédie

2 theatricals *npl* (**a**) *Theat* théâtre *m* d'amateur

(**b**) *Fig* cinéma *m*, comédie *f*; **I'm fed up with all her theatricals** j'en ai assez de son cinéma

►► ***theatrical agent*** agent *m* (de théâtre); ***theatrical producer*** producteur(trice) *m,f* de théâtre

theatrically [θɪ'ætrɪklɪ] *adv* théâtralement

thebaine ['θi:bəi:n] *n Pharm* thébaïne *f*

Theban ['θi:bən] **1** *n* Thébain(e) *m,f*

2 *adj* thébain

Thebes [θi:bz] *n* Thèbes

theca ['θi:kə] *n* (**a**) *Bot* loge *f* (**b**) *Zool* thèque *f*

thee [ði:] *pron Bible & Arch* te; *(after prep)* toi; **we beseech thee** nous te supplions

theft [θeft] *n* vol *m*; **to commit theft** commettre un vol; **to be charged with theft** être inculpé de vol

their [ðeə(r), *unstressed* ðə(r)] *adj (singular)* leur; *(plural)* leurs; **their car** leur voiture; **their clothes** leurs vêtements; **their father and mother** leur père et leur mère, leurs père et mère; **their eyes are blue** ils ont les yeux bleus; **somebody's left their umbrella behind** quelqu'un a oublié son parapluie; **a house of their own** leur propre maison, une maison à eux; **everyone must bring their own book** chacun doit apporter son livre; **nobody in their right mind would do such a thing!** personne de sensé ne ferait une chose pareille!; **Their Highnesses the King and the Queen** Leurs Majestés le roi et la reine

theirs [ðeəz] *pron* (**a**) *(gen* → *singular)* le leur (la leur) *m,f*; *(*→ *plural)* les leurs *mfpl*; **our car is sturdier than theirs** notre voiture est plus solide que la leur; **I like that painting of theirs** j'aime leur tableau; **I really can't stand that dog of theirs** je ne supporte pas leur sacré chien; **a friend of theirs** un ami à eux/elles, un de leurs amis; **is this yours or theirs?** est-ce que ceci est à vous ou à eux?; **it is not theirs to choose** ce n'est pas à eux de choisir, le choix ne leur appartient pas; **if anyone hasn't got theirs, they can use mine** si quelqu'un n'a pas le sien, il pourra utiliser le mien

(**b**) *Fam (their house, flat* → *gen)* chez eux ❑; *(*→ *female household)* chez elles ❑

theism ['θi:ɪzəm] *n Rel* théisme *m*

theist ['θi:ɪst] *Rel* **1** *adj* théiste

2 *n* théiste *mf*

theistic ['θi:ɪstɪk] *adj Rel* théiste

them [ðem, *unstressed* ðəm] **1** *pron* (**a**) *(direct object)* les; **I met them last week** je les ai rencontrés la semaine dernière

(**b**) *(indirect object)* leur; **we bought/gave them some flowers** nous leur avons acheté/donné des fleurs

(**c**) *(after preposition)* **it's for them** c'est pour eux; **the yacht belongs to them** le yacht leur appartient; **both of them are wool** ils sont tous les deux en laine; **she's brighter than them** elle est plus intelligente qu'eux; **neither of them is happy** ils ne sont heureux ni l'un ni l'autre; **I don't want any of them** je n'en veux aucun; **a few of them seemed genuinely interested** quelques-uns d'entre eux semblaient vraiment intéressés; **all of them came** ils sont tous venus; **most of them are busy** la plupart d'entre eux sont occupés; **it was good of them to come** c'était gentil de leur part *ou* à eux de venir

(**d**) *Fam (as indefinite pronoun)* **when anyone comes she says to them...** quand quelqu'un vient elle lui dit... ❑

2 *adj Fam (those)* ces; **them shoes/kids** ces bouquins/gamins

thematic [θɪ'mætɪk] *adj* thématique

►► *Mktg* ***thematic apperception test*** test *m* d'aperception thématique

theme [θi:m] *n* (**a**) *(subject, topic)* thème *m*, sujet *m*

(**b**) *Mus* thème *m*; **theme and variations** thème *m* et variations *fpl*

(**c**) *Gram & Ling* thème *m*

►► ***theme music*** *Rad & TV (of programme)* générique *m*; *Cin (in film)* thème *m* principal de la musique d'un/du film; ***theme park*** parc *m* à thème; ***theme pub*** bar *m* à thème; ***theme song*** *(from film)* chanson *f* (de film); *Am (signature tune)* indicatif *m*; **the theme song from 'The Graduate'** la chanson du film 'Le Lauréat'; ***theme tune*** *(from film)* musique *f* (de film); *Br (signature tune)* indicatif *m*; **the theme tune from 'Brookside'** l'indicatif de 'Brookside'

themed [θi:md] *adj (pub, restaurant)* à thème

►► ***themed evening, themed night*** soirée *f* thématique

Themis ['θi:mɪs] *pr n Myth* Thémis

Themistocles [θə'mɪstəkli:z] *pr n Antiq* Thémistocle

themselves [ðəm'selvz] *pron* (**a**) *(reflexive use)* **they hurt themselves** ils se sont fait mal; **the girls enjoyed themselves** les filles se sont bien amusées; **the children could see themselves in the mirror** les enfants se voyaient dans la glace

(**b**) *(emphatic use)* eux-mêmes (elles-mêmes) *mpl,fpl*; **they had to come themselves** ils ont dû venir eux-mêmes *ou* en personne; **they painted the house themselves** ils ont peint la maison eux-mêmes; **they came by themselves** ils sont venus tout seuls

(**c**) *(referring to things)* eux-mêmes (elles-mêmes) *mpl,fpl*; **the boxes themselves aren't very heavy** les boîtes (en) elles-mêmes ne sont pas très lourdes; **the details in themselves are not important** ce ne sont pas les détails en eux-mêmes qui sont importants

(**d**) *Fam (indefinite use)* **if anybody hurts themselves** si quelqu'un se fait mal ❑

then [ðen] **1** *adv* (**a**) *(at a particular time)* alors, à ce moment-là; *(in distant past)* à l'époque, à cette époque, à cette époque-là; **we were very young then** nous étions très jeunes à l'époque; **we can talk about it then** nous pourrons en parler à ce moment-là; **Marilyn, or Norma Jean as she then was known** Marilyn, ou Norma Jean comme elle s'appelait alors; **by then** *(in future)* d'ici là; *(in past)* entre-temps; **from then on** à partir de ce moment-là; **since then** depuis (lors); **until then** *(in future)* jusque-là; *(in past)* jusqu'alors, jusqu'à ce moment-là

(**b**) *(afterwards, next)* puis, ensuite; **we went shopping, then we had lunch** nous avons fait des courses, puis nous avons déjeuné; **do your homework first, then you can watch TV** fais d'abord tes devoirs, et ensuite tu pourras regarder la télé; **on the left the church, then a few old houses** à gauche l'église, puis *ou* ensuite quelques vieilles maisons; **you then take the sliced onions...** prenez ensuite les oignons émincés...

(**c**) *(so, in that case)* donc, alors; **what do you suggest then?** qu'est-ce que vous suggérez alors?; **you were right then!** mais alors, vous aviez raison!; **I'll see you at 6 then** bon, je te retrouve à 6 heures alors; **right then, anyone for more tea?** bon alors, qui d'autre veut du thé?; **if... then...** si... alors...; **if x equals 10 then y...** si x égale 10 alors y...; **if it's not in my bag, then look in the cupboard** si ce n'est pas dans mon sac, regarde dans le placard

(**d**) *(also)* et puis; **then there's Peter to invite** et puis il faut inviter Peter

(**e**) *(therefore)* donc; **these then are the main problems** voici donc les principaux problèmes; **its significance, then, is twofold** sa signification, donc, est double

2 *adj* d'alors, de l'époque; **the then head of department** le chef du département d'alors *ou* de l'époque

3 then again *adv* **and then again, you may prefer to forget it** mais enfin peut-être que vous préférez ne plus y penser; **but then again, no one can be sure** mais après tout, on ne sait jamais

thenar ['θi:nə(r)] *n Anat* (**a**) *(base of thumb)* thénar *m* (**b**) *(palm)* paume *f*

►► ***thenar eminence*** éminence *f* thénar, thénar *m*

thence [ðens] *adv Literary or Formal* (**a**) *(from that place)* de là, de ce lieu, de ce lieu-là (**b**) *(from that time)* depuis lors (**c**) *(therefore)* par conséquent

thenceforth [,ðens'fɔ:θ], **thenceforward** [,ðens'fɔ:wəd] *adv Literary or Formal* dès lors, désormais

theobromine [,θi:ə'brəʊmi:n] *n Pharm* théobromine *f*

theocentric [θɪə'sentrɪk] *adj* théocentrique

theocracy [θɪ'ɒkrəsɪ] (*pl* **theocracies**) *n* théocratie *f*

theocrat ['θɪəkræt] *n* théocrate *mf*

theocratic [,θɪə'krætɪk] *adj* théocratique

theocratically [,θɪə'krætɪklɪ] *adv* théocratiquement

Theocritus [θɪ'ɒkrɪtəs] *pr n* Théocrite

theodolite [θɪ'ɒdəlaɪt] *n* théodolite *m*

Theodosius [,θɪə'dəʊsɪəs] *pr n* Théodose

theolinguistics [,θi:əʊlɪŋ'gwɪstɪks] *n (UNCOUNT)* étude *f* du langage religieux

theologian [,θɪə'ləʊdʒən] *n* théologien(enne) *m,f*

theological [,θɪə'lɒdʒɪkəl] *adj* théologique

►► ***theological college*** séminaire *m*

theologically [,θɪə'lɒdʒɪklɪ] *adv* théologiquement; *(from a theological point of view)* d'un point de vue théologique

theology [θɪ'ɒlədʒɪ] (*pl* **theologies**) *n* théologie *f*

theomachy [θɪ'ɒməkɪ] (*pl* **theomachies**) *n* guerre *f* des dieux

theomancy ['θɪəmænsɪ] *n* théomancie *f*

theomania [,θɪə'meɪnɪə] *n Med* théomanie *f*

theomaniac [,θɪə'meɪnɪæk] *n Med* théomaniaque *mf*

theophobia [,θɪə'fəʊbɪə] *n* théophobie *f*

Theophrastus [,θi:ə'fræstəs] *pr n Antiq* Théophraste

theorbo [θɪ'ɔ:bəʊ] (*pl* **theorbos**) *n Mus* téorbe *m*, théorbe *m*

theorem ['θɪərəm] *n* théorème *m*

theorematic [,θɪərə'mætɪk] *adj* théorématique

theoretical [,θɪə'retɪkəl] *adj* théorique

►► ***theoretical physics*** physique *f* théorique

theoretically [,θɪə'retɪklɪ] *adv* théoriquement, en principe

theoretician [,θɪərə'tɪʃən] *n* théoricien(enne) *m,f*

theoretics [,θɪə'retɪks] *n (UNCOUNT)* théorétique *f*; **theoretics and practice** la théorie et la pratique

theorist ['θɪərɪst] *n* théoricien(enne) *m,f*

theorization [,θɪəraɪ'zeɪʃən] *n* théorisation *f*

theorize, -ise ['θɪə,raɪz] **1** *vi* (**a**) *(speculate)* théoriser, faire des théories; **analysts have theorized about the reasons for this** les analystes ont émis toutes sortes de théories pour expliquer cela; **it's no use theorizing, we have to make a decision** ça ne sert à rien de faire de grandes théories, il faut qu'on prenne une décision

(**b**) *(scientist)* élaborer des théories

2 *vt* **scientists theorized that the space probe would disintegrate** les scientifiques émirent l'hypothèse que la sonde spatiale se désintégrerait

theorizer ['θɪə,raɪzə(r)] *n* théoricien(enne) *m,f*

theorizing ['θɪə,raɪzɪŋ] *n* théorisation *f*

theory ['θɪərɪ] (*pl* **theories**) **1** *n* (**a**) *(hypothesis)* théorie *f*; **I have a theory about his disappearance** j'ai mon idée sur sa disparition; **the theory of evolution** la théorie de l'évolution; **the theory of relativity** la théorie de la relativité (**b**) *(principles, rules)* théorie *f*; **musical theory** théorie *f* musicale

2 in theory *adv* en théorie, théoriquement, en principe

theosophical [ˌθɪəˈsɒfɪkəl] *adj* théosophique

theosophist [θɪˈɒsəfɪst] *n* théosophe *mf*

theosophy [θɪˈɒsəfɪ] *n* théosophie *f*

therapeutic [ˌθerəˈpjuːtɪk] *adj* thérapeutique; *Fig* **she finds gardening therapeutic** elle trouve que le jardinage lui fait beaucoup de bien

▸▸ ***therapeutic community*** communauté *f* thérapeutique

therapeutically [ˌθerəˈpjuːtɪklɪ] *adv* **used therapeutically** utilisé comme thérapeutique

therapeutics [ˌθerəˈpjuːtɪks] *n (UNCOUNT) Med* thérapeutique *f*

therapist [ˈθerəpɪst] *n* thérapeute *mf*

therapy [ˈθerəpɪ] *(pl* **therapies***) n* thérapie *f*; **to go for** *or* **to be in therapy** suivre une thérapie

THERE [ðeə(r), *unstressed* ðə(r)]

là	▸ **1 (a) – (d)**
y	▸ **1 (a)**
il y a	▸ **2**

1 *adv* (**a**) *(in or to a particular place)* là, y; **they aren't there** ils ne sont pas là, ils n'y sont pas; **we never go there** nous n'y allons jamais; **we're there!** nous voilà arrivés!; **who's there?** qui est là?; **is Margot there?** est-ce que Margot est là?; **see that woman there? that's Marlene** tu vois cette femme là-bas? c'est Marlene; **so there we were/I was** donc, on était/j'étais là; **she got there in the end** *(reached a place)* elle a fini par arriver; *(completed a task)* elle a fini par y arriver; **put it there** mets-le là; *(shake my hand)* serre-moi la main; **it's there on the desk** c'est là sur le bureau; **she just sat/stood there** elle était assise/debout là; **move along there, please!** circulez, s'il vous plaît; **we go to Paris and from there to Rome** nous allons à Paris et de là à Rome, **here and there** çà et là, **there it is** le voilà; **it's around there somewhere** c'est quelque part par là; **back there** là-bas; **in there** là-dedans; **on there** là-dessus; **over there** là-bas; **under there** là-dessous; **that car there** cette voiture-là; **those cars there** ces voitures-là; **your friend there** votre ami; *Fam Fig* **I've been there** je suis passé par là, j'ai connu ça; *Fam* **I've been there before** non merci, j'ai déjà donné; *Fam* **been there, done that (got the T-shirt)** non merci, j'ai déjà donné

(**b**) *(available)* là; **it's there if you need it** c'est là si tu en as besoin; **she's always been there for me** elle a toujours été là quand j'avais besoin d'elle

(**c**) *(in existence)* là; **I couldn't believe he was really there** je n'arrivais pas à croire qu'il était vraiment là; **the central problem is still there** le principal problème est toujours là

(**d**) *(on or at a particular point)* là; **we disagree there, there we disagree** nous ne sommes pas d'accord là-dessus; **there's** *or* **there lies the difficulty** voilà le problème, le problème est là; **there you're wrong** là vous vous trompez; **you're right there** là vous avez raison; **let's leave it there** restons-en là; **we'll have to stop there for today** nous nous arrêterons là pour aujourd'hui; **could I just stop you there?** puis-je vous interrompre ici?; **as for the food, I've no complaints there** pour ce qui est de la nourriture, là je n'ai pas à me plaindre; *Fam* **you've got me there!** là, je ne sais pas quoi vous répondre *ou* dire!

(**e**) *(drawing attention to someone or something)* **hello** *or* **hi there!** salut!; **hey there!** hep, vous là-bas!; **there they are!** les voilà!; **there they come** les voilà (qui arrivent); **there you go again!** ça y est, vous recommencez!; **there she goes, complaining again!** voilà qu'elle recommence à se plaindre!; **there's the bell, I must be going** tiens ça sonne, je dois partir; *Ironic* **there's gratitude for you** c'est beau la reconnaissance!; **now finish your homework, there's a good boy** maintenant sois un grand garçon et finis tes devoirs

(**f**) *(idiom)* **he's not all** *or* **not quite there** *(stupid)* il n'a pas toute sa tête; *(senile)* il n'a plus toute sa tête

2 *pron* **there is** *(used before singular noun)* il y a; **there are** *(used before plural noun)* il y a; **there was/were** il y avait; **there will be** il y aura; **there is** *or* **there's a book on the table** il y a un livre sur la table; **there are some books on the table** il y a des livres sur la table; **there isn't any** il n'y en a pas; **there's a bus coming** il y a un bus qui arrive; **well, there's that girl I was telling you about before...** il y a bien cette fille dont je t'ai déjà parlé...; **what happens if there's a change of plan?** qu'est-ce qui se passe si on change d'idée?; **there must have been a mistake** il a dû y avoir une erreur; **there was once a king** il était *ou* il y avait une fois un roi; **there was singing and dancing** on a chanté et dansé; **there were some pieces missing** il manquait des pièces; **there weren't any more, were there?** il n'en restait pas, si?; **there's one slice left** il reste une tranche; **there are** *or Fam* **there's two slices left** il reste deux tranches; **there's nothing we can do to help them** on ne peut rien faire pour les aider; **there's no stopping her** rien ne peut l'arrêter; **there's no knowing what he'll do next** il est impossible de prévoir ce qu'il fera ensuite; **there was no denying it** c'était indéniable; **there now follows a party political broadcast** = formule annonçant la diffusion télévisée des messages électoraux des différents partis; **there comes a time when you have to slow down** il arrive un moment où il faut ralentir le rythme; **there still remain several points to be resolved** il reste encore plusieurs problèmes à résoudre; **there arose a murmur of disapproval** un murmure de désapprobation s'éleva

3 *exclam* (**a**) *(soothing)* **there now, don't cry!** allons *ou* là! ne pleure pas!; **there, that wasn't so bad, was it?** voilà, ça n'était pas si terrible que ça, si?; **there, there!** allez!

(**b**) *(aggressive)* **there (now), what did I say?** voilà, qu'est-ce que je t'avais dit?; **there, now you've made me lose count!** et voilà, tu m'as fait perdre le compte!

(**c**) *(finishing task)* **there (now), that's done!** là! voilà qui est fait!

(**d**) *(after all)* **but, there, it's not surprising** mais enfin, ce n'est pas surprenant

4 so there *exclam* voilà!

5 there again *adv* après tout; **but there again, no one really knows** mais après tout, personne ne sait vraiment

6 there and back *adv* **we did the trip there and back in three hours** nous avons fait l'aller retour en trois heures; **it will take you about an hour/cost you about £50 there and back** l'aller retour vous prendra à peu près une heure/vous coûtera environ 50 livres

7 there and then, then and there *adv* sur-le-champ; **I decided there and then to have no more to do with him** j'ai tout de suite décidé de ne plus avoir affaire à lui

8 there you are, there you go *adv* (**a**) *(never mind)* **it wasn't the ideal solution, but there you are** *or* **go** ce n'était pas l'idéal, mais enfin *ou* mais qu'est-ce que vous voulez

(**b**) *(it's done)* **just press the button and there you are** *or* **go!** vous n'avez qu'à appuyer sur le bouton et ça y est!

(**c**) *(I told you so)* voilà, ça y est

(**d**) *(here you are)* tenez, voilà

thereabouts [ˈðeərəbaʊts], *Am* **thereabout** [ˈðeərəbaʊt] *adv* (**a**) *(indicating place)* par là, dans les environs, pas loin; **somewhere thereabouts** quelque part par là (**b**) *(indicating quantity, weight)* à peu près, environ (**c**) *(indicating price)* environ; **£10 or thereabouts** 10 livres environ (**d**) *(indicating time)* aux alentours de; **at 10 p.m. or thereabouts** aux alentours de 22 heures, vers 10 heures du soir

thereafter [ˌðeərˈɑːftə(r)] *adv Formal* (**a**) *(subsequently)* par la suite (**b**) *(below)* ci-dessous

thereat [ˌðeərˈæt] *adv Arch or Formal* (**a**) *(of place)* là (**b**) *(of time)* alors

thereby [ˌðeəˈbaɪ] *adv* (**a**) *Formal* de ce fait, ainsi (**b**) *(idiom)* **thereby hangs a tale!** c'est une longue histoire!

therefore [ˈðeəfɔː(r)] *adv* donc, par conséquent; **I think, therefore I am** je pense, donc je suis

therefrom [ˌðeəˈfrɒm] *adv Arch or Formal* de là

therein [ˌðeərˈɪn] *adv Law or Formal* (**a**) *(within)* à l'intérieur; **the box and all that is contained therein** la boîte et son contenu (**b**) *(in that respect)* là; **therein lies the difficulty** là est la difficulté; **therein you are mistaken** en cela vous vous trompez

thereinafter [ˌðeərɪnˈɑːftə(r)] *adv Law* ci-après

thereof [ˌðeərˈɒv] *adv Arch or Formal* de cela, en; **all citizens of the republic are subject to the laws thereof** tous les citoyens de la république doivent se soumettre aux lois de celle-ci; **he ate thereof** il en mangea

thereon [ˌðeərˈɒn] *adv Arch or Formal* (**a**) *(on that subject)* là-dessus (**b**) *(then)* sur ce

there's = **there is**

thereto [ˌðeəˈtuː] *adv Law or Formal* **the letter attached thereto** la lettre ci-jointe; **a copy of the Bill and the amendments thereto** une copie du projet de loi et de ses amendements

theretofore [ˌðeətuːˈfɔː(r)] *adv Law or Formal* jusqu'alors, avant cela

thereunder [ðeərˈʌndə(r)] *adv Law or Formal* là-dessous, en dessous

thereupon [ˌðeərəˈpɒn] *adv* (**a**) *Formal (then)* sur ce (**b**) *Law or Formal (on that subject)* à ce sujet, là-dessus

therewith [ˌðeəˈwɪð] *adv* (**a**) *Law (with)* avec cela; *(in addition)* en outre (**b**) *Arch (then)* sur ce

therm [θɜːm] *n Br* $\simeq$ 1,055 x 10^8 joules *(unité de chaleur)*

thermal [ˈθɜːməl] **1** *adj* (**a**) *Phys (energy, insulation)* thermique; *(conductor, unit)* thermique, de chaleur

(**b**) *(stream)* thermal

(**c**) *(underwear)* en Thermolactyl®

2 *n Aviat & Met* thermique *m*, ascendance *f* thermique

3 thermals *npl (thermal underwear)* sous-vêtements *mpl* en Thermolactyl®

▸▸ ***thermal baths*** thermes *mpl*; ***thermal imager*** caméra *f* thermique; ***thermal imaging*** thermographie *f*; *Comput* ***thermal paper*** papier *m* thermique *ou* thermosensible; *Comput* ***thermal printer*** imprimante *f* thermique *ou* thermoélectrique; ***thermal reactor*** réacteur *m* thermique; ***thermal shield*** bouclier *m* thermique; ***thermal springs*** eaux *fpl ou* sources *fpl* thermales

thermic [ˈθɜːmɪk] *adj Phys* thermique

thermion [ˈθɜːmɪən] *n Phys* thermion *m*

thermionic [ˌθɜːmɪˈɒnɪk] *Phys* **1** *adj* thermoïonique, thermoélectronique

2 thermionics étude *f* des émissions thermoïoniques *ou* thermoélectroniques

▸▸ ***thermionic emission*** émission *f* thermoïonique; *Am* ***thermionic tube***, *Br* ***thermionic valve*** tube *m* thermoïonique *ou* thermoélectronique

thermistor [θɜːˈmɪstə(r)] *n* thermistor *m*

thermobarometer [ˌθɜːməʊbəˈrɒmɪtə(r)] *n* thermobaromètre *m*

thermochemical [ˌθɜːməʊˈkemɪkəl] *adj* thermochimique

thermochemist [ˌθɜːməʊˈkemɪst] *n* thermochimiste *mf*

thermochemistry [ˌθɜːməʊˈkemɪstrɪ] *n* thermochimie *f*

thermocouple [ˈθɜːməʊkʌpəl] *n* thermocouple *m*

thermodynamic [ˌθɜːməʊdaɪˈnæmɪk] *adj* thermodynamique

thermodynamics [ˌθɜːməʊdaɪˈnæmɪks] *n (UNCOUNT)* thermodynamique *f*

thermoelectric [ˌθɜːməʊɪˈlektrɪk], **thermoelectrical** [ˌθɜːməʊɪˈlektrɪkəl] *adj* thermoélectrique

thermoelectricity [ˌθɜːməʊɪlekˈtrɪsətɪ] *n* thermoélectricité *f*

thermoelectron [ˌθɜːməʊɪˈlektrɒn] *n* électron *m* thermique

▸▸ ***thermoelectron emission*** émission *f* thermionique

thermograph [ˌθɜːməʊˈgrɑːf] *n* thermographe *m*

thermography [θɜːˈmɒgrəfɪ] *n* thermographie *f*

thermoluminescence [θɜːməʊˌluːmɪˈnesəns] *n* thermoluminescence *f*

▸▸ *Archeol* ***thermoluminescence dating*** datation *f* par thermoluminescence

thermomagnetic [ˌθɜːməʊmægˈnetɪk] *adj Phys* thermomagnétique

the–the

thermomagnetism [ˌθɜːməʊˈmægnɪˌtɪzəm] *n Phys* thermomagnétisme *m*

thermometer [θəˈmɒmɪtə(r)] *n* thermomètre *m*

thermometry [θəˈmɒmɪtrɪ] *n Phys* thermométrie *f*

thermonuclear [ˌθɜːməʊˈnjuːklɪə(r)] *adj* thermonucléaire

thermophile [ˈθɜːməʊfaɪl], **thermophil** [ˈθɜːməʊfɪl] *Biol* **1** *adj* thermophile
2 *n* thermophile *m*

thermopile [ˈθɜːməʊpaɪl] *n* thermopile *f*

thermoplastic [ˌθɜːməʊˈplæstɪk] **1** *adj* thermoplastique
2 *n* thermoplastique *m*

Thermos® [ˈθɜːmɒs] *n* Thermos® *m ou f*
►► ***Thermos® flask*** (bouteille *f*) Thermos® *m ou f*

thermoscope [ˈθɜːməʊskəʊp] *n* thermoscope *m*

thermoscopic [ˌθɜːməʊˈskɒpɪk] *adj* thermoscopique

thermosensitive [ˌθɜːməʊˈsensɪtɪv] *adj* thermosensible

thermosetting [ˈθɜːməʊˌsetɪŋ] *adj* thermodurcissable

thermosphere [ˈθɜːməʊsfɪə(r)] *n* thermosphère *f*

thermostat [ˈθɜːməʊstæt] *n* thermostat *m*

thermostatic [ˌθɜːməʊˈstætɪk] *adj* thermostatique

thermostatically [ˌθɜːməʊˈstætɪklɪ] *adv* **thermostatically controlled** contrôlé par thermostat

thermotaxis [ˌθɜːməʊˈtæksɪs] *n* thermotaxie *f*

thermotherapy [ˌθɜːməʊˈθerəpɪ] *n* thermothérapie *f*

thesaurus [θɪˈsɔːrəs] (*pl* **thesauri** [-raɪ] *or* **thesauruses** [-sɪz]) *n* (**a**) *(book of synonyms)* ≃ dictionnaire *m* analogique (**b**) *Comput* thésaurus *m*

these [ðiːz] *pl of* **this**

Theseus [ˈθiːsɪəs] *pr n Myth* Thésée

thesis [ˈθiːsɪs] (*pl* **theses** [-siːz]) *n (gen) & Univ* thèse *f*

thesp [θesp] *n Br Fam* acteur(trice)❑ *m,f*

thespian [ˈθespɪən] *Formal or Hum* **1** *adj* dramatique, de théâtre
2 *n* acteur(trice) *m,f*

Thessalonians [ˌθesəˈləʊnɪənz] *npl* Thessaloniciens *mpl*; **the Epistle of Paul to the Thessalonians** l'Épître *f* de saint Paul aux Thessaloniciens

Thessaly [ˈθesəlɪ] *n* Thessalie *f*; **in Thessaly** en Thessalie

theta [ˈθiːtə] *n* thêta *m*

theurgy [ˈθiːɜːdʒɪ] (*pl* **theurgies**) *n* théurgie *f*

thew [θjuː] *n* (**a**) *(tendon)* tendon *m*; *(muscle)* muscle *m*; **he has thews of steel** il a des nerfs d'acier (**b**) *Fig* **thews** ardeur *f*, vigueur *f*

they [ðeɪ] *pron* (**a**) *(subject)* ils (elles) *mpl,fpl*; *(stressed form)* eux (elles) *mpl,fpl*; **they've left** ils sont partis; **THEY bought the flowers** ce sont eux qui ont acheté les fleurs; **oh, there they are!** ah, les voilà!; **they say that she married him for his money** on prétend qu'elle l'a épousé pour son argent
(**b**) *Fam (after indefinite pronoun or to replace "he/she")* **nobody ever admits they're wrong** on ne veut jamais reconnaître qu'on a tort; **each candidate must be told that they should...** chaque candidat doit être informé qu'il doit...

they'd [ðeɪd] (**a**) = **they had** (**b**) = **they would**

they'll [ðeɪl] = **they will**

they're [ðeə(r)] = **they are**

they've [ðeɪv] = **they have**

thiamin [ˈθaɪəmɪn], **thiamine** [ˈθaɪəmiːn] *n* thiamine *f*

thiazole [ˈθaɪəzəʊl], **thiazol** [ˈθaɪəzɒl] *n* thiazole *m*

thick [θɪk] **1** *adj* (**a**) *(wall, slice, writing)* épais(aisse), gros(grosse); *(print)* gras(grasse); *(lips)* épais(aisse), charnu; *(shoes, boots)* gros (grosse); **the boots have a thick fur lining** les bottes sont doublées de fourrure épaisse; **the snow was thick on the ground** il y avait une épaisse couche de neige sur le sol; **the boards are 20 cm thick** les planches ont une épaisseur de 20 cm, les planches font 20 cm d'épaisseur; *Br Fam* **to give sb a thick ear** donner une gifle à qn; *Br Fam* **he got a thick ear** il a reçu une bonne gifle
(**b**) *(hair)* épais(aisse); *(beard, eyebrows)* épais(aisse), touffu; *(grass, forest, crowd)* épais(aisse), dense; *(carpet)* épais(aisse); **pubs are not very thick on the ground round here** les pubs sont plutôt rares par ici
(**c**) *(soup, cream, sauce)* épais(aisse); **to become** *or* **to get thick** épaissir
(**d**) *(fog, smoke)* épais(aisse), dense; *(clouds)* épais(aisse); *(darkness, night)* profond; **the air is rather thick in here** on respire mal ici; *Fam* **my head feels a bit thick this morning** j'ai un peu mal au crâne *ou* aux cheveux ce matin
(**e**) *(covered, full)* **the shelves were thick with dust** les étagères étaient recouvertes d'une épaisse couche de poussière; **the air was thick with smoke** *(from smokers)* la pièce était enfumée; *(from fire, guns)* l'air était empli d'une épaisse fumée; **the streets were thick with police** les rues étaient pleines de policiers
(**f**) *(voice → with emotion)* voilé; *(→ after late night, drinking)* pâteux; **in a voice thick with emotion** d'une voix voilée par l'émotion
(**g**) *(accent)* fort, prononcé
(**h**) *Fam (intimate)* intime❑, très lié❑; **he's very thick with the boss** il est très bien avec le chef, lui et le chef sont comme les deux doigts de la main; **those two are as thick as thieves** ces deux-là s'entendent comme larrons en foire
(**i**) *Br Fam (stupid)* bête❑, débile; **to be as thick as two short planks** être bête comme ses pieds *ou* bête à manger du foin; **will you get that into your thick skull!** tu vas te mettre ça dans la tête, oui ou non?
(**j**) *Br Fam (unreasonable)* **that's a bit thick!** c'est un peu fort!; **it's a bit thick expecting us to take them to the airport!** ils exagèrent de compter sur nous pour les conduire à l'aéroport!❑
2 *adv (spread)* en couche épaisse; *(cut)* en tranches épaisses, en grosses tranches; **the snow lay thick on the ground** il y avait une épaisse couche de neige sur le sol; **the grass grows thick at the bottom of the hill** l'herbe pousse dru en bas de la colline; **arrows started falling thick and fast around them** les flèches pleuvaient (dru) autour d'eux; **invitations/phone calls began to come in thick and fast** il y eut une avalanche d'invitations/de coups de téléphone; **the questions/jokes came** *or* **flew thick and fast** les questions/blagues fusaient; *Fam* **to lay it on thick** exagérer❑, en rajouter
3 *n* **to stick** *or* **to stay with sb through thick and thin** rester fidèle à qn contre vents et marées *ou* quoi qu'il arrive
4 in the thick of *prep* au milieu *ou* cœur de, en plein, en plein milieu de; **in the thick of the battle** en plein milieu *ou* au plus fort de la bataille; **in the thick of the discussion** en pleine discussion; **he's really in the thick of it** *(dispute, activity)* il est vraiment dans le feu de l'action; **we soon found ourselves in the thick of things** nous nous sommes vite retrouvés au cœur de l'action

thicken [ˈθɪkən] **1** *vi* (**a**) *(fog, clouds, smoke)* s'épaissir, devenir plus épais(aisse); *(bushes, forest)* s'épaissir (**b**) *(sauce)* épaissir; *(jam, custard)* durcir (**c**) *(crowd)* grossir (**d**) *(mystery)* s'épaissir; **the plot thickens** les choses se compliquent *ou* se corsent, l'histoire se corse
2 *vt (sauce, soup)* épaissir

thickener [ˈθɪkənə(r)] *n (for sauce, soup)* liant *m*; *(for oil, paint)* épaississant *m*

thickening [ˈθɪkənɪŋ] **1** *n* (**a**) *(of fog, clouds, smoke)* épaississement *m*; *(of sauce)* liaison *f* (**b**) *Culin (thickener)* liant *m*
2 *adj (agent)* épaississant; *(process)* d'épaississement

thicket [ˈθɪkɪt] *n* fourré *m*

thickhead [ˈθɪkhed] *n Fam* bêta(asse) *m,f*, andouille *f*

thickheaded [ˌθɪkˈhedɪd] *adj Fam* obtus❑, bouché

thickie [ˈθɪkɪ] *n Br Fam* bêta(asse) *m,f*, andouille *f*

thickish [ˈθɪkɪʃ] *adj* assez épais(aisse)

thick-lipped *adj* aux lèvres épaisses *ou* charnues, lippu

thickly [ˈθɪklɪ] *adv* (**a**) *(spread)* en couche épaisse; *(cut)* en tranches épaisses; **the windows were thickly covered in** *or* **with ice** les vitres étaient recouvertes d'une épaisse couche de givre; **thickly buttered toast** pain grillé avec une épaisse couche de beurre; **thickly carpeted rooms** des pièces au sol couvert de moquette épaisse
(**b**) *(densely)* dru; **to grow thickly** *(vegetation, beard)* pousser dru; **thickly wooded** très boisé; **thickly populated** très peuplé, à forte densité de population; **the snow fell thickly** la neige tombait dru
(**c**) *(speak)* d'une voix rauque *ou* pâteuse

thickness [ˈθɪknɪs] *n* (**a**) *(of wall, snow, layer)* épaisseur *f*; *(of string, bolt)* épaisseur *f*, grosseur *f* (**b**) *(of beard, hair)* épaisseur *f*, abondance *f*; *(of lips)* épaisseur *f* (**c**) *(of fog, smoke, forest)* épaisseur *f*, densité *f* (**d**) *(layer → of paper etc)* couche *f*

thicko [ˈθɪkəʊ] (*pl* **thickos**) *n Br Fam* bêta(asse) *m,f*, andouille *f*

thickset [ˌθɪkˈset] *adj* trapu, costaud

thick-skinned *adj* peu sensible, qui a la peau dure; **she's very thick-skinned** elle est capable de supporter beaucoup de choses

thick-sliced *adj (bread)* coupé en tranches épaisses

thicky (*pl* **thickies**) = **thickie**

thief [θiːf] (*pl* **thieves** [θiːvz]) *n* voleur(euse) *m,f*; **stop thief!** au voleur!; *Prov* **set a thief to catch a thief** à malin, malin et demi; **like a thief in the night** *(leave, depart)* comme un voleur
►► ***thieves' kitchen*** repaire *m* de brigands

thieve [θiːv] **1** *vt* voler
2 *vi* voler

thievery [ˈθiːvərɪ] *n* vol *m*

thieves [θiːvz] *pl of* **thief**

thieving [ˈθiːvɪŋ] **1** *adj* voleur; *Fam* **keep your thieving hands off!** pas touche!, bas les pattes!
2 *n (UNCOUNT)* vol *m*, vols *mpl*

'The Thieving Magpie' *Rossini* 'La Pie voleuse'

thigh [θaɪ] *n* cuisse *f*
►► ***thigh boots*** cuissardes *fpl*

thighbone [ˈθaɪbəʊn] *n* fémur *m*

thigh-high *adj* à hauteur de cuisse; **the grass was thigh-high** l'herbe m'arrivait/nous arrivait/etc jusqu'aux cuisses
►► ***thigh-high boots*** cuissardes *fpl*

thigh-length *adj (dress, coat)* qui descend jusqu'à mi-cuisse
►► ***thigh-length boots*** cuissardes *fpl*

thimble [ˈθɪmbəl] *n* dé *m* à coudre

thimbleful [ˈθɪmbəlfʊl] *n Fig (of liquid)* doigt *m*, goutte *f*

thin [θɪn] (*compar* **thinner,** *superl* **thinnest,** *pt & pp* **thinned,** *cont* **thinning**) **1** *adj* (**a**) *(layer, wire)* mince, fin; *(wall)* mince, peu épais(aisse); *(person → skinny)* maigre; *(→ lean)* mince; *(leg, neck)* maigre; *(lips, book)* mince; *(clothing, blanket)* léger, fin; *(carpet)* ras; *(crowd)* peu nombreux, épars; **to become** *or* **to get** *or* **to grow thin** *(person)* maigrir; **he's as thin as a** *Br* **rake** *or Am* **rail** il est maigre comme un clou *ou* sec comme un coup de trique; **it's the thin end of the wedge** cela ne fait que commencer et ne présage rien de bon; **the move appears to be the thin end of the wedge of eventual privatisation** cette mesure est vraisemblablement le prélude à une privatisation à venir; **cheap hotels are thin on the ground** les hôtels bon marché sont rares; **honest people are thin on the ground** les gens honnêtes sont rares *ou* ne courent pas les rues
(**b**) *(sparse → beard, hair)* clairsemé; **he's getting a bit thin on top** il commence à perdre ses cheveux, il se dégarnit
(**c**) *(in consistency → soup, sauce)* clair; *(→ cream)* liquide; *(→ paint, ink)* délayé, dilué; *(→ blood)* appauvri, anémié
(**d**) *(smoke, clouds, mist)* léger; *(air)* raréfié; **to grow** *or* **become thinner** *(air)* se raréfier; *(ozone layer)* diminuer, s'amincir; **she seemed to vanish into thin air** elle semblait s'être volatilisée; **to conjure sth out of thin air** sortir qch de nulle part
(**e**) *(feeble, lame → excuse, argument)* mince, peu convaincant; *(→ joke, plot, majority)* faible; **the report is rather thin on facts** le rapport

ne présente pas beaucoup de faits concrets

(**f**) *(profits)* maigre; **to have a thin time of it** *(go through difficult time)* traverser une période difficile; *(not enjoy oneself)* s'ennuyer, s'embêter; **there are thin times ahead for the coal industry** une période de vaches maigres s'annonce pour l'industrie houillère; *St Exch* **trading was thin** le marché était calme

(**g**) *(voice)* grêle; *(smile)* petit

2 *adv (spread)* en fine couche, en couche mince; *(cut)* en tranches minces *ou* fines

3 *vt (sauce, soup)* allonger, délayer, éclaircir

4 *vi (crowd)* s'éclaircir, se disperser; *(fog)* se lever, devenir moins dense *ou* épais(aisse); *(smoke)* devenir moins dense *ou* épais(aisse); *(population)* se réduire; **his hair is thinning** il perd ses cheveux

▸▸ *Electron* ***thin film transistor*** transistor *m* en couche mince

▸**thin down** **1** *vt sep (sauce, soup)* allonger, éclaircir, délayer; *(paint)* délayer, diluer

2 *vi (person)* maigrir

▸**thin out** **1** *vt sep (plants)* éclaircir; *(hair)* éclaircir, désépaissir

2 *vi (crowd)* se disperser; *(population)* se réduire, diminuer; *(fog)* se lever

'The Thin Red Line' *Malick* 'La Ligne rouge'

thine [ðaɪn] *Bible or Arch* **1** *possessive adj (with singular possession)* ton (ta); *(with plural possession)* tes

2 *pron (replacing singular possession)* le tien (la tienne) *m,f*; *(replacing plural possession)* les tiens (les tiennes) *mpl, fpl*; **for thee and thine** pour toi et les tiens

THING [θɪŋ]

chose(s)	▸ **1A (a), (b); B (a) – (d); 2 (b) – (d)**
objet	▸ **1A (a)**
créature	▸ **1A (d)**
idée	▸ **1B (a)**
question	▸ **1B (b)**
idéal	▸ **1C (c)**
mode	▸ **1C (d)**
effets	▸ **2 (a)**
affaires	▸ **2 (a)**

1 *n* **A.** (**a**) *(object, item)* chose *f*, objet *m*; **what's that yellow thing on the floor?** qu'est-ce que c'est que ce truc jaune par terre?; **what's that thing for?** à quoi ça sert, ça?; **what's this knob thing for?** à quoi sert cette espèce de bouton?; **where's my hat? I can't find the thing anywhere** où est mon chapeau? je ne le trouve nulle part; **the only thing I could hear was a dripping tap** la seule chose que j'entendais c'était un robinet qui fuyait; **any idea how to work this thing?** tu sais comment ça marche?; **I had to rewrite the whole thing** j'ai dû tout réécrire; **the thing he loves most is his pipe** ce qu'il aime le plus, c'est sa pipe; **I need a few things from the shop** j'ai besoin de faire quelques courses; **she loves books and posters and things, she loves things like books and posters** elle aime les livres, les posters, ce genre de choses; **he likes making things with his hands** il est très manuel; **she enjoys the good things in life** elle apprécie les bonnes choses de la vie; **I must be seeing things** je dois avoir des visions; **I must be hearing things** je dois rêver, j'entends des voix; *Hum* **things that go bump in the night** les choses qui font du bruit la nuit; **they were treated as things not people** on les traitait comme des choses, pas comme des êtres humains

(**b**) *(activity, event)* chose *f*; **he likes things like gardening** il aime le jardinage et les choses dans ce goût-là; *Fam* **she's still into this art thing in a big way** elle est encore très branchée art; **the thing to do is to pretend you're asleep** vous n'avez qu'à faire semblant de dormir; **the first thing to do is (to) ring the police** la première chose à faire, c'est d'appeler la police; **the only thing left is to...** il ne reste plus qu'à...; **the next thing on the agenda** le point suivant à l'ordre du jour; **it's the best thing to do** c'est ce qu'il y a de mieux à faire; **that was a silly thing to do!** ce n'était pas la chose à faire!; **how could you do such a thing?** comment avez-vous pu faire une chose pareille?; **I have lots of things to do** j'ai des tas de choses à faire; **she certainly gets things done** avec elle, ça ne traîne pas

(**c**) *(in negative clauses)* **I don't know a thing about what happened** j'ignore tout de ce qui s'est passé; **I don't know a thing about algebra** je n'y connais absolument rien en algèbre; **not a thing was overlooked** pas un détail n'a été négligé; **I didn't understand a thing she said** je n'ai rien compris à ce qu'elle disait, je n'ai pas compris un mot de ce qu'elle disait; **we couldn't do a thing about it** nous n'y pouvions absolument rien; **I couldn't do a thing to help** je n'ai rien pu faire pour me rendre utile; **it doesn't mean a thing to me** *(I don't understand it at all)* je n'y comprends (absolument) rien; *(it isn't at all familiar to me)* ça ne me dit absolument rien; *(it doesn't concern me at all)* ça ne me concerne pas; **she hadn't got a thing on** elle était entièrement nue; **I haven't got a thing to wear** je n'ai rien à me mettre sur le dos

(**d**) *(creature, being)* créature *f*, être *m*; **the thing he loves most is his dog** ce qu'il aime le plus, c'est son chien; **there wasn't a living thing around** il n'y avait pas âme qui vive; **what a sweet little thing!** quel amour!; **she's a dear old thing** c'est une charmante petite vieille; **you silly thing** espèce d'idiot; **poor thing!** *(said about somebody)* le/la pauvre!; *(said to somebody)* mon/ma pauvre!; *(animal)* (la) pauvre bête!

(**e**) *(monster)* **the thing from outer space** le monstre de l'espace

B. (**a**) *(idea, notion)* idée *f*, chose *f*; **the best thing would be to ask them** le mieux serait de leur demander; **it would be a good thing if we all went together** ce serait une bonne chose que nous y allions tous ensemble; **it's a good thing (for you) no one knew** heureusement (pour vous) que personne ne savait; **to be on to a good thing** être sur une bonne affaire; **to know a thing or two about sth** s'y connaître en qch; **I could show him a thing or two about hang gliding** je pourrais lui apprendre une ou deux petites choses en deltaplane

(**b**) *(matter, question)* chose *f*, question *f*; **the thing is, we can't really afford it** le problème, c'est qu'on n'a pas vraiment les moyens; **the thing is, will she want to come?** le problème c'est qu'on ne sait pas si elle voudra venir; **the main thing is to succeed** ce qui importe, c'est de réussir; **the important thing is not to stop** ce qui compte, c'est de ne pas arrêter; **the thing to remember is that...** ce dont il faut se souvenir est que...; **it's one thing to talk but quite another to act** parler est une chose, agir en est une autre; **that's quite another thing** ça, c'est tout autre chose; **and another thing** en plus; **we talked of one thing and another** nous avons parlé de choses et d'autres; **what with one thing and another, I haven't had time** avec tout ce qu'il y avait à faire, je n'ai pas eu le temps; **if it's not one thing, it's another, it's one thing after another** [illegible]; **taking one thing with another** à tout prendre, somme toute

(**c**) *(remark)* **that's not a very nice thing to say** ce n'est pas très gentil de dire ça; **she said some nasty things about him** elle a dit des méchancetés sur lui; **how can you say such a thing?** comment pouvez-vous dire une chose pareille?; **the things you say!** les choses que tu peux dire parfois!; **I said no such thing!** je n'ai rien dit de tel!; **I said the first thing that came into my head** j'ai dit la première chose qui m'est venue à l'esprit

(**d**) *(quality, characteristic)* chose *f*; **one of the things I like about her is her sense of humour** une des choses que j'aime chez elle, c'est son sens de l'humour; **the town has a lot of things going for it** la ville a beaucoup de bons côtés

C. (**a**) *Fam (strong feeling)* **to have a thing about sb/sth** *(like)* avoir un faible pour qn/qch ❑; *(dislike)* avoir horreur de qn/qch ❑; **I have a thing about seafood** *(like)* j'aime vraiment les fruits de mer ❑; *(dislike)* je n'aime vraiment pas les fruits de mer ❑; **he has a thing about red hair** *(likes)* il adore les cheveux roux ❑; *(dislikes)* il a quelque chose contre les cheveux roux ❑; **it's a bit of a thing with me** *(like)* j'aime assez ça ❑; *(dislike)* c'est ma bête noire

(**b**) *Fam (interest)* **it's not really my thing** ce n'est pas vraiment mon truc; **he went off to the States to do his own thing** il est parti aux États-Unis vivre sa vie ❑

(**c**) *(what is needed, required)* idéal *m*; **hot cocoa is just the thing on a winter's night** un chocolat chaud, c'est l'idéal les soirs d'hiver; **that's the very thing** c'est juste ce qu'il faut; **that's the very thing for my bad back!** c'est juste ce dont j'avais besoin pour mon mal de dos!

(**d**) *(fashion)* mode *f*; **it's the latest thing in swimwear** c'est la dernière mode en matière de maillots de bain; **it's quite the thing** c'est très à la mode; **natural food is the thing just now** les aliments biologiques sont la grande mode en ce moment; **a thing of the past** une chose du passé

(**e**) *(fuss)* **to make a big thing about sth** faire (tout) un plat de qch; **he made a big thing out of my not going** il a fait tout un plat parce que je n'y allais pas; **there's no need to make a big thing out of it!** ce n'est pas la peine d'en faire tout un plat *ou* toute une montagne!

(**f**) *Fam (relationship)* **to have a thing with sb** avoir une liaison avec qn ❑

(**g**) *Fam (penis)* chose *f*

2 things *npl* (**a**) *(belongings)* effets *mpl*, affaires *fpl*; *(clothes)* affaires *fpl*; *(equipment)* affaires *fpl*, attirail *m*; *(tools)* outils *mpl*, ustensiles *mpl*; **put your things away** ramassez vos affaires; **take your wet things off** enlevez vos affaires humides; **you can take your things off in the bedroom** vous pouvez vous déshabiller dans la chambre; **have you brought your fishing/swimming things?** avez-vous apporté votre attirail de pêche/vos affaires de piscine?; **have you washed the breakfast things?** as-tu fait la vaisselle du petit déjeuner?; **to take the tea things away** desservir la table (après le thé); **to pack (up) one's things** faire ses valises

(**b**) *(situation, circumstances)* choses *fpl*; *Fam* **how's** *or* **how are things?** comment ça va?; **things are getting better** les choses vont mieux; **things are going badly** ça va mal; **things began to get rather dangerous** les choses ont commencé à devenir assez dangereuses; **I feel rather out of things** je n'ai pas l'impression d'être vraiment dans le bain; **you take things too seriously** vous prenez les choses trop au sérieux; **I need time to think things over** j'ai besoin de temps pour réfléchir; **as things are** *or* **stand** dans l'état actuel des choses; **things being what they are** les choses étant ce qu'elles sont; **it's just one of those things** ce sont des choses qui arrivent

(**c**) *(specific aspect of life)* choses *fpl*; **things of the mind** les choses *fpl* de l'esprit; **she's interested in all things French** elle s'intéresse à tout ce qui est français; **moderation in all things** de la modération en tout; **she wants to be an airline pilot of all things!** elle veut être pilote de ligne, non mais vraiment!

(**d**) *(facts, actions etc)* choses *fpl*; **they did terrible things to their prisoners** ils ont fait des choses atroces à leurs prisonniers; **I've heard good things about his work** on dit du bien de son travail

(**e**) *Law (property)* biens *mpl*

3 for one thing *adv* (tout) d'abord; **for one thing... and for another thing** (tout) d'abord... et puis; **well for one thing, we can't afford it** pour commencer, nous n'en avons pas les moyens

thingahoochie ['θɪŋə,huːtʃɪ] *n Am Fam* truc *m*

thingumabob ['θɪŋəmɪbɒb], **thingumajig** ['θɪŋəmɪdʒɪg], **thingummy** ['θɪŋəmɪ], **thingy** [,θɪŋɪ] *n Fam (person)* Bidule *mf*, Machin(e) *m,f*; *(thing)* truc *m*, machin *m*; **have you seen the thingy for the food processor?** tu as vu le machin du robot de cuisine?; **I saw thingy who you used to work with last week** la semaine dernière, j'ai vu Machin-Chose avec qui tu travaillais dans le temps

THINK [θɪŋk]

penser	▸ **1 (a), (b), (d); 2 (b), (f)**
raisonner	▸ **1 (a)**
réfléchir	▸ **1 (b); 3**
(s')imaginer	▸ **1 (c); 2 (d)**
croire	▸ **1 (d); 2 (b)**
juger	▸ **2 (c)**
considérer	▸ **2 (c)**
penser à	▸ **2 (a), (e)**
réfléchir à	▸ **2 (a)**
se rappeler	▸ **2 (e)**
s'attendre à	▸ **2 (f)**

(*pt & pp* **thought** [θɔːt]) **1** *vi* (**a**) *(reason)* penser, raisonner; **to think for oneself** se faire ses propres opinions; **sorry, I wasn't thinking clearly** désolé, je n'avais pas les idées claires; **to think aloud** penser tout haut; *Fam* **to think big** voir les choses en grand ❑; **she always thinks big** elle voit toujours les choses en grand; **think big!** sois ambitieux! ❑; **to think on one's feet** réfléchir vite; **you couldn't hear yourself think** il n'était pas possible de se concentrer; **I can't think straight with this headache** ce mal de tête m'embrouille les idées

(**b**) *(ponder, reflect)* penser, réfléchir; **he thought for a moment** il a réfléchi un instant; **she doesn't say much but she thinks a lot** elle ne dit pas grand-chose, mais elle n'en pense pas moins; **think before you speak** réfléchissez avant de parler; **think again!** *(reconsider)* repensez-y!; *(guess)* vous n'y êtes pas, réfléchissez donc!; **you just don't think, do you!** *(are inconsiderate, careless etc)* jamais tu ne réfléchis, hein!; **let me think** laisse-moi réfléchir; **think carefully before deciding** réfléchissez bien avant de vous décider; **I thought hard** j'ai beaucoup réfléchi; **I thought twice before accepting** j'ai réfléchi à deux fois avant d'accepter; **to act without thinking** agir sans réfléchir; **I'm sorry, I wasn't thinking** désolé, je l'ai fait/dit sans réfléchir; **it makes you think** ça vous fait réfléchir; **that's what set me thinking** c'est ce qui m'a fait réfléchir

(**c**) *(imagine)* (s')imaginer; **if you think I'd lend you my car again...** si tu t'imagines que je te prêterai encore ma voiture...; **just think!** imaginez(-vous) un peu!; **just think, you might have married him!** imagine(-toi) que tu aurais pu l'épouser!

(**d**) *(believe, have as opinion)* penser, croire; **she thinks as I do** elle pense comme moi; **to her way of thinking** à son avis; **it's a lot harder than I thought** c'est beaucoup plus difficile que je ne croyais

2 *vt* (**a**) *(ponder, reflect on)* penser à, réfléchir à; **he was thinking what they could do next** il se demandait ce qu'ils allaient pouvoir faire ensuite; **I'm thinking how to go about it** je me demande comment il faudrait s'y prendre; **I was just thinking how ironic it all is** je pensais simplement à l'ironie de la chose; **guess what we're thinking** essaye de deviner à quoi nous pensons; **I kept thinking "why me?"** je n'arrêtais pas de me dire: pourquoi moi?; **I'm happy to think she's not all alone** je suis content de savoir qu'elle n'est pas toute seule; **to think deep/evil thoughts** avoir des pensées profondes/de mauvaises pensées

(**b**) *(believe)* penser, croire; **I think so** je crois; **I don't think so, I think not** je ne crois pas; **he's a crook – I thought so** *or* **I thought as much** c'est un escroc – je m'en doutais; **I should think so!** je crois bien!; **do you think they'll agree? – I should think so** croyez-vous qu'ils accepteront? – je pense que oui; **he's going to apologize – I should think so (too)!** il va s'excuser – j'espère bien!; **he apologized – I should think so (too)!** il s'est excusé – ce n'est pas trop tôt!; **I shouldn't think so** je ne crois pas; **I think you mean Johnson, not Boswell** je crois que tu veux dire Johnson, pas Boswell; **more tea? – I don't think I will, thank you** encore un peu de thé? – non merci, je ne pense pas; **she didn't think he would actually leave** elle ne pensait pas qu'il partirait vraiment; **she thinks you should leave town** elle croit que tu devrais quitter la ville; **they asked me what I thought** ils m'ont demandé mon avis; **what does he think I should do?** que pense-t-il *ou* croit-il que je doive faire?; **he wants cream walls – what do you think?** il veut des murs crème – qu'est-ce que tu en penses?; **I thought I heard a noise** j'ai cru *ou* il m'a semblé entendre un bruit; **it's expensive, don't you think?** c'est cher, tu ne trouves pas?; *Fam* **oh, he's so honest, I don't think!** honnête, mon œil, oui!; **I don't know what to think** je ne sais pas quoi penser; **he thinks he knows everything** il croit tout savoir; **she thinks she's talented** elle se croit *ou* se trouve douée; **that's what you think!** tu te fais des illusions!; **what will people think?** qu'en dira-t-on?, qu'est-ce que les gens vont penser?; **it is thought that...** on suppose que... + *indicative*; **anyone would think he owned the place** on croirait que c'est lui le propriétaire; **anybody would think it was Sunday** on dirait un dimanche; **(just) who does he think he is?** (mais) pour qui se prend-il?; **you always think the best/the worst of everyone** vous avez toujours une très bonne/mauvaise opinion de tout le monde

(**c**) *(judge, consider)* juger, considérer; **we think the rule unfair** nous trouvons le règlement injuste; **you must think me very nosy** vous devez me trouver très curieux; **everyone thought he was mad** on le tenait pour fou; **she is thought to be one of the best** on dit qu'elle fait partie des meilleurs; **you thought her (to be) a fool** vous l'avez prise pour une sotte; **if you think it necessary** si vous le jugez nécessaire; **I hardly think it likely that...** il me semble peu probable que... + *subjunctive*

(**d**) *(imagine)* (s')imaginer; **I can't think why he refused** je ne vois vraiment pas pourquoi il a refusé; **you'd think she'd be pleased** elle devrait être contente; **one would have thought that...** c'était à croire que... + *indicative*; **who'd have thought he'd become president!** qui aurait dit qu'elle serait un jour président!; **who'd have thought it!** qui l'eût cru!; **just think what we can do with all that money!** imaginez ce qu'on peut faire avec tout cet argent!; **I can't think what you mean** je n'arrive pas à comprendre *ou* voir ce que vous voulez dire; **and to think she did it all by herself** et dire *ou* quand on pense qu'elle a fait cela toute seule

(**e**) *(remember)* penser à, se rappeler; **I can't think what his name is** je n'arrive pas à me rappeler son nom, son nom m'échappe; **he couldn't think which countries belonged to the EU** il n'arrivait pas à se rappeler quels pays étaient membres de l'UE; **to think to do sth** penser à faire qch; **they didn't think to invite her** ils n'ont pas pensé à l'inviter; **did you think to buy some bread?** as-tu pensé à acheter du pain?

(**f**) *(expect)* penser, s'attendre à; **I don't think she'll come** je ne pense pas qu'elle viendra *ou* vienne; **I didn't think to find you here** je ne m'attendais pas à vous trouver ici; **I little thought I would see him again** je ne m'attendais guère à le revoir

(**g**) *(have as intention)* **I think I'll go for a walk** je crois que je vais aller me promener; *esp Literary* **I only thought to help you** ma seule pensée était de vous aider

(**h**) *(in requests)* **do you think you could help me?** pourriez-vous m'aider?

(**i**) *Fam (have as main concern)* **designers are thinking pink** le rose, c'est la couleur in chez les stylistes; **the company is thinking expansion** le maître mot dans la société, c'est expansion ❑; **think thin!** pensez minceur!

3 *n* **to have a think** réfléchir; **we've had a think about it** nous y avons réfléchi; **she had a good think about their offer** elle a bien réfléchi à leur proposition; **I'll have another think about it** je vais encore y réfléchir; *Fam* **you've got another think coming!** tu te fais des illusions!

▸▸ ***think tank*** groupe *m* de réflexion

▸**think about** *vt insep* (**a**) *(ponder, reflect on)* **to think about sth/doing sth** penser à qch/à faire qch; **what are you thinking about?** à quoi pensez-vous?; **we were just thinking about the holidays** nous pensions justement aux vacances; **I've thought about your proposal** j'ai réfléchi à votre proposition; **it's not a bad idea, if you think about it** ce n'est pas une mauvaise idée, si tu réfléchis bien; **that's worth thinking about** cela mérite réflexion; **she's thinking about starting a business** elle pense à *ou* envisage de monter une affaire; **we'll think about it** nous allons y penser *ou* réfléchir; **she has a lot to think about just now** elle est très préoccupée en ce moment; **there's so much to think about when you buy a house** il y a tant de choses à prendre en considération quand on achète une maison; **the conference gave us much to think about** la conférence nous a donné matière à réflexion; **I'll give you something to think about!** je vais te donner de quoi réfléchir!

(**b**) *(consider seriously)* penser à; **all he thinks about is money** il n'y a que l'argent qui l'intéresse; **he's always thinking about food – what else is there to think about?** il ne pense qu'à manger – c'est ce qu'il y a de plus intéressant, non?; **I've got my family/future to think about** il faut que je pense à ma famille/mon avenir

(**c**) *(have opinion about)* penser de; **what do you think about him?** que pensez-vous de lui?; **what do you think about it?** qu'en pensez-vous?

▸**think ahead** *vi* prévoir; **you have to learn to think ahead** il faut apprendre à prévoir

▸**think back** *vi* **to think back to sth** se rappeler qch; **think back to that night** essayez de vous souvenir de *ou* vous rappeler cette nuit-là; **I thought back over the years** j'ai repensé aux années passées; **when I think back** quand j'y repense

▸**think of** *vt insep* (**a**) *(have as tentative plan)* penser à, envisager de; **she's thinking of starting a business** elle pense à *ou* envisage de monter une affaire; **what were you thinking of giving her?** que pensais-tu lui donner?

(**b**) *(have in mind)* penser à; **we're thinking of you** nous pensons à toi; **I was thinking of how much times have changed** je songeais combien les temps ont changé; **whatever were you thinking of?** où avais-tu la tête?; **come to think of it, that's not a bad idea** à la réflexion, ce n'est pas une mauvaise idée; **we wouldn't think of letting our daughter travel alone** il ne nous viendrait pas à l'esprit de laisser notre fille voyager seule; **I couldn't think of it!** c'est impossible!

(**c**) *(remember)* penser à, se rappeler; **I can't think of the address** je n'arrive pas à me rappeler l'adresse; **he couldn't think of the name** il ne se rappelait pas le nom, le nom ne lui venait pas; **that makes me think of my childhood** ça me rappelle mon enfance

(**d**) *(come up with → idea, solution)* **she's the one who thought of double-checking it** c'est elle qui a eu l'idée de le vérifier; **it's the only way they could think of doing it** ils ne voyaient pas d'autre façon de s'y prendre; **try every method you can think of** essayez toutes les méthodes que vous puissiez imaginer; **I thought of the answer** j'ai trouvé la réponse; **I've just thought of something, she'll be out** j'avais oublié *ou* je viens de me rappeler, elle ne sera pas là; **I've just thought of something else** il y a autre chose *ou* ce n'est pas tout; **I'd never have thought of that** je n'y aurais jamais pensé; **why didn't you phone? – I didn't think of it** pourquoi n'avez-vous pas téléphoné? – je n'y ai pas pensé; **whatever will they think of next?** qu'est-ce qu'ils vont bien pouvoir trouver ensuite?; **think of a number between 1 and 10** pensez à un chiffre entre 1 et 10; **I thought better of it** je me suis ravisé; **to think better of sb for doing sth** estimer qn davantage d'avoir *ou* pour avoir fait qch; **he thought nothing of leaving the baby alone for hours at a time** il trouvait (ça) normal de laisser le bébé seul pendant des heures; **thank you – think nothing of it!** merci – mais je vous en prie *ou* mais c'est tout naturel!

(**e**) *(judge, have as opinion)* **what do you think of the new teacher?** comment trouvez-vous le *ou* que pensez-vous du nouveau professeur?; **what do you think of it?** qu'en pensez-vous?; **she thinks very highly of** *or* **very well of him** elle a une très haute opinion de lui; **he thinks of**

himself as an artist il se prend pour un artiste; **to think a great deal of oneself, to think too much of oneself** avoir une haute idée de soi-même *ou* de sa personne; **as a doctor she is very well thought of** elle est très respectée en tant que médecin; **I hope you won't think badly of me if I refuse** j'espère que vous ne m'en voudrez pas si je refuse; **I don't think much of that idea** cette idée ne me dit pas grand-chose; **he doesn't think much of his brother** il n'a pas une haute opinion de son frère; **I told her what I thought of her** je lui ai dit son fait

(**f**) *(imagine)* penser à, imaginer; **I always thought of her as being blonde** je la croyais blonde; **just think of it, me as president!** imaginez un peu: moi président!, vous m'imaginez président?; **when I think of how things might have turned out** quand je pense à la manière dont les choses auraient pu finir; **when I think of what might have happened!** quand je pense à ce qui aurait pu arriver!; **you might have married him, think of that!** tu aurais pu l'épouser, imagine un peu!

(**g**) *(take into consideration)* penser à, considérer; **I have my family to think of** il faut que je pense à ma famille; **she never thinks of anyone but herself** elle ne pense qu'à elle-même; **think of your mother's feelings** pense un peu à ta mère; **he never thinks of her** il n'a aucun égard *ou* aucune considération pour elle; **you never think of the expense** tu ne regardes jamais à la dépense; **think of how much it will cost!** pense un peu à ce que ça va coûter!, **you can't think of everything** on ne peut pas penser à tout

▸**think out** *vt sep (plan)* élaborer, préparer; *(problem)* bien étudier *ou* examiner; *(solution)* bien étudier; **it needs thinking out** cela demande mûre réflexion; **he likes to think things out for himself** il aime juger des choses par lui-même; **a carefully thought-out answer** une réponse bien pesée; **a well-thought-out plan** un projet bien conçu *ou* ficelé

▸**think over** *vt sep* bien examiner, bien réfléchir à; **we'll have to think it over** il va falloir que nous y réfléchissions; **this needs thinking over** cela mérite réflexion; **think the offer over carefully** réfléchissez bien à cette proposition; **on thinking things over we've decided not to sell the house** réflexion faite, on a décidé de ne pas vendre la maison; **I need some time to think things over** j'ai besoin de temps pour réfléchir

▸**think through** *vt sep (plan etc)* bien considérer; **the scheme has not been properly thought through** le plan n'a pas été considéré suffisamment en détail

▸**think up** *vt sep (excuse, plan, solution)* trouver

---

thinkable [ˈθɪŋkəbəl] *adj* pensable, concevable, imaginable; **it is scarcely** *or* **barely thinkable that...** il est difficilement concevable *ou* imaginable que... + *subjunctive*

thinker [ˈθɪŋkə(r)] *n* penseur(euse) *m,f*

'The Thinker' *Rodin* 'Le Penseur'

---

thinking [ˈθɪŋkɪŋ] **1** *adj (person)* pensant, rationnel, qui réfléchit; **it's the thinking man's answer to pulp fiction** c'est un roman de hall de gare en plus intelligent; *Br Fam Hum* **the thinking man's/woman's crumpet** la petite préférée/le petit préféré des intellos; *Fam Fig* **to put on one's thinking cap** se mettre à réfléchir□, cogiter□

2 *n* (**a**) *(act)* pensée *f*, pensées *fpl*, réflexion *f*; **I've done some serious** *or* **hard thinking about the situation** j'ai bien *ou* sérieusement *ou* mûrement réfléchi à la situation; **his life was saved thanks to the nurses' quick thinking** la réaction rapide des infirmières lui a sauvé la vie

(**b**) *(opinion, judgment)* point *m* de vue, opinion *f*, opinions *fpl*; **my thinking on disarmament has changed** mes opinions sur le désarmement ont changé; **she finally came round to my way of thinking** elle s'est finalement ralliée à mon point de vue; **to his way of thinking it was wrong** pour lui, ce n'était pas bien

▸▸ *Aut* ***thinking distance*** temps *m* de réaction

thin-lipped *adj* aux lèvres minces

thinly [ˈθɪnlɪ] *adv (spread)* en couche mince; *(cut)* en fines tranches; **a thinly disguised insult** une insulte à peine voilée; **a thinly veiled allusion** une allusion à peine voilée; **a thinly clad child** un enfant insuffisamment *ou* trop légèrement vêtu; **the area is thinly populated** la région n'est pas très peuplée

thinner [ˈθɪnə(r)] **1** *compar of* **thin**

2 *n (solvent)* diluant *m*

thinness [ˈθɪnnɪs] *n* (**a**) *(of layer)* minceur *f*, finesse *f*; *(of wall)* minceur *f*, faible épaisseur *f*; *(of person → skinniness)* maigreur *f*; *(→ leanness)* minceur *f*; *(of lips)* minceur *f*; *(of wire)* finesse *f*; *(of clothing, blanket, carpet)* légèreté *f*, finesse *f*

(**b**) *(of beard, hair)* finesse *f*, rareté *f*

(**c**) *(of excuse)* faiblesse *f*, insuffisance *f*; *(of joke, storyline, plot)* faiblesse *f*; **because of the thinness of their majority** à cause de leur faible majorité

(**d**) *(of air)* raréfaction *f*

thinning [ˈθɪnɪŋ] *adj* **his thinning hair** ses cheveux qui commencent à se clairsemer

▸▸ ***thinning agent*** diluant *m*

thinnish [ˈθɪnɪʃ] *adj* (**a**) *(layer, wire etc)* assez mince; *(person → skinny)* maigrichon(onne), maigrelet(ette); *(→ lean)* assez mince; *(clothing)* assez léger, assez fin; *(crowd)* assez peu nombreux (**b**) *(hair, beard)* assez clairsemé (**c**) *(soup, sauce)* un peu clair; *(paint, ink)* un peu dilué *ou* délayé (**d**) *(mist)* assez léger (**e**) *(voice)* assez grêle

thin-skinned *adj Fig* susceptible

thin-sliced *adj (bread)* coupé en tranches fines, finement coupé

thionic [θaɪˈɒnɪk] *adj Chem* thionique

thiosulphate [ˌθaɪəʊˈsʌlfeɪt] *n Chem* thiosulfate *m*, hyposulfite *m*

thiosulphuric [ˌθaɪəʊsʌlˈfjʊərɪk] *n Chem* thiosulfurique, hyposulfureux

third [θɜːd] **1** *n* (**a**) *(fraction)* tiers *m*

(**b**) *(in series)* troisième *mf*

(**c**) *(of month)* trois *m inv*

(**d**) *Mus* tierce *f*

(**e**) *Aut* troisième *f*; **in third** en troisième

(**f**) *Br Univ* ≃ licence *f* sans mention

2 *adj* troisième; **third time lucky** la troisième fois sera la bonne

3 *adv* troisièmement; *(in contest)* en troisième position, à la troisième place; *see also* **fifth**

▸▸ ***third base*** *(in baseball)* troisième but *m*; ***third class*** **1** *n* (**a**) *(for travel)* troisième classe *f*; *(for accommodation)* troisième catégorie *f* (**b**) *Am (for mail)* ≃ tarif *m* "imprimés", ≃ tarif *m* lent **2** *adv* (**a**) *(travel)* en troisième classe (**b**) *Am* **to mail a package third class** ≃ envoyer un colis au tarif lent; *Fam* ***third degree*** interrogatoire *m* serré□; **to get the third degree** subir un interrogatoire; **to give sb the third degree** *(torture)* passer qn à tabac; *(interrogate)* cuisiner qn; *Hist* ***the Third Estate*** le Tiers état; ***third finger*** majeur *m*; *Aut* ***third gear*** troisième vitesse *f*; *Am Sch* ***third grade*** = classe du primaire pour les 7–8 ans, *Can* 3ème année; ***third party*** tierce personne *f*, tiers *m*; *Gram* ***third person*** troisième personne *f*; **in the third person** à la troisième personne; *Fin* ***third quarter*** *(of financial year)* troisième trimestre *m*; *Pol* ***third reading*** *(of bill)* = dernière lecture; *Hist* ***the Third Reich*** le Troisième Reich; *Br Pol* ***the Third Way*** la troisième voie *(politique consensuelle prêchée par le parti travailliste réformé de Tony Blair, censée dépasser les clivages traditionnels droite-gauche de façon à rassembler toutes les classes sociales)*; ***the Third World*** le tiers-monde

'The Third Man' *Greene, Reed* 'Le Troisième homme'

---

third-class *adj* (**a**) *(ticket, compartment)* de troisième classe; *(hotel, accommodation)* de troisième catégorie (**b**) *(inferior → merchandise)* de qualité inférieure, de pacotille; *(→ restaurant)* de qualité inférieure (**c**) *Am (mail)* ≃ au tarif "imprimés", ≃ au tarif lent

▸▸ *Br Univ* ***third-class degree*** ≃ licence *f* sans mention

third-degree burn *n* brûlure *f* au troisième degré

thirdhand [ˌθɜːdˈhænd] **1** *adj (car, information)* de troisième main

2 *adv (buy)* en troisième main

third-level education *n Ir* enseignement *m* supérieur

thirdly [ˈθɜːdlɪ] *adv* troisièmement, en troisième lieu, tertio

third-party *adj*

▸▸ *Ins* ***third-party insurance*** assurance *f* au tiers; *Ins* ***third-party liability*** responsabilité *f* au tiers

third-rate *adj* de qualité inférieure

Third-World *adj* du tiers-monde

thirst [θɜːst] **1** *n also Fig* soif *f*; **all that hard work has given me a thirst** ça m'a donné soif de travailler dur comme ça; **he has a thirst for adventure** il a soif d'aventure; **to have a thirst for knowledge** avoir soif de connaissances

2 *vi also Fig* **to thirst for sth** avoir soif de qch; **he was thirsting for a beer** il avait envie d'une bière; **a jealous husband thirsting for revenge** un mari jaloux assoiffé de vengeance; **to thirst for knowledge** être avide de connaissances

thirstily [ˈθɜːstɪlɪ] *adv* avidement

thirstiness [ˈθɜːstɪnɪs] *n* soif *f*

thirst-quenching [-kwentʃɪŋ] *adj* désaltérant

thirsty [ˈθɜːstɪ] *(compar* **thirstier**, *superl* **thirstiest**) *adj* (**a**) *(wanting a drink)* qui a soif, assoiffé; **to be thirsty** avoir soif; **I feel very thirsty** j'ai très soif; **salted peanuts make you thirsty** les cacahuètes salées donnent soif; **it's thirsty work** ça donne soif

(**b**) *Fig (for knowledge, adventure)* assoiffé; **to be thirsty for** avoir soif de, être assoiffé de; **she was thirsty for revenge** elle était assoiffée de vengeance

(**c**) *(plant)* qui a besoin de beaucoup d'eau; *(soil)* desséché

thirteen [ˌθɜːˈtiːn] **1** *n* treize *m inv*

2 *pron* treize

3 *adj* treize; *see also* **five**

thirteenth [ˌθɜːˈtiːnθ] **1** *n* (**a**) *(fraction)* treizième *m* (**b**) *(in series)* treizième *mf* (**c**) *(of month)* treize *m inv*

2 *adj* treizième

3 *adv* treizièmement; *(in contest)* en treizième position, à la treizième place; *see also* **fifth**

thirtieth [ˈθɜːtɪəθ] **1** *n* (**a**) *(fraction)* trentième *m* (**b**) *(in series)* trentième *mf* (**c**) *(of month)* trente *m inv*

2 *adj* trentième

3 *adv* trentièmement; *(in contest)* en trentième position, à la trentième place; *see also* **fifth**

thirty [ˈθɜːtɪ] *(pl* **thirties**) **1** *n* trente *m inv*

2 *pron* trente; **about thirty** une trentaine

3 *adj* trente; *see also* **fifty**

▸▸ *Hist* ***the Thirty Years' War*** la guerre de Trente Ans

'The Thirty-Nine Steps' *Buchan, Hitchcock* 'Les Trente-neuf marches'

---

thirty-second note *n Am Mus* triple croche *f*

thirty-second rest *n Am Mus* huitième *m* de soupir

thirty-sixmo [-ˈsɪksməʊ] *Typ* **1** *adj* in-trente-six *(inv)*

2 *n* in-trente-six *m inv*

thirtysomething [ˈθɜːtɪsʌmθɪŋ] **1** *n (person in his/her thirties → gen)* trentenaire *mf*; *(→ yuppie)* trentenaire *mf* qui a réussi dans la vie

2 *adj (of person in his/her thirties → gen)* trentenaire *mf*; *(→ yuppie)* = (caractéristique) du trentenaire qui a réussi dans la vie

thirty-three *n (record)* trente-trois tours *m inv*

thirty-twomo [-ˈtuːməʊ] *Typ* **1** *adj* in-trente-deux *(inv)*

2 *n* in-trente-deux *m inv*

THIS [ðɪs]

ceci	▸ 1 (a)
ce	▸ 1 (a); 2 (a)
celui-ci	▸ 1 (b)
ce...-ci	▸ 2 (b)
aussi	▸ 3
si	▸ 3

(*pl* **these** [ðiːz]) **1** *demonstrative pron* (**a**) *(person, situation, statement, thing indicated → subject)* ceci, ce; *(→ object)* ce; **what's this?** qu'est-ce que c'est (que ça)?; **who's this?** *(gen)* qui est-ce?; *(on phone)* qui est à l'appareil?; **this is for you** tiens, c'est pour toi; **this is Mr Smith speaking** *(on phone)* M. Smith à l'appareil, c'est M. Smith; **this is my mother** *(in introduction)* je vous présente ma mère; *(in picture)* c'est ma mère; **these are my children** voici mes enfants; **these are things we cannot do without** ce sont des choses dont on ne peut se passer; **this is the place I was talking about** c'est *ou* voici l'endroit dont je parlais; **this is terrible** c'est affreux; **this is what he told me** voici ce qu'il m'a dit; **this is where I live** c'est ici que j'habite; **listen to this** écoutez bien ceci; **eat/drink some of this** mangez-/buvez-en un peu; **what's this I hear about your leaving?** on me dit que vous partez?; **what's all this?** *(these objects)* qu'est-ce que c'est que tout ça?; *(what's happening?)* qu'est-ce qu'il y a?, qu'est-ce qui se passe?; **it was like this** voici comment les choses se sont passées; **do it like this** voici comment il faut faire; **I didn't want it to end like this** je ne voulais pas que ça finisse *ou* se termine comme ça; **that it should come to this** qu'on en arrive là; **and there's no way she could live with you? – well, this is it** et elle ne pourrait pas vivre avec toi? – non, justement; **this is it, wish me luck** voilà, souhaite-moi bonne chance; **this is it, the moment we've all been waiting for!** nous y voilà, c'est le moment que nous attendons tous!; **I'll tell you this...** je vais te dire une chose...; **after/before this** après/avant ça; **at** *or* **with this, he left the room** là-dessus *ou* sur ce, il a quitté la pièce; **what did you talk about? – oh, this and that** de quoi avez-vous parlé? – oh, de choses et d'autres; **they sat chatting about this, that and the other** ils étaient là, assis, à bavarder de choses et d'autres; **it's always John this and John that** c'est John par-ci, John par-là

(**b**) *(contrasted with that)* celui-ci (celle-ci) *m,f*; **these** ceux-ci (celles-ci) *mpl, fpl*; **this is a rose, that is a peony** ceci est une rose, ça c'est une pivoine; **I want these, not those!** je veux ceux-ci, pas ceux-là!; **is this more expensive than that?** celui-ci est-il plus cher que celui-là?

2 *demonstrative adj* (**a**) *(referring to a particular person, idea, time or thing)* ce (cette); **these** ces; **this man** cet homme; **these ideas** ces idées; **this plan of yours won't work** votre projet ne marchera pas; **this book you wanted** le livre que vous vouliez; **he's lived in this country for years** ça fait des années qu'il vit dans ce pays; **this way please** par ici, s'il vous plaît; **this funny little man came up to me** un petit bonhomme à l'air bizarre est venu vers moi; **there were these two Germans...** il y avait ces deux Allemands...; **who's this friend of yours?** c'est qui, cet ami?; *Fam* **this here bicycle** ce vélo-ci ❑; **this morning** ce matin; **by this time tomorrow he'll be gone** demain à cette heure-ci, il sera parti; **this time last week** la semaine dernière à la même heure; **this time next year** l'année prochaine à la même époque; **this coming week** la semaine prochaine *ou* qui vient; **saving money isn't easy these days** faire des économies n'est pas facile aujourd'hui *ou* de nos jours; **he's worked hard these last two months** il a beaucoup travaillé ces deux derniers mois; **I've been watching you this past hour** ça fait une heure *ou* voici une heure que je vous regarde; **what are you doing this Christmas?** qu'est-ce que vous faites pour Noël cette année?; *Fam* **I've known him these three years** je le connais depuis trois ans ❑

(**b**) *(contrasted with "that")* ce ...-ci (cette ... -ci); **these** ces ...-ci; **this table over here** cette table-ci; **which do you prefer, this one or that one?** lequel tu préfères, celui-ci ou celui-là?; **this dress is cheaper than that one** cette robe-ci est moins chère que celle-là *ou* que l'autre; **people ran this way and that** les gens couraient dans tous les sens

3 *adv* aussi, si; **it was this high** c'était haut comme ça; **we've come this far, we might as well go on** *(on journey)* nous sommes venus jusqu'ici, alors autant continuer; *(on project)* maintenant que nous en sommes là, autant continuer

thistle ['θɪsəl] *n* chardon *m*

THISTLE

Le chardon est l'emblème de l'Écosse. La légende veut qu'il acquit ce statut symbolique pendant l'invasion de l'Écosse par les Vikings: un soldat viking, qui venait de marcher sur un chardon, hurla de douleur, alertant ainsi les Écossais qui vainquirent promptement les Vikings.

thistledown ['θɪsəldaʊn] *n* duvet *m* de chardon

thistly ['θɪslɪ] *adj* couvert de chardons

thither ['ðɪðə(r)] *adv Formal or Literary* là; **go thither** allez-y

thitherto [ˌðɪðə'tuː] *adv Formal or Literary* jusqu'alors

thixotropy [θɪk'sɒtrəpɪ] *n Phys* thixotropie *f*

tho, tho' = **though**

thole [θəʊl], **tholepin** ['θəʊlpɪn] *n Naut* tolet *m*, dame *f* de nage

thong [θɒŋ] **1** *n* (**a**) *(strip → of leather, rubber)* lanière *f* (**b**) *(underwear)* cache-sexe *m*; *(swimwear)* tanga *m*

2 thongs *npl Am & Austr (flip-flops)* tongs *fpl*

Thor [θɔː(r)] *pr n Myth* Thor

thoraces ['θɔːrəsiːz] *pl of* **thorax**

thoracic [θɔː'ræsɪk] *adj* thoracique

▸▸ ***thoracic duct*** canal *m* thoracique

thoracoplasty ['θɔːrəkəʊˌplæstɪ] *n Med* thoracoplastie *f*

thoracoscopy [ˌθɔːrə'kɒskəpɪ] *n Med* thoracoscopie *f*

thoracotomy [ˌθɔːrə'kɒtəmɪ] *n Med* thoracotomie *f*

thorax ['θɔːræks] (*pl* **thoraxes** *or* **thoraces** [-rəsiːz]) *n* thorax *m*

thorium ['θɔːrɪəm] *n Chem* thorium *m*

▸▸ ***thorium series*** famille *f* du thorium

thorn [θɔːn] *n* (**a**) *(prickle)* épine *f*; *Fig* **it's a thorn in his side** *or* **flesh** c'est une source d'irritation constante pour lui, c'est sa bête noire (**b**) *(tree, shrub)* arbuste *m* épineux; *(hawthorn)* aubépine *f*

▸▸ ***thorn apple*** stramoine *f*

thornback ['θɔːnbæk] *n Ich* raie *f* bouclée

thornbill ['θɔːnbɪl] *n Orn* colibri *m*

thornbird ['θɔːnbɜːd] *n Orn* annumbi *m*

thornbush ['θɔːnbʊʃ] *n* buisson *m* épineux

thornless ['θɔːnlɪs] *adj* sans épines

thorny ['θɔːnɪ] (*compar* **thornier**, *superl* **thorniest**) *adj also Fig* épineux

thorough ['θʌrə] *adj* (**a**) *(complete → inspection, research)* minutieux, approfondi; **to give sth a thorough cleaning/dusting** nettoyer/épousseter qch à fond; **she has a thorough knowledge of her subject** elle a une connaissance parfaite de son sujet, elle connaît son sujet à fond *ou* sur le bout des doigts; **she was subjected to a thorough cross-examination** elle a subi un contre-interrogatoire minutieux; **it needs a thorough revision** il faut réviser ça en profondeur; **they were given a thorough telling-off** ils ont reçu un bon savon

(**b**) *(meticulous → work, worker)* minutieux; **he did a very thorough job** il a fait un travail très minutieux

(**c**) *(as intensifier)* absolu, complet(ète); **what a thorough bore this book is!** qu'est-ce qu'il est ennuyeux, ce livre!; **the man is a thorough scoundrel!** c'est une crapule finie!; **it's a thorough nuisance!** c'est vraiment très embêtant!; **to make a thorough nuisance of oneself** se rendre complètement insupportable

thoroughbred ['θʌrəbred] **1** *adj (horse)* pur-sang *(inv)*; *(animal → gen)* de race

2 *n* (**a**) *(horse)* pur-sang *m inv*; *(animal → gen)* bête *f* de race (**b**) *(person)* **she's a thoroughbred** elle a de la classe, elle est racée

thoroughfare ['θʌrəfeə(r)] *n* voie *f* de communication; **one of the main thoroughfares of the town** une des rues principales *ou* une des artères de la ville; **no thoroughfare** *(no entry)* passage interdit; *(cul-de-sac)* voie sans issue; **public thoroughfare** voie *f* publique

thoroughgoing ['θʌrəˌgəʊɪŋ] *adj (search, investigation)* minutieux, approfondi, complet(ète); **he's a thoroughgoing nuisance** il est vraiment pénible

thoroughly ['θʌrəlɪ] *adv* (**a**) *(minutely, in detail → search)* à fond, de fond en comble; *(→ examine)* à fond, minutieusement; **the carpet has been thoroughly cleaned** le tapis a été nettoyé à fond; **read all the questions thoroughly** lisez très attentivement toutes les questions

(**b**) *(as intensifier)* tout à fait, absolument; **it's thoroughly disgraceful** c'est absolument honteux, c'est un véritable scandale, c'est une honte; **to be thoroughly bored** s'ennuyer mortellement; **I thoroughly agree** je suis tout à fait d'accord

thoroughness ['θʌrənɪs] *n* minutie *f*; **the thoroughness of his knowledge** ses connaissances très complètes; **the thoroughness of his work** la minutie qu'il apporte à son travail

thorow-wax ['θɒrəʊ-] *n Bot* buplèvre *m* à feuilles rondes

those [ðəʊz] *pl of* **that**

thou¹ [ðaʊ] *pron NEng or Arch or Literary* tu; *(stressed form)* toi

thou² [θaʊ] (*pl* **inv** *or* **thous**) *n* (**a**) *Fam (abbr* **thousand**) mille ❑ *m inv* (**b**) *(abbr* **thousandth of an inch**) millième *m* de pouce

though [ðəʊ] **1** *conj* bien que + *subjunctive*, quoique + *subjunctive*; **though young, she's very mature** bien qu'elle soit jeune *ou* quoique jeune, elle est très mûre; **though it's a difficult language, I intend to persevere** bien que ce soit une langue difficile, j'ai l'intention de persévérer; **he enjoyed the company though not the food** il appréciait les gens avec qui il était mais pas ce qu'il mangeait; **kind though she was, we never really got on** malgré sa gentillesse, nous ne nous sommes jamais très bien entendus; **though not handsome, he was attractive** sans être beau, il avait du charme; **it's an excellent book, though I say so myself** c'est un très bon livre, sans fausse modestie; **strange though it may seem** aussi étrange que cela puisse paraître

2 *adv* pourtant; **he's a difficult man; I like him though** il n'est pas facile à vivre; pourtant je l'aime bien; **it's nice, though, isn't it?** c'est joli quand même, tu ne trouves pas?; *Fam* **did she though!** elle a dit/fait cela? ❑

thought [θɔːt] **1** *pt & pp of* **think**

2 *n* (**a**) *(UNCOUNT) (reflection)* pensée *f*, réflexion *f*; **to give a problem much** *or* **a lot of thought** bien réfléchir à un problème; **after much thought** après mûre réflexion, après avoir mûrement réfléchi; **we gave some thought to the matter** nous avons réfléchi à la question; **this problem needs careful thought** nous devons bien réfléchir à ce problème; **she was lost** *or* **deep in thought** elle était absorbée par ses pensées *ou* plongée dans ses pensées; **capable of thought** capable de penser

(**b**) *(consideration)* considération *f*, pensée *f*; **have you given my proposal a single thought?** avez-vous pensé un seul instant à ma proposition?; **I haven't given it a thought** je n'y ai pas pensé; **don't give it another thought** n'y pensez plus; **to collect one's thoughts** rassembler ses esprits; **my thoughts were elsewhere** j'avais l'esprit ailleurs; **my thoughts went back to the time I had spent in Tunisia** j'ai repensé au temps où j'étais en Tunisie; **she accepted the job with no thought of her family** elle a accepté le travail sans tenir compte de sa famille; **he had no thought for his own safety** il ne pensait pas à sa propre sécurité; **our thoughts are with you** nos pensées vous accompagnent

(**c**) *(idea, notion)* idée *f*, pensée *f*; **happy thought** heureuse idée *f*; **dark** *or* **gloomy thoughts** idées *fpl* noires; **the thought occurred to me that you might like to come** l'idée m'est venue *ou* je me suis dit que cela vous ferait peut-être plaisir de venir; **I had to give up all thought** *or* **thoughts of finishing on time** j'ai dû finalement renoncer à l'idée de terminer à temps; **the mere thought of it makes me feel ill** rien que d'y penser, ça me rend malade; **that's a thought!** ça, c'est une idée!; **what an awful thought!** quelle horreur!; **what a kind thought!** quelle aimable attention!; **now there's a thought!** voilà une idée!

(**d**) *(intention)* idée *f*, intention *f*; **we have thoughts of going to Australia** nous avons dans l'idée d'aller *ou* nous songeons à aller en Australie; **her one thought was to reach the top** sa seule idée était d'atteindre le sommet; **I have no thought of resigning** je n'ai pas l'intention de démissionner; **you must give up all thought** *or* **thoughts of seeing him** il faut renoncer à le voir, il ne faut plus penser à le voir; **it's the thought that counts** c'est l'intention qui compte

(**e**) *(opinion)* opinion *f*, avis *m*; **we'd like your thoughts on the matter** nous aimerions savoir ce que vous en pensez

(**f**) *(UNCOUNT) (doctrine, ideology)* pensée *f*; **contemporary political thought** la pensée politique contemporaine

(**g**) *Old-fashioned (small amount)* **a thought too salty** un tout petit peu trop salé

►► ***thought police*** police *f* de la pensée; ***thought transference*** transmission *f* de pensée

thoughtful ['θɔːtfʊl] *adj* (**a**) *(considerate, kind)* prévenant, attentionné; **it was a thoughtful gesture** c'était un geste plein de délicatesse; **be more thoughtful next time** pensez un peu plus aux autres la prochaine fois; **it was very thoughtful of them to send the flowers** c'est très gentil de leur part d'avoir envoyé les fleurs (**b**) *(pensive)* pensif (**c**) *(reasoned → decision, remark, essay)* réfléchi; *(→ study)* sérieux

thoughtfully ['θɔːtfʊlɪ] *adv* (**a**) *(considerately, kindly)* avec prévenance *ou* délicatesse, gentiment; **she very thoughtfully offered to help me** elle a très gentiment proposé de m'aider (**b**) *(pensively)* pensivement (**c**) *(with careful thought)* d'une manière réfléchie; **it's a thoughtfully written article** c'est un article écrit de façon réfléchie

thoughtfulness ['θɔːtfʊlnɪs] *n* (**a**) *(kindness)* prévenance *f*, délicatesse *f*, gentillesse *f* (**b**) *(pensiveness)* air *m* pensif

thoughtless ['θɔːtlɪs] *adj* (**a**) *(inconsiderate → person)* qui manque d'égards pour autrui, qui se soucie peu des autres; *(→ act, behaviour)* qui dénote un manque d'égards *ou* de considération pour autrui; *(→ remark)* indélicat; **it was thoughtless of me** ce n'était pas très délicat de ma part; **what a thoughtless thing to do!** quel manque de délicatesse!

(**b**) *(hasty, rash → person)* irréfléchi; *(→ action, remark)* irréfléchi, inconsidéré

thoughtlessly ['θɔːtlɪslɪ] *adv* (**a**) *(without consideration)* sans aucun égard, sans aucune considération; **to treat sb thoughtlessly** manquer d'égards envers qn; **he very thoughtlessly left it locked** il l'a laissé fermé sans se soucier le moins du monde des autres; **she had thoughtlessly thrown out all their notes** elle avait jeté toutes leurs notes sans s'inquiéter de savoir s'ils pouvaient en avoir besoin

(**b**) *(without forethought)* sans réfléchir

thoughtlessness ['θɔːtlɪsnɪs] *n (UNCOUNT)* (**a**) *(lack of consideration)* manque *m* d'égards *ou* de prévenance (**b**) *(lack of forethought)* irréflexion *f*, étourderie *f*

thought-provoking *adj* qui pousse à la réflexion, stimulant

thousand ['θaʊzənd] **1** *adj* mille; **a thousand years** mille ans, un millénaire; **five thousand people** cinq mille personnes; **I've already told you a thousand times** je te l'ai déjà dit mille fois; **I've got a thousand and one things to ask you/to do** j'ai mille choses à vous demander/à faire

2 *n* mille *m inv*; **in the year two thousand** en l'an deux mille; **there were thousands of people** il y avait des milliers de personnes; **how many people were there? – about a thousand** combien de gens étaient là? – un millier; **she's one in a thousand** c'est la femme entre mille

►► ***Thousand Island dressing*** = sauce à base de mayonnaise, de ketchup et de cornichons hachés

---

'The Thousand and One Nights' 'Les Mille et une nuits'

---

thousandfold ['θaʊzəndfəʊld] **1** *adj* multiplié par mille

2 *adv* mille fois autant

thousandth ['θaʊzəntθ] **1** *adj* millième

2 *n* (**a**) *(fraction)* millième *m* (**b**) *(in series)* millième *mf*

Thrace [θreɪs] *n* la Thrace

thraldom, *Am* **thralldom** ['θrɔːldəm] *n Formal* servitude *f*, esclavage *m*

thrall [θrɔːl] *n Formal* (**a**) *(state)* servitude *f*, esclavage *m*; **to be in thrall to sb** être l'esclave de qn; *Fig* être sous l'emprise de qn; **to be in thrall to sth** être l'esclave de qch; **the government are in thrall to big business** le gouvernement est inféodé aux grandes entreprises; **a people in thrall to a colonial power** un peuple sous le joug colonialiste; *Fig* **to hold sb in thrall** fasciner qn (**b**) *(person)* esclave *mf*

thralldom *Am* = **thraldom**

thrash [θræʃ] **1** *n* (**a**) *Br Fam (party)* fiesta *f*

(**b**) *(music)* thrash *m* (metal)

2 *vt* (**a**) *(as a punishment)* rouer de coups, rosser; *Fam (defeat)* battre à plate(s) couture(s); **he thrashed the hedge with a stick** il donna des grands coups de bâton dans la haie; **the horse reared and thrashed the air with its hooves** le cheval se cabra et fouetta l'air de ses sabots; *Fam* **Liverpool thrashed Arsenal** Liverpool a battu Arsenal à plate(s) couture(s); **to thrash sb soundly** *(as punishment)* donner une bonne raclée à qn; *Fam (defeat)* battre qn à plate(s) couture(s)

(**b**) *(move vigorously)* **to thrash one's arms/legs** agiter violemment les bras/jambes; **the dolphin thrashed its tail and disappeared** le dauphin donna de grands coups de queue et disparut

(**c**) *(thresh → corn)* battre

3 *vi (move violently)* se débattre; **a sea of thrashing limbs** une mer de bras et de jambes qui s'agitaient; **the waves thrashed against the rocks/boat** les vagues battaient violemment contre les rochers/le bateau

►► ***thrash metal*** *(music)* thrash *m* (metal)

►**thrash about, thrash around** **1** *vi (person, fish)* se débattre; **she was thrashing about in bed** elle se débattait dans le lit; **he thrashed about to free himself** il se débattait pour se libérer; **he was thrashing about in the undergrowth with his stick** il battait les broussailles de son bâton

2 *vt sep (stick)* agiter; **to thrash one's arms and legs about** se débattre des mains et des pieds

►**thrash out** *vt sep (problem)* débattre de; *(agreement)* finir par trouver; **we'll thrash it out over lunch** on démêlera *ou* éclaircira cette affaire pendant le repas

thrasher ['θræʃə(r)] *n Orn* moqueur *m*

thrashing [ˌθræʃɪŋ] *n* (**a**) *(beating)* volée *f*; *(punishment)* correction *f*, **to give sb a thrashing** donner une volée à qn; *(as a punishment)* donner une bonne correction à qn; **to get a thrashing** prendre une volée (**b**) *Fam (defeat)* déculottée *f*, raclée *f*; **to give sb a thrashing** battre qn à plate(s) couture(s) (**c**) *(of corn)* battage *m*

thread [θred] **1** *n* (**a**) *Sewing & Med* fil *m*; **gold thread** fil *m* d'or; **polyester thread** fil *m* polyester; *Fig* **his life hung by a thread** sa vie ne tient qu'à un fil

(**b**) *Fig (of water, smoke)* filet *m*; *(of light)* mince rayon *m*; *(of story, argument)* fil *m*; **I've lost the thread of what I was saying** j'ai perdu le fil de ce que je disais; **it's difficult to follow the thread of her argument** il est difficile de suivre le fil de ses idées; **she gradually began to pick up the threads of her life again** elle a lentement commencé à reconstruire sa vie

(**c**) *Tech (of screw)* pas *m*, filetage *m*

(**d**) *Comput (in newsgroup)* fil *m* de discussion

2 *vt* (**a**) *(needle, beads, cotton)* enfiler; **she threaded black cotton through the needle** elle a enfilé une aiguillée de coton noir; **she threaded the needle** elle a enfilé l'aiguille; **she quickly threaded the film into the projector** elle a vite monté le film sur le projecteur; **you have to thread the elastic through the loops** il faut enfiler *ou* faire passer l'élastique dans les boucles; *Fig* **her hair was threaded with grey** elle avait quelques fils blancs dans les cheveux, *Literary* ses cheveux étaient semés de fils d'argent; **she threaded her way through the crowd/market** elle s'est faufilée parmi la foule/à travers le marché

(**b**) *Tech (screw)* tarauder, fileter

3 *vi (needle, cotton)* s'enfiler; **the tape threads through the slot** la bande passe dans la fente

4 threads *npl Fam (clothes)* fringues *fpl*

►► ***thread mark*** filigrane *m (des billets de banque)*

►**thread together** *vt sep (beads)* enfiler

threadbare ['θredbeə(r)] *adj* (**a**) *(carpet, clothing)* usé, râpé; **he lived a threadbare existence** il menait une existence miséreuse (**b**) *(joke, excuse, argument)* usé, rebattu

threadlike ['θredlaɪk] *adj* filiforme

threadworm ['θredwɜːm] *n* oxyure *m*

threat [θret] *n also Fig* menace *f*; **to make threats against sb** proférer des menaces contre qn; **they got what they wanted by threats** ils ont obtenu ce qu'ils voulaient par la menace; **terrorist attacks are a constant threat to our security** les attentats terroristes représentent une menace constante pour notre sécurité; **he's a threat to our security** il constitue une menace pour notre sécurité; **political unrest poses a threat to peace in the area** l'agitation politique menace la paix dans la région; **he is under threat of death** il est menacé de mort; **the country lives under (the) threat of war** le pays vit sous la menace de la guerre

threaten ['θretən] **1** *vt* (**a**) *(make threats against → person)* menacer; **to threaten to do sth** menacer de faire qch; **he threatened her with a gun** il l'a menacée avec un pistolet; **he started threatening me** il s'est fait menaçant, il s'est mis à me menacer; **we were threatened with the sack** on nous a menacés de licenciement; *Law* **to threaten proceedings against sb, to threaten sb with proceedings** menacer de poursuivre qn, menacer qn de poursuites

(**b**) *(of danger, unpleasant event)* menacer; **the species is threatened with extinction** l'espèce est menacée *ou* en voie de disparition; **our jobs are threatened** nos emplois sont menacés; **the threatened strike didn't come off** cette menace de grève n'a pas abouti; **it's threatening to rain/to snow** la pluie/la neige menace

(**c**) *(be a danger for → society, tranquillity)* menacer, être une menace pour

2 *vi (danger, storm)* menacer

threatened ['θretənd] *adj* menacé

threatening ['θretənɪŋ] *adj (danger, sky, storm, person)* menaçant; *(letter)* de menaces; *(gesture)* menaçant, de menace; **she gave me a threatening look** elle m'a lancé un regard menaçant; **to use threatening language** prononcer des paroles menaçantes

►► *Law* ***threatening behaviour*** menaces *fpl*, comportement *m* menaçant

threateningly ['θretənɪŋlɪ] *adv (behave, move)* de manière menaçante, d'un air menaçant; *(say)* d'un ton *ou* sur un ton menaçant

three [θriː] **1** *n (number, numeral)* trois *m inv*; *Pol & Hist* **the Big Three** les Trois Grands *mpl*

2 *pron* trois

3 *adj* trois; *see also* **five**

►► ***Three Mile Island*** Three Mile Island *(théâtre d'un accident dans une centrale nucléaire aux États-Unis en 1979)*

'The Three Musketeers' *Dumas* 'Les Trois mousquetaires'

'Three Men in a Boat' *Jerome* 'Trois hommes dans un bateau'

Three pipe problem

Dans certaines histoires de *Sherlock Holmes*, de Conan Doyle, le célèbre détective emploie l'expression **a three pipe problem** ("un problème à trois pipes") à propos de certaines énigmes particulièrement difficiles à résoudre, qui nécessitent une période de réflexion correspondant au temps qu'il faut pour fumer trois pipes afin d'élaborer une stratégie. On emploie cette expression par allusion à Sherlock Holmes à propos de tout problème ardu qui demande beaucoup de réflexion.

three-button mouse *n Comput* souris *f* à trois boutons

three-card trick *n* bonneteau *m*

three-colour, three-coloured, *Am* **three-color, three-colored** *adj* tricolore; *Phot* trichrome
▸▸ ***three-colour process, three-coloured process*** trichromie *f*

three-cornered *adj* triangulaire
▸▸ ***three-cornered discussion*** débat *m* à trois; ***three-cornered hat*** tricorne *m*

three-course *adj (meal)* à trois plats

3-D, three-D, three-dimensional *adj* (**a**) *(object)* à trois dimensions, tridimensionnel; *(film)* en relief; *(image)* en trois dimensions (**b**) *(character → in book, play etc)* qui semble réel

three-day *adj*
▸▸ *Horseriding* ***three-day event*** = concours hippique sur trois jours; *Ind* ***three-day week*** semaine *f* de trois jours

threefold [ˈθriːfəʊld] **1** *adj* triple; **a threefold increase in the membership figures** une augmentation au triple du nombre d'adhérents
2 *adv* trois fois autant; **to increase threefold** tripler

three-four *adj*
▸▸ *Mus* ***three-four time*** trois-quatre *m inv*; **in three-four time** en trois-quatre

three-handed *adj*
▸▸ *Cards etc* ***three-handed game*** partie *f* à trois

three-legged *adj (stool, table)* à trois pieds; *(animal)* à trois pattes
▸▸ ***three-legged race*** = course où les participants courent par deux, la jambe gauche de l'un attachée à la droite de l'autre

three-line whip *n Br Pol* = convocation urgente d'un député par un "whip" à un vote lors d'une séance parlementaire

threepence [ˈθrepəns, ˈθrʌpəns] *n Br* trois (anciens) pence *mpl*

threepenny [ˈθrepənɪ, ˈθrʌpənɪ] *Br* **1** *n* = ancienne pièce de trois pence
2 *adj* à trois pence, coûtant trois pence
▸▸ ***threepenny bit, threepenny piece*** = ancienne pièce de trois pence

'The Threepenny Opera' *Brecht & Weill* 'L'Opéra de quat' sous'

three-phase *adj Elec* triphasé

three-piece *adj*
▸▸ *Mus* ***three-piece band*** trio *m*; *Am* ***three-piece set*** salon *m* trois pièces *(canapé et deux fauteuils)*; ***three-piece suit*** (costume *m*) trois-pièces *m inv*; *Br* ***three-piece suite*** salon *m* trois pièces *(canapé et deux fauteuils)*

three-pin *adj*
▸▸ ***three-pin plug*** prise *f* à trois fiches

three-ply 1 *n (wool)* laine *f* à trois fils; *(wood)* contreplaqué *m (à trois épaisseurs)*
2 *adj (wool)* à trois fils; *(rope)* à trois brins
▸▸ ***three-ply wood*** contre-plaqué *m (à trois épaisseurs)*

three-point *adj*
▸▸ *Aviat* ***three-point landing*** atterrissage *m* trois points; *Aut* ***three-point turn*** demi-tour *m* en trois manœuvres

three-quarter 1 *adj (sleeve)* trois-quarts *(inv)*; *(portrait)* de trois-quarts; **three-quarter (length) jacket** veste *f* trois-quarts
2 *n (in rugby)* trois-quart *m inv*
▸▸ ***three-quarter back*** *(in rugby)* trois-quart *m inv*; ***three-quarter line*** *(in rugby)* ligne *f* des trois-quarts

three-quarters 1 *npl* trois quarts *mpl*
2 *adv* aux trois quarts; **the tank is three-quarters full** le réservoir est aux trois quarts plein

three-ring circus *n Am* cirque *m* à trois pistes; *Fig* **it's a real three-ring circus** c'est un véritable cirque

threescore [ˌθriːˈskɔː(r)] *Literary* **1** *adj* soixante; **threescore years and ten** soixante-dix ans
2 *n* soixante *m*

three-sided *adj (shape)* à trois côtés *ou* faces; *(discussion)* à trois

threesome [ˈθriːsəm] *n* (**a**) *(group)* groupe *m* de trois personnes; **we went as a threesome** nous y sommes allés à trois (**b**) *(in cards, golf)* partie *f ou* jeu *m* à trois; **she came along to make up a threesome** elle est venue pour que nous soyons trois (joueurs) (**c**) *Fam (for sex)* partouze *f* à trois

three-speed *adj* à trois vitesses
▸▸ ***three-speed gearbox*** boîte *f* trois vitesses

three-star *adj* trois étoiles

three-storey, three-storeyed, *Am* **three-story, three-storied** *adj (house)* à trois étages

three-way *adj (discussion, conversation)* à trois; *(division)* en trois; *(switch)* à trois voies *ou* directions
▸▸ *Aut* ***three-way catalytic convertor*** catalyseur *m* à trois voies; *Br Pol* ***three-way marginal*** = circonscription où trois candidats ont d'égales chances de succès

three-wheeled vehicle *n* trois-roues *m*

three-wheeler *n (tricycle)* tricycle *m*; *(car)* voiture *f* à trois roues

thremmatology [θreməˈtɒlədʒɪ] *n Bot & Zool* science *f* des cultures et de l'élevage

threnody [ˈθrenədɪ] *(pl* **threnodies***)* *n* thrène *m*, chant *m* funèbre

threonine [ˈθrɪənaɪn] *n Biol & Chem* thréonine *f*

thresh [θreʃ] *vt (corn, wheat)* battre

thresher [ˈθreʃə(r)] *n* (**a**) *Agr (person)* batteur(-euse) *m,f* (**b**) *Agr (machine)* batteuse *f* (**c**) *Ich* renard *m* marin
▸▸ *Ich* ***thresher shark*** renard *m* marin

threshing [ˈθreʃɪŋ] *n* battage *m*
▸▸ ***threshing floor*** aire *f* de battage; ***threshing machine*** batteuse *f*

threshold [ˈθreʃhəʊld] **1** *n* (**a**) *(doorway)* seuil *m*, pas *m* de la porte; **to cross the threshold** franchir le seuil
(**b**) *Fig* seuil *m*, début *m*; **on the threshold of** *(era, new century, millennium)* au seuil de, à la veille de; **we are on the threshold of new discoveries** nous sommes sur le point de faire de nouvelles découvertes; **she is on the threshold of a new career** elle débute une nouvelle carrière
(**c**) *Econ & Fin* limite *f*, seuil *m*; **the government has raised tax thresholds in line with inflation** le gouvernement a relevé les tranches de l'impôt pour tenir compte de l'inflation
(**d**) *Anat & Psy* seuil *m*; **to have a low boredom threshold** être prédisposé à l'ennui, s'ennuyer facilement; **to have a high/low pain threshold** avoir un seuil de tolérance à la douleur élevé/peu élevé; **below the threshold of consciousness** au niveau du subconscient, au niveau subliminal
2 *comp Elec (current, voltage)* de seuil
▸▸ *Physiol* ***threshold of audibility, threshold of hearing*** seuil *m* d'audibilité; *Ling* ***threshold level*** niveau *m* seuil; *Fin* ***threshold price*** prix *m* du seuil; *Br Econ* ***threshold (wage) agreement*** accord *m* d'indexation des salaires sur les prix; *Br Econ* ***threshold (wage) policy*** politique *f* d'indexation des salaires sur les prix

threw [θruː] *pt of* **throw**

thrice [θraɪs] *adv Literary or Arch* trois fois

thrift [θrɪft] *n* (**a**) *(care with money)* économie *f*, esprit *m* d'économie (**b**) *Am (savings bank)* caisse *f* d'épargne
▸▸ *Am* ***thrift institution*** caisse *f* d'épargne; *Am* ***thrift shop*** = magasin vendant des articles d'occasion au profit d'œuvres charitables

thriftily [ˈθrɪftɪlɪ] *adv* avec économie; *(live)* frugalement

thriftiness [ˈθrɪftɪnɪs] *n* sens *m* de l'économie

thriftless [ˈθrɪftlɪs] *adj* dépensier, peu économe

thriftlessness [ˈθrɪftlɪsnɪs] *n* tendance *f* au gaspillage

thrifty [ˈθrɪftɪ] *(compar* **thriftier,** *superl* **thriftiest***)* *adj* économe, peu dépensier

thrill [θrɪl] **1** *n (feeling of excitement)* frisson *m*; *(exciting experience, event)* sensation *f*, (vive) émotion *f*; **he felt a thrill of anticipation** un délicieux frisson le parcourut à l'idée du plaisir qui l'attendait; **it was a real thrill to meet the president** j'ai ressenti une grande émotion à rencontrer le président; **the film gave the audience plenty of thrills** le film a procuré aux spectateurs beaucoup de sensations fortes; **the touch of his hand sent a thrill through her** le contact de sa main la fit frissonner de plaisir; **he gets a thrill out of gambling/driving fast** le jeu/la vitesse lui procure des sensations fortes; **he gets a thrill out of humiliating people** il éprouve du plaisir à humilier les gens; **they got quite a thrill out of the experience** ils ont été ravis *ou* enchantés de l'expérience; **the thrill of the chase** le frisson de la poursuite; **what a thrill for you!** quelle émotion vous avez dû ressentir!; *Fam* **go on, give us a thrill, let's see you dance!** allez, fais-nous plaisir *ou* montre-nous ce que tu sais faire, danse!❑; *Fam* **all the thrills and spills of the circus/the hunt** tous les frissons que procure le cirque/la chasse❑
2 *vt (person)* ravir, transporter de joie; *(audience)* électriser; **the news thrilled her** la nouvelle l'a ravie; *(stronger)* la nouvelle l'a transportée de joie; **the magician thrilled the audience with his tricks** le prestidigitateur a électrisé les spectateurs avec ses tours; **the sight of the pyramids thrilled us** le spectacle des pyramides nous a procuré une vive émotion; **a novel/film that will thrill you** un roman/film qui vous passionnera
3 *vi (with joy)* tressaillir, frissonner; **they thrilled to the sound of the drums** le bruit des tambours les fit frissonner; **I thrilled at the sight** à la vue de ce spectacle, j'ai ressenti une vive émotion

thrilled [θrɪld] *adj* ravi; **she was thrilled to be chosen** elle était ravie d'avoir été choisie; **I was thrilled with the new chairs** j'étais ravi des nouvelles chaises; *Fam* **to be thrilled to bits** être aux anges

thriller [ˈθrɪlə(r)] *n (film)* thriller *m*, film *m* à suspense; *(book)* thriller *m*, roman *m* à suspense

thrilling [ˈθrɪlɪŋ] *adj (adventure, film, story)* palpitant, passionnant; *(speech)* exaltant; **what a thrilling experience!** quelle expérience excitante!

thrillingly [ˈθrɪlɪŋlɪ] *adv (narrated)* de façon passionnante; *(acted)* merveilleusement

thrips [θrɪps] *(pl* **inv***)* *n Entom* thrips *m*

thrive [θraɪv] *(pt* **thrived** *or* **throve** [θrəʊv], *pp* **thrived** *or* **thriven** [ˈθrɪvən]) *vi* (**a**) *(plant)* pousser (bien); *(child)* grandir, se développer; *(adult)* se porter bien, respirer la santé; **the plants thrive in peaty soil** les plantes poussent bien dans un sol tourbeux; **she thrived on the mountain air** l'air des montagnes lui réussissait très bien; **young children thrive on affection** les enfants ont besoin d'affection pour s'épanouir; **some people thrive on stress** il y a certaines personnes à qui le stress réussit; **to thrive on danger** aimer le danger, se complaire dans les situations dangereuses; **to thrive on other people's misfortunes** se repaître de la misère d'autrui; **do I like it? I thrive on it!** si j'aime ça? j'adore!
(**b**) *(business, company)* prospérer, être florissant; *(businessman)* prospérer, réussir

thriving [ˈθraɪvɪŋ] *adj* (**a**) *(person)* florissant de santé, vigoureux; *(animal)* vigoureux; *(plant)* robuste, vigoureux (**b**) *(business, company)* prospère, florissant; *(businessman)* prospère

thro' *Literary* = **through**

throat [θrəʊt] **1** *n* gorge *f*; **the back of the throat** le fond de la gorge, l'arrière-gorge *f*; **to have a sore throat** avoir mal à la gorge; **to cut sb's throat** couper la gorge à qn, égorger qn; **he was wearing a scarf round his throat** il portait une écharpe autour du cou; *Hum* **get this drink/medicine down your throat!** avalez-moi cette boisson/ce médicament!; **he grabbed him by the throat** il l'a pris à la gorge; **to clear one's throat** s'éclaircir la voix; **the two brothers are always at each other's throats** les deux frères sont toujours en train de se battre; *Fam* **she's always jumping down my throat** elle est toujours à me crier dessus; *Fam* **he never misses the chance to ram** *or* **to shove his success down my throat** il ne manque jamais une occasion de me rebattre les oreilles avec sa réussite
2 *comp (cancer)* de la gorge
▸▸ ***throat infection*** angine *f*

throatily [ˈθrəʊtɪlɪ] *adv* d'une voix rauque

throatiness [ˈθrəʊtɪnɪs] *n* **the throatiness of his voice** sa voix rauque

throatlash [ˈθrəʊtlæʃ], **throatlatch** [ˈθrəʊtlætʃ] *n Horseriding* sous-gorge *f inv*, sougorge *f*

throat-microphone, throat-mike *n* laryngophone *m*

throaty ['θrəʊtɪ] *(compar* **throatier,** *superl* **throatiest)** *adj (voice, whisper, laugh, cough)* rauque

throb [θrɒb] *(pt & pp* **throbbed,** *cont* **throbbing) 1** *vi* **(a)** *(music)* vibrer; *(drums)* battre (rythmiquement); *(engine, machine)* vrombir, vibrer; **a city throbbing with activity** une ville palpitante d'activité

(b) *(heart)* battre fort, palpiter

(c) *(with pain)* lanciner; **my head is throbbing** j'ai très mal à la tête; **my finger still throbs where I hit it** j'ai encore des élancements dans le doigt là où je l'ai cogné

2 *n* **(a)** *(of music, drums)* rythme *m*, battement(s) *m(pl)* rythmique(s); *(of engine, machine)* vibration(s) *f(pl)*, vrombissement(s) *m(pl)*

(b) *(of heart)* battement(s) *m(pl)*, pulsation(s) *f(pl)*

(c) *(of pain)* élancement *m*

throbbing ['θrɒbɪŋ] *adj* **(a)** *(rhythm)* battant; *(drum)* qui bat rythmiquement; *(engine, machine)* vibrant, vrombissant **(b)** *(heart)* battant, palpitant **(c)** *(pain)* lancinant; **I've got a throbbing headache** j'ai un mal de tête lancinant

throes [θrəʊz] **in the throes of** *prep* **in the throes of war/illness** en proie à la guerre/la maladie; **a country in the throes of revolution** un pays en proie à la révolution *ou* dans la tourmente de la révolution; **to be in the throes of doing sth** être en train de faire qch; **they are in the throes of moving house** ils sont en plein déménagement

thrombi ['θrɒmbaɪ] *pl of* **thrombus**

thrombin ['θrɒmbɪn] *n Biol & Chem* thrombine *f*

thrombocyte ['θrɒmbəʊsaɪt] *n Physiol* thrombocyte *m*

thrombophlebitis [ˌθrɒmbəʊflɪ'baɪtɪs] *n Med* thrombophlébite *f*

thromboplastic [ˌθrɒmbəʊ'plæstɪk] *adj Med* thromboplastique

thrombosis [θrɒm'bəʊsɪs] *(pl* **thromboses** [-si:z]) *n Med* thrombose *f*, thromboses *fpl*

thrombus ['θrɒmbəs] *(pl* **thrombi** [-baɪ]) *n Med* thrombus *m*, caillot *m* de sang

throne [θrəʊn] **1** *n* trône *m*; **to come to** *or* **ascend** *or* **mount the throne** monter sur le trône, accéder au trône; **the heir to the throne** l'héritier *m* au trône; **on the throne** sur le trône; *Euph* **to be on the throne** *(on the toilet)* être là où le roi va seul

2 *vt (monarch)* mettre sur le trône; *(bishop)* introniser

►► ***throne room*** salle *f* du trône

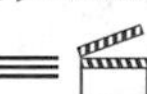

'Throne of Blood' *Kurosawa* 'Le Trône du sang'

throng [θrɒŋ] **1** *n* foule *f*, multitude *f*; **throngs of people were doing their Christmas shopping** une foule de gens faisaient leurs achats de Noël *ou* faisait ses achats de Noël

2 *vt* **demonstrators thronged the streets** des manifestants se pressaient dans les rues; **the shops were thronged with people** les magasins grouillaient de monde *ou* étaient bondés

3 *vi* affluer, se presser; **crowds of people thronged towards the stadium** les gens se dirigeaient en masse vers le stade; **people thronged into the square to get a glimpse of the president** les gens se sont pressés sur la place pour apercevoir le président

thronging ['θrɒŋɪŋ] *adj* **a thronging mass** une foule grouillante

throstle ['θrɒsəl] *n* **(a)** *Literary Orn* grive *f* musicienne **(b)** *Tex* métier *m* continu

throttle ['θrɒtəl] **1** *n (of car)* accélérateur *m*; *(of motorcycle)* poignée *f* d'accélération *ou* des gaz; *(of aircraft)* commande *f* des gaz; **to open/to close the throttle** mettre/réduire les gaz; **at full throttle** (à) pleins gaz

2 *vt* **(a)** *(strangle)* étrangler; **I could throttle you!** je pourrais t'étrangler!

(b) *(engine)* mettre au ralenti

►► ***throttle cable*** câble *m* d'accélération; ***throttle valve*** papillon *m* des gaz, soupape *f* d'étranglement

►**throttle back, throttle down 1** *vi (slow engine)* mettre le moteur au ralenti; *(cut, close off fuel)* couper *ou* fermer les gaz; **the pilot/rider gradually throttled back** le pilote/motard coupa les gaz progressivement

2 *vt sep (engine)* mettre au ralenti

throttling ['θrɒtlɪŋ] *n* **(a)** *(strangling)* étranglement *m* **(b)** *(of engine)* **throttling (back** *or* **down)** ralenti *m*

►► ***throttling valve*** papillon *m* des gaz, soupape *f* d'étranglement

THROUGH [θru:]

à travers	► **1 (a) – (c)**
dans	► **1 (b)**
à	► **1 (d)**
par	► **1 (e)**
grâce à	► **1 (e)**
à cause de	► **1 (f)**

1 *prep* **(a)** *(from one end or side to the other of)* à travers; **to walk through the streets** se promener dans *ou* à travers les rues; **they drove through the countryside** ils ont roulé à travers la campagne; **we travelled through America** nous avons parcouru les États-Unis; **I was wandering through the garden/trees** j'errais dans le jardin/parmi les arbres; **he swam quickly through the water** il nageait rapidement; **the river flows through a deep valley** le fleuve traverse une vallée profonde; **to go through a tunnel** passer dans un tunnel; **the police let them through the roadblock** la police les a laissés passer à travers le barrage routier; **the bullet went straight through his shoulder** la balle lui a traversé l'épaule de part en part; **we went through a door** nous avons passé une porte; **water poured through the hole** l'eau coulait par le trou; **he could see her through the window** il pouvait la voir par la fenêtre; **can you see through it?** est-ce que tu peux voir au travers?; **I can't see much through the fog** je ne vois pas grand-chose à travers le brouillard; **what can you see through the telescope?** qu'est-ce que vous voyez dans *ou* à travers le télescope?; **I could hear them through the wall** je les entendais à travers le mur; **she couldn't feel anything through her gloves** elle ne sentait rien à travers ses gants; **a shiver ran through him** il fut parcouru d'un frisson; **he drove through a red light** il a brûlé un feu rouge; *also Fig* **to slip through the net** passer à travers les mailles du filet; **he goes through his money very quickly** l'argent lui brûle les doigts; **she ate her way through a whole box of chocolates** elle a mangé toute une boîte de chocolats

(b) *(in)* dans, à travers; **he got a bullet through the leg** une balle lui a traversé la jambe; **she was shot through the heart** on lui a tiré une balle dans le cœur; **the bull had a ring through its nose** le taureau avait un anneau dans le nez; **to make a hole through sth** percer un trou à travers qch

(c) *(from beginning to end of)* à travers; **through the ages** à travers les âges; **all through his life** durant *ou* pendant toute sa vie; **halfway through the performance** à la moitié *ou* au milieu de la représentation; **I'm halfway through this book** [illegible]; **she has lived through some difficult times** elle a connu *ou* traversé des moments difficiles; *Fam* **he's been through it** *or* **through a lot** il en a bavé, il en a vu de dures; **we had to sit through a boring lecture** nous avons dû rester à écouter une conférence ennuyeuse; **I slept through the storm** l'orage ne m'a pas réveillé; **will he live through the night?** passera-t-il la nuit?; **the war lasted all through 1914 to 1918** la guerre a duré de 1914 jusqu'en 1918; **she maintained her dignity through it all** elle a toujours gardé sa dignité

(d) *Am (to, until)* **80 through 100** de 80 à 100; **Monday through Friday** de lundi à vendredi, du lundi au vendredi; **April through July** d'avril jusqu'en juillet, d'avril à juillet

(e) *(by means of)* par, grâce à; **I sent it through the post** je l'ai envoyé par la poste; **she can only be contacted through her secretary** on ne peut la contacter que par l'intermédiaire de sa secrétaire; **it was only through his intervention that we were allowed out** c'est uniquement grâce à son intervention qu'on nous a laissés sortir; **I met a lot of people through him** il m'a fait rencontrer beaucoup de gens; **she was interviewed through an interpreter** on l'a interviewée par l'intermédiaire d'un interprète; **change must be achieved through peaceful means** le changement doit être obtenu par des moyens pacifiques

(f) *(because of)* à cause de; **through no fault of his own, he lost his job** il a perdu son emploi sans que ce soit de sa faute; **through ignorance** par ignorance; **absent through illness** absent par suite *ou* pour cause de maladie; **it all came about through a misunderstanding** tout est arrivé à cause d'un malentendu; **through failing to lock the door...** pour n'avoir pas fermé la porte à clé...

2 *adv* **(a)** *(from one end or side to the other)* **please go through into the lounge** passez dans le salon, s'il vous plaît; **I couldn't get through** je ne pouvais pas passer; **we shoved our way through** nous nous sommes frayé un chemin en poussant; **the police let us through** la police nous a laissés passer; **the rain was coming through** la pluie passait au travers; **the nail had gone right through** le clou était passé au travers; **her trousers are through at the knees** son pantalon est déchiré aux genoux

(b) *(from beginning to end)* **I slept through until 8 o'clock** j'ai dormi (sans me réveiller) jusqu'à 8 heures; **I slept the whole night through** j'ai dormi d'un trait jusqu'au matin; **I saw the film all the way through** j'ai vu le film jusqu'au bout; **I read the letter through** j'ai lu la lettre jusqu'au bout; **I left halfway through** je suis parti au milieu; **England are through to the semi-final** l'Angleterre s'est qualifiée pour *ou* jouera la demi-finale

(c) *(directly)* **the train goes through to Paris without stopping** le train va directement à Paris *ou* est sans arrêt jusqu'à Paris; **to book through to Paris** prendre un billet direct pour Paris; **can you get a bus right through to the port?** est-ce qu'il y a un bus direct pour le port?

(d) *(completely)* **to be wet through** être complètement trempé; **she's an aristocrat through and through** c'est une aristocrate jusqu'au bout des ongles

(e) *Tel* **can you put me through to Elaine/to extension 363?** pouvez-vous me passer Elaine/le poste 363?; **I'm putting you through now** je vous passe votre correspondant *ou* communication; **I tried ringing him, but I couldn't get through** j'ai essayé de l'appeler mais je n'ai pas réussi à l'avoir; **you're through now** vous êtes en ligne

3 *adj* **(a)** *(direct* · *train, ticket)* direct; *(traffic)* en transit, de passage; **all through passengers must remain seated** tous les passagers en transit doivent garder leur place; **a through train to London** un train direct pour Londres; *Br* **no through road,** *Am* **not a through street** *(sign)* voie sans issue

(b) *(finished)* **are you through?** avez-vous fini?, c'est fini?; **he's through with his work at last** il a enfin terminé tout son travail; **I'll be through reading the newspaper in a minute** j'aurai fini de lire le journal dans un instant; **I'm through with smoking** la cigarette, c'est fini; **she's through with him** elle en a eu assez de lui; **we're through** c'est fini entre nous; **you can do your own typing, I'm through!** tu n'as qu'à le taper toi-même, moi c'est fini *ou* j'en ai assez!

'Through the Looking Glass' *Carroll* 'De l'autre côté du miroir'

throughout [θru:'aʊt] **1** *prep* **(a)** *(in space)* partout dans; **throughout the world** dans le monde entier, partout dans le monde; **throughout Europe** à travers *ou* dans toute l'Europe, partout en Europe

(b) *(in time)* **throughout the year** pendant toute l'année; **throughout my life** (durant) toute ma vie; **throughout this period** pendant toute cette période

2 *adv* **(a)** *(everywhere)* partout; **the house has**

been repainted throughout la maison a été entièrement repeinte

(**b**) *(all the time)* (pendant) tout le temps; **she remained silent throughout** elle est restée silencieuse du début jusqu'à la fin

throughput ['θru:pʊt] *n Comput* capacité *f* de traitement

throughway = **thruway**

throve [θrəʊv] *pt of* **thrive**

THROW [θrəʊ]

lancer	▸ 1 (a), (e); 2; 3 (a)
jeter	▸ 1 (a), (e)
projeter	▸ 1 (c), (e)
plonger	▸ 1 (d)
jet	▸ 3 (a)
coup	▸ 3 (b)
tour	▸ 3 (b)

(*pt* **threw** [θru:], *pp* **thrown** [θrəʊn]) **1** *vt* (**a**) *(stone)* lancer, jeter; *(ball)* lancer; *Sport (discus, javelin etc)* lancer; *(dice)* jeter; *(coal onto fire)* mettre; **throw me the ball, throw the ball to me** lance-moi le ballon; **he threw the ball over the wall** il a lancé *ou* envoyé le ballon par-dessus le mur; **a bomb was thrown into the crowded waiting room** une bombe a été lancée dans la salle d'attente bondée; **could you throw me my lighter?** peux-tu me lancer mon briquet?; **she threw the serviette into the bin** elle a jeté la serviette à la poubelle; **children were throwing bread to the birds** les enfants jetaient *ou* lançaient du pain aux oiseaux; **he threw his jacket over a chair** il a jeté sa veste sur une chaise; **to throw a sheet over sth** couvrir qch d'un drap; **she threw a few clothes into a suitcase** elle a jeté quelques affaires dans une valise; **I threw some cold water on my face** je me suis aspergé la figure avec de l'eau froide; **a group of rioters threw stones at the police/the car** un groupe de manifestants a lancé *ou* jeté des pierres sur les policiers/la voiture; **he threw two sixes** *(with dice)* il a jeté deux six; **to throw sb into prison** *or* **jail** jeter qn en prison; **to throw sb to the lions** jeter qn aux lions; *Fig* jeter qn en pâture

(**b**) *(opponent, rider)* jeter (par *ou* à terre); **his opponent threw him to the ground** *(in fight)* son adversaire l'a jeté à terre; *(in wrestling match)* son adversaire l'a envoyé au sol *ou* au tapis; **the horse threw him** le cheval le désarçonna *ou* le jeta à terre

(**c**) *(with force, violence)* projeter; **she was thrown clear** *(in car accident)* elle a été éjectée; **the force of the explosion threw them against the wall** la force de l'explosion les a projetés contre le mur; **to throw open** ouvrir en grand *ou* tout grand; **she threw open the door/windows** elle a ouvert la porte/les fenêtres en grand; *Fig* **the House of Commons has been thrown open to the television cameras** la Chambre des communes a été ouverte aux caméras de télévision; **she threw herself into an armchair** elle s'est jetée dans un fauteuil; **he threw himself at her feet** il s'est jeté à ses pieds; **she threw herself at him** *(attacked)* elle s'est jetée *ou* s'est ruée sur lui; *(as lover)* elle s'est jetée sur lui *ou* à sa tête; *Fig* **he threw himself on the mercy of the king** il s'en est remis au bon vouloir du roi

(**d**) *(plunge)* plonger; **the news threw them into confusion/a panic** les nouvelles les ont plongés dans l'embarras/les ont affolés; **the scandal has thrown the country into confusion** le scandale a semé la confusion dans le pays; **to throw oneself into one's work** se plonger dans son travail; **she threw herself into the job of organizing the wedding** elle s'est plongée avec enthousiasme dans l'organisation des noces

(**e**) *(direct, aim → look, glance)* jeter, lancer; *(→ accusation, reproach)* lancer, envoyer; *(→ punch)* lancer, porter; *(cast → light, shadows)* projeter; **to throw sb a kiss** envoyer un baiser à qn; **to throw a question at sb** poser une question à brûle-pourpoint à qn; **don't throw that one at me!, don't throw that in my face!** ne me faites pas ce reproche!, ne me jetez pas ça à la figure!; *Theat* **to throw one's voice** projeter sa voix; *Constr* **to throw a bridge over a river** jeter un pont sur une rivière

(**f**) *(confuse)* désarçonner, dérouter, déconcerter; **that question really threw me!** cette question m'a vraiment désarçonné!, je ne savais vraiment pas quoi répondre à cette question!; **I was completely thrown for a few seconds** je suis resté tout interdit pendant quelques secondes

(**g**) *(activate → switch, lever, clutch)* actionner

(**h**) *Sport (race, match)* perdre délibérément

(**i**) *(silk)* tordre; **to throw a pot** *(potter)* tourner un vase

(**j**) *Vet (of cat, pig)* **to throw a litter** mettre bas

2 *vi* **she can throw a hundred metres** elle est capable de lancer à cent mètres; **I can't throw straight** je n'arrive pas à lancer droit

3 *n* (**a**) *(of ball, javelin)* jet *m*, lancer *m*; *(of dice)* lancer *m*; **his whole fortune depended on a single throw of the dice** toute sa fortune dépendait d'un seul coup de dés; **it's your throw** c'est ton tour, (c'est) à toi; *Sport* **a free throw** un lancer franc; **that was a good throw!** vous avez bien visé!

(**b**) *Fam (go, turn)* coup□ *m*, tour□ *m*; **10p a throw** 10 pence le coup; **at £20 a throw I can't afford it** à 20 livres chaque fois, je ne peux pas me l'offrir□; **give me another throw** laissez-moi encore une chance□

(**c**) *(cover)* couverture *f*; *(piece of fabric)* jeté *m* de fauteuil *ou* de canapé

▸▸ *Am* ***throw pillow*** coussin *m*

▸**throw about, throw around** *vt sep* (**a**) *(toss)* lancer; *(scatter)* jeter, éparpiller; **the boys were throwing a ball about** les garçons jouaient à la balle; **don't throw your books/toys about like that** ne lance pas tes livres/jouets comme ça; **to throw one's money about** gaspiller son argent; **to be thrown about** être ballotté

(**b**) *(move violently)* **to throw oneself about** s'agiter, se débattre; **she was throwing her arms about wildly** elle agitait frénétiquement les bras

▸**throw aside** *vt sep (unwanted object)* rejeter, laisser de côté; *(friend, work)* laisser tomber, laisser de côté; *(idea, suggestion)* rejeter, repousser; *(prejudices, fears, hatred etc)* se débarrasser de

▸**throw away** **1** *vt sep* (**a**) *(old clothes, rubbish)* jeter

(**b**) *Fig (waste → advantage, opportunity, talents)* gaspiller, gâcher; *(→ affection, friendship)* perdre; **don't throw your money away on expensive toys** ne gaspille pas ton argent à acheter des jouets coûteux; **you're throwing away your only chance of happiness** vous êtes en train de gâcher votre seule chance de bonheur; **his presents are just thrown away on her** elle ne sait pas apprécier les cadeaux qu'il lui fait; **to throw away one's life** *(waste)* gâcher sa vie; *(sacrifice for nothing)* se sacrifier inutilement; **don't throw yourself away on a waster like him** ne gâche pas ta vie pour un bon à rien pareil

(**c**) *Theat (line, remark)* laisser tomber

2 *vi (in cards)* se défausser

▸**throw back** *vt sep* (**a**) *(gen)* relancer, renvoyer; *(fish)* rejeter (à l'eau); *Fig (image, light)* réfléchir, renvoyer; *(heat)* réverbérer; **she threw his words of love back at him** elle lui a jeté tous ses mots d'amour à la tête; *Fig* **to throw sth back in sb's face** jeter qch à la figure de qn

(**b**) *(hair, head)* rejeter en arrière; *(shoulders)* redresser, jeter en arrière

(**c**) *(curtains)* ouvrir; *(shutters)* repousser, ouvrir tout grand; *(bedclothes)* repousser

(**d**) *(idiom) (force to rely on)* **we were thrown back on our own resources** on a dû se rabattre sur nos propres ressources

▸**throw down** *vt sep* (**a**) *(to lower level)* jeter; **can you throw the towel down to me?** pouvez-vous me lancer la serviette?; **she threw her bag down on the floor** elle a jeté son sac par terre; **to throw oneself down on the ground/on one's knees** se jeter par terre/à genoux; **he threw his cards down on the table** il a jeté ses cartes sur la table; **I threw the money down on the counter** j'ai jeté l'argent sur le comptoir

(**b**) *(weapons)* jeter, déposer; **they threw down their arms** ils ont déposé les armes

(**c**) *Fig (challenge)* lancer

(**d**) *Br Fam (idiom)* **it's throwing it down** *(raining)* il pleut à verse□, il tombe des cordes

▸**throw in** **1** *vt sep* (**a**) *(into box, cupboard etc)* jeter; *(through window)* jeter, lancer; *also Fig* **to throw in the towel** jeter l'éponge; *also Fig* **to throw in one's hand** abandonner la partie

(**b**) *(interject → remark, suggestion)* placer; **she threw in a few comments about housing problems** elle a placé quelques remarques sur les problèmes de logement

(**c**) *(include)* **breakfast is thrown in** le petit déjeuner est compris; **the salesman said he'd throw in a free door if we bought new windows** le vendeur nous a promis une porte gratuite pour l'achat de fenêtres neuves; **with a special trip to Stockholm thrown in** avec en prime une excursion à Stockholm

(**d**) *Sport (ball)* remettre en jeu

2 *vi Am* **to throw in with sb** s'associer à *ou* avec qn

▸**throw off** *vt sep* (**a**) *(discard → clothes)* enlever *ou* ôter (à la hâte); *(→ mask, disguise)* jeter; **he threw off his shirt and dived into the water** il enleva sa chemise et plongea dans l'eau

(**b**) *(get rid of → habit, inhibition)* se défaire de, se débarrasser de; *(→ burden)* se libérer de, se débarrasser de; *(→ cold, infection)* se débarrasser de

(**c**) *(elude → pursuer)* perdre, semer; **he managed to throw the dogs off the trail** il a réussi à dépister les chiens

(**d**) *(write hastily → poem etc)* composer au pied levé

▸**throw on** *vt sep (clothes)* enfiler *ou* passer (à la hâte); **she threw on some make-up/an old coat** elle s'est maquillée/a enfilé un vieux manteau à la hâte

▸**throw out** *vt sep* (**a**) *(rubbish, unwanted items)* jeter, mettre au rebut

(**b**) *(eject → from building)* mettre à la porte, jeter dehors; *(→ from night club)* jeter dehors, vider; *(evict → from accommodation)* expulser; *(expel → from school, army)* renvoyer, expulser; **we were thrown out of our jobs** on s'est fait mettre à la porte; **the takeover will throw a lot of people out of work** le rachat va mettre beaucoup de monde au chômage

(**c**) *(reject → bill, proposal)* rejeter, repousser

(**d**) *(extend → arms, leg)* tendre, étendre; **to throw out one's chest** bomber le torse

(**e**) *(make → remark, suggestion)* émettre, laisser tomber; **to throw out a challenge** lancer un défi

(**f**) *(disturb → person)* déconcerter, désorienter; *(upset → calculation, results)* fausser

(**g**) *(emit → light)* émettre, diffuser; *(→ smoke, heat)* émettre, répandre

▸**throw over** *vt sep Fam (girlfriend, boyfriend)* quitter□, laisser tomber□; *(plan)* abandonner□, renoncer à□; **she threw me over for another guy** elle m'a laissé tomber pour un autre

▸**throw together** *vt sep* (**a**) *Fam (make quickly → equipment, table)* fabriquer à la hâte□, bricoler; **he managed to throw a meal together** il a réussi à improviser un repas□; **the film looks as if it's been thrown together** le film semble bâclé; **she threw the report together the night before** elle a rédigé le rapport en vitesse la veille au soir□

(**b**) *(gather)* rassembler à la hâte; **she threw a few things together and rang for a taxi** elle a jeté quelques affaires dans un sac et a appelé un taxi

(**c**) *(by accident)* réunir par hasard; **Fate had thrown them together** le destin les avait réunis

▸**throw up** **1** *vt sep* (**a**) *(above one's head)* jeter *ou* lancer en l'air; **can you throw me up my towel?** peux-tu me lancer ma serviette?; **they threw their hats up into the air** ils ont lancé leur chapeau en l'air; **she threw up her hands in horror** elle a levé les bras en signe d'horreur

(**b**) *(produce → problem)* produire, créer; *(→ evidence)* mettre à jour; *(→ dust, dirt)* soulever; *(→ artist)* produire; **the discussion threw up some new ideas** la discussion a amené de nouvelles idées

(**c**) *(abandon → career, studies)* abandonner, laisser tomber; *(→ chance, opportunity)* laisser passer, gaspiller

(**d**) *Pej (construct → building)* construire *ou* bâtir en moins de deux
(**e**) *Fam (vomit)* dégobiller
2 *vi Fam* vomir□, rendre; **it makes you want to throw up** c'est à vomir

throwaway ['θrəʊə,weɪ] **1** *adj (line, remark)* fait comme par hasard *ou* comme si de rien n'était; **it was just a throwaway remark** il a/elle a/*etc* dit ça comme ça; **we live in a throwaway culture** *or* **society** nous vivons dans une société de gaspillage
2 *n* (**a**) *(bottle)* bouteille *f* sans consigne; *(container)* emballage *m* perdu *ou* jetable
(**b**) *Am (handbill)* prospectus *m*
3 *comp (bottle, carton etc)* jetable, à jeter, à usage unique

throwback ['θrəʊbæk] *n* (**a**) *(anthropological) & Biol* régression *f* atavique; **he's a throwback to his great-grandfather** il a hérité (des caractéristiques) de son arrière-grand-père (**b**) *(of fashion, custom)* **those new hats are a throwback to the 1930s** ces nouveaux chapeaux marquent un retour aux années 30 *ou* sont inspirés des années 30

thrower ['θrəʊə(r)] *n* lanceur(euse) *m,f*

throw-in *n Ftbl* rentrée *f* en touche

thrown [θrəʊn] *pp of* **throw**

thru *Am* = **through**

thrum [θrʌm] **1** *vi* (**a**) *(engine, machine)* vibrer, vrombir; *(rain)* tambouriner (**b**) *(guitarist)* gratter les cordes; **to thrum on a guitar** gratter de la guitare
2 *vt* (**a**) *(repeat)* réciter *ou* répéter d'une manière monotone (**b**) *(guitar)* gratter de, taquiner; **to thrum a tune on the guitar** racler un air sur la guitare

thrush [θrʌʃ] *n* (**a**) *Orn* grive *f* (**b**) *(UNCOUNT) Med (oral)* muguet *m*; *(vaginal)* mycose *f*, candidose *f*

thrust [θrʌst] *(pt & pp* **thrust**) **1** *vt* (**a**) *(push, shove → finger)* enfoncer; *(→ handkerchief)* fourrer; *(→ knife)* plonger, planter, enfoncer; **he thrust his finger/elbow into my ribs** il m'a enfoncé le doigt/le coude dans les côtes; **I thrust the stick into the jar** j'ai plongé le bâton dans le pot; **he thrust his sword into its scabbard** il a glissé son épée dans son fourreau; **to thrust one's hands into one's pockets** enfoncer *ou* fourrer les mains dans ses poches; **he thrust her into the cell** il l'a poussée violemment dans la cellule; **she thrust the money towards him** elle a brusquement poussé l'argent vers lui; **she thrust the money into his hands/into his bag** elle lui a fourré l'argent dans les mains/dans le sac; **I had a gun thrust at me** on m'a mis un revolver sous le nez; **she thrust me to the front** elle m'a poussé devant; **to thrust one's way through the crowd/to the front** se frayer un chemin à travers la foule/pour être devant
(**b**) *(force → responsibility, fame)* imposer; **the job was thrust upon me** on m'a imposé ce travail; **to be thrust into a position of responsibility** être parachuté à un poste à responsabilités; **fame was thrust upon her overnight** la gloire lui est tombée dessus du jour au lendemain; **he was thrust into the limelight** il a été mis en vedette; **to thrust oneself on** *or* **upon sb** imposer sa présence à qn, s'imposer à qn
2 *vi* (**a**) *(push)* **he thrust past her** *(rudely)* il l'a bousculée en passant devant elle; *(quickly)* il est passé devant elle comme une flèche; *Fig* **towers thrusting upwards into the sky** des tours qui s'élancent vers le ciel
(**b**) *Fencing* allonger *ou* porter une botte; **he thrust at him with a knife** il a essayé de lui donner un coup de couteau
3 *n* (**a**) *(lunge)* poussée *f*; *(stab)* coup *m*; **with a single thrust of his sword** d'un seul coup d'épée
(**b**) *Fig (remark)* pointe *f*; **a few well-aimed thrusts at the opposition parties** quelques pointes bien senties contre les partis de l'opposition
(**c**) *(UNCOUNT) (force → of engine)* poussée *f*; *Fig (drive)* dynamisme *m*, élan *m*
(**d**) *(of argument, story)* sens *m*, idée *f*; *(of policy)* idée *f* directrice; *(of research)* aspect *m* principal; **the main thrust of her argument** l'idée maîtresse de son raisonnement
(**e**) *(UNCOUNT) Archit & Geol* poussée *f*

▸**thrust aside** *vt sep (person, thing)* écarter brusquement; *(suggestion)* écarter *ou* rejeter brusquement

▸**thrust away** *vt sep* repousser

▸**thrust forward** *vt sep* pousser en avant brusquement; **to thrust oneself forward** se frayer un chemin; *Fig* se mettre en avant

▸**thrust in** **1** *vi (physically)* s'introduire de force
2 *vt sep (finger, pointed object)* enfoncer; **she thrust her hand in** elle a brusquement mis la main dedans; **to thrust one's way in** se frayer un passage pour entrer

▸**thrust out** *vt sep* (**a**) *(arm, leg)* allonger brusquement; *(hand)* tendre brusquement; *(chin)* projeter en avant; **she thrust her head out of the window** elle a brusquement passé la tête par la fenêtre; **to thrust out one's chest** bomber la poitrine; **to thrust one's way out** se frayer un chemin pour sortir
(**b**) *(eject)* pousser dehors

▸**thrust up** *vi* s'élancer, jaillir

thruster ['θrʌstə(r)] *n* (**a**) *Astron (rocket)* micropropulseur *m* (**b**) *(dynamic person)* personne *f* dynamique *ou* plein d'allant; *Pej (pushy person)* arriviste *mf*; **he's a bit of a thruster** il va toujours de l'avant; *Pej* il se met toujours en avant, c'est le genre arriviste

thrusting ['θrʌstɪŋ] *adj Br (dynamic)* dynamique, entreprenant, plein d'entrain; *Pej (pushy)* qui se fait valoir, qui se met en avant; **one of these thrusting young salesmen** un de ces jeunes vendeurs qui cherchent à se mettre en avant

thruway ['θru:weɪ] *n Am* ≃ autoroute *f (à cinq ou six voies)*

Thucydides [θu:'sɪdɪdi:z] *pr n* Thucydide

thud [θʌd] *(pt & pp* **thudded**, *cont* **thudding**) **1** *vi* (**a**) *(make noise → gen)* faire un bruit sourd; *(→ falling object)* tomber en faisant un bruit sourd; **we could hear the cannon thudding in the distance** on entendait gronder les canons au loin
(**b**) *(walk or run heavily)* **to thud across/in/past** traverser/entrer/passer à pas pesants; **his feet went thudding along the corridor** ses pas résonnaient sourdement dans le couloir; **we could hear people thudding about in the flat above** on entendait les gens du dessus marcher à pas lourds; **footsteps thudded up the stairs** quelqu'un montait l'escalier d'un pas lourd
(**c**) *(heart)* battre fort
2 *n* bruit *m* sourd; **the book fell to the floor with a thud** le livre est tombé par terre avec un bruit sourd

thug [θʌg] *n (hooligan)* voyou *m*; *(brutal person)* brute *f*; **a gang of thugs** une bande de voyous

thuggery ['θʌgərɪ] *n* brutalité *f*, violence *f*

thulium ['θu:lɪəm] *n Chem* thulium *m*

thumb [θʌm] **1** *n* pouce *m*; *Fig* **to be under sb's thumb** être sous la coupe de qn; **his mother's really got him under her thumb** sa mère a vraiment de l'emprise sur lui *ou* en fait vraiment ce qu'elle veut; **to be all (fingers and) thumbs** être maladroit; **to stick out like a sore thumb** *(be obvious)* crever les yeux; *(be obtrusive)* faire tache; **that factory sticks out like a sore thumb** cette usine fait tache
2 *vt* (**a**) *(book, magazine)* feuilleter, tourner les pages de; *(pages)* tourner; **the catalogue has been well thumbed** les pages du catalogue sont bien écornées
(**b**) *(hitch)* **to thumb a** *Br* **lift** *or Am* **ride** faire du stop *ou* de l'auto-stop; **they thumbed a lift to Exeter** ils sont allés à Exeter en stop; **I had to thumb a lift home** j'ai dû rentrer (chez moi) en stop; **she thumbed a lift from a passing motorist** elle a réussi à se faire prendre en stop par une voiture qui passait
(**c**) *(idiom)* **to thumb one's nose at sb** faire un pied de nez à qn
3 *vi Am Fam* faire du stop *ou* de l'auto-stop
▸▸ ***thumb index*** répertoire *m* à onglets

▸**thumb through** *vt insep (book, magazine)* feuilleter; *(files)* consulter rapidement; *(pages)* tourner

thumb-indexed *adj (book)* à onglets

thumbnail ['θʌmneɪl] *n* (**a**) *(on finger)* ongle *m* du pouce (**b**) *Comput* vignette *f*
▸▸ ***thumbnail sketch*** *(of plan)* aperçu *m*, croquis *m* rapide; *(of personality)* bref portrait *m*

thumbprint ['θʌmprɪnt] *n* empreinte *f* du pouce

thumbscrew ['θʌmskru:] *n* (**a**) *Tech* vis *f* à papillon *ou* à ailettes (**b**) *(instrument of torture)* = instrument de torture servant à écraser les pouces des prisonniers

thumbs-down *n* **he gave her the thumbs-down as he came out** en sortant, il lui a fait signe que cela avait mal marché; **my proposal was given the thumbs-down** ma proposition a été rejetée

thumbstall ['θʌmstɔ:l] *n* poucier *m*

thumbs-up *n* **to give sb the thumbs-up** *(all OK)* faire signe à qn que tout va bien; *(in encouragement)* faire signe à qn pour l'encourager; **he gave her the thumbs-up as he came out** en sortant, il lui a fait signe que cela avait bien marché; **they've given them the thumbs-up for the project** ils leur donné le feu vert pour le projet

thumbtack ['θʌmtæk] *n Am* punaise *f*

thump [θʌmp] **1** *vt* donner un coup de poing à, frapper d'un coup de poing; **he thumped me in the stomach/on the head** il m'a donné un coup de poing à l'estomac/à la tête; **to thump sb on the back** donner une grande tape dans le dos à qn; **he thumped his fist on the table** il a frappé du poing sur la table
2 *vi* (**a**) *(bang)* cogner; **he thumped on the door/wall** il a cogné à la porte/contre le mur; **she was thumping away on the piano** elle tapait sur le piano comme une sourde; **my heart was thumping with fear/excitement** la peur/l'émotion me faisait battre le cœur
(**b**) *(run or walk heavily)* **to thump in/out/past** entrer/sortir/passer à pas lourds; **heavy boots thumped up the stairs** on entendait de lourds bruits de bottes dans l'escalier
3 *n* (**a**) *(blow → gen)* coup *m*; *(→ with fist)* coup *m* de poing; *(→ with stick)* coup *m* de bâton; **to give sb a thump** assener un coup de poing à qn; **he got a thump in the stomach** il a reçu un coup de poing à l'estomac
(**b**) *(sound)* bruit *m* sourd; **the log fell to the ground with a thump** la bûche est tombée par terre lourdement *ou* avec un bruit sourd
4 *adv Fam* **to go thump** faire boum

▸**thump out** *vt sep* **to thump out a tune on the piano** marteler un air au piano

thumper ['θʌmpə(r)] *n Fam Old-fashioned* (**a**) *(big thing)* chose *f* maousse; **isn't it a thumper!** il/elle est de taille! (**b**) *(lie)* **to tell thumpers** en conter de fortes; **that's a thumper!** en voilà une forte!

thumping ['θʌmpɪŋ] *Br Fam* **1** *adj (success)* énorme□, immense□, phénoménal; *(difference)* énorme□
2 *adv Old-fashioned (as intensifier)* **a thumping great meal** un repas énorme□; **that was a thumping good show!** ce spectacle était formidable!; **a thumping big lie** un gros mensonge□

thunder ['θʌndə(r)] **1** *n* (**a**) *Met* tonnerre *m*; **clap of thunder** coup *m* de tonnerre; **there was a lot of thunder last night** il a beaucoup tonné la nuit dernière; **there's thunder in the air** le temps est à l'orage; **to be as black as thunder** *(angry)* être dans une colère noire; **his voice was like thunder** il avait une voix de tonnerre
(**b**) *(of applause, guns)* tonnerre *m*; *(of engine, traffic)* bruit *m* de tonnerre; *(of hooves)* fracas *m*; **we could hear the thunder of the waves crashing on the rocks below** on entendait le fracas des vagues qui s'écrasaient sur les rochers en contre-bas
(**c**) *Br Old-fashioned* **by thunder!** tonnerre!
2 *vi* (**a**) *Met* tonner; **it's thundering** il tonne, ça tonne
(**b**) *(guns, waves)* tonner, gronder; *(hooves)* retentir; **a train thundered past** le train est passé dans un grondement de tonnerre
(**c**) *(shout)* **to thunder at sb/against sth** tonner contre qn/contre qch
3 *vt (order, threat)* lancer d'une voix tonitruante *ou* tonnante; **"damn them!", he thundered** "qu'ils aillent au diable!", tonna-t-il; **the audience thundered their delight** *(applauded)* le public manifesta son plaisir par un tonnerre d'applaudissements
▸▸ *Theat* ***thunder sheet*** = plaque de métal servant à imiter le bruit du tonnerre

thr–thu

▸**thunder out** *vt sep (order)* lancer d'une voix tonitruante

Thunderbird ['θʌndəbɜːd] *n (car)* Thunderbird *f (nom d'un modèle de Ford des années 50)*

thunderbolt ['θʌndəbəʊlt] *n Met* foudre *m*; *Fig* coup *m* de tonnerre; **the news came like a thunderbolt** cette nouvelle m'a/l'a/*etc* stupéfait

thunderbox ['θʌndəbɒks] *n Fam Hum* petit coin *m*, cabinets *mpl*

thunderclap ['θʌndəklæp] *n* coup *m* de tonnerre

thundercloud ['θʌndəklaʊd] *n Met* nuage *m* orageux; *Fig* nuage *m* noir

Thunderer ['θʌndərə(r)] *n* (**a**) *Myth* **the Thunderer** Jupiter (**b**) *Br Press* **the Thunderer** = surnom du 'Times'

thunderflash ['θʌndəflæʃ] *n* grand pétard *m*

thunderhead ['θʌndəhed] *n esp Am Met* cumulonimbus *m*

thundering ['θʌndərɪŋ] *Br Fam Old-fashioned* **1** *adj* (**a**) *(terrible)* **to be in a thundering temper** *or* **rage** être dans une colère noire❑ *ou* hors de soi❑; **it's a thundering nuisance!** quelle barbe! (**b**) *(superb → success)* foudroyant❑, phénoménal

2 *adv* **it's a thundering good read** c'est un livre formidable

thunderingly ['θʌndərɪŋlɪ] *adv Br Fam Old-fashioned (extremely)* joliment, excessivement❑

thunderous ['θʌndərəs] *adj (shouts, noise)* retentissant; **there was thunderous applause** il y eut un tonnerre d'applaudissements

thundershower ['θʌndəˌʃaʊə(r)] *n* pluie *f* d'orage

thunderstorm ['θʌndəstɔːm] *n* orage *m*

thunderstruck ['θʌndəstrʌk] *adj* foudroyé, abasourdi; **she was thunderstruck by the news** la nouvelle la foudroya

thunderthighs ['θʌndəθaɪz] *n Fam Hum* = femme aux grosses cuisses

thundery ['θʌndərɪ] *adj* orageux; **thundery weather is forecast** la météo prévoit de l'orage

▸▸ ***thundery shower*** averse *f* accompagnée de tonnerre

Thur *(written abbr* **Thursday**) jeu

thurible ['θjʊərɪbəl] *n* encensoir *m*

thurifer ['θjʊərɪfə(r)] *n* thuriféraire *m*

Thuringia [θjʊ'rɪndʒɪə] *n* la Thuringe; **in Thuringia** en Thuringe

Thurs *(written abbr* **Thursday**) jeu

Thursday ['θɜːzdɪ] *n* jeudi *m*; *see also* **Friday**

thus [ðʌs] *adv (so)* ainsi, donc; *(as a result)* ainsi, par conséquent; *(in this way)* ainsi; **thus far** *(in present)* jusqu'ici; *(in past)* jusque-là; **it was ever thus** il en a toujours été ainsi

thwack [θwæk] **1** *n* (**a**) *(blow)* grand coup *m*; *(slap)* claque *f*; **he gave the hedge a thwack with his stick** il donna un grand coup de canne dans la haie (**b**) *(sound)* claquement *m*, coup *m* sec

2 *vt* donner un coup sec à; *(slap → person)* gifler; **the player thwacked the ball into the crowd** *(footballer)* le joueur envoya la balle dans le public d'un vigoureux coup de pied; *(with racket)* le jouer envoya la balle dans le public

thwart [θwɔːt] *vt (plan)* contrecarrer, contrarier; *(plot, scheme)* déjouer; *(person → in efforts)* contrarier les efforts de; *(→ in plans)* contrarier les projets de; *(→ in attempts)* déjouer les tentatives de; **I was thwarted in my attempts to leave the country** j'ai tenté vainement de quitter le pays, toutes les tentatives que j'ai faites pour quitter le pays ont échoué

thy [ðaɪ] *adj NEng or Arch or Literary (singular)* ton (ta); *(plural)* tes

thyme [taɪm] *n* thym *m*

thymine ['θaɪmiːn] *n Biol & Chem* thymine *f*

thymol ['θaɪmɒl] *n Chem* thymol *m*

thymus ['θaɪməs] *(pl* **thymuses** *or* **thyme**) *n Anat* thymus *m*

thyristor [θaɪ'rɪstə(r)] *n Elec* thyristor *m*

thyroid ['θaɪrɔɪd] *Anat* **1** *n* thyroïde *f*

2 *adj* thyroïde

▸▸ *Anat* ***thyroid cartilage*** cartilage *m* thyroïde; *Physiol* ***thyroid hormone*** hormone *f* thyroïdienne

thyroidectomy [ˌθaɪrɔɪ'dektəmɪ] *n Med* thyroïdectomie *f*

thyroiditis [ˌθaɪrɔɪ'daɪtɪs] *n Med* thyroïdite *f*; **ligneous thyroiditis** maladie *f* (ligneuse) de Riedel

thyroxin [θaɪ'rɒksɪn], **thyroxine** [θaɪ'rɒksiːn] *n* thyroxine *f*

thyself [ðaɪ'self] *pron NEng or Arch or Literary (reflexive)* te; *(intensifier)* toi-même

ti = **te**

Tiananmen Square ['tjænənmen-] *n* la place Tian'anmen

tiara [tɪ'ɑːrə] *n (gen)* diadème *m*; *Rel* tiare *f*

Tiber ['taɪbə(r)] *n* **the (River) Tiber** le Tibre

Tiberias [taɪ'bɪərɪæs] *n* **Lake Tiberias** le lac de Tibériade

Tiberius [taɪ'bɪərɪəs] *pr n* Tibère

Tibesti [tɪ'bestɪ] *n* **the Tibesti (Massif)** le Tibesti

Tibet [tɪ'bet] *n* le Tibet; **in Tibet** au Tibet

Tibetan [tɪ'betən] **1** *n* (**a**) *(person)* Tibétain(e) *m,f* (**b**) *Ling* tibétain *m*

2 *adj* tibétain

tibia ['tɪbɪə] *(pl* **tibias** *or* **tibiae** [-bɪiː]) *n Anat* tibia *m*

tibial ['tɪbɪəl] *adj Anat* tibial

tic [tɪk] *n* **(nervous) tic** tic *m* (nerveux)

tich [tɪtʃ] *n Br Fam (person)* microbe *m*; **he's a real tich** il est haut comme trois pommes

tichy ['tɪtʃɪ] *adj Br Fam* minuscule❑, tout petit❑

Ticino [tɪ'tʃiːnəʊ] *n* Tessin *m*

tick [tɪk] **1** *vi (clock, time-bomb)* faire tic-tac; *Fig* **I wonder what makes him tick** *(what motivates him)* je me demande ce qui le motive; *(what goes on in his mind)* je me demande ce qui se passe dans sa tête

2 *vt Br (mark → name, item)* cocher, pointer; *(→ box, answer)* cocher; *Sch (→ as correct)* marquer juste

3 *n* (**a**) *(of clock)* tic-tac *m*

(**b**) *Br Fam (moment)* instant❑ *m*; **just a tick!** un instant!; **I'll be ready in a tick/in a couple of ticks** je serai prêt dans une seconde❑/en moins de deux; **I'll only be a tick** j'en ai pour une seconde❑

(**c**) *Br (mark)* coche *f*; **to put a tick against sth** cocher qch

(**d**) *Entom* tique *f*

(**e**) *Br Fam (credit)* crédit❑ *m*; **to buy sth on tick** acheter qch à crédit

(**f**) *Tex (ticking)* toile *f* à matelas; *(covering → for mattress)* housse *f* (de matelas); *(→ for pillow)* housse *f* (d'oreiller), taie *f*

▸**tick away** *vi* (**a**) *(clock)* faire tic-tac; *(taximeter)* tourner

(**b**) *(time)* passer; **the minutes ticked away** les minutes passaient

▸**tick by** *vi* = **tick away** (**b**)

▸**tick off** *vt sep* (**a**) *(name, item)* cocher

(**b**) *Fig (count → reasons, chapters)* compter, énumérer; **he ticked off the EU countries on his fingers** il compta les pays de Union européenne sur ses doigts

(**c**) *Br Fam (scold)* attraper, passer un savon à; **she got ticked off for being late** elle s'est fait attraper pour être arrivée en retard

(**d**) *Am Fam (annoy)* prendre la tête à; **to be ticked off (with)** en avoir marre (de)

▸**tick over** *vi* (**a**) *Br (car engine)* tourner au ralenti; *(taximeter)* tourner

(**b**) *Fig (business, production)* tourner doucement; **everything's ticking over nicely** tout tourne bien; **it keeps my brain ticking over** ça fait travailler ma cervelle

ticked [tɪkt] *adj Am Fam (annoyed)* en rogne

ticker ['tɪkə(r)] *n* (**a**) *Am (printer)* téléscripteur *m*, téléimprimeur *m* (**b**) *Fam (heart)* palpitant *m*, cœur❑ *m* (**c**) *Fam (watch)* tocante *f*, toquante *f*

tickertape ['tɪkəteɪp] *n* (**a**) *(tape)* bande *f* de téléscripteur *ou* de téléimprimeur (**b**) *Am* **to get a tickertape reception** *or* **welcome** être accueilli sous une pluie de serpentins; *Fig* recevoir un accueil triomphal

▸▸ ***tickertape parade*** = aux États-Unis, défilé où l'on accueille un héros national sous une pluie de serpentins

ticket ['tɪkɪt] **1** *n* (**a**) *(for travel → on coach, plane, train)* billet *m*; *(→ on bus, underground)* billet *m*, ticket *m*; *(for entry → to cinema, theatre, match)* billet *m*; *(→ to car park)* ticket *m* (de parking); *(for membership → of library)* carte *f*; **to buy a ticket** prendre *ou* acheter un billet; **this play's the hottest ticket in town** c'est le spectacle dont tout le monde parle en ce moment

(**b**) *(receipt → in shop)* ticket *m* (de caisse), reçu *m*; *(→ for left-luggage, cloakroom)* ticket *m* (de consigne); *(→ from pawnshop)* reconnaissance *f*

(**c**) *(label)* étiquette *f*

(**d**) *Aut (fine)* P-V *m*, contravention *f*, amende *f*; **to give sb a ticket** mettre un P-V *ou* une contravention à qn; **to get a ticket** avoir un P-V

(**e**) *Am Pol (platform)* programme *m*; *(list)* liste *f*; **he fought the election on a Democratic ticket** il a basé son programme électoral sur les principes du Parti démocrate; **to run on a presidential ticket** être candidat à la vice-présidence

(**f**) *Fam Naut (certificate)* brevet❑ *m*

(**g**) *Br Fam Mil slang* **to get one's ticket** être libéré des obligations militaires❑

(**h**) *Fam (idiom)* **that's (just) the ticket!** voilà exactement ce qu'il faut!❑

2 *vt* (**a**) *(label)* étiqueter

(**b**) *(earmark)* désigner, destiner

(**c**) *Am (issue with a ticket)* donner un billet à; **I'm ticketed on the 7.30 flight** j'ai un billet pour le vol de 7 heures 30

(**d**) *Am (issue with a parking ticket)* mettre un P-V à

▸▸ ***ticket agency*** *Theat* agence *f* de spectacles; *Rail* agence *f* de voyages; ***ticket barrier*** portillon *m* automatique; *Rail* ***ticket collector*** contrôleur(-euse) *m,f*, *Belg* accompagnateur(trice) *m,f* de train; *Br St Exch* ***ticket day*** jour *m* de la déclaration des noms; ***ticket desk*** guichet *m*; ***ticket holder*** personne *f* munie d'un billet; *Br Rail* ***ticket inspector*** contrôleur(euse) *m,f*, *Belg* accompagnateur(trice) *m,f* de train; *Br Hist* ***ticket of leave*** = libération conditionnelle autrefois accordée pour bonne conduite aux forçats; ***ticket machine*** distributeur *m* de tickets, billetterie *f* automatique; ***ticket office*** bureau *m* de vente des billets, guichet *m*; *Am* ***ticket taker*** contrôleur(euse) *m,f*; *Br* ***ticket tout*** revendeur(-euse) *m,f* de billets *(sur le marché noir)*; ***ticket window*** guichet *m*

ticketless ['tɪkɪtlɪs] *adj*

▸▸ *Aviat* ***ticketless travel*** = vol avec reçu de paiement tenant lieu de billet

tickety-boo [ˌtɪkɪtɪ'buː] *adj Br Fam Old-fashioned* au poil; **everything's tickety-boo** tout baigne dans l'huile, tout est au poil

ticking ['tɪkɪŋ] *n* (**a**) *(of clock)* tic-tac *m* (**b**) *Tex* toile *f* (à matelas)

▸▸ *Br Fam* ***ticking off*** engueulade *f*; **to give sb a ticking off** enguirlander qn, tirer les oreilles à qn; **she got a ticking off for being late** elle s'est fait enguirlander parce qu'elle était en retard; **he needs a good ticking off** il a besoin qu'on lui tire les oreilles *ou* qu'on lui passe un bon savon

tickle ['tɪkəl] **1** *vt* (**a**) *(by touching)* chatouiller; **don't tickle my feet!** ne me chatouille pas les pieds!; **to tickle sb in the ribs/under the chin** chatouiller les côtes/le menton à qn; **the blanket tickled her nose** la couverture lui chatouillait le nez

(**b**) *Fig (curiosity, vanity)* chatouiller; **to tickle the palate** *(of food, wine)* chatouiller le palais

(**c**) *Fig (amuse)* amuser, faire rire; *(please)* faire plaisir à; **she was really tickled by the news** *(amused)* la nouvelle l'a vraiment amusée; *(pleased)* la nouvelle lui a vraiment fait plaisir; **this idea tickled her fancy** cette idée lui a plu *ou* l'a séduite; **to be tickled pink** *or* **to death** être ravi *ou* aux anges; **he was tickled pink at becoming a grandfather** il était ravi de devenir grand-père; **she was tickled to death to think he actually liked her** elle était enchantée de penser qu'en fait il l'aimait bien

2 *vi (person, blanket)* chatouiller; *(beard)* piquer; **don't tickle!** ne me chatouille pas!

3 *n (on body)* chatouillement *m*; *(in throat)* picotement *m*, chatouillement *m*; **to give sb a tickle** chatouiller qn, faire des chatouilles à qn; **I've got an awful tickle in my throat** j'ai des picotements vraiment désagréables dans la gorge

tickler ['tɪklə(r)] *n* (**a**) *Fam (question)* colle *f*; *(problem)* casse-tête *m inv*; *(situation)* situation *f* délicate❑ *ou* épineuse❑ (**b**) *Am (memorandum book)* pense-bête *m*

tickling ['tɪklɪŋ] **1** *n (UNCOUNT) (of person)* chatouilles *fpl*; *(of blanket)* picotement *m*

2 *adj (throat)* qui gratouille *ou* picote; *(cough)* d'irritation, qui gratte la gorge; **you get a tickling sensation in your feet** on a une sensation de picotement dans les pieds

ticklish ['tɪklɪʃ] *adj* (**a**) *(person, feet)* chatouilleux; *(sensation)* de chatouillement (**b**) *Fam (touchy)* chatouilleux; **she's very ticklish about certain subjects** il y a des sujets qu'il ne faut pas aborder avec elle ❑ (**c**) *Fam (delicate → situation, topic)* délicat ❑, épineux ❑; *(→ moment)* crucial ❑; *(→ negotiations)* délicat ❑

ticklishness ['tɪklɪʃnɪs] *n* (**a**) *(of person)* sensibilité *f* au chatouillement (**b**) *Fam (of situation, topic, negotiations)* délicatesse ❑ *f*

tickly ['tɪklɪ] *adj (sensation)* de chatouillis; *(blanket)* qui chatouille; *(beard)* qui pique; **a tickly throat** une irritation dans la gorge

ticktack = **tic tac**

ticktack man = **tic tac man**

tick-tack-toe = **tic-tac-toe**

ticktock ['tɪktɒk] *n (of clock)* tic-tac *m*

ticky-tacky ['tɪkɪˌtækɪ] *Fam* **1** *adj* de pacotille

2 *n* pacotille *f*

tic tac ['tɪkˌtæk] *n* (**a**) *Br (sign language)* gestuelle *f* des bookmakers *(pour indiquer la cote)* (**b**) *Am (of clock)* tic-tac *m*

►► *Br* ***tic tac man*** = sur un terrain de courses, bookmaker qui donne des renseignements à des collègues en faisant des signaux avec les mains et les bras

tic-tac-toe *n Am (game)* morpion *m*, *Can* tictato *m*

tidal ['taɪdəl] *adj (estuary, river)* qui a des marées; *(current, cycle, force)* de la marée; *(ferry)* dont les horaires sont fonction de la marée

►► ***tidal basin*** bassin *m* à flot; ***tidal bore*** mascaret *m*; ***tidal energy, tidal power*** énergie *f* marémotrice; ***tidal wave*** raz-de-marée *m inv*; *Fig (of sympathy, enthusiasm, emotion)* vague *f*

tidbit ['tɪdbɪt] *Am* = **titbit**

tiddledywink, tiddledywinks ['tɪdəldɪwɪŋks] *Am* = **tiddlywink, tiddlywinks**

tiddler ['tɪdlə(r)] *n Fam* (**a**) *(fish)* petit poisson ❑ *m*; *(minnow)* fretin ❑ *m*; *(stickleback)* épinoche ❑ *f* (**b**) *Br (child)* mioche *mf*

tiddly ['tɪdlɪ] *(compar* **tiddlier**, *superl* **tiddliest**) *adj Br Fam* (**a**) *(tiny)* tout petit ❑, minuscule ❑ (**b**) *(tipsy)* éméché, paf

tiddlywink ['tɪdlɪwɪŋk], *Am* **tiddledywink** ['tidəldɪwɪŋk] **1** *n* pion *m* (du jeu de puce)

2 tiddlywinks, *Am* **tiddledywinks** *n* jeu *m* de puce

tide [taɪd] *n* (**a**) *(of sea)* marée *f*; **at high/low tide** à marée haute/basse; **high tide is at 17.29** la mer est haute à 17 heures 29, la marée haute est à 17 heures 29; **the raft was swept out to sea on the tide** la marée a emporté le radeau au large; **they left on the first tide** ils sont partis avec la première marée

(**b**) *Fig (of opinion)* courant *m*; *(of discontent, indignation)* vague *f*; *(of events)* cours *m*, marche *f*; **the tide has turned** la chance a tourné; *Fig* **the tide had turned against them** les événements se sont retournés contre eux; **the rising tide of discontent** la vague croissante du mécontentement; **there is a rising tide of unrest amongst the workforce** il y a une agitation grandissante parmi le personnel; **attempts to turn back the tide of progress/secularization** des efforts pour renverser la marche du progrès/de la sécularisation

►► ***tide gauge*** marégraphe *m*; ***tide race*** courant *m* de marée rapide; ***tide table*** échelle *f ou* table *f* des marées, almanach *m* (des marées)

►**tide over** *vt sep* dépanner; **to tide sb over a difficult patch** dépanner qn qui se trouve en difficulté; **here's £20 to tide you over until Monday** voici 20 livres pour vous dépanner jusqu'à lundi

tideland ['taɪdlænd] *n Am* laisse *f* (de la marée)

tideless ['taɪdlɪs] *adj* sans marée

tideline ['taɪdlaɪn] *n (on shore)* laisse *f* de haute mer

tidemark ['taɪdmɑːk] *n* (**a**) *(on shore)* laisse *f* de haute mer (**b**) *Fig Hum (round bath, neck)* traînée *f* de crasse

tidewaiter ['taɪdˌweɪtə(r)] *n Hist* douanier *m* (de port)

tidewater ['taɪdˌwɔːtə(r)] *n (UNCOUNT)* (**a**) *Br (water)* (eaux *fpl* de) marée *f* (**b**) *Am (land)* côte *f* (baignée par des eaux de marée)

tideway ['taɪdweɪ] *n (channel)* lit *m* de la marée; *(part of river)* estuaire *m*, aber *m*

tidily ['taɪdɪlɪ] *adv (pack, fold)* soigneusement, avec soin; **tidily dressed** *(adult)* bien habillé *ou* mis; *(child)* habillé proprement; **her hair was tied back tidily** ses cheveux étaient soigneusement attachés; **put your books/clothes away tidily** range bien tes livres/habits

tidiness ['taɪdɪnɪs] *n* (**a**) *(of drawer, desk, room, house)* ordre *m*; *(of garden)* bon entretien *m*; *(of town)* propreté *f* (**b**) *(of appearance)* aspect *m* soigné (**c**) *(of person)* goût *m* de l'ordre; *(of work, exercise book)* propreté *f*; *(of writing)* netteté *f*

tidings ['taɪdɪŋz] *npl Arch or Literary* nouvelles *fpl*; **we bring you tidings of great joy** nous vous apportons de joyeuses nouvelles

tidy ['taɪdɪ] *(compar* **tidier**, *superl* **tidiest**, *pl* **tidies**, *pt & pp* **tidied**) **1** *adj* (**a**) *(room, house, desk, drawer)* bien rangé, en ordre; *(garden)* bien entretenu; *(town)* propre; **neat and tidy** propre et net; **he keeps his flat very tidy** il tient son appartement bien rangé; **can't you make the room a bit tidier?** tu ne peux pas mettre un peu (plus) d'ordre dans cette pièce?

(**b**) *(in appearance → person, clothes, hair)* soigné

(**c**) *(work, writing)* soigné, net

(**d**) *(in character → person)* ordonné, méthodique; **she has a very tidy mind** elle a l'esprit très méthodique

(**e**) *Fam (sum, profit)* joli, coquet; **a tidy part of my income goes in tax** une bonne partie de mes revenus part en impôts ❑

2 *n* (**a**) *(receptacle)* vide-poches *m inv*

(**b**) *Am (on chair)* têtière *f*

3 *vt (room)* ranger, mettre de l'ordre dans; *(desk, clothes, objects)* ranger; **to tidy one's hair** se recoiffer; **tidy those books into a cupboard** range ces livres dans un placard

►**tidy away** *vt sep* ranger, ramasser

►**tidy out** *vt sep (drawer, wardrobe, garden shed)* ranger de fond en comble, mettre de l'ordre dans; *(newspapers)* ranger, trier; **go and tidy out your room** va mettre de l'ordre dans *ou* ranger ta chambre

►**tidy up 1** *vi* (**a**) *(in room)* tout ranger; **after the last guests had gone she was left to tidy up** elle a dû tout remettre en ordre *ou* tout ranger après le départ des derniers invités

(**b**) *(in appearance)* s'arranger; **you'd better tidy up before they arrive** tu ferais mieux de t'arranger un peu avant qu'ils arrivent

2 *vt sep (room, clothes)* ranger, mettre de l'ordre dans; *(desk)* ranger; **to tidy oneself up** s'arranger; **tidy your things up** *(make tidy)* range tes affaires; *(put away)* range *ou* ramasse tes affaires

tidy-out *n Fam* **to have a tidy-out** *(make tidy)* faire du (grand) rangement ❑; *(clear out)* faire le rangement par le vide ❑; **we gave the room a good tidy-out** on a rangé la pièce de fond en comble ❑

tidy-up *n Fam* **to have a tidy-up** faire du rangement ❑; **we'll have to give the place a tidy-up before the guests arrive** il va falloir mettre de l'ordre ❑ *ou* faire du rangement dans la maison avant l'arrivée des invités

TIE [taɪ]

cravate	► **1 (a)**
attache	► **1 (b), (c)**
lien	► **1 (c)**
entrave	► **1 (d)**
égalité	► **1 (e)**
match nul	► **1 (e)**
match	► **1 (f)**
attacher	► **2 (a), (b)**
s'attacher	► **3 (a)**
être à égalité	► **3 (b)**

1 *n* (**a**) *(necktie)* cravate *f*

(**b**) *(fastener → gen)* attache *f*; *(→ on apron)* cordon *m*; *(→ for curtain)* embrasse *f*; *(→ on shoes)* lacet *m*

(**c**) *(bond, link)* lien *m*, attache *f*; **emotional ties** liens *mpl* affectifs; **family ties** liens *mpl* de parenté *ou* familiaux; **there are strong ties between the two countries** les deux pays entretiennent d'étroites relations; **he has no ties to the place** il n'y a rien qui l'attache à cet endroit

(**d**) *(restriction)* entrave *f*; **pets/young children can be a tie** les animaux/les jeunes enfants peuvent être une entrave

(**e**) *Sport (draw)* égalité *f*; *(drawn match)* match *m* nul; *(in competition)* = compétition dont les gagnants sont ex aequo; *Pol* égalité *f* de voix; **the match ended in a tie** les deux équipes ont fait match nul; **it was a tie for first/second place** il y avait deux premiers/seconds ex aequo; **the election resulted in a tie** les candidats ont obtenu le même nombre de voix *ou* étaient à égalité des voix

(**f**) *Ftbl (match)* match *m*; **a championship tie** un match de championnat; **a European cup tie** un match de la coupe européenne

(**g**) *Mus* liaison *f*

(**h**) *Am Rail* traverse *f*, *Can* dormant *m*

(**i**) *Constr* tirant *m*

2 *vt* (**a**) *(with string, rope → parcel)* attacher, ficeler; **is it tied properly?** est-ce que c'est bien attaché?; **they tied him to a tree** il l'ont attaché *ou* ligoté à un arbre; **his hands and feet were tied** ses mains et ses pieds étaient ligotés

(**b**) *(necktie, scarf, shoelaces)* attacher, nouer; **to tie one's shoelaces** attacher *ou* nouer ses lacets (de chaussures); **to tie a scarf round one's neck** nouer une écharpe autour de son cou; **why not tie some string to the handle?** pourquoi ne pas attacher une ficelle à la poignée?; **she tied the ribbon in a bow** elle a fait un nœud au ruban; **she tied a bow/a ribbon in her hair** elle s'est mis un nœud/un ruban dans les cheveux; **to tie a knot in sth, to tie sth in a knot** faire un nœud à qch; *Fig* **he's still tied to his mother's apron strings** il n'a pas encore quitté les jupes de sa mère

(**c**) *(confine → of responsibility, job etc)* **she's tied to the house** *(unable to get out)* elle est clouée à la maison; *(kept busy)* la maison l'accapare beaucoup; **the job keeps me very much tied to my desk** mon travail m'oblige à passer beaucoup de temps devant mon bureau; **they're tied to** *or* **by the conditions of the contract** ils sont liés par les conditions du contrat

(**d**) *(link)* **to be tied to** avoir un lien avec

(**e**) *Mus* lier

3 *vi* (**a**) *(apron, shoelace etc)* s'attacher, se nouer; **the dress ties at the back** la robe s'attache par derrière

(**b**) *(draw → players)* être à égalité; *(→ in match)* faire match nul; *(→ in exam, competition)* être ex aequo; *(→ in election)* obtenir le même score *ou* nombre de voix; **they tied for third place in the competition** ils étaient troisième ex aequo au concours

►► *Constr* ***tie beam*** longrine *f*; ***tie clasp, tie clip*** fixe-cravate *m*; *Tel* ***tie line*** ligne *f* interautomatique; ***tie pin*** épingle *f* de cravate; ***tie rack*** porte-cravates *m inv*; *Am* ***tie tack*** fixe-cravate *m*

►**tie back** *vt sep (hair)* attacher (en arrière); *(curtains, plant)* attacher; **her hair was tied back in a bun** ses cheveux étaient ramassés en chignon

►**tie down** *vt sep* (**a**) *(with string, rope → person, object)* attacher; **they had to tie him down** ils ont dû l'attacher

(**b**) *Fig (restrict)* accaparer; **she doesn't want to feel tied down** elle ne veut pas perdre sa liberté; **children can really tie you down** il arrive que les enfants vous accaparent totalement; **I'd rather not be tied down to a specific time** je préférerais qu'on ne fixe pas une heure précise; **we must tie them down to the terms of the contract** il faut les obliger à respecter les termes du contrat

►**tie in 1** *vi* (**a**) *(be connected)* être lié *ou* en rapport; **everything seems to tie in** tout semble se tenir; **this ties in with what I said before** cela rejoint ce que j'ai dit avant

(**b**) *(correspond)* correspondre, concorder; **the evidence doesn't tie in with the facts** les indices dont nous disposons ne correspondent pas aux faits *ou* ne cadrent pas avec les faits

2 *vt sep* **how is this tied in with your previous**

experiments? quel est le lien *ou* le rapport avec vos expériences antérieures?; **she's trying to tie her work experience in with her research** elle essaie de faire coïncider son expérience professionnelle et ses recherches

►**tie on** *vt sep* (**a**) *(attach)* attacher, nouer; **she had a basket tied on to the handlebars** elle avait un panier attaché à son guidon

(**b**) *Am Fam* **to tie one on** *(get drunk)* prendre une cuite, se cuiter

►**tie together 1** *vi* **it all ties together** tout se tient; **his story doesn't tie together very well** son histoire ne tient pas vraiment debout

2 *vt sep (papers, sticks)* attacher (ensemble); **to tie sb's hands/feet together** attacher les mains/les pieds de qn; **the letters had been tied together in bundles** les lettres avaient été mises en liasses

►**tie up 1** *vt sep* (**a**) *(parcel, papers)* ficeler; *(plant, animal)* attacher; *(prisoner)* attacher, ligoter; *(boat)* attacher, arrimer; *(shoelace, hair)* nouer, attacher; **the letters were tied up in bundles** les lettres étaient ficelées en liasses; **the dog was tied up to a post** le chien était attaché à un poteau

(**b**) *(usu passive) (money, supplies)* immobiliser; **their money is all tied up in shares** leur argent est entièrement investi dans des actions; **her inheritance is tied up until her 21st birthday** elle ne peut toucher à son héritage avant son 21ème anniversaire

(**c**) *(connect → company, organization)* lier par des accords

(**d**) *(complete, finalize → deal)* conclure; *(→ terms of contract)* fixer; **I'd like to get everything tied up before the holidays** je voudrais arriver à tout régler avant les vacances; **there are still a few loose ends to tie up** il y a encore quelques points de détail à régler

(**e**) *(impede → traffic)* bloquer; *(→ progress, production)* freiner, entraver

2 *vi* (**a**) *(be connected)* être lié; **how does this tie up with the Chicago gang killings?** quel est le rapport avec les assassinats du gang de Chicago?; **it's all beginning to tie up** tout commence à s'expliquer

(**b**) *Naut* accoster

---

tieback ['taɪbæk] *n (cord)* embrasse *f* (de rideaux); *(curtain)* rideau *m (retenu par une embrasse)*

tiebreak ['taɪbreɪk], **tiebreaker** ['taɪbreɪkə(r)] *n Sport (in tennis)* tie-break *m*; *(in game, contest)* épreuve *f* subsidiaire; *(in quiz)* question *f* subsidiaire

tied [taɪd] *adj* (**a**) *Sport* **to be tied** *(players)* être à égalité; *(game)* être nul

(**b**) *(person → by obligation, duties)* pris, occupé; **he doesn't want to feel tied** il ne veut pas s'engager; **she feels very tied by the new baby** elle est très prise par le nouveau bébé; **she isn't tied by any family obligations** elle n'a *ou* elle n'est tenue par aucune obligation familiale

(**c**) *Mus (note)* lié

►► *Fin* ***tied agent*** agent *m* lié; *Br* ***tied cottage*** = logement attaché à une ferme et occupé par un employé agricole; ***tied house*** *(pub)* = pub lié par contrat à une brasserie qui l'approvisionne; *(house)* logement *m* de fonction; *Fin* ***tied loan*** prêt *m* conditionnel *ou* à condition; *Mktg* ***tied outlet*** concession *f* exclusive, magasin *m* sous franchise exclusive

tied up *adj* (**a**) *(busy)* **to be tied up** être occupé *ou* pris; **she's tied up with the children every Wednesday** elle est prise par les enfants tous les mercredis; **he's tied up in a meeting until five o'clock** il est en réunion jusqu'à cinq heures; **I'll be tied up all weekend writing these wretched reports** je vais devoir passer tout le week-end à rédiger ces maudits rapports

(**b**) **to be tied up with sth** *(connected)* être lié à qch; **it's tied up with the increase in the interest rate** c'est lié à l'augmentation des taux d'intérêt

tie-dye *vt* teindre en nouant *(pour obtenir une teinture non uniforme)*

tie-dyeing *n* = procédé de teinture qui consiste à nouer le tissu pour qu'il prenne la couleur de manière irrégulière

tie-in *n* (**a**) *(connection)* lien *m*, rapport *m* (**b**) *Am Com (sale)* vente *f* par lots; *(items)* lot *m* (**c**) *(film from book)* = film tiré d'un livre; *(book from film, TV series)* = livre tiré d'un film *ou* d'un feuilleton; **there may be a film tie-in** on pourrait en tirer un film

►► ***tie-in promotion*** promotion *f* collective

tie-on *adj (label)* à œillet

tier [tɪə(r)] **1** *n* (**a**) *(row of seats → in theatre, stadium)* gradin *m*, rangée *f*; *(level)* étage *m*; **to arrange seats in tiers** disposer des sièges en gradins; **the seats rose in tiers** les sièges étaient disposés en gradins

(**b**) *Admin* échelon *m*, niveau *m*; **a five-tier system** un système à cinq niveaux; **a two-tier education system/health service** un système éducatif/de santé à deux vitesses

(**c**) *(of cake)* étage *m*; **a three-tier wedding cake** un gâteau de mariage à trois étages

2 *vt (seating)* disposer en gradins

tierce [tɪəs] *n* (**a**) *Rel (tierce)* tierce *f* (**b**) *Cards* tierce *f* (**c**) *Fencing* tierce *f*

tiered ['tɪəd] *adj (seating)* en gradins; *(system)* à plusieurs niveaux; **three-tiered cake** pièce montée *f* à trois étages; **three-tiered stand** *(for cakes etc)* étagère *f* à trois tablettes; **a tiered dress/skirt** une robe/jupe à volants

tie-rod *n Aut* tirant *m*

Tierra del Fuego [tɪˌerədel'fweɪgəʊ] *n* Terre de Feu *f*; **in Tierra del Fuego** en Terre de Feu

tie-up *n* (**a**) *(connection)* lien *m*, rapport *m* (**b**) *Com (merger)* (absorption-)fusion *f*, unification *f*; *(joint venture)* coentreprise *f*, joint-venture *m* (**c**) *Am (stoppage)* arrêt *m*, interruption *f* (**d**) *Am (traffic jam)* embouteillage *m*, bouchon *m*

TIF [ˌtiːaɪ'ef] *n Rail (abbr* **transport international ferroviaire***)* TIF *m*

TIFF [tɪf] *n Comput (abbr* **Tagged Image File Format***)* format *m* TIFF

tiff [tɪf] *n Br Fam* prise *f* de bec; **they've had a bit of a tiff** ils se sont un peu disputés ❑; **a lover's tiff** une dispute d'amoureux ❑

tiffany ['tɪfənɪ] *n Tex* gaze *f*

tiffin ['tɪfɪn] *n Br Old-fashioned* repas *m* de midi *(dans l'Inde coloniale)*

tig [tɪg] *n* (jeu *m* du) chat *m*; **to play tig** jouer à chat

tiger ['taɪgə(r)] *n* tigre *m*; **to hunt tiger** aller à la chasse au tigre; **to fight like a tiger** se battre comme un tigre; **to get off the tiger** *or* **the tiger's back** se tirer d'embarras; **to have a tiger by the tail** se trouver pris dans une situation dont on n'est plus maître; **to ride the tiger** vivre dangereusement

►► ***tiger cub*** petit *m* du tigre; ***tiger economy*** = pays à l'économie très performante; **the (Asian) tiger economies** les dragons *mpl ou* les tigres *mpl* asiatiques; ***tiger lily*** lis *m* tigré; *Entom* ***tiger moth*** écaille *f*; ***tiger prawn*** crevette *f* tigrée; ***tiger shark*** requin-tigre *m*; ***tiger snake*** vipère-tigre *f*

Tiger balm® *n* baume *m* du tigre *(pommade mentholée utilisée comme panacée)*

tigerish ['taɪgərɪʃ] *adj* (**a**) *(appearance, eyes)* de tigre (**b**) *Fig (combative)* redoutable (**c**) *Fig (cruel)* cruel (comme un tigre); *(fierce)* féroce (comme un tigre)

tiger's-eye *n (stone)* œil-de-tigre *m*

tight [taɪt] **1** *adj* (**a**) *(garment, footwear)* serré, étroit; **these shoes are a bit tight** ces chaussures sont un peu trop serrées; **it's a tight fit** c'est trop serré *ou* juste; **tight jeans** *(too small)* un jean trop serré; *(close-fitting)* un jean moulant; **a tight skirt** *(too small)* une jupe trop serrée; *(close-fitting)* une jupe moulante; **my tie is too tight** ma cravate est trop serrée

(**b**) *(stiff → drawer, door)* dur à ouvrir; *(→ tap)* dur à tourner; *(→ lid)* dur à enlever; *(→ screw)* serré; *(constricted)* pesant; **I've got a tight feeling across my chest** j'ai comme un poids sur la poitrine; **it was a tight squeeze but we got everyone in** on a eu du mal mais on a réussi à faire entrer tout le monde; *Fig* **to be in a tight corner** *or* **spot** être dans une situation difficile

(**c**) *(taut → rope)* raide, tendu; *(→ bow)* tendu; *(→ net, knitting, knot)* serré; *(→ skin)* tiré; *(→ group)* serré; **her face looked tight and drawn** elle avait les traits tirés; **they marched in tight formation** ils marchaient en ordre serré

(**d**) *(firm)* **to hold sb in a tight embrace** serrer qn fort dans ses bras; **to keep a tight hold** *or* **grasp on sth** bien tenir qch; **she kept a tight hold on the rail** elle s'agrippait à la balustrade; *Fig* **she kept a tight hold on the expenses** elle surveillait les dépenses de près; **you should keep a tighter rein on the children/your emotions** il faudrait surveiller les enfants de plus près/mieux maîtriser vos émotions

(**e**) *(sharp → bend, turn)* brusque; **we had to make a tight turn to avoid the car** nous avons dû effectuer un virage serré pour éviter la voiture

(**f**) *(strict → control, restrictions)* strict, sévère; *(→ security)* strict; **to run a tight ship** mener son monde à la baguette

(**g**) *(limited → budget, credit)* serré, resserré; **to work on a tight budget** travailler avec un budget serré; **money is a bit tight** *or* **things are a bit tight at the moment** l'argent manque un peu en ce moment

(**h**) *(close → competition)* serré; **it should be a tight finish** *(in race)* l'arrivée devrait être serrée

(**i**) *(busy → schedule)* serré, chargé; **it was tight but I made it in time** c'était juste, mais je suis arrivé à temps

(**j**) *Fam (mean)* radin, pingre ❑; **he's very tight with his money** il est très près de ses sous

(**k**) *Fam (drunk)* pompette; **he gets tight on one glass of wine** un verre de vin suffit à le soûler

(**l**) *Mus (group, band)* très au point

2 *adv (close, fasten)* bien; **packed tight** *(bag)* bien rempli *ou* plein; *(pub, room)* bondé; **hold tight!** tenez-vous bien!, accrochez-vous bien!; **she held the rabbit tight in her arms** elle serrait le lapin dans ses bras; **pull the thread tight** tirez *ou* tendez bien le fil; **is that window shut tight?** cette fenêtre est-elle bien fermée?; **it needs to be turned/screwed tight** il faut le serrer/le visser à fond

3 tights *npl* **(pair of) tights** collant *m*, collants *mpl*

►► ***tight end*** *(in American football)* receveur *m* rapproché; *Econ* ***tight money*** argent *m* rare

tight-arsed [-ɑːst], *Am* **tight-assed** [-æst] *adj very Fam (uptight)* coincé, constipé

tighten ['taɪtən] **1** *vt* (**a**) *(belt, strap)* resserrer; **he tightened his grasp on the rail** il agrippa plus fermement la balustrade; **to tighten one's belt** resserrer sa ceinture; *Fig* se serrer la ceinture; *Fig* **the army/government has tightened its grip on the region** l'armée/le gouvernement a renforcé son emprise sur la région

(**b**) *(nut, screw)* serrer, bien visser; *(knot)* serrer; *(cable, rope)* serrer, tendre

(**c**) *(control, security, regulations)* renforcer; *(credit)* resserrer

2 *vi* (**a**) *(grip)* **his finger tightened on the trigger** son doigt se serra sur la gâchette; **her grasp tightened on my arm** elle serra mon bras plus fort

(**b**) *(nut, screw, knot)* se resserrer; *(cable, rope)* se raidir, se tendre

(**c**) *(control, security, regulation)* être renforcé; *(credit)* se resserrer

(**d**) *(throat, stomach)* se nouer; **her lips tightened** elle serra les lèvres

►**tighten up** *vt sep* (**a**) *(nut, screw)* resserrer

(**b**) *(control, security, regulation, blockade)* renforcer; **the law on drug peddling has been tightened up** la loi sur le trafic de drogue a été renforcée

►**tighten up on** *vt insep* **to tighten up on discipline/security** renforcer la discipline/la sécurité; **the government are tightening up on drug pushers/tax evasion** le gouvernement renforce la lutte contre les revendeurs de drogue/la fraude fiscale

tightener ['taɪtənə(r)] *n Tech (device)* tendeur *m*, raidisseur *m*; **belt tightener** tendeur *m* de courroie; **stay tightener** tendeur *m* de haubans

tightening ['taɪtənɪŋ] *n (of screw, credit)* resserrement *m*; *(of control, regulation, blockade)* renforcement *m*; **he felt a tightening in his throat** il sentit sa gorge se nouer

tight-fisted [-'fɪstɪd] *adj Fam* radin, pingre ❑

tight-fistedness [-'fɪstɪdnɪs] *n Fam* radinerie *f*, pingrerie ❑ *f*

tight-fitting *adj (skirt, trousers)* moulant; *(suit, joint)* bien ajusté; *(lid)* qui ferme bien

tight-head prop *n (in rugby)* pilier *m* droit

tight-knit *adj (community, family)* (très) uni

tight-lipped [-'lɪpt] *adj* **he sat tight-lipped and pale** il était assis, pâle et muet; **she sat in tight-lipped silence** elle se tenait assise, sans desserrer les dents

tightly ['taɪtlɪ] *adv* (**a**) *(firmly → hold, fit, screw)* (bien) serré; *(→ seal, shut)* hermétiquement; **he held his daughter tightly to him** il serrait sa fille tout contre lui; **hold on tightly** tenez-vous *ou* accrochez-vous bien; **we held on tightly to the rail** nous nous sommes agrippés fermement à la balustrade; **make sure the lid fits tightly** vérifiez que le couvercle est bien fermé; **the cases were tightly sealed** les caisses étaient bien scellées *ou* hermétiquement fermées; **her eyes were tightly shut** elle avait les yeux bien fermés; **news is tightly controlled** les informations sont soumises à un contrôle rigoureux; **tightly curled hair** des cheveux frisés

(**b**) *(densely)* **the lecture hall was tightly packed** l'amphithéâtre était bondé *ou* plein à craquer

tightness ['taɪtnɪs] *n* (**a**) *(of garment, shoes)* étroitesse *f*

(**b**) *(stiffness → of drawer, screw, tap)* dureté *f*

(**c**) *(tautness → of bow, rope)* raideur *f*; *(firmness → of grip, embrace)* force *f*; **he felt a sudden tightness in his throat** il sentit soudain sa gorge se nouer; **he felt a sudden tightness in his chest** *(physical)* il ressentit soudain une douleur dans la poitrine; *(emotional)* il sentit soudain son cœur se serrer

(**d**) *(strictness → of control, regulation)* rigueur *f*, sévérité *f*; *(→ of security)* rigueur *f*

tightrope ['taɪtrəʊp] *n* corde *f* raide; **to walk the tightrope** marcher sur la corde raide; *Fig* **she's walking a political tightrope** elle s'est aventurée sur un terrain politique glissant *ou* dangereux

►► ***tightrope walker*** funambule *mf*

tightwad ['taɪtwɒd] *n Am Fam Pej* radin(e) *m,f*; **he's a real tightwad** il est vraiment grippe-sou

tigon ['taɪgən] *n Zool* tigron *m*

Tigré ['tiːgreɪ] *n* le Tigré; **in Tigré** dans le Tigré

tigress ['taɪgrɪs] *n Zool & Fig* tigresse *f*

Tigris ['taɪgrɪs] *n* **the (River) Tigris** le Tigre

TIG welding [tɪg-] *n Tech* (*abbr* **tungsten-electrode inert gas**) soudure *f* à l'arc au tungstène

tike = **tyke**

tikka ['tiːkə] *n Culin* **chicken/lamb tikka** poulet *m*/agneau *m* tikka *(mariné dans une sauce légèrement épicée puis cuit en ragoût)*; **chicken/lamb tikka masala** poulet/agneau tikka masala *(mariné aux épices et cuit au four)*

tilapia [tɪ'læpɪə] *n Ich* tilapie *m*, tilapia *m*

tilde ['tɪldə] *n Ling* tilde *m*

tile [taɪl] **1** *n (for roof)* tuile *f*; *(for wall, floor)* carreau *m*; *Br Fam* **to have a night (out) on the tiles** faire la noce

2 *vt* (**a**) *(roof)* couvrir de tuiles; *(floor, wall)* carreler (**b**) *Comput (windows)* afficher en mosaïque

tiled [taɪld] *adj (floor, wall)* carrelé

►► ***tiled bathroom*** salle *f* de bains carrelée; ***tiled floor*** sol *m* carrelé; ***tiled roof*** toit *m* de tuiles

tiler ['taɪlə(r)] *n (of roof)* couvreur *m (de toits en tuiles)*; *(of floor, wall)* carreleur *m*

tiling ['taɪlɪŋ] *n (UNCOUNT)* (**a**) *(putting on tiles → on roof)* pose *f* des tuiles; *(→ on floor, in bathroom)* carrelage *m* (**b**) *(tiles → on roof)* tuiles *fpl*; *(→ on floor, wall)* carrelage *m*, carreaux *mpl*

till [tɪl] **1** *conj & prep* = **until**

2 *n* (**a**) *(cash register)* caisse *f* (enregistreuse); *(drawer)* tiroir-caisse *m*; *Fig* **to be caught with one's fingers** *or* **hands in the till** être pris en flagrant délit *ou* la main dans le sac; **pay at the till** payez à la caisse (**b**) *(money)* caisse *f*

3 *vt Agr* labourer; **to till the soil** labourer la terre

►► ***till receipt*** ticket *m* de caisse

tillage ['tɪlɪdʒ] *n* (**a**) *(act)* labour *m*, labourage *m* (**b**) *(land)* labour *m*, pièce *f* labourée

tiller ['tɪlə(r)] *n* (**a**) *Naut* barre *f*, gouvernail *m* (**b**) *Bot* pousse *f*, talle *f*

tilt [tɪlt] **1** *vt* (**a**) *(lean)* pencher, incliner; **to tilt one's chair (back)** se balancer sur sa chaise; **he tilted his head to one side** il pencha *ou* inclina la tête sur le côté; **to tilt one's head back** renverser la tête en arrière; **her hat was tilted over one eye** son chapeau était penché sur le côté; *Fig* **this may tilt the odds in our favour** cela peut faire pencher la balance de notre côté

(**b**) *(cover → gen)* bâcher; *Naut* tauder

2 *vi* (**a**) *(lean → person)* se pencher, s'incliner; *(→ building, picture etc)* pencher; **to tilt backwards/forwards** pencher vers l'arrière/l'avant; **don't tilt back on your chair** ne te balance pas sur ta chaise

(**b**) *Hist (joust)* jouter; **to tilt at sb** diriger un coup de lance contre qn; *Fig* lancer des piques à qn; *Fig* **to tilt at windmills** se battre contre des moulins à vent

3 *n* (**a**) *(angle)* inclinaison *f*; *(slope)* pente *f*; **the room has a definite tilt to it** la pièce penche nettement; **she wore her hat at a tilt** elle portait son chapeau incliné; **I'm sure that picture's on a tilt** je suis sûr que le tableau penche

(**b**) *Hist (joust)* joute *f*; *(thrust)* coup *m* de lance; *Fig* **to have a tilt at sb** s'en prendre à qn, décocher des pointes à qn; *Fig* **that was obviously a tilt at you** c'était une pointe qui vous était destinée

(**c**) *(awning)* store *m* (de toile), bâche *f*; *Naut* taud *m*

4 full tilt *adv* à toute vitesse, **he ran full tilt into her** il lui est rentré en plein dedans; **he ran full tilt into the door** il est rentré en plein dans la porte

►**tilt over** *vi* (**a**) *(slant)* pencher

(**b**) *(overturn)* se renverser, basculer

tilt-and-slide sunroof *n* toit *m* ouvrant entrebâillant et coulissant

tilt-and-turn window *n* fenêtre *f* basculante

tilted ['tɪltɪd] *adj* incliné, penché

tilth [tɪlθ] *n (act of tilling)* labourage *m*; *(soil)* terre *f* arable

tilting ['tɪltɪŋ] **1** *adj* (**a**) *(at an angle)* incliné, penché (**b**) *(able to be tilted)* inclinable

2 *n Hist (jousting)* joute *f*

Timaeus [tɪ'meɪəs] *pr n Antiq* Timée

timbale [tæm'bæl] *n Culin* timbale *f*

timber ['tɪmbə(r)] **1** *n* (**a**) *(wood → for building work)* bois *m* de construction *ou* de charpente; *(→ for carpentry)* bois *m* de menuiserie

(**b**) *(UNCOUNT) (trees)* arbres *mpl*, bois *m*; **to fell timber** abattre *ou* couper des arbres; **land under timber** terre *f* boisée; **to put land under timber** boiser un terrain; **standing timber** bois *m* sur pied

(**c**) *(beam)* madrier *m*, poutre *f*; *(on ship)* membrure *f*

2 *comp (roof, fence)* en bois

3 *vt (tunnel)* boiser

4 *exclam* attention!

►► *Naut* ***timber hitch*** nœud *m* de bois *ou* d'anguille; *Br* ***timber merchant*** marchand *m* de bois; ***timber trade*** commerce *m* du bois; ***timber wolf*** loup *m* gris

timbered ['tɪmbəd] *adj (region, land)* boisé; *(house)* en bois

timberhead ['tɪmbəhed] *n Naut* bitte *f* (d'amarrage), bollard *m*

timbering ['tɪmbərɪŋ] *n* (**a**) *(of region)* boisage *m* (**b**) *(of mine shaft)* boisage *m*, cuvelage *m*

timberland ['tɪmbəlænd] *n Am* terre *f ou* région *f* boisée *(pour l'abattage)*

timberline ['tɪmbəlaɪn] *n* limite *f* des arbres

timberwork ['tɪmbəwɜːk] *n* structure *f* en bois

timberyard ['tɪmbəjɑːd] *n* chantier *m* de bois

timbre ['tæmbrə, 'tɪmbə(r)] *n Ling & Mus* timbre *m*

timbrel ['tɪmbrəl] *n Mus* tambourin *m*

Timbuktu [,tɪmbʌk'tuː] *n* Tombouctou *m*

TIME [taɪm]

temps	► **1 (a) – (e), (m), (o)**
durée	► **1 (e)**
heure	► **1 (f), (g), (m)**
moment	► **1 (i), (j)**
fois	► **1 (k)**
époque	► **1 (o)**
fin	► **1 (r)**
mesure	► **1 (u)**
chronométrer	► **2 (a)**
fixer l'heure de	► **2 (b)**
choisir le moment de	► **2 (c)**
régler	► **2 (d)**

1 *n* (**a**) *(continuous stretch of time)* temps *m*; **as time goes by** avec le temps; **the price has gone up over time** le prix a augmenté avec le temps; **it's only a matter** *or* **a question of time** ce n'est qu'une question de temps; **these things take time** cela ne se fait pas du jour au lendemain; **to have time on one's hands** *or* **time to spare** avoir du temps; **time hangs heavy on his hands** le temps lui pèse, il trouve le temps long; **since the dawn of time** depuis la nuit des temps; **time flies** le temps passe vite; **doesn't time fly!** comme le temps passe vite!; **time heals all wounds** le temps guérit tout; **only time will tell** seul l'avenir nous le dira; **time will prove me right** l'avenir me donnera raison; **it's a race against time** c'est une course contre la montre; **they're working against time to save her** ils ne disposent que de très peu de temps pour la sauver; **time is on our side** le temps joue en notre faveur; **time out of mind** de temps immémorial, de toute éternité; **time is money** le temps, c'est de l'argent; *Prov* **time and tide wait for no man** les événements n'attendent personne

(**b**) *(period of time spent on particular activity)* temps *m*; **there's no time to lose** il n'y a pas de temps à perdre; **he lost no time in telling me** il s'est empressé de me le dire; **to make up for lost time** rattraper le temps perdu; **to make good/poor time doing sth** mettre peu de temps/longtemps à faire qch; **I passed the time reading** j'ai passé mon temps à lire; **take your time** prenez votre temps; **take your good time over it** prenez le temps qu'il faudra; **it took me all my time just to get here!** avec le temps que j'ai mis pour arriver ici!; **you took your time about it!** tu en as mis du temps!; **she took the time to explain it to us** elle a pris le temps de nous l'expliquer; **she made the time to read the report** elle a pris le temps de lire le rapport; **I can always make time for you** pour vous, je suis toujours là; **I spend half/all my time cleaning up** je passe la moitié de/tout mon temps à faire le ménage; **half the time he doesn't know what he's doing** la moitié du temps il ne sait pas ce qu'il fait, **most of the time** la plupart du temps; **he was ill part** *or* **some of the time** il a été malade une partie du temps; **it rained part** *or* **some of the time** il a plu par moments; **we spend the better part of our time working** nous passons le plus clair de notre temps à travailler; **I start in three weeks' time** je commence dans trois semaines; **they'll have finished the project in three weeks' time** ils auront terminé le projet dans trois semaines; **all in good time!** chaque chose en son temps!; **I'll finish it in my own good time** je le finirai quand bon me semblera; **in no time (at all), in next to no time** en un rien de temps, en moins de rien

(**c**) *(available period of time)* temps *m*; **I haven't (the) time to do the shopping** je n'ai pas le temps de faire les courses; **I've no time for gossip** je n'ai pas de temps à perdre en bavardages; **I've no time for that sort of attitude** je ne supporte pas ce genre de mentalité; **he has no time for sycophants/for laziness** il n'a pas de temps à perdre avec les flatteurs/les paresseux; **my time is my own** mon temps m'appartient, **my time is not my own** je ne suis pas libre de mon temps; **we've just got time to catch the train** on a juste le temps d'attraper le train; **that doesn't leave them much time to get ready** cela ne leur laisse guère de temps pour se préparer; **you'll have to find the time to see her** il faut que tu trouves le temps de la voir; **you have plenty of time to finish it** vous avez largement le temps de le finir; **we've got plenty of time** *or* **all the time in the world** nous avons tout le temps

(**d**) *(while)* temps *m*; **after a time** après un (certain) temps; **a long time** longtemps; **a long time ago** il y a longtemps; **it's a long time since we've been out for a meal together** ça fait longtemps que nous ne sommes pas sortis dîner ensemble; **she's been dreaming of this for a long time now** voilà longtemps qu'elle en rêve; **he waited for a long time** il a attendu longtemps; **I worked for a long time as a translator** j'ai travaillé (pendant) longtemps comme traducteur; **for a long time he refused to eat**

tig–tim

meat il a (pendant) longtemps refusé de manger de la viande; **it'll be a long time before I do that again** je ne suis pas près de recommencer, je ne recommencerai pas de si tôt *ou* de sitôt; **the car takes a long time to warm up** la voiture met longtemps à chauffer; **you took a long time!** tu en as mis du temps!, il t'en a fallu du temps!; *Fam* **long time no see!** ça faisait longtemps!; **a short time** peu de temps; **after a short time** peu (de temps) après; **a short time before their wedding** peu avant leur mariage; **she's going to stay with us for a short time** elle va rester avec nous pendant quelque temps; **in the shortest possible time** dans les plus brefs délais, le plus vite *ou* tôt possible; **after some time** au bout de quelque temps, après un certain temps; **some time after their trip** quelque temps après leur voyage; **some time ago** il y a quelque temps; **for some time past** depuis quelque temps; **for some time (to come)** pendant quelque temps; **it's the best film I've seen for some time** c'est le meilleur film que j'aie vu depuis un moment; **it will take (quite) some time to repair** il va falloir pas mal de temps pour le réparer; **all this time** pendant tout ce temps

(**e**) *(time taken or required to do something)* temps *m*, durée *f*; **the flying time to Madrid is two hours** la durée du vol pour Madrid est de deux heures; **the cooking time is two hours** le temps de cuisson est de deux heures; **the winner's time was under four minutes** le gagnant a fait un temps de moins de quatre minutes; **1 minute 34 seconds is her best/a good time** 1 minute 34 secondes, c'est son meilleur temps/un bon temps; **it takes time** cela prend du temps; **how much time will it take?** combien de temps cela prendra-t-il?; **she finished in half the time it took me to finish** elle a mis deux fois moins de temps que moi pour finir

(**f**) *(by clock)* heure *f*; **what time is it?, what's the time?** quelle heure est-il?; **what time do you make it?** quelle heure avez-vous?; **do you have the time?** vous avez l'heure?; **have you got the right time on you?** avez-vous l'heure juste?; **the time is twenty past three** il est trois heures vingt; **what time are we leaving?** à quelle heure partons-nous?; **do you know how to tell the time?** est-ce que tu sais lire l'heure?; **could you tell me the time?** pourriez-vous me dire l'heure (qu'il est)?; **have you seen the time?** avez-vous vu l'heure?; **I looked at the time** j'ai regardé l'heure; **this old watch still keeps good time** cette vieille montre est toujours à l'heure *ou* exacte; **at this time of day** à cette heure de la journée; **we'll have to keep an eye on the time** il faudra surveiller l'heure; **it is almost time to leave/for my bus** il est presque l'heure de partir/de mon bus; **it's time I was going** il est temps que je parte; **it's dinner time, it's time for dinner** c'est l'heure de dîner; **there you are, it's about time!** te voilà, ce n'est pas trop tôt!; **I wouldn't give him the time of day** je ne lui dirais même pas bonjour; **to pass the time of day with sb** échanger quelques mots avec qn

(**g**) *(system)* **local time** heure *f* locale; **it's 5 o'clock Tokyo time** il est 5 heures, heure de Tokyo

(**h**) *(schedule)* **is the bus running to time?** est-ce que le bus est à l'heure?; **within the required time** dans les délais requis

(**i**) *(particular point in time)* moment *m*; **at that time I was in Madrid** à ce moment-là, j'étais à Madrid *ou* j'étais alors à Madrid; **I worked for her at one time** à un moment donné j'ai travaillé pour elle; **at the present time** en ce moment, à présent; **he is president at the present time** il est actuellement président; **at the time of delivery** au moment de la livraison; **at a later time** plus tard; **at a given time** à un moment donné; **at any one time** à la fois; **there's room for 15 people at any one time** il y a de la place pour 15 personnes à la fois; **an inconvenient time** un moment inopportun; **you called at a most inconvenient time** vous avez appelé à un très mauvais moment; **there are times when I could scream** il y a des moments où j'ai envie de hurler; **at the best of times** même quand tout va bien; **even at the best of times he is not that patient** même dans ses bons moments il n'est pas particulièrement patient; **at no time did I agree to that** je n'ai jamais donné mon accord pour cela; **by the time you get this...** le temps que tu reçoives ceci..., quand tu auras reçu ceci...; **by that time it will be too late** à ce moment-là il sera trop tard; **by that time we'll all be dead** d'ici là nous serons tous morts; **by this time next week** d'ici une semaine, dans une semaine; **this time next week** la semaine prochaine à cette heure-ci; **this time last week** il y a exactement une semaine; **from that time on we had nothing to do with them** à partir de ce moment-là, nous avons refusé d'avoir affaire à eux; **in between times** entre-temps; **some time or other** un jour ou l'autre; **some time next month** dans le courant du mois prochain; **until such time as I hear from them** jusqu'à ce que *ou* en attendant que j'aie de leurs nouvelles

(**j**) *(suitable moment)* moment *m*; **she chose her time badly** elle a mal choisi son moment; **this is no time for you to leave** ce n'est pas le moment de partir; **now's our time to tell her** c'est maintenant que nous devrions *ou* voici venu le moment de le lui dire; **now is the time to invest** c'est maintenant qu'il faut investir; **when the time comes** le moment venu, quand le moment sera venu; **we'll talk about that when the time comes** nous en parlerons en temps utile; **the time has come to make a stand** c'est le moment d'avoir le courage de ses opinions; **the time for talking is past** ce n'est plus le moment de parler; **it's about time we taught her a lesson** il est grand temps que nous lui donnions une bonne leçon; **there's no time like the present** *(let's do it now)* faisons-le maintenant; **there's a time and a place for everything** il y a un temps et un lieu pour *ou* à tout

(**k**) *(occasion, instance)* fois *f*; **I'll forgive you this time** je vous pardonne cette fois-ci *ou* pour cette fois; **each** *or* **every time** chaque fois; **she succeeds every time** elle réussit à chaque fois; **the last time he came** la dernière fois qu'il est venu; **the time before** la fois précédente *ou* d'avant; **another** *or* **some other time** une autre fois; **I called her three times** je l'ai appelée trois fois; **many times** bien des fois, très souvent; **many a time I've wondered...** je me suis demandé plus d'une *ou* bien des fois...; **several times** plusieurs fois; **several times in the past** plusieurs fois déjà; **he asked me several times if...** il m'a demandé plusieurs fois si...; **it costs 15 cents a time** ça coûte 15 cents à chaque fois; **the one time I'm winning, he wants to stop playing** pour une fois que je gagne, il veut arrêter de jouer; **nine times out of ten the machine doesn't work** neuf fois sur dix la machine ne marche pas; **we'll have to decide some time or other** tôt ou tard *ou* un jour ou l'autre il va falloir nous décider; **do you remember that time we went to Germany?** tu te rappelles la fois où nous sommes allés en Allemagne?; **there's always a first time** il y a un début à tout; **I've told you a hundred times!** je te l'ai dit vingt *ou* cent fois!; **give me a good detective story every time!** rien ne vaut un bon roman policier!

(**l**) *(experience)* **to have a good time** bien s'amuser; **she's had a terrible time of it** elle a beaucoup souffert; **I had the time of my life** jamais je ne me suis si bien *ou* autant amusé; **we had an awful time at the picnic** nous nous sommes ennuyés à mourir au pique-nique; **it was a difficult time for all of us** c'était une période difficile pour nous tous; **she had a hard time bringing up five children alone** ça a été difficile pour elle d'élever cinq enfants seule; **to give sb a hard** *or* **rough** *or* **tough time** en faire voir de dures à qn, en faire voir de toutes les couleurs à qn; **what a time I had with him!** *(fun)* qu'est-ce que j'ai pu m'amuser avec lui!; *(trouble)* qu'est-ce qu'il m'en a fait voir!

(**m**) *(hours of work)* **to put in time** faire des heures (de travail); **to work part/full time** travailler à temps partiel/à plein temps; *Br* **in company time,** *Am* **on company time** pendant les heures de travail; *Br* **in your own time,** *Am* **on your own time** pendant votre temps libre, en dehors des heures de travail

(**n**) *(hourly wages)* **we pay time and a half on weekends** nous payons les heures du week-end une fois et demie le tarif normal; **overtime is paid at double time** les heures supplémentaires sont payées *ou* comptées double

(**o**) *(usu plural) (era)* époque *f*, temps *m*; **in Victorian times** à l'époque victorienne; **in the time of Henry IV** à l'époque d'Henri IV, du temps d'Henri IV; **in times past, in former times** autrefois, jadis; **in times to come** à l'avenir; **at one time, things were different** autrefois *ou* dans le temps les choses étaient différentes; **the house has seen better times** la maison a connu des jours meilleurs; **in happier times** en un *ou* des temps plus heureux; **in time** *or* **times of need/war** en temps de pénurie/de guerre; **time was when doctors made house calls** il fut un temps où les médecins faisaient des visites à domicile; **those were happy times!** c'était le bon (vieux) temps!; **times are hard** les temps sont durs; **in our time** de nos jours; **the times we live in** l'époque *f* où nous vivons; **in my time children didn't talk back** de mon temps, les enfants ne répondaient pas; **she was probably a good singer in her time** en son temps, c'était sûrement une bonne chanteuse; **it was a very popular car in its time** c'était une voiture très populaire à l'époque (où elle est sortie); **very advanced for its time** très en avance sur son temps *ou* sur l'époque; **to be ahead of** *or* **before one's time** être en avance sur son époque *ou* sur son temps; **to be behind the times** être en retard sur son époque *ou* sur son temps; **to keep up with the times** vivre avec son temps; **to move with the times** évoluer avec son temps; **times have changed** autres temps, autres mœurs

(**p**) *(lifetime)* **I've heard some odd things in my time!** j'en ai entendu, des choses, dans ma vie!; **it won't happen in our time** nous ne serons pas là pour voir ça; **if I had my time over again** si j'avais à recommencer (ma vie); **at my time of life** à mon âge; **that was before your time** *(birth)* vous n'étiez pas encore né; *(arrival)* vous n'étiez pas encore là; **her time has come** *(childbirth)* elle arrive à son terme; *(death)* son heure est venue *ou* a sonné; *(success)* son heure est venue; **he died before his time** il est mort avant l'âge

(**q**) *(season)* **it's hot for the time of year** il fait chaud pour la saison

(**r**) *(end of period)* fin *f*; **time's up** *(on exam, visit)* c'est l'heure; *(on meter, telephone)* le temps est écoulé; *Br* **time (gentlemen), please!** *(in pub)* on ferme!; *Sport* **the referee called time** l'arbitre a sifflé la fin du match

(**s**) *Am Com (credit)* **to buy sth on time** acheter qch à tempérament *ou* à terme *ou* à crédit

(**t**) *Fam (in prison)* **to do time** faire de la taule; **he's serving time for murder** il est en taule pour meurtre

(**u**) *Mus (tempo)* mesure *f*; *(note value)* valeur *f (d'une note)*; **to keep time, to be in time** être en mesure; **he beat time with his foot** il battait *ou* marquait la mesure du pied; **in triple** *or* **three-part time** à trois temps

(**v**) *Rad & TV* espace *m*; **to buy/to sell time on television** acheter/vendre de l'espace publicitaire à la télévision

(**w**) *Am Fam (idiom)* **to make time with sb** *(pursue)* draguer qn; *(be with)* être avec qn ❑ *(en couple)*; *(have sex with)* s'envoyer en l'air avec qn

2 *vt* (**a**) *(on clock → runner, worker, race)* chronométrer; **they timed her at four minutes a mile** ils l'ont chronométrée *ou* ils ont chronométré son temps à quatre minutes au mille; **time how long she takes to finish** regardez combien de temps elle met pour finir; **he timed his speech to last twenty minutes** il a fait en sorte que son discours dure vingt minutes; **to time an egg** minuter le temps de cuisson d'un œuf

(**b**) *(schedule)* fixer *ou* prévoir (l'heure de); *Phot (exposure)* calculer; **they timed the attack for 6 o'clock** l'attaque était prévue pour 6 heures

(**c**) *(choose right moment for)* choisir *ou* calculer le moment de; **she timed her entrance well** elle a bien choisi le moment pour faire son entrée; **he timed the blow perfectly** il a frappé au bon moment; **your remark was perfectly/badly timed** votre observation est venue au bon/au mauvais moment

(**d**) *(synchronize)* régler, ajuster; **she tried to**

time her steps to the music elle essayait de régler ses pas sur la musique

3 times 1 *npl (indicating degree)* fois *f*; **she's ten times cleverer than** *or* **as clever as he is** elle est dix fois plus intelligente que lui; **he ate four times as much cake as I did** il a mangé quatre fois plus de gâteau que moi **2** *prep Math* **3 times 2 is 6** 3 fois 2 font *ou* égalent 6; **1 times 6 is 6** une fois six fait *ou* égale six

4 ahead of time *adv* en avance; **I'm ten minutes ahead of time** j'ai dix minutes d'avance

5 all the time *adv* **he talked all the time we were at lunch** il a parlé pendant tout le déjeuner; **he's been watching us all the time** il n'a pas cessé de nous regarder; **I knew it all the time** je le savais depuis le début

6 any time *adv* n'importe quand; **come over any time** venez quand vous voulez; **you're welcome any time** vous serez toujours le bienvenu; **thanks for all your help – any time** merci de votre aide – de rien

7 at a time *adv* **for days at a time** pendant des journées entières, des journées durant; **to do two things at a time** faire deux choses à la fois; **take one book at a time** prenez les livres un par un *ou* un (seul) livre à la fois; **she ran up the stairs two at a time** elle a monté les marches quatre à quatre

8 at all times *adv* à tous moments

9 at any time *adv* à toute heure; **hot meals at any time** repas chauds à toute heure; **at any time of day or night** à n'importe quelle heure du jour ou de la nuit; **at any time during office hours** n'importe quand pendant les heures de bureau; **he could die at any time** il peut mourir d'un moment à l'autre; **if at any time...** si à l'occasion...

10 at the same time *adv* (**a**) *(simultaneously)* en même temps; **they all spoke at the same time** ils se sont mis à parler tous en même temps; **they arrived at the same time (as) he did** ils sont arrivés en même temps que lui

(**b**) *(yet)* en même temps; **she was pleased but at the same time a bit concerned** elle était contente mais en même temps un peu inquiète

(**c**) *(nevertheless)* pourtant, cependant; **at the same time, we must not forget...** pourtant *ou* cependant, il ne faut pas oublier...

11 at the time *adv* **at the time of their wedding** au moment de leur mariage; **I didn't pay much attention at the time** sur le moment, je n'ai pas fait vraiment attention

12 at times *adv* parfois, par moments

13 behind time *adv* en retard; **we're a bit behind time** nous sommes légèrement en retard; **the project was running behind time** le projet avait du retard

14 for a time *adv* pendant un (certain) temps; **for a time, he was unable to walk** pendant un certain temps, il n'a pas pu marcher

15 for all time *adv* pour toujours

16 for the time being *adv* pour le moment

17 from time to time *adv* de temps en temps, de temps à autre

18 in time *adv* (**a**) *(eventually)* **she'll come to her senses in time** elle finira par revenir à la raison; **he'll forget about it in (the course of) time** il finira par l'oublier (avec le temps)

(**b**) *(not too late)* **let me know in (good) time** prévenez-moi (bien) à l'avance; **she arrived in time for the play** elle est arrivée à l'heure pour la pièce; **you're just in time to greet our guests** tu arrives juste à temps pour accueillir nos invités; **I'll be back in time for the film** je serai de retour à temps pour le film

(**c**) *Mus* en mesure; **to be** *or* **keep in time (with the music)** être en mesure (avec la musique)

19 in (next to) no time, in no time at all *adv* en un rien de temps

20 of all time *adv* de tous les temps

21 of all times *adv* **why now of all times?** pourquoi faut-il que ce soit juste maintenant?

22 on time *adv* à l'heure; **to run on time** *(trains etc)* être à l'heure; **she arrived right on time** elle est arrivée juste à l'heure; **is the bus on time?** est-ce que le bus est à l'heure?

23 out of time *adv Mus* **he got out of time** il a perdu la mesure

24 time after time, time and (time) again *adv* maintes et maintes fois

25 time off *n* temps *m* libre; **what do you do in your time off?** qu'est-ce que vous faites de votre temps libre?

26 time out *n* (**a**) *Sport* temps *m* mort; *(in chess match)* temps *m* de repos; *Sport* **to take time out** faire un temps mort

(**b**) *(break)* **I took time out to travel** *(from work)* je me suis mis en congé pour voyager; *(from studies)* j'ai interrompu mes études pour voyager; **she took time out to read the report** elle a pris le temps de lire le rapport

►► ***time of arrival*** heure *f* d'arrivée; *St Exch* ***time bargain*** marché *m* à terme; *Fin* ***time bill*** traite *f* à terme; *also Fig* ***time bomb*** bombe *f* à retardement; *Fig* **a demographic time bomb** une situation démographique qui menace d'exploser; **the situation is like a time bomb ticking away** la situation est explosive; *Fig* **they're sitting on a time bomb** ils sont assis sur un volcan; ***time capsule*** capsule *f* témoin *(qui doit servir de témoignage historique aux générations futures)*; *Ind* ***time card*** carte *f ou* fiche *f* de pointage; ***time chart*** *(showing time zones)* carte *f* des fuseaux horaires; *(showing events)* table *f* d'événements historiques; *(showing planning)* calendrier *m*, planning *m*; ***time check*** *(on radio)* rappel *m* de l'heure; *(in cycling, skiing, motor racing)* contrôle *m* du temps intermédiaire; *Gram* ***time clause*** proposition *f* temporelle; *Ind* ***time clock*** pointeuse *f*; ***time code*** code *m* temporel; ***time of departure*** heure *f* de départ; *Am Fin* ***time deposit*** dépôt *m* à terme; ***time difference*** décalage *m* horaire; *Fin* ***time draft*** traite *f* à terme; ***time exposure*** *(of film)* (temps *m* de) pose *f*; *(photograph)* photo *f* prise en pose; ***time frame*** délai *m*; **what's our time frame?** de combien de temps disposons-nous?; ***time fuse*** détonateur *m ou* fusée *f* à retardement; ***time lag*** *(delay)* décalage *m* dans le temps; *(in time zones)* décalage *m* horaire; ***time lapse*** intervalle *m*, laps *m* de temps; ***time limit*** *(gen)* délai *m*, date *f* limite; *Law* délai *m* de forclusion; **there is a strict time limit for applications** il y a un délai impératif *ou* de rigueur pour la remise des dossiers de candidature; **we'll have to set ourselves a time limit for the work** il va falloir nous imposer un délai pour finir ce travail; **the work must be completed within the time limit** le travail doit être terminé avant la date limite; *Fin* ***time loan*** emprunt *m* à terme; ***time machine*** machine *f* à voyager dans le temps; ***time management*** gestion *f* du temps de travail; *Mktg* ***time pricing*** fixation *f* des prix en fonction du moment; ***time sheet*** feuille *f* de présence; *Rad* ***time signal*** signal *m ou* top *m* horaire; *Mus* ***time signature*** indication *f* de la mesure; *Comput* ***time slice*** tranche *f* de temps; *Comput* ***time slicing*** temps *m* partagé; ***time slot*** créneau *m ou* tranche *f* horaire; ***time switch*** *(for oven, heating)* minuteur *m*; *(for lighting)* minuterie *f*; ***time travel*** voyage *m* dans le temps; ***time traveller*** personne *f* qui voyage dans le temps; *Sport* ***time trial*** course *f* contre la montre, contre-la-montre *m inv*; *Tel* ***time unit*** unité *f*; ***time value*** *Mus* valeur *f (d'une note)*; *Fin* valeur *f* temporelle; ***time warp*** *(in science fiction)* faille *f* spatio-temporelle; **it's like living in a time warp** c'est comme si on vivait hors du temps; **the country seems to have entered a time warp** le temps semble s'être arrêté dans le pays; **the house/company seems to be caught in a 19th century time warp** la maison/la société semble ne pas avoir changé depuis le XIXème siècle; ***time zone*** fuseau *m* horaire

---

'The Time Machine' *Wells* 'La Machine à explorer le temps'

I may be some time

Ce sont les mots ("je risque d'en avoir pour un certain temps") qu'aurait prononcés le capitaine Oates lorsqu'il sortit de la tente qu'il occupait avec le capitaine Scott au cours de leur expédition de 1912 au pôle sud. Oates souffrait de gelures multiples et afin de ne pas ralentir la progression de ses camarades, il décida de se sacrifier en disparaissant dans la tourmente. Cet épisode est censé symboliser les qualités d'héroïsme et d'abnégation associées au caractère britannique. Aujourd'hui, on emploie cette formule par allusion à Oates sur le mode humoristique lorsque l'on sort d'une pièce ou bien lorsqu'on va aux toilettes.

time-and-date signal *n* signal *m* horodateur

time-and-date stamp *n* horodateur *m*

time-and-motion *n*

►► ***time-and-motion expert*** expert *m* en productivité, spécialiste *mf* de l'organisation scientifique du travail; ***time-and-motion studies*** *(science)* organisation *f* scientifique du travail, OST *f*; ***time-and-motion study*** étude *f* de productivité *(qui porte sur l'organisation scientifique du travail)*

time-consuming *adj (task, work, activity)* qui prend beaucoup de temps

time-critical *adj* aux délais très serrés

time-efficient *adj Am* efficace

time-expired *adj (soldier etc)* qui a fait *ou* servi son temps

time-fill *Comput* **1** *n* temporisation *f*

2 *vi* temporiser

time-filler *n* **I'm just doing this job as a time-filler** je fais ce travail uniquement pour tuer le temps

time-filling *n Comput* temporisation *f*

time-honoured [-ˌɒnəd] *adj* consacré (par l'usage)

timekeeper ['taɪmˌkiːpə(r)] *n* (**a**) *(watch)* montre *f*; *(clock)* horloge *f*, *(stopwatch)* chronomètre *m*; **this watch is a good timekeeper** cette montre est toujours à l'heure (**b**) *(supervisor)* pointeau *m* (**c**) *(employee, friend)* **he's a good timekeeper** il est toujours à l'heure, il est toujours très ponctuel; **he's a bad timekeeper** il n'est jamais à l'heure (**d**) *Sport (official)* chronométreur(euse) *m,f* officiel(elle)

timekeeping ['taɪmˌkiːpɪŋ] *n* (**a**) *(of employee)* ponctualité *f*; **bad timekeeping** manque *m* de ponctualité, non-respect *m* des horaires; **he was sacked for bad timekeeping** il a été renvoyé pour manque de ponctualité *ou* non-respect des horaires (**b**) *Sport etc (calculation of time)* chronométrage *m*

time-lapse photography *n* accéléré *m*

timeless ['taɪmlɪs] *adj* éternel, hors du temps, intemporel

timelessness ['taɪmlɪsnɪs] *n* intemporalité *f*

timeline ['taimˌlaɪn] *n* frise *f* chronologique

timeliness ['taɪmlɪnɪs] *n (of remark)* à-propos *m*, opportunité *f*; *(of visit)* opportunité *f*

timely ['taɪmlɪ] *adj (remark, intervention, warning)* qui tombe à point nommé, opportun; *(visit)* opportun; **he made a timely escape** il s'est échappé juste à temps

timepiece ['taɪmpiːs] *n Formal or Old-fashioned (watch)* montre *f*; *(clock)* horloge *f*, pendule *f*

timer ['taɪmə(r)] *n* (**a**) *Culin* minuteur *m*; **(egg) timer** sablier *m*, compte-minutes *m inv* (**b**) *(counter)* compteur *m* (**c**) *(for lighting)* minuterie *f* (**d**) *(stopwatch)* chronomètre *m* (**e**) *Sport (official)* chronométreur(euse) *m,f* (**f**) *Aut* distributeur *m* d'allumage (**g**) *(on time bomb)* minuterie *f*

time-saver *n* **a dishwasher is a great time-saver** on gagne beaucoup de temps avec un lave-vaisselle, un lave-vaisselle permet de gagner beaucoup de temps

time-saving 1 *adj (device, method)* qui économise *ou* fait gagner du temps; **it's a time-saving device** cet appareil fait gagner du temps

2 *n* gain *m* de temps

timescale ['taɪmskeɪl] *n* période *f* (de temps); **the overall timescale** la durée totale; **what sort of timescale were you thinking of?** *(for completing the job, being absent from work etc)* de combien de temps allez-vous avoir besoin?; **the timescale of a novel** la période sur laquelle s'échelonne un roman

time-sensitive *adj* qui requiert un minutage très précis

time-served [-sɜːvd] *adj (toolmaker etc)* qui a fait son apprentissage

time-server *n* (**a**) *(opportunist)* opportuniste *mf* (**b**) *(employee)* tire-au-flanc *m inv*

time-serving 1 *adj* opportuniste
2 *n* opportunisme *m*

time-share 1 *n* **to buy a time-share in a flat** acheter un appartement en multipropriété
2 *adj (flat)* en multipropriété; *(computer)* en temps partagé

time-sharing *n* **(a)** *(of flat, villa)* multipropriété *f* **(b)** *Comput* partage *m* de temps

timespan ['taɪmspæn] *n* intervalle *m* de temps

timetable ['taɪm,teɪbəl] **1** *n* **(a)** *(for transport)* horaire *m*; **bus timetable** indicateur *m ou* horaire *m* des autobus
(b) *(schedule)* emploi *m* du temps; **I have a very full timetable** j'ai un emploi du temps très chargé
(c) *(calendar)* calendrier *m*; **exam timetable** dates *fpl ou* calendrier *m* des examens
2 *vt (meeting → during day)* fixer une heure pour; *(→ during week, month)* fixer une date pour; *Sch (classes, course)* établir un emploi du temps pour; **the train is timetabled to arrive at six o'clock** l'arrivée du train est prévue à six heures; **her visit is timetabled to coincide with the celebrations** sa visite est prévue pour coïncider avec les festivités

timewaster ['taɪm,weɪstə(r)] *n* fainéant(e) *m,f*; **no timewasters please** *(in advertisement)* pas sérieux s'abstenir

timewasting ['taɪm,weɪstɪŋ] *n* perte *f* de temps; **the team was accused of timewasting** on a reproché à l'équipe d'avoir joué la montre

timework ['taɪmwɜːk] *n (hourly)* travail *m* payé à l'heure; *(daily)* travail *m* payé à la journée; **to be on timework** *(hourly)* être payé *ou* travailler à l'heure; *(daily)* être payé *ou* travailler à la journée

timeworker ['taɪm,wɜːkə(r)] *n (paid hourly)* horaire *mf*; *(paid daily)* journalier(ère) *m,f*

timeworn ['taɪmwɔːn] *adj (object)* usé par le temps, vétuste; *Fig (idea, phrase)* rebattu, éculé

timid ['tɪmɪd] *adj* timide

timidity [tɪ'mɪdətɪ] *n* timidité *f*

timidly ['tɪmɪdlɪ] *adv* timidement

timidness ['tɪmɪdnɪs] *n* timidité *f*

timing ['taɪmɪŋ] *n* **(a)** *(of actor)* minutage *m* (du débit); *(of musician)* sens *m* du rythme; *(of tennis player)* timing *m*; *(of stunt driver)* synchronisation *f*; **you need a good sense of timing, you need to get the timing right** il faut savoir choisir le bon moment; **cooking such a big meal requires careful timing** pour préparer un si grand repas, il faut organiser son temps avec soin; **that was good timing!** voilà qui était bien calculé!; **he has no sense of timing** *(of what is suitable)* il n'a aucun sens de l'à-propos
(b) *(chosen moment → of operation, visit)* moment *m* choisi; **they're still discussing the timing of the election** ils sont encore en train de discuter de la date des élections; **the timing of the election to coincide with...** la date des élections choisie pour coïncider avec...; **the timing of the statement was unfortunate** cette déclaration est vraiment tombée à un très mauvais moment
(c) *Sport* chronométrage *m*
(d) *Aut* réglage *m* de l'allumage
▸▸ ***timing device*** *(for bomb)* mécanisme *m* d'horlogerie; *(for lights)* minuterie *f*; ***timing mechanism*** *(for bomb, in clock)* mécanisme *m* d'horlogerie

timocracy [taɪ'mɒkrəsɪ] *n* timocratie *f*

timocratic [,taɪmə'krætɪk] *adj* timocratique

Timor ['tiːmɔː(r)] *n* Timor *m*; **East Timor** le Timor-Oriental

Timorese [tiːmɔː'riːz] *(pl* **inv)** **1** *npl* **the Timorese** les Timorais *mpl*; **the East Timorese** les Timorais *mpl* de l'Est
2 *n (person)* Timorais(e) *m,f*; **East Timorese** Timorais(e) *m,f* de l'Est
3 *adj* timorais; **East Timorese** du Timor-Oriental

timorous ['tɪmərəs] *adj* timoré, craintif

timorously ['tɪmərəslɪ] *adv* craintivement

timorousness ['tɪmərəsnɪs] *n* caractère *m* timoré *ou* craintif

Timothy ['tɪməθɪ] *pr n Bible* Timothée

timothy grass ['tɪməθɪ-] *n Bot* fléole *f* des prés

timpani ['tɪmpənɪ] *npl Mus* timbales *fpl*

timpanist ['tɪmpənɪst] *n Mus* timbalier *m*

tin [tɪn] *(pt & pp* **tinned**, *cont* **tinning)** **1** *n* **(a)** *(metal)* étain *m*; **tin (plate)** fer-blanc *m*; **the tin** *(of squash court)* la plaque de faute
(b) *Br (can)* boîte *f* (en fer-blanc); *(containing food)* boîte *f* de conserve; **tins of beans/of food** des boîtes *fpl* de haricots/de conserve; **a tin of paint** un pot de peinture; **to live out of tins** se nourrir de conserves
(c) *(for storing)* boîte *f* en fer; **biscuit tin** *(empty)* boîte *f* à biscuits; *(full)* boîte *f* de biscuits
(d) *(for cooking meat)* plat *m*; *(for cooking bread, cakes etc)* moule *m*
2 *adj (made of tin)* en étain; *(made of tinplate)* en fer-blanc; *(box)* en fer; *(roof)* en tôle; *Am* **he's got a tin ear** il n'a pas l'oreille musicale
3 *vt* **(a)** *Br (food)* mettre en conserve *ou* en boîte
(b) *(plate)* étamer
▸▸ ***tin can*** boîte *f* (en fer-blanc); ***tin god*** **(a)** *(petty dictator)* petit chef *m*, chefaillon *m*; **he's nothing but a little tin god** il est très imbu de sa personne, il se croit sorti de la cuisse de Jupiter **(b)** *(object of veneration)* idole *f* de pacotille; *Br* ***tin hat*** casque *m* (militaire); *Fam* ***tin lizzie*** vieille guimbarde *f*; ***tin mine*** mine *f* d'étain; *Br* ***tin opener*** ouvre-boîte *m*, ouvre-boîtes *m inv*; ***Tin Pan Alley*** = le monde de la musique populaire; **he works in Tin Pan Alley** il travaille dans la musique pop; ***tin soldier*** soldat *m* de plomb; ***tin whistle*** flûtiau *m*, pipeau *m*

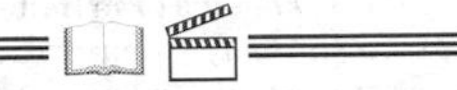

'The Tin Drum' *Grass, Schlöndorff* 'Le Tambour'

Does exactly what it says on the tin
Il s'agit du slogan d'une publicité britannique pour la marque de peinture et de vernis Ronseal. Le message de la publicité est direct et simple et vise à donner une impression de fiabilité: "fait exactement ce qui est écrit sur la boîte". Aujourd'hui, on emploie cette expression en anglais britannique lorsqu'une chose correspond exactement à ce que l'on en attendait. On dira par exemple **the Comprehensive Guide to Pop Trivia website is really cool – it does exactly what it says on the tin, it's got everything** ("le site web du Guide complet de la musique pop est vraiment chouette – le titre ne ment pas: il est vraiment complet").

tinamou ['tɪnəmuː] *n Orn* tinamou *m*

tinctorial [tɪŋk'tɔːrɪəl] *adj* tinctorial

tincture ['tɪŋktʃə(r)] **1** *n* **(a)** *Chem & Pharm* teinture *f*; **tincture of iodine** teinture *f* d'iode **(b)** *(colour, tint)* teinte *f*, nuance *f* **(c)** *Literary (trace, hint)* teinte *f*, touche *f*
2 *vt also Fig* teinter

tinder ['tɪndə(r)] *n (UNCOUNT) (in tinderbox)* amadou *m*; *(dry wood)* petit bois *m*; *(dry grass)* herbes *fpl* sèches; *Fig* **his words were tinder to the mob's fury** ses paroles ont eu un effet incendiaire sur la foule en colère

tinderbox ['tɪndəbɒks] *n* **(a)** *(lighter)* briquet *m* à amadou **(b)** *(dry place)* endroit *m* sec **(c)** *Fig (explosive situation)* poudrière *f*, situation *f* explosive; **the country is a tinderbox** le pays est une poudrière

tinder-dry *adj* très sec (sèche)

tindery ['tɪndərɪ] *adj* hautement inflammable, sec (sèche) (comme de l'amadou)

tine [taɪn] *n (of fork)* dent *f*; *(of antler)* andouiller *m*

tinea ['tɪnɪə] *n Med* teigne *f*

tinfoil ['tɪnfɔɪl] *n* papier *m* d'aluminium

ting [tɪŋ] **1** *onomat* ding
2 *vi* tinter
3 *vt* faire tinter

ting-a-ling 1 *onomat (of phone, doorbell, bike)* dring-dring
2 *n* dring-dring *m*

tinge [tɪndʒ] **1** *n* teinte *f*, nuance *f*; **a tinge of irony** une pointe *ou* une note d'ironie
2 *vt* teinter; **sky tinged with pink** ciel teinté de rose; *Fig* **her smile was tinged with sadness** son sourire était empreint de tristesse

tingle ['tɪŋgəl] **1** *vi* **(a)** *(with heat, cold → ears, cheeks, hands)* fourmiller, picoter; **the cold wind made my face/blood tingle** le vent froid me piquait le visage/me fouettait le sang; **his cheeks were tingling** les joues lui picotaient; **my whole body was tingling** j'avais des picotements *ou* des fourmis dans tout le corps; **my face still tingled from the blow** le visage me cuisait encore à cause du coup que j'avais reçu; **it makes my tongue tingle** ça me pique la langue
(b) *(with excitement, pleasure)* frissonner, frémir; **she was tingling with excitement** elle tremblait d'excitation; **the insult left me tingling with indignation** l'insulte me fit frémir d'indignation
2 *n* **(a)** *(stinging)* picotements *mpl*, fourmillements *mpl*
(b) *(thrill)* frisson *m*, frémissement *m*; **he felt a tingle of excitement** il sentit un frisson d'excitation le parcourir

tingling ['tɪŋglɪŋ] **1** *n (stinging)* picotement *m*, fourmillement *m*; *(from excitement)* frisson *m*, frémissement *m*
2 *adj (sensation)* de picotement, de fourmillement

tingly ['tɪŋglɪ] *adj (sensation)* de picotement, de fourmillement; **my fingers have gone all tingly** j'ai des fourmis dans les doigts; **the cold shower made me (feel) tingly all over** la douche froide m'a fouetté le sang

tinhorn ['tɪnhɔːn] *Fam* **1** *n Am* petit(e) prétentieux(-euse) *m,f*
2 *adj* de pacotille, clinquant

tininess ['taɪnɪnɪs] *n* petitesse *f* (extrême)

tinker ['tɪŋkə(r)] **1** *n* **(a)** *(pot mender)* rétameur *m* (ambulant); *(gipsy)* romanichel(elle) *m,f*; *Fam* **I don't give a tinker's cuss** *or Br* **damn!** je m'en fiche comme de ma première chemise!; *Fam* **it's not worth a tinker's cuss** ça vaut des clopinettes; **tinker, tailor, soldier, sailor...** *(child's rhyme)* = comptine pour découvrir quel genre d'homme on épousera ou ce qu'on fera comme métier plus tard
(b) *Br Fam (child)* voyou *m*, garnement *m*; **you little tinker!** petit garnement!
(c) *(act of tinkering)* bricolage *m*
2 *vi* **to tinker about** bricoler; **he spends hours tinkering with that car** il passe des heures à bricoler cette voiture; **he's forever tinkering with the radio** *(fiddling with it)* il n'arrête pas de tripoter la radio; *(repairing it)* il passe des heures à rafistoler le poste de radio; **who's been tinkering with the thermostat?** qui a touché au thermostat?; **someone has tinkered with this report** quelqu'un a trafiqué ce rapport; **so far you've only been tinkering with the problem** pour l'instant, tu n'as fait qu'effleurer le problème

tinkering ['tɪŋkərɪŋ] *n (doing odd jobs)* bricolage *m*

tinkle ['tɪŋkəl] **1** *vi* **(a)** *(bell)* tinter **(b)** *Fam (urinate)* faire pipi
2 *vt (small bell)* faire tinter
3 *n* **(a)** *(ring)* tintement *m*; **I heard the tinkle of a bell** j'ai entendu tinter une sonnette **(b)** *Br Fam (phone call)* **to give sb a tinkle** donner *ou* passer un coup de fil à qn **(c)** *Br Fam (act of urinating)* **to go for a tinkle** aller faire pipi

tinkling ['tɪŋklɪŋ] **1** *n* tintement *m*
2 *adj (bell)* qui tinte; *(water)* qui murmure

tinkly ['tɪŋklɪ] = **tinkling** *adj*

tinned [tɪnd] *adj Br (preserved in tins)* en boîte, en conserve
▸▸ ***tinned food*** conserves *fpl*

tinniness ['tɪnɪnɪs] *n* **(a)** *(of sound)* timbre *m* métallique **(b)** *Fam (poor quality)* mauvaise qualité *f*

tinnitus [tɪ'naɪtəs] *n (UNCOUNT) Med* acouphène *m*

tinny ['tɪnɪ] *(compar* **tinnier**, *superl* **tinniest)** *adj* **(a)** *(sound)* métallique, de casserole; *(music)* grêle; **tinny piano** = piano qui fait un bruit de casserole **(b)** *Fam (poor quality → radio, car)* de camelote, de quatre sous

tinplate ['tɪnpleɪt] *n* fer-blanc *m*

tin-plate *vt* étamer

tinpot ['tɪnpɒt] *adj Br Fam* **(a)** *(worthless → car, machine)* qui ne vaut rien **(b)** *(insignificant, hopeless)* médiocre; **a tinpot regime/dictator** un régime/un dictateur de pacotille; **a tinpot**

frontier town une petite ville frontalière sans importance□

tinsel ['tɪnsəl] (*Br pt & pp* **tinselled,** *cont* **tinselling,** *Am pt & pp* **tinseled,** *cont* **tinseling**) **1** *n (UNCOUNT)* (**a**) *(for Christmas tree)* guirlandes *fpl* de Noël; *(in fine strands)* cheveux *mpl* d'ange (**b**) *Fig* clinquant *m*

2 *vt (tree)* orner *ou* décorer de guirlandes

▸▸ *Hum Pej* ***Tinsel Town*** = surnom donné à Hollywood

tinsmith ['tɪnsmɪθ] *n* étameur *m*, ferblantier *m*

tint [tɪnt] **1** *n* (**a**) *(colour, shade)* teinte *f*, nuance *f*; **red with a blue tint** rouge avec une nuance de bleu (**b**) *(hair dye)* shampooing *m* colorant (**c**) *(in engraving, printing)* hachure *f*, hachures *fpl*

2 *vt* teinter; **blue-tinted walls** des murs bleutés; **tinted lenses** verres *mpl* teintés; **to tint one's hair** se faire un shampooing colorant; **she tints her hair** elle se teint les cheveux

tintack ['tɪntæk] *n* clou *m* de tapissier, semence *f*

tinting ['tɪntɪŋ] *n* coloration *f*

tintinnabulation ['tɪntɪˌnæbjʊ'leɪʃən] *n Literary* tintamarre *m*

Tintoretto [ˌtɪntə'retəʊ] *pr n* le Tintoret; **a painting by Tintoretto** un tableau du Tintoret

tintype ['tɪntaɪp] *n Phot* photographie *f* sur ferrotype

tinware ['tɪnweə(r)] *n (UNCOUNT)* articles *mpl* en fer-blanc

tinwork ['tɪnwɜːk] *n* ferblanterie *f (ustensiles)*

tinworks ['tɪnwɜːks] (*pl* **inv**) *n* ferblanterie *f (usine)*

tiny ['taɪnɪ] (*compar* **tinier,** *superl* **tiniest**) *adj* tout petit, minuscule; **a tiny baby** un tout petit bébé; **a tiny bit** un tout petit peu; **the meat is a tiny bit overdone** la viande est un tantinet trop cuite

▸▸ ***tiny tot*** petit(e) enfant *m,f*; **games for tiny tots** des jeux pour les tout-petits

tip [tɪp] (*pt & pp* **tipped,** *cont* **tipping**) **1** *n* (**a**) *(extremity → of ear, finger, nose)* bout *m*; *(→ of tongue)* bout *m*, pointe *f*; *(→ of cigarette, wing)* bout *m*; *(→ of blade, knife, fork)* pointe *f*; **stand on the tips of your toes** mettez-vous sur la pointe des pieds; **from tip to toe** de la tête aux pieds; **six metres from tip to tip** six mètres d'envergure *ou* de long; **his name is on the tip of my tongue** j'ai son nom sur le bout de la langue

(**b**) *(of island, peninsula)* extrémité *f*, pointe *f*; *Fig* **it's just the tip of the iceberg** ce n'est que la partie émergée de l'iceberg

(**c**) *(cap → on walking stick, umbrella)* embout *m*; *(→ on snooker cue)* procédé *m*; **steel tip** *(of shoe)* bout *m* ferré

(**d**) *Br (dump → for rubbish)* décharge *f*, dépôt *m* d'ordures; *(→ for coal)* terril *m*; *Fam Fig* **your room is a real tip!** quel bazar, ta chambre!; *Fam Fig* **the house is a bit of a tip** la maison est un vrai dépotoir

(**e**) *(hint → for stock market, race)* tuyau *m*; *(advice)* conseil *m*; **to give sb a tip** *(for race)* donner un tuyau à qn; *(for repairs, procedure)* donner un tuyau *ou* un conseil à qn; **to take a tip from sb** suivre le conseil de qn; **if you take my tip, you'll wait a bit longer before selling** si vous voulez un bon conseil, attendez encore un peu avant de vendre; **any tips for the 4.30?** avez-vous un tuyau pour la course de 16h30?; **Orlando's my tip** je pense qu'Orlando va gagner; **'Handy Tips for Successful Gardening'** *(book title)* 'Comment réussir votre jardin'

(**f**) *(money)* pourboire *m*; **to give sb a tip** donner un pourboire à qn; **how big a tip shall I leave?** combien de pourboire dois-je laisser?

2 *vt* (**a**) *(cane)* mettre un embout à; *(snooker cue)* mettre un procédé à; **an ivory-tipped cane** une canne à pommeau d'ivoire; **arrows tipped with poison** des flèches empoisonnées

(**b**) *(tilt, lean)* incliner, pencher; **she tipped her head to one side** elle a penché la tête sur le côté; **to tip one's hat to sb** saluer qn d'un coup de chapeau; **to tip one's hat over one's eyes** rabattre son chapeau sur ses yeux; **the boxer tipped the scales at 80 kg** le boxeur pesait 80 kg; *Fig* **to tip the scales in sb's favour** faire pencher la balance en faveur de qn; **the election tipped the balance of power** avec les élections, l'équilibre des forces politiques a été inversé

(**c**) *(upset, overturn)* renverser, faire chavirer; **I was tipped off my stool/into the water** on m'a fait tomber de mon tabouret/dans l'eau

(**d**) *Br (empty, pour)* verser; *(unload)* déverser, décharger; **she tipped the sugar into the bowl** elle a versé *ou* vidé le sucre dans le bol; **the lorry tipped the rubbish into the field** le camion a déchargé *ou* déversé les déchets dans le champ

(**e**) *(winning horse)* pronostiquer; **Orlando is tipped for the 2.30** *or* **to win the 2.30** Orlando est donné gagnant dans la course de 14h30; **he tipped the winner** il a pronostiqué *ou* donné le cheval gagnant; *Fig* **you've tipped a winner there** vous avez trouvé un bon filon; **he's tipped to be the next president** *or* **as the next president** on prédit *ou* pronostique qu'il sera le prochain président; **he is strongly tipped to become Home Secretary** il est donné comme favori pour le poste de ministre de l'Intérieur; *Fam* **to tip sb the wink** avertir qn□, prévenir qn□

(**f**) *(porter, waiter)* donner un pourboire à; **she tipped him £1** elle lui a donné une livre de pourboire

3 *vi* (**a**) *Br (tilt)* incliner, pencher; **to tip to the left** pencher à gauche

(**b**) *Br (overturn)* basculer, se renverser

(**c**) *Br (dump rubbish)* **no tipping** *(sign)* défense de déposer des ordures

(**d**) *(give money)* laisser un pourboire; **how much do you usually tip?** combien de pourboire laissez-vous habituellement?

▸▸ ***tip cart*** tombereau *m*

▸**tip back 1** *vi* se rabattre en arrière, s'incliner en arrière; **don't tip back on your chair** ne te balance pas sur ta chaise

2 *vt sep* faire basculer (en arrière); **don't tip your chair back too far** ne te penche pas trop en arrière sur ta chaise

▸**tip down** *Br Fam* **1** *vi* **the rain is tipping down, it's tipping down (with rain)** il pleut des cordes

2 *vt sep (idiom)* **it's tipping it down** il pleut des cordes

▸**tip in** *vt sep* (**a**) *(in basketball)* **to tip the ball in** claquer (le ballon) dans le panier (**b**) *Typ* monter en hors-texte

▸**tip off** *vt sep* avertir, prévenir; **the police had been tipped off about the robbery** la police avait été avertie que le hold-up aurait lieu; **someone must have tipped them off** quelqu'un a dû les prévenir

▸**tip out** *vt sep Br* (**a**) *(empty → liquid, small objects)* vider, verser; *(→ rubbish, larger objects)* déverser, décharger; **tip the tea out into the sink** vide *ou* verse le thé dans l'évier; **she tipped the coins out into my hand** elle a fait tomber les pièces dans ma main

(**b**) *(overturn, toss)* faire basculer; **we were tipped out of the cart into the water** on nous a fait basculer de la charrette pour nous faire tomber dans l'eau

▸**tip over 1** *vi* (**a**) *(tilt)* pencher

(**b**) *(overturn → boat)* chavirer, se renverser

2 *vt sep* faire basculer, renverser

▸**tip up 1** *vi* (**a**) *(cinema seat)* se rabattre; *(bunk, plank, cart)* basculer; **the table tipped up when I sat on it** la table a basculé quand je me suis assis dessus

(**b**) *(bucket, cup, vase)* se renverser

2 *vt sep* (**a**) *(seat, table)* faire basculer, rabattre

(**b**) *(upside down → bottle, barrel)* renverser

tip-in *n* (**a**) *(in basketball)* claquette *f* au rebond (**b**) *Typ* hors-texte *m*

tip-off *n* (**a**) *Fam* **to give sb a tip-off** *(hint)* filer un tuyau à qn; *(warning)* avertir qn□, prévenir qn□; **a tip-off to the police led to his arrest** quelqu'un l'a donné *ou* dénoncé à la police (**b**) *(in basketball)* entre-deux *m*

tipped ['tɪpt] *adj* (**a**) **tipped with felt/steel** à bout feutré/ferré (**b**) *(cigarettes)* (à) bout filtre *(inv)*

-tipped [tɪpt] *suff* à bout...; **steel/felt-tipped** à bout ferré/feutré; **a felt-tipped pen** un crayon-feutre, un feutre

tipper ['tɪpə(r)] *n* (**a**) *(truck)* camion *m* à benne (basculante) (**b**) *(tipping device)* benne *f* (basculante) (**c**) *(customer)* **he's a generous tipper** il laisse toujours de bons pourboires

▸▸ ***tipper truck*** camion *m* à benne (basculante)

Tipperary [ˌtɪpə'reərɪ] *n* (**a**) *(town)* Tipperary *m* (**b**) *(county)* le comté de Tipperary, = comté dans le sud de la République d'Irlande; **in Tipperary** dans le comté de Tipperary

tippet ['tɪpɪt] *n (cape → gen)* pèlerine *f*; *(→ of fur)* étole *f*; *(→ worn by clergyman)* étole *f*

Tipp-Ex® ['tɪpeks] *n Br* correcteur *m* liquide, Tipp-Ex® *m*

▸**Tipp-Ex**® **out** *vt sep* effacer (avec du Tipp-Ex®)

tipping ['tɪpɪŋ] **1** *adj (wagon etc)* basculant, à bascule

2 *n (giving money)* distribution *f* de pourboires; *(system)* (système *m* des) pourboires *mpl*

tipple ['tɪpəl] **1** *vi Fam* picoler

2 *n* (**a**) *Fam (drink)* **he likes a tipple now and then** il aime boire un coup de temps à autre; **what's your tipple then?** qu'est-ce que vous prendrez?□; **gin was my tipple** je buvais du gin à l'époque□ (**b**) *Mining (device)* culbuteur *m*; *(place → for loading)* aire *f* de chargement; *(→ for unloading)* aire *f* de déchargement

tippler ['tɪplə(r)] *n Fam* picoleur(euse) *m,f*

tippy-toe ['tɪpɪ-] *Am* = **tiptoe**

tipsily ['tɪpsɪlɪ] *adv Fam* **he got tipsily to his feet** il s'est levé en titubant□

tipsiness ['tɪpsɪnɪs] *n Fam* (légère) ivresse□ *f*

tipstaff ['tɪpstɑːf] *n* (**a**) *Br Law (official)* huissier *m* (**b**) *(staff)* bâton *m* ferré (cérémonial)

tipster ['tɪpstə(r)] *n* **(racing) tipster** pronostiqueur(euse) *m,f*

tipsy ['tɪpsɪ] (*compar* **tipsier,** *superl* **tipsiest**) *adj Fam* éméché, pompette; **to get tipsy** se griser; **white wine makes me tipsy** le vin blanc me monte à la tête□

▸▸ *Br* ***tipsy cake*** gâteau *m* imbibé d'alcool

tip-tilted *adj* à bout relevé; *(nose)* retroussé

tiptoe ['tɪptəʊ] **1** *n* **on tiptoe** sur la pointe des pieds

2 *vi* marcher sur la pointe des pieds; **to tiptoe in/out** entrer/sortir sur la pointe des pieds; **he tiptoed downstairs** il est descendu sur la pointe des pieds *ou* sans faire de bruit

tip-top *adj Fam* de premier ordre□, de toute première qualité□; **in tip-top condition** en excellent état□

tip-up *adj*

▸▸ ***tip-up seat*** *(in cinema, theatre)* siège *m* rabattable, strapontin *m*; *(in metro)* strapontin *m*; *Br* ***tip-up truck*** camion *m* à benne (basculante)

TIR [ˌtiːaɪ'ɑː(r)] *n Transp (abbr* **transports internationaux routiers**) TIR *m*

tirade [taɪ'reɪd] *n* diatribe *f*; **a tirade of abuse** une bordée d'injures; **he launched into a long tirade against bureaucrats** il s'est lancé dans une longue diatribe contre les bureaucrates

Tirana, Tiranë [tɪ'rɑːnə] *n* Tirana *f*

tire ['taɪə(r)] **1** *vi* (**a**) *(become exhausted)* se fatiguer; **she tires easily** elle est vite fatiguée

(**b**) *(become bored)* se fatiguer, se lasser; **he soon tired of her/of her company** il se lassa vite d'elle/de sa compagnie; **he never tires of talking about the war** il ne se lasse jamais de parler de la guerre

2 *vt* (**a**) *(exhaust)* fatiguer

(**b**) *(bore)* fatiguer, lasser

3 *n Am* = **tyre**

▸**tire out** *vt sep* épuiser, éreinter; **the long walk had tired us all out** cette longue marche nous avait tous épuisés; **I'm tired out!** je n'en peux plus!; **you'll tire yourself out moving all those boxes** vous allez vous épuiser à déplacer toutes ces caisses

tired ['taɪəd] *adj* (**a**) *(exhausted)* fatigué; **to feel tired** se sentir fatigué; **to get tired** se fatiguer; **the walk made me tired** la marche m'a fatigué; **I'm so tired I could drop** je tombe de sommeil; **my eyes are tired** j'ai les yeux fatigués; **in a tired voice** d'une voix lasse; *Hum Euph* **to be tired and emotional** *(drunk)* être dans les vignes du Seigneur

(**b**) *(fed up)* fatigué, las; **to be tired of sb/sth** en avoir assez de qn/qch; **I'm tired of their excuses** j'en ai assez de leurs excuses; **I'm tired of telling them** j'en ai assez de le leur répéter; **she soon got tired of him** elle se fatigua *ou* se lassa vite de lui; **I got rather tired of playing cards** j'en ai eu assez de jouer aux cartes; **the children make me tired with their constant**

whining les enfants me fatiguent avec leur pleurnicheries continuelles; **tired of arguing, he consented** de guerre lasse, il a donné son consentement

(**c**) *(hackneyed)* rebattu

(**d**) *Fig (old → skin)* desséché; *(→ vegetable)* défraîchi, flétri; *(→ upholstery, springs, car)* fatigué

tiredly ['taɪədlɪ] *adv (say)* d'une voix lasse; *(move, walk)* avec lassitude

tiredness ['taɪədnɪs] *n* (**a**) *(exhaustion)* fatigue *f*; **tiredness began to set in** la fatigue commença à se faire sentir (**b**) *(tedium)* fatigue *f*, lassitude *f*

tireless ['taɪəlɪs] *adj (person)* infatigable, inlassable; *(effort, campaign)* soutenu; *(energy)* inépuisable

tirelessly ['taɪəlɪslɪ] *adv* infatigablement, inlassablement, sans ménager ses efforts

tirelessness ['taɪəlɪsnɪs] *n* infatigabilité *f*

Tiresias [taɪ'riːsɪæs] *pr n Myth* Tirésias

tiresome ['taɪəsəm] *adj (irritating)* agaçant, ennuyeux; *(boring)* assommant, ennuyeux; **how tiresome!** que c'est ennuyeux!; **you're being very tiresome!** tu m'ennuies!, tu es vraiment agaçant!

tiresomely ['taɪəsəmlɪ] *adv* d'une façon ennuyeuse

tiring ['taɪərɪŋ] *adj* fatigant

tiro = **tyro**

Tirol = **Tyrol**

'tis [tɪz] *Arch, Hum or Ir* = **it is**

tisane [tiː'zæn] *n* tisane *f*

tissue ['tɪʃuː] *n* (**a**) *Anat & Bot* tissu *m* (**b**) *Tex* voile *m*; *Fig* **a tissue of lies** un tissu de mensonges (**c**) *(paper handkerchief)* mouchoir *m* en papier; *(toilet paper)* papier *m* hygiénique

►► *Biol* ***tissue culture*** culture *f* de tissus; ***tissue paper*** papier *m* de soie; *Biol* ***tissue type*** groupe *m* tissulaire

tit [tɪt] *n* (**a**) *Orn* mésange *f* (**b**) *very Fam (breast)* nichon *m*, robert *m*; *Br* **to get on sb's tits** courir sur le haricot à qn, taper sur le nerfs à qn (**c**) *Br very Fam Pej (person)* con (conne) *m,f*; **I felt a right tit** je me suis senti tout con (**d**) *(idiom)* **it's tit for tat!** c'est un prêté pour un rendu!

Titan ['taɪtən] *n Astron* Titan *m*; *Myth* Titan *m*; **the Titans** les Titans *mpl*; *Fig* **a Titan of the motor industry** un géant de l'industrie automobile

titanic [taɪ'tænɪk] *adj* (**a**) *(huge)* titanesque, colossal (**b**) *Chem* au titane

►► ***titanic acid*** acide *m* de titane

titanium [taɪ'teɪnɪəm] *n Chem* titane *m*

titanous ['taɪtənəs] *adj Chem* titaneux

titbit ['tɪtbɪt], *Am* **tidbit** ['tɪdbɪt] *n* (**a**) *Culin* bon morceau *m*, morceau *m* de choix (**b**) *(of information, scandal)* détail *m* croustillant; **titbit of gossip** potin *m*, racontar *m*

titch = **tich**

titchy = **tichy**

titer *Am* = **titre**

titfer ['tɪtfə(r)] *n SEng Fam Old-fashioned (rhyming slang* **tit for tat** = **hat**) galurin *m*

tit-for-tat *adj (killing, expulsions etc)* fait en représailles *ou* en riposte

tithe [taɪð] **1** *n* (**a**) *Hist* dîme *f*; **to pay tithes** payer la dîme (**b**) *(percentage of income)* = montant équivalant à un dixième du revenu, versé par les membres de certaines Églises

2 *vt* (**a**) *Hist* lever la dîme sur (**b**) *(income)* = verser à l'Église

►► ***tithe barn*** = grange où l'on mettait les recettes de la dîme

tithing ['taɪðɪŋ] *n Hist* (**a**) *(paying of tithes)* paiement *m* de la dîme (**b**) *(exacting of tithes)* prélèvement *m* de la dîme (**c**) *(administrative division)* = en Angleterre, ancienne division administrative d'un comté

Titian ['tɪʃən] *pr n* (le) Titien

titian ['tɪʃən] *adj* blond vénitien *(inv)*

Titianesque [,tɪʃə'nesk] *adj* titianesque

Titicaca [,tɪtɪ'kɑːkɑː] *n* **Lake Titicaca** le lac Titicaca

titillate ['tɪtɪleɪt] **1** *vt* titiller

2 *vi* titiller les sens

titillating ['tɪtɪ,leɪtɪŋ] *adj* titillant

titillation [,tɪtɪ'leɪʃən] *n* titillation *f*

titivate ['tɪtɪveɪt] *Fam Hum* **1** *vi* se bichonner, se pomponner

2 *vt* **to titivate oneself** se bichonner, se pomponner

titivation [,tɪtɪ'veɪʃən] *n Fam* bichonnage *m*

titlark ['tɪtlɑːk] *n Orn* pipit *m* (des prés)

title ['taɪtəl] **1** *n* (**a**) *(indicating rank, status)* titre *m*; **he has the title of Chief Executive Officer** son titre officiel est directeur général; **to give sb a title** donner un titre à qn, titrer qn; **to have a title** *(nobleman)* avoir un titre de noblesse, être titré; **the monarch bears the title of Defender of the Faith** le monarque porte le titre de défenseur de la foi

(**b**) *(nickname)* surnom *m*; **she earned the title "Iron Lady"** on l'a surnommée "la Dame de Fer"

(**c**) *(of book, film, play, song)* titre *m*; *(of newspaper article)* titre *m*, intitulé *m*

(**d**) *Typ (book)* titre *m*; **they published 200 titles last year** ils ont publié 200 titres l'an dernier

(**e**) *Sport* titre *m*; **to win the title** remporter le titre; **he holds the world heavyweight boxing title** il détient le titre de champion du monde de boxe des poids lourds

(**f**) *Law* droit *m*, titre *m*

2 *comp (music)* du générique

3 *vt (book, chapter, film)* intituler

4 titles *npl Cin & TV (credits)* générique *m*

►► *Comput* ***title bar*** barre *f* de titre; *Law* ***title deed*** titre *m* de propriété; *Boxing* ***title fight*** combat *m* comptant pour le titre; ***title page*** page *f* de titre; ***title role*** rôle-titre *m*; **with Vanessa Redgrave in the title role** avec Vanessa Redgrave dans le rôle-titre; ***title track*** morceau *m* qui donne son titre à l'album

titled ['taɪtəld] *adj (person, family)* titré; **the titled classes** les classes *fpl* titrées

titleholder ['taɪtəl,həʊldə(r)] *n* détenteur(trice) *m,f* du titre; *Sport* tenant(e) *m,f* du titre

titmouse ['tɪtmaʊs] *(pl* **titmice** [-maɪs]) *n Zool* mésange *f*

Titoism ['tiːtəʊɪzəm] *n Pol* titisme *m*

Titoist ['tiːtəʊɪst] *Pol* **1** *adj* titiste

2 *n* titiste *mf*

titrate [*Br* 'taɪtreɪt, *Am* taɪ'treɪt] *vt Chem* titrer

titration [taɪ'treɪʃən] *n Chem* titrage *m*

titre, *Am* **titer** ['taɪtə(r)] *n Biol & Chem* titre *m*

titter ['tɪtə(r)] **1** *vi* rire bêtement *ou* sottement, glousser

2 *n* petit rire *m* bête *ou* sot, gloussement *m*

tittering ['tɪtərɪŋ] *n (UNCOUNT)* petits rires *mpl*

tittivate, tittivation = **titivate, titivation**

tittle ['tɪtəl] *n Typ* signe *m* diacritique, iota *m*

tittle-tattle [-,tætəl] **1** *n (UNCOUNT)* potins *mpl*, cancans *mpl*

2 *vi* jaser, cancaner

titty ['tɪtɪ] *n very Fam* (**a**) *(breast)* nichon *m*, robert *m* (**b**) **tough titty!** dur! dur!

titubation [,tɪtjʊ'beɪʃən] *n Med* titubation *f*

titular ['tɪtjʊlə(r)] *adj* nominal

titularly ['tɪtjʊləlɪ] *adv* nominalement

titulary ['tɪtjʊlərɪ] *adj* nominal

Titus ['taɪtəs] *pr n* (**a**) *Antiq* Titus (**b**) *Bible* Tite

tizz [tɪz], **tizzy** ['tɪzɪ] *n Fam* panique □ *f*; **to be in a tizzy** être dans tous ses états, ne pas savoir où donner de la tête; **don't get into a tizzy about it** ne t'affole pas pour ça

T-joint *n* assemblage *m* en T

T-junction *n Br* intersection *f* en T

TKO [,tiːkeɪ'əʊ] *n Boxing (abbr* **technical knockout**) K-O *m* technique

TLC [,tiːel'siː] *n Fam (abbr* **tender loving care**) affection □ *f*; **she just needs a bit of TLC** elle a juste besoin d'un peu d'affection

Tlingit ['tlɪŋgɪt] *n* (**a**) *(tribe)* Tlingit *mpl* (**b**) *(member of tribe)* Tlingit *mf inv*

TLS [,tiːel'es] *n Press (abbr* **Times Literary Supplement**) = supplément littéraire du 'Times'

T lymphocyte *n* lymphocyte *m* T

TM[1] [,tiː'em] *n (abbr* **transcendental meditation**) MT *f*

TM[2] *(written abbr* **trademark**) MD

tmesis ['tmiːsɪs] *n* tmèse *f*

TN *(written abbr* **Tennessee**) Tennessee *m*

TNT [,tiːen'tiː] *n Chem (abbr* **trinitrotoluene**) TNT *m*

TO [tuː, *unstressed* tə]

à	► **1A (a) – (c), (e); B (b); D (a), (l)**
en	► **1A (c)**
jusqu'à	► **1A (d); B (b)**
contre	► **1A (e)**
pour	► **1C (f), (g); D (b)**
de	► **1D (i)**

1 *prep* **A.** (**a**) *(indicating direction)* **to go to school/the cinema** aller à l'école/au cinéma; **let's go to town** allons en ville; **he climbed to the top** il est monté jusqu'au sommet *ou* jusqu'en haut; **she ran to where her mother was sitting** elle a couru (jusqu')à l'endroit où sa mère était assise; **we've been to it before** nous y sommes déjà allés; **the vase fell to the ground** le vase est tombé par *ou* à terre; **I invited them to dinner** je les ai invités à dîner; **he returned to his work** il est retourné à son *ou* il a repris son travail; **let's go to Susan's** allons chez Susan; **to go to the doctor** *or* **doctor's** aller chez le médecin; **he pointed to the door** il a pointé son doigt vers la porte; **the road to the south** la route du sud; **our house is a mile to the south** notre maison est à un mile au sud; **it's 12 miles to the nearest town** *(from here)* nous sommes à 12 miles de la ville la plus proche; *(from there)* c'est à 12 miles de la ville la plus proche; **what's the best way to the station?** quel est le meilleur chemin pour aller à la gare?; **she turned his photograph to the wall** elle a retourné sa photo contre le mur; **I sat with my back to her** j'étais assis lui tournant le dos; **tell her to her face** dites-le-lui en face

(**b**) *(indicating location, position)* à; **the street parallel to this one** la rue parallèle à celle-ci; **she lives next door to us** elle habite à côté de chez nous; **to one side** d'un côté; **to the left/right** à gauche/droite; **the rooms to the back** les chambres de derrière; **to leave sth to one side** laisser qch de côté

(**c**) *(with geographical names)* **to Madrid** à Madrid; **to Le Havre** au Havre; **to France** en France; **to Argentina** en Argentine; **to Japan** au Japon; **to the United States** aux États-Unis; **I'm off to Paris** je pars à *ou* pour Paris; **the road to Chicago** la route de Chicago; **on the way to Milan** en allant à Milan, sur la route de Milan; **planes to and from Europe** les vols à destination et en provenance de l'Europe

(**d**) *(indicating age, amount or level reached)* jusqu'à; **the snow came (up) to her knees** la neige lui arrivait aux genoux; **unemployment is up to nearly 9 percent** le (taux de) chômage atteint presque les 9 pour cent; **they cut expenses down to a minimum** ils ont réduit les frais au minimum; **she can count (up) to one hundred** elle sait compter jusqu'à cent; **it's accurate to the millimetre** c'est exact au millimètre près; **it weighs 8 to 9 pounds** ça pèse entre 8 et 9 livres; **moderate to cool temperatures** des températures douces ou fraîches; **to live to a great age** vivre jusqu'à un âge avancé

(**e**) *(so as to make contact with)* à, contre; **she pinned the brooch to her dress** elle a épinglé la broche sur sa robe; **they sat in bumper-to-bumper traffic** ils étaient coincés pare-chocs contre pare-chocs; **they danced cheek to cheek** ils dansaient joue contre joue; **he clutched the baby to his chest** il a serré l'enfant contre lui

B. (**a**) *(before the specified hour or date)* **it's ten minutes to three** il est trois heures moins dix; **we left at a quarter to six** nous sommes partis à six heures moins le quart; **it's twenty to** il est moins vingt; **how long is it to dinner?** on dîne dans combien de temps?; **there are only two weeks to Christmas** il ne reste que deux semaines avant Noël

(**b**) *(up to and including)* (jusqu')à; **from Tuesday night to Thursday morning** du mardi soir (jusqu')au jeudi matin; **from morning to night** du matin au soir; **from March to June** de mars (jusqu')à juin; **a nine-to-five job** des horaires *mpl* de fonctionnaire; **it was three years ago to the day since I saw her last** il y a trois ans jour pour jour que je l'ai vue pour la dernière fois; **to this day** jusqu'à ce jour, jusqu'à aujourd'hui; **he**

was brave (up) to the last il a été courageux jusqu'au bout *ou* jusqu'à la fin; **from day to day** de jour en jour; **I read it from beginning to end** je l'ai lu du début (jusqu')à la fin; **from bad to worse** de mal en pis; **I do everything from scrubbing the floor to keeping the books** je fais absolument tout, depuis le ménage jusqu'à la comptabilité

C. (**a**) *(before infinitive)* **to talk** parler; **to open** ouvrir; **to answer** répondre

(**b**) *(after verb)* **she lived to be a hundred** elle a vécu jusqu'à cent ans; **we are to complete the work by Monday** nous devons finir le travail pour lundi; **she went on to become a brilliant guitarist** elle est ensuite devenue une excellente guitariste; **I finally accepted, (only) to find that they had changed their mind** lorsque je me suis décidé à accepter, ils avaient changé d'avis; **she turned round to find him standing right in front of her** lorsqu'elle s'est retournée, elle s'est retrouvée nez à nez avec lui; **he left the house never to return to it again** il quitta la maison pour ne plus y revenir; **he dared to speak out against injustice** il a osé s'élever contre l'injustice; **you can leave if you want to** vous pouvez partir si vous voulez; **why? – because I told you to** pourquoi? – parce que je t'ai dit de le faire; **would you like to come? – we'd love to** voulez-vous venir? – avec plaisir *ou* oh, oui!; **you ought to** vous devriez le faire; **we shall have to** il le faudra bien, nous serons bien obligés

(**c**) *(after noun)* **I have a lot to do** j'ai beaucoup à faire; **I have a letter to write** j'ai une lettre à écrire; **that's no reason to leave** ce n'est pas une raison pour partir; **I haven't got money to burn** je n'ai pas d'argent à jeter par les fenêtres; **the first to complain** le premier à se plaindre; **the house to be sold** la maison à vendre; **there was not a sound to be heard** on n'entendait pas le moindre bruit; **he isn't one to forget his friends** il n'est pas homme à oublier ses amis; **that's the way to do it** voilà comment il faut faire

(**d**) *(after adjective)* **I'm happy/sad to see her go** je suis content/triste de la voir partir; **pleased to meet you** enchanté (de faire votre connaissance); **difficult/easy to do** difficile/facile à faire; **it was strange to see her again** c'était bizarre de la revoir; **she's too proud to apologize** elle est trop fière pour s'excuser; **he's old enough to understand** il est assez grand pour comprendre

(**e**) *(after "how", "which", "where" etc)* **do you know where to go?** savez-vous où aller?; **he told me how to get there** il m'a dit comment y aller; **can you tell me when to get off?** pourriez-vous me dire quand je dois descendre?; **she can't decide whether to go or not** elle n'arrive pas à décider si elle va y aller ou non

(**f**) *(indicating purpose)* pour; **I did it to annoy her** je l'ai fait exprès pour l'énerver; **to answer that question, we must…** pour répondre à cette question, il nous faut…

(**g**) *(introducing statement)* pour; **to be honest/frank** pour être honnête/franc; **to put it another way** en d'autres termes

(**h**) *(in exclamations)* **oh, to be in England!** ah, si je pouvais être en Angleterre!; **and to think I nearly married him!** quand je pense que j'ai failli l'épouser!

(**i**) *(in headlines)* **unions to strike** les syndicats s'apprêtent à déclencher la grève; **Russia to negotiate with Baltic States** la Russie va négocier avec les pays Baltes

D. (**a**) *(indicating intended recipient, owner)* à; **I showed the picture to her** je lui ai montré la photo; **I showed it to her** je le lui ai montré; **show it to her** montrez-le-lui; **the person I spoke to** la personne à qui j'ai parlé; **that book belongs to her** ce livre lui appartient; **be kind to him/to animals** soyez gentil avec lui/bon envers les animaux; **what's it to him?** qu'est-ce que cela peut lui faire?; **it doesn't matter to her** ça lui est égal; **did you have a room to yourself?** avais-tu une chambre à toi *ou* pour toi tout seul?; **to keep sth to oneself** garder qch pour soi; **I said to myself** je me suis dit; **he is known to the police** il est connu de la police

(**b**) *(in the opinion of)* pour; **$2 is a lot of money to some people** il y a des gens pour qui 2 dollars représentent beaucoup d'argent; **it sounds suspicious to me** cela me semble bizarre; **it didn't make sense to him** ça n'avait aucun sens pour lui

(**c**) *(indicating intention)* **with a view to clarifying matters** dans l'intention d'éclaircir la situation; **it's all to no purpose** tout cela ne sert à rien *ou* est en vain

(**d**) *(indicating resulting state)* **the light changed to red** le feu est passé au rouge; **the noise drove him to distraction** le bruit le rendait fou; **the rain turned to snow** la pluie avait fait place à la neige; **her admiration turned to disgust** son admiration s'est transformée en dégoût; **(much) to my relief/surprise/delight** à mon grand soulagement/mon grand étonnement/ma grande joie; **(much) to my horror, I found the money was missing** c'est avec horreur que je me suis rendu compte que l'argent avait disparu; **the meat was done to perfection** la viande était cuite à la perfection; **smashed to pieces** brisé en mille morceaux; **moved to tears** ému (jusqu')aux larmes; **he was beaten to death** il a été battu à mort; **they starved to death** ils sont morts de faim; **the court sentenced him to death** le juge l'a condamné à mort; **she rose rapidly to power** elle est arrivée au pouvoir très rapidement; **she sang the baby to sleep** elle a chanté jusqu'à ce que le bébé s'endorme

(**e**) *(as regards)* **the answer to your question** la réponse à votre question; **a hazard to your health** un danger pour votre santé; **what's your reaction to all this?** comment réagissez-vous à tout ça?; **no one was sympathetic to his ideas** ses idées ne plaisaient à personne; **what would you say to a game of bridge?** que diriez-vous d'un bridge?, si on faisait un bridge?; **that's all there is to it** c'est aussi simple que ça; **there's nothing to it** il n'y a rien de plus simple; **there's nothing** *or* **there isn't a lot to these cameras** ils ne sont pas bien compliqués, ces appareils photos; *Com* **to translating annual report: $300** *(on bill)* traduction du rapport annuel: 300 dollars; **to services rendered** *(on bill)* pour services rendus

(**f**) *(indicating composition or proportion)* **there are 16 ounces to a pound** il y a 16 onces dans une livre; **there are 6 francs to the dollar** un dollar vaut 6 francs; **there are 25 chocolates to a box** il y a 25 chocolats dans chaque *ou* par boîte; **one cup of sugar to every three cups of fruit** une tasse de sucre pour trois tasses de fruits; **three is to six as six is to twelve** trois est à six ce que six est à douze; **Milan beat Madrid by 4 (points) to 3** Milan a battu Madrid 4 (points) à 3; **I'll bet 100 to 1** je parierais 100 contre 1; **the odds are 1000 to 1 against it happening again** il y a 1 chance sur 1000 que cela se produise à nouveau; **the vote was 6 to 3** il y avait 6 voix contre 3

(**g**) *(per)* **how many miles do you get to the gallon?** ≃ vous faites combien de litres au cent?

(**h**) *(indicating comparison)* **inferior to** inférieur à; **they compare her to Callas** on la compare à (la) Callas; **that's nothing (compared) to what I've seen** ce n'est rien à côté de ce que j'ai vu; **inflation is nothing (compared) to last year** l'inflation n'est rien à côté de *ou* en comparaison de l'année dernière; **as a cook she's second to none** comme cuisinière on ne fait pas mieux; **to prefer sth to sth** préférer qch à qch

(**i**) *(of)* de; **the key to this door** la clé de cette porte; **he's secretary to the director/to the committee** c'est le secrétaire du directeur/du comité; **she's assistant to the president** c'est l'adjointe du président; **the French ambassador to Algeria** l'ambassadeur français en Algérie; **ambassador to the King of Thailand** ambassadeur auprès du roi de Thaïlande; **she's interpreter to the president** c'est l'interprète du président; **Susan, sister to Mary** Susan, sœur de Mary; **he's been like a father to me** il est comme un père pour moi

(**j**) *(in accordance with)* **to his way of thinking, to his mind** à son avis; **to hear him talk, you'd think he was an expert** à l'entendre parler, on croirait que c'est un expert; **to my knowledge, she never met him** elle ne l'a jamais rencontré (pour) autant que je sache; **it's to your advantage to do it** c'est (dans) ton intérêt de le faire; **the climate is not to my liking** le climat ne me plaît pas; **add salt to taste** salez selon votre goût *ou* à volonté; **she made out a cheque to the amount of £15** elle a fait un chèque de 15 livres

(**k**) *(indicating accompaniment, simultaneity)* **we danced to live music** nous avons dansé sur la musique d'un orchestre; **in time to the music** en mesure avec la musique

(**l**) *(in honour of)* à; **let's drink to his health** buvons à sa santé; **(here's) to your health!** à la vôtre!; **(here's) to the bride!** à la mariée!; **to my family** *(in dedication)* à ma famille; **his book is dedicated to his mother** son livre est dédié à sa mère; **a monument to the war dead** un monument aux morts

E. (**a**) *(indicating addition)* **add flour to the list** ajoutez de la farine sur la liste; **add 3 to 6** additionnez 3 et 6, ajoutez 3 à 6; **in addition to Charles, there were three women** en plus de Charles, il y avait trois femmes

(**b**) *Math* **to the power…** à la puissance…; **2 to the 3rd power, 2 to the 3rd** 2 (à la) puissance 3

2 *adv* (**a**) *(closed)* fermé; **the wind blew the door to** un coup de vent a fermé la porte

(**b**) *(back to consciousness)* **to come to** revenir à soi, reprendre connaissance

(**c**) *Naut* **to bring a ship to** mettre un bateau en panne

3 to and fro *adv* **to go to and fro** aller et venir, se promener de long en large; *(shuttle bus etc)* faire la navette; **to swing to and fro** se balancer d'avant en arrière

---

toad [təʊd] *n* (**a**) *(animal)* crapaud *m* (**b**) *Fam Fig (man)* sale bonhomme *m*, crapule□ *f*; *(woman)* sale bonne femme, crapule□ *f*; **you lying toad!** sale menteur!

toadfish ['təʊdfɪʃ] *(pl* **inv** *or* **toadfishes***)* *n Ich* poisson-crapaud *m*

toadflax ['təʊdflæks] *n Bot* linaire *f*, lin *m* sauvage

toad-in-the-hole *n Br Culin* = plat composé de saucisses cuites au four dans une sorte de pâte à crêpes

toadstool ['təʊdstu:l] *n* champignon *m* (vénéneux)

toady ['təʊdɪ] *(pl* **toadies**, *pt & pp* **toadied***)* *Pej* **1** *n* flatteur(euse) *m,f*

2 *vi* être flatteur; **to toady to sb** passer de la pommade à qn

toadying ['təʊdɪɪŋ] *n Pej* flagornerie *f*

toadyism ['təʊdɪɪzəm] *n Pej* flagornerie *f*

to-and-fro *adj* **a to-and-fro movement** un mouvement de va-et-vient

toast [təʊst] **1** *n* (**a**) *(bread)* pain *m* grillé; **a piece** *or* **slice of toast** une tartine grillée, un toast; **three slices** *or* **rounds of toast** trois tartines grillées; **don't burn the toast** ne brûle pas le pain; **cheese/sardines on toast** fromage fondu/sardines sur du pain grillé; **as warm as toast** bien chaud

(**b**) *(drink)* toast *m*; **to drink a toast to sb** porter un toast à qn, boire à la santé de qn; **we drank a toast to their success/future happiness** on a bu à leur succès/bonheur futur; **to propose a toast (to sb)** porter un toast (à qn); **she was the toast of the town** elle était la coqueluche de la ville

(**c**) *Fam* **to be toast** *(in trouble)* être foutu; *(exhausted)* être naze *ou* crevé; **if Mum finds out, you're toast** si Maman s'en rend compte, t'es mort *ou* foutu!

2 *vt* (**a**) *(grill)* griller; *Fig* **he was toasting himself/his feet by the fire** il se chauffait/il se rôtissait les pieds devant la cheminée

(**b**) *(drink to → person)* porter un toast à, boire à la santé de; *(→ success, win)* arroser; **to toast sb's success** arroser la réussite de qn; **to toast sb's health** boire à la santé de qn; **they toasted her victory in champagne** ils ont arrosé sa victoire au champagne

3 *vi (bread)* griller; **it toasts well** ça fait du bon pain grillé

►► *Br* ***toast rack*** porte-toasts *m inv*

toasted ['təʊstɪd] *adj*

►► ***toasted cheese*** fromage *m* fondu; ***toasted cheese sandwich*** ≃ croque-monsieur *m inv*; ***toasted sandwich*** sandwich *m* grillé

toaster ['təʊstə(r)] *n* grille-pain *m inv* (électrique), toaster *m*

toastie ['təʊstɪ] *n Fam* sandwich *m* grillé ❑

toasting fork ['təʊstɪŋ-] *n* fourchette *f* à griller le pain

toastmaster ['təʊst,mɑːstə(r)] *n* animateur *m (qui annonce les toasts ou les discours lors d'une réception)*

toasty ['təʊstɪ] *(pl* **toasties***) Fam* **1** *adj (warm)* **it's toasty in here** il fait bon ici ❑, on est bien au chaud ici ❑

2 *n (sandwich)* sandwich *m* grillé ❑

tobacco [tə'bækəʊ] *(pl* **tobaccos***)* **1** *n* **(a)** *(for smoking)* tabac *m* **(b)** *Bot (plant)* (pied *m* de) tabac *m*

2 *comp (leaf, plantation, smoke)* de tabac; *(industry)* du tabac

▸▸ ***tobacco brown*** *n* couleur *f* tabac; *Bot* ***tobacco plant*** pied *m* de tabac *m*; ***tobacco pouch*** blague *f* à tabac; ***tobacco tin*** boîte *f* à tabac, tabatière *f*

'Tobacco Road' *Caldwell* 'La Route au tabac'

tobacco-brown *adj* tabac *(inv)*

tobacconist [tə'bækənɪst] *n* marchand(e) *m,f* de tabac, buraliste *mf*; *(shop)* (bureau *m* de) tabac *m*

▸▸ ***tobacconist's shop*** bureau *m* de tabac

Tobago [tə'beɪgəʊ] *see* **Trinidad and Tobago**

-to-be [tə'biː] *suff* **mother-to-be** future mère *f*; **father-to-be** futur père *m*

toboggan [tə'bɒgən] **1** *n* luge *f*

2 *comp (race)* de luge

3 *vi* **(a)** *(person)* faire de la luge; **they tobogganed down the slope** ils ont descendu la pente en luge **(b)** *Am (prices, sales)* dégringoler

▸▸ ***toboggan run*** piste *f* de luge

tobogganer [tə'bɒgənə(r)] *n* lugeur(euse) *m,f*

tobogganing [tə'bɒgənɪŋ] *n* luge *f*; **to go tobogganing** faire de la luge

tobogganist [tə'bɒgənɪst] *n* lugeur(euse) *m,f*

Tobruk [tə'brʊk] *n* Tobrouk *m*

toby jug ['təʊbɪ-] *n* = tasse ou cruche en forme d'homme assis portant un tricorne et fumant la pipe

toccata [tə'kɑːtə] *n Mus* toccata *f*

tocology [tɒ'kɒlədʒɪ] *n Med* tocologie *f*

tocopherol [tɒ'kɒfərɒl] *n Chem* tocophérol *m*

tocsin ['tɒksɪn] *n* tocsin *m*

tod [tɒd] *n Br Fam (rhyming slang* **Tod Sloan** = **own***)* **to be on one's tod** être tout seul ❑

today [tə'deɪ] **1** *adv* aujourd'hui; **she's arriving a week today** elle arrive aujourd'hui en huit; **they arrived a week ago today** ils sont arrivés il y a huit jours; **they've been here a week today** ils sont là depuis exactement une semaine; **he died 5 years ago today** cela fait 5 ans aujourd'hui qu'il est mort; **she's more popular today than she was 10 years ago** elle est plus populaire aujourd'hui qu'il y a 10 ans; **here today and gone tomorrow** ça va ça vient; **many new bands are here today and gone tomorrow** beaucoup de groupes disparaissent aussi vite qu'ils sont apparus

2 *n* aujourd'hui *m*; **what's today's date?** quelle est la date d'aujourd'hui?; **what day is it today?** quel jour est-on (aujourd'hui)?; **today is 17 March** aujourd'hui, on est le 17 mars; **it's Monday today** on est lundi aujourd'hui; **a week from today** dans une semaine aujourd'hui; **three weeks from today** dans trois semaines; **as from today** à partir d'aujourd'hui; **have you seen today's paper?** as-tu vu le journal d'aujourd'hui?; **the youth of today, today's youth** la jeunesse d'aujourd'hui; **today's the day!** c'est le grand jour!

toddle ['tɒdəl] **1** *vi* **(a)** *(start to walk → child)* faire ses premiers pas; *(walk unsteadily)* marcher d'un pas chancelant; **he's just started to toddle** il vient de commencer à marcher; **he managed to toddle across the room** il a réussi à faire quelques pas dans la pièce

(b) *Fam (go)* aller ❑; *(stroll)* se balader ❑; *(go away)* s'en aller ❑, partir ❑; **she toddled along after him** elle trottinait derrière lui; **could you just toddle down to the shops for me?** pourrais-tu faire une ou deux courses pour moi? ❑

2 *n Fam* **I'm just going for a toddle** je vais faire un tour *ou* une balade

▸**toddle off** *vi Fam (go)* aller ❑; *(go away)* s'en aller ❑, partir bien gentiment; **she toddled off somewhere on her own** elle est partie faire un tour toute seule ❑; **he toddled off to the pub** il est allé au bistrot

toddler ['tɒdlə(r)] *n* tout(e) petit(e) *m,f (qui fait ses premiers pas)*; **he's just a toddler** il est encore tout petit; **their children are still toddlers** leurs enfants sont tout juste en âge de marcher

toddy ['tɒdɪ] *(pl* **toddies***) n* **(a)** *(drink)* **(hot) toddy** ≃ grog *m* **(b)** *(sap)* sève *f* de palmier *(utilisée comme boisson)*

to-die-for *adj Fam* craquant

to-do *n Fam* **(a)** *(fuss)* remue-ménage *m inv*, tohu-bohu *m inv*; **she made a great to-do about it** elle en a fait tout un plat; **there was a great to-do over her wedding** son mariage a fait grand bruit; **what a to-do!** quelle affaire!, quelle histoire! **(b)** *Am (party)* bringue *f*

toe [təʊ] **1** *n* **(a)** *Anat* orteil *m*, doigt *m* de pied; **big/little toe** gros/petit orteil *m*; **to stand on one's toes** se dresser sur la pointe des pieds; *also Fig* **to step** *or* **to tread on sb's toes** marcher sur les pieds de qn; *Fig* **she kept us on our toes** elle ne nous laissait aucun répit

(b) *(of sock, shoe)* bout *m*; **there's a hole in the toe** le bout est troué; *Fig* **the toe of Italy** le bout de l'Italie

2 *vt* **(a)** *(ball)* toucher du bout du pied

(b) *(idioms)* **to toe the line** *or Am* **mark** se mettre au pas, obtempérer; *Pol* **to toe the party line** s'aligner sur le *ou* suivre la ligne du parti

▸▸ ***toe clip*** cale-pied *m*; ***toe loop*** *(in figure skating)* boucle *f* piquée

toecap ['təʊkæp] *n* bout *m* renforcé *(de soulier)*; **steel toecap** bout *m* ferré

-toed [təʊd] *suff* **six-toed** à six orteils; **square-/pointed-toed** *(shoes)* à bouts carrés/pointus

toehold ['təʊhəʊld] *n* prise *f* de pied; **to get** *or* **to gain a toehold** *(climber)* trouver une prise (pour le pied); *Fig* prendre pied, s'implanter; *Fig* **the company now has a toehold in the foreign market** l'entreprise a désormais un pied sur le marché étranger

toe-in *n Aut* pincement *m* des roues avant

toeless ['təʊlɪs] *adj* **(a)** *Anat* sans orteil/orteils **(b)** *(sock, shoe)* (à bout) ouvert

toenail ['təʊneɪl] **1** *n* **(a)** *(on foot)* ongle *m* de pied **(b)** *Carp* clou *m* enfoncé de biais

2 *vt Carp* fixer avec un clou enfoncé de biais

toe-out *n Aut* ouverture *f*, pincement *m* négatif

toe-piece *n (of ski)* butée *f*

toerag ['təʊræg] *n Br very Fam Pej* ordure *f*

toe-strap *n* lanière *f* de gros orteil

toff [tɒf] *n Br Fam Pej* rupin(e) *m,f*

toffee ['tɒfɪ] *Br* **1** *n* caramel *m* (au beurre); *Fam* **he can't dance for toffee** il danse comme un pied; *Fam* **I can't speak Italian for toffee** je suis incapable de parler italien ❑

2 *comp (yogurt, ice cream)* au caramel

▸▸ ***toffee apple*** pomme *f* d'amour *(confiserie)*

toffee-nosed *adj Br Fam Pej* bêcheur, snob

tofu ['təʊfuː] *n Culin* tofu *m inv*

tog [tɒg] *(pt & pp* **togged**, *cont* **togging***)* **1** *n Br (measurement of warmth)* = unité servant à mesurer l'indice d'isolation thermique d'une couette

2 togs *npl* **(a)** *Fam (clothes)* fringues *fpl*; *Sport* affaires ❑ *fpl*

(b) *Old-fashioned or Ir* **(swimming) togs** maillot *m* de bain

▸▸ *Br* ***tog number*** indice *m* de PA

▸**tog out, tog up** *vt sep Fam* nipper, fringuer; **she was all togged up in her best clothes** elle était super sapée; **he hates getting togged up for special occasions** il a horreur de se saper pour les grandes occasions; **they were all togged out for the match** ils s'étaient tous mis en tenue pour le match

toga ['təʊgə] *n* toge *f*

together [tə'geðə(r)] **1** *adv* **(a)** *(with each other)* ensemble; **we went shopping together** nous sommes allés faire des courses ensemble; **are you together?** êtes-vous ensemble?; **they get on well together** ils s'entendent bien; **we're all in this together!** on est tous logés à la même enseigne!; **those colours go well together** ces couleurs vont bien ensemble; **the family will all be together at Christmas** la famille sera réunie à Noël; **they were together for six years before getting married** ils ont été ensemble six ans avant de se marier; **they're back together** ils sont de nouveau ensemble

(b) *(jointly)* **she's cleverer than both of them put together** elle est plus intelligente qu'eux deux réunis; **even taken together, their efforts don't amount to much** même si on les considère dans leur ensemble, leurs efforts ne représentent pas grand-chose; **together we can change things** ensemble, nous pouvons changer les choses

(c) *(indicating proximity)* **tie the two ribbons together** attachez les deux rubans l'un à l'autre; **she tried to bring the two sides together** elle a essayé de rapprocher les deux camps; **we were crowded together into the room** on nous a tous entassés dans la pièce; **they were bound together by their beliefs** leurs convictions les unissaient

(d) *(at the same time)* à la fois, en même temps, ensemble; **all together now!** *(pull)* tous ensemble!, ho hisse!; *(sing, recite)* tous ensemble *ou* en chœur!

(e) *(consecutively)* **for ten hours together** pendant dix heures d'affilée *ou* de suite

2 *adj Fam (person)* équilibré ❑, bien dans sa peau; **the band weren't very together** *(didn't play in unison)* le groupe ne jouait pas vraiment ensemble ❑

3 together with *conj (as well as)* ainsi que; *(at the same time as)* en même temps que; **together with the French, the Swedes objected** les Suédois émirent une objection, de même que les Français; **pick up a leaflet together with an entry form** prenez un imprimé et une feuille d'inscription

togetherness [tə'geðənɪs] *n (unity)* unité *f*; *(solidarity)* solidarité *f*; *(comradeship)* camaraderie *f*; **the earlier feeling of togetherness had gone out of their relationship** le sentiment de former un couple uni qu'ils avaient éprouvé auparavant avait disparu; **the feeling of togetherness generated by a family Christmas** ce sentiment de chaleureuse communion que l'on ressent lors des Noëls passés en famille

toggle ['tɒgəl] **1** *n* **(a)** *(peg)* cheville *f*

(b) *Sewing* olive *f*, bouton *m* de duffle-coat

(c) *Naut* cabillot *m*

2 *vt Naut* attacher avec un cabillot

3 *vi Comput* basculer; **to toggle between two applications** alterner entre deux applications

▸▸ *Tech* ***toggle joint*** genouillère *f*; *Comput* ***toggle key*** touche *f* à bascule; ***toggle switch*** *Elec* interrupteur *m* à bascule; *Comput* commande *f* à bascule

Togo ['təʊgəʊ] *n* le Togo; **in Togo** au Togo

Togoland ['təʊgəʊlænd] *n Hist* le Togo

Togolese [,təʊgə'liːz] *(pl* **inv***)* **1** *n* Togolais(e) *m,f*

2 *adj* togolais

3 *comp (embassy, history)* du Togo

toil [tɔɪl] **1** *vi* **(a)** *(labour)* travailler dur, peiner; **he toiled over his essay for weeks** il a peiné *ou* il a sué sur sa dissertation pendant des semaines

(b) *(as verb of movement)* avancer péniblement; **they toiled up the hill on their bikes/on foot** ils montèrent péniblement la colline à vélo/à pied; **they toiled on over the rough ground** ils poursuivirent péniblement leur chemin sur le terrain accidenté

(c) *(make difficult progress)* **to be toiling** peiner; **I'm toiling to finish this drink as it is** j'ai déjà assez de mal à finir ce verre

2 *vt* **he toiled his way through a mass of papers** il a dû laborieusement lire tout un tas de documents

3 *n* labeur *m*, travail *m* (pénible)

▸**toil away** *vi* travailler dur, peiner

toile [twɑːl] *n Tex* toile *f*

toiler ['tɔɪlə(r)] *n* travailleur(euse) *m,f*

toilet ['tɔɪlɪt] *n* **(a)** *(lavatory)* toilettes *fpl*; **to go to the toilet** aller aux toilettes *ou* aux cabinets; **he's still in** *or Fam* **on the toilet** il est encore aux toilettes; **the toilet won't flush** la chasse d'eau

ne marche pas; **he threw it down the toilet** il l'a jeté dans les toilettes; **Public Toilets** *(sign)* Toilettes, W-C Publics
(**b**) *Formal or Old-fashioned (washing and dressing)* toilette *f*; **to make** *or* **perform one's toilet** faire sa toilette; **to be at one's toilet** être à sa toilette
(**c**) *Fam Fig (filthy place)* endroit *m* dégueulasse
(**d**) *Fam* **to go down the toilet** *(plan, career, work)* être foutu en l'air; **that's our holidays down the toilet!** on peut faire une croix sur nos vacances!
►► ***toilet bag*** trousse *f* de toilette; ***toilet block*** bloc *m* sanitaire; ***toilet bowl*** cuvette *f* (de W-C); ***toilet humour*** humour *m* scatologique; ***toilet paper*** papier *m* hygiénique; ***toilet roll*** *(roll)* rouleau *m* de papier hygiénique; *(paper)* papier *m* hygiénique; ***toilet roll holder*** porte-papier *m inv*; ***toilet seat*** siège *m* des cabinets *ou* W-C *ou* toilettes; ***toilet soap*** savon *m* de toilette; ***toilet tank*** réservoir *m* de chasse d'eau; ***toilet tissue*** papier *m* hygiénique; ***toilet training*** apprentissage *m* de la propreté *(pour un enfant)*; ***toilet water*** eau *f* de toilette

toiletries ['tɔɪlɪtrɪz] *npl* articles *mpl* de toilette

toilette [twɑː'let] *n Formal or Old-fashioned* toilette *f*

toilet-train *vt* **to toilet-train a child** apprendre à un enfant à être propre

toilet-trained [-ˌtreɪnd] *adj* propre

toils [tɔɪlz] *npl Literary* rets *mpl*, filets *mpl*

toilsome ['tɔɪlsəm] *adj* pénible, laborieux

to-ing and fro-ing [ˌtuːɪŋən'frəʊɪŋ] *n (UNCOUNT) Fam* allées et venues ❑ *fpl*

tokamak ['təʊkəmæk] *n Phys* tokamak *m*

Tokay [təʊ'kaɪ] *n (wine)* tokay *m*, tokaj *m*

tokay ['təʊkeɪ] *n Zool* tokeh *m*; **red-spotted tokay** tokeh *m* à taches rouges

toke [təʊk] *Fam* **1** *n (of cigarette, joint)* taffe *f*; **to take a toke** prendre une taffe
2 *vi* **to toke on a cigarette/joint** prendre une taffe d'une cigarette/d'un joint

token ['təʊkən] **1** *n* (**a**) *(of affection, appreciation, esteem etc)* marque *f*, témoignage *m*; **as a token of** *or* **in token of my gratitude** en témoignage *ou* en gage de ma reconnaissance; **a love token** un gage d'amour; **as a token of our love** en gage de notre amour
(**b**) *(souvenir, gift)* souvenir *m*; **we'd like you to accept this little token to remind you of your visit** nous aimerions que vous acceptiez ce petit cadeau en souvenir de votre visite
(**c**) *(for machine)* jeton *m*
(**d**) *(voucher)* bon *m*
(**e**) *(indication)* signe *m*; **in token** *or* **as a token of sincerity** en signe *ou* en témoignage de bonne foi
(**f**) *Ling* occurrence *f*
2 *adj (gesture, effort)* symbolique, pour la forme; *(increase, protest)* symbolique, de pure forme; **a token black person/token woman** un noir/une femme qui est là pour la forme; **they only pay a token rent** ils ne paient qu'un loyer symbolique; **to put up a token resistance** opposer une résistance symbolique
3 by the same token *adv* de même, pareillement
►► *Fin* ***token money*** monnaie *f* fiduciaire; ***token payment*** paiement *m* symbolique (d'intérêts); *Comput* ***token ring*** anneau *m* à jeton; *Comput* ***token ring network*** réseau *m* en anneau à jeton; ***token strike*** grève *f* symbolique *ou* d'avertissement; ***token vote*** vote *m* symbolique

tokenism ['təʊkənɪzəm] *n* = pratique qui consiste à nommer un ou deux membres d'une minorité (femmes, Noirs etc) pour donner l'impression d'une libéralisation; **the appointment of a woman to the board was nothing but tokenism** ils ont nommé une femme au conseil d'administration uniquement pour la forme

Tok Pisin [ˌtɒk'pɪzɪn] *n* pidgin-english *m* de Papouasie-Nouvelle-Guinée

Tokyo ['təʊkjəʊ] *n* Tokyo *m*

tola ['təʊlə] *n Bot* tola *m*

tolbooth ['təʊlbuːð] = **tollbooth**

told [təʊld] *pt & pp of* **tell**

Toledo [tɒ'leɪdəʊ] *n* Tolède *m*

tolerable ['tɒlərəbəl] *adj* (**a**) *(pain, situation, behaviour)* tolérable; *(standard)* admissible (**b**) *(not too bad)* pas trop mal, passable

tolerably ['tɒlərəblɪ] *adv* passablement; **she performed tolerably (well)** elle n'a pas trop mal joué; **I'm tolerably well** je me porte assez bien; **they were tolerably pleased with the results** ils étaient assez contents des résultats

tolerance ['tɒlərəns] *n* (**a**) *(of behaviour, beliefs, opinions)* tolérance *f*; **they showed great tolerance** ils ont fait preuve de beaucoup de tolérance, ils ont été très tolérants; **religious/racial tolerance** tolérance *f* religieuse/raciale
(**b**) *Physiol & Med (to alcohol)* tolérance *f*; *(to cold)* résistance *f*, tolérance *f*; **to develop (a) tolerance to a drug** développer une accoutumance à un médicament; **they have little tolerance to cold** ils ont peu de résistance au froid
(**c**) *Tech* tolérance *f*; **a tolerance of a thousandth of a millimetre** une tolérance d'un millième de millimètre

tolerant ['tɒlərənt] *adj* tolérant; **he's not very tolerant of others** il n'est pas très tolérant envers les autres; **she's not very tolerant of criticism** elle ne supporte pas bien les critiques; *Phys* **tolerant to heat/cold** résistant à la chaleur/au froid

tolerantly ['tɒlərəntlɪ] *adv* avec tolérance

tolerate ['tɒləreɪt] *vt* (**a**) *(permit)* tolérer (**b**) *(put up with → person, behaviour)* supporter; *(withstand → drug, cold, climate, medical treatment)* supporter

toleration [ˌtɒlə'reɪʃən] *n* tolérance *f*

toll [təʊl] **1** *n* (**a**) *(on bridge, road)* péage *m*
(**b**) *(of victims)* nombre *m* de victimes; *(of casualties)* nombre *m* de blessés; *(of deaths)* nombre *m* de morts; **the epidemic took a heavy toll of** *or* **among the population** l'épidémie a fait beaucoup de morts *ou* de victimes parmi la population; **the years have taken their toll** les années ont laissé leurs traces; **her illness took its toll on her family** sa maladie a ébranlé sa famille
(**c**) *(of bell)* sonnerie *f*
(**d**) *Am & NZ Tel* frais *mpl* d'interurbain
2 *vt (bell)* sonner; **to toll sb's death** sonner le glas pour qn; **the church clock tolled midday** l'horloge de l'église a sonné midi
3 *vi (bell)* sonner; **to toll for the dead** sonner pour les morts
►► ***toll bar*** barrière *f* (de péage); ***toll bridge*** pont *m* à péage; *Am & NZ Tel* ***toll call*** communication *f* interurbaine; ***toll charge*** (**a**) *(for bridge)* (coût *m* du) péage *m* (**b**) *NZ Tel* tarif *m* interurbain

tollage ['təʊlɪdʒ] *n* péage *m*

tollbooth ['təʊlbuːð] *n* (**a**) *(for collecting toll)* (poste *m* de) péage *m* (**b**) *Scot Arch (town hall)* hôtel *m* de ville; *(prison)* prison *f*

toll-free *adv Am* **to call toll-free** appeler un numéro vert *ou Can* sans frais
►► ***toll-free number*** ≃ numéro *m* vert

tollgate ['təʊlgeɪt] *n* (barrière *f* de) péage *m*

tollhouse ['təʊlhaʊs, *pl* -haʊzɪz] *n* (bureau *m* de) péage *m*
►► *Am* ***tollhouse cookie*** cookie *m* aux pépites de chocolat

tollroad ['təʊlrəʊd] *n* route *f* à péage

tollway ['təʊlweɪ] *n Am* autoroute *f* à péage

Tolstoy ['tɒlstɔɪ] *pr n* **Léo Tolstoy** Léon Tolstoï

tolu ['təʊljuː] *n* tolu *m*

toluene ['tɒljʊiːn] *n Chem* toluène *m*

Tom [tɒm] *pr n* **any** *or* **every Tom, Dick or Harry** n'importe qui, le premier venu
►► ***Tom Collins*** *(drink)* Tom Collins *m (boisson glacée au gin et au jus de citron)*

tom [tɒm] *n (cat)* matou *m*

tomahawk ['tɒməhɔːk] *n* tomahawk *m*

tomalley [tə'mælɪ] *n Culin* = partie crémeuse du homard
►► ***tomalley sauce*** = sauce faite avec la partie crémeuse du homard

tomato [*Br* tə'mɑːtəʊ, *Am* tə'meɪtəʊ] (*pl* **tomatoes**) **1** *n* tomate *f*
2 *comp (salad, soup)* de tomates
►► ***tomato juice*** jus *m* de tomates; ***tomato ketchup*** ketchup *m*; ***tomato plant*** (pied *m* de) tomate *f*; ***tomato purée*** concentré *m ou* purée *f* de tomates; ***tomato sauce*** sauce *f* tomate; *(ketchup)* ketchup *m*

tomb [tuːm] *n* tombeau *m*, tombe *f*; **the Tomb of the Unknowns** = la tombe des soldats inconnus des deux guerres mondiales, des guerres de Corée et du Vietnam, au cimetière d'Arlington, en Virginie

tombac ['tɒmbæk] *n Metal* tombac *m*

tombola [tɒm'bəʊlə] *n Br* tombola *f*

tombolo ['tɒmbələʊ] (*pl* **tombolos**) *n Geog* tombolo *m*, flèche *f* isthme

tomboy ['tɒmbɔɪ] *n* garçon *m* manqué; **she looks a bit of a tomboy** elle fait un peu garçon manqué

tomboyish ['tɒmbɔɪɪʃ] *adj* de garçon manqué, garçonnier

tombstone ['tuːmstəʊn] *n* pierre *f* tombale

tomcat ['tɒmkæt] *n* chat *m*, matou *m*
►**tomcat around** *vi Am Fam* courir les filles

tome [təʊm] *n* gros volume *m*

tomfool [ˌtɒm'fuːl] *Fam* **1** *n* imbécile ❑ *mf*
2 *adj* imbécile ❑

tomfoolery [tɒm'fuːlərɪ] *n (UNCOUNT) Fam (words, behaviour)* bêtises ❑ *fpl*

Tommy ['tɒmɪ] (*pl* **Tommies**) *n Br Fam Old-fashioned* = surnom donné autrefois aux soldats britanniques

tommy gun ['tɒmɪ-] *n Fam* mitraillette ❑ *f*

tommyrot ['tɒmɪrɒt] *n (UNCOUNT) Br Fam Old-fashioned* balivernes ❑ *fpl*, bêtises ❑ *fpl*; **tommyrot!** mon œil!

tomography [tə'mɒgrəfɪ] *n Med* tomographie *f*

tomorrow [tə'mɒrəʊ] **1** *adv* demain; **tomorrow morning/evening** demain matin/soir; **see you tomorrow!** à demain!; **a week tomorrow** dans une semaine demain; **they arrived/they will have been here a week tomorrow** ça fera huit jours demain qu'ils sont arrivés/qu'ils sont là
2 *n* (**a**) *(the day after today)* demain *m*; **what's tomorrow's date?** le combien serons-nous demain?; **what day is it** *or* **will it be tomorrow?** quel jour serons-nous demain?; **tomorrow is** *or* **will be 17 March** demain, on sera le 17 mars; **tomorrow is Monday** demain, c'est lundi; **a week from tomorrow** dans une semaine demain; **three weeks from tomorrow** dans trois semaines demain; **the day after tomorrow** après-demain, dans deux jours; **tomorrow may never come** qui sait où nous serons demain; **tomorrow never comes** demain n'arrive jamais; **tomorrow is another day** demain il fera jour; *Prov* **never put off till tomorrow what you can do today** il ne faut pas remettre au lendemain ce que l'on peut faire le jour même
(**b**) *Fig (future)* demain *m*; **we look forward to a bright tomorrow** nous espérons des lendemains qui chantent; **tomorrow's world** le monde de demain; *Fam* **he spends money like there was no tomorrow** il dépense sans se soucier du lendemain *ou* sans souci du lendemain ❑

tomtit ['tɒmtɪt] *n Orn* mésange *f*

tom-tom *n* tam-tam *m*

ton [tʌn] **1** *n* (**a**) *(weight)* tonne *f*; *Br* **(long) ton** tonne *f* longue (= 1016 kg); *Am* **(short** *or* **net) ton** tonne *f* courte (= 907 kg); **(metric) ton** tonne *f* (métrique) (= 1000 kg); *Naut* **(register) ton** tonneau *m*; **a 35-ton lorry** un 35 tonnes; *Fig* **it's a ton weight!** ça pèse une tonne!; *Fam* **this suitcase weighs a ton!** cette valise pèse une tonne!
(**b**) *Fam (100 mph)* vitesse *f* de cent miles à l'heure ❑; *(score of 100)* cent ❑ *m*; *(£100)* cent livres ❑ *fpl*; **to do a ton** *(vehicle, driver)* faire du cent miles à l'heure
2 tons *npl Fam (lots)* **tons of money** des tas *mpl ou* des tonnes *fpl* d'argent; **tons of people** des tas *mpl* de gens; **tons better** beaucoup mieux ❑

tonal ['təʊnəl] *adj* tonal

tonality [tə'nælətɪ] (*pl* **tonalities**) *n Mus* tonalité *f*

tondo ['tɒndəʊ] (*pl* **tondi** ['tɒndiː]) *n Art* tondo *m*

tone [təʊn] **1** *n* (**a**) *(way of speaking)* ton *m* (de la voix); **don't (you) speak to me in that tone (of voice)!** ne me parle pas sur ce ton!; **I don't like your tone!** je n'aime pas votre ton!; **I didn't much like the tone of her remarks** je n'ai pas beaucoup aimé le ton de ses remarques; **it was the tone of the letter I didn't like** c'est le ton de cette lettre qui ne m'a pas plu; **I knew by the tone of his voice** j'ai compris au ton *ou* timbre de sa voix; **to raise/to lower the tone of one's voice** hausser/baisser le ton; **he spoke to me in**

soft tones *or* **in a soft tone** il m'a parlé d'une voix douce

(**b**) *(sound → of voice, musical instrument)* sonorité *f*; *(→ of singer)* timbre *m* (de la voix); **the rich bass tones of his voice** la richesse de sa voix dans les tons graves; **the stereo has an excellent tone** la stéréo a une excellente sonorité; *Hum* **I thought I recognized those dulcet tones** j'ai cru reconnaître cette douce voix

(**c**) *Mus (interval)* ton *m*

(**d**) *Ling* ton *m*; **rising/falling tone** ton *m* ascendant/descendant

(**e**) *Tel* tonalité *f*; **please speak after the tone** veuillez parler après le signal sonore

(**f**) *(control → of amplifier, radio)* tonalité *f*

(**g**) *(shade)* ton *m*; **in matching tones of red and gold** dans des tons rouge et or assortis; **soft blue tones** des tons bleu pastel; **a two-tone colour scheme** une palette de couleurs à deux tons

(**h**) *(style, atmosphere → of poem, article)* ton *m*; **to set the tone** donner le ton; **to give a serious tone to a discussion** donner un ton sérieux à une discussion

(**i**) *(classiness)* chic *m*, classe *f*; **to give/to lend tone to sth** donner de la classe/apporter un plus à qch; **it lowers/raises the tone of the neighbourhood** cela rabaisse/rehausse le standing du quartier

(**j**) *Fin (of market)* tenue *f*

(**k**) *Physiol (of muscle, nerves)* tonus *m*

(**l**) *Am Mus (note)* note *f*

2 *vi (colour)* s'harmoniser; **the wallpaper doesn't tone well with the carpet** le papier peint n'est pas bien assorti à la moquette

3 *vt (body, muscles)* tonifier

►► ***tone arm*** bras *m* de lecture; ***tone colour*** timbre *m*; ***tone control*** bouton *m* de tonalité; ***tone deafness*** manque *m* d'oreille; *Ling* ***tone language*** langue *f* à tons; *Mus* ***tone poem*** poème *m* symphonique

►**tone down** *vt sep* (**a**) *(colour, contrast)* adoucir

(**b**) *(sound, voice)* atténuer, baisser

(**c**) *(moderate → language, statement, views)* tempérer, modérer; *(→ effect)* adoucir, atténuer; **his article had to be toned down for publication** son article a dû être édulcoré avant d'être publié

►**tone in** *vi* s'harmoniser, s'assortir; **the curtains tone in well with the carpet** les rideaux sont bien dans le ton du tapis

►**tone up 1** *vt sep (body, muscles)* tonifier

2 *vi (body, muscles)* se tonifier

tone-deaf *adj* **to be tone-deaf** ne pas avoir d'oreille

toneless ['təʊnlɪs] *adj (voice)* blanc (blanche), sans timbre; *(colour)* terne

tonelessly ['təʊnlɪslɪ] *adv (say, speak)* d'une voix blanche

tonelessness ['təʊnlɪsnɪs] *n (of voice)* absence *f* de timbre; *(of colour)* aspect *m* terne

toneme ['təʊniːm] *n Ling* tonème *m*

toner ['təʊnə(r)] *n* (**a**) *(for hair)* colorant *m*; *(for skin)* lotion *f* tonique (**b**) *Phot & Comput* toner *m*, encre *f*

►► ***toner cartridge*** cartouche *f* de toner

tonetic [təʊ'netɪk] *adj Ling* à tons

tonetics [təʊ'netɪks] *n Ling* tonétique *f*

tong [tɒŋ] *vt (hair)* friser au fer

Tonga ['tɒŋgə] *n* Tonga *mfpl*; **in Tonga** à Tonga

Tongan ['tɒŋgən] **1** *n* (**a**) *(person)* Tongan(e) *m,f*

(**b**) *(language)* tongan *m*

2 *adj* tongan

3 *comp (embassy, history)* de Tonga; *(teacher)* de tongan

tongs [tɒŋz] *npl* **(pair of) tongs** pinces *fpl*; *(for hair)* fer *m* à friser; **fire tongs** pincettes *fpl*; **(sugar) tongs** pince *f* (à sucre)

tongue [tʌŋ] **1** *n* (**a**) *Anat* langue *f*; **to put** *or* **to stick one's tongue out (at sb)** tirer la langue (à qn); *Fig* **his tongue was practically hanging out** *(in eagerness)* il en salivait littéralement; *(in thirst)* il était pratiquement mort de soif; *Br very Fam Hum* **to give someone a tongue sandwich** rouler une pelle *ou* un patin à qn

(**b**) *Fig (for speech)* langue *f*; **to lose/to find one's tongue** perdre/retrouver sa langue; **hold your tongue!** tenez votre langue!, taisez-vous!; **try to keep a civil tongue in your head!** essayez de rester courtois *ou* correct!; *Br* **I can't get my tongue round his name** je n'arrive pas à prononcer correctement son nom; **to have a sharp tongue** avoir la langue acérée; **she has a quick tongue** elle n'a pas sa langue dans sa poche; **tongues will wag** les langues iront bon train, ça va jaser; **the news set tongues wagging** la nouvelle a fait jaser (les gens); **tongue in cheek** ironiquement; **she said it tongue in cheek** *or* **with her tongue in her cheek** elle l'a dit avec une ironie voilée, il ne faut pas prendre au sérieux ce qu'elle a dit

(**c**) *Formal or Literary (language)* langue *f*; *Rel* **to speak in tongues** avoir le don des langues

(**d**) *(UNCOUNT) Culin* langue *f* (de bœuf)

(**e**) *(of shoe)* languette *f*; *(of bell)* battant *m*; *(of buckle)* ardillon *m*; *Tech* langue *f*, languette *f*

(**f**) *(of flame, land, sea)* langue *f*

2 *vt* (**a**) *Mus (note)* détacher; *(phrase)* détacher les notes de

(**b**) *Carp* langueter

►► *Am Med* ***tongue depressor*** abaisse-langue *m*

tongue-and-groove *Carp* **1** *n (joint, edge)* assemblage *m* à languette; *(wood)* lattes *fpl* à languette

2 *vt (boards, slats)* pratiquer des languettes et des rainures sur

►► ***tongue-and-groove joint*** assemblage *m* à languette

tongue-in-cheek *adj (remark, article)* ironique

tongue-lashing *n Fam* **to give sb a tongue-lashing** sonner les cloches à qn

tongue-tied *adj Fig* muet; **she was completely tongue-tied** elle semblait avoir perdu sa langue

tongue-twister *n* = mot ou phrase très difficile à prononcer; **his name's a real tongue-twister** son nom est impossible à prononcer

tonguing ['tʌŋɪŋ] *n Mus* coup *m* de langue

tonic ['tɒnɪk] **1** *n* (**a**) *Med* tonique *m*, fortifiant *m*; *Fig* **the news was a tonic to us all** la nouvelle nous a remonté le moral à tous; **it's a tonic to see you looking so happy** ça me fait du bien *ou* me remonte le moral de te voir si heureux; **he's a tonic** il vous remonte le moral, il est stimulant

(**b**) *(cosmetic)* lotion *f* tonique; **hair tonic** lotion *f* capillaire

(**c**) *(drink)* ≃ Schweppes® *m*

(**d**) *Mus* tonique *f*

(**e**) *Ling* syllabe *f* tonique *ou* accentuée

2 *adj* (**a**) *Med* tonique; **the tonic effect of sea air** l'effet *m* tonique *ou* vivifiant de l'air marin

(**b**) *Ling* tonique

►► *Mus* ***tonic sol-fa*** solfège *m*; *Physiol* ***tonic spasm*** convulsion *f* tonique; *Ling* ***tonic stress*** accent *m* tonique; *Ling* ***tonic syllable*** syllabe *f* tonique; ***tonic water*** ≃ Schweppes® *m*; ***tonic wine*** vin *m* tonique

tonicity [tə'nɪsətɪ] *n (gen)* tonicité *f*; *Physiol* tonus *m*

tonight [tə'naɪt] **1** *n (this evening)* ce soir; *(this night)* cette nuit; **in tonight's newspaper** dans le journal de ce soir; **tonight's the night** c'est le grand soir

2 *adv (this evening)* ce soir; *(this night)* cette nuit *f*; **shall we go dancing tonight?** si on allait danser ce soir?; **I hope I sleep well tonight** j'espère que je dormirai bien cette nuit

> **Not tonight, Josephine**
> On raconte en Grande-Bretagne que Napoléon Bonaparte aurait prononcé ces mots en réponse à sa femme Joséphine qui l'invitait à la rejoindre au lit. Aujourd'hui, on emploie cette expression ("pas ce soir, Joséphine") pour plaisanter et en prenant l'accent français dans des circonstances similaires ou bien lorsqu'on décline une invitation, comme dans l'exemple suivant: **Do you want to go out for a drink? – not tonight, Josephine** ("est-ce que tu veux aller prendre un verre ce soir? – pas ce soir Joséphine").

toning ['təʊnɪŋ] *n Phot* virage *m*

►► ***toning lotion*** lotion *f* tonifiante

Tonkin ['tɒŋkɪn] *n Formerly* le Tonkin

Tonkinese [,tɒŋkɪ'niːz] **1** *adj* tonkinois

2 *n* (**a**) *(person)* Tonkinois(e) *m,f* (**b**) *Ling* tonkinois *m*

Tonking ['tɒŋkɪŋ] *n Formerly* le Tonkin

tonnage ['tʌnɪdʒ] *n* (**a**) *(total weight)* poids *m* total (**b**) *(capacity → of ship)* tonnage *m*, jauge *f*; *(→ of port)* tonnage *m*

►► ***tonnage certificate*** certificat *m* de jaugeage

tonne [tʌn] *n* tonne *f* (métrique)

tonneau ['tɒnəʊ] *(pl* **tonneaus** *or* **tonneaux** [-əʊz]) *n* (**a**) *Aut* capote *f* (**b**) *(of wine)* tonneau *m*

►► *Aut* ***tonneau cover*** bâche *f*

-tonner ['tʌnə(r)] *suff* **a thousand-tonner** un navire de mille tonneaux

tonometer [təʊ'nɒmɪtə(r)] *n Med & Mus* tonomètre *m*

tonometric [,tɒnə'metrɪk] *adj Med & Mus* tonométrique

tonometry [təʊ'nɒmɪtrɪ] *n Med & Mus* tonométrie *f*

tonsil ['tɒnsəl] *n (usu pl)* amygdale *f*; **enlarged tonsils** des amygdales *fpl* hypertrophiées; **your tonsils are inflamed** vous avez une inflammation des amygdales; **to have one's tonsils out** se faire opérer des amygdales; *Fam Hum* **to play tonsil hockey** se rouler des pelles *ou* des patins

tonsillectomy [,tɒnsɪ'lektəmɪ] *(pl* **tonsillectomies**) *n Med* amygdalectomie *f*

tonsillitis [,tɒnsɪ'laɪtɪs] *n (UNCOUNT)* angine *f*, *Spec* amygdalite *f*; **to have tonsillitis** avoir une angine *ou Spec* une amygdalite

tonsillotomy [,tɒnsɪ'lɒtəmɪ] *(pl* **tonsillotomies**) *n Med* amygdalotomie *f*, tonsillectomie *f*

tonsorial [tɒn'sɔːrɪəl] *adj Hum* de coiffeur, capillaire

tonsure ['tɒnʃə(r)] **1** *n* tonsure *f*

2 *vt* tonsurer

tontine [tɒn'tiːn] *n Fin* tontine *f*

ton-up boy *n Br Fam* fou *m* de moto

tonus ['təʊnəs] *n Physiol* tonus *m*

Tony (Award) ['təʊnɪ] *n Theat* Tony Award *m* *(distinction honorifique décernée chaque année aux États-Unis dans le domaine du théâtre)*

tony ['təʊnɪ] *(compar* **tonier**, *superl* **toniest**) *adj Am Fam* chic❏, de grande classe❏; **a tony neighborhood** un quartier élégant❏

too [tuː] *adv* (**a**) *(as well)* aussi, également; **I like Thai food – I do too** *or* **me too** j'aime la cuisine thaïlandaise – moi aussi; **he's a professor too** *(as well as something else)* il est également professeur; *(as well as someone else)* lui aussi est professeur; **stylistically, too, they are similar** du point de vue du style également, ils se ressemblent; *Literary* **would I too fail?** allais-je échouer moi aussi?

(**b**) *(excessively)* trop; **it's too difficult** c'est trop difficile; **too difficult a job** un travail trop difficile; **she works too hard** elle travaille trop; **I have one apple too many** j'ai une pomme de trop; **that's too bad** c'est vraiment dommage; *Ironic* tant pis!; **too little money** trop peu d'argent; **too few people** trop peu de gens; **50p too much** 50p de trop; **she's too tired to go out** elle est trop fatiguée pour sortir; **all too soon we had to go home** très vite, nous avons dû rentrer; *Fig* **you're going too far** tu exagères, tu vas trop loin; **you're too kind** vous êtes trop aimable; **I know her all** *or* **only too well** je ne la connais que trop

(**c**) *(with negatives)* trop; **the first ski slope wasn't too bad** la première descente n'était pas trop difficile; **I wasn't too happy about it** ça ne me réjouissait pas trop; **she hasn't been too well** elle ne va pas trop bien depuis quelque temps

(**d**) *(moreover)* en outre, en plus; **he's so silly! – and a grown man too!** qu'est-ce qu'il peut être bête! – et il en a passé l'âge en plus!

(**e**) *(for emphasis)* **and quite right too!** tu as/il a/*etc* bien fait; **about time too!** ce n'est pas trop tôt!; **I should think so too!** j'espère bien!; **too true!** ça, c'est vrai!

(**f**) *Am (indeed)* **you didn't do your homework – I did too!** tu n'as pas fait tes devoirs – si!; **you will too behave!** si, tu vas être sage!

toodle-oo [,tuːdəl'uː], **toodle-pip** *exclam Br Fam Old-fashioned* salut!

took [tʊk] *pt of* **take**

tool [tuːl] **1** *n* (**a**) *(instrument)* outil *m*; **set of tools** outillage *m*; **the tools of the trade** les instruments *mpl* de travail; **you have to learn the tools of your trade** on ne peut pratiquer un métier sans apprentissage; **the computer has**

become an essential tool for most businesses l'ordinateur est devenu un outil essentiel pour la plupart des entreprises; **to down tools** cesser le travail, se mettre en grève, débrayer

(**b**) *Fig (means, instrument)* instrument *m*; **to use sb as a tool** utiliser qn; **he was nothing but a tool of the government** *(dupe)* il n'était que le jouet *ou* l'instrument du gouvernement

(**c**) *Typ* fer *m* de reliure

(**d**) *very Fam (penis)* engin *m*

(**e**) *Br very Fam Crime slang (gun)* flingue *m*

(**f**) *very Fam (man)* con *m*, connard *m*

2 *vt (decorate → wood)* travailler, façonner; *(→ stone)* sculpter; *(→ book cover)* ciseler; **tooled leather** cuir *m* repoussé

3 *vi Fam* rouler ❑ *(en voiture)*; **I was tooling along at 30 mph** je roulais peinardement à 50 km/h

►► *Comput* **tool bar** barre *m* d'outils; **tool rack** râtelier *m* à outils

►**tool around** *vi Am Fam* traîner ❑; **all I ever did in high school was tool around with the guys** je n'ai jamais rien fait au lycée à part traîner avec les copains

►**tool up 1** *vi* s'équiper

2 *vt sep* (**a**) *(equip with tools)* outiller, équiper; **they are preparing to tool up the new factory** ils s'apprêtent à outiller *ou* équiper la nouvelle usine

(**b**) *Br very Fam Crime slang* **to be tooled up** *(carrying weapons)* être armé ❑

toolbag ['tu:lbæg] *n* trousse *f* à outils

toolbox ['tu:lbɒks] *(pl* **toolboxes***) n* boîte *f* à outils

toolcase ['tu:lkeɪs] *n* caisse *f* à outils

toolchest ['tu:ltʃest] *n* coffre *m* à outils

toolholder ['tu:lˌhəʊldə(r)] *n* porte-outil *m*

tooling ['tu:lɪŋ] *n* (**a**) *(decoration → on wood)* façonnage *m*; *(→ on leather)* repoussé *m*; *(→ on stone)* ciselure *f* (**b**) *(equipment)* outillage *m*

toolkit ['tu:lkɪt] *n* jeu *m* d'outils

toolmaker ['tu:lˌmeɪkə(r)] *n* outilleur *m*

toolmaking ['tu:lˌmeɪkɪŋ] *n* fabrication *f* d'outils

toolroom ['tu:lrʊm] *n* atelier *m* d'outillage

toolshed ['tu:lʃed] *n* remise *f*, resserre *f*

toot [tu:t] **1** *vi* (**a**) *(car)* klaxonner; *(train)* siffler

(**b**) *Fam (sniff cocaine)* sniffer de la coke

2 *vt* (**a**) **to toot a horn/a trumpet** sonner du cor/de la trompette; *Aut* **he tooted his horn** il a klaxonné *ou* donné un coup de klaxon

(**b**) *Fam (cocaine)* sniffer

3 *n* (**a**) *(sound)* appel *m*; **the tugboat gave a toot** le remorqueur a donné un coup de sirène; *Aut* **a toot of the horn** un coup de Klaxon ❑

(**b**) *Fam (of cocaine)* prise *f* de coke

(**c**) *Am Fam (drinking spree)* **to go on the toot** prendre une cuite

4 *adv Fam* **toot sweet** tout de suite ❑, illico

tooth [tu:θ] *(pl* **teeth***)* **1** *n* (**a**) *Anat* dent *f*; **permanent teeth** dents *fpl* permanentes; **a set of teeth** une denture, une dentition; **a false tooth** une fausse dent; **a set of false teeth** un dentier; **to have a tooth out** se faire arracher une dent; **to have good/bad teeth** avoir de bonnes/mauvaises dents; *also Fig* **to bare** *or* **to show one's teeth** montrer les dents; **to have no teeth** être édenté; *Fig* manquer de force; **the amendment will give the law some teeth** l'amendement renforcera quelque peu le pouvoir de la loi

(**b**) *(of comb, file, cog, saw)* dent *f*

(**c**) *(idioms) Fam* **to be fed up** *or* **sick to the back teeth (with sb/sth)** en avoir plein le dos *ou* ras le bol (de qn/qch); **armed to the teeth** armé jusqu'aux dents; **to fight tooth and nail** se battre bec et ongles; *Fig* **to cut one's teeth on sth** se faire les dents sur qch; **to get one's teeth into sth** se mettre à fond à qch; **she needs something to get her teeth into** elle a besoin de quelque chose qui la mobilise; **the play gives you nothing to get your teeth into** la pièce manque de substance; *Fam* **it was a real kick in the teeth** ça m'a fichu un sacré coup; *Fam* **it's better than a kick in the teeth** c'est mieux que rien ❑; *Fig* **to set sb's teeth on edge** faire grincer qn des dents; **she's a bit long in the tooth** elle n'est plus toute jeune

2 *vi (cogwheels)* s'engrener

3 in the teeth of *prep* malgré; **he acted in the teeth of fierce opposition** il a agi malgré une opposition farouche

►► **tooth decay** carie *f* dentaire; **the tooth fairy** ≃ la petite souris; **tooth glass** verre *m* à dents; **tooth mug** verre *m* à dents; **tooth powder** poudre *f* dentifrice

toothache ['tu:θeɪk] *n* mal *m* de dents; **to have toothache** *or Am* **a toothache** avoir mal aux dents

toothbrush ['tu:θbrʌʃ] *(pl* **toothbrushes***) n* brosse *f* à dents

toothed [tu:θt] *adj (wheel)* denté

►► *Bot* **toothed medick** luzerne *f* polymorphe

-toothed [tu:θt] *suff* **gap-toothed** aux dents écartées

toothless ['tu:θlɪs] *adj* (**a**) *(person)* édenté, sans dents (**b**) *Fig* sans pouvoir *ou* influence; **the committee has been criticized for being toothless** on a reproché son impuissance à la commission

toothlessness ['tu:θlɪsnɪs] *n* édentement *m*; *Fig* impuissance *f*

toothpaste ['tu:θpeɪst] *n* dentifrice *m*, pâte *f* dentifrice; **a tube of toothpaste** un tube de dentifrice

►► **toothpaste dispenser** doseur *m* de dentifrice

toothpick ['tu:θpɪk] *n* cure-dents *m inv*

toothsome ['tu:θsəm] *adj Literary or Hum* (**a**) *(food)* appétissant (**b**) *(person)* séduisant

toothy ['tu:θɪ] *(compar* **toothier**, *superl* **toothiest***) adj Fam* **a toothy grin** un sourire tout en dents

►► **toothy pegs** *(in children's language)* dents *fpl*

tooting ['tu:tɪŋ] *n (UNCOUNT) Aut* coups *mpl* de Klaxon ❑

tootle ['tu:təl] *Fam* **1** *vi* (**a**) *(on musical instrument)* jouer un petit air; **he was tootling on a recorder** il jouait un petit air sur sa flûte

(**b**) *Br (drive)* **we were tootling along quite nicely until the tyre burst** nous suivions notre petit bonhomme de chemin lorsque le pneu a éclaté; **I'm going to tootle into town this afternoon** je vais aller faire un petit tour en ville cet après-midi; **well, I'll tootle along now** bon, je vais me mettre en route

2 *n* (**a**) *(on musical instrument)* petit air *m*

(**b**) *Br (drive)* petit tour *m* en voiture

toots [tʊts] *n Fam (term of address)* chéri(e) ❑ *m,f*

tootsie ['tʊtsɪ] *n Fam* (**a**) *(in children's language → foot)* pied ❑ *m*, peton *m*; *(→ toe)* doigt *m* de pied ❑, orteil ❑ *m* (**b**) *(term of address)* chéri(e) ❑ *m,f*

tootsie-wootsie [-'wʊtsɪ] *n Fam* petit peton *m*

tootsy *(pl* **tootsies***)* = **tootsie**

TOP [tɒp]

haut	► **1 (a), (h)**
sommet	► **1 (a)**
dessus	► **1 (b)**
couvercle	► **1 (d)**
couvrir	► **2 (a)**
dépasser	► **2 (c)**
être en tête de	► **2 (d)**
du dessus	► **3 (a)**
du haut	► **3 (a)**
premier	► **3 (b)**

(pt & pp **topped**, *cont* **topping***)* **1** *n* (**a**) *(highest point)* haut *m*, sommet *m*; *(of tree)* sommet *m*, cime *f*; **carrot tops** fanes *fpl* de carottes; **top of the milk** crème *f* du lait; **at the top of the stairs/tree** en haut de l'escalier/l'arbre; **he searched the house from top to bottom** il a fouillé la maison de fond en comble; *Br* **from top to toe** de la tête aux pieds; **she filled the jar right to the top** elle a rempli le bocal à ras bord; **the page number is at the top of the page** la numérotation se trouve en haut de la page; *St Exch* **to buy at the top and sell at the bottom** acheter au plus haut et vendre au plus bas

(**b**) *(surface)* dessus *m*, surface *f*; **he's getting thin on top** il commence à se dégarnir; **just put it on top** mets-le sur le dessus; **a cake with a cherry on top** un gâteau avec une cerise dessus

(**c**) *(end)* **at the top of the street** au bout de la rue; **at the top of the garden** au fond du jardin

(**d**) *(cap, lid)* couvercle *m*; **where's the top to my pen?** où est le capuchon de mon stylo?; **bottle top** *(screw-on)* bouchon *m* (de bouteille); *(on beer bottle)* capsule *f* (de bouteille)

(**e**) *(highest degree)* **he is at the top of his form** il est au meilleur de sa forme; **at the top of one's voice** à tue-tête

(**f**) *(most important position) Br* **at the top of the table** à la place d'honneur; **she's top of her class** elle est première de sa classe; **someone who has reached the top in their profession** quelqu'un qui est arrivé en haut de l'échelle dans sa profession; **it went right to the top** *(complaint, request etc)* cela est remonté jusqu'au sommet; *Theat* **to be (at the) top of the bill** être en tête d'affiche; **to reach the top of the tree** arriver en haut de l'échelle; **it's tough at the top!** c'est la rançon de la gloire!; **this car is the top of the range** c'est une voiture haut de gamme; *Ir* **top of the morning!** bien le bonjour!

(**g**) *Br Aut (fourth gear)* quatrième *f*; *(fifth gear)* cinquième *f*; **she changed into top** elle a enclenché la quatrième/la cinquième; **in top** en quatrième/cinquième

(**h**) *(garment)* haut *m*; **does this top go with my skirt?** est-ce que ce haut va avec ma jupe?

(**i**) *(beginning)* **play it again from the top** reprends au début; **let's take it from the top** commençons par le commencement; **at the top of the fifth (inning)** *(in baseball)* au début de la cinquième manche

(**j**) *(toy)* toupie *f*; **to spin a top** lancer *ou* fouetter une toupie; *Br* **to sleep like a top** dormir comme un loir

(**k**) *(idioms)* **to come out on top** avoir le dessus; *Br Fam* **he doesn't have much up top** il n'est pas très futé; **the soldiers went over the top** les soldats sont montés à l'assaut; *Fam* **to blow one's top** piquer une crise, exploser

2 *vt* (**a**) *(form top of)* couvrir, recouvrir; **a cake topped with chocolate** un gâteau recouvert de chocolat; **snow topped the mountains** les sommets (des montagnes) étaient recouverts de neige

(**b**) *Br (trim)* écimer, étêter; **she was topping the carrots** elle coupait les fanes des carottes; **to top and tail gooseberries** équeuter des groseilles

(**c**) *(exceed)* dépasser; **production topped five tons last month** le mois dernier, la production a dépassé les cinq tonnes; **he topped her offer** il a renchéri sur son offre; **his score tops the world record** avec ce score, il bat le record du monde; **his story topped them all** son histoire était la meilleure de toutes; **and to top it all** et pour comble (de malheur), et en plus de tout cela; *Br* **that tops the lot!** ça, c'est le bouquet!

(**d**) *(be at the top of)* **the book topped the best-seller list** ce livre est arrivé en tête des best-sellers; **she topped the polls in the last election** aux dernières élections, elle est arrivée en tête de scrutin; **topping the bill tonight we have...** le clou de cette soirée est...; **to top the charts** *(record, singer)* être à la première place *ou* en tête des hit-parades

(**e**) *Br Fam (kill)* buter, zigouiller; **to top oneself** se suicider ❑, se foutre en l'air

3 *adj* (**a**) *(highest)* du dessus, du haut, d'en haut; **the top floor** *or* **storey** le dernier étage; **the top shelf** l'étagère du haut; **the top button of her dress** le premier bouton de sa robe; **in the top right-hand corner** dans le coin en haut à droite; **the top speed of this car is 150 mph** la vitesse maximum de cette voiture est de 240 km/h; **to travel at top speed** *(plane, train etc)* aller à sa vitesse maximale; **to be on top form** être en pleine forme; *Br Fam* **the top brass** les officiers *mpl* supérieurs ❑, les gros bonnets *mpl*; *Fam* **to pay top dollar** *or Br* **whack for sth** payer qch au prix fort ❑; *Br Fam* **I can offer you £20 top whack** je vous en donne 20 livres, c'est mon dernier prix ❑

(**b**) *(best, major)* premier; **she got the top mark** *or* **came top in history** elle a eu la meilleure note en histoire; **the top people** *(prominent people)* les gens *mpl* en vue; *(in an organization)* les gros bonnets *mpl*; **all the top people in New York eat there** c'est un restaurant où se retrouve toute l'élite new-yorkaise; **the country's top ten companies** les dix premières sociétés du pays; **one of the world's top ten players** un des dix meilleurs joueurs mondiaux; **top management** la direction générale;

Br Fam **a family right out of the top drawer** une famille de la haute

4 **on top of** *prep* sur; **the wreckage floated on top of the water** l'épave flottait sur l'eau; **suddenly the lorry was on top of him** d'un seul coup, il a réalisé que le camion lui arrivait dessus; **we're living on top of each other** nous vivons les uns sur les autres; *Fig* **on top of everything else** pour couronner le tout; **it's just one thing on top of another** ça n'arrête pas; **don't worry, I'm on top of things** ne t'inquiète pas, je m'en sors très bien; **it's all getting on top of him** il est dépassé par les événements; **to feel on top of the world** avoir la forme

►► *Fam* ***top banana*** *(person)* huile *f*, gros bonnet *m*, grosse légume *f*; *Br* ***top boots*** bottes *fpl* hautes; *Br* ***top copy*** original *m*; *Fam* ***top dog*** chef *m*; **he's top dog around here** c'est lui qui commande ici; *Br* ***top gear*** vitesse *f* supérieure; ***top hat*** (chapeau *m*) haut-de-forme *m*; ***top pupil*** premier(ère) *m,f* de la classe; ***top rate*** *(of tax)* taux *m* maximum; *Sport* ***top scorer*** *(gen)* meilleur(e) marqueur(euse) *m,f*; *Ftbl* meilleur(e) buteur(euse) *m,f*; ***top table*** *(at wedding)* table *f* d'honneur; ***top ten*** = hit parade des dix meilleures ventes de disques pop et rock

►**top off** *vt sep* (**a**) *Br (conclude)* terminer, couronner; **and to top off a miserable day, it started to rain** et pour conclure cette triste journée, il s'est mis à pleuvoir; **topped off with a cherry** garni d'une cerise

(**b**) *Am (fill to top)* remplir

►**top out** *vt insep (building)* fêter l'achèvement de

►**top up** *Br* **1** *vt sep (fill up)* remplir; **can I top up your drink** *or* **top you up?** encore une goutte?; *Aut* **to top up the tank** faire le plein; *Aut* **to top up the battery** ajouter de l'eau dans la batterie; **to top up one's life assurance premium** augmenter les versements de son assurance-vie; **the government tops up the rest** *(pays the balance)* le gouvernement met l'argent qui manque *ou* rajoute la différence

2 *vi Aut (with petrol)* faire le plein

topaz [ˈtəʊpæz] *n* topaze *f*; **a topaz bracelet** un bracelet de topazes

top-bracket *adj* de première catégorie

top-class *adj* excellent

topcoat [ˈtɒpkəʊt] *n* (**a**) *(clothing)* pardessus *m*, manteau *m* (**b**) *(of paint)* couche *f* de finition

top-down *adj* hiérarchisé; *(management)* contrôlé par le haut

►► *Mktg* ***top-down forecasting*** prévisions *fpl* hiérarchisées

top-drawer *adj Br Fam* de tout premier rang□; **he's a top-drawer musician** c'est un musicien de haute volée□

top-dress *vt Agr* fumer en surface

top-dressing *n Agr* fumure *f* en surface

tope [təʊp] *vi Arch or Literary* boire

topee [ˈtəʊpiː] *n Br* casque *m* colonial *(des Indes)*

toper [ˈtəʊpə(r)] *n Literary* alcoolique *mf*, buveur(-euse) *m,f*

top-flight *adj* de premier ordre

topgallant [ˌtɒpˈgælənt, təˈgælənt] *n Naut (mast)* mât *m* de perroquet; *(sail)* voile *f* de perroquet

top-hatted [-ˈhætɪd] *adj* qui porte un haut-de-forme

top-heavy *adj* (**a**) *(unbalanced)* trop lourd du haut, déséquilibré (**b**) *Fig (company, organization → with too many senior staff)* où il y a trop de cadres; *(→ over-capitalized)* surcapitalisé (**c**) *Fam (big-breasted)* **to be top-heavy** avoir de gros seins□

top-hole *adj Br Fam Old-fashioned* épatant, formidable□

topi [ˈtəʊpɪ] = **topee**

topiary [ˈtəʊpjərɪ] **1** *n (art)* art *m* topiaire; *(garden)* = jardin d'arbustes taillés en formes diverses

2 *adj* topiaire

topic [ˈtɒpɪk] *n (theme)* sujet *m*, thème *m*; **tonight's topic for debate is unemployment** le débat de ce soir porte sur le chômage

topical [ˈtɒpɪkəl] *adj* (**a**) *(current)* actuel; **a topical question** une question d'actualité; **matters of topical interest** des questions *fpl* d'actualité; **it's very topical** c'est tout à fait d'actualité; **a few topical references in the text** quelques références à l'actualité dans le texte; **a timely and topical report** un rapport qui vient à point nommé (**b**) *Med* topique, à usage local

topicality [ˌtɒpɪˈkælɪtɪ] *(pl* **topicalities**) *n* actualité *f*

topically [ˈtɒpɪklɪ] *adv (write, speak)* sur des thèmes d'actualité

topknot [ˈtɒpnɒt] *n* (**a**) *(of hair)* chignon *m*; *(of ribbons)* ornement *m* fait de rubans; *(of feathers)* aigrette *f* (**b**) *Ich* pleuronectidé *m*

topless [ˈtɒplɪs] *adj (sunbather, dancer)* aux seins nus; **to go topless** ne pas porter de haut

►► ***topless bar*** bar *m* topless

top-level *adj* de très haut niveau

top-loader *n (washing machine)* machine *f* à laver à chargement par le haut

topmast [ˈtɒpmɑːst] *n Naut* mât *m* de hune

topmost [ˈtɒpməʊst] *adj* le plus haut, le plus élevé

top-notch *adj Fam* excellent□

top-of-the-range *adj* haut de gamme

topographer [təˈpɒgrəfə(r)] *n* topographe *mf*

topographic [ˌtɒpəˈgræfɪk], **topographical** [ˌtɒpəˈgræfɪkəl] *adj* topographique

topographically [ˌtɒpəˈgræfɪklɪ] *adv* topographiquement

topography [təˈpɒgrəfɪ] *(pl* **topographies**) *n* topographie *f*

topologic [ˌtɒpəˈlɒdʒɪk], **topological** [ˌtɒpəˈlɒdʒɪkəl] *adj* topologique

topology [təˈpɒlədʒɪ] *n* topologie *f*

toponym [ˈtɒpənɪm] *n* toponyme *m*

toponymic [ˌtɒpəˈnɪmɪk] *adj* toponymique

toponymy [təˈpɒnəmɪ] *n* toponymie *f*

-topped [tɒpt] *suff Literary* **cloud-topped peaks** sommets *mpl* couronnés de nuages; **ivory-topped walking stick** canne *f* à pommeau d'ivoire

topper [ˈtɒpə(r)] *n Br Fam (top hat)* (chapeau *m*) haut-de-forme□ *m*

topping [ˈtɒpɪŋ] **1** *n* dessus *m*; *Culin (for dessert, pizza etc)* garniture *f*; **ice-cream with raspberry topping** glace recouverte d'un coulis de framboises; **the dish has a cheese and breadcrumb topping** le plat est garni de fromage et de chapelure

2 *adj Br Fam Old-fashioned* épatant, formidable□

topple [ˈtɒpəl] **1** *vi (fall)* basculer; *(totter)* vaciller; **the whole pile toppled over** toute la pile s'est effondrée; **he toppled over backwards** il a perdu l'équilibre et est tombé en arrière; **he toppled into the pool/over the edge of the cliff** il a culbuté dans la piscine/par-dessus la falaise

2 *vt* (**a**) *(cause to fall)* faire tomber, faire basculer

(**b**) *Fig* renverser; **the scandal almost toppled the government** ce scandale a failli faire tomber le gouvernement

top-quality *adj* de qualité supérieure

top-ranking *adj* de premier rang, haut placé; **a top-ranking official** un haut fonctionnaire

top-rope *n (in mountaineering)* moulinette *f*

TOPS [tɒps] *n Br (abbr* **Training Opportunities Scheme**) = programme du recyclage professionnel en Grande-Bretagne

tops [tɒps] *Fam* **1** *n Old-fashioned* **it's the tops!** c'est bath!

2 *adv Fam (at the most)* maxi; **it'll cost a fiver tops** ça coûtera cinq livres maxi *ou* à tout casser

topsail [ˈtɒpsəl, ˈtɒpseɪl] *n Naut* hunier *m*

top-secret *adj* top secret *(inv)*, ultraconfidentiel

top-security *adj* de haute sécurité

►► ***top-security prison*** ≃ quartier *m* de haute sécurité

top-shelf *adj*

►► *Br* ***top-shelf magazines*** revues *fpl* érotiques

topshell [ˈtɒpʃel] *n Zool* troque *m*, troche *m*

topside [ˈtɒpsaɪd] **1** *n Br (of beef)* tende-de-tranche *m*

2 topsides *npl Naut* accastillage *m*

topsider [ˈtɒpsaɪdə(r)] *n (shoe)* chaussure *f* bateau

topsoil [ˈtɒpsɔɪl] *n* terre *f* superficielle, couche *f* arable

topspin [ˈtɒpspɪn] **1** *n* effet *m* accéléré; *(in tennis)* lift *m*; **to put topspin on a ball** lifter une balle

2 *adj (in tennis)* lifté

►► ***topspin lob*** lob *m* lifté

topsy-turvy [ˌtɒpsɪˈtɜːvɪ] **1** *adj* sens dessus dessous; **a topsy-turvy world** le monde à l'envers; **everything is topsy-turvy** tout est sens dessus dessous

2 *adv* **the war turned their lives topsy-turvy** la guerre a bouleversé leur vie

top-up *n Br* **can I give you a top-up?** je vous ressers?, encore une goutte?

►► ***top-up card*** *(for mobile phone)* recharge *f*; *Fin* ***top-up finance*** fonds *m* complémentaire; *Fin* ***top-up loan*** prêt *m* complémentaire

toque [təʊk] *n (brimless hat)* toque *f*; *Can (knitted hat)* bonnet *m*

tor [tɔː(r)] *n* colline *f* rocailleuse *(notamment dans le sud-ouest de l'Angleterre)*

Torah [ˈtɔːrə] *n* Torah *f*

torch [tɔːtʃ] *(pl* **torches**) **1** *n* (**a**) *Br (electric)* lampe *f* de poche (**b**) *(flaming stick)* torche *f*, flambeau *m*; **to put a torch to sth** mettre le feu à qch; *Fig* **to carry a torch for sb** en pincer pour qn (**c**) *Tech (for welding, soldering)* chalumeau *m*

2 *vt* mettre le feu à; **they torched the old barn** ils ont mis le feu à la vieille grange

►► ***torch song*** chanson *f* d'amour triste

torchbearer [ˈtɔːtʃˌbeərə(r)] *n* porteur(euse) *m,f* de flambeau

torchlight [ˈtɔːtʃlaɪt] *n* lumière *f* de flambeau *ou* de torche; *(of electric torch)* lumière d'une/de la torche électrique; **by torchlight** à la lueur des flambeaux; *(electric torch)* à la lumière d'une torche électrique

►► ***torchlight procession*** retraite *f* aux flambeaux

tore [tɔː(r)] *pt of* **tear**

toreador [ˈtɒrɪədɔː(r)] *n* torero *m*, toréador *m*

►► ***toreador pants*** pantalon *m* corsaire

torero [tɒˈreərəʊ] *(pl* **toreros**) *n* torero *m*

tori [ˈtɔːraɪ] *pl of* **torus**

torment 1 *n* [ˈtɔːment] (**a**) *(suffering)* supplice *m*, *Literary* tourment *m*; **to be in torment** être au supplice; **her face showed her inner torment** son tourment intérieur se lisait sur son visage; **to suffer torment** souffrir le martyre

(**b**) *(ordeal)* rude épreuve *f*

(**c**) *(pest)* démon *m*; **that child is a real torment** cet enfant est vraiment insupportable

2 *vt* [tɔːˈment] (**a**) *(cause pain to)* torturer; **tormented by doubt** harcelé de doutes

(**b**) *(harass)* tourmenter, harceler; **stop tormenting your sister!** laisse ta sœur tranquille!

tormentil [ˈtɔːməntɪl] *n Bot* tormentille *f*

tormentor [tɔːˈmentə(r)] *n* persécuteur(trice) *m,f*, bourreau *m*

torn [tɔːn] *pp of* **tear**

tornado [tɔːˈneɪdəʊ] *(pl* **tornados** *or* **tornadoes**) *n (storm)* tornade *f*; *Fig (person, thing)* ouragan *m*

toroid [ˈtɒrɔɪd] *n Geom* tore *m*

Toronto [təˈrɒntəʊ] *n* Toronto *m*

torose [tɒˈrəʊs], **torous** [ˈtɔːrəs] *adj Biol* qui présente des protubérances, noueux

torpedo [tɔːˈpiːdəʊ] *(pl* **torpedoes**, *pt & pp* **torpedoed**) **1** *n* (**a**) *Mil* torpille *f* (**b**) *Am (firework)* pétard *m* (**c**) *Ich (fish)* (poisson *m*) torpille *f*

2 *vt* (**a**) *Mil* torpiller (**b**) *Fig (destroy → plan)* faire échouer, torpiller

►► ***torpedo boat*** torpilleur *m*, vedette *f* lance-torpilles; *Ich* ***torpedo fish*** poisson *m* torpille; ***torpedo tube*** tube *m* lance-torpilles

torpid [ˈtɔːpɪd] *adj Formal* léthargique; **a torpid mind** un esprit engourdi

torpidity [tɔːˈpɪdɪtɪ], **torpidness** [ˈtɔːpɪdnɪs] *n Formal* torpeur *f*, léthargie *f*, engourdissement *m*; *Naut* **torpidity of the compass** stagnation *f* du compas

torpor [ˈtɔːpə(r)] *n Formal* torpeur *f*, léthargie *f*, engourdissement *m*

torque [tɔːk] *n* (**a**) *(rotational force) Tech* moment *m* de torsion; *Aut* couple *m* moteur (**b**) *Hist (collar)* torque *m* (**c**) *(necklace)* collier *m* ras de cou

►► ***torque converter*** convertisseur *m* de couple; ***torque plate*** plateau *m* absorbeur de couple; ***torque wrench*** clé *f* dynamométrique

torqued [tɔːkt] *adj Am Fam* (**a**) *(angry)* furibard, furax (**b**) *(drunk)* bourré, fait

torquemeter ['tɔːkˌmiːtə(r)] *n* torsiomètre *m*, complemètre *m*

torr [tɔː(r)] *n Phys* torr *m*

torrefaction [ˌtɒrɪ'fækʃən] *n* torréfaction *f*

torrefy ['tɒrɪfaɪ] *vt* torréfier

torrent ['tɒrənt] *n* (**a**) *(of liquid)* torrent *m*; **the rain came down in torrents** il pleuvait à torrents *ou* à verse (**b**) *(of emotion, abuse etc)* torrent *m*; **a torrent of insults** un torrent *ou* flot d'injures

torrential [tə'renʃəl] *adj* torrentiel; **we've had torrential rain all week** il y a eu des pluies torrentielles toute la semaine

torrentially [tə'renʃəlɪ] *adv* torrentiellement, à torrents

Torres Strait ['tɔːrɪz-] *n* **the Torres Strait** le détroit de Torres

▸▸ ***Torres Strait islander*** indigène *mf* des îles du détroit de Torres

torrid ['tɒrɪd] *adj* (**a**) *(hot)* torride; *Geog* **the torrid zone** la zone intertropicale (**b**) *(passionate)* passionné, ardent, torride

torridity [tɒ'rɪdɪtɪ], **torridness** ['tɒrɪdnɪs] *n (heat)* chaleur *f* torride; *(torrid nature)* caractère *m* passionné

torsade [tɔː'seɪd] *n* torsade *f*

torsion ['tɔːʃən] *n* torsion *f*

▸▸ ***torsion balance*** balance *f* de torsion; ***torsion bar*** barre *f* de torsion

torsional ['tɔːʃənəl] *adj* de torsion

▸▸ ***torsional deflection*** déformation *f* due à la *ou* par torsion; ***torsional stiffness*** rigidité *f ou* raideur *f* à la torsion; ***torsional strain, torsional stress*** effort *m* de torsion; ***torsional strength*** resistance *f* à la torsion

torso ['tɔːsəʊ] (*pl* **torsos**) *n (human)* torse *m*; *(sculpture)* buste *m*

tort [tɔːt] *n Law* délit *m*, préjudice *m*

▸▸ *Am* ***torts lawyer*** avocat(e) *m,f* spécialisé(e) en responsabilité délictuelle

torte [tɔːt] *n* gâteau *m*

tortellini [tɔːtə'liːnɪ] *npl Culin* tortellinis *mpl*

torticollis [tɔːtɪ'kɒlɪs] *n Med* torticolis *m*

tortilla [tɔː'tiːjə] *n Culin* tortilla *f (galette de maïs)*

▸▸ ***tortilla chips*** tortilla chips *fpl*

tortious ['tɔːʃəs] *adj Law* dommageable, préjudiciable

tortiously ['tɔːʃəslɪ] *adv Law* d'une façon préjudiciable

tortoise ['tɔːtəs] *n* tortue *f*

tortoiseshell ['tɔːtəsʃel] **1** *n* (**a**) *(substance)* écaille *f* (de tortue) (**b**) *(cat)* chat *m* écaille de tortue (**c**) *(butterfly)* vanesse *f*

2 *adj* (**a**) *(comb, ornament)* en écaille (**b**) *(cat)* écaille de tortue *(inv)*

Tortuga [tɔː'tuːgə] *n Geog* **Isle of Tortuga, Tortuga Island** la Tortue

tortuous ['tɔːtjʊəs] *adj* (**a**) *(path)* tortueux, sinueux (**b**) *(argument, piece of writing)* contourné, tarabiscoté; *(mind)* tortueux, retors

tortuously ['tɔːtjʊəslɪ] *adv* tortueusement, de manière tortueuse

tortuousness ['tɔːtjʊəsnɪs] *n (of path, thinking etc)* caractère *m* tortueux

torture ['tɔːtʃə(r)] **1** *n* (**a**) *(cruelty)* torture *f*, supplice *m*; **to be subjected to torture** être torturé, subir des tortures; **instruments of torture** instruments *mpl* de torture

(**b**) *Fig* torture *f*, tourment *m*; **wearing these shoes is torture** c'est un vrai supplice de porter ces chaussures; **the waiting was sheer torture!** cette attente fut un vrai supplice!

2 *vt* (**a**) *(inflict pain on)* torturer; **they tortured her until she confessed** ils l'ont torturée jusqu'à ce qu'elle avoue

(**b**) *Fig (torment)* torturer; **tortured by remorse** tenaillé par le remords

(**c**) *Fig (distort)* **she tortures the Spanish language** elle écorche la langue espagnole; **to torture a song** massacrer une chanson

▸▸ ***torture chamber*** chambre *f* de torture

torturer ['tɔːtʃərə(r)] *n* tortionnaire *mf*, bourreau *m*

torus ['tɔːrəs] (*pl* **tori** [-raɪ]) *n* (**a**) *Phys* tore *m* (**b**) *Geom* tore *m* (**c**) *Bot* réceptacle *m*

Tory ['tɔːrɪ] (*pl* **Tories**) **1** *n Pol* tory *m*, membre *m* du parti conservateur

2 *adj (party, MP)* tory, conservateur

Toryism ['tɔːrɪɪzəm] *n Pol* torysme *m*

tosh [tɒʃ] *Br Fam* **1** *n* foutaises *fpl*; **that's a load of tosh!** c'est des foutaises!

2 *exclam* n'importe quoi!

toss [tɒs] **1** *vt* (**a**) *(throw)* lancer, jeter; **she tossed him the ball** elle lui a lancé la balle; **I tossed some herbs into the soup** j'ai ajouté une poignée de fines herbes à la soupe; **the horse nearly tossed its rider into the ditch** le cheval a failli faire tomber son cavalier dans le fossé; **he was tossed by the bull** le taureau l'a projeté en l'air; *Br* **to toss pancakes** faire sauter des crêpes; **to toss a coin** jouer à pile ou face; **she tossed back her head with a laugh** elle rejeta la tête en arrière en riant; **who's going to pay? – I'll toss you for it** qui va payer? – décidons-le à pile ou face

(**b**) *Culin* mélanger; **to toss a salad** remuer *ou* retourner une salade; **toss the carrots in butter** ajoutez du beurre et mélangez aux carottes

2 *vi* s'agiter; **to toss and turn (in bed)** avoir le sommeil agité; **I tossed and turned all night** je me suis tourné et retourné dans mon lit toute la nuit; **the trees were tossing in the wind** le vent secouait les arbres; **to pitch and toss** *(boat)* tanguer; **shall we toss for it?** on joue à pile ou face?

3 *n* (**a**) *(throw → gen)* lancer *m*, lancement *m*; *(→ of a coin)* coup *m* de pile ou face; *Sport* tirage *m* au sort; **to win/to lose the toss** gagner/perdre à pile ou face; **our team won the toss** notre équipe a gagné au tirage au sort; *Br* **to argue the toss** ergoter, chicaner; *Br Fam* **I don't give a toss** je m'en fiche; *Br Fam* **who gives a toss?** qu'est-ce que ça peut foutre?

(**b**) *(of head)* mouvement *m* brusque

(**c**) *(fall from horse)* chute *f*; **to take a toss** être désarçonné, faire une chute

▸**toss about, toss around 1** *vt sep* (**a**) *(rock, buffet)* ballotter, secouer; **we were tossed about by the bumpy road** nous avons été ballottés sur cette route cahoteuse; **the boat was tossed about by the waves** les vagues faisaient tanguer le bateau

(**b**) *(ball)* lancer; *Fig* **they were tossing ideas about** ils lançaient toutes sortes d'idées; **figures of £5,000 were being tossed around** on avançait allègrement des chiffres de l'ordre de 5000 livres

2 *vi* s'agiter

▸**toss off 1** *vt sep* (**a**) *(task, essay, article)* expédier; **to toss off a letter** écrire une lettre au pied levé

(**b**) *(drink)* boire d'un coup, lamper

(**c**) *Br very Fam (masturbate)*; **to toss sb off** branler qn; **to toss oneself off** se branler

2 *vi Br very Fam (masturbate)* se branler

▸**toss up 1** *vt sep* lancer, jeter; **she tossed the ball up into the air** elle a lancé le ballon en l'air

2 *vi* jouer à pile ou face

tosser ['tɒsə(r)] *n Br very Fam* tache *f*, branque *m*

tossing ['tɒsɪŋ] *n (UNCOUNT) (of boat)* ballottement *m*

tosspot ['tɒspɒt] *n* (**a**) *Arch or Literary (drunk)* ivrogne *mf* (**b**) *very Fam (stupid person)* connard (connasse) *m,f*

toss-up *n* (**a**) *(with coin)* coup *m* de pile ou face; **in the event of a tie the winner will be decided by a toss up** en cas d'égalité, on tirera à pile ou face pour désigner le gagnant

(**b**) *Fam* **in the end it was a toss-up between Majorca and Rhodes** finalement, nous avons dû choisir entre Majorque et Rhodes□; **it's a toss-up which is best** il est impossible de dire quel est le meilleur□; **I don't know, it's a toss-up** je ne sais pas, c'est kif-kif

tot [tɒt] (*pt & pp* **totted**, *cont* **totting**) *n* (**a**) *(child)* petit(e) enfant□ *m,f*; **tiny tots** les tout petits□ *mpl* (**b**) *Br (of alcohol)* goutte *f*; **a tot of rum** un petit verre de rhum

▸**tot up** *Br* **1** *vt sep* additionner; **I'll tot up your bill** je vais vous faire l'addition

2 *vi* **that tots up to £3** ça fait 3 livres en tout

total ['təʊtəl] (*Br pt & pp* **totalled**, *cont* **totalling**, *Am pt & pp* **totaled**, *cont* **totaling**) **1** *adj* (**a**) *(amount, number)* total; **the total gains/losses** le total des profits/pertes; **the total cost** le coût total; **marketing the product accounts for 20 percent of the total costs** le coût de commercialisation du produit revient à 20 pour cent du coût total

(**b**) *(as intensifier)* complet(ète); **total silence** un silence absolu; **we are in total disagreement** nous ne sommes pas d'accord du tout; **that's total nonsense!** c'est complètement absurde!; **he was a total stranger to me** je ne le connaissais ni d'Ève ni d'Adam

2 *n* total *m*; **there are a total of thirteen inspectors in the whole country** au total, il y a treize inspecteurs dans tout le pays; **she wrote a total of ten books** elle a écrit dix livres en tout; **that comes to a total of £2** ça fait 2 livres en tout; **a total of 102 hours/people** un total de 102 heures/personnes; **the total payable** le total à payer

3 *vt* (**a**) *(add up)* additionner, faire le total de

(**b**) *(amount to)* s'élever à; **the groceries total £10** la note d'épicerie s'élève à 10 livres; **the collection totalled 50 cars** cette collection comptait 50 voitures en tout

(**c**) *Am Fam (wreck)* démolir□; **he totaled his car** sa voiture est bonne pour la casse

4 in total *adv* au total; **there are three hundred students in total** au total, il y a trois cents étudiants

▸▸ *Fin* ***total annual expenses*** consommations *fpl* de l'exercice; *Fin* ***total assets*** total *m* de l'actif; *Fin* ***total asset value*** valeur *f* de bilan; *Astron* ***total eclipse*** éclipse *f* totale; *Fin* ***total gross income*** revenu *m* brut global; *Fin* ***total insured value*** valeur *f* totale assurée; *Fin* ***total liabilities*** total *m* du passif; *Fin* ***total loss*** perte *f* totale; *Fin* ***total net income*** revenu *m* net global; *Com* ***total quality control*** contrôle *m* de la qualité totale; *Com* ***total quality management*** qualité *f* totale; ***total recall*** mémoire *f* très précise; **to have total recall of sth** avoir un souvenir très précis de qch, se souvenir de qch dans les moindres détails

totalitarian [ˌtəʊtælɪ'teərɪən] *adj* totalitaire

totalitarianism [ˌtəʊtælɪ'teərɪənɪzəm] *n* totalitarisme *m*

totality [təʊ'tælətɪ] (*pl* **totalities**) *n* (**a**) *(completeness, complete amount)* totalité *f*; **in its totality** dans sa totalité, intégralement (**b**) *Astron* occultation *f* totale

totalizator ['təʊtəlaɪzeɪtə(r)] *n* (**a**) *(adding machine)* totalisateur *m*, machine *f* totalisatrice (**b**) *Br (in betting)* pari *m* mutuel

totalize, -ise ['təʊtəlaɪz] *vt* totaliser, additionner

totalizer ['təʊtəlaɪzə(r)] = **totalizator**

totalling, *Am* **totaling** ['təʊtəlɪŋ] *n* totalisation *f*

totally ['təʊtəlɪ] *adv* (**a**) *(completely)* totalement, entièrement, complètement; **do you agree? – yes, totally** êtes-vous d'accord? – oui, tout à fait (**b**) *(expressing agreement)* absolument (**c**) *Am Fam (a lot)* vachement; **I don't smoke but my parents totally smoke** moi je fume pas, mais mes parents fument vachement

tote[1] [təʊt] **1** *n (bag)* grand sac *m*, fourre-tout *m inv*

2 *vt Fam* porter□; **I've been toting that thing around all day** j'ai trimballé ce truc toute la journée; **he was toting a gun** il avait un fusil sur lui

▸▸ ***tote bag*** grand sac *m*, fourre-tout *m inv*

tote[2] *n Br Horseracing* (*abbr* **totalizator**) pari *m* mutuel

▸▸ ***tote board*** tableau *m* électronique

totem ['təʊtəm] *n* totem *m*

▸▸ ***totem pole*** mât *m* totémique

totemic [təʊ'temɪk] *adj* totémique

totemism ['təʊtəˌmɪzəm] *n* totémisme *m*

totemist ['təʊtəmɪst] *n* totémiste *mf*

totemistic [ˌtəʊtə'mɪstɪk] *adj* totémistique

t'other, tother ['tʌðə(r)] *Fam or Hum* = **the other**

toto ['təʊtəʊ] **in toto** *adv Formal* entièrement, complètement

totter ['tɒtə(r)] **1** *vi* (**a**) *(person)* chanceler, tituber; *(pile, vase)* chanceler; **he tottered down the stairs** il descendit les escaliers en chancelant; **the child tottered into/out of the room** l'enfant est entré dans/sorti de la pièce d'un pas mal assuré

(**b**) *Fig (government, company)* chanceler, être dans une mauvaise passe

2 *n* vacillement *m*; *(gait)* démarche *f* titubante *ou* chancelante; **with a totter** d'un pas chancelant, en chancelant

tottering ['tɒtərɪŋ], **tottery** ['tɒtərɪ] *adj* chancelant;

(building) branlant; *(government)* chancelant, déstabilisé; **with tottering steps** en titubant

totting ['tɒtɪŋ] *n Br Fam* = recherche d'objets récupérables dans les décharges

totty ['tɒtɪ] *n Br Fam (attractive women)* belles nanas *fpl*, belles gonzesses *fpl*

toucan ['tu:kən] *n Orn* toucan *m*

TOUCH [tʌtʃ]

toucher	▸ 1 (a), (b), (h); 2 (a), (e), (g)
contact	▸ 1 (b), (g)
effleurement	▸ 1 (b)
touche	▸ 1 (c), (i)
coup	▸ 1 (e)
pointe	▸ 1 (f)
toucher à	▸ 2 (b), (d)
jouxter	▸ 2 (c)
émouvoir	▸ 2 (e)
concerner	▸ 2 (g)
se toucher	▸ 3 (a), (b)

(*pl* **touches**) **1** *n* (**a**) *(sense)* toucher *m*; **sense of touch** sens *m* du toucher; **soft to the touch** doux au toucher

(**b**) *(physical contact)* toucher *m*, contact *m*; *(light brushing)* effleurement *m*, frôlement *m*; **she felt the touch of his hand** elle a senti le frôlement de sa main; **she felt a touch on her shoulder** elle sentit qu'on lui touchait l'épaule; **the machine works at the touch of a button** il suffit de toucher un bouton pour mettre en marche cet appareil

(**c**) *(style)* touche *f*; **this painting has the Hopper touch** on reconnaît dans ce tableau la patte de Hopper; **the pianist has a light touch** ce pianiste a le toucher léger; *Fig* **to give sth a personal touch** ajouter une note personnelle à qch; **to have the right touch with sb/sth** savoir s'y prendre avec qn/qch; **the house needed a woman's touch** il manquait dans cette maison une présence féminine; **the cook has lost his touch** le cuisinier a perdu la main

(**d**) *(detail)* **to put the final** *or* **finishing touches to sth** apporter la touche finale à qch; **that logo in the bottom corner is a nice touch** c'est une bonne idée d'avoir mis ce logo dans le coin en bas

(**e**) *(slight mark)* coup *m*; **with a touch of the pen** d'un coup de stylo; **to add a few touches to a picture** faire quelques retouches à un tableau

(**f**) *(small amount, hint)* pointe *f*, note *f*; **a touch of garlic** une pointe *ou* un soupçon d'ail; **a touch of madness** un grain de folie; **there's a touch of spring in the air** ça sent le printemps; **he answered with a touch of bitterness** il a répondu avec une pointe d'amertume; **I got a touch of sunstroke** j'ai eu une petite insolation; **I've got a touch of flu** je suis un peu grippé, j'ai une petite grippe; **to add a touch of class to sth** rendre qch plus distingué; **there was a touch too much pepper in the soup** le potage était un petit peu trop poivré

(**g**) *(contact)* **to be/to keep in touch with sb** être/rester en contact avec qn; **I'll be in touch!** je te contacterai!; **keep** *or* **stay in touch!** donne-nous de tes nouvelles!; **to get in touch with sb** contacter qn; **you can get in touch with me at this address** vous pouvez me joindre à cette adresse; **he put me in touch with the director** il m'a mis en relation avec le directeur; **she is** *or* **keeps in touch with current events** elle se tient au courant de l'actualité; **I'll keep in touch with developments** je me tiendrai au courant de la situation; **I am out of touch with her now** je ne suis plus en contact avec elle; **she is out of touch with politics** elle ne suit plus l'actualité politique; **they lost touch long ago** ils se sont perdus de vue il y a longtemps; **he has lost touch with reality** il a perdu le sens des réalités; **the President has lost touch with the electorate** le Président a perdu le contact avec son électorat

(**h**) *(of an instrument)* toucher *m*; *(of a typewriter)* frappe *f*; **a keyboard with a light touch** un clavier à frappe légère

(**i**) *Sport* touche *f*; **to kick the ball into touch** mettre le ballon en touche; **the ball landed in touch** le ballon est sorti en touche; *Fig* **to kick sth into touch** mettre qch au rencart; *Br Fam Fig* **to kick sb into touch** mettre qn sur la touche

(**j**) *(idiom) Fam* **to be an easy** *or* **soft touch** être un pigeon *ou* une poire

2 *vt* (**a**) *(make contact with)* toucher; **to touch lightly** frôler, effleurer; **his arm touched hers** son bras a touché le sien; **to touch sb on the shoulder** toucher qn à l'épaule; **she touched it with her foot** elle l'a touché du pied; **he loved to touch her hair** il adorait lui caresser les cheveux; **a smile touched her lips** un sourire effleura ses lèvres; **he touched his hat to her** il a porté la main à son chapeau pour la saluer; **since they met, her feet haven't touched the ground** depuis leur rencontre, elle est sur un nuage; **can you touch the bottom?** as-tu pied?; **the boat touched land** le bateau a accosté; **the law can't touch him** la loi ne peut rien contre lui

(**b**) *(handle)* toucher à; **don't touch her things** ne dérangez pas ses affaires; **I didn't touch it!** je n'y ai pas touché!; **don't touch anything until I get home** ne touchez à rien avant mon retour; **he swears he never touched her** il jure qu'il ne l'a jamais touchée; **I didn't touch him!** je n'ai pas touché à un cheveu de sa tête!; **nobody will touch him these days** personne ne veut plus rien avoir à faire avec lui; **stolen, are they, sorry, can't touch them** elles sont volées, hein, désolé, je ne veux rien avoir à faire avec ça; **if it's against the law, we won't touch it** si c'est illégal, nous ne nous en mêlerons pas

(**c**) *(adjoin)* jouxter; **Alaska touches Canada** l'Alaska et le Canada sont limitrophes

(**d**) *(usu neg) (eat, drink)* toucher à; **I never touch meat** je ne mange jamais de viande; **she didn't touch her vegetables** elle n'a pas touché aux légumes

(**e**) *(move emotionally)* émouvoir, toucher; **he touched the right note** il a touché la corde sensible; **he was very touched by her generosity** il a été très touché par sa générosité; **his remark touched a (raw) nerve** sa réflexion a touché un point sensible; *Br* **to touch sb to the quick** toucher qn au vif

(**f**) *(damage)* **fruit touched by frost** fruits abîmés par le gel; **the fire didn't touch the pictures** l'incendie a épargné les tableaux; **the war didn't touch this area** cette région a été épargnée par la guerre

(**g**) *(concern)* concerner, toucher; **the problem touches us all** ce problème nous concerne tous

(**h**) *(usu neg) Fam (rival)* valoir❑, égaler❑; **nothing can touch butter for cooking** rien ne vaut la cuisine au beurre; **no professor can touch him** c'est un professeur sans égal❑

(**i**) *Am (dial)* **touch 645** faites le 645

(**j**) *(idiom) Fam* **to touch sb for a loan** taper qn; **to touch sb for a fiver** taper qn de cinq livres

3 *vi* (**a**) *(be in contact)* se toucher

(**b**) *(adjoin → properties, areas)* se toucher, être contigus

(**c**) *(handle)* **do not touch!** *(sign)* défense de toucher

(**d**) *Naut* **the ship touches at Hong Kong** le navire fait escale à Hong Kong

▸▸ *Am* ***touch football*** = sorte de football sans tacles; ***touch hole*** *(in cannon)* lumière *f*; ***touch judge*** *(in rugby)* juge *m* de touche; ***touch kick*** *(in rugby)* coup *m* de pied en touche; ***touch rugby*** = sorte de rugby sans placage; ***touch screen*** écran *m* tactile; ***touch screen computer*** ordinateur *m* à écran tactile

▸**touch down 1** *vi* (**a**) *(aeroplane, spacecraft → on land)* atterrir; *(→ on sea)* amerrir

(**b**) *(in rugby)* marquer un essai

2 *vt sep (in rugby)* **to touch the ball down** marquer un essai

▸**touch off** *vt sep (explosive)* faire exploser, faire détoner; *Fig* déclencher, provoquer; **the ruling touched off widespread rioting** cette décision a provoqué une vague d'émeutes

▸**touch on** *vt insep* aborder; **his speech barely touched on the problem of unemployment** son discours a à peine effleuré le problème du chômage

▸**touch up** *vt sep* (**a**) *(painting, photograph)* faire des retouches à, retoucher; *(paintwork)* refaire; **to touch up one's make-up** rafraîchir son maquillage

(**b**) *Br very Fam (sexually)* peloter; **to touch oneself up** se toucher

'A Touch of Evil' *Welles* 'La Soif du mal'

touch-and-go *adj* **a touch-and-go situation** une situation dont l'issue est incertaine; **it was touch-and-go with him** il revient de loin; **it was touch-and-go whether we'd make it in time** nous avons bien failli ne pas arriver à temps; **right up to the minute they signed it was touch-and-go** jusqu'au moment où ils ont signé, rien n'était sûr

touchback ['tʌtʃbæk] *n (in American football)* touche *f* (derrière son propre but)

touchdown ['tʌtʃdaʊn] *n* (**a**) *(on land)* atterrissage *m*; *(on sea)* amerrissage *m* (**b**) *(in American football)* essai *m*

touché ['tu:ʃeɪ] *exclam* (**a**) *(in fencing)* touché! (**b**) *Fig* très juste!

touched [tʌtʃt] *adj* (**a**) *(with gratitude)* touché; **she was touched by his thoughtfulness** elle était touchée par sa délicatesse (**b**) *Br Fam (mad)* toqué, timbré, cinglé

touchily ['tʌtʃɪlɪ] *adv* avec susceptibilité

touchiness ['tʌtʃɪnɪs] *n* susceptibilité *f*

touching ['tʌtʃɪŋ] **1** *adj* touchant, émouvant

2 *prep Literary* touchant

3 *n* **touching is not allowed, no touching!** il est défendu de toucher

touchingly ['tʌtʃɪŋlɪ] *adv* d'une manière touchante

touch-in goal *n (in rugby)* en-but *m*

touchline ['tʌtʃlaɪn] *n Sport* ligne *f* de touche

touch-me-not *n Bot* impatiens *f*, balsamine *f*

touchpaper ['tʌtʃ,peɪpə(r)] *n* papier *m* nitraté

touch-sensitive *adj Comput (screen)* tactile; *(key, switch)* à effleurement

touchstone ['tʌtʃstəʊn] *n Miner & Fig* pierre *f* de touche

touch-tone *adj*

▸▸ ***touch-tone telephone*** téléphone *m* à touches

touch-type *vi* taper au toucher

touch-typing *n* dactylographie *f* au toucher

touch-up *n Art & Phot* retouche *f*; *(of object)* restauration *f*

touchwood ['tʌtʃwʊd] *n* amadou *m*

touchy ['tʌtʃɪ] (*compar* **touchier**, *superl* **touchiest**) *adj* (**a**) *(oversensitive)* susceptible, ombrageux; **she's touchy about her weight** elle est susceptible *ou* chatouilleuse sur la question de son poids; **he's very touchy** il se froisse *ou* se vexe pour un rien (**b**) *(matter, situation)* délicat, épineux

touchy-feely ['fi:lɪ] *adj Pej* qui affectionne les contacts physiques

tough [tʌf] **1** *adj* (**a**) *(resilient → person)* solide, résistant, robuste; *(→ meat)* dur, coriace; *(→ animal, plant)* résistant, robuste; *(→ substance, fabric)* solide, résistant; **you have to be tough to make it here** il faut être solide pour s'en tirer ici; **she's tough enough to win** elle a assez d'endurance pour gagner; *Br* **he's as tough as old boots** il est coriace; **this steak is as tough as old boots** ce n'est pas du bifteck, c'est de la semelle

(**b**) *(difficult)* dur, pénible; **a tough problem** un problème épineux; **it's tough on him** c'est un coup dur pour lui; **she made it tough for him** elle lui a mené la vie dure; **that's a tough act to follow** c'est difficile de faire mieux; **I gave them a tough time** je leur en ai fait voir de toutes les couleurs; **they had a tough time when their parents died** ils en ont connu de dures quand leurs parents sont morts; **it's tough work** c'est un travail pénible; **she had a tough life** elle n'a pas eu une vie facile; **he had a tough time passing the exam** il a eu du mal à réussir son examen; **Wall Street is a tough environment** Wall Street est un milieu très dur

(**c**) *(severe)* sévère; *(resolute)* dur, inflexible; **a tough economic policy** une politique économique draconienne; **a tough boss** un patron sévère; **to get tough with sb** se montrer dur avec qn; **the boss takes a tough line with people who are late** le patron ne plaisante pas avec les retardataires; **she's a tough person to deal with** elle ne fait pas de concessions; *Fam* **he's a tough cookie** il n'est pas commode; *Fam* **they're tough customers** ce sont des durs à cuire

(**d**) *(rough, hardened)* dur; **a tough criminal** un criminel endurci; *Fam* **a real tough guy** un vrai dur; **stay out of the tough neighbourhoods** évitez les quartiers dangereux

(**e**) *Fam (unfortunate)* malheureux❑; **that's really tough** ça, c'est vraiment vache; **it's tough for him, great for us** c'est dur pour lui, mais génial pour nous; **tough luck!** pas de pot!; **that's your tough luck!** tant pis pour vous!

2 *adv Fam* **to talk/act tough** jouer au dur

3 *vt (idiom) Fam* **to tough it out** tenir bon

4 *n Fam* dur(e) *m,f*

►► ***tough love*** = attitude stricte adoptée vis-à-vis d'un drogué, d'un alcoolique etc, dans le but de l'aider à se désaccoutumer

'Tough Guys Don't Dance' *Mailer* 'Les Vrais durs ne dansent pas'

toughen ['tʌfən] **1** *vt (metal, leather)* rendre plus solide, renforcer; *(person)* endurcir; *(conditions)* rendre plus sévère

2 *vi (metal, glass, leather)* durcir; *(person)* s'endurcir

►**toughen up** *vt sep & vi* = **toughen**

toughened ['tʌfənd] *adj (glass)* trempé

toughie ['tʌfɪ] *n Fam (person)* dur(e) *m,f*; *(problem)* casse-tête *m*; **question 5 was a real toughie** la question 5 était une horreur

toughly ['tʌflɪ] *adv (fight)* avec acharnement, âprement; *(speak)* durement, sans ménagement

tough-minded *adj* **he's a tough-minded man** il a la tête froide

toughness ['tʌfnɪs] *n* (**a**) *(of fabric, glass, leather)* solidité *f*; *(of meat)* dureté *f*; *(of metal)* ténacité *f*, résistance *f* (**b**) *(of job)* difficulté *f*; *(of struggle)* acharnement *m*, âpreté *f* (**c**) *(of character → strength)* force *f*, résistance *f*; *(→ hardness)* dureté *f*; *(→ severity)* inflexibilité *f*, sévérité *f*

toupee ['tu:peɪ] *n* postiche *m*

tour [tʊə(r)] **1** *n* (**a**) *(trip)* voyage *m*; **to go on a tour of the Highlands** partir en voyage dans les Highlands; **we're going on a tour of Eastern Europe** nous allons visiter les pays de l'Est; **a day tour** une excursion (d'un jour); **she's on a walking tour in Wales** elle fait une randonnée à pied dans le pays de Galles; **they're off on a world tour** ils sont partis faire le tour du monde

(**b**) *(of a building)* visite *f*; **we went on a tour of the factory** nous avons visité l'usine; **would you like a tour of the garden?** voulez-vous que je vous fasse visiter le jardin?

(**c**) *(by entertainer, band, sports team)* tournée *f*; **the dance company is on tour** la troupe de danseurs est en tournée; **to go on tour** faire une tournée; **is he taking the team on tour?** est-ce qu'il emmène l'équipe en tournée?; **she's taking the play on tour** elle donne la pièce en tournée

(**d**) *Sport (circuit)* circuit *m*

(**e**) *(in cycling)* tour *m*; **the Tour de France** le Tour de France; **the Tour of Italy** le Tour d'Italie, le Giro; **the Tour of Spain** le Tour d'Espagne, la Vuelta

2 *vt* (**a**) *(visit)* visiter; **they're touring Italy** ils visitent l'Italie, ils font du tourisme en Italie

(**b**) *(of entertainer, band, sports team)* faire une tournée dans; **the orchestra is touring the provinces** l'orchestre est en tournée en province; **they'll be touring the country later this year** ils feront une tournée dans tous le pays cette année

3 *vi* (**a**) *(tourist)* voyager, faire du tourisme; **we're just touring around** nous ne faisons que visiter la région; **we decided to tour through the Loire Valley** nous avons décidé de visiter la Vallée de la Loire

(**b**) *(entertainer, band, sports team)* être en tournée; **we spend most of the year touring** nous passons la plus grande partie de l'année en tournée; **we go touring every summer** nous partons en tournée tous les étés

►► ***tour brochure*** brochure *f ou* catalogue *m* de voyages; ***tour bus*** car *m* de tournée, car *m* aménagé pour les tournées; *Am* ***tour conductor, tour director*** *(courier)* accompagnateur(trice) *m,f*; *Mil* ***tour of duty*** service *m*; ***tour de force*** tour *m* de force; ***tour group*** groupe *m* (de touristes); ***tour guide*** *(person)* guide *mf*; *(book)* guide *m* touristique; ***tour of inspection*** tournée *f* d'inspection; ***tour leader,*** *Am* ***tour manager*** accompagnateur(trice) *m,f*; ***tour operator*** *(travel agency)* tour-opérateur *m*, voyagiste *m*; *(bus company)* compagnie *f* de cars *(qui organise des voyages)*; ***tour package*** forfait *m* voyage

tourer ['tʊərə(r)] *n* voiture *f* de tourisme

Tourette's syndrome [tʊə'rets-] *n Med* maladie *f* de Gilles de La Tourette

touring ['tʊərɪŋ] **1** *adj* **we had a touring holiday in the North of Italy** pour nos vacances nous avons visité le Nord de l'Italie

2 *n (UNCOUNT)* tourisme *m*, voyages *mpl* touristiques; **to do some touring** faire du tourisme

►► ***touring bicycle*** vélo *m* de randonnée; ***touring car*** voiture *f* de tourisme; *Theat* ***touring company*** *(permanently)* troupe *f* ambulante; *(temporarily)* troupe *f* en tournée; *Sport* ***touring party*** équipe *f* en tournée

tourism ['tʊərɪzəm] *n* tourisme *m*

tourism-generated *adj* généré par le tourisme

tourist ['tʊərɪst] **1** *n* touriste *mf*; *Sport* **the tourists** les visiteurs *mpl*

2 *comp (agency, centre)* de tourisme; *(information, ticket)* touristique; *(restaurant, pub)* pour touristes

►► ***tourist area*** zone *f* touristique; ***tourist attraction*** attrait *m ou* attraction *f ou* site *m* touristique; ***tourist board*** comité *m* du tourisme; *Br* ***tourist class*** classe *f* touriste; ***tourist destination*** destination *f* touristique; ***tourist guide*** *(book)* guide *m* touristique; *(person)* guide *mf* (touristique); ***tourist industry*** industrie *f* touristique; ***tourist (information) centre*** *or* ***office*** office *m* de tourisme, syndicat *m* d'initiative; ***tourist route*** itinéraire *m* touristique; ***tourist season*** saison *f* touristique; ***tourist trade*** tourisme *m*; **the country relies on its tourist trade** le pays vit du tourisme; ***tourist traffic*** flot *m* des touristes; ***tourist trap*** attrape-touristes *m inv*; ***Tourist Trophy*** = courses de moto sur l'île de Man; ***tourist visa*** visa *m* de touriste

touristic [tʊə'rɪstɪk] *adj* touristique

touristy ['tʊərɪstɪ] *adj Fam Pej* trop touristique❑

tourmaline ['tɔ:məli:n] *n Miner* tourmaline *f*

tournament ['tɔ:nəmənt] *n* tournoi *m*

tournedos ['tʊənədəʊ] *n Culin* tournedos *m*

tourney ['tʊənɪ] *n Hist & Am Sport* tournoi *m*

tourniquet ['tʊənɪkeɪ] *n* garrot *m*

tousle ['taʊzəl] *vt (hair)* ébouriffer; *(clothes)* friper, froisser

tousled ['taʊzəld] *adj (hair)* ébouriffé; *(clothes)* fripé, froissé; **his tousled appearance** son aspect débraillé

tout [taʊt] *Br* **1** *n* (**a**) **(ticket) tout** revendeur(euse) *m,f* de billets *(au marché noir)*

(**b**) *(in racing)* vendeur(euse) *m,f* de tuyaux

2 *vt* (**a**) *(peddle → tickets)* revendre *(au marché noir)*; *(→ goods)* vendre *(en vantant sa marchandise)*; **the cries of the market traders touting their wares** les cris des marchands essayant de racoler *ou* raccrocher les clients; **he's been touting those records around for days** ça fait des jours qu'il essaie de revendre ces disques; **she had touted her article around all the newspapers** elle avait fait le tour de tous les journaux pour essayer de placer son article

(**b**) *(promote)* **he is being touted as a future prime minister** on veut faire de lui un futur premier ministre

3 *vi* (**a**) **salesmen touting for custom** des vendeurs qui essaient d'attirer les clients; **they've been touting around for work/business** ils essayaient de trouver du travail/de se constituer une clientèle

(**b**) *(in racing → sell information)* vendre des pronostics; *(→ spy)* espionner

touting ['taʊtɪŋ] *n* (**a**) *(by salesmen)* racolage *m*, raccrochage *m* (**b**) *(in racing → selling information)* vente *f* de pronostics; *(→ spying)* espionnage *m*

tow [təʊ] **1** *vt* tirer; *(boat)* remorquer, touer; *(car)* remorquer; *(barge)* haler; **the ship was towed out of harbour** le navire a été remorqué hors du port; **they were towing a trailer** leur voiture tirait une remorque

2 *n* (**a**) *(action)* remorquage *m*; *(vehicle)* véhicule *m* en remorque; **to be** *Br* **on** *or Am* **under tow** être en remorque; **to give sb/sth a tow** remorquer qn/qch; **he took my car in tow** il a pris ma voiture en remorque; *Fam* **he always has his family in tow** il trimbale toujours toute sa famille avec lui; *Fam* **with six assistants in tow** avec six assistants dans son sillage

(**b**) *(line)* câble *m* de remorquage

(**c**) *Tex* filasse *f*, étoupe *f*

►► *Am* ***tow truck*** dépanneuse *f*

►**tow away** *vt sep* remorquer, prendre en remorque; *(of police)* emmener à la fourrière; **the police towed my car away** la police a emmené ma voiture à la fourrière; **you'll get towed away** tu vas te retrouver à la fourrière

towage ['təʊɪdʒ] *n (UNCOUNT) (act)* remorquage *m*; *(fee)* frais *mpl* de remorquage

toward [tə'wɔ:d] **1** *prep esp Am* = **towards**

2 *adj Arch (in progress)* en cours; *(imminent)* imminent

towards [tə'wɔ:dz], *esp Am* **toward** [tə'wɔ:d] *prep* (**a**) *(in the direction of)* dans la direction de, vers; **he turned towards her** il s'est tourné vers elle; **we headed towards Chicago** nous avons pris la direction de Chicago; **she was standing with her back towards him** elle lui tournait le dos; *Fig* **the negotiations are a first step towards peace** les négociations sont un premier pas sur le chemin de la paix; **they are working towards a solution** ils cherchent une solution; **'Towards a New Humanism'** *(book title)* 'Vers un nouvel humanisme'

(**b**) *(indicating attitude)* envers; **she's very hostile towards me** elle est très hostile à mon égard; **the public's attitude towards crime** l'attitude de l'opinion publique face à la criminalité; **his feelings towards her** ses sentiments pour elle, les sentiments qu'il éprouve pour elle

(**c**) *(as contribution to)* pour; **the money is going towards a new car** l'argent contribuera à l'achat d'une nouvelle voiture; **I'll give you something towards your expenses** je vous donnerai quelque chose pour payer une partie de vos frais

(**d**) *(near → in time)* vers; *(→ in space)* près de; **towards the end of his life** vers *ou* sur la fin de sa vie; **towards the end of the century** vers la fin du siècle; **towards the middle** vers le milieu

tow-away zone *n Am* = zone de ramassage des véhicules en infraction

towbar ['təʊbɑ:(r)] *n* barre *f* de remorquage

towboat ['təʊbəʊt] *n* remorqueur *m*

tow-coloured *adj* (blond) filasse *(inv)*

towel ['taʊəl] (*Br pt & pp* **towelled,** *cont* **towelling,** *Am pt & pp* **toweled** *or* **towelled,** *cont* **toweling** *or* **towelling**) **1** *n* serviette *f* (de toilette); *(for hands)* essuie-mains *m inv*; *(for glasses)* essuie-verres *m inv*; (*Br* **tea** *or Am* **dish) towel** torchon *m* à vaisselle

2 *vt* frotter avec une serviette; **to towel oneself dry** *or* **down** s'essuyer *ou* se sécher avec une serviette

►► *Am* ***towel bar,*** *Br* ***towel rail*** porte-serviettes *m inv*; ***towel ring*** porte-serviettes *m inv*

►**towel off** *vi* se sécher

towelette [taʊə'let] *n Am* lingette *f*

towelhead ['taʊəlhed] *n Fam (Arab)* raton *m*, bicot *m*, = terme injurieux désignant un Arabe

towelling, *Am* **toweling** ['taʊəlɪŋ] **1** *n* (**a**) *(material)* tissu *m* éponge (**b**) *(drying)* **to give sb a towelling (down)** frictionner qn avec une serviette

2 *comp (robe, shirt)* en tissu éponge

tower ['taʊə(r)] **1** *n* (**a**) *(building)* tour *f*; **church tower** clocher *m*; *Fig* **he's a tower of strength** c'est un roc; **you've been a tower of strength to me** ton soutien m'a été précieux

(**b**) *Comput* boîtier *m* vertical, tour *f*

(**c**) *(for camera)* échafaudage *m* pour caméra

2 *vi* **to tower above** *or* **over sth** dominer qch; **the skyscraper towers above** *or* **over the city** le gratte-ciel domine la ville; **he towered above** *or* **over me** j'étais tout petit à côté de lui; *Fig* **she**

towers above *or* **over her contemporaries** elle domine de loin ses contemporains

►► ***the Tower of Babel*** la tour de Babel; *Br* ***tower block*** tour *f* d'habitation; ***Tower Bridge*** Tower Bridge *m*; ***tower crane*** grue *f* à pylône; ***the Tower of London*** la Tour de Londres; *Comput* ***tower system*** système *m* à boîtier vertical, système *m* à tour

towering ['taʊərɪŋ] *adj* (**a**) *(very high → skyscraper, tree, statue)* très haut, imposant; *(→ person)* très grand; *(→ ambitions)* sans bornes; **a towering great figure of a man** un géant (**b**) *(excessive)* démesuré; **in a towering rage** dans une colère noire

'The Towering Inferno' *Guillermin* 'La Tour infernale'

tow-headed *adj Br* aux cheveux (blond) filasse

towing ['təʊɪŋ] *n* remorque *f*, remorquage *m*, touage *m*; *(from towpath)* halage *m*; *Aut* **suspended towing** remorquage *m* suspendu

►► ***towing charge*** (droit *m ou* frais *mpl* de) remorquage *m*; ***towing pole*** timon *m* de remorquage; ***towing rod*** barre *f* de remorquage; ***towing rope*** câble *m* de remorquage; ***towing weight*** charge *f* remorquable; *Admin* ***towing zone*** zone *f* de touage

towline ['təʊlaɪn] *n* câble *m* de remorque; *(to towpath)* câble *m* de halage

town [taʊn] *n* (**a**) *(urban area)* ville *f*; **a country town** une ville de province; **to live in a small town** habiter une *ou* dans une petite ville; **she's going into town** elle va en ville; **he's out of town this week** il n'est pas là *ou* il est en déplacement cette semaine; *Am* **we're from out of town** nous ne sommes pas d'ici; **the best pizzas in town** les meilleures pizzas de la ville; **it's the talk of the town** toute la ville en parle; **town and gown** = expression désignant collectivement les habitants et les étudiants de certaines villes universitaires et soulignant les différences de culture entre les deux milieux

(**b**) *(main shopping or business area)* centre-ville *m*; **to go into town** aller en ville; **I work in town** je travaille en ville; *Fam* **they went out on the town last night** hier soir, ils ont fait une virée en ville; *Fam* **to have a night (out) on the town** faire la noce *ou* la java en ville; *Fam* **to go to town** *(make great effort)* se mettre en quatre; *Fam* **they really went to town on the stadium** pour le stade ils n'ont pas fait les choses à moitié *ou* ils ont vraiment mis le paquet

►► *Fam Pej* ***town bike*** *(promiscuous woman)* Marie-couche-toi-là *f*; **she's the town bike** il n'y a que le train qui ne lui est pas passé dessus; ***town centre*** centre-ville *m*; *Hist* ***town clerk*** secrétaire *mf* de mairie; ***town council*** conseil *m* municipal; ***town councillor*** conseiller(ère) *m,f* municipal(e); ***town crier*** garde-champêtre *m*; *Br* ***town dweller*** citadin(e) *m,f*; ***town gas*** gaz *m* de ville; ***town hall*** hôtel *m* de ville, mairie *f*; ***town house*** *(gen)* maison *f* en ville; *(aristocratic mansion)* ≃ hôtel *m* particulier; *Am (semi-detached house)* maison *f* mitoyenne (en ville); *Am* ***town meeting*** = assemblée générale des habitants d'une ville; ***town planner*** urbaniste *mf*; ***town planning*** urbanisme *m*

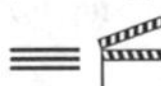

'Mr Deeds Goes to Town' *Capra* 'L'Extravagant Mr Deeds'

townee ['taʊniː] *n Fam Pej* citadin(e)[❑] *m,f*, rat *m* des villes

townhome ['taʊnhəʊm] *n Am* maison *f* mitoyenne

townie = **townee**

townscape ['taʊnskeɪp] *n* paysage *m* urbain

townsfolk ['taʊnzfəʊk] *npl* citadins *mpl*

township ['taʊnʃɪp] *n* (**a**) *(gen)* commune *f* (**b**) *(in South Africa)* township *f* (**c**) *Br Hist* = division d'une paroisse (**d**) *(in Canada, US)* canton *m* (**e**) *(in Australia)* petite agglomération *f*

►► ***township violence*** la violence dans les ghettos noirs

townsman ['taʊnzmən] *(pl* **townsmen** [-mən]) *n* citadin *m*; **my fellow townsmen** mes concitoyens

townspeople ['taʊnz,piːpəl] *npl* citadins *mpl*

townswoman ['taʊnz,wʊmən] *(pl* **townswomen** [-,wɪmɪn]) *n* habitante *f* de la ville, citadine *f*

towny *(pl* **townies**) = **townee**

towpath ['təʊpɑːθ, *pl* -pɑːðz] *n* chemin *m* de halage

towrope ['təʊrəʊp] *n* câble *m* de remorque; *(to towpath)* câble *m* de halage

tow-start *n* **to give sb a tow-start** faire démarrer qn en remorque

toxaemia, *Am* **toxemia** [tɒk'siːmɪə] *n Med* toxémie *f*

toxic ['tɒksɪk] *adj* toxique

►► *Med* ***toxic shock syndrome*** syndrome *m* du choc toxique; ***toxic waste*** déchets *mpl* toxiques

toxicant ['tɒksɪkənt] **1** *adj* toxique

2 *n* toxique *m*

toxicity [tɒk'sɪsətɪ] *n* toxicité *f*

toxicogenic [,tɒksɪkəʊ'dʒenɪk] *adj* toxicogène

toxicological [,tɒksɪkə'lɒdʒɪkəl] *adj* toxicologique

toxicologist [,tɒksɪ'kɒlədʒɪst] *n* toxicologue *mf*

toxicology [,tɒksɪ'kɒlədʒɪ] *n* toxicologie *f*

toxicosis [,tɒksɪ'kəʊsɪs] *(pl* **toxicoses** [-siːz]) *n Med* toxicose *f*

toxin ['tɒksɪn] *n* toxine *f*

toxocara [tɒksə'kɑːrə] *n Zool* toxocara *f*

toxocariasis [tɒksəkə'raɪəsɪs] *n Med* toxocarose *f*

toxoid ['tɒksɔɪd] *n Med* toxoïde *m*, anatoxine *f*

toxoplasmosis [,tɒksəʊplæz'məʊsɪs] *n Med* toxoplasmose *f*

toy [tɔɪ] **1** *n* jouet *m*

2 *comp* (**a**) *(car, train)* miniature

(**b**) *(box, chest, drawer)* à jouets

►► ***toy dog*** chien *m* nain; ***toy poodle*** caniche *m* nain; ***toy shop*** magasin *m* de jouets; ***toy soldier*** soldat *m* de plomb; ***toy theatre*** théâtre *m* de marionnettes; ***toy trumpet*** trompette *f* d'enfant

►**toy with** *vt insep* jouer avec; **to toy with one's food** manger du bout des dents; **she toyed with the idea of going home** elle jouait avec l'idée de rentrer chez elle; **he was toying with her affections** il jouait avec ses sentiments

toyboy ['tɔɪbɔɪ] *n Br Fam* = jeune amant d'une femme plus âgée; **she's got herself a toyboy** elle s'est déniché un petit jeune *ou* un jeune amant

toymaker ['tɔɪ,meɪkə(r)] *n* fabricant *m* de jouets

tpi *Comput (written abbr* **tracks per inch**) pistes *fpl* par pouce

TQC [,tiːkjuː'siː] *n (abbr* **total quality control**) QG *f*

TQM [,tiːkjuː'em] *n (abbr* **total quality management**) gestion *f* de la QG

trabecula [trə'bekjʊlə] *n Anat* trabécule *f*

trace [treɪs] **1** *n* (**a**) *(sign)* trace *f*; **to disappear** *or* **to sink without trace** disparaître sans laisser de traces; **there is no trace of it now** il n'en reste plus aucune trace; **there's not a trace of your wallet anywhere in the house** ton portefeuille n'est nulle part dans la maison; **we've lost all trace of her** nous ignorons ce qu'elle est devenue

(**b**) *(small amount)* trace *f*, **traces of cocaine were found in his blood** l'analyse de son sang a révélé des traces de cocaïne; **without a trace of fear** sans la moindre peur; **there was the trace of a smile on her face** il y avait l'ombre d'un sourire sur son visage

(**c**) *(trail)* trace *f* de pas, piste *f*; *Am (path)* piste *f*, sentier *m*

(**d**) *(drawing)* tracé *m*

(**e**) *Tech* **a radar trace** la trace d'un spot

(**f**) *(harness)* trait *m*; **in the traces** attelé; *Fig* **to kick over the traces** *(person → rebel)* ruer dans les brancards; *(→ break free)* s'émanciper

2 *vt* (**a**) *(follow trail of)* suivre la trace de; *(track down → object)* retrouver; **she traced him as far as New York** elle a suivi sa piste jusqu'à New York; **I can't trace any reference to that letter** je ne trouve aucune mention de cette lettre; **they traced the murder to him** ils ont finalement établi qu'il était le meurtrier; **they traced the lost shipment** ils ont retrouvé la cargaison égarée; **we eventually traced the problem to a computer error** nous avons finalement découvert que le problème était dû à une erreur de l'ordinateur

(**b**) *(follow development of)* suivre; **the film traces the rise to power of a gangland boss** ce film relate l'ascension d'un chef de gang

(**c**) *(mark outline of)* tracer, dessiner; *(with tracing paper)* décalquer; **he traced (out) a map in the sand with his finger** avec son doigt, il a dessiné un plan sur le sable

►► ***trace element*** oligo-élément *m*; ***trace fossil*** trace *f* fossile

►**trace back 1** *vt sep* **to trace sth back to its source** retrouver l'origine de qch; **she can trace her ancestry back to the 15th century** sa famille remonte au XVème siècle; **he traced the rumour back to her** il a découvert qu'elle était à l'origine de cette rumeur; **the cause of the epidemic was traced back to an infected water supply** on a découvert que l'épidémie était due à la contamination de l'alimentation en eau

2 *vi Am* (**a**) *(go back)* **to trace back to** remonter à; **his family traces back to the Norman Conquest** sa famille remonte à la conquête de l'Angleterre par les Normands

(**b**) *(be due to)* être dû à

traceability [,treɪsə'bɪlɪtɪ] *n (of meat, product)* traçabilité *f*; *(of parcel)* suivi *m*

traceable ['treɪsəbəl] *adj (gen)* dont on peut retrouver l'origine; *(meat, product)* traçable, dont on peut établir l'origine; *(parcel)* qu'on peut suivre; **to be traceable to** remonter à

tracer ['treɪsə(r)] *n* (**a**) *(person)* traceur(euse) *m,f*; *(device)* traçoir *m* (**b**) *Chem* traceur *m*

►► ***tracer bullet*** balle *f* traçante

traceried ['treɪsərɪd] *adj Archit* à réseau, à remplage

tracery ['treɪsərɪ] *(pl* **traceries**) *n* (**a**) *(design)* filigrane *m*, dentelles *fpl*; *(on leaf, insect wing)* nervures *fpl* (**b**) *Archit* réseau *m*

trachea [trə'kiːə] *(pl* **tracheae** [-'kiːiː] *or* **tracheas**) *n* trachée *f*

tracheal [trə'kiːəl] *adj Anat* trachéal

tracheate [trə'kiːeɪt] *Zool* **1** *adj* trachéate

2 *n* trachéate *m*

►► ***tracheate arthropod*** trachéate *m*

tracheitis [,trækɪ'aɪtɪs] *n Med* trachéite *f*

tracheoscopy [,trækɪ'ɒskəpɪ] *n Med* trachéoscopie *f*

tracheostomy [,trækɪ'ɒstəmɪ] *(pl* **tracheostomies**) *n Med* trachéostomie *f*

tracheotomy [,trækɪ'ɒtəmɪ] *(pl* **tracheotomies**) *n Med* trachéotomie *f*

trachoma [trə'kəʊmə] *n Med* trachome *m*

trachyte ['trækaɪt] *n Miner* trachyte *m*

tracing ['treɪsɪŋ] *n (process)* calquage *m*; *(result)* calque *m*

►► ***tracing paper*** papier-calque *m inv*, papier *m* à décalquer

track [træk] **1** *n* (**a**) *(path, route)* chemin *m*, sentier *m*; *(of planet, star, aeroplane)* trajectoire *f*; **a mountain track** un sentier de montagne; **a farm track** un chemin de campagne; *Fig* **to be on the right track** être sur la bonne voie; *Fig* **he's on the wrong track** il fait fausse route; *Fam* **you're way off track!** tu es complètement à côté de la plaque!

(**b**) *Sport (for running)* piste *f*; *Br* **motor-racing track** autodrome *m*; **track and field** athlétisme *m*; **track and field events** épreuves *fpl* d'athlétisme; *Cycling* **to do a track stand** faire du surplace

(**c**) *Rail* voie *f*, rails *mpl*; **the train jumped the tracks** le train a déraillé *ou* a quitté les rails; *esp Am* **to live on the right/wrong side of the tracks** habiter un bon/mauvais quartier; *esp Am* **to come from the wrong side of the tracks** être issu d'un milieu défavorisé

(**d**) *(mark, trail)* trace *f*, piste *f*; *(of animal, person)* piste *f*; *(of boat)* sillage *m*; **to be on sb's track** *or* **tracks** être sur la piste de qn; **the terrorists had covered their tracks well** les terroristes n'avaient pas laissé de traces; **to throw sb off the track** dépister qn; **that should throw them off my track** avec ça, je devrais arriver à les semer; **to keep track of** suivre; **it's hard to keep track of her, she moves around so much** il est difficile de rester en contact avec elle, elle bouge tout le temps; **we like to keep track of current events** nous aimons nous tenir au courant de l'actualité; **why can't you keep track of your things?** tu ne peux pas faire attention où tu mets tes affaires?; **we'll have to keep track of the time!** il ne faudra pas oublier l'heure!; **don't lose track of those files** n'égarez pas ces dossiers; **they've lost track of the situation** ils ne suivent plus *ou* ne sont plus au courant de ce qui se passe; **I lost track of them years ago** j'ai perdu le contact avec eux *ou* je les ai perdus de vue il y a des années; **she lost all track of time** elle a perdu toute notion du temps; **he lost track of what he was saying** il a perdu le fil de ce qu'il disait; *Fam* **to make tracks** mettre les voiles; **she made tracks for home** elle a filé chez elle

(**e**) *(on CD, LP, tape)* morceau *m*; *Comput (of disk)* piste *f*; *Comput* **tracks per inch** pistes *fpl* par pouce

(**f**) *Aut (of tracked vehicle)* chenille *f*; *(tyre tread)* chape *f*; *(space between wheels)* écartement *m*

(**g**) *Am Sch* classe *f* de niveau

(**h**) *Fam Drugs slang* trace *f* de piqûre

2 *vt* (**a**) *(follow → animal)* suivre à la trace, filer; *(→ rocket)* suivre la trajectoire de; *(→ criminal)* traquer

(**b**) *Am* **don't track mud into the house!** ne traîne pas de boue dans la maison!

3 *vi* (**a**) *(stylus)* suivre le sillon

(**b**) *(with camera)* faire un traveling *ou* travelling

►► *Aut* ***track arm*** bras *m* de direction; *Rail* ***track bed*** plate-forme *f*; *Sport* ***track event*** épreuve *f* sur piste; *Am Sport* ***track meet*** rencontre *f* d'athlétisme; *Sport* ***track racing*** *(UNCOUNT)* courses *fpl* sur piste; *Sport & Fig* ***track record*** *(past record, career to date)* antécédents *mpl*; *(list of achievements)* palmarès *m*; **she has a good track record** elle a fait ses preuves; **he doesn't have a very good track record for punctuality** il n'est pas réputé pour sa ponctualité; **in view of his track record of getting home late every Friday night...** vu l'habitude qu'il a de rentrer tard tous les vendredis soirs...; **a company with a good/poor track record in winning export orders** une entreprise avec un bon/mauvais palmarès sur le plan des commandes à l'exportation; **no wonder the insurance is high with your track record!** pas étonnant que l'assurance soit chère avec ton palmarès!; **given the government's track record in the field of cutting benefits** vu les antecedents du gouvernement en matière de réduction des prestations sociales; *Br Aut* ***track rod*** biellette *f* de connexion; *Sport* ***track shoe*** chaussure *f* d'athlétisme; *Sport* ***track star*** star *f* de l'athlétisme; *Am Sch* ***track system*** = répartition des élèves en sections selon leurs aptitudes; ***track vehicle*** véhicule *m* chenillé

►**track down** *vt sep* retrouver, localiser; *(animal, criminal)* traquer et capturer

trackball ['trækbɔːl] *n Comput* boule *f* de commande, trackball *m ou f*

tracked [trækt] *adj (vehicle)* chenillé, à chenilles

tracker ['trækə(r)] *n* (**a**) *(person → gen)* poursuivant(e) *m,f*; *(→ in hunting)* traqueur(euse) *m,f* (**b**) *(device)* appareil *m* de poursuite (**c**) *TV* machiniste *m* de travelling

►► ***tracker dog*** chien *m* policier; *Fin* ***tracker fund*** fonds *m* indiciel *ou* à gestion indicielle

tracking ['trækɪŋ] **1** *n* (**a**) *(following)* poursuite *f*; *(of missile)* repérage *m* (**b**) *Am Sch* = répartition des élèves en sections selon leurs aptitudes

2 *comp (radar, satellite)* de poursuite

►► *Cin & TV* ***tracking shot*** traveling *m*, travelling *m*; *Astron* ***tracking station*** station *f* d'observation

tracklayer ['træk,leɪə(r)] *n Am* poseur *m* de rails

tracklaying ['træk,leɪɪŋ] *adj*

►► ***tracklaying vehicle*** véhicule *m* à chenilles

trackless ['trækləs] *adj* (**a**) *(forest)* sans chemins, sans sentiers (**b**) *(vehicle)* sans chenilles

tracklist ['træklɪst] *n* liste *f* des morceaux *ou* des chansons

trackman ['trækmən] (*pl* **trackmen** [-mən]) *n Am Rail* = responsable de l'entretien de la voie

trackpad ['trækpæd] *n Comput* tablette *f* tactile

tracksuit ['træksuːt] *n* survêtement *m*

tract [trækt] *n* (**a**) *(pamphlet)* tract *m* (**b**) *(large area)* étendue *f*; *Am (housing estate)* lotissement *m*; *Mining* gisement *m*; **a tract house** un pavillon (**c**) *Anat* **respiratory/digestive tract** appareil *m* respiratoire/digestif

tractability [,træktə'bɪlɪtɪ] *n (of person, animal)* caractère *m* accommodant; *(of material)* malléabilité *f*; *(of problem)* caractère *m* soluble

tractable ['træktəbəl] *adj (person, animal)* accommodant; *(material)* malléable; *(problem)* soluble, facile à résoudre

tractableness ['træktəbəlnɪs] = **tractability**

Tractarianism [træk'teərɪənɪzəm] *n Rel* le mouvement *m* d'Oxford

tractate ['trækteɪt] *n Formal* traité *m*

traction ['trækʃən] *n* (**a**) *Tech* traction *f*; **electric/steam traction** traction *f* électrique/à vapeur; (**b**) *Med* **to be in traction** être en extension; **traction of the tongue** *(artificial respiration)* tractions *fpl* rythmées de la langue

►► ***traction cable*** câble *m* tracteur; *Aut* ***traction control*** contrôle *m* de traction; ***traction engine*** locomotive *f*; *Med* ***traction splint*** attelle *f* d'extension; ***traction wheels*** roues *fpl* motrices

tractive ['træktɪv] *adj Tech* tractif

►► ***tractive force*** effort *m* de traction

tractor ['træktə(r)] *n (on farm)* tracteur *m*; *Tech* locomobile *f*

►► *Comput* ***tractor feed*** dispositif *m* d'entraînement à picots; ***tractor holes*** *(on tractor wheel)* trous *mpl* à ergots; ***tractor pin*** *(in tractor wheel)* ergot *m* de tracteur; ***tractor wheel*** *(on printer etc)* roue *f* d'entraînement

tractor-drawn *adj* tracté

tractor-trailer *n Am* semi-remorque *m*

trad [træd] *Fam* **1** *adj* traditionnel ❑

2 *n Mus* jazz *m* traditionnel des années 30 ❑

►► *Mus* ***trad jazz*** jazz *m* traditionnel des années 30 ❑

trade [treɪd] **1** *n* (**a**) *(UNCOUNT) Com* commerce *m*, affaires *fpl*; **the clothing trade** la confection, l'industrie *f* de la confection; **she is in the tea trade** elle est dans le commerce du thé, elle est négociante en thé; **trade is brisk** les affaires vont bien; **to do a good** *or* **roaring trade** faire des affaires en or; **it's good for trade** cela fait marcher le commerce; **domestic/foreign trade** commerce *m* intérieur/extérieur; **retail/wholesale trade** commerce *m* de détail/de gros

(**b**) *(illicit dealings)* trafic *m*; **the drug trade** le trafic de drogue

(**c**) *(vocation, occupation)* métier *m*; **she is an electrician by trade** elle est électricienne de son métier *ou* de son état; **to be in the trade** être du métier; **everyone to his trade** chacun son métier; **as we say in the trade** comme on dit dans le métier; **open to members of the trade only** pour les membres de la profession seulement

(**d**) *(exchange)* échange *m*; **to do a trade** faire un échange; **fair trade** échange *m* équitable

(**e**) *(regular customers)* clientèle *f*

(**f**) *Am (transaction)* marché *m*, affaire *f*

2 *vt (exchange)* échanger, troquer; **he traded a marble for a toffee** il a échangé *ou* troqué une bille contre un caramel; **they traded insults over the dinner table** ils ont échangé des insultes pendant le dîner

3 *vi* (**a**) *(businessman, country)* faire du commerce, commercer ; **he trades in clothing** il est négociant en confection, il est dans la confection; **what name do you trade under?** quel est votre raison sociale?; **to trade at a loss** vendre à perte; **to trade with sb** avoir *ou* entretenir des relations commerciales avec qn; **they stopped trading with Iran** ils ont arrêté toute relation commerciale avec l'Iran

(**b**) *Am (private individual)* faire ses achats; **to trade at** *or* **with** faire ses courses à *ou* chez

(**c**) *Fin (shares, commodity, currency)* se négocier, s'échanger (**at** à); **corn is trading at £25** le maïs se négocie à 25 livres

4 trades *npl (winds)* alizés *mpl*

►► ***trade advertising*** publicité *f* auprès des intermédiaires; ***trade agreement*** accord *m* commercial; ***trade allowance*** remise *f* entre professionnels; ***trade association*** association *f* professionnelle; ***trade balance*** balance *f* commerciale; ***trade ban*** interdiction *f* de commerce; ***trade barriers*** barrières *fpl* douanières; ***trade bills*** effets *mpl* de commerce; ***trade body*** syndicat *m* professionnel; *Acct* ***trade credit*** crédit *m* fournisseur *ou* commercial; *Acct* ***trade creditor*** créancier(ère) *m,f* d'exploitation; ***trade cycle*** cycle *m* de commercialisation; *Acct* ***trade debt*** dettes *fpl* d'exploitation; *Acct* ***trade debtor*** compte *m ou* créance *f* client; ***trade deficit*** balance *f* commerciale déficitaire, déficit *m* extérieur *ou* commercial; ***trade delegation*** délégation *f* commerciale; *Br* ***the Trade Descriptions Act*** = loi qui empêche la publicité mensongère; ***trade directory*** annuaire *m* de commerce; ***trade discount*** *(to customer)* escompte *m* commercial, escompte *m* d'usage; *(to retailer)* escompte *m* professionnel, remise *f* professionnelle; ***trade embargo*** embargo *m* commercial; ***trade exhibition*** foire-exposition *f*, exposition *f* commerciale; *Br* ***trade fair*** foire *f* commerciale, salon *m*; ***trade figures*** chiffre *m* d'affaires; ***trade gap*** déficit *m* commercial; ***trade journal*** journal *m* professionnel, revue *f* professionnelle; ***trade marketing*** marketing *m* commercial, trade marketing *m*; ***trade mission*** mission *f* commerciale; ***trade name*** *(of product)* nom *m* de marque; *(of firm)* raison *f* commerciale; ***trade paper*** revue *f* spécialisée; *Br Aut* ***trade plate*** plaque *f* d'immatriculation provisoire; ***trade policy*** politique *f* commerciale; ***trade press*** presse *f* spécialisée, presse *f* professionnelle; ***trade price*** *Com* prix *m* marchand; *St Exch* prix *m* de négociation; ***trade promotion*** promotion *f* auprès des intermédiaires; ***trade publication*** revue *f* spécialisée *ou* professionnelle; ***trade register*** registre *m* du commerce; ***trade route*** route *f* commerciale; ***trade secret*** secret *m* de fabrication; *Hum* **she won't tell me her recipe, she says it's a trade secret!** elle ne veut pas me donner sa recette, elle dit que c'est un secret!; ***trade show*** salon *m* (professionnel); ***trade ticket*** avis *m* d'opéré, avis *m* d'opération sur titres; *Br* ***the Trades Union Congress*** = la Confédération des syndicats britanniques; ***trade(s) union*** syndicat *m*; **to join a trade(s) union** se syndiquer; **the workers formed a trade(s) union** les ouvriers ont formé un syndicat; **I am in the trade(s) union** je suis syndiqué, j'appartiens au syndicat; ***trade unionism*** syndicalisme *m*; ***trade(s) unionist*** syndicaliste *mf*; ***trade union tariff*** tarif *m* syndical; ***trade wind*** alizé *m*

►**trade down** *vi* (**a**) *St Exch* acheter des valeurs basses

(**b**) *(car owner)* changer pour un modèle moins cher

►**trade in** *vt sep* **I traded my television/car in for a new one** ils ont repris mon vieux téléviseur/ma vieille voiture quand j'ai acheté le nouveau/la nouvelle

►**trade off 1** *vt sep (exchange)* échanger, troquer; *(as a compromise)* accepter en compensation; **to trade sth off against sth** laisser *ou* abandonner qch pour qch; **they have traded off quality against speed** ils ont fait primer la rapidité sur la qualité; **you can't ask me to trade off reputation against profit** vous ne pouvez pas me demander de choisir entre ma réputation et un profit

2 *vi Am* **they trade off every year for first place** ils sont premiers chacun leur tour tous les ans

►**trade on** *vt insep* exploiter, profiter de; **he trades on her gullibility** il profite de sa crédulité; **I'd hate to trade on your kindness** je ne voudrais pas abuser de votre gentillesse

►**trade up** *vi* (**a**) *St Exch* acheter des valeurs hautes

(**b**) *(car owner)* changer pour un modèle plus cher

tradeable ['treɪdəbəl] *adj St Exch* négociable

traded option ['treɪdɪd-] *n St Exch* option *f* négociable, option *f* cotée

trade-in *n* reprise *f*; **will he accept a trade-in?** acceptera-t-il la reprise?; **they took my old refrigerator as a trade-in** ils ont repris mon vieux réfrigérateur

►► ***trade-in allowance*** (valeur *f* de) reprise *f*; ***trade-in facility*** facilité *f* de reprise; ***trade-in price*** prix *m* à la reprise; ***trade-in value*** valeur *f* de reprise

trademark ['treɪdmɑːk] **1** *n* marque *f* (de fabrique); *Fig* signe *m* caractéristique; *Fig* **these close-up shots are her trademark** ces gros-plans sont sa marque *ou* sa signature; *Fig* **his trademark moustache** ses fameuses moustaches

2 *vt (product → label)* apposer une marque sur; *(→ register)* déposer

trade-off *n (exchange)* échange *m*; *(compromise)* compromis *m*; **there's always a trade-off between speed and accuracy** il faut toujours faire un compromis entre la vitesse et la précision
▸▸ *Mktg* ***trade-off analysis*** analyse *f* conjointe

trader ['treɪdə(r)] *n* **(a)** *(gen)* commerçant(e) *m,f*, marchand(e) *m,f*; *(on large scale)* négociant(e) *m,f* **(b)** *(ship)* navire *m* marchand *ou* de commerce **(c)** *St Exch* opérateur(trice) *m,f*

tradescantia [,trædɪ'skæntɪə] *n Bot* tradescantia *m*, tradescantie *f*

tradesman ['treɪdzmən] (*pl* **tradesmen** [-mən]) *n* **(a)** *(trader)* commerçant *m*, marchand *m* **(b)** *(skilled workman)* ouvrier *m* qualifié
▸▸ ***tradesman's entrance*** entrée *f* de service *ou* des fournisseurs; *Br Vulg (anus)* entrée *f* de service

tradespeople ['treɪdz,pi:pəl] *npl esp Br* commerçants *mpl*

trading ['treɪdɪŋ] **1** *n (buying and selling)* commerce *m*, négoce *m*; *(illicit dealing)* trafic *m*; **trading on the Stock Exchange was heavy** le volume de transactions à la Bourse était important
2 *comp (partner)* commercial; **France is our most important trading partner** la France est notre principal partenaire commercial
▸▸ *Acct* ***trading account*** compte *m* d'exploitation générale; ***trading bank*** banque *f* commerciale; ***trading capital*** capital *m* engagé *ou* de roulement; ***trading company*** société *f* commerciale; *St Exch* ***trading day*** jour *m* de Bourse; *Br* ***trading estate*** zone *f* artisanale et commerciale; *St Exch* ***trading floor*** corbeille *f*, parquet *m*; ***trading hours*** heures *fpl* d'ouverture; *St Exch* horaires *fpl* des criées; *St Exch* ***trading instrument*** outil *m* de spéculation; ***trading licence*** carte *f* de commerce; ***trading loss*** perte *f*; **trading losses for the past year were heavy** les pertes subies pour l'exercice de l'année écoulée ont été lourdes; *St Exch* ***trading member*** intermédiaire *m* négociateur; *St Exch* ***trading month*** mois *m* d'échéance; ***trading nation*** nation *f* commerçante; *St Exch* ***trading order*** ordre *m* de négociation; *Am* ***trading post*** *(store)* comptoir *m* commercial; *St Exch* parquet *m*, corbeille *f*; *Com* ***trading profit*** bénéfice(s) *m(pl)* d'exploitation; *Acct* ***trading and profit and loss account*** compte *m* de résultat; *St Exch* ***trading range*** écart *m* de prix, fourchette *f* de cotation; **prices are stuck in a trading range** les prix ne varient pas beaucoup; *St Exch* ***trading rate*** cours *m*; ***trading results*** résultats *mpl* de l'exercice; *St Exch* ***trading room*** salle *f* des changes *ou* des marchés; *St Exch* ***trading session*** séance *f* boursière; ***trading stamp*** timbre-prime *m*, vignette-épargne *f*; ***trading standards*** normes *fpl* de conformité; ***trading standards office*** ≃ Direction *f* de la consommation et de la répression des fraudes; ***trading year*** année *f* d'exploitation, exercice *m*

tradition [trə'dɪʃən] *n* tradition *f*, coutume *f*; **it's in the best tradition of New Year's Eve parties** c'est dans la plus pure tradition des réveillons du Nouvel An; **tradition has it that...** la tradition veut que...; **the tradition that...** la tradition selon laquelle... *ou* qui veut que...; **a comedian in the tradition of Chaplin** un comédien dans la lignée de Chaplin; **to break with tradition** rompre avec la tradition

traditional [trə'dɪʃənəl] *adj* traditionnel; **it is traditional to sing Auld Lang Syne at New Year** il est de tradition de chanter Auld Lang Syne au Nouvel An; **this school is a very traditional one** cette école est très traditionnelle
▸▸ ***traditional dress*** costume *m* traditionnel

traditionalism [trə'dɪʃənəlɪzəm] *n* traditionalisme *m*

traditionalist [trə'dɪʃənəlɪst] **1** *n* traditionaliste *mf*
2 *adj* traditionaliste

traditionally [trə'dɪʃənəlɪ] *adv* traditionnellement

traduce [trə'dju:s] *vt Formal (malign)* calomnier, diffamer

traffic ['træfɪk] (*pt & pp* **trafficked**, *cont* **trafficking**) **1** *n* **(a)** *(on roads)* circulation *f*; *(rail, air, maritime)* trafic *m*; **holiday traffic** *(outward)* la circulation des grands départs; *(homeward)* la circulation des grands retours; **the traffic is heavy/light** la circulation est dense/fluide; **traffic is building up** la circulation augmente; **there is a great deal of traffic on the roads** les routes sont encombrées; **traffic in and out of the city** circulation à destination et en provenance de la ville; **watch out for traffic when crossing!** (fais) attention aux voitures en traversant!; **road closed to heavy traffic** route interdite aux poids lourds; **eastbound traffic** circulation *f* ouest-est; **the cyclist weaved through the traffic** le cycliste se faufila entre les voitures; *Fig* **the resort experiences heavy ski traffic in winter** il y a beaucoup de skieurs en hiver dans cette station
(b) *Com* commerce *m*; *(illicit)* trafic *m*; *Am (customers)* clientèle *f*; **the traffic in arms/drugs** le trafic des armes/de drogue
(c) *Br (dealings)* échange *m*; **you should have no traffic with these people** évitez d'avoir affaire à ces gens
2 *vi* **to traffic in** faire le commerce de; **organizations trafficking in arms/drugs** des organisations spécialisées dans le trafic d'armes/de drogue; *Fig* **reporters who traffic in human misery** journalistes qui exploitent la misère humaine
▸▸ *Mktg* ***traffic builder*** *(product)* article *m* d'appel; ***traffic calming*** contrôle *m* de la circulation; *Am* ***traffic circle*** rond-point *m*, sens *m* giratoire; ***traffic cone*** cône *m* de signalisation (pour la circulation routière); ***traffic control*** régulation *f* de la circulation; *Aviat, Naut & Rail* contrôle *m* du trafic; *Aviat* ***traffic controller*** contrôleur(-euse) *m,f* de la navigation aérienne, aiguilleur *m* du ciel; *Aviat* ***traffic control tower*** tour *f* de contrôle; *Am Fam* ***traffic cop*** agent *m* de la circulation ☐; *Am* ***traffic court*** = tribunal chargé des infractions au code de la route; ***traffic island*** refuge *m*; *Br* ***traffic jam*** embouteillage *m*, bouchon *m*; ***traffic lights*** feu *m* de signalisation; **the traffic lights are (at) green** le feu est (au) vert; **carry on to the next set of traffic lights** continuez jusqu'aux prochains feux; ***traffic offence*** infraction *f* au code de la route; ***traffic patrol*** patrouille *f* de la circulation (routière); *Aviat* ***traffic pattern*** couloir *m* ou position *f* d'approche; ***traffic police*** *(for speeding, safety)* police *f* de la route; *(on point duty)* agents *mpl* de la circulation; ***traffic policeman*** agent *m* de police; *(on point duty)* agent *m* de la circulation; ***traffic sign*** panneau *m* de signalisation, poteau *m* indicateur; ***traffic signal*** feu *m* de signalisation; *Am* ***traffic violation*** infraction *f* au code de la route; *Br* ***traffic warden*** contractuel(elle) *m,f*

TRAFFIC WARDEN

En Grande-Bretagne, les contractuels sont habilités à dresser les procès-verbaux mais aussi à régler la circulation.

trafficator ['træfɪkeɪtə(r)] *n Br Old-fashioned* flèche *f* de direction

trafficker ['træfɪkə(r)] *n* trafiquant(e) *m,f*; **drug trafficker** trafiquant *m* de drogue

tragacanth ['trægəkænθ] *n Bot* tragacanthe *f*

tragedian [trə'dʒi:dɪən] *n (author)* auteur *m* tragique; *(actor)* tragédien *m*

tragedienne [trə,dʒi:dɪ'en] *n* tragédienne *f*

tragedy ['trædʒədɪ] (*pl* **tragedies**) *n (gen) & Theat* tragédie *f*; **to make a tragedy out of sth** prendre qch au tragique; **it's a tragedy that this should happen to her** c'est tragique que ça lui arrive à elle; **what a tragedy!** quel malheur!, quelle tragédie!

tragic ['trædʒɪk] *adj* tragique
▸▸ ***tragic actor*** tragédien *m*; ***tragic actress*** tragédienne *f*; ***tragic hero*** héros *m* tragique; ***tragic irony*** ironie *f* tragique

tragically ['trædʒɪklɪ] *adv* tragiquement; **the trip went tragically wrong** le voyage a tourné au drame; **he died at a tragically early age** c'est tragique qu'il soit mort si jeune

tragicomedy [,trædʒɪ'kɒmədɪ] (*pl* **tragicomedies**) *n* tragi-comédie *f*

tragicomic [,trædʒɪ'kɒmɪk] *adj* tragi-comique

tragopan ['trægəpæn] *n Orn* tragopan *m*

trail [treɪl] **1** *n* **(a)** *(path)* sentier *m*, chemin *m*; *(through jungle)* piste *f*; **to break a trail** faire la trace, tracer; *Fig* **he hit the campaign trail** il est parti en campagne (électorale); *Am* **the end of the trail** le bout de la piste *(nom donné à la Californie par les pionniers américains)*; *Am Hist* **the trail of tears** le chemin des larmes
(b) *(traces of passage)* piste *f*, trace *f*; **to be on the trail of sb/sth** être sur la piste de qn/qch; **the police were on his trail** la police était sur sa trace; **the trail was cold by then** la piste était déjà froide; **a false trail** une fausse piste; **the storm left a trail of destruction** l'orage a tout détruit sur son passage; *Fig* **she leaves a trail of broken hearts behind her** elle laisse beaucoup de cœurs brisés derrière elle
(c) *(of blood, smoke)* traînée *f*; *(of comet)* queue *f*
(d) *(of gun)* crosse *f ou* flèche *f* d'affût
2 *vt* **(a)** *(follow)* suivre, filer; *(track)* suivre la piste de; *(animal, criminal)* traquer
(b) *(drag behind, tow)* traîner; *(boat, trailer)* tirer, remorquer; **she trailed her hand in the water** elle laissait traîner sa main dans l'eau; **he was trailing a sack of coal behind him** il traînait *ou* tirait un sac de charbon derrière lui; *Fig* **to trail one's coat** chercher la bagarre
(c) *(lag behind)* être en arrière par rapport à; **he trails all his classmates** il est en retard par rapport aux autres élèves
(d) *(gun)* porter à la main
(e) *Cin, Rad & TV (advertise → film, programme)* annoncer *(en diffusant un extrait)*
3 *vi* **(a)** *(long garment)* traîner; *(plant)* ramper; **smoke trailed from the chimney** de la fumée sortait de la cheminée; **your skirt is trailing (on the ground)** votre jupe traîne (par terre)
(b) *(move slowly)* traîner; **he trailed along at a snail's pace** il avançait comme un escargot; **the prisoners trailed slowly past** les prisonniers passaient lentement à la queue leu leu; *Sport* **he trailed in last** il est arrivé bon dernier
(c) *(lag behind)* être à la traîne; **he's trailing in the polls** il est à la traîne dans les sondages; **our team is trailing at the bottom of the league** notre équipe se traîne en fin de classement
(d) *(follow)* suivre, filer; **with five children trailing behind her** avec cinq enfants dans son sillage
▸▸ ***trail bike*** moto *f* de cross; ***trail mix*** = mélange de cacahuètes et de fruits secs; *Fishing* ***trail net*** traîne *f*, chalut *m*, traîneau *m*
▸**trail away** *vi* s'estomper; **his voice trailed away to a whisper** sa voix ne fut plus qu'un murmure
▸**trail off** *vi* s'estomper; **he trailed off in mid sentence** il n'a pas terminé sa phrase

THE TRAIL OF TEARS

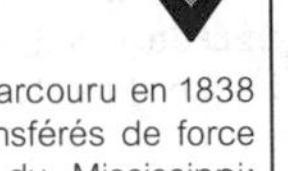

On donna ce nom au chemin parcouru en 1838 par les Indiens d'Amérique transférés de force dans des réserves à l'ouest du Mississippi: nombre d'entre eux succombèrent à la maladie et aux mauvais traitements.

trailblazer ['treɪl,bleɪzə(r)] *n Fig* pionnier(ère) *m,f*

trailblazing ['treɪl,bleɪzɪŋ] *adj* de pionnier

trailer ['treɪlə(r)] *n* **(a)** *Aut* remorque *f*; *Am (mobile home)* camping-car *m* **(b)** *Cin & TV* bande-annonce *f*; *Rad* aperçu *m* **(c)** *(end of film roll)* amorce *f*
▸▸ *Am* ***trailer court*** = terrain aménagé pour les camping-cars; *Am* ***trailer hitch*** timon *m* de remorque; *Am* ***trailer home*** caravane *f*; *Am* ***trailer park*** = terrain aménagé pour les camping-cars; ***trailer tent*** tente *f* remorque; *Am Fam Pej* ***trailer trash*** prolos *mpl (qui vivent dans des caravanes)*

trailer-truck *n Am* semi-remorque *f*

trailing ['treɪlɪŋ] *adj (long garment)* traînant; *(plant)* rampant
▸▸ *Aut* ***trailing arm*** bras *m* tiré; *Aut* ***trailing brake shoe*** segment *m* de frein secondaire; *Aviat* ***trailing edge*** *(of wing)* bord *m* de fuite; *Mktg* ***trailing firm*** entreprise *f* à la traîne; *Aut* ***trailing shoe*** segment *m* secondaire; *Comput* ***trailing spaces*** espaces *mpl* à droite; *Comput* ***trailing zeroes*** zéros *mpl* à droite

train [treɪn] **1** *n* **(a)** *(on railway)* train *m*; *(on underground)* métro *m*, rame *f*; **to go by train**

prendre le train, aller en train; **the 5 o'clock train** le train de 5 heures; **the Cardiff train, the train to Cardiff** le train de Cardiff; **I met a friend on the train** j'ai rencontré un ami dans le train; **to transport goods by train** transporter des marchandises par voie ferrée *ou* rail; **to the trains** *(sign)* accès aux quais

(**b**) *(procession → of vehicles)* file *f*, cortège *m*; *(→ of mules)* file *f*; *(→ of camels)* caravane *f*; *Mil* convoi *m*; *(retinue)* suite *f*, équipage *m*; *Mil* équipage *m*; **the famine brought disease in its train** la maladie succéda à la famine; **the evils that follow in the train of war** les maux que la guerre engendre

(**c**) *(of dress)* traîne *f*

(**d**) *(connected sequence)* suite *f*, série *f*; **in an unbroken train** en succession ininterrompue; **a train of events** une suite d'événements; **a train of thought** un enchaînement d'idées; **my remark interrupted her train of thought** ma remarque a interrompu le fil de sa pensée *ou* ses pensées; **to follow sb's train of thought** suivre le raisonnement de qn

(**e**) *Tech* train *m*; **train of gears** train *m* d'engrenage

(**f**) *Formal (progress)* **in train** en marche; **to set sth in train** mettre qch en marche

(**g**) *(fuse)* amorce *f*; *(of gunpowder)* traînée *f* (de poudre)

2 *comp (dispute, strike)* des cheminots, des chemins de fer; *(reservation, ticket)* de train; **there is a good train service to the city** la ville est bien desservie par le train; **there is an hourly train service** il y a des trains toutes les heures

3 *vt* (**a**) *(employee, soldier)* former; *(voice)* travailler; *(ear)* exercer; *(animal)* dresser; *(mind)* former; *Sport* entraîner; **he is training sb to take over from him** il forme son successeur; **to train sb in a trade** apprendre un métier à qn, préparer qn à un métier; **she was trained in economics** elle a reçu une formation d'économiste; **he was trained at Sandhurst** il a fait ses classes à Sandhurst; **to train sb to use sth** apprendre à qn à utiliser qch; **he has been trained in the use of explosives** il a été formé au maniement des explosifs; **the dogs have been trained to detect explosives** les chiens ont été dressés pour détecter les explosifs

(**b**) *(direct, aim)* braquer; **he trained his gun on us** il a braqué son arme sur nous

(**c**) *(plant → by pruning)* tailler; *(→ by tying)* palisser; *(climbing plant)* diriger, faire grimper

(**d**) *Fam* **we trained it down to the South of France** nous sommes allés en train jusque dans le Midi de la France❑

4 *vi* (**a**) *(do professional training)* recevoir une formation; **I trained as a translator** j'ai reçu une formation de traducteur; **she's training as a teacher** elle suit une formation pédagogique; **where did you train?** où avez-vous reçu votre formation?

(**b**) *Sport* s'entraîner, se préparer

►► ***train set*** train *m* électrique; ***train station*** gare *f (de chemin de fer)*; ***train surfing*** = pratique dangereuse qui consiste pour des jeunes à sauter sur le marche-pied d'un train qui démarre et sauter à nouveau sur le quai quand le train arrive au bout du quai

►**train up** *vt sep* [illegible]

trainbearer ['treɪn,beərə(r)] *n* = personne qui porte la traîne d'un dignitaire; *(at wedding)* demoiselle *f ou* dame *f* d'honneur; *(boy)* garçon *m* d'honneur

trained [treɪnd] *adj* (**a**) *(person)* compétent, qualifié; *(engineer)* breveté, diplômé; *(nurse, translator)* diplômé, qualifié; **he's not trained for this job** il n'est pas qualifié *ou* n'a pas la formation requise pour ce poste; **we need a well-trained employee** il nous faut quelqu'un qui ait une bonne formation; *Hum* **she has her boss well trained!** elle a bien dressé son patron!; **a trained eye** un œil exercé; **a trained ear** une oreille exercée; **he has a trained voice** il a travaillé sa voix

(**b**) *(animal)* dressé; **a trained parrot** un perroquet savant; **a well trained horse** un cheval bien dressé

trainee [treɪ'niː] **1** *n* stagiaire *mf*; **sales trainee** stagiaire *mf* de vente

2 *adj* stagiaire, en stage; *(in trades)* en apprentissage; **trainee computer programmer** élève *mf* programmeur(euse); **trainee journalist** journaliste *mf* stagiaire

traineeship [treɪ'niːʃɪp] *n* stage *m*

trainer ['treɪnə(r)] *n* (**a**) *Sport* entraîneur(euse) *m,f* (**b**) *(of animal)* dresseur(euse) *m,f*; *(of racehorses)* entraîneur(euse) *m,f*; *(of lion)* dompteur(euse) *m,f* (**c**) *Aviat (simulator)* simulateur *m*; *(aircraft)* avion-école *m* (**d**) *Br (shoe)* chaussure *f* de sport

►► ***trainer aircraft*** avion-école *m*

training ['treɪnɪŋ] *n* (**a**) *(of employee)* formation *f*; *(of soldier)* instruction *f*; *(of animal)* dressage *m*; **he is a carpenter by training** il est menuisier de formation; **I have had some business training** j'ai suivi une petite formation commerciale; *Mil* **to do one's basic training** faire ses classes; *Fig* **it's good training for when you're a parent** ça vous prépare pour quand vous aurez des enfants

(**b**) *Sport* entraînement *m*, préparation *f*; **to be in training** être en cours d'entraînement *ou* de préparation; **I'm out of training** j'ai perdu la forme; **to be in training for sth** s'entraîner pour *ou* se préparer à qch

►► *Br* ***Training Agency*** = organisme créé en 1989 qui propose des stages de formation et de recyclage; *Mil* ***training base*** base *f* école; ***training camp*** camp *m* d'entraînement; *Mil* base *f* école; ***training centre*** centre *m* de formation; ***training college*** école *f* spécialisée *ou* professionnelle; ***training course*** stage *m* de formation; *Br* ***Training and Enterprise Council*** = centre d'emploi et de formation; ***training manual*** manuel *m* d'utilisation, manuel *m* d'instruction; *Br* ***Training Opportunities Scheme*** = programme du recyclage professionnel; ***training period*** stage *m*, stage *m* de formation; ***training programme*** programme *m* de formation; ***training scheme*** plan *m* de formation; ***training session*** entraînement *m*; ***training ship*** navire-école *m*; ***training shoes*** chaussures *fpl* de sport; ***training video*** vidéo *f* d'entraînement; *Am* ***training wheels*** stabilisateurs *mpl*

trainload ['treɪnləʊd] *n* **trainload of coal** train *m* chargé de houille; **trainload of tourists** train *m* plein de touristes; **they were arriving by the trainload** ils arrivaient par trains entiers

trainsick ['treɪnsɪk] *adj* **to be** *or* **to get trainsick** être malade en train

trainspotter ['treɪn,spɒtə(r)] *n Br* (**a**) *(who notes train numbers)* = amateur de trains dont la passion consiste à relever les numéros des locomotives (**b**) *Fam (unfashionable person)* ringard(e) *m,f*

trainspotting ['treɪn,spɒtɪŋ] *n Br* = activité consistant à relever les numéros des locomotives

traipse [treɪps] *Fam* **1** *vi* **we all traipsed off to the shops** nous sommes tous partis traîner dans les magasins; **she came traipsing in** elle est entrée en traînassant; **to traipse about** *or* **around** se balader, vadrouiller; **they traipsed from one museum to another** ils ont fait tous les musées; **we had to traipse all the way back to the station** il a fallu qu'on se retape tout le trajet jusqu'à la gare

2 *n* longue promenade❑; **it's quite a traipse** ça fait une trotte

trait [treɪt] *n* trait *m*

traitor ['treɪtə(r)] *n* traître *mf*; **a traitor to his country** un traître envers son pays; **you're a traitor to your country/to the cause** vous trahissez votre pays/la cause; **he turned traitor** *(gen)* il s'est mis à trahir; *(soldier, spy)* il est passé *ou* s'est vendu à l'ennemi

traitorous ['treɪtərəs] *adj Formal* traître, perfide

traitorously ['treɪtərəslɪ] *adv Formal* traîtreusement

traitorousness ['treɪtərəsnɪs] *n Formal* traîtrise *f*, perfidie *f*

traitress ['treɪtrɪs] *n* traîtresse *f*

Trajan ['treɪdʒən] *pr n Antiq* Trajan

trajectory [trə'dʒektərɪ] *(pl* **trajectories**) *n* trajectoire *f*

tra-la [trɑː'lɑː], **tra-la-la** [,trɑːlɑː'lɑː] *onomat* = refrain de chanson sans sens particulier

TRAM [træm] *n Comput (abbr* **transputer module**) module *m* de transputer

tram [træm] *n Br* (**a**) *(in street)* tram *m*, tramway *m*; **to go by tram** prendre le tram; **the trams** *(system)* le réseau des tramways; **to work on the trams** travailler dans les tramways (**b**) *(in mine)* berline *f*, benne *f* roulante

►► ***tram driver*** conducteur(trice) *m,f* de tramway

tramcar ['træmkɑː(r)] *n Br* tram *m*, tramway *m*

tramline ['træmlaɪn] **1** *n Br (rails)* voie *f* de tramway; *(route)* ligne *f* de tramway

2 **tramlines** *npl* (**a**) *(in tennis, badminton)* lignes *fpl* de côté (**b**) *Fam Drugs slang (on arm)* traces *fpl* de piquouses

trammel ['træməl] *(Br pt & pp* **trammelled**, *cont* **trammelling**, *Am pt & pp* **trammeled**, *cont* **trammeling**) **1** *vt also Fig* entraver

2 *n* (**a**) *Literary (hindrance)* **the trammels of society/routine** les entraves *fpl* de la société/de la routine (**b**) *Fishing* tramail *m*, trémail *m*

tramontana [,træmɒn'tɑːnə] *n* tramontane *f*

tramontane [trə'mɒnteɪn] **1** *adj (region, wind)* ultramontain, d'outre-monts

2 *n (wind)* tramontane *f*

tramp [træmp] **1** *n* (**a**) *(vagabond)* clochard(e) *m,f*, *Old-fashioned* chemineau *m*

(**b**) *(sound)* bruit *m* de pas; **I could hear the tramp of soldiers' feet** j'entendais le pas lourd des soldats

(**c**) *(long walk)* randonnée *f* (à pied), promenade *f*; **it's a long tramp into town** il y a un bon bout de chemin à faire jusqu'à la ville

(**d**) *(ship)* **tramp (steamer)** tramp *m*

(**e**) *Fam Pej (promiscuous woman)* traînée *f*

2 *vi* (**a**) *(hike)* marcher, se promener; **we tramped along in silence for a while** nous avons poursuivi notre chemin en silence pendant un moment

(**b**) *(walk heavily)* marcher d'un pas lourd; **to tramp up and down** faire les cent pas; **to tramp on sth** piétiner *ou* écraser qch; **I wish you'd stop tramping on my foot!** j'aimerais bien que tu arrêtes de m'écraser le pied!

3 *vt* parcourir; **he tramped the streets in search of work** il a battu le pavé pour trouver du travail

►**tramp down, tramp in** *vt sep* tasser du pied

trampet, trampette [træm'pet] *n* trampoline *m*

trample ['træmpəl] **1** *vt* piétiner, fouler aux pieds; *Fig (somebody's feelings)* bafouer; **the crowd trampled the man to death** l'homme est mort piétiné par la foule; **he trampled my arguments underfoot** il a piétiné *ou* pulvérisé mes arguments

2 *vi* marcher d'un pas lourd

3 *n (action)* piétinement *m*; *(sound)* bruit *m* de pas

►**trample on, trample over** *vt insep* piétiner; *Fig (somebody's feelings)* bafouer; *(objections)* passer outre à

trampoline ['træmpəliːn] **1** *n* trampoline *m*

2 *vi* faire du trampoline

trampolining [træmpə'liːnɪŋ] *n* trampoline *m*; **to go trampolining** faire du trampoline

tramway ['træmweɪ] *n Br (rails)* voie *f* de tramway; *(route)* ligne *f* de tramway

trance [trɑːns] *n* transe *f*; *Med* catalepsie *f*; **to go** *or* **to fall into a trance** entrer en transe; *Med* tomber en catalepsie; **he put me into a trance** il m'a hypnotisé, il m'a fait entrer en transe; **he's been wandering around in a trance ever since his wife left him** il erre en transe *ou* dans un état de transe depuis que sa femme l'a quitté

tranche [trɑ̃ʃ] *n (of loan, payment, shares)* tranche *f*

trannie, tranny ['trænɪ] *(pl* **trannies**) *n Br Fam* (**a**) *Old-fashioned (transistor radio)* transistor❑ *m* (**b**) *(transvestite)* travelo *m*

tranquil ['træŋkwɪl] *adj* tranquille, paisible

tranquillity, *Am* **tranquility** [træŋ'kwɪlɪtɪ] *n* tranquillité *f*, calme *m*

tranquillization, *Am* **tranquilization** [,træŋkwɪlaɪ'zeɪʃən] *n* apaisement *m*; *Med* mise *f* sous tranquillisants

tranquillize, -ise, *Am* **tranquilize** ['træŋkwɪ,laɪz] *vt* calmer, apaiser; *Med* mettre sous tranquillisants

tranquillizer, *Am* **tranquilizer** ['træŋkwɪ,laɪzə(r)] *n* tranquillisant *m*, calmant *m*

tranquillizing, *Am* **tranquilizing** ['træŋkwɪ,laɪzɪŋ] *adj* tranquillisant, calmant

tranquilly ['træŋkwɪlɪ] *adv* tranquillement, paisiblement

trans. (*written abbr* **translated, translation**) trad.

transact [træn'zækt] *vt* traiter, régler; **to transact business with sb** faire des affaires avec qn; **the deal was successfully transacted** l'affaire a été conclue avec brio

transactinide [trænz'æktɪnaɪd] *adj*
▸▸ *Chem* ***transactinide element*** transactinide *m*

transaction [træn'zækʃən] **1** *n* (**a**) *Com & Fin* transaction *f*; *St Exch* opération *f*; **cash transaction** transaction *f* en liquide; **cash transactions have increased** les mouvements d'espèces ont augmenté; **Stock Exchange transactions** opérations *fpl* de Bourse
(**b**) *(act of transacting)* conduite *f*, gestion *f*; **transaction of business will continue as normal** la conduite des affaires se poursuivra comme à l'accoutumée
(**c**) *Comput* mouvement *m*
2 transactions *npl (proceedings of organization)* travaux *mpl*; *(minutes)* actes *mpl*
▸▸ *St Exch* ***transaction costs*** frais *mpl* de Bourse; *St Exch* ***transaction tax*** impôt *m* de Bourse

transactional [træn'zækʃənəl] *adj* transactionnel
▸▸ *Psy* ***transactional analysis*** analyse *f* transactionnelle

transactor [træn'zæktə(r)] *n* négociateur(trice) *m,f*

transafrican [ˌtrænz'æfrɪkən] *adj* transafricain

transalpine [ˌtrænz'ælpaɪn] *adj* transalpin

transamerican [ˌtrænzə'merɪkən] *adj* transaméricain

transaminase [ˌtrænz'æmɪneɪz] *n Biol & Chem* transaminase *f*

transatlantic [ˌtrænzət'læntɪk] *adj* transatlantique
▸▸ ***transatlantic carrier*** transporteur *m* transatlantique

transaxle ['trænzæksəl] *n Aut* boîte-pont *f*

Transcaucasia [ˌtrænskɔː'keɪzɪə] *n* la Transcaucasie

Transcaucasian [ˌtrænskɔː'keɪzɪən] *adj* transcaucasien

transceiver [træn'siːvə(r)] *n* émetteur-récepteur *m*

transcend [træn'send] *vt* (**a**) *(go beyond)* transcender, dépasser; *Phil & Rel* transcender; **the issue transcends party loyalties** le problème dépasse les clivages partisans (**b**) *(surpass)* surpasser

transcendence [træn'sendəns], **transcendency** [træn'sendənsɪ] *n* transcendance *f*

transcendent [træn'sendənt] *adj* transcendant

transcendental [ˌtrænsen'dentəl] *adj* transcendantal
▸▸ ***transcendental meditation*** méditation *f* transcendantale; *Math* ***transcendental number*** nombre *m* transcendant

transcendentalism [ˌtrænsen'dentəlɪzəm] *n Phil* transcendantalisme *m*

transcendentalist [ˌtrænsen'dentəlɪst] *n Phil* transcendantaliste *mf*

transcoder [trænz'kəʊdə(r)] *n* transcodeur *m*

transcontinental ['trænzˌkɒntɪ'nentəl] *adj* transcontinental
▸▸ ***the Transcontinental Railroad*** la Transcontinentale

THE TRANSCONTINENTAL RAILROAD

Cette voie de chemin de fer traverse les États-Unis d'est en ouest. Achevée en 1869, elle fut construite par deux compagnies: la "Union Pacific" et la "Central Pacific", qui, parties respectivement de la côte est et de la côte ouest, se rejoignirent dans l'Utah.

transcribe [træn'skraɪb] *vt* (**a**) *(write out)* copier, transcrire; *(shorthand)* traduire; *Acct* **to transcribe entries** transcrire des écritures (**b**) *Mus (for another instrument)* transcrire (**c**) *TV (record)* enregistrer; *(broadcast)* retransmettre en différé (**d**) *Comput (data)* transcrire

transcriber [træn'skraɪbə(r)] *n* transcripteur *m*, copiste *mf*

transcript ['trænskrɪpt] *n* transcription *f*; *Am Sch* livret *m* scolaire; *Am Univ* = liste officielle des notes obtenues dans chaque matière

transcriptase [træn'skrɪpteɪz] *n Biol* transcriptase *f*

transcription [træn'skrɪpʃən] *n* transcription *f*

transdermal [ˌtræns'dɜːməl] *adj* transdermique
▸▸ ***transdermal patch*** timbre *m* autocollant transdermique

transduce [trænz'djuːs] *vt* transformer, convertir

transducer [trænz'djuːsə(r)] *n* transducteur *m*

transduction [trænz'dʌkʃən] *n* transduction *f*

transect [træn'sekt] *vt* sectionner transversalement

transection [træn'sekʃən] *n* coupe *f ou* section *f* transversale

transept ['trænsept] *n* transept *m*

transfer 1 *vt* [træns'fɜː(r)] (**a**) *(move)* transférer; *(employee, civil servant)* transférer, muter; *(soldier)* muter; *Br (player)* transférer; *(passenger)* transférer, transborder; *(object, goods)* transférer, transporter; **can this ticket be transferred to another airline?** peut-on utiliser ce billet d'avion sur une autre compagnie?
(**b**) *Fin & Banking (money)* virer; **I transferred the funds to my bank account** j'ai fait virer l'argent sur mon compte bancaire
(**c**) *(convey → property, ownership)* transmettre, transférer, *Law* faire cession de, céder; *(→ power, responsibility)* passer; **she will transfer the rights over to him** elle va lui céder *ou* passer les droits
(**d**) *Tel* **I'm transferring you now** *(operator)* je vous mets en communication; *Br* **I'd like to transfer the charges** je voudrais téléphoner en PCV; *Br* **transferred charge call** communication *f* en PCV
(**e**) *(displace → design, picture)* reporter, décalquer; **to transfer a design from one surface to another** décalquer un dessin d'un support sur un autre; *Fig* **she transferred her affection/allegiance to him** elle a reporté son affection/sa fidélité sur lui
(**f**) *Acct (debt)* transporter; *(entry)* contre-passer
2 *vi* [træns'fɜː(r)] (**a**) *(move)* être transféré; *(employee, civil servant)* être muté *ou* transféré; *(soldier)* être muté; *Br (player)* être transféré; *Am* **she transferred to another school** elle a changé d'école; **I'm transferring to history** je me réoriente en histoire
(**b**) *(change mode of transport)* être transféré *ou* transbordé; **they had to transfer to a train** ils ont dû changer et prendre le train
3 *n* ['trænsfɜː(r)] (**a**) *(gen)* transfert *m*; *(of employee, civil servant)* mutation *f*; *(of passenger)* transfert *m*, transbordement *m*; *Br (of player)* transfert *m*; *(of goods, objects)* transfert *m*, transport *m*; **he has asked for a transfer** il a demandé son transfert *ou* à être muté; *Br (player)* il a demandé son transfert
(**b**) *Fin & Banking (of funds, capital)* virement *m*, transfert *m*
(**c**) *Law* transmission *f*, cession *f*; **transfer of ownership from sb to sb** transfert *m ou* translation *f* de propriété de qn à qn; **application for transfer of proceedings** demande *f* de renvoi devant une autre juridiction
(**d**) *Br (design, picture)* décalcomanie *f*; *(rub-on)* autocollant *m*; *(sew-on)* décalque *m*
(**e**) *(change of mode of travel)* transfert *m*; *(at airport, train station)* correspondance *f*; **free transfer** transfert *m* gratuit
(**f**) *(ticket)* billet *m* de correspondance
(**g**) *Comput (of data)* transfert *m*
(**h**) *Acct (of debt)* transport *m*; *(of entry)* contre-passation *f*; **transfer of charges** transfert *m* de charges
(**i**) *St Exch (of shares)* transfert *m*; *(document)* (feuille *f* de) transfert *m*; **transfer by endorsement** transmission *f* par endossement
▸▸ ***transfer advice*** avis *m* de virement; ***transfer bus*** navette *f*; *Br Tel* ***transfer charge call*** communication *f* en PCV; ***transfer cheque*** chèque *m* de virement; *Law* ***transfer deed*** acte *m* de cession; ***transfer desk*** *(at airport)* guichet *m* de transit; ***transfer duty*** droits *mpl* de transfert; ***transfer fee*** (**a**) *Br Sport* indemnité *f* de transfert (**b**) *Fin* frais *mpl* de transfert; ***transfer form*** formule *f* de transfert; *Br Sport* ***transfer list*** liste *f* des joueurs transférables; *Br* ***transfer lounge*** *(at airport)* salle *f* de transit; ***transfer order*** ordre *m ou* mandat *m* de virement; *Br* ***transfer passenger*** *(between flights)* voyageur(-euse) *m,f* en transit; *Pol* ***transfer of power*** passation *f* de pouvoir; *Comput* ***transfer rate*** taux *m* de transfert; *Biol* ***transfer RNA*** ARN *m* de transfert; *Comput* ***transfer speed*** vitesse *f* de transfert; *Br* ***transfer tax*** droits *mpl* de succession; *(between living persons)* droit *m* de mutation; ***transfer ticket*** billet *m* de correspondance

transferability [ˌtrænsfərə'bɪlɪtɪ] *n* transmissibilité *f*, transférabilité *f*; *Law* cessibilité *f*

transferable [træns'fɜːrəbəl] *adj* transmissible, transférable; *Law* cessible; **this ticket is not transferable** ce billet est strictement personnel
▸▸ ***transferable bond*** obligation *f* transmissible *ou* transférable; ***transferable credit*** crédit *m* transférable; ***transferable document*** document *m* transmissible; ***transferable letter of credit*** crédit *m* transférable; ***transferable securities*** valeurs *fpl* négociables *ou* mobilières; ***transferable share*** action *f* au porteur; ***transferable vote*** = voix pouvant se reporter sur un autre candidat

transferase ['trænsfəreɪs] *n Biol* transférase *f*

transferee [ˌtrænsfɜː'riː] *n Law & Fin* cessionnaire *mf*, bénéficiaire *mf*

transference ['trænsfərəns] *n (gen) & Psy* transfert *m*; *(of employee, civil servant)* mutation *f*; *(of money)* virement *m*; *(of power)* passation *f*; *(of ownership)* transfert *m ou* translation *f* de propriété

transferential [ˌtrænsfə'renʃəl] *adj Psy* transférentiel

transfer-listed *adj Br Sport* **to be transfer-listed** être sur la liste des joueurs transférables

transferor, transferrer [træns'fɜːrə(r)] *n Law* cédant(e) *m,f*; *Fin (of shares, funds, capital)* vendeur(euse) *m,f*

transfiguration [ˌtrænsfɪgə'reɪʃən] *n* transfiguration *f*; *Rel* **the Transfiguration** la Transfiguration

transfigure [træns'fɪgə(r)] *vt* transfigurer

transfinite [træns'faɪnaɪt] *adj* transfini

transfix [træns'fɪks] *vt* transpercer; *Fig* pétrifier; **to be transfixed with fear** être paralysé par la peur; **she stood transfixed** elle est restée clouée sur place

transfixion [træns'fɪkʃən] *n* transpercement *m*; *Med* transfixion *f*

transform [træns'fɔːm] **1** *vt* (**a**) *(change → gen)* transformer; **to transform sth into sth** transformer qch en qch; **her year abroad has completely transformed her** son année à l'étranger l'a complètement transformée *ou* l'a métamorphosée (**b**) *Elec* transformer; *Chem, Math & Phys* transformer, convertir (**c**) *Ling* transformer
2 *n* (**a**) *Ling* transformation *f* (**b**) *Math* transformée *f*

transformable [træns'fɔːməbəl] *adj* transformable (**into** en)

transformation [ˌtrænsfə'meɪʃən] *n* (**a**) *(change)* transformation *f*, métamorphose *f* (**b**) *Elec, Math, Chem & Phys* transformation *f* (**c**) *Ling* transformation *f*

transformational grammar [ˌtrænsfə'meɪʃənəl-] *n Ling* grammaire *f* transformationnelle

transformer [træns'fɔːmə(r)] *n Elec* transformateur *m*
▸▸ ***transformer station*** station *f* de transformation; ***transformer unit*** bloc *m* transformateur

transfuse [træns'fjuːz] *vt (gen) & Med* transfuser; *Literary* **in a voice transfused with emotion** d'une voix emplie d'émotion

transfusion [træns'fjuːʒən] *n (gen) & Med* transfusion *f*; **they gave him a transfusion** ils lui ont fait une transfusion

transgender [ˌtræns'dʒendə(r)] *n* transsexuel(-elle) *m,f*

transgenic [ˌtrænz'dʒenɪk] *adj* transgénique
▸▸ ***transgenic animal*** animal *m* transgénique

transgress [trænz'gres] *Formal* **1** *vt (law etc)* transgresser, enfreindre
2 *vi* enfreindre la loi; *(sin)* pécher

transgression [trænz'greʃən] *n Formal (of law etc)* transgression *f*, infraction *f* (**of** à); *(sin)* péché *m*

transgressive [trænz'gresɪv] *adj* (**a**) *Formal*

(breaking law) transgressif (**b**) *Geol (deposit)* transgressif

▸▸ *Geol* ***transgressive stratification*** stratification *f* transgressive

transgressor [trænz'gresə(r)] *n Formal (of law etc)* transgresseur *m*; *(sinner)* pécheur(eresse) *m,f*

tranship = **transship**

transhipment = **transshipment**

transhumance [ˌtræns'hju:məns] *n Agr* transhumance *f*

transience ['trænzɪəns], **transiency** ['trænzɪənsɪ] *n (temporariness)* caractère *m* transitoire *ou* passager; *(fleetingness)* caractère *m* éphémère

transient ['trænzɪənt] **1** *adj (temporary)* transitoire, passager; *(fleeting)* éphémère

2 *n* (**a**) *(person)* voyageur(euse) *m,f* en transit (**b**) *(goods)* marchandise *f* en transit

transiently ['trænzɪəntlɪ] *adv (temporarily)* transitoirement, passagèrement; *(fleetingly)* de façon éphémère

transire [træn'saɪə(r)] *n Com* passavant *m*, laissez-passer *m inv*

transistor [træn'zɪstə(r)] *n* transistor *m*

▸▸ ***transistor radio*** transistor *m*

transistorize, -ise [træn'zɪstəraɪz] *vt* transistoriser

▸▸ ***transistorized circuit*** circuit *m* à transistors

transit ['trænsɪt] **1** *n* (**a**) *(of goods, passengers)* transit *m*; **in transit** en transit; **goods lost in transit** marchandises *fpl* égarées pendant le transport

(**b**) *Astron* passage *m*

2 *comp (goods, passengers)* en transit; *(documents, port)* de transit

3 *vt* (**a**) *(goods, passengers)* transiter

(**b**) *Astron* passer sur

▸▸ *Am* ***transit authority*** régie *f* des transports (en commun); ***transit bill*** passavant *m*; ***transit camp*** camp *m* de transit; *Com* ***transit declaration*** déclaration *f* de transit; ***transit duty*** droit *m* de transit; ***transit hotel*** hôtel *m* de passage *ou* de transit; *Opt* ***transit instrument*** instrument *m* méridien; ***transit lounge*** salle *f* de transit; ***transit passenger*** passager(ère) *m,f* en transit; ***transit visa*** visa *m* de transit

transition [træn'zɪʃən] **1** *n* transition *f*, passage *m*; **the transition from childhood to maturity** le passage de l'enfance à l'âge adulte

2 *comp (period)* de transition

▸▸ *Chem* ***transition element*** élément *m* de transition

transitional [træn'zɪʃənəl] *adj* de transition, transitoire

▸▸ *Br Admin* ***transitional relief*** = aide financière de l'État pour faciliter la mise en place d'une réforme administrative

transitive ['trænzɪtɪv] *adj Gram* transitif

transitively ['trænzɪtɪvlɪ] *adv Gram* transitivement

transitory ['trænzɪtərɪ] *adj* transitoire, passager

Transjordan [ˌtrænz'dʒɔ:dən], **Transjordania** [ˌtrænzdʒɔ:'deɪnɪə] *n Hist* la Transjordanie

Transjordanian [ˌtrænzdʒɔ:'deɪnɪən] *adj Hist* transjordanien

Transkei [træn'skaɪ] *n* Transkei *m*

translatable [træns'leɪtəbəl] *adj* traduisible

translate [træns'leɪt] **1** *vt* (**a**) *(word, text, book)* traduire; **to translate sth from Spanish into English** traduire qch de l'espagnol en anglais; **how do you translate "hunger"?** comment traduit-on "hunger"?; **it can be translated as...** on peut le traduire par...; **translated into Fahrenheit** exprimé *ou* converti en Fahrenheit; **we can now translate these figures into a graph** nous pouvons maintenant traduire ces chiffres en un graphe; *Fig* **he translated her silence as a refusal** il a interprété son silence comme un refus; **to translate ideas into action** traduire des idées en actes

(**b**) *Rel (transfer → cleric, relics)* transférer; *(convey to heaven)* ravir

2 *vi* (**a**) *(word, text, book)* se traduire; **it doesn't translate** c'est intraduisible; *Fig* **how does that translate into economic reality?** comment est-ce que ça se traduit sur le plan économique?

(**b**) *(person)* traduire; **she translates for the EU** elle fait des traductions pour l'Union européenne

translation [træns'leɪʃən] *n* (**a**) *(of word, text, book)* traduction *f*; *Sch* version *f*; **to read sth in translation** lire une traduction de qch; **the book is a translation from (the) Chinese** le livre est traduit du chinois; **the text loses something in (the) translation** le texte perd quelque chose à la traduction

(**b**) *Rel (of cleric, relics)* translation *f*; *(conveying to heaven)* ravissement *m*

▸▸ ***translation agency*** bureau *m ou* agence *f* de traduction; ***translation company*** cabinet *m ou* société *f* de traduction; *Comput* ***translation table*** table *f* de traduction

translational [træns'leɪʃənəl] *adj Tech (movement)* de translation

translator [træns'leɪtə(r)] *n* traducteur(trice) *m,f*

transliterate [trænz'lɪtəreɪt] *vt* translitérer, translittérer

transliteration [ˌtrænzlɪtə'reɪʃən] *n* translitération *f*, translittération *f*

translocate [ˌtrænzləʊ'keɪt] *vt* déplacer; *Biol* transloquer

translocation [ˌtrænzləʊ'keɪʃən] *n* déplacement *m*; *Biol* translocation *f*; **police translocation** relégation *f*

translucence [trænz'lu:səns] *n* translucidité *f*

translucent [trænz'lu:sənt] *adj* translucide, diaphane

transmigrate [ˌtrænzmaɪ'greɪt] *vi (soul)* transmigrer; *(people)* émigrer

transmigration [ˌtrænzmaɪ'greɪʃən] *n (of souls)* transmigration *f*; *(of people)* émigration *f*

transmissibility [trænzˌmɪsɪ'bɪlɪtɪ] *n* transmissibilité *f*

transmissible [trænz'mɪsəbəl] *adj* transmissible

transmission [trænz'mɪʃən] *n* (**a**) *(gen)* transmission *f*; *Tel* transmission *f*, émission *f*; *TV & Rad (of programme)* diffusion *f* (**b**) *Aut* transmission *f*

▸▸ ***transmission brake*** frein *m* sur transmission; ***transmission shaft*** arbre *m* de transmission; ***transmission speed*** vitesse *f* de transmission

transmissive [trænz'mɪsɪv] *adj* (**a**) *(relating to transmission)* transmetteur (**b**) *(transmissible)* transmissible

transmissivity [ˌtrænzmɪ'sɪvɪtɪ] *n Phys* transmissivité *f*

transmit [trænz'mɪt] (*pt & pp* **transmitted**, *cont* **transmitting**) **1** *vt (gen)* transmettre; *Tel* transmettre, émettre; *TV & Rad (programme)* diffuser

2 *vi Rad, Tel & TV* émettre, diffuser

transmittable [trænz'mɪtəbəl] *adj* transmissible

transmittal [trænz'mɪtəl] *n* transmission *f*

transmittance [trænz'mɪtəns] *n Phys* transmittance *f*; **radiant transmittance** transmittance *f* radiante; **spectral transmittance** transmittance *f* spectrale

transmittancy [trænz'mɪtənsɪ] *n Phys* coefficient *m* de transmittance

transmitter [trænz'mɪtə(r)] *n* transmetteur *m*; *Rad & TV* émetteur *m*; *(in telephone)* microphone *m* (téléphonique)

▸▸ *Tel & Rad* ***transmitter receiver*** émetteur-récepteur *m*; *TV & Rad* ***transmitter van*** car *m* de transmission

transmitting [trænz'mɪtɪŋ] **1** *adj Tel* émetteur

2 *n* transmission *f*

transmogrify [trænz'mɒgrɪfaɪ] (*pt & pp* **transmogrified**) *vt Hum* métamorphoser, changer

transmutable [trænz'mju:təbəl] *adj* transmuable, transmutable

transmutation [ˌtrænzmju:'teɪʃən] *n* transmutation *f*

transmute [trænz'mju:t] *vt* transmuer, transmuter; **the process transmutes the metal into gold** le processus transforme *ou* transmute le métal en or

transnational [ˌtrænz'næʃənəl] *adj* transnational

transoceanic [ˌtrænzəʊsɪ'ænɪk] *adj* transocéanien

transom ['trænsəm] *n* (**a**) *(in window)* petit bois *m* horizontal; *(above door)* traverse *f* d'imposte (**b**) *Am (fanlight)* imposte *f* (semi-circulaire)

▸▸ *Am* ***transom window*** imposte *f* (semi-circulaire)

transonic [træn'sɒnɪk] *adj* transsonique

transpacific [ˌtrænzpə'sɪfɪk] *adj* transpacifique

transparency [træns'pærənsɪ] (*pl* **transparencies**) *n* (**a**) *(quality)* transparence *f* (**b**) *(for overhead projector)* transparent *m*; *esp Br (slide)* diapositive *f*

transparent [træns'pærənt] *adj* transparent

transparently [træns'pærəntlɪ] *adv (obviously)* de toute évidence; **that's transparently obvious** c'est clair comme de l'eau de roche

transpersonal [træns'pɜ:sənəl] *adj Psy* transpersonnel

transpiration [ˌtrænspɪ'reɪʃən] *n Bot & Physiol* transpiration *f*

transpire [træn'spaɪə(r)] **1** *vi* (**a**) *(be discovered, turn out)* apparaître; **it transpired that he had been embezzling funds** on a appris *ou* on s'est aperçu qu'il avait détourné des fonds (**b**) *(happen)* se passer, arriver; **the events that transpired later that day** les événements intervenus plus tard dans la journée (**c**) *Bot & Physiol* transpirer

2 *vt Bot (water, vapour)* dégager

transplant **1** *vt* [træns'plɑ:nt] (**a**) *Bot (plant)* transplanter; *(seedling)* repiquer (**b**) *Med (organ)* greffer, transplanter; *(tissue)* greffer (**c**) *(population)* transplanter

2 *n* ['trænsˌplɑ:nt] *Med (organ)* transplant *m*; *(tissue, operation)* greffe *f*; **she's had a kidney transplant** on lui a fait une greffe du rein; **she's had a heart transplant** on lui a greffé un cœur

transplantable [træns'plɑ:ntəbəl] *adj* transplantable

transplantation [ˌtrænsplɑ:n'teɪʃən] *n* (**a**) *Bot (of plant)* transplantation *f*; *(of seedling)* repiquage *m* (**b**) *Fig (of people)* transplantation *f*

transponder [træn'spɒndə(r)] *n* transpondeur *m*

transport **1** *n* ['trænspɔ:t] (**a**) *(UNCOUNT) Br (system)* transport *m*, transports *mpl*; **the Transport and General Workers' Union** = le plus grand syndicat interprofessionnel britannique

(**b**) *(means)* moyen *m* de transport *ou* de locomotion; *Br Fam* **have you got transport for tonight?** tu as un moyen de locomotion pour ce soir?

(**c**) *(of goods)* transport *m*

(**d**) *Literary (of joy)* transport *m*; *(of anger)* accès *m*; **he went into transports of delight** il fut transporté de joie

2 *vt* [træn'spɔ:t] transporter

▸▸ ***transport advertising*** affichage *m* transport; ***transport allowance*** prime *f* de transport; *Br* ***transport café*** ≃ routier *m (restaurant)*; ***transport company*** entreprise *f ou* société *f* de transport; ***transport costs*** frais *mpl* de transport; ***transport cover*** garantie *f* transport; ***transport document*** titre *m ou* document *m* de transport; ***transport facilities*** moyens *mpl* de transport; ***Transport House*** = bâtiment à Londres abritant le siège de la TGWU et, jusqu'en 1980, le parti travailliste; ***transport museum*** musée *m* des transports; ***transport plane*** avion *m* de transport; *Br* ***transport police*** = service d'ordre des chemins de fer; ***transport ship*** navire *m* de transport

transportable [træn'spɔ:təbəl] *adj* transportable

transportation [ˌtrænspɔ:'teɪʃən] *n* (**a**) *Am (transport)* transport *m*; **public transportation** transports *mpl* publics; **transportation system** système *m* des transports; *Pol* **Secretary of Transportation** ministre *m* des Transports

(**b**) *(of criminals)* transportation *f*

▸▸ *Am* ***transportation advertising*** affichage *m* transport; *Am* ***transportation agreement*** contrat *m* de transport; *Am* ***transportation desk*** *(in hotel)* bureau *m* de voyages; *Am* ***transportation insurance*** assurance *f* transport

transporter [træn'spɔ:tə(r)] *n* (**a**) *Mil (for troops → lorry)* camion *m* de transport; *(→ ship)* navire *m* de transport; *(for tanks)* camion *m* porte-char (**b**) *(for cars → lorry)* camion *m* pour transport d'automobiles; *(→ train)* wagon *m* pour transport d'automobiles

▸▸ ***transporter bridge*** pont *m* transbordeur

transposable [træns'pəʊzəbəl] *adj* transposable

transpose [træns'pəʊz] *vt* transposer

transposing instrument [træns'pəʊzɪŋ-] *n Mus* transpositeur *m*

transposition [ˌtrænspə'zɪʃən] *n* transposition *f*

transpositional [ˌtrænspə'zɪʃənəl], **transpositive** [træns'pɒzɪtɪv] *adj* transpositif

transposon [ˌtræns'pəʊzɒn] *n Biol* transposon *m*

transputer [træns'pju:tə(r)] *n Comput* transputer *m*

transsexual [trænsˈsekʃʊəl] *n* transsexuel(elle) *m,f*

transship [trænsˈʃɪp] (*pt & pp* **transshipped,** *cont* **transshipping**) *vt* transborder

transshipment [trænsˈʃɪpmənt] *n* transbordement *m*
►► ***transshipment bill of lading*** connaissement *m* de transbordement

Trans-Siberian [ˈtrænz-] *adj* **the Trans-Siberian (Railway)** le Transsibérien

transsonic = **transonic**

transubstantiate [ˌtrænsəbˈstænʃɪeɪt] **1** *vt* transmuer, transmuter
2 *vi Rel* subir la transsubstantiation

transubstantiation [ˈtrænsəbˌstænʃɪˈeɪʃən] *n Rel* transsubstantiation *f*

transude [trænˈsjuːd] *vi Physiol* transuder

transuranic [ˌtrænsjʊˈrænɪk] *adj Chem* transuranien

Transvaal [ˈtrænzvɑːl] *n* le Transvaal; **in the Transvaal** au Transvaal

transversal [ˌtrænzˈvɜːsəl] **1** *adj* transversal
2 *n Geom* transversale *f*

transversally [ˌtrænzˈvɜːsəlɪ] *adv* transversalement

transverse [ˈtrænzvɜːs] **1** *adj (beam, line)* transversal; *Anat* transverse
2 *n (gen)* partie *f* transversale; *Geom* axe *m* transversal *(d'une hyperbole)*
►► *Constr* ***transverse beam*** traverse *f*; *Aut* ***transverse engine*** moteur *m* transversal; *Geom* ***transverse line*** transversale *f*; *Phys* ***transverse wave*** onde *f* transversale

transversely [ˌtrænzˈvɜːslɪ] *adv* transversalement

transverter [trænzˈvɜːtə(r)] *n Rad* émetteur-récepteur *m* additionnel

transvestism [trænzˈvestɪzəm] *n* travestisme *m*, transvestisme *m*

transvestite [trænzˈvestaɪt] *n* travesti(e) *m,f*

Transylvania [ˌtrænsɪlˈveɪnɪə] *n* Transylvanie *f*; **in Transylvania** en Transylvanie

Transylvanian [ˌtrænsɪlˈveɪnɪən] **1** *n* Transylvanien(enne) *m,f*
2 *adj* transylvanien

trap [træp] (*pt & pp* **trapped,** *cont* **trapping**) **1** *n* (**a**) *(snare)* piège *m*; *(dug in ground)* trappe *f*; *(gin-trap)* collet *m*; **to set** *or* **to lay a trap (for sth)** tendre un piège (à qch); **the badger was caught in a trap** le blaireau était pris dans un piège
(**b**) *Fig* piège *m*, traquenard *m*; **to set** *or* **to lay a trap for sb** tendre un piège à qn; **they fell into the trap** ils sont tombés dans le piège; **the poverty trap** le piège de la pauvreté
(**c**) *Tech (for water, oil etc)* collecteur *m*; *(in drain)* siphon *m*
(**d**) *(in dog racing)* box *m* de départ; *(for trapshooting)* ball-trap *m*
(**e**) *Golf* bunker *m* (de sable)
(**f**) *(carriage)* cabriolet *m*, charrette *f* anglaise
(**g**) *(trapdoor)* trappe *f*
(**h**) *very Fam (mouth)* gueule *f*, clapet *m*; **shut your trap!** ta gueule!, ferme-la!; **you would have to go and open your big trap!** il a fallu que tu ouvres ta grande gueule!; **to keep one's trap shut** la fermer, la boucler
2 *vt* (**a**) *(animal)* prendre au piège, piéger
(**b**) *Fig (person)* piéger; **now you're trapped!** maintenant vous êtes piégé *ou* pris!; **to trap sb into saying sth** faire dire qch à qn en usant de ruse; **he trapped me into thinking I was safe** il m'a piégé en me faisant croire que j'étais hors de danger; **we got trapped into going** on s'est fait piéger et on a dû y aller; **she trapped him into marrying her** elle l'a piégé en le forçant à l'épouser
(**c**) *(immobilize, catch)* bloquer, immobiliser; *Sport (ball)* bloquer; **they were trapped** *or* **they got trapped in the lift** ils ont été bloqués *ou* coincés dans l'ascenseur; **we were trapped by the incoming tide** on a été surpris par la marée montante; **I trapped my leg** *or* **my leg got trapped under the table** je me suis coincé la jambe *ou* j'avais la jambe coincée sous la table; **she trapped her fingers in the door** elle s'est pris les doigts dans la porte; **the window blew shut and trapped my hand** un coup de vent a fermé la fenêtre et ma main est restée coincée; **they were trapped in the rubble** ils étaient coincés *ou* immobilisés sous les décombres; **to feel trapped** *(in relationship)* se sentir coincé
(**d**) *(hold back → water, gas)* retenir; **there's a grid to trap dead leaves** il y a une grille pour retenir les feuilles mortes

trapdoor [ˈtræpdɔː(r)] *n* trappe *f*
►► *Entom* ***trapdoor spider*** cténize *f*, mygale *f* maçonne

trapes = **traipse**

trapeze [trəˈpiːz] *n* trapèze *m (de cirque)*
►► ***trapeze artist*** trapéziste *mf*

trapezium [trəˈpiːzɪəm] (*pl* **trapeziums** *or* **trapezia** [-zɪə]) *n* (**a**) *Geom Br (with no parallel sides)* trapèze *m*; *Am (with two parallel sides)* quadrilatère *m* trapézoïdal (**b**) *Anat* trapèze *m*

trapezius [trəˈpiːzjəs] *n Anat (muscle)* muscle *m* trapèze
►► *Anat* ***trapezius muscle*** muscle *m* trapèze

trapezoid [ˈtræpɪzɔɪd] **1** *n* (**a**) *Geom Br* quadrilatère *m* trapézoïdal; *Am* trapèze *m* (**b**) *Anat* trapézoïde *m*
2 *adj* trapézoïde

trapper [ˈtræpə(r)] *n* trappeur *m*

trapping [ˈtræpɪŋ] *n* **1** *Typ* recouvrement *m* (des couleurs), prise *f*
2 trappings *npl* (**a**) *(accessories)* ornements *mpl*; **the trappings of power** les signes *mpl* extérieurs du pouvoir (**b**) *(harness)* harnachement *m*, carapaçon *m*

Trappist [ˈtræpɪst] **1** *n* trappiste *m*
2 *comp (monk, monastery)* de la Trappe

traps [træps] *npl (luggage)* bagages *mpl*, affaires *fpl*

trapshooter [ˈtræpˌʃuːtə(r)] *n* tireur(euse) *m,f* de ball-trap

trapshooting [ˈtræpˌʃuːtɪŋ] *n* ball-trap *m*; **to go trapshooting** faire du ball-trap

trash [træʃ] **1** *n (UNCOUNT)* (**a**) *(nonsense)* bêtises *fpl*, âneries *fpl*; **he talks/writes a lot of trash** il dit/écrit beaucoup d'âneries; **what utter trash!** c'est vraiment n'importe quoi!; **how can you watch that trash?** comment peux-tu regarder de telles nullités *ou* idioties?
(**b**) *(goods, objects)* camelote *f*; **they sell a lot of trash** ils vendent beaucoup de camelote
(**c**) *Am (waste)* ordures *fpl*; **to put something in the trash** mettre qch à la poubelle
(**d**) *Fam (people)* racaille *f*; **they're just trash** c'est de la racaille
(**e**) *Am Comput* poubelle *f*
2 *vt Fam* (**a**) *(reject)* jeter, bazarder; **they trashed all my ideas** ils ont rejeté toutes mes idées ❑
(**b**) *(criticize)* débiner, éreinter, démolir
(**c**) *(vandalize)* foutre en l'air, bousiller
(**d**) *Am Sport (opponent)* démolir
►► *Am* ***trash bag*** sac *m* poubelle; *Am* ***trash barrel*** (grande) poubelle *f*; *Am* ***trash compactor*** compacteur *m* d'ordures ménagères; *Am* ***trash heap*** tas *m* d'ordures; *Am Comput* ***trash icon*** icône *f* de la corbeille

trashcan [ˈtræʃkæn] *n Am* poubelle *f*

trashed [træʃt] *adj Fam (drunk)* rond, fait, bourré; *(on drugs)* défoncé, raide

trasher [ˈtræʃə(r)] *n Am* vandale ❑ *m*, voyou ❑ *m*

trashiness [ˈtræʃɪnɪs] *n (of goods)* mauvaise qualité *f*; *(of book, idea, programme)* nullité *f*

trashman [ˈtræʃmæn] (*pl* **trashmen** [-men]) *n Am* éboueur *m*

trashy [ˈtræʃɪ] (*compar* **trashier,** *superl* **trashiest**) *adj (goods)* de pacotille; *(magazine, book)* de quatre sous; *(idea, article)* qui ne vaut rien; *(programme)* lamentable, au-dessous de tout

trauma [*Br* ˈtrɔːmə, *Am* ˈtraʊmə] (*pl* **traumas** *or* **traumata** [-mətə]) *n (gen) & Psy* traumatisme *m*, *Spec* trauma *m*; *Med* traumatisme *m*

traumatic [*Br* trɔːˈmætɪk, *Am* traʊˈmætɪk] *adj (gen) & Psy* traumatisant; *Med* traumatique

traumatism [*Br* ˈtrɔːmətɪzəm, *Am* ˈtraʊmətɪzəm] *n* traumatisme *m*

traumatize, -ise [*Br* ˈtrɔːmətaɪz, *Am* ˈtraʊmətaɪz] *vt* traumatiser

travail [ˈtræveɪl] *Arch or Literary* **1** *n* (**a**) *(work)* labeur *m* (**b**) *(in childbirth)* douleurs *fpl* de l'enfantement, travail *m*
2 *vi* (**a**) *(work)* peiner (**b**) *(in childbirth)* être en travail *ou* en couches
3 travails *npl (hardship)* vicissitudes *fpl*

travel [ˈtrævəl] (*Br pt & pp* **travelled,** *cont* **travelling,** *Am pt & pp* **traveled,** *cont* **traveling**) **1** *vi* (**a**) *(journey)* voyager; *(journey around)* faire des voyages; **to travel by air/car** voyager en avion/en voiture; **they travelled to Greece by boat** ils sont allés en Grèce en bateau; **they've travelled a lot together** ils ont beaucoup voyagé ensemble; **to travel round the world** faire le tour du monde; **she's travelling (about** *or* **around) somewhere in Asia** elle est en voyage quelque part en Asie; **we travelled across France by train** nous avons traversé la France en train; **they've travelled far and wide** ils ont voyagé partout dans le monde; **to travel light** voyager avec peu de bagages; **to travel back** revenir, rentrer; **let's travel back in time to 1940** retournons en 1940
(**b**) *Com* être représentant(e) *m,f* de commerce; *Br* **he travels in confectionery** il est représentant en confiserie
(**c**) *(go, move → person)* aller; *(→ vehicle, train)* aller, rouler; *(→ piston, shuttle)* se déplacer; *(→ light, sound)* se propager; **the train travelled at high speed through the countryside** le train roulait à toute vitesse à travers la campagne; **we were travelling at an average speed of 60 mph** on faisait du 96 km/h de moyenne; **the signals travel along different routes** les signaux suivent des trajets différents; **the components travel along a conveyor belt** les pièces détachées sont transportées sur un tapis roulant
(**d**) *Fam (go very fast)* rouler (très) vite ❑; **we were really travelling** on roulait vraiment très vite; **this car certainly travels!** elle bombe, cette voiture!
(**e**) *Fig (thoughts, mind)* **my mind travelled back to last June** mes pensées m'ont ramené au mois de juin dernier
(**f**) *(news, rumour)* se répandre, se propager, circuler; **news travels fast** les nouvelles vont vite
(**g**) *(food)* supporter le voyage; *(humour)* bien passer les frontières
(**h**) *(in basketball)* marcher
2 *vt* (**a**) *(distance)* faire, parcourir; **I travelled 50 miles to get here** j'ai fait 80 km pour venir ici
(**b**) *(area, road)* parcourir; **I've travelled these roads for years** j'ai parcouru ces routes pendant des années; **we travelled the country from west to east** on a parcouru *ou* traversé le pays d'ouest en est
3 *n (UNCOUNT) (journeys)* voyage *m*, voyages *mpl*; **travel broadens the mind** les voyages ouvrent l'esprit; **I've done a lot of foreign travel** j'ai beaucoup voyagé à l'étranger; **travel was slower in those days** on voyageait plus lentement à cette époque; **what do you spend on travel?** à combien vous reviennent vos déplacements?
4 *comp (guide, brochure)* touristique; *(writer)* qui écrit des récits de voyage
5 travels *npl (journeys)* voyages *mpl*; *(comings and goings)* allées et venues *fpl*; **I met them on my travels in China** je les ai rencontrés au cours de mes voyages en Chine; *Fam* **did you see my glasses on your travels?** tu n'as pas vu mes lunettes quelque part? ❑
►► ***travel agency*** agence *f* de voyages; ***travel agent*** agent *m* de voyages; ***travel agent's*** agence *f* de voyages; ***travel allowance*** indemnité *f* de déplacement; ***travel book*** récit *m* de voyages; ***travel brochure*** dépliant *m* touristique; ***travel bureau*** agence *f* de voyages; ***travel company*** voyagiste *mf*; ***travel documents*** documents *mpl* de voyage; ***travel expenses*** frais *mpl* de déplacement; ***travel firm*** voyagiste *mf*; ***travel guide*** guide *m* touristique; ***travel insurance*** assurance-voyage *f*; **to take out travel insurance** prendre une assurance-voyage; ***travel literature*** documentation *f* touristique; ***travel programme*** *(travelogue)* émission *f* sur les voyages; ***travel rug*** plaid *m*; *Br* ***travel sickness*** mal *m* des transports; ***travel writer*** auteur *m* de récits de voyage

'Gulliver's Travels' *Swift* 'Les Voyages de Gulliver'

travelator [ˈtrævəleɪtə(r)] *n* tapis *m ou* trottoir *m* roulant

Travelcard ['trævəlkɑːd] *n Br* carte *f* d'abonnement *(pour les transports en commun à Londres)*
traveled, traveler *etc Am* = **travelled, traveller** *etc*
travelled, *Am* **traveled** ['trævəld] *adj* (**a**) *(person)* qui a beaucoup voyagé; **he's a well-travelled man** il a beaucoup voyagé (**b**) *(road, path)* fréquenté; **this is a much travelled road** c'est une route très fréquentée
traveller, *Am* **traveler** ['trævələ(r)] *n* (**a**) *(gen)* voyageur(euse) *m,f*; **I'm not a good traveller** je supporte mal les voyages (**b**) *(salesman)* voyageur(euse) *m,f* de commerce (**c**) *(gipsy)* bohémien(enne) *m,f*
►► ***traveller's cheque*** chèque *m* de voyage, traveller's cheque *m*; *Bot* ***traveller's joy*** clématite *f* des haies, clématite *f* vigne blanche
travelling, *Am* **traveling** ['trævəlɪŋ] **1** *n (UNCOUNT)* (**a**) *(gen)* voyage *m*, voyages *mpl*; **to do a lot of travelling** beaucoup voyager; **there isn't a lot of travelling in this job** on ne voyage pas beaucoup dans ce travail
(**b**) *(in basketball)* marché *m*
2 *adj (companion, bag)* de voyage; *(preacher, musician)* itinérant; *(crane)* mobile
►► ***travelling allowance*** indemnité *f* de déplacement; ***travelling circus*** cirque *m* forain; ***travelling clock*** réveil *m* de voyage; ***travelling companion*** compagnon *m* de voyage; ***travelling expenses*** frais *mpl* de déplacement; ***travelling library*** ≃ bibliobus *m*; ***travelling people*** gens *mpl* du voyage; *Cin* ***travelling platform*** travelling *m*; *Br* ***travelling rug*** plaid *m*; ***travelling salesman*** représentant *m ou* voyageur *m* de commerce; ***travelling scholarship*** bourse *f* de voyage; *Cin* ***travelling shot*** prise *f* de vue en travelling, plan *m* travelling
travelogue, *Am* **travelog** ['trævəlɒg] *n (lecture, book)* récit *m* de voyage; *(film)* film *m* de voyage
travel-sick *adj Br* **to be travel-sick** *(in car)* avoir mal au cœur en voiture, avoir le mal de la route; *(in boat)* avoir le mal de mer; *(in plane)* avoir le mal de l'air; **to get travel-sick** souffrir du mal des transports, être malade en voyage
travel-size *adj (shampoo etc)* de voyage
travel-stained *adj* sali par le voyage *ou* les voyages
travel-weary *adj* fatigué par le voyage *ou* les voyages
traversable ['trævəsəbəl, trə'vɜːsəbəl] *adj Formal* traversable
traverse ['trævəs, ˌtrə'vɜːs] **1** *vt* (**a**) *Formal (go over)* traverser (**b**) *Arch or Literary (plan, opinion)* contrarier, traverser
2 *vi (in climbing, skiing)* faire une traversée, traverser
3 *n* (**a**) *(beam)* traverse *f* (**b**) *Geom* (ligne *f*) transversale *f*; *(in surveying)* cheminement *m* (**c**) *(in mountaineering, skiing → across face of escarpment)* vire *f* (**d**) *(gallery)* galerie *f* transversale
travertine ['trævətɪn] *n Geol* travertin *m*
travesty ['trævəstɪ] (*pl* **travesties,** *pt & pp* **travestied**) **1** *n (parody)* parodie *f*, pastiche *m*; *Pej (mockery, pretence)* simulacre *m*, parodie *f*; **the trial was a travesty of justice** le procès n'était qu'un simulacre de justice, c'était une parodie de procès
2 *vt (justice)* bafouer
►► *Theat* ***travesty role*** rôle *m* travesti
travolator = **travelator**
trawl [trɔːl] **1** *n* (**a**) *Fishing (net)* chalut *m*
(**b**) *(search)* recherche *f*; **to do a trawl through the Internet** faire une recherche *ou* des recherches sur Internet
2 *vi* (**a**) *Fishing* pêcher au chalut; **to trawl for mackerel** pêcher le maquereau au chalut
(**b**) *(search)* chercher; **to trawl for information** chercher des renseignements, aller à la pêche (aux renseignements)
3 *vt (net)* traîner, tirer; *(sea)* pêcher dans; *Fig* **she trawled the small-ads for bargains** elle épluchait les petites annonces à la recherche de bonnes affaires; **he trawled the singles bars** il écumait les bars pour célibataires
►► *Fishing* ***trawl line*** palangre *f*; *Fishing* ***trawl net*** chalut *m*
trawler ['trɔːlə(r)] *n (boat, fisherman)* chalutier *m*
trawlerman ['trɔːləmən] (*pl* **trawlermen** [-mən]) *n* chalutier *m*
trawling ['trɔːlɪŋ] *n Fishing* pêche *f* au chalut, chalutage *m*
tray [treɪ] *n* (**a**) *(for carrying)* plateau *m*; *(for selling ice cream etc)* éventaire *m*; **a tray of sandwiches** un plateau de sandwichs (**b**) *(for papers)* casier *m* (de rangement); *(for mail)* corbeille *f*; *(of printer)* bac *m*; **in/out tray** *(for mail)* corbeille *f* arrivée/départ (**c**) *(in box of chocolates)* supports *mpl* alvéolés
traycloth ['treɪklɒθ] *n* napperon *m* (de plateau)
trayful ['treɪfʊl] *n* plein plateau *m*
treacherous ['tretʃərəs] *adj* (**a**) *(disloyal → ally)* traître, perfide; *Fig (memory)* infidèle (**b**) *(dangerous → water, current, ice)* traître; **the roads are treacherous** les routes sont très glissantes
treacherously ['tretʃərəslɪ] *adv (act)* traîtreusement; **the currents are treacherously strong** les courants sont traîtres tellement ils sont forts
treacherousness ['tretʃərəsnɪs] *n* (**a**) *(of ice, current, roads)* caractère *m* dangereux (**b**) *(disloyalty)* perfidie *f*, traîtrise *f*
treachery ['tretʃərɪ] (*pl* **treacheries**) *n* perfidie *f*, traîtrise *f*
treacle ['triːkəl] *n Br (molasses)* mélasse *f*; *(golden syrup)* mélasse *f* raffinée
►► ***treacle pudding*** pudding *m* à la mélasse; ***treacle tart*** tarte *f* à la mélasse
treacly ['triːklɪ] *adj (sweet)* sirupeux; *Fig (sentimental)* mièvre, sirupeux
tread [tred] (*pt* **trod** [trɒd], *pp* **trod** *or* **trodden** ['trɒdən]) **1** *vt* (**a**) *(walk)* **a path had been trodden through the grass** les pas des marcheurs avaient tracé un chemin dans l'herbe; **she trod the streets looking for him** elle a battu le pavé *ou* parcouru la ville à sa recherche; **the path had been trodden by generations of hikers** des générations de randonneurs avaient foulé ce chemin; *Theat* **to tread the boards** monter sur les planches
(**b**) *(trample)* fouler; **to tread grapes** fouler du raisin; **to tread sth underfoot** fouler qch aux pieds, piétiner qch; **to tread water** nager sur place; *Fig* faire du surplace
(**c**) *(stamp)* enfoncer, écraser; **she trod the cigarette into the sand** elle a écrasé du pied le mégot dans le sable; **to tread mud/dirt into the carpet** mettre de la boue/de la terre sur le tapis (avec ses chaussures); **don't tread the crumbs into the carpet** ne piétinez pas les miettes sur la moquette
2 *vi* (**a**) *(walk)* marcher; **to tread lightly** marcher d'un pas léger; *Fig* **to tread carefully** *or* **warily** y aller doucement *ou* avec précaution
(**b**) *(step)* **to tread on sth** *(accidentally)* marcher sur qch; *(deliberately)* marcher (exprès) sur qch; **I must have trodden in something** j'ai dû marcher sur *ou* dans quelque chose; **he trod on my foot** il m'a marché sur le pied; *Fig* **to tread on sb's heels** talonner qn, suivre qn de près; *also Fig* **to tread on sb's toes** marcher sur les pieds de qn
3 *n* (**a**) *(footstep)* pas *m*; *(sound of steps)* bruit *m* de pas; **to walk with a heavy tread** marcher d'un pas lourd; **she could hear the measured tread of his footsteps** elle entendait le bruit régulier de ses pas
(**b**) *(of stairs)* marche *f*, *Spec* giron *m*
(**c**) *(of shoe)* semelle *f*; *(of tyre → depth)* bande *f* de roulement, chape *f*; *(→ pattern)* sculptures *fpl*; **there's no tread left** *(on shoe)* la semelle est usée; *(on tyre)* le pneu est lisse
►**tread down** *vt sep* tasser (du pied)
►**tread in** *vt sep (plant)* tasser la terre autour de
treading ['tredɪŋ] *n (of grapes)* foulage *m*
treadle ['tredəl] **1** *n* pédale *f (sur un tour ou sur une machine à coudre)*
2 *vi* actionner la pédale
treadmill ['tredmɪl] *n* (**a**) *Hist (gen)* = roue ou manège mus par un homme; *(driven by horse)* trépigneuse *f*; *Fig* **I feel like I'm on a treadmill** je ne supporte pas cette routine; **the same old treadmill** le train-train quotidien (**b**) *(in gym)* tapis *m* de jogging, tapis *m* de course
treas. *(written abbr* **treasurer***)* trés
treason ['triːzən] *n* trahison *f*
treasonable ['triːzənəbəl] *adj (action, statement)* qui constitue une trahison
treasure ['treʒə(r)] **1** *n* (**a**) *(valuables)* trésor *m*
(**b**) *(art)* joyau *m*, trésor *m*; **the museum has many treasures of Renaissance art** le musée contient de nombreux joyaux de la Renaissance
(**c**) *Fam (person)* trésor *m*, ange *m*; **come here, my little treasure** viens là, mon (petit) trésor; **she's a real treasure** *(cleaning lady, servant etc)* c'est une vrai perle
2 *vt* (**a**) *(friendship, possession)* tenir beaucoup à
(**b**) *(gift)* garder précieusement, être très attaché à; *(memory)* conserver précieusement, *Formal* chérir; *(moment)* chérir
►► ***treasure house*** *(museum)* trésor *m (lieu)*; *(room, library)* mine *f*, trésor *m*; *Fig* **she's a treasure house of information** c'est un puits de science *ou* une mine de renseignements; ***treasure hunt*** chasse *f* au trésor; ***the Treasure State*** = surnom donné au Montana; *Law* ***treasure trove*** trésor *m (qu'on a découvert)*; *Fig* **the museum is a real treasure trove** le musée est une véritable caverne d'Ali-Baba; **the book was a treasure trove of anecdotes** le livre était une mine d'anecdotes

'Treasure Island' *Stevenson* 'L'Île au trésor'

treasurer ['treʒərə(r)] *n* (**a**) *(of club)* trésorier(-ère) *m,f* (**b**) *Am (of company)* directeur(trice) *m,f* financier(ère)
treasury ['treʒərɪ] (*pl* **treasuries**) *n* (**a**) *(building)* trésorerie *f*
(**b**) *Fig (of information)* mine *f*; *(of poems)* recueil *m*
(**c**) *Admin (funds)* trésor *m* (public); **the Treasury** *(government department)* la Trésorerie, ≃ le ministère des Finances; *Am* **Secretary/Department of the Treasury** ≃ ministre *m*/ministère *m* des Finances
►► *Br* ***Treasury bench*** banc *m* des ministres *(au Parlement britannique)*; *Fin* ***Treasury bill, Treasury bond*** certificat *m* de trésorerie, ≃ bon *m* du Trésor; *Fin* ***Treasury note*** billet *m* de trésorerie; *Fin* ***Treasury scrip*** inscription *f* sur le grand-livre; *Fin* ***Treasury swap*** échange *m* cambiste; *Fin* ***Treasury warrant*** mandat *m* du Trésor
treat [triːt] **1** *vt* (**a**) *(deal with)* traiter; **to treat sb well** bien traiter qn; **to treat sb badly** mal traiter qn, ne pas bien traiter qn; **the hostages said that they had been well treated** les otages ont déclaré qu'ils avaient été bien traités; **he treats them with contempt** il est méprisant envers eux; **teachers expect to be treated with respect by their pupils** les professeurs exigent que leurs élèves se conduisent respectueusement envers eux; **you shouldn't treat them like children** vous ne devriez pas les traiter comme des enfants; **you treat this place like a hotel!** ce n'est pas un hôtel ici!
(**b**) *(handle → substance, object)* utiliser, se servir de; *(→ claim, request)* traiter; **the weedkiller needs to be treated with great care** il faut se servir du désherbant avec beaucoup de précaution
(**c**) *(consider → problem, question)* traiter, considérer; **the whole episode was treated as a joke** on a pris *ou* on a considéré tout cet épisode comme une plaisanterie; **she treated the subject rather superficially** elle a traité le sujet assez superficiellement
(**d**) *Med (patient, illness)* soigner, traiter; **she's being treated for cancer** on la soigne pour un cancer
(**e**) *(fruit, timber, crops)* traiter; **the land has been treated with fertilizer** la terre a été traitée aux engrais
(**f**) *(buy)* **to treat sb to sth** offrir *ou* payer qch à qn; **she treated them all to ice cream** elle a payé *ou* offert une glace à tout le monde; **I treated myself to a new coat** je me suis offert *ou* payé un manteau neuf; **go on, treat yourself!** vas-y, gâte-toi *ou* fais-toi plaisir!; *Ironic* **he treated us to a fair old display of petulance** nous avons eu droit à une belle démonstration de mauvaise humeur; *Ironic* **they were treated to a graphic description of her symptoms** ils ont eu droit à une description de ses symptômes dans tous les détails
2 *vi Formal* (**a**) **to treat of** *(deal with)* traiter de; **the book treats of love** le livre traite de l'amour

(**b**) *(negotiate)* **to treat with sb** traiter avec qn; **the government refuses to treat with terrorists** le gouvernement refuse de traiter avec les terroristes; **to treat with the enemy** pactiser avec l'ennemi

3 *n* (**a**) *(on special occasion → enjoyment)* gâterie *f*, (petit) plaisir *m*; *(→ surprise)* surprise *f*; *(→ present)* cadeau *m*; *(→ outing)* sortie *f*; **as a special treat we went to the planetarium** on nous a offert tout spécialement une visite au planétarium; **these chocolates are a real treat** ces chocolats sont un véritable délice *ou* un vrai régal; **I've got a treat for you** j'ai une bonne surprise pour toi; **to give oneself a treat** s'offrir un petit plaisir, se faire plaisir; **let's give her a treat** faisons-lui un petit plaisir, gâtons-la un peu; **this is my treat** c'est moi qui offre *ou* régale; **you've got a treat in store** on te réserve une bonne surprise, attends-toi à une bonne surprise; **it used to be a real treat to travel by train** autrefois, on se faisait une vraie fête de voyager en train

(**b**) *(pleasure)* plaisir *m*; **it's a treat for us to see you looking so happy** cela nous fait vraiment plaisir *ou* pour nous c'est une grande joie de vous voir si heureuse

4 a treat *adv Br Fam* à merveille ❑; **he's coming on a treat** il fait de sacrés progrès; **the idea worked a treat** l'idée a marché à merveille; **to go down a treat** être très apprécié ❑

treatable ['tri:təbəl] *adj* traitable

treatise ['tri:tɪs] *n* traité *m*; **a treatise on racism** un traité sur le racisme

'A Treatise of Human Nature' *Hume* 'Traité de la nature humaine'

treatment ['tri:tmənt] *n* (**a**) *(of person)* traitement *m*; **we complained of ill treatment** nous nous sommes plaints d'avoir été mal traités; **they gave him preferential treatment** ils lui ont accordé un traitement préférentiel *ou* de faveur; **I got very good treatment** on m'a très bien traité; *Fam* **to give sb the (full) treatment** *(treat well)* traiter qn avec tous les égards ❑; *(beat up)* rosser qn

(**b**) *(UNCOUNT) Med* soins *mpl*, traitement *m*; **a course of treatment** un traitement; **she was sent to Madrid for treatment** on l'a envoyée se faire soigner à Madrid; **to receive/to undergo treatment** recevoir/suivre un traitement; **is he responding to treatment?** est-ce qu'il réagit au traitement?; **no doctor has the right to refuse treatment** aucun médecin n'a le droit de refuser ses soins à un malade; **cancer treatment** traitement *m* du cancer; **X-ray treatment** traitement *m* par rayons X

(**c**) *(of subject)* traitement *m*, façon *f* de traiter; **Cézanne's treatment of colour** la façon dont Cézanne traite les couleurs

(**d**) *(of crops, timber)* traitement *m*

(**e**) *(chemical)* produit *m* chimique

(**f**) *Cin* traitement *m*

treaty ['tri:tɪ] (*pl* **treaties**) *n* (**a**) *Pol* traité *m*; **to sign a treaty (with sb)** signer *ou* conclure un traité (avec qn); **there is a treaty between the two countries** les deux pays sont liés par traité

(**b**) *Law (between individuals)* accord *m*; *(contract)* contrat *m*; **they sold the property by private treaty** ils ont vendu la propriété par accord privé

►► *Hist* ***the Treaty of Brest-Litovsk*** le traité de Brest-Litovsk; *Hist* ***the Treaty of Rome*** le traité de Rome; *Hist* ***the Treaty of Versailles*** le traité de Versailles

treble ['trebəl] **1** *adj* (**a**) *(triple)* triple; *Br* **my phone number is seventy treble four** mon numéro de téléphone est le soixante-dix, quatre cent quarante-quatre

(**b**) *Mus (voice)* de soprano; *(part)* pour voix de soprano

2 *n* (**a**) *Mus (part, singer)* soprano *m*

(**b**) *(UNCOUNT) (in hi-fi)* aigus *mpl*

3 *vt* tripler

4 *vi* tripler

5 *adv* trois fois plus; **treble the number** le triple; **treble the amount** trois fois plus; *Mus* **to sing treble** chanter dans un registre de soprano

►► *Br* ***treble chance*** = méthode de pari en football; *Mus* ***treble clef*** clef *f* de sol

trebly ['treblɪ] *adv* triplement, trois fois plus; **trebly difficult** trois fois plus difficile

trebuchet ['trebjʊʃet, ˌtreɪbu:'ʃeɪ] *n Mil & Hist* trébuchet *m*

trecentist [treɪ'tʃentɪst] *n Art & Literature* trécentiste *m*

trecento [treɪ'tʃentəʊ] *n Art & Literature* **the trecento** le XIVème siècle

tree [tri:] **1** *n* (**a**) *Bot* arbre *m*; **fruit tree** arbre *m* fruitier; *Bible* **the Tree of Knowledge/Life** l'arbre *m* de la science du bien et du mal/de vie; *Fig* **to be at the top of the tree** être au sommet; *Fig* **to get to the top of the tree** arriver au sommet de sa profession; *Am Fam* **to be up a tree** être dans une impasse ❑; *Fam* **to be out of one's tree** *(mad)* être cinglé *ou* givré; *(drunk)* être rond *ou* rétamé *ou* bourré; *(on drugs)* être défoncé *ou* raide; *Fam* **money doesn't grow on trees!** l'argent ne pousse pas sur les arbres!; *Fam* **good proofreaders don't grow on trees** les bons correcteurs ne courent pas les rues

(**b**) *(diagram)* **tree (diagram)** représentation *f* en arbre *ou* arborescente, arborescence *f*

(**c**) *(for shoes)* embauchoir *m*, forme *f*

(**d**) *(of saddle)* arçon *m*

2 *vt* (**a**) *(hunter, animal)* forcer *ou* obliger à se réfugier dans un arbre

(**b**) *Am Fam Fig (trap)* piéger ❑

►► *Orn* ***tree duck*** dendrocygne *m*; *Bot* ***tree fern*** fougère *f* arborescente; *Zool* ***tree fox*** urocyon *m*; *Zool* ***tree frog*** rainette *f*; *Entom* ***tree hopper*** membracide *m*; *Pej* ***tree hugger*** écologiste *mf* fanatique; *Zool* ***tree kangaroo*** dendrolague *m*, kangourou *m* arboricole; ***tree line*** limite *f* des arbres; *Orn* ***tree pipit*** pipit *m* des arbres; ***tree ring*** cercle *m* d'arbres; *Zool* ***tree shrew*** tupaïa *m*, tupaja *m*; ***tree snake*** serpent *m* arboricole; *Orn* ***tree sparrow*** (moineau *m*) friquet *m*; *Comput* ***tree structure*** arborescence *f*, structure *f* arborescente; ***tree surgeon*** arboriculteur(-trice) *m,f (qui s'occupe de soigner et d'élaguer les arbres)*; ***tree surgery*** arboriculture *f (traitement des arbres malades)*; ***tree trunk*** tronc *m* d'arbre

treecreeper ['tri:kri:pə(r)] *n Orn* grimpereau *m* (des bois)

treehouse ['tri:haʊs, *pl* -haʊzɪz] *n* = cabane construite dans un arbre

treeless ['tri:lɪs] *adj* sans arbres, dénudé

tree-lined *adj* bordé d'arbres

treenail ['tri:neɪl] *n Tech* cheville *f*

treestump ['tri:stʌmp] *n* souche *f*

treetop ['tri:tɒp] *n* cime *f ou* haut *m ou* faîte *m* d'un arbre; **in the treetops** au faîte *ou* au sommet des arbres; *Aviat* **to skim the treetops** voler en rase-mottes

trefa ['treɪfə] *adj Rel* tréfa

trefoil ['trefɔɪl] *n Archit & Bot* trèfle *m*

trek [trek] (*pt & pp* **trekked**, *cont* **trekking**) **1** *n* (**a**) *(walk)* marche *f*; *(hike)* randonnée *f*; **to go on a trek** faire une marche/une randonnée; **a long trek** un trajet long et pénible *(à pied)*; **it was a real trek to get here** ç'a été une véritable expédition pour arriver ici; **it's a bit of a trek to the shops** ça fait une trotte jusqu'aux magasins *ou* pour aller aux magasins

(**b**) *SAfr Hist* voyage *m* en char à bœufs

2 *vi* (**a**) *(walk)* avancer avec peine; *(hike)* faire de la randonnée; *Fig (drag oneself)* se traîner; **we had to trek across fields to get here** il a fallu passer à travers champs pour arriver ici; **they trekked all the way out here to see us** ils ont fait tout ce chemin pour venir nous voir; **I can't be bothered to trek over to the supermarket again** je n'ai pas le courage de refaire tout ce chemin jusqu'au supermarché

(**b**) *SAfr Hist* voyager en char à bœufs

3 *vt SAfr (load)* tirer, traîner

Trekkie ['trekɪ] *n Fam* fan *mf* de Star Trek

trekking ['trekɪŋ] *n (as holiday activity)* randonnée *f*, trekking *m*; **I went on a trekking holiday in Nepal** j'ai été faire de la randonnée au Népal pour mes vacances

trellis ['trelɪs] **1** *n* treillage *m*, treillis *m*

2 *vt (wood strips)* faire un treillage de; *(plant)* treillager

trelliswork ['trelɪs,wɜ:k] *n* treillage *m*

trematode ['tremətəʊd] *n Zool (ver m)* trématode *m*

tremble ['trembəl] **1** *vi* (**a**) *(person → with cold)* trembler, frissonner; *(→ from fear, excitement, rage)* trembler, frémir; *(hands)* trembler; **to tremble with fear** trembler de peur; **to tremble like a leaf** trembler comme une feuille

(**b**) *(voice → from emotion)* trembler, vibrer; *(→ from fear)* trembler; *(→ from infirmity, old age)* trembler, chevroter; **her voice trembled with emotion** sa voix tremblait d'émotion

(**c**) *(bridge, house, ground)* trembler; *(engine)* vibrer

(**d**) *Fig (be anxious)* frémir; **she trembled at the thought** elle frémissait à cette seule pensée; **he trembled for their safety** il tremblait pour eux; **where are they? – I tremble to think!** où sont-ils? – je n'ose y penser!

2 *n* (**a**) *(from fear)* tremblement *m*; *(from excitement, rage)* frémissement *m*; *(from cold)* frissonnement *m*; *Fam* **to be all of a tremble** être tout tremblant

(**b**) *(in voice)* frémissement *m*, frisson *m*

trembling ['tremblɪŋ] **1** *adj* (**a**) *(body → with cold)* frissonnant, grelottant; *(→ in fear, excitement)* frémissant, tremblant; *(hands)* tremblant

(**b**) *(voice → with emotion)* vibrant; *(→ with fear)* tremblant; *(→ because of old age)* chevrotant; **with a trembling voice** *(speaker)* d'une *ou* la voix tremblante; *(singer)* d'une *ou* la voix chevrotante

2 *n (from cold)* tremblement *m*, frissonnement *m*; *(from fear)* tremblement *m*, frémissement *m*; **in fear and trembling** tout tremblant

►► *Bot* ***trembling poplar*** (peuplier *m*) tremble *m*

tremendous [trɪ'mendəs] *adj* (**a**) *(number, amount)* énorme, très grand; *(cost, speed)* très élevé, vertigineux; *(building, arch)* énorme; *(height)* vertigineux, très grand; *(undertaking)* énorme, monumental; *(admiration, disappointment, pride)* très grand, extrême; *(crash, noise)* terrible, épouvantable; **the fair was a tremendous success** la foire a été une très grande réussite; **there's been a tremendous improvement in her work** son travail s'est énormément amélioré; **there was a tremendous crowd** il y avait un monde fou *ou* une foule énorme; **you've been a tremendous help** vous m'avez été d'une aide précieuse

(**b**) *(wonderful)* sensationnel, formidable; **I had a tremendous time** je me suis amusé comme un fou; **she looks tremendous in black** elle a beaucoup d'allure en noir; **he scored a tremendous goal** il a marqué un but sensationnel

tremendously [trɪ'mendəslɪ] *adv (as intensifier)* extrêmement; **we heard a tremendously loud explosion** on a entendu une formidable explosion; **we enjoyed it tremendously** cela nous a énormément plu; **he did tremendously well** il a extrêmement bien réussi; **I'm not tremendously keen on his plays** je n'aime pas vraiment ses pièces

tremendousness [trɪ'mendəsnɪs] *n (of success, sacrifice)* énormité *f*; *(of crash, explosion)* intensité *f*

tremolo ['treməlәʊ] (*pl* **tremolos**) *n Mus* trémolo *m*

►► ***tremolo arm*** = levier sur une guitare électrique qui sert à varier le ton d'une note

tremor ['tremə(r)] *n* (**a**) *Geol* secousse *f* (sismique) (**b**) *(in voice)* frémissement *m*, frisson *m*, tremblement *m* (**c**) *(of fear, thrill)* frisson *m*; **a tremor of anticipation ran through the audience** à l'idée de ce qui allait suivre, la salle fut parcourue d'un frisson

tremulous ['tremjʊləs] *adj Literary* (**a**) *(with fear)* tremblant; *(with excitement, nervousness)* frémissant; *(handwriting)* tremblé; **he was tremulous with emotion/fear** il tremblait d'émotion/de peur; **her voice was tremulous with joy** sa voix vibrait de joie (**b**) *(timid → person, manner)* timide, craintif; *(→ animal)* craintif, effarouché; *(→ smile)* timide

tremulously ['tremjʊləslɪ] *adv Literary* (**a**) *(with fear, emotion)* en tremblant; **to sing/to answer tremulously** chanter/répondre d'une voix tremblante (**b**) *(timidly)* timidement, craintivement

tremulousness ['tremjʊləsnɪs] *n Literary* (**a**) *(of voice, limbs, body)* tremblotement *m*; **the tremulousness of his handwriting** son écriture tremblée (**b**) *(timidity)* timidité *f*

trench [trentʃ] **1** *n (gen) & Constr & Mil* tranchée *f*; *(ditch)* fossé *m*; **life in the trenches** la vie dans les tranchées; **my grandfather fought in the trenches** mon grand-père a fait la guerre des tranchées

2 *vt (field)* creuser une tranchée *ou* des tranchées dans; *Mil* retrancher

3 *vi* creuser une tranchée *ou* des tranchées

►► ***trench coat*** trench-coat *m*; *Med* ***trench fever*** rickettsiose *f*; *Med* ***trench foot*** = gelure au pied due au froid ou à l'humidité; *Mil* ***trench mortar*** engin *m ou* pièce *f* de tranchée; *Med* ***trench mouth*** angine *f* ulcéreuse *ou* de Vincent; ***trench warfare*** guerre *f* de tranchées

trenchancy ['trentʃənsɪ] *n* mordant *m*

trenchant ['trentʃənt] *adj* incisif, tranchant

trenchantly ['trentʃəntlɪ] *adv (speak)* d'un ton tranchant *ou* incisif; *(write)* d'une manière incisive

trencher ['trentʃə(r)] *n* tranchoir *m*

trencherman ['trentʃəmən] (*pl* **trenchermen** [-mən]) *n Literary or Hum* gros mangeur *m*; **he's a good/great trencherman** il a un bon coup de fourchette

trend [trend] **1** *n (tendency)* tendance *f*; *(fashion)* mode *f*; **the trend is towards shorter skirts** la tendance est aux jupes plus courtes; **there is a trend away from going abroad for holidays** on a tendance à délaisser les vacances à l'étranger; **political/electoral trends** tendances *fpl* politiques/électorales; **the general trend of the market** les tendances *fpl* du marché; **house prices are on an upward trend again** le prix des maisons est de nouveau à la hausse; **if present trends continue** si les tendances actuelles se poursuivent; **the trend of events** le cours *ou* la tournure des événements; **the latest trends** la dernière mode; **to set a/the trend** *(style)* donner un/le ton; *(fashion)* lancer une/la mode

2 *vi (extend* → *mountain range)* s'étendre; *(veer* → *coastline)* s'incliner; *(turn* → *prices, opinion)* s'orienter

►► *Mktg* ***trend analysis*** analyse *f* des tendances; *Mktg* ***trend reversal*** renversement *m* de tendance

trendily ['trendɪlɪ] *adv Br Fam (dress)* branché; **the decor was trendily minimalist** le décor minimaliste était très tendance

trendiness ['trendɪnɪs] *n Br Fam* côté *m* branché *ou* à la mode; **the trendiness of his haircut/views** sa coupe *f*/ses idées *fpl* à la mode; **the trendiness of the decor** le décor branché

trendsetter ['trend,setə(r)] *n (person* → *in style)* personne *f* qui donne le ton; *(*→ *in fashion)* personne *f* qui lance une mode

trendsetting ['trend,setɪŋ] **1** *adj (person)* qui lance une mode; *(idea, garment)* d'avant-garde

2 *n* lancement *m* d'une mode

trendy ['trendɪ] (*compar* **trendier,** *superl* **trendiest,** *pl* **trendies**) *Br Fam* **1** *adj (music, appearance, clothes)* branché; *(ideas, place, resort)* à la mode, branché; **he's a very trendy dresser** il est toujours habillé à la dernière mode

2 *n Pej* branché(e) *m,f*

►► [illegible]

Trent [trent] *n* (**a**) *(river)* **the (River) Trent** le Trent (**b**) *(city)* Trente; *Hist* **the Council of Trent** le concile de Trente

Trento ['trentəʊ] *n* Trente

trepan [trɪ'pæn] (*pt & pp* **trepanned,** *cont* **trepanning**) **1** *vt* (**a**) *Mining* forer (**b**) *Med* trépaner

2 *n* (**a**) *Mining* foreuse *f*; *(for metal, plastic)* foret *m* (**b**) *Med* trépan *m*

trepang [trɪ'pæŋ] *n Ich* tripang *m*, trépang *m*

trephine [trɪ'fi:n, trɪ'faɪn] *Med* **1** *n* tréphine *f*

2 *vt* trépaner

trepidation [,trepɪ'deɪʃən] *n* (**a**) *(alarm)* appréhension *f*; **with great trepidation** avec une vive appréhension; **he stood there in trepidation before the headmaster** il se tenait tout tremblant devant le directeur de l'école; **he picked up the phone and, not without trepidation, dialled** il saisit l'écouteur et, non sans appréhension, composa le numéro (**b**) *(excitement)* agitation *f*

trespass ['trespəs] **1** *vi* (**a**) *(on property)* pénétrer sans autorisation *ou* s'introduire dans une propriété privée; *Law* se rendre coupable d'une violation de propriété; **you're trespassing** vous êtes sur une propriété privée; **to trespass on sb's land** s'introduire *ou* entrer sans autorisation dans une propriété privée; **no trespassing** *(sign)* défense d'entrer, propriété privée

(**b**) *Fig (encroach)* **I don't want to trespass on your time/hospitality** je ne veux pas abuser de votre temps/hospitalité; **he's trespassing on my area of responsibility** il empiète sur mon terrain; **to trespass on sb's rights** violer *ou* enfreindre les droits de qn

(**c**) *Bible* **to trespass against sb** offenser qn; **as we forgive those that trespass against us** comme nous pardonnons à ceux qui nous ont offensés; **to trespass against the law** enfreindre la loi (divine)

2 *n* (**a**) *(UNCOUNT)* entrée *f* non autorisée; *Law* violation *f* de propriété; **to commit trespass** s'introduire dans une propriété privée

(**b**) *Bible* péché *m*; **forgive us our trespasses** pardonne-nous nos offenses

trespasser ['trespəsə(r)] *n* (**a**) *Law* intrus(e) *m,f* *(dans une propriété privée)*; **trespassers will be prosecuted** *(sign)* défense d'entrer sous peine de poursuites (**b**) *Bible* pécheur(eresse) *m,f*

trespassing ['trespəsɪŋ] *n (on sb's land)* violation *f* de propriété (foncière); **no trespassing** *(sign)* défense d'entrer

tress [tres] *n Literary* **a tress (of hair)** une mèche *ou* une boucle de cheveux; **her golden tresses** sa blonde chevelure *f*

trestle ['tresəl] *n* (**a**) *(for table)* tréteau *m* (**b**) *Constr* chevalet *m*

►► ***trestle bridge*** pont *m* sur chevalets; ***trestle table*** table *f* à tréteaux

trews [tru:z] *npl Scot Old-fashioned* pantalon *m* en tissu écossais

trey [treɪ] *n (on cards, dice)* trois *m*

triable ['traɪəbəl] *adj Law (case)* susceptible d'être porté en justice

triacid [traɪ'æsɪd] *n Chem* triacide *m*

triad ['traɪæd] *n* (**a**) *(group of three)* triade *f* (**b**) *(Chinese secret society)* triade *f* (**c**) *Mus* accord *m* parfait (**d**) *Chem (element)* élément *m* trivalent; *(atom)* atome *m* trivalent; *(ion)* ion *m* trivalent

triadic [traɪ'ædɪk] *adj* triadique

triage ['tri:ɑ:ʒ] *n Med* triage *m (des malades, des blessés)*

trial ['traɪəl] **1** *n* (**a**) *Law* procès *m*; **he pleaded guilty at the trial** il a plaidé coupable à son procès *ou* devant le tribunal; **many witnesses were brought forward at the trial** de nombreux témoins sont venus à la barre au cours du procès; **to be** *or* **to go on trial for sth, to stand trial for sth** passer en jugement *ou* en justice pour qch; **he was put on** *or* **sent for trial for murder** il a été jugé pour meurtre; **to bring sb to trial** faire passer *ou* traduire qn en justice; **his case comes up for trial in September** son affaire passe en jugement en septembre; **trial by jury** jugement *m* par jury; **famous trials** causes *fpl* célèbres

(**b**) *(test)* essai *m*; *(for a drug, a process)* test *m*; **to give sth a trial** [illegible] qch; **to be on trial** être à l'essai; **give her a month's trial before you take her on** prenez-la un mois à l'essai avant de l'embaucher; **it was a trial of strength** c'était une épreuve de force; **by trial and error** par tâtonnements, de façon empirique; **it was just trial and error** on a/ils ont/*etc* procédé par tâtonnements

(**c**) *(hardship, adversity)* épreuve *f*; **the trials of married life** les vicissitudes *fpl* de la vie conjugale; **trials and tribulations** tribulations *fpl*; **after all your trials and tribulations** après tout ce que vous avez dû souffrir; **her arthritis was a great trial to her** son arthrite l'a beaucoup fait souffrir; **he's always been a trial to his parents** il a toujours donné du souci à ses parents

(**d**) *(competition)* concours *m*; *(for selection* → *match)* match *m* de sélection; *(*→ *race)* épreuve *f* de sélection

2 *adj (test* → *flight)* d'essai; *(*→ *marriage)* à l'essai; **on a trial basis** à titre d'essai

3 *vt (new product)* tester

4 trials *npl (competition)* concours *m*; *(for selection* → *match)* match *m* de sélection; *(*→ *race)* épreuve *f* de sélection; **sheepdog trials** concours *m* de chiens de berger

►► *Am Law* ***trial attorney*** avocat *m*; *Acct* ***trial balance*** balance *f* d'inventaire; *also Fig* ***trial balloon*** ballon *m* d'essai; ***trial court*** tribunal *m* de première instance; *Sport* ***trial game*** match *m* de sélection; ***trial judge*** ≃ juge *m* d'instance; ***trial jury*** jury *m*; *Am Law* ***trial lawyer*** avocat *m*; ***trial offer*** offre *f* d'essai; *Mktg* ***trial order*** commande *f* d'essai; ***trial period*** période *f* d'essai; **to be on a trial period** *(of employee)* être en période d'essai; ***trial run*** essai *m*; **to give sth a trial run** essayer qch, faire un essai avec qch; **we'll have a trial run before we record** on fera un essai avant d'enregistrer; ***trial separation*** séparation *f* à l'essai

trialist ['traɪəlɪst] *n Sport* concurrent(e) *m,f* dans les épreuves de sélection

trial-sized *adj (pack, box)* d'essai

triangle ['traɪæŋgəl] *n* (**a**) *Geom* triangle *m* (**b**) *Am (set square)* équerre *f* (**c**) *Mus* triangle *m*

►► *Phys* ***triangle of forces*** triangle *m* des forces

triangular [traɪ'æŋgjʊlə(r)] *adj* triangulaire

triangulate [traɪ'æŋgjʊleɪt] *vt* (**a**) *Geom* diviser en triangles (**b**) *Geog (region)* trianguler

triangulation [traɪ,æŋgjʊ'leɪʃən] *n* triangulation *f*

►► ***triangulation station*** point *m* géodésique

Triassic [traɪ'æsɪk] *Geol* **1** *n* trias *m*

2 *adj* triasique

triathlete [traɪ'æθli:t] *n* triathlète *mf*

triathlon [traɪ'æθlɒn] *n* triathlon *m*

triatomic [,traɪə'tɒmɪk] *adj Chem* triatomique

►► ***triatomic oxygen*** ozone *m*

triaxial [traɪ'æksɪəl] *adj* à trois axes

tribade ['trɪbəd] *n* tribade *f*

tribadism ['trɪbədɪzəm] *n* tribadisme *m*

tribal ['traɪbəl] *adj (society, system)* tribal; *(warfare)* tribal, entre tribus; *(people)* qui vit en tribu; *(leader)* de tribu; *(loyalty)* à la tribu

tribalism ['traɪbəlɪzəm] *n* tribalisme *m*

tribalistic [,traɪbə'lɪstɪk] *adj* tribal

tribally ['traɪbəlɪ] *adv (to live)* en tribu; *(to be organized)* par tribus

tribe [traɪb] *n* (**a**) *(gen)* tribu *f*; **the twelve tribes of Israel** les douze tribus *fpl* d'Israël; **the lost tribe of Israel** la tribu perdue d'Israël (**b**) *Fam Fig* tribu *f*, smala *f*

tribesman ['traɪbzmən] (*pl* **tribesmen** [-mən]) *n* membre *m* d'une tribu; *(of particular tribe)* membre *m* de la tribu

tribespeople ['traɪbz,pi:pəl] *npl (tribes)* tribus *fpl*; *(members of particular tribe)* membres *mpl* de la tribu; **the Negrito tribespeople** les membres *mpl* de la tribu des Négritos, les Négritos *mpl*

tribeswoman ['traɪbz,wʊmən] (*pl* **tribeswomen** [-wɪmən]) *n* membre *m* d'une tribu; *(of particular tribe)* membre *m* de la tribu

triboelectricity ['traɪbəʊ,ɪlek'trɪsətɪ] *n* triboélectricité *f*

tribology [traɪ'bɒlədʒɪ] *n Tech* tribologie *f*

triboluminescence ['traɪbəʊ,lu:mɪ'nesəns] *n Phys* triboluminescence *f*

triboluminescent ['traɪbəʊ,lu:mɪ'nesənt] *adj Phys* triboluminescent

tribometer [traɪ'bɒmɪtə(r)] *n Tech* tribomètre *m*

tribometry [illegible]

tribrach ['trɪbræk] *n Literature* tribraque *m*

tribulation [,trɪbjʊ'leɪʃən] *n Literary* affliction *f*, tourment *m*; **in times of tribulation** en temps de malheurs

tribunal [traɪ'bju:nəl] *n (gen) & Law* tribunal *m*; *Fig* **the tribunal of public opinion** le jugement de l'opinion publique; **military tribunal** tribunal *m* militaire

►► ***tribunal of inquiry*** commission *f* d'enquête

tribunate ['trɪbjʊnət] *n Antiq* tribunat *m*

tribune ['trɪbju:n] *n* (**a**) *Antiq* tribun *m* (**b**) *(platform)* tribune *f*; *Fig* **the newspaper provides a tribune for the views of young people** le journal offre une tribune à des jeunes pour faire connaître leurs points de vue (**c**) *(defender)* tribun *m*

►► *Pol* ***the Tribune Group*** = le groupe des députés de gauche du parti travailliste britannique

tributary ['trɪbjʊtrɪ] (*pl* **tributaries**) **1** *n* (**a**) *(ruler, state)* tributaire *m* (**b**) *Geog (stream)* affluent *m*

2 *adj* tributaire

tribute ['trɪbju:t] *n* (**a**) *(mark of respect)* hommage *m*; **to pay tribute to sb** rendre hommage à qn; **to pay a last tribute to sb** rendre à qn les derniers devoirs; **we stood in silent tribute** nous lui avons rendu un hommage silencieux
(**b**) *(indication of efficiency)* témoignage *m*; **it is a tribute to their organizational skills that everything went so smoothly** si tout a si bien marché, c'est grâce à leurs qualités d'organisateurs
(**c**) *Hist & Pol* tribut *m*
►► ***tribute band*** = groupe qui joue uniquement des reprises d'un groupe très connu

tricameral [traɪ'kæmərəl] *adj* tricaméral

trice [traɪs] **1** *n (moment)* **in a trice** en un clin d'œil, en un rien de temps
2 *vt Naut (sail)* hisser

tricentenary [,traɪsen'ti:nərɪ], *esp Am* **tricentennial** [,traɪsen'tenɪəl] **1** *adj* tricentenaire; *(celebrations)* du tricentenaire
2 *n* tricentenaire *m*

triceps ['traɪseps] (*pl* **tricepses** [-sɪz]) *n* triceps *m*

triceratops [traɪ'serətɒps] *n* tricératops *m*

trichiasis [trɪ'kaɪəsɪs] *n Med* trichiasis *m*

trichina ['trɪkɪnə, trɪ'kaɪnə] *n Biol* trichine *f*

trichinosis [,trɪkɪ'nəʊsɪs] *n Med* trichinose *f*

trichlorethylene [,traɪklɔ:r'eθɪli:n] *n Chem* trichloréthylène *m*

trichloride [traɪ'klɔ:raɪd] *n* trichlorure *m*

trichloroethanal [traɪ,klɔ:rəʊ'eθənəl] *n Chem* chloral *m*

trichloroethylene [traɪ,klɔ:rəʊ'eθɪli:n] *n Chem* trichloréthylène *m*

trichologist [trɪ'kɒlədʒɪst] *n* spécialiste *mf* de trichologie

trichology [trɪ'kɒlədʒɪ] *n* trichologie *f*

trichome ['trɪkəʊm] *n Bot* trichome *m*

trichomonad [,trɪkəʊ'mɒnəd] *n Biol* trichomonas *m*

trichomoniasis [,trɪkəʊmə'naɪəsɪs] *n Med* trichomonase *f*, trichomonose *f*

trichopteron [traɪ'kɒptərɒn] *n Entom* trichoptère *m*

trichosis [trɪ'kəʊsɪs] *n Med* trichose *f*

trichotomous [traɪ'kɒtəməs] *adj* trichotome, trichotomique

trichotomy [traɪ'kɒtəmɪ] (*pl* **trichotomies**) *n* trichotomie *f*

trichroic [traɪ'krəʊɪk] *adj* trichroïte

trichromat [traɪ'krəʊmæt] *n* trichromate *mf*

trichromatic [,traɪkrəʊ'mætɪk] *adj* trichrome

trichromatism [traɪ'krəʊmətɪzəm] *n* trichromie *f*

trick [trɪk] **1** *n* (**a**) *(deception, ruse)* ruse *f*, astuce *f*; **it's just a trick to get you to open the door** c'est une ruse *ou* une astuce pour vous amener à ouvrir la porte; **a trick of the light** un effet d'optique
(**b**) *(joke, prank)* tour *m*, farce *f*, blague *f*; **to play a trick on sb** faire une farce *ou* jouer un tour à qn; **my eyes must have been playing tricks on me** *or* **playing me tricks** mes yeux ont dû me jouer des tours, j'ai dû avoir la berlue; **what a dirty** *or* **mean** *or* **nasty trick to play!** quel sale tour!; **"trick or treat"** "une gâterie ou une farce" *(phrase rituelle des enfants déguisés qui font la quête la veille de la fête de Halloween)*
(**c**) *(usu pl) (silly behaviour)* bêtise *f*; **none of your tricks!** et pas de bêtises, hein!; **he's up to his old tricks again** il fait encore des siennes
(**d**) *(knack)* truc *m*, astuce *f*; *(in conjuring, performance)* tour *m*; **conjuring trick** tour *m* de prestidigitation *ou* de passe-passe; **there, that should do the trick** voilà, ça fera l'affaire; **he knows a trick or two** il a plus d'un tour dans son sac, c'est un malin; **to teach a dog tricks** apprendre des tours à un chien; **she still has a few tricks up her sleeve** il lui reste plus d'un tour dans son sac; **she doesn't miss a trick** rien ne lui échappe; **the tricks of the trade** les trucs *mpl ou* les astuces *fpl* du métier; **it's one of the tricks of the trade** c'est une vieille ficelle *ou* un truc du métier
(**e**) *(habit)* habitude *f*, manie *f*; *(particularity)* particularité *f*; *(gift)* don *m*; *(mannerism)* manie *f*, tic *m*; **he has a trick of turning up at mealtimes** il a le chic pour arriver à l'heure des repas
(**f**) *(in card games)* pli *m*, levée *f*; **to make** *or* **to take a trick** faire un pli *ou* une levée
(**g**) *Am very Fam (prostitute's client)* micheton *m*; **to turn a trick** faire une passe
(**h**) *Naut* tour *m* de barre
(**i**) *(idiom) Fam* **how's tricks?** comment va?, quoi de neuf?
2 *adj* (**a**) *(for jokes)* d'attrape, faux (fausse), de farces et attrapes; **trick soap** savon *m* d'attrape, faux savon *m*
(**b**) *(deceptive → lighting)* truqué
(**c**) *Am (weak → knee)* faible; *(→ leg)* boiteux
3 *vt (deceive)* tromper, rouler; *(swindle)* escroquer; *(catch out)* attraper; **you've been tricked!** vous vous êtes fait rouler!; **to trick sb into doing sth** amener qn à faire qch en usant de ruse; **I was tricked into leaving** on a manœuvré pour me faire partir; **to trick sb out of sth** *(of opportunity etc)* frustrer qn de qch; *(of money, inheritance)* escroquer qch à qn
►► ***trick cyclist*** *(in circus)* cycliste *mf* acrobate; *Br Fam (psychiatrist)* psy *mf*; ***trick photograph*** photo *f* truquée; ***trick photography*** trucages *mpl*; ***trick question*** question-piège *f*
►**trick out, trick up** *vt sep Literary* parer; **they were tricked out to look like circus performers** ils étaient déguisés en artistes de cirque; **she was tricked out in all her finery** elle était parée de ses plus beaux atours, elle était sur son trente et un

trickery ['trɪkərɪ] *n* ruse *f*, supercherie *f*; **through** *or* **by trickery** par la ruse

trickiness ['trɪkɪnɪs] *n (of job, problem, negotiations)* difficulté *f*; *(of situation)* délicatesse *f*

trickle ['trɪkəl] **1** *vi* (**a**) *(liquid)* couler goutte à goutte; **rainwater trickled from the gutters** un mince filet d'eau de pluie s'échappait des gouttières; **I felt the blood trickle slowly down my leg** je sentis le sang couler doucement le long de ma jambe; **water trickled down the window pane** un filet d'eau coulait *ou* dégoulinait le long de la vitre; **tears trickled down his face** les larmes coulaient *ou* dégoulinaient sur son visage
(**b**) *Fig* **information began to trickle out from behind enemy lines** les informations commencèrent à filtrer depuis l'arrière des lignes ennemies; **news is beginning to trickle through** *or* **out from the devastated area** on commence à recevoir peu à peu des nouvelles de la région sinistrée; **cars began to trickle over the border** la circulation a repris progressivement à la frontière; **the ball trickled into the goal** le ballon roula tranquillement dans les buts
2 *vt* (**a**) *(liquid)* faire couler goutte à goutte; **he trickled a few drops of milk into the flour** il a versé quelques gouttes de lait dans la farine; **she trickled some oil out of the can** elle a versé un peu d'huile de la boîte
(**b**) *(sand, salt)* faire glisser *ou* couler; **to trickle sand through one's fingers** faire glisser *ou* couler du sable entre ses doigts
3 *n* (**a**) *(liquid)* filet *m*; **the flow from the spring dwindled to a trickle** la source ne laissait plus échapper qu'un mince filet d'eau; **the trickle of lava soon became a torrent** le filet de lave se transforma bientôt en torrent; **there was only a trickle of water from the tap** un maigre filet d'eau coulait du robinet
(**b**) *Fig* **a trickle of applications began to come in** les candidatures commencèrent à arriver au compte-gouttes; **there was only a trickle of visitors** il n'y avait que quelques rares visiteurs, les visiteurs étaient rares
►► ***trickle charger*** chargeur *m* à régime lent
►**trickle away** *vi* (**a**) *(liquid)* s'écouler lentement; **the water trickled away down the plughole** l'eau s'écoulait lentement dans le trou de l'évier
(**b**) *Fig (money, savings)* disparaître petit à petit; *(crowd)* se disperser petit à petit; *(people)* s'en aller progressivement
►**trickle in** *vi* (**a**) *(rain)* entrer goutte à goutte
(**b**) *(spectators)* entrer par petits groupes
(**c**) *Fig* **offers of help began to trickle in** quelques offres d'aide commençaient à arriver; **information on the disaster only trickled in at first** au début les informations sur le désastre arrivaient au compte-gouttes

trickle-down *adj*
►► ***trickle-down economics, trickle-down theory*** = théorie selon laquelle les richesses accumulées par un petit nombre bénéficieront à tous les membres de la société

trickling ['trɪklɪŋ] *n* écoulement *m* goutte à goutte

trickster ['trɪkstə(r)] *n (swindler)* filou *m*, escroc *m*

tricksy ['trɪksɪ] (*compar* **tricksier**, *superl* **tricksiest**) *adj* (**a**) *(mischievous)* espiègle (**b**) *(sly)* malin(igne), rusé

tricky ['trɪkɪ] (*compar* **trickier**, *superl* **trickiest**) *adj* (**a**) *(complex, delicate → job, situation, negotiations)* difficile, délicat; *(→ problem)* épineux, difficile; **the path is tricky in places** le chemin est difficile *ou* peu praticable par endroits (**b**) *(sly → person)* rusé, fourbe

triclinic [traɪ'klɪnɪk] *adj Miner* triclinique

tricolour, *Am* **tricolor** ['trɪkələ(r)] *n* drapeau *m* tricolore

tricoloured, *Am* **tricolored** ['traɪkʌləd] *adj* tricolore

tricorn, tricorne ['traɪkɔ:n] **1** *adj* **tricorn hat** tricorne *m*
2 *n* tricorne *m*

trictrac, tricktrack ['trɪk,træk] *n* trictrac *m*

tricuspid [traɪ'kʌspɪd] *adj* tricuspide

tricycle ['traɪsɪkəl] **1** *n* tricycle *m*
2 *vi* faire du tricycle

tricyclist ['traɪsɪklɪst] *n* tricycliste *mf*

tridactyl [traɪ'dæktɪl], **tridactylous** [traɪ'dæktɪləs] *adj Zool* tridactyle

trident ['traɪdənt] **1** *n* trident *m*
2 Trident *n Mil* Trident *m*
3 *comp (missile, submarine)* Trident *(inv)*

tridental [traɪ'dentəl], **tridentate** [traɪ'denteɪt] *adj* tridenté

Tridentine Mass [trɪ'dentaɪn-] *n* messe *f* traditionnelle en latin

tried [traɪd] *pt & pp of* **try**

triennial [traɪ'enɪəl] **1** *adj* triennal; *Bot* trisannuel
2 *n* (**a**) *(anniversary)* troisième anniversaire *m* (**b**) *(period)* période *f* de trois ans (**c**) *Bot* plante *f* trisannuelle

triennially [traɪ'enɪəlɪ] *adv* tous les trois ans

triennium [traɪ'enɪəm] (*pl* **triennia** [-nɪə] *or* **trienniums**) *n* triennat *m*

Trier ['trɪə(r)] *n* Trèves

trier ['traɪə(r)] *n* **to be a trier** être persévérant; **he's a real trier** il ne se laisse jamais décourager

Trieste [tri:'est] *n* Trieste

trifecta [traɪ'fektə] *n Horseracing* tiercé *m (avec gagnants dans l'ordre)*

trifid ['traɪfɪd] *adj Biol* trifide

trifle ['traɪfəl] **1** *n* (**a**) *(unimportant thing, small amount)* bagatelle *f*, broutille *f*, rien *m*; **don't waste your time on trifles** ne perdez pas votre temps à des bagatelles; **she doesn't worry over trifles like money** l'argent est le cadet de ses soucis; **they quarrel over trifles** il se disputent pour un oui pour un non *ou* pour un rien; **I bought it for a trifle** je l'ai acheté pour une bouchée de pain *ou* pour trois fois rien; **£100 is a mere trifle to them** 100 livres, c'est peu de chose pour eux
(**b**) *Culin* = dessert où alternent une couche de génoise imbibée d'alcool et de fruits en gelée et une couche de crème anglaise, le tout recouvert de chantilly
2 a trifle *adv* un peu, un tantinet; **a trifle too wide/too short** un tantinet trop large/trop court; **it's a trifle easier than it was** c'est un peu *ou* un rien plus facile qu'avant
►**trifle with** *vt insep* **to trifle with sb's affections** jouer avec les sentiments de qn; **he's not a man to be trifled with** avec lui, on ne plaisante pas

trifling ['traɪflɪŋ] *adj* insignifiant; **that's a trifling matter** ce n'est qu'une bagatelle *ou* une broutille; *Ironic* **the trifling sum of 10,000 francs** la bagatelle de 10 000 francs

trifocal [traɪ'fəʊkəl] **1** *adj (lens)* à triple foyer
2 *n (lens)* lentille *f* à triple foyer
3 trifocals *npl (spectacles)* lunettes *fpl* à triple foyer

trifoliate [traɪ'fəʊlɪɪt] *adj* à trois feuilles; *Bot* trifolié

trifoliated [traɪ'fəʊlɪeɪtɪd] *adj Archit (arch)* tréflé

triforium [traɪ'fɔ:rɪəm] (*pl* **triforia** [-rɪə]) *n* triforium *m*

triform ['traɪfɔ:m] *adj* en *ou* à trois parties

trifurcate [traɪ'fɜ:keɪt] *adj* trifurqué

trig [trɪg] *n Fam (abbr* **trigonometry***)* trigo *f*
►► ***trig point*** station *f* géodésique

trigeminal [traɪ'dʒemɪnəl] *adj Anat* trijumeau
►► ***trigeminal nerve*** nerf *m* trijumeau; *Med* ***trigeminal neuralgia*** névralgie *f* du trijumeau *ou* faciale

trigeminus [traɪ'dʒemɪnəs] *n Anat* trijumeau *m*

trigger ['trɪgə(r)] **1** *n* (**a**) *(in gun)* gâchette *f*, détente *f*; **to pull** *or* **to squeeze the trigger** appuyer sur la gâchette; **he's fast** *or* **quick on the trigger** il tire vite; *Fig* il réagit vite
(**b**) *Fig (initiator)* déclenchement *m*; **the strike was the trigger for nationwide protests** la grève a donné le signal d'un mouvement de contestation dans tout le pays
2 *vt (mechanism, explosion, reaction)* déclencher; *(revolution, protest)* déclencher, provoquer, soulever
►► ***trigger action*** déclenchement *m*; ***trigger finger*** index *m (avec lequel on appuie sur la gâchette)*; ***trigger spray*** spray *m* à pompe

►**trigger off** *vt sep* = **trigger** *vt*

triggerfish ['trɪgəfɪʃ] *n Ich* baliste *m*

trigger-happy *adj Fam (individual)* qui a la gâchette facile; *(country)* va-t-en-guerre *(inv)*

triglyceride [traɪ'glɪsəraɪd] *n Biol & Chem* triglycéride *m*

triglyph ['traɪglɪf] *n Archit* triglyphe *m*

trigon ['traɪgɒn] *n (gen) & Anat & Astron* trigone *m*

trigonal ['traɪgənəl] *adj* (**a**) *(triangular → gen) & Biol* trigone (**b**) *Geol (in crystallography)* trigonal, rhombohédrique

trigonometric [,trɪgənə'metrɪk], **trigonometrical** [,trɪgənə'metrɪkəl] *adj* trigonométrique
►► ***trigonometrical point*** station *f* géodésique

trigonometrically [,trɪgənə'metrɪklɪ] *adv* trigonométriquement

trigonometry [,trɪgə'nɒmətrɪ] *n* trigonométrie *f*

trig point *n* station *f* géodésique

trigram ['traɪgræm] *n* trigramme *m*

trigraph ['traɪgrɑːf] *n* trigramme *m*

trihedral [traɪ'hiːdrəl] **1** *adj* trièdre
2 *n* (angle *m*) trièdre *m*

trihedron [traɪ'hiːdrən] *(pl* **trihedra** [-drə] *or* **trihedrons***)* *n* (angle *m*) trièdre *m*

trike [traɪk] *n Fam* tricycle ▫ *m*

trilateral [,traɪ'lætərəl] *adj* trilatéral, à trois côtés

trilby ['trɪlbɪ] *n Br (hat)* (chapeau *m* en) feutre *m*
►► ***trilby hat*** chapeau *m* en feutre

trilinear [traɪ'lɪnɪə(r)] *adj* trilinéaire

trilingual [traɪ'lɪŋgwəl] *adj* trilingue

trill [trɪl] **1** *n Mus & Orn* trille *m*; *Ling* consonne *f* roulée
2 *vi* triller, faire des trilles
3 *vt* (**a**) *(note, word)* triller; **"I'm up here", she trilled** "je suis en haut", dit-elle d'une voix flûtée (**b**) *Ling (consonant)* rouler

trillion ['trɪljən] *n Br* trillion *m*; *Am* billion *m*; **trillions of stars** des milliards *mpl* d'étoiles

trillium ['trɪlɪəm] *n Bot* trillium *m*

trilobate [traɪ'ləʊbaɪt] *adj Bot* trilobé

trilobite ['traɪləʊbaɪt] *n Zool* trilobite *m*

trilogy ['trɪlədʒɪ] *(pl* **trilogies***)* *n* trilogie *f*

trim [trɪm] *(compar* **trimmer,** *superl* **trimmest,** *pt & pp* **trimmed,** *cont* **trimming***)* **1** *adj* (**a**) *(neat → appearance)* net, soigné; *(→ person)* d'apparence soignée; *(→ garden, flowerbed)* bien entretenu; *(→ ship)* en bon ordre; **the garden is looking very trim** le jardin a l'air très bien entretenu
(**b**) *(svelte → figure)* svelte, mince
(**c**) *(fit)* en bonne santé, en forme
2 *vt* (**a**) *(cut → roses)* tailler, couper; *(→ hair, nails)* couper; *(→ beard)* tailler; *(→ candle wick)* tailler, moucher; *(→ paper, photo)* rogner; **to trim one's nails** se couper les ongles; **I had my hair trimmed** je me suis fait raccourcir les cheveux; **trim the frayed edges off** égalisez les bords du tissu
(**b**) *(edge)* orner, garnir; *(decorate)* décorer; **a hat trimmed with fur** un chapeau bordé *ou* orné de fourrure; **the collar was trimmed with lace** le col était bordé *ou* garni de dentelle; **we trimmed the Christmas tree with tinsel** on a décoré le sapin de Noël avec des guirlandes
(**c**) *Aviat & Naut (plane, ship)* équilibrer; *(sails)* régler; *Fig* **to trim one's sails** réviser son jugement
(**d**) *(cut back → budget, costs)* réduire, limiter; **they were able to trim several thousand pounds from the budget** ils ont pu réduire le budget de plusieurs milliers de livres
(**e**) *Comput (database)* supprimer les espaces blancs inutiles de
3 *n* (**a**) *(neat state)* **to be in good trim** être en bon état; **the garden doesn't look in very good trim** le jardin a l'air un peu à l'abandon
(**b**) *(fit condition → of person)* **to get in** *or* **into trim** se remettre en forme; **are you in (good) trim for the match?** êtes-vous en forme pour le match?; **in fighting trim** prêt pour le combat
(**c**) *(cut)* coupe *f*, taille *f*; *(of hair etc)* coupe *f* d'entretien; **she gave the hedge a trim** elle a taillé la haie; **she gave her nails a trim** elle s'est coupé les ongles; **to have a trim** *(at hairdresser's)* se faire raccourcir les cheveux; **just a trim, please** vous me les raccourcissez juste un peu, s'il vous plaît
(**d**) *(UNCOUNT) (moulding, decoration)* moulures *fpl*; *(on car)* aménagement *m* intérieur, finitions *fpl* intérieures; *(on dress)* garniture *f*; *Am (in shop window)* composition *f* d'étalage; *Aut* **interior trim** finitions *fpl* intérieures, garnissage *m*; **seat trim** habillage *m* des sièges
(**e**) *Naut (of sails)* orientation *f*, réglage *m*
(**f**) *Cin* coupe *f*
►► ***trim track, trim trail*** parcours-santé *m*

►**trim down 1** *vt sep* (**a**) *(wick)* tailler, moucher
(**b**) *(budget, costs)* réduire
2 *vi (spend less)* réduire ses dépenses; *(shed staff)* réduire ses effectifs

►**trim off** *vt sep (edge)* enlever, couper; *(hair)* couper; *(branch)* tailler; *(jagged edges)* ébarber; **to trim the fat off the meat** enlever le gras de la viande

trimaran ['traɪməræn] *n* trimaran *m*

trimer ['traɪmə(r)] *n Chem* trimère *m*

trimerous ['traɪmərəs] *adj Bot* trimère

trimester [traɪ'mestə(r)] *n* (**a**) *Am* trimestre *m* (**b**) *(gen)* trois mois *mpl*

trimestrial [traɪ'mestrɪəl] *adj* trimestriel

trimeter ['trɪmɪtə(r)] *n Literature* trimètre *m*

trimmer ['trɪmə(r)] *n* (**a**) *Constr* linçoir *m*, linsoir *m* (**b**) *(for timber)* trancheuse *f (pour le bois)*; *(in papermaking, bookbinding etc)* massicot *m*; **(hedge) trimmer** taille-haie *m* (**c**) *Electron* trimmer *m*, condensateur *m* ajustable (**d**) *Pej (person)* opportuniste *mf*

trimming ['trɪmɪŋ] **1** *n* (**a**) *Sewing* parement *m*; *(lace, ribbon)* passement *m*; **trimmings** *(on garment etc)* passementerie *f*
(**b**) *Culin* garniture *f*, accompagnement *m*; **turkey with all the trimmings** la dinde avec sa garniture habituelle; *Fig* **with all the trimmings** avec tout le tralala
(**c**) *(accessory)* accessoire *m*; **it's the trimmings you pay for** ce sont les accessoires que vous payez
(**d**) *Am Fam (defeat)* raclée *f*; **to get a trimming** prendre une raclée, se faire battre à plate(s) couture(s)
(**e**) *(cutting → of hedges, trees)* taille *f*; *(→ of edges of book)* ébarbage *m*, rognage *m*
(**f**) *(reduction → of expenses etc)* réduction *f*
2 trimmings *npl (scraps)* chutes *fpl*, rognures *fpl*

trimness ['trɪmnɪs] *n (of person, garden, ship)* aspect *m* soigné; *(of figure)* sveltesse *f*

trimolecular [,traɪmə'lekjʊlə(r)] *adj* trimoléculaire

trimonthly [traɪ'mʌnθlɪ] *adj* trimestriel

trimorphism [traɪ'mɔːfɪzəm] *n Biol* trimorphisme *m*

trimurti [trɪ'mʊətɪ] *n Rel* trimurti *f*

trinary ['traɪnərɪ] *adj* ternaire

trine [traɪn] **1** *n* (**a**) *Astrol* trin aspect *m* (**b**) *(group of three)* triade *f*
2 *adj (triple)* triple

Trinidad ['trɪnɪdæd] *n* (l'île *f* de) la Trinité *f*; **in Trinidad** à la Trinité

Trinidad and Tobago [-tə'beɪgəʊ] *n* Trinité-et-Tobago; **in Trinidad and Tobago** à Trinité-et-Tobago

Trinidadian [,trɪnɪ'dædɪən, ,trɪnɪ'deɪdɪən] **1** *n* Trinidadien(enne) *m,f*, habitant(e) *m,f* de la Trinité
2 *adj* trinidadien, de la Trinité

Trinitarian [,trɪnɪ'teərɪən] *Rel* **1** *n* trinitaire *mf*
2 *adj* trinitaire

trinitroglycerin [traɪ,naɪtrəʊ'glɪsəriːn] *n* nitroglycérine *f*

trinitrotoluene [traɪ,naɪtrəʊ'tɒljʊiːn] *n* trinitrotoluène *m*

trinity ['trɪnɪtɪ] *(pl* **trinities***)* **1** *n Formal or Literary* trio *m*, groupe *m* de trois
2 Trinity *n Rel* (**a**) *(union)* **the Trinity** la Trinité (**b**) *(feast)* (la fête de) la Trinité; **the first Sunday after Trinity** le premier dimanche après la Trinité
►► ***Trinity House*** = association chargée de la construction et de l'entretien des phares sur les côtes britanniques; ***Trinity Sunday*** (la fête de) la Trinité; *Univ* ***Trinity term*** troisième trimestre *m* (universitaire) *(à Oxford, Cambridge et au Trinity College de Dublin)*

trinket ['trɪŋkɪt] *n (bauble)* bibelot *m*, babiole *f*; *(jewel)* colifichet *m*; *(on bracelet)* breloque *f*

trinomial [traɪ'nəʊmɪəl] **1** *n* trinôme *m*
2 *adj* à trois termes

trio ['triːəʊ] *(pl* **trios***)* *n* (**a**) *Mus* trio *m (morceau)* (**b**) *(group)* trio *m*, groupe *m* de trois; *Mus* trio *m (joueurs)*
►► ***trio sonata*** sonate *f* en trio

triode ['traɪəʊd] *n* triode *f*

trioecious [traɪ'iːʃəs] *adj Bot* qui présente une triécie

triolet ['triːəʊlet] *n* triolet *m*

trioxide [traɪ'ɒksaɪd] *n Chem* trioxyde *m*

trip [trɪp] *(pt & pp* **tripped,** *cont* **tripping***)* **1** *n* (**a**) *(journey)* voyage *m*; **to go on a trip** faire un voyage, partir en voyage; **he's away on a business trip** il est parti en voyage d'affaires; **we went on a long bus trip** on a fait un long voyage en bus; **I had to make three trips into town** j'ai dû aller trois fois en ville *ou* faire trois voyages en ville; **to make a trip to the dentist's** aller chez le dentiste
(**b**) *(excursion)* promenade *f*, excursion *f*; *(outing)* promenade *f*, sortie *f*; **we had a lovely trip to Devon** nous avons fait une très belle promenade dans le Devon; **she took the children on a trip to the seaside** elle a emmené les enfants en promenade au bord de la mer; **school trip** voyage *m* scolaire
(**c**) *(stumble)* faux pas *m*; *Sport (foul)* croc-en-jambe *m*, croche-pied *m*
(**d**) *very Fam Drugs slang* trip *m*; **an LSD trip** un trip au LSD; **to have a bad trip** faire un mauvais trip
(**e**) *Fig (experience)* **he seems to be on some kind of nostalgia trip** il semble être en pleine crise de nostalgie; **to be on a guilt trip** culpabiliser; **to be on a power trip** être en plein trip mégalo; **to be on an ego trip** se faire mousser
2 *vt* (**a**) *(person → make stumble)* faire trébucher; *(→ make fall)* faire tomber; *(intentionally)* faire un croche-pied *ou* un croc-en-jambe à; **he tripped me** il m'a fait un croche-pied
(**b**) *(switch, alarm)* déclencher
(**c**) *(idiom) Hum* **to trip the light fantastic** danser
3 *vi* (**a**) *(stumble)* trébucher; **I tripped and fell** j'ai trébuché et je suis tombé; **she tripped on** *or* **over the wire** elle s'est pris le pied dans le fil; **I tripped on a pile of books** j'ai buté contre *ou* trébuché sur une pile de livres
(**b**) *(step lightly)* **to trip in/out** entrer/sortir d'un pas léger; **she tripped down the lane** elle descendit le chemin d'un pas léger; *Fig* **her name doesn't exactly trip off the tongue** son nom n'est pas très facile à prononcer
(**c**) *very Fam Drugs slang* faire un trip, triper; **to trip on acid** faire un trip à l'acide
►► *Aut* ***trip recorder*** compteur *m* journalier, totalisateur *m* partiel; ***trip switch*** interrupteur *m*

►**trip out** *vi very Fam Drugs slang* faire un trip

►**trip over 1** *vi* trébucher, faire un faux pas
2 *vt insep* buter sur *ou* contre, trébucher sur *ou* contre; *Fig* **you can't go anywhere without tripping over celebrities** par ici on ne peut pas faire un pas sans se heurter à une célébrité

►**trip up 1** *vt sep* (**a**) *(cause to fall)* faire trébucher; *(deliberately)* faire un croche-pied à
(**b**) *(trap)* désarçonner; **her questions are often designed to trip people up** ses questions sont souvent conçues pour désarçonner les gens

tri–tri

2 *vi* (**a**) *(fall)* trébucher; **I tripped up on a stone** j'ai trébuché *ou* buté contre une pierre

(**b**) *(make a mistake)* gaffer, faire une gaffe; **I tripped up badly there** j'ai fait une grosse gaffe, là

tripartite [ˌtraɪˈpɑːtaɪt] *adj (division, agreement)* tripartite, triparti

tripe [traɪp] *n (UNCOUNT)* (**a**) *Culin* tripes *fpl* (**b**) *Fam (nonsense)* foutaises *fpl*, conneries *fpl*; **don't talk tripe!** dis pas n'importe quoi!, raconte pas de conneries!; **what a load of tripe!** n'importe quoi!; **the film is absolute tripe!** il vaut pas un clou, ce film!

triphammer [ˈtrɪpˌhæmə(r)] *n* marteau *m* à bascule

triphase [ˈtraɪfeɪz] *adj Elec* triphasé

trip-hop *n Mus* trip-hop *m*

triphthong [ˈtrɪfθɒŋ] *n* triphtongue *f*

triplane [ˈtraɪpleɪn] *n* triplan *m*

triple [ˈtrɪpəl] **1** *adj* (**a**) *(in three parts)* triple; **she has a triple role of actress, director and producer** elle a le triple rôle d'actrice, de metteur en scène et de productrice; **the organization serves a triple purpose** le but de l'organisation est triple; **in triple time** à trois temps

(**b**) *(treble)* triple; **a triple brandy** un triple cognac; **a triple murder** un triple meurtre; **triple the usual amount** trois fois la dose habituelle

2 *n* triple *m*

3 *vt* tripler

4 *vi* tripler

▸▸ *Hist* ***the Triple Alliance*** *(1668)* la Triple Alliance; *(1882-1914)* la Triple-Alliance, la Triplice; *Med* ***triple (combination) therapy*** trithérapie *f*; ***Triple Crown*** *(in rugby)* = fait de battre, dans une même saison, les trois autres participants au championnat britannique de rugby; *Horseracing* = fait de remporter, dans une même saison, le Two Thousand Guineas, le Derby et le St Leger; ***triple glazing*** triple vitrage *m*; ***triple jump*** triple saut *m*; *Phys* ***triple point*** point *m* triple

triple-A rating *n St Exch* notation *f* AAA

triple-nerved *adj Bot* triplinervé

triplet [ˈtrɪplɪt] *n* (**a**) *(child)* triplé(e) *m,f*; **triplets** des triplés *mpl*, des triplées *fpl* (**b**) *Mus* triolet *m*; *Literature* tercet *m*

Triplex® [ˈtrɪpleks] *n Br (glass)* Triplex® *m*, *(verre m)* Sécurit® *m*

▸▸ ***Triplex® glass*** Triplex® *m*, verre *m* Sécurit® *m*; ***Triplex® windscreen*** pare-brise *m inv* en (verre) Sécurit®

triplex [ˈtrɪpleks] **1** *adj (triple)* triple

2 *n Am (apartment)* triplex *m*

triplicate 1 *adj* [ˈtrɪplɪkət] en trois exemplaires, en triple exemplaire

2 *n* [ˈtrɪplɪkət] (**a**) *(document)* **in triplicate** en trois exemplaires, en triple exemplaire (**b**) *(third copy)* triplicata *m*

3 *vt* [ˈtrɪplɪkeɪt] multiplier par trois, tripler

triplication [ˌtrɪplɪˈkeɪʃən] *n* multiplication *f* par trois

triplicity [trɪˈplɪsɪtɪ] *n* triplicité *f*

triploid [ˈtrɪplɔɪd] *adj Biol* triploïde

triply [ˈtrɪplɪ] *adv* triplement

tripod [ˈtraɪpɒd] *n* trépied *m*

Tripoli [ˈtrɪpəlɪ] *n* Tripoli

tripos [ˈtraɪpɒs] *n* = examen de licence ("BA") à l'université de Cambridge

tripper [ˈtrɪpə(r)] *n Br (on day trip)* excursionniste *mf*; *(on holiday)* vacancier(ère) *m,f*

trippy [ˈtrɪpɪ] *adj Fam* psychédélique ❑

triptane [ˈtrɪpteɪn] *n Chem* triptane *m*

triptych [ˈtrɪptɪk] *n* triptyque *m*

tripwire [ˈtrɪpwaɪə(r)] *n* fil *m* de détente

trireme [ˈtraɪriːm] *n* trirème *f*, trière *f*

trisect [traɪˈsekt] *vt* diviser en trois parties égales

trisecting [traɪˈsektɪŋ], **trisection** [traɪˈsekʃən] *n* trisection *f*

trishaw [ˈtraɪʃɔː] *n* vélo-pousse *m*

triskaidekaphobia [ˌtrɪskaɪdekəˈfəʊbɪə] *n Psy* triskaïdékaphobie *f*

triskele [ˈtrɪskiːl], **triskelion** [trɪsˈkelɪən] *(pl* **triskelia** [-lɪə]*)* *n* triquètre *f*, triskèle *f*

trismus [ˈtrɪzməs] *n Med* trisme *m*, trismus *m*

trisomic [traɪˈsəʊmɪk] **1** *adj* trisomique

2 *n* organisme *m* trisomique

trisomy [ˈtraɪsəʊmɪ] *n Med* trisomie *f*

Tristan da Cunha [ˌtrɪstəndəˈkuːnjə] *n* (îles *fpl*) Tristan da Cunha

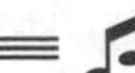

'Tristan and Iseult' 'Tristan et Iseut'

'Tristan and Isolde' *Wagner* 'Tristan et Isolde'

tristichous [ˈtrɪstɪkəs] *adj Bot* tristique

trisyllabic [ˌtraɪsɪˈlæbɪk] *adj* trisyllabique, trisyllabe

trisyllable [ˌtraɪˈsɪləbəl] *n* trisyllabe *m*

trite [traɪt] *adj (theme, picture)* banal; **trite remarks** banalités *fpl*, lieux *mpl* communs; **I know it sounds a bit trite, but I do care** je sais que ça peut paraître banal de dire ça, mais vraiment je me sens concernée

tritely [ˈtraɪtlɪ] *adv* banalement

triteness [ˈtraɪtnɪs] *n* banalité *f*

tritheism [ˈtraɪθiːɪzəm] *n Rel* trithéisme *m*

tritiate [ˈtrɪtɪeɪt] *vt Chem* modifier par tritiation

triticum [ˈtrɪtɪkəm] *n Bot* céréale *f* de la famille Triticum

tritium [ˈtrɪtɪəm] *n Chem* tritium *m*

triton 1 *n* (**a**) [ˈtraɪtən] *Zool* triton *m* (**b**) [ˈtraɪtɒn] *Phys* triton *m*

2 Triton [ˈtraɪtɒn] *pr n Myth* Triton

tritone [ˈtraɪtəʊn] *n Mus* triton *m*

triturate [ˈtrɪtjʊreɪt] *vt* triturer

trituration [ˌtrɪtjʊˈreɪʃən] *n* trituration *f*

triumph [ˈtraɪəmf] **1** *n* (**a**) *(jubilation)* (sentiment *m* de) triomphe *m*; **to return in triumph** rentrer triomphalement; **a look of triumph** un air triomphant

(**b**) *(victory)* victoire *f*, triomphe *m*; *(success)* triomphe *m*, (grande) réussite *f*; **the musical was an absolute triumph** la comédie musicale a été *ou* a fait un véritable triomphe; **the triumph of reason over passion** le triomphe de la raison sur la passion; **the agreement will be seen as a personal triumph for the President** cet accord sera considéré comme un triomphe personnel pour le président

(**c**) *(in ancient Rome)* triomphe *m*

2 *vi* triompher; **to triumph over difficulties/a disability** triompher des difficultés/d'une infirmité, vaincre les difficultés/une infirmité

triumphal [traɪˈʌmfəl] *adj* triomphal; **the king's/army's triumphal entry into the city** l'entrée triomphale du roi/de l'armée dans la ville

▸▸ *Archit* ***triumphal arch*** arc *m* de triomphe; ***triumphal procession*** triomphe *m*

triumphalism [traɪˈʌmfəlɪzəm] *n* triomphalisme *m*

triumphalist [traɪˈʌmfəlɪst] **1** *adj* triomphaliste

2 *n* triomphaliste *mf*

triumphant [traɪˈʌmfənt] *adj (team)* victorieux, triomphant; *(return)* triomphal; *(cheer, smile)* de triomphe, triomphant; *(success)* triomphal

triumphantly [traɪˈʌmfəntlɪ] *adv (march)* en triomphe, triomphalement; *(cheer, smile)* triomphalement; *(announce)* d'un ton triomphant, triomphalement; *(look)* d'un air triomphant, triomphalement

triumvir [traɪˈʌmvə(r)] *(pl* **triumvirs** *or* **triumviri** [-vɪˌriː]*)* *n* triumvir *m*

triumviral [traɪˈʌmvɪrəl] *adj* triumviral

triumvirate [traɪˈʌmvɪrət] *n* triumvirat *m*

triune [ˈtraɪjuːn] *adj Rel* trin

trivalent [traɪˈveɪlənt] *adj* trivalent

trivet [ˈtrɪvɪt] *n (when cooking)* trépied *m*, chevrette *f*; *(for table)* dessous-de-plat *m inv*

trivia [ˈtrɪvɪə] *npl (trifles)* bagatelles *fpl*, futilités *fpl*; *(details)* détails *mpl*; **to get bogged down in trivia** s'embarrasser de futilités; **the trivia of everyday life** les petites choses de la vie quotidienne; **he has an amazing memory for trivia** il a une mémoire remarquable pour les choses sans importance

trivial [ˈtrɪvɪəl] *adj* (**a**) *(insignificant → sum, reason)* insignifiant, dérisoire; **it's only a trivial offence** ce n'est qu'une peccadille, c'est sans gravité (**b**) *(pointless → discussion, question)* sans intérêt, insignifiant (**c**) *(banal → story, conversation)* banal

triviality [ˌtrɪvɪˈælətɪ] *(pl* **trivialities***)* *n* (**a**) *(of sum)* insignifiance *f*, caractère *m* insignifiant; *(of discussion)* insignifiance *f*, caractère *m* oiseux; *(of film)* banalité *f* (**b**) *(trifle)* futilité *f*, bagatelle *f*; **don't waste your time on trivialities** ne perdez pas votre temps à des bagatelles

trivialization [ˌtrɪvɪəlaɪˈzeɪʃən] *n* banalisation *f*

trivialize, -ise [ˈtrɪvɪəlaɪz] *vt (make insignificant)* banaliser, dévaloriser; **her work's very important to her, don't trivialize it** son travail est très important pour elle, ne le dévalorisez pas; **the tabloids trivialize even the most important events** la presse populaire banalise même les événements les plus importants

trivially [ˈtrɪvɪəlɪ] *adv (to deal with)* de façon inconséquente; **a trivially small amount** une somme insignifiante

trivium [ˈtrɪvɪəm] *n Hist* trivium *m*

triweekly [traɪˈwiːklɪ] *(pl* **triweeklies***)* **1** *adv* (**a**) *(every three weeks)* toutes les trois semaines (**b**) *(three times a week)* trois fois par semaine

2 *adj (newspaper)* qui paraît toutes les trois semaines; *(visit, class)* qui se produit trois fois par semaine

3 *n* journal *m* qui paraît toutes les trois semaines

t-RNA [ˌtiːɑːˌrenˈeɪ] *n Biol* (*abbr* **transfer RNA**) ARN *m* de transfert

TRO [ˌtiːɑːˈrəʊ] *n Law* (*abbr* **temporary restraining order**) injonction *f* du tribunal

trocar [ˈtrəʊkɑː(r)] *n Med* trocart *m*

trochaic [trəʊˈkeɪɪk] *adj* trochaïque

trochal [ˈtrəʊkəl] *adj Zool* rotiforme

trochanter [trəʊˈkæntə(r)] *n Anat & Zool* trochanter *m*

troche [trəʊʃ] *n Pharm* tablette *f*, pastille *f*

trochee [ˈtrəʊkiː] *n* trochée *m*

trochlea [ˈtrɒklɪə] *n Anat* trochlée *f*

trochlear [ˈtrɒklɪə(r)] *adj Anat* trochléen

trochoid [ˈtrəʊkɔɪd] **1** *n Geom* cycloïde *f*

2 *adj* (**a**) *Geom* cycloïdal (**b**) *Anat* trochoïde

trod [trɒd] *pt & pp of* **tread**

trodden [ˈtrɒdən] *pp of* **tread**

trog [trɒg] *(pt & pp* **trogged,** *cont* **trogging***)* *vi Br Fam* se traîner

trogloditic [ˌtrɒgləˈdɪtɪk] *adj* troglodytique

troglodyte [ˈtrɒglədaɪt] **1** *n* troglodyte *m*

2 *adj* troglodytique

trogon [ˈtrəʊgɒn] *n Orn* trogon *m*, trogonidé *m*

troika [ˈtrɔɪkə] *n* troïka *f*

troilism [ˈtrɔɪlɪzəm] *n* triolisme *m*

Trojan [ˈtrəʊdʒən] **1** *adj* troyen

2 *n* Troyen(enne) *m,f*; **to work like a Trojan** travailler comme un forçat

▸▸ *Hist & Fig* ***Trojan Horse*** cheval *m* de Troie; ***Trojan War*** guerre *f* de Troie; ***Trojan work*** travail *m* de titan

troll [trəʊl] **1** *n (goblin)* troll *m*

2 *vi* (**a**) *Fishing* pêcher à la traîne; **to troll for mackerel/pike** pêcher le maquereau/le brochet à la traîne (**b**) *Br Fam (stroll)* se balader (**c**) *Arch (sing)* chanter vigoureusement

trolley [ˈtrɒlɪ] *n* (**a**) *(handcart)* chariot *m*; *(two-wheeled)* diable *m*; *(for child)* poussette *f*; *(in supermarket)* chariot *m*, caddie® *m*; *(in restaurant)* chariot *m*; **(dinner** *or* **tea) trolley** table *f* roulante; **dessert trolley** chariot *m* à desserts; **drinks trolley** chariot *m* à boissons; *Br Fam* **to be off one's trolley** être cinglé

(**b**) *(on rails → in mine)* wagonnet *m*, benne *f*

(**c**) *Elec (for tram)* trolley *m*

(**d**) *Am (tram)* tramway *m*, tram *m*

▸▸ *Am* ***trolley car*** tramway *m*, tram *m*; *Br Fam Pej* ***trolley dolly*** *(air hostess)* hôtesse *f* de l'air ❑

trolleybus [ˈtrɒlɪbʌs] *n* trolleybus *m*, trolley *m*

trolling [ˈtrəʊlɪŋ] *n Fishing* pêche *f* à la traîne

trollop [ˈtrɒləp] *n Old-fashioned Pej (prostitute)* catin *f*; *(slut)* souillon *f*

trombone [trɒmˈbəʊn] *n* trombone *m (instrument)*

trombonist [trɒmˈbəʊnɪst] *n* tromboniste *mf*, trombone *m (musicien)*

trommel [ˈtrɒməl] *n Mining* trommel *m*, trieur *m*

trompe l'oeil [ˈtrɒmplɜɪ] *n Art* trompe-l'œil *m inv*

troop [truːp] **1** *n (band → of schoolchildren)* bande *f*, groupe *m*; *(→ of scouts)* troupe *f*; *(→ of animals)* troupe *f*; *Mil (of cavalry, artillery)* escadron *m*

2 *vi* **to troop by** *or* **past** passer en troupe; **to troop in/out** entrer/sortir en troupe; **the children trooped back to school** les enfants sont repartis à l'école en bande

3 *vt Br Mil* **to troop the colour** faire le salut au drapeau

4 troops *npl (gen) & Mil* troupes *fpl*

►► ***troop carrier*** *(ship)* transport *m* de troupes; *(plane)* avion *m* de transport militaire; *(vehicle)* véhicule *m* de transport de troupes; ***troop train*** train *m* militaire; *Mil* ***troop transport*** transport *m* de troupes

trooper ['tru:pə(r)] *n* (**a**) *(soldier)* soldat *m* de cavalerie; *Fam Fig* **he's a real trooper** il répond toujours présent à l'appel, on peut toujours compter sur lui (**b**) *Am & Austr (mounted policeman)* membre *m* de la police montée; **(state) trooper** ≃ gendarme *m* (**c**) *Br Mil (ship)* transport *m* de troupes

trooping ['tru:pɪŋ] *n Br* **trooping (of) the colour** salut *m* au drapeau; **Trooping the Colour** = défilé de régiments ayant lieu chaque année le jour officiel de l'anniversaire de la reine d'Angleterre

troopship ['tru:pʃɪp] *n* navire *m* de transport

tropaeolum [trəʊ'pi:ələm] *(pl* **tropaeolums** *or* **tropaeola** [-lə]) *n Bot* tropéolum *m*

trope [trəʊp] *n* trope *m*

trophic ['trɒfɪk] *adj* trophique

trophy ['trəʊfɪ] *(pl* **trophies**) *n* trophée *m*

►► *Hum Pej* ***trophy wife*** = épouse considérée comme un signe extérieur de réussite sociale

tropic ['trɒpɪk] **1** *n* tropique *m*

2 *adj Literary* = **tropical**

3 tropics *npl* **the tropics** les tropiques *mpl*; **in the tropics** sous les tropiques

►► ***the Tropic of Cancer*** le tropique du Cancer; ***the Tropic of Capricorn*** le tropique du Capricorne

'Tropic of Cancer' *Henry Miller* 'Tropique du Cancer'

tropical ['trɒpɪkəl] *adj (region)* des tropiques, tropical; *(weather, forest, medicine)* tropical

►► ***tropical rainforest*** forêt *f* tropicale humide

tropically ['trɒpɪkəlɪ] *adv* comme sous les tropiques

tropicbird ['trɒpɪkbɜ:d] *n Orn* phaéton *m*, paille-en-queue *m*

tropism ['trəʊpɪzəm] *n* tropisme *m*

tropophyte ['trɒpəfaɪt] *n Bot* tropophyte *f*

troposphere ['trɒpəsfɪə(r)] *n* troposphère *f*

Trot [trɒt] *n Fam Pej Pol (abbr* **Trotskyist**) trotskiste ❑ *mf*

trot [trɒt] *(pt & pp* **trotted**, *cont* **trotting**) **1** *n* (**a**) *(of horse)* trot *m*; **to set off at a trot** partir au trot; **to go at a trot** aller au trot, trotter

(**b**) *(of person)* **he went off at a trot** il est parti au pas de course

(**c**) *(ride)* promenade *f* à cheval; *Fam (run)* petite course ❑ *f*; **to go for a trot** *(on horseback)* aller faire une promenade à cheval; *Fam (on foot)* aller faire une balade; *Br Fam* **on the trot** *(busy)* affairé ❑; *(in succession)* d'affilée, de suite; **they kept me on the trot all afternoon** ils m'ont fait courir tout l'après-midi; **he conducted ten interviews on the trot (that morning)** (ce matin-là,) il a fait dix interviews d'affilée *ou* de suite

(**d**) *Am Fam (crib)* antisèche *f*

2 *vi* (**a**) *(horse, rider)* trotter; **he trotted up to us** il est venu vers nous au trot

(**b**) *(on foot)* **to trot in/out/past** entrer/sortir/passer en courant; **can you trot down to the shops for me?** peux-tu faire un saut pour moi jusqu'aux magasins?

3 *vt (horse)* faire trotter

4 trots *npl Br Fam* courante *f*; **to have the trots** avoir la courante

►**trot along** *vi* (**a**) *(horse)* trotter, aller au trot

(**b**) *Fam (person)* filer, se sauver; **I must be trotting along** il faut que je file *ou* que je me sauve; **trot along now** sauve-toi *ou* file maintenant

►**trot away** *vi* (**a**) *(horse)* partir au trot

(**b**) *Fam (person)* partir au pas de course

►**trot out** *vt sep Br Fam (excuse, information)* débiter; *(story, list)* débiter, réciter; **she trotted out the usual excuses** elle débita *ou* sortit les excuses habituelles

►**trot over** *vi* (**a**) *(rider)* venir à cheval

(**b**) *Fam (person)* faire un saut; **why don't you trot over to see me some time?** viens donc faire un saut un de ces jours; **she trotted over to the shops** elle a fait un saut jusqu'aux magasins

troth [trəʊθ] *n Arch* **by my troth!** ma foi!, pardieu!; **in troth** en vérité

trotline ['trɒtlaɪn] *n Fishing* = ligne qui traverse une rivière et à laquelle on suspend des hameçons

Trotsky ['trɒtskɪ] *pr n* Trotski

Trotskyism ['trɒtskɪɪzəm] *n* trotskisme *m*

Trotskyist ['trɒtskɪɪst] **1** *adj* trotskiste

2 *n* trotskiste *mf*

Trotskyite ['trɒtskɪaɪt] **1** *adj* trotskiste

2 *n* trotskiste *mf*

trotter ['trɒtə(r)] *n* (**a**) *(horse)* trotteur(euse) *m,f*

(**b**) *Culin* **pig's trotters** pieds *mpl* de porc

troubadour ['tru:bədɔ:(r)] *n* troubadour *m*

TROUBLE ['trʌbəl]

ennui(s)	► **1 (a), (b), (e), (f), (h)**
problème(s)	► **1 (a), (d) – (f), (h)**
difficultés	► **1 (b)**
mal	► **1 (b), (c)**
peine	► **1 (c)**
défaut	► **1 (d)**
troubles	► **1 (g)**
inquiéter	► **2 (a)**
troubler	► **2 (a), (e)**
gêner	► **2 (b)**
déranger	► **2 (c), (d)**
se déranger	► **3 (a)**

1 *n* (**a**) *(UNCOUNT) (conflict)* ennuis *mpl*, problèmes *mpl*; *(discord)* discorde *f*; **to be in trouble** avoir des ennuis; **you're really in trouble now!** tu es dans de beaux draps *ou* te voilà bien maintenant!; **I've never been in trouble with the police** je n'ai jamais eu d'ennuis *ou* d'histoires avec la police; **to get into trouble** s'attirer des ennuis, se faire attraper; **to get into trouble with the police** avoir affaire à la police; **her sharp tongue often gets her into trouble** sa causticité lui attire souvent des ennuis; **he got into trouble for stealing apples** il s'est fait attraper pour avoir volé des pommes; **he got his friends into trouble** il a causé des ennuis à ses amis; **to get sb out of trouble** tirer qn d'affaire; **to keep out of trouble** éviter les ennuis; **to keep sb out of trouble** éviter des ennuis à qn; **he's just looking** *or* **asking for trouble** il cherche les ennuis; **it's asking for trouble driving without insurance** on cherche les histoires quand on conduit sans assurance; **there's trouble brewing** ça sent le roussi; **she caused a lot of trouble between them** elle a semé la discorde entre eux; **this means trouble** ça va mal se passer; **there'll be trouble if he finds out** je vais/tu vas/on va/*etc* avoir des ennuis s'il s'en rend compte

(**b**) *(UNCOUNT) (difficulties, problems)* difficultés *fpl*, ennuis *mpl*, mal *m*; **to make** *or* **to create trouble for sb** causer des ennuis à qn; **to make trouble for oneself** se créer des ennuis; **he's given his parents a lot of trouble** *(hard time)* il a donné du fil à retordre à ses parents; *(worry)* il a donné beaucoup de soucis à ses parents; **the baby hardly gives me any trouble** le bébé ne me donne pratiquement aucun mal; **this machine's been** *or* **given nothing but trouble** cette machine ne m'a/ne nous a apporté que des problèmes; **my eyes have been giving me some trouble** mes yeux me donnent quelques soucis; **what's the trouble?** qu'est-ce qu'il y a?, quel est le problème?; **you'll have trouble with him** il va vous causer des difficultés *ou* des ennuis; **to have trouble (in) doing sth** avoir du mal *ou* des difficultés à faire qch; **to be in/to get into trouble** *(climber, swimmer, business)* être/se trouver en difficulté; *Br Euph* **to get a girl into trouble** mettre une fille dans une position intéressante; *Fam* **he's got woman/she's got man trouble** ça ne va pas très bien pour lui/elle côté cœur

(**c**) *(inconvenience, bother)* mal *m*, peine *f*; **to go** *or* **to put oneself to the trouble to do** *or* **of doing sth** prendre *ou* se donner la peine de faire qch; **to go** *or* **to put oneself to a lot of trouble to do** *or* **doing sth** se donner beaucoup de mal *ou* de peine pour faire qch; **she went to considerable trouble to get the tickets** elle s'est donné énormément de mal pour obtenir les billets; **you shouldn't have gone to all this trouble** il ne fallait pas vous donner tout ce mal *ou* tant de peine; **I went to a lot of trouble for nothing** je me suis donné beaucoup de mal pour rien; **to put sb to trouble** donner du mal à qn, déranger qn; **I hope we're not putting you to too much trouble** j'espère que nous ne vous donnons pas trop de mal; **he didn't even take the trouble to read the instructions** il ne s'est même pas donné *ou* il n'a même pas pris la peine de lire les instructions; **I don't want to be any trouble** je ne veux pas vous déranger; **if it's no trouble** si ça ne vous dérange pas; **it's no trouble (at all)** cela ne me dérange pas (du tout); **nothing is too much trouble for her** elle se donne vraiment beaucoup de mal; **it's not worth the trouble, it's more trouble than it's worth** cela n'en vaut pas la peine, le jeu n'en vaut pas la chandelle

(**d**) *(drawback)* problème *m*, défaut *m*; **the trouble with him is that he's too proud** le problème avec lui, c'est qu'il est trop fier; **the only trouble with your solution is that it's expensive** ta solution n'a qu'un défaut, c'est qu'elle revient cher; **the trouble is that no one understands him** l'ennui *ou* le problème, c'est que personne ne le comprend; **that's the trouble** c'est ça le problème

(**e**) *(UNCOUNT) (mechanical failure)* ennuis *mpl*, problèmes *mpl*; **I'm having a bit of engine trouble** j'ai des problèmes de moteur; **they've had trouble with the new dishwasher, the new dishwasher has given them trouble** ils ont eu des problèmes avec leur nouveau lave-vaisselle; **have you found out what the trouble is?** avez-vous trouvé d'où vient la panne?; **what seems to be the trouble?** qu'est-ce qui ne va pas?

(**f**) *(worry, woe)* ennui *m*, souci *m*, problème *m*; **money troubles** ennuis *mpl* d'argent; **at last your troubles are over** enfin vos soucis sont terminés; **her troubles are not at an end yet** elle n'est pas encore au bout de ses peines; *SEng Fam Hum* **the trouble and strife** *(rhyming slang* **= wife)** ma légitime; *Fam* **here comes trouble!** tiens, voilà les ennuis qui arrivent!

(**g**) *(UNCOUNT) (friction)* troubles *mpl*, conflits *mpl*; *(disorder, disturbance)* troubles *mpl*, désordres *mpl*; **the trouble began when the police arrived** l'agitation a commencé quand la police est arrivée; **industrial** *or* **labour troubles** conflits *mpl* sociaux; **there will be trouble** il va y avoir du grabuge; **there's some sort of trouble down at the mine** il y a de l'agitation à la mine; **there was trouble on the pitch/on the terraces** il y a eu des histoires sur le terrain/dans les gradins

(**h**) *(UNCOUNT) Med* ennuis *mpl*, problèmes *mpl*; **I have kidney/back trouble** j'ai des ennuis rénaux/des problèmes de dos; **stomach trouble** troubles *mpl* digestifs; **to have heart trouble** être malade du cœur

2 *vt* (**a**) *(worry)* inquiéter; *(upset)* troubler; **what troubles me is that we've had no news** ce qui m'inquiète, c'est que nous n'avons pas eu de nouvelles; **he didn't want to trouble her with bad news** il ne voulait pas l'inquiéter en lui annonçant de mauvaises nouvelles; **don't let it trouble you!** que cela ne vous inquiète pas!, ne vous tourmentez pas à ce sujet!; **nothing seems to trouble him** il ne s'en fait jamais, il ne se fait jamais de souci; **her conscience was troubling her** elle avait des problèmes de conscience

(**b**) *(cause pain to)* gêner; **his back is troubling him** il a des problèmes de dos; **how long has this cough been troubling you?** depuis combien de temps souffrez-vous de cette toux?; **she's often troubled by nightmares** elle est sujette aux cauchemars

(**c**) *(bother, disturb)* déranger; **I won't trouble you with the details just now** je vous ferai grâce des *ou* épargnerai les détails pour l'instant; **he didn't even trouble himself to phone** il ne s'est même pas donné la peine de téléphoner; **don't trouble yourself!** ne vous dérangez pas!; *Ironic* ne vous dérangez surtout pas!

(**d**) *(in polite phrases)* déranger; **can I trouble you to open the window?** est-ce que je peux vous demander d'ouvrir la fenêtre?; **I'm sorry to**

trouble you, but could I have the newspaper? excusez-moi de vous déranger, mais puis-je avoir le journal?; **could I trouble you a minute?** excusez-moi, vous auriez une minute?; **may I trouble you for a light/the salt?** puis-je vous demander du feu/le sel?; *Br* **I'll trouble you to be more polite next time!** *(in reproach)* vous allez me faire le plaisir d'être plus poli la prochaine fois!
(**e**) *Literary (disturb → water)* troubler; **a light breeze troubled the surface of the lake** une légère brise troublait la surface du lac
3 *vi* (**a**) *(bother)* se déranger; **don't trouble to do the washing-up now** ne faites pas la vaisselle maintenant, ce n'est pas la peine
(**b**) *(worry)* se faire du souci, s'en faire; **don't trouble about it** ne vous faites pas de souci *ou* ne vous en faites pas (pour ça)
4 Troubles *npl* **the Troubles** = le conflit politique en Irlande du Nord
►► ***trouble spot*** point *m* chaud *ou* de conflit

troubled [ˈtrʌbəld] *adj* (**a**) *(worried → mind, look)* inquiet(ète), préoccupé; **he seems troubled about something** il semble préoccupé par quelque chose; **he's got a troubled conscience** il n'a pas la conscience tranquille
(**b**) *(disturbed → sleep, night, breathing)* agité; *(→ water)* troublé; *(→ person)* tourmenté; *(turbulent → marriage, life)* agité, mouvementé; **we live in troubled times** nous vivons une époque troublée *ou* agitée
►► *Fig* ***troubled waters*** eaux *fpl* troubles; **the troubled waters of Middle Eastern politics** les troubles *mpl* politiques qui agitent le Moyen-Orient; *(stronger)* la tourmente politique au Moyen-Orient
trouble-free *adj (journey, equipment)* sans problème, sans histoires; *(period of time, visit)* sans histoires; *(life)* sans soucis, sans histoires; *(industry)* sans grèves
troublemaker [ˈtrʌbəlˌmeɪkə(r)] *n* provocateur(-trice) *m,f*
troubleshoot [ˈtrʌbəlʃuːt] *vi* (**a**) *(overseer, envoy)* régler un problème (**b**) *(mechanic)* localiser une panne
troubleshooter [ˈtrʌbəlˌʃuːtə(r)] *n* (**a**) *(in crisis)* expert *m (appelé en cas de crise)*; *Ind & Pol (in conflict)* médiateur(trice) *m,f* (**b**) *(mechanic)* dépanneur(euse) *m,f*
troubleshooting [ˈtrʌbəlˌʃuːtɪŋ] *n* (**a**) *(in crisis)* médiation *f* (**b**) *gen & Comput (in mechanism)* dépannage *m*
troublesome [ˈtrʌbəlsəm] *adj* (**a**) *(annoying → person, cough)* gênant, pénible; **he was always a troublesome child** il a toujours été un enfant difficile (**b**) *(difficult → situation)* difficile; *(→ request)* gênant, embarrassant; *(→ job)* difficile, pénible
troubling [ˈtrʌbəlɪŋ] *adj (news etc)* inquiétant
troublous [ˈtrʌbləs] *adj Literary* agité
►► ***troublous times*** époque *f* troublée *ou* agitée
trough [trɒf] *n* (**a**) *(for animals → drinking)* abreuvoir *m*; *(→ eating)* auge *f* (**b**) *(depression → in land)* dépression *f*; *(→ between waves)* creux *m* (**c**) *Met* dépression *f*, zone *f* dépressionnaire; **a trough of low pressure** une zone de basse pression (**d**) *(on graph, in cycle)* creux *m*; *Fin* creux *m*, dépression *f* (**e**) *(gutter)* gouttière *f*; *(channel)* chenal *m*
trounce [traʊns] *vt (defeat)* écraser, battre à plate couture *ou* plates coutures; **to get trounced** être battu à plates coutures
trouncing [ˈtraʊnsɪŋ] *n* **we gave Rovers a real trouncing** nous avons écrasé les Rovers, nous avons battu les Rovers à plate(s) couture(s)
troupe [truːp] *n Theat* troupe *f*
trouper [ˈtruːpə(r)] *n* acteur(trice) *m,f (de théâtre)*; **he's an old trouper** c'est un vieux de la vieille
trousers [ˈtraʊzəz] *npl Br* pantalon *m*; **(a pair of) trousers** un pantalon; **I need some new trousers** il me faut un pantalon neuf; *Fig* **she wears the trousers** c'est elle qui porte la culotte; *Fam* **to be caught with one's trousers down** être pris au dépourvu
►► *Br* ***trouser press*** presse *f* à pantalons; *Br* ***trouser suit*** tailleur-pantalon *m*
trousseau [ˈtruːsəʊ] *(pl* **trousseaus** *or* **trousseaux** [-əʊz]) *n* trousseau *m (de jeune mariée)*
trout [traʊt] *(pl* **inv** *or* **trouts**) *n* truite *f*; *Fam (woman)* **(old) trout** vieille bique *f*
►► ***trout farm*** élevage *m* de truites; ***trout fishing*** la pêche à la truite; ***trout river*** rivière *f* à truites
trove [trəʊv] *n see* **treasure trove**
trover [ˈtrəʊvə(r)] *n Formerly Law* (**a**) *(taking possession of property)* = appropriation illicite du bien d'autrui (**b**) *(action to recover property)* **(action for) trover** = action en restitution de biens illégalement détenus
trow [trəʊ] *Arch* **1** *vt* croire
2 *vi* croire
trowel [ˈtraʊəl] *n (for garden)* déplantoir *m*; *(for cement, plaster)* truelle *f*; *Fam Fig* **to lay it on with a trowel** en faire trop
Troy [trɔɪ] *n* Troie
troy [trɔɪ] *n* **troy (weight)** troy *m*, troy-weight *m*
truancy [ˈtruːənsɪ] *n* absentéisme *m* (scolaire); **they were punished for truancy** ils ont été punis pour avoir manqué l'école
truant [ˈtruːənt] **1** *n* élève *mf* absentéiste; **to play truant** faire l'école buissonnière
2 *vi Admin* manquer les cours
3 *adj Literary (thought)* vagabond
►► *Br* ***truant officer*** = responsable municipal chargé de résoudre les problèmes touchant à la vie des établissements scolaires (absentéisme, discipline etc)
truce [truːs] *n* trêve *f*; **to call a truce** conclure *ou* établir une trêve; *Fig* faire la paix
Trucial States [ˈtruːʃəl-] *npl Formerly* Trucial States *mpl*
truck [trʌk] **1** *n* (**a**) *esp Am (lorry)* camion *m*; **the sheep were taken away by truck** les moutons ont été emmenés *ou* transportés en camion
(**b**) *Br (open lorry)* camion *m* à plate-forme; *(van)* camionnette *f*
(**c**) *Br Rail* wagon *m* ouvert, truck *m*; **cattle truck** fourgon *m* à bestiaux
(**d**) *(UNCOUNT) (dealings)* **to have no truck with sb/sth** refuser d'avoir quoi que ce soit à voir avec qn/qch; **they refused to have any truck with him** ils ont refusé d'avoir affaire à lui
(**e**) *(UNCOUNT) Am (produce)* produits *mpl* maraîchers
(**f**) *(barter)* troc *m*, échange *m*
(**g**) *Br (payment)* paiement *m* en nature; **I was paid in truck** on m'a payé en nature
2 *vt Am (goods, animals)* camionner, transporter par *ou* en camion
3 *vi Am* aller *ou* rouler en camion; **keep on trucking!** bon courage!
►► *esp Am* ***truck driver*** camionneur *m*, (chauffeur *m*) routier *m*; *Am* ***truck farm*** jardin *m* maraîcher; *Am* ***truck farmer*** maraîcher(ère) *m,f*; *Am* ***truck garden*** jardin *m* maraîcher; *Am* ***truck gardener*** maraîcher(ère) *m,f*; *Am* ***truck gardening*** maraîchage *m*; *Am* ***truck stop*** (relais *m*) routier *m*
truckage [ˈtrʌkɪdʒ] *n Am* camionnage *m*
trucker [ˈtrʌkə(r)] *n Am* (**a**) *(driver)* (chauffeur *m*) routier *m*, camionneur *m* (**b**) *Agr* maraîcher(-ère) *m,f*
trucking [ˈtrʌkɪŋ] *n Am* camionnage *m*, transport *m* par camion
►► *Am* ***trucking company*** entreprise *f* de transports routiers
truckle [ˈtrʌkəl] **1** *n (castor)* roulette *f*
2 *vt (furniture)* déplacer sur des roulettes
3 *vi Literary* **to truckle to sb** s'abaisser *ou* s'humilier devant qn
►► ***truckle bed*** lit *m* gigogne
truckload [ˈtrʌkləʊd] *n* (**a**) *esp Am (lorryload)* cargaison *f (d'un camion)*; **a truckload of soldiers** un camion de soldats; **medical aid arrived by the truckload** l'aide médicale arriva par camions entiers (**b**) *Fam Fig* **a truckload of** un tas de
truckman [ˈtrʌkmən] *(pl* **truckmen** [-mən]) *n Am* (chauffeur *m*) routier *m*, camionneur *m*
truculence [ˈtrʌkjʊləns], **truculency** [ˈtrʌkjʊlənsɪ] *n* agressivité *f*
truculent [ˈtrʌkjʊlənt] *adj* belliqueux, agressif
truculently [ˈtrʌkjʊləntlɪ] *adv* agressivement
trudge [trʌdʒ] **1** *vi* marcher péniblement *ou* en traînant les pieds; **we trudged wearily along the path** nous avons marché *ou* avancé péniblement le long du chemin; **the prisoners trudged past** les prisonniers passaient en traînant les pieds; **she trudged home through the snow** elle rentra chez elle en marchant péniblement dans la neige; **we trudged from shop to shop** nous nous sommes traînés de magasin en magasin
2 *vt* **to trudge the streets** se traîner de rue en rue
3 *n* marche *f* pénible; **they began the long trudge up the hill** ils ont entrepris la longue ascension de la colline
true [truː] **1** *adj* (**a**) *(factual → statement, story)* vrai, véridique; *(→ account, description)* exact, véridique; **it's a true story** c'est une histoire vraie; **the film is based on a true story** le film est tiré d'une histoire vraie *ou* d'une histoire vécue; **the true adventures of a Second World War spy** les aventures véridiques d'un espion pendant la Deuxième Guerre mondiale; **is it true that they were lovers?** c'est vrai qu'ils étaient amants?; **is it true about Michael?** c'est vrai ce qu'on dit à propos de Michael?; **it is not true that he has disappeared** ce n'est pas vrai qu'il a disparu; **I can't believe it's true** je n'arrive pas à le croire; **if it were true that she was innocent** si elle était vraiment innocente; **can it be true?** est-ce possible?; **he's a complete idiot – (that's) true, but he's very lovable** il est complètement idiot – ça c'est vrai, mais il est très sympathique; **the same is** *or* **holds true for many people** il en va de même pour *ou* c'est vrai pour beaucoup de gens; **to come true** *(dream)* se réaliser; *(prophecy)* se réaliser, se vérifier; **too true!** c'est vrai ce que vous dites!, ah oui alors!; *Fam* **he's so stingy, it's not true!** ce n'est pas possible d'être aussi radin!
(**b**) *(precise, exact → measurement)* exact, juste; *Mus (→ note, voice)* juste; *(→ copy)* conforme; *Constr (wall)* vertical, d'aplomb; *(beam)* droit; **I certify that this is a true copy of the diploma** je certifie que ceci est une copie conforme du diplôme; **he's not a genius in the true sense of the word** ce n'est pas un génie au vrai sens du terme; *also Fig* **his aim is true** il vise juste
(**c**) *(genuine → friendship, feelings)* vrai, authentique; *(→ friend, love)* vrai, véritable; *(real, actual → nature, motive)* réel, véritable; **she was a true democrat** c'était une démocrate dans l'âme; **he's a true Irishman** *(conforms to stereotype)* il est bien irlandais; *(by birth)* c'est un Irlandais, un vrai; **a story of true love** l'histoire d'un grand amour; **to find true love** trouver le grand amour; **to get a true idea of the situation** se faire une idée juste de la situation; **it's not a true amphibian** ce n'est pas vraiment un amphibien; **spoken like a true soldier!** voilà qui est bien dit!
(**d**) *(faithful → lover)* fidèle; *(→ portrait)* fidèle, exact; **a true likeness** une ressemblance parfaite; **to be true to sb** être fidèle à *ou* loyal envers qn; **to be true to oneself** être fidèle à soi-même; **to be true to one's ideals/principles** être fidèle à ses idéaux/principes; **she was true to her word** elle a tenu parole; **true to life** *(story, situation)* qui correspond bien à la réalité; **the painting is very true to life** le tableau est très ressemblant; **to be** *or* **to run true to type** être typique; **she was an accountant, and true to type she...** elle était comptable, et bien entendu elle...; **true to form, he arrived half an hour late** fidèle à son habitude *ou* comme à son habitude, il est arrivé avec une demi-heure de retard; **the horse hasn't been running true to form lately** ces derniers temps, le cheval n'a pas couru comme à son habitude *ou* comme on pouvait s'y attendre
2 *adv* (**a**) *(aim, shoot, sing)* juste; *Biol* **to breed true** se reproduire dans la conformité de l'espèce; **it doesn't ring true** cela sonne faux
(**b**) *Literary (truly)* **tell me true** dites-moi la vérité; **love me true** aime-moi fidèlement
3 *vt* aligner, ajuster
4 out of true *adj Br (wall)* hors d'aplomb; *(beam)* tordu; *(wheel)* voilé; *(axle)* faussé; *(painting)* de travers
►► *Fin* ***true discount*** escompte *m* en dedans; *Acct* ***true and fair view*** *(of accounts)* image *f* fidèle; ***true north*** vrai nord *m*, nord *m* géographique; *Mktg* ***true sample*** échantillon *m* représentatif
►**true up** *vt sep* aligner, ajuster

true-blue *adj* (**a**) *(loyal)* loyal (**b**) *esp Br Pol* conservateur, tory; **true-blue Tories** des fidèles *mpl* du parti conservateur

trueborn ['truː,bɔːn] *adj* véritable, authentique; **a trueborn Englishman** un vrai Anglais d'Angleterre

truebred ['truː,bred] *adj* de race pure

true-false *adj*
▸▸ ***true-false test*** questionnaire *m* auquel on répond par "vrai" ou "faux"

truehearted [,truː'hɑːtɪd] *adj Literary* loyal, sincère

true-life *adj* vrai, vécu; **a true-life story** une histoire vécue

truelove ['truːlʌv] *n Literary* bien-aimé(e) *m,f*

truffle ['trʌfəl] *n* truffe *f*; **chocolate truffles** truffes *fpl* au chocolat

trug [trʌg] *n Br* corbeille *f* de jardinier

truism ['truːɪzəm] *n* truisme *m*, lapalissade *f*; **it is a truism that...** c'est un lieu commun de dire que... + *indicative*

truly ['truːlɪ] *adv* (**a**) *Formal (really)* vraiment, réellement; **I'm truly sorry for what I've done** je suis vraiment navré de ce que j'ai fait; **they truly believe they'll succeed** ils croient réellement qu'ils vont réussir; **he really said yes? – truly he did** il a vraiment dit oui? – vraiment, je te le jure; **truly it was the last thing on my mind** je vous assure que j'étais loin de penser à ça; **tell me truly now, do you want the job?** maintenant, dites-moi sincèrement, voulez-vous ce travail?
(**b**) *(as intensifier)* vraiment, absolument; **it was a truly awful film** c'était absolument épouvantable comme film; **the meal was truly delicious** le repas était vraiment délicieux; **hers is a truly amazing talent** elle a vraiment un talent étonnant
(**c**) *(in letter-writing) Am* **yours truly, Kathryn Schmidt** je vous prie d'agréer, Monsieur *ou* Madame, l'expression de mes sentiments respectueux, Kathryn Schmidt; *Fam Hum* **yours truly** *(myself)* mézigue; **meanwhile yours truly had left** entretemps mézigue était parti

trumeau ['truːməʊ] *n Archit* trumeau *m*

trump [trʌmp] **1** *n* (**a**) *(in cards)* atout *m*; *Fig* atout *m*, carte *f* maîtresse; **to play a trump** jouer (un) atout; **what's trumps?** quel est l'atout?; **diamonds are trumps** (c'est) atout carreau; **the six of trumps** le six d'atout; **no trump** sans-atout *m inv*; **to hold all the trumps** avoir tous les atouts dans son jeu *ou* en main; *Br* **to turn up** *or* **to come up trumps** sauver la situation
(**b**) *Bible (trumpet)* trompette *f*; **the last trump** la trompette du Jugement dernier
2 *vt* (**a**) *(card)* couper, jouer atout sur; *(trick)* remporter avec un atout
(**b**) *(outdo → remark, action)* renchérir sur
▸▸ *also Fig* ***trump card*** atout *m*; *Fig* **to play one's trump card** jouer ses atouts

▸**trump up** *vt sep (invent → excuse)* forger *ou* inventer de toutes pièces; **to trump up a charge against sb** forger une accusation contre qn

trumped-up [trʌmpt-] *adj (charge)* forgé de toutes pièces; *(story)* inventé de toutes pièces

trumpery ['trʌmpərɪ] (*pl* **trumperies**) *Literary* **1** *n* (**a**) *(nonsense)* bêtises *fpl* (**b**) *(trinkets)* pacotille *f*
2 *adj* (**a**) *(flashy)* tapageur, criard (**b**) *(worthless)* sans valeur, insignifiant

trumpet ['trʌmpɪt] **1** *n* (**a**) *(instrument)* trompette *f*; **Armstrong is on trumpet** Armstrong est à la trompette
(**b**) *(trumpeter)* trompettiste *mf*; *(in military band)* trompette *f*
(**c**) *(of elephant)* barrissement *m*
(**d**) *(hearing aid)* (**ear**) **trumpet** cornet *m* acoustique
2 *vi (elephant)* barrir
3 *vt (secret, news)* claironner; **there's no need to trumpet it abroad** il n'est pas nécessaire de le crier sur les toits; **the government's much trumpeted land reforms** la réforme agraire annoncée à grand renfort de publicité par le gouvernement
▸▸ *Mus* ***trumpet call*** sonnerie *f* de trompette; *Fig (appeal)* appel *m*; *Fig* **a trumpet call to liberty** un appel vibrant à la liberté; *Mil* ***trumpet major*** trompette-major *m*; ***trumpet voluntary*** solo *m* pour trompette et orgue *(joué en prélude à une cérémonie religieuse)*

trumpeter ['trʌmpɪtə(r)] *n* (**a**) *(musician)* trompettiste *mf*; *(in orchestra)* trompette *m* (**b**) *Orn* agami *m*; **trumpeter finch** bouvreuil *m* githagine

trumpeting ['trʌmpɪtɪŋ] *n* (**a**) *(of elephant)* barrissement *m*, barrissements *mpl* (**b**) *Mus* coup *m ou* coups *mpl* de trompette

truncate [trʌŋ'keɪt] *vt (gen) & Comput* tronquer

truncated [trʌŋ'keɪtɪd] *adj (body, text)* tronqué; *(meeting, journey)* écourté
▸▸ *Geom* ***truncated cone*** cône *m* tronqué

truncation [trʌŋ'keɪʃən] *n (gen) & Ling* troncation *f*; *(d'un cristal)* troncature *f*

truncheon ['trʌntʃən] **1** *n* matraque *f*
2 *vt* matraquer

trundle ['trʌndəl] **1** *vi (heavy equipment, wheelbarrow)* avancer *ou* rouler lentement; *(person)* aller *ou* avancer tranquillement; **to trundle in/out/past** entrer/sortir/passer tranquillement; **the lorry trundled slowly along** le camion avançait lentement; **I could hear the wheelbarrow trundling down the path** j'entendais quelqu'un pousser bruyamment la brouette sur le chemin; *Br Hum* **do you fancy trundling down to the pub?** ça vous dit d'aller faire un tour au pub?
2 *vt (push)* pousser (avec effort); *(pull)* traîner (avec effort); *(wheel)* faire rouler bruyamment; **he trundled the trolley along behind him** il traînait le chariot derrière lui; **she trundled the piano across the room** elle a fait rouler le piano bruyamment à travers la pièce
3 *n Fam Hum (walk)* balade *f*
▸▸ ***trundle bed*** lit *m* gigogne

▸**trundle out** *vt sep (old bicycle, theory etc)* ressortir

trunk [trʌŋk] **1** *n* (**a**) *(of tree, body)* tronc *m* (**b**) *(of elephant)* trompe *f* (**c**) *(case)* malle *f*; *(metal)* cantine *f* (**d**) *Am Aut* coffre *m*
2 trunks *npl (for swimming)* maillot *m ou* slip *m* de bain; *(underwear)* slip *m* (d'homme)
▸▸ *Br Old-fashioned* ***trunk call*** appel *m* interurbain; ***trunk line*** (**a**) *Old-fashioned Tel* inter *m*, interurbain *m* (**b**) *Rail* grande ligne *f*; *Br* ***trunk road*** (route *f*) nationale *f*; ***trunk roads*** grandes routes *fpl*

trunnion ['trʌnjən] *n* tourillon *m*

truss [trʌs] **1** *vt* (**a**) *(prisoner, animal)* ligoter; *(poultry)* trousser; *(hay)* botteler (**b**) *Constr* armer, renforcer
2 *n* (**a**) *(of hay)* botte *f*; *(of fruit)* grappe *f* (**b**) *Constr* ferme *f* (**c**) *Med* bandage *m* herniaire
▸▸ ***truss bridge*** pont *m* à fermes

▸**truss up** *vt sep (prisoner)* ligoter; *(poultry)* trousser; **trussed up like a chicken** ficelé comme un poulet

trust [trʌst] **1** *vt* (**a**) *(have confidence in → person)* faire confiance à, avoir confiance en; *(→ method, feelings, intuition)* faire confiance à, se fier à; *(→ judgment, memory, instincts)* se fier à; **you can trust me** vous pouvez me faire confiance *ou* avoir confiance en moi; **she's not to be trusted** *(not trustworthy)* on ne peut pas lui faire confiance; *(unreliable)* on ne peut pas se fier à elle; **can we trust his account of events?** peut-on se fier à sa version des faits?; **to trust sb to do sth** faire confiance à qn *ou* compter sur qn pour faire qch; **we're trusting you to save the company** nous comptons sur vous pour sauver la société; **I can't trust him to do the job properly** je ne peux pas compter sur lui pour faire le travail correctement; **he can't be trusted out of your sight** impossible de le lâcher des yeux, on ne peut pas lui faire confiance; *Hum* **trust Mark to put his foot in it!** pour mettre les pieds dans le plat, on peut faire confiance à Mark!; **trust you!** cela ne m'étonne pas de toi!; **I couldn't trust myself not to say anything** je ne pourrais pas résister à l'envie de dire quelque chose; **I wouldn't trust her as far as I could throw her!** je ne lui ferais absolument pas confiance!
(**b**) *(entrust)* **to trust sb with sth** confier qch à qn; **I certainly wouldn't trust him with any of my personal secrets** je ne lui confierais certainement pas un secret; **I don't trust you with money** je ne te confierais pas mon argent
(**c**) *Formal (suppose)* supposer; *(hope)* espérer; **I trust (that) everyone enjoyed themselves** j'espère que tout le monde s'est bien amusé;
I trust not j'espère que non
2 *vi* (**a**) *(believe)* **to trust in God** croire en Dieu
(**b**) *(have confidence)* **I want someone I can trust in** il me faut une personne de confiance; **to trust to luck** s'en remettre à la chance; **we'll just have to trust to luck that it doesn't rain** espérons qu'avec un peu de chance il ne pleuvra pas
3 *n* (**a**) *(confidence, faith)* confiance *f*, foi *f*; **to betray sb's trust** trahir la confiance de qn; **to place** *or* **to put one's trust in sb** placer *ou* mettre sa confiance en qn; **to place** *or* **to put one's trust in sth** avoir confiance en qch, se fier à qch; **to take sth on trust** prendre *ou* accepter qch en toute confiance *ou* les yeux fermés; **you can't take everything he says on trust** on ne peut pas croire sur parole tout ce qu'il dit; **I bought the machine on trust** j'ai acheté la machine les yeux fermés; **the garage lent me the car on trust** au garage on m'a prêté la voiture parce qu'on me fait confiance
(**b**) *(responsibility)* responsabilité *f*; **he has a position of trust** il a un poste de confiance *ou* à responsabilités
(**c**) *(care)* charge *f*; **to give** *or* **to place sth into sb's trust** confier qch aux soins de qn
(**d**) *Fin & Law (group of trustees)* administrateurs *mpl*; *(investment)* fidéicommis *m*; **the scholarship is run by a trust** la gestion de la bourse (d'études) a été confiée à un groupe d'administrateurs; **to set up a trust for sb** instituer un fidéicommis pour qn; **to leave money in trust for sb** faire administrer un legs par fidéicommis pour qn; **the money was held in trust until her eighteenth birthday** l'argent a été administré par fidéicommis jusqu'à ses dix-huit ans
(**e**) *(cartel)* trust *m*, cartel *m*
▸▸ *Fin* ***trust account*** compte *m* en fidéicommis; *Fin* ***trust bank*** banque *f* de gestion de patrimoine; *Fin* ***trust company*** société *f* fiduciaire; *Fin* ***trust deed*** document *m* de fidéicommis; *Fin* ***trust fund*** fonds *m* en fidéicommis; ***trust hospital*** = hôpital britannique ayant opté pour l'auto-gestion mais qui reçoit toujours son budget de l'État; ***trust territory*** territoire *m* sous tutelle

trustafarian [,trʌstə'feərɪən] *n Br Fam* = jeune anglais blanc de milieu relativement aisé qui cultive une image rasta

trustbuster ['trʌst,bʌstə(r)] *n Am* = fonctionnaire chargé de veiller à l'application des lois anti-trust

trustbusting ['trʌst,bʌstɪŋ] *Am* **1** *n* démantèlement *m* des trusts
2 *adj* qui a trait au démantèlement des trusts

trusted ['trʌstɪd] *adj (method)* éprouvé; *(figures)* fiable; **he's a trusted friend** c'est un ami en qui j'ai entièrement confiance
▸▸ *Comput* ***trusted third party*** *(for Internet transactions)* tierce partie *f* de confiance

trustee [trʌs'tiː] *n* (**a**) *Fin & Law* fidéicommissaire *m*; *(proxy)* mandataire *mf*, fondé(e) *m,f* de pouvoir; *(for minor)* curateur(trice) *m,f*; *(in bankruptcy)* syndic *m* (**b**) *Admin* *(of* [illegible] *charity, company, life assurance policy)* administrateur(trice) *m,f*; **board of trustees** conseil *m* d'administration

trusteeship [,trʌs'tiːʃɪp] *n* (**a**) *Fin & Law* fidéicommis *m*; *(for minor)* curatelle *f* (**b**) *Admin* poste *m* d'administrateur; **she accepted the trusteeship** elle a accepté d'être administratrice (**c**) *Pol (of territory)* tutelle *f*

trustful ['trʌstfʊl] = **trusting**

trustfully ['trʌstfʊlɪ] *adv* avec confiance

trusting ['trʌstɪŋ] *adj (nature, person)* qui a confiance; *(look)* confiant; **he's too trusting of people** il fait trop confiance aux gens

trustingly ['trʌstɪŋlɪ] *adv* en toute confiance; **he looked at me trustingly** il m'a lancé un regard confiant

trustworthiness ['trʌst,wɜːðɪnɪs] *n* (**a**) *(reliability → of person)* loyauté *f*, sérieux *m*; *(→ of information, source, report, figures)* fiabilité (**b**) *(honesty)* honnêteté *f*

trustworthy ['trʌst,wɜːðɪ] *adj* (**a**) *(reliable →*

tru–tru

person) sur qui on peut compter, à qui on peut faire confiance; *(→ information, source)* sûr, fiable; *(→ report, figures)* fiable (**b**) *(honest)* honnête

trusty ['trʌstɪ] (*compar* **trustier**, *superl* **trustiest**, *pl* **trusties**) **1** *adj Arch or Hum (steed, sword)* loyal, fidèle; *Hum* **my trusty typewriter** ma bonne vieille machine à écrire

2 *n (prisoner)* = détenu bénéficiant d'un régime de faveur

truth [tru:θ] (*pl* **truths** [tru:ðz]) **1** *n* (**a**) *(true facts)* vérité *f*; **I then discovered the truth about Neil** j'ai alors découvert la vérité sur Neil; **there isn't a grain** *or* **an ounce of truth in what he says** il n'y a pas une once de vérité dans ce qu'il dit; **there's some truth in what he says** il y a du vrai dans ce qu'il dit; **there is no truth in the rumour** il n'y a rien de vrai dans cette rumeur; **the truth of the matter is I really don't care any more** la vérité c'est que maintenant je m'en fiche vraiment; **... and that's the truth** ... et voilà la vérité; **to tell the truth** dire la vérité; **to tell (you) the truth** à vrai dire, à dire vrai; *Literary* **truth to tell** à dire vrai; **truth is the first casualty (of war)** toute guerre s'accompagne de son cortège de mensonges; *Law* **the truth, the whole truth, and nothing but the truth** la vérité, toute la vérité, rien que la vérité; *Prov* **(the) truth will out** = la vérité finit toujours par se savoir

(**b**) *(fact, piece of information)* vérité *f*; **he learned some important truths about himself** on lui a dit ses quatre vérités; **universal truths** vérités *fpl* universelles

2 in truth *adv* en vérité

▸▸ ***truth drug*** sérum *m* de vérité; *Math & (in logic)* ***truth set*** = ensemble qui n'a pas de solution unique; ***truth table*** table *f ou* matrice *f* de vérité

truth-condition *n Phil & (in logic)* condition *f* nécessaire et préalable

truthful ['tru:θfʊl] *adj (person)* qui dit la vérité; *(character)* honnête; *(article, statement)* fidèle à la réalité, vrai; *(story)* véridique, vrai; *(portrait)* fidèle

truthfully ['tru:θfʊlɪ] *adv (answer, speak)* honnêtement, sans mentir; *(portray)* fidèlement

truthfulness ['tru:θfʊlnɪs] *n (of person)* honnêteté *f*; *(of portrait)* fidélité *f*; *(of story, statement)* véracité *f*

truth-function *n Phil & (in logic)* fonction *f* véri-conditionnelle

truth-value *n Phil & (in logic)* valeur *f* de vérité

TRY [traɪ]

essayer	▸ **1 (a) – (f); 2**
goûter à	▸ **1 (c)**
juger	▸ **1 (g)**
éprouver	▸ **1 (h)**
essai	▸ **3 (a) – (c)**
tentative	▸ **3 (a)**

(*pt & pp* **tried**, *pl* **tries**) **1** *vt* (**a**) *(attempt)* essayer; **to try an experiment** tenter une expérience; **to try to do** *or* **doing sth** essayer *ou* tâcher de faire qch, chercher à faire qch; **I've tried to give up smoking before** j'ai déjà essayé d'arrêter de fumer; **try phoning later** essaie de rappeler plus tard; **she tried not to think about it** elle essaya de ne pas y penser *ou* d'éviter d'y penser; **I tried hard to understand** j'ai tout fait pour essayer de comprendre, j'ai vraiment cherché à comprendre; **to try one's best** *or* **hardest** faire de son mieux; **he tried his best to explain** il a essayé d'expliquer de son mieux; **I'm willing to try anything once!** je suis prêt à tout essayer au moins une fois!; **I'd like to see you try it!** je voudrais bien t'y voir!; **it's trying to rain** on dirait qu'il va pleuvoir; *Fam* **and don't try any funny business!** et pas d'entourloupe!; **just you try it!** *(as threat)* essaie un peu pour voir!

(**b**) *(test → method, approach, car)* essayer; **have you tried acupuncture?** avez-vous essayé l'acupuncture?; **tried and tested** *(remedy, method, friend)* éprouvé, qui a fait ses preuves; **the method has been tried and tested** la méthode a fait ses preuves; **he has been tried and found wanting** il ne s'est pas montré à la hauteur; *Fam* **(just) try me!** essaie toujours!; **to try one's strength against sb** se mesurer à qn; **to try one's luck (at sth)** tenter sa chance (à qch)

(**c**) *(sample → recipe, wine)* essayer, goûter à; *(→ clothes, product)* essayer; **try it, you'll like it** essayez *ou* goûtez-y donc, vous aimerez; **just try the dress and see if it suits you** essaie donc la robe, pour voir si elle te va; **try this for size** *(garment)* essayez ceci pour voir la taille; *(shoe)* essayez ceci pour voir la pointure; *Fig* essayez ceci pour voir si ça va

(**d**) *(attempt to open → door, window)* essayer; **we tried the door, but it was locked** on a essayé la porte, mais elle était fermée à clé

(**e**) *Tel* essayer; **try the number again** refaites le numéro; *Fam* **try him later** essayez de le rappeler plus tard

(**f**) *(visit)* essayer; **I've tried six shops already** j'ai déjà essayé six magasins; **try Jane** *(ask)* demande à Jane; **he tried the embassy first** il a d'abord essayé l'ambassade

(**g**) *Law (person, case)* juger; **he was tried for murder** il a été jugé pour meurtre

(**h**) *(tax, strain → patience)* éprouver, mettre à l'épreuve; **these things are sent to try us!** c'est le ciel qui nous envoie ces épreuves!; **it's enough to try the patience of a saint** même un ange n'aurait pas la patience; *Literary or Hum* **to be sorely tried** être durement éprouvé

2 *vi* essayer; **to try and do sth** essayer de faire qch; **try again** refaites un essai, recommencez; **try later** essayez plus tard; **we can but try** on peut toujours essayer; **you can do it if you try** quand on veut, on peut; **just (you) try!** essaie un peu pour voir!; **I'd like to see you try!** *(answer to threat, challenge)* je voudrais bien t'y voir!; **... and she wasn't even trying** ... et elle l'a fait sans le moindre effort

3 *n* (**a**) *(attempt)* essai *m*, tentative *f*; **to have a try at sth/at doing sth** essayer qch/de faire qch; **good try!** bel effort!; **it's worth a try** cela vaut la peine d'essayer; **I managed it at the first try** j'ai réussi du premier coup; **can I have a try?** (est-ce que) je peux essayer?; **he had several tries at opening the box** il a essayé plusieurs fois d'ouvrir la boîte

(**b**) *(test, turn)* essai *m*; **to give sth a try** essayer qch; **do you want a try on my bike?** veux-tu essayer mon vélo?

(**c**) *Sport (in rugby)* essai *m*; **to score a try** marquer un essai; *Sport* **the try scorer** celui qui a marqué l'essai; **France's leading try scorer** celui qui a marqué le plus d'essais pour la France

▸▸ *Tech* ***try square*** équerre *f* de menuisier, équerre *f* à chapeau

▸**try for** *vt insep (attempt to obtain)* tâcher d'obtenir; **to try for a job** poser sa candidature à un emploi; **he's trying for (a place at) music school** il essaie d'obtenir une place à l'école de musique; **she's trying for the record/a gold medal** elle essaie de battre le record/ décrocher une médaille d'or; **they're trying for a baby** ils essaient d'avoir un enfant

▸**try on** *vt sep* (**a**) *(garment)* essayer; **try it on for size** essayez-le pour voir la taille

(**b**) *Br Fam (idiom)* **to try it on with sb** essayer de voir jusqu'où on peut pousser qn ☐; *(flirt)* essayer de flirter avec qn; *(attempt to deceive)* essayer d'embobiner qn; *(attempt to seduce)* faire des avances à qn ☐; *(test someone's tolerance)* faire le coup à qn; **he's just trying it on to see how far he can go** il essaie juste de voir jusqu'où il peut aller; **don't you try anything on with me!** *(gen)* ne fais pas le malin avec moi!; *(flirt)* n'essaie pas de flirter avec moi!

▸**try out 1** *vt sep (new car, bicycle)* essayer, faire un essai avec; *(method, chemical, recipe)* essayer; *(employee)* mettre à l'essai; **to try sth out on sb** essayer *ou* expérimenter qch sur qn

2 *vi Am* **to try out for a team** faire un essai pour se faire engager dans une équipe

▸**try over** *vt sep (music)* jouer à titre d'essai

trying ['traɪɪŋ] *adj (experience)* pénible, éprouvant; *(journey, job)* ennuyeux, pénible; *(person)* fatigant, pénible; **he had a very trying time** *(moment)* il a passé un moment très difficile; *(period)* il a vécu une période très difficile; *(experience)* il a vécu une expérience très pénible *ou* éprouvante

try-on *n Br Fam* **it's a try-on** c'est du bluff

try-out *n* essai *m*; *Am Theat* audition *f*; *Sport* épreuve *f* de sélection

trypanosome ['trɪpənə,səʊm] *n Biol* trypanosome *m*

trypanosomiasis [,trɪpənəsə'maɪəsɪs] *n Med* trypanosomiase *f*

trypsin ['trɪpsɪn] *n Biol & Chem* trypsine *f*

tryptophan ['trɪptəfæn] *n Biol & Chem* tryptophane *m*

trysail ['traɪsəl] *n* voile *f* goélette

tryst [trɪst] *n Literary* rendez-vous *m* galant; **to keep tryst** venir à un rendez-vous; **to break tryst** manquer à un rendez-vous

trysting place ['trɪstɪŋ-] *n Literary* (lieu *m* de) rendez-vous *m*

tsar [zɑ:(r)] *n* tsar *m*, tzar *m*, czar *m*

tsarevitch ['zɑ:rəvɪtʃ] *n* tsarévitch *m*, tzarévitch *m*

tsarina [zɑ:'ri:nə] *n* tsarine *f*, tzarine *f*

tsarism ['zɑ:rɪzəm] *n* tsarisme *m*

tsarist ['zɑ:rɪst] **1** *adj* tsariste

2 *n* tsariste *mf*

T-section *n* profil *m* en T

tsetse fly ['tsetsɪ-] *n Entom* (mouche *f*) tsé-tsé *f*

T-shaped *adj* en forme de T

T-shirt *n* tee-shirt *m*, t-shirt *m*; *Hum* **been there, done that, got the T-shirt** je connais déjà

tsp. (*written abbr* **teaspoon(ful)**) cc

T-square *n* équerre *f* en T, té *m*, T *m (règle)*

TSS [,ti:es'es] *n Med* (*abbr* **toxic shock syndrome**) SCT *m*

T-stop *n Phot* diaphragme *m*

T-strap *n (on shoe)* fermeture *f* en té

tsunami [tsu:'nɑ:mɪ] *n* tsunami *m*

Tswana ['tswɑ:nə] **1** *n* (**a**) *(person)* Tswana *mf inv*; **the Tswana** les Tswana *mpl* (**b**) *(language)* tswana *m*

2 *adj* tswana *(inv)*

TT [,ti:'ti:] **1** *adj* (*abbr* **teetotal**) qui ne boit jamais d'alcool

2 *n Sport* (*abbr* **Tourist Trophy**) **the TT races** = courses de moto sur l'île de Man

TTL [,ti:ti:'el] *adj Phot* (*abbr* **through the lens**)

▸▸ ***TTL flash*** flash *m* TTL; ***TTL measurement*** mesure *f* TTL *ou* à travers l'objectif

TTP [,ti:ti:'pi:] *n Comput* (*abbr* **trusted third party**) *(for Internet transactions)* TPC *f*

TU [,ti:'ju:] *n Ind* (*abbr* **trade union**) syndicat *m*

Tuareg ['twɑ:reg] (*pl* **inv** *or* **Tuaregs**) **1** *n* (**a**) *(person)* Touareg(ègue) *m,f* (**b**) *Ling* touareg *m*

2 *adj* touareg

tuatara [,tu:ə'tɑ:rə] *n Zool* sphénodon *m*

tub [tʌb] *n* (**a**) *(container → for liquid)* cuve *f*, bac *m*; *(→ for flowers)* bac *m*; *(→ for washing clothes)* baquet *m*; *(→ in washing machine)* cuve *f* (**b**) *(contents → of washing powder)* baril *m*; *(→ of wine, beer)* tonneau *m*; *(→ of ice cream, yoghurt)* pot *m* (**c**) *Fam (bathtub)* **a hot tub** *(bath)* un bain chaud ☐; **he's in the tub** il prend un bain ☐ (**d**) *Fam (boat)* rafiot *m*

tuba ['tju:bə] *n* tuba *m*

tubal ['tju:bəl] *adj Anat & Med (relating to the Fallopian tubes)* tubaire; *(relating to eustachian tubes)* tubaire; *(relating to the bronchial tubes)* des bronches

▸▸ ***tubal breathing*** souffle *m* tubaire; ***tubal ligation*** ligature *f* des trompes (de Fallope); ***tubal pregnancy*** grossesse *f* tubaire; ***tubal respiration*** souffle *m* tubaire

tubby ['tʌbɪ] (*compar* **tubbier**, *superl* **tubbiest**) *adj Fam* dodu, rondelet

tube [tju:b] **1** *n* (**a**) *(pipe)* tube *m*; **he was fed through a tube** on l'a nourri à la sonde

(**b**) *Anat* tube *m*, canal *m*

(**c**) *(of glue, toothpaste, paint)* tube *m*

(**d**) *(in tyre)* **(inner) tube** chambre *f* à air

(**e**) *Fam (television)* **what's on the tube tonight?** qu'est-ce qu'il y a à la télé ce soir?; **(cathode-ray) tube** tube *m* (cathodique)

(**f**) *Br (underground)* **the tube** le métro londonien; **to go by tube, to take the tube** aller en métro, prendre le métro

(**g**) *Fam* **to have one's tubes tied** *(be sterilized)* se faire ligaturer les trompes ☐

(**h**) *Fam (idioms)* **to go down the tubes** tomber à l'eau; **he watched his marriage/life's work go down the tubes** il a vu son mariage/le travail de toute une vie tourner en eau de boudin; **that's**

£500 down the tubes ça fait 500 livres de foutus en l'air

2 *comp (map, station)* de métro

▸▸ *Br* ***tube dress*** robe *f* tube; *Br* ***tube skirt*** jupe *f* tube

tubectomy [tʃuː'bektəmɪ] *(pl* **tubectomies***)* *n Med* ablation *f* d'une trompe de Fallope

tube-feed *vt* nourrir à la sonde

tube-feeding *n Med* gavage *m*

tubeless ['tjuːblɪs] *adj*

▸▸ *Br* ***tubeless tyre*** pneu *m* sans chambre (à air)

tubelike ['tjuːblaɪk] *adj (gen)* tubulaire; *Anat* fistulaire

tuber ['tjuːbə(r)] *n Anat & Bot* tubercule *m*

tubercle ['tjuːbəkəl] *n* tubercule *m*

tubercular [tjuː'bɜːkjʊlə(r)] *adj* tuberculeux

tuberculate [tjuː'bɜːkjʊleɪt] *adj* tuberculé

tuberculin [tjuː'bɜːkjʊlɪn] *n* tuberculine *f*

tuberculin-tested [-'testɪd] *adj (cow)* tuberculinisé, tuberculiné

▸▸ ***tuberculin-tested milk*** ≃ lait *m* certifié

tuberculosis [tjuːˌbɜːkjʊ'ləʊsɪs] *n (UNCOUNT)* tuberculose *f*; **he has tuberculosis** il a la tuberculose, il est tuberculeux

tuberculous [tjuː'bɜːkjʊləs] *adj* tuberculeux

tuberose ['tjuːbərəʊs] *Bot* **1** *n* tubéreuse *f*

2 *adj* tubéreux

tuberous ['tjuːbərəs] *adj Bot* tubéreux

tubful ['tʌbfʊl] *n* cuvée *f*, plein baquet *m*

tubing ['tjuːbɪŋ] *n (UNCOUNT)* tubes *mpl*, tuyaux *mpl*; **a piece of plastic tubing** un tube en plastique

tub-thumper [-'θʌmpə(r)] *n Br Fam* orateur(-trice) *m,f* démagogue ❑

tub-thumping *Br Fam* **1** *n* démagogie ❑ *f*

2 *adj* démagogique ❑

Tubuai Islands [ˌtuːbuː'aɪ-] *npl* **the Tubuai Islands** les îles *fpl* Australes

tubular ['tjuːbjʊlə(r)] *adj* (**a**) *(furniture, shape)* tubulaire (**b**) *Am Fam (excellent)* génial, super *(inv)*, géant

▸▸ *Mus* ***tubular bells*** carillon *m* d'orchestre

tubule ['tʃuːbjuːl] *n Bot & Zool* tubule *m*

TUC [ˌtiːjuː'siː] *n Br Ind (abbr* **Trades Union Congress***)* = confédération des syndicats britanniques; **the TUC annual conference** le congrès annuel des syndicats

tuck [tʌk] **1** *vt* (**a**) *(shirt)* rentrer; *(sheet)* rentrer, border; **he tucked his shirt into his trousers** il rentra sa chemise dans son pantalon; **she tucked the sheets under the mattress** elle borda le lit

(**b**) *(put)* mettre; *(slip)* glisser; **she tucked the book under the bedclothes** elle glissa le livre sous les draps; **he had a newspaper tucked under his arm** il avait un journal sous le bras; **she tucked her arm in(to) mine** elle a passé son bras sous le mien; **she tucked her hair behind her ears** elle ramena ses cheveux derrière ses oreilles; **his mother came to tuck him into bed** sa mère est venue le border dans son lit

2 *n* (**a**) *Sewing* rempli *m*; **to put** *or* **to make a tuck in sth** faire un rempli dans qch

(**b**) *(in diving)* plongeon *m* groupé

(**c**) *Br Fam* boustifaille *f*

▸▸ *Br Sch* ***tuck box*** gamelle *f (d'écolier)*; ***tuck position*** *(in skiing)* [illegible]; *Br Sch* ***tuck shop*** = petite boutique où les écoliers achètent bonbons, gâteaux etc

▸**tuck away** *vt sep* (**a**) *(hide)* cacher; *(put)* mettre, ranger; **the house was tucked away in the hills** la maison était cachée dans les collines

(**b**) *Fam (food)* s'enfiler, avaler; **he tucked away three helpings** il s'est enfilé trois portions; **she really can tuck it away!** *(eat a lot)* qu'est-ce qu'elle peut bouffer!

▸**tuck in** **1** *vt sep* (**a**) *(shirt, stomach)* rentrer

(**b**) *(child)* border; **he tucked her in for the night** il la borda pour la nuit

2 *vi Fam (eat)* **we tucked in to a lovely meal** nous avons attaqué un excellent repas; **don't wait for me, tuck in!** ne m'attendez pas, attaquez!

▸**tuck up** *vt sep* (**a**) *(person)* border (dans son lit); **all the children were safely tucked up in bed** les enfants étaient tous bien bordés dans leurs lits

(**b**) *(skirt, sleeves)* remonter; *(hair)* rentrer

(**c**) *(legs)* replier, rentrer

tucker ['tʌkə(r)] **1** *n* (**a**) *(on dress)* fichu *m* (**b**) *Austr & NZ Fam (food)* bouffe *f*

2 *vt Am Fam (exhaust)* crever; **you look tuckered out!** tu as l'air complètement crevé!

tuck-in *n Br Fam* **we had a great tuck-in** on a super bien bouffé

Tudor ['tjuːdə(r)] **1** *adj (family, period)* des Tudor; *(monarch, architecture)* Tudor *(inv)*

2 *n* Tudor *m inv*, membre *m* de la famille des Tudor

▸▸ ***Tudor rose*** = rose stylisée adoptée comme emblème par Henri VII et très utilisée comme motif ornemental à l'époque des Tudor

Tue., Tues. *(written abbr* **Tuesday***)* mar

Tuesday ['tjuːzdɪ] *n* mardi *m*; *see also* **Friday**

tufa ['tjuːfə] *n* tuf *m* calcaire

tuff [tʌf] *n Geol* tuf *m* volcanique

tuffaceous [tʌ'feɪʃəs] *adj Geol* tufacé

tuffet ['tʌfɪt] *n Arch* (**a**) *(of grass)* touffe *f* d'herbe (**b**) *(stool)* petit tabouret *m*

tuft [tʌft] *n* (**a**) *(of hair, grass)* touffe *f*; **tuft of bristles** *(in paint etc brush)* loquet *m* de soies (**b**) *Orn* **tuft (of feathers)** huppe *f*, aigrette *f*

tufted ['tʌftɪd] *adj* (**a**) *(bird)* huppé (**b**) *(grass)* en touffe *ou* touffes (**c**) *(carpet)* tufté

▸▸ *Orn* ***tufted duck*** (fuligule *f*) morillon *m*; *Orn* ***tufted heron*** héron *m* à aigrette, aigrette *f*

tug [tʌg] *(pt & pp* **tugged**, *cont* **tugging***)* **1** *n* (**a**) *(pull)* petit coup *m*; **to give sth a tug** tirer sur qch d'un coup sec; **give the rope a tug, will you?** tire un peu sur la corde, tu veux?; **he felt a tug at his sleeve** il sentit qu'on le tirait par la manche

(**b**) *Naut* remorqueur *m*

2 *vt* (**a**) *(handle, sleeve)* tirer sur; *(load)* tirer, traîner; **he tugged the heavy crate along the path** il traîna la lourde caisse le long de l'allée

(**b**) *Naut* remorquer

3 *vi* **to tug at** *or* **on sth** tirer sur qch; *Fig* **the music tugged at her heartstrings** cette musique l'émouvait

tugboat ['tʌgbəʊt] *n* remorqueur *m*

tug-of-love *n Br Fam* = conflit entre des parents en instance de divorce pour avoir la garde d'un enfant

▸▸ ***tug-of-love children*** = enfants dont les parents se disputent la garde

tug-of-war *n Sport* lutte *f* à la corde; *Fig* lutte *f* acharnée

tugrik ['tʌgrɪk] *n* tugrik *m*

tui ['tuːɪ] *n Orn* prosthemadère *m*

tuition [tjuː'ɪʃən] *n (UNCOUNT)* (**a**) *Br (instruction)* cours *mpl*; **I give tuition in Spanish** je donne des cours d'espagnol (**b**) *Univ (fees)* frais *mpl* de scolarité

▸▸ *Univ* ***tuition fees*** frais *mpl* de scolarité

tularaemia, *Am* **tularemia** [tuːlə'riːmɪə] *n Med & Vet* tularémie *f*

tulip ['tjuːlɪp] *n* tulipe *f*

▸▸ ***tulip glass*** (verre *m*) tulipe *f*; ***tulip tree*** tulipier *m*

tulle [tjuːl] *n Tex* tulle *m*

tum [tʌm] *n Br Fam* ventre ❑ *m*

tumble ['tʌmbəl] **1** *vi* (**a**) *(fall → person)* tomber, faire une chute; *(→ ball, objects)* tomber; **he tumbled down the stairs** il a dégringolé *ou* il est tombé dans l'escalier; **to tumble head over heels** faire une culbute *ou* un roulé-boulé; **the bottles came tumbling off the shelf** les bouteilles ont dégringolé *ou* sont tombées de l'étagère; **to tumble into bed** se jeter dans son lit; **to tumble out of bed** tomber du lit; **they were tumbling over one another** ils se bousculaient

(**b**) *(collapse → prices)* dégringoler, s'effondrer; **the Chancellor's resignation sent share prices tumbling** la démission du ministre des Finances a fait dégringoler *ou* chuter le cours des actions

(**c**) *(rush)* se précipiter; **the children tumbled into the kitchen** les enfants se ruèrent *ou* se précipitèrent dans la cuisine; **they came tumbling after me** ils se sont lancés à ma poursuite

(**d**) *(perform somersaults)* faire des cabrioles *ou* des culbutes

2 *vt (knock, push → person)* renverser, faire tomber *ou* dégringoler; **she tumbled me into the pool** elle m'a fait tomber dans la piscine; **she tumbled the books onto the table** elle a fait tomber les livres sur la table

3 *n (fall)* chute *f*, culbute *f*, roulé-boulé *m*; *(somersault)* culbute *f*, cabrioles *fpl*; **he had a bad tumble on the ice** il a fait une mauvaise chute sur la glace; **to take a tumble** faire une chute *ou* une culbute; *Fig* **his pride took a tumble** son orgueil a souffert; **share prices took a tumble today** le prix des actions s'est effondré aujourd'hui; **they had a tumble in the hay** ils ont batifolé dans le foin, ils se sont roulés dans le foin

▸**tumble about** **1** *vi (children)* gambader, batifoler; *(acrobat)* faire des cabrioles; *(swimmer)* s'ébattre; *(water)* clapoter

2 *vt sep* mettre en désordre; **the waves tumbled us about** nous étions ballotés par les vagues

▸**tumble down** *vi (person)* faire une culbute, dégringoler; *(pile)* dégringoler; *(wall, building)* s'effondrer; **the whole building came tumbling down** tout l'édifice s'est effondré *ou* écroulé

▸**tumble out** **1** *vi* (**a**) *(person → from tree, loft)* dégringoler; *(→ from bus, car)* se jeter, sauter; *(possessions, contents)* tomber (en vrac); **the apples tumbled out of her basket** les pommes ont roulé de son panier; **the tablets tumbled out onto the table** les comprimés ont roulé sur la table; **he tumbled out of bed at midday** il est tombé du lit à midi; **the van doors flew open and the children came tumbling out** les portes de la camionnette se sont ouvertes et les enfants se sont rués à l'extérieur

(**b**) *(news, confession)* s'échapper; **all their secrets came tumbling out** ils ont déballé tous leurs secrets

2 *vt sep* faire tomber en vrac *ou* en tas

▸**tumble over** **1** *vi (person)* culbuter, faire une culbute; *(pile, vase)* se renverser

2 *vt sep* renverser, faire tomber

▸**tumble to** *vt insep Br Fam (fact, secret, joke)* piger, saisir; **I finally tumbled to their little game** j'ai enfin compris leur petit manège

tumbledown ['tʌmbəldaʊn] *adj* en ruines, délabré

tumble-drier *n* sèche-linge *m inv*

tumble-dry *vt* faire sécher dans le sèche-linge

tumbler ['tʌmblə(r)] *n* (**a**) *(glass)* verre *m* (droit); *(beaker)* gobelet *m*, timbale *f*; **a tumbler of orange (juice)** un verre de jus d'orange

(**b**) *(acrobat)* acrobate *mf*

(**c**) *(in lock)* gorge *f* (de serrure)

(**d**) *(tumble-drier)* sèche-linge *m inv*

(**e**) *(pigeon)* pigeon *m* culbutant

▸▸ ***tumbler switch*** interrupteur *m* à bascule

tumblerful ['tʌmbləfʊl] *n* plein verre *m* (**of** de)

tumbleweed ['tʌmbəlwiːd] *n* = espèce d'amarante (qui, en séchant, casse et est emportée par le vent)

tumbling ['tʌmbəlɪŋ] **1** *n Sport* tumbling *m*

2 *adj Literary* **tumbling billows** flots *mpl* agités

tumbrel ['tʌmbrəl], **tumbril** ['tʌmbrɪl] *n* tombereau *m*

tumefaction [ˌtjuːmɪ'fækʃən] *n* tuméfaction *f*

tumefy ['tjuːmɪfaɪ] **1** *vt* tuméfier

2 *vi* se tuméfier

tumescence [tju:'mesəns] *n* tumescence *f*

tumescent [tjuː'mesənt] *adj* tumescent

tumid ['tjuːmɪd] *adj* (**a**) *Med* tuméfié (**b**) *Literary (style)* ampoulé, boursouflé

tumidity [tjuː'mɪdɪtɪ] *n* (**a**) *Med* tuméfaction *f* (**b**) *Literary (of style)* boursouflure *f*, enflure *f*

tummy ['tʌmɪ] *Fam n* ventre ❑ *m*; **to have (a) tummy ache** avoir mal au ventre

▸▸ *Br* ***tummy button*** nombril ❑ *m*

tumor *Am* = **tumour**

tumoral ['tjuːmərəl] *adj Med* tumoral

tumorous ['tjuːmərəs] *adj Med* tumoral; *(affected with tumours)* affecté de tumeurs

tumour, *Am* **tumor** ['tjuːmə(r)] *n* tumeur *f*

tumuli ['tjuːmjʊlaɪ] *pl of* **tumulus**

tumult ['tjuːmʌlt] *n* (**a**) *(noise)* tumulte *m*; *(agitation)* tumulte *m*, agitation *f*; **in (a) tumult** *(auditorium, meeting)* tumultueux; *(person, feeling)* en émoi (**b**) *Formal or Literary (of feelings)* émoi *m*

tumultuous [tjuː'mʌltjʊəs] *adj (crowd, noise)* tumultueux; *(applause)* frénétique; *(period)* mouvementé, agité; **he got a tumultuous welcome** il a reçu un accueil enthousiaste

tumultuously [tjuːˈmʌltjʊəslɪ] *adv* tumultueusement; *(applaud)* frénétiquement

tumultuousness [tjuːˈmʌltjʊəsnɪs] *n (of crowd)* agitation *f*; *(of applause)* frénésie *f*; *(of period)* caractère *m* mouvementé

tumulus [ˈtjuːmjʊləs] *(pl* **tumuli** [-laɪ]*)* *n* tumulus *m*

tun [tʌn] *n* fût *m*, tonneau *m*

tuna [*Br* ˈtjuːnə, *Am* ˈtuːnə] *n* thon *m*

►► ***tuna fish*** thon *m*

tundra [ˈtʌndrə] *n* toundra *f*

tune [tjuːn] **1** *n (melody)* air *m*, mélodie *f*; **give us a tune on the mouth organ** joue-nous un petit air d'harmonica; **the band played some old Irish tunes** l'orchestre joua de vieilles mélodies irlandaises; **they marched to the tune of the Marseillaise** ils défilèrent aux accents de la Marseillaise; **it's got no tune to it** ça manque de mélodie, ce n'est pas mélodieux; *Br Fam Fig* **to call the tune** faire la loi; *Fig* **to change one's tune** changer de discours

2 *vt* **(a)** *(musical instrument)* accorder; **the strings are tuned to the key of G** les cordes sont en sol

(b) *(regulate → engine, machine)* mettre au point, régler

(c) *(radio, television)* régler; **the radio is tuned to BBC4** la radio est réglée sur "BBC4"; **we can't tune our TV to Channel 5** nous ne pouvons pas capter "Channel 5" sur notre télé; **stay tuned!** restez à l'écoute!

(d) *(adapt)* **politicians always tune their remarks to suit their audience** les hommes politiques se mettent toujours au diapason de leur auditoire, les hommes politiques adaptent toujours leurs commentaires à leur auditoire

3 in tune 1 *adj (instrument)* accordé, juste; *(singer)* qui chante juste; **the violins are not in tune with the piano** les violons ne sont pas accordés avec le piano; *Fig* **to be in tune with** être en accord avec; **he is completely in tune with current political thinking** il est complètement en accord avec la pensée politique actuelle **2** *adv* juste; **to play/to sing in tune** jouer/chanter juste

4 out of tune 1 *adj (instrument)* faux (fausse), désaccordé; *(singer)* qui chante faux; *Fig* **to be out of tune with** être en désaccord avec; **the MP was out of tune with the rest of his party** le député n'était pas sur la même longueur d'onde que les autres membres de son parti *ou* était en désaccord avec les autres membres de son parti **2** *adv* faux; **to play/to sing out of tune** jouer/chanter faux

5 to the tune of *prep* **they were given grants to the tune of £100,000** on leur a accordé des subventions qui s'élevaient à 100 000 livres

►**tune in 1** *vi Rad & TV* se mettre à l'écoute; **don't forget to tune in again tomorrow** n'oubliez pas de nous rejoindre *ou* de vous mettre à l'écoute demain; **I tuned in to Radio Ultra** je me suis mis sur Radio Ultra

2 *vt sep* **(a)** *(radio, television)* régler sur

(b) *Fam Fig* **to be tuned in to sth** être branché sur qch

►**tune out** *Am* **1** *vi (refuse to listen)* faire la sourde oreille; *(stop listening)* décrocher

2 *vt sep* **(a)** *(remark)* ignorer

(b) *(radio)* éteindre; *Fam Fig* **he is completely tuned out** il n'est pas du tout branché

►**tune up 1** *vi Mus (player)* accorder son instrument; *(orchestra)* accorder ses instruments

2 *vt sep* **(a)** *Mus* accorder

(b) *Aut* mettre au point, régler

tuned-in [tjuːnd-] *adj Fam (aware)* branché; **she's very tuned-in to other people's needs** elle est toujours consciente des besoins des gens

tuneful [ˈtjuːnfʊl] *adj (song, voice)* mélodieux; *(singer)* à la voix mélodieuse

tunefully [ˈtjuːnfʊlɪ] *adv* mélodieusement

tunefulness [ˈtjuːnfʊlnɪs] *n* qualité *f* mélodieuse

tuneless [ˈtjuːnlɪs] *adj* peu mélodieux, discordant

tunelessly [ˈtjuːnlɪslɪ] *adv (with no tune)* de manière peu mélodieuse; *(out of tune)* faux

tuner [ˈtjuːnə(r)] *n* **(a)** *(of piano)* accordeur(-euse) *m,f* **(b)** *Rad & TV* tuner *m*, *Spec* syntoniseur *m*

►► ***tuner amplifier*** ampli-tuner *m*

tune-up *n Aut* réglage *m*, mise *f* au point; **to have a tune-up** faire faire une mise au point *ou* un réglage

tung [tʌŋ] *n Bot* abrasin *m*

►► ***tung oil*** huile *f* d'abrasin, huile *f* de Canton; *Bot* ***tung tree*** abrasin *m*

tungsten [ˈtʌŋstən] *n* tungstène *m*

►► ***tungsten carbide*** carbure *m* de tungstène; ***tungsten steel*** acier *m* au tungstène

tungsten-halogen *n* tungstène-halogène *m*

►► ***tungsten-halogen lamp*** lampe *f* tungstène-halogène, lampe *f* au tungstène

Tungus [ˈtʊŋʊs, ˈtʊŋgʊs] **1** *npl* **the Tungus** *(people)* les Evenke *mpl*

2 *n* **(a)** *(member)* Evenke *mf inv* **(b)** *(language)* toungouse *m*, toungouze *m*

tunic [ˈtjuːnɪk] *n (gen) & Bot* tunique *f*

tunicle [ˈtjuːnɪkəl] *n* tunique *f*, tunicelle *f*

tuning [ˈtjuːnɪŋ] *n* **(a)** *Mus* accord *m* **(b)** *Rad & TV* réglage *m* **(c)** *Aut* réglage *m*, mise *f* au point

►► ***tuning fork*** diapason *m*; ***tuning hammer*** accordoir *m*, clef *f* d'accordeur; ***tuning key*** accordoir *m*; ***tuning knob*** bouton *m* de réglage

Tunis [ˈtjuːnɪs] *n* Tunis

Tunisia [tjuːˈnɪzɪə] *n* Tunisie *f*; **in Tunisia** en Tunisie

Tunisian [tjuːˈnɪzɪən] **1** *n* Tunisien(enne) *m,f*

2 *adj* tunisien

3 *comp (embassy)* de Tunisie; *(history)* de la Tunisie

tunnage = **tonnage**

tunnel [ˈtʌnəl] *(Br pt & pp* **tunnelled,** *cont* **tunnelling,** *Am pt & pp* **tunneled,** *cont* **tunneling***)* **1** *n (gen & Rail)* tunnel *m*; *Mining* galerie *f*; *(of mole, badger)* galerie *f*; **to make** *or* **to dig a tunnel** *(gen)* percer *ou* creuser un tunnel; *Mining* percer *ou* creuser une galerie; **to drive a tunnel through a mountain** percer un tunnel à travers *ou* sous une montagne

2 *vt (hole, passage)* creuser, percer; *Constr* **to tunnel one's way through the earth** creuser un tunnel dans la terre; **the prisoners tunnelled their way to freedom** les prisonniers se sont évadés en creusant un tunnel

3 *vi (person)* creuser *ou* percer un tunnel *ou* des tunnels; *(badger, mole)* creuser une galerie *ou* des galeries; **they tunnelled into the mountain** *Constr* ils ont percé un tunnel dans la montagne; *Mining* ils ont percé une galerie dans la montagne; **the machines had to tunnel through granite** les machines ont dû creuser dans le granit

►► ***tunnel effect*** effet *m* tunnel; ***tunnel vision*** *Opt* rétrécissement *m* du champ visuel; *Fig* esprit *m* borné; **to have tunnel vision** avoir des vues étroites, voir les choses par le petit bout de la lorgnette

tunnelling, *Am* **tunneling** [ˈtʌnəlɪŋ] *n* percement *m* d'un tunnel/de tunnels

►► ***tunnelling equipment*** équipement *m* pour le percement d'un tunnel; ***tunnelling machine*** foreuse *f*

tunnel-of-love *n* train *m* fantôme

tunny [ˈtʌnɪ] = **tuna**

tup [tʌp] *(pt & pp* **tupped,** *cont* **tupping***)* **1** *n* **(a)** *Br (ram)* bélier *m* **(b)** *(on pile-driver)* mouton *m*

2 *vt (of ram)* s'accoupler à; *(ram)* accoupler

tupelo [ˈtjuːpɪləʊ] *(pl* **tupelos***)* *n Bot* nyssa *m*, tupélo *m*

tupik [ˈtuːpɪk] *n* tente *f* esquimaude en peau

tuppence [ˈtʌpəns] *n Br* deux pence *mpl*; *Fam* **the picture isn't worth tuppence** *(in price)* le tableau ne vaut pas un rond *ou* ne vaut rien; *(in quality)* le tableau ne vaut pas un clou; *Fam* **I don't care tuppence for your opinion** je me fiche pas mal de votre opinion *ou* de ce que vous pensez

tuppenny [ˈtʌpnɪ] *adj Br* de *ou* à deux pence; *Fam* **I don't give a tuppenny damn** je m'en fiche (et je m'en contrefiche)

tuppenny-ha'penny [ˈtʌpnɪˌheɪpnɪ] *adj Br Fam* de rien du tout, de quatre sous

Tupperware® [ˈtʌpəweə(r)] **1** *n* Tupperware® *m*

2 *comp* en Tupperware®

►► ***Tupperware***® ***party*** réunion *f* Tupperware®

tuque [tuːk] *n* tuque *f*

turaco [ˈtʊərəkəʊ] *(pl* **turacos***)* *n Orn* touraco *m*

turban [ˈtɜːbən] *n* turban *m*

turbaned [ˈtɜːbənd] *adj (person)* en turban; *(head)* coiffé d'un turban, enturbanné

turbary [ˈtɜːbərɪ] *(pl* **turbaries***)* *n* **(a)** *(land)* tourbière *f* **(b)** *Law (right)* droit *m* de prendre la tourbe

turbellarian [ˌtɜːbəˈleərɪən] *n Zool* turbellarié *m*

turbid [ˈtɜːbɪd] *adj* turbide, trouble

turbidity [tɜːˈbɪdɪtɪ], **turbidness** [ˈtɜːbɪdnɪs] *n* état *m* trouble, turbidité *f*

turbinate [tɜːˈbɪnɪt] *adj Anat, Bot & Zool* turbiné

turbine [ˈtɜːbaɪn] *n* turbine *f*; **gas/steam turbine** turbine *f* à gaz/à vapeur

turbit [ˈtɜːbɪt] *n Orn* pigeon *m* cravaté *ou* à cravate

turbo [ˈtɜːbəʊ] *(pl* **turbos***)* *n* **(a)** *Aut* turbo *m* **(b)** *(turbine)* turbine *f*

►► *Comput* ***turbo button*** bouton *m* de turbo; *Aut* ***turbo diesel*** turbodiesel *m*; *Aut* ***turbo diesel engine*** moteur *m* turbodiesel

turbocharged [ˈtɜːbəʊtʃɑːdʒd] *adj* turbo *(inv)*

turbocharger [ˈtɜːbəʊtʃɑːdʒə(r)] *n* turbocompresseur *m*

turboelectric [ˌtɜːbəʊɪˈlektrɪk] *adj* turboélectrique

turbofan [ˈtɜːbəʊfæn] *adj*

►► ***turbofan engine*** turboventilateur *m*, turbofan *m*

turbogenerator [ˌtɜːbəʊˈdʒenəreɪtə(r)] *n* turbogénérateur *m*

turbojet [ˌtɜːbəʊˈdʒet] *n (engine)* turboréacteur *m*; *(plane)* avion *m* à turboréacteur

turbomarketing *n Mktg* turbo-marketing *m*

turboprop [ˌtɜːbəʊˈprɒp] *n (engine)* turbopropulseur *m*; *(plane)* avion *m* à turbopropulseur

turbosupercharger [ˌtɜːbəʊˈsuːpəˌtʃɑːdʒə(r)] *n* turbocompresseur *m* de suralimentation

turbot [ˈtɜːbət] *(pl* **inv** *or* **turbots***)* *n Ich* turbot *m*

turbulence [ˈtɜːbjʊləns] *n* **(a)** *(unrest)* turbulence *f*, agitation *f* **(b)** *(in air)* turbulence *f*; *(in sea)* agitation *f* **(c)** *Phys* turbulence *f*

turbulent [ˈtɜːbjʊlənt] *adj (crowd, period, emotions)* tumultueux; *(sea)* agité

turbulently [ˈtɜːbjʊləntlɪ] *adv (gen)* d'une manière turbulente; *(flow)* en bouillonnant

Turco- [ˈtɜːkəʊ] *pref* turco-; **Turco-Persian** turco-persan

turd [tɜːd] *n very Fam* **(a)** *(excrement)* merde *f* **(b)** *(person)* ordure *f*

tureen [təˈriːn] *n* soupière *f*

turf [tɜːf] *(pl* **turfs** *or* **turves** [tɜːvz]*)* **1** *n* **(a)** *(grass)* gazon *m*

(b) *(sod)* motte *f* de gazon

(c) *Sport* turf *m*; **to follow the turf** être turfiste

(d) *Ir (peat)* tourbe *f*

(e) *Am Fam (field of expertise, authority)* domaine❑ *m*; **that's not my turf** c'est pas mon rayon

(f) *Fam (of gang)* territoire *m* réservé, chasse *f* gardée

2 *vt* **(a)** *(with grass)* **turf (over)** gazonner

(b) *Br Fam (throw)* balancer, flanquer, jeter; **she turfed the old magazines into the box** elle a balancé les vieux magazines dans la boîte

3 *comp (fire)* de tourbe

►► *Br Formal* ***turf accountant*** bookmaker *m*; ***turf war*** conflit *m* pour le contrôle d'un territoire

►**turf out** *vt sep Br Fam (eject, evict → person)* vider, flanquer à la porte; *(remove → furniture, possessions)* sortir❑, enlever❑; *(throw away → rubbish)* bazarder; **he turfed everything out of the cupboard** il a tout sorti du placard, il a bazardé tout ce qu'il y avait dans le placard; **he was turfed out of the club** il s'est fait virer *ou* vider du club

turfman [ˈtɜːfmən] *(pl* **turfmen** [-mən]*)* *n Am* turfiste *m*

Turgenev [tɜːˈgeɪnjev] *pr n* Tourgueniev

turgid [ˈtɜːdʒɪd] *adj* **(a)** *(style, prose)* ampoulé, boursouflé **(b)** *Med* enflé, gonflé

turgidity [tɜːˈdʒɪdɪtɪ] *n* **(a)** *(of style, prose)* boursouflure *f* **(b)** *Med* enflure *f*, gonflement *m*

turgidly [ˈtɜːdʒɪdlɪ] *adv (written etc)* dans un style ampoulé *ou* boursouflé

turgor [ˈtɜːgə(r)] *n Bot* turgescence *f*

Turin [tjʊəˈrɪn] *n* Turin

►► ***the Turin Shroud*** le saint suaire

Turing ['tjʊərɪŋ] *n Comp* ***Turing machine*** machine *f* de Turing; ***Turing test*** test *m* de Turing

turion ['tjʊərɪən] *n Bot* turion *m*

Turk [tɜːk] *n* Turc (Turque) *m,f*

►► *Bot* ***Turk's cap*** martagon *m*; ***Turk's head*** *(knot)* nœud *m* de tête de Turc

Turkestan, Turkistan [ˌtɜːkɪ'stɑːn] *n* Turkistan *m*; **in Turkestan** au Turkistan

Turkey ['tɜːkɪ] *n* Turquie *f*; **in Turkey** en Turquie

turkey ['tɜːkɪ] (*pl* **inv** *or* **turkeys**) *n* (**a**) *(bird → cock)* dindon *m*; *(→ hen)* dinde *f*

(**b**) *Culin* dinde *f*

(**c**) *Am Fam (person)* crétin(e) *m,f*, andouille *f*, courge *f*

(**d**) *Am Fam (unsuccessful film, book)* bide *m*; *Theat* four *m*

(**e**) *Fam (idioms) Am* **to talk turkey** *(get down to business)* passer aux choses sérieuses; *(speak frankly)* parler franc; **it's like turkeys voting for Christmas** c'est le monde à l'envers

►► ***turkey cock*** dindon *m*; *Fam Fig* crâneur(-euse) *m,f*; ***turkey hen*** dinde *f*; ***Turkey red*** rouge *m* d'Andrinople, rouge *m* turc; *Am* ***turkey shoot*** partie *f* de chasse au dindon; *Am Fig* **it was a real turkey shoot** c'était gagné d'avance; *Orn* ***turkey vulture*** vautour *m* aura

Turki ['tɜːkɪ] **1** *n* (**a**) *(person)* membre *m* d'un peuple turcique (**b**) *Ling* langues *fpl* turques

2 *adj* turcique

Turkic ['tɜːkɪk] **1** *n Ling* langues *fpl* turques

2 *adj* turcique

Turkish ['tɜːkɪʃ] **1** *n (language)* turc *m*

2 *adj* turc

3 *comp (embassy)* de Turquie, *(history)* de la Turquie; *(teacher)* de turc

►► ***Turkish bath*** bain *m* turc; ***Turkish coffee*** café *m* turc; ***Turkish delight*** loukoum *m*; ***Turkish towel*** serviette *f* éponge

Turkman ['tɜːkmən] (*pl* **Turkmans** *or* **Turkmen** [-men]) **1** *n* (**a**) *(person)* Turkmène *mf* (**b**) *(language)* turkmène *m*

2 *adj* turkmène

3 *comp (embassy, history)* du Turkménistan; *(teacher)* de turkmène

Turkmen ['tɜːkmən] *n (language)* turkmène *m*

Turkmenian [ˌtɜːk'menɪən] *adj* turkmène

Turkmenistan [ˌtɜːkmenɪ'stɑːn] *n* Turkménistan *m*; **in Turkmenistan** au Turkménistan

Turks and Caicos Islands [-'keɪkəs-] *npl* **the Turks and Caicos Islands** les îles *fpl* Turks et Caïcos; **in the Turks and Caicos Islands** aux îles Turks et Caïcos

turmeric ['tɜːmərɪk] *n* curcuma *m*, safran *m* des Indes

►► ***turmeric paper*** papier *m* (de) curcuma

turmoil ['tɜːmɔɪl] *n* (**a**) *(confusion)* agitation *f*, trouble *m*, chaos *m*; **the country was in turmoil** le pays était en ébullition *ou* en effervescence (**b**) *(emotional)* trouble *m*, émoi *m*; **her mind was in (a) turmoil** elle était dans le désarroi, la confusion régnait dans son esprit

TURN [tɜːn]

tourner	► 1A (a); B (a), (d); C (d); 2 (a), (b), (f)
faire tourner	► 1A (a)
[illegible]	[illegible]
changer	► 1C (a)
faire devenir	► 1C (a)
se tourner	► 2 (a)
se retourner	► 2 (b)
devenir	► 2 (d)
se changer	► 2 (e)
tour	► 3 (a), (d), (f), (g)
tournant	► 3 (b), (c)
virage	► 3 (b), (c)
tournure	► 3 (d)

1 *vt* **A.** (**a**) *(cause to rotate, move round)* tourner; *(shaft, axle)* faire tourner, faire pivoter; *(direct)* diriger; **she turned the key in the lock** *(to lock)* elle a donné un tour de clé (à la porte), elle a fermé la porte à clé; *(to unlock)* elle a ouvert la porte avec la clé; **turn the wheel all the way round** faites faire un tour complet à la roue; *Aut* **to turn the (steering) wheel** tourner le volant; **turn the knob to the right** tournez le bouton vers la droite; **turn the knob to "record"** mettez le bouton en position "enregistrer"; **she turned the oven to its highest setting** elle a allumé *ou* mis le four à la température maximum; **she turned her chair towards the window** elle a tourné sa chaise face à la fenêtre; **he turned the car into the drive** il a engagé la voiture dans l'allée; **we turned our steps homeward** nous avons dirigé nos pas vers la maison; **turn your head this way** tournez la tête de ce côté

(**b**) *Fig (change orientation of)* **she turned the conversation to sport** elle a orienté la conversation vers le sport; **their votes could turn the election in his favour** leurs voix pourraient faire basculer les élections en sa faveur; **he would not be turned from his decision to resign** il n'y a pas eu moyen de le faire revenir sur sa décision de démissionner; **nothing would turn the rebels from their cause** rien ne pourrait détourner les rebelles de leur cause; **you've turned my whole family against me** vous avez monté toute ma famille contre moi; **we turned his joke against him** nous avons retourné la plaisanterie contre lui; **let's turn our attention to the matter in hand** occupons-nous de l'affaire en question; **she turned her attention to the problem** elle s'est concentrée sur le problème; **to turn one's thoughts to God** tourner ses pensées vers Dieu; **research workers have turned the theory to practical use** les chercheurs ont mis la théorie en pratique; **how can we turn this policy to our advantage** *or* **account?** comment tirer parti de cette politique?, comment tourner cette politique à notre avantage?; **to turn one's back on sb** tourner le dos à qn; **she looked at the letter the minute his back was turned** dès qu'il a eu le dos tourné, elle a jeté un coup d'œil à la lettre; **how can you turn your back on your own family?** comment peux-tu abandonner ta famille?; **she turned her back on her friends** elle a tourné le dos à ses amis; **to turn one's back on the past** tourner la page, tourner le dos au passé; **she was so pretty that she turned heads wherever she went** elle était si jolie que tout le monde se retournait sur son passage; **success had not turned his head** la réussite ne lui avait pas tourné la tête, il ne s'était pas laissé griser par la réussite; **all their compliments had turned her head** tous leurs compliments lui étaient montés à la tête *ou* lui avaient tourné la tête; **to turn the tables on sb** reprendre l'avantage sur qn; *Fig* **now the tables are turned** maintenant les rôles sont renversés

B. (**a**) *(flip over → page)* tourner; *(→ collar, mattress, sausages, soil, hay)* retourner; **the very thought of food turns my stomach** l'idée même de manger me soulève le cœur; **to turn sth on its head** bouleverser qch, mettre qch sens dessus dessous; **recent events have turned the situation on its head** les événements récents ont retourné la situation

(**b**) *(send away)* **he turned the beggar from his door** il a chassé le mendiant; **they turned the poachers off their land** ils ont chassé les braconniers de leurs terres

(**c**) *(release, let loose)* **he turned the cattle into the field** il a fait rentrer le bétail dans le champ

(**d**) *(go round → corner)* tourner

(**e**) *(reach → in age, time)* passer, franchir; **I had just turned twenty** je venais d'avoir vingt ans; **she's turned thirty** elle a trente ans passés, elle a dépassé le cap de la trentaine; **it has only just turned four o'clock** il est quatre heures passées de quelques secondes

(**f**) *(do, perform)* faire; **the skater turned a circle on the ice** la patineuse a décrit un cercle sur la glace; **to turn a cartwheel** faire la roue

(**g**) *(ankle)* tordre; **I've turned my ankle** je me suis tordu la cheville

C. (**a**) *(transform, change)* changer, transformer; *(make)* faire devenir, rendre; **to turn sth into sth** transformer *ou* changer qch en qch; **bitterness turned their love into hate** l'amertume a transformé leur amour en haine; **she turned the remark into a joke** elle a tourné la remarque en plaisanterie; **they're turning the book into a film** ils adaptent le livre pour l'écran; **the sight turned his heart to ice** le spectacle lui a glacé le cœur *ou* l'a glacé; *St Exch* **you should turn your shares into cash** vous devriez réaliser vos actions; **time had turned the pages yellow** le temps avait jauni les pages

(**b**) *(make bad, affect)* **the lemon juice turned the milk (sour)** le jus de citron a fait tourner le lait

(**c**) *Am Com (goods)* promouvoir la vente de; *(money)* gagner; **to turn a good profit** faire de gros bénéfices; **he turns an honest penny** il gagne sa vie honnêtement; *Fam* **he was out to turn a fast buck** il cherchait à gagner *ou* faire du fric facilement

(**d**) *Tech (shape)* tourner, façonner au tour; **a well-turned leg** une jambe bien faite; *Fig* **to turn a phrase** faire des phrases

2 *vi* (**a**) *(move round → handle, key, wheel)* tourner; *(→ shaft)* tourner, pivoter; *(→ person)* se tourner; **to turn on an axis** tourner autour d'un axe; **the crane turned (through) 180°** la grue a pivoté de 180°; **the key won't turn** la clé ne tourne pas; **he turned right round** il a fait volte-face; **they turned towards me** ils se sont tournés vers moi *ou* de mon côté; **they turned from the gruesome sight** ils se sont détournés de cet horrible spectacle; **turn (round) and face the front** tourne-toi et regarde devant toi

(**b**) *(flip over → page)* tourner; *(→ car, person, ship)* se retourner; *Fig* **the smell made my stomach turn** l'odeur m'a soulevé le cœur

(**c**) *(change direction → person)* tourner; *(→ vehicle)* tourner, virer; *(→ luck, wind)* tourner, changer; *(→ river, road)* faire un coude; *(→ tide)* changer de direction; **turn (to the) right** *(walking)* tournez à droite; *(driving)* tournez *ou* prenez à droite; *Mil* **right turn!** à droite!; **we turned towards town** nous nous sommes dirigés vers la ville; **he turned (round) and went back** il a fait demi-tour et est revenu sur ses pas; **the road turns south** la route tourne vers le sud; **the car turned into our street** la voiture a tourné dans notre rue; **we turned onto the main road** nous nous sommes engagés dans *ou* nous avons pris la grand-route; **we turned off the main road** nous avons quitté la grand-route; *St Exch* **the market turned downwards/upwards** le marché était à la baisse/à la hausse; *Fig* **I don't know where** *or* **which way to turn** je ne sais plus quoi faire

(**d**) *(with adj or noun complement) (become)* devenir; **it's turning cold** il commence à faire froid; **the weather's turned bad** le temps s'est gâté; **the argument turned nasty** la dispute s'est envenimée; **she turned angry when he refused** elle s'est mise en colère quand il a refusé; **to turn red/blue** virer au rouge/bleu; **he turned red** il a rougi; **a lawyer turned politician** un avocat devenu homme politique; **to turn professional** passer *ou* devenir professionnel; **the whole family turned Muslim** toute la famille s'est convertie à l'islam

(**e**) *(transform)* se changer, se transformer; **the pumpkin turned into a carriage** la citrouille s'est transformée en carrosse; **the rain turned to snow** la pluie s'est transformée en neige; **the little girl had turned into a young woman** la petite fille était devenue une jeune femme; **their love turned to hate** leur amour se changea en haine *ou* fit place à la haine

(**f**) *(leaf)* tourner, jaunir; *(milk)* tourner; **the weather has turned** le temps a changé

3 *n* (**a**) *(revolution, rotation)* tour *m*; **he gave the handle a turn** il a tourné la poignée; **give the screw another turn** donnez un autre tour de vis; **with a turn of the wrist** avec un tour de poignet

(**b**) *(change of course, direction)* tournant *m*; *(in skiing)* virage *m*; **to make a right turn** *(walking)* tourner à droite; *(driving)* tourner *ou* prendre à droite; **take the second turn on the right** prenez la deuxième à droite; **no right turn** *(sign)* défense de tourner à droite; *Fig* **at every turn** à tout instant, à tout bout de champ

(**c**) *(bend, curve in road)* virage *m*, tournant *m*; **there is a sharp turn to the left** la route fait un brusque virage *ou* tourne brusquement à gauche

(**d**) *(change in state, nature)* tour *m*, tournure *f*; **the conversation took a new turn** la conversation a pris une nouvelle tournure; **it was an unexpected turn of events** les événements ont pris une tournure imprévue; **things took a turn**

for the worse/better les choses se sont aggravées/améliorées; **the patient took a turn for the worse/better** l'état du malade s'est aggravé/amélioré; **the situation took a tragic turn** la situation a tourné au tragique

(**e**) *(time of change)* **at the turn of the year** vers la fin de l'année; **at the turn of the century** au tournant du siècle

(**f**) *(in game, order, queue)* tour *m*; **it's my turn** c'est à moi, c'est mon tour; **whose turn is it?** *(in queue)* (c'est) à qui le tour?; *(in game)* c'est à qui de jouer?; **it's his turn to do the dishes** c'est à lui *ou* c'est son tour de faire la vaisselle; **you'll have to wait your turn** il faudra attendre ton tour; **they laughed and cried by turns** ils passaient tour à tour du rire aux larmes; **to take it in turns to do sth** faire qch à tour de rôle; **let's take it in turns to drive** relayons-nous au volant; **we took turns sleeping on the floor** nous avons dormi par terre à tour de rôle; **turn and turn about** à tour de rôle

(**g**) *(action, deed)* **to do sb a good/bad turn** rendre service/jouer un mauvais tour à qn; **he did them a bad turn** il leur a joué un mauvais tour; **I've done my good turn for the day** j'ai fait ma bonne action de la journée; *Prov* **one good turn deserves another** = un service en vaut un autre, un service rendu en appelle un autre

(**h**) *Fam (attack of illness)* crise *f*, attaque *f*; **she had one of her (funny) turns this morning** elle a eu une de ses crises ce matin

(**i**) *Fam (shock)* **you gave me quite a turn!** tu m'as fait une sacrée peur!, tu m'as fait une de ces peurs!; **it gave me such a turn!** j'ai eu une de ces peurs!

(**j**) *Old-fashioned (short trip, ride, walk)* tour *m*; **let's go for** *or* **take a turn in the garden** allons faire un tour dans le jardin

(**k**) *(tendency, style)* **to have an optimistic turn of mind** être optimiste de nature *ou* d'un naturel optimiste; **he has a strange turn of mind** il a une drôle de mentalité; **to have a good turn of speed** rouler vite; **turn of phrase** tournure *f ou* tour *m* de phrase; **she has a witty turn of phrase** elle est très spirituelle *ou* pleine d'esprit

(**l**) *(purpose, requirement)* exigence *f*, besoin *m*; **this book has served its turn** ce livre a fait son temps

(**m**) *Mus* doublé *m*

(**n**) *St Exch (transaction)* transaction *f (qui comprend l'achat et la vente)*; *Br (difference in price)* écart *m* entre le prix d'achat et le prix de vente

(**o**) *Br Theat* numéro *m*; **a comedy turn** un numéro de comédie

(**p**) *Br Culin* **done to a turn** cuit à point; *Fam Hum (tanned)* tout bronzé

4 in turn *adv* **she interviewed each of us in turn** elle a eu un entretien avec chacun de nous l'un après l'autre; **I told Sarah and she in turn told Paul** je l'ai dit à Sarah qui, à son tour, l'a dit à Paul; **I worked in turn as a waiter, an actor and a teacher** j'ai travaillé successivement *ou* tour à tour comme serveur, acteur et enseignant

5 on the turn *adj* **to be on the turn** être sur le point de changer; **the tide is on the turn** c'est le changement de marée; *Fig* le vent tourne; **the milk is on the turn** le lait commence à tourner

6 out of turn *adv* **don't play out of turn** attends ton tour pour jouer; *Fig* **to speak out of turn** faire des remarques déplacées, parler mal à propos

►► *(shift)* ***turn of duty*** *(gen)* tour *m* de service; *Mil* tour *m* de garde; *Am* ***turn signal*** clignotant *m*, *Belg* clignoteur *m*, *Suisse* signofil(e) *m*; *Am* ***turn signal lever*** (manette *f* de) clignotant *m*

►**turn against** *vt insep* se retourner contre, s'en prendre à

►**turn around** = **turn round**

►**turn aside 1** *vi (move to one side)* s'écarter; *also Fig (move away)* se détourner; **she turned aside to blow her nose** elle se détourna pour se moucher

2 *vt sep also Fig* écarter, détourner

►**turn away 1** *vt sep* (**a**) *(avert)* détourner; **she turned her head away from him** elle s'est détournée de lui

(**b**) *(reject → person)* renvoyer; *(stronger)* chasser; **the college turned away hundreds of applicants** l'université a refusé des centaines de candidats; **she turned the salesman away** elle chassa le représentant; **to turn people away** *(in theatre etc)* refuser du monde; **we've been turning business away** nous avons refusé du travail

2 *vi* se détourner; **he turned away from them in anger** en *ou* de colère, il leur a tourné le dos

►**turn back 1** *vi* (**a**) *(return → person)* revenir, rebrousser chemin; *(→ vehicle)* faire demi-tour; **it was getting dark so we decided to turn back** comme il commençait à faire nuit, nous avons décidé de faire demi-tour; **my mind is made up, there is no turning back** ma décision est prise, je ne reviendrai pas dessus

(**b**) *(go back in book)* **turn back to chapter one** revenez *ou* retournez au premier chapitre

2 *vt sep* (**a**) *(force to return)* faire faire demi-tour à; *(refugee)* refouler

(**b**) *(fold → collar, sheet)* rabattre; *(→ sleeves)* remonter, retrousser; *(→ corner of page)* corner

(**c**) *(idiom)* **to turn the clock back** remonter dans le temps, revenir en arrière

►**turn down 1** *vt sep* (**a**) *(heating, lighting, sound)* baisser

(**b**) *(fold → sheet)* rabattre, retourner; *(→ collar)* rabattre; **to turn down the corner of a page** corner une page; **to turn down the bed** ouvrir le lit

(**c**) *(reject → offer, request, suitor)* rejeter, repousser; *(→ candidate, job)* refuser; **they offered him a job but he turned them down** ils lui ont proposé un emploi mais il a rejeté leur offre; *Fam* **she turned me down flat** elle m'a envoyé balader

2 *vi (move downwards)* tourner vers le bas; **the corners of his mouth turned down** il a fait la moue *ou* une grimace désapprobatrice

►**turn in 1** *vt sep* (**a**) *(return, give in → borrowed article, equipment, piece of work)* rendre, rapporter; *(→ criminal)* livrer à la police; **they turned the thief in** *(took him to the police)* ils ont livré le voleur à la police; *(informed on him)* ils ont dénoncé le voleur à la police

(**b**) *(fold in)* **turn in the edges** rentrez les bords

(**c**) *(produce)* **the actor turned in a good performance** l'acteur a très bien joué; **the company turned in record profits** l'entreprise a fait des bénéfices record

2 *vi* (**a**) *(feet, toes)* **my toes turn in** j'ai les pieds en dedans

(**b**) *(go through entrance off road etc)* **he turned in at the gate** arrivé à la porte, il est entré

(**c**) *Fam (go to bed)* se coucher[❑]

(**d**) *(idiom)* **to turn in on oneself** se replier sur soi-même

►**turn off 1** *vt sep* (**a**) *(switch off → light)* éteindre; *(→ heater, radio, television)* éteindre, fermer; *(cut off at mains)* couper; *(tap)* fermer; **she turned the ignition/engine off** elle a coupé le contact/arrêté le moteur

(**b**) *Fam (fail to interest)* rebuter[❑]; *(sexually)* couper l'envie à; *(repulse)* débecter; **her superior attitude really turns me off** son air suffisant me rebute

2 *vi* (**a**) *(leave road)* tourner; **we turned off at junction 5** nous avons pris la sortie d'autoroute 5

(**b**) *(switch off)* s'éteindre; **the heater turns off automatically** l'appareil de chauffage s'éteint *ou* s'arrête automatiquement

►**turn on 1** *vt sep* (**a**) *(switch on → electricity, heating, light, radio, television)* allumer; *(→ engine)* mettre en marche; *(→ water)* faire couler; *(→ tap)* ouvrir; *(open at mains)* ouvrir; *Fig* **she can turn on the charm/the tears whenever necessary** elle sait faire du charme/pleurer quand il le faut

(**b**) *Fam (person → interest)* intéresser[❑]; *(→ sexually)* exciter; *(→ introduce to drugs)* initier à la drogue[❑]; **to be turned on** *(sexually)* être excité; **the movie didn't turn me on at all** le film ne m'a vraiment pas emballé; **he turned us on to this new pianist** il nous a fait découvrir ce nouveau pianiste

2 *vt insep (attack)* attaquer; **the dogs turned on him** les chiens l'ont attaqué *ou* se sont jetés sur lui; **his colleagues turned on him and accused him of stealing** ses collègues s'en sont pris à lui et l'ont accusé de vol

3 *vi (take drugs)* se droguer

4 *vi* (**a**) *(switch on)* s'allumer; **the oven turns on automatically** le four s'allume automatiquement

(**b**) *(depend, hinge on)* dépendre de, reposer sur; **the whole case turned on** *or* **upon this detail** toute l'affaire reposait sur ce détail; **everything turns on whether he continues as president** tout dépend s'il reste président ou non

►**turn out 1** *vt sep* (**a**) *(switch off → light)* éteindre; *(→ gas)* éteindre, couper

(**b**) *(point outwards)* **she turns her toes out when she walks** elle marche en canard

(**c**) *(dismiss, expel)* mettre à la porte; *(tenant)* expulser, déloger; **he turned his daughter out of the house** il a mis sa fille à la porte *ou* a chassé sa fille de la maison; **he was turned out of his job** il a été renvoyé

(**d**) *(empty → container, pockets)* retourner, vider; *(→ contents)* vider; *(→ jelly)* verser; **turn the cake out onto a plate** démoulez le gâteau sur une assiette

(**e**) *Br (clean)* nettoyer à fond; **to turn out a room** faire une pièce à fond

(**f**) *(produce)* produire, fabriquer; **he turns out a book a year** il écrit un livre par an; **few schools turn out the kind of people we need** peu d'écoles forment le type de gens qu'il nous faut

(**g**) *(police, troops)* envoyer; **turn out the guard!** faites sortir la garde!

(**h**) *(usu passive) (dress)* habiller; **nicely** *or* **smartly turned out** élégant; **he was turned out in a suit and a tie** il portait un costume-cravate; **she always turns her children out beautifully** elle habille toujours bien ses enfants

2 *vi* (**a**) *(show up)* venir, arriver; *Mil (guard)* (aller) prendre la faction; *(troops)* aller au rassemblement; **thousands turned out for the concert** des milliers de gens sont venus *ou* ont assisté au concert; **the doctor had to turn out in the middle of the night** le docteur a dû se déplacer au milieu de la nuit

(**b**) *(car, person)* sortir, partir; **the car turned out of the car park** la voiture est sortie du parking

(**c**) *(point outwards)* **my feet turn out** j'ai les pieds en canard *ou* en dehors

(**d**) *(prove)* se révéler, s'avérer; **his statement turned out to be false** sa déclaration s'est révélée fausse; **her story turned out to be true** ce qu'elle a raconté était vrai; **he turned out to be a scoundrel** il s'est révélé être un vaurien, on s'est rendu compte que c'était un vaurien; **it turns out that...** il se trouve que... + *indicative*

(**e**) *(end up)* **I don't know how it turned out** je ne sais pas comment cela a fini; **how did the cake turn out?** le gâteau était-il réussi?; **the story turned out happily** l'histoire s'est bien terminée *ou* a bien fini; **the evening turned out badly** la soirée a mal tourné; **everything will turn out fine** tout va s'arranger *ou* ira bien; **as it turns out, he needn't have worried** en l'occurrence *ou* en fin de compte, ce n'était pas la peine de se faire du souci

(**f**) *Br Fam (get out of bed)* se lever[❑], sortir du lit[❑]

►**turn over 1** *vt sep* (**a**) *(playing card, mattress, person, stone)* retourner; *(page)* tourner; *(vehicle)* retourner; *(boat)* faire chavirer; **I was turning over the pages of the magazine** je feuilletais la revue; *Fig* **to turn over a new leaf** s'acheter une conduite; *Agr* **to turn over the soil** retourner la terre

(**b**) *(consider)* réfléchir à *ou* sur; **I was turning the idea over in my mind** je tournais et retournais *ou* ruminais l'idée dans ma tête

(**c**) *(hand over, transfer)* rendre, remettre; **he turned the responsibility over to his deputy** il s'est déchargé de la responsabilité sur son adjoint; **to turn sb over to the authorities** livrer qn aux autorités

(**d**) *(change)* transformer, changer; **he's turning the land over to cattle farming** il reconvertit sa terre dans l'élevage du bétail

(**e**) *Com* **the store turns over £1,000 a week** la boutique fait un chiffre d'affaires de 1000 livres par semaine

(**f**) *(search through)* fouiller

(**g**) *Br Fam (rob → person)* voler[❑], dévaliser[❑];

(→ store) dévaliser❑; *(→ house)* cambrioler❑
 2 *vi* (**a**) *(roll over → person)* se retourner; *(→ vehicle)* se retourner, faire un tonneau; *(→ boat)* se retourner, chavirer
 (**b**) *(engine)* commencer à tourner
 (**c**) *(when reading)* tourner; **please turn over** *(in letter)* TSVP
 (**d**) *TV (change channel)* changer de chaîne
 (**e**) *Com (merchandise)* s'écouler, se vendre

▸**turn round** **1** *vi Br* (**a**) *(rotate → person)* se retourner; *(→ object)* tourner; **she turned round and waved goodbye** elle se retourna et dit au revoir de la main; **the dancers turned round and round** les danseurs tournaient *ou* tournoyaient (sur eux-mêmes)
 (**b**) *(face opposite direction → person)* faire volte-face, faire demi-tour; *(→ vehicle)* faire demi-tour; *Fig* **she turned round and accused us of stealing** elle s'est retournée contre nous et nous a accusés de vol
 2 *vt sep* (**a**) *(rotate → head)* tourner; *(→ object, person)* tourner, retourner; *(→ vehicle)* faire faire demi-tour à; **could you turn the car round please?** tu peux faire demi-tour, s'il te plaît?
 (**b**) *(quantity of work)* traiter
 (**c**) *(change nature of)* **to turn a situation round** renverser une situation; *Com* **to turn a company round** sauver une entreprise de la faillite
 (**d**) *(sentence, idea)* retourner

▸**turn to** *vt insep* (**a**) *(person)* se tourner vers; *(→ page)* aller à; **turn to chapter one** allez au premier chapitre
 (**b**) *(seek help from)* s'adresser à, se tourner vers; **to turn to sb for advice** consulter qn, demander conseil à qn; **I don't know who to turn to** je ne sais pas à qui m'adresser *ou* qui aller trouver; **he turned to his mother for sympathy** il s'est tourné vers sa mère pour qu'elle le console; **she won't turn to me for help** elle ne veut pas me demander de l'aide; **he turned to the bottle** il s'est mis à boire
 (**c**) *Fig (shift, move on to)* **her thoughts turned to her sister** elle se mit à penser à sa sœur; **the discussion turned to the war** on se mit à discuter de la guerre
 (**d**) *(address → subject, issue etc)* aborder, traiter; **we shall now turn to the problem of housing** nous allons maintenant aborder le problème du logement; **let us turn to another topic** passons à un autre sujet

▸**turn up** **1** *vt sep* (**a**) *(heat, lighting, radio, TV)* mettre plus fort; **to turn the sound up** augmenter *ou* monter le volume; **she turned the oven up** elle a mis *ou* réglé le four plus fort, elle a augmenté la température du four; *Br very Fam* **turn it up!** la ferme!
 (**b**) *(find, unearth)* découvrir, dénicher; *(buried object)* déterrer; **her research turned up some interesting new facts** sa recherche a révélé de nouveaux détails intéressants
 (**c**) *(point upwards)* remonter, relever; **she has a turned-up nose** elle a le nez retroussé
 (**d**) *(collar)* relever; *(trousers)* remonter; *(sleeve)* retrousser, remonter; *(in order to shorten)* raccourcir en faisant un ourlet
 (**e**) *(uncover → card)* retourner
 2 *vi* (**a**) *(appear)* apparaître; *(arrive)* arriver; **she turned up at my office this morning** elle s'est présentée à mon bureau ce matin; **he'll turn up again one of these days** il reviendra bien un de ces jours; **I'll take the first job that turns up** je prendrai le premier poste qui se présentera
 (**b**) *(be found)* être trouvé *ou* retrouvé; **her bag turned up eventually** elle a fini par retrouver son sac
 (**c**) *(happen)* se passer, arriver; **don't worry, something will turn up** ne t'en fais pas, tu finiras par trouver quelque chose; **until something better turns up** en attendant mieux

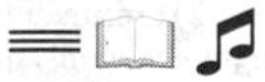

'The Turn of the Screw' *James, Britten* 'Le Tour d'écrou'

turnabout ['tɜːnəbaʊt] *n* revirement *m*

turnaround ['tɜːnəraʊnd] *n* (**a**) *(of passenger ship, plane)* temps *m* nécessaire au débarquement et à l'embarquement (de nouveaux passagers); *(for freight)* temps *m* nécessaire au déchargement et au chargement (d'une nouvelle cargaison) (**b**) *(time taken to complete round trip)* temps *m* de rotation (**c**) *Comput* temps *m* de rotation (**d**) = **turnabout**
 ▸▸ ***turnaround time*** (**a**) *(for job)* temps *m* d'exécution (**b**) = **turnaround** (**a**) – (**c**)

turn-around ['tɜːnəraʊnd] *adj*
 ▸▸ ***turn-around jump shot*** *(in basketball)* tir *m* en suspension *(exécuté tout en se retournant)*

turncoat ['tɜːnkəʊt] *n* renégat(e) *m,f*, transfuge *mf*

turndown ['tɜːndaʊn] **1** *n* (**a**) *(rejection)* refus *m* (**b**) *(in prices)* tendance *f* à la baisse; *(in the economy)* (tendance *f* à la) baisse *f*
 2 *adj (collar)* rabattu; *(edge)* à rabattre

turned [tɜːnd] *adj (milk)* tourné
 ▸▸ *Typ* ***turned comma*** ≃ guillemet *m*; ***turned period*** point *m* décimal, ≃ virgule *f*

turned-on *adj Fam* (**a**) *(up-to-date)* branché, câblé (**b**) *(aroused)* excité; **to get turned-on** s'exciter

turned-up *adj (collar etc)* relevé; *(nose)* retroussé

turner ['tɜːnə(r)] *n* (**a**) *(lathe operator)* tourneur *m* (**b**) *Am (gymnast)* gymnaste *mf*

turnery ['tɜːnərɪ] *(pl* **turneries***)* *n* atelier *m* de tournage

turning ['tɜːnɪŋ] *n* (**a**) *Br (side road)* route *f* transversale; *(side street)* rue *f* transversale, petite rue *f*; **take the third turning on the right** prenez la troisième à droite
 (**b**) *Br (bend → in road)* virage *m*; *(→ in river, staircase)* coude *m*; *(fork)* embranchement *m*, carrefour *m*
 (**c**) **the turning of the tide** le changement *ou* renversement de la marée; *Fig* le renversement de tendances
 (**d**) *Ind* tournage *m*
 ▸▸ *Br Aut* ***turning circle*** rayon *m* de braquage; ***turning point*** *(decisive moment)* moment *m* décisif; *(change)* tournant *m*; **1989 marked a turning point in my career** l'année 1989 marqua un tournant dans ma carrière; **it was a turning point in her life** ce fut un tournant dans sa vie; *Am* ***turning radius*** rayon *m* de braquage

turnip ['tɜːnɪp] *n* navet *m*

turnkey ['tɜːnkiː] **1** *n Arch (jailer)* geôlier(ère) *m,f*
 2 *adj Constr (project, factory, plant)* clés en main
 ▸▸ *Comput* ***turnkey system*** système *m* clés en main

turn-off *n* (**a**) *(road)* sortie *f* (de route), route *f* transversale, embranchement *m* (**b**) *Fam* **it's a real turn-off** *(gen)* c'est vraiment à vous dégoûter; *(sexual)* ça vous coupe vraiment l'envie

turn-of-the-century *adj* du début du siècle; **turn-of-the-century London** le Londres du début du siècle

turn-on *n Fam* **what a turn-on!** c'est excitant!; **he finds leather a turn-on** il trouve le cuir excitant, le cuir l'excite

turnout ['tɜːnaʊt] *n* (**a**) *(attendance → at meeting, concert)* assistance *f*; *Pol (at election)* (taux *m* de) participation *f*; **there was a good turnout** *(gen)* il y avait beaucoup de monde, beaucoup de gens sont venus; *Pol* il y avait un fort taux de participation; **low turnouts at elections** faible participation *f* aux élections
 (**b**) *(dress)* mise *f*, tenue *f*
 (**c**) *Br (clearout)* **we had a good turnout of the attic** on a nettoyé *ou* fait le grenier à fond; **I had a turnout of my old clothes for the jumble sale** j'ai trié mes vieux vêtements pour la vente de charité
 (**d**) *Am Aut* refuge *m (pour se laisser doubler)*

turnover ['tɜːn,əʊvə(r)] *n* (**a**) *Br Fin (of company)* chiffre *m* d'affaires; *(of capital)* rotation *f*; **his turnover is £100,000 per annum** il fait 100 000 livres de chiffre d'affaires par an
 (**b**) *(of staff, tenants)* renouvellement *m*; **the (staff) turnover there is very high** le taux de renouvellement du personnel y est très élevé; **there is a high turnover of tenants** les locataires changent souvent
 (**c**) *Am (of stock)* vitesse *f* de rotation, écoulement *m*; *(of shares)* mouvement *m*; **computer magazines have a high turnover** les revues d'informatique se vendent bien
 (**d**) *Culin* **apple turnover** chausson *m* aux pommes
 (**e**) *Sport (in basketball, American football)* perte *f* de balle
 ▸▸ *Com* ***turnover rate*** taux *m* de rotation; *Fin* ***turnover tax*** impôt *m ou* taxe *f* sur le chiffre d'affaires

turnpike ['tɜːnpaɪk] *n* (**a**) *(barrier)* barrière *f* de péage (**b**) *Am (road)* autoroute *f* à péage

turnround ['tɜːnraʊnd] *n esp Br* (**a**) *(of passenger ship, plane)* temps *m* nécessaire au débarquement et à l'embarquement (de nouveaux passagers); *(for freight)* temps *m* nécessaire au déchargement et au chargement (d'une nouvelle cargaison)
 (**b**) *(time taken to complete round trip)* temps *m* de rotation
 (**c**) *Comput* temps *m* de rotation
 (**d**) *(reversal → of fortunes)* retournement *m*, renversement *m*; *(→ of opinions)* revirement *m*
 ▸▸ ***turnround time*** = **turnround** (**a**) – (**c**)

turnspit ['tɜːnspɪt] *n* tournebroche *m (personne)*

turnstile ['tɜːnstaɪl] *n* tourniquet *m (barrière)*

turnstone ['tɜːnstəʊn] *n Orn* tourne-pierre *m*

turntable ['tɜːn,teɪbəl] *n* (**a**) *(on record player)* platine *f* (**b**) *Rail* plaque *f* tournante (**c**) *(on microscope)* platine *f* (**d**) *Austr (turning space)* endroit *m* pour manœuvrer
 ▸▸ ***turntable ladder*** échelle *f* pivotante *(des pompiers)*

turn-up *n Br* (**a**) *(on trousers)* revers *m* (**b**) *Fam (surprise)* surprise❑ *f*; **that's a turn-up for the book** *or* **books** c'est une sacrée surprise

turpentine ['tɜːpəntaɪn] *n (UNCOUNT) Br* (essence *f* de) térébenthine *f*
 ▸▸ ***turpentine substitute*** white-spirit *m*; *Bot* ***turpentine tree*** térébinthe *m*

turpeth ['tɜːpɪθ] *n Bot & Pharm* turbith *m*

turpitude ['tɜːpɪtjuːd] *n* turpitude *f*

turps [tɜːps] *n (UNCOUNT) Br Fam* (essence *f* de) térébenthine❑ *f*

turquoise ['tɜːkwɔɪz] **1** *n* (**a**) *(gem)* turquoise *f* (**b**) *(colour)* turquoise *m inv*
 2 *adj* (**a**) *(bracelet, ring)* de *ou* en turquoise (**b**) *(in colour)* turquoise *(inv)*

turret ['tʌrɪt] *n Archit, Mil & Tech* tourelle *f*
 ▸▸ *Mil* ***turret gun*** canon *m* de tourelle; *Tech* ***turret lathe*** tour *m* revolver

turreted ['tʌrɪtɪd] *adj Archit (castle)* à tourelles

turtle ['tɜːtəl] *n* (**a**) *(in sea)* tortue *f* marine; *Am (on land)* tortue *f* (**b**) *Comput* tortue *f* (**c**) *(idiom)* **to turn turtle** se renverser
 ▸▸ *Culin* ***turtle soup*** consommé *m* à la tortue

turtleback ['tɜːtəlbæk] *n Naut* pont *m* en carapace de tortue

turtledove ['tɜːtəldʌv] *n Orn* tourterelle *f*; **young turtledove** tourtereau *m*

turtleneck ['tɜːtəlnek] **1** *adj (sweater, dress)* à col montant, à encolure montante; *Am* à col roulé
 2 *n* col *m* montant, encolure *f* montante; *Am* (pull *m* à) col *m* roulé

turves [tɜːvz] *pl of* **turf**

Tuscan ['tʌskən] **1** *n* (**a**) *(person)* Toscan(e) *m,f* (**b**) *Ling* toscan *m*
 2 *adj* toscan

Tuscany ['tʌskənɪ] *n* Toscane *f*; **in Tuscany** en Toscane

tush¹ [tʊʃ] *n Am Fam (buttocks)* fesses *fpl*

tush² *exclam Old-fashioned* bah!, taratata!

tusk [tʌsk] *n (of elephant, boar)* défense *f*

tusker ['tʌskə(r)] *n (elephant)* éléphant *m (adulte)*; *(boar)* sanglier *m (adulte)*

tusser ['tʌsə(r)] *n* (**a**) *Tex* tussor *m*, tussore *m* (**b**) *Zool* ver *m* à soie sauvage

tussive ['tʌsɪv] *adj Med (relating to coughing)* de la toux; *(caused by coughing)* causé par la toux

tussle ['tʌsəl] **1** *n* (**a**) *(scuffle)* mêlée *f*, bagarre *f*; **to have a tussle with sb** se battre contre qn, en venir aux mains avec qn
 (**b**) *(struggle)* lutte *f*; **it was quite a tussle to get him to agree** il a fallu pas mal lutter *ou* faire des pieds et des mains pour qu'il accepte
 (**c**) *(quarrel)* dispute *f*; **to have a tussle with sb** se disputer avec qn
 2 *vi (scuffle, fight)* se battre; **I tussled with her for the ball** je me suis battu avec elle pour avoir la balle, on s'est disputé la balle; **the kids were tussling over the toy** les gosses se disputaient le jouet

tussock ['tʌsək] *n* touffe *f* d'herbe
▸▸ *Bot* ***tussock grass*** pâturin *m*; *Entom* ***tussock moth*** orgyie *f*

tussore ['tʌsɔː(r)] *n* (**a**) *Tex* tussor *m*, tussore *m* (**b**) *Zool* ver *m* à soie sauvage

tut [tʌt] (*pt & pp* **tutted,** *cont* **tutting**) **1** *exclam* **tut!, tut-tut!** *(in disapproval)* allons donc!; *(in annoyance)* zut!
2 *vi (in disapproval)* pousser une exclamation désapprobatrice; *(in annoyance)* exprimer son mécontentement; **she tutted with disapproval** elle eut une exclamation désapprobatrice

Tutankhamen [ˌtuːtənˈkɑːmən], **Tutankhamun** [ˌtuːtənkɑːˈmuːn] *pr n* Toutankhamon

tutelage ['tjuːtɪlɪdʒ] *n Formal* tutelle *f*; **under his tutelage** sous sa tutelle

tutelary ['tjuːtɪlərɪ] *adj Formal* tutélaire

tutor ['tjuːtə(r)] **1** *n* (**a**) *(teacher)* professeur *m* particulier; *(full-time)* précepteur(trice) *m,f*; **piano tutor** professeur *m* de piano; **she has a private German tutor** elle prend des cours particuliers avec un professeur d'allemand
(**b**) *Br Univ (teacher)* directeur(trice) *m,f* d'études; *Br Sch* professeur *m* principal *(surtout dans les écoles privées)*
(**c**) *Scot Law (guardian)* tuteur(trice) *m,f*
2 *vt* (**a**) *(instruct)* donner des cours (particuliers) à; **I'm tutoring her in maths** je lui donne des cours particuliers de maths
(**b**) *Br Univ* diriger les études de
(**c**) *Scot Law* être le tuteur de
3 *vi* (**a**) *(pupil)* suivre des cours particuliers
(**b**) *(teacher)* donner des cours particuliers

tutorial [tjuːˈtɔːrɪəl] **1** *n* (**a**) *Univ* (séance *f* de) travaux *mpl* dirigés, TD *mpl*; **a maths tutorial** des TD *mpl* de maths (**b**) *Comput* didacticiel *m*
2 *adj (duties)* de directeur d'études; **tutorial work** travaux *mpl* dirigés; **the tutorial system** = le système d'enseignement où les étudiants sont supervisés par un directeur d'études
▸▸ *Comput* ***tutorial program*** didacticiel *m*

tutoring ['tjuːtərɪŋ] *n* leçons *fpl* particulières; **to do tutoring** donner des cours particuliers

tutorship ['tjuːtəʃɪp] *n Br Univ* direction *f* d'études; *Br Sch* fonction *f* de professeur principal; **private tutorship** préceptorat *m*

tutsan ['tʌtsən] *n Bot* toute-saine *f*, androsème *m*

tutti frutti [ˌtuːtɪˈfruːtɪ] (*pl* **tutti fruttis**) **1** *n* plombières *f*, tutti frutti *m*
2 *adj (ice cream, flavour)* tutti frutti *(inv)*

tut-tut = **tut**

tutty ['tʌtɪ] *n Miner* cadmie *f*

tutu ['tuːtuː] *n* tutu *m*

Tuvalu [tuːˈvɑːluː] *n* Tuvalu *m*

tu-whit tu-whoo [təˈwɪttəˈwuː] *onomat* hou-hou

tux [tʌks] *n Fam* (*abbr* **tuxedo**) smoking ❑ *m*

tuxedo [tʌkˈsiːdəʊ] (*pl* **tuxedos**) *n Am* smoking *m*

TV[1] [ˌtiːˈviː] (*abbr* **television**) **1** *n* TV *f*
2 *comp (programme, set)* de télé; *(star)* de la télé
▸▸ ***TV advertisement*** publicité *f* télévisée; ***TV advertising*** publicité *f* télévisée; ***TV campaign*** campagne *f* télévisuelle; ***TV commercial*** spot *m*; ***TV dinner*** plateau-repas *m*, repas *m* tout prêt *ou* prêt à consommer *(que l'on mange devant la télé)*; ***TV movie*** téléfilm *m*; *Mktg* ***TV viewing panel*** panel *m* de téléspectateurs

TV[2] *n Fam* (*abbr* **transvestite**) travelo *m*

TVM [ˌtiːviːˈem] *n* (*abbr* **television movie**) téléfilm *m*

TVP [ˌtiːviːˈpiː] *n Culin* (*abbr* **textured vegetable protein**) protéine *f* végétale texturée

twaddle ['twɒdəl] *n (UNCOUNT) Br Fam* bêtises *fpl*, âneries *fpl*, imbécillités ❑ *fpl*; **what a load of twaddle!** n'importe quoi!; **to talk twaddle** dire *ou* débiter des bêtises *ou* des âneries

twain [tweɪn] *n Literary* **the twain** les deux; **never** *or* **ne'er the twain shall meet** *(gen)* les deux sont inconciliables; *(of people)* les deux ne pourront jamais se mettre d'accord

twang [twæŋ] **1** *n* (**a**) *(of wire, guitar)* son *m* de corde pincée (**b**) *(in voice)* ton *m* nasillard; **she speaks with a twang** elle parle du nez, elle nasille (**c**) *(accent)* accent *m*; **he has a slight Australian twang** il a un léger accent australien
2 *vt (string instrument)* pincer les cordes de
3 *vi (arrow, bow, wire)* vibrer; **the arrow twanged through the air** la flèche a traversé l'air en vibrant

'twas [twɒz] *Literary or Fam* = **it was**

twat [twæt] *n very Fam* (**a**) *(woman's genitals)* chatte *f*, chagatte *f* (**b**) *(person)* tache *f*, taré(e) *m,f*

tweak [twiːk] **1** *vt* (**a**) *(twist → ear, nose)* tordre (doucement), pincer; *(pull)* tirer (sur) (**b**) *Aut* mettre au point; *Fig (text)* apporter quelques petites modifications à, mettre au point; *Comput* peaufiner, mettre au point
2 *n* (petit) coup *m* sec; **he gave my ear a tweak** il m'a tiré l'oreille

twee [twiː] *adj Br Fam Pej (person)* chichiteux; *(idea, sentiment)* mièvre ❑; *(village, decor)* cucul *(inv)*

tweed [twiːd] **1** *n (cloth)* tweed *m*
2 *comp (jacket, skirt)* de tweed, en tweed
3 tweeds *npl (clothes)* vêtements *mpl* de *ou* en tweed; *(suit)* costume *m* de *ou* en tweed; **a smart lady in tweeds** une femme élégante en tailleur de tweed

tweedy ['twiːdɪ] *(compar* **tweedier,** *superl* **tweediest**) *adj* (**a**) *(fabric)* qui ressemble au tweed (**b**) *Pej (man)* qui a le genre gentleman-farmer; *(woman)* qui fait bourgeoise de campagne

'tween [twiːn] *Literary* = **between**

tweenager ['twiːnˌeɪdʒə(r)] *n Fam* = terme utilisé par les professionnels de la vente pour désigner les enfants de 7 à 12 ans envisagés comme consommateurs

'tween decks ['twiːndeks] *Naut* **1** *n* faux-pont *m*, entrepont *m*
2 *adj* dans l'entrepont
3 *adv* dans l'entrepont

tweeness ['twiːnɪs] *n Br Fam Pej (of person)* côte *m* chichiteux *f*; *(of idea, sentiment)* mièvrerie ❑ *f*; *(of village, decor)* côté *m* cucul

tweeny ['twiːnɪ] (*pl* **tweenies**) *n Fam* (**a**) *Br Old-fashioned (maid)* bonne ❑ *f (qui aide la cuisinière et la femme de chambre)* (**b**) = **tweenager**

tweet [twiːt] **1** *n* pépiement *m*
2 *onomat* cui-cui
3 *vi* pépier

tweeter ['twiːtə(r)] *n* tweeter *m*, haut-parleur *m* d'aigus

tweeze [twiːz] *vt (eyebrows)* épiler

tweezers ['twiːzəz] *npl* **(pair of) tweezers** pince *f* à épiler

twelfth [twelfθ] **1** *n* (**a**) *(fraction)* douzième *m*
(**b**) *(in series)* douzième *mf*
(**c**) *(of month)* douze *m inv*; **the twelfth of July** = célébration de la victoire des protestants sur les catholiques (le 12 juillet 1690) en Irlande, donnant lieu à des défilés d'Orangistes en Irlande du Nord
(**d**) *Mus* douzième *f*
2 *adj* douzième
3 *adv* douzièmement; *(in contest)* en douzième position, à la douzième place; *see also* **fifth**
▸▸ *Am Sch* ***twelfth grade*** = classe de lycée pour les 17–18 ans, ≃ (classe *f* de) terminale *f*; ***twelfth man*** *(in cricket)* joueur *m* de réserve; ***Twelfth Night*** la fête des Rois

'Twelfth Night' *Shakespeare* 'La Nuit des rois'

twelfthly ['twelfθlɪ] *adv* douzièmement, en douzième lieu

twelve [twelv] **1** *n (number, numeral)* douze *m inv*
2 *pron* douze; **about twelve** une douzaine
3 *adj* douze; **about twelve people** une douzaine de personnes; **the Twelve Apostles** les douze apôtres *mpl*; *see also* **five**

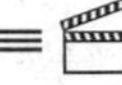

'Twelve Angry Men' *Lumet* 'Douze hommes en colère'

twelve-hour clock *n* = indication de l'heure selon un système qui divise la journée en deux parties de douze heures chacune

twelve-inch *n* maxi single *m*
▸▸ ***twelve-inch single*** maxi single *m*

twelvemo ['twelvməʊ] (*pl* **twelvemos**) *Typ* **1** *adj* in-douze *(inv)*, in-12 *(inv)*
2 *n* in-douze *m inv*, in-12 *m inv*

twelvemonth ['twelvmʌnθ] *n Br Arch or Literary* année *f*, an *m*

twelve-tone *adj Mus* dodécaphonique
▸▸ ***twelve-tone system*** dodécaphonisme *m*

twentieth ['twentɪəθ] **1** *n* (**a**) *(fraction)* vingtième *m* (**b**) *(in series)* vingtième *mf* (**c**) *(of month)* vingt *m inv*
2 *adj* vingtième
3 *adv* vingtièmement; *(in contest)* en vingtième position, à la vingtième place; *see also* **fifth**

twenty ['twentɪ] **1** *n* (*pl* **twenties**) vingt *m inv*
2 *pron* vingt; **about twenty** une vingtaine
3 *adj* vingt; *see also* **fifty**

'20,000 Leagues under the Sea' *Verne, Fleischer* '20 000 Lieues sous les mers'

twenty-first *n (birthday)* vingt-et-unième anniversaire *m (anniversaire considéré comme un rite de passage à l'âge adulte, particulièrement fêté en Grande-Bretagne)*

twenty-four *adj* **a twenty-four-hour petrol station** une station-service ouverte jour et nuit *ou* vingt-quatre heures sur vingt-quatre; **open twenty-four hours a day** ouvert vingt-quatre heures sur vingt-quatre
▸▸ ***twenty-four hour clock*** = indication de l'heure selon un système qui va de 0 à 24; ***twenty-four-hour service*** service *m* vingt-quatre heures sur vingt-quatre *ou* jour et nuit

twenty-four/seven *adv Fam* sans arrêt ❑

twenty-one *n (pontoon)* vingt-et-un *m inv (jeu)*

twenty-twenty vision *n* **to have twenty-twenty vision** avoir dix dixièmes à chaque œil

'twere [twɜː(r)] *Literary or Fam* = **it were**

twerp [twɜːp] *n Br Fam* courge *f*, nouille *f*

twice [twaɪs] **1** *adv* (**a**) *(with noun)* deux fois; **twice 3 is 6** deux fois 3 font 6
(**b**) *(with verb)* deux fois; **I've already told you twice** je te l'ai déjà dit deux fois, je te l'ai déjà répété; **they didn't need to be asked** *or* **told twice** ils ne se sont pas fait prier, ils ne se le sont pas fait dire deux fois; **to think twice before doing sth** y regarder *ou* réfléchir à deux fois avant de faire qch; **to think twice before saying sth** réfléchir avant de parler; **she didn't have to think twice before accepting** elle a accepté sans hésiter
(**c**) *(with adjective or adverb)* **twice weekly/daily** deux fois par semaine/jour; **she can run twice as fast as me** elle court deux fois plus vite que moi; **it's twice as good** c'est deux fois mieux; **twice as much time/as many apples** deux fois plus de temps/de pommes
2 *predet* deux fois; **twice a day** deux fois par jour; **twice the price** deux fois plus cher; **he's almost twice your height** il est presque deux fois plus grand que vous; **since the operation he is twice the man he was** depuis son opération il est transformé *ou* en pleine forme; **he's twice the man you are!** il vaut deux fois mieux que toi!

Twickenham [twɪkenəm] *n* Twickenham *m*, = stade de rugby londonien où joue l'équipe d'Angleterre

Twickers ['twɪkəz] *n Br Fam* = **Twickenham**

twiddle ['twɪdəl] **1** *vt (knob, dial)* tourner, manier; *(moustache)* tripoter, jouer avec; *also Fig* **to twiddle one's thumbs** se tourner les pouces
2 *vi* **to twiddle with the knob** tourner le bouton; **to twiddle with the radio** jouer avec la radio; **she sat there twiddling with a ruler** elle était assise là à jouer avec une règle
3 *n* **give the knob a twiddle** tournez le bouton

twig [twɪg] (*pt & pp* **twigged,** *cont* **twigging**) **1** *vi Br Fam (understand)* piger
2 *vt Br Fam (understand)* piger
3 *n (for fire)* brindille *f*; *(on tree)* petite branche *f*

twilight ['twaɪlaɪt] **1** *n* (**a**) *(in evening)* crépuscule *m*; *(in morning)* aube *f*; **at twilight** *(evening)* au crépuscule; *(morning)* à l'aube
(**b**) *(half-light)* pénombre *f*, obscurité *f*, demi-jour *m*; **I could hardly see you in the twilight** je vous voyais à peine dans la pénombre
(**c**) *Fig (last stages, end)* crépuscule *m*; **in the twilight of his life** au crépuscule de sa vie
2 *adj* **the twilight hours** le crépuscule; **a**

twilight world un monde nébuleux; **his twilight years** les dernières années *fpl* de sa vie
▸▸ *Med* ***twilight sleep*** demi-sommeil *m* provoqué; ***twilight zone*** *(in city)* quartier *m* délabré *(qui entoure un quartier commercial)*; *(in ocean)* zone *f* crépusculaire; *Fig* zone *f* d'ombre, zone *f* floue

twill [twɪl] *n* sergé *m*

'twill [twɪl] *Literary or Fam* = **it will**

twin [twɪn] *(pt & pp* **twinned**, *cont* **twinning**) **1** *n* jumeau(elle) *m,f*; **she gave birth to twins** elle a donné naissance à des jumeaux
2 *adj* (**a**) *(child, sibling)* **they have twin boys/girls** ils ont des jumeaux/des jumelles; **my twin sister** ma sœur jumelle
(**b**) *(dual → spires, hills)* double, jumeau; *(→ aims)* double; **the twin towers overlooking the bay** les deux tours qui surplombent la baie; **the Twin Cities** = surnom des villes voisines de Saint-Paul et Minneapolis
3 *vt (town)* jumeler; **our town is twinned with Hamburg** notre ville est jumelée avec Hambourg
▸▸ ***twin beds*** lits *m* jumeaux; *Am Fam* ***twin bill*** *Cin* = séance avec deux longs métrages à la suite; *TV* = programmation de deux longs métrages à la suite; *Med* ***twin birth*** accouchement *m* de jumeaux; ***twin camshaft*** double arbre *m* à cames; ***twin carburettor*** carburateur *m* double-corps; ***twin cylinder*** **1** *n* moteur *m* à deux cylindres **2** *adj* à deux cylindres; ***twin room*** chambre *f* à deux lits; ***twin town*** ville *f* jumelée *ou* jumelle; ***twin tub*** machine *f* à laver à deux tambours

twin-bedded [-'bedɪd] *adj (room)* à deux lits

twin-cam *n* double arbre *m* à cames

twine [twaɪn] **1** *vt* (**a**) *(wind → hair, string)* entortiller, enrouler; **she twined the rope round a post** elle enroula la corde autour d'un poteau; **the honeysuckle had twined itself around the tree** le chèvrefeuille s'était enroulé autour de l'arbre
(**b**) *(weave)* tresser
2 *vi* (**a**) *(stem, ivy)* s'enrouler; **the honeysuckle had twined around the tree** le chèvrefeuille s'était enroulé autour de l'arbre
(**b**) *(path, river)* serpenter
3 *n (UNCOUNT)* (grosse) ficelle *f*

twin-engined [-'endʒɪnd] *adj* bimoteur

twiner ['twaɪnə(r)] *n* (**a**) *Bot* plante *f* volubile (**b**) *Tex* retordoir *m*, retorsoir *m*

twinge [twɪndʒ] *n* (**a**) *(of guilt, shame)* sentiment *m*; *(of jealousy, regret, envy)* pointe *f*; **to have** *or* **to feel a twinge of remorse** éprouver un certain remords; **he watched her leave with a twinge of sadness** il la regarda partir avec (une certaine) tristesse (**b**) *(of pain)* élancement *m*, tiraillement *m*; **she felt a twinge in her back** elle ressentit une petite douleur dans le dos

twining ['twaɪnɪŋ] *adj (plant)* volubile

twinjet ['twɪndʒet] *n* biréacteur *m*

twinkie ['twɪŋkɪ] **1** *n Am Fam (homosexual)* homo *m*
2 Twinkie® *n Am (cake)* = petit gâteau fourré à la crème

twinkle ['twɪŋkəl] **1** *vi* (**a**) *(star, diamond)* briller, scintiller (**b**) *(eyes)* briller, pétiller; **her eyes twinkled with excitement** ses yeux brillaient d'excitation
2 *n* (**a**) *(of star, diamond, light)* scintillement *m* (**b**) *(in eye)* pétillement *m*; **he had a mischievous twinkle in his eye** il avait les yeux pétillants de malice; *Hum* **when you were just a twinkle in your father's eye** bien avant que tu ne fasses ton entrée dans le monde; **in a twinkle (of an eye)** en un clin d'œil

twinkling ['twɪŋklɪŋ] **1** *adj* (**a**) *(star, gem, sea)* scintillant, brillant (**b**) *(eyes)* pétillant, brillant (**c**) *Fig (feet)* agile
2 *n (UNCOUNT)* (**a**) *(of star, light, gem)* scintillement *m* (**b**) *(in eyes)* pétillement *m*; **in the twinkling of an eye** en un clin d'œil

twinky ['twɪŋkɪ] *n Am Fam (homosexual)* homo *m*

twin-lens reflex *n Phot* appareil *m* reflex à deux objectifs
▸▸ ***twin-lens reflex camera*** appareil *m* reflex à deux objectifs

twinning ['twɪnɪŋ] *n (of towns)* jumelage *m*

twin-screw *adj (boat)* à deux hélices

twinset ['twɪn,set] *n* twin set *m*; *Br Fam Pej* **she's a bit twinset and pearls** ≃ elle fait un peu foulard Hermès et collier de perles, elle fait plutôt BCBG

twirl [twɜːl] **1** *vt* (**a**) *(spin → stick, parasol, lasso)* faire tournoyer; *(handle)* tourner; **she twirled the stick (round) in the air** elle jeta le bâton en l'air en le faisant tournoyer
(**b**) *(twist → moustache, hair)* tortiller, friser
2 *vi (dancer, lasso)* tournoyer; **she twirled round to face us** elle se tourna pour nous faire face, elle fit volte-face vers nous
3 *n* (**a**) *(whirl → of body, stick)* tournoiement *m*; *(pirouette)* pirouette *f*; **I gave the top/wheel a twirl** j'ai fait tourner la toupie/la roue; **to do a twirl** tourner sur soi-même, faire une pirouette
(**b**) *(written flourish)* fioriture *f*

Give us a twirl

Le jeu télévisé britannique *The Generation Game*, diffusé depuis les années 70, fut présenté pendant de nombreuses années par Bruce Forsyth. Il prononçait ces mots ("retourne-toi!") au début de chaque émission lorsqu'apparaissait sa jeune et séduisante assistante Anthea Redfern vêtue d'une nouvelle robe. Il lui demandait de faire un tour sur elle-même pour que le public puisse l'admirer. On emploie cette expression par allusion au *Generation Game* en guise de compliment à une femme élégamment vêtue.

twirling ['twɜːlɪŋ] *n* tournoiement *m*

twirp = **twerp**

TWIST [twɪst]

tourner	▸ **1 (a) – (c)**
tordre	▸ **1 (a), (d)**
tresser	▸ **1 (b)**
enrouler	▸ **1 (b)**
déformer	▸ **1 (e)**
serpenter	▸ **2 (a)**
s'enrouler	▸ **2 (b)**
se tortiller	▸ **2 (c)**
se tordre	▸ **2 (d)**
tour	▸ **3 (a), (e)**
torsion	▸ **3 (a)**
tournant	▸ **3 (b)**
virage	▸ **3 (b)**

1 *vt* (**a**) *(turn → round and round)* tourner; *(→ round axis)* tourner, visser; *(→ tightly)* tordre; **try twisting the dial to the left** essaie de tourner le cadran vers la gauche; **you have to twist the lid off** il faut dévisser le couvercle dans le sens des aiguilles d'une montre; **she twisted her hankie nervously** elle tordait nerveusement son mouchoir; **to twist sth into a ball** faire une boule de qch; **he twisted the wire into the shape of a dog** il a tordu le fil pour lui donner la forme d'un chien; **the railings were twisted out of shape** les grilles étaient toutes tordues; **he twisted the keys from my hand** il m'a arraché les clés des mains
(**b**) *(twine)* tresser, entortiller; *(wind)* enrouler, tourner; **she twisted her hair into a bun** elle s'est coiffée en chignon, elle a torsadé ses cheveux pour faire un chignon; **the seat-belt got twisted** la ceinture (de sécurité) a été entortillée; **the wires got twisted** les fils se sont entortillés; **he twisted the threads into a rope** il a tressé *ou* torsadé les fils pour en faire une corde
(**c**) *(body, part of body)* tourner; **I twisted my head (round) to the left** j'ai tourné la tête vers la gauche; **he twisted himself free** il s'est dégagé en se tortillant; *Fig* **her face was twisted with pain** ses traits étaient tordus par la douleur, la douleur lui tordait le visage; **to twist sb's arm** tordre le bras à qn; *Fig* forcer la main à qn; **if you twist his arm, he'll agree to go** si tu insistes un peu, il voudra bien y aller
(**d**) *(sprain → ankle, wrist)* tordre, fouler; **I've twisted my ankle** je me suis tordu *ou* foulé la cheville; **I seem to have twisted my neck** je crois que j'ai attrapé un torticolis
(**e**) *(distort → words)* déformer; *(→ argument)* déformer, fausser; **don't twist the facts to suit your argument** ne déformez pas les faits pour étayer votre argument; **she twists everything I say** elle déforme tout ce que je dis
(**f**) *Br Fam (cheat, swindle)* arnaquer; **I've been twisted** je me suis fait avoir
2 *vi* (**a**) *(road, stream)* serpenter; **the path twisted and turned through the forest** le chemin zigzaguait à travers la forêt
(**b**) *(become twined)* s'enrouler; **the ivy twisted round the tree** le lierre s'enroulait autour de l'arbre
(**c**) *(body, part of body)* se tortiller; **he twisted and turned to get himself free** il s'est tortillé tant qu'il a pu pour se dégager; **the dog twisted out of my arms** le chien s'est dégagé de mes bras en se tortillant; **his mouth twisted into a smile** il eut un rictus
(**d**) *(be sprained → ankle)* se tordre, se fouler; *(→ knee)* se tordre
(**e**) *(dance)* twister
(**f**) *(in pontoon)* **twist!** encore une carte!
3 *n* (**a**) *(turn, twirl)* tour *m*, torsion *f*; **to give sth a twist** *(dial, handle, lid)* (faire) tourner qch; *(wire)* tordre qch; **with a twist of the wrist** en un tour de main; **there's a twist in the tape** la bande est entortillée; **to get (oneself) into a twist about sth** *(get angry)* se fâcher *ou* s'énerver au sujet de qch; *(get upset)* prendre qch au tragique, se mettre dans tous ses états à cause de qch; **the string is in an awful twist** la ficelle est tout emmêlée
(**b**) *(in road)* tournant *m*, virage *m*; *(in river)* coude *m*; *(in staircase)* tournant *m*; *Fig (in thinking)* détour *m*; **the road has many twists and turns** la route a beaucoup de tournants et de virages *ou* fait de nombreux tours et détours; **it's difficult to follow the twists and turns of his argument/of government policy** il est difficile de suivre les méandres de son argumentation/de la politique gouvernementale
(**c**) *(coil → of tobacco)* rouleau *m*; *(→ of paper)* tortillon *m*
(**d**) *Culin* **a twist of lemon** un zeste de citron
(**e**) *(in story, plot)* tour *m*; **the film has an exciting twist at the end** le film se termine par un coup de théâtre passionnant; **there is an ironic twist to the story** l'histoire comporte un tour ironique; **the book gives a new twist to the old story** le livre donne une nouvelle tournure *ou* un tour nouveau à cette vieille histoire; **by a strange twist of fate, we met again years later in Zimbabwe** par un hasard extraordinaire *ou* un caprice du destin, nous nous sommes retrouvés au Zimbabwe des années après
(**f**) *(dance)* twist *m*; **to do** *or* **to dance the twist** twister
(**g**) *Br Fam (cheat)* arnaque *f*; **it's a real twist!** c'est vraiment de l'arnaque *ou* du vol!; **what a twist!** on s'est bien fait avoir!
(**h**) *Br Fam (idiom)* **to be completely round the twist** être complètement dingue *ou* cinglé; **to go round the twist** devenir dingue *ou* cinglé, perdre la boule; **to drive sb round the twist** rendre qn chèvre *ou* dingue!; **they're driving me round the twist!** ils me rendent chèvre *ou* dingue!
▸▸ ***twist grip*** *(accelerator)* poignée *f* d'accélération; *(gear change)* poignée *f* de changement de vitesses

▸**twist about, twist around** *vi* (**a**) *(wire, rope)* s'entortiller, s'emmêler
(**b**) *(road)* serpenter, zigzaguer

▸**twist off** **1** *vt sep (lid)* dévisser; *(cork)* enlever en tournant; *(branch)* enlever *ou* arracher en tordant
2 *vi (cap, lid)* se dévisser

▸**twist out** *vt sep (nail, cork)* enlever en tournant

▸**twist round** *Br* **1** *vt sep (rope, tape)* enrouler; *(lid)* visser; *(handle)* (faire) tourner; *(swivel chair)* faire tourner *ou* pivoter; *(hat, head)* tourner; **I twisted myself round on my chair** je me suis retourné sur ma chaise
2 *vi* (**a**) *(person)* se retourner
(**b**) *(strap, rope)* s'entortiller; *(swivel chair)* pivoter
(**c**) *(path)* serpenter, zigzaguer

▸**twist together** *vt sep (threads)* tresser, enrouler; *(wires)* enrouler

▸**twist up** **1** *vt sep (threads, wires)* enrouler, emmêler
2 *vi* (**a**) *(threads, wires)* s'emmêler, s'enchevêtrer
(**b**) *(smoke)* monter en volutes

twisted ['twɪstɪd] *adj* (**a**) *(piece of metal)* tordu; *(piece of string)* entortillé; **the twisted wreckage of the plane/car** l'épave *f* tordue de l'avion/de la voiture
(**b**) *(personality, smile)* tordu; *(mind)* tordu, mal tourné
(**c**) *(logic, argument)* faux (fausse), tordu; **by a kind of twisted logic** selon une sorte de logique tordue
(**d**) *(dishonest)* malhonnête; *(politician, lawyer, businessman)* malhonnête, véreux
(**e**) *Fam (crazy)* tordu
►► *Archit* ***twisted pillar*** colonne *f* torse

twisted-pair cable *n* câble *m* en paire torsadée

twister ['twɪstə(r)] *n Fam* (**a**) *Br (crook)* arnaqueur(euse) *m,f* (**b**) *(tornado)* tornade ❑ *f*

twisting ['twɪstɪŋ] *adj (path)* tortueux

twisty ['twɪstɪ] *adj (road, river)* sinueux, qui serpente

twit [twɪt] **1** *vt Old-fashioned (tease)* taquiner; **they twitted him about his hat** ils l'ont taquiné sur *ou* à propos de son chapeau
2 *n Br Fam (idiot)* courge *f*, nouille *f*; **you silly twit!** espèce d'idiot *ou* de crétin!

twitch [twɪtʃ] **1** *vi* (**a**) *(jerk → once)* avoir un mouvement convulsif; *(→ habitually)* avoir un tic; *(muscle)* se contracter convulsivement; **his hands twitched nervously** ses mains se contractaient nerveusement; **his right eye twitches** il a un tic à l'œil droit; **the rabbit's nose twitched** le lapin a remué le nez
(**b**) *(wriggle)* s'agiter, se remuer; **stop twitching about on your chair!** arrête de t'agiter *ou* de te tortiller sur ta chaise!
2 *vt (ears, nose)* remuer, bouger; *(curtain, rope)* tirer d'un coup sec, donner un coup sec à; **to twitch its tail** *(of cat)* remuer la queue; **she twitched my sleeve** elle tira ma manche d'un petit coup sec; **she twitched the scarf out of my hands** elle m'arracha l'écharpe des mains
3 *n* (**a**) *(nervous tic)* tic *m*; *(muscular spasm)* spasme *m*; **to have a (nervous) twitch** avoir un tic (nerveux); **the rabbit's ears gave a twitch** le lapin a remué les oreilles
(**b**) *(tweak, pull → on hair, rope)* coup *m* sec, saccade *f*; **a twitch of the whip** un petit coup de fouet
►► *Bot* ***twitch grass*** chiendent *m* officinal *ou* des boutiques

twitcher ['twɪtʃə(r)] *n Fam Pej* dingue *mf* d'ornithologie

twitching ['twɪtʃɪŋ] *n* (**a**) *(action → of face, hands)* contraction *f* nerveuse (**b**) *(nervous tic)* tic *m*

twitchy ['twɪtʃɪ] *adj (person)* agité, nerveux

twite [twaɪt] *n Orn* linotte *f* à bec jaune, linotte *f* montagnarde

twitter ['twɪtə(r)] **1** *vi* (**a**) *(bird)* gazouiller, pépier (**b**) *Pej (person → chatter)* jacasser; **she's always twittering (on) about her daughter** elle ne parle que de sa fille
2 *n* (**a**) *(of bird)* gazouillement *m*, pépiement *m* (**b**) *Pej (of person)* bavardage *m* (**c**) *Fam (agitation)* état *m* d'agitation ❑; **to be all of a** *or* **in a twitter about sth** être dans tous ses états *ou* sens dessus dessous à cause de qch

twittering ['twɪtərɪŋ] **1** *adj (bird)* gazouillant; *Pej (person, voice)* piaillant
2 *n (of bird)* gazouillement *m*; *Pej (talk)* jacassement *m*

'twixt [twɪkst] *Literary* = **betwixt**

two [tu:] **1** *n (pl* **twos***)* (**a**) *(number, numeral)* deux *m inv*; **to cut sth in two** couper qch en deux; **in twos, two by two** deux par deux; **in twos and threes** par (groupes de) deux ou trois; **two at a time** deux à la fois
(**b**) *(idioms)* **to put two and two together** faire le rapport (entre deux choses) et tirer ses conclusions; **she put two and two together, and made five** elle en a tiré des conclusions erronées; **they're two of a kind** ils sont du même genre, ils se ressemblent tous les deux; **that makes two of us** vous n'êtes pas le seul, moi c'est pareil; **two's company, three's a crowd** deux ça va, trois c'est trop; **she blames him but it takes two to tango** elle dit que c'est de sa faute à lui, mais ils ont tous les deux leur part de responsabilité
2 *pron* deux
3 *adj* deux; *see also* **five**

►► ***the Two Thousand Guineas*** = course de chevaux qui se déroule à Newmarket, en Angleterre

two-bit *adj Am Fam Pej* de pacotille

two-by-four **1** *n* = bois d'œuvre de 2 pouces sur 4 de section
2 *adj Am Fam (small)* exigu ❑; *(worthless)* minable

two-chamber system *n Pol* système *m* bicaméral

twocker ['twɒkə(r)] *n Br Fam* voleur(euse) *m,f* de voitures ❑

two-colour, *Am* **two-color** *adj* de deux couleurs, bicolore; *(print ribbon)* bicolore
►► *Typ* ***two-colour process*** bichromie *f*

two-cycle *adj Am (engine)* à deux temps

two-cylinder *adj* à deux cylindres

two-dimensional *adj* (**a**) *(figure, drawing)* à deux dimensions (**b**) *(simplistic → character)* sans profondeur, simpliste

two-door *adj (car)* à deux portes

two-edged *adj (sword, policy, argument)* à double tranchant

two-faced *adj* hypocrite

twofold ['tu:fəʊld] **1** *adj* double; **their aims are twofold** ils ont deux objectifs *ou* un objectif double; **there has been a twofold increase in attendance** le nombre de personnes présentes a doublé
2 *adv (increase)* au double; **prices have risen twofold** les prix ont doublé

two-four time *n Mus* mesure *f* à deux temps, deux-quatre *m inv*

two-handed *adj* (**a**) *(tool)* à deux poignées; *(saw)* à deux mains, forestière; *(sword)* à deux mains (**b**) *(game)* qui se joue à deux, pour deux joueurs (**c**) *(in tennis)* à deux mains; **a two-handed backhand** un revers à deux mains

two-headed *adj* bicéphale; *Her (eagle)* double, à deux têtes

two-horse *adj (carriage)* à deux chevaux; *Br Fig* **a two-horse race** une épreuve/élection qui ne comprend que deux concurrents

two-lane *adj Am (highway)* à deux voies

two-legged *adj* bipède

two-level *adj* à deux niveaux

two-line whip *n Br Pol* = convocation d'un député par un "whip" à un débat ou à un vote lors d'une séance parlementaire

two-liter *n Am (bottle)* bouteille *f* de deux litres

two-masted *adj* à deux mâts

two-minute silence *n Br* = deux minutes de silence observées à onze heures lors du "Remembrance Day" en souvenir des morts des deux guerres mondiales

two-one *n Br Univ* ≃ licence *f* avec mention bien

two-party *adj (coalition, system)* biparti, bipartite

twopence ['tʌpəns] *n Br* deux pence *mpl*; *Fam* **I don't give twopence for what he thinks** je me moque bien *ou* je me fiche pas mal de ce qu'il pense

twopenny ['tʌpnɪ] *adj Br* à *ou* de deux pence; *Fam Fig (worthless)* de quatre sous, qui ne vaut pas un clou

twopenny-halfpenny *adj Fam* qui ne vaut pas un clou; *(solicitor, system)* à la gomme

two-phase *adj Elec* diphasé, biphasé

two-piece **1** *adj* en deux parties
2 *n (bikini)* deux-pièces *m*; *(man's suit)* costume *m* deux-pièces; *(woman's suit)* tailleur *m*
►► ***two-piece suit*** *(man's)* costume *m* deux-pièces; *(woman's)* tailleur *m*; ***two-piece swimming costume*** (maillot *m* de bain) deux-pièces *m*

two-pin *adj*
►► *Elec* ***two-pin plug*** prise *f* à deux fiches; ***two-pin socket*** prise *f* à deux douilles

two-ply **1** *n (wool)* laine *f* à deux fils
2 *adj (wool)* à deux fils; *(rope)* à deux brins; *(tissue)* double, à double épaisseur; *(wood)* à deux épaisseurs

two-seater **1** *adj* à deux places
2 *n (plane)* avion *m* à deux places; *(car)* voiture *f* à deux places

two-sided *adj* (**a**) *(problem)* qui a deux aspects; *(argument)* discutable, qui comporte deux points de vue (**b**) *(copy)* en recto-verso

twosome ['tu:səm] *n* (**a**) *(pair)* paire *f*; *(of friends etc)* couple *m* (**b**) *(match)* partie *f* à deux

two-speed *adj also Fig* à deux vitesses
►► ***two-speed monetary union*** union *f* monétaire à deux vitesses; ***two-speed wiper*** essuie-glace *m* à deux vitesses

two-star **1** *adj* (**a**) *(restaurant, hotel)* deux étoiles (**b**) *Br (petrol)* ordinaire
2 *n Br (petrol)* (essence *f*) ordinaire *m*

two-step *n (dance, music)* pas *m* de deux

two-storey *adj* à deux étages

two-stroke *adj Br (engine)* à deux temps

two-tier *adj (cake)* à deux étages; *(management structure)* à deux niveaux; *(education system, health service)* à deux vitesses

two-time *vt Fam (lover)* tromper ❑, être infidèle à ❑

two-timer *n Fam* personne *f* infidèle ❑

two-timing *adj Fam* infidèle ❑; **you two-timing bastard!** espèce de salaud!

two-tone *adj (in colour)* à deux tons; *(in sound)* de deux tons

two-two *n Br Univ* ≃ licence *f* avec mention assez bien

'twould [twʊd] *Literary or Hum* = **it would**

two-up *n Austr* = pile ou face avec deux pièces donnant lieu à des paris

two-way *adj (traffic, trade)* dans les deux sens; *(street)* à double sens; *(agreement, process)* bilatéral; **a relationship has got to be a two-way thing** en amour comme en amitié, il faut savoir prendre et donner
►► ***two-way mirror*** glace *f* sans tain; *Tel* ***two-way radio*** émetteur-récepteur *m*; *Elec* ***two-way switch*** va-et-vient *m inv*

two-wheeler *n (motorbike)* deux-roues *m*; *(bicycle)* bicyclette *f*, deux-roues *m*

TX *(written abbr* **Texas***)* Texas *m*

tychism ['taɪkɪzəm] *n Phil* tychisme *m*

tycoon [taɪ'ku:n] *n* homme *m* d'affaires important, magnat *m*; **oil/newspaper tycoon** magnat *m* du pétrole/de la presse

'The Last Tycoon' *Fitzgerald* 'Le Dernier Nabab'

tyke [taɪk] *n Fam* (**a**) *(dog)* chien *m* bâtard ❑ (**b**) *(child)* morveux(euse) *m,f*, môme *mf* (**c**) *Br (coarse person)* lourdaud(e) *m,f*

Tylenol® ['taɪlənɒl] *n* = marque d'analgésique

tylopod ['taɪləpɒd] *n Zool* tylopode *m*

tympan ['tɪmpən] *n Archit, Typ & Tech* tympan *m*
►► ***tympan paper*** (papier *m* de) décharge *f*, papier *m* intercalaire; *Typ* ***tympan sheet*** marge *f*

tympani = **timpani**

tympanic [tɪm'pænɪk] *n Anat* (os *m*) tympanal *m*
►► ***tympanic bone*** os *m* tympanal; ***tympanic membrane*** membrane *f* tympanique *ou* du tympan

tympanist = **timpanist**

tympanites [,tɪmpə'naɪti:z] *n Med* tympanisme *m*, tympanite *f*

tympanitic [,tɪmpə'nɪtɪk] *adj*
►► *Med* ***tympanitic resonance*** son *m* tympanique, tympanisme *m*

tympanitis [,tɪmpə'naɪtʌɪs] *n Med* (**a**) *(inflammation of eardrum)* tympanite *f*, otite *f* moyenne (**b**) *(distension of abdomen)* tympanisme *m*, tympanite *f*

tympanum ['tɪmpənəm] *(pl* **tympana** [-nə] *or* **tympanums***)* *n* (**a**) *Anat, Archit & Zool* tympan *m* (**b**) *Mus* tymbale *f*

Tyne and Wear [,taɪnən'wɪə(r)] *n* le Tyne et Wear, = comté du nord-est de l'Angleterre; **in Tyne and Wear** dans le Tyne and Wear

Tynwald ['tɪnwəld, 'taɪnwəld] *n Parl* **the Tynwald** = le Parlement de l'île de Man

type [taɪp] **1** *n* (**a**) *(gen & Biol)* **blood/hair type** type *m* sanguin/de cheveux
(**b**) *(sort, kind)* sorte *f*, genre *m*, espèce *f*; *(make → of coffee, shampoo etc)* marque *f*; *(model → of car, plane, equipment etc)* modèle *m*; **what type of washing powder do you use?** quelle (marque de) lessive utilisez-vous?; **what type of car do you drive?** qu'est-ce que vous avez comme voiture?, quel modèle de voiture avez-vous?; **a new type of warship/of phone** un nouveau modèle de navire de guerre/de téléphone
(**c**) *(referring to person)* genre *m*, type *m*; **she's not that type (of person)** ce n'est pas son genre;

she's not the type to gossip elle n'est pas du genre à faire des commérages; **he's not my type** ce n'est pas mon genre *ou* type (d'homme); **men of his type** les hommes *mpl* de son genre *ou* son espèce; **I know his/their type** je connais les gens de son espèce/de leur espèce, je connais le genre; **the blond fair-skinned type** le type cheveux blonds et peau blanche; **she's one of those sporty types** elle est du genre sportif
(**d**) *(typical example)* type *m*, exemple *m*
(**e**) *(UNCOUNT) Typ (single character)* caractère *m*; *(block of print)* caractères *mpl* (d'imprimerie); **to set type** composer
2 *vt* (**a**) *(of typist)* taper (à la machine), dactylographier; **to type sth into a computer** saisir qch à l'ordinateur; **to type a letter** taper une lettre
(**b**) *Med (blood sample)* classifier
3 *vi (typist)* taper (à la machine); **I can only type with two fingers** je ne tape qu'avec deux doigts
►► *Biol **type genus*** genre *m* type; ***type library*** typothèque *f*; *Typ **type size*** taille *f* des caractères, corps *m*
►**type in** *vt sep* taper
►**type out** *vt sep* (**a**) *(letter)* taper (à la machine) (**b**) *(error)* effacer (à la machine)
►**type over** *vt insep Comput* écraser
►**type up** *vt sep (report, notes)* taper (à la machine)
-type [taɪp] *suff* du type, genre; **western-type governments** les gouvernements *mpl* du type occidental; **collie-type dogs** des chiens *mpl* genre colley
typebar ['taɪpbɑ:(r)] *n* barre *f* porte-caractères, barre *f* d'impression
typecase ['taɪpkeɪs] *n Typ* casse *f*
typecast ['taɪpkɑ:st] *(pt & pp* **typecast**) *vt (actor)* enfermer dans le rôle de; **she was being typecast as a dumb blonde** elle était cantonnée aux rôles de blondes écervelées; **he is always typecast as a villain** on lui fait toujours jouer des rôles de bandit
typeface ['taɪpfeɪs] *n* (**a**) *Typ (printing surface)* œil *m* du caractère (**b**) *Typ (type family)* famille *f* de caractères; *Comput* police *f* (de caractères); **try another typeface** essaie avec un autre caractère
typefounder ['taɪp,faʊndə(r)] *n* fondeur *m* en caractères d'imprimerie, fondeur *m* typographe
typeover ['taɪp,əʊvə(r)] *n* (mode *m*) écraser *m*
typescript ['taɪpskrɪpt] *n* texte *m* dactylographié, tapuscrit *m*
typeset ['taɪpset] *(pt & pp* **typeset,** *cont* **typesetting**) *vt Typ* composer
typesetter ['taɪp,setə(r)] *n Typ (worker)* compositeur(trice) *m,f*; *(company)* compositeur *m*; *(machine)* linotype® *f*; *Comput (in DTP)* photocomposeuse *f*
typesetting ['taɪp,setɪŋ] *n Typ* composition *f*
typewrite ['taɪpraɪt] **1** *vi* taper à la machine
2 *vt* taper à la machine
typewriter ['taɪp,raɪtə(r)] **1** *n* machine *f* à écrire
2 *comp (ribbon)* de machine à écrire; *(rubber)* pour machine à écrire
typewriting ['taɪp,raɪtɪŋ] *n* dactylographie *f*
typewritten ['taɪp,rɪtən] *adj* dactylographié, tapé à la machine
typhlitis [tɪf'laɪtɪs] *n Med* typhlite *f*
typhlology [tɪf'lɒlədʒɪ] *n* soin *m* des aveugles
typhoid ['taɪfɔɪd] **1** *n (UNCOUNT)* typhoïde *f*
2 *comp (injection)* antityphoïdique; *(symptoms)* de la typhoïde
►► ***typhoid fever*** (fièvre *f*) typhoïde *f*; *Am **typhoid Mary*** source *f* d'un fléau; ***typhoid-paratyphoid A and B*** (vaccin *m*) TAB *m*
typhoidal [taɪ'fɔɪdəl] *adj Med* typhoïque, typhoïdique
typhoon [taɪ'fu:n] *n* typhon *m*
typhus ['taɪfəs] *n* typhus *m*
typical ['tɪpɪkəl] *adj* typique, caractéristique; **such behaviour is typical of young people nowadays** un tel comportement est typique *ou* caractéristique des jeunes d'aujourd'hui; **it was typical of him to offer to pay** c'était bien son genre de proposer de payer; **it's a typical example of Aztec pottery** c'est un exemple type de poterie aztèque; **in a typical day you can earn £300** en une journée normale vous pouvez gagner 300 livres; **the typical American** l'Américain *m* typique *ou* type; *Pej* **that's typical of her!** c'est bien d'elle!; **your letter took six days to get here – typical!** ta lettre a mis six jours pour arriver – ça c'est typique! *ou* ça ne m'étonne pas!; **he said with typical self-deprecation** dit-il avec son humilité habituelle; **typical man!** c'est bien un homme!
typically ['tɪpɪklɪ] *adv* (**a**) *(normally)* d'habitude; **we typically deal with 20 phone calls a day** d'habitude nous répondons à 20 appels téléphoniques par jour; **it was a typically sunny day** c'était une journée ensoleillée, comme d'habitude
(**b**) *(characteristically)* typiquement; **she's typically English** elle est typiquement anglaise, c'est l'Anglaise type *ou* typique; **it's a typically French scene** c'est une scène bien française *ou* typiquement française; **a group of typically noisy schoolboys** un groupe de lycéens bruyants comme le sont tous les lycéens; **typically, she changed her mind at the last minute** comme à son habitude, elle a changé d'avis au dernier moment; **employees typically work a 40-hour week** les employés travaillent en moyenne 40 heures par semaine
typify ['tɪpɪfaɪ] *(pt & pp* **typified**) *vt* (**a**) *(be typical of)* être typique *ou* caractéristique de; **the building typifies the Baroque style** l'édifice est typique *ou* caractéristique du style baroque
(**b**) *(embody, symbolize)* symboliser, être le type même de; **she typifies the modern career woman** c'est le type même de la femme moderne qui poursuit une carrière
typing ['taɪpɪŋ] *n* (**a**) *(typing work)* **he had 10 pages of typing to do** il avait 10 pages à taper *ou* dactylographier (**b**) *(typescript)* tapuscrit *m*, texte *m* dactylographié (**c**) *(skill)* dactylo *f*, dactylographie *f*
►► ***typing error*** faute *f* de frappe; ***typing paper*** papier *m* machine; ***typing pool*** bureau *m ou* pool *m* des dactylos; ***typing skills*** compétences *fpl* en dactylographie; ***typing speed*** vitesse *f* de frappe; **I have a typing speed of 30 words a minute** je tape 30 mots à la minute
typist ['taɪpɪst] *n* dactylo *mf*, dactylographe *mf*
typo ['taɪpəʊ] *(pl* **typos**) *n Fam (in typescript)* faute *f* de frappe ❏; *(in printed text)* coquille ❏ *f*
typographer [taɪ'pɒgrəfə(r)] *n* typographe *mf*
typographic [,taɪpə'græfɪk], **typographical** [,taɪpə'græfɪkəl] *adj* typographique
typographically [,taɪpə'græfɪklɪ] *adv* typographiquement
typography [taɪ'pɒgrəfɪ] *n* typographie *f*
typological [,taɪpə'lɒdʒɪkəl] *adj* typologique
typology [taɪ'pɒlədʒɪ] *n* typologie *f*
tyramine ['taɪrəmi:n] *n* tyramine *f*
tyrannical [tɪ'rænɪkəl] *adj* tyrannique
tyrannically [tɪ'rænɪklɪ] *adv* tyranniquement, avec tyrannie
tyrannicide [tɪ'rænɪsaɪd] *n* (**a**) *(person)* tyrannicide *mf* (**b**) *(act)* tyrannicide *m*
tyrannize, -ise ['tɪrənaɪz] **1** *vt* tyranniser
2 *vi* **to tyrannize over sb** tyranniser qn
tyrannosaur [tɪ'rænəsɔ:(r)], **tyrannosaurus** [tɪ,rænə'sɔ:rəs] *n* tyrannosaure *m*
tyrannous ['tɪrənəs] *adj* tyrannique
tyrannously ['tɪrənəslɪ] *adv* tyranniquement, en tyran
tyranny ['tɪrənɪ] *(pl* **tyrannies**) *n* tyrannie *f*
tyrant ['taɪrənt] *n* tyran *m*; **to be a domestic tyrant** être un tyran domestique
Tyre ['taɪə(r)] *n* Tyr
tyre, *Am* **tire** ['taɪə(r)] *n* pneu *m*
►► ***tyre centre*** centre *m* de vente et réparation de pneus; ***tyre chain*** chaîne *f* (de pneu); ***tyre fitter*** monteur *m* de pneus; ***tyre gauge*** manomètre *m (pour pneus)*; ***tyre iron, tyre lever*** démonte-pneu *m*; ***tyre pressure*** pression *f* des pneus; ***tyre pump*** pompe *f* (pour gonfler les pneus); ***tyre valve*** valve *f* de gonflage
Tyrian ['tɪrɪən] **1** *n* tyrien(enne) *m,f*
2 *adj* tyrien
tyro ['taɪrəʊ] *(pl* **tyros**) *n Formal* débutant(e) *m,f*, novice *mf*
Tyrol [tɪ'rəʊl] *n* Tyrol *m*; **in the Tyrol** dans le Tyrol
Tyrolean [tɪrə'lɪən], **Tyrolese** [,tɪrə'li:z] **1** *n* Tyrolien(enne) *m,f*
2 *adj* tyrolien
►► ***Tyrolean hat*** chapeau *m* tyrolien
tyrosinase [taɪ'rɒsɪneɪz] *n Biol & Chem* tyrosinase *f*
tyrosine ['taɪrəsi:n] *n Biol & Chem* tyrosine *f*
Tyrrhenian Sea [tɪ'ri:nɪən-] *n* **the Tyrrhenian Sea** la mer Tyrrhénienne
tzar, tzarevitch *etc* = **tsar, tsarevitch** *etc*
tzatziki [tsæt'si:ki:] *n Culin* tzatziki *m*
tzetze fly = **tsetse fly**
tzigane [tsɪ'gɑ:n] *n* tzigane *mf*
T-zone *n* zones *fpl* grasses du visage *(front, nez, menton)*

U¹, u [juː] **1** *n (letter)* U, u *m inv*; **two u's** deux u; **U for umbrella** ≃ U comme Ursule

2 *adj Br Fam Old-fashioned (upper-class → expression, activity)* distingué ❑; **U/non-U language** langage *m* distingué/vulgaire ❑

U² [juː] *n Cin (abbr* **universal***)* = désigne un film tous publics en Grande-Bretagne

U³ *(written abbr* **unionist***)* unioniste

UAE [ˌjuːeɪ'iː] *n (abbr* **United Arab Emirates***)* EAU *mpl*

uakari [uːæ'kɑːrɪ] *n Zool* ouakari *m*

UAR [ˌjuːeɪ'ɑː(r)] *n (abbr* **United Arab Republic***)* RAU *f*

UAW [ˌjuːeɪ'dʌbəljuː] *n Am (abbr* **United Automobile Workers***)* = syndicat américain de l'industrie automobile

UB40 [ˌjuːbiː'fɔːtɪ] *n Br Formerly (abbr* **unemployment benefit form 40***) (card)* = carte de pointage pour bénéficier de l'allocation de chômage; *Fam (person)* chômeur(euse) ❑ *m,f*

U-bend *n* **(a)** *(in pipe)* coude *m*; *(under sink)* siphon *m* **(b)** *Br (in road)* virage *m* en épingle à cheveux

über- ['uːbə(r)] *pref Fam* super-; **überbabe** super-canon *m*

ubiquinone [jʊ'bɪkwɪnəʊn] *n Biol & Chem* ubiquinone *f*

ubiquitous [juː'bɪkwɪtəs] *adj (gen)* omniprésent, que l'on trouve partout; *(person)* doué d'ubiquité, omniprésent

ubiquity [juː'bɪkwətɪ] *n* ubiquité *f*, omniprésence *f*

U-boat *n* sous-marin *m* allemand

U-bolt *n* agrafe *f* filetée, étrier *m*

UBR [ˌjuːbiː'ɑː(r)] *n Fin (abbr* **uniform business rate***)* = taxe assise sur la valeur des locaux commerciaux, ≃ taxe *f* professionnelle

UCAS ['juːkæs] *n Br (abbr* **University and College Admissions Service***)* = organisme centralisant les demandes d'inscription dans les universités britanniques

UCATT ['juːkæt] *n Br (abbr* **Union of Construction, Allied Trades and Technicians***)* = syndicat britannique des employés du bâtiment

UCCA ['ʌkə] *n Br Formerly (abbr* **Universities Central Council on Admissions***)* = organisme centralisant les demandes d'inscription dans les universités britanniques

UCITS [ˌjuːsiːaɪˌtiː'es] *n Fin (abbr* **undertakings for collective investment in transferables***)* OPCVM *m*

UCL [ˌjuːsiː'el] *n Br (abbr* **University College, London***)* = l'une des facultés de l'Université de Londres

UCLA ['ʌklə] *n Am (abbr* **University of California at Los Angeles***)* UCLA *f*, = partie de l'université de Californie située à Los Angeles, célèbre pour la qualité de ses équipes de sport

UCW [ˌjuːsiː'dʌbəljuː] *n Br (abbr* **Union of Communication Workers***)* = syndicat britannique des communications

UDA [ˌjuːdiː'eɪ] *n (abbr* **Ulster Defence Association***)* = organisation paramilitaire protestante d'Irlande du Nord, déclarée hors la loi en 1992

UDC [ˌjuːdiː'siː] *n Br Admin (abbr* **Urban District Council***)* = conseil d'une communauté urbaine

udder ['ʌdə(r)] *n* mamelle *f*, pis *m*

UDI [ˌjuːdiː'aɪ] *n (abbr* **Unilateral Declaration of Independence***)* = déclaration unilatérale d'indépendance

UDM [ˌjuːdiː'em] *n Br (abbr* **Union of Democratic Mineworkers***)* = syndicat britannique de mineurs

udometer [juː'dɒmɪtə(r)] *n Met* udomètre *m*, pluviomètre *m*

UDR [ˌjuːdiː'ɑː(r)] *n Br Formerly (abbr* **Ulster Defence Regiment***)* = ancien régiment de réservistes d'Irlande du Nord qui fait aujourd'hui partie du "Royal Irish Regiment"

UEFA [juː'eɪfə] *n (abbr* **Union of European Football Associations***)* UEFA *f*

UFC [ˌjuːef'siː] *n Br (abbr* **Universities Funding Council***)* = organisme répartissant les crédits entre les universités en Grande-Bretagne

UFO [ˌjuːef'əʊ, 'juːfəʊ] *n (abbr* **unidentified flying object***)* OVNI *m*, ovni *m*

ufologist [juː'fɒlədʒɪst] *n* spécialiste *mf* d'ufologie

ufology [juː'fɒlədʒɪ] *n* ufologie *f*

Uganda [juː'gændə] *n* Ouganda *m*; **in Uganda** en Ouganda

Ugandan [juː'gændən] **1** *n* Ougandais(e) *m,f*

2 *adj* ougandais

3 *comp (embassy)* d'Ouganda; *(history)* de l'Ouganda

UGC [ˌjuːdʒiː'siː] *n Br (abbr* **University Grants Committee***)* = organisme répartissant les crédits entre les universités en Grande-Bretagne

ugh [ʌg] *exclam* beurk!, berk!, pouah!

ugli® ['ʌglɪ] *(pl* **uglis** *or* **uglies***) n* **ugli**® **(fruit)** tangelo *m*

uglification [ˌʌglɪfɪ'keɪʃən] *n Fam* enlaidissement ❑ *m*

uglify ['ʌglɪfaɪ] *(pt & pp* **uglified***) vt Fam (city, building)* enlaidir ❑

ugliness ['ʌglɪnɪs] *n* laideur *f*

ugly ['ʌglɪ] *(compar* **uglier,** *superl* **ugliest***) adj* **(a)** *(in appearance → person, face, building)* laid; **it was an ugly sight** ce n'était pas beau à voir; **as ugly as sin** laid à faire peur; *(person)* laid comme un pou

(b) *(unpleasant, nasty → habit)* sale, désagréable; *(→ behaviour)* répugnant; *(→ quarrel)* mauvais; *(→ clouds, weather)* vilain, sale; *(→ bruise, wound, scar)* vilain, méchant; *(→ rumour, word)* vilain; *(→ situation)* fâcheux, mauvais; **there were some ugly scenes** il y a eu du vilain; **the ugly truth is...** la vérité, dans toute son horreur, c'est que...; **he was in an ugly mood** il était d'une humeur massacrante, il était de très mauvaise humeur; **she gave me an ugly look** elle m'a regardé d'un sale œil; **he's an ugly customer** c'est un sale individu; **to turn** *or* **to get ugly** *(situation)* dégénérer, mal tourner; **things took an ugly turn** les choses ont mal tourné

▶▶ ***Ugly American*** touriste *mf* américain moyen (sans culture et sans tact); ***ugly duckling*** vilain petit canard *m*; ***Ugly Sisters*** = les sœurs de Cendrillon, personnages de la "pantomime" anglaise

'The Ugly Duckling' *Andersen* 'Le vilain petit canard'

Ugrian ['juːgrɪən], **Ugric** ['juːgrɪk] **1** *adj* ougrien

2 *n* **(a)** *(person)* Ougrien(enne) *m,f* **(b)** *Ling* langue *f* ougrienne

UHF [ˌjuːeɪtʃ'ef] *n (abbr* **ultra-high frequency***)* UHF *f*

uh-huh [ʌ'hʌ] *exclam Fam* **uh-huh!** *(as conversation filler)* ah ah!; *(in assent)* oui oui!, OK!; **uh-huh?** *(in question)* ah ha?; *(in surprise)* ah bon?, ah ouais?

uhlan ['uːlɑːn, 'juːlɑːn] *n Hist* uhlan *m*

UHT [ˌjuːeɪtʃ'tiː] *adj (abbr* **ultra-heat-treated***)* UHT

uh-uh ['ʌʌ] *exclam Fam (no)* non non!; *(in warning)* hé!

uitlander ['eɪtlændə(r), 'ɔɪtlændə(r)] *n SAfr* étranger(ère) *m,f*

UK [ˌjuː'keɪ] *(abbr* **United Kingdom***)* **1** *n* Royaume-Uni *m*; **in the UK** au Royaume-Uni

2 *comp* du Royaume-Uni

UKAEA [ˌjuːkeɪˌeɪiː'eɪ] *n Br (abbr* **United Kingdom Atomic Energy Authority***)* = commissariat britannique à l'énergie atomique

ukase [juː'keɪz] *n* ukase *m*, oukase *m*

uke [juːk] *n Fam (abbr* **ukulele***)* guitare *f* hawaïenne ❑, ukulélé ❑ *m*

ukelele = **ukulele**

Ukraine [juː'kreɪn] *n* **(the) Ukraine** Ukraine *f*; **in (the) Ukraine** en Ukraine

Ukrainian [juː'kreɪnjən] **1** *n* **(a)** *(person)* Ukrainien(enne) *m,f* **(b)** *(language)* ukrainien *m*

2 *adj* ukrainien

3 *comp (embassy)* d'Ukraine; *(history)* de l'Ukraine; *(teacher)* d'ukrainien

▶▶ ***the Ukrainian Soviet Socialist Republic*** la République soviétique d'Ukraine

ukulele [ˌjuːkə'leɪlɪ] *n* guitare *f* hawaïenne, ukulélé *m*

ulama ['uːləmə] *n Rel* **(a)** *(body of Muslim scholars)* ulémas *mpl*, oulémas *mpl* **(b)** *(Muslim scholar)* uléma *m*, ouléma *m*

Ulan Bator [ʊˌlɑːn'bɑːtɔː(r)] *n* Oulan-Bator

ulcer ['ʌlsə(r)] *n* **(a)** *Med (in stomach)* ulcère *m*; *(in mouth)* aphte *m* **(b)** *Fig* plaie *f*

ulcerate ['ʌlsəreɪt] **1** *vt* ulcérer

2 *vi* s'ulcérer

ulcerated ['ʌlsəreɪtɪd] *adj* ulcéreux

ulceration [ˌʌlsə'reɪʃən] *n* ulcération *f*

ulcerative ['ʌlsərətɪv] *adj Med* ulcératif

ulcerogenic [ˌʌlsərəʊ'dʒenɪk] *adj Med* ulcérogène

ulcerous ['ʌlsərəs] *adj* **(a)** *(ulcerated)* ulcéreux **(b)** *(causing ulcers)* ulcératif

ulema = **ulama**

ullage ['ʌlɪdʒ] *n* **(a)** *(in transport)* = quantité de liquide perdue par évaporation ou par des fuites au cours du transport **(b)** *(in wine bottle)* = espace entre le bouchon et le vin

'ullo ['ʌˌləʊ] *exclam Fam (greeting)* salut!; *(doubtful)* tiens, tiens!

ulna ['ʌlnə] *(pl* **ulnae** [-niː] *or* **ulnas***) n* cubitus *m*

ulotrichous [jʊ'lɒtrɪkəs] *adj* ulotrique

Ulster ['ʌlstə(r)] *n* **(a)** *(province)* Ulster *m*; **in Ulster** dans l'Ulster

(b) *(Northern Ireland)* Irlande *f* du Nord, Ulster *m*

▶▶ ***Ulster Defence Association*** = organisation paramilitaire protestante d'Irlande du Nord, déclarée hors la loi en 1992; *Br Formerly* ***Ulster Defence Regiment*** = ancien régiment de réservistes d'Irlande du Nord qui fait aujourd'hui partie du "Royal Irish Regiment"; ***Ulster Democratic Unionist Party*** = parti politique essentiellement protestant exigeant le maintien de l'Irlande du Nord au sein du Royaume-Uni; ***Ulster Unionists*** = parti politique essentiellement protestant, favorable au maintien de l'Irlande du Nord au sein du Royaume-Uni; ***Ulster Volunteer Force*** = organisation paramilitaire déclarée hors la loi, favorable au maintien de l'Irlande du Nord au sein du Royaume-Uni

ulster ['ʌlstə(r)] *n (coat)* = gros pardessus

Ulsterman ['ʌlstəmən] *(pl* **Ulstermen** [-mən]*) n* Ulstérien *m*, habitant *m* de l'Irlande du Nord

Ulsterwoman ['ʌlstə,wʊmən] *(pl* **Ulsterwomen** [-,wɪmɪn]) *n* Ulstérienne *f*, habitante *f* de l'Irlande du Nord

ult *Old-fashioned (written abbr* **ultimo**) du mois dernier

ulterior [ʌl'tɪərɪə(r)] *adj (hidden, secret)* secret(ète), dissimulé

▸▸ ***ulterior motive*** arrière-pensée *f*

ultima ['ʌltɪmə] *n Ling* dernière syllabe *f* d'un mot

ultimata [,ʌltɪ'meɪtə] *pl of* **ultimatum**

ultimate ['ʌltɪmət] **1** *adj* (**a**) *(eventual, final → ambition, power, responsibility)* ultime; *(→ cost, destination, objective)* ultime, final; *(→ solution, decision, answer)* final, définitif; **her tragic illness and ultimate death deprived the world of a great artist** sa mort survenue à l'issue d'une tragique maladie a privé le monde d'une grande artiste; **I believe in the party's ultimate victory** je crois que le parti finira par gagner; **they regard nuclear weapons as the ultimate deterrent** ils considèrent les armes nucléaires comme l'ultime moyen de dissuasion

(**b**) *(basic, fundamental → cause)* fondamental, premier; *(→ truth)* fondamental, élémentaire; **the ultimate constituents of matter** les constituants fondamentaux de la matière; **the ultimate meaning of life** le sens fondamental de la vie

(**c**) *(extreme, supreme → authority, insult)* suprême; *(→ cruelty, stupidity)* suprême, extrême; **the ultimate double-glazing** le meilleur double vitrage; **it's their idea of the ultimate holiday** c'est leur conception des vacances idéales; **the ultimate sound system** la meilleure sono qui soit; **the ultimate sacrifice** le sacrifice suprême; *Fam* **he really is the ultimate incompetent!** plus incompétent que lui tu meurs!

(**d**) *(furthest)* le plus éloigné; **the ultimate origins of mankind** les origines premières de l'homme

2 *n* comble *m*, summum *m*; **the ultimate in comfort** le summum du confort; **the ultimate in hi-fi** le nec plus ultra de la hi-fi

▸▸ *Mktg* ***ultimate consumer*** utilisateur(trice) *m,f* final(e)

ultimately ['ʌltɪmətlɪ] *adv* (**a**) *(eventually, finally)* finalement, en fin de compte, à la fin; *(later)* par la suite; **a solution will ultimately be found** on finira bien par trouver une solution; **ultimately there will be peace** tôt ou tard, il y aura la paix

(**b**) *(basically)* en dernière analyse, en fin de compte; **ultimately, the problem is a shortage of money** en dernière analyse, le problème est lié à un manque d'argent; **responsibility ultimately lies with you** en fin de compte c'est vous qui êtes responsable

ultimatum [,ʌltɪ'meɪtəm] *(pl* **ultimatums** *or* **ultimata** [-tə]) *n* ultimatum *m*; **to give** *or* **to issue** *or* **to deliver an ultimatum to sb** adresser un ultimatum à qn

ultimo ['ʌltɪməʊ] *adv Old-fashioned* du mois dernier; **the 16th ultimo** le 16 du mois dernier

ultimogeniture [,ʌltɪməʊ'dʒenɪtʃə(r)] *n Law* ultimogéniture *f*

ultra ['ʌltrə] *(pl* **ultras**) **1** *adj* ultra, extrémiste

2 *n* ultra *mf*

ultra- ['ʌltrə] *pref* ultra-, hyper-; *Fam* **ultra-trendy** hyper-branché; **ultra-right-wing** d'extrême [illegible]

ultrabasic [,ʌltrə'beɪsɪk] *adj Geol* ultrabasique

ultracentrifugation [,ʌltrə,sentrɪfjʊ'geɪʃən] *n* ultracentrifugation *f*

ultracentrifuge [,ʌltrə'sentrɪfju:dʒ] *n* ultracentrifugeur *m*, ultracentrifugeuse *f*

ultraclean [,ʌltrə'kli:n] *adj* hyper-propre

ultraconservative [,ʌltrəkən'sɜ:vətɪv] **1** *adj* ultraconservateur

2 *n* ultraconservateur(trice) *m,f*

ultra-fashionable *adj* ultra-chic

ultrafiche ['ʌltrəfi:ʃ] *n* microfiche *f*

ultra-high frequency *n* ultra haute fréquence *f*

ultraism ['ʌltrəɪzəm] *n* ultraïsme *m*, ultracisme *m*

ultraist ['ʌltrəɪst] *n* ultra *mf*

ultraleft [,ʌltrə'left] *Pol* **1** *adj* d'extrême gauche

2 *n* extrême gauche *f*

ultralight **1** *adj* [,ʌltrə'laɪt] ultraléger

2 *n* ['ʌltrəlaɪt] ULM *m*, ultraléger *m* motorisé

ultramarine [,ʌltrəmə'ri:n] **1** *n* bleu *m* outremer

2 *adj* bleu outremer *(inv)*

ultramicroscope [,ʌltrə'maɪkrəskəʊp] *n* ultramicroscope *m*

ultramicroscopic ['ʌltrə,maɪkrə'skɒpɪk] *adj* ultramicroscopique

ultramodern [,ʌltrə'mɒdən] *adj* ultramoderne

ultramontane [,ʌltrə'mɒnteɪn] *Geog & Rel* **1** *adj* ultramontain

2 *n* ultramontain(e) *m,f*

ultramontanism [,ʌltrə'mɒntənɪzəm] *n Rel* ultramontanisme *m*

ultramontanist [,ʌltrə'mɒntənɪst] *n Rel* ultramontain(e) *m,f*

ultramundane [,ʌltrə'mʌndeɪn] *adj* ultramondain

ultranationalist [,ʌltrə'næʃnəlɪst] **1** *n* ultranationaliste *mf*

2 *adj* ultranationaliste

ultraright [,ʌltrə'raɪt] *Pol* **1** *adj* d'extrême droite

2 *n* extrême droite *f*

ultrasensitive [,ʌltrə'sensɪtɪv] *adj* ultrasensible

ultrashort [,ʌltrə'ʃɔ:t] *adj* ultracourt

ultrasonic [,ʌltrə'sɒnɪk] **1** *adj* ultrasonique

2 ultrasonics *n (UNCOUNT)* science *f* des ultrasons

ultrasound ['ʌltrəsaʊnd] *n* ultrason *m*

▸▸ ***ultrasound scan*** échographie *f*

ultrastructure ['ʌltrə,strʌktʃə(r)] *n Biol* ultrastructure *f*

ultraviolet [,ʌltrə'vaɪələt] **1** *adj* ultraviolet

2 *n* ultraviolet *m*

▸▸ ***ultraviolet rays*** rayons *mpl* ultraviolets; *Med* ***ultraviolet treatment*** traitement *m* aux (rayons) ultraviolets

ultra vires [-'vaɪəri:z] **1** *adj* au-delà des pouvoirs

2 *adv* au-delà des pouvoirs

ultravirus [,ʌltrə'vaɪərəs] *n* ultravirus *m*

ululate ['ju:ljʊleɪt] *vi Formal (owl)* ululer, hululer; *(wolf, dog)* hurler

ululation [,ju:ljʊ'leɪʃən] *n Formal (of owl)* ululement *m*, hululement *m*; *(of wolf, dog)* hurlement *m*

Uluru ['u:lʊru:] *n Geog* Uluru

Ulysses [ju:'lɪsi:z] *pr n* Ulysse

'Ulysses' *Joyce* 'Ulysse'

---

um [ʌm] *(pt & pp* **ummed**, *cont* **umming**) *Fam* **1** *exclam* euh

2 *vi* dire euh; **to um and ah** tergiverser, hésiter; **he's always umming and ahing** il n'arrive jamais à se décider

umbel ['ʌmbəl] *n Bot* ombelle *f*

umbellifer [ʌm'belɪfə(r)] *n Bot* ombellifère *f*

umbelliferous [,ʌmbe'lɪfərəs] *adj Bot* ombellifère

umber ['ʌmbə(r)] **1** *adj (colour, paint)* terre d'ombre *(inv)*

2 *n (clay)* terre *f* d'ombre *ou* de Sienne

umbilical [ʌm'bɪlɪkəl, ʌmbɪ'laɪkəl] *adj* ombilical

▸▸ *Anat* ***umbilical cord*** cordon *m* ombilical

umbilicate [ʌm'bɪlɪkeɪt] *adj* (**a**) *(with a navel)* ombiliqué (**b**) *(navel-like)* déprimé en ombilic

umbilicus [ʌm'bɪlɪkəs, ʌmbɪ'laɪkəs] *(pl* **umbilici** [-saɪ]) *n Anat* ombilic *m*, nombril *m*

umbles ['ʌmbəlz] *npl Arch* entrailles *fpl*, abats *mpl*

[illegible] **bos**) (**a**) *(of shield)* ombon *m*, umbo *m* (**b**) *Zool* umbo *m*, crochet *m* (**c**) *Anat* manche *m* du marteau (**d**) *Bot* protubérance *f*

umbra ['ʌmbrə] *(pl* **umbras** *or* **umbrae** [-bri:]) *n Astron* ombre *f*

umbrage ['ʌmbrɪdʒ] *n* (**a**) *(offence)* **to take umbrage at sth** prendre ombrage de qch, s'offenser de qch (**b**) *Arch or Literary (shadow)* ombrage *m*

umbrageous [ʌm'breɪdʒəs] *adj Arch or Literary* (**a**) *(shady → tree)* ombreux; *(→ place)* ombragé, ombreux (**b**) *(quick to take offence)* ombrageux

umbrella [ʌm'brelə] **1** *n* (**a**) *(device)* parapluie *m*; **to put up** *or* **open an umbrella** ouvrir un parapluie; **to put down** *or* **to close an umbrella** fermer un parapluie

(**b**) *Fig (protection, cover)* protection *f*; **under the umbrella of the United Nations** sous la protection des Nations Unies

(**c**) *Mil* écran *m ou* rideau *m* de protection

(**d**) *(of jellyfish)* ombrelle *f*

(**e**) *Am Fam Mil slang (parachute)* parachute ☐ *m*, pépin *m*

2 *comp (term)* général

▸▸ *Orn* ***umbrella bird*** céphaloptère *m*; ***umbrella committee*** comité *m* de coordination; *Fin* ***umbrella fund*** fonds *m* de consolidation; ***umbrella group, umbrella organization*** organisation *f* qui en regroupe plusieurs autres; ***umbrella pine*** pin *m* parasol; ***umbrella plant*** laîche *f*, carex *m*; ***umbrella stand*** porte-parapluies *m inv*; *Mktg* ***umbrella trademark*** marque *f* ombrelle; ***umbrella tree*** magnolia *m* parasol

Umbria ['ʌmbrɪə] *n* Ombrie *f*

Umbrian ['ʌmbrɪən] **1** *n* Ombrien(enne) *m,f*

2 *adj* ombrien

umiak ['u:mɪæk] *n* oumiac *m*, oumiak *m*

UMIST ['ju:mɪst] *n Br (abbr* **University of Manchester Institute of Science and Technology**) = institut de science et de technologie de l'université de Manchester, en Grande-Bretagne

umlaut ['ʊmlaʊt] *n (in Germanic languages)* umlaut *m*, inflexion *f* vocalique; *(diaeresis)* tréma *m*

ump [ʌmp] *n Am Fam* arbitre ☐ *m*

umph [hm] *exclam (in disbelief, displeasure)* hum!, hmm!

umpire ['ʌmpaɪə(r)] **1** *n* arbitre *m*

2 *vt (match, contest)* arbitrer

3 *vi* servir d'arbitre, être arbitre

umpiring ['ʌmpaɪərɪŋ] *n* arbitrage *m*

umpteen [,ʌmp'ti:n] *Fam* **1** *adj* je ne sais combien de, des tas de; **she's got umpteen dresses** elle a je ne sais combien de robes *ou* des tas de robes; **I've told you umpteen times** je te l'ai dit trente-six fois *ou* cent fois; **umpteen people** des dizaines de gens, des tas de gens

2 *pron* **there were umpteen of them** il y en avait des tas *ou* je ne sais combien

umpteenth [,ʌmp'ti:nθ] *adj Fam* énième, nième; **for the umpteenth time** pour la nième fois

UMW [,ju:em'dʌbəlju:] *n Am (abbr* **United Mineworkers of America**) = syndicat américain de mineurs

UN [,ju:'en] *(abbr* **United Nations**) **1** *n* **the UN** l'ONU *f*, l'Onu *f*

2 *comp* de l'ONU

▸▸ ***UN peacekeeping forces*** les casques *mpl* bleus; ***UN resolution*** résolution *f* de l'ONU; ***the UN security council*** le Conseil de sécurité de l'ONU

'un [ʌn] *pron Fam* **he's only a young 'un** ce n'est qu'un petit gars; **the little 'uns** les petiots *mpl*; **the young 'uns** les jeunots *mpl*; **he's a bad 'un** c'est un sale type

unabashed [,ʌnə'bæʃt] *adj* (**a**) *(undeterred)* nullement décontenancé *ou* déconcerté, imperturbable; **she was quite unabashed by the criticism** elle ne se laissa pas intimider *ou* elle ne fut nullement décontenancée par les critiques; **to carry on unabashed** continuer sans se démonter *ou* décontenancer (**b**) *(unashamed)* sans honte, qui n'a pas honte

unabashedly [,ʌnə'bæʃtlɪ] *adv* (**a**) *(without being discouraged)* sans se laisser décontenancer, sans se démonter (**b**) *(unashamedly)* sans aucune honte

unabated [,ʌnə'beɪtɪd] **1** *adv* [illegible] diminuer; **the storm/the noise continued unabated for most of the night** la tempête/le bruit a continué sans répit pendant une grande partie de la nuit

2 *adj* non diminué; **their enthusiasm was unabated** leur enthousiasme ne diminuait pas, ils montraient toujours autant d'enthousiasme

unabbreviated [,ʌnə'bri:vɪeɪtɪd] *adj (word)* sans abréviation; **in its unabbreviated form** sous sa forme non abrégée, en toutes lettres

unable [,ʌn'eɪbəl] *adj* **to be unable to do sth** *(gen)* ne pas pouvoir faire qch; *(not know how to)* ne pas savoir faire qch; *(be incapable of)* être incapable de faire qch; *(not be in a position to)* ne pas être en mesure de faire qch; *(be prevented from)* être dans l'impossibilité de faire qch; **children who are unable to read/swim** les enfants qui ne savent pas lire/nager; **he seems totally unable to understand** il semble tout à fait incapable de comprendre; **he was unable to pay** il n'était pas en mesure de payer;

unfortunately I'm unable to come malheureusement, je ne peux pas venir *ou* il m'est impossible de venir

unabridged [ˌʌnəˈbrɪdʒd] *adj (text, version, edition)* intégral; **the film is unabridged** le film est dans sa version intégrale

unabsorbed cost [ˌʌnəbzɔːbd-] *n Fin* coût *m* non-absorbé

unacademic [ˌʌnækəˈdemɪk] *adj (person)* peu doué pour les études; *(writing)* peu intellectuel

unaccented [ˌʌnəkˈsentɪd], **unaccentuated** [ˌʌnəkˈsentjʊeɪtɪd] *adj Ling (syllable)* non accentué, atone; *Mus* **unaccented beat** temps *m* faible

unacceptability [ˌʌnəkˈseptəbɪlɪtɪ] *n* caractère *m* intolérable *ou* inadmissible

unacceptable [ˌʌnəkˈseptəbəl] *adj* (**a**) *(intolerable → violence, behaviour)* inadmissible, intolérable; *(→ language)* inacceptable; **it is unacceptable that anyone should have to** *or* **for anyone to have to sleep rough** il est inadmissible que des gens soient obligés de coucher dehors; **the unacceptable face of capitalism** la face honteuse du capitalisme (**b**) *(gift, proposal)* inacceptable

unacceptably [ˌʌnəkˈseptəblɪ] *adv (noisy, rude)* à un point inacceptable *ou* inadmissible; **the film was unacceptably violent** le film était d'une violence inacceptable

unaccommodating [ˌʌnəˈkɒmədeɪtɪŋ] *adj (person)* peu accommodant

unaccompanied [ˌʌnəˈkʌmpənɪd] *adj* (**a**) *(child, traveller)* non accompagné, seul; *(baggage)* non accompagné; **unaccompanied by an adult** non accompagné par un adulte (**b**) *Mus (singing)* sans accompagnement, a capella; *(singer)* non accompagné, a capella; *(song)* sans accompagnement; *(choir)* a capella; **for unaccompanied violin** pour violon seul

unaccomplished [ˌʌnəˈkʌmplɪʃt] *adj* (**a**) *(incomplete → task)* inachevé, inaccompli (**b**) *(unfulfilled → wish, plan)* non réalisé, non accompli (**c**) *(untalented → actor, player)* sans grand talent, médiocre; *(→ performance)* médiocre

unaccountable [ˌʌnəˈkaʊntəbəl] *adj* (**a**) *(inexplicable → disappearance, reason)* inexplicable (**b**) *(not accountable)* qui n'a de comptes à rendre à personne; **to be unaccountable to sb** ne pas avoir à répondre devant qn, ne pas avoir de comptes à rendre à qn; **representatives who are unaccountable to the general public** les représentants qui ne sont pas responsables devant la population

unaccountably [ˌʌnəˈkaʊntəblɪ] *adv* inexplicablement, de manière inexplicable; **she was unaccountably delayed** elle a été retardée sans que l'on sache (trop) pourquoi

unaccounted [ˌʌnəˈkaʊntɪd] **unaccounted for** *adj* (**a**) *(money)* qui manque; **there is still a lot of money unaccounted for** il manque encore beaucoup d'argent; **these sixty pounds are unaccounted for in the balance sheet** ces soixante livres ne figurent pas au bilan (**b**) *(person)* qui manque, qui a disparu; *(plane)* qui n'est pas rentré; **by nightfall, two children were still unaccounted for** à la tombée de la nuit, il manquait encore deux enfants

unaccredited [ˌʌnəˈkredɪtɪd] *adj (agent etc)* non accrédité, sans pouvoirs

unaccustomed [ˌʌnəˈkʌstəmd] *adj* (**a**) *(not used to → person)* **he is unaccustomed to wearing a tie** il n'a pas l'habitude de mettre des cravates; **unaccustomed as I am to public speaking** bien que je n'aie guère l'habitude de prendre la parole en public (**b**) *(unusual, uncharacteristic → rudeness, light-heartedness)* inhabituel, inaccoutumé

unachievable [ˌʌnəˈtʃiːvəbəl] *adj (project etc)* irréalisable, inexécutable

unacknowledged [ˌʌnəkˈnɒlɪdʒd] *adj* (**a**) *(unrecognized → truth, fact)* non reconnu; *(→ qualities, discovery)* non reconnu, méconnu; **he's an unacknowledged genius** c'est un génie méconnu (**b**) *(ignored → letter)* resté sans réponse; **you shouldn't let his letter go unacknowledged** tu ne devrais pas laisser sa lettre sans réponse

unacquainted [ˌʌnəˈkweɪntɪd] *adj* **to be unacquainted with sb/sth** ne pas connaître qn/qch; **I am unacquainted with her** je ne la connais pas, je n'ai pas fait sa connaissance; **we are not unacquainted with pressure** nous n'ignorons pas ce que c'est que le stress

unadapted [ˌʌnəˈdæptɪd] *adj* mal adapté, peu adapté (**to** à)

unaddressed [ˌʌnəˈdrest] *adj (letter, parcel, envelope)* sans adresse, qui ne porte pas d'adresse

unadjusted [ˌʌnəˈdʒʌstɪd] *adj* **unadjusted data** données *fpl* brutes; **figures unadjusted for inflation** des chiffres qui ne tiennent pas compte de l'inflation

unadmired [ˌʌnədˈmaɪəd] *adj* méconnu

unadmitted [ˌʌnədˈmɪtɪd] *adj Law (fault etc)* inavoué

unadopted [ˌʌnəˈdɒptɪd] *adj* (**a**) *Br (road)* non pris en charge *ou* entretenu par la commune (**b**) *(resolution, bill)* non adopté, rejeté (**c**) *(child)* qui n'est pas adopté

unadorned [ˌʌnəˈdɔːnd] *adj (undecorated)* sans ornement, naturel, simple; *esp Literary* **her unadorned beauty** sa beauté sans parure *ou* sans fard; **the unadorned truth** la vérité pure *ou* toute nue

unadulterated [ˌʌnəˈdʌltəreɪtɪd] *adj* (**a**) *(milk, flour)* pur, naturel; *(wine)* non frelaté (**b**) *(pleasure, joy)* pur (et simple), parfait; **the unadulterated truth** la vérité pure et simple; **unadulterated by Western influences** non corrompu par les influences occidentales; **it's unadulterated rubbish!** c'est de la pure bêtise!

unadventurous [ˌʌnədˈventʃərəs] *adj (person)* qui ne prend pas de risques, qui manque d'audace; *(lifestyle)* conventionnel, banal; *(performance)* terne; *(holiday)* banal; **she is an unadventurous cook** c'est une cuisinière qui manque d'imagination

unadventurously [ˌʌnədˈventʃərəslɪ] *adv (produced, designed)* peu audacieusement; *(decide, choose)* sans prendre de risques; **we very unadventurously chose beige carpets again** nous n'avons pas pris de risques et avons encore choisi des moquettes beiges

unadvertised [ˌʌnˈædvətaɪzd] *adj (job)* non affiché, pour lequel il n'y a pas eu d'annonce; *(meeting, visit)* discret(ète), sans publicité

unadvisable [ˌʌnədˈvaɪzəbəl] *adj* imprudent, à déconseiller; **it is unadvisable for her to travel** les voyages lui sont déconseillés, il vaut mieux qu'elle évite de voyager

unadvised [ˌʌnədˈvaɪzd] *adj (unwise)* imprudent

unaesthetic, *Am* **unesthetic** [ˌʌniːsˈθetɪk] *adj* inesthétique

unaffected [ˌʌnəˈfektɪd] *adj* (**a**) *(resistant)* non affecté, qui résiste; **unaffected by cold** qui n'est pas affecté par le *ou* qui résiste au froid; **unaffected by heat** qui résiste à la chaleur

(**b**) *(unchanged, unaltered)* qui n'est pas touché *ou* affecté; **we were unaffected by the war** nous n'avons pas été affectés *ou* touchés par la guerre; **children cannot remain unaffected by TV violence** il est impossible que les enfants ne soient pas affectés *ou* marqués par la violence qu'ils voient à la télé; **there's snow almost everywhere, but the north-west is unaffected** il y a de la neige presque partout, mais le nord-ouest n'est pas touché

(**c**) *(indifferent)* indifférent, insensible; **he seems quite unaffected by his loss** sa perte ne semble pas l'émouvoir, sa perte n'a pas du tout l'air de le toucher

(**d**) *(natural → person, manners, character)* simple, naturel, sans affectation; *(→ style)* simple, sans recherche

►► *Med* ***unaffected carrier*** porteur *m* sain

unaffectedly [ˌʌnəˈfektɪdlɪ] *adv (speak, behave)* sans affectation; *(write, dress)* simplement, sans recherche

unaffectionate [ˌʌnəˈfekʃənət] *adj (person)* froid, qui n'est pas affectueux; *(kiss)* froid, forcé

unaffiliated [ˌʌnəˈfɪlɪeɪtɪd] *adj (unions)* indépendant

unaffordable [ˌʌnəˈfɔːdəbəl] *adj* inabordable

unafraid [ˌʌnəˈfreɪd] *adj* sans peur, qui n'a pas peur; **he was quite unafraid** il n'avait pas du tout peur

unaggressive [ˌʌnəˈgresɪv] *adj* qui n'a rien d'agressif, pacifique

unaided [ˌʌnˈeɪdɪd] **1** *adj* sans aide (extérieure); **it is his own unaided work** c'est un travail qu'il a fait tout seul *ou* sans l'aide de personne; **an impossible task for an unaided person** une tâche qu'il est impossible d'accomplir seul *ou* sans se faire aider

2 *adv (work)* tout seul, sans être aidé; **he did it unaided** il l'a fait tout seul *ou* à lui seul

unaired [ˌʌnˈeəd] *adj* (**a**) *(room)* non aéré (**b**) *(opinions)* non exprimé

unalarmed [ˌʌnəˈlɑːmd] *adj* (**a**) *(not anxious)* pas inquiet (**b**) *(vehicle, building)* non équipé d'une alarme

unaligned [ˌʌnəˈlaɪnd] *adj* (**a**) *(wheels, posts)* non aligné, qui n'est pas aligné (**b**) *Pol* non-aligné

unalike [ˌʌnəˈlaɪk] *adj* différent, peu ressemblant; **the two sisters are quite unalike** les deux sœurs ne se ressemblent pas du tout, les deux sœurs sont très différentes; **they look** *or* **seem quite unalike** ils ne se ressemblent absolument pas

unallayed [ˌʌnəˈleɪd] *adj (grief)* inapaisé; *(desire)* insatisfait; *(joy)* sans mélange; **their fears/suspicions were unallayed by these revelations** ces révélations n'ont en rien dissipé leurs craintes/soupçons

unalleviated [ˌʌnəˈliːvɪeɪtɪd] *adj* sans répit; **unalleviated boredom** ennui *m* mortel

unallocated [ˌʌnˈæləkeɪtɪd] *adj (rooms, places)* non assigné; *(money, grants)* non alloué

unallotted [ˌʌnəˈlɒtɪd] *adj St Exch (shares)* non réparti

unalloyed [ˌʌnəˈlɔɪd] *adj* (**a**) *Literary (joy, enthusiasm)* sans mélange, parfait (**b**) *(metal)* pur, sans alliage

unalterable [ˌʌnˈɔːltərəbəl] *adj (fact)* immuable; *(decision)* irrévocable; *(truth)* certain, immuable

unalterably [ˌʌnˈɔːltərəblɪ] *adv* immuablement

unaltered [ˌʌnˈɔːltəd] *adj* inchangé, non modifié; **the original building remains unaltered** le bâtiment d'origine reste tel quel *ou* n'a pas subi de modifications

unambiguous [ˌʌnæmˈbɪgjʊəs] *adj (wording, rule)* non ambigu, non équivoque; *(thinking)* clair

unambiguously [ˌʌnæmˈbɪgjʊəslɪ] *adv* sans ambiguïté, sans équivoque

unambitious [ˌʌnæmˈbɪʃəs] *adj* sans ambition, peu ambitieux

unambitiously [ˌʌnæmˈbɪʃəslɪ] *adv* (en) faisant preuve d'un manque d'ambition

unambivalent [ˌʌnæmˈbɪvələnt] *adj (person)* clair; *(message)* sans équivoque; *(reply)* sans équivoque, catégorique; *(support)* catégorique

unamended [ˌʌnəˈmendɪd] *adj Law & Parl* sans amendement

un-American *adj* (**a**) *(uncharacteristic)* peu américain; **it's very un-American** ce n'est pas du tout américain (**b**) *(anti-American)* antiaméricain

unamplified [ʌnˈæmplɪfaɪd] *adj (sound)* non amplifié

unamused [ˌʌnəˈmjuːzd] *adj* qui n'est pas amusé; **she was distinctly unamused** visiblement, cela ne l'amusait pas

unamusing [ˌʌnəˈmjuːzɪŋ] *adj* peu amusant; **the story was not unamusing** l'histoire ne manquait pas d'humour *ou* n'était pas sans humour

unanimity [juːnəˈnɪmətɪ] *n* unanimité *f*; **there must be unanimity on the issue** il faut qu'il y ait unanimité à ce sujet

unanimous [juːˈnænɪməs] *adj* unanime; **passed by a unanimous vote** voté à l'unanimité; **we must give him our unanimous support** il faut que nous soyons unanimes à le soutenir; **the audience was unanimous in its approval** le public a approuvé à l'unanimité; **to reach a unanimous decision** se prononcer à l'unanimité

unanimously [juːˈnænɪməslɪ] *adv (decide, agree)* à l'unanimité, unanimement; *(vote)* à l'unanimité

unannounced [ˌʌnəˈnaʊnst] **1** *adj (arrival, event)* inattendu; **their unannounced arrival caused some confusion** leur arrivée inattendue a provoqué une certaine confusion

2 *adv (unexpectedly)* de manière inattendue,

sans se faire annoncer; *(suddenly)* subitement; **he turned up unannounced** il est arrivé à l'improviste

unanswerable [ˌʌn'ɑːnsərəbəl] *adj* (**a**) *(impossible → question, problem)* auquel il est impossible de répondre (**b**) *(irrefutable → argument, logic)* irréfutable, incontestable

unanswered [ˌʌn'ɑːnsəd] **1** *adj* (**a**) *(question)* qui reste sans réponse; *(prayer)* inexaucé; **my main argument was left unanswered** on n'a toujours pas réfuté mon argument principal; *Law* **an unanswered charge** une accusation non réfutée *ou* irréfutée

(**b**) *(unsolved → mystery, puzzle)* non résolu

(**c**) *(letter, question)* (resté) sans réponse; **I have 6 unanswered letters to deal with** il y a 6 lettres auxquelles je n'ai pas encore répondu; **I had to leave two questions unanswered** j'ai dû laisser deux questions sans réponse

(**d**) *Literary* **unanswered love** amour *m* non partagé

2 *adv* **to go unanswered** rester sans réponse

unanticipated [ˌʌnæn'tɪsɪpeɪtɪd] *adj (success, arrival)* inattendu; *(situation, event, result, outcome)* imprévu, inattendu; *(announcement)* inattendu, surprenant

unapologetic [ˌʌnəpɒlə'dʒetɪk] *adj* **he's an unapologetic royalist/admirer of Hitler** il ne se cache pas d'être royaliste/d'être un admirateur d'Hitler; **they're unapologetic about it** ils estiment qu'il n'ont pas à s'excuser

unapologetically [ˌʌnəpɒlə'dʒetɪkəlɪ] *adv (react, behave)* sans manifester le moindre regret, sans présenter la moindre excuse; **the article is unapologetically biased** l'auteur de l'article ne prétend pas du tout à l'objectivité

unapparent [ˌʌnə'pærənt] *adj* peu apparent, non évident

unappealing [ˌʌnə'piːlɪŋ] *adj* peu attrayant, peu attirant

unappealingly [ˌʌnə'piːlɪŋlɪ] *adv* de façon peu attrayante *ou* attirante

unappeasable [ˌʌnə'piːzəbəl] *adj Literary (hunger, desire)* inassouvissable; *(pain)* inapaisable

unappeased [ˌʌnə'piːzd] *adj Literary (hunger, desire)* inassouvi; *(pain)* inapaisé

unappetizing [ˌʌn'æpɪtaɪzɪŋ] *adj* peu appétissant

unappreciated [ˌʌnə'priːʃɪeɪtɪd] **1** *adj (person, talents)* méconnu, incompris; *(efforts, kindness)* non apprécié, qui n'est pas apprécié

2 *adv* **her efforts go unappreciated** le mal qu'elle se donne n'est pas apprécié à sa juste valeur

unappreciative [ˌʌnə'priːʃɪətɪv] *adj (audience)* froid, indifférent; **to be unappreciative of sth** être indifférent à qch

unapprehensive [ˌʌnæprɪ'hensɪv] *adj Literary* sans appréhension (**of** de); **to be unapprehensive of danger** ne pas appréhender le danger, être insouciant du danger

unapprised [ˌʌnə'praɪzd] *adj Literary* non informé, ignorant (**of** de)

unapproachable [ˌʌnə'prəʊtʃəbəl] *adj* (**a**) *(person)* inabordable, d'un abord difficile (**b**) *(place)* inaccessible, inabordable; **unapproachable by road** inaccessible par la route

unappropriated [ˌʌnə'prəʊprɪeɪtɪd] *adj Fin (money)* inutilisé, disponible

►► ***unappropriated profits*** bénéfices non distribués

unapproved [ˌʌnə'pruːvd] *adj* (**a**) *(method, practice)* non reconnu, non admis (**b**) *(not officially authorized)* non approuvé, non agréé

unarguable [ˌʌn'ɑːgjʊəbəl] *adj* incontestable

unarguably [ˌʌn'ɑːgjʊəblɪ] *adv* incontestablement

unarmed [ˌʌn'ɑːmd] *adj* (**a**) *(person, vehicle)* sans armes, non armé; **I'm not going in there unarmed** je n'entre pas là-dedans sans arme (**b**) *Bot* sans épines

►► ***unarmed combat*** combat *m* à mains nues

unarmoured [ˌʌn'ɑːməd] *adj Mil* non blindé

unarticulated [ˌʌnɑː'tɪkjəleɪtɪd] *adj* non exprimé

unartistic [ˌʌnɑː'tɪstɪk] *adj (decor)* peu artistique; *(person)* peu artiste

unartistically [ˌʌnɑː'tɪstɪkəlɪ] *adv (arranged, decorated)* avec un manque de sens esthétique

unary ['juːnərɪ] *adj* unaire, monadique

unashamed [ˌʌnə'ʃeɪmd] *adj (curiosity, gaze)* sans gêne; *(greed, lie, hypocrisy)* effronté, sans scrupule; *(person)* sans honte; **to be unashamed about doing sth** ne pas avoir honte de faire qch; **he was quite unashamed about** *or* **of his huge wealth** il ne se cachait pas de son immense richesse, il étalait son immense richesse sans vergogne *ou* sans pudeur; **with unashamed relief** avec un soulagement non dissimulé

unashamedly [ˌʌnə'ʃeɪmɪdlɪ] *adv (brazenly)* sans honte, sans scrupule; *(openly)* sans honte, sans se cacher; **George was unashamedly in favour of the war** George se déclarait ouvertement en faveur de la guerre; **she lied quite unashamedly** elle mentait absolument sans vergogne, c'était une menteuse tout à fait éhontée; **he is unashamedly greedy** il est d'une gourmandise éhontée

unasked [ˌʌn'ɑːskt] **1** *adj (question)* que l'on n'a pas posé; **the central question is still unasked** la question essentielle reste à poser

2 *adv* **he came unasked** il est venu sans avoir été invité; **they did the job unasked** ils ont fait le travail sans qu'on le leur ait demandé *ou* spontanément

unasked-for *adj (gift)* spontané, qu'on n'a pas demandé; *(advice)* non sollicité

unaspirated [ˌʌn'æspɪreɪtɪd] *adj Ling* non aspiré

unassailable [ˌʌnə'seɪləbəl] *adj (fort, city)* imprenable, inébranlable; *(certainty, belief)* inébranlable; *(reputation)* inattaquable; *(argument, reason)* inattaquable, irréfutable; **to be in an unassailable position** être dans une position inattaquable

unassertive [ˌʌnə'sɜːtɪv] *adj (person)* qui manque d'assurance, qui ne sait pas s'imposer

unassertively [ˌʌnə'sɜːtɪvlɪ] *adv (behave)* sans savoir s'imposer; *(say)* d'un ton mal assuré

unassertiveness [ˌʌnə'sɜːtɪvnɪs] *n* manque *m* d'assurance

unassigned [ˌʌnə'saɪnd] *adj (office, room → for person)* non attribué; *(→ for purpose)* non affecté; *(task)* non assigné

►► *Fin* ***unassigned revenue*** recettes *fpl* non gagées

unassimilated [ˌʌnə'sɪmɪleɪtɪd] *adj* inassimilé; **unassimilated knowledge** connaissances *fpl* mal assimilées

unassisted [ˌʌnə'sɪstɪd] **1** *adv* sans aide, tout seul

2 *adj* **to be unassisted** ne pas être aidé

unassociated [ˌʌnə'səʊʃɪeɪtɪd] *adj (facts, events)* sans lien entre eux

unassuaged [ˌʌnə'sweɪdʒd] *adj Literary (grief, pain, person)* inapaisé; *(hunger, thirst)* inassouvi

unassuming [ˌʌnə'sjuːmɪŋ] *adj* modeste, sans prétention(s)

unassumingly [ˌʌnə'sjuːmɪŋlɪ] *adv* modestement, sans prétention(s)

unattached [ˌʌnə'tætʃt] *adj* (**a**) *(unconnected → building, part, group)* indépendant (**b**) *(wire)* à attacher sôi-même (**c**) *(not in relationship)* libre, sans attaches

unattackable [ˌʌnə'tækəbəl] *adj (place, position)* inattaquable

unattainable [ˌʌnə'teɪnəbəl] *adj (goal, place)* inaccessible

unattempted [ˌʌnə'temptɪd] *adj* jamais tenté

unattended [ˌʌnə'tendɪd] *adj* (**a**) *(vehicle, luggage)* laissé sans surveillance; **do not leave small children unattended** ne laissez pas de jeunes enfants sans surveillance *ou* tout seuls; **do not leave luggage unattended** ne laissez pas vos bagages sans surveillance

(**b**) *(person)* sans escorte, seul; **I can't even go to the toilet unattended** je ne peux même pas aller aux toilettes seul; **don't leave the guests unattended (to)** ne négligez pas les invités, occupez-vous des invités

unattested [ˌʌnə'testɪd] *adj (fact)* non attesté; *Law (certificate etc)* non légalisé

unattractive [ˌʌnə'træktɪv] *adj (room, wallpaper, decor)* peu attrayant, assez laid; *(smile, face, person)* peu attirant, dépourvu de charme; *(habit)* peu attrayant, désagréable, déplaisant; *(personality)* déplaisant, peu sympathique; *(prospect)* désagréable, peu attrayant, peu agréable

unattractively [ˌʌnə'træktɪvlɪ] *adv (dressed, furnished)* d'une façon peu attrayante

unattractiveness [ˌʌnə'træktɪvnɪs] *n (of face, town, landscape)* manque *m* d'attrait; *(of room, wallpaper, decor)* laideur *f*; *(of person)* manque *m* de charme; **the unattractiveness of his habits** ses habitudes déplaisantes

unattributable [ˌʌnə'trɪbjʊtəbəl] *adj (words, text, quotation)* de source inconnue

unattributed [ˌʌnə'trɪbjʊtɪd] *adj* de source inconnue

unau ['juːnɔː] *n Zool* unau *m*

unaudited [ˌʌn'ɔːdɪtɪd] *adj (accounts)* non vérifié

unauthentic [ˌʌnɔː'θentɪk] *adj* (**a**) *(not genuine)* non authentique (**b**) *(not believable)* peu vraisemblable

unauthenticated [ˌʌnɔː'θentɪkeɪtɪd] *adj (story)* non vérifié; *(painting, handwriting)* non authentifié; *(evidence)* non établi

unauthoritative [ˌʌnɔː'θɒrɪtətɪv] *adj* (**a**) *(manner, person)* sans autorité (**b**) *(article, report)* qui manque de sérieux

unauthorized [ˌʌn'ɔːθəraɪzd] *adj (absence, entry)* non autorisé, fait sans autorisation

►► *Comput* ***unauthorized access*** accès *m* non autorisé

unavailability [ˌʌnəveɪlə'bɪlɪtɪ] *n* indisponibilité *f*

unavailable [ˌʌnə'veɪləbəl] *adj (person)* indisponible, qui n'est pas libre; *(resources)* indisponible, qu'on ne peut se procurer; **the book is unavailable** *(in library, bookshop)* le livre n'est pas disponible; *(from publisher)* le livre est épuisé; **Mr Fox is unavailable** M. Fox n'est pas disponible *ou* libre; **the minister was unavailable for comment** le ministre s'est refusé à tout commentaire

unavailing [ˌʌnə'veɪlɪŋ] *adj (effort, attempt)* vain, inutile; *(method)* inefficace

unavailingly [ˌʌnə'veɪlɪŋlɪ] *adv* en vain, sans succès

unavenged [ˌʌnə'vendʒd] *adv* **it won't go unavenged** cela ne restera pas impuni; **the unavenged death of his sister** la mort de sa sœur qui n'a pas été vengée

unavoidable [ˌʌnə'vɔɪdəbəl] *adj (accident, delay)* inévitable; **it is unavoidable that...** il est inévitable que... + *subjunctive*

►► *Fin* ***unavoidable costs*** coûts *mpl* induits

unavoidably [ˌʌnə'vɔɪdəblɪ] *adv (happen)* inévitablement; *(detain)* malencontreusement; **I was unavoidably delayed** j'ai été retardé malgré moi *ou* pour des raisons indépendantes de ma volonté

unavowed [ˌʌnə'vaʊd] *adj* inavoué

unawakened [ˌʌnə'weɪkənd] *adj* non encore éveillé

unaware [ˌʌnə'weə(r)] *adj (ignorant)* inconscient, qui ignore; **to be unaware of** *(facts)* ignorer, ne pas être au courant de; *(danger)* être inconscient de, ne pas avoir conscience de; **I was unaware that they had arrived** j'ignorais *ou* je ne savais pas qu'ils étaient arrivés; **her husband was totally unaware of what was going on** son mari ne se rendait absolument pas compte de ce qui se passait; **he continued unaware of what was happening** il a continué, ignorant de ce qui se passait *ou* sans [illegible] qui se passait; **she is politically unaware** elle n'a aucune conscience politique, elle ignore tout de la politique; **he seemed quite unaware that he was being watched** il semblait tout à fait ignorer qu'on l'observait, il ne semblait pas du tout remarquer qu'on l'observait; **we are not unaware of the need for reform** nous avons conscience de la nécessité d'une réforme

unawares [ˌʌnə'weəz] *adv* (**a**) *(by surprise)* au dépourvu, à l'improviste; **to catch** *or* **to take sb unawares** prendre qn à l'improviste *ou* au dépourvu; **the photographer caught us unawares** le photographe nous a pris sans que nous nous en rendions compte *ou* à notre insu (**b**) *(unknowingly)* inconsciemment (**c**) *(by accident)* par mégarde, par inadvertance

unawed [ˌʌn'ɔːd] *adj Literary* aucunement intimidé

unbaked [ˌʌn'beɪkt] *adj* (**a**) *(brick etc)* cru (**b**) *Culin* pas encore cuit

unbalance [ˌʌn'bæləns] **1** *vt* déséquilibrer

2 *n* déséquilibre *m*

una–unb

unbalanced [ˌʌnˈbælənst] *adj* (**a**) *(load)* mal équilibré (**b**) *(person, mind)* déséquilibré, désaxé (**c**) *(reporting)* tendancieux, partial (**d**) *Fin (economy)* déséquilibré; *Acct (account)* non soldé (**e**) *Elec (circuit, load)* déséquilibré

unbandage [ˌʌnˈbændɪdʒ] *vt (wound)* débander

unbankable [ˌʌnˈbæŋkəbəl] *adj Fin (bill)* non bancable
▸▸ ***unbankable paper*** papier *m* non bancable

unbanked [ʌnˈbæŋkt] *adj (cheque)* qui n'a pas encore été déposé à la banque

unbaptized [ˌʌnbæpˈtaɪzd] *adj* non baptisé

unbar [ˌʌnˈbɑː(r)] *(pt & pp* **unbarred,** *cont* **unbarring**) *vt* (**a**) *(door, gate)* enlever la barre de (**b**) *Fig (path, road)* ouvrir; **the decision could unbar the way to a lasting solution** cette décision pourrait bien ouvrir la voie à une solution durable

unbearable [ˌʌnˈbeərəbəl] *adj* insupportable

'The Unbearable Lightness of Being' *Kundera, Kaufman* 'L'Insoutenable légèreté de l'être'

unbearably [ˌʌnˈbeərəblɪ] *adv* insupportablement; **he is unbearably conceited** il est d'une vanité insupportable; **it's unbearably hot** il fait une chaleur insupportable; **he's unbearably arrogant** son arrogance est insupportable

unbeatable [ˌʌnˈbiːtəbəl] *adj (champion, prices)* imbattable; **it's unbeatable value for money** le rapport qualité-prix est imbattable

unbeaten [ˌʌnˈbiːtən] *adj (fighter, team)* invaincu; *(record, price)* non battu; **the record has remained unbeaten for 20 years** le record n'a pas été battu depuis 20 ans

unbecoming [ˌʌnbɪˈkʌmɪŋ] *adj* (**a**) *(garment, colour, hat)* peu seyant, qui ne va pas; **that coat is rather unbecoming** ce manteau ne lui/te/*etc* va pas (**b**) *(behaviour)* malséant

unbefitting [ˌʌnbɪˈfɪtɪŋ] *adj* peu convenable, peu seyant; **in a manner unbefitting a member of parliament** d'une façon qui ne sied pas à un député

unbeknown [ˌʌnbɪˈnəʊn], **unbeknownst** [ˌʌnbɪˈnəʊn(st)] *adv* **unbeknown to** à l'insu de; **unbeknown to him** à son insu, sans qu'il le sache

unbelief [ˌʌnbɪˈliːf] *n* (**a**) *(incredulity)* incrédulité *f* (**b**) *Rel* incroyance *f*

unbelievable [ˌʌnbɪˈliːvəbəl] *adj* (**a**) *(extraordinary)* incroyable; **it's unbelievable that they should want to marry so young** il est incroyable *ou* je n'arrive pas à croire qu'ils veuillent se marier si jeunes; **she has an unbelievable number of clothes** elle a une quantité incroyable de vêtements; **unbelievable stupidity** stupidité *f* incroyable; **unbelievable good fortune** chance *f* insolente *ou* incroyable
(**b**) *(implausible)* incroyable, invraisemblable; **his story was totally unbelievable** son histoire était totalement incroyable *ou* à dormir debout

unbelievably [ˌʌnbɪˈliːvəblɪ] *adv* (**a**) *(extraordinarily)* incroyablement, extraordinairement; **unbelievably beautiful/cruel** d'une beauté/cruauté incroyable *ou* extraordinaire; **unbelievably, he agreed** aussi incroyable que cela puisse paraître, il a accepté (**b**) *(implausibly)* invraisemblablement, incroyablement

unbeliever [ˌʌnbɪˈliːvə(r)] *n Rel* incroyant(e) *m,f*

unbelieving [ˌʌnbɪˈliːvɪŋ] *adj (gen)* incrédule, sceptique; *Rel* incroyant

unbelievingly [ˌʌnbɪˈliːvɪŋlɪ] *adv (look, speak)* d'un air incrédule

unbelt [ˌʌnˈbelt] *vt* défaire la ceinture de

unbelted [ˌʌnˈbeltɪd] *adj* sans ceinture

unbend [ˌʌnˈbend] *(pt & pp* **unbent** [-ˈbent]) **1** *vt (fork, wire)* redresser, détordre
2 *vi (relax)* se détendre

unbending [ˌʌnˈbendɪŋ] *adj* (**a**) *(will, attitude)* intransigeant, inflexible; **she remained unbending on the issue** elle est restée intransigeante sur la question; **his unbending puritanism** son puritanisme rigide (**b**) *(pipe, metal)* rigide, non flexible

unbiased, unbiassed [ˌʌnˈbaɪəst] *adj* impartial

unbiblical [ˌʌnˈbɪblɪkəl] *adj* qui n'est pas conforme à la bible

unbiddable [ˌʌnˈbɪdəbəl] *adj Br* désobéissant, indocile

unbidden [ˌʌnˈbɪdən] *adv Literary* spontanément, sans que l'on demande; **she did it unbidden** elle l'a fait de son propre chef *ou* sans qu'on le lui ait demandé; **she entered unbidden** elle est entrée sans y avoir été invitée; **the thought came unbidden to my mind** l'idée m'est venue spontanément

unbind [ˌʌnˈbaɪnd] *(pt & pp* **unbound** [-ˈbaʊnd]) *vt (prisoner)* délier; *(bandage)* défaire, dérouler

unbleached [ˌʌnˈbliːtʃt] *adj (fabric)* écru

unblemished [ˌʌnˈblemɪʃt] *adj (purity, skin, colour, reputation)* sans tache, sans défaut; **an unblemished record** un parcours sans faute

unblended [ˌʌnˈblendɪd] *adj (gen)* pur; *(whisky)* pur malt

unblinking [ˌʌnˈblɪŋkɪŋ] *adj (impassive)* impassible; *(fearless)* impassible, imperturbable; **she stared at me with unblinking eyes** elle me regarda fixement *ou* sans ciller

unblock [ˌʌnˈblɒk] *vt (sink, pipe)* déboucher; *(road, path, traffic jam)* dégager

unblushing [ˌʌnˈblʌʃɪŋ] *adj* éhonté

unblushingly [ˌʌnˈblʌʃɪŋlɪ] *adv* sans rougir

unbolt [ˌʌnˈbəʊlt] *vt (door)* déverrouiller, tirer le verrou de; *(scaffolding)* déboulonner

unbonded warehouse [ˌʌnˈbɒndɪd-] *n* entrepôt *m* fictif

unborn [ˌʌnˈbɔːn] *adj (child)* qui n'est pas encore né

unbosom [ˌʌnˈbʊzəm] *vt Literary (secret, emotions)* confesser; **to unbosom oneself to sb** ouvrir son cœur à qn, se confier à qn

unbothered [ˈʌnˈbɒðəd] *adj* **we're/they're unbothered about it** ça nous/leur est égal, ça ne nous/les dérange pas

unbound [ˌʌnˈbaʊnd] **1** *pt & pp of* **unbind**
2 *adj* (**a**) *(prisoner, hands)* non lié (**b**) *(book, periodical)* non relié (**c**) *Ling (morpheme)* libre

unbounded [ˌʌnˈbaʊndɪd] *adj (gratitude, admiration)* illimité, sans borne; *(pride, greed)* démesuré

unbowed [ˌʌnˈbaʊd] *adj* insoumis, invaincu; **they stood with their heads unbowed** ils étaient debout, la tête haute

unbranded [ˌʌnˈbrændɪd] *adj Mktg* sans marque

unbreakable [ˌʌnˈbreɪkəbəl] *adj* (**a**) *(crockery)* incassable (**b**) *(habit)* dont on ne peut pas se débarrasser (**c**) *(promise)* sacré; *(will, spirit)* inébranlable, que l'on ne peut briser

unbreathable [ˌʌnˈbriːðəbəl] *adj (air)* irrespirable

unbribable [ˌʌnˈbraɪbəbəl] *adj* incorruptible

unbridled [ˌʌnˈbraɪdəld] *adj (horse)* débridé, sans bride; *(anger, greed)* sans retenue, effréné; *(passion, enthusiasm)* débridé

unbridgeable [ˌʌnˈbrɪdʒəbəl] *adj (gap)* impossible à combler

un-British *adj* peu britannique; **with a rather un-British loss of self-control** avec un manque de sang-froid assez peu britannique

unbroken [ˌʌnˈbrəʊkən] *adj* (**a**) *(line)* continu; *(surface, expanse)* continu, ininterrompu; *(sleep, tradition, peace)* ininterrompu; **the peace remained unbroken for ten years** la paix n'a pas été troublée pendant dix ans
(**b**) *(crockery, eggs)* intact, non cassé; *(fastening, seal)* intact, non brisé; *(record)* non battu
(**c**) *Fig (promise)* tenu, non rompu; *(rules)* toujours observé *ou* respecté; **despite all her troubles, her spirit remains unbroken** malgré tous ses ennuis, elle garde le moral *ou* elle ne se laisse pas abattre
(**d**) *(voice)* qui n'a pas (encore) mué
(**e**) *(horse)* indompté

unbrotherly [ˌʌnˈbrʌðəlɪ] *adj* peu fraternel

unbruised [ˌʌnˈbruːzd] *adj (person)* indemne; *(fruit)* sans meurtrissures; *Fig (pride)* intact; **he escaped unbruised** il s'en est sorti indemne

unbuckle [ˌʌnˈbʌkəl] *vt (belt)* déboucler, dégrafer; *(shoe)* défaire la boucle de

unbuilt [ʌnˈbɪlt, ˈʌnbɪlt] *adj (ground, plot)* vague, non construit

unbundle [ˌʌnˈbʌndəl] *vt* (**a**) *Com (company)* dégrouper; *(products, services)* détailler, tarifer séparément (**b**) *Comput* décompresser

unbundling [ˌʌnˈbʌndəlɪŋ] *n Com (of company)* dégroupage *m*; *(of products, services)* tarification *f* séparée

unburden [ˌʌnˈbɜːdən] *vt* (**a**) *Formal* décharger (d'un fardeau); **can I unburden you of your bags?** puis-je vous décharger de vos sacs? (**b**) *Fig (heart)* livrer, épancher, soulager; *(grief, guilt)* se décharger de; *(conscience, soul)* soulager; **to unburden oneself to sb** se confier à qn, s'épancher auprès de qn; **she unburdened her heart to me** elle s'est confiée à moi, elle m'a ouvert son cœur

unburied [ˌʌnˈberɪd] *adj* non enterré, non enseveli

unburned [ˌʌnˈbɜːnd], **unburnt** [ˌʌnˈbɜːnt] *adj* non brûlé

unbusinesslike [ˌʌnˈbɪznɪslaɪk] *adj (person)* peu commerçant, qui n'a pas le sens des affaires; *(procedure, handling)* peu professionnel; **to conduct one's affairs in an unbusinesslike way** mal mener ses affaires

unbuttered [ˌʌnˈbʌtəd] *adj* sans beurre

unbutton [ˌʌnˈbʌtən] **1** *vt (shirt, jacket)* déboutonner
2 *vi Fam Fig* se déboutonner

unbuttoned [ˌʌnˈbʌtənd] *adj Fam (relaxed)* décontracté

uncaged [ˌʌnˈkeɪdʒd] *adj* en liberté

uncalculated [ˌʌnˈkælkjʊleɪtɪd] *adj (unintentional)* non délibéré

uncallable [ˌʌnˈkɔːləbəl] *adj Fin (bond)* non remboursable

uncalled [ˌʌnˈkɔːld] *adj Fin (capital)* non appelé

uncalled-for *adj (rudeness, outburst, rebuke)* qui n'est pas nécessaire, injustifié; *(remark)* mal à propos, déplacé; **that was quite uncalled-for!** c'était tout à fait injustifié!

uncannily [ˌʌnˈkænɪlɪ] *adv (accurate, familiar)* étrangement; *(quiet)* mystérieusement, étrangement

uncanny [ˌʌnˈkænɪ] *(compar* **uncannier,** *superl* **uncanniest**) *adj* (**a**) *(strange → accuracy, likeness, ability)* troublant, étrange; **it's uncanny how you always know what I'm thinking** c'est curieux *ou* bizarre ce don que tu as de toujours savoir ce que je pense (**b**) *(eerie → place)* sinistre, qui donne le frisson; *(→ noise)* mystérieux, sinistre; *(→ atmosphere)* étrange, sinistre

uncanonical [ˌʌnkəˈnɒnɪkəl] *adj Rel (text)* non canonique; *(practice)* contraire aux canons (de l'église)

uncap [ˌʌnˈkæp] *(pt & pp* **uncapped,** *cont* **uncapping**) *vt (bottle, jar)* décapsuler, déboucher

uncared-for [ˌʌnˈkeəd-] *adj (appearance)* négligé, peu soigné; *(house, bicycle)* négligé, (laissé) à l'abandon; *(child)* laissé à l'abandon, délaissé

uncaring [ˌʌnˈkeərɪŋ] *adj (unfeeling)* insensible, dur

uncarpeted [ˌʌnˈkɑːpɪtɪd] *adj* sans tapis, sans moquette

uncashed [ˌʌnˈkæʃt] *adj* non encaissé

uncatalogued [ˌʌnˈkætəlɒgd] *adj* qui n'est pas catalogué

uncaught [ˌʌnˈkɔːt] *adj (escapee)* qui n'a pas été appréhendé

unceasing [ˌʌnˈsiːsɪŋ] *adj* incessant, continuel

unceasingly [ˌʌnˈsiːsɪŋlɪ] *adv* sans cesse, continuellement

uncelebrated [ˌʌnˈselɪbreɪtɪd] *adj (birthday, success)* non célébré *ou* fêté

uncensored [ˌʌnˈsensəd] *adj (correspondance)* non censuré; *(text)* non expurgé, non censuré

uncensured [ˌʌnˈsenʃəd] *adj* sans blâme

unceremonious [ˈʌnˌserɪˈməʊnɪəs] *adj* (**a**) *(abrupt)* brusque; **after his unceremonious departure from politics** après qu'il eut peu glorieusement abandonné la politique (**b**) *(without ceremony)* sans façon; **his unceremonious dismissal** son brusque renvoi; **he was packed off in a very unceremonious way to stay with his uncle in Australia** on l'a envoyé très cavalièrement *ou* sans aucune cérémonie chez son oncle en Australie

unceremoniously [ˈʌnˌserɪˈməʊnɪəslɪ] *adv* (**a**) *(abruptly)* avec brusquerie, brusquement (**b**) *(without ceremony)* sans cérémonie; **they were pushed unceremoniously into the back of the**

police van on les a poussés brutalement à l'arrière de la voiture cellulaire

uncertain [ˌʌn'sɜːtən] *adj* (**a**) *(unsure)* incertain; **we were uncertain whether to continue** *or* **we should continue** nous ne savions pas trop si nous devions continuer; **they were uncertain how to begin** ils ne savaient pas trop comment commencer; **I feel uncertain about him** j'ai des doutes à son sujet; **to be uncertain about sth** être inquiet au sujet de *ou* incertain de qch
(**b**) *(unpredictable → result, outcome)* incertain, aléatoire; *(→ weather)* incertain; **it's uncertain whether we'll succeed or not** il n'est pas sûr *ou* certain que nous réussissions; **in no uncertain terms** en termes on ne peut plus clairs, sans mâcher ses mots
(**c**) *(unknown)* inconnu, incertain; **the cause of her death is still uncertain** la cause de sa mort reste inconnue, on ignore encore la cause de sa mort
(**d**) *(unsteady → voice, steps)* hésitant, mal assuré
(**e**) *(undecided → plans)* incertain, pas sûr

uncertainly [ˌʌn'sɜːtənlɪ] *adv* avec hésitation, d'une manière hésitante

uncertainty [ˌʌn'sɜːtəntɪ] *(pl* **uncertainties***)* *n* incertitude *f*, doute *m*; **to be in a state of uncertainty** être dans le doute; **I am in some uncertainty as to whether I should tell him** je ne sais pas trop *ou* je ne suis pas trop sûre si je dois le lui dire ou non; **there's still some uncertainty as to what was actually said** il reste quelque incertitude sur ce qui s'est réellement dit; **to remove any uncertainty** pour dissiper toute équivoque; **is there any uncertainty about what to do?** est-ce que quelqu'un a des doutes sur ce qu'il faut faire?; **financial uncertainties** incertitudes *fpl* financières
►► *Phys* ***uncertainty principle*** principe *m* d'incertitude *ou* d'indétermination de Heisenberg

uncertificated [ˌʌnsə'tɪfɪkeɪtɪd] *adj* sans diplôme, non diplômé

uncertified [ˌʌn'sɜːtɪfaɪd] *adj (copy)* non certifié; *(doctor, teacher)* non diplômé
►► *Am* ***uncertified teacher*** ≃ maître *m* auxiliaire

unchain [ˌʌn'tʃeɪn] *vt (door, dog)* enlever *ou* défaire les chaînes de, désenchaîner; *(emotions)* déchaîner

unchallengeable [ˌʌn'tʃælɪndʒəbəl] *adj (argument)* irréfutable; *(right)* incontestable; *Law (evidence, proof)* irrécusable; **to be in an unchallengeable position** *(runner, team, politician etc)* être hors d'atteinte

unchallenged [ˌʌn'tʃælɪndʒd] **1** *adj* (**a**) *(authority, leader)* incontesté, indiscuté; *(version)* non contesté; **his position/his authority remains unchallenged** sa position/son autorité reste incontestée
(**b**) *Law (witness)* non récusé; *(evidence)* non contesté
2 *adv* (**a**) *(unquestioned)* sans discussion, sans protestation; **her decisions always go unchallenged** ses décisions ne sont jamais contestées *ou* discutées; **that remark cannot go unchallenged** on ne peut pas laisser passer cette remarque sans protester
(**b**) *(unchecked)* sans rencontrer d'opposition; **he walked into the army base unchallenged** il est entré dans la base militaire sans être interpellé *ou* sans rencontrer d'opposition

unchangeable [ˌʌn'tʃeɪndʒəbəl] *adj* immuable, invariable

unchanged [ˌʌn'tʃeɪndʒd] *adj* inchangé; *Med* **his condition remains unchanged** son état est stationnaire

unchanging [ˌʌn'tʃeɪndʒɪŋ] *adj* invariable, immuable

unchaperoned [ˌʌn'ʃæpərəʊnd] *adj (young woman)* qui n'est pas chaperonnée, non accompagnée

uncharacteristic ['ʌnˌkærəktə'rɪstɪk] *adj* peu caractéristique, peu typique; **it's uncharacteristic of him** cela ne lui ressemble pas; **it's uncharacteristic for her to make a mistake like that** ce n'est pas dans son habitude de faire une erreur pareille

uncharacteristically ['ʌnˌkærəktə'rɪstɪklɪ] *adv* d'une façon peu caractéristique

uncharitable [ˌʌn'tʃærɪtəbəl] *adj (unkind)* peu charitable, peu indulgent

uncharitably [ˌʌn'tʃærɪtəblɪ] *adv* peu charitablement, sans charité

uncharted [ˌʌn'tʃɑːtɪd] *adj* (**a**) *(unmapped → region, forest, ocean)* dont on n'a pas dressé la carte; *(not on map)* qui n'est pas sur la carte (**b**) *Fig* **we're moving into uncharted waters** nous faisons un saut dans l'inconnu; **we're sailing in uncharted waters** nous ne savons pas où nous allons; **the uncharted regions of the mind** les profondeurs inexplorées de l'esprit

unchaste [ˌʌn'tʃeɪst] *adj Literary* impudique, non chaste

unchastened [ˌʌn'tʃeɪsənd] *adj (person)* aucunement repentant, nullement assagi; **he was unchastened by his experience** son expérience n'a rien rabattu de ses prétentions

unchecked [ˌʌn'tʃekt] **1** *adj* (**a**) *(unrestricted → growth, expansion, tendency)* non maîtrisé; *(anger, instinct)* non réprimé, auquel on laisse libre cours
(**b**) *(unverified → source, figures)* non vérifié; *(proofs)* non relu
2 *adv* (**a**) *(grow, expand)* continuellement, sans arrêt; *(continue)* impunément, sans opposition; **such rudeness can't go unchecked** on ne peut pas laisser passer une telle impolitesse *ou* grossièreté; **the growth of industry continued unchecked** la croissance industrielle s'est poursuivie de façon constante
(**b**) *(advance)* sans rencontrer d'opposition

unchivalrous [ˌʌn'ʃɪvəlrəs] *adj* peu galant, discourtois

unchosen [ˌʌn'tʃəʊzən] *adj* qui n'a pas été choisi; **to be left unchosen** ne pas avoir été choisi, être laissé de côté

unchristian [ˌʌn'krɪstʃən] *adj* (**a**) *Rel* peu chrétien (**b**) *Fig* barbare; **this is an unchristian hour to phone someone!** ce n'est pas une heure pour téléphoner aux gens!

unchurch [ˌʌn'tʃɜːtʃ] *vt (person)* excommunier; *(building)* déconsacrer

uncial ['ʌnsɪəl] **1** *adj* oncial
2 *n* onciale *f*

uncircumcised [ˌʌn'sɜːkəmsaɪzd] *adj* incirconcis

uncivil [ˌʌn'sɪvəl] *adj* impoli, grossier; **to be uncivil to sb** être impoli envers *ou* à l'égard de qn

uncivilized [ˌʌn'sɪvɪlaɪzd] *adj* (**a**) *(people, tribe)* non civilisé (**b**) *(primitive, barbaric → behaviour, conditions)* barbare; *(→ people)* barbare, inculte; **it's very uncivilized of him to keep us waiting like this** ce n'est pas correct de sa part de nous faire attendre comme ça (**c**) *Fig (ridiculous)* impossible, extraordinaire; **the plane arrives at the uncivilized hour of 4 a.m.** l'avion arrive à une heure indue, 4 heures du matin

unclad [ˌʌn'klæd] *adj Literary* sans vêtements, nu

unclaimed [ˌʌn'kleɪmd] *adj (property, reward, dividend)* non réclamé; *(rights)* non revendiqué

unclamp [ˌʌn'klæmp] *vt* (**a**) *(remove clamps from)* ôter les pinces de; *Tech* ôter les crampons de (**b**) *(loosen → vice etc)* desserrer

unclasp [ˌʌn'klɑːsp] *vt (hands)* ouvrir; *(bracelet)* dégrafer, défaire; **he was continually clasping and unclasping his hands** il n'arrêtait pas de se tordre les mains nerveusement

unclassifiable [ˌʌnklæsɪ'faɪəbəl] *adj* inclassable

unclassified [ˌʌn'klæsɪfaɪd] *adj* (**a**) *(not sorted → books, papers)* non classé (**b**) *Br (road)* non classé (**c**) *(information)* non secret

uncle ['ʌŋkəl] *n* (**a**) *(relative)* oncle *m*; **hello, Uncle** bonjour mon oncle, bonjour tonton; **Uncle Peter** l'oncle Peter, tonton Peter; *Am Fam* **to cry** *or* **to say uncle** s'avouer vaincu[❑], se rendre[❑] (**b**) *Br Fam Old-fashioned (pawnbroker)* prêteur *m* sur gages
►► ***Uncle Sam*** l'Oncle *m* Sam *(personnification des États-Unis)*; *Am very Fam Pej* ***Uncle Tom*** = Noir qui se comporte de façon obséquieuse avec les Blancs

'Uncle Vanya' *Chekhov* 'L'Oncle Vania'

'Uncle Tom's Cabin' *Beecher Stowe* 'La Case de l'oncle Tom'

unclean [ˌʌn'kliːn] *adj* (**a**) *(dirty → water, habits)* sale (**b**) *Rel* impur; **to feel unclean** se sentir souillé

unclear [ˌʌn'klɪə(r)] *adj* (**a**) *(confused, ambiguous → thinking, purpose, reason)* pas clair, pas évident; **the instructions were unclear** les instructions n'étaient pas claires; **I'm still unclear about what exactly I have to do** je ne sais pas encore très bien ce que je dois faire exactement
(**b**) *(uncertain → future, outcome)* incertain; **it is now unclear whether the talks will take place or not** nous ne savons plus très bien si la conférence va avoir lieu
(**c**) *(indistinct → sound, speech)* indistinct, inaudible; *(→ outline)* flou

uncleared [ˌʌn'klɪəd] *adj* (**a**) *(ground)* non défriché (**b**) *Fin (debt)* non liquidé; *(cheque)* non compensé, non crédité (**c**) *(goods)* non dédouané

unclearly [ˌʌn'klɪəlɪ] *adv (see)* peu clair, mal; *(hear, speak)* indistinctement; *(describe, explain)* peu clairement, peu précisément; *(think)* peu clairement, peu lucidement

unclench [ˌʌn'klentʃ] *vt (fist, teeth)* desserrer

unclimbable [ˌʌn'klaɪməbəl] *adj (mountain)* impossible à escalader

unclimbed [ˌʌn'klaɪmd] *adj (mountain, peak)* invaincu

uncloak [ˌʌn'kləʊk] *vt (mystery)* dévoiler; *(plans)* découvrir; *(impostor)* démasquer

unclog [ˌʌn'klɒg] *(pt & pp* **unclogged**, *cont* **unclogging***)* *vt (drain)* déboucher; *(wheel, machine)* débloquer

unclothe [ˌʌn'kləʊð] *vt (strip)* déshabiller; *(uncover)* découvrir

unclothed [ˌʌn'kləʊðd] *adj* dévêtu, nu

unclouded [ˌʌn'klaʊdɪd] *adj* (**a**) *(sky)* dégagé, sans nuages; *Fig (thinking)* limpide; *(mind, vision)* clair; **a future unclouded by financial worries** un avenir sans soucis financiers (**b**) *(liquid)* clair, limpide

uncluttered [ˌʌn'klʌtəd] *adj (room)* dépouillé, simple; *(style of writing)* sobre; *(design)* dépouillé; *(mind, thinking)* clair, net; **the room is spacious and uncluttered** la pièce est spacieuse et simple; **the diagram should be neat and uncluttered** le diagramme devrait être net et concis

unco ['ʌŋkəʊ] *Scot Arch* **1** *adj* (**a**) *(strange)* étrange (**b**) *(great)* grand (**c**) *(remarkable)* remarquable
2 *adv* très

uncoil [ˌʌn'kɔɪl] **1** *vt* dérouler
2 *vi* se dérouler

uncollectable [ˌʌnkə'lektəbəl] *adj (tax)* non percevable

uncollected [ˌʌnkə'lektɪd] *adj (luggage)* non réclamé; *(tax)* non perçu

uncoloured, *Am* **uncolored** [ʌn'kʌləd] *adj* non coloré; *Fig* **an uncoloured account of sth** un rapport impartial sur qch

uncombed [ʌn'kəʊmd] *adj (hair)* mal peigné, ébouriffé; *(wool)* non peigné

uncomely [ˌʌn'kʌmlɪ] *adj* peu joli

uncomfortable [ˌʌn'kʌmftəbəl] *adj* (**a**) *(physically → chair, bed, clothes)* inconfortable, peu confortable; *(→ position)* inconfortable, peu commode; **this chair is very uncomfortable** cette chaise n'est pas du tout confortable, on est très mal sur cette chaise; **I feel most uncomfortable perched on this stool** je ne me sens pas du tout à l'aise perché sur ce tabouret
(**b**) *Fig (awkward, uneasy → person)* mal à l'aise, gêné; *(difficult, embarrassing → situation, truth)* difficile, gênant; *(unpleasant)* désagréable; **I feel uncomfortable about the whole thing** je me sens mal à l'aise avec tout ça; **to make sb (feel) uncomfortable** mettre qn mal à l'aise; **I've an uncomfortable feeling this isn't going to work** je ne peux pas m'empêcher de penser que ça ne va pas marcher; **to make life** *or* **things (very) uncomfortable for sb** créer des ennuis à qn; **I'd feel uncomfortable (about) asking my parents for money** ça me gênerait de demander de l'argent à mes parents; **it's a very uncomfortable feeling, knowing you could easily have been killed** c'est un sentiment très déplaisant de savoir que tu aurais très

unc–unc

bien pu mourir; **there was an uncomfortable silence** il y eut un silence gêné

uncomfortably [ˌʌn'kʌmftəblɪ] *adv* (**a**) *(lie, sit, stand)* inconfortablement, peu confortablement; *(dressed)* mal, inconfortablement
(**b**) *(unpleasantly → heavy, hot)* désagréablement; **the train was uncomfortably crowded** le train était désagréablement bondé; **he came uncomfortably close to discovering the truth** il a été dangereusement près de découvrir la vérité; **I was uncomfortably aware of him watching me** j'étais désagréablement conscient du fait qu'il me regardait
(**c**) *(uneasily)* avec gêne; **he shifted uncomfortably in his seat** il bougeait avec embarras sur son siège

uncomfy [ˌʌn'kʌmfɪ] *adj Fam (chair, bed, clothes)* pas confortable

uncommercial [ˌʌnkə'mɜːʃəl] *adj* peu commercial

uncommissioned [ˌʌnkə'mɪʃənd] *adj* non commissionné, non délégué (**to do sth** pour faire qch)

uncommitted [ˌʌnkə'mɪtɪd] *adj (person, literature)* non engagé; **he remains politically uncommitted** il reste neutre politiquement; **an uncommitted relationship** une relation libre
▸▸ *Comput* ***uncommitted logic array*** réseau *m* logique non programmé

uncommon [ˌʌn'kɒmən] **1** *adj* (**a**) *(rare, unusual → disease, species)* rare, peu commun; **it's not uncommon for the heating to break down** il n'est pas rare que le chauffage soit en panne (**b**) *Formal (exceptional)* singulier, extraordinaire; **a child of uncommon abilities** un enfant aux dons singuliers
2 *adv Arch Fam* singulièrement, exceptionnellement

uncommonly [ˌʌn'kɒmənlɪ] *adv* (**a**) *(rarely)* rarement, inhabituellement (**b**) *Formal (exceptionally → clever, cold, polite)* singulièrement, exceptionnellement; **he took an uncommonly long time over it** il a mis exceptionnellement longtemps à le faire

uncommonness [ˌʌn'kɒmənnɪs] *n* (**a**) *(rarity)* rareté *f* (**b**) *Formal (exceptional nature)* singularité *f*

uncommunicative [ˌʌnkə'mjuːnɪkətɪv] *adj* peu communicatif, taciturne; **to be uncommunicative about sth** se montrer réservé sur qch

uncompanionable [ˌʌnkəm'pænjənəbəl] *adj Literary* peu sociable, insociable

uncompassionate [ˌʌnkəm'pæʃənət] *adj* peu compatissant

uncompetitive [ˌʌnkəm'petɪtɪv] *adj (person)* qui n'a pas l'esprit de compétition; *(price, product)* peu compétitif

uncomplaining [ˌʌnkəm'pleɪnɪŋ] *adj* qui ne se plaint pas; **he has a calm and uncomplaining wife** il a une femme calme et résignée

uncomplainingly [ˌʌnkəm'pleɪnɪŋlɪ] *adv* sans se plaindre

uncompleted [ˌʌnkəm'pliːtɪd] *adj* inachevé

uncomplicated [ˌʌn'kɒmplɪkeɪtɪd] *adj* peu compliqué, simple

uncomplimentary ['ʌnˌkɒmplɪ'mentərɪ] *adj* peu flatteur; **he was very uncomplimentary about you** ce qu'il a dit de vous était loin d'être flatteur

uncomprehending ['ʌnˌkɒmprɪ'hendɪŋ] *adj* qui ne comprend pas; **to give sb an uncomprehending look** regarder qn sans comprendre; **in uncomprehending amazement** ahuri

uncomprehendingly ['ʌnˌkɒmprɪ'hendɪŋlɪ] *adv* sans comprendre

uncompromising [ˌʌn'kɒmprəmaɪzɪŋ] *adj (rigid → attitude, behaviour)* rigide, intransigeant, inflexible; *(committed → person)* convaincu, ardent; **a man of uncompromising principles** un homme aux principes très stricts; **we took an uncompromising stance on this** nous avons adopté une position inflexible à ce sujet

uncompromisingly [ˌʌn'kɒmprəmaɪzɪŋlɪ] *adv* sans concession, de manière intransigeante; **uncompromisingly honest** d'une honnêteté absolue

unconcealed [ˌʌnkən'siːld] *adj (joy, anger)* évident, non dissimulé

unconcern [ˌʌnkən'sɜːn] *n* (**a**) *(indifference)* indifférence *f*; **your unconcern for others/for danger** ton indifférence envers les autres/au danger (**b**) *(calm)* sang-froid *m inv*; **she continued with apparent unconcern** elle poursuivit avec un sang-froid apparent

unconcerned [ˌʌnkən'sɜːnd] *adj* (**a**) *(unworried, calm)* qui ne s'inquiète pas, insouciant; **he seemed quite unconcerned about the exam/her health** il ne semblait pas du tout s'inquiéter pour l'examen/pour sa santé (**b**) *(uninterested)* indifférent; **she's unconcerned with political matters** elle est indifférente aux questions politiques

unconcernedly [ˌʌnkən'sɜːnɪdlɪ] *adv* (**a**) *(calmly)* sans s'inquiéter, sans se laisser troubler (**b**) *(uninterestedly)* avec indifférence *ou* insouciance

unconditional [ˌʌnkən'dɪʃənəl] *adj* (**a**) *(support, submission)* inconditionnel, sans condition (**b**) *Math (equality)* sans conditions
▸▸ *Law* ***unconditional discharge*** libération *f* inconditionnelle; *Fin* ***unconditional order*** ordre *m* (de payer) pur et simple; ***unconditional surrender*** reddition *f* inconditionnelle

unconditionality [ˌʌnkənˌdɪʃə'nælɪtɪ] *n* inconditionnalité *f*

unconditionally [ˌʌnkən'dɪʃənəlɪ] *adv (accept, surrender)* inconditionnellement, sans condition

unconditioned [ˌʌnkən'dɪʃənd] *adj* (**a**) *Psy (reflex)* inconditionnel (**b**) *Phil* absolu, inconditionné
▸▸ *Psy* ***unconditioned response*** réponse *f* inconditionnelle; *Psy* ***unconditioned stimulus*** stimulus *m* inconditionnel

unconfident [ˌʌn'kɒnfɪdənt] *adj* (**a**) *(not self-assured)* peu sûr de soi, qui manque d'assurance (**b**) *(uncertain)* peu confiant

unconfined [ˌʌnkən'faɪnd] *adj Literary* illimité, sans bornes; **let joy be unconfined** que la joie éclate

unconfirmed [ˌʌnkən'fɜːmd] *adj* non confirmé; **the report remains unconfirmed** la nouvelle n'a pas encore été confirmée
▸▸ *Fin* ***unconfirmed letter of credit*** lettre *f* de crédit révocable

unconformable [ˌʌnkən'fɔːməbəl] *adj* (**a**) *(not conforming)* non conforme (**b**) *Geol* discordant

uncongenial [ˌʌnkən'dʒiːnɪəl] *adj (surroundings, atmosphere, work)* peu agréable; *(person)* antipathique; *(climate)* peu favorable (**to** à)

uncongeniality [ˌʌnkənˌdʒiːnɪ'ælɪtɪ] *n (of surroundings, atmosphere, work)* caractère *m* peu agréable; *(of person)* caractère *m* antipathique; *(of climate)* caractère *m* peu favorable (**to** à)

unconnected [ˌʌnkə'nektɪd] *adj (unrelated → facts, incidents)* sans rapport; *(→ ideas, thoughts)* sans suite, décousu; **the riot was unconnected with food prices** l'émeute n'avait pas de rapport *ou* était sans rapport avec les prix alimentaires; **the two events are totally unconnected** les deux événements n'ont aucun rapport entre eux; **the two incidents are not unconnected** les deux incidents ne sont pas sans lien

unconquerable [ˌʌn'kɒŋkərəbəl] *adj (opponent, mountain)* invincible; *(obstacle, problem)* insurmontable; *(instinct, will)* irrépressible

unconquered [ˌʌn'kɒŋkəd] *adj (nation, territory)* qui n'a pas été conquis; *(mountain)* invaincu

unconscientious [ˌʌnkɒnʃɪ'enʃəs] *adj* peu consciencieux

unconscientiously [ˌʌnkɒnʃɪ'enʃəslɪ] *adv* peu consciencieusement

unconscionable [ˌʌn'kɒnʃənəbəl] *adj Formal* (**a**) *(liar)* sans scrupules (**b**) *(demand)* déraisonnable; *(time)* extraordinaire

unconscionably [ˌʌn'kɒnʃənəblɪ] *adv Formal* (**a**) *(shamelessly)* sans vergogne *ou* scrupules (**b**) *(excessively)* excessivement, démesurément

unconscious [ˌʌn'kɒnʃəs] **1** *adj* (**a**) *(in coma)* sans connaissance; *(in faint)* évanoui, sans connaissance; **to knock sb unconscious** assommer qn; **he lay unconscious for 5 days** il est resté sans connaissance pendant 5 jours; **she remained unconscious for some minutes** elle est restée évanouie *ou* sans connaissance pendant quelques minutes
(**b**) *(unaware)* inconscient; **to be unconscious of doing sth** ne pas se rendre compte qu'on fait qch; **to be unconscious of sth** ne pas avoir conscience de qch, ne pas se rendre compte de qch; **she seemed unconscious of all the noise around her** elle semblait ne pas avoir conscience de tout le bruit autour d'elle; **they are unconscious of the fact** ils n'en sont pas conscients
(**c**) *(unintentional)* inconscient, involontaire; **it was an unconscious pun** c'était un jeu de mots involontaire; **there was an unconscious bias in his selection of candidates** il y avait un parti pris involontaire dans son choix de candidats
(**d**) *Psy (motives)* inconscient; **the unconscious mind** l'inconscient *m*
2 *n Psy* inconscient *m*; **the unconscious** l'inconscient *m*

unconsciously [ˌʌn'kɒnʃəslɪ] *adv* inconsciemment, sans s'en rendre compte; **I think, unconsciously, she resents me** je crois qu'inconsciemment, elle ne m'apprécie pas

unconsciousness [ˌʌn'kɒnʃəsnɪs] *n (UNCOUNT)* (**a**) *Med (coma)* perte *f* de connaissance; *(fainting)* évanouissement *m*; **in a state of unconsciousness** sans connaissance (**b**) *(lack of awareness)* inconscience *f*

unconsecrated [ˌʌn'kɒnsɪkreɪtɪd] *adj* non consacré

unconsidered [ˌʌnkən'sɪdəd] *adj* (**a**) *(thought, action)* irréfléchi (**b**) *Formal (object)* sans importance

unconsolidated [ˌʌnkən'sɒlɪdeɪtɪd] *adj Fin (debt)* non consolidé

unconstitutional [ˌʌnkɒnstɪ'tjuːʃənəl] *adj* inconstitutionnel

unconstitutionality ['ʌnkɒnstɪˌtjuːʃə'nælɪtɪ] *n* inconstitutionnalité *f*

unconstitutionally [ˌʌnkɒnstɪ'tjuːʃənəlɪ] *adv* inconstitutionnellement

unconstrained [ˌʌnkən'streɪnd] *adj (feelings)* sans contrainte, non contraint; *(action)* spontané; *(manner)* aisé; **he is unconstrained by inhibitions** les inhibitions ne l'arrêtent pas; **unconstrained laughter** hilarité *f* débordante

unconstricted [ˌʌnkən'strɪktɪd] *adj (opening, passage)* large; *(breathing, movement)* sans gêne

unconsummated [ˌʌn'kɒnsəmeɪtɪd] *adj (marriage)* non consommé

uncontaminated [ˌʌnkən'tæmɪneɪtɪd] *adj* non contaminé

uncontested [ˌʌnkən'testɪd] *adj (position, authority)* non disputé, incontesté; *Pol* **the seat was uncontested** il n'y avait qu'un candidat pour le siège

uncontrived [ˌʌnkən'traɪvd] *adj* naturel

uncontrollable [ˌʌnkən'trəʊləbəl] *adj* (**a**) *(fear, desire, urge)* irrésistible, irrépressible; *(stammer)* que l'on ne peut maîtriser *ou* contrôler; **to be seized by uncontrollable laughter/anger** être pris d'un fou rire/d'un accès de colère; **I had an uncontrollable urge to slap her** j'ai eu une envie irrépressible de la gifler (**b**) *(animal)* indomptable; *(child)* impossible à discipliner (**c**) *(inflation)* qui ne peut être freiné, galopant

uncontrollably [ˌʌnkən'trəʊləblɪ] *adv* (**a**) *(helplessly)* irrésistiblement; **he was laughing uncontrollably** il avait le fou rire; **I shook uncontrollably** je tremblais sans pouvoir m'arrêter (**b**) *(out of control)* **the boat rocked uncontrollably** on n'arrivait pas à maîtriser le tangage du bateau (**c**) *(fall, rise)* irrésistiblement; **prices are rising uncontrollably** les prix augmentent irrésistiblement

uncontrolled [ˌʌnkən'trəʊld] *adj* (**a**) *(unrestricted → fall, rise)* effréné, incontrôlé; *(→ population growth)* non contrôlé; *(→ anger, emotion)* incontrôlé, non retenu; **inflation cannot remain uncontrolled** l'inflation ne peut demeurer incontrôlée; **scenes of uncontrolled violence** des scènes de violence incontrôlée *ou* d'une extrême violence (**b**) *(unverified → experiment)* non contrôlé

uncontroversial ['ʌnˌkɒntrə'vɜːʃəl] *adj* qui ne prête pas à controverse, incontestable

unconventional [ˌʌnkən'venʃənəl] *adj* non conformiste

unconventionally [ˌʌnkən'venʃənəlɪ] *adv (live, think)* d'une manière originale *ou* peu conventionnelle; *(dress)* d'une manière originale
unconverted [ˌʌnkən'vɜːtɪd] *adj Rel* inconverti
unconvicted [ˌʌnkən'vɪktɪd] *adj* qui n'a pas été reconnu coupable
unconvinced [ˌʌnkən'vɪnst] *adj* incrédule, sceptique; **I'm unconvinced** je ne suis pas convaincu, je reste sceptique; **to be/to remain unconvinced by sth** être/rester sceptique à l'égard de qch
unconvincing [ˌʌnkən'vɪnsɪŋ] *adj* peu convaincant
unconvincingly [ˌʌnkən'vɪnsɪŋlɪ] *adv (argue, lie)* d'un ton *ou* d'une manière peu convaincante, peu vraisemblablement
uncooked [ˌʌn'kʊkt] *adj* non cuit, cru
uncool [ˌʌn'kuːl] *adj Fam* (**a**) *(unfashionable, unsophisticated)* ringard; **it's a really uncool place** c'est vraiment ringard comme endroit; **what an uncool thing to do!** c'est vraiment nul de faire un truc pareil! (**b**) *(not allowed, not accepted)* mal vu ❑; **I think it's a bit uncool to smoke in here** je pense pas que ça soit très bien vu de fumer ici (**c**) *(upset)* **she was a bit uncool about me moving in with them** elle tenait pas trop à ce que je m'installe chez eux
uncooperative [ˌʌnkəʊ'ɒpərətɪv] *adj* peu coopératif
uncooperatively [ˌʌnkəʊ'ɒpərətɪvlɪ] *adv* de manière peu coopérative
uncooperativeness [ˌʌnkəʊ'ɒpərətɪvnɪs] *n* manque *m* de coopération
uncoordinated [ˌʌnkəʊ'ɔːdɪneɪtɪd] *adj* (**a**) *(movements)* mal coordonné; **her hand and eye movements are uncoordinated** les mouvements de ses yeux et de ses mains ne sont pas coordonnés (**b**) *(clumsy)* maladroit (**c**) *(unorganized → efforts, attack, undertaking)* qui manque de coordination, mal organisé
uncork [ˌʌn'kɔːk] *vt (bottle)* déboucher; *Fig (emotions)* déchaîner
uncorrected [ˌʌnkə'rektɪd] *adj (exercise, proof)* non corrigé; *(error)* non rectifié *ou* corrigé
uncorroborated [ˌʌnkə'rɒbəreɪtɪd] *adj* non corroboré
uncorrupted [ˌʌnkə'rʌptɪd] *adj (person)* non corrompu
uncountable [ˌʌn'kaʊntəbəl] *adj* (**a**) *(numberless)* incalculable, innombrable (**b**) *Gram* indénombrable, non comptable
uncountably [ʌn'kaʊntəblɪ] *adv Gram* de façon indénombrable; **this noun can only be used uncountably** on ne peut utiliser ce nom que de façon indénombrable
uncounted [ˌʌn'kaʊntɪd] *adj* (**a**) *(not counted)* non compté (**b**) *Literary (numberless)* incalculable, innombrable
uncouple [ˌʌn'kʌpəl] *vt (engine)* découpler; *(carriage)* dételer; *(cart, trailer)* détacher
uncouth [ˌʌn'kuːθ] *adj* grossier, fruste
uncouthly [ˌʌn'kuːθlɪ] *adv* grossièrement
uncouthness [ˌʌn'kuːθnɪs] *n* grossièreté *f*
uncovenanted [ˌʌn'kʌvənəntɪd] *adj* non stipulé par contrat
uncover [ˌʌn'kʌvə(r)] **1** *vt* (**a**) *(furniture, swimming pool)* découvrir; *(saucepan)* enlever le couvercle de (**b**) *(evidence, plot, conspiracy)* découvrir (**c**) *Chess (piece)* découvrir, dégarnir
2 *vi Arch* se découvrir
uncovered [ˌʌn'kʌvəd] *adj* (**a**) *(without a cover)* découvert; **food should not be left uncovered** la nourriture ne doit pas rester à l'air (**b**) *Fin* sans couverture; *(purchase, sale)* à découvert; *(cheque)* sans provision
►► *Fin* ***uncovered advance*** avance *f* à découvert; *Fin* ***uncovered balance*** découvert *m*; *St Exch* ***uncovered position*** position *f* non couverte
uncreasable [ˌʌn'kriːsəbəl] *adj (fabric)* infroissable
uncreative [ˌʌnkriː'eɪtɪv] *adj* peu créatif
uncritical [ˌʌn'krɪtɪkəl] *adj (naïve)* dépourvu d'esprit critique, non critique; *(unquestioning)* inconditionnel; *(audience)* peu exigeant; **to be uncritical of sb/sth** ne faire preuve d'aucun sens *ou* esprit critique à l'égard de qn/qch
uncritically [ˌʌn'krɪtɪkəlɪ] *adv (accept)* sans se poser la moindre question; *(support)* inconditionnellement
uncross [ˌʌn'krɒs] *vt* décroiser
uncrossed [ˌʌn'krɒst] *adj* (**a**) *(cheque)* non barré (**b**) *(legs)* décroisé
uncrowded [ˌʌn'kraʊdɪd] *adj (beach, streets)* où il n'y a pas trop de monde; *(road)* peu encombré
uncrowned [ˌʌn'kraʊnd] *adj* sans couronne, non couronné; **the uncrowned king of rock 'n' roll** le roi sans couronne du rock'n'roll
uncrumple [ˌʌn'krʌmpəl] *vt* défroisser
uncrunch [ˌʌn'krʌntʃ] *vt Comput* décompresser, décompacter
uncrushable [ˌʌn'krʌʃəbəl] *adj (fabric)* infroissable
uncrushed [ˌʌn'krʌʃt] *adj (ice)* non pilé; *(garlic)* non écrasé, entier; *(hat, box)* non écrasé; *(clothes)* non froissé
UNCSTD [ˌjuːensiːˌestiː'diː] *n* (*abbr* **United Nations Conference on Science and Technology for Development**) CSTD *f*
UNCTAD ['ʌŋktæd] *n* (*abbr* **United Nations Conference on Trade and Development**) CNUCED *f*
unction ['ʌŋkʃən] *n* (**a**) *Rel* onction *f* (**b**) *Formal (unctuousness)* manières *fpl* onctueuses (**c**) *Literary* onguent *m*
unctuous ['ʌŋktjʊəs] *adj Formal* mielleux, onctueux
unctuously ['ʌŋktjʊəslɪ] *adv Formal* mielleusement, onctueusement
unctuousness ['ʌŋktjʊəsnɪs] *n (UNCOUNT) Formal* manières *fpl* mielleuses *ou* onctueuses
uncultivated [ˌʌn'kʌltɪveɪtɪd] *adj* (**a**) *(land)* inculte, en friche (**b**) *(person)* inculte; *(manners, accent, speech)* qui manque de raffinement
uncultured [ˌʌn'kʌltʃəd] *adj (person)* inculte; *(manners, accent, speech)* qui manque de raffinement
uncurbed [ʌn'kɜːbd] *adj (authority)* sans restriction; *(passion)* déchaîné; **if these tendencies are allowed to go uncurbed** si on ne met pas un frein à ces tendances
uncured [ˌʌn'kjʊəd] *adj* (**a**) *(meat, fish)* non traité (**b**) *(illness)* non guéri
uncurl [ˌʌn'kɜːl] **1** *vt (rope)* dérouler; *(body, toes)* étirer; **to uncurl oneself** s'étirer
2 *vi (leaf)* s'ouvrir; *(cat)* s'étirer; *(snake)* se dérouler
uncurtained [ˌʌn'kɜːtənd] *adj (window)* sans rideaux
uncut [ˌʌn'kʌt] *adj* (**a**) *(hair, nails)* non coupé; *(hedge, stone)* non taillé; *(diamond)* non taillé, brut; *(corn, wheat)* non récolté, sur pied; *(pages)* non rogné (**b**) *(uncensored → film, text)* intégral, sans coupures; **the uncut version** la version longue (**c**) *(drugs)* pur
undamaged [ˌʌn'dæmɪdʒd] *adj* (**a**) *(car, contents, merchandise, building, roof)* indemne, intact, non endommagé (**b**) *Fig (reputation)* intact
undamped [ˌʌn'dæmpt] *adj* (**a**) *(enthusiasm, feelings)* intact, non affaibli (**b**) *(piano string)* non étouffé (**c**) *Rad (oscillation)* non amorti, entretenu
undated [ˌʌn'deɪtɪd] *adj* non daté, sans date
undaunted [ˌʌn'dɔːntɪd] *adj* (**a**) *(not discouraged)* qui ne se laisse pas décourager *ou* démonter; **she was undaunted by their criticism** leurs critiques ne la décourageaient pas; **he carried on undaunted** il a continué sans se laisser décourager (**b**) *(fearless)* sans peur
undecagon [ˌʌn'dekəgən] *n* hendécagone *m*
undecaying [ˌʌndɪ'keɪɪŋ] *adj Literary* impérissable; **undecaying beauty** beauté *f* toujours jeune
undeceive [ˌʌndɪ'siːv] *vt Literary* détromper
undecided [ˌʌndɪ'saɪdɪd] *adj (person, issue)* indécis; *(outcome)* incertain; **to be undecided about sth** être indécis à propos de qch; **he is undecided whether to stay or go** il n'a pas décidé s'il restera ou s'il partira; **the matter is still undecided** *(not settled)* la question n'a pas encore été tranchée; *(not yet decided)* aucune décision n'a encore été prise à ce sujet
undecipherable [ˌʌndɪ'saɪfərəbəl] *adj (writing)* indéchiffrable, illisible; *(code)* indéchiffrable
undeclared [ˌʌndɪ'kleəd] *adj (goods, income, war)* non déclaré; *(love)* non avoué
undefeated [ˌʌndɪ'fiːtɪd] *adj* invaincu
undefended [ˌʌndɪ'fendɪd] *adj* (**a**) *Mil (fort, town)* sans défense (**b**) *Law (lawsuit)* où on ne présente pas de défense
undefiled [ˌʌndɪ'faɪld] *adj* sans souillure, immaculé; **undefiled by any contact with Western society** non corrompu par la civilisation occidentale
undefinable [ˌʌndɪ'faɪnəbəl] *adj* indéfinissable, impossible à définir
undefined [ˌʌndɪ'faɪnd] *adj (term etc)* non défini; *(vague → feeling etc)* indéterminé, vague
undelete [ˌʌndɪ'liːt] *vt Comput* restaurer
undelivered [ˌʌndɪ'lɪvəd] *adj (letter)* non remis, non distribué; **if undelivered please return to sender** en cas de non-distribution, prière de retourner à l'expéditeur
undemanding [ˌʌndɪ'mɑːndɪŋ] *adj (person)* facile à vivre, qui n'est pas exigeant; *(work)* simple, qui n'est pas astreignant
undemocratic ['ʌnˌdemə'krætɪk] *adj* antidémocratique, peu démocratique
undemonstrative [ˌʌndɪ'mɒnstrətɪv] *adj* réservé, peu démonstratif
undeniable [ˌʌndɪ'naɪəbəl] *adj* indéniable, incontestable
undeniably [ˌʌndɪ'naɪəblɪ] *adv (true)* incontestablement, indiscutablement; **he's undeniably a very clever man** c'est incontestablement un homme très intelligent
undenominational ['ʌndɪˌnɒmɪ'neɪʃənəl] *adj* non confessionnel
undependable [ˌʌndɪ'pendəbəl] *adj (machine, trains, person)* peu fiable

UNDER ['ʌndə(r)]

sous	► **1 (a), (d) – (g)**
moins de	► **1 (b)**
au-dessous de	► **1 (b)**
sous le poids de	► **1 (c)**
conformément à	► **1 (h)**
en cours de	► **1 (i)**
dessous	► **2 (a)**

1 *prep* (**a**) *(beneath, below)* sous; **the newspaper was under the chair/cushion** le journal était sous la chaise/le coussin; **the pantry is under the stairs** le garde-manger est sous l'escalier; **I can't see anything under it** je ne vois rien (en) dessous; **put it under that** mettez-le là-dessous; **there is a coat of paint under the wallpaper** il y a une couche de peinture sous le papier peint; **the body was lying under a sheet** le cadavre était étendu sous un drap; **he wore a white shirt under his jacket** il portait une chemise blanche sous sa veste; **he pulled a wallet from under his jersey** il a sorti un portefeuille de sous son pull; **he was carrying a paper under his arm** il portait un journal sous le bras; **hold your hand under the tap** mettez votre main sous le robinet; **stand under my umbrella** mettez-vous sous mon parapluie; **we took shelter under a tree** nous nous sommes abrités sous un arbre; **to be born under Aries/Leo** être né sous le signe du Bélier/du Lion; **it can only be seen under a microscope** on ne peut le voir qu'au microscope; **we had to crawl under the barbed wire** on a dû passer sous les barbelés en rampant; **you have to crawl under it** il faut ramper dessous; **the tunnel ran under the sea** le tunnel passait sous la mer; **she was swimming under water/under the bridge** elle nageait sous l'eau/sous le pont; **it's unlucky to walk under a ladder** ça porte malheur de passer sous une échelle
(**b**) *(less than)* moins de, au-dessous de; **under £7,000** moins de 7000 livres; **everything is under £5** tout est à moins de 5 livres; **is she under 16?** est-ce qu'elle a moins de 16 ans?; **children under ten** les enfants au-dessous *ou* de moins de dix ans; **in under ten minutes** en moins de dix minutes
(**c**) *(weighed down by)* sous le poids de; **he staggered under his heavy load** il chancelait sous le poids de son lourd chargement; *Fig* **to sink under the weight of one's debts** sombrer sous le poids de ses dettes
(**d**) *(indicating conditions or circumstances)* sous, dans; **we had to work under appalling conditions** on a dû travailler dans des conditions épouvantables; **she was murdered under strange circumstances** elle a été tuée dans

d'étranges circonstances; **under the circumstances** vu les circonstances

(**e**) *(subject to)* sous; **under duress/threat** sous la contrainte/la menace

(**f**) *Med* sous; **under sedation/treatment** sous calmants/traitement

(**g**) *(directed, governed by)* sous (la direction de); **he studied under Fox** il a été l'élève de Fox; **she has two assistants under her** elle a deux assistants sous ses ordres; *Mus* **the Bristol Chamber Orchestra under Martin Davenport** l'orchestre de (musique de) chambre de Bristol sous la direction de Martin Davenport; **I served under General White** j'ai servi sous le général White; **the book describes Uganda under Amin** le livre décrit l'Ouganda sous (le régime d')Amin Dada; **to come under (the authority of) the Home Office** relever du ministère de l'Intérieur; **under her management, the firm prospered** sous sa direction, l'entreprise a prospéré; **under fascism, many groups were outlawed** sous le régime fasciste, de nombreux groupes furent interdits

(**h**) *(according to)* conformément à, en vertu de, selon; **under the new law, all this will change** avec la nouvelle loi, tout cela va changer; **under the new law, elections will be held every four years** en vertu de *ou* selon la nouvelle loi, les élections auront lieu tous les quatre ans; **under the Emergency Powers Act** conformément à la loi instituant l'état d'urgence; **under this system, the President has little real power** dans ce système, le Président a peu de pouvoir véritable; **under (the terms of) his will/the agreement** selon (les termes de) son testament/l'accord

(**i**) *(in the process of)* en cours de; **under construction** en cours de construction; **the matter is under consideration/discussion** on est en train d'étudier/de discuter la question

(**j**) *Agr* **under wheat/barley** en blé/orge

(**k**) *(in classification)* **you'll find the book under philosophy** vous trouverez le livre sous la rubrique philosophie; **you'll find my number under Magee** vous trouverez mon numéro sous Magee; **she writes under the name of Heidi Croft** elle écrit sous le nom de Heidi Croft; **few singers perform under their own name** peu de chanteurs gardent leur vrai nom

2 *adv* (**a**) *(below ground, water, door etc)* **to slide** *or* **to slip under** se glisser dessous; **to pass under** passer dessous; **to stay under** *(under water)* rester sous l'eau

(**b**) *Med (anaesthetized)* sous l'effet de l'anesthésie

(**c**) *(less → in age, price)* **you have to be 16 or under to enter** il faut avoir 16 ans ou moins pour se présenter; **items at £20 and under** des articles à 20 livres et au-dessous

'Under Milk Wood' *Thomas* 'Au bois lacté'

'Under Western Eyes' *Conrad* 'Sous les yeux de l'Occident'

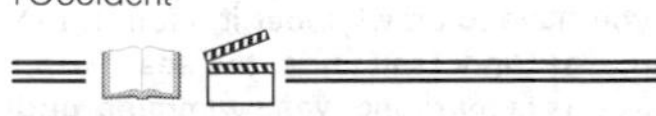

'Under the Volcano' *Lowry, Huston* 'Au-dessous du volcan'

under- [ˈʌndə(r)] *pref* (**a**) *(below)* sous-; **holidays for the under-30s** vacances pour les moins de 30 ans (**b**) *(junior)* sous-; **under-gardener** sous-jardinier(ère) *m,f*

under-18 *n* personne *f* de moins de 18 ans, mineur(e) *m,f*

underachieve [ˌʌndərəˈtʃiːv] *vi* ne pas obtenir les résultats escomptés; **he constantly underachieves** il n'obtient jamais les résultats dont il est capable

underachiever [ˌʌndərəˈtʃiːvə(r)] *n (gen)* = personne ou élève qui n'obtient pas les résultats escomptés; **he's always been an underachiever** il a toujours été en deçà de ses possibilités

underact [ˌʌndəˈrækt] **1** *vt (part, role → act with insufficient conviction)* jouer sans conviction; *(act in understated way)* jouer tout en nuances

2 *vi (act with insufficient conviction)* jouer sans conviction; *(act in understated way)* avoir un jeu *ou* jouer tout en nuances

underactive [ˌʌndeˈræktɪv] *adj* **to have an underactive thyroid** faire de l'hypothyroïdie

under-age *adj (person)* mineur

▸▸ ***under-age drinking*** consommation *f* d'alcool par les mineurs; ***under-age sex*** rapports *mpl* sexuels avant l'âge légal

underarm [ˈʌndərɑːm] **1** *adv Sport (bowl, hit, serve)* (par) en dessous

2 *adj* (**a**) *(deodorant)* pour les aisselles; *(hair)* sous les bras *ou* les aisselles (**b**) *Sport (bowl, throw, serve)* par en dessous

underbelly [ˈʌndəˌbelɪ] *(pl* **underbellies***)* *n* (**a**) bas-ventre *m* (**b**) *Fig* point *m* faible; **the soft underbelly of society** le point faible de la société

underbid [ˌʌndəˈbɪd] *(pt & pp* **underbid,** *cont* **underbidding***)* **1** *n Cards (in bridge)* annonce *f* au-dessous de sa force

2 *vt* (**a**) *Com* **to underbid sb** faire des soumissions *ou* offrir des conditions plus avantageuses que qn (**b**) *Cards (in bridge)* **to underbid one's hand** annoncer au-dessous de sa force

3 *vi* (**a**) *Cards (in bridge)* annoncer au-dessous de sa force (**b**) *(in auction)* ne pas offrir assez, faire une enchère insuffisamment élevée

underblanket [ˈʌndəˌblæŋkɪt] *n* protège-matelas *m*; *(waterproof)* alaise *f*

underbody [ˈʌndəˌbɒdɪ] *n* (**a**) *(of animal)* ventre *m* (**b**) *(of car)* dessous *m* de caisse

underborrow [ˌʌndəˈbɒrəʊ] *vi Fin (company)* ne pas emprunter assez

underborrowed [ˌʌndəˈbɒrəʊd] *adj Fin (company)* sous-endetté

underborrowing [ˌʌndəˈbɒrəʊɪŋ] *n Fin (of company)* sous-endettement *m*

underbred **1** *n* [ˈʌndəbred] *(animal)* animal *m* croisé; *(person)* personne *f* mal élevée, mal élevé(e) *m,f*

2 *adj* [ˌʌndəˈbred] *(animal)* croisé; *(person)* mal élevé

underbrush [ˈʌndəbrʌʃ] *n (UNCOUNT) Am* sous-bois *m*, broussailles *fpl*

undercapitalization [ˈʌndəˌkæpɪtəlaɪˈzeɪʃən] *n Econ* sous-capitalisation *f*

undercapitalized [ˌʌndəˈkæpɪtəlaɪzd] *adj (entrepreneur, company)* sous-capitalisé

undercarriage [ˈʌndəˌkærɪdʒ] *n (of aeroplane)* train *m* d'atterrissage; *(of vehicle)* châssis *m*; **to get the undercarriage down** sortir le train d'atterrissage

undercharge [ˌʌndəˈtʃɑːdʒ] *vt* (**a**) *(customer)* faire payer insuffisamment *ou* moins cher à; **I was undercharged** on m'a fait payer moins cher, on ne m'a pas fait payer le prix indiqué; **she undercharged him by £6** elle lui a fait payer 6 livres de moins que le prix (**b**) *(gun)* charger insuffisamment

underclass [ˈʌndəklɑːs] *n* **the underclass** le sous-prolétariat, les exclus *mpl*

underclassman [ˈʌndəˌklɑːsmən] *(pl* **underclassmen** [-mən]*)* *n Am Univ* étudiant *m* de première ou deuxième année

underclasswoman [ˈʌndəˌklɑːsˌwʊmən] *(pl* **underclasswomen** [-ˌwɪmɪn]*)* *n Am Univ* étudiante *f* de première ou deuxième année

undercliff [ˈʌndəklɪf] *n* = remblai créé par les débris d'érosion au bas d'une falaise

undercloth [ˈʌndəklɒθ] *n (on table)* sous-nappe *f*

underclothes [ˈʌndəkləʊðz] *npl* sous-vêtements *mpl*; *(for women)* lingerie *f*, dessous *mpl*

underclothing [ˈʌndəˌkləʊðɪŋ] *n (UNCOUNT)* = **underclothes**

undercoat [ˈʌndəkəʊt] **1** *n (of paint)* sous-couche *f*; *(of anti-rust treatment)* couche *f* d'antirouille

2 *vt (with paint)* poser une sous-couche sur; *(with anti-rust treatment)* poser une couche d'antirouille sur

undercook [ˌʌndəˈkʊk] *vt* ne pas assez cuire; **the potatoes were undercooked** les pommes de terre n'étaient pas assez cuites *ou* n'avaient pas cuit assez longtemps

undercover [ˈʌndəˌkʌvə(r)] **1** *adj (methods, work)* secret(ète), clandestin

2 *adv* clandestinement

▸▸ ***undercover agent*** agent *m* secret

undercroft [ˌʌndəkrɒft] *n* salle *f* souterraine

undercurrent [ˈʌndəˌkʌrənt] *n* (**a**) *(in sea)* courant *m* sous-marin; *(in river)* courant *m* (**b**) *Fig (feeling)* sentiment *m* sous-jacent; **there was an undercurrent of hostility throughout the discussion** il y eut une hostilité sous-jacente tout au long de la discussion

undercut [ˌʌndəˈkʌt] *(pt & pp* **undercut,** *cont* **undercutting***)* **1** *vt* (**a**) *Com (competitor)* vendre moins cher que; *(prices)* casser (**b**) *(undermine → efforts, principle)* amoindrir (**c**) *Sport (ball)* lifter

2 *n* (**a**) *Sport* lift *m* (**b**) *Culin (meat)* (morceau *m* de) filet *m*

underdeveloped [ˌʌndədɪˈveləpt] *adj* (**a**) *(country, society)* sous-développé; *(area)* insuffisamment mis en valeur; *(resources)* sous-exploité (**b**) *(stunted → foetus, plant)* qui n'est pas complètement développé *ou* formé; *(→ child)* peu développé; *(→ muscle)* pas assez développé (**c**) *Fig (argument, idea)* insuffisamment développé *ou* exposé (**d**) *Phot (film, print)* insuffisamment développé

underdevelopment [ˌʌndədɪˈveləpmənt] *n* (**a**) *(of country, society)* sous-développement *m*; *(of resources)* sous-exploitation *f* (**b**) *Phot* développement *m* insuffisant

underdo [ˌʌndəˈduː] *(pt & pp* **underdone** [-ˈdʌn]*)* *vt (food)* faire cuire insuffisamment

underdog [ˈʌndədɒg] *n* **the underdog** *(in fight, contest)* celui (celle) *m,f* qui risque de perdre *ou* qui part perdant(e); *(in society)* le laissé-pour-compte (la laissée-pour-compte) *m,f*, l'opprimé(e) *m,f*; **he's always been one to side with the underdog** il prend toujours le parti du perdant; **the underdogs won 5–2** ceux qui étaient donnés perdants d'avance ont gagné 5 à 2

underdone [ˌʌndəˈdʌn] *adj (accidentally)* pas assez cuit; *(deliberately → meat)* saignant; *(→ vegetable, cake)* pas trop cuit

underdrawers [ˈʌndəˌdrɔːz] *npl Am* caleçon *m* (d'homme)

underdrawing [ˈʌndəˌdrɔːɪŋ] *n Art* croquis *m* préliminaire

underdressed [ˌʌndəˈdrest] *adj (too lightly)* trop légèrement vêtu; *(too informally)* habillé trop sport; **I feel really underdressed in these jeans** avec ce jean, je me trouve très mal habillé pour la circonstance

underemphasize, -ise [ˌʌndəˈremfəsaɪz] *vt* ne pas insister assez sur

underemployed [ˌʌndərɪmˈplɔɪd] *adj (worker, equipment)* sous-employé; *(resources)* sous-exploité; **he feels underemployed** il trouve qu'il n'a pas assez de travail

underemployment [ˌʌndərɪmˈplɔɪmənt] *n (of workers)* sous-emploi *m*; *(of resources)* sous-exploitation *f*

underequipped [ˌʌndərɪˈkwɪpt] *adj (country etc)* sous-équipé

underestimate **1** *vt* [ˌʌndəˈrestɪmeɪt] *(size, strength)* sous-estimer; *(person, value)* sous-estimer, mésestimer

2 *n* [ˌʌndəˈrestɪmət] sous-estimation *f*

underestimation [ˈʌndərˌestɪˈmeɪʃən] *n* sous-estimation *f*

underexpose [ˌʌndərɪkˈspəʊz] *vt* (**a**) *Phot (print, film)* sous-exposer (**b**) *(underpublicize → person, film, event)* ne pas faire assez de publicité pour

underexposed [ˈʌndərɪkˈspəʊzd] *adj Phot* sous-exposé

underexposure [ˌʌndərɪkˈspəʊʒə(r)] *n* (**a**) *Phot (lack of exposure)* sous-exposition *f*; *(photo, print)* photo *f* sous-exposée (**b**) *(to publicity)* manque *m* de publicité; **the campaign suffered from underexposure in the media** la campagne a souffert d'un manque de publicité dans les médias (**c**) *(social)* **underexposure to other children may inhibit development** le manque de contact avec d'autres enfants peut freiner le développement

underfed [ˌʌndəˈfed] **1** *pt & pp of* **underfeed**

2 *adj (person)* sous-alimenté

underfeed [ˌʌndəˈfiːd] *(pt & pp* **underfed** [-ˈfed]*)* *vt* sous-alimenter

underfeeding [ˌʌndəˈfiːdɪŋ] *n* sous-alimentation *f*

underfelt [ˈʌndəfelt] *n* thibaude *f*

underfinance [ˌʌndəˈfaɪnæns] *vt* financer insuffisamment

underfinanced [ˌʌndəˈfaɪnænst] *adj (business, scheme, school)* qui ne dispose pas de fonds suffisants

underfloor [ˈʌndəflɔː(r)] *adj (pipes, wiring)* qui se trouve sous le plancher

►► ***underfloor heating*** chauffage *m* par le sol

underflow [ˈʌndəfləʊ] *n* (**a**) *(current → in sea)* courant *m* sous-marin (**b**) *Comput* dépassement *m* par valeurs inférieures

underfoot [ˌʌndəˈfʊt] *adv* sous les pieds; **the grass is wet underfoot** l'herbe est humide; **I felt the gravel crunch underfoot** j'ai senti les graviers crisser sous mes pieds; *also Fig* **to trample sb/sth underfoot** *(of person)* fouler qn/qch aux pieds; *(of animal)* piétiner qn/qch

underfund [ˌʌndəˈfʌnd] *vt (gen)* ne pas doter de fonds suffisants; *Fin* sous-capitaliser; **the health system in this country has been underfunded for years** le système de santé de ce pays pâtit d'un manque de fonds depuis des années

underfunded [ˌʌndəˈfʌndɪd] *adj (gen)* qui ne dispose pas de fonds suffisants; *Fin* sous-capitalisé

underfunding [ˌʌndəˈfʌndɪŋ] *n (gen)* financement *m* insuffisant; *Fin* sous-capitalisation *f*

underfur [ˈʌndəfɜː(r)] *n* bourre *f*, duvet *m*

under-gardener *n* aide-jardinier(ère) *m,f*

undergarment [ˈʌndəˌgɑːmənt] *n* sous-vêtement *m*

underglaze [ˈʌndəgleɪz] *n* sous-couche *f*

undergo [ˌʌndəˈgəʊ] *(pt* **underwent** [-ˈwent], *pp* **undergone** [-ˈgɒn]) *vt* (**a**) *(experience → change)* subir; *(→ hardship)* subir, éprouver (**b**) *(test, trials)* subir, passer; *(training)* suivre (**c**) *(be subject to)* subir; **the building/the system is undergoing modernization** l'immeuble/le système est en cours de modernisation (**d**) *Med* **to undergo an operation** subir une intervention chirurgicale; **to undergo treatment** suivre un traitement

undergrad [ˈʌndəgræd] *n Fam* étudiant(e) *m,f (qui prépare une licence)*

undergraduate [ˌʌndəˈgrædʒʊət] **1** *n* étudiant(e) *m,f (qui prépare une licence)*; **she was an undergraduate at Manchester** elle était en licence à Manchester

2 *adj (circles, life)* estudiantin, étudiant; *(course)* pour les étudiants de licence; *(accommodation, grant)* pour étudiants; *(humour)* d'étudiant

►► ***undergraduate student*** étudiant(e) *m,f* en licence

underground 1 *adj* [ˈʌndəgraʊnd] (**a**) *(subterranean → explosion, pipe, lake, cable)* souterrain; *(→ car park)* en sous-sol, souterrain

(**b**) *(secret)* secret(ète), clandestin; **they joined an underground movement** *(clandestine)* ils sont entrés dans un mouvement clandestin; *(resistance)* ils sont entrés dans un mouvement de résistance; **the underground press** la presse clandestine

(**c**) *(unofficial → literature, theatre)* d'avant-garde, underground *(inv)*; *(→ institutions)* parallèle

(**d**) *(illegal → methods)* illégal

2 *n* [ˈʌndəgraʊnd] (**a**) *Mil & Pol (resistance)* résistance *f*; *(secret army)* armée *f* secrète

(**b**) *Art, Mus & Theat* avant-garde *f*, underground *m inv*

(**c**) *Br (railway)* métro *m*; **to go by underground** aller en métro; **the London/Glasgow underground** le métro de Londres *ou* londonien/de Glasgow

3 *adv* [ˌʌndəˈgraʊnd] (**a**) *(below surface)* sous (la) terre

(**b**) *(in hiding)* **to go underground** passer dans la clandestinité, prendre le maquis

►► ***underground economy*** économie *f* souterraine; *Hist* ***the Underground Railroad*** = réseau clandestin qui permettait aux fugitifs noirs des États esclavagistes de rejoindre le nord des États-Unis ou le Canada; ***underground railway*** métro *m*; ***underground station*** station *f* de métro; ***underground train*** rame *f* de métro

undergrown [ˌʌndəgrəʊn] *adj (person, plant)* qui n'a pas atteint une taille normale, dont la croissance est insuffisante

undergrowth [ˈʌndəgrəʊθ] *n (UNCOUNT)* sous-bois *m*; *(scrub)* broussailles *fpl*

underhand [ˌʌndəˈhænd] **1** *adj* (**a**) *(action)* en dessous, en sous-main; *(person)* sournois; **in an underhand way** sournoisement (**b**) *Sport* par en dessous

2 *adv* sournoisement

underhanded [ˌʌndəˈhændɪd] *adj* (**a**) = **underhand** *adj* (**b**) *(shorthanded)* qui manque de personnel

underhandedly [ˌʌndəˈhændɪdlɪ] *adv* en dessous, sournoisement

underhung [ˌʌndəˈhʌŋ] *adj* (**a**) *(jaw)* prognathe, saillant (**b**) *(door)* à coulisse

underinsure [ˌʌndərɪnˈʃɔː(r)] *vt* sous-assurer

underinsured [ˌʌndərɪnˈʃɔːd] *adj* sous-assuré

underinvestment [ˌʌndərɪnˈvestmənt] *n* insuffisance *f* d'investissement

underlaid [ˌʌndəˈleɪd] *pt & pp of* **underlay**

underlain [ˌʌndəˈleɪn] *pp of* **underlie**

underlay 1 [ˌʌndəˈleɪ] *pt of* **underlie**

2 *vt* [ˌʌndəˈleɪ] *(pt & pp* **underlaid** [-ˈleɪd]) *(carpet)* doubler

3 *n* [ˈʌndəleɪ] *(felt)* thibaude *f*; *(foam)* doublure *f*

underlie [ˌʌndəˈlaɪ] *(pt* **underlay** [-ˈleɪ], *pp* **underlain** [-ˈleɪn]) *vt* sous-tendre, être à la base de

underline [ˌʌndəˈlaɪn] *vt also Fig* souligner

underling [ˈʌndəlɪŋ] *n Pej* subalterne *mf*, sous-fifre *m*

underlining [ˌʌndəˈlaɪnɪŋ] *n* soulignage *m*

underlying [ˌʌndəˈlaɪɪŋ] *adj* sous-jacent

►► *Fin* ***underlying asset*** actif *m* sous-jacent; *St Exch* ***underlying futures contract*** contrat *m* à terme sous option; *Fin* ***underlying mortgage*** hypothèque *f* sous-jacente; *Fin* ***underlying security*** titre *m* sous-jacent

undermanager [ˈʌndəˌmænɪdʒə(r)] *n* sous-chef *m*, sous-directeur(trice) *m,f*

undermanned [ˌʌndəˈmænd] *adj* qui manque de main-d'œuvre; *Naut* qui manque d'hommes d'équipage

undermanning [ˌʌndəˈmænɪŋ] *n* manque *m ou* pénurie *f* de main-d'œuvre; *Naut* manque *m* d'hommes d'équipage

undermentioned [ˌʌndəˈmenʃənd] *adj Formal* ci-dessous (mentionné)

undermine [ˌʌndəˈmaɪn] *vt* (**a**) *(cliff, coast, wall)* miner, saper (**b**) *(authority, person, principle)* saper; *(health)* user; *(confidence)* ébranler; **to undermine the foundations of society** attaquer les bases de la société; **to undermine democracy** fragiliser la démocratie; **stop undermining me!** arrête de me rabaisser!

undermost [ˈʌndəməʊst] **1** *adj (in heap)* le dernier, le plus bas; *(in depth)* le plus profond *ou* bas

2 *adv* tout en bas

undernamed [ˌʌndəˈneɪmd] *(pl* **inv**) **1** *n* personne *f* nommée ci-dessous *ou* dont le nom suit

2 *adj* nommé ci-dessous

underneath [ˌʌndəˈniːθ] **1** *prep* sous, au-dessous de, en dessous de; **the cat slipped underneath the fence** le chat s'est glissé *ou* est passé sous *ou* par-dessous le grillage; **she was wearing two pullovers underneath her coat** elle portait deux pullovers sous son manteau; **the noise was coming from underneath the floorboards** le bruit venait de sous le plancher

2 *adv* (**a**) *(in space)* (en) dessous, au-dessous; **I've got a pullover on underneath** j'ai un pull dessous

(**b**) *(within oneself)* **he smiled, but underneath he felt afraid/helpless** il a souri, mais dans le fond *ou* en son for intérieur il avait peur/il se sentait impuissant

3 *n* dessous *m*; **what's written on the underneath?** qu'est-ce qui est écrit sur le dessous?; **the underneath of the box is black** le dessous de la boîte est noir

4 *adj* de dessous, d'en dessous

undernourished [ˌʌndəˈnʌrɪʃt] *adj* sous-alimenté

undernourishment [ˌʌndəˈnʌrɪʃmənt] *n* sous-alimentation *f*

underpaid [ˌʌndəˈpeɪd] **1** *pt & pp of* **underpay**

2 *adj* sous-payé

underpants [ˈʌndəpænts] *npl* (**a**) *(for men)* slip *m (d'homme)*; **a pair of underpants** un slip, un caleçon (**b**) *Am (for women)* culotte *f*

underpart [ˈʌndəpɑːt] **1** *n* (**a**) *Zool (underside)* dessous *m*, partie *f* inférieure (**b**) *Theat* rôle *m* secondaire

2 underparts *npl (abdomen)* ventre *m*

underpass [ˈʌndəpɑːs] *n* (**a**) *(subway)* passage *m* souterrain (**b**) *(road)* route *f* inférieure

underpay [ˌʌndəˈpeɪ] *(pt & pp* **underpaid** [-ˈpeɪd]) *vt* sous-payer

underpeopled [ˌʌndəˈpiːpəld] *adj* sous-peuplé

underperform [ˌʌndəpəˈfɔːm] *vi* rester en deçà de ses possibilités; *St Exch (shares)* avoir un cours trop bas

underpin [ˌʌndəˈpɪn] *(pt & pp* **underpinned,** *cont* **underpinning**) *vt also Fig* soutenir, étayer; **the principles which underpin Marxism-Leninism** les principes de base du marxisme-léninisme

underpinning [ˌʌndəˈpɪnɪŋ] *n* soutien *m*, étayage *m*

underplay [ˌʌndəˈpleɪ] **1** *vt* (**a**) *(minimize → importance)* minimiser; *(→ event)* réduire *ou* minimiser l'importance de; **to underplay one's hand** *(in cards)* jouer volontairement une petite carte; *Fig* cacher son jeu (**b**) *Theat (role)* jouer avec retenue

2 *vi (in cards)* jouer volontairement une petite carte

underpopulated [ˌʌndəˈpɒpjʊleɪtɪd] *adj* sous-peuplé

underpowered [ˌʌndəˈpaʊəd] *adj* qui manque de puissance; *Fig* **an underpowered performance** un jeu qui manque de puissance

underprice [ˌʌndəˈpraɪs] *vt* mettre en vente au-dessous de sa valeur réelle

underpriced [ˌʌndəˈpraɪst] *adj* très bon marché (par rapport à sa valeur réelle); **at £15.99 it's definitely underpriced** à 15,99 livres c'est vraiment donné

underpricing [ˌʌndəˈpraɪsɪŋ] *n* fixation *f* de prix trop bas

underprivileged [ˌʌndəˈprɪvɪlɪdʒd] **1** *adj (person, social class)* défavorisé, déshérité

2 *npl* **the underprivileged** les défavorisés *mpl*

underproduce [ˌʌndəprəˈdjuːs] **1** *vt* produire insuffisamment de

2 *vi* produire insuffisamment

underproduction [ˌʌndəprəˈdʌkʃən] *n* sous-production *f*

underqualified [ˌʌndəˈkwɒlɪfaɪd] *adj* sous-qualifié

underquote [ˌʌndəˈkwəʊt] *vt* (**a**) *(goods, securities, services)* = proposer à un prix inférieur à celui du marché (**b**) *(competitor)* vendre moins cher que

underrate [ˌʌndəˈreɪt] *vt* sous-estimer

underrated [ˌʌndəˈreɪtɪd] *adj* sous-estimé; *(person)* méconnu

underrehearsed [ˌʌndərɪˈhɜːst] *adj Mus & Theat* insuffisamment répété

underrepresent [ˌʌndərepriˈzent] *vt* minimiser, ne pas donner assez d'importance à

underrepresentation [ˈʌndəˌreprɪzenˈteɪʃən] *n (gen) & Pol* sous-représentation *f*

underrepresented [ˌʌndərepriˈzentɪd] *adj (gen) & Pol* sous-représenté

underripe [ˌʌndəˈraɪp] *adj* pas mûr

underscore [ˌʌndəˈskɔː(r)] **1** *vt also Fig* souligner

2 *n* soulignage *m*, soulignement *m*

undersea [ˈʌndəsiː] **1** *adj* sous-marin

2 *adv* sous la mer

underseal [ˈʌndəsiːl] *Br Aut* **1** *n* (**a**) *(product)* produit *m* antirouille (**b**) *(act, result)* couche *f* antirouille

2 *vt* traiter contre la rouille

underseas [ˌʌndəˈsiːz] *adv* sous la mer

undersecretary [ˌʌndəˈsekrətərɪ] *(pl* **undersecretaries**) *n Pol* (**a**) *Br (in department)* chef *m* de cabinet (**b**) *(politician)* sous-secrétaire *m*; **undersecretary of state** sous-secrétaire d'État

undersell [ˌʌndəˈsel] *(pt & pp* **undersold** [-ˈsəʊld]) **1** *vt (competitor)* vendre moins cher que; *(goods)* vendre au-dessous de la valeur de; *Fig* **to undersell oneself** se sous-estimer; *Fig* **don't undersell yourself at the interview** essaie de bien te vendre lors de l'entretien

2 *vi (goods)* se vendre mal

undersexed [ˌʌndəˈsekst] *adj* qui manque de libido

undersheet [ˈʌndəʃiːt] *n* alaise *f*

undershield [ˈʌndəʃiːld] *n Aut* bouclier *m* inférieur

undershirt [ˈʌndəʃɜːt] *n Am* maillot *m ou* tricot *m* de corps

undershoot [ˌʌndəˈʃuːt] (*pt & pp* **undershot** [ˈʃɒt]) *vt* **the plane undershot the runway** l'avion s'est posé avant d'atteindre la piste d'atterrissage; **he undershot the target** son coup n'a pas atteint la cible

undershorts [ˈʌndəʃɔːts] *npl Am* caleçon *m*, slip *m*

undershot [ˌʌndəˈʃɒt] **1** *pt & pp of* **undershoot**
2 *adj* (**a**) *(jaw)* proéminent, saillant (**b**) *(waterwheel)* à aubes

underside [ˈʌndəsaɪd] *n* **the underside** le dessous, la face inférieure

undersigned [ˈʌndəsaɪnd] (*pl* **inv**) *Formal* **1** *n* **the undersigned** le soussigné, la soussignée; **I, the undersigned** je soussigné
2 *adj* soussigné

undersize(d) [ˌʌndəˈsaɪz(d)] *adj* trop petit

underskirt [ˈʌndəskɜːt] *n* jupon *m*

underslung [ˌʌndəˈslʌŋ] *adj* très bas; *Aut* surbaissé

undersoil [ˈʌndəsɔɪl] *n Agr* sous-sol *m*

undersold [ˌʌndəˈsəʊld] *pt & pp of* **undersell**

understaffed [ˌʌndəˈstɑːft] *adj* qui manque de personnel

understaffing [ˌʌndəˈstɑːfɪŋ] *n* manque *m ou* pénurie *f* de personnel

understand [ˌʌndəˈstænd] (*pt & pp* **understood** [-ˈstʊd]) **1** *vt* (**a**) *(meaning)* comprendre; **I understand what you mean** je comprends ce que vous voulez dire; **is that understood?** est-ce compris?; **to make oneself understood** se faire comprendre; **do I make myself understood?** *(as threat)* est-ce que je me suis bien fait comprendre?; **she didn't understand a single word** elle n'a pas compris un traître mot; **I can't understand it!** je ne comprends pas!, cela me dépasse!
(**b**) *(subject, theory)* comprendre, entendre; **I don't understand a thing about economics** je ne comprends rien à l'économie
(**c**) *(character, person)* comprendre; **he claims his wife doesn't understand him** il affirme que sa femme ne le comprend pas; **I understand your need to be independent** je comprends bien que vous ayez besoin d'être indépendant; **we understand each other perfectly** nous nous comprenons parfaitement; **she didn't understand why no one was interested** elle ne comprenait pas pourquoi personne n'était intéressé
(**d**) *(believe)* comprendre, croire; **I understand you need a loan** j'ai cru comprendre que *ou* si j'ai bien compris, vous avez besoin d'un prêt; **I understood that I was to be paid for my work** j'ai cru comprendre que je devais être payé pour mon travail; **am I to understand that they refused?** dois-je comprendre qu'ils ont refusé?; **they are understood to have fled the country** il paraît qu'ils ont fui le pays; **we were given to understand that he was very ill** on nous a fait comprendre *ou* donné à entendre qu'il était très malade; **so I understand** c'est ce que j'ai compris
(**e**) *(interpret)* entendre; **what do you understand by "soon"?** qu'est-ce que vous entendez par "bientôt"?; **as I understand it, there's nothing to pay** d'après ce que j'ai compris, il n'y a rien à payer
(**f**) *(leave implicit)* entendre, sous-entendre; **she let it be understood that she preferred to be alone** elle a laissé entendre *ou* donné à entendre qu'elle préférait être seule; *Gram* **the object of the sentence is understood** l'objet de la phrase est sous-entendu
2 *vi* comprendre; **of course, I understand** bien sûr, je comprends (bien); **if you do that once more you're out, understand?** faites ça encore une fois et vous êtes viré, compris?; **they understand about international finance** ils s'y connaissent en finance internationale

understandable [ˌʌndəˈstændəbəl] *adj* compréhensible; **that's perfectly understandable** cela se comprend parfaitement

understandably [ˌʌndəˈstændəblɪ] *adv* (**a**) *(naturally)* naturellement; **they were, understandably (enough), deeply embarrassed** ils étaient profondément gênés, ce qui se comprend parfaitement (**b**) *(speak, write)* de manière compréhensible

understanding [ˌʌndəˈstændɪŋ] **1** *n* (**a**) *(UNCOUNT) (comprehension)* compréhension *f*; *(intelligence)* intelligence *f*; *(knowledge)* connaissance *f*, connaissances *fpl*; **it is our understanding that they have now left the country** d'après ce que nous avons compris, ils ont quitté le pays à présent; **they have little understanding of what the decision involves** ils ne comprennent pas très bien ce que la décision entraînera; **it's beyond all understanding!** cela dépasse l'entendement!, c'est à n'y rien comprendre!
(**b**) *(agreement)* accord *m*, arrangement *m*; **to come to** *or* **reach an understanding about sth (with sb)** s'entendre (avec qn) sur qch; **there's some kind of understanding between them** il y a quelque arrangement entre eux
(**c**) *(interpretation)* compréhension *f*, interprétation *f*; *(conception)* conception *f*; **my understanding of the matter is that he's resigned** d'après ce que j'ai compris, il a démissionné; **my understanding was that the venue would be paid for by the organizers** j'avais compris que les organisateurs paieraient pour la location des locaux
(**d**) *(relationship → between people)* bonne intelligence *f*, entente *f*; *(→ between nations)* entente *f*
(**e**) *(sympathy)* **he showed great understanding** il a fait preuve de beaucoup de compréhension
(**f**) *(condition)* condition *f*
2 *adj* compréhensif, bienveillant
3 on the understanding that *conj* à condition que; **on the understanding that the money is given to charity** à condition que l'argent soit donné à des bonnes œuvres

understandingly [ˌʌndəˈstændɪŋlɪ] *adv* avec compréhension, avec bienveillance

understate [ˌʌndəˈsteɪt] *vt* (**a**) *(minimize)* minimiser (l'importance de); **the deliberately understated figures in the foreground** les silhouettes volontairement estompées au premier plan (**b**) *(state with restraint)* dire avec retenue, modérer l'expression de

understated [ˌʌndəˈsteɪtɪd] *adj* discret(ète); **the acting was very understated** le jeu des acteurs était très sobre

understatement [ˌʌndəˈsteɪtmənt] *n* euphémisme *m*; *Ling & Literature* litote *f*; **that's a bit of an understatement!** c'est peu dire!; **to say it's expensive is an understatement** dire que c'est cher est un euphémisme; **calling him lazy is something of an understatement** le traiter de paresseux, c'est peu dire; *Hum* **that's the understatement of the year!** c'est le moins qu'on puisse dire!; **with typical British understatement** avec un sens de l'euphémisme tout britannique

understeer [ˈʌndəˌstɪə(r)] *vi Aut* sous-virer

understeering [ˈʌndəˌstɪərɪŋ] *n Aut* sous-virage *m*, comportement *m* sous-vireur

understock [ˌʌndəˈstɒk] *vt (shop)* mal approvisionner; **the farm is understocked** la ferme manque de bétail

understood [ˌʌndəˈstʊd] *pt & pp of* **understand**

understudy [ˈʌndəˌstʌdɪ] (*pl* **understudies**, *pt & pp* **understudied**) **1** *n Theat* doublure *f*
2 *vt (role)* apprendre un rôle en tant que doublure; *(actor)* doubler

undersubscribed [ˌʌndəsʌbˈskraɪbd] *adj Fin & St Exch (issue, share)* non-souscrit

undertake [ˌʌndəˈteɪk] (*pt* **undertook** [-ˈtʊk], *pp* **undertaken** [-ˈteɪkən]) **1** *vt* (**a**) *Formal (take up → job, project, journey)* entreprendre; *(→ experiment)* entreprendre, se lancer dans; *(→ responsibility)* assumer, se charger de; *(→ change)* entreprendre, mettre en œuvre
(**b**) *Formal (agree, promise)* s'engager à; **he undertook to pay half the costs** il s'est engagé à payer la moitié des frais
(**c**) *Fam (vehicle)* doubler par l'intérieur ❑
2 *vi Fam (driver, vehicle)* doubler par l'intérieur ❑

undertaker [ˈʌndəˌteɪkə(r)] *n* entrepreneur *m* des pompes funèbres; **we'd better call the undertakers** il faut appeler les pompes funèbres

undertaking [ˌʌndəˈteɪkɪŋ] *n* (**a**) *(promise)* engagement *m*; **to give a written undertaking to do sth** s'engager par écrit à faire qch; **she gave an undertaking that she wouldn't intervene** elle a promis de ne pas intervenir (**b**) *(enterprise)* entreprise *f*; **it's quite an undertaking** c'est toute une affaire (**c**) *Fam (of vehicle)* dépassement *m* par l'intérieur ❑

undertax [ˌʌndəˈtæks] *vt (goods, product)* taxer insuffisamment; *(person)* ne pas faire payer assez d'impôts à

under-the-counter *Fam* **1** *adj (agreement, offer, sale)* en douce, clandestin ❑; **an under-the-counter payment** un dessous-de-table
2 *adv* clandestinement ❑, sous le manteau; **to sell sth under-the-counter** vendre qch sous le manteau

underthings [ˈʌndəθɪŋz] *npl Fam* dessous *mpl*, sous-vêtements ❑ *mpl*

underthrust [ˌʌndəθrʌst] *n Geol* sous-charriage *m*

undertip [ˌʌndəˈtɪp] (*pt & pp* **undertipped**, *cont* **undertipping**) *vi* donner un pourboire trop petit

undertone [ˈʌndətəʊn] *n* (**a**) *(in speech)* voix *f* basse; **to speak in an undertone** parler à voix basse *ou* à mi-voix (**b**) *(of feeling)* nuance *f*; **the situation had comic undertones** au fond, la situation avait quelque chose de comique; **all her poetry has a tragic undertone** toute sa poésie a un fond de tragique (**c**) *(in colour)* nuance *f*; **grey with blue undertones** gris nuancé de bleu

undertook [ˌʌndəˈtʊk] *pt of* **undertake**

undertow [ˈʌndətəʊ] *n* courant *m* sous-marin *(causé par le reflux de la vague)*; *Fig* **I sensed an undertow of resentment in her words** je sentais un vague ressentiment dans ses paroles

undertrick [ˈʌndətrɪk] *n Cards (in bridge)* = trick qui ne remplit pas le contrat

undertrump [ˌʌndəˈtrʌmp] *vi Cards* = jouer un atout inférieur à un autre déjà joué

underuse 1 *n* [ˌʌndəˈjuːs] *(gen)* sous-utilisation *f*; *(of resources, land)* sous-exploitation *f*
2 *vt* [ˌʌndəˈjuːz] *(gen)* sous-utiliser; *(resources, land)* sous-exploiter

underused [ˌʌndəˈjuːzd] *adj (gen)* sous-utilisé, insuffisamment utilisé; *(resources, land)* sous-exploité

underutilization [ˈʌndəˌjuːtɪlaɪˈzeɪʃən] *n (gen)* sous-utilisation *f*; *(of resources, land)* sous-exploitation *f*

underutilize, -ise [ˌʌndəˈjuːtɪlaɪz] *vt (gen)* sous-utiliser; *(resources, land)* sous-exploiter

underutilized [ˌʌndəˈjuːtɪlaɪzd] *adj (gen)* sous-utilisé, insuffisamment utilisé; *(resources, land)* sous-exploité

undervaluation [ˌʌndəvæljʊˈeɪʃən] *n (object, goods)* sous-évaluation *f*

undervalue [ˌʌndəˈvæljuː] *vt (object, goods)* sous-évaluer, sous-estimer; *(person, help)* sous-estimer

undervest [ˈʌndəvest] *n Br* tricot *m ou* maillot *m* de corps

underwater 1 *adj* [ˈʌndəwɔːtə(r)] sous-marin; *Am St Exch (share prices)* décoté
2 *adv* [ˌʌndəˈwɔːtə(r)] sous l'eau
►► *Am St Exch* ***underwater option*** option *f* à prix glissant à la baisse

underwear [ˈʌndəweə(r)] *n (UNCOUNT)* sous-vêtements *mpl*

underweight [ˌʌndəˈweɪt] *adj* (**a**) *(person)* qui ne pèse pas assez, trop maigre; **to be underweight** être en dessous de son poids normal; **I'm half a stone underweight** je devrais peser trois kilos de plus (**b**) *(goods)* d'un poids insuffisant; **all the packets are 20 grams underweight** il manque 20 grammes à chaque paquet

underwent [ˌʌndəˈwent] *pt of* **undergo**

underwhelm [ˌʌndəˈwelm] *vt Hum* décevoir; **she felt rather underwhelmed by it all** elle a été plutôt déçue par tout ça; **your generosity underwhelms me** votre générosité me renverse; **he was obviously underwhelmed by his present** le cadeau l'avait laissé manifestement indifférent; **the critics were underwhelmed by his next film** son nouveau film fut accueilli avec un enthousiasme très relatif par la critique

underwhelming [ˌʌndəˈwelmɪŋ] *adj Hum* décevant; **I found the whole affair distinctly underwhelming** j'ai trouvé toute l'affaire vraiment décevante

underwired [ˈʌndəˌwaɪəd] *adj (bra)* avec armature

underwood [ˈʌndəwʊd] *n (UNCOUNT)* sous-bois *m*; *(scrub)* broussailles *fpl*

underworld [ˈʌndəˌwɜːld] **1** *n* (**a**) *(of criminals)* pègre *f*, milieu *m* (**b**) *Myth* **the underworld** les Enfers *mpl*

2 *comp (activity)* du milieu; *(contact)* dans *ou* avec le milieu

'Underworld' *DeLillo* 'Outremonde'

underwrite [ˈʌndəraɪt] *(pt* **underwrote** [-ˈrəʊt], *pp* **underwritten** [-ˈrɪtən]) *vt* (**a**) *Ins (policy)* garantir; *(risk)* garantir, assurer contre (**b**) *St Exch (new issue)* garantir, souscrire (**c**) *(support → financially)* soutenir *ou* appuyer financièrement; *(→ by agreement)* soutenir, souscrire à

underwriter [ˈʌndəˌraɪtə(r)] *n* (**a**) *Ins (of policy, risk)* assureur *m* (**b**) *St Exch (of new issue)* syndicataire *mf*; **the underwriters** le syndicat de garantie

►► *St Exch* ***underwriter agent*** agent *m* souscripteur; ***Underwriters' Laboratories*** = organisme américain contrôlant la sécurité des appareils électriques

underwriting [ˈʌndəˌraɪtɪŋ] *n Ins (of policy, risk)* garantie *f*; **marine underwriting** assurance *f* maritime

►► *St Exch* ***underwriting agent*** agent *m* souscripteur; *Ins* ***underwriting commission*** commission *f* de garantie; *Ins* ***underwriting fee*** commission *f* de placement

underwritten [ˌʌndəˈrɪtən] *pp of* **underwrite**

underwrote [ˌʌndəˈrəʊt] *pt of* **underwrite**

undescended [ˌʌndɪˈsendɪd] *adj Anat (testis)* qui n'est pas descendu

undeserved [ˌʌndɪˈzɜːvd] *adj* immérité, injuste

undeservedly [ˌʌndɪˈzɜːvɪdlɪ] *adv* injustement, indûment

undeserving [ˌʌndɪˈzɜːvɪŋ] *adj (person)* peu méritant; *(cause)* peu méritoire; **he is quite undeserving of such praise** il est parfaitement indigne de *ou* il ne mérite pas du tout de telles louanges

undesirable [ˌʌndɪˈzaɪərəbəl] **1** *adj* indésirable; **highly undesirable** tout à fait inopportun; **to have an undesirable influence on sb** avoir une mauvaise influence sur qn

2 *n* indésirable *mf*

►► ***undesirable alien*** étranger(ère) *m,f* indésirable

undesired [ˌʌndɪˈzaɪəd] *adj (effect, result)* non souhaité

undesirous [ˌʌndɪˈzaɪərəs] *adj Literary* peu désireux (**of** de); **to be undesirous of doing sth** n'avoir aucun désir de faire qch

undetected [ˌʌndɪˈtektɪd] *adj (error)* non détecté, non décelé; *(disease)* non détecté, non dépisté; **to go undetected** passer inaperçu

undetermined [ˌʌndɪˈtɜːmɪnd] *adj* (**a**) *(unknown)* inconnu, indéterminé; **an artefact of undeter-** [illegible] nue; **for an undetermined sum of money** pour une somme d'argent non fixée (**b**) *(hesitant)* irrésolu, indécis

undeterred [ˌʌndɪˈtɜːd] *adj* sans se laisser décourager; **she was undeterred by this setback** elle ne s'est pas laissé décourager par ce revers; **undeterred by the weather, he went out for a walk** en dépit du mauvais temps, il est sorti se promener

undeveloped [ˌʌndɪˈveləpt] *adj* (**a**) *(ideas, suggestions)* non développé; *(country)* en développement; *(muscles, organs)* non formé; *(land, resources)* non exploité (**b**) *(immature)* immature (**c**) *Phot (film)* non développé

undeviating [ˌʌnˈdiːvɪeɪtɪŋ] *adj (course, path)* droit, direct; *(faithfulness)* qui ne se dément pas

undid [ˌʌnˈdɪd] *pt of* **undo**

undies [ˈʌndɪz] *npl Fam* (*abbr* **underwear**) sous-vêtements *mpl* féminins

undifferentiated [ˌʌndɪfəˈrenʃɪeɪtɪd] *adj* indifférencié

►► *Mktg* ***undifferentiated marketing*** marketing *m* indifférencié

undigested [ˌʌndɪˈdʒestɪd] *adj* mal digéré, non digéré

undignified [ˌʌnˈdɪgnɪfaɪd] *adj (behaviour, person)* qui manque de dignité; **to be undignified** manquer de dignité; **their business venture came to an undignified end** leur entreprise a échoué de façon lamentable

undiluted [ˌʌndaɪˈljuːtɪd] *adj* (**a**) *(liquid)* non dilué; *(acid)* concentré (**b**) *Fig (emotion)* sans mélange, parfait; **it's pure, undiluted malice** c'est de la méchanceté à l'état pur

undiminished [ˌʌndɪˈmɪnɪʃt] *adj* intact, non diminué; **my respect for him remains undiminished** mon respect pour lui n'a pas diminué *ou* est resté intact; **thirty years later, the appeal of the film remains undiminished** trente ans plus tard, le film n'a rien perdu de son intérêt

undimmed [ˌʌnˈdɪmd] *adj Literary* (**a**) *(light, faculty)* non diminué (**b**) *Fig (fame, lustre)* non terni; *(memory)* intact

undine [ˈʌndiːn] *n Myth* ondine *f*

undiplomatic [ˌʌndɪpləˈmætɪk] *adj (action)* peu diplomatique; *(person)* peu diplomate, qui manque de diplomatie

undiplomatically [ˌʌndɪpləˈmætɪklɪ] *adv* de manière peu diplomatique

undipped [ˌʌnˈdɪpt] *adj Br Aut* **to drive with undipped headlights** rouler en pleins phares

undirected [ˌʌndɪˈrektɪd] *adj* (**a**) *(effort)* sans but (**b**) *(mail)* sans adresse

undiscerned [ˌʌndɪˈsɜːnd] *adj* inaperçu

undiscerning [ˌʌndɪˈsɜːnɪŋ] *adj (eater, winedrinker)* peu raffiné, peu connaisseur; *(mind)* peu pénétrant; **to be undiscerning** *(person)* manquer de discernement

undischarged [ˌʌndɪsˈtʃɑːdʒd] *adj Fin & Law (bankrupt)* non réhabilité, non déchargé; *(debt)* non liquidé

undisciplined [ʌnˈdɪsɪplɪnd] *adj* indiscipliné

undisclosed [ˌʌndɪsˈkləʊzd] *adj* non divulgué; **for an undisclosed sum** pour une somme dont le montant n'a pas été révélé

►► *Com* ***undisclosed principal*** acheteur *m* non identifié *ou* anonyme

undiscountable [ˌʌndɪsˈkaʊntəbəl] *adj Fin* inescomptable

undiscovered [ˌʌndɪˈskʌvəd] *adj* non découvert; **the manuscript lay undiscovered for centuries** le manuscrit est resté inconnu des siècles durant; **an undiscovered land** une terre inconnue

undiscriminating [ˌʌndɪsˈkrɪmɪˌneɪtɪŋ] *adj* qui manque de discernement

undiscriminatingly [ˌʌndɪsˈkrɪmɪˌneɪtɪŋlɪ] *adv* sans discernement

undisguised [ˌʌndɪsˈgaɪzd] *adj (hatred, contempt, pleasure)* non dissimulé

undisguisedly [ˌʌndɪsˈgaɪzɪdlɪ] *adv* ouvertement

undismayed [ˌʌndɪsˈmeɪd] *adj* qui ne se laisse pas décourager; **he seemed quite undismayed by his defeat** sa défaite ne semblait pas du tout l'avoir découragé

undisputed [ˌʌndɪˈspjuːtɪd] *adj* incontesté

undisputedly [ˌʌndɪˈspjuːtɪdlɪ] *adj* incontestablement

undissolved [ˌʌndɪˈzɒlvd] *adj (salt, sugar, chemical substance)* non dissous

undistinguishable [ˌʌndɪˈstɪŋgwɪʃəbəl] *adj (alike)* impossible à distinguer

undistinguished [ˌʌndɪˈstɪŋgwɪʃt] *adj* (**a**) *(person)* peu distingué, sans distinction (**b**) *(style, taste)* banal, quelconque

undistributed [ˌʌndɪsˈtrɪbjətəd] *adj Fin (money, earnings)* non distribué

►► ***undistributed profits*** bénéfices *mpl* non distribués

undisturbed [ˌʌndɪˈstɜːbd] *adj* (**a**) *(in peace)* tranquille; **I want to be left undisturbed for a while** je veux qu'on me laisse tranquille un moment

(**b**) *(unchanged, untroubled)* inchangé, tranquille; **village life has gone on here undisturbed for centuries** la vie du village se poursuit tranquillement depuis des siècles; **the population remained largely undisturbed by the war** en général, la population n'a pas été affectée par la guerre

(**c**) *(untouched → body, ground, papers)* non dérangé, non déplacé

undivided [ˌʌndɪˈvaɪdɪd] *adj* (**a**) *(whole)* entier; **this job requires your undivided attention** ce travail nécessite toute votre attention *ou* votre entière attention; **you have my undivided love** vous avez tout mon amour (**b**) *(unanimous)* unanime

undivulged [ˌʌndaɪˈvʌldʒd] *adj* non divulgué

undo [ˌʌnˈduː] *(pt* **undid** [-ˈdɪd], *pp* **undone** [-ˈdʌn]) **1** *vt* (**a**) *(bow, knot, button, knitting)* défaire; *(tie, lace)* défaire, dénouer; *(fastening)* défaire; *(screw)* desserrer; *(parcel)* défaire, déficeler; *(shoes)* délacer; *(garment, belt)* défaire

(**b**) *(ruin → work)* détruire; *(→ effect)* annuler; *(→ plan)* mettre en échec; **you can't undo the past** ce qui est fait est fait

(**c**) *(repair → wrong, mistake)* réparer

(**d**) *Comput (command)* annuler, défaire; **can't undo** impossible d'annuler; **undo changes** annuler les révisions; **undo last** annuler dernière opération

(**e**) *Literary or Hum (hope, plan)* ruiner, anéantir; *(person)* être la ruine de

2 *vi (tie, bra, belt, lace, knot)* se défaire; *(zip)* s'ouvrir; *(blouse)* se déboutonner

►► *Comput* ***undo command*** commande *f* d'annulation

undock [ˌʌnˈdɒk] **1** *vt Astron* larguer

2 *vi* (**a**) *Astron* se séparer (**b**) *Naut* quitter le quai

undocking [ˌʌnˈdɒkɪŋ] *n Astron* largage *m*

►► *Astron* ***undocking manoeuvre*** manœuvre *f* de largage

undocumented [ˌʌnˈdɒkjʊmentɪd] *adj* non documenté

undoing [ˌʌnˈduːɪŋ] *n* perte *f*; **that man will be her undoing** cet homme la conduira à sa perte; **his indecision proved to be his undoing** son indécision a causé sa perte

undomesticated [ˌʌndəˈmestɪˌkeɪtɪd] *adj (animal)* non domestiqué; *(person)* sans talent pour les travaux ménagers; **she's completely undomesticated** elle ne sait rien faire dans la maison

undone [ˌʌnˈdʌn] **1** *pp of* **undo**

2 *adj* (**a**) *(button, hair)* défait; *(fastening)* défait; *(blouse)* déboutonné; *(flies)* ouvert; **to come undone** se défaire (**b**) *(task)* non accompli; **we had to leave it undone** nous n'avons pas pu le terminer; **we have left undone those things that we ought to have done** nous n'avons pas fait les choses que nous aurions dû faire (**c**) *Literary or Hum (hope, plan)* ruiné, anéanti; **we are undone!** nous sommes perdus!

undoubted [ˌʌnˈdaʊtɪd] *adj* indubitable

undoubtedly [ˌʌnˈdaʊtɪdlɪ] *adv* indubitablement

undrained [ˌʌnˈdreɪnd] *adj (land, marsh)* non drainé, non asséché

undramatic [ˌʌndrəˈmætɪk] *adj (lacking in interest)* pas très intéressant; **this seemingly undramatic incident...** cet incident apparemment anodin...

undrawn [ˌʌnˈdrɔːn] *adj* (**a**) *(cheque)* qu'on n'a pas tiré (**b**) *(curtains)* ouvert

undreamed-of [ˌʌnˈdriːmd-], **undreamt-of** [ˌʌnˈdremt-] *adj* inconcevable, impensable, auquel on ne songe pas

undress [ˌʌnˈdres] **1** *vt* déshabiller

2 *vi* se déshabiller

3 *n Hum* **in a state of undress** en petite tenue

undressed [ˌʌnˈdrest] *adj* (**a**) *(person)* déshabillé; **to get undressed** se déshabiller (**b**) *(wound)* non pansé (**c**) *(lobster, crab)* nature; *(salad)* non assaisonné (**d**) *(cloth)* inapprêté; *(wood)* en grume; *(stone)* non taillé

undrinkable [ˌʌnˈdrɪŋkəbəl] *adj* (**a**) *(bad-tasting)* imbuvable (**b**) *(unfit for drinking)* non potable

undubbed [ˌʌnˈdʌbd] *adj Cin & TV* non doublé; **the undubbed version of the film** la version originale du film

undue [ˌʌnˈdjuː] *adj* excessif; **with undue haste** avec une hâte excessive

undulant fever [ˈʌndjʊlənt-] *n Med* fièvre *f* ondulante

undulate [ˈʌndjʊleɪt] *vi* onduler

undulating [ˈʌndjʊleɪtɪŋ] *adj (curves, hills)* onduleux

undulation [ˌʌndjʊ'leɪʃən] *n* ondulation *f*

undulatory ['ʌndjʊlətrɪ] *adj (gen)* ondulant; *Phys* ondulatoire

unduly [ˌʌn'djuːlɪ] *adv* excessivement, trop; **not unduly expensive/concerned** pas excessivement cher/inquiet; **he worries unduly** *or* **he's unduly worried about his health** sa santé le préoccupe trop

undutiful [ˌʌn'djuːtɪfʊl] *adj (person)* qui ne remplit pas ses devoirs; *(child)* insoumis

undyed [ˌʌn'daɪd] *adj (fabric, wool)* non teint; *(hair)* non teint; *(foodstuff)* sans colorants

undying [ˌʌn'daɪɪŋ] *adj (faith)* éternel; **to swear one's undying love (for sb)** jurer un amour éternel (à qn)

unearned [ˌʌn'ɜːnd] *adj* (**a**) *(undeserved → fame, privilege)* non mérité, immérité (**b**) *Econ* non gagné en travaillant *ou* par le travail

►► ***unearned income*** *(UNCOUNT)* revenus *mpl* non professionnels, rentes *fpl*; *Econ* ***unearned increment*** plus-value *f*

unearth [ˌʌn'ɜːθ] *vt* (**a**) *(dig up)* déterrer (**b**) *Fig (find → object, equipment, fact)* dénicher, trouver; *(→ old ideas)* ressortir, ressusciter

unearthly [ˌʌn'ɜːθlɪ] *adj* (**a**) *(weird)* étrange; *(unnatural)* surnaturel; *(mysterious)* mystérieux; *(sinister)* sinistre (**b**) *Fig* **at an unearthly hour** à une heure indue; **unearthly din** vacarme *m* de tous les diables; **for some unearthly reason** pour une raison absurde

unease [ˌʌn'iːz] *n Literary* (**a**) *(of mind)* inquiétude *f*, malaise *m*; *(embarrassment)* malaise *m*, gêne *f*; **I tried to ignore my growing unease** j'essayais d'ignorer mon malaise grandissant (**b**) *Pol (unrest)* troubles *mpl*; *(tension)* tension *f*

uneasily [ˌʌn'iːzɪlɪ] *adv* (**a**) *(anxiously → wait, watch)* anxieusement, avec inquiétude; *(→ sleep)* d'un sommeil agité (**b**) *(with embarrassment)* avec gêne, mal à l'aise

uneasiness [ˌʌn'iːzɪnɪs] *n* (**a**) *(anxiety)* inquiétude *f*, malaise *m*; *(of conscience)* trouble *m*; *(of sleep)* agitation *f*; **she felt a growing uneasiness** elle sentait une inquiétude croissante (**b**) *(embarrassment)* malaise *m*, gêne *f*

uneasy [ˌʌn'iːzɪ] *(compar* **uneasier,** *superl* **uneasiest**) *adj* (**a**) *(troubled → person)* inquiet(ète); *(→ sleep)* agité; **I had the uneasy feeling we were being followed** j'avais la désagréable impression que l'on nous suivait; **I've just got an uneasy feeling that it won't work** j'ai la fâcheuse impression que ça ne marchera pas; **she was uneasy in her mind** elle se sentait inquiète; **to feel uneasy about sth/doing sth** se sentir inquiet à l'idée de qch/de faire qch; **I had an uneasy conscience** je n'avais pas la conscience tranquille

(**b**) *(embarrassed → person)* mal à l'aise, gêné; *(→ silence)* gêné; **I feel uneasy in her presence** je me sens mal à l'aise en sa présence

(**c**) *(uncertain → peace, situation)* précaire

uneatable [ˌʌn'iːtəbəl] *adj* immangeable

uneaten [ˌʌn'iːtn] *adj* qui n'a pas été mangé; **he left his meal uneaten** il n'a pas touché à son repas

uneconomic ['ʌnˌiːkə'nɒmɪk] *adj* (**a**) *(expensive)* peu économique (**b**) *(wasteful)* peu rentable

uneconomical ['ʌnˌiːkə'nɒmɪkəl] *adj (wasteful)* peu rentable

unedifying [ˌʌn'edɪfaɪɪŋ] *adj* peu édifiant

unedited [ˌʌn'edɪtɪd] *adj Cin & TV* non monté; *(speech, text)* non édité, non révisé

uneducable [ˌʌn'edjʊkəbəl] *adj Formal* non éducable, impossible à éduquer

uneducated [ˌʌn'edjʊkeɪtɪd] *adj* (**a**) *(person)* sans instruction (**b**) *(behaviour, manners)* sans éducation, inculte; *(writing)* informe; *(speech, accent)* populaire

UNEF ['juːnef] *n (abbr* **United Nations Emergency Force**) FUNU *f*

unelectable [ˌʌnɪ'lektəbəl] *adj (person)* inéligible; *(party)* incapable de remporter des élections

unelected [ˌʌnɪ'lektɪd] *adj* non élu

unemancipated [ˌʌnɪ'mænsɪpeɪtɪd] *adj* non émancipé

unembarrassed [ˌʌnɪm'bærəst] *adj* peu embarrassé, peu gêné

unembellished [ˌʌnɪm'belɪʃt] *adj (garment, building)* sans embellissements, sans ornements; *(account, story)* sans enjolivements, sans fioritures

unemotional [ˌʌnɪ'məʊʃənəl] *adj (person)* impassible; *(behaviour, reaction)* qui ne trahit aucune émotion; *(voice)* neutre; *(account, style)* sans passion, neutre

unemotionally [ˌʌnɪ'məʊʃənəlɪ] *adv* froidement

unemphatic [ˌʌnɪm'fætɪk] *adj* (**a**) *(gesture)* sans emphase; *(speaker, manner, tone)* peu énergique, peu vigoureux (**b**) *Ling (syllable)* non accentué

unemployable [ˌʌnɪm'plɔɪəbəl] *adj (person)* inapte au travail, que l'on ne peut pas embaucher; **I'm 65 but does that make me unemployable?** j'ai 65 ans mais est-ce que je suis inapte à travailler pour autant?

unemployed [ˌʌnɪm'plɔɪd] **1** *npl* **the unemployed** les chômeurs *mpl*, les demandeurs *mpl* d'emploi

2 *adj* (**a**) *(person)* en *ou* au chômage; **she was unemployed for months** elle est restée au chômage pendant des mois (**b**) *Fin (capital, funds)* inactif

unemployment [ˌʌnɪm'plɔɪmənt] **1** *n* chômage *m*

2 *comp (compensation)* de chômage

►► *Br Formerly* ***unemployment benefit*** allocation *f* (de) chômage; *Am* ***unemployment compensation*** allocation *f* (de) chômage; ***unemployment figures*** les chiffres *mpl* du chômage; ***unemployment fund*** caisse *f* de chômage; ***unemployment insurance*** assurance *f* chômage; ***unemployment level, unemployment rate*** taux *m* de chômage

unemptied [ˌʌn'emptɪd] *adj* non vidé

unenclosed [ˌʌnɪn'kləʊzd] *adj (land, field)* sans clôture

unencumbered [ˌʌnɪn'kʌmbəd] *adj (passage)* dégagé, non encombré; *(person)* non encombré; **unencumbered by children or mortgage** sans enfants ni emprunt immobilier à rembourser

►► *Law* ***unencumbered estate*** propriété *f* franche d'hypothèques

unending [ˌʌn'endɪŋ] *adj* sans fin, interminable

unendingly [ˌʌn'endɪŋlɪ] *adv* sans fin, interminablement

unendorsed [ˌʌnɪn'dɔːst] *adj Fin (cheque)* non endossé

unendowed [ˌʌnɪn'daʊd] *adj (institution)* sans dotation, qui ne jouit d'aucune dotation

unendurable [ˌʌnɪn'djʊərəbəl] *adj* intolérable

unendurably [ˌʌnɪn'djʊərəblɪ] *adv* **it was unendurably hot** il faisait une chaleur insupportable; **he found the film was unendurably long** il avait l'impression que le film ne finirait jamais

unenforceable [ˌʌnɪn'fɔːsəbəl] *adj* inapplicable

un-English *adj* peu anglais; **he's very un-English** ce n'est pas du tout l'Anglais type

unenjoyable [ˌʌnɪn'dʒɔɪəbəl] *adj (gen)* peu agréable; *(meal, film, book, match)* pas très bon; **I had a rather unenjoyable day** j'ai passé une journée pas très agréable

unenlightened [ˌʌnɪn'laɪtənd] *adj (person)* ignorant, peu éclairé; *(practice)* arriéré; **an unenlightened age** une époque où règne/régnait l'ignorance; **I remained completely unenlightened** je suis resté dans l'ignorance la plus totale

unenlightening [ˌʌnɪn'laɪtənɪŋ] *adj (comment)* qui n'apporte pas grand-chose

unenterprising [ˌʌn'entəpraɪzɪŋ] *adj (person)* peu entreprenant; *(measure)* timoré

unenthusiastic [ˌʌnɪnθjuːzɪ'æstɪk] *adj* peu enthousiaste; **she seemed rather unenthusiastic about it** ça n'avait pas l'air de l'enthousiasmer

unenthusiastically [ˌʌnɪnθjuːzɪ'æstɪklɪ] *adv (say)* sans enthousiasme; *(welcome)* tièdement

unenviable [ˌʌn'envɪəbəl] *adj (conditions, situation, task)* peu enviable

unequal [ˌʌn'iːkwəl] *adj* (**a**) *(amount, number, result)* inégal (**b**) *(contest, struggle)* inégal, non équilibré (**c**) *Formal (incapable)* **to be unequal to a job/to a task** ne pas être à la hauteur d'un travail/d'une tâche

unequalled, *Am* **unequaled** [ˌʌn'iːkwəld] *adj* inégalé, sans pareil

unequally [ˌʌn'iːkwəlɪ] *adv* inégalement

unequipped [ˌʌnɪ'kwɪpt] *adj (factory)* non équipé, non outillé; *(person)* non équipé; *(laboratory, kitchen)* non installé, non équipé; *(person, army, soldier, ship)* non équipé; **he is unequipped to teach children of primary-school age** il est mal préparé pour enseigner dans une école primaire

unequivocal [ˌʌnɪ'kwɪvəkəl] *adj* sans équivoque

unequivocally [ˌʌnɪ'kwɪvəklɪ] *adv* sans équivoque, clairement

unerring [ˌʌn'ɜːrɪŋ] *adj* infaillible, sûr; *(aim)* sûr

unerringly [ˌʌn'ɜːrɪŋlɪ] *adv* infailliblement

UNESCO [juː'neskəʊ] *n (abbr* **United Nations Educational, Scientific and Cultural Organization**) Unesco *f*

unescorted [ˌʌnɪs'kɔːtɪd] *adj* non accompagné; **an unescorted woman** une femme non accompagnée

unessential [ˌʌnɪ'senʃəl] *adj* non essentiel

unesthetic *Am* = **unaesthetic**

unethical [ˌʌn'eθɪkəl] *adj* contraire à l'éthique

unethically [ˌʌn'eθɪkəlɪ] *adv* contrairement à l'éthique

un-European *adj* non-européen

uneven [ˌʌn'iːvən] *adj* (**a**) *(line)* irrégulier, qui n'est pas droit; *(surface)* irrégulier, rugueux; *(ground)* raboteux, accidenté; *(edge)* inégal; **she has uneven teeth** ses dents sont irrégulières; **the floorboards are uneven** les lattes du plancher ne sont pas toutes au même niveau (**b**) *(unequal → contest, quality, distribution)* inégal; *Fig* **his performance was very uneven** il a joué de façon très inégale (**c**) *(number)* impair

unevenly [ˌʌn'iːvənlɪ] *adv* (**a**) *(divide, spread)* inégalement; **the contestants are unevenly matched** les adversaires ne sont pas de force égale (**b**) *(cut, draw)* irrégulièrement (**c**) *(breathe)* irrégulièrement

unevenness [ˌʌn'iːvnnɪs] *n* (**a**) *(of line, surface, ground, edge)* irrégularité *f* (**b**) *(of contest, quality, distribution)* inégalité *f*

uneventful [ˌʌnɪ'ventfʊl] *adj (day)* sans événement marquant, sans histoires; *(career)* sans histoires; *(journey)* sans histoires, sans encombre; **to lead an uneventful life** mener une vie sans histoires *ou* paisible

uneventfully [ˌʌnɪ'ventfʊlɪ] *adv* sans incidents

unexamined [ˌʌnɪg'zæmɪnd] *adj* (**a**) *(records, files etc)* non examiné; *(passport)* non contrôlé; *(in customs → baggage)* non fouillé, non examiné (**b**) *Law (witness)* non entendu; *(suspect)* non interrogé, qui n'a pas subi d'interrogatoire

unexampled [ˌʌnɪg'zɑːmpəld] *adj Formal or Literary* sans exemple, sans pareil

unexceptionable [ˌʌnɪk'sepʃnəbəl] *adj Formal* irréprochable

unexceptional [ˌʌnɪk'sepʃənəl] *adj* qui n'a rien d'exceptionnel, banal

unexchangeable [ˌʌnɪks'tʃeɪndʒəbəl] *adj Fin (securities)* impermutable, inéchangeable

unexcitable [ˌʌnɪk'saɪtəbəl] *adj (person)* flegmatique

unexcited [ˌʌnɪk'saɪtɪd] *adj* calme, tranquille; **he was quite unexcited about the good news** ces bonnes nouvelles l'ont laissé assez indifférent

unexciting [ˌʌnɪk'saɪtɪŋ] *adj (life)* peu passionnant; *(film)* sans grand intérêt; *(food)* quelconque; *(person, orator, etc)* terne

unexpected [ˌʌnɪk'spektɪd] **1** *adj (gen)* inattendu, imprévu; *(pleasure, gift)* inattendu; *(success)* inattendu, inespéré; *(departure, death)* inopiné; **their marriage was totally unexpected** leur mariage était totalement inattendu; **it was completely unexpected** on ne s'y attendait pas du tout; **this is all so unexpected!** tout est si inattendu!

2 *n* **the unexpected** l'imprévu *m*

unexpectedly [ˌʌnɪk'spektɪdlɪ] *adv* (**a**) *(arrive)* à l'improviste, de manière imprévue; *(fail, succeed)* contre toute attente, de manière inattendue (**b**) *(surprisingly)* étonnamment

unexpectedness [ˌʌnɪk'spektɪdnɪs] *n (of event etc)* caractère *m* inattendu

unexpiated [ˌʌn'ekspɪeɪtɪd] *adj* inexpié

unexpired [ˌʌnɪk'spaɪəd] *adj (lease)* non expiré; *(passport, ticket)* non périmé, encore valable

unexplainable [ˌʌnɪk'spleɪnəbəl] *adj* inexplicable

unexplained [ˌʌnɪk'spleɪnd] *adj* inexpliqué

unexploded [ˌʌnɪk'spləʊdɪd] *adj* non explosé
unexploited [ˌʌnɪk'splɔɪtɪd] *adj* inexploité
unexplored [ˌʌnɪk'splɔːd] *adj* inexploré, inconnu; *(solution, possibility)* inexploré
unexposed [ˌʌnɪk'spəʊzd] *adj* (**a**) *Phot (film)* vierge (**b**) *(criminal)* non démasqué (**c**) *(not subject to)* **she has been unexposed to the influences of the outside world** elle n'a pas été en contact avec le monde extérieur; **unexposed to the influence of TV** qui n'est pas soumis à l'influence de la télévision
unexpressed [ˌʌnɪk'sprest] *adj* inexprimé
unexpurgated [ˌʌn'ekspəgeɪtɪd] *adj* non expurgé, intégral
unfaded [ˌʌn'feɪdɪd] *adj (colour)* non fané; *(feeling, pleasure)* non diminué; *(memory)* intact
unfading [ˌʌn'feɪdɪŋ] *adj (colour, feeling, pleasure)* toujours vif *(malgré le temps)*; *(memory)* toujours vif, ineffaçable
unfailing [ˌʌn'feɪlɪŋ] *adj (courage, good mood, loyalty, support)* inébranlable, à toute épreuve; *(means, remedy, memory)* infaillible; *(zeal)* infatigable; *(energy, supply)* intarissable, inépuisable; *(interest)* constant; *(kindness)* inaltérable
unfailingly [ˌʌn'feɪlɪŋlɪ] *adv* inlassablement, toujours
unfair [ˌʌn'feə(r)] *adj (advantage, decision, treatment)* injuste; *(system)* injuste, inique; *(judgement)* inique; *(competition, play)* déloyal; **to be unfair to sb** se montrer injuste envers qn; **to have an unfair advantage over everybody else** être injustement avantagé par rapport à tous les autres; **he has been put at an unfair disadvantage** il a été désavantagé
▸▸ *Com* ***unfair competition*** concurrence *f* déloyale; *Ind* ***unfair dismissal*** licenciement *m* abusif; **he's claiming unfair dismissal** il prétend avoir fait l'objet d'un licenciement abusif
unfairly [ˌʌn'feəlɪ] *adv (treat)* inéquitablement, injustement; *(compete)* déloyalement; *Ind* **to be unfairly dismissed** être victime d'un licenciement abusif
unfairness [ˌʌn'feənɪs] *n (UNCOUNT)* injustice *f*
unfaithful [ˌʌn'feɪθfʊl] *adj* infidèle; **to be unfaithful to sb** être infidèle à qn
unfaithfully [ˌʌn'feɪθfʊlɪ] *adv* infidèlement
unfaithfulness [ˌʌn'feɪθfʊlnɪs] *n* infidélité *f*
unfaltering [ʌn'fɔːltərɪŋ] *adj (speech, voice, steps)* ferme, assuré; **she was unfaltering in her support of the reform** elle soutenait fermement la réforme
unfalteringly [ʌn'fɔːltərɪŋlɪ] *adv (speak)* d'une voix ferme *ou* assurée; *(walk)* d'un pas ferme *ou* assuré
unfamiliar [ˌʌnfə'mɪljə(r)] *adj* (**a**) *(not known → face, person, surroundings)* inconnu; *(→ ideas)* peu familier, que l'on connaît mal (**b**) *(strange)* étrange; **the unfamiliar sounds of the language** les sonorités étranges de cette langue (**c**) **to be unfamiliar with sth** *(of person)* ne pas connaître *ou* mal connaître qch, ne pas être au fait de qch; **I'm unfamiliar with his writings** je connais mal ses écrits
unfamiliarity ['ʌnfəˌmɪlɪ'ærətɪ] *n* (**a**) *(strangeness → of faces, ideas, surroundings)* aspect *m* peu familier, étrangeté *f* (**b**) *(lack of knowledge)* ignorance *f* (**with** de); **my unfamiliarity with the city put me at a disadvantage** mon inexpérience de la ville a été un handicap
unfancied [ˌʌn'fænsɪd] *adj (player, team, racehorse etc)* peu coté
unfashionable [ˌʌn'fæʃənəbəl] *adj* (**a**) *(clothes, ideas)* démodé (**b**) *(area, restaurant)* pas très chic; *(term)* démodé; *(writer)* qui n'est plus à la mode
unfashionably [ˌʌn'fæʃənəblɪ] *adv (dress)* sans se préoccuper de la mode; **unfashionably long skirts** des jupes trop longues pour être à la mode; **he has unfashionably conservative views** il a des opinions conservatrices assez démodées; **unfashionably romantic films** des films romantiques comme on n'en fait plus
unfasten [ˌʌn'fɑːsən] *vt (garment, tie, lace, knot, belt, button, bracelet)* défaire; *(gate)* ouvrir
unfathered [ˌʌn'fɑːðəd] *adj* (**a**) *(without a father)* sans père (**b**) *Formal (source, origin)* obscur
unfatherly [ˌʌn'fɑːðəlɪ] *adj* peu paternel
unfathomable [ˌʌn'fæðəməbəl] *adj* insondable
unfathomed [ˌʌn'fæðəmd] *adj* inexploré, insondé
unfavourable, *Am* **unfavorable** [ˌʌn'feɪvrəbəl] *adj (gen)* défavorable; *(terms)* désavantageux
unfavourably, *Am* **unfavorably** [ˌʌn'feɪvrəblɪ] *adv* défavorablement; **to be unfavourably disposed towards sb/sth** être mal disposé envers qn/qch; **his work compares unfavourably with his brother's** son travail supporte mal la comparaison avec celui de son frère
unfazed [ˌʌn'feɪzd] *adj Fam* pas du tout impressionné; **he was totally unfazed by the prospect of having to speak in front of thousands of people** l'idée d'avoir à prendre la parole devant des milliers de personnes ne l'inquiétait pas le moins du monde
unfeasible [ˌʌn'fiːzəbəl] *adj (plan, suggestion)* peu faisable, irréalisable
unfeasibly [ˌʌn'fiːzəblɪ] *adv* (**a**) *(impracticably)* **the project turned out to be unfeasibly expensive** le projet s'est révélé être beaucoup trop cher (**b**) *(unbelievably)* incroyablement; **he drives an unfeasibly large car** il conduit une énorme voiture
unfed [ˌʌn'fed] *adj* qui n'a pas mangé; **she had left the cat unfed** elle n'avait pas donné à manger au chat, elle n'avait pas nourri le chat
unfeeling [ˌʌn'fiːlɪŋ] *adj* insensible, dur
unfeelingly [ˌʌn'fiːlɪŋlɪ] *adv* avec dureté, sans pitié
unfeigned [ˌʌn'feɪnd] *adj* non feint, réel
unfeminine [ˌʌn'femɪnɪn] *adj* qui manque de féminité, peu féminin
unfenced [ˌʌn'fenst] *adj (land etc)* sans clôture
unfermented [ˌʌnfə'mentɪd] *adj* non fermenté
unfertilized [ˌʌn'fɜːtɪlaɪzd] *adj (egg)* non fécondé
unfetter [ˌʌn'fetə(r)] *vt Formal (slave, prisoner)* désenchaîner; *(horse)* débarrasser de ses entraves
unfettered [ˌʌn'fetəd] *adj Formal (action)* sans contrainte, sans entrave; *(imagination, violence)* débridé; **unfettered by moral constraints** libre de toute contrainte morale
unfilial [ˌʌn'fɪlɪəl] *adj* peu filial
unfilmable [ˌʌn'fɪlməbəl] *adj* impossible à adapter au cinéma
unfiltered [ˌʌn'fɪltəd] *adj (water, light)* non filtré; *(cigarette)* sans filtre
unfinished [ˌʌn'fɪnɪʃt] *adj* (**a**) *(incomplete)* incomplet(ète), inachevé; **an unfinished piece of work** un travail inachevé (**b**) *(rough → furniture)* brut, non fini; *(→ material)* sans apprêt; *(→ wood)* brut
▸▸ ***unfinished business*** affaires *fpl* à régler; *Fig* questions *fpl* à régler

'The Unfinished Symphony' *Schubert* 'La Symphonie inachevée'

unfired [ˌʌn'faɪəd] *adj (bullet)* qui n'a pas été tiré; *(gun, cannon, torpedo)* qui n'a pas été déchargé; *(arrow)* qui n'a pas été décoché
unfished [ˌʌn'fɪʃt] *adj (water)* dans lequel personne ne pêche
unfit [ˌʌn'fɪt] *(pt & pp* **unfitted,** *cont* **unfitting)** **1** *adj* (**a**) *(unsuited → permanently)* inapte; *(→ temporarily)* qui n'est pas en état; **he is unfit for life in the army** il est inapte à la vie militaire; **unfit for human consumption** impropre à la consommation; **unfit for publication** impubliable; **she is unfit for social work** *or* **to be a social worker** elle n'est pas faite pour être assistante sociale; **he's still unfit for work** il n'est toujours pas en état de reprendre le travail; **this house is unfit for habitation** cette maison est inhabitable
(**b**) *(unhealthy → person)* qui n'est pas en forme, qui est en mauvaise forme; *(→ condition)* mauvais; **three of our star players have been declared unfit** trois de nos joueurs vedettes ont été déclarés hors d'état de jouer
2 *vt Formal* rendre inapte; **his past record unfitted him for public office** sa conduite passée lui interdisait toute fonction officielle
unfitness [ˌʌn'fɪtnɪs] *n* (**a**) *(unsuitability)* inaptitude *f*; **his unfitness for public office** son inaptitude à toute fonction officielle (**b**) *(lack of health, physical fitness)* mauvaise forme *f*
unfitted [ˌʌn'fɪtɪd] *adj Formal (unprepared)* mal préparé; *(unsuitable)* inapte; **to be unfitted to do sth** être inapte à faire qch; **unfitted for** inapte à; **he is quite unfitted for a job in management** il est totalement inapte à un poste de direction
unfitting [ˌʌn'fɪtɪŋ] *adj (remarks)* déplacé, inconvenant; *(behaviour)* inconvenant
unfittingly [ʌn'fɪtɪŋlɪ] *adv (say, remark)* mal à propos; *(behave)* de manière peu convenable
unfix [ˌʌn'fɪks] *vt (bayonet)* remettre
unflagging [ˌʌn'flægɪŋ] *adj (courage)* infatigable, inlassable; *(enthusiasm)* inépuisable; **with unflagging interest** avec un intérêt toujours soutenu
unflaggingly [ˌʌn'flægɪŋlɪ] *adv* infatigablement, inlassablement
unflappability [ˌʌnflæpə'bɪlɪtɪ] *n Fam* imperturbabilité *f*
unflappable [ˌʌn'flæpəbəl] *adj Fam* imperturbable, qui ne se laisse pas démonter
unflattering [ˌʌn'flætərɪŋ] *adj (gen)* peu flatteur; *(clothes, hat)* qui n'arrange pas; **her hat was most unflattering** son chapeau ne la mettait certes pas en valeur; **it shows him in an unflattering light** ça le montre sous un jour défavorable; **he was rather unflattering about your playing** il ne s'est pas montré très flatteur quant à votre jeu
unflatteringly [ˌʌn'flætərɪŋlɪ] *adv* d'une manière peu flatteuse; **her dress was unflatteringly tight** sa robe, trop étroite, ne la flattait guère; **she spoke rather unflatteringly about him** elle a parlé de lui en termes assez peu flatteurs
unflavoured, *Am* **unflavored** [ˌʌn'fleɪvəd] *adj* sans parfum
unfledged [ˌʌn'fledʒd] *adj* (**a**) *(bird)* sans plumes (**b**) *Fig* inexpérimenté, novice
unflinching [ˌʌn'flɪntʃɪŋ] *adj (person)* intrépide, qui ne bronche pas; *(resolve, courage)* inébranlable
unflinchingly [ˌʌn'flɪntʃɪŋlɪ] *adv* stoïquement, sans broncher
unflustered [ˌʌn'flʌstəd] *adj* impassible
unfocused, unfocussed [ˌʌn'fəʊkəst] *adj (gaze, photo)* flou; *Fig* **unfocused energy** énergie sans but
unfold [ˌʌn'fəʊld] **1** *vt* (**a**) *(spread out → cloth, map)* déplier
(**b**) *(reveal → intentions, plans)* exposer, révéler; *(→ story)* raconter, dévoiler; *(→ secret)* dévoiler; *(→ reasons)* faire connaître
(**c**) **to unfold one's arms** décroiser les bras
2 *vi* (**a**) *(cloth, map)* se déplier; *(wings)* se déployer
(**b**) *(truth, story)* être révélé; *(events)* se dérouler; *(view)* se dérouler, s'étendre; **the drama unfolded before our eyes** le drame se déroulait devant nos yeux; **a spectacular view unfolded before us** un spectaculaire panorama s'étendait devant nous
unforced [ˌʌn'fɔːst] *adj* qui n'est pas forcé, spontané
▸▸ *Sport* ***unforced error*** faute *f* directe; ***unforced laugh*** rire *m* franc
unforeseeable [ˌʌnfɔː'siːəbəl] *adj* imprévisible
unforeseen [ˌʌnfɔː'siːn] *adj* imprévu, inattendu
▸▸ ***unforeseen expenses*** dépenses *fpl* non prévues au budget
unforgettable [ˌʌnfə'getəbəl] *adj* inoubliable
unforgettably [ˌʌnfə'getəblɪ] *adv* inoubliablement
unforgivable [ˌʌnfə'gɪvəbəl] *adj* impardonnable; **it's unforgivable of me** je suis impardonnable
unforgivably [ˌʌnfə'gɪvəblɪ] *adv* impardonnablement
unforgiven [ˌʌnfə'gɪvən] *adj* non pardonné

'Unforgiven' *Eastwood* 'Impitoyable'

unforgiving [ˌʌnfə'gɪvɪŋ] *adj* implacable, impitoyable, sans merci; *(garment)* qui révèle toutes les imperfections
unforgotten [ˌʌnfə'gɒtən] *adj* inoublié
unformatted [ˌʌn'fɔːmætɪd] *adj Comput (disk)* non formaté; *(text)* non mis en forme
▸▸ ***unformatted capacity*** *(of disk)* capacité *f* brute

unformed [ˌʌnˈfɔːmd] *adj* (**a**) *(undeveloped)* non formé; *(mind)* inculte; *(idea)* en gestation (**b**) *(shapeless)* informe, sans forme

unformulated [ˌʌnˈfɔːmjʊˌleɪtɪd] *adj* informulé

unforthcoming [ˌʌnfɔːθˈkʌmɪŋ] *adj* **he was very unforthcoming about the date of the elections** il s'est montré très discret sur la date des élections

unfortified [ˌʌnˈfɔːtɪfaɪd] *adj* non fortifié, sans fortifications

unfortunate [ʌnˈfɔːtʃnət] **1** *adj* (**a**) *(unlucky)* malheureux, malchanceux; **hundreds of unfortunate people are now homeless** des centaines de malheureux sont maintenant sans abri; **he's been most unfortunate** il n'a vraiment pas eu de chance

(**b**) *(regrettable → incident, situation)* fâcheux, regrettable; *(→ joke, remark)* malencontreux; **it's just unfortunate things turned out this way** il est malheureux *ou* regrettable que les choses se soient passées ainsi; **an unfortunate choice of words** un choix de mots peu heureux; **an unfortunate state of affairs** une situation regrettable *ou* fâcheuse; **in unfortunate circumstances** dans des circonstances regrettables

2 *n Euph Formal* malheureux(euse) *m,f*

3 *npl* **the unfortunate** les infortunés *mpl*

unfortunately [ʌnˈfɔːtʃnətlɪ] *adv* malheureusement; **unfortunately not** malheureusement pas; **unfortunately for him** malheureusement pour lui

unfounded [ˌʌnˈfaʊndɪd] *adj* infondé, dénué de fondement

unframed [ˌʌnˈfreɪmd] *adj* sans cadre

unfranked [ˌʌnˈfræŋkt] *adj Br* non affranchi

unfreeze [ˌʌnˈfriːz] *(pt* **unfroze** [-ˈfrəʊz], *pp* **unfrozen** [-ˈfrəʊzən]) **1** *vt* (**a**) *(de-ice)* dégeler (**b**) *Fin (credit, rent)* débloquer, dégeler

2 *vi* (se) dégeler

unfrequented [ˌʌnfrɪˈkwentɪd] *adj* peu fréquenté

unfriendliness [ˌʌnˈfrendlɪnɪs] *n* froideur *f*

unfriendly [ˌʌnˈfrendlɪ] *(compar* **unfriendlier,** *superl* **unfriendliest**) *adj (person)* froid, peu sympathique; *(welcome, tone)* froid; *(behaviour, gesture, remark)* inamical; **to be unfriendly to** *or* **towards sb** traiter qn avec froideur

►► *Mil* ***unfriendly action*** action *f* hostile

unfrightened [ˌʌnˈfraɪtənd] *adj* qui n'a pas peur; **to be unfrightened of sb/sth** ne pas avoir peur de qn/qch

unfrock [ˌʌnˈfrɒk] *vt* défroquer

unfroze [ˌʌnˈfrəʊz] *pt of* **unfreeze**

unfrozen [ˌʌnˈfrəʊzən] *pp of* **unfreeze**

unfruitful [ˌʌnˈfruːtfʊl] *adj* (**a**) *(barren)* stérile, improductif (**b**) *Fig (efforts, search)* infructueux, vain

unfulfilled [ˌʌnfʊlˈfɪld] *adj (person)* insatisfait, frustré; *(dream)* non réalisé; *(ambition, hopes)* inaccompli; *(promise)* non tenu; **to feel unfulfilled** éprouver un sentiment d'insatisfaction

unfunded [ˌʌnˈfʌndɪd] *adj* sans subvention

►► *Fin* ***unfunded debt*** dette *f* flottante *ou* non consolidée

unfunny [ˌʌnˈfʌnɪ] *adj (experience, joke, situation)* qui n'a rien d'amusant; **I find that most unfunny** je ne trouve pas ça amusant du tout

unfurl [ˌʌnˈfɜːl] **1** *vt (flag, sail)* déferler, déployer

2 *vi* se déployer

unfurnished [ˌʌnˈfɜːnɪʃt] *adj (flat, room)* non meublé

unfussy [ˌʌnˈfʌsɪ] *adj (clothes, manners, person)* simple, pas compliqué; *(design, furniture)* simple

ungainliness [ˌʌnˈgeɪnlɪnɪs] *n* maladresse *f*, gaucherie *f*

ungainly [ˌʌnˈgeɪnlɪ] *(compar* **ungainlier,** *superl* **ungainliest**) *adj (in movement)* maladroit, gauche; *(in appearance)* dégingandé, disgracieux

ungallant [ˌʌnˈgælənt] *adj* peu galant, discourtois

ungeared [ˌʌnˈgɪəd] *adj Fin* sans endettement

►► ***ungeared balance sheet*** bilan *m* sans emprunts *ou* à faible endettement

ungenerous [ˌʌnˈdʒenərəs] *adj* (**a**) *(allowance, person)* peu généreux; **the offer was not ungenerous** l'offre n'était pas peu généreuse (**b**) *(criticism, remark)* mesquin

ungenerously [ˌʌnˈdʒenərəslɪ] *adv* (**a**) *(parcimoniously)* peu généreusement (**b**) *(unkindly)* mesquinement

ungenial [ˌʌnˈdʒiːnɪəl] *adj (unfriendly → person)* peu aimable, peu affable; *(→ expression, voice)* peu cordial, peu chaleureux; *(→ face)* inamical

ungentlemanly [ˌʌnˈdʒentəlmənlɪ] *adj (attitude, conduct, remark)* peu galant, discourtois

ungetatable [ˌʌngetˈætəbəl] *adj Fam* inaccessible❑, hors de portée❑

ungifted [ˌʌnˈgɪftɪd] *adj (person)* peu doué

ungird [ˌʌnˈgɜːd] *(pt & pp* **ungirt** [ˌʌnˈgɜːt]) *vt (sword)* détacher

unglamorous [ˌʌnˈglæmərəs] *adj* (**a**) *(unalluring → person)* sans apprêt; *(→ clothing)* inélégant; **an unglamorous but highly talented actress** une actrice sans apprêt mais pleine de talent (**b**) *(unexciting → lifestyle)* sans éclat; *(→ career)* sans éclat, peu prestigieux; *(→ show, place)* sans attrait

unglazed [ʌnˈgleɪzd] *adj* (**a**) *(window)* sans vitres (**b**) *(paper)* mat, non glacé (**c**) *Cer* non verni, non émaillé; *(brick)* non vitrifié

►► ***unglazed porcelain*** biscuit *m*; *Phot* ***unglazed print*** épreuve *f* mate

ungloved [ˌʌnˈglʌvd] *adj* déganté, sans gant(s); **ungloved hand** main *f* nue *ou* dégantée

ungodliness [ˌʌnˈgɒdlɪnɪs] *n* impiété *f*

ungodly [ˌʌnˈgɒdlɪ] *adj* (**a**) *Literary* irréligieux, impie (**b**) *Hum Fig (noise)* infernal; **at an ungodly hour** à une heure impossible *ou* indue

ungovernable [ˌʌnˈgʌvənəbəl] *adj* (**a**) *(feelings, temper)* irrépressible (**b**) *(country)* ingouvernable

ungraceful [ˌʌnˈgreɪsfʊl] *adj* sans grâce, gauche

ungracefully [ˌʌnˈgreɪsfʊlɪ] *adv* sans grâce, gauchement

ungracious [ˌʌnˈgreɪʃəs] *adj* désobligeant; **it would be ungracious of me to refuse** j'aurais mauvaise grâce à refuser

ungraciously [ˌʌnˈgreɪʃəslɪ] *adv* de mauvaise grâce

ungraciousness [ˌʌnˈgreɪʃəsnɪs] *n* mauvaise grâce *f*

ungrammatical [ˌʌngrəˈmætɪkəl] *adj* agrammatical, non grammatical

ungrammatically [ˌʌngrəˈmætɪklɪ] *adv* incorrectement

ungrateful [ʌnˈgreɪtfʊl] *adj* (**a**) *(person)* ingrat; **to be ungrateful to sb** manquer de reconnaissance envers qn (**b**) *Formal or Literary (task)* ingrat

ungratefully [ʌnˈgreɪtfʊlɪ] *adv* de manière ingrate, avec ingratitude

ungratefulness [ʌnˈgreɪtfʊlnɪs] *n* ingratitude *f*

ungratified [ˌʌnˈgrætɪfaɪd] *adj (desire)* inassouvi

ungreen [ˌʌnˈgriːn] *adj Ecol (lacking consideration for the environment)* peu respectueux de l'environnement; *(harmful to the environment)* nuisible à l'environnement

ungrounded [ˌʌnˈgraʊndɪd] *adj (belief)* infondé, sans fondement

ungrudging [ˌʌnˈgrʌdʒɪŋ] *adj (expense, help)* généreux

ungrudgingly [ˌʌnˈgrʌdʒɪŋlɪ] *adv* généreusement, de bon cœur

ungual [ˈʌŋgwəl] **1** *n* (**a**) *Anat* phalangette *f* (**b**) *Zool (nail)* ongle *m*; *(claw)* griffe *f*; *(hoof)* sabot *m*

2 *adj* (**a**) *Anat* unguéal (**b**) *Zool (relating to a nail)* unguéal; *(relating to a claw)* de la griffe; *(relating to a hoof)* du sabot

unguarded [ˌʌnˈgɑːdɪd] *adj* (**a**) *(house)* non surveillé, non gardé; *(suitcase)* sans surveillance, non surveillé; *(town)* sans défense (**b**) *(fire)* sans pare-feu (**c**) *(machinery, mechanism)* sans dispositif de protection (**d**) *(remark)* irréfléchi; **in an unguarded moment** dans un moment d'inattention (**e**) *(feelings)* franc (franche); **she gave unguarded support for the scheme** elle n'a pas hésité à soutenir ce projet

unguent [ˈʌŋgwənt] *n Literary* onguent *m*, pommade *f*

unguiculate [ˌʌnˈgwɪkjʊlət] **1** *n Anat & Zool* onguiculé *m*

2 *adj* (**a**) *Bot* onguiculé (**b**) *Anat & Zool* onguiculé

unguided [ˌʌnˈgaɪdɪd] *adj* sans guide

unguis [ˈʌŋgwɪs] *n* (**a**) *Bot* onglet *m* (**b**) *Anat & Zool (nail)* ongle *m*; *(claw)* griffe *f*

ungulate [ˈʌŋgjʊleɪt] **1** *adj* ongulé

2 *n* ongulé *m*

unhallowed [ˌʌnˈhæləʊd] *adj* (**a**) *Rel (ground)* non consacré (**b**) *(ungodly → act, behaviour)* impie

unhampered [ˌʌnˈhæmpəd] *adj* non entravé, libre

unhand [ˌʌnˈhænd] *vt Arch or Hum* lâcher; **unhand me, sir!** monsieur, lâchez-moi!

unhandy [ˌʌnˈhændɪ] *adj* (**a**) *(unwieldy)* peu commode, peu pratique (**b**) *(unskilled)* peu adroit de ses mains

unhappily [ʌnˈhæpɪlɪ] *adv* (**a**) *(sadly)* tristement; **she looked at me unhappily** elle me regarda d'un air triste *ou* malheureux; **they're unhappily married** ils ne sont pas heureux en ménage (**b**) *Formal (unfortunately)* malheureusement; **unhappily, all her friends had left** malheureusement *ou* par malheur tous ses amis étaient partis

unhappiness [ʌnˈhæpɪnɪs] *n* (**a**) *(sadness)* chagrin *m*, peine *f*; **her departure caused me great unhappiness** son départ m'a fait beaucoup de peine; **there's so much unhappiness in the world** il y a tellement de misère dans le monde (**b**) *(disaffection)* mécontentement *m*; **their unhappiness with the situation at work is growing** leur insatisfaction au travail est de plus en plus grande

unhappy [ʌnˈhæpɪ] *(compar* **unhappier,** *superl* **unhappiest**) *adj* (**a**) *(sad)* triste, malheureux; **to make sb unhappy** rendre qn malheureux; **he had an unhappy time abroad** il a fait un mauvais séjour à l'étranger

(**b**) *Formal (unfortunate → coincidence)* malheureux, regrettable; *(→ remark)* malheureux, malencontreux; **an unhappy turn of phrase** une tournure malheureuse; **it's a most unhappy state of affairs** c'est une situation tout à fait regrettable *ou* fâcheuse; *Br* **the unhappy fellow drowned** le pauvre malheureux s'est noyé

(**c**) *(displeased)* mécontent; **to be unhappy about** *or* **with sth** être mécontent de qch; **she was unhappy about me spending so much money** elle n'aimait pas que je dépense tant d'argent

(**d**) *(worried)* inquiet(ète); **I'm unhappy about leaving the house empty** je n'aime pas laisser *ou* ça m'inquiète de laisser la maison vide

unhardened [ˌʌnˈhɑːdənd] *adj (snow, skin, substance)* non durci; *(steel)* non trempé

unharmed [ˌʌnˈhɑːmd] *adj* (**a**) *(person)* sain et sauf, indemne; **to escape unharmed** s'en sortir indemne; **they released two boys unharmed** ils ont relâché deux garçons sains et saufs (**b**) *(object)* intact; *(house, paintwork)* non endommagé

unharmful [ˌʌnˈhɑːmfʊl] *adj* (**a**) *(person, influence)* non nuisible, non malfaisant (**b**) *(chemicals)* non nocif; *(effects)* non nuisible

unharmonious [ˌʌnhɑːˈməʊnɪəs] *adj* peu harmonieux

unharness [ˌʌnˈhɑːnɪs] *vt (remove harness from)* déharnacher; *(unhitch)* dételer

unharvested [ˌʌnˈhɑːvɪstɪd] *adj (wheat etc)* non moissonné, non récolté

unhatched [ˌʌnˈhætʃt] *adj (egg)* non éclos

UNHCR [ˌjuːenˌeɪtʃsiːˈɑː(r)] *n (abbr* **United Nations High Commission for Refugees**) HCR *m*

unhealthily [ˌʌnˈhelθɪlɪ] *adv* d'une manière malsaine; **to be unhealthily thin** être d'une maigreur malsaine

unhealthiness [ˌʌnˈhelθɪnɪs] *n* (**a**) *(of person)* mauvaise santé *f*; **the unhealthiness of her complexion** son teint maladif (**b**) *(of air, place)* insalubrité *f* (**c**) *Fig (of curiosity, interest)* caractère *m* malsain *ou* morbide; *(of influence, relationship)* caractère *m* malsain

unhealthy [ˌʌnˈhelθɪ] *(compar* **unhealthier,** *superl* **unhealthiest**) *adj* (**a**) *(person)* malade; *(complexion)* maladif; **he had an unhealthy look about him** il avait un air maladif; *Fam* **the car's sounding rather unhealthy** la voiture fait un drôle de bruit (**b**) *(air, place)* malsain, insalubre (**c**) *Fig (curiosity, interest)* malsain, morbide; *(influence, relationship)* malsain

unheard [ˌʌnˈhɜːd] *adj* (**a**) *(voice, complaints)* non entendu; **his cries for help went unheard** personne n'a entendu ses appels à l'aide; **the opinions of the immigrant population go**

unheard personne ne tient compte des opinions des immigrés (**b**) *Law (case)* non jugé; **to be judged unheard** être jugé sans être entendu

unheard-of *adj* (**a**) *(extraordinary)* inouï, sans précédent; **unheard-of cruelty** une cruauté inouïe
(**b**) *(unprecedented)* inconnu, sans précédent; **such an occurrence is quite unheard of** pareil événement n'est pratiquement jamais arrivé
(**c**) *(unknown)* inconnu, ignoré; **several previously unheard-of painters were included in the exhibition** plusieurs peintres inconnus jusqu'alors ont participé à l'exposition; **it was unheard-of in my day** de mon temps ça n'existait pas

unheated [ˌʌnˈhiːtɪd] *adj* sans chauffage

unheeded [ˌʌnˈhiːdɪd] *adj (ignored → message, warning)* ignoré, dont on ne tient pas compte; *(unnoticed)* inaperçu; **his instructions went** *or* **were unheeded** ses instructions n'ont pas été suivies; **the announcement went unheeded** on n'a pas tenu compte de l'annonce

unheeding [ˌʌnˈhiːdɪŋ] *adj* (**a**) *(unconcerned)* insouciant, indifférent (**b**) *(inattentive)* inattentif

unhelped [ˌʌnˈhelpt] *adv* sans l'aide de personne

unhelpful [ˌʌnˈhelpfʊl] *adj (person)* peu secourable *ou* serviable; *(instructions, map)* qui n'est d'aucun secours; *(advice)* inutile; **you're being deliberately unhelpful** vous faites exprès de ne pas nous aider

unhelpfully [ˌʌnˈhelpfʊlɪ] *adv* (**a**) *(act)* sans aider, sans coopérer; **someone very unhelpfully left the disk on a radiator** quelqu'un de très négligent a laissé la disquette sur un radiateur (**b**) *(advise, say, suggest)* inutilement; **she unhelpfully suggested that I go and see a clairvoyant** elle n'a rien trouvé de mieux que de me conseiller d'aller voir un voyant

unhelpfulness [ˌʌnˈhelpfʊlnɪs] *n* inutilité *f*; *(of person)* manque *m* d'obligeance

unheralded [ˌʌnˈherəldɪd] *adj (unannounced)* non annoncé; *(unexpected)* inattendu

unheroic [ˌʌnhɪˈrəʊɪk] *adj* peu héroïque

unheroically [ˌʌnhɪˈrəʊɪkəlɪ] *adv* de façon peu héroïque

unhesitating [ʌnˈhezɪteɪtɪŋ] *adj (reaction, reply)* immédiat, spontané; *(belief)* résolu, ferme; *(person)* résolu, qui n'hésite pas

unhesitatingly [ʌnˈhezɪteɪtɪŋlɪ] *adv* sans hésitation

unhewn [ˌʌnˈhjuːn] *adj (stone etc)* non taillé

unhindered [ʌnˈhɪndəd] *adj* sans entrave *ou* obstacle; **we crossed the border unhindered** nous avons passé la frontière sans encombre; **unhindered by all that luggage** sans être encombré par tous ces bagages; **unhindered by petty regulations** sans être gêné par des règlements tatillons; **unhindered by any moral scruples** nullement encombré de scrupules

unhinge [ˌʌnˈhɪndʒ] *vt* (**a**) *(door, window)* démonter, enlever de ses gonds (**b**) *Fig (mind, person)* déséquilibrer, déranger

unhinged [ˌʌnˈhɪndʒd] *adj* déséquilibré

unhip [ˌʌnˈhɪp] *adj Fam* ringard

unhistorical [ˌʌnhɪsˈtɒrɪkəl] *adj (fact)* non historique

unhitch [ˌʌnˈhɪtʃ] *vt* (**a**) *(rope)* détacher, décrocher (**b**) *(horse, etc)* dételer

unholiness [ˌʌnˈhəʊlɪnɪs] *n* impiété *f*

unholy [ˌʌnˈhəʊlɪ] *(compar* **unholier,** *superl* **unholiest**) *adj* (**a**) *Rel* profane, impie; *Fig* **an unholy alliance** une alliance *f* contre nature (**b**) *Fam (awful → noise, mess)* impossible ☐, invraisemblable ☐; **at an unholy hour** à une heure impossible *ou* indue

unhook [ˌʌnˈhʊk] **1** *vt* (**a**) *(remove, take down)* décrocher (**b**) *(garment)* dégrafer, défaire
2 *vi (garment)* se dégrafer

unhoped-for [ʌnˈhəʊpt-] *adj* inespéré

unhopeful [ʌnˈhəʊpfʊl] *adj* (**a**) *(person)* pessimiste, sans illusion (**b**) *(situation)* décourageant

unhorse [ˌʌnˈhɔːs] *vt* (**a**) *Horseriding* démonter, désarçonner (**b**) *Fig (from power)* faire tomber, renverser

unhoused [ˌʌnˈhaʊzd] *adj (person)* sans logement

unhuman [ˌʌnˈhjuːmən] *adj* inhumain

unhung [ˌʌnˈhʌŋ] *adj (picture)* non exposé

unhurried [ʌnˈhʌrɪd] *adj (person)* qui ne se presse pas; *(manner)* tranquille, serein; **we enjoyed an unhurried lunch** nous avons pris plaisir à déjeuner sans nous presser

unhurriedly [ʌnˈhʌrɪdlɪ] *adv* calmement, sans se presser

unhurt [ˌʌnˈhɜːt] *adj* indemne, sans blessure; **to escape unhurt** sortir sain et sauf *ou* indemne

unhygienic [ˌʌnhaɪˈdʒiːnɪk] *adj* antihygiénique, non hygiénique

unhyphenated [ˌʌnˈhaɪfɪneɪtɪd] *adj* sans trait d'union

uni [ˈjuːnɪ] *n Fam* (**a**) *Br (abbr* **university**) fac *f*, *Suisse* Uni *f*; **he's doing law at uni** il fait une fac de droit (**b**) *Am (abbr* **uniform**) uniforme ☐ *m*

Uniat [ˈjuːnɪət], **Uniate** [ˈjuːnɪɪt, ˈjuːnɪeɪt] *Rel* **1** *n* uniate *m*
2 *adj* uniate

uniaxial [ˌjuːnɪˈæksɪəl] *adj* (**a**) *Bot* unicaule (**b**) *(crystal)* uniaxe

unicameral [ˌjuːnɪˈkæmərəl] *adj* monocaméral

unicameralism [ˌjuːnɪˈkæmərəlɪzəm] *n* monocamérisme

UNICEF [ˈjuːnɪsef] *(abbr* **United Nations International Children's Emergency Fund**) *n* Unicef *m*

unicellular [ˌjuːnɪˈseljʊlə(r)] *adj* unicellulaire

unicorn [ˈjuːnɪkɔːn] *n Myth & Her* licorne *f*

unicycle [ˈjuːnɪsaɪkəl] *n* monocycle *m*

unidentifiable [ˌʌnaɪˈdentɪfaɪəbəl] *adj* non identifiable

unidentified [ˌʌnaɪˈdentɪfaɪd] *adj* non identifié
►► ***unidentified flying object*** objet *m* volant non identifié

unidimensional [ˌjuːnɪdaɪˈmenʃənəl] *adj* unidimensionnel

unidiomatic [ˌʌnɪdɪəˈmætɪk] *adj* peu idiomatique

unidirectional [ˌjuːnɪdɪˈrekʃənəl] *adj* unidirectionnel

UNIDO [juːˈniːdəʊ] *n (abbr* **United Nations Industrial Development Organization**) ONUDI *f*

unification [ˌjuːnɪfɪˈkeɪʃən] *n* unification *f*; **the Unification Church** = nom officiel de la secte mooniste

unified [ˈjuːnɪfaɪd] *adj* unifié
►► *Phys* ***unified field theory*** théorie *f* unifiée

uniflorous [ˌjuːnɪˈflɔːrəs] *adj Bot* uniflore

unifoliate [ˌjuːnɪˈfəʊlɪeɪt] *adj Bot* unifolié

uniform [ˈjuːnɪfɔːm] **1** *n* uniforme *m*; **in uniform** *(gen)* en uniforme; *Mil* sous les drapeaux; **in school uniform** en uniforme d'école; **to wear uniform** porter l'uniforme
2 *adj (identical)* identique, pareil; *(constant)* constant; *(unified)* uniforme; **these boxes are all of uniform size** ces boîtes sont toutes de la même grandeur
►► *Acct* ***uniform accounting*** comptabilité *f* uniforme; *Com* ***uniform business rate*** = taxe assise sur la valeur des locaux commerciaux, ≃ taxe *f* professionnelle; ***uniform rate*** taux *m* uniforme

uniformed [ˈjuːnɪfɔːmd] *adj (gen)* en uniforme; *(policeman, soldier)* en tenue

uniformitarianism [ˌjuːnɪfɔːmɪˈteərɪənɪzəm] *n Geol* uniformitarisme *m*

uniformity [ˌjuːnɪˈfɔːmətɪ] *(pl* **uniformities**) *n* uniformité *f*

uniformly [ˈjuːnɪfɔːmlɪ] *adv* uniformément

UNIFI [ˈjuːnɪfaɪ] *n* = syndicat britannique des employés du domaine financier

unify [ˈjuːnɪfaɪ] *(pt & pp* **unified**) *vt* (**a**) *(unite → country)* unifier (**b**) *(make uniform → legislation, prices)* uniformiser

unifying [ˈjuːnɪfaɪɪŋ] *adj* unificateur

unignorable [ˌʌnɪgˈnɔːrəbəl] *adj* que l'on ne peut ignorer

unilateral [ˌjuːnɪˈlætərəl] *adj* (**a**) *(action, decision)* unilatéral; **unilateral declaration of independence** déclaration *f* unilatérale d'indépendance (**b**) *Med (paralysis)* hémiplégique
►► ***unilateral disarmament*** désarmement *m* unilatéral

unilateralism [ˌjuːnɪˈlætərəlɪzəm] *n* doctrine *f* du désarmement unilatéral

unilateralist [ˌjuːnɪˈlætərəlɪst] *n* partisan *m* du désarmement unilatéral

unilaterally [ˌjuːnɪˈlætərəlɪ] *adv* (**a**) *(act, decide)* unilatéralement (**b**) *Med* **to be paralysed unilaterally** être paralysé d'un seul côté, être hémiplégique

unilingual [ˌjuːnɪˈlɪŋgwəl] *adj* monolingue, unilingue

unilluminated [ˌʌnɪˈluːmɪneɪtɪd] *adj (sign, notice)* non illuminé

unilluminating [ˌʌnɪˈluːmɪneɪtɪŋ] *adj (speech, interview, comparison, remark, example)* qui n'éclaire rien; *(book, programme)* qui n'apprend rien

unillustrated [ˌʌnˈɪləstreɪtɪd] *adj* non illustré

unimaginable [ˌʌnɪˈmædʒɪnəbəl] *adj* inimaginable, inconcevable

unimaginably [ˌʌnɪˈmædʒɪnəblɪ] *adv* incroyablement, invraisemblablement

unimaginative [ˌʌnɪˈmædʒɪnətɪv] *adj* manquant d'imagination, peu imaginatif; **they're very unimaginative about their holidays** ils ne font preuve d'aucune imagination pour ce qui est de partir en vacances; **you're so unimaginative!** vous n'avez aucune imagination!

unimaginatively [ˌʌnɪˈmædʒɪnətɪvlɪ] *adv* sans imagination

unimaginativeness [ˌʌnɪˈmædʒɪnətɪvnɪs] *n* manque *m* d'imagination

unimagined [ˌʌnɪˈmædʒɪnd] *adj* inimaginé

unimpaired [ˌʌnɪmˈpeəd] *adj (faculty, strength)* intact; *(health)* non altéré; **her political prestige remains unimpaired** son prestige politique demeure intact

unimpassioned [ˌʌnɪmˈpæʃənd] *adj* sans passion

unimpeachable [ˌʌnɪmˈpiːtʃəbəl] *adj Formal (source, evidence)* incontestable; *(reputation, honesty, character)* irréprochable

unimpeded [ˌʌnɪmˈpiːdɪd] *adj* sans obstacle, libre

unimportance [ˌʌnɪmˈpɔːtəns] *n* (**a**) *(of detail, matter, question)* manque *m ou* peu *m* d'importance, insignifiance *f* (**b**) *(of person)* manque *m ou* peu *m* d'importance

unimportant [ˌʌnɪmˈpɔːtənt] *adj* (**a**) *(detail, matter, question)* sans importance, insignifiant (**b**) *(person)* sans importance

unimposing [ˌʌnɪmˈpəʊzɪŋ] *adj* (**a**) *(unimpressive)* peu imposant *ou* impressionnant (**b**) *(insignificant)* insignifiant

unimpressed [ˌʌnɪmˈprest] *adj* non impressionné; **I was unimpressed by her** elle ne m'a pas fait une grosse impression; **they were unimpressed by your threats** vos menaces ne les ont pas impressionnés

unimpressionable [ˌʌnɪmˈpreʃənəbəl] *adj* peu impressionnable

unimpressive [ˌʌnɪmˈpresɪv] *adj* guère impressionnant; **their record is unimpressive** leur dossier n'est pas très impressionnant *ou* est très quelconque

unimproved [ˌʌnɪmˈpruːvd] *adj* (**a**) *(no better)* non amélioré; **his condition is unimproved** son état ne s'est pas amélioré (**b**) *(land)* non amendé; *(resources)* inexploité, inutilisé; **unimproved value** valeur *f* non bâtie *(d'un terrain)*

unincorporated [ˌʌnɪnˈkɔːpəreɪtɪd] *adj* (**a**) *(not included)* non incorporé *ou* intégré (**b**) *Com & Law* non enregistré

unindexed [ˌʌnˈɪndekst] *adj (book)* sans index

uninfected [ˌʌnɪnˈfektɪd] *adj* (**a**) *(wound, organ, person, animal)* non infecté (**b**) *(food, water, area, clothing)* non contaminé (**c**) *Comput (file)* non infecté

uninflamed [ˌʌnɪnˈfleɪmd] *adj Med* non enflammé, non irrité

uninflammable [ˌʌnɪnˈflæməbəl] *adj* ininflammable

uninflected [ˌʌnɪnˈflektɪd] *adj Gram (word)* sans flexion; *(language)* non flexionnel

uninfluenced [ˌʌnˈɪnflʊənst] *adj* **to be uninfluenced by sb/sth** ne pas être influencé par qn/qch

uninfluential [ˌʌnɪnflʊˈenʃəl] *adj* sans influence

uninformative [ˌʌnɪnˈfɔːmətɪv] *adj (book, leaflet, person)* qui n'apprend rien; *(conversation)* qui n'est pas très instructif

uninformed [ˌʌnɪnˈfɔːmd] *adj (person)* non informé; *(opinion)* mal informé; *(reader)* non averti; **uninformed critics** critiques *mpl* non avertis; **to make an uninformed guess** deviner au hasard

uninhabitable [ˌʌnɪnˈhæbɪtəbəl] *adj* inhabitable

uninhabited [ˌʌnɪnˈhæbɪtɪd] *adj* inhabité

uninhibited [ˌʌnɪnˈhɪbɪtɪd] *adj (person)* sans inhibition *ou* inhibitions; *(behaviour, reaction)* non réfréné, non réprimé; *(laughter)* franc et massif, sans retenue

uninitialized [ʌnɪˈnɪʃəlaɪzd] *adj Comput* non initialisé

uninitiated [ˌʌnɪˈnɪʃɪeɪtɪd] **1** *npl* **the uninitiated** les profanes *mpl*, les non-initiés *mpl*; **to** *or* **for the uninitiated** pour le profane

2 *adj* non initié

uninjured [ˌʌnˈɪndʒəd] *adj (person)* indemne, sain et sauf; **miraculously she was uninjured** par miracle, elle était indemne

uninspired [ˌʌnɪnˈspaɪəd] *adj* qui manque d'inspiration; **an uninspired performance** un spectacle peu passionnant

uninspiring [ˌʌnɪnˈspaɪərɪŋ] *adj (dull)* qui n'inspire pas; *(mediocre)* médiocre; *(unexciting)* qui n'est pas passionnant; *(uninteresting)* sans intérêt

uninstall [ˌʌnɪnˈstɔːl] *vt Comput* désinstaller, supprimer

uninstructed [ˌʌnɪnˈstrʌktɪd] *adj* sans instruction

uninstructive [ˌʌnɪnˈstrʌktɪv] *adj* non instructif, ininstructif

uninsured [ˌʌnɪnˈʃʊəd] *adj* non assuré (**against** contre)

unintegrated [ˌʌnˈɪntɪgreɪtɪd] *adj* non intégré

unintellectual [ˌʌnɪntəˈlektjʊəl] *adj* peu intellectuel

unintelligent [ˌʌnɪnˈtelɪdʒənt] *adj* inintelligent, qui manque d'intelligence; **he's not an unintelligent lad** ce garçon n'est pas bête

unintelligible [ˌʌnɪnˈtelɪdʒəbəl] *adj* inintelligible

unintelligibly [ˌʌnɪnˈtelɪdʒəblɪ] *adv* inintelligiblement

unintended [ˌʌnɪnˈtendɪd] *adj (outcome, consequence)* non recherché, non voulu; *(pun, irony)* involontaire

unintentional [ˌʌnɪnˈtenʃənəl] *adj* involontaire, non intentionnel; **it was quite unintentional** ce n'était pas fait exprès

unintentionally [ˌʌnɪnˈtenʃnəlɪ] *adv* sans le vouloir, involontairement; **he did it quite unintentionally** il ne l'a pas fait exprès

uninterested [ˌʌnˈɪntrəstɪd] *adj (indifferent)* indifférent; **to be uninterested in sb/sth** être indifférent à qn/qch

uninteresting [ˌʌnˈɪntrəstɪŋ] *adj (subject)* inintéressant, sans intérêt; *(book)* inintéressant, ennuyeux; *(person)* ennuyeux

uninterestingly [ˌʌnˈɪntrəstɪŋlɪ] *adv* d'une manière peu intéressante

uninterrupted [ˈʌnˌɪntəˈrʌptɪd] *adj* continu, ininterrompu

uninterruptedly [ˈʌnˌɪntəˈrʌptɪdlɪ] *adv* de façon ininterrompue, sans interruption

uninventive [ˌʌnɪnˈventɪv] *adj (person, mind)* peu inventif; *(plan, solution)* peu ingénieux

uninvited [ˌʌnɪnˈvaɪtɪd] *adj* (**a**) *(person)* qu'on n'a pas invité; **an uninvited guest** un invité inattendu; **he turned up uninvited at the party** il a débarqué à la soirée sans y avoir été invité

(**b**) *(comment)* non sollicité

uninviting [ˌʌnɪnˈvaɪtɪŋ] *adj (place)* peu accueillant; *(prospect)* peu attrayant; *(smell)* peu attirant; *(food)* peu appétissant

uninvolved [ˌʌnɪnˈvɒlvd] *adj* **to be uninvolved (in sth)** ne pas être impliqué (dans qch); **he preferred to remain uninvolved** il préférait ne pas s'impliquer

uninvolving [ˌʌnɪnˈvɒlvɪŋ] *adj* pas très passionnant

union [ˈjuːnɪən] **1** *n* (**a**) *(act of linking, uniting)* union *f*; *Com* regroupement *m*, fusion *f*

(**b**) *Ind* syndicat *m*; **to join a union** se syndiquer; **to form a union** créer un syndicat; **unions and management** les syndicats *mpl* et la direction, les partenaires *mpl* sociaux

(**c**) *(association)* association *f*, union *f*; *Fig* **a union of French and British skills** un mariage entre le savoir-faire français et britannique

(**d**) *(marriage)* union *f*, mariage *m*

(**e**) *Math* union *f*

(**f**) *Univ (premises)* ≃ foyer *m* des étudiants; *Br (organization)* syndicat *m ou* union *f* des étudiants

2 *comp (dues, leader, meeting)* syndical

3 Union *n Hist* **the Union** *Br (between Scotland and England)* l'Union *f* de l'Angleterre et de l'Écosse; *(between Great Britain and Northern Ireland)* l'Union *f* de la Grande Bretagne et de l'Irlande du Nord; *Am* les États *mpl* de l'Union

►► ***union agreement*** convention *f* collective; ***union card*** carte *f* syndicale; ***union catalogue*** = catalogue des publications commun à plusieurs bibliothèques; ***the Union Flag*** *Br* l'Union Jack *m*; *Am Hist* = drapeau des nordistes pendant la guerre de Sécession; ***the Union Jack*** l'Union Jack *m (drapeau officiel du Royaume-Uni)*; ***union member*** *(in general)* membre *m* d'un syndicat, syndiqué(e) *m,f*; *(of particular union)* membre *m* du syndicat, syndiqué(e) *m,f*; *Tech* ***union nut*** écrou *m* de raccord; ***union regulations*** règles *fpl* syndicales; ***union representative*** délégué(e) *m,f ou* représentant(e) *m,f* syndical(e); *Am* ***union shop*** atelier *m* d'ouvriers syndiqués, union shop *m*; *Formerly* ***the Union of South Africa*** la République d'Afrique du Sud; *Formerly* ***the Union of Soviet Socialist Republics*** l'Union *f* des républiques socialistes soviétiques; *Am* ***union suit*** combinaison *f*

union-bashing *n Br* antisyndicalisme *m*

unionism [ˈjuːnjənɪzəm] *n* (**a**) *Ind* syndicalisme *m* (**b**) *Pol* unionisme *m*

unionist [ˈjuːnjənɪst] **1** *adj Ind* syndicaliste

2 *n* (**a**) *Ind* syndicaliste *mf* (**b**) *Pol* unioniste *mf*; *(in American Civil War)* nordiste *mf*

unionize, -ise [ˈjuːnjənaɪz] **1** *vi* se syndicaliser, se syndiquer

2 *vt* syndicaliser, syndiquer

unionized [ˈjuːnɪənaɪzd] *adj* syndiqué

uniparous [juːˈnɪpərəs] *adj* unipare

uniped [ˈjuːnɪped] **1** *n (person → with one leg)* unijambiste *m*; *(→ with one foot)* = personne qui n'a qu'un pied; *(creature)* unipède *m*

2 *adj (person → with one leg)* unijambiste; *(→ with one foot)* qui n'a qu'un pied; *(creature)* unipède

unipod [ˈjuːnɪpɒd] *n Phot* monopode *m*

unipolar [ˌjuːnɪˈpəʊlə(r)] *adj Elec* unipolaire

►► *Biol* ***unipolar cell*** cellule *f* unipolaire; *Pol* ***unipolar coalition*** coalition *f* unipolaire

uniprocessor [ˌjuːnɪˈprəʊsesə(r)] *n Comput* monoprocesseur *m*

uniprogramming [ˌjuːnɪˈprəʊgræmɪŋ] *n Comput* monoprogrammation *f*

unique [juːˈniːk] *adj* (**a**) *(sole, single)* unique; *(particular)* particulier, propre; **a problem unique to this region** un problème propre à cette région; **to be unique in doing sth** être le seul à faire qch; **you're not unique** ton cas n'est pas unique, tu n'es pas le seul

(**b**) *(exceptional)* exceptionnel, remarquable; **his work is quite unique** son travail est tout à fait exceptionnel

►► *Mktg* ***unique proposition*** proposition *f* unique; *Mktg* ***unique selling point, unique selling proposition*** proposition *f* unique de vente

uniquely [juːˈniːklɪ] *adv (particularly)* particulièrement; *(remarkably)* exceptionnellement, remarquablement; **he is uniquely placed to get this information** il est exceptionnellement bien placé pour obtenir ce renseignement

uniqueness [juːˈniːknɪs] *n* originalité *f*

unironed [ʌnˈaɪənd] *adj* non repassé

unisex [ˈjuːnɪseks] *adj* unisexe

UNISON [ˈjuːnɪsn] *n* = "super-syndicat" de la fonction publique en Grande-Bretagne

unison [ˈjuːnɪsən] *n* unisson *m*; **in unison** à l'unisson (**with** de)

unissued [ˌʌnˈɪʃuːd] *adj St Exch (shares, share capital)* non encore émis

unit [ˈjuːnɪt] **1** *n* (**a**) *(constituent, component)* unité *f*; **administrative unit** unité *f* administrative; **the parish is the basic church unit** la paroisse est l'unité de base de l'Église

(**b**) *(group)* unité *f*; *(team)* équipe *f*, unité *f*; **army unit** unité *f* de l'armée; **family unit** cellule *f* familiale; **production unit** unité *f* de production

(**c**) *(department → in hospital)* service *m*; *(→ in school, university, company)* groupe *m*, section *f*; *(centre)* centre *m*; *(building)* locaux *mpl*; *(offices)* bureaux *mpl*; **child care unit** service *m* de pédiatrie; **operating unit** bloc *m* opératoire

(**d**) *(in amounts, measurement)* unité *f*; **each batch contains a hundred units** chaque lot contient cent unités; **a glass of wine equals one unit of alcohol** un verre de vin compte pour une unité d'alcool; **unit of length/time** unité *f* de longueur/de temps; *Med* **two units of morphine** deux unités de morphine

(**e**) *(part → of furniture)* élément *m*; *(→ of mechanism, system)* bloc *m*, élément *m*; **the knives are in the unit there** les couteaux sont dans ce placard

(**f**) *Austr (apartment)* appartement *m*

(**g**) *Sch (lesson)* unité *f*; **unit 5** unité 5

2 units *npl Math* **the units** les unités *fpl*

►► *Fin* ***unit of account*** unité *f* de compte; *Tel* ***unit charge*** taxe *f* unitaire; *Constr* ***unit construction*** préfabrication *f*; *Com & Ind* ***unit cost*** coût *m* unitaire; ***unit of currency*** unité *f* monétaire; ***unit furniture*** mobilier *m* par éléments; ***unit of length*** unité *f* de longueur; ***unit price*** prix *m* unitaire *ou* à l'unité; ***unit of time*** unité *f* de temps; *Br St Exch* ***unit trust*** fonds *m* commun de placement, ≃ SICAV *f*

unitard [ˈjuːnɪtɑːd] *n* combinaison *f* moulante

Unitarian [ˌjuːnɪˈteərɪən] **1** *n Rel* unitaire *mf*, unitarien(enne) *m,f*

2 *adj* unitaire, unitarien

Unitarianism [ˌjuːnɪˈteərɪənɪzəm] *n Rel* unitarisme *m*

unitary [ˈjuːnɪtrɪ] *adj* (**a**) *(united, single)* unitaire (**b**) *(government)* centralisé

unite [juːˈnaɪt] **1** *vt* (**a**) *(join, link → forces)* unir, rassembler

(**b**) *(unify → country, party)* unifier, unir; **more unites us than separates us** ce qui nous unit est plus fort que ce qui nous divise; **common interests that unite two countries** intérêts communs qui unissent deux pays

(**c**) *(bring together → people, relatives)* réunir

(**d**) *Formal (marry)* unir (en mariage)

2 *vi* s'unir; **they united in their efforts to defeat the enemy** ils ont conjugué leurs efforts pour vaincre l'ennemi; **the two countries united in opposing** *or* **to oppose oppression** les deux pays se sont unis pour s'opposer à l'oppression; **they seem to have united against me** ils semblent s'être unis contre moi

united [juːˈnaɪtɪd] *adj (family)* uni; *(efforts)* conjugué; *(country, party)* uni, unifié; **to present a united front** montrer un front uni; **to be united against sb/sth** être uni contre qn/qch; **we are united in our aims** nous sommes d'accord dans nos objectifs, nous partageons les mêmes objectifs; *Sport* **Melchester United** Melchester United; *Prov* **united we stand, divided we fall** l'union fait la force

►► ***the United Arab Emirates*** les Émirats *mpl* arabes unis; **in the United Arab Emirates** dans les Émirats arabes unis; ***the United Arab Republic*** la République arabe unie; **in the United Arab Republic** dans la République arabe unie; ***United Farm Workers*** = syndicat américain d'ouvriers agricoles; ***the United Kingdom*** le Royaume-Uni; **in the United Kingdom** au Royaume-Uni; ***the United Nations*** les Nations *fpl* unies; ***United Nations Organization*** Organisation *f* des Nations unies; ***United Provinces*** les Provinces-Unies *fpl*; **in the United Provinces** dans les Provinces-Unies; ***the United Reformed Church*** = église fondée en 1972 par la réunion de l'Église presbytérienne et l'Église congrégationnaliste; ***the United States*** les États-Unis *mpl*; **in the United States** aux États-Unis; ***the United States of America*** les États-Unis *mpl* d'Amérique; ***United Way*** = association caritative américaine

unity [ˈjuːnətɪ] (*pl* **unities**) *n* (**a**) *(union)* unité *f*, union *f*; **national/political unity** unité *f* nationale/politique; **strength lies in unity** l'union fait la force (**b**) *(identity → of purpose)* identité *f*; *(→ of views)* unité *f* (**c**) *(harmony)* harmonie *f*; **to live in unity** vivre en harmonie (**d**) *Theat* unité *f*; **the dramatic unities** les unités *fpl* dramatiques (**e**) *Math* unité *f*

Univ. (*written abbr* **university**) Univ.

univalent [ˌjuːnɪˈveɪlənt] **1** *adj Biol & Chem* univalent, monovalent

2 *n* chromosome *m* univalent

univalve [ˈjuːnɪvælv] **1** *adj Zool* univalve

2 *n* mollusque *m* univalve

universal [ˌjuːnɪˈvɜːsəl] **1** *adj* (**a**) *(concerning all* *people, things)* universel; **topics of universal interest** sujets *mpl* qui intéressent tout le monde

(**b**) *(widespread)* unanime; **this proposal met with universal rejection** la proposition a été unanimement rejetée; **to meet with universal agreement** faire l'unanimité; **to meet with universal acclaim** être applaudi par tout le monde

2 *n* (**a**) *(truth)* vérité *f* universelle; *(proposition)* proposition *f* universelle

(**b**) *Ling & Phil* **universals** universaux *mpl*

►► ***the Universal Declaration of Human Rights*** la Déclaration universelle des droits de l'homme; ***universal grammar*** grammaire *f* universelle; *Chem* ***universal indicator*** indicateur *m* universel de pH; *Tech* ***universal joint*** (joint *m* de) cardan *m*; *Am* ***universal product code*** code *m* barres; *Comput* ***universal serial bus*** norme *f* USB, port *m* série universel

universalism [ˌjuːnɪ'vɜːsəlɪzəm] *n Rel & Phil* universalisme *m*

universalist [ˌjuːnɪ'vɜːsəlɪst] *n Rel & Phil* universaliste *mf*

universality [ˌjuːnɪvɜː'sælətɪ] *n* universalité *f*

universalization ['juːnɪˌvɜːsəlaɪ'zeɪʃən] *n* universalisation *f*

universalize, -ise [ˌjuːnɪ'vɜːsəlaɪz] *vt* universaliser, généraliser

universally [ˌjuːnɪ'vɜːsəlɪ] *adv* universellement; **a universally held opinion** une opinion qui prévaut partout; **he is universally liked/admired** tout le monde l'aime bien/l'admire

universe ['juːnɪvɜːs] *n* (**a**) *(space)* univers *m*; **in the universe** dans l'univers (**b**) *Mktg (number of people in group or segment)* univers *m*

university [ˌjuːnɪ'vɜːsətɪ] (*pl* **universities**) **1** *n* université *f*; **to go to university** aller à l'université, faire des études universitaires; **to be at university** être à l'université *ou* en faculté; **she studied at Cambridge university** elle était à l'université de Cambridge; *Fig* **I studied at the university of life** je me suis formé à l'école de la vie

2 *comp (building, campus, team)* universitaire; *(professor, staff)* d'université; *(education, studies)* supérieur, universitaire

►► ***university fees*** frais *mpl* d'inscription à l'université; ***university student*** étudiant(e) *m,f (à l'université)*; *Belg & Suisse* universitaire *mf*; ***university town*** ville *f* universitaire

univocal [ˌjuːnɪ'veʊkəl] **1** *adj (message, term, text)* univoque

2 *n Ling* mot *m* univoque

UNIX® ['juːnɪks] *n Comput (abbr* **Uniplexed Information and Computing System**) UNIX® *m*

UNIX®-based *adj Comput* basé sur UNIX®

unjust [ˌʌn'dʒʌst] *adj* injuste

unjustifiable [ˌʌndʒʌstɪ'faɪəbəl] *adj (behaviour)* injustifiable, inexcusable; *(claim)* que l'on ne peut justifier; *(error)* injustifié

unjustifiably [ˌʌndʒʌstɪ'faɪəblɪ] *adv* sans justification

unjustified [ˌʌn'dʒʌstɪfaɪd] *adj* (**a**) *(unwarranted)* injustifié; **unjustified absences** absences *fpl* sans motif valable; **such accusations are unjustified** de telles plaintes sont sans fondement *ou* sont injustifiées (**b**) *Typ* non justifié

unjustly [ˌʌn'dʒʌstlɪ] *adv* injustement, à tort

unjustness [ˌʌn'dʒʌstnɪs] *n* injustice *f*

unkempt [ˌʌn'kempt] *adj (hair)* mal peigné, en bataille; *(beard)* hirsute; *(appearance, person)* négligé, débraillé; *(garden)* mal entretenu, en friche

unkind [ʌn'kaɪnd] *adj* (**a**) *(person)* peu aimable, qui n'est pas gentil; *(manner)* peu aimable; *(thought)* vilain, méchant; *(remark)* désobligeant, méchant; **he was rather unkind to me** il n'a pas été très gentil à mon égard *ou* avec moi; **to say unkind things to sb** dire des méchancetés à qn; **to be unkind to animals** être cruel avec les animaux; *Literary* **the unkindest cut of all** la pire des trahisons (**b**) *(climate)* rigoureux, rude

unkindly [ʌn'kaɪndlɪ] **1** *adv (cruelly)* méchamment, cruellement; *(roughly)* sans ménagement; **to take unkindly to sth** mal accepter qch; **she didn't mean it unkindly** elle n'a voulu blesser *ou* offenser personne

2 *adj Literary* (**a**) *(person)* peu aimable *ou* gentil; *(action)* vilain; *(remark)* désobligeant (**b**) *(temps)* peu favorable; *(climat)* rude

unkindness [ʌn'kaɪndnɪs] *n* (**a**) *(of person)* manque *m* de gentillesse, méchanceté *f*; *(of behaviour, manner)* méchanceté *f* (**b**) *(of climate)* rigueur *f*

unknit [ˌʌn'nɪt] (*pt & pp* **unknitted,** *cont* **unknitting**) *vt* (**a**) *(pullover)* défaire, détricoter (**b**) *Fig Literary (alliance, friendship)* rompre

unknot [ˌʌn'nɒt] (*pt & pp* **unknotted,** *cont* **unknotting**) *vt* dénouer

unknowable [ˌʌn'nəʊəbəl] **1** *adj* inconnaissable

2 *n* inconnaissable *m*

unknowing [ˌʌn'nəʊɪŋ] *adj* inconscient; **they went, all unknowing, to their deaths** ils allaient, sans le savoir, au-devant de leur mort

unknowingly [ˌʌn'nəʊɪŋlɪ] *adv* à mon/son/*etc* insu, sans m'en/s'en/*etc* apercevoir

unknown [ˌʌn'nəʊn] **1** *adj* (**a**) *(not known)* inconnu; **for reasons unknown to us** pour des raisons que nous ignorons *ou* qui nous sont inconnues; **these drugs are unknown to most family doctors** ces médicaments sont inconnus de la plupart des généralistes; *Law* **verdict against person or persons unknown** verdict *m* contre inconnu

(**b**) *(obscure → cause)* inconnu, mystérieux; *(→ place)* inconnu; *(→ actor, writer)* inconnu, méconnu

2 *n* (**a**) *(person)* inconnu(e) *m,f*

(**b**) *(place, situation)* inconnu *m*; **the great unknown** le grand inconnu, l'inconnu *m*; **the explorers set off into the unknown** les explorateurs se lancèrent vers l'inconnu

(**c**) *Math & (logic)* inconnue *f*

3 *adv* **unknown to his son, he sold the house** à l'insu de son fils *ou* sans que son fils le sache, il a vendu la maison; **unknown to us, the bus had already gone** nous ne le savions pas, mais le bus était déjà parti

►► *Math & Fig* ***unknown quantity*** inconnue *f*; **the new minister is a bit of an unknown quantity** le nouveau ministre est un personnage dont on ne sait pas grand-chose; **the new drug is an unknown quantity** on ne sait pas grand-chose des effets de ce nouveau médicament; ***the Unknown Soldier, the Unknown Warrior*** le Soldat inconnu

unlabelled [ˌʌn'leɪbəld] *adj* non étiqueté, sans étiquette

unlaboured, *Am* **unlabored** [ˌʌn'leɪbəd] *adj (style)* aisé, coulant

unlace [ˌʌn'leɪs] *vt (bodice, shoe)* délacer

unladen [ˌʌn'leɪdən] *adj* (**a**) *(goods)* déchargé (**b**) *(lorry, ship)* à vide

►► ***unladen weight*** poids *m* à vide

unladylike [ˌʌn'leɪdɪlaɪk] *adj (girl)* mal élevé; *(behaviour, posture)* peu distingué; **it's unladylike to whistle** une jeune fille bien élevée ne siffle pas

unlaid [ˌʌn'leɪd] **1** *pt & pp of* **unlay**

2 *adj* **the table was still unlaid** la table n'était pas encore mise

unlamented [ˌʌnlə'mentɪd] *adj* regretté de personne; **his death was unlamented, he died unlamented** personne n'a pleuré sa mort

unlash [ˌʌn'læʃ] *vt (cargo)* désarrimer

unlatch [ˌʌn'lætʃ] **1** *vt (door)* soulever le loquet de, ouvrir; **the door was left unlatched** la porte est restée entrouverte, on n'avait pas fermé le loquet de la porte

2 *vi (door)* s'ouvrir

unlawful [ˌʌn'lɔːfʊl] *adj* illicite, illégal; **it is unlawful to use a television set without a licence** il est interdit d'utiliser une télévision sans payer de redevance; **their marriage was deemed unlawful** leur mariage fut jugé illégitime

►► ***unlawful arrest*** arrestation *f* illégale; *Law* ***unlawful assembly*** réunion *f* illégale, attroupement *m* illégal; ***unlawful detention*** détention *f* abusive; ***unlawful killing*** meurtre *m*

unlawfully [ˌʌn'lɔːfʊlɪ] *adv* illicitement, illégalement

unlawfulness [ˌʌn'lɔːfʊlnɪs] *n* illégalité *f*

unlay [ˌʌn'leɪ] (*pt & pp* **unlaid** [ʌn'leɪd]) *vt (rope, cable)* décommettre, décorder

unleaded [ˌʌn'ledɪd] *adj (petrol)* sans plomb

unlearn [ˌʌn'lɜːn] (*pt & pp* **unlearned** *or* **unlearnt** [-'lɜːnt]) *vt* désapprendre

unlearned *adj* (**a**) [ˌʌn'lɜːnɪd] *(person)* non instruit, ignorant (**b**) [ˌʌn'lɜːnd] *(lesson)* non appris; *(reflex)* inné, non acquis

unlearnt [ˌʌn'lɜːnt] *adj (lesson)* non appris; *(reflex)* inné, non acquis

unleash [ˌʌn'liːʃ] *vt* (**a**) *(dog)* lâcher (**b**) *Fig (anger, violence)* déchaîner; *(wave of repression)* provoquer, déclencher; **she unleashed a stream of invective** elle lâcha une bordée d'injures

unleavened [ˌʌn'levənd] *adj Culin* sans levain; *Rel* azyme; *Literary* **the speech was unleavened by even a trace of humour** le discours n'était même pas égayé par une pointe d'humour

unless [ən'les] *conj* à moins que + *subjunctive*, à moins de + *infinitive*; **I'll go unless he phones first** j'irai, à moins qu'il (ne) téléphone d'abord; **unless I'm very much mistaken** à moins que je ne me trompe; **unless he pays me tomorrow, I'm leaving** s'il ne m'a pas payé demain, je m'en vais; **we won't get there on time unless we leave now** nous ne serons pas à l'heure à moins de partir maintenant; **I would always be back by 6.15, unless I was working late** je rentrais toujours à 6 heures 15 au plus tard, sauf quand je travaillais tard; **you won't win unless you practise** vous ne gagnerez pas si vous ne vous entraînez pas; **they won't agree unless I go myself** ils n'accepteront pas si je n'y vais pas moi-même; **don't speak unless spoken to** ne parle que lorsqu'on t'adresse la parole; **unless I hear otherwise** *or* **to the contrary** sauf avis contraire, sauf contrordre; **unless otherwise stated** sauf indication contraire

unlet [ˌʌn'let] *adj (house, flat)* non loué

unlettable [ˌʌn'letəbəl] *adj (house, flat)* non louable

unlettered [ˌʌn'letəd] *adj Literary (uneducated)* sans instruction; *(illiterate)* illettré, analphabète

unliberated [ˌʌn'lɪbəreɪtɪd] *adj* non libéré; **unliberated slaves** les esclaves non émancipés; **the unliberated woman** la femme non libérée

unlicensed [ˌʌn'laɪsənst] *adj (parking, sale)* illicite, non autorisé; *(fishing, hunting)* sans permis, illicite; *(car)* sans vignette; *(premises)* qui n'a pas de licence de débit de boissons

unlighted [ˌʌn'laɪtɪd] *adj* (**a**) *(fire)* non allumé (**b**) *(corridor etc)* non éclairé, sans lumière

unlikable [ˌʌn'laɪkəbəl] *adj (person)* peu sympathique; *(place, thing)* peu agréable

unlike [ˌʌn'laɪk] **1** *adj (dissimilar)* dissemblable; *(different)* différent; *(showing no likeness)* peu ressemblant; *(unequal)* inégal; **the two sisters are quite unlike each other** les deux sœurs ne se ressemblent pas du tout

2 *prep* (**a**) *(different from)* différent de, qui ne ressemble pas à; **he's quite unlike his brother** il ne ressemble pas à son frère; **she is not unlike your sister in looks** elle n'est pas sans ressembler à votre sœur; **your situation is quite unlike mine** votre situation est très différente de la mienne

(**b**) *(uncharacteristic of)* **that's (very) unlike him!** cela ne lui ressemble pas (du tout)!

(**c**) *(in contrast to)* à la différence de, contrairement à; **unlike you, I prefer a quiet life** contrairement à vous, je préfère une vie tranquille

unlikeable = **unlikable**

unlikelihood [ˌʌn'laɪklɪhʊd], **unlikeliness** [ˌʌn'laɪklɪnɪs] *n* improbabilité *f*

unlikely [ˌʌn'laɪklɪ] *adj* (**a**) *(improbable → event, outcome)* improbable, peu probable; **it is very** *or* **most unlikely that it will rain** il est très peu probable qu'il pleuve, il y a peu de chances pour qu'il pleuve; **in the unlikely event of my winning** au cas improbable où je gagnerais

(**b**) *(person)* peu susceptible, qui a peu de chances; **he is unlikely to come/to fail** il est peu probable qu'il vienne/échoue, il est peu susceptible de venir/d'échouer; **she is unlikely to choose him** il est peu probable qu'elle le choisisse, il y a peu de chances pour qu'elle le choisisse

(**c**) *(implausible → excuse, story)* invraisemblable

(**d**) *(unexpected → situation, undertaking, costume etc)* extravagant, invraisemblable; *(→*

person) peu indiqué; **he turns up at the most unlikely times** il débarque à des heures invraisemblables; **the manager chose the most unlikely person to run the department** on ne s'attendait pas du tout à ce que le directeur choisissent cette personne pour diriger le service; **we found the ring in a most unlikely place** nous avons retrouvé la bague dans un endroit auquel nous n'aurions jamais pensé

unlimber [ˌʌn'lɪmbə(r)] *vt (gun)* décrocher l'avant-train de

unlimited [ˌʌn'lɪmɪtɪd] *adj (possibilities, space)* illimité, sans limites; *(power)* illimité, sans bornes; *(time)* infini, illimité; *Mktg (guarantee, warranty)* illimité; **there was unlimited coffee** il y avait du café à volonté; **he has an unlimited fund of stories** il a un stock d'histoires inépuisable

▸▸ *Br Fin* ***unlimited company*** société *f* à responsabilité illimitée *ou* infinie; *Comput* ***unlimited e-mail addresses*** nombre *m* d'adresses électroniques illimité; ***unlimited liability*** responsabilité *f* illimitée; ***unlimited travel*** nombre *m* de voyages illimité

unlimited-access highway *n Am* = autoroute pour tous les véhicules, y compris les poids lourds

unlined [ˌʌn'laɪnd] *adj* (**a**) *(paper)* non réglé, uni (**b**) *(curtain, clothes)* sans doublure (**c**) *(face)* sans rides

unlisted [ʌn'lɪstɪd] *adj* (**a**) *(not on list → name)* qui ne paraît pas sur la liste; **she was unlisted in the standard reference works** son nom ne figurait pas dans les livres de référence classiques (**b**) *Am Tel* qui est sur la liste rouge (**c**) *St Exch* non coté (en Bourse), non inscrit à la cote

▸▸ *St Exch* ***unlisted market*** Bourse *f* coulisse; *St Exch* ***unlisted securities market*** marché *m* hors cote, second marché *m*

unlit [ˌʌn'lɪt] *adj* (**a**) *(candle, fire)* non allumé (**b**) *(room, street)* non éclairé

unliterary [ˌʌn'lɪtərərɪ] *adj* non littéraire

unlivable, unliveable [ˌʌn'lɪvəbəl] *adj (life)* impossible, insupportable

unload [ˌʌn'ləʊd] **1** *vt* (**a**) *(remove load from → gun, ship, truck)* décharger; **have you unloaded the washing machine?** avez-vous enlevé le linge de la machine?

(**b**) *(remove → cargo, furniture)* décharger; *(→ film)* enlever; **to unload bricks from a cart** décharger les briques d'une charrette

(**c**) *Fam (get rid of)* se débarrasser de❑, se défaire de❑

(**d**) *Fig (responsibility, worries)* décharger; **to unload one's problems onto sb** se décharger de ses problèmes sur qn

2 *vi* (**a**) *(ship, truck)* décharger

(**b**) *Am Mktg (flood market)* inonder le marché

unloaded [ˌʌn'ləʊdɪd] *adj* (**a**) *(lorry, ship → with load removed)* déchargé; *(→ without a load)* non chargé, sans chargement (**b**) *(gun, camera)* non chargé; **don't worry, the gun's unloaded** n'aie pas peur, le fusil n'est pas chargé

unloading [ˌʌn'ləʊdɪŋ] **1** *n* déchargement *m*

2 *comp (platform, permit)* de déchargement

▸▸ ***unloading dock*** quai *m* de déchargement

unlock [ˌʌn'lɒk] **1** *vt* (**a**) *(door)* ouvrir (**b**) *Fig (mystery, puzzle)* résoudre, donner la clé de; *(secret)* dévoiler (**c**) *Comput (file, diskette, keyboard)* déverrouiller (**d**) *Fin (assets)* débloquer

2 *vi* s'ouvrir

unlocked [ˌʌn'lɒkt] *adj (door)* qui n'est pas fermé à clef

unlooked-for [ˌʌn'lʊkt-] *adj* inattendu, imprévu

unloose[1] [ˌʌn'luːs] = **unleash**

unloose[2], **unloosen** [ˌʌn'luːsən] *vt (belt, grip)* relâcher, desserrer

unlovable [ˌʌn'lʌvəbəl] *adj* peu attachant

unloved [ˌʌn'lʌvd] *adj* privé d'affection, aimé de personne; **to feel unloved** ne pas se sentir aimé, se sentir mal aimé

unlovely [ˌʌn'lʌvlɪ] *adj* laid, déplaisant

unloving [ˌʌn'lʌvɪŋ] *adj* peu affectueux

unluckily [ˌʌn'lʌkɪlɪ] *adv* malheureusement; **unluckily for us, it rained** malheureusement pour nous, il a plu

unluckiness [ˌʌn'lʌkɪnɪs] *n* malchance *f*, malheur *m*

unlucky [ˌʌn'lʌkɪ] *(compar* **unluckier,** *superl* **unluckiest**) *adj* (**a**) *(person)* malchanceux; *(day)* de malchance; **she was rather unlucky** elle a été plutôt malchanceuse; **we were unlucky enough to get caught in a jam** nous avons eu la malchance d'être pris dans un embouteillage; **it was unlucky for him that she arrived just at that moment** malheureusement pour lui, elle est arrivée à cet instant précis; **to be unlucky in love** être malheureux en amour

(**b**) *(colour, number)* qui porte malheur; *(omen)* funeste, mauvais; **it's supposed to be unlucky to break a mirror** c'est censé porter malheur de casser un miroir

unmade [ˌʌn'meɪd] **1** *pt & pp of* **unmake**

2 *adj* (**a**) *(bed)* défait (**b**) *Br (road)* non goudronné

unmade-up *adj (face)* non maquillé, sans maquillage

unmaintainable [ˌʌnmeɪn'teɪnəbəl] *adj (attitude, opinion, position)* insoutenable, indéfendable

unmake [ˌʌn'meɪk] *(pt & pp* **unmade** [-'meɪd]) *vt* (**a**) *(bed)* défaire (**b**) *Formal or Literary (reputation)* démolir, ruiner; *(man)* briser, ruiner; *(ruler)* déposer

unmalleable [ˌʌn'mælɪəbəl] *adj (substance)* peu malléable; *(person)* peu influençable, peu malléable

unmalted [ˌʌn'mɔːltɪd] *adj* non malté

unman [ˌʌn'mæn] *(pt & pp* **unmanned,** *cont* **unmanning)** *vt* (**a**) *Naut* renvoyer l'équipage de (**b**) *Literary (person)* faire perdre courage à

unmanageable [ˌʌn'mænɪdʒəbəl] *adj* (**a**) *(vehicle, ship)* difficile à manœuvrer; *(object)* peu maniable, difficile à manier; **the trailer was of an unmanageable length** à cause de sa longueur, la caravane était difficile à manœuvrer (**b**) *(animal)* difficile, indocile; *(children)* difficile, impossible (**c**) *(situation)* difficile à gérer; **the problem has become unmanageable** le problème est devenu impossible à gérer *ou* à régler (**d**) *(hair)* difficile à coiffer, rebelle

unmanfully [ˌʌn'mænfəlɪ] *adj* lâchement

unmanliness [ˌʌn'mænlɪnɪs] *n* (**a**) *(effeminacy)* manque *m* de virilité (**b**) *(cowardice)* lâcheté *f*

unmanly [ˌʌn'mænlɪ] *adj* (**a**) *(effeminate)* efféminé, peu viril (**b**) *(cowardly)* lâche

unmanned [ˌʌn'mænd] *adj (without crew → plane, ship)* sans équipage; *(→ spacecraft, flight)* inhabité; *Rail (→ station)* sans personnel; *(→ level crossing)* non gardé, automatique; **the border post/switchboard was unmanned** il n'y avait personne au poste frontière/au standard; **the control centre was left unmanned** le centre de contrôle est resté sans surveillance

▸▸ ***unmanned space travel*** vols *mpl* spatiaux non habités

unmannerliness [ˌʌn'mænəlɪnɪs] *n Formal* manque *m* de courtoisie, impolitesse *f*

unmannerly [ˌʌn'mænəlɪ] *adj Formal* discourtois, impoli

unmapped [ˌʌn'mæpt] *adj (area)* pour lequel il n'existe pas de carte, dont on n'a pas dressé la carte

unmarked [ˌʌn'mɑːkt] *adj* (**a**) *(face, furniture, page)* sans marque, sans tache

(**b**) *(without identifying features)* **the radioactive waste was carried in unmarked drums** les déchets radioactifs étaient transportés dans des barils non identifiés; **an unmarked police car** une voiture de police banalisée; **to be buried in an unmarked grave** être enterré dans une tombe anonyme

(**c**) *(without name tag, label)* sans nom, non marqué

(**d**) *(essay)* non corrigé

(**e**) *Ling* non marqué

(**f**) *Sport (player)* démarqué

unmarketable [ˌʌn'mɑːkɪtəbəl] *adj* invendable

unmarred [ˌʌn'mɑːd] *adj Literary* non abîmé; *(reputation)* sans tache, entier

unmarriageable [ˌʌn'mærɪdʒəbəl] *adj* immariable

unmarried [ˌʌn'mærɪd] *adj* non marié, célibataire

▸▸ ***unmarried mother*** mère *f* célibataire; ***unmarried state*** célibat *m*

unmask [ˌʌn'mɑːsk] *vt (person)* démasquer; *(plot, conspiracy)* dévoiler

unmatchable [ˌʌn'mætʃəbəl] *adj* inégalable

unmatched [ˌʌn'mætʃt] *adj* inégalé, sans égal *ou* pareil; **she is unmatched as a novelist** comme romancière, elle n'a pas sa pareille

unmatriculated [ˌʌnmə'trɪkjʊleɪtɪd] *adj* non inscrit

unmatured [ˌʌnmə'tʃʊəd] *adj (wine, spirits)* jeune; *(cheese)* frais, non affiné

unmeasurable [ˌʌn'meʒərəbəl] *adj* incommensurable

unmeasured [ˌʌn'meʒəd] *adj* (**a**) *(gen)* sans mesure, démesuré (**b**) *Mus* sans mesure, non mesuré

unmechanized [ˌʌn'mekənaɪzd] *adj Ind* non mécanisé

unmelodious [ˌʌnmə'ləʊdɪəs] *adj* peu mélodieux

unmelted [ˌʌn'meltɪd] *adj (ice etc)* pas encore fondu

unmemorable [ˌʌn'memərəbəl] *adj (event, speech etc)* peu mémorable, peu remarquable

unmentionable [ˌʌn'menʃənəbəl] **1** *adj (subject)* dont il ne faut pas parler, interdit; *(word)* qu'il ne faut pas prononcer, interdit

2 the unmentionable *n (forbidden subject)* le sujet interdit *ou* dont il ne faut pas parler; *(taboo)* le sujet tabou

3 unmentionables *npl Euph Hum (underwear)* dessous *mpl*, sous-vêtements *mpl*

unmentioned [ˌʌn'menʃənd] *adj* dont on ne parle/parlait/*etc* pas; **the event went unmentioned** personne n'a parlé de l'événement; **the incident went unmentioned by national newspapers** la presse nationale n'a pas parlé de l'incident

unmercenary [ˌʌn'mɜːsənərɪ] *adj* désintéressé

unmerciful [ʌn'mɜːsɪfʊl] *adj* impitoyable, sans pitié; **to be unmerciful to** *or* **towards sb** être sans pitié pour qn

unmercifully [ʌn'mɜːsɪfʊlɪ] *adv (treat)* impitoyablement, sans pitié; *(tease)* sans répit

unmerited [ˌʌn'merɪtɪd] *adj (undeserved)* immérité; *(unjust)* injuste

unmet [ˌʌn'met] *adj (target, quota)* non atteint; *(demands, needs)* non satisfait; **to go unmet** *(demands, needs)* ne pas être satisfait

unmethodical [ˌʌnmɪ'θɒdɪkəl] *adj* peu méthodique

unmetrical [ˌʌn'metrɪkəl] *adj (verse)* boiteux

unmilitary [ˌʌn'mɪlɪtərɪ] *adj (behaviour)* peu digne d'un soldat

unmindful [ˌʌn'maɪndfʊl] *adj Formal (uncaring)* peu soucieux; *(forgetful)* oublieux; *(inattentive)* inattentif; **he is unmindful of other people's feelings** il est peu soucieux des sentiments des autres, il ne tient pas compte des sentiments des autres

unmined [ˌʌn'maɪnd] *adj* (**a**) *Mil (channel etc)* non miné (**b**) *Mining & Fig* inexploité

unmissable [ˌʌn'mɪsəbəl] *adj (TV programme, film)* à ne pas manquer

unmistakable [ˌʌnmɪ'steɪkəbəl] *adj (distinctive)* aisément reconnaissable, caractéristique; *(clear, obvious)* indubitable, manifeste, évident; **the unmistakable sound of bagpipes** le son caractéristique de la cornemuse; **these symptoms are unmistakable** on ne peut pas se tromper sur ces symptômes; **she began to show unmistakable signs of fatigue** elle commença à montrer des signes évidents de fatigue

unmistakably [ˌʌnmɪ'steɪkəblɪ] *adv* (**a**) *(undeniably)* indéniablement, sans erreur possible; **the style is unmistakably French** le style est français, il n'y a pas à s'y tromper (**b**) *(visibly)* visiblement, manifestement

unmistakeable = **unmistakable**

unmitigated [ˌʌn'mɪtɪgeɪtɪd] *adj* (**a**) *(total → disaster, chaos)* total; *(→ horror)* absolu; *(→ stupidity)* pur, total; **the whole project was an unmitigated disaster** tout le projet a été un véritable désastre (**b**) *(undiminished)* non mitigé

unmixed [ˌʌn'mɪkst] *adj* non mélangé, pur

unmodernized [ˌʌn'mɒdənaɪzd] *adj* non modernisé, qui n'a pas été modernisé

unmodified [ˌʌn'mɒdɪfaɪd] *adj Tech* non modifié

▸▸ *Comput* ***unmodified instruction*** instruction *f* sous forme initiale

unmolested [ˌʌnməˈlestɪd] *adj* sans encombre; **to leave sb unmolested** *(not bother)* laisser qn en paix

unmonitored [ˌʌnˈmɒnɪtəd] *adj*
►► *Electron* ***unmonitored control system*** système *m* de commande à boucle ouverte

unmoor [ˌʌnˈmɔː(r)] *vt Naut* (**a**) *(free from moorings)* démarrer, désamarrer (**b**) *(reduce mooring of)* lever une des ancres d'affourche de

unmortgaged [ˌʌnˈmɔːgɪdʒd] *adj Fin* libre d'hypothèques

unmotherly [ˌʌnˈmʌðəlɪ] *adj* peu maternel

unmotivated [ˌʌnˈməʊtɪveɪtɪd] *adj* sans mobile; *(person)* non motivé; *(without ambition)* dépourvu d'ambition; **his actions were unmotivated by any desire for personal glory** ses actes n'étaient pas motivés par un quelconque désir de gloire personnelle

unmounted [ˌʌnˈmaʊntɪd] *adj* (**a**) *(rider)* sans monture (**b**) *(photograph)* non monté (**c**) *(jewel)* non serti

unmourned [ˌʌnˈmɔːnd] *adj* **he died unmourned** personne ne l'a pleuré

unmovable, unmoveable [ˌʌnˈmuːvəbəl] *adj* impossible à déplacer

unmoved [ˌʌnˈmuːvd] *adj* indifférent, insensible; **to be unmoved by sth** rester insensible à qch; **the music left me unmoved** la musique ne m'a pas ému; **he remained unmoved** il est resté de marbre

unmoving [ˌʌnˈmuːvɪŋ] *adj* (**a**) *(stationary)* immobile (**b**) *(not touching)* qui n'émeut pas

unmown [ˌʌnˈməʊn] *adj* *(hay)* non coupé; *(lawn)* non tondu

unmusical [ˌʌnˈmjuːzɪkəl] *adj* (**a**) *(sound)* peu mélodieux (**b**) *(person)* peu musicien; **to my unmusical ear it sounds like...** pour mon oreille peu musicienne ça ressemble à...

unmusically [ˌʌnˈmjuːzɪkəlɪ] *adv* de façon peu musicale

unmuzzle [ˌʌnˈmʌzəl] *vt* (**a**) *(dog, horse)* démuseler (**b**) *Fig (press)* débâillonner, démuseler

unnameable [ˌʌnˈneɪməbəl] *adj* innommable, sans nom

unnamed [ˌʌnˈneɪmd] *adj* (**a**) *(anonymous)* anonyme; *(unspecified)* non précisé (**b**) *(having no name → child)* sans nom, qui n'a pas reçu de nom; *(→ desire, fear)* inavoué

unnatural [ˌʌnˈnætʃərəl] *adj* (**a**) *(affected → behaviour, manner, tone)* affecté, peu naturel; *(→ laughter)* peu naturel, forcé (**b**) *(odd, abnormal → circumstances, state)* anormal; *(→ phenomenon)* surnaturel; **it's unnatural for him (to)** cela ne lui ressemble pas (de) (**c**) *(perverse → love, passion)* contre nature

unnaturally [ˌʌnˈnætʃərəlɪ] *adv (behave, laugh, walk)* bizarrement, de façon peu naturelle; **it was unnaturally hot** il faisait anormalement chaud; **he not unnaturally decided to resign** naturellement, il a décidé de démissionner; **the text reads very unnaturally** ce texte est très forcé

unnaturalness [ˌʌnˈnætʃərəlnɪs] *n* (**a**) *(affectedness → of behaviour, manner, tone)* manque *m* de naturel, affectation *f* (**b**) *(abnormality → of circumstances, state)* caractère *m* anormal, anormalité *f*; *(→ of phenomenon)* caractère *m* surnaturel (**c**) *(perversity → of love, passion)* perversité *f*

unnavigable [ˌʌnˈnævɪgəbəl] *adj* non navigable

unnavigated [ˌʌnˈnævɪgeɪtɪd] *adj (waters)* inexploré

unnecessarily [*Br* ʌnˈnesəsərɪlɪ, *Am* ˌʌnnesəˈserəlɪ] *adv (worry)* sans raison; *(do, say)* inutilement; **the questions were unnecessarily complicated** les questions étaient inutilement compliquées; **you're being unnecessarily hard on yourself** tu te fais du mal pour rien; **she works unnecessarily hard** elle n'a pas besoin de travailler aussi dur

unnecessary [ˌʌnˈnesəsərɪ] *adj* superflu, inutile; **it's quite unnecessary for you all to attend** il n'est vraiment pas nécessaire *ou* utile que vous y alliez tous; **it's a lot of unnecessary fuss** c'est beaucoup d'agitation pour rien

unneeded [ˌʌnˈniːdɪd] *adj* inutile

unnegotiable [ˌʌnnɪˈgəʊʃəbəl] *adj Fin (cheque, bill)* non négociable

unneighbourly, *Am* **unneighborly** [ˌʌnˈneɪbəlɪ] *adj (unfriendly)* peu obligeant, qui n'agit pas en bon voisin; *(unhelpful)* peu serviable

unnerve [ˌʌnˈnɜːv] *vt* déconcerter, troubler

unnerving [ˌʌnˈnɜːvɪŋ] *adj (event, experience)* déconcertant, perturbant

unnervingly [ˌʌnˈnɜːvɪŋlɪ] *adv* **he can be unnervingly flippant** il est parfois d'une désinvolture déconcertante; **there was something unnervingly peaceful about the village** le calme qui régnait dans le village avait quelque chose de troublant

unnilennium [ˌʌnɪlˈenɪəm] *n Chem* unnilennium *m*

unnilhexium [ˌʌnɪlˈheksɪəm] *n Chem* unnilhexium *m*

unniloctium [ˌʌnɪlˈɒktɪəm] *n Chem* unniloctium *m*

unnilpentium [ˌʌnɪlˈpentɪəm] *n Chem* unnilpentium *m*

unnilquadium [ˌʌnɪlˈkwɒdɪəm] *n Chem* unnilquadium *m*

unnilseptium [ˌʌnɪlˈseptɪəm] *n Chem* unnilseptium *m*

unnoted [ˌʌnnəʊtɪd] *adj* inaperçu; **to go unnoted** passer inaperçu

unnoticeable [ˌʌnˈnəʊtɪsəbəl] *adj* qui ne se remarque pas

unnoticed [ˌʌnˈnəʊtɪst] *adj* inaperçu; **to go** *or* **pass unnoticed** passer inaperçu; **she left the party unnoticed** elle a quitté la soirée sans que personne ne s'en rende compte *ou* ne s'en aperçoive

unnumbered [ˌʌnˈnʌmbəd] *adj* (**a**) *(seats, tickets, copies)* non numéroté; *(house)* sans numéro (**b**) *Fig Formal (descendants, followers, stars)* innombrable, sans nombre

UNO [ˈjuːnəʊ, ˌjuːenˈəʊ] *n* (*abbr* **United Nations Organization**) ONU *f*

unobjectionable [ˌʌnəbˈdʒekʃnəbəl] *adj (idea, activity)* acceptable; *(behaviour, person)* qui ne peut être critiqué

unobliging [ˌʌnəˈblaɪdʒɪŋ] *adj* pas serviable *ou* obligeant

unobscured [ˌʌnəbˈskjʊəd] *adj (view)* dégagé; **to be unobscured by sth** ne pas être caché par *ou* masqué par

unobservable [ˌʌnəbˈzɜːvəbəl] *adj* inobservable

unobservant [ˌʌnəbˈzɜːvənt] *adj* peu observateur; **you're so unobservant!** tu n'es vraiment pas observateur!

unobserved [ˌʌnəbˈzɜːvd] *adj* inaperçu; **she crept past unobserved** elle s'est faufilée sans se faire remarquer

unobstructed [ˌʌnəbˈstrʌktɪd] *adj* (**a**) *(view, road, entry, passage)* dégagé; *(tube, pipe)* non bouché (**b**) *(activity, progress)* sans obstacle

unobtainable [ˌʌnəbˈteɪnəbəl] *adj* (**a**) *(goods, item)* introuvable; *(tickets)* impossible à obtenir; *Tel (number)* qui n'est pas en service (**b**) *(person)* inaccessible
►► *Br Tel* ***unobtainable tone*** = tonalité continue indiquant qu'un numéro n'est pas en service

unobtrusive [ˌʌnəbˈtruːsɪv] *adj (person)* discret(ète), effacé; *(object)* discret(ète), pas trop visible; *(smell)* discret(ète); **he always tried to remain unobtrusive** il cherchait toujours à s'effacer

unobtrusively [ˌʌnəbˈtruːsɪvlɪ] *adv* discrètement; **she stood unobtrusively in a corner** elle se tenait dans un coin sans se faire remarquer

unoccupied [ˌʌnˈɒkjʊpaɪd] *adj* (**a**) *(person)* qui ne fait rien, oisif (**b**) *(house)* inoccupé, inhabité; *(hotel room)* libre; *(seat)* libre (**c**) *Mil (territory)* non occupé; **the unoccupied zone** *(in WW2 France)* la zone libre

unoffended [ˌʌnəˈfendɪd] *adj* **to be unoffended** ne pas se vexer

unofficial [ˌʌnəˈfɪʃəl] *adj* (**a**) *(unconfirmed → report)* officieux, non officiel (**b**) *(informal → appointment)* non officiel, privé; **in an unofficial capacity** à titre privé; **from an unofficial source** de source officieuse
►► *Ind* ***unofficial strike*** grève *f* sauvage

unofficially [ˌʌnəˈfɪʃəlɪ] *adv (informally)* officieusement; *(in private)* en privé

unofficious [ˌʌnəˈfɪʃɪs] *adj (unzealous)* peu zélé, peu empressé

unoiled [ˌʌnˈɔɪld] *adj (hinge)* non huilé; *(machine)* non lubrifié, non graissé

unopened [ˌʌnˈəʊpənd] *adj* (**a**) *(letter, bottle)* non ouvert, qui n'a pas été ouvert; **the letters lay unopened on the table** les lettres étaient sur la table, non décachetées (**b**) *Bot* non éclos

unopposed [ˌʌnəˈpəʊzd] *adj* sans opposition; *(to advance)* sans rencontrer d'opposition *ou* de résistance; **we cannot allow this sort of thing to go unopposed** on ne peut pas laisser faire ce genre de choses; **she was elected unopposed** elle était la seule candidate (et elle a été élue)

unordained [ˌʌnəˈdeɪnd] *adj Rel* qui n'a pas été ordonné

unorganized [ˌʌnˈɔːgənaɪzd] *adj (event, group, person etc)* non organisé; *(disorganized)* désorganisé
►► *Ind* ***unorganized labour*** main-d'œuvre *f* non syndiquée

unoriginal [ˌʌnəˈrɪdʒənəl] *adj* sans originalité

unornamented [ˌʌnˈɔːnəmentɪd] *adj* sans ornements

unorthodox [ˌʌnˈɔːθədɒks] *adj* non orthodoxe, pas très orthodoxe; *Rel* hétérodoxe

unostentatious [ˌʌnɒstenˈteɪʃəs] *adj (person, behaviour, house, party)* simple; *(dress)* sobre, simple

unostentatiously [ˌʌnɒstenˈteɪʃəslɪ] *adv (act)* simplement; *(dressed)* simplement, sobrement

unostentatiousness [ˌʌnɒstenˈteɪʃəsnɪs] *n (of person, lifestyle, house etc)* absence *f* d'ostentation, simplicité *f*

unoxidized [ˌʌnˈɒksɪdaɪzd] *adj Chem* non oxydé

unpack [ˌʌnˈpæk] **1** *vt* (**a**) *(bag, suitcase)* défaire; *(books, clothes, shopping)* déballer; *(car)* décharger; **to get unpacked** défaire ses bagages; **can you unpack the cases from the boot?** pouvez-vous sortir les valises du coffre? (**b**) *Comput* décompresser

2 *vi (after travelling)* défaire ses bagages; *(after moving)* déballer *ou* vider ses cartons

unpacking [ˌʌnˈpækɪŋ] *n* déballage *m*; **to do the unpacking** déballer ses affaires

unpaged [ˌʌnˈpeɪdʒd] *adj (book)* non paginé, non folioté

unpaid [ˌʌnˈpeɪd] *adj* (**a**) *(helper, job)* bénévole, non rémunéré (**b**) *(bill, salary)* impayé; *(employee)* non payé; **the money is still unpaid** l'argent n'a toujours pas été versé
►► ***unpaid holiday, unpaid leave*** congé *m* sans solde

unpainted [ˌʌnˈpeɪntɪd] *adj* non peint

unpaired [ˌʌnˈpeəd] *adj* (**a**) *Anat (organ)* impair (**b**) *Phys (electron)* non apparié

unpalatable [ˌʌnˈpælətəbəl] *adj (food)* immangeable; *Fig (idea)* dérangeant; *(truth)* désagréable à entendre

unpapered [ˌʌnˈpeɪpəd] *adj (wall)* non tapissé

unparalleled [ˌʌnˈpærəleld] *adj (unequalled)* sans pareil; *(unprecedented)* sans précédent

unpardonable [ˌʌnˈpɑːdənəbəl] *adj* impardonnable, inexcusable

unpardonably [ˌʌnˈpɑːdənəblɪ] *adv* de manière inexcusable; **he was unpardonably rude** il a été d'une impolitesse inexcusable *ou* impardonnable

unparliamentary [ˈʌnˌpɑːləˈmentərɪ] *adj (language, action)* contraire aux règles du parlement
►► *Br Pol* ***unparliamentary language*** langage *m* grossier

unpasteurized [ˌʌnˈpɑːstʃəraɪzd] *adj (beer)* non pasteurisé; *(milk)* cru

unpatented [ˌʌnˈpeɪtəntɪd] *adj* non breveté

unpatriotic [*Br* ˌʌnpætrɪˈɒtɪk, *Am* ˌʌnpeɪtrɪˈɒtɪk] *adj (person)* peu patriote; *(sentiment, song)* peu patriotique

unpatriotically [*Br* ˌʌnpætrɪˈɒtɪklɪ, *Am* ˌʌnpeɪtrɪˈɒtɪklɪ] *adv (act)* de manière peu patriotique

unpatronizing [ˌʌnˈpætrənaɪzɪŋ] *adj (tone, manner)* sans trace de condescendance; *(person)* qui ne se montre pas condescendant

unpaved [ˌʌnˈpeɪvd] *adj (street)* non pavé

unpayable [ˌʌnˈpeɪəbəl] *adj (debt)* impossible à rembourser

unpeaceful [ˌʌnˈpiːsfʊl] *adj* agité, turbulent

unpeg [ˌʌnˈpeg] *vt* (*pt & pp* **unpegged,** *cont* **unpegging**) *(washing on line)* décrocher; *(tent)* enlever les piquets de; *(remove dowel/dowels from)* ôter la cheville/les chevilles de

unpeople [ˌʌnˈpiːpəl] *vt (area)* vider de ses habitants

unpeopled [ˌʌnˈpiːpəld] *adj* inhabité

unperceived [ˌʌnpəˈsiːvd] *adj* non perçu

unperceptive [ˌʌnpəˈseptɪv] *adj (person)* peu perspicace; *(remark)* peu judicieux; *(analysis, article)* sans finesse

unperforated [ˌʌnˈpɜːfəreɪtɪd] *adj* non perforé, non percé

unperformed [ˌʌnpəˈfɔːmd] *adj* (**a**) *(task)* inexécuté, inaccompli (**b**) *(play)* non joué, non représenté; *(piece of music)* non joué, non exécuté

unperfumed [*Br* ˌʌnˈpɜːfjuːmd, *Am* ˌʌnpərˈfjuːmd] *adj* non parfumé, sans parfum

unperplexed [ˌʌnpəˈplekst] *adj (person)* nullement troublé

unperson [ˈʌnpɜːsən] *n Pol* non-personne *f*

unpersuadable [ˌʌnpəˈsweɪdəbəl] *adj* qui ne se laisse pas persuader; **he remained unpersuadable** il ne s'est pas laissé persuader, il est resté inflexible

unpersuasive [ˌʌnpəˈsweɪzɪv] *adj (manner, speaker, argument)* peu convaincant

unperturbed [ˌʌnpəˈtɜːbd] *adj* imperturbable, impassible; **to be unperturbed by sth** rester imperturbable face à qch; **he remained unperturbed** il est resté impassible

unphilosophical [ˌʌnfɪləˈsɒfɪkəl] *adj (person, attitude)* peu philosophe

unpick [ˌʌnˈpɪk] *vt (seam, hem)* défaire; *(garment)* découdre

unpierced [ˌʌnˈpɪəst] *adj (ears)* non percé

unpin [ˌʌnˈpɪn] *(pt & pp* **unpinned,** *cont* **unpinning**) *vt (seam)* enlever les épingles de

unpitying [ˌʌnˈpɪtɪɪŋ] *adj (look, tone)* sans pitié

unplaced [ˌʌnˈpleɪst] *adj (horse, competitor)* non placé

unplait [ˌʌnˈplæt] *vt* dénatter

unplaned [ˌʌnˈpleɪnd] *adj* non raboté

unplanned [ˌʌnˈplænd] *adj (visit, activity)* imprévu; *(child)* non prévu

unplanted [ˌʌnˈplɑːntɪd] *adj (area, field)* non planté

unplastered [ˌʌnˈplɑːstəd] *adj (wall, surface)* non plâtré

unplayable [ˌʌnˈpleɪəbəl] *adj (pitch)* impraticable; *(ball, shot → in tennis, squash etc)* impossible à rattraper; *(→ in golf)* injouable; *(music)* injouable

unpleasant [ʌnˈplezənt] *adj (person)* désagréable; *(smell, taste, weather)* désagréable, mauvais; *(remark)* désagréable, désobligeant; *(memory)* pénible; **it was a most unpleasant experience** ce fut une expérience extrêmement désagréable; **the boss was most unpleasant to her** le patron était très désagréable avec elle

unpleasantly [ʌnˈplezəntlɪ] *adv* désagréablement, de façon déplaisante; **the wine was unpleasantly sweet** le vin était tellement sucré que c'en était désagréable; **her remarks were unpleasantly close to the truth** ses remarques tombaient si juste que c'en était désagréable

unpleasantness [ʌnˈplezəntnɪs] *n* (**a**) *(of person)* côté *m* désagréable; *(of food)* caractère *m* peu appétissant; **the unpleasantness of the experience** cette expérience désagréable; **the unpleasantness of the weather** le mauvais temps (**b**) *(discord)* friction *f*, dissension *f*; **the disputes caused a lot of unpleasantness** le conflit a provoqué beaucoup de frictions; **there was some unpleasantness between them** il y avait des frictions *ou* tensions entre eux

unpleasing [ˌʌnˈpliːzɪŋ] *adj* déplaisant, désagréable

unpleasurable [ˌʌnˈpleʒərəbəl] *adj* déplaisant, désagréable

unpledged revenue [ˌʌnˈpledʒd-] *n Fin* recettes *fpl* non gagées

unpliable [ˌʌnˈplaɪəbəl] *adj (material)* rigide

unploughed, *Am* **unplowed** [ˌʌnˈplaʊd] *adj (field)* non labouré

unplug [ʌnˈplʌg] *(pt & pp* **unplugged,** *cont* **unplugging**) *vt* (**a**) *Elec* débrancher (**b**) *(opening, pipe)* déboucher

unplugged [ˌʌnˈplʌgd] *adj (concert, album)* acoustique

unplumbed [ˌʌnˈplʌmd] *adj (depths, area of knowledge)* insondé

unpoetic [ˌʌnpəʊˈetɪk], **unpoetical** [ˌʌnpəʊˈetɪkəl] *adj* peu poétique

unpoetically [ˌʌnpəʊˈetɪkəlɪ] *adv* de façon peu poétique

unpointed [ˌʌnˈpɔɪntɪd] *adj* (**a**) *(not sharp → blade)* émoussé; *(→ pencil)* épointé (**b**) *Constr (brickwork, masonry)* non jointoyé

unpolarized [ˌʌnˈpəʊləraɪzd] *adj Phys* non polarisé

unpoliced [ˌʌnpəˈliːst] *adj (gen → area)* non surveillé; *(without policemen → area, event)* sans présence policière

unpolished [ˌʌnˈpɒlɪʃt] *adj* (**a**) *(furniture, brass)* non poli; *(floor, shoes)* non ciré (**b**) *Fig (person)* qui manque de savoir-vivre; *(manners, style)* peu raffiné, peu élégant

unpolitical [ˌʌnpəˈlɪtɪkəl] *adj* (**a**) *(not relating to politics)* non politique (**b**) *(not interested in politics)* apolitique

unpolled [ˌʌnˈpəʊld] *adj (who has not voted)* qui n'a pas voté; *(who has not been included in opinion poll)* qui n'a pas été sondé

unpolluted [ˌʌnpəˈluːtɪd] *adj* non pollué

unpopular [ˌʌnˈpɒpjʊlə(r)] *adj* impopulaire, peu populaire; **this style is unpopular with the younger generation** ce style est peu populaire chez les jeunes, les jeunes n'aiment pas beaucoup ce style; **an unpopular make of car** une marque de voiture qui n'est pas très populaire; **at school she had been an unpopular child** quand elle était à l'école les autres enfants ne l'aimaient pas beaucoup; **I'm rather unpopular with the bosses** je ne suis pas très bien vu des patrons; **to make oneself unpopular** se rendre impopulaire

unpopularity [ˈʌnˌpɒpjʊˈlærətɪ] *n* impopularité *f*

unpopulated [ˌʌnˈpɒpjʊleɪtɪd] *adj* désert, non peuplé

unposed [ˌʌnˈpəʊzd] *adj (photograph)* pris sur le vif

unposted [ˌʌnˈpəʊstɪd] *adj (letter, parcel)* non posté

unpracticable [ˌʌnˈpræktɪkəbəl] *adj* (**a**) *(unfeasible)* peu réalisable, peu praticable; *(impossible)* impossible (**b**) *(road)* impraticable

unpractical [ˌʌnˈpræktɪkəl] *adj* (**a**) *(person)* peu pratique; **he's completely unpractical** il n'a aucun sens pratique (**b**) *(plan)* irréalisable

unpractised, *Am* **unpracticed** [ˌʌnˈpræktɪst] *adj* inexpérimenté; **to be unpractised in the art of public speaking** ne pas avoir l'habitude de parler en public; **to the unpractised ear/eye** pour les oreilles non exercées/l'œil non exercé

unprecedented [ʌnˈpresɪdəntɪd] *adj* sans précédent; **this was quite unprecedented in the continent's history** c'était du jamais vu dans l'histoire du continent

unpredictability [ˌʌnprɪdɪktəˈbɪlətɪ] *n* imprévisibilité *f*

unpredictable [ˌʌnprɪˈdɪktəbəl] *adj (person, behaviour, mood)* imprévisible; *(weather)* incertain

unpredictableness [ˌʌnprɪˈdɪktəbəlnɪs] *n* imprévisibilité *f*

unpredictably [ˌʌnprɪˈdɪktəblɪ] *adv* de façon imprévisible

unpredicted [ˌʌnprɪˈdɪktɪd] *adv* imprévu

unprejudiced [ˌʌnˈpredʒʊdɪst] *adj* impartial, sans parti pris

unpremeditated [ˌʌnprɪˈmedɪteɪtɪd] *adj* non prémédité

unprepared [ˌʌnprɪˈpeəd] *adj* (**a**) *(food etc)* non préparé; *(speech)* improvisé, impromptu; **to find everything unprepared** ne rien trouver de prêt; **the hall was quite unprepared for the party** la salle n'était pas du tout prête pour la soirée

(**b**) *(person)* **to be unprepared for sth** ne pas s'attendre à qch; **to go into an undertaking unprepared** faire qch sans être préparé; **I was quite unprepared for the exam** *(hadn't studied for it)* je n'étais pas du tout préparé à l'examen

unpreparedness [ˌʌnprɪˈpeərɪdnɪs] *n* manque *m* de préparation

unprepossessing [ˈʌnˌpriːpəˈzesɪŋ] *adj (place)* peu attrayant; *(person, appearance, smile)* peu avenant *ou* engageant

unprescribed [ˌʌnprɪˈskraɪbd] *adj (medication)* non prescrit

unpresentable [ˌʌnprɪˈzentəbəl] *adj (person, room)* qui n'est pas présentable; *(clothes)* immettable

unpressed [ˌʌnˈprest] *adj (garment)* non repassé

unpressurized [ˌʌnˈpreʃəraɪzd] *adj (container)* non pressurisé; *(liquid, gas)* qui n'est pas sous pression

unpretentious [ˌʌnprɪˈtenʃəs] *adj (person)* sans prétention, simple; *(tastes, house)* simple

unpretentiously [ˌʌnprɪˈtenʃəslɪ] *adv* simplement

unpriced [ˌʌnˈpraɪst] *adj* non étiqueté, qui n'a pas d'étiquette de prix

unprincipled [ʌnˈprɪnsɪpəld] *adj (person)* dénué de principes, peu scrupuleux; *(behaviour)* sans scrupules

unprintable [ˌʌnˈprɪntəbəl] *adj* (**a**) *(language)* grossier; **her reply was unprintable** la décence m'empêche de rapporter sa réponse (**b**) *(article)* impubliable

unprinted [ˌʌnˈprɪntɪd] *adj* non imprimé, inimprimé

unprivileged [ˌʌnˈprɪvɪlɪdʒd] **1** *adj (person)* défavorisé; **he comes from an unprivileged background** il vient d'un milieu défavorisé

2 *npl* **the unprivileged** les milieux *mpl* défavorisés

unprized [ˌʌnˈpraɪzd] *adj Literary* peu estimé, mésestimé

unproblematic [ˈʌnˌprɒbləˈmætɪk], **unproblematical** [ˈʌnˌprɒbləˈmætɪkəl] *adj* sans problèmes; **so far it's all been unproblematic** jusqu'ici, il n'y a eu aucun problème

unprocessed [ʌnˈprəʊsest] *adj* (**a**) *(food, wool)* non traité, naturel (**b**) *Phot (film)* non développé (**c**) *(data)* brut

unprocurable [ˌʌnprəˈkjʊərəbəl] *adj (goods)* introuvable

unproductive [ˌʌnprəˈdʌktɪv] *adj (land)* improductif, stérile; *(discussion, weekend, worker)* improductif

unprofessional [ˌʌnprəˈfeʃənəl] *adj (attitude, conduct)* peu professionnel; **it looks unprofessional not to send a covering letter** ça ne fait pas très professionnel de ne pas envoyer une lettre de motivation

unprofessionally [ˌʌnprəˈfeʃənəlɪ] *adv (do job, work, carry out contract, behave)* de manière peu professionnelle; **he dealt with the whole situation rather unprofessionally** la façon dont il s'est occupé de l'affaire n'était pas très professionnelle

unprofitable [ˌʌnˈprɒfɪtəbəl] *adj* (**a**) *(business)* peu rentable (**b**) *(discussions)* peu profitable; *(action)* inutile

unprofitably [ˌʌnˈprɒfɪtəblɪ] *adv* sans profit

Unprofor [ˈʌnprəʊfɔː(r)] *n (abbr* **United Nations Protection Force**) FORPRONU *f*

unprogressive [ˌʌnprəˈgresɪv] *adj (backward-looking)* rétrograde

unprohibited [ˌʌnprəʊˈhɪbɪtɪd] *adj* non prohibé, non interdit

unpromising [ˌʌnˈprɒmɪsɪŋ] *adj* peu prometteur; **the weather looks unpromising** on dirait qu'il ne va pas faire beau; **that's an unpromising start** c'est un mauvais départ *ou* un départ qui augure mal de la suite

unprompted [ˌʌnˈprɒmptɪd] *adj (action, words)* spontané; **that was quite unprompted by any self-interest** ce n'était motivé par aucun intérêt personnel

unpronounceable [ˌʌnprəˈnaʊnsəbəl] *adj* imprononçable

unpropitious [ˌʌnprəˈpɪʃɪs] *adj Formal* peu propice, peu favorable

unprotected [ˌʌnprəˈtektɪd] *adj* (**a**) *(person)* sans protection, non défendu; **children over 15 are unprotected by the legislation** les enfants de plus de 15 ans ne sont pas protégés par la législation (**b**) *(machinery)* sans protection, non protégé (**c**) *(wood)* non traité (**d**) *(exposed)* exposé (aux intempéries); **the house is unprotected from the east wind** la maison est exposée aux vents d'est

►► ***unprotected sex*** rapports *mpl* non protégés

unprotesting [ˌʌnprəʊˈtestɪŋ] *adj (person)* docile, qui ne proteste pas; **he was led, unprotesting, to the exit** il s'est laissé conduire à la sortie sans protester

unproved [ˌʌn'pruːvd], **unproven** [ˌʌn'pruːvən] *adj* non prouvé

unprovided-for [ˌʌnprə'vaɪdɪd-] *adj (family)* sans ressources; *(eventuality)* non prévu; **he left his family unprovided-for in his will** il n'a rien laissé à sa famille dans son testament

unprovoked [ˌʌnprə'vəʊkt] *adj (attack, insult)* injustifié

unpublicized [ˌʌn'pʌblɪsaɪzd] *adj* dont on n'a pas parlé

unpublishable [ˌʌn'pʌblɪʃəbəl] *adj* impubliable

unpublished [ˌʌn'pʌblɪʃt] *adj (manuscript, book)* inédit, non publié

unpunctual [ˌʌn'pʌŋktʃʊəl] *adj* peu ponctuel

unpunctuality ['ʌnˌpʌŋktʃʊ'ælɪtɪ] *n* manque *m* de ponctualité

unpunctuated [ˌʌn'pʌŋktʃʊeɪtɪd] *adj* sans ponctuation

unpunished [ˌʌn'pʌnɪʃt] *adj* impuni; **he can't be allowed to go unpunished** il ne peut pas rester impuni

unpurified [ˌʌn'pjʊərɪfaɪd] *adj (water, oil)* inépuré, non épuré

unputdownable [ˌʌnpʊt'daʊnəbəl] *adj Br Fam (book, novel)* passionnant❑, auquel on a du mal à s'arracher❑; **I found it absolutely unputdownable** je ne pouvais pas m'arrêter de lire❑

unqualified [ˌʌn'kwɒlɪfaɪd] *adj* (**a**) *(unskilled)* non qualifié; *(without diploma)* qui n'a pas les diplômes requis; *(unsuitable)* qui n'a pas les qualités requises; **he is unqualified for the job of chairman** il n'est pas qualifié pour le poste de président
(**b**) *(not competent)* non qualifié *ou* compétent; **she is unqualified to decide** elle n'est pas qualifiée pour décider
(**c**) *(unrestricted → admiration, approval, support)* inconditionnel, sans réserve; *(→ praise)* sans réserve; *(→ success)* complet(ète)

unquantifiable [ʌnˌkwɒntɪ'faɪəbəl] *adj* impossible à quantifier

unquantified [ˌʌn'kwɒntɪfaɪd] *adj* (**a**) *(unestimated)* non quantifié (**b**) *Gram* sans quantifieur *ou* quantificateur (**c**) *(logic)* non quantifié

unquenchable [ˌʌn'kwentʃəbəl] *adj Literary (curiosity, desire)* insatiable, inassouvissable; *(thirst)* impossible à étancher

unquenched [ˌʌn'kwentʃt] *adj (fire)* non éteint; *Literary (desire, curiosity, passion)* inassouvi; **unquenched thirst** soif *f* non étanchée

unquestionable [ˌʌn'kwestʃənəbəl] *adj* (**a**) *(undeniable)* incontestable, indubitable (**b**) *(above suspicion)* qui ne peut être mis en question

unquestionably [ʌn'kwestʃənəblɪ] *adv* indéniablement, incontestablement

unquestioned [ʌn'kwestʃənd] *adj (decision, leader, principle)* indiscuté, incontesté; **to let a statement pass** *or* **go unquestioned** laisser passer une affirmation sans la relever

unquestioning [ʌn'kwestʃənɪŋ] *adj (faith, love, obedience, belief)* absolu, aveugle

unquestioningly [ʌn'kwestʃənɪŋlɪ] *adv* aveuglément

unquiet [ˌʌn'kwaɪət] *adj Literary (person)* troublé, inquiet(ète), tourmenté; *(mind)* perturbé, tourmenté; *(period)* troublé, agité; *Fig* **she lies in an unquiet grave** elle ne repose pas en paix

unquote [ˌʌn'kwəʊt] *adv* fin de citation; *(in dictation)* fermez les guillemets

unquoted [ˌʌn'kwəʊtɪd] *adj St Exch* non coté
►► *Br* ***unquoted company*** société *f* non cotée (en Bourse); ***unquoted securities*** valeurs *fpl* non cotées (en Bourse); ***unquoted shares*** actions *fpl* non cotées (en Bourse)

unratified [ˌʌn'rætɪfaɪd] *adj* non ratifié

unravel [ˌʌn'rævəl] *(Br pt & pp* **unravelled,** *cont* **unravelling,** *Am pt & pp* **unraveled,** *cont* **unraveling**) **1** *vt* (**a**) *(knitting)* défaire; *(textile)* effiler, effilocher (**b**) *(untangle → knots, string)* démêler; *Fig (→ mystery)* débrouiller, éclaircir; *(→ plot)* dénouer, démêler
2 *vi (knitting)* se défaire; *(textile)* s'effilocher

unreachable [ˌʌn'riːtʃəbəl] *adj* (**a**) *(town, goal, destination)* inaccessible (**b**) *(person)* injoignable

unreactive [ˌʌnrɪ'æktɪv] *adj (gen, Chem & Phys)* non réactif; *Psy* non réactionnel

unread [ˌʌn'red] *adj* (**a**) *(person)* qui a peu lu (**b**) *(book, report)* qui n'a pas été lu; **he left the magazine on the table unread** il a laissé la revue sur la table sans l'avoir lue

unreadable [ˌʌn'riːdəbəl] *adj* (**a**) *(handwriting, signature)* illisible (**b**) *(book, report)* illisible, ennuyeux (**c**) *Comput (file, data)* illisible

unreadiness [ˌʌn'redɪnɪs] *n* (**a**) *(unpreparedness)* manque *m* de préparation (**b**) *(unwillingness)* manque *m* d'empressement; **their unreadiness to contribute** la mauvaise volonté qu'ils ont mise à contribuer; *(refusal)* leur refus de contribuer

unready [ˌʌn'redɪ] *adj* (**a**) *(unprepared)* non préparé, qui n'est pas prêt (**b**) *(unwilling)* peu disposé

unreal [ˌʌn'rɪəl] *adj* (**a**) *(appearance, feeling)* **it all seems so unreal** tout paraît si irréel; **an unreal situation** une situation artificielle (**b**) *Fam (unbelievable)* pas possible, pas croyable, dingue; **his arrogance is unreal!** il est d'une arrogance pas possible *ou* pas croyable *ou* dingue! (**c**) *Fam (excellent)* dément, super *(inv)*, génial

unrealism [ˌʌn'rɪəlɪzəm] *n* irréalisme *m*

unrealistic [ˌʌnrɪə'lɪstɪk] *adj* irréaliste, peu réaliste

unrealistically [ˌʌnrɪə'lɪstɪklɪ] *adv* **his hopes were unrealistically high** ses espoirs étaient trop grands pour être réalistes

unreality [ˌʌnrɪ'ælətɪ] *n* irréalité *f*

unrealizable [ˌʌnrɪə'laɪzəbəl] *adj (aim, dream)* irréalisable; *(fact, situation, state)* inconcevable; *Fin (capital, assets)* non réalisable

unrealized [ˌʌn'rɪəlaɪzd] *adj* (**a**) *(hope, wish)* irréalisé (**b**) *Fin (capital)* non réalisé
►► ***unrealized gain*** gain *m* latent; ***unrealized loss*** perte *f* latente

unreason [ˌʌn'riːzən] *n Formal* déraison *f*, folie *f*

unreasonable [ˌʌn'riːzənəbəl] *adj* (**a**) *(absurd, preposterous)* déraisonnable; *(unfair)* injuste; **you're being unreasonable** vous n'êtes pas raisonnable; **it's unreasonable to stay up so late** ce n'est pas raisonnable de veiller si tard; **surely it's not unreasonable to expect that...** on peut tout de même raisonnablement s'attendre à ce que...; **at this unreasonable hour** à cette heure indue (**b**) *(excessive)* excessif, déraisonnable

unreasonableness [ˌʌn'riːzənəbəlnɪs] *n* (**a**) *(absurdity)* absurdité *f* (**b**) *(excessiveness)* caractère *m* excessif

unreasonably [ˌʌn'riːzənəblɪ] *adv (behave)* de manière *ou* façon déraisonnable; **that's unreasonably expensive** c'est excessivement cher; **they asked, and not altogether unreasonably, that in future they should be kept informed about such matters** ils ont demandé, ce qui est tout à fait raisonnable *ou* légitime, que dorénavant on les tienne au courant de ces choses

unreasoned [ˌʌn'riːzənd] *adj (contrary to reason)* irrationnel; *(not controlled by reason)* irraisonné

unreasoning [ʌn'riːzənɪŋ] *adj (fear, hatred)* irrationnel

unreceptive [ˌʌnrɪ'septɪv] *adj* peu réceptif; **to be unreceptive to sth** [illegible]

unreciprocated [ˌʌnrɪ'sɪprəkeɪtɪd] *adj (love, feelings)* qui n'est pas réciproque; **his love was unreciprocated** il n'était pas aimé en retour

unreclaimed [ˌʌnrɪ'kleɪmd] *adj* (**a**) *(belongings, parcel)* non réclamé (**b**) *(land)* non défriché, laissé en friche; *(marshes)* non asséché

unrecognizable ['ʌnˌrekəg'naɪzəbəl] *adj* méconnaissable

unrecognizably ['ʌnˌrekəg'naɪzəblɪ] *adv* **they are unrecognizably alike** il est impossible de les distinguer l'un de l'autre; **the fog had unrecognizably blurred the outlines** le brouillard en avait estompé les contours et les avait rendus méconnaissables

unrecognized [ˌʌn'rekəgnaɪzd] *adj* (**a**) *(without being recognized)* **he slipped out unrecognized** il s'est glissé vers la sortie sans être reconnu (**b**) *(not acknowledged → talent, achievement)* méconnu; **he is unrecognized by the scientific community** il n'est pas reconnu par la communauté scientifique; **her discoveries went largely unrecognized** ses découvertes sont restées méconnues pour la plupart

unrecommended [ˌʌnrekə'mendɪd] *adj* qui n'est pas recommandé, non recommandé

unreconciled [ˌʌnrekən'saɪld] *adj (enemies)* jurés, irréductibles; **they are still unreconciled enemies** ce sont des ennemis irréductibles

unreconstructed ['ʌnˌriːkən'strʌktɪd] *adj (traditional → politician, feminist, man)* rétrograde

unrecorded [ˌʌnrɪ'kɔːdɪd] *adj* (**a**) *(remark, fact)* qui n'a pas été enregistré; **to go unrecorded** *(crime, incident)* ne pas être signalé; **the details of the case went unrecorded** il n'y a pas eu de trace écrite sur les détails de l'affaire (**b**) *(music)* qui n'a pas encore été enregistré

unrecoverable [ˌʌnrɪ'kʌvərəbəl] *adj* (**a**) *Comput* irrécouvrable (**b**) *Fin (debt)* inexigible

unredeemable [ˌʌnrɪ'diːməbəl] *adj (error)* irréparable; *(sin, crime)* inexpiable; *(sinner)* que rien ne peut racheter

unredeemed [ˌʌnrɪ'diːmd] *adj* (**a**) *(from pawn)* non dégagé *ou* racheté (**b**) *(promise)* non tenu; *(obligation)* non rempli (**c**) *(sinner)* impénitent; *(sin)* inexpié, non racheté; *Fig* **the town's ugliness is unredeemed by any charm whatsoever** la ville n'a aucun charme qui puisse racheter sa laideur (**d**) *Fin (loan)* non amorti, non remboursé; *(draft)* non honoré; *(mortgage)* non purgé

unreel [ˌʌn'riːl] **1** *vt* dérouler
2 *vi* se dérouler

unrefined [ˌʌnrɪ'faɪnd] *adj* (**a**) *(petrol)* brut, non raffiné; *(sugar)* non raffiné; *(flour)* non bluté (**b**) *(person, manners)* peu raffiné, fruste

unreflecting [ˌʌnrɪ'flektɪŋ] *adj* (**a**) *(person, action, behaviour)* irréfléchi (**b**) *(surface)* non réfléchissant

unreflective [ˌʌnrɪ'flektɪv] *adj* (**a**) *(surface)* non réfléchissant (**b**) *(mind, person)* qui n'est pas porté à la réflexion

unreformed [ˌʌnrɪ'fɔːmd] *adj (person)* qui ne s'est pas corrigé; *(law)* non amendé; **to remain unreformed** *(person)* rester incorrigible

unrefreshed [ˌʌnrɪ'freʃt] *adj* encore fatigué, non reposé

unrefreshing [ˌʌnrɪ'freʃɪŋ] *adj (drink)* qui n'est pas rafraîchissant, qui ne rafraîchit pas; *(atmosphere, sleep)* qui n'est pas reposant

unregarded [ˌʌnrɪ'gɑːdɪd] *adj (gen → ignored)* dont on ne tient pas compte, ignoré; *(→ underrated)* dont on fait peu de cas; *(writer, artist)* méconnu; **to go unregarded** *(grievance, complaint)* être ignoré; *(remark, sarcasm)* passer inaperçu; *(writer, artist)* être méconnu

unregenerate [ˌʌnriː'dʒenərət] *adj* (**a**) *(unrepentant, unreformed)* impénitent, invétéré (**b**) *(adhering to personal opinions)* obstiné, entêté

unregistered [ˌʌn'redʒɪstəd] *adj* (**a**) *(luggage, complaint)* non enregistré (**b**) *(mail)* non recommandé (**c**) *(car)* non immatriculé (**d**) *(voter, student)* non inscrit; *(birth)* non déclaré
►► *Br* ***unregistered childminder*** nourrice *f* non agréée

unregretted [ˌʌnrɪ'gretɪd] *adj* que l'on ne regrette pas; **she died unregretted** personne n'a regretté sa mort

unregulated [ˌʌn'regjʊleɪtɪd] *adj* non réglementé

unrehearsed [ˌʌnrɪ'hɜːst] *adj* (**a**) *(improvised)* improvisé, spontané (**b**) *Mus & Theat* sans répétition, qui n'a pas été répété

unrelated [ˌʌnrɪ'leɪtɪd] *adj* (**a**) *(unconnected)* sans rapport; **the two incidents are unrelated** les deux incidents sont sans rapport l'un avec l'autre; **his answer was completely unrelated to the question** sa réponse n'avait absolument aucun rapport *ou* absolument rien à voir avec la question (**b**) *(people)* sans lien de parenté

unreleased [ˌʌnrɪ'liːst] *adj (film, album, recording)* qui n'est pas encore sorti

unrelenting [ˌʌnrɪ'lentɪŋ] *adj* (**a**) *(relentless → activity, effort)* soutenu, continuel; *(→ struggle, criticism)* acharné; *(→ pressure, rain)* incessant (**b**) *(person → tenacious)* tenace, obstiné; *(→ merciless)* implacable; **he was unrelenting** *(would not be persuaded, influenced)* il restait inflexible; *(merciless)* il était implacable

unrelentingly [ˌʌnrɪ'lentɪŋlɪ] *adv* sans répit; **the film is unrelentingly grim** le film est sinistre du début à la fin

unreliability [ˈʌnrɪˌlaɪəˈbɪlətɪ] *n* (**a**) *(of person)* manque *m* de sérieux (**b**) *(of method, machine)* manque *m* de fiabilité

unreliable [ˌʌnrɪˈlaɪəbəl] *adj* (**a**) *(person)* peu fiable, sur qui on ne peut pas compter; **he's too unreliable** on ne peut vraiment pas compter sur lui *ou* lui faire confiance (**b**) *(car, machinery)* peu fiable (**c**) *(service)* peu fiable, peu sûr; *(business, company)* qui n'inspire pas confiance (**d**) *(information, memory)* peu fiable

unreliably [ˌʌnrɪˈlaɪəblɪ] *adv* de manière peu fiable

unrelieved [ˌʌnrɪˈliːvd] *adj* (**a**) *(unvarying → gloom, misery)* constant, permanent; *(→ boredom)* mortel; *(→ black)* uniforme; *(→ landscape, routine)* monotone; **vast expanses of grey, unrelieved by any bright colour** de vastes étendues de gris qu'aucune couleur vive ne vient égayer (**b**) *(pain)* sans rémission, sans répit

unreligious [ˌʌnrɪˈlɪdʒɪs] *adj* (**a**) *(person)* non croyant (**b**) *(secular)* laïque

unremarkable [ˌʌnrɪˈmɑːkəbəl] *adj* peu remarquable, quelconque

unremarked [ˌʌnrɪˈmɑːkt] *adj* inaperçu

unremitting [ˌʌnrɪˈmɪtɪŋ] *adj* *(activity, rain)* incessant, ininterrompu; *(demands, efforts)* inlassable, infatigable; *(opposition)* implacable, opiniâtre; **they were unremitting in their efforts to find a solution** ils se sont efforcés avec assiduité de trouver une solution

unremittingly [ˌʌnrɪˈmɪtɪŋlɪ] *adv* *(work)* sans cesse, inlassablement; *(rain)* sans cesse, sans interruption; *(hostile, opposed)* implacablement, opiniâtrement

unremorseful [ˌʌnrɪˈmɔːsfʊl] *adj* *(person)* qui n'éprouve aucun remords

unremunerative [ˌʌnrɪˈmjuːnərətɪv] *adj* peu rémunérateur

unrenowned [ˌʌnrɪˈnaʊnd] *adj* peu connu, peu célèbre

unrepairable [ˌʌnrɪˈpeərəbəl] *adj* irréparable, impossible à réparer

unrepealed [ˌʌnrɪˈpiːld] *adj* *(law etc)* non abrogé

unrepeatable [ˌʌnrɪˈpiːtəbəl] *adj* (**a**) *(remark)* qu'on n'ose pas répéter, trop grossier pour être répété; **what he said was quite unrepeatable** ce qu'il a dit n'est pas répétable (**b**) *(offer, performance)* exceptionnel, unique

unrepentant [ˌʌnrɪˈpentənt] *adj* impénitent; **to die unrepentant** mourir dans le péché; **she was unrepentant about what she had done** *(gen)* elle ne regrettait pas du tout ce qu'elle avait fait; *(about sin)* elle ne se repentissait aucunement de ce qu'elle avait fait

unreported [ˌʌnrɪˈpɔːtɪd] *adj* non signalé *ou* mentionné; **the accident went unreported** l'accident n'a pas été signalé

unrepresentative [ˌʌnreprɪˈzentətɪv] *adj* non représentatif; **it's completely unrepresentative of the style of the period** ce n'est pas du tout représentatif du style de l'époque; **his opinions are unrepresentative of the group** ses opinions ne représentent pas celles du groupe

unrepresented [ˌʌnreprɪˈzentɪd] *adj Pol* qui n'est pas représenté

unreproachful [ˌʌnrɪˈprəʊtʃfʊl] *adj* *(voice, look, attitude, tone)* sans trace de reproche; *(words)* qui n'exprime aucun reproche

unreproved [ˌʌnrɪˈpruːvd] *adj* non réprimandé

unrequested [ˌʌnrɪˈkwestɪd] *adj* non sollicité

unrequited [ˌʌnrɪˈkwaɪtɪd] *adj Literary* non réciproque, non partagé

▸▸ ***unrequited love*** amour *m* non partagé

unresentful [ˌʌnrɪˈzentfʊl] *adj* sans ressentiment

unreserved [ˌʌnrɪˈzɜːvd] *adj* (**a**) *(place)* non réservé (**b**) *(unqualified)* sans réserve, entier; **to be unreserved in one's praise of sth** ne pas tarir d'éloges à propos de qch

unreservedly [ˌʌnrɪˈzɜːvɪdlɪ] *adv* (**a**) *(without qualification)* sans réserve, entièrement; **to trust sb unreservedly** avoir pleine confiance en qn (**b**) *(frankly)* sans réserve, franchement

unresisting [ˌʌnrɪˈzɪstɪŋ] *adj* soumis, docile

unresolvable [ˌʌnrɪˈzɒlvəbəl] *adj* insoluble

unresolved [ˌʌnrɪˈzɒlvd] *adj* *(issue, problem)* non résolu

unresponsive [ˌʌnrɪˈspɒnsɪv] *adj* (**a**) *(without reaction)* qui ne réagit pas; *Aut & Tech (steering)* qui ne répond pas bien; *(engine)* qui manque de nervosité; **management was unresponsive to workers' demands** l'administration n'a pas répondu aux exigences des ouvriers; **the patient has been unresponsive to medical treatment** le traitement n'a pas agi sur le malade, le malade n'a pas réagi au traitement; **the disease has been unresponsive to medical treatment** le traitement n'a pas agi *ou* n'a eu aucun effet sur la maladie
(**b**) *(mentally → gen)* insensible; *(→ audience)* passif; *(sexually → woman)* frigide; **she complains that her husband is unresponsive in bed** elle se plaint du fait que son mari manque d'enthousiasme au lit

unrest [ˌʌnˈrest] *n (UNCOUNT)* agitation *f*, troubles *mpl*; **labour** *or* **industrial unrest** agitation *f* ouvrière; **social unrest** *(discontent)* malaise *m* social; *(disorder)* troubles *mpl* sociaux

unrestrained [ˌʌnrɪˈstreɪnd] *adj* (**a**) *(anger, growth, joy)* non contenu; **the unrestrained use of force** l'usage sans limites de la force (**b**) *Literary* **unrestrained by our presence, he continued to talk** aucunement gêné par notre présence, il a continué de parler

unrestrainedly [ˌʌnrɪˈstreɪnɪdlɪ] *adv* librement, sans contrainte

unrestricted [ˌʌnrɪˈstrɪktɪd] *adj* *(access, parking)* libre; *(number, time)* illimité; *(power)* absolu

unrevealed [ˌʌnrɪˈviːld] *adj* non révélé

unrevealing [ˌʌnrɪˈviːlɪŋ] *adj* (**a**) *(interview, comment)* peu révélateur; *(examination, investigation)* qui n'a pas donné grand-chose (**b**) *(dress)* qui ne laisse rien deviner; *(neckline)* pudique

unrevoked [ˌʌnrɪˈvəʊkt] *vt* *(decision)* non annulé; *(measure, law)* non abrogé, non annulé, non révoqué; *(will)* non révoqué, non annulé; *(title, diploma, licence, permit, right)* non retiré

unrewarded [ˌʌnrɪˈwɔːdɪd] *adj* *(person)* non récompensé; *(effort, search)* vain, infructueux; **our efforts went unrewarded** nos efforts sont restés sans récompense

unrewarding [ˌʌnrɪˈwɔːdɪŋ] *adj* (**a**) *(financially)* pas très intéressant financièrement (**b**) *Fig (work, experience)* ingrat

unrhythmical [ˌʌnˈrɪðmɪkəl] *adj* *(person)* qui n'a pas le sens du rythme; *(music)* peu rythmé

unrhythmically [ˌʌnˈrɪðmɪkəlɪ] *adj* *(play, sing, dance)* sans aucun sens du rythme

unriddle [ˌʌnˈrɪdəl] *vt* *(riddle, mystery)* résoudre

unrig [ˌʌnˈrɪg] (*pt & pp* **unrigged**, *cont* **unrigging**) *vt Naut (ship)* dégréer

unrighteous [ˌʌnˈraɪtʃəs] *npl Literary* **the unrighteous** *(not pious)* les impies *mpl*; *(sinful)* les pécheurs *mpl*

unripe [ˌʌnˈraɪp] *adj* vert

unrivalled, *Am* **unrivaled** [ʌnˈraɪvəld] *adj* sans égal *ou* pareil, incomparable

unroadworthy [ˌʌnˈrəʊdˌwɜːðɪ] *adj* *(vehicle)* qui n'est pas en état de rouler

unroll [ˌʌnˈrəʊl] *vt* dérouler

unromantic [ˌʌnrəˈmæntɪk] *adj* *(person → unsentimental)* peu romantique; *(→ down-to-earth)* prosaïque, terre à terre *(inv)*; *(ideas, place)* peu romantique

unrope [ˌʌnˈrəʊp] *vi* *(in mountaineering)* se détacher (de la cordée)

unrounded [ˌʌnˈraʊndɪd] *adj Ling* étiré

unruffled [ˌʌnˈrʌfəld] *adj* (**a**) *(person)* imperturbable, qui ne perd pas son calme; **she remained completely unruffled** elle n'a pas sourcillé *ou* bronché (**b**) *(hair)* lisse; *(water)* calme, lisse

unruled [ˌʌnˈruːld] *adj* *(paper)* blanc (blanche), non réglé

unruliness [ˌʌnˈruːlɪnɪs] *n* *(of child)* indiscipline *f*, turbulence *f*; *(of mob)* agitation *f*; *(of horse)* caractère *m* fougueux

unruly [ˌʌnˈruːlɪ] *adj* (**a**) *(children)* indiscipliné, turbulent; *(mob)* incontrôlé; *(horse)* fougueux (**b**) *(hair)* indiscipliné

unrumpled [ˌʌnˈrʌmpəld] *adj* *(clothes)* qui n'est pas froissé; *(hair)* bien coiffé; *(fur)* lisse

unsaddle [ˌʌnˈsædəl] *vt* *(horse)* desseller; *(rider)* désarçonner

unsafe [ˌʌnˈseɪf] *adj* (**a**) *(dangerous → machine, neighbourhood)* peu sûr, dangereux; *(→ building, bridge)* peu solide, dangereux; **the water is unsafe to drink** l'eau n'est pas potable; **it's unsafe to leave it near the fire** c'est dangereux de le laisser près du feu (**b**) *(endangered)* en danger; **I feel very unsafe here** je ne me sens pas du tout en sécurité ici

▸▸ ***unsafe sex*** rapports *mpl* non protégés

unsaid [ˌʌnˈsed] **1** *pt & pp of* **unsay**
2 *adj* non dit, inexprimé; **a lot was left unsaid** beaucoup de choses ont été passées sous silence; **there was a lot that was left unsaid between them** il y a eu beaucoup de non-dits entre eux; **some things are better left unsaid** parfois il faut savoir se taire

unsalable [ˌʌnˈseɪləbəl] *adj* *(goods)* invendable

unsalaried [ˌʌnˈsælərɪd] *adj* *(position)* non rémunéré; *(person)* non salarié

unsaleable [ˌʌnˈseɪləbəl] *adj* *(goods)* invendable

unsalted [ˌʌnˈsɔːltɪd] *adj* non salé

▸▸ ***unsalted butter*** beurre *m* doux

unsanctioned [ˌʌnˈsæŋkʃənd] *adj* (**a**) *(action)* non autorisé, non approuvé (**b**) *(law, decree)* non sanctionné, non ratifié

unsanitary [ˌʌnˈsænɪtərɪ] *adj* insalubre, malsain

unsatisfactorily [ˌʌnsætɪsˈfæktərɪlɪ] *adv* d'une manière peu satisfaisante

unsatisfactoriness [ˌʌnsætɪsˈfæktərɪnɪs] *n* caractère *m* peu satisfaisant

unsatisfactory [ˌʌnsætɪsˈfæktərɪ] *adj* peu satisfaisant, qui laisse à désirer; **this situation is most unsatisfactory** cette situation n'est pas du tout satisfaisante

unsatisfiable [ˌʌnsætɪsˈfaɪəbəl] *adj* *(desire, curiosity, passion)* insatiable, inassouvissable

unsatisfied [ˌʌnˈsætɪsfaɪd] *adj* (**a**) *(person → unhappy)* insatisfait, mécontent; *(→ unconvinced)* non convaincu; **they remain unsatisfied with her work** ils sont toujours mécontents de son travail (**b**) *(desire)* insatisfait, inassouvi; *(appetite)* non rassasié

unsatisfying [ˌʌnˈsætɪsfaɪɪŋ] *adj* (**a**) *(activity, task)* peu gratifiant, ingrat (**b**) *(unconvincing)* peu convaincant (**c**) *(meal → insufficient)* insuffisant, peu nourrissant; *(→ disappointing)* décevant

unsaturated [ˌʌnˈsætʃəreɪtɪd] *adj* non saturé

▸▸ ***unsaturated fats*** graisses *fpl* insaturées

unsavouriness, *Am* **unsavoriness** [ˌʌnˈseɪvərɪnɪs] *n* (**a**) *(of behaviour, habits)* caractère *m* peu ragoûtant; *(of place)* caractère *m* louche; *(of reputation, film, novel)* caractère *m* douteux (**b**) *(of food)* mauvais goût *m*

unsavoury, *Am* **unsavory** [ˌʌnˈseɪvərɪ] *adj* (**a**) *(behaviour, habits)* peu ragoûtant, très déplaisant; *(person)* peu recommandable; *(place)* louche; *(reputation, film, novel)* douteux (**b**) *(smell)* fétide, nauséabond; *(food)* mauvais; **the food looked unsavoury** la nourriture était peu ragoûtante

unsay [ˌʌnˈseɪ] (*pt & pp* **unsaid** [-ˈsed]) *vt* retirer, revenir sur; **what's said cannot be unsaid** ce qui est dit est dit

unscarred [ˌʌnˈskɑːd] *adj* *(physically)* sans cicatrices; **his difficult childhood has left him remarkably unscarred** chose surprenante, son enfance difficile l'a peu marqué; **she was unscarred by the experience** l'expérience ne l'a pas affectée

unscathed [ˌʌnˈskeɪðd] *adj* *(physically)* indemne, sain et sauf; *(psychologically)* non affecté; **luckily he emerged unscathed from the experience** heureusement, il est sorti indemne de cette aventure; **the city survived the bombing relatively unscathed** la ville a survécu au bombardement sans trop de dégâts

unscented [ˌʌnˈsentɪd] *adj* *(soap etc)* sans parfum, non parfumé

unscheduled [*Br* ˌʌnˈʃedjuːld, *Am* ˌʌnˈskedʒʊld] *adj* imprévu

unscholarly [ˌʌnˈskɒləlɪ] *adj* *(not appropriate for a scholar)* qui n'est pas digne d'un intellectuel; *(not written etc in a scholarly way)* peu académique

unschooled [ˌʌnˈskuːld] *adj Formal* (**a**) *(person)* qui n'a pas d'instruction; **he is unschooled in such matters** il est ignorant en la matière, il n'a jamais été initié à ces choses (**b**) *(talent)* inné, naturel

unscientific [ˌʌnsaɪənˈtɪfɪk] *adj* *(method, approach)* non *ou* peu scientifique

unscientifically [ˌʌnsaɪənˈtɪfɪklɪ] *adv* peu scientifiquement

unscramble [ˌʌnˈskræmbəl] *vt (code, message)* déchiffrer; *Tel* désembrouiller; *Fig (problem)* résoudre

unscrambler [ˌʌnˈskræmblə(r)] *n* décodeur *m*

unscreened [ˌʌnˈskriːnd] *adj* (**a**) *(unsheltered → place)* exposé, non abrité (**b**) *(without a screen)* sans écran; *Elec (condenser etc)* non blindé (**c**) *(coal)* non criblé (**d**) *(employees)* non filtré (**e**) *(film, television programme)* pas encore diffusé

unscrew [ˌʌnˈskruː] **1** *vt* dévisser
2 *vi* se dévisser

unscripted [ˌʌnˈskrɪptɪd] *adj (play, speech)* improvisé; *(item, subject)* non programmé

unscrupulous [ˌʌnˈskruːpjʊləs] *adj (person)* sans scrupules, peu scrupuleux; *(behaviour, methods)* malhonnête, peu scrupuleux

unscrupulously [ˌʌnˈskruːpjʊləslɪ] *adv* sans scrupules, peu scrupuleusement

unscrupulousness [ˌʌnˈskruːpjʊləsnɪs] *n (of person)* manque *m* de scrupules, malhonnêteté *f*; *(of behaviour, methods)* malhonnêteté *f*

unseal [ˌʌnˈsiːl] *vt (open → letter)* ouvrir, décacheter; *(→ deed, testament)* desceller; *Fig* **to unseal one's lips** rompre le silence, parler

unsealed [ˌʌnˈsiːld] *adj (letter)* ouvert, décacheté; *(deed, testament)* descellé

unseasonable [ˌʌnˈsiːzənəbəl] *adj* (**a**) *(clothing, weather)* qui n'est pas de saison; **this weather's very unseasonable** ce n'est pas un temps de saison (**b**) *Literary (inopportune)* **an unseasonable request** une demande inopportune

unseasonably [ˌʌnˈsiːzənəblɪ] *adv* **an unseasonably cold night** une nuit fraîche pour la saison

unseasoned [ˌʌnˈsiːzənd] *adj* (**a**) *(food)* non assaisonné (**b**) *(wood)* vert

unseat [ˌʌnˈsiːt] *vt (rider)* désarçonner; *(government, king)* faire tomber; *Parl (Member of Parliament)* faire perdre son siège à

unseaworthy [ˌʌnˈsiːwɜːðɪ] *n (ship)* innavigable

unsecured [ˌʌnsɪˈkjʊəd] *adj* (**a**) *(door, window → unlocked)* qui n'est pas fermé à clé; *(→ open)* mal fermé (**b**) *Fin (loan, overdraft)* sans garantie, non garanti
▸▸ *Fin* ***unsecured advance*** avance *f* à découvert; *Fin* ***unsecured creditor*** créancier(ère) *m,f* ordinaire *ou* chirographaire; *Fin* ***unsecured debenture*** obligation *f* non garantie; *Fin* ***unsecured debt*** créance *f* chirographaire *ou* sans garantie

unseeded [ˌʌnˈsiːdɪd] *adj Sport* non classé

unseeing [ˌʌnˈsiːɪŋ] *adj Literary* aveugle; **he looked at her with unseeing eyes** il l'a regardée sans (vraiment) la voir

unseemliness [ˌʌnˈsiːmlɪnɪs] *n Literary (of behaviour, dress)* inconvenance *f*

unseemly [ˌʌnˈsiːmlɪ] *adj Literary (improper → behaviour)* inconvenant, déplacé; *(→ dress)* inconvenant, peu convenable; *(rude)* indécent, grossier

unseen [ˌʌnˈsiːn] **1** *adj* (**a**) *(invisible)* invisible; *(unnoticed)* inaperçu; **she passed unseen through the crowd** elle est passée inaperçue dans la foule (**b**) *(not seen previously)* **to buy sth sight unseen** acheter qch sans l'avoir vu; *Br Sch & Univ* **an unseen translation** une traduction sans préparation *ou* à vue
2 *n Br Sch & Univ* traduction *f* sans préparation *ou* à vue

unsegregated [ˌʌnˈsegrɪˌgeɪtɪd] *adj* où la ségrégation n'est pas appliquée

unselective [ˌʌnsɪˈlektɪv] *adj (person)* qui manque de discernement; *(method)* qui ne fait pas le tri; **to be unselective in one's choice** choisir sans discernement; **to have an unselective approach** ne pas faire le tri, prendre tout en vrac; **to be unselective in one's reading habits** lire n'importe quoi

unselfconscious [ˌʌnselfˈkɒnʃəs] *adj (charm)* naturel; *(laugh)* spontané; *(person → spontaneous)* naturel; *(→ uninhibited)* sans complexes; **he's got a big scar on his face but he's quite unselfconscious about it** il a une grande cicatrice sur le visage mais n'est pas complexé; **she's quite unselfconscious about speaking up** elle n'a vraiment pas peur de dire ce qu'elle pense, elle dit ce qu'elle pense sans aucun complexe

unselfconsciously [ˌʌnselfˈkɒnʃəslɪ] *adv (spontaneously)* avec naturel; *(uninhibitedly)* sans complexes

unselfconsciousness [ˌʌnselfˈkɒnʃəsnɪs] *n (spontaneity)* naturel *m*; *(lack of inhibition)* absence *f* de complexes

unselfish [ˌʌnˈselfɪʃ] *adj (person, act)* généreux, désintéressé

unselfishly [ˌʌnˈselfɪʃlɪ] *adv* généreusement, sans penser à soi

unselfishness [ˌʌnˈselfɪʃnɪs] *n (of person, act)* générosité *f*, désintéressement *m*

unsellable [ˌʌnˈseləbəl] *adj* invendable

unsentimental [ˌʌnsentɪˈmentəl] *adj (person)* qui ne fait pas de sentiment; *(book, description)* qui ne tombe pas dans le sentimental, sans sentimentalisme; **to be unsentimental about animals** ne pas faire de sentiment au sujet des animaux; **the film remains unsentimental throughout** le film ne fait jamais dans le mélo

unserviceable [ˌʌnˈsɜːvɪsəbəl] *adj* inutilisable

unset [ˌʌnˈset] *adj (diamond, emerald)* non serti, non enchâssé

unsettle [ˌʌnˈsetəl] *vt* (**a**) *(person)* inquiéter, troubler (**b**) *(stomach)* déranger

unsettled [ˌʌnˈsetəld] *adj* (**a**) *(unstable → conditions, situation)* instable, incertain; *(→ person)* troublé, perturbé, inquiet(ète); *(→ stomach)* dérangé; *(→ weather)* incertain, changeant; **I feel unsettled in my job** je ne suis pas bien dans mon travail (**b**) *(unfinished → issue, argument, dispute)* qui n'a pas été réglé (**c**) *(account, bill)* non réglé, impayé (**d**) *(area, region)* inhabité, sans habitants

unsettling [ˌʌnˈsetəlɪŋ] *adj (disturbing)* troublant, perturbateur

unsex [ˌʌnˈseks] *vt Literary (woman)* faire perdre sa féminité à; *(man)* faire perdre sa virilité à

unsexy [ˌʌnˈseksɪ] *adj* pas sexy

unshackle [ˌʌnˈʃækəl] *vt* désenchaîner, ôter ses fers à; *Fig* libérer, émanciper

unshackled [ˌʌnˈʃækəld] *adj* sans entraves, libre; **to be unshackled by convention** ne pas porter le poids des conventions

unshakeable [ˌʌnˈʃeɪkəbəl] *adj (conviction, faith)* inébranlable; *(decision)* ferme

unshakeably [ˌʌnˈʃeɪkəblɪ] *adv* irréductiblement

unshaken [ˌʌnˈʃeɪkən] *adj* inébranlable

unshapely [ˌʌnˈʃeɪplɪ] *(compar* **unshapelier**, *superl* **unshapeliest**) *adj (body, legs)* vilain; *(woman)* mal faite; **I look rather unshapely in this dress** j'ai l'air d'un sac dans cette robe, cette robe ne m'avantage guère

unshaven [ˌʌnˈʃeɪvən] *adj* non rasé

unsheathe [ˌʌnˈʃiːð] *vt* dégainer

unsheltered [ˌʌnˈʃeltəd] *adj* non abrité, non protégé (**from** contre)

unship [ˌʌnˈʃɪp] *vt (pt & pp* **unshipped**, *cont* **unshipping**) *Naut* décharger, débarquer

unshockable [ˌʌnˈʃɒkəbəl] *adj* imperturbable, impassible

unshod [ˌʌnˈʃɒd] *adj* (**a**) *(horse)* qui n'est pas ferré (**b**) *(person)* sans chaussures; *(having removed shoes)* déchaussé

unshuttered [ˌʌnˈʃʌtəd] *adj (window → with open shutters)* dont les volets ne sont pas fermés; *(→ without shutters)* sans volets

unsighted [ˌʌnˈsaɪtɪd] *adj* (**a**) *(with one's view blocked)* **I didn't see what happened, I was unsighted** je n'ai pas vu ce qui s'est passé, quelqu'un bloquait ma vue; **the goalkeeper was unsighted** quelqu'un empêchait le gardien de but de voir le ballon (**b**) *(sightless)* aveugle

unsightliness [ʌnˈsaɪtlɪnɪs] *n* laideur *f*, aspect *m* disgracieux

unsightly [ʌnˈsaɪtlɪ] *adj* disgracieux, laid

unsigned [ˌʌnˈsaɪnd] *adj* non signé, sans signature

unsinkable [ˌʌnˈsɪŋkəbəl] *adj (boat)* insubmersible; *Fig (person)* qui ne se démonte pas facilement

unsisterly [ˌʌnˈsɪstəlɪ] *adj (person)* peu comme une sœur; *(behaviour → gen)* indigne d'une sœur; *(→ not feminist)* = qui fait preuve de peu de solidarité avec les autres femmes

unskilful, *Am* **unskillful** [ˌʌnˈskɪlfʊl] *adj (lacking skill)* malhabile; *(clumsy)* maladroit

unskilfully, *Am* **unskillfully** [ˌʌnˈskɪlfʊlɪ] *adv (without skill)* malhabilement; *(clumsily)* maladroitement

unskilled [ˌʌnˈskɪld] *adj* (**a**) *(worker)* sans formation professionnelle, non spécialisé, non qualifié (**b**) *(job, work)* qui ne nécessite pas de connaissances professionnelles (**c**) *(person)* inexpérimenté; **to be unskilled in** *or* **at doing sth** ne pas être doué pour faire qch
▸▸ *Br* ***unskilled labourer*** ouvrier *m* non spécialisé, ouvrière *f* non spécialisée

unskillful, unskillfully *Am* = **unskilful, unskilfully**

unskimmed [ʌnˈskɪmd] *adj (milk)* entier

unsleeping [ˌʌnˈsliːpɪŋ] *adj Literary* toujours en éveil, vigilant

unslept-in [ˌʌnˈslept-] *adj (bed)* non défait

unsliced [ˌʌnˈslaɪst] *adj* entier

unsling [ˌʌnˈslɪŋ] *(pt & pp* **unslung** [-ˈslʌŋ]) *vt* dégréer; *(hammock)* décrocher; **to unsling one's rifle** enlever son fusil de l'épaule

unsmiling [ˌʌnˈsmaɪlɪŋ] *adj (person, face)* austère, sérieux

unsmoked [ʌnˈsməʊkt] *adj* non fumé

unsnarl [ˌʌnˈsnɑːl] *vt* démêler

unsociable [ˌʌnˈsəʊʃəbəl] *adj (person)* sauvage, peu sociable; *(place)* peu accueillant; **to feel unsociable** ne pas avoir envie de voir du monde; **don't be so unsociable!** ne sois pas si sauvage!

unsocial [ˌʌnˈsəʊʃəl] *adj* **she works unsocial hours** elle travaille en dehors des heures normales

unsold [ˌʌnˈsəʊld] *adj* invendu

unsoldierly [ˌʌnˈsəʊldʒəlɪ] *adj* peu militaire

unsolicited [ˌʌnsəˈlɪsɪtɪd] *adj (comment)* non sollicité; *(contribution)* volontaire; *(application)* spontané; **unsolicited manuscript** manuscrit *m* non commandé; **to do sth unsolicited** faire qch spontanément

unsolicitous [ˌʌnsəˈlɪsɪtəs] *adj (inattentive)* peu attentionné; *(unconcerned)* indifférent

unsolvable [ˌʌnˈsɒlvəbəl] *adj* insoluble

unsolved [ˌʌnˈsɒlvd] *adj (mystery)* non résolu, inexpliqué; *(problem)* non résolu

unsophisticated [ˌʌnsəˈfɪstɪkeɪtɪd] *adj* (**a**) *(person → in dress, tastes)* simple; *(→ in attitude)* simple, naturel
(**b**) *(dress, style)* simple, qui n'est pas sophistiqué
(**c**) *(device, machine, technology)* simple; *(approach, method)* rudimentaire, *Pej* simpliste
(**d**) *(novice, inexperienced)* inexpérimenté; **unsophisticated users/investors** les utilisateurs/investisseurs inexpérimentés; **guidelines for the financially unsophisticated** des conseils pour ceux qui ne sont pas très au fait *ou* manquent d'expérience en matière de finances

unsorted [ˌʌnˈsɔːtɪd] *adj (clothing, mail)* non trié; *(documents)* non classé

unsought [ˌʌnˈsɔːt] *adj (advice, compliment)* non sollicité, non recherché

unsound [ˌʌnˈsaʊnd] *adj* (**a**) *(argument, conclusion, reasoning)* mal fondé, peu pertinent; *(advice, decision)* peu judicieux, peu sensé; *(enterprise, investment)* peu sûr, risqué; *(business)* peu sûr, précaire; **the project is economically unsound** le projet n'est pas sain *ou* viable sur le plan économique; **ideologically/politically unsound** *(theory, beliefs, system)* pas valable sur le plan idéologique/politique; **he's ideologically unsound** son idéologie est suspecte; **scientifically unsound** qui ne repose *ou* s'appuie pas sur des bases scientifiques solides; **this method of waste disposal is environmentally unsound** ce système de traitement des ordures est nuisible à l'environnement
(**b**) *(building, bridge)* peu solide, dangereux; **the building is structurally unsound** le bâtiment n'est pas solide
(**c**) *(idiom)* **to be of unsound mind** ne pas jouir de toutes ses facultés mentales

unsoundness [ˌʌnˈsaʊndnɪs] *n* (**a**) *(of argument, conclusion, reasoning)* manque *m* de pertinence; *(of advice, decision)* caractère *m* peu judicieux; *(of enterprise, investment)* caractère *m* risqué; *(business)* caractère *m* précaire (**b**) *(of building, bridge)* manque *m* de solidité (**c**) **unsoundness of mind** faiblesse *f* d'esprit

unsparing [ˌʌnˈspeərɪŋ] *adj* (**a**) *(generous)* généreux, prodigue; **to be unsparing of one's time/with one's advice** ne pas être avare de son temps/de conseils; **they were unsparing in**

their efforts to help us ils n'ont pas ménagé leurs efforts pour nous aider (**b**) *(harsh)* sévère

unsparingly [ʌn'speərɪŋlɪ] *adv* (**a**) *(lavishly)* généreusement, libéralement (**b**) *(criticize, mock)* sévèrement, sans mâcher ses mots

unspeakable [ˌʌn'spiːkəbəl] *adj* (**a**) *(crime, pain)* épouvantable, atroce (**b**) *(beauty, joy)* indicible, ineffable

unspeakably [ˌʌn'spiːkəblɪ] *adv (cruel, rude)* épouvantablement, atrocement; *(beautiful)* indiciblement, ineffablement

unspecialized [ˌʌn'speʃəlaɪzd] *adj (equipment)* non spécialisé; *(skills, knowledge)* général

unspecified [ˌʌn'spesɪfaɪd] *adj* non spécifié; **certain unspecified persons** certaines personnes, dont on taira les noms

unspectacular [ˌʌnspek'tækjʊlə(r)] *adj* peu spectaculaire

unspent [ˌʌn'spent] *adj* non dépensé, restant

unspoiled [ˌʌn'spɔɪld], **unspoilt** [ˌʌn'spɔɪlt] *adj* (**a**) *(person)* (qui est resté) naturel; **they were unspoiled by fame** ils étaient simples *ou* naturels malgré leur succès, le succès ne leur était pas monté à la tête (**b**) *(beauty, town)* intact (**c**) *(flavour)* naturel

unspoken [ˌʌn'spəʊkən] *adj* (**a**) *(agreement)* tacite (**b**) *(thought, wish)* inexprimé; *(word)* non prononcé; **although his name remained unspoken…** bien que son nom n'ait pas été prononcé…; **her unspoken thought was that…** intérieurement elle pensait que…

unsporting [ˌʌn'spɔːtɪŋ] *adj (person)* déloyal; *(behaviour → gen)* déloyal; *(→ in sport)* peu sportif, peu fair-play *(inv)*; **it was unsporting of him not to help us** ce n'était pas très chic de sa part de ne pas nous aider; **he was suspended for unsporting behaviour** il a été suspendu pour conduite indigne d'un sportif

unsportsmanlike [ʌn'spɔːtsmənlaɪk] *adj* peu sportif, peu fair-play *(inv)*

unsprung [ˌʌn'sprʌŋ] *adj* (**a**) *(mattress)* sans ressorts (**b**) *(trap)* qui ne s'est pas déclenché

unstable [ˌʌn'steɪbəl] *adj* (**a**) *(chair, government, price, situation)* instable (**b**) *(marriage)* peu solide (**c**) *(person)* déséquilibré, instable

unstaffed [ˌʌn'stɑːft] *adj* sans personnel; **the office is unstaffed between twelve o'clock and two o'clock** il n'y a personne au bureau entre midi et deux heures

unstained [ˌʌn'steɪnd] *adj* (**a**) *(reputation)* sans tache (**b**) *(wood)* non teinté

unstamped [ˌʌn'stæmpt] *adj (letter)* non affranchi, non timbré; *(document)* non tamponné

unstarched [ˌʌn'stɑːtʃt] *adj* non amidonné

unstated [ˌʌn'steɪtɪd] *adj* (**a**) *(agreement)* tacite (**b**) *(desire)* inexprimé

unstatesmanlike [ˌʌn'steɪtsmənlaɪk] *adj (behaviour)* peu digne d'un homme d'État

unsteadily [ˌʌn'stedɪlɪ] *adv (walk)* d'un pas chancelant *ou* incertain, en titubant; *(speak)* d'une voix mal assurée; *(hold, write)* d'une main tremblante

unsteadiness [ˌʌn'stedɪnɪs] *n (of step, voice, writing)* manque *m* d'assurance; *(of table)* manque *m* de stabilité *f*

unsteady [ˌʌn'stedɪ] *(compar* **unsteadier**, *superl* **unsteadiest**) *adj* (**a**) *(chair, ladder)* instable, branlant (**b**) *(step, voice)* mal assuré, chancelant; *(hand)* tremblant; **to be unsteady on one's feet** *(from illness, tiredness, drink)* ne pas tenir très bien sur ses jambes (**c**) *(rhythm, speed, temperature)* irrégulier; *(flame)* vacillant (**d**) *Fin (prices)* variable; *(market)* agité

unsterilized [ˌʌn'sterɪlaɪzd] *adj* non stérilisé

unstick [ˌʌn'stɪk] *(pt & pp* **unstuck** [-'stʌk]) **1** *vt* décoller

2 *vi* se décoller

unstinted [ˌʌn'stɪntɪd] *adj* (**a**) *(supplies)* abondant (**b**) *(praise, admiration)* sans réserve

unstinting [ˌʌn'stɪntɪŋ] *adj (care)* infini; *(help)* généreux; *(efforts)* incessant, illimité; *(support)* sans réserve, inconditionnel; *(person)* généreux, prodigue; **the firm has been unstinting in its efforts to help us** l'entreprise ne ménage pas ses efforts pour nous aider; **to be unstinting in one's praise of sb/sth** ne pas tarir d'éloges au sujet de qn/qch; **to give unstinting praise** ne pas ménager ses louanges

unstintingly [ˌʌn'stɪntɪŋlɪ] *adv* généreusement; *(to help, work)* sans se ménager; *(to support)* sans réserve, inconditionnellement; **to praise sb unstintingly** ne pas tarir d'éloges sur qn

unstitch [ˌʌn'stɪtʃ] *vt* découdre; **the hem came unstitched** l'ourlet s'est décousu

unstop [ˌʌn'stɒp] *(pt & pp* **unstopped**, *cont* **unstopping**) *vt (drain, sink)* déboucher

unstoppable [ˌʌn'stɒpəbəl] *adj* qu'on ne peut pas arrêter; *(force)* irrésistible; *Sport (shot)* imparable; **the unstoppable rise in property prices** la hausse inexorable des prix de l'immobilier; **he's unstoppable now** désormais rien ne peut l'arrêter

unstopped [ˌʌn'stɒpt] *adj Ling* constrictif

unstrap [ˌʌn'stræp] *(pt & pp* **unstrapped**, *cont* **unstrapping**) *vt* défaire les sangles de; **to unstrap sth from sth** détacher qch de qch

unstreamed [ˌʌn'striːmd] *adj Sch (class)* où les élèves ne sont pas séparés en groupes de niveaux

unstressed [ˌʌn'strest] *adj Ling* inaccentué, atone

unstring [ˌʌn'strɪŋ] *(pt & pp* **unstrung** [-'strʌŋ]) *vt* (**a**) *(bow)* débander; **to unstring a violin** ôter les cordes d'un violon (**b**) *(beads etc)* ôter le fil de

unstructured [ˌʌn'strʌktʃəd] *adj (activity, essay)* non structuré; *(group)* non organisé; *Mktg (interview)* non structuré, libre

unstrung [ˌʌn'strʌŋ] **1** *pt & pp of* **unstring**

2 *adj (musical instrument → without strings)* sans cordes; *(→ with relaxed strings)* dont les cordes sont détendues

unstuck [ˌʌn'stʌk] **1** *pt & pp of* **unstick**

2 *adj (envelope, label)* décollé; **to come unstuck** se décoller; *Fig (plan, policy)* tomber à l'eau; *(person)* se casser la figure

unstudied [ˌʌn'stʌdɪd] *adj (natural)* naturel; *(spontaneous)* spontané

unstuffy [ˌʌn'stʌfɪ] *adj (relaxed → person)* simple, naturel; *(→ atmosphere, reception)* détendu

unstylish [ˌʌn'staɪlɪʃ] *adj (clothes)* sans chic, peu élégant; *(person)* qui manque d'élégance; *(neighbourhood)* pas très chic

unsubdued [ˌʌnsəb'djuːd] *adj* indompté

unsubscribed [ˌʌnsəb'skraɪbd] *adj Fin (capital)* non souscrit

unsubsidized [ˌʌn'sʌbsɪdaɪzd] *adj* non subventionné

unsubstantiated [ˌʌnsəb'stænʃɪeɪtɪd] *adj (report, story)* non confirmé *ou* corroboré; *(accusation)* non fondé

unsubtle [ˌʌn'sʌtəl] *adj (person, remark)* peu subtil, sans finesse; *(joke)* gros (grosse); **how could anyone be so unsubtle!** comment peut-on manquer de subtilité à ce point!

unsuccessful [ˌʌnsək'sesfʊl] *adj (plan, project)* qui est un échec, qui n'a pas réussi; *(attempt)* vain, infructueux; *(person)* qui n'a pas de succès; *(demand)* refusé, rejeté; *(marriage, outcome)* malheureux; **after several unsuccessful attempts** après plusieurs essais infructueux; **to be unsuccessful** échouer; **I was unsuccessful in my attempts to find her** je n'ai pas réussi *ou* je ne suis pas arrivé à la trouver, je l'ai cherchée en vain *ou* sans succès; **to be unsuccessful in an exam** échouer *ou* ne pas être reçu à un examen; **your application has been unsuccessful** votre candidature n'a pas été retenue; **unsuccessful applications will not be acknowledged** nous ne répondrons pas aux personnes dont les candidatures n'ont pas été retenues; **unsuccessful candidate** *(at election)* candidat *m* non élu

unsuccessfully [ˌʌnsək'sesfʊlɪ] *adv* en vain, sans succès

unsuitability [ˌʌnsuːtə'bɪlɪtɪ] *n (of person)* inaptitude *f* (**for sth** à qch); *(of behaviour, language)* caractère *m* inconvenant; **due to the unsuitability of the climate…** *(for person)* le climat étant peu indiqué…; *(for plants)* le climat ne convenant pas…; **the unsuitability of the clothes he was wearing** les vêtements *mpl* inadéquats qu'il portait; **this seems proof of his unsuitability for the job** ceci semble indiquer qu'il n'est pas la personne qu'il faut pour ce poste; **he pointed out the unsuitability of that date for the meeting** il a fait remarquer que cette date ne convenait pas pour la réunion; **the unsuitability of the tools meant that the job took twice as long** le travail a pris deux fois plus longtemps parce que les outils ne convenaient pas

unsuitable [ˌʌn'suːtəbəl] *adj (arrangement, candidate, qualities, tool)* qui ne convient pas; *(behaviour, language)* inconvenant; *(moment, time)* inopportun; *(clothing)* peu approprié, inadéquat; *(friend, people)* peu recommandable; *(climate → for person)* peu indiqué; *(→ for plants)* qui ne convient pas; **he chose an unsuitable time to call** il a mal choisi le moment pour appeler; **this is an unsuitable time to bring the matter up** ce n'est pas le moment de parler de cela; **unsuitable for children** *(on packaging)* ne convient pas aux enfants; **the land is unsuitable for farming** le sol n'est pas propice aux cultures *ou* n'est pas cultivable; **he's quite unsuitable for the job** ce n'est pas la personne qu'il faut pour ce poste; **unsuitable for the occasion** qui ne convient pas à la circonstance

unsuitably [ˌʌn'suːtəblɪ] *adv (behave)* de façon inconvenante; *(dress)* de façon inappropriée; **they're unsuitably matched** *(of couple)* ils sont mal assortis

unsuited [ˌʌn'suːtɪd] *adj (person)* inapte; *(machine, tool)* mal adapté, impropre; **he is unsuited to politics** il n'est pas fait pour la politique; **as a couple they seem totally unsuited** ils forment un couple mal assorti, ils ne vont pas du tout ensemble

unsullied [ˌʌn'sʌlɪd] *adj Literary* sans souillure, sans tache; **her reputation was unsullied by…** sa réputation n'a pas souffert de…

unsung [ˌʌn'sʌŋ] *adj Literary (deed, hero)* méconnu

unsupervised [ʌn'suːpəvaɪzd] *adj (child)* non surveillé; **unsupervised minors not admitted** *(sign)* interdit aux enfants non accompagnés

unsupported [ˌʌnsə'pɔːtɪd] *adj* (**a**) *(argument, theory)* non vérifié; *(accusation, statement)* non fondé; **the theories were unsupported by any evidence** ces théories n'ont été étayées par aucune preuve (**b**) *(wall, aperture)* sans support; **to walk unsupported** *(invalid)* marcher sans se faire aider (**c**) *Fig (person → financially, emotionally)* **to be unsupported** n'avoir aucun soutien

unsupportive [ˌʌnsə'pɔːtɪv] *adj (person, attitude)* qui n'est d'aucun soutien

unsuppressed [ˌʌnsə'prest] *adj (emotion)* non contenu; *(laughter)* franc (franche)

unsure [ˌʌn'ʃɔː(r)] *adj (lacking self-confidence)* qui manque d'assurance, qui n'est pas sûr de soi; *(hesitant)* incertain; **to be unsure of oneself** manquer d'assurance, ne pas être sûr de soi; **I'm unsure about going** je ne suis pas certain d'y aller; **they were unsure of his reaction** ils ignoraient quelle serait sa réaction

unsurpassable [ˌʌnsə'pɑːsəbəl] *adj* insurpassable

unsurpassed [ˌʌnsə'pɑːst] *adj* sans égal *ou* pareil

unsurprised [ˌʌnsə'praɪzd] *adj* non surpris; **I was unsurprised by his decision** je n'ai pas été surpris par sa décision

unsurprising [ˌʌnsə'praɪzɪŋ] *adj* peu surprenant

unsurprisingly [ˌʌnsə'praɪzɪŋlɪ] *adv* bien entendu, évidemment; **unsurprisingly, this suggestion was rejected** évidemment *ou* comme on pouvait s'y attendre, cette suggestion fut rejetée

unsuspected [ˌʌnsə'spektɪd] *adj* insoupçonné

unsuspecting [ˌʌnsə'spektɪŋ] *adj* qui ne soupçonne rien, qui ne se doute de rien

unsuspectingly [ˌʌnsə'spektɪŋlɪ] *adv* sans se douter de rien, sans se méfier

unsuspicious [ˌʌnsəs'pɪʃəs] *adj* peu soupçonneux

unsustainable [ˌʌnsə'steɪnəbəl] *adj* non viable

unsustained [ˌʌnsə'steɪnd] *adj* non viable

unsweetened [ˌʌn'swiːtənd] *adj* sans sucre, non sucré

unswerving [ˌʌn'swɜːvɪŋ] *adj (devotion, loyalty)* indéfectible, à toute épreuve; *(determination)* inébranlable

unswervingly [ˌʌn'swɜːvɪŋlɪ] *adv* **unswervingly loyal** d'une loyauté à toute épreuve

unsympathetic [ʌn,sɪmpə'θetɪk] *adj* (**a**) *(unfeeling)* insensible, incompréhensif; **to be unsympathetic to a cause** être opposé *ou* hostile à une cause; **they were very unsympathetic about our problems** nos problèmes les laissaient complètement indifférents; **he was generally unsympathetic to modern art** *(didn't like)* de manière générale il appréciait peu l'art moderne; *(made critical statements about)* il n'était généralement pas tendre avec l'art moderne; **the idea met with an unsympathetic reception** l'idée a reçu un accueil plutôt froid

(**b**) *(unlikeable)* antipathique; **I find the characters of this novel unsympathetic** les personnages de ce roman me sont peu sympathiques

unsympathetically ['ʌn,sɪmpə'θetɪklɪ] *adv* *(speak)* froidement, sans compassion; *(behave)* sans compassion; **"tough!", she said unsympathetically** "tant pis pour vous!", dit-elle froidement

unsystematic [,ʌnsɪstə'mætɪk] *adj* non systématique, non méthodique

unsystematically [,ʌnsɪstə'mætɪklɪ] *adv* sans méthode

untainted [,ʌn'teɪntɪd] *adj (water)* pur; *Fig (reputation)* sans tache; **his work is untainted by commercialism** son œuvre n'est pas commerciale

untalented [,ʌn'tæləntɪd] *adj* peu doué

untamable, untameable [,ʌn'teɪməbəl] *adj* indomptable, inapprivoisable

untamed [,ʌn'teɪmd] *adj* (**a**) *(animal → undomesticated)* sauvage, inapprivoisé; *(→ untrained)* non dressé; *(lion, tiger)* indompté (**b**) *(land)* sauvage (**c**) *(person)* insoumis, indompté; *(spirit)* indompté, rebelle

untangle [,ʌn'tæŋgəl] *vt (hair, necklace, rope)* démêler; *Fig (mystery)* débrouiller, éclaircir

untanned [,ʌn'tænd] *adj (skin, face)* blanc (blanche), non bronzé

untapped [,ʌn'tæpt] *adj* inexploité

untarnished [,ʌn'tɑːnɪʃt] *adj (silver)* non terni; *Fig (reputation)* non terni, sans tache

untasted [,ʌn'teɪstɪd] *adj* auquel on n'a pas goûté; **he sent the wine back untasted** il a renvoyé le vin sans y avoir goûté *ou* touché

untaught [,ʌn'tɔːt] *adj* (**a**) *(person)* sans instruction, ignorant (**b**) *(skill)* inné, naturel

untaxable [,ʌn'tæksəbəl] *adj Fin* non imposable

untaxed [,ʌn'tækst] *adj Fin (items)* non imposé, exempt de taxes, non taxé; *(income)* non imposable, exempt d'impôt, exonéré d'impôt, *(car)* = sans vignette

unteachable [,ʌn'tiːtʃəbəl] *adj (person)* à qui on ne peut rien apprendre; *(skill)* impossible à enseigner *ou* à inculquer

untempered [,ʌn'tempəd] *adj Metal (metal)* non trempé

untenability [,ʌntenə'bɪlɪtɪ] *n (of argument, theory)* caractère *m* indéfendable; *(of position)* caractère *m* intenable

untenable [,ʌn'tenəbəl] *adj (argument, theory)* indéfendable; *(position)* intenable

untenableness [,ʌn'tenəbəlnɪs] *n (of argument, theory)* caractère *m* indéfendable; *(of position)* caractère *m* intenable

untenanted [,ʌn'tenəntɪd] *adj* inoccupé, sans locataire

untended [,ʌn'tendɪd] *adj (sick person)* non soigné, sans soins; *(garden)* non entretenu; *(sheep)* sans surveillance

untested [,ʌn'testɪd] *adj (employee, method, theory)* qui n'a pas été mis à l'épreuve; *(invention, machine, product)* qui n'a pas été essayé; *(drug)* non encore expérimenté

unthinkable [,ʌn'θɪŋkəbəl] *adj* impensable, inconcevable; **it's unthinkable that...** il est inconcevable que... + *subjunctive*; **if the unthinkable should happen** si l'inconcevable se produisait

unthinking [,ʌn'θɪŋkɪŋ] *adj (action, remark)* irréfléchi, inconsidéré; *(person)* irréfléchi, étourdi

unthinkingly [,ʌn'θɪŋkɪŋlɪ] *adv* sans réfléchir, inconsidérément

unthread [,ʌn'θred] *vt (beads)* ôter le fil de

unthreatening [,ʌn'θretənɪŋ] *adj (gesture, behaviour)* inoffensif; **to appear unthreatening** avoir l'air inoffensif

untidily [,ʌn'taɪdɪlɪ] *adv* sans soin, d'une manière négligée; **the children's clothes were strewn untidily across the floor** les vêtements des enfants jonchaient le plancher; **she stuffed everything untidily into a drawer** elle a tout fourré pêle-mêle dans un tiroir

untidiness [,ʌn'taɪdɪnɪs] *n (of dress)* manque *m* de soin, débraillé *m*; *(of room)* désordre *m*; *(of person → in appearance)* aspect *m* négligé; *(→ characteristic)* manque *m* d'ordre

untidy [,ʌn'taɪdɪ] (*compar* **untidier**, *superl* **untidiest**) *adj (cupboard, desk, room)* mal rangé, en désordre; *(appearance)* négligé, débraillé; *(person → as characteristic)* désordonné; **untidy appearance** tenue *f* débraillée; **his room/desk always gets untidy** sa chambre/son bureau est toujours en désordre; **his playing is untidy** *(of musician)* son jeu manque de netteté

untie [,ʌn'taɪ] *vt (string)* dénouer; *(knot)* défaire; *(bonds)* défaire, détacher; *(package)* défaire, ouvrir; *(prisoner)* détacher, délier

untied [,ʌn'taɪd] *adj* **your shoes are untied** tes lacets sont défaits; **to come untied** se défaire

until [ən'tɪl] **1** *prep* (**a**) *(up to)* jusqu'à; **until midnight/Monday** jusqu'à minuit/lundi; **until 1989** jusqu'en 1989; **stay on the motorway until junction 13** restez sur l'autoroute jusqu'à la sortie 13; **until such time as you are ready** jusqu'à ce que *ou* en attendant que vous soyez prêt; **she was here (up) until February** elle était ici jusqu'en février; **(up) until now** jusqu'ici, jusqu'à présent; **(up) until then** jusque-là

(**b**) *(with negative → before)* **not until tomorrow** pas avant demain; **they didn't arrive until 8 o'clock** ils ne sont arrivés qu'à 8 h; **your car won't be ready until next week** votre voiture ne sera pas prête avant la semaine prochaine; **I've never seen it until now** c'est la première fois que je le vois

2 *conj* (**a**) *(up to the specified moment → in present)* jusqu'à ce que + *subjunctive*; *(→ in past)* avant que + *subjunctive*, jusqu'à ce que + *subjunctive*; **I'll wait here until you come back** j'attendrai ici jusqu'à ce que tu reviennes; **wait until she says hello** attendez qu'elle dise bonjour; **they stayed until everybody had gone** ils sont restés jusqu'à ce que tout le monde soit parti; **I laughed until I cried** j'ai ri aux larmes

(**b**) *(with negative main clause)* **until she spoke I didn't realize she was Spanish** jusqu'à ce qu'elle commence à parler, je ne m'étais pas rendu compte qu'elle était espagnole; **she won't go to sleep until her mother comes home** elle ne s'endormira pas avant que sa mère (ne) soit rentrée *ou* tant que sa mère n'est pas rentrée; **he can't leave hospital until the wound has completely healed** il ne peut pas quitter l'hôpital tant que sa blessure n'est pas complètement guérie; **don't sign anything until the boss gets there** ne signez rien avant que le patron n'arrive, attendez le patron pour signer quoi que ce soit; **the play didn't start until everyone was seated** la pièce n'a commencé qu'une fois que tout le monde a été assis

untilled [,ʌn'tɪld] *adj (uncultivated)* non cultivé; *(not ploughed)* non labouré

untimeliness [,ʌn'taɪmlɪnɪs] *n* (**a**) *(prematureness → of death)* caractère *m* prématuré (**b**) *(inopportuneness → of remark)* inopportunité *f*; [illegible]

untimely [,ʌn'taɪmlɪ] *adj* (**a**) *(premature)* prématuré, précoce; **an untimely death** une mort prématurée; **to meet** *or* **to come to an untimely end** *(person)* mourir avant l'âge; *(reign, project)* connaitre une fin prématurée (**b**) *(inopportune → remark)* inopportun, déplacé; *(→ moment)* inopportun, mal choisi; *(→ visit)* intempestif

untiring [,ʌn'taɪərɪŋ] *adj (efforts)* inlassable, infatigable; **they were untiring in their efforts** ils n'ont pas ménagé leurs efforts

untiringly [,ʌn'taɪərɪŋlɪ] *adv* inlassablement, infatigablement

untitled [,ʌn'taɪtəld] *adj (painting)* sans titre; *(person)* non titré

unto ['ʌntuː] *prep Arch or Literary* (**a**) *(to)* à; *Bible* **unto us a child is born** un enfant nous est né; *Bible* **and I say unto you...** en vérité je vous le dis...; **do unto others as you would have them do unto you** ne faites pas à autrui ce que vous ne voudriez pas qu'il vous fît (**b**) *(until)* jusqu'à; **unto death** jusqu'à la mort

untogether [,ʌntə'geðə(r)] *adj Fam* **he's very untogether** *(in work)* il est très mal organisé ❑; *(emotionally)* il est vraiment mal dans sa peau

untold [,ʌn'təʊld] *adj* (**a**) *(tale)* jamais raconté; *(secret)* jamais dévoilé; **the story remains untold** cette histoire reste secrète *ou* n'a jamais été racontée (**b**) *(great → joy, suffering)* indicible, indescriptible; *(→ amount, number)* incalculable; **the war caused untold suffering** la guerre a causé des souffrances indicibles

untouchable [,ʌn'tʌtʃəbəl] **1** *adj* intouchable

2 *n (in India)* intouchable *mf*; *Fig* paria *m*

untouched [,ʌn'tʌtʃt] *adj* (**a**) *(not changed)* auquel on n'a pas touché, intact; **he'd left the meal untouched** il n'avait pas touché à son repas

(**b**) *(unaffected)* **to be untouched by the influence of television** ne pas avoir subi l'influence de la télévision; **these artefacts have lain untouched by human hand for thousands of years** ces objets sont restés inconnus de l'homme pendant des milliers d'années

(**c**) *(unharmed → person)* indemne, sain et sauf; *(→ thing)* indemne, intact; **most of the city centre has remained untouched** une grande partie du centre ville est resté intact

(**d**) *(unmoved → person)* indifférent, insensible (**by** à)

untouristy [,ʌn'tʊərɪstɪ] *adj Fam* pas très touristique ❑

untoward [,ʌntə'wɔːd] *adj Formal (unfortunate → circumstances)* fâcheux, malencontreux; *(→ effect)* fâcheux, défavorable; **I hope nothing untoward has happened** j'espère qu'il n'est rien arrivé de fâcheux

untraceable [,ʌn'treɪsəbəl] *adj* introuvable

untradable [,ʌn'treɪdəbəl] *adj St Exch* incotable

untraditional [,ʌntrə'dɪʃənəl] *adj (method, approach)* peu conventionnel

untrained [,ʌn'treɪnd] *adj (person)* sans formation; *(ear)* inexercé; *(mind)* non formé; *(voice)* non travaillé; *(dog, horse)* non dressé; **to the untrained eye** pour un œil inexercé

untrammelled, *Am* **untrammeled** [,ʌn'træməld] *adj Literary* sans contrainte, sans entraves; **untrammelled by convention** libre de toute convention

untransferable [,ʌntræns'fɜːrəbəl] *adj* non transmissible; *Law (right, property)* incessible

untranslatable [,ʌntræns'leɪtəbəl] *adj* intraduisible

untravelled, *Am* **untraveled** [,ʌn'trævəld] *adj* *(road)* peu utilisé *ou* fréquenté; *(person)* qui n'a pas beaucoup voyagé

untreatable [,ʌn'triːtəbəl] *adj* incurable

untreated [,ʌn'triːtɪd] *adj* (**a**) *(unprocessed → food, wood)* non traité; *(→ sewage)* brut (**b**) *(infection, tumour)* non traité, non soigné; **her condition will worsen if left untreated** son état empirera si elle ne reçoit pas de traitement

untrendy [,ʌn'trendɪ] *adj Fam* pas branché, pas à la mode

untried [,ʌn'traɪd] *adj* (**a**) *(method, recruit, theory)* qui n'a pas été mis à l'épreuve; *(invention, product)* qui n'a pas été essayé (**b**) *Law (prisoner, case)* qui n'a pas encore été jugé

untrimmed [,ʌn'trɪmd] *adj (hair)* qui a besoin d'une coupe; *(beard, moustache, hedge)* qui a besoin d'être taillé

untrodden [,ʌn'trɒdən] *adj (ground, wilderness)* inexploré, vierge; *(path)* non utilisé *ou* fréquenté

►► ***untrodden snow*** neige *f* immaculée *ou* vierge

untroubled [,ʌn'trʌbəld] *adj* tranquille, paisible; **they seemed untroubled by the situation** la situation ne paraissait pas les inquiéter

untrue [,ʌn'truː] *adj* (**a**) *(incorrect → belief, statement)* faux (fausse), erroné; *(→ measurement, reading)* erroné, inexact (**b**) *(disloyal)* **to be untrue to sb** être déloyal envers *ou* infidèle à qn; **to be untrue to oneself** trahir ses principes

untruss [,ʌn'trʌs] *vt (gen)* détacher; *(person)* défaire les liens de; **untruss the chicken** coupez les ficelles qui attachent le poulet

untrusting [,ʌn'trʌstɪŋ] *adj* méfiant

untrustworthiness [,ʌn'trʌst,wɜːðɪnɪs] *n (of information, machine)* manque *m* de fiabilité; **he**

uns–unt

was noted for his untrustworthiness il avait la réputation de quelqu'un à qui on ne peut pas faire confiance

untrustworthy [ˌʌn'trʌstˌwɜːðɪ] *adj (person)* qui n'est pas digne de confiance; *(information, machine)* peu fiable

untruth [ˌʌn'truːθ] *n Euph Formal (lie)* mensonge *m*, invention *f*; **to tell an untruth** mentir, dire un mensonge

untruthful [ˌʌn'truːθfʊl] *adj (statement)* mensonger; *(person)* menteur; **to say untruthful things** mentir, dire des mensonges

untruthfully [ˌʌn'truːθfʊlɪ] *adv* d'une façon mensongère

untruthfulness [ˌʌn'truːθfʊlnɪs] *n (of evidence)* caractère *m* mensonger; **he was notorious for his untruthfulness** c'était un menteur notoire

untuck [ˌʌn'tʌk] *vt (person)* découvrir; *(bedclothes)* défaire

untuned [ˌʌn'tjuːnd] *adj (instrument)* non accordé; *(engine)* qui n'est pas réglé

untuneful [ˌʌn'tjuːnfʊl] *adj (song, voice)* peu mélodieux

untutored [ˌʌn'tjuːtəd] *adj* (**a**) *(person)* sans instruction; *(eye, ear)* inexercé; *(voice)* non travaillé; *(mind)* non formé (**b**) *(skill, talent)* inné, naturel

untwine [ˌʌn'twaɪn] *vt* détordre, détortiller

untwist [ˌʌn'twɪst] *vt* détordre

untypable [ˌʌn'taɪpəbəl] *adj Med (blood)* inclassifiable

untypical [ˌʌn'tɪpɪkəl] *adj* peu typique; **it's very untypical of her** ce n'est pas d'elle, ça ne lui ressemble pas du tout

untypically [ˌʌn'tɪpɪklɪ] *adj* anormalement; **it was an untypically sunny day** il faisait anormalement beau; **untypically for him, he didn't complain** il ne s'est pas plaint, ce qui n'est pas dans ses habitudes *ou* ce qui ne lui ressemble guère; **untypically, she didn't win** elle n'a pas gagné, ce qui était très inattendu

unusable [ˌʌn'juːzəbəl] *adj* inutilisable

unused *adj* (**a**) [ˌʌn'juːzd] *(not in use)* inutilisé; *(new → machine, material)* neuf, qui n'a pas servi; *(→ clothing, shoes)* neuf, qui n'a pas été porté (**b**) [ʌn'juːst] *(unaccustomed)* **to be unused to sth** ne pas avoir l'habitude de qch, ne pas être habitué à qch; **I'm unused to (eating) spicy food** je n'ai pas l'habitude de manger *ou* je ne suis pas habitué à manger épicé

unusual [ˌʌn'juːʒəl] *adj (uncommon)* peu commun, inhabituel; *(odd)* insolite, étrange, bizarre; **it's unusual for her to be so brusque** il est rare qu'elle soit si brusque, ça ne lui ressemble pas *ou* ce n'est pas son genre d'être aussi brusque; **it's not unusual to see flooding in these parts** il n'est pas rare *ou* il arrive assez fréquemment qu'il y ait des inondations par ici; **what do you think of my new haircut? – well, it's certainly unusual!** que penses-tu de ma nouvelle coupe de cheveux? – ah pour ça c'est original!; **nothing unusual** rien d'anormal

unusually [ˌʌn'juːʒəlɪ] *adv* (**a**) *(exceptionally)* exceptionnellement, extraordinairement; **she is unusually intelligent** elle est d'une intelligence exceptionnelle (**b**) *(abnormally)* exceptionnellement, anormalement; **he was unusually silent that day** il était étrangement *ou* anormalement silencieux ce jour-là; **unusually, it wasn't raining** chose rare, il ne pleuvait pas

unutterable [ˌʌn'ʌtərəbəl] *adj Formal (misery, pain)* indicible, indescriptible; *(boredom)* mortel; *(joy)* inexprimable; **he's an unutterable fool!** c'est vraiment un imbécile fini!

unutterably [ˌʌn'ʌtərəblɪ] *adv Formal (miserable, tired)* terriblement, horriblement; *(happy)* extrêmement, extraordinairement; **he's unutterably stupid** il est d'une stupidité invraisemblable *ou* inouïe

unuttered [ˌʌn'ʌtəd] *adj* inexprimé

unvanquishable [ˌʌn'væŋkwɪʃəbəl] *adj* invicible

unvanquished [ˌʌn'væŋkwɪʃt] *adj* invaincu

unvaried [ˌʌn'veərɪd] *adj* qui manque de variété, monotone; **an unvaried diet** une alimentation peu variée

unvarnished [ˌʌn'vɑːnɪʃt] *adj* (**a**) *(furniture)* non verni; *(pottery)* non vernissé (**b**) *Fig (plain, simple)* simple, sans fard; **the plain unvarnished truth** la vérité pure et simple *ou* toute nue

unvarying [ˌʌn'veərɪɪŋ] *adj* invariable, uniforme

unvaryingly [ˌʌn'veərɪŋlɪ] *adv* invariablement

unveil [ˌʌn'veɪl] *vt (painting, statue, plaque)* dévoiler, inaugurer; *(new car → at a show)* présenter; *Fig (secret, details, plans)* révéler, dévoiler; *(profits)* annoncer

unveiling [ˌʌn'veɪlɪŋ] *n (of painting, statue, car)* inauguration *f*; *(of secret, details, plans, proposals)* révélation *f*

►► ***unveiling ceremony*** (cérémonie *f* d')inauguration *f*

unventilated [ˌʌn'ventɪleɪtɪd] *adj (room)* non aéré

unverifiable ['ʌnˌverɪ'faɪəbəl] *adj* invérifiable

unverified [ˌʌn'verɪfaɪd] *adj* non vérifié

unversed [ˌʌn'vɜːst] *adj Formal* peu versé; **to be unversed in sth** être peu versé dans qch

unviable [ˌʌn'vaɪəbəl] *adj* inviable, non viable

unvisited [ˌʌn'vɪzɪtɪd] *adj* non visité

unvoiced [ˌʌn'vɔɪst] *adj* (**a**) *(desire, objection)* inexprimé (**b**) *Ling (sound)* non voisé, sourd

unwaged [ˌʌn'weɪdʒd] **1** *adj (unsalaried)* non salarié; *(unemployed)* sans emploi, au chômage

2 *npl* **the unwaged** les sans-emploi *mpl*

unwanted [ˌʌn'wɒntɪd] *adj (child, pregnancy)* non désiré, non souhaité; *(books, clothing)* dont on n'a plus besoin, dont on veut se séparer; **unwanted hair** poils *mpl* superflus; **to feel unwanted** *(in the way)* se sentir de trop; *(unloved)* se sentir mal-aimé

unwarily [ˌʌn'weərɪlɪ] *adv* imprudemment

unwarlike [ˌʌn'wɔːlaɪk] *adj* non belliqueux

unwarrantable [ˌʌn'wɒrəntəbəl] *adj* injustifiable

unwarrantably [ˌʌn'wɒrəntəblɪ] *adv* d'une manière injustifiable

unwarranted [ˌʌn'wɒrəntɪd] *adj (concern, criticism)* injustifié; *(remark, interference)* déplacé

unwary [ˌʌn'weərɪ] *adj (person, animal)* qui n'est pas méfiant *ou* sur ses gardes; **an unwary reader** un lecteur non averti; **unwary consumers** les consommateurs non avertis

unwashed [ˌʌn'wɒʃt] **1** *adj (dishes, feet, floor)* non lavé; *(person)* qui ne s'est pas lavé

2 *npl Br Hum Pej* **the great unwashed** la populace

unwatchable [ˌʌn'wɒtʃəbəl] *adj (film, TV programme, videotape → bad)* minable; *(→ because of bad reception)* qu'on ne peut pas regarder tellement l'image est mauvaise

unwavering [ˌʌn'weɪvərɪŋ] *adj (devotion, support)* indéfectible, à toute épreuve; *(look)* fixe; *(person)* inébranlable, ferme; **they were unwavering in their belief** ils étaient inébranlables dans leur conviction

unwaveringly [ˌʌn'weɪvərɪŋlɪ] *adv (believe, support)* sans réserve, fermement; *(look)* fixement

unwaxed [ˌʌn'wækst] *adj (floor)* non ciré; *(lemon)* non traité à la cire alimentaire

unweaned [ˌʌn'wiːnd] *adj (child, kitten)* non sevré

unwearable [ˌʌn'weərəbəl] *adj* pas mettable

unwearying [ˌʌn'wɪərɪɪŋ] *adj* inlassable, infatigable

unwed [ˌʌn'wed] *adj* célibataire

unweighed [ˌʌn'weɪd] *adj* non pesé

unweighted [ˌʌn'weɪtɪd] *adj Econ (index)* non pondéré; **unweighted figures** chiffres *mpl* bruts

unwelcome [ˌʌn'welkəm] *adj (advances, attention)* importun; *(advice)* non sollicité; *(visit)* inopportun; *(visitor)* importun, gênant; *(news, situation)* fâcheux; **he made his mother feel unwelcome** il a donné l'impression à sa mère qu'elle gênait; **her news could not have been more unwelcome** les nouvelles qu'elle apportait n'auraient pas pu être plus fâcheuses; **the extra £50 was not unwelcome** les 50 livres supplémentaires ne tombaient pas mal du tout

unwelcoming [ˌʌn'welkəmɪŋ] *adj (person, look)* hostile, froid; *(place)* peu accueillant

unwell [ˌʌn'wel] *adj (indisposed)* souffrant, *Formal* indisposé; *(ill)* malade

unwholesome [ˌʌn'həʊlsəm] *adj (climate)* malsain, insalubre; *(activity, habits, thoughts)* malsain, pernicieux; *(fascination, interest)* malsain, morbide; *(drink, food)* peu sain, nocif

unwieldiness [ˌʌn'wiːldɪnɪs] *n* (**a**) *(of piece of furniture, package)* caractère *m* encombrant (**b**) *(of argument, method)* maladresse *f*; *(of bureaucracy, system)* lourdeur *f*

unwieldy [ˌʌn'wiːldɪ] *adj* (**a**) *(piece of furniture, package)* encombrant (**b**) *(argument, method)* maladroit; *(bureaucracy, system)* lourd

unwilling [ˌʌn'wɪlɪŋ] *adj (helper, student)* réticent, peu enthousiaste; **he was unwilling to cooperate** il n'était pas vraiment disposé à coopérer; **I was unwilling that my wife should know** *or* **for my wife to know** je ne voulais pas que ma femme le sache; **I was their unwilling accomplice** j'étais leur complice malgré moi *ou* à mon corps défendant

unwillingly [ˌʌn'wɪlɪŋlɪ] *adv* à contrecœur, contre son gré

unwillingness [ˌʌn'wɪlɪŋnɪs] *n* manque *m* d'enthousiasme, réticence *f*; **she showed her usual unwillingness to compromise** comme d'habitude, elle s'est montrée réticente à accepter le compromis

unwind [ˌʌn'waɪnd] *(pt & pp* **unwound** [-'waʊnd]*)*
1 *vt* dérouler

2 *vi* (**a**) *(ball of yarn, cord)* se dérouler (**b**) *Fig (relax)* se détendre, se relaxer

unwise [ˌʌn'waɪz] *adj (action, decision)* peu judicieux, imprudent; **it would be unwise of you to go** vous auriez tort *ou* il serait imprudent de votre part d'y aller

unwisely [ˌʌn'waɪzlɪ] *adv* imprudemment

unwitting [ˌʌn'wɪtɪŋ] *adj Formal (accomplice)* involontaire, malgré soi; *(insult)* non intentionnel, involontaire

unwittingly [ˌʌn'wɪtɪŋlɪ] *adv* involontairement, sans (le) faire exprès

unwomanly [ˌʌn'wʊmənlɪ] *adj* peu féminin

unwonted [ˌʌn'wəʊntɪd] *adj Formal (event)* exceptionnel; *(generosity, kindness)* inaccoutumé, inhabituel

unworkable [ˌʌn'wɜːkəbəl] *adj (idea, plan)* impraticable, impossible à réaliser; **your project is unworkable** votre projet ne marchera pas *ou* est infaisable

unworldliness [ˌʌn'wɜːldlɪnɪs] *n* (**a**) *(lack of materialism)* détachement *m* de ce monde (**b**) *(naivety)* simplicité *f*, candeur *f*

unworldly [ˌʌn'wɜːldlɪ] *adj* (**a**) *(not materialistic → person)* détaché de ce monde, indifférent aux biens de ce monde; *(→ existence)* détaché de ce monde (**b**) *(naive)* naïf, ingénu (**c**) *(otherworldly → beauty)* surnaturel, céleste, qui n'est pas de ce monde

unworn [ˌʌn'wɔːn] *adj (clothing)* qui n'a pas été porté, (comme) neuf; *(carpet)* qui n'est pas usé

unworthiness [ˌʌn'wɜːðɪnɪs] *n (of person)* indignité *f*, manque *m* de mérite; *(of action)* indignité *f*

unworthy [ˌʌn'wɜːðɪ] *adj (unbefitting)* indigne; *(undeserving)* indigne, peu méritant; **he felt unworthy of such praise** il se croyait indigne de *ou* il ne croyait pas mériter de telles louanges; **such behaviour is unworthy of you!** une telle conduite est indigne de vous!; **such details are unworthy of her attention** de tels détails ne méritent pas son attention

unwound [ˌʌn'waʊnd] **1** *pt & pp of* **unwind**

2 *adj* **to come unwound** se dérouler

unwounded [ˌʌn'wuːndɪd] *adj* non blessé, indemne

unwrap [ˌʌn'ræp] *(pt & pp* **unwrapped,** *cont* **unwrapping)** *vt (parcel)* défaire; *(goods)* déballer

unwrinkled [ˌʌn'rɪŋkəld] *adj* sans rides, lisse; *(face)* sans rides

unwritten [ˌʌn'rɪtən] *adj (legend, story)* non écrit; *(agreement)* verbal, tacite; **an unwritten rule** une règle tacitement admise

►► *Law* ***unwritten law*** droit *m* coutumier

unyielding [ˌʌn'jiːldɪŋ] *adj (ground, material)* très dur; *(person)* inflexible, intransigeant; *(determination, principles)* inébranlable

unyoke [ˌʌn'jəʊk] *vt* dételer

unzip [ˌʌn'zɪp] *(pt & pp* **unzipped,** *cont* **unzipping)**
1 *vt* (**a**) *(garment, bag etc)* défaire la fermeture Éclair® de (**b**) *Comput (file)* dézipper, décompresser

2 *vi* **it unzips at the side** il y a une fermeture Éclair® sur le côté

UP [juː'piː] *n (abbr* **unit price)** PU *m*

UP [ʌp] *(pt & pp* **upped,** *cont* **upping)** **1** *adv* **A. (a)** *(towards a higher position or level)* en haut; **all the way up, the whole way up, right up (to the top)** *(of stairs, hill)* jusqu'en haut; **he's on his way up** il monte; **they had coffee sent up** ils ont fait monter du café; **hang it higher up** accrochez-le plus haut; **wait till the moon comes up** attends que la lune se lève; *Fam* **he doesn't have very much up top** c'est pas une lumière, il a pas inventé l'eau chaude *ou* le fil à couper le beurre; *Fam* **she's got plenty up top** elle en a dans le ciboulot

(b) *(in a higher position, at a higher level)* **she wears her hair up** elle porte ses cheveux relevés; **hold your head up high!** redressez la tête!; **heads up!** attention!; **up above** au-dessus; **the glasses are up above the plates** les verres sont au-dessus des assiettes; **up in the air** en l'air; **look at the kite up in the sky** regardez le cerf-volant (là-haut) dans le ciel; **I live eight floors up** j'habite au huitième (étage); **she lives three floors up from us** elle habite trois étages au-dessus de chez nous; **she's up in her room** elle est en haut dans sa chambre; **we spend our holidays up in the mountains** nous passons nos vacances à la montagne; **from up on the mountain** du haut de la montagne; **do you see her up on that hill?** la voyez-vous en haut de *ou* sur cette colline?; **what are you doing up there?** qu'est-ce que vous faites là-haut?; **the captain is up on deck** le capitaine est en haut sur le pont; **have you ever been up in a plane?** avez-vous déjà pris l'avion?; **up the top** tout en haut; **it's up on top of the wardrobe** c'est sur le dessus de l'armoire; *Fig* **she's up there with the best (of them)** elle est parmi *ou* dans les meilleurs

(c) *(in a raised position)* levé; **Charles has his hand up** Charles a la main levée; **wind the window up** *(in car)* remontez la vitre; **put your hood up** relève *ou* mets ta capuche; **she turned her collar up** elle a relevé son col

(d) *(into an upright position)* debout; **up you get!** debout!; **he helped me up** il m'a aidé à me lever *ou* à me mettre debout; **sit up straight!** tiens-toi droit!; **the trunk was standing up on end** la malle était debout; *Fam* **up and at them!** grouillez-vous!

(e) *(out of bed)* **get up!** debout!; **she got up late this morning** elle s'est levée tard ce matin; **she's always up and doing** elle n'arrête jamais

(f) *(facing upwards)* **the body was lying face up** le corps était couché sur le dos; **I turned the poster right side up** j'ai mis l'affiche dans le bon sens *ou* à l'endroit; **put it the other way up** retournez-le; **he turned his hand palm up** il a tourné la main paume vers le haut; **fragile – this way up** *(on packaging)* fragile – haut; *Fam Fig* **he doesn't know which end is up** il est bête comme ses pieds

(g) *(erected, installed)* **they're putting up a new hotel there** ils construisent un nouvel hôtel là-bas; **help me get the curtains/the pictures up** aide-moi à accrocher les rideaux/les tableaux

(h) *(on wall)* **up on the blackboard** au tableau; **I saw an announcement up about it** je l'ai vu sur une affiche

(i) *(removed)* **careful, we've got some of the floorboards up** attention au plancher, il manque des lattes; **when we've got the carpet up...** quand nous aurons enlevé la moquette...

B. (a) *(towards north)* **they came up for the weekend** ils sont venus pour le week-end; **it's cold up here** il fait froid ici; **up there** là-bas; **up north** dans le nord

(b) *(in, to or from a larger place)* **up in Madrid** à Madrid; **she's up in Maine for the week** elle passe une semaine dans le Maine; **we're up from Munich** nous venons *ou* arrivons de Munich; **he was on his way up to town** il allait en ville

(c) *Br (at university)* **he's up at Oxford** il est à Oxford

(d) *(further)* **there's a café up ahead** il y a un café plus loin; **the sign up ahead says 10 miles** la pancarte là-bas indique 10 miles

(e) *(in phrasal verbs)* **the clerk came up to him** le vendeur s'est approché de lui *ou* est venu vers lui; **a car drew up at the petrol pump** une voiture s'est arrêtée à la pompe à essence; **up came a small, blonde child** un petit enfant blond s'est approché

(f) *(close to)* **up close** de près; **I like to sit up front** j'aime bien m'asseoir devant; **when you get right up to her** quand vous la voyez de près; **they stood up close to one another** ils se tenaient l'un contre l'autre *ou* tout près l'un de l'autre

C. (a) *(towards a higher level)* **prices have gone up by 10 percent** les prix ont augmenté *ou* monté de 10 pour cent; **bread has gone up again** le pain a encore augmenté; **the temperature soared up into the thirties** la température est montée au-dessus de trente degrés; **they can cost anything from £750 up** ils coûtent au moins 750 livres, on en trouve à partir de 750 livres; **suitable for children aged seven and up** convient aux enfants âgés de sept ans et plus; **all ranks from sergeant up** tous les rangs à partir de celui de sergent

(b) *(more loudly, intensely)* plus fort; **speak up** parlez plus fort; **he turned the radio up** il a mis la radio plus fort

D. (a) *(indicating completion)* **drink up!** finissez vos verres!; **eat up your greens** finis tes légumes; **the river had dried up** la rivière s'était asséchée

(b) *(into small pieces)* **he ripped the shirt up** il a mis la chemise en lambeaux; **I tore up the letter** j'ai déchiré la lettre (en petits morceaux)

(c) *(together)* **add these figures up** additionnez ces chiffres; **the teacher gathered up his notes** le professeur a ramassé ses notes

E. (a) *(before an authority)* **he came up before the judge for rape** il a comparu devant le juge pour viol; **the murder case came up before the court today** le meutre a été jugé aujourd'hui; **she comes up before the board tomorrow** elle paraît devant le conseil demain

(b) *Fam (indicating support)* **up (with) the Revolution!** vive la Révolution!; *Sport* **up the Lakers!** allez les Lakers!

2 *adj* **A. (a)** *(at or moving towards higher level)* haut; **the river is up** le fleuve est en crue; **the tide is up** la marée est haute; **before the sun was up** avant le lever du soleil; **prices are up on last year** les prix ont augmenté par rapport à l'année dernière; **the temperature is up in the twenties** la température a dépassé les vingt degrés

(b) *(in a raised position)* levé; **the blinds are up** les stores sont levés; **keep the windows up** *(in car)* n'ouvrez pas les fenêtres; **her hair was up (in a bun)** elle avait un chignon; **her hood was up so I couldn't see her face** sa capuche était relevée, si bien que je ne voyais pas sa figure; *Fig* **his defences were up** il était sur ses gardes

(c) *(in an upwards direction)* **the up escalator** l'escalier roulant qui monte

(d) *Br Rail (heading for a larger city)* **the up train** le train qui va en ville; **the up platform** le quai où l'on prend le train qui va en ville

(e) *(out of bed)* **is she up yet?** est-elle déjà levée *ou* debout?; **we're normally up at 6** d'habitude nous nous levons à 6 heures; **she was up late last night** elle s'est couchée *ou* elle a veillé tard hier soir; **they were up all night** ils ne se sont pas couchés de la nuit, ils ont passé une nuit blanche

(f) *(in tennis)* **was the ball up?** la balle était-elle bonne?

B. (a) *(road)* en travaux; **road up** *(sign)* travaux

(b) *(erected, installed)* **these buildings haven't been up long** ça ne fait pas longtemps que ces immeubles ont été construits; **are the new curtains up yet?** les nouveaux rideaux ont-ils été posés?; **when the tent's up** quand la tente sera montée

(c) *(on wall)* **are the results up yet?** les résultats sont-ils déjà affichés?

C. (a) *(finished, at an end)* terminé; **time is up!** *(on exam, visit)* c'est l'heure!; *(in game, on meter)* le temps est écoulé!; **when the month was up he left** à la fin du mois, il est parti

(b) *(ahead) Sport* **Madrid was two goals up** Madrid menait de deux buts; *Sport* **Georgetown was 13 points up on Baltimore** Georgetown avait 13 points d'avance sur Baltimore; *Golf* **to be one hole up** avoir un trou d'avance; *Fam* **I'm $50 up on you** j'ai 50 dollars de plus que vous □; *Fam* **to be one up on sb** avoir un avantage sur qn □

(c) *Fam (ready)* prêt □; **dinner's up** le dîner est prêt

(d) *(in operation)* **the computer's up again** l'ordinateur fonctionne à nouveau

D. *Fam* **(a)** *(cheerful)* gai □; **he seemed very up when I saw him** il avait l'air en pleine forme quand je l'ai vu

(b) *(well-informed)* **to be up on sth** être au fait de qch □; **he's really up on history** il est fort *ou* calé en histoire □; **she's always up with the latest trends** elle est toujours au courant de la dernière mode □

E. (a) to be up *(before an authority)* comparaître; **to be up before a court/a judge** comparaître devant un tribunal/un juge; **she's up before the board tomorrow** elle comparaît devant le conseil demain

(b) *Fam (idioms)* **something's up** *(happening)* il se passe quelque chose □; *(wrong)* quelque chose ne va pas □; **what's up?** *(happening)* qu'est-ce qui se passe? □; *(wrong)* qu'est-ce qu'il y a? □; *Am (as greeting)* quoi de neuf?; **what's up with you?** *(happening)* quoi de neuf?; *(wrong)* qu'est-ce que tu as? □; **do you know what's up?** est-ce que tu sais ce qui se passe? □; **something's up with Mum** il y a quelque chose qui ne va pas chez maman □, maman a quelque chose □; **there's something up with the TV** la télé débloque

3 *prep* **(a)** *(indicating motion to a higher place or level)* **we carried our suitcases up the stairs** nous avons monté nos valises; **he ran up the stairs** il a monté l'escalier en courant; **she was up and down stairs all day** elle montait et descendait les escaliers toute la journée; **I climbed up the ladder** je suis monté à l'échelle; **the cat climbed up the tree** le chat a grimpé dans l'arbre; **the smoke went up my nose** la fumée m'est montée par le nez; **the gas goes up this pipe** le gaz monte par ce tuyau; **further up the wall** plus haut sur le mur; *Literary* **up hill and down dale** par monts et par vaux

(b) *(at or to the top of)* **her flat is up those stairs** son appartement est en haut de cet escalier; **the cat is up a tree** le chat est (perché) sur un arbre; **we walked up the street** nous avons monté la rue; **she pointed up the street** elle a montré le haut de la rue; **she lives up this street** elle habite dans cette rue; **the café is just up the road** le café se trouve plus loin *ou* plus haut dans la rue

(c) *(towards the source of)* **up the river** en amont; **a voyage up the Amazon** une remontée de l'Amazone

(d) *Br Fam (at, to)* à □; **he's up the pub** il est au pub; **I'm going up the shops** je vais faire les courses □

(e) *(idiom) very Fam* **up yours!** va te faire voir!

4 *vt* **(a)** *(increase)* augmenter; **they have upped their prices by 25 percent** ils ont augmenté leurs prix de 25 pour cent; *also Fig* **to up the stakes** monter la mise

(b) *(promote)* lever, relever; **the boss upped him to district manager** le patron l'a bombardé directeur régional

(c) *(idiom)* **to up sticks** plier bagages

5 *vi Fam* **she upped and left** elle a fichu le camp; **he just upped and hit him** tout à coup il (s'est levé et) l'a frappé; **he upped and married her** en moins de deux, il l'a épousée

6 *n* **(a)** *(high point)* haut *m*; **ups and downs** *(in land, road)* accidents *mpl*; *(of market)* fluctuations *fpl*; **I've had a lot of ups and downs in my life** j'ai connu des hauts et des bas; **we all have our ups and downs** nous avons tous des hauts et des bas

(b) *(increase)* **the market is on the up** le marché est à la hausse; **prices are on the up** les prix sont en hausse

(c) *Fam (drug)* amphet *f*, amphé *f*

7 up against *prep* **(a)** *(touching)* contre; **lean the ladder up against the window** appuyez l'échelle contre la fenêtre

(b) *(in competition or conflict with)* **you're up against some good candidates** vous êtes en compétition avec de bons candidats; **they don't know what they're up against!** ils ne se rendent pas compte de ce qui les attend!; **to be up against the law** être dans l'illégalité; *Fam* **to be up against it** être dans le pétrin

8 up and about, up and around *adj* **I've been up and about since 7 o'clock** *(gen)* je suis levé depuis 7 heures; **so you're up and about again?** *(after illness)* alors tu n'es plus alité?

9 up and down 1 *adv* (**a**) *(upwards and downwards)* **he was jumping up and down** il sautait sur place; **she looked us up and down** elle nous a regardés de haut en bas; **the bottle bobbed up and down on the waves** la bouteille montait et descendait sur les vagues; **I was up and down all night** *(in and out of bed)* je n'ai pas arrêté de me lever la nuit dernière (**b**) *(to and fro)* de long en large; **I could hear him walking up and down** je l'entendais faire les cent pas *ou* marcher de long en large; **she walked up and down the platform** elle faisait les cent pas sur le quai (**c**) *(in all parts of)* **up and down the country** dans tout le pays **2** *adj* **she's been very up and down lately** elle a eu beaucoup de hauts et de bas ces derniers temps

10 up for *prep* (**a**) *(under consideration, about to undergo)* à; **the house is up for sale** la maison est à vendre; **the project is up for discussion** on va discuter du projet; **she's up for election** elle est candidate *ou* elle se présente aux élections

(**b**) *(due to be tried for)* **he's up for murder/speeding** il va être jugé pour meurtre/excès de vitesse

(**c**) *Fam (interested in, ready for)* **are you still up for supper tonight?** tu veux toujours qu'on dîne ensemble ce soir?❑; **he's up for anything** il est toujours partant❑; **was she up for it?** *(willing to have sex)* elle a bien voulu coucher?

11 up to *prep* (**a**) *(as far as)* jusqu'à; **he can count up to 100** il sait compter jusqu'à 100; **the river is up to 25 feet wide** le fleuve a jusqu'à 25 pieds de largeur; **the bus can take up to 50 passengers** le bus peut accueillir jusqu'à 50 passagers; **I'm up to page 120** j'en suis à la page 120; **up to and including Saturday** jusqu'à samedi inclus; **up to here** jusqu'ici; **up to** *or* **up until now** jusqu'à maintenant, jusqu'ici; **up to** *or* **up until then** jusqu'alors, jusque-là; **we were up to our knees in mud** nous avions de la boue jusqu'aux genoux

(**b**) *(the responsibility of)* **should he attend the meeting? – that's up to him** est-ce qu'il doit assister à la réunion? – il fait ce qu'il veut *ou* c'est à lui de voir; **which film do you fancy? – it's up to you** quel film est-ce que tu veux voir? – c'est comme tu veux; **it's entirely up to you whether you go or not** il ne tient qu'à toi de rester ou de partir; **if it were up to me...** si c'était moi qui décidais *ou* à moi de décider...; **it's up to them to pay damages** c'est à eux *ou* il leur appartient de payer les dégâts

(**c**) *(capable of)* **to be up to doing sth** être capable de faire qch; **he's not up to heading the team** il n'est pas capable de diriger l'équipe; **my German is not up to translating novels** mon niveau d'allemand ne me permet pas de traduire des romans; **he's not up to it** *(not good enough)* il n'est pas capable de le faire; **are you going out tonight? – no, I don't feel up to it** tu sors ce soir? – non, je n'en ai pas tellement envie; **he's not up to the journey** il n'est pas à même de faire le voyage; **are you up to working** *or* **to work?** êtes-vous capable de *ou* en état de travailler?; **I'm not up to going back to work** je ne suis pas encore en état de reprendre le travail; *Fam* **the football team isn't up to much** l'équipe de foot ne vaut pas grand-chose; *Fam* **I don't feel up to much** je ne me sens pas en super forme

(**d**) *(as good as)* **his work is not up to his normal standard** son travail n'est pas aussi bon que d'habitude; **the levels are up to standard** les niveaux sont conformes aux normes; **I don't feel up to par** je ne me sens pas en forme

(**e**) *(engaged in, busy with)* **let's see what she's up to** allons voir ce qu'elle fait *ou* fabrique; **what have you been up to lately?** qu'est-ce que tu deviens?; **what's he been up to now?** qu'est-ce qu'il a encore inventé?; **what's he up to with that ladder?** qu'est-ce qu'il fabrique avec cette échelle?; **what are you up to with my girlfriend?** qu'est-ce que tu lui veux à ma copine?; **they're up to something** ils manigancent quelque chose; **she's up to no good** elle prépare un mauvais coup; **the things we got up to in our youth!** qu'est-ce qu'on *ou* ce qu'on ne faisait pas quand on était jeunes!

►► *Comput* ***up arrow*** flèche *f* vers le haut; ***up arrow key*** touche *f* de déplacement vers le haut

---

up-and-coming *adj (athlete, star, politician)* qui monte; **the up-and-coming generation of politicians** la nouvelle génération d'hommes politiques

up-and-down *adj* (**a**) *(movement)* qui monte et qui descend, ascendant et descendant (**b**) *(unstable)* **his career has been very up-and-down** sa carrière a connu des hauts et des bas; *Br* **I've been very up-and-down lately** j'ai eu des hauts et des bas ces derniers temps

up-and-over *adj*

►► ***up-and-over door*** porte *f* basculante *(d'un garage etc)*

up-and-under *n (in rugby)* chandelle *f*

up-and-up *n (idiom)* **to be on the up-and-up** *Br (improving)* aller de mieux en mieux; *Am (honest)* être honnête

upbeat [ˈʌpbiːt] **1** *adj (mood, person)* optimiste; *(music)* entraînant

2 *n Mus* levé *m*

upbraid [ˌʌpˈbreɪd] *vt Formal* réprimander

upbringing [ˈʌpˌbrɪŋɪŋ] *n* éducation *f*; **to rebel against one's upbringing** se révolter contre son éducation; **he had a strict upbringing** il a eu une éducation très stricte

upchuck [ˈʌpˌtʃʌk] *vi Fam Hum* dégobiller, dégueuler

upcoming [ˈʌpˌkʌmɪŋ] *adj (event)* à venir, prochain; *(book)* à paraître, qui va paraître; *(film)* qui va sortir; **Ford's upcoming film** le prochain film de Ford; **the upcoming elections** les élections qui vont bientôt avoir lieu

►► ***upcoming attractions*** *(film, theatre advertisement)* prochainement

up-country 1 *adj (inland)* de l'intérieur; *Pej (unsophisticated)* provincial

2 *n* intérieur *m*

3 *adv (go, move)* vers l'intérieur; *(live)* dans l'intérieur

update 1 *vt* [ˌʌpˈdeɪt] *(information, record)* mettre à jour; *Comput (computer software)* mettre à jour, actualiser; *(army, system)* moderniser; *(person)* mettre au courant; **could you update me on what's been happening?** pourriez-vous me mettre au courant de ce qui s'est passé?; **it hasn't been updated since 1933** il n'a pas été remis à jour depuis 1933

2 *n* [ˈʌpdeɪt] *(of information, record)* mise *f* à jour; *Comput (of software package)* mise *f* à jour, actualisation *f*; *(of army, system)* modernisation *f*; **a dictionary should have an update at least every 5 years** un dictionnaire devrait être remis à jour au minimum tous les 5 ans; **an update on the situation** une mise au point sur la situation; **to give sb an update on sth** mettre qn au courant de qch

updated [ˌʌpˈdeɪtɪd] *adj (records)* mis à jour; *(army, system)* modernisé

updating [ˌʌpˈdeɪtɪŋ] *n* mise *f* à jour

up-draught, *Am* **up-draft** *n Aviat* courant *m* d'air ascendant

upend [ˌʌpˈend] *vt* (**a**) *(object)* mettre debout; *(person)* mettre la tête en bas (**b**) *Fig (upset)* bouleverser

upfront [ˌʌpˈfrʌnt] **1** *adj Fam* (**a**) *(frank → person)* franc (franche)❑, ouvert❑; *(→ remark)* franc (franche)❑, direct❑ (**b**) *(payment)* d'avance❑

2 up front *adv (pay)* d'avance

upgradability [ˈʌpˌgreɪdəˈbɪlɪtɪ] *n Comput* possibilités *fpl* d'extension

upgradable [ˌʌpˈgreɪdəbəl] *adj Comput (hardware, system)* évolutif; *(memory)* extensible

upgrade 1 *vt* [ˌʌpˈgreɪd] (**a**) *(improve)* améliorer; *(increase)* augmenter; **I was upgraded to business class** *(on plane)* on m'a mis en classe affaires

(**b**) *Comput (system)* optimiser; *(software)* améliorer, perfectionner; *(hardware)* mettre à niveau

(**c**) *(job)* revaloriser; *(employee)* promouvoir; **I was upgraded** je suis monté en grade; **she was upgraded to sales manager** elle a été promue directrice des ventes

2 *vi* [ˌʌpˈgreɪd] **we've upgraded to a more powerful system** on est passés à un système plus puissant

3 *n* [ˈʌpgreɪd] (**a**) *Am (slope)* pente *f* ascendante; *(of railway line)* montée *f*

(**b**) *Comput (of software)* mise *f* à jour, actualisation *f*; *(of hardware, system)* mise *f* à niveau

(**c**) *(idiom)* **to be on the upgrade** *(price, salary)* augmenter, être en hausse; *(business, venture)* progresser, être en bonne voie; *(sick person)* être en voie de guérison; **his career is on the upgrade** sa carrière est en bonne voie

►► ***upgrade kit*** ensemble *m* de mise à niveau

upgradeability = **upgradability**

upgradeable = **upgradable**

upgrading [ˌʌpˈgreɪdɪŋ] *n* (**a**) *(of system)* amélioration *f*; *(of person)* avancement *m*; **the upgrading of the polytechnic to university status** le reclassement de l'IUT au rang d'université (**b**) *Comput (of software)* mise *f* à jour, actualisation *f*; *(of hardware, system)* mise *f* à niveau

upheaval [ˌʌpˈhiːvəl] *n (emotional, political etc)* bouleversement *m*; *(social unrest)* agitation *f*, perturbations *fpl*; **the war brought a lot of upheaval** la guerre a entraîné de nombreux bouleversements; **the great political/social upheavals of the twentieth century** les grands bouleversements politiques/sociaux du vingtième siècle

upheld [ˌʌpˈheld] *pt & pp of* **uphold**

uphill [ˌʌpˈhɪl] **1** *adj* (**a**) *(road, slope)* qui monte (**b**) *Fig (task)* ardu, pénible; *(battle)* rude, acharné; **it's uphill all the way** ça monte tout le long du chemin; *Fig* c'est une lutte permanente; **it was an uphill struggle convincing him** j'ai eu beaucoup de mal à le convaincre

2 *adv* **to go uphill** *(car, person)* monter (la côte); *(road)* monter; **to ski uphill** skier en amont

►► ***uphill ski*** ski *m* amont

uphold [ˌʌpˈhəʊld] *(pt & pp* **upheld** [-ˈheld]) *vt* (**a**) *(right)* défendre, faire respecter; *(law, rule)* faire respecter *ou* observer (**b**) *Law (conviction, decision)* maintenir, confirmer

upholder [ˌʌpˈhəʊldə(r)] *n* défenseur *m*; **an upholder of law and order** un défenseur de l'ordre public

upholster [ˌʌpˈhəʊlstə(r)] *vt (cover)* recouvrir, tapisser; *(pad)* capitonner, rembourrer; **upholstered in leather** garni de cuir; *Hum* **to be well upholstered** être bien rembourré

upholsterer [ˌʌpˈhəʊlstərə(r)] *n* tapissier(ère) *m,f (en ameublement)*

upholstery [ˌʌpˈhəʊlstərɪ] *n (UNCOUNT)* (**a**) *(covering → fabric)* tissu *m* d'ameublement; *(padding)* capitonnage *m*, rembourrage *m*; *(→ leather)* cuir *m*; *(→ in car)* garniture *f* (**b**) *(trade)* tapisserie *f*

►► ***upholstery tack*** clou *m* de tapissier

upkeep [ˈʌpkiːp] *n (UNCOUNT) (maintenance)* entretien *m*; *(cost)* frais *mpl* d'entretien; **he paid nothing towards the upkeep of the children** il ne donnait pas d'argent pour subvenir aux besoins matériels des enfants

upland [ˈʌplənd] **1** *n* **the upland** *or* **uplands** les hautes terres *fpl*

2 *adj (landscape, stream, farm)* de montagne

►► ***upland areas*** hautes terres *fpl*

uplift 1 *vt* [ʌpˈlɪft] *(person → spiritually)* élever (l'âme de); *(→ morally)* édifier; **to uplift sb's spirits** remonter le moral à qn, redonner du cœur à qn; **he was uplifted by the news** la nouvelle lui a remonté le moral *ou* lui a redonné du cœur

2 *n* [ˈʌplɪft] (**a**) *(in the economy)* nouvel essort *m* (**b**) *(of person)* **spiritual uplift** élévation *f* de l'esprit; **moral uplift** édification *f* (**c**) *Geol* soulèvement *m*

►► ***uplift bra*** soutien-gorge *m* de maintien

uplifted [ʌpˈlɪftɪd] *adj* (**a**) *(of hand)* levé (**b**) *(person)* **she was spiritually uplifted** cela lui a élevé l'âme; **they left the cinema feeling**

uplifted ils se sentaient plus gais en sortant du cinéma

uplifting [ʌp'lɪftɪŋ] *adj (experience, sermon)* édifiant; *(film, book)* qui remonte le moral

uplighter ['ʌplaɪtə(r)] *n* = applique ou lampadaire diffusant la lumière vers le haut

uplink receiver ['ʌplɪŋk-] *n* récepteur *m* de liaison terre/satellite

upload *Comput* **1** *n* ['ʌpləʊd] téléchargement *m (vers le serveur)*

2 *vt* [ˌʌp'ləʊd] télécharger *(vers le serveur)*

upmarket 1 *adj* ['ʌpmɑːkɪt] *(goods, service, area)* haut de gamme, de première qualité; *(restaurant)* haut de gamme; *(neighbourhood)* riche; *(newspaper, television programme)* qui vise un public cultivé; *(audience)* cultivé

2 *adv* [ˌʌp'mɑːkɪt] **to move upmarket** *(company)* se repositionner à la hausse; **she's moved upmarket** elle fait dans le haut de gamme maintenant

upmost ['ʌpməʊst] = **uppermost**

upon [ə'pɒn] *prep* (**a**) *Formal (indicating position or place)* **upon the grass/the table** sur la pelouse/la table; **she had a sad look upon her face** elle avait l'air triste; **the ring upon her finger** la bague à son doigt

(**b**) *Formal (indicating person or thing affected)* **attacks upon old people are on the increase** les attaques contre les personnes âgées sont de plus en plus fréquentes; **you brought it upon yourself** ne t'en prends qu'à toi-même!

(**c**) *Formal (immediately after)* à; **upon our arrival in Rome** à notre arrivée à Rome; **upon hearing the news, he rang home** lorsqu'il a appris la nouvelle, il a appelé chez lui; **upon request** sur simple demande

(**d**) *(indicating large amount)* et; **mile upon mile of desert** des kilomètres et des kilomètres de désert; **we receive thousands upon thousands of offers each year** nous recevons plusieurs milliers de propositions chaque année

(**e**) *(indicating imminence)* **the holidays are nearly upon us** les vacances approchent

(**f**) *(idiom) Old-fashioned* **upon my word!** ma parole!

upper ['ʌpə(r)] **1** *adj* (**a**) *(physically higher)* supérieur, plus haut *ou* élevé; *(top)* du dessus, du haut; **temperatures are in the upper 30s** la température dépasse 30 degrés; **the upper atmosphere** les couches supérieures de l'atmosphère; **companies operating at the upper end of the market** sociétés spécialisées dans le haut de gamme; **models at the upper end of the range** modèles haut de gamme; **to have the upper hand** avoir le dessus; **to get** *or* **to gain the upper hand** prendre le dessus *ou* l'avantage; **to let sb get the upper hand** laisser qn prendre le dessus, laisser qn dominer

(**b**) *(higher in order, rank)* supérieur; **the upper echelons of the civil service** les plus hauts échelons de l'administration

(**c**) *Geog (inland)* haut; **the upper valley of the Nile** la haute vallée du Nil; **the upper Rhine** le haut Rhin

2 *n* (**a**) *(of shoe)* empeigne *f*; *Br Fam* **to be on one's uppers** manger de la vache enragée, être fauché

(**b**) *Fam Drugs* [illegible] *f*

▸▸ ***Upper Canada*** le haut Canada; ***upper case*** *Typ* haut *m* de casse; *Comput* majuscule *f*; ***upper class, the upper classes*** = l'aristocratie et la haute bourgeoisie; ***Upper Egypt*** la Haute-Égypte; ***the Upper House*** *(gen)* la Chambre haute; *(the House of Lords)* la Chambre des lords; ***upper limit*** plafond *m*; ***upper lip*** lèvre *f* supérieure; ***upper middle class*** = classe sociale réunissant les professions libérales, les universitaires, les cadres de l'industrie et les hauts fonctionnaires; ***upper reaches*** *(of river)* amont *m*; *Br* ***the upper school*** les grandes classes *fpl*; *Br Sch* ***upper sixth*** terminale *f*; ***Upper Volta*** Haute-Volta *f*; **in Upper Volta** en Haute-Volta

upper-case *adj* **an upper-case letter** une majuscule

upper-class *adj* (**a**) *(accent, family)* aristocratique (**b**) *Am Univ (student)* = de troisième ou quatrième année

▸▸ *Fam Pej* ***upper-class twit*** = aristocrate bête et prétentieux

upper-crust *adj Fam* aristo, de la haute

uppercut ['ʌpəkʌt] *(pt & pp* **uppercut,** *cont* **uppercutting**) **1** *n* uppercut *m*

2 *vt* frapper d'un uppercut

uppermost ['ʌpəməʊst] **1** *adj* (**a**) *(part, side)* le plus haut *ou* élevé; *(drawer, storey)* du haut, du dessus (**b**) *(most prominent)* le plus important; **it's not uppermost in my mind** ce n'est pas ma préoccupation essentielle en ce moment; **human rights are uppermost on his list of priorities** les droits de l'homme sont en tête de ses priorités

2 *adv (most prominently)* **the question that comes uppermost in my mind** la question que je me pose en premier *ou* avant toute autre

uppity ['ʌpɪtɪ], **uppish** ['ʌpɪʃ] *adj Fam* bêcheur, arrogant; **he's getting very uppity** il se croit quelqu'un; **you don't have to get so uppity about it!** inutile de le prendre de si haut!; **don't you get uppity with me!** ne joue pas les arrogants avec moi!

Uppsala ['ʌpsɑːlə] *n* Uppsala

upraise ['ʌpreɪz] *vt Literary* lever

upraised [ʌp'reɪzd] *adj* levé

upright ['ʌpraɪt] **1** *adj* (**a**) *(erect)* droit (**b**) *(honest)* droit, honnête

2 *adv* (**a**) *(sit, stand)* droit; **he sat bolt upright** il se redressa (sur son siège) (**b**) *(put)* droit, debout; **to put** *or* **to stand sth upright** mettre qch debout *ou* d'aplomb

3 *n* (**a**) *(of door, bookshelf)* montant *m*, portant *m*; *(of goal post)* montant *m* du but; *Archit* pied-droit *m* (**b**) *(piano)* piano *m* droit (**c**) *(vacuum cleaner)* aspirateur-balai *m*

▸▸ ***upright freezer*** congélateur *m* armoire; ***upright piano*** piano *m* droit; ***upright vacuum cleaner*** aspirateur-balai *m*

uprightly ['ʌpraɪtlɪ] *adv* droitement, honnêtement

uprightness ['ʌpraɪtnɪs] *n* droiture *f*, honnêteté *f*

uprising ['ʌpˌraɪzɪŋ] *n* soulèvement *m*, révolte *f*

upriver [ˌʌp'rɪvə(r)] **1** *adj* (situé) en amont, d'amont

2 *adv (be)* en amont; *(move)* vers l'amont; *(row, swim)* contre le courant

uproar ['ʌprɔː(r)] *n (noise)* tumulte *m*, vacarme *m*; *(protest)* protestations *fpl*, tollé *m*; **his speech caused quite an uproar** *(protests)* son discours a déclenché un tollé; *(shouting)* son discours a déclenché le tumulte; **the town was in (an) uproar over the new taxes** la ville entière s'est élevée contre le nouvel impôt; **the recent uproar in the press about...** le tollé qui s'est élevé récemment dans la presse au sujet de...

uproarious [ʌp'rɔːrɪəs] *adj (crowd, group)* hilare; *(film, joke)* hilarant, désopilant; *(laughter)* tonitruant

uproariously [ʌp'rɔːrɪəslɪ] *adv (laugh)* aux éclats; **uproariously funny** désopilant, tordant

uproot [ˌʌp'ruːt] *vt also Fig* déraciner; **to feel uprooted** se sentir déraciné

uprush ['ʌprʌʃ] *n (of water)* montée *f* soudaine; *(of oil)* jaillissement *m*; *(of air, gas)* bouffée *f* (montante)

UPS [ˌjuːpiː'es] *n Comput (abbr* **uninterruptible power supply**) onduleur *m*

upsadaisy *Br Fam* = **upsydaisy**

upscale ['ʌpskeɪl] *adj Am* haut de gamme

upset *(pt & pp* **upset,** *cont* **upsetting**) **1** *vt* [ʌp'set] (**a**) *(overturn → chair, pan)* renverser; *(→ milk, paint)* renverser, répandre; *(→ boat)* faire chavirer

(**b**) *(disturb → plans, routine)* bouleverser, déranger; *(→ procedure)* bouleverser; *(→ calculations, results)* fausser; *(→ balance)* rompre, fausser

(**c**) *(person → annoy)* contrarier, ennuyer; *(→ offend)* fâcher, vexer; *(→ worry)* inquiéter, tracasser; *(→ distress)* faire de la peine à, blesser; **the least little thing upsets her** un rien la contrarie; **it's not worth upsetting yourself over** ce n'est pas la peine de te mettre dans tous tes états

(**d**) *(make ill → stomach)* déranger; *(→ person)* rendre malade; **seafood always upsets me** *or* **my stomach** les fruits de mer me rendent toujours malade

2 *adj* [ʌp'set] (**a**) *(annoyed)* contrarié, ennuyé; *(offended)* vexé, fâché; *(worried)* inquiet(ète); *(grieved)* peiné; *(distressed)* bouleversé; **there's no reason to get so upset** il n'y a pas de quoi en faire un drame; **he's upset about losing the deal** il est contrarié d'avoir perdu l'affaire; **I was most upset that she left** j'ai été très peiné qu'elle parte; **what are you so upset about?** qu'est-ce qui te met dans cet état?; **she was clearly upset by the pictures** *(distraught, moved)* ces images l'avaient manifestement bouleversée; **he was so upset he couldn't speak** *(distressed)* il était tellement bouleversé qu'il n'arrivait pas à parler; *(offended)* il était tellement fâché qu'il n'arrivait pas à parler

(**b**) *(stomach)* dérangé; **to have an upset stomach** avoir une indigestion

3 *n* ['ʌpset] (**a**) *(in plans)* bouleversement *m*; *(of government)* renversement *m*; *(of team)* défaite *f*; **the result caused a major political upset** le résultat a entraîné de grands bouleversements politiques

(**b**) *(emotional)* bouleversement *m*

(**c**) *(of stomach)* indigestion *f*; **he often gets stomach upsets** il a souvent des indigestions

▸▸ *Am & Scot* ***upset price*** mise *f* à prix

upsetting [ʌp'setɪŋ] *adj (annoying)* ennuyeux, contrariant; *(offensive)* vexant; *(saddening)* attristant, triste; *(worrying)* inquiétant; *(disturbing)* perturbant, troublant; *(more seriously)* bouleversant; **viewers might find some of these scenes upsetting** certaines des scènes qui vont suivre peuvent être de nature à perturber les téléspectateurs; **I didn't find the experience in the least upsetting** l'expérience ne m'a pas du tout perturbé

upshift ['ʌpʃɪft] *n (of gears)* passage *m* à la vitesse supérieure

upshot ['ʌpʃɒt] *n* résultat *m*, conséquence *f*; **what will be the upshot of it?** cela finira comment?; **the upshot of it all was that he resigned** le résultat, c'est qu'il a donné sa démission

upside ['ʌpsaɪd] **1** *n* (**a**) *(surface)* dessus *m* (**b**) *(of situation)* avantage *m*, bon côté *m*

2 *prep Am Fam* **to go upside sb's head** filer un coup sur le ciboulot à qn

▸▸ *St Exch* ***upside potential*** potentiel *m* de hausse; ***upside risk*** risque *m* de hausse

upside down 1 *adj* (**a**) *(cup, glass)* à l'envers, retourné; *(person, animal)* la tête en bas

(**b**) *(room, house)* sens dessus dessous

2 *adv* (**a**) *(in inverted fashion)* à l'envers; **to hold sth upside down** tenir qch à l'envers; **she hung upside down from the bar** elle s'est suspendue à la barre la tête en bas; **to read sth upside down** lire qch à l'envers

(**b**) *(in disorderly fashion)* sens dessus dessous; **we turned the house upside down looking for the keys** nous avons mis la maison sens dessus dessous en cherchant les clés; **the news turned our world upside down** la nouvelle a bouleversé notre univers

▸▸ ***upside down cake*** gâteau *m* renversé; *Fig* ***upside down logic*** raisonnement *m* tordu

upsilon ['ʌpsɪlɒn, juːp'saɪlən] *n* upsilon *m*

upstage [ˌʌp'steɪdʒ] **1** *adv (move)* vers le fond de la scène; *(enter, exit)* par le fond de la scène; *(stand)* au fond de la scène

2 *vt Fig* éclipser, voler la vedette à

upstairs 1 *adv* [ˌʌp'steəz] (**a**) en haut, à l'étage; **there are three bedrooms upstairs** il y a trois chambres en haut *ou* à l'étage; **to go upstairs** monter (à l'étage); **she ran back upstairs** elle est remontée en courant; **he chased me upstairs** il m'a poursuivi dans l'escalier; **I'll take your bags upstairs** je monterai vos bagages; **let me show you upstairs** permettez que je vous fasse monter; *Fig* **he hasn't got much upstairs** il n'a pas grand-chose dans le crâne

(**b**) *(in house with masters and servants)* chez les maîtres

2 *adj* ['ʌpsteəz] *(room, window)* du haut, (situé) à l'étage; *(flat, neighbour)* du dessus

3 *n* ['ʌpsteəz] étage *m*; **we rent out the upstairs** nous louons (les pièces de) l'étage

▸▸ *esp Am* ***upstairs maid*** femme *f* de chambre

upstanding [ˌʌp'stændɪŋ] *adj* (**a**) *(in character)* intègre, droit; *(in build)* bien bâti; **a fine upstanding young man** un jeune homme bien comme il faut (**b**) *Formal (on one's feet)* **be upstanding** levez-vous

upl–ups

upstart ['ʌpstɑːt] *n Pej* parvenu(e) *m,f*; **that young upstart!** ce petit morveux!

upstate [,ʌp'steɪt] *Am* **1** *adv (live)* dans le nord (de l'État); *(move)* vers le nord (de l'État); **he moved upstate** il est allé s'installer dans le nord (de l'État)

2 *adj* au nord (de l'État); **upstate New York** = la partie nord de l'État de New York

upstream [,ʌp'striːm] **1** *adv* (**a**) *(live)* en amont; *(move)* vers l'amont; *(row, swim)* contre le courant (**b**) *Econ* en amont

2 *adj* (**a**) *(gen)* d'amont, (situé) en amont (**b**) *Econ* en amont

upstroke ['ʌpstrəʊk] *n (of pen)* délié *m*; *(of piston)* mouvement *m* ascendant

upsurge ['ʌpsɜːdʒ] *n (gen)* mouvement *m* vif; *(of anger, enthusiasm)* vague *f*, montée *f*; *(of interest)* recrudescence *f*, regain *m*; *(in production, sales)* forte augmentation *f*

upswept ['ʌpswept] *adj Aut & Aviat* profilé

▶▶ ***upswept hair(style)*** coiffure *f* en hauteur

upswing ['ʌpswɪŋ] *n* (**a**) *(movement)* mouvement *m* ascendant, montée *f* (**b**) *(improvement)* amélioration *f*, **the stock market is on the upswing** la Bourse est en hausse; **there's been an upswing in sales** il y a eu une progression des ventes

upsydaisy [,ʌpsə'deɪzɪ] *exclam Fam* **upsydaisy!** allez, hop!

uptake ['ʌpteɪk] *n* (**a**) *(of air)* admission *f*, *(of water)* prise *f*, adduction *f*; *Physiol (of oxygen, calcium etc)* assimilation *f* (**b**) *(of offer, allowance)* **a campaign to improve the uptake of child benefit** une campagne pour inciter les gens à réclamer leurs allocations familiales (**c**) *(idioms)* **to be quick on the uptake** avoir l'esprit vif *ou* rapide, comprendre vite; **to be slow on the uptake** être lent à comprendre *ou* à saisir

up-tempo *Mus* **1** *adj* vif

2 *adv* vivement

upthrust ['ʌpθrʌst] *n (of piston)* poussée *f* ascendante; *Geol* soulèvement *m*

uptight [,ʌp'taɪt] *adj Fam* (**a**) *(tense)* tendu ❑, crispé; *(irritable)* irritable ❑, énervé ❑; *(nervous)* nerveux ❑, inquiet(ète) ❑; **he gets so uptight whenever I mention it** *(tense)* il se crispe chaque fois que j'en parle; *(annoyed)* il s'énerve chaque fois que j'en parle (**b**) *(repressed, prudish)* coincé, collet monté *(inv)*; **he's very uptight about sex** il est très coincé quand il s'agit de sexe (**c**) *Am (excellent)* super *(inv)*, génial

uptime ['ʌptaɪm] *n Comput* temps *m* de bon fonctionnement

up-to-date *adj* (**a**) *(information, report → updated)* à jour; *(→ most current)* le plus récent; **I try to keep up-to-date on the news** j'essaie de me tenir au courant de l'actualité; **to bring sb up-to-date on sth** mettre qn au courant de qch; **they brought the reports up-to-date** ils ont mis les rapports à jour (**b**) *(modern → machinery, methods)* moderne

up-to-the-minute *adj* le plus récent

▶▶ ***up-to-the-minute news reporting*** bulletins *mpl* (d'information) de dernière minute

uptown *Am* **1** *adj* ['ʌptaʊn] des quartiers résidentiels

2 *adv* [,ʌp'taʊn] *(be, live)* dans les quartiers résidentiels; *(move)* vers les quartiers résidentiels

3 *n* ['ʌptaʊn] les quartiers *mpl* résidentiels

uptrend ['ʌptrend] *n Com* tendance *f* à la hausse

upturn 1 *n* ['ʌptɜːn] *(in economy, situation)* amélioration *f*; *(in production, sales)* progression *f*, reprise *f*; **there's been an upturn in the market** il y a eu une progression du marché

2 *vt* [ʌp'tɜːn] *(turn over)* retourner; *(turn upside down)* mettre à l'envers; *(overturn)* renverser

upturned [ʌp'tɜːnd] *adj* (**a**) *(nose)* retroussé; **he gazed down at her upturned face** il contemplait son visage, qu'elle tenait levé vers lui (**b**) *(upside down)* retourné, renversé

upward ['ʌpwəd] **1** *adj (movement)* ascendant; *Fin (trend)* à la hausse

2 *adv Am* = **upwards**

▶▶ ***upward mobility*** ascension *f* sociale

upward-compatible *adj Comput* compatible vers le haut

upwardly mobile ['ʌpwədlɪ-] *adj (moving up)* qui s'élève rapidement sur l'échelle sociale; *(in a position to move)* qui peut s'élever rapidement sur l'échelle sociale

upwards ['ʌpwədz] **1** *adv* (**a**) *(move, climb)* vers le haut; **to slope upwards** monter; **we looked upwards** nous avons levé les yeux *ou* regardé vers le haut; **if you look upwards you can see...** si vous levez la tête *ou* les yeux, vous voyez...; **prices are moving upwards** les prix sont à la hausse

(**b**) *(facing up)* **she placed the photos (face) upwards on the table** elle a posé les photos à l'endroit sur la table; **he lay on the floor face upwards** il était allongé par terre sur le dos

(**c**) *(onwards)* **from 15 years upwards** à partir de 15 ans; **from her youth upwards** depuis sa jeunesse

2 upwards of *prep* **upwards of 100 candidates applied** plus de 100 candidats se sont présentés; **they can cost upwards of £150** ils peuvent coûter 150 livres et plus

upwind [,ʌp'wɪnd] **1** *adv* du côté du vent, contre le vent

2 *adj* dans le vent, au vent; **to be upwind of sth** être dans le vent *ou* au vent par rapport à qch

Ur [ɜː(r)] *n* Our, Ur

uracil ['jʊərəsɪl] *n Biol & Chem* uracile *m*

uraemia, *Am* **uremia** [jʊ'riːmɪə] *n* urémie *f*

uraemic, *Am* **uremic** [jʊ'riːmɪk] *adj* urémique

Ural ['jʊərəl] *adj*

▶▶ ***the Ural Mountains*** les monts *mpl* Oural, l'Oural *m*; ***the Ural River*** l'Oural *m*

Ural-Altaic [-æl'teɪk] **1** *n Ling* ouralo-altaïque *m*

2 *adj Ling & Geog* ouralo-altaïque

Uralian [jʊ'reɪlɪən], **Uralic** [jʊ'rælɪk] *adj Geog* ouralien

Urals ['jʊərəlz] *npl* **the Urals** l'Oural *m*; **in the Urals** dans l'Oural

Uranian [jʊə'reɪnɪən] *adj Astron* uranien

uraninite [jʊ'rænənaɪt] *n Miner* uraninite *f*

uranite ['jʊərənaɪt] *n* uranite *f*

uranium [jʊ'reɪnjəm] *n* uranium *m*

▶▶ ***uranium series*** série *f* uranique

uranography [,jʊərə'nɒgrəfɪ] *n Astron* uranographie *f*

uranometry [,jʊərə'nɒmɪtrɪ] *n Astron* uranométrie *f*

Uranus ['jʊərənəs] **1** *n Astron* Uranus *f*

2 *pr n Myth* Uranus

uranyl ['jʊərənɪl] *n Chem* uranyle *m*

urate ['jʊəreɪt] *n Chem* urate *m*

urban ['ɜːbən] *adj* urbain

▶▶ ***urban area*** zone *f* urbaine, agglomération *f*; ***urban blight*** dégradation *f* urbaine; ***urban centre*** centre *m* urbain, agglomération *f* urbaine; ***urban decay*** dégradation *f* urbaine; *Br Admin* ***urban district*** district *m* urbain; *Br Admin* ***urban district council*** conseil *m* de district urbain; ***urban guerrilla*** guérillero *m* urbain; ***the urban jungle*** la jungle de la ville; ***urban legend*** *or* ***myth*** légende *f*, faux fait *m* divers; ***urban planner*** urbaniste *mf*; ***urban renewal*** rénovations *fpl* urbaines; ***urban sprawl*** étalement *m* urbain; **the urban sprawl of the London suburbs** l'étalement tentaculaire de la banlieue de Londres; ***urban studies*** études *fpl* d'urbanisme; ***urban unemployment*** chômage *m* en zones urbaines

urbane [ɜː'beɪn] *adj (person)* courtois, d'une politesse raffinée; *(manner)* poli, raffiné

urbanely [ɜː'beɪnlɪ] *adv* avec mondanité

urbanism ['ɜːbənɪzəm] *n* urbanisme *m*

urbanite ['ɜːbənaɪt] *n* citadin(e) *m,f*

urbanity [ɜː'bænətɪ] *n* savoir-vivre *m inv*, *Formal* urbanité *f*

urbanization [,ɜːbənaɪ'zeɪʃən] *n* urbanisation *f*

urbanize, -ise ['ɜːbənaɪz] *vt* urbaniser

Urbino [ɜː'biːnəʊ] *n Hist* **Duchy of Urbino** duché *m* d'Urbin

urceolate ['ɜːsɪəleɪt] *adj Biol* urcéolé

urchin ['ɜːtʃɪn] *n* galopin *m*, polisson(onne) *m,f*

▶▶ ***urchin cut*** coupe *f ou* coiffure *f* à la garçonne

Urdu ['ʊəduː] *n* ourdou *m*, urdu *m*

urea ['jʊərɪə] *n Biol & Chem* urée *f*

▶▶ *Chem* ***urea resin*** résine *f* urée-formaldéhyde

urea-formaldehyde *n Chem* urée-formaldéhyde *f*

urease ['jʊərɪeɪs] *n Biol & Chem* uréase *f*

ureide ['jʊərɪaɪd] *n Chem* uréide *m*

uremia, uremic *Am* = **uraemia, uraemic**

ureter [jʊ'riːtə(r)] *n* uretère *m*

ureteric [,jʊrɪ'terɪk] *adj* urétérique

ureteritis [,jʊriːtə'raɪtɪs] *n Med* urétérite *f*

urethane ['jʊərəθeɪn] *n Chem* uréthane *m*

urethra [jʊ'riːθrə] *n* urètre *m*

urethral [jʊ'riːθrəl] *adj* urétral

urethritis [,jʊərɪ'θraɪtɪs] *n (UNCOUNT) Med* urétrite *f*

urethroscope [jʊ'riːθrəskəʊp] *n Med* urétroscope *m*

urethroscopy [,jʊriː'θrɒskəpɪ] *n Med* urétroscopie *f*

urge [ɜːdʒ] **1** *n* forte envie *f*, désir *m*; *Psy* pulsion *f*; **I felt** *or* **I had a sudden urge to tell her** j'avais tout à coup très envie de lui dire; **I'll let you know if I ever get the urge** je te le dirai si j'en ai envie *ou* si ça me chante; **the sexual urge** les pulsions *fpl* sexuelles

2 *vt* (**a**) *(person → incite)* exhorter, presser; **I urge you to reconsider** je vous conseille vivement de reconsidérer votre position; **she urged us not to sell the house** elle nous a vivement déconseillé de vendre la maison; **he urged them to revolt** il les a incités à la révolte *ou* à se révolter

(**b**) *(course of action)* conseiller vivement, préconiser; *(need, point)* insister sur; **they urged the need for new schools** ils ont insisté sur la nécessité de construire de nouvelles écoles; **we urged caution** nous avons préconisé la prudence

(**c**) *(goad, encourage etc)* **to urge a horse forward** pousser un cheval; **he urged his men into battle** il poussa ses hommes dans la bataille

▸**urge on** *vt sep* talonner, presser; *(person, troops)* faire avancer; **to urge sb on to do sth** inciter qn à faire qch

urgency ['ɜːdʒənsɪ] *n* urgence *f*, **it's a matter of great urgency** c'est une affaire très urgente; **there's no great urgency** cela n'est pas urgent *ou* ne presse pas; **could you do this as a matter of the utmost urgency?** pourriez-vous faire ceci de toute urgence?; **there was a note of urgency in her voice** il y avait quelque chose de pressant dans sa voix

urgent ['ɜːdʒənt] *adj* (**a**) *(matter, need)* urgent, pressant; *(message)* urgent; **it's not urgent** ce n'est pas urgent, ça ne presse pas; **is it urgent?** est-ce urgent?; **the roof is in urgent need of repair** le toit a un besoin urgent d'être réparé; **I was in urgent need of a drink** il me fallait absolument quelque chose à boire; **just how urgent is it that you should be there tomorrow?** qu'y a-t-il de si urgent qui exige que tu y sois demain?

(**b**) *(manner, voice)* insistant; **he was urgent in his demands for help** il a insisté pour qu'on lui vienne en aide

urgently ['ɜːdʒəntlɪ] *adv* d'urgence, de toute urgence; **they appealed urgently for help** ils ont demandé du secours avec insistance; **the matter is urgently in need of attention** l'affaire demande à être traitée immédiatement *ou* sans délais; **supplies are urgently needed** un ravitaillement est absolument nécessaire

Uriah Heep [jʊ'raɪə,hiːp] *pr n* = personnage cruel dans 'David Copperfield' de Charles Dickens

urial ['ʊərɪəl] *n Zool* urial *m*

uric ['jʊərɪk] *adj* urique

▶▶ ***uric acid*** acide *m* urique

uridine ['jʊərɪdiːn] *n Biol & Chem* uridine *f*

urinal ['jʊərɪnəl] *n (fitting)* urinal *m*; *(building)* urinoir *m*

urinalysis [,jʊərɪ'nælɪsɪs] *n* analyse *f* d'urine

urinary ['jʊərɪnərɪ] *adj* urinaire

▶▶ ***urinary tract*** appareil *m* urinaire

urinate ['jʊərɪ,neɪt] *vi* uriner

urination [,jʊərɪ'neɪʃən] *n* urination *f*

urine ['jʊərɪn] *n* urine *f*

urinogenital [,jʊərɪnəʊ'dʒenɪtəl] = **urogenital**

urinometer [,jʊərɪ'nɒmɪtə(r)] *n Med* urinomètre *m*, pèse-urine *m*

urinous ['jʊərɪnəs] *adj* urineux

URL [,juːɑː'rel] *n Comput* (*abbr* **uniform resource locator**) (adresse *f*) URL *m*

urn [ɜːn] *n* (**a**) *(container → gen)* urne *f* (**b**) *(for ashes)* urne *f* (funéraire) (**c**) *(for coffee, tea)* fontaine *f*

urnfield ['ɜːnfiːld] *n Archeol* champ *m* d'urnes
urodele ['jʊərəʊdiːl] *n Zool* urodèle *m*
urogenital [ˌjʊərəʊ'dʒenɪtəl] *adj* urogénital
urography [jʊə'rɒgrəfɪ] *n Med* urographie *f*
urological [ˌjʊərə'lɒdʒɪkəl] *adj* urologique
urologist [jʊə'rɒlədʒɪst] *n* urologue *mf*
urology [jʊə'rɒlədʒɪ] *n* urologie *f*
uropygium [ˌjʊərə'pɪdʒɪəm] *n Orn* uropyge *m*, uropygium *m*
uroscopy [jʊ'rɒskəpɪ] *n Med* uroscopie *f*
urostyle ['jʊərəʊstaɪl] *n Zool* urostyle *m*
Ursa ['ɜːsə] *n Astron* **Ursa Major/Minor** la Grande/Petite Ourse
ursine ['ɜːsaɪn] *adj Zool* ursin, oursin
Ursuline ['ɜːsjʊlaɪn, 'ɜːsjʊlɪn] *n* ursuline *f*
►► ***Ursuline convent*** couvent *m* d'ursulines; *Fam (school)* ursulines ❑ *fpl*; ***Ursuline nun*** ursuline *f*
urtica ['ɜːtɪkə] *n Bot* ortie *f*
urticaria [ˌɜːtɪ'keərɪə] *n Med* urticaire *f*
urticate ['ɜːtɪkeɪt] **1** *vt* produire une urtication sur
2 *vi* piquer
urtication [ˌɜːtɪ'keɪʃən] *n* urtication *f*
Uruguay ['jʊərəgwaɪ] *n* Uruguay *m*; **in Uruguay** en Uruguay
Uruguayan [jʊərʊ'gwaɪən] **1** *n* Uruguayen(-enne) *m,f*
2 *adj* uruguayen
3 *comp (embassy)* d'Uruguay; *(history)* de l'Uruguay
US [juː'es] *(abbr* **United States***)* **1** *n* **the US** les USA *mpl*, les États-Unis *mpl*; **in the US** aux USA, aux États-Unis
2 *comp* des États-Unis, américain
us [ʌs] **1** *pron* **(a)** *(object form of we)* nous; **tell us the truth** dites-nous la vérité; **it's us!** c'est nous!; **it's us she's looking for** c'est nous qu'elle cherche; **most of us are students** nous sommes presque tous des étudiants; **all four of us went** nous y sommes allés tous les quatre; **there are three of us** nous sommes trois; **those of us who were left...** ceux d'entre nous qui restaient...; **they're with us** ils sont avec nous; **between them and us** entre eux et nous; **as for us Scotsmen** quant à nous autres Écossais
(b) *Fam (me → direct object)* me ❑; *(→ indirect object)* me ❑, moi ❑; **give us a kiss!** embrasse-moi!; **give us a chance, I've only just got here!** je t'en prie, je viens d'arriver! ❑
2 *n Fam* **is there still an us?** *(in relationship)* est-ce que nous sommes encore un couple? ❑
USA [juːes'eɪ] *n* **(a)** *(abbr* **United States of America***)* **the USA** les USA *mpl*, les États-Unis *mpl*; **in the USA** aux USA, aux États-Unis; *Am Press* **USA Today** = quotidien américain de qualité **(b)** *(abbr* **United States Army***)* = armée des États-Unis
usable ['juːzəbəl] *adj* utilisable
USAF [juːesˌeɪ'ef] *n (abbr* **United States Air Force***)* = armée de l'air des États-Unis
usage ['juːzɪdʒ] *n* **(a)** *(custom, practice)* coutume *f*, usage *m*; **sanctified** *or* **hallowed by usage** consacré par l'usage
(b) *(of term, word)* usage *m*; **accepted usage** le bon usage; **the term is in common usage** le terme est employé couramment; **that phrase has long since dropped out of usage** cette expression n'est plus usitée depuis longtemps
(c) *(employment)* usage *m*, emploi *m*; *(treatment → of material, tool)* manipulation *f*; *(→ of person)* traitement *m*; **designed for rough usage** conçu pour résister aux chocs; **these books are not meant for rough usage** ces livres ne sont pas faits pour être malmenés; **directions** *or* **instructions for usage** mode *m* d'emploi
USAID [juːesˌeɪaɪ'diː] *n (abbr* **United States Agency for International Development***)* = agence américaine d'aide au développement
usance ['juːzəns] *n Banking & Fin (time limit)* usance *f*; **at thirty days' usance** à usance de trente jours
►► ***usance bill*** effet *m* à usance
USB [juːes'biː] *n Comput (abbr* **universal serial bus***)* norme *f* USB, port *m* série universel
USCG [juːesˌsiː'dʒiː] *n (abbr* **United States Coast Guard***)* = service de surveillance côtière américain
USDA [juːesˌdiː'eɪ] *n (abbr* **United States Department of Agriculture***)* = ministère américain de l'Agriculture
USDAW ['ʌzdɔː] *n (abbr* **Union of Shop, Distributive and Allied Workers***)* = syndicat britannique des personnels de la distribution
USDI [juːesˌdiː'aɪ] *n (abbr* **United States Department of the Interior***)* = ministère américain de l'Intérieur

USE

utilisation	► **1 (a), (b)**
emploi	► **1 (a), (c)**
consommation	► **1 (a)**
usage	► **1 (a) – (d), (f), (g)**
besoin	► **1 (d)**
se servir de	► **2 (a), (b)**
utiliser	► **2 (a), (c)**
employer	► **2 (a)**
prendre	► **2 (a), (e)**
profiter de	► **2 (b)**
consommer	► **2 (c)**
finir	► **2 (c)**

1 *n* [juːs] **(a)** *(utilization → of materials)* utilisation *f*, emploi *m*; *(consumption → of water, resources etc)* consommation *f*; *(being used, worn etc)* usage *m*; **the use of brick in building** l'emploi *ou* l'utilisation de la brique dans la construction; **to stretch (out) with use** se détendre à l'usage; **to wear out with use** s'user; **the dishes are for everyday use** c'est la vaisselle de tous les jours; **ready for use** prêt à l'emploi; **directions** *or* **instructions for use** *(on packaging)* mode d'emploi; **for your personal use** *(on packaging)* pour votre usage personnel; **for customer use only** *(sign)* réservé à notre clientèle; *Med* **for external/internal use only** *(on packaging)* à usage externe/interne; **for use in case of emergency** *(sign)* à utiliser en cas d'urgence; **the film is for use in teaching** le film est destiné à l'enseignement; **in use** *(machine, system)* en usage, utilisé; *(lift, cash point)* en service; *(phrase, word)* usité; **in general use** d'emploi courant, d'utilisation courante; **not in use, out of use** *(machine, system)* hors d'usage; *(lift, cash point)* hors service; **the phrase is no longer in use** l'expression est inusitée *ou* ne s'utilise plus; **to come into use** entrer en service; **to go out of use** *(machine)* être mis au rebut; **steam engines went out of use in 1950** on a cessé d'utiliser *ou* d'employer les machines à vapeur en 1950; **to make use of sth** se servir de *ou* utiliser qch; **schools are making increasing use of audio-visual aids** les écoles se servent de plus en plus de supports audiovisuels; **to make good use of, to put to good use** *(machine, money)* faire bon usage de; *(opportunity, experience)* tirer profit de
(b) *(ability or right to use)* usage *m*, utilisation *f*; **we gave them the use of our car** nous leur avons laissé l'usage de notre voiture; **he only has the use of one arm** il n'a l'usage que d'un bras; **she lost the use of her legs** elle a perdu l'usage de ses jambes; **the old man still has the full use of his faculties** le vieil homme jouit encore de toutes ses facultés
(c) *(practical application)* usage *m*, emploi *m*; **this tool has many uses** cet outil a de nombreux usages *ou* emplois; **we found a use for the old fridge** nous avons trouvé un emploi pour le vieux frigo; *Hum* **I have my uses** il m'arrive de servir à quelque chose
(d) *(need)* besoin *m*, usage *m*; **do you have any use for this book?** avez-vous besoin de ce livre?; **to have no use for sth** ne pas avoir besoin de qch; *Fig* n'avoir que faire de qch; **I have no use for idle gossip** je n'ai que faire des cancans; **this department has no use for slackers** il n'y a pas de place pour les fainéants dans ce service
(e) *(usefulness)* **to be of use (to sb)** être utile (à qn), servir (à qn); **this dictionary might be of use to you** ce dictionnaire pourrait vous être utile *ou* vous servir; **were the instructions (of) any use?** est-ce que le mode d'emploi a servi à quelque chose?; **I found his advice to be of little use, his advice was of little use to me** je n'ai pas trouvé ses conseils très utiles; **the book would be of more use if it had illustrations** le livre serait plus utile s'il contenait des illustrations; **it's not much use** cela ne sert pas à grand-chose; **he's not much use as a secretary** il n'est pas brillant comme secrétaire; **to be (of) no use** *(thing)* ne servir à rien; *(person)* n'être bon à rien; **they were no use at all during the move** ils n'ont rien fait pendant le déménagement; **you're no use!** tu n'es bon à rien!; **it's** *or* **there's no use complaining** inutile de *ou* ça ne sert à rien de se plaindre; **there's no use shouting** ça ne sert à rien de crier, (c'est) inutile de crier; **it's no use, we might as well give up** c'est inutile *ou* ça ne sert à rien, autant abandonner; **I tried to convince her but it was no use** j'ai essayé de la convaincre mais il n'y avait rien à faire; **is it any use calling her?** est-ce que ça servira à quelque chose de l'appeler?; **what's the use of waiting?** à quoi bon attendre?, à quoi ça sert d'attendre?; **oh, what's the use?** à quoi bon?; *Fam Ironic* **that's a fat lot of use!** ça nous fait une belle jambe!
(f) *Ling* usage *m*; **that's an old-fashioned use** c'est un usage vieilli
(g) *Rel* usage *m*
2 *vt* [juːz] **(a)** *(put into action → service, tool, skills)* se servir de, utiliser; *(→ product, name)* utiliser; *(→ method, phrase, word)* employer; *(→ vehicle, form of transport)* prendre; **these are the notebooks he used** ce sont les cahiers dont il s'est servi *ou* qu'il a utilisés; **is anyone using this book?** est-ce que quelqu'un se sert de *ou* a besoin de ce livre?; **it's very easy to use** c'est très facile à utiliser; **it's no longer used** *(machine, tool)* ça ne sert plus; *(word, expression)* ça n'est plus usité; **am I using the term correctly?** est-ce comme ça qu'on utilise le terme?; **I'd like to use my language skills more** j'aimerais utiliser davantage mes connaissances en langues; **I always use public transport** je prends toujours les transports en commun; **we use this room as an office** nous nous servons de cette pièce comme bureau, cette pièce nous sert de bureau; **what is this used for** *or* **as?** à quoi cela sert-il?; **it's used for identifying the blood type** cela sert à identifier le groupe sanguin; **I use it for opening** *or* **to open letters** je m'en sers *ou* je l'utilise pour ouvrir les lettres; **I used the money to rebuild my garage** j'ai utilisé *ou* employé l'argent pour reconstruire mon garage; **what battery does this radio use?** quelle pile faut-il pour cette radio?; **my car uses unleaded petrol** ma voiture marche à l'essence sans plomb; **may I use the phone?** puis-je téléphoner?; **he asked to use the** *Br* **toilet** *or Am* **bathroom** il a demandé à aller aux toilettes; **to use force/violence** avoir recours à la force/violence; **the police often use tear gas** la police a souvent recours au gaz lacrymogène; **to use one's intelligence/intuition** faire marcher son intelligence/intuition; **to use diplomacy** user de diplomatie; **to use discretion** agir avec discrétion; **to use one's influence** user de son influence; **use your imagination!** utilise ton imagination!; **use your initiative!** fais preuve d'initiative!; **use your head** *or* **your brains!** réfléchis un peu!; **use your eyes!** ouvrez l'œil!; *Fam* **he could certainly use some help** un peu d'aide ne lui ferait pas de mal; *Fam* **we could all use a holiday!** nous aurions tous bien besoin de vacances! ❑
(b) *(exploit, take advantage of → opportunity)* profiter de; *(→ person)* se servir de; **use it to your advantage!** profitez-en!; **he's only using you to get ahead** il ne fait que se servir de toi pour avancer; **I feel used** j'ai l'impression qu'on s'est servi de moi
(c) *(consume)* consommer, utiliser; *(finish, use up)* finir, épuiser; **the car's using a lot of oil** la voiture consomme beaucoup d'huile; **have you used all the shampoo?** as-tu utilisé tout le shampooing?
(d) *Formal (treat physically)* traiter; *(behave towards)* agir envers; **they used the workers well** ils ont bien traité les ouvriers, ils ont bien agi envers les ouvriers; **I consider I was ill used** je considère qu'on ne m'a pas traité comme il faut; **how's the world been using you?** comment ça va?
(e) *Fam (drug)* prendre ❑

3 *v aux* [juːz] *(only in past tense)* **they used to live here** (avant) ils habitaient ici; **he used to drink a lot** il buvait beaucoup avant; **it used to be true** c'était vrai autrefois; **it used to be a pleasant town to live in** autrefois c'était une ville agréable; **things aren't what they used to be** les choses ne sont plus ce qu'elles étaient; **she can't get about the way she used to** elle ne peut plus se déplacer comme avant; **she never used to smoke** elle ne fumait pas avant; **we used not** *or* **we didn't use to eat meat** avant, nous ne mangions pas de viande; **did he use to visit her?** venait-il la voir avant?; **do you travel much? – I used to** vous voyagez beaucoup? – autrefois, oui

4 *vi* [juːz] *Fam (use drugs)* se camer

▸**use up** *vt sep (consume)* consommer, prendre; *(exhaust → paper, soap)* finir; *(→ patience, energy, supplies)* épuiser; **she used up the leftovers to make the soup** elle a utilisé les restes pour faire un potage; **did you use up all your money?** as-tu dépensé tout ton argent?; **the paper was all used up** il ne restait plus de papier

---

use-by date *n* date *f* de péremption

used¹ [juːzd] *adj (book, car)* d'occasion; *(clothing)* d'occasion, usagé; *(glass, linen)* sale, qui a déjà servi; *(stamp)* oblitéré, qui a déjà servi; **hardly used** presque neuf

used² [juːst] *adj (accustomed)* **to be used to (doing) sth** avoir l'habitude de *ou* être habitué à (faire) qch; **I'm used to working alone** j'ai l'habitude de *ou* je suis habitué à travailler tout seul; **they're not used to it** ils n'y sont pas habitués, ils n'en ont pas l'habitude; **to be used to sb** être habitué à qn; **to get used to sth** s'habituer à qch; **he can't get used to it** il n'arrive pas à s'y habituer; **I'm not used to being spoken to like that!** je n'ai pas l'habitude qu'on me parle comme ça!; **you'll soon get used to the idea** tu te feras à l'idée

useful ['juːsfʊl] *adj* (**a**) *(handy → book, information, machine)* utile, pratique; *(→ discussion, experience)* utile, profitable; *(→ method)* utile, efficace; **does it serve any useful purpose?** est-ce utile?, est-ce que cela sert à quelque chose?; **I felt as if I was doing something useful** j'avais l'impression de faire quelque chose d'utile *ou* de me rendre utile; **it will come in very useful** cela rendra bien service; **you could be useful to the director** vous pourriez rendre service au directeur; **the information was useful to us in making a decision** les renseignements nous ont aidés à prendre une décision; **make yourself useful and help me tidy up** rends-toi utile et aide-moi à ranger; **it's useful to know** c'est bon à savoir; **she's a useful person to know** c'est une femme qu'il est bon de connaître; **he's very useful around the house** il est très utile *ou* il rend beaucoup de services dans la maison; **they're useful when it comes to financial affairs** ils sont très compétents dans le domaine financier; **this map could be very useful** cette carte pourrait être très utile *ou* d'une grande utilité

(**b**) *Fam (satisfactory → performance, score)* honorable; **he's a very useful player** c'est un joueur très compétent

(**c**) *Fam (skilful)* **to be useful with one's fists** savoir se servir de ses poings; **to be useful with a gun** savoir manier un fusil

▸▸ ***useful life*** vie *f* utile; **this machine has a useful life of ten years** cette machine a une durée de vie de dix ans

usefully ['juːsfʊlɪ] *adv* utilement; **his free time was usefully employed in improving his languages** il a employé utilement son temps libre à améliorer ses connaissances en langues; **you could usefully devote a further year's study to the subject** tu pourrais consacrer avec profit une année d'étude supplémentaire au sujet; **his work might usefully be compared to that of Joyce** il est intéressant de comparer son œuvre à celle de Joyce

usefulness ['juːsfʊlnɪs] *n* utilité *f*; **it's outlived its usefulness** ça a fait son temps, ça ne sert plus à rien

useless ['juːslɪs] *adj* (**a**) *(bringing no help → book, information, machine)* inutile; *(→ discussion, experience)* vain, qui n'apporte rien; *(→ advice, suggestion)* qui n'apporte rien, qui ne vaut rien; *(→ attempt, effort)* inutile, vain; *(→ remedy)* inefficace; *(unusable)* inutilisable; **the contract is useless to them** le contrat ne leur est d'aucune utilité; **it's useless trying to reason with him, it's useless to try and reason with him** ça ne sert à rien *ou* c'est inutile d'essayer de lui faire entendre raison; **the computer is useless without the instructions** l'ordinateur est inutilisable *ou* on ne peut pas se servir de l'ordinateur sans mode d'emploi

(**b**) *Fam (incompetent)* nul; **she makes me feel useless** elle me donne l'impression d'être nul *ou* bon à rien; **I'm useless at history/maths** je suis nul en histoire/math; **she's useless as a navigator** elle est nulle *ou* elle ne vaut rien en tant que navigatrice; **her brother is absolutely useless** son frère est nul *ou* bon à rien

uselessly ['juːslɪslɪ] *adv* inutilement

uselessness ['juːslɪsnɪs] *n* inutilité *f*; *(of remedy)* inefficacité *f*; *Fam (of person)* nullité *f*

Usenet ['juːznet] *n Comput* Usenet *m*

user ['juːzə(r)] *n (of computer, machine, product, dictionary)* utilisateur(trice) *m,f*; *(of telephone)* abonné(e) *m,f*; *(of airline, public service, road)* usager *m*; *(of electricity, gas, oil)* usager *m*, utilisateur(trice) *m,f*; *(of drugs)* consommateur(trice) *m,f*; **users of public transport** usagers *mpl* des transports en commun

▸▸ *Comput* ***user ID, user identification*** identification *f* de l'utilisateur; *Comput* ***user interface*** interface *f* utilisateur; *Comput* ***user language*** langage *m* utilisateur; *Comput* ***user manual*** manuel *m* d'utilisation; *Comput* ***user name*** nom *m* de l'utilisateur; *Comput* ***user network*** réseau *m* d'utilisateurs; *Mktg* ***user panel*** panel *m* d'utilisateurs; *Comput* ***user software*** logiciel *m* utilisateur; *Comput* ***user support*** assistance *f* à l'utilisateur

user-definable *adj Comput (characters, keys)* définissable par l'utilisateur

user-friendliness *n (gen) & Comput* convivialité *f*

user-friendly *adj (gen) & Comput* convivial, facile à utiliser

user-interface *n Comput & Fig* interface *f* utilisateur

user-programmable *adj Comput* programmable par l'utilisateur

USES [juːesˌiː'es] *n* (*abbr* **United States Employment Service**) = services américains de l'emploi

U-shaped *adj* en U

usher ['ʌʃə(r)] **1** *vt* conduire, accompagner; **I ushered them to their seats** je les ai conduits à leur place; **he ushered us into/out of the living room** il nous a fait entrer au/sortir du salon

2 *n* (**a**) *(at concert, theatre, wedding)* placeur(euse) *m,f* (**b**) *(doorkeeper)* portier *m*; *Law* huissier *m*

▸**usher in** *vt sep Fig* inaugurer, marquer le début de; **the printing press ushered in a new era** l'imprimerie a marqué le début d'une ère nouvelle

usherette [ˌʌʃə'ret] *n* ouvreuse *f*

USIA [juːesˌaɪ'eɪ] *n* (*abbr* **United States Information Agency**) = agence américaine de renseignements

USM [juːes'em] *n* (**a**) *Am* (*abbr* **United States Mail**) ≃ la Poste *(aux États-Unis)* (**b**) *Am* (*abbr* **United States Mint**) ≃ la Monnaie *(aux États-Unis)* (**c**) *St Exch* (*abbr* **unlisted securities market**) marché *m* hors cote, second marché *m*

USMC [juːesˌem'siː] *n* (*abbr* **United States Marine Corps**) = corps des marines américains

USN [juːes'en] *n* (*abbr* **United States Navy**) = marine de guerre des États-Unis

USO [juːes'əʊ] *n* (*abbr* **United Service Organization**) = organisme organisant des activités culturelles pour les forces armées américaines

USP [juːes'piː] *n Mktg* (*abbr* **unique selling point** *or* **proposition**) proposition *f* unique de vente

USPHS [juːesˌpiːeɪtʃ'es] *n* (*abbr* **United States Public Health Service**) = direction américaine des Affaires sanitaires et sociales

USS [juːes'es] *n* (*abbr* **United States Ship**) = initiales précédant le nom des navires américains; **the USS Washington** le Washington

USSR [juːesˌes'ɑː(r)] *n Formerly* (*abbr* **Union of Soviet Socialist Republics**) **the USSR** l'URSS *f*; **in the USSR** en URSS

usu. (*written abbr* **usually**) d'habitude

usual ['juːʒʊəl] **1** *adj (customary → activity, place)* habituel; *(→ practice, price)* habituel, courant; *(→ expression, word)* courant, usité; *(→ doctor)* habituel, traitant; **we sat at our usual table** nous nous sommes assis à notre table habituelle; **they asked the usual questions** ils ont posé les questions habituelles; **I didn't get my usual bus this morning** je n'ai pas pris le bus que je prends d'habitude ce matin; **my usual diet consists of fish and vegetables** généralement *ou* d'habitude je mange du poisson et des légumes; **let's meet at the usual time** retrouvons-nous à l'heure habituelle *ou* à la même heure que d'habitude; **6 o'clock is the usual time he gets home** d'habitude *ou* en général il rentre à 18 heures; **later than usual** plus tard que d'habitude; **he drank more than usual** il a bu plus que d'habitude; **she was her usual cheery self** elle était gaie comme d'habitude; **she's her usual self again** elle est redevenue elle-même; **with her usual optimism** avec son optimisme habituel, avec l'optimisme qui est le sien *ou* qui la caractérise; **it's not usual for him to be so bitter** il est rarement si amer, c'est rare qu'il soit si amer; **it's the usual story** c'est toujours la même histoire; **it's quite usual to see flooding in the spring** il y a souvent des inondations au printemps; **it's usual to pay in advance** il est d'usage de payer d'avance; **I believe it's the usual practice** je crois que c'est ce qui se fait d'habitude; **as is usual with young mothers** comme d'habitude avec les jeunes mamans

2 *n Fam (drink, meal)* **what will you have? – the usual, please** que prends-tu? – comme d'habitude, s'il te plaît

3 as usual, as per usual *adv* comme d'habitude; **as usual, the opposition objected** comme d'habitude *ou* comme toujours, l'opposition a élevé une objection; **life goes on as usual** la vie continue; **business as usual** *(during building work)* le magasin reste ouvert pendant la durée des travaux; **despite recent events it was business as usual** malgré les récents événements, la vie continuait comme si de rien n'était

> **Round up the usual suspects**
> Il s'agit de l'ordre que le policier interprété par Claude Raines donne à ses hommes dans le film *Casablanca*. On emploie fréquemment cette formule ("allez me chercher les suspects habituels") par allusion au film lorsqu'on demande à quelqu'un de rassembler des gens, ou bien, dans sa version tronquée, pour parler d'un groupe de personnes déterminé, comme dans l'exemple suivant: **all the usual suspects were there at the party** ("il y avait la bande habituelle à la soirée").

usually ['juːʒəlɪ] *adv* d'habitude, généralement, d'ordinaire; **I usually get to work early** généralement *ou* d'habitude j'arrive tôt au bureau; **she's not usually late** il est rare qu'elle soit en retard, elle est rarement en retard; **we don't usually eat dessert** d'habitude nous ne mangeons pas de dessert; **what route do you usually take?** quelle route prenez-vous d'habitude *ou* d'ordinaire?; **the roads were more than usually busy** il y avait encore plus de circulation que d'habitude *ou* d'ordinaire *ou* de coutume sur les routes

usufruct ['juːsjʊˌfrʌkt] *n Law* usufruit *m*

usufructuary [juːsjʊ'frʌktjʊərɪ] *Law* **1** *n* usufruitier(ère) *m,f*

2 *adj* usufruitier

▸▸ ***usufructuary right*** droit *m* usufructuaire

usurer ['juːʒərə(r)] *n* usurier(ère) *m,f*

usurious [juː'ʒʊərɪəs] *adj (interest etc)* usuraire

usurp [juː'zɜːp] *vt* usurper

usurpation [ˌjuːzɜː'peɪʃən] *n* usurpation *f*

usurpatory [juː'zɜːpətərɪ] *adj* usurpatoire

usurper [juː'zɜːpə(r)] *n* usurpateur(trice) *m,f*

usury ['juːʒʊrɪ] *n* usure *f (intérêt)*

USW [juːes'dʌbəljuː] *n Rad* (**a**) (*abbr* **ultrashort wave**) OUC *f* (**b**) (*abbr* **ultrasonic wave**) onde *f* ultrasonore

UT *(written abbr* **Utah**) Utah *m*

Utah ['ju:tɑ:] *n* l'Utah *m*; **in Utah** dans l'Utah

Ute [ju:t] *n* (**a**) *(tribe)* **the Ute(s)** les Utes *mpl* (**b**) *(member of tribe)* Ute *mf*

utensil [ju:'tensəl] *n* ustensile *m*, outil *m*; **cooking utensils** ustensiles *mpl* de cuisine

uterine ['ju:tərain] *adj* utérin

uterogestation [,ju:tərəʊdʒes'teɪʃən] *n Physiol* gestation *f* utérine

uterus ['ju:tərəs] *(pl* **uteri** [-raɪ] *or* **uteruses**) *n* utérus *m*

utilitarian [,ju:tɪlɪ'teərɪən] **1** *adj* (**a**) *(functional)* utilitaire, fonctionnel (**b**) *Phil* utilitariste

2 *n* utilitariste *mf*

utilitarianism [,ju:tɪlɪ'teərɪənɪzəm] *n* utilitarisme *m*

utility [ju:'tɪlətɪ] *(pl* **utilities**) **1** *n* (**a**) *(usefulness)* utilité *f* (**b**) *(service)* service *m*; **they plan to improve (public) utilities** ils ont l'intention d'améliorer les services publics (**c**) *Comput* utilitaire *m*, programme *m* utilitaire (**d**) *Am (room)* ≃ buanderie *f*

2 *adj (fabric, furniture)* utilitaire, fonctionnel; *(vehicle)* utilitaire

►► *Am* ***utility man*** *(worker)* ouvrier *m* polyvalent; *(for gas, electricity)* = employé des services publics; *(actor)* = acteur qui joue les utilités; *Sport* ***utility player*** joueur(euse) *m,f* polyvalent; *Am* ***utility pole*** = poteau pour câbles électriques et téléphoniques; *Comput* ***utility program*** (logiciel *m*) utilitaire *m*; ***utility room*** ≃ buanderie *f*; *Am St Exch* ***utility stocks*** valeurs *fpl* de services publics

utilizable [,ju:tɪ'laɪzəbəl] *adj* utilisable

utilization [,ju:tɪlaɪ'zeɪʃən] *n* utilisation *f*

utilize, -ise ['ju:tɪlaɪz] *vt (use)* utiliser, se servir de; *(make best use of)* exploiter; **you could have utilized your time better** vous auriez pu tirer meilleur parti de votre temps *ou* mieux profiter de votre temps

utmost ['ʌtməʊst] **1** *adj* (**a**) *(greatest)* le plus grand; **it's a matter of the utmost seriousness** c'est une affaire extrêmement sérieuse; **in the utmost secrecy** dans le plus grand secret; **it's of the utmost importance that I see him** il est extrêmement important *ou* il est d'une importance capitale que je le voie; **with the utmost respect, I cannot agree with your conclusions** avec tout le respect que je vous dois, je ne peux pas partager vos conclusions; **it was only with the utmost difficulty that we were able to persuade them** nous avons eu toutes les peines du monde à les convaincre

(**b**) *(farthest)* **to the utmost ends of the earth** au bout du monde

2 *n* (**a**) *(maximum)* maximum *m*, plus haut degré *m*; **at the utmost** au grand maximum; **to do sth to the utmost of one's abilities** faire qch au maximum de ses capacités; **to live life to the utmost** profiter pleinement de la vie; **the utmost in comfort** ce qui se fait de mieux en matière de confort

(**b**) *(best effort)* **we did our utmost to fight the new taxes** nous avons fait tout notre possible *ou* tout ce que nous pouvions pour lutter contre les nouveaux impôts; **she tried her utmost** elle a fait de son mieux

utopia, Utopia [ju:'təʊpɪə] *n* utopie *f*

'Utopia' *More* 'L'Utopie'

---

utopian, Utopian [ju:'təʊpɪən] **1** *adj* utopique

2 *n* utopiste *mf*

utopianism, Utopianism [ju:'təʊpɪənɪzəm] *n* utopisme *m*

Utrecht [ju:'trekt] *n* Utrecht

utricle ['ju:trɪkəl] *n Anat, Bot & Zool* utricule *m*

utricular [ju:'trɪkjʊlə(r)] *adj Anat & Zool* utriculaire; *Bot* utriculé, utriculeux

utter ['ʌtə(r)] **1** *vt* (**a**) *(pronounce → word)* prononcer, proférer; *(→ cry, groan)* pousser; **he didn't utter a sound** il n'a pas ouvert la bouche, il n'a pas soufflé mot; **never utter his name in her presence** il ne faut jamais prononcer son nom devant elle

(**b**) *Law (libel)* publier; *(counterfeit money)* émettre, mettre en circulation

2 *adj (amazement, bliss)* absolu, total; *(fool)* parfait, fini; **he shows an utter disregard for his family's welfare** il affiche une indifférence absolue pour le bien-être de sa famille; **he's talking utter rubbish** ce qu'il dit n'a aucun sens *ou* est absolument idiot; **it's an utter scandal** c'est un véritable scandale; **it's utter madness** c'est de la folie totale *ou* pure; **an utter fool** un parfait crétin, un crétin fini; **to her utter amazement** à sa plus grande stupéfaction

utterance ['ʌtərəns] *n* (**a**) *(statement)* déclaration *f*; *Ling* énoncé *m*; **they taped the child's first utterances** ils ont enregistré les premiers mots de l'enfant; **his recent utterances in the national press** ses récentes déclarations dans la presse nationale (**b**) *(expression)* expression *f*, énonciation *f*; **to give utterance to sth** exprimer qch

utterly ['ʌtəlɪ] *adv* complètement, tout à fait

uttermost ['ʌtəməʊst] = **utmost**

U-tube *n* tube *m* en U

U-turn *n* (**a**) *Aut* demi-tour *m*; **to make a U-turn** faire (un) demi-tour; **no U-turns** *(sign)* défense de faire demi-tour (**b**) *Fig* volte-face *f inv*, revirement *m*; **the government were accused of making a U-turn on health policy** le gouvernement a été accusé de faire volte-face en matière de politique de santé

UV [,ju:'vi:] *n (abbr* **ultra-violet**) UV *m*

UV-A, UVA [,ju:vi:'eɪ] *n (abbr* **ultra-violet-A**) UVA *m*

uvarovite [u:'vɑ:rəvaɪt] *n Miner* ouvarovite *f*, ouwarowite *f*

UV-B, UVB [,ju:vi:'bi:] *n (abbr* **ultra-violet-B**) UVB *m*

UVF [,ju:vi:'ef] *n (abbr* **Ulster Volunteer Force**) = organisation paramilitaire déclarée hors la loi, favorable au maintien de l'Irlande du Nord au sein du Royaume-Uni

uvula ['ju:vjʊlə] *(pl* **uvulas** *or* **uvulae** [-li:]) *n* luette *f*, *Spec* uvule *f*, *Spec* uvula *f*

uvular ['ju:vjʊlə(r)] *adj* uvulaire

UWIST ['ju:wɪst] *n Br (abbr* **University of Wales Institute of Science and Technology**) = institut de science et de technologie de l'université du pays de Galles

uxoricide [ʌk'sɔ:rɪsaɪd] *n* uxoricide *m*

uxorious [ʌk'sɔ:rɪəs] *adj Formal* (**a**) *(devoted to one's wife)* excessivement dévoué à sa femme; **an uxorious husband** un mari dévoué (**b**) *(submissive to one's wife)* soumis à sa femme; **an uxorious husband** un mari soumis

uxoriousness [ʌk'sɔ:rɪəsnɪs] *n Formal (devotion to one's wife)* dévotion *f* excessive (à sa femme); *(submission to one's wife)* soumission *f* (à sa femme)

Uzbek ['ʊzbek] *n* (**a**) *(person)* Ouzbek *mf* (**b**) *(language)* ouzbek *m*

Uzbekistan [ʊz,bekɪ'stɑ:n] *n* Ouzbékistan *m*; **in Uzbekistan** en Ouzbékistan

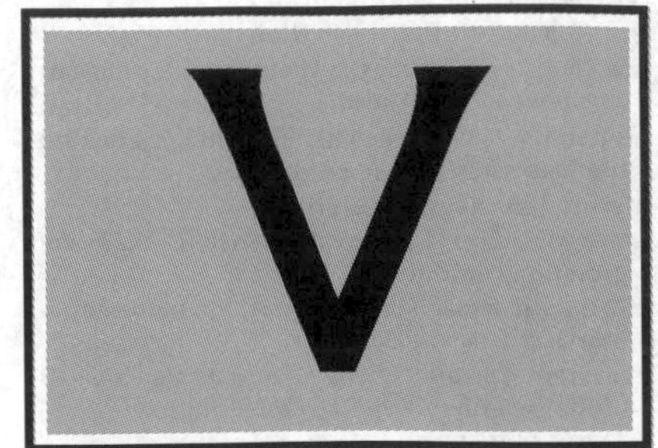

V[1], v[1] [viː] *n* (**a**) *(letter)* V, v *m inv*; **two v's** deux v; **V for Victor** V comme Victor; **V-1 (bomb)** V1 *m*; **V-2 (rocket)** V2 *m*; **V-8 (engine)** moteur *m* à huit cylindres en V (**b**) *(Roman numeral)* V V *m*

V[2] *(written abbr* **volt**) V

v[2] (**a**) *(written abbr* **velocity**) v (**b**) *(written abbr* **verb**) v (**c**) *(written abbr* **verse**) v (**d**) *(written abbr* **versus**) contre (**e**) *(written abbr* **vide**) v

VA[1] [ˌviːˈeɪ] *n Am (abbr* **Veterans Administration**) Bureau *m* des anciens combattants

VA[2] *(written abbr* **Virginia**) Virginie *f*

vac [væk] *n Br Fam (abbr* **vacation**) vacances❑ *fpl*; **the Easter vac** les vacances *fpl* de Pâques

vacancy [ˈveɪkənsɪ] *(pl* **vacancies**) *n* (**a**) *(job)* poste *m* vacant *ou* libre, vacance *f*; **do you have any vacancies?** avez-vous des postes à pourvoir?, est-ce qu'il y a de l'embauche?; **we have a vacancy for a sales clerk** nous avons un poste de vendeur à pourvoir, nous cherchons un vendeur; **the vacancy has been filled** le poste a été pourvu; **no vacancies** *(sign)* pas d'embauche; **vacancies for waitresses** *(sign)* cherchons serveuses

(**b**) *(in hotel)* chambre *f* libre; **no vacancies** *(sign)* complet

(**c**) *(lack of intelligence)* ineptie *f*, esprit *m* vide; **he had a look of utter vacancy on his face** il avait l'air complètement idiot

(**d**) *(emptiness)* vide *m*

vacant [ˈveɪkənt] *adj* (**a**) *(house, room → to rent)* libre, à louer; *(→ empty)* inoccupé; *(seat)* libre, inoccupé; **is this seat vacant?** y a-t-il quelqu'un à cette place?, est-ce que cette place est libre?; **the room becomes vacant tomorrow** la chambre sera libérée *ou* disponible demain; **apartments sold with vacant possession** appartements vendus avec jouissance immédiate

(**b**) *(job, position)* vacant, libre; **there are several vacant places to be filled** il y a plusieurs postes à pourvoir; **I found the job through the "situations vacant" column** j'ai trouvé le poste grâce à la rubrique des offres d'emploi; **a secretarial job became** *or* **fell vacant** un poste de secrétaire est devenu disponible *ou* vacant

(**c**) *(empty → mind, look)* vide; *(stupid → person, expression)* niais, idiot; **I asked a question and she just looked vacant** j'ai posé une question et elle a eu l'air de ne pas comprendre

(**d**) *(time)* de loisir, perdu; *(hour)* creux, de loisir

►► *Am* ***vacant lot*** terrain *m* vague; *Br* ***vacant possession*** libre possession *f*; **apartments sold with vacant possession** appartements libres à la vente

vacantly [ˈveɪkəntlɪ] *adv (expressionlessly)* d'un air absent *ou* vague; *(stupidly)* d'un air niais *ou* idiot; **he looked at us vacantly** *(expressionlessly)* il nous a regardés avec des yeux vides *ou* sans expression; *(stupidly)* il nous a regardés bêtement; **she stared vacantly into space** elle avait le regard perdu dans le vague

vacate [vəˈkeɪt] *vt (hotel room)* libérer, quitter; *(flat, house)* quitter, déménager de; *(job)* démissionner de; **they vacated the premises yesterday** ils ont quitté *ou* libéré les lieux hier

vacation [vəˈkeɪʃən] **1** *n* (**a**) *Br Univ (recess)* vacances *fpl*; *Law* vacations *fpl*, vacances *fpl* judiciaires; **over the vacation** pendant les vacances

(**b**) *Am (holiday)* vacances *fpl*; **to be on vacation** être en vacances; **they went to Italy on vacation** ils ont passé leurs vacances en Italie; **when are you going on** *or* **taking vacation?** quand est-ce que vous prenez vos vacances?

2 *comp Am (job)* de vacances

3 *vi Am* passer des vacances; **they're vacationing in the mountains** ils sont en vacances à la montagne

►► *Am* ***vacation center*** club *m* de vacances; *Univ* ***vacation course*** cours *mpl* d'été; ***vacation home*** résidence *f* secondaire; *Admin* ***vacation leave*** congé *m* annuel; *Am* ***vacation resort*** camp *m* de vacances; ***vacation work*** travail *m* effectué pendant les vacances *(par un étudiant)*

vacationer [vəˈkeɪʃənə(r)], **vacationist** [vəˈkeɪʃənɪst] *n Am* vacancier(ère) *m,f*

vaccinate [ˈvæksɪneɪt] *vt* vacciner; **to get vaccinated** se faire vacciner; **have you been vaccinated against polio?** est-ce que vous êtes vacciné *ou* est-ce que vous vous êtes fait vacciner contre la polio?

vaccination [ˌvæksɪˈneɪʃən] *n* vaccination *f*; **polio vaccination, vaccination against polio** vaccination *f* contre la polio; **the children all had vaccinations against polio** les enfants étaient tous vaccinés contre la polio

vaccine [*Br* ˈvæksiːn, *Am* vækˈsiːn] *n* vaccin *m*; **smallpox vaccine** vaccin *m* contre la variole

vaccinee [ˌvæksɪˈniː] *n Am* personne *f* vaccinée

vaccinia [vækˈsɪnɪə] *n Vet & Med* vaccine *f*

vaccinium [vækˈsɪnɪəm] *n Bot* vaccinier *m*

vacillate [ˈvæsəleɪt] *vi* hésiter

vacillating [ˈvæsəleɪtɪŋ] **1** *adj (behaviour)* indécis, irrésolu

2 *n* indécision *f*

vacillation [ˌvæsəˈleɪʃən] *n* hésitation *f*, indécision *f*

vacuity [væˈkjuːətɪ] *(pl* **vacuities**) *n Formal* (**a**) *(of person, reasoning)* vacuité *f* (**b**) *(statement)* ânerie *f*, niaiserie *f*

vacuolar [ˈvækjʊələ(r)] *adj Biol* vacuolaire

vacuolate [ˈvækjʊəleɪt], **vacuolated** [ˈvækjʊəˌleɪtɪd] *adj Biol* vacuolaire

vacuole [ˈvækjʊəʊl] *n Biol* vacuole *f*

vacuous [ˈvækjʊəs] *adj Formal (eyes, look)* vide, sans expression; *(remark)* sot (sotte), niais; *(film, novel)* idiot, dénué de tout intérêt; *(life)* vide de sens; **he's completely vacuous** il n'a rien dans la tête

vacuously [ˈvækjʊəslɪ] *adv Formal (to gaze)* sans expression; *(to say)* niaisement

vacuousness [ˈvækjʊəsnɪs] *n Formal (of laugh)* bêtise *f*, niaiserie *f*; *(of remark, debate)* vacuité *f*

vacuum [ˈvækjʊəm] *(pl* **vacuums** *or* **vacua** [-jʊə]) **1** *n* (**a**) *(void)* vide *m*; **his death left a vacuum in her life** sa mort a laissé un vide dans sa vie; **a cultural/political vacuum** un vide sur le plan culturel/politique

(**b**) *Phys* vacuum *m*

(**c**) *(machine)* **vacuum (cleaner)** aspirateur *m*; **I gave the room a quick vacuum** j'ai passé l'aspirateur en vitesse dans la pièce

2 *vt (carpet)* passer l'aspirateur sur; *(flat, room)* passer l'aspirateur dans

►► ***vacuum advance*** avance *f* à dépression; *Am* ***vacuum bottle*** (bouteille *f*) Thermos® *f*; ***vacuum brake*** frein *m* à vide; ***vacuum chamber*** chambre *f* à dépression; ***vacuum cleaner*** aspirateur *m*; ***vacuum cleaner accessories*** accessoires *mpl* d'aspirateur *ou* pour aspirateur; *Br* ***vacuum flask*** (bouteille *f*) Thermos® *f*; ***vacuum pack*** emballage *m* sous vide; *Ind & Com* ***vacuum packing*** emballage *m* sous vide; ***vacuum pump*** pompe *f* à vide; *Am* ***vacuum tube*** tube *m* électronique *ou* à vide

vacuum-clean = **vacuum** *vt*

vacuuming [ˈvækjʊəmɪŋ] *n* **to do the vacuuming** passer l'aspirateur

vacuum-packed *adj* emballé sous vide

VAD [ˌviːeɪˈdiː] *n (abbr* **Voluntary Aid Detachment**) = infirmières britanniques volontaires pendant la Première Guerre mondiale

vade mecum [ˌvɑːdɪˈmeɪkʊm] *(pl* **vade mecums**) *n* vade-mecum *m inv*

vadose [ˈveɪdəʊs] *adj*

►► *Geol* ***vadose water*** eaux *fpl* d'infiltration

vag [veɪg] *n Am Fam (abbr* **vagrant**) clodo *mf*

vagabond [ˈvægəbɒnd] **1** *n (wanderer)* vagabond(e) *m,f*; *(tramp)* clochard(e) *m,f*

2 *adj* vagabond, errant

vagal [ˈveɪgəl] *adj Anat* vagal

vagary [ˈveɪgərɪ] *(pl* **vagaries**) *n* caprice *m*; **the vagaries of fashion/the weather** les caprices de la mode/du temps

vagina [vəˈdʒaɪnə] *(pl* **vaginas** *or* **vaginae** [-niː]) *n* vagin *m*

vaginal [vəˈdʒaɪnəl] *adj* vaginal

►► ***vaginal discharge*** pertes *fpl* blanches; ***vaginal smear*** frottis *m* vaginal

vaginate [ˈvædʒɪneɪt] *adj* vaginé, engainé

vaginismus [ˌvædʒɪˈnɪzməs] *n* vaginisme *m*

vaginitis [ˌvædʒɪˈnaɪtɪs] *n* vaginite *f*

vagrancy [ˈveɪgrənsɪ] *n (gen) & Law* vagabondage *m*

vagrant [ˈveɪgrənt] **1** *n (wanderer)* vagabond(e) *m,f*; *(tramp)* clochard(e) *m,f*; *(beggar)* mendiant(e) *m,f*

2 *adj* vagabond

vague [veɪg] *adj* (**a**) *(imprecise → promise, statement)* vague, imprécis; *(→ person)* vague; **she had only a vague idea of what he meant** elle ne comprenait que vaguement ce qu'il voulait dire; **he made a vague gesture toward the office** d'un geste vague il désigna le bureau; **don't be so vague** précisez ce que vous voulez dire, soyez plus précis; **his instructions were vague** ses instructions manquaient de précision; **they were vague about their activities** *(imprecise)* ils n'ont pas précisé la nature de leurs activités; *(evasive)* ils sont restés vagues sur la nature de leurs activités; **I'm still vague about how to get there** *(unsure)* je ne comprends toujours pas comment y aller; **I haven't the vaguest idea** je n'en ai pas la moindre idée

(**b**) *(dim → memory, feeling)* vague, confus; **I have a vague recollection of summers spent in Greece** je me rappelle vaguement les étés passés en Grèce

(**c**) *(indistinct → shape)* flou, indistinct

(**d**) *(absent-minded)* distrait; **she looked vague** elle avait un air distrait

vaguely [ˈveɪglɪ] *adv* (**a**) *(not clearly → promise, say)* vaguement; *(→ remember, understand)* vaguement, confusément; **I vaguely remember dining here before** j'ai le vague souvenir *ou* je me souviens vaguement d'avoir déjà mangé ici

(**b**) *(a bit)* vaguement, peu; **it tastes vaguely like coffee** cela a vaguement un goût de café; **she resembles her sister only vaguely** elle ne ressemble pas beaucoup à sa sœur

(**c**) *(absent-mindedly)* distraitement; **he looked vaguely around him** il regardait autour de lui d'un air vague *ou* distrait

vagueness [ˈveɪgnɪs] *n* (**a**) *(imprecision → of instructions, statement)* imprécision *f*, manque *m* de clarté (**b**) *(of memory)* imprécision *f*, manque *m* de précision; *(of feeling)* vague *m*, caractère *m* vague *ou* indistinct (**c**) *(of shape)* flou *m*, caractère *m* indistinct (**d**) *(absent-mindedness)* distraction *f*

vagus ['veɪgəs] (*pl* **vagi** [-dʒaɪ]) *n* nerf *m* vague *ou* pneumogastrique, pneumogastrique *m*

vail [veɪl] *Arch* **1** *vt* **to vail one's bonnet/cap** se découvrir; **to vail one's pride** rabattre son orgueil

2 *vi (bow)* s'incliner (**to sb** devant qn); *Fig (yield)* céder (**to sb** à qn)

vain [veɪn] **1** *adj* (**a**) *(conceited)* vaniteux; **he's very vain about his looks** il s'occupe beaucoup de sa petite personne

(**b**) *(unsuccessful → attempt, effort)* vain, inutile; *(→ hope, plea, search)* vain, futile

(**c**) *(idle → promise)* vide, en l'air; *(→ word)* creux, en l'air

2 in vain *adv (unsuccessfully)* en vain, inutilement; **they tried in vain to free the driver** ils ont essayé sans succès *ou* en vain de libérer le conducteur; **all their efforts were in vain** leurs efforts n'ont servi à rien *ou* ont été vains; **it was all in vain** c'était peine perdue; **to take sb's name in vain** *(show disrespect)* manquer de respect envers le nom de qn; *(mention name)* parler de qn en son absence; *Hum* **are you taking my name in vain again?** vous parlez encore de moi derrière mon dos?

vainglorious [ˌveɪn'glɔːrɪəs] *adj Literary (proud)* vaniteux, orgueilleux; *(boastful)* vantard

vaingloriously [ˌveɪn'glɔːrɪəslɪ] *adv Literary (proudly)* vaniteusement, orgueilleusement; *(boastfully)* en se vantant

vainglory [ˌveɪn'glɔːrɪ] *n Literary (pride)* vanité *f*, orgueil *m*; *(boastfulness)* vantardise *f*

vainly ['veɪnlɪ] *adv* (**a**) *(conceitedly)* avec vanité, vaniteusement (**b**) *(unsuccessfully → try)* en vain, inutilement; *(→ hope)* en vain

vair [veə(r)] *n Her* vair *m*; **vair ancient/in pale** vair *m* antique/en pal

Vaisya ['vaɪsjə] *n* vaishya *m inv*

valance ['væləns] *n (round bed frame)* frange *f* de lit; *(round shelf, window)* lambrequin *m*, frange *f*

valanced sheet ['vælənst-] *n* housse *f* cache-sommier

vale [veɪl] *n Literary* vallée *f*, val *m*; *Fig* **this vale of tears** cette vallée de larmes

valediction [ˌvælɪ'dɪkʃən] *n* (**a**) *(act)* adieux *mpl*; (**b**) *Am Sch & Univ (at graduation)* discours *m* d'adieu; **to give the valediction** prononcer le discours d'adieu

valedictorian [ˌvælɪdɪk'tɔːrɪən] **1** *adj* d'adieu

2 *n Am Sch & Univ* = major de la promotion (qui prononce le discours d'adieu)

valedictory [ˌvælɪ'dɪktərɪ] (*pl* **valedictories**) *Formal* **1** *adj (mass, service, ceremony, speech)* d'adieu; **the valedictory tone of his final novel** le ton qui faisait de son dernier roman le roman de l'adieu; **the valedictory mood of the meeting** l'ambiance de la réunion, qui annonçait la fin

2 *n Am Sch & Univ (at graduation)* discours *m* d'adieu

valence ['veɪləns] *n* (**a**) *Am Chem* valence *f* (**b**) *(bonding capacity)* atomicité *f*

Valencia [və'lenʃɪə] *n* Valence

valency ['veɪlənsɪ] (*pl* **valencies**) *n Chem* valence *f*

Valentine ['væləntaɪn] *pr n* **(Saint) Valentine's Day** la Saint-Valentin; *Am Hist* **the Saint Valentine's Day Massacre** le massacre de la Saint-Valentin

THE SAINT VALENTINE'S DAY MASSACRE

On désigne ainsi le massacre particulièrement sanglant de cinq membres d'un gang de Chicago par une bande rivale, le 14 février 1929. Bien que sa culpabilité n'ait jamais pu être prouvée, Al Capone fut soupçonné d'en avoir été l'instigateur.

valentine ['væləntaɪn] *n* (**a**) *(card)* carte *f* de la Saint-Valentin (**b**) *(recipient of card)* = celui/celle qui reçoit une carte envoyée le jour de la Saint-Valentin; **will you be my valentine?** = phrase écrite sur les cartes de la Saint-Valentin pour exprimer ses sentiments amoureux à l'égard du/de la destinataire; **George is my valentine** c'est George que j'aime

►► ***valentine card*** carte *f* de la Saint-Valentin

Valerian [və'lɪərɪən] *pr n* Valérien

valerian [və'lɪərɪən] *n Bot* valériane *f*

valeric [və'lerɪk] *adj Chem (acid)* valérique

valet 1 *n* ['væleɪ] (**a**) *(manservant)* valet *m* de chambre (**b**) *(clothing rack)* valet *m*

2 *vt* ['vælɪt] **can I have my suit valeted?** puis-je faire nettoyer mon costume?; *Aut* **to have one's car valeted** faire faire un lavage-route à sa voiture

►► ***valet parking*** *(sign)* service de voiturier; ***valet service*** *(in hotel)* pressing *m* de l'hôtel

valeting ['vælɪtɪŋ] *n Aut* lavage-route *m*

Valetta = **Valletta**

valetudinarian [ˌvælɪtjuːdɪ'neərɪən] *Arch or Literary* **1** *adj* valétudinaire

2 *n* valétudinaire *mf*

valgus ['vælgəs] *Med* **1** *adj* valgus

2 *n* valgus *m inv*

Valhalla [væl'hælə] *n Myth* Walhalla *m*

valiance ['væljəns] *n Literary* vaillance *f*, bravoure *f*

valiant ['væljənt] *adj (person)* vaillant, courageux; *(behaviour, deed)* courageux, brave; **she made a valiant attempt to put out the fire** elle a tenté avec courage *ou* courageusement d'éteindre l'incendie; **he made a valiant effort not to cry out** il a fait un gros effort pour ne pas crier

valiantly ['væljəntlɪ] *adv* vaillamment, courageusement

valid ['vælɪd] *adj* (**a**) *(argument, reasoning)* valable, bien fondé; *(excuse)* valable (**b**) *(contract, passport)* valide, valable; **a valid driving licence** un permis de conduire valable *ou* valide *ou* en règle; **my driver's licence is no longer valid** mon permis de conduire est périmé; **valid for two months** *(on train ticket)* valable deux mois

validate ['vælɪdeɪt] *vt* (**a**) *(argument, claim)* confirmer, prouver la justesse de; *Am* **to validate an election** valider une élection (**b**) *(document)* valider (**c**) *Comput* valider

validation [ˌvælɪ'deɪʃən] *n* (**a**) *(of argument, claim)* confirmation *f*, preuve *f* (**b**) *(of document)* validation *f*

validity [və'lɪdətɪ] *n* (**a**) *(of argument, reasoning)* justesse *f*, solidité *f* (**b**) *(of document)* validité *f*

validly ['vælɪdlɪ] *adv* avec raison

valine ['veɪliːn] *n* valine *f*

valise [*Br* və'liːz, *Am* və'liːs] *n Old-fashioned or Am (case)* mallette *f*; *(bag)* sac *m* de voyage

Valium® ['vælɪəm] (*pl* **inv**) *n* Valium® *m*; **to be on Valium**® être sous Valium®

►► *Am Fam St Exch* ***valium picnic*** *(quiet day on New York Stock Exchange)* séance *f* morne

Valkyrie [væl'kɪərɪ] *n* Walkyrie *f*, Valkyrie *f*

vallecula [væ'lekjʊlə] (*pl* **valleculae** [-liː]) *n* (**a**) *Anat* fosse *f*; *(of cerebellum)* scissure *f* médiane (**b**) *Bot* vallécule *f*

Valletta [və'letə] *n* La Valette

valley ['vælɪ] *n* vallée *f*; *(small)* vallon *m*; **the Valleys** = le sud du pays de Galles; **the Loire/Rhone valley** la vallée de la Loire/du Rhône

Valley Forge *n* Valley Forge *f*

VALLEY FORGE

C'est dans cette vallée de l'État de Pennsylvanie que l'armée de George Washington prit ses quartiers d'hiver en 1777–78, pendant la guerre d'Indépendance américaine. Le courage des troupes face aux difficiles conditions de vie dans les campements a fait de cette vallée un lieu hautement symbolique.

vallisneria [ˌvælɪs'nɪərɪə] *n Bot* vallisnérie *f*

vallum ['væləm] *n Archeol* vallum *m*

valonia [və'ləʊnɪə] *n Bot* vélanèdes *fpl*

valor *Am* = **valour**

valorization [ˌvæləraɪ'zeɪʃən] *n* valorisation *f*

valorize, -ise ['væləraɪz] *vt* valoriser

valorous ['vælərəs] *adj Literary* valeureux, vaillant

valorously ['vælərəslɪ] *adv Literary* valeureusement, vaillamment

valour, *Am* **valor** ['vælə(r)] *n Literary* vaillance *f*, bravoure *f*

Valparaiso [ˌvælpə'raɪzəʊ] *n* Valparaiso

valuable ['væljʊəbəl] **1** *adj* (**a**) *(of monetary worth)* de (grande) valeur; **a valuable antique** un objet ancien de grande valeur (**b**) *(advice, friendship, time)* précieux; **she has given years of valuable service** elle a donné des années de bons et loyaux services

2 *n (usu pl)* **valuables** objets *mpl* de valeur; **take your valuables with you** emportez tous vos objets de valeur; **do not leave valuables in your car** ne pas laisser des objets de valeur dans la voiture

valuate ['væljʊeɪt] *vt Am* estimer, expertiser; **the house was valuated at $100,000** la maison a été expertisée *ou* estimée *ou* évaluée à 100 000 dollars

valuation [ˌvæljʊ'eɪʃən] *n (act)* évaluation *f*, estimation *f*, expertise *f*; *(price)* évaluation *f*; **to get a valuation of sth** faire évaluer *ou* estimer *ou* expertiser qch; **to make a valuation of sth** évaluer *ou* estimer *ou* expertiser qch; **we asked for a valuation of the house** nous avons fait expertiser *ou* estimer la maison; **the valuation of** *or* **the valuation (put) on the business is £50,000** l'affaire a été estimée *ou* évaluée à 50 000 livres

►► *Fin* ***valuation charge*** taxation *f* à la valeur

valuator ['væljʊeɪtə(r)] *n* expert *m (en expertise de biens)*

value ['væljuː] **1** *n* (**a**) *(monetary worth)* valeur *f*; **to be of value** avoir de la valeur; **they own nothing of value** ils ne possèdent rien de valeur *ou* rien qui ait de la valeur; **this necklace is of great value** ce collier vaut cher; **this necklace is of little value** ce collier ne vaut pas grand-chose *ou* a peu de valeur; **it's of no value** c'est sans valeur; **to be good/poor value (for money)** être d'un bon/mauvais rapport qualité-prix; **it's excellent value for money** le rapport qualité-prix est excellent; **it's good value at £10** ce n'est pas cher à 10 livres; **we got good value for our money** nous en avons eu pour notre argent; **he gives you value for money** il vous en donne pour votre argent; **which of the brands gives the best value?** laquelle des marques est la plus avantageuse?; **the airline paid her the value of the lost luggage** la compagnie aérienne l'a dédommagée de la perte de ses bagages; **to go up/down in value** prendre/perdre de la valeur; **property is going up/down in value** l'immobilier prend/perd de la valeur; **to depreciate in value** se déprécier; **the increase in value** la hausse de valeur, l'appréciation *f*; **the loss in value** la perte de valeur, la dépréciation; **to set** *or* **to put a value on sth** estimer la valeur de qch; **they put a value of £80,000 on the house** ils ont estimé *ou* expertisé la maison à 80 000 livres; **of no commercial value** sans valeur commerciale; **she bought goods to the value of £400** elle a acheté pour 400 livres de marchandise; **goods to the value of £50 or more are subject to duty** les marchandises d'une valeur égale ou supérieure à £50 sont soumis à une taxe; **what will this do to the value of property?** quel effet est-ce que ça va avoir sur le prix de l'immobilier?

(**b**) *(merit, importance → of method, work)* valeur *f*; *(→ of person)* valeur *f*, mérite *m*; **he had nothing of value to add** il n'avait rien d'important *ou* de valable à ajouter; **these books may be of value to them** ces livres peuvent leur servir, ils peuvent avoir besoin de ces livres; **they place little/a high value on punctuality** ils font peu de cas/grand cas de l'exactitude, ils attachent peu d'importance/beaucoup d'importance à l'exactitude; **your help/contribution was of great value** votre aide/contribution a été très précieuse; **she has been of great value to the company** elle a apporté une contribution précieuse à l'entreprise

(**c**) *(usu pl) (principles)* **values** valeurs *fpl*; **sense of values** sens *m* des valeurs; **moral values** valeurs *fpl* morales; **he has old-fashioned values** il est très traditionaliste

(**d**) *(feature)* particularité *f*

(**e**) *(of colour)* valeur *f*

(**f**) *Ling, Math & Mus* valeur *f*

2 *vt* (**a**) *(assess worth of)* expertiser, estimer, évaluer; **to have sth valued** faire évaluer *ou* estimer *ou* expertiser qch; **we had our paintings**

valued nous avons fait expertiser *ou* estimer *ou* évaluer nos tableaux; **they valued the company at $10 billion** ils ont estimé la valeur de la société à 10 milliards de dollars; **they valued the house at £50,000** ils ont estimé *ou* évalué la maison à 50 000 livres

(**b**) *(have high regard for → friendship)* apprécier, estimer; *(→ honesty, punctuality)* faire grand cas de; **if you value your freedom/your life you'd better leave** si vous tenez à votre liberté/à la vie, vous feriez mieux de partir; **we greatly value your help** nous apprécions beaucoup *ou* nous vous sommes très reconnaissants de votre aide; **does he value your opinion?** votre opinion lui importe-t-elle?

►► *Banking* ***value in account*** valeur *f* en compte; *Fin* ***value added*** valeur *f* ajoutée; *Fin* ***value analysis*** analyse *f* de valeur; *Fin* ***value below rate*** décote *f*; *Mktg* ***value brand*** marque *f* de valeur; *Com* ***value chain*** chaîne *f* de valeur; *Fin* ***value for collection*** valeur *f* à l'encaissement; *Fin* ***value date*** date *f* de valeur; *Fin* ***value day*** jour *m* de valeur; *Fin* ***value engineering*** analyse *f* de valeur; *Fin* ***value in exchange*** valeur *f* d'échange, contre-valeur *f*; *Banking* ***value in gold currency*** valeur-or *f*; ***value judgement*** jugement *m* de valeur; *Fin* ***value at liquidation*** valeur *f* de liquidation *ou* liquidative; *Fin* ***value at maturity*** valeur *f* à l'échéance; *Fin* ***value for money audit*** = estimation des performances d'une société à but non lucratif ou d'un service gouvernemental; *Fin* ***value in use*** valeur *f* d'usage

value-added tax *n Br Fin* taxe *f* sur la valeur ajoutée, *Can* taxe *f* sur les ventes

valued ['væljuːd] *adj (opinion)* estimé; *(advice, friend)* précieux

►► *Ins* ***valued policy*** assurance *f* forfaitaire

valueless ['væljʊlɪs] *adj* sans valeur

valuer ['væljʊə(r)] *n* expert *m (en expertise de biens)*; **official valuer** commissaire-priseur *m*

valvate ['vælveɪt] *adj Bot* valvé, valvaire

►► ***valvate dehiscence*** déhiscence *f* valvaire

valve [vælv] *n* (**a**) *(in pipe, tube, air chamber)* valve *f*; *(in machine)* soupape *f*, valve *f* (**b**) *Anat* valve *f*; *(small)* valvule *f* (**c**) *Bot & Zool* valve *f* (**d**) *Mus (of brass instrument)* piston *m* (**e**) *Elec (of radio)* lampe *f*, valve *f*

valved [vælvd] *adj Tech (pipe, tube, air chamber)* à valve(s); *(machine)* à valve(s), à soupape(s); *Mus (instrument)* à pistons

valvula ['vælvjʊlə] *(pl* **valvulae** [-liː]) *n Anat* valvule *f*

valvular ['vælvjʊlə(r)] *adj* (**a**) *(machine)* à soupapes *ou* valves (**b**) *Anat, Bot & Zool* valvulaire (**c**) *Mus (instrument)* à pistons

valvulitis [,vælvjʊ'laɪtɪs] *n Med* valvulite *f*

vamoose [və'muːs] *vi Am Fam* décamper, filer; **vamoose!** fiche le camp!

vamp [væmp] **1** *n* (**a**) *Fam (woman)* vamp *f*

(**b**) *(piecing together)* rafistolage *m*

(**c**) *(of story)* enjolivement *m*

(**d**) *Mus* improvisation *f*

(**e**) *(of shoe)* devant *m*

2 *vt* (**a**) *Fam (seduce)* vamper

(**b**) *(repair)* rafistoler; *(renovate)* rénover

(**c**) *(story)* enjoliver

(**d**) *Mus (piece, song)* improviser des accompagnements à; *(accompaniment)* improviser

(**e**) *Fam (of woman)* vamper

3 *vi Fam* (**a**) *(woman)* jouer la vamp

(**b**) *Am (leave)* se casser, se tirer

►**vamp up** *vt sep* = **vamp** *vt* (**b**) – (**d**)

vampire ['væmpaɪə(r)] *n (bat, monster)* vampire *m*; *(person)* vampire *m*, sangsue *f*

►► *Zool* ***vampire bat*** vampire *m*

vampiric [væm'pɪrɪk] *adj* vampirique

vampirism ['væmpaɪərɪzəm] *n* vampirisme *m*

vampish ['væmpɪʃ] *adj Fam Old-fashioned (looks, dress)* de vamp, de femme fatale

VAN [væn] *n Comput (abbr* **value-added network**) réseau *m* à valeur ajoutée

van [væn] *n* (**a**) *(small vehicle)* camionnette *f*, fourgonnette *f*; *(large vehicle)* camion *m*, fourgon *m* (**b**) *Br Rail* fourgon *m*, wagon *m* (**c**) *(caravan)* caravane *f* (**d**) *Br Fam (advantage → in tennis)* avantage[□] *m*; **van in/out** avantage dedans/dehors (**e**) *Mil (vanguard)* avant-garde *f*; **in the van** en tête; *Fig* **in the van of abstract art** à l'avant-garde de l'art abstrait

►► *Am* ***van pool*** = covoiturage *m* en minibus *(souvent aux frais de l'entreprise)*

vanadinite [və'nædɪnaɪt] *n Miner* vanadinite *f*

vanadium [və'neɪdɪəm] *n Chem* vanadium *m*

Van Allen [,væn'ælən] *pr n*

►► ***Van Allen (radiation) belts*** ceintures *f ou* zones *f* de Van Allen

Vancouver [væn'kuːvə(r)] *n* Vancouver

V and A [,viːən'eɪ] *n Br (abbr* **Victoria and Albert Museum**) = grand musée londonien des arts décoratifs

vandal ['vændəl] **1** *n (hooligan)* vandale *mf*

2 Vandal *n Hist* Vandale *mf*

vandalism ['vændəlɪzəm] *n* vandalisme *m*; **act of vandalism** acte *m* de vandalisme

vandalize, -ise ['vændəlaɪz] *vt (building, telephone etc)* saccager; **several pictures have been vandalized** plusieurs tableaux ont été mutilés (par des vandales)

Van de Graaff [,vændə'grɑːf] *pr n*

►► *Phys* ***Van de Graaff generator*** générateur *m* Van de Graaff

Van der Waals [,vændə'wɑːlz] *pr n*

►► *Phys* ***Van der Waals equation of state*** équation *f* de l'état de Van der Waals; *Phys* ***Van der Waals forces*** forces *f* Van der Waals

Van Diemen's Land [,væn'diːmənslænd] *n Hist* la Terre de Van Diemen

van driver *n* chauffeur *m* de camionnette

Vandyke [,væn'daɪk] *n (beard)* barbiche *f*, bouc *m*

►► ***Vandyke beard*** barbiche *f*, bouc *m*

vane [veɪn] *n* (**a**) *(blade → of propeller)* pale *f*; *(→ of windmill)* aile *f*; *(→ of turbine)* aube *f*; *(→ of bomb, torpedo)* ailette (**b**) **(weather) vane** girouette *f* (**c**) *Orn (of feather)* barbe *f*

vanguard ['vængɑːd] *n Mil* avant-garde *f*; **in the vanguard of the division** en tête de la division; *Fig* **to be in the vanguard of a movement** être un des pionniers d'un mouvement; **in the vanguard of progress** à l'avant-garde *ou* à la pointe du progrès

vanguardism ['vængɑːdɪzəm] *n* avant-gardisme *m*

vanilla [və'nɪlə] **1** *n (plant)* vanillier *m*; *(flavour)* vanille *f*; **flavoured with vanilla, vanilla flavoured** vanillé, (parfumé) à la vanille

2 *comp* **vanilla ice cream/flavour** glace *f* /parfum *m* à la vanille

►► ***vanilla bean*** gousse *f* de vanille; ***vanilla essence*** extrait *m* de vanille; ***vanilla pod*** gousse *f* de vanille; ***vanilla sugar*** sucre *m* vanillé; *St Exch* ***vanilla swap*** swap *m* vanilla

vanillin ['vænɪlɪn] *n* vanilline *f*

vanish ['vænɪʃ] *vi (object, person, race)* disparaître; *(hopes, worries)* s'évanouir, disparaître; **the aeroplane vanished from sight** l'avion a disparu; **the sun vanished behind the mountains** le soleil a disparu derrière les montagnes; **she vanished into the crowd** elle s'est perdue dans la foule; **entire species have vanished from the face of the earth** des espèces entières ont disparu de la surface du globe; **elephants are vanishing from the earth** les éléphants sont en voie de disparition; **just when you need him he vanishes!** dès que vous avez besoin de lui, il s'éclipse!

vanishing ['vænɪʃɪŋ-] *adj Fig* **she did a vanishing act** elle s'est éclipsée

►► *Old-fashioned* ***vanishing cream*** crème *f* de jour; ***vanishing point*** point *m* de fuite; *Fig* **profits have dwindled to vanishing point** les bénéfices se sont trouvés réduits à néant; ***vanishing trick*** tour *m* de passe-passe; *Fig* **he did a vanishing trick** *(disappeared)* il a disparu

vanitas ['vænɪtæs] *n Art* vanité *f*

vanity ['vænətɪ] *(pl* **vanities**) *n* (**a**) *(conceit)* vanité *f*, orgueil *m*; **she refused to use a walking stick out of (sheer) vanity** par (pure) vanité elle a refusé d'utiliser une canne; **I think I can without vanity claim to be the most competent** sans vanité *ou* sans vouloir me vanter, je peux prétendre être le plus compétent (**b**) *Formal or Literary (futility)* futilité *f*, insignifiance *f*, *Literary* vanité *f*; **all is vanity** tout n'est que vanité (**c**) *Am (dressing table)* coiffeuse *f*, table *f* de toilette

►► ***vanity bag*** trousse *f* de toilette *(pour femme)*; ***vanity case*** mallette *f* de toilette, vanity-case *m*; ***vanity mirror*** miroir *m* de courtoisie; *Am* ***vanity plate*** plaque *f* d'immatriculation personnalisée; ***vanity press*** maison *f* d'édition à compte d'auteur; ***vanity publishing*** publication *f* à compte d'auteur; ***vanity table*** coiffeuse *f*, table *f* de toilette; ***vanity unit*** = meuble de salle de bains avec lavabo encastré

'Vanity Fair' *Thackeray* 'La Foire aux vanités'

vanner[1] ['vænə(r)] *n Mining (person, machine)* vanneur *m*

vanner[2] *n* (**a**) *(horse)* cheval *m* de trait léger (**b**) *Am (van owner)* camionneur *m*

vanning ['vænɪŋ] *n Mining* vannage *m*

►► ***vanning machine*** vanneur *m*; ***vanning shovel*** pelle *f* à vanner, van *m*

vanquish ['væŋkwɪʃ] *vt* vaincre

vanquisher ['væŋkwɪʃə(r)] *n* vainqueur *m*

vanquishing ['væŋkwɪʃɪŋ] **1** *adj* vainqueur

2 *n* victoire *f* (**of** sur)

vantage ['vɑːntɪdʒ] *n* (**a**) *(advantageous situation)* avantage *m*, supériorité *f*; **point of vantage** point de vue *m* privilégié (**b**) *(in tennis)* avantage *m*

►► ***vantage ground*** *(gen)* point de vue *m* (privilégié); *Mil* position *f* stratégique; ***vantage point*** point de vue *m* (privilégié), position *f* (avantageuse); **from our vantage point we could see...** de la position avantageuse où nous étions nous voyions...; *Fig* **from the vantage point of the twentieth century, it is easy to...** avec le recul qui nous est possible au vingtième siècle, il est facile de...

Vanuatu ['vænuː,ætuː] *n Geog* Vanuatu

vapid ['væpɪd] *adj (conversation, remark)* fade, insipide; *(style)* fade, plat; *(person)* fade, terne

vapidity [væ'pɪdətɪ] *n (of conversation)* insipidité *f*; *(of style)* platitude *f*, caractère *m* plat; *(of person)* fadeur *f*

vapor *Am* = **vapour**

vaporetto [væpə'retəʊ] *(pl* **vaporettos** *or* **vaporetti** [-tɪ]) *n* vaporetto *m*

vaporization [,veɪpəraɪ'zeɪʃən] *n* vaporisation *f*

vaporize, -ise ['veɪpəraɪz] **1** *vt* vaporiser

2 *vi* se vaporiser

vaporizer ['veɪpəraɪzə(r)] *n* (**a**) *(gen)* vaporisateur *m*; *(for perfume, spray)* atomiseur *m*, pulvérisateur *m* (**b**) *Med (inhaler)* inhalateur *m*; *(for throat)* pulvérisateur *m*

vaporous ['veɪpərəs] *adj* vaporeux

vapour, *Am* **vapor** ['veɪpə(r)] **1** *n* vapeur *f*; *(on window)* buée *f*

2 *vi* (**a**) *Phys* s'évaporer (**b**) *Am Fam (brag)* se vanter[□], fanfaronner

3 vapours *npl Arch* **to have (an attack of) the vapours** avoir des vapeurs

►► *Constr* ***vapour barrier*** coupe-vapeur *m inv*; ***vapour bath*** bain *m* de vapeur; ***vapour density*** densité *f* de vapeur; ***vapour lock*** bouchon *m* de vapeur; ***vapour pressure*** pression *f ou* tension *f* de vapeur; *Aviat* ***vapour trail*** traînée *f* de condensation

varactor [və'ræktə(r)] *n Electron* varactor *m*

varan ['værən] *n Zool* varan *m*

variability [,veərɪə'bɪlətɪ] *n* variabilité *f*

variable ['veərɪəbəl] **1** *adj* (**a**) *(weather)* variable, changeant; *(quality)* variable, inégal; *(performance, work)* de qualité inégale, inégal; **the combinations are infinitely variable** les combinaisons peuvent varier à l'infini (**b**) *Comput & Math* variable

2 *n* variable *f*

►► *Fin* ***variable budget*** budget *m* variable *ou* flexible; *Fin* ***variable costs*** coûts *mpl* variables, frais *mpl* variables; ***variable interest rate*** taux *m* d'intérêt variable; *Banking* ***variable rate*** taux *m* variable; ***variable star*** étoile *f* variable

variable-income *adj Fin (bond, investment)* à revenu variable

variableness ['veərɪəbəlnɪs] *n* variabilité *f*

variable-rate interest *n* intérêt *m* variable

variable-rate security *n* valeur *f* à revenu variable

variable-yield *adj Fin (investments, securities)* à revenu variable

val–var

variably ['veərɪəblɪ] *adv* variablement

variance ['veərɪəns] *n* (**a**) *(in statistics)* variance *f*; *(in law)* divergence *f*, différence *f*
(**b**) *Acct* variance *f*, écart *m*; **variance analysis** analyse *f* des écarts
(**c**) *Chem & Math* variance *f*
(**d**) *(idioms)* **to be at variance with sb** être en désaccord avec qn; **to be at variance with sth** ne pas cadrer avec *ou* ne pas concorder avec qch; **she is at variance with her colleagues on** *or* **over this issue** elle est en désaccord avec ses collègues à ce sujet; **this announcement is at variance with his previous statements** cette annonce est en contradiction avec *ou* ne s'accorde pas avec ses déclarations antérieures

variant ['veərɪənt] **1** *n (gen) & Ling* variante *f*
2 *adj* (**a**) *(different)* autre, différent; **variant interpretation** *or* **reading** interprétation *f ou* lecture *f* différente; **a variant spelling** une variante orthographique (**b**) *(various)* varié, divers (**c**) *Ling* variant

variate ['veərɪeɪt] *n Math (in statistics)* variable *f* aléatoire

variation [,veərɪ'eɪʃən] *n* (**a**) *(change, modification)* variation *f*, modification *f*; **variations in temperature** variations *fpl ou* changements *mpl* de température; **the level of demand is subject to considerable variation** le niveau de la demande peut varier considérablement; **variation between two readings** *(using scientific instrument)* écart *m* entre deux lectures
(**b**) *Mus* variation *f*; **theme and variations** thème *m* et variations *fpl*
(**c**) *(different version)* variation *f*; **another variation on the same theme** une autre variation sur le même thème; **the different legends are variations of the same basic story** ces différentes légendes sont des variantes de la même histoire originelle
(**d**) *Biol* variation *f*
►► *Ins* ***variation of risk*** modification *f* de risque

variational [,veərɪ'eɪʃənəl] *adj* sujet à des variations, variationnel

varicella [,værɪ'selə] *n Med* varicelle *f*

varicoloured, *Am* **varicolored** ['veərɪ,kʌləd] *adj* multicolore, aux couleurs variées, bigarré; *Fig* divers

varicose ['værɪkəʊs] *adj (ulcer)* variqueux; **to have** *or* **to suffer from varicose veins** avoir des varices

varicosity [,værɪ'kɒsɪtɪ] *n Med* (**a**) *(varicose state)* état *m* variqueux (**b**) *(varicose vein)* varice *f*

varicotomy [,værɪ'kɒtəmɪ] *(pl* **varicotomies***) n Med* varicectomie *f*

varied ['veərɪd] *adj* varié, divers

variegate ['veərɪgeɪt] *vt* panacher, bigarrer

variegated ['veərɪgeɪtɪd] *adj* (**a**) *(gen)* bigarré (**b**) *Bot* panaché

variegation [,veərɪ'geɪʃən] *n* bigarrure *f*

varietal [və'raɪətəl] *adj* variétal

variety [və'raɪətɪ] *(pl* **varieties***)* **1** *n* (**a**) *(diversity)* variété *f*, diversité *f*; **there isn't much variety in the menu** le menu n'est pas très varié *ou* n'offre pas un grand choix; **he needs more variety in his diet** il a besoin d'un régime plus varié; **the work lacks variety** le travail manque de variété *ou* n'est pas assez varié; **meeting lots of different people adds variety to the job** les rencontres avec des tas de gens différents mettent de la variété dans le travail; *Prov* **variety is the spice of life** = la diversité est le sel de la vie
(**b**) *(number, assortment)* nombre *m*, quantité *f*; **for a variety of reasons** *(various)* pour diverses raisons; *(many)* pour de nombreuses raisons; **in a variety of ways** de diverses manières; **the dresses come in a variety of sizes** les robes sont disponibles dans un grand nombre de tailles; **there is a wide variety of colours/styles to choose from** il y a un grand choix de couleurs/styles
(**c**) *(type)* espèce *f*, genre *m*; **different varieties of cheese** différentes sortes *fpl* de fromage, des fromages *mpl* variés
(**d**) *Bot & Zool (strain)* variété *f*
(**e**) *(UNCOUNT) Theat & TV* variétés *fpl*
2 *comp (artiste, show, theatre)* de variétés, de music-hall
►► *Am* ***variety meat*** abats *mpl*; *Am* ***variety store*** grand magasin *m*

varifocals [veərɪ'fəʊkəlz] *npl* lunettes *fpl* à verres progressifs

variform ['veərɪfɔːm] *adj* dont la forme est variable, diversiforme

variola [və'raɪələ] *n Med* variole *f*, petite vérole *f*

variolar [və'raɪələ(r)] *adj Med* variolaire

variole ['veərɪəʊl] *n* (**a**) *(cavity)* petite cavité *f*, petit trou *m* (**b**) *Miner* sphérolithe *m* (dans la variolite)

variolite ['veərɪəlaɪt] *n Miner* variolite *f*

variometer [,veərɪ'ɒmɪtə(r)] *n Phys, Electron & Aviat* variomètre *m*

variorum [,veərɪ'ɔːrəm] **1** *n* (édition *f*) variorum *m inv*
2 *adj* variorum *(inv)*

various ['veərɪəs] *adj* (**a**) *(diverse)* divers, différent; *(several)* plusieurs; **she writes under various names** elle écrit sous divers pseudonymes; **at various times in his life** à différents moments *ou* à plusieurs reprises dans sa vie; **at various intervals** de temps à autre (**b**) *(varied, different)* varié; **his reasons were many and various** ses raisons étaient nombreuses et variées

variously ['veərɪəslɪ] *adv (in different ways)* diversement, de différentes *ou* diverses façons; **variously estimated at...** estimé par diverses sources à...; **he is variously known as soldier, king and emperor** on le connaît à la fois comme soldat, roi et empereur

variscite ['værɪsaɪt] *n Miner* variscite *f*

varistor [və'rɪstə(r)] *n Electron* varistance *f*, varistor *m*

varix ['veərɪks] *(pl* **varices** ['værɪ,siːz]*) n (on shell) & Med* varice *f*

varlet ['vɑːlɪt] *n* (**a**) *Arch (servant)* valet *m* (**b**) *Pej Literary* fripon *m*, gredin *m*

varmint ['vɑːmɪnt] *n Fam Old-fashioned* coquin(e) *m,f*, vaurien(enne) *m,f*

varnish ['vɑːnɪʃ] **1** *n also Fig* vernis *m*
2 *vt (nails, painting, wood)* vernir; *(pottery)* vernir, vernisser; **to varnish one's (finger)nails** se mettre du vernis à ongles; *Fig* **to varnish (over) the truth** maquiller la vérité

varnisher ['vɑːnɪʃə(r)] *n* vernisseur *m*

varnishing ['vɑːnɪʃɪŋ] *n* vernissage *m*
►► *Art* ***varnishing day*** (jour *m* du) vernissage *m*

varoom [və'ruːm] *exclam* vroum!

varsity ['vɑːsətɪ] *(pl* **varsities***) Fam* **1** *n Br Old-fashioned* université *f*, fac *f*
2 *adj Am Sport* = qui représente l'université au plus haut niveau
►► ***varsity match*** match *m* interuniversitaire *(entre Oxford et Cambridge)*

varus ['veərəs] *adj Med* varus

varve [vɑːv] *n Geol* varve *f*

vary ['veərɪ] **1** *vi* (**a**) *(be different)* varier; **opinions on this question vary** les opinions varient sur ce sujet; **the students vary considerably in ability** les étudiants ont des niveaux très différents; **they vary in size from small to extra large** ils vont de la plus petite taille à la plus grande; **to vary from year to year/place to place** varier d'une année à l'autre *ou* selon les années/d'un lieu à l'autre *ou* selon les lieux
(**b**) *(change, alter)* changer, se modifier; **his mood varies with the weather** il est très lunatique; **the colour of the wood varies with age** ce bois change de couleur en vieillissant
2 *vt (diet, menu)* varier; *(temperature)* faire varier

varying ['veərɪɪŋ] *adj* variable, qui varie; **with varying degrees of success** avec plus ou moins de succès

vas [væs] *(pl* **vasa** ['veɪsə]*) n Anat & Biol* canal *m*; *(for blood)* vaisseau *m*

vasal ['veɪsəl] *adj Anat* des canaux; *(of blood vessel)* vasculaire

vascular ['væskjʊlə(r)] *adj* vasculaire
►► *Bot* ***vascular bundle*** faisceau *m* fibro-vasculaire; *Med* ***vascular disease*** maladie *f* vasculaire; *Anat* ***vascular tissue*** tissu *m* vasculaire

vascularization [,væskjʊləraɪ'zeɪʃən] *n Med* vascularisation *f*

vascularize, -ise ['væskjʊlə,raɪz] *vt Med* vasculariser

vas deferens ['væs'defərenz] *(pl* **vasa deferentia** ['veɪsədefə'renʃɪə]*) n Anat* canal *m* déférent

vase [*Br* vɑːz, *Am* veɪz] *n* vase *m*

vasectomy [væ'sektəmɪ] *(pl* **vasectomies***) n* vasectomie *f*; **to have a vasectomy** subir une vasectomie

Vaseline® ['væsəliːn] **1** *n* vaseline *f*
2 *vt* enduire de vaseline, vaseliner
►► ***Vaseline® jelly*** vaseline *f*

vasoconstriction [,veɪzəʊkən'strɪkʃən] *n Med* vasoconstriction *f*

vasoconstrictor [,veɪzəʊkən'strɪktə(r)] *n* vasoconstricteur *m*

vasodilation [,veɪzəʊdaɪ'leɪʃən] *n Med* vasodilatation *f*

vasodilator [,veɪzəʊdaɪ'leɪtə(r)] *n* vasodilatateur *m*

vasomotor [,veɪzəʊ'məʊtə(r)] *adj* vasomoteur

vasopressin [,veɪzəʊ'presɪn] *n Physiol* vasopressine *f*

vasopressor [,veɪzəʊ'presə(r)] *n Med* vasopresseur *m*

vassal ['væsəl] **1** *adj* vassal
2 *n* vassal *m*
►► ***vassal state*** pays *m* vassal

vassalage ['væsəlɪdʒ] *n* vassalité *f*, vasselage *m*

vast [vɑːst] *adj* vaste, immense, énorme; **vast sums of money** des sommes *fpl* énormes, énormément d'argent; **it's a vast improvement on his last performance** c'est infiniment mieux que sa dernière interprétation; **she has vast experience in this area** elle a beaucoup d'expérience dans ce domaine

vastly ['vɑːstlɪ] *adv (wealthy)* extrêmement, immensément; *(grateful)* infiniment; *(different)* extrêmement; **the show was vastly successful** le spectacle a eu un immense succès; **he is vastly improved** *(in health)* il va infiniment mieux; *(in work, performance)* il est infiniment meilleur

vastness ['vɑːstnɪs] *n* immensité *f*

VAT [væt, ,viːeɪ'tiː] *n Br Fin (abbr* **value added tax***)* TVA *f*; **exclusive of** *or* **excluding VAT** hors TVA; **subject to VAT** soumis à la TVA; **to be VAT registered** être assujetti à la TVA
►► ***VAT credit*** crédit *m* de TVA; ***VAT man*** = inspecteur *m* de la TVA; ***VAT rate*** taux *m* de TVA; ***VAT registration number*** code *m* assujetti TVA; ***VAT return*** déclaration *f* de TVA; ***VAT statement*** état *m* TVA

vat [væt] *n* cuve *f*, bac *m*
►► ***vat dye*** matière *f* colorante insoluble

vatful ['vætfʊl] *n (quantity)* cuvée *f*

Vatican ['vætɪkən] **1** *n* **the Vatican** le Vatican; **in the Vatican** au Vatican
2 *comp (edict, bank, policy)* du Vatican; **the First/Second Vatican council** le premier/deuxième concile du Vatican
►► ***Vatican City*** l'État *m* de la cité du Vatican, le Vatican; **in Vatican City** au Vatican; *Fam Hum* ***Vatican roulette*** = méthode de contraception basée sur l'abstinence périodique

Vaticanism ['vætɪkə,nɪzəm] *n* ultramontanisme *m*

Vaticanist ['vætɪkənɪst] *n* ultramontain(e) *m,f*

vatman ['vætmæn] *(pl* **vatmen** [-men]*) n Br Fam* **the vatman** le service de la TVA

vaudeville ['vɔːdəvɪl] **1** *n Am* vaudeville *m*
2 *comp (artiste, theatre)* de vaudeville, de music-hall

vault [vɔːlt] **1** *n* (**a**) *Archit* voûte *f*; *Fig* **the vault of heaven** la voûte céleste
(**b**) *Anat* voûte *f*
(**c**) *(cellar)* cave *f*, cellier *m*; *(burial chamber)* caveau *m*; **a family vault** un caveau de famille
(**d**) *(in bank)* chambre *f* forte; **a bank vault** les coffres *mpl* d'une banque, la salle des coffres; **the money is safely deposited in the vaults of the bank** l'argent est en sécurité dans les coffres de la banque
(**e**) *(jump)* (grand) saut *m*; *Sport* saut *m* (à la perche)
2 *vi (jump)* sauter; *Sport* sauter (à la perche); **he vaulted over the fence** il a sauté par-dessus la clôture
3 *vt* (**a**) *Archit* voûter, cintrer
(**b**) *(jump)* sauter par-dessus

vaulted ['vɔːltɪd] *adj Archit* voûté, en voûte

vaulting ['vɔːltɪŋ] **1** *n* (**a**) *Archit* voûte *f*, voûtes *fpl* (**b**) *Sport* saut *m* à la perche
2 *adj* (**a**) *Sport (pole)* de saut (**b**) *Fig Literary (arrogance)* outrecuidant; *(ambition)* démesuré
►► ***vaulting horse*** cheval-d'arçons *m inv*

var–vau

vaunt [vɔːnt] *Literary* **1** *vt* vanter, se vanter de; **her much vaunted charms** ses charmes tant vantés
2 *vi* se vanter, fanfaronner

vaunting ['vɔːntɪŋ] **1** *adj* vantard
2 *n* vantardise *f*, *Literary* jactance *f*

vavasour ['vævəsʊə(r)] *n Hist* vavasseur *m*, vassal *m*

va-va-voom [ˌvævæ'vuːm] *n Fam (of person)* punch *m*; *(of car)* nerf *m*; **the car has plenty of va-va-voom** c'est une voiture nerveuse

VC [ˌviː'siː] *n* **(a)** *Br Mil (abbr* **Victoria Cross***)* Victoria Cross *f* **(b)** *Br Univ (abbr* **vice-chancellor***)* ≃ président *m* d'université **(c)** *(abbr* **vice-chairman***)* VP *m* **(d)** *Am Hist (abbr* **Vietcong***)* Viêt-cong *mf*

V-chip *n Comput & TV* puce *f* anti-violence

vCJD [ˌviːsiːˌdʒeɪ'diː] *n Med (abbr* **new-variant Creutzfeldt-Jakob disease***)* vMCJ *m*

VCR [ˌviːsiː'ɑː(r)] *n (abbr* **video cassette recorder***)* magnétoscope *m*

VCT [ˌviːsiː'tiː] *n Fin (abbr* **venture capital trust***)* FCPR *m*

VD [ˌviː'diː] *n (UNCOUNT) (abbr* **venereal disease***)* MST *f*
►► ***VD clinic*** centre *m* de traitement des maladies vénériennes

VDT [ˌviːdiː'tiː] *n Comput (abbr* **visual display terminal***)* moniteur *m*

VDU [ˌviːdiː'juː] *n Comput (abbr* **visual display unit***)* moniteur *m*
►► *Comput* ***VDU operator*** personne *f* travaillant sur écran

veal [viːl] **1** *n* veau *m (viande)*
2 *comp* de veau

vealer ['viːlə(r)] *n* veau *m* de boucherie

Vectian ['vektɪən] *adj Geol* de l'île de Wight

vector ['vektə(r)] **1** *n* **(a)** *Math & Med* vecteur *m* **(b)** *Aviat* direction *f*
2 *comp Math* vectoriel
3 *vt Aviat* radioguider
►► *Comput* ***vector graphics*** image *f* vectorielle

vectorial [vek'tɔːrɪəl] *adj* vectoriel

VED [ˌviːiː'diː] *n (abbr* **vehicle excise duty***)* taxe *f*, impôt *m* direct

Veda ['veɪdə] *n Rel* Veda *mpl*

Vedaism ['veɪdəɪzəm] *n* védisme *m*

VE day [ˌviː'iː-] *n (abbr* **Victory in Europe Day***)* = jour de l'armistice du 8 mai 1945

Vedda ['vedə] *n* Vedda *mf*; **the Vedda** les Veddas *mpl*

vedette [vɪ'det] *n Mil & Naut* vedette *f*

Vedic ['veɪdɪk] *adj* védique

veduta [ve'duːtə] *n Art* veduta *f*, perspective *f* naturelle

vee [viː] *n* = objet en forme de V

veep [viːp] *n Am Fam* vice-président(e) ❑ *m,f*

veer [vɪə(r)] **1** *vi* **(a)** *(vehicle, road)* virer, tourner; *(ship)* virer de bord; *(wind)* tourner, changer de direction; **the car veered (over) to the left** la voiture a viré vers la *ou* à gauche; **the wind has veered (round) to the east** le vent a tourné à l'est; **the deer veered away from us** le cerf s'est éloigné de nous; **the car veered off into the ditch** la voiture a quitté la route et a basculé dans le fossé; **to veer off course** *(car)* quitter sa route; *(boat, plane, wind-surfer)* quitter sa trajectoire
(b) *Fig* **the conversation veered round to the elections** la conversation a dévié sur les élections; **the speaker kept veering off the subject** l'orateur s'éloignait sans cesse du sujet; **her mood veers between euphoria and black depression** son humeur oscille entre l'euphorie et un profond abattement *ou* va de l'euphorie à un profond abattement
2 *vt* **(a)** *(ship, car)* faire virer
(b) *(cable)* filer
►**veer round** *vi (vehicle, person)* faire demi-tour; *(wind)* changer de direction; *Fig (person)* se ranger à l'opinion contraire

veery ['vɪːrɪ] *n Orn* grive *f* fauve

veg [vedʒ] *Fam* **1** *npl (vegetables)* légumes ❑ *mpl*; **you should eat plenty of fruit and veg** il faut manger beaucoup de fruits et de légumes
2 *vi* traîner, glandouiller; **I just feel like vegging in front of the TV tonight** j'ai envie de m'installer devant la télé ce soir
►**veg out** *vi Fam* traîner, glandouiller

Vega ['viːgə] *n Astron* Véga *m*

vegan ['viːgən] **1** *n* végétalien(enne) *m,f*
2 *adj* végétalien

veganism ['viːgənɪzəm] *n* végétalisme *m*

vegeburger ['vedʒɪˌbɜːgə(r)] *n* hamburger *m* végétarien

vegetable ['vedʒtəbəl] **1** *n* **(a)** *Culin & Hort* légume *m*; *Bot (plant)* végétal *m*; **early vegetables** primeurs *mpl*; **green vegetables** légumes *mpl* verts; **root vegetables** racines *fpl (comestibles)*
(b) *Fam Fig (person)* légume *m*; **the accident has left her a vegetable** depuis son accident, elle est comme un légume
2 *comp (matter)* végétal; *(soup)* de légumes; **he's reduced to a vegetable existence** il est réduit à un état végétatif
►► ***vegetable butter*** beurre *m* végétal; ***vegetable dish*** plat *m* à légumes, légumier *m*; ***vegetable garden*** (jardin *m*) potager *m*; ***vegetable knife*** couteau *m* à légumes, éplucheur *m*; ***vegetable marrow*** courge *f*; ***vegetable oil*** huile *f* végétale; ***vegetable peeler*** couteau *m* à légumes, éplucheur *m*; ***vegetable slicer*** coupe-légumes *m inv*; ***vegetable wax*** cire *f* végétale

vegetal ['vedʒɪtəl] *adj* végétal

vegetarian [ˌvedʒɪ'teərɪən] **1** *n* végétarien(enne) *m,f*
2 *adj* végétarien

vegetarianism [ˌvedʒɪ'teərɪənɪzəm] *n* végétarisme *m*

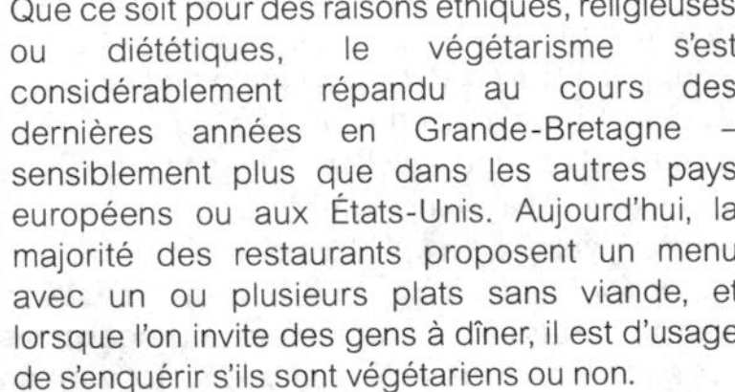

VEGETARIANISM

Que ce soit pour des raisons éthiques, religieuses ou diététiques, le végétarisme s'est considérablement répandu au cours des dernières années en Grande-Bretagne – sensiblement plus que dans les autres pays européens ou aux États-Unis. Aujourd'hui, la majorité des restaurants proposent un menu avec un ou plusieurs plats sans viande, et lorsque l'on invite des gens à dîner, il est d'usage de s'enquérir s'ils sont végétariens ou non.

vegetate ['vedʒɪteɪt] *vi also Fig* végéter

vegetation [ˌvedʒɪ'teɪʃən] *n* végétation *f*

vegetative ['vedʒɪtətɪv] *adj also Fig* végétatif
►► *Physiol* ***vegetative nervous system*** système *m* nerveux végétatif; *Bot* ***vegetative propagation*** multiplication *f* végétative

vegetatively ['vedʒɪtətɪvlɪ] *adv* végétativement

veggie ['vedʒɪ] *Fam (abbr* **vegetarian***)* **1** *n* végétarien(enne) ❑ *m,f*
2 *adj* végétarien ❑

veggieburger ['vedʒɪˌbɜːgə(r)] *n* hamburger *m* végétarien

vehemence ['viːɪməns] *n (of emotions)* ardeur *f*, véhémence *f*; *(of actions, gestures)* violence *f*, véhémence *f*; *(of language)* véhémence *f*, passion *f*

vehement ['viːɪmənt] *adj (emotions)* ardent, passionné, véhément; *(actions, gestures)* violent, véhément; *(language)* véhément, passionné; **she launched a vehement attack on the government** elle s'est lancée dans une attaque véhémente contre *ou* elle a violemment attaqué le gouvernement

vehemently ['viːɪməntlɪ] *adv (speak)* avec passion, avec véhémence; *(deny)* avec véhémence; *(attack)* avec violence; *(gesticulate)* frénétiquement

vehicle ['viːɪkəl] *n* **(a)** *(gen) & Aut* véhicule *m*; **heavy vehicles turning** *(sign)* passage d'engins; **vehicle emissions** gaz *mpl* d'échappement
(b) *Pharm* véhicule *m*
(c) *Fig* véhicule *m*; **the newspaper is merely a vehicle for state propaganda** le journal n'est qu'un véhicule de la propagande gouvernementale; **the play is merely a vehicle for him/his talents** la pièce n'est qu'un moyen de le mettre en valeur/de mettre ses talents en valeur
►► ***vehicle excise duty*** taxe *f*, impôt *m* direct; ***vehicle identification number*** numéro *m* d'immatriculation

vehicular [vɪ'hɪkjʊlə(r)] *adj (gen) & Aut* de véhicules, de voitures
►► ***vehicular access*** accès *m* aux véhicules; ***vehicular traffic*** circulation *f* automobile

veil [veɪl] **1** *n* **(a)** *(over face)* voile *m*; *(on hat)* voilette *f*; **she was wearing a veil** elle était voilée **(b)** *Fig* voile *m*; **to draw a veil over sth** mettre un voile sur qch; **under the veil of secrecy** sous le voile du secret; **a veil of mist/of silence** un voile de brume/de silence **(c)** *Rel* **to take the veil** prendre le voile
2 *vt* **(a)** *(face)* voiler, couvrir d'un voile; **to veil oneself** se voiler **(b)** *Fig (truth, feelings, intentions)* voiler, dissimuler, masquer

veiled [veɪld] *adj* **(a)** *(wearing a veil)* voilé **(b)** *(hidden, disguised → expression, meaning)* voilé, caché; *(→ allusion, insult)* voilé; *(→ hostility)* sourd

veiling ['veɪlɪŋ] *n* **(a)** *Tex* voilage *m* **(b)** *Fig (of truth)* dissimulation *f*

vein [veɪn] *n* **(a)** *Anat* veine *f*; **she has Polish blood in her veins** elle a du sang polonais dans les veines
(b) *(on insect wing)* veine *f*; *(on leaf)* nervure *f*
(c) *(in cheese, wood, marble)* veine *f*; *(of ore, mineral)* filon *m*, veine *f*; **a rich vein of irony runs through the book** le livre est parcouru d'une ironie sous-jacente
(d) *(mood)* esprit *m*; *(style)* veine *f*, style *m*; **in a more frivolous vein** dans un esprit plus frivole; **in the same vein** dans le même style *ou* la même veine; **written in an imaginative vein** écrit dans un style plein d'imagination

veined [veɪnd] *adj* **(a)** *(hand, skin)* veiné **(b)** *(leaf)* nervuré **(c)** *(cheese, stone)* marbré, veiné; **green-veined marble** marbre *m* veiné de vert

veining ['veɪnɪŋ] *n (UNCOUNT)* **(a)** *Anat* veines *fpl* **(b)** *Bot (on leaf)* nervures *fpl* **(c)** *(in wood, marble, cheese)* veines *fpl*

veiny ['veɪnɪ] *adj (leaf, wood)* veineux

velamen [və'leɪmən] *n Bot* voile *m*

velar ['viːlə(r)] *adj Anat & Ling* vélaire

velarium [vɪ'leərɪəm] *(pl* **velaria** [-rɪə]*)* *n Antiq* vélarium *m*

velarization [ˌviːləraɪ'zeɪʃən] *n Ling* vélarisation *f*

velarize, -ise ['viːləraɪz] *vt Ling* vélariser

Velcro® ['velkrəʊ] *n (bande f)* Velcro® *m*

veld, veldt [velt] *n* veld *m*, veldt *m*

vellum ['veləm] **1** *n* vélin *m*
2 *adj* de vélin
►► ***vellum paper*** papier *m* vélin

veloce [və'ləʊtʃeɪ] *Mus* **1** *adj* veloce
2 *adv* veloce

velocipede [vɪ'lɒsɪpiːd] *n* vélocipède *m*

velocity [vɪ'lɒsətɪ] *(pl* **velocities***)* *n* vélocité *f*

velodrome ['velədrəʊm] *n* vélodrome *m*

velour, velours [və'lʊə(r)] *(pl* **velours** [-'lʊəz]*)* **1** *n* velours *m*
2 *comp* de *ou* en velours

velum ['viːləm] *n Anat* voile *m* du palais

velvet ['velvɪt] **1** *n* **(a)** *(material)* velours *m*; **as smooth as velvet** *(skin)* doux comme du *ou* le velours; *(drink)* velouté; *Fam Fig* **to be on velvet** jouer sur le velours
(b) *Am Fam (profit)* bénef *m*; *(easy money)* argent *m* facile ❑
2 *comp (curtains, dress)* de *ou* en velours; *Fig (skin, voice)* velouté, de velours; **to walk with a velvet tread** marcher à pas de velours *ou* à pas feutrés; *Fig* **an iron hand in a velvet glove** une main de fer dans un gant de velours
►► *Entom* ***velvet ant*** mutille *f*; *Hist* ***the Velvet Revolution*** la Révolution de Velours; *Orn* ***velvet scoter*** macreuse *f* brune

velveteen [ˌvelvɪ'tiːn] **1** *n* veloutine *f*
2 *adj* en *ou* de veloutine

velvety ['velvɪtɪ] *adj (cloth, complexion, texture)* velouteux, velouté; *Fig (cream, voice)* velouté

vena cava [ˌviːnə'keɪvə] *(pl* **venae cavae** [ˌviːnɪ'keɪviː]*)* *n Anat* veine *f* cave

venal ['viːnəl] *adj* vénal

venality [viː'nælətɪ] *n* vénalité *f*

venation [vɪ'neɪʃən] *n Bot & Zool* nervation *f*, nervulation *f*

vend [vend] *vt Law or Formal* vendre

vendace ['vendeɪs] *n Ich* corégone *m* blanc

Vendean [ven'diːən] *Hist & Geog* **1** *adj* vendéen
2 *n* Vendéen(enne) *m,f*

vendee [ven'diː] *n Law* acquéreur *m*

vendetta [ven'detə] *n* vendetta *f*; **to wage a vendetta against sb** mener une vendetta contre qn

vendible ['vendɪbəl] *adj Formal* commercialisable, vendable

vending ['vendɪŋ] *n Law or Formal* vente *f*
▸▸ ***vending machine*** distributeur *m* automatique

vendor ['vendɔ:(r)] *n* (**a**) *Com* marchand(e) *m,f*; **ice-cream vendor** marchand *m* de glaces (**b**) *(machine)* distributeur *m* automatique (**c**) *Law & Fin* vendeur(euse) *m,f* (**d**) *Comput* fournisseur *m*
▸▸ *Law & Fin* ***vendor's lien*** privilège *m* du vendeur; *Law & Fin* ***vendor's shares*** actions *fpl* d'apport *ou* de fondation

vendue ['vendju:] *n Am* vente *f* aux enchères

veneer [və'nɪə(r)] **1** *n* (**a**) *(of wood)* placage *m* (de bois); **walnut veneer** placage *m* noyer (**b**) *Fig* vernis *m*, masque *m*, apparence *f*; **a veneer of politeness/respectability** un vernis de politesse/respectabilité
2 *vt* plaquer; **veneered in** *or* **with walnut** plaqué noyer

veneering [və'nɪərɪŋ] *n* (**a**) *(process)* placage *m* (**b**) *(layer of wood)* placage *m*, revêtement *m*; *(wood)* bois *m* de placage
▸▸ ***veneering hammer*** marteau *m* à plaquer; ***veneering press*** presse *f* à plaquer; ***veneering wood*** bois *m* de placage

venepuncture ['venɪ,pʌŋktʃə(r)] *n Med* ponction *f* d'une veine

venerability [,venərə'bɪlɪtɪ] *n* vénérabilité *f*

venerable ['venərəbəl] *adj (gen) & Rel* vénérable

venerableness ['venərəbəlnɪs] *n* vénérabilité *f*

venerate ['venəreɪt] *vt* vénérer

veneration [,venə'reɪʃən] *n* vénération *f*

venereal [vɪ'nɪərɪəl] *adj* vénérien
▸▸ ***venereal disease*** maladie *f* vénérienne

venereologist [vɪ,nɪərɪ'ɒlədʒɪst] *n* vénéréologue *mf*, vénérologue *mf*

venereology [vɪ,nɪərɪ'ɒlədʒɪ] *n* vénérologie *f*, vénéréologie *f*

venerologist [vɪ,nɪə'rɒlədʒɪst] *n* vénérologue *mf*, vénéréologue *mf*

venerology [vɪ,nɪə'rɒlədʒɪ] *n* vénérologie *f*, vénéréologie *f*

venery ['venərɪ] *n Arch* (**a**) *(hunting)* vénerie *f*, chasse *f*; **hounds of venery** chiens *mpl* courants (**b**) *(sexual pleasure)* plaisirs *mpl* sexuels

venesection ['venɪsekʃən] *n Med* phlébotomie *f*

Venetian [vɪ'ni:ʃən] **1** *n* Vénitien(enne) *m,f*
2 *adj* vénitien, de Venise
▸▸ ***Venetian blind*** store *m* vénitien; ***Venetian glass*** verre *m ou* cristal *m* de Venise; *Archit* ***Venetian window*** (fenêtre *f*) serlienne *f*

Veneto ['venətəʊ] *n* Vénétie *f*

Venezuela [,venɪ'zweɪlə] *n* Venezuela *m*; **in Venezuela** au Venezuela

Venezuelan [,venɪ'zweɪlən] **1** *n* Vénézuélien(enne) *m,f*
2 *adj* vénézuélien
3 *comp (embassy, history)* du Venezuela

vengeance ['vendʒəns] *n* (**a**) *(revenge)* vengeance *f*; **to take** *or* **to wreak vengeance on** *or* **upon sb (for sth)** se venger de qn (pour qch); **to seek vengeance for sth** vouloir tirer vengeance de qch, chercher à se venger de qch (**b**) *(idiom)* **with a vengeance** très fort; **by then it was raining with a vengeance** à ce moment-là, la pluie tombait à torrents; **to work with a vengeance** travailler d'arrache-pied *ou* à un rythme d'enfer; **she's back with a vengeance** elle fait un retour en force

vengeful ['vendʒfʊl] *adj* vindicatif

vengefully ['vendʒfʊlɪ] *adv* d'une manière vindicative

vengefulness ['vendʒfʊlnɪs] *n (of action)* caractère *m* vindicatif; *(of person)* esprit *m* de vengeance

venial ['vi:nɪəl] *adj (gen) & Rel* véniel

veniality [,vi:nɪ'ælətɪ] *n* caractère *m* véniel

Venice ['venɪs] *n* Venise

venipuncture = **venepuncture**

venire [vɪ'naɪrɪ] *n Law* (**a**) *(writ)* injonction *f* d'assigner un jury (**b**) *Am (list of jurors)* tableau *m ou* liste *f* des jurés assignés

venisection ['venɪsekʃən] *n* phlébotomie *f*

venison ['venɪzən] *n* venaison *f*; **haunch of venison** quartier *m* de chevreuil

Venn diagram [ven-] *n* diagramme *m* de Venn

vennel ['venəl] *n Scot* ruelle *f*, vennelle *f*

venom ['venəm] *n also Fig* venin *m*; *Fig* **with venom** d'une manière venimeuse

venomous ['venəməs] *adj* venimeux; *Fig (remark, insult)* venimeux, malveillant; *(look)* haineux, venimeux; **he has a venomous tongue** il a une langue de vipère

venomously ['venəməslɪ] *adv* d'une manière venimeuse

venose ['vi:nəʊs] *adj (hand, arm)* aux veines saillantes

venous ['vi:nəs] *adj* veineux

vent [vent] **1** *n* (**a**) *(outlet → for air, gas, liquid)* orifice *m*, conduit *m*; *(→ in chimney)* conduit *m*, tuyau *m*; *(→ in volcano)* cheminée *f*; *(→ in barrel)* trou *m*; *(→ for ventilation)* conduit *m* d'aération; *Ich & Orn (of fish, bird)* orifice *m* anal
(**b**) *(in jacket, skirt)* fente *f*
(**c**) *(idiom)* **to give vent to sth** donner *ou* laisser libre cours à qch; **he gave full vent to his feelings** il a donné *ou* laissé libre cours à ses émotions; **she gave vent to her anger** elle a laissé échapper sa colère
2 *vt* (**a**) *(barrel)* pratiquer un trou dans, trouer; *(pipe, radiator)* purger
(**b**) *(release → smoke)* laisser échapper; *(→ gas)* évacuer
(**c**) *Fig (express → anger)* décharger; **to vent one's anger/one's spleen on sb** décharger sa colère/sa bile sur qn

vented ['ventɪd] *adj* pourvu d'orifices

venter ['ventə(r)] *n* (**a**) *Arch (womb)* ventre *m*; *Law* **his two sons by another venter** ses deux fils d'un autre lit (**b**) *Anat (of bone)* dépression *f* (**c**) *Bot (of archegonium)* ventre *m*

ventifact ['ventɪfækt] *n Geol* caillou *m* éolisé

ventil ['ventɪl] *n Mus (in wind instrument, organ)* anche *f*

ventilate ['ventɪleɪt] *vt* (**a**) *(room)* ventiler, aérer; **a well/badly ventilated room** une pièce bien/mal aérée (**b**) *Fig (controversy, question)* agiter (au grand jour); *(grievance)* étaler (au grand jour) (**c**) *Med (blood)* oxygéner

ventilating ['ventɪ,leɪtɪŋ] **1** *adj* aérant, aérateur
2 *n* ventilation *f*, aération *f*, aérage *m*
▸▸ ***ventilating engine*** machine *f* à ventiler; ***ventilating fan*** ventilateur *m*; ***ventilating pipe*** manche *f* à vent *ou* à air; *Bot* ***ventilating tissue*** parenchyme *m* aérifère

ventilation [,ventɪ'leɪʃən] *n* aération *f*, ventilation *f*; **a ventilation shaft** un conduit d'aération *ou* de ventilation

ventilator ['ventɪ,leɪtə(r)] *n* (**a**) *(in room, building)* ventilateur *m*; *Aut* déflecteur *m* (**b**) *Med* respirateur *m* (artificiel); **to be on a ventilator** être sur respirateur

Ventimiglia [,ventɪ'mɪlɪə] *n* Vintimille

venting screw ['ventɪŋ-] *n Aut* vis *f* de mise à l'air libre *ou* de purge

ventral ['ventrəl] *adj* ventral
▸▸ *Ich* ***ventral fin*** nageoire *f* pelvienne, nageoire *f* abdominale

ventrally ['ventrəlɪ] *adv* ventralement

ventricle ['ventrɪkəl] *n Anat* ventricule *m*

ventricose ['ventrɪkəʊs] *adj Bot & Zool* bombé, renflé

ventricular [ven'trɪkjʊlə(r)] *adj Anat* ventriculaire

ventriloquism [ven'trɪləkwɪzəm] *n* ventriloquie *f*

ventriloquist [ven'trɪləkwɪst] *n* ventriloque *mf*; **ventriloquist's dummy** marionnette *f* de ventriloque

ventriloquy [ven'trɪləkwɪ] = **ventriloquism**

venture ['ventʃə(r)] **1** *n* (**a**) *(undertaking)* entreprise *f* périlleuse *ou* risquée; *(adventure)* aventure *f*; *(project)* projet *m*, entreprise *f*; **his latest film venture** sa dernière entreprise cinématographique; **it's his first venture into politics** c'est la première fois qu'il s'aventure dans la politique; **this venture into advertising/fiction** cette incursion dans la publicité/fiction
(**b**) *Com & Fin (firm)* entreprise *f*; **a business venture** une entreprise commerciale, un coup d'essai commercial
(**c**) *(idiom)* **at a venture** au hasard
2 *vt* (**a**) *(risk → fortune, life)* hasarder, risquer; **he ventured a glance at her** il risqua un coup d'œil dans sa direction; *Prov* **nothing ventured nothing gained** qui ne risque rien n'a rien
(**b**) *(proffer → opinion, suggestion)* hasarder, avancer, risquer; **she didn't dare venture an opinion on the subject** elle n'a pas osé exprimer sa pensée à ce sujet; **if I may venture a guess/an opinion** si je peux me permettre d'avancer une hypothèse/une opinion
(**c**) *(dare)* oser; **to venture to do sth** s'aventurer *ou* se hasarder à faire qch; **he ventured to contradict her** il a osé la contredire
3 *vi* (**a**) *(embark)* se lancer; **the government has ventured on a new defence policy** le gouvernement s'est lancé dans *ou* a entrepris une nouvelle politique de défense; **to venture into politics** se lancer dans la politique
(**b**) *(go)* **to venture in/out** prendre le risque d'entrer/de sortir, se risquer à entrer/à sortir; **I wouldn't venture out of doors in this weather** je ne me risquerais pas à sortir par ce temps; **don't venture too far across the ice** ne va pas trop loin sur la glace; **don't venture too far from the beach** ne t'éloigne pas trop de la plage; **he ventured into the woods** il s'est hasardé dans les bois; *Literary* **the explorers ventured forth into the jungle** les explorateurs se sont lancés dans la jungle
▸▸ *Fin* ***venture capital*** capital-risque *m*; ***venture capital company*** société *f* à capital-risque; ***venture capital trust*** fonds *m* commun de placement à risques; *Fin* ***venture capitalist*** pourvoyeur(euse) *m,f* de capital-risque, spécialiste *mf* de la prise de risques *(dans la finance)*; *Br* **Venture Scout** éclaireur *m (de grade supérieur)*

venturer ['ventʃərə(r)] *n* (**a**) *(adventurer)* aventurier(ère) *m,f*; **venturers into unknown lands** ceux qui s'aventurent en pays inconnus (**b**) *Hist (trader)* marchand *m* aventurier

venturesome ['ventʃəsəm] *adj Literary* (**a**) *(daring → nature, person)* aventureux, entreprenant (**b**) *(hazardous → action, journey)* hasardeux, risqué

Venturi [ven'tjʊərɪ] *n Phys* venturi *m*
▸▸ ***Venturi tube*** venturi *m*

venue ['venju:] *n* (**a**) *(setting)* lieu *m* (de rendez-vous *ou* de réunion); *(for football match)* terrain *m*; *(for tennis)* court *m*; **he hasn't decided on a venue for the concert** il n'a pas décidé où le concert aura lieu; **they've changed the venue for tonight's meeting** ils ont changé le lieu de réunion de ce soir; **the band have played at all of the biggest London venues** l'orchestre a joué dans toutes les grandes salles (de concert) de Londres (**b**) *Law* lieu *m* du procès; **to lay the venue** désigner la cour qui sera saisie de l'affaire

venule ['venju:l] *n Anat* veinule *f*

Venus ['vi:nəs] **1** *n Astron* Vénus *f*
2 *pr n Myth* Vénus
▸▸ *Bot* ***Venus's comb*** peigne *m* de Vénus; *Zool* ***Venus's flowerbasket*** euplectelle *f*; ***Venus flytrap*** dionée *f*; *Zool* ***Venus shell*** Vénus *m*

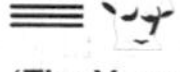

'The Venus de Milo' 'la Vénus de Milo'

Venusian [vɪ'nju:zɪən] **1** *n* Vénusien(ienne) *m,f*
2 *adj* vénusien

veracious [və'reɪʃəs] *adj* véridique

veracity [və'ræsɪtɪ], **veraciousness** [və'reɪʃəsnɪs] *n* véracité *f*

veranda, verandah [və'rændə] *n* véranda *f*

veratrine ['verətri:n] *n Chem etc* vératrine *f*

veratrum [və'reɪtrəm] *n Bot & Pharm* vératre *m*

verb [vɜ:b] *n* verbe *m*
▸▸ ***verb phrase*** syntagme *m ou* groupe *m* verbal

verbal ['vɜ:bəl] **1** *adj* (**a**) *(spoken → account, agreement, promise)* verbal, oral; *(→ confession)* oral; *Fam* **to have verbal** *Br* **diarrhoea** *or Am* **diarrhea** être atteint de diarrhée verbale
(**b**) *(literal → copy, translation)* mot à mot, littéral, textuel
(**c**) *Gram* verbal
2 *n Br Fam* **to give sb verbal** *(shout at)* engueuler qn; **they were given some verbal** ils se sont fait engueuler
3 *vt Br Fam (of police)* = impliquer dans un crime en citant devant la cour un prétendu aveu
4 verbals *npl Law* aveux *mpl* faits oralement *ou* de vive voix

►► **verbal memory** mémoire *f* auditive; *Gram* **verbal noun** nom *m* verbal; **verbal skills** aptitudes *fpl* à l'oral

verbalism ['vɜːbəˌlɪzəm] *n* (**a**) *(expression)* expression *f*, locution *f* (**b**) *(cliché)* cliché *m* (**c**) *(overemphasis on words)* verbalisme *m*

verbalization [ˌvɜːbəlaɪ'zeɪʃən] *n (of feelings, ideas)* verbalisation *f*

verbalize, -ise ['vɜːbəlaɪz] *vt (feelings, ideas)* verbaliser, exprimer par des mots

verbally ['vɜːbəlɪ] *adv* (**a**) *(orally)* verbalement, oralement; **to be verbally abused** se faire insulter verbalement; **to agree verbally to do sth** se mettre d'accord verbalement pour faire qch; **verbally deficient** illettré, analphabète (**b**) *(as a verb)* en tant que verbe

verbatim [vɜː'beɪtɪm] **1** *adj* mot pour mot

2 *adv* textuellement; **to report a speech verbatim** rendre compte mot à mot d'un discours

►► **verbatim report** procès-verbal *m (d'une réunion)*

verbena [vɜː'biːnə] *n (herb, plant)* verveine *f*; *(genus)* verbénacées *fpl*

verbiage ['vɜːbɪɪdʒ] *n* verbiage *m*

verbigeration [vɜːˌbɪdʒə'reɪʃən] *n Med* verbigération *f*

verbomania [ˌvɜːbə'meɪnɪə] *n Psy* verbomanie *f*

verbose [vɜː'bəʊs] *adj* verbeux, prolixe

verbosely [vɜː'bəʊslɪ] *adv* avec verbosité, verbeusement; **verbosely worded** verbeux

verbosity [vɜː'bɒsətɪ] *n* verbosité *f*

verdancy ['vɜːdənsɪ] *n Literary* verdure *f*

verdant ['vɜːdənt] *adj Literary* verdoyant

verd-antique [vɜːd-] *n Miner* vert *m* antique, vert *m* de Florence

verdict ['vɜːdɪkt] *n* (**a**) *Law* verdict *m*; **to reach a verdict** arriver à un verdict; **a verdict of guilty/not guilty** un verdict de culpabilité/non-culpabilité; **the jury returned a verdict of not guilty/guilty** le jury a déclaré l'accusé non coupable/coupable; **open verdict** *(at inquest)* = jugement qui ne formule aucune conclusion sur les circonstances dans lesquelles la mort a eu lieu

(**b**) *Fig (conclusion)* verdict *m*, jugement *m*; **to give one's verdict on sth** se prononcer sur qch; **what is your/the verdict?** quel est votre/le verdict?

verdigris ['vɜːdɪgrɪs] **1** *n* vert-de-gris *m inv*

2 *adj* vert-de-grisé

verdin ['vɜːdɪn] *n Orn* auripare *m* verdin

verdure ['vɜːdʒə(r)] *n Literary* verdure *f*

verge [vɜːdʒ] **1** *n* (**a**) *(edge → of lawn)* bord *m*; *(→ of forest)* orée *f*; *Br (→ by roadside)* accotement *m*, bas-côté *m*; **grass verge** *(round flowerbed)* bordure *f* en gazon; *(by roadside)* herbe *f* au bord de la route; *(in park, garden)* bande *f* d'herbe; *Br Aut* **soft verges** *(road sign)* accotement instable; **the car skidded onto the verge** la voiture a dérapé et est montée sur l'accotement *ou* sur le bas-côté

(**b**) *Fig (brink)* bord *m*; *(threshold)* seuil *m*; **to be on the verge of tears** être au bord des larmes; **to be on the verge of bankruptcy/of a nervous breakdown** être au bord de la faillite/de la dépression nerveuse; **to be on the verge of adolescence/old age** être au seuil de l'adolescence/de la vieillesse; **to be on the verge of doing sth** être sur le point de faire qch; **I was on the verge of telling him** j'étais sur le point de lui dire, j'étais à deux doigts de lui dire; **he's on the verge of sixty** il frôle *ou* frise la soixantaine; **the country has been brought to the verge of civil war** le pays a été amené au seuil de la guerre civile

2 *vt (road, lawn)* border

►**verge on, verge upon** *vt insep (be close to)* côtoyer, s'approcher de; **they are verging on bankruptcy** ils sont au bord de la faillite, la faillite les menace; **his feeling was one of panic verging on hysteria** il ressentait une sorte de panique proche de l'hystérie *ou* qui frôlait l'hystérie; **she's verging on thirty** elle frise la trentaine; **green verging on blue** du vert qui tire sur le bleu

vergency ['vɜːdʒənsɪ] *n Opt* vergence *f*

verger ['vɜːdʒə(r)] *n Rel* bedeau *m*, suisse *m*; *(at ceremony)* huissier *m* à verge, massier *m*

Vergil = **Virgil**

veridical [və'rɪdɪkəl] *adj* véridique

verifiability [ˌverɪfaɪə'bɪlɪtɪ] *n* vérifiabilité *f*

verifiable [ˌverɪ'faɪəbəl] *adj* vérifiable

verifiableness [ˌverɪ'faɪəbəlnɪs] *n* vérifiabilité *f*

verification [ˌverɪfɪ'keɪʃən] *n* vérification *f*

verifier ['verɪˌfaɪə(r)] *n* (**a**) *(person)* vérificateur(-trice) *m,f* (**b**) *Comput (machine)* vérificatrice *f*, vérifieuse *f*

►► **verifier operator** vérificateur(trice) *m,f*, vérifieur(euse) *m,f*

verify ['verɪfaɪ] *(pt & pp* **verified***) vt (prove → information, rumour)* vérifier; *(confirm → truth)* vérifier, confirmer; **this verifies my worst suspicions** ceci vérifie *ou* confirme mes pires soupçons; **I have witnesses who can verify what I have said** j'ai des témoins qui peuvent confirmer mes dires

verily ['verəlɪ] *adv Arch* vraiment, véritablement

verisimilar [ˌverɪ'sɪmɪlə(r)] *adj Formal* vraisemblable

verisimilitude [ˌverɪsɪ'mɪlɪtjuːd] *n Formal* vraisemblance *f*

verism ['vɪərɪzəm] *n* vérisme *m*

veritable ['verɪtəbəl] *adj* véritable; **he is a veritable genius** c'est un véritable *ou* un vrai génie

veritably ['verɪtəblɪ] *adv* véritablement

verity ['verətɪ] *(pl* **verities***) n Formal* vérité *f*

verjuice ['vɜːdʒuːs] *n* verjus *m*; *Fig* **she looked vinegar and verjuice** *(manner)* elle avait l'air acariâtre; *(gaze)* elle eut un regard aigre

►► **verjuice grape** verjus *m*

vermicelli [ˌvɜːmɪ'selɪ] *n (UNCOUNT)* vermicelle *m*, vermicelles *mpl*

vermicide ['vɜːmɪsaɪd] *n* vermicide *m*

vermicular [vɜː'mɪkjʊlə(r)] *adj* (**a**) *(worm-like)* vermiculaire (**b**) *Med* vermiculaire (**c**) *Archit* vermiculé

vermiculated [vɜː'mɪkjʊˌleɪtɪd] *adj* (**a**) *(worm-eaten)* vermoulu, piqué des vers (**b**) *Archit & Zool* vermiculé

vermiculite [vɜː'mɪkjʊlaɪt] *n Miner* vermiculite *f*

vermiculture ['vɜːmɪkʌltʃə(r)] *n* vermiculture *f*

vermiform ['vɜːmɪfɔːm] *adj* vermiforme

vermifugal [ˌvɜːmɪ'fjuːgəl] *adj* vermifuge

vermifuge ['vɜːmɪfjuːdʒ] *n* vermifuge *m*

vermilion, vermillion [və'mɪlɪən] **1** *n* vermillon *m*

2 *adj* vermillon *(inv)*

►► *Orn* **vermilion flycatcher** tyran *m* écarlate

vermin ['vɜːmɪn] *npl* (**a**) *(rodents)* animaux *mpl* nuisibles; *(insects)* vermine *f* (**b**) *Pej (people)* vermine *f*, racaille *f*

verminous ['vɜːmɪnəs] *adj* (**a**) *(place)* infesté de vermine *ou* d'animaux nuisibles, pouilleux; *(clothes)* pouilleux, couvert de vermine; *Med (disease)* vermineux (**b**) *Pej (person)* infect, ignoble

vermis ['vɜːmɪs] *(pl* **vermes** [-miːz]*) n Anat* vermis *m*

Vermont [vɜː'mɒnt] *n* le Vermont; **in Vermont** dans le Vermont

vermouth [vɜː'muːθ] *n* vermouth *m*

vernacular [və'nækjʊlə(r)] **1** *n* (**a**) *Ling* (langue *f*) vernaculaire *m*; *Ling* **in the vernacular** en langue vernaculaire; *(everyday language)* en langage courant; *(not Latin)* en langue vulgaire (**b**) *(jargon)* jargon *m*; **the sporting vernacular** le jargon sportif (**c**) *Bot & Zool* nom *m* vernaculaire (**d**) *Archit* style *m* typique (du pays)

2 *adj* (**a**) *Bot, Ling & Zool* vernaculaire (**b**) *(architecture, style)* indigène

vernal ['vɜːnəl] *adj Literary (flowers, woods, breeze)* printanier

►► **vernal equinox** équinoxe *m* de printemps

vernalization [ˌvɜːnəlaɪ'zeɪʃən] *n Agr & Hort* vernalisation *f*

vernation [vɜː'neɪʃən] *n Bot* vernation *f*, préfoliation *f*

vernier ['vɜːnɪə(r)] *n* vernier *m*

Verona [və'rəʊnə] *n* Vérone

veronal ['verənəl] *n Pharm* véronal *m*

Veronese [ˌverə'neɪzɪ] *pr n* Véronèse

veronica [və'rɒnɪkə] *n Bot* véronique *f*

verruca [və'ruːkə] *(pl* **verrucas** *or* **verrucae** [-kaɪ]*) n* verrue *f* (plantaire)

versant ['vɜːsənt] *n (of mountain)* versant *m*

versatile ['vɜːsətaɪl] *adj* (**a**) *(person)* aux talents variés, doué dans tous les domaines; *(mind)* souple; *(tool)* polyvalent, à usages multiples; *(dress, jacket → which can be worn anywhere)* passe-partout; *(→ which has detachable parts, is reversible etc)* polyvalent; **a politician has to be very versatile** un politicien doit avoir des talents variés (**b**) *Bot* versatile (**c**) *Zool* mobile, pivotant

versatility [ˌvɜːsə'tɪlətɪ] *n* (**a**) *(of person)* faculté *f* d'adaptation, variété *f* de talents; *(of mind)* souplesse *f*; *(of tool)* polyvalence *f* (**b**) *Bot & Zool* versatilité *f*

verse [vɜːs] **1** *n* (**a**) *(stanza → of poem)* strophe *f*; *(→ of song)* couplet *m*; *(→ in bible)* verset *m* (**b**) *(UNCOUNT) (poetry)* vers *mpl*, poésie *f*; **in verse** en vers; **free verse** vers *mpl* libres

2 *comp (line, epic)* en vers

versed [vɜːst] *adj* **versed in** *(knowledgeable)* versé dans; *(experienced)* rompu à; **he is well/not very well versed in current affairs** il est/n'est pas très au courant de l'actualité, *Formal* il est très/peu versé dans les questions d'actualité; **I am well versed in his ways** je le connais bien, je sais bien comment il est

►► *Math* **versed sine** sinus *m* verse

versicle ['vɜːsɪkəl] *n* (**a**) *Rel* verset *m* (**b**) *(short verse)* vers *m* court

versicoloured, *Am* **versicolored** ['vɜːsɪˌkʌləd] *adj* versicolore

versification [ˌvɜːsɪfɪ'keɪʃən] *n* versification *f*

versifier ['vɜːsɪˌfaɪə(r)] *n Pej* versificateur(trice) *m,f*

versify ['vɜːsɪfaɪ] *(pt & pp* **versified***)* **1** *vt* versifier, mettre en vers

2 *vi* rimer, faire des vers

versifying ['vɜːsɪˌfaɪɪŋ] *n* versification *f*, mise *f* en vers

versin ['vɜːsɪn], **versine** ['vɜːsaɪn] *n Math* sinus *m* verse

version ['vɜːʃən] *n* (**a**) *(account of events)* version *f*; **her version differs from mine** sa version des faits diffère de la mienne

(**b**) *(form → of book, song)* version *f*; **did you see the film in the original version?** est-ce que vous avez vu le film dans sa *ou* en version originale?; **the screen** *or* **film version of the book** l'adaptation cinématographique du livre; *Fig* **he looks like a younger version of his father** c'est l'image de son père en plus jeune

(**c**) *(model → of car, plane)* modèle *m*, version *f*

(**d**) *(translation)* version *f*

verso ['vɜːsəʊ] *(pl* **versos***) n (of page)* verso *m*; *(of coin, medal)* revers *m*

versus ['vɜːsəs] *prep* (**a**) *(against)* contre; **it's the government versus the trade unions** c'est le gouvernement contre les syndicats, c'est une lutte entre le gouvernement et les syndicats; *Sport* **Italy versus France** Italie-France; *Law* **Dickens versus Dickens** Dickens contre Dickens

(**b**) *(compared with)* par rapport à, par opposition à; **country versus city life** la vie à la campagne par opposition à *ou* par rapport à la vie citadine; **the advantages of living in a house versus (living in) a flat** les avantages d'une maison par rapport à un appartement; **the advantage of a higher salary versus the loss of security** l'avantage d'un salaire plus élevé en contrepartie d'une sécurité moindre

vertebra ['vɜːtɪbrə] *(pl* **vertebras** *or* **vertebrae** [-briː]*) n* vertèbre *f*

vertebral ['vɜːtɪbrəl] *adj* vertébral

►► **vertebral column** colonne *f* vertébrale

vertebrate ['vɜːtɪbreɪt] **1** *adj* vertébré

2 *n* vertébré *m*

vertex ['vɜːteks] *(pl* **vertexes** *or* **vertices** [-tɪsiːz]*) n Math* sommet *m*; *Astron* apex *m*; *Anat* vertex *m*

vertical ['vɜːtɪkəl] **1** *adj* (**a**) *(gen) & Geom* vertical; **a vertical cliff** une falaise à pic *ou* qui s'élève à la verticale; **a vertical line** une ligne verticale; **a vertical drop** une descente *ou* une pente verticale

(**b**) *Fig (structure, organization)* vertical

2 *n* verticale *f*; **out of the vertical** écarté de la verticale, hors d'aplomb

►► *Geom* **vertical angles** angles *mpl* de pointe; *Astron* **vertical circle** vertical *m*; *Fin* **vertical equity** équité *f* verticale; *Am* **vertical file** *(cabinet)* = casier des documents qui ne font pas partie de la collection permanente d'une bibliothèque; *(documents)* = documents qui ne font pas partie de la collection permanente d'une bibliothèque; *TV* ***vertical hold*** bouton *m* de commande de synchronisme vertical; *Com* ***vertical integration*** intégration *f* verticale; *Comput* ***vertical justification*** justification *f* verticale; *Fin* ***vertical spread*** écart *m* vertical; ***vertical takeoff*** décollage *m* vertical; ***vertical takeoff aircraft*** avion *m* à décollage vertical; ***vertical takeoff and landing*** *(system)* décollage *m* et atterrissage *m* vertical; *Am* ***vertical union*** confédération *f* syndicale

verticality [ˌvɜːtɪ'kælɪtɪ] *n* verticalité *f*

vertically ['vɜːtɪklɪ] *adv* verticalement; *Aviat* **to take off vertically** décoller à la verticale

verticil ['vɜːtɪsɪl] *n Bot* verticille *m*

vertiginous [vɜː'tɪdʒɪnəs] *adj Formal* vertigineux

vertigo ['vɜːtɪgəʊ] *n (UNCOUNT)* vertige *m*; **to suffer from** *or* **to have vertigo** avoir le vertige; **heights give me vertigo** l'altitude me donne le vertige

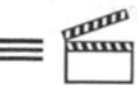

'Vertigo' *Hitchcock* 'Sueurs froides'

verumontanum [ˌverʊmɒn'teɪnəm] *n Anat* vérumontanum *m*

vervain ['vɜːveɪn] *n Bot* verveine *f*

verve [vɜːv] *n* verve *f*, brio *m*

vervet ['vɜːvɪt] *n Zool* **vervet (monkey)** vervet *m*

Very ['vɪərɪ-] *n*

►► ***Very light*** fusée *f* éclairante; ***Very pistol*** pistolet *m* lance-fusées

VERY ['verɪ] *(compar* **verier**, *superl* **veriest**) **1** *adv* (**a**) *(with adj or adv)* très, bien; **it was very pleasant** c'était très *ou* bien agréable; **was the pizza good? – very/not very** la pizza était-elle bonne? – très/pas très; **I'm not very impressed with the results** je ne suis pas très *ou* tellement impressionné par les résultats; **be very careful** faites très *ou* bien attention; **he was very hungry/thirsty** il avait très faim/soif; **I very nearly fell** j'ai bien failli tomber; **very few/little** très peu; **so very little** si peu; **there were very few of them** *(people)* ils étaient très peu nombreux; *(objets)* il y en avait très peu; **he takes very little interest in what goes on** il s'intéresse très peu à ce qui se passe; **there's very little one can do to help** on ne peut pas faire grand-chose pour aider; **there weren't very many people** il n'y avait pas beaucoup de gens, il n'y avait pas grand monde; **it isn't so very difficult** ce n'est pas tellement difficile, ce n'est pas si difficile que ça; **very good!, very well!** *(expressing agreement, consent)* très bien!; **you can't very well ask outright** tu ne peux pas vraiment demander directement; **that's all very well but...** tout ça, c'est très bien mais...

(**b**) *(with superlative - emphatic use)* **our very best wine** notre meilleur vin; **the very best of friends** les meilleurs amis du monde; **it's the very worst thing that could have happened** c'est bien ce qui pouvait arriver de pire; **the very latest designs** les créations les plus récentes; **at the very latest** au plus tard; **at the very least/most** tout au moins/plus; **the very first/last person** la (toute) première/dernière personne; **the very next day** le lendemain même, dès le lendemain; **the very next person I met was his brother** la première personne que j'ai rencontrée était son frère; **we'll stop at the very next town** nous nous arrêterons à la prochaine ville; **it's nice to have your very own car** *or* **a car of your very own** c'est agréable d'avoir sa voiture à soi; **it's my very own** c'est à moi; **the very same day** le jour même; **on the very same date** exactement à la même date; *Rel* **the Very Reverend Alan Scott** le très révérend Alan Scott

2 *adj* (**a**) *(extreme, far)* **at the very end** *(of street, row etc)* tout au bout; *(of story, month etc)* tout à la fin; **to the very end** *(in space)* jusqu'au bout; *(in time)* jusqu'à la fin; **at the very beginning** au tout début; **at the very back** tout au fond; **at the very top/bottom of the page** tout en haut/en bas de la page; **at the very bottom of the sea** au plus profond de la mer

(**b**) *(exact)* **at that very moment** juste à ce moment-là; **the very man I need** juste l'homme qu'il me faut; **those were his very words** ce sont ses propos mêmes, c'est exactement ce qu'il a dit; **this is the very room where they were murdered** c'est dans cette pièce même qu'ils ont été tués; **it was a year ago to the very day** c'était il y a un an jour pour jour; **by its very nature** par sa nature même

(**c**) *(emphatic use)* **the very idea!** quelle idée!; **the very thought of it makes me shiver** je frissonne rien que d'y penser; **it happened before my very eyes** cela s'est passé sous mes yeux; *Arch* **the veriest trifle** la moindre petite chose; *Arch* **the veriest fool could do it** le premier imbécile venu pourrait le faire

3 very much 1 *adv* (**a**) *(greatly)* beaucoup, bien; **I like French cinema very much** j'aime beaucoup le cinéma français; **I very much hope to be able to come** j'espère bien que je pourrai venir; **very much better/bigger** beaucoup mieux/plus grand; **unless I'm very much mistaken** à moins que je ne me trompe; **were you impressed? – very much so** ça vous a impressionné? – beaucoup (**b**) *(to a large extent)* **the situation remains very much the same** la situation n'a guère évolué; **it's very much a question of who to believe** la question est surtout de savoir qui on doit croire **2** *adj* beaucoup de; **there wasn't very much wine** il n'y avait pas beaucoup de vin

3 *pron* beaucoup; **she doesn't say very much** elle parle peu, elle ne dit pas grand-chose

►► ***very high frequency*** très haute fréquence *f*, (gamme *f* des) ondes *fpl* métriques; ***very low frequency*** très basse fréquence *f*

vesica ['vesɪkə] *(pl* **vesicae** [-kiː]) *n Anat & Zool* vessie *f*

►► *Ich* ***vesica natatoria*** vessie *f* natatoire, vésicule *f* aérienne; *Art* ***vesica piscis*** amande *f* mystique, auréole *f* elliptique

vesical ['vesɪkəl] *adj Anat & Med* vésical

vesicant ['vesɪkənt] **1** *n* vésicant *m*

2 *adj* vésicant

vesicate ['vesɪkeɪt] **1** *vt (skin)* produire des vésicules *ou* des ampoules sur

2 *vi (vesicant)* produire des ampoules *ou* des vésicules; *(skin)* s'ampouler

vesicle ['vesɪkəl] *n (sac)* vésicule *f*; *(blister)* ampoule *f*

vesicular [ve'sɪkjʊlə(r)] *adj Med* vésiculaire

Vespasian [ves'peɪʒən] *pr n* Vespasien

vesperal ['vespərəl] *n Rel* vespéral *m*

vespers ['vespəz] *npl* vêpres *fpl*

vessel ['vesəl] *n* (**a**) *Literary (container)* récipient *m*; **a drinking vessel** une timbale, un gobelet (**b**) *Naut* vaisseau *m* (**c**) *Anat & Bot* vaisseau *m*

vest [vest] **1** *n* (**a**) *Br (singlet → for boy, man)* maillot *m* de corps, tricot *m* de peau; *(→ for woman)* chemise *f*

(**b**) *Am (waistcoat)* gilet *m* (de costume)

2 *vt Formal* investir; **to vest sb with the power to do sth** investir qn du pouvoir de faire qch; **to vest sth in sb** assigner *ou* attribuer qch à qn; **the power vested in the government** le pouvoir dont le gouvernement est investi; **the president is vested with the power to veto the government** le président a le pouvoir d'opposer son veto aux projets du gouvernement; **legislative authority is vested in Parliament** le Parlement est investi du pouvoir législatif

vestal ['vestəl] *Antiq* **1** *adj (relating to Vesta)* de Vesta; *(relating to the vestal virgins)* de vestale, des vestales

2 *n* vestale *f*

►► ***vestal virgin*** vestale *f*

vested interest ['vestɪd-] **1** *n* intérêt *m* (direct *ou* personnel); **to have a vested interest in doing sth** avoir directement intérêt à faire qch; **she has a vested interest in keeping it secret/in the success of the venture** elle a tout intérêt à garder le secret/à ce que l'entreprise réussisse; *Fin* **to have a vested interest in a business** avoir des capitaux investis dans une entreprise, être intéressé dans une entreprise

2 vested interests *npl (rights)* droits *mpl* acquis; *(investments)* capitaux *mpl* investis; *(advantages)* intérêts *mpl*; **there are vested interests in industry opposed to trade union reform** ceux qui ont des intérêts dans l'industrie s'opposent à la réforme des syndicats; **that case will never come to trial, there are too many vested interests** cette affaire ne sera jamais jugée, cela dérange trop de gens

vestibular [ve'stɪbjʊlə(r)] *adj Anat & Med* vestibulaire

vestibule ['vestɪbjuːl] *n* (**a**) *(in house, church)* vestibule *m*; *(in hotel)* vestibule *m*, hall *m* d'entrée (**b**) *Anat* vestibule *m* (**c**) *Am Rail* sas *m*

vestige ['vestɪdʒ] *n* (**a**) *(remnant)* vestige *m*; **he clung on to the last vestiges of power** il s'accrochait aux derniers vestiges de son pouvoir; **not a vestige of the original building remains** il ne reste plus un seul vestige de l'édifice d'origine; **there's not a vestige of truth in the story** il n'y a pas un grain *ou* une once de vérité dans cette histoire (**b**) *Anat & Zool* organe *m* rudimentaire; **the vestige of a tail** une queue rudimentaire

vestigial [ve'stɪdʒɪəl] *adj* (**a**) *(remaining)* résiduel; **some vestigial sense of decency prevented him from doing it** le peu de décence qui lui restait l'a empêché de le faire (**b**) *Anat & Zool (organ, tail)* rudimentaire, atrophié

vestiture ['vestɪtʃə(r)] *n Zool & Bot* revêtement *m*

vestment ['vestmənt] *n* habit *m* de cérémonie; *Rel* vêtement *m* sacerdotal

vest-pocket *Am* **1** *n* poche *f* de gilet

2 *adj (book, object)* de poche; *Fig* minuscule, tout petit

vestry ['vestrɪ] *(pl* **vestries**) *n* (**a**) *(room)* sacristie *f* (**b**) *(committee)* conseil *m* paroissial

vesture ['vestʃə(r)] *n Literary* vêtements *mpl*

Vesuvius [vɪ'suːvɪəs] *n* **(Mount) Vesuvius** le Vésuve

vet[1] [vet] *n (abbr* **veterinary surgeon, veterinarian**) vétérinaire *mf*

vet[2] *Am Fam (abbr* **veteran**) **1** *n* ancien combattant ❑ *m*, vétéran ❑ *m*

2 *adj (association, rally)* d'anciens combattants ❑

vet[2] *(pt & pp* **vetted**, *cont* **vetting**) *vt* (**a**) *(check → application)* examiner minutieusement, passer au crible; *(→ claims, facts, figures)* vérifier soigneusement, passer au crible; *(→ documents)* contrôler; *(→ person)* enquêter sur; **she was thoroughly vetted for the job** ils ont soigneusement examiné sa candidature avant de l'embaucher; **all sources must be carefully vetted before publication** toutes les sources doivent être soigneusement vérifiées avant publication; **the committee has to vet any expenditure exceeding £100** le comité doit approuver toute dépense au-delà de 100 livres; **all his girlfriends were vetted by his mother** toutes ses copines devaient recevoir l'approbation maternelle

(**b**) *Vet (examine)* examiner; *(treat)* soigner

vetch [vetʃ] *n Bot* vesce *f*

vetchling ['vetʃlɪŋ] *n Bot* **(yellow) vetchling** gesse *f* des prés; **hairy vetchling** gesse *f* velue

veteran ['vetərən] **1** *n* (**a**) *Mil* ancien combattant *m*, vétéran *m*

(**b**) *(experienced person)* vétéran *m*, ancien(-enne) *m,f*

(**c**) *(car)* voiture *f* ancienne *ou* d'époque; *(machinery)* vieille machine *f*

2 *adj (experienced)* expérimenté, chevronné; **she's a veteran campaigner for civil rights** c'est une ancienne de la campagne pour les droits civiques

►► *Am* ***Veterans Affairs*** = organisme de soutien aux anciens combattants; ***Veterans Association*** association *f* d'anciens combattants; *Br* ***veteran car*** voiture *f* de collection *(normalement antérieure à 1905)*; *Am* ***Veterans Day*** fête *f* de l'armistice *(le 11 novembre)*, *Can* le Jour du Souvenir; ***veteran soldier*** vieux soldat *m*

veterinarian [ˌvetərɪ'neərɪən] *n Am* vétérinaire *mf*

veterinary ['vetərɪnrɪ] *adj (medicine, science)* vétérinaire

►► *Br* ***veterinary surgeon*** vétérinaire *mf*

vetiver ['vetɪvə(r)] *n Bot* vétiver *m*

veto ['viːtəʊ] *(pl* **vetoes**) **1** *n* (**a**) *(UNCOUNT) (power)* droit *m* de veto; **to use one's veto** exercer son droit de veto (**b**) *(refusal)* veto *m*; **to put a veto on sth** mettre *ou* opposer son veto à qch

2 *vt Pol & Fig* mettre *ou* opposer son veto à; **he vetoed it** il y a mis *ou* opposé son veto

vetting ['vetɪŋ] *n (UNCOUNT) (of things)* contrôle *m*; *(of people)* enquête *f* (**of sur**); **to undergo positive vetting** être soumis à une enquête de sécurité; **security vetting** enquêtes *fpl* de sécurité

vex [veks] *vt* contrarier, ennuyer

vexation [vek'seɪʃən] *n Formal* (**a**) *(anger)* ennui *m*, agacement *m*; **she threw it down in vexation** elle le jeta avec agacement (**b**) *(difficulty, annoyance)* ennui *m*, tracasserie *f*; **one of life's vexations** une de ces contrariétés que nous réserve la vie

vexatious [vek'seɪʃəs] *adj Formal* contrariant, ennuyeux

vexed [vekst] *adj Formal* (**a**) *(annoyed)* fâché, ennuyé, contrarié; **to become vexed** se fâcher; **to be vexed with sb** être fâché contre qn, en vouloir à qn; **she was vexed at his behaviour** elle était contrariée par son comportement, son comportement l'avait contrariée; **she was vexed to discover that she had left her purse behind** elle a été contrariée quand elle a réalisé qu'elle avait oublié son porte-monnaie

(**b**) *(question, issue → controversial)* controversé; *(→ difficult)* épineux; **the vexed question of crime and punishment** le problème constamment débattu du crime et du châtiment; **it remains a vexed question** c'est un sujet qui continue à soulever les controverses; **it is a vexed question whether this policy will work** cette politique va-t-elle fonctionner? c'est une question qui soulève les controverses; **it's a very vexed period in our history** c'est une période délicate de notre histoire

vexillum [vek'sɪləm] *(pl* **vexilla** [-lə]*) n* (**a**) *Antiq (standard)* vexille *m*, enseigne *f*; *(soldiers)* troupe *f* vexillaire (**b**) *Rel* écharpe *f* (de crosse d'évêque) (**c**) *Bot* étendard *m* (**d**) *Orn (of feather)* vexille *m*

vexing ['veksɪŋ] *adj* (**a**) *(annoying)* contrariant, ennuyeux, fâcheux (**b**) *(frustrating → issue, riddle)* frustrant

VFD [ˌviːef'diː] *n Am (abbr* **voluntary fire department**) = pompiers bénévoles aux États-Unis

VG *(written abbr* **very good**) TB

VGA [ˌviːdʒiː'eɪ] *n Comput (abbr* **Video Graphics Array**) VGA *m*

▸▸ ***VGA monitor*** moniteur *m* VGA

vgc *(written abbr* **very good condition**) tbe

VHF [ˌviːeɪtʃ'ef] *n (abbr* **very high frequency**) VHF *f*

VHS [ˌviːeɪt'es] *n (abbr* **video home system**) VHS *m*

VI *(written abbr* **Virgin Islands**) îles *fpl* Vierges

via ['vaɪə] *prep* (**a**) *(by way of)* via, par; **they travelled from Paris to Rome via Florence** ils ont voyagé de Paris à Rome via *ou* en passant par Florence; **the trip is shorter if you travel via Calais** le trajet est plus court par Calais

(**b**) *(by means of)* par, au moyen de; **contact me via this number/via my secretary** contactez-moi à ce numéro/par l'intermédiaire de ma secrétaire; **she sent him the letter via her sister** elle lui a envoyé la lettre par l'intermédiaire de sa sœur; **these pictures come via satellite** ces images arrivent par satellite; **the best way to get into films is via drama school** le meilleur moyen d'entrer dans le monde du cinéma est de passer par une école d'art dramatique; **the patient was fed via a tube** le malade était alimenté au moyen d'un tube

viability [ˌvaɪə'bɪlətɪ] *n (UNCOUNT)* (**a**) *Econ (of company, state)* viabilité *f* (**b**) *(of plan, programme, scheme)* chances *fpl* de réussite, viabilité *f* (**c**) *Med & Bot* viabilité *f*

viable ['vaɪəbəl] *adj* (**a**) *Econ (company, economy, state)* viable (**b**) *(practicable → plan, programme)* viable, qui a des chances de réussir; **there is no viable alternative** il n'y a pas d'autre solution viable; **it's not a viable proposition** cette proposition n'est pas viable (**c**) *Med & Bot* viable

Via Dolorosa ['viːəˌdɒlə'rəʊsə] *n Rel* Chemin *m* de la Croix

viaduct ['vaɪədʌkt] *n* viaduc *m*

Viagra® [ˌvaɪ'ægrə] *n* Viagra® *m*

vial ['vaɪəl] *n Literary* fiole *f*; *Pharm* ampoule *f*

viand ['vaɪənd] **1** *n Arch or Literary* friandise *f*

2 viands *npl Arch* aliments *mpl*

viaticum [vaɪ'ætɪkəm] *(pl* **viaticums** *or* **viatica** [-kə]*) n* viatique *m*

vibes [vaɪbz] *npl Fam* (**a**) *Mus (abbr* **vibraphone**) vibraphone❑ *m* (**b**) *(abbr* **vibrations**) atmosphère❑ *f*, ambiance❑ *f*; **they give off really good/bad vibes** avec eux le courant passe vraiment bien/ne passe vraiment pas; **I get really bad vibes from her** je la sens vraiment mal; **I don't like the vibes in this place** je n'aime pas l'ambiance ici

vibex ['vaɪbeks] *(pl* **vibices** [-siːz]*) n Med* vergeture *f*; **vibices** vibices *fpl*

vibraharp ['vaɪbrəhɑːp] *Am* = **vibraphone**

vibrancy ['vaɪbrənsɪ] *n (of person, painting, description)* vivacité *f*; *(of style)* vigueur *f*; *(of new company)* dynamisme *m*; *(of colour)* éclat *m*; *(of sound, voice)* caractère m vibrant

vibrant ['vaɪbrənt] **1** *adj* (**a**) *(vigorous, lively → person, painting, description)* plein de vie; *(→ town, cultural scene, atmosphere)* très animé; *(→ style)* plein de vigueur; *(→ speech)* vibrant; *(→ new company)* très dynamique; **to be vibrant with life** être plein de vie; **city vibrant with activity** ville palpitante d'activité (**b**) *(resonant → sound, voice)* vibrant (**c**) *(bright → colour, light)* éclatant

2 *n Ling* vibrante *f*

vibraphone ['vaɪbrəfəʊn] *n* vibraphone *m*

vibrate [vaɪ'breɪt] *vi* (**a**) *(shake, quiver)* vibrer (**b**) *(sound)* vibrer, retentir (**c**) *Phys (oscillate)* osciller, vibrer

vibrating [vaɪ'breɪtɪŋ] *adj* vibrant

vibration [vaɪ'breɪʃən] **1** *n* vibration *f*

2 vibrations *npl Fam (feeling)* ambiance❑ *f*; **good vibrations** une bonne ambiance

vibrational [vaɪ'breɪʃənəl] *adj* vibratoire

▸▸ ***vibrational energy*** énergie *f* de vibration; ***vibrational spectrum*** spectre *m* de vibration

vibrato [vɪ'brɑːtəʊ] *(pl* **vibratos**) *Mus* **1** *n* vibrato *m*

2 *adv* avec vibrato

vibrator [vaɪ'breɪtə(r)] *n* (**a**) *Elec* vibrateur *m* (**b**) *(for massage, sexual)* vibromasseur *m*

vibratory ['vaɪbrətrɪ] *adj* vibratoire

vibrio ['vaɪbrɪəʊ] *(pl* **vibrios**), **vibrion** ['vaɪbrɪən] *(pl* **vibriones** [-'əʊniːz]*) n Biol* vibrion *m*

vibriosis [ˌvaɪbrɪ'əʊsɪs] *(pl* **vibrioses** [-siːz]*) n Vet* vibriose *f*

vibrissa [vaɪ'brɪsə] *n* vibrisse *f*

viburnum [vaɪ'bɜːnəm] *n* viorne *f*

vicar ['vɪkə(r)] *n* pasteur *m (de l'Église anglicane)*; **the Vicar of Christ** le vicaire de Jésus-Christ

▸▸ ***vicar apostolic*** vicaire *m* apostolique; ***vicar general*** vicaire *m* général

vicarage ['vɪkərɪdʒ] *n* presbytère *m*

vicarial [vɪ'keərɪəl] *adj* (**a**) *Rel* pastoral (**b**) *(delegated → power, authority)* délégué

vicarious [vɪ'keərɪəs] *adj* (**a**) *(indirect, second-hand → feeling, pride, enjoyment)* indirect, par procuration *ou* contrecoup; **to lead a vicarious existence** vivre par procuration; **they got vicarious satisfaction from their son's success** le succès de leur fils les a satisfaits par procuration (**b**) *(punishment)* (fait) pour autrui; *(suffering, pain)* subi pour autrui (**c**) *(power, authority)* délégué (**d**) *Physiol* vicariant

▸▸ *Rel* ***vicarious sacrifice*** le sacrifice du Christ mort pour racheter les hommes

vicariously [vɪ'keərɪəslɪ] *adv* (**a**) *(experience)* indirectement; **she lived vicariously through her reading** elle vivait par procuration à travers ses lectures (**b**) *(authorize)* par délégation, par procuration

vicariousness [vɪ'keərɪəsnɪs] *n Physiol* vicariance *f*

vice 1 *n* [vaɪs] (**a**) *(depravity)* vice *m*

(**b**) *(moral failing)* vice *m*; *(less serious)* défaut *m*; *Hum* **it's my only vice** c'est mon seul vice

(**c**) *Tech* étau *m*; **he had a grip like a vice** il avait une poigne de fer

(**d**) *Am* brigade *f* des mœurs, brigade *f* mondaine

2 *prep* ['vaɪsɪ] *Formal (instead of)* à la place de, en remplacement de

▸▸ ***vice ring*** organisation *f* criminelle *(impliquée dans la prostitution/le trafic de drogue/etc)*; ***vice squad*** brigade *f* des mœurs, brigade *f* mondaine

vice- [vaɪs] *pref* vice-

vice-admiral *n* vice-amiral *m* d'escadre

vice-chairman *n* vice-président(e) *m,f*

vice-chairmanship *n* vice-présidence *f*

vice-chamberlain *n* adjoint *m* au grand chambellan

vice-chancellor *n Br Univ* ≃ président(e) *m,f* d'université

vice-chancellorship *n Br Univ* ≃ présidence *f* d'université

vice-consul *n* vice-consul *m*

vice-consulate *n (post or premises)* vice-consulat *m*

vicegerent [vaɪs'dʒerənt] *n* représentant(e) *m,f*, délégué(e) *m,f*

vicelike ['vaɪslaɪk] *adj* **held in a vicelike grip** serré dans une poigne de fer, serré comme dans un étau

vicennial [vɪ'senɪəl] *adj* vicennal

Vicenza [viː'tʃentsə] *n* Vicence

vice-premier *n* vice-premier ministre *m*

vice-presidency *n* vice-présidence *f*

vice-president *n* vice-président(e) *m,f*

vice-presidential *adj* vice-présidentiel

▸▸ ***vice-presidential candidate*** candidat *m* à la vice-présidence

vice-principal *n Sch* directeur(trice) *m,f* adjoint(e)

viceregal [ˌvaɪs'riːgəl] *adj* de *ou* du vice-roi

vicereine [ˌvaɪs'reɪn] *n* vice-reine *f*

viceroy ['vaɪsrɔɪ] *n* vice-roi *m*

viceroyalty [ˌvaɪs'rɔɪəltɪ] *n* vice-royauté *f*

vice versa [ˌvaɪsɪ'vɜːsə] *adv* vice versa, inversement

Vichy ['viːʃiː] *n* Vichy

▸▸ ***Vichy water*** eau *f* de Vichy

Vichyist ['viːʃɪɪst] **1** *adj* vichyste

2 *n* vichyste *mf*

vichyssoise [ˌviːʃiː'swɑːz] *n* **vichyssoise (soup)** vichyssoise *f*

vicinity [vɪ'sɪnətɪ] *(pl* **vicinities**) *n* (**a**) *(surrounding area)* environs *mpl*, alentours *mpl*; *(neighbourhood)* voisinage *m*, environs *mpl*; *(proximity)* proximité *f*; **is there a good school in the vicinity?** est-ce qu'il y a une bonne école dans les alentours *ou* dans le quartier?; **he's somewhere in the vicinity** il est quelque part dans les environs *ou* dans le coin; **in the vicinity of the town centre** *(in the area)* dans les environs du centre-ville; *(close)* à proximité du centre-ville; **in the immediate vicinity** dans les environs immédiats; *Formal* **one good thing about the house is its vicinity to the station** un des bons côtés de la maison, c'est qu'elle est située tout près de la gare

(**b**) *(approximate figures, amounts)* **his salary is in the vicinity of £18,000** son salaire est aux alentours de *ou* de l'ordre de 18 000 livres; **its weight is in the vicinity of £500 lb** cela pèse dans les 500 livres

vicious ['vɪʃəs] *adj* (**a**) *(cruel, savage → attack, blow)* brutal, violent; **a vicious wind** un vent violent (**b**) *(malevolent → criticism, gossip, remarks)* méchant, malveillant; **he has a vicious tongue** il a une langue de vipère (**c**) *(dog)* méchant; *(horse)* vicieux, rétif (**d**) *(perverse → behaviour, habits)* vicieux pervers

▸▸ ***vicious circle*** cercle *m* vicieux

viciously ['vɪʃəslɪ] *adv (attack, beat)* brutalement, violemment; *(criticize)* avec malveillance, méchamment

viciousness ['vɪʃəsnɪs] *n (of attack, beating)* brutalité *f*, violence *f*; *(of criticism, gossip)* méchanceté *f*, malveillance *f*

vicissitude [vɪ'sɪsɪtjuːd] *n Formal* vicissitude *f*

vicissitudinous [vɪˌsɪsɪ'tjuːdɪnəs] *adj Formal (subject to vicissitude)* sujet à des vicissitudes; *(characterized by vicissitude)* marqué par des vicissitudes

victim ['vɪktɪm] *n* (**a**) *(physical sufferer)* victime *f*; *(of earthquake, floods, disaster)* sinistré(e) *m,f*; **to fall victim to sth** être victime de qch; **the fire claimed many victims** l'incendie a fait de nombreuses victimes; **road are accident victims** les victimes *ou* les accidentés de la route; **a fund for victims of cancer** des fonds pour les cancéreux *ou* les malades du cancer

(**b**) *Fig* victime *f*; **to fall victim to sb's charms** succomber aux charmes de qn; **the game fell victim to the weather** le match a été annulé à cause du temps; **many people fall victim to these fraudulent schemes** beaucoup de gens se font avoir par ces combines frauduleuses; **he was a victim of his own ambition/success** il a été victime de sa propre ambition/de son propre succès; **education is always the first victim of government spending cuts** l'éducation est toujours la première à souffrir des réductions des dépenses publiques

victimhood [ˌvɪktɪmʊd] *n* mentalité *f* de victime

victimization [ˌvɪktɪmaɪ'zeɪʃən] *n (for beliefs, race, differences)* persécution *f*; *(reprisals)* représailles *fpl*; **there must be no further victimization of workers** il ne doit pas y avoir d'autres représailles contre les ouvriers

victimize, -ise ['vɪktɪmaɪz] *vt (make victim of)* persécuter; *(take reprisals against)* exercer des *ou* user de représailles sur; **she was victimized at school because of her accent/of her colour** elle a été victime de brimades à l'école à cause de son accent/de la couleur de sa peau; **immigrant workers are being victimized by some of the foremen** les travailleurs immigrés sont pris pour victimes *ou* pour cibles par certains contremaîtres; **the strikers feel they are being victimized** les grévistes estiment qu'ils sont victimes de représailles; **it victimizes the lower paid** cela constitue un traitement discriminatoire à l'égard des petits salaires, ce sont les petits salaires qui en souffrent; **he felt that he was being victimized** il avait l'impression d'être victime d'un traitement discriminatoire

victimless crime ['vɪktɪmlɪs-] *n* délit *m* sans victime

victimology [vɪktɪ'mɒlədʒɪ] *n* victimologie *f*

victor ['vɪktə(r)] *n* vainqueur *m*; **Labour were the victors in the election** le Parti travailliste a remporté la victoire aux élections

Victoria [vɪk'tɔːrɪə] **1** *pr n (person)* **Queen Victoria** la reine Victoria

2 *n* (**a**) *(state)* le Victoria; **in Victoria** dans le Victoria (**b**) *(lake)* **Lake Victoria** le lac Victoria

▸▸ *Mil* ***Victoria Cross*** Victoria Cross *f (en Grande-Bretagne, la plus haute décoration militaire)*; ***Victoria Day*** *(Canada)* = fête *f* de Victoria *(jour férié en mai)*; ***Victoria Falls*** les chutes *fpl* Victoria; *Culin* ***Victoria sponge (cake)*** gâteau *m* de Savoie *(à la confiture, à la chantilly etc)*

victoria [vɪk'tɔːrɪə] *n* (**a**) *(carriage)* victoria *f* (**b**) *(plum)* = grosse prune rouge

▸▸ ***victoria plum*** = grosse prune rouge

Victorian [vɪk'tɔːrɪən] **1** *adj* victorien; **a return to Victorian values** un retour aux valeurs victoriennes *ou* de l'époque victorienne

2 *n* Victorien(enne) *m,f*

VICTORIAN VALUES

Le sens du devoir et la stricte moralité qui caractérisèrent le règne (1837–1901) de la reine Victoria symbolisent traditionnellement le puritanisme du XIXème siècle britannique. Ceci coïncidait avec l'apogée de l'Empire et de la prospérité économique britanniques. Dans les années 80, Margaret Thatcher, en s'employant à radicalement transformer le paysage politique du pays, invoquait les vertus victoriennes du travail et de l'auto-suffisance économique. Son successeur John Major utilisa lors de sa campagne électorale le slogan "Back to Basics", mais cette tentative d'un retour aux valeurs traditionnelles de l'ère victorienne (esprit d'initiative, esprit d'entreprise et importance de la famille) comme antidote à la permissivité héritée des années 60, se retourna contre le gouvernement lorsqu'une série de scandales compromettant des ministres éclata au grand jour.

Victoriana [ˌvɪktɔːrɪ'ɑːnə] *n (UNCOUNT)* antiquités *fpl* victoriennes, objets *mpl* de l'époque victorienne

victorious [vɪk'tɔːrɪəs] *adj (army, campaign, party)* victorieux; *(army)* vainqueur; *(cry)* de victoire; **to be victorious over sb** être victorieux de qn, remporter la victoire sur qn

victoriously [vɪk'tɔːrɪəslɪ] *adv* victorieusement

victory ['vɪktərɪ] *(pl* **victories***)* *n* victoire *f*; **to gain** *or* **to win a victory over sb** remporter la victoire sur qn; **he described the decision as a victory for common sense** il a décrit la décision comme une victoire du bon sens

▸▸ ***Victory in Europe Day*** = jour de l'armistice du 8 mai 1945; *Am* ***victory garden*** = jardin potager cultivé pendant la Seconde Guerre mondiale pour permettre au pays d'envoyer plus de nourriture aux alliés; ***victory parade*** défilé *m* de la victoire, défilé *m* pour célébrer une victoire; *Mil Aviat* ***victory roll*** = looping pour marquer une victoire; ***victory sign*** V *m* de la victoire

victual ['vɪtəl] *(pt & pp* **victualled,** *cont* **victualling***)* *Arch* **1** *vt* ravitailler, approvisionner

2 *vi* se ravitailler, s'approvisionner

3 victuals *npl Arch* victuailles *fpl*

victualler ['vɪtlə(r)] *n* fournisseur *m* (de provisions)

vicuna [vɪ'kjuːnə] *n Zool* vigogne *f*

vide ['vaɪdiː] *impersonal vb (in text)* voir, cf

videlicet [vɪ'diːlɪset] *adv Formal* à savoir

video ['vɪdɪəʊ] *(pl* **videos***)* **1** *n* (**a**) *(medium)* vidéo *f*; **I use video a lot in my teaching** j'utilise beaucoup la vidéo pendant mes cours

(**b**) *(VCR)* magnétoscope *m*; **have you set the video?** est-ce que tu as mis le magnétoscope en marche *ou* programmé le magnétoscope?; **they recorded the series on video** ils ont enregistré le feuilleton au magnétoscope

(**c**) *(cassette)* vidéocassette *f*; *(recording)* vidéo *f*; *(for pop-song)* clip *m*, vidéoclip *m*; **they rented a video for the night** ils ont loué une vidéo *ou* vidéocassette pour la soirée; **we've got a video of the film** on a le film en vidéocassette

(**d**) *Am Fam (television)* télé *f*

2 *comp* (**a**) *(film, version)* (en) vidéo; *(services, equipment, signals)* vidéo *(inv)*; **a video shop** un magasin vidéo

(**b**) *Am (on TV)* télévisé

3 *vt* (**a**) *(film, programme)* enregistrer sur magnétoscope, magnétoscoper

(**b**) *(using camcorder)* filmer (à la caméra vidéo); **they didn't know they were being videoed** ils ne savaient pas qu'ils étaient filmés

▸▸ *Comput* ***video accelerator card*** carte *f* vidéo accélératrice; ***video arcade*** salle *f* de jeux vidéo; ***video art*** art *m* vidéo; *Comput* ***video board*** carte *f* vidéo; ***video camera*** caméra *f* vidéo; *Comput* ***video card*** carte *f* vidéo; ***video cartridge*** cartouche *f* vidéo; ***video cassette*** vidéocassette *f*; ***video cassette recorder*** magnétoscope *m*; ***video clip*** clip *m*, vidéoclip *m*, clip *m* vidéo; ***video club*** club *m* vidéo; ***video conference*** vidéoconférence *f*, visioconférence *f*; ***video conferencing*** vidéoconférences *fpl*; ***video diary*** journal *m* vidéo; ***video frequency*** vidéofréquence *f*; ***video game*** jeu *m* vidéo; ***video installation*** installation *f* vidéo; *Fam* ***video jock*** présentateur(trice) *m,f* de vidéoclips[□]; ***video jockey*** présentateur(trice) *m,f* de vidéoclips; ***video library*** vidéothèque *f*; ***video link*** liaison *f* vidéo; ***video machine*** magnétoscope *m*; *Br Fam* ***video nasty*** = film vidéo à caractère violent et souvent pornographique; ***video piracy*** duplication *f* pirate de cassettes vidéo; ***video player*** magnétoscope *m*; ***video projector*** vidéoprojecteur *m*; ***video recording*** enregistrement *m* sur magnétoscope; ***video telephone*** vidéophone; ***video wall*** mur *m* d'écrans de télévision

videodisc ['vɪdɪəʊdɪsk] *n* vidéodisque *m*

videofit ['vɪdɪəʊfɪt] *n* = portrait capté par une caméra de surveillance

video-on-demand *n* vidéo *f* à la demande

videophone ['vɪdɪəʊfəʊn] *n* vidéophone *m*

▸▸ ***videophone conference*** visioconférence *f*

video-record *vt* enregistrer sur magnétoscope, magnétoscoper

videorecorder ['vɪdɪəʊrɪˌkɔːdə(r)] *n* magnétoscope *m*

videotape ['vɪdɪəʊteɪp] **1** *n* bande *f* vidéo

2 *vt* enregistrer sur magnétoscope, magnétoscoper

videotext ['vɪdɪəʊtekst] *n* vidéotex *m*, vidéographie *f* interactive

vidimus ['vaɪdɪməs] *n Law* vidimus *m*

vie [vaɪ] *(pt & pp* **vied,** *cont* **vying***)* *vi* rivaliser, lutter; **to vie with sb for sth** disputer qch à qn; **the two children vied with each other for attention** les deux enfants rivalisaient pour attirer l'attention; **several companies were vying with each other to sponsor the event** plusieurs firmes se battaient pour parrainer l'évènement

Vienna [vɪ'enə] **1** *n* Vienne

2 *comp* viennois, de Vienne

▸▸ ***Vienna bread*** pain *m* viennois; ***Vienna roll*** ≃ pain *m* au lait

Viennese [ˌvɪə'niːz] *(pl* **inv***)* **1** *n* Viennois(e) *m,f*

2 *adj* viennois

Vietcong [ˌvjet'kɒŋ] *(pl* **inv***)* *n* Viêt-cong *mf*

Vietnam [*Br* ˌvjet'næm, *Am* ˌvjet'nɑːm] *n* Viêt-nam *m*; **in Vietnam** au Viêt-nam

▸▸ ***the Vietnam War*** la guerre du Viêt-nam

THE VIETNAM WAR 

Ce conflit opposa, de 1954 à 1975, le Viêt-nam du Nord communiste au Viêt-nam du Sud, soutenu militairement par les États-Unis. Aussitôt critiqué par l'opinion publique nationale, l'effort de guerre américain s'intensifia considérablement au milieu des années 60, sans parvenir pour autant à faire basculer l'issue du conflit. À partir de 1970, sous la présidence de R. Nixon, un processus de cessez-le-feu fut engagé, aboutissant au retrait des troupes américaines en 1973. Un an plus tard, le sud du pays passa aux mains des communistes. Véritable traumatisme national, la guerre du Viêt-nam est l'un des épisodes les plus pénibles de l'histoire des États-Unis. La longueur du conflit, les atrocités commises de part et d'autre, le nombre très élevé de victimes, mais surtout les interrogations sur la finalité de cette guerre remirent radicalement en question la légitimité de l'intervention américaine et provoquèrent chez les jeunes Américains de l'époque un mouvement antimilitariste d'une ampleur sans précédent.

Vietnamese [ˌvjetnə'miːz] *(pl* **inv***)* **1** *n* (**a**) *(person)* Vietnamien(enne) *m,f* (**b**) *(language)* vietnamien *m*

2 *adj* vietnamien

3 *comp (embassy, history)* du Viêt-nam; *(teacher)* de vietnamien

Viet Vet [vɪet'vet] *n Am Fam Mil* ancien *m* du Viêt-nam[□]

view [vjuː] **1** *n* (**a**) *(sight)* vue *f*; **to come into view** apparaître; **we came into view of the shore** nous sommes arrivés en vue du rivage, nous avons aperçu le rivage; **he turned the corner and disappeared from view** il a tourné au coin et on l'a perdu de vue *ou* il a disparu; **it happened in full view of the television cameras/police** cela s'est passé juste devant les caméras de télévision/sous les yeux de la police; **to be on view** *(house)* être ouvert aux visites; *(picture)* être exposé; **the woods are within view of the house** de la maison on voit les bois; **to hide sth from view** *(accidentally)* cacher qch; *(deliberately)* cacher qch aux regards; **to keep sth in view** ne pas perdre qch de vue

(**b**) *(prospect)* vue *f*; **the house has a good view of the sea** la maison a une belle vue sur la mer; **a room with a view** une chambre avec vue; **there's a nice view from the window** de la fenêtre il y a une très belle vue; **there are nice views of the coast from that hill** de cette colline on a de belles vues sur la côte; **from here we have a side view of the cathedral** d'ici nous avons une vue de profil de la cathédrale; **you get a better view from here** on voit mieux d'ici; **the man in front of me blocked my view of the stage** l'homme devant moi m'empêchait de voir la scène; *Fig* **a comprehensive view of English literature** une vue d'ensemble de la littérature anglaise

(**c**) *(future perspective)* **in view** en vue; **there appears to be no solution in view** il semble n'y avoir aucune solution en vue; **what do you have in view as regards work?** quelles sont vos intentions en ce qui concerne le travail?; **with this (end) in view** avec *ou* dans cette intention; **she has in view the publication of a new book** elle envisage de publier un nouveau livre; **to take the long view of sth** voir qch à long terme

(**d**) *(aim, purpose)* but *m*, intention *f*; **with a view to doing sth** en vue de faire qch, dans l'intention de faire qch; **they bought the house**

with a view to their retirement ils ont acheté la maison en pensant à leur retraite

(**e**) *(interpretation)* vue *f*; **an overall view** une vue d'ensemble; **he has** *or* **takes a gloomy view of life** il a une vue pessimiste de la vie, il envisage la vie d'une manière pessimiste

(**f**) *(picture, photograph)* vue *f*; **views of Venice** vues de Venise; **an aerial view of New York** une vue aérienne de New York

(**g**) *(opinion)* avis *m*, opinion *f*; **in my view** à mon avis; **in the view of many of our colleagues** de l'avis de beaucoup de nos collègues; **I respect her political views** je respecte ses opinions politiques; **that seems to be the generally accepted view** ceci semble être l'opinion générale *ou* courante; **that's the official view** c'est le point de vue officiel; **everybody has their own view of the situation** chacun comprend la situation à sa façon, chacun a sa propre façon de voir la situation; **he takes the view that they are innocent** il pense *ou* estime qu'ils sont innocents; **I don't take that view** je ne partage pas cet avis; **she took a poor** *or* **dim view of his behaviour** elle n'appréciait guère son comportement; **what is your view on the matter?** quelle est votre opinion sur la question?; **she holds** *or* **has strong views on the subject** elle a des opinions *ou* des idées bien nettes sur le sujet; **he's changed his views on disarmament** il a changé d'avis sur le désarmement

2 *vt* (**a**) *(look at)* voir, regarder; *(film, programme)* regarder; **viewed from above/from afar/from the outside** vu d'en haut/de loin/de l'extérieur

(**b**) *(examine → slides)* visionner; *(→ through microscope)* regarder; *(→ flat, showhouse)* visiter, inspecter; *(exhibition, paintings)* voir; **the house may be viewed at weekends only** on peut visiter la maison pendant les week-ends uniquement

(**c**) *Fig (consider, judge)* considérer, envisager; **the committee viewed his application favourably** la commission a porté un regard favorable sur sa candidature; **he was viewed as a dangerous maniac** on le considérait comme un fou dangereux; **how do you view this matter?** quel est votre avis sur cette affaire?; **the government views the latest international developments with alarm** le gouvernement porte un regard inquiet sur les derniers développements internationaux; **I would view his departure with equanimity** j'envisagerais son départ avec sérénité; **when viewed in this light** vu sous cet angle

(**d**) *Hunt (fox)* apercevoir

(**e**) *Comput (codes, document)* visualiser, afficher

3 *vi TV* regarder la télévision

4 in view of *prep* étant donné, vu; **in view of his age** étant donné son âge, vu son âge; **in view of what has happened** en raison de *ou* étant donné ce qui s'est passé; **in view of this** ceci étant

viewable area ['vjuːəbəl-] *adj Comput (of monitor)* zone *f* d'affichage

Viewdata® ['vjuːˌdeɪtə] *n* vidéotex *m*, vidéographie *f* interactive

viewer ['vjuːə(r)] *n* (**a**) *TV* téléspectateur(trice) *m,f*; **the programme has** *or* **attracts a lot of women viewers/young viewers** l'émission est très regardée par les femmes/les jeunes (**b**) *Phot (for slides)* visionneuse *f*; *(viewfinder)* viseur *m* (**c**) *Comput (program)* visualiseur *m*

viewership ['vjuːəʃɪp] *n Am TV* public *m*

viewfinder ['vjuːˌfaɪndə(r)] *n Phot* viseur *m*

view-halloo [-hə'luː] *n Hunt* vue *f*

viewing ['vjuːɪŋ] **1** *n (UNCOUNT)* (**a**) *TV* programme *m*, programmes *mpl*, émissions *fpl*; **late-night viewing on BBC2** émissions de fin de soirée sur BBC2; **his latest film makes exciting viewing** son dernier film est un spectacle passionnant; **a good evening's viewing** une soirée passée devant de bons programmes de télévision

(**b**) *(of showhouse, exhibition)* visite *f*; **viewing at weekends only** visites uniquement le week-end

(**c**) *Astron* observation *f*

2 *comp* (**a**) *TV (time, patterns)* d'écoute; **a young viewing audience** de jeunes téléspectateurs

(**b**) *Astron & Met (conditions)* d'observation

►► *TV* ***viewing figures*** taux *m ou* indice *m* d'écoute; *TV* ***viewing hours*** heures *fpl* d'écoute; **at peak viewing hours** aux heures de grande écoute

viewless ['vjuːlɪs] *adj* (**a**) *(site, windows)* qui n'offre pas de vue (**b**) *(person)* sans opinion *ou* opinions

viewphone ['vjuːfəʊn] *n* vidéophone *m*, visiophone *m*

viewpoint ['vjuːpɔɪnt] *n* (**a**) *(opinion)* point *m* de vue (**b**) *(viewing place)* point *m* de vue, panorama *m*

vig [vɪg] *n Am Fam* intérêts□ *mpl*

vigesimal [vaɪ'dʒesɪməl] *adj* vicésimal

vigil ['vɪdʒɪl] *n* (**a**) *(watch)* veille *f*; *(in sickroom)* veillée *f*; *(for dead person)* veillée *f* funèbre; **to keep (an all-night) vigil by sb's bedside** veiller (toute la nuit) au chevet de qn (**b**) *(demonstration)* manifestation *f* silencieuse (nocturne) (**c**) *Rel* vigile *f*

vigilance ['vɪdʒɪləns] *n* vigilance *f*

►► *Am* ***vigilance committee*** groupe *m* d'autodéfense

vigilant ['vɪdʒɪlənt] *adj* vigilant, éveillé

vigilante [ˌvɪdʒɪ'læntɪ] *n* = membre d'un groupe d'autodéfense

►► ***vigilante group*** groupe *m* d'autodéfense

vigilantism [ˌvɪdʒɪ'læntɪzəm] *n* = attitude agressive typique des groupes d'autodéfense

vigilantly ['vɪdʒɪləntlɪ] *adv* avec vigilance, attentivement

vignette [vɪ'njet] **1** *n (illustration)* vignette *f*; *Art & Phot* portrait *m* en buste dégradé; *Literature* esquisse *f* de caractère, portrait *m*; *Fig* **this ten-minute vignette of city life** cet aperçu de dix minutes de la vie dans une grande ville

2 *vt (picture, photograph)* dégrader, estomper; *(character)* esquisser; *(book, page)* orner de vignettes

vigor *Am* = **vigour**

vigorish ['vɪgərɪʃ] *n Am Fam (percentage of winnings)* = pourcentage des gains payable au bookmaker; *(interest on loan)* taux *m* d'intérêt exorbitant□

vigorous ['vɪgərəs] *adj* (**a**) *(robust → person, plant)* vigoureux; *(enthusiastic → person)* enthousiaste (**b**) *(forceful → opposition, campaign, support)* vigoureux, énergique; *(→ denial)* formel (**c**) *(energetic → exercise)* énergique

vigorously ['vɪgərəslɪ] *adv* vigoureusement, énergiquement; **he nodded his head vigorously** il acquiesça vivement de la tête

vigour, *Am* **vigor** ['vɪgə(r)] *n* (**a**) *(physical vitality)* vigueur *f*, énergie *f*, vitalité *f*; *(mental vitality)* vigueur *f*, vivacité *f*; **he is no longer in the full vigour of youth** il n'a plus toute la vigueur de la jeunesse (**b**) *(of attack, style)* vigueur *f*; *(of storm)* violence *f* (**c**) *Am Law* **in vigour** en vigueur

Viking ['vaɪkɪŋ] **1** *adj* viking

2 *n* Viking *mf*

►► ***Viking ship*** drakkar *m*

vile [vaɪl] *adj* (**a**) *(morally wrong → deed, intention, murder)* vil, ignoble, infâme; **to be vile to sb** être ignoble envers qn; **he made some vile accusations** il a porté des accusations ignobles *ou* infâmes

(**b**) *(disgusting → person, habit, taste)* abominable, exécrable; *(→ food)* infect, exécrable; *(→ smell)* infect, nauséabond; **it smells vile!** ça pue!; **spitting is a vile habit** cracher est une sale habitude; **he used some vile language** il a employé des termes ignobles

(**c**) *(very bad → temper)* exécrable, massacrant; *(→ weather)* exécrable; **to be in a vile temper** être d'une humeur massacrante; **what vile weather!** quel sale temps!

(**d**) *Arch or Literary* sans valeur; **they dreamt of changing vile metals into gold** ils rêvaient de changer en or les métaux vils

'Vile Bodies' *Waugh* 'Diableries' *ou* 'Ces Corps vils'

vilely ['vaɪllɪ] *adv* (**a**) *(basely, despicably)* vilement, bassement (**b**) *(decorated etc)* d'une manière abominable *ou* exécrable

vileness ['vaɪlnɪs] *n* (**a**) *(of deed, intention)* vilenie *f*, bassesse *f* (**b**) *(of smell, taste, weather)* caractère *m* exécrable *ou* abominable (**c**) *Literary (of metal)* vileté *f*

vilification [ˌvɪlɪfɪ'keɪʃən] *n Formal* diffamation *f*, calomnie *f*

vilify ['vɪlɪfaɪ] (*pt & pp* **vilified**) *vt Formal* diffamer, calomnier

villa ['vɪlə] *n (in country)* maison *f* de campagne; *(by sea)* villa *f*; *Br (in town)* villa *f ou* pavillon *m* (de banlieue); *Hist* villa *f*

village ['vɪlɪdʒ] **1** *n* village *m*; *Am* **the Village** = surnom de Greenwich Village, quartier de New York

2 *comp* du village

►► *Br* ***village green*** = pelouse se trouvant au centre du village; ***village hall*** salle *f* des fêtes; ***village idiot*** idiot *m* du village; *Orn* ***village weaver*** tisserin *m* à capuchon

VILLAGE GREEN

Souvent situé au centre du village, le "village green" accueille en Grande-Bretagne les kermesses et des manifestations sportives.

villager ['vɪlɪdʒə(r)] *n* villageois(e) *m,f*

villain ['vɪlən] *n* (**a**) *(ruffian, scoundrel)* scélérat(e) *m,f*, vaurien(enne) *m,f*; *(in film, story)* méchant(e) *m,f*, traître(esse) *m,f*; *Theat & Fig* **the villain of the piece** le méchant, le coupable (**b**) *Fam (rascal)* coquin(e) *m,f*, vilain(e) *m,f*; **you little villain!** petit coquin!, vilain! (**c**) *Fam Crime slang (criminal)* bandit *m*, malfaiteur *m* (**d**) *Hist (free)* vilain(e) *m,f*; *(unfree)* serf *m*, serve *f*

villainous ['vɪlənəs] *adj* (**a**) *(evil → act, person)* vil, ignoble, infâme; **a villainous deed** une infamie, une bassesse (**b**) *(foul → food, weather)* abominable, exécrable

villainously ['vɪlənəslɪ] *adv* d'une manière infâme *ou* ignoble

villainy ['vɪlənɪ] (*pl* **villainies**) *n* infamie *f*, bassesse *f*

villanelle [ˌvɪlə'nel] *n Literature* villanelle *f*

villein ['vɪlɪn] *n Hist (free)* vilain(e) *m,f*; *(unfree)* serf (serve) *m,f*

villiform ['vɪlɪfɔːm] *adj Zool* villiforme

villus ['vɪləs] (*pl* **villi** [-laɪ]) *n Bot* poil *m*; *Anat & Zool* villosité *f*

Vilnius ['vɪlnɪəs] *n* Vilnious

vim [vɪm] *n Fam* énergie□ *f*, entrain□ *m*; **full of vim (and vigour)** plein d'entrain□

VIN [ˌviːaɪ'en] *n (abbr* **vehicle identification number**) numéro *m* d'immatriculation

vinaceous [vaɪ'neɪʃəs] *adj* vineux, couleur de vin

vinaigrette [ˌvɪnɪ'gret] *n Culin* vinaigrette *f*

vincible ['vɪnsɪbəl] *adj* qui peut être dompté, pas invincible

vinculum ['vɪŋkjʊləm] (*pl* **vincula** [-lə]) *n* (**a**) *(tie, bond)* lien *m* (**b**) *Anat (of tongue etc)* frein *m*, filet *m* (**c**) *Math* trait *m* horizontal

vindaloo [ˌvɪndə'luː] *n* vindaloo *m (plat indien au curry très épicé)*

vindicate ['vɪndɪkeɪt] *vt* (**a**) *(justify)* justifier; **this vindicates my faith in him** ceci prouve que j'avais raison d'avoir confiance en lui, ceci prouve que la confiance que j'avais en lui était justifiée (**b**) *(show to be correct → opinions, theory)* confirmer; *(→ person)* donner raison à (**c**) *(uphold → claim, right)* faire valoir, revendiquer (**d**) *Law (exonerate → person)* innocenter

vindication [ˌvɪndɪ'keɪʃən] *n* justification *f*; **he spoke in vindication of his behaviour** il s'expliqua pour justifier son comportement

vindicatory ['vɪndɪˌkeɪtərɪ] *adj* (**a**) *(justifying)* justificatif; *Rel* apologétique (**b**) *(avenging)* vindicatif, vengeur(eresse)

►► ***vindicatory justice*** justice *f* vindicative

vindictive [vɪn'dɪktɪv] *adj* vindicatif

►► *Law* ***vindictive damages*** dommages-intérêts *mpl* à titre punitif

vindictively [vɪn'dɪktɪvlɪ] *adv (say)* vindicativement; *(act)* par esprit de vengeance; **he had quite vindictively made sure she would not get the job** par esprit de vengeance, il avait tout fait pour qu'elle n'obtienne pas le poste

vindictiveness [vɪn'dɪktɪvnɪs] *n* caractère *m*

vindicatif; **she did it out of sheer vindictiveness** elle l'a fait par esprit de vengeance

vine [vaɪn] **1** *n* (**a**) *(grapevine)* vigne *f* (**b**) *(plant → climbing)* plante *f* grimpante; *(→ creeping)* plante *f* rampante

2 *comp (leaf)* de vigne; *(disease)* de la vigne

3 vines *npl Am Fam (clothes)* fringues *fpl*

▸▸ ***vine fruit*** raisin *m*; ***vine grower*** viticulteur(-trice) *m,f*, vigneron(onne) *m,f*; ***vine growing*** viticulture *f*; ***vine harvest*** vendange *f*, vendanges *fpl*

vinegar ['vɪnɪgə(r)] *n* vinaigre *m*

▸▸ ***vinegar fly*** mouche *f* du vinaigre

vinegary ['vɪnɪgərɪ] *adj* (**a**) *(smell, taste)* de vinaigre; *(wine)* qui a un goût de vinaigre (**b**) *Fig (tone, reply)* acide, acerbe; *(temper)* acide, acariâtre

vineleaf [vaɪnliːf] *(pl* **vineleaves** [-liːvz]*)* *n* feuille *f* de vigne

vinery ['vaɪnərɪ] *(pl* **vineries***)* *n (hothouse)* = serre où l'on cultive la vigne

vineyard ['vɪnjəd] *n* (champ *m* de) vigne *f*; *(commercially exploited)* vignoble *m*

viniculture ['vɪnɪkʌltʃə(r)] *n* viniculture *f*

vinification [ˌvɪnɪfɪ'keɪʃən] *n* vinification *f*

vino ['viːnəʊ] *(pl* **vinos***)* *n Fam* pinard *m*

vinous ['vaɪnəs] *adj* vineux

vint [vɪnt] *vt (wine)* faire

vintage ['vɪntɪdʒ] **1** *n* (**a**) *(wine)* vin *m* de cru; *(year)* cru *m*, millésime *m*; **this claret is an excellent vintage** ce bordeaux est un très grand cru; **1982 was a good vintage** 1982 a été une bonne année pour le vin; **a 1983 vintage** un vin de 1983; **what vintage is this wine?** quel est le millésime *ou* quelle est l'année de ce vin?

(**b**) *(crop)* récolte *f*; *(harvesting)* vendange *f*, vendanges *fpl*

(**c**) *(period)* époque *f*; **an old radio of pre-war vintage** une vieille radio d'avant-guerre; **our parents are of the same vintage** nos parents sont de la même génération

2 *adj* (**a**) *(old)* antique, ancien

(**b**) *(classic, superior)* classique; **a season of vintage films** une saison de films classiques; **it was vintage Agatha Christie** c'était de l'Agatha Christie du meilleur style *ou* cru

(**c**) *(champagne)* millésimé; *(port)* vieux

3 *vt* vendanger

▸▸ *Br* ***vintage car*** voiture *f* de collection *(normalement construite entre 1919 et 1930)*; ***vintage model*** modèle *m ou* pièce *f* d'époque; ***vintage wine*** vin *m* millésimé; ***vintage year*** *(for wine)* grand millésime *m*, grande année *f*; *(for books, films)* très bonne année *f*; **it was a vintage year for the British film industry** ce fut une excellente année pour l'industrie cinématographique britannique

vintner ['vɪntnə(r)] *n* négociant *m* en vins

vinyl ['vaɪnɪl] **1** *n* vinyle *m*

2 *adj (wallpaper, tiles, coat)* de *ou* en vinyle; *(paint)* vinylique

viol ['vaɪəl] *n* viole *f*

▸▸ ***viol player*** violiste *mf*

viola [vɪ'əʊlə] *n* (**a**) *Mus* alto *m* (**b**) *Bot (genus)* violacée *f*; *(flower)* pensée *f*, violette *f*

▸▸ ***viola player*** altiste *mf*

viola da gamba [-də'gæmbə] *(pl* **viole da gamba** [vɪˌəʊle-]*)* *n* viole *f* de gambe

viola d'amore [-dæ'mɔːrɪ] *(pl* **viole d'amore** [vɪˌəʊle-]*)* *n* viole *f* d'amour

violate ['vaɪəleɪt] *vt* (**a**) *(promise, secret, treaty)* violer; *(law)* violer, enfreindre; *(rights)* violer, bafouer (**b**) *(frontier, property)* violer; **to violate a country's territorial waters** violer les eaux territoriales d'un pays (**c**) *(peace, silence)* troubler, rompre; **to violate sb's privacy** violer l'intimité de qn (**d**) *(sanctuary, tomb)* violer, profaner (**e**) *Formal (rape)* violer, violenter

violation [ˌvaɪə'leɪʃən] *n* (**a**) *(of promise, rights, secret)* violation *f* (**of** de); *(of law)* violation (**of** de), infraction *f* (**of** à); *Sport* faute *f*; **they acted in violation of the treaty** ils ont contrevenu au traité

(**b**) *(of frontier, property)* violation *f*; **it's a violation of my privacy** c'est une atteinte à ma vie privée; **violation of territorial waters** violation *f* des eaux territoriales

(**c**) *Admin* **violation of the peace** trouble *m* de l'ordre public

(**d**) *(of sanctuary, tomb)* profanation *f*, violation *f*

(**e**) *Am Law (offence)* infraction *f*

(**f**) *Formal (rape)* viol *m*

violator ['vaɪəleɪtə(r)] *n* (**a**) *(gen)* violateur *m* (**b**) *Am Law (offender)* contrevenant *m*

violence ['vaɪələns] *n (UNCOUNT)* (**a**) *(physical)* violence *f*; **acts/scenes of violence** actes *mpl*/scènes *fpl* de violence; **football/TV violence** la violence sur les terrains de football/à la télévision; **the men of violence** *(terrorists)* les terroristes *mpl*; **violence broke out in the streets** il y a eu de violents incidents *ou* des bagarres ont éclaté dans les rues

(**b**) *Law* violences *fpl*; **crimes of violence** crimes *mpl* de violence; **robbery with violence** vol *m* avec coups et blessures

(**c**) *(of language, passion, storm)* violence *f*

(**d**) *(idiom)* **to do violence to** faire violence à

violent ['vaɪələnt] *adj* (**a**) *(attack, crime, person, behaviour)* violent; **by violent means** par la violence; **to be violent with sb** se montrer *ou* être violent avec qn; **he began to get violent** il a commencé à se montrer violent; **he gave the door a violent kick** il a donné un violent coup de pied dans la porte; **to die a violent death** mourir de mort violente

(**b**) *(intense → pain)* violent, aigu(uë); *(furious → temper)* violent; *(strong, great → contrast, change)* violent, brutal; *(→ explosion, storm)* violent; **she took a violent dislike to him** elle s'est prise d'une vive aversion à son égard; **to be in a violent temper** être furieux; **I've got a violent toothache/headache** j'ai une rage de dents/un mal de tête atroce

(**c**) *(forceful, impassioned → argument, language, emotions)* violent

(**d**) *(wind, weather)* violent

(**e**) *(colour)* criard, voyant; **the walls had been painted a violent red** on avait peint les murs d'un rouge criard

violently ['vaɪələntlɪ] *adv (attack, shake, struggle)* violemment; *(act, react)* violemment, avec violence; **to behave violently** avoir un comportement violent; **he was violently sick** il fut pris de vomissements violents; **he was shaking/shivering violently** il était secoué de tremblements/de frissons violents

violet ['vaɪələt] **1** *n* (**a**) *Bot* violette *f* (**b**) *(colour)* violet *m*

2 *adj* violet

violin [ˌvaɪə'lɪn] **1** *n* violon *m*

2 *comp (concerto)* pour violon; *(lesson)* de violon

▸▸ ***violin case*** étui *m* à violon; ***violin maker*** luthier *m*

violinist [ˌvaɪə'lɪnɪst] *n* violoniste *mf*

violist *n* (**a**) ['vaɪəlɪst] *(viol player)* joueur(euse) *m,f* de viole, violiste *mf* (**b**) [vɪ'əʊlɪst] *(viola player)* joueur(euse) *m,f* d'alto, altiste *mf*

violoncellist [ˌvaɪələn'tʃelɪst] *n* violoncelliste *mf*

violoncello [ˌvaɪələn'tʃeləʊ] *(pl* **violoncellos***)* *n* violoncelle *m*

violone ['vaɪələʊn] *n Mus* violone *f*

VIP [ˌviːaɪ'piː] *(abbr* **very important person***)* **1** *n* VIP *mf*, personnalité *f*, personnage *m* de marque

2 *comp (guests, visitors)* de marque, éminent, très important; **to give sb the VIP treatment** traiter qn comme un personnage de marque; **we got VIP treatment** on nous a réservé un accueil princier, on nous a traités comme des rois

▸▸ ***VIP lounge*** *(in airport)* = salon d'accueil réservé aux personnages de marque

viper ['vaɪpə(r)] *n Zool & Fig* vipère *f*; *Fig* **a vipers' nest** un nœud de vipères

▸▸ *Bot* ***viper's bugloss*** vipérine *f*

viperish ['vaɪpərɪʃ], **viperous** ['vaɪpərəs] *adj* vipérin, de vipère; *(person)* qui a une langue de vipère; *Fig* **a viperish tongue** une langue de vipère

viraemia [vaɪ'riːmɪə] *n Br Med* virémie *f*

virago [vɪ'rɑːgəʊ] *(pl* **viragoes** *or* **viragos***)* *n* mégère *f*, virago *f*

viral ['vaɪrəl] *adj* viral; **a viral infection** une infection virale

▸▸ *Med* ***viral load*** charge *f* virale

viremia [vaɪ'riːmjə] *n Med* virémie *f*

virescence [vɪ'resəns] *n* (**a**) *Bot* virescence *f* (**b**) *Literary* couleur *f* verte, verdure *f (du printemps)*

virescent [vɪ'resənt] *adj Literary* verdoyant

virga ['vɜːgə] *(pl* **virgae** [-giː]*)* *n Met* virga *f*

virgate ['vɜːgeɪt] *adj Bot* en verge, élancé

Virgil ['vɜːdʒɪl] *pr n* Virgile

Virgilian [vɜː'dʒɪlɪən] *adj* virgilien

virgin ['vɜːdʒɪn] **1** *n (girl)* vierge *f*, pucelle *f*; *(boy)* puceau *m*

2 *adj* (**a**) *(sexually)* vierge (**b**) *(forest, soil, wool)* vierge; *(fresh)* virginal; **virgin white sheets** draps d'un blanc immaculé

3 Virgin *pr n Rel* **the Virgin** la Vierge

▸▸ *Rel* ***the Virgin birth*** l'Immaculée Conception *f*; ***virgin birth*** *(parthenogenesis)* parthénogenèse *f*; ***the Virgin Islands*** les îles *fpl* Vierges; **in the Virgin Islands** dans les îles Vierges; *Bible* ***the Virgin Mary*** la Vierge Marie; ***The Virgin Queen*** la reine *f* vierge *(Élisabeth Ire)*; ***virgin snow*** neige *f* fraîche; ***virgin territory*** territoire *m* vierge; *Fig* **this market is virgin territory for the company** ce marché constitue un territoire vierge pour la société

virginal ['vɜːdʒɪnəl] **1** *n Mus* **virginals** virginal *m*

2 *adj* virginal

Virginia [və'dʒɪnjə] *n* la Virginie; **in Virginia** en Virginie

▸▸ *Bot* ***Virginia creeper*** vigne *f* vierge; *Orn* ***Virginia rail*** râle *m* de Virginie; ***Virginia stock*** malcolmia *m*; ***Virginia tobacco*** virginie *m*, tabac *m* de Virginie

Virginian [və'dʒɪnjən] **1** *n* Virginien(enne) *m,f*

2 *adj* virginien

virginity [və'dʒɪnɪtɪ] *n* virginité *f*; **to lose one's virginity** perdre sa virginité

Virgo ['vɜːgəʊ] **1** *n* (**a**) *Astron* Vierge *f* (**b**) *Astrol* Vierge *f*; **he's a Virgo** il est (du signe de la) Vierge

2 *adj Astrol* de la Vierge; **he's Virgo** il est (du signe de la) Vierge

Virgoan ['vɜːgəʊən] *Astrol* **1** *n* **to be a Virgoan** être (du signe de la) Vierge

2 *adj* de la Vierge; **the Virgoan male** l'homme Vierge

virgule ['vɜːgjuːl] *n Typ* barre *f* oblique

viridescent [ˌvɪrɪ'desənt] *adj* verdâtre; *(leaves, vegetation etc)* verdoyant

viridian [vɪ'rɪdɪən] *n Art* vert *m* Guignet

virile ['vɪraɪl] *adj* viril

virilism ['vɪrɪˌlɪzəm] *n Med* virilisme *m*

virility [vɪ'rɪlɪtɪ] *n* virilité *f*

virion ['vaɪrɪən] *n Biol* virion *m*

virological [ˌvaɪrə'lɒdʒɪkəl] *adj* virologique

virologist [ˌvaɪ'rɒlədʒɪst] *n* virologue *mf*, virologiste *mf*

virology [ˌvaɪ'rɒlədʒɪ] *n* virologie *f*

virtual ['vɜːtʃʊəl] *adj* (**a**) *(near, as good as)* **the country is in a state of virtual anarchy** c'est pratiquement l'anarchie dans le pays; **the strike led to a virtual halt in production** la grève a provoqué une interruption quasi totale de la production; **it's a virtual impossibility/dictatorship** c'est une quasi-impossibilité/une quasi-dictature; **he's a virtual prisoner** il est quasiment prisonnier; **the virtual extinction of this species** la disparition quasi-totale de cette espèce

(**b**) *(actual, effective)* **they are the virtual rulers of the country** en fait, ce sont eux qui dirigent le pays, ce sont eux les dirigeants de fait du pays

(**c**) *Comput & Phys* virtuel

▸▸ *Phys* ***virtual image*** image *f* virtuelle; *Comput* ***virtual memory*** mémoire *f* virtuelle; ***virtual reality*** réalité *f* virtuelle; ***virtual reality helmet*** casque *m* de réalité virtuelle; *Comput* ***virtual reality simulator*** simulateur *m* de réalité virtuelle; *Comput* ***virtual storage*** mémoire *f* virtuelle

virtuality [ˌvɜːtʃʊ'ælɪtɪ] *n* virtualité *f*

virtually ['vɜːtʃʊəlɪ] *adv* (**a**) *(almost)* pratiquement, quasiment; **it's virtually impossible** c'est pratiquement *ou* quasiment impossible; **it's virtually finished** c'est presque *ou* quasiment fini; **I'm virtually certain** je suis pratiquement certain; **she virtually insulted me** elle m'a pratiquement insulté; **virtually every country in Europe** chaque pays européen ou presque

(**b**) *(actually, in effect)* en fait; **he is virtually**

the manager en fait *ou* en pratique, c'est lui le directeur

virtue ['vɜːtjuː] **1** *n* **(a)** *(goodness)* vertu *f*; **to make a virtue of necessity** faire de nécessité vertu; **a woman of easy virtue** une femme de petite vertu; *Prov* **virtue is its own reward** = la vertu est sa propre récompense

(b) *(merit)* mérite *m*, avantage *m*; **she at least has the virtue of being discreet** elle a au moins le mérite d'être discrète; **the flat has the virtue of being centrally heated** l'appartement a l'avantage d'avoir le chauffage central

(c) *(power)* vertu *f*; **the healing virtues of certain plants** les vertus curatives de certaines plantes

2 by virtue of *prep* en vertu *ou* en raison de; **by virtue of her age** en vertu *ou* en raison de son âge; **by virtue of being the eldest** en vertu *ou* en raison du fait qu'il est l'aîné

virtuosity [ˌvɜːtjʊ'ɒsɪtɪ] *n* virtuosité *f*

virtuoso [ˌvɜːtjʊ'əʊzəʊ] *(pl* **virtuosos** *or* **virtuosi** [-ziː]) **1** *n (gen) & Mus* virtuose *mf*

2 *adj* de virtuose; **it was a virtuoso performance** *Mus* c'était une interprétation de virtuose; *Fig* c'était un tour de force

virtuous ['vɜːtʃʊəs] *adj* vertueux

virtuously ['vɜːtʃʊəslɪ] *adv* vertueusement

virtuousness ['vɜːtjʊəsnɪs] *n* vertu *f*

virulence ['vɪrʊləns] *n* virulence *f*

virulent ['vɪrʊlənt] *adj Med & Fig* virulent

virulently ['vɪrʊləntlɪ] *adv* avec virulence

virus ['vaɪrəs] *n* **(a)** *Med* virus *m*; **the flu virus** le virus de la grippe; *Fam* **the virus** *(AIDS)* le sida ❑

(b) *Comput* virus *m*; **to disable a virus** désactiver un virus

►► *Comput* ***virus check*** détection *f* de virus; **to run a virus check on a disk** faire tourner le programme détecteur de virus sur une disquette; *Comput* ***virus detection*** détection *f* de virus; *Comput* ***virus detector*** détecteur *m* de virus; *Med* ***virus infection*** infection *f* virale; *Comput* ***virus program*** programme *m* virus

virus-free *adj Comput* dépourvu de virus

virus-infected *adj Comput* contaminé par un/des virus

Visa® ['viːzə] *n* carte Visa® *f*; **to pay by Visa**® payer par carte Visa®

►► ***Visa*® *card*** carte *f* Visa®

visa ['viːzə] **1** *n* visa *m*; **he has applied for an American visa** il a demandé un visa pour l'Amérique

2 *vt Admin* viser

visage ['vɪzɪdʒ] *n Literary* visage *m*, figure *f*

vis-à-vis [ˌviːzɑː'viː] *(pl* **inv**) **1** *prep* **(a)** *(in relation to)* par rapport à **(b)** *(opposite)* vis-à-vis de

2 *adv* vis-à-vis

3 *n* **(a)** *(person or thing opposite)* vis-à-vis *m inv* **(b)** *(counterpart)* homologue *mf*

viscacha [vɪ'skætʃə] *n Zool* viscache *f*

viscera ['vɪsərə] *npl* viscères *mpl*

visceral ['vɪsərəl] *adj* viscéral

viscid ['vɪsɪd] *adj* visqueux

viscidity [vɪ'sɪdɪtɪ] *n* viscosité *f*

viscose ['vɪskəʊs] **1** *n* viscose *f*

2 *adj* visqueux

viscosity [vɪ'skɒsɪtɪ] *(pl* **viscosities**) *n* viscosité *f*

viscount ['vaɪkaʊnt] *n* vicomte *m*

viscountcy ['vaɪkaʊntsɪ] *n* vicomté *f*

viscountess ['vaɪkaʊntɪs] *n* vicomtesse *f*

viscounty ['vaɪkaʊntɪ] = **viscountcy**

viscous ['vɪskəs] *adj* visqueux, gluant

viscus ['vɪskəs] *n Med* viscère *m*

vise [vaɪs] *Am* = **vice** *n* **(c)**

Vishnu ['vɪʃnuː] *pr n Rel* Vishnou

Vishnuism ['vɪʃnuːɪzəm] *n Rel* vishnouisme *m*

visibility [ˌvɪzɪ'bɪlɪtɪ] *n* visibilité *f*; **good/poor visibility** bonne/mauvaise visibilité *f*; **visibility is down to a few yards** la visibilité est réduite à quelques mètres

visible ['vɪzəbəl] *adj* **(a)** *(gen) & Opt* visible; **to become visible** devenir visible; **clearly visible to the naked eye** clairement visible à l'œil nu; **only visible under a microscope** seulement visible au microscope; **the beach is not visible from the road** on ne peut pas voir la plage de la route, la plage n'est pas visible de la route

(b) *(evident)* visible, apparent, manifeste; **his nervousness was clearly visible** sa nervosité était manifeste *ou* évidente; **it serves no visible purpose** on n'en voit pas vraiment l'utilité, on ne voit pas vraiment à quoi cela sert; *Admin* **with no visible means of support** sans ressources apparentes

►► *Com* ***visible balance*** balance *f* visible; *Com* ***visible defects*** défauts *mpl* apparents; ***visible horizon*** horizon *m*; *Phys* ***visible spectrum*** spectre *m* visible; *Com* ***visible trade*** commerce *m* de biens

visibly ['vɪzɪblɪ] *adv* visiblement; **he was visibly surprised/annoyed** il était visiblement surpris/ennuyé, sa surprise/son ennui était manifeste

Visigoth ['vɪzɪˌgɒθ] *n* Visigoth(e) *m,f*, Wisigoth(e) *m,f*

Visigothic [ˌvɪzɪ'gɒθɪk] *adj* visigoth, wisigoth

vision ['vɪʒən] *n* **(a)** *(UNCOUNT) Opt (sight)* vision *f*, vue *f*; **to suffer from defective vision** avoir mauvaise vue; **outside/within one's field of vision** hors de/en vue

(b) *(insight)* vision *f*, clairvoyance *f*; **a man of vision** un visionnaire; **we need people with vision and imagination** nous avons besoin de gens inspirés et imaginatifs

(c) *(dream, fantasy)* vision *f*; *Rel* **to have a vision** avoir une vision; *Med & Psy* **to have visions** avoir des visions; **he has visions of being rich and famous** il se voit riche et célèbre; **I had visions of you lying in a hospital bed** je vous voyais couché dans un lit d'hôpital; **I had visions of having to walk all the way into town** je me suis vu devoir aller jusqu'en ville à pied

(d) *(conception)* vision *f*, conception *f*; **what is your vision of the new town centre?** comment voyez-vous *ou* comment concevez-vous le nouveau centre-ville?

(e) *(apparition)* vision *f*, apparition *f*; *(lovely sight)* magnifique spectacle *m*; **she was a vision in white lace** elle était ravissante en dentelle blanche; **a vision of loveliness** une apparition de charme

(f) *TV* image *f*

►► ***vision mixer*** *TV (equipment)* mixeur *m*, mélangeur *m* de signaux; *(person)* opérateur(-trice) *m,f* de mixage; *TV* ***vision mixing*** mixage *m* d'images

'The Vision of Piers the Plowman' *Langland* 'La Vision de Pierre le Laboureur'

visionary ['vɪʒənərɪ] *(pl* **visionaries**) **1** *adj* visionnaire

2 *n* visionnaire *mf*

visit ['vɪzɪt] **1** *n* **(a)** *(call)* visite *f*; **to pay sb a visit** rendre visite à qn; **I haven't paid a visit to the cathedral yet** je n'ai pas encore visité *ou* je ne suis pas encore allé voir la cathédrale; **I had a visit from your aunt last week** j'ai eu la visite de ta tante la semaine dernière; **you must pay them a return visit** il faut leur rendre leur visite; **she met him on a return visit to her home town** elle l'a rencontré quand elle est retournée en visite dans sa ville natale; *Br Fam Euph* **to pay a visit** aller au petit coin

(b) *(stay)* visite *f*, séjour *m*; *(trip)* voyage *m*, séjour *m*; **she's on a visit to her aunt's** elle est en visite chez sa tante; **she's on a visit to Amsterdam** elle fait un séjour à Amsterdam; **did you enjoy your visit to California?** avez-vous fait un bon séjour en Californie?; **the President is on an official visit to Australia** le président est en visite officielle en Australie; **this is my first visit to your country** c'est la première fois que je viens dans votre pays

(c) *Am (chat)* causette *f*, bavardage *m*

2 *vt* **(a)** *(person → go to see)* rendre visite à, aller voir; *(→ stay with)* rendre visite à, séjourner chez; **she went to visit her aunt in hospital** elle est allée rendre visite à sa tante *ou* allée voir sa tante à l'hôpital; **to visit the doctor/dentist** aller voir le médecin/le dentiste, aller chez le médecin/le dentiste; **not many people come to visit her** il n'y a pas beaucoup de gens qui viennent lui rendre visite; **to visit the sick** visiter les malades; **he's away visiting friends at the moment** il séjourne chez des amis en ce moment

(b) *(museum, town)* visiter, aller voir; **in the afternoon they went to visit Pisa** l'après-midi, ils sont allés voir *ou* visiter Pise

(c) *(inspect → place, premises)* visiter, inspecter, faire une visite d'inspection à; *Law* **to visit the scene of the crime** se rendre sur les lieux du crime

(d) *Literary (inflict)* **to visit a punishment on sb** punir qn; **the sins of the fathers are visited upon their sons** les fils sont punis pour les péchés de leurs pères; **the city was visited by the plague in the 17th century** la ville a été atteinte par la peste au XVIIème siècle

3 *vi* être de passage; **we're just visiting** nous sommes simplement de passage

►**visit with** *vt insep Am (call on)* passer voir; *(talk with)* bavarder avec

visitant ['vɪzɪtənt] *n* **(a)** *Literary (ghost)* revenant *m*, fantôme *m* **(b)** *(bird)* oiseau *m* migrateur *ou* de passage

visitation [ˌvɪzɪ'teɪʃən] **1** *n* **(a)** *(official visit, inspection)* visite *f ou* tour *m* d'inspection; *Rel (of bishop)* visite *f* épiscopale *ou* pastorale; *Hum* **we're having a visitation from the managing director next week** le directeur général nous fait l'honneur de sa visite la semaine prochaine

(b) *(social visit)* visite *f*; *Hum (prolonged)* visite *f* trop prolongée

(c) *Formal (affliction)* punition *f* du ciel; *(reward)* récompense *f* divine

2 Visitation *n Rel* **the Visitation** la Visitation

visitatorial [ˌvɪzɪtə'tɔːrɪəl] *adj (right, duty etc)* de visite, d'inspection

visiting ['vɪzɪtɪŋ] *adj (circus, performers)* de passage; *(lecturer)* invité; *(birds)* de passage, migrateur; *Sport* **the visiting team** les visiteurs *mpl*

►► *Br* ***visiting card*** carte *f* de visite; *Am Fam* ***visiting fireman*** visiteur *m* de marque ❑; ***visiting hours*** heures *fpl* de visite; *Am* ***visiting nurse*** infirmier(ère) *m,f* à domicile; *Univ* ***visiting professor*** professeur *m* associé *ou* invité; *Law* ***visiting rights*** *(of divorced parent)* droit *m* de visite; ***visiting time*** heures *fpl* de visite

visitor ['vɪzɪtə(r)] *n* **(a)** *(caller → at hospital, house, prison)* visiteur(euse) *m,f*; **you have a visitor** vous avez de la visite; **I rarely have visitors** c'est rare que j'aie de la visite; **they are not allowed any visitors after 10 p.m.** ils n'ont pas le droit de recevoir des visiteurs *ou* des visites après 22 heures

(b) *(guest → at private house)* visiteur(euse) *m,f*, invité(e) *m,f*; *(→ at hotel)* client(e) *m,f*; **we have visitors** on a du monde *ou* des invités

(c) *(tourist)* visiteur(euse) *m,f*, touriste *mf*; **visitors to the exhibition are requested not to smoke** il est demandé aux personnes visitant l'exposition de ne pas fumer; **we had 40,000 visitors last year** on a eu 40 000 visiteurs l'an dernier; **we get lots of American visitors in the town** nous avons énormément de visiteurs américains dans la ville

(d) *Orn* oiseau *m* passager; **this bird is a visitor to these shores** cet oiseau est seulement de passage sur ces côtes; **this species is a winter visitor to Britain** cette espèce vient passer l'hiver en Grande-Bretagne

►► ***visitors' book*** *(in house, museum)* livre *m* d'or; *(in hotel)* registre *m*; ***visitor centre*** *(in park, at tourist attraction etc)* centre *m* d'accueil pour les visiteurs; ***visitors' gallery*** tribune *f* du public; ***visitor's passport*** passeport *m* temporaire

visor ['vaɪzə(r)] *n (on hat)* visière *f*; *(in car)* pare-soleil *m inv*

VISTA ['vɪstə] *n Am (abbr* **Volunteers in Service to America**) = programme américain d'aide aux personnes les plus défavorisées

vista ['vɪstə] *n* **(a)** *(view)* vue *f*, perspective *f*; **a mountain vista** une vue sur les montagnes, une perspective de montagnes **(b)** *Fig (perspective)* perspective *f*, horizon *m*; *(image → of past)* vue *f*, vision *f*; *(→ of future)* perspective *f*, vision *f*; **to open up new vistas** ouvrir de nouvelles perspectives *ou* de nouveaux horizons

►► ***vista point*** point *m* de vue

vistadome ['vɪstədəʊm] *n Am Rail* vistadôme *m*

Vistula ['vɪstjʊlə] *n Geog* **the Vistula** la Vistule

visual ['vɪʒʊəl] **1** *adj* **(a)** *(gen) & Opt (image, impression, faculty)* visuel; **her comedy is very visual** son comique repose sur les effets visuels **(b)** *Aviat (landing, navigation)* à vue

2 visuals *npl* supports *mpl* visuels

►► ***visual aid*** support *m* visuel; ***visual arts*** arts *mpl* plastiques; ***visual display terminal, visual display unit*** visuel *m*, écran *m* de visualisation; ***visual field*** champ *m* visuel; ***visual handicap*** handicap *m* visuel; ***visual memory*** mémoire *f* visuelle

visualization [ˌvɪʒʊəlaɪ'zeɪʃən] *n* (**a**) *(visual presentation)* visualisation *f* (**b**) *(imagination)* visualisation *f*, évocation *f*

visualize, -ise ['vɪʒʊəlaɪz] *vt* (**a**) *(call to mind → scene)* se représenter, évoquer; *(imagine)* s'imaginer, visualiser, se représenter; **I remember the name but I can't visualize his face** je me souviens de son nom mais je ne revois plus son visage; **he tried to visualize what it would be like** il essaya de s'imaginer comment ce serait; **she tried to visualize herself travelling through the Amazon** elle essayait de se représenter *ou* de s'imaginer en train de traverser l'Amazone

(**b**) *(foresee)* envisager, prévoir; **I can't visualize things getting any better** je n'envisage aucune amélioration

(**c**) *Tech (make visible)* visualiser; *Med* rendre visible par radiographie

visually ['vɪʒʊəlɪ] *adv* visuellement; **visually handicapped, visually impaired** malvoyant, *Spec* amblyope; **the visually handicapped** les malvoyants *mpl*

vital ['vaɪtəl] **1** *adj* (**a**) *(essential → information, services, supplies)* vital, essentiel, indispensable; **of vital importance** d'une importance capitale; **this drug is vital to the success of the operation** ce médicament est indispensable au succès de l'opération; **it's vital that I know the truth** il est indispensable que je sache la vérité; **to play a vital role** jouer un rôle capital *ou* primordial

(**b**) *(very important → decision, matter)* vital, fondamental; **tonight's match is vital** le match de ce soir est décisif

(**c**) *Biol (function, organ)* vital

(**d**) *(energetic)* plein d'entrain, dynamique

2 vitals *npl* (**a**) *Anat or Hum* organes *mpl* vitaux

(**b**) *(essential elements)* parties *fpl* essentielles

►► *Med* ***vital capacity*** capacité *f* thoracique; ***vital force*** force *f* vitale; *Med* ***vital signs*** = température, rythme cardiaque et respiration; ***vital statistics*** *(demographic)* statistiques *fpl* démographiques; *Fam (of woman)* mensurations *fpl*

vitalism ['vaɪtəˌlɪzəm] *n Biol* vitalisme *m*

vitalist ['vaɪtəlɪst] *n Biol* vitaliste *mf*

vitalistic [ˌvaɪtə'lɪstɪk] *adj Biol* vitaliste

vitality [vaɪ'tælɪtɪ] *n* vitalité *f*

vitalize, -ise ['vaɪtəlaɪz] *vt* vivifier, dynamiser

vitalizing ['vaɪtəˌlaɪzɪŋ] *adj (power, influence etc)* dynamisant, vivifiant

vitally ['vaɪtəlɪ] *adv* absolument; **it's vitally important that you attend this meeting** il est extrêmement important *ou* il est essentiel que vous assistiez à cette réunion; **this question is vitally important** cette question est d'une importance capitale; **supplies are vitally needed** on a un besoin vital de vivres; **vitally for the British, the European Commission has agreed** la Commission Européenne a accepté, ce qui est vital *ou* capital pour les Britanniques

vitamin [*Br* 'vɪtəmɪn, *Am* 'vaɪtəmɪn] *n* vitamine *f*; **vitamin C/E** vitamine C/E; **with added vitamins** vitaminé

►► ***vitamin deficiency*** *(gen)* carence *f* vitaminique; *(disease)* avitaminose *f*; ***vitamin pill*** comprimé *m* de vitamines

vitaminization [*Br* ˌvɪtəmɪnaɪ'zeɪʃən, *Am* ˌvaɪtəmɪnaɪ'zeɪʃən] *n* vitaminisation *f*

vitaminized [*Br* 'vɪtəmɪnaɪzd, *Am* 'vaɪtəmɪnaɪzd] *adj* vitaminé

vitaminizing [*Br* 'vɪtəmɪnaɪzɪŋ, *Am* 'vaɪtəmɪnaɪzɪŋ] *n* vitaminisation *f*

vitiate ['vɪʃɪeɪt] *vt Formal* vicier

vitiated ['vɪʃɪeɪtɪd] *adj Formal (air, taste etc)* vicié

vitiating ['vɪʃɪeɪtɪŋ] *adj Formal* viciateur

vitiation [ˌvɪʃɪ'eɪʃən] *n Formal* viciation *f*

viticultural [ˌvɪtɪ'kʌltʃərəl] *adj* viticole

viticulture ['vɪtɪˌkʌltʃə(r)] *n* viticulture *f*

vitiligo [ˌvɪtɪ'laɪgəʊ] *n Med* vitiligo *m*

vitreous ['vɪtrɪəs] *adj* (**a**) *(china, rock)* vitreux; *(enamel)* vitrifié (**b**) *Anat* vitré

►► ***vitreous body*** *(in eye)* corps *m* vitré; ***vitreous humour*** humeur *f* vitrée

vitrescent [vɪ'tresənt] *adj* vitrescible, vitreux

vitrifaction [ˌvɪtrɪ'fækʃən], **vitrification** [ˌvɪtrɪfɪ'keɪʃən] *n* vitrification *f*

vitrified ['vɪtrɪfaɪd] *adj* vitrifié

vitriform ['vɪtrɪfɔːm] *adj* vitreux, qui a l'apparence du verre

vitrify ['vɪtrɪfaɪ] (*pt & pp* **vitrified**) **1** *vt* vitrifier

2 *vi* se vitrifier

vitriol ['vɪtrɪəl] *n Chem & Fig* vitriol *m*

vitriolic [ˌvɪtrɪ'ɒlɪk] *adj* (**a**) *Chem* de vitriol (**b**) *(attack, description, portrait)* au vitriol; *(tone)* venimeux

►► ***vitriolic criticism*** critique *f* mordante

vitriolize, -ise ['vɪtrɪəlaɪz] *vt* vitrioler

vitta ['vɪtə] (*pl* **vittae** [-tiː]) *n* (**a**) *Bot* canal *m* résinifère (**b**) *Zool* bande *f* (de couleur), raie *f*

vittle *Arch* = **victual**

vituperate [vɪ'tjuːpəreɪt] *Literary* **1** *vt* vitupérer (contre), vilipender

2 *vi* vitupérer; **to vituperate against sb/sth** vitupérer (contre) qn/qch

vituperation [vɪˌtjuːpə'reɪʃən] *n (UNCOUNT)* vitupérations *fpl*

vituperative [vɪ'tjuːpərətɪv] *adj* injurieux

viva¹ ['viːvə] **1** *exclam* vive!

2 *n* vivat *m*

viva² ['vaɪvə] = **viva voce** *n*

vivace [vɪ'vɑːtʃɪ] *Mus* **1** *adj* vivace

2 *adv* vivace

vivacious [vɪ'veɪʃəs] *adj* (**a**) *(manner, person)* enjoué, plein de vivacité (**b**) *Bot* vivace

vivaciously [vɪ'veɪʃəslɪ] *adv* avec vivacité

vivacity [vɪ'væsɪtɪ] *n (in action)* vivacité *f*; *(in speech)* verve *f*

Vivaldi [vɪ'vældɪ] *pr n* Vivaldi

vivarium [vaɪ'veərɪəm] (*pl* **vivariums** *or* **vivaria** [-rɪə]) *n* vivarium *m*

vivat ['vaɪvæt] **1** *n* vivat *m*

2 *exclam* vivat!

viva voce [ˌvaɪvə'vəʊtʃɪ] **1** *n Br Univ (gen)* épreuve *f* orale, oral *m*; *(for thesis)* soutenance *f* de thèse

2 *adj* oral

3 *adv* de vive voix, oralement

vivid ['vɪvɪd] *adj* (**a**) *(bright → colour, light)* vif, éclatant; *(→ clothes)* voyant; **vivid green paint** peinture d'un vert éclatant

(**b**) *(intense → feeling)* vif

(**c**) *(lively → personality)* vif, vivant; *(→ imagination)* vif; *(→ language)* coloré; **it was a very vivid performance** c'était une interprétation pleine de verve

(**d**) *(graphic → account, description)* vivant; *(→ memory)* vif, net; *(→ example)* frappant; *(→ imagery)* saisissant; **he paints a vivid picture of 18th century life** il dresse un tableau très vivant de la vie au XVIIIème siècle

vividly ['vɪvɪdlɪ] *adv* (**a**) *(coloured)* de façon éclatante; *(painted, decorated)* avec éclat, de façon éclatante (**b**) *(describe)* de façon frappante *ou* vivante; **I can vividly remember the day we first met** j'ai un vif souvenir du jour où nous nous sommes rencontrés

vividness ['vɪvɪdnɪs] *n* (**a**) *(of colour, light)* éclat *m*, vivacité *f* (**b**) *(of description, language)* vivacité *f*; *(of memory)* clarté *f*; **she could remember him with great vividness** elle se souvenait très nettement de lui; **the vividness of the imagery in this poem** les images saisissantes dans ce poème

vivification [ˌvɪvɪfɪ'keɪʃən] *n* vivification *f*

vivify ['vɪvɪfaɪ] (*pt & pp* **vivified**) *vt* vivifier

vivifying ['vɪvɪˌfaɪɪŋ] *adj* vivifiant

viviparity [ˌvɪvɪ'pærɪtɪ] *n Biol* viviparité *f*

viviparous [vɪ'vɪpərəs] *adj Biol* vivipare

vivisect [ˌvɪvɪ'sekt] *vt* pratiquer la vivisection sur

vivisection [ˌvɪvɪ'sekʃən] *n* vivisection *f*

vivisectionist [ˌvɪvɪ'sekʃənɪst] *n* (**a**) *(practitioner)* vivisecteur(trice) *m,f* (**b**) *(advocate)* partisan(e) *m,f* de la vivisection

vivisector ['vɪvɪˌsektə(r)] *n* vivisecteur(trice) *m,f*

vixen ['vɪksən] *n* (**a**) *Zool* renarde *f* (**b**) *Pej (woman)* mégère *f*

vixenish ['vɪksənɪʃ] *adj Pej (woman)* acariâtre, méchante; *(character)* de mégère

Viyella® [vaɪ'elə] *n* = tissu mélangé (laine et coton)

viz [vɪz] *adv (abbr* **videlicet**) c.-à-d.

vizcacha = **viscacha**

vizier [vɪ'zɪə(r)] *n* vizir *m*

vizor = **visor**

vizsla ['vɪʒlə] *n (dog)* vizsla *m*

VJ [ˌviː'dʒeɪ] *n (abbr* **Video Jockey**) présentateur(trice) *m,f* de (vidéo)clips

VJ Day *n (abbr* **Victory in Japan Day**) = jour de la victoire des alliés sur le Japon, le 15 août 1945

VLF [ˌviːel'ef] *n (abbr* **very low frequency**) VLF *f*

VLSI [ˌviːelˌes'aɪ] *n Comput (abbr* **very large-scale integration**) VLSI *f*

V-neck 1 *n* encolure *f* en V

2 *adj* à encolure en V

V-necked *adj* à encolure en V

VOA [ˌviːəʊ'eɪ] *n Am Rad (abbr* **Voice of America**) = station de radio américaine émettant dans le monde entier

vocab ['vəʊkæb] *n Fam* vocabulaire[□] *m*

vocable ['vəʊkəbəl] *n* vocable *m*

vocabulary [və'kæbjʊlərɪ] (*pl* **vocabularies**) **1** *n* vocabulaire *m*; *Ling* vocabulaire *m*, lexique *m*

2 *comp (test, guide, book)* de vocabulaire

vocal ['vəʊkəl] **1** *adj* (**a**) *Anat* vocal; **the vocal organs** les organes *mpl* vocaux

(**b**) *(oral → communication)* oral, verbal

(**c**) *(outspoken → person, minority)* qui se fait entendre; **the most vocal member of the delegation** le membre de la délégation qui s'est fait le plus entendre *ou* qui s'est exprimé le plus énergiquement; **one of privatisation's/the government's most vocal critics** l'un de ceux qui critiquent la privatisation/le gouvernement avec le plus de véhémence; **he is very vocal about…** il se fait entendre souvent au sujet de…

(**d**) *(noisy → assembly, meeting)* bruyant

(**e**) *Mus* vocal

(**f**) *Ling (sound)* vocalique; *(consonant)* voisé

2 *n Ling* son *m* vocalique

3 vocals *npl Mus* chant *m*, musique *f* vocale; **Lucy Johnston on vocals** au chant: Lucy Johnston

►► ***vocal cords*** cordes *fpl* vocales; **false vocal cords** fausses cordes *fpl* vocales, bandes *fpl* ventriculaires; **true vocal cords** (vraies) cordes *fpl* vocales; ***vocal score*** partition *f* chorale

vocalic [və'kælɪk] *adj* vocalique

vocalism ['vəʊkəˌlɪzəm] *n Ling & Mus* vocalisme *m*

vocalist ['vəʊkəlɪst] *n* chanteur(euse) *m,f (de groupe pop)*; **backing vocalist** choriste *mf*

vocalization [ˌvəʊkəlaɪ'zeɪʃən] *n* vocalisation *f*

vocalize, -ise ['vəʊkəlaɪz] **1** *vt* (**a**) *(gen → articulate)* exprimer (**b**) *Ling (sound)* vocaliser (**c**) *(text)* vocaliser, marquer des points-voyelles sur

2 *vi Mus* vocaliser, faire des vocalises

vocally ['vəʊkəlɪ] *adv* vocalement; *(protest)* à haute voix

vocation [vəʊ'keɪʃən] *n (gen) & Rel* vocation *f*; **he has no vocation for teaching/acting** il n'a pas la vocation de l'enseignement/du théâtre; **to miss one's vocation** manquer sa vocation

vocational [vəʊ'keɪʃənəl] *adj* professionnel

►► ***vocational course*** *(short)* stage *m* de formation professionnelle; *(longer)* enseignement *m* professionnel; ***vocational guidance*** orientation *f* professionnelle; *Am & Ir* ***vocational school*** lycée *m* professionnel; ***vocational training*** formation *f* professionnelle

vocationalism [vəʊ'keɪʃənəˌlɪzəm] *n Sch* enseignement *m* professionnel

vocationally [vəʊ'keɪʃənəlɪ] *adv* **vocationally oriented** à vocation professionnelle; **vocationally relevant subjects** matières à vocation professionnelle

vocative ['vɒkətɪv] *Gram* **1** *n* vocatif *m*; **in the vocative** au vocatif

2 *adj* **the vocative case** le vocatif

vociferate [və'sɪfəreɪt] *vi* vociférer, hurler

vociferation [vəˌsɪfə'reɪʃən] *n (shout)* cri *m*; *(shouting)* vociférations *fpl*, cris *mpl*

vociferous [və'sɪfərəs] *adj* bruyant, véhément; **to be vociferous in one's criticism of sth** critiquer qch avec véhémence

vociferously [və'sɪfərəslɪ] *adv (argue, complain)* bruyamment; *(criticize, protest, condemn)* avec véhémence

vocoder ['vəʊˌkəʊdə(r)] *n* vocodeur *m*

VOD [ˌviːəʊ'diː] *n* (*abbr* **video on demand**) vidéo *f* à la demande

vodka ['vɒdkə] *n* vodka *f*; **vodka and orange** vodka-orange *f*

vogue [vəʊg] **1** *n* (*fashion*) vogue *f*, mode *f*; **to come into vogue** devenir à la mode; **that hairstyle was much in vogue in the 1930s** cette coiffure était très en vogue *ou* très à la mode dans les années trente; **the vogue for long hair is on the way out** les cheveux longs passent de mode; **mini skirts are back in vogue** les mini-jupes sont de nouveau à la mode

2 *adj* (*style, word*) en vogue, à la mode

voice [vɔɪs] **1** *n* (**a**) (*speech*) voix *f*; **in a low voice** à voix basse; **in a loud voice** d'une voix forte; **to have a good speaking voice** avoir une bonne voix; **we heard the sound of voices** on entendait des gens parler; **he likes the sound of his own voice** (*is talkative*) il parle beaucoup; (*is conceited*) il s'écoute parler; **to shout at the top of one's voice** crier à tue-tête; **to give voice to sth** exprimer qch; **to hear voices** entendre des voix; **keep your voices down** ne parlez pas si fort; **to raise one's voice** (*speak louder*) parler plus fort; (*get angry*) hausser le ton; **don't you raise your voice at** *or* **to me!** ne prenez pas ce ton-là avec moi!; **several voices were raised in protest** plusieurs voix se sont élevées pour protester; **to make one's voice heard** se faire entendre; *Fig* **the voice of conscience/reason** la voix de la conscience/de la raison; **a little voice inside her told her it was wrong** (*her conscience told her*) une petite voix en elle lui dit que c'était mal; **with one voice** d'une seule voix; **the government must be seen to speak with one voice** le gouvernement doit donner l'impression qu'il parle d'une seule voix; *Am Rad* **Voice of America** = station de radio américaine émettant dans le monde entier

(**b**) (*of singer*) voix *f*; **to have a good (singing) voice** avoir une belle voix; **to be in good voice** être bien en voix

(**c**) (*say*) voix *f*; **we have no voice in the matter** nous n'avons pas voix au chapitre; **did you have a voice in deciding who should be invited?** avez-vous participé à l'élaboration de la liste des invités?; **proportional representation would give small parties a greater voice** la représentation proportionnelle donnerait davantage voix au chapitre aux petits partis

(**d**) *Gram* voix *f*; **in the active/passive voice** à la voix active/passive

2 *vt* (**a**) (*express → feelings*) exprimer, formuler; (*→ opposition, support*) exprimer; **to voice one's anxieties** exprimer ses angoisses

(**b**) *Ling* (*consonant*) voiser, sonoriser

(**c**) *Mus* (*organ*) harmoniser

▸▸ *Tel* ***voice bank*** boîte *f* vocale; ***voice box*** larynx *m*; *Comput* ***voice input*** entrée *f* vocale; ***voice mail*** messagerie *f* vocale; *Mus* ***voice part*** partie *f* vocale; *Comput* ***voice recognition*** reconnaissance *f* de la parole; *Comput* ***voice recognition software*** logiciel *m* de reconnaissance vocale; *Comput* ***voice response*** réponse *f* vocale; *Comput* ***voice synthesizer*** synthétiseur *m* de paroles; ***voice test*** audition *f*; ***voice training*** (*UNCOUNT*) *Mus* cours *mpl* de chant; *Theat* cours *mpl* de diction *ou* d'élocution; *Am Pol* ***voice vote*** vote *m* par acclamation

voice-activated *adj* à commande vocale

voiced [vɔɪst] *adj Ling* (*consonant*) sonore, voisé

-voiced [vɔɪst] *suff* **low/soft-voiced** à voix basse/douce

voice-driven *adj* à commande vocale

voiceless ['vɔɪslɪs] *adj* (**a**) *Med* aphone (**b**) (*with no say*) sans voix; **the voiceless masses** les masses sans voix *ou* qui ne peuvent pas s'exprimer (**c**) *Ling* (*consonant*) non-voisé, sourd

voice-over *n Cin & TV* voix *f* off

voiceprint ['vɔɪsprɪnt] *n* empreinte *f* vocale

void [vɔɪd] **1** *n* (**a**) *Phys & Astron* vide *m*

(**b**) (*chasm*) vide *m*

(**c**) (*emptiness*) vide *m*; **to fill a void** combler un vide; **her husband's death left an aching void in her life** la mort de son mari a laissé un grand vide *ou* un vide douloureux dans sa vie

2 *adj* (**a**) (*empty*) vide; **void of interest** dépourvu d'intérêt, sans aucun intérêt

(**b**) *Law* (*deed, contract*) **(null and) void** nul; **to make sth void** annuler *ou* rendre nul qch

(**c**) (*vacant → position*) vacant

3 *vt* (**a**) *Formal* (*empty*) vider; (*discharge → bowels*) évacuer

(**b**) *Law* annuler, rendre nul

voidance ['vɔɪdəns] *n Law* résiliation *f*

voidness ['vɔɪdnɪs] *n* (**a**) (*emptiness*) vide *m*, vacuité *f* (**b**) *Law* nullité *f*

voile [vɔɪl, vwɑːl] *n Tex* voile *m*

Vojvodina ['vɔɪvɒdiːnə] *n* Vojvodine *f*

vol. (*written abbr* **volume**) vol

volant ['vəʊlənt] *adj* (**a**) *Zool* volant (**b**) *Her* volant, essorant

volatile [*Br* 'vɒlətaɪl, *Am* 'vɒlətəl] **1** *adj* (**a**) *Chem* volatil (**b**) (*person → changeable*) versatile, inconstant; (*→ temperamental*) lunatique (**c**) (*unstable → situation*) explosif, instable; (*→ market*) instable; (*→ Stock Exchange*) volatil (**d**) *Literary* (*transitory*) fugace (**e**) *Comput* (*memory*) volatil

2 *n Chem* substance *f* volatile

volatility [ˌvɒlə'tɪlɪtɪ] *n* (**a**) *Chem* volatilité *f* (**b**) (*of person → changeability*) versatilité *f*, inconstance *f* (**c**) (*of situation, market*) caractère *m* explosif, instabilité *f*; (*of Stock Exchange*) volatilité *f*

volatilization [vɒˌlætɪlaɪ'zeɪʃən] *n* volatilisation *f*

volatilize, -ise [vɒ'lætɪlaɪz] **1** *vt* volatiliser

2 *vi* se volatiliser, s'évaporer

vol-au-vent ['vɒləʊvɑ̃] *n Culin* vol-au-vent *m inv*

volcanic [vɒl'kænɪk] *adj* volcanique

volcanically [vɒl'kænɪklɪ] *adv* volcaniquement, de façon volcanique

volcanicity [ˌvɒlkə'nɪsɪtɪ] *n* vulcanicité *f*

volcanism ['vɒlkəˌnɪzəm] *n* volcanisme *m*, vulcanisme *m*

volcano [vɒl'keɪnəʊ] (*pl* **volcanoes** *or* **volcanos**) *n* volcan *m*

volcanologic [ˌvɒlkənə'lɒdʒɪk], **volcanological** [ˌvɒlkənə'lɒdʒɪkəl] *adj* volcanologique, vulcanologique

volcanologist [ˌvɒlkə'nɒlədʒɪst] *n* volcanologue *mf*, vulcanologue *mf*

volcanology [ˌvɒlkə'nɒlədʒɪ] *n* volcanologie *f*, vulcanologie *f*

vole [vəʊl] *n Zool* campagnol *m*

Volga ['vɒlgə] *n* **the (River) Volga** la Volga

volition [və'lɪʃən] *n* (*gen*) & *Phil* volition *f*, volonté *f*; **of one's own volition** de son propre gré

volitional [və'lɪʃənəl], **volitionary** [və'lɪʃənərɪ] *adj* volitif

volitive ['vɒlɪtɪv] *adj Formal* volitif

volley ['vɒlɪ] **1** *n* (**a**) (*of gunshots*) volée *f*, salve *f*; (*of arrows, missiles, stones*) volée *f*, grêle *f*; (*of blows*) volée *f*

(**b**) (*of insults, curses*) bordée *f*, torrent *m*; (*of questions*) feu *m* roulant; (*of applause*) salve *f*

(**c**) *Sport* volée *f*; **half volley** (*in tennis*) demi-volée *f*

2 *vt* (**a**) (*missile, shot*) tirer une volée *ou* une salve de

(**b**) (*curses, insults*) lâcher une bordée *ou* un torrent de

(**c**) *Sport* reprendre de volée

3 *vi* (**a**) *Mil* tirer par salves

(**b**) *Sport* (*in tennis*) volleyer, reprendre la balle de volée; (*in football*) reprendre le ballon de volée

volleyball ['vɒlɪbɔːl] *n* volley-ball *m*, volley *m*

▸▸ ***volleyball player*** volleyeur(euse) *m,f*

volleyer ['vɒlɪə(r)] *n Sport* (*in tennis*) volleyeur(-euse) *m,f*

volplane ['vɒlpleɪn] *vi Aviat* (*fly*) faire du vol plané, planer; (*fly down*) descendre en vol plané; **to volplane to the ground** atterrir en vol plané

volt[1] [vəʊlt] *n Elec* volt *m*

volt[2] [vɒlt, vəʊlt] *n Fencing* volte *f*; **to make a volt** volter

Volta ['vɒltə] *n* Volta *f*; **the Black Volta** la Volta Noire; **the White Volta** la Volta Blanche

voltage ['vəʊltɪdʒ] *n* voltage *m*, *Spec* tension *f*; **high/low voltage** haute/basse tension *f*

voltaic [vɒl'teɪɪk] *adj* voltaïque

▸▸ ***voltaic pile*** pile *f* voltaïque

Voltairean, Voltairian [vɒl'teərɪən] **1** *adj* voltairien

2 *n* voltairien(enne) *m,f*

voltameter [vɒl'tæmɪtə(r)] *n* voltamètre *m*

volt-ampere *n* voltampère *m*

volte-face [ˌvɒlt'fɑːs] *n* volte-face *f inv*; **the speech represents a complete volte-face** ce discours marque un revirement complet *ou* représente une véritable volte-face

voltmeter ['vəʊltˌmiːtə(r)] *n* voltmètre *m*

volubility [ˌvɒljʊ'bɪlɪtɪ] *n* volubilité *f*

voluble ['vɒljʊbəl] *adj* volubile, loquace

volubly ['vɒljʊblɪ] *adv* avec volubilité

volume ['vɒljuːm] *n* (**a**) (*gen*) & *Phys* volume *m*; (*capacity*) volume *m*, capacité *f*; (*amount*) volume *m*, quantité *f*; **to increase in volume** augmenter de volume; **the volume of traffic has greatly increased** le volume de la circulation a beaucoup augmenté; **a huge volume of work** une énorme quantité de travail; **the volume of business/imports** le volume des affaires/des importations; **this shampoo gives the hair more volume** ce shampoing donne du volume aux cheveux

(**b**) (*acoustics*) volume *m*; **to turn the volume up/down** augmenter/baisser le volume; *Rad* **at full volume** à fond, à plein volume

(**c**) (*book*) volume *m*, tome *m*; **volume one** volume *m ou* tome *m* premier, premier volume *m*; **an encyclopedia in twenty volumes** une encyclopédie en vingt volumes; **the third volume of his memoirs** le troisième tome *ou* volume de ses mémoires; **a rare volume** un exemplaire *ou* un livre rare; *Fig* **to speak volumes (about)** (*of action, remark etc*) en dire long (sur), être révélateur (de)

(**d**) (*of hair*) volume *m*

▸▸ *Rad & TV* ***volume control*** bouton *m* de réglage du volume; *Mktg* ***volume mailing*** multipostage *m*, publipostage *m* groupé

volumetric [ˌvɒljʊ'metrɪk], **volumetrical** [ˌvɒljʊ'metrɪkəl] *adj* volumétrique

▸▸ ***volumetric analysis*** analyse *f* volumétrique

volumetrically [ˌvɒljʊ'metrɪkəlɪ] *adv* volumétriquement

voluminosity [vəˌluːmɪ'nɒsɪtɪ] *n* = **voluminousness**

voluminous [və'luːmɪnəs] *adj* (*gen*) volumineux; (*garment*) ample; (*correspondence*) abondant

voluminously [və'luːmɪnəslɪ] *adv* (*write*) abondamment

voluminousness [və'luːmɪnəsnɪs] *n* (*of garment*) ampleur *f*; (*of documents*) grande quantité *f*; **the voluminousness of her correspondence** son abondante correspondance

voluntarily [*Br* 'vɒləntrɪlɪ, *Am* ˌvɒlən'terəlɪ] *adv* (**a**) (*willingly*) volontairement, de son plein gré (**b**) (*without payment*) bénévolement

voluntariness ['vɒləntrɪnɪs] *n* (*of act*) nature *f* volontaire, spontanéité *f*

voluntarism ['vɒləntəˌrɪzəm] *n* (**a**) *Phil* volontarisme *m* (**b**) *Rel* = **voluntaryism**

voluntarist ['vɒləntərɪst] *Phil* **1** *adj* volontariste

2 *n* volontariste *mf*

voluntaristic [ˌvɒləntə'rɪstɪk] *adj Phil* volontariste

voluntary ['vɒləntrɪ] (*pl* **voluntaries**) **1** *adj* (**a**) (*freely given → statement, donation, gift*) volontaire, spontané

(**b**) (*optional*) facultatif; **attendance on the course is purely voluntary** la participation au cours est facultative

(**c**) (*unpaid → help, service*) bénévole; **the shop is run on a voluntary basis** le personnel du magasin se compose de bénévoles, le magasin est tenu par des bénévoles

(**d**) *Physiol* volontaire

2 *n* (**a**) *Rel & Mus* morceau *m* d'orgue

(**b**) (*unpaid work*) travail *m* bénévole, bénévolat *m*

▸▸ ***voluntary agency*** organisme *m* bénévole; *Br Fin* ***voluntary arrangement*** = arrangement entre une entreprise et ses créanciers de façon à éviter la mise en liquidation; ***voluntary body*** organisme *m* bénévole; *Br Com* ***voluntary liquidation*** liquidation *f* volontaire; **to go into voluntary liquidation** déposer son bilan; *Law* ***voluntary manslaughter*** homicide *m* volontaire; *Anat* ***voluntary muscle*** muscle *m* strié *ou* squelettique; *Br* ***voluntary redundancy*** départ *m* volontaire; **he decided to take voluntary redundancy** il a accepté d'être licencié en échange d'indemnités; ***voluntary school*** = école privée qui reçoit une aide de l'État mais garde un certain pouvoir de décision, notamment sur le contenu des cours d'instruction religieuse et le choix des enseignants; ***voluntary service*** service *m* volontaire; ***Voluntary Service Overseas*** = coopération technique à l'étranger (non rémunérée); ***voluntary shop*** magasin *m* tenu par des bénévoles; ***voluntary work*** travail *m* bénévole, bénévolat *m*; ***voluntary worker*** bénévole *mf*

voluntary-aided school *n Br* = école financée principalement par l'État mais également par l'Église, ce qui donne à celle-ci un droit de regard sur l'instruction religieuse

voluntary-controlled school *n Br* école *f* publique

voluntaryism ['vɒləntrɪˌɪzəm] *n Rel* = principe de la séparation de l'Église et de l'État et du soutien de l'Église par contributions volontaires

volunteer [ˌvɒlən'tɪə(r)] **1** *n* (**a**) *(gen) & Mil* volontaire *mf*; **can I have a volunteer from the audience?** y a-t-il une personne dans la salle qui voudrait bien venir sur scène?
(**b**) *(unpaid worker)* bénévole *mf*
2 *comp* (**a**) *(army, group)* de volontaires
(**b**) *(work, worker)* bénévole
3 *vt* (**a**) *(advice, information, statement)* donner *ou* fournir spontanément; *(help, services)* donner *ou* proposer volontairement; **he volunteered his services as a guide** il s'est offert *ou* s'est proposé comme guide; **to volunteer to do sth** se proposer pour *ou* offrir de faire qch
(**b**) *(say)* dire spontanément; **"I saw them yesterday", she volunteered** "je les ai vus hier", dit-elle spontanément; **she seemed unwilling to volunteer anything more than this** elle n'avait pas l'air de vouloir en dire plus
4 *vi (gen)* se porter volontaire; *Mil* s'engager comme volontaire; **to volunteer for extra work/guard duty** se porter volontaire pour (faire) du travail supplémentaire/pour être de garde; **why not volunteer for the Marines?** pourquoi ne pas vous engager comme volontaire dans la marine?
►► ***the Volunteer State*** = surnom donné au Tennessee

voluptuary [və'lʌptʃʊərɪ] (*pl* **voluptuaries**) *Literary* **1** *n* voluptueux(euse) *m,f*, sybarite *mf*
2 *adj* voluptueux, sensuel

voluptuous [və'lʌptʃʊəs] *adj* voluptueux, sensuel

voluptuously [və'lʌptʃʊəslɪ] *adv* voluptueusement

voluptuousness [və'lʌptʃʊəsnɪs] *n* volupté *f*, sensualité *f*

volute [və'lu:t] *n* volute *f*

voluted [və'lu:tɪd] *adj* en volute

volution [və'lu:ʃən] *n* enroulement *m*

volva ['vɒlvə] (*pl* **volvas** *or* **volvae** [-vi:]) *n* volve *f*

vom [vɒm] *Fam* **1** *n* dégueulis *m*
2 *vi* dégueuler, gerber

vomit ['vɒmɪt] **1** *n* vomissement *m*, vomi *m*
2 *vt also Fig* vomir; **to vomit blood** vomir du sang

►**vomit out, vomit up** *vt sep* vomir

vomiting ['vɒmɪtɪŋ] *n* (*UNCOUNT*) vomissements *mpl*

vomitorium [ˌvɒmɪ'tɔ:rɪəm] (*pl* **vomitoria** [-rɪə]) *n Antiq* vomitoire *m*

vomitory ['vɒmɪtərɪ] (*pl* **vomitories**) **1** *adj Med* vomitif *m*
2 *n* (**a**) *Med* vomitif *m* (**b**) *Antiq* vomitoire *m*

voodoo ['vu:du:] (*pl* **voodoos**) **1** *n* vaudou *m*
2 *adj* vaudou *(inv)*
3 *vt* envoûter, ensorceler
►► *Am* ***voodoo economics*** = politique économique qui tient de l'illusionnisme

voodooism ['vu:du:ɪzəm] *n* vaudou *m*

voracious [və'reɪʃəs] *adj (appetite, energy, person)* vorace; *(reader)* avide

voraciously [və'reɪʃəslɪ] *adv (consume, eat)* voracement, avec voracité; *(read)* avec voracité, avidement

voracity [vɒ'ræsɪtɪ] *n* voracité *f*

vortex ['vɔ:teks] (*pl* **vortexes** *or* **vortices** [-tɪsi:z]) *n (of water, gas)* vortex *m*, tourbillon *m*; *Fig* tourbillon *m*, maelström *m*

vortical ['vɔ:tɪkəl] **1** *adj* tourbillonnaire, en tourbillon
2 *n Phys* mouvement *m* tourbillonnaire
►► *Phys* ***vortical motion*** mouvement *m* tourbillonnaire

Vorticism ['vɔ:tɪsɪzəm] *n Art* vorticisme *m*

Vorticist ['vɔ:tɪsɪst] *n Art* vorticiste *m*

vorticist ['vɔ:tɪsɪst] *n Phys & Phil* tourbillonniste *m*

votary ['vəʊtərɪ] (*pl* **votaries**) *n Rel & Fig* fervent(e) *m,f*

vote [vəʊt] **1** *n* (**a**) *(ballot)* vote *m*; **to have a vote on sth** voter sur qch, mettre qch aux voix; **to put a question to the vote** mettre une question aux voix; **let's put it to the vote** votons; **to take a vote on sth** *(gen)* voter sur qch; *Admin & Pol* procéder au vote de qch; **if it comes to a** *or* **the vote, I know where I stand** s'il est procédé à un vote, je sais quelle est ma position; **vote of thanks** discours *m* de remerciement; **I propose a vote of thanks to our charming hostesses** je propose que l'on remercie chaleureusement nos charmantes hôtesses
(**b**) *(in parliament)* vote *m*, scrutin *m*; **seventy MPs were present for the vote** soixante-dix députés étaient présents pour le vote; **the vote went in the government's favour/against the government** les députés se sont prononcés en faveur du/contre le gouvernement; **vote of confidence** vote *m* de confiance; **vote of no confidence** motion *f* de censure
(**c**) *(individual choice)* vote *m*, voix *f*; **to give one's vote to sb** voter pour qn; **they've got my vote** je vote pour eux; **to count the votes** *(gen)* compter les votes *ou* les voix; *Pol* dépouiller le scrutin; **the candidate got 15,000 votes** le candidat a recueilli 15 000 voix; **to be elected by one vote** être élu à une voix de majorité; **one member, one vote** = système de scrutin "un homme, une voix"
(**d**) *(ballot paper)* bulletin *m* de vote
(**e**) *(suffrage)* droit *m* de vote; **to have the vote** avoir le droit de vote; **to give the vote to sb** accorder le droit de vote à qn; **the suffragettes campaigned for votes for women** les suffragettes ont fait campagne pour qu'on accorde le droit de vote aux femmes
(**f**) *(UNCOUNT) (collectively → voters)* vote *m*, voix *fpl*; *(→ votes cast)* voix *fpl* exprimées; **they hope to win the working-class vote** ils espèrent gagner les voix des ouvriers; **the Scottish vote went against the government** le vote écossais a été défavorable au gouvernement; **they won 40 percent of the vote** ils ont remporté 40 pour cent des voix *ou* des suffrages; **they increased their vote by 12 percent** ils ont amélioré leurs résultats de 12 pour cent
(**g**) *Br Pol (grant)* vote *m* de crédits; **a vote of £100,000** un vote de crédits de 100 000 livres
2 *vt* (**a**) *(in election)* voter; **vote Malone!** votez Malone!; **to vote Labour/Republican** voter travailliste/républicain; **our family have always voted Conservative** notre famille a toujours voté conservateur *ou* pour le parti conservateur
(**b**) *(in parliament, assembly → motion, law, money)* voter; **they voted that the sitting (should) be suspended** ils ont voté la suspension de la séance
(**c**) *(elect)* élire; *(appoint)* nommer; **she was voted president** elle a été élue présidente
(**d**) *(declare)* proclamer; **the party was voted a great success** de l'avis de tous, la soirée a été un grand succès
(**e**) *(suggest)* proposer; **I vote we all go to bed** je propose qu'on aille tous se coucher
3 *vi* voter; **France is voting this weekend** la France va aux urnes ce week-end; **how did the country vote?** comment est-ce que le pays a voté?; **to vote for/against sb** voter pour/contre qn; **I'm going to vote for Barron** je vais voter (pour) Barron *ou* donner ma voix à Barron; **most of the delegates voted against the chairman** la plupart des délégués ont voté contre le président; **to vote in favour of/against sth** voter pour/contre qch; **the party conference voted on the question of nuclear disarmament** le congrès du parti a voté sur la question du désarmement nucléaire; **let's vote on it!** mettons cela aux voix!; **to vote by a show of hands** voter à main levée; *Fig* **to vote with one's feet** *(by leaving)* manifester *ou* signifier son mécontentement en partant; *(by not turning up)* manifester *ou* signifier son mécontentement par le boycott

►**vote down** *vt sep (bill, proposal)* rejeter *(par le vote)*

►**vote in** *vt sep (person, government)* élire; *(new law)* voter, adopter

►**vote out** *vt sep (suggestion)* rejeter; *(minister)* relever de ses fonctions; **the bill was voted out** le projet de loi n'a pas été adopté *ou* a été rejeté

►**vote through** *vt sep (bill, reform)* voter, ratifier

vote-catcher *n* politique *f* électoraliste

vote-catching *adj (plan, strategy)* électoraliste

vote-loser *n* politique *f* qui risque de faire perdre des voix, politique *f* peu populaire

voter ['vəʊtə(r)] *n* électeur(trice) *m,f*; **the voters** l'électorat *m*; **French voters go to the polls tomorrow** les Français vont aux urnes demain
►► ***voter registration*** inscription *f* sur les listes électorales

voting ['vəʊtɪŋ] **1** *n* vote *m*, scrutin *m*; **voting takes place on Sunday** le scrutin a lieu dimanche, les électeurs vont aux urnes dimanche; **I don't know how the voting will go** je ne sais pas comment les gens vont voter
2 *adj (assembly, member)* votant
►► ***voting booth*** isoloir *m*; *Am* ***voting machine*** machine *f* pour enregistrer les votes; ***voting paper*** bulletin *m* de vote; *Am* ***voting precinct*** circonscription *f* électorale; *Fin* ***voting rights*** droits *mpl* de vote; ***voting shares*** actions *fpl* donnant droit au vote

votive ['vəʊtɪv] *adj* votif
►► ***votive offering*** ex-voto *m inv*

vouch [vaʊtʃ] *vi* **to vouch for sb/sth** se porter garant de qn/qch, répondre de qn/qch; **he needs somebody to vouch for his honesty** il lui faut quelqu'un qui se porte garant de son honnêteté; **I can vouch for the truth of her story** je peux attester *ou* témoigner de la véracité de sa déclaration

voucher ['vaʊtʃə(r)] *n* (**a**) *Br (for restaurant, purchase, petrol)* bon *m*; **(gift) voucher** bon-cadeau *m*; **when you've collected five vouchers, you get a free car wash** quand vous avez réuni cinq bons, vous avez droit à un lavage auto gratuit
(**b**) *(receipt)* reçu *m*, récépissé *m*
(**c**) *Law* pièce *f* justificative
(**d**) *Acct* pièce *f* comptable
►► *Br Sch* ***voucher scheme*** = système de bons permettant aux parents "d'acheter" la scolarité de leur enfant dans un établissement de leur choix, public ou privé

vouchsafe [vaʊtʃ'seɪf] *vt Formal* (**a**) *(grant → help, support)* accorder, octroyer; *(→ answer)* accorder; **he vouchsafed us no reply** il n'a pas daigné nous répondre (**b**) *(undertake)* **to vouchsafe to do sth** *(willingly)* accepter gracieusement de faire qch; *(reluctantly)* condescendre à *ou* daigner faire qch

voussoir ['vu:swɑ:(r)] *n Archit* voussoir *m*, claveau *m*; **centre voussoir** clef *f* (de voûte)

vow [vaʊ] **1** *n* (**a**) *(promise)* serment *m*, promesse *f*; **to make** *or* **to take a vow to do sth** faire serment *ou* jurer de faire qch; **I'm under a vow of silence** j'ai fait serment *ou* j'ai juré de ne rien dire; **she took a solemn vow to return once a year** elle a juré solennellement de revenir une fois par an
(**b**) *Rel* vœu *m*; **to take one's vows** prononcer ses vœux; **to take a vow of poverty/of chastity** faire vœu de pauvreté/de chasteté; **to take a vow of silence** *(monk etc)* faire vœu de silence
2 *vt (swear → gen)* jurer; *(→ to oneself)* se jurer; **to vow to do sth** jurer de faire qch; **to vow obedience/secrecy** jurer obéissance/de garder le secret; **to vow revenge on sb** faire serment *ou* jurer de se venger de qn; **she vowed never to return** *or* **that she would never return** elle s'est juré de ne jamais revenir

vowel ['vaʊəl] **1** *n* voyelle *f*
2 *comp (harmony, pattern, sound)* vocalique
►► ***vowel gradation*** alternance *f* vocalique, ablaut *m*; ***vowel point*** point-voyelle *m*; ***vowel shift*** mutation *f* vocalique

vowelize, -ise ['vaʊəlaɪz] *vt* (**a**) *(consonant)* vocaliser (**b**) *(Hebrew text)* mettre les points-voyelles à

vox pop [ˌvɒks'pɒp] *n Br Fam* micro-trottoir *m*
vox populi [vɒks'pɒpjʊlaɪ] *n* **the vox populi** la voix du peuple, la vox populi
voyage ['vɔɪɪdʒ] **1** *n* voyage *m*; **a transatlantic voyage** un voyage *ou* une traversée transatlantique; **to go on a voyage** partir en voyage; **a round-the-world voyage** un voyage autour du monde; **a voyage into the unknown** un voyage dans l'inconnu; **a voyage to Jupiter** un voyage vers Jupiter; **great voyages of discovery** grands voyages d'exploration
2 *vt Naut* traverser, parcourir
3 *vi* (**a**) *Naut* voyager par mer; **they voyaged across the Atlantic/the desert** ils ont traversé l'Atlantique/le désert; **to voyage round the world** voyager autour du monde
(**b**) *Am Aviat* voyager par avion
voyager ['vɔɪɪdʒə(r)] *n* (**a**) *(traveller)* voyageur(-euse) *m,f* (**b**) *(explorer)* navigateur(trice) *m,f*
voyeur [vwɑː'jɜː(r)] *n* voyeur(euse) *m,f*
voyeurism [vwɑː'jɜːrɪzəm] *n* voyeurisme *m*
voyeuristic [ˌvɔɪə'rɪstɪk] *adj* voyeuriste
VP [ˌviː'piː] *n (abbr* **vice-president**) VP *m*
VPL [ˌviːpiː'el] *n (abbr* **visible panty line**) = contours du slip visibles sous les vêtements
VR [ˌviː'ɑː(r)] *Br (abbr* **Victoria Regina**) la Reine Victoria
VRAM ['viːræm] *n Comput (abbr* **video random access memory**) VRAM *f*
VRML [ˌviːɑːˌrem'el] *n Comput (abbr* **virtual reality modelling language**) VRML *m*
vs *(written abbr* **versus**) contre
V-shaped *adj* en (forme de) V
V-sign *n* **to give the V-sign** *(for victory, approval)* faire le V de la victoire; *Br* **to give sb the V-sign** *(as insult)* ≃ faire un bras d'honneur à qn

VSO [ˌviːes'əʊ] *n Br (abbr* **Voluntary Service Overseas**) = coopération technique à l'étranger (non rémunérée)
VSOP [ˌviːesˌəʊ'piː] *n (abbr* **very special old pale**) VSOP
VT, Vt *(written abbr* **Vermont**) Vermont *m*
VTOL ['viːtɒl] *n Aviat (abbr* **vertical takeoff and landing**) *(system)* décollage *m* et atterrissage *m* vertical; *(plane)* ADAV *m*
VTR [ˌviːtiː'ɑː(r)] *n (abbr* **video tape recorder**) magnétoscope *m*
Vulcan ['vʌlkən] *pr n Myth* Vulcain
vulcanite ['vʌlkənaɪt] *n* ébonite *f*
vulcanization [ˌvʌlkənaɪ'zeɪʃən] *n* vulcanisation *f*
vulcanize, -ise ['vʌlkənaɪz] *vt* vulcaniser
vulcanological [ˌvʌlkənə'lɒdʒɪkəl] *adj* volcanologique, vulcanologique
vulcanologist [ˌvʌlkə'nɒlədʒɪst] *n* volcanologue *mf*, vulcanologue *mf*
vulcanology [ˌvʌlkə'nɒlədʒɪ] *n* volcanologie *f*, vulcanologie *f*
vulgar ['vʌlgə(r)] *adj* (**a**) *(rude)* vulgaire, grossier (**b**) *(common – person, taste, decor)* vulgaire, commun; **the vulgar tongue** la langue commune
►► ***vulgar fraction*** fraction *f* ordinaire; ***Vulgar Latin*** latin *m* vulgaire
vulgarian [vʌl'geərɪən] *n* personne *f* vulgaire
vulgarism ['vʌlgərɪzəm] *n* (**a**) *(uneducated language)* vulgarisme *m*; *(rude word)* grossièreté *f* (**b**) *(vulgarity)* vulgarité *f*
vulgarity [vʌl'gærɪtɪ] *n* vulgarité *f*
vulgarization [ˌvʌlgəraɪ'zeɪʃən] *n* vulgarisation *f*
vulgarize, -ise ['vʌlgəraɪz] *vt* (**a**) *(appearance, language)* rendre vulgaire (**b**) *(popularize)* vulgariser, populariser
vulgarly ['vʌlgəlɪ] *adv* (**a**) *(coarsely)* vulgairement, grossièrement (**b**) *(commonly)* vulgairement, communément
Vulgate ['vʌlgeɪt] *n* Vulgate *f*
vulnerability [ˌvʌlnərə'bɪlɪtɪ] *n* vulnérabilité *f*
vulnerable ['vʌlnərəbəl] *adj* (**a**) *(gen)* vulnérable; **to be vulnerable to sth** être vulnérable à qch; **that's her vulnerable spot** c'est son point faible *ou* son talon d'Achille; **the vulnerable spot in our defences** le point faible de nos défenses; **this left them vulnerable on their eastern border** cela les a laissés dans une position vulnérable sur leur frontière est (**b**) *Cards (in bridge)* vulnérable
vulnerary ['vʌlnərərɪ] *(pl* **vulneraries**) *Pharm* **1** *n* vulnéraire *m*
2 *adj* vulnéraire
vulpine ['vʌlpaɪn] *adj* vulpin; *Fig Literary* sournois
vulture ['vʌltʃə(r)] *n also Fig* vautour *m*
vulturine ['vʌltʃəraɪn] *adj Orn* du vautour; *Fig Literary (rapacious)* rapace
►► ***vulturine fish eagle*** vautour-pêcheur *m*; ***vulturine guinea fowl*** pintade *f* vulturine
vulva ['vʌlvə] *(pl* **vulvas** *or* **vulvae** [-viː]) *n Anat* vulve *f*
vulval ['vʌlvəl], **vulvar** ['vʌlvə(r)] *adj Anat* vulvaire
vulvitis [vʌl'vaɪtɪs] *n Med* vulvite *f*
vv (**a**) *(written abbr* **verses**) v. (**b**) *(written abbr* **versus**) contre
vying ['vaɪɪŋ] *n* rivalité *f*

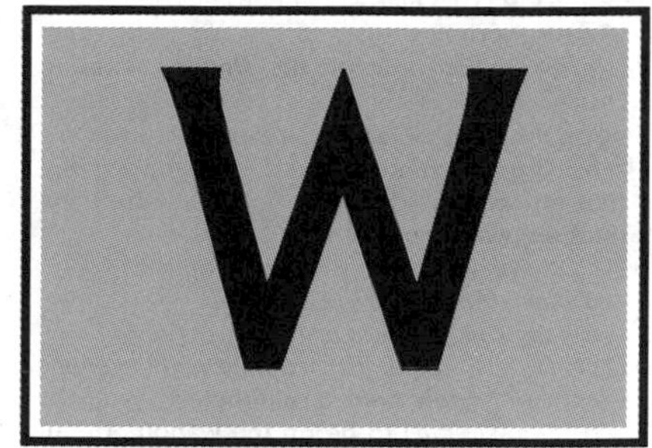

W¹, w ['dʌbəl,juː] *n (letter)* W, w *m inv*; **two w's** deux w; **W for William** W comme William

W² (**a**) *(written abbr* **west**) O (**b**) *(written abbr* **watt**) w

W2 [,dʌbəljuː'tuː] *n Am (form)* récapitulatif *m* annuel de paie
►► *Am* ***W2 form*** récapitulatif *m* annuel de paie

W3 [,dʌbəljuː'θriː] *n Comput (abbr* **World Wide Web**) W3 *m*, le Web *m*

WA (**a**) *(written abbr* **Washington (State)**) État *m* de Washington (**b**) *(written abbr* **Western Australia**) Australie-Occidentale *f*

WAAC [wæk] *n Br Hist (abbr* **Women's Army Auxiliary Corps**) = pendant la Seconde Guerre mondiale, section féminine auxiliaire de l'armée de terre britannique

WAAF [wæf] *n Br Hist (abbr* **Women's Auxiliary Air Force**) = pendant la Seconde Guerre mondiale, section féminine auxiliaire de l'armée de l'air britannique

wack ['wæk] *Fam* **1** *n Br (in Liverpool and the Midlands)* **hiya wack!** salut, mon pote!
2 *adj Am* (**a**) *(worthless)* nul (**b**) *(mad)* cinglé, toqué (**c**) *(stupid)* débile

wackily ['wækɪlɪ] *adv Fam* **to behave wackily** faire des loufoqueries

wackiness ['wækɪnɪs] *n Fam* loufoquerie *f*

wacko ['wækəʊ] *(pl* **wackos**) *Fam* **1** *n* cinglé(e) *m,f*, dingue *mf*
2 *adj* cinglé, dingue

wacky ['wækɪ] *(compar* **wackier**, *superl* **wackiest**) *adj Fam* loufoque, farfelu
►► *Hum* ***wacky baccy*** *(marijuana)* herbe *f*

wad [wɒd] *(pt & pp* **wadded**, *cont* **wadding**) **1** *n* (**a**) *(of cotton wool, paper)* tampon *m*, bouchon *m*; *(of tobacco)* chique *f*; *(of straw)* bouchon *m*; *(of gum)* boulette *f*; *Mil (for cannon, gun)* bourre *f*
(**b**) *(of letters, documents)* liasse *f*, paquet *m*; **he pulled out a thick wad of banknotes** il a sorti une grosse liasse de billets; **to shoot one's wad** *Fam (spend all one's money)* claquer tout son fric; *esp Am Vulg (have orgasm)* décharger, envoyer la sauce
2 *vt* (**a**) *(cloth, paper)* faire un tampon de; *(tobacco, chewing gum)* faire une boulette de
(**b**) *(hole, aperture)* boucher (avec un tampon); *Mil (barrel, cannon)* bourrer
(**c**) *(quilt, garment)* ouater; **a wadded jacket** une veste ouatée *ou* doublée d'ouate

Waddenzee ['wædənzeɪ] *n* **the Waddenzee** la mer des Wadden

wadding ['wɒdɪŋ] *n* (**a**) *Mil (in gun, cartridge)* bourre *f* (**b**) *(stuffing → for furniture, packing)* rembourrage *m*, capitonnage *m*; *(→ for clothes)* ouate *f*, ouatine *f*

waddle ['wɒdəl] **1** *vi (duck, person)* se dandiner; **to waddle along/in** avancer/entrer en se dandinant
2 *n* dandinement *m*; **to walk with a waddle** *(of person)* marcher en se dandinant

wade [weɪd] **1** *vi* avancer, marcher; **they waded across the stream** ils ont traversé le ruisseau à pied; **we waded into the water** nous sommes entrés dans l'eau; **she waded out to the boat** elle s'avança dans l'eau vers le bateau
2 *vt (river)* passer *ou* traverser à pied
►**wade in** *vi Br (in fight, quarrel)* s'en mêler
►**wade into** *vt insep Br (work, task)* attaquer, s'atteler à, se mettre à; *(meal)* attaquer, entame; *(person → verbally)* s'attaquer à, s'en prendre à; *(→ physically)* attaquer, se jeter sur; **critics have waded into his latest film** la critique a démoli son dernier film
►**wade through** *vt insep* avancer *ou* marcher dans; **to wade through piles of dirty clothing** *(walk through them)* se tailler un chemin à travers des piles de linge sale; *Fig* **I'm still wading through 'War and Peace'** je suis toujours aux prises avec 'Guerre et paix'; **it took me a month to wade through that book** il m'a fallu un mois pour venir à bout de ce livre; **she's got a 100-page report to wade through** elle a un rapport de 100 pages à lire, elle doit se taper un rapport de 100 pages

wader ['weɪdə(r)] *n Orn* échassier *m*

waders ['weɪdəz] *npl* cuissardes *fpl (de pêcheur)*

wadge [wɒdʒ] *n Br Fam* paquet ❑ *m*; **wadges of notes** des liasses ❑ *fpl* de billets

wadi ['wɒdɪ] *n Geog* oued *m*

wading ['weɪdɪŋ] *n (in water)* marche *f* dans l'eau
►► ***wading bird*** échassier *m*; *Am* ***wading pool*** *(in swimming pool)* petit bassin *m*; *(inflatable)* piscine *f* gonflable

Waf [wæf] *n* = soldat ou officier féminin de l'armée de l'air américaine

wafer ['weɪfə(r)] **1** *n* (**a**) *Culin* gaufrette *f*, *Belg* galette *f* (**b**) *Rel* hostie *f* (**c**) *(seal)* cachet *m* (de papier rouge) (**d**) *Comput & Tech* tranche *f*
2 *vt* (**a**) *(seal)* cacheter (avec du papier rouge) (**b**) *Comput & Tech* diviser en tranches

wafer-thin, wafery ['weɪfərɪ] *adj* mince comme une feuille de papier à cigarette *ou* comme une pelure d'oignon; **a wafer-thin majority** une majorité infime

waffle ['wɒfəl] **1** *n* (**a**) *Culin* gaufre *f*
(**b**) *Br Fam (spoken)* baratin *m*, bla-bla *m inv*; *(written)* remplissage *m*, baratin *m*; **it's just a load of waffle** ce n'est que du baratin; **cut the waffle and get to the point** arrêtez de parler pour ne rien dire et venez-en au fait
2 *vi Fam (in speaking)* baratiner, parler pour ne rien dire; *(in writing)* faire du remplissage; **what did you say to that? – I just waffled** qu'est-ce que tu as répondu à ça? – j'ai baratiné; **he's been waffling away for over an hour** cela fait plus d'une heure qu'il raconte son baratin; *Br* **to waffle on** bavarder, faire des laïus; **she's always waffling on about her children** elle n'arrête pas de parler de ses enfants ❑
►► *Culin* ***waffle iron*** gaufrier *m*

waffler ['wɒflə(r)] *n Br Fam* baratineur(euse) *m,f*

waffling ['wɒflɪŋ] *n Br Fam (spoken)* baratin *m*, bla-bla *m inv*; *(written)* baratin *m*, remplissage *m*

waffly ['wɒflɪ] *adj Fam (speech, essay)* plein de baratin

waft [wɑːft, wɒft] **1** *vt (scent, sound)* porter, transporter; **the breeze wafted the curtains gently to and fro** le vent léger faisait ondoyer les rideaux
2 *vi (scent, sound)* flotter; **a delicious smell wafted into the room** une délicieuse odeur envahit la pièce; **the papers wafted off the table** un souffle d'air emporta les papiers qui étaient sur la table; **her voice wafted gently down the stairs** sa voix douce parvenait jusqu'en bas de l'escalier; *Fig* **Vanessa wafted into/out of the room** Vanessa entra dans/sortit de la pièce d'un pas léger
3 *n (of smoke, air)* bouffée *f*

wag [wæg] *(pt & pp* **wagged**, *cont* **wagging**) **1** *vt (tail, finger)* agiter, remuer; **the dog wagged its tail enthusiastically** le chien agita la queue de contentement; **she wagged her finger at him** elle le menaça du doigt
2 *vi (tail)* remuer, frétiller; **tongues were wagging about her behaviour** son comportement faisait jaser *ou* parler les gens; **if you carry on like this tongues will begin to wag** si tu continues comme ça, les gens vont jaser
3 *n* (**a**) *(of tail)* remuement *m*, frétillement *m*; **with a wag of its tail** en agitant *ou* en remuant la queue
(**b**) *Br (person)* plaisantin *m*, farceur(euse) *m,f*

wage [weɪdʒ] **1** *n* (**a**) *(pay → of worker)* salaire *m*, paye *f*, paie *f*; *(→ of servant)* gages *mpl*; **her wage is** *or* **her wages are only £100 a week** elle ne gagne que 100 livres par semaine; **his employers took it out of his wages** ses employeurs l'ont prélevé sur sa paie; *Br* **a wages and prices** *or* **a wage-price spiral** une spirale des prix et des salaires; *Hum* **I'm fed up with being a wage slave** j'en ai assez d'être obligé de gagner ma vie
(**b**) *(reward)* salaire *m*, récompense *f*; *Bible* **the wages of sin is death** la mort est le prix du péché
2 *comp (claim, demand, settlement)* salarial; *(increase, incentive)* de salaire
3 *vt* **to wage war on** *or* **against** faire la guerre contre; **the government have decided to wage war on drug trafficking** le gouvernement a résolu de partir en guerre contre les trafiquants de drogue; **to wage a campaign for/against sth** faire campagne pour/contre qch
►► ***wage attachment order*** ordre *m* de saisie sur salaire *(émis par le fisc)*; ***wage bargaining*** *(UNCOUNT)* négociations *fpl* salariales; ***wage bill*** masse *f* salariale, charges *fpl* salariales; ***wage bracket*** fourchette *f* de salaire; ***wage ceiling*** salaire *m* plafonné; ***wage claim*** revendication *f* salariale; ***wage cut*** réduction *f* de salaire, réduction *f* salariale; *Br* ***wage differential*** écart *m* salarial; ***wage earner*** salarié(e) *m,f*; **they are both wage earners** ils sont salariés tous les deux, ils ont tous les deux un salaire; ***wage freeze*** gel *m ou* blocage *m* des salaires; ***wage inflation*** inflation *f* des salaires; *Acct* ***wages ledger*** journal *m* de paie; *Br* ***wage packet*** *(envelope)* paie *f* en espèces; *(money)* paie *f*, salaire *f*; ***wage policy*** politique *f* salariale *ou* des salaires; ***wage pyramid*** pyramide *f* des salaires; ***wage rise*** augmentation *f* de salaire; ***wage scale*** échelle *f* des salaires; ***wage slip*** fiche *f* de paie, bulletin *m* de salaire; ***wage structure*** structure *f* des salaires

wager ['weɪdʒə(r)] **1** *vt* parier; **I'll wager £10 that he'll come** je parie 10 livres qu'il viendra
2 *vi* parier, faire un pari
3 *n* pari *m*; **to make** *or* **to lay a wager** faire un pari

wageworker ['weɪdʒ,wɜːkə(r)] *n Am* salarié(e) *m,f*

waggery ['wægərɪ] *(pl* **waggeries**) *n* (**a**) *(joking)* facétie(s) *f(pl)* (**b**) *(joke)* **(piece of) waggery** facétie *f*

waggish ['wægɪʃ] *adj* facétieux

waggishly ['wægɪʃlɪ] *adv* d'un ton facétieux, facétieusement

waggishness ['wægɪʃnɪs] *n* caractère *m* facétieux

waggle ['wægəl] **1** *vt (tail)* agiter, remuer; *(pencil)* agiter; *(loose tooth, screw)* faire jouer; *(ears, nose)* remuer
2 *vi (tail)* bouger, frétiller; *(loose tooth, screw)* bouger, branler; **the knob waggles if you touch it** le bouton bouge si on y touche
3 *n* **to give sth a waggle** agiter *ou* remuer qch

waggon, waggonette *etc Br* = **wagon, wagonette** *etc*

Wagner ['vɑːgnə(r)] *pr n* Wagner

Wagnerian [vɑːgˈnɪərɪən] **1** *adj* wagnérien
2 *n* wagnérien(enne) *m,f*

Wagon [ˈwægən] *n Astron* **the Wagon** la Grande Ourse

wagon [ˈwægən] *n* **(a)** *(horse-drawn)* chariot *m* **(b)** *(truck)* camionnette *f*, fourgon *m*; *Am* **(patrol) wagon** fourgon *m* cellulaire; *Am* **(station) wagon** break *m*
(c) *Br Rail* wagon *m* (de marchandises)
(d) *Am (drinks trolley)* chariot *m*
(e) *Fam (lorry)* bahut *m*
(f) *Ir very Fam Pej (unpleasant woman)* connasse *f*; *(ugly woman)* mocheté *f*
(g) *Fam (idiom)* **to be on the wagon** être au régime sec; **to be off** *or* **have fallen off the wagon** s'être remis à boire ❑
▸▸ ***wagon train*** convoi *m* de chariots *(en particulier de colons américains)*

wagoner [ˈwægənə(r)] *n* charretier *m*

wagonette [ˌwægəˈnet] *n* break *m* (attelé)

wagonload [ˈwægənləʊd] *n Agr* charretée *f*; *Rail* wagon *m*

wagtail [ˈwægteɪl] *n Orn* hochequeue *m*, bergeronnette *f*

Wahhabi [wəˈhɑːbɪ] **1** *adj* wahhabite
2 *n* Wahhabite *mf*

wahine [wæˈhiːneɪ] *n* vahiné *f*

wahoo [wæˈhuː] *n* **(a)** *Bot* fusain *m* de l'Est **(b)** *Ich* wahoo *m*, thazard *m* bâtard

wah-wah [ˈwɑːˌwɑː] *n* effet *m* wah-wah *ou* wa-wa
▸▸ *Mus* ***wah-wah pedal*** pédale *f* wah-wah

waif [weɪf] *n* **(a)** *(child → neglected)* enfant *mf* malheureux(euse); *(→ homeless)* enfant *mf* abandonné(e); **waifs and strays** *(children)* enfants *mpl* abandonnés; *(animals)* animaux *mpl* errants **(b)** *(excessively thin person)* squelette *m*, personne *f* famélique; **the waif look is fashionable again this year** le look famélique est très à la mode cette année

waiflike [ˈweɪflaɪk] *adj* famélique; **the waiflike look of some models** la maigreur famélique de certains mannequins

wail [weɪl] **1** *vi* **(a)** *(person → whine, moan)* gémir, pousser des gémissements; *(baby → shout)* hurler; *(→ weep)* pleurer bruyamment; **what's he wailing about now?** de quoi se plaint-il maintenant?
(b) *(wind)* gémir; *(siren)* hurler
2 *vt* dire en gémissant, gémir; **"you've broken it!" she wailed** "tu l'as cassé!" gémit-elle
3 *n* **(a)** *(of person)* gémissement *m*; **he gave a loud wail** il poussa un profond gémissement; **"he's gone!" she said with a wail** "il est parti!" dit-elle en gémissant
(b) *(of wind)* gémissement *m*; *(of siren)* hurlement *m*

wailing [ˈweɪlɪŋ] **1** *n (UNCOUNT) (of person)* gémissements *mpl*, plaintes *fpl*; *(of wind)* gémissements *mpl*, plainte *f*; *(of siren)* hurlement *m*, hurlements *mpl*
2 *adj (person)* gémissant; *(sound)* plaintif
▸▸ ***the Wailing Wall*** le mur des Lamentations

wailingly [ˈweɪlɪŋlɪ] *adv* plaintivement, en gémissant

wain [weɪn] **1** *n Literary* chariot *m (de ferme)*
2 Wain *n Astron* **the Wain** le Grand Chariot, la Grande Ourse

wainscot [ˈweɪnskət] *n* lambris *m (en bois)*

wainscoting, wainscotting [ˈweɪnskətɪŋ] *n Br* lambrissage *m (en bois)*

wainwright [ˈweɪnraɪt] *n Br* charron *m*

waist [weɪst] *n* **(a)** *(of person, garment)* taille *f*; **he measures 80 cm around the waist, his waist measures 80 cm** il fait 80 cm de tour de taille, son tour de taille est de 80 cm; **he put his arm around her waist** il l'a prise par la taille; **it's too tight at** *or* **round the waist** ça serre à la taille; **he was up to the** *or* **his waist in water** l'eau lui arrivait à la ceinture *ou* à la taille
(b) *(of ship, plane)* partie *f* centrale; *(of violin)* partie *f* resserrée de la table; *(of pipe)* rétrécissement *m*
▸▸ ***waist lock*** *(in wrestling)* ceinture *f*; ***waist measurement, waist size*** tour *m* de taille

waistband [ˈweɪstbænd] *n* ceinture *f (d'un vêtement)*

waistbelt [ˈweɪstbelt] *n Old-fashioned* ceinture *f*; *Mil* ceinturon *m*

waistcoat [ˈweɪskəʊt] *n Br* gilet *m (de costume)*

waist-deep *adj* **he was waist-deep in water** l'eau lui arrivait à la ceinture *ou* à la taille; **the water was waist-deep** l'eau arrivait à la ceinture

waisted [ˈweɪstɪd] *adj (coat, jacket)* cintré

-waisted [ˈweɪstɪd] *suff* **a low/high-waisted dress** une robe à taille basse/haute; **to be slim/thick-waisted** avoir la taille fine/épaisse

waist-high *adj (grass)* à hauteur de la taille

waistline [ˈweɪstlaɪn] *n* taille *f*; **to watch one's waistline** surveiller sa ligne

wait [weɪt] **1** *vi* **(a)** *(person, bus, work)* attendre; **I've been waiting for half an hour/since Easter** j'attends depuis une demi-heure/depuis Pâques; **just you wait!** *(as threat)* attends un peu, tu vas voir!, tu ne perds rien pour attendre!; *(you'll see)* vous verrez!; **we'll just have to wait and see** on verra bien; **wait and see!** attends voir!; **he didn't wait to be told twice** il ne se l'est pas fait dire deux fois; **letters waiting to be delivered** lettres qui attendent d'être distribuées, *Admin* lettres en souffrance; **we're waiting to be served** nous attendons qu'on nous serve *ou* qu'on s'occupe de nous; **to keep sb waiting** faire attendre qn; **you shouldn't keep people waiting** vous ne devriez pas vous faire attendre *ou* faire attendre les gens; **they do it while you wait** ils le font devant vous; **repairs while you wait** *(sign)* réparations minute; **keys cut while you wait** *(sign)* clés minute; *Prov* **everything comes to him** *or* **to he who waits** tout vient à point à qui sait attendre
(b) *(with "can")* **it can wait** cela peut attendre; **he can wait** laisse-le attendre; *also Ironic* **I can't wait!** je brûle d'impatience!; **it can't wait** cela ne peut pas attendre, c'est très urgent; **I can hardly wait to see them again** j'ai hâte de les revoir; **I can't wait for the weekend (to arrive)** j'attends le week-end avec impatience!, vivement le week-end!
(c) *(with "until" or "till")* **wait until I've finished** attendez que j'aie fini; **wait until the film is over** attendez la fin du film; **you'll have to wait until you're old enough** il va falloir attendre que tu sois plus grand; **can't that wait until tomorrow?** cela ne peut pas attendre jusqu'à demain?; **just wait till your parents hear about it** attends un peu que tes parents apprennent cela
(d) *(serve)* servir, faire le service; **to wait** *Br* **at** *or Am* **on table** servir à table, faire le service
2 *vt* **(a)** *(period of time)* attendre; **I waited half an hour** j'ai attendu (pendant) une demi-heure; **I waited all day for the repairman to come** j'ai passé toute la journée à attendre le réparateur; **wait a minute!** (attendez) une minute *ou* un instant!; **wait your turn!** attendez votre tour!
(b) *Am (delay)* **don't wait dinner for me** ne m'attendez pas pour vous mettre à table
(c) *Am (serve at)* **to wait tables** servir à table, faire le service
3 *n* attente *f*; **we had a long wait** nous avons dû attendre (pendant) longtemps; **she had a half hour** *or* **half hour's wait at Gatwick** il a fallu qu'elle attende une demi-heure *ou* elle a eu une demi-heure d'attente à Gatwick; **there was an hour's wait between trains** il y avait une heure de battement *ou* d'attente entre les trains; **it was worth the wait** ça valait la peine d'attendre; **to lie in wait for** être à l'affût de, guetter; **the foxes lay in wait for the hares** les renards étaient à l'affût des lièvres; **the gunmen were lying in wait for the convoy** les bandits guettaient l'arrivée du convoi; **the detective was lying in wait for her outside her house** *(arrival)* le détective guettait son arrivée à la maison; *(departure)* le détective guettait son départ de la maison
4 waits *npl Br Mus* chanteurs *mpl* de Noël
▸▸ *Comput* ***wait loop*** boucle *f* d'attente; *Comput* ***wait state*** état *m* d'attente

▸**wait about** *vi Br* traîner, faire le pied de grue; **to wait about for sb** attendre qn, faire le pied de grue en attendant qn; **don't keep me waiting about** ne me fais pas attendre; **I can't stand all this waiting about** cela m'énerve d'être obligé d'attendre *ou* de traîner comme ça; **I can't wait about all evening until he comes home** je ne peux pas traîner toute la soirée à attendre qu'il rentre

▸**wait around** = **wait about**

▸**wait behind** *vi* rester; **to wait behind for sb** rester pour attendre qn; **they waited behind after the meeting** ils sont restés après la réunion

▸**wait for** *vt insep* **to wait for sb/sth** attendre qn/qch; **I'm waiting for the children/for the next train** j'attends les enfants/le prochain train; **I'm waiting for the bank to open** j'attends que la banque soit ouverte, j'attends l'ouverture de la banque; **wait for the signal** attendez le signal; **that was worth waiting for** cela valait la peine d'attendre; **what are you waiting for?** qu'est-ce que vous attendez?; *Br Hum* **wait for it!** tiens-toi bien!

▸**wait in** *vi* rester à la maison; **I waited in all evening for her** je suis resté chez moi toute la soirée à l'attendre

▸**wait on** *vt insep* **(a)** *(serve)* **I'm not here to wait on you!** *(male)* je ne suis pas ton serviteur!; *(female)* je ne suis pas ta servante *ou* ta bonne! **to wait on sb hand and foot** être aux petits soins pour qn; **he expects to be waited on hand and foot** il veut que tout le monde soit à son service *ou* à ses petits soins **(b)** *Am (in restaurant)* **to wait on tables** faire le service, servir à table

▸**wait out** *vt sep (war, stoum)* attendre la fin de; *(concert, film)* rester jusqu'à la fin *ou* jusqu'au bout de, attendre la fin de

▸**wait up** *vi* **(a)** *(at night)* rester debout, veiller; **I'll be late so don't wait up (for me)** je rentrerai tard, ne veillez pas pour moi *ou* couchez-vous sans m'attendre; **her parents always wait up for her** ses parents ne se couchent jamais avant qu'elle soit rentrée *ou* attendent toujours qu'elle rentre pour se coucher; **the children were allowed to wait up until midnight** on a permis aux enfants de veiller jusqu'à minuit
(b) *Fam (wait)* **hey, wait up!** attendez-moi! ❑

▸**wait upon** = **wait on (a)**

'Waiting for Godot' *Beckett* 'En attendant Godot'

wait-and-see *adj (approach)* attentiste
▸▸ ***wait-and-see policy*** politique *f* attentiste, attentisme *m*

Waitangi Day [waɪˈtʌŋɪ-] *n* = fête nationale de la Nouvelle-Zélande, le 6 février, qui commémore le traité de 1840 avec les Maoris

waiter [ˈweɪtə(r)] *n* **(a)** *(in restaurant)* serveur *m*, garçon *m*; **waiter!** s'il vous plaît!, monsieur! **(b)** *St Exch* coursier *m*
▸▸ ***waiter service*** service *m* à table

waiting [ˈweɪtɪŋ] **1** *n* attente *f*; **after two hours of waiting** après deux heures d'attente, après avoir attendu deux heures; **this waiting is nerve-wracking** c'est angoissant d'avoir à attendre, cette attente est angoissante; **no waiting** *(sign)* stationnement interdit; **to be in waiting on sb** être au service de qn
2 *adj (person, taxi)* qui attend; **to play a waiting game** *Mil & Pol* mener une politique d'attentisme; *Fig* jouer la montre, attendre son heure
▸▸ ***waiting list*** liste *f* d'attente; **to be on the waiting list** être sur la liste d'attente; **there's a two-month waiting list for an operation** il faut attendre deux mois pour une opération; ***waiting period*** période *f* d'attente; ***waiting room*** *(in office, surgery, airport, station)* salle *f* d'attente

waitlist [ˈweɪtlɪst] *vt Am* mettre sur la liste d'attente; **I'm waitlisted for the next flight** je suis sur la liste d'attente pour le prochain vol

waitperson [ˈweɪtpɜːsən] *n Am* serveur(euse) *m,f*

waitress [ˈweɪtrɪs] *n* serveuse *f*; **waitress!** s'il vous plaît!, mademoiselle!
▸▸ ***waitress service*** service *m* à table

waive [weɪv] *vt (condition, requirement)* ne pas insister sur, abandonner; *(law, rule)* déroger à; *(claim, right)* renoncer à, abandonner

waiver [ˈweɪvə(r)] *n (of condition, requirement)* abandon *m*; *(of law, rule)* dérogation *f*; *(of claim, right)* renonciation *f*, abandon *m*

wake [weɪk] (*pt* **woke** [wəʊk] *or* **waked**, *pp* **woken** [ˈwəʊkən] *or* **waked**) **1** *vi (stop sleeping)* se réveiller, s'éveiller; **the baby woke at six** le bébé s'est réveillé à six heures; **he woke to the news that war had broken out** à son réveil *ou* en se réveillant, il a appris que la guerre avait éclaté; **they woke to find themselves famous**

du jour au lendemain, ils se sont retrouvés célèbres

2 *vt* (**a**) *(rouse from sleep)* réveiller, tirer *ou* sortir du sommeil; **wake me at seven** réveillez-moi à sept heures; **the noise was enough to wake the dead** il y avait un bruit à réveiller les morts

(**b**) *(arouse → curiosity, jealousy)* réveiller, éveiller, exciter; *(→ memories)* réveiller, éveiller, ranimer

(**c**) *(alert)* éveiller l'attention de

3 *n* (**a**) *(vigil)* veillée *f* (mortuaire); **to have a wake for sb** organiser une veillée de commémoration en souvenir de qn; *Fig* **it is too soon to hold a wake for the ideal of European unity** il est encore trop tôt pour enterrer l'idéal de l'unité européenne

(**b**) *(of ship)* sillage *m*, eaux *fpl*; *Fig* sillage *m*; **famine followed in the wake of the drought** la famine a suivi la sécheresse; **he always brings trouble in his wake** il amène toujours des ennuis (dans son sillage); **to follow in sb's wake** marcher sur les traces *ou* dans le sillage de qn; **Steven followed in his father's wake and became a lawyer** Steven a suivi l'exemple de son père et est devenu avocat; **since then many other countries have followed in our wake** depuis lors bon nombre d'autres pays nous ont suivis; **he left the other athletes trailing in his wake** il a laissé les autres athlètes à la traîne *ou* loin derrière lui; **in the wake of the storm** après l'orage

(**c**) = **wakes**

4 wakes *npl (in Northern England)* = congé annuel (dans le Nord de l'Angleterre)

▸▸ ***wakes week*** *(in Northern England)* = la semaine de congé annuel (dans le Nord de l'Angleterre)

▸**wake up 1** *vi* (**a**) *(stop sleeping)* se réveiller, s'éveiller; **wake up!** réveille-toi!; **they woke up to find themselves famous** du jour au lendemain, ils se sont retrouvés célèbres

(**b**) *(become alert)* se réveiller, prendre conscience; **wake up and do some work!** réveille-toi *ou* secoue-toi et mets-toi au travail!

(**c**) *(become aware of truth, reality)* ouvrir les yeux; **it's time you woke up to the truth** il est temps que tu regardes la vérité en face; **it took him a while to wake up to what was going on** il lui fallut un certain temps pour comprendre *ou* pour réaliser ce qui se passait; **oh, wake up (and smell the roses** *or* **the coffee)!** ouvre les yeux!

2 *vt sep* (**a**) *(rouse from sleep)* réveiller, tirer *ou* sortir du sommeil; **wake me up at seven** réveillez-moi à sept heures

(**b**) *(make alert)* réveiller, secouer; **a little exercise will wake you up!** un peu d'exercice va vous réveiller!; **the accident woke us up to the dangers of nuclear power** l'accident a attiré *ou* éveillé notre attention sur les dangers de l'énergie nucléaire

(**c**) *(make aware of truth, reality)* ouvrir les yeux à qn; **that woke her up to what was going on** ça lui a ouvert les yeux sur ce qui se passait

wakeboarding ['weɪkbɔːdɪŋ] *n* monoski *m* nautique

wakeful ['weɪkfʊl] *adj* (**a**) *(person → unable to sleep)* qui ne dort pas, éveillé; *(→ alert)* vigilant (**b**) *(night, week)* sans sommeil; **I had** *or* **I spent a wakeful night** j'ai passé une nuit blanche

wakefully ['weɪkfʊlɪ] *adv (without sleeping)* sans dormir; *(alertly)* vigilamment, avec vigilance

wakefulness ['weɪkfʊlnɪs] *n (sleeplessness)* insomnie *f*; *(alertness)* vigilance *f*

waken ['weɪkən] *Literary* **1** *vi* se réveiller, s'éveiller; **to waken from sleep** se réveiller, s'éveiller, sortir du sommeil

2 *vt* réveiller, tirer *ou* sortir du sommeil

wake-up call *n* réveil *m* téléphonique

wakey wakey [ˌweɪkɪ'weɪkɪ] *exclam Br Fam* réveille-toi! ❑, debout! ❑

waking ['weɪkɪŋ] **1** *adj (hours)* de veille; **she spends all her waking hours reading** elle passe tout son temps à lire; **a waking dream** une rêverie, une rêvasserie

2 *n (state)* (état *m* de) veille *f*

waky waky *Fam* = **wakey wakey**

Waldensian [wɒl'densɪən] *Rel & Hist* **1** *adj* vaudois

2 *n* vaudois(e) *m,f*

Waldorf salad ['wɔːldɔːf-] *n* = salade composée de pommes, de céleri et de noix, assaisonnée avec de la mayonnaise

wale [weɪl] *n* (**a**) *(on skin)* zébrure *f*, marque *f* de coup (**b**) *(on cloth)* côte *f* (**c**) *Naut* plat-bord *m*

Wales [weɪlz] *n* pays *m* de Galles; **in Wales** au pays de Galles

WALK [wɔːk]

marcher	▸ **1 (a)**
se promener	▸ **1 (a)**
aller à pied	▸ **1 (b)**
faire à pied	▸ **2 (a)**
accompagner	▸ **2 (b)**
faire marcher	▸ **2 (c)**
promener	▸ **2 (c)**
promenade	▸ **3 (b), (d)**
randonnée	▸ **3 (b)**
démarche	▸ **3 (c)**

1 *vi* (**a**) *(gen)* marcher; *(go for a walk)* se promener; **walk, don't run!** ne cours pas!; *Am* **walk!/don't walk!** *(traffic sign)* (piétons) passez!/attendez!; **he walked along the beach** il marchait *ou* se promenait le long de la plage; **we walked down/up the street** nous avons descendu/monté la rue à pied; **to walk across** *or* **over the street to speak to sb** traverser la rue pour parler à qn; **they walked through the park** ils ont traversé le parc à pied; **he walked slowly towards the door** il s'est dirigé lentement vers la porte; **she walked back and forth** elle marchait de long en large, elle faisait les cent pas; **let's walk a little** si nous marchions un peu?; **walk with me to the shop** accompagnez-moi au magasin; **he walks in his sleep** il est somnambule; **he walked downstairs in his sleep** il a descendu l'escalier en dormant; **to walk on one's hands** marcher sur les mains, faire l'arbre fourchu; *Fig* **you have to walk before you can run** il faut apprendre petit à petit; **I'm walking on air!** je suis aux anges!; **to walk on water** marcher sur l'eau; **as far as the party faithful are concerned, he can walk on water** aux yeux des fidèles du parti, il est capable de miracles; *Am* **he's walking tall** il marche la tête haute

(**b**) *(as opposed to drive, ride)* aller à pied; **to walk home** rentrer à pied; **I walk to work** je vais au travail à pied; **did you walk all the way?** avez-vous fait tout le chemin à pied?, **is it too far to walk?** est-ce trop loin pour y aller à pied?

(**c**) *(horse, rider)* aller au pas

(**d**) *(go free)* être relâché

(**e**) *Fam (disappear, be stolen → money, object)* disparaître ❑; **the money seems to have walked** l'argent semble s'être envolé

2 *vt* (**a**) *(cover on foot)* faire à pied; **we walk 3 km a day** nous faisons 3 km (de marche) à pied par jour; **you can walk it in 10 minutes** il faut 10 minutes (pour y aller) à pied; **I can't walk another step** je ne peux pas faire un pas de plus; **she walks this road every day** elle passe à pied par cette rue tous les jours; **to walk the streets** *(wander)* se promener dans les rues; *(looking for something)* arpenter les rues, battre le pavé; *(as prostitute)* faire le trottoir; **to walk a beat** *(policeman)* faire sa ronde

(**b**) *(escort)* accompagner, marcher avec; **I'll walk you to the station** je vais vous accompagner (à pied) à la gare; **may I walk you home?** puis-je vous raccompagner?

(**c**) *(take for walk → person)* faire marcher; *(→ dog)* promener; *(→ horse)* conduire à pied; **his friend walked him up and down the room** son ami l'a fait marcher en long et en large dans la pièce; **she walked her mother round the garden** elle a fait faire un tour de jardin à sa mère; **they walked him forcibly to the door** ils l'ont dirigé de force vers la porte; **she walked the bike up the hill** elle a poussé le vélo dans la côte; *Br Fam* **she has walked me off my feet** elle m'a fait tellement marcher que je ne tiens plus debout ❑

(**d**) *Fam (idiom)* **to walk it** *(succeed easily)* gagner les doigts dans le nez

3 *n* (**a**) *(movement)* **she slowed to a walk** elle a ralenti et s'est mise à marcher; **they moved along at a brisk walk** ils marchaient d'un pas rapide

(**b**) *(stroll)* promenade *f*; *(long)* randonnée *f*; **to go for** *or* **to take a walk** aller se promener, faire une promenade *ou* un tour; **we had a long walk through the woods** nous avons fait une grande promenade *ou* balade en forêt; **it'll be a nice walk for you** cela vous fera une belle promenade; **I take a 5 km walk each day** je fais chaque jour une promenade de 5 km; **it's a long walk to the office** ça fait loin pour aller à pied au bureau; **the station is a five-minute walk from here** la gare est à cinq minutes de marche *ou* à cinq minutes à pied d'ici; **I took my mother for a walk** j'ai emmené ma mère en promenade *ou* faire un tour; **did you take the dog for a walk?** as-tu promené *ou* sorti le chien?; *Fam* **it was a walk in the park** c'était un jeu d'enfant; *Am Fam* **take a walk!** dégage!

(**c**) *(gait)* démarche *f*, façon *f* de marcher; **you'll recognize her from her walk** tu la reconnaîtras à sa démarche *ou* à sa façon de marcher *ou* à la façon dont elle marche; **his walk reminds me of Groucho Marx** quand il marche, il me fait penser à Groucho Marx

(**d**) *(path)* promenade *f*; *(in garden)* allée *f*; *(in forest)* sentier *m*, chemin *m*; **a coastal walk** un chemin côtier; *Am* **the front walk** l'allée *f (devant la maison)*

(**e**) *(occupation)* **I meet people from all walks** *or* **from every walk of life** je rencontre des gens de tous milieux

(**f**) *Am (sidewalk)* trottoir *m*

▸**walk about** *vi Br* se promener, se balader

▸**walk across 1** *vi* traverser (à pied)

2 *vt sep* faire traverser (à pied)

▸**walk around** = **walk about**

▸**walk away** *vi* partir, s'en aller; **she walked away from the group** elle s'est éloignée du groupe, elle a quitté le groupe; **he walked away from the accident** il est sorti de l'accident indemne; *Fig* **to walk away from trouble/a problem** éviter une situation difficile/un problème; **you can't just walk away from the situation** tu ne peux pas te désintéresser comme ça de la situation

▸**walk away with** *vt insep* **to walk away with sth** emporter qch; *Fig (win easily)* remporter *ou* gagner qch haut la main; **I walked away with an antique dressing table for just thirty pounds** j'ai réussi à avoir une coiffeuse ancienne pour seulement trente livres; **he walked away with a small fine** il s'en est tiré avec une petite amende; **she walked away with all the credit** c'est elle qui a reçu tous les honneurs

▸**walk back 1** *vi (return)* revenir *ou* retourner (à pied)

2 *vt sep* raccompagner (à pied)

▸**walk in 1** *vi* entrer; **she walked in and started complaining** elle est entrée et a commencé à se plaindre; **we walked in on her as she was getting dressed** nous sommes entrés sans prévenir alors qu'elle s'habillait

2 *vt sep* faire entrer

▸**walk into** *vt insep* (**a**) *(enter → house, room)* entrer dans; *(→ job)* obtenir (sans problème); *(→ situation)* se retrouver dans; *(→ trap)* tomber dans; *Fam* **you walked right into that one!** tu t'es bien fait piéger! (**b**) *(bump into → chair, wall)* se cogner à, rentrer dans; *(→ person)* rentrer dans; **he walked right into me/it** il m'est rentré en plein dedans/il est rentré en plein dedans

▸**walk off 1** *vi* partir, s'en aller

2 *vt sep (get rid of → headache)* faire passer en marchant; *(→ weight)* perdre en faisant de la marche; **to walk off one's lunch** faire une promenade pour digérer

▸**walk off with** *vt insep* **to walk off with sth** *(take)* emporter qch; *(steal)* voler qch; **he walked off with all the prizes** il a remporté *ou* il a gagné tous les prix (haut la main)

▸**walk out** *vi* (**a**) *(go out)* sortir; *(leave)* partir, s'en aller; **we walked out of the meeting** nous avons quitté la réunion *ou* nous sommes partis de la réunion en signe de protestation (**b**) *(worker)* se mettre en grève (**c**) *Br Old-fashioned (court)* **to walk out with sb** faire la cour à qn, courtiser qn

►**walk out on** *vt insep (family, lover)* quitter

►**walk over 1** *vt insep (bridge)* traverser; *Sport* **to walk over the course** inspecter le terrain (avant l'épreuve); *Fig* **don't let them walk all over you** ne vous laissez pas avoir, ne vous laissez pas marcher sur les pieds

2 *vi* aller, faire un saut; **I'll walk over to her place tomorrow** je ferai un saut *ou* je passerai chez elle demain; **the boss walked over to congratulate him** le patron s'est approché de lui pour le féliciter

►**walk round** *vt insep (museum, shops etc)* faire le tour de

►**walk through** *vt insep (one's exams etc)* réussir sans effort

►**walk up** *vi* (**a**) *(go upstairs)* monter (**b**) *(come close)* s'approcher; **a complete stranger walked up to her** un inconnu s'est approché d'elle

walkable ['wɔːkəbəl] *adj* **it's walkable** on peut y aller à pied

walkabout ['wɔːkə,baʊt] *n* (**a**) *Br* **to go on a walkabout** *(of celebrity, politician, member of royal family)* prendre un bain de foule (**b**) *Austr (of Aborigine)* = excursion périodique dans la brousse; **to go walkabout** partir dans la brousse (**c**) *Fam* **to go walkabout** *(become mislaid)* disparaître ❑

walkaway ['wɔːkə,weɪ] *n Am Fam* victoire *f* facile ❑; **the race was a walkaway for him** il a gagné la course haut la main *ou* dans un fauteuil

walker ['wɔːkə(r)] *n* (**a**) *(person → stroller)* promeneur(euse) *m,f*, marcheur(euse) *m,f*; *(→ in mountains)* randonneur(euse) *m,f*; *Sport* marcheur(euse) *m,f*; **are you a keen walker?** êtes-vous bon marcheur?, aimez-vous la marche?; **she's a fast/slow walker** elle marche vite/lentement (**b**) *(apparatus → for babies)* trotte-bébé *m*; *(→ for invalids)* déambulateur *m*

walkies ['wɔːkɪz] *n Br Fam* **(let's go) walkies!** *(said to dog)* allez, on va se promener! ❑; **my pen has gone walkies** mon stylo a disparu ❑

walkie-talkie [,wɔːkɪ'tɔːkɪ] *(pl* **walkie-talkies***)* *n* (poste *m*) émetteur-récepteur *m* portatif, talkie-walkie *m*

walk-in 1 *n (customer in hotel)* client(e) *m,f* sans réservation; *esp Am (patient)* patient(e) *m,f* sans rendez-vous

2 *adj* (**a**) *(safe, wardrobe)* de plain-pied; **the flat is in walk-in condition** l'appartement est libre d'occupation (**b**) *Am Fam (victory)* facile ❑

►► ***walk-in closet*** *or* ***cupboard*** *(gen)* débarras *m*; *(for clothes)* dressing *m*; ***walk-in fridge*** armoire *f* réfrigérante

walking ['wɔːkɪŋ] **1** *n* (**a**) *(activity → gen)* marche *f* (à pied), promenade *f*, promenades *fpl*; *(→ hiking)* randonnée *f*; *Sport* marche *f* (athlétique); **walking is the best form of exercise** la marche est le meilleur des exercices

(**b**) *(in basketball)* marcher *m*

2 *adj (clothing, shoes)* de marche; **at walking pace** au pas; **is it within walking distance?** est-ce qu'on peut y aller à pied?; **a walking holiday in the Vosges** un séjour de randonnée dans les Vosges; **we went on a walking tour of the Alps** nous avons fait de la randonnée dans les Alpes; **the walking wounded** les blessés qui peuvent encore marcher; *Fam* **she's a walking dictionary/encyclopedia** c'est un dictionnaire/une encyclopédie ambulant(e); **that man's a walking disaster area!** ce type est une catastrophe ambulante!; *Am Fam* **to hand** *or* **to give sb their walking papers** *(employee)* renvoyer qn ❑, flanquer qn à la porte; *(lover)* plaquer qn; **to get one's walking papers** *(of employee)* se faire mettre à la porte; *(of lover)* se faire plaquer

►► ***walking frame*** déambulateur *m*; ***walking race*** épreuve *f* de marche; ***walking shoes*** chaussures *fpl* de marche; ***walking stick*** (**a**) *(cane)* canne *f* (**b**) *Am (stick insect)* phasme *m*

walking-out dress *n Mil* tenue *f* de ville

Walkman® ['wɔːkmən] *(pl* **Walkmans***)* *n* Walkman® *m*, *Offic* baladeur *m*

walk-on *n* rôle *m* de figurant

►► ***walk-on part*** rôle *m* de figurant

walkout ['wɔːkaʊt] *n (of members, spectators)* départ *m* (en signe de protestation); *(of workers)* grève *f*; **to stage a walkout** *(negotiators, students)* partir (en signe de protestation); *(workers)* se mettre en grève

walkover ['wɔːk,əʊvə(r)] *n* (**a**) *Br Fam (victory)* victoire *f* dans un fauteuil; **the race was a walkover for the German team** l'équipe allemande a gagné la course haut la main *ou* dans un fauteuil (**b**) *(in horseracing)* walk-over *m inv*

walk-through *n* (**a**) *Theat* répétition *f* (**b**) *Comput* guide *m* détaillé

walk-up *Am* **1** *adj (apartment)* situé dans un immeuble sans ascenseur; *(building)* sans ascenseur

2 *n (apartment, office)* = appartement ou bureau situé dans un immeuble sans ascenseur; *(building)* = immeuble sans ascenseur; **they live in a fifth-floor walk-up** ils habitent un quatrième étage sans ascenseur

walkway ['wɔːkweɪ] *n (path)* sentier *m*, chemin *m*; *(passage)* passage *m ou* passerelle *f (pour piétons, entre deux bâtiments)*

walky-talky *(pl* **walky-talkies***)* = **walkie-talkie**

WALL [wɔːl] *n Comput (abbr* **Web-assisted language learning***)* enseignement *m* des langues assisté par la Toile

wall [wɔːl] **1** *n* (**a**) *(of building, room)* mur *m*; *(round field, garden)* mur *m* de clôture; *(round castle, city)* murs *mpl*, murailles *fpl*, remparts *mpl*; **the city walls of Langres** les remparts *ou* murs de Langres; **within the city walls** dans les murs, dans la ville, intra-muros; **the prisoners went over the wall** les prisonniers ont fait le mur; **people like him should be put up against a wall and shot** les gens comme lui méritent la peine de mort; *Fam* **to drive** *or* **to send sb up the wall** rendre qn fou *ou* dingue; *Fam* **I'll go up the wall if I have to work with her** je vais devenir fou si je dois travailler avec elle; **this is between you, me and these four walls** garde ça pour toi, que ça reste entre nous; *Br* **to go to the wall** *(business)* faire faillite; *(employee)* perdre la partie; **walls have ears** les murs ont des oreilles

(**b**) *(side → of box, cell, vein, cave, tunnel)* paroi *f*; *(→ of tyre)* flanc *m*

(**c**) *(of mountain)* paroi *f*, face *f*

(**d**) *Fig* **a wall of fire** une muraille de feu; **a wall of silence** un mur de silence

2 *vt (garden, land)* clôturer, entourer d'un mur; *(city)* fortifier

►► ***wall bars*** espalier *m (pour exercices)*; ***wall bracket*** support *m* mural; ***wall clock*** pendule *f* murale; ***wall covering*** tapisserie *f*, revêtement *m* mural; *Orn* ***wall creeper*** grimpereau *m ou* tichodrome *m* des murailles; ***wall cupboard*** placard *m* mural; ***wall game*** = sorte de football pratiqué à Eton; ***wall hanging*** tenture *f* murale; ***wall lamp, wall light*** applique *f (lampe)*; ***wall lighting*** éclairage *m* par appliques; ***wall painting*** peinture *f* murale; ***wall socket*** prise *f* murale; *Bot* ***wall speedwell*** véronique *f* des champs; ***Wall Street*** Wall Street *(quartier de la Bourse de New York)*; **according to Wall Street...** selon la Bourse de New York..., selon Wall Street...; **a Wall Street broker** un courtier de la Bourse de New York; ***the Wall Street Crash*** le krach de Wall Street; *Am Press* ***Wall Street Journal*** = quotidien financier américain; ***wall unit*** élément *m* mural

►**wall in** *vt sep (garden)* clôturer, entourer d'un mur; **the park was walled in on all four sides by giant buildings** le parc était bordé sur les quatre côtés par des immeubles gigantesques; *Fig* **she felt walled in by social convention** elle se sentait prisonnière des convenances

►**wall off** *vt sep* séparer par un mur *ou* par une cloison; **part of the garden was walled off from the rest** une partie du jardin était isolée du reste par un mur

►**wall up** *vt sep (door, window)* murer, condamner; *(body, treasure)* emmurer

THE WALL STREET CRASH

Ce krach financier, survenu à la Bourse de New York le 24 octobre 1929 ("jeudi noir"), entraîna la ruine de plusieurs milliers de personnes, acculant même certains au suicide. Cet événement est considéré comme le point de départ de la crise économique qu'allaient vivre les États-Unis pendant dix ans (la grande dépression).

wallaby ['wɒləbɪ] *(pl* **wallabies***)* *n Zool* wallaby *m*

wallah ['wɒlə] *n Fam Old-fashioned* préposé ❑ *m*; **the tea wallah** le préposé au thé

wallboard ['wɔːlbɔːd] *n* plaque *f* de plâtre

wallchart ['wɔːltʃɑːt] *n* panneau *m* mural

walled [wɔːld] *adj (city)* fortifié; *(garden)* clos

wallet ['wɒlɪt] *n* portefeuille *m*

walleye ['wɔːl,aɪ] *n* (**a**) *(squint)* strabisme *m*; **to have a walleye** loucher, avoir un strabisme (**b**) *(eye)* œil *m* vairon (**c**) *Am Ich* doré *m* jaune

walleyed ['wɔːl,aɪd] *adj (person, eyes)* qui louche

►► *Ich* ***walleyed pike*** doré *m* jaune

wallflower ['wɔːl,flaʊə(r)] *n* (**a**) *Bot* giroflée *f* (**b**) *Fam (person)* **I'm tired of being a wallflower** j'en ai assez de faire tapisserie

Wallis and Futuna Islands ['wɒlɪsənfuː,tjuːnə-] *npl* **the Wallis and Futuna Islands** Wallis-et-Futuna; **in the Wallis and Futuna Islands** à Wallis-et-Futuna

wall-mounted *adj (clock, telephone)* mural

Wallonia [wɒ'ləʊnɪə] *n* Wallonie *f*

Walloon [wɒ'luːn] **1** *n* (**a**) *(person)* Wallon(onne) *m,f* (**b**) *Ling* wallon *m*

2 *adj* wallon

wallop ['wɒləp] *Fam* **1** *vt* (**a**) *(hit → person)* flanquer un coup à, cogner sur; *(→ ball)* donner un grand coup dans ❑; **she walloped him on the jaw** elle lui a flanqué son poing sur la figure; **wallop him one!** fiche-lui une beigne!

(**b**) *(defeat)* mettre une raclée à

2 *n* (**a**) *(blow)* beigne *f*; **to give sb a wallop** flanquer *ou* filer une beigne à qn; **she gave him a wallop across the face** elle lui a flanqué *ou* filé une beigne; **he packs a real wallop** il a du punch; **give it a wallop with the hammer** mets-y un coup de marteau

(**b**) *(impact)* **she fell down with a wallop** et vlan! elle est tombée par terre

(**c**) *Br Fam (beer)* bière ❑ *f*

3 *adv Br* **to run wallop into sth** rentrer en plein dans qch

walloping ['wɒləpɪŋ] *Fam* **1** *adj* énorme, phénoménal; **a walloping great lie** un gros *ou* énorme mensonge

2 *adv* vachement

3 *n* (**a**) *(beating)* raclée *f*; **his mother gave him a good walloping** sa mère lui a flanqué une raclée (**b**) *(defeat)* raclée *f*; **they gave our team a walloping** ils ont flanqué une raclée à notre équipe

wallow ['wɒləʊ] **1** *vi* (**a**) *(roll about)* se vautrer, se rouler

(**b**) *(indulge)* se vautrer, se complaire; **to wallow in a bath** se prélasser dans un bain; **to wallow in misery** se complaire dans la tristesse; **to wallow in self-pity** s'apitoyer sur soi-même

(**c**) *Naut* être ballotté

2 *n* (**a**) *(mud)* boue *f*, bourbe *f*; *(place)* mare *f* bourbeuse

(**b**) *Fam (act of wallowing)* **there's nothing like a wallow in a warm bath to unwind** rien de tel qu'un bon bain pour se détendre; **to have a wallow in the mud** se vautrer dans la boue; **we all enjoy a good wallow in nostalgia** tout le monde aime se laisser aller à la nostalgie de temps en temps

wallpaper ['wɔːl,peɪpə(r)] **1** *n (gen) & Comput* papier *m* peint

2 *vt* tapisser (de papier peint)

►► ***wallpaper paste*** colle *f* badigeon

wallpapering ['wɔːl,peɪpərɪŋ] *n* **wallpapering is easy** poser du papier peint est facile

►► ***wallpapering brush*** *(for applying paste)* pinceau *m* à encoller le papier peint; *(for smoothing paper)* balai *m* de colleur

wallposter ['wɔːl,pəʊstə(r)] *n* affiche *f* murale

wall-to-wall *adj (widespread, complete)* **wall-to-wall sound** son enveloppant; **the room was wall-to-wall with people** la pièce était bondée

►► ***wall-to-wall carpet, wall-to-wall carpeting*** moquette *f*

wally ['wɒlɪ] *(pl* **wallies***)* *n Br Fam* imbécile ❑ *mf*, andouille *mf*; **I felt a bit of a wally** je me suis senti un peu idiot ❑; **he looked a real** *or* **a right wally** il avait vraiment l'air d'un imbécile ❑

walnut ['wɔːlnʌt] **1** *n (tree, wood)* noyer *m*; *(fruit)* noix *f*

2 *comp (furniture)* de *ou* en noyer; *(oil)* de noix; *(cake)* aux noix

Walpurgis [væl'pɜːdʒɪs] *pr n*

►► ***Walpurgis Night*** nuit *f* de Walpurgis *(nuit du 30 avril au 1er mai)*

walrus ['wɔːlrəs] *(pl* **inv** *or* **walruses)** *n Zool* morse *m*

►► ***walrus moustache*** moustache *f* à la gauloise

Walter Mitty [,wɔːltə'mɪtɪ] *adj* **to lead a Walter Mitty existence** vivre dans un monde imaginaire; **a Walter Mitty character** un rêveur

> **Walter Mitty**
>
> Il s'agit d'une allusion au personnage principal du roman de l'écrivain américain James Thurber, *The Secret Life of Walter Mitty* (1947). Ce personnage, homme tout à fait ordinaire mais doté d'une imagination très vive, essaie continuellement d'échapper à sa vie monotone en s'imaginant être le héros de toutes sortes d'aventures, au point de vivre davantage dans un monde imaginaire que dans la réalité.
>
> On évoque son nom pour désigner toute personne au caractère rêveur qui essaie de compenser la monotonie de la vie quotidienne par son imagination.

waltz [wɔːls] **1** *n* valse *f*

2 *vi* (**a**) *(dancer)* valser, danser une valse

(**b**) *(move)* danser; **she waltzed in/out of his office** *(jauntily)* elle est entrée dans/sortie de son bureau d'un pas joyeux; *(brazenly)* elle est entrée dans/sortie de son bureau avec effronterie; **he waltzed right up to the boss** il s'est approché du patron sans hésitation; **to waltz off** partir, s'en aller; **he waltzed off with her purse** il lui a volé son sac à main; **they waltzed off with first prize** ils ont remporté le premier prix haut la main

3 *vt* (**a**) *(dance)* valser avec, faire valser; **he waltzed her round the room** il s'est mis à valser *ou* danser avec elle à travers la chambre

(**b**) *(propel)* pousser, propulser

waltzer ['wɔːlsə(r)] *n* (**a**) *(dancer)* valseur(euse) *m,f* (**b**) *(at fairground)* Mont-Blanc *m*

Waltzing Matilda ['wɔːltsɪŋmə'tɪldə] *n* = chanson populaire australienne

Walworth Road ['wɒlwəθ-] *n* = rue de Londres où se trouve le siège du parti travailliste

wampum ['wɒmpəm] *n (UNCOUNT)* (**a**) *(beads)* wampum *m* (**b**) *Am Fam (money)* pognon *m*

WAN [wæn] *n Comput* (*abbr* **wide area network**) réseau *m* longue distance

wan [wɒn] *(compar* **wanner,** *superl* **wannest)** *adj Literary (person → pale)* pâle, blême, blafard; *(→ sad)* triste; *(smile)* pâle, faible; *(light, star)* pâle

wand [wɒnd] *n (of fairy, magician)* baguette *f* (magique)

wander ['wɒndə(r)] **1** *vi* (**a**) *(meander → person)* errer, flâner; *(→ stream)* serpenter, faire des méandres; **she wandered into a café** elle est entrée dans un café d'un pas nonchalant; **we wandered round the town** nous avons flâné en ville, nous nous sommes promenés au hasard dans la ville; **I'll just wander down to the beach later** j'irai faire un tour *ou* je descendrai à la plage plus tard; **her eyes wandered over the crowd** elle a promené son regard sur la foule

(**b**) *(stray → person)* s'égarer; **he's wandered off somewhere** il est parti mais il n'est pas loin; **the tourists wandered into the red light district** les touristes se sont retrouvés par hasard dans le quartier chaud; **don't wander too far, the bus will be here in ten minutes** ne t'éloigne pas trop, le bus sera là dans dix minutes; **don't wander off the path** ne vous écartez pas du chemin

(**c**) *(mind, thoughts)* vagabonder, errer; **he wandered off the topic** il s'est écarté du sujet; **her attention began to wander** elle commença à être de moins en moins attentive; **his eyes wandered over the scene** ses regards se promenaient sur cette scène; **I can't concentrate, my mind keeps wandering** je ne peux pas me concentrer, je suis trop distrait; **my mind wandered back to when we first met** mes pensées se sont reportées à l'époque où nous nous sommes connus; **her thoughts wandered to her holiday plans** sa pensée erra sur ses projets de vacances

(**d**) *(become confused)* divaguer, déraisonner; **her mother's mind** *or* **her mother has begun to wander** sa mère commence à divaguer

2 *vt* errer dans, parcourir (au hasard); **their children wander the streets at night** leurs enfants errent dans les rues *ou* courent les rues le soir; **the nomads wander the desert** les nomades parcourent le désert; **he spent his life wandering the world** il a passé sa vie à parcourir le monde

3 *n* promenade *f*, tour *m*; **we went for a wander round the town** nous sommes allés faire un tour dans la ville

►**wander about, wander around** *vi (without destination)* errer, aller sans but; *(without hurrying)* flâner, aller sans se presser

wanderer ['wɒndərə(r)] *n* vagabond(e) *m,f*; *Fig* **she's a bit of a wanderer** elle n'aime pas trop se fixer; *Hum* **the wanderer returns** voilà un revenant!

wandering ['wɒndərɪŋ] **1** *adj* (**a**) *(roaming → person)* errant, vagabond; *(→ tribe)* nomade; *(→ stream)* qui serpente, qui fait des méandres

(**b**) *(distracted → mind, thoughts, attention)* distrait, vagabond

(**c**) *(confused → mind, person)* qui divague, qui délire; *(→ thoughts)* incohérent

2 *n* (**a**) *(roaming)* vagabondage *m*, voyages *mpl*

(**b**) *(of mind)* délire *m*

3 wanderings *npl (roaming)* vagabondage *m*, voyages *mpl*; **during his wanderings** pendant ses voyages

►► *Orn* ***wandering albatross*** albatros *m* hurleur; *Fam* ***wandering hands*** mains *fpl* baladeuses; ***the Wandering Jew*** le Juif errant; *Bot* ***wandering Jew*** misère *f*; ***wandering minstrels*** ménestrels *mpl*

wanderlust ['wɒndəlʌst] *n* envie *f* de voyager

wanderoo [,wɒndə'ruː] *n Zool* (**a**) *(langur)* langur *m* du Sri Lanka (**b**) *(macaque monkey)* macaque *m* ouanderou

Wandsworth Prison ['wɒnzwəθ-] *n* = la plus grande prison de Grande-Bretagne, à Londres

wane [weɪn] **1** *vi (moon)* décroître, décliner; *(interest, power, popularity, influence)* diminuer; *(civilization, empire)* décliner, être en déclin; *(beauty)* se faner

2 *n* **to be on the wane** *(moon)* décroître, décliner; *(interest, power, popularity, influence)* diminuer; *(civilization, empire)* décliner, être en déclin; *(beauty)* se faner

wangle ['wæŋgəl] *Fam* **1** *n* combine *f*, embrouille *f*, truc *m*

2 *vt (obtain → through cleverness)* se débrouiller pour avoir; *(→ through devious means)* resquiller, carotter; **can you wangle me an invitation?** est-ce que tu peux m'avoir *ou* me dégotter une invitation?; **can you wangle it?** est-ce que tu peux arranger ça?; **he wangled his way into the job** c'est par combine qu'il a décroché le poste; **I wangled myself a trip to Rome** je me suis débrouillé pour resquiller un voyage à Rome; **they wangled their way out of paying the fine** ils se sont débrouillés pour ne pas payer l'amende

wangler ['wæŋglə(r)] *n Fam* resquilleur(euse) *m,f*

wangling ['wæŋglɪŋ] *n Fam* resquillage *m*, carottage *m*; **with a bit of wangling I managed to get myself a ticket** j'ai eu mon ticket en faisant marcher le système D; **it just needs a bit of wangling** il suffit de resquiller un peu

waning ['weɪnɪŋ] **1** *n (of moon)* décroissement *m*; *(of interest, power)* diminution *f*; *(of empire)* déclin *m*

2 *adj (moon)* décroissant, à son déclin; *(interest, power)* qui diminue; *(empire)* sur son déclin, en déclin

wank [wæŋk] *Br Vulg* **1** *vi* se branler

2 *n* (**a**) *(masturbation)* branlette *f*; **to have a wank** se faire une branlette (**b**) *Fig (nonsense)* conneries *fpl*; **he was talking a load of wank** il disait que des conneries

►**wank off** *Br Vulg* **1** *vi* se branler

2 *vt sep* **to wank oneself off** se branler; **to wank sb off** branler qn

Wankel engine ['wæŋkəl-] *n Aut* moteur *m* wankel

wanker ['wæŋkə(r)] *n Br Vulg* connard *m*

wanly ['wɒnlɪ] *adv* (**a**) *(answer, smile)* faiblement, tristement (**b**) *(shine)* faiblement, avec une pâle *ou* une faible clarté

wanna ['wɒnə] *Fam* (**a**) = **want to** (**b**) = **want a**

wannabe ['wɒnə,biː] *n Fam* = se dit de quelqu'un qui veut être ce qu'il ne peut pas être; **a James Dean wannabe** un clone de James Dean

wanness ['wɒnnɪs] *n (of person → paleness)* pâleur *f*; *(→ sadness)* tristesse *f*; *(of light)* pâleur *f*, manque *m* de clarté

WANT [wɒnt]

vouloir	► 1 (a)
désirer	► 1 (a), (b)
avoir envie de	► 1 (a), (b)
demander	► 1 (c)
vouloir voir	► 1 (c)
(re)chercher	► 1 (d)
avoir besoin de	► 1 (e)
désir	► 3 (a)
envie	► 3 (a)
besoin	► 3 (b)
manque	► 3 (c)

1 *vt* (**a**) *(expressing a wish or desire)* vouloir, désirer; **to want sth badly** avoir très envie de qch; **what do you want?** qu'est-ce que vous voulez?; **what do you want now?** qu'est-ce que tu veux encore?; **what more do you want?** que voulez-vous de plus?; **I want a cup of coffee** je veux *ou* voudrais une tasse de café; **I want my Mummy!** je veux ma maman!; **all he wants is to go to bed** tout ce qu'il veut, c'est aller se coucher; **to want to do sth** avoir envie de *ou* vouloir faire qch; **they want to go to Spain on holiday** ils ont envie d'aller *ou* ils veulent aller en vacances en Espagne; **she doesn't want to go** elle n'a pas envie d'y aller, elle ne veut pas y aller; **she doesn't want to** elle n'en a pas envie; **he doesn't want to know** il ne veut rien savoir; **I want you to wait here** je veux que tu attendes ici; **I don't want it known** je ne veux pas que cela se sache; **what do you want done?** que désirez-vous qu'on fasse?; **I don't want you turning everything upside down** je ne veux pas que vous mettiez tout sens dessus dessous; **they never wanted (to have) children** ils n'ont jamais eu envie d'avoir des enfants, ils n'ont jamais voulu (avoir) d'enfants; **I don't want (to have) any trouble** je ne veux pas d'ennuis; **how much** *or* **what do you want for this table?** combien voulez-vous pour cette table?; **what do you want with her?** qu'est-ce que tu lui veux?; **what do you want from her?** que voulez-vous d'elle?; *Ironic* **she doesn't want much!** elle n'est pas difficile, elle au moins; *Fig* **now I've got you where I want you!** je te tiens!

(**b**) *(desire sexually)* désirer, avoir envie de

(**c**) *(require to be present)* demander, vouloir voir; **you're wanted** on vous demande; **the boss wants you** le patron vous demande *ou* veut vous voir *ou* demande à vous voir; **someone wants you** *or* **you're wanted on the phone** quelqu'un vous demande au téléphone; **what does he want me for?** qu'est-ce qu'il me veut?; **where do you want this wardrobe?** où voulez-vous qu'on mette cette armoire?; **you won't be wanted this afternoon** on n'aura pas besoin de vous cet après-midi; **they don't want (to have) me** ils ne veulent pas de moi; **go away, you're not wanted here** va-t-en, tu n'es pas le bienvenu ici; **I know when I'm not wanted** je sais quand je suis de trop

(**d**) *(hunt, look for)* chercher, rechercher; **to be wanted by the police** être recherché par la police; **he's wanted for armed robbery** il est recherché pour attaque à main armée

(**e**) *(need → of person)* avoir besoin de; *(→ of task, thing)* avoir besoin de, nécessiter; **do you have everything you want?** avez-vous tout ce qu'il vous faut?; **I have more than I want** j'en ai plus qu'il n'en faut; **I've had all I want(ed)** j'en ai eu assez; **that's the very thing I want, that's just what I want** c'est juste ce qu'il me faut, cela fera parfaitement mon affaire; **this room wants a fresh coat of paint** cette pièce a besoin d'une nouvelle couche de peinture; **that child wants a good hiding** cet enfant a besoin d'une bonne correction; **this coat wants cleaning very badly** ce manteau a besoin d'un bon nettoyage; **your hair wants cutting** tu as besoin de te faire couper les cheveux, tu devrais te faire couper les cheveux; **there are still a couple of things that want doing** il y a encore quelques petites choses à faire *ou* qu'il faut faire; **what do you want with a car that size?** qu'allez-vous faire d'une voiture de cette taille?; **wanted: a good cook** *(advertisement)* on demande *ou* recherche une bonne cuisinière

(**f**) *Fam (ought)* **you want to see a doctor about that leg** vous devez montrer *ou* il faut que vous montriez cette jambe à un médecin ❏; **she wants to watch out, the boss is looking for her** elle devrait faire attention, le patron la cherche ❏

(**g**) *Literary (lack → food, shelter)* manquer de

2 *vi Fam* **the cat wants in/out** le chat veut entrer ❏/sortir ❏; *Fig* **he wants in (on the deal)** il veut une part du gâteau; **I want out!** je ne suis plus de la partie! ❏

3 *n* (**a**) *(desire, wish)* désir *m*, envie *f*; **to satisfy sb's wants** satisfaire les envies *ou* les désirs de qn

(**b**) *(requirement)* besoin *m*; **I have few wants, my wants are few** j'ai peu de besoins, j'ai besoin de peu; **she attends to all his wants** elle pourvoit à tous ses besoins

(**c**) *(lack)* manque *m*; **a want of generosity** un manque de générosité; **there's certainly no want of goodwill** ce ne sont certainement pas les bonnes volontés qui manquent; **to be in want of sth** avoir besoin de qch

(**d**) *(poverty)* misère *f*, besoin *m*; **to be in want** être dans le besoin *ou* dans la misère

4 for want of *prep* faute de; **I'll take this novel for want of anything better** faute de mieux, je vais prendre ce roman; **for want of anything better to do, she went for a walk** n'ayant rien de mieux à faire, elle est allée se promener; **the project fell through for want of funding** faute de financement, le projet est tombé à l'eau; **if we failed, it wasn't for want of trying** nous avons échoué mais ce n'est pas faute d'avoir essayé

►► *Am* ***want ad*** petite annonce *f*

►**want for** *vt insep* manquer de; **they never wanted for friends** ils n'ont jamais manqué d'amis; **he wants for nothing** il ne manque de rien

---

wanted [ˈwɒntɪd] *adj* (**a**) *(in advertisements)* **carpenter/cook wanted** on recherche (un) charpentier/(un) cuisinier; **accommodation wanted** cherche appartement (**b**) *(murderer, thief)* recherché; **wanted for armed robbery** *(sign)* recherché pour vol à main armée

►► ***wanted notice*** avis *m* de recherche

wanting [ˈwɒntɪŋ] *adj* (**a**) *(inadequate)* **to be found wanting** *(person)* ne pas convenir, ne pas faire l'affaire; *(machine)* ne pas convenir, ne pas être au point (**b**) *(lacking)* manquant; **to be wanting in sth** manquer de qch; **there is something wanting** le compte n'y est pas (**c**) *Euph (weak-minded)* simple d'esprit

wanton [ˈwɒntən] **1** *adj* (**a**) *(malicious → action, cruelty)* gratuit, injustifié; *(→ destroyer)* vicieux (**b**) *Formal (immoral → behaviour, thoughts)* licencieux; *(→ person)* dévergondé (**c**) *Arch or Literary (uncontrolled → vegetation)* abondant, exubérant (**d**) *Arch or Literary (playful → breeze)* capricieux

2 *n Literary (man)* dévergondé *m*; *(woman)* dévergondée *f*, femme *f* légère

wantonly [ˈwɒntənlɪ] *adv* (**a**) *(maliciously)* gratuitement, sans justification (**b**) *Formal (immorally)* licencieusement (**c**) *Arch or Literary (playfully)* capricieusement (**d**) *Literary (grow → vegetation)* surabondamment, profusément

wantonness [ˈwɒntənnɪs] *n* (**a**) *(of action, cruelty)* gratuité *f* (**b**) *Formal (immorality)* libertinage *m*

WAP [wæp] *n Comput & Tel (abbr* **wireless application protocol**) WAP *m*

►► ***WAP phone*** téléphone *f* WAP

wapiti [ˈwɒpɪtɪ] *n Zool* wapiti *m*

Wapping [ˈwɒpɪŋ] *n* = quartier de l'Est de Londres où se trouvent les sièges de plusieurs journaux détenus par Rupert Murdoch

war [wɔː(r)] *(pt & pp* **warred,** *cont* **warring**) **1** *n* (**a**) *(armed conflict)* guerre *f*; **to be at war/to go to war with sb** être en guerre/entrer en guerre avec qn; **Japan was at war with Russia** le Japon était en guerre avec la Russie; **Israel went to war with Syria over border disagreements** Israël est entré en guerre avec *ou* contre la Syrie pour des problèmes territoriaux; **the Allies waged war against** *or* **on the Axis** les Alliés ont fait la guerre aux puissances de l'Axe; **he fought in the war** il a fait la guerre; **the troops went off to war** les troupes sont parties pour *ou* sont allées à la guerre; *Fam Hum* **you've been through the wars!** on dirait que tu reviens de la guerre!, tu t'es bien arrangé!; *Fam Hum* **that carpet (looks like it) has been through the wars!** cette moquette est dans un état lamentable!; **to have a good war** *(soldier)* être vaillant au combat; **the war to end all wars** la der des der; *Literary* **to let loose the dogs of war** déchaîner les fureurs de la guerre; **war of attrition** guerre *f* d'usure; **war of nerves** guerre *f* des nerfs; **the American War of Independence** la guerre d'Indépendance américaine; **the War between the States, the War of Secession** la guerre de Sécession; **the Wars of the Roses** la guerre des Deux-Roses

(**b**) *(conflict, struggle)* guerre *f*, lutte *f*; **to declare** *or* **to wage war on sth** partir en guerre contre *ou* déclarer la guerre à qch; **a war of nerves/words** une guerre des nerfs/des mots; **the war against crime/drugs** la lutte contre le crime/la drogue

2 *comp (diary, hero, pension)* de guerre; **during the war years** pendant la guerre; **the war effort** l'effort *m* de guerre

3 *vi* faire la guerre; **to war with sb** faire la guerre à qn

►► ***war baby*** = enfant né pendant la guerre; ***war bond*** titre *m* d'emprunt de guerre *(émis pendant la Seconde Guerre mondiale)*; ***war bride*** mariée *f* de la guerre; ***war cabinet*** cabinet *m* de guerre; ***war cemetery*** cimetière *m* militaire; ***war chest*** caisse *f* spéciale *(affectée à une guerre)*; *Fig* caisse *f* spéciale *(d'un parti politique, d'hommes d'affaires etc)*; ***war clouds*** nuages *mpl ou* signes *mpl* précurseurs de guerre; **the war clouds are gathering** la guerre menace; ***war correspondent*** correspondant(e) *m,f* de guerre; ***war crime*** crime *m* de guerre; ***war criminal*** criminel(elle) *m,f* de guerre; *also Fig* ***war cry*** cri *m* de guerre; ***war dance*** danse *f* de guerre *ou* guerrière; ***war film*** film *m* de guerre; ***war game*** *Mil (simulated battle with maps)* kriegspiel *m*, wargame *m*; *(manoeuvres)* manœuvres *fpl* militaires; *(game)* wargame *m*; ***war grave*** = tombeau d'un soldat tombé au champ d'honneur; *Br* ***war loan*** titre *m* d'emprunt de guerre; ***war machine*** machine *f* de guerre; ***war memorial*** monument *m* aux morts; ***war museum*** musée *m* de la guerre; ***the War Office*** = ancien nom du ministère de la Défense britannique; ***war record*** passé *m* militaire; **he has a good war record** il s'est conduit honorablement pendant la guerre; **what's his war record?** qu'est-ce qu'il a fait pendant la guerre?; ***war risk*** *(in insurance)* risques *mpl* de guerre; ***war victims*** victimes *fpl* de guerre; ***war widow*** veuve *f* de guerre; **a war widow's pension** une pension de veuve de guerre; ***war wound*** blessure *f* de guerre; ***war zone*** zone *f* de guerre

'War and Peace' *Tolstoy* 'Guerre et paix'

'The War of the Worlds' *Wells* 'La Guerre des mondes'

THE WARS OF THE ROSES

Au XVème siècle, ces guerres opposèrent les deux familles pouvant prétendre au trône d'Angleterre: la maison d'York, dont l'emblème était une rose blanche, et la maison de Lancastre, représentée par une rose rouge. La guerre des Deux-Roses prit fin en 1485 avec la victoire d'un Lancastre, qui devint Henri VII et réconcilia les deux familles en épousant Élisabeth d'York.

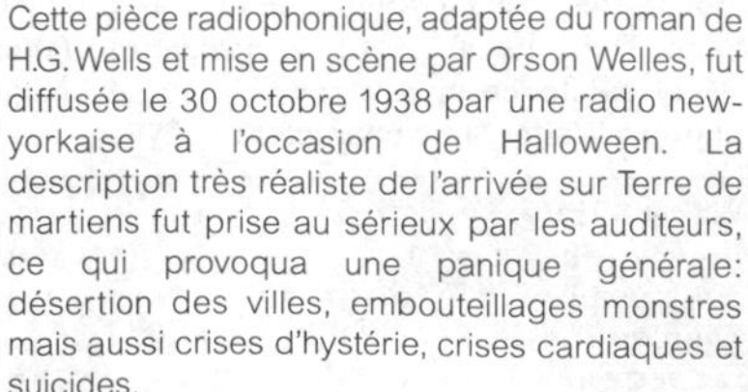

THE WAR OF THE WORLDS

Cette pièce radiophonique, adaptée du roman de H.G. Wells et mise en scène par Orson Welles, fut diffusée le 30 octobre 1938 par une radio new-yorkaise à l'occasion de Halloween. La description très réaliste de l'arrivée sur Terre de martiens fut prise au sérieux par les auditeurs, ce qui provoqua une panique générale: désertion des villes, embouteillages monstres mais aussi crises d'hystérie, crises cardiaques et suicides.

War. = **Warks**

waratah [ˈwɒrətæ] *n Bot* waratah *m*

warble[1] [ˈwɔːbəl] **1** *vi (bird)* gazouiller; *(person)* chanter (avec des trilles)

2 *vt (of bird)* gazouiller; *(of person)* chanter (avec des trilles)

3 *n* gazouillis *m*, gazouillement *m*

warble[2] *n Vet* (**a**) *(on horse)* cors *m* (**b**) *(of cattle)* varron *m*

►► *Entom* ***warble fly*** hypoderme *m* (du bœuf)

warbler [ˈwɔːblə(r)] *n Orn* fauvette *f*, pouillot *m*

warbling [ˈwɔːblɪŋ] **1** *n* gazouillis *m*, gazouillement *m*

2 *adj (bird)* gazouillant; *(sound)* mélodieux

ward [wɔːd] *n* (**a**) *(of hospital → room)* salle *f*; *(→ section)* pavillon *m*; *(of prison)* quartier *m*

(**b**) *Pol (district)* circonscription *f* électorale

(**c**) *Law (person)* pupille *mf*; *(guardianship)* tutelle *f*; **to be in ward** être sous tutelle judiciaire; **she was placed in ward** elle a été placée sous tutelle judiciaire

►► *Law* ***ward of court*** pupille *mf* sous tutelle judiciaire; *Am Pol* ***ward heeler*** agent *m* électoral *(qui sollicite des voix)*

►**ward off** *vt sep (danger, disease)* éviter; *(blow)* parer, éviter

warden [ˈwɔːdn] *n* (**a**) *(director → of building, institution)* directeur(trice) *m,f*; *Am (→ of prison)* directeur(trice) *m,f* (**b**) *(public official → of fortress, town)* gouverneur *m*; *(→ of park, reserve)* gardien(enne) *m,f*; *Br* **Warden of the Cinque Ports** gouverneur des Cinq Ports (**c**) *Br Univ* portier *m*

warder [ˈwɔːdə(r)] *n Br (prison guard)* gardien(enne) *m,f*, surveillant(e) *m,f*

wardress [ˈwɔːdrɪs] *n Br (prison guard)* gardienne *f*, surveillante *f*

wardrobe [ˈwɔːdrəʊb] *n* (**a**) *(cupboard)* armoire *f*, penderie *f*

(**b**) *(clothing)* garde-robe *f*; *Theat* costumes *mpl*; *Cin & Theat* **Elizabeth Taylor's wardrobe by...** Elizabeth Taylor est habillée par..., les costumes d'Elizabeth Taylor sont de chez...; **this is my summer wardrobe** c'est ma garde-robe d'été; **to have a large wardrobe** avoir une garde-robe importante; **she brought half her wardrobe with her** elle a emporté la moitié de sa garde-robe; *Theat* **to work in wardrobe** être costumier/costumière, s'occuper des costumes

►► ***wardrobe mistress*** costumière *f*; ***wardrobe trunk*** malle *f (penderie)*

wardroom [ˈwɔːdrʊm] *n Naut (quarters)* quartiers *mpl* des officiers *(excepté le capitaine)*; *(officers)* officiers *mpl (excepté le capitaine)*

wardship [ˈwɔːdʃɪp] *n* tutelle *f*

warehouse 1 *n* [ˈweəhaʊs, *pl* -haʊzɪz] entrepôt *m*, dépôt *m* de marchandises; *(for furniture)* garde-meuble *m*

2 *vt* [ˈweəhaʊz] entreposer, mettre en entrepôt

►► *Com* ***warehouse charges*** frais *mpl* d'entreposage; *Com* ***warehouse club*** club *m* de gros; ***warehouse manager*** responsable *mf* d'entrepôt; ***warehouse party*** = soirée house dans un local désaffecté; *Com* ***warehouse warrant*** certificat *m* d'entreposage

warehouseman [ˈweəhaʊsmən] *(pl* **warehousemen** [-mən]) *n* magasinier *m*

warehousing [ˈweəˌhaʊzɪŋ] *n* (**a**) *(of goods)* entreposage *m* (**b**) *(of shares)* parcage *m*

►► ***warehousing company*** société *f* d'entrepôts; ***warehousing costs*** frais *mpl* d'entreposage

wares [weəz] *npl* marchandises *fpl*

warfare [ˈwɔːfeə(r)] *n Mil* guerre *f*; *Fig* lutte *f*, guerre *f*; **class warfare** lutte *f* des classes;

economic warfare guerre *f* économique; *Mil & Fig* **open warfare** guerre *f* ouverte

warfarin ['wɔːfərɪn] *n Med* warfarine *f*

warfaring ['wɔːfeərɪŋ] *adj* militant, qui combat; **warfaring nation** nation *f* militante *ou* guerrière

warhead ['wɔːhed] *n* ogive *f*

warhorse ['wɔːhɔːs, *pl* -hɔːsɪz] *n* (**a**) *Hist (horse)* cheval *m* de bataille (**b**) *Fam Fig (person)* dur(e) *m,f* à cuire; **he's an old warhorse of the party** c'est un vétéran du parti (**c**) *Mktg* cheval *m* de bataille

warily ['weərɪlɪ] *adv (carefully)* prudemment, avec prudence *ou* circonspection; *(distrustfully)* avec méfiance; **the soldiers advanced warily through the forest** les soldats avançaient avec prudence dans la forêt; **they eyed him warily as he continued his explanation** ils le regardaient avec méfiance alors qu'il poursuivait son explication

wariness ['weərɪnɪs] *n (caution)* prudence *f*, circonspection *f*; *(distrust)* méfiance *f*

Warks (*written abbr* **Warwickshire**) Warwickshire *m*

warlike ['wɔːlaɪk] *adj* guerrier, belliqueux

warlock ['wɔːlɒk] *n* sorcier *m*

warlord ['wɔːlɔːd] *n* seigneur *m* de la guerre

warm [wɔːm] **1** *adj* (**a**) *(moderately hot)* chaud; **to be warm** *(of water)* être chaud; *(of person)* avoir chaud; *Met* **a warm front** un front chaud; **a warm oven** un four moyen; **warm milk** lait *m* chaud; **I can't wait for the warm weather** j'ai hâte qu'il fasse chaud; **it's getting warmer** *(of weather)* il commence à faire plus chaud; **this soup is barely warm** cette soupe est à peine chaude *ou* est tiède; **will you keep dinner warm for me?** peux-tu me garder le dîner au chaud?; **does that coat keep you warm?** est-ce que ce manteau te tient chaud?; **it's a difficult house to keep warm** c'est une maison difficile à chauffer; **are you warm enough?** avez-vous assez chaud?; **I can't seem to get warm** je n'arrive pas à me réchauffer; **the room is too warm** il fait trop chaud *ou* on étouffe dans cette pièce; **the bedroom was nice and warm** il faisait bon *ou* agréablement chaud dans la chambre; **am I right? – you're getting warmer!** est-ce que j'y suis? – tu chauffes!

(**b**) *(clothing)* chaud, qui tient chaud

(**c**) *(work)* qui donne chaud

(**d**) *(affectionate → feelings)* chaud, chaleureux; *(→ personality)* chaleureux; **he's a very warm person, he has a warm heart** il est très chaleureux; **she has a warm relationship with her mother** elle a une relation très affectueuse avec sa mère; **give my warmest wishes to your wife** toutes mes amitiés à votre femme

(**e**) *(hearty → greeting, welcome)* chaleureux, cordial; *(→ thanks)* vif; *(→ admirer, support)* ardent, enthousiaste; *(→ applause)* chaleureux, enthousiaste; *(→ smile)* accueillant

(**f**) *(colour, sound)* chaud; *(voice)* chaud, chaleureux

(**g**) *(scent, trail)* récent

2 *vt* (**a**) *(heat → person, room)* réchauffer; *(→ food)* (faire) chauffer; **she warmed her hands by the fire** elle s'est réchauffé les mains audessus du feu; **come and warm yourself at the fire** viens te chauffer *ou* te réchauffer près du feu; **the sight was enough to warm the cockles of your heart!** c'était un spectacle à vous chauffer *ou* réchauffer *ou* réjouir le cœur!

(**b**) *(reheat)* (faire) réchauffer

3 *vi* (**a**) *(food)* chauffer

(**b**) *Fig* **to warm to** *or* **towards** *(person)* se prendre de sympathie pour; *(idea, topic)* s'enthousiasmer pour; **they warmed to one another immediately** ils se sont pris de sympathie immédiatement; **you'll soon warm to the idea** tu verras, cette idée finira par te plaire; **the speaker began to warm to his subject** le conférencier s'est laissé entraîner par son sujet; **"then…", he continued, warming to his theme** "puis…", poursuivit-il, entraîné par son sujet

4 *n Fam* **come into the warm** viens au chaud *ou* où il fait chaud ☐; **to give sth a warm** réchauffer qch ☐; **I'll give the coffee a warm** je vais réchauffer le café; **give your hands a warm at the fire** réchauffe-toi les mains devant le feu

▸▸ *Comput* ***warm boot*** redémarrage *m* à chaud; *Comput* ***warm start*** redémarrage *m* à chaud

▸**warm down** *vi (after physical effort)* = faire des étirements après un échauffement intense

▸**warm over** *vt sep Am* (**a**) *(food)* (faire) réchauffer (**b**) *Pej (idea)* ressasser

▸**warm through** *vt sep* (faire) réchauffer complètement

▸**warm up 1** *vt sep* (**a**) *(heat → person, room)* réchauffer; *(→ food)* (faire) chauffer; *(→ engine, machine)* faire chauffer

(**b**) *(reheat)* (faire) réchauffer

(**c**) *(animate → audience)* mettre en train, chauffer

2 *vi* (**a**) *(become hotter → person)* se chauffer, se réchauffer; *(→ room, engine, food)* se réchauffer; *(→ weather)* devenir plus chaud, se réchauffer

(**b**) *(get ready → athlete, comedian)* s'échauffer, se mettre en train; *(→ audience)* commencer à s'animer

(**c**) *(debate, discussion)* s'animer; **the party began to warm up** la soirée commençait à s'animer

warm-blooded [-'blʌdɪd] *adj Zool* à sang chaud; *Fig (ardent)* ardent, qui a le sang chaud

warm-hearted [-'hɑːtɪd] *adj (kindly)* chaleureux, bon; *(generous)* généreux

warm-heartedly [-'hɑːtɪdlɪ] *adv (kindly)* chaleureusement, avec chaleur; *(generously)* généreusement

warming ['wɔːmɪŋ] **1** *adj (drink)* qui réchauffe; *(thought)* réconfortant

2 *n* réchauffage *m*

▸▸ ***warming pan*** bassinoire *f*; ***warming up*** (**a**) *(of food)* réchauffage *m* (**b**) *Sport* échauffement *m*; **warming-up exercises** exercices *mpl* d'échauffement

warmly ['wɔːmlɪ] *adv* (**a**) *(dress)* chaudement; **the sun shone warmly** le soleil chauffait

(**b**) *(greet, smile, welcome)* chaleureusement, chaudement; *(recommend, thank)* vivement, chaudement; *(support)* avec enthousiasme, ardemment; *(applaud)* avec enthousiasme, chaleureusement; **his suggestion was not warmly received** sa proposition n'a pas été chaudement accueillie; **the film was warmly received by the critics** le film a été accueilli par la critique avec enthousiasme

warmonger ['wɔːˌmʌŋgə(r)] *n* belliciste *mf*

warmongering ['wɔːˌmʌŋgərɪŋ] **1** *n (UNCOUNT) (activities)* activités *fpl* bellicistes; *(attitude)* bellicisme *m*; *(propaganda)* propagande *f* belliciste

2 *adj* belliciste

warmth [wɔːmθ] *n* (**a**) *(of temperature)* chaleur *f*; **we huddled together for warmth** nous nous sommes blottis les uns contre les autres pour nous tenir chaud

(**b**) *(of greeting, welcome)* chaleur *f*, cordialité *f*; *(of recommendation, thanks)* chaleur *f*, vivacité *f*; *(of applause, support)* enthousiasme *m*

(**c**) *(of colour)* chaleur *f*

(**d**) *(anger)* emportement *m*, vivacité *f*; **…she said with some warmth** …dit-elle d'un ton vif

warm-up *n (gen)* préparation *f*, préparations *fpl*; *(of athlete, singer)* échauffement *m*; *(of audience)* mise *f* en train; **they get a ten-minute warm-up** ils ont dix minutes d'échauffement

▸▸ ***warm-up exercises*** exercices *mpl* d'échauffement; ***warm-up man*** personne *f* chargée de chauffer la salle; ***warm-up match*** match *m* préparatoire *ou* d'entraînement; *esp Am* ***warm-up suit*** survêtement *m*

warmups ['wɔːmʌps] *npl Am* survêtement *m*

warn [wɔːn] *vt* (**a**) *(inform)* avertir, prévenir; **I warned them of the danger** je les ai avertis *ou* prévenus du danger; **warn them that the bridge is unsafe** prévenez-les *ou* avertissez-les que le pont n'est pas sûr; **she warned them that she would be late** elle les a prévenus qu'elle serait en retard; **you've been warned!** te voilà averti *ou* prévenu!; **warn the police!** alertez la police!; **don't say I didn't warn you!** je t'aurai prévenu!; **I'm warning you for the last time** je te préviens pour la dernière fois; *Hum* **my parents warned me about people like you!** mes parents m'avaient bien dit de me méfier des gens comme toi!

(**b**) *(advise)* conseiller, recommander; **he warned her about** *or* **against travelling at night, he warned her not to travel at night** il lui a déconseillé de voyager la nuit, il l'a mise en garde contre les voyages de nuit; **he warned me not to do it** il m'a déconseillé de le faire

▸**warn off** *vt sep* (**a**) *(tell to leave)* **to warn sb off** demander à qn de quitter les lieux; **he warned them off his land** il leur demanda instamment de quitter ses terres; **the signs are meant to warn people off** les panneaux sont là pour interdire aux gens d'entrer

(**b**) *(advise against)* **to warn sb off sth** déconseiller qch à qn; **to warn sb off doing sth** déconseiller à qn de faire qch; **the doctor has warned him off alcohol** le médecin lui a vivement déconseillé l'alcool

warning ['wɔːnɪŋ] **1** *n* (**a**) *(caution)* avertissement *m*; **let that be a warning to you** que cela vous serve d'avertissement; **thanks for the warning** merci de m'avoir prévenu *ou* m'avoir averti; **this is your last warning** *(to child)* c'est la dernière fois que je te le dis; *(to worker)* c'est votre dernier avertissement; **there was a note of warning in her voice** il y avait comme un avertissement dans sa voix; **the police gave him a warning (about speeding)** la police lui a donné un avertissement (pour excès de vitesse); **to issue a warning against sth** mettre qn en garde contre qch

(**b**) *(advance notice)* avis *m*, préavis *m*; **we only received a few days' warning** nous n'avons été prévenus que quelques jours à l'avance; **the boss visited the office without (any) warning** le patron est venu visiter le bureau inopinément *ou* à l'improviste; **he left without any warning** il est parti sans prévenir; **they gave us advance warning of the meeting** ils nous ont prévenus de la réunion

(**c**) *(alarm, signal)* alerte *f*, alarme *f*

(**d**) *(advice)* conseil *m*; **he gave them a stern warning about the dangers of smoking** il les a sévèrement mis en garde contre les dangers du tabac

2 *adj* d'avertissement; **they fired a warning shot** *(gen) & Mil* ils ont tiré une fois en guise d'avertissement; *Naut* ils ont tiré un coup de semonce

▸▸ ***warning beep*** signal *m* sonore; ***warning bell*** sonnette *f ou* sonnerie *f* d'alarme; ***warning buzzer*** avertisseur *m* sonore; *Zool* ***warning coloration*** coloration *f* aposématique; ***warning device*** avertisseur *m*; ***warning light*** voyant *m* (avertisseur), avertisseur *m* lumineux; *Comput* ***warning message*** message *m* d'avertissement; ***warning notice*** avis *m*, avertissement *m*; ***warning sign*** panneau *m* avertisseur; *Fig* **he's going to go crazy, I've seen all the warning signs** il va perdre la tête, ça se voit; **diabetes is often a warning sign of heart disease** le diabète est souvent un signe avant-coureur des maladies cardio-vasculaires; ***warning signal*** *(gen)* signal *m* d'alarme *ou* d'alerte; *Aut* signal *m* de détresse; *Ind* ***warning strike*** grève *f* d'avertissement; ***warning system*** système *m ou* dispositif *m* d'alarme; *Br Aut* ***warning triangle*** triangle *m* de signalisation

War On Want *n* = association caritative britannique luttant pour les pays défavorisés

warp [wɔːp] **1** *vt* (**a**) *(wood)* gauchir, voiler; *(metal, plastic)* voiler (**b**) *Fig (person, character, mind)* pervertir; *(thinking)* fausser, pervertir

2 *vi (wood)* gauchir, se voiler; *(metal, plastic)* se voiler

3 *n* (**a**) *(fault → in wood)* gauchissement *m*, voilure *f*; *(→ in metal, plastic)* voilure *f* (**b**) *Tex (of yarn)* chaîne *f*; *(for tapestry)* lisse *f*, lice *f*

warpaint ['wɔːpeɪnt] *n (of Indian)* peinture *f* de guerre; *Fig Hum (make-up)* maquillage *m*, peinture *f* de guerre

warpath ['wɔːpɑːθ] *n* **to be on the warpath** être sur le sentier de la guerre; *Fig* **be careful, the boss is on the warpath** fais attention, le patron est d'une humeur massacrante

warped [wɔːpt] *adj* (**a**) *(wood)* gauchi, voilé; *(metal, plastic)* voilé (**b**) *Fig (person, character, mind)* perverti; *(thinking, view)* faux (fausse), perverti; **you've got a warped mind!, your mind is warped!** tu as l'esprit tordu!; **what a warped sense of humour!** quel humour tordu!; **you**

must be a bit warped if you think that's funny! tu dois être un peu tordu pour trouver ça drôle!

warplane [ˈwɔːpleɪn] *n* avion *m* de guerre

warrant [ˈwɒrənt] **1** *n* (**a**) *Law (written order)* mandat *m*; **there's a warrant (out) for his arrest** il y a un mandat d'arrêt contre lui

(**b**) *Com & Fin (for payment)* bon *m*; *(guarantee)* garantie *f*; *(for shares)* bon *m* de souscription d'actions; *(for goods)* certificat *m* d'entrepôt

(**c**) *Mil* brevet *m*

2 *vt* (**a**) *(justify)* justifier; **the situation warrants a new approach** la situation demande que l'on s'y prenne autrement; **costs are too high to warrant further investment** les frais sont trop élevés pour permettre *ou* pour justifier d'autres investissements

(**b**) *Old-fashioned (declare with certainty)* assurer, certifier; **I'll warrant (you) that's the last we see of her** c'est la dernière fois qu'on la voit, je vous le garantie

(**c**) *Com (goods)* warranter

▸▸ ***warrant officer*** adjudant *m (auxiliaire d'un officier)*

warrantable [ˈwɒrəntəbəl] *adj (justifiable)* justifiable

warrantee [ˌwɒrənˈtiː] *n Law* titulaire *mf* d'une garantie

warrantor, warranter [ˈwɒrəntɔː(r)] *n Law* garant(e) *m,f*, débiteur(trice) *m,f*

warranty [ˈwɒrəntɪ] (*pl* **warranties**) *n* (**a**) *(guarantee)* garantie *f*; **a one-year warranty** une garantie d'un an; **this computer has a five-year warranty** cet ordinateur est garanti cinq ans; **under warranty** sous garantie; **is it still under warranty?** est-ce que c'est encore sous garantie? (**b**) *Law* garantie *f*

▸▸ ***warranty certificate*** certificat *m* de garantie

Warren *pr n*

▸▸ ***the Warren Commission*** la commission Warren *(qui publia le rapport du même nom)*; ***the Warren Report*** = rapport sur l'assassinat de John F. Kennedy qui récusa la thèse de la conspiration

warren [ˈwɒrən] *n* (**a**) *(of rabbit)* terriers *mpl*, garenne *f* (**b**) *Fig (maze of passageways)* labyrinthe *m*, dédale *m*

warrigal [ˈwɒrɪgəl] *n Austr Zool* (**a**) *(wild dog)* dingo *m* (**b**) *(wild horse)* cheval *m* sauvage

warring [ˈwɔːrɪŋ] *adj (nations, tribes)* en guerre; *Fig (beliefs)* en conflit; *(interests)* contradictoire, contraire; **warring factions within the Labour Party** des factions adverses au sein du Labour Party

warrior [ˈwɒrɪə(r)] *n* guerrier(ère) *m,f*

Warsaw [ˈwɔːsɔː] *n* Varsovie

▸▸ *Hist* ***the Warsaw Ghetto*** le ghetto de Varsovie; ***the Warsaw Pact*** le pacte de Varsovie; ***Warsaw Pact countries*** pays *mpl* (membres) du pacte de Varsovie

war-scarred *adj (city, country)* dévasté par la guerre

warship [ˈwɔːʃɪp] *n* navire *m ou* bâtiment *m* de guerre

wart [wɔːt] *n* (**a**) *Med* verrue *f*; *Fig* **a biography of Charles de Gaulle, warts and all** une biographie de Charles de Gaulle écrite sans complaisance *ou* qui ne fait pas de cadeaux; *Fig* **she'll have to accept him as he is, warts and all** il faudra qu'elle l'accepte comme il est, avec tous ses défauts (**b**) *Bot* excroissance *f*

warthog [ˈwɔːthɒg] *n Zool* phacochère *m*

wartime [ˈwɔːtaɪm] **1** *n* période *f* de guerre; **in wartime** en temps de guerre

2 *comp* de guerre; **wartime London** le Londres des années de guerre

▸▸ ***wartime rations*** rations *fpl* de guerre

war-torn *adj* déchiré par la guerre

warty [ˈwɔːtɪ] (*compar* **wartier**, *superl* **wartiest**) *adj* couvert de verrues, *Spec* verruqueux

war-weary *adj* las de la guerre

Warwickshire [ˈwɒrɪkʃɪə(r)] *n* le Warwickshire, = comté du centre de l'Angleterre; **in Warwickshire** dans le Warwickshire

wary [ˈweərɪ] (*compar* **warier**, *superl* **wariest**) *adj (prudent → person)* prudent, sur ses gardes; *(→ look)* prudent; *(→ smile)* hésitant; *(distrustful)* méfiant; **I'm wary about promoting these ideas** j'hésite à promouvoir ces idées; **the people were wary of the new regime** les gens se méfiaient du nouveau régime; **he kept a wary eye on the dog** il surveillait le chien attentivement

was [wɒz, *unstressed* wəz] *pt of* **be**

wasabi [wæˈsɑːbɪ] *n Culin* wasabi *m*

Wash[1] [wɒʃ] *n Geog* **the Wash** = grande baie sur la côte est de l'Angleterre

Wash[2] (*written abbr* **Washington**) Washington *f*

WASH [wɒʃ]

laver	▸ **1 (a); 2 (c)**
baigner	▸ **1 (b)**
emporter	▸ **1 (b)**
se laver	▸ **2 (a), (b)**
faire sa toilette	▸ **2 (a)**
être lavable	▸ **2 (b)**
nettoyage	▸ **3 (a)**
lessive	▸ **3 (b)**
remous	▸ **3 (c)**

1 *vt* (**a**) *(clean)* laver; **to wash oneself** *(person)* se laver, faire sa toilette; *(cat, dog)* faire sa toilette; **go and wash your hands** va te laver les mains; **she washed her hair** elle s'est lavé la tête *ou* les cheveux; **he washed the walls clean** il a bien lavé *ou* nettoyé les murs; **to wash the dishes** faire *ou* laver la vaisselle; **to wash clothes** faire la lessive; **wash in cold/hot water** *(on clothing label)* laver à l'eau froide/chaude; **I wash my hands of the whole affair** je me lave les mains de toute cette histoire; **she washed her hands of him** elle s'est désintéressée de lui

(**b**) *(of current, river, waves → move over)* baigner; *(→ carry away)* emporter, entraîner; **the waves washed the shore** les vagues baignaient la côte; **the body was washed ashore** le cadavre s'est échoué *ou* a été rejeté sur la côte; **the crew was washed overboard** l'équipage a été emporté par une vague; **he was washed out to sea** il a été emporté par la mer

(**c**) *(coat, cover)* badigeonner

(**d**) *Mining (gold, ore)* laver

2 *vi* (**a**) *(clean oneself → person)* se laver, faire sa toilette; **have you washed properly?** est-ce que tu as bien fait ta toilette?

(**b**) *(be washable)* se laver, être lavable; **this dress doesn't wash very well** cette robe ne supporte pas bien le lavage; *Br Fam* **his story just doesn't wash with me** son histoire ne marche pas avec moi, il ne me fera pas avaler cette histoire

(**c**) *(do dishes)* **you wash and I'll dry** tu laves et j'essuie

(**d**) *(waves, sea)* **the waves washed against the cliff** les vagues baignaient la falaise

3 *n* (**a**) *(act of cleaning)* nettoyage *m*; **this floor needs a good wash** ce plancher a bien besoin d'être lavé *ou* nettoyé; **your hair needs a wash** il faut que tu te laves la tête; **give your face a wash** lave-toi le visage; **I gave the car a wash** j'ai lavé la voiture; **he's having a wash** il se lave, il fait sa toilette; **I could do with a quick wash and brush-up** j'aimerais faire un brin de toilette *ou* me débarbouiller

(**b**) *(clothes to be washed)* lessive *f*, linge *m* sale; **your shirt is in the wash** *(laundry basket)* ta chemise est au (linge) sale; *(machine)* ta chemise est à la lessive; **the stain came out in the wash** la tache est partie au lavage; *Br* **it'll all come out in the wash** *(become known)* ça finira par se savoir; *(turn out for the best)* tout cela finira par s'arranger

(**c**) *(movement of water → caused by current)* remous *m*; *(→ caused by ship)* sillage *m*, remous *m*; *(sound of water)* clapotis *m*

(**d**) *(of paint)* badigeon *m*

(**e**) *Med (lotion)* solution *f*, lotion *f*

(**f**) *Art (of watercolour)* lavis *m*

4 *adj Am* lavable

▸▸ *Art* ***wash drawing*** dessin *m* au lavis; *Am St Exch* ***wash sale*** vente *f* fictive

▸**wash away** *vt sep (carry off → boat, bridge, house)* emporter; *(→ river bank, soil)* éroder; **the rain washed away the road** la route s'est effondrée sous l'action de la pluie; *Fig* **to wash one's sins away** laver ses péchés

▸**wash down** *vt sep* (**a**) *(clean)* laver (à grande eau)

(**b**) *(food)* arroser; *(tablet)* faire descendre; **roast beef washed down with Burgundy wine** rosbif arrosé d'un bourgogne

▸**wash off 1** *vt sep (remove → with soap)* enlever *ou* faire partir au lavage; *(→ with water)* enlever *ou* faire partir à l'eau

2 *vi (disappear → with soap)* s'en aller *ou* partir au lavage; *(→ with water)* s'en aller *ou* partir à l'eau; **the paint won't wash off** la peinture ne s'en va pas *ou* ne part pas

▸**wash out 1** *vt sep* (**a**) *(remove → with soap)* enlever *ou* faire partir au lavage; *(→ with water)* enlever *ou* faire partir à l'eau

(**b**) *(clean)* laver

(**c**) *(carry away → bridge)* emporter; *(→ road)* dégrader

(**d**) *(cancel, prevent)* **the game was washed out** le match a été annulé à cause de la pluie

2 *vi* = **wash off**

▸**wash over** *vt insep (of waves)* balayer; *Fig (have no effect on)* ne faire aucun effet à; **anything I say just washes over her** rien de ce que je lui dis ne lui fait le moindre effet

▸**wash up 1** *vi* (**a**) *Br (wash dishes)* faire *ou* laver la vaisselle

(**b**) *Am (wash oneself)* se laver, faire sa toilette

2 *vt sep* (**a**) *Br (glass, dish)* laver; **whose turn is it to wash up the dishes?** à qui le tour de faire *ou* de laver la vaisselle?

(**b**) *(of sea)* rejeter; **several dolphins were washed up on shore** plusieurs dauphins se sont échoués sur la côte

---

washable [ˈwɒʃəbəl] *adj* lavable, lessivable

wash-and-wear *adj* qui ne nécessite aucun repassage

washbag [ˈwɒʃbæg] *n* trousse *f* de toilette

washbasin [ˈwɒʃˌbeɪsən] *n (basin)* cuvette *f*, bassine *f*; *(sink)* lavabo *m*

washboard [ˈwɒʃbɔːd] *n* planche *f* à laver

▸▸ *Fam* ***washboard stomach*** ventre *m* plat ❑

washbowl [ˈwɒʃbəʊl] *n Am (basin)* cuvette *f*, bassine *f*; *(sink)* lavabo *m*

washcloth [ˈwɒʃklɒθ] *n (for dishes)* lavette *f*; *Am (face flannel)* ≃ gant *m* de toilette

washday [ˈwɒʃdeɪ] *n* jour *m* de lessive

washed-out [ˌwɒʃt-] *adj* (**a**) *(faded → colour)* délavé; *(→ curtain, jeans)* décoloré, délavé (**b**) *Fam (exhausted)* épuisé ❑, lessivé; *(pale)* pâle de fatigue ❑

washed-up [ˌwɒʃt-] *adj Fam* fichu; **he's washed-up as a singer** sa carrière de chanteur est fichue *ou* est finie ❑; **their marriage is washed-up** leur mariage est fichu *ou* se casse la figure

washer [ˈwɒʃə(r)] *n* (**a**) *Constr* joint *m*, rondelle *f*; *(in tap)* joint *m* (**b**) *(washing machine)* machine *f* à laver, lave-linge *m inv*

washer-dryer, washer-drier *n* machine *f* à laver séchante

washer-up (*pl* **washers-up**), **washer-upper** (*pl* **washer-uppers**) *n Br Fam (gen)* laveur(euse) *m,f* de vaisselle ❑; *(in restaurant)* plongeur(-euse) ❑ *m,f*

washerwoman [ˈwɒʃəˌwʊmən] (*pl* **washerwomen** [-ˌwɪmɪn]) *n* blanchisseuse *f*

wash-hand basin *Br* = **washbasin**

washhouse [ˈwɒʃhaʊs, *pl* -haʊzɪz] *n* lavoir *m*

washing [ˈwɒʃɪŋ] *n* (**a**) *(act → of car, floors)* lavage *m*; *(→ of laundry)* lessive *f*; *Rel (of feet, hands)* lavement *m*

(**b**) *(laundry)* linge *m*, lessive *f*; **a pile of dirty washing** une pile de linge sale; **to do the washing** faire la lessive, laver le linge; **where can I hang the washing?** où puis-je étendre le linge?; **do you have a lot of washing to do?** avez-vous beaucoup de lessive *ou* une grande lessive à faire?

▸▸ ***washing day*** jour *m* de lessive; ***washing line*** corde *f* à linge; ***washing liquid*** lessive *f* liquide; ***washing machine*** machine *f* à laver, lave-linge *m inv*; ***washing powder*** lessive *f ou* détergent *m (en poudre)*; ***washing soda*** cristaux *mpl* de soude

Washington [ˈwɒʃɪŋtən] *n* (**a**) *(state)* **Washington (State)** l'État *m* de Washington; **in Washington** dans l'État de Washington (**b**) *(town)* **Washington (DC)** Washington *f*

▸▸ ***the Washington Monument*** = monument à la mémoire de George Washington, à Washington; *Am Press* ***Washington Post*** = quotidien américain de qualité

washing-up *n Br* vaisselle *f (à laver)*; **to do the washing-up** faire la vaisselle
►► ***washing-up bowl*** cuvette *f*, bassine *f*; *Br* ***washing-up liquid*** produit *m* pour la vaisselle, liquide *m* vaisselle

wash-leather *n Br* peau *f* de chamois

washline ['wɒʃlaɪn] *n* corde *f* à linge

washload ['wɒʃləʊd] *n (washing capacity)* capacité *f* de lavage; *(items to be washed)* lessive *f*

washout ['wɒʃaʊt] *n Fam (party, plan)* fiasco *m*; *(person)* raté(e) *m,f*; **the whole thing's a washout** c'est une perte sèche

washrag ['wɒʃræg] *n Am* lavette *f*

washroom ['wɒʃrʊm] *n* (**a**) *(for laundry)* buanderie *f* (**b**) *Am Euph (lavatory)* toilettes *fpl*

washstand ['wɒʃstænd] *n* table *f* de toilette

washtub ['wɒʃtʌb] *n (for laundry)* bassine *f*, cuvette *f*

wash-wipe *n Aut* lavage-balayage *m*

wasn't [wɒzənt] = **was not**

Wasp, WASP [wɒsp] *n Am (abbr* **White Anglo-Saxon Protestant**) = Blanc d'origine anglo-saxonne et protestante, appartenant aux classes aisées et influentes

wasp [wɒsp] *n* guêpe *f*; **a wasp's nest** un guêpier; *Fig* **to have a wasp waist** avoir une taille de guêpe

'The Wasp Factory' *Banks* 'Le Seigneur des guêpes'

waspish ['wɒspɪʃ] *adj (person → by nature)* méchant; *(→ in bad mood)* qui est de mauvaise humeur; *(reply, remark)* acerbe, mordant, méchant

waspishly ['wɒspɪʃlɪ] *adv (say)* d'un ton acerbe *ou* mordant, méchamment

waspishness ['wɒspɪʃnɪs] *n* méchanceté *f*

wasp-waisted *adj* à la taille de guêpe

wassail ['wɒseɪl] *Arch & Literary* **1** *n* (**a**) *(drink → beer)* bière *f* épicée; *(→ wine)* vin *m* chaud (**b**) *(festivity)* beuverie *f* (**c**) *(toast)* toast *m*
2 *vi* chanter (des chants de Noël); **to go wassailing** aller chanter des noëls de maison en maison

wassailer ['wɒseɪlə(r)] *n Arch & Literary* (**a**) *(reveller)* noceur(euse) *m,f* (**b**) *(carol singer)* chanteur(euse) *m,f* de noëls *(qui va de maison en maison)*

Wassermann's reaction, Wassermann's test ['væsəmænz-] *n Med* réaction *f* de Bordet-Wassermann

wast [wɒst, *unstressed* wəst] *Arch* = **(you) were**

wastage ['weɪstɪdʒ] *n (UNCOUNT)* (**a**) *(loss → of materials, money)* gaspillage *m*, gâchis *m*; *(→ of heat)* déperdition *f*, perte *f*; *(→ of time)* perte *f*; *(→ through leakage)* fuites *fpl*, pertes *fpl* (**b**) *(what is wasted)* déchets *mpl*, rebuts *mpl* (**c**) *(in numbers, workforce)* réduction *f*; **many students are lost by wastage** beaucoup d'étudiants abandonnent en cours de route

waste [weɪst] **1** *vt* (**a**) *(misuse → materials, money)* gaspiller; *(→ time)* perdre; *(→ life)* gâcher; **very little is wasted in this family** on ne gaspille pas dans cette famille; **I hate wasting food** j'ai horreur de gâcher la nourriture; **don't waste your life hanging around pubs** ne gâche pas ta vie à traîner dans les pubs; **I wasted an hour at the post office** j'ai perdu une heure à la poste; **don't waste your time worrying about her** ne t'en fais pas pour elle, tu perds ton temps; **she wasted no time in telling us about it** elle s'est empressée de nous le raconter; *Fam* **you didn't waste any time, did you!** tu n'as pas perdu de temps, hein?; **expensive wine is wasted on me** je suis incapable d'apprécier le bon vin; **a beautiful house like that is wasted on such people** une belle maison comme ça, c'est trop beau pour des gens pareils; **the joke was wasted on him** il n'a pas compris la plaisanterie; **you're wasting your energy** vous vous dépensez inutilement; **you're wasting your breath!** tu uses ta salive pour rien!; **don't waste your breath trying to convince them** ne te fatigue pas *ou* ne perds pas ton temps à essayer de les convaincre; *Prov* **waste not, want not** = l'économie protège du besoin
(**b**) *(wear away → limb, muscle)* atrophier; *(→ body, person)* décharner; **her body was completely wasted by cancer** son corps était complètement miné par le cancer
(**c**) *Fam (attack)* casser la gueule à, démonter le portrait à; *(kill)* buter, refroidir, zigouiller; **to waste sb's face** casser *ou* défoncer la gueule à qn, faire une tête au carré à qn
2 *n* (**a**) *(misuse → of materials, money)* gaspillage *m*, gâchis *m*; *(→ of time)* perte *f*; **what a waste!** quel gâchis *ou* gaspillage!; **it's a waste of breath arguing about it** ce n'est pas la peine d'en discuter; **that book was a complete waste of money** ce livre, c'était de l'argent jeté par les fenêtres; **it's a waste of time talking to her** tu perds ton temps à discuter avec elle; **what a waste of time!** que de temps perdu!; **our trip was a waste of time and energy** notre voyage a été une perte de temps et d'énergie; **it's an enormous waste of talent** c'est énormément de talent gâché; **to go to waste** *(gen)* se perdre, être gaspillé; *(land)* tomber en friche; **don't let all this food go to waste!** ne laissez pas *ou* n'allez pas laisser tout ça se perdre!; **I'm not going to let the opportunity go to waste** je ne vais pas laisser passer l'occasion; *Fam* **he's a waste of space** il est nul
(**b**) *(UNCOUNT) (refuse → gen)* déchets *mpl*; *(→ household)* ordures *fpl* (ménagères); *(→ water)* eaux *fpl* usées; **industrial waste** déchets *mpl* industriels
(**c**) *(land)* terrain *m* vague
(**d**) *(idiom)* **to lay waste to sth, to lay sth waste** ravager *ou* dévaster qch
3 *adj* (**a**) *(paper)* de rebut; *(energy)* perdu; *(water)* sale, usé; *(food)* qui reste
(**b**) *(ground)* en friche; *(region)* désert, désolé; **the children were playing on waste ground** les enfants jouaient sur un terrain vague
4 wastes *npl* terres *fpl* désolées, désert *m*; **the polar wastes** le désert polaire
►► *Br* ***waste bin*** *(in kitchen)* poubelle *f*, boîte *f* à ordures; *(for paper)* corbeille *f* (à papier); ***waste collection*** ramassage *m* des ordures; ***waste disposal*** élimination *f ou* destruction *f* des déchets *ou* des ordures; ***waste disposal site*** dépôt *m* d'ordures; ***waste disposal unit*** broyeur *m* d'ordures; ***waste heat*** chaleur *f* perdue; ***waste heat recovery*** récupération *f* de la chaleur perdue; ***waste material*** déchets *mpl*; ***waste matter*** déchets *mpl*; ***waste paper*** *(UNCOUNT)* papier *m ou* papiers *mpl* de rebut; ***waste pipe*** (tuyau *m* de) vidange *f*; ***waste product*** *Ind* déchet *m* de production *ou* de fabrication; *Physiol* déchet *m (de l'organisme)*; ***waste segregation*** tri *m* sélectif (des ordures ménagères)
►**waste away** *vi* dépérir

'The Waste Land' *Eliot* 'La Terre Gaste' *ou* 'La Terre vaine'

wastebasket [weɪstbæskɪt] *n esp Am* corbeille *f* (à papier); *Comput* poubelle *f*

wasted ['weɪstɪd] *adj* (**a**) *(material, money)* gaspillé; *(energy, opportunity, time)* perdu; *(attempt, effort)* inutile, vain; *(food)* inutilisé; **a wasted journey** un voyage raté; **she's wasted in that job** cet emploi est bien au-dessous de ses capacités
(**b**) *(figure, person)* décharné; *(limb → emaciated)* décharné; *(→ enfeebled)* atrophié
(**c**) *Fam (drunk)* pété, bourré, fait; *(on drugs)* défoncé

wasteful ['weɪstfʊl] *adj (habits)* de gaspillage; *(person)* gaspilleur; *(procedure)* inefficace, peu rentable; **a wasteful use of natural resources** un gaspillage des ressources naturelles

wastefully ['weɪstfʊlɪ] *adv* en gaspillant; **we spend our time so wastefully** on gaspille un temps fou

wastefulness ['weɪstfʊlnɪs] *n (of person)* gaspillage *m*, manque *m* d'économie; *(of procedure)* inefficacité *f*

wasteheap ['weɪsthiːp] *n* tas *m* de déchets; *Mining* halde *f* de déblais

wasteland ['weɪstlænd] *n (land → disused)* terrain *m* vague; *(→ uncultivated)* terres *fpl* en friche *ou* abandonnées; *(of desert, snow)* désert *m*; *Fig* **a cultural wasteland** un désert culturel

wastepaper basket [,weɪst'peɪpə(r)-] *n Br* corbeille *f* (à papier)

waster ['weɪstə(r)] *n* (**a**) *(wasteful person)* gaspilleur(euse) *m,f*; *(who wastes money)* dépensier(-ère) *m,f* (**b**) *Br (good-for-nothing)* bon *m* à rien, bonne *f* à rien

wasting ['weɪstɪŋ] *n* (**a**) *(of resources, time)* gaspillage *m* (**b**) *(of body)* dépérissement *m*, amaigrissement *m*; *(of limb)* atrophie *f*
►► *Acct* ***wasting asset*** actif *m* qui se déprécie; ***wasting disease*** maladie *f* qui ronge

wastrel ['weɪstrəl] = **waster**

WATCH [wɒtʃ]

regarder	► **1 (a); 2 (a)**
observer	► **1 (a), (b); 2 (a)**
surveiller	► **1 (b), (c)**
faire attention à	► **1 (d)**
suivre de près	► **1 (d)**
veiller	► **2 (b)**
montre	► **3 (a)**
surveillance	► **3 (b)**
garde	► **3 (c), (d)**

1 *vt* (**a**) *(look at, observe → event, film)* regarder; *(→ animal, person)* regarder, observer; **they watch a lot of television** ils regardent beaucoup la télévision; **is there anything worth watching on TV?** est-ce qu'il y a quelque chose de bien (à regarder) à la télévision?; **I watched her working** je la regardais travailler; **the crowds were watching the lions being fed** la foule regardait les lions qu'on était en train de nourrir; **we sat outside watching the world go by** nous étions assis dehors à regarder les gens passer; **watch how I do it, watch me** regardez *ou* observez comment je fais; **I bet he ignores us, just you watch!** je parie qu'il va nous ignorer, tu vas voir!; *Prov* **a watched pot never boils** = inutile de s'inquiéter, ça ne fera pas avancer les choses
(**b**) *(spy on → person)* surveiller, observer; *(→ activities, suspect)* surveiller; **you'd better watch him** vous feriez bien de le surveiller *ou* de l'avoir à l'œil; **I think we're being watched** *(gen)* j'ai l'impression qu'on nous observe *ou* qu'on nous surveille; *(by police, thieves)* j'ai l'impression qu'on nous surveille
(**c**) *(guard, tend → children, pet)* surveiller, s'occuper de; *(→ belongings, house)* surveiller, garder; *Mil* monter la garde devant, garder
(**d**) *(pay attention to → health, weight)* faire attention à; *(→ development, situation)* suivre de près; **watch where you're going!** regardez devant vous!; **watch what you're doing!** faites bien attention (à ce que vous faites)!; **watch you don't spill the coffee** fais attention à *ou* prends garde de ne pas renverser le café; **can you watch the milk?** peux-tu surveiller le lait?; **I'm watching the classifieds for any job opportunities** je regarde les petites annonces pour les offres d'emploi; **watch you don't break anything** faites attention à ne rien casser; **we'd better watch the time** il faut que nous surveillions l'heure; **stop watching the clock and do some work!** arrêtez de surveiller la pendule et travaillez un peu!; **watch this space** [illegible] d'une publicité ou d'informations à paraître; **watch your head!** attention *ou* gare à votre tête!; **watch your language!** surveille ton langage!; **watch it!** *(warning)* (fais) attention!; *(threat)* attention!, gare à vous!; *also Fig* **watch your step** faites attention *ou* regardez où vous mettez les pieds; **you should watch your step** *or* **watch yourself with the boss** vous feriez bien de vous surveiller quand vous êtes avec le patron
2 *vi* (**a**) *(observe)* regarder, observer; **I watched to see how she would react** j'ai attendu pour voir quelle serait sa réaction; **he watched closely as I removed the bandage** il a regardé *ou* observé attentivement quand j'ai enlevé le bandage; **I just came to watch** je suis simplement venu regarder, je suis venu en simple spectateur
(**b**) *(keep vigil)* veiller; **his mother watched by his bedside** sa mère a veillé à son chevet
3 *n* (**a**) *(timepiece)* montre *f*; **it's six o'clock by my watch** il est six heures à ma montre

(**b**) *(lookout)* surveillance *f*; *Br* **be on the watch for pickpockets** faites attention *ou* prenez garde aux voleurs à la tire; *Br* **tax inspectors are always on the watch for fraud** les inspecteurs des impôts sont toujours à l'affût des fraudeurs; **a sentry was on watch** *or* **kept watch** une sentinelle montait la garde; **to keep watch by sb's bed** veiller au chevet de qn; **the police kept a close watch on the suspect** la police a surveillé le suspect de près; **we'll keep watch on your house during your absence** nous surveillerons votre maison pendant votre absence; **we're keeping a watch on inflation rates** nous surveillons de près les taux d'inflation

(**c**) *(person on guard → gen) & Mil* sentinelle *f*; *Naut* homme *m* de quart; *(group of guards → gen) & Mil* garde *f*; *Naut* quart *m*

(**d**) *(period of duty → gen) & Mil* garde *f*; *Naut* quart *m*; **who's on watch?** *(gen) & Mil* qui monte la garde?; *Naut* qui est de quart?

(**e**) *Literary (period of the night)* **in the slow watches of the night** pendant les longues nuits sans sommeil

►► ***watch chain*** chaîne *f* de montre; ***watch crystal*** verre *m* de montre; ***watch night*** nuit *f* de la Saint-Sylvestre; ***watch night service*** messe *f* (de minuit) de la Saint-Sylvestre; ***watch pocket*** gousset *m*

►**watch for** *vt insep* guetter, surveiller; **he watched for a chance to approach the President** il attendait une occasion d'approcher le Président; **watch for any sudden changes in temperature** surveillez toute variation soudaine de la température; **something to watch for this month is the London marathon** la chose à ne pas rater ce mois-ci, c'est le marathon de Londres

►**watch out** *vi* faire attention, prendre garde; **watch out!** *(warning)* (faites) attention!; **you'd better watch out, the boss knows** tu devrais te méfier, le patron est au courant; **to watch out for sth** *(be on lookout for)* guetter qch; *(be careful of)* faire attention *ou* prendre garde à qch; **watch out for the bus** guettez le bus; **watch out for the fine print** faites bien attention à toutes les clauses; **watch out for Ronnie!** gare à Ronnie!

►**watch over** *vt insep* garder, surveiller; **the shepherds were watching over their flocks** les bergers gardaient *ou* surveillaient leurs troupeaux; **she watched over the children while we were gone** elle a surveillé les enfants *ou* elle s'est occupée des enfants pendant notre absence; **God will watch over you** Dieu vous protégera

---

watchable ['wɒtʃəbəl] *adj* (**a**) *(able to be watched)* que l'on peut regarder (**b**) *(enjoyable to watch)* qui se laisse regarder

watchband ['wɒtʃˌbænd] *n Am* bracelet *m* de montre

watchcase ['wɒtʃkeɪs] *n* étui *m* de montre

watchdog ['wɒtʃdɒg] **1** *n (dog)* chien(enne) *m,f* de garde; *Fig (person)* gardien(enne) *m,f*; *(organization)* organisme *m* de surveillance *ou* de contrôle; **the committee acts as watchdog on environmental issues** le comité veille aux problèmes d'environnement

2 *comp (body, committee)* de surveillance

►► *Comput* ***watchdog program*** programme *m* sentinelle

watcher ['wɒtʃə(r)] *n* observateur(trice) *m,f*; *(spectator)* spectateur(trice) *m,f*; *(idle onlooker)* curieux(euse) *m,f*; **Downing Street/Kremlin watchers** les observateurs de Downing Street/du Kremlin

watchful ['wɒtʃfʊl] *adj* vigilant, attentif; **he was watchful for any unusual behaviour** il était attentif à tout comportement inhabituel; **under the watchful eye of her mother** sous l'œil vigilant de sa mère; **to keep a watchful eye on sb/sth** avoir qn/qch à l'œil; **she kept a watchful eye on the situation** elle a suivi la situation de près

watchfully ['wɒtʃfʊlɪ] *adv* avec vigilance, d'un œil attentif

watchfulness ['wɒtʃfʊlnɪs] *n* vigilance *f*

watchglass ['wɒtʃglɑːs] *n* verre *m* de montre

watching brief ['wɒtʃɪŋ-] *n* **to have a watching brief** avoir un mandat de contrôle

watchmaker ['wɒtʃˌmeɪkə(r)] *n* horloger(ère) *m,f*

watchmaking ['wɒtʃˌmeɪkɪŋ] *n* horlogerie *f*

watchman ['wɒtʃmən] *(pl* **watchmen** [-mən]*) n* gardien *m*

watchout ['wɒtʃaʊt] *n Am* **to keep a watchout for sb/sth** faire attention à qn/qch

watchstrap ['wɒtʃstræp] *n* bracelet *m* de montre

watchtower ['wɒtʃˌtaʊə(r)] *n* tour *f* de guet

watchword ['wɒtʃwɜːd] *n (password)* mot *m* de passe; *(slogan)* mot *m* d'ordre

water ['wɔːtə(r)] **1** *n* (**a**) *(gen)* eau *f*; **I took a drink of water** j'ai bu de l'eau *ou* un verre d'eau; **is the water safe to drink?** est-ce que l'eau est potable?; **hot and cold running water** eau *f* courante chaude et froide; **turn on the water** *(at main)* ouvre l'eau; *(at tap)* ouvre le robinet; **prisoners were put on bread and water** on mit les prisonniers au pain (sec) et à l'eau; **they held his head under water** ils lui ont tenu la tête sous l'eau; **the cellar is under 2 metres of water** il y a 2 mètres d'eau dans la cave; **my shoes let in water** mes chaussures prennent l'eau; **the water** *or* **waters of the Seine** l'eau *ou* les eaux de la Seine; **the ship was making water** le bateau prenait l'eau *ou* faisait eau; *Fig* **they're in rough financial waters** ils sont dans une situation financière difficile; **that idea won't hold water** cette idée ne tient pas debout; *Fam* **you're in hot water now** tu vas avoir de gros ennuis[□], tu es dans de beaux draps; *Fam* **her statement got us into hot water** sa déclaration nous a mis dans le pétrin *ou* dans de beaux draps; *Fam* **I'm trying to keep my head above water** *or* **to stay above water** j'essaye de me maintenir à flot *ou* de faire face; **the wine flowed like water** le vin coulait à flots; **to spend money like water** jeter l'argent par les fenêtres; **they poured** *or* **threw cold water on our suggestion** ils n'ont pas été enthousiasmés par notre suggestion; **it's like water off a duck's back** ça glisse comme sur les plumes d'un canard; **it's water under the bridge** c'est du passé; **a lot of water has passed under the bridge since then** il a coulé beaucoup d'eau sous les ponts depuis; *Br Formal* **he's an artist of the first water** c'est un artiste de premier ordre

(**b**) *(body of water)* eau *f*; **the children played at the water's edge** les enfants ont joué au bord de l'eau; **she fell in the water** elle est tombée à l'eau; **they sent the goods by water** ils ont envoyé la marchandise par bateau

(**c**) *(tide)* marée *f*; **at high/low water** à marée haute/basse

(**d**) *Euph (urine)* urine *f*; **to make** *or* **to pass water** uriner

(**e**) *Med* **water on the brain** hydrocéphalie *f*; **the baby has water on the brain** le bébé est hydrocéphale; **to have water on the knee** avoir un épanchement de synovie

(**f**) *Tex (of cloth)* moiré *m*

2 *vt* (**a**) *(land, plants)* arroser; **the land here is watered by the Seine** ici, la terre est arrosée *ou* irriguée par la Seine

(**b**) *(animal)* donner à boire à, faire boire

(**c**) *(dilute → alcohol)* couper (d'eau)

(**d**) *Tex (cloth)* moirer

3 *vi* (**a**) *(eyes)* larmoyer

(**b**) *(mouth)* **the smell made my mouth water** l'odeur m'a fait venir l'eau à la bouche

4 waters *npl* (**a**) *(territorial)* eaux *fpl*; **in Japanese waters** dans les eaux (territoriales) japonaises

(**b**) *(spa water)* **to take the waters** prendre les eaux, faire une cure thermale

(**c**) *(of pregnant woman)* poche *f* des eaux; **her waters broke** elle a perdu les eaux, la poche des eaux s'est rompue

(**d**) *Prov* **to cast one's bread upon the waters** = se comporter de façon altruiste

►► *Bot* ***water avens*** benoîte *f* des ruisseaux; ***water bag*** outre *f* à eau; *Br* ***water bailiff*** garde-pêche *m (personne)*; ***water bed*** lit *m* à matelas d'eau; *Entom* ***water beetle*** *(whirligig beetle)* gyrin *m*, tourniquet *m*; ***water bird*** oiseau *m* aquatique; ***water birth*** accouchement *m* sous l'eau; *Br* ***water biscuit*** = biscuit salé croquant; ***water blister*** ampoule *f*, *Spec* phlyctène *f*; *Br Admin* ***water board*** service *m* des eaux; *Entom* ***water boatman*** notonecte *f*; ***water bomb*** bombe *f* à eau; ***water bottle*** *(gen)* bouteille *f* d'eau; *(soldier's, worker's)* bidon *m* à eau; *(in leather)* gourde *f*; ***water buffalo*** *(in India)* buffle *m* d'Inde; *(in Malaysia)* karbau *m*, kérabau *m*; *(in Asia)* buffle *m* d'Asie; *Entom* ***water bug*** *(water scorpion)* nèpe *f*; ***water bus*** navette *f (sur eau)*; ***water butt*** citerne *f* (à eau de pluie); ***water cannon*** canon *m* à eau; ***water carrier*** *(container)* bidon *m* à eau; *(person)* porteur(euse) *m,f* d'eau; *Astrol & Astron* ***the Water Carrier*** le Verseau; ***water cart*** *(to sprinkle water)* arroseuse *f*; *(to sell water)* voiture *f* de marchand d'eau; ***water chestnut*** châtaigne *f* d'eau; *Bot* ***water chickweed*** mouron *m* des fontaines; ***water chute*** *(in swimming-pool)* toboggan *m*; ***water clock*** horloge *f* à eau, clepsydre *f*; *Old-fashioned* ***water closet*** W-C *mpl*, toilettes *fpl*, cabinets *mpl*; ***water cooler*** distributeur *m* d'eau fraîche; *Fam TV* ***water cooler show*** émission *f* dont tout le monde parle[□]; ***water cooling*** refroidissement *m* par eau; *Am* ***water cracker*** = biscuit salé craquant; *Geog* ***water cycle*** cycle *m* de l'évaporation; ***water damage*** dégâts *mpl* des eaux; *Bot* ***water dock*** oseille *f* aquatique; *Bot* ***water flag*** flambe *f* d'eau; *Entom* ***water flea*** daphnie *f*, puce *f* d'eau; ***water fountain*** *(for decoration)* jet *m* d'eau; *(for drinking)* distributeur *m* d'eau fraîche; ***water gas*** gaz *m* à l'eau; ***water gauge*** jauge *f* d'eau; ***water glass*** *(for drinking out of)* verre *m* à eau; *(water gauge)* jauge *f* d'eau; *Chem* silicate *m* de potasse; ***water gun*** pistolet *m* à eau; ***water hammer*** *(in pipes)* cognements *mpl* dans la canalisation; ***water heater*** chauffe-eau *m inv*; *Bot* ***water hemlock*** ciguë *f* vireuse; ***water hen*** poule *f* d'eau; *Br* ***water ice*** sorbet *m*; ***water jacket*** chemise *f* d'eau; *Aut* ***water jet*** gicleur *m* d'eau; ***water jump*** brook *m*; ***water level*** *(of river, sea)* niveau *m* de l'eau; *(in tank)* niveau *m* d'eau; *Bot* ***water lily*** nénuphar *m*; ***water main*** conduite *f* d'eau; ***water mattress*** matelas *m* à eau; ***water meadow*** prairie *f (souvent inondée)*; ***water meter*** compteur *m* d'eau; *Bot* ***water milfoil*** volant *m* d'eau, myriophylle *m*; *Bot* ***water mint*** menthe *f* aquatique; ***water nymph*** naïade *f*; *Orn* ***water ouzel*** cincle *m* plongeur, merle *m* d'eau; *Zool* ***water ox*** *(in India)* buffle *m* d'Inde; *(in Malaysia)* karbau *m*, kérabau *m*; *(in Asia)* buffle *m* d'Asie; ***water park*** parc *m* aquatique; *Bot* ***water pepper*** renouée *f* poivre-d'eau; ***water pipe*** *Constr* conduite *f ou* canalisation *f* d'eau; *(hookah)* narguilé *m*; *Orn* ***water pipit*** pipit *m* spioncelle; ***water pistol*** pistolet *m* à eau; ***water plant*** plante *f* aquatique; *Bot* ***water plantain*** plantain *m* d'eau; *Ecol* ***water pollution*** pollution *f* des eaux; ***water polo*** water-polo *m*; ***water power*** énergie *f* hydraulique, houille *f* blanche; ***water pump*** pompe *f* à eau; *Orn* ***water rail*** râle *m* d'eau; *Zool* ***water rat*** rat *m* d'eau; *Br* ***water rate*** taxe *f* sur l'eau; *Astrol* ***water sign*** signe *m* d'eau; ***water ski*** ski *m* nautique; ***water skier*** skieur(euse) *m,f* nautique; ***water skiing*** ski *m* nautique; *Zool* ***water snail*** hélice *f* aquatique; *Zool* ***water snake*** serpent *m* d'eau; ***water softener*** adoucisseur *m* d'eau; ***water spaniel*** épagneul *m (qui chasse du gibier d'eau)*; *Entom* ***water spider*** araignée *f* d'eau; ***water sports*** *(water skiing, windsurfing etc)* sports *mpl* nautiques; *Vulg* = pratique sexuelle qui consiste à uriner sur son ou sa partenaire; *Myth* ***water sprite*** ondin(e) *m,f*; ***water supply*** *(for campers, troops)* provision *f* d'eau; *(to house)* alimentation *f* en eau; *(to area, town)* distribution *f* des eaux, approvisionnement *m* en eau; **the water supply has been cut off** l'eau a été coupée; ***water table*** niveau *m* de la nappe phréatique; ***water tank*** réservoir *m* d'eau, citerne *f*; ***water torture*** supplice *m* de l'eau; ***water tower*** château *m* d'eau; ***water transport*** transport *m* par voie d'eau; ***water vapour*** vapeur *f* d'eau; *Bot* ***water violet*** hottonie *f* des marais; *Zool* ***water vole*** rat *m* d'eau

►**water down** *vt sep* (**a**) *(alcohol)* couper (d'eau) (**b**) *Fig (speech)* édulcorer; *(complaint, criticism)* atténuer

water-based *adj* à l'eau

waterborne ['wɔːtəbɔːn] *adj (vehicle)* flottant; *(commerce, trade)* effectué par voie d'eau; *(disease)* d'origine hydrique

waterbuck ['wɔːtəbʌk] *n Zool* kob *m*, cob *m*

watercolour, *Am* **watercolor** ['wɔːtəˌkʌlə(r)] **1** *n (paint)* couleur *f* pour aquarelle; *(painting)* aquarelle *f*; **painted in watercolour** peint à l'aquarelle

2 *adj (paint)* pour aquarelle, à l'eau; *(landscape, portrait)* à l'aquarelle

►► ***watercolour artist*** aquarelliste *mf*

watercolourist, *Am* **watercolorist** ['wɔːtəˌkʌlərɪst] *n* aquarelliste *mf*

water-cooled [-ˌkuːld] *adj* à refroidissement par eau

watercourse ['wɔːtəkɔːs] *n (river, stream)* cours *m* d'eau; *(bed)* lit *m (d'un cours d'eau)*

watercress ['wɔːtəkres] *n* cresson *m* (de fontaine)

water-diviner *n* sourcier(ère) *m,f*, radiesthésiste *mf*

water-driven *adj* hydromoteur

watered ['wɔːtəd] *adj*

►► *Tex* ***watered silk*** soie *f* moirée; *Fin* ***watered stock*** titres *mpl* dilués

watered-down *adj (alcohol)* coupé (d'eau); *(speech)* édulcoré; *(complaint, criticism)* atténué

waterfall ['wɔːtəfɔːl] *n* cascade *f*, chute *f* d'eau

waterfinder ['wɔːtəˌfaɪndə(r)] *Am* = **water-diviner**

Waterford ['wɔːtəfəd] *n* (**a**) *(town)* Waterford (**b**) *(county)* le comté de Waterford, = comté du sud de la République d'Irlande; **in Waterford** dans le comté de Waterford

►► ***Waterford crystal*** = cristal fabriqué à Waterford, en Irlande

waterfowl ['wɔːtəfaʊl] *(pl* **inv** *or* **waterfowls***) n (bird)* oiseau *m* aquatique; *(collectively)* gibier *m* d'eau

waterfront ['wɔːtəfrʌnt] *n (at harbour)* quais *mpl*; *(seafront)* front *m* de mer; **on the waterfront** *(at harbour)* sur les quais; *(on seafront)* face à la mer

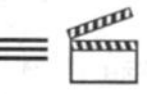

'On the Waterfront' *Kazan* 'Sur les quais'

Watergate ['wɔːtəgeɪt] *n* le Watergate

WATERGATE

Ce scandale politique entraîna en août 1974 la démission du président américain républicain Richard Nixon, impliqué dans un vol de documents au siège du parti démocrate (situé dans l'immeuble de Watergate à Washington) et dans une affaire d'écoute clandestine. Alors que plusieurs de ses collaborateurs furent jugés et condamnés, R. Nixon démissionna avant sa mise en accusation, ce qui contribua à ébranler la confiance des Américains dans leur gouvernement.

waterhole ['wɔːtəhəʊl] *n* point *m* d'eau; *(in desert)* oasis *f*

wateriness ['wɔːtərɪnɪs] *n (of ground, soil)* excès *m* d'eau; *(of coffee, tea)* manque *m* de goût; *(of soup)* insipidité *f*, fadeur *f*; *(of beer)* insipidité *f*; *(of light)* faiblesse *f*; *(of colour)* ton *m* délavé

watering ['wɔːtərɪŋ] *n* (**a**) *(of garden, plants)* arrosage *m*; *(of crops, fields)* irrigation *f*; **azaleas need daily watering** il faut arroser les azalées chaque jour

(**b**) *(of animals)* abreuvage *m*

(**c**) *Tex (of silk)* moirage *m*

►► ***watering can*** arrosoir *m*; ***watering hole*** *(for animals)* point *m* d'eau; *Fam Hum (pub)* troquet *m*; ***watering place*** *(waterhole)* point *m* d'eau; *Br (spa)* station *f* thermale; *Br (seaside resort)* station *f* balnéaire; ***watering pot*** arrosoir *m*

waterland ['wɔːtəlænd] *n*

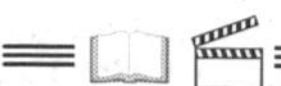

'Waterland' *Graham Swift, Gyllenhaal* 'Le Pays des eaux'

waterless ['wɔːtəlɪs] *adj* sans eau; *(region etc)* aride

waterline ['wɔːtəlaɪn] *n* (**a**) *(left by river)* ligne *f* des hautes eaux; *(left by tide)* laisse *f* de haute mer (**b**) *Naut (on ship)* ligne *f* de flottaison

waterlogged ['wɔːtəlɒgd] *adj (land, soil)* détrempé; *(boat)* plein d'eau; *(clothing, shoes, carpet)* saturé d'eau, trempé

Waterloo [ˌwɔːtə'luː] *n* (**a**) *Geog* Waterloo; *Hist* **the Battle of Waterloo** la bataille de Waterloo (**b**) *Fig* **to meet one's Waterloo** essuyer un revers

waterman ['wɔːtəmən] *(pl* **watermen** [-mən]) *n* batelier *m*

watermark ['wɔːtəmɑːk] **1** *n* (**a**) *(left by river)* ligne *f* des hautes eaux; *(left by tide)* laisse *f* de haute mer (**b**) *(on paper)* filigrane *m*

2 *vt* filigraner

watermarked ['wɔːtəmɑːkt] *adj (paper)* à filigrane

watermelon ['wɔːtəˌmelən] *n* pastèque *f*

watermill ['wɔːtəmɪl] *n* moulin *m* à eau

waterproof ['wɔːtəpruːf] **1** *adj (clothing, material)* imperméable; *(container, wall, watch)* étanche

2 *n* imperméable *m*; **waterproofs** vêtements *mpl* imperméables

3 *vt (clothing, material)* imperméabiliser; *(barrel, wall)* rendre étanche

waterproofing ['wɔːtəpruːfɪŋ] *n (process → for clothing, material)* imperméabilisation *f*; *(→ for barrel, wall)* action *f* de rendre étanche; *(coating)* imperméabilisation *f*

water-repellent *adj* imperméable, hydrofuge

water-resistant *adj (material)* semi-imperméable; *(lotion)* qui résiste à l'eau; *(ink)* indélébile, qui résiste à l'eau

watershed ['wɔːtəʃed] *n* (**a**) *Geog (line)* ligne *f* de partage des eaux; *Am (area)* bassin *m* hydrographique

(**b**) *Fig (event)* grand tournant *m*; **the concert was a watershed in her career as a singer** ce concert fut un moment décisif *ou* un grand tournant dans sa carrière de chanteuse; **at this watershed in her life** à ce moment critique de sa vie

(**c**) *TV* **the watershed** = l'heure après laquelle l'émission de programmes destinés aux adultes est autorisée

waterside ['wɔːtəsaɪd] **1** *n* bord *m* de l'eau

2 *adj (house, path)* au bord de l'eau; *(flower)* du bord de l'eau; **waterside residents** riverains *mpl*

►► *Am* ***waterside workers*** dockers *mpl*

water-ski *vi* faire du ski nautique

water-soluble *adj* soluble dans l'eau

waterspout ['wɔːtəspaʊt] *n* (**a**) *(pipe)* (tuyau *m* de) descente *f* (**b**) *Met* trombe *f*

watertight ['wɔːtətaɪt] *adj* (**a**) *(box, door)* étanche (**b**) *Fig (argument, reasoning)* inattaquable, indiscutable; *(alibi)* en béton

►► *Naut* ***watertight bulkhead*** cloison *f* étanche

waterway ['wɔːtəweɪ] *n* cours *m* d'eau, voie *f* navigable

waterweed ['wɔːtəwiːd] *n* élodée *f*

waterwheel ['wɔːtəwiːl] *n* roue *f* hydraulique

waterwings ['wɔːtəwɪŋz] *npl* brassards *mpl*, flotteurs *mpl*

waterworks ['wɔːtəwɜːks] *(pl* **inv**) **1** *n (establishment)* station *f* hydraulique; *(system)* système *m* hydraulique

2 *npl* (**a**) *(fountain)* jet *m* d'eau (**b**) *Br Fam Euph (urinary system)* voies *fpl* urinaires ❑; **he has problems with his waterworks** il a des problèmes de vessie ❑ (**c**) *Fam Hum (tears)* **she turned on the waterworks** elle s'est mise à pleurer comme une Madeleine

waterwort ['wɔːtəwɜːt] *n Bot* élatine *f*

watery ['wɔːtərɪ] *adj* (**a**) *(surroundings, world)* aquatique; *(ground, soil)* détrempé, saturé d'eau; **the sailors found a watery grave** les marins ont été ensevelis par les eaux

(**b**) *(eyes)* larmoyant, humide

(**c**) *(coffee, tea)* trop léger; *(soup)* trop liquide; *(milk)* qui a trop d'eau; *(vegetables, beer)* insipide; *(taste)* fade, insipide

(**d**) *(light, sun, smile)* faible; *(colour)* délavé, pâle; *(sky)* chargé de pluie

Watling Street ['wɒtlɪŋ-] *n* = route romaine de l'ouest de l'Angleterre

WATS [wɒts] *n Tel (abbr* **Wide Area Telephone Service**) = service téléphonique qui propose un forfait pour les appels longue distance

watt [wɒt] *n* watt *m*

wattage ['wɒtɪdʒ] *n* puissance *f ou* consommation *f* (en watts)

watt-hour *n* wattheure *m*

wattle ['wɒtəl] *n* (**a**) *(of bird, lizard)* caroncule *f* (**b**) *(sticks)* clayonnage *m*

►► ***wattle and daub*** clayonnage *m* enduit de torchis; ***wattle walls*** murs *mpl* en clayonnage

wattled ['wɒtəld] *adj (fence, door etc)* clayonné; *(branches, reeds etc)* entrelacé, tressé

►► ***wattled wall*** mur *m* en clayonnage

wattmeter ['wɒtˌmiːtə(r)] *n* wattmètre *m*

wave [weɪv] **1** *n* (**a**) *(in sea)* vague *f*, lame *f*; *(on lake)* vague *f*; **the waves** les flots *mpl*; *Fig* **don't make waves** ne faites pas de vagues, ne créez pas de remous

(**b**) *(of earthquake, explosion)* onde *f*; *Fig (of crime, panic, pain, disgust)* vague *f*; *(of anger)* bouffée *f*; **the refugees arrived in waves** les réfugiés sont arrivés par vagues; *Mil* **there were several waves of attack** il y eut plusieurs vagues d'assaut

(**c**) *(in hair)* cran *m*, ondulation *f*; **her hair has a natural wave to it** ses cheveux ondulent naturellement

(**d**) *(gesture)* geste *m ou* signe *m* de la main; **our neighbour gave us a friendly wave** notre voisin nous a fait un signe amical; **with a wave of the hand** d'un geste *ou* d'un signe de la main; **with a wave of her magic wand** d'un coup de baguette magique

(**e**) *Phys & Rad (electric, magnetic)* onde *f*

2 *vi* (**a**) *(gesture)* faire un signe *ou* un geste de la main; **his sister waved at** *or* **to him** *(greeted)* sa sœur l'a salué d'un signe de la main; *(signalled)* sa sœur lui a fait signe de la main; **he waved to us as he left** il nous fit au revoir de la main en partant; **she waved at** *or* **to them to come in** elle leur a fait signe d'entrer; **he waved vaguely towards the door** il a montré vaguement la porte d'un geste de la main

(**b**) *(move → flag)* flotter; *(→ wheat)* onduler, ondoyer; *(→ branch)* être agité

3 *vt* (**a**) *(brandish → flag)* agiter, brandir; *(→ pistol, sword)* brandir; **to wave a magic wand** donner un coup de baguette magique; *Fig* **I can't just wave a magic wand!** je ne peux pas faire de miracle!, je n'ai pas de baguette magique!

(**b**) *(gesture)* **his mother waved him away** sa mère l'a écarté d'un geste de la main; **the guard waved us back/on** le garde nous a fait signe de reculer/d'avancer; **the policeman waved us through the crossroads** le policier nous a fait signe de traverser le carrefour; **we waved goodbye** nous avons fait au revoir de la main; *Fam Fig* **you can wave goodbye to your promotion!** tu peux dire adieu à ta promotion!

(**c**) *(hair)* onduler

►► ***wave band*** bande *f* de fréquences; ***wave energy*** énergie *f* des vagues; ***wave function*** fonction *f* d'onde; ***wave machine*** machine *f* à vagues; ***wave mechanics*** *(UNCOUNT)* mécanique *f* ondulatoire; ***wave power*** énergie *f* des vagues

►**wave about 1** *vi (move → flag)* flotter; *(→ wheat)* onduler, ondoyer; *(→ branch)* être agité

2 *vt sep Br (flag, sign)* agiter, brandir; *(pistol, sword)* brandir; **he was waving his hands about** il gesticulait

►**wave aside** *vt sep (person)* écarter *ou* éloigner d'un geste; *(protest)* écarter; *(help, suggestion)* refuser, rejeter

►**wave down** *vt sep* **to wave sb/a car down** faire signe à qn/à une voiture de s'arrêter

waveform ['weɪvfɔːm] *n* courbe *f* d'onde

waveguide ['weɪvgaɪd] *n* guide *m* d'ondes

wavelength ['weɪvleŋθ] *n Phys & Rad* longueur *f* d'onde; *Fig* **we're just not on the same wavelength** nous ne sommes pas sur la même longueur d'onde

wavelet ['weɪvlɪt] *n* vaguelette *f*

waver ['weɪvə(r)] *vi* (**a**) *(person)* vaciller, hésiter; *(confidence, courage)* vaciller, faiblir; **they didn't waver in their loyalty to the cause** leur attachement à la cause n'a pas faibli (**b**) *(flame, light)* vaciller, osciller; *(temperature)* osciller; **the price wavered around the £46 per kilo mark** le prix tournait autour des 46 livres le kilo (**c**) *(voice)* trembloter, trembler

waverer ['weɪvərə(r)] *n* irrésolu(e) *m,f*, indécis(e) *m,f*

wavering ['weɪvərɪŋ] **1** *adj* (**a**) *(person)* irrésolu, indécis; *(confidence, courage)* vacillant, défaillant

(**b**) *(flame, light)* vacillant, oscillant; *(steps)* vacillant, chancelant; *(temperature)* oscillant
(**c**) *(voice)* tremblotant, tremblant
2 *n* (**a**) *(of person)* irrésolution *f*, indécision *f*; *(of confidence, courage)* défaillance *f*
(**b**) *(of flame, light)* vacillement *m*, oscillation *f*; *(of temperature)* oscillation *f*
(**c**) *(of voice)* tremblement *m*

waveringly ['weɪvərɪŋlɪ] *adv (act)* avec indécision, en hésitant; *(speak)* d'une voix tremblotante *ou* tremblante

waviness ['weɪvɪnɪs] *n (of line, surface)* ondulation *f*; *(of hair)* ondulations *fpl* naturelles

waving ['weɪvɪŋ] *adj (fields, corn)* ondulant, ondoyant

wavy ['weɪvɪ] (*compar* **wavier,** *superl* **waviest**) *adj (line, surface, hair)* ondulé

wavy-haired *adj* aux cheveux ondulés

wax [wæks] **1** *n* (**a**) *(for car, floor, furniture)* cire *f*; *(in ear)* cérumen *m*; *(for skis)* fart *m*
(**b**) *Br Fam Old-fashioned* **to be in a wax** être en rogne *ou* en colère ▫
2 *comp (candle, figure)* de *ou* en cire
3 *vt* (**a**) *(floor, table)* cirer, encaustiquer; *(skis)* farter; *(car)* enduire de cire
(**b**) *(legs)* épiler (à la cire); **to wax one's legs** s'épiler les jambes (à la cire)
4 *vi* (**a**) *(moon)* croître; *Fig (influence, power)* croître, augmenter; **to wax and wane** *(moon)* croître et décroître; *Fig (influence, power)* croître et décliner
(**b**) *Arch (become)* devenir; **he waxed poetic/sentimental** il se fit poète/sentimental; *Hum* **she waxed eloquent** *or* **lyrical on the subject of country life** elle s'est montrée éloquente sur le thème de la vie à la campagne
▸▸ *Am* ***wax beans*** haricots *mpl* beurre; ***wax crayons*** crayons *mpl* gras; ***wax jacket*** veste *f* en toile huilée; ***wax museum*** musée *m* de cire; *Bot* ***wax myrtle*** symphorine *f*; *Bot* ***wax palm*** *(Copernica Cerifera)* palmier *m* à cire; *(Ceroxylon Andicola)* céroxyle *m*, ceroxylon *m*; ***wax paper*** papier *m* paraffiné *ou* sulfurisé; *Bot* ***wax plant*** hoya *f*; *Bot* ***wax tree*** *(Chinese)* troène *m* de Chine; *(Japanese)* arbre *m* à cire, sumac *m* cirier

waxberry ['wæksberɪ] (*pl* **waxberries**) *n Bot* symphorine *f*

waxbill ['wæksbɪl] *n Orn* astrild *m*, sénégali *m*, bengali *m*

waxed [wækst] *adj (floor, tablecloth)* ciré; *(thread)* poissé; *(moustache)* gominé; *(lemon)* traité à la cire alimentaire
▸▸ ***waxed cotton*** coton *m* ciré; ***waxed jacket*** veste *f* en toile huilée; ***waxed paper*** papier *m* paraffiné *ou* sulfurisé

waxen ['wæksən] *adj* (**a**) *(made of wax → candle, figure)* de *ou* en cire (**b**) *(resembling wax → complexion, face)* cireux

waxwing ['wækswɪŋ] *n Orn* jaseur *m*

waxwork ['wækswɜːk] *n (object)* objet *m* de *ou* en cire; *(statue of person)* statue *f* de cire

waxworks ['wækswɜːks] (*pl* **inv**) *n* musée *m* de cire

waxy ['wæksɪ] (*compar* **waxier,** *superl* **waxiest**) *adj (complexion, texture)* cireux; *(colour)* cireux, jaunâtre; *(potato)* ferme, pas farineux
▸▸ *Bot* ***waxy cap*** hygrophore *m*

WAY [weɪ]

chemin	▸ **1A (a) – (c)**
voie	▸ **1A (a)**
route	▸ **1A (a), (c)**
direction	▸ **1A (d)**
sens	▸ **1A (d), (e)**
parages	▸ **1A (f)**
moyen	▸ **1B (a)**
méthode	▸ **1B (a)**
façon	▸ **1B (b)**
manière	▸ **1B (b), (c)**
coutume	▸ **1B (c)**
habitude	▸ **1B (c)**
égard	▸ **1B (f)**
rapport	▸ **1B (f)**

1 *n* **A.** (**a**) *(thoroughfare, path)* chemin *m*, voie *f*; *(for cars)* rue *f*, route *f*; **we took the way through the woods** nous avons pris le chemin qui traverse le bois; **they're building a way across the desert** ils ouvrent une route à travers le désert; **they live across** *or* **over the way from the school** ils habitent en face de l'école; **the house/the people over** *or* **across the way** la maison/les gens d'en face; **pedestrian way** voie *f ou* rue *f* piétonne; **private/public way** voie *f* privée/publique; *Rel* **the Way of the Cross** le chemin de Croix
(**b**) *(route leading to a specified place)* chemin *m*; **this is the way to the library** la bibliothèque est par là; **could you tell me the way to the library?** pouvez-vous me dire comment aller à la bibliothèque?; **what's the shortest** *or* **quickest way to town?** quel est le chemin le plus court pour aller en ville?; **that's the way to ruin** c'est le chemin de la ruine; **we took the long way (round)** nous avons pris le chemin le plus long; **which way does this bus go?** par où passe ce bus?; **I had to ask the** *or* **my way** il a fallu que je demande mon chemin; **she knows the way to school** elle connaît le chemin de l'école; **to know one's way about a place** connaître un endroit; **you'll soon find your way about** tu trouveras bientôt ton chemin tout seul; **they went the wrong way** ils se sont trompés de chemin, ils ont pris le mauvais chemin; **to lose one's way** s'égarer, perdre son chemin; *Fig* s'égarer, se fourvoyer; **to know one's way around** savoir s'orienter; *Fig* savoir se débrouiller; **the way to a man's heart is through his stomach** = pour conquérir le cœur d'un homme, il faut lui faire de bons petits plats
(**c**) *(route leading in a specified direction)* chemin *m*, route *f*; **the way back** le chemin *ou* la route du retour; **I got lost on the way back home** je me suis perdu sur le chemin du retour; **he couldn't find the way back home** il n'a pas trouvé le chemin pour rentrer (à la maison); **on our way back we stopped for dinner** au retour *ou* sur le chemin du retour, nous nous sommes arrêtés pour dîner; **she showed us the easiest way down/up** elle nous a montré le chemin le plus facile pour descendre/monter; **the way up is difficult but the way down will be easier** la montée est difficile mais la descente sera plus facile; **do you know the way down/up?** savez-vous par où on descend/on monte?; **the way in** l'entrée *f*; **the way out** la sortie; **we looked for a way in/out** nous cherchions un moyen d'entrer/de sortir; **I took the back way out** je suis sorti par derrière; **can you find your way out?** vous connaissez le chemin pour sortir?; **I can find my own way out** je trouverai mon chemin; **way in** *(sign)* entrée; **way out** *(sign)* sortie; *Fig* **miniskirts are on the way back in** la minijupe est de retour; **miniskirts are on the way out** la minijupe n'est plus tellement à la mode; **the director is on the way out** le directeur ne sera plus là très longtemps; **they found a way out of the deadlock** ils ont trouvé une solution pour sortir de l'impasse; **is there no way out of this nightmare?** n'y a-t-il pas moyen de mettre fin à ce cauchemar?; **their decision left her no way out** leur décision l'a mise dans une impasse; **he left himself a way out** il s'est ménagé une porte de sortie
(**d**) *(direction)* direction *f*, sens *m*; **come this way** venez par ici; **he went that way** il est allé par là; **is this the way?** c'est par ici?; **this way to the chapel** *(sign)* vers la chapelle; **this way and that** de-ci de-là, par-ci par-là; **look this way** regarde par ici; **I never looked their way** je n'ai jamais regardé dans leur direction; **to look the other way** détourner les yeux; *Fig* fermer les yeux; **he didn't know which way to look** *(embarrassed)* il ne savait plus où se mettre; **which way is the library from here?** par où faut-il passer pour aller à la bibliothèque?; **which way did you come?** par où êtes-vous venu?; **which way did she go?** par où est-elle passée?; **which way is the wind blowing?** d'où vient le vent?; *Fig* **I could tell which way the wind was blowing** je voyais très bien ce qui allait se passer; **which way does the tap turn?** dans quel sens faut-il tourner le robinet?; **which way do I go from here?** où est-ce que je vais maintenant?; *Fig* qu'est-ce que je fais maintenant?; **get in, I'm going your way** montez, je vais dans la même direction que vous; **they set off, each going his own way** ils sont partis chacun de leur côté; **to go one's own way** *(follow own wishes)* faire à sa guise; *(differ from others)* faire bande à part, suivre son chemin; **we each went our separate ways** *(on road)* nous sommes partis chacun de notre côté; *(in life)* chacun de nous a suivi son propre chemin; **he went the wrong way** il a pris la mauvaise direction; *(down one-way street)* il a pris la rue en sens interdit; **to come one's way** se présenter; **any job that comes my way** n'importe quel travail qui se présente; **if ever the opportunity comes your way** si jamais l'occasion se présente; *Fam* **everything's going my way** tout marche comme je veux en ce moment; **the vote went our way** le vote nous a été favorable; **the vote couldn't have gone any other way** les résultats du vote étaient donnés d'avance; **to go one's own way** n'en faire qu'à sa tête, vivre à sa guise; **to go the way of all flesh** *or* **of all things** mourir
(**e**) *(side)* sens *m*; **stand the box the other way up** posez le carton dans l'autre sens; **this way up** *(on packaging)* haut; **hold the picture the right way up** tenez le tableau dans le bon sens; **is it the right way round?** est-ce qu'il est à l'endroit?; **it's the wrong way up** c'est dans le mauvais sens; **it's the wrong way round** c'est dans le mauvais sens; **the curtains are the wrong way round** les rideaux sont à l'envers *ou* dans le mauvais sens; **your sweater is the right/wrong way out** votre pull est à l'endroit/à l'envers; **try it the other way round** essayez dans l'autre sens; **cats hate having their fur brushed the wrong way** les chats détestent qu'on les caresse à rebrousse-poil; **SHE insulted him? you've got it the wrong way round** elle, elle l'a insulté? mais c'est le contraire; **he invited her tonight, last time it was the other way round** ce soir c'est lui qui l'a invitée, la dernière fois c'était l'inverse
(**f**) *(area, vicinity)* parages *mpl*; **call in when you're up our way** passez nous voir quand vous êtes dans le coin *ou* dans les parages; **I was out** *or* **over your way yesterday** j'étais près de *ou* du côté de chez vous hier; **the next time you're that way** la prochaine fois que vous passerez par là; **the blast came from Chicago way** l'explosion venait du côté de Chicago; **the village is rather out of the way** le village est un peu isolé
(**g**) *(distance)* **we came part of the way by foot** nous avons fait une partie de la route à pied; **to go part of the way with sb** faire un bout de chemin avec qn; **they were one-third of the way through their trip** ils avaient fait un tiers de leur voyage; **we've come most of the way** nous avons fait la plus grande partie du chemin; **he talked the entire** *or* **whole way** il a parlé pendant tout le trajet; **he can swim quite a way** il peut nager assez longtemps; **a long way off** *or* **away** loin; **a little** *or* **short way off** pas très loin, à courte distance; **Susan sat a little way off** Susan était assise un peu plus loin; **I saw him from a long way off** je l'ai aperçu de loin; **it's a long way to Berlin** Berlin est loin; **it's a long way from Paris to Berlin** la route est longue de Paris à Berlin; **we're a long way from home** nous sommes loin de chez nous; **we've come a long way** *(from far away)* nous venons de loin; *(made progress)* nous avons fait du chemin; **we've a long way to go** *(far to travel)* il nous reste beaucoup de route à faire; *(a lot to do)* nous avons encore beaucoup à faire; *(a lot to collect, pay)* nous sommes encore loin du compte; **he has a long way to go to be ready for the exam** il est loin d'être prêt pour l'examen
(**h**) *(in time)* **it's a long way to Christmas** Noël est encore loin; **you have to go back a long way** il faut remonter loin; *Fig* **I'm a long way from trusting him** je suis loin de lui faire confiance; **you're a long way off** *or* **out** *(in guessing)* vous n'y êtes pas du tout; **that's a long way from what we thought** ce n'est pas du tout ce qu'on croyait; **she'll go a long way** elle ira loin; **the scholarship will go a long way towards helping with expenses** la bourse va beaucoup aider à faire face aux dépenses; **a little goodwill goes a long way** un peu de bonne volonté facilite bien les choses; **you can make a little meat go a long way by doing this** utilisez au mieux un petit

morceau de viande en faisant ceci; **she makes her money go a long way** elle sait ménager son argent; **a little bit goes a long way** il en faut très peu; *Hum* **a little of him goes a long way** il est sympa, mais à petites doses

(**i**) *(space in front of person, object)* **you're in the way** tu gênes le passage; *Fig* tu gênes, tu me/nous/*etc* déranges; **a tree was in the way** un arbre bloquait *ou* barrait le passage; **a car was in his way** une voiture lui barrait le passage *ou* l'empêchait de passer; **I can't see, the cat is in the way** je ne vois pas, le chat me gêne; **is the lamp in your way?** la lampe vous gêne-t-elle?; **put the suitcases under the bed out of the way** rangez les valises sous le lit pour qu'elles ne gênent pas; **to get out of the way** s'écarter (du chemin); **we got out of his way** nous l'avons laissé passer; **out of my way!** pousse-toi!, laisse-moi passer!; **the cars got out of the ambulance's way** les voitures ont laissé passer l'ambulance; **to get sb out of the way** se débarrasser de qn, écarter *ou* éloigner qn; **to get sth out of the way** enlever *ou* pousser qch; *Fig* **let's get the subject of holidays out of the way first** réglons d'abord la question des vacances; **keep out of the way!** ne reste pas là!; **make way!** écartez-vous!; **make way for the parade!** laissez passer le défilé!; **make way for the President!** faites place au Président!; **to get in one another's way** se gêner (les uns les autres); *Fig* **her social life got in the way of her studies** ses sorties l'empêchaient d'étudier; **I don't want to get in the way of your happiness** je ne veux pas entraver votre bonheur; **I kept out of the boss's way** j'ai évité le patron; *Fam* **he wants his boss out of the way** il veut se débarrasser de son patron ❑; *Fam* **once the meeting is out of the way** dès que nous serons débarrassés de la réunion; **he is retiring to make way for a younger man** il prend sa retraite pour céder la place à un plus jeune; **they tore down the slums to make way for blocks of flats** ils ont démoli les taudis pour pouvoir construire des immeubles; **to clear** *or* **prepare the way for sth** préparer la voie à qch; **to put difficulties in sb's way** créer des difficultés à qn; **couldn't you see your way (clear) to doing it?** ne trouveriez-vous pas moyen de le faire?

(**j**) *(indicating a progressive action)* **the acid ate its way through the metal** l'acide est passé à travers le métal; **I fought** *or* **pushed my way through the crowd** je me suis frayé un chemin à travers la foule; **we made our way towards the train** nous nous sommes dirigés vers le train; **to make one's way home** rentrer; **I made my way back to my seat** je suis retourné à ma place; **they made their way across the desert** ils ont traversé le désert; **they made their way down/up the hill** ils ont descendu/monté la colline; **she made her way up through the hierarchy** elle a gravi les échelons de la hiérarchie un par un; **she had to make her own way in the world** elle a dû faire son chemin toute seule; **she talked her way out of it** elle s'en est sortie avec de belles paroles; **he worked** *or* **made his way through the pile of newspapers** il a lu les journaux un par un; **I worked my way through college** j'ai travaillé pour payer mes études; **however did it find its way into print?** comment en est-on venu à l'imprimer?

B. (**a**) *(means, method)* moyen *m*, méthode *f*; **in what way can I help you?** comment *ou* en quoi puis-je vous être utile?; **there are several ways to go** *or* **of going about it** il y a plusieurs façons *ou* plusieurs moyens de s'y prendre; **I do it this way** voilà comment je fais; **in one way or another** d'une façon ou d'une autre; **they thought they would win that way** ils pensaient pouvoir gagner comme ça; **he's going to handle it his way** il va faire ça à sa façon; **she has her own way of cooking fish** elle a sa façon à elle de cuisiner le poisson; **the right/wrong way to do it** la bonne/mauvaise façon de le faire; **you're doing it the right/wrong way** c'est comme ça/ce n'est pas comme ça qu'il faut (le) faire; **do it the usual way** faites comme d'habitude; **there's no way** *or* **I can't see any way we'll finish on time** nous ne finirons jamais *ou* nous n'avons aucune chance de finir à temps; *Pol* **ways and means** financement *m*; **there are ways and means** il y a des moyens; **to find a way of doing sth** trouver (le) moyen de faire qch; *Hum* **love will find a way** l'amour finit toujours par triompher; **that's the way to do it!** c'est comme ça qu'il faut faire!, voilà comment il faut faire!; *Am Fam* **well done! that's the way (to go)!** bravo! c'est bien! ❑; **what a way to go!** *(manner of dying)* quelle belle mort!; *(congratulations)* bravo!

(**b**) *(particular manner, fashion)* façon *f*, manière *f*; **in this way** de cette façon; **in a friendly way** gentiment; **he spoke in a general way about the economy** il a parlé de l'économie d'une façon générale; **she doesn't like the way he is dressed** elle n'aime pas la façon dont il est habillé; **he doesn't speak the way his family does** il ne parle pas comme sa famille; **they see things in the same way** ils voient les choses de la même façon; **in their own (small) way they fight racism** à leur façon *ou* dans la limite de leurs moyens, ils luttent contre le racisme; **in the same way, we note that...** de même, on notera que...; **that's one way to look at it** *or* **of looking at it** c'est une façon *ou* manière de voir les choses; **my way of looking at it** mon point de vue sur la question; **that's not my way (of doing things)** ce n'est pas mon genre, ce n'est pas ma façon de faire; **try to see it my way** mettez-vous à ma place; **way of speaking/writing** façon de parler/d'écrire; **to her way of thinking** à son avis; **the way she feels about him** les sentiments qu'elle éprouve à son égard; **I didn't think you would take it this way** je ne pensais pas que vous le prendriez comme ça; **if that's the way you feel about it!** si c'est comme ça que vous le prenez!; **the American way of life** la manière de vivre des Américains, le mode de vie américain; **being on the move is a way of life for the gypsy** le voyage est un mode de vie pour les gitans; **dieting has become a way of life with some people** certaines personnes passent leur vie à faire des régimes; **yearly strikes have become a way of life** les grèves annuelles sont devenues une habitude

(**c**) *(custom)* coutume *f*, usage *m*; *(habitual manner of acting)* manière *f*, habitude *f*; **we soon got used to her ways** nous nous sommes vite habitués à ses manières; **I know his little ways** je connais ses petites manies; **the ways of God and men** les voies de Dieu et de l'homme; **he knows nothing of their ways** il les connaît très mal, il ne les comprend pas du tout; **she has a way of tossing her head when she laughs** elle a une façon *ou* manière de rejeter la tête en arrière quand elle rit; **they're happy in their own way** ils sont heureux à leur manière; **he's a genius in his way** c'est un génie dans son genre; **it's not my way to criticize** ce n'est pas mon genre *ou* ce n'est pas dans mes habitudes de critiquer; **he's not in a bad mood, it's just his way** il n'est pas de mauvaise humeur, c'est sa façon d'être habituelle; **she got into/out of the way of rising early** elle a pris/perdu l'habitude de se lever tôt; **you'll get into the way of it** vous vous y ferez

(**d**) *(facility, knack)* **she has a (certain) way with her** elle a le chic; **he has a way with children** il sait (comment) s'y prendre *ou* il a le chic avec les enfants; **she has a way with words** elle a le chic pour s'exprimer; **trouble has a way of showing up when least expected** les ennuis ont le chic pour se manifester quand on ne s'y attend pas

(**e**) *(indicating a condition, state of affairs)* **let me tell you the way it was** laisse-moi te raconter comment ça s'est passé; **we can't invite him given the way things are** on ne peut pas l'inviter étant donné la situation; **we left the flat the way it was** nous avons laissé l'appartement tel qu'il était *ou* comme il était; **is he going to be staying here? – it looks that way** est-ce qu'il va loger ici? – on dirait (bien); **it's not the way it looks!** ce n'est pas ce que vous pensez!; **it's not the way it used to be** ce n'est pas comme avant; **that's the way things are** c'est comme ça; **that's the way of the world** ainsi va le monde; **business is good and we're trying to keep it that way** les affaires vont bien et nous faisons en sorte que ça dure; **the train is late – that's always the way** le train est en retard – c'est toujours comme ça *ou* pareil; **that's always the way with him** il est toujours comme ça, c'est toujours comme ça avec lui; **life goes on (in) the same old way** la vie va son train *ou* suit son cours; **I don't like the way things are going** je n'aime pas la tournure que prennent les choses; **we'll never finish the way things are going** au train où vont les choses, on n'aura jamais fini; **to be in a bad way** être en mauvais état; **he's in a bad way** il est dans un triste état; **their business is in a bad/good way** leurs affaires marchent mal/bien; **she's in a fair way to succeed/to becoming president** elle est bien partie pour réussir/pour devenir président

(**f**) *(respect, detail)* égard *m*, rapport *m*; **in what way?** à quel égard?, sous quel rapport?; **in this way** à cet égard, sous ce rapport; **it's important in many ways** c'est important à bien des égards; **in some ways** à certains égards, par certains côtés; **the job suits her in every way** le poste lui convient à tous égards *ou* à tous points de vue; **I'll help you in every possible way** je ferai tout ce que je peux pour vous aider; **she studied the problem in every way possible** elle a examiné le problème sous tous les angles possibles; **useful in more ways than one** utile à plus d'un égard; **these two books, each interesting in its (own) way** ces deux livres, qui sont intéressants chacun dans son genre; **he's clever that way** sur ce plan-là, il est malin; **in one way** d'un certain point de vue; **in a way you're right** en un sens vous avez raison; **I see what you mean in a way** d'un certain point de vue *ou* d'une certaine manière, je vois ce que tu veux dire; **I am in no way responsible** je ne suis absolument pas *ou* aucunement responsable; **this in no way changes your situation** ceci ne change en rien votre situation; **without wanting in any way to criticize** sans vouloir le moins du monde critiquer

(**g**) *(scale)* **to do things in a big way** faire les choses en grand; **she went into politics in a big way** elle s'est lancée à fond dans la politique; **they're in the arms business in a big way** ils font de grosses affaires dans l'armement; **they helped out in a big way** ils ont beaucoup aidé; **a grocer in a big/small way** un gros/petit épicier; **we live in a small way** nous vivons modestement; **the restaurant is doing quite well in a small way** le restaurant marche bien à son échelle; **it does change the situation in a small way** ça change quand même un peu la situation

(**h**) *(usu pl) (part, share)* **we divided the money four ways** nous avons partagé l'argent en quatre; **the committee was split three ways** le comité était divisé en trois groupes

(**i**) *Naut* **we're gathering/losing way** nous prenons/perdons de la vitesse; **the ship has way on** le navire a de l'erre

(**j**) *(idioms)* **she always gets** *or* **has her (own) way** elle arrive toujours à ses fins; **he only wants it his way** il n'en fait qu'à sa tête; **I'm not going to let you have it all your (own) way** je refuse de te céder en tout; **if I had my way, he'd be in prison** si cela ne tenait qu'à moi, il serait en prison; **I refuse to go – have it your (own) way** je refuse d'y aller – fais ce que *ou* comme tu veux; **no, it was 1789 – have it your (own) way** non, c'était en 1789 – soit; **you can't have it both ways** il faut choisir; **I can stop too, it works both ways** je peux m'arrêter aussi, ça marche dans les deux sens; **there are no two ways about it** il n'y a pas le choix; **no two ways about it, he was rude** il n'y a pas à dire, il a été grossier; *Hum* **to have one's (wicked) way with sb** coucher avec qn

2 *adv Fam* (**a**) *(far → in space, time)* très loin ❑; **they live way over yonder** ils habitent très loin par là-bas; **way up the mountain** très haut dans la montagne ❑; **way down south** là-bas dans le sud ❑; **way back in the distance** au loin derrière ❑; **way back in the 1930s** déjà dans les années 30 ❑

(**b**) *Fig* **we know each other from way back, we go way back** nous sommes amis depuis très longtemps ❑; **you're way below the standard** tu es bien en-dessous du niveau voulu ❑; **he's way over forty** il a largement dépassé la quarantaine ❑; **she's way ahead of her class** elle est très en avance sur sa classe□; **he's way off** *or* **out in his guess** il est loin d'avoir deviné□

(**c**) *(very)* vachement; **he is way crazy** il est vachement atteint

3 ways *npl Naut (in shipbuilding)* cale *f*

4 all the way *adv* **the baby cried all the way** le bébé a pleuré tout le long du chemin; **don't close the curtains all the way** ne fermez pas complètement les rideaux; **prices go all the way from 200 to 1,000 dollars** les prix vont de 200 à 1000 dollars; *Fig* **I'm with you all the way** je vous suis *ou* je vous soutiens jusqu'au bout; *Fam* **to go all the way (with sb)** aller jusqu'au bout (avec qn)

5 along the way *adv* en route; **I stopped several times along the way** je me suis arrêté plusieurs fois en (cours de) route; *Fig* **their project had some problems along the way** leur projet a connu quelques problèmes en cours de route

6 by a long way *adv* **I prefer chess by a long way** je préfère de loin *ou* de beaucoup les échecs; **this is bigger by a long way** c'est nettement *ou* beaucoup plus grand; **he's not as capable as you are by a long way** il est loin d'être aussi compétent que toi; **is your project ready? – not by a long way!** ton projet est-il prêt? – loin de là!

7 by the way 1 *adv (incidentally)* à propos; **by the way, where did he go?** à propos, où est-il allé?; **by the way, her brother sings much better** soit dit en passant, son frère chante beaucoup mieux; **I bring up this point by the way** je signale ce point au passage *ou* en passant **2** *adj (incidental)* secondaire; **that point is quite by the way** ce détail est tout à fait secondaire

8 by way of *prep* (**a**) *(via)* par, via; **to go by way of Brussels** passer par Bruxelles

(**b**) *(as a means of)* **by way of illustration** à titre d'exemple; **she outlined the situation by way of introduction** elle a présenté un aperçu de la situation en guise d'introduction; **by way of introducing himself, he gave us his card** en guise de présentation, il nous a donné sa carte; **they receive money by way of grants** ils reçoivent de l'argent sous forme de bourses

9 either way *adv* (**a**) *(in either case)* dans les deux cas; **either way I lose** dans les deux cas, je suis perdant; **shall we take the car or the bus? – it's fine by me** *or* **I don't mind either way** tu préfères prendre la voiture ou le bus? – n'importe, ça m'est égal

(**b**) *(more or less)* en plus ou en moins; **a few days either way could make all the difference** quelques jours en plus ou en moins pourraient tout changer

(**c**) *(indicating advantage)* **the match could have gone either way** le match était ouvert; **there's nothing in it either way** c'est pareil

10 in such a way as to *conj* de façon à ce que; **she answered in such a way as to make me understand** elle a répondu de façon à ce que je comprenne

11 in such a way that *conj* de telle façon *ou* manière que

12 in the way of *prep* (**a**) *(in the form of)* **she receives little in the way of salary** son salaire n'est pas bien gros; **what is there in the way of food?** qu'est-ce qu'il y a à manger?; **do you need anything in the way of paper?** avez-vous besoin de papier?; **he doesn't have much in the way of brains** il n'a rien dans la tête

(**b**) *(within the context of)* **we met in the way of business** nous nous sommes rencontrés dans le cadre du travail; **they put me in the way of making some money** ils m'ont indiqué un moyen de gagner de l'argent

13 no way *adv Fam* pas question; **will you do it for me? – no way!** tu feras ça pour moi? – pas question!; **no way am I going to tell him!** (il n'est) pas question que je le lui dise!; **there's no way that's Jeanne Moreau!** tu rigoles?, ce n'est pas Jeanne Moreau!

14 on one's way, on the way *adj & adv* (**a**) *(along the route)* **it's on my way** c'est sur mon chemin; **you pass it on your way to the office** vous passez devant en allant au bureau; **I'll catch up with you on the way** je te rattraperai en chemin *ou* en route; **to stop on the way** s'arrêter en chemin; **on the way to work** en allant au bureau; **I'm on my way!** j'y vais!; **she's on her way home** elle rentre chez elle; **he's on his way to Paris** il est en route pour Paris; **on his way to town he met his father** en allant en ville, il a rencontré son père; **we must be on our way** il faut que nous y allions; **to go one's way** repartir, reprendre son chemin

(**b**) *Fig* **she has a baby on the way** elle attend un bébé; **her second book is on the way** *(being written)* elle a presque fini d'écrire son deuxième livre; *(being published)* son deuxième livre est sur le point de paraître; **she's on the way to success** elle est sur le chemin de la réussite; **the patient is on the way to recovery** le malade est en voie de guérison; **she's (well) on the way to becoming president** elle est en bonne voie de devenir présidente; **the new school is well on the way to being finished** la nouvelle école est presque terminée

15 one way and another *adv* en fin de compte; **I've done quite well for myself one way and another** je me suis plutôt bien débrouillé en fin de compte

16 one way or the other, one way or another *adv* (**a**) *(by whatever means)* d'une façon ou d'une autre; **one way or the other I'm going to get that job!** d'une façon ou d'une autre, j'aurai ce boulot!

(**b**) *(expressing impartiality or indifference)* **I've nothing to say one way or the other** je n'ai rien à dire, ni pour ni contre; **it doesn't matter to them one way or another** ça leur est égal

(**c**) *(more or less)* **a month one way or the other** un mois de plus ou de moins

17 out of one's way *adv* **to go out of one's way** s'écarter de son chemin, dévier de sa route, faire un détour; **I don't want to take you out of your way** je ne veux pas vous faire faire un détour; *Fig* **don't go out of your way for me!** ne vous dérangez pas pour moi!; *Fig* **she went out of her way to find me a job** elle s'est donné du mal pour me trouver du travail

18 under way 1 *adj* **to be under way** *(person, vehicle)* être en route; *Fig (meeting, talks)* être en cours; *(plans, project)* être en train; **the meeting was already under way** la réunion avait déjà commencé; **the project is well under way** le projet est en bonne voie de réalisation; *Naut* **the ship is under way** le navire est en route **2** *adv* **to get under way** *(person, train)* se mettre en route, partir; *(car)* se mettre en route, démarrer; *Fig (meeting, plans, talks)* démarrer; **they got the plans under way** ils ont mis le projet en route; **the captain got (the ship) under way** le capitaine a appareillé; **the ship got under way** le navire a appareillé *ou* a levé l'ancre

►► *Am* ***way station*** *Rail* petite gare *f*; *Fig* étape *f*; **a way station on the road to success** une étape sur la route du succès

---

'The Way of the World' *Congreve* 'Ainsi va le monde'

> **We have ways of making you talk**
>
> Il s'agit de la formule prononcée par les membres de la Gestapo dans les films de guerre anglais des années 50 et 60 lorsqu'ils interrogent des prisonniers de guerre britanniques.
>
> Aujourd'hui, on emploie cette expression ("nous avons les moyens de vous faire parler") pour plaisanter en prenant l'accent allemand lorsqu'on veut obtenir une information de quelqu'un.

-way [weɪ] *suff* **one-way street** rue *f* à sens unique; **a four-way discussion** une discussion à quatre participants; **there was a three-way split of the profits** les bénéfices ont été divisés en trois

waybill ['weɪbɪl] *n* feuille *f* de route, lettre *f* de voiture

wayfarer ['weɪfeərə(r)] *n* voyageur(euse) *m,f*

wayfaring ['weɪfeərɪŋ] **1** *n (UNCOUNT)* voyages *mpl*

2 *adj* voyageur; **a wayfaring life** une vie de voyages; **wayfaring man** voyageur *m* (à pied)

►► *Bot* ***wayfaring tree*** viorne *f* cotonneuse *ou* flexible

waylay [ˌweɪ'leɪ] *(pt & pp* **waylaid** [-'leɪd]) *vt (attack)* attaquer, assaillir; *(stop)* intercepter, arrêter (au passage); **sorry I'm late, I got waylaid** excuse mon retard, quelqu'un m'a arrêté au passage, excuse mon retard, je me suis fait harponner

waymark ['weɪmɑːk] *n (on trail, path, walk)* indication *f*, balise *f*

waymarked ['weɪmɑːkt] *adj (trail, path, walk)* balisé

way-out *adj Fam* (**a**) *(unusual → film, style)* bizarre□, curieux□; *(→ person)* excentrique□, bizarre□ (**b**) *Old-fashioned (excellent)* géant

Ways and Means Committee *n* = commission américaine du budget à la Chambre des représentants

wayside ['weɪsaɪd] **1** *n* bord *m ou* côté *m* de la route

2 *adj* au bord de la route; **a wayside inn** une auberge au bord de la route; **wayside flowers** les fleurs qui bordent la route

wayward ['weɪwəd] *adj* (**a**) *(person → wilful)* entêté, têtu; *(→ unpredictable)* qui n'en fait qu'à sa tête, imprévisible; *(behaviour)* imprévisible; *(horse)* rétif (**b**) *(fate)* fâcheux, malencontreux (**c**) *(shot, pass)* manqué

waywardly ['weɪwədlɪ] *adv (wilfully)* avec entêtement; *(unpredictably)* de façon imprévisible

waywardness ['weɪwədnɪs] *n (wilfulness)* entêtement *m*; *(unpredictability)* caractère *m* imprévisible; **a certain waywardness became apparent in his character** il est apparu comme quelqu'un qui n'en faisait qu'à sa tête

wazoo [wɑː'zuː] *n Am Fam* fesses□ *fpl*

WBA [ˌdʌbəljuːbiː'eɪ] *n (abbr* **World Boxing Association**) WBA *f*

WBC [ˌdʌbəljuːbiː'siː] *n (abbr* **World Boxing Council**) WBC *m*

WBO [ˌdʌbəljuːbiː'əʊ] *n (abbr* **World Boxing Organization**) WBO *f*

WC [ˌdʌbəljuː'siː] *n (abbr* **water closet**) W-C *mpl*

WCC [ˌdʌbəljuːsiː'siː] *n (abbr* **World Council of Churches**) COE *m*

we [wiː] *pron* (**a**) *(oneself and others)* nous; **we went for a walk** nous sommes allés nous promener; **we all stood up** nous nous sommes tous levés; **we both thank you** nous vous remercions tous (les) deux; **we, the people** nous, le peuple; **we Democrats believe that...** nous, les démocrates, croyons que...; **as we say back home** comme on dit chez nous; **as we will see in chapter two** comme nous le verrons *ou* comme on le verra dans le chapitre deux; **you don't think that WE did it!** vous ne pensez pas que c'est nous qui l'avons fait?; **we all make mistakes** tout le monde peut se tromper

(**b**) *Formal (royal)* nous; **the royal we** le nous *ou* le pluriel de majesté

(**c**) *Fam (you)* **and how are we today, John?** alors, comment ça va aujourd'hui, John?

w/e *(written abbr* **week ending**) semaine se terminant

weak [wiːk] **1** *adj* (**a**) *(physically → animal, person)* faible; *(→ health)* fragile, délicat; *(→ eyes, hearing)* faible, mauvais; **to become** *or* **to get** *or* **to grow weak** *or* **weaker** s'affaiblir; **we were weak with** *or* **from hunger** nous étions affaiblis par la faim; **he felt weak with fear** il avait les jambes molles de peur; **I went weak at the knees** mes jambes se sont dérobées sous moi, j'avais les jambes en coton; *Br* **it's always the weakest who go to the wall** ce sont toujours les plus faibles qui trinquent; *Pej* **the weaker sex** le sexe faible

(**b**) *(morally, mentally)* mou (molle), faible; **he's far too weak to be a leader** il est beaucoup trop mou pour être un meneur; **in a weak moment** dans un moment de faiblesse; **to be weak in the head** être faible d'esprit

(**c**) *(feeble → argument, excuse)* faible, peu convaincant; *(→ army, government, institution)* faible, impuissant; *(→ structure)* fragile, peu solide; *(→ light, signal, currency, economy)* faible; *(market)* en baisse, baissier; **she managed a weak smile** elle a réussi à sourire faiblement; **she answered in a weak voice** elle répondit d'une voix faible; **to have a weak**

hand *(in cards)* avoir des cartes faibles; **he's the weak** *or* **weakest link (in the chain)** c'est lui le maillon faible de la chaîne

(**d**) *(deficient, poor → pupil, subject)* faible; **I'm weak in geography, geography is my weak subject** je suis faible en géographie; **she's rather weak on discipline** elle est plutôt laxiste

(**e**) *(chin)* fuyant; *(mouth)* tombant

(**f**) *(acid, solution)* faible; *(drink, tea)* léger; *Aut & Tech (mixture)* pauvre

(**g**) *Gram & Ling (verb)* faible, régulier; *(syllable)* faible, inaccentué

2 *npl* **the weak** les faibles *mpl*

weaken ['wi:kən] **1** *vt* (**a**) *(person)* affaiblir; *(heart)* fatiguer; *(health)* miner

(**b**) *(government, institution, team)* affaiblir

(**c**) *(argument)* enlever du poids *ou* de la force à; *(position)* affaiblir; *(determination)* affaiblir, faire fléchir

(**d**) *(structure)* affaiblir, rendre moins solide; *(foundations, cliff)* miner, saper

(**e**) *Fin (currency)* affaiblir, faire baisser; *(market, prices)* faire fléchir

2 *vi* (**a**) *(person → physically)* s'affaiblir, faiblir; *(→ morally)* faiblir; *(voice, health, determination)* faiblir; **her resolution began to weaken** sa détermination commençait à faiblir; **he finally weakened and gave in** il s'est finalement laissé fléchir et a cédé

(**b**) *(influence, power)* diminuer, baisser

(**c**) *(structure)* faiblir, devenir moins solide

(**d**) *Fin (currency)* s'affaiblir, baisser; *(market, prices)* fléchir; **the pound has weakened against the dollar** la livre est en baisse par rapport au dollar

weakening ['wi:kənɪŋ] **1** *adj* (**a**) *(debilitating)* affaiblissant (**b**) *(losing strength)* faiblissant

2 *n* (**a**) *(of person, resolve)* affaiblissement *m* (**b**) *(of structure)* fléchissement *m*, affaiblissement *m* (**c**) *Fin (of currency)* fléchissement *m*, affaiblissement *m*

weak-kneed [-ni:d] *adj Fam* mou (molle)❑, lâche❑

weakling ['wi:klɪŋ] *n* (**a**) *(physically)* gringalet *m*, petite nature *f* (**b**) *(morally)* faible *mf*, mauviette *f*

weakly ['wi:klɪ] **1** (*compar* **weaklier**, *superl* **weakliest**) *adj (person)* débile, chétif

2 *adv (get up, walk)* faiblement; *(speak, protest)* faiblement, mollement

weak-minded *adj* (**a**) *(not intelligent)* faible *ou* simple d'esprit (**b**) *(lacking willpower)* faible, irrésolu

weakness ['wi:knɪs] *n* (**a**) *(of person → physical)* faiblesse *f*; *(→ moral)* point *m* faible; **in a moment of weakness** dans un moment de faiblesse; **sweets are one of his weaknesses** la confiserie est un de ses points faibles; **he has a weakness for sports cars** il a un faible pour les voitures de sport

(**b**) *(of government, institution)* faiblesse *f*, fragilité *f*

(**c**) *(of structure)* fragilité *f*

(**d**) *Fin (of currency)* faiblesse *f*

weak-willed *adj* faible, velléitaire

weal [wi:l] *n* (**a**) *(mark)* marque *f* de coup, [illegible] le dos couvert de traces de coups (**b**) *Arch or Literary (wellbeing)* bien *m*, bonheur *m*; **the common** *or* **public weal** le bien public

Weald [wi:ld] *n (region)* **the Weald** = région du sud-est de l'Angleterre

weald [wi:ld] *n Br Arch (open country)* pays *m* découvert; *(wooded country)* pays *m* boisé

wealth [welθ] *n (UNCOUNT)* (**a**) *(richness → of family, person)* richesse *f*, richesses *fpl*, fortune *f*; *(→ of nation)* richesse *f*, prospérité *f*; **a young woman of great wealth** une jeune femme très fortunée; **they have acquired considerable wealth** ils ont acquis une fortune considérable *ou* des biens considérables

(**b**) *(large amount → of details, ideas)* abondance *f*, profusion *f*; **he showed a wealth of knowledge about Egyptian art** il fit preuve d'une profonde connaissance de l'art égyptien; **this job offers a wealth of opportunity for travel** cet emploi offre de nombreuses occasions de voyage; **she has had a wealth of opportunities to prove it** elle a eu une quantité d'occasions de le prouver

►► ***wealth creation*** création *f* de richesses; *Fin* ***wealth tax*** impôt *m* de solidarité sur la fortune

wealth-creating [-kri:,eɪtɪŋ] *adj* générateur de richesses

wealthy ['welθɪ] (*compar* **wealthier**, *superl* **wealthiest**) **1** *adj (person)* riche, fortuné; *(country)* riche; **a wealthy heiress** une riche héritière

2 *npl* **the wealthy** les riches *mpl*

wean[1] [wi:n] *vt (baby)* sevrer; **youngsters today are being weaned on computers** les jeunes d'aujourd'hui sont nourris d'informatique; **she had been weaned on Mozart** elle a grandi sur les airs de Mozart

►**wean off** *vt sep* **to wean sb off sth** détourner qn de qch; **he was trying to wean himself off cigarettes** il essayait de se passer peu à peu de la cigarette

wean[2] [weɪn] *n Scot Fam (child)* gosse *mf*, môme *mf*

weaner ['wi:nə(r)] *n (pig)* = porcelet venant d'être sevré et pesant moins de 40 kg

weaning ['wi:nɪŋ] **1** *n* sevrage *m*

2 *adj (animal)* en sevrage

weanling ['wi:nlɪŋ] *n* = nourrisson ou jeune animal qui vient d'être sevré

weapon ['wepən] *n also Fig* arme *f*; **weapons of mass destruction** armes *fpl* de destruction massive; **carrying a weapon is illegal** le port d'armes est illégal; *Fig* **patience is your best weapon in this situation** la patience est votre meilleure arme dans cette situation; **high interest rates are seen as a weapon against inflation** des taux d'intérêt élevés sont considérés comme une arme contre l'inflation

►► ***weapons grade uranium*** = uranium utilisé dans l'armement; ***weapon system*** dispositif *m ou* système *m* militaire

weaponless ['wepənlɪs] *adj* sans armes

weaponry ['wepənrɪ] *n (UNCOUNT)* armes *fpl*; *Mil* matériel *m* de guerre, armements *mpl*

WEAR [weə(r)]

porter	► 1 (a)
avoir	► 1 (b)
afficher	► 1 (b)
user	► 1 (c)
durer	► 2 (a)
s'user	► 2 (b)
passer	► 2 (c)
usage	► 3 (b)
usure	► 3 (c)

(*pt* **wore** [wɔ:(r)], *pp* **worn** [wɔ:n]) **1** *vt* (**a**) *(beard, spectacles, clothing etc)* porter; **what shall I wear?** qu'est-ce que je vais mettre?; **I haven't a thing to wear** je n'ai rien à me mettre; **she wore a miniskirt** elle portait une minijupe, elle était en minijupe; *Aut* **to wear a seat belt** mettre la ceinture (de sécurité); **to wear black** porter du noir; **the miniskirt is being worn again this year** la minijupe se porte de nouveau cette année; **he always wears good clothes** il est toujours bien habillé, il s'habille toujours bien; **he was wearing slippers/a dressing gown** il était en chaussons/en robe de chambre; **he wears a beard** il porte la barbe; **she wore a ribbon in her hair** elle portait *ou* avait un ruban dans les cheveux; **she wears her hair in a bun** elle a un chignon; **he wears his hair long** il a les cheveux longs; **do you always wear make-up?** tu te maquilles tous les jours?; **she wore lipstick** elle s'était mis *ou* elle avait mis du rouge à lèvres; **I often wear perfume/aftershave** je mets souvent du parfum/de la lotion après-rasage

(**b**) *(expression)* avoir, afficher; *(smile)* arborer; **she wore an anxious look** son regard exprimait l'inquiétude, elle avait un air inquiet; **he wore a frown** il fronçait les sourcils

(**c**) *(make by rubbing)* user; **to wear holes in sth** trouer *ou* percer peu à peu qch; **her shoes were worn thin** ses chaussures étaient complètement usées; **he wore his coat threadbare** il a usé son manteau jusqu'à la corde; **a path had been worn across the lawn** un sentier avait été creusé à travers la pelouse par le passage des gens; **the wheel had worn a groove in the wood** la roue avait creusé le bois

(**d**) *Br Fam (accept → argument, behaviour)* supporter❑, tolérer❑; **I won't wear it!** je ne marcherai pas!

(**e**) *(idioms)* **to wear oneself to a frazzle** *or* **a shadow** s'éreinter

2 *vi* (**a**) *(endure, last)* durer; **wool wears better than cotton** la laine résiste mieux à l'usure *ou* fait meilleur usage que le coton; **this coat has worn well** ce manteau a bien servi; **this rug should wear for years** ce tapis devrait durer *ou* faire des années; **it will wear forever** cela durera pour toujours, c'est inusable; *Fig* **their friendship has worn well** leur amitié est restée intacte malgré le temps; **the film has not worn well** le film n'a pas bien vieilli; *Br Fam* **she's worn well** elle est bien conservée

(**b**) *(be damaged through use)* s'user; **this rug has worn badly in the middle** ce tapis est très usé au milieu; **the carpet had worn thin** le tapis était usé *ou* élimé; **the stone had worn smooth** la pierre était polie par le temps; *Fig* **her patience was wearing thin** elle était presque à bout de patience; **his excuses are wearing a bit thin** ses excuses ne prennent plus; **his jokes are wearing a bit thin** ses plaisanteries ne sont plus drôles

(**c**) *Literary (time)* passer; **as morning wore into afternoon** comme la matinée passait *ou* l'après-midi approchait; **as the year wore to its close** comme l'année tirait à sa fin

3 *n (UNCOUNT)* (**a**) *(of clothes)* **for everyday wear** pour porter tous les jours; **clothes suitable for evening wear** tenue *f* de soirée; **a suit for business wear** un costume pour le bureau; **women's wear** vêtements *mpl* pour femmes; **winter wear** vêtements *mpl* d'hiver

(**b**) *(use)* usage *m*; **these shoes will stand hard wear** ces chaussures feront un bon usage *ou* résisteront bien à l'usure; **there's still plenty of wear in that dress** cette robe est encore très portable; **to get a lot of wear from** *or* **out of sth** faire durer qch; **is there any wear left in them?** feront-ils encore de l'usage?

(**c**) *(deterioration)* **wear (and tear)** usure *f*; **fair** *or* **normal wear and tear** usure *f* normale; **living in the big city puts a lot of wear and tear on people** les grandes villes sont une source de stress pour leurs habitants; **the sheets are beginning to show signs of wear** les draps commencent à être un peu usés *ou* fatigués

►**wear away 1** *vt sep (soles)* user; *(cliff, land)* ronger, éroder; *(stone)* éroder; *(paint, design)* effacer

2 *vi (metal)* s'user; *(land)* être rongé, s'éroder; *(grass, topsoil)* disparaître *(par usure)*; *(stone)* s'éroder; *(design)* s'effacer

►**wear down 1** *vt sep (steps)* user; *Fig (patience, strength)* épuiser petit à petit; *(courage, resistance)* saper, miner; **in the end she wore me down** *(I gave in to her)* elle a fini par me faire céder; **the busy schedule finally wore her down** son emploi du temps chargé a fini par l'épuiser *ou* l'exténuer

2 *vi (pencil, steps, tyres)* s'user; *(courage)* s'épuiser; **the heels have worn down** les talons sont usés

►**wear off 1** *vi* (**a**) *(marks, design)* s'effacer, disparaître

(**b**) *(excitement)* s'apaiser, passer; *(anaesthetic, effects)* se dissiper, disparaître; *(pain)* se calmer, passer; **the novelty soon wore off** l'attrait de la nouveauté a vite passé

2 *vt sep* effacer par l'usure, user

►**wear on** *vi (day, season)* avancer lentement; *(battle, discussion)* se poursuivre lentement; **as time wore on** au fur et à mesure que le temps passait

►**wear out 1** *vt sep* (**a**) *(clothing, machinery)* user

(**b**) *(patience, strength, reserves)* épuiser; **to wear out one's welcome** abuser de l'hospitalité de ses hôtes

(**c**) *(tire)* épuiser; **you're wearing yourself out working so hard** tu t'épuises *ou* tu t'exténues à tant travailler; **to be worn out** être exténué *ou* éreinté; **worn out from arguing, he finally accepted their offer** de guerre lasse, il a fini par accepter leur offre; **their constant bickering wears me out** leurs chamailleries continuelles me fatiguent *ou* m'épuisent

2 *vi (clothing, shoes)* s'user; **this material will never wear out** ce tissu est inusable

▸**wear through 1** *vt sep* trouer, percer

2 *vi* se trouer; **my jeans have worn through at the knees** mon jean est troué aux genoux

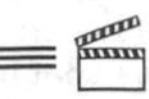

'She Wore a Yellow Ribbon' *Ford* 'La Charge héroïque'

wearable ['weərəbəl] *adj* portable

wearer ['weərə(r)] *n* **good news for wearers of glasses** bonnes nouvelles pour les personnes qui portent des lunettes; **designed with the wearer's comfort in mind** conçu pour le confort de celui qui le portera

wearily ['wɪərɪlɪ] *adv* avec lassitude; **"all right, if I must", she said wearily** "bien, s'il le faut", dit-elle d'un ton las; **he smiled wearily** il sourit d'un air fatigué; **we shuffled wearily along the platform** nous traînions les pieds sur le quai avec lassitude

weariness ['wɪərɪnɪs] *n* **(a)** *(tiredness)* lassitude *f*, fatigue *f* **(b)** *(discontent)* lassitude *f*, ennui *m*

wearing ['weərɪŋ] *adj* fatigant, épuisant; **their company is rather wearing** je trouve leur présence assez pénible

wearisome ['wɪərɪsəm] *adj* **(a)** *(tiring)* fatigant, épuisant **(b)** *(annoying)* ennuyeux, lassant

weary ['wɪərɪ] (*compar* **wearier**, *superl* **weariest**, *pt & pp* **wearied**) **1** *adj* **(a)** *(tired → physically, morally)* las, lasse, fatigué; **she grew weary of reading** elle s'est lassée de lire; **I'm weary of his silly jokes** j'en ai assez de ses plaisanteries stupides; **he gave a weary sigh** il a soupiré d'un air las; **he spoke in a weary voice** il parlait d'une voix lasse; **I'm weary of life** j'en ai assez *ou* je suis las de la vie

(b) *(tiring → day, journey)* fatigant, lassant

2 *vt (tire)* fatiguer, lasser; *(annoy)* lasser, agacer; **they weary me with all their complaining** ils m'ennuient avec leurs plaintes continuelles

3 *vi* se lasser; **she began to weary of life in the country** elle commença à se lasser de la vie à la campagne

wearying ['wɪərɪɪŋ] *adj* fatigant, ennuyeux; **I find her quite wearying** je la trouve très pénible; **I find it very wearying** cela me fatigue beaucoup

weasel ['wi:zəl] **1** *n* **(a)** *Zool* belette *f* **(b)** *Pej (person)* fouine *f*

2 *vi Am* ruser; *(in speaking)* parler d'une façon ambiguë

3 *vt* **he weaseled his way into the conversation** il s'est insinué dans la conversation

▸▸ ***weasel words*** paroles *fpl* ambiguës *ou* équivoques, discours *m* ambigu *ou* équivoque

▸**weasel out** *vi Am Fam* **to weasel out of sth** se tirer de qch; **he weaseled out of the contract** il s'est débrouillé pour se dégager du contrat; **she always weasels out of doing the dishes** elle se débrouille toujours pour échapper à la vaisselle

weasel-faced *adj (person)* à figure de fouine

weather ['weðə(r)] **1** *n* **(a)** *Met* temps *m*; **what's the weather like?** quel temps fait-il?; **it's beautiful/terrible weather** il fait beau/mauvais; **the weather is awful** *or* **foul** il fait un temps de chien; **weather permitting** si le temps le permet; **surely you're not going out in this weather?** vous n'allez tout de même pas sortir par un temps pareil?; **we had good weather for the time of year** nous avons eu du beau temps pour la saison; **in hot weather** par temps chaud, en période de chaleur; **in all weathers** par tous les temps; **there was a change in the weather** il y eut un changement de temps, le temps changea

(b) *Rad & TV* **weather (forecast)** (bulletin *m*) météo *f*; **did you listen to the weather?** as-tu écouté la météo?

(c) *(idioms) Fam* **to feel under the weather** ne pas être dans son assiette; *Fam* **keep your weather eye open!** veillez au grain!; *Fam* **I'll keep a weather eye on the kids** je vais surveiller les enfants ▫

2 *comp (conditions)* climatique, atmosphérique

3 *vt* **(a)** *(survive → storm)* réchapper à; *(→ crisis)* survivre à, réchapper à; **the ship weathered the storm** le navire a traversé la tempête; *Fig* **will he weather the storm?** va-t-il se tirer d'affaire *ou* tenir le coup?

(b) *(wood)* exposer aux intempéries; *(rock)* éroder; **the rocks had been weathered by wind and rain** le vent et la pluie avaient érodé les rochers

4 *vi (bronze, wood)* se patiner; *(rock)* s'éroder; **this paint weathers well** cette peinture vieillit bien *ou* résiste bien aux intempéries; **the brickwork has weathered to a pleasant shade of pink** la brique a pris une jolie couleur rose avec le temps

▸▸ ***weather balloon*** ballon-sonde *m*; ***weather bulletin*** bulletin *m* météorologique; *Am* ***weather bureau*** ≃ office *m* national de la météorologie; *Br* ***weather centre*** ≃ centre *m* météorologique régional; **the London weather centre** la station de météorologie de Londres; ***weather chart*** carte *f* météorologique; ***weather deck*** *(on ship)* pont *m* découvert; *(on bus)* impériale *f* découverte; ***weather forecast*** prévisions *fpl* météorologiques, météo *f*; **what's the weather forecast for tomorrow?** quelle est la météo pour demain?; ***weather house*** = sorte de baromètre décoratif représentant une petite maison d'où sortent deux figurines, l'une par beau temps, l'autre par mauvais temps; ***weather map*** carte *f* météorologique; ***weather report*** bulletin *m* météorologique; ***weather satellite*** satellite *m* météorologique; ***weather ship*** navire *m* météorologique; ***weather side*** *(of house etc)* côté exposé au vent; *Naut* bord du vent; ***weather station*** station *f ou* observatoire *m* météorologique; ***weather strip*** *(for door, window)* bourrelet *m* isolant, calfeutrage *m*; ***weather vane*** girouette *f*; ***weather warning*** alerte *f* météorologique; **to issue a weather warning** lancer une alerte météorologique

weather-beaten *adj (face, person)* buriné; *(building, stone)* dégradé par les intempéries

weatherboard ['weðəbɔ:d] *n* **(a)** *(UNCOUNT) (on outer walls)* planche *f ou* planches *fpl* à recouvrement **(b)** *(on door)* planche *f* de recouvrement

weatherboarding ['weðəbɔ:dɪŋ] *n (UNCOUNT)* planches *fpl* à recouvrement

weather-bound *adj (aircraft, ship)* immobilisé par le mauvais temps; *(event)* reporté pour cause de mauvais temps

weathercock ['weðəkɒk] *n also Fig* girouette *f*

weathered ['weðəd] *adj (bronze, wood)* patiné par le temps; *(building, stone)* érodé par le temps, usé par les intempéries; *(face)* buriné

weathergirl ['weðəgɜ:l] *n* présentatrice *f* de la météo

weatherglass ['weðəglɑ:s] *n* baromètre *m*

weathering ['weðərɪŋ] *n* désagrégation *f*, érosion *f*

weatherly ['weðəlɪ] *adj* qui tient bien près du vent; **a weatherly ship** un bateau ardent

Weatherman ['weðəmæn] *n Am* = groupe révolutionnaire américain des années 70

weatherman ['weðəmæn] (*pl* **weathermen** [-men]) *n* **the weatherman** le météorologue, le météorologiste; *Rad & TV* le journaliste météo

weatherproof ['weðəpru:f] **1** *adj (paint, coating)* résistant à l'eau; *(clothing)* imperméable; *(building, windows)* étanche; *(equipment, machinery)* qui résiste aux intempéries

2 *vt (paint, coating, clothing)* imperméabiliser; *(building, windows)* rendre étanche; *(equipment, machinery)* traiter à l'antirouille

weatherworn ['weðəwɔ:n] *adj (face, person)* buriné; *(building, stone)* dégradé par le temps

weave [wi:v] (*vt senses* **(a)**, **(b)**, **(c)** *& vi senses* **(a)** *&* **(b)** *pt* **wove** [wəʊv], *pp* **woven** ['wəʊvən], *vt sense* **(d)** *& vi sense* **(c)** *pt & pp* **weaved**)

1 *vt* **(a)** *(cloth, web)* tisser; *(basket, garland)* tresser; **she wove the strands together into a necklace** elle a tressé *ou* entrelacé les fils pour en faire un collier

(b) *(story)* tramer, bâtir; *(plot)* tisser, tramer; *also Fig* **to weave a spell over sb** ensorceler qn; **the witch wove a spell to make sure that they could not escape** la sorcière leur a jeté un sort pour les empêcher de s'échapper; **a tightly woven plot** une intrigue bien ficelée

(c) *(introduce)* introduire, incorporer; **he managed to weave all the facts together to make a fascinating report** il a réussi à incorporer tous les faits dans un rapport passionnant; **political elements have been woven into the plot** des éléments politiques ont été introduits dans *ou* intégrés à l'intrigue

(d) *(as verb of movement)* **he weaved his way across the room/towards the bar** il s'est frayé un chemin à travers la salle/vers le bar; **I had to weave my way through the crowd** j'ai dû me frayer un chemin à travers la foule; **the cyclist weaved his way through the traffic** le cycliste se faufilait entre les voitures

2 *vi* **(a)** *Tex* tisser

(b) *(road, river)* serpenter

(c) *(as verb of movement)* se faufiler, se glisser; **he weaved unsteadily across the street** il a traversé la rue en titubant *ou* en zigzaguant; **to weave through the traffic** se faufiler entre les voitures; **to weave in and out of the crowd** se faufiler dans la foule *ou* parmi la foule; **the boxer ducked and weaved** le boxeur a esquivé tous les coups; *Fam* **come on, get weaving!** allons, grouillez-vous!

3 *n* tissage *m*; **the basket has a loose/tight weave** le panier a un tissage lâche/serré

weaver ['wi:və(r)] *n* **(a)** *Tex* tisserand(e) *m,f* **(b)** *Orn* tisserin *m*

weaverbird ['wi:vəbɜ:d] *n Orn* tisserin *m*

weaving ['wi:vɪŋ] **1** *n* **(a)** *(of cloth)* tissage *m*; *(of baskets, garlands)* tressage *m* **(b)** *(of story)* récit *m*; *(of plot)* trame *f*

2 *comp (industry, mill)* de tissage

Web [web] *n Comput* **the Web** le Web, *Offic* la Toile

▸▸ ***Web authoring*** création *f* de pages Web; ***Web authoring program*** programme *m* de création de pages Web; ***Web authoring tool*** outil *m* de création de pages Web; ***Web browser*** navigateur *m*, logiciel *m* de navigation; ***Web cam*** caméra *f* Internet; ***Web consultancy*** société *f* conseil pour la création et l'administration de sites Web; ***Web design agency*** société *f* spécialisée dans la conception de sites Web; ***Web designer*** concepteur(trice) *m,f* de sites Web; ***Web hosting*** hébergement *m* de sites Web; ***Web master*** Webmaster *m*, Webmestre *m*, responsable *mf* de site Web; ***Web page*** page *f* Web; ***Web server*** serveur *m* Web; ***Web site*** site *m* Web; ***Web space*** espace *m* Web

web [web] *n* **(a)** *(of fabric, metal)* tissu *m*; *(of spider)* toile *f*; *Fig (of lies)* tissu *m*; *(of intrigue)* réseau *m* **(b)** *(on feet → of duck, frog)* palmure *f*; *(→ of humans)* palmature *f*

webbed [webd] *adj* palmé; **to have webbed feet** *or* **toes** *(duck, frog)* avoir les pattes palmées; *(human)* avoir une palmature

webbing ['webɪŋ] *n (UNCOUNT)* **(a)** *Tex (material)* toile *f* à sangles; *(on chair)* sangles *fpl* **(b)** *Anat (animal)* palmure *f*; *(human)* palmature *f*

webcast ['webkɑ:st] *Comput* **1** *n* = émission, concert etc diffusés en direct sur Internet

2 *vt* diffuser sur Internet

weber ['veɪbə(r)] *n Phys* weber *m*

web-fed *adj (printer)* à alimentation de papier en continu

webfoot ['webfʊt] (*pl* **webfeet** [-fi:t]) *n* **(a)** *(foot → of animal)* patte *f* palmée; *(→ of human)* palmature *f* **(b)** *(kind of animal)* palmipède *m*

web-footed [-'fʊtɪd] *adj (animal)* palmipède, qui a les pattes palmées; *(human)* qui a une palmature

webmaster ['web,mɑ:stə(r)] = **Web master**

web-offset printing *n* impression *f* (offset) continue

website ['websaɪt] *n* = **Web site**

webzine ['webzi:n] *n Comput* webzine *m*

Wed. *(written abbr* **Wednesday***)* mer

wed [wed] (*pt & pp* **wed** *or* **wedded**, *cont* **wedding**) **1** *vt Literary* **(a)** *(marry)* épouser, se marier avec; **to get wed** se marier

(b) *(of clergyman)* marier

(c) *(usu passive) (unite, combine)* allier; **intelligence wedded to beauty** l'intelligence alliée à la beauté; **he's wedded to the cause** il est véritablement marié à cette cause; **the fate of the project was wedded to that of the Chairman** la destinée du projet était liée à celle du Président

2 *vi (in headline)* se marier; **PM's son to wed** le fils du Premier ministre se marie

we'd [wi:d] (**a**) = **we would** (**b**) = **we had**

wedded ['wedɪd] *adj (person)* marié; *(bliss, life)* conjugal; **her lawful wedded husband** son époux légitime; **the newly wedded couple** les jeunes mariés *mpl*

wedding ['wedɪŋ] **1** *n* (**a**) *(marriage)* mariage *m*, noces *fpl*; **to have a church wedding** se marier à l'église; **we had a quiet wedding** nous nous sommes mariés *ou* nous avons célébré le mariage dans l'intimité

(**b**) *(uniting)* union *f*

2 *comp (night)* de noces; *(ceremony, photograph, present)* de mariage; **the wedding guests** les invités *mpl* (au mariage)

▸▸ ***wedding anniversary*** anniversaire *m* de mariage; **our tenth wedding anniversary** notre dixième anniversaire de mariage; ***wedding band*** alliance *f*, anneau *m* de mariage; ***wedding breakfast*** repas *m* de noces; ***wedding cake*** gâteau *m* de noces, ≃ pièce *f* montée; ***wedding day*** jour *m* du mariage; **on their wedding day** le jour de leur mariage; ***wedding dress*** robe *f* de mariée; ***wedding invitation*** invitation *f* de mariage; ***wedding list*** liste *f* de mariage; ***wedding march*** marche *f* nuptiale; ***wedding reception*** réception *f* de mariage; ***wedding ring*** alliance *f*, anneau *m* de mariage; *Fam Hum* ***wedding tackle*** *(man's genitals)* bijoux *mpl* de famille

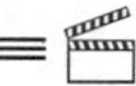

'Four Weddings and a Funeral' *Newell* 'Quatre mariages et un enterrement'

wedeln ['veɪdəln] *Ski* **1** *n* godille *f*

2 *vi* descendre en godille

wedge [wedʒ] **1** *n* (**a**) *(under door, wheel)* cale *f*; **put a wedge under the door** calez la porte, mettez une cale sous la porte; *Fig* **their political differences drove a wedge between the two friends** les deux amis se sont brouillés à cause de leurs divergences politiques

(**b**) *(for splitting wood)* coin *m*

(**c**) *(of cheese, cake, pie)* morceau *m*, part *f*

(**d**) *(golf club)* cale *f*

(**e**) *(for climber)* coin *m*

(**f**) *(shoe heel)* semelle *f* compensée

(**g**) *Br Fam (money)* fric *m*, flouze *m*, pognon *m*

2 *vt* (**a**) *(make fixed or steady)* caler; **the window was wedged open** la fenêtre était maintenue ouverte à l'aide d'une cale; **I wedged the door open/shut** j'ai maintenu la porte ouverte/fermée par une cale; **wedge the table with something, it's wobbling** mets une cale sous la table, elle est branlante

(**b**) *(squeeze, push)* enfoncer; **to wedge sth apart** fendre *ou* forcer qch; **he wedged his foot in the door** il a bloqué la porte avec son pied; **she sat wedged between her two aunts** elle était assise coincée entre ses deux tantes; **I found the ring wedged down behind the cushion** j'ai trouvé la bague enfoncée derrière le coussin

▸▸ ***wedge heel*** semelle *f* compensée

▸**wedge in** *vt sep (object)* faire rentrer, enfoncer; *(person)* faire rentrer; **she was wedged in between two Italians** elle était coincée entre deux Italiens; **I wedged myself in at the back of the crowded hall** je me suis glissé au fond de la salle bondée; **the photo was wedged in between two books** la photo était glissée entre deux livres

wedge-heeled [-hi:ld] *adj* à semelle compensée

▸▸ ***wedge-heeled shoe*** chaussure *f* à semelle compensée

wedge-shaped *adj* en forme de coin

wedgie ['wedʒi:] *n Fam* (**a**) *(shoe)* chaussure *f* à semelle compensée❑ (**b**) *Hum* **to give sb a wedgie** = tirer le slip de qn pour le lui faire rentrer dans les fesses; **I've got a wedgie** j'ai mon slip coincé entre les fesses

wedlock ['wedlɒk] *n Formal* mariage *m*; **to be born out of wedlock** être un enfant naturel, être né hors du mariage

Wednesday ['wenzdɪ] *n* mercredi *m*; *see also* **Friday**

wee [wi:] **1** *adj esp Scot* petit; **a wee bit** un peu; **a wee drop of whisky** une larme de whisky; **in the wee (small) hours of the morning** au petit matin, aux premières heures du jour; **a wee boy** un petit garçon; **the Wee Free** = surnom de la "Free Church of Scotland"

2 *vi Fam* faire pipi

3 *n Fam* pipi *m*; **to have a wee** faire pipi

weed [wi:d] **1** *n* (**a**) *(plant)* mauvaise herbe *f*; **that plant grows like a weed** cette plante pousse comme du chiendent

(**b**) *Pej (person → physically)* gringalet *m*; *(→ in character)* mauviette *f*

(**c**) *Fam (tobacco)* **the weed** le tabac❑; **I've given up the weed** j'ai arrêté de fumer❑

(**d**) *Fam Drugs slang (marijuana)* herbe *f*

2 *vt* désherber, arracher les mauvaises herbes de; *(with hoe)* sarcler

3 *vi* désherber, arracher les mauvaises herbes; *(with hoe)* sarcler

4 **weeds** *npl* vêtements *mpl* de deuil; **in widow's weeds** en deuil

▸▸ *Am* ***Weed Whacker***® débroussailleuse *f* (à fil)

▸**weed out** *vt sep* éliminer; *(troublemakers)* expulser; **to weed out the bad from the good** faire le tri

weedgie ['wi:dʒɪ] *n Scot Fam Pej (inhabitant of Glasgow)* habitant(e) *m,f* de Glasgow❑; *(native of Glasgow)* originaire *mf* de Glasgow❑

weediness ['wi:dɪnɪs] *n* (**a**) *(of ground)* **look at the weediness of those fields** regardez-moi ces champs, comme ils sont couverts de mauvaises herbes! (**b**) *Fam Pej (of person → physical)* constitution *f* malingre❑; *(→ in character)* faiblesse❑*f*, mollesse *f*

weeding ['wi:dɪŋ] *n* désherbage *m*; *(with hoe)* sarclage *m*; **he does a little weeding every day** il désherbe un peu *ou* il enlève quelques mauvaises herbes tous les jours

weedkiller ['wi:d,kɪlə(r)] *n* herbicide *m*, désherbant *m*

weedy ['wi:dɪ] *(compar* **weedier**, *superl* **weediest**) *adj* (**a**) *(ground)* couvert de *ou* envahi par les mauvaises herbes (**b**) *Fam Pej (person → physically)* gringalet, malingre❑; *(→ in character)* faible❑, mou

Weejun® ['wi:dʒən] *n Am* mocassin *m*

week [wi:k] *n* semaine *f*; **next/last week** la semaine prochaine/dernière; **see you next week** à la semaine prochaine; **in one week, in one week's time** dans huit jours, d'ici une semaine; **two weeks ago** il y a deux semaines *ou* quinze jours; **a week ago today** il y a (aujourd'hui) huit jours; **within a week** *(gen)* dans la semaine, d'ici une semaine; *Admin & Com* sous huitaine; **week ending March 25** la semaine du 21 mars; **a week (from) today** d'ici huit jours; **a week (from) tomorrow** demain en huit; **yesterday week, a week yesterday** il y a eu une semaine hier; **Monday week, a week on Monday** lundi en huit; **twice a week** deux fois par semaine; **week in week out, week after week** semaine après semaine; **from week to week** de semaine en semaine; **it rained for weeks on end** il a plu pendant des semaines; **I haven't seen you in** *or* **for weeks** ça fait des semaines que je ne t'ai pas vu; **we're taking a week's holiday** nous prenons huit jours de congé; **the working week** la semaine de travail; **a forty-hour/five-day week** une semaine de quarante heures/de cinq jours; **she's paid by the week** elle est payée à la semaine; **this dress cost me a week's wages** cette robe m'a coûté une semaine de salaire; **I lost a week's pay** j'ai perdu une semaine de salaire

weekday ['wi:k,deɪ] **1** *n* jour *m* de la semaine; *Admin & Com* jour *m* ouvrable; **on weekdays** en semaine; **weekdays only** sauf samedi et dimanche

2 *comp (activities)* de la semaine; **on weekday mornings** le matin en semaine

weekend [,wi:k'end] **1** *n* week-end *m*, fin *f* de semaine; *Br* **at** *or Am* **on the weekend** le week-end; **have a good weekend!** bon week-end!, bonne fin de semaine!; **I'll do it at the weekend** je le ferai pendant le week-end; **what do you do at weekends?** que fais-tu (pendant) le week-end *ou* les week-ends?; **what are you doing at the weekend?** qu'est-ce que tu fais ce week-end?; **he's staying with them for the weekend** il passe le week-end chez eux; **I'm going away for the weekend** je pars pour le week-end; **a long weekend** un week-end prolongé; **as Thursday is a bank holiday, I'm taking Friday off and making a long weekend of it** jeudi est férié alors je fais le pont

2 *comp (schedule, visit)* de *ou* du week-end; *(golfer, rugby player)* qui ne joue que le week-end

3 *vi* passer le week-end

▸▸ ***weekend bag*** sac *m* de voyage, mallette *f*; ***weekend break*** = séjour d'un week-end; ***weekend case*** sac *m* de voyage, mallette *f*; ***weekend cottage*** maison *f* secondaire *ou* de campagne *(où on passe le week-end)*; *Br Rail* ***weekend return*** = billet aller-retour valable du vendredi au dimanche soir

Anything for the weekend, sir?

Cette formule ("vous désirez quelque chose pour le week-end, Monsieur?") était jadis utilisée en Grande-Bretagne par les coiffeurs pour hommes pour proposer des préservatifs à leurs clients.

Cette expression ou sa version tronquée **something for the weekend** ("quelque chose pour le week-end") s'emploie aujourd'hui lorsqu'il est question de s'adonner à une activité particulière pendant le week-end ou bien pour évoquer une certaine lubricité qui serait typique du caractère britannique.

weekender [,wi:k'endə(r)] *n* = personne en voyage pour le week-end; **he's one of the weekenders who come here to ski** il fait partie des gens qui viennent skier ici le week-end; **most of the cottages belong to weekenders** la plupart des maisons sont des résidences secondaires

weekly ['wi:klɪ] *(pl* **weeklies**) **1** *adj (visit, meeting)* de la semaine, hebdomadaire; *(publication, payment, wage)* hebdomadaire; *(tenant)* à la semaine; **these incidents were an almost weekly occurrence** ces incidents avaient lieu presque chaque semaine

2 *n* hebdomadaire *m*; **the weeklies** la presse hebdomadaire

3 *adv (once a week)* chaque semaine, une fois par semaine; *(each week)* chaque semaine, tous les huit jours; **twice weekly** deux fois par semaine; **he's paid weekly** il est payé à la semaine

weeknight ['wi:knaɪt] *n* soir *m* de la semaine; **I can't go out on weeknights** je ne peux pas sortir le soir en semaine

ween [wi:n] *vt Arch or Literary* **I ween** j'imagine, je crois; **weenst thou that...?** croyez-vous que...?

weenie ['wi:nɪ] *n Am Fam* (**a**) *(frankfurter)* saucisse *f* (de Francfort)❑ (**b**) *(penis)* zizi *m*; **to play hide the weenie** *(have sex)* s'envoyer en l'air (**c**) *(person)* imbécile *mf*

▸▸ ***weenie stand*** = kiosque où l'on vend des hot dogs

weeny ['wi:nɪ] *(compar* **weenier**, *superl* **weeniest**) *adj Fam* tout petit❑, minuscule❑; **would you like a brandy? – just a weeny one** voulez-vous un cognac? – (j'en prendrai) juste un tout petit

weenybopper ['wi:nɪ,bɒpə(r)] *n Fam* = gamine férue de musique pop

weep [wi:p] *(pt & pp* **wept** [wept]) **1** *vi* (**a**) *(person)* pleurer, verser des larmes; **to weep for joy/with vexation** pleurer de joie/de dépit; **she wept for her lost youth** elle pleurait sa jeunesse perdue; **to weep for sb** pleurer qn; **the little girl wept over her broken doll** la petite fille pleurait sur sa poupée cassée; **he wept to see her so ill** il a pleuré de la voir si malade; **that's nothing to weep about** *or* **over** il n'y a pas de quoi pleurer; *Hum* **it's enough to make you weep!** c'est à faire pleurer!; **I could have wept!** j'en aurais pleuré!

(**b**) *(walls, wound)* suinter

2 *vt (tears)* verser, pleurer; **he wept bitter tears** il pleura amèrement

3 *n* **to have a weep** pleurer, verser quelques larmes; **she had a little weep** elle a versé quelques larmes

weeping ['wi:pɪŋ] **1** *adj (person)* qui pleure; *(walls, wound)* suintant

2 *n (UNCOUNT)* larmes *fpl*, pleurs *mpl*; **a fit of weeping, a weeping fit** une crise de larmes; **we could hear weeping from the next room** on

pouvait entendre quelqu'un qui pleurait dans la pièce d'à côté

►► ***weeping willow*** saule *m* pleureur

weepy ['wiːpɪ] (*compar* **weepier**, *superl* **weepiest**, *pl* **weepies**) **1** *adj* (**a**) *(tone, voice)* larmoyant; *(person)* qui pleure; **she is** *or* **feels weepy** elle a envie de pleurer, elle est au bord des larmes (**b**) *(film, story)* sentimental, larmoyant

2 *n Br Fam (film)* mélo *m*, film *m* sentimental ❑; *(book)* mélo *m*, roman *m* à l'eau de rose

weever ['wiːvə(r)] *n Ich* vive *f*

weevil ['wiːvəl] *n Entom* charançon *m*

wee-wee *Br Fam* **1** *n* pipi *m*; **to go (for a) wee-wee** faire pipi

2 *vi* faire pipi

weft [weft] *n Tex* trame *f*

weigh [weɪ] **1** *vt* (**a**) *(person, thing)* peser; **to weigh oneself** se peser; **to weigh sth in one's hand** soupeser qch

(**b**) *(consider)* considérer, peser; **let's weigh the evidence** considérons les faits; **to weigh the consequences** calculer les conséquences; **she weighed her words carefully** elle a bien pesé ses mots; **you have to weigh the pros and cons** il faut peser le pour et le contre; **to weigh one thing against another** mettre deux choses en balance

(**c**) *Naut* **to weigh anchor** lever l'ancre

2 *vi* (**a**) *(person, object)* peser; **how much do you weigh?** combien est-ce que tu pèses?, quel poids fais-tu?; **the fish weighs one kilo** le poisson pèse un kilo; **he doesn't weigh much** il ne pèse pas lourd

(**b**) *(influence)* **his silence began to weigh (heavy)** son silence commençait à devenir pesant; **the facts weigh heavily against him** les faits plaident lourdement en sa défaveur; **her qualifications weighed in her favour** ses qualifications ont fait pencher la balance en sa faveur *ou* ont joué en sa faveur

3 under weigh *adj Naut* appareillé, en marche

►**weigh down** *vt sep* (**a**) faire plier, courber; **the branches were weighed down with snow** les branches ployaient sous le poids de la neige; **she was weighed down with suitcases** elle pliait sous le poids des valises

(**b**) *Fig* **she's weighed down with financial problems** elle est en proie à des *ou* accablée de problèmes financiers; **weighed down with debts/with sorrow** accablé de dettes/de tristesse

►**weigh in** *vi* (**a**) *Boxing & Horseracing* se faire peser *(avant une épreuve)*; **the boxer weighed in at 85 kilos** le boxeur faisait 85 kilos avant le match; **the jockey weighed in at 45 kilos** le jockey pesait 45 kilos avant la course

(**b**) *(join in)* intervenir; **he always has to weigh in with his opinions** il faut toujours qu'il intervienne pour imposer ses opinions

►**weigh on** *vt insep* peser; **his worries weighed heavily on him** ses soucis lui pesaient beaucoup; **the exam weighed on his mind** l'examen le préoccupait *ou* tracassait

►**weigh out** *vt sep* peser; **weigh out 200 grams of flour for me** pèse-moi 200 grammes de farine

►**weigh up** *vt sep* (**a**) *(consider)* examiner, calculer; *(compare)* mettre en balance; **to weigh up the situation** peser la situation; **I'm weighing up whether to take the job or not** je me demande si je dois prendre le poste; **to weigh up one's chances of doing sth** calculer ses chances de faire qch; **to weigh up the pros and cons** peser le pour et le contre

(**b**) **to weigh sb up** *(their character)* estimer la valeur de qn; *(their intentions)* estimer les intentions de qn; **I looked round, weighing up the opposition** je me suis retourné pour mesurer l'adversaire

weighbridge ['weɪbrɪdʒ] *n* pont-bascule *m*

weigh-in *n Boxing & Horseracing* pesage *m*, pesée *f*

weighing machine ['weɪɪŋ-] *n (for people)* balance *f*; *(for loads)* bascule *f*

weight [weɪt] **1** *n* (**a**) *(of person, package, goods)* poids *m*; **she tested** *or* **felt the weight of the package** elle a soupesé le paquet; **what's your normal weight?** combien pesez-vous *ou* quel poids faites-vous normalement?; **my weight is 50 kg, I'm 50 kilos in weight** je pèse *ou* je fais 50 kilos; **we're the same weight** nous faisons le même poids; **he's twice your weight** il pèse deux fois plus lourd que toi; **to gain** *or* **to put on weight** grossir, prendre du poids; **to lose weight** maigrir, perdre du poids; **she's watching her weight** elle fait attention à sa ligne; **what a weight!** *(person)* qu'il est lourd!; *(stone, parcel)* que c'est lourd!; **that case must be quite a weight** cette valise doit être drôlement lourde; **don't lift any heavy weights** ne soulève pas trop de poids; **to sell sth by weight** vendre qch au poids; **she's worth her weight in gold** elle vaut son pesant d'or; *Hum* **take the weight off your feet** assieds-toi un peu; *Horseracing* **to carry weight** être handicapé

(**b**) *(force)* poids *m*; **he put his full weight behind the blow** il a frappé de toutes ses forces; *Fig* **to pull one's weight** faire sa part du travail, y mettre du sien; *Fig* **to throw one's weight about** *or* **around** bousculer les gens

(**c**) *(burden)* poids *m*; **the weight of years** le poids des années; **he quailed under the weight of responsibility** le poids de la responsabilité l'a effrayé; **that's a weight off my mind** je suis vraiment soulagé

(**d**) *(importance, influence)* poids *m*, influence *f*; **the facts lend considerable weight to her argument** les faits donnent un poids considérable à son raisonnement; **their opinion carries quite a lot of weight** leur opinion a un poids *ou* une autorité considérable; **she put** *or* **threw all her weight behind the candidate** elle a apporté tout son soutien au candidat; **she carries little weight with the authorities** elle n'a pas beaucoup d'influence *ou* de poids auprès de l'administration

(**e**) *(for scales)* poids *m*; **weights and measures** poids *mpl* et mesures *fpl*; **a set of weights** une série de poids; **a one-kilogramme weight** un poids d'un kilogramme

(**f**) *Sport* poids *m*; **to lift weights** soulever des poids *ou* des haltères

(**g**) *(of clock)* poids *m*; *(for fishing net)* lest *m*

(**h**) *Phys* pesanteur *f*, poids *m*

2 *comp* **to have a weight problem** avoir un problème de poids

3 *vt* (**a**) *(put weights on)* lester

(**b**) *(hold down)* retenir *ou* maintenir avec un poids

(**c**) *Econ (index, average)* pondérer; *Fig* **the circumstances are weighted in his favour** les circonstances jouent en sa faveur *ou* lui sont favorables; **the system is weighted in favour of the wealthy** le système est favorable aux riches *ou* privilégie les riches; **the electoral system was weighted against him** le système électoral lui était défavorable *ou* jouait contre lui

►► ***weight allowance*** *(in aeroplane)* poids *m* de bagages autorisé; ***weight charge*** taxation *f* au poids; ***weight loss*** perte *f* de poids; ***weight training*** entraînement *m* aux haltères

►**weight down** *vt sep* (**a**) *(body, net)* lester (**b**) *(papers, tarpaulin)* maintenir avec un poids

weighted ['weɪtɪd] *adj* (**a**) *(body, net)* lesté (**b**) *(index, average)* pondéré

►► *Fin* ***weighted average*** moyenne *f* pondérée; *Acct* ***weighted average cost*** coût *m* moyen pondéré; *Mktg* ***weighted distribution*** distribution *f* valeur

weightily ['weɪtɪlɪ] *adv (reason)* puissamment, avec force

weightiness ['weɪtɪnɪs] *n* (**a**) *(heaviness)* lourdeur *f*, pesanteur *f* (**b**) *(importance → of reasoning, argument)* poids *m*, force *f*; *(→ of problem)* importance *f*, gravité *f*

weighting ['weɪtɪŋ] *n* (**a**) *(extra salary)* indemnité *f*, allocation *f* (**b**) *(of statistics)* pondération *f*; *Sch* coefficient *m*

weightless ['weɪtlɪs] *adj* très léger; *Astron* en état d'apesanteur

weightlessness ['weɪtlɪsnɪs] *n* extrême légèreté *f*; *Astron* apesanteur *f*

weightlifter ['weɪtˌlɪftə(r)] *n* haltérophile *mf*

weightlifting ['weɪtˌlɪftɪŋ] *n* haltérophilie *f*

weightwatcher ['weɪtˌwɒtʃə(r)] *n (person → on diet)* personne *f* qui suit un régime; *(→ figure-conscious)* personne *f* qui surveille son poids

weighty ['weɪtɪ] (*compar* **weightier**, *superl* **weightiest**) *adj* (**a**) *(heavy)* lourd, pesant (**b**) *(important → responsibility)* lourd; *(→ problem)* important, grave; *(→ argument, reasoning)* probant, de poids; **we're not qualified to consider such weighty matters** nous n'avons pas les compétences requises pour examiner des questions aussi importantes

weir [wɪə(r)] *n* barrage *m (sur un cours d'eau)*

weird [wɪəd] *adj* (**a**) *(mysterious)* mystérieux, surnaturel (**b**) *Fam (odd)* bizarre ❑, étrange ❑; **he has some weird ideas** il a de drôles d'idées ❑; **he went a bit weird after his parents died** il est devenu un peu bizarre après la mort de ses parents

►**weird out** *vt sep Am Fam* **to weird sb out** faire flipper qn

weirdie ['wɪədɪ] *n Fam* drôle d'oiseau *m ou* de zèbre *m*

weirdly ['wɪədlɪ] *adv* (**a**) *(mysteriously)* mystérieusement (**b**) *(oddly)* bizarrement, singulièrement

weirdness ['wɪədnɪs] *n* étrangeté *f*, singularité *f*

weirdo ['wɪədəʊ] (*pl* **weirdos**) *Fam* **1** *n* drôle d'oiseau *m ou* de zèbre *m*

2 *comp (hairdo, clothes)* extravagant ❑; *(habits, ideas)* bizarre ❑

Weismannism ['vaɪsmæˌnɪzəm] *n Biol* théorie *f* de Weismann

weka ['wekə] *n Orn* ocydrome *m*

welch = **welsh**

WELCOME ['welkəm]

accueillir	► 1 (a)
être heureux d'avoir	► 1 (b)
accueil	► 2
bienvenu	► 3 (a), (b); 4
opportun	► 3 (b)

1 *vt* (**a**) *(greet, receive → people)* accueillir; **I welcomed her warmly** je lui ai fait bon accueil *ou* un accueil chaleureux; **they welcomed me in** ils m'ont chaleureusement invité à entrer; **we welcomed him with open arms** nous l'avons accueilli à bras ouverts; **a dinner to welcome the new members** un dîner pour accueillir les nouveaux membres; **the dog welcomes them home every evening** le chien leur fait la fête chaque soir lorsqu'ils rentrent; **would you please welcome Melissa Harte!** *(to audience)* voulez-vous applaudir Melissa Harte!

(**b**) *(accept gladly)* être heureux d'avoir, recevoir avec plaisir; **I welcomed the opportunity to speak to her** j'étais content d'avoir l'occasion de lui parler; **he welcomed the news** il s'est réjoui de la nouvelle, il a accueilli la nouvelle avec joie; **she welcomed any comments** elle accueillait volontiers les remarques que l'on pouvait lui faire; **his efforts weren't welcomed** ses efforts ont reçu peu d'encouragement; **we'd welcome a cup of coffee** nous prendrions volontiers une tasse de café

2 *n* accueil *m*; **she said a few words of welcome** elle a prononcé quelques mots de bienvenue; **we bid them welcome** nous leur souhaitons la bienvenue; **they gave him a warm welcome** ils lui ont fait bon accueil *ou* réservé un accueil chaleureux; **we gave her a big welcome home** nous lui avons fait fête à son retour à la maison; **let's give a warm welcome to Louis Armstrong!** *(to audience)* applaudissons très fort Louis Armstrong!; **to overstay** *or* **to outstay one's welcome** abuser de l'hospitalité de ses hôtes; **I don't want to outstay my welcome** je ne veux pas abuser de sa/votre/*etc* hospitalité

3 *adj* (**a**) *(person)* bienvenu; **to be welcome** être le bienvenu; **she's always welcome here** elle est toujours la bienvenue ici; **they made us very welcome** ils nous ont fait un très bon accueil; **she didn't feel very welcome** elle s'est sentie de trop; **the card is welcome in over 1,000 outlets** la carte est acceptée dans plus de 1000 points de vente

(**b**) *(pleasant, desirable → arrival)* bienvenu; *(→ change, interruption, remark)* opportun; **a welcome cup of coffee** une bonne tasse de café; **that's welcome news** nous sommes heureux de l'apprendre; **that would be most welcome** *(food, drink)* ça me ferait le plus grand bien; **their offer was most welcome** leur suggestion m'a fait grand plaisir; **this cheque is most welcome** ce chèque arrive opportunément *ou* tombe bien; **that's a welcome sight!** c'est un spectacle à réjouir le cœur!; **a helping hand is always welcome** un coup de main est toujours le bienvenu *ou* ne fait jamais de mal; **the news came as a welcome relief to him** la nouvelle a été un vrai soulagement pour lui, il a été vraiment soulagé d'apprendre la nouvelle; **the holiday came as a welcome break** les vacances ont été une coupure bienvenue *ou* appréciable; **the laid-back atmosphere of the village made a welcome change from London** l'atmosphère détendue du village nous changeait en bien de Londres

(**c**) *(permitted)* **you're welcome to join us** n'hésitez pas à vous joindre à nous; **he's welcome to borrow my book** qu'il n'hésite pas à emprunter mon livre; **I don't need it, she's welcome to it** je n'en ai pas besoin, elle peut bien le prendre *ou* je le lui donne volontiers; **you're welcome to anything you need** servez-vous si vous avez besoin de quelque chose; **they're welcome to stay with us** ils peuvent venir chez nous; **you're welcome to try** je vous en prie, essayez; **he's welcome to try!** *(grudgingly)* libre à lui d'essayer!, qu'il essaie donc!; **she's welcome to him!** je ne le lui envie pas!; **take it and welcome!** je te le donne bien volontiers!

(**d**) *(acknowledgment of thanks)* **you're welcome!** je vous en prie!, il n'y a pas de quoi!, *Suisse* service!; **tell her she's welcome** dis-lui que ce n'est rien

4 *exclam* soyez le bienvenu!; **welcome back** *or* **home!** content de vous revoir!; *Rad & TV* **welcome back!** *(after commercial)* re-bonjour!/re-bonsoir!; **welcome to my home!** bienvenue chez moi *ou* à la maison!; **welcome to Wales** *(sign)* bienvenue au pays de Galles

►► ***welcome committee*** comité *m* d'accueil; ***welcome mat*** paillasson *m*; *Fig* **they put out the welcome mat for him** ils l'ont accueilli à bras ouverts; *Comput* ***welcome message*** message *m* d'accueil; ***welcome pack*** *(at conference, in hotel)* documentation *f (remise à l'accueil)*; ***welcome reception*** réception *f* de bienvenue

►**welcome back** *vt sep* accueillir (à son retour); **we welcomed her back after her illness** nous lui avons fait fête *ou* l'avons accueillie chaleureusement après sa maladie; *Rad & TV* **I am pleased to welcome back Billy Bragg** j'ai le plaisir d'accueillir à nouveau Billy Bragg

---

welcoming ['welkəmɪŋ] *adj (person, greeting, smile, atmosphere)* accueillant; *(ceremony, committee)* d'accueil; **the welcoming party took them to their hotel** la délégation venue les accueillir les a conduits à leur hôtel

weld [weld] **1** *vt* (**a**) *Tech* souder; **to weld parts together** souder des pièces ensemble; **he welded the bracket onto the shelf** il a soudé le support à l'étagère

(**b**) *(unite)* amalgamer, réunir; **to weld employees into a team** réunir des employés en une équipe bien soudée; **a set of policies that will weld the party into a united political force** un ensemble de mesures qui cimentera le parti et en fera une force politique unie

2 *vi* souder

3 *n* (**a**) soudure *f*

(**b**) *Bot* réséda *m* des teinturiers

►► ***weld spot*** point *m* de soudure

welder ['weldə(r)] *n (person)* soudeur(euse) *m,f*; *(machine)* soudeuse *f*, machine *f* à souder

welding ['weldɪŋ] *n Tech* soudage *m*; *(of groups)* union *f*

►► ***welding helmet*** casque *m* de soudeur; ***welding machine*** soudeuse *f*, machine *f* à souder; ***welding mask*** masque *m* de soudeur; ***welding rod*** baguette *f* de soudure; ***welding torch*** chalumeau *m*

welfare ['welfeə(r)] **1** *n* (**a**) *(wellbeing)* bien-être *m*; **the welfare of the nation** le bien public; **the physical and spiritual welfare of the people** le bien-être physique et moral du peuple; **I am concerned about** *or* **for her welfare** je m'inquiète pour elle; **she's looking after his welfare** elle s'occupe de lui

(**b**) *Am (state aid)* aide *f* sociale; **his family is on welfare** sa famille touche l'aide sociale; **to live on welfare** vivre de l'aide sociale; **people on welfare** les personnes *ou* ceux qui touchent l'aide sociale

2 *comp (meals, milk)* gratuit; **the welfare lines are lengthening** la masse des gens qui touchent le chômage augmente; **to stand in the welfare line** recevoir les allocations chômage

►► *Am* ***welfare benefits*** avantages *mpl* sociaux; ***welfare centre*** ≃ centre *m* d'assistance sociale; *Am* ***welfare check*** (chèque *m* d') allocations *fpl*; ***welfare economics*** économie *f* du bien-être; ***welfare hotel*** foyer *m* d'accueil; ***welfare officer*** = travailleur social ayant la charge d'une personne mise en liberté surveillée; ***welfare payments*** prestations *fpl* sociales; ***welfare service*** ≃ service *m* d'assistance sociale; ***the Welfare State*** *(concept)* l'État *m* providence; **the government wants to cut back on the Welfare State** le gouvernement veut réduire les dépenses d'aide sociale; ***welfare work*** travail *m* social; ***welfare worker*** assistant *m* social, assistante *f* sociale

welfare-to-work *n Pol* = principe selon lequel les bénéficiaires de l'allocation de chômage doivent fournir un travail en échange

welfarism ['welfeə,rɪzəm] *n* théorie *f* de l'État providence

welfarist ['welfeərɪst] *n* partisan(e) *m,f* de l'État providence

well[1] [wel] **1** *n* (**a**) *(for water, oil)* puits *m* (**b**) *(for lift, staircase)* cage *f*; *(between buildings)* puits *m*, cheminée *f* (**c**) *Br Law* barreau *m (au tribunal)* (**d**) *Literary* source *f*, fontaine *f*

2 *vi* = **well up**

►**well out** *vi (water)* jaillir

►**well up** *vi (blood, spring, tears)* monter, jaillir; **tears welled up in her eyes** les larmes lui montèrent aux yeux; **joy welled up within her** la joie monta en elle

---

WELL[2] *(compar* **better** ['betə(r)], *superl* **best** [best]) **1** *adv* (**a**) *(satisfactorily, successfully)* bien; **she speaks French very well** elle parle très bien (le) français; **he plays the piano well** il joue bien du piano; **she came out of it rather well** elle s'en est plutôt bien sortie; **it's extremely well done** c'est vraiment très bien fait; **everything is going well** tout se passe bien; **the meeting went well** la réunion s'est bien passée; **those colours go really well together** ces couleurs vont vraiment bien ensemble; **the machine/system works well** la machine/le système marche bien; **things have worked out well** les choses se sont bien passées; **does she work as well as I do?** fait elle son travail aussi bien que moi?; **to do well** s'en sortir; **she's doing very well** elle s'en sort très bien; **he did very well for a beginner** il s'est très bien débrouillé pour un débutant; **you did quite well in the exam** vous vous en êtes assez bien sorti à l'examen; **to do well for oneself** bien se débrouiller; **to do well out of sb/sth** bien s'en sortir avec qn/qch; **that boy will do well!** ce garçon ira loin!; **the patient is doing well** le malade se rétablit bien *ou* est en bonne voie de guérison; **we would do well to keep quiet** nous ferions bien de nous taire; **well done!** bravo!; **well said!** bien dit!; **it was money well spent** ce n'était pas de l'argent gaspillé; *Arch* **well met!** heureuse rencontre!, vous arrivez bien à propos!

(**b**) *(favourably, kindly)* bien; **she treats her staff very well** elle traite très bien son personnel; **everyone speaks well of you** tout le monde dit du bien de vous; **his action speaks well of his courage** son geste montre bien son courage; **she won't take it well** elle ne va pas apprécier; **she thinks well of you** elle a de l'estime pour vous; **he wished her well** il lui souhaita bonne chance; **it's a card from someone wishing you well** c'est une carte de quelqu'un qui vous veut du bien; **to do well by sb** traiter qn comme il se doit

(**c**) *(easily, readily)* bien; **he could well decide to leave** il se pourrait tout à fait qu'il décide de partir; **I couldn't very well accept** je ne pouvais guère accepter; **you may well be right** il se peut bien que tu aies raison; **I can well believe it** je le crois facilement *ou* sans peine; **she was angry, and well she might be** elle était furieuse, et à juste titre

(**d**) *(to a considerable extent or degree)* bien; **she's well over** *or* **past forty** elle a bien plus de quarante ans; **he's well into his seventies** il a largement dépassé les soixante-dix ans; **there were well over 5,000 demonstrators** il y avait bien plus de 5000 manifestants; **he's well on in years** il n'est plus tout jeune; **well on into the morning** jusque tard dans la matinée; **the fashion lasted well into the 1960s** cette mode a duré une bonne partie des années 60; **it's well above/within the limit** c'est bien au-dessus de/inférieur à la limite; **it's well after midday** il est bien plus de midi; **the play went on until well after midnight** la partie s'est prolongée bien au-delà de minuit; **I woke well before dawn** je me suis réveillé bien avant l'aube; **let me know well in advance** prévenez-moi longtemps à l'avance; **the team finished well up the league** l'équipe a fini parmi les premières de sa division

(**e**) *(thoroughly)* bien; **shake/stir well** bien secouer/remuer; **be sure to cook it well** veillez à ce que ce soit bien cuit; **well cooked** *or* **done** bien cuit; **let it dry well first** attendez d'abord que ce soit bien sec; **I know her well** je la connais bien; **you know your subject well** vous connaissez bien votre sujet; **I know only too well how hard it is** je ne sais que trop bien à quel point c'est difficile; **how well I understand her feelings!** comme je comprends ce qu'elle ressent!; **I'm well aware of the problem** je suis bien conscient *ou* j'ai bien conscience du problème; **he was well annoyed** il était vraiment contrarié; *Ironic* **I bet he was well pleased!** il devait être content!; **I like him well enough** il ne me déplaît pas; **we got well and truly soaked** nous nous sommes fait tremper jusqu'aux os; **it's well and truly over** c'est bel et bien fini; **it's well worth the money** ça vaut largement la dépense; **it's well worth trying** ça vaut vraiment la peine d'essayer; *Fam* **he was well annoyed** il était super-énervé

(**f**) *(idioms)* **to be well away** *(making good progress)* être sur la bonne voie; *(drunk)* être complètement parti; **to be well in with sb** être bien avec qn; **she's well in with all the right people** elle est très bien avec tous les gens qui peuvent servir; **to be well out of it** s'en sortir à bon compte; **you're well out of it** tu as bien fait de partir; **she's well rid of him/it!** quel bon débarras pour elle!; **to be well up on sth** s'y connaître en qch; **she's well up on European law** elle s'y connait en droit européen; **to leave** *or* **let well alone** *(equipment)* ne pas toucher; *(situation)* ne pas s'occuper de; *(person)* laisser tranquille

2 *adj* (**a**) *(good)* bien, bon; **all is not well with them** il y a quelque chose qui ne va pas chez eux; **owning a home is all very well but...** c'est bien beau d'être propriétaire mais...; **it's all very well pretending you don't care but...** c'est bien beau de dire que ça t'est égal mais...; **it is all very well for you to say that** tu peux bien dire ça, toi; *Mil* **all's well!** rien à signaler!

(**b**) *(advisable)* bien; **it would be well to start soon** nous ferions bien de commencer bientôt; *Br* **you'd be just as well to tell him** tu ferais mieux de (le) lui dire

(**c**) *(in health)* **to be well** aller *ou* se porter bien; **how are you? – well, thank you** comment allez-vous? – bien, merci; **he's been ill but he's better now** il a été malade mais il va mieux (maintenant); **I don't feel well** je ne me sens pas bien; **she's not very well** elle ne va pas très bien; **to get well** se remettre, aller mieux; **get well soon** *(on card)* bon rétablissement; **I hope you're well** j'espère que vous allez bien; **you're looking** *or* **you look well** vous avez l'air en forme; **are you okay?, you don't sound very well** ça va?, tu n'as pas l'air bien; **he's not a well man** il ne se porte pas bien

3 *exclam* (**a**) *(indicating start or continuation of speech)* bon, bien; **well, I would just say one thing** bon, je voudrais simplement dire une chose; **well, let me just add that...** alors, laissez-moi simplement ajouter que...; **well, here we are again!** et nous y revoilà!

(**b**) *(indicating change of topic or end of conversation)* **well, as I was saying...** donc, je disais que..., je disais donc que...; **right, well, let's move on to the next subject** bon, alors passons à la question suivante; **well thank you Mr Alderson, I'll be in touch** eh bien merci M. Alderson, je vous contacterai

(**c**) *(softening a statement)* **well, obviously I'd like to come but...** disons que, bien sûr, j'aimerais venir mais...; **he was, well, rather unpleasant really** il a été, disons, assez désagréable, c'est le mot

(**d**) *(expanding on or explaining a statement)* **he was rather fat, well stout might be a better word** il était plutôt gros, enfin disons corpulent; **I've known her for ages, well at least three years** ça fait des années que je la connais, enfin au moins trois ans; **you know John? well I saw him yesterday** tu connais John? eh bien je l'ai vu hier

(**e**) *(expressing hesitation or doubt)* ben, eh bien; **did you ask? – well... I didn't dare actually** as-tu demandé? – eh bien *ou* ben, je n'ai pas osé; **are you ready? – well, I should really stay in and work** tu viens? – eh bien, il vaudrait mieux que je reste à la maison pour travailler

(**f**) *(asking a question)* eh bien, alors; **well, who was it?** alors *ou* eh bien, qui était-ce?; **well, what of it?** et alors?; **well then, why worry about it?** eh bien *ou* alors, pourquoi se faire du mauvais sang?

(**g**) *(expressing surprise or anger)* **well, look who's here!** ça alors, regardez qui est là!; **well, well, well** tiens, tiens; **well, really!** ça alors!; *Fam* **well I never!** ça par exemple!; **(well,) well, what do you know!** eh bien *ou* ça alors, qui l'aurait cru!

(**h**) *(in relief)* eh bien; **well, at least that's over!** eh bien, en tout cas, c'est terminé!

(**i**) *(in resignation)* bon; **(oh) well, it can't be helped** bon tant pis, on n'y peut rien; **(oh) well, that's life** bon enfin, c'est la vie; **(oh) well, all right** bon allez, d'accord; **can I come too? – oh, very well, if you must** je peux venir aussi? – bon allez, si tu y tiens

4 *npl* **the well** ceux *mpl* qui sont en bonne santé

5 all well and good *adv* tout ça, c'est très bien; **so you want to go to drama school, all well and good, but...** alors comme ça, tu veux faire une école de théâtre? tout ça, c'est très bien mais...

'The Well-Tempered Clavier' *Bach* 'Le Clavier bien tempéré'

> **Didn't he/she do well?**
> Le jeu télévisé britannique *The Generation Game* fut présenté pendant de nombreuses années par un nommé Bruce Forsyth. Cette expression ("il/elle s'est bien débrouillé(e), vous ne trouvez pas?") était l'une des petites phrases qu'il employait immanquablement au cours de l'émission. Il utilisait cette formule en s'adressant au public lorsqu'un concurrent venait de terminer une épreuve.
> Aujourd'hui, on emploie cette expression pour féliciter quelqu'un sur un ton légèrement condescendant.

we'll [wi:l] (**a**) = **we shall** (**b**) = **we will**

well-adjusted *adj (person → psychologically)* équilibré; *(→ to society, work)* bien adapté

well-advised *adj* sage, prudent; **he would be well-advised to leave** il aurait intérêt à partir

well-aimed [-eɪmd] *adj (shot)* bien ajusté; *(criticism, remark)* qui porte

well-appointed [-ə'pɔɪntɪd] *adj Br Formal (house)* bien équipé; *(hotel)* de catégorie supérieure

well-argued [-'ɑ:gju:d] *adj* bien argumenté; **a well-argued case** un point de vue bien argumenté

well-attended [-ə'tendɪd] *adj* **the meeting was well-attended** il y avait beaucoup de monde à la réunion; **the classes were not well-attended** les cours étaient peu suivis

well-balanced *adj (person)* équilibré, posé; *(diet)* bien équilibré; *(sentence)* bien construite

well-behaved [-bɪ'heɪvd] *adj (person)* bien élevé; *(animal)* bien dressé

wellbeing [ˌwel'bi:ɪŋ] *n* bien-être *m inv*; **the general wellbeing of the population** le bien-être général de la population; **he felt a sense of wellbeing** il éprouvait une impression de bien-être; **for your own wellbeing** pour votre bien

well-beloved *adj Literary* bien-aimé

well-born *adj* de bonne famille; **she was not sufficiently well-born to marry him** elle n'était pas assez bien née pour l'épouser

well-bred *adj* (**a**) *(well-behaved)* bien élevé (**b**) *(from good family)* de bonne famille (**c**) *(animal)* de (bonne) race; *(horse)* pur-sang *(inv)*

well-brought-up *adj* bien élevé

well-built *adj* (**a**) *(person)* bien bâti (**b**) *(building)* bien construit

well-chilled *adj (wine)* frais (fraîche)

well-chosen *adj (present, words)* bien choisi

well-conducted *adj (business, operation)* bien mené

well-connected *adj (of good family)* de bonne famille; *(having influential friends)* qui a des relations

well-defined [-dɪ'faɪnd] *adj* (**a**) *(distinct → colour, contrasts, shape)* bien défini, net (**b**) *(precise → problem)* bien défini, précis; **within well-defined limits** dans des limites bien définies

well-deserved [-dɪ'zɜ:vd] *adj* bien mérité

well-designed [-dɪ'zaɪnd] *adj* bien conçu

well-developed *adj* (**a**) *(person)* bien fait; *(body, muscles)* bien développé (**b**) *(scheme)* bien développé; *(idea)* bien exposé

welldigger ['welˌdɪgə(r)] *n* puisatier *m*

well-disposed [-dɪ'spəʊzd] *adj* bien disposé; **to be well-disposed to** *or* **towards sb** être bien disposé envers qn; **to be well-disposed to** *or* **towards sth** voir qch d'un bon œil

well-documented [-'dɒkjʊmentɪd] *adj* bien documenté

well-done *adj (work)* bien fait; *(meat)* bien cuit

well-dressed *adj* bien habillé

well-earned [-ɜ:nd] *adj* bien mérité

well-educated *adj* cultivé, instruit

well-endowed [-ɪn'daʊd] *adj Euph Fig* **a well-endowed young man/woman** un jeune homme bien doté/une jeune femme bien dotée par la nature; **she's well-endowed!** elle a une belle poitrine!, il y a du monde au balcon!

well-equipped [-ɪ'kwɪpt] *adj (garage, kitchen, person)* bien équipé; *(with tools)* bien outillé; **the vans are well-equipped to deal with any emergency** les camionnettes sont équipées pour faire face à toute urgence

well-established *adj* bien établi

well-favoured *adj Arch* beau (belle)

well-fed *adj (animal, person)* bien nourri

well-fixed *adj Am Fam* à l'aise ❑

well-formed *adj (gen) & Ling* bien formé

well-founded [-'faʊndɪd] *adj (doubt, suspicion)* fondé, légitime

well-groomed *adj (person)* soigné; *(hair)* bien coiffé; *(horse)* bien pansé; *(garden, lawn)* bien entretenu

well-grounded *adj* fondé

wellhead ['welhed] *n also Fig* source *f*

well-heeled [-hi:ld] *adj Fam* à l'aise ❑

well-hung *adj* (**a**) *(game)* bien faisandé (**b**) *very Fam (man)* bien monté

wellie = **welly**

well-in *adj Fam* (**a**) *Br* **to be well-in with sb** être bien avec qn ❑ (**b**) *Austr (rich)* à l'aise ❑

well-informed *adj (having information)* bien informé *ou* renseigné; *(knowledgeable)* instruit; **in well-informed circles** dans les milieux bien informés; **he's very well-informed about current affairs** il est très au courant de l'actualité

Wellington ['welɪŋtən] **1** *n Geog* Wellington *f*

2 *npr* Wellington

wellington ['welɪŋtən] *n Br (boot)* botte *f* (en caoutchouc)

►► ***wellington boot*** botte *f* en caoutchouc

Wellingtonia [ˌwelɪŋ'təʊnɪə] *n Bot* séquoia *m*, wellingtonia *m*

well-intentioned [-ɪn'tenʃənd] *adj* bien intentionné

well-judged [-'dʒʌdʒd] *adj (remark)* bien vu, judicieux; *(shot, throw)* bien jugé; *(estimate)* juste; *(moment)* opportun

well-kept *adj* (**a**) *(hands, nails)* soigné; *(hair)* bien coiffé; *(house)* bien tenu; *(garden)* bien entretenu (**b**) *(secret)* bien gardé

well-knit *adj (person, body)* bien bâti; *(argument)* bien enchaîné

well-known *adj (person)* connu, célèbre; *(fact)* bien connu; **it is well-known** *or* **it is a well-known fact that she disagrees with the policy** tout le monde sait qu'elle n'est pas d'accord avec cette politique; **what is less well-known is that she's an accomplished actress** ce qu'on sait moins, c'est que c'est une très bonne actrice

well-liked [-laɪkt] *adj* apprécié

well-loved *adj* très aimé

well-made *adj (furniture)* bien fait, de fabrication soignée; *(garment)* de coupe soignée; *(play)* bien construit

►► *Theat* ***well-made play*** pièce *f* bien faite

well-mannered *adj* qui a de bonnes manières, bien élevé

well-matched *adj (couple)* faits l'un pour l'autre; *(teams)* de force égale

well-meaning *adj* bien intentionné

well-meant *adj (action, remark)* bien intentionné

well-nigh *adv* presque; **it's well-nigh impossible** c'est presque *ou* quasi impossible

well-off 1 *adj* (**a**) *(financially)* aisé (**b**) *(in a good position)* **they were still well-off for supplies** ils avaient encore largement assez de provisions; *Fig* **you don't know when you're well-off** vous ne connaissez pas votre bonheur

2 *npl* **the well-off** les riches *mpl*; **the less well-off** ceux qui ont des moyens modestes

well-oiled *adj* (**a**) *(machinery)* bien graissé; **the operation ran like a well-oiled machine** l'opération s'est parfaitement déroulée (**b**) *Fam (drunk)* pompette

well-ordered *adj (life)* bien réglé; *(place)* bien tenu

well-padded *adj Fam Euph* bien enveloppé

well-paid *adj* bien payé

well-placed [-pleɪst] *adj* bien placé; **to be well-placed to do sth** être bien placé pour faire qch

well-prepared *adj* bien préparé

well-preserved [-prɪ'zɜ:vd] *adj (person, building)* bien conservé

well-proportioned [-prə'pɔ:ʃənd] *adj* bien proportionné

well-read [-red] *adj* cultivé, érudit; **she's very well-read** elle est très cultivée

well-respected *adj* respecté

well-rounded *adj* (**a**) *(complete → education)* complet(ète); *(→ life)* bien rempli (**b**) *(figure)* rondelet (**c**) *(style)* harmonieux; *(sentence)* bien tourné

well-spent *adj (time)* bien utilisé, qui n'est pas perdu; *(money)* utilement dépensé, que l'on n'a pas gaspillé; **it's money well-spent** c'est un bon investissement

well-spoken *adj (person)* qui s'exprime bien

well-spoken-of *adj* **she's very well-spoken-of in business circles** on dit beaucoup de bien d'elle dans le milieu des affaires

wellspring ['welsprɪŋ] *n* source *f*; *Fig* source *f* intarissable

well-stacked *adj Br very Fam (woman)* qui a de gros nichons; **she's well-stacked** il y a du monde au balcon

well-stocked [-stɒkt] *adj (shop)* bien approvisionné

well-thought-of *adj* bien considéré

well-thought-out *adj* bien conçu

well-thumbed [-θʌmd] *adj (magazine)* qui a été beaucoup feuilleté; *(book)* lu et relu

well-timed [-'taɪmd] *adj (arrival, remark)* opportun, qui tombe à point; *(blow)* bien calculé

well-to-do 1 *adj* aisé, riche

2 *npl* **the well-to-do** les nantis *mpl*

well-travelled *adj* qui a beaucoup voyagé

well-tried *adj* éprouvé, qui a fait ses preuves

well-trodden *adj* **a well-trodden path** un chemin très fréquenté; *Fig* **a well-trodden path to fame** le parcours classique vers la célébrité

well-turned *adj (ankle)* fin; *(leg)* bien galbé; *Br (sentence)* bien tourné

well-upholstered [-ʌp'həʊlstəd] *adj Fam Euph (person)* bien rembourré

wel–wel

well-versed *adj* **to be well-versed in sth** bien connaître qch

well-wisher [-ˌwɪʃə(r)] *n (gen)* personne *f* qui offre son soutien; *(of cause, group)* sympathisant(e) *m,f*, partisan *m*; **surrounded by well-wishers** entouré d'admirateurs

well-woman clinic *n* centre *m* de santé pour femmes

well-worn *adj* (**a**) *(carpet, clothes)* usé, usagé (**b**) *(path)* battu (**c**) *(expression, joke)* rebattu; **a well-worn phrase** une banalité, un lieu commun

welly ['welɪ] *(pl* **wellies**) *n Br Fam* (**a**) *(boot)* botte *f* (en caoutchouc)❑ (**b**) *(idiom)* **give it some welly!** du nerf!

Welsh [welʃ] **1** *npl* **the Welsh** les Gallois *mpl*

2 *n Ling* gallois *m*

3 *adj* gallois

►► ***the Welsh Assembly*** l'Assemblée *f* galloise *ou* du pays de Galles; ***Welsh dresser*** vaisselier *m*; ***the Welsh Guards*** = régiment de l'armée britannique; ***Welsh harp*** harpe *f* galloise; ***the Welsh Office*** = secrétariat d'État aux affaires galloises; *Br* ***Welsh rabbit, Welsh rarebit*** ≃ toast *m* au fromage

WELSH

Jusqu'au milieu du XIXème siècle, pratiquement la moitié de la population du pays de Galles parlait gallois; un siècle plus tard, son usage avait décliné de façon spectaculaire. Aujourd'hui, grâce à la politique mise en place suite au développement d'un important mouvement nationaliste dans les années 60, le gallois est la langue celtique la plus parlée. On estime que le gallois est la première ou la seconde langue d'environ 20 pour cent des trois millions de Gallois. Des organisations, telle la "Society for the Welsh Language", se sont battues pour donner au gallois le statut de langue officielle, au même titre que l'anglais. De nos jours, beaucoup d'écoles choisissent le gallois comme langue d'enseignement et il existe plusieurs chaînes de télévision et de radio galloises.

THE WELSH ASSEMBLY

L'assemblée nationale du pays de Galles fut établie dans le cadre de la décentralisation (voir aussi l'encadré à **devolution**) engagée par le gouvernement travailliste et fut inaugurée à Cardiff en mai 1999. Les soixante membres de l'assemblée forment le "Welsh Cabinet" et siègent sous la houlette du "First Secretary" qui représente les intérêts gallois au parlement de Westminster. L'assemblée nationale du pays de Galles, la première depuis six siècles, a toutefois moins de pouvoirs que le parlement écossais mis en place en même temps.

welsh [welʃ] *vi Br Fam* décamper sans payer; **to welsh on a debt** décamper sans payer une dette; **to welsh on a promise** ne pas tenir une promesse❑

Welshman ['welʃmən] *(pl* **Welshmen** [-mən]) *n* Gallois *m*

Welshwoman ['welʃwʊmən] *(pl* **Welshwomen** [-ˌwɪmɪn]) *n* Galloise *f*

welt [welt] *n* (**a**) *(on skin)* zébrure *f* (**b**) *(on garment)* bordure *f*; *(on shoe)* trépointe *f*

welted ['weltɪd] *adj (shoe, sole)* à trépointes

►► ***welted joint*** *(in plumbing)* agrafe *f*; ***welted pocket*** poche *f* passepoilée, poche *f* à patte de gilet

welter ['weltə(r)] **1** *vi Literary* se vautrer, se rouler

2 *n* confusion *f*; **a welter of detail** une profusion de détails; **a welter of conflicting information** une avalanche d'informations contradictoires

welterweight ['weltəweɪt] *Boxing* **1** *n* poids *m* welter

2 *comp (champion)* des poids welter; *(fight, title)* de poids welter

Wembley ['wemblɪ] *n (stadium)* Wembley *m (stade londonien)*

►► ***Wembley Arena*** = salle de concert londonienne; ***Wembley Stadium*** Wembley *m (stade londonien)*

wen [wen] *n* (**a**) *Med* loupe *f*, *Spec* kyste *m* sébacé (**b**) *(city)* **the great wen** Londres *f*

Wenceslas ['wensɪsləs] *pr n* Venceslas

wench [wentʃ] **1** *n* (**a**) *Arch or Hum (young woman)* jeune fille *f*, jeune femme *f* (**b**) *Arch* **(serving) wench** *(in inn)* serveuse *f* (**c**) *Arch (prostitute)* fille *f* de joie

2 *vi Arch* **to go wenching** aller courir le jupon

wencher ['wentʃə(r)] *n Arch or Hum* coureur *m* de jupons

wend [wend] *vt Literary* s'acheminer; **to wend one's way home** s'acheminer vers chez soi; **he wended his way through the forest** il s'achemina à travers la forêt

Wendy house ['wendɪ-] *n Br* = maison en miniature dans laquelle les jeunes enfants peuvent jouer

Wensleydale ['wenzlɪdeɪl] *n* = fromage anglais à pâte dure originaire de Wensleydale

went [went] *pt of* **go**

wentletrap ['wentəlˌtræp] *n Zool* scalaire *f*

wept [wept] *pt & pp of* **weep**

were [wɜː(r)] *pt of* **be**

we're [wɪə(r)] = **we are**

weren't [wɜːnt] = **were not**

werewolf ['wɪəwʊlf] *(pl* **werewolves** [-wʊlvz]) *n* loup-garou *m*

wert [wɜːt] *NEng or Arch or Literary* = **were**

Wesleyan ['wezlɪən] *Rel* **1** *adj* de Wesley, wesleyen

2 *n* disciple *m* de Wesley

►► ***Wesleyan Methodists*** méthodistes *mpl* wesleyens

west [west] **1** *n* (**a**) *Geog* ouest *m*; **in the west** à l'ouest, dans l'ouest; **the house lies to the west (of the town)** la maison se trouve à l'ouest (de la ville); **two miles to the west** trois kilomètres à l'ouest; **look towards the west** regardez vers l'ouest; **I was born in the west** je suis né dans l'Ouest; **in the west of Austria** dans l'ouest de l'Autriche; **on the west of the island** à l'ouest de l'île; **the wind is in the west** le vent est à l'ouest; **the wind is coming from the west** le vent vient *ou* souffle de l'ouest; **the West** *(the Occident)* l'Occident *m*, les pays *mpl* occidentaux; *(in US)* l'Ouest *m (États situés à l'ouest du Mississippi)*

(**b**) *Cards* ouest *m*

2 *adj* (**a**) *Geog* ouest *(inv)*, de l'ouest; *(country)* de l'Ouest; *(wall)* exposé à l'ouest; **the west coast** la côte ouest; **in west London** dans l'ouest de Londres; **on the west side** du côté ouest

(**b**) *(wind)* d'ouest

3 *adv* à l'ouest; *(travel)* vers l'ouest, en direction de l'ouest; **the village lies west of Manchester** le village est situé à l'ouest de Manchester; **the living room faces west** la salle de séjour est exposée à l'ouest; **the path heads (due) west** le chemin va *ou* mène (droit) vers l'ouest; **drive west until you come to a main road** roulez vers l'ouest jusqu'à ce que vous arriviez à une route principale; **I travelled west** je suis allé vers l'ouest; **he travelled west for three days** pendant trois jours, il a voyagé en direction de l'ouest; **to sail west** naviguer cap sur l'ouest; **it's 20 miles west of Edinburgh** c'est à 32 kilomètres à l'ouest d'Édimbourg; **west by north/by south** ouest-quart-nord-ouest/ouest-quart-sud-ouest; **the school lies further west of the town hall** l'école se trouve plus à l'ouest de la mairie; **to go west** aller à *ou* vers l'ouest; *Fam Hum (person)* passer l'arme à gauche; *(thing)* tomber à l'eau; *Fam* **there's another job gone west!** encore un emploi de perdu!

►► ***West Africa*** Afrique *f* occidentale; ***West African*** **1** *n* habitant(e) *m,f* de l'Afrique occidentale **2** *adj (languages, states)* de l'Afrique occidentale, ouest-africain; ***the West Bank*** la Cisjordanie; **on the West Bank** en Cisjordanie; *Formerly* ***West Berlin*** Berlin *m* Ouest; *Formerly* ***West Berliner*** habitant(e) *m,f* de Berlin Ouest; *Ir Fam Pej* ***West Brit*** = terme péjoratif désignant les Irlandais qui cherchent à s'angliciser par l'accent, le mode de vie etc; ***the West Coast*** la côte ouest *(des États-Unis)*; ***the West Country*** = le sud-ouest de l'Angleterre (Cornouailles, Devon et Somerset); **in the West Country** dans le sud-ouest de l'Angleterre; ***the West End*** *n (in general)* les quartiers *mpl* ouest; *(of London)* le West End *(centre touristique et commercial de la ville de Londres connu pour ses théâtres)*; **in the West End** dans le West End; *Formerly* ***West German*** **1** *n* Allemand(e) *m,f* de l'Ouest **2** *adj* ouest-allemand; *Formerly* ***West Germany*** Allemagne *f* de l'Ouest; **in West Germany** en Allemagne de l'Ouest; ***West Glamorgan*** le West Glamorgan, = comté du sud-ouest du pays de Galles; **in West Glamorgan** dans le West Glamorgan; ***West Highland terrier*** terrier *m* écossais, West Highland terrier *m*; ***West Indian*** **1** *n* Antillais(e) *m,f* **2** *adj* antillais; ***the West Indies*** les Antilles *fpl*; **in the West Indies** aux Antilles; **the French West Indies** les Antilles françaises; **the Dutch West Indies** les Antilles néerlandaises; ***the West Midlands*** les West Midlands *mpl*, = comté du centre de l'Angleterre; **in the West Midlands** dans les West Midlands; ***West Point*** = importante école militaire américaine; *Am* ***the West Side*** les quartiers *mpl* ouest de New York; ***West Sussex*** le Sussex occidental, = comté du sud de l'Angleterre; **in West Sussex** dans le Sussex occidental; ***West Virginia*** la Virginie-Occidentale; **in West Virginia** en Virginie-Occidentale; ***West Yorkshire*** le West Yorkshire, = comté du nord de l'Angleterre; **in West Yorkshire** dans le West Yorkshire

'Once Upon a Time in the West' *Leone* 'Il était une fois dans l'ouest'

Go West young man

On attribue cette phrase ("va vers l'Ouest, jeune homme") à John Soule, journaliste américain de l'Indiana qui l'aurait employée pour la première fois en 1851. Il s'agit d'une allusion à la colonisation de l'ouest américain mais on emploie cette formule dans d'autres contextes, lorsque quelqu'un part en voyage vers l'Ouest, quel que soit le pays où il se trouve, ou bien en l'adaptant en remplaçant ouest par un autre terme. On utilise aussi cette expression pour encourager quelqu'un à faire preuve d'ambition et à se déplacer de façon à trouver du travail.

westbound ['westbaʊnd] *adj (traffic)* en direction de l'ouest; *(lane, carriageway)* de l'ouest; *(road)* qui va vers l'ouest; **westbound traffic is subject to delays** la circulation est ralentie dans le sens ouest; *Br* **the westbound carriageway of the motorway is closed** l'axe ouest de l'autoroute est fermé (à la circulation); **there are roadworks on the westbound carriageway of the motorway** il y a des travaux sur l'autoroute en direction de l'ouest; **there's a jam on the westbound carriageway** il y a un bouchon en direction de l'ouest

wester ['westə(r)] *vi (sun, moon)* passer à l'ouest

westering ['westərɪŋ] *adj Literary* qui passe à l'ouest; **the westering sun** le soleil couchant

westerly ['westəlɪ] *(pl* **westerlies**) **1** *adj* (**a**) *Geog* ouest *(inv)*, de l'ouest; **to travel in a westerly direction** aller vers l'ouest; **westerly point** point *m* situé à l'ouest *ou* vers l'ouest; **the most westerly point on the island** le point le plus à l'ouest de l'île; **a room with a westerly aspect** une pièce exposée à l'ouest; *Naut* **to steer a westerly course** faire route vers l'ouest; *(when setting out)* mettre le cap à l'ouest

(**b**) *(wind)* d'ouest

2 *adv* vers l'ouest, en direction de l'ouest

3 *n* vent *m* d'ouest

western ['westən] **1** *adj* (**a**) *Geog* ouest *(inv)*, de l'ouest; *(of West)* occidental; **the western wing of the castle** l'aile ouest du château; **in western Spain** dans l'ouest de l'Espagne; **the western side of the country** la partie ouest du pays

(**b**) *(wind)* d'ouest

(**c**) *Pol (powers, technology, world)* occidental

2 *n (film)* western *m*; *(book)* roman-western *m*

►► ***Western Australia*** l'Australie-Occidentale *f*; **in Western Australia** en Australie-Occidentale; ***the Western Church*** l'Église *f* d'Occident *ou* latine; ***Western Europe*** Europe *f* occidentale; ***Western Isles*** les Hébrides *fpl*; **in the Western Isles** aux Hébrides; *Sport* ***western roll*** rouleau *m* costal; ***Western Sahara*** le Sahara occidental; **in** the **Western Sahara** au Sahara occidental; ***Western Samoa*** Samoa *fpl* occidentales; **in Western Samoa** dans les Samoa occidentales; ***Western Union*** = compagnie américaine privée des télégraphes

Westerner ['westənə(r)] *n* habitant(e) *m,f* de l'ouest; *Pol* Occidental(e) *m,f*

westernization [,westənaɪ'zeɪʃən] *n* occidentalisation *f*

westernize, -ise ['westənaɪz] *vt* occidentaliser; **Japan is becoming increasingly westernized** le Japon s'occidentalise de plus en plus

westernmost ['westənməʊst] *adj* le plus à l'ouest

west-facing *adj (house, wall)* (exposé) à l'ouest *ou* au couchant

Westie ['westɪ] *n Fam (West Highland Terrier)* terrier *m* écossais ❑, West Highland terrier ❑ *m*

westing ['westɪŋ] *n Naut* chemin *m* ouest

Westmeath [,west'miːð] *n* le comté de Westmeath, = comté du centre de la République d'Irlande; **in Westmeath** dans le comté de Westmeath

Westminster ['westmɪnstə(r)] *n* = quartier du centre de Londres où se trouvent le Parlement et le palais de Buckingham

►► ***Westminster Abbey*** l'abbaye *f* de Westminster

WESTMINSTER

C'est dans ce quartier que se trouvent le Parlement et le palais de Buckingham. Le nom de "Westminster" est également employé pour désigner le Parlement lui-même.

westmost ['westməʊst] *adj* le plus à l'ouest

west-north-west 1 *n* ouest-nord-ouest *m*

2 *adj* (**a**) *Geog* ouest-nord-ouest *(inv)*, de l'ouest-nord-ouest (**b**) *(wind)* d'ouest-nord-ouest

3 *adv* à l'ouest-nord-ouest; *(travel)* vers l'ouest-nord-ouest, en direction de l'ouest-nord-ouest

Westphalia [west'feɪlɪə] *n* Westphalie *f*

Westphalian [west'feɪlɪən] **1** *adj* westphalien

2 *n* Westphalien(enne) *m,f*

west-south-west 1 *n* ouest-sud-ouest *m*

2 *adj* (**a**) *Geog* ouest-sud-ouest *(inv)*, de l'ouest-sud-ouest (**b**) *(wind)* d'ouest-sud-ouest

3 *adv* à l'ouest-sud-ouest; *(travel)* vers l'ouest-sud-ouest, en direction de l'ouest-sud-ouest

westward ['westwəd] **1** *adj* vers l'ouest, en direction de l'ouest

2 *adv* vers l'ouest, en direction de l'ouest; **to sail westward** naviguer cap sur l'ouest

3 *n* ouest *m*

westwardly ['westwədlɪ] **1** *adj* vers l'ouest, en direction de l'ouest

2 *adv* vers l'ouest, en direction de l'ouest

westwards ['westwədz] *adv* en direction de *ou* vers l'ouest; **to sail westwards** naviguer cap sur l'ouest

wet [wet] *(compar* **wetter,** *superl* **wettest,** *pt & pp* **wet** *or* **wetted,** *cont* **wetting) 1** *adj* (**a**) *(ground, person, umbrella → gen)* mouillé; *(→ damp)* humide; *(→ soaked)* trempé; **to get wet** se mouiller; **I got my jacket wet** j'ai mouillé ma veste; **I got my feet wet** je me suis mouillé les pieds; **try not to get your shoes wet** essaie de ne pas mouiller tes chaussures; **to be wet through** *(person)* être trempé jusqu'aux os *ou* complètement trempé; *(clothes, towel)* être complètement trempé; **her eyes were wet with tears** elle avait les yeux baignés de larmes; **the roads can be slippery when wet** les routes mouillées peuvent être glissantes; *Fig* **to be (still) wet behind the ears** manquer d'expérience

(**b**) *(ink, paint, concrete)* frais (fraîche); **wet paint!** *(sign)* peinture fraîche!

(**c**) *(climate, weather → damp)* humide; *(→ rainy)* pluvieux; *(day)* pluvieux, de pluie; **it's going to be very wet all weekend** il va beaucoup pleuvoir tout ce week-end; **the wettest summer on record** l'été le plus humide dont on se souvienne; **in wet weather** par temps de pluie, quand il pleut; **the wet season** la saison des pluies

(**d**) *Br Fam (feeble)* faible ❑, mou (molle); **don't be so wet!** tu es une vraie lavette!; **he thinks it's wet to discuss emotions** il trouve ça mièvre de parler des sentiments ❑

(**e**) *Br Pol* modéré, mou (molle) *(du parti conservateur)*

(**f**) *Am Fam (wrong)* **to be all wet** avoir tort ❑

(**g**) *Am (state, town)* = où l'on peut acheter librement des boissons alcoolisées

2 *vt (hair, sponge, towel)* mouiller; **to wet oneself** *or* **one's pants** mouiller sa culotte; **to wet the bed** faire pipi au lit; **to wet one's lips** s'humecter les lèvres; **to wet oneself** *(from worry)* se faire de la bile; *(from laughter)* rire aux larmes; *Fam* **to wet one's whistle** boire un coup; *Fam Fig* **we'll have to wet the baby's head** il faudra qu'on arrose la naissance du bébé ❑

3 *n* (**a**) *Br (rain)* pluie *f*; *(damp)* humidité *f*; **to go out in the wet** sortir sous la pluie; **let's get in out of the wet** entrons, ne restons pas sous la pluie; **he left his bike out in the wet** il a laissé son vélo dehors sous la pluie

(**b**) *Austr* **the wet** la saison des pluies

(**c**) *Br Pol* modéré(e) *m,f*, mou (molle) *m,f (du parti conservateur)*

(**d**) *Br Fam Pej (feeble person)* lavette *f*

►► *Am* ***wet bar*** = minibar avec un petit évier; *Fam* ***wet blanket*** rabat-joie *m inv*; ***wet dock*** bassin *m* à flot; ***wet dream*** éjaculation *f ou* pollution *f* nocturne; ***wet fish*** poisson *m* frais; ***wet lease*** *(for aircraft)* location *f* d'avion avec équipage; ***wet nurse*** nourrice *f*; *Med* ***wet pack*** = traitement qui consiste à envelopper le malade dans des draps humides; ***wet rot*** *(UNCOUNT)* moisissure *f* humide; ***wet suit*** combinaison *f ou* ensemble *m* de plongée

wet and dry *n* = toile d'émeri très fine

wetback ['wetbæk] *n Am* = terme injurieux désignant un ouvrier mexicain entré illégalement aux États-Unis

wether ['weðə(r)] *n* bélier *m* châtré, mouton *m*

wetland ['wetlənd] *n* marécage *m*, marais *m*

wet-look 1 *adj (garment)* brillant; *(hairstyle)* luisant *(après application de gel)*; **a wet-look dress** une robe qui brille

2 *n* aspect *m* brillant

wetness ['wetnɪs] *n* humidité *f*; **the area is renowned for the wetness of its climate** la région est connue pour son climat pluvieux

wet-nurse *vt* servir de nourrice à, élever au sein

wetting agent ['wetɪŋ-] *n Chem* (agent *m*) mouillant *m*

wetting solution ['wetɪŋ-] *n (for contact lenses)* solution *f* de rinçage

wetware ['wetweə(r)] *n Fam* utilisateurs ❑ *mpl (d'un système informatique)*

wet-weather tyre *n* pneu *m* pluie

WEU [,dʌbəljuːiː'juː] *n Pol (abbr* **Western European Union)** UEO *f*

we've [wiːv] = **we have**

Wexford ['weksfəd] *n* (**a**) *(town)* Wexford (**b**) *(county)* le comté de Wexford, = comté du sud-est de la République d'Irlande; **in Wexford** dans le comté de Wexford

WFP [,dʌbəljuːef'piː] *n (abbr* **World Food Programme)** PAM *m*

WFTU [,dʌbəljuːef,tiː'juː] *n (abbr* **World Federation of Trade Unions)** FSM *f*

whack [wæk] *Fam* **1** *n* (**a**) *(thump)* claque *f*, grand coup ❑ *m*; *(sound)* claquement ❑ *m*, coup *m* sec ❑; **to give sb/sth a whack** donner un grand coup à qn/qch

(**b**) *(try)* essai *m*; **to have a whack at sth** essayer qch

(**c**) *Br (share)* part ❑ *f*; **he paid more than his whack** il a payé plus que sa part; **she didn't do her fair whack** elle n'a pas fait sa part du travail

(**d**) *(amount, rate)* **you're already earning the top whack for this job** tu gagnes déjà le maximum pour ce travail; **I'll pay 50 pounds, top whack** je paierai 50 livres, et pas un sou de plus; **we can offer you £50,000, top whack** nous pouvons vous offrir 50 000 livres, dernier prix *ou* grand maximum

(**e**) *Am (idiom)* **out of the whack** déglingué

2 *vt* (**a**) *(person → hit)* donner un coup *ou* des coups à ❑; *(→ spank)* donner une claque sur les fesses à; *(ball → hit)* donner un grand coup dans ❑; *(→ kick)* donner un grand coup de pied dans ❑; **to whack sb over the head** frapper qn sur la tête ❑; **to whack sb with a stick/a ruler** donner un coup de bâton/de règle à qn ❑ (**b**) *Br (defeat)* flanquer une dérouillée *ou* raclée à

3 *vi* **to whack at sth with a stick** donner un coup de bâton à qch

4 *exclam* vlan!

►**whack off** *vi Vulg* se branler

whacked [wækt] *adj Br Fam* vanné, crevé

whacker ['wækə(r)] *n Br Fam* (**a**) *(large object)* **he caught a real whacker** *(fish)* il a attrapé un poisson super géant; **he's got a whacker of a nose** il a un nez énorme ❑; **that sandwich is a real whacker** c'est un énorme sandwich *ou* un sandwich gigantesque ❑; **what a whacker!** il est gigantesque! (**b**) *Old-fashioned (lie)* gros mensonge *m*

whacking ['wækɪŋ] *Fam* **1** *adj Br* énorme ❑, colossal ❑

2 *adv* vachement; **a whacking great dog/house** un chien/une maison absolument énorme ❑

3 *n* (**a**) *(beating)* rossée *f*, raclée *f*; **his father gave him a whacking** son père lui a donné une raclée; **to get a whacking** prendre une raclée

(**b**) *(defeat)* **we gave them a whacking** on leur a mis la pâtée; **to get a whacking** prendre une raclée *ou* une déculottée

whacko [,wæk'əʊ] *exclam Fam Old-fashioned* épatant!, bath!

whacky *(compar* **whackier,** *superl* **whackiest)** = **wacky**

whale [weɪl] **1** *n* (**a**) *(mammal)* baleine *f*

(**b**) *Fam (idioms)* **we had a whale of a time** on s'est drôlement bien amusés; **a whale of a difference** une différence énorme ❑

2 *vi* (**a**) *(hunt whales)* pêcher la baleine

(**b**) *Am Fam* **to whale away at sth** s'en prendre à qch ❑

3 *vt Am Fam* (**a**) *(thump)* mettre une raclée à, rosser; **I'll whale the living daylights out of you!** je vais te mettre une de ces raclées!

(**b**) *(defeat)* mettre une raclée à

►► ***whale calf*** baleineau *m*; ***whale hunter*** baleinier *m*; ***whale oil*** huile *f* de baleine; ***whale shark*** requin-baleine *m*

whaleboat ['weɪlbəʊt] *n* baleinière *f*

whalebone ['weɪlbəʊn] *n* fanon *m* de baleine; *(in corset, dress)* baleine *f*

whaler ['weɪlə(r)] *n* (**a**) *(person)* pêcheur *m* de baleine (**b**) *(ship)* baleinier *m*

whaling ['weɪlɪŋ] **1** *n* (**a**) *(industry)* pêche *f* à la baleine (**b**) *Am Fam (thrashing)* rossée *f*, raclée *f*

2 *comp (industry, port)* baleinier; **International Whaling Commission** Commission *f* internationale baleinière

►► ***whaling ship*** baleinier *m*

wham [wæm] *(pt & pp* **whammed,** *cont* **whamming)** *Fam* **1** *n* **we hit the wall with a wham** et vlan! on est rentrés dans le mur

2 *exclam* vlan!; **it was wham, bam, thank you ma'am** il a tiré son coup et il s'est cassé

3 *vt* (**a**) *(hit → person)* donner une raclée à; *(→ ball)* donner un grand coup dans; **she whammed the ball over the net** d'un grand coup, elle a envoyé la balle par-dessus le filet

(**b**) *(crash → heavy object, vehicle)* rentrer dans ❑

4 *vi* **to wham into sth** rentrer dans qch ❑; **the ball whammed into the back of the net** le ballon a filé dans les buts; **her fist whammed into his face** son poing s'est écrasé sur son visage; **she whammed into the wall** elle s'est écrasée contre le mur; **the car whammed into the lamppost** la voiture est rentrée dans le réverbère

whammy ['wæmɪ] *n Fam Am* **to put the whammy on sb** mettre des bâtons dans les roues à qn

whang [wæŋ] *Fam* **1** *vt* cogner, battre (d'un coup retentissant) ❑

2 *n* coup *m* retentissant ❑; **I fell (with a) whang on the pavement** vlan! je suis tombé sur le trottoir

wharf [wɔːf] *(pl* **wharves** [wɔːvz] *or* **wharfs) 1** *n* quai *m*

2 *vt* (**a**) *(goods → store)* entreposer sur le quai; *(→ unload)* débarquer (**b**) *(ship)* amarrer à quai

3 *vi (ship)* venir à quai, amarrer à quai

wharfage ['wɔːfɪdʒ] *n* droits *mpl* de quai

WHAT [wɒt]

qu'est-ce qui	▸ **1 (a)**
que	▸ **1 (a)**
qu'est-ce que	▸ **1 (a)**
quoi	▸ **1 (a), (b), (d), (f)**
ce qui	▸ **1 (b), (f)**
ce que	▸ **1 (b), (f), (g)**
comment	▸ **1 (c)**
combien	▸ **1 (e)**
quel	▸ **2 (a); 3**

1 *pron* (**a**) *(in direct questions → as subject)* qu'est-ce qui, que; *(→ as object)* (qu'est-ce) que, quoi; *(→ after preposition)* quoi; **what do you want?** qu'est-ce que tu veux?, que veux-tu?; **what's happening?** qu'est-ce qui se passe?, que se passe-t-il?; **what's new?** quoi de neuf?; *Fam* **what's up?** qu'est-ce qu'il y a?❑; *Am (as greeting)* quoi de neuf?; **what's that for?** à quoi cela sert-il?, à quoi ça sert?; **what's the matter?, what is it?** qu'est-ce qu'il y a?; *Fam* **what's it to you?** qu'est-ce que ça peut te faire?; **what's that?** qu'est-ce que c'est que ça?; *(what did you say)* quoi?; **what's that building?** qu'est-ce que c'est que ce bâtiment?; **what's your phone number?** quel est votre numéro de téléphone?; **what's her name?** comment s'appelle-t-elle?; **what's the Spanish for "light"?** comment dit-on "light" en espagnol?; **what's the boss like?** comment est le patron?; **what is life without friends?** que vaut la vie sans amis?; *Fam* **what's up with him?** qu'est-ce qu'il a?❑; **what did I tell you?** *(gen)* qu'est-ce que je vous ai dit?; *(I told you so)* je vous l'avais bien dit!; **she must be, what, 50?** elle doit avoir, quoi, 50 ans?; **Mum? – what? – can I go out?** Maman? – quoi? – est-ce que je peux sortir?; **what are you thinking about?** à quoi pensez-vous?; **what did he die of?** de quoi est-il mort?; **what do you take me for?** pour qui me prenez-vous?; **what could be more beautiful?** quoi de plus beau?; *Formal or Hum* **to what do I owe this honour?** qu'est-ce qui me vaut cet honneur?

(**b**) *(in indirect questions → as subject)* ce qui; *(→ as object)* ce que, quoi; **tell us what happened** dites-nous ce qui s'est passé; **I wonder what she was thinking about!** je me demande ce qui lui est passé par la tête!; **I asked what it was all about** j'ai demandé de quoi il était question; **he didn't understand what I said** il n'a pas compris ce que j'ai dit; **I don't know what to do** je ne sais pas quoi faire; **I don't know what to do to help him** je ne sais pas quoi faire pour l'aider; **I don't know what that building is** je ne sais pas ce qu'est ce bâtiment

(**c**) *(asking someone to repeat something)* comment; **what's that?** qu'est-ce que tu dis?; **they bought what?** quoi, qu'est-ce qu'ils ont acheté?

(**d**) *(expressing surprise)* quoi; **what, another new dress?** quoi, encore une nouvelle robe?; **what, no coffee!** comment *ou* quoi? pas de café?; **he's going into the circus – what!** il va travailler dans un cirque – quoi?; **I found $350 – you what!** j'ai trouvé 350 dollars – quoi?; **I told her to leave – you did what!** je lui ai dit de partir – tu lui as dit quoi?

(**e**) *(how much)* **what's 17 minus 4?** combien *ou* que fait 17 moins 4?; **what does it cost?** combien est-ce que ça coûte?; **what do I owe you?** combien vous dois-je?; **do you know what he was asking for it?** savez-vous combien il en demandait?

(**f**) *(that which → as subject)* ce qui; *(→ as object)* ce que, quoi; **what you need is a hot bath** ce qu'il vous faut, c'est un bon bain chaud; **they spent what amounted to a week's salary** ils ont dépensé l'équivalent d'une semaine de salaire; **she has what it takes to succeed** elle a ce qu'il faut pour réussir; **that's what life is all about!** c'est ça la vie!; **education is not what it used to be** l'enseignement n'est plus ce qu'il était; **what is most remarkable is that...** ce qu'il y a de plus remarquable c'est que...; **it was pretty much what we expected** c'était plus ou moins ce qu'on avait imaginé; **what's done cannot be undone** ce qui est fait est fait; **and what is worse...** et ce qui est pire...

(**g**) *(whatever, everything that)* **they rescued what they could** ils ont sauvé ce qu'ils ont pu; **say what you will** vous pouvez dire *ou* vous direz tout ce que vous voudrez; **say what you will, I don't believe you** racontez tout ce que vous voulez, je ne vous crois pas; **come what may** advienne que pourra

(**h**) *Br Fam Old-fashioned (inviting agreement)* n'est-ce pas❑; **an interesting book, what?** un livre intéressant, n'est-ce pas *ou* pas vrai?

(**i**) *(idioms)* **I'll tell you what...** écoute!; **you know what...?** tu sais quoi...?; **I know what** j'ai une idée; **you'll never guess what** tu ne devineras jamais (quoi); *Fam* **documents, reports and what have you** *or* **and what not** des documents, des rapports et je ne sais quoi encore❑; *Fam* **and I don't know what** et que sais-je encore❑; *Fam* **and God knows what** et Dieu sait quoi; **have you got a flat, rooms or what?** vous avez un appartement, une chambre ou quoi?; **look, do you want to come or what?** alors, tu veux venir ou quoi?; **a trip to Turkey? – what next!** un voyage en Turquie? – et puis quoi encore!; **what have we here?** mais que vois-je?; **what then?** et après?; *Old-fashioned* **what ho!** eh! ho!; *(as greeting)* salut!; *Fam* **we need to find out what's what** il faut qu'on sache où en sont les choses; *Fam* **she told me what was what** elle m'a mis au courant; *Fam* **they know what's what in art** ils s'y connaissent en art❑; *Fam* **I'll show him what's what!** je vais lui montrer de quel bois je me chauffe!

2 *adj* (**a**) *(in questions → singular)* quel (quelle); *(→ plural)* quels (quelles); **what books did you buy?** quels livres avez-vous achetés?; **what colour/size is it?** de quelle couleur/taille c'est?; **(at) what time will you be arriving?** à quelle heure arriverez-vous?; **what day is it?** quel jour sommes-nous?; **what good** *or* **use is this?** à quoi ça sert?

(**b**) *(as many as, as much as)* **I gave her what money I had** je lui ai donné le peu d'argent que j'avais; **he gathered what strength he had** il a rassemblé le peu de forces qui lui restaient; **what time we had left was spent (in) packing** on a passé le peu de temps qui nous restait à faire les valises; **they stole what little money she had** ils lui ont volé le peu d'argent qu'elle avait; **I gave her what comfort I could** je l'ai consolée autant que j'ai pu

3 *predet (expressing an opinion or a reaction)* **what a suggestion!** quelle idée!; **what a strange thing!** comme c'est bizarre!; **what a pity!** comme c'est *ou* quel dommage!; **what an idiot he is!** comme il est bête!, qu'il est bête!; **what lovely children you have!** quels charmants enfants vous avez!; **what a lot of people!** que de gens!, que de monde!; **you can't imagine what a time we had getting here** vous ne pouvez pas vous imaginer le mal qu'on a eu à venir jusqu'ici

4 *adv (in rhetorical questions)* **what do I care?** qu'est-ce que ça peut me faire?; **what does it matter?** qu'est-ce que ça peut faire?; **well, what of it?** et bien?, et après?

5 what about *adv* **what about lunch?** et si on déjeunait?; **when shall we go? – what about Monday?** quand est-ce qu'on y va? – (et si on disait) lundi!; **what about your promise? – what about my promise?** et ta promesse? – ben quoi, ma promesse?; *Fam* **what about it?** et alors?; **do you remember Lauryn? – what about her?** tu te souviens de Lauryn? – oui, et alors?; **and what about you?** et vous donc?

6 what for *adv (why)* pourquoi?; **what did you say that for?** pourquoi as-tu dit cela?; **I'm leaving town – what for?** je quitte la ville – pourquoi?

7 what if *conj* **what if we went to the beach?** et si on allait à la plage?; **he won't come – and what if he doesn't?** *(supposing)* il ne va pas venir – et alors?

8 what with *conj* **what with work and the children I don't get much sleep** entre le travail et les enfants, je ne dors pas beaucoup; **what with paying for dinner and the cab he was left with no cash** après avoir payé le dîner et le taxi, il n'avait plus d'argent; **what with one thing and another I never got there** pour un tas de raisons je n'y suis jamais allé

whatchamacallit ['wɒtʃəmə͵kɔːlɪt] *n Fam (thing)* machin *m*, truc *m*

what-d'ye-call-her ['wɒtjəkɔːlə(r)] *n Fam (person)* Machine *f*

what-d'ye-call-him ['wɒtjəkɔːlɪm] *n Fam (person)* Machin *m*

what-d'ye-call-it ['wɒtjəkɔːlɪt] *n Fam (thing)* machin *m*, truc *m*

whate'er [wɒt'eə(r)] *Literary* = **whatever**

whatever [wɒt'evə(r)] **1** *pron* (**a**) *(anything, everything)* tout ce que; **do whatever he asks you** faites tout ce qu'il vous demande; **take whatever you need** prenez tout ce dont vous avez besoin; **I'll do whatever is necessary** je ferai le nécessaire; **whatever you like** ce que tu veux

(**b**) *(no matter what)* quoi que + *subjunctive*; **whatever I say, he always disagrees** quoi que je dise, il n'est jamais d'accord; **whatever happens, stay calm** quoi qu'il arrive, restez calme; **whatever you do, don't tell her what I said** surtout, ne lui répète pas ce que je t'ai dit; **whatever it may be** quoi que ce soit; **whatever the reason** quelle que soit la raison; **the doctors must operate whatever the risk** les médecins doivent opérer quel que soit le risque; **whatever it costs, I want that house** je veux cette maison à tout prix; **I won't do it, whatever you say** vous aurez beau dire *ou* vous pouvez dire tout ce que vous voulez, je ne le ferai pas; **whatever you say, whatever you think best** comme tu voudras; **whatever you may think, I am telling the truth** vous pouvez penser ce que vous voulez, mais je dis la vérité

(**c**) *(indicating surprise)* **whatever can that mean?** qu'est-ce que ça peut bien vouloir dire?; **whatever do you want to do that for?** et pourquoi donc voulez-vous faire ça?; **he wants to join the circus – whatever next!** il veut travailler dans un cirque – et puis quoi encore!

(**d**) *(indicating uncertainty)* **it's an urban regeneration area, whatever that means** c'est une zone de rénovation urbaine, si tu sais ce qu'ils entendent par là

(**e**) *Fam (some similar thing or things)* **they sell newspapers, magazines and whatever** ils vendent des journaux, des revues et ainsi de suite *ou* et que sais-je encore; **I don't want to study English or philosophy or whatever** je ne veux étudier ni l'anglais, ni la philosophie, ou que sais-je encore

(**f**) *Fam (indicating lack of interest)* **shall I take the red or the green? – whatever** je prends le rouge ou le vert? – n'importe; **I'll call you next week – whatever** je t'appellerai la semaine prochaine – comme tu veux

2 *adj* (**a**) *(any, all)* tout, n'importe quel; **she read whatever books she could find** elle lisait tous les livres qui lui tombaient sous la main; **he gave up whatever ambitions he still had** il a abandonné ce qui lui restait d'ambition; **I'll take whatever fruit you have** je prendrai ce que vous avez comme fruits

(**b**) *(no matter what)* **for whatever reason, he changed his mind** pour une raison quelconque, il a changé d'avis; **she likes all films, whatever subject they have** elle aime tous les films quel qu'en soit le sujet

3 *adv* **choose any topic whatever** choisissez n'importe quel sujet; **I have no doubt whatever** je n'ai pas le moindre doute; **I see no reason whatever to go** je ne vois absolument aucune raison d'y aller; **we have no intention whatever of giving up** nous n'avons pas la moindre intention d'abandonner; **he knew nothing whatever about it** il n'en savait absolument rien *ou* rien du tout; **she has no money whatever** elle n'a pas un sou

what-for *n Fam* **to give sb what-for** *(physically)* foutre une raclée à qn; *(verbally)* passer un savon à qn; **to get what-for** *(physically)* prendre une raclée; *(verbally)* se faire passer un savon

what-ho *exclam Br Old-fashioned* (**a**) *(in surprise)* eh bien!, tiens! (**b**) *(greeting)* bonjour!, salut!

whatnot ['wɒtnɒt] *n* (**a**) *(furniture)* étagère *f* (**b**) *Fam (idiom)* **and whatnot** et ainsi de suite; **there was champagne, caviar and whatnot** il y avait du champagne, du caviar et tout le tralala

what's [wɒts] (**a**) = **what is** (**b**) = **what has**

whatshername ['wɒtsənem] *n Fam* Machine *f*; **Mrs whatshername** Madame Machin

whatshisname ['wɒtsɪznem] *n Fam* Machin *m*, Machin Chouette *m*; **Mr whatshisname** Monsieur Machin

whatsit ['wɒtsɪt] *n Fam* machin *m*, truc *m*

whatsitsname ['wɒtsɪtsnem] *n Fam* machin *m*, truc *m*

whatsoever [ˌwɒtsəʊ'evə(r)] *pron* **none whatsoever** aucun; **he gave us no encouragement whatsoever** il ne nous a pas prodigué le moindre encouragement

What's On *n Br Press* = magazine d'informations culturelles

wheat [wi:t] **1** *n* blé *m*; **to separate the wheat from the chaff** séparer le bon grain de l'ivraie

2 *comp (flour)* de blé, de froment; *(field)* de blé

▸▸ ***wheat beer*** biére *f* blanche; ***wheat germ*** germe *m* de blé; ***wheat rust*** rouille *f* du blé

wheatear ['wi:tˌɪə(r)] *n Orn* traquet *m* (motteux)

wheaten ['wi:tən] *adj* (**a**) *(bread)* de blé, de froment (**b**) *(colour)* blond comme les blés

wheatmeal ['wi:tmi:l] *n (flour)* farine *f* complète

▸▸ ***wheatmeal flour*** farine *f* complète

wheatsheaf ['wi:tʃi:f] *n* gerbe *f* de blé

Wheatstone bridge ['wi:tstən-] *n Phys* pont *m* de Wheatstone

whee [wi:] *exclam* ooooh!

wheedle ['wi:dəl] *vt* enjôler; **to wheedle sb into doing sth** convaincre qn de faire qch à force de cajoleries; **to wheedle sth out of sb** obtenir qch de qn par des cajoleries; **he wheedled his way into the old lady's confidence** il s'est assuré la confiance de la vieille dame à force de cajoleries

wheedler ['wi:dlə(r)] *n* enjôleur(euse) *m,f*

wheedling ['wi:dlɪŋ] **1** *n (UNCOUNT)* cajolerie *f*, cajoleries *fpl*

2 *adj* cajoleur, enjôleur; **a wheedling voice** une voix pateline

wheel [wi:l] **1** *n* (**a**) *(of bicycle, car, train)* roue *f*; *(smaller)* roulette *f*; *(for potter)* tour *m*; **on wheels** sur roues/roulettes; *Fig* **the wheel has come full circle** la boucle est bouclée; **the wheel of fortune** la roue de la fortune; *Fig* **the wheels have come off** les choses ont commencé à mal tourner

(**b**) *Aut* **(steering) wheel** volant *m*; **to be at the wheel** être au volant; *Fig* être aux commandes; **to get behind** *or* **to take the wheel** se mettre au *ou* prendre le volant; **the City on Wheels** = surnom de Los Angeles

(**c**) *Naut* barre *f*, gouvernail *m*; **at the wheel** à la barre

(**d**) *Hist (of torture)* roue *f*; **to break sb on the wheel** rouer qn

2 *vi* (**a**) *(birds)* tournoyer; *(procession)* faire demi-tour; *Mil (column)* effectuer une conversion; **to wheel to the left** tourner sur la gauche; *Mil* **left wheel!** à gauche!

(**b**) *(idiom) Fam* **to wheel and deal** *(do business)* brasser des affaires; *Pej* magouiller

3 *vt (bicycle, trolley, barrow)* pousser; *(suitcase)* tirer; **she wheeled the baby around the park** elle a promené le bébé dans le parc; **she wheeled in a trolley full of cakes** elle entra en poussant un chariot plein de gâteaux; *Fig* **they wheeled on** *or* **out the usual celebrities** ils ont ressorti les mêmes célébrités

4 wheels *npl* (**a**) *(workings)* rouages *mpl*; **the wheels of government** les rouages du gouvernement; **there are wheels within wheels** c'est plus compliqué que ça n'en a l'air

(**b**) *Fam (car)* bagnole *f*; **he's got a new set of wheels** il a une nouvelle bagnole

▸▸ *Aut* ***wheel alignment*** parallélisme *m* des roues; *Aut* ***wheel arch*** passage *m* de roue; *Aut* ***wheel bolt*** boulon *m* de roue; ***wheel brace*** clef *f* en croix; *Aut* ***wheel chain*** chaîne *f* (de pneu); *Aut* ***wheel cover*** enjoliveur *m*; *Aut* ***wheel cylinder*** cylindre *m* de roue; *Aut* ***wheel disc*** enjoliveur *m*; *Aut* ***wheel hop*** rebond *m* des roues; *Aut* ***wheel lock(-up)*** blocage *m* des roues; *Aut* ***wheel nut*** écrou *m* de roue; *Aut* ***wheel rim*** jante *f* de roue; *Aut* ***wheel shimmy*** phénomène *m* de shimmy; *Aut* ***wheel track*** alignement *m* des roues; *Aut* ***wheel trim*** enjoliveur *m* de roues; *Aut* ***wheel wobble*** flottement *m* des roues

▸**wheel about, wheel around 1** *vi* (**a**) *(turn)* faire demi-tour *ou* se retourner (brusquement); *(procession)* faire demi-tour; *(horse)* pirouetter; *(birds)* tournoyer; **she wheeled around to face him** elle s'est retournée brusquement pour lui faire face

(**b**) *(circle)* tourner en rond *ou* en cercle, tournoyer; **vultures wheeling about in the sky** des vautours qui tournoient dans le ciel

2 *vt sep (turn)* tourner; *(dancing partner)* faire tourner

wheelbarrow ['wi:lˌbærəʊ] *n* brouette *f*

wheelbase ['wi:lbeɪs] *n Aut* empattement *m*

wheelchair ['wi:lˌtʃeə(r)] *n* fauteuil *m* roulant; **she'll be in a wheelchair for the rest of her life** elle sera dans un fauteuil roulant pour le reste de ses jours

▸▸ ***wheelchair access*** accès *m* aux handicapés; ***the Wheelchair Olympics*** les jeux *mpl* Olympiques handisport *ou* pour handicapés; ***wheelchair ramp*** rampe *f* d'accès pour les handicapés; ***wheelchair user*** handicapé(e) *m,f*

wheelclamp ['wi:lklæmp] **1** *n* sabot *m* de Denver

2 *vt* **my car was wheelclamped** on a mis un sabot à ma voiture

wheeled [wi:ld] *adj* à roues, muni de roues

-wheeled [wi:ld] *suff* à roues; **four-wheeled** à quatre roues

wheeler ['wi:lə(r)] *n* (**a**) *(wheelmaker)* charron *m* (**b**) *(horse)* timonier *m*

-wheeler [wi:lə(r)] *suff* à roues; **three-wheeler** véhicule *m* à trois roues

wheeler-dealer *n Fam Pej* magouilleur(euse) *m,f*

wheelhorse ['wi:lhɔ:s] *n* timonier *m*

wheelhouse ['wi:lhaʊs, *pl* -haʊzɪz] *n Naut* timonerie *f*

wheelie ['wi:lɪ] *n Fam* **to do a wheelie** faire une roue arrière, cabrer

▸▸ ***wheelie bin*** poubelle *f (avec des roues)*

wheeling and dealing ['wi:lɪŋ-] *n (UNCOUNT) Fam* combines *fpl*, manigances *fpl*

wheelspin ['wi:lspɪn] *n Aut* patinage *m*

wheelwright ['wi:lraɪt] *n* charron *m*

wheesht [wi:ʃt] *Scot Fam* **1** *exclam* chut!

2 *n* **hold your wheesht!** retiens ta langue!❑, tais-toi!❑

wheeze [wi:z] **1** *vi (person)* respirer bruyamment, avoir une respiration sifflante; *(animal)* souffler

2 *vt* dire d'une voix rauque; **the old accordion can still wheeze out a note or two** on peut encore tirer quelques notes du vieil accordéon

3 *n* (**a**) *(sound of breathing)* respiration *f* bruyante *ou* sifflante

(**b**) *Br Fam (trick)* combine *f*; **the government's latest wheeze for cutting unemployment** la dernière trouvaille du gouvernement pour réduire le chômage

(**c**) *Br Fam (joke)* blague *f*

(**d**) *Am (saying)* dicton *m*

wheezily ['wi:zɪlɪ] *adv (breathe)* bruyamment, en sifflant; *(say)* d'une voix rauque

wheezing ['wi:zɪŋ] *n (of person)* respiration *f* bruyante *ou* sifflante, *Med* sibilance *f* respiratoire

wheezy ['wi:zɪ] (*compar* **wheezier**, *superl* **wheeziest**) *adj (person)* asthmatique; *(voice, chest)* d'asthmatique; *(musical instrument, horse)* poussif; **she's still a little bit wheezy after her cold** elle a encore un peu de mal à respirer après son rhume; *Fig* **a wheezy old barrel organ** un vieil orgue de Barbarie asthmatique

whelk [welk] *n* bulot *m*, buccin *m*

whelp [welp] **1** *n* (**a**) *(animal)* petit(e) *m,f* (**b**) *Pej (youth)* petit(e) morveux(euse) *m,f*

2 *vi (animals)* mettre bas

WHEN [wen]

quand	▸ 1; 2 (a) – (g)
lorsque	▸ 2 (c)
dès que	▸ 2 (d)
après que	▸ 2 (d)
chaque fois que	▸ 2 (f)
étant donné que	▸ 2 (g)
alors que	▸ 2 (h)
où	▸ 3 (a), (c)

1 *adv* quand; **when are we leaving?** quand partons-nous?; **when is the next bus?** à quelle heure est *ou* quand passe le prochain bus?; **when did the war end?** quand la guerre s'est-elle terminée?; **when did the accident happen?** quand l'accident a-t-il eu lieu?; **when was the Renaissance?** à quand remonte l'époque de la Renaissance?; **when will the wedding be?** à quand le mariage?; **when do you start your new job?** quand commencez-vous votre nouveau travail?; **when do you use the subjunctive?** quand emploie-t-on le subjonctif?; **you're open until when?** vous êtes ouvert jusqu'à quand?; **when did you last see her?** quand l'avez-vous vue pour la dernière fois?; **when do the Easter holidays begin?** quand est-ce que commencent les vacances de Pâques?; **when is the best time to call?** quel est le meilleur moment pour appeler?; **the homework is due when?** quand doit-on rendre les devoirs?

2 *conj* (**a**) *(how soon)* quand; **I don't know when we'll see you again** je ne sais pas quand nous vous reverrons; **do you remember when we met?** te souviens-tu du jour où nous nous sommes connus?; **do you know when he was born?** savez-vous quand il est né?, connaissez-vous sa date de naissance?; **I wonder when the shop opens** je me demande à quelle heure ouvre le magasin; **your contract states when you will be paid** votre contrat spécifie quand vous serez payé; **we don't agree on when it should be done** nous ne sommes pas d'accord sur le moment où il faudrait le faire

(**b**) *(at which time)* quand; **come back next week when we'll have more time** revenez la semaine prochaine quand nous aurons plus de temps; **he returned in the autumn, when the leaves were beginning to turn** il est revenu à l'automne, alors que les feuilles commençaient à jaunir; **the prince will arrive on the 10th, when he will open the new university** le prince arrivera le dix et inaugurera la nouvelle université

(**c**) *(indicating a specific point in time)* quand, lorsque; **he turned round when she called his name** il s'est retourné quand *ou* lorsqu'elle l'a appelé; **when she's gone, he's unhappy** quand *ou* lorsqu'elle n'est pas là, il est malheureux; **when I was a student** lorsque j'étais *ou* à l'époque où j'étais étudiant; **will you still love me when I'm old?** m'aimeras-tu encore quand je serai vieux?; **she's only happy when she's writing** elle n'est heureuse que lorsqu'elle écrit; **they were talking when he came in** ils étaient en train de discuter quand il est entré; **she's thinner than when I last saw her** elle a maigri depuis la dernière fois que je l'ai vue; **he left town when he was twenty** il a quitté la ville quand il avait *ou* à l'âge de vingt ans; **when she was a child** quand *ou* lorsqu'elle était enfant; **on Sunday, when I go to the market** *(this week)* dimanche, quand j'irai au marché; *(every week)* le dimanche, quand je vais au marché; **I had just walked in the door/he was about to go to bed when the phone rang** je venais juste d'arriver/il était sur le point de se coucher quand le téléphone a sonné; **we hadn't been gone five minutes when Susan wanted to go home** ça ne faisait pas cinq minutes que nous étions partis et Susan voulait déjà rentrer

(**d**) *(as soon as)* quand, dès que; *(after)* quand, après que; **put your pencils down when you have finished** posez votre crayon quand vous avez terminé; **when completed, the factory will employ 100 workers** une fois terminée, l'usine emploiera 100 personnes; **when he starts drinking, he can't stop** une fois qu'il a commencé à boire, il ne peut plus s'arrêter; **I'll answer any questions when the meeting is over** quand la réunion sera terminée, je répondrai à toutes vos questions; *Culin* **when cool, turn out onto a dish** une fois refroidi, démouler sur un plat; **when I had read my report, she suggested we take a break** après mon exposé, elle a suggéré qu'on fasse une pause; **when they had finished dinner, he offered to take her home** quand *ou* après qu'ils eurent dîné, il lui proposa de la ramener; **when you see her you'll understand** quand vous la verrez vous comprendrez; **when she had talked to him, she left** après lui avoir parlé, elle est partie

(**e**) *(the time that)* **remember when a coffee cost 10 cents?** vous souvenez-vous de l'époque où un café coûtait 10 cents?; **he talked about when he was a soldier** il parlait de l'époque où il était soldat; **that's when it snowed so hard** c'est quand il a tant neigé; **that's when he got up and left** c'est à ce moment-là *ou* c'est alors qu'il s'est levé et qu'il est parti; **that's when the shops close** c'est l'heure où les magasins ferment; *Fig* **now is when we should stand up and be counted** c'est le moment d'avoir le courage de nos opinions

(**f**) *(whenever)* quand, chaque fois que; **when it's sunny, the children play outside** quand il y a du soleil, les enfants jouent dehors; **when I hear that song, I think of her** chaque fois que *ou* quand j'entends cette chanson, je pense à elle; **when I think of what she must have suffered!** quand je pense à ce qu'elle a dû souffrir!; **I get very irritated when talking to her** je m'énerve chaque fois que je lui parle; **I try to avoid seeing him when possible** j'essaie de l'éviter quand c'est possible

(**g**) *(since, given that)* quand, étant donné que; **what good is it applying when I don't qualify for the job?** à quoi bon me porter candidat quand *ou* si je n'ai pas les capacités requises pour faire ce travail?; **how can you treat her so badly when you know she loves you?** comment pouvez-vous la traiter si mal quand *ou* alors que vous savez qu'elle vous aime?; **why change jobs when you like what you do?** pourquoi changer de travail quand *ou* puisque vous aimez ce que vous faites?; **fancy having soup when you could have had caviar!** pourquoi manger de la soupe quand on peut manger du caviar?

(**h**) *(whereas)* alors que; **she described him as being lax when in fact he's quite strict** elle l'a décrit comme étant négligent alors qu'en réalité il est assez strict

3 *relative pron* (**a**) *(at which time)* **an age when men were men** une époque où les hommes étaient des hommes; **in a period when business was bad** à une période où les affaires allaient mal; **she was president until 1980, when she left the company** elle fut présidente jusqu'en 1980, année où elle a quitté l'entreprise

(**b**) *(which time)* **she started her job in May, since when she has had no free time** elle a commencé à travailler en mai et elle n'a pas eu de temps libre depuis; **the new office will be ready in January, until when we use the old one** le nouveau bureau sera prêt en janvier, jusque là *ou* en attendant, nous utiliserons l'ancien

(**c**) *(that)* où; **do you remember the year when we went to Alaska?** tu te rappelles l'année où on est allés en Alaska?; **what about the time when she didn't show up?** et la fois où elle n'est pas venue?; **one day when he was out** un jour où il était sorti *ou* qu'il était sorti; **it was only a minute later when he heard a scream** à peine une minute plus tard, il entendait un cri; **on Monday, the day when I was supposed to start work** lundi, le jour où je devais commencer à travailler; **it's one of those days when everything goes wrong** c'est un de ces jours où tout va de travers; **there were times when she didn't know what to do** il y avait des moments où elle ne savait plus quoi faire

4 *n* **the when and the how of it** quand et comment cela s'est-il passé/se passera-t-il/*etc*

whence [wens] *Formal* **1** *adv* d'où

2 *pron* d'où

whene'er [wen'eə(r)] *Literary* = **whenever**

whenever [wen'evə(r)] **1** *conj* (**a**) *(every time that)* quand, chaque fois que; **whenever we go on a picnic, it rains** chaque fois qu'on part en pique-nique, il pleut; **whenever it snows there's chaos on the roads** chaque fois qu'il neige, c'est la panique sur les routes; **he can come whenever he likes** il peut venir quand il veut; **I go to visit her whenever I can** je vais la voir dès que je peux; **whenever there is an eclipse** à chaque éclipse

(**b**) *(at whatever time)* quand; **call me whenever you need me** appelez-moi si vous avez besoin de moi; **you can leave whenever you're ready** vous pouvez partir dès que vous serez prêt; **they try to help whenever possible** ils essaient de se rendre utiles quand c'est possible

2 *adv* (**a**) *(expressing surprise)* quand; **whenever did you find the time?** mais quand donc avez-vous trouvé le temps?

(**b**) *(referring to an unknown or unspecified time)* **I'll pick you up at six o'clock or whenever is convenient** je te prendrai à six heures ou quand ça te convient; *Fam* **let's assume he started work in April or whenever** supposons qu'il ait commencé à travailler en avril ou quelque chose comme ça; *Fam* **we could have lunch on Thursday or Friday or whenever** on pourrait déjeuner ensemble jeudi, vendredi ou un autre jour

whensoever [ˌwensəʊ'evə(r)] *Literary* = **whenever**

WHERE [weə(r)]

où	► **1 (a); 2 (a); 3 (a)**
là où	► **2 (a) – (d)**
là que	► **2 (b)**
quand	► **2 (c)**
alors que	► **2 (d)**

1 *adv* (**a**) *(at, in, to what place)* où; **where is the restaurant?** où est le restaurant?; **where are we going?** où allons-nous?; **where are you from?** d'où est-ce que vous venez?, d'où êtes-vous?; **where did you put them?** où les avez-vous mis?; **where is the entrance?** où est l'entrée?; **the school is near where?** l'école est près d'où?; **where does this road lead?** où va cette route?

(**b**) *(at what stage, position)* **where are you in your work/in the book?** où en êtes-vous dans votre travail/dans votre lecture?; **where were we?** où en étions-nous?; **where do you stand on this issue?** quelle est votre position *ou* opinion sur cette question?; **where do you stand with the boss?** quels sont vos rapports avec le patron?; **where do I come into it?** qu'est-ce que j'ai à faire là-dedans, moi?; **where would I be without you?** que serais-je devenu sans toi?

2 *conj* (**a**) *(the place at or in which)* (là) où; **it rains a lot where we live** il pleut beaucoup là où nous habitons; **she told me where to go** *(gave me directions)* elle m'a dit où (il fallait) aller; *(was rude)* elle m'a envoyé promener; **there is a factory where I used to go to school** il y a une usine là où *ou* à l'endroit où j'allais autrefois à l'école; **how did you know where to find me?** comment avez-vous su où me trouver?; **I wonder where my keys are** je me demande où sont mes clés; **you'll find your key where you left it** tu trouveras ta clé (là) où tu l'as laissée; **sit where you like** asseyez-vous où vous voulez *ou* voudrez; **turn left where the two roads meet** tournez à gauche au croisement; **where the Doubs meets the Saône** au confluent du Doubs et de la Saône; *Fig* **I just don't know where to begin** je ne sais vraiment pas par où commencer

(**b**) *(the place that)* là que, là où; **this is where I work** c'est là que je travaille; **so that's where I left my coat!** voilà où j'ai laissé mon manteau!; **he showed me where the students live** il m'a montré l'endroit où habitent les étudiants; **this is where we get off the bus** c'est là que nous descendons; **the child ran up to where her mother was sitting** l'enfant a couru jusqu'à l'endroit où sa mère était assise; **we can't see well from where we're sitting** nous ne voyons pas bien d'où *ou* de là où nous sommes assis; *Fig* **I see where I went wrong** je vois où je me suis trompé; **that's where she's mistaken** c'est là qu'elle se trompe, voilà son erreur; **this is where you have to make up your mind** là, il faut que tu te décides

(**c**) *(whenever, wherever)* quand, là où; **the judge is uncompromising where drugs are concerned** le juge est intraitable lorsqu'il *ou* quand il s'agit de drogue; **the situation is hopeless where defence is concerned** pour la défense, la situation est sans espoir; **he can't be objective where she's concerned** il ne peut pas être objectif lorsqu'il s'agit d'elle; *Math* **where x equals y** où x égale y; **where possible** là où *ou* quand c'est possible; **delete where inapplicable** *(on form)* rayer les mentions inutiles; *Prov* **where there's life, there's hope** tant qu'il y a de la vie, il y a de l'espoir

(**d**) *(whereas, while)* là où, alors que; **where others see a horrid brat, I see a shy little boy** là où les autres voient un affreux moutard, je vois un petit garçon timide

3 *relative pron* (**a**) *(in which, at which)* où; **the place where we went on holiday** l'endroit où nous sommes allés en vacances; **the room where he was working** la pièce où *ou* dans laquelle il travaillait; **the table where they were sitting** la table où *ou* à laquelle ils étaient assis; **it was the kind of restaurant where tourists go** c'était le genre de restaurant que fréquentent les touristes; *Fig* **I'm at the part where they discover the murder** j'en suis au moment où ils découvrent le meurtre; **it's reached a stage where I'm finding it difficult to work** ça en est au point où travailler me devient pénible

(**b**) *(in or at which place)* **Boston, where I was born** Boston, où je suis né, Boston, ma ville natale; **they went to Paris, where they stayed a week** ils sont allés à Paris et y sont restés huit jours; **sign at the bottom, where I've put a cross** signez en bas, là où j'ai mis une croix

4 *n* **they discussed the where and how of his accident** ils ont parlé en détail des circonstances de son accident; **the where and the when** le lieu et la date/l'heure; **you can find that any old where** vous pouvez trouver cela n'importe où

whereabouts 1 *adv* [ˌweərə'baʊts] où; **whereabouts are you from?** d'où êtes-vous?; **I used to live in Cumbria – oh, really, whereabouts?** j'habitais dans le Cumbria – vraiment? où ça *ou* dans quel coin?; **do you know whereabouts the town hall is?** savez-vous de quel côté se trouve l'hôtel de ville?; **whereabouts in France do you live?** où est-ce que tu habites en France?

2 *npl* ['weərəbaʊts] **to know the whereabouts of sb/sth** savoir où se trouve qn/qch; **her exact whereabouts are unknown** personne ne sait exactement où elle se trouve

whereafter [weər'ɑːftə(r)] *conj Arch or Formal* après quoi

whereas [weər'æz] *conj* (**a**) *(gen)* alors que, tandis que (**b**) *Law or Formal* attendu que, considérant que

whereat [weər'æt] *Arch or Formal* **1** *conj* sur *ou* après quoi, sur ce

2 *adv* où

whereby [weə'baɪ] *relative pron Formal* par lequel, au moyen duquel; **there's a new system whereby everyone gets one day off a month** il y a un nouveau système qui permet à tout le monde d'avoir un jour de congé par mois

wherefore ['weəfɔː(r)] **1** *adv Arch or Formal* pourquoi, pour quelle raison

2 *conj Arch or Formal* pour cette raison, donc

3 *n see* **why**

wherein [weər'ɪn] *Arch or Formal* **1** *relative pron* où, dans lequel (laquelle)

2 *adv* en quoi, dans quoi

3 *conj* en quoi, dans quoi

whereof [weər'ɒv] *Arch or Formal* **1** *relative pron* *(person)* dont, de qui; *(thing)* dont, duquel (de laquelle)

2 *adv* de quoi

whereon [weər'ɒn] *Arch or Formal* **1** *relative pron* sur quoi, sur lequel (laquelle)

2 *adv* sur quoi

wheresoever [ˌweəsəʊ'evə(r)] *Formal or Literary* = **wherever**

whereto [weə'tuː] *Arch or Formal* **1** *relative pron* vers quoi

2 *adv* (vers) où

whereupon [ˌweərə'pɒn] **1** *conj* sur *ou* après quoi, sur ce; **whereupon he left us** sur quoi il nous a quittés

2 *adv Arch* sur quoi

wherever [weər'evə(r)] **1** *conj* (**a**) *(every place)* partout où; *(no matter what place)* où que; **wherever you go in Europe, you meet other tourists** où que vous alliez en Europe, vous rencontrez d'autres touristes; **wherever you go it's the same thing** c'est la même chose où que vous alliez, c'est partout pareil; **wherever we went, he complained about the food** partout où nous sommes allés, il s'est plaint de la nourriture

(**b**) *(anywhere, in whatever place)* (là) où; **he can sleep wherever he likes** il peut dormir (là) où il veut; **we'll have to sit wherever there's room** il faudra s'asseoir là où il y aura de la place; **she works wherever she's needed** elle travaille là où on a besoin d'elle; **he takes on work wherever he can find it** il accepte du travail où il en trouve; **we can go wherever we please** nous pouvons aller où bon nous semble; **wherever there is poverty there are social problems** là où il y a de la misère, il y a des problèmes sociaux; **they're from Little Pucklington, wherever that is** ils viennent d'un endroit qui s'appelle Little Pucklington

(**c**) *(in any situation)* quand; **I wish, wherever possible, to avoid job losses** je souhaite éviter toute perte d'emploi quand c'est possible; **grants are given wherever needed** des bourses sont accordées à chaque fois que c'est nécessaire

2 *adv Fam* (**a**) *(indicating surprise)* mais où donc; **wherever did you get that idea?** mais d'où sors-tu cette idée?; **wherever have you been?** où étais-tu donc passé?

(**b**) *(indicating unknown or unspecified place)* **they're holidaying in Marbella or Malaga or wherever** ils passent leurs vacances à Marbella ou à Malaga ou Dieu sait où

wherewith [weə'wɪθ] *conj Formal Literary* avec quoi, avec lequel (laquelle)

wherewithal ['weəwɪðɔːl] *n Br* **the wherewithal** les moyens *mpl*; **I don't have the wherewithal to buy a new coat** je n'ai pas les moyens de me payer un manteau neuf

wherry ['werɪ] (*pl* **wherries**) *n* esquif *m*; *(for fishing)* canot *m*

whet [wet] (*pt & pp* **whetted**, *cont* **whetting**) *vt (cutting tool)* affûter, aiguiser; *(appetite)* aiguiser, ouvrir; **to whet sb's appetite** ouvrir l'appétit à qn; *Fig* **her few days in Spain only whetted her appetite for more** ces quelques jours passés en Espagne n'ont fait que lui donner envie d'y revenir

whether ['weðə(r)] *conj* (**a**) *(if)* si; **I asked whether I could come** j'ai demandé si je pouvais venir; **I don't know whether she's ready or not** je ne sais pas si elle est prête ou non; **I don't know now whether it's such a good idea** je ne suis plus sûr que ce soit vraiment une bonne idée; **I doubt whether he'll come** je doute qu'il vienne; **the question now is whether you want the job or not** la question est maintenant de savoir si tu veux cet emploi ou pas

(**b**) *(no matter if)* **whether it rains or not** qu'il pleuve ou non; **whether you want to or not** que tu le veuilles ou non; **whether they open it now or later, it doesn't matter** qu'ils l'ouvrent maintenant ou plus tard, cela n'a pas d'importance; **whether by accident or design** que ce soit par hasard ou fait exprès; **everyone, whether rich or poor, needs it** chacun, qu'il soit riche ou pauvre, en a besoin

whetstone ['wetstəʊn] *n* pierre *f* à aiguiser

whew [hwjuː] *exclam (in relief)* ouf!; *(admiration)* oh là là!; **whew! I'm glad that's over!** ouf! je suis bien content que ça soit fini!

whey [weɪ] *n* petit-lait *m*

whey-faced *adj* pâle

WHICH [wɪtʃ]

quel	▸ 1 (a)
lequel	▸ 2 (a)
celui qui	▸ 2 (b)
celui que	▸ 2 (b)
qui	▸ 3 (a)
que	▸ 3 (a)
ce qui	▸ 3 (b)
ce que	▸ 3 (b)

1 *adj* (**a**) *(in questions → singular)* quel (quelle); *(→ plural)* quels (quelles); **which book did you buy?** quel livre as-tu acheté?; **which candidate are you voting for?** pour quel candidat allez-vous voter?; **which one?** lequel?/laquelle?; **which ones?** lesquels?/lesquelles?; **which one of you spoke?** lequel de vous a parlé?; **which one of the twins got married?** lequel des jumeaux s'est marié?; **I saw several films – which ones?** j'ai vu plusieurs films – lesquels?; **I wonder which route would be best** je me demande quel serait le meilleur chemin; **which way should we go?** par où devrions-nous aller?; **keep track of which employees come in late** notez le nom des employés qui arrivent en retard

(**b**) *(referring back to preceding noun or statement)* **he may miss his plane, in which case he'll have to wait** il est possible qu'il rate son avion, auquel cas il devra attendre; **she arrives at 5 p.m. at which time I'll still be at the office** elle arrive à 17 heures, heure à laquelle je serai encore au bureau; **they lived in Madrid for one year, during which time their daughter was born** ils ont habité Madrid pendant un an, et c'est à cette époque que leur fille est née

2 *pron* (**a**) *(in questions → singular)* lequel (laquelle) *m,f*; *(→ plural)* lesquels (lesquelles) *mpl, fpl*; **which of the houses do you live in?** dans quelle maison habitez-vous?; **which of these books is yours?** lequel de ces livres est le tien?; **which is the freshest?** quel est le plus frais?; **which is the more interesting of the two films?** lequel de ces deux films est-il le plus intéressant?; **which of you saw the accident?** qui de vous a vu l'accident?; **which of you three is the oldest?** lequel de vous trois est le plus âgé?, qui est le plus âgé de vous trois?; **she's from Chicago or Boston, I don't remember which** elle vient de Chicago ou de Boston, je ne sais plus laquelle des deux; **we can play bridge or poker, I don't care which** on peut jouer au bridge ou au poker, peu m'importe; **I can't tell which is which** je n'arrive pas à les distinguer (l'un de l'autre); **which is which?** lequel est-ce?

(**b**) *(the one or ones that → as subject) (singular)* celui qui (celle qui) *m,f*; *(plural)* ceux qui (celles qui) *mpl,fpl*; *(→ as object) (singular)* celui que (celle que) *m,f*; *(plural)* ceux que (celles que) *mpl,fpl*; **show me which you prefer** montrez-moi celui que vous préférez; **tell her which is yours** dites-lui lequel est le vôtre

3 *relative pron* (**a**) *(adding further information → as subject)* qui; *(→ as object)* que; **the house, which is very old, needs urgent repairs** la maison, qui est très vieille, a besoin d'être réparée sans plus attendre; **the vases, each of which held white roses, were made of crystal** les vases, qui contenaient chacun des roses blanches, étaient en cristal; **the hand with which I write** la main avec laquelle j'écris; **the office in which she works** le bureau dans lequel *ou* où elle travaille; **the hotels at which they stayed** les hôtels où ils sont allés *ou* descendus; **the house of which I am speaking** la maison dont je parle; **the countries to which we are going** *or* **which we're going to** les pays où nous allons

(**b**) *(commenting on previous statement → as subject)* ce qui; *(→ as object)* ce que; **it took her an hour, which isn't bad really** elle a mis une heure, ce qui n'est pas mal en fait; **he looked like a military man, which in fact he was** il avait l'air d'un militaire, et en fait c'en était un; **he says it was an accident, which I don't believe for an instant** il dit que c'était un accident, ce que je ne crois absolument pas *ou* mais je ne le crois pas un seul instant; **he's getting married, which surprises me** il va se marier, ce qui m'étonne; **I don't like it when rents go up, which they often do** je n'aime pas que les loyers augmentent, ce qui arrive souvent; **then they arrived, after which things got better** puis ils sont arrivés, après quoi tout est allé mieux; **she lied about the letter, from which I guessed she was up to something** elle a menti au sujet de la lettre, d'où j'ai deviné qu'elle combinait quelque chose; **he insists that actors should have talent, in which he is right** il exige que les acteurs aient du talent, (ce) en quoi il a raison; **he started shouting, upon which I left the room** il s'est mis à crier, sur quoi *ou* et sur ce j'ai quitté la pièce

4 Which? *n Press* = magazine de l'Union des consommateurs britanniques connu pour ses essais comparatifs

whichever [wɪtʃ'evə(r)] **1** *pron* (**a**) *(the one or ones that → as subject) (singular)* celui (celle) qui *m,f*; *(plural)* ceux (celles) qui *mpl,fpl*; *(→ as object) (singular)* celui (celle) que *m,f*; *(plural)* ceux (celles) que *mpl,fpl*; **choose whichever most appeals to you** choisissez celui/celle qui vous plaît le plus; **choose whichever most appeal to you** choisissez ceux/celles qui vous plaisent le plus; **will whichever of you arrives first turn on the heating?** celui d'entre vous qui arrivera le premier pourra-t-il allumer le chauffage?; **take whichever is (the) cheapest** prenez (celui qui est) le moins cher; **shall we go to the cinema or the theatre? – whichever you prefer** on va au cinéma ou au théâtre? – choisis ce que tu préfères; **let's meet at 3.30 or 4, whichever is best for you** donnons-nous rendez-vous à 3h30 ou 4h, comme cela vous arrange le mieux; **we will reimburse half the value or $1,000, whichever is the greater** nous vous rembourserons la moitié de la valeur ou 1000 dollars, soit la somme la plus avantageuse

(**b**) *(no matter which one)* **whichever of the routes you choose, allow about two hours** quel que soit le chemin que vous choisissiez, comptez environ deux heures; **whichever of the houses you buy it will be a good investment** quelle que soit la maison que vous achetiez, ce sera un bon investissement; **whichever of the computers you buy will be installed free of charge** quel que soit l'ordinateur que vous achetiez, l'installation sera gratuite; **I'd like to speak either to Mr Brown or Mr Jones, whichever is available** j'aimerais parler à M. Brown ou à M. Jones, celui des deux qui est disponible

2 *adj* (**a**) *(indicating the specified choice or preference)* **grants will be given to whichever students most need them** des bourses seront accordées à ceux des étudiants qui en ont le plus besoin; **I'll buy whichever car does the best mileage** je prendrai la voiture qui consomme le moins (, peu importe laquelle); **take whichever seat you like** asseyez-vous (là) où vous voulez; **we'll travel by whichever train is fastest** nous prendrons le train le plus rapide(, peu importe lequel); **keep whichever one appeals to you most** gardez celui/celle qui vous plaît le plus

(**b**) *(no matter what → as subject)* quel que soit… qui; *(→ as object)* quel que soit… que; **whichever job you take, it will mean a lot of travelling** quel que soit le poste que vous preniez, vous serez obligé de beaucoup voyager; **whichever party is in power** quel que soit le parti au pouvoir; **we'll still be late whichever way we go** nous serons en retard de toute façon quel que soit le chemin que nous prenions; **whichever way you look at it, it's not fair** peu importe la façon dont on considère la question, c'est vraiment injuste

whichsoever [ˌwɪtʃsəʊ'evə(r)] *Formal or Literary* = **whichever**

whichways ['wɪtʃweɪz] *adv Am* où; **she left the papers lying every whichways** elle a laissé les papiers traîner partout

whiff [wɪf] **1** *n* (**a**) *(inhalation)* bouffée *f*; *Fam* **one whiff of this gas and you'd be out cold** une seule bouffée de ce gaz et vous tombez dans les pommes

(**b**) *(smell)* odeur *f*; **he got a sudden whiff of her perfume/of rotten eggs** il sentit soudain l'odeur de son parfum/une odeur d'œufs pourris; *Fam* **get a whiff of this!** sens-moi un peu ça!; *Fig* **a whiff of scandal** une odeur de scandale; **he had caught a whiff of something suspicious** il avait senti que quelque chose de louche était dans l'air; *Fig Literary* **there has always been a whiff of sulphur about him** il a toujours eu une réputation sulfureuse

2 *vi Fam* schlinguer

whiffle ['wɪfəl] *vi* (**a**) *(blow)* souffler par bouffées légères *ou* soudaines (**b**) *Fig (person)* se conduire capricieusement

whiffy ['wɪfɪ] (*compar* **whiffier**, *superl* **whiffiest**) *adj Fam* qui schlingue; **the dog's a bit whiffy** le chien schlingue un peu; **it's a bit whiffy in here,**

don't you think? ça schlingue ici, tu ne trouves pas?

Whig [wɪg] *Pol* **1** *adj* whig

2 *n* whig *m*

Whiggery ['wɪgərɪ] *n Pol* whiggisme *m*

Whiggish ['wɪgɪʃ] *adj Pol* des whigs

while [waɪl] **1** *conj* (**a**) *(during the time that)* pendant que; **he read the paper while he waited** il lisait le journal en attendant; **while (you're) in London you should visit the British Museum** pendant que vous serez à Londres *ou* pendant votre séjour à Londres, il faut visiter le British Museum; **she fell asleep while on duty** elle s'est endormie pendant le service; **he cut himself while (he was) shaving** il s'est coupé en se rasant; **while this was going on** pendant ce temps-là; **heels repaired/keys cut while you wait** *(sign)* talons/clés minute; **while you're up could you fetch me some water?** puisque tu es debout, peux-tu aller me chercher de l'eau?; **while you're at** *or* **about it, could you photocopy this too?** pendant que tu y es, peux-tu aussi me photocopier cela?

(**b**) *(although)* bien que, quoique; **while I admit it's difficult, it's not impossible** j'admets que c'est difficile, mais ce n'est pas impossible; **while comprehensive, the report lacked clarity** bien que détaillé le rapport manquait de clarté

(**c**) *(whereas)* alors que, tandis que; **while he loves opera, I prefer jazz** il adore l'opéra alors que moi je préfère le jazz; **she's left-wing, while he's rather conservative** elle est de gauche tandis que lui est plutôt conservateur

2 *n* **to wait a while** attendre (un peu); **after a while** au bout de quelque temps; **for a while/a long while I believed her** pendant un certain temps/pendant assez longtemps je l'ai crue; **it took me a while to realize what she meant** j'ai mis un certain temps à comprendre ce qu'elle voulait dire; **a long while ago** il y a longtemps; **I was in the States a short while ago** j'étais aux États-Unis il y a peu (de temps); **she was in the garden a short while ago** elle était dans le jardin il y a un instant; **it's been a good while since I've seen her** ça fait pas mal de temps que je ne l'ai pas vue; **it will be a good while before you see him again** vous ne le reverrez pas de si tôt; **it takes quite a while to get there** il faut un certain temps pour y aller; **all the while** (pendant) tout ce temps; **once in a while** de temps en temps, de temps à autre

►**while away** *vt sep* faire passer; **to while away the time** passer le temps; **she whiled away the hours reading until he returned** elle passa le temps à lire jusqu'à son retour

while-you-wait *adj* **while-you-wait heel repairs** *(sign)* talons minute

whilst [waɪlst] *Br* = **while** *conj*

whim [wɪm] *n* caprice *m*, fantaisie *f*; **it's just one of his little whims** ce n'est qu'une de ses petites lubies; **arrangements are altered at the whim of the King** les préparatifs sont changés sur un simple caprice du roi; **she indulges his every whim** elle lui passe tous ses caprices; **whenever the whim takes him** chaque fois que l'idée lui prend; **on a sudden whim I telephoned her mother** tout à coup, l'idée m'a pris de téléphoner à sa mère

whimbrel ['wɪmbrəl] *n Orn* courlieu *m*

whimper ['wɪmpə(r)] **1** *vi (person)* gémir, geindre; *Pej* pleurnicher; *(dog)* gémir, pousser des cris plaintifs

2 *vt* gémir

3 *n* gémissement *m*, geignement *m*; **"don't" he said with a whimper** "non" dit-il d'un ton larmoyant *ou* gémit-il; **I don't want to hear a whimper out of you** je ne veux pas t'entendre te plaindre; **she did it without a whimper** elle l'a fait sans se plaindre

whimpering ['wɪmpərɪŋ] **1** *n (UNCOUNT)* gémissements *mpl*, plaintes *fpl*; **stop your whimpering!** arrête de pleurnicher!

2 *adj (voice)* larmoyant; *(person)* qui pleurniche; *(dog)* qui gémit

whimsical ['wɪmzɪkəl] *adj (person → capricious)* capricieux, fantasque; *(→ playful)* malicieux; *(behaviour, sense of humour, story, remark)* farfelu; *(smile)* malicieux

whimsicality [wɪmzɪ'kælɪtɪ] *n (of person → capriciousness)* caractère *m* capricieux *ou* fantasque; *(→ playfulness)* malice *f*; *(of behaviour, sense of humour, story, remark)* caractère *m* farfelu

whimsically ['wɪmzɪkəlɪ] *adv (capriciously)* capricieusement; *(playfully)* malicieusement; *(directed, written)* de façon farfelue; *(smile)* malicieusement

whimsy ['wɪmzɪ] *(pl* **whimsies***) n* (**a**) *(whimsicality)* caractère *m* fantasque *ou* fantaisiste; **a piece of pure whimsy** de la pure fantaisie; **full of whimsy** plein de fantaisie *ou* de malice (**b**) *(idea)* caprice *m*, fantaisie *f*

whin [wɪn] *n* ajonc *m*

whinchat [wɪntʃæt] *n Orn* traquet *m* tarier

whine [waɪn] **1** *vi* (**a**) *(in pain, discomfort → person)* gémir, geindre; *(→ dog)* gémir, pousser des gémissements

(**b**) *(complain)* se lamenter, se plaindre; **to whine about sth** se plaindre de qch; **don't come whining to me about it** ne viens pas t'en plaindre à moi

2 *vt* dire en gémissant; **"I'm hungry", she whined** "j'ai faim", dit-elle d'une voix plaintive

3 *n* (**a**) *(from pain, discomfort)* gémissement *m*

(**b**) *(complaint)* plainte *f*

(**c**) *(of machinery, engine)* bruit *m* strident

whiner ['waɪnə(r)] *n Fam Pej* pleurnichard(e) *m,f*

whinge [wɪndʒ] *(cont* **whingeing***) Br & Austr Fam Pej* **1** *vi* geindre❑, pleurnicher❑; **he's always whingeing about something** il est toujours à pleurnicher à propos de quelque chose; **don't come whingeing to me about your problems** ne venez pas vous plaindre à moi de vos problèmes

2 *n* plainte❑ *f*, pleurnicherie❑ *f*; **to have a whinge about sth** se plaindre (à propos) de qch❑

whingeing ['wɪndʒɪŋ] *Br & Austr Fam* **1** *n (UNCOUNT)* pleurnicherie❑*f*, plainte❑*f*

2 *adj (person)* pleurnicheur❑; *(voice)* plaintif❑

whinger [wɪndʒə(r)] *n Br & Austr Fam* râleur(-euse) *m,f*

whining ['waɪnɪŋ] **1** *n (UNCOUNT)* (**a**) *(of person)* gémissements *mpl*, pleurnicheries *fpl*; *(of dog)* gémissements *mpl*; **I've had enough of your whining!** j'en ai assez de tes pleurnicheries *ou* de tes jérémiades! (**b**) *(of machinery, engine)* gémissement *m*

2 *adj (person)* geignard, pleurnicheur; *(voice)* geignard; *(dog)* qui gémit

whinny ['wɪnɪ] *(pt & pp* **whinnied,** *pl* **whinnies***)* **1** *vi* hennir

2 *n* hennissement *m*

whinnying ['wɪnɪɪŋ] **1** *n* hennissement *m*

2 *adj* **a whinnying laugh** un rire hennissant; **he gave a whinnying laugh** il eut un rire hennissant

whinstone ['wɪnstəʊn] *n Geol* trapp *m*

whiny ['waɪnɪ] *(compar* **whinier,** *superl* **whiniest***) adj* pleurnichard

whip [wɪp] *(pt & pp* **whipped,** *cont* **whipping***)* **1** *vt* (**a**) *(person, animal)* fouetter; **the cold wind whipped her face** le vent glacial lui fouettait le visage; **the wind whipped her hair about** le vent agitait sa chevelure

(**b**) *Fam (defeat)* vaincre❑, battre❑; **I know when I'm whipped** je sais quand déclarer forfait❑

(**c**) *Culin* fouetter, battre au fouet

(**d**) *(move quickly)* **she whipped it out of sight** elle l'a caché d'un mouvement rapide; **she was whipped into hospital** elle a été transportée à l'hôpital de toute urgence

(**e**) *Fig* **his speech whipped them all into a frenzy** son discours les a tous rendus frénétiques; **I'll soon whip the team into shape** j'aurai bientôt fait de mettre l'équipe en forme; **I need time to whip the project into shape** il me faut du temps pour donner forme au projet; **to whip sb into line** mettre qn au pas

(**f**) *Br Fam (steal)* faucher, piquer; **someone's whipped my wallet** on m'a piqué mon portefeuille

(**g**) *Sewing* surfiler

(**h**) *(cable, rope)* surlier

2 *vi* (**a**) *(lash)* fouetter; **the rain whipped against the windows** la pluie fouettait *ou* cinglait les vitres; **the flags whipped about in the wind** les drapeaux claquaient au vent

(**b**) *(move quickly)* aller vite, filer; **the car whipped along the road** la voiture filait sur la route; **she whipped around the corner** elle a pris le virage sur les chapeaux de roue; **the sound of bullets whipping through the air** le bruit des balles qui sifflaient; **the ball whipped past him into the net** la balle est passée devant lui comme un éclair pour finir au fond du filet; **I'll just whip down to the shop** je vais juste faire un saut au magasin; **can you whip round to the library for me?** est-ce que tu peux faire un saut à la bibliothèque pour moi?

3 *n* (**a**) *(lash)* fouet *m*; *(for riding)* cravache *f*; *Fig* **to have the whip hand** être le maître; **to have the whip hand over sb** avoir le dessus sur qn

(**b**) *Pol (MP)* = parlementaire chargé de la discipline de son parti et qui veille à ce que ses députés participent aux votes

(**c**) *Br Pol (summons)* convocation *f*

(**d**) *Br Pol (paper)* = calendrier des travaux parlementaires envoyé par le "whip" aux députés de son parti

(**e**) *(dessert → with cream)* crème *f*; *(→ with egg whites)* mousse *f*; **pineapple whip** *(with cream)* crème *f* à l'ananas; *(with egg whites)* mousse *f* à l'ananas

►► *Entom* ***whip scorpion*** pédipalpe *m*

►**whip away** *vt sep (of wind)* emporter brusquement; **a sudden gust whipped my hat away** une rafale de vent a emporté mon chapeau

►**whip in 1** *vt sep* (**a**) *Hunt* ramener, rassembler (**b**) *Br Pol (in parliament)* battre le rappel de *(pour voter)* (**c**) *(supporters)* rallier

2 *vi* (**a**) *(rush in)* entrer précipitamment (**b**) *Hunt* être piqueur

►**whip off** *vt sep (take off → jacket, shoes)* se débarrasser de; *(write quickly → letter, memo)* écrire en vitesse

►**whip on** *vt sep (horse)* cravacher

►**whip out 1** *vt sep* (**a**) *(take out)* sortir vivement; **he whipped a notebook out of his pocket** il a vite sorti un carnet de sa poche; **she whipped out a gun** elle a soudain sorti un pistolet; **they had to whip out his appendix** on a dû l'opérer d'urgence de l'appendicite

(**b**) *(grab)* **someone whipped my bag out of my hand** quelqu'un m'a arraché mon sac des mains

2 *vi* sortir précipitamment; **I'm just whipping out to the library** je file à la bibliothèque

►**whip round** *vi (person)* se retourner vivement, faire volte-face

►**whip through** *vt insep Fam (book)* parcourir en vitesse❑; *(task)* expédier❑, faire en quatrième vitesse

►**whip up** *vt sep* (**a**) *(curiosity, emotion)* attiser; *(support)* obtenir; **to whip up an audience** galvaniser *ou* exalter un public (**b**) *(typhoon)* susciter, provoquer; *(dust)* soulever (des nuages de) (**c**) *Culin* battre au fouet, fouetter; *(egg whites)* battre à la neige; *Fam* **I'll whip up some lunch** je vais préparer de quoi déjeuner en vitesse

whipcord ['wɪpkɔːd] **1** *n* (**a**) *(cord)* mèche *f* de fouet (**b**) *Tex (fabric)* whipcord *m*

2 *comp* en whipcord

whipgraft ['wɪpgrɑːft] *vt Hort* greffer en fente anglaise

whiplash ['wɪplæʃ] *n (stroke of whip)* coup *m* de fouet

►► *Med* ***whiplash effect*** effet *m* du coup du lapin; ***whiplash injury*** coup *m* du lapin, *Spec* syndrome *m* cervical traumatique

whipped [wɪpt] *adj (cream)* fouetté

whipper-in [,wɪpə(r)-] *(pl* **whippers-in***) n Hunt* piqueur *m*

whippersnapper ['wɪpə,snæpə(r)] *n Old-fashioned* freluquet *m*

whippet ['wɪpɪt] *n* whippet *m*

whipping ['wɪpɪŋ] *n* (**a**) *(as punishment → child)* correction *f*; *(→ prisoner)* coups *mpl* de fouet; **his father gave him a good whipping** son père lui a donné une bonne correction (**b**) *Fam (defeat)* raclée *f*; **the team got a whipping** l'équipe a pris une raclée

►► ***whipping boy*** bouc *m* émissaire; ***whipping cream*** ≃ crème *f* fraîche (à fouetter); ***whipping post*** poteau *m* *(auquel étaient attachés les condamnés au fouet)*; ***whipping top*** toupie *f*

whippletree ['wɪpəltri:] *n* palonnier *m*

whippoorwill ['wɪp,pʊəwɪl] *n Orn* engoulevent *m* d'Amérique du Nord

whippy ['wɪpɪ] *adj (stick, cane)* flexible, souple

whip-round *n Br Fam* collecte❑ *f*; **they had a whip-round for her** ils ont fait une collecte pour elle

whipsaw ['wɪpsɔ:] **1** *n* scie *f* à chantourner

2 *vt* chantourner; *Am Fig* **the candidate whipsawed his opponent** le candidat a battu son adversaire sur un double plan

whir = **whirr**

whirl [wɜ:l] **1** *vi* **(a)** *(person, skater)* tourner, tournoyer; **she whirled round the ice rink** elle a fait le tour de la piste en tourbillonnant

(b) *(leaves, smoke)* tourbillonner, tournoyer; *(dust, water)* tourbillonner; *(spindle, top)* tournoyer; *(propeller)* tourner; **snowflakes whirled past the window** des flocons de neige passaient devant la fenêtre en tourbillonnant; **the water whirled away down the sink** l'eau s'est écoulée en tourbillonnant dans l'évier

(c) *(head, ideas)* tourner; **my head is whirling** (j'ai) la tête (qui) me tourne; **the news made her mind whirl** les nouvelles lui ont fait tourner la tête

(d) *(move quickly)* aller à toute vitesse; **the houses whirled past us** les chevaux sont passés devant nous à toute allure

2 *vt* **(a)** *(dancer, skater)* faire tourner; **he whirled his partner around the floor** il faisait tournoyer sa partenaire autour de la piste

(b) *(leaves, smoke)* faire tourbillonner *ou* tournoyer; *(dust, sand)* faire tourbillonner; **the wind whirled the leaves about** le vent faisait tourbillonner les feuilles

(c) *(take rapidly)* **she whirled us off on a trip round Europe** elle nous a embarqués pour un tour d'Europe

3 *n* **(a)** *(of dancers, leaves, events)* tourbillon *m*; *Fig* **my head's in a whirl** la tête me tourne; **her thoughts were in a whirl** tout tourbillonnait dans sa tête; *Hum* **the mad social whirl** la folle vie mondaine; **the kitchen was a whirl of activity** la cuisine bourdonnait d'activité

(b) *Fam (try)* **to give sth a whirl** s'essayer à qch❑; **why don't you give it a whirl?** pourquoi n'essayez-vous pas?

(c) *Fam (trip)* promenade❑ *f*, tour❑ *m*

►**whirl round 1** *vi* **(a)** *(person)* se retourner brusquement; *(dancer, skater)* pirouetter; **she whirled round and round in the middle of the dance floor** elle tournait et tournait au milieu de la piste de danse **(b)** *(leaves)* tourbillonner, tournoyer

2 *vt sep* **to whirl sb round** faire tournoyer qn

whirligig ['wɜ:lɪgɪg] *n Br* **(a)** *(top)* toupie *f*; *(toy windmill)* moulin *m* à vent *(jouet)* **(b)** *(merry-go-round)* manège *m* **(c)** *(of activity, events)* tourbillon *m*

►► *Entom* ***whirligig beetle*** tourniquet *m*, gyrin *m*

whirling ['wɜ:lɪŋ] *adj (dancer, skater, leaves, smoke)* tourbillonnant, tournoyant; *(dust, water)* tourbillonnant; *(top)* tournoyant; *(propeller)* tournant

►► ***whirling dervish*** derviche *m* tourneur

whirlpool ['wɜ:lpu:l] *n also Fig* tourbillon *m*

►► ***whirlpool bath*** bain *m* à remous, Jacuzzi® *m*

whirlwind ['wɜ:lwɪnd] *n* tornade *f*, trombe *f*; *Fig* **he went through the office accounts like a whirlwind** il a passé les comptes de la société en revue en un rien de temps

►► ***whirlwind romance*** aventure *f* enivrante; ***whirlwind tour*** visite *f* éclair

whirlybird ['wɜ:lɪbɜ:d] *n Fam Old-fashioned* hélico *m*

whirr [wɜ:(r)] **1** *n (of wings)* bruissement *m*; *(of camera, machinery)* bruit *m*, ronronnement *m*; *(of helicopter, propeller)* bruit *m*, vrombissement *m*; **we could hear the whirr of the cameras** on entendait le ronronnement des caméras

2 *vi (wings)* bruire; *(camera, machinery)* ronronner; *(propeller)* vrombir

whirring ['wɜ:rɪŋ] **1** *adj (camera, machinery)* ronronnant; *(propeller)* vrombissant; *(wings)* bruissant

2 *n* = **whirr** *n*

whish [wɪʃ] = **swish** *vi & n*

whisht [hwi:ʃt] *Scot* **1** *exclam* chut!

2 *n* **hold your whisht!** retiens ta langue!❑, taistoi!❑

whisk [wɪsk] **1** *vt* **(a)** *(put or take quickly)* **we whisked the money into the tin/off the counter** nous avons vite fait disparaître l'argent dans la boîte/du comptoir; **she whisked the gun back into her bag** elle remit vivement le pistolet dans son sac; **the car whisked us to the embassy** la voiture nous emmena à l'ambassade à toute allure; **she whisked the children out of the room** elle emmena rapidement les enfants hors de la pièce

(b) *Culin (cream, eggs)* battre; *(egg whites)* battre en neige; **whisk in the cream** incorporer la crème avec un fouet

(c) *(flick)* **the horse/the cow whisked its tail** le cheval/la vache agitait la queue

2 *vi (move quickly)* aller vite; **she just whisked in and out** elle n'a fait qu'entrer et sortir; **the train whisked through the countryside** le train filait *ou* roulait à vive allure à travers la campagne

3 *n* **(a)** *(of tail, stick, duster)* coup *m*; **the horse gave a whisk of its tail** le cheval agita la queue *ou* donna un coup de queue; **give the bedroom a quick whisk with a duster** passez un coup de chiffon dans la chambre

(b) *(for sweeping)* époussette *f*; *(for flies)* chasse-mouches *m inv*

(c) *Culin* fouet *m*; *(electric)* batteur *m*; **give the batter a good whisk** bien travailler la pâte au fouet

►**whisk away** *vt sep* **(a)** *(dust)* enlever, chasser; *(dishes, tablecloth)* faire disparaître; *(flies → with fly swatter)* chasser à coups de chasse-mouches; *(→ with tail)* chasser d'un coup de queue

(b) *(take off)* **the president was whisked away in a helicopter** le président a été emmené à toute vitesse en hélicoptère; **he was whisked away to hospital in an ambulance** il a été transporté de toute urgence en ambulance à l'hôpital; **a car whisked us away to the embassy** *(immediately)* une voiture nous emmena sur-le-champ à l'ambassade; *(quickly)* une voiture nous emmena à toute allure à l'ambassade

►**whisk off** *vt sep (quickly)* empouter *ou* emmener à vive allure; *(suddenly, immediately)* conduire sur-le-champ; **the bus whisked us off to the airport** le bus nous emmena rapidement jusqu'à l'aéroport; **we were whisked off to the police station** on nous emmena sur-le-champ au poste de police

whisker ['wɪskə(r)] **1** *n* poil *m*; *Fam* **she won the contest by a whisker** elle a gagné le concours de justesse❑; *Fam* **he came within a whisker of discovering the truth** il s'en est fallu d'un cheveu *ou* d'un poil qu'il apprenne la vérité

2 whiskers *npl (beard)* barbe *f*; *(moustache)* moustache *f*; *(on animal)* moustaches *fpl*

whiskered ['wɪskəd] *adj (bearded)* qui a une barbe; *(with moustache)* qui a une moustache; *(animal)* qui a des moustaches

►► *Orn* ***whiskered tern*** guifette *f* à moustaches

whiskery ['wɪskərɪ] = **whiskered**

whiskey ['wɪskɪ] *(pl* **whiskeys***) Am & Ir* = **whisky**

whisky ['wɪskɪ] *(pl* **whiskies***)* *n* whisky *m*; **a whisky and soda** un whisky soda; **a whisky on the rocks** un whisky avec des glaçons

►► ***whisky company*** société *f* de fabrication de whisky; ***whisky distillery*** distillerie *f* de whisky; ***whisky glass*** verre *m* à whisky; ***whisky mac*** = boisson à base de whisky et d'alcool au gingembre; ***whisky sour*** = cocktail à base de whisky et de jus de citron

'Whisky Galore' *Mackenzie, MacKendrick*
'Whisky à gogo'

whisper ['wɪspə(r)] **1** *vi* **(a)** *(person)* chuchoter, parler à voix basse; **to whisper to sb** parler *ou* chuchoter à l'oreille de qn; **stop whispering!** arrêtez de chuchoter!; **what are you whispering about?** qu'est-ce que vous avez à chuchoter?

(b) *(leaves)* bruire; *(water, wind)* murmurer

2 *vt* **(a)** *(person)* chuchoter, dire à voix basse; **to whisper sth to sb** chuchoter qch à qn; **I whispered the answer to her** je lui ai soufflé la réponse; **to whisper sweet nothings to sb** susurrer des mots doux à l'oreille de qn

(b) *Br (rumour)* **it's whispered that her husband's left her** le bruit court *ou* on dit que son mari l'a quittée; **I've heard it whispered that he's lost his fortune** j'ai entendu dire qu'il avait perdu toute sa fortune

3 *n* **(a)** *(of voice)* chuchotement *m*; **to speak in a whisper** parler tout bas *ou* à voix basse; **we never raised our voices above a whisper** nous n'avons fait que murmurer; **...she said in a loud whisper** ...chuchota-t-elle assez fort; *Fig* **not a whisper of this to anyone!** n'en soufflez mot à personne!

(b) *(of leaves)* bruissement *m*; *(of water, wind)* murmure *m*

(c) *Br (rumour)* rumeur *f*, bruit *m*; **there are whispers of his leaving** le bruit court *ou* on dit qu'il va partir; **I've heard whispers that they're getting married** j'ai entendu dire qu'ils allaient se marier

whisperer ['wɪspərə(r)] *n* chuchoteur(euse) *m,f*

whispering ['wɪspərɪŋ] **1** *n* **(a)** *(of voices)* chuchotement *m*, chuchotements *mpl*

(b) *(of leaves)* bruissement *m*; *(of water, wind)* murmure *m*

(c) *(usu pl) Br (rumour)* rumeur; **I've heard whisperings about the new president's private life** j'ai entendu toutes soutes de rumeurs sur la vie privée du nouveau président

2 *adj* **(a)** *(voice)* qui chuchote

(b) *(leaves, tree)* qui frémit *ou* murmure; *(water, wind)* qui murmure

►► ***whispering campaign*** campagne *f* de diffamation; *Archit* ***whispering gallery*** galerie *f* à écho

whist [wɪst] *n* whist *m*; **to have a game of whist** faire une partie de whist; **to play whist** jouer au whist

►► ***whist drive*** tournoi *m* de whist

whistle ['wɪsəl] **1** *vi* **(a)** *(person → using lips)* siffler; *(→ using whistle)* donner un coup de sifflet, siffler; **he walked in whistling happily** il est entré en sifflant joyeusement; **to whistle to sb** siffler qn; **I whistled to my dog** j'ai sifflé mon chien; **the porter whistled for a taxi** le portier a sifflé un taxi; **he whistles at all the girls** il siffle toutes les filles; **the audience booed and whistled** le public a hué et sifflé; *Br Fam* **you can whistle for it!** tu peux toujours courir *ou* te brosser!; *Br* **let him whistle for his lunch!** il peut toujours l'attendre, son repas!; *Fig* **to whistle in the dark** essayer de se donner du courage

(b) *(bird, kettle, train)* siffler; **bullets whistled past him** des balles passaient près de lui en sifflant; **the wind whistled through the trees** le vent gémissait dans les arbres

2 *vt (tune)* siffler, siffloter; **the coach whistled them off the field** l'entraîneur a sifflé pour qu'ils quittent le terrain; **the players were whistled off the field by the crowd** les joueurs ont quitté le terrain sous les sifflements de la foule

3 *n* **(a)** *(whistling → through lips)* sifflement *m*; *(→ from whistle)* coup *m* de sifflet; **the cheers and whistles of the crowd** les acclamations et les sifflements de la foule; **if you need me, just give a whistle** tu n'as qu'à siffler si tu as besoin de moi

(b) *(of bird, kettle, train)* sifflement *m*

(c) *(instrument → of person, on train)* sifflet *m*; **to blow a whistle** donner un coup de sifflet; **the whistle blew for the end of the shift** le sifflet a signalé la fin du service; **the referee blew his whistle for half-time** l'arbitre a sifflé la mi-temps; **to be as clean as a whistle** briller comme un sou neuf; *Fig* **it's got all the bells and whistles** il a tous les accessoires possibles et imaginables

(d) *Mus* **(penny** *or* **tin) whistle** flûtiau *m*, pipeau *m*

(e) *SEng Fam (rhyming slang* **whistle and flute** = **suit)** costard *m*

►**whistle up** *vt sep Br* **(a)** *(by whistling)* siffler; **I'll whistle up a cab** je vais siffler un taxi **(b)** *(find)* dénicher, dégoter; **I managed to whistle up a van for the move** j'ai réussi à dégoter un camion pour le déménagement; **I can't whistle up a sofa just like that!** je ne peux pas faire apparaître un canapé comme par enchantement!

whistle-blower *n Fam* = personne qui vend la mèche; **we need a few more whistle-blowers like her** il faudrait d'autres personnes comme elle pour tirer sur la sonnette d'alarme

whistler ['wɪslə(r)] *n* (**a**) *(person)* siffleur(euse) *m,f* (**b**) *(bird)* oiseau *m* siffleur (**c**) *(animal)* siffleur *m*, marmotte *f* canadienne, *Can* siffleux *m*

whistle-stop 1 *n Am Rail* arrêt *m* facultatif; *(town)* village *m* perdu

2 *vi Am Pol* = faire une tournée électorale en passant par des petites villes

3 *adj* **he made a whistle-stop tour of the West** il a fait une tournée rapide dans l'ouest

►► ***whistle-stop town*** village *m* perdu

whistling ['wɪslɪŋ] *n* sifflement *m*

►► *Orn* ***whistling duck*** dendrocygne *m*

Whit [wɪt] **1** *n* Pentecôte *f*

2 *comp (holidays, week)* de Pentecôte

►► ***Whit Monday*** lundi *m* de Pentecôte; ***Whit Sunday*** dimanche *m* de Pentecôte

whit [wɪt] *n Literary* petit peu *m*; **he hasn't changed a whit** il n'a absolument pas changé; **I don't care a whit what people think** je me moque éperdument de ce que les gens pensent; **it won't make a whit of difference** ça ne changera rien à rien; **it doesn't matter a whit** ça n'a aucune espèce d'importance

white [waɪt] **1** *adj* (**a**) *(in colour)* blanc (blanche); **he painted his house white** il a peint sa maison en blanc; **she wore a dazzling white dress** elle portait une robe d'un blanc éclatant; **his hair has turned white** ses cheveux ont blanchi; **he went white overnight** ses cheveux sont devenus blancs du jour au lendemain

(**b**) *(pale)* **she was white with fear/with rage** elle était verte de peur/blanche de colère; **his face suddenly went white** il a blêmi tout d'un coup; **whiter than white** plus blanc que blanc; *Fig* sans tache; **you're as white as a ghost/as a sheet** vous êtes pâle comme la mort/comme un linge; **as white as snow** blanc comme neige

(**c**) *(flour, rice, sugar)* blanc (blanche); **(a loaf of) white bread** du pain blanc

(**d**) *(race)* blanc (blanche); **a white man** un Blanc; **a white woman** une Blanche; **white man's justice** la justice des Blancs; **an all-white neighbourhood** un quartier blanc; **white schools** écoles *fpl* pour les Blancs

(**e**) *(coffee)* au lait; **do you take your coffee white?** tu prends du lait dans ton café?

2 *n* (**a**) *(colour)* blanc *m*; **the bride wore white** la mariée était en blanc; **he was dressed all in white** il était tout en blanc; **dazzling white** blanc éclatant

(**b**) *Anat (of eye)* blanc *m*; *Fig* **don't shoot until you see the whites of their eyes** ne tirez qu'au dernier moment

(**c**) *Culin (of egg)* blanc *m*

(**d**) *(Caucasian)* Blanc *m*, Blanche *f*; **whites only** *(sign)* réservé aux Blancs; **they're trying to set white against black** ils essaient de monter les Blancs contre les Noirs

(**e**) *Chess* **White** les blancs *mpl*

(**f**) *(in snooker, pool)* **the white** la blanche

3 *vt Arch* blanchir

4 *vi Arch* blanchir

5 whites *npl (sportswear)* tenue *f* de sport blanche; *(linen)* blanc *m*

►► *Entom* ***white admiral*** = papillon aux ailes marron marquées de blanc; *Am* ***White Anglo-Saxon Protestant*** = Blanc d'origine anglo-saxonne et protestante, appartenant aux classes aisées et influentes; ***white ant*** fourmi *f* blanche, termite *m*; *Hist* ***the White Army*** les armées *fpl* blanches; ***white ball*** *(in snooker, pool)* blanche *f*; *Biol* ***white blood cell*** globule *m* blanc; ***white chocolate*** chocolat *m* blanc; ***white Christmas*** Noël *m* sous la neige; ***white coffee*** café *m* au lait; *Bot* ***white dead-nettle*** ortie *f* blanche; *Astron* ***white dwarf*** naine *f* blanche; ***white elephant*** *(useless construction)* = réalisation de prestige dont l'utilité ne justifie pas le coût; **the new submarine has turned out to be a complete white elephant** le nouveau sous-marin s'est révélé être un luxe tout à fait superflu; *Br* ***white elephant stall*** *(at fair, jumble sale)* stand *m* de bibelots; ***White Ensign*** = pavillon de la marine royale britannique; *Br Hist* ***white feather*** = symbole de lâcheté; **to show the white feather** battre en retraite; *Br* ***white fish*** = poisson à chair blanche; ***white flag*** drapeau *m* blanc; *Am* ***white flight*** exode *m* des Blancs *(quand les Noirs viennent habiter leur quartier)*; *Am* ***white folks*** les Blancs *mpl*; *Rel* ***White Friar*** carme *m*; ***white gold*** or *m* blanc; ***white goods*** *(household equipment)* appareils *mpl* ménagers; *(linen)* linge *m* de maison, blanc *m*; *Phys & Fig* ***white heat*** chaleur *f* incandescente; **in the white heat of passion** au plus fort de la passion; **anti-war feelings have reached white heat** les sentiments d'hostilité par rapport à la guerre ont atteint un paroxysme; ***white hope*** espoir *m*; **he's the (great) white hope of British athletics** c'est le grand espoir de l'athlétisme britannique; ***white horses*** *(waves)* moutons *mpl*; ***the White House*** la Maison-Blanche; *Fig* ***white knight*** sauveur *m*, chevalier *m* blanc; ***white lead*** blanc *m* de céruse *ou* de plomb; ***white lie*** pieux mensonge *m*; ***white light*** lumière *f* blanche; *Fam* ***white lightning*** tord-boyaux *m inv (distillé illégalement)*; ***white line*** *(on road)* ligne *f* blanche; ***white magic*** magie *f* blanche; ***white man's burden*** = obligation pour les Blancs d'assurer l'instruction des habitants noirs de leurs colonies; *Anat* ***white matter*** substance *f* blanche; ***white meat*** viande *f* blanche; *(of poultry)* blanc *m*; *Orn* ***white melilot*** mélilot *m* blanc; ***white metal*** métal *m* blanc; *Br* ***white meter*** = système économique de chauffage qui utilise l'électricité pendant les heures où elle coûte moins cher; ***the White Nile*** le Nil Blanc; ***white noise*** bruit *m* de fond; *Am* ***White Out***® correcteur *m* liquide; ***white owl*** harfang *m*, chouette *f* blanche; *Am* ***the White Pages*** l'annuaire *m* (du téléphone); *Br* ***white paper*** *(government report)* livre *m* blanc; ***white pepper*** poivre *m* blanc; *Bot* ***white poplar*** ypréau *m*; *Culin* ***white pudding*** boudin *m* blanc; ***White Russia*** Russie *f* Blanche; ***White Russian 1*** *adj* (**a**) *Ling & Geog* biélorusse (**b**) *Hist (soldier)* russe blanc (blanche); **the White Russian Army** les armées *fpl* blanches **2** *n* (**a**) *Hist (person)* Russe *m* blanc, Russe *f* blanche (**b**) *Ling & Geog* biélorusse *m* (**c**) *(cocktail)* = cocktail à base de Kahlua, de vodka et de crème fraîche; *Am* ***white sale*** promotion *f* sur le blanc; ***white sauce*** sauce *f* blanche; ***the White Sea*** la mer Blanche; ***white shark*** requin *m* blanc; ***white slave*** victime *f* de la traite des Blanches; ***white slavery, white slave trade*** traite *f* des Blanches; ***white space*** *(on page)* espace *m* blanc; ***white spirit*** white-spirit *m*; *Orn* ***white stork*** cigogne *f* blanche; ***white stick*** *(of blind person)* canne *f* blanche; ***white supremacist*** partisan(e) *m,f* de la suprématie blanche; ***white supremacy*** suprématie *f* blanche; *Fam Aviat* ***white tail*** = avion n'appartenant encore à aucune compagnie aérienne; ***white tie*** *(formal clothes)* habit *m*; *(on invitation)* ≃ tenue de soirée exigée; *Pej* ***white trash*** Blancs *mpl* pauvres; *Br Fam* ***white van man*** = jeune ouvrier en camionnette à la conduite agressive; ***white water*** eau *f* vive; ***white wedding*** mariage *m* en blanc; **she's having a white wedding** elle se marie en blanc; ***white whale*** bélouga *m*, béluga *m*; ***white wine*** vin *m* blanc; ***white witch*** = sorcière qui a recours à la magie blanche

►**white out** *vt sep* effacer (au correcteur liquide); **can you white out this word?** peux-tu effacer ce mot?

'The White Devil' *Webster* 'Le Diable blanc'

The white man's burden

Cette expression provient du titre d'un poème de l'écrivain anglais Rudyard Kipling publié en 1899, dans lequel il fait l'éloge du colonialisme, justifié selon lui par la supériorité culturelle de l'empire britannique. Le "fardeau" auquel le titre fait référence est la mission civilisatrice de l'homme blanc colonisateur. Le titre du poème devint le slogan des impérialistes de l'époque. L'expression est aujourd'hui souvent utilisée de façon ironique pour désigner l'attitude raciste et condescendante des impérialistes.

whitebait ['waɪtbeɪt] *n (for fishermen)* blanchaille *f*; *Culin* petite friture *f*

whitebeam ['waɪtbiːm] *n Bot* alisier *m* blanc, allouchier *m*

whitebean ['waɪtbiːn] *n* cormier *m*

whiteboard ['waɪtbɔːd] *n* tableau *m* blanc

whitebread ['waɪtbred] *adj Am Fam Pej* conventionnel ❑

whitecaps ['waɪtkæps] *npl (waves)* moutons *mpl*

white-collar *adj*

►► ***white-collar crime*** délits *mpl* financiers; ***white-collar job*** poste *m* d'employé de bureau; ***white-collar union*** syndicat *m* d'employés de bureau; ***white-collar workers*** les employés *mpl* de bureau, les cols *mpl* blancs

whited sepulchre ['waɪtɪd-] *n Formal* hypocrite *mf*

white-eye *n Orn* zostérops *m*, oiseau *m* à lunettes

white-faced *adj* au visage pâle

whitefish ['waɪtfɪʃ] (*pl* **inv** *or* **whitefishes**) *n Ich* corégone *m*

whitefly ['waɪtflaɪ] (*pl* **whiteflies**) *n Entom* aleurode *m*

white-fronted goose [-'frʌntɪd-] *n Orn* oie *f* rieuse

white-haired *adj (person)* aux cheveux blancs; *(animal)* aux poils blancs; **his white-haired old mother** sa vieille mère aux cheveux blancs

►► *Am Fig* ***white-haired boy*** chouchou *m*

Whitehall ['waɪthɔːl] *n* = rue du centre de Londres

WHITEHALL

De nombreux services gouvernementaux ont leurs bureaux dans cette rue londonienne dont le nom est souvent employé pour désigner le gouvernement lui-même.

white-hat hacker *n Fam Comput* = personne habilitée de par sa fonction à se livrer au piratage informatique

whitehead ['waɪthed] *n* bouton *m*

white-headed *adj (person)* aux cheveux blancs; *(animal, bird)* à la tête blanche

►► *Am Fig* ***white-headed boy*** chouchou *m*

white-hot *adj Phys & Fig* chauffé à blanc

white-knuckle *adj*

►► ***white-knuckle ride*** tour *m* de manège terrifiant; *Fig* **the film was a bit of a white-knuckle ride** le film était palpitant

whiteleg ['waɪtleg] *n Med* leucophlegmasie *f*

white-livered [-lɪvəd] *adj Fig (person)* poltron

whiten ['waɪtən] **1** *vt* (**a**) *(hair, linen, shoes)* blanchir (**b**) *(with whitewash)* blanchir à la chaux, badigeonner de chaux

2 *vi* blanchir; *(with fear, rage)* pâlir, blêmir

whitener ['waɪtənə(r)] *n* agent *m* blanchissant; *(for coffee)* succédané *m* de lait en poudre

whiteness ['waɪtnɪs] *n* (**a**) *(gen)* blancheur *f*; *(of skin)* blancheur *f*, pâleur *f* (**b**) *Literary* innocence *f*, pureté *f*

whitening ['waɪtənɪŋ] *n* (**a**) *(substance)* blanc *m* (**b**) *(process → of walls)* blanchiment *m*; *(→ of linen, shoes)* blanchissage *m*; *(of hair)* blanchissement *m*

white-on-black *n Typ* noir *m* au blanc

whiteout ['waɪtaʊt] *n* voile *m* blanc; **in whiteout conditions** dans des conditions de visibilité nulle

white-slaver *n* = personne qui se livre à la traite des Blanches

white-tailed *adj*

►► *Zool* ***white-tailed deer*** cerf *m* de Virginie; *Orn* ***white-tailed sea eagle*** pygargue *m* à queue blanche

white-tail plane *n Fam Aviat* = avion n'appartenant encore à aucune compagnie aérienne

whitethorn ['waɪtθɔːn] *n Bot* aubépine *f*

whitethroat ['waɪtθrəʊt] *n Orn* fauvette *f* grisette

white-tie *adj* habillé; **it was a white tie dinner** c'était un dîner habillé

whitewall ['waɪtwɔːl] *n* pneu *m* à flanc blanc

whitewash ['waɪtwɒʃ] **1** *n* (**a**) *(substance)* lait *m* de chaux (**b**) *Fig (cover-up)* **the police report was simply a whitewash** le rapport de police visait seulement à étouffer l'affaire (**c**) *Sport (crushing defeat)* défaite *f* cuisante

2 *vt* (**a**) *(building, wall)* blanchir à la chaux (**b**)

Fig (cover up) blanchir, étouffer; **the minister tried to whitewash the affair** le ministre essaya d'étouffer l'affaire (**c**) *Sport (defeat)* écraser

whitewashed ['waɪtwɒʃt] *adj* (**a**) *(wall, house)* blanchi à la chaux (**b**) *(furniture, wood, frame)* cérusé

whitewashing ['waɪt,wɒʃɪŋ] *n* (**a**) *(painting)* peinture *f* à la chaux, badigeonnage *m* (**b**) *Fig (of reputation)* blanchiment *m*

whitewater rafting ['waɪt,wɔːtə-] *n* descente *f* en eau vive, rafting *m*

white-winged black tern *n Orn* guifette *f* à ailes blanches

whitewood ['waɪtwʊd] *n* bois *m* blanc

whitey ['waɪtɪ] *n Am very Fam Pej* = terme injurieux désignant un Blanc

whither ['wɪðə(r)] *Arch or Literary* **1** *adv* (vers) où; **whither Christianity?** *(in headlines, titles)* où va le christianisme?

2 *conj* (vers) où; **I shall go whither fate leads me** j'irai là où me mènera le destin

whiting ['waɪtɪŋ] *n* (**a**) *Ich* merlan *m* (**b**) *(colouring agent)* blanc *m* d'Espagne

whitish ['waɪtɪʃ] *adj* blanchâtre; **her hair was whitish blond** ses cheveux étaient d'un blond presque blanc

whitlow ['wɪtləʊ] *n* panaris *m*

►► *Bot* ***whitlow grass*** drave *f* printanière

Whitney system ['wɪtnɪ-] *n (in hotel)* planning *m* Whitney

Whitsun ['wɪtsən], **Whitsuntide** ['wɪtsəntaɪd] *n* Pentecôte *f*; **at Whitsun** à la Pentecôte

whitter = **witter**

whittle ['wɪtəl] **1** *vt* tailler (au couteau); **he whittled an arrow from an old stick, he whittled an old stick into an arrow** il a taillé une flèche dans un vieux bâton

2 *vi* tailler (au couteau)

►**whittle away 1** *vt sep Fig* amoindrir, diminuer; **they whittled away his resistance** ils ont amoindri sa résistance

2 *vi (with knife)* tailler; **he sat there whittling away at a piece of wood** il était assis à tailler un morceau de bois avec un couteau; *Fig* **their constant teasing whittled away at his patience** leurs moqueries constantes ont mis sa patience à bout

►**whittle down** *vt sep (with knife)* tailler (au couteau); *Fig* amenuiser, amoindrir; **rising fuel costs have whittled down our profits** l'augmentation du prix du pétrole a fait baisser nos bénéfices; **we've whittled down the number of candidates** nous avons réduit le nombre des candidats

Whitworth thread ['wɪtwəθ-] *n Tech* filetage *m* Whitworth

whity *Am* = **whitey**

whizz [wɪz] *(pt & pp* **whizzed**, *cont* **whizzing)** **1** *vi* (**a**) *(rush)* filer; **a car whizzed past** une voiture est passée à toute allure; **I'll whizz down to the shops** je vais faire un saut dans les magasins; **the holiday has just whizzed by** les vacances ont passé à toute vitesse

(**b**) *(hiss)* **bullets whizzed around** *or* **past him** des balles sifflaient tout autour *ou* passaient près de lui en sifflant

2 *n* (**a**) *(hissing sound)* sifflement *m*

(**b**) *Fam (swift movement)* **I'll just have a (quick) whizz round with the Hoover®/the duster** je vais juste passer un petit coup d'aspirateur/de chiffon

(**c**) *Fam (bright person)* as *m*; **she's a whizz at chemistry** c'est un as en chimie; **she's a real computer whizz** c'est vraiment un as de l'informatique; **he's a real whizz in the kitchen** il cuisine comme un chef

(**d**) *Br Fam Drugs slang (amphetamines)* amphés *fpl*, amphets *fpl*

(**e**) *Am Fam* **to take a whizz** *(urinate)* faire pipi

►► *Fam* ***whizz kid*** jeune prodige□ *m*; **she's a computer whizz kid** c'est un vrai génie de l'informatique

►**whizz through** *vt insep Fam (work)* faire à toute vitesse□; *(meal)* avaler□; *(book)* lire à toute vitesse□

whizz-bang *Fam* **1** *n* (**a**) *Mil (shell)* obus□ *m (utilisé pendant la Première Guerre mondiale)* (**b**) *(fireworks)* pétard□ *m*

2 *adj (first-rate)* champion

WHO [,dʌbəljuːeɪtʃ'əʊ] *n (abbr* **World Health Organization)** OMS *f*

who [huː] **1** *pron (what person or persons → as subject)* (qui est-ce) qui; *(→ as object)* qui est-ce que, qui; **who are you?** qui êtes-vous?; **who is it?** *(at door)* qui est-ce?, qui est là?; **who's speaking?** *(on telephone)* qui est à l'appareil?; *(asking for third person)* c'est de la part de qui?; **who's going with you?** qui est-ce qui *ou* qui t'accompagne?; **it's Michael – who?** c'est Michael – qui ça?; **I told him who I was** je lui ai dit qui j'étais; **find out who they are** voyez qui c'est *ou* qui sont ces gens; **bring who you want** amenez qui vous voulez; **who do you think you are?** vous vous prenez pour qui?; **who do you think you are, giving me orders?** de quel droit est-ce que vous me donnez des ordres?; **who did you say was coming to the party?** qui avez-vous dit qui viendrait à la soirée?; **who did they invite?** qui est-ce qu'ils ont invité?, qui ont-ils invité?; **you'll have to tell me who's who** il faudra que tu me dises qui est qui; **who is the film by?** de qui est le film?; **who is the letter from?** la lettre est de qui?, de qui est la lettre?; **who did he go with?** avec qui y est-il allé?; **who were you talking to?** à qui parliez-vous?

2 *relative pron* qui; **the family who lived here moved away** la famille qui habitait ici a déménagé; **those of you who were late** ceux d'entre vous qui sont arrivés en retard; **anyone who so wishes may leave** ceux qui le souhaitent peuvent partir; **any reader who finds the story lacks imagination...** les lecteurs qui trouvent que l'histoire n'est pas très originale...; **Charles, who is a policeman, lives upstairs** Charles, qui est policier, vit en haut; **my mother, who I believe you've met...** ma mère, que vous avez déjà rencontrée je crois...

whoa [wəʊ] *exclam* ho!, holà!; *Fam (to person)* doucement!, attendez!

who'd [huːd] (**a**) = **who had** (**b**) = **who would**

whodunit, whodunnit [,huː'dʌnɪt] *n Fam* série *f* noire□; **to read/to write whodunits** lire/écrire des romans de série noire

whoe'er [huː'eə(r)] *pron Literary* celui qui (celle qui), quiconque

whoever [huː'evə(r)] *pron* (**a**) *(any person who)* qui; **whoever wants it can have it** celui qui le veut peut le prendre; **I'll give it to whoever needs it** je le donnerai à qui en a besoin; **invite whoever you like** invitez qui vous voulez

(**b**) *(the person who)* celui qui (celle qui) *m,f*; *(the people who)* ceux qui (celles qui) *mpl,fpl*; **whoever answered the phone had a nice voice** la personne qui a répondu au téléphone avait une voix agréable; **contact whoever found the body** contactez celui qui *ou* la personne qui a trouvé le corps

(**c**) *(no matter who)* **come out, whoever you are!** montrez-vous, qui que vous soyez!; **whoever gets the job will find it a real challenge** celui qui obtiendra cet emploi n'aura pas la tâche facile; **whoever you vote for, make sure he's honest** quel que soit celui pour qui vous votez, assurez-vous qu'il est honnête; **it's from Sandy Campbell, whoever he is** c'est de la part d'un certain Sandy Campbell, si ça te dit quelque chose; **ask Mark or Paul or whoever** demande à Mark ou à Paul ou à n'importe qui

(**d**) *(emphatic use)* qui donc; **whoever can that be?** qui cela peut-il bien être?

whole [həʊl] **1** *adj* (**a**) *(entire, complete) (with singular nouns)* entier, tout; *(with plural nouns)* entier; **it took me a whole day to paint the kitchen** j'ai mis une journée entière *ou* toute une journée pour peindre la cuisine; **I didn't read the whole book** je n'ai pas lu tout le livre *ou* le livre en entier; **I've never seen anything like it in my whole life** je n'ai jamais vu une chose pareille de toute ma vie; **that was the whole point of going there** c'est uniquement pour ça que j'y suis allé; **she said nothing the whole time we were there** elle n'a rien dit tout le temps que nous étions là; **he spent the whole time watching television** il a passé tout son temps à regarder la télévision; **I never saw her the whole evening** je ne l'ai pas vue de (toute) la soirée; **the whole truth** toute la vérité; **the whole world was watching** le monde entier regardait; **do you have to tell the whole world?** est-ce que tu tiens à ce que tout le monde le sache?; **whole cities were devastated** des villes entières furent dévastées; **there are two whole months still to go** il reste deux mois entiers; **she won the whole lot** elle a gagné le tout; **the whole thing** *or* **the whole business was a farce** ce fut un véritable fiasco; **I had to start the whole thing over again** j'ai dû tout recommencer; **forget the whole thing** n'en parlons plus

(**b**) *(as intensifier)* tout; *Fam* **a whole pile of records** tout un tas de disques; **he's got a whole collection of old photographs** il a toute une collection de vieilles photographies; **a whole new way of living** une façon de vivre tout à fait nouvelle

(**c**) *(unbroken → china, egg yolk)* intact; *(unhurt → person)* indemne, sain et sauf; **the cups were still whole** les tasses étaient toujours intactes; *Arch or Bible* **to make whole** sauver; **thy faith hath made thee whole** ta foi t'a sauvé

(**d**) *Culin (milk)* entier; *(grain)* complet(ète)

(**e**) *(brother, sister)* **whole brothers** des frères qui ont les mêmes parents

2 *n* (**a**) *(complete thing, unit)* ensemble *m*; **the whole of which this is just a part** l'ensemble dont ceci n'est qu'une partie; **the whole is greater than the sum of its parts** le tout est plus grand que la somme des parties

(**b**) *(as quantifier)* **the whole of** tout; **it will be cold over the whole of England** il fera froid sur toute l'Angleterre; **we spent the whole of August at the seaside** nous avons passé tout le mois d'août au bord de la mer; **she spent the whole of her fortune on paintings** elle a dépensé toute sa fortune *ou* sa fortune toute entière en tableaux; **can you pay the whole of the amount?** pouvez-vous payer toute la somme *ou* l'intégralité de la somme?

3 *adv* **cook the fish whole** faites cuire le poisson entier; **to swallow sth whole** avaler qch en entier; *Fam Fig* **he swallowed her story whole** il a gobé tout ce qu'elle lui a dit

4 as a whole *adv* (**a**) *(as a unit)* entièrement; **as a whole or in part** entièrement ou en partie

(**b**) *(overall)* dans son ensemble; **is it true of America as a whole?** est-ce vrai pour toute l'Amérique *ou* l'Amérique en général?; **considered as a whole, the festival was a remarkable success** dans son ensemble, le festival a été un vrai succès

5 a whole lot *adv Fam* beaucoup□; **he's a whole lot younger than his wife** il est beaucoup plus jeune que sa femme; **I don't think it will make a whole lot of difference** je ne pense pas que ça fasse une énorme différence; **there's a whole lot of things that need explaining** il y a beaucoup de choses qui doivent être expliquées; **for a whole lot of reasons** pour tout un tas de raisons

6 on the whole *adv* dans l'ensemble; **on the whole he made a good impression** dans l'ensemble, il a fait bonne impression; **I agree with that on the whole** je suis d'accord dans l'ensemble

►► *Am Mus* ***whole note*** *(semibreve)* ronde *f*; *Math* ***whole number*** *(integer)* nombre *m* entier; *Am Mus* ***whole rest*** pause *f*

wholefood ['həʊlfuːd] *n* aliment *m* complet; **the wholefood section of the supermarket** le rayon diététique du supermarché; **wholefood shop** magasin *m* diététique

wholegrain ['həʊlgreɪn] *adj (bread, flour)* complet(ète)

wholehearted [,həʊl'hɑːtɪd] *adj (unreserved)* sans réserve; **she gave them her wholehearted support** elle leur a donné un soutien sans réserve *ou* sans faille; **you have my wholehearted sympathy** je compatis de tout mon cœur à votre peine; **he is a wholehearted supporter of our cause** il est dévoué corps et âme à notre cause

wholeheartedly [,həʊl'hɑːtɪdlɪ] *adv (unreservedly)* de tout cœur; **I agree wholeheartedly** j'accepte de tout (mon) cœur; **he flung himself wholeheartedly into his new job** il s'est jeté corps et âme dans son nouveau travail

wholemeal ['həʊlmiːl] *adj Br (bread, flour)* complet(ète)

wholeness ['həʊlnɪs] *n (indivisibility)* intégrité *f*, intégralité *f*

wholesale ['həʊlseɪl] **1** *n* (vente *f* en) gros *m*; **wholesale and retail** le gros et le détail

2 *adj* (**a**) *(business, price, shop)* de gros
(**b**) *Fig (indiscriminate)* en masse; **there was a wholesale massacre of civilians** il y a eu un massacre en masse de civils

3 *adv* (**a**) *(buy, sell)* en gros; **they only sell wholesale** ils vendent uniquement en gros; **I can get it for you wholesale** je peux vous le procurer au prix de gros
(**b**) *Fig (in entirety)* **to reject sth wholesale** rejeter qch en bloc; **communities have been destroyed wholesale** des communautés entières ont été détruites

▸▸ *Fin* ***wholesale bank*** banque *f* de gros; ***wholesale co-operative*** coopérative *f* d'achats; ***wholesale customer*** client(e) *m,f* qui achète en gros; ***wholesale dealer*** grossiste *mf*; ***wholesale distribution*** distribution *f* en gros; ***wholesale goods*** marchandises *fpl* de gros; ***wholesale manufacture*** fabrication *f* en série; *Banking* ***wholesale market*** marché *m* de gré à gré entre banques; ***wholesale price*** prix *m* de gros; ***wholesale price index*** indice *m* des prix de gros; ***wholesale trade*** commerce *m* de gros; ***wholesale trader*** grossiste *mf*

wholesaler ['həʊl,seɪlə(r)] *n* grossiste *mf*, commerçant(e) *m,f* en gros

▸▸ ***wholesaler margin*** marge *f* du grossiste

wholesaling ['həʊl,seɪlɪŋ] *n* vente *f* en gros

wholesome ['həʊlsəm] *adj (healthy → food, attitude, image, life)* sain; *(→ air, climate, environment)* salubre, salutaire; *(advice)* salutaire; **a wholesome-looking boy** un garçon sain d'aspect

wholesomeness ['həʊlsəmnɪs] *n (of food, attitude, image, life)* nature *f* saine; *(of air, climate, environment)* salubrité *f*; **the wholesomeness of her appearance** son côté rangé *ou* (bien) comme il faut

wholewheat ['həʊlwiːt] *adj (bread, flour)* complet(ète)

who'll [huːl] (**a**) = **who will** (**b**) = **who shall**

wholly ['həʊlɪ] *adv* entièrement; **you will be wholly compensated for the damage** les dommages vous seront intégralement remboursés

wholly-owned subsidiary *n Com* filiale *f* à cent pour cent; **the firm has two wholly-owned subsidiaries** la société a deux filiales à cent pour cent

whom [huːm] *Formal* **1** *pron (in questions)* qui; **whom did you contact?** qui avez-vous contacté?; **whom did she see?** qui a-t-elle vu?; **for whom was the book written?** pour qui le livre a-t-il été écrit?

2 *relative pron* (**a**) *(as object of verb)* que; **she is the person whom I most admire** c'est la personne que j'admire le plus; **she saw two men, neither of whom she recognized** elle a vu deux hommes mais elle n'a reconnu ni l'un ni l'autre
(**b**) *(after preposition)* **the person to whom I am writing** la personne à qui *ou* à laquelle j'écris; **a composer about whom little is known** un compositeur sur qui *ou* sur lequel on sait peu de choses

whomever [huːm'evə(r)] *Formal or Literary* **1** *pron (in questions)* **whomever did you get that from?** [illegible]

2 *relative pron* **you may go with whomever you like** vous pouvez y aller avec qui vous voudrez; **he greeted whomever he met** il saluait tous ceux qu'il rencontrait

whomp [wɒmp] *vt Am Fam* (**a**) *(hit)* tabasser, cogner; **shut up or I'll whomp you one** tais-toi ou je t'en colle une (**b**) *(defeat)* mettre une raclée à; **the White Sox got whomped last night** les White Sox ont pris une raclée hier soir

whomsoever [,huːmsəʊ'evə(r)] *Formal or Literary* = **whomever** *relative pron*

whoop [wuːp] **1** *n* (**a**) *(yell)* cri *m*; **whoops of delight came from the nursery** il y avait des cris de joie venant de la garderie (**b**) *Med* quinte *f* de toux

2 *vi* (**a**) *(yell)* **she whooped with joy** elle poussa un cri de joie (**b**) *Med* avoir un accès de toux coquelucheuse

▸**whoop up** *vt sep Fam* **to whoop it up** *(celebrate)* faire la noce bruyamment

whoopee *Fam* **1** *exclam* [wʊ'piː] youpi!

2 *n* ['wʊpiː] **to make whoopee** *(celebrate)* faire la noce; *(have sex)* faire l'amour❑

▸▸ ***whoopee cushion*** coussin-péteur *m*

whooper swan [hʊːpə-] *n* cygne *m* chanteur *ou* sauvage

whooping ['huːpɪŋ] *adj*

▸▸ *Med* ***whooping cough*** coqueluche *f*; *Orn* ***whooping crane*** grue *f* blanche américaine

whoops [wʊps], **whoops-a-daisy** *exclam Fam* houp-là!

whoosh [wʊʃ] *Fam* **1** *n* **a whoosh of air** une bouffée d'air❑; **with a whoosh he was off** il est parti comme une flèche

2 *vi* **fighter planes whooshed by overhead** des avions de combat passèrent en trombe au-dessus de nous; **the car whooshed through the puddles** la voiture passa en trombe dans les flaques

3 *exclam* zoum!

whop [wɒp] *(pt & pp* **whopped**, *cont* **whopping**) *Fam* **1** *vt (beat)* rosser; *(defeat)* écraser

2 *n (blow)* coup❑ *m*

whopper ['wɒpə(r)] *n Fam* (**a**) *(large object)* **he caught a real whopper** *(fish)* il a attrapé un poisson super géant; **he's got a whopper of a nose** il a un nez énorme❑; **that sandwich is a real whopper** c'est un énorme sandwich❑ *ou* un sandwich gigantesque; **what a whopper!** il est gigantesque!
(**b**) *(lie)* gros mensonge❑ *m*, mensonge *m* énorme❑; **to tell a whopper** dire un mensonge gros comme une maison

whopping ['wɒpɪŋ] *Fam* **1** *adj* énorme❑, géant; **inflation increased to a whopping 360 percent** l'inflation a atteint le taux colossal de 360 pour cent

2 *adv* **a whopping great lie** un mensonge énorme; **a whopping great fish** un poisson super géant

3 *n (beating, defeat)* raclée *f*

whore [hɔː(r)] *Pej* **1** *n* putain *f*; *Bible (sinner)* pécheresse *f*

2 *vi* (**a**) **to go whoring** *(prostitute oneself)* se prostituer; *(frequent prostitutes)* fréquenter les prostituées, courir la gueuse (**b**) *Fig* **to whore after sth** se prostituer pour obtenir qch

▸**whore around** *vi Fam Pej* se conduire comme une putain

who're ['huːə(r)] = **who are**

whorehouse ['hɔːhaʊs, *pl* -haʊzɪz] *n Fam* maison *f* close❑

whoremonger ['hɔː,mʌŋgə(r)] *n Arch or Bible* vicieux *m*, fornicateur *m*

whoring ['hɔːrɪŋ] *n Old-fashioned & Literary* (**a**) *(by woman)* prostitution *f* (**b**) *(by man)* **because of all his whoring** parce qu'il n'arrêtait pas de fréquenter les prostituées

whorish ['hɔːrɪʃ] *adj Pej* dissolu, dépravé

whorl [wɜːl] *n* (**a**) *(on shell)* spire *f*; *(on finger)* sillon *m*; **whorls of smoke rose from the chimney** la fumée montait en spirale de la cheminée, des volutes de fumée s'échappaient de la cheminée (**b**) *Bot* verticille *m*

whorled [wɜːld] *adj (flower)* verticillé; *(shell)* convoluté

whortleberry ['wɜːtəl,berɪ] *(pl* **whortleberries**) *n* myrtille *f*

who's [huːz] (**a**) = **who is** (**b**) = **who has**

whose [huːz] **1** *possessive pron* à qui; **whose is it?** à qui est-ce?; **whose could it be?** à qui pourrait-il bien être?; **whose was the winning number?** à qui était le numéro gagnant?

2 *possessive adj* (**a**) *(in a question)* à qui, de qui; **whose car was he driving?** à qui était la voiture qu'il conduisait?; **whose child is she?** de qui est-elle l'enfant?; **whose side are you on?** de quel côté êtes-vous?; **whose fault is it?** à qui la faute?; **on whose authority are you acting?** au nom de quelle autorité agissez-vous?
(**b**) *(in a relative clause)* dont; **isn't that the man whose photograph was in the newspaper?** n'est-ce pas l'homme qui était en photo dans le journal?; **the girl, both of whose parents had died, lived with her aunt** la fille, dont les parents étaient morts, vivait avec sa tante; **they had twins neither of whose names I can remember** ils avaient des jumeaux mais je ne me souviens pas de leurs prénoms

whoso ['huːsəʊ] *pron Arch* celui qui, quiconque

whosoever [,huːsəʊ'evə(r)] *pron Formal or Literary* celui (celle) qui, quiconque

Who's Who *n* ≃ le Bottin® mondain

who've [huːv] = **who have**

WH question *n* = en anglais, question commençant par un "WH word"

WH word *n* = en anglais, mot commençant par les lettres "wh" et servant à demander un renseignement (what, when, where, who, why)

why [waɪ] **1** *adv* pourquoi; **why am I telling you this?** pourquoi est-ce que je vous dis ça?; **why is it that he never phones?** pourquoi est-ce qu'il ne téléphone jamais?; **why continue the war at all?** pourquoi *ou* à quoi bon continuer la guerre?; **why pay more?** pourquoi payer davantage?; **why the sudden panic?** pourquoi toute cette agitation?; **why not?** pourquoi pas?; **why not join us?** vous pourriez vous joindre à nous, joignez-vous donc à nous; **why me?** pourquoi moi?

2 *conj* pourquoi; **I can't imagine why she isn't here** je ne comprends pas pourquoi elle n'est pas ici; **I wonder why he left** je me demande pourquoi il est parti; **that's why he dislikes you** c'est pour ça qu'il *ou* voilà pourquoi il ne vous aime pas; **is that why she hasn't written?** est-ce pour ça qu'elle n'a pas écrit?; **they've gone, I can't think why** ils sont partis, je ne sais pas pourquoi

3 *relative pron (after reason)* **the reason why I lied was that I was scared** j'ai menti parce que j'avais peur; **he didn't tell me the reason why** il ne m'a pas dit pourquoi; **this is the reason why I lied** voilà pourquoi j'ai menti; **there is no (good) reason why she shouldn't come** il n'y a pas de raison qu'elle ne vienne pas

4 *exclam (expressing surprise, indignation etc)* **why, it's your sister!** tiens, c'est ta sœur!; **why, Mr Ricks, how kind of you to call!** M. Ricks! comme c'est gentil à vous de téléphoner!; **why, there's nothing to it!** oh, il n'y a rien de plus simple!; **why, he's an impostor!** mais enfin, c'est un imposteur!

5 *n* **the whys and wherefores** le pourquoi et le comment

whydah ['wɪdə] *n Orn* **whydah (bird)** veuve *f*

WI[1] [,dʌbəljuː'aɪ] **1** *n (abbr* **Women's Institute**) = association britannique de femmes particulièrement active en milieu rural, à qui l'on prête une image démodée

2 *npl (abbr* **West Indies**) Antilles *fpl*

WI[2] *(written abbr* **Wisconsin**) Wisconsin *m*

wick [wɪk] *n* (**a**) *(for candle, lamp)* mèche *f* (**b**) *very Fam* **to dip one's wick** *(have sex)* tremper son biscuit (**c**) *Br Fam (idiom)* **to get on sb's wick** taper sur les nerfs à qn

wicked ['wɪkɪd] **1** *adj* (**a**) *(evil → person, action, thought)* mauvais, méchant; *(immoral, indecent)* vicieux; **he's a wicked man** c'est un méchant *ou* un mauvais homme; **it was a wicked thing to do** ce n'était pas gentil; **what a wicked thing to say!** quelle méchanceté!; **she felt as if she had done something very wicked** elle avait le sentiment d'avoir fait quelque chose de très mal; *Fig* **it's a wicked waste of natural resources** c'est un gâchis scandaleux de ressources; [illegible] sorcière *f*; *Hum* **to have one's wicked way with sb** séduire qn
(**b**) *(very bad → weather)* épouvantable; *(→ temper)* mauvais, épouvantable; **he's got a wicked temper** il a très mauvais caractère; **there are some wicked bends on those mountain roads** il y a quelques méchants virages sur ces routes de montagne; **they're asking a wicked price for their house** ils ont mis leur maison en vente à un prix exorbitant; *Fam* **prices have gone up something wicked** les prix ont augmenté quelque chose de bien
(**c**) *(mischievous → person)* malicieux; *(→ smile, look, sense of humour)* malicieux, coquin; **you're a wicked little boy** tu es un petit coquin; **a wicked remark** une réflexion malicieuse *ou* espiègle
(**d**) *Fam (skilful → goal, shot)* super; **she has a wicked forehand** elle a un sacré coup droit; **that was a wicked goal** c'était un sacré *ou* super but
(**e**) *Fam (very good)* génial; **she makes a wicked curry** elle fait un curry d'enfer

2 *adv Am Fam* vachement; **this bed is wicked comfortable** il est vachement confortable, ce lit
3 *exclam Fam* génial!
4 *npl* **the wicked** les méchants *mpl*; *Hum* **(there's) no rest for the wicked** pas de repos pour les braves
wickedly ['wɪkɪdlɪ] *adv* (**a**) *(with evil intent)* méchamment, avec méchanceté (**b**) *(mischievously)* malicieusement
wickedness ['wɪkɪdnɪs] *n* (**a**) *Rel (sin, evil)* iniquité *f*, vilenie *f*; *(cruelty → of action, crime)* méchanceté *f*; *(→ of thought)* méchanceté *f*, vilenie *f*; **he spoke of the wickedness in the world** il parla du mal qui règne dans le monde (**b**) *(mischievousness → of look, sense of humour, smile)* caractère *m* malicieux *ou* espiègle, malice *f*
wicker ['wɪkə(r)] **1** *n* osier *m*; **made of wicker** en osier
2 *adj (furniture)* en osier
►► ***wicker basket*** panier *m* en osier
wickerwork ['wɪkəwɜːk] **1** *n (material)* osier *m*; *(objects)* vannerie *f*; **is the chair made of wickerwork?** est-ce que la chaise est en osier?; **they sell wickerwork** ils vendent de la vannerie
2 *comp (furniture)* en osier; *(shop)* de vannerie
wicket ['wɪkɪt] *n* (**a**) *Am (window)* guichet *m* (**b**) *(gate)* (petite) porte *f*, portillon *m* (**c**) *(in cricket → stumps)* guichet *m*; *(→ area of grass)* terrain *m* (entre les guichets); **to keep wicket** garder les guichets; **to take a wicket** éliminer un batteur; **they were 275 for six wickets** le score était de 275 pour six guichets
wicketkeeper ['wɪkɪtkiːpə(r)] *n* gardien *m* de guichet
Wicklow ['wɪkləʊ] *n* (**a**) *(town)* Wicklow (**b**) *(county)* le comté de Wicklow, = comté de l'est de la République d'Irlande; **in Wicklow** dans le comté de Wicklow
wide [waɪd] **1** *adj* (**a**) *(broad)* large; **how wide is it?** cela fait combien (de mètres) de large?, quelle largeur ça fait?; **do you know how wide it is?** savez-vous combien ça fait de large?; **the road is thirty metres wide** la route fait trente mètres de large; **they're making the street wider** ils élargissent la route; **wide hips/shoulders** hanches/épaules larges; **a wide forehead** un large front; **he gave a wide grin** il a fait un large sourire; **there are wider issues at stake here** des problèmes plus vastes sont ici en jeu; **we need to see the problem in a wider context** il faut que nous envisagions le problème dans un contexte plus général; **I'm using the word in its widest sense** j'emploie ce mot au sens le plus large; **to disappear into the wide blue yonder** disparaître, s'évanouir dans la nature
(**b**) *(fully open → eyes)* grand ouvert; **she watched with wide eyes** elle regardait les yeux grands ouverts; **his eyes were wide with terror** ses yeux étaient agrandis par l'épouvante
(**c**) *(extensive, vast)* étendu, vaste; **a wide plain** une vaste plaine; **to travel the wide world** parcourir le vaste monde; **she has wide experience in this area** elle a une longue *ou* une grande expérience dans ce domaine; **he has very wide interests** il a des centres d'intérêt très larges; **he has a wide knowledge of music** il a de vastes connaissances *ou* des connaissances approfondies en musique; **there are wide gaps in her knowledge** il y a des lacunes importantes dans ses connaissances; **the incident received wide publicity** l'événement a été largement couvert par les médias; *Com* **a wide range of products** une gamme importante de produits; **a wide range of views was expressed** des points de vue très différents furent exprimés; **a wide variety of colours** un grand choix de couleurs
(**d**) *(large → difference)* **the gap between rich and poor remains wide** l'écart (existant) entre les riches et les pauvres demeure considérable
(**e**) *Sport* **the ball was wide** la balle est passée à côté; **the shot was wide** le coup est passé à côté; *Br* **to be wide of the mark** rater *ou* être passé loin de la cible; *Fig* être loin de la vérité *ou* du compte
2 *adv* (**a**) *(to full extent)* **open (your mouth) wide** ouvrez grand votre bouche; **she opened the windows wide** elle ouvrit les fenêtres en grand; **he flung his arms wide** il a ouvert grand les bras; **place your feet wide apart** écartez bien les pieds
(**b**) *(away from target)* à côté; **the missile went wide** le missile est tombé à côté
3 *n (in cricket)* balle *f* écartée *ou* qui passe hors de la portée du batteur
►► *Comput* ***wide area network*** réseau *m* longue distance; *Br Fam Pej* ***wide boy*** escroc ❑ *m*, fricoteur *m*; *Cin* ***wide screen*** grand écran *m*, écran *m* panoramique
-wide [waɪd] *suff* **state-wide** à travers tout l'État, dans l'ensemble de l'État; **world-wide** à travers le monde (entier)
wide-angle *adj*
►► ***wide-angle lens*** grand-angle *m*, grand-angulaire *m*; *Cin & TV* ***wide-angle shot*** panoramique *m*
wide-awake *adj* tout éveillé; *Fig (alert)* éveillé, vif
wide-body *adj* **a wide-body aircraft** avion *m* à fuselage élargi, gros-porteur *m*
wide-eyed *adj* (**a**) *(with fear, surprise)* les yeux agrandis *ou* écarquillés; **he looked at me in wide-eyed astonishment** il me regarda, les yeux écarquillés d'étonnement; **she watched wide-eyed** elle regardait, les yeux écarquillés (**b**) *(naive)* candide, ingénu; **he listened with wide-eyed innocence** il écoutait avec une innocence (tout) ingénue
wide-lapelled, *Am* **wide-lapeled** [-lə'peld] *adj (jacket, shirt)* à larges revers
widely ['waɪdlɪ] *adv* (**a**) *(broadly)* **to smile widely** faire un grand sourire; **to yawn widely** bâiller profondément; **the houses were widely scattered/spaced** les maisons étaient très dispersées/espacées
(**b**) *(extensively)* **she has travelled widely** elle a beaucoup voyagé; **the talk ranged widely over a variety of topics** la discussion embrassa des sujets très variés; **the drug is now widely available/used** le médicament est maintenant largement répandu/utilisé; **it was widely believed that war was inevitable** il était largement *ou* communément admis que la guerre était inévitable; **the truth about the incident is not widely known** la vérité sur l'incident n'est pas connue du grand public; **widely held beliefs/opinions** des croyances/des opinions très répandues; **widely held views** des points de vue très répandus; **to be widely read** *(writer, book)* être très lu, avoir un grand public; *(person)* avoir beaucoup lu, être très cultivé; **she is widely read in history** elle a beaucoup lu en histoire
(**c**) *Fig (significantly)* **prices vary widely** les prix varient très sensiblement; **the two versions differed widely** les deux versions étaient sensiblement différentes; **the students came from widely differing backgrounds** les étudiants venaient d'horizons très différents
widen ['waɪdən] **1** *vt* élargir, agrandir; *Fig (experience, influence, knowledge)* accroître, étendre; **the tax reform will widen the gap between rich and poor** la réforme fiscale va accentuer *ou* agrandir l'écart entre les riches et les pauvres; **I've widened my study to include recent events** j'ai développé mon étude afin d'y inclure les derniers événements
2 *vi* s'élargir; *(eyes)* s'agrandir; *(smile)* s'accentuer; **the gulf between skilled and unskilled workers is widening** l'écart entre les travailleurs qualifiés et non qualifiés va en s'accentuant; **turn left where the road widens out** tournez à gauche à l'endroit où la route s'élargit
wideness ['waɪdnɪs] *n* largeur *f*
widening ['waɪdənɪŋ] *n* (**a**) *(of road, channel)* élargissement *m* (**b**) *(of influence)* extension *f*
wide-open *adj* (**a**) *(extensive)* grand ouvert; **the wide-open spaces of Australia** les grands espaces de l'Australie (**b**) *(fully open)* **she stood there with her eyes/mouth wide open** elle était là, les yeux écarquillés/bouche bée (**c**) *Fig (vulnerable)* exposé; **he left himself wide open to attack/to criticism** il prêtait ainsi le flanc aux attaques/aux critiques (**d**) *Am (town)* ouvert
wide-ranging [-'reɪndʒɪŋ] *adj* (**a**) *(extensive)* large, d'une grande ampleur; **she has wide-ranging interests** elle a des intérêts variés; **a wide-ranging cross-section of public opinion** un échantillon très large de l'opinion publique; **a wide-ranging report/survey** un rapport/une étude de grande envergure
(**b**) *(far-reaching → effect)* de grande portée; **the opposition called for wide-ranging reforms** l'opposition réclama des réformes de grande portée *ou* de grande envergure
wide-screen *adj* grand écran *(inv)*; **a wide-screen epic** un film à grand spectacle
widespread ['waɪdspred] *adj* (**a**) *(arms)* en croix; *(wings)* déployé; **she stood there arms wide-spread** elle se tenait là, les bras en croix (**b**) *(extensive)* (très) répandu; **there has been widespread public concern** l'opinion publique se montre extrêmement préoccupée
wide-wale *adj*
►► *Am* ***wide-wale corduroy*** velours *m* côtelé à côtes épaisses
widgeon = **wigeon**
widget ['wɪdʒɪt] *n* (**a**) *Fam (thing, gadget)* truc *m*, machin *m* (**b**) *(in beer can)* = dispositif fixé au fond des canettes de bière afin de produire de la mousse lorsque le contenu est versé dans le verre
widow ['wɪdəʊ] **1** *n* (**a**) *(woman)* veuve *f*; **she's a widow** elle est veuve; *Arch* **Widow Thomas** Madame veuve Thomas; *Br Fam Hum* **a golf widow** = une femme que son mari délaisse pour le golf; *Bible* **the widow's mite** le denier de la veuve
(**b**) *Typ & Comput* (ligne *f*) veuve *f*
(**c**) *Cards* = main de cartes placée sur la table, la face en dessous
2 *vt (usu passive)* **he was widowed last year** il a perdu sa femme l'année dernière; **she was widowed last year** elle a perdu son mari l'année dernière; **she is recently widowed** elle est veuve depuis peu, elle a perdu son mari il n'y a pas longtemps; **he is twice widowed** il est deux fois veuf
►► ***widow's peak*** = ligne de cheveux sur le front en forme de v; ***widow's pension*** allocation *f* veuvage; ***widow's weeds*** deuil *m* de veuve
widowed ['wɪdəʊd] *adj (man)* veuf; *(woman)* veuve; **his widowed mother** sa mère qui est/était veuve
widower ['wɪdəʊə(r)] *n* veuf *m*
widowhood ['wɪdəʊhʊd] *n* veuvage *m*
width [wɪdθ] *n* (**a**) *(breadth)* largeur *f*; **the room was ten metres in width** la pièce faisait dix mètres de largeur; **she swam the entire width of the river** elle a parcouru toute la largeur du fleuve à la nage (**b**) *(of swimming pool)* largeur *f*; **she swam two widths** elle a fait deux largeurs de piscine (**c**) *Tex* laize *f*, lé *m*; **half a width of cloth** une demi-laize *ou* un demi-lé de tissu
widthways ['wɪdθweɪz], **widthwise** ['wɪdθwaɪz] *adv* dans le sens de la largeur
wield [wiːld] *vt* (**a**) *(weapon)* brandir; *(pen, tool)* manier (**b**) *(influence, power)* exercer, user de
Wiener ['viːnə(r)] *n*
►► *Culin* ***Wiener schnitzel*** escalope *f* viennoise
wiener ['wiːnə(r)] *n Am (frankfurter)* saucisse *f* de Francfort
wife [waɪf] *(pl* **wives** [waɪvz]) *n* (**a**) *(spouse)* femme *f*, épouse *f*; *Admin* conjointe *f*; *Arch* **to take a wife** prendre femme; *Formal* **do you take this woman to be your lawful, wedded wife?** prenez-vous cette femme pour épouse légitime?; *Arch* **to take sb to wife** prendre qn pour femme; **she's his second wife** elle est sa deuxième femme, il l'a épousée en secondes noces; **she's been a good wife to him** elle a été une bonne épouse pour lui; **the farmer's wife** la fermière; *Br Fam* **the wife** la ménagère, la bourgeoise
(**b**) *Arch or Fam (woman)* femme *f*
wifely ['waɪflɪ] *adj* de bonne épouse
wife-swapping *n* échangisme *m*
►► ***wife-swapping party*** soirée *f* échangiste
wifey ['waɪfɪ] *n Fam (wife)* épouse ❑ *f*; **the wifey** la ménagère, la bourgeoise
wifie ['waɪfɪ] *n Scot Fam (in Edinburgh, Fife) (any woman)* bonne femme *f*
wig [wɪg] *(pt & pp* **wigged**, *cont* **wigging**) *n* perruque *f*; *(hairpiece)* postiche *m*; *Br (for lawyers)* perruque *f*
►**wig out** *vi esp Am Fam (get angry)* piquer une

crise, péter les plombs; *(go mad)* devenir cinglé, perdre la boule; *(get excited)* devenir dingue

wigeon ['wɪdʒən] *n Orn* canard *m* siffleur

wigged [wɪgd] *adj* à perruque

wigger ['wɪgə(r)] *n Am Fam Pej* = Blanc qui cherche à copier le mode de vie des Noirs

wigging ['wɪgɪŋ] *n Br Fam Old-fashioned (scolding)* savon *m*; **to get a (good) wigging** se faire disputer, se faire passer un savon; **to give sb a (good) wigging** passer un savon à qn

wiggle ['wɪgəl] **1** *vt* remuer; *(hips)* remuer, tortiller; **to wiggle one's toes** remuer les orteils; **to wiggle one's hips** tortiller les hanches

2 *vi (person)* (se) remuer, frétiller; *(loose object)* branler

3 *n* (**a**) *(movement)* tortillement *m*; **he gave his toes a wiggle** il remua ses orteils (**b**) *(wavy line)* trait *m* ondulé

wiggly ['wɪglɪ] *(compar* **wigglier,** *superl* **wiggliest)** *adj* frétillant, qui remue; **a wiggly line** un trait ondulé

wiggy ['wɪgɪ] *(compar* **wiggier,** *superl* **wiggiest)** *adj Am Fam (mad)* cinglé, tapé; *(eccentric)* loufoque, allumé

wight [waɪt] *n Arch* être *m*

wigmaker ['wɪg,meɪkə(r)] *n* perruquier(ère) *m,f*

wigwam ['wɪgwæm] *n* wigwam *m*

wilco ['wɪlkəʊ] *exclam Tel* j'exécute

wild [waɪld] **1** *adj* (**a**) *(undomesticated)* sauvage; *(untamed)* farouche; **a wild beast** une bête sauvage; *Fig* une bête féroce; **a pack of wild dogs** une meute de chiens féroces *ou* sauvages; **a wild rabbit** un lapin de garenne

(**b**) *(uncultivated → fruit)* sauvage; *(→ flower, plant)* sauvage, des champs; **wild strawberries** fraises *fpl* des bois; **many parts of the country are still wild** beaucoup de régions du pays sont encore à l'état sauvage

(**c**) *(violent)* **wild weather** du gros temps; **a wild wind** un vent violent *ou* de tempête; **a wild sea** une mer très agitée; **it was a wild night** ce fut une nuit de tempête

(**d**) *(mad)* fou (folle), furieux; **to be wild with grief/happiness/jealousy** être fou de douleur/ de joie/de jalousie; **that noise is driving me wild** ce bruit me rend fou; **he had wild eyes** *or* **a wild look in his eyes** il avait une lueur de folie dans le regard

(**e**) *(dishevelled → appearance)* débraillé; *(→ hair)* en bataille, ébouriffé; **a wild-looking young man** un jeune homme à l'air farouche

(**f**) *(enthusiastic)* **the speaker received wild applause** l'orateur reçut des applaudissements frénétiques; *Fam* **to be wild about sb** être dingue de qn; *Fam* **to be wild about sth** être dingue de qch, être emballé par qch; **I'm not really wild about modern art** l'art moderne ne m'emballe pas vraiment

(**g**) *(outrageous → idea, imagination)* insensé, fantaisiste; *(→ promise)* insensé; *(→ rumour)* délirant; *(→ plan)* extravagant; **he has some wild scheme for getting rich quick** il a un projet farfelu *ou* abracadabrant pour devenir riche en peu de temps; **the book's success was beyond his wildest dreams** le succès de son livre dépassait ses rêves les plus fous

(**h**) *(reckless)* fou (folle); **they're always having wild parties** ils organisent toujours des soirées démentes; **that was in my wild youth** c'était au temps de ma folle jeunesse; **we had some wild times together** nous en avons fait des folies ensemble; **there was a lot of wild talk about revolution/going to court** on a beaucoup parlé de révolution/de porter l'affaire devant les tribunaux

(**i**) *(random)* **to take a wild swing at sth** lancer le poing au hasard pour atteindre qch; **to make a wild guess (at the answer)** répondre à tout hasard *ou* à l'aveuglette; **at a wild guess** à vue de nez; *Cards* **aces are wild** les as sont libres; *Fig* **to play a wild card** prendre un risque

(**j**) *Fam Euph* **to sow one's wild oats** jeter sa gourme

(**k**) *Fam (idiom)* **wild and woolly** *(idea, plan)* peu réfléchi ❑; *(place)* sauvage ❑, primitif ❑

2 *n* **in the wild** en liberté; **the call of the wild** l'appel *m* de la nature; **he spent a year living in the wild** *or* **the wilds** il a passé un an dans la brousse; **the wilds of northern Canada** le fin fond du nord du Canada

3 *adv* (**a**) *(grow, live)* en liberté; **strawberries grow wild in the forest** des fraises poussent à l'état sauvage dans la forêt; **the deer live wild in the hills** les cerfs vivent en liberté dans les collines

(**b**) *(emotionally)* **to go wild with joy/rage** devenir fou de joie/de colère; **when he came on stage the audience went wild** les spectateurs hurlèrent d'enthousiasme quand il arriva sur le plateau

(**c**) *(unconstrained)* **to run wild** *(animals)* courir en liberté; *(children)* être déchaîné; **they let their children run wild** ils laissent leurs enfants traîner dans la rue; *Fig* ils ne disciplinent pas du tout leurs enfants; **they've left the garden to run wild** ils ont laissé le jardin à l'abandon *ou* revenir à l'état sauvage

►► *Bot* ***wild angelica*** angélique *f* sauvage; *Zool* ***wild boar*** sanglier *m*; ***wild card*** *(in card games)* joker *m*; *Comput* joker *m*; *Sport (player)* = sportif invité à participer à une compétition sans s'être qualifié; *(in American football)* = équipe qualifiée pour la finale sans pour autant avoir remporté sa poule; *Comput* ***wild card character*** caractère *m* joker; *Bot* ***wild carrot*** carotte *f* sauvage; ***wild cherry*** *(fruit)* merise *f*; *(tree)* merisier *m*; *Bot* ***wild chicory*** chicorée *f* sauvage, mignonnette *f*; *Zool* ***wild goat*** chèvre *f* sauvage; *(ibex)* bouquetin *m*; ***wild horse*** cheval *m* sauvage; *Fig* **wild horses couldn't drag it out of me** je serai muet comme une tombe; *Bot* ***wild hyacinth*** jacinthe *f* des bois; *Bot* ***wild madder*** garance *f* voyageuse; ***wild man*** *(savage)* sauvage *m*; *Bot* ***wild mignonette*** réséda *m* jaune; *Bot* ***wild pansy*** petite jacée *f*; *Culin* ***wild rice*** zizania *m*, riz *m* sauvage; ***wild rose*** *(dog rose)* églantine *f*; *(sweetbrier)* églantier *m* odorant; ***wild silk*** soie *f* sauvage; *Bot* ***wild thyme*** serpolet *m*; ***Wild West*** Far West *m*; **a Wild West show** = un spectacle sur le thème du Far West

'Wild Strawberries' *Bergman* 'Les Fraises sauvages'

'Wild at Heart' *Lynch* 'Sailor et Lula'

'The Wild Bunch' *Peckinpah* 'L'Équipée sauvage'

wildcat ['waɪldkæt] *(pl sense* (**a**) **inv** *or* **wildcats,** *sense* (**b**)) **1** *n* (**a**) *Zool* chat *m* sauvage; *Fig* **she's a real wildcat** c'est une vraie tigresse (**b**) *Am (product, company)* dilemme *m*

2 *adj (imprudent, ill-considered)* aléatoire, hasardeux

3 *vi Petr* creuser un puits d'exploration

►► ***wildcat strike*** grève *f* sauvage

wildcatter ['waɪld,kætə(r)] *n Am Petr (company)* entrepreneur *m* de forage d'exploration; *(driller)* ouvrier *m* qui creuse des puits d'exploration

Wildean ['waɪldɪən] *adj (of Wilde)* de Wilde; *(characteristic of Wilde)* à la manière de Wilde

wildebeest ['wɪldɪbiːst] *(pl* **inv** *or* **wildebeests)** *n Zool* gnou *m*

wilderness ['wɪldənɪs] **1** *n* (**a**) *(uninhabited area)* pays *m* désert, région *f* sauvage; *Bible* désert *m*; **a wilderness of snow and ice** une région *ou* une étendue de neige et de glace; **his warnings came like a voice in the wilderness** ses avertissements étaient comme une voix dans le désert; *Fig* **she's been relegated to the political wilderness** elle en est réduite à une traversée du désert sur le plan politique; **a concrete wilderness** un désert de béton; *Fig* **a cultural wilderness** un désert culturel

(**b**) *(overgrown piece of land)* jungle *f*; **the garden's like a wilderness** le jardin est une véritable jungle

2 *adj (region)* reculé; *Fig* **the wilderness years** la traversée du désert; **the party believes that the wilderness years may be about to end** le parti pense que sa traversée du désert touche à sa fin

►► ***wilderness area*** *(gen)* région *f* déserte; *Am (protected area)* parc *m* naturel; ***wilderness permit*** = dans les parcs naturels américains, autorisation de se rendre dans les parties les plus sauvages

wild-eyed *adj* (**a**) *(crazed)* au regard fou; **she watched in wild-eyed terror** elle regardait, les yeux remplis de terreur (**b**) *(impractical)* extravagant

wildfire ['waɪld,faɪə(r)] *n* **to spread like wildfire** se répandre comme une traînée de poudre; **news of the attack spread like wildfire** la nouvelle de l'attaque s'est répandue comme une traînée de poudre

wildfowl ['waɪldfaʊl] *npl* oiseaux *mpl* sauvages; *Hunt (collectively)* sauvagine *f*, gibier *m* à plume

wildfowler ['waɪld,faʊlə(r)] *n* chasseur *m* à la sauvagine

wildfowling ['waɪld,faʊlɪŋ] *n* chasse *f* à la sauvagine

wild-goose chase *n* fausse piste *f*; **to go on a wild-goose chase** faire fausse piste; **you're on a wild-goose chase** tu es sur une fausse piste, tu perds ton temps; **I was sent on a wild-goose chase** on m'a envoyé courir au diable pour rien

wilding ['waɪldɪŋ] *n* (**a**) *(crab apple)* pomme *f* sauvage (**b**) *(wild plant)* plante *f* sauvage (**c**) *(wild animal)* animal *m* sauvage (**d**) *Am Fam* = actes de violence extrême effectués par une bande de voyous contre des personnes

wildlife ['waɪldlaɪf] **1** *n (UNCOUNT) (wild animals)* faune *f*; *(wild animals and plants)* la faune et la flore

2 *comp* de la vie sauvage; *(photographer)* de la nature; *(programme)* sur la nature *ou* la vie sauvage; *(expert, enthusiast)* de la faune et de la flore

►► ***wildlife park*** réserve *f* naturelle; ***wildlife sanctuary*** réserve *f* animale

wildly ['waɪldlɪ] *adv* (**a**) *(violently)* violemment, furieusement; **waves beat wildly against the rocks** les vagues venaient se heurter furieusement contre les rochers; **she struggled wildly to free herself** elle se débattait furieusement pour tenter de se libérer

(**b**) *(enthusiastically)* frénétiquement; **the crowd applauded wildly** la foule applaudissait frénétiquement

(**c**) *(randomly)* au hasard; **"you're a Scorpio, aren't you" I said, guessing wildly** "tu es Scorpion, non?" ai-je demandé au hasard; **to swing wildly at sb/sth** lancer le poing au hasard en direction de qn/qch; **he dashed about wildly** il s'agitait frénétiquement; **exchange rates fluctuated wildly** les taux de change fluctuaient de façon aberrante

(**d**) *(extremely)* excessivement; **the reports are wildly inaccurate** les comptes rendus sont complètement faux; **to be wildly excited** être surexcité; **wildly expensive** follement cher; **he is wildly funny!** il est d'un drôle!; **his stories are wildly funny** ses histoires sont à mourir de rire; **to be wildly jealous/happy** être fou de jalousie/ de bonheur; **I'm not wildly happy about the decision** cette décision ne m'enchante pas spécialement; **it's not wildly encouraging** ça il est pas franchement encourageant; **I'm not wildly enthusiastic about it** je ne suis pas franchement emballé

(**e**) *(recklessly)* avec témérité; **he talked wildly of joining the foreign legion** il parlait avec témérité de s'engager dans la légion étrangère

wildness ['waɪldnɪs] *n* (**a**) *(of country, animal)* état *m* sauvage; *(of region, landscape)* aspect *m* sauvage

(**b**) *(violence, intensity → of storm)* violence *f*; *(of wind, waves)* fureur *f*, violence *f*; *(→ of applause)* frénésie *f*; *(→ of imagination)* caractère *m* insensé *ou* fantaisiste

(**c**) *(disorderliness → of party)* ambiance *f* démente; **the wildness of the atmosphere** l'ambiance démente; **the wildness of her appearance** son apparence débraillée

(**d**) *(madness)* **the wildness of his eyes** la lueur de folie qui brillait dans son regard

(**e**) *(outrageousness → of ideas, words)* extravagance *f*

wildwood ['waɪldwʊd] *n Literary* bois *m* sauvage

wiles [waɪlz] *npl* ruses *fpl*; **he fell victim to her feminine wiles** il se laissa prendre à ses ruses de femme

wilful, *Am* **willful** ['wɪlfʊl] *adj* (**a**) *(deliberate)* délibéré; *(damage)* volontaire, délibéré; **he rebuked her for wilful disobedience** il l'a réprimandée pour avoir désobéi délibérément *ou* à dessein (**b**) *(obstinate)* entêté, obstiné

wilfully, *Am* **willfully** ['wɪlfʊlɪ] *adv* (**a**) *(deliberately)* délibérément; **he wilfully disregarded my advice** il n'a délibérément *ou* sciemment tenu aucun compte de mes conseils (**b**) *(obstinately)* obstinément, avec entêtement; **she has behaved quite wilfully over this issue** elle n'en a fait qu'à sa tête à ce sujet

wilfulness, *Am* **willfulness** ['wɪlfʊlnɪs] *n* (**a**) *(deliberateness)* caractère *m* délibéré; *(of damage)* caractère *m* intentionnel (**b**) *(obstinacy)* obstination *f*, entêtement *m*

wiliness ['waɪlɪnɪs] *n (of person)* ruse *f*, caractère *m* rusé; *(of scheme, trick)* habileté *f*

WILL[1] [wɪl]

On trouve généralement **I/you/he/***etc* **will** sous leurs formes contractées **I'll/you'll/he'll/***etc*. La forme négative correspondante est **won't** que l'on écrira **will not** dans des contextes formels.

modal aux v (**a**) *(indicating the future)* **what time will you be home tonight?** à quelle heure rentrez-vous ce soir?; **the next meeting will be held in July** la prochaine réunion aura lieu en juillet; **I will be there before ten o'clock** j'y serai avant dix heures; **I don't think he will** *or* **he'll come today** je ne pense pas qu'il vienne *ou* je ne crois pas qu'il viendra aujourd'hui; **do you think she'll marry him? – I'm sure she will/she won't** est-ce que tu crois qu'elle va se marier avec lui? – je suis sûr que oui/non; **he doesn't think he'll be able to fix it** il ne pense pas pouvoir *ou* il ne croit pas qu'il pourra le réparer; **she's sure she'll have to work next weekend** elle est sûre qu'elle devra *ou* elle est sûre de devoir travailler le week-end prochain; **while he's on holiday his wife will be working** pendant qu'il sera en vacances, sa femme travaillera; **when they come home the children will be sleeping** quand ils rentreront, les enfants dormiront *ou* seront endormis

(**b**) *(indicating probability)* **that'll be the postman** ça doit être *ou* c'est sans doute le facteur; **they'll be wanting their dinner** ils doivent attendre *ou* ils attendent sans doute leur dîner; **she'll be grown up by now** elle doit être grande maintenant; **it won't be ready yet** ce n'est sûrement pas prêt

(**c**) *(indicating resolution, determination)* **I'll steal the money if I have to** je volerai l'argent s'il le faut; **I won't go!** je n'irai pas!; **I won't have it!** je ne supporterai *ou* je n'admettrai pas ça!; **you must come! – I won't!** il faut que vous veniez! – je ne viendrai pas!; **I won't go – oh yes you will!** je n'irai pas – oh (que) si!; **he can't possibly win – he will!** il ne peut pas gagner – mais si!

(**d**) *(indicating willingness)* **I'll carry your suitcase** je vais porter votre valise; **who'll volunteer? – I will!** qui se porte volontaire? – moi!; **will you marry me? – yes, I will/no, I won't** veux-tu m'épouser? – oui/non; **my secretary will answer your questions** ma secrétaire répondra à vos questions; **our counsellors will help you to solve your financial difficulties** nos conseillers vous aideront à résoudre vos difficultés financières; *Fam* **will do!** d'accord! ❑

(**e**) *(in requests, invitations)* **will you please stop smoking?** pouvez-vous éteindre votre cigarette, s'il vous plaît?; **you won't forget, will you?** tu n'oublieras pas, n'est-ce pas?; **you WILL remember to lock the door, won't you?** tu n'oublieras pas de fermer à clef, hein?; **won't you join us for lunch?** vous déjeunerez bien avec nous?; **if you will come with me** si vous voulez bien venir avec moi

(**f**) *(in orders)* **stop complaining, will you!** arrête de te plaindre, tu veux!; **he'll do as he's told** il fera ce qu'on lui dira; **you'll stop arguing this minute!** vous allez arrêter de vous disputer tout de suite!; **you'll be here at three** soyez ici à trois heures; **will you be quiet!** vous allez vous taire!

(**g**) *(indicating basic ability, capacity)* **the machine will wash up to 5 kilos of laundry** la machine peut laver jusqu'à 5 kilos de linge; **this car won't do more than 75 miles per hour** ≃ cette voiture ne peut pas faire plus de 120 kilomètres à l'heure; **this hen will lay up to six eggs a week** cette poule pond jusqu'à six œufs par semaine

(**h**) *(indicating temporary state or capacity)* **the car won't start** la voiture ne veut pas démarrer; **it will start, but it dies after a couple of seconds** elle démarre, mais elle s'arrête tout de suite; **the television won't switch on** la télévision ne veut pas s'allumer

(**i**) *(indicating habitual action)* **she'll play in her sandpit for hours** elle peut jouer des heures dans son bac à sable

(**j**) *(indicating obstinacy)* **she WILL insist on calling me Uncle Roger** elle insiste pour *ou* elle tient à m'appeler Oncle Roger; **it WILL keep on doing that** ça n'arrête pas de faire ça; **she WILL have the last word** il faut toujours qu'elle ait le dernier mot; **accidents WILL happen** on ne peut pas éviter les accidents

(**k**) *(used with "have")* **another ten years will have gone by** dix autres années auront passé

(**l**) *(expressing probability)* **she'll have finished by now** elle doit avoir fini maintenant; **you'll be tired** vous devez être fatigué

will[2] 1 *n* (**a**) *(desire, determination)* volonté *f*; **he has a weak/a strong will** il a peu/beaucoup de volonté; **she succeeded by force of will** elle a réussi à force de volonté; **a battle of wills** une lutte d'influences; **she no longer has the will to live** elle n'a plus envie de vivre; **you must have the will to win/to succeed** il faut avoir envie de gagner/de réussir; **it is the will of the people that…** le peuple veut que…; **his death was the will of God** sa mort était la volonté de Dieu; *Bible* **thy will be done** que ta volonté soit faite; **to have a will of iron** *or* **an iron will** avoir une volonté de fer; **to have a will of one's own** n'en faire qu'à sa tête, être très indépendant; **with the best will in the world** avec la meilleure volonté du monde; *Prov* **where there's a will there's a way** quand on veut on peut

(**b**) *Law* testament *m*; **last will and testament** dernières volontés *fpl*; **to make a will** faire un testament; **did he leave me anything in his will?** m'a-t-il laissé quelque chose dans son testament?

2 *vt* (**a**) *(using willpower)* **I was willing her to say yes** j'espérais qu'elle allait dire oui; **she willed herself to keep walking** elle s'est forcée à poursuivre sa marche; **I could feel the crowd willing me on** je sentais que la foule me soutenait; **you can't just will these things to happen** on ne peut pas faire arriver ces choses par un simple acte de volonté

(**b**) *(bequeath)* léguer; **she willed her entire fortune to charity** elle a légué toute sa fortune à des œuvres de charité

(**c**) *Literary (wish, intend)* vouloir; **the Lord so willed it** le Seigneur a voulu qu'il en soit ainsi; **say what you will, you won't be believed** quoi que vous disiez, on ne vous croira pas; **you can will the struggle, but you cannot will the outcome** vous pouvez décider de vous battre, mais il ne vous appartient pas de décider qui va gagner

3 *vi Arch or Literary (wish)* vouloir; **as you will** comme vous voulez

4 against one's will *adv* contre sa volonté; **he left home against his father's will** il est parti de chez lui contre la volonté de son père

5 at will *adv* à sa guise; **they can come and go at will here** ils peuvent aller et venir à leur guise ici; **fire at will!** feu à volonté!

6 with a will *adv* avec ardeur, avec acharnement; **we set to with a will** nous nous attelâmes à la tâche avec ardeur

-willed [wɪld] *suff* **a strong-willed woman** une femme qui a beaucoup de volonté *ou* très volontaire; **a weak-willed boy** un garçon qui manque de volonté

willet ['wɪlɪt] *n Orn* symphémie *f* semi-palmée

willful, willfully *etc Am* = **wilful, wilfully** *etc*

William ['wɪlɪəm] *pr n* **William of Orange** Guillaume d'Orange; **William Rufus** Guillaume le Roux; **William Tell** Guillaume Tell; **William the Conqueror** Guillaume le Conquérant

►► ***William and Mary*** = style de mobilier du règne du roi Guillaume III d'Angleterre et de la reine Marie, vers la fin du XVIIème siècle

willie = **willy**

willies ['wɪlɪz] *npl Fam* **he/it gives me the willies** il/ça me fiche la trouille

willing ['wɪlɪŋ] *adj* (**a**) *(ready, prepared)* **are you willing to cooperate with us?** êtes-vous prêt à collaborer avec nous?; **he isn't even willing to try** il ne veut même pas essayer; **to be willing and able (to do sth)** avoir l'envie et les moyens (de faire qch); **he's more than willing to change jobs** il ne demande pas mieux que de changer d'emploi; **willing or not, they must lend a hand** qu'ils le veuillent ou non, ils devront nous aider

(**b**) *(compliant)* **he's a willing victim** c'est une victime complaisante

(**c**) *(eager, enthusiastic → helper)* bien disposé, plein de bonne volonté; **she's a willing pupil** c'est une élève pleine de bonne volonté

(**d**) *(idiom)* **to show willing** faire preuve de bonne volonté

willingly ['wɪlɪŋlɪ] *adv* (**a**) *(eagerly, gladly)* de bon cœur, volontiers; **they willingly gave up their time** ils n'ont pas été avares de leur temps; **I'll do it willingly, I'll willingly do it** je le ferai volontiers (**b**) *(voluntarily)* volontairement, de plein gré; **I bet he didn't do it willingly** je parie qu'il ne l'a pas fait de bon cœur; **he came along quite willingly** il est venu de son plein gré

willingness ['wɪlɪŋnɪs] *n* (**a**) *(enthusiasm)* **he set to with great willingness** il s'est attelé à la tâche avec un grand enthousiasme (**b**) *(readiness)* **the soldiers were surprised at the enemy's willingness to fight** les soldats furent surpris que l'ennemi veuille se battre; **he admired her willingness to sacrifice her own happiness** il admirait le fait qu'elle soit prête à sacrifier son propre bonheur

will-o'-the-wisp *n also Fig* feu *m* follet

willow ['wɪləʊ] **1** *n* (**a**) *Bot* saule *m* (**b**) *Fam Old-fashioned (in cricket)* **the willow** la batte ❑

2 *comp* de saule

►► *Orn* ***willow grouse*** lagopède *m* des saules; ***willow pattern*** = motif de céramique; ***willow pattern plates*** des assiettes à motifs chinois; *Orn* ***willow tit*** mésange *f* boréale; ***willow tree*** saule *m*; *Orn* ***willow warbler*** pouillot *m* fitis

WILLOW PATTERN

Ce motif de céramique, généralement bleu sur fond blanc, représente une scène chinoise avec des personnages, un saule et un pont sur une rivière.

willowherb ['wɪləʊhɜːb] *n Bot* épilobe *m*

willowy ['wɪləʊɪ] *adj (figure, person)* élancé, svelte; *(object)* souple, flexible

willpower ['wɪlˌpaʊə(r)] *n* volonté *f*; **he lacks the willpower to diet** il n'a pas suffisamment de volonté pour se mettre au régime; **he gave up smoking through sheer willpower** il a arrêté de fumer par la seule force de sa volonté

willy ['wɪlɪ] (*pl* **willies**) *n Br Fam (penis)* zizi *m*

willy-nilly [-'nɪlɪ] *adv* (**a**) *(without order, randomly)* au hasard; **the editor just altered a few words willy-nilly** le rédacteur a simplement changé quelques mots au hasard (**b**) *(willingly or not)* bon gré mal gré

wilt[1] [wɪlt] *NEng or Arch or Literary 2nd pers sing of* **will[1]**

wilt[2] 1 *vi* (**a**) *(flower, plant)* se faner, se flétrir (**b**) *(person → with heat, fatigue)* languir, s'alanguir; *(→ lose courage)* se dégonfler; **I'm beginning to wilt** je commence à fatiguer; **to wilt under pressure** fléchir sous la pression; **he wilted under her fierce gaze** il perdit contenance sous son regard furieux

2 *vt (flower, plant)* faner, flétrir

Wilts *(written abbr* **Wiltshire***)* Wiltshire *m*

Wiltshire ['wɪltʃɪə(r)] *n* le Wiltshire, = comté du sud de l'Angleterre; **in Wiltshire** dans le Wiltshire

wily ['waɪlɪ] *(compar* **wilier,** *superl* **wiliest**) *adj (person)* rusé, malin(igne); *(scheme, trick)* habile, astucieux; **a wily old devil** *or* **fox** un vieux malin *ou* rusé

wimble ['wɪmbəl] **1** *n* vrille *f*

2 *vt* vriller

WIMP [wɪmp] *n Comput (abbr* **window, icon, mouse, pointer**) interface *f* WIMP

wimp [wɪmp] *n Fam Pej (person → physically weak)* mauviette *f*; *(→ morally weak, irresolute)* mou (molle), pâte *f* molle; **don't be such a wimp!** quel mollasson tu fais!

►**wimp out** *vi Fam* se dégonfler; **he wimped out of the fight** il s'est dégonflé au dernier moment et a refusé de se battre; **he wimped out of telling her the truth** finalement, il a eu la trouille de lui dire la vérité

wimpish ['wɪmpɪʃ] *adj Fam Pej* mollasson; **stop being so wimpish!** quel mollasson tu fais!

wimple ['wɪmpəl] *n* guimpe *f*

wimpy ['wɪmpɪ] *(compar* **wimpier,** *superl* **wimpiest**) *adj Fam Pej (physically weak)* malingre ❏; *(morally weak)* poule mouillée *(inv)*

win [wɪn] *(pt & pp* **won** [wʌn], *cont* **winning**) **1** *vi (in competition)* gagner; **she always wins at tennis** elle gagne toujours au tennis; **they're winning three nil** ils gagnent trois à zéro; **he won by only one point** il a gagné d'un point seulement; **did you win at cards?** avez-vous gagné aux cartes?; **who do you think will win?** à votre avis, qui va gagner *ou* l'emporter?; **he won by a length** *(in horseracing)* il a gagné d'une longueur; **to let sb win** laisser gagner qn; **OK, you win!** bon, d'accord!; **I (just) can't win!** j'ai toujours tort!; **to win hands down** gagner haut la main

2 *vt* (**a**) *(award, prize, race, competition)* gagner; *(scholarship)* obtenir; *(contract)* gagner, remporter; **he won first prize** il a gagné *ou* il a eu le premier prix; **he won £100 at poker** il a gagné 100 livres au poker; **win yourself a dream holiday!** gagnez des vacances de rêve!; **she won a gold medal in the Olympics** elle a obtenu une médaille d'or aux jeux Olympiques; **his superior finishing speed won him the race** il a gagné la course grâce à sa vitesse supérieure dans la dernière ligne *ou* au finish; *Br* **to win a place at university** obtenir une place à l'université; *Fig* **he has won his place in history** il s'est fait un nom dans l'histoire; **the Greens have won ten seats** les Verts ont gagné dix sièges; **they won the seat from Labour** ils ont enlevé le siège aux travaillistes; **we have won a great victory** nous avons remporté une grande victoire; **this offensive could win them the war** cette offensive pourrait leur faire gagner la guerre

(**b**) *(acquire, secure → friendship, love)* gagner; *(→ sympathy)* s'attirer; *(→ popularity)* acquérir; **to win sb's heart** gagner *ou* conquérir le cœur de qn; **to win the right to do sth** obtenir le droit de faire qch; *Arch* **to win sb's hand** obtenir la main de qn; **she was desperate to win his favour** elle cherchait désespérément à attirer ses bonnes grâces; **intransigence has won him many enemies** son intransigeance lui a valu de nombreux ennemis; **his impartiality has won him the respect of his colleagues** son impartialité lui a valu *ou* fait gagner le respect de ses collègues; **he has finally won recognition for his work** son travail a finalement été reconnu; **you've just won yourself a friend** tu viens juste de te faire un ami

(**c**) *Mining* extraire

(**d**) *Formal or Literary (reach)* **we finally won the shore after three days at sea** nous avons fini par gagner le rivage après trois jours de mer

(**e**) *Arch or Literary (earn)* **to win one's living** *or* **one's daily bread** gagner sa vie *ou* son pain quotidien

3 *n* (**a**) *Sport* victoire *f*; **they've had an unprecedented run of wins** ils ont eu une série de victoires sans précédent; **we haven't had one win all season** nous n'avons pas remporté une seule victoire de toute la saison

(**b**) *Am Horseracing* **win, place, show** gagnant, placé et troisième

►**win back** *vt sep (money, trophy)* reprendre, recouvrer; *(land)* reprendre, reconquérir; *(loved one)* reconquérir; *(esteem, respect, support)* retrouver, recouvrer; *Pol (votes, voters, seats)* récupérer, recouvrer; **they were determined to win back the Cup from the Australians** ils étaient décidés à reprendre la Coupe aux Australiens; **I won every penny back from him** je lui ai repris jusqu'au dernier centime; **you won't win back your wife with threats** tu ne vas pas reconquérir *ou* retrouver l'amour de ta femme avec des menaces

►**win out** *vi* triompher; **the need for peace won out over the desire for revenge** le besoin de paix triompha du désir de revanche

►**win over** *vt sep (convert, convince)* rallier; **he has won several of his former opponents over to his ideas** il a rallié plusieurs de ses anciens adversaires à ses idées; **the report won her over to the protesters' cause** le rapport l'a gagnée à la cause des protestataires; **we won him over in the end** nous avons fini par le convaincre; **I won him round to my point of view** j'ai réussi à le rallier à mon point de vue

►**win round** *Br* = **win over**

►**win through** *vi* remporter; **the striking rail workers won through in the end** les cheminots en grève ont fini par obtenir gain de cause

wince [wɪns] **1** *vi (from pain)* crisper le visage, grimacer; **she didn't even wince** elle n'a pas fait la moindre grimace; **to wince with pain** grimacer de douleur; *Fig* grimacer (de dégoût); **she winced at the thought** cette pensée l'a fait grimacer de dégoût

2 *n* grimace *f*

winceyette [,wɪnsɪ'et] *Br* **1** *n* flanelle *f* de coton

2 *comp (nightdress, pyjamas, sheets)* en flanelle de coton

winch [wɪntʃ] **1** *n* treuil *m*

2 *vt* **to winch sb/sth up/down** monter/descendre qn/qch au treuil; **the survivors were winched to safety** à l'aide d'un treuil, on a hissé les rescapés hors de danger

Winchester disk ['wɪntʃestə-] *n Comput* disque *m* (dur) Winchester

wind[1] [wɪnd] **1** *n* (**a**) *Met* vent *m*; **there's quite a wind** il y a beaucoup de vent; **the wind has risen/dropped** le vent s'est levé/est tombé; **the wind is changing** le vent tourne; *Naut* **into the wind** contre le vent; *Naut* **off the wind** dans le sens du vent; *Naut* **before the wind** le vent en poupe; *Fig* **the winds of change are blowing** il y a du changement dans l'air; *Fig* **with a fair wind** si tout va bien; **the cold wind of recession** le vent glacial de la récession; **to get wind of sth** avoir vent de qch; **to run like the wind** courir comme le vent; **to be scattered to the four winds** être éparpillés aux quatre vents; **there's something in the wind** il se prépare quelque chose; **to take the wind out of sb's sails** couper l'herbe sous le pied à qn; **let's wait and see which way the wind blows** attendons de voir quelle tournure les événements vont prendre

(**b**) *(breath)* souffle *m*; **to get one's wind back** reprendre haleine *ou* son souffle; **to get one's second wind** reprendre haleine *ou* son souffle; *Sport* **he had the wind knocked out of him** on lui a coupé le souffle, on l'a mis hors d'haleine; **the fall knocked the wind out of her** la chute lui a coupé le souffle; *Fam* **to put the wind up sb** flanquer la frousse à qn; *Fam* **to have the wind up** avoir la frousse

(**c**) *Fam (empty talk)* vent *m*; **his speech was just a lot of wind** son discours n'était que du vent

(**d**) *(UNCOUNT) (air in stomach)* vents *mpl*, gaz *mpl*; **broad beans give me wind** les fèves me donnent des vents *ou* des gaz; **I've got terrible wind** j'ai de terribles vents; **to break wind** lâcher des vents; **to get a baby's wind up** faire faire son renvoi à un bébé

(**e**) *Mus* **the wind (section)** les instruments *mpl* à vent, les vents *mpl*; **the wind is** *or* **are too loud** les instruments à vent sont trop forts

2 *vt* (**a**) *(make breathless)* **to wind sb** couper le souffle à qn; **the blow winded him** le coup l'a mis hors d'haleine *ou* lui a coupé le souffle; **she was quite winded by the walk uphill** la montée de la côte l'a essoufflée *ou* lui a coupé le souffle; **don't worry, I'm only winded** ne t'inquiète pas, j'ai la respiration coupée, c'est tout

(**b**) *(horse)* laisser souffler

(**c**) *(baby)* faire faire son renvoi à

(**d**) *Hunt (prey)* avoir vent de

►► **wind chimes** carillon *m* éolien; **wind cone** manche *f* à air; **wind energy** énergie *f* éolienne; **wind farm** champ *m* d'éoliennes; **wind gauge** anémomètre *m*; *Mus* **wind harp** harpe *f* éolienne; *Mus* **wind instrument** instrument *m* à vent; *Theat* **wind machine** machine *f* à souffler le vent; **wind power** énergie *f* du vent *ou* éolienne; **wind pump** éolienne *f*; **wind rose** rose *f* des vents; *Aviat* **wind sleeve** manche *f* à air; **wind speed** vitesse *f* du vent; **wind tunnel** tunnel *m* aérodynamique; **wind turbine** éolienne *f*

wind[2] [waɪnd] *(pt & pp* **wound** [waʊnd]) **1** *vi (bend → procession, road)* serpenter; *(coil → thread)* s'enrouler; **the river winds through the valley** le fleuve décrit des méandres dans la vallée *ou* traverse la vallée en serpentant

2 *vt* (**a**) *(wrap → bandage, rope)* enrouler; **I wound a scarf round my neck** j'ai enroulé une écharpe autour de mon cou; **wind the string into a ball** enrouler la ficelle pour en faire une pelote; **the snake had wound itself around the man's arm** le serpent s'était enroulé autour du bras de l'homme; *Literary* **to wind sb in one's arms** enlacer qn; **to wind sb round** *or* **around one's little finger** mener qn par le bout du nez

(**b**) *(clock, watch, toy)* remonter; *(handle)* tourner, donner un tour de; **have you wound your watch?** avez-vous remonté votre montre?

(**c**) *Arch or Hum (travel)* **to wind one's way home** prendre le chemin du retour

3 *n* (**a**) *Tech* **give the clock/the watch a wind** remontez l'horloge/la montre; **she gave the handle another wind** elle tourna la manivelle encore une fois, elle donna un tour de manivelle de plus

(**b**) *(bend → of road)* tournant *m*, courbe *f*; *(→ of river)* coude *m*

►**wind back** *vt sep* rembobiner

►**wind down 1** *vi* (**a**) *(person)* se détendre, décompresser (**b**) *(party, meeting)* tirer à sa fin; **the party didn't begin to wind down until nearly 4 a.m.** la fête a continué à battre son plein jusqu'à environ 4 heures du matin (**c**) *Tech (clock, watch)* ralentir

2 *vt sep* (**a**) *Tech (lower)* faire descendre; *(car window)* baisser (**b**) *(bring to an end → business)* mener (doucement) vers sa fin

►**wind forward** *vt sep* (faire) avancer

►**wind off** *vt sep* dérouler; *(from a spool or reel)* dévider

►**wind on** *vt sep* enrouler

►**wind up 1** *vt sep* (**a**) *(conclude → meeting)* terminer; *(→ account, business)* liquider; **the chairman wound up the debate** le président a clos le *ou* mis fin au débat; **the business will be wound up by the end of the year** l'entreprise sera liquidée avant la fin de l'année

(**b**) *(raise)* monter, faire monter; *(car window)* monter, fermer

(**c**) *(string, thread)* enrouler; *(on a spool)* dévider

(**d**) *Tech (clock, watch, toy)* remonter; *Fam Fig* **to be wound up (about sth)** être à cran (à cause de qch)

(**e**) *Br Fam (annoy)* asticoter; *(tease)* faire marcher; *(fool)* mettre en boîte; **they're only winding you up** ils te font marcher, ils essaient seulement de te mettre en boîte; **don't you know when you're being wound up?** tu ne te rends même pas compte quand on te fait marcher *ou* quand on essaie de te mettre en boîte?

2 *vi* (**a**) *Fam (end up)* finir ❏; **he wound up in jail** il a fini *ou* s'est retrouvé en prison; **she'll wind up begging in the streets** elle finira par mendier dans la rue; **he wound up with a broken nose** il a fini avec le nez cassé; **we usually wind up back at my place** généralement, nous finissons chez moi; **we wound up working for the same company** nous nous sommes retrouvés à travailler pour la même compagnie

(**b**) *(end speech, meeting)* conclure; **I'd like to wind up by saying...** je voudrais conclure en disant...

windbag ['wɪndbæg] *n Fam Pej* moulin *m* à paroles, jaseur(euse) *m,f*

windbill ['wɪndbɪl] *n Fin* billet *m* de complaisance, effet *m* de complaisance

windblown [ˈwɪndbləʊn] *adj (hair)* ébouriffé par le vent; *(trees)* fouetté *ou* cinglé par le vent

windborne [ˈwɪndbɔːn] *adj* transporté par le vent

windbreak [ˈwɪndbreɪk] *n* abri-vent *m*, coupe-vent *m inv*

windbreaker® [ˈwɪnd,breɪkə(r)] *n Am* anorak *m*, coupe-vent *m inv*

windbroken [ˈwɪnd,brəʊkən] *adj (horse)* poussif

windburn [ˈwɪndbɜːn] *n* rougeurs *fpl* cutanées *(occasionnées par l'exposition au vent)*

windcheater [ˈwɪnd,tʃiːtə(r)] *n Br* anorak *m*, coupe-vent *m inv*

windchill factor [ˈwɪndtʃɪl-] *n* facteur *m* de refroidissement au vent

wind-down [waɪnd-] *n* mise *f* en sommeil, ralentissement *m*

winder [ˈwaɪndə(r)] *n (for clock)* remontoir *m*; *(for car window)* lève-vitre *m*, lève-glace *m*; *(for thread, yarn)* dévidoir *m*

windfall [ˈwɪndfɔːl] **1** *n* (**a**) *(fruit)* fruit *m* tombé
(**b**) *Fig (unexpected gain)* (bonne) aubaine *f*; **I've had a bit of a windfall from my aunt** j'ai eu la chance d'hériter d'un peu d'argent de ma tante
2 *adj (fruit)* tombé *ou* abattu par le vent
▸▸ ***windfall dividends*** dividendes *mpl* exceptionnels; ***windfall profits*** bénéfices *mpl* exceptionnels; ***windfall revenues*** revenus *mpl* inespérés *ou* exceptionnels; ***windfall tax*** impôt *m* sur les bénéfices exceptionnels

windfallen [ˈwɪnd,fɔːlən] *adj (fruit)* abattu par le vent

Windhoek [ˈwɪndhʊk] *n* Windhoek

windhover [ˈwɪnd,hɒvə(r)] *n Orn* (faucon *m*) crécerelle *f*

winding [ˈwaɪndɪŋ] **1** *adj (road, street)* tortueux, sinueux; *(river)* sinueux; *(staircase)* en hélice, en colimaçon
2 *n* (**a**) *(process)* enroulement *m*; *Elec (wire)* bobinage *m*, enroulement *m*
(**b**) *(in a river)* méandres *mpl*, coudes *mpl*; *(in a road)* zigzags *mpl*
▸▸ ***winding gear*** *(of lift)* treuil *m*; *Mining* appareils *mpl ou* machine *f* d'extraction; ***winding sheet*** linceul *m*

winding-up *n (of account, meeting)* clôture *f*; *(of business)* liquidation *f*
▸▸ ***winding-up arrangement*** *(in bankruptcy)* concordat *m*

windjammer [ˈwɪnd,dʒæmə(r)] *n* (**a**) *Naut* grand voilier *m* marchand (**b**) *Br (light jacket)* anorak *m*, coupe-vent *m inv*

windlass [ˈwɪndləs] **1** *n* treuil *m*; *Naut* guindeau *m*
2 *vt (raise)* monter au treuil; *(haul)* tirer au treuil

windless [ˈwɪndləs] *adj Literary* sans vent

windmill [ˈwɪndmɪl] **1** *n* (**a**) *(building)* moulin *m* à vent; *(toy)* moulinet *m* (**b**) *(wind turbine)* aéromoteur *m*, éolienne *f*
2 *vi* (**a**) *(arms)* tourner en moulinet (**b**) *Aviat (propeller, rotor)* tourner par la force du vent

window [ˈwɪndəʊ] **1** *n* (**a**) *(in room)* fenêtre *f*; *(in car)* vitre *f*, glace *f*; *(in front of shop)* vitrine *f*, devanture *f*; *(in church)* vitrail *m*; *(at ticket office)* guichet *m*; *(on envelope)* fenêtre *f*; **she looked out of** *or* **through the window** elle regarda par la fenêtre; **he jumped out of the window** il a sauté par la fenêtre; **to break a window** casser une vitre *ou* un carreau; **can I try on that dress in the window?** puis-je essayer la robe qui est dans la *ou* en vitrine?; *Fam* **all our plans have gone out the window** tous nos projets sont partis en fumée; *Fam* **that's my chances of promotion out the window** je peux faire une croix sur mon avancement
(**b**) *Comput* fenêtre *f*
(**c**) *(in diary)* créneau *m*, moment *m* libre; **a window of opportunity** une chance; **to create a window of opportunity for sth** créer une conjoncture favorable à qch; **they saw this as a window of opportunity to advance the cause of human rights** ils ont vu là l'occasion de faire progresser la cause des droits de l'homme
(**d**) *(insight)* **a window on the world of finance** un aperçu des milieux financiers
(**e**) *(opportune time) Astron* **launch window** fenêtre *f ou* créneau *m* de lancement; **weather window** accalmie *f (permettant de mener à bien des travaux)*
2 *comp* de fenêtre
▸▸ ***window box*** jardinière *f*; ***window cleaner*** *(person)* laveur(euse) *m,f* de vitres *ou* de carreaux; *(substance)* nettoyant *m* pour vitres; ***window display*** étalage *m*; ***window envelope*** enveloppe *f* à fenêtre; ***window frame*** châssis *m* de fenêtre; ***window ledge*** *(inside)* appui *m* de fenêtre; *(outside)* rebord *m* de fenêtre; *Am* ***window roller*** *(in car)* lève-vitre *m*; ***window sash*** = cadre vitré d'une fenêtre à guillotine; ***window seat*** *(in room)* banquette *f* sous la fenêtre; *(in train, plane)* place *f* côté fenêtre; *Am* ***window shade*** store *m*; ***window tab*** *(on suspension file)* onglet *m* à fenêtre; *Aut* ***window winder*** lève-vitre *m*

window-dress *vt Acct (accounts, balance sheet)* camoufler, habiller

window-dresser étalagiste *mf*

window-dressing (**a**) *(merchandise on display)* présentation *f* de l'étalage; *(activity)* art *m* de l'étalage; **they need someone to do the window-dressing** ils ont besoin de quelqu'un pour composer *ou* pour faire l'étalage (**b**) *Fig (facade)* façade *f*; **that's just window-dressing** ce n'est qu'une façade; **no amount of window-dressing can hide the fact that the party is in crisis** rien ne pourra camoufler l'état de crise dans lequel se trouve le parti (**c**) *Acct* habillage *m* de bilan

windowing [ˈwɪndəʊɪŋ] *n Comput* fenêtrage *m*

windowless [ˈwɪndəʊlɪs] *adj* sans fenêtres

windowpane [ˈwɪndəʊpeɪn] *n* carreau *m*, vitre *f*

window-shop *vi* faire du lèche-vitrines

window-shopper *n* = personne qui fait du lèche-vitrines; **the streets were full of window-shoppers** les rues étaient pleines de gens en train de faire du lèche-vitrines

window-shopping *n* lèche-vitrines *m inv*; **to go window-shopping** faire du lèche-vitrines

windowsill [ˈwɪndəʊsɪl] *n* rebord *m* de fenêtre

windpipe [ˈwɪndpaɪp] *n* trachée *f*

wind-pollinated [ˈwɪndˈpɒləneɪtɪd] *adj* pollinisé par le vent

wind-pollination [ˈwɪnd-] *n* pollinisation *f* par le vent

windproof [ˈwɪndpruːf] *adj* protégeant du vent

windrow [ˈwɪndrəʊ] *n Agr* andain *m*

Windscale [ˈwɪndskeɪl] *n* = ancien nom de la centrale nucléaire de Sellafield

windscreen [ˈwɪndskriːn] *n Br* pare-brise *m inv*
▸▸ ***windscreen washer*** lave-glace *m*; ***windscreen wiper*** essuie-glace *m*

windshield [ˈwɪndʃiːld] *n Am* pare-brise *m inv*
▸▸ ***windshield wiper*** essuie-glace *m*

windsock [ˈwɪndsɒk] *n Aviat* manche *f* à air

Windsor [ˈwɪnzə(r)] **1** *n* **Windsor Castle** le château de Windsor
2 *pr n* **the Windsors** la famille royale britannique, les Windsor

windstorm [ˈwɪndstɔːm] *n* (vent *m* de) tempête *f*

windsurf [ˈwɪndsɜːf] *vi* faire de la planche à voile

windsurfer [ˈwɪnd,sɜːfə(r)] *n (board)* planche *f* à voile; *(person)* véliplanchiste *mf*, planchiste *mf*

windsurfing [ˈwɪnd,sɜːfɪŋ] *n* planche *f* à voile; **to go windsurfing** faire de la planche à voile

windswept [ˈwɪndswept] *adj (place)* balayé par le vent; *(hair)* ébouriffé par le vent; **you're looking very windswept** tu as l'air tout ébouriffé par le vent

wind-up [waɪnd-] **1** *adj (mechanism)* **a wind-up toy/watch** un jouet/une montre à remontoir
2 *n* (**a**) *Br Fam (joke)* **is this a wind-up?** est-ce qu'on veut me faire marcher? (**b**) *(conclusion)* conclusion *f*

windward [ˈwɪndwəd] *Naut* **1** *adj* **on the windward side** du côté du vent
2 *n* côté *m* du vent; **to windward** au vent, contre le vent
3 *adv* contre le vent; **to sail windward** avoir le vent debout

Windward Islands *npl* **the Windward Islands** les îles *fpl* du Vent; **in the Windward Islands** aux îles du Vent

windy [ˈwɪndɪ] *(compar* **windier**, *superl* **windiest**) *adj* (**a**) *Met* **it's windy today** il y a du vent aujourd'hui; **tomorrow it will be very windy everywhere** demain, il fera *ou* il y aura du vent *ou* le vent soufflera partout; **it was terribly windy up on deck** il y avait un vent terrible *ou* le vent soufflait terriblement sur le pont; **a cold, windy morning** un matin froid et de grand vent; **it's a very wet and windy place** c'est un endroit très pluvieux et très venteux
(**b**) *Fam (pompous, verbose)* ronflant, pompeux❑
(**c**) *Fam Old-fashioned (nervous)* **to be** *or* **to get windy about sth** paniquer à propos de qch
▸▸ ***the Windy City*** = surnom de Chicago

wine [waɪn] **1** *n* (**a**) *(drink)* vin *m*; **a bottle/a glass of wine** une bouteille/un verre de vin; **red/white wine** vin rouge/blanc; **the wines of Spain** les vins espagnols; **wine and cheese evening** = petite fête où l'on déguste du vin et du fromage; **wines and spirits** *(shop sign)* vins et spiritueux
(**b**) *(colour)* lie *f* de vin
2 *comp (bottle, glass)* à vin
3 *vt* **to wine and dine sb** inviter qn dans les bons restaurants
4 *vi* **to go out wining and dining** faire la fête au restaurant
5 *adj (colour)* lie-de-vin *(inv)*
▸▸ ***wine bar*** *(drinking establishment)* bistrot *m*; ***wine box*** Cubitainer® *m*; ***wine cellar*** cave *f* (à vin), cellier *m*; ***wine cooler*** *(container)* seau *m* à rafraîchir (le vin); *Am (drink)* = mélange de vin, de jus de fruit et d'eau gazeuse; *Br* ***wine gum*** = bonbon gélifié aux fruits; ***wine lake*** excédent *m* de vin; ***wine list*** carte *f* des vins; ***wine merchant*** *(shopkeeper)* marchand(e) *m,f* de vin(s); *(wholesaler)* négociant(e) *m,f* en vin(s); ***wine rack*** casier *m* à vin; ***wine shop*** magasin *m* de vin(s); **to go to the wine shop** aller chez le marchand de vins; ***wine taster*** *(person)* dégustateur(trice) *m,f*; *(cup)* tâte-vin *m inv*, taste-vin *m inv*; ***wine tasting*** dégustation *f* (de vins); ***wine vinegar*** vinaigre *m* de vin; ***wine waiter*** sommelier *m*

winebibber [ˈwaɪn,bɪbə(r)] *n Literary Hum* ivrogne *mf*, grand amateur *m* de vin

wine-coloured *adj* lie-de-vin *(inv)*; **a wine-coloured dress** une robe lie-de-vin

wineglass [ˈwaɪnglɑːs] *n* verre *m* à vin

wineglassful [ˈwaɪnglɑːsfʊl] *n* plein verre *m* à vin

winegrower [ˈwaɪn,grəʊə(r)] *n* viticulteur(trice) *m,f*, vigneron(onne) *m,f*

winegrowing [ˈwaɪn,grəʊɪŋ] **1** *n* viticulture *f*
2 *adj (area, industry)* vinicole, viticole

winepress [ˈwaɪnpres] *n* pressoir *m* à vin

winery [ˈwaɪnərɪ] *(pl* **wineries**) *n Am* établissement *m* vinicole

wineskin [ˈwaɪnskɪn] *n* outre *f* à vin

wing [wɪŋ] **1** *n* (**a**) *(of bird, insect)* aile *f*; *Literary* **to take wing** prendre son envol *ou* son essor; **my heart took wing** mon cœur s'emplit de joie; *Literary* **to be on the wing** être en (plein) vol; **he shot the bird on the wing** il tira l'oiseau en vol; *Literary* **desire gave** *or* **lent him wings** le désir lui donnait des ailes; **to take sb under one's wing** prendre qn sous son aile
(**b**) *Aviat* aile *f*; *Fig* **on a wing and a prayer** en s'en remettant à la Providence
(**c**) *Br (of car)* aile *f*
(**d**) *Pol* aile *f*; **the radical wing of the party** l'aile *ou* la fraction radicale du parti; **the left/right wing** l'aile gauche/droite
(**e**) *(of building)* aile *f*; *(of hospital)* pavillon *m*; *(of door)* battant *m*; **the west wing** l'aile ouest
(**f**) *Sport (of field)* aile *f*; *(player)* ailier *m*; **she plays on the wing** elle est ailier
(**g**) *(of nut)* oreille *f*, ailette *f*
(**h**) *Mil & Aviat (unit)* escadre *f* aérienne
(**i**) *(of windmill)* aile *f*
(**j**) *(of armchair)* oreille *f*
2 *vt* (**a**) *(wound → bird)* blesser, toucher à l'aile; *(→ person)* blesser *ou* toucher légèrement
(**b**) *(fly) also Fig* **to wing one's way** voler; **while the letters were winging their way over the ocean** pendant que les lettres survolaient l'océan; **my report should be winging its way towards you now** mon rapport devrait te parvenir incessamment sous peu
(**c**) *Literary (cause to fly → arrow)* darder, décocher
(**d**) *Fam* **to wing it** *(improvise)* improviser❑
3 *vi Literary (fly)* **the plane winged over the mountains** l'avion survola les montagnes

4 wings *npl* (**a**) *Theat* coulisse *f*, coulisses *fpl*; *also Fig* **to wait in the wings** se tenir dans la coulisse *ou* dans les coulisses; *Fig* **younger politicians are waiting in the wings to seize power** les jeunes politiciens se tiennent dans la coulisse *ou* dans les coulisses en attendant de prendre le pouvoir

(**b**) *Am (for non-swimmer)* brassards *mpl*, flotteurs *mpl*

(**c**) *Aviat (badge)* **to win one's wings** faire ses preuves, prendre du galon

►► ***wing back*** *(in football)* arrière *m* d'aile; *Zool* ***wing case*** élytre *m*; ***wing chair*** bergère *f* à oreilles; ***wing collar*** col *m* cassé; ***wing commander*** ≃ lieutenant-colonel *m*; ***wing flap*** *(of plane)* volet *m*; ***wing forward*** *(in rugby)* ailier *m*; ***wing mirror*** rétroviseur *m* extérieur; ***wing nut*** papillon *m*, écrou *m* à ailettes; ***wing three-quarter*** *(in rugby)* trois-quarts aile *m*; ***wing tip*** *(of plane, bird)* bout *m* de l'aile

'The Wings of the Dove' *James* 'Les Ailes de la colombe'

'Wings of Desire' *Wenders* 'Les Ailes du désir'

wingding ['wɪŋdɪŋ] *n Am Fam (party)* fête❑ *f*, bringue *f*; **we had a real wingding** on a vraiment fait la bringue

winge (*cont* **wingeing**) = **whinge**

winged [wɪŋd] *adj* (**a**) *(possessing wings)* ailé (**b**) *(wounded → bird, animal)* blessé à l'aile; *(→ person)* blessé légèrement

►► *Literary* ***winged words*** paroles *fpl* ailées

'The Winged Victory' 'La Victoire de Samothrace'

-winged [wɪŋd] *suff* **white-winged** aux ailes blanches

winger ['wɪŋə(r)] *n Sport* ailier *m*

wingless ['wɪŋlɪs] *adj* sans ailes; *(insect)* aptère

winglet ['wɪŋlɪt] *n* (**a**) *Aviat* cloison *f* d'extrémité de voilure (**b**) *Orn* aile *f* bâtarde, alula *f*

wingspan ['wɪŋspæn] *n* envergure *f*

wingspread ['wɪŋspred] *n* envergure *f*

wingtips ['wɪŋtɪps] *npl Am* = chaussures assez lourdes ornées de petits trous

wink [wɪŋk] **1** *vi* (**a**) *(person)* faire un clin d'œil; **to wink at sb** faire un clin d'œil à qn; *Fig* **to wink at sth** fermer les yeux sur qch; **it's as easy as winking** c'est simple comme bonjour

(**b**) *Literary (light, star)* clignoter; **the water sparkled and winked** l'eau miroitait et scintillait

2 *vt* **to wink an eye at sb** faire un clin d'œil à qn

3 *n* clin *m* d'œil; **she gave them a knowing wink** elle leur a fait un clin d'œil entendu; **"hello darling" he said with a big wink** "bonjour chérie" dit-il en faisant un grand clin d'œil; **I didn't get a wink of sleep** *or* **I didn't sleep a wink last night** je n'ai pas fermé l'œil de la nuit; **(as) quick as a wink** en un clin d'œil; **it was all over in the wink of an eye** c'était fini en un clin d'œil

winker ['wɪŋkə(r)] *n Br Aut Fam* clignotant❑ *m*

winking ['wɪŋkɪŋ] **1** *adj (lights)* clignotant

2 *n* (**a**) *(of an eye)* clins *mpl* d'œil; **it was all over in the winking of an eye** c'était fini en un clin d'œil (**b**) *(of lights, stars)* clignotement *m*

winkle ['wɪŋkəl] *n Br* (**a**) *(shellfish)* bigorneau *m*, vigneau *m* (**b**) *Fam (penis)* zizi *m*

►**winkle out** *vt sep Fam (information)* arracher; *(person)* déloger; **to winkle information out of sb** arracher des informations à qn; **we finally managed to winkle him out of his room** nous avons finalement réussi à l'extirper de sa chambre

winkle-pickers *npl Br Fam* chaussures *fpl* pointues❑

Winnebago® [,wɪnɪ'beɪgəʊ] *n* camping-car *m*

winner ['wɪnə(r)] *n* (**a**) *(of prize, competition, race)* gagnant(e) *m,f*; *(of battle, war)* vainqueur *m*; *(of match)* vainqueur *m*, gagnant(e) *m,f*; **there will be neither winners nor losers in this war** il n'y aura ni vainqueurs ni vaincus dans cette guerre; **to back a winner** *Horseracing* jouer un cheval gagnant; *Fig* jouer gagnant, bien miser

(**b**) *Sport (winning point)* **he scored the winner** c'est lui qui a marqué le but décisif; **he played a winner** *(successful shot)* il a joué un coup gagnant

(**c**) *(successful person)* gagneur(euse) *m,f*; *(successful thing)* succès *m*; **she's one of life's winners** c'est une gagneuse, elle est de celles qui gagnent; **her latest book is a sure winner** son dernier livre va faire un vrai tabac; **to be onto a winner** tirer le bon numéro, être parti pour gagner

Winnie the Pooh [,wɪnɪðə'puː] *pr n* Winnie l'ourson

winning ['wɪnɪŋ] **1** *adj* (**a**) *(successful)* gagnant; *Sport (goal, stroke)* décisif; **to be on a winning streak** remporter victoire sur victoire; **winning number** *(in lottery)* numéro *m* gagnant *ou* sortant

(**b**) *(charming)* engageant, charmant; **that child has a winning way with her** cette enfant est très gracieuse

2 winnings *npl* gains *mpl*

►► ***winning post*** poteau *m* d'arrivée

winningmost ['wɪnɪŋməʊst] *adj Am (player, team)* qui a gagné le plus de matchs

winnow ['wɪnəʊ] **1** *vt Agr* vanner; *Fig (separate)* démêler, trier; **to winnow the chaff from the grain** *or* **the wheat** vanner; *Fig* séparer le bon grain de l'ivraie; **to winnow out fact from fiction** démêler le réel d'avec l'imaginaire

2 *n (machine)* tarare *m*, vanneuse *f*

winnower ['wɪnəʊə(r)] *n* (**a**) *(person)* vanneur(-euse) *m,f* (**b**) *(machine)* tarare *m*, vanneuse *f*

winnowing ['wɪnəʊɪŋ] *n Agr* vannage *m*; *Fig* examen *m* minutieux; **winnowings** *(of grain)* vannure *f*

►► ***winnowing basket*** van *m*

wino ['waɪnəʊ] (*pl* **winos**) *n Fam* poivrot(e) *m,f*

winsome ['wɪnsəm] *adj (person)* charmant, gracieux; *(smile)* engageant, charmeur

winsomely ['wɪnsəmlɪ] *adv* de façon charmante

winsomeness ['wɪnsəmnɪs] *n* charme *m*

winter ['wɪntə(r)] **1** *n* hiver *m*; **it never snows here in (the) winter** il ne neige jamais ici en hiver; **she was born in the winter of 1913** elle est née pendant l'hiver 1913; **we spent the winter in Nice** nous avons passé l'hiver à Nice; **a cold winter's day** une froide journée d'hiver; *Literary* **a man of seventy-five winters** un homme qui a vu passer soixante-quinze hivers; **the winter of discontent** = l'hiver 1978-79, marqué en Grande-Bretagne par de graves conflits sociaux

2 *comp (clothing, holiday)* d'hiver

3 *vi Formal (spend winter)* passer l'hiver, hiverner

4 *vt (farm animals)* hiverner

►► *Bot* ***winter aconite*** aconit *m* d'hiver; ***winter barley*** escourgeon *m*; *Bot* ***winter cherry*** alkékenge *f*, coqueret *m*; ***winter corn*** semis *m* d'hiver; *Bot* ***winter cress*** barbarée *f*; ***winter depression*** dépression *f* hivernale *ou* saisonnière; ***winter garden*** *(conservatory)* jardin *m* d'hiver; ***the Winter Olympics*** les jeux *mpl* Olympiques d'hiver; ***winter resort*** station *f* de sports d'hiver; ***winter season*** saison *f* d'hiver; ***winter solstice*** solstice *m* d'hiver; ***winter sports*** sports *mpl* d'hiver; ***winter wheat*** blé *m* d'hiver; *Orn* ***winter wren*** roitelet *m*

'The Winter's Tale' *Shakespeare* 'Le Conte d'hiver'

THE WINTER OF DISCONTENT

Cette allusion à la première phrase de la pièce *Richard III* de Shakespeare désigne souvent l'hiver 1978–79 en Grande-Bretagne, marqué par de graves conflits sociaux qui amenèrent le gouvernement travailliste à tenir des élections qu'il perdit. L'expression est parfois utilisée pour désigner des hivers plus récents présentant les mêmes caractéristiques.

winterfeed ['wɪntəfiːd] (*pt & pp* **winterfed** [-fed]) *vt* nourrir en hiver

winter-flowering *adj* hibernal

wintergreen ['wɪntəgriːn] *n Bot* gaulthérie *f*; **oil of wintergreen** essence *f* de wintergreen

winterize, -ise ['wɪntəraɪz] *vt Am* aménager pour l'hiver

winter-plough, *Am* **winter-plow** *vt Agr* entrehiverner

wintertide ['wɪntətaɪd] *n Literary* hiver *m*

wintertime ['wɪntətaɪm] *n* hiver *m*; **in (the) wintertime** en hiver

winterweight ['wɪntəweɪt] *adj (clothes)* d'hiver

wintery, wintry ['wɪntrɪ] *adj* hivernal; *Fig (look, smile)* glacial; **it's quite wintery, this morning** c'est presque un jour d'hiver, ce matin; **because of the wintery conditions** parce qu'il fait/faisait un temps d'hiver

winy ['waɪnɪ] (*compar* **winier,** *superl* **winiest**) *adj* vineux

winze [wɪnz] *adj Mining* descenderie *f*

WIP [,dʌbəljuːaɪ'piː] *n Acct* (*abbr* **work in progress**) travail *m* en cours, encours *m* de production de biens

wipe [waɪp] **1** *vt* (**a**) *(with cloth)* essuyer; **he wiped the plate dry** il a bien essuyé l'assiette; **go and wipe your hands** va t'essuyer les mains; **to wipe one's feet** s'essuyer les pieds; **to wipe one's nose** se moucher; **to wipe one's bottom** s'essuyer; **she wiped the sweat from his brow** elle essuya la sueur de son front; **she wiped her knife clean** elle nettoya son couteau (d'un coup de torchon); *Fam* **to wipe the floor with sb** réduire qn en miettes; **he wiped the floor with me** il m'a complètement démoli; **to wipe the slate clean** passer l'éponge, tout effacer; *Br Vulg* **it's not fit to wipe your arse with** tu peux te torcher avec

(**b**) *(delete → from written record, magnetic tape)* effacer; **the remark was wiped from the minutes** l'observation fut retirée du compte-rendu; **the tape has been wiped** la bande a été effacée

2 *vi* essuyer; **she wiped round the sink with a wet cloth** elle a essuyé l'évier avec un chiffon humide

3 *n* (**a**) *(action of wiping)* **give the table a wipe** donne un coup d'éponge sur la table; **he gave the plate a quick wipe** il essuya rapidement l'assiette d'un coup de torchon

(**b**) *(moist tissue)* lingette *f*; **antistatic wipe** chiffon *m* antistatique

(**c**) *TV & Cin* volet *m*

►**wipe away** *vt sep (blood, tears)* essuyer; *(dirt, dust)* enlever; **he wiped the mud away with a cloth** il enleva *ou* il ôta la boue avec un chiffon

►**wipe down** *vt sep (paintwork, walls)* lessiver

►**wipe off 1** *vt sep* (**a**) *(remove)* enlever; *Fam* **wipe that smile** *or* **that grin off your face!** enlève-moi ce sourire idiot!; *Fam* **that'll wipe the smile off his face** ça n'a rien de drôle

(**b**) *(erase)* effacer; *Rad & TV* **he wiped off half the programme by accident** il a effacé la moitié de l'émission par mégarde

(**c**) *Fin (debt)* annuler; **several millions of pounds were wiped off the value of shares** la valeur des actions a baissé de plusieurs millions de livres

2 *vi (stain)* s'enlever

►**wipe out** *vt sep* (**a**) *(clean)* nettoyer

(**b**) *(erase)* effacer; *Fig (insult, disgrace)* effacer, laver

(**c**) *(debt)* liquider, amortir; **his gambling debts wiped out his entire fortune** ses dettes de jeu ont eu raison de toute sa fortune; **many small traders were wiped out in the recession** de nombreux petits commerçants ont été balayés par la récession

(**d**) *(destroy)* anéantir, décimer; **whole families were wiped out by the disease** des familles entières ont été exterminées par la maladie; **the fire wiped out the whole district** l'incendie a détruit tout le quartier

(**e**) *Fam (exhaust)* crever; **that match really wiped me out** le match m'a complètement crevé

►**wipe up 1** *vt sep* éponger, essuyer

2 *vi Br* essuyer (la vaisselle)

wiped (out) [waɪpt-] *adj Fam (exhausted)* crevé

wipeout ['waɪpaʊt] *n Fam* (**a**) *(in surfing)* chute❑ *f* (**b**) *(failure, disaster)* cata *f*

wiper ['waɪpə(r)] *n* (**a**) *Aut* essuie-glace *m* (**b**) *Electron* balai *m*

wire ['waɪə(r)] **1** *n* (**a**) *(of metal)* fil *m* (métallique *ou* de fer); **a wire fence** un grillage; **they've cut the telephone wires** ils ont coupé les fils téléphoniques; *Fig* **he got his application in just under the wire** sa candidature est arrivée juste à temps; *Fam* **we got our wires crossed** nous ne nous sommes pas compris ❑, il y a eu un malentendu ❑

(**b**) *Old-fashioned (telegram)* télégramme *m*; **news has just come through on the wire that...** *(on telex)* on vient de nous informer par télex que...

(**c**) *esp Am Horseracing (finishing line)* ligne *f* d'arrivée; *Fig* **down to the wire** jusqu'à la dernière minute; *Fig* **to just get in under the wire** *(of application etc)* arriver de justesse; *Fig* **the peace talks went right down to the wire** les pourparlers de paix se sont poursuivis jusqu'à la toute dernière minute

(**d**) *Am Fam (hidden microphone)* micro *m* caché

2 *vt* (**a**) *(attach with wire)* relier avec du fil de fer; *(jaw)* mettre en place avec du fil de fer; *(flowers etc)* monter sur fil de fer; *(opening, fence)* grillager

(**b**) *Elec (building, house)* mettre l'électricité dans, faire l'installation électrique de; *(connect electrically)* brancher; **the lamp is wired to the switch on the wall** la lampe est branchée sur *ou* reliée à l'interrupteur placé sur le mur; **the room had been wired (up) for sound** la pièce avait été sonorisée

(**c**) *(send telegram to → person)* envoyer un télégramme à, télégraphier à; *(send by telegram → money, information)* envoyer par télégramme, télégraphier

(**d**) *Am Fam (police officer, detective)* munir d'un micro

►► ***wire brush*** brosse *f* métallique; ***wire gauge*** calibre *m* pour fils métalliques; ***wire gauze*** toile *f* métallique; ***wire glass*** verre *m* armé; ***wire mesh, wire netting*** grillage *m*, treillis *m* métallique; ***wire photo*** phototélégraphie *f*, bélinogramme *m*; ***wire rope*** câble *m* métallique; *Am* ***wire service*** agence *f* de presse *(envoyant des dépêches télégraphiques)*; *Aut* ***wire wheel*** roue *f* avec jante à rayons; ***wire wool*** éponge *f* métallique

►**wire into** *vt insep Fam* **to wire into sb** *(scold)* engueuler qn; **to wire into sth** attaquer qch; **he wired into his colleagues about their failure to keep him informed** il a engueulé ses collègues parce qu'ils ne l'avaient pas tenu au courant; **they wired into the food as if they hadn't eaten for days** ils ont attaqué la nourriture comme s'ils n'avaient pas mangé depuis des jours; **they got wired into the backlog of work** ils se sont attaqués au travail en retard

►**wire together** *vt sep* relier avec du fil de fer

►**wire up** *vt sep* (**a**) *(attach with wire)* relier avec du fil de fer; *(jaw)* mettre en place avec du fil de fer; *(flowers etc)* monter sur fil de fer; *(opening, fence)* grillager

(**b**) *Am Fam (make nervous)* énerver ❑; **he gets all wired up before exams** il est à cran avant les examens

wirecoated [ˌwaɪə'kəʊtɪd] *adj* à poils durs

wirecutter ['waɪəˌkʌtə(r)], **wirecutters** ['waɪəˌkʌtəz] *n* coupe-fil *m inv*, pince *f* coupante

wired ['waɪəd] *adj* (**a**) *Elec (to an alarm)* relié à un système d'alarme (**b**) *(wiretapped)* mis sur écoute (**c**) *(bra)* à tiges métalliques (**d**) *Fam (highly strung)* sur les nerfs, à cran; *(after taking drugs)* défoncé *(après avoir pris de la cocaïne ou des amphétamines)*

wiredraw ['waɪədrɔː] *(pt* **wiredrew** [-druː], *pp* **wiredrawn** [-drɔːn]) *vt Metal* tréfiler

wire-haired *adj (dog)* à poils durs

wireless ['waɪəlɪs] **1** *n Br Old-fashioned* TSF *f*; **wireless (set)** poste *m* de TSF; **on the wireless** à la TSF; **he sent us a message by wireless** il nous envoya un message par sans-fil

2 *comp (broadcast, waves)* de TSF

►► *Comput* ***wireless mouse*** souris *f* sans fil; *Old-fashioned* ***wireless operator*** opérateur(trice) *m,f* de TSF, radiotélégraphiste *mf*; *Old-fashioned* ***wireless room*** cabine *f* radio *(inv)*; *Old-fashioned* ***wireless set*** poste *m* de TSF, TSF *f*

wireman ['waɪəmən] *(pl* **wiremen** [-mən]) *n Am* câbleur *m*

wirepuller ['waɪəˌpʊlə(r)] *n Am Fam* personne *f* qui a du piston

wirepulling ['waɪəˌpʊlɪŋ] *n Am Fam* piston *m*; **he did some wirepulling for me** il m'a pistonné

wirestripper ['waɪəˌstrɪpə(r)] *n* dénudeur *m* de fils électriques

wiretap ['waɪətæp] *(pt & pp* **wiretapped,** *cont* **wiretapping**) **1** *vt* mettre sur écoute

2 *vi* mettre un téléphone sur écoute

3 *n* **they put a wiretap on his phone** ils ont mis son téléphone sur écoute

wiretapping ['waɪəˌtæpɪŋ] *n* mise *f* sur écoute des lignes téléphoniques

wirework ['waɪəwɜːk] *(pl* **inv**) **1** *n (UNCOUNT)* (**a**) *(making wire)* tréfilage *m* (**b**) *(wire netting)* grillage *m*, treillis *m* métallique

2 wireworks *n* tréfilerie *f*

wireworm ['waɪəwɜːm] *n* larve *f* de taupin

wiriness ['waɪərɪnɪs] *n* (**a**) *(of person)* constitution *f* mince et musclée; *(of animal)* vigueur *f* (**b**) *(of hair)* toucher *m* rêche (**c**) *Med (of pulse)* caractère *m* filiforme

wiring ['waɪərɪŋ] *n* installation *f* électrique; **the house needs new wiring** il faut refaire l'installation électrique de *ou* l'électricité dans la maison

►► ***wiring diagram*** schéma *m* de branchement, schéma *m* de câblage

Wirral ['wɪrəl] *n* **the Wirral** = promontoire entre les embouchures de la Mersey et de la Dee

wiry ['waɪərɪ] *(compar* **wirier,** *superl* **wiriest**) *adj* (**a**) *(person)* sec (sèche) et musclé; *(animal)* nerveux, vigoureux (**b**) *(hair)* rêche (**c**) *(grass)* élastique, flexible (**d**) *Med (pulse)* filiforme

Wis *(written abbr* **Wisconsin**) Wisconsin *m*

Wisconsin [wɪs'kɒnsɪn] *n* le Wisconsin; **in Wisconsin** dans le Wisconsin

wisdom ['wɪzdəm] *n* (**a**) *(advisability, judgement)* sagesse *f*; **I have my doubts about the wisdom of moving house this year** j'ai des doutes sur l'opportunité de déménager cette année

(**b**) *(store of knowledge)* sagesse *f*

(**c**) *(opinion)* avis *m* (général), jugement *m*; **(the) received** *or* **conventional wisdom** les idées *fpl* reçues; *Hum* **Donald, in his wisdom, decided we should cancel** Donald, toujours prudent, décida que nous devions annuler

►► ***wisdom tooth*** dent *f* de sagesse

wise [waɪz] **1** *adj* (**a**) *(learned, judicious)* sage; **a wise man** un sage; **you'd be wise to take my advice** vous seriez sage de suivre mes conseils; **do you think it's wise to invite his wife?** crois-tu que ce soit prudent d'inviter sa femme?

(**b**) *(clever, shrewd)* habile, astucieux; **a wise move** *(in board games)* un coup habile *ou* astucieux; **the president made a wise move in dismissing the attorney general** le président a été bien avisé de renvoyer le ministre de la Justice; **it's always easy to be wise after the event** c'est toujours facile d'avoir raison après coup; **the Three Wise Men** les Rois Mages *mpl*; **to be none the wiser** ne pas être plus avancé; **do it while he's out, he'll be none the wiser** fais-le pendant qu'il est sorti et il n'en saura rien; *Fam* **to be wise to sth** être au courant de qch; **I'm wise to you** *or* **to your schemes** je sais ce que tu manigances; *Fam* **to get wise to sb** percer qn à jour; *Fam* **you'd better get wise to what's going on** vous feriez bien d'ouvrir les yeux sur ce qui se passe; *Fam* **to put sb wise to sth** avertir qn de qch ❑; *Fam* **to put sb wise to sb** prévenir qn contre qn ❑

2 *n Literary (way)* manière *f*, façon *f*; **he is in no wise** *or* **not in any wise satisfied with his new position** il n'est point *ou* aucunement satisfait de son nouveau poste

►► *Fam* ***wise guy*** malin(igne) *m,f*; **don't be a wise guy!** ne fais pas le malin!; **OK, wise guy, what would you do?** OK, gros malin, qu'est-ce que tu ferais?

►**wise up** *Fam* **1** *vi* **he'd better wise up!** il ferait bien de se mettre dans le coup!; **to wise up to sb** voir qn sous son vrai jour ❑; **to wise up to sth** se rendre compte de qch ❑; **she finally wised up to the fact that she'd never be a great musician** elle a enfin compris qu'elle ne serait jamais une grande musicienne ❑

2 *vt sep Am* mettre dans le coup

-wise [waɪz] *suff* (**a**) *(in the direction of)* dans le sens de; **length-wise** dans le sens de la longueur (**b**) *(in the manner of)* à la manière de, comme; **he edged crab-wise up to the bar** il s'approcha du bar en marchant de côté comme un crabe (**c**) *Fam (as regards)* côté; **money-wise the job leaves a lot to be desired** le poste laisse beaucoup à désirer côté argent

wiseacre ['waɪzˌeɪkə(r)] *n Pej* bel esprit *m*

wiseass ['waɪzæs] *n Am Fam* je-sais-tout *mf inv*

wisecrack ['waɪzkræk] *n Fam* sarcasme ❑ *m*

wisecracking ['waɪzˌkrækɪŋ] *adj Fam* blagueur

wisely ['waɪzlɪ] *adv* sagement, avec sagesse

wisenheimer ['waɪzɪnˌhaɪmə(r)] *n Am* je-sais-tout *m inv*

wisent ['wiːzənt] *n Zool* aurochs *m*

WISH [wɪʃ]

souhaiter	► 1 (a), (c), (d); 2 (a)
vouloir	► 1 (c); 2 (a)
faire un vœu	► 2 (b)
souhait	► 3 (a)
vœu	► 3 (a), (c)
désir	► 3 (b)
amitiés	► 3 (c)

1 *vt* (**a**) *(expressing something impossible or unlikely)* souhaiter; **to wish sb dead** souhaiter la mort de qn; **I wish I were a bird!** je voudrais être un oiseau!; **she wished herself far away** elle aurait souhaité être loin; *Fam* **I wish I were** *or Br* **was somewhere else** j'aimerais bien être ailleurs; **wish you were here** *(on postcard)* j'aimerais bien que tu sois là; **I wish you didn't have to leave** j'aimerais que tu ne sois pas *ou* ce serait bien si tu n'étais pas obligé de partir; **I wish you hadn't said that** tu n'aurais pas dû dire ça; **I wish I'd never come!** je n'aurais jamais dû venir; **I wish I'd thought of that before** je regrette de n'y avoir pas pensé plus tôt; **why don't you come with us? – I wish I could** pourquoi ne venez-vous pas avec nous? – j'aimerais bien

(**b**) *(expressing criticism, reproach)* **I wish you'd be more careful** j'aimerais que vous fassiez plus attention; **I wish you wouldn't talk so much!** tu ne peux pas te taire un peu?; **I wish you wouldn't play that music so loud** j'aimerais bien que tu ne mettes pas la musique aussi fort

(**c**) *Formal (want)* souhaiter, vouloir; **I don't wish to appear rude, but...** je ne voudrais pas paraître grossier mais...; **he no longer wishes to discuss it** il ne veut *ou* il ne souhaite plus en parler; **do you wish to see me?** désirez-vous me voir?; **how do you wish to pay?** comment désirez-vous payer?

(**d**) *(in greeting, expressions of goodwill)* souhaiter; **I wished her a pleasant journey** je lui ai souhaité (un) bon voyage; **he wished them success in their future careers** il leur a souhaité de réussir dans leur carrière; **he wished us good day** il nous a souhaité le bonjour; **I wish you no harm** je ne vous veux pas de mal; **I wish you well** j'espère que tout ira bien pour vous; **I wish you (good) luck** je vous souhaite bonne chance; **to wish sb joy of sth** souhaiter bien du plaisir à qn pour qch

2 *vi* (**a**) *Formal (want, like)* vouloir, souhaiter; **may I see you again? – if you wish** puis-je vous revoir? – si vous le voulez *ou* le souhaitez; **do as you wish** faites comme vous voulez; *Ironic* **did you get a pay rise/go on holiday this year? – I wish!** tu as eu une augmentation/tu es allé en vacances cette année? – tu parles!

(**b**) *(make a wish)* faire un vœu; **close your eyes and wish hard** ferme les yeux et fais un vœu; *Literary* **to wish upon a star** faire un vœu en regardant une étoile

3 *n* (**a**) *(act of wishing, thing wished for)* souhait *m*, vœu *m*; **make a wish!** fais un souhait *ou* un vœu!; **to grant a wish** exaucer un vœu; **he got his wish, his wish came true** son vœu s'est réalisé

(**b**) *(desire)* désir *m*; **to express a wish for sth** exprimer le désir de qch; *Formal* **it is my (dearest) wish that...** c'est mon vœu le plus cher que...; **it was his last wish** c'était sa dernière volonté; *Literary or Hum* **your wish is my command** vos désirs sont des ordres; *Formal* **I have no wish to appear melodramatic, but...** je ne voudrais pas avoir l'air de dramatiser mais...; **she had no great wish to travel** elle n'avait pas très envie de voyager; **to respect sb's wishes** respecter les vœux de qn; **she went against my wishes** elle a agi contre ma volonté; **he joined the navy against** *or* **contrary to my wishes** il s'est engagé dans la marine contre mon gré *ou* ma volonté

(**c**) *(regards)* **give your wife my best wishes** transmettez toutes mes amitiés à votre épouse; **my parents send their best wishes** mes parents vous font toutes leurs amitiés; **with every good wish** *(in card)* avec mes meilleurs vœux; **best wishes for the coming year** meilleurs vœux pour la nouvelle année; **best wishes for a Merry Christmas** joyeux Noël; **best wishes on your graduation (day)** toutes mes/nos félicitations à l'occasion de l'obtention de votre diplôme; **(with) best wishes** *(in letter)* bien amicalement, toutes mes amitiés

►► *Psy* ***wish fulfilment*** accomplissement *m* d'un désir; ***wish list*** liste *f* de vœux; **the unions presented a wish list of their conditions** les syndicats ont présenté une liste de conditions

►**wish away** *vt sep* **you can't simply wish away the things you don't like** on ne peut pas faire comme si les choses qui nous déplaisent n'existaient pas

►**wish for** *vt insep* souhaiter; **what did you wish for?** quel était ton vœu?; **what more could a man/a woman wish for?** que peut-on souhaiter de plus?

►**wish on** *vt sep* (**a**) *(fate, problem)* souhaiter à; **I wouldn't wish this headache on anyone** je ne souhaite à personne d'avoir un mal de tête pareil (**b**) *(foist on)* **it's a terribly complicated system wished on us by head office** c'est un système très compliqué dont nous a fait cadeau la direction; **he'll probably wish the children on us for the afternoon** il nous fera sans doute cadeau des enfants pour l'après-midi

---

wishbone ['wɪʃbəʊn] *n* (**a**) *(bone)* bréchet *m*, fourchette *f*; **to pull a wishbone with sb** = tirer à deux sur le bréchet en faisant un vœu *(le vœu de celui qui casse le plus long morceau sera exaucé)* (**b**) *(in windsurfing)* wishbone *m*

►► *Aut* ***wishbone suspension*** suspension *f* triangulée

wishful thinking [wɪʃfʊl-] *n* **I suppose it was just wishful thinking** je prenais mes rêves pour la réalité; **he thinks a peace deal can be achieved but that's just wishful thinking** il pense qu'un accord de paix peut être conclu mais ce n'est pas réaliste; **they dismissed her predictions as mere wishful thinking** ils ont qualifié ses prédictions d'irréalistes

wishing well ['wɪʃɪŋ-] *n* = puits où l'on jette une pièce en faisant un vœu

wishy-washy ['wɪʃɪ,wɒʃɪ] *adj Fam (behaviour)* mou (molle); *(person)* sans personnalité □; *(colour)* délavé □; *(taste)* fadasse

wisp [wɪsp] *n* (**a**) *(of grass, straw)* brin *m*; *(of hair)* petite mèche *f*; *(of smoke, steam)* ruban *m*; *Fig* **a wisp of a girl** un petit bout de fillette (**b**) *Literary (hint, trace)* soupçon *m*, pointe *f*; **there wasn't a wisp of a cloud** il n'y avait pas le moindre nuage

wispy ['wɪspɪ] (*compar* **wispier**, *superl* **wispiest**) *adj (beard)* effilé; *(hair)* épars; *(person)* (tout) menu

wisteria [wɪ'stɪərɪə] *n* glycine *f*

wistful ['wɪstfʊl] *adj* mélancolique, nostalgique; **he sounded wistful when he spoke of her** il parlait d'elle avec une nuance de regret dans la voix

wistfully ['wɪstfʊlɪ] *adv* d'un air triste et rêveur

wit [wɪt] **1** *n* (**a**) *(humour)* esprit *m*; **to have a quick/a ready wit** avoir de la vivacité d'esprit/beaucoup d'esprit; **her prose sparkles with wit** sa prose est pétillante d'esprit

(**b**) *(humorous person)* bel esprit *m*, homme *m*/femme *f* d'esprit; **he was a great wit** c'était un homme plein d'esprit

(**c**) *(intelligence)* esprit *m*, intelligence *f*; *Fam* **he didn't have the wit to keep his mouth shut** il n'a pas eu l'intelligence de *ou* il n'a pas été assez futé pour fermer son bec; **she has quick wits** elle a l'esprit fin, elle est très fine; **you need your wits about you in this job** il faut avoir de la présence d'esprit dans ce métier; **keep your wits about you while you're travelling** sois prudent *ou* attentif pendant que tu voyages; **to live by one's wits** vivre d'expédients; **to collect** *or* **to gather one's wits** se ressaisir, reprendre ses esprits; **I was at my wits' end** je ne savais plus quoi faire; **you frightened me out of my wits** *or* **the wits out of me!** tu m'as fait une de ces peurs!

(**d**) *Arch or Literary (faculty)* sens *m*; **one's five wits** les cinq sens

2 to wit *adv Formal* à savoir

witch [wɪtʃ] **1** *n (sorceress)* sorcière *f*; *Fig* **it's that old witch of a landlady** c'est cette vieille sorcière de propriétaire; *Fam* **you little witch!** petite garce!; *Am Fam* **it's as cold as a witch's tit** *or* **titty** ça caille; **witches' Sabbath** sabbat *m* (de sorcières)

2 *vt (bewitch)* envoûter

►► *Bot* ***witch elm*** orme *m* blanc *ou* de montagne

witchcraft ['wɪtʃkrɑːft] *n (UNCOUNT)* sorcellerie *f*; **he claimed to have been a victim of witchcraft** il a prétendu qu'on lui avait jeté un sort

witchdoctor ['wɪtʃ,dɒktə(r)] *n* sorcier *m* (de tribu), shaman *m*

witchery ['wɪtʃərɪ] *n Literary* (**a**) *(witchcraft)* sorcellerie *f* (**b**) *(charm, enchantment)* ensorcellement *m*

witch-hazel *n Bot* hamamélis *m*

witch-hunt *n* chasse *f* aux sorcières; *Fig* chasse *f* aux sorcières, persécution *f* (politique)

witching hour ['wɪtʃɪŋ-] *n* **the witching hour** l'heure *f* fatale

---

WITH [wɪð]

avec	► (a), (c), (g), (j), (k)
à	► (b), (e)
chez	► (d), (e), (k)
de	► (h), (j), (l)

1 *prep* (**a**) *(by means of)* avec; **she broke it with her hands** elle l'a cassé avec ses *ou* les mains; **what did you fix it with?** avec quoi l'as-tu réparé?; **I've got nothing/I need something to open this can with** je n'ai rien pour/j'ai besoin de quelque chose pour ouvrir cette boîte; **she painted the wall with a roller** elle a peint le mur avec un *ou* au rouleau; **they fought with swords** ils se sont battus à l'épée; **she filled the vase with water** elle a rempli le vase d'eau; **his eyes filled with tears** ses yeux se remplirent de larmes; **covered/furnished/lined with** couvert/meublé/doublé de

(**b**) *(describing a feature or attribute)* à; **a boy with green eyes** un garçon aux yeux verts; **a woman with long hair** une femme aux cheveux longs; **which boy? – the one with the torn jacket** quel garçon? – celui qui a la veste déchirée; **a man with one eye/a hump/a limp** un homme borgne/bossu/boiteux; **with his/her hat on** le chapeau sur la tête; **the house with the red roof** la maison au toit rouge; **a table with three legs** une table à trois pieds; **an old woman with no teeth** une vieille femme édentée; **a child with no home** un enfant sans foyer *ou* sans famille; **she was left with nothing to eat or drink** on l'a laissée sans rien à manger ni à boire

(**c**) *(accompanied by, in the company of)* avec; **she went out with her brother** elle est sortie avec son frère; **she came in with a suitcase** elle est entrée avec une valise; **I'm sorry I don't have a handkerchief with me** je suis désolé, je n'ai pas de mouchoir; **can I go with you?** puis-je aller avec vous *ou* vous accompagner?; **I have no one to go with** je n'ai personne avec qui aller; **she stayed with him all night** *(gen)* elle est restée avec lui toute la nuit; *(sick person)* elle est restée auprès de lui toute la nuit; **are you with him?** *(accompanying)* êtes-vous avec lui?; **to leave a child with sb** laisser un enfant à la garde de qn; **I'll be with you in a minute** je suis à vous dans une minute; **are you with me?** *(supporting)* vous êtes avec moi?; *(understanding)* vous me suivez?; **I'm with you there** là, je suis d'accord avec toi; **I'm with you one hundred per cent** *or* **all the way** je suis complètement d'accord avec vous; **I'm not with you** *(don't understand)* je ne vous suis pas; **this is a problem that will always be with us** ce problème sera toujours d'actualité

(**d**) *(in the home of)* chez; **I'm (staying) with friends** je suis *ou* je loge chez des amis; **he stayed with a family** il a logé dans une famille; **she lives with her mother** elle vit chez sa mère; **I live with a friend** je vis avec un ami

(**e**) *(an employee of)* **she's with the UN** elle travaille à l'ONU; **isn't he with Ford any more?** ne travaille-t-il plus chez Ford?

(**f**) *(a client of)* **we're with the Galena Building Society** nous sommes à la Galena Building Society; **she's decided to stay** *or* **to stick with her present accountant** elle a décidé de garder le même comptable

(**g**) *(indicating joint action)* avec; **to correspond with sb** correspondre avec qn; **who did you dance with?** avec qui as-tu dansé?; **stop fighting with your brother** arrête de te battre avec ton frère

(**h**) *(indicating feelings towards someone else)* **angry/furious/at war with** fâché/furieux/en guerre contre; **in love/infatuated with** amoureux/entiché de; **pleased with** content de

(**i**) *(including)* **does the meal come with wine?** est-ce que le vin est compris dans le menu?; **the bill came to £16 with the tip** l'addition était de 16 livres service compris; **the radio didn't come with batteries** la radio était livrée sans piles; **coffee with milk** café *m* au lait; **duck with orange sauce** canard *m* à l'orange; **some cheese to eat with it** du fromage pour manger avec

(**j**) *(indicating manner)* de, avec; **he knocked the guard out with one blow** il assomma le gardien d'un (seul) coup; **he spoke with ease** il s'exprima avec aisance; **with a cry** en poussant un cri; **she hit him with all her might** elle le frappa de toutes ses forces; **"you'll be late again", she said with a smile** "tu vas encore être en retard", dit-elle avec un sourire *ou* en souriant; **with these words** *or* **with that he left** sur ces mots, il partit

(**k**) *(as regards, concerning)* **you never know with him** avec lui, on ne sait jamais; **all is well with her** elle va bien; **it's an obsession with her** c'est une manie chez elle; *Fam* **what's with you?, what's wrong with you?** qu'est-ce qui te prend?; **he isn't very good with animals** il ne sait pas vraiment s'y prendre avec les bêtes

(**l**) *(because of, on account of)* de; **white with fear** vert de peur; **sick** *or* **ill with malaria** atteint du paludisme; *Fig* **I was sick with worry** j'étais malade d'inquiétude; **with crime on the increase, more elderly people are afraid to go out** avec l'augmentation du taux de criminalité, de plus en plus de personnes âgées ont peur de sortir; **what will happen to her with both her parents dead?** *(now that they are dead)* que va-t-elle devenir maintenant que son père et sa mère sont morts?; **I can't draw with you watching** je ne peux pas dessiner si tu me regardes; **with your intelligence you'll easily guess what followed** intelligent comme vous l'êtes, vous devinerez facilement la suite; **he'll never stop smoking with his friends offering him cigarettes all the time** il n'arrêtera jamais de fumer si ses amis continuent à lui proposer des cigarettes

(**m**) *(in spite of) Fam* **with all his money he's so stingy** il a beau avoir beaucoup d'argent, il est vraiment radin; **with all his bragging he's just a coward** il a beau se vanter, ce n'est qu'un lâche; **with all his faults** malgré tous ses défauts □

2 with it *adj Fam* (**a**) *(alert)* réveillé □; **she's not really with it this morning** elle n'est pas très bien réveillée ce matin; **get with it!** réveille-toi!, secoue-toi!

(**b**) *Old-fashioned (fashionable)* dans le vent

---

withal [wɪ'ðɔːl] *adv Literary (as well, besides)* de plus, en outre; *(nevertheless)* néanmoins

withdraw [wɪð'drɔː] (*pt* **withdrew**, *pp* **withdrawn**) **1** *vt* (**a**) *(remove)* retirer; **they have withdrawn their support/their offer** ils ont retiré leur soutien/leur offre; **the car has been withdrawn (from sale)** la voiture a été retirée de la vente;

he withdrew his hand from his pocket il a retiré la main de sa poche

(**b**) *(money)* retirer; **I withdrew £500 from my account** j'ai retiré 500 livres de mon compte

(**c**) *(bring out → diplomat)* rappeler; *(→ troops)* retirer

(**d**) *(statement, remark)* retirer, rétracter; *Law (charge)* retirer; **he withdrew his previous statements** il est revenu sur *ou* il a retiré ses déclarations antérieures; *Formal* **to withdraw one's labour** faire la grève; **the right to withdraw one's labour** le droit de grève

2 *vi* (**a**) *(retire)* se retirer; **the waiter withdrew discreetly** le serveur s'est discrètement retiré; **she has decided to withdraw from politics** elle a décidé de se retirer de la politique

(**b**) *(retreat)* se retirer; *(move back)* reculer; **he withdrew ten paces** il a reculé de dix pas; **the troops withdrew to a new position** les troupes se sont retirées vers une nouvelle position; **he tends to withdraw into himself** il a tendance à se replier sur lui-même; **she often withdrew into a fantasy world** elle se réfugiait souvent dans un monde imaginaire

(**c**) *(back out → candidate, competitor)* se retirer, se désister; *(→ partner)* se rétracter, se dédire

(**d**) *(after sex)* se retirer

withdrawal [wɪð'drɔːəl] *n* (**a**) *(removal → of funding, support, troops)* retrait *m*; *(→ of envoy)* rappel *m*; *(→ of candidate)* retrait *m*, désistement *m*; *(→ of love)* privation *f*; **I support withdrawal from NATO** je soutiens notre retrait de l'OTAN

(**b**) *(of statement, remark)* rétraction *f*; *Law (of charge)* retrait *m*, annulation *f*

(**c**) *Psy* repli *m* sur soi-même, introversion *f*; **the boy is showing signs of withdrawal** le jeune garçon présente des signes de repli sur lui-même

(**d**) *Med (from drugs)* état *m* de manque; **to experience withdrawal** être en (état de) manque

(**e**) *(of money)* retrait *m*; **to make a withdrawal** faire un retrait

►► *Banking* ***withdrawal limit*** plafond *m* (d'autorisation) de retrait; ***withdrawal method*** *(of contraception)* coït *m* interrompu; *Banking* ***withdrawal notice*** avis *m* de retrait; *Banking* ***withdrawal slip*** bordereau *m* de retrait; ***withdrawal symptoms*** symptômes *mpl* de manque; **to have** *or* **to suffer from withdrawal symptoms** être en (état de) manque

withdrawn [wɪð'drɔːn] **1** *pp of* **withdraw**

2 *adj (shy)* renfermé, réservé

withdrew [wɪð'druː] *pt of* **withdraw**

withe [wɪθ, wɪð, waɪð] *n (twig)* pleyon *m*

wither ['wɪðə(r)] **1** *vi* (**a**) *(flower, plant)* se flétrir, se faner; *(body → from age)* se ratatiner; *(→ from sickness)* s'atrophier; *Fig* **to wither on the vine** *(project)* ne rien donner, ne pas aboutir; **this new initiative must not be allowed to wither on the vine** il ne faut pas que cette nouvelle initiative finisse par tomber dans l'oubli

(**b**) *Fig (beauty)* se faner; *(hope, optimism)* s'évanouir; *(memory)* s'étioler; **without the steel industry the region will simply wither and die** sans l'industrie sidérurgique, la région va mourir lentement; **the party gradually withered and died** le parti s'est peu à peu éteint

2 *vt* (**a**) *(plant)* flétrir, faner; *(body → of age)* ratatiner; *(→ of sickness)* atrophier; *Fig* **to wither sb with a look** foudroyer qn du regard

(**b**) *Fig (beauty)* altérer

►**wither away** *vi (flower, plant)* se dessécher, se faner; *(beauty)* se faner, s'évanouir; *(hope, optimism)* s'évanouir; *(memory)* disparaître, s'atrophier

withered ['wɪðəd] *adj* (**a**) *(flower, plant)* flétri, fané; *(face, cheek)* fané, flétri; **he was old and withered** il était vieux et complètement desséché (**b**) *(arm)* atrophié

withering ['wɪðərɪŋ] **1** *adj (heat, sun)* desséchant; *(criticism, remark)* cinglant, blessant; **she gave me a withering look** elle m'a lancé un regard méprisant, elle m'a foudroyé du regard; **she spoke of him with withering scorn** elle parlait de lui avec un mépris cinglant

2 *n (of plant)* flétrissure *f*; *(of arm)* atrophie *f*; *(of beauty)* déclin *m*; *(of hope, optimism)* évanouissement *m*

witheringly ['wɪðərɪŋlɪ] *adv* avec un profond mépris

witherite ['wɪðəraɪt] *n Miner* withérite *f*

withers ['wɪðəz] *npl* garrot *m* (du cheval)

withershins ['wɪðəʃɪnz] *adv Scot* à contre-sens

withhold [wɪð'həʊld] *(pt & pp* **withheld** [-'held]) *vt* (**a**) *(refuse → love, permission, support, loan)* refuser; *(refuse to pay → rent, tax)* refuser de payer; **to withhold payment** refuser de payer; **he withheld his consent** il a refusé son consentement

(**b**) *(keep back → criticism, news)* taire, cacher; *(→ information, facts)* ne pas divulguer; **to withhold the truth from sb** cacher la vérité à qn; **I managed to withhold my indignation/my laughter** j'ai réussi à contenir mon indignation/mon rire; **they withhold 2 percent of the profits** ils retiennent 2 pour cent des bénéfices

withholding [wɪð'həʊldɪŋ] *n* (**a**) *(refusal)* **the withholding of payments** le refus de payer; **the withholding of taxes** le refus de payer les impôts; **the government's withholding of aid to developing countries** le refus du gouvernement d'aider les pays en voie de développement (**b**) *(of information, facts)* rétention *f*

►► *Fin* ***withholding tax*** retenue *f* à la source, retenue *f* fiscale

within [wɪ'ðɪn] **1** *prep* (**a**) *(inside → place)* à l'intérieur de, dans; *Fig (→ group, system)* à l'intérieur de, au sein de; *(→ person)* en; **he lived and worked within these four walls** il a vécu et travaillé entre ces quatre murs; **a play within a play** une pièce dans une pièce; **new forces are at work within our society** des forces nouvelles sont à l'œuvre dans notre société; **the man's role within the family is changing** le rôle de l'homme au sein de la famille est en train de changer; **a small voice within her** une petite voix intérieure *ou* au fond d'elle-même

(**b**) *(inside the limits of)* dans les limites de; **you must remain within the circle** tu dois rester dans le *ou* à l'intérieur du cercle; **to be within the law** être dans les limites de la loi; **within the framework of the agreement** dans le cadre de l'accord; **it is not within the bounds of possibility** ça dépasse le cadre du possible; **to live within one's means** vivre selon ses moyens; **the car is well within his price range** la voiture est tout à fait dans ses prix *ou* dans ses moyens; **within reason** dans des limites raisonnables

(**c**) *(before the end of a specified period of time)* en moins de; **within the hour** *or* **an hour she had finished** en moins d'une heure, elle avait fini; **I'll let you know within a week** je vous dirai ce qu'il en est dans le courant de la semaine; **within the required time** dans le délai prescrit; **within twenty-four hours** dans les vingt-quatre heures; **use within two days of purchase** *(on packaging)* à consommer dans les deux jours suivant la date d'achat; **within a week of taking the job, she knew it was a mistake** moins d'une semaine après avoir accepté cet emploi, elle sut qu'elle avait fait une erreur; **within the next five years, within five years from now** d'ici cinq ans

(**d**) *(indicating distance, measurement)* **they were within 10 km of Delhi** ils étaient à moins de 10 km de Delhi; **we are within walking distance of the shops** nous pouvons aller faire nos courses à pied; **accurate to within 0.1 of a millimetre** précis au dixième de millimètre près; **within a radius of ten kilometres** dans un rayon de dix kilomètres; **she came within seconds of beating the record** elle a failli battre le record à quelques secondes près; **we were within sight of the shore** nous avions la côte en vue

(**e**) *(during)* **enormous changes have taken place within a single generation** de grands changements ont eu lieu en l'espace d'une seule génération; **did the accident take place within the period covered by the insurance?** l'accident a-t-il eu lieu pendant la période couverte par l'assurance?

2 *adv* dedans, à l'intérieur; **enquire within** *(sign)* renseignements à l'intérieur; **from within** de l'intérieur; **the appointment will be made from within** la nomination se fera au sein de l'entreprise

without [wɪ'ðaʊt] **1** *prep* sans; **three nights without sleep** trois nuits sans dormir; **we couldn't have done it without you** on n'aurait pas pu le faire sans vous; **without milk or sugar** sans lait ni sucre; **with or without chocolate sauce?** avec ou sans sauce au chocolat?; **to be without fear/shame** ne pas avoir peur/honte; **not without irony** non sans ironie; **he took it without so much as a thank you** il l'a pris sans même dire merci; **without any difficulty** sans aucune difficulté; **not without difficulty** non sans difficulté; **the rumour is without foundation** la rumeur est dénuée de fondement *ou* n'est pas fondée; **she did it without asking/being asked** elle l'a fait sans demander/sans qu'on le lui demande; **without looking up** sans lever les yeux; **I knocked without getting a reply** j'ai frappé sans obtenir de réponse; **leave the house without anybody knowing** quittez la maison sans que personne le sache

2 *adv Literary* au dehors, à l'extérieur; **a voice from without** une voix de l'extérieur

3 *conj NEng (unless)* **without they go themselves** à moins qu'ils y aillent eux-mêmes

with-pack premium *n Mktg* prime *f* directe

with-profits *adj Fin (pension fund)* avec participation aux bénéfices

withstand [wɪð'stænd] *(pt & pp* **withstood** [-'stʊd]) *vt (heat, punishment)* résister à; **to withstand the test of time** résister à l'épreuve du temps

withy ['wɪðɪ] *(pl* **withies**) *n* brin *m ou* lien *m* d'osier

witless ['wɪtlɪs] *adj* sot (sotte), stupide; *Fam* **to scare sb witless** faire une peur bleue à qn

witness ['wɪtnɪs] **1** *n* (**a**) *(onlooker)* témoin *m*; **the police are asking for witnesses of** *or* **to the accident** la police recherche des témoins de l'accident

(**b**) *Law (in court, to signature, will, document)* témoin *m*; **to call sb as (a) witness** citer qn comme témoin; **witness for the prosecution/defence** témoin à charge/à décharge; **two people must be witnesses to my signature/will** deux personnes doivent signer comme témoins de ma signature/de mon testament; **will you act as a witness at our wedding?** est-ce que vous voulez bien être témoin à notre mariage?

(**c**) *(testimony)* **in witness of sth** en témoignage de qch; **to be** *or* **to bear witness to sth** témoigner de qch; **to give witness on behalf of sb** témoigner en faveur de qn; *Literary* **his vast bulk was witness to his gluttony** son énorme corpulence témoignait de sa gourmandise

(**d**) *Rel* témoignage *m*; **to bear false witness** porter un faux témoignage

2 *vt* (**a**) *(see)* être témoin de, témoigner de; **did she witness the accident?** a-t-elle été témoin de l'accident?; **millions witnessed the first moon landing** des millions de gens ont vu le premier atterrissage sur la lune; **I witnessed the whole thing** j'ai assisté à tout ce qui s'est passé; **this house has witnessed many deaths** cette maison a vu de nombreux décès; **we are witnessing a historic event** nous assistons à un événement historique; **he had witnessed the entire scene from his window** il avait vu *ou* il avait assisté à toute la scène depuis sa fenêtre; **never in my entire life have I witnessed such stupidity** je n'ai jamais, de ma vie entière, vu une telle stupidité

(**b**) *(signature)* être témoin de; *(will, document)* signer comme témoin

(**c**) *(experience → change)* voir, connaître; **the 19th century witnessed many revolutions** le XIXème siècle a connu beaucoup de révolutions

3 *vi (gen) & Law* témoigner, être témoin; **to witness to sth** témoigner de qch; **to witness against sb** témoigner contre qn; **she witnessed to finding the body** elle a témoigné avoir découvert le cadavre

►► *Br* ***witness box*** barre *f* des témoins; **in the witness box** à la barre; ***witness protection programme*** service *m* de protection pour témoins en danger; *Am* ***witness stand*** barre *f* des témoins; **to take the witness stand** venir à la barre

-witted ['wɪtɪd] *suff* **quick-witted** à l'esprit vif; **dim-witted** à l'esprit lent

witter ['wɪtə(r)] *vi Br Fam Pej* **they were wittering**

on about diets ils parlaient interminablement de régimes□; **do stop wittering on** arrête de parler pour ne rien dire, arrête tes jacasseries; **he's always wittering on about the army** il n'en finit pas de parler de l'armée

wittering ['wɪtərɪŋ] *n Br Fam Pej* jacasseries *fpl*; **his constant wittering gets on my nerves** ses jacasseries constantes me tapent sur les nerfs

Wittgensteinian [ˌvɪtgən'ʃtaɪnɪən] *adj (of Wittgenstein)* de Wittgenstein; *(characteristic of Wittgenstein)* à la manière de Wittgenstein

witticism ['wɪtɪsɪzəm] *n* bon mot *m*, trait *m* d'esprit

wittily ['wɪtɪlɪ] *adv* spirituellement, avec beaucoup d'esprit

wittiness ['wɪtɪnɪs] *n* esprit *m*, humour *m*

wittingly ['wɪtɪŋlɪ] *adv Formal* en connaissance de cause, sciemment

witty ['wɪtɪ] (*compar* **wittier**, *superl* **wittiest**) *adj* spirituel, plein d'esprit; **a witty observation** un bon mot, une remarque spirituelle

wives [waɪvz] *pl of* **wife**

wiz [wɪz] *n Fam* as□ *m*, crack *m*

wizard ['wɪzəd] **1** *n* (**a**) *(magician)* enchanteur *m*, sorcier *m*

(**b**) *Fig (expert)* génie *m*; **she's a wizard with animals** elle sait vraiment s'y prendre avec les animaux; **she's a real wizard at drawing** elle est vraiment douée en dessin; **she's a wizard with computers** c'est un champion de l'ordinateur; **a financial wizard** un génie de la finance

(**c**) *Comput* assistant *m*

2 *adj Br Fam Old-fashioned* épatant; **he's a wizard card player** il est épatant comme joueur de cartes; **she's got a wizard bike!** son vélo est génial!

3 *exclam Br Fam Old-fashioned* épatant!

'The Wizard of Oz' *Baum, Fleming* 'Le Magicien d'Oz'

wizardry ['wɪzədrɪ] *n* (**a**) *(magic)* magie *f*, sorcellerie *f* (**b**) *Fig (genius)* génie *m*; **financial wizardry** le génie de la finance; **they've installed a new piece of technical wizardry in the office** ils ont installé une nouvelle merveille de la technique dans le bureau; **that was sheer wizardry with the ball** c'était un jeu purement et simplement génial

wizened ['wɪzənd] *adj (skin, hands)* desséché; *(old person)* desséché, ratatiné; *(face, fruit, vegetables)* ratatiné

wk *(written abbr* **week**) sem

Wm. *(written abbr* **William**) William

WNW *(written abbr* **west-north-west**) O-NO

WO [ˌdʌbəljuː'əʊ] *n Br Mil (abbr* **warrant officer**) adjt

wo = **whoa**

woad [wəʊd] *n* guède *f*

wobbegong ['wɒbɪgɒŋ] *n Zool* wobbegong *m*

wobble ['wɒbəl] **1** *vi* (**a**) *(hand, jelly, voice)* trembler; *(chair, table)* branler, être branlant *ou* bancal; *(compass needle)* osciller; *(drunkard)* tituber, chanceler; *(building, tooth)* bouger; *(cyclist)* aller de travers, aller en zigzag; **the stone wobbled as I stood on it** la pierre a oscillé quand je suis monté dessus; **the pile of books wobbled dangerously** la pile de livres oscilla dangereusement; **the tightrope walker wobbled and almost fell** le funambule oscilla et faillit tomber; **the child wobbled across the room** l'enfant traversa la pièce en chancelant; **she wobbled off/past on her bike** elle partit/passa sur son vélo, en équilibre instable

(**b**) *Fig (hesitate, dither)* hésiter

2 *vt* faire bouger; **don't wobble the table when I'm writing** ne fais pas bouger la table quand j'écris

3 *n* **the chair has got a bit of a wobble** la chaise est légèrement bancale *ou* branlante; **there is a slight wobble in the front wheel of the bike** la roue avant du vélo a un léger jeu; **after a few wobbles, he finally got going** après avoir cherché son équilibre, il se mit enfin en route

wobbly ['wɒblɪ] (*compar* **wobblier**, *superl* **wobbliest**, *pl* **wobblies**) **1** *adj* (**a**) *(table, chair)* branlant, bancal; *(pile)* chancelant; *(jelly)* qui tremble; **that pile looks a bit wobbly** cette pile a l'air d'être en équilibre plutôt instable

(**b**) *(hand, voice)* tremblant; **I feel a bit wobbly** je me sens un peu faible; **she's rather wobbly on her feet** elle flageole un peu *ou* elle ne tient pas très bien sur ses jambes

(**c**) *(line)* qui n'est pas droit; *(handwriting)* tremblé

2 *n Br Fam (idiom)* **to throw a wobbly** piquer une crise

wodge [wɒdʒ] *n Br Fam* gros bloc *m*, gros morceau *m*; **great wodges of paper** de gros blocs de papier

woe [wəʊ] *Literary or Hum* **1** *n* malheur *m*, infortune *f*; **a tale of woe** une histoire pathétique; **tell me your woes** raconte-moi tes malheurs, dis-moi ce qui ne va pas; **woe betide anyone who lies to me** malheur à celui qui me raconte des mensonges; **a cry of woe** un cri de détresse

2 *exclam* hélas; **woe is me!** pauvre de moi!

woebegone ['wəʊbɪˌgɒn] *adj Literary or Hum* désolé, abattu

woeful ['wəʊfʊl] *adj* (**a**) *(sad → person, look, news, situation)* malheureux, très triste; *(→ scene, tale)* affligeant, très triste (**b**) *(very poor)* lamentable, épouvantable, consternant; **it shows a woeful lack of imagination** cela démontre un manque d'imagination consternant

woefully ['wəʊfʊlɪ] *adv* (**a**) *(sadly → look, smile)* très tristement (**b**) *(badly → perform, behave)* lamentablement; **he is woefully lacking in common sense** le bon sens lui fait cruellement défaut; **our funds are woefully inadequate** nous manquons cruellement de fonds; **the garden was woefully neglected for several years** le jardin avait été très négligé pendant plusieurs années

wog [wɒg] *n Br very Fam* nègre (négresse) *m,f*, = terme raciste désignant un Noir

woggle ['wɒgəl] *n Br* bague *f* en cuir *(pour cravate de scout)*

wok [wɒk] *n* wok *m (poêle chinoise)*

woke [wəʊk] *pt of* **wake**

woken ['wəʊkən] *pp of* **wake**

wold [wəʊld] *n* haute plaine *f*, plateau *m*

wolf [wʊlf] (*pl* **wolves** [wʊlvz]) **1** *n* (**a**) *(animal)* loup *m*; *also Fig* **the big bad wolf** le grand méchant loup; **he is a wolf in sheep's clothing** c'est un loup déguisé en brebis; **it helps keep the wolf from the door** ça me/le/*etc* met à l'abri du besoin; **to throw sb to the wolves** sacrifier qn

(**b**) *Fam (seducer)* tombeur *m*

2 *vt Fam (food)* engloutir□, dévorer□

►► ***wolf child*** enfant *m* sauvage; *Br Fam Old-fashioned* ***Wolf Cub*** *(scout)* louveteau *m*; ***wolf cub*** *(animal)* louveteau *m*; ***wolf pack*** meute *f* de loups; *Entom* ***wolf spider*** lycose *f*, araignée-loup *f*; ***wolf whistle*** sifflement *m (au passage d'une femme)*

►**wolf down** *vt sep Fam (food)* engloutir□, dévorer□

wolffish ['wʊlffɪʃ] *n Ich* loup *m* de l'Atlantique

wolfhound ['wʊlfhaʊnd] *n* chien-loup *m*

wolfish ['wʊlfɪʃ] *adj (appearance)* de loup; *(appetite)* vorace

wolfishly ['wʊlfɪʃlɪ] *adv* voracement

wolfram ['wʊlfrəm] *n* tungstène *m*, wolfram *m*

wolfsbane ['wʊlfsbeɪn] *n* aconit *m* jaune

wolf-whistle *vt* siffler *(une femme)*

Wolverine [wʊlvəriːn] *n Am* habitant(e) *m,f* du Michigan

►► ***the Wolverine State*** = surnom donné au Michigan

wolverine ['wʊlvəriːn] (*pl* **inv** *or* **wolverines**) *n Zool* glouton *m*

wolves [wʊlvz] *pl of* **wolf**

woman ['wʊmən] (*pl* **women** ['wɪmɪn]) *n* (**a**) *(gen)* femme *f*; **a single/married woman** une femme célibataire/mariée; **a young woman** une jeune femme; **an old woman** une vieille femme; *Fam Pej* **he's an old woman** il fait des histoires pour rien; **come here, young woman** venez-là, mademoiselle; **she's quite the young woman now** elle fait très jeune fille maintenant; **women and children first** les femmes et les enfants d'abord; **man's perception of woman** la façon dont les hommes voient les femmes, la vision de la femme qu'a l'homme; **women live longer than men** les femmes vivent plus longtemps que les hommes; *Prov* **a woman's work is never done** = quand on est une femme, on a toujours quelque chose à faire; **I don't even know the woman!** je ne sais même pas qui elle est *ou* qui c'est!; **oh, damn the woman!** quelle idiote!; **a woman of letters** une femme de lettres; **a woman of the world** *(cultivated)* une femme du monde; *(worldly-wise)* une femme d'expérience; **she's a working/career woman** elle travaille/elle a une carrière; **the women's page** *(in newspaper)* la page des lectrices; **a woman's** *or* **women's magazine** un magazine féminin

(**b**) *(employee)* femme *f*; **a woman minds the children for me** j'ai une femme qui me garde les enfants; **the factory women left for work** les ouvrières sont parties travailler; **(cleaning) woman** femme *f* de ménage

(**c**) *Fam (wife)* femme *f*; *(girlfriend, mistress)* nana *f*; **he's bringing his new woman with him** il amène sa nouvelle copine; **the little woman** ma *ou* la petite femme; **the other woman** *(mistress)* l'autre femme

(**d**) *Fam (patronizing term of address) Old-fashioned* **my good woman** ma petite dame; **that's enough, woman!** assez, femme!

►► ***woman doctor*** (femme *f*) médecin *m*; ***woman driver*** conductrice *f*; ***woman friend*** amie *f*; ***woman police constable*** femme *f* agent de police; *Euph* ***women's problems*** problèmes *mpl* de femmes; ***woman teacher*** professeur *m* (femme); **they have a woman teacher** leur professeur est une femme

'Women in Love' *Lawrence, Russell* 'Femmes amoureuses' (roman), 'Love' (film)

'A Woman of No Importance' *Wilde* 'Une Femme sans importance'

woman-hater *n* misogyne *mf*

womanhood ['wʊmənhʊd] *n (UNCOUNT)* (**a**) *(female nature)* féminité *f*; **to reach womanhood** devenir une femme (**b**) *(women collectively)* les femmes *fpl*

womanish ['wʊmənɪʃ] *adj Pej (man)* efféminé; *(characteristic)* de femme, féminin

womanize, -ise ['wʊmənaɪz] *vi* courir les femmes

womanizer ['wʊmənaɪzə(r)] *n* coureur *m* de jupons

womanizing ['wʊmənaɪzɪŋ] **1** *n* **she was fed up with his womanizing** elle en avait assez qu'il coure le jupon

2 *adj (ways, habits)* de coureur de jupon; **her womanizing husband** son coureur de jupon de mari

womankind [ˌwʊmən'kaɪnd] *n* les femmes *fpl*

womanlike ['wʊmənlaɪk] *adj* féminin

womanliness ['wʊmənlɪnɪs] *n* féminité *f*

womanly ['wʊmənlɪ] *adj (virtue, figure)* féminin, de femme; *(act)* digne d'une femme, féminin

womb [wuːm] *n* (**a**) *Anat* utérus *m*; **in his mother's womb** dans le ventre de sa mère (**b**) *Fig* sein *m*, entrailles *fpl*

wombat ['wɒmbæt] *n Zool* wombat *m*

women ['wɪmɪn] *pl of* **woman**

►► ***women's group*** *(campaigning organization)* groupe *m* féministe; *(social club)* groupe *m* de femmes; ***Women's Institute*** = association britannique de femmes particulièrement active en milieu rural, à qui l'on prête une image démodée; ***Women's Lib*** MLF *m*, mouvement *m* de libération de la femme; ***Women's Libber*** féministe *f*; ***Women's Liberation*** mouvement *m* de libération de la femme, MLF *m*; ***Women's Movement*** mouvement *m* féministe; ***women's refuge*** centre *m* d'accueil pour les femmes; ***women's rights*** droits *mpl* de la femme; *Am* ***women's room*** toilettes *fpl* des femmes; ***Women's Royal Naval Service*** = section féminine de la marine de guerre britannique; ***women's shelter*** centre *m* d'accueil pour les femmes; ***women's studies*** = discipline universitaire ayant pour objet la sociologie et l'histoire des femmes, la création littéraire féminine etc

womenfolk ['wɪmɪnfəʊk] *npl* **the womenfolk** les femmes *fpl*

won[1] [wʌn] *pt & pp of* **win**

won[2] [wɒn] *n (currency)* won *m*

wonder ['wʌndə(r)] **1** *n* (**a**) *(marvel)* merveille *f*; **the seven wonders of the world** les sept merveilles du monde; **the wonders of science** les miracles de la science; **the wonders of nature** les merveilles de la nature; **to work** *or* **to do wonders** *(person)* faire des merveilles; *(action, event)* faire merveille; **a hot bath worked wonders for her aching body** un bain chaud la soulagea à merveille de ses douleurs

(**b**) *(amazing event or circumstances)* **the wonder (of it) is that he manages to get any work done at all** le plus étonnant dans tout cela, c'est qu'il arrive à travailler; **it's a wonder that anyone can work in such awful conditions** cela me semble incroyable qu'on puisse travailler dans des conditions aussi épouvantables; **it's a wonder (that) she didn't resign on the spot** c'est étonnant qu'elle n'ait pas démissionné sur-le-champ; **no wonder they refused** ce n'est pas étonnant qu'ils aient refusé; **no wonder!** ce n'est pas étonnant!, cela vous étonne?; **is it any wonder that he got lost?** cela vous étonne qu'il se soit perdu?; **it's little** *or* **small wonder no one came** ce n'est guère étonnant que personne ne soit venu; *Hum* **wonders will never cease!** on n'a pas fini d'être étonné!

(**c**) *(awe)* émerveillement *m*; **the children were filled with wonder** les enfants étaient émerveillés; **they looked on, lost in wonder** ils regardaient, totalement émerveillés *ou* éblouis; **there was a look of wonder in his eyes** il avait les yeux pleins d'étonnement

(**d**) *(prodigy)* prodige *m*, génie *m*; **a boy wonder** un petit prodige *ou* génie

2 *comp (drug, detergent)* miracle; *(child)* prodige

3 *vt* (**a**) *(ask oneself)* se demander; **I wonder where she's gone** je me demande où elle est allée; **I wonder how he managed it** je me demande comment il s'y est pris; **I wonder why** je me demande bien pourquoi; **I wonder who invented that** je suis curieux de savoir qui a inventé cela; **it makes you wonder how safe these power stations are** on en vient à se demander si ces centrales électriques sont vraiment sûres; **I often wonder that myself** je me pose souvent la question; **I wonder whether** *or* **if she'll come** je me demande si elle viendra

(**b**) *(in polite requests)* **I was wondering if you were free tomorrow** est-ce que par hasard vous êtes libre demain?; **I wonder if you could help me** pourriez-vous m'aider, s'il vous plaît?

(**c**) *(be surprised)* s'étonner; **I wonder that he wasn't hurt** je m'étonne *ou* cela m'étonne qu'il n'ait pas été blessé; **I shouldn't wonder if he were already married** cela ne m'étonnerait pas *ou* cela ne me surprendrait pas qu'il soit déjà marié; **she knows a lot more, I shouldn't wonder** cela ne m'étonnerait pas qu'elle en sache beaucoup plus long que ça

4 *vi* (**a**) *(think, reflect)* penser, réfléchir; **it makes you wonder** cela donne à penser *ou* à réfléchir; **his remarks set me wondering** ses remarques m'ont laissé songeur *ou* m'ont donné à réfléchir; **I'm wondering about going tomorrow** je me demande si je ne vais pas y aller demain; **I was wondering about it too** je me posais la même question; **the war will be over in a few days – I wonder** la guerre sera finie dans quelques jours – je n'en suis pas si sûr; **why? – oh, I just wondered** pourquoi? – oh, pour rien, comme ça

(**b**) *(marvel, be surprised)* s'étonner, s'émerveiller; **to wonder at sth** s'émerveiller de qch; **the people wondered at the magnificent sight** les gens s'émerveillaient de ce magnifique spectacle; **I don't wonder (that) you're annoyed** cela ne m'étonne pas que vous soyez contrarié; **I don't wonder** cela ne m'étonne pas

Wonderbra® ['wʌndəbrɑː] *n* Wonderbra® *m*

wonderful ['wʌndəfʊl] *adj (enjoyable)* merveilleux, formidable; *(beautiful)* superbe, magnifique; *(delicious)* excellent; *(astonishing)* étonnant, surprenant; **it was a wonderful sight** c'était un spectacle merveilleux *ou* magnifique; **we had a wonderful time/holiday** nous avons passé des moments/des vacances formidables; **the weather was wonderful** il a fait un temps superbe; **what wonderful news!** quelle nouvelle formidable!; **she has some wonderful ideas** elle a des idées formidables; **that's wonderful!** c'est merveilleux!; **you've been wonderful** vous avez été formidable; **you look wonderful** tu es superbe

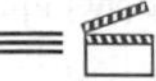

'It's a Wonderful Life' *Capra* 'La Vie est belle'

wonderfully ['wʌndəfʊlɪ] *adv* (**a**) *(with adj or adv)* merveilleusement, admirablement; **you look wonderfully well** vous avez une mine superbe; **she was wonderfully kind** elle était d'une gentillesse merveilleuse

(**b**) *(with verb)* merveilleusement, à merveille; **they got on wonderfully** ils s'entendirent à merveille; **I slept wonderfully** j'ai dormi à merveille, j'ai merveilleusement bien dormi; **she plays wonderfully** elle joue merveilleusement bien

wondering ['wʌndərɪŋ] *adj (pensive)* songeur, pensif; *(surprised)* étonné; **she looked at him with wondering eyes** elle le regarda d'un air perplexe

wonderingly ['wʌndərɪŋlɪ] *adv (look → pensively)* d'un air songeur; *(→ in surprise)* d'un air étonné; *(speak)* avec étonnement

wonderland ['wʌndəlænd] *n* pays *m* des merveilles; **it's like wonderland** on se croirait au pays des merveilles; **a winter wonderland** un paysage hivernal féerique

wonderment ['wʌndəmənt] *n (wonder)* émerveillement *m*; *(surprise)* étonnement *m*; **he looked around in wonderment** il regarda autour de lui émerveillé

wonderworker ['wʌndə,wɜːkə(r)] *n* **he's a real wonderworker** il accomplit des vrais miracles

wondrous ['wʌndrəs] *Literary* **1** *adj* merveilleux

2 *adv* merveilleusement

wondrously ['wʌndrəslɪ] *adv Literary* merveilleusement

wonga ['wɒŋgə] *n Br Fam (money)* fric *m*, flouze *m*, pognon *m*

wonk [wɒŋk] *n Am Fam* (**a**) *(student)* bûcheur(-euse) *m,f* (**b**) *(intellectual, expert)* intello *mf (qui ne s'intéresse qu'à sa discipline)*

wonky ['wɒŋkɪ] *(compar* **wonkier**, *superl* **wonkiest**) *adj Br Fam (table, chair)* bancal ❑, branlant ❑; *(bicycle)* détraqué; *(gadget, zip, switch)* qui débloque; *(radio, TV)* déréglé ❑, détraqué; *(line)* qui n'est pas bien droit ❑; *(collar, picture)* de travers ❑; **your tie is a bit wonky** ta cravate est un peu de travers; **I've got a wonky leg** j'ai une jambe faible ❑; **the floorboards are a bit wonky** le plancher est un peu branlant; **the little girl did a rather wonky drawing of a cow** la petite fille a fait un dessin maladroit d'une vache; **this sentence is a bit wonky** il y a quelque chose qui cloche dans cette phrase

wont [wəʊnt] *Literary* **1** *n* coutume *f*, habitude *f*; **as was his/her wont** comme de coutume

2 *adj* **to be wont to do sth** avoir l'habitude *ou* coutume de faire qch; **he is wont to panic** il a tendance à paniquer, il panique facilement

won't [wəʊnt] = **will not**

wonted ['wəʊntɪd] *adj Literary* coutumier

won ton ['wɒntɒn] *n Culin* won ton *m*

woo [wuː] *(pt & pp* **wooed**) *vt* (**a**) *Old-fashioned (court)* courtiser, faire la cour à

(**b**) *(attract → customers, voters)* chercher à plaire à, rechercher les faveurs de; **they tried to woo the voters with promises of lower taxes** ils cherchaient à s'attirer les faveurs de l'électorat en promettant de baisser les impôts; **they wooed him away from their rivals by promising him more money** ils lui ont fait quitter leurs concurrents en lui promettant plus d'argent

wood [wʊd] **1** *n* (**a**) *(timber)* bois *m*; **the stove burns wood and coal** le poêle fonctionne au bois et au charbon; **a piece of wood** un bout de bois; *Br* **to touch** *or Am* **to knock on wood** toucher du bois; *Br* **touch wood!**, *Am* **knock on wood!** touchons du bois!

(**b**) *(group of trees)* bois *m*; **we went for a walk in the woods** nous sommes allés nous promener dans les bois; *Fig* **he can't see the wood for the trees** les arbres lui cachent la forêt; *Fig* **we're not out of the woods yet** on n'est pas encore sortis de l'auberge, on n'est pas encore tirés d'affaire

(**c**) *(casks, barrels)* tonneau *m*; **matured in the wood** vieilli au tonneau; **drawn from the wood** tiré au tonneau

(**d**) *(in bowls)* boule *f*

(**e**) *Golf* bois *m*; **a (number) 3 wood** un bois 3

(**f**) *Am Fam* **to put the wood to sb** *(beat up)* tabasser qn; *(defeat)* battre qn à plates coutures

(**g**) *Vulg* **to get wood** *(erection)* bander; **to put the wood to sb** *(have sex with)* tringler qn

2 *comp* (**a**) *(wooden → floor, table, house)* en bois, de bois

(**b**) *(for burning wood → stove)* à bois; *(→ fire)* de bois

3 woods *npl Mus* bois *mpl*

▸▸ ***wood alcohol*** esprit-de-bois *m*, alcool *m* méthylique; *Bot* ***wood anemone*** anémone *f* des bois; ***wood ant*** fourmi *f* rousse; *Bot* ***wood avens*** benoîte *f*; *Bot* ***wood ash*** cendre *f* de bois; ***wood carver*** sculpteur *m* sur bois; ***wood chisel*** ciseau *m* à bois; *Bot* ***wood crane's bill*** géranium *m* des bois; ***wood fibre*** fibre *f* de bois; ***wood nymph*** nymphe *f* des bois, dryade *f*; ***wood panelling*** boiserie *f*; *Orn* ***wood pigeon*** ramier *m*; ***wood pulp*** pâte *f* à papier; *Zool* ***wood rat*** rat *m* des bois; *Orn* ***wood sandpiper*** chevalier *m* sylvain; ***wood screw*** vis *f* à bois; *Bot* ***wood sorrel*** oxalis *m*, oxalide *f*; *Bot* ***wood speedwell*** véronique *f* des montagnes; ***wood spirit*** esprit-de-bois *m*; *Bot* ***wood spurge*** euphorbe *f* des bois; ***wood stain*** teinture *f* pour bois; *Orn* ***wood stork*** tantale *m* d'Amérique; ***wood stove*** poêle *m* à bois; ***wood tar*** goudron *m* de bois; *Orn* ***wood warbler*** pouillot *m* siffleur

woodbine ['wʊdbaɪn] *n Bot (honeysuckle)* chèvrefeuille *m*; *Am (Virginia creeper)* vigne *f* vierge

woodblock ['wʊdblɒk] *n* (**a**) *(for printing)* bois *m* de graveur (**b**) *(for floor)* pavé *m* de bois

wood-burning *adj (stove, boiler)* à bois

woodcarving ['wʊd,kɑːvɪŋ] *n* (**a**) *(craft)* sculpture *f* sur bois (**b**) *(object)* sculpture *f* en bois

woodchat (shrike) ['wʊdtʃæt-] *n Orn* pie-grièche *f* rousse

woodchip ['wʊdtʃɪp] *n (wallpaper)* = revêtement mural de papier avec copeaux de bois incorporés

woodchuck ['wʊdtʃʌk] *n* marmotte *f* d'Amérique

woodcock ['wʊdkɒk] *(pl* **inv** *or* **woodcocks**) *n Orn* bécasse *f*

woodcraft ['wʊdkrɑːft] *n Am* (**a**) *(in woodland)* connaissance *f* des bois et des forêts (**b**) *(artistry)* art *m* de travailler le bois

woodcut ['wʊdkʌt] *n* gravure *f* sur bois

woodcutter ['wʊd,kʌtə(r)] *n* bûcheron(onne) *m,f*

woodcutting ['wʊd,kʌtɪŋ] *n* (**a**) *(in forest)* abattage *m* des arbres (**b**) *(engraving)* gravure *f* sur bois

wooded ['wʊdɪd] *adj* boisé; **densely wooded** très boisé

wooden ['wʊdən] *adj* (**a**) *(made of wood)* en bois, de bois; **a wooden leg** une jambe de bois; *Am Fam* **to try to sell sb wooden nickels** essayer de rouler qn; **the Wooden Horse of Troy** le cheval de Troie

(**b**) *Fig (stiff → gesture, manner)* crispé, raide; *(→ performance, actor)* raide, qui manque de naturel

▸▸ *Fam Hum* ***wooden overcoat*** *(coffin)* costume *m* de sapin; ***wooden spoon*** cuillère *f* en bois; *Br Sport* **to win the wooden spoon** gagner la cuillère de bois

woodenhead ['wʊdən,hed] *n Fam* idiot(e) *m,f*, imbécile ❑ *mf*

woodenheaded ['wʊdən,hedɪd] *adj Fam (stupid)* stupide ❑, bouché

woodenly ['wʊdənlɪ] *adv (perform, move, smile, speak)* avec raideur

woodenness ['wʊdənnɪs] *n Fig (of gesture, manner)* raideur *f*; *(of performance, actor)* manque *m* de naturel

woodhouse ['wʊdhaʊs, *pl* -haʊzɪz] *n* bûcher *m (abri)*

woodie ['wʊdɪ] *n Am very Fam (erection)* érection ❑ *f*, bandaison *f*; **to have a woodie** bander

woodland ['wʊdlənd] **1** *n* région *f* boisée
2 *adj (fauna)* des bois; **woodland walks** promenades *fpl* à travers bois

woodlander ['wʊd,ləndə(r)] *n* habitant(e) *m,f* des bois

woodlark ['wʊdlɑːk] *n Orn* alouette *f* des bois, lulu *m*

woodlouse ['wʊdlaʊs] (*pl* **woodlice** [-laɪs]) *n Entom* cloporte *m*

woodman ['wʊdmən] (*pl* **woodmen** [-mən]) *n* forestier *m*

woodmite ['wʊdmaɪt] *n Entom* oribate *m*, oribatidé *m*

woodpecker ['wʊd,pekə(r)] *n Orn* pic *m*, pivert *m*

woodpile ['wʊdpaɪl] *n* tas *m* de bois

woodruff ['wʊdrʌf] *n Bot* aspérule *f* odorante

woodshed ['wʊdʃed] *n* bûcher *m (abri)*; *Fig* **there's something nasty in the woodshed** il y a quelque chose de pas catholique là-dessous

> **Something nasty in the woodshed**
> Il s'agit d'une allusion à un roman comique anglais, *Cold Comfort Farm* (1932), de Stella Gibbons. Parmi les personnages excentriques qui figurent dans le roman se trouve une vieille dame, Aunt Ada Doom, qui répète sans cesse la phrase "I saw something nasty in the woodshed"("J'ai vu quelque chose d'horrible dans le bûcher"), en se remémorant une expérience traumatisante qui a eu lieu dans son enfance. La nature de cette expérience reste inexpliquée. L'expression est couramment utilisée, souvent de façon humoristique, pour désigner une chose ou un événement mal élucidé mais dont on soupçonne la nature louche ou néfaste.

woodsman ['wʊdzmən] (*pl* **woodsmen** [-mən]) *n Am* forestier *m*

woodstack ['wʊdstæk] *n* tas *m* de bois

woodsy ['wʊdzɪ] (*compar* **woodsier,** *superl* **woodsiest**) *adj Am Fam (flowers)* des bois; *(smell)* du bois; *(area)* boisé

woodwind ['wʊdwɪnd] **1** *adj (music)* pour les bois
2 *n* (**a**) *(single instrument)* bois *m* (**b**) *(UNCOUNT) (family of instruments)* bois *mpl*
▸▸ ***woodwind instruments, woodwind section*** bois *mpl*

woodwork ['wʊdwɜːk] *n (UNCOUNT)* (**a**) *(craft → carpentry)* menuiserie *f*; *(→ cabinet-making)* ébénisterie *f*; *(school subject)* menuiserie *f* (**b**) *(in building → doors, window frames)* boiseries *fpl*; *(→ beams)* charpente *f*; *Fam* **to come** *or* **to crawl out of the woodwork** sortir d'un peu partout (**c**) *Fam Ftbl (goalposts and crossbar)* poteaux *mpl*

woodworker ['wʊd,wɜːkə(r)] *n (carpenter)* menuisier *m*; *(joiner)* menuisier *m*; *(cabinet-maker)* ébéniste *m*

woodworking ['wʊd,wɜːkɪŋ] = **woodwork** (**a**)

woodworm ['wʊdwɜːm] *n* (**a**) *(insect)* ver *m* de bois (**b**) *(infestation)* **a chair affected** *or* **damaged by woodworm** une chaise vermoulue *ou* mangée aux vers; **the sideboard has got woodworm** le buffet est vermoulu

woody ['wʊdɪ] (*compar* **woodier,** *superl* **woodiest**) *adj* (**a**) *(plant, vegetation)* ligneux (**b**) *(countryside)* boisé (**c**) *(taste, texture)* de bois; *(smell)* boisé

woodyard ['wʊdjɑːd] *n* chantier *m* de bois

wooer ['wuːə(r)] *n Old-fashioned* prétendant *m*

woof[1] [wuːf] *n Tex* trame *f*

woof[2] [wʊf] **1** *n (bark)* aboiement *m*
2 *vi* (**a**) *(animal)* aboyer (**b**) *Am Fam (boast, bluff)* frimer, flamber
3 *onomat* ouah! ouah!

woofer ['wʊfə(r)] *n* haut-parleur *m* de graves, woofer *m*

woofter ['wʊftə(r)] *n Br Fam* pédé *m*, = terme injurieux désignant un homosexuel

wool [wʊl] **1** *n* laine *f*; **pure new wool** pure laine vierge; **a ball of wool** une pelote de laine; **she can't wear wool next to her skin** elle ne peut pas porter de laine à même la peau; *Am Fam* **all wool and a yard wide** de première classe, de premier ordre; **to pull the wool over sb's eyes** berner *ou* duper qn
2 *adj* (**a**) *(made of wool → cloth)* de laine; *(→ socks, dress)* en laine (**b**) *(relating to wool)* **the wool industry** l'industrie *f* lainière; **wool shop** magasin *m* de laines
▸▸ ***wool fat*** lanoline *f*; ***wool stapler*** *(dealer)* négociant(e) *m,f* en laine; *(sorter)* = ouvrier qui trie les toisons

woolen *Am* = **woollen**

woolgatherer ['wʊl,gæðərə(r)] *n* rêvasseur(-euse) *m,f*, rêveur(euse) *m,f*

woolgathering ['wʊl,gæðərɪŋ] *n* **to be** *or* **to go woolgathering** rêvasser

woolgrower ['wʊl,grəʊə(r)] *n* éleveur(euse) *m,f* de moutons *(à laine)*

woollen, *Am* **woolen** ['wʊlən] **1** *adj* (**a**) *(fabric)* de laine; *(jacket, gloves, blanket)* en laine (**b**) *(industry)* lainière; *(manufacture)* de lainages
2 woollens, *Am* **woolens** *npl* lainages *mpl*, vêtements *mpl* de laine
▸▸ ***woollen cloth*** lainage *m*, étoffe *f* de laine; ***woollen mill*** lainerie *f*

woolliness, *Am* **wooliness** ['wʊlɪnɪs] *n* (**a**) *(of reasoning, ideas, style)* flou *m*, caractère *m* confus; *(of outline)* manque *m* de netteté, flou *m* (**b**) *(resemblance to wool)* nature *f* laineuse (**of** de)

woolly, *Am* **wooly** ['wʊlɪ] (*Br pl* **woollies**, *Am pl* **woolies**) **1** *adj* (**a**) *(socks, hat)* en laine (**b**) *(sheep)* laineux (**c**) *(clouds)* cotonneux; *(hair)* frisé (**d**) *(vague → reasoning, ideas, style)* confus, flou (**e**) *(outline)* flou, peu net
2 *n Br Fam (jumper)* tricot *m*, lainage *m*; **winter woollies** lainages *mpl* d'hiver
▸▸ *Zool* ***woolly bear*** hérissonne *f*; *Zool* ***woolly monkey*** singe *m* laineux

woolly-headed, *Am* **wooly-headed** *adj (person)* écervelé; *(ideas)* vague, confus

woolly-minded, *Am* **wooly-minded** *adj* à l'esprit confus

woolpack ['wʊlpæk] *n* balle *f* de laine

woolsack ['wʊlsæk] *n Br Parl* **the woolsack** *(seat)* = coussin rouge sur lequel s'assoit le Lord Chancellor (à la Chambre des lords); *(office)* = le siège du Lord Chancellor (à la Chambre des lords)

woolshed ['wʊlʃed] *n Austr & NZ* hangar *m* pour la tonte

wooly *Am* = **woolly**

woomera ['wuːmərə] *n Austr* arme *f* de jet

woops = **whoops**

woozy ['wuːzɪ] (*compar* **woozier,** *superl* **wooziest**) *adj Fam* (**a**) *(dazed)* hébété ❑, dans les vapes (**b**) *(sick)* **to feel woozy** avoir mal au cœur ❑ (**c**) *(from drink)* éméché, pompette

wop [wɒp] *n very Fam* macaroni *mf*, = terme injurieux désignant un Italien

Worcester sauce ['wʊstə-] *n* sauce *f* Worcestershire, = sauce épicée au soja et au vinaigre

Worcs (*written abbr* **Worcestershire**) Worcestershire *m*

WORD [wɜːd]

mot	▸ 1 (a) – (c)
parole	▸ 1 (a), (b), (d)
nouvelle(s)	▸ 1 (c)
message	▸ 1 (c)
promesse	▸ 1 (d)
conseil	▸ 1 (e)
bruit	▸ 1 (f)
ordre	▸ 1 (g)
rédiger	▸ 2 (a)

1 *n* (**a**) *(gen → written)* mot *m*; *(→ spoken)* mot *m*, parole *f*; **the words of a song** les paroles d'une chanson; *Ironic* **(what) fine words!** quelles belles paroles!; **what is the Russian word for "head"?, what is the word for "head" in Russian?** comment dit-on "head" en russe?; **the Japanese don't have a word for it** les Japonais n'ont pas de mot pour dire cela; **she can't put her ideas/her feelings into words** elle ne trouve pas les mots pour exprimer ses idées/ce qu'elle ressent; **I can't find (the) words to tell you how glad I am!** je ne saurais vous dire à quel point je suis content!; **there are no words to describe** *or* **words cannot describe how I feel** aucun mot ne peut décrire ce que je ressens; **they left without (saying) a word** ils sont partis sans (dire) un mot; **with these words they left** sur ces mots *ou* là-dessus, ils sont partis; **lazy isn't the word for it!** paresseux, c'est peu dire!; **idle would be a better word** oisif serait plus juste; *Fig* **he doesn't know the meaning of the word "generosity"** il ne sait pas ce que veut dire le mot "générosité"; **he's mad, there's no other word for it** il est fou, il n'y a pas d'autre mot; **there's a word for people like you, it's "thief"** les gens dans ton genre, on les appelle des voleurs; **I didn't understand a word of the lecture** je n'ai pas compris un mot de la conférence; **he doesn't know a word of German** il ne sait pas un mot d'allemand; **I don't believe a word of it!** je n'en crois pas un mot!; **that's my last** *or* **my final word on the matter** c'est mon dernier mot (sur la question); **those were his dying words** ce sont les dernières paroles qu'il a prononcées avant de mourir; **she said a few words of welcome** elle a dit quelques mots de bienvenue; **I gave him a few words of advice** je lui ai donné quelques conseils; **I gave him a few words of encouragement** je lui ai dit quelques mots d'encouragement; **can I give you a word of warning/of advice?** puis-je vous mettre en garde/vous conseiller?; **he didn't say a word** il n'a rien dit, il n'a pas dit un mot; **I can't get a word out of her** je ne peux pas en tirer un mot; **and now a word from our sponsors** et maintenant, voici un message publicitaire de nos sponsors; **I'm a woman of few words** je ne suis pas quelqu'un qui fait de grands discours; **he's a man of few words** c'est un homme peu loquace, c'est quelqu'un qui n'aime pas beaucoup parler; **in the words of Shelley** comme l'a dit Shelley; **in the words of his boss, he's a layabout** à en croire son patron *ou* d'après (ce que dit) son patron, c'est un fainéant; **tell me in your own words** dites-le moi à votre façon *ou* avec vos propres mots; **he told me in so many words that I was a liar** il m'a dit carrément *ou* sans mâcher ses mots que j'étais un menteur; **she didn't say it in so many words but her meaning was quite clear** elle n'a pas dit exactement cela, mais c'était sous-entendu; **a six-hundred-word article** un article de six cents mots; **by** *or* **through word of mouth** oralement; **the news spread by word of mouth** la nouvelle se répandit de bouche à oreille; **too beautiful for words** d'une beauté extraordinaire; **too stupid for words** vraiment trop bête; **word for word** *(translate)* littéralement, mot à mot; *(repeat)* mot pour mot; **from the word go** dès le départ; **(upon) my word!** ma parole!, oh la la!; **not a word!** pas un mot!, bouche cousue!; **don't put words into my mouth** ne me faites pas dire ce que je n'ai pas dit; **he took the words out of my mouth** il a dit exactement ce que j'allais dire; **words fail me!** j'en perds la parole!, je suis stupéfait!; **he never has a good word to say about anyone** personne ne trouve jamais grâce à ses yeux; **to put in a (good) word for sb** glisser un mot en faveur de qn; **to have the last word** avoir le dernier mot; *Br* **it's the last word in comfort** c'est ce qui se fait de mieux en matière de confort; *Br* **it's the last word in luxury** c'est ce qu'on fait de plus luxueux

(**b**) *(talk)* mot(s) *m(pl)*, parole(s) *f(pl)*; **to have a word with sb about sth** toucher un mot *ou* deux mots à qn au sujet de qch; **can I have a word with you about the meeting?** est-ce que je peux vous dire deux mots à propos de la réunion?; **can I have a word?** je voudrais vous parler un instant

(**c**) *(UNCOUNT) (news)* nouvelle(s) *f(pl)*; *(message)* message *m*, mot *m*; **the word got out that there had been a coup** la nouvelle d'un coup d'État a circulé; **word came from Tokyo that the strike was over** la nouvelle arriva de Tokyo que la grève était terminée; **she brought them word of Tom** elle leur a apporté des nouvelles de Tom; **have you had any word from him?** avez-vous eu de ses nouvelles?; **we have had no word from him** nous sommes sans nouvelles de lui; **she left word for us to follow** elle nous a laissé un message pour dire que nous devions la suivre; **to spread the word** *(proselytize)* annoncer la bonne parole; **spread the word that Mick's back in town** faites passer la nouvelle *ou* faites dire que Mick est de retour en ville; **he sent word to say he had arrived**

safely il a envoyé un mot pour dire qu'il était bien arrivé

(**d**) *(promise)* parole *f*, promesse *f*; **he gave his word that we wouldn't be harmed** il a donné sa parole qu'il ne nous ferait aucun mal; **I give you my word on it** je vous en donne ma parole; **she gave her solemn word** elle a juré *ou* elle a promis solennellement; **to break one's word** manquer à sa parole; **to go back on one's word** revenir sur sa parole; **we held** *or* **we kept her to her word** nous l'avons obligée à tenir sa parole; **to keep one's word** tenir parole, tenir (sa) promesse; **he was as good as his word** il a tenu parole; **she's a woman of her word** c'est une femme de parole; **I'm a man of my word** je suis un homme de parole; **word of honour!** parole d'honneur!; **we only have his word for it** il n'y a que lui qui le dit, personne ne peut prouver le contraire; **you can take my word for it** vous pouvez me croire sur parole; **we'll have to take your word for it** nous sommes bien obligés de vous croire; **take my word (for it), it's a bargain!** croyez-moi, c'est une affaire!; **I took her at her word** je l'ai prise au mot; **it's your word against mine** c'est votre parole contre la mienne; **my word is my bond** je n'ai qu'une parole, je tiens toujours parole

(**e**) *(advice)* conseil *m*; **a word to travellers, watch your luggage!** un petit conseil aux voyageurs, surveillez vos bagages!; **a quick word in your ear** je vous glisse un mot à l'oreille; **a word to the wise** à bon entendeur, salut

(**f**) *(rumour)* bruit *m*; **(the) word went round that he was dying** le bruit a couru qu'il était sur le point de mourir

(**g**) *(order)* ordre *m*; **he gave the word to march** il a donné l'ordre *ou* le signal de se mettre en marche; **his word is law** c'est lui qui fait la loi; **just give** *or* **say the word and we'll be off** vous n'avez qu'à donner le signal et nous partons

(**h**) *(watchword)* mot *m* d'ordre; *(password)* mot *m* de passe; **the word now is "democracy"** le mot d'ordre maintenant, c'est "démocratie"

2 *vt* (**a**) *(letter, document)* rédiger, formuler; *(contract)* rédiger; **they worded the petition carefully** ils ont choisi les termes de la pétition avec le plus grand soin; **we sent a strongly worded protest** nous avons envoyé une lettre de protestation bien sentie

(**b**) *Austr Fam (advise)* conseiller□; *(inform)* informer□

3 *exclam Am Fam* **word (up)!** *(I agree)* parfaitement!□; *(it's true)* sans dec!

4 Word *n Rel* **the Word** le Verbe; **the Word of God** la parole de Dieu

5 words *npl Br Fam (argument)* dispute□ *f*; **to have words** se disputer□, avoir des mots; **they had words about her drinking** ils se sont disputés sur le fait qu'elle boit□

6 in a word *adv* en un mot

7 in other words *adv* autrement dit, en d'autres termes

►► ***word association*** association *f* d'idées par les mots; *Ling* ***word class*** classe *f* de mots; *Comput* ***word count*** nombre *m* des mots; **to do a word count** compter les mots; ***word count facility*** fonction *f* de comptage de mots; ***word game*** = jeu de lettres; ***word group*** groupe *m* de mots, membre *m* de phrase; ***word order*** ordre *m* des mots; ***word picture*** description *f* imagée *ou* pittoresque; *(of person)* portrait *m* en prose; ***word processing*** traitement *m* de texte; ***word processor*** logiciel *m* de traitement de texte; *Typ* ***word split*** coupure *f* de mot; *Comput* ***word wrap*** retour *m* à la ligne automatique

word-blind *adj Br* dyslexique

word-blindness *n Br* dyslexie *f*

wordbook ['wɜːdbʊk] *n* lexique *m*, vocabulaire *m*

wordfinder ['wɜːdfaɪndə(r)] *n* dictionnaire *m* de synonymes, dictionnaire *m* analogique

word-for-word *adj (repetition, imitation)* mot pour mot; *(translation)* littéral; **it's a word-for-word translation** c'est une traduction littérale, c'est du mot à mot

wordiness ['wɜːdɪnɪs] *n* verbosité *f*

wording ['wɜːdɪŋ] *n (UNCOUNT)* (**a**) *(of letter, speech)* termes *mpl*, formulation *f*; *(of contract)* termes *mpl*; **I think you should change the wording of the last sentence** je crois que vous devriez reformuler la dernière phrase; **the new wording sounds better** la nouvelle formulation sonne mieux; **the wording is rather strange** c'est bizarrement formulé

(**b**) *Admin & Law* rédaction *f*; **I don't really understand the wording of the contract** je ne comprends pas vraiment les termes du contrat

wordless ['wɜːdlɪs] *adj* (**a**) *Literary (silent → admiration)* muet (**b**) *(without words → music)* sans paroles

wordlessly ['wɜːdlɪslɪ] *adv* sans dire un mot

wordlist ['wɜːdlɪst] *n (in notebook, textbook)* lexique *m*, liste *f* de mots; *(in dictionary)* nomenclature *f*

word-of-mouth *adj (account)* oral, verbal

►► *Mktg* ***word-of-mouth advertising*** publicité *f* de bouche à oreille

word-perfect *adj (recitation)* que l'on connaît parfaitement *ou* sur le bout des doigts; **she rehearsed her speech until she was word-perfect** elle a répété son discours jusqu'à le connaître parfaitement *ou* sur le bout des doigts

wordplay ['wɜːdpleɪ] *n (UNCOUNT)* jeu *m* de mots

word-process 1 *vi* travailler sur traitement de texte

2 *vt (text)* réaliser par traitement de texte

word-processing program *n Comput* logiciel *m* de traitement de texte

wordsmith ['wɜːdsmɪθ] *n* manieur *m* de mots; **he's a real wordsmith** il sait manier les mots

Wordsworthian [ˌwɜːdz'wɜːðɪən] *adj (of Wordsworth)* de Wordsworth; *(characteristic of Wordsworth)* à la manière de Wordsworth

wordy ['wɜːdɪ] *(compar* **wordier**, *superl* **wordiest)** *adj* verbeux

wore [wɔː(r)] *pt of* **wear**

WORK [wɜːk]

travail	► 1 (a) – (e), (g)
œuvre	► 1 (a), (f)
besogne	► 1 (b)
emploi	► 1 (c)
ouvrage	► 1 (f)
recherches	► 1 (g)
travailler	► 2A (a) – (e); 3A (b), (c), (e); 3C (a)
fonctionner	► 2B (a)
marcher	► 2B (a), (b)
réussir	► 2B (b)
agir	► 2B (c), (d)
faire travailler	► 3A (a)
faire marcher	► 3B (a)
façonner	► 3C (a)
mécanisme	► 4 1 (a)
travaux	► 4 1 (b)
usine	► 4 2 (a)

1 *n* (**a**) *(effort, activity)* travail *m*, œuvre *f*; **computers take some of the work out of filing** les ordinateurs facilitent le classement; **this report needs more work** il y a encore du travail à faire sur ce rapport, ce rapport demande plus de travail; **she's done a lot of work for charity** elle a beaucoup travaillé pour des associations caritatives; **it will take a lot of work to make a team out of them** ça va être un drôle de travail de faire d'eux une équipe; **keep up the good work!** continuez comme ça!; **nice** *or* **good work!** c'est du bon travail!, bravo!; **that's fine work** *or* **a fine piece of work** c'est du beau travail; **your work has been useful** vous avez fait du travail utile; **work on the tunnel is to start in March** *(existing tunnel)* les travaux sur le tunnel doivent commencer en mars; *(new tunnel)* la construction du tunnel doit commencer en mars; **work in progress** *Admin* travail en cours; *Acct* travaux *mpl* en cours, inventaire *m* de production; *(sign)* travaux en cours; **she put a lot of work into that book** elle a beaucoup travaillé sur ce livre; **to make work for sb** compliquer la vie à qn; **to start work, to set to work** se mettre au travail; **she set** *or* **she went to work on the contract** elle a commencé à travailler sur le contrat; **he set to work undermining their confidence** il a entrepris de saper leur confiance; **I set him to work (on) painting the kitchen** je lui ai donné la cuisine à peindre; **they put him to work in the kitchen** ils l'ont mis au travail dans la cuisine; **let's get (down) to work!** (mettons-nous) au travail!; *Prov* **all work and no play makes Jack a dull boy** beaucoup de travail et peu de loisirs ne réussissent à personne

(**b**) *(duty, task)* travail *m*, besogne *f*; **I've got loads of work to do** j'ai énormément de travail à faire; **she gave us too much work** elle nous a donné trop de travail; **he's trying to get some work done** il essaie de travailler un peu; **they do their work well** ils travaillent bien, ils font du bon travail; **it's hard work** c'est du travail, ce n'est pas facile; **it's thirsty work** ça donne soif; **to make short** *or* **light work of sth** expédier qch; *Fig* **to make short work of sb** ne faire qu'une bouchée de qn; *Fam* **it's nice work if you can get it!** c'est une bonne planque, encore faut-il la trouver!

(**c**) *(paid employment)* travail *m*, emploi *m*; **what (kind of) work do you do?** qu'est-ce que vous faites dans la vie?, quel travail faites-vous?; **I do translation work** je suis traducteur, je fais des traductions; **to find work** trouver du travail; **to look for work** chercher du travail *ou* un emploi; **to be in work** travailler, avoir un emploi; **to be out of work** être au chômage *ou* sans travail *ou* sans emploi; **he had a week off work** *(holiday)* il a pris une semaine de vacances; *(illness)* il n'est pas allé au travail pendant une semaine; **to take time off work** prendre des congés; **she's off work today** elle ne travaille pas aujourd'hui; **to do a full day's work** faire une journée entière de travail; **people out of work** *(gen)* les chômeurs *mpl*; *Admin & Econ* les inactifs *mpl*

(**d**) *(place of employment)* travail *m*; *Admin* lieu *m* de travail; **I go to work by bus** je vais au travail en bus; **I'm late for work** je suis en retard pour le travail; **he's a friend from work** c'est un collègue; **where is your (place of) work?** où travaillez-vous?, quel est votre lieu de travail?; **on her way home from work** en rentrant du travail

(**e**) *(papers, material etc being worked on)* travail *m*; **to take work home** prendre du travail à la maison; **her work was all over the table** son travail était étalé sur la table

(**f**) *(creation, artefact etc)* œuvre *f*; *(on smaller scale)* ouvrage *m*; *Sewing* ouvrage *m*; **it's all my own work** j'ai tout fait moi-même; **it's an interesting piece of work** *(gen)* c'est un travail intéressant; *Art, Literature & Mus* c'est une œuvre intéressante; **very detailed/delicate work** *(embroidery, carving etc)* ouvrage très détaillé/délicat; **these formations are the work of the wind** ces formations sont l'œuvre du vent; **the silversmith sells much of his work to hotels** l'orfèvre vend une grande partie de ce qu'il fait *ou* de son travail à des hôtels; **the complete works of Shakespeare** les œuvres complètes *ou* l'œuvre de Shakespeare; **a new work on Portugal** un nouvel ouvrage sur le Portugal; **a work of art** une œuvre d'art; **works of fiction** des ouvrages de fiction

(**g**) *(research)* travail *m*, recherches *fpl*; **there hasn't been a lot of work done on the subject** peu de travail a été fait *ou* peu de recherches ont été faites sur le sujet

(**h**) *(deed)* œuvre *f*, acte *m*; **good works** bonnes œuvres *fpl*; **each man will be judged by his works** chaque homme sera jugé selon ses œuvres; **charitable works** actes *mpl* de charité, actes *mpl* charitables; **the murder is the work of a madman** le meurtre est l'œuvre d'un fou

(**i**) *(effect)* effet *m*; **wait until the medicine has done its work** attendez que le médicament ait agi *ou* ait produit son effet

(**j**) *Phys* travail *m*

2 *vi* **A.** (**a**) *(exert effort on a specific task, activity etc)* travailler; **we worked for hours cleaning the house** nous avons passé des heures à faire le ménage; **they worked in the garden** ils ont fait du jardinage; **we work hard** nous travaillons dur; **she's working on a novel just now** elle travaille à un roman en ce moment; **a detective is working on this case** un détective est sur cette affaire; **he works at** *or* **on keeping**

himself fit il fait de l'exercice pour garder la forme; **we have to work to a deadline** nous devons respecter des délais dans notre travail; **we have to work to a budget** nous devons travailler avec un certain budget; **I've worked with the handicapped before** j'ai déjà travaillé avec les handicapés; **I work with the Spanish on that project** je travaille (en collaboration) avec les Espagnols sur ce projet

(**b**) *(be employed)* travailler; **he works as a teacher** il a un poste d'enseignant; **I work in advertising** je travaille dans la publicité; **who do you work for?** chez qui est-ce que vous travaillez?; **she works in** *or* **for a bank** elle travaille dans *ou* pour une banque; **I work a forty-hour week** je travaille quarante heures par semaine, je fais une semaine de quarante heures; **to work for a living** travailler pour gagner sa vie; *Ind* **to work to rule** faire la grève du zèle

(**c**) *(strive for a specific goal or aim)* **to work for a good cause** travailler pour une bonne cause; **they're working for better international relations** ils s'efforcent d'améliorer les relations internationales

(**d**) *(study)* travailler, étudier; **you're going to have to work if you want to pass the exam** il va falloir que tu travailles *ou* que tu étudies si tu veux avoir ton examen

(**e**) *(use a specified substance)* travailler; **this sculptor works in** *or* **with copper** ce sculpteur travaille avec le cuivre; **she has always worked in** *or* **with watercolours** elle a toujours travaillé avec de la peinture à l'eau

B. (**a**) *(function, operate → machine, brain, system)* fonctionner, marcher; **the lift doesn't work at night** l'ascenseur ne marche pas la nuit; **the lift never works** l'ascenseur est toujours en panne; **the radio works off batteries** la radio fonctionne avec des piles; **a pump worked by hand** une pompe actionnée à la main *ou* manuellement; **they soon got** *or* **had it working** ils sont vite parvenus à le faire fonctionner; **she sat still, her brain** *or* **her mind working furiously** elle était assise immobile, le cerveau en ébullition; *Fig* **everything worked smoothly** tout s'est déroulé comme prevu; **your idea just won't work** ton idée ne peut pas marcher; **this relationship isn't working** cette relation ne marche pas; **that argument works both ways** ce raisonnement est à double tranchant; **how does the law work exactly?** comment la loi fonctionne-t-elle exactement?

(**b**) *(produce results, succeed)* marcher, réussir; **it worked brilliantly** ça a très bien marché; **their scheme didn't work** leur complot a échoué; **that/flattery won't work with me** ça/la flatterie ne prend pas avec moi

(**c**) *(drug, medicine)* agir, produire *ou* faire son effet

(**d**) *(act)* agir; **the acid works as a catalyst** l'acide agit comme *ou* sert de catalyseur; **events have worked against us/in our favour** les événements ont agi contre nous/en notre faveur; **I'm working on the assumption that they'll sign the contract** je pars du principe qu'ils signeront le contrat

C. (**a**) *(reach a condition or state gradually)* **to work loose** se desserrer; **to work free** se libérer; **the nail worked through the sole of my shoe** le clou est passé à travers la semelle de ma chaussure

(**b**) *(face, mouth)* se contracter, se crisper

(**c**) *(ferment)* fermenter

3 *vt* **A.** (**a**) *(worker, employee, horse)* faire travailler; **the boss works his staff hard** le patron exige beaucoup de travail de ses employés; **you work yourself too hard** tu te surmènes; **to work oneself to death** se tuer à la tâche; **to work one's fingers to the bone** s'user au travail

(**b**) *(pay for with labour or service)* **they worked their passage to India** ils ont payé leur passage en Inde en travaillant; **I worked my way through college** j'ai travaillé pour payer mes études à l'université

(**c**) *(carry on activity in)* **he works the southern sales area** il travaille pour le service commercial de la région sud; **the pollster worked both sides of the street** le sondeur a enquêté des deux côtés de la rue; *Fig* **the candidate worked the crowd** le candidat s'efforçait de soulever l'enthousiasme de la foule; **a real-estate agent who works the phones** un agent immobilier qui fait de la prospection par téléphone; **she works the bars** *(prostitute)* elle travaille dans les bars

(**d**) *(achieve, accomplish)* **the new policy will work major changes** la nouvelle politique opérera *ou* entraînera des changements importants; **the story worked its magic** *or* **its charm on the public** l'histoire a enchanté le public; **to work a spell on sb** jeter un sort à qn; **to work miracles** faire *ou* accomplir des miracles; **to work wonders** faire merveille; **she has worked wonders with the children** elle a fait des merveilles avec les enfants

(**e**) *(make use of, exploit → land)* travailler, cultiver; *(→ mine, quarry)* exploiter, faire valoir

B. (**a**) *(operate)* faire marcher, faire fonctionner; **this switch works the furnace** ce bouton actionne *ou* commande la chaudière; **he knows how to work the drill** il sait se servir de la perceuse

(**b**) *(manoeuvre)* **I worked the handle up and down** j'ai remué la poignée de haut en bas; **to work one's hands free** parvenir à dégager ses mains; **she worked the ropes loose** elle a réussi à desserrer les cordes petit à petit

(**c**) *(by slow progression)* **I worked my way along the ledge** j'ai longé la saillie avec précaution; **he worked his way down/up the cliff** il a descendu/monté la falaise lentement; **the beggar worked his way towards us** le mendiant s'est approché de nous; **they worked their way through the list** ils ont traité chaque élément de la liste tour à tour; **he's worked his way through the whole grant** il a épuisé toute la subvention; **a band of rain working its way across the country** un front de pluie qui traverse le pays; **they have worked themselves into a corner** ils se sont mis dans une impasse

(**d**) *Fam (contrive)* s'arranger; **she managed to work a few days off** elle s'est arrangée *ou* s'est débrouillée pour avoir quelques jours de congé; **I worked it** *or* **worked things so that she's never alone** j'ai fait en sorte qu'elle *ou* je me suis arrangé pour qu'elle ne soit jamais seule

C. (**a**) *(shape → leather, metal, stone)* travailler, façonner; *(→ clay, dough)* travailler, pétrir; *(→ object, sculpture)* façonner; *Sewing (design, initials)* broder; **she worked the silver into earrings** elle a travaillé l'argent pour en faire des boucles d'oreilles; **she worked a figure out of the wood** elle a sculpté une silhouette dans le bois; **the flowers are worked in silk** les fleurs sont brodées en soie; **work the putty into the right consistency** travaillez le mastic pour lui donner la consistance voulue

(**b**) *(rub)* **gently work the cream into your hands** massez-vous les mains pour faire pénétrer la crème; **work the dye into the surface of the leather** faites pénétrer la teinture dans le cuir

(**c**) *(excite, provoke)* **the orator worked the audience into a frenzy** l'orateur a enflammé *ou* a galvanisé le public; **she worked herself into a rage** elle s'est mise dans une colère noire

4 works 1 *npl* (**a**) *(mechanism)* mécanisme *m*, rouages *mpl*; *(of clock)* mouvement *m*; *Fam* **to foul up** *or* **to gum up the works** tout foutre en l'air (**b**) *Constr* travaux *mpl*; *(installation)* installations *fpl*; **road works** travaux *mpl*; *(sign)* travaux; **Minister/Ministry of Works** ministre *m*/ministère *m* des Travaux publics **2** *n* (**a**) *Ind (factory)* usine *f*; **a printing works** une imprimerie; **a gas works** une usine à gaz; **price ex works** prix *m* sortie usine (**b**) *Fam (everything)* **the (whole) works** tout le bataclan *ou* le tralala; **they had eggs, bacon, toast, the works** ils mangeaient des œufs, du bacon, du pain grillé, tout, quoi!; *Am* **to shoot the works** jouer le grand jeu; *Am* **we shot the works on the project** nous avons mis le paquet sur le projet; **to give sb the works** *(special treatment)* dérouler le tapis rouge pour qn; *(beating)* passer qn à tabac

5 at work 1 *adj* (**a**) *(person)* **to be at work on sth/(on) doing sth** travailler (à) qch/à faire qch; **he's at work on a new book** il travaille à un nouveau livre; **they're hard at work painting the house** ils sont en plein travail, ils repeignent la maison (**b**) *(having an effect)* **there are several factors at work here** il y a plusieurs facteurs qui entrent en jeu *ou* qui jouent ici; **there are evil forces at work** des forces mauvaises sont en action **2** *adv (at place of work)* **she's at work** *(gen)* elle est au travail; *(office)* elle est au bureau; *(factory)* elle est à l'usine; **I'll phone you at work** je t'appellerai au travail; **we met at work** on s'est connus au travail

►► ***work area*** *(in school, home)* coin *m* de travail; *Comput* zone *f* de travail; ***works band*** fanfare *m (d'une entreprise)*; ***work camp*** *(prison)* camp *m* de travail; *(voluntary)* chantier *m* de travail; *Am* ***work coat*** blouse *f*; ***works committee, works council*** comité *m* d'entreprise; ***work ethic*** = exaltation des valeurs liées au travail; ***work experience*** stage *m* (en entreprise); **the course includes two months' work experience** le programme comprend un stage en entreprise de deux mois; *Am* ***work farm*** = camp de travail forcé où les détenus travaillent la terre; *Comput* ***work file*** fichier *m* de travail; ***work flow*** déroulement *m* des opérations; ***work group*** groupe *m* de travail; ***works manager*** directeur(trice) *m,f* d'usine; ***work party*** *(of soldiers)* escouade *f*; *(of prisoners)* groupe *m* de travail; ***work permit*** permis *m* de travail; *Comput* ***work sheet*** feuille *f* de travail; ***work space*** *(at home)* coin-travail *m*; *(in office)* & *Comput* espace *m* de travail; **I need more work space** j'ai besoin de plus d'espace pour travailler; ***work surface*** surface *f* de travail; *Am* ***work week*** semaine *f* de travail

►**work away** *vi* travailler; **while he worked away at fixing the furnace** tandis qu'il travaillait à réparer la chaudière; **we worked away all evening** nous avons passé la soirée à travailler

►**work down** *vi* glisser; **her socks had worked down around her ankles** ses chaussettes étaient tombées sur ses chevilles

►**work in** *vt sep* (**a**) *(incorporate)* incorporer; **work the ointment in thoroughly** faites bien pénétrer la pommade; *Culin* **work the butter into the flour** incorporez le beurre à la farine

(**b**) *(insert)* faire entrer *ou* introduire petit à petit; **he worked in a few sly remarks about the boss** il a réussi à glisser quelques réflexions sournoises sur le patron; **I'll try and work the translation in some time this week** *(into schedule)* j'essayerai de (trouver le temps de) faire la traduction dans le courant de la semaine

►**work off** *vt sep* (**a**) *(dispose of → fat, weight)* se débarrasser de, éliminer; *(→ anxiety, frustration)* passer, assouvir; **I worked off my excess energy chopping wood** j'ai dépensé mon trop-plein d'énergie en cassant du bois; **he worked off his tensions by running** il s'est défoulé en faisant du jogging; **to work off one's anger on sb** passer sa colère sur qn

(**b**) *(debt, obligation)* **it took him three months to work off his debt** il a dû travailler trois mois pour rembourser son emprunt

►**work on 1** *vt insep* (**a**) *(person)* essayer de convaincre; **we've been working on him but he still won't go** nous avons essayé de le [illegible] **I'll work on her** je vais m'occuper d'elle

(**b**) *(task, problem)* **the police are working on who stole the jewels** la police s'efforce de retrouver celui qui a volé les bijoux; **he's been working on his breaststroke/emotional problems** il a travaillé sa brasse/essayé de résoudre ses problèmes sentimentaux; **have you got any ideas? – I'm working on it** as-tu des idées? – je cherche

(**c**) *(use as basis)* **have you any data to work on?** avez-vous des données sur lesquelles vous fonder?

2 *vi (continue to work)* continuer à travailler

►**work out 1** *vt sep* (**a**) *(discharge fully)* acquitter en travaillant; **to work out one's notice** faire son préavis

(**b**) *(calculate → cost, distance, sum)* calculer; *(→ answer, total)* trouver; **I work it out at £22** d'après mes calculs, ça fait 22 livres

(**c**) *(solve → calculation, problem)* résoudre; *(→ puzzle)* faire, résoudre; *(→ code)* déchiffrer; **have they worked out their differences?** est-ce qu'ils ont réglé *ou* résolu leurs différends?; **I'm sure we can work this thing out** *(your problem)* je suis sûr que nous pouvons arranger ça; *(our argument)* je suis sûr que nous finirons par nous mettre d'accord; **things will work themselves out** les choses s'arrangeront toutes seules *ou* d'elles-mêmes

(**d**) *(formulate → idea, plan)* élaborer, combiner; *(→ agreement, details)* mettre au point; **to work out a solution** trouver une solution; **have you worked out yet when it's due to start?** est-ce que tu sais quand ça doit commencer?; **she had it all worked out** elle avait tout planifié; **we worked out an easier route** nous avons trouvé un itinéraire plus facile

(**e**) *(figure out)* arriver à comprendre; **I finally worked out why he was acting so strangely** j'ai enfin découvert *ou* compris pourquoi il se comportait si bizarrement; **the dog had worked out how to open the door** le chien avait compris comment ouvrir la porte; **I can't work her out** je n'arrive pas à la comprendre; **I can't work their relationship out** leurs rapports me dépassent

(**f**) *(mine, well)* épuiser

2 *vi* (**a**) *(happen)* se passer; **it depends on how things work out** ça dépend de la façon dont les choses se passent; **the trip worked out as planned** le voyage s'est déroulé comme prévu; **I wonder how it will all work out** je me demande comment tout cela va s'arranger; **it all worked out for the best** tout a fini par s'arranger pour le mieux; **but it didn't work out that way** mais il en a été tout autrement; **it worked out badly for them** les choses ont mal tourné pour eux

(**b**) *(have a good result → job, plan)* réussir; *(→ problem, puzzle)* se résoudre; **she worked out fine as personnel director** elle s'est bien débrouillée comme directeur du personnel; **are things working out for you OK?** est-ce que ça se passe bien pour toi?; **did the new job work out?** ça a marché pour le nouveau boulot?; **it didn't work out between them** les choses ont plutôt mal tourné entre eux; **their project didn't work out** leur projet est tombé à l'eau

(**c**) *(amount to)* **how much does it all work out at?** ça fait combien en tout?; **the average price for an apartment works out to** *or* **at $5,000 per square metre** le prix moyen d'un appartement s'élève *ou* revient à 5000 dollars le mètre carré; **that works out at three hours a week** ça fait trois heures par semaine; **electric heating works out expensive** le chauffage électrique revient cher

(**d**) *(exercise)* faire de l'exercice; *(professional athlete)* s'entraîner

►**work over** *vt sep* (**a**) *Am (revise)* revoir, réviser (**b**) *Fam (beat up)* tabasser, passer à tabac

►**work round 1** *vi* (**a**) *(turn)* tourner; **the wind worked round to the north** le vent a tourné au nord petit à petit (**b**) *Fig (in conversation)* **he finally worked round to the subject of housing** il a fini par aborder le sujet du logement; **what's she working round to?** où veut-elle en venir?

2 *vt sep (bring round)* **I worked the conversation round to my salary** j'ai amené la conversation sur la question de mon salaire

►**work through 1** *vt sep* (**a**) *(insert)* faire passer à travers

(**b**) *(progress through)* **we worked our way through the crowd** nous nous sommes frayé un chemin à travers la foule; **he worked his way through the book** il a lu le livre du début à la fin; *Fig* **I worked the problem through** j'ai étudié le problème sous tous ses aspects

2 *vt insep* (**a**) *(continue to work)* **she worked through lunch** elle a travaillé pendant l'heure du déjeuner

(**b**) *(resolve)* **he worked through his emotional problems** il a réussi à assumer ses problèmes affectifs

►**work up 1** *vt sep* (**a**) *(stir up, rouse)* exciter, provoquer; **he worked up the crowd** il a excité la foule; **he worked the crowd up into a frenzy** il a rendu la foule frénétique; **he works himself up** *or* **he gets himself worked up over nothing** il s'énerve pour rien; **she had worked herself up into a dreadful rage** elle s'était mise dans une rage terrible

(**b**) *(develop)* développer; **I want to work these ideas up into an article** je veux développer ces idées pour en faire un article; **to work up an appetite** se mettre en appétit; **we worked up a sweat/a thirst playing tennis** jouer au tennis nous a donné chaud/soif; **I can't work up any enthusiasm for this work** je n'arrive pas à avoir le moindre enthousiasme pour ce travail; **he tried to work up an interest in the cause** il a essayé de s'intéresser à la cause

(**c**) *(idiom)* **to work one's way up** faire son chemin; **she worked her way up from secretary to managing director** elle a commencé comme secrétaire et elle a fait son chemin jusqu'au poste de P-DG; **I worked my way up from nothing** je suis parti de rien

2 *vi* (**a**) *(clothing)* remonter

(**b**) *(build up)* **the film was working up to a climax** le film approchait de son point culminant; **things were working up to a crisis** une crise se préparait, on était au bord d'une crise; **she's working up to what she wanted to ask** elle en vient à ce qu'elle voulait demander; **what are you working up to?** où veux-tu en venir?

---

workability [ˌwɜːkəˈbɪlɪtɪ] *n* (**a**) *(of plan)* caractère *m* réalisable (**b**) *(of mine, field)* caractère *m* exploitable

workable [ˈwɜːkəbəl] *adj* (**a**) *(plan, proposal)* réalisable, faisable; **do you really think it's workable?** croyez-vous vraiment que c'est faisable *ou* que ça va marcher? (**b**) *(mine, field)* exploitable

workaday [ˈwɜːkədeɪ] *adj (clothes, routine)* de tous les jours; *(man)* ordinaire, banal; *(incident)* courant, banal; **the workaday world of the office** la routine du bureau

workaholic [ˌwɜːkəˈhɒlɪk] *n Fam* bourreau *m* de travail

workbag [ˈwɜːkbæg] *n* sac *m* à ouvrage

workbasket [ˈwɜːkˌbɑːskɪt] *n* corbeille *f* à ouvrage

workbench [ˈwɜːkbentʃ] *n* établi *m*

workbook [ˈwɜːkbʊk] *n* (**a**) *Sch (exercise book)* cahier *m* d'exercices; *(record book)* cahier *m* de classe (**b**) *(manual)* manuel *m*

workbox [ˈwɜːkbɒks] *n* boîte *f* à ouvrage

workday [ˈwɜːkdeɪ] **1** *n* (**a**) *(day's work)* journée *f* de travail (**b**) *(working day)* jour *m* ouvré *ou* où l'on travaille; **Sunday is a workday for some people** il y a des gens qui travaillent le dimanche

2 *adj* = **workaday**

worked up [ˌwɜːkt-] *adj* énervé, dans tous ses états; **to get worked up** s'énerver, se mettre dans tous ses états

worker [ˈwɜːkə(r)] *n* (**a**) *Ind (gen)* travailleur(-euse) *m,f*, employé(e) *m,f*; *(manual)* ouvrier(-ère) *m,f*, travailleur(euse) *m,f*; **relations between workers and management** les relations entre les travailleurs *ou* les employés et la direction; **he's a fast worker!** il travaille vite!; **she's a good worker** elle travaille bien; **she's a hard worker** elle travaille dur

(**b**) *Entom* ouvrière *f*

►► ***worker ant*** (fourmi *f*) ouvrière *f*; ***worker bee*** (abeille *f*) ouvrière *f*; ***worker director*** = ouvrier qui fait partie du conseil d'administration; ***worker participation*** participation *f* ouvrière; ***worker representation*** représentation *f* du personnel

worker-priest *n* prêtre-ouvrier *m*

workfare [ˈwɜːkfeə(r)] *n Pol* = principe selon lequel les bénéficiaires de l'allocation de chômage doivent fournir un travail en échange

workflow [ˈwɜːkfləʊ] *n* rythme *m* de travail

►► ***workflow schedule*** plan *m* de travail

workforce [ˈwɜːkfɔːs] *n* main-d'œuvre *f*, effectifs *mpl*

work-harden *vt Metal* écrouir

work-hardening *n Metal* écrouissage *m*

workhorse [ˈwɜːkhɔːs, *pl* -hɔːsɪz] *n* (**a**) *(horse)* cheval *m* de labour (**b**) *Fig (worker)* bourreau *m* de travail; *(machine, vehicle)* bonne mécanique *f*

workhouse [ˈwɜːkhaʊs, *pl* -haʊzɪz] *n* (**a**) *Hist (in UK)* asile *m* des pauvres (**b**) *(in US → prison)* maison *f* de correction

work-in *n* = occupation d'une entreprise par le personnel (avec poursuite du travail)

working [ˈwɜːkɪŋ] **1** *adj* (**a**) *(mother)* qui travaille; *(population)* actif; **ordinary working people** les travailleurs ordinaires; **the party of the working man** le parti des travailleurs

(**b**) *(day, hours)* de travail; **working day** *(gen)* journée *f* de travail; *Admin* jour *m* ouvrable; **during a normal working day** pendant la journée de travail; **Sunday is not a working day** le dimanche est chômé, on ne travaille pas le dimanche; **a working week of forty hours** une semaine de quarante heures; **he spent his entire working life with the firm** il a travaillé toute sa vie dans l'entreprise; **to be of working age** être en âge de travailler; **a working breakfast/lunch** un petit déjeuner/un déjeuner d'affaires

(**c**) *(clothes, conditions)* de travail; **a relaxed working environment** un milieu professionnel détendu; **we have a close working relationship** nous travaillons bien ensemble

(**d**) *(functioning → farm, factory)* qui marche; **in (good) working order** en (bon) état de marche;

(**e**) *(theory, definition)* de travail; *(majority)* suffisant; *(agreement)* de circonstance; *(knowledge)* adéquat, suffisant; **working agreement** modus vivendi *m*; **to have a working knowledge of French/the law** posséder une connaissance suffisante du français/du droit

2 *n* (**a**) *(work)* travail *m*

(**b**) *(operation → of machine)* fonctionnement *m*

(**c**) *(of mine)* exploitation *f*; *(of clay, leather)* travail *m*

3 workings *npl* (**a**) *(mechanism)* mécanisme *m*; *Fig (of government, system)* rouages *mpl*; **it's difficult to understand the workings of his mind** il est difficile de savoir ce qu'il a dans la tête *ou* ce qui se passe dans sa tête

(**b**) *Mining* chantier *m* d'exploitation; **old mine workings** anciennes mines *fpl*

►► *Fin* ***working account*** compte *m* d'exploitation; *Acct* ***working assets*** actif *m* circulant; *Fin* ***working capital*** *(UNCOUNT)* fonds *mpl* de roulement, capital *m* de roulement; *Fin* ***working capital cycle*** cycle *m* du besoin en fonds de roulement; *Fin* ***working capital fund*** compte *m* d'avances; ***the working class, the working classes*** la classe ouvrière, le prolétariat; ***working copy*** *(of document, text)* copie *f* de travail; ***working drawing*** épure *f*; ***working expenses*** frais *mpl* généraux, frais *mpl* d'exploitation; *Comput* ***working file*** fichier *m* de travail; ***working girl*** *(prostitute)* professionnelle *f*; ***working group*** *(committee → for study)* groupe *m* de travail; *(→ for enquiry)* commission *f* d'enquête; ***working hypothesis*** hypothèse *f* de travail; ***working interest*** participation *f* d'exploitation; ***working lunch*** déjeuner *m* d'affaires *ou* de travail; ***working majority*** majorité *f* suffisante; *Br* ***working man*** ouvrier *m*; ***working men's club*** = club d'ouvriers, comportant un bar et une scène où sont présentés des spectacles; ***working model*** modèle *m* qui fonctionne; *Math* ***working out*** *(of problem)* résolution *f*; **show all working out** *(in exam paper)* montrez les étapes de votre raisonnement; ***working party*** *(committee → for study)* groupe *m* de travail; *(→ for enquiry)* commission *f* d'enquête; *(group → of prisoners, soldiers)* groupe *m* de travail; ***working speed*** vitesse *f* de régime; *Br Law* ***working time directive*** loi *f* sur le temps de travail; ***working title*** titre *m* provisoire; ***working woman*** *(worker)* ouvrière *f*, employée *f*; *(woman with job)* femme *f* qui travaille

working-class *adj (district, origins)* ouvrier; *(accent)* des classes populaires; **she's working-class** elle appartient à la classe ouvrière; **a working class hero** un héros de la classe ouvrière *ou* du prolétariat

workless [ˈwɜːklɪs] **1** *adj* sans travail

2 *npl* **the workless** les chômeurs *mpl*

workload [ˈwɜːkləʊd] *n* travail *m* à effectuer, charge *f* de travail; **my workload has eased off a bit** j'ai un peu moins de travail en ce moment; **I still have a heavy workload** je suis encore surchargé de travail

workman [ˈwɜːkmən] (*pl* **workmen** [-mən]) *n* (**a**) *(manual worker)* ouvrier *m*; **the workmen came**

to fix the drainpipe les ouvriers sont venus réparer la gouttière; *Am* **workmen's compensation** indemnité *f* pour accident de travail; *Prov* **a bad workman always blames his tools** les mauvais ouvriers ont toujours de mauvais outils (**b**) *(craftsman)* artisan *m*; **he is a good workman** il travaille bien, il fait du bon travail

workmanlike ['wɜːkmənlaɪk] *adj* (**a**) *(efficient → approach, person)* professionnel; **she did the job in a workmanlike way** elle a fait du très bon travail (**b**) *(well made → artefact)* bien fait, soigné; **he wrote a workmanlike report** il a fait un compte rendu très sérieux (**c**) *(serious → attempt, effort)* sérieux

workmanship ['wɜːkmənʃɪp] *n (UNCOUNT)* (**a**) *(skill)* métier *m*, maîtrise *f*; **he was famous for his workmanship** il était connu pour la finesse de son travail

(**b**) *(quality)* exécution *f*, fabrication *f*; *(of clothes)* façon *f*; **she admired the fine workmanship of the carving** elle admira le ciselage délicat; **it was a shoddy piece of workmanship** c'était du travail mal fait *ou* bâclé; **you don't get any workmanship these days** la qualité n'est plus ce qu'elle était

workmate ['wɜːkmeɪt] *n* camarade *mf* de travail

workout ['wɜːkaʊt] *n* séance *f* d'entraînement; **to have a workout** s'entraîner physiquement, faire une séance d'entraînement

workpeople ['wɜːkˌpiːpəl] *npl* travailleurs *mpl*

workplace ['wɜːkpleɪs] *n* lieu *m* de travail; **in the workplace** sur le lieu de travail

workroom ['wɜːkrʊm] *n* salle *f* de travail

workshare ['wɜːkʃeə(r)] *n* travail *m* en temps partagé; *(person)* travailleur(euse) *m,f* en temps partagé; **workshares are becoming more common** le partage du travail devient de plus en plus courant

worksharing ['wɜːkˌʃeərɪŋ] *n* partage *m* du travail; **we have a worksharing arrangement** nous avons un système de partage du travail; **worksharing is becoming popular** le partage du travail est de plus en plus courant

workshop ['wɜːkʃɒp] *n* (**a**) *Ind (gen)* atelier *m* (**b**) *(study group)* atelier *m*, groupe *m* de travail

workshy ['wɜːkʃaɪ] *adj* fainéant, tire-au-flanc *(inv)*

workstation ['wɜːkˌsteɪʃən] *n Comput* poste *m ou* station *f* de travail

work-study *n Ind* étude *f* des cadences

worktable ['wɜːkˌteɪbəl] *n* table *f* de travail

worktop ['wɜːktɒp] *n (in kitchen)* plan *m* de travail, *Can* comptoir *m* de cuisine

work-to-rule *n Br* grève *f* du zèle

WORLD [wɜːld] **1** *n* **A.** (**a**) *(earth)* monde *m*; **to travel round the world** faire le tour du monde, voyager autour du monde; **to see the world** voir du pays, courir le monde; **throughout the world** dans le monde entier; **in this part of the world** dans cette région; **the best in the world** le meilleur du monde; **I'm the world's worst photographer** il n'y a pas pire photographe que moi; **there isn't a nicer spot in the whole world** il n'y a pas d'endroit plus agréable au monde; **the world over, all over the world** dans le monde entier, partout dans le monde; **love is the same the world over** l'amour, c'est la même chose partout dans le monde; **it's a small world!** (que) le monde est petit!

(**b**) *(planet)* monde *m*; **there may be other worlds out there** il existe peut-être d'autres mondes quelque part

(**c**) *(universe)* monde *m*, univers *m*; **since the world began** depuis que le monde existe

B. (**a**) *(part of the world) & Hist & Pol* monde *m*; **the Arab World** le monde arabe; **the developing world** les pays *mpl* en voie de développement; **the Gaelic-speaking world** les régions où l'on parle le gaélique; **the Spanish-speaking world** le monde hispanophone

(**b**) *(society)* monde *m*; **she wants to change the world** elle veut changer le monde; **in the modern world** dans le monde moderne; **she's gone up in the world** elle a fait du chemin; **he's gone down in the world** il a connu de meilleurs jours; **to come into the world** venir au monde; **to bring a child into the world** mettre un enfant au monde; **they hesitated to bring children into the world** ils hésitaient à avoir des enfants; **to be alone in the world** être seul au monde; **to make one's way in the world** faire son chemin; **you have to take the world as you find it** il faut prendre les choses comme elles viennent; **what's the world coming to?** où allons-nous?, où va le monde?

(**c**) *(general public)* monde *m*; **the world awaits the outcome of the talks** le monde entier attend le résultat des pourparlers; **the news shook the world** la nouvelle a ébranlé le monde entier; **the singer had the world at her feet** la chanteuse avait tout le monde à ses pieds

(**d**) *(people in general)* **we don't want the whole world to know** nous ne voulons pas que tout le monde le sache; *Fam Fig* **(all) the world and his wife** le monde entier

C. (**a**) *(existence, particular way of life)* monde *m*, vie *f*; **a whole new world opened up to me** un monde nouveau s'ouvrit à moi; **we live in different worlds** nous ne vivons pas sur la même planète; **it's a different world up north** c'est complètement différent au nord; **to be worlds apart** *(in lifestyle)* avoir des styles de vie complètement différents; *(in opinions)* avoir des opinions complètement différentes

(**b**) *(realm)* monde *m*; **he lives in a world of his own** il vit dans un monde à lui; **a nightmare/a fantasy world** un monde de cauchemar/de rêve; **the child's world** l'univers *m* des enfants; **they knew nothing of the world outside** ils ignoraient tout du monde extérieur; **the underwater world** le monde sous-marin

(**c**) *(field, domain)* monde *m*, milieu *m*, milieux *mpl*; **she is well known in the theatre world** elle est connue dans le milieu du théâtre; **the publishing world** le monde de l'édition

(**d**) *(group of living things)* monde *m*; **the animal/the plant world** le règne animal/végétal

(**e**) *Rel* monde *m*; **to renounce the world** renoncer au monde; **in this world and the next** dans ce monde(-ci) et dans l'autre; **he isn't long for this world** il n'en a pas pour longtemps; *Arch or Bible* **world without end** pour les siècles des siècles

(**f**) *(idioms)* **a holiday will do you a** *or* **the world of good** des vacances vous feront le plus grand bien; **it made a world of difference** ça a tout changé; **there's a world of difference between them** il y a un monde entre eux; **he thinks the world of his daughter** il a une admiration sans bornes pour sa fille; **it means the world to me** c'est quelque chose qui me tient beaucoup à cœur

2 *comp (champion, championship, record)* mondial, du monde; *(language, history, religion)* universel; *(population)* mondial; **on a world scale** à l'échelle mondiale

3 for all the world *adv* exactement; **she behaved for all the world as if she owned the place** elle faisait exactement comme si elle était chez elle

4 for (anything in) the world *adv* **I wouldn't hurt her for (anything in) the world** je ne lui ferais de mal pour rien au monde

5 in the world *adv* (**a**) *(for emphasis)* **nothing in the world would change my mind** rien au monde ne me ferait changer d'avis; **I felt as if I hadn't a care in the world** je me sentais libre de tout souci; **we've got all the time in the world** nous avons tout le *ou* tout notre temps; **all the good intentions in the world won't bring her back** on ne la ramènera pas, même avec les meilleures intentions du monde; **I wouldn't do it for all the money in the world!** je ne le ferais pas pour tout l'or du monde!

(**b**) *(expressing surprise, irritation, frustration)* **who in the world will believe you?** qui donc va vous croire?; **where in the world have you put it?** où l'avez-vous donc mis?; **what in the world made you do it?** pourquoi donc avez-vous fait ça?; **why in the world didn't you tell me?** pourquoi donc ne me l'as-tu pas dit?

6 out of this world *adj Fam* extraordinaire, sensationnel

►► *Am* ***the World Almanac*** = publication annuelle qui recense les événements de l'année; ***the World Bank*** la Banque mondiale; ***the World Council of Churches*** le Conseil œcuménique des Églises; ***the World Cup*** la Coupe du monde; ***world domination*** domination *f* du monde; ***world economy*** conjoncture *f* économique mondiale; ***World Fair*** exposition *f* universelle; ***the World Health Organization*** l'Organisation *f* mondiale de la santé; ***world language*** langue *f* internationale; ***world map*** carte *f* du monde; *(in two hemispheres)* mappemonde *f*; *Com* ***world market*** marché *m* mondial *ou* international; ***world music*** world music *f*; ***world opinion*** l'opinion internationale; ***world peace*** la paix mondiale; ***world power*** puissance *f* mondiale; *Fin* ***world reserves*** réserves *fpl* mondiales; ***world rights*** droits *mpl* d'exploitation pour le monde entier; ***World Series*** = le championnat américain de base-ball; *Rad* ***the World Service*** = service étranger de la BBC; ***world television*** mondovision *f*; ***world tour*** voyage *m* autour du monde; ***world trade*** commerce *m* international; ***the World Trade Center*** le World Trade Center; ***the World Trade Organization*** l'Organisation *f* mondiale du commerce; ***world view*** = vue métaphysique du monde; ***world war*** guerre *f* mondiale; ***World War I, the First World War*** la Première Guerre mondiale; ***World War II, the Second World War*** la Seconde Guerre mondiale; *Fam* ***world war three*** la troisième guerre mondiale; ***the World Wide Fund for Nature*** le Fonds international pour la protection de la nature; *Comput* ***the World Wide Web*** le World Wide Web

world-beater *n Fam (person)* champion(onne) *m,f*; *Fig* **this new car is going to be a world-beater** cette nouvelle voiture va faire un tabac

world-beating *adj Fam (performance, achievement)* inégalé, qui supasse tous les autres; **of world-beating quality** d'une qualité inégalée; **the new world-beating X52** le X52, nouveau leader mondial

world-class *adj (player, runner)* parmi les meilleurs du monde, de classe internationale

world-famous *adj* de renommée mondiale, célèbre dans le monde entier

worldliness ['wɜːldlɪnɪs] *n* (**a**) *(materialism)* matérialisme *m* (**b**) *(experience of the world)* mondanité *f*; **there was an air of worldliness about her** elle avait l'air de quelqu'un qui a l'expérience du monde

worldly ['wɜːldlɪ] *(compar* **worldlier**, *superl* **worldliest**) *adj* (**a**) *(material → possessions, pleasures, matters)* matériel, de ce monde, terrestre; *Rel* temporel, de ce monde; **he is not interested in worldly things** les choses de ce monde ne l'intéressent pas; **all my worldly goods** tout ce que je possède au monde; **worldly wisdom** la sagesse du monde *ou* du siècle

(**b**) *(materialistic → person, outlook)* matérialiste

(**c**) *(sophisticated → person)* qui a l'expérience du monde; *(→ attitude, manner)* qui démontre une expérience du monde; **she was very worldly for one so young** elle avait une bien grande expérience du monde pour quelqu'un d'aussi jeune

worldly-wise *adj* qui a l'expérience du monde

world-shaking, world-shattering *adj (event, news)* bouleversant, renversant

world-weariness *n* dégoût *m* du monde, ennui *m*

world-weary *adj (person)* las du monde

worldwide ['wɜːldwaɪd] **1** *adj (depression, famine, reputation)* mondial, global

2 *adv* partout dans le monde, dans le monde entier; **this product is now sold worldwide** ce produit se vend maintenant dans le monde entier

►► ***worldwide rights*** droits *mpl* d'exploitation pour le monde entier

WORM [wɜːm] *Comput (abbr* **write once read many times**) WORM

worm [wɜːm] **1** *n* (**a**) *(in earth, garden)* ver *m* (de terre); *(in fruit)* ver *m*; *(for fishing)* ver *m*, asticot *m*; *Br Fig* **the worm has turned** j'en ai eu/il en a eu/*etc* assez de se faire marcher dessus; *Fig* **the worm in the bud** le ver dans le fruit

(**b**) *(parasite → in body)* ver *m*; **to have worms** avoir des vers (**c**) *Fam Fig (person)* minable *mf*; **what a worm!** quel minable!

(**d**) *Literary (troublesome thing)* tourment *m*, tourments *mpl*; **the worm of jealousy** les affres *fpl* de la jalousie

(**e**) *Tech (of screw)* filet *m*; **worm and roller steering** direction *f* à vis et galet

2 *vt* (**a**) *(move)* **to worm one's way under sth** passer sous qch à plat ventre *ou* en rampant; **she wormed her way through a gap in the fence** en se tortillant, elle s'est faufilée par une ouverture dans la palissade; **he managed to worm his way to the front** il a réussi à se faufiler jusqu'à l'avant

(**b**) *Pej (sneak)* **they have wormed their way into our party** ils se sont infiltrés *ou* immiscés dans notre parti; **he wormed his way into her affections** il a trouvé le chemin de son cœur *(par sournoiserie)*

(**c**) *(dog, sheep)* débarrasser de ses vers

►► ***worm cast*** déjections *fpl* de ver; *Tech* ***worm drive*** transmission *f* par vis sans fin; *Tech* ***worm gear*** engrenage *m* de vis sans fin; ***worm powder*** poudre *f* à vers, poudre *f* vermifuge; ***worm tablets*** comprimés *mpl* vermifuges

►**worm out** *vt sep (information)* soutirer; **I tried to worm the truth out of him** j'ai essayé de lui soutirer la vérité; **he'll worm it out of her eventually** il finira par lui tirer les vers du nez; **stop trying to worm it out of me!** arrête d'essayer de me tirer les vers du nez!; **I'd like to see her worm her way out of that one** j'aimerais bien voir comment elle va s'en tirer

worm-eaten *adj (apple)* véreux; *(furniture)* vermoulu, mangé aux vers; *Fig (ancient)* désuet(-ète), antédiluvien

wormhole ['wɜːmhəʊl] *n* trou *m* de ver

worming tablets ['wɜːmɪŋ-] *npl* comprimés *mpl* vermifuges

worm's-eye view *n (from below)* perspective *f* vue d'en bas; *Phot & Cin* contre-plongée *f*; *(from lowly position)* perspective *f* au ras des pâquerettes; **to get a worm's-eye view of the theatre/catering industry** voir le monde du théâtre/de la restauration au ras des pâquerettes *ou* d'un point de vue restreint; **he presents a worm's-eye view of events** il nous présente les événements vus par les humbles

wormwood ['wɜːmwʊd] *n* (**a**) *(plant)* armoise *f* (**b**) *Literary (bitterness)* fiel *m*, amertume *f*; **life to him was gall and wormwood** la vie pour lui n'était qu'amertume et dégoût

Wormwood Scrubs ['wɜːmwʊd-] *n* = grande prison pour hommes de Londres

wormy ['wɜːmɪ] *(compar* **wormier**, *superl* **wormiest**) *adj* (**a**) *(apple)* véreux; *(furniture)* vermoulu, piqué aux vers (**b**) *(soil)* plein de vers (**c**) *(in shape)* vermiculaire

worn [wɔːn] **1** *pp of* **wear**

2 *adj* (**a**) *(shoes, rug, tyre)* usé (**b**) *(weary → person)* las (lasse)

worn-out *adj* (**a**) *(shoes, tyre)* complètement usé; *(rug, dress)* usé jusqu'à la corde; *(battery)* usé (**b**) *(person)* épuisé, éreinté

worried ['wʌrɪd] *adj (person, look)* inquiet(ète) *m,f*; **I'm worried that they may get lost** *or* **in case they get lost** j'ai peur qu'ils ne se perdent; **to be worried about sb/sth** être inquiet pour qn/qch; **she's worried about the future** elle est inquiète pour l'avenir; **a worried frown** un froncement inquiet des sourcils; **I'm worried about him** je suis inquiet *ou* je m'inquiète pour lui; **to be worried sick** *or* **to death (about sb)** être fou *ou* malade d'inquiétude (pour qn); **you had me worried for a minute** vous m'avez fait peur pendant une minute; **I'm not worried either way** ça m'est égal; **I was worried it would be the wrong size** j'avais peur que ce ne soit pas la bonne taille

worriedly ['wʌrɪdlɪ] *adv (say)* avec un air inquiet

worrier ['wʌrɪə(r)] *n* anxieux(euse) *m,f*, inquiet(-ète) *m,f*; **he's a born worrier** c'est un éternel inquiet; **don't be such a worrier** arrête de t'inquiéter comme ça

worriment ['wʌrɪmənt] *n Am Fam* inquiétude *f*

worrisome ['wʌrɪsəm] *adj Old-fashioned* inquiétant

worry ['wʌrɪ] *(pt & pp* **worried**, *pl* **worries**) **1** *vt* (**a**) *(make anxious)* inquiéter, tracasser; **you really worried me** je me suis vraiment inquiété à cause de toi; **he was worried by her sudden disappearance** il était inquiet de sa disparition subite; **I sometimes worry that they'll never be found** parfois, je crains qu'on ne les retrouve jamais; **that boiler worries me, suppose it blows up?** la chaudière m'inquiète, si elle explosait?; **she is worrying herself sick** *or* **to death about it** elle en est malade d'inquiétude; **something is worrying her** il y a quelque chose qui la préoccupe *ou* qui la travaille; **nothing seems to worry her** rien ne semble l'inquiéter *ou* la tracasser; **what's worrying you?** qu'est-ce qui vous tracasse?; **it doesn't worry me if you want to waste your life** cela m'est égal *ou* ne me gêne pas si vous voulez gâcher votre vie; *Fam* **don't worry your head** *or* **yourself about the details** ne vous inquiétez pas pour les détails

(**b**) *(disturb, bother)* inquiéter, ennuyer; **why worry him with your problems?** pourquoi l'ennuyer avec vos problèmes?; **he doesn't want to be worried with these minor details** il ne veut pas être embêté par ces petits détails; **it doesn't seem to worry you if other people get hurt** que d'autres souffrent ne semble pas te préoccuper

(**c**) *(of dog → bone, ball)* secouer dans la gueule; *(→ sheep)* harceler

2 *vi* s'inquiéter, se faire du souci, se tracasser; **don't tell them, they'll only worry** ne le leur dis pas, ça ne fera que les inquiéter; **to worry about** *or* **over sth** s'inquiéter pour *ou* au sujet de qch; **she has enough to worry about** elle a assez de soucis comme ça; **there's nothing to worry about** il n'y a pas lieu de s'inquiéter; **it's only a scratch, nothing to worry about** ce n'est qu'une égratignure, pas de quoi s'inquiéter; **don't worry** ne vous inquiétez *ou* ne vous tracassez pas; **they'll be found, don't you worry** on va les trouver, ne t'en fais pas; **stop worrying!** ne t'en fais donc pas!; **not to worry!** ce n'est pas grave!; **what's the use of worrying?** à quoi bon se tourmenter?; *Ironic* **YOU should worry** ce n'est pas votre problème, il n'y a pas de raisons de vous en faire

3 *n* (**a**) *(anxiety)* inquiétude *f*, souci *m*; **money is a constant source of worry** l'argent est un perpétuel souci *ou* une perpétuelle source d'inquiétude; **her sons are a constant worry to her** ses fils lui causent constamment des soucis *ou* du souci; **he was sick with worry about her** il se rongeait les sangs pour elle *ou* à son sujet

(**b**) *(concern)* sujet *m* d'inquiétude, souci *m*; *(problem)* problème *m*; **my greatest worry is my health** mon plus grand souci, c'est ma santé; **he doesn't seem to have any worries** il n'a pas l'air d'avoir de soucis; **it's a real worry for her** cela la tracasse vraiment; **that's my worry** c'est mon problème; **that's the least of my worries** c'est le moindre *ou* le cadet *ou* le dernier de mes soucis; *Austr Fam* **no worries!** pas de problème!

►► ***worry beads*** ≃ komboloï *m*

►**worry at** *vt insep Br* = **worry** *vt* (**c**)

►**worry out** *vt sep Br (problem)* résoudre à force de considérer sous tous ses aspects; *(answer)* trouver à force de chercher

worryguts ['wʌrɪgʌts] *n Br Fam* anxieux(euse)[□] *m,f*, éternel(elle) inquiet(ète) *m,f*

worrying ['wʌrɪɪŋ] **1** *adj* inquiétant; **the worrying thing is that it could happen again** ce qu'il y a d'inquiétant *ou* ce qui est inquiétant, c'est que cela pourrait se reproduire

2 *n* inquiétude *f*; **worrying won't solve anything** cela ne résoudra rien de se faire du souci

worryingly ['wʌrɪɪŋlɪ] *adv* **the project is worryingly late** le projet a pris un retard inquiétant; **worryingly, I haven't seen him for weeks** je ne l'ai pas vu depuis des semaines, ça m'inquiète; **even more worryingly, the interest rates are predicted to rise again** ce qui est encore plus inquiétant, c'est qu'on prévoit une nouvelle hausse des taux d'intérêt; **there are worryingly high levels of radioactivity in the area** il y a un niveau *ou* un taux de radioactivité inquiétant dans la région

worrywart ['wʌrɪwɔːt] *Am Fam* = **worryguts**

WORSE [wɜːs]

pire	► 1 (a); 3
plus mauvais	► 1 (a)
plus mal	► 1 (b); 2 (a)
moins bien	► 2 (a)

1 *adj (compar of* **bad**) (**a**) *(not as good, pleasant as)* pire, plus mauvais; **I'm a worse player than he is** je joue plus mal que lui; **you're bad at French but he's worse** tu es mauvais en français mais il est plus mauvais que toi; **the news is even worse than we expected** les nouvelles sont encore plus mauvaises que nous ne pensions; **your writing is worse than mine** votre écriture est pire que la mienne; **my writing is bad, but yours is worse** j'écris mal, mais vous, c'est pire; **things are worse than you imagine** les choses vont plus mal que vous l'imaginez; **it could have been worse!** ça aurait pu être pire!; **I lost my money, and worse still** *or* **and what's worse, my passport** j'ai perdu mon argent, et ce qui est plus grave, mon passeport; **worse than before/than ever** pire qu'avant/que jamais; **how are things? – no worse than before** comment ça va? – pas plus mal qu'avant; **the rain is worse than ever** il pleut de plus en plus; **worse than useless** complètement inutile; **to get** *or* **to grow worse** empirer, s'aggraver; **to get worse and worse** aller de mal en pis; **conditions got worse** les conditions se sont aggravées *ou* détériorées; **his drug problem got worse** son problème de drogue ne s'est pas arrangé; **things will get worse before they get better** les choses ne sont pas près de s'améliorer; **his memory is getting worse** sa mémoire est de moins en moins bonne; **you're only making things** *or* **matters worse** vous ne faites qu'aggraver les choses; **she's only making things** *or* **matters worse for herself** elle ne fait qu'aggraver son cas; **and, to make matters worse, he swore at the policeman** et pour tout arranger, il a insulté le policier; **to make things worse, I lost my camera** et pour tout arranger, j'ai perdu mon appareil photo; **there's nothing worse than arriving too early** il n'y a rien de pire que d'arriver trop tôt; **worse things happen at sea!** on a vu pire!, ce n'est pas la fin du monde!; *Fam* **worse luck!** quelle poisse!

(**b**) *(in health)* plus mal; **I feel worse** je me sens encore plus mal *ou* encore moins bien; **her headache got worse** son mal de tête s'est aggravé; **you'll only get worse if you go out in this awful weather** ton état ne peut que s'aggraver si tu sors par ce temps

(**c**) *(idioms)* **this carpet is looking rather the worse for wear** cette moquette est plutôt défraîchie; **he's looking/feeling rather the worse for wear** *(tired, old)* il n'a pas l'air/il ne se sent pas très frais; *(drunk)* il a l'air/il se sent plutôt éméché; *(ill)* il n'a pas l'air/il ne se sent pas très bien; **he was rather the worse for drink** il était plutôt éméché

2 *adv (compar of* **badly**) (**a**) *(less well)* plus mal, moins bien; **he behaved worse than ever** il ne s'est jamais aussi mal conduit; **he is worse off than before** *(in worse situation)* sa situation a empiré; *(even poorer)* il est encore plus pauvre qu'avant; **you could** *or* **you might do worse than (to) marry him** l'épouser, ce n'est pas ce que vous pourriez faire de pire; **she doesn't think any the worse of her for it** elle ne l'en estime pas moins pour ça

(**b**) *(more severely → snow, rain)* plus fort; **the noise went on worse than ever** le vacarme a repris de plus belle

3 *n* pire *m*; **there's worse to come, worse is to come** *(in situation)* le pire est à venir; *(in story)* il y a pire encore; **worse was to follow** le pire était encore à venir; **I have seen worse** j'en ai vu bien d'autres, j'ai vu pire; **there's been a change for the worse** les choses se sont aggravées; **to take a turn for the worse** *(health, situation)* se détériorer, se dégrader; **the economy has taken a turn for the worse** la situation économique s'est aggravée; **the patient has taken a turn for the worse** l'état du patient s'est aggravé; *Am* **if worse comes to worse** au pire, dans le pire des cas

4 none the worse *adj* pas plus mal; **he's**

wor–wor

apparently none the worse for his drinking session last night il n'a pas l'air de se ressentir de sa beuverie d'hier soir; **the little girl is none the worse for the experience** la petite fille ne se ressent pas de son expérience

worsen ['wɜːsən] **1** *vi (depression, crisis, pain, illness)* empirer, s'aggraver; *(weather, situation)* se gâter, se détériorer
2 *vt (situation)* empirer, rendre pire; *(crisis, infection, bad mood)* aggraver; *(relations, driving conditions)* rendre plus difficile

worsening ['wɜːsənɪŋ] **1** *adj (situation)* qui empire; *(health)* qui se détériore; *(weather)* qui se gâte, qui se détériore
2 *n* aggravation *f*, détérioration *f*

worse-off 1 *adj* (**a**) *(financially)* moins riche, plus pauvre; **tax increases mean we are worse-off than before** les augmentations d'impôts signifient que nous avons moins d'argent qu'auparavant; **I am worse-off than I was** ma situation financière est pire *ou* moins bonne qu'avant
(**b**) *(in worse state)* dans une situation moins favorable; **the country is no worse-off for having a coalition government** le pays ne se porte pas plus mal d'avoir un gouvernement de coalition
2 *npl* **the worse-off** les pauvres *mpl*, les moins nantis *mpl*

worship ['wɜːʃɪp] *(Br pt & pp* **worshipped**, *cont* **worshipping**, *Am pt & pp* **worshiped**, *cont* **worshiping**) **1** *n* (**a**) *Rel (service)* culte *m*, office *m*; *(liturgy)* liturgie *f*; *(adoration)* adoration *f*; **church worship** office *m* religieux; **an act of worship** *(veneration)* un acte de dévotion; *(service)* un culte, un office; **freedom of worship** la liberté de culte; **place of worship** lieu *m* de culte; **hours of worship** heures *fpl* des offices
(**b**) *Fig (veneration)* adoration *f*, culte *m*; **the rock star has become an object of worship** la rock star est devenue un véritable objet de culte; **the worship of wealth and power** le culte de l'argent et du pouvoir
2 *vt* (**a**) *Rel* adorer, vénérer; **worship the Lord!** adorez *ou* vénérez le Seigneur!; **they worshipped Venus** ils rendaient un culte à Vénus, ils adoraient Vénus
(**b**) *(person)* adorer, vénérer; *(money, possessions)* vouer un culte à, avoir le culte de; **he worships his mother** il adore sa mère; **they worshipped the ground she walked on** ils vénéraient jusqu'au sol sur lequel elle marchait
3 *vi* faire ses dévotions; **the church where she worshipped for ten years** l'église où elle a fait ses dévotions pendant dix ans; **they worshipped at the temple of Apollo** ils faisaient leurs dévotions au temple d'Apollon; *Fig* **to worship at the altar of success** vouer un culte au succès
4 Worship *n Br Formal (in titles)* **His Worship the Mayor** monsieur le Maire; **Your Worship** *(to judge)* monsieur le Juge; *(to mayor)* monsieur le Maire

worshiper *Am* = **worshipper**

worshipful ['wɜːʃɪpfʊl] *adj* (**a**) *(respectful)* respectueux (**b**) *Br Formal (in titles)* **the Worshipful Mayor of Portsmouth** monsieur le Maire de Portsmouth; **the Worshipful Company of Mercers** l'honorable compagnie des marchands de tissus

worshipper, *Am* **worshiper** ['wɜːʃɪpə(r)] *n* (**a**) *Rel* adorateur(trice) *m,f*, fidèle *mf*; **thousands of worshippers came to the shrine** des milliers d'adorateurs sont venus au lieu saint; **the worshippers take off their shoes** les fidèles enlèvent leurs chaussures (**b**) *Fig (of possessions, person)* adorateur(trice) *m,f*

WORST [wɜːst]

le pire	► **1 (a); 3 (a), (b)**
le plus mauvais	► **1 (a)**
le plus grave	► **1 (b)**
le plus mal	► **2**

1 *adj (superl of* **bad**) (**a**) *(least good, pleasant etc)* le pire, le plus mauvais; **it's the worst book I've ever read** c'est le plus mauvais livre que j'aie jamais lu; **this is the worst thing that could have happened** c'est la pire chose qui pouvait arriver; **the worst thing about it was the heat** le pire, c'était la chaleur; **it has happened at the worst possible time** c'est arrivé au plus mauvais moment; **and, worst of all, I lost my keys** et le pire de tout, c'est que j'ai perdu mes clés; **we came off worst** *(in deal)* c'est nous qui étions perdants; *(in fight)* c'est nous qui avons reçu le plus de coups; **I felt worst of all just after the operation** c'est juste après l'opération que je me suis senti le plus mal
(**b**) *(most severe, serious → disaster, error)* le plus grave; *(→ winter)* le plus rude; **the fighting was worst near the border** les combats les plus violents se sont déroulés près de la frontière
2 *adv (superl of* **badly**) **out of all of us I played worst** j'ai joué le plus mal de nous tous; **that frightened me worst of all** c'est ce qui m'a fait le plus peur; **they are the worst paid** ce sont les plus mal payés; **the worst affected** le plus affecté, le plus touché
3 *n* (**a**) *(thing)* **the worst** le pire; **the worst that can happen** le pire qui puisse arriver; **the worst of it is she knew all along** le pire, c'est qu'elle le savait depuis le début; **that's the worst of cheap shoes** c'est l'inconvénient des chaussures bon marché; **money brings out the worst in people** l'argent réveille les pires instincts (chez les gens); **to expect/to be prepared for the worst** s'attendre/être préparé au pire; **I fear the worst** je crains le pire; **the worst is still to come** le pire est encore à venir; **the worst was yet to come** le pire restait à venir; **the worst is over** le plus mauvais moment est passé; **if the worst comes to the worst, if it comes to the worst** au pire, dans le pire des cas; **he got the worst of it** c'est lui qui s'en est le moins bien sorti; **and that's not the worst of it!** et ce n'est pas le pire!, et il y a pire encore!; *Hum* **do your worst!** allez-y, je suis prêt; **the fever was at its worst last night** la fièvre était à son paroxysme hier soir; **when the storm was at its worst** au plus fort de l'orage; **when the situation was at its worst** alors que la situation était désespérée; **things** *or* **matters were at their worst** les affaires étaient au plus mal, les choses ne pouvaient pas aller plus mal; **I'm at my worst in the morning** le matin est mon plus mauvais moment de la journée; **even at her worst she is still a brilliant player** même quand elle joue mal, elle reste une joueuse fantastique
(**b**) *(person)* **the worst** le (la) pire de tous; **to be the worst in the class** être le (la) dernier(-ère) de la classe; **when it comes to dancing, he's the world's worst** pour ce qui est de danser, il n'y a pas pire que lui
4 *vt Literary (opponent, rival)* battre, avoir le dessus sur
5 at (the) worst *conj* au pire, dans le pire des cas

worst- [wɜːst] *pref* **the worst-dressed** le moins bien habillé; **the worst-behaved** le moins sage; **to be the worst-off** *(financially)* être le moins riche; *(in situation)* s'en sortir le moins bien

worst-case *adj* **the worst-case scenario** le scénario catastrophe; **the worst-case scenario is that we lose all the money** dans le pire des cas ou au pire, nous perdrions tout l'argent

worsted ['wʊstɪd] **1** *n* worsted *m*, laine *f* peignée
2 *adj (suit)* en worsted, en laine peignée
►► ***worsted cloth*** worsted *m*, laine *f* peignée

wort [wɜːt] *n (in brewing)* moût *m*

WORTH [wɜːθ] **1** *adj* (**a**) *(financially, in value)* **to be worth £40,000** valoir 40 000 livres; **how much is the picture worth?** combien vaut le tableau?; **it isn't worth much** cela ne vaut pas grand-chose; **£10 isn't worth much nowadays** 10 livres ne valent pas *ou* ne représentent pas grand-chose de nos jours; **to be worth a lot of money** *(thing)* valoir cher, avoir beaucoup de valeur; *(person)* être riche; **his uncle is worth several million pounds** la fortune de son oncle s'élève à plusieurs millions de livres; **it was worth every penny** ça en valait vraiment la peine; **what's it worth to you?** vous êtes prêt à y mettre combien?; *Fig* **it isn't worth the paper it's written on** ça ne vaut pas le papier sur lequel c'est écrit; **to be worth one's weight in gold** valoir son pesant d'or; *Br* **any proofreader worth his salt would have spotted the mistake** n'importe quel correcteur digne de ce nom aurait relevé l'erreur
(**b**) *(emotionally)* **it's worth a lot to me** j'y attache beaucoup de valeur *ou* de prix; **the bracelet is worth a lot to me** j'attache beaucoup de prix au bracelet; **their friendship is worth a lot to her** leur amitié a beaucoup de prix pour elle; **she's worth ten of you** elle en vaut dix comme toi; **it's more than my job's worth to cause a fuss** je ne veux pas risquer ma place en faisant des histoires; **I can't do it, it's more than my life is worth** je ne peux absolument pas prendre le risque de faire cela
(**c**) *(valid, deserving)* **the church is (well) worth a visit** l'église vaut la peine d'être visitée *ou* vaut le détour; **it's worth a try** *or* **trying** cela vaut la peine d'essayer; **it wasn't worth the effort** *or* **the trouble** cela ne valait pas la peine de faire un tel effort, ça n'en valait pas la peine; **it's not worth waiting for him** cela ne vaut pas la peine de l'attendre; **is the film worth seeing?** est-ce que le film vaut la peine d'être vu?; **without you, life wouldn't be worth living** sans toi, la vie ne vaudrait pas la peine d'être vécue; **it's worth thinking about** cela mérite réflexion; **it's worth knowing** c'est bon à savoir; **don't bother to phone, it isn't worth it** inutile de téléphoner, cela n'en vaut pas la peine; **don't get upset, he isn't worth it** ne te rends pas malade, il n'en vaut pas la peine; *Prov* **if something's worth doing, it's worth doing well** = si une chose vaut la peine d'être faite, elle vaut la peine d'être bien faite; *Br Fam* **the game isn't worth the candle** le jeu n'en vaut pas la chandelle
(**d**) *(idioms)* **it would be worth your while to check** *or* **checking** vous auriez intérêt à vérifier; **it's not worth (my) while waiting** cela ne vaut pas la peine d'attendre *ou* que j'attende; **I'll make it worth your while** je vous récompenserai de votre peine; **she was running for all she was worth** elle courait de toutes ses forces *ou* aussi vite qu'elle pouvait; **I tried/I shouted for all I was worth** j'ai essayé du mieux/crié aussi fort que j'ai pu; **for what it's worth** pour ce que cela vaut
2 *n* (**a**) *(in money, value)* valeur *f*; **of great/little/no worth** de grande/de peu de/d'aucune valeur; **£2,000 worth of damage** pour 2000 livres de dégâts, des dégâts qui se montent à 2000 livres; **he sold £50 worth of ice cream** il a vendu pour 50 livres de glaces
(**b**) *(of person)* valeur *f*; **she knows her own worth** elle sait ce qu'elle vaut, elle connaît sa propre valeur
(**c**) *(equivalent value)* équivalent *m*; **he got a day's worth of work out of me for nothing** j'ai travaillé pour lui l'équivalent d'une journée, pour rien; **a week's worth of supplies** suffisamment de provisions pour une semaine

worthily ['wɜːðɪlɪ] *adv (live, behave)* dignement; *(donate, sacrifice)* honorablement

worthiness ['wɜːðɪnɪs] *n (dignity)* caractère *m* digne; *(praiseworthiness)* caractère *m* louable

worthless ['wɜːθlɪs] *adj* (**a**) *(goods, land etc)* sans valeur, qui ne vaut rien (**b**) *(useless → attempt)* inutile; *(→ advice, suggestion)* inutile, sans valeur (**c**) *(person)* incapable, qui ne vaut rien; **he's a worthless wretch!** c'est un bon à rien!

worthlessness ['wɜːθlɪsnɪs] *n* (**a**) *(of goods, land etc)* absence *f* totale de valeur (**b**) *(of attempt, advice, suggestion)* inutilité *f* (**c**) *(of person)* nullité *f*

worthwhile [ˌwɜːθ'waɪl] *adj* (**a**) *(useful → action, visit)* qui vaut la peine; *(→ job)* utile, qui a un sens; **they didn't think it was worthwhile buying** *or* **to buy a new car** ils ne pensaient pas que ça valait la peine d'acheter une nouvelle voiture (**b**) *(deserving → cause, project, organization)* louable, méritoire (**c**) *(interesting → book)* qui vaut la peine d'être lu; *(→ film)* qui vaut la peine d'être vu

worthy ['wɜːðɪ] *(compar* **worthier**, *superl* **worthiest**, *pl* **worthies**) **1** *adj* (**a**) *(deserving → person)* digne, méritant; *(→ cause)* louable, digne; **to be worthy of sth** être digne de *ou* mériter qch; **to be worthy to do sth** être digne *ou* mériter de faire qch; **they are worthy of praise/of respect**

ils sont dignes d'éloges/de respect, ils méritent des éloges/le respect; **her remarks are worthy of contempt** ses remarques sont dignes de mépris; **surely my letter was at least worthy of an answer?** ma lettre méritait quand même une réponse, non?; **she was a worthy winner** elle méritait bien de gagner; **it is worthy of note that...** il est intéressant de remarquer *ou* de noter que...; **the town has no museum worthy of the name** la ville n'a aucun musée digne de ce nom

(**b**) *Hum* excellent, brave; **the worthy captain** l'excellent *ou* le brave capitaine

2 *n (important person)* notable *mf*; *Hum* brave citoyen(enne) *m,f*

We are not worthy!
Cette formule ("nous ne méritons pas cet honneur") vient du film comique américain de 1992 *Wayne's World*. Tout comme dans le film, on emploie cette expression sur le mode humoristique en se prosternant pour exprimer son admiration pour quelqu'un, le plus souvent une vedette de la musique pop ou du sport.

wot [wɒt] **1** *Br Fam* = **what**

2 *vt Arch* savoir

3 *vi Arch* **God wot** Dieu sait

wotcha, wotcher ['wɒtʃə] *exclam Br Fam* salut!

WOULD [wʊd] **1** *pt of* **will**

2 *modal aux v*

On trouve généralement **I/you/he/***etc* **would** sous leurs formes contractées **I'd/you'd/he'd/** *etc*. La forme négative correspondante est **wouldn't** que l'on écrira **would not** dans des contextes formels.

A. (**a**) *(speculating, hypothesizing)* **I'm sure they would come if you asked them** je suis sûr qu'ils viendraient si vous le leur demandiez; **he would if he could** il le ferait s'il le pouvait; **he would be thirty now if he had lived** il aurait trente ans maintenant s'il avait vécu; **I wouldn't do that if I were you** je ne ferais pas ça si j'étais vous *ou* à votre place; **you would think they had better things to do** on pourrait penser qu'ils ont mieux à faire; **I thought he would understand** je pensais qu'il comprendrait; **they wouldn't have come if they'd known** ils ne seraient pas venus s'ils avaient su; **he wouldn't have finished without your help** il n'aurait pas terminé sans votre aide; **she would have been sixteen by now** elle aurait seize ans maintenant

(**b**) *(making polite offers, requests)* **would you please be quiet!** voulez-vous vous taire, s'il vous plaît!; **would you pass the mustard please?** voudriez-vous bien me passer la moutarde?; **would you mind driving me home?** est-ce que cela vous dérangerait de me reconduire chez moi?; **would you like to see her?** aimeriez-vous *ou* voudriez-vous la voir?; **would you like another cup?** en voulez-vous encore une tasse?; **I'll do it for you – would you?** je vais m'en occuper – vraiment?

(**c**) *(expressing preferences, desires)* **I would prefer to go** *or* **I would rather go alone** j'aimerais mieux *ou* je préférerais y aller seul; **I would have preferred to go** *or* **I would rather have gone alone** j'aurais mieux aimé *ou* j'aurais préféré y aller seul; **I would love to go** je serais ravi d'y aller

B. (**a**) *(indicating willingness, responsiveness → of person, mechanism)* **they would give their lives for the cause** ils donneraient leur vie pour la cause; **she wouldn't touch alcohol** elle refusait de toucher à l'alcool; **I couldn't find anyone who would lend me a torch** je n'ai trouvé personne pour me prêter une lampe électrique; **the light wouldn't work** la lumière ne marchait pas; **the car wouldn't start** la voiture ne voulait pas démarrer

(**b**) *(indicating habitual or characteristic behaviour)* **he would smoke a cigar after dinner** il fumait un cigare après le dîner; **she would often complain about the neighbours** elle se plaignait souvent des voisins; **they would go and break something!** il fallait qu'ils aillent casser quelque chose!; **I didn't really enjoy the fish – you wouldn't, would you?** je n'ai pas tellement aimé le poisson – ça m'aurait étonné!; **he would!** c'est bien de lui!; **he would say that, wouldn't he** il fallait qu'il dise ça

(**c**) *(expressing opinions)* **I would disagree there** je crains de n'être pas d'accord sur ce point; **I would imagine it's warmer than here** j'imagine qu'il fait plus chaud qu'ici; **I would think he'd be pleased** j'aurais cru que ça lui ferait plaisir; **I wouldn't know** *(I don't know)* je ne saurais dire

(**d**) *(giving advice)* **I would have a word with her about it(, if I were you)** moi, je lui en parlerais (à votre place)

(**e**) *(expressing surprise, incredulity)* **you wouldn't think she was only fifteen, would you?** on ne dirait pas qu'elle n'a que quinze ans, n'est-ce pas?; **who would have thought it?** qui l'aurait cru?; **I wouldn't have thought it possible** je ne l'aurais pas cru possible; **would you credit it!** tu te rends compte!

(**f**) *(indicating likelihood, probability)* **there was a woman there – that would be his wife** il y avait une femme – ça devait être sa femme; **would that be your cousin you have in mind?** c'est à votre cousin que vous pensez?

C. (**a**) *(in reported speech)* **it was to be the last time I would see him before he left** c'était la dernière fois que je le voyais avant son départ

(**b**) *(used with "have")* **they would have been happy if it hadn't been for the war** ils auraient vécu heureux si la guerre n'était pas survenue; *Am* **if you would have told the truth, this would never have happened** si tu m'avais dit la vérité, ça ne serait jamais arrivé

(**c**) *(subjunctive use) Formal or Literary (expressing wishes)* **would that it were true!** si seulement c'était vrai!; **would to God that I still had it!** plût à Dieu que je l'eusse encore!; **what would you have me do?** que voulez-vous que je fasse?

would-be *adj* (**a**) *(hopeful)* **a would-be writer/MP** une personne qui veut être écrivain/député; **troops seized the would-be assassin** les militaires ont attrapé l'assassin avant qu'il ne commette le crime; **the would-be burglar was tied up to a chair** le cambrioleur, pris sur le fait, était attaché à une chaise (**b**) *Pej (so-called)* prétendu, soi-disant *(inv)*

wouldn't ['wʊdənt] = **would not**

wouldst [wʊdst] *Arch 2nd pers sing of* **would**

would've ['wʊdəv] = **would have**

wound[1] [wuːnd] **1** *n* (**a**) *(physical injury)* blessure *f*, plaie *f*; **a bullet wound** une blessure par balle; **she had three bullet wounds** elle avait été blessée par trois balles; **she had three knife wounds** elle avait reçu trois coups de couteau; **they had serious head wounds** ils avaient été gravement blessés à la tête; **to dress a wound** panser une blessure *ou* une plaie

(**b**) *Fig (emotional or moral)* blessure *f*; **he was still suffering from deep psychological wounds** il souffrait encore de graves blessures psychologiques; **to reopen an old wound** rouvrir une plaie

2 *vt* (**a**) *(physically)* blesser; **the children were wounded by flying glass** les enfants ont été blessés par des éclats de verre; **she was wounded in the shoulder** elle a été blessée à l'épaule

(**b**) *Fig (emotionally)* blesser; **he was deeply wounded by their criticism** il a été profondément blessé par leurs critiques; **to wound sb's pride** heurter l'amour-propre de qn, blesser qn dans son amour-propre

3 *vi* causer une blessure

wound[2] [waʊnd] *pt & pp of* **wind**

wounded ['wuːndɪd] **1** *adj* (**a**) *(soldier, victim)* blessé; **a wounded woman** une blessée (**b**) *Fig (feelings, pride)* blessé

2 *npl* **the wounded** les blessés *mpl*

Wounded Knee *n* Wounded Knee *(lieu situé dans le Dakota du Sud, où, le 29 décembre 1890, 146 Indiens sioux détenus par des soldats américains furent abattus)*

wounding ['wuːndɪŋ] *adj Fig (hurtful)* blessant

wound-up [waʊnd-] *adj* (**a**) *(clock)* remonté; *(car window)* remonté, fermé (**b**) *Fam (tense → person)* à cran

woundwort ['wuːndwɜːt] *n Bot* (**a**) *(Stachys)* stachys *m* (**b**) *(kidney vetch)* (anthyllide *f*) vulnéraire *f*

wove [wəʊv] *pt of* **weave**

woven ['wəʊvən] *pp of* **weave**

wow [waʊ] *Fam* **1** *exclam* oh là là!, la vache!

2 *n* (**a**) **it's a real wow!** c'est vraiment super!; **he's a wow at hockey** c'est un super joueur de hockey (**b**) *(acoustics)* pleurage *m*

3 *vt (impress)* impressionner❑, emballer; **she wowed them with her piano playing** elle les a emballés quand elle a joué du piano

wowser ['waʊzə(r)] *n Austr* puritain(e) *m,f* à outrance, rabat-joie *mf inv*

WP[1] [ˌdʌbəljuː'piː] *n* (**a**) *(abbr* **word processing***)* TTX *m*, traitement *m* de texte (**b**) *(abbr* **word processor***)* machine *f* à traitement de texte

WP[2] *(written abbr* **weather permitting***)* si le temps le permet

WPC [ˌdʌbəljuːpiː'siː] *n Br (abbr* **woman police constable***)* = femme agent de police; **WPC Roberts** l'agent Roberts

wpm *(written abbr* **words per minute***)* mots/min

WRAC [ræk] *n Br (abbr* **Women's Royal Army Corps***)* = section féminine de l'armée de terre britannique

wrack [ræk] *n* (**a**) *(seaweed)* varech *m* (**b**) = **rack** (**g**)

WRAF [ræf] *n Br (abbr* **Women's Royal Air Force***)* = section féminine de l'armée de l'air britannique

wraith [reɪθ] *n Literary* apparition *f*, spectre *m*

wraithlike ['reɪθlaɪk] *adj Literary* spectral

wrangle ['ræŋgəl] **1** *vi* se disputer, se chamailler; **to wrangle about** *or* **over sth** se disputer à propos de qch; **they were wrangling over who should pay** ils se disputaient pour savoir qui devait payer; **to wrangle with sb** se disputer *ou* se chamailler avec qn

2 *vt Am (cattle, horses)* garder

3 *n* dispute *f*; **a long legal wrangle over the amount of damages** une longue dispute juridique sur le montant des dommages-intérêts

wrangler ['ræŋglə(r)] *n* (**a**) *Am (cowboy)* cowboy *m* (**b**) *Br Univ* ≃ major *m (candidat en mathématiques à Cambridge qui reçoit une mention très bien)* (**c**) *Cin* = personne chargée de s'occuper des animaux participant au tournage d'un film

wrangling ['ræŋglɪŋ] *n (UNCOUNT)* disputes *fpl*, querelles *fpl*; **there has been a lot of wrangling over who to give the job to** il y a eu beaucoup de querelles pour décider à qui donner le poste; **stop all this wrangling!** arrêtez toutes ces chamailleries!

wrap [ræp] *(pt & pp* **wrapped***)* **1** *vt* (**a**) *(goods, parcel, gift, food)* emballer, envelopper; **the fish was wrapped in foil** le poisson était enveloppé dans du papier d'aluminium; **would you like it wrapped?** *(gift)* c'est pour offrir?; **she wrapped the scarf in tissue paper** elle a emballé *ou* enveloppé l'écharpe dans du papier de soie

(**b**) *(cocoon, envelop)* envelopper, emmailloter; **the baby was wrapped in a blanket** le bébé était enveloppé dans une couverture; **her head was wrapped in a thick scarf** elle avait la tête enveloppée dans une grosse écharpe; *Fig* **her visit was wrapped in mystery** sa visite était entourée de mystère

(**c**) *(twist, wind)* **to wrap round** *or* **around** enrouler; **she had a towel wrapped round her head** sa tête était enveloppée dans une serviette; **she had a towel wrapped round her body** elle s'était enveloppée dans une serviette; **wrap this blanket round you/your shoulders** enroule cette couverture autour de toi/de tes épaules; **he wrapped the bandage round her hand** il lui a enroulé la main dans une bande; **he wrapped his arms round her** il l'a prise dans ses bras; *Fam Fig* **he wrapped the car round a tree** il s'est payé un arbre

2 *vi Comput (lines)* se boucler

3 *n* (**a**) *(housecoat)* peignoir *m*; *(shawl)* châle *m*; *(over ballgown)* sortie-de-bal *f*; *(blanket, rug)* couverture *f*

(**b**) *Cin* **it's a wrap!** c'est dans la boîte!

(**c**) *Culin (sandwich)* = tortilla fourrée

4 wraps *npl Fig* **to keep a plan/one's feelings under wraps** garder un plan secret/ses sentiments secrets; **when the wraps eventually came off** lorsque tout a été dévoilé; **the wraps**

were taken off the new car today la voiture a été montrée au public pour la première fois aujourd'hui

►**wrap up** **1** *vt sep* (**a**) *(goods, parcel, gift, food)* envelopper, emballer, empaqueter; **he wrapped the sandwiches up in foil** il a enveloppé les sandwiches dans du papier d'aluminium

(**b**) *(person → in clothes, blanket)* envelopper; **wrap him up in a blanket** enveloppez-le dans une couverture; **she was well wrapped up in a thick coat** elle était bien emmitouflée dans un épais manteau; **wrap yourself up warmly** couvrez-vous bien

(**c**) *Fig* **politicians are skilled at wrapping up bad news in an acceptable form** les politiciens s'y connaissent pour présenter les mauvaises nouvelles sous un jour acceptable; **his meaning was wrapped up in diplomatic jargon** il enrobait ce qu'il disait de jargon diplomatique

(**d**) *Fam (conclude → job)* terminer❑, conclure❑; *(→ deal, contract)* conclure❑, régler❑; **that wraps up business for today** c'est fini pour aujourd'hui❑; **let's get this matter wrapped up** finissons-en avec cette question❑

(**e**) *(engross)* **to be wrapped up in sth** être absorbé par qch; **he's very wrapped up in his work** il est très absorbé par son travail; **they're wrapped up in their children** ils ne vivent que pour leurs enfants; **she's very wrapped up in herself** elle est très repliée sur elle-même; **she is too wrapped up in her own problems** elle est trop préoccupée par ses propres problèmes

(**f**) *(implicate)* **he was wrapped up in some shady dealings** il a été impliqué dans des transactions louches

(**g**) *Am (summarize)* résumer; **she wrapped up her talk with three points** elle a résumé son discours en trois points

2 *vi* (**a**) *(dress)* s'habiller, se couvrir; **wrap up warmly** *or* **well!** couvrez-vous bien!

(**b**) *Br Fam (be quiet)* la fermer; **wrap up!** la ferme!

wraparound ['ræpə,raʊnd] **1** *adj (dress, skirt)* portefeuille *(inv)*

2 *n* (**a**) *(skirt)* jupe *f* portefeuille (**b**) *Comput* mise à la ligne *f* automatique des mots

3 wraparounds *npl (sunglasses)* lunettes *fpl* de soleil panoramiques

►► *Aut* ***wraparound bumper*** pare-chocs *m* enveloppant; *Aut* ***wraparound rear window*** lunette *f* arrière panoramique; ***wraparound sunglasses*** lunettes *fpl* de soleil panoramiques

wrapover ['ræp,əʊvə(r)] **1** *n (skirt)* jupe *f* portefeuille

2 *adj (dress, skirt)* portefeuille *(inv)*

wrapped [ræpt] *adj (bread, cheese)* préemballé

wrapper ['ræpə(r)] *n* (**a**) *(for sweet)* papier *m*; *(for parcel)* papier *m* d'emballage; *(of cigar)* emballage *m*; **her pocket was full of old sweet wrappers** sa poche était pleine de vieux papiers de bonbons (**b**) *(cover → on book)* jaquette *f*; *(→ on magazine, newspaper)* bande *f* (**c**) *(housecoat)* peignoir *m*

wrapping ['ræpɪŋ] *n (on parcel)* papier *m* d'emballage; *(on sweet)* papier *m*; **she tore the plastic wrapping from the box** elle a déchiré *ou* arraché l'emballage en plastique de la boîte

►► ***wrapping paper*** *(for gift)* papier *m* cadeau; *(for parcel)* papier *m* d'emballage

wrapround ['ræpraʊnd] *n (in word processing)* bouclage *m*, renouement *m* (des mots)

►► *Aut* ***wrapround rear window*** lunette *f* arrière panoramique; ***wrapround windscreen*** pare-brise *m* panoramique

wrasse [ræs] *n Ich* labre *m*, vieille *f*

wrath [rɒθ] *n Literary* colère *f*, courroux *m*; **the wrath of God** la colère de Dieu

wrathful ['rɒθfʊl] *adj Literary* en colère, courroucé

wrathfully ['rɒθfʊlɪ] *adv Literary* avec colère, avec courroux

wrathfulness ['rɒθfʊlnɪs] *n Literary* colère *f*, courroux *m*

wreak [ri:k] *(pt & pp sense* (**a**) **wreaked** *or* **wrought** [rɔ:t]) *vt* (**a**) *(cause → damage, chaos)* causer, provoquer; **the damage wreaked by the explosion** les dommages provoqués par l'explosion; **to wreak havoc** faire des ravages, tout mettre sens dessus dessous; **the storm wreaked havoc with telephone communications** la tempête a sérieusement perturbé les communications téléphoniques; *Fig* **it wreaked havoc with my holiday plans** cela a bouleversé mes projets de vacances

(**b**) *(inflict → revenge, anger)* assouvir; **to wreak vengeance on sb** assouvir sa vengeance sur qn

wreath [ri:θ] *(pl* **wreaths** [ri:ðz]) *n* (**a**) *(for funeral)* couronne *f*; **the President laid a wreath at the war memorial** le Président a déposé une gerbe au monument aux morts; *Mil* **the laying of wreaths** le dépôt *m* de gerbes (**b**) *(garland)* guirlande *f*; **a holly wreath** une guirlande de houx; **a laurel wreath** une couronne de laurier (**c**) *Fig (of mist)* nappe *f*; *(of smoke)* volute *f*

wreathe [ri:ð] **1** *vt* (**a**) *(shroud)* envelopper; **the mountain top was wreathed in mist** le sommet de la montagne était enveloppé *ou* disparaissait dans la brume; **he sat wreathed in smoke** il était assis dans un nuage de fumée; *Fig* **to be wreathed in smiles** être rayonnant

(**b**) *(with flowers → person)* couronner; *(→ grave, window)* orner; **a cross wreathed with chrysanthemums** une croix ornée de chrysanthèmes

2 *vi (smoke)* monter en volutes

wreck [rek] **1** *n* (**a**) *(wrecked remains → of ship)* épave *f*; *(→ of plane)* avion *m* accidenté, épave *f*; *(→ of train)* train *m* accidenté; *(→ of car, lorry, bus)* véhicule *m* accidenté, épave *f*; **the car was a wreck** la voiture était une épave; **the burnt-out wreck of a bus** les restes calcinés d'un bus

(**b**) *(wrecking → of ship)* naufrage *m*; *(→ of plane, car)* accident *m*; *(→ of train)* déraillement *m*

(**c**) *Fam (dilapidated car)* guimbarde *f*; *(old bike)* clou *m*

(**d**) *Fam (person)* épave *f*, loque *f*; **a human wreck** une loque humaine; **he's a wreck** *(physically)* c'est une épave; *(mentally)* il est à bout; **I must look a wreck** je dois avoir une mine de déterré; **I'm a nervous wreck** je suis à bout; **the man's an emotional wreck** le type est une loque, au niveau émotionnel

(**e**) *Fig (of hopes, plans)* effondrement *m*, anéantissement *m*

2 *vt* (**a**) *(in accident, explosion → ship)* provoquer le naufrage de; *(→ car, plane)* détruire totalement; *(→ building)* démolir; **the tanker was wrecked off the African coast** le pétrolier a fait naufrage au large des côtes africaines; **the car was completely wrecked in the accident** la voiture a été totalement détruite dans l'accident; **the store was wrecked by a bomb blast** une bombe a fait sauter le magasin, le magasin a été détruit par l'explosion d'une bombe

(**b**) *(damage → furniture)* casser, démolir; *(→ mechanism)* détruire, détraquer; **he wrecked the room in a fit of rage** il a tout cassé dans la pièce dans un accès de rage

(**c**) *(upset → marriage, relationship)* briser; *(→ hopes, chances)* anéantir; *(→ health)* briser, ruiner; *(→ negotiations)* faire échouer, saboter; **she's wrecked my plans** elle a ruiné mes plans; **this defeat has wrecked the team's chances** cette défaite a anéanti les chances de l'équipe; **the accident wrecked her hopes** l'accident a anéanti ses espoirs; **you've wrecked my life!** tu as brisé ma vie!

wreckage ['rekɪdʒ] *n* (**a**) *(UNCOUNT) (debris → from ship, car)* débris *mpl*; *(→ from building)* décombres *mpl*; **pieces of wreckage from the building lay in the street** les décombres du bâtiment jonchaient la rue; **a body was found in the wreckage of the plane** un corps a été trouvé dans les débris de l'avion; **to pull sb from the wreckage** tirer qn des décombres; **wreckage has been washed up on the beach** la marée a déposé des débris sur la plage

(**b**) *(wrecked ship)* épave *f*, navire *m* naufragé; **he clung to the wreckage** il s'agrippa à l'épave

(**c**) *Fig (of hopes, relationship)* anéantissement *m*

wrecked [rekt] *adj* (**a**) *(ship)* naufragé; *(car, plane)* complètement détruit; *(house)* complètement démoli; **wrecked cars** épaves *fpl* d'automobiles, voitures *fpl* accidentées (**b**) *Fig (relationship, hopes)* anéanti (**c**) *Fam (drunk)* bourré, pété, beurré, fait; *(on drugs)* défoncé, raide (**d**) *Fam (exhausted)* crevé, naze

►► ***wrecked remains*** *(of ship)* épave *f*; *(of train, car)* débris *mpl*; *(of building)* décombres *mpl*

wrecker ['rekə(r)] *n* (**a**) *(destroyer)* destructeur(-trice) *m,f*, démolisseur(euse) *m,f*; **marriage-wrecker** briseur(euse) *m,f* de ménages (**b**) *Am (demolition man → for buildings)* démolisseur *m*; *(→ for cars)* ferrailleur *m*, casseur *m* (**c**) *Am (breakdown van)* dépanneuse *f* (**d**) *Hist (of ships)* naufrageur *m*

wrecking ['rekɪŋ] *n* (**a**) *(of ship)* naufrage *m*; *(of train)* déraillement *m*; *(of car, plane)* destruction *f* totale (**b**) *Fig (of relationship, hopes)* anéantissement *m*

►► ***wrecking ball*** boulet *m* de démolition; ***wrecking bar*** pied-de-biche *m*; ***wrecking car*** camion *m* de dépannage, dépanneuse *f*; *Am* ***wrecking service*** service *m* de dépannage; *Am* ***wrecking truck*** camion *m* de dépannage, dépanneuse *f*

Wren [ren] *n Br* = membre du "Women's Royal Naval Service"; **the Wrens** = section féminine de la marine britannique

wren [ren] *n Orn* roitelet *m*

wrench [rentʃ] **1** *vt* (**a**) *(pull)* tirer violemment sur; **she wrenched the door open** elle a ouvert la porte d'un geste violent; **we'll have to wrench the lid off** nous allons être obligés de forcer le couvercle pour l'ouvrir; **someone wrenched the bag out of my hands** *or* **from my grasp** quelqu'un m'a arraché le sac des mains; **to wrench oneself free** se dégager d'un mouvement violent; **she wrenched herself free of my grasp** elle s'est dégagée brusquement de mon étreinte

(**b**) *(eyes, mind)* arracher, détacher; **I couldn't wrench my gaze (away) from the horrible sight** je ne pouvais pas détacher mon regard de cet horrible spectacle; **nothing could wrench her away from her book** rien ne pouvait l'arracher à son livre

(**c**) *(ankle, arm)* se faire une entorse à; **I've wrenched my shoulder** je me suis foulé l'épaule; **to wrench one's back** se donner *ou* se faire un tour de reins

2 *vi* **he wrenched free of his bonds** il s'est dégagé de ses liens d'un mouvement violent; *Fig* il s'est libéré de ses liens

3 *n* (**a**) *(tug, twist)* mouvement *m* violent *(de torsion)*; **with a sudden wrench she pulled herself free** elle se dégagea d'un mouvement brusque; **he gave the handle a wrench** il a tiré brusquement *ou* violemment sur la poignée; **with a sudden wrench, she threw the door open** d'un mouvement brusque, elle ouvrit la porte

(**b**) *(to ankle, knee)* entorse *f*; **I gave my ankle a wrench** je me suis fait une entorse à *ou* je me suis foulé la cheville; **I gave my back a wrench** je me suis donné *ou* fait un tour de reins

(**c**) *Fig (emotional)* déchirement *m*; **it was a terrible wrench for me to leave home** ce fut un déchirement terrible pour moi de quitter la maison

(**d**) *Tech (spanner)* clé *f*, clef *f*; *(adjustable)* clé *f* anglaise; *(for wheels)* clé *f* en croix; *Am* **he threw a wrench into the works** il nous a mis des bâtons dans les roues

wrest [rest] *vt Literary* (**a**) *(grab → object)* arracher violemment; **he wrested the gun from me** *or* **from my grasp** il m'a arraché violemment le fusil des mains; **they wrested the stick out of my hands** ils m'ont arraché violemment le bâton des mains

(**b**) *(extract → truth, secret)* arracher; **he wrested the truth from her** il lui a arraché la vérité; **they just manage to wrest a living from the land** ils réussissent tout juste à vivre de la terre; **we could wrest no meaning from the coded message** nous n'avons rien pu tirer du message codé

(**c**) *(control, power)* ravir, arracher; **to wrest power from sb** ravir le pouvoir à qn; **the Liberals wrested two seats from the Conservatives** les libéraux ont ravi *ou* ont arraché deux sièges aux conservateurs; **we wrested victory from the jaws of defeat** nous avons arraché la victoire des mains de l'ennemi

wrestle ['resəl] **1** *vi* (**a**) *(fight)* lutter, pratiquer la lutte; *Sport (in freestyle wrestling)* catcher, pratiquer le catch; **to wrestle with sb** lutter (corps à corps) avec qn, se battre avec qn; **the two men wrestled briefly** les deux hommes ont brièvement lutté

(**b**) *Fig (struggle)* se débattre, lutter; **he died after wrestling with a long illness** il mourut après avoir lutté contre une longue maladie; **she wrestled with her conscience** elle se débattait avec sa conscience; **I wrestled with the problem all evening** je me suis débattu avec ce problème toute la soirée

(**c**) *(try to control)* **to wrestle with sth** se débattre avec qch; **the woman wrestled to keep control of the car** la femme luttait pour garder le contrôle de la voiture

2 *vt (fight → intruder, enemy)* lutter contre; *Sport (in Greek wrestling, in Sumo wrestling)* rencontrer à la lutte; *(in freestyle wrestling)* rencontrer au catch; **he wrestled his attacker to the ground** luttant avec son agresseur, il réussit à le clouer au sol

3 *n* lutte *f*; **to have a wrestle with sb** lutter avec *ou* contre qn; **after a wrestle with the knot, she was free** après s'être débattue avec le nœud, elle était libre; *Fig* **after a wrestle with his conscience, he agreed** après une lutte avec sa conscience, il a accepté

wrestler ['reslə(r)] *n Sport* lutteur(euse) *m,f*; *(in freestyle wrestling)* catcheur(euse) *m,f*

wrestling ['reslɪŋ] *Sport* **1** *n* lutte *f*; *(freestyle)* catch *m*

2 *comp (hold, match)* de lutte; *(in freestyle wrestling)* de catch

wretch [retʃ] *n* (**a**) *(unfortunate person)* pauvre diable *m*, malheureux(euse) *m,f*; **the poor wretch** le pauvre malheureux (**b**) *Literary or Hum (scoundrel)* scélérat(e) *m,f*, misérable *mf*; **the wretch who stole my bag** le scélérat qui m'a volé mon sac (**c**) *(child)* vilain(e) *m,f*, coquin(e) *m,f*; **you little wretch!** petit coquin!

wretched ['retʃɪd] **1** *adj* (**a**) *(poor → dwelling, clothes)* misérable; **she had a wretched existence** elle a eu une existence misérable; **their living conditions are wretched** leurs conditions de vie sont misérables *ou* sont épouvantables; **she receives a wretched wage** elle touche un salaire de misère

(**b**) *(unhappy)* malheureux; *(depressed)* déprimé, démoralisé; **he was** *or* **felt wretched about what he had said** il se sentait coupable à cause de ce qu'il avait dit; **I felt cold and wretched** j'avais froid et je me sentais malheureux

(**c**) *(ill)* malade; **the flu made me feel really wretched** je me sentais vraiment très mal avec cette grippe

(**d**) *Fam (as expletive)* fichu, maudit; **keep your wretched money!** garde-le, ton fichu argent!

(**e**) *(abominable → behaviour, performance, weather)* lamentable; **what wretched luck!** quelle déveine!; **I'm a wretched singer/writer** je suis un piètre chanteur/écrivain; **it's a wretched business** c'est une affaire *ou* une histoire lamentable

2 *npl* **the wretched** les déshérités *mpl*

> **Wretched refuse**
>
> Ces mots (que l'on pourrait traduire par "le rebut") sont extraits du poème *New Colossus* (1883) de la poétesse américaine Emma Lazarus. Ce poème est inscrit sur le piédestal de la Statue de la Liberté, à l'entrée du port de New York. Y figurent également les vers **Give me your tired, your poor, Your huddled masses yearning to breathe free** ("donnemoi tes exténués, tes pauvres, qui en rangs pressés aspirent à vivre libres"). On emploie cette formule en anglais américain à propos des immigrants des siècles passés mais également à propos de ceux d'aujourd'hui.

wretchedly ['retʃɪdlɪ] *adv* (**a**) *(poorly → live, dress)* misérablement, pauvrement (**b**) *(unhappily → cry, look)* pitoyablement, misérablement; **he apologized wretchedly** il a fait des excuses pitoyables (**c**) *(abominably → behave)* abominablement; *(→ play, perform)* très mal, lamentablement; **a wretchedly small amount** une somme absolument dérisoire

wretchedness ['retʃɪdnɪs] *n* (**a**) *(poverty → of living conditions)* extrême pauvreté *f*, misère *f* (**b**) *(unhappiness)* tristesse *f*, malheur *m* (**c**) *(meanness → of behaviour)* mesquinerie *f*; *(→ of sum, wage)* caractère *m* dérisoire (**d**) *(in quality → of performance, of weather, of meal)* médiocrité *f*

wrick [rɪk] *Br* = **rick** *vt* (**b**) & *n* (**b**)

wriggle ['rɪgəl] **1** *vt (toes, fingers)* tortiller; **he wriggled his way under the fence** il est passé sous la clôture en se tortillant *ou* à plat ventre; **the worm was wriggling its way across the grass** le ver avançait dans l'herbe en se tortillant; *Fig* **I'd like to see him wriggle his way out of that!** j'aimerais bien voir comment il va se sortir de cette situation!

2 *vi (person)* remuer, gigoter; *(snake, worm)* se tortiller; *(fish)* frétiller; **stop wriggling!** arrête de t'agiter!; **the children were wriggling in their seats** les enfants gigotaient sur leur siège; **to wriggle along** *(person)* avancer en rampant *ou* à plat ventre; *(snake)* avancer en se tortillant; **the fish/the little boy wriggled from her grasp** le poisson/le petit garçon réussit à s'échapper de ses mains en se tortillant; **he wriggled past the guards** il est passé devant les gardes en se glissant à plat ventre; **she wriggled under the fence** elle est passée sous la clôture à plat ventre *ou* en se tortillant; **she wriggled under the blankets** elle s'est enfoncée sous les couvertures en se tortillant; **to wriggle free** se libérer en se tortillant; *Fig* s'en sortir

3 *n* **to give a wriggle** *(snake)* se tortiller; *(fish)* frétiller; *(person)* se tortiller; **with a wriggle the rabbit shook itself free from the trap** en se tortillant, le lapin parvint à se dégager du piège

►**wriggle about, wriggle around** *vi (eel, worm)* se tortiller; *(fish)* frétiller; *(person)* gigoter, se trémousser; **stop wriggling about!** arrête de gigoter comme ça!

►**wriggle out** *vi* (**a**) *(fish, snake)* sortir; **the fish wriggled out from under a rock** le poisson est sorti en frétillant de sous un rocher; **the fish wriggled out of the net** le poisson s'est échappé du filet en se tortillant

(**b**) *(person)* se dégager (en se tortillant); **the little boy wriggled out of my grasp** le petit garçon s'est dégagé de mon étreinte en se tortillant

►**wriggle out of** *vt insep (evade)* **to wriggle out of a task** se dérober à *ou* esquiver une tâche; **I managed to wriggle out of the situation** j'ai réussi à me sortir de cette situation; **to wriggle out of doing sth** se débrouiller pour éviter de faire qch; **he wriggled out of paying** il a trouvé un moyen d'éviter de payer; **wriggle out of that one if you can!** à toi de t'en sortir!

wriggler ['rɪgələ(r)] *n* (**a**) *(person)* **he's a terrible wriggler** il n'arrête pas de gigoter, il ne se tient jamais tranquille (**b**) *Entom* larve *f* de moustique

wriggling ['rɪgəlɪŋ] **1** *adj* = **wriggly**

2 *n* tortillement *m*; **a wriggling movement** un tortillement

wriggly ['rɪgəlɪ] (*compar* **wrigglier**, *superl* **wriggliest**) *adj (eel, snake, worm)* qui se tortille; *(fish)* frétillant; *(person)* remuant, qui gigote

wring [rɪŋ] (*pt & pp* **wrung** [rʌŋ]) **1** *vt* (**a**) *(wet cloth, clothes)* essorer, tordre; **he wrung the towel dry** il a essoré la serviette en la tordant; **she wrung the water from the sponge** elle a exprimé l'eau de l'éponge

(**b**) *(neck)* tordre; **she wrung the chicken's neck** elle a tordu le cou au poulet; *Fig* **I'll wring his neck!** je vais lui tordre le cou!

(**c**) *(hand → in handshake)* serrer; **he wrung her hand** il lui a serré la main vigoureusement; **to wring one's hands (in despair)** se tordre les mains (de désespoir); *Fig* **it's no use sitting there wringing your hands** cela ne sert à rien de rester assis à vous désespérer

(**d**) *(extract → confession)* arracher; *(→ money)* extorquer; **she wrung every last detail from him** elle a réussi à lui extorquer tous les renseignements; **I'll wring the truth out of them** je vais leur arracher la vérité; **the blackmailer wrung £5,000 from her** le maître chanteur lui a extorqué 5000 livres; **he's wringing the maximum publicity from the situation** il profite de la situation pour en tirer le maximum de publicité

(**e**) *Fig (heart)* fendre; **her efforts to cope with four children on her own wrung my heart** ses efforts pour se débrouiller toute seule avec quatre enfants me fendaient le cœur

2 *vi* essorer; **do not wring** *(on label)* ne pas essorer

3 *n* **give the cloth a wring** essorez la serpillière

►**wring out** *vt sep (wet cloth, clothes)* essorer, tordre; **wring those wet clothes out for me** essore *ou* tords ces habits mouillés, s'il te plaît

wringer ['rɪŋə(r)] *n* essoreuse *f* (à rouleaux); **to put clothes through the wringer** essorer des vêtements (à la machine); *Fig* **he's really been through the wringer** on lui en a fait voir de toutes les couleurs

wringing ['rɪŋɪŋ] **1** *n* (**a**) *(of washing)* tordage *m*; *(by machine)* essorage *m* (**b**) *(of hands)* **she told us the news, with much wringing of hands** elle nous a annoncé la nouvelle, en se tordant les mains

2 *adj* **wringing (wet)** *(clothes)* complètement trempé; *(person)* complètement trempé, trempé jusqu'aux os; **the shirt was wringing with sweat** la chemise était trempée de sueur

wrinkle ['rɪŋkəl] **1** *vt* (**a**) *(nose)* froncer; *(brow)* plisser

(**b**) *(paper, rug, cloth)* froisser

2 *vi* (**a**) *(skin, hands)* se rider; *(brow)* se contracter, se plisser; *(nose)* se froncer, se plisser; *(fruit)* se ratatiner, se rider

(**b**) *(skirt, stocking)* faire des plis

3 *n* (**a**) *(on skin, fruit)* ride *f*

(**b**) *(in paper, carpet)* pli *m*; *(in cloth)* faux pli *m*; *Fig* **there are still some wrinkles in the plan which need ironing out** il reste encore quelques difficultés à aplanir

(**c**) *Br Fam Old-fashioned (trick)* combine *f*; *(hint)* tuyau *m*

►**wrinkle up** *vi & vt sep* = **wrinkle** *vi & vt*

wrinkled ['rɪŋkəld] *adj* (**a**) *(skin, hands)* ridé; *(brow, nose)* plissé, froncé; *(fruit)* ridé, ratatiné; **a wrinkled old man** un vieillard ratatiné (**b**) *(rug, skirt)* qui fait des plis; *(stockings, tights)* en accordéon

wrinkly ['rɪŋklɪ] (*compar* **wrinklier**, *superl* **wrinkliest**, *pl* **wrinklies**) **1** *adj* (**a**) *(skin, hands)* ridé; *(after bath)* fripé; *(fruit)* ridé, ratatiné (**b**) *(stockings, tights)* en accordéon

2 *n Br Fam Pej* croulant(e) *m,f*

wrist [rɪst] *n* poignet *m*

►► ***wrist loop*** *(of ski pole, ice axe, umbrella)* dragonne *f*; *Tech* ***wrist pin*** *Br* goujon *m*; *Am* goupille *f*; *Comput* ***wrist rest*** repose-poignets *m inv*

wristband ['rɪstbænd] *n (on shirt, blouse)* poignet *m*; *(sweatband)* poignet *m*; *(of watch)* bracelet *m*

wristbone ['rɪstbəʊn] *n Anat* os *m* du carpe

wristlet ['rɪstlɪt] *n* bracelet *m*

wristlock ['rɪstlɒk] *n (in wrestling)* clef *f* de poignet; **to put a wristlock on sb** faire une clef de poignet à qn

wristwatch ['rɪstwɒtʃ] *n* montre-bracelet *f*

wristy ['rɪstɪ] *adj Sport (stroke etc)* de poignet

writ [rɪt] **1** *pt & pp Arch see* **write**

2 *n* (**a**) *Law* ordonnance *f*; **to issue a writ against sb** *(for arrest)* lancer un mandat d'arrêt contre qn; *(for libel)* assigner qn en justice; **to serve a writ on sb, to serve sb with a writ** assigner qn (en justice)

(**b**) *Pol (for elections)* ordonnance *f (émanant du président de la Chambre des communes et convoquant les députés pour un vote)*

3 *adj (idiom)* **capitalism writ large** le capitalisme avec un grand C; **astonishment was writ large on everybody's face** l'étonnement se lisait sur tous les visages

►► ***writ of attachment*** ordonnance *f* de saisie; ***writ of execution*** titre *m* exécutoire; ***writ of possession*** envoi *m* en possession; ***writ of subpoena*** assignation *f ou* citation *f* en justice

write [raɪt] (*pt* **wrote** [rəʊt], *pp* **written** ['rɪtən], *pt & pp Arch* **writ** [rɪt]) **1** *vt* (**a**) *(letter)* écrire; *(address, name)* écrire, inscrire; *(initials)* écrire, tracer; *(prescription, cheque)* écrire, faire; *(will)* faire; *(application form)* compléter, rédiger; **to write a letter to sb** écrire *ou* envoyer une lettre à qn; **write her a letter** envoyez-lui une lettre, écrivez-lui; **I have some letters to write** j'ai du courrier à faire; **they wrote me a letter of thanks** ils m'ont écrit pour me remercier; **he wrote her a postcard** il lui a envoyé une carte postale; **can I write you a cheque (for it)?** est-ce que je peux vous faire un chèque?; *Am* **to write sb** écrire à qn; *Am* **she wrote me about her father's illness** elle m'a écrit au sujet de la maladie de son père; **he can't speak Italian very well, but he can write it** il ne parle pas très bien l'italien mais il peut l'écrire; **it is written in the Bible "thou shalt love thy neighbour as thyself"** il est écrit dans la bible "tu aimeras ton prochain comme toi-même"; *Fig* **perplexity was written all over his face** la perplexité se lisait sur son visage; *Fig* **he had success written all over him** on voyait bien qu'il avait réussi; **he's got journalist written all over him** on voit tout de suite que c'est un journaliste

(**b**) *(book)* écrire; *(article, report)* écrire, faire; *(essay)* faire; *(music)* écrire, composer; **well written** bien écrit; **written for brass ensemble** écrit pour ensemble de cuivres

(**c**) *(send letter about)* écrire; **he wrote that he was getting married** il a écrit (pour annoncer) qu'il se mariait

(**d**) *(spell)* écrire; **I never know how to write her name** je ne sais jamais comment s'écrit son nom

(**e**) *Comput (program)* écrire; *(CD-ROM)* graver, enregistrer; *(data → store)* stocker, sauvegarder; *(→ transfer)* transférer; **to write sth to disk** écrire qch sur disque

2 *vi* (**a**) *(gen)* écrire; **to write in pencil/in ink** écrire au crayon/à l'encre; **to learn to read and write** apprendre à lire et à écrire; **I don't write very well** je n'ai pas une belle écriture

(**b**) *(send letter)* écrire; **to write to sb** écrire à qn; **we still write** *(to each other)* nous nous écrivons toujours; **to write to thank/to invite sb** écrire pour remercier/pour inviter qn; **have you written to let her know?** lui avez-vous écrit pour l'avertir?; **she wrote and told me about it** elle m'a écrit pour me le raconter; **please write (again) soon** écris-moi vite (à nouveau), s'il te plaît; **at the time of writing** au moment où j'écris; **they wrote (to him) asking** *or* **to ask for permission** ils (lui) ont écrit pour demander l'autorisation; **I've written for a catalogue** j'ai écrit pour demander *ou* pour qu'on m'envoie un catalogue

(**c**) *(professionally → as author)* écrire, être écrivain; *(→ as journalist)* écrire, être journaliste; **he writes on home affairs for 'The Economist'** il fait des articles de politique intérieure dans 'The Economist'; **she writes for the 'Independent'** elle écrit dans 'The Independent'; **she writes for children's television** elle fait des émissions pour les enfants à la télévision; **she writes under a pseudonym** elle écrit sous un pseudonyme; **he writes on** *or* **about archeology** il écrit sur l'archéologie, il traite de questions d'archéologie; **they wrote about their experiences in the Amazon** ils ont décrit leurs expériences en Amazonie

(**d**) *(pen, typewriter)* écrire; **this pen doesn't write very well** ce stylo n'écrit pas *ou* ne marche pas très bien

►► *Comput* ***write access*** accès *m* en écriture; *Comput* ***write area*** zone *f* d'écriture; *Comput* ***write density*** densité *f* d'écriture; *Tech* **write** [illegible] d'enregistrement; *Comput* ***write protection*** protection *f* contre l'écriture *ou* en écriture; *Comput* ***write speed*** vitesse *f* d'écriture

►**write away** *vi* (**a**) *(correspond)* écrire; **I had to write away to the publisher** j'ai dû écrire à la maison d'édition (**b**) *(order by post)* **I wrote away for a catalogue** j'ai écrit pour demander *ou* pour qu'on m'envoie un catalogue; **I had to write away for spare parts** j'ai dû écrire pour commander des pièces

►**write back** *vi (answer)* répondre (à une lettre); **please write back soon** réponds-moi vite, s'il te plaît; **he wrote back to say he couldn't come** il a répondu qu'il ne pouvait pas venir; **he wrote back rejecting their offer** il a renvoyé une lettre refusant leur offre

►**write down** *vt sep* (**a**) *(note)* écrire, noter; *(put in writing)* mettre par écrit; **unless you write the number down, you'll forget it** si vous ne notez pas le numéro *ou* si vous ne mettez pas le numéro par écrit, vous allez l'oublier; *Fig* **I had them written down as layabouts** je les considérais comme des bons à rien

(**b**) *Fin & Com (in price)* réduire le prix de; *(in value)* réduire la valeur de; *(undervalue)* sous-évaluer; *(asset)* déprécier

►**write in 1** *vi* écrire; **to write in for a refund** écrire pour demander un remboursement; **hundreds wrote in to complain** des centaines de personnes ont écrit pour se plaindre

2 *vt sep* (**a**) *(on list, document → word, name)* ajouter, insérer (**b**) *Am Pol (add → name)* ajouter, inscrire *(sur un bulletin de vote)*; *(vote for → person)* voter pour *(en ajoutant le nom sur le bulletin de vote)*

►**write off 1** *vt sep* (**a**) *Fin (capital, stock)* amortir; *(bad debt, asset)* passer aux profits et pertes

(**b**) *(consider lost, useless)* faire une croix sur, considérer comme perdu; *(cancel)* renoncer à, annuler; **the plan had to be written off** le projet a dû être abandonné; **three months' hard work was simply written off** on a perdu trois mois de travail acharné; **he was written off as a failure** on a considéré qu'il n'y avait rien de bon à en tirer

(**c**) *(in accident → of insurance company)* considérer comme irréparable, mettre à la casse; *(→ of driver)* rendre inutilisable; *Br* **she wrote off her new car** elle a complètement démoli sa voiture neuve; *Br* **his car has been written off** sa voiture a été mise à la casse

(**d**) *(letter, poem)* écrire en vitesse

2 *vi* = **write away**

►**write out** *vt sep* (**a**) *(report)* écrire, rédiger; *(list, cheque)* faire, établir; *(prescription)* rédiger; **can you write the amount out in full?** pouvez-vous écrire la somme en toutes lettres? (**b**) *(copy up → notes)* recopier, mettre au propre (**c**) *Rad & TV (character)* faire disparaître

►**write up** *vt sep* (**a**) *(diary, impressions)* écrire, rédiger; *Press (event)* faire un compte rendu de, rendre compte de; **the demonstration was written up in the local newspaper** le journal local a fait un compte rendu de la manifestation; **he wrote up his ideas in a report** il a consigné ses idées dans un rapport

(**b**) *(copy up → notes, data)* recopier, mettre au propre

(**c**) *Fin & Com (in price)* augmenter le prix de; *(in value)* augmenter la valeur de; *(overvalue)* surévaluer; *(asset)* revaloriser

write-back *n Acct* **write-back of provisions** reprises *fpl* sur provisions

write-down *n Fin* dépréciation *f*

write-in *n Am Pol (on ballot paper → addition of name)* inscription *f*, rajout *m*; *(→ name added)* nom *m* rajouté

write-off *n* (**a**) *Fin* annulation *f* par écrit, passation *f* par pertes et profits (**b**) **to be a write-off** *(motor vehicle)* être irréparable *ou* bon pour la casse; *(garment)* être bon à jeter; *(business venture)* être une perte de temps et d'argent

write-protect *vt Comput* protéger contre l'écriture *ou* en écriture

write-protected *adj Comput (disk)* protégé contre l'écriture *ou* en écriture

writer ['raɪtə(r)] *n* (**a**) *(of novel, play)* écrivain *m*, auteur *m*; *(of letter)* [illegible] **writer of novels/of poetry** un romancier/poète connu; **she's a fine writer** c'est un excellent écrivain; **technical writer** rédacteur(trice) *m,f* technique; **I'm a bad letter-writer** je suis un mauvais correspondant

(**b**) *(in handwriting)* **to be a good writer** avoir une belle écriture; **to be a bad writer** écrire mal

(**c**) *Scot Law* notaire *m*; **Writer to the Signet** ≃ avoué *m*

►► ***writer's block*** angoisse *f* de la page blanche; ***writer's cramp*** crampe *f* de l'écrivain

write-up *n* (**a**) *(review)* compte rendu *m*, critique *f*; **the play got a good write-up** la pièce a eu une bonne critique *ou* a été bien accueillie par la critique; **the guide contains write-ups of several ski resorts** le guide contient des notices descriptives sur plusieurs stations de ski (**b**) *Acct* augmentation *f* (**c**) *Am (of assets)* surestimation *f*

writhe [raɪð] *vi* (**a**) *(person → in pain)* se tordre, se contorsionner; *(snakes, worms)* se tortiller; **to writhe in** *or* **with agony** se tordre de douleur, être en proie à d'atroces souffrances

(**b**) *Fig* **her remarks made him writhe** *(in disgust)* ses remarques l'ont fait frémir; *(in embarrassment)* ses remarques l'ont atrocement gêné; **the memory still makes me writhe with embarrassment** ce souvenir me fait encore rougir; **they writhed under his criticism** ils ont vivement ressenti ses critiques

►**writhe about, writhe around** *vi* se tortiller; **the fish writhed about in the grass** le poisson se tortillait dans l'herbe; **to writhe about in pain** se tordre de douleur

writhing ['raɪðɪŋ] *n* contorsions *fpl*

writing ['raɪtɪŋ] **1** *n* (**a**) *(of books, letters)* écriture *f*; **to take up writing** *(author)* commencer à écrire; **to devote one's time to writing** se consacrer à l'écriture; **writing as a career** la carrière *ou* le métier d'écrivain; **it's a good piece of writing** c'est bien écrit; **this is clear, concise writing** c'est un style clair et concis, c'est écrit avec clarté et concision; **the report was four years in the writing** il a fallu quatre ans pour rédiger le rapport; **at the time of writing** au moment où j'écris/il écrit/*etc*; *Press* à l'heure où nous mettons sous presse

(**b**) *(handwriting)* écriture *f*; **I can't read your writing** je ne peux pas déchiffrer votre écriture *ou* ce que vous avez écrit

(**c**) *(written text)* **there was writing all over the board** il n'y avait plus de place pour écrire quoi que ce soit sur le tableau noir; *Fig* **the writing's on the wall** l'issue est inéluctable; **the writing was on the wall for the Roman Empire** la fin de l'empire romain était imminente; **I could see the writing on the wall** je savais ce qui allait arriver

(**d**) *Sch (spelling)* orthographe *f*; *(written language)* écriture *f*; **to learn reading and writing** apprendre à lire et à écrire, apprendre la lecture et l'écriture

2 writings *npl (written works)* œuvre *f*, écrits *mpl*; **the writings of Karl Marx** les écrits *mpl ou* l'œuvre *m* de Karl Marx; **selected writings** morceaux *mpl* choisis

3 in writing *adv* par écrit; **to put sth in writing** mettre qch par écrit; **can we have that in writing?** pouvons-nous avoir cela par écrit?; **you need her agreement in writing** il vous faut son accord écrit; **I won't be satisfied until I see it in writing** je ne serai pas satisfait tant que ce ne sera pas écrit noir sur blanc

►► ***writing block*** bloc *m* de papier à lettres; ***writing case*** nécessaire *m* de correspondance; ***writing desk*** secrétaire *m (meuble)*; ***writing materials*** matériel *m* nécessaire pour écrire; ***writing pad*** bloc-notes *m*; ***writing paper*** papier *m* à lettres; ***writing table*** secrétaire *m (meuble)*

writing off *n Acct (of debt)* amortissement *m*

written ['rɪtən] **1** *pp of* **write**

2 *adj (form, text, examination)* écrit; *(confirmation, consent)* par écrit; **to make a written request** faire une demande par écrit; **written language** écrit *m*; **written law** loi *f* écrite; **the written word** l'écrit *m*; **her written French is not as good as her oral French** elle parle le français mieux qu'elle ne l'écrit

[illegible], **written-down value** *n Fin* valeur *f* amortie

WRNS [renz] *n Br* (*abbr* **Women's Royal Naval Service**) = section féminine de la marine de guerre britannique

WRONG [rɒŋ]

mauvais	► **1 (a), (c)**
faux	► **1 (a)**
erroné	► **1 (a)**
tort	► **1 (b); 3 (b) – (d)**
mal	► **1 (d); 2; 3 (a)**
injuste	► **1 (d)**
faire du tort à	► **4**

1 *adj* (**a**) *(incorrect → address, answer, information)* mauvais, faux (fausse), erroné; *(→ decision)* mauvais; *Mus (note)* faux (fausse); *Tel (number)* faux (fausse); **to get things in the wrong order** mettre les choses dans le mauvais ordre; **these cups are in the wrong place** ces tasses ne sont pas à leur place; **they came on**

the wrong day ils se sont trompés de jour pour leur venue; **to take the wrong road/train** se tromper de route/de train; **this is the wrong road for Munich** ce n'est pas la bonne route pour aller à Munich; **to drive on the wrong side of the road** conduire du mauvais côté de la route; **she went to the wrong address** elle s'est trompée d'adresse; **you've put your shoes on the wrong feet** vous vous êtes trompé (de pied) en mettant vos chaussures; **to be (the) wrong side up** être à l'envers; **the biscuit went down the wrong way** j'ai avalé le gâteau de travers; **it was a wrong number** c'était une erreur; **to dial the wrong number** se tromper de numéro; **I'm sorry, you've got the wrong number** désolé, vous vous êtes trompé de numéro *ou* vous faites erreur; **you've got the wrong man, Jack Taylor isn't a murderer** vous faites erreur, Jack Taylor n'est pas un meurtrier; **the clock/my watch is wrong** le réveil/ma montre n'est pas à l'heure; **the clock has always shown the wrong time** la pendule n'a jamais été à l'heure *ou* n'a jamais indiqué l'heure exacte

(**b**) *(mistaken → person)* **to be wrong (about sth)** avoir tort *ou* se tromper (à propos de qch); **you were wrong to lose your temper** vous avez eu tort de vous emporter; **you were wrong to accuse him, it was wrong of you to accuse him** vous avez eu tort de l'accuser, vous n'auriez pas dû l'accuser; **to be wrong about sb** se tromper sur (le compte de) qn; **how wrong can you be!** comme quoi on peut se tromper!; **that's just where you are wrong** c'est justement ce qui vous trompe, c'est justement là que vous vous trompez; **I hope he won't get the wrong idea about me** j'espère qu'il ne se fera pas de fausses idées sur mon compte; **I hope you won't take this the wrong way, but...** ne le prends pas mal mais...

(**c**) *(unsuitable)* mauvais, mal choisi; **you've got the wrong attitude** vous n'avez pas l'attitude qu'il faut *ou* la bonne attitude; **it was the wrong thing to do/to say** ce n'était pas la chose à faire/à dire; **I said all the wrong things** j'ai dit tout ce qu'il ne fallait pas dire; **his ideas are all wrong** il a des idées tout de travers; **you're going about it in the wrong way** vous vous y prenez mal; **it's the wrong way to deal with the situation** ce n'est pas comme cela qu'il faut régler la situation; **to come at the wrong time** venir à un mauvais moment *ou* mal à propos; **he's the wrong man for the job** ce n'est pas l'homme qu'il faut pour ce poste; **I'm the wrong person to ask** il ne faut pas me demander ça à moi; **I think you're in the wrong job** je pense que ce n'est pas le travail qu'il vous faut; *Hum* vous vous êtes trompé de métier!; **she was wearing the wrong shoes for a long walk** elle n'avait pas les chaussures qui conviennent *ou* elle n'avait pas les bonnes chaussures pour une randonnée; **this village is the wrong place for a nightclub** ce village n'est pas l'endroit qui convient *ou* n'est pas le bon endroit pour une boîte de nuit

(**d**) *(immoral, bad)* mal; *(unjust)* injuste; **cheating is wrong** c'est mal de tricher; **slavery is wrong** l'esclavage est inacceptable; **it was wrong of him to take the money** ce n'était pas bien de sa part de prendre l'argent; **what's wrong with reading comics?** qu'est-ce qu'il y a de mal à lire des bandes dessinées?; **what's wrong with that?** qu'est-ce qu'il y a de mal à ça?; **there's nothing wrong with it** il n'y a rien à redire à cela, il n'y a pas de mal à cela; **it's wrong that anyone should have to live in poverty** il est injuste que des gens soient obligés de vivre dans la misère

(**e**) *(amiss)* **something is wrong** *or* **there's something wrong with the lamp** la lampe ne marche pas bien *ou* a un défaut; **something is wrong** *or* **there's something wrong with my elbow** j'ai quelque chose au coude; **there's something wrong with me** *(ill)* j'ai quelque chose qui ne va pas; **there must be something wrong with me** *(that people don't like me)* il doit y avoir quelque chose qui ne va pas chez moi; **there must be something seriously wrong** il doit y avoir un gros problème; **there's something wrong somewhere** il y a quelque chose qui ne va pas quelque part; **I hope there's nothing wrong** j'espère qu'il n'est rien arrivé; **there's nothing at all wrong with the clock** la pendule marche parfaitement bien; **there's nothing wrong with your work** votre travail est très bon; **there's nothing wrong with her decision/her reasoning** sa décision/son raisonnement est parfaitement valable; **there's nothing wrong about wanting a holiday without the kids** il n'y a pas de mal à vouloir des vacances sans les enfants; **there's nothing wrong with you** vous vous êtes en parfaite santé; **there's nothing wrong, thank you** tout va bien, merci; **there's nothing wrong with your eyes/your hearing!** vous avez de bons yeux/de bonnes oreilles!; **what's wrong?** qu'est-ce qui ne va pas?; **what's wrong with the car?** qu'est-ce qu'elle a, la voiture?; **what's wrong with your elbow?** qu'est-ce qu'il a, votre coude?; **what's wrong with you?** qu'est-ce que vous avez?; **what's wrong with these people?** *(that they don't understand)* qu'est-ce qu'ils ont qui ne va pas, ces gens?; **what's wrong with going to France?** quel mal y a-t-il à aller en France?; **there's very little wrong with you** dans l'ensemble, vous êtes en très bonne santé; **there wasn't much wrong with the car** la voiture n'avait pas grand-chose; *Br Fam* **to be wrong in the head** avoir la tête fêlée *ou* le cerveau fêlé, être fêlé *ou* timbré

(**f**) *Tex* **the wrong side of the fabric** l'envers *m* du tissu; **wrong side out** à l'envers

(**g**) *(idioms)* **he got hold of the wrong end of the stick** il a tout compris de travers; *Br* **to be caught on the wrong foot** être pris au dépourvu; **they got off on the wrong foot** ils se sont mal entendus au départ; *Br* **I'm (on) the wrong side of fifty** j'ai cinquante ans bien sonnés; **to get out of bed on the wrong side** se lever du pied gauche; **to get on the wrong side of sb** se faire mal voir de qn

2 *adv* mal; **you did wrong** vous avez mal agi; **I guessed wrong** je suis tombé à côté, je me suis trompé; **you've spelt the word wrong** vous avez mal écrit *ou* mal orthographié ce mot; **she got the time/address/name wrong** *(was mistaken about)* elle s'est trompée d'heure/d'adresse/de nom; *(misunderstood)* elle a mal compris l'heure/l'adresse/le nom; **I got the answer wrong** je n'ai pas donné la bonne réponse; **to get one's sums wrong** *Math* faire des erreurs dans ses opérations; *Fig* se tromper dans ses calculs; **she's got her facts wrong** elle se trompe, ce qu'elle avance est faux; **you've got it wrong, I never said that** vous vous trompez *ou* vous n'avez pas compris, je n'ai jamais dit cela; **don't get me wrong** comprenez-moi bien; **you've got her all wrong** vous vous trompez complètement sur son compte; **to go wrong** *(person)* se tromper; *(plan)* mal marcher, mal tourner; *(deal)* tomber à l'eau; *(machine)* tomber en panne; **something has gone wrong with the TV** la télé est tombée en panne; **something went wrong with her eyesight** elle a eu des ennuis avec sa vue; **the space flight went disastrously wrong** le vol spatial a tourné à la catastrophe; **we must have gone wrong somewhere** nous avons dû nous tromper quelque part; **you can't go wrong** vous ne pouvez pas vous tromper, c'est très simple; **you won't go far wrong if you follow her advice** vous ne risquez guère de vous tromper si vous suivez ses conseils; **you can't go wrong with a pair of jeans** vous êtes tranquille avec un jean; **you can't go wrong with a good book** *(for reading)* vous ne risquez pas de vous ennuyer avec un bon livre; *(as present)* un bon livre, cela plaît toujours; **where I went wrong was in being too kind to him** là où j'ai commis une erreur, c'est en me montrant trop gentil avec lui; **when did things start going wrong?** quand est-ce que les choses ont commencé à se gâter?; **she used to be a normal, happy little girl, but something went wrong** c'était une petite fille normale et heureuse mais quelque chose a mal tourné; **everything that could go wrong went wrong** tout ce qui pouvait aller de travers est allé de travers; **to turn out wrong** *(event)* mal (se) terminer; *(calculation)* se révéler faux; *(person)* mal tourner

3 *n* (**a**) *(immorality, immoral act)* mal *m*; **to know the difference between right and wrong** savoir distinguer le bien du mal; **I did no wrong** je n'ai rien fait de mal; *Prov* **two wrongs don't make a right** = on ne répare pas une injustice par une autre

(**b**) *(harm)* tort *m*, injustice *f*; **to suffer wrong** subir une injustice; **to do sb wrong** faire du tort à *ou* se montrer injuste envers qn; **he did them a great wrong** il leur a fait subir une grave injustice, il leur a fait (un) grand tort

(**c**) *(error)* tort *m*, erreur *f*; **he can do no wrong in her eyes** tout ce qu'il fait trouve grâce à ses yeux

(**d**) *Law* tort *m*

4 *vt* faire du tort à, traiter injustement; **he wronged his wife by accusing her of being unfaithful** il a traité injustement sa femme en l'accusant d'infidélité; **she felt deeply wronged** elle se sentait gravement lésée; **she has been badly wronged** *(by words)* on a dit à tort beaucoup de mal d'elle; *(by actions)* on a agi de manière injuste envers elle

5 in the wrong 1 *adj* dans son tort; **to be in the wrong** être dans son tort, avoir tort **2** *adv* **to put sb in the wrong** mettre qn dans son tort

---

wrongdoer [ˌrɒŋ'duːə(r)] *n* (**a**) *(delinquent)* malfaiteur *m*, délinquant(e) *m,f* (**b**) *(sinner)* pécheur(eresse) *m,f*

wrongdoing [ˌrɒŋ'duːɪŋ] *n* mal *m*, méfait *m*; **a sense of wrongdoing** le sentiment de mal faire; **his many wrongdoings** ses nombreux méfaits

wrong-foot *vt Sport* prendre à contre-pied; *Fig* prendre au dépourvu

wrongful ['rɒŋfʊl] *adj (unjust)* injuste; *(unjustified)* injustifié; *(illegal)* illégal, illicite

►► *Law* ***wrongful arrest*** arrestation *f* arbitraire; *Ind* ***wrongful dismissal*** renvoi *m* injustifié; ***wrongful imprisonment*** emprisonnement *m* injustifié; ***wrongful trading*** = situation dans laquelle une société poursuit ses opérations en dépit du fait que la mise en liquidation est inévitable

wrongfully ['rɒŋfʊlɪ] *adv* injustement; *Ind* **I was wrongfully dismissed** j'ai été renvoyé à tort

wrongheaded [ˌrɒŋ'hedɪd] *adj (person)* buté; *(idea)* insensé

wrongheadedly [ˌrɒŋ'hedɪdlɪ] *adv (wrongly, mistakenly)* à tort; *(obstinately)* avec une obstination que rien ne justifie

wrongheadedness [ˌrɒŋ'hedɪdnɪs] *n (of person)* persistance *f* dans l'erreur; *(of idea)* absurdité *f*

wrongly ['rɒŋlɪ] *adv* (**a**) *(unjustly)* à tort, injustement; **to be wrongly accused** être accusé à tort *ou* injustement accusé

(**b**) *(incorrectly)* à tort, mal; **to be wrongly informed** être mal renseigné; **this word is spelt wrongly** ce mot est mal écrit *ou* mal orthographié; **I guessed wrongly** je suis tombé à côté, je me suis trompé; **the cat was wrongly described as a Siamese** le chat a été décrit à tort comme un siamois

(**c**) *(by mistake)* par erreur, à tort; **he was wrongly assigned to the night shift** il a été affecté par erreur *ou* à tort à l'équipe de nuit

wrongness ['rɒŋnɪs] *n* (**a**) *(error)* erreur *f* (**b**) *(injustice)* injustice *f* (**c**) *(immorality)* immoralité *f*, mal *m*

wrote [rəʊt] *pt of* **write**

wrought [rɔːt] **1** *(pt & pp Arch see* **work***)* **the havoc wrought by the hurricane** les ravages causés par l'ouragan; **the changes wrought by industrialization** les (profonds) changements occasionnés par la révolution industrielle

2 *adj (silver, gold)* travaillé, ouvragé, façonné; *(metal)* ouvré, forgé; *(copper)* martelé; *Literary* **wheels wrought by hand** des roues façonnées *ou* fabriquées à la main; **carefully wrought prose** prose *f* finement ciselée

►► ***wrought iron*** fer *m* forgé; *Tex* ***wrought silk*** soie *f* ouvragée

wrought-iron *adj* en fer forgé

wrought-up *adj* énervé

WRU [ˌdʌbəljuːɑː'juː] *n Sport (abbr* **Welsh Rugby Union***)* = association galloise de rugby à quinze

wrung [rʌŋ] *pt & pp of* **wring**

WRVS [ˌdʌbəljuːɑːˌviː'es] *n Br (abbr* **Women's Royal Voluntary Service***)* = association de femmes au service des déshérités

wry [raɪ] *(compar* **wrier** *or* **wryer**, *superl* **wriest** *or*

wryest) *adj* (**a**) *(ironic → comment, smile)* ironique, désabusé; **wry humour** ironie *f*; **the film is a wry comedy** le film est plein d'ironie (**b**) *(expression, glance → of distaste)* désabusé; **she made a wry face** elle a fait la grimace

wrybill ['raɪbɪl] *n Orn* pluvier *m* anarhynque

wryly ['raɪlɪ] *adv* de manière désabusée, ironiquement; **he smiled back at me wryly** il m'a répondu par un sourire ironique *ou* désabusé; **her wryly observed portrait** son portrait ironique

wryneck ['raɪnek] *n* (**a**) *Med* torticolis *m* (**b**) *Orn* torcol *m*

wryness ['raɪnɪs] *n* ironie *f*

WSW (*written abbr* **west-south-west**) O-SO

wt (*written abbr* **weight**) poids

wt. (*written abbr* **weight**) poids

WTO [ˌdʌbəljuːtiːˈəʊ] *n* (*abbr* **World Trade Organization**) OMC *f*

wulfenite ['wʊlfənaɪt] *n Miner* wulfénite *f*

wunderkind ['wʌndəkɪnd] *n* enfant *mf* prodige

wurst [wɜːst] *n* = grosse saucisse allemande

wuss [wʊs] *n Fam* mauviette *f*, lavette *f*

wussy ['wʊsɪ] *Fam* **1** *n* mauviette *f*, lavette *f*
2 *adj* mou (molle), mollasson

WV, WVa (*written abbr* **West Virginia**) Virginie-Occidentale *f*

WW (*written abbr* **World War**) guerre *f* mondiale

WWF [ˌdʌbəljuːdʌbəljuːˈef] *n* (*abbr* **Worldwide Fund for Nature**) WWF *m*

WWJD [ˌdʌbəljuːdʌbəljuːˌdʒeɪˈdiː] *Am* (*abbr* **what would Jesus do?**) = slogan souvent arboré sur un bracelet, exhortant celui qui le porte à faire le bien dans ses actions quotidiennes

WWW [ˌdʌbəljuːdʌbəljuːˈdʌbəljuː] *n Comput* (*abbr* **world wide web**) WWW, W3

WY (*written abbr* **Wyoming**) Wyoming *m*

Wyandot, Wyandotte ['waɪəndɒt] *n* (**a**) *(tribe)* **the Wyandot(s)** *or* **Wyandotte(s)** les Wyandottes *mpl* (**b**) *(member of tribe)* Wyandotte *mf*
►► ***wyandotte chicken*** wyandotte *f*

wych elm [wɪtʃ-] *n Bot* orme *m* blanc

wye [waɪ] *n* (**a**) *(letter)* y *m* (**b**) *(in plumbing)* branche *f* culotte

wynd [waɪnd] *n Scot* allée *f*

Wyo (*written abbr* **Wyoming**) Wyoming *m*

Wyoming [waɪˈəʊmɪŋ] *n* le Wyoming; **in Wyoming** dans le Wyoming

WYSIWYG ['wɪzɪwɪg] *n & adj Comput* (*abbr* **what you see is what you get**) tel écran-tel écrit *m*, tel-tel *m*, Wysiwyg *m*
►► ***WYSIWYG display*** affichage *m* tel écran-tel écrit *ou* tel-tel *ou* Wysiwyg

wyvern ['waɪvən] *n Her* dragon *m* ailé à deux pattes

X[1], x[1] [eks] *n (letter)* X, x *m inv*; **two x's** deux x; **X for xylophone** ≃ X comme Xavier

X[2] *(pt & pp* **X-ed** *or* **X'd**) **1** *n (unknown factor)* X *m*; **X marks the spot** l'endroit est marqué d'une croix; **Mr X** monsieur X; **for X number of years** pendant x années

2 *vt* marquer d'une croix

►► *Br Formerly Cin* ***X certificate*** = signalait (jusqu'en 1982) un film interdit aux moins de dix-huit ans; *Br Formerly Cin* ***X (certificate) film*** = film *m* interdit aux moins de dix-huit ans *(remplacé en 1982 par "18")*; ***X chromosome*** chromosome *m* X

►**X out** *vt sep* biffer, rayer (avec des croix)

X[3] (**a**) *(written abbr* **kiss**) = formule affectueuse placée après la signature à la fin d'une lettre (**b**) *(written abbr* **Christ**) Christ *m*

x[2] *n Math* x *m*

xanthene ['zænθiːn] *n Chem* xanthène *m*

xanthin ['zænθɪn], **xanthine** ['zænθaɪn] *n Chem* xanthine *f*

xanthoma [zæn'θəʊmə] *n Med* xanthoma *m*, xanthome *m*

x-axis *n Math* axe *m* des X, abscisse *f*

x-coordinate *n Math* abscisse *f*

xenogenic [zenəʊ'dʒenɪk] *adj Med* xénogénique

xenoglossia [zenəʊ'glɒsɪə] *n* xénoglossie *f*

xenolith ['zenəlɪθ] *n Geol* enclave *f*

xenon ['ziːnɒn] *n Chem* xénon *m*

xenophilous [ze'nɒfɪləs] *adj* xénophile

xenophobe ['zenəfəʊb] *n* xénophobe *mf*

xenophobia [ˌzenə'fəʊbɪə] *n* xénophobie *f*

xenophobic [ˌzenə'fəʊbɪk] *adj* xénophobe

Xenophon ['zenəfɒn] *pr n Antiq* Xénophon

xenotransplant ['zenəʊtrænsplɑːnt] *n Med* (**a**) *(UNCOUNT) (procedure)* xénogreffe *f*, hétérotransplantation *f* (**b**) *(transplanted organ)* xénogreffe *f*, greffe *f* xénogénique

xenotransplantation [zenəʊtrænsplɑːn'teɪʃən] = **xenotransplant** (**a**)

xerographic [ˌzɪərə'græfɪk] *adj* de photocopie

►► ***xerographic equipment*** copieur *m*, photocopieuse *f*

xerography [ˌzɪə'rɒgrəfɪ] *n (UNCOUNT)* photocopie *f*, *Spec* électrocopie *f*

xerophilous [zɪə'rɒfɪləs] *adj* xérophile

xerophthalmia [ˌzɪərɒf'θælmɪə] *n Med* xérophtalmie *f*

xerophyte ['zɪərəfaɪt] *n Bot* xérophyte *m*

xerophytic [ˌzɪərə'fɪtɪk] *adj Bot* xérophyte, xérophytique

Xerox® ['zɪərɒks] *n* (**a**) *(machine)* copieur *m*, photocopieuse *f* (**b**) *(process, copy)* photocopie *f*

xerox ['zɪərɒks] *vt* photocopier

Xerxes ['zɜːksiːz] *pr n Myth* Xerxès

x-height *n Comput & Typ* hauteur *f* d'œil

Xhosa ['kəʊsə, 'kɔːsə] **1** *adj* xhosa

2 *n* Xhosa *mf*; **the Xhosa** les Xhosa *mpl*, les Xhosas *mpl*

xiphoid ['zɪfɔɪd] *Anat* **1** *adj* **xiphoid appendage** *or* **cartilage** *or* **process** appendice *m* xiphoïde

2 *n* appendice *m* xiphoïde

XL [ˌeks'el] *n (abbr* **extra-large**) XL *m*

Xmas *(written abbr* **Christmas**) Noël *m*

XML [ˌeksem'el] *n Comput (abbr* **Extensible Markup Language**) XML *m*

X-rated [-reɪtɪd] *adj Formerly Cin (film)* interdit aux mineurs *ou* aux moins de dix-huit ans

x-ray, X-ray 1 *vt* (**a**) *Med (examine → chest, ankle)* radiographier, faire une radio de; *(→ patient)* faire une radio à

(**b**) *(inspect → luggage)* passer aux rayons X

(**c**) *(treat)* traiter aux rayons X

2 *n* (**a**) *Med* radio *f*; **to have an x-ray** passer une radio; **to take an x-ray of sth** radiographier qch, faire une radiographie de qch

(**b**) *Phys* rayon *m* X

3 *comp* (**a**) *Med (examination)* radioscopique; *(treatment)* radiologique, par rayons X

(**b**) *Phys (astronomy, tube)* à rayons X

►► *Phys* ***x-ray crystallography*** radiocristallographie *f*; *Med* ***x-ray diagnosis*** radiodiagnostic *m*; *Phys* ***x-ray diffraction*** radiodiffraction *f*; *Med* ***x-ray photograph*** radiographie *f*, radio *f*; *Astron* ***x-ray star*** = étoile émettant un rayonnement radioélectrique; *Med* ***x-ray therapy*** radiothérapie *f*; *Med* ***x-ray unit*** service *m* de radiologie

xylem ['zaɪlem] *n Bot* xylème *m*

xylene ['zaɪliːn] *n Chem* xylène *m*

xylograph ['zaɪləˌgrɑːf] **1** *n* xylographie *f*

2 *vt (drawing, text)* tirer à partir d'une gravure sur bois

xylographic [ˌzaɪlə'græfɪk] *adj* xylographique

xylography [zaɪ'lɒgrəfɪ] *n (UNCOUNT)* xylographie *f*

xylol ['zaɪlɒl] *n Chem* xylol *m*

xylophone ['zaɪləfəʊn] *n* xylophone *m*

xylophonist [zaɪ'lɒfənɪst] *n* joueur(euse) *m,f* de xylophone

xylopia [zaɪ'ləʊpɪə] *n Bot* xylopia *m*

xylose ['zaɪləʊs] *n Chem* xylose *m*

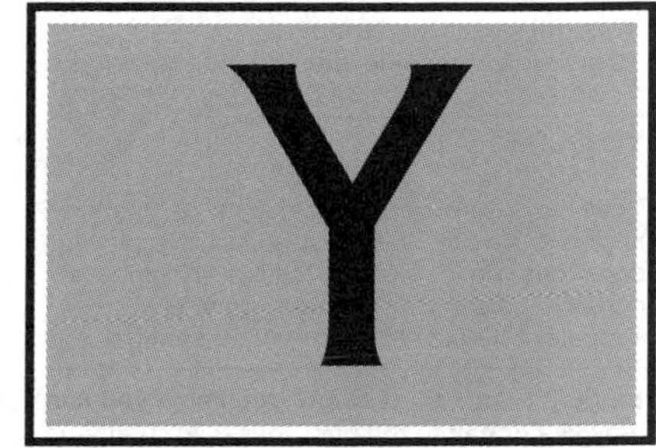

Y¹, y¹ [waɪ] *n (letter)* Y, y *m inv*; **two y's** deux y; **Y for yellow** ≃ Y comme Yvonne
►► ***Y chromosome*** chromosome *m* Y

Y² (**a**) (*written abbr* **yen**) y (**b**) (*written abbr* **yuan**) yuan

y² *n Math* y *m*

Y2K [ˌwaɪtuːˈkeɪ] (*abbr* **year 2000**) **1** *n* l'an *m* 2000
2 *adj Comput* **Y2K compatible, Y2K compliant** conforme à l'an 2000

yabber [ˈjæbə(r)] *Austr Fam* **1** *vi* jacasser
2 *n* bavardage *m*, jacassement *m*

yacht [jɒt] **1** *n (sailing boat)* voilier *m*; *(pleasure boat)* yacht *m*
2 *comp (race)* de voiliers
3 *vi* faire du yachting; **to go yachting** faire du yachting
►► ***yacht club*** yacht-club *m*

yachting [ˈjɒtɪŋ] **1** *n* yachting *m*, navigation *f* de plaisance
2 *comp (holiday)* en yacht, sur l'eau; *(magazine)* de voile; *(cap)* de marin

yachtsman [ˈjɒtsmən] (*pl* **yachtsmen** [-mən]) *n* yachtman *m*, yachtsman *m*

yachtswoman [ˈjɒtsˌwʊmən] (*pl* **yachtswomen** [-ˌwɪmɪn]) *n* yachtwoman *f*

yack [jæk] = **yak** *n* (**b**) *& vi*

yackety-yak [ˌjækətɪˈjæk] *Fam* **1** *vi* jacasser
2 *n (UNCOUNT)* jacasserie *f*
3 *adv* **to go yackety-yack** jacasser

yah [jɑː] **1** *exclam Fam* beurk!
2 *n Br Fam Pej* **(OK) yah** bourge *mf*

yahoo [jɑːˈhuː] (*pl* **yahoos**) *n* rustre *m*, butor *m*

Yahveh [ˈjɑːveɪ], **Yahweh** [ˈjɑːweɪ] *pr n* Jahvé *m*, Yahvé *m*

yak [jæk] (*pt & pp* **yakked**, *cont* **yakking**) **1** *n* (**a**) *Zool* yak *m*, yack *m* (**b**) *(UNCOUNT) Fam* papotage *m*; **to have a yak** papoter; **it's ages since we've had a really good yak** ça fait longtemps qu'on ne s'est pas taillé une bonne bavette
2 *vi Fam* (**a**) *(chat)* jacasser; **it's yak, yak, yak all day long with that woman!** cette femme n'arrête pas de jacasser toute la journée! (**b**) *Am (vomit)* gerber, dégueuler

Yakut [jæˈkʊt] **1** *adj* iakoute, yakoute
2 *n* Iakoute *mf*, Yakoute *mf*

Yale [jeɪl] *n* Yale *(prestigieuse université du Connecticut)*
►► ***Yale lock***® serrure *f* de sécurité *(à cylindre)*

y'all [jɑːl] = **you-all**

Yalta [ˈjæltə] *n* Yalta *f*; **the Yalta Conference** la conférence de Yalta

yam [jæm] *n* (**a**) *(plant, vegetable)* igname *f* (**b**) *Am Culin* patate *f* douce

yammer [ˈjæmə(r)] *vi Fam (person → whine)* pleurnicher, geindre; *(→ chatter)* jacasser; **what are you yammering about?** qu'est-ce que tu as à jacasser comme ça?

yang [jæŋ] *n* yang *m*

Yangtze [ˈjæŋtsɪ] *n* **the Yangtze** le Yang-tseu-kiang, le Yangzi Jiang

Yank [jæŋk] *Fam* **1** *n* (**a**) *Am (inhabitant of New England)* habitant(e) *m,f* de la Nouvelle Angleterre; *(native of New England)* originaire *mf* de Nouvelle Angleterre; *(inhabitant of Northern US)* habitant(e) *m,f* du Nord (des États-Unis); *(native of Northern US)* originaire *mf* du Nord (des États-Unis) (**b**) *Br Fam Pej* Yankee *mf*, Amerloque *mf*
2 *adj* (**a**) *Am* yankee (**b**) *Br Fam Pej* yankee, amerloque

yank [jæŋk] **1** *vt (hair, sleeve)* tirer brusquement (sur), tirer d'un coup sec; **he was yanked to his feet** on l'a tiré brutalement pour l'obliger à se lever; **I yanked the lever back** j'ai tiré le levier en arrière d'un coup sec
2 *n* coup *m* sec; **I gave the wire/her hair a yank** j'ai tiré d'un coup sec sur le fil/sur ses cheveux

►**yank off** *vt sep (button, cover)* arracher; **she yanked the cloth off the table** elle a enlevé la nappe de la table d'un coup sec

►**yank out** *vt sep (nail, tooth)* arracher

Yankee [ˈjæŋkɪ] **1** *n* (**a**) *Am (inhabitant of New England)* habitant(e) *m,f* de la Nouvelle Angleterre; *(native of New England)* originaire *mf* de la Nouvelle Angleterre; *(inhabitant of Northern US)* habitant(e) *m,f* du Nord (des États-Unis); *(native of Northern US)* originaire *mf* du Nord (des États-Unis)
(**b**) *Hist (in the American Civil War)* Nordiste *m*
(**c**) *Br Fam Pej* Yankee *mf*, Amerloque *mf*
2 *adj* (**a**) *Am* yankee
(**b**) *Br Fam Pej* yankee, amerloque
►► *Am Fin* ***Yankee bond*** obligation *f* Yankee; ***Yankee Doodle*** (**a**) *(song)* = air populaire de la guerre d'Indépendance devenu chanson traditionnelle des États-Unis (**b**) *Fam Pej* Amerloque *mf*

'A Connecticut Yankee in King Arthur's Court'
Twain, Garnett 'Un Yankee à la cour du roi Arthur'

Yankeeism [ˈjæŋkɪɪzəm] *n Ling* américanisme *m*

Yaoundé [jɑːˈʊndeɪ] *n* Yaoundé *f*

yap [jæp] (*pt & pp* **yapped**, *cont* **yapping**) **1** *vi* (**a**) *(dog)* japper
(**b**) *Fam Fig (person)* jacasser; **the shop assistants were yapping away instead of serving** les vendeuses jacassaient au lieu de servir la clientèle
2 *n* (**a**) *(yelp)* jappement *m*
(**b**) *Fam (mouth)* clapet *m*, gueule *f*; **shut your yap!** ferme ton clapet!, la ferme!
(**c**) *Am Fam (idiot)* andouille *f*, truffe *f*; *(country bumpkin)* péquenaud(e) *m,f*

yapping [ˈjæpɪŋ] **1** *adj (dog)* jappeur
2 *n (UNCOUNT)* (**a**) *(of dog)* jappement *m*; **I wish that dog would stop its yapping!** si ce chien pouvait arrêter ses jappements! (**b**) *Fam Fig (of person)* jacasseries *fpl*

yappy [ˈjæpɪ] (*compar* **yappier**, *superl* **yappiest**) *adj* (**a**) *(dog)* jappeur (**b**) *Fam (person)* jacasseur

yarborough [ˈjɑːbərə] *n Cards (in bridge, whist)* = main de treize cartes sans honneurs

yard [jɑːd] *n* (**a**) *(of factory, farm, house, school)* cour *f*; **parked in the yard** garé dans la cour
(**b**) *(work site)* chantier *m*; **builder's yard** chantier *m* de construction; *Naut* **repair yard** chantier *m* de radoub
(**c**) *(for storage)* dépôt *m*
(**d**) *Rail* voies *fpl* de garage
(**e**) *(for animals → enclosure)* enclos *m*; *(→ pasture)* pâturage *m*
(**f**) *Br Fam* **the Yard** Scotland Yard; **Wilson of the Yard** Wilson de Scotland Yard
(**g**) *Am (backyard)* cour *f*; *(garden)* jardin *m*
(**h**) *(unit of measurement)* = 0,914m, yard *m*; *(in Canada)* verge *f*; **square yard** = 0,836m², yard *m* carré; **it was about ten yards away** c'était à environ dix mètres; **it was ten yards wide** il avait dix mètres de large; **to buy cloth by the yard** acheter le tissu au mètre; *Fig* **we still have yards of green velvet** nous avons toujours des quantités de velours vert; *Fig* **his calculations were yards out** il s'était complètement trompé dans ses calculs; **his face was a yard long** il en faisait une tête, il faisait une tête d'enterrement
(**i**) *Old-fashioned Sport* **the 100 yards, the 100 yards' dash** le cent mètres; **she won the 3,000 yards' steeplechase** elle a gagné le 3000 mètres steeple
(**j**) *Naut* vergue *f*
►► ***yard of ale*** *(container)* = long récipient à bière d'une contenance d'environ un litre et demi; **to do the yard of ale** = boire un litre et demi de bière d'une seule traite dans un "yard of ale"; *Sport* ***yard line*** *(in American football)* = l'une des deux lignes horizontales qui divisent le terrain en yards; *Am* ***yard sale*** vide-grenier *m*; ***yard work*** jardinage *m*

yardage [ˈjɑːdɪdʒ] *n Tex* ≃ métrage *m*

yardarm [ˈjɑːdɑːm] *n* extrémité *f* d'une vergue carrée; *Fam Hum* **the sun's over the yardarm** c'est l'heure de l'apéro

yardbird [ˈjɑːdbɜːd] *n Am very Fam Mil slang* bleu *m*, bidasse *m (empoté)*

Yardie [ˈjɑːdɪ] *n* truand *m* d'origine jamaïcaine

yardman [ˈjɑːdmæn] *n Am* jardinier *m*

yardstick [ˈjɑːdstɪk] *n* (**a**) *(instrument)* mètre *m (en bois ou en métal)* (**b**) *Fig* critère *m*, point *m* de référence; *Fig* **salary seems to be a yardstick for success** il semble que le salaire soit un critère de réussite

yarmulka, yarmulke [ˈjɑːməlkə] *n Rel* kippa *f*

yarn [jɑːn] **1** *n* (**a**) *(UNCOUNT) Tex* fil *m (à tricoter ou à tisser)* (**b**) *(tall story)* histoire *f* à dormir debout; *(long story)* longue histoire *f*
2 *vi (tell tall stories)* raconter des histoires; *(tell long stories)* raconter de longues histoires

yarrow [ˈjærəʊ] *n Bot* mille-feuille *f*, achillée *f*

yashmak [ˈjæʃmæk] *n* litham *m*, litsam *m*

yataghan [ˈjætəgən] *n* yatagan *m*

yatter [ˈjætə(r)] *vi Fam* bavarder

yaw [jɔː] **1** *vi* (**a**) *(ship)* être déporté, faire une embardée (**b**) *(plane, missile)* faire un mouvement de lacet
2 *vt* faire dévier de sa trajectoire
3 *n* (**a**) *(of ship)* écart *m*, embardée *f* (**b**) *(of plane, missile)* mouvement *m* de lacet

yawl [jɔːl] *n* (**a**) *(sailing boat)* yawl *m* (**b**) *(carried on ship)* chaloupe *f* (**c**) *(fishing boat)* yole *f*

yawn [jɔːn] **1** *vi* (**a**) *(person)* bâiller
(**b**) *(chasm, opening)* être béant, s'ouvrir; **the gulf yawned at his feet** le gouffre s'ouvrait *ou* béait à ses pieds
2 *vt (utter with yawn)* dire en bâillant; *Fam* **she was yawning her head off** elle bâillait à se décrocher la mâchoire
3 *n* (**a**) *(of person)* bâillement *m*; **to give a big yawn** bâiller (bruyamment) la bouche grande ouverte
(**b**) *Fam Fig* **to be a yawn** *(meeting)* être ennuyeux; *(film, book)* être rasoir; **what a yawn!** qu'est-ce que c'est rasoir!

yawning [ˈjɔːnɪŋ] **1** *adj* (**a**) *(person)* qui bâille (**b**) *(gap, chasm)* béant
2 *n (UNCOUNT)* bâillement *m*, bâillements *mpl*

yawningly [ˈjɔːnɪŋlɪ] *adv* en bâillant

yawp [jɔːp] *Am Fam* **1** *vi* (**a**) *(yawn)* bâiller bruyamment (**b**) *(bawl)* gueuler (**c**) *(bark)* aboyer
2 *n* (**a**) *(bark)* aboiement *m* (**b**) *(shout)* cri *m*

yaws [jɔːz] *n (UNCOUNT) Med* pian *m*

y-axis *n Math* axe *m* des Y *ou* des ordonnées

yay [jeɪ] *n Am Fam Drugs slang (cocaine)* coco *f*, neige *f*

y-coordinate *n Math* ordonnée *f*

yd (*written abbr* **yard**) yd

ye [ji:] **1** *pron Arch or Bible* vous; **ye who weep** vous qui versez des larmes
2 *def art Arch* **ye olde inne** la vieille hostellerie

> **YE OLDE**
>
> Cette expression, qui représente la graphie ancienne de "the old", est souvent employée dans des dénominations pseudo-historiques: certains salons de thé de villes anciennes s'appellent "ye olde tea shoppe", par exemple.

yea [jeɪ] **1** *adv* (**a**) *(yes)* oui; **you know you can say yea or nay to the plan** vous savez bien que vous avez la faculté d'accepter ou de refuser ce projet (**b**) *Arch or Literary (indeed)* voire, vraiment
2 *n (in vote)* oui *m*; **the yeas and nays** les oui et les non, les voix pour et contre

yeah [jeə] *Fam adv (yes)* ouais; *Ironic* **yeah, right!** oui, c'est ça!

year [jɪə(r)] *n* (**a**) *(period of time)* an *m*, année *f*; **this year** cette année; **last year** l'an dernier, l'année dernière; **next year** l'année prochaine; **the year after next** dans deux ans; **year by year** d'année en année; **year after year** année après année; **all (the) year round** (pendant) toute l'année; **year in year out** année après année; **it was five years last Christmas** ça a fait cinq ans à Noël; **we'll have been here five years next Christmas** cela fera cinq ans à Noël que nous sommes là; **after ten years in politics** après dix ans passés dans la politique; **he spent many years working for the same company** il a passé de nombreuses années dans la même société; **in a few years, in a few years' time** dans quelques années; **in ten years, in ten years' time** dans dix ans; **in years to come** dans les années à venir; **in all my years as a social worker** au cours de toutes mes années d'assistante sociale; **I haven't seen her for years** je ne l'ai pas vue depuis des années; **for a few years** pendant quelques années; **I haven't been home for two long years** cela fait deux longues années que je ne suis pas rentré chez moi; **for years and years** pendant des années; **she'll be busy writing her memoirs for years** elle en a pour des années de travail à écrire ses mémoires; **two years ago** il y a deux ans; **that was many years ago** cela remonte à bien des années; **the batteries last (for) years** les piles durent des années; **it took me years to build up the collection** cela m'a demandé des années pour *ou* j'ai mis des années à rassembler cette collection; **he earns over £40,000 a year** il gagne plus de 40 000 livres par an; **it cost me a year's salary** cela m'a coûté un an de salaire; **it costs at least £5,000 a year to run a car** rouler en voiture coûte au moins 5000 livres par an
(**b**) *(in calendar)* an *m*, année *f*; **in the year 1607** en (l'an) 1607; **in the year of grace 1900** en l'an de grâce 1900; *Br* **since the year dot,** *Am* **since year one** depuis une éternité, de tout temps; *Fin* **the year under review** l'exercice écoulé; *Fin* **year ended 31 December 2002** exercice clos le 31 décembre 2002
(**c**) *(in age)* **he is fifteen years old** *or* **of age** il a quinze ans; **the foundations are 4,000 years old** les fondations sont vieilles de 4000 ans; **a man of eighty years** un homme (âgé) de quatre-vingts ans; **a man of your years** un homme de votre âge; **she died in her fiftieth year** elle est morte dans sa cinquantième année; **she's young for her years** elle fait jeune pour son âge, elle ne fait pas son âge; **to be old for one's years** *(of child)* être précoce; *(of adult)* faire plus vieux que son âge; **I'm getting on in years** je prends de l'âge; **the experience put years on/took years off her** l'expérience l'a beaucoup vieillie/rajeunie; **smoking can take years off your life** fumer peut raccourcir la durée de votre vie; **that dress takes years off her** cette robe la fait paraître des années plus jeune *ou* la rajeunit beaucoup; **the carpet is beginning to show its years** la moquette commence à trahir son âge
(**d**) *Br (as student)* année *f*; **he's in the first year** *(at school)* ≃ il est en sixième; *(at college, university)* il est en première année; **first-year students** les étudiants de première année; **all the third year** tous les élèves de troisième année, tous les troisième année; **he was in my year** *(at school)* il était dans ma classe; *(at university)* il est de ma promotion; **she was in the year above/below me** elle était dans la classe au-dessus/en dessous de la mienne
(**e**) *(for wine, coin)* année *f*; **1965 was a good year** 1965 fut une bonne année *ou* un bon millésime
►► *Fin* ***year of assessment*** année *f* d'imposition; *Fin* ***year end*** fin *f* d'exercice

'The Year of Living Dangerously' *Weir* 'L'Année de tous les dangers'

year-2000 compatible, year-2000 compliant *adj Comput* conforme à l'an 2000

yearbook ['jɪəbʊk] *n* annuaire *m*, recueil *m* annuel

> **YEARBOOK**
>
> Aux États-Unis, les écoles, les universités et certaines colonies de vacances ont un "yearbook" qui rassemble photos et adresses, mais aussi des anecdotes, sur l'année ou l'été écoulé.

year-end 1 *adj Acct* de fin d'année, de fin d'exercice
2 *n* **at the year-end** à la fin de l'année, en fin d'année
►► ***year-end accounts*** compte *m* de résultats; ***year-end audit*** vérification *f* comptable de fin d'exercice; ***year-end closing of accounts*** clôture *f* annuelle des livres; ***year-end loss*** perte *f* de fin d'exercice; ***year-end profits*** bénéfices *mpl* de fin d'exercice; ***year-end report*** rapport *m* annuel

yearling ['jɪəlɪŋ] **1** *n Zool* petit *m* d'un an; *Horse-riding* yearling *m*
2 *adj Zool* (âgé) d'un an

yearlong [jɪə'lɒŋ] *adj* de toute une année; **a yearlong drought** une sécheresse qui a duré toute une année

yearly ['jɪəlɪ] (*pl* **yearlies**) **1** *adj* annuel
2 *adv* annuellement
3 *n Press* publication *f* annuelle
►► *Acct* ***yearly accounts*** comptes *mpl* annuels

yearn [jɜ:n] *vi* (**a**) **to yearn for** *(freedom, peace)* aspirer à; *(child, somebody's company)* désirer ardemment; **she yearned for love** *or* **to be loved** elle aspirait à l'amour, elle avait très envie d'être aimée; **to yearn to do sth** brûler de faire qch; **he was yearning to see her again** il brûlait de la revoir; **she yearned to see her home again, she yearned for home** elle avait la nostalgie du pays
(**b**) *Literary (be moved → person)* s'attendrir, s'émouvoir; *(→ heart)* s'attendrir

yearning ['jɜ:nɪŋ] *n (longing)* désir *m* ardent; *(pining)* nostalgie *f*; **he feels a constant yearning to see his old friends** *or* **for his old friends** il n'aspire qu'à une chose, revoir ses vieux amis; **I felt a sudden yearning for company** j'ai eu un soudain désir *ou* besoin de compagnie

yearningly ['jɜ:nɪŋlɪ] *adv (longingly)* avec désir, avec envie; *(piningly)* avec nostalgie; **to look at sth yearningly** couver qch des yeux

year-round *adj (activity)* qui dure toute l'année, sur toute l'année; *(facility)* qui fonctionne toute l'année

yeast [ji:st] **1** *n* levure *f*
2 *vi* mousser
►► *Am* ***yeast cake*** bloc *m* de levure; *Culin* ***yeast extract*** extrait *m* de levure; *Med* ***yeast infection*** *(vaginal thrush)* mycose *f* vaginale; ***yeast plant*** levure *f*

yeasty ['ji:stɪ] (*compar* **yeastier**, *superl* **yeastiest**) *adj* (**a**) *(in taste)* qui a un goût de levure; *(in smell)* à l'odeur de levure (**b**) *(frothy)* écumeux, qui mousse (**c**) *Br (trivial, frivolous)* frivole, superficiel

yecch [jek] *exclam Am Fam* berk!

yegg [jeg] *n Am very Fam (robber)* cambrioleur(euse) *m,f*

yell [jel] **1** *vi* hurler; **to yell at sb** hurler après qn; **to yell about sth** brailler au sujet de qch; **to yell with pain/with laughter** hurler de douleur/de rire; **to yell at the top of one's voice** crier à tue-tête; **if you need me, just yell** si vous avez besoin de moi, vous n'avez qu'à crier
2 *vt (shout out)* hurler; *(proclaim)* clamer, crier; *Fam* **he was yelling his head off** il beuglait comme un veau
3 *n* (**a**) *(shout)* hurlement *m*; **to give a yell of terror** pousser un hurlement de terreur; **I heard a yell outside** j'ai entendu un hurlement dehors
(**b**) *Am (from students, supporters)* cri *m* de ralliement; **the Buffstone yell** *(from students)* le cri de ralliement des étudiants de Buffstone; *(from supporters)* le cri de ralliement des supporters de Buffstone

yelling ['jelɪŋ] *n (UNCOUNT)* hurlements *mpl*; **stop that yelling!** cesse de hurler comme ça!

yellow ['jeləʊ] **1** *adj* (**a**) *(in colour)* jaune; **the papers had gone** *or* **turned yellow with age** les papiers avaient jauni avec le temps; **yellow cab** = taxi new-yorkais
(**b**) *Fam (cowardly)* lâche[❑], trouillard; **he says you're yellow!** il dit que tu n'es qu'un trouillard *ou* qu'un lâche!; **we all have a yellow streak** on est tous un peu lâches; **to turn** *or* **to go yellow** se dégonfler
2 *n* (**a**) *(colour)* jaune *m*
(**b**) *(yolk)* jaune *m* (d'œuf)
(**c**) *(in snooker)* boule *f* jaune
3 *vi* jaunir; **to yellow with age** jaunir avec le temps
4 *vt* jaunir; **newspapers yellowed with age** des journaux jaunis par le temps
►► ***yellow alert*** alerte *f* orange; ***yellow card*** *(in football, rugby)* carton *m* jaune, *Belg* carte *f* jaune; ***yellow fever*** fièvre *f* jaune; *Naut* ***yellow flag*** pavillon *m* de quarantaine; *Bot* ***yellow iris*** iris *m* jaune *ou* de marais, flambe *f* d'eau; *Am* ***yellow jacket*** guêpe *f*; *Cycling* ***yellow jersey*** *(in Tour de France)* maillot *m* jaune; *Am* ***yellow light*** feu *m* orange; ***yellow line*** bande *f* jaune; **to park on a yellow line** ≃ se mettre en stationnement irrégulier; **double yellow line** *or* **yellow lines** double ligne *f* jaune; ***yellow metal*** *(brass)* cuivre *m* jaune, laiton *m*; *(gold)* métal *m* jaune, or *m*; ***yellow ochre*** ocre *f* jaune; ***Yellow Pages***® les Pages *fpl* Jaunes; *Old-fashioned* ***yellow peril, Yellow Peril*** péril *m* jaune; *Bot* ***yellow pimpernel*** lysamique *f*; *Old-fashioned* ***yellow press*** presse *f* à sensation; *Bot* ***yellow rattle*** (rhinanthe *m*) crête-de-coq *f*; *Am* ***yellow ribbon*** = ruban jaune arboré en signe de patriotisme et de solidarité avec ceux qui sont au combat, prisonniers politiques etc; ***the Yellow River*** le fleuve Jaune; ***the Yellow Sea*** la mer Jaune; *Zool* ***yellow wagtail*** bergeronnette *f* printanière flavéole; *Bot* ***yellow water flag*** flambe *f* d'eau

> **YELLOW LINES**
>
> En Grande-Bretagne, une ligne jaune parallèle au trottoir signifie "arrêt autorisé réglementé"; une double ligne jaune signifie "stationnement interdit".

yellowback ['jeləʊ,bæk] *n* = roman bon marché et à sensation du XIXème siècle

yellow-bellied [-'belɪd] *adj Fam* trouillard

yellow-belly (*pl* **yellow-bellies**) *n Fam* trouillard(e) *m,f*

yellow-billed tropic bird *n Orn* paille-en-queue *m* à bec jaune

yellow-dog-contract *n Am Old-fashioned* = contrat qui interdisait à l'employé de se syndiquer

yellowhammer ['jeləʊ,hæmə(r)] *n Orn* (**a**) *(European bunting)* bruant *m* jaune (**b**) *Am (American woodpecker)* colapte *m* doré
►► ***the Yellowhammer State*** = surnom donné à l'Alabama

yellowing ['jeləʊɪŋ] *adj* jaunissant

yellowlegs ['jeləʊlegz] *n Orn* **greater/lesser yellowlegs** grand/petit chevalier *m* à pattes jaunes

yellowish ['jeləʊɪʃ] *adj* jaunâtre, qui tire sur le jaune

yellowness ['jeləʊnɪs] *n* (**a**) *(colour)* couleur *f* jaune; *(of person, complexion)* teint *m* jaune; **judging by the yellowness of her skin** à en juger par son teint jaune (**b**) *Fam (cowardice)* lâcheté[□] *f*, poltronnerie *f*

Yellowstone National Park ['jeləʊstəʊn-] *n* le parc national de Yellowstone

yellowweed ['jeləʊwi:d] *n Bot (ragwort)* jacobée *f*, herbe *f* de Saint-Jacques; *(goldenrod)* verge *f* d'or, solidago *m*

yellowwood ['jeləʊwʊd] *n Bot* (**a**) *(American yellowwood)* cladrastis *m* tinctoria (**b**) *(Cape yellowwood)* podocarpe *m* Thunbergii (**c**) *(yellow sandalwood)* santal *m* citrin (de Cochinchine)

yellowy ['jeləʊɪ] *adj* un peu jaune, qui tire sur le jaune

yelp [jelp] **1** *vi (dog)* japper, glapir; *(person)* crier, glapir; **to yelp in** *or* **with pain** *(dog)* glapir de douleur; *(person)* crier de douleur

2 *n (of dog)* jappement *m*, glapissement *m*; *(of person)* cri *m*, glapissement *m*

yelping ['jelpɪŋ] *n (of dog)* jappements *mpl*, glapissements *mpl*; *(of person)* cris *mpl*, glapissements *mpl*

Yeltsin ['jeltsɪn] *pr n* **Boris Yeltsin** Boris Eltsine

Yemen ['jemən] *n* Yémen *m*; **in (the) Yemen** au Yémen; **the Yemen Arab Republic** la République arabe du Yémen; **the People's Democratic Republic of Yemen** la République démocratique et populaire du Yémen; **the Yemen Republic** la République du Yémen

Yemeni ['jemənɪ], **Yemenite** ['jemənaɪt] **1** *n* Yéménite *mf*

2 *adj* yéménite

3 *comp (embassy, history)* du Yemen

yen [jen] *(pl sense* (**a**) **inv**) *n* (**a**) *(currency)* yen *m* (**b**) *Fam (desire)* envie *f*; **to have a yen for sth/to do sth** avoir très envie de *ou* mourir d'envie de qch/faire qch

Yenisei [,jenɪ'seɪ] *n* **the (River) Yenisei** l'Ienisseï *m*

yeoman ['jəʊmən] *(pl* **yeomen** [-mən]) *n* (**a**) *Hist (small freeholder)* franc-tenancier *m*; *Fig* **to do yeoman service** rendre des services inestimables (**b**) *Br Mil & Hist* soldat *m* du "yeomanry"; **Yeoman of the Guard** yeoman *m* de la garde (**c**) *Mil & Naut (petty officer)* quartier-maître *m*

▸▸ ***yeoman farmer*** franc-tenancier *m*

yeomanry ['jəʊmənrɪ] *n (UNCOUNT)* (**a**) *Hist (small freeholders)* francs-tenanciers *mpl* (**b**) *Br Mil & Hist* = corps de cavalerie composé de volontaires

yep [jep] *exclam Fam* ouais!

yer [jə(r)] *Fam* = **your**

yes [jes] **1** *adv* (**a**) *(gen)* oui; *(in answer to negatives)* si; *(answering knock on door)* oui (entrez); *(answering phone)* allô, oui; *(encouraging a speaker to continue)* oui, et puis?, oui, et alors?; **to say/to vote yes** dire/voter oui; **is it raining? – yes (it is)** est-ce qu'il pleut? – oui; **will you tell her? – yes (I will)** le lui direz-vous? – oui (je vais le faire); **are you hungry? – yes (I am)** avez-vous faim?– oui; **yes? what do you want?** oui? que voulez-vous?; **did they enjoy the cruise? – oh, yes!** ont-ils aimé leur croisière? – oh, oui!; **oh yes?** *(doubtful)* c'est vrai?; **you don't like me, do you? – yes I do!** vous ne m'aimez pas, n'est-ce pas? – mais si (voyons)!; **yes please** oui, s'il vous plaît; **yes of course, yes certainly** oui, bien sûr

(**b**) *(introducing a contrary opinion)* **yes but...** oui *ou* d'accord mais...

(**c**) *(in response to command or call)* oui; **yes, sir** oui *ou* bien, monsieur; **James! – yes?** James! – oui?

(**d**) *(indeed)* en effet, vraiment; **she was rash, yes, terribly rash** elle a été imprudente, vraiment très imprudente

2 *n (person, vote)* **to count the yeses** compter les oui *ou* les votes pour; **there are ten yeses and sixteen noes** il y a dix oui et seize non

3 yes and no *adv* oui et non; **do you like him? – well, yes and no** vous l'aimez bien?– ben, oui et non

▸▸ ***yes vote*** vote *m* pour; **to give a yes vote** voter pour

yeshiva [jə'ʃi:və] *n Rel* yeshiva *f*

yes-man *n Fam* béni-oui-oui *m inv*

yes/no question *n (in survey)* question *f* fermée

yesterday ['jestədɪ] **1** *adv* (**a**) *(the day before today)* hier; **he came yesterday** il est venu hier; **yesterday morning/afternoon** hier matin/après-midi; **a week yesterday, a week ago yesterday,** *Br* **yesterday week** il y a huit jours; **I wasn't born yesterday** je ne suis pas né de la dernière pluie

(**b**) *(in the past)* hier, naguère

2 *n* (**a**) *(day before)* hier *m*; **yesterday was Monday** hier c'était lundi; **yesterday's programme** l'émission d'hier; **the day before yesterday** avant-hier; **it seems like (only) yesterday** c'est comme si c'était hier

(**b**) *(former times)* temps *mpl* passés *ou* anciens; **yesterday's fashions** la mode d'hier *ou* d'autrefois; *Pej* **yesterday's men/designers** les hommes/les designers qui appartiennent au passé; **all our yesterdays** tout notre passé

yesternight ['jestənaɪt] *adv Arch* la nuit dernière, hier soir

yesteryear ['jestjə(r)] *n Formal or Literary* temps *m* jadis; **the heroes of yesteryear** les héros d'antan

yet [jet] **1** *adv* (**a**) *(up to now)* déjà; **is he here yet?** est-il déjà là?; **has he arrived yet?** est-il déjà arrivé?; **have you been to London yet?** êtes-vous déjà allés à Londres?; *Am* **did you go to the zoo yet?** êtes-vous déjà allés au zoo?; **not as yet** pas encore; **as yet unexplored jungle** jungle pas encore explorée

(**b**) *(at the present time)* **not yet** pas encore; **not just yet** pas tout de suite; **she isn't here yet** elle n'est pas encore là; **I haven't finished yet** je n'ai pas encore fini; **they haven't had any answer yet** ils n'ont pas encore (reçu) de réponse; **it isn't time for a break yet** il n'est pas encore l'heure de faire une pause

(**c**) *(in affirmative statements) (still)* encore, toujours; **I have yet to meet her** je ne l'ai pas encore rencontrée; **the manuscripts have yet to be deciphered** les manuscrits n'ont pas encore été déchiffrés; **the best is yet to come** le meilleur est encore à venir *ou* reste à venir; **there are another ten miles to go yet** il reste encore une quinzaine de kilomètres; **I won't be ready for another hour yet** j'en ai encore pour une heure; **they won't be here for another hour yet** ils ne seront pas là avant une heure; **they may yet be found** on peut encore les retrouver, il se peut encore qu'on les retrouve; **they may yet be alive** ils sont peut-être encore *ou* toujours en vie

(**d**) *(with comparatives and superlatives) (even)* encore, même; **yet more expensive** encore plus cher; **yet more snow was expected** on prévoyait encore de la neige; **yet higher interest rates** des taux d'intérêt encore plus élevés; **a life of parties and yet more parties** une existence qui consiste à aller de fête en fête; *Literary* **he is not handsome, nor yet well-dressed** il n'est pas beau, ni même bien habillé

(**e**) *(emphasizing amount, frequency etc)* **yet another bomb** encore une bombe; **yet again** encore une fois

(**f**) *(so far → in present)* jusqu'ici, jusque-là; *(→ in past)* jusque-là; **it's her best play yet** c'est sa meilleure pièce

(**g**) *(despite everything)* après tout, quand même; **she may yet surprise you all** elle va peut-être vous surprendre tous autant que vous êtes; **I'll manage it yet!** j'y arriverai quand même!; **I shall catch him yet!** je finirai bien par l'attraper!

2 *conj (nevertheless)* néanmoins, toutefois; *(however)* cependant, pourtant; *(but)* mais; **they had no income yet they still had to pay taxes** ils n'avaient pas de revenus et pourtant ils devaient payer des impôts; **he was firm yet kind** il était sévère mais juste

yeti ['jetɪ] *n* yéti *m*

yew [ju:] *n* (**a**) *(tree)* if *m* (**b**) *(wood)* (bois d') if *m*

▸▸ ***yew tree*** if *m*

Y-fronts® *npl* slip *m* kangourou

YHA [,waɪeɪtʃ'eɪ] *n Br (abbr* **Youth Hostels Association**) = fédération unie des auberges de jeunesse

yid, Yid [jɪd] *n very Fam* youpin(e) *m,f*, = terme antisémite désignant un juif

Yiddish ['jɪdɪʃ] **1** *n* yiddish *m*

2 *adj* yiddish

yield [ji:ld] **1** *vi* (**a**) *(person → give in)* céder; *(→ surrender)* se rendre; **he refused to yield** il a refusé de céder *ou* de se laisser fléchir; **to yield to** *(argument)* céder *ou* s'incliner devant; *(criticism, force)* céder devant; *(blackmail, demand)* céder à; *(pressure, threat)* céder sous; *(desire, temptation)* succomber à, céder à; **to yield to reason** se rendre à la raison; **I had to yield to them on that point** j'ai dû leur céder sur ce point; **the city yielded after a month-long siege** la ville a capitulé après un mois de siège; **I yield to nobody in my appreciation of his work** personne plus que moi n'apprécie son œuvre; **the countryside has had to yield to suburbia** la campagne a dû reculer au profit de la banlieue

(**b**) *(break, bend → under weight, force)* céder, fléchir; **the ice yielded under his weight** la glace céda sous son poids; **the window catch eventually yielded** le loqueteau de la fenêtre a fini par céder; **the door began to yield under the pressure** la porte a commencé à céder sous la pression

(**c**) *Am Aut* céder le passage *ou* la priorité; **yield** *(sign)* cédez le passage; **yield to pedestrians** *(sign)* priorité aux piétons

(**d**) *Agr (field)* rapporter, rendre; *(crop)* rapporter

2 *vt* (**a**) *(produce, bring in → gen)* produire, rapporter; *(→ land, crops)* produire, rapporter, donner; *(→ results)* donner; *Fin (→ dividend, interest)* rapporter; *(→ income)* créer; **the orchard yielded plentiful amounts of fruit** le verger a produit *ou* a donné des fruits à profusion; **to yield a profit** rapporter *ou* dégager un bénéfice; **the investment bond will yield 11 percent** le bon d'épargne rapportera 11 pour cent; **their research has yielded some interesting results** leur recherche a fourni *ou* a donné quelques résultats intéressants; **these remarks yield an insight into his motives** ces remarques donnent une idée de ses motifs

(**b**) *(relinquish, give up)* céder, abandonner; *Mil & Fig* **to yield ground** céder du terrain; **he was forced to yield control of the party** il a dû céder le contrôle du parti; *Mil* **to yield a position** abandonner une position; **to yield a point to sb** céder à qn sur un point, concéder un point à qn

(**c**) *Am Aut* **to yield right of way** céder la priorité

3 *n* (**a**) *Agr & Ind (output)* rendement *m*, rapport *m*; *(of wheat, fruit)* récolte *f*; *(of crops)* rendement *m*; **high-yield crops** récoltes *fpl* à rendement élevé; **rice yield** récolte *f* de riz; **yield per acre** ≃ rendement *m* à l'hectare

(**b**) *Fin (from investments)* rapport *m*, rendement *m*; *(profit)* bénéfice *m*, bénéfices *mpl*; *(from tax)* recette *f*, rapport *m*; **an 8 percent yield on investments** des investissements qui rapportent 8 pour cent

▸▸ *Fin* ***yield capacity*** productivité *f*; *Fin* ***yield gap*** prime *f* de risque; *Tech* ***yield point*** limite *f* d'élasticité; *Am* ***yield sign*** panneau *m* de priorité

▸**yield up** *vt sep Br* (**a**) *(surrender → town, prisoner)* livrer; **he yielded himself up to the police** il s'est livré à la police (**b**) *(reveal → treasure, secret)* livrer; **divers have made the ocean yield up its treasures** les plongeurs ont fait livrer ses trésors à l'océan

yielding ['ji:ldɪŋ] **1** *adj* (**a**) *(soft → ground)* mou (molle) (**b**) *(flexible → material, metal)* flexible, extensible (**c**) *(person)* complaisant, accommodant; *(character)* docile

2 *n (of town)* reddition *f*; *(of rights, control)* cession *f*

yikes [jaɪks] *exclam Fam* mince!

yikker ['jɪkə(r)] *vi (bird)* piailler

yin [jɪn] *n* **yin and yang** le yin et le yang

yippee [*Br* jɪ'pi:, *Am* 'jɪpɪ] *exclam Fam* hourra!

yips [jɪps] *npl Fam Golf* **the yips** tremblements *mpl* involontaires des mains au putting

Y-junction *n* fourche *f*

ylang-ylang [ɪ,læŋɪ'læŋ] *n Bot* ilang-ilang *m*, ylang-ylang *m*

ylem ['aɪləm] *n Phys* ylem *m*

YMCA [,waɪem,si:'eɪ] *n (abbr* **Young Men's Christian Association**) = association chrétienne de jeunes gens (surtout connue pour ses centres d'hébergement)

yo [jəʊ] *exclam esp Am Fam* salut!

yob [jɒb] *n Br Fam Pej* voyou m, loubard *m*; **the yob culture that prevails in this country today** l'agressivité et l'anti-intellectualisme qui règnent aujourd'hui dans notre pays

yobbish ['jɒbɪʃ] *adj Br Fam* de voyou, de loubard; **it makes you look yobbish** ça te donne l'air d'un voyou *ou* d'un loubard; **don't be so yobbish** arrête de jouer les voyous *ou* les loubards

yobbo ['jɒbəʊ] (*pl* **yobbos**) = **yob**

yod [jɒd] *n* yod *m*

yodel ['jəʊdəl] (*Br pt & pp* **yodelled,** *cont* **yodelling,** *Am pt & pp* **yodeled,** *cont* **yodeling**) **1** *vi* jodler, iodler

2 *n* tyrolienne *f*

yodeller, yodler, *Am* **yodeler, yodler** ['jəʊdələ(r)] *n* jodleur(euse) *m,f*, iodleur(euse) *m,f*

yoga ['jəʊgə] **1** *n* yoga *m*; **to do yoga** faire du yoga

2 *comp (class, teacher)* de yoga

yoghourt, yoghurt [*Br* 'jɒgət, *Am* 'jəʊgərt] *n* yaourt *m*, yogourt *m*, yoghourt *m*

yogi ['jəʊgɪ] *n* yogi *m*

yogic ['jəʊgɪk] *adj (exercise etc)* de yoga

yogini [jəʊ'gɪnɪ] *n* yogini *f*

yogurt = **yoghourt**

yohimbine [jəʊ'hɪmbiːn] *n Pharm* yohimbine *f*

YOI [ˌwaɪəʊ'aɪ] *n Br (abbr* **Young Offenders' Institution**) = centre de détention pour mineurs

yoke [jəʊk] **1** *n* (**a**) *(frame → for hitching oxen)* joug *m*; *(→ for carrying buckets)* joug *m*, palanche *f*

(**b**) *Fig (burden, domination)* joug *m*; **under the yoke of tyranny** sous le joug de la tyrannie; **a country struggling to cast off the yoke of foreign domination** un pays qui lutte pour briser le joug de la domination étrangère

(**c**) *(pair of animals)* attelage *m*, paire *f*

(**d**) *(of dress, skirt, blouse)* empiècement *m*

(**e**) *Constr (for beams)* moise *f*, lien *m*

(**f**) *Literary* **the yoke of marriage** les liens *mpl* du mariage

(**g**) *Ir Fam (thing, object)* truc *m*, machin *m*

2 *vt* (**a**) *(oxen)* atteler; **to yoke (up) oxen/bullocks to a plough** atteler des bouvillons/des bœufs à une charrue

(**b**) *(ideas, qualities)* lier, joindre

yokel ['jəʊkəl] *n Pej* péquenot *m*

Yokohama [ˌjəʊkə'hɑːmə] *n* Yokohama *f*

yolk [jəʊk] *n* (**a**) **(egg) yolk** jaune *m* (d'œuf) (**b**) *Biol* vitellus *m*

►► ***yolk bag, yolk sac*** membrane *f* vitelline

yolkless ['jəʊklɪs] *adj (egg)* nain

Yom Kippur [ˌjɒm'kɪpʊə(r)] *n Rel* Yom Kippour *m inv*

yomp [jɒmp] *vi Br Fam Mil slang* crapahuter

yon [jɒn] *adj Scot & NEng or Arch* ce ...-là; **yon tree** cet arbre-là, l'arbre là-bas

yonder ['jɒndə(r)] *Literary* **1** *adj* **yonder tree** l'arbre là-bas

2 *adv* là-bas; **way over yonder** loin là-bas

yonks [jɒŋks] *n Br Fam* **I haven't been there for yonks** il y a une paie *ou* ça fait un bail que je n'y suis pas allé

yoof [juːf] *adj Br Fam (television, programme)* pour jeunes ▫

yoo-hoo ['juːˌhuː] *exclam* ohé!

YOP [jɒp] *n Br (abbr* **Youth Opportunities Programme**) *(programme)* ≃ TUC *mpl*; *(worker)* ≃ tuciste *mf*

yore [jɔː(r)] *n Arch or Literary* **in days of yore** au temps jadis

yorkie ['jɔːkɪ] = **Yorkshire terrier**

Yorkist ['jɔːkɪst] *n Hist* partisan(e) *m,f* de la maison d'York

Yorks. *(written abbr* **Yorkshire**) Yorkshire *m*

Yorkshire ['jɔːkʃə(r)] *n* le Yorkshire; **the Yorkshire Moors** les Landes *fpl* du Yorkshire

►► ***Yorkshire pudding*** = crêpe épaisse salée traditionnellement servie avec du rôti de bœuf; ***Yorkshire Ripper*** = l'éventreur du Yorkshire, accusé en 1981 du meurtre de treize femmes; ***Yorkshire terrier*** yorkshire-terrier *m*, yorkshire *m*

Yorkshireman ['jɔːkʃəmən] (*pl* **Yorkshiremen** [-mən]) *n (inhabitant)* habitant *m* du Yorkshire; *(native)* natif *m* du Yorkshire

Yoruba ['jɒrʊbə] **1** *n* (**a**) *(person)* Yoruba *mf*, Yorouba *mf* (**b**) *Ling* yoruba *m*, yorouba *m*

2 *adj* yoruba, yorouba

you [juː] *pron* (**a**) *(as plural subject)* vous; *(as singular subject → polite use)* vous; *(→ familiar use)* tu; *(as plural object)* vous; *(as singular object → polite use)* vous; *(→ familiar use)* te; **you didn't ask** vous n'avez pas/tu n'as pas demandé; **don't you dare!** je te le déconseille!; **you and I will go together** vous et moi/toi et moi irons ensemble; **would you like a drink?** voulez-vous boire/veux-tu boire quelque chose?; **you and yours** vous et les vôtres/toi et les tiens; **you there!** vous là-bas/toi là-bas!; **don't you say a word** je t'interdis de dire quoi que ce soit; **did he see you?** est-ce qu'il vous a vu/t'a vu?; **I'll get you some dinner** je vais vous/te préparer à manger; **she gave you the keys** elle vous a donné/elle t'a donné les clés

(**b**) *(after preposition)* vous; *(familiar use)* toi; **all of you** vous tous; **with you** avec vous/toi; **for you** pour vous/toi; **that's men for you** ah! les hommes!; **she gave the keys to you** elle vous a donné/elle t'a donné les clés; **between you and me** entre nous; **now there's a singer for you!** ah, voilà un chanteur!; **now there's a typical politician for you** voilà un politicien type; **now there's manners for you!** ça au moins, c'est quelqu'un de bien élevé/ce sont des gens bien élevés!; *Ironic* en voilà des manières!

(**c**) *(before noun or adjective) very Fam* **you bloody fool!** espèce de crétin!; **you sweetie!** oh, le mignon/la mignonne!; **you Americans are all the same** vous les Américains *ou* vous autres Américains, vous êtes tous pareils

(**d**) *(emphatic use)* vous; *(familiar form)* toi; **you mean they chose you** tu veux dire qu'ils t'ont choisi toi; **you wouldn't do that, would you?** vous ne feriez pas cela/tu ne ferais pas cela, n'est-ce pas?; **silly/lucky (old) you!** quel gros bêta/veinard tu fais!; *Fam* **that jacket/job wasn't you** cette veste/ce travail n'était pas ton style; **just you try!** essaye un peu pour voir!

(**e**) *(impersonal use)* **you never know** on ne sait jamais; **a hot bath does you a world of good** un bon bain chaud vous fait un bien immense; **you take the first on the left** prenez la première à droite

you-all *pron Am Fam (in southern states)* vous (tous)

you'd [juːd] (**a**) = **you had** (**b**) = **you would**

you-know-what *n Fam Euph* **does he know about the you-know-what?** est-ce qu'il est au courant du... tu vois de quoi je veux parler *ou* ce que je veux dire?; **they were doing you-know-what** ils étaient en train de... tu vois ce que je veux dire?

you-know-who *n Fam Euph* qui tu sais/qui vous savez

you'll [juːl] = **you will**

young [jʌŋ] (*compar* **younger** ['jʌŋgə(r)], *superl* **youngest** ['jʌŋgɪst]) **1** *adj* (**a**) *(in age, style, ideas → person, clothes)* jeune; **the young men and women of today** les jeunes gens et les jeunes femmes d'aujourd'hui; **a young woman** une jeune femme; **young people** les jeunes *mpl*, la jeunesse *f*; **the younger generation** la jeune génération; **families with young children** les familles qui ont des enfants en bas âge; **my younger brother** mon frère cadet, mon petit frère; **I'm ten years younger than she is** j'ai dix ans de moins qu'elle; **I'm not as young as I was!** je n'ai plus (mes) vingt ans!; **he is young for such responsibility** il est bien jeune pour de telles responsabilités; **you're only young once!** la jeunesse ne dure qu'un temps!; **in my younger days** dans ma jeunesse, quand j'étais jeune; *Br* **how is young Christopher?** comment va le jeune Christopher?; **the young Mr Ford, Mr Ford the younger** le jeune M. Ford, M. Ford fils; **now listen here young man!** écoutez-moi bien, jeune homme!; *Old-fashioned* **her young man** son petit ami, son amoureux; *Old-fashioned* **his young lady** sa petite amie, son amoureuse; **young lady!** mademoiselle!; **she's quite a young lady now** c'est une vraie jeune fille maintenant; **what do you have to say for yourself, young lady?** qu'avez-vous à dire, mademoiselle?

(**b**) *(youthful)* jeune; **he is young for forty-five** il fait jeune pour quarante-cinq ans; **she is a young forty-five** elle a quarante-cinq ans, mais elle ne les fait pas; **he's young for his age** il est jeune pour son âge, il ne fait pas son âge; **to be young at heart** avoir la jeunesse du cœur

(**c**) *(recent → grass, plant)* nouveau(elle); *(→ wine)* jeune, vert; *Geol (→ rock formation)* jeune, récent; **a young country/company** un pays/une société de création récente

2 *npl* (**a**) *(people)* **the young** les jeunes (gens) *mpl*, la jeunesse; **a game suitable for young and old alike** un jeu pour les jeunes et les moins jeunes

(**b**) *(of animal)* petits *mpl*; **a lioness and her young** une lionne et ses petits; **to be with young** *(animal)* être pleine *ou* grosse

►► ***young blood*** *(new attitudes, ideas, people)* sang *m* nouveau *ou* neuf; *Br Pol* ***Young Conservatives*** jeunes conservateurs *mpl*; *Br* ***Young Offenders' Institution*** = centre de détention pour mineurs; *Hist* ***the Young Pretender*** le jeune Prétendant *(surnom de Charles Stuart, l'un des deux prétendants au trône)*; *Hist & Fig* ***Young Turk*** jeune-turc (jeune-turque) *m,f*

youngish ['jʌŋɪʃ] *adj* plutôt jeune

young-looking *adj* d'allure jeune

Young's modulus *n Tech* module *m* de Young, module *m* d'élasticité

youngster ['jʌŋstə(r)] *n* (**a**) *(young person)* jeune *mf* (**b**) *Horseriding* jeune cheval *m*

your [jɔː(r)] *adj* (**a**) *(with singular possession → familiar use)* ton (ta); *(→ familiar plural, polite use)* votre; *(with plural possession → familiar use)* tes; *(→ familiar plural, polite use)* vos; **your book** votre/ton livre; **your car** votre/ta voiture; **your books** vos/tes livres; **your father and mother** votre père et votre mère/ton père et ta mère; **I object to your visiting the children** je m'oppose à ce que tu rendes visite aux enfants

(**b**) *(with parts of body, clothes)* **don't put your hands in your pockets** ne mets pas tes mains dans les poches; **why are you scratching your head?** pourquoi est-ce que tu te grattes la tête?; **hold on to your hat!** tenez-bien votre chapeau!; **I think you've broken your finger** je crois que vous vous êtes cassé le doigt; **does your wrist hurt?** est-ce que tu as mal au poignet?

(**c**) *(emphatic form)* **is this your book or his?** est-ce que c'est votre livre ou le sien?; **oh it's YOUR book, is it?** ah, c'est à toi ce livre!; **that's YOUR problem** c'est TON problème

(**d**) *(impersonal use)* **if you don't stand up for your rights, no one else will** si vous ne défendez pas vos droits vous-même, personne ne le fera à votre place; **swimming is good for your heart and lungs** la natation est un bon exercice pour le cœur et les poumons; **where are your Churchills and your De Gaulles when you need them?** où sont vos Churchill et vos De Gaulle quand vous avez besoin d'eux?; **it's not a film for your average cinema goer** ce n'est pas un film pour n'importe quel public; **I like your London buses** j'aime bien les bus que vous avez à Londres

(**e**) *(in titles)* **Your Highness** Votre Majesté *(à un roi, une reine, un prince ou une princesse)*; **Your Holiness** Très Saint Père; **Your Honour** Votre Honneur; **Your Majesty** Votre Majesté *(à un roi ou une reine uniquement)*

you're [jɔː(r)] = **you are**

yours [jɔːz] *pron* (**a**) *(replacing singular possession → familiar use)* le tien (la tienne) *m,f*; *(→ familiar plural, polite use)* le vôtre (la vôtre) *m,f*; *(replacing plural possession → familiar use)* les tiens (les tiennes) *mpl, fpl*; *(→ familiar plural, polite use)* les vôtres *mfpl*; **is this book yours?** est-ce que ce livre est à vous/toi?; **is this car yours?** c'est votre/ta voiture?; **are these books yours?** ces livres sont-ils à vous/toi?; **is he a friend of yours?** est-ce un de vos/tes amis?; **yours is an unenviable task** votre tâche est peu enviable; **can't you control that wretched dog of yours?** vous ne pouvez pas retenir votre satané chien?; **the bathroom's all yours** la salle de bains est libre maintenant; **can I use your telephone? – it's all yours** est-ce que je peux utiliser ton téléphone? – vas-y

(**b**) *(up to you)* **it is not yours to decide** ce n'est pas à vous *ou* il ne vous appartient pas de décider

(**c**) *Br Fam (in offering drinks)* **what's yours?** qu'est-ce que vous buvez/tu bois?, qu'est-ce que je vous/te sers?

(**d**) *Fam (your house, flat)* chez vous/chez toi, votre/ta maison; **let's go to yours** allons chez vous/chez toi

(**e**) *(in letter)* **yours, Peter** ≃ bien à vous *ou* à bientôt, Peter; **yours sincerely, yours faithfully** *(in letters)* ≃ je vous prie d'agréer, Madame/Monsieur, l'expression de mes sentiments distingués

yourself [jɔː'self] *(pl* **yourselves** [-'selvz]) *pron* (**a**) *(personally → polite use)* vous-même; *(→ familiar use)* toi-même; **do it yourself** faites-le vous-même/fais-le toi-même; **do it yourselves** faites-le vous-mêmes; **you've kept the best seats for yourselves** vous avez gardé les meilleures places pour vous; **sort it out among yourselves** débrouillez-vous entre vous; **see for yourself** tu n'as qu'à voir par toi-même; **tell us something about yourself** parle-nous de toi/parlez-nous de vous; **did you come by yourself?** vous êtes venu tout seul?/tu es venu tout seul?; **did you mend the fuse (by) yourself?** vous avez remplacé le fusible tout seul?/tu as remplacé le fusible tout seul?; **did you make it yourself?** l'avez-vous fait vous-même?/l'as-tu fait toi-même?; **you don't look quite yourself** vous n'avez pas l'air dans votre assiette/tu n'as pas l'air dans ton assiette; **just be yourself** sois naturel/soyez naturel

(**b**) *(reflexive use)* **did you hurt yourself?** est-ce que vous vous êtes/tu t'es fait mal?; **did you enjoy yourself?** est-ce que c'était bien?; **you were talking to yourself** tu parlais tout seul/vous parliez tout seul; **speak for yourself!** parle pour toi!; **just look at yourself!** regarde-toi donc! **you don't seem yourself today** tu n'as pas l'air dans ton assiette aujourd'hui/vous n'avez pas l'air dans votre assiette aujourd'hui

(**c**) *(emphatic use)* **you told me yourself, you yourself told me** vous me l'avez dit vous-même, c'est vous-même qui me l'avez dit/tu me l'as dit toi-même, c'est toi-même qui me l'as dit; **you must have known yourself that they wouldn't accept** vous-même, vous auriez dû savoir qu'ils n'accepteraient pas/toi-même, tu aurais dû savoir qu'ils n'accepteraient pas

(**d**) *(impersonal use)* **you have to know how to look after yourself in the jungle** dans la jungle, il faut savoir se défendre tout seul *ou* se débrouiller soi-même; **you're supposed to help yourself** on est censé se servir soi-même

yours truly *pron Fam* bibi, mézigue

youth [juːθ] *(pl* **youths** [juːðz]) **1** *n* (**a**) *(young age)* jeunesse *f*; **in my youth** dans ma jeunesse, quand j'étais jeune; **in his early youth** dans sa première jeunesse; **he is no longer in his first youth** il n'est plus de la première jeunessse; **the optimism of youth** l'optimisme de la jeunesse; *Prov* **youth will have its way** *or* **its fling** il faut bien que jeunesse se passe

(**b**) *(young man)* adolescent *m*, jeune *m*

2 *npl (young people)* **the youth of today** les jeunes *mpl ou* la jeunesse d'aujourd'hui; **the youth of the nation** la jeunesse du pays

3 *comp* **to go youth hostelling** passer ses vacances en auberges de jeunesse

▸▸ *Br* ***youth club*** ≃ maison *f* des jeunes; ***youth culture*** culture *f* des jeunes; *Br* ***youth custody*** détention *f* de mineurs, éducation *f* surveillée; *Br* ***youth custody centre*** = centre de détention pour jeunes délinquants (jusqu'en 1988) *(aujourd'hui appelé "Young Offenders' Institution")*; ***youth hostel*** auberge *f* de jeunesse; ***youth hosteller*** habitué(e) *m,f* des auberges de jeunesse; ***Youth Hostels Association*** association *f* des auberges de jeunesse; *Mktg* ***youth market*** marché *m* de la jeunesse; *Mktg* ***youth marketing*** marketing *m* de la classe des jeunes, marketing *m* des juniors; ***youth orchestra*** orchestre *m* de jeunes; ***youth worker*** éducateur(trice) *m,f*

youthful ['juːθfʊl] *adj* (**a**) *(young → person)* jeune; *(→ appearance)* d'allure jeune; **to look youthful** avoir l'air jeune; **youthful good looks** *(of men)* air *m* de jeune homme; **he is a youthful fifty-two** il est jeune pour ses cinquante-deux ans (**b**) *(typical of youth → idea, error)* de jeunesse; *(→ enthusiasm, expectations, attitude)* juvénile; **youthful good humour** bonne humeur *f* juvénile *ou* propre à la jeunesse

youthfully ['juːθfʊlɪ] *adv (dressed)* jeune; **she's youthfully slim** elle a une silhouette de jeune fille

youthfulness ['juːθfʊlnɪs] *n (of person)* jeunesse *f*; *(of appearance)* allure *f* jeune; *(of mind, ideas)* jeunesse *f*, fraîcheur *f*

you've [juːv] = **you have**

yowl [jaʊl] **1** *vi (cat)* miauler (fort); *(dog, person)* hurler; **to yowl in pain** *(cat)* miauler de douleur; *(dog, person)* hurler de douleur

2 *n (of cat)* miaulement *m* (déchirant); *(of dog, person)* hurlement *m*

yo-yo ['jəʊjəʊ] *(pl* **yo-yos**) **1** *n* (**a**) *(toy)* Yo-Yo® *m inv*; *Fam* **he was jumping up and down like a yo-yo** il sautait sur place comme s'il était monté sur un ressort; *Fam* **I've been up and down the stairs like a yo-yo all day** je n'ai pas arrêté de monter et de descendre l'escalier toute la journée (**b**) *Am very Fam (fool)* couillon *m*

2 *vi Fam* fluctuer

yr *(written abbr* **year**) année *f*

YT *(written abbr* **Yukon Territory**) territoire *m* du Yukon

YTS [ˌwaɪtiː'es] *n Br (abbr* **Youth Training Scheme**) *(programme)* = programme gouvernemental britannique d'insertion des jeunes dans la vie professionnelle; *(person)* = personne participant au programme "YTS"

ytterbium [ɪ'tɜːbɪəm] *n Chem* ytterbium *m*

yttriferous [ɪ'trɪfərəs] *adj Miner* yttrifère

yttrium ['ɪtrɪəm] *n Chem* yttrium *m*

yuan [juː'ɑːn] *(pl* **inv**) *n* yuan *m*

Yucatan [ˌjuːkə'tɑːn] *n* le Yucatan

Yucatecan [ˌjuːkə'tekən] *adj* yucatèque

yucca ['jʌkə] *n* yucca *m*

yuck [jʌk] *exclam Fam* berk!, beurk!

yucky ['jʌkɪ] *(compar* **yuckier**, *superl* **yuckiest**) *adj Fam* dégueulasse

Yugoslav ['juːgəʊˌslɑːv] **1** *n* Yougoslave *mf*

2 *adj* yougoslave

Yugoslavia [ˌjuːgəʊ'slɑːvɪə] *n Formerly* Yougoslavie *f*; **in Yugoslavia** en Yougoslavie

Yugoslavian [ˌjuːgəʊ'slɑːvɪən] **1** *n* Yougoslave *mf*

2 *adj* yougoslave

yuk = **yuck**

yukky *(compar* **yukkier**, *superl* **yukkiest**) = **yucky**

Yukon ['juːkɒn] *n* **the Yukon (Territory)** le territoire du Yukon; **in the Yukon (Territory)** dans le territoire du Yukon

yule, Yule [juːl] *n Arch or Literary* Noël *m*

▸▸ ***yule log*** bûche *f* de Noël

yuletide, Yuletide ['juːltaɪd] *Literary* **1** *n* (époque *f* de) Noël *m*; **at yuletide** à Noël

2 *comp (greetings, festivities)* de Noël

yum, [jʌm], **yummy** ['jʌmɪ] *(compar* **yummier**, *superl* **yummiest**) *Fam* **1** *adj (food)* succulent ❑, délicieux ❑

2 *exclam* miam-miam!

yum-yum **1** *exclam Fam* miam-miam!

2 *n Br (cake)* chichi *m*

Yunnan [juː'næn] *n* Yunnan *m*

yup [jʌp] *adv Am Fam* ouais

yuppie ['jʌpɪ] *(abbr* **young upwardly mobile professional**) **1** *n* yuppie *mf*, ≃ jeune cadre *m* dynamique

2 *adj (club)* pour jeunes cadres dynamiques; *(lifestyle, neighbourhood)* de yuppies

▸▸ ***yuppie flu*** encéphalomyélite *f* myalgique

yuppiedom ['jʌpɪdəm] *n (state)* vie *f* de yuppie; *(milieu)* le milieu yuppie

yuppify ['jʌpɪfaɪ] *(pt & pp* **yuppified**) *vt* **to become yuppified** s'embourgeoiser

yuppy *(pl* **yuppies**) = **yuppie**

YWCA [ˌwaɪdʌbəljuːˌsiː'eɪ] *n (abbr* **Young Women's Christian Association**) = association chrétienne de jeunes filles (surtout connue pour ses centres d'hébergement)

Z

Z, z [*Br* zed, *Am* ziː] *n (letter)* Z, z *m inv*; **two z's** deux z; **Z for zebra** ≃ Z comme Zoé; *Am Fam* **to get** *or* **score some z's** faire une petite somme
►► *Ind & Math* ***Z chart*** = table statistique de données journalières, hebdomadaires et mensuelles pour une année
zabaglione [ˌzæbælɪ'əʊnɪ] *n Culin* sabayon *m*
Zachariah [ˌzækə'raɪə], **Zacharias** [ˌzækə'raɪəs], **Zachary** ['zækərɪ] *pr n Bible* Zacharie
Zagreb ['zɑːgreb] *n* Zagreb *m*
Zaïre [zɑː'ɪə(r)] *n* Zaïre *m*; **in Zaïre** au Zaïre
Zaïrean [zɑː'ɪərɪən] **1** *n* Zaïrois(e) *m,f*
2 *adj* zaïrois
Zaïrese [ˌzɑːɪə'riːz] **1** *n* Zaïrois(e) *m,f*
2 *adj* zaïrois
Zambesi, Zambezi [zæm'biːzɪ] *n* **the Zambesi** le Zambèze
►► *Zool* ***Zambesi shark*** requin *m* bouledogue
Zambia ['zæmbɪə] *n* Zambie *f*; **in Zambia** en Zambie
Zambian ['zæmbɪən] **1** *n* Zambien(enne) *m,f*
2 *adj* zambien
3 *comp (embassy)* de Zambie; *(history)* de la Zambie
zamia ['zeɪmɪə] *n Bot* zamia *m*, zamier *m*
zanily ['zeɪnɪlɪ] *adv Fam* d'une manière loufoque
zaniness ['zeɪnɪnɪs] *n Fam* loufoquerie *f*
zany ['zeɪnɪ] (*compar* **zanier,** *superl* **zaniest,** *pl* **zanies**) *Fam* **1** *adj* farfelu, loufoque
2 *n Theat* bouffon *m*, zani *m*, zanni *m*
Zanzibar [ˌzænzɪ'bɑː(r)] *n* Zanzibar *m*; **in Zanzibar** au Zanzibar
zap [zæp] (*pt & pp* **zapped,** *cont* **zapping**) *Fam* **1** *vi* (**a**) *(go quickly)* courir; **I'll zap over to see her** je file la voir, je vais faire un saut chez elle
(**b**) *(send quickly)* **zap it in the microwave** passe-le vite fait au micro-ondes; **we'll zap it across to you by courier** on vous l'enverra *ou* expédiera vite fait par coursier
(**c**) *TV* zapper; **stop zapping!** arrête de zapper!
2 *vt* (**a**) *(destroy by bombing → town)* ravager ☐, bombarder ☐; *(→ target)* atteindre ☐
(**b**) *(kill → victim)* tuer ☐, descendre; *(→ in video game)* éliminer
(**c**) *Comput (display, data)* effacer, supprimer; *(file)* écraser
3 *n (energy)* pêche *f*, punch *m*
4 *exclam* vlan!
►**zap up** *vt sep Fam (make more exciting)* **to zap up one's style** rendre son style plus coloré *ou* plus vivant; **to zap up the colour scheme** *(in house etc)* rehausser les couleurs
Zapotec ['zæpəʊtek] **1** *adj* zapotèque
2 *n* Zapotèque *mf*
zapped [zæpt] *adj Fam (exhausted)* crevé, claqué
zapper ['zæpə(r)] *n Fam (for TV)* télécommande ☐ *f*
zapping ['zæpɪŋ] *n (changing TV channels)* zapping *m*
zappy ['zæpɪ] (*compar* **zappier,** *superl* **zappiest**) *adj Br Fam* qui a la pêche, plein de punch; **a zappy little car** une petite voiture nerveuse
Zarathustra [ˌzærə'θuːstrə] *pr n* Zarathoustra

'Thus Spake Zarathustra' *Nietzsche, Richard Strauss* 'Ainsi parlait Zarathoustra'

Zarathustrian [ˌzærə'θuːstrɪən] **1** *adj* zoroastrien
2 *n* zoroastrien(enne) *m,f*
zarzuela [zɑː'zweɪlə] *n Literature* zarzuela *f*
z-axis *n Math* axe *m* des Z
ZBB [*Br* ˌzedbiː'biː, *Am* ˌziːbiː'biː] *n Fin* (*abbr* **zero-base budgeting**) BBZ *m*
Z-bed *n Br* lit *m* pliant
Z-car *n Br Old-fashioned* voiture *f* pie *(de la police)*
zeal [ziːl] *n* zèle *m*, ferveur *f*, ardeur *f*; **full of zeal** plein de zèle; **she undertook the work with great zeal** elle a entrepris le travail avec beaucoup de zèle; **political/religious zeal** ferveur politique/religieuse
Zealand ['ziːlənd] *n* Zélande *f*
Zealot ['zelət] *n Hist* zélote *mf*
zealot ['zelət] *n (fanatic)* fanatique *mf*, zélateur(-trice) *m,f*; **religious zealots** fanatiques *mpl* religieux
Zealotism ['zelətɪzəm] *n Hist* zélotisme *m*
zealotry ['zelətrɪ] *n* fanatisme *m*
zealous ['zeləs] *adj (worker, partisan)* zélé, actif; *(opponent)* zélé, acharné; **she is zealous in carrying out her duties** elle fait ce qu'elle a à faire avec beaucoup de zèle *ou* d'ardeur
zealously ['zeləslɪ] *adv* avec zèle *ou* ardeur
Zebedee ['zebədiː] *pr n Bible* Zébédée
zebra [*Br* 'zebrə, *Am* 'ziːbrə] (*pl* **inv** *or* **zebras**) *n* (**a**) *(animal)* zèbre *m* (**b**) *Am Fam (in American football)* arbitre ☐ *m*
►► *Br* ***zebra crossing*** passage *m* clouté *ou* pour piétons
zebroid ['ziːbrɔɪd] *n* zébroïde *m*, zébrule *m*
zebu ['ziːbuː] *n Zool* zébu *m*
Zechariah [ˌzekə'raɪə] *pr n Bible* Zacharie
zed [zed] *n Br* (lettre *f*) z *m inv*; *Fam* **to catch some zeds** piquer un roupillon
zedoary ['zedəʊərɪ] *n Bot* zédoaire *m*
zee [ziː] *Am* = **zed**
Zeeland ['ziːlənd] *n* Zélande *f*
zeitgeist, Zeitgeist ['zaɪtgaɪst] *n* esprit *m* de l'époque
Zen [zen] **1** *n* zen *m*
2 *adj* zen *(inv)*
►► ***Zen Buddhism*** les préceptes *mpl* du zen, le bouddhisme zen; ***Zen Buddhist*** bouddhiste *mf* zen
zenana [ze'nɑːnə] *n* zénana *m*, harem *m*
►► *Tex* ***zenana cloth*** zénana *m*
zenith [*Br* 'zenɪθ, *Am* 'ziːnəθ] *n* (**a**) *Astron* zénith *m*; **the sun at its zenith** le soleil en son zénith
(**b**) *(peak)* zénith *m*; **at the zenith of his fame** à l'apogée *ou* au sommet de sa gloire; **she had reached the zenith of her career** elle était au sommet *ou* au faîte *ou* à l'apogée de sa carrière; **when the British Empire was at its zenith** lorsque l'empire britannique était à son apogée, à l'apogée de l'empire britannique
zenithal [*Br* 'zenɪθəl, *Am* 'ziːnəθəl] *adj Astron* zénithal
►► *Geog* ***zenithal projection*** projection *f* azimutale
Zeno ['ziːnəʊ] *pr n Antiq* Zénon
zeolite ['ziːəlaɪt] *n Miner* zéolite *f*
zephyr ['zefə(r)] *n* (**a**) *Literary (wind)* zéphyr *m* (**b**) *Tex* zéphyr *m*
Zephyrus ['zefɪrəs] *n Myth* Zéphyr *m*
zeppelin ['zepəlɪn] *n* zeppelin *m*
zero ['zɪərəʊ] (*pl* **zeros** *or* **zeroes**) **1** *n* (**a**) *Math* zéro *m*
(**b**) *(in temperature)* zéro *m*; **40 below zero** 40 degrés au-dessous de zéro, moins 40
(**c**) *Sport* **to win three zero** gagner trois (à) zéro
(**d**) *(nothing, nought)* **our chances have been put at zero** on considère que nos chances sont nulles
(**e**) *Fam (person)* nul (nulle) *m,f*
2 *comp (altitude)* zéro *(inv)*; *(visibility)* nul; **the project has zero interest for me** le projet ne présente aucun intérêt pour moi; **he's got zero intelligence/charm** il n'a aucune intelligence/aucun charme
3 *vt (instrument)* régler sur zéro
►► *Fin* ***zero coupon bond*** obligation *f* à coupon zéro; ***zero gravity*** apesanteur *f*; *Agr* ***zero grazing*** = système d'élevage intensif dans lequel les animaux enfermés sont nourris à l'herbe; ***zero growth*** croissance *f* zéro; ***zero hour*** heure *f* H; *Pol* ***the zero option*** l'option *f* zéro; ***zero sum*** somme *f* nulle; **a zero sum game** un match nul; ***zero tolerance*** = politique d'intransigeance à l'égard de toute infraction à la loi ou au règlement; **to have a zero tolerance approach to crime/to vagrancy** ne rien tolérer *ou* ne rien laisser passer en matière de délinquance/de vagabondage
►**zero in on** *vt insep* (**a**) *Mil (aim for)* se diriger *ou* piquer droit sur; *(aim weapon at)* régler le tir sur; *Fam* **the police zeroed in on the terrorists' hideout** la police a investi la cachette des terroristes (**b**) *Fam (concentrate on)* se concentrer sur ☐ (**c**) *Fam (pinpoint)* mettre le doigt sur
zero-base budgeting *n Fin* budget *m* base zéro, budgétisation *f* base zéro
zeroed ['zɪərəʊd] *adj (milometer)* à zéro
zeroing ['zɪərəʊɪŋ] *n Comput* initialisation *f* du compteur
zero-rated *adj* **zero-rated (for VAT)** exempt de TVA, exonéré de TVA; **in Britain, books are zero-rated** en Grande-Bretagne, les livres sont exempts *ou* exonérés de TVA
zero-rating *n Fin* taux *m* zéro
zeroth ['zɪərəʊθ] *adj Math* zéro
zest [zest] **1** *n* (**a**) *(piquancy)* piquant *m*, saveur *f*; **to add zest to a situation** ajouter du sel *ou* du piquant à une situation (**b**) *(enthusiasm)* enthousiasme *m*, entrain *m*; **with zest** *(fight etc)* avec élan, avec entrain; *(eat)* avec appétit, de bon appétit; **zest for life** joie *f* de vivre (**c**) *Culin (of orange, lemon)* zeste *m*
2 *vt (orange, lemon)* zester
zester [zestə(r)] *n* zesteur *m*
zestful ['zestfʊl] *adj (person)* enthousiaste; *(performance)* plein de vie
zeta ['ziːtə] *n* zêta *m*
zeugma ['zjuːgmə] *n Ling* zeugma *m*, zeugme *m*
zeugmatic [zjuːg'mætɪk] *adj Ling (sentence)* qui contient un zeugma
Zeus [zjuːs] *pr n Myth* Zeus
ziff [zɪf] *n Austr & NZ Fam (beard)* barbichette *f*
ziggurat ['zɪgʊræt] *n Archeol* ziggourat *f*
zigzag ['zɪgzæg] (*pt & pp* **zigzagged,** *cont* **zigzagging**) **1** *vi (walker, vehicle)* avancer en zigzags, zigzaguer; *(road)* zigzaguer; *(river)* serpenter; **to zigzag across/up the road** traverser/monter la rue en zigzaguant; **the road zigzags through the valley** la route traverse la vallée en zigzaguant *ou* serpente à travers la vallée
2 *n (in design)* zigzag *m*; *(on road)* lacet *m*; *(in river)* boucle *f*
3 *adj (path, line)* en zigzag; *(pattern)* à zigzag, à zigzags; **the path follows a zigzag course across the fields** le chemin traverse les champs en zigzaguant
4 *adv* en zigzag
zilch [zɪltʃ] *n Fam* que dalle
zillion ['zɪlɪən] (*pl* **inv** *or* **zillions**) *Fam* **1** *n* foultitude *f*; **they earn/cost zillions** ils gagnent/coûtent des milliards; **we got zillions of replies**

nous avons eu des tas et des tas *ou* des tonnes de réponses

 2 *adj* **for a zillion reasons** pour des tas et des tas *ou* une foultitude de raisons

Zimbabwe [zɪm'bɑːbwɪ] *n* Zimbabwe *m*; **in Zimbabwe** au Zimbabwe

Zimbabwean [zɪm'bɑːbwɪən] **1** *n* Zimbabwéen(-enne) *m,f*

 2 *adj* zimbabwéen

 3 *comp (embassy, history)* du Zimbabwe

Zimmer (frame)® ['zɪmə(r)-] *n* déambulateur *m*

zinc [zɪŋk] **1** *n* zinc *m*

 2 *comp (chloride, sulphate, sulphide)* de zinc; *(ointment)* à l'oxyde de zinc

 ►► ***zinc blende*** blende *f*; ***zinc ointment*** pommade *f* à l'oxyde de zinc; ***zinc oxide*** oxyde *m* de zinc; ***zinc white*** blanc *m* de zinc, oxyde *m* de zinc

zinciferous [zɪŋ'kɪfərəs] *adj* zincifère

zincite ['zɪŋkaɪt] *n Geol* zincite *f*

zinckiferous = **zinciferous**

zincography [zɪŋ'kɒgrəfɪ] *n* zincographie *f*, photogravure *f* sur zinc; **to reproduce by zincography** zincographier

zineb ['zɪnəb] *n Agr* zinèbe *m*

Zinfandel ['zɪnfəndel] *n* zinfandel *m*

zing [zɪŋ] *Fam* **1** *onomat* zim!

 2 *n* (**a**) *(of bullet)* sifflement *m*

 (**b**) *(of person)* punch *m*; **this drink's got real zing!** cette boisson est vraiment costaud!

 3 *vi* (**a**) *(projectile)* siffler, passer dans un sifflement; **the bullet zinged past me** la balle est passée à côté de moi dans un sifflement

 (**b**) *Am Fam (tease)* vanner, chambrer

zinger ['zɪŋə(r)] *n Am Fam* (**a**) *(pointed remark)* pique *f*, vanne *f* (**b**) *(impressive thing)* **it was a real zinger** c'était dingue; **a real zinger of a black eye** un œil au beurre noir pas croyable

zinkiferous = **zinciferous**

zinnia ['zɪnɪə] *n Bot* zinnia *m*

Zion ['zaɪɒn] *n* Sion

Zionism ['zaɪənɪzəm] *n* sionisme *m*

Zionist ['zaɪənɪst] **1** *n* sioniste *mf*

 2 *adj* sioniste

zip [zɪp] *(pt & pp* **zipped**, *cont* **zipping**) **1** *n* (**a**) *(fastener)* fermeture *f* Éclair® *ou* à glissière

 (**b**) *(sound of bullet)* sifflement *m*

 (**c**) *Fam (liveliness)* vivacité *f*, entrain *m*; **put some zip into it!** mets-y du nerf!; **your style needs more zip** ton style a besoin d'un peu plus de punch

 (**d**) *Am (zip code)* code *m* postal

 (**e**) *Am Fam (nothing)* rien *m*

 2 *vi* (**a**) *(with zip fastener)* **to zip open/shut** s'ouvrir/se fermer à l'aide d'une fermeture Éclair® *ou* à glissière

 (**b**) *Fam (verb of movement)* **to zip past** passer comme une flèche; **to zip upstairs** monter l'escalier quatre à quatre; **she zipped out to get a paper** elle a filé chercher un journal; **I zipped through the book/my work** j'ai lu ce livre/j'ai fait mon travail en quatrième vitesse

 (**c**) *(arrow, bullet)* siffler; **bullets zipped past us** des balles sifflaient à nos oreilles

 3 *vt* (**a**) *(with zip fastener)* **to zip sth open/shut** fermer/ouvrir la fermeture Éclair® *ou* à glissière de qch; **I zipped myself into my sleeping bag** je me suis mis dans mon sac de couchage et j'ai tiré la fermeture

 (**b**) *Fam (do quickly)* **I'll just zip this cake into the oven** je glisse en vitesse ce gâteau dans le four

 (**c**) *Fam* **to zip it** *(be quiet)* la fermer, la boucler; **zip it!** la ferme!

 (**d**) *Comput (file)* zipper, compresser

 ►► *Am* ***zip code, ZIP code*** code *m* postal; *Br* ***zip fastener*** fermeture *f* Éclair® *ou* à glissière; *Am Fam* ***zip gun*** pistolet *m* rudimentaire *(à ressort)*

►**zip on 1** *vt sep* attacher (avec une fermeture à glissière)

 2 *vi* s'attacher avec une fermeture Éclair® *ou* à glissière

►**zip up 1** *vt sep* (**a**) *(clothing, sleeping bag)* fermer avec la fermeture Éclair® *ou* à glissière (**b**) *(of person)* fermer la fermeture Éclair® *ou* à glissière de; **zip me up** remonte ma fermeture

 2 *vi (dress)* se fermer avec une fermeture Éclair® *ou* à glissière

Zip® **disk** *n Comput* cartouche *f* Zip®

Zip® **drive** *n Comput* lecteur *m* Zip®

zip-on *adj (flap, hood)* qui s'attache avec une fermeture Éclair® *ou* à glissière

zipper ['zɪpə(r)] *Am* = **zip** *n* (**a**)

zipping ['zɪpɪŋ] *n (with tape)* avance *f* rapide

zippy ['zɪpɪ] *(compar* **zippier**, *superl* **zippiest**) *adj Fam (person)* vif; *(car)* nerveux

zip-up *adj (bag, coat)* à fermeture Éclair®, zippé

zircon ['zɜːkɒn] *n Miner* zircon *m*

zirconia [zɜː'kəʊnɪə] *n Chem* zircone *f*

zirconite ['zɜːkənaɪt] *n Miner* zirconite *f*

zirconium [zɜː'kəʊnɪəm] *n Chem* zirconium *m*

 ►► ***zirconium oxide*** zircone *f*

zit [zɪt] *n Fam* bouton ❑ *m (sur la peau)*

zither ['zɪðə(r)] *n* cithare *f*

zizania [zɪ'zeɪnɪə] *n Bot* zizanie *f*

zizz [zɪz] *n Br Fam* **to have a zizz** faire un somme

zloty ['zlɒtɪ] *n* zloty *m*

zodiac ['zəʊdɪæk] *n* zodiaque *m*

zodiacal [zəʊ'daɪəkəl] *adj* zodiacal

zoetrope ['zəʊɪtrəʊp] *n* zootrope *m*

zombie ['zɒmbɪ] *n Rel & Fig* zombi(e) *m*; **he walks about like a zombie** il a tout le temps l'air abruti *ou* l'air d'un zombi

zonal ['zəʊnəl] *adj* zonal

zonate ['zəʊneɪt] *adj* zoné

zone [zəʊn] **1** *n* (**a**) *(area)* zone *f*, secteur *m*; *Mil* **the occupied zone** la zone occupée; *Mil* **battle/war zone** zone *f* des combats/de guerre

 (**b**) *(sphere)* zone *f*, domaine *m*

 (**c**) *Geog & Met* zone *f*

 (**d**) *Fam Sport* **to be in the zone** être au top de sa forme

 (**e**) *Am Fam* **to be in a zone** *(dazed)* être dans le coaltar; *(after taking drugs)* être raide, planer

 2 *vt* (**a**) *(partition)* diviser en zones

 (**b**) *(classify)* désigner; **to zone an area as industrial/residential** classer un secteur zone industrielle/résidentielle

 ►► ***zone defence*** *(in basketball)* défense *f* de zone

zoned [zəʊnd] *adj Am Fam* **to be zoned (out)** *(dazed)* être dans le coaltar; *(after taking drugs)* être raide, planer

zoning ['zəʊnɪŋ] *n* zonage *m*

 ►► *Am* ***zoning board*** = comité chargé du zonage

zonked [zɒŋkt] *adj Fam* (**a**) *(exhausted)* vanné, claqué (**b**) *(drunk)* bourré; *(on drugs)* défoncé

zonure ['zəʊnjʊə(r)] *n Zool* zonure *m*

zoo [zuː] *(pl* **zoos**) *n* zoo *m*, jardin *m* zoologique

zooflagellate [,zəʊə'flædʒəlet] *n Biol* zooflagellé *m*

zoogamete [,zəʊə'gæmiːt] *n Bot* zoogamète *m*

zoogeography [,zəʊədʒɪ'ɒgrəfɪ] *n* zoogéographie *f*

zoogloea [,zəʊə'gliːə] *n Biol* zooglée *f*

zoographic [,zəʊə'græfɪk], **zoographical** [,zəʊə'græfɪkəl] *adj* zoographique

zookeeper ['zuː,kiːpə(r)] *n* gardien(enne) *m,f* de zoo

zoolater [zəʊ'ɒlətə(r)] *n* zoolâtre *mf*

zoolatrous [zəʊ'ɒlətrəs] *adj* zoolâtre

zoolatry [zəʊ'ɒlətrɪ] *n* zoolâtrie *f*

zoological [,zəʊə'lɒdʒɪkəl] *adj* zoologique

 ►► ***zoological gardens*** jardin *m ou* parc *m* zoologique

zoologically [,zəʊə'lɒdʒɪkəlɪ] *adv* zoologiquement

zoologist [zəʊ'ɒlədʒɪst] *n* zoologiste *mf*

zoology [zəʊ'ɒlədʒɪ] *n* zoologie *f*

zoom [zuːm] **1** *vi* (**a**) *(verb of movement)* **the car zoomed up/down the hill** la voiture a monté/descendu la côte à toute allure *ou* en trombe; **the rocket zoomed up into the clouds** la fusée est montée en chandelle dans les nuages; **I'm just going to zoom into town to get some food** je vais faire un saut en ville pour acheter de quoi manger

 (**b**) *(prices, costs, sales)* monter en flèche; **inflation zoomed up** *or* **upwards** l'inflation est montée en flèche

 (**c**) *(engine)* vrombir

 (**d**) *Aviat (climb steeply)* monter en chandelle

 2 *vt Am Fam* (**a**) *(fool, deceive)* se foutre de (**b**) *(flirt with)* faire du rentre-dedans à

 3 *n* (**a**) *(of engine)* vrombissement *m*

 (**b**) *Phot (lens, effect)* zoom *m*

 4 *onomat* vroum!

 ►► *Comput* ***zoom box*** case *f* zoom; ***zoom lens*** zoom *m*

►**zoom in** *vi Phot* faire un zoom; **the camera zoomed in on the laughing children** la caméra a fait un zoom sur les enfants en train de rire

►**zoom off** *vi* filer; **they're zooming off on holiday tomorrow** ils filent en vacances demain

►**zoom out** *vi Phot* faire un zoom arrière

zoomorphic [,zəʊə'mɔːfɪk] *adj* zoomorphe

zoomorphism [,zəʊə'mɔːfɪzəm] *n* zoomorphisme *m*

zoonosis [,zəʊɪ'nəʊsɪs] *n Med & Vet* zoonose *f*

zoophagous [,zəʊ'ɒfəgəs] *adj* zoophage

zoophyte ['zəʊəfaɪt] *n* zoophyte *m*

zoophile ['zəʊəfaɪl] *n* zoophile *mf*

zoophilic [,zəʊə'fɪlɪk] *adj* zoophile

zoophilia [,zəʊə'fɪlɪə] *n* zoophilie *f*

zoophobia [,zəʊə'fəʊbɪə] *n* zoophobie *f*

zooplankton [,zəʊə'plæŋktən] *n* zooplancton *m*

zoosperm ['zəʊəspɜːm] *n* zoosperme *m*, spermatozoïde *m*

zoospore ['zəʊəspɔː(r)] *n Biol* zoospore *f*

zooted ['zuːtɪd] *adj Am Fam* (**a**) *(drunk)* bourré, pété (**b**) *(on drugs)* raide, défoncé

zootrope ['zəʊətrəʊp] *n* zootrope *m*

zoot suit [zuːt-] *n* costume *m* zazou *(des années quarante)*

zorbing ['zɔːbɪŋ] *n Sport* zorbing *m*

zorille ['zɒrɪl] *n Zool* zorille *f*

Zoroaster [,zɒrəʊ'æstə(r)] *pr n* Zoroastre

Zoroastrian [,zɒrəʊ'æstrɪən] *Rel* **1** *adj* zoroastrien

 2 *n* zoroastrien(enne) *m,f*

Zoroastrianism [,zɒrəʊ'æstrɪə,nɪzəm] *n Rel* zoroastrisme *m*

zoster ['zɒstə(r)] *n Med* zona *m*

zounds [zaʊndz] *exclam Arch* morbleu!, sacrebleu!

zowie ['zaʊɪ] *exclam Am Fam* oh là là!, la vache!

zucchetto [tsʊ'ketəʊ] *(pl* **zucchettos**) *n Rel* calotte *f* (de prêtre)

zucchini [zuː'kiːnɪ] *(pl* **inv** *or* **zucchinis**) *n Am* courgette *f*

Zug [zuːg] *n (town, canton)* Zug

zugzwang ['zuːgzwæŋ] *Chess* **1** *n* = situation du joueur qui ne peut déplacer une pièce qu'à son désavantage

 2 *vt (opponent)* = mettre dans une situation où tout déplacement entraîne un gros désavantage

Zulu ['zuːluː] *(pl* **inv** *or* **Zulus**) **1** *n* (**a**) *(person)* Zoulou(e) *m,f* (**b**) *Ling* zoulou *m*

 2 *adj* zoulou

Zululand ['zuːluːlænd] *n* Zoulouland *m*

Zuni ['zuːnɪ] *n* (**a**) *(tribe)* **the Zuni(s)** les Zūnis *mpl* (**b**) *(member of tribe)* Zūni(e) *m,f*

Zürich ['zjʊərɪk] *n* Zurich *m*

zurna ['zɜːnə] *n Mus* zourna *m*

zwieback® ['zwiːbæk] *n Am* biscotte *f*, *Suisse* zwieback *m*

Zwinglian ['tsvɪŋglɪən] *Rel* **1** *n* zwinglien(enne) *m,f*

 2 *adj* zwinglien

Zwinglianism ['tsvɪŋglɪənɪzəm] *n Rel* zwinglianisme *m*

zwitterion ['tsvɪtə,raɪən] *n Chem* zwitterion *m*

zygodactyl [,zaɪgəʊ'dæktɪl] *Orn* **1** *adj* zygodactyle

 2 *n* zygodactyle *m*

zygoma [zaɪ'gəʊmə] *(pl* **zygomata** [-mətə]) *n Anat* zygoma *m*, os *m* malaire

zygomatic [,zaɪgəʊ'mætɪk] *adj Anat* zygomatique

 ►► ***zygomatic arch*** zygoma *m*, os *m* malaire

zygomorphic [,zaɪgəʊ'mɔːfɪk], **zygomorphous** [,zaɪgəʊ'mɔːfəs] *adj Bot* zygomorphe

zygomycete [,zaɪgəʊ'maɪsiːt] *n Bot* zygomycète *m*

zygote ['zaɪgəʊt] *n Biol* zygote *m*

zymase ['zaɪmeɪs] *n Chem* zymase *f*

zymogen ['zaɪmədʒen] *n Biol & Chem* zymogène *m*

zymology [zaɪ'mɒlədʒɪ] *n Chem* zymologie *f*

zymotic [zaɪ'mɒtɪk] *adj* (**a**) *Chem* zymotique (**b**) *Old-fashioned Med* zymotique

zythum ['zɪθəm] *n Hist* zythum *m*

Supplement
Appendice

Chronology/Chronologie

Note: Historical events are marked with a solid lozenge (◆), cultural events are marked with an empty lozenge (◇).

Les événements historiques et culturels sont signalés respectivement par un losange noir (◆) et un losange blanc (◇).

English/Anglais

◆55 av. J.-C. L'invasion romaine: Jules César (100 ou 101 – 44 av. J.-C.) conquiert l'île de Bretagne.
◇Vers l'an 8 ap. J.-C. C'est à cette époque qu'est écrite l'épopée de *Beowulf*, vaillant héros et pourfendeur de dragon. Un manuscrit sur toile datant de la fin du 10ème siècle survit encore.
◆122 – 128 Construction du mur d'Hadrien dans le nord de l'Angleterre actuelle, destiné à repousser les invasions des Pictes et autres tribus venant de ce qui est maintenant l'Écosse. Ce mur marquait la frontière septentrionale de l'empire romain.
◆162 Les Romains ont perdu le contrôle de l'Écosse et se sont retranchés en deçà du mur d'Hadrien.

Français/French

◆53 BC Vercingetorix (72 – 46 BC), chief of the Gauls.
◆52 BC Defeat of Vercingetorix by Caesar at Alésia.

◇50 AD The Pont du Gard and the Théâtre des Chorégies at Orange are built by the Romans.

◆352 Frankish invasions of Gaul.

400

◆Vers 400 – 410 Le mur d'Hadrien cesse d'être un mur de défense.

◆406 Great invasion of Germanic tribes.

428 – 751 The Merovingians

◆476 Fall of the Roman Empire in the West.
◆481 Reign of Clovis, king of the Franks (466 – 511).
◆496 Conversion of Clovis to Christianity.

500

◆Vers 500 Les envahisseurs nordiques (principalement Angles et Saxons) s'installent dans l'île de Bretagne et refoulent plusieurs tribus celtes vers le Pays de Galles et la Cornouailles où leurs descendants sont encore très nombreux.

◇563 Le missionnaire irlandais St Columba fonde un monastère sur l'île écossaise d'Iona. Aujourd'hui encore cette île reste un lieu de pèlerinage.

◆507 Clovis beats back the Visigoths at Vouillé (Charentes).
◇507 Foundation by Clovis of the Basilica of the Apostles (later Sainte-Geneviève).
◆511 Clovis publishes the Salic Law (legal code of the Salian Franks) which included a clause preventing women from inheriting land. Death of Clovis.
◇543 Foundation of the Abbey of Saint-Germain-des-Prés (543 – 556).
◆558 Clotaire becomes king of the Franks (497 – 561). On his death, his sons divide up his kingdom.
◆579 The Bretons invade the regions of Rennes and Nantes.

600

◇Vers 634 St Aidan d'Iona fonde un monastère sur l'île de Lindisfarne ou Holy Island (l'Île Sainte). Lindisfarne, qui compte St Cuthbert parmi ses évêques les plus célèbres, devient un foyer d'érudition et de christianisation. C'est là que sont enluminés les *Lindisfarne Gospels* (Évangiles de Lindisfarne) entre 690 et 700.
◇Vers 650 Rédaction du *Book of Durrow* (Le Livre de Durrow). C'est le plus ancien exemple connu du nouvel art chrétien celte.

◆629 Dagobert I (ca. 600 – ca. 638) becomes king of the Franks. Saint-Eloi is his principal counsellor.

◇654 Foundation of the Abbey of Jumièges.
◇660 Foundation of the Abbey of Chelles.

700

◇ca. 700 Latin disappears as a spoken language in Gaul.
◆732 Charles Martel (688 – 741) checks Arab expansion at the Battle of Poitiers.
◆738 Saracen invasions in Provence.
◆742 – 743 Last great plague epidemic of the Early Middle Ages.

751 – 987 The Carolingians

◆751 Pepin the Short (Pépin le Bref) (741 – 768) is made king of the Franks at Soissons.
◇754 Pepin imposes the Latin liturgy on all the States of his Empire. Growth of Gregorian Chant.
◆771 Charlemagne (742 – 814) inherits the kingdom of the Franks.
◆778 Charlemagne is ambushed at Roncevaux in the Pyrenees.
◇782 Creation of the Palatine school of Aix-la-Chapelle (Aachen).

800

◆Vers 800 Fin de la rédaction du *Book of Kells*, manuscrit des Évangiles somptueusement enluminé par des moines irlandais sur l'île [illegible]

◆843 Kenneth MacAlpin bat les Pictes et devient le premier roi de toute l'Écosse.

◆871 Règne du roi Alfred the Great (Alfred le Grand) (849 – 899). Il bat les Pictes, organise une armée et une flotte. Il fait renaître la religion, favorise l'instruction et la littérature et traduit plusieurs ouvrages latins en anglais.

◆800 Charlemagne is anointed Emperor of the West (empereur [illegible]) in [illegible] Basilica in Rome. His kingdom includes Gaul, Germania, and parts of modern-day Spain and Italy. His reign witnesses a flowering of the arts and the spread of Christianity.
◆814 Reign of Louis the Pious (Louis le Pieux) (778 – 840).
◇842 The Strasbourg Oaths (Serments de Strasbourg), which seal the alliance between Charles the Bald (Charles le Chauve) and Louis the German (Louis le Germanique), written in 'Roman' and German, considered the oldest document in French.
◆843 The Treaty of Verdun formally divides the empire into three kingdoms; Francia Occidentalis, the future France, is given to Charles the Bald (823 – 877).
Royal power begins to decline in favour of the nobility; creation of large duchies (Normandy, Burgundy, Flanders, Aquitaine) as the territory under the control of the King is gradually reduced to just the Île de France.
◇846 First Bible of Charles the Bald illuminated at the Abbey of Saint-Martin at Tours.
◆877 Charles signs the charter of Kiersy-sur-Oise, which promulgates the heredity of fiefs and seigneurial benefices.
Reign of Louis II the Stammerer (Louis II le Bègue) (846 – 879).
◆879 Reigns of Louis III (863 – 882) and Carloman (867 – 884).
◇881 The *Séquence de Sainte Eulalie*, the first poem in langue d'oïl to be preserved, marks the beginnings of French literature.

English/Anglais	French/Français
	◆898 Reign of Charles the Simple (Charles le Simple) (879 – 929), son of Louis the Stammerer (Louis le Bègue).

900

English/Anglais	French/Français
◇Vers 909 Naissance du prélat anglo-saxon St Dunstan (mort en 988). Réformateur de la vie monastique, il fait de Glastonbury un centre de culture chrétienne. ◆924 – 939 Règne du roi anglo-saxon Athelstan (v. 895 – 939). Ce règne marque une période d'unification pour l'Angleterre. En 927 Athelstan envahit la Northumbrie et devient le premier roi de toute l'Angleterre. En 937, à la bataille de Brunanburh, il défait les Danois alliés aux Écossais et aux Gallois, renforçant ainsi son contrôle sur l'Angleterre. ◇975 *L'Exeter Book* (Le Livre d'Exeter), l'un des plus importants recueils de poèmes en vieil anglais, est copié et plus tard offert à la cathédrale d'Exeter. ◆978 Début du règne d'Ethelred II (the Unready) (968 – 1016). Il forge le premier lien dynastique entre la France et l'Angleterre par son mariage avec Emma, fille du duc de Normandie. Mais chassé de son trône par les Vikings en 1013, il doit s'exiler.	◇ca. 910 Foundation of the monastery of Cluny by William I of Aquitaine (Guillaume d'Aquitaine). ◆911 Beginning of the Feudal period (10th–12th century). Viking invasions in Normandy. Creation of autonomous regions (notably Anjou, Maine, and Toulouse). ◇ca. 915 – 917 Building of the First Abbey Church of Cluny, centre for the spread of Benedictine reform across Europe. ◆936 Reign of Louis IV d'Outremer (921 – 954), son of Charles the Simple. ◇949 First written account of the pilgrimage to Santiago de Compostela (Saint-Jacques-de-Compostelle). ◆954 Reign of Lothaire (941 – 986). ◇966 Richard I of Normandy founds the abbey of Mont-Saint-Michel, entrusted to the Benedictines. ◆985 Reign of Louis V (967 – 987). **987 – 1328 The Capetians** ◆987 Reign of Hugo Capet (Hugues Capet) (987 – 996). ◇990 Building of the keep of the château of Langeais.

1000

English/Anglais	French/Français
◆1009 Les Danois envahissent l'Angleterre. ◆1014 Défaite des Vikings à la bataille de Clontarf, en Irlande. ◆1016 Mort du roi Ethelred the Unready. Canut bat Edmond II Côte-de-Fer (Edmund Ironside) à la bataille d'Ashington; Edmond règne sur l'Écosse pendant une courte période, jusqu'à sa mort. Canute devient alors souverain de toute l'Angleterre. ◇Vers 1020 Mort d'Aelfric dit 'the Grammarian' (le Grammairien), abbé et érudit anglo-saxon. Sa prose, écrite en langue vulgaire, en fait le plus grand écrivain de son époque. On lui doit entre autres les *Lives of the Saints* (Vies de saints). ◆1028 Canut, roi d'Angleterre et du Danemark, conquiert la Norvège. ◆1031 Canut oblige Malcolm, roi des Écossais, à reconnaître sa suzeraineté. ◆1040 Macbeth assassine Duncan Ier, roi des Écossais, et monte sur le trône. ◆1042 Fin de la période de domination danoise. Le Saxon Édouard le Confesseur (Edward the Confessor) devient roi. Fils d'Ethelred the Unready et d'Emma, il est le dernier souverain de la vieille lignée royale anglaise. C'est sa grande piété qui lui a valu son surnom. ◇1065 Consécration de l'abbaye de Westminster, abbaye de style roman construite sur les ordres d'Édouard le Confesseur.	◆1060 Reign of Philip I (1053 – 1108). ◇1060 Building of the abbey church of Sainte-Foy de Conques (on the pilgrims' route to Santiago de Compostela).
1066 – 1154 L'Angleterre normande ◆1066 'La Conquête Normande' (The Norman Conquest): la victoire de Guillaume le Conquérant (William the Conqueror) (1028 – 1087), duc de Normandie, sur Harold II à Hastings, lui assure la couronne d'Angleterre.	◆1066 William the Conqueror (Guillaume le Conquérant) (1028 – 1087), Duke of Normandy, lands in England and defeats Harold at the Battle of Hastings. He has himself crowned king.
◇1066 Début de la transformation radicale de la langue anglaise au contact du français, langue maternelle des Normands. Pendant les trois siècles qui suivront (les Angevins succédant aux Normands à la couronne d'Angleterre), le français sera la langue du droit, la langue du parlement, ainsi que la langue maternelle des rois d'Angleterre. ◇1067 Début des travaux de construction de la Tour de Londres, conçue pour être à la fois palais et forteresse. ◆1072 Guillaume le Conquérant étend sa conquête à l'Écosse. ◇1077 La tapisserie de Bayeux (tapisserie de la reine Mathilde, épouse de Guillaume le Conquérant), brodée en Angleterre, est terminée. Elle représente les événements qui ont précédé la conquête de l'Angleterre par les Normands ainsi que la bataille d'Hastings en 1066. ◇1086 *Domesday* ou *Doomsday Book* (t. orig. Livre du jugement dernier): ce recensement de toutes les terres d'Angleterre est réalisé sur l'ordre de Guillaume le Conquérant, probablement pour permettre au souverain d'estimer la capacité fiscale et militaire des nouveaux fiefs. ◆1087 Guillaume le Conquérant meurt. Son fils Guillaume II le Roux (William II) (v. 1056 – 1100) lui succède. ◆1091 Signature du Traité de Caen entre Guillaume II le Roux et son frère qui se disputaient la Normandie. Aux termes de ce traité, les terres du premier à décéder reviendront au survivant. ◆1093 Malcolm, roi d'Écosse, est tué au cours de l'invasion d'Alnwick dans le Northumberland. ◆1096 Le frère de Guillaume II le Roux, Robert, part pour la première croisade. Son départ expose la Normandie aux convoitises de Guillaume.	◆1096 Peter the Hermit (Pierre l'Hermite) (1050 – 1115) advocates a crusade to aid the Christians of the East. ◇1098 Foundation of the Abbey of Cîteaux (Cistercian order) by Robert of Molesme. ◇ca. 1098 – 99 Beginning of the *Chanson de Roland* (Song of Roland), the oldest chanson de geste. An historical event (the defeat of Charlemagne at Roncevaux in 778) is turned into an heroic epic. ◆1099 Under the leadership of Godfrey of Bouillon (Godefroy de Bouillon) (1061 – 1100), Duke of Lorraine, the crusaders take Jerusalem. ◇1099 Foundation in Jerusalem of the Hospitaliers de Saint-Jean.

1100

English/Anglais	French/Français
◆1100 Henri Ier Beauclerc (1068 – 1135) succède à son frère aîné Guillaume après la mort suspecte de ce dernier, tué par une flèche au cours d'une chasse. ◆1106 Henri Ier l'emporte sur son frère Robert II Courteheuse (Robert Curthose) à la bataille de Tinchebrai et devient duc de Normandie. Son but est de faire de l'Angleterre et de la Normandie un seul royaume.	◆1108 Reign of Louis VI the Fat (Louis VI le Gros) (1081 – 1137). ◇1108 Abelard (1079 – 1142) disputes the 'querelle des Universaux' (doctrine of Universals). ◇1110 The Tympanum of the Apocalypse is sculpted on the portal of the church at Moissac.

English/Anglais

◆1124 David Ier, personnage influent, devient roi d'Écosse. Il compte de nombreux amis anglo-normands et de plus épouse une riche héritière normande. David est en position de force en Écosse et dans une partie du nord de l'Angleterre. Il établit une nouvelle aristocratie de langue française dans le sud de l'Écosse.
◇Vers 1125 Adélard de Bath traduit le traité de géometrie d'Euclide, *Éléments*, de l'arabe en latin.
◆1128 Mathilde, fille d'Henri I, épouse Geoffroi le Bel (dit Plantagenêt), comte d'Anjou.

◆1135 À la mort du roi Henri I, son neveu Étienne de Blois (Stephen) (v.1090 – 1154) s'empare du trône à la place de Mathilde. Début de la guerre civile qui oppose ses partisans à ceux de Mathilde.
◇Vers 1136 Geoffroi de Monmouth (Geoffrey of Monmouth) écrit son *Historia Regum Britanniae* (Histoire des Bretons). Cette œuvre fait entrer la légende d'Arthur dans la littérature européenne.

◆1141 Après une série d'attaques contre l'Angleterre, David Ier d'Écosse réussit à s'emparer d'une partie de la Northumbrie.

◆1147 – 1149 Deuxième croisade.

◆1153 Le roi Étienne (King Stephen), resté sans héritier, désigne comme successeur à la couronne d'Angleterre Henri Plantagenêt (1113-1189), (fils de Mathilde et de Geoffroi le Bel) alors duc de Normandie, comte d'Anjou, et duc d'Aquitaine (depuis son mariage avec Aliénor d'Aquitaine en 1152).

1154 – 1485 Les Plantagenêts

◆1154 Henri Plantagenêt est couronné roi d'Angleterre et devient Henri II d'Angleterre. Premier souverain de la dynastie des Plantagenêts, il règne sur le grand empire angevin.
◇1154 Adrien IV (Nicholas Breakspear) (v.1100 – 1159) devient pape. Il demeure le seul pape anglais.
◇1155 Le poète anglo-nomand Robert Wace (v.1115 – 1183) termine son *Roman de Brut*, adaptation de l'Histoire des Bretons de Geoffroi de Monmouth.
◇Entre 1155 et 1170 Le poète anglo-normand Thomas d'Angleterre compose sa version de *Tristan et Iseut* en français.
◆1164 Signature des Constitutions de Clarendon qui définissent les pouvoirs de l'Église et de l'État.
◇Vers 1167 Henri II ayant interdit aux Anglais d'étudier à Paris, l'université d'Oxford se développe rapidement.
◆1170 Assassinat de Thomas Becket, archevêque de Cantorbéry, dans sa cathédrale. Il s'était opposé à la politique religieuse du roi qui voulait soumettre la justice ecclésiastique à la justice royale.
◆1171 Henri II mène une expédition victorieuse contre l'Irlande et annexe l'île.
◆1173 – 1174 Le fils d'Henri II, nommé lui aussi Henri, se révolte contre son père, soutenu par Guillaume Ier d'Écosse, Louis VII de France et le comte Philippe de Flandre.
◇1173 Thomas Becket est canonisé.
◇1176 Premier Eisteddfod (festival d'arts) au Pays de Galles.
◇Vers 1187 Première mention de l'utilisation d'une boussole comme instrument de navigation dans *De utensilibus* d'Alexander Neckham.
◆1189 Les fils d'Henri II, Richard et Jean (John), s'emparent du Maine et de la Touraine. Henri accepte de reconnaître Richard comme son seul héritier. Richard Ier Cœur de Lion (the Lionheart) (1157 – 1199) devient roi d'Angleterre.
◆1189 – 1192 Troisième croisade, conduite par Richard Cœur de Lion et Philippe Auguste. Prise de Chypre et de Saint-Jean-d'Acre.
◇Vers 1190 Le poète anglo-normand Béroul compose sa version de *Tristan et Iseut* en français.
◆1199 Jean sans Terre (John Lackland) (1167 – 1216) devient roi d'Angleterre.

French/Français

William of Aquitaine (Guillaume d'Aquitaine) (1071 – 1126), Count of Poitiers is the first troubadour; birth of the ideal of courtly love.
◇1115 Reform of the Cistercian order by Saint Bernard of Clairvaux (1090 – 1153).
◇1119 Foundation in Jerusalem of the Order of the Templars (Ordre des Templiers).

◆1132 Abbot Suger of Saint-Denis (1081 – 1151) is political and religious advisor to Louis VI the Fat, then to Louis VII the Young (Louis VII le Jeune).
◆1137 Reign of Louis VII the Young (1120 – 1180). He marries Eleanor of Aquitaine (Aliénor d'Aquitaine) (1122 – 1204).
◇1137 Rebuilding (1137 – 1144) of the chancel of the abbey church of Saint-Denis directed by abbot Suger: emergence of the Gothic style.

◇1145 The Royal Portal of Chartres Cathedral is built (1145 – 1150).
◆1146 Bernard of Clairvaux (1090 – 1153) argues for the second crusade (1147 – 1149), which fails at Damas.
◇ca. 1150 *Raoul de Cambrai*, chanson de geste on the feudal revolt and treachery between barons.
The court of Eleanor marks the apogee of courtly love. The troubadours Bernard de Ventadour, Marcabru, Jaufre Rudel in residence.
◆1152 Eleanor of Aquitaine, repudiated by Louis VII, marries Henry Plantagenet (son of Geoffrey the Fair, and Duke of Normandy and Count of Anjou), which makes him Duke of Aquitaine.

◆1154 Henry Plantagenet is crowned Henry II, King of England, which becomes part of the possessions of the Angevins.

◇1162 – 1182 The work of Chrétien de Troyes (1135 – 1183).
◇1163 The building of Notre-Dame de Paris begins.
◇1168 *Lancelot ou le chevalier à la charrette* (Lancelot or the Knight of the Cart) by Chrétien de Troyes.

◇1170 *Le Roman de Renart* (1170 – 1205), an anonymous satirical romance, is started.

◆1180 Philippe II Augustus (Philippe Auguste) (1165 – 1223) accedes to the throne of France. He will strengthen the power of the royalty and enlarge the territory under royal control.
◇1180 *Perceval ou le conte du Graal* (Percival or the Story of the Holy Grail) by Chrétien de Troyes.
◆1189 Beginning of the third crusade (1189 – 1192), led by Philippe II Augustus and Richard I (the Lionheart). Cyprus and Acre are taken.

1200

English/Anglais

◆1200 Traité du Goulet : les Français reconnaissent les possessions françaises du roi Jean sans Terre.
◇Vers 1200 L'arc de guerre est couramment utilisé par les forces anglaises.
◆1202 – 1204 Quatrième croisade et prise de Constantinople.

◆1204 La France reprend la Normandie à l'Angleterre.

◆1209 Jean sans Terre est excommunié par le pape.
◇1209 À la suite d'émeutes à Oxford, plusieurs membres de l'université quittent cette ville pour aller s'installer à Cambridge où ils fondent une nouvelle université.
Construction du premier pont en pierre de Londres.
◇Vers 1214 Naissance du théologien et philosophe anglais Roger Bacon (mort en 1292). Il publie de nombreux ouvrages de mathématiques, de philosophie et de logique dont l'importance ne sera reconnue que beaucoup plus tard.
◆1215 Les barons imposent *The Magna Carta* (la Grande Charte) à Jean sans Terre à Runnymede. Garantie contre l'arbitraire royal, cette charte fondamentale marque le début de l'évolution de l'Angleterre vers un régime parlementaire. Elle servira de modèle à d'autres systèmes de gouvernement basés sur le système anglais.
◆1216 Plusieurs barons anglais abandonnent leur roi et invitent le futur Louis VIII de France à monter sur le trône d'Angleterre.
Mort soudaine de Jean sans Terre. Son fils Henri III lui succède.

French/Français

◇ca. 1200 *Aucassin et Nicolette*, first romance in prose and verse.

◆1202 Fourth crusade (1202 – 1204). Th[illegible] Constantinople.

◆1204 England loses Normandy to France.

◆1209 Crusade (1209 – 1229) against the Albigenses (Cathar heretics).

◆1214 Victory of Philippe Augustus at the Battle of Bouvines against Otto IV (Otton IV) (Emperor of the Holy Roman Empire) and his allies including English King John Lackland.
◇1215 *Le Livre de Lancelot du Lac*, by Chrétien de Troyes. Prose romance.

English/Anglais

◆1217 Louis et ses partisans sont chassés d'Angleterre après leur défaite à la bataille de Douvres.
◆1217 – 1221 Cinquième croisade.

◆1228 Sixième croisade et prise de Jérusalem.

◆Vers 1240 C'est vers cette date que l'on commence à utiliser le terme 'Parlement' pour désigner le Grand Conseil, réuni pour la première fois en 1224.
◆1242 Henri III tente vainement de reprendre le Poitou et autres fiefs français confisqués à son père, Jean sans Terre.
◇1245 Reconstruction de l'abbaye de Westminster dans le style gothique anglais.
◆1248 – 1254 Septième croisade, conduite par Louis IX de France (Saint-Louis).
◇1249 Fondation d'University College à Oxford.
◆1254 Le pape donne le contrôle du royaume de Sicile à Henri III.
◆1258 Traité de Paris : Henri III abandonne ses prétentions sur les provinces annexées par Philippe Auguste et reconnaît sa vassalité pour ses fiefs du sud-ouest de la France.
◇1259 Mort du chroniqueur et moine bénédictin Matthew Paris (né v. 1200). Ses *Chronica Majora*, qui relatent les événements survenus entre 1236 et 1259, en font le meilleur chroniqueur de son époque.
◇Vers 1265 Naissance du théologien et philosophe franciscain John Duns Scotus (Duns Scot) (mort en 1308). Il est, avec Thomas d'Aquin, le plus grand théologien du Moyen Âge.
◆1266 'The Dictum of Kenilworth' (la paix de Kenilworth) met fin à la guerre des barons (menés par Simon de Montfort) dont la cause avait été le refus du roi d'appliquer les 'Provisions d'Oxford' qui demandaient une réunion périodique du 'Parlement'. Le roi recouvre le pouvoir mais doit s'engager à respecter les articles de la Grande Charte.

◆1270 – 1272 Huitième croisade.
◆1272 Mort d'Henri III. Son fils Édouard Ier (1239 – 1307) lui succède. Édouard reste en Sicile jusqu'en 1274. Pendant cette période le pays est gouverné par des régents.
◆Vers 1274 Naissance de William Wallace, chef écossais et champion de l'indépendance de l'Écosse.
◆1276 Début de la première guerre galloise.

◆1284 Édouard Ier soumet les Gallois et annexe le Pays de Galles.

◆1290 L'opinion publique se retourne contre les Juifs qui sont expulsés d'Angleterre.
◆1290 – 1292 Le trône d'Écosse est vacant pendant cette période.
◆1291 Édouard Ier impose sa suzeraineté sur l'Écosse.
◆1295 Formation d'une alliance franco-écossaise.
◆1296 Édouard Ier bat les Écossais à Dunbar et gouverne l'Écosse après l'abdication de John Balliol (John Bailleul) d'Écosse. Il fait transporter la pierre du couronnement des rois écossais ('the Stone of Destiny') du palais de Scone à l'abbaye de Westminster, marquant sa souveraineté par ce geste symbolique.
◆1297 Les Écossais, menés par William Wallace, battent les Anglais à Stirling Bridge.
◆1298 Édouard Ier bat William Wallace à Falkirk.

French/Français

◆1217 Fifth crusade (1217 – 1221) against Egypt.

◆1223 Reign of Louis VIII (1187 – 1226).

◆1226 Reign of Louis IX (known as Saint-Louis) (1226 – 1270). During his reign he establishes the main bodies of central government.

◆1228 Sixth crusade (1228 – 1229). Jerusalem is taken.

◆1229 End of the crusade against the Albigenses.
◇ca. 1235 First part of the *Roman de la Rose* (Romance of the Rose) by Guillaume de Lorris (1200 – 1240).

◇1241 Saint-Louis has the Sainte-Chapelle (1241 – 1248) built in Paris.

◆1248 – 1254 Seventh crusade led by Saint-Louis.

◇1257 Foundation of the Sorbonne.
◆1258 The Treaty of Paris: Henry III renounces the French provinces he has lost and becomes a vassal of the French king for his remaining fiefs in the south-west of France.

◆1270 – 1272 Eighth crusade. Death of Saint-Louis near Tunis. Reign of Philip III the Bold (Philippe III le Hardi) (1245 – 1285).
◇ca. 1275 Second part of the *Roman de la Rose*, by Jean de Meung (1240 – 1305).

◆1285 Reign of Philip IV the Fair (Philippe IV le Bel) (1268 – 1314).

◇1290 Beginning of the composition of *La Légende Dorée* (The Golden Legend), by Jacques de Voragine (1228 – 1298).

◆1295 Formation of an alliance between France and Scotland.

1300

English/Anglais

◆1305 L'Écossais William Wallace est arrêté et pendu par les Anglais.
◆1306 Robert Bruce (1274 – 1329) est couronné roi d'Écosse à Scone mais, vaincu par les Anglais à la bataille de Methven, il est contraint de s'enfuir en Irlande.
◆1307 Robert Bruce (Robert the Bruce) revient d'exil et bat les Anglais à Loudoun Hill.
Édouard Ier meurt. Son fils Édouard II (1284 – 1327) lui succède.
◆1314 Sous Robert Bruce les Écossais remportent une victoire décisive sur les forces anglaises d'Édouard II à la bataille de Bannockburn.
◆1314 – 1317 Une série de récoltes désastreuses entraîne une famine et une forte hausse des prix de la nourriture en Angleterre.
◆1319 Conclusion d'une trêve entre l'Angleterre et l'Écosse.
◆1327 Édouard II est assassiné dans sa prison. Son fils Édouard III lui succède et parvient à restaurer le pouvoir de la monarchie.
Renouvellement de l'alliance franco-écossaise au traité de Corbeil.

◆1328 Le traité de Northampton reconnaît l'indépendance de l'Écosse et le droit de Robert Bruce à la couronne d'Écosse.
◆1331 Édouard III confirme qu'il doit hommage lige à la France pour ses fiefs continentaux et discute des termes d'une paix durable entre les deux pays.
◆1332 Première mention de la coupure du Parlement en deux chambres, les Lords et les Commoners (les Communes).

◆1337 Édouard III revendique la couronne de France. A la même époque Philippe VI s'empare de l'Aquitaine, alors possession anglaise. Ces événements déclenchent le long conflit auquel sera donné le nom de Guerre de Cent Ans (1337 – 1453).

French/Français

◆1309 Pope Clement V (? – 1314) establishes the papacy in Avignon.
◇1309 *Livre des saintes paroles et des bon faits de notre roi Louis* (Life of Saint-Louis), by Jean de Joinville (1224 – 1317).
◆1314 Reign of Louis X the Stubborn (Louis X le Hutin) (1289 – 1316).
◆1316 Reign of Philip V the Tall (Philippe V le Long) (1293 – 1322).

◆1322 Reign of Charles IV the Fair (Charles IV le Bel) (1295 – 1328), last of the Capetian kings.

◆1327 Renewal of the alliance between France and Scotland with the treaty of Corbeil.
◇1327 The poet Petrarch (Pétrarque) (1304 – 1374) undertakes the writing of his *Canzoniere* at the court of the popes of Avignon.

1328 – 1589 The Valois

◆1328 Accession of Philip VI de Valois (1293 – 1350) to the throne of France, by virtue of the Salic Law, containing a clause which excluded women from succession to the throne of France.
◆1337 Philip VI confiscates Aquitaine from the king of England; at the same time Edward III lays claim to the French Crown. These events mark the beginning of the Hundred Years War (1337 – 1453).

English/Anglais

♦1340 Édouard III détruit la flotte française à la bataille de Sluys. À Gand il revêt le blason de France et se proclame roi de ce pays.
◇Vers 1342 Naissance de Julian of Norwich (Julienne de Norwich), mystique et récluse anglaise (morte en 1413). Son ouvrage *Sixteen Revelations of Divine Love* (Seize révélations de l'amour divin) influencera longtemps les théologiens.
♦1346 Édouard III défait les troupes françaises à la bataille de Crécy. C'est la première fois que les Anglais utlisent l'arc de guerre sur le continent. Les Écossais attaquent dans le nord de l'Angleterre et sont battus près de Durham. Leur roi, David II, est fait prisonnier.

♦1347 Calais se rend aux Anglais.
◇1347 La première monnaie d'or anglaise est frappée pour célébrer la capitulation de Calais.
♦1348 – 1350 Une épidémie de peste noire ('The Black Death' ou 'Great Plague') se propage à travers l'Angleterre et l'Écosse.
◇Vers 1349 Mort du philosophe et théologien anglais William of Ockham (Guillaume D'Occam) (né v.1285) dont la pensée exercera une profonde influence.

♦1356 Les Français sont vaincus par les Anglais à Poitiers et leur roi, Jean II le Bon, est fait prisonnier.
♦1360 Le traité de Brétigny entre la France et l'Angleterre met fin a la première phase de la Guerre de Cent Ans. Par ce traité, en plus d'une énorme rançon en échange de sa liberté, Jean II le Bon abandonne à l'Angleterre de nombeux territoires français.
♦1361 – 1362 Deuxième épidémie de peste en Angleterre.
◇1362 L'anglais remplace le français comme langue officielle au Parlement et dans les tribunaux ('The Statute of Pleading').
◇Vers 1375 Un auteur inconnu écrit l'un des plus grands poèmes de cette période *Sir Gawain and the Green Knight* (Sire Gauvain et le Chevalier Vert).
♦1376 Premier cas d'impeachment de l'histoire de l'Angleterre : au cours de la réunion du 'Good Parliament' (le Bon Parlement), certains individus sont nommés et mis en accusation.
♦1377 Édouard III meurt. Son petit-fils âgé de 10 ans, Richard II (1367 – 1400), devient roi.
La première capitation ('poll tax'), impôt levé sur chaque adulte, est introduite en Angleterre.
Tout comme les futures capitations, cet impôt est fort mal accueilli par l'opinion et nombreux sont ceux qui se soustraient à son paiement.
◇1380 Geoffrey Chaucer (v. 1345 – 1400) entame les *Contes de Cantorbéry* (The Canterbury Tales).
♦1381 La mutiplication des impôts entre 1377 et 1381 provoque la Révolte des Paysans, menée par Wat Tyler, dans le sud de l'Angleterre. Cette révolte est rapidement réprimée.
◇1384 Mort du théologien et réformateur anglais John Wycliffe (né v. 1330). Précurseur de la Réformation, il prêche le retour à la Bible comme seule autorité en matière de foi. Il est l'auteur de la première traduction anglaise de la Bible.
◇1385 William Langland commence à écrire son poème allégorique *The Vision of Piers Plowman* (La Vision de Pierre le Laboureur).
♦1388 – 1399 Le règne de Richard II est marqué par une série de conflits avec le Parlement et se termine par son abdication.

1399 – 1461 Les Lancastres

♦1399 Richard abdique en faveur d'Henri IV (1366 – 1413) mettant ainsi la maison de Lancastre sur le trône. C'est seulement sous le règne de Henri IV que le roi d'Angleterre parle l'anglais comme langue maternelle et non plus le français (depuis Guillaume le Conquérant).

French/Français

♦1346 Edward III defeats the French troops at the battle of Crécy. Beginning of the Black Death ('la Peste noire' or 'Grande Peste'), which ravages the whole of Europe and decimates a third of the French population.

♦1347 Calais surrenders to the English troops.

◇1349 Guillaume de Machaut (1300 – 1377) composes the *Messe Notre-Dame*: advent of polyphony.
♦1350 Reign of John II the Good (Jean II le Bon) (1319 – 1364).
♦1356 The French are defeated by the English at the Battle of Poitiers, and the French king, John II, is captured.
♦1358 Etienne Marcel (1316 – 1358), provost of the merchants of Paris, leads an uprising against the Dauphin (future Charles V). Overburdened by taxes, the peasants (Jacques) rise up in Île-de-France, an episode known as the Jacquerie.
♦1360 France and England sign the Treaty of Brétigny, which ends the first stage of the Hundred Years War. Under the Treaty, Edward III makes great territorial gains on France, and exacts a huge ransom for the French king's release.
♦1364 Charles V the Wise (Charles V le Sage) (1338 – 1380) succeeds John II the Good.
♦1367 Pope Urban V (1310 – 1370) leaves Avignon for Rome, then returns to Avignon (1370).
♦1369 Bertrand Du Guesclin (1320 – 1380), military commander, takes back the lands ceded by the Treaty of Brétigny as a ransom for the abduction of John the Good.

◇1378 Start of the Great Western Schism (1378 – 1417): Pope Clement VII (1342 – 1394) takes up residence in Avignon.

♦1380 Reign of Charles VI (1368 – 1422). His uncles the dukes of Anjou and Bourgogne act as regents (1380 – 1388).

♦1392 Charles VI is declared mad. His uncles take back power. Start of the war between the Armagnacs, on the side of the Dauphin (future Charles VII), and the Burgundians, on the side of the English.

1400

English/Anglais

♦1400 Henri IV attaque l'Écosse mais est battu.
♦1401 Les Gallois, conduits par Owen Glendower, se révoltent contre Henri IV.
♦1403 Henri IV bat les Écossais, alliés aux Gallois et au comte Henry 'Hotspur' Percy, à Shrewsbury.
♦1404 Les Français s'allient au Gallois Owen Glendower.
◇1408 Mort de John Gower, le dernier des poètes anglo-normands, auteur de poèmes en latin, en français et en anglais.
◇1411 Fondation de l'université de St Andrews, la plus ancienne d'Écosse.
♦1413 Henri IV meurt. Son fils Henri V (1387 – 1422) lui succède.
♦1415 Henri V, qui veut reconquérir la couronne de France, bat les Français à Azincourt.

♦1420 Signature de la 'paix perpétuelle' de Troyes. Henri V recouvre la plus grande partie de la Normandie et est reconnu comme Régent de France et héritier de la couronne de France.
♦1422 Henri VI (1421 – 1471) succède à son père à l'âge de neuf mois. Bien que couronné roi de France en 1431, les territoires conquis par son père lui échappent peu à peu.
♦1423 Les Anglais, alliés aux Bourguignons, remportent la victoire de Verneuil sur les forces franco-écossaises.

♦1431 Jeanne d'Arc (Joan of Arc) est brûlée vive. Toutefois son action avait mis fin à l'hégémonie des Anglais en France.

French/Français

♦1407 Murder of Louis of Orléans (brother of King Charles VI) by the duke of Burgundy, John the Fearless (Jean sans Peur) (1371 – 1419). Start of the Civil War (1407 – 1435) between Armagnacs and Burgundians (allies of the English).
◇1408 *Les Très Riches Heures* (The Very Rich Hours) by the duke of Berry, a manuscript illuminated by the Limbourg brothers.

♦1415 Defeat by the English under [illegible]
[illegible] End of the Great Western Schism.
♦1418 Flight of the Dauphin to Bourges.
♦1419 Murder of John the Fearless. Philip the Good (Philippe le Bon) (1396 – 1467) becomes duke of Burgundy.
♦1420 The 'perpetual peace' of Troyes is concluded. Henry has regained control of most of Normandy, and is recognized as heir to the French throne and Regent of France.

♦1422 Death of Charles VI. The Dauphin proclaims himself king and becomes Charles VII (1403 – 1461).
♦1423 An allied force of English and Burgundian troops defeat a French-Scottish army at Verneuil.

♦1429 Joan of Arc (Jeanne d'Arc) (1412 – 1431) fights in the siege of Orléans. Charles VII crowned at Reims.
♦1430 Joan of Arc is taken prisoner at Compiègne.
♦1431 Trial and execution of Joan of Arc.

English/Anglais

◇1440 Henri VI fonde le collège d'Eton, public school pour garçons. Mort de la mystique anglaise Margery Kempe (née v. 1373). Elle est l'auteur d'une des premières autobiographies, *The Book of Margery Kempe* (Le Livre de Margery Kempe), dictée entre 1432 et 1436.

◆1445 Une épidémie de peste se déclare en Angleterre.

◆1453 La bataille de Châtillon met fin à la Guerre de Cent Ans. Les Anglais ne conservent que Calais (qu'ils perdront en 1558) et les îles de la Manche.
◇1453 Mort du compositeur anglais John Dunstable (né v. 1390).
◆1455 Début de la guerre des Deux-Roses, guerre civile en Angleterre, dont la cause est la lutte pour le pouvoir entre les deux branches rivales de la maison des Plantagenêts : la maison d'York qui a pour emblème la rose blanche, et la maison de Lancastre dont l'emblème est la rose rouge.

1461 – 1485 Les Yorks

◆1461 Henri VI est détrôné par Édouard IV de la maison d'York (1442 – 1483).
◇1471 Mort de l'écrivain anglais Sir Thomas Mallory. Son chef-d'œuvre, *Le Morte d'Arthur* est une adaptation en prose de la geste d'Arthur.
◇1475 L'imprimeur et traducteur anglais William Caxton (v. 1422 – 1491) publie à Bruges le premier livre imprimé en anglais *The Recuyell of the Historyes of Troye.*
◇1476 William Caxton établit une imprimerie à Westminster et publie le premier livre imprimé en Angleterre, *The Sayings of the Philosophers.*

◇1480 Caxton imprime *The Chronicles of England* (Chroniques d'Angleterre).
◆1483 Le jeune Édouard V (1470 – 1483) occupe le trône pendant une courte période avant d'être emprisonné dans la Tour de Londres où il est probablement assassiné.
◆1483 – 1485 Règne du roi Richard III (1452 – 1485), dernier roi de la dynastie des Plantagenêts.

1485 – 1603 Les Tudors

◆1485 La bataille de Bosworth Field où Richard III, vaincu, trouve la mort, met fin à la guerre des Deux-Roses. Henri VII (1457 – 1509), le vainqueur, devient le premier souverain de la dynastie des Tudors. Pendant son règne, il réussit à rétablir la paix et la prospérité en Angleterre.
◆1490 Renouvellement de l'alliance franco-écossaise: en cas de guerre entre la France et l'Angleterre, l'Écosse s'engage à attaquer l'Angleterre.
◆1497 Jean Cabot, navigateur gênois au service de l'Angleterre, découvre les terres d'Amérique septentrionale (île du Cap-Breton et Nouvelle-Écosse).

French/Français

◆1435 Treaty of Arras which brings to an end the war between the Armagnacs and the Burgundians. Reconquest of France by Charles VII.
◇1440 Trial of Gilles de Rais or Retz (1400 – 1440): this comrade in arms of Joan of Arc is condemned and executed for having indulged in satanic worship.

◇1445 *Portrait of Charles VII* by Jean Fouquet (1415 – 1480).

◇1450 In Strasbourg, Johannes Gutenberg invents a mould for casting movable type and the first printing press.
◆1453 End of the Hundred Years War, with the Battle of Châtillon. Only Calais (regained in 1558) and the Channel Islands remain English territories.

◆1461 Reign of Louis XI (1423 – 1483).
◇1461 The *Testaments* by François Villon (1431 – 1463).

◇1476 Nicolas Froment (1425 – 1483) paints the *Triptyque du Buisson Ardent* (Moses and the Burning Bush).
◆1477 Acquisition of the duchy of Burgundy by Louis XI.

◆1483 Reign of Charles VIII (1470 – 1498).

◆1498 Reign of Louis XII of Orléans (1462 – 1515), cousin of Charles VIII.
◇1498 *Mémoires*, historical chronicles by Philippe de Commynes (1447 – 1511).

1500

English/Anglais

◇1500 L'ouverture d'une imprimerie par Wynkyn de Worde dans Fleet Street à Londres marque le début de la longue association entre cette rue et les métiers de l'imprimerie.
◆1509 Henri VIII (1491 – 1547) succède à Henri VII.

◆1512 Henri VIII envahit la France et remporte la victoire des Spurs (1513).
◆1513 Les forces franco-écossaises sont vaincues à la bataille de Flodden.

◇1516 L'humaniste et homme politique anglais Sir Thomas More écrit *Utopia* (L'Utopie).
◇1518 Le médecin et humaniste anglais Thomas Linacre (v.1460 – 1524) fonde le Royal College of Medecine (Collège Royal de médecine).

◇1525 William Tyndale imprime à Cologne sa traduction en anglais du Nouveau Testament.

◆1534 L'Acte de Suprématie (the Act of Supremacy) met fin à l'autorité du pape et établit le roi comme chef unique et suprême de l'Église d'Angleterre.

◆1540 La dissolution des monastères commence en Angleterre.

◆1545 – 1563 Le pape convoque le Concile de Trente qui se réunit en trois périodes pour examiner et redéfinir certains points du dogme. Ce concile fait partie de la Contre-Réforme.

French/Français

◆1515 Reign of Francis I (François I) (1494 – 1547). Francis I wins the battle of Marignano (Marignan) and gains control of Milan for the French.
◇1516 Francis I brings Leonardo da Vinci (Léonard de Vinci) to the Court of France.
◇1519 Building of the château of Chambord (1519 – 1537), the last of the great châteaux of the Loire.

◆1525 The French army is defeated by the Spanish at the battle of Pavia: Francis I is taken prisoner (freed in 1526).
◇1530 Francis I founds the Collège de France, on the advice of Guillaume Budé (1467 – 1540).
◆1532 By the Edict of Union, Brittany is linked indissolubly with France.
◇1532 *Pantagruel*, by Rabelais (1494 – 1553).
◆1534 First voyage of Jacques Cartier (1491 – 1557) to Canada, on behalf of Francis I.
France lays claim to Canada.
◇1534 *Gargantua*, by Rabelais.
◆1535 The Frenchman John Calvin (Jean Calvin, 1509 – 1564) goes into exile in Basle.
The Reformation begins in Switzerland.
Second voyage of Jacques Cartier to Canada. Exploration of the Saint Lawrence river, which opens the way to French colonization of Canada.
◇1535 First Protestant bible in French.
◇1537 Requirement for every publisher to place a copy of every book in the royal Library (origin of the registration of copyright).
◇1539 Francis I signs the Edict of Villers-Cotterêts which confirms the primacy of French as official and legal language.
◆1541 Third voyage of Jacques Cartier to Canada.
◇1542 *Délie* (Delia), a collection of love poems, is published by Maurice Scève (1501 – 1560).
◇1545 Ambroise Paré's (1509 – 1590) *Traité de chirurgie* marks the birth of modern surgery.

English/Anglais

◆1547 Édouard VI, fervent protestant, devient roi d'Angleterre. Sous son règne la Réforme se développe.

◆1553 Lady Jane Grey monte sur le trône mais est renversée neuf jours plus tard par Marie Ière Tudor qui, fervente catholique, ramène l'Angleterre au catholicisme le plus intransigeant. Sa persécution des protestants lui vaut le surnom de 'Marie la Sanglante' (Bloody Mary).
◆1558 Élisabeth (1533 – 1603), demi-sœur protestante de Marie, devient reine. Son règne est marqué par l'essor général du pays ainsi que par une période de paix entre la France et l'Angleterre.
◇1558 Mort du mathématicien anglais Robert Recorde (né v.1510). Il est l'auteur des premiers manuels anglais d'arithmétique élémentaire et d'algèbre. C'est lui qui a introduit le signe d'égalité en mathématiques.
◆1559 Élisabeth devient chef de l'Église d'Angleterre.
◆1560 John Knox établit l'Église presbytérienne d'Écosse qui est restée l'Église nationale de cette province.
◆1562 Francis Drake et John Hawkins entreprennent le commerce des esclaves avec l'Amérique.

◇1564 Naissance de Shakespeare, auteur dramatique, poète et acteur anglais (mort en 1616).
◆1567 Élisabeth emprisonne Marie Ière Stuart, reine d'Écosse, au château de Loch Leven près de Kinross en Écosse.

◇1578 – 1580 Le romancier et auteur dramatique anglais, John Lyly (v.1554-1606) écrit *Euphueus*, roman allégorique qui connaît un énorme succès. Le maniérisme du style, sa préciosité, ont donné naissance au terme 'euphuisme'.
◆1580 Francis Drake revendique la Californie pour l'Angleterre et revient dans son pays après avoir doublé le cap de Bonne-Espérance.
◇1582 Le pape Grégoire XIII introduit le calendrier grégorien qui ne sera adopté en Grande-Bretagne qu'en 1752.
◆1583 Sir Humphrey Gilbert prend possession de Terre-Neuve pour l'Angleterre. C'est la première colonie anglaise.

◆1587 Élisabeth fait exécuter Marie Ière Stuart (1542 – 1587).
◆1588 Défaite de l'Invincible Armada, flotte envoyée par Philippe II d'Espagne avec pour mission d'envahir l'Angleterre.
◇1590 Publication des trois premiers livres de *The Faerie Queene* (La Reine des Fées), du poète anglais Edmund Spenser (v. 1552 – 1599).
◇1593 L'auteur dramatique anglais Christopher Marlowe (né en 1564) meurt poignardé au cours d'une rixe dans une taverne. Parmi ses œuvres, il faut citer *Tamburlaine the Great* (Tamerlan), *The Tragic History of Dr. Faustus* (La Tragique Histoire du docteur Faust), et *The Jew of Malta* (Le Juif de Malte).
◆1595 Sir Walter Raleigh s'embarque pour les Indes espagnoles d'où il ramène le tabac et la pomme de terre.

◇1599 Ouverture du Globe Theatre à Londres avec la représentation d'une pièce de Shakespeare, *Henry V.*

1600

◆1600 Fondation de la Compagnie des Indes Orientales (East India Company). D'abord formée pour assurer à l'Angleterre le monopole du commerce avec les Indes, elle acquerra plus tard des pouvoirs territoriaux, y compris le droit de lever des impôts.
◇1600 Le médecin et physicien anglais William Gilbert (1544 – 1603) publie son traité sur le magnétisme terrestre *De Magnete.*

1603 – 1649 Les Stuarts

◆1603 Jacques VI (James VI) d'Écosse, fils de Marie Stuart, devient également Jacques Ier d'Angleterre à la mort d'Elisabeth Ière, restée sans descendant. Sous son règne la Grande-Bretagne devient une réalité politique.
◆1605 Échec de la Conspiration des Poudres (The Gunpowder Plot), complot formé par des catholiques (dont Guy Fawkes). C'est le dernier complot catholique important.
◆1606 [illegible] dit 'Union Jack' qui porte les croix des trois saints patrons de l'Angleterre, de l'Écosse et de l'Irlande.
◇1606 L'auteur dramatique anglais Ben Jonson (1572 – 1637) écrit *Volpone.*
◆1607 La Virginie devient la première colonie anglaise d'Amérique du Nord.
◆1611 Des colons anglais et écossais s'établissent en Ulster (nord de l'Irlande).
◇1611 Publication de la Bible anglaise *The Authorized Version* ou *King James' Bible.*
◇1614 Le mathématicien écossais John Napier (1550 – 1617) publie sa découverte des logarithmes dans son traité *Mirifici Logarithmorum Canonis Descriptio.*
◇1617 Le mathématicien anglais Henry Briggs établit les tables de logarithmes décimaux qui simplifient énormement les calculs numériques.
◆1620 Les Pères Pèlerins (Pilgrim Fathers), embarqués à bord du Mayflower, fondent la colonie de Plymouth en Amérique.
◇1621 Le mathématicien anglais William Oughtred (1575 – v. 1660) invente la première règle à calcul.
Parution du premier journal anglais '*The Corante*'.

French/Français

◇1546 Francis I puts Pierre Lescot in charge of building the new Louvre (1546 – 1559).
◆1547 Reign of Henry II (1519 – 1559).
◇1549 *Fontaine des Innocents* (Fountain of the Innocents) by Jean Goujon (Paris).
Défense et illustration de la langue française (Defence and Illustration of the French Language), by Joachim du Bellay (1522 – 1560).

◇1552 *Les Amours* is published by Ronsard (1524 – 1585).
◇1555 Poet Louise Labé (1524 – 1566) publishes *Débat de folie et d'amour* (Debate Between Folly and Love).

◆1559 Reign of Francis II (François II) (1544 – 1560).
The Treaty of Cateau-Cambresis ends the Franco-Spanish War.
◇1559 *L'Heptaméron* by the queen of Navarre, Margaret of Angoulême, sister of Francis I (1553 – 1615).
◆1560 Reign of Charles IX (1550 – 1574). Beginning of the regency of Catherine de Médicis (1519 – 1589).
◇1560 Jean Nicot (1530 – 1600) introduces tobacco into France.
◆1562 Massacre of the Protestants at Wassy. First War of Religion (1562 – 1563).
◇1564 Reform of the calendar; the year now begins on 1 January instead of 25 March.

◆1572 On Saint Bartholomew's Eve (24 August), the Catholics massacre the Protestants in Paris and in the provinces (le massacre de la Saint-Barthélémy). Fourth War of Religion (1572 – 1573).
◆1574 Reign of Henry III (1551 – 1589).

◇1580 *Essais* (Essays) (1580 – 1588) by Michel de Montaigne (1533 – 1592).

◆1585 Eighth War of Religion (1585 – 1598).

1589 – 1792 The Bourbons

◆1589 Assassination of Henry III (without issue), last of the Valois. Accession of Henry IV of Bourbon (1553 – 1610), leader of the Protestants.
◆1590 Victory of Henry IV at the Battle of Ivry, near Evreux, on 14 March 1590, against the Holy Catholic League.
◆1593 Henry IV abjures Protestantism and enters Paris.

◆1596 Sully (1559 – 1641), counsellor to Henry IV, advocates the development of agriculture.
◆1598 Henry IV issues the Edict of Nantes (which allows freedom of worship to the Protestants) and so brings an end to the Wars of Religion and re-establishes peace in the kingdom.

◆1600 Marriage of Henry IV and Marie de Médicis (1573 – 1642).
◇1600 The Grande Galerie du Louvre (1600 – 1608) is designed by the architect Jacques II Androuet du Cerceau (1550 – 1614).
◇1602 Henry IV founds the tapestry-making company Les Gobelins in Paris; Flemish artisans are invited to introduce new techniques.

◆1608 French navigator and Governor of New France Samuel de Champlain (ca. 1570 – 1635) founds Quebec.
◆1610 Assassination of Henry IV.
Louis XIII (1601 – 1643) becomes king of France.
Regency of Marie de Médicis (1573 – 1642) and Concini (1575 – 1617).

◇1616 *Les Tragiques*, by Agrippa d'Aubigné (1552 – 1630), poem glorifying Protestantism.

◇1622 Marie de Médicis commissions from Rubens the paintings for the Gallery of the Luxembourg Palace in Paris.

English/Anglais

◇1623 Sept ans après la mort de Shakespeare, deux acteurs de sa troupe, John Heminges et Henry Condell, rassemblent et publient 36 de ses pièces dans le *Premier Folio*.
L'auteur dramatique anglais John Webster (né v.1580 – mort v.1625) écrit *The Duchess of Malfi* (La Duchesse de Malfi).
◆1624 Les Hollandais chassent les Anglais de l'archipel des Moluques.
◇1624 Naissance de George Fox (mort en 1691), fondateur de la 'Société des Amis' ou secte des 'Quakers'.
◆1625 Charles Ier monte sur le trône.
La peste noire fait plus de 40 000 morts à Londres.
◇1626 Mort de Francis Bacon, philosophe et homme d'État anglais. Son ouvrage *Novum Organum* pose les principes d'une méthode inductive et expérimentale.
◆1627 L'Angleterre déclare la guerre à la France.
◇1628 Le médecin anglais William Harvey (1578 – 1657) publie son *Exertitatio Anatomica de Motu Cordis et Sanguinis* qui contient la première description de la circulation du sang.
◆1629 L'aventurier David Kirke prend possession de Québec pour la Grande-Bretagne.
◆1630 Début d'un fort courant d'émigration de l'Angleterre vers le Massachusetts.
◇1631 Mort du poète anglais John Donne (né v. 1572).
◆1632 Le traité de Saint-Germain-en-Laye rend Québec à la France.
◇1632 Naissance de Christopher Wren, architecte de la cathédrale de Saint Paul, du Royal Exchange et de l'Observatoire de Greenwich.
◆1635 Fondation de la colonie américaine de Rhode Island.
◇1635 Inauguration d'un service postal public entre Édimbourg et Londres.
◆1636 Fondation de la colonie américaine du Connecticut.
◇1637 En Écosse, l'Église d'Angleterre tente de s'imposer face à l'Église d'Écosse, presbytérienne et calviniste; la première lecture du *Revised Prayer Book* (nouvelle version du Livre de Prières des Anglicans) dans la cathédrale de St Giles, à Édimbourg, provoque de violentes émeutes.

◆1641 Des milliers de colons protestants périssent au cours d'un soulèvement en Ulster.
◆1642 – 1648 Guerre civile en Angleterre entre les Parlementaristes, inquiets de la croissance de l'absolutisme royal, et les partisans de Charles Ier.
◆1643 Batailles de Edgehill et de Newbury.
◆1644 Batailles de Marston Moor et de Naseby.

1649 – 1659 le Commonwealth ou Protectorat de Cromwell

◆1649 Exécution de Charles Ier d'Angleterre (né en 1600) et abolition de la monarchie. Oliver Cromwell (1599 – 1658) institue un nouveau régime, le Commonwealth.
Les niveleurs (the Levellers), républicains qui s'opposent aux tendances autoritaires de Cromwell et réclament une représentation populaire accrue, sont vaincus à la bataille de Burford.
◇1651 Le philosophe anglais Thomas Hobbes (1588 – 1679) expose ses théories philosophiques et politiques dans le plus important de ses ouvrages *Leviathan* (Le Léviathan).
◆1652 – 1674 Guerres anglo-hollandaises, trois guerres navales dues essentiellement à des rivalités commerciales et coloniales entre les deux pays.
◆1654 Annexation de l'Irlande. Le parti républicain irlandais s'oppose à la domination anglaise.

1660 – 1688 Restauration: retour des Stuarts

◆1660 Restauration de la monarchie. Charles II, de la maison écossaise des Stuarts, monte sur le trône.
◇1660 L'Anglais Samuel Pepys (1633 – 1673), fonctionnaire à l'Amirauté, commence la rédaction de son célèbre *Journal*.
◇1662 Le physicien et chimiste irlandais Robert Boyle (1627 – 1691) énonce la loi de Boyle, selon laquelle, à temperature constante, la pression d'un gaz est inversement proportionnelle à son volume.
◆1664 Les Anglais s'emparent de la colonie hollandaise de New Amsterdam qu'ils rebaptisent New York.
◇1665 Le poète anglais John Milton (1608 – 1674) termine *Paradise Lost* (le Paradis Perdu), son œuvre la plus célèbre.
◆1666 Le Grand Incendie de Londres (the Great Fire of London) éclate dans une boulangerie de Pudding Lane et, favorisé par les constructions en bois, fait de terribles ravages dans le centre de la ville. La cathédrale médiévale de St Paul est détruite.
◆1668 Sir William Temple (1628 – 1699) conclut la Triple Alliance (Grande-Bretagne, Hollande et Suède) contre la France.
◇1668 La nomination du poète John Dryden (1631 – 1700) au poste de 'Poet Laureate' inaugure la tradition des 'poètes officiels de la Cour'.
◆1670 Fondation de la Compagnie de la baie d'Hudson, établie pour le commerce des fourrures. Fondation des colonies de Caroline du Nord et du Sud en Amérique.
Signature des deux traités de Douvres, l'un secret et l'autre public, entre Charles II et Louis XIV. Charles II s'engage à se convertir au catholicisme, engagement qu'il ne tient d'ailleurs pas. Il est maintenant tenu de soutenir Louis XIV, en particulier contre les Hollandais.

French/Français

◆1624 Richelieu (1585 – 1642) becomes minister of Louis XIII. His programme consists of reducing the power of the nobles, destroying the Huguenots and fighting Austria.

◆1628 Capitulation of La Rochelle, a Protestant refuge, after a year-long siege by Richelieu.

◆1630 Day of the Dupes: Richelieu triumphs over the supporters of Marie de Médicis.
◇1631 Théophraste Renaudot (1586 – 1653) founds the *Gazette*, which marks the beginning of journalism.
◆1632 The treaty of Saint-Germain-en-Laye returns Quebec to France.
◇1634 Richelieu founds the Académie Française.

◇1636 Corneille (1606 – 1684) publishes *le Cid*.
◆1637 Uprising of the Croquants (peasants) of the Limousin.
◇1637 Descartes (1596 – 1650) writes *Discours de la méthode* (Discourse on Method).
Claude Gelée, also known as Lorrain, (1600 – 1682), paints *Port au soleil couchant* (Seaport at Sunset).
◆1638 The French take the island of Réunion.
◆1639 Uprising of the va-nu-pieds (Bare Feet) (1639 – 1641) in Normandy.
◇1640 Nicolas Poussin painter-in-ordinary to the king.
◆1642 Mazarin (1602 – 1661) becomes minister to Louis XIII.
◇1642 Building of the château of Maisons (Maisons-Laffitte) by François Mansart (1598 – 1666).
Pascal (1623 – 1662) invents a calculating machine.
◆1643 Reign of Louis XIV (1638 – 1715). Regency of Anne of Austria (1601 – 1666) and Mazarin.
◇1643 Molière (1622 – 1673) founds the Illustre Théâtre.
◇1645 Building of the Val-de-Grâce, by Mansart.
◇1647 Vaugelas (1585 – 1650) publishes *Remarques sur la langue française* (Remarks on the French Language).
◆1648 At the end of the Thirty Years War, the Treaty of Westphalia transfers to the king of France the rights of the Habsburgs in Alsace and proclaims the independence and neutrality of the Swiss Confederation.
◆1648 First Fronde (1648 – 1649) (insurrection) against Mazarin.
◆1650 Second Fronde (1650 – 53) led by parliament against Mazarin.

◇1654 Correspondence between Fermat, Pascal and Huyghens, on the origin of the calculation of probabilities.

◇1656 Pascal publishes *Les Provinciales* (Provincial Letters), a work in which he attacks the Jesuits and defends the Jansenists.
◆1659 Treaty of the Pyrenees: victory of France over Spain; France keeps among others Artois and Roussillon.
Creation of Saint-Louis, a French trading post in Africa (Senegal).
◆1661 Louis XIV reigns without a regent. Colbert (1619 – 1683) and Louvois (1639 – 1691) are ministers.
◇1661 The building of the palace of Versailles entrusted to Le Vau, Le Brun and Le Nôtre.
◆1664 Foundation of the Compagnie Française des Indes.
◇1664 Molière's *Tartuffe* is staged at Versailles and immediately banned.
◇1665 Molière writes *Dom Juan*.
La Rochefoucauld (1613 – 1680) publishes *Maximes*.

◇1667 Racine's (1639 – 1699) *Andromaque* is performed.
◇1668 Molière's *L'Avare* (The Miser) is performed. Jean de La Fontaine (1621 – 1695) publishes *Fables*.
◇1669 Molière's *Tartuffe* is finally permitted to be performed.
Racine writes *Britannicus*.
◆1670 Treaty of Dover creating an alliance between Louis XIV and Charles II.
◇1670 Pascal's *Pensées* is published posthumously.
◆1673 Expedition of Jolliet and Père Marquette up the Mississippi valley.
◇1673 Molière's *Le Malade imaginaire* (The Imaginary Invalid) is performed.

English/Anglais

◇1676 Inauguration de l'Observatoire de Greenwich conçu par Christopher Wren. Construit sur le méridien origine, il sert de base au temps solaire moyen de Greenwich.
♦1678 Sous la pression de l'opinion publique, Charles II conclut une alliance avec les Hollandais contre la France.
◇1678 L'écrivain anglais John Bunyan termine la première partie du *Pilgrim's Progress* (Le Voyage du Pèlerin).
Mort du poète et métaphysicien Andrew Marvell (né en 1621).
◇1680 L'astronome anglais Edmund Halley (1656 – 1742) prédit le retour d'une comète dont le passage au périhalie avait été observé en 1583 (comète de Halley) pour 1758, 1835 et 1910.
Introduction d'un service postal, le Penny Post, à Londres.
♦1681 Charles II octroie un territoire en Amérique à William Penn qui le nomme Pennsylvania en l'honneur de son père.
◇1684 Le mathématicien, physicien, astronome et penseur Sir Isaac Newton (1642 – 1727) expose sa théorie de la gravitation universelle dans *De Motu Corporum*.
♦1685 Jacques II d'Angleterre (Jacques VII d'Écosse) monte sur le trône.
◇1687 Isaac Newton publie son œuvre maîtresse *Philosophiae Naturalis Principia Mathematica* qui contient ses trois lois de la mécanique.

1688: La Révolution Glorieuse

♦1688 En Angleterre, la Révolution Glorieuse (The Glorious Revolution) oblige Jacques II à s'enfuir en France.
◇1688 Aphra Behn (1604 – 1689), sans doute le premier auteur féminin professionnel en Angleterre, publie son roman *Oroonoko*.
♦1689 Le protestant Guillaume d'Orange (Guillaume III d'Angleterre, Guillaume Ier d'Écosse) partage la couronne avec son épouse Marie II, fille de Jacques II.
◇1689 Mort du médecin anglais Thomas Sydenham (né en 1624). Ses ouvrages, avec leurs descriptions de maladies, seront traduits et réimprimés pendant tout le 18ème siècle.
Le compositeur anglais Henry Purcell (1659 – 1695) termine le premier opéra anglais, *Dido and Aeneas* (Didon et Enée).
♦1690 Guillaume d'Orange remporte la victoire de la Boyne en Irlande sur Jacques II qui s'enfuit en France.
◇1690 Le philosophe empiriste John Locke (1632 – 1704) publie son *Essay concerning Human Understanding* (Essai sur l'entendement humain).
♦1691 Guillaume d'Orange assiège Limerick, en Irlande. Traité de Limerick.
♦1692 À Glencoe, en Écosse, les Macdonald, partisans de Jacques II, sont massacrés par le clan rival des Campbell.
Jacques II et Louis XIV rassemblent des troupes en Normandie pour envahir l'Angleterre. Leurs tentatives échouent.
◇1692 Procès des sorcières de Salem dans la colonie du Massachusetts. Dix-neuf personnes sont accusées de sorcellerie et exécutées avant d'être reconnues innocentes.
♦1694 Après la mort de sa femme, la reine Marie, Guillaume d'Orange règne seul jusqu'à sa mort en 1702.
Création de la banque d'Angleterre.
♦1698 Le Parlement sanctionne la traite des Noirs. Entre 1680 et 1786, les marchands d'esclaves anglais transportent près de deux millions d'esclaves d'Afrique en Amérique où ils serviront de main d'œuvre dans les nouvelles plantations de sucre et de café.
◇1698 Thomas Savery (v. 1650 – 1715) invente la première machine utilisant la vapeur d'eau comme force motrice pour pomper l'eau dans les mines de charbon.

French/Français

♦1678 Alsace becomes a French territory.
In the Treaty of Nimègues, Spain cedes Franche-Comté to France.
◇1678 Mme de La Fayette (1634 – 1693) writes *La Princesse de Clèves* (The Princess of Clèves), first novel of modern sentiments.
◇1680 The Comédie-Française is founded.
Richelet publishes *Dictionnaire français des mots et des choses*, the first French dictionary.
♦1681 Strasbourg is annexed by France.
♦1682 Louis XIV moves the Court to Versailles.
René Robert Le Cavelier de La Salle (1643 – 1687) sails down the Mississippi and founds Louisiana in honour of Louis XIV.
◇1684 Furetière publishes *Essai d'un dictionnaire universel*.
♦1685 Louis XIV decrees the Revocation of the Edict of Nantes which leads to the exile of Protestants.
♦1686 De Troyes and Le Moyne D'Uberville take three English trading posts on James Bay, in Canada.
◇1688 La Bruyère (1645 – 1696) publishes *Les Caractères*, anthology of psychological and social portraits.
First report on the use of steam, by Denis Papin.
◇1690 François Couperin composes *Works for organ*.
◇1691 Racine writes *Athalie*.
◇1697 Charles Perrault (1628 – 1703) publishes his *Contes de ma mère l'oye*, the first collection of fairy tales in literature.
Pierre Bayle publishes his *Dictionnaire historique et critique*.

1700

English/Anglais

◇1701 L'agriculteur anglais Jethro Tull (1674 – 1740) invente la machine à semer en sillons.
♦1702 Anne, fille de Jacques II, devient reine d'Angleterre, d'Écosse et d'Irlande.
♦1704 Les Anglais s'emparent de Gibraltar, jusqu'alors possession espagnole.
◇1704 Le savant anglais Sir Isaac Newton publie *Opticks*.
♦1707 L'Acte d'Union unit l'Angleterre à l'Écosse.
◇1709 Le métallurgiste anglais Abraham Darby (v. 1678 – 1717) utilise pour la première fois le coke pour l'extraction du fer par fusion.
♦1713 Le Traité d'Utrecht établit la paix entre la France et la Grande-Bretagne et donne à celle-ci de vastes territoires au Canada.

1714 - 1901 Les Hanovre

♦1714 George Ier, roi protestant de la maison de Hanovre, devient roi de Grande-Bretagne et d'Irlande.
♦1715 Révolte des Jacobites (partisans de Jacques II et de la maison des Stuarts) en Grande-Bretagne contre la succession protestante hanovrienne.
◇1719 L'écrivain anglais Daniel Defoe (1660 – 1731) publie *Robinson Crusoe*.
♦1720 'The South Sea Bubble': l'effondrement des valeurs de la Compagnie des Mers du Sud après une période de spéculation effrénée entraîne une crise financière et la ruine de nombreux actionnaires.
◇1724 L'Anglais Thomas Longman fonde la maison d'édition qui porte toujours son nom.
◇1726 Jonathan Swift, pasteur et satiriste anglo-irlandais, publie *Gulliver's Travels* (Les Voyages de Gulliver).
♦1727 George II (1683 – 1760) devient roi de Grande-Bretagne et d'Irlande.
♦1733 La Géorgie devient colonie britannique par Charte Royale. C'est la dernière des treize colonies anglaises d'Amérique du Nord à être fondée.
◇1733 La mécanisation de l'industrie textile progresse grâce à l'invention de la navette volante par John Kay (1701 – 1764).

French/Français

◇1707 Denis Papin builds a boat propelled by paddle wheels.
♦1713 The Treaty of Utrecht establishes peace between Britain and France, and gives Britain large areas of what is now Canada.
♦1715 Reign of Louis XV (1710 – 1774). The French take Mauritius.
♦1718 Founding of New Orleans (La Nouvelle-Orléans).
◇1721 Montesquieu (1689 – 1755) writes *Lettres Persanes* (Persian Letters).
♦1723 Louis XV comes of age and rules without a regent.
◇1728 Abbé Prévost publishes *Manon Lescaut*.
◇1730 Marivaux publishes *Le Jeu de l'amour et du hasard* (Love in Livery).
◇1734 Voltaire (1694 – 1778) publishes *Lettres philosophiques*.
◇1735 Scientific voyage (1735 – 1744) of La Condamine and Bouger to South America to measure the length of a degree of meridian at the equator.

English/Anglais

◇1739 Le philosophe écossais David Hume (1711 – 1776) publie *A Treatise of Human Nature* (Traité de la nature humaine).
◇1740 Le romancier anglais Samuel Richardson (1689 – 1761) publie *Pamela*, un roman épistolaire.
◇1742 Le compositeur allemand naturalisé britannique Georg Friedrich Haendel compose son *Messie* (Messiah).
◆1745 Deuxième révolte jacobite importante.
◆1746 La défaite des partisans de Jacques II face aux forces de George II (de la maison de Hanovre) à Culloden met fin aux ambitions jacobites. Début d'une campagne de répression féroce dans les Highlands d'Écosse, qui marque la fin du système des clans.

◇1750 Le philosophe écossais David Hume commence la rédaction des *Dialogues concerning Natural Religion* (Dialogues sur la religion naturelle).
◇1752 Adoption du calendrier grégorien en Grande-Bretagne.

◆1755 Au Canada, expulsion des Acadiens par les Anglais (Le Grand Dérangement). Certains d'entre eux s'installeront en Louisiane (les Cajuns).
◇1755 L'écrivain anglais Samuel Johnson (1709 – 1784) publie son *Dictionnaire de la langue anglaise.*
◆1757 Les forces britanniques conduites par Robert Clive (1725 – 1774) remportent la victoire de Plassey sur Siraj ud-Daula (v.1732 – 1757), nabab du Bengale. Cette victoire constitue une étape importante de l'acquisition du Bengale par la Grande-Bretagne.
◆1759 Le général britannique James Wolfe (1727 – 1759) l'emporte sur les Français aux Plaines d'Abraham, près de Québec.
◆1760 George III (1738 – 1820) accède au trône.
◇1760 Le peintre anglais Joshua Reynolds (1723 – 1792) exécute son *Portrait de Georgiana comtesse Spencer et sa fille.*
◆1763 Par le traité de Paris (marquant la fin de la guerre de sept ans), la France cède tout le Canada à la Grande-Bretagne et perd ses possessions en Inde à l'exception de cinq comptoirs.
◇1763 Les géomètres britanniques Charles Mason (1730 – 1787) et Jeremiah Dixon (mort en 1777) entreprennent la délimitation de la frontière entre la Pennsylvanie et le Maryland (Ligne Mason-Dixon). Cette frontière est considérée comme la ligne de démarcation entre le Nord et le Sud.
◇1764 L'anglais James Hargreaves (1720 – 1778) invente la première machine à filer à plusieurs broches, dite 'spinning jenny'.
◆1765 – 1766 La crise du Stamp Act (Loi du Timbre) reflète le mécontentement grandissant des colons américains face aux exigences financières de la Grande-Bretagne.
◇1765 L'ingénieur écossais James Watt (1736 – 1819) perfectionne le moteur à vapeur.
◇1766 Le chimiste anglais Henry Cavendish (1731 – 1810) découvre l'hydrogène.

◆1770 Le capitaine James Cook (1728 – 1779), navigateur anglais, découvre Botany Bay en Australie.
◇1770 Le peintre anglais Thomas Gainsborough (1727 – 1788) exécute son célèbre *Blue Boy.*
◆1773 La 'Boston Tea Party': en réponse aux taxes instituées par la Grande-Bretagne, les colons américains jettent les cargaisons de thé de la Compagnie des Indes à la mer.
◆1774 Une communauté de chrétiens revivalistes, les 'Shakers', s'installe près d'Albany, dans l'État de New York.
◇1774 Le pasteur et chimiste anglais Joseph Priestley (1733 – 1804) découvre l'oxygène.
◆1775 Début de la Guerre d'Indépendance dans les colonies anglaises d'Amérique du Nord.
◆1776 Le Congrès continental américain adopte la Déclaration d'Indépendance qui rejette l'autorité du roi d'Angleterre le 4 juillet.

◆1778 La France et la Hollande soutiennent les colons américains et l'Angleterre déclare la guerre à la France.

◆1783 La Paix de Paris reconnaît l'existence de la République fédérée des États-Unis.
Le Second Pitt (William Pitt the Younger) (1759 – 1806) devient Premier ministre du Royaume-Uni. Son premier ministère est marqué par d'importantes réformes et une politique influencée par les théories libérales de l'économiste Adam Smith.
◇1785 Le pasteur anglais John Cartwright (1743 – 1823) invente le métier mécanique pour la filature du coton.
◇1786 Le poète écossais Robert Burns (1759 – 1796) publie ses *Poems, Chiefly in the Scottish Dialect* (Poèmes, pour la plupart en langue écossaise).
◆1787 George Washington devient le premier Président des États-Unis.
◆1788 Les premiers colons anglais débarquent à Botany Bay, en Nouvelle-Galles du Sud, en Australie.

French/Français

◇1735 Rameau composes *Les Indes galantes.*
◇1736 Scientific voyage (1736 – 1739) of Maupertuis to Lapland to measure the length of a degree of meridian which will lead to confirmation of Newton's theories on the flattening-out of the earth at the poles.
◇1737 Marivaux publishes *Les Fausses Confidences.*
◇1739 Le duc de Saint-Simon (1675 – 1755) begins his *Mémoires.*
◇1743 D'Alembert (1717 – 1783) publishes *Traité de dynamique.*

◇1751 Denis Diderot (1713 – 1784) begins the publication (1751 – 1772) of *l'Encyclopédie ou Dictionnaire raisonné des sciences, des arts et des techniques* (Encyclopedia, or Critical Dictionary of Sciences, Arts and Trades), which represents the full spirit of the Enlightenment.
◇1754 The architect J.A. Gabriel (1698 – 1782) builds the Place de la Concorde, the Royal Military Academy and the Petit Trianon at Versailles.
◆1755 Expulsion of the French population from Acadia by the English (the Grand Dérangement). Some of their descendants will settle in Louisiana and become the Cajuns.

◆1759 The British under the leadership of General James Wolfe (1727 – 1759) defeat the French on the Plains of Abraham, near Quebec.
◇1759 Voltaire writes *Candide.*
◇1762 Rousseau (1712 – 1778) writes *Emile* and the *Contrat social* (Social Contract).
◆1763 At the end of the Seven Years War, in the Treaty of Paris, France cedes Quebec with all of Canada to England, and the French Indies are reduced to five trading posts.

◇1770 Joseph Cugnot builds the first steam-powered vehicle.

◆1774 Reign of Louis XVI (1754 – 1793). Turgot (1727 – 1781) becomes Comptroller-General of Finance.
The English government grants Canada a statute (Quebec Act) which provides legislative and political guarantees for the French Quebecois, whilst reinforcing the authority of London.
◆1775 A terrible food shortage in Paris leads to the fall of the Minister of Finance, Turgot.
◇1776 Jouffroy d'Abbans (1751 – 1832) sails the first steam boat on the Doubs.
◆1777 The physiocrat Necker (1732 – 1804) becomes Comptroller-General of Finance.
◇1777 The chemist Lavoisier (1743 – 1794) explains the role of oxygen in the respiratory system.
◆1778 – 1782 France sends troops to fight against the British in the American War of Independence. General de La Fayette (1757 – 1834) plays a leading role in the war.
◇1781 Rousseau publishes *Confessions.*
◇1782 Choderlos de Laclos (1741 – 1803) publishes the novel *Les Liaisons dangereuses* (Dangerous Liaisons).
◇1784 Beaumarchais (1732 – 1799) writes the play *Le Mariage de Figaro* (The Marriage of Figaro).
Rivarol (1753 – 1801) publishes *Discours sur l'universalité de la langue française.*
◆1785 – 1786 The affair of queen Marie-Antoinette's diamond necklace, a swindle instigated by the adventurer Cagliostro, brings discredit upon the queen.
◇1785 Scientific expedition led by La Pérouse (1741 – 1788) in the Pacific Ocean. He is killed in 1788.
◆1788 Popular riots in Paris and the provinces. Calling of the Estates General.

1789: The French Revolution

◆1789 Beginning of the French Revolution.
The Estates General proclaim themselves a National Assembly. Parisians storm the Bastille on 14 July.
The abolition of Privileges is decreed (on the night of 4 August), and the Declaration of the Rights of Man and of the Citizen is passed. The property of the clergy is confiscated by the Nation.

English/Anglais

◇1792 Thomas Paine (1737 – 1809), auteur politique anglais, publie *The Rights of Man* (Les Droits de l'homme).
◇1793 L'Américain Eli Whitney (1765 – 1825) invente l'égreneuse qui sépare les graines des fibres de coton.

◆1794 Publication de *Chants d'expérience* (Songs of Experience), du poète William Blake (1757 – 1827).

◇1796 Le médecin anglais Edward Jenner (1749 – 1823) découvre le principe de la vaccination et réussit à immuniser un enfant contre la variole.

◆1798 Échec d'un soulèvement en Irlande. William Pitt propose une union législative suivie de l'émancipation des catholiques.
Victoire de Nelson contre Bonaparte à la bataille d'Aboukir.
◇1798 *Lyrical Ballads* (Ballades lyriques) de Coleridge et Wordsworth, véritable manisfeste du romantisme.

French/Français

◇1789 David (1748 – 1825) paints *Le Serment du Jeu de Paume* (The Tennis Court Oath).
◆1790 Division of France into 83 departments. 14 July is established as the 'fête de la Fédération' (French national day).
◇1790 Jussieu (1748 – 1836) develops the Jardin des Plantes botanical gardens in Paris.
◆1791 Flight and arrest of the king at Varennes. Passing of the Constitution.
In Canada, a constitutional bill separates Canada into two regions: French-speaking Quebec forms Lower Canada.

1792 – 1804 The First Republic

◆1792 Uprising in Paris and overthrow of the king. Abolition of royalty and proclamation of the First Republic on 21 September. Beginning of the king's trial.
◇1792 Rouget de Lisle (1760 – 1836) composes *La Marseillaise.*
◆1793 Execution of Louis XVI on 21 January.
Promulgation of the 1793 Constitution known as Year II.
France at war with England, Holland, Austria, Russia, Prussia, Spain and Portugal, who want to crush the revolution.
Trial and execution of Marie-Antoinette.
◆1794 Robespierre (1758 – 1794) has the Great Terror decreed, but his adversaries have it thrown out and he is guillotined along with his allies.
◇1794 Creation of the École Polytechnique.
Creation of the National Archives. Creation of the École Normale Supérieure.
French becomes obligatory in all public documents.
◆1795 Promulgation of the Constitution of Year III. Following an insurrection on 5 October (13 Vendémiaire in the revolutionary calendar), Bonaparte (1769 – 1821) crushes the royalists and establishes the Directory.
◇1795 Creation of the Écoles Centrales. Creation of the School of oriental languages.
Institution of the metric system
◆1796 Bonaparte, head of the French army in Italy, is victorious in the first Italy campaign at Lodi, Arcole, Rivoli and Mantua (1797).
◇1796 Laplace (1749 – 1827) publishes *Exposition du système du monde* (The System of the World), his nebular hypothesis of planetary origin.
◆1797 Bonaparte concludes his Italian victories by the Treaty of Campo Formio which sanctions the defeats of Austria. Belgium is ceded to France.
◇1797 Lamarck (1744 – 1829) publishes *Mémoires de physique.*
◆1798 Reuniting of Mulhouse and Geneva with France.
The French give a constitution to Holland and to the Swiss Cantons.
Bonaparte leads the Egypt expedition: victorious in the battle of the Pyramids, he takes Cairo, but is defeated at the battle of Aboukir by Admiral Nelson, who destroys the French fleet.
◇1798 Bonaparte founds the Cairo Institute.
◆1799 Following his coup d'état on 9 November (18 Brumaire in the revolutionary calendar), Bonaparte becomes Consul for three years and promulgates the Constitution of Year VIII, which brings the French Revolution to an end and marks the beginning of the Consulate (1799 – 1804).
◇1799 Monge (1746 – 1718) publishes *Traité de géométrie descriptive* (Treatise on Descriptive Geometry).

1800

English/Anglais

◆1800 Thomas Jefferson (1743 – 1826) est élu à la présidence des États-Unis (1800 – 1808). Il fut le principal auteur de la Déclaration d'indépendance en 1776.
Les Anglais s'emparent de Malte.

◆1803 L'achat de la Louisiane à la France donne aux États-Unis le contrôle de toute la vallée du Mississippi.

◆1804 William Clark (1770 – 1838) et Meriwether Lewis (1774 – 1809) entament leur voyage d'exploration à l'ouest du Mississippi.

◆1805 Bataille de Trafalgar. Nelson y remporte une éclatante victoire sur la flotte franco-espagnole mais y trouve la mort.
◇1805 J.M.W. Turner (1775 – 1851) peint *Shipwreck.*

French/Français

◆1800 Foundation of the Bank of France. The second Italy campaign imposes peace on Austria through the Treaty of Lunéville (1801), concluded by the victory of Marengo.
◆1801 Bonaparte brings an end to the civil and religious wars by signing the Concordat with Pius VII (Pie VII).
◆1802 Bonaparte is appointed Consul for Life by plebiscite; he promulgates the Constitution of Year X.
◇1802 Chateaubriand (1768 – 1848) writes *Le Génie du christianisme* (The Beauties of Christianity or The Genius of Christianity).
Bichat (1771 – 1802) publishes *Anatomie générale*: Bichat is the first anatomist to establish that each organ is composed of tissues.
Creation of the Lycées and of the Legion of Honour.
◆1803 Napoleon sells Louisiana (which at the time represented a third of present-day America) to the United States.
◇1803 Jean-Baptiste Say publishes *Traité d'économie politique* (A Treatise on Political Economy).

1804 – 1814 The Napoleonic Empire

◆1804 Promulgation of the Civil Code. Napoleon has himself proclaimed Emperor, and anointed by Pope Pius VII on 2 December. Promulgation of the Constitution of Year XII. Beginning of the First Empire.
◇1804 Cuvier publishes *Leçons d'anatomie générale* (Lessons of Comparative Anatomy).
◆1805 Third coalition (Anglo-Austro-Russian) against Napoleon. Resumption of the war with the English and defeat at Trafalgar by Nelson. The Grand Army crosses the Rhine. Napoleon is victorious over Austria and Russia at Austerlitz.
◇1805 Invention of the Jacquard loom (1752 – 1834).
Chateaubriand writes *René.*
◆1806 Victorious in the battle of Jena over Prussia, Napoleon takes Berlin and Warsaw.
◇1806 Building of the Vendôme Column and start of the construction of the Arc de Triomphe on the Place de l'Étoile in Paris.

English/Anglais	French/Français

English/Anglais

◆1807 Abolition de la traite des esclaves dans l'ensemble de l'empire britannique, à la suite du mouvement lancé par le député réformiste William Wilberforce (1759 – 1834).
◇1807 Publication de *Ode on Intimations of Immortality*, de William Wordsworth (1770 – 1850).
Début de l'éclairage au gaz à Londres.
◆1808 – 1814 Guerre d'Espagne entre la France et la Grande-Bretagne pour le contrôle de péninsule ibérique.
◆1809 Défaite de la Grande-Bretagne face à la France à La Corogne.

French/Français

◆1807 Napoleon continues his conquests with victories over Russia at Eylau and Friedland and forces Tsar Alexander I to sign the Tilsit peace treaty. The Great Empire is established.
◇1807 Studies by Gay-Lussac (1778 – 1850) on the expansion of gases.
David paints *Le Sacre* (Anointing of Napoleon).
◆1808 Creation of the imperial nobility. Conspiracy of Talleyrand (1754 – 1838) and Fouché (1759 – 1820).
◆1809 The 5th coalition against Napoleon, led by Austria, is defeated at Wagram. Repudiation of Joséphine de Beauharnais (1763 – 1814).
◇1809 J.B. Lamarck publishes *Philosophie zoologique* (Zoological Philosophy), the first great theory of the evolution of the species (Lamarckism).

1810

English/Anglais

◇1810 Le poète et romancier écossais Sir Walter Scott (1771 – 1832) publie *The Lady of the Lake* (La Dame du lac).
L'architecte britannique John Nash (1752 – 1835) entame la conception du Royal Pavilion de Brighton.
◆1811 – 1812 En Angleterre, des ouvriers de l'industrie textile (les Luddites) détruisent de nouveaux métiers à tisser en réaction contre les bas salaires et la menace du chômage.
◇1811 La romancière anglaise Jane Austen (1775 – 1817) publie *Sense and Sensibility* (Raison et Sensibilité).
◇1812 La publication du premier volume du chef-d'œuvre du poète britannique George Gordon, Lord Byron (1788 – 1824) *Childe Harold's Pilgrimage* (Le Chevalier Harold) connaît un vif succès. Childe Harold, personnage mélancolique et révolté, reste le type du héros romantique 'byronien'.
◇1813 Publication de *Orgueil et préjugé* (Pride and Prejudice), de Jane Austen.
◆1815 Battu à Waterloo par Wellington et Blucher, Napoléon abdique pour la deuxième fois et est deporté à Sainte-Hélène.
Le gouvernement de Lord Liverpool impose les 'Corn Laws', droits élevés sur les importations de blé étranger.
◆1818 Les États-Unis et la Grande-Bretagne décident de fixer la frontière entre le Canada et les États-Unis au 49ème parallèle.
◇1818 Publication de *Frankenstein*, de Mary Shelley (1797 – 1851).
◆1819 Sir Stamford Raffles (1781 – 1826) acquiert Singapour pour la compagnie des Indes Orientales.
Mort de onze personnes lors de l'intervention de la police au cours d'un meeting sur la réforme parlementaire à St Peter's Fields, à Manchester. Cet épisode est connu sous le nom de Peterloo Massacre (jeu de mots avec Waterloo).
L'Espagne vend la Floride aux États-Unis.
◇1819 Publication de *Prométhée délivré* (Prometheus Unbound), de Percy Bysshe Shelley (1792 – 1822).

French/Français

◆1810 Marriage of Napoleon to Marie Louise (1791 – 1847), daughter of the Emperor of Austria. Publication of the Penal Code.
◆1811 Birth of the king of Rome, son of Napoleon and Marie Louise, nicknamed the Eagle (l'Aiglon). He is to die in 1832.
◇1811 J. Fourier (1768 – 1830) introduces the expansion of functions in trigonometric series.
◆1812 Napoleon marches on Moscow. After the taking of Vilna and Vitebsk and the victory of Borodino, the Grand Army has to retreat because of the winter which has reduced its ranks to one tenth their numbers: this is the rout of Berezina.
◇1812 Laplace publishes *Théorie analytique des probabilités.*
Cuvier (1773 – 1838) starts writing his *Recherches sur les ossements fossiles*, the founding work of palaeontology.
◆1813 Napoleon is forced to retreat from Germany following defeat at Leipzig.

1814 - 1830 The Restoration of the Bourbon monarchy

◆1814 The France Campaign (January–March) ends in the invasion of the country and leads to the abdication of Napoleon and the restoration of Louis XVIII (1755 – 1824).
◇1814 Ingres (1780 – 1867) paints the *Grande Odalisque.*
Ampère (1775 – 1836) discovers electromagnetism and invents the galvanometer and the electromagnet.
◆1815 The Hundred Days (from March to June). Napoleon leaves the Island of Elba and marches on Paris. After his defeat by Wellington and Blucher at Waterloo, he abdicates and is deported to Saint Helena, leaving Louis XVIII to reign over France until 1824.
At the end of the Battle of Waterloo, England conceives the plan of making Belgium a buffer state to contain the territorial ambitions of France: Belgium and the Netherlands are united and the Prince of Orange is called to the crown. But Belgium is Catholic whilst the Netherlands are Reformist (Calvinists).
The Federal Pact ratifies the membership of 22 Cantons of the Swiss Confederation, reproclaimed neutral and independent by the Congress of Vienna.
◇1816 The physicist Nicéphore Niepce (1765 – 1833) invents the technique of photography.
Benjamin Constant (1767-1830) publishes *Adolphe.*
◇1819 Théodore Géricault (1791 – 1824) paints *Le Radeau de la Méduse* (The Raft of the Medusa).

1820

English/Anglais

◆1820 Le Compromis de Missouri: le parallèle 36 30 sépare les états esclavagistes des états non esclavagistes.
En Grande-Bretagne, George IV (1762 – 1830) accède au trône.
◇1820 Le poète anglais John Keats publie *Lamia and Other Poems* qui contient ses œuvres les plus connues, dont les *Odes.*
◆1821 Le physicien et chimiste anglais Michael Faraday (1791 – 1867) invente le moteur électromagnétique ainsi qu'une génératrice à courant continu.
◇1821 Le peintre paysagiste anglais John Constable (1776 – 1837) exécute *The Haywain* (La charrette de foin).
◇1822 Publication des *Confessions d'un mangeur d'opium anglais* (Confessions of an English Opium Eater), de Thomas de Quincey (1785 – 1859).
◆1823 La 'Doctrine de Monroe' affirme l'opposition des États-Unis à toute ingérence européenne sur le continent américain.
◇1825 Inauguration de la première ligne de chemin de fer avec traction à vapeur pour le transport des voyageurs, entre Stockton et Darlington, dans le nord-est de l'Angleterre.
◇1826 Publication du *Dernier des Mohicans* (The Last of the Mohicans), du romancier américain James Fenimore Cooper (1789 – 1851).
◇1828 Le lexicographe américain Noah Webster (1758 – 1843) publie *An American Dictionary of the English Language* (Dictionnaire américain de la langue anglaise).
◆1829 La totalité du territoire australien est déclarée dépendance britannique.
Le ministre de l'Intérieur Robert Peel fait adopter l'acte d'émancipation des catholiques; il crée la police londonienne (d'où les surnoms de 'Peelers' ou 'Bobbies' donnés aux policiers).
◇1829 Première course entre les universités d'Oxford et de Cambridge sur la Tamise.

French/Français

◆1820 After the assassination of the duke of Berry (1778 – 1820), heir to the throne, the Ultras (non-liberal royalists) return to power under minister Villèle (1773 – 1854) from 1821 to 1827.
◇1820 Lamartine (1790 – 1869) publishes *Méditations poétiques.*
Ampère (1775 – 1836) discovers electrodynamics.
Arago (1786 – 1853) succeeds in magnetizing iron using electricity.
◆1821 Death of Napoleon at St Helena.
◇1821 Saint-Simon (1760 – 1825) develops in *Le Système industriel* a liberal version of industrial progress that is the precursor of an enlightened socialism, which will form the basis of Saint-Simonism.
◇1822 Champollion (1790 – 1832), the founder of Egyptology, deciphers the Egyptian hieroglyphs.
◇1823 Lamartine publishes *Nouvelles méditations.*
Saint-Simon publishes *Le Catéchisme des industriels.*
◆1824 The Chambre retrouvée: triumph of the Ultras at the legislative elections and reign of Charles X (1757 – 1836), who tries to restore the Ancien Régime.
◇1824 Arago (1786 – 1853) discovers the magnetism of rotation. Carnot (1796 – 1832) publishes his *Réflexions sur la puissance motrice du feu* (Reflections on the Motive Power of Fire), which is the foundation of thermodynamics.
◆1825 France recognizes the independence of Haiti.
◆1826 Having failed to re-establish the law of primogeniture, Charles X promulgates a more liberal Constitution.
◇1826 Brillat-Savarin (1755 – 1826) publishes his gastronomic treatise *Physiologie du Goût* (The Physiology of Taste).
◇1827 Victor Hugo (1802 – 1885) publishes his *Préface de Cromwell* (Preface to Cromwell), which marks the beginning of Romantic theatre, for which it is a manifesto.
◇1828 Berlioz (1803 – 1869) composes *La Symphonie fantastique.*
Delacroix (1798 – 1863) paints *La Mort de Sardanapale.*

1830

English/Anglais

◆1830 Guillaume IV (William IV) (1765 – 1837) accède au trône.
Les premiers colons américains s'installent en Californie, alors territoire mexicain.
◇1831 Le naturaliste anglais Charles Darwin (1809 – 1882) s'embarque à bord du Beagle. Il basera sa théorie de l'origine des espèces sur les observations qu'il effectuera au cours de son expédition.

French/Français

1830 - 1848 The July Monarchy

◆1830 The July Revolution (26–28 July) overthrows Charles X and heralds the reign of Louis Philippe I (1773 – 1850) of Valois.

English/Anglais

◇1832 William Chambers, auteur et libraire écossais, lance le *Chambers Edinburgh Journal* et peu après fonde avec son frère la maison d'édition W. & R. Chambers.
◆1833 Naissance de l'Oxford Movement (Le Mouvement d'Oxford), qui veut réformer l'Église anglicane en la rapprochant de la doctrine et des usages catholiques.
Abolition de l'esclavage dans l'empire britannique.
Le mathématicien anglais Charles Babbage (1792 – 1871) conçoit, sans la réaliser, une machine à calculer analytique qui peut être considérée comme l'ancêtre de l'ordinateur.
Des ouvriers agricoles du Dorset (les Tolpuddle Martyrs) organisent le premier syndicat. Ils sont condamnés à la déportation vers l'Australie.
◇1833 – 1834 L'homme de lettres écossais Thomas Carlyle publie son ouvrage de philosophie sociale *'Sartor Resartus'*.
◇1835 Enregistrement du brevet du revolver Colt, de Samuel Colt (1814 – 1862).
◆1836 Début de la grande migration des Boers (The Great Trek) qui quittent la colonie du Cap pour échapper à la domination anglaise.
◇1836 Début de la publication par épisodes du premier roman de Charles Dickens (1812 – 1870), *The Pickwick Papers* (Les Aventures de M. Pickwick).
◆1837 Victoria (1819 – 1901) accède au trône.
◇1837 Sir Charles Wheatstone (1802 – 1875) fait breveter son télégraphe électrique.
Publication d'*Oliver Twist*, de Charles Dickens.
L'Américain Samuel Morse (1791 – 1872) invente le morse.
◇1839 L'inventeur américain Charles Goodyear (1800 – 1860) découvre la vulcanisation du caoutchouc.
L'Anglais William Fox-Talbot invente le calotype, procédé photographique qui fut le précurseur des procédés actuels car il donnait un négatif et permettait de tirer plusieurs positifs.
◆1839 Des émeutes éclatent en Grande-Bretagne, provoquées par le mouvement d'émancipation ouvrière des chartistes.

French/Français

The ideas of the revolution in France open the way to the idea of Nation in Belgium: the States General proclaim the separation of the North and South, and the neutrality of Belgium, against the decision of the Congress of Vienna.
Beginning of the colonial conquest of Algeria. Taking of Algiers and Oran.
◇1830 Start of publication of the *Cours de philosophie positive* (1830 – 1848) by Auguste Comte (1798 – 1857), the founder of Positivism.
Lamartine (1790 – 1869) publishes *Harmonies Poétiques* (Poetical and Religious Harmonies).
Stendhal (1783 – 1842) writes *Le Rouge et le Noir* (Scarlet and Black).
Delacroix paints *La Barricade*.
Delacroix paints *La Liberté guidant le peuple* (Liberty Guiding the People).
◆1831 Revolt of the 'canuts' (silk workers) of Lyon.
The Independence of Belgium is ratified by the London Conference.
Léopold de Saxe-Coburg-Gotha is proposed as King of Belgium.
◇1831 Victor Hugo writes *Notre Dame-de-Paris* (The Hunchback of Notre Dame).
Michelet (1798 – 1874) publishes *Introduction à l'Histoire Universelle*.
◆1833 Guizot Law (1787 – 1874) on primary education paid for by the communes for the most impoverished. Ozanam founds the Saint-Vincent-de-Paul charity.
◇1833 Michelet publishes *Histoire de France* (1833 – 1867).
Balzac writes *Eugénie Grandet*.
Musset (1810 – 1857) writes *Les Caprices de Marianne*.
◆1834 In Algiers, the emir Abd-el-Kader (1808 – 1883) leads the resistance against the French conquest.
◇1834 Musset publishes *Lorenzaccio* and *On ne badine pas avec l'amour*.
Balzac writes *Le Père Goriot*.
Daumier (1808 – 1879) creates the lithograph *La rue Transnonain*.
◆1835 Failed assassination attempt against Louis Philippe.
Abd-el-Kader is defeated at the battle of Makta.
◇1835 Alexis de Tocqueville (1805 – 1859) publishes *De la Démocratie en Amérique* (1837 – 1840).
◆1836 Ministry of Adolphe Thiers (1797 – 1877). First attempted insurrection by Louis-Napoleon Bonaparte.
◆1837 Taking of Constantine in Algeria.
Revolts (1837 – 1838) in French-speaking Lower Canada (present-day Quebec) in favour of a parliamentary system. The revolts are harshly suppressed.
◇1837 Balzac publishes *Les Illusions perdues* (Lost Illusions).
Berlioz (1803 – 1869) composes his *Requiem*.
Chopin (1810 – 1849) composes *24 préludes opus 28*.
◇1838 L.J.M. Daguerre (1787 – 1851) produces the first daguerreotypes.

1840

English/Anglais

◆1840 La Grande-Bretagne annexe la Nouvelle-Zélande.

◆1842 La Grande-Bretagne acquiert Hongkong.
◆1843 Les Britanniques s'emparent du Natal, alors tenu par les Boers.

◆1845 Entrée du Texas dans l'Union, ce qui provoque la guerre contre le Mexique (1846 – 1848).
◆1845 – 1851 Une famine causée par la maladie de la pomme de terre prive l'Irlande de la moitié de sa population, par mort ou émigration.

◆1846 Le Premier ministre Robert Peel abroge les Corn Laws, provoquant la scission de son parti. Benjamin Disraeli (1804 – 1881), adversaire de Peel, s'impose sur la scène politique.
◇1846 Fondation de la Smithonian Institution, à Washington.

◇1847 Publication de *Jane Eyre*, de Charlotte Brontë (1816 – 1855).
Publication des *Hauts de Hurlevent* (Wuthering Heights), d'Emily Brontë (1818 – 1848).

◆1848 Ruée vers l'or en Californie.
Le parlement britannique abroge la loi qui interdisait l'usage du français au Canada.
◇1848 Le physicien britannique William Kelvin (qui deviendra Lord Kelvin) (1824 – 1907) établit une échelle théorique des températures (température absolue).
Création de la Confrérie des Préraphaélites, mouvement visant à renouveler l'art victorien.
Publication de *La Foire aux vanités* (Vanity Fair), de William Thackeray (1811 – 1863).

French/Français

◆1840 France annexes Mayotte and Nossi-Bé (1840 – 1842) in the Comoros islands.
In the South Antarctic, Dumont d'Urville (1790 – 1842) takes possession of Adelie Land.
Act of Union of the two Canadas (present-day Quebec and Ontario) to form United Canada.
French ceases to be an official language in Canada.
◇1840 Pierre Joseph Proudhon (1809 – 1865), theoretician of socialism, publishes *Qu'est-ce que la propriété* (What is Property?).
◇1842 Eugène Sue (1804 – 1857) publishes *Les Mystères de Paris* in serial form.
◆1843 Taking of the retinue of chief Abd-el-Kader by the troops of the duke of Aumale (1822 – 1897).
Tahiti (Polynesia) becomes a French protectorate after conquest by Admiral Dupetit-Thouars (1793 – 1864).
◆1844 Franco-Moroccan war: bombing of Tangiers.
◇1844 Alexandre Dumas père (1802 – 1870) writes *Les Trois mousquetaires* (The Three Musketeers), an historical adventure story.
Prosper Mérimée (1803 – 1870) writes *Carmen*.
◇1846 Expedition of Père Huc (1813 – 1860) to Tibet and China.
◆1847 In Paris, the prohibition, during the electoral campaign, of banquets organized by the opponents to the regime of Louis-Philippe serves as a catalyst for the revolution that is to break out in 1848.
In Algeria, the surrender of Abd-el-Kader marks the beginning of French colonial rule.
The passing of a new Constitution transforms the Swiss Confederation into a genuine Federal State.
◇1847 Beginning of the publication (1847 – 1853) of Michelet's *L'Histoire de la Révolution Française*.
The painters Théodore Rousseau and Jean François Millet settle in Barbizon, where Corot and Courbet also spent periods of time. The Barbizon School is formed.

1848 – 1852 The Second Republic

◆1848 February French Revolution: the democratically and socially inspired popular Paris uprising brings about the fall of Louis-Philippe and the proclamation of the Second Republic (1848 – 1852) by a provisional government including figures such as Lamartine.
Decree on the abolition of slavery in the French colonies.
Canada: the British Parliament abrogates the article of the Act of Union that banned the French language.
Taking advantage of the Revolution, Louis-Napoleon Bonaparte (1808 – 1873) has himself made President of the Republic on 10 December and promulgates a new Constitution. From this moment, he methodically prepares the coup d'état which will make him Emperor of France.
◇1848 René de Chateaubriand (1768 – 1848) writes *Mémoires d'Outre-Tombe* (Memoires from Beyond the Tomb) (1848 – 1850).
A. Dumas fils (1824 – 1895) writes *La Dame aux Camélias* (The Lady of the Camelias).

English/Anglais	French/Français

◇1849 The physicist H. Fizeau (1819 – 1896) determines the speed of light and observes the infrared spectrum.

1850

◇1850 Publication de *David Copperfield*, de Charles Dickens.
◆1851 La Grande Exposition de Londres célèbre l'essor de l'industrie britannique. Elle se tient au Crystal Palace, construit à cette occasion.
Ruée vers l'or en Australie.
◇1851 L'auteur américain Herman Melville (1819 – 1891) publie *Moby Dick* qui est considéré comme l'un des plus grands romans américains.

◇1852 William Holman Hunt (1827 – 1910) peint *The Light of the World*.
L'Américaine Harriet Beecher Stowe (1811 – 1896) publie *La Case de l'oncle Tom* (Uncle Tom's Cabin), roman qui contribuera à mobiliser l'opinion publique contre l'esclavage.

◆1854 – 1856 Guerre de Crimée: l'Angleterre et la France luttent aux côtés de la Turquie contre la Russie.
◆1854 Épisode de la charge de la brigade légère (the Charge of the Light Brigade). Florence Nightingale organise les hôpitaux de campagne. Victoires de l'Alma et d'Inkerman (avec les Français), et de Balaklava.
◇1855 L'auteur anglais Anthony Trollope publie *The Warden*, premier volume de sa Chronique des Barset.
Walt Whitman (1819 – 1891) publie *Leaves of Grass* (Feuilles d'herbe).
◆1856 L'explorateur britannique David Livingstone (1813 – 1873) traverse l'Afrique d'Est en Ouest et 'découvre' les chutes qu'il baptise Victoria Falls (les chutes Victoria).
◇1856 L'Américain Elisha Otis (1811 – 1861) invente l'ascenseur.
◆1856 – 1858 Révolte des Cipayes ('the Indian Mutiny'): en Inde, les soldats indigènes recrutés par les Britanniques se soulèvent. La Compagnie des Indes Orientales transfère le contrôle de ses territoires à la Couronne.

◆1858 – 1864 Ruée vers l'or dans le Colorado et au Névada.

◇1859 Le philosophe utilitariste anglais J.S.Mill (1806 – 1873) publie *On Liberty* (La Liberté).
Charles Darwin publie *The Origin of Species* (De l'origine des espèces au moyen de la sélection naturelle).

◇1850 At the 1850 Salon, Gustave Courbet (1819 – 1877) exhibits his painting *L'Enterrement à Ornans* (Burial at Ornans), the 'realism' of which scandalizes the critics.
◆1851 Coup d'état of the Prince-President Louis-Napoleon Bonaparte.
◇1851 Eugène Labiche's (1815 – 1888) *Le Chapeau de paille d'Italie* is performed (marking the birth of light comedy theatre).
Claude Bernard (1813 – 1878) discovers the glycogenic function of the liver.

1852 – 1870 The Second Empire

◆1852 Louis-Napoleon Bonaparte has himself proclaimed Emperor and becomes Napoleon III. He is to be deposed in 1870.
◇1852 The physicist Foucault (1819 – 1868) determines the velocity of light by the revolving mirror method. He goes on to demonstrate the rotation of the Earth with a pendulum.
Establishment of the first department store in Paris, the Bon Marché on the left bank.
◆1853 Haussmann (1809 – 1891) is appointed prefect of the Seine. He revolutionizes the design of Paris and other cities of France with a view to modernizing the city and moving the working population away, largely to allow the police and army to exert control when needed.
France occupies New Caledonia.
Gobineau (1816 – 1882), diplomat and writer, sets forth in his *Essai sur l'inégalité des races* (The Inequality of Human Races) doctrines that are to become the inspiration of various racist theoreticians.
◆1854 Faidherbe (1818 – 1889) is appointed Governor General of Senegal (1854-1865).
Crimean war: France and Britain fight alongside Turkey against Russia.
A Franco-British coalition defeats the Russians at the battles of Alma and Inkerman.
◇1854 Gérard de Nerval (1808 – 1855) publishes his poems *Les Chimères*. Some of his work prefigures the surrealist experiments of the 20th century.
◆1855 Ferdinand de Lesseps (1805 – 1894) obtains permission to build the Suez Canal from the viceroy of Egypt.
◇1855 Paris Universal Exhibition.
Courbet paints *L'Atelier du Peintre* (Studio of the Painter).
◆1857 Surrender of Kabylia (Algeria). Faidherbe founds the port of Dakar (Africa). French occupation of Canton (China).
◇1857 Gustave Flaubert (1821 – 1880) writes *Madame Bovary*.
The anthology of poetry by Charles Baudelaire (1821 – 1867), *Les Fleurs du Mal* (Flowers of Evil), results in censorship and makes his name as a caustic and morbid critic of modern society.
◆1858 Creation of the first Ministry for Algeria in Paris.
◇1858 First aerial photograph (in a balloon) taken by F. Tournachon, known as Nadar (1820 – 1910). He goes on to immortalize the celebrities of his time.
Visions of Bernadette Soubirous at Lourdes, which turn the town into a place of pilgrimage.
◆1859 War of Italy between Austria and Piedmont allied with France. Victories at the battles of Magenta and Solferino. Napoleon III and the Emperor of Austria sign the armistice of Villafranca, which completes the Austrian defeat.
First French occupation of Saigon, which marks the beginning of its involvement in Indochina.
Foundation of the bank Société Générale.

1860

◆1860 Robert Burke (1820 – 1861) et William Wills (1834 – 1861) dirigent la première expédition à travers l'Australie (du Nord au Sud).
◇1860 Publication du *Moulin sur la Floss* (The Mill on the Floss) de Mary Ann Evans (1819 – 1880), alias George Eliot.
◆1860 – 1861 Aux États-Unis, onze États du Sud qui s'opposent à l'abolition de l'esclavage font sécession et forment une Conféderation.
◆1861 Abraham Lincoln, antiesclavagiste, est élu à la présidence des États-Unis. Début de la guerre de Sécession (American Civil War) entre le Nord et le Sud.
À la première bataille de Bull Run, victoire sudiste sous le commandement du général Thomas 'Stonewall' Jackson.
◇1862 Herbert Spencer (1820 – 1822), philosophe évolutionniste adepte des théories de Darwin, publie le premier volume de son *System of Synthetic Philosophy* (Système de philosophie synthétique). C'est lui qui a forgé l'expression 'the survival of the fittest' (la survie du plus fort).
L'Américaine Julia Ward Howe (1819 – 1910) écrit *The Battle Hymn of the Republic*, hymne nordiste.
◆1863 Aux États-Unis, Abraham Lincoln abolit l'esclavage.
La victoire des nordistes à la bataille de Gettysburg marque un tournant décisif dans la guerre de Sécession.
Sur les lieux de la bataille, Lincoln prononce son fameux discours, la Gettysburg address.
◇1863 Inauguration de la première ligne de métro à Londres.
◇1864 Henry Newman (1801 – 1890), théologien, cardinal et l'une des principales figures du Mouvement d'Oxford, publie son autobiographie spirituelle *Apologia Pro Vita Sua*.
Le mathématicien écossais James Maxwell (1831 – 1879) publie ses recherches sur le lien entre lumière et électricité.
◆1865 Reddition des confédérés du général Lee aux troupes nordistes du général Grant à Appomattox, en Virginie. Fin de la guerre de Sécession.
Assassinat de Lincoln dans un théâtre de Washington par John Wilkes Booth.

◆1860 In recognition of the French intervention in Italy, Piedmont cedes Savoy and Nice to France.
In Lebanon, the French intervention against the Druze during the massacres of Damas leads to the first French occupation of Syria (1860 – 1861).
◇1860 Invention of the internal combustion engine by Lenoir (1822 – 1900).
◇1861 Charles Garnier (1825 – 1898) begins the building of the Paris Opera House (1862 – 1874).
◆1862 Annam (Indochina) cedes Cochin China to France which completes its conquest in 1867. French expedition to Mexico (1862 – 1867).
◇1862 Hugo publishes his novel *Les Misérables*. Flaubert publishes *Salâmmbo*.
◆1863 France imposes its protectorate on Cambodia.
Foundation of the bank Crédit Lyonnais.
◇1863 Édouard Manet (1832 – 1883) paints *Déjeuner sur l'herbe* and *Olympia*.
◆1864 Foundation of the International Red Cross in Geneva (Geneva Convention), at the initiative of the philanthropist Henri Dunant (1828 – 1910). He is awarded the first Nobel Peace Prize in 1901.
◇1864 Alfred de Vigny (1797 – 1863) publishes *Les Destinées*. Gounod (1818 – 1893) composes the opera *Mireille*. Offenbach (1819 – 1880) composes the opera *La Belle Hélène*.
Jules Verne (1828 – 1905) writes *Voyage au centre de la terre* (A Journey to the Centre of the Earth).
◇1865 Cl. Bernard (1813 – 1878) writes *Introduction à la médecine expérimentale* (Introduction to the Study of Experimental Medicine).
◇1866 Offenbach composes the opera *La Vie Parisienne* (Parisian Life).
The *Grand Dictionnaire Universel du XIXème siècle* (1866 – 1876) is published by Pierre Larousse (1817 – 1875).
◆1867 Retreat of French troops from Mexico.

English/Anglais	French/Français

◇1865 Publication d'*Alice au pays des merveilles* (Alice in Wonderland), de Charles Dodgson (1832 – 1898), alias Lewis Carroll.
◆1867 Les États-Unis achètent l'Alaska à la Russie.
Création du dominion du Canada qui a désormais sa propre constitution.
◆1868 L'Anglais William Gladstone, chef du parti libéral, devient Premier ministre. Pendant son premier mandat il sépare l'Église de l'État en Irlande et généralise l'enseignement primaire.
Création du British Trades Union Congress (Congrès des Syndicats Britanniques).
◇1868 Publication du roman autobiographique *Les Quatre filles du Dr March* (Little Women), de la romancière américaine Louisa May Alcott (1832 – 1888).
◆1869 La jonction des voies ferroviaires des compagnies du Central Pacific et de l'Union Pacific établit la première ligne transcontinentale aux États-Unis.

Canada: coming into force of the Canadian Constitution. Article 133 gives French the status of official language in the Parliaments of Ottawa and Quebec and before the federal and Quebec courts.
◇1867 Gounod composes *Roméo et Juliette*. J.-F. Millet (1814 – 1875) paints *L'Angelus*.
J.-B. Clément's song *Le Temps des cerises* becomes an emblem of popular song.
Universal Exhibition in Paris.
◇1868 A. Daudet (1840 – 1897) publishes *Le Petit Chose* (Young What's His Name).
Discovery of the first remains of Cro-Magnon man at Eyzies-de-Tayac (Dordogne).
◇1869 Daudet publishes *Les lettres de mon moulin* (Letters from my Mill).
Flaubert writes *L'Éducation sentimentale* (Sentimental Education).

1870

◆1870 Succeeding the Empire, the Government of National Defence headed by Léon Gambetta (1838 – 1882) proclaims the Third Republic (1870 – 1940), but is unable to prevent the Franco-Prussian War, which ends in the Defeat of Sedan and the Siege of Paris.
◇1870 Léo Delibes (1836 – 1891) composes *Coppelia*.

1871 – 1940 The Third Republic

◇1871 L'Américain James Whistler (1834 – 1903) peint le *Portrait de la mère de l'artiste* (Arrangement in Grey and Black – the Artist's Mother), influencé par l'art japonais.
◆1874 – 1880 Benjamin Disraeli, conservateur, est Premier ministre. C'est pour la Grande-Bretagne une période de réformes sociales et de succès diplomatiques.
◆1875 La Grande-Bretagne achète le canal de Suez.
◇1875 Publication des *Aventures de Tom Sawyer* (The Adventures of Tom Sawyer), de Mark Twain (1835 – 1910).
◆1876 La reine Victoria est proclamée impératrice des Indes.
Bataille de Little Bighorn contre les Sioux de Sitting Bull: Custer et son régiment sont tués.
◇1876 L'inventeur américain d'origine écossaise Alexander Graham Bell (1847 – 1922) fait breveter son téléphone.
◇1877 Création de l'Armée du salut (The Salvation Army) à Londres par l'Anglais William Booth (1829 – 1912).
L'inventeur américain Thomas Edison (1847 – 1931) fait breveter le phonographe.
◆1879 En Afrique du Sud, défaite des Zoulous face aux Britanniques.

◆1871 Government leader Adolphe Thiers signs the Frankfurt Peace Treaty which completes the French defeat with the loss of Alsace-Lorraine. The success of the monarchists in the legislative elections provokes the insurrection of the Commune in Paris (March to May), supported by the working classes. It is brutally repressed in the 'Semaine Sanglante' by the troops of the Thiers government from its seat at Versailles.
◇1871 Émile Zola (1840 – 1902) publishes his sociological novel, *La Fortune des Rougon* (The Fortunes of the Rougons), the first part of his novelistic work on the Rougon-Macquart family which forms the basis of naturalism in France.
◆1873 Marshall MacMahon (1808 – 1893), a legitimist, becomes President, but is forced to resign in 1879. Occupation of Hanoi by France.
◇1873 Arthur Rimbaud (1854 – 1891) publishes *Une saison en enfer* (A Season in Hell), poems in prose that are revolutionary both in spirit and tone.
Jules Verne publishes *Le Tour du monde en quatre-vingts jours* (Around the World in Eighty Days).
◇1874 At the Nadar studio, Claude Monet (1840 – 1926) exhibits *Impression, soleil levant* (Impression: Sunrise), which gives its name to the Impressionist movement.
Verlaine publishes the poems *Romances sans paroles* (Romances Without Words).
◇1875 Georges Bizet (1838 – 1875) composes the opera *Carmen*.
Camille Saint-Saëns (1835 – 1921) composes *Danse macabre*.
◇1876 Auguste Renoir (1841 – 1919) paints *Le Moulin de la Galette* (The Ball at the Moulin de la Galette).
Start of construction (1876 – 1912) of the Sacré-Cœur Basilica in Paris, built to atone for the Commune's revolt.
◇1877 Zola writes *L'Assommoir* (The Drunkard).
Saint-Saëns composes the opera *Samson et Dalila*.
◆1879 Jules Grévy (1807 – 1891) is elected President of the Republic (1879 – 1887).
◇1879 Pasteur (1822 – 1895) discovers the principle of vaccine by inoculating with microbes.

1880

◆1880 – 1881 En Afrique du Sud, la première guerre des Boers (guerre du Transvaal) contre la domination anglaise se termine par la défaite des troupes britanniques à Majuba Hill.
◆1880 Le hors-la-loi Ned Kelly (1854 – 1881) est exécuté en Australie.
◇1880 Adoption du temps solaire moyen de Greenwich en Grande-Bretagne.
◆1881 Le hors-la-loi 'Billy the Kid' (William Bonney (1858 – 1881)) est abattu au Nouveau-Mexique.
Fusillade à OK Corral à Tombstone, dans l'Arizona, dont Wyatt Earp (1848 – 1929) sort vainqueur.
◇1881 Publication d'*Un Portrait de femme* (Portrait of a Lady), de l'Américain Henry James (1843 – 1916).
◆1883 Paul Kruger (1825 – 1904) devient président de la république du Transvaal.
◇1883 Publication de *L'Île au trésor* (Treasure Island), de l'auteur écossais Robert Louis Stevenson (1850 – 1894).
Sir Hiram Maxim (1840 – 1916), Américain devenu citoyen britannique, invente le premier fusil automatique, le fusil Maxim.
◇1884 Parution de la première partie de *l'Oxford English Dictionary*.
◆1885 Fondation du Congrès National Indien, dont le but est d'affranchir le pays de la domination britannique.
Le général Gordon est tué à Khartoum, au Soudan, après avoir soutenu un siège de 10 mois.
Le Britannique Cecil Rhodes (1853 – 1902) s'empare du Bechuanaland (aujourd'hui le Botswana), en Afrique australe.
◆1886 En Grande-Bretagne, le gouvernement de Gladstone essaie d'introduire le 'Home Rule' (projet de gouvernement autonome de l'Irlande). Le projet échoue et provoque la chute de Gladstone et la scission du parti libéral.
◇1886 La Statue de la Liberté (*La Liberté éclairant le monde*) cadeau de la France aux États-Unis, est installée dans le port de New York.

◆1880 Government of Jules Ferry.
◇1880 Guy de Maupassant (1850 – 1893) writes *Boule de Suif* (Ball of Tallow).
Zola writes *Nana*.
Rodin (1840 – 1917) completes the sculpture *Le Penseur* (The Thinker).
◆1881 Jules Ferry (1832 – 1893) has laws passed on freedom of assembly, of the press and trade union rights, and gives his name to educational legislation providing compulsory, free and non-religious primary schooling.
France establishes the protectorate of Tunisia, brought in by the Treaty of Bardo.
Ferdinand de Lesseps begins work on the Panama Canal.
◇1881 Édouard Manet (1832 – 1883) paints *Un bar aux Folies-Bergères* (A Bar at the Folies-Bergère).
The mathematician Henri Poincaré (1854 – 1912) discovers a general method for resolving differential equations.
◆1883 The second Jules Ferry cabinet (1883 – 1885) pursues a policy of colonial expansion, marked by the establishment of a French protectorate over Annam, the occupation of Madagascar and the foundation of Bamako (now Mali).
◇1883 Maupassant publishes *Une vie* (A Woman's Life).
The Egyptologist Gaston Maspéro (1846 – 1916) begins exploration of the Temple at Luxor and the Sphinx at Gîza.
◆1884 The Waldeck-Rousseau (1846 – 1904) law legalizes trade unions.
◇1884 Georges Seurat (1859 – 1891) radicalizes Impressionism with his painting *Un dimanche après-midi à la Grande-Jatte* (Sunday Afternoon on the Island of La Grande Jatte).
◆1885 Resignation of Jules Ferry following a setback in Tonkin.
The Republic resists as best it can the Boulangist crisis (1885 – 1889) instigated by the agitation of nationalists and monarchists led by General Boulanger (1837 – 1891) who is forced into exile in Belgium following an aborted attempt at a coup d'etat.
The Congo, personal property of Leopold II, becomes a Belgian possession. Universal suffrage is introduced in Belgium.
◇1885 Pasteur produces the first vaccine against rabies.

English/Anglais

◇1887 Publication de la première histoire de Sherlock Holmes, de l'Écossais Conan Doyle (1859 – 1930).
◇1888 L'industriel américain George Eastman (1854 – 1932) met au point le premier appareil photo portatif Kodak.
Le vétérinaire écossais John Dunlop (1840 – 1921) invente le pneu.

♦1889 Création de la Rhodésie (aujourd'hui la Zambie et le Zimbabwe) à partir de territoires occupés par la British South Africa Company de Cecil Rhodes.

French/Français

Zola publishes *Germinal*.
◇1886 Rodin sculpts *Le Baiser* (The Kiss).
Bartholdi (1834 – 1904) creates *La Liberté éclairant le monde* (Statue of Liberty) (a gift from France to the United States).
♦1887 Marie François Sadi Carnot (1837 – 1894) is elected President of the Republic.
Creation of French-English joint sovereignty over the New Hebrides.
Creation of the Union of Indochina.
◇1887 Gabriel Fauré composes *Requiem*.
♦1888 Issue of the first Russian loan in Paris.
◇1888 Vincent Van Gogh (1853 – 1890) paints *La chambre de Vincent à Arles* (Vincent's Room, Arles).
Opening of the Pasteur Institute.
◇1889 Henri Bergson (1859 – 1941) publishes *Essai sur les données immédiates de la conscience* (Time and Freewill).
The engineer Gustave Eiffel (1832 – 1923) builds the Eiffel Tower for the Paris World Exhibition.
Vincent Van Gogh paints *Autoportrait à l'oreille coupée* (Self-Portrait with Bandaged Ear).

1890

English/Anglais

♦1890 Massacre d'Indiens d'Amérique à Wounded Knee par l'armée américaine.
Première exécution à la chaise électrique aux États-Unis.
◇1891 Publication du *Portrait de Dorian Gray* (The Picture of Dorian Gray), de l'auteur irlandais Oscar Wilde (1854 – 1900).
L'auteur anglais Thomas Hardy (1840 – 1928) publie *Tess of the d'Urbervilles* (Tess d'Urberville).

♦1892 L'Écossais Keir Hardie (1856 – 1915) devient le premier député travailliste.

♦1893 Deuxième projet de loi sur le 'Home Rule' (voir 1896), adopté par la Chambre des communes mais rejeté par la Chambre des lords.

◇1894 Publication du *Livre de la jungle* (The Jungle Book), de Rudyard Kipling (1865 – 1936).

◇1895 Première représentation de *The Importance of being Earnest* (De l'importance d'être constant), pièce de l'écrivain irlandais Oscar Wilde.

◇1896 Publication d'*Un Gars du Shropshire* (A Shropshire Lad), du poète anglais A. E. Housman (1859 – 1936).

♦1898 À la fin de la guerre hispano-américaine, les États-Unis annexent Porto Rico et les Philippines.
Annexion de Hawaii.

♦1899 - 1902 Deuxième guerre du Transvaal en Afrique du Sud.
◇1899 Le compositeur anglais Edward Elgar (1857 – 1934) achève ses *Enigma Variations*.
♦1899 Un accord franco-anglais consacre le renoncement de la France sur le Nil en faveur des Britanniques.

French/Français

♦1890 Establishment of a French-English colonial agreement over Madagascar, Zanzibar and the Sudan.
1 May is made international labour day at the congress of the second Socialist International in Paris.
◇1890 E.J. Marey (1830 – 1904) devises the first sequential photography, from which cinema develops.
Clément Ader makes the first aeroplane flight.
♦1891 The Panama financial scandal (1891 – 1893) gives rise to a wave of protests orchestrated by the opposition.
Strengthening of the labour movement, in spite of the bloody repression of a workers' strike in favour of the 8-hour day at Fourmies, on 1 May.
◇1891 First petrol-driven car built by R. Panhard and his partner É. Levassor.
Toulouse-Lautrec creates the poster *La Goulue au Moulin-Rouge* (Moulin Rouge, La Goulue).
'Scélérates' laws: repression of anarchist ideas and the anarchist movement.
◇1892 Toulouse-Lautrec paints *Jeanne-Avril dansant* (Jeanne Avril Dancing).
Paul Cézanne (1839 – 1906) paints *Les Joueurs de cartes* (The Card Players)
♦1893 Siam cedes the left bank of the Mekong to France. French protectorate over Laos.
◇1893 Marey builds the first cinema projector.
Émile Durkheim (1858 – 1917), one of the founders of sociology, publishes *De la division du travail social* (The Division of Labour in Society).
♦1894 President Sadi Carnot is assassinated by an anarchist.
Establishment of the French protectorate over Dahomey (now Benin).
The Dreyfus Affair: the officer Alfred Dreyfus (1859 – 1935) is unjustly accused of spying for Germany. He is dismissed and deported to Guyana.
♦1895 Félix Faure (1841 – 1899) becomes President of the Republic until 1899. Foundation of the national trades congress, the Confédération Générale du Travail (C.G.T.).
Organization of French West Africa consisting of Senegal, Mauritania, Sudan (Mali), Upper Volta (Burkina Faso), Niger, Ivory Coast and Dahomey. Annexation of Madagascar (1895 – 96).
◇1895 The Lumière brothers, Louis (1864 – 1948) and Auguste (1862 – 1954), invent cinematography: *L'Arrivée d'un train en gare de La Ciotat*, *L'arroseur arrosé*.
♦1896 Departure of the Marchand expedition (1863 – 1934) to link the Nile with the Congo. J. B. Marchand reaches the Nile at Fashoda.
Madagascar becomes a French colony.
Constitution of French Indochina.
◇1896 Alfred Jarry (1873 – 1907) writes the play *Ubu Roi*, a forerunner of the Theatre of the Absurd.
Henri Becquerel (1852 – 1908) discovers radioactivity.
◇1897 Stéphane Mallarmé publishes the poem *Un coup de dés jamais n'abolira le hasard* (A Throw of Dice Will Never Abolish the Hazard).
André Gide (1869 – 1951) publishes *Les Nourritures terrestres* (Fruits of the Earth).
♦1898 Publication of *J'accuse* (I accuse): Émile Zola's plea on behalf of Dreyfus is published in the newspaper *L'Aurore*, and brings the affair into public debate. At the same time, the French extreme right founds Action Française.
◇1898 Pierre (1859 – 1906) and Marie (1867 – 1934) Curie discover polonium and radium.
Edmond Rostand (1868 – 1918) writes the play *Cyrano de Bergerac*.
♦1899 Émile Loubet (1838 – 1929) is President of the Republic (1899 – 1906). Formation of the Bloc des Gauches which pursues an anticlerical policy.
Second trial of Dreyfus, sentenced to ten years' imprisonment on 9 September, and pardoned on the 19th.
France concludes the agreement granting British authority over the Nile basin.

1900

English/Anglais

1901 - 1917 Les Saxe-Cobourg-Gotha

♦1901 La reine Victoria meurt après 64 ans de règne. Son fils aîné Édouard VII (Édouard Ier d'Écosse) lui succède. Il reste le seul souverain de la maison de Saxe-Cobourg. Malgré une conduite dissipée avant son accession au trône, il se montre habile diplomate.

French/Français

♦1900 The French gain possession of the Rabah Empire in Chad.
◇1900 Claude Debussy (1862 – 1918) composes *Trois nocturnes*.
Colette (1873 – 1954) publishes *Claudine à l'école* (first novel in the Claudine series).
World Exhibition and Summer Olympic Games held in Paris.
Opening of the Paris metro.

English/Anglais

Un acte du Parlement impérial crée le Commonwealth d'Australie avec pour capitale Canberra.
Le premier message transatlantique par télégraphie sans fil, la lettre 'S', est transmis de Cornouailles à Terre-Neuve.
◆1902 Victoire des Anglais contre les Boers lors de la seconde guerre du Transvaal.
◇1902 Le philosophe américain William James (1842 – 1910) publie *The Varieties of Religious Experience* (Les Variétés de l'expérience religieuse). La même année, son frère Henry James (1843 – 1916) écrit *The Wings of a Dove* (Les Ailes de la colombe).
Rudyard Kipling (1865 – 1936) publie un recueil d'histoires pour enfants *Just So Stories* (Histoires comme ça).
◇1903 Les frères Wright, Orville (1871 – 1948) et Wilbur (1867 – 1912), effectuent le premier vol mécanique à Kitty Hawk en Caroline du Sud.
◆1904 Signature de l'Entente Cordiale par la France et la Grande-Bretagne.
◇1904 Première représentation de *Peter Pan*, de J.M. Barrie (1860 – 1937).
Première représentation de *Man and Superman* (L'Homme et le Surhomme) et *Major Barbara* (La Commandante Barbara) de George Bernard Shaw (1856 – 1950).
Les jeux Olympiques ont lieu à Saint Louis, aux États-Unis.

◇1905 Albert Einstein (1879 – 1947), physicien allemand naturalisé américain, publie un mémoire sur sa théorie de la relativité restreinte.

◆1906 Le British Labour Representation Committee adopte le nom de 'Labour Party'. La même année ce parti réclame le droit de vote pour les femmes.
Tremblement de terre et incendie de San Francisco.

◆1907 Triple Entente entre la France, la Grande-Bretagne et la Russie.

◇1907 La première représentation de la pièce *The Playboy of the Western World* (Le Baladin du monde occidental) de J.M. Synge (1871 – 1909) provoque des scènes d'émeute à Dublin.
L'Anglais Rudyard Kipling (1865 – 1936) remporte le prix Nobel de littérature.
◇1908 L'ingénieur automobile américain John Ford (1863 – 1947) lance son Modèle T, première voiture construite en série.
Le romancier anglais E.M. Forster (1879 – 1970) publie *A Room with a View* (Une chambre d'où l'on voit), œuvre dans laquelle il examine la bourgeoisie anglaise.
Les jeux Olympiques ont lieu à Londres.

French/Français

◆1901 Promulgation of the law on non-profit-making organizations: full freedom, with the exception of congregations.

◇1902 Debussy composes *Pelléas et Mélisande*.
Georges Méliès (1861 – 1938), *Le Voyage dans la lune* (A Trip to the Moon) (film).
First Lépine award, for inventors of all kinds.

◇1903 The first Tour de France cycle race.
Marie Curie wins the Nobel Prize for physics.

◆1904 Signature of the Entente Cordiale treaty between France and Great Britain.
◇1904 Monet paints *Vues de Londres* (Views of London).
Jean Jaurès founds the newspaper *l'Humanité*.
◆1905 Formation of the SFIO, the French socialist party founded by Jean Jaurès (1859 – 1914) and Jules Guesde.
Culmination of the anticlerical policy of the Bloc des Gauches, the law separating Church and State is promulgated.
◇1905 Rodin completes the sculpture *Victor Hugo*.
Appearance of the term fauvism to describe the paintings of Braque, Matisse, Vlaminck, Derain, Dufy and Van Dongen.
◆1906 Armand Fallières (1841 – 1931) is elected President of the Republic (1906 – 1913).
Georges Clemenceau (1841 – 1929), leader of the Radicals, becomes Prime Minister. Dreyfus' name is finally cleared by the Bloc des Gauches.
◇1906 Bergson publishes *L'évolution créatrice* (Creative Evolution).
Paul Claudel, *Partage de Midi* (play).
Opening of the Simplon tunnel in the Swiss Alps.
◆1907 Formation of the Triple Entente between Great Britain, France and Russia.
Law on freedom of worship in France.
◇1907 Picasso (1881 – 1973) finishes his *Demoiselles d'Avignon* (The Young Ladies of Avignon).
◆1908 Leopold II, King of the Belgians, cedes the Congo, his personal property, to Belgium.
◆1909 Aristide Briand (1862 – 1932) succeeds Clemenceau. The repressive policies of Clemenceau and Briand lead to disunity on the left and to ministerial instability.
◇1909 Louis Blériot (1872 – 1936) makes the first aeroplane flight across the English Channel.
Henri Matisse (1869 – 1954), leader of the Fauves, begins his fresco *La Danse* (Dance).
Foundation of the Ballets Russes by Sergei Diaghilev (1872 – 1929) in Paris.

1910

English/Anglais

◆1910 À la mort d'Édouard VII, son fils George V (1865 – 1936) lui succède.
L'Union d'Afrique du Sud (réunion de plusieurs provinces autonomes) devient un dominion.

◆1912 Naufrage du Titanic.
◇1912 L'explorateur anglais R.F. Scott entreprend une expédition dans l'Antarctique. Il atteint le pôle Sud où le Norvégien Amundsen l'avait devancé de 35 jours, mais périt avec ses hommes au retour de ce raid.

◇1913 *Sons and Lovers* (Fils), roman semi-autobio[illegible] romancier anglais D.H. Lawrence (1885 – 1930) connaît un immense succès. Deux plus tard, l'auteur sera poursuivi pour obscénité après la publication de *The Rainbow* (L'Arc-en-ciel) qui examine les rapports amoureux du couple.

◆1914 Les troupes allemandes violent la neutralité belge garantie par le traité de Londres de 1839.
La Grande-Bretagne déclare la guerre à l'Allemagne et se bat aux côtés de la France.
Ouverture du canal de Panama. Construit par le corps des ingénieurs américains, il relie l'océan Atlantique au Pacifique.
◆1915 Échec de l'offensive franco-anglaise aux Dardanelles.
Torpillage du Lusitania.

French/Français

◆1910 Organization of French Equatorial Africa (A.E.F.) which includes Gabon, Middle Congo (Congo), Ubangi-Shari (Central African Republic) and Chad.
◇1910 Raymond Roussel (1877 – 1933) publishes *Impressions d'Afrique* (Impressions of Africa), a novel that is to inspire surrealism.
Georges Feydeau (1862 – 1921) revives farce with *On purge bébé*.
Charles Péguy (1873 – 1914) publishes his poems *Le mystère de la charité de Jeanne d'Arc* (The Mystery of Joan of Arc's Charity).
◆1911 The Agadir Coup marks the second Moroccan crisis between Germany and France. The settlement of the crisis in favour of France leads to its occupation of Fez the same year.
◇1911 Marie Curie wins the Nobel Prize for chemistry.
◆1912 Raymond Poincaré (1860 – 1934) is Prime Minister. He establishes the French protectorate over Morocco.
Arrest of the criminals of Bonnot's gang, consisting of a group of anarchists specializing in organized crime.
◇1912 Claudel (1868 – 1955) writes the play *L'Annonce faite à Marie* (The Annunciation).
Anatole France publishes his novel *Les dieux ont soif* (The Gods will have Blood).
The choreography of Nijinsky (1889 – 1950) for Debussy's *L'Après-midi d'un faune* (Prelude to the Afternoon of a Faun) marks the beginning of modern ballet and causes scandal in the Paris press.
Marcel Duchamp (1887 – 1968) revolutionizes contemporary art with his *Nu descendant l'escalier* (Nude Descending a Staircase).
◆1913 R. Poincaré becomes President of the Republic (1913 – 1920).
◇1913 Marcel Proust (1871 – 1922) publishes *Du côté de chez Swann*, (Swann's Way), the first section of *À la recherche du temps perdu* (Remembrance of Things Past) (1913 – 1927).
Guillaume Apollinaire (1880 – 1918) publishes the poems *Alcools*.
Alain-Fournier (1886 – 1914) publishes *Le Grand Meaulnes* (The Lost Domain).
Louis Feuillade (1873 – 1925) releases *Fantômas* (first in a series of five films).
In Gabon, Albert Schweitzer (1875 – 1965) founds the hospital of Lambaréné.
Rolland Garros (1888 – 1918) makes the first aeroplane flight across the Mediterranean.
◆1914 On the same day as the assassination of Jaurès (31 July), Germany lays down its ultimatum to France. On 1 August France orders general mobilization. On 3 August Germany declares war on France.
The Sacred Union (l'Union sacrée) between the parties is urged by Poincaré.
The War begins with victory at the Battle of the Marne.
◆1915 Failure of the French and British Dardanelles naval expedition.

English/Anglais

◇1915 Sortie du film *The Birth of a Nation* (Naissance d'une nation) du réalisateur et novateur américain D.W. Griffith (1875 – 1948) qui marque une étape dans l'histoire du cinéma tant par la technique que par l'esthétique, en dépit d'une idéologie profondément raciste.
◆1916 Première utilisation du char de combat par les troupes britanniques pendant la bataille de la Somme. 420 000 soldats britanniques trouvent la mort au cours de cette série d'offensives et contre-offensives.
À Dublin, les nationalistes irlandais (Sinn Féin) s'insurgent contre la domination anglaise ('the Easter Rising'). Les rebelles proclament un gouvernement provisoire, mais le soulèvement est réprimé au bout de cinq jours et 14 de ses meneurs sont exécutés.

1917 – Les Windsor

◆1917 L'entrée en guerre des États-Unis vient soulager la Grande-Bretagne, fortement éprouvée par la pénurie de vivres causée par la présence des sous-marins allemands.
Le Premier ministre britannique, Lloyd George, annonce un projet de loi pour donner le droit de vote aux femmes mariées âgées de plus de 30 ans.
Déclaration Balfour : le ministre des Affaires étrangères, Arthur Balfour (1848 – 1930) promet aux Sionistes la création d'un foyer national pour les Juifs en Palestine.
La famille royale britannique change son nom en "Windsor," "Saxe-Cobourg-Gotha" étant jugé trop germanique.
◆1918 Fin de la première guerre mondiale.
Les femmes votent pour la première fois aux élections législatives en Grande-Bretagne
◇1918 En Grande-Bretagne, Marie Stopes (1880 – 1958) publie *Married Life* qui remet en cause la condition de la femme.
Elle se battra toute sa vie pour les droits de la femme et l'accès à la contraception.
◆1919 La Société des Nations (the League of Nations) pour le maintien de la paix et de la sécurité naît du traité de Versailles. Elle a son siège à Genève. Ses membres fondateurs comprennent la plupart des Alliés victorieux mais les États-Unis n'en font pas partie.
◇1919 Les aviateurs anglais John Alcock (1892 – 1919) et Arthur Brown (1886 – 1948) effectuent le premier vol transatlantique. La même année, Alcock trouve la mort dans un accident d'avion.

French/Français

◆1916 Allied offensive on the Somme.
Pétain (1856 – 1951) wins the Battle of Verdun.
◇1916 In his novel *Le Feu* (Under Fire), Henri Barbusse (1873 – 1935) recounts the atrocities of trench warfare.
Foundation of the Dadaist movement in Zurich, around Tristan Tzara and Jean Arp.

◆1917 The failure of the Nivelle offensive at the Chemin des Dames propels Pétain to the rank of supreme commander. He restores the morale of the troops and prepares the counter-offensive of 1918.
◇1917 Paul Valéry (1871 – 1945) publishes the poems *La jeune Parque* (The Young Fate). His poetic and epistemological work is to lead to a chair of poetry being created for him at the Collège de France.
◆1918 The allied counter-offensives sound the German retreat. The Rethondes armistice is signed on 11 November, bringing the First World War to an end.
◇1918 Apollinaire (1880 – 1918) publishes *Calligrammes*, poems consisting of objects freely arranged on the page, the form of which represents the subject.
André Gide publishes *La Symphonie pastorale* (Two Symphonies).
◆1919 The Peace Conference meeting in Paris redraws the maps of Europe, and the signing of the Treaty of Versailles between Germany and the Allies reincorporates Alsace and Lorraine into France.
Creation of the League of Nations (la Société des Nations) which has its headquarters in Geneva.
◇1919 Roland Dorgelès (1885 – 1973) publishes *Les Croix de bois* (The Wooden Crosses), a novel about the horrors of trench warfare.
Marcel Proust publishes *À l'ombre des jeunes filles en fleurs* (Within a Budding Grove).

1920

◇1920 Publication posthume des *Poems* de Wilfred Owen (1893 – 1918), tué sur le front de l'Ouest une semaine avant l'armistice de 1918. Ces poèmes, édités par son ami Siegfried Sassoon, expriment toute l'horreur de la guerre des tranchées.
◆1921 Pour tenter d'apaiser la situation en Irlande, Lloyd George signe le traité de partage (the Irish Free State settlement) qui crée l'État libre d'Irlande. Six des neuf comtés de l'Ulster obtiennent une autonomie partielle et forment la province d'Irlande du Nord.
◇1922 Le logicien et philosophe anglais d'origine autrichienne Ludwig Wittgenstein (1889 – 1951) publie son *Tractatus Logico-philosophicus*, rédigé alors qu'il était dans l'armée pendant la première guerre mondiale. Cet ouvrage exercera une profonde influence sur la philosophie britannique du XXème siècle.
James Joyce (1882 – 1941), écrivain irlandais, publie *Ulysses* (Ulysse) à Paris. Cette œuvre va renouveler la structure du roman au XXème siècle. Toutefois, jugée obscène en Grande-Bretagne et aux USA, elle ne paraîtra dans ces pays qu'en 1936.
Publication de *The Waste Land* (La Terre gaste), de T.S. Eliot (1888 – 1965).
◇1923 Le poète et dramaturge irlandais W.B. Yeats (1865 – 1939) reçoit le prix Nobel de littérature.
◆1924 Élection du premier gouvernement travailliste avec à sa tête Ramsay MacDonald qui ne reste que onze mois au pouvoir.
Les Indiens des États-Unis obtiennent le droit à la citoyenneté américaine.
◇1924 L'Américain George Gershwin (1898 – 1937) compose sa *Rhapsody in Blue*, œuvre dont le romantisme s'exprime dans le style jazz.
◇1925 *The Great Gatsby* (Gatsby le magnifique) de Scott Fitzgerald (1896 – 1940).
The Gold Rush (La ruée vers l'or), de Charlie Chaplin (1889 – 1977).
L'auteur irlandais George Bernard Shaw (1856 – 1950) reçoit le prix Nobel de littérature.
◆1926 Par solidarité avec les mineurs qui protestent contre une diminution des salaires, le Trades Union Congress lance un appel à la grève générale. Cette grève est vite brisée, laissant les mineurs isolés.
◇1926 L'ingénieur et physicien écossais John Logie Baird (1888 – 1946) fait sa première démonstration de transmission d'image télévisée.
◇1927 L'aviateur américain Charles Lindbergh (1902 – 1955) effectue le premier vol transatlantique sans escale, seul sur son monoplan 'The Spirit of St Louis'.
La compagnie Warner Bros produit le premier film avec passages parlants ou chantants *The Jazz Singer* (Le Chanteur de jazz).
La BBC reçoit le monopole de la radiodiffusion britannique.
To the Lighthouse (La Promenade au phare), de Virginia Woolf (1882 – 1941).
◇1928 Le bactériologiste écossais Alexander Fleming (1881 – 1955) découvre la pénicilline. Toutefois, son manque de connaissances en chimie ne lui permet pas d'isoler ce bactéricide et ce n'est que onze ans plus tard que deux de ses collègues en feront une étude qui mènera à la production industrielle de cet antibiotique.
D.H. Lawrence achève son roman *Lady Chatterley's Lover* (L'Amant de Lady Chatterley) qui fait scandale et sera interdit en Grande-Bretagne jusqu'en 1960.
◆1929 La crise financière déclenchée par le krach boursier de New York (the Wall Street Crash) entraîne une dépression mondiale (the Great Depression).

◆1920 At the Congress of Tours, the split between the socialists and communists is followed by the foundation of the French Communist Party (P.C.F.).
Syria and Lebanon are made French mandates by the League of Nations.
◇1920 In music, the critics create the term 'Les Six' for the new generation of young composers: Georges Auric, Arthur Honegger, Germaine Taillefer, Darius Milhaud, Louis Durey and Francis Poulenc.
◆1921 The end of Belgian neutrality: French and Belgian troops occupy the Ruhr.
◇1921 Albert Calmette (1863 – 1933) and Camille Guérin (1872 – 1961) introduce the first vaccine against tuberculosis (BCG).
Coco Chanel creates the 'little black dress'.
◇1922 Charles Dullin (1885 – 1949) founds the Atelier theatre, and Firmin Gémier (1869 – 1933), the Théâtre National Populaire (TNP).
◇1923 Raymond Radiguet (1903 – 1923) publishes his novel *Le Diable au corps* (The Devil in the Flesh).
Louis de Broglie (1892 – 1987) sets out the principles of wave mechanics in physics.
Creation of the Le Mans 24-hour motor race.
◆1924 Election of the Cartel of the Left made up of Socialists, Communists and Radicals, opposed by the business and industry circles that constituted the Wall of Money.
◇1924 André Breton (1896 – 1966) publishes with Aragon (1897 – 1982), Soupault (1897 – 1990), Eluard (1895 – 1952) and Desnos (1900 – 1945), *Le Manifeste du Surréalisme* (The Surrealist Manifesto), the founding deed of this literary and artistic movement.
The Summer Olympic Games are held in Paris, and the Winter Olympics in Chamonix.
◇1925 Blaise Cendrars (1887 – 1961) writes the novel *L'Or* (Sutter's Gold).
André Gide publishes *Les Faux-Monnayeurs* (The Counterfeiters).
◆1926 Birth of Algerian nationalism with Messali Hadj, leader of the Étoile du Nord movement.
In Paris, constitution of a government of national Union led by Poincaré (1926 – 29).
◇1926 Louis Aragon publishes *Le Paysan de Paris* (The Night Walker), the first surrealist novel conceived as a journey through Paris of the industrial era.
Paul Éluard publishes the poems *Capitale de la douleur* (The Capital of Pain).
◆1927 Building of the Maginot Line (1927 – 36), a defensive structure built on the NE border of France. The Germans were to bypass it in 1940 when they invaded France through Belgium.
◇1927 François Mauriac (1885 – 1970) writes *Thérèse Desqueyroux*.
The film director Abel Gance (1889 – 1981) makes the silent film *Napoléon*.
Georges Bernanos (1888 – 1948) writes the novel *Sous le soleil de Satan* (Under Satan's Sun).
◆1928 In Paris, Poincaré devalues and stabilizes the franc, which becomes known as the Poincaré Franc.
◇1928 André Breton writes the surrealist novel *Nadja*. Marcel Pagnol (1895 – 1974) writes the play *Topaze*.
Maurice Ravel composes *Le Boléro*.
The Winter Olympic Games are held in St Moritz, Switzerland.
◇1929 Paul Claudel writes the play *Le Soulier de satin* (The Satin Slipper).

English/Anglais

◇1929 *The Sound and the Fury* (Le Bruit et la fureur) de William Faulkner (1897–1962).

French/Français

First appearance of the Tintin character created by the Belgian cartoonist, Georges Rémi, known as Hergé (1907 – 1983).

1930

◇1930 L'astronome américain Clyde Tombaugh (1906 – 1997) découvre Pluton, la plus petite planète du système solaire.
American Gothic, du peintre américain Grant Wood, portrait d'un fermier du Midwest et de sa fille.
L'Américain Sinclair Lewis (1885 – 1951) reçoit le prix Nobel de littérature.
◆1930–36 L'Américain John Dos Passos (1896 – 1970) publie sa trilogie *USA*.
◆1931 L'Afrique du Sud devient un état souverain au sein du Commonwealth.
Pour faire face à la crise qui s'abat sur la Grande-Bretagne, durement touchée par la dépression, Ramsay MacDonald forme un gouvernement d'Union nationale.
◇1932 Ouverture du pont du port de Sydney.
Publication du roman de l'auteur anglais Aldous Huxley (1894 – 1963) *Brave New World* (Le Meilleur des Mondes) qui exprime une vision pessimiste d'un avenir dans lequel les êtres humains sont créés en laboratoire.
Le romancier britannique John Galsworthy (1867 – 1933) reçoit le prix Nobel de littérature.
Jeux Olympiques d'été à Los Angeles, jeux Olympiques d'hiver à Lake Placid, aux États-Unis.
◇1934 Parution de *Tropic of Cancer* (Tropique du Cancer), roman de l'écrivain américain Henry Miller (1891 – 1980). Publié à Paris, ce roman fait scandale en Grande-Bretagne et aux USA où il est interdit.
◇1935 Le physicien écossais Robert Watson-Watt (1892 – 1945) met au point l'ancêtre du radar.
◆1936 Édouard VIII (Édouard II d'Écosse) (1894 – 1972) accède au trône mais abdique un an plus tard en faveur de son frère George VI (1895 – 1952) afin d'épouser Wallis Simpson, une Américaine deux fois divorcée.
Des mineurs et des ouvriers des chantiers navals frappés par le chômage organisent une marche de la faim (the Jarrow March) depuis le comté de Durham jusqu'à Londres pour protester contre la pauvreté qui règne dans le nord de l'Angleterre.
◇1936 La BBC, financée par la redevance, diffuse ses premières émissions télévisées.
L'architecte américain Frank Lloyd Wright (1867 – 1959) crée la maison de *Falling Water*.
Le dramaturge américain Eugene O'Neill (1888 – 1953) reçoit le prix Nobel de littérature.
◇1937 L'ingénieur aéronautique britannique Frank Whittle (1907 – 1996) invente le turboréacteur.
Sortie de *Snow White and the Seven Dwarfs* (Blanche-Neige et les sept nains) de Walt Disney (1901 – 1966); c'est le premier dessin animé de long métrage de l'histoire du cinéma.
◆1938 Conférence de Munich; la France et la Grande-Bretagne n'interviendront pas en faveur de la Tchécoslovaquie face à Hitler. De retour, le premier ministre britannique Neville Chamberlain prononce son fameux 'I believe it is peace for our time'.
◇1938 La romancière américaine Pearl Buck (1892 – 1973) reçoit le prix Nobel de littérature.
◆1939 Début de la deuxième guerre mondiale: Hitler ayant envahi la Pologne, la France et la Grande-Bretagne déclarent la guerre à l'Allemagne. 1 200 000 personnes doivent quitter leur foyer pour échapper aux bombardements aériens.
◇1939 Sortie du western *Stagecoach* (La Chevauchée fantastique) de John Ford (1895 – 1973), premier grand rôle de John Wayne (1907 – 1979).
Victor Fleming (1889 – 1949) réalise *The Wizard of Oz* (Le Magicien d'Oz) et *Gone with the Wind* (Autant en emporte le vent).

◆1930 France promulgates a Constitution in Syria.
◆1931 Paul Doumer (1857 – 1932) is elected President of the Republic against Briand. He is assassinated the following year by a Russian émigré.
◇1931 Pierre Drieu La Rochelle (1893 – 1945) publishes the novel *Le Feu Follet* (The Fire Within).
◆1932 Albert Lebrun (1871 – 1950) becomes President of the Republic. In Africa, Upper Volta is divided between French Sudan (Mali), the Ivory Coast and Niger.
◇1932 Mauriac writes *Le Nœud de vipères* (The Vipers' Tangle).
Louis-Ferdinand Céline (1894 – 1961) publishes *Voyage au bout de la nuit* (Journey to the End of Night), an iconoclastic novel shattering the myth of the heroism of war to show its atrocity and wretchedness.
◆1933 Rise in extremism of the right, including the Croix-de-Feu (Flaming Cross) movement of extreme right-wing militia, created by Colonel de La Rocque (1885 – 1946).
◇1933 André Malraux (1901 – 1976) publishes the novel *La Condition humaine* (Man's Estate).
◆1934 The Stavisky affair, named after the French financier who embezzled money and was found shot dead, causes a great stir and fuels the anti-parliamentarianism of the extreme right.
A violent demonstration by the extreme right on 6 February leaves 20 dead.
In Belgium, King Leopold III supports Flemish nationalism.
◇1934 Irène (1897 – 1956) and Frédéric Joliot-Curie (1900 – 1958) discover artificial radioactivity.
Jean Vigo (1905 – 1934) makes *L'Atalante*, a film with Michel Simon.
◇1935 Jean Giono (1895 – 1970) writes the novel *Que ma joie demeure* (Joy of Man's Desiring).
Jean Giraudoux (1882 – 1944) writes the play *La Guerre de Troie n'aura pas lieu* (Tiger at the Gates).
◆1936 The Popular Front (1936 – 1938): Socialists, Communists and Radicals come together under the premiership of Léon Blum (1872 – 1950), heir to the French Socialist Party of Jaurès: wage rises, guaranteed trade union rights, 40-hour week, paid holidays, nationalization of armament factories.
◇1936 Georges Bernanos (1888 – 1948) publishes *Le Journal d'un curé de campagne* (Diary of a Country Priest).
◆1937 Creation of the SNCF, the French national railway company.
◇1937 Julien Duvivier (1896 – 1967) makes *Pépé le Moko*, a film with Jean Gabin.
Pablo Picasso (1881 – 1973) paints *Guernica*.
◆1938 Daladier government.
Munich conference and agreements: capitulation before Hitler. France and Britain will let Hitler invade Czechoslovakia.
◇1938 Malraux writes the novel *L'Espoir* (Man's Hope).
Jean-Paul Sartre (1905 – 1980) writes the novel *La Nausée* (Nausea).
Jean Cocteau (1889 – 1963) writes the play *Les Parents terribles*.
Marcel Carné's (1906 – 1996) film *Le Quai des Brumes* (Port of Shadows) is released.
◆1939 General mobilization (1 September).
Britain declares war on Germany, followed by France (3 September).
Beginning of the phoney war (la drôle de guerre).
◇1939 Jean Renoir's (1894 – 1979) film *La règle du jeu* (The Rules of the Game) is released.
Marcel Carné's film *Le jour se lève* (Daybreak) is released.
Nathalie Sarraute (1900 – 1999) publishes the novel *Tropismes* (Tropisms).

1940

◆1940 Évacuation de Dunkerque.
Sir Winston Churchill (1874 – 1965) forme un gouvernement de coalition qui siègera pendant toute la durée de la guerre. Churchill donne le ton de la résistance dans son célèbre discours 'Je n'ai rien d'autre à offrir que du sang, des efforts, des larmes et de la sueur' ('blood, toil, tears and sweat').
L'impôt sur le revenu est porté au taux record de 50% et le rationnement alimentaire est introduit.
Bataille d'Angleterre: la victoire de la RAF (aviation de chasse britannique) sur la Luftwaffe oblige Hitler à renoncer à sa tentative d'invasion de l'Angleterre.
◇1940 Ernest Hemingway (1899 – 1961) publie *For Whom the Bell Tolls* (Pour qui sonne le glas), sur la guerre d'Espagne.
◆1941 L'attaque japonaise de la base navale américaine de Pearl Harbor aux îles Hawaii fait entrer les États-Unis dans la guerre aux côtés de la Grande-Bretagne et de la France.
◇1941 Sortie de *Citizen Kane*, chef d'œuvre du cinéma réalisé par l'américain Orson Welles (1915 – 1985).

◆1940 German invasion of the Netherlands, Belgium and Luxembourg, then of France.
Evacuation of Dunkirk (6 June).
Fall of Paris (14 June).
Beginning of the Occupation.
The government withdraws to the free zone (Tours, then Bordeaux and Vichy). Paul Reynaud (1878 – 1966) resigns from the Presidency of the Council.
17 June: Pétain calls for the cessation of fighting.
18 June: Call from General de Gaulle from London urging the French to continue fighting the enemy.
Small resistance groups are formed.
22 June: Signature of the French-German armistice. Marshal Pétain is elected by the National Assembly as head of the French State.
28 June: De Gaulle is recognized as the leader of Free France by Britain.
2 July: The State locates itself in Vichy.

July 1940 – Aug. 1944 The Vichy regime

◆10 July: Pétain is elected head of the government.
August: French Equatorial Africa and Cameroon join forces with General de Gaulle.
24 October: Pétain and Hitler meet at Montoire. Policy of collaboration.
30 November: Alsace-Lorraine is officially annexed by Germany.
◇1940 Chance discovery by two adolescents of prehistoric wall paintings in a cave in Lascaux (Dordogne).
◆1941 Admiral Darlan (1881 – 1942) is appointed leader of the Pétain government: he sets up a policy of collaboration with the occupying forces.
The Free French Forces grant independence to Syria and Lebanon.

English/Anglais

◆1942 La victoire britannique d'El Alamein (sous le commandement du Maréchal Montgomery), en Égypte, sur les forces allemandes de l'Afrikakorps marque un tournant dans la campagne d'Afrique du Nord, campagne qui avait débuté par l'invasion italienne de l'Égypte en 1940.
◇1942 Le physicien américain d'origine italienne Enrico Fermi (1901 – 1954) construit la première pile atomique. C'est en grande partie sous son influence que le gouvernement américain décide d'adopter l'énergie nucléaire.
Sortie du film *Casablanca*, de l'Américain Michael Curtiz (1888 – 1962).

◆1943 Conférence de Téhéran avec Churchill, Roosevelt et Staline. Projet de débarquement en Provence.

◆1944 Le débarquement de Normandie le 6 juin (D-Day) marque le début de la libération de l'Europe par les Alliés. Paris est libéré le 25 août.
◇1944 Première représentation de *The Glass Menagerie* (La Ménagerie de verre), de Tennessee Williams (1911 – 1983).

◆1945 L'Allemagne se rend aux Alliés en mai. En août, les bombes atomiques américaines lâchées sur Hiroshima et Nagasaki obligent le Japon à capituler.
En Grande-Bretagne, Clement Attlee (1883 – 1967) devient Premier ministre après la victoire travailliste aux élections; il entreprend la nationalisation des secteurs principaux de l'industrie et de l'énergie.
◇1945 L'auteur anglais George Orwell (pseudonyme d'Eric Blair) (1903 – 1950) publie *Animal Farm* (La Ferme des animaux), satire du totalitarisme stalinien.
Sortie du film *Brief Encounter* (Brève Rencontre) du britannique David Lean (1908 – 1991).
◆1946 Churchill prononce son célèbre discours de Fulton (États-Unis) dans lequel il parle du rideau de fer qui divise l'Europe.
Début de la Guerre froide.
◆1947 Le Président américain Harry Truman (1884 – 1972) promet l'aide économique et militaire des États-Unis aux pays menacés par le communisme (doctrine Truman).
La Nouvelle-Zélande acquiert son indépendance au sein du Commonwealth.
Le pilote d'essai américain Charles 'Chuck' Yeager (1923 –) effectue le premier vol à vitesse supersonique (1 078 km/h) à bord du Bell X-1, avion propulsé par un moteur-fusée.
◇1947 Création du festival international d'Édimbourg qui se déroule sur trois semaines en août-septembre (concerts, opéra, art dramatique). Durant cette période, le festival alternatif offre des milliers de spectacles moins prestigieux.
◇1947 – 1956 Le peintre américain Jackson Pollock (1912 – 1956) produit une série de toiles en utilisant la technique du dripping.
◆1948 L'Inde devient indépendante.
Création du National Health Service, financé par le gouvernement et les impôts locaux. Ce service de santé national promet la gratuité des soins et des médicaments.
◇1948 L'invention du transistor aux États-Unis améliore la réception des postes de radio et de télévision et constitue un événement d'importance majeure pour le développement de l'informatique.
L'Américain Alfred Kinsey (1894 – 1956) publie son rapport *Sexual Behaviour in the Human Male*.
Première représentation de *A Streetcar Named Desire* (Un Tramway nommé Désir), de Tennessee Williams (1911 – 1983).
Le poète américain T.S. Eliot (1888 – 1965) reçoit le prix Nobel de littérature.
Les jeux Olympiques ont lieu à Londres.
◇1949 George Orwell (1903 – 1950) publie son roman *1984*.
William Faulkner (1897 – 1962) reçoit le prix Nobel de littérature.
Sortie de *The Third Man* (Le Troisième homme) du cinéaste britannique Carol Reed (1906 – 1976) d'après un roman de Graham Greene (1904 – 1991).

French/Français

◇1941 Robert Brasillach (1909 – 1945), director of the collaborationist journal *Je suis partout*, publishes *Notre avant-guerre*, a Nazi propaganda essay, whilst the composer Olivier Messiaen (1908 – 1992) writes a *Quatuor pour la fin du temps* (Quartet for the End of Time).
◆1942
17 April: Pierre Laval (1883 – 1945) becomes head of the Vichy government.
May: Requirement for Jews to wear the yellow star in the occupied zone.
21 – 22 July: The rounding up of Jews in the Paris Vélodrome d'Hiver: 13,000 Jews arrested by the French police.
8 November: Allied landings in North Africa.
11 November: The Germans occupy the free zone, in the south of France.
◇1942 Francis Ponge (1899 – 1988) publishes the poems *Le Parti pris des choses* (The Voice of Things).
Albert Camus writes *L'Étranger* (The Outsider).
Marcel Carné's film *Les Visiteurs du soir* (The Devil's Envoys) is released.
◆1943
January: Law setting up the Milice, to hunt down the Resistance.
February: Introduction of the STO (forced labour service).
Setting up of the National Council of the Resistance by Jean Moulin (1899 – 1943) who manages to unify the political movements around General de Gaulle.
The Teheran Conference between Churchill, Roosevelt and Stalin decides on the Allied landing in Provence.
De Gaulle visits Algiers; formation of the French Committee of National Liberation (CFLN).
◇1943 Jean-Paul Sartre publishes *L'Être et le Néant* (Being and Nothingness), the founding work of Sartre's existentialism.
Antoine de Saint-Exupéry (1900 – 1944) publishes *Le Petit Prince* (The Little Prince).
Henri-Georges Clouzot (1907 – 1977) makes *Le Corbeau* (The Raven), a detective film in which the subject and ambience reflect the atmosphere of the Occupation and its practices of denunciation.
Marcel Carné's film *Les Enfants du paradis* (Children of Paradise) is released.

June 1944 – 1946 Provisional Government of the French Republic

◆1944
6 June: Allied landings in Normandy in which the French Forces of the Interior (F.F.I.) take part.
19 – 25 August: Liberation of Paris by the forces under General Leclerc. Procession up the Champs-Élysées.
5 October: The right to vote is granted to women.
◇1944 First issue of the newspaper *Le Monde*, edited by Hubert Beuve-Méry (1902 – 1989).
Jean Anouilh (1910 – 1987) writes the play *Antigone*.
◆1945 Germany surrenders to the Allies.
Marshal Pétain's death sentence is commuted to life imprisonment.
Creation of the French Social Security system.
Ho Chi Min's Indochina and Laos declare their independence, which is not recognized by France.
Belgium is liberated.
◇1945 Foundation of the monthly *Les Temps Modernes* (Modern Times) by Jean-Paul Sartre, Simone de Beauvoir (1908 – 1986), Maurice Merleau-Ponty (1908 – 1961) and Raymond Aron (1905 – 1983).
The pro-Nazi writer Robert Brasillach is sentenced to death and executed in Febuary.

1946 – 1958 The Fourth Republic

◆1946 De Gaulle leaves the provisional government when the Constitution of the Fourth Republic is promulgated (1946 – 1958).
Creation of the French Union, which includes colonial possessions and creates the Overseas Départements (DOM).
Beginning of the conflict in Indochina (1946 – 1954) with the bombing of the Bay of Haiphong.
◇1946 Opening of the first Cannes International Film Festival.
Jean Cocteau and René Clément's film *La Belle et la Bête* (Beauty and the Beast) is released.
◆1947 Vincent Auriol (1884 – 1956) becomes President of the Republic (1947 – 54).
General de Gaulle founds the RPF (Rassemblement du peuple français).
France accepts the Marshall Plan for American aid in the reconstruction of Europe.
Insurrection in Madagascar.
In The Hague, signature of the customs protocol between Belgium, Holland and Luxembourg (Benelux).
◇1947 André Gide awarded the Nobel Prize for literature.
Albert Camus publishes *La Peste* (The Plague).
Aimé Césaire (1913 –), a poet from Martinique writing about black experience and culture, publishes the collection of poems *Cahier d'un retour au pays natal* (Notebook of a Return to my Native Land).
Jean Vilar (1912 – 1971) sets up the Festival of Avignon.
Édith Piaf (1915 – 1963) sings *La vie en rose*.
Le Corbusier (1887 – 1965) builds La Cité Radieuse, a housing complex in Marseille.
◇1948 Hervé Bazin (1911 – 1996) publishes the novel *Vipère au poing* (Viper in the Fist).
The Winter Olympic Games are held in St Moritz, Switzerland.
◆1949 Belgium signs the North Atlantic Treaty.
A world congress of the Peace movement is held in Paris, for which Picasso paints the dove of peace.
◇1949 Simone de Beauvoir publishes *Le Deuxième sexe* (The Second Sex), the founding text of feminism.
Creation of the magazine *Paris-Match*.

English/Anglais	French/Français

1950

◆1950 – 1953 Guerre de Corée. Les forces de l'ONU défendent la Corée du Sud contre l'invasion communiste de la Corée du Nord et de la Chine. Période du maccartisme.

◆1951 Winston Churchill est de nouveau Premier ministre.
◇1951 L'écrivain américain J.D. Salinger (1919 –) publie *Catcher in the Rye* (L'Attrape-Cœur). Son roman raconte les aventures d'un adolescent qui se rebelle contre un monde adulte et bourgeois.
◆1952 Premiers essais de la bombe à hydrogène aux États-Unis.
Mort de Georges VI. Élisabeth II (1926 –) devient reine du Royaume-Uni et chef du Commonwealth.
La Grande-Bretagne se dote de la bombe atomique.
◇1952 *High Noon* (Le Train sifflera trois fois), film de l'Américain Fred Zinnemann (1907 – 1997).
Le poète gallois Dylan Thomas (1914 – 1953) écrit *Under Milk Wood* (Au bois lacté).
Winston Churchill reçoit le prix Nobel de littérature.
◆1953 Dwight Eisenhower (1890 – 1969), rendu populaire par sa réussite de la difficile coordination des forces alliées, en particulier en Afrique du Nord, devient Président des États-Unis. La résistance au communisme et les contacts directs avec les chefs d'États étrangers sont les traits dominants de sa présidence.
◇1953 Découverte de la structure en double hélice de la molécule d'ADN par le biochimiste anglais Francis Crick (1916 –) et le biologiste américain James Watson (1928 –) au laboratoire de Cavendish à Cambridge.
Première représentation de *The Crucible* (Les Sorcières de Salem), allégorie du maccartisme, du dramaturge américain Arthur Miller.
◇1954 *Lord of the Flies* (Sa Majesté des Mouches) de l'auteur anglais William Golding (1911 – 1993).
Kingsley Amis (1922 – 1995) publie son roman comique *Lucky Jim*.
Ernest Hemingway (1899 – 1961) reçoit le prix Nobel de littérature.
◇1954 – 1955 J.R.R. Tolkien (1892 – 1973) publie sa trilogie *The Lord of the Rings* (Le Seigneur des anneaux).
◆1954 – 1968 Lutte pour les droits civiques aux États-Unis.

◆1955 Anthony Eden (1897 – 1977), conservateur, succède à Churchill comme Premier ministre.
À Montgomery, dans l'Alabama, début du boycott des autobus organisé par Martin Luther King, à la suite de l'arrestation de Rosa Parks, une Noire qui s'était installée dans la section réservée aux blancs.
◇1955 *Rock Around the Clock* de Bill Haley (1925 – 1981) et les Comets est l'un des premiers grands succès de l'époque du rock and roll.
Rebel Without a Cause (La Fureur de vivre), de Nicholas Ray, avec James Dean (1931 – 1955).

◆1956 Crise de Suez. L'Égypte nationalise le canal de Suez; la France et la Grande-Bretagne, malgré les critiques, occupent la zone du canal, mais la crainte d'une intervention de la Russie et des USA les obligent à évacuer leurs troupes.
◇1956 Le philosophe britannique A.J. Ayer (1910 – 1989) publie *The Problem of Knowledge* (Le Problème de la Connaissance).
Première représentation de *Look Back in Anger* (La Paix du dimanche), pièce de l'auteur dramatique anglais John Osborne (1929 – 1994), chef de file des Angry Young Men (Jeunes Gens en colère).
Sortie de *Heartbreak Hotel*, grand succès d'Elvis Presley (1935 – 1977), devenu le chanteur le plus populaire aux États-Unis.
Première démonstration du magnétoscope par les ingénieurs américains Raymond Dolby (1933 –) et Charles Ginsburg.
Première représentation de *A Long Day's Journey into Night* (Long Voyage vers la nuit) du dramaturge américain Eugene O'Neill, qui remportera le prix Pullitzer l'année suivante.
Jeux Olympiques d'été à Melbourne, en Australie.
◆1957 Harold Macmillan (1894 – 1986), conservateur, devient Premier ministre en Grande-Bretagne. La popularité de ses mesures sociales et de sa politique étrangère lui vaudra d'être réélu en 1959.
◇1957 L'auteur américain Jack Kerouac (1922 – 1969) publie *On the Road* (Sur la route). Dans ce roman, il se fait le porte-parole de la 'Beat Generation' en révolte contre le conformisme bourgeois et la société de consommation.
◆1959 L'Alaska et Hawaï deviennent respectivement les 49ème et 50ème états des États-Unis.
◇1959 Vladimir Nabokov (1899 – 1977) publie *Lolita*, récit de la passion d'un quadragénaire pour une nymphette.
Some Like it Hot (Certains l'aiment chaud), film de l'Américain Billy Wilder (1906–) avec Marilyn Monroe (1926 – 1962).

◆1950 Creation of the SMIG (guaranteed minimum wage).
Internationalization of the France-Vietnam conflict: the Americans provide support for the French against the Viet Minh forces and Ho Chi Minh.
◇1950 Eugène Ionesco (1912 – 1994) writes *La Cantatrice chauve* (The Bald Prima Donna), a play that marks the emergence of the Theatre of the Absurd.
◆1951 In Belgium, beginning of the reign of Baudoin I (1930 – 1993).
Treaty of Paris, establishing the European Coal and Steel Community (ECSC). Provided for by the Schuman plan, the ECSC is developed by R. Schuman (1886 – 1963) and Jean Monnet (1888 – 1979), the 'fathers of Europe'.
◇1951 Albert Camus publishes the essay *L'Homme révolté* (The Rebel): dispute with Sartre.
Jean Vilar takes over the management of the TNP.
François Mauriac wins the Nobel Prize for literature.
◆1953 In Morocco, France deposes sultan Mohammed V, who personifies the desire for independence of his country.
◇1953 Samuel Beckett's (1906 – 1989) play *En attendant Godot* (Waiting for Godot) is first performed. The English version is first performed in 1955.
Roland Barthes publishes *Le Degré zéro de l'écriture* (Writing Degree Zero).
◆1954 René Coty (1882 – 1962) becomes President of the Republic (1954 – 1958).
In Indochina, the disaster of Dien-Bien-Phu brings to an end the France-Vietnam war through the Geneva accords, which divide Vietnam into the democratic Republic in the North (governed by Ho Chi Minh) and the Republic of South Vietnam, led by Bao Dai, and confirm the independence of Laos and Cambodia.
In Algeria, insurrection in Kabylia and in the Aurès region, driven by the National Liberation Front (F.L.N.) founded by Ahmed Ben Bella, which marks the beginning of the War of Algeria (1954 – 1962).
◇1954 Françoise Sagan (1935 –) publishes *Bonjour Tristesse*. This novel by the young French writer creates a scandal and meets with immediate success.
On the radio, Henri Grouès, known as Abbé Pierre (1912 –), launches an appeal on behalf of the destitute and homeless, helping them through the creation of the Companions of Emmaus community (1949).
Truffaut's *Manifesto* is published in the *Cahiers du cinéma*.
◆1955 End of the French protectorate in Morocco and reinstatement of Mohammed V.
Riots and violent repression in Algeria.
◇1955 Claude Lévi-Strauss (1908 –) publishes *Tristes Tropiques* (A World on the Wane), an autobiographical essay by the renowned anthropologist.
Pierre Boulez composes *Le Marteau sans maître* (The Hammer without a Master), based on words by the poet René Char.
Alain Resnais releases *Nuit et brouillard* (Night and Fog), a film about the Nazi concentration camps.
◆1956 Guy Mollet, President of the Council, goes to Algiers where he is met by a demonstration of Pieds-Noirs (French settlers in Algeria).
End of the protectorate in Tunisia; French trading posts are returned to India.
Creation of the Overseas Territories (Territoires d'outre-mer or T.O.M.) prepared by Gaston Defferre (1910 – 1986), to lead to the independence of French West Africa and French East Africa.
The Suez crisis: France and Britain occupy the Suez Canal zone after it is nationalized by Nasser. They are forced to evacuate their troops after the operation is strongly condemned by both the USA and the USSR.
◇1956 Commander Jacques Cousteau (1910 – 1997) produces *Le Monde du silence* (The Silent World) with Louis Malle.
◆1957 Signature of the two Treaties of Rome setting up the European Economic Community (EEC), then known as the Common Market, and of Euratom. The founding countries form the Europe of the Six (France, West Germany, Italy, the Netherlands, Belgium and Luxembourg).
Declaration of independence by Morocco and Tunisia.
◇1957 Albert Camus wins the Nobel Prize for literature.
Samuel Beckett writes the play *Fin de partie* (Endgame).
Michel Butor (1926 –) publishes the 'new' novel *La Modification* (Second Thoughts).

1958 The Fifth Republic

◆1958 The insurrection in Algiers brings General de Gaulle back to power. President of the Council, he is given emergency powers and goes to Algiers. By referendum (direct consultation of the citizens of France), he has the Constitution of the Fifth Republic approved and is elected President. The Community of French-speaking Africa succeeds the French Union. It is rejected by Guinea, which becomes independent.
◇1958 Marguerite Duras (1914 – 1996) publishes the novel *Moderato Cantabile*.
◆1959 De Gaulle is President of the Republic.
He announces a policy of self-determination in Algeria.
◇1959 Raymond Queneau publishes *Zazie dans le métro* (Zazie), a novel adapted for the cinema by Louis Malle in 1960.
François Truffaut's film *Les 400 coups* (The 400 Blows) is released.
Le Sacre du printemps (The Rite of Spring), choreography by Maurice Béjart (1927–), music by Igor Stravinsky.

1960

◇1960 Le physicien américain Theodore Maiman (1927 –) réalise le premier laser optique.
◆1960 John Updike (1932 –), romancier américain, publie *Rabbit, Run*.
Psycho (Psychose), d'Alfred Hitchcock (1899 – 1980).

◆1960 A week of street riots in Algiers fuelled by the opposition to self-determination of the population of French extraction.

English/Anglais	French/Français

Les jeux Olympiques d'hiver ont lieu à Squaw Valley, en Californie.
◆1961 Devant l'opposition internationale à son régime de discrimination raciale (l'apartheid), l'Afrique du Sud se retire du Commonwealth et forme une république indépendante.
Élection de John F. Kennedy (1917 – 1963): il est le premier Président catholique des USA et le plus jeune. Parlant d'une 'nouvelle frontière', il met en place un programme de réformes sociales et d'intégration raciale.
◇1961 Le romancier américain Joseph Heller obtient un succès immédiat avec la publication de son roman *Catch 22* dont le titre est passé dans la langue pour désigner une situation sans issue.
◆1962 Crise des missiles de Cuba : la découverte de bases de fusées soviétiques à Cuba suscite une vive inquiétude internationale. Les États-Unis établissent le blocus de l'île. Kennedy finit par obtenir que l'URSS évacue ses fusées.
◇1962 Sortie de *Dr No*, premier d'une série de films à grand succès dont le héros est l'agent secret James Bond, rôle tenu à plusieurs reprises par Sean Connery.
Les Beatles obtiennent leur premier grand succès avec la chanson *Love Me Do*. Ils déclenchent un enthousiasme populaire quasi hystérique.
Le peintre américain Andy Warhol (v.1926 – 1987) réalise le *Marilyn Diptych*, photos colorées de Marilyn Monroe.
Le romancier britannique Anthony Burgess (1917 – 1993) publie *A Clockwork Orange* (Orange mécanique) dans lequel il dénonce la violence de la société moderne.
Le romancier américain John Steinbeck (1902 – 1968) reçoit le prix Nobel de littérature.
◆1963 John Kennedy est assassiné à Dallas, au Texas, à son arrivée en visite officielle. Lyndon Johnson (1908 – 1973), son Vice-Président, lui succède.
Martin Luther King prononce son discours 'I have a dream' au cours d'un rassemblement pour les droits civiques, à Washington.
Suite à la démission d'Harold Macmillan, Alec Douglas-Home (1903 – 1995) renonce à ses titres nobiliaires et devient Premier ministre du Royaume-Uni.
◇1963 L'Américaine Betty Friedan (1921 –) publie son livre *The Feminine Mystique* (La Femme mystifiée), un des ouvrages phares du mouvement féministe.
Affaire Profumo en Grande-Bretagne: John Profumo, ministre de la guerre, démissionne à la suite de révélations concernant sa liaison avec une jeune femme également liée à un officier russe.
◆1964 Harold Wilson, leader des travaillistes, devient Premier ministre de Grande-Bretagne. Son programme économique est compromis par une grave crise financière.
Aux USA, Lyndon Johnson, poursuivant la politique d'intégration raciale de Kennedy, fait voter le 'Civil Rights Act' (loi sur les droits civils).
◆1964 – 1975 Les États-Unis envoient des troupes au Viêt-nam pour soutenir le régime anti-communiste du Sud contre ses adversaires communistes du Nord.
◇1964 Martin Luther King obtient le prix Nobel de la paix.
◆1965 Une loi électorale apporte une nouvelle amélioration au statut des Noirs américains.
◇1965 *The Sound of Music* (La Mélodie du bonheur), film de l'Américain Robert Wise (1914 –).
◇1966 L'Angleterre gagne la Coupe du monde de football.
Cathy Come Home, film de Ken Loach (1936 –) qui traite du problème des sans-logis; c'est à la suite de sa diffusion que sera créée l'association d'aide aux SDF Shelter.
◇1967 En Afrique du Sud, le chirurgien Christian Barnard (1922 –) réalise la premiere greffe du cœur. Le patient survivra 18 jours.
Sortie de l'album des Beatles *Sergeant Pepper's Lonely Hearts Club Band*.
◆1968 Martin Luther King est assassiné à Memphis, au Tennessee.
◇1968 *2001: A Space Odyssey* (2001: l'Odyssée de l'espace), film du cinéaste américain Stanley Kubrick (1928 – 1999).

◆1969 L'Irlande du Nord entre dans une période de violents affrontements entre catholiques et protestants. L'armée britannique envoie des troupes pour tenter de maintenir la paix.
Richard Nixon (1913 – 1994) est élu à la présidence des USA.
◇1969 L'astronaute américain Neil Armstrong, commandant d'Apollo 11, est le premier homme à mettre pied sur la Lune.
Premier vol du supersonique franco-britannique Concorde.
Festival pop de Woodstock, aux États-Unis.

The States of Africa which are members of the Community of French-speaking Africa or under French trusteeship become independent: Mauritania, Upper Volta, Niger, Chad, Senegal, Mali, Ivory Coast, Togo, Dahomey (Benin), Cameroon, Gabon, Congo, Central African Republic, Madagascar. Belgium proclaims the independence of Congo-Kinshasa (formerly the Belgian Congo, and now the Democratic Republic of Congo).
France has the atomic bomb.
Creation of the New Franc.
◇1960 The poet Saint-John Perse (1887 – 1975) wins the Nobel Prize for literature.
Jean-Luc Godard (1930 –), film critic for *Cahiers du Cinéma* and young filmmaker representative of the New Wave, films *A bout de souffle* (Breathless).
Pop music: start of the yé-yé wave around the magazine *Salut les copains*. Among its leading figures are Johnny Hallyday, Sylvie Vartan, Françoise Hardy, Claude François and Eddy Mitchell.
◆1961 After the proclamation by De Gaulle of the self-determination of the Algerian people, the French population of Algeria and army officers try to oppose it with an attempted coup d'état by senior army officers (which fails) supported by the OAS (Organisation Armée secrète), which commits several terrorist attacks in Algeria and France.
Canada: creation of the French language office (Office de la langue française).
◇1961 Jean Genêt (1910 – 1986) writes the play *Les Paravents* (The Screens).
Édith Piaf sings *Non, je ne regrette rien*.
◆1962 Amendment of the Constitution introducing the election of the President of the Republic by universal suffrage.
Death of 8 people at the Charonne metro station during an anti-OAS demonstration. Signature of the Evian Agreements recognizing Algerian independence and bringing the war to an end. Mass exodus of French people from Algeria (the Pieds-Noirs).
Ruanda-Urundi (under Belgian trusteeship) becomes independent and splits into two States: Rwanda and Burundi.
◇1962 The Mont Blanc tunnel is built.
◆1963 Addis Ababa Conference, which sets up the Organization of African Unity (OAU).
◇1963 *Le Mépris* (Contempt), film by Jean-Luc Godard, with Brigitte Bardot.
◆1964 France withdraws from the integrated military organization of NATO.
◇1964 Sartre refuses the Nobel Prize.
Jacques Demy's (1931 – 1990) musical film *Les Parapluies de Cherbourg* (The Umbrellas of Cherbourg) is released.
◆1965 Re-election of De Gaulle to the Presidency of the Republic.
Mehdi Ben Barka, leader of the forces of opposition to King Hassan II, is abducted and never seen again. This becomes known as the Ben Barka Affair.
◇1965 François Jacob, Jacques Monod and André Lwof, receive the Nobel Prize for medicine for their work on the genetic code.
◇1966 Publication of *Écrits* (The Language of the Self: The Function of Language in Psychoanalysis) by Jacques Lacan (1901 – 1981), who reinterprets the theoretical approach of Freudian psychoanalysis.
Jean Genêt's *Les Paravents* (The Screens) is performed: the event of the theatre season.
Jean-Luc Godard's film *Pierrot le Fou* is released.
◆1967 De Gaulle travels to Canada where Quebec is experiencing a revival of French Canadian nationalism. In Montreal, he utters a resounding 'Vive le Québec libre!' (Long Live Free Quebec).
◆1968 In France, student demonstrations at the University of Nanterre spark off the May Events, leading to widespread social and political protests.
General strike on an unprecedented scale.
France has the H bomb.
◇1968 Albert Cohen (1895 – 1981) publishes the novel *Belle du Seigneur*.
The Winter Olympic Games are held in Grenoble.
◆1969 Resignation of General de Gaulle.
Georges Pompidou (1911 – 1974) is elected President of the Republic.
◇1969 First flight of the supersonic plane Concorde.
Marcel Ophuls (1927 –) makes *Le Chagrin et la Pitié* (The Sorrow and the Pity), a documentary about life in a French village during the Occupation.

1970

◆1970 Edward Heath (1916 –), conservateur, est le nouveau Premier ministre en Grande-Bretagne.
◇1970 Publication d'une nouvelle version de la Bible, *The New English Bible*. Écrite dans un anglais littéraire moderne, elle tient compte des tout derniers travaux de recherche.
L'universitaire féministe australienne Germaine Greer publie *The Female Eunuch* (La Femme eunuque).
Le peintre britannique David Hockney (1937 –) présente *Mr and Mrs Clark and Percy*.
◆1971 Introduction du système décimal dans la monnaie britannique.
◆1972 Épisode du dimanche sanglant (Bloody Sunday) à Londonderry, en Irlande du Nord: 13 manifestants catholiques sont abattus par des soldats de l'armée britannique.
Visite de Nixon en Chine.
◇1972 *The Godfather* (Le Parrain), film du cinéaste américain Francis Ford Coppola (1939 –).
◆1973 La Grande-Bretagne et la République d'Irlande entrent dans la Communauté économique européenne.
Grève des mineurs en Grande-Bretagne.
Désengagement des troupes américaines au Viêt-nam sous la pression d'une opinion publique de plus en plus hostile à la guerre.

◆1970 October crisis in Quebec: the Quebec Liberation Front kidnaps a British diplomat and a minister of the Quebec government, executing the latter. The army is brought in, as is the law on war measures.
Death of General de Gaulle.
◆1971 Creation of the Socialist Party at the Epinay Congress. François Mitterrand (1916 – 1996) is elected first secretary.
◇1971 Start of the building (1971 – 1975) in Paris of the Georges Pompidou Centre, by Renzo Piano and Richard Rogers.
◆1972 The left (François Mitterrand's Socialist Party, Georges Marchais' Communist Party, Robert Fabre's Radical Party) present a joint government programme.
◆1973 At the Lip watchmaking factory, striking workers decide in opposition to the management to resume work and to set up self-management of the factory.
◇1973 Birth of the newspaper *Libération*, under the aegis of Jean-Paul Sartre (edited by Serge July after 1974).
◆1974 Death of Georges Pompidou.
After the interim government of Alain Poher, Valéry Giscard-d'Estaing (1926 –) is elected President of the Republic (1974 – 1981).

English/Anglais	French/Français

Nixon et Kissinger annoncent 'la paix dans l'honneur' et Nixon promet le versement de plus de 3 milliards de dollars en réparations au Viêt-nam, somme qui ne sera jamais payée.
Insurrection indienne à Wounded Knee, dans le Dakota du Sud, aux États-Unis.
La Cod War (Guerre de la morue), dispute entre la Grande-Bretagne et l'Islande à propos des zones de pêche.
◇1973 Le romancier américain Thomas Pynchon (1937 –) publie *Gravity's Rainbow*, roman controversé et d'un surréalisme obscur.
The Exorcist (L'Exorciste) de l'Américain William Friedkin (1939 –).
Le romancier australien Patrick White (1912 – 1990) reçoit le prix Nobel de littérature.
◆1974 Démission du Président américain Richard Nixon menacé d''impeachment' (mise en accusation) suite à l'affaire de Watergate. Gerald Ford (1913 –) lui succède, mais la 'grâce' qu'il accorde à Nixon le rend impopulaire.
Harold Wilson revient au pouvoir mais se heurte bientôt à de graves dissensions internes au sujet du maintien de la Grande-Bretagne dans la CEE.
En Angleterre, Lord Lucan, membre de la chambre des Lords, disparaît à la suite du meurtre de la nourrice de ses enfants.
Pendant environ deux mois, la semaine de travail est réduite à trois jours en raison d'une pénurie de carburant.
◆1976 Après la démission d'Harold Wilson, James Callaghan (1912 –), nouveau chef des travaillistes, lui succède.
Fête du bicentenaire de l'Indépendance aux États-Unis.
◇1976 *Taxi Driver*, film de Martin Scorsese (1942 –) avec Robert De Niro (1943 –).
Le romancier Saul Bellow (1915 –) reçoit le prix Nobel de littérature.
Les jeux Olympiques ont lieu à Montréal.
◆1977 Élection du Démocrate Jimmy Carter (1924 –) à la présidence des États-Unis.
La Grande-Bretagne fête le Silver Jubilee de la reine d'Angleterre, marquant 25 ans de règne.
◇1977 Sortie de *Star Wars* (La Guerre des étoiles), superproduction de science-fiction réalisée par l'Américain George Lucas (1944 –).
Mort d'Elvis Presley 'Roi du rock and roll'. Il est pleuré par des millions de personnes.
◆1978 Série de grèves en Grande-Bretagne: le Winter of Discontent.
◇1978 Naissance en Grande-Bretagne de Louise Brown, premier 'bébé-éprouvette' (c.à.d. conçu par fécondation in-vitro).
Le romancier américain Isaac Bashevis Singer (1904 – 1991) reçoit le prix Nobel de littérature.
◆1979 Margaret Thatcher (1925 –), chef du parti conservateur, devient la première femme Premier ministre de Grande-Bretagne. Elle triomphera de nouveau aux élections législatives de 1983 et 1987. Durant ses trois mandats, elle pousuivra une politique générale de dénationalisation et de privatisation et diminuera le rôle des administrations locales. Sa personnalité et sa politique lui vaudront le surnom d''Iron Lady' (la dame de fer).
◇1979 *Apocalypse Now*, film de l'Américain Francis Ford Coppola (1939–), sur la guerre du Viêt-Nam, avec Marlon Brando (1924 –).
◆1979 – 1981 Crise des otages de l'Iran: des étudiants islamiques prennent en otage le personnel de l'ambassade des USA à Téhéran. Ils demandent en échange que le Shah en exil leur soit livré par les États-Unis pour être jugé par un tribunal islamique. Malgré des sanctions économiques, les 52 otages ne seront libérés qu'au bout de 444 jours de captivité.

The minimum voting age is lowered from 21 to 18. Simone Veil (1927 –), Minister of Health, secures the legalization of abortion in a law that bears her name.
◇1974 *Les Valseuses*, film by Bertrand Blier starring Gérard Depardieu, Patrick Dewaere and Miou-Miou.
◆1975 Declaration of the independence of the Comoros; only Mayotte chooses to remain French.
◇1975 Michel Colucci, known as Coluche (1944 – 1986), makes his debut at the Café de la Gare. Here he ushers in, with the group of comedians Le Splendid, a new style of comedy.
Bernard Pivot launches the literary television programme *Apostrophes*.
◆1976 At its 22nd Congress, the PCF abandons the doctrine of the dictatorship of the proletariat.
In Quebec, the separatist party (Parti Québécois) of René Levesque attains power.
The Summer Olympic Games are held in Montreal.
◇1976 *Monsieur Klein* (Mr Klein), film by Joseph Losey with Alain Delon.
Michel Foucault (1926 – 1984) publishes *Histoire de la sexualité* (History of Sexuality).
◆1977 Belgium is divided into three regions: Wallonia, Flanders and Brussels.
The Republic of Djibouti (formerly the French Territory of the Afars and Issas) gains independence.
In Quebec, Law 101 establishes French as the official language.
◇1977 Opening of the Georges Pompidou Centre.
◆1978 The Swiss Confederation creates the canton of Jura, which combines three French-speaking regions.
◇1978 Oil slick in Brittany following the sinking of the Liberian tanker Amoco-Cadiz.
In *Le Monde*, Robert Faurisson publishes the article *Le problème des chambres à gaz, ou la rumeur d'Auschwitz* (The question of the gas chambers or the rumour of Auschwitz) which marks the beginning of revisionism, or denial of genocide.
Béate and Serge Klarsfeld publish the essay *Mémorial de la déportation des juifs de France.*
◆1979 The satirical newspaper *Le Canard enchaîné* publishes an article on the diamonds given by Emperor Bokassa (of the Central African Republic) to Valéry Giscard d'Estaing.
◇1979 First successful launch of the Ariane rocket.
Jean Fourastié (1907 – 1990) publishes *Les Trente Glorieuses*, a book about the thirty years of unprecedented economic prosperity in post-war France.

1980

◆1980 Siège de l'ambassade d'Iran à Londres; un commando de l'armée donne l'assaut et libère les otages.
◇1980 John Lennon, auteur-interprète, ancien membre des Beatles, est assassiné à New York.
Représentation à Londres de la pièce de théâtre *Romans in Britain* de Howard Brenton (1942 –), une allégorie sur la présence de l'armée britannique en Irlande du Nord. Le metteur en scène Michael Bogdanov est poursuivi à cause du caractère sexuellement explicite de l'une des scènes.
Le poète américain Czeslaw Milosz (1911 –) reçoit le prix Nobel de littérature.
Les jeux Olympiques d'hiver ont lieu à Lake Placid, dans l'État de New York.
◆1981 Ronald Reagan (1911 –), est élu à la présidence des USA. Il lance un important programme de réformes économiques pour lutter contre l'inflation et réduire les dépenses publiques. Dans le domaine de la politique étrangère, il adopte une attitude résolument anti-communiste.
Grève de la faim de [illegible] membres de l'IRA en Irlande du Nord, qui revendiquent le statut de prisonniers politiques. Mort de 10 d'entre eux, dont Bobby Sands, qui avait été élu député.
◇1981 Premier vol expérimental avec deux astronautes à bord de la navette spatiale américaine mise au point par la NASA. Lancée comme une fusée, cette navette réutilisable atterrit sur une piste commme un avion.
À Londres, première représentation de *Cats*, comédie musicale d'Andrew Lloyd Webber (1948 –).
◆1982 Guerre des Malouines (les Falklands en anglais). L'Argentine revendique cette colonie britannique. Suite à la rupture des pourparlers, elle occupe l'archipel. Les Britanniques attaquent la flotte argentine et après le débarquement de leurs troupes et deux mois de durs combats, ils obligent les Argentins à capituler. Cette victoire fait remonter l'indice de popularité du gouvernement.
'Canada Act': avec l'accord de Londres, la Constitution du Canada ne dépend plus que du gouvernement fédéral.
◇1982 *Blade Runner*, film de science-fiction de Ridley Scott, avec Harrison Ford (1942 –).
L'américaine Alice Walker (1944 –) publie *The Color Purple* (La Couleur pourpre), et remporte le prix Pullitzer l'année suivante.
◆1983 Intervention américaine à la Grenade.

◆1980 In a referendum, the Quebecois vote against independence for the province.
◇1980 Attack on a synagogue in the rue Copernic in Paris.
The Belgian writer Marguerite Yourcenar (1903 – 1987) is elected to the Académie Française.
Le Père Noël est une ordure, alternative theatre success by the Le Splendid group of comedians.
Bernard Kouchner founds Médecins du Monde.
The first TGV (high-speed train) comes into operation.
◆1981 François Mitterrand is elected President of the Republic.
Abolition of the death penalty.
◆1982 Laws on nationalizations, decentralization, the 39-hour week and retirement at 60.
◇1982 Amandine, the first French test-tube baby, is born.
An antisemitic attack in the rue des Rosiers in Paris leaves 6 dead and 22 injured.
◆1983 The ex-Nazi Klaus Barbie, extradited from Bolivia, arrives in France where he is charged with crimes against humanity.

English/Anglais	French/Français

239 soldats américains sont tués dans un attentat à Beyrouth, au Liban.
◇1983 Le romancier britannique William Golding (1911 – 1993) reçoit le prix Nobel de littérature.
◆1984 Une bombe de l'IRA explose au Grand Hotel de Brighton pendant la conférence annuelle du parti conservateur, et fait quatre morts et de nombreux blessés.
Grève des mineurs en Grande-Bretagne, menés par Arthur Scargill, en réaction à la fermeture annoncée de nombreux puits. Violentes confrontations entre grévistes et forces de l'ordre.
◇1984 Les jeux Olympiques ont lieu à Los Angeles.
◆1985 Émeutes raciales à Londres (Brixton et Tottenham) et à Birmingham (Handsworth).
Drame du Heysel à Bruxelles: 41 personnes trouvent la mort au cours d'émeutes provoquées par les supporters de Liverpool. Les clubs britanniques sont exclus des compétitions européennes.
Premiers cas d'encéphalopathie bovine spongiforme (maladie de la vache folle) en Grande-Bretagne.
◇1985 Mort de Robert Graves (1895 – 1985), poète et romancier anglais, auteur de *I, Claudius* (Moi, Claude), de *Claudius the God* (Le Dieu Claude), ainsi que de recueils de poèmes.

◆1986 Scandale de l'Irangate aux États-Unis: découverte de ventes secrètes d'armes à l'Iran – peut-être autorisées par le Président – pour tenter d'obtenir la libération d'otages américains détenus au Liban, et afin de financer la guerre et les opérations terroristes menées par les Contras contre l'état nicaraguayen dont les réformes économiques déplaisent à Washington.
Des bombardiers américains basés en Grande-Bretagne bombardent la Libye à la suite d'attentats attribués au Colonel Khadafi.
Explosion en vol de la navette Challenger.
◇1986 Avènement de l'ordinateur personnel Apple Macintosh.
Mort d'Henry Moore, sculpteur anglais semi-abstrait. L'une de ses œuvres les plus célèbres, *Madonna and Child* (La Vierge et l'Enfant) se trouve dans l'église de St Matthew à Northampton.
◆1987 Début des travaux de creusement du tunnel sous la Manche (il sera terminé en 1994) entre Cheriton, près de Folkestone en Angleterre, et Sangatte, près de Calais.
Nouveau krach boursier aux États-Unis.
◇1987 Le poète américain Joseph Brodsky (1940 – 1996) reçoit le prix Nobel de littérature.
◆1988 150 travailleurs trouvent la mort dans l'incendie de la plate-forme pétrolière Piper Alpha en mer du Nord.
Un Boeing 747 de la Pan Am explose au dessus de Lockerbie, en Écosse, provoquant la mort des 270 passagers et de 11 villageois.
Bicentennaire de l'arrivée des premiers colons européens en Australie.
◇1988 *A Brief History of Time* (Brève Histoire du Temps), ouvrage de cosmologie du savant anglais Stephen Hawking (1942 –) est un bestseller.
Salman Rushdie publie *The Satanic Verses* (Les Versets sataniques), ouvrage jugé blasphématoire par de nombreux musulmans et qui lui vaut d'être l'objet d'une fatwa.
Jeux Olympiques d'hiver à Calgary, au Canada.
◆1989 Le Républicain George Bush (1924 –) accède à la présidence des États-Unis. Son mandat marque la fin de la guerre froide entre l'URSS et les États-Unis.
Intervention américaine au Panama.
En Angleterre, 95 supporters de Liverpool meurent écrasés au stade de Hillsborough, à Sheffield, à la suite d'un mouvement de foule non contrôlé.
◇1989 Mort du grand acteur et metteur en scène anglais Laurence Olivier (1907 – 1989). Célèbre avant tout pour son interprétation du théâtre shakespearien, il avait également mené une carrière d'acteur de cinéma et de télévision.

58 French soldiers are killed in a bomb attack in Beirut.
◇1983 Nathalie Sarraute publishes *Enfance* (Childhood).
The tennis player Yannick Noah is the first French winner of the French Open since 1946.
Professor Luc Montagnier (1932 –) of the Pasteur Institute identifies the HIV virus responsible for AIDS.
◆1984 Laurent Fabius (1946 –) becomes Prime Minister (1984 – 1986).
Jacques Delors (1925 –) becomes President of the European Commission.
◇1984 Marguerite Duras writes the novel *L'Amant* (The Lover).
France wins the Football European Cup.
◆1985 Presentation of the Pisani Plan for a new more independent status for New Caledonia.
The tiny extreme-left group, Action Directe, claims responsibility for the murder of René Audran, Director of International Affairs at the Ministry of Defence.
On the initiative of Coluche, opening of the first Resto du cœur soup kitchen in Paris.
Scandal of the Rainbow Warrior: the French secret services are implicated in the attack (in which one person dies) on a Greenpeace ship in New Zealand.
◇1985 Claude Simon (1913 –) receives the Nobel Prize for literature. He is the author of *La Route des Flandres* (The Flanders Road).
Shoah, documentary film by Claude Lanzmann on the extermination of the Jews.
Agnès Varda's film *Sans toit ni loi* (Vagabonde) is released.
Beginning of the building of the Grande Arche at La Défense, by O. von Spreckelsen.
◆1986 Following the legislative elections, Jacques Chirac's RPR and Valéry Giscard d'Estaing's UDF obtain the majority of seats in the National Assembly; this is the start of the first 'cohabitation': Jacques Chirac (1932–) becomes Prime Minister (1986 – 1988).
Assassination of Georges Besse, manager of the state-controlled car manufacturers Renault; responsibility is claimed by Action Directe.
Series of fatal bomb attacks in Paris.
◇1986 Death of Coluche and Thierry Le Luron, the two most popular comedians of the decade.
L'Identité de la France (The Identity of France), essay by the historian of human behaviour, Fernand Braudel.
◆1987 Arrest of the leaders of Action Directe.
Trial of Klaus Barbie in Lyon where he lived during the Occupation; he is sentenced to life imprisonment for crimes against humanity.
In response to the zero option (withdrawal of medium-range missiles in Europe) proposed by Mikhail Gorbatchev, President Mitterrand reasserts France's position on maintaining the nuclear deterrent.
Referendum on self-determination for New Caledonia in favour of independence.
◇1987 Jean-Marie Lehn (1939 –) wins the Nobel Prize for chemistry.
The medieval historian Georges Duby (1919 – 1996), is elected to the Académie Française.
Louis Malle's film *Au revoir les enfants* (Goodbye Children) is released.
Sous le soleil de Satan (Under Satan's Sun) by Maurice Pialat wins the Palme d'or at the Cannes Film Festival.
◆1988 François Mitterrand is re-elected President of the Republic (1988 – 1995).
Introduction of the RMI (minimum welfare payment funded by the wealth tax).
Prime Minister Michel Rocard (1930 –) negotiates the Matignon Accords in Paris with Jean-Marie Tjibaou (FLNKS, separatist party) and Jacques Lafleur (RPCR, against independence) on the future of New Caledonia.
◇1988 Maurice Allais (1911 –) wins the Nobel Prize for economics.
Monsignor Lefebvre (1905 – 1991) is excommunicated by Pope John Paul II, for having ordained four bishops without the authority of the Vatican.
◆1989 Assassination in New Caledonia of Jean-Marie Tjibaou and Yeiwéné-Yeiwéné (FLNKS).
Third summit of French-speaking countries in Dakar: François Mitterrand announces the cancellation of part of the debt of 35 African countries to France.
◇1989 Celebration of the Bicentennary of the French Revolution.
Opening of the Grand Louvre (with the glass pyramid).

1990

◆1990 L'introduction de la poll tax en Angleterre et au pays de Galles provoquent de graves émeutes, notamment à Londres.
L'attitude 'eurosceptique' de Margaret Thatcher divise les Conservateurs. Elle démissionne lorsqu'elle n'obtient pas la majorité qualifiée lors du renouvellement statutaire du leader de son parti, cédant la place à John Major (1943 –).
En Afrique du Sud, libération de Nelson Mandela après 27 ans d'incarcération.
Les équipes française et britannique opèrent la jonction du tunnel sous la Manche.
De violentes tempêtes provoquent de graves dégâts en Angleterre et au pays de Galles.
◆1991 Guerre du Golfe: le Conseil de sécurité de l'ONU autorise l'intervention d'une force multinationale coordonnée par les Américains pour chasser les Iraquiens du Koweït. Destruction d'une grande partie des armements de l'Iraq.
◇1991 La romancière sud-africaine Nadine Gordimer (1923 –) reçoit le prix Nobel de littérature.
◆1992 Graves émeutes à Los Angeles à la suite de l'acquittement d'un policier accusé d'avoir violemment battu un automobiliste noir.
L'ouragan Andrew provoque d'importants dégâts en Floride.
◇1992 Michael Ondaatje (1943 –), écrivain canadien d'origine sri-lankaise, obtient le prix Booker ex-aequo pour son roman *The English Patient* (Le Patient anglais).

◆1990 The two Eurotunnel construction sites meet beneath the Channel.
◇1990 Opening of the Opéra at Bastille.
◆1991 Beginning of the Gulf War to which France sends an armoured division.
Vigipirate plan: enhanced measures to combat terrorist attacks.
◇1991 Scandal involving infected blood: the blood transfusion centre continued, knowingly, to use blood infected with the AIDS virus.
◆1992 Pierre Bérégovoy (1925 – 1993) succeeds Édith Cresson as Prime Minister (1992 – 1993).
◇1992 Infected blood affair: conviction of the managers of the blood transfusion organization.
Georges Charpak (1924 –) wins the Nobel Prize for physics.
Les Nuits fauves (Savage Nights), a film by Cyril Collard makes AIDS a subject for mainstream cinema.

English/Anglais	French/Français

Le poète antillais de langue anglaise Derek Walcott (1930 –) reçoit le prix Nobel de littérature.
♦1993 Aux États-Unis, les Républicains cèdent la place aux Démocrates après 12 années au pouvoir. Le nouveau président, Bill Clinton (1946 –), promet le retour à la prospérité.
Une bombe explose au World Trade Center à New York; l'attentat est attribué à des fondamentalistes islamiques.
Fusillade et incendie meurtriers à Waco, au Texas, au cours de l'intervention armée du FBI contre la secte de David Koresh.
◇1993 L'artiste britannique Damien Hirst (1965 –) présente son œuvre *Mother and Child Divided*, une vache coupée en deux dans du formol.
La romancière américaine Toni Morrison (1931 –) reçoit le prix Nobel de littérature.
Jurassic Park, film de l'américain Steven Spielberg (1947 –).
♦1994 Nelson Mandela (1918 –), condamné à la prison à vie en 1964 puis libéré en 1990, devient le premier président noir de l'Afrique du Sud.
Ouverture du tunnel sous la Manche.
♦1995 L'explosion d'une bombe dans un bâtiment du gouvernement fédéral à Oklahoma City fait 168 morts.
◇1995 Le poète irlandais Seamus Heaney (1939 –) reçoit le prix Nobel de littérature.
Toy Story, produit par les studios Disney et réalisé par John Lasseter, premier long métrage comprenant uniquement des images de synthèse.
♦1996 Bill Clinton est réélu à la présidence des États-Unis.
Les autorités britanniques annoncent qu'il existerait un lien entre le nouveau variant de la maladie de Creutzfeldt-Jacob et l'encéphalopathie bovine spongiforme. Début de l'embargo européen sur la viande bovine britannique.
◇1996 Sortie du film *Trainspotting*, du britannique Danny Boyle (1956 –), d'après l'œuvre du romancier écossais Irvine Welsh (1961 –).
La romancière anglaise JK Rowling (1965 –) publie *Harry Potter and the Philosopher's Stone* (Harry Potter à l'école des sorciers). Cet ouvrage et les trois suivants sont des succès de librairie phénoménaux.
Les jeux Olympiques ont lieu à Atlanta, aux États-Unis. L'explosion d'une bombe fait une victime.
♦1997 Hong-Kong, qui avait été cédée à la Grande-Bretagne pour une période de 99 ans, est rendue à la Chine.
Élection des travaillistes en Grande-Bretagne, après 18 ans de pouvoir conservateur. Tony Blair est Premier ministre.
La princesse Diana est tuée dans un accident de voiture à Paris.
◇1997 Premier clonage d'un animal ('Dolly', une brebis) à Roslin, près d'Édimbourg.
Sortie du film *Titanic*, réalisé par l'Américain James Cameron (1954 –); plus gros succès commercial de l'histoire du cinéma à ce jour.
♦1998 Signature d'un accord de paix en Irlande du Nord (Good Friday agreement).
L'Écosse et le pays de Galles votent en faveur de davantage d'autonomie au cours de référendums.
L'ouragan Georges provoque d'importants dégâts en Floride.
◇1998 *The Angel of the North*, sculpture métallique géante du Britannique Anthony Gormley, est érigée à Gateshead, à côté de Newcastle.
♦1999 Inauguration du parlement écossais et de l'assemblée du pays de Galles.
L'ouragan Floyd dévaste les côtes de Caroline du Nord.
◇1999 Mort de Yehudi Menuhin, grand violoniste anglais né en 1916 aux États-Unis.

First broadcasts of Arte, Franco-German cultural television channel.
The Winter Olympic Games are held in Albertville.
♦1993 The defeat of the socialists in the legislative elections brings an RPR-UDF government back into power (1993 – 1995), with Edouard Balladur (1929 –) as Prime Minister; this is the beginning of the second period of 'cohabitation'.
In Belgium, a constitutional review transforms unitary Belgium into a federal State accompanied by decentralized powers. Albert II succeeds Baudoin I.
In Quebec, an amendment to Law 101 authorizes a limited use of English in advertising displays.
♦1994 Indictment of Ministers Georgina Dufoix, Edmond Hervé and Laurent Fabius for their involvement in the infected blood affair. Mme Dufoix declares herself to be responsible, but not guilty.
Paul Touvier, an official in the Pétain government, is sentenced to life imprisonment.
The Channel Tunnel is opened.
◇ 1994 The first map of the entire human genome is drawn up by the French Généthon team.
♦1995 Election of Jacques Chirac to the Presidency of the Republic (1995—2002). He calls on Alain Juppé (1945 –) as Prime Minister (1995 – 1997).
President Chirac acknowledges the wrongs committed by the French State against the Jews in the Second World War.
The Quebecois decide by a small majority against independence for the province.
◇1995 Cardinal Lustiger is elected to the Académie Française.
La Haine (Hate) is released, a film by Mathieu Kassovitz on the lives of three teenagers living in a deprived Paris suburb.
♦1996 Death of François Mitterrand on 8 January.
The Corsican issue is at the forefront of domestic French politics.
Assassination of seven French monks in Tibérine, Algeria.
Illegal Malian immigrants asking for asylum are taken in by the Saint-Bernard church in Paris: this marks the beginning of the affair of the 'sans-papiers' (people without work or residence permits).
♦1997 Massive mobilization in Europe against the French government's decision to close the Vilvorde Renault factory in Belgium.
President Chirac decides unexpectedly to dissolve the National Assembly, offering a victory to the left which makes Lionel Jospin (1937 –) Prime Minister.
Beginning of the Papon trial in Bordeaux: Maurice Papon, a former senior civil servant in the Vichy government, is accused of crimes against humanity.
◇1997 Claude Cohen-Tannoudji (1933 –) wins the Nobel Prize for physics.
♦1998 Beginning of the Elf affair: publication in the press of the investigation into the Elf affair, in which Roland Dumas, president of the Constitutional Council, is implicated.
Assassination of Claude Erignac, Prefect of Corsica, in Ajaccio.
Maurice Papon is sentenced to ten years imprisonment.
The referendum on self-determination for New Caledonia achieves a 72% vote in favour.
◇1998 France (which is also the host country) wins the Football World Cup.
♦1999 Passing of the PACS (pacte civil de solidarité), a contract for people in a long-term relationship, which considerably extends the rights of unmarried couples and homosexuals.
Passing of the law on the 35-hour week.
◇1999 Violent storms cause considerable damage in France.

2000

♦2000 Élection controversée du Républicain George W. Bush à la présidence des États-Unis.
◇2000 Les jeux Olympiques ont lieu à Sydney, en Australie.
♦2001 Réélection du travailliste Tony Blair en Grande-Bretagne.

♦2000 In a referendum, a majority of voters declare themselves in favour of the five-year period for the presidency of the Republic.
◇2000 France wins the Football European Cup.
♦2001 Roland Dumas, former president of the Constitutional Council and foreign minister under Mitterrand, is sentenced to 6 months' imprisonment for accepting bribes from the oil company Elf.

Guide de communication en anglais

La correspondance

La présentation d'une lettre doit toujours être soignée, qu'il s'agisse d'un courrier commercial ou privé. Chaque pays a ses normes et conventions à respecter. Ce guide a pour objectif de vous aider à rédiger un courrier en anglais : vous y trouverez des conseils sur la mise en page, les formules d'appel et de politesse, la rédaction de l'adresse ainsi que de nombreux modèles de lettres et suggestions de tournures à employer dans la correspondance privée ou commerciale, le courrier électronique et les documents transmis par télécopie.

Présentation de la lettre

Il existe deux types de présentations. La présentation traditionnelle, réservée aux lettres manuscrites de la correspondance privée, veut que chaque paragraphe commence par un alinéa. Dans la deuxième présentation, plus répandue et utilisée dans toutes les lettres dactylographiées, les paragraphes sont alignés à gauche et séparés par une ligne de blanc (voir les modèles et les notes ci-dessous).

Style

La correspondance administrative ou commerciale, influencée par le fax et le courrier électronique, exige l'emploi d'un style direct et concis. On emploiera de préférence un ton amical mais respectueux en évitant les abréviations ou les contractions telles que **don't, I've** et **she'd** pour **do not, I have,** et **she had/would** qui doivent être réservées au courrier privé ou à la communication orale. La correspondance privée, tout comme le courrier électronique ou le fax, se caractérise par un style plus spontané et une langue moins soutenue.

Organisation

Chaque paragraphe doit comporter un maximum de trois ou quatre phrases et traiter d'un seul sujet. On veillera à ne pas mélanger passé et présent à l'intérieur d'une même phrase et à respecter les règles de la concordance des temps.

Lorsque l'on répond à une lettre, il peut être utile d'utiliser l'original pour y relever les points essentiels développés par l'expéditeur ainsi que les formules à reprendre.

Formules d'appel et formules de politesse

La formule de politesse varie en fonction de la formule d'appel utilisée. Voir le tableau au verso.

▪ formule d'appel	▪ formule de politesse

Lorsqu'on ne connaît pas le nom de la personne à qui l'on s'adresse :

Dear Sir
Dear Madam

Lorsqu'on ne sait pas s'il s'agit d'un homme ou d'une femme :
Dear Sir or Madam

ou
Dear Sir/Madam

Lorsqu'on s'adresse à une société ou à un organisme sans préciser le nom du destinataire :
Dear Sirs [Br]
Gentlemen [Am]

Yours faithfully [Br]

En anglais américain, la formule de politesse est toujours inversée :
Faithfully yours [Am]

Lorsqu'on connaît le nom de la personne à qui l'on s'adresse :

Dear Mr Jameson
Dear Mrs Lucas
Dear Miss Crookshaw
Dear Ms Greening

[L'abréviation Ms est de plus en plus employée lorsqu'on s'adresse à une femme car elle permet de ne pas préciser s'il s'agit d'une femme mariée [Mrs] ou non [Miss].]

Dear Dr Illingworth

Aux États-Unis, l'abréviation est généralement suivie d'un point : Mr., Mrs., Ms., Dr.

Lorsqu'on s'adresse au rédacteur en chef d'un journal :
Sir

à un conseiller :
Dear Councillor Henderson
Dear Councillor Mr/Mrs/Ms Adams

à un député :
Dear Mr/Mrs Brown

à un gouverneur :
Dear Governor Almanza

à un représentant ou membre du Congrès :
Sir/Madam
Dear Congressman/Congresswoman Fox
Dear Senator Mitcham

au Premier ministre :
Dear Sir/Madam
Dear Prime Minister

Au président des États-Unis :
Sir/Madam
Dear Mr/Madam President

Yours sincerely [Br]
Sincerely yours [Am]
Sincerely [Am]

Ton plus amical :
Yours very sincerely [Br]

Style moins soutenu :
With best wishes
With kind regards
Kindest regards

Plus rare :
Yours respectfully [Br]
Respectfully yours [Am]
Respectfully [Am]

Lorsqu'on s'adresse à de la famille ou à des amis :

Dear Bill
Dear Marjorie
Dear Graham and Barbara
Dear all
Dear Mum and Dad
Dear Uncle Ralph/Auntie Ann
My dear Hector
Dearest/My dearest Jill

Très familier :
Hi John!
Hello there

With love
Love
Love from
Love and best wishes

Plus affectueux :
With all my/our love
Much love

Plus familier :
Lots of love

Plus soutenu :
Yours
All the best [Br]
Best wishes
Regards

Familier :
See you soon
Cheers [Br]
Bye for now

Présentation d'une lettre dactylographiée

Les paragraphes sont alignés à gauche, sans retrait, et séparés par une ligne de blanc.

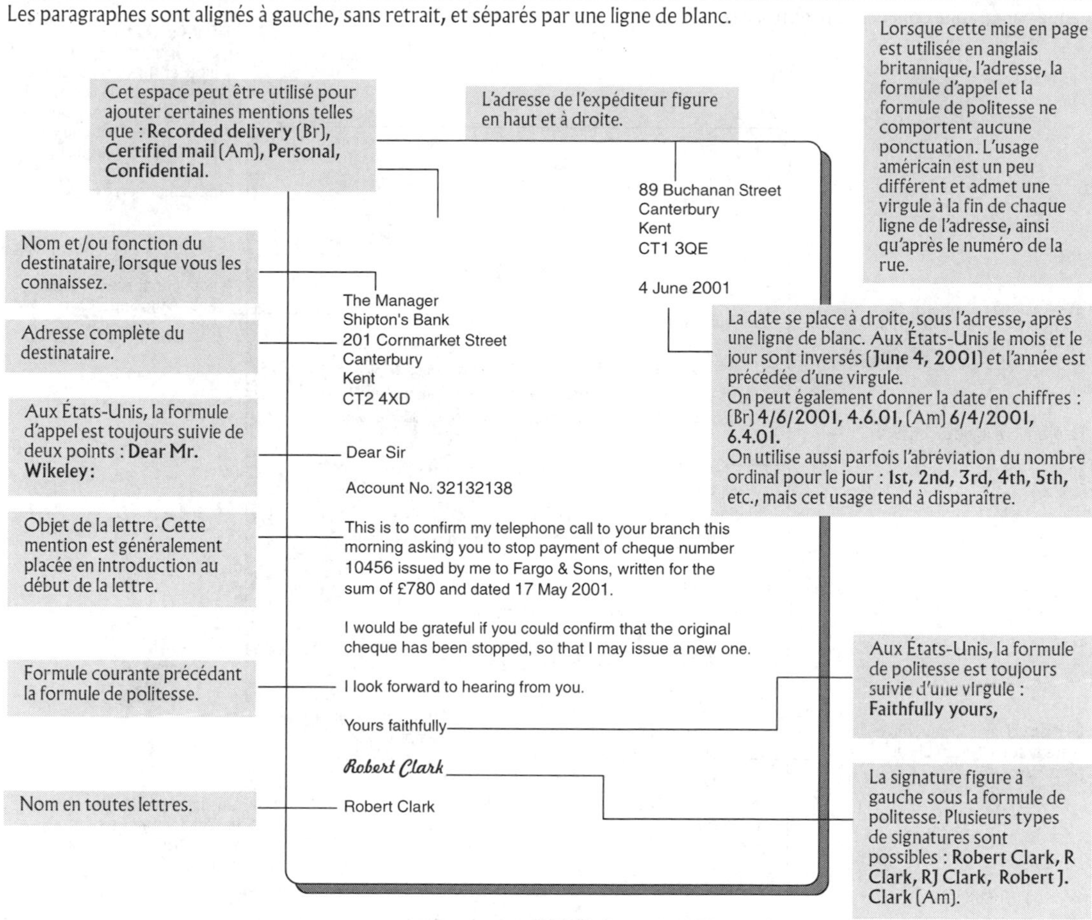

Cet espace peut être utilisé pour ajouter certaines mentions telles que : **Recorded delivery** (Br), **Certified mail** (Am), **Personal, Confidential.**
L'adresse de l'expéditeur figure en haut et à droite.
Lorsque cette mise en page est utilisée en anglais britannique, l'adresse, la formule d'appel et la formule de politesse ne comportent aucune ponctuation. L'usage américain est un peu différent et admet une virgule à la fin de chaque ligne de l'adresse, ainsi qu'après le numéro de la rue.
Nom et/ou fonction du destinataire, lorsque vous les connaissez.
Adresse complète du destinataire.
La date se place à droite, sous l'adresse, après une ligne de blanc. Aux États-Unis le mois et le jour sont inversés (**June 4, 2001**) et l'année est précédée d'une virgule. On peut également donner la date en chiffres : (Br) **4/6/2001, 4.6.01,** (Am) **6/4/2001, 6.4.01.** On utilise aussi parfois l'abréviation du nombre ordinal pour le jour : **1st, 2nd, 3rd, 4th, 5th,** etc., mais cet usage tend à disparaître.
Aux États-Unis, la formule d'appel est toujours suivie de deux points : **Dear Mr. Wikeley:**
Objet de la lettre. Cette mention est généralement placée en introduction au début de la lettre.
Formule courante précédant la formule de politesse.
Aux États-Unis, la formule de politesse est toujours suivie d'une virgule : **Faithfully yours,**
La signature figure à gauche sous la formule de politesse. Plusieurs types de signatures sont possibles : **Robert Clark, R Clark, RJ Clark, Robert J. Clark** (Am).
Nom en toutes lettres.

89 Buchanan Street
Canterbury
Kent
CT1 3QE

4 June 2001

The Manager
Shipton's Bank
201 Cornmarket Street
Canterbury
Kent
CT2 4XD

Dear Sir

Account No. 32132138

This is to confirm my telephone call to your branch this morning asking you to stop payment of cheque number 10456 issued by me to Fargo & Sons, written for the sum of £780 and dated 17 May 2001.

I would be grateful if you could confirm that the original cheque has been stopped, so that I may issue a new one.

I look forward to hearing from you.

Yours faithfully

Robert Clark

Robert Clark

Présentation d'une lettre sur papier à en-tête

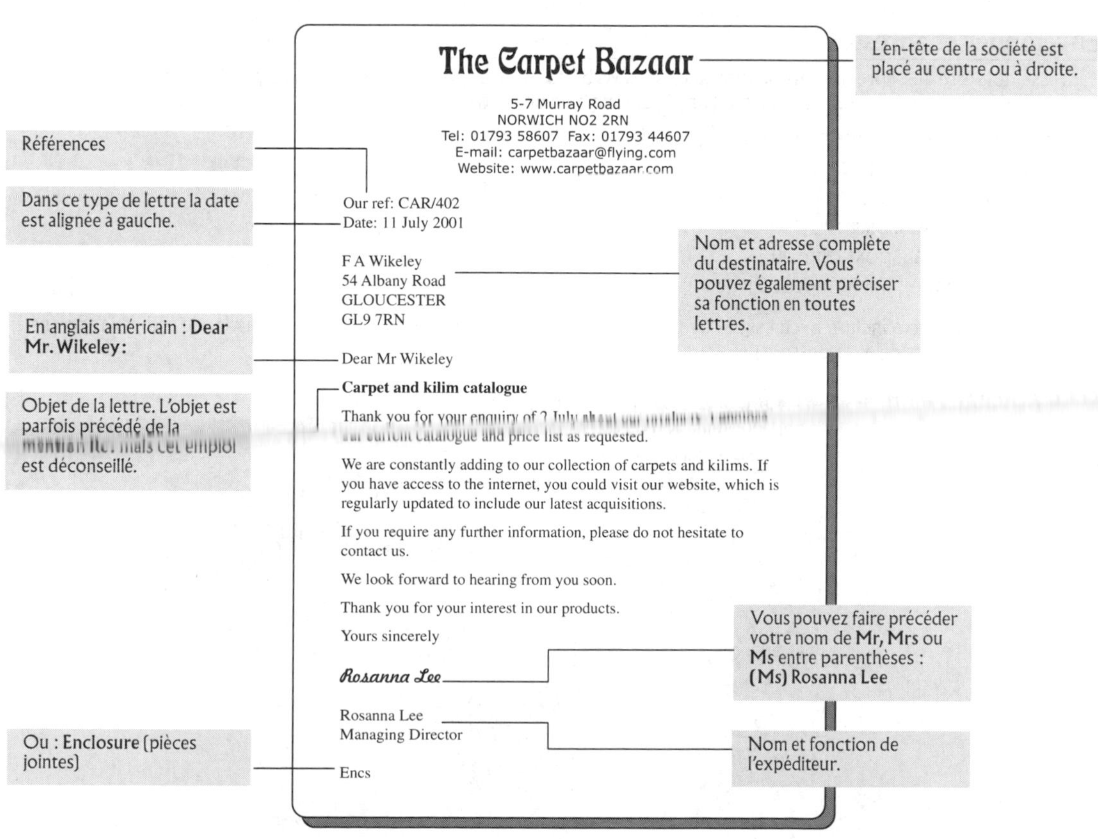

L'en-tête de la société est placé au centre ou à droite.

Dans ce type de lettre la date est alignée à gauche.

Objet de la lettre. L'objet est parfois précédé de la mention [illegible] mais cet emploi est déconseillé.
Vous pouvez faire précéder votre nom de **Mr, Mrs** ou **Ms** entre parenthèses : **(Ms) Rosanna Lee**
Ou : **Enclosure** (pièces jointes)

The Carpet Bazaar

5-7 Murray Road
NORWICH NO2 2RN
Tel: 01793 58607 Fax: 01793 44607
E-mail: carpetbazaar@flying.com
Website: www.carpetbazaar.com

Our ref: CAR/402
Date: 11 July 2001

F A Wikeley
54 Albany Road
GLOUCESTER
GL9 7RN

Dear Mr Wikeley

Carpet and kilim catalogue

Thank you for your enquiry of ? July [illegible] current catalogue and price list as requested.

We are constantly adding to our collection of carpets and kilims. If you have access to the internet, you could visit our website, which is regularly updated to include our latest acquisitions.

If you require any further information, please do not hesitate to contact us.

We look forward to hearing from you soon.

Thank you for your interest in our products.

Yours sincerely

Rosanna Lee

Rosanna Lee
Managing Director

Encs

Présentation d'une lettre manuscrite à un ami

Chaque paragraphe commence par un alinéa.

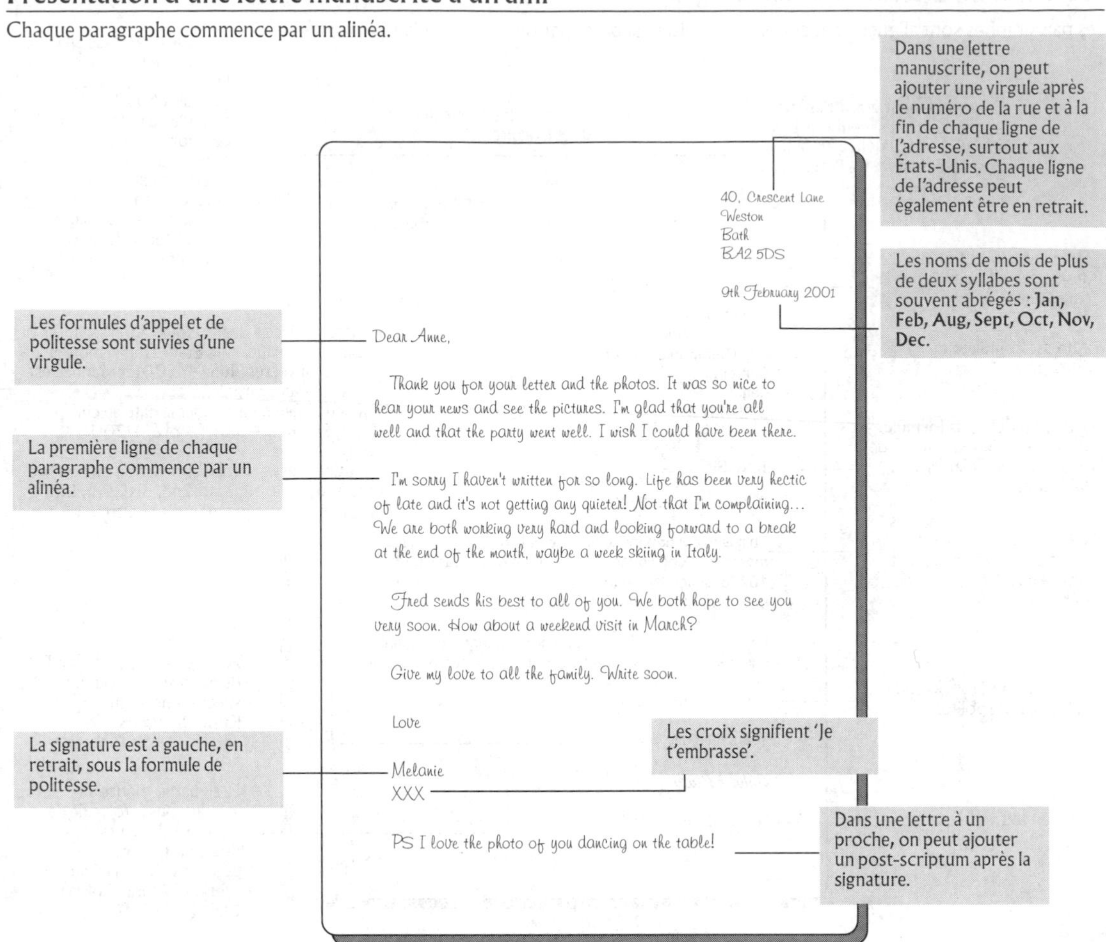

Dans une lettre manuscrite, on peut ajouter une virgule après le numéro de la rue et à la fin de chaque ligne de l'adresse, surtout aux États-Unis. Chaque ligne de l'adresse peut également être en retrait.
40, Crescent Lane
Weston
Bath
BA2 5DS
9th February 2001
Les noms de mois de plus de deux syllabes sont souvent abrégés : **Jan, Feb, Aug, Sept, Oct, Nov, Dec.**
Les formules d'appel et de politesse sont suivies d'une virgule.
Dear Anne,
Thank you for your letter and the photos. It was so nice to hear your news and see the pictures. I'm glad that you're all well and that the party went well. I wish I could have been there.
La première ligne de chaque paragraphe commence par un alinéa.
I'm sorry I haven't written for so long. Life has been very hectic of late and it's not getting any quieter! Not that I'm complaining... We are both working very hard and looking forward to a break at the end of the month, maybe a week skiing in Italy.
Fred sends his best to all of you. We both hope to see you very soon. How about a weekend visit in March?
Give my love to all the family. Write soon.
Love
Les croix signifient 'Je t'embrasse'.
La signature est à gauche, en retrait, sous la formule de politesse.
Melanie
XXX
PS I love the photo of you dancing on the table!
Dans une lettre à un proche, on peut ajouter un post-scriptum après la signature.

Enveloppes et adresses

L'adresse doit être aussi précise que possible. Les sites Web des services postaux des différents pays peuvent être utiles pour trouver l'adresse complète d'un particulier, d'un organisme ou d'une entreprise, y compris le code postal précis.

Royaume-Uni : www.royalmail.com
Canada : www.canadapost.ca
Irlande : www.anpost.ie
États-Unis : www.usps.gov
Australie : www.auspost.com.au
Nouvelle-Zélande : www.nzpost.co.nz

Il est recommandé de n'inclure aucun signe de ponctuation et, surtout aux États-Unis et au Canada, de rédiger l'adresse en majuscules (voir les modèles ci-dessous).

- **Au Royaume-Uni :**

Mr (Mrs, Ms, Dr, etc.), prénom (ou initiale), nom de famille
(Dénomination du lieu et/ou) Numéro, nom de la rue
Localité (ville, village)
COMTÉ ou GRANDE VILLE
CODE POSTAL

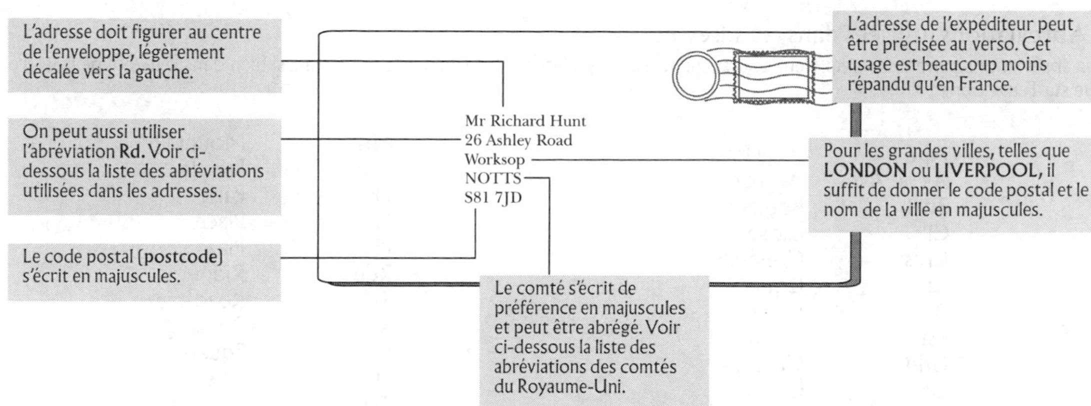

L'adresse doit figurer au centre de l'enveloppe, légèrement décalée vers la gauche.
On peut aussi utiliser l'abréviation **Rd.** Voir ci-dessous la liste des abréviations utilisées dans les adresses.
Le code postal (**postcode**) s'écrit en majuscules.
Mr Richard Hunt
26 Ashley Road
Worksop
NOTTS
S81 7JD
L'adresse de l'expéditeur peut être précisée au verso. Cet usage est beaucoup moins répandu qu'en France.
Pour les grandes villes, telles que **LONDON** ou **LIVERPOOL**, il suffit de donner le code postal et le nom de la ville en majuscules.
Le comté s'écrit de préférence en majuscules et peut être abrégé. Voir ci-dessous la liste des abréviations des comtés du Royaume-Uni.

- **Aux États-Unis :**

Mr. (Mrs., Ms., Dr., etc.), PRÉNOM (et/ou INITIALE), NOM
(DÉNOMINATION DU LIEU et/ou) NUMÉRO, NOM DE LA RUE
LOCALITÉ (ville, village), ÉTAT et CODE POSTAL

La ville, l'abréviation de l'État et le code postal (ZIP code) se suivent sur la même ligne.

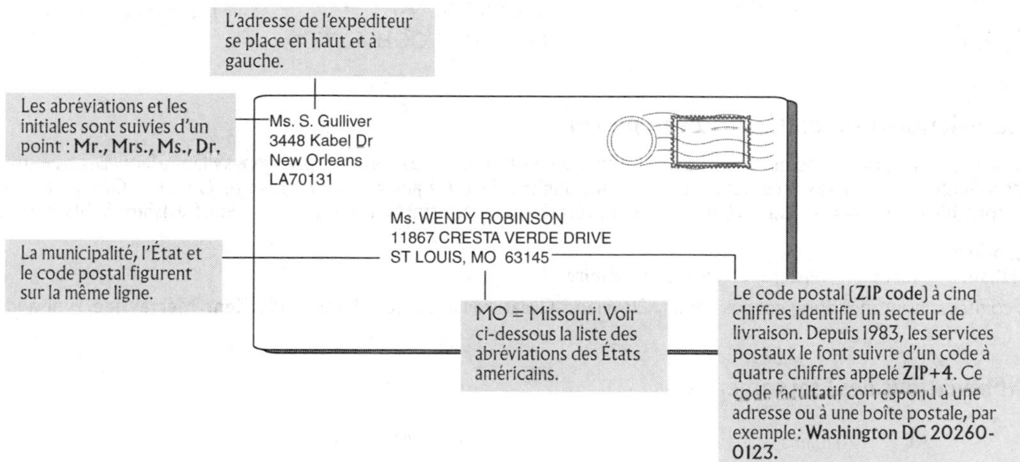

L'adresse de l'expéditeur se place en haut et à gauche.
Les abréviations et les initiales sont suivies d'un point : **Mr., Mrs., Ms., Dr.**
Ms. S. Gulliver
3448 Kabel Dr
New Orleans
LA70131
Ms. WENDY ROBINSON
11867 CRESTA VERDE DRIVE
ST LOUIS, MO 63145
La municipalité, l'État et le code postal figurent sur la même ligne.
MO = Missouri. Voir ci-dessous la liste des abréviations des États américains.
Le code postal (**ZIP code**) à cinq chiffres identifie un secteur de livraison. Depuis 1983, les services postaux le font suivre d'un code à quatre chiffres appelé **ZIP+4**. Ce code facultatif correspond à une adresse ou à une boîte postale, par exemple: **Washington DC 20260-0123.**

- **Adresse en Irlande :**

Mrs Kathleen Ryan
48 The Glen
Roden Park
Rathfarnham
Dublin 14
(Ireland)

Ou : **Republic of Ireland.**

Il n'y a pas de code postal en Irlande, sauf à Dublin où l'on utilise un chiffre entre 1 et 18 pour désigner les différents secteurs de la ville. Pour les adresses rurales, on emploie l'abréviation **Co.** pour désigner le comté où le destinataire est domicilié : par exemple, **Co. Clare** pour le comté de Clare.

- **Adresse au Canada :**

Mr & Mrs Fitzgerald
28 Alpine Boulevard
St Albert AB T8N 2M7
(Canada)

AB = Alberta. Voir ci-dessous la liste des abréviations des provinces et des territoires du Canada.

Les deux premières lettres du code postal canadien représente la province ou le territoire.

- **Adresse en Australie :**

Gareth Connolly
[illegible] Elizabeth Street
Potts Point
NSW 2020
(Australia)

Abréviation de l'État ou du territoire (voir la liste ci-dessous).

- **Adresse en Nouvelle-Zélande :**

Mr J Hall
3 Bridge Avenue
Te Atatu
Auckland 8
(New Zealand)

▪ Abréviations utilisées dans les adresses

Les abréviations suivantes s'emploient couramment dans les adresses. Elles peuvent figurer aussi bien dans l'en-tête de la lettre que sur l'enveloppe.

Apt	Apartment
Av ou **Ave**	Avenue
Blvd	Boulevard
Cl	Close
Cres	Crescent
Ct	Court
Dr	Drive
Est	Estate
Gdns	Gardens
Gr	Grove
Hts	Heights
La	Lane
Mtn	Mountain
Pde	Parade
Pk	Park
Pl	Place
Plz	Plaza
Rdg	Ridge
Rd	Road
Rm	Room
Sq	Square
St	Street
Ter	Terrace

Les abréviations **N** (North), **S** (South), **W** (West), **E** (East), **NE** (Northeast), **NW** (Northwest), **SE** (Southeast) et **SW** (Southwest) sont également très courantes, notamment dans les adresses américaines et canadiennes.

Par exemple, à New York :

351 W 32ND ST
NEW YORK, NY 10001

Cette adresse se lit : **three hundred and fifty-one West Thirty-second Street**

à Montréal :

123 MAIN ST NW
MONTREAL QC H3Z 2Y7

Cette adresse se lit : **one hundred and twenty-three Main Street Northwest**

▪ Abréviations des comtés au Royaume-Uni

En règle générale, pour les noms des comtés se terminant en **-shire**, on ne garde que la première syllabe à laquelle on ajoute un **'s'** : **Beds = Bedfordshire, Berks = Berkshire, Bucks = Buckinghamshire, Cambs = Cambridgeshire, Gloucs = Gloucester, Herts = Hertfordshire, Lancs = Lancashire, Lincs = Lincolnshire, Notts = Nottinghamshire, Staffs = Staffordshire, Wilts = Wiltshire.**

Exceptions :
Northants = Northamptonshire, Oxon = Oxfordshire

Les comtés suivants ne s'abrègent pas : **Avon, Cleveland, Greater Manchester, Humberside, Kent, Merseyside, Tyne and Wear.**

▪ Abréviations des États américains

AL	Alabama
AK	Alaska
AZ	Arizona
AR	Arkansas
CA	California
CO	Colorado
CT	Connecticut
DE	Delaware
DC	District of Columbia
FL	Florida
GA	Georgia
HI	Hawaii
ID	Idaho
IL	Illinois
IN	Indiana
IA	Iowa
KS	Kansas
KY	Kentucky
LA	Louisiana
ME	Maine
MD	Maryland
MA	Massachusetts
MI	Michigan
MN	Minnesota
MS	Mississippi
MO	Missouri
MT	Montana
NE	Nebraska
NV	Nevada
NH	New Hampshire
NJ	New Jersey
NM	New Mexico
NY	New York
NC	North Carolina
ND	North Dakota
OH	Ohio
OK	Oklahoma
OR	Oregon
PA	Pennsylvania
RI	Rhode Island
SC	South Carolina
SD	South Dakota
TN	Tennessee
TX	Texas
UT	Utah
VT	Vermont
VA	Virginia
WA	Washington
WV	West Virginia
WI	Wisconsin
WY	Wyoming

- **Abréviations des provinces et des territoires du Canada**

AB	Alberta
BC	British Columbia
MB	Manitoba
NB	New Brunswick
NF	Newfoundland
NT	Northwest Territories
NS	Nova Scotia
NU	Nunavut
ON	Ontario
PE	Prince Edward Island
QC	Quebec
SK	Saskatchewan
YT	Yukon

- **Abréviations des États et territoires australiens**

ACT	Australian Capital Territory
NSW	New South Wales
NT	Northern Territory
QLD	Queensland
SA	South Australia
TAS	Tasmania
VIC	Victoria
WA	Western Australia

Modèles de lettres

Lettre à un ami

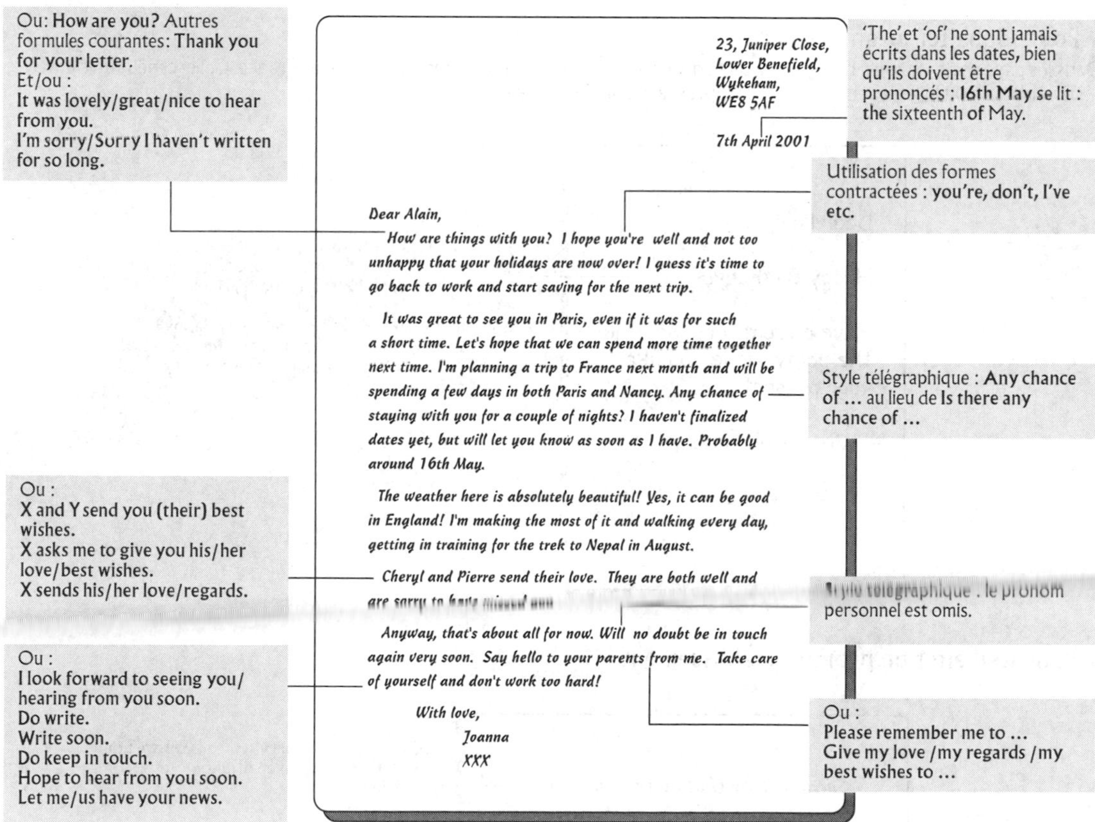

Ou: **How are you?** Autres formules courantes: **Thank you for your letter.**
Et/ou :
It was lovely/great/nice to hear from you.
I'm sorry/Sorry I haven't written for so long.

'The' et 'of' ne sont jamais écrits dans les dates, bien qu'ils doivent être prononcés : **16th May** se lit : the sixteenth of May.

Utilisation des formes contractées : **you're, don't, I've** etc.

Style télégraphique : **Any chance of ...** au lieu de **Is there any chance of ...**

Ou :
X and Y send you (their) best wishes.
X asks me to give you his/her love/best wishes.
X sends his/her love/regards.

Style télégraphique : le pronom personnel est omis.

Ou :
I look forward to seeing you/hearing from you soon.
Do write.
Write soon.
Do keep in touch.
Hope to hear from you soon.
Let me/us have your news.

Ou :
Please remember me to ...
Give my love /my regards /my best wishes to ...

23, Juniper Close,
Lower Benefield,
Wykeham,
WE8 5AF

7th April 2001

Dear Alain,

How are things with you? I hope you're well and not too unhappy that your holidays are now over! I guess it's time to go back to work and start saving for the next trip.

It was great to see you in Paris, even if it was for such a short time. Let's hope that we can spend more time together next time. I'm planning a trip to France next month and will be spending a few days in both Paris and Nancy. Any chance of staying with you for a couple of nights? I haven't finalized dates yet, but will let you know as soon as I have. Probably around 16th May.

The weather here is absolutely beautiful! Yes, it can be good in England! I'm making the most of it and walking every day, getting in training for the trek to Nepal in August.

Cheryl and Pierre send their love. They are both well and are sorry to have missed you.

Anyway, that's about all for now. Will no doubt be in touch again very soon. Say hello to your parents from me. Take care of yourself and don't work too hard!

With love,
Joanna
XXX

Cartes postales

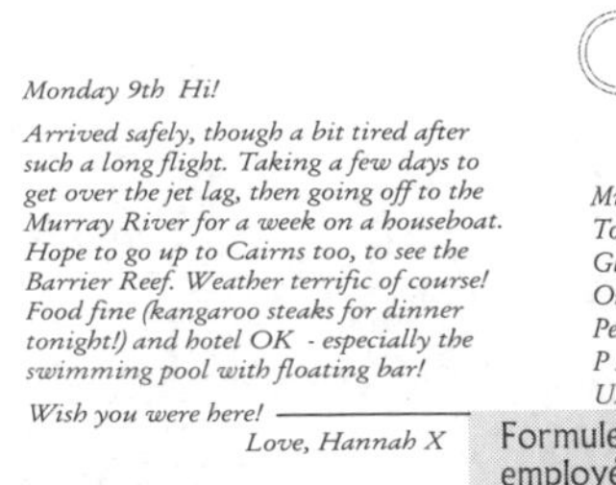

Monday 9th Hi!

Arrived safely, though a bit tired after such a long flight. Taking a few days to get over the jet lag, then going off to the Murray River for a week on a houseboat. Hope to go up to Cairns too, to see the Barrier Reef. Weather terrific of course! Food fine (kangaroo steaks for dinner tonight!) and hotel OK - especially the swimming pool with floating bar!

Wish you were here!

Love, Hannah X

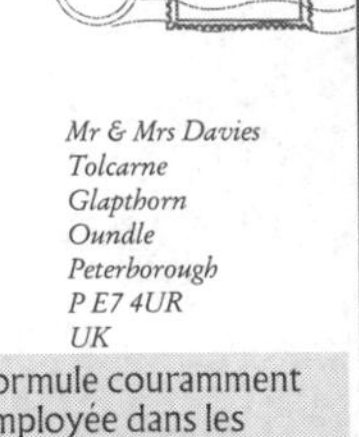

Mr & Mrs Davies
Tolcarne
Glapthorn
Oundle
Peterborough
P E7 4UR
UK

Formule couramment employée dans les cartes postales.

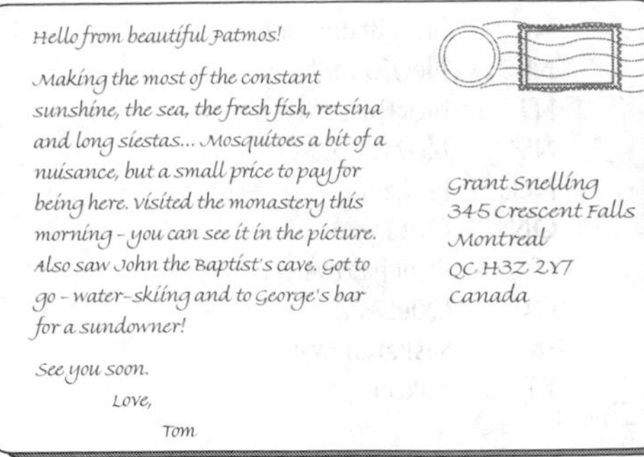

Hello from beautiful Patmos!

Making the most of the constant sunshine, the sea, the fresh fish, retsina and long siestas... Mosquitoes a bit of a nuisance, but a small price to pay for being here. Visited the monastery this morning - you can see it in the picture. Also saw John the Baptist's cave. Got to go - water-skiing and to George's bar for a sundowner!

See you soon.

Love,

Tom

Grant Snelling
345 Crescent Falls
Montreal
QC H3Z 2Y7
Canada

Cartes de vœux

Dans les pays anglo-saxons, les cartes de vœux s'envoient au mois de décembre, avant Noël, et non en janvier comme en France.

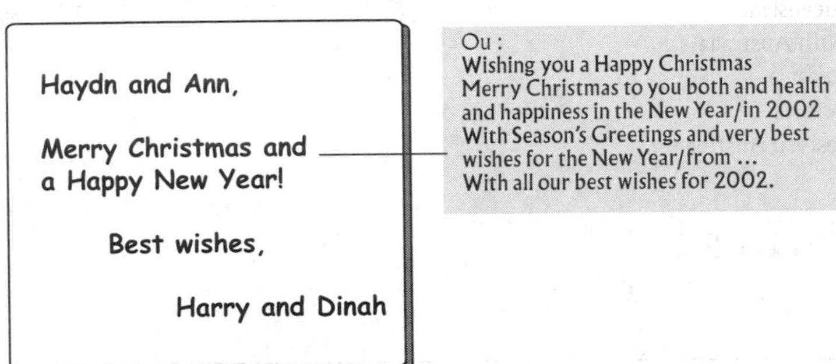

Haydn and Ann,

Merry Christmas and a Happy New Year!

Best wishes,

Harry and Dinah

Ou :
Wishing you a Happy Christmas
Merry Christmas to you both and health and happiness in the New Year/in 2002
With Season's Greetings and very best wishes for the New Year/from ...
With all our best wishes for 2002.

▪ Pour souhaiter un anniversaire

Dans les pays anglo-saxons, l'usage de la carte d'anniversaire est beaucoup plus répandu qu'en France. Celle-ci peut être envoyée au destinataire ou lui être remis en mains propres, avec ou sans cadeau.

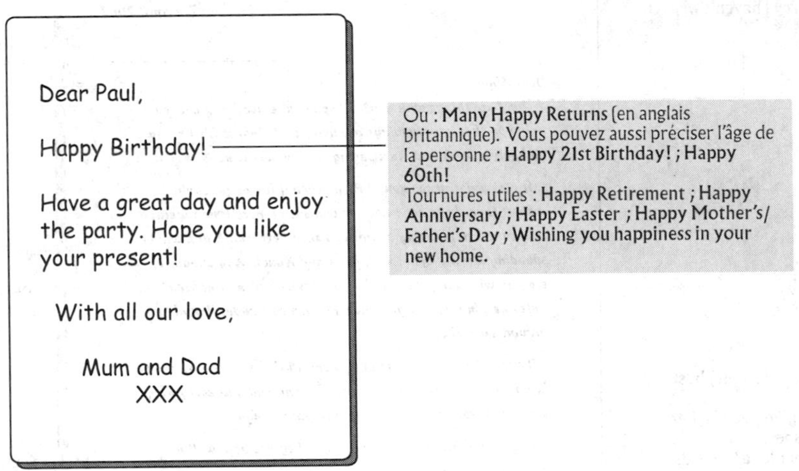

Dear Paul,

Happy Birthday!

Have a great day and enjoy the party. Hope you like your present!

With all our love,

Mum and Dad
XXX

Ou : **Many Happy Returns** (en anglais britannique). Vous pouvez aussi préciser l'âge de la personne : **Happy 21st Birthday! ; Happy 60th!**
Tournures utiles : **Happy Retirement ; Happy Anniversary ; Happy Easter ; Happy Mother's/ Father's Day ; Wishing you happiness in your new home.**

▪ Pour souhaiter un prompt rétablissement

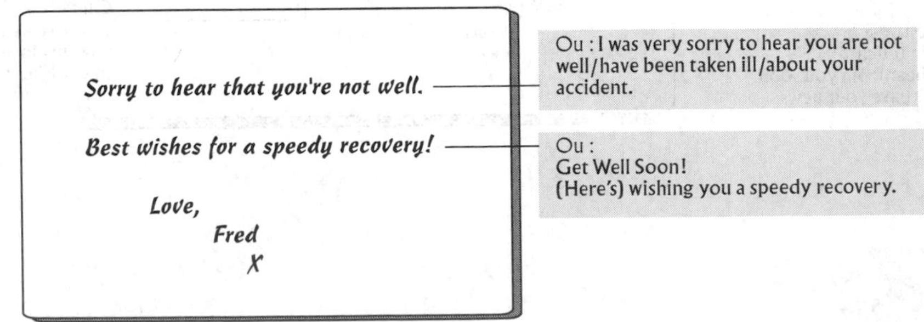

Sorry to hear that you're not well.

Best wishes for a speedy recovery!

Love,
Fred
X

Ou : I was very sorry to hear you are not well/have been taken ill/about your accident.

Ou :
Get Well Soon!
(Here's) wishing you a speedy recovery.

- **Pour souhaiter bonne chance**

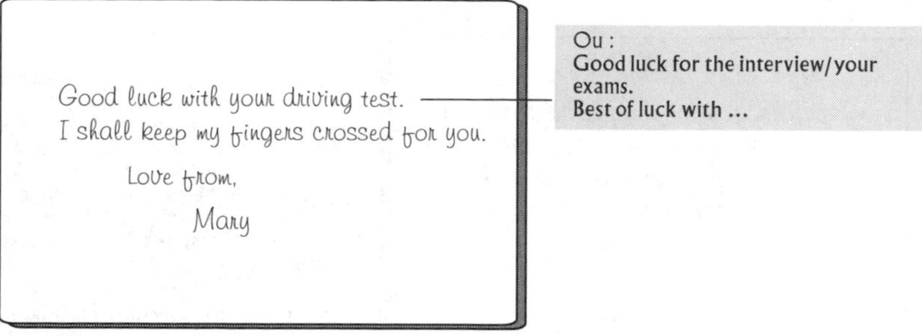

Good luck with your driving test.
I shall keep my fingers crossed for you.
Love from,
Mary

Ou :
Good luck for the interview/your exams.
Best of luck with ...

- **Pour féliciter**

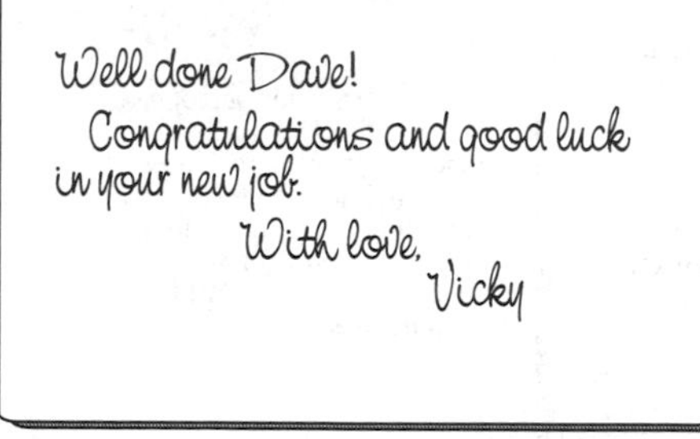

Well done Dave!
Congratulations and good luck in your new job.
With love,
Vicky

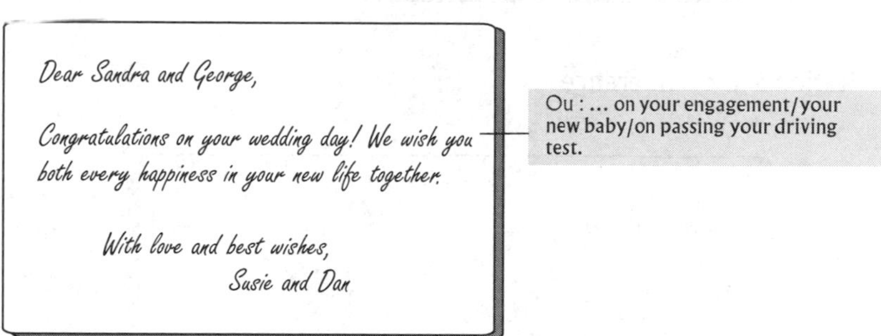

Dear Sandra and George,

Congratulations on your wedding day! We wish you both every happiness in your new life together.

With love and best wishes,
Susie and Dan

Ou : **... on your engagement/your new baby/on passing your driving test.**

Invitations et réponses

- **Carton d'invitation à un mariage**

Une invitation à un événement important peut se faire sur un carton imprimé ou sur papier libre.

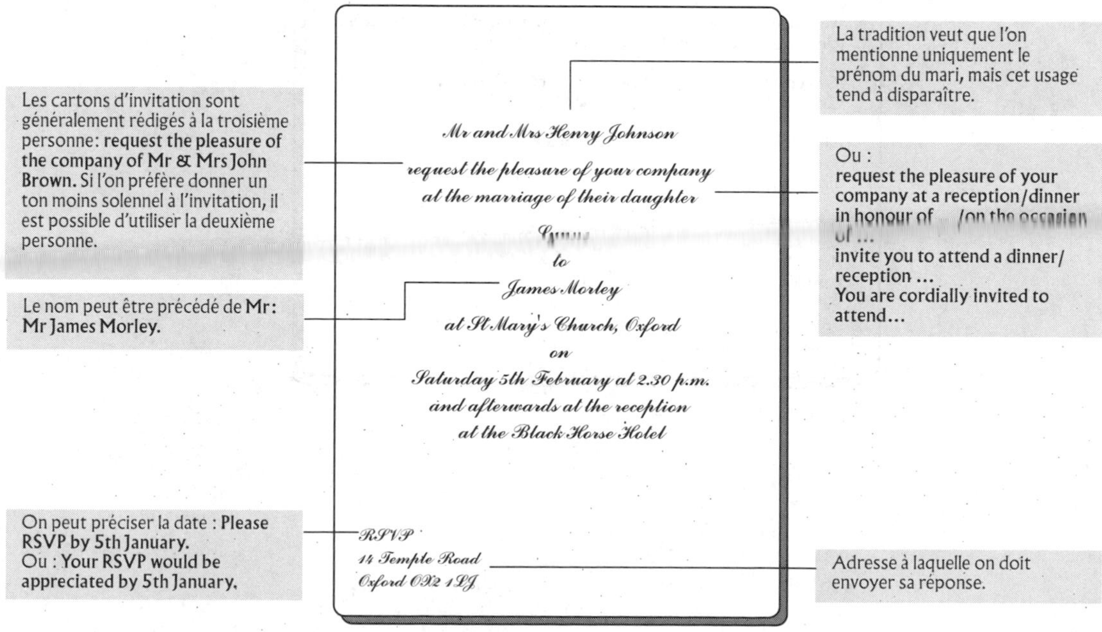

Mr and Mrs Henry Johnson
request the pleasure of your company
at the marriage of their daughter
[illegible]
to
James Morley
at St Mary's Church, Oxford
on
Saturday 5th February at 2.30 p.m.
and afterwards at the reception
at the Black Horse Hotel

RSVP
14 Temple Road
Oxford OX2 4LJ

La tradition veut que l'on mentionne uniquement le prénom du mari, mais cet usage tend à disparaître.

Les cartons d'invitation sont généralement rédigés à la troisième personne: **request the pleasure of the company of Mr & Mrs John Brown.** Si l'on préfère donner un ton moins solennel à l'invitation, il est possible d'utiliser la deuxième personne.

Ou :
request the pleasure of your company at a reception/dinner in honour of [illegible]/on the occasion of ...
invite you to attend a dinner/reception ...
You are cordially invited to attend...

Le nom peut être précédé de **Mr: Mr James Morley.**

On peut préciser la date : **Please RSVP by 5th January.**
Ou : **Your RSVP would be appreciated by 5th January.**

Adresse à laquelle on doit envoyer sa réponse.

Pour accepter une invitation officielle

La réponse doit toujours être manuscrite.

We thank you for your kind invitation to the marriage of your daughter Lynne on 5th February, and to the reception afterwards. We have great pleasure in accepting.

Lorsque l'on répond à ce type d'invitation, il n'est pas nécessaire d'indiquer la date ni de signer. Si l'invitation est rédigée à la troisième personne, il faut utiliser la troisième personne dans la réponse: **Mr & Mrs George Adams thank Mr & Mrs Henry Johnson for their kind invitation to the marriage of their daughter Lynne on 5th February, and to the reception afterwards. They have great pleasure in accepting.**

Ou : **It is with great/much pleasure that we/they accept.**

Pour refuser une invitation officielle

We thank you for your kind invitation to your daughter's wedding, and to the reception afterwards, but regret that we are unable to attend.

Ou, à la troisième personne : **Mr and Mrs Hall thank Mr and Mrs Johnson for their kind invitation to their daughter's wedding, and to the reception afterwards, but regret that they will be unable to attend.**

Lettre d'invitation à une conférence

November 11, 2001

Mr. Faraday Peters
114 Roanoke Drive
Blacksburg,
VA 23501

Dear Mr. Peters,

On behalf of the Virginia Arthurian Society, I would like to extend to you an invitation to speak at our seminar during the VAS annual conference in Chicago on Saturday, February 8 from 10:00am to 12:00pm.

We would like you to speak about your latest research and your recent publications. You would have up to 20 minutes to speak.

If you have any questions, please contact me by email at vas@excalibur.edu or by telephone at (540) 567-1123.

I look forward to hearing from you soon.

Sincerely,

Henry Hunt

Henry Hunt
President, Virginia Arthurian Society

Ou :
I would like to invite you to ...
You are cordially invited to ...

- Carton d'invitation : soirée entre amis

> James and Fiona
>
> INVITE YOU TO
> a house-warming party
>
> ON: Friday 13th September
> AT: 45 Rowan Crescent
> FROM: 8pm onwards
>
> Please bring a bottle RSVP

Ou :
We're giving a dinner party/cocktail party/birthday party next Friday and hope you will be able to come.
We are celebrating our engagement by holding a dinner dance at the ... on ..., and would be delighted if you could join us.
I'm having/planning a party - come along, and bring a friend.

- Réponse à une invitation : soirée entre amis

> 46 Hatton Street
> Bath
> BA5 2GA
>
> 23 August 2001
>
> Dear James and Fiona,
>
> Thank you so much for the invitation to your house-warming party. I'd love to come. It will be great to see you and, of course, your new home.
>
> If you need any help with food, I'd be only too glad to bring something along, as well as a bottle, of course!
>
> Thanks once again for the kind invitation. I look forward to seeing you.
>
> Love,
>
> Emily

Ou :
I'd love to come to your party. It was good of you to invite me.
Thank you for your invitation to dinner/for the weekend - I look forward to it very much.
Thank you so much for your invitation, but I'm afraid I/we won't be able to come.
I was/We were delighted to get your invitation but unfortunately I/we can't come.

Remerciements

- Pour un séjour chez des amis

> *40 The Crescent*
> *5152 Crafers*
> *SA Australia*
>
> *2 September 2001*
>
> *Dear Mrs Hepplewhite*
>
> *I am writing to thank you for extending such a warm welcome to myself and my wife during our recent stay with you in Edinburgh. We greatly appreciated your help and advice, not to mention your hospitality and your cooking!*
>
> *We were both very taken with the city and enjoyed the festival immensely. Thank you so much for guiding us through both the streets and the festival programme. We are already planning to return next year.*
>
> *I hope you and your family are all well. Remember you are always more than welcome to come and stay with us in Australia. We would love the opportunity to return your hospitality and of course we have the Adelaide Festival to tempt you with.*
>
> *We look forward to hearing from you and thank you once again for everything.*
>
> *With best wishes*
>
> *Tony and Diana Sedgwick*

Ou:
I am writing to say thank you for... ;
I would like to thank you for...

Ou:
for your hospitality.
for the hospitality you showed myself and my wife/you showed to me ...

Ou:
Your help and advice were much appreciated.

Ou:
Thanking you once again for all your help. We look forward to ...

Ou:
Best wishes. Le ton de ces formules est amical. Elles peuvent être suivies ou bien remplacées par la formule **Yours sincerely,** plus impersonnelle.

- Pour un cadeau

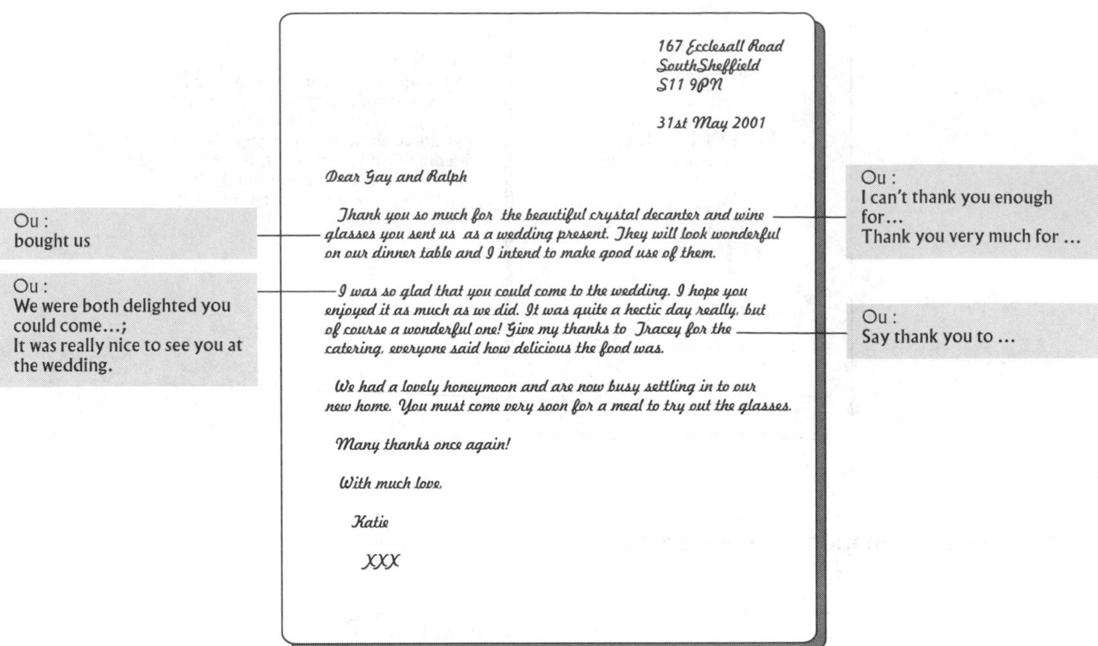

167 Ecclesall Road
South Sheffield
S11 9PN

31st May 2001

Dear Gay and Ralph

Thank you so much for the beautiful crystal decanter and wine glasses you sent us as a wedding present. They will look wonderful on our dinner table and I intend to make good use of them.

I was so glad that you could come to the wedding. I hope you enjoyed it as much as we did. It was quite a hectic day really, but of course a wonderful one! Give my thanks to Tracey for the catering, everyone said how delicious the food was.

We had a lovely honeymoon and are now busy settling in to our new home. You must come very soon for a meal to try out the glasses.

Many thanks once again!

With much love,

Katie

XXX

Ou :
bought us

Ou :
We were both delighted you could come…;
It was really nice to see you at the wedding.

Ou :
I can't thank you enough for…
Thank you very much for …

Ou :
Say thank you to …

Condoléances

Pour présenter ses condoléances, il est préférable d'envoyer une courte lettre, écrite à la main. On peut également envoyer une carte imprimée, à laquelle on ajoute un petit mot manuscrit.

- À une connaissance, un collègue

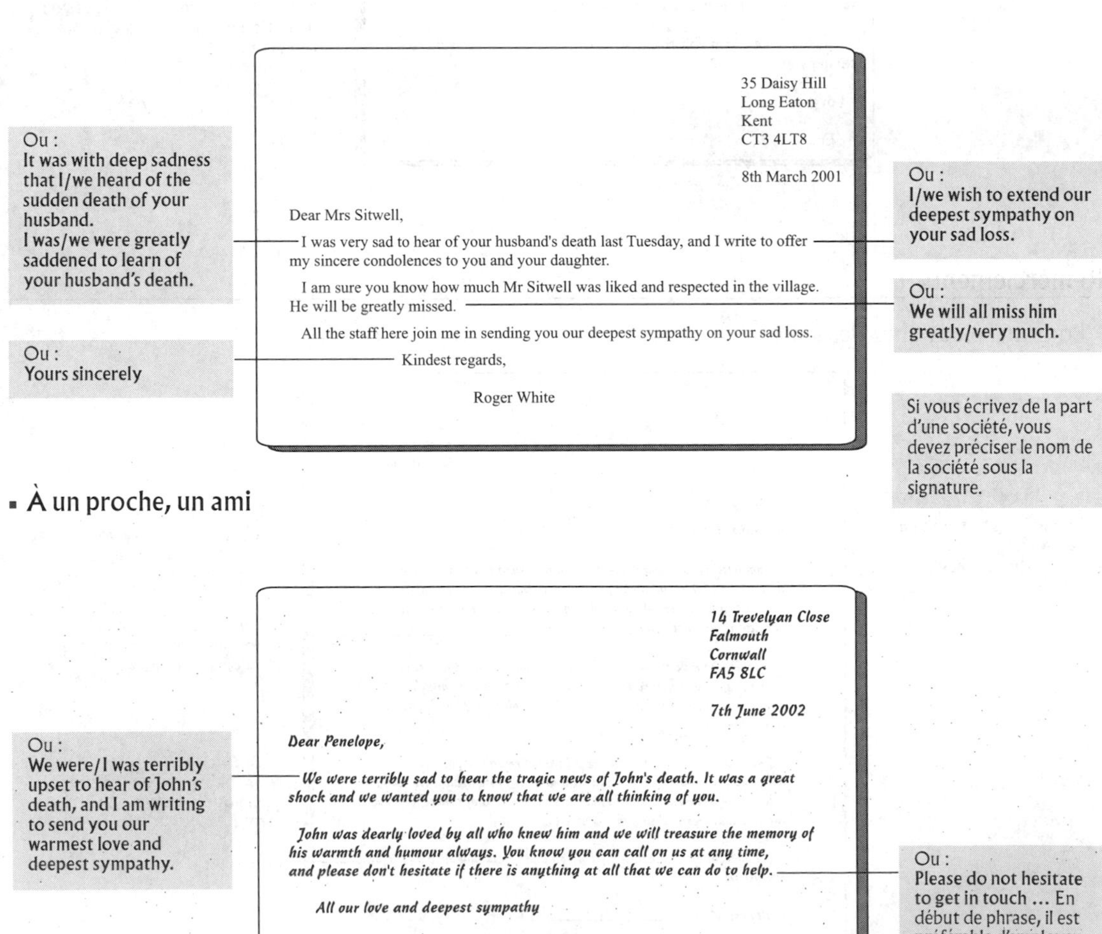

35 Daisy Hill
Long Eaton
Kent
CT3 4LT8

8th March 2001

Dear Mrs Sitwell,

I was very sad to hear of your husband's death last Tuesday, and I write to offer my sincere condolences to you and your daughter.

I am sure you know how much Mr Sitwell was liked and respected in the village. He will be greatly missed.

All the staff here join me in sending you our deepest sympathy on your sad loss.

Kindest regards,

Roger White

Ou :
It was with deep sadness that I/we heard of the sudden death of your husband.
I was/we were greatly saddened to learn of your husband's death.

Ou :
Yours sincerely

Ou :
I/we wish to extend our deepest sympathy on your sad loss.

Ou :
We will all miss him greatly/very much.

Si vous écrivez de la part d'une société, vous devez préciser le nom de la société sous la signature.

- À un proche, un ami

14 Trevelyan Close
Falmouth
Cornwall
FA5 8LC

7th June 2002

Dear Penelope,

We were terribly sad to hear the tragic news of John's death. It was a great shock and we wanted you to know that we are all thinking of you.

John was dearly loved by all who knew him and we will treasure the memory of his warmth and humour always. You know you can call on us at any time, and please don't hesitate if there is anything at all that we can do to help.

All our love and deepest sympathy

Sandra and Derek

Ou :
We were/I was terribly upset to hear of John's death, and I am writing to send you our warmest love and deepest sympathy.

Ou :
Please do not hesitate to get in touch … En début de phrase, il est préférable d'employer do not plutôt que la forme contractée don't.

Réservations

Les réservations de billets ou de chambres d'hôtel se font de plus en plus par Internet et par courrier électronique. Pour toute réservation faite par téléphone, il est recommandé de confirmer par écrit. Qu'il s'agisse d'une lettre ou d'un message électronique, le corps du texte reste le même. Il est important de préciser par écrit toutes les conditions : date, nombre de nuits, type et nombre de chambres/billets, etc.

▪ Lettre de réservation

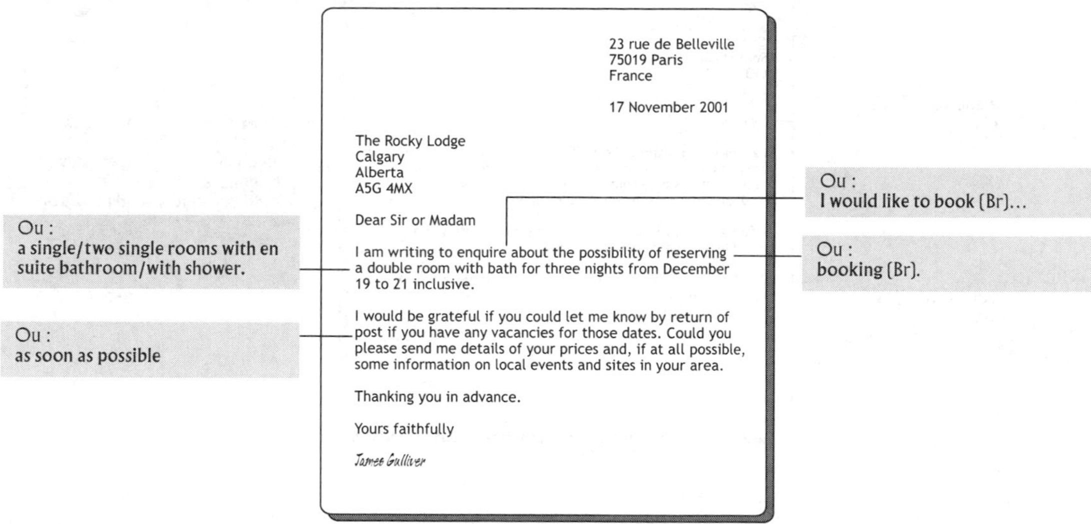

23 rue de Belleville
75019 Paris
France

17 November 2001

The Rocky Lodge
Calgary
Alberta
A5G 4MX

Dear Sir or Madam

I am writing to enquire about the possibility of reserving a double room with bath for three nights from December 19 to 21 inclusive.

I would be grateful if you could let me know by return of post if you have any vacancies for those dates. Could you please send me details of your prices and, if at all possible, some information on local events and sites in your area.

Thanking you in advance.

Yours faithfully

James Gulliver

▪ Pour confirmer une réservation

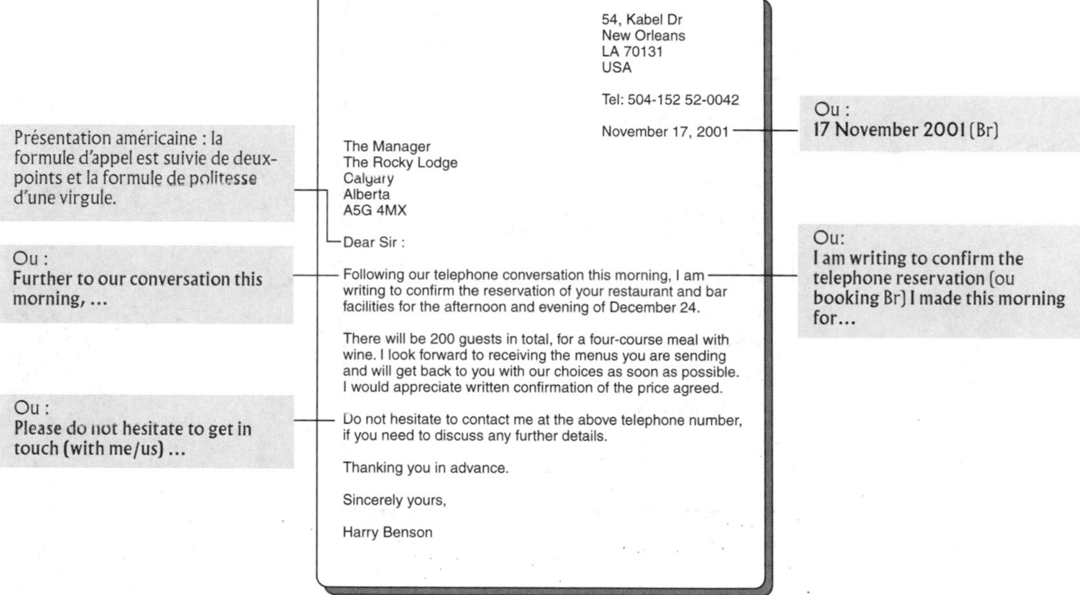

54, Kabel Dr
New Orleans
LA 70131
USA

Tel: 504-152 52-0042

November 17, 2001

The Manager
The Rocky Lodge
Calgary
Alberta
A5G 4MX

Dear Sir :

Following our telephone conversation this morning, I am writing to confirm the reservation of your restaurant and bar facilities for the afternoon and evening of December 24.

There will be 200 guests in total, for a four-course meal with wine. I look forward to receiving the menus you are sending and will get back to you with our choices as soon as possible. I would appreciate written confirmation of the price agreed.

Do not hesitate to contact me at the above telephone number, if you need to discuss any further details.

Thanking you in advance.

Sincerely yours,

Harry Benson

▪ Pour annuler une réservation

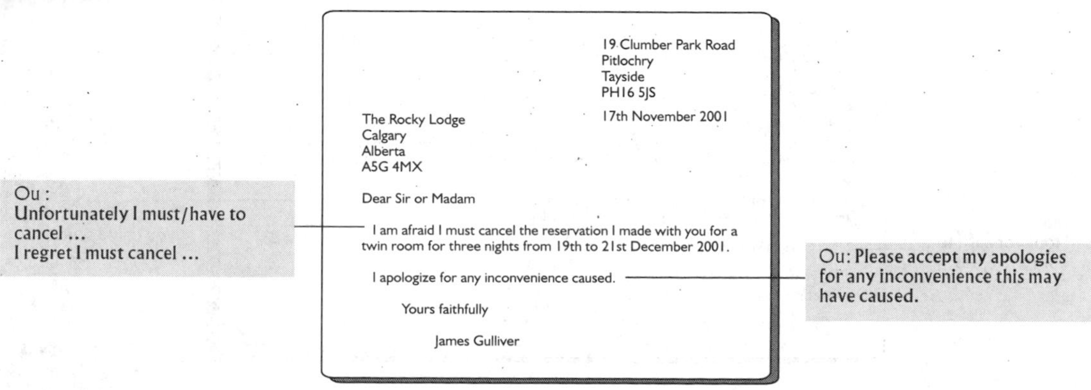

19 Clumber Park Road
Pitlochry
Tayside
PH16 5JS

17th November 2001

The Rocky Lodge
Calgary
Alberta
A5G 4MX

Dear Sir or Madam

I am afraid I must cancel the reservation I made with you for a twin room for three nights from 19th to 21st December 2001.

I apologize for any inconvenience caused.

Yours faithfully

James Gulliver

Ou :
Unfortunately I must/have to cancel ...
I regret I must cancel ...
Ou: Please accept my apologies for any inconvenience this may have caused.

Demande de renseignements

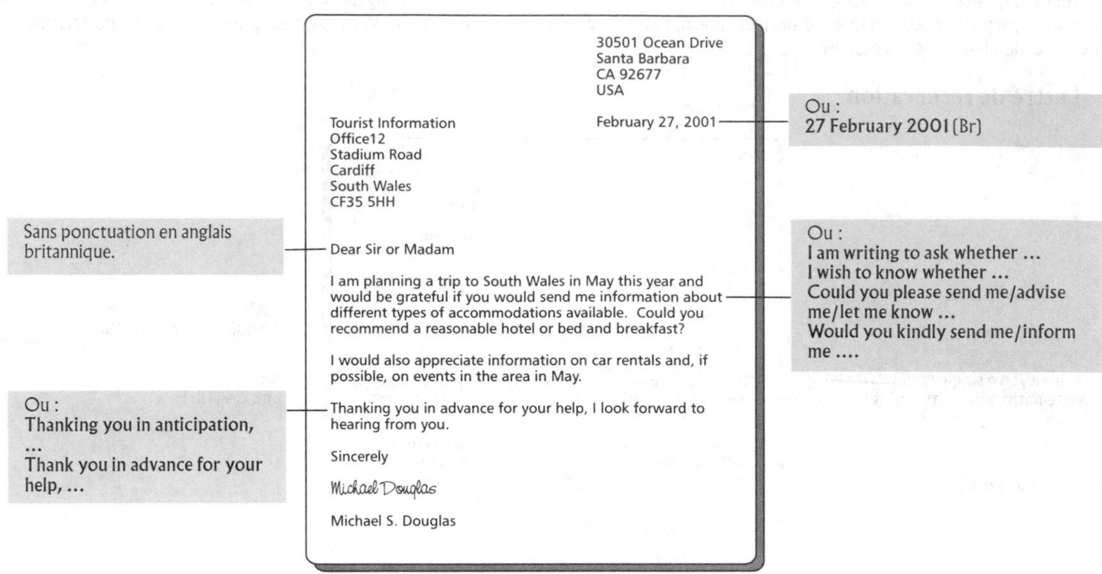

30501 Ocean Drive
Santa Barbara
CA 92677
USA

Tourist Information
Office12
Stadium Road
Cardiff
South Wales
CF35 5HH

February 27, 2001

Dear Sir or Madam

I am planning a trip to South Wales in May this year and would be grateful if you would send me information about different types of accommodations available. Could you recommend a reasonable hotel or bed and breakfast?

I would also appreciate information on car rentals and, if possible, on events in the area in May.

Thanking you in advance for your help, I look forward to hearing from you.

Sincerely

Michael Douglas

Michael S. Douglas

Ou :
27 February 2001 (Br)
Sans ponctuation en anglais britannique.
Ou :
I am writing to ask whether ...
I wish to know whether ...
Could you please send me/advise me/let me know ...
Would you kindly send me/inform me ....
Ou :
Thanking you in anticipation, ...
Thank you in advance for your help, ...

Demande de catalogue

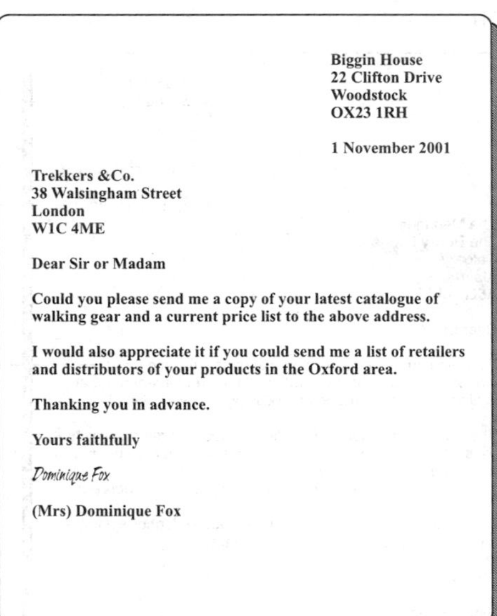

Biggin House
22 Clifton Drive
Woodstock
OX23 1RH

1 November 2001

Trekkers &Co.
38 Walsingham Street
London
W1C 4ME

Dear Sir or Madam

Could you please send me a copy of your latest catalogue of walking gear and a current price list to the above address.

I would also appreciate it if you could send me a list of retailers and distributors of your products in the Oxford area.

Thanking you in advance.

Yours faithfully

Dominique Fox

(Mrs) Dominique Fox

Demande de devis

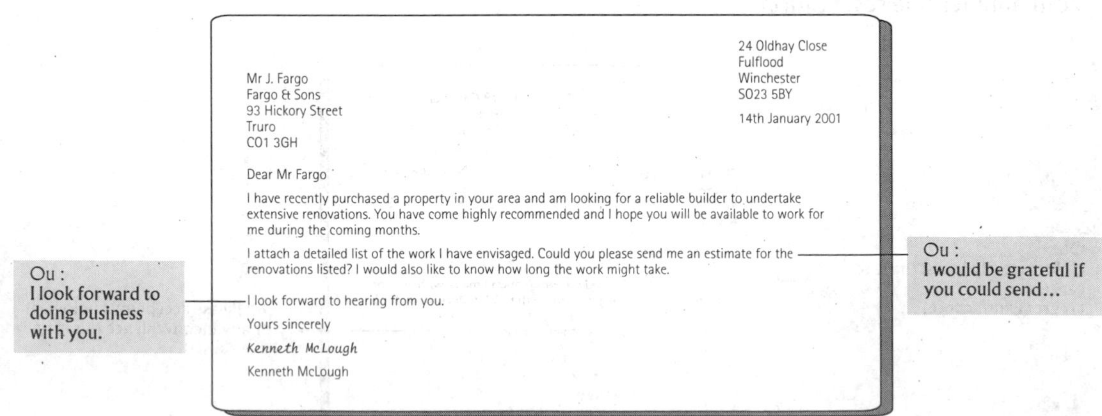

24 Oldhay Close
Fulflood
Winchester
SO23 5BY

Mr J. Fargo
Fargo & Sons
93 Hickory Street
Truro
CO1 3GH

14th January 2001

Dear Mr Fargo

I have recently purchased a property in your area and am looking for a reliable builder to undertake extensive renovations. You have come highly recommended and I hope you will be available to work for me during the coming months.

I attach a detailed list of the work I have envisaged. Could you please send me an estimate for the renovations listed? I would also like to know how long the work might take.

I look forward to hearing from you.

Yours sincerely

Kenneth McLough

Kenneth McLough

Ou :
I look forward to doing business with you.
Ou :
I would be grateful if you could send...

Si vous ne connaissez pas le nom du destinataire, adressez votre lettre au **Customer Services Manager**. Pour les plus petites entreprises ou les entreprises familiales, vous pouvez adresser votre lettre au directeur: **The Manager**.

12, Biggles Close
Woodbridge
Suffolk
CB12 3DF

The Customer Services Manager
East Coast Trains
King's Cross Station
London
NO1 4YY

4th August 2000

Dear Sir or Madam

I am writing to complain about the inconvenience caused to me last week by your company's inadequate performance.

I was travelling on the 9.30 train from London to York on 1st August. The train was due to arrive in York at midday. It did not arrive until 5 o'clock in the afternoon, making me miss an important meeting. Added to this inconvenience, there were too few announcements informing passengers of what was happening.

I am more than disappointed with the service I received and feel I am entitled to compensation that reflects adequately the inconvenience suffered.

I look forward to receiving your response within the next 14 days.

Yours faithfully

G. Roberts

Mr G. Roberts

Ou:
I wish to complain about...
I wish to complain most strongly about...

Ou:
The service I received was extremely unsatisfactory...
I am extremely unhappy with the service I received...

Ou :
I trust/hope that you will see your way to offering adequate compensation for the inconvenience suffered/caused.

Ou :
I look forward to receiving a reasonable offer of compensation.

Il est recommandé de préciser le délai dans lequel vous souhaitez obtenir une réponse.

3 Pennybrook Lane
Dollis Hill
London
NW2 6HG

The Customer Services Manager
Blotto & Co.
34 Vine Street
Ashford
Kent
KE8 5HB

1st September 2001

Dear Sir or Madam

Order 324B

I received the above order from you on 30 August 2001. I regret to inform you that there were several items missing from the shipment and other items do not correspond to the original order.

I enclose a list of the wines I have received, as well as a photocopy of the original order form and invoice.I trust you will remedy the situation as quickly as possible.

I look forward to hearing from you within the next 7 days.

Yours faithfully

Jackson Brattel

Mr Jackson Brattel

Objet de la plainte : préciser le numéro de commande, le code du modèle ou les informations nécessaires pour identifier la marchandise.

Ou :
The goods I received were badly damaged.
The goods you sent me were damaged in transit/were damaged on receipt.
The goods you sent me had the following defects: ...

La correspondance commerciale

La correspondance commerciale exige l'emploi d'un style direct, concis et courtois. L'orthographe et la grammaire doivent être impeccables.

Dans les pays anglo-saxons, la lettre d'affaires est toujours dactylographiée. Les paragraphes sont alignés à gauche, sans retrait, et séparés par une ligne de blanc. En anglais britannique, la date, les adresses, les formules d'appel et de politesse ne comportent aucun signe de ponctuation. En anglais américain, on insère une virgule avant l'année dans la date, un point après les abréviations Mr., Ms., etc., deux-points après la formule d'appel et une virgule après la formule de politesse.

Pour prendre rendez-vous

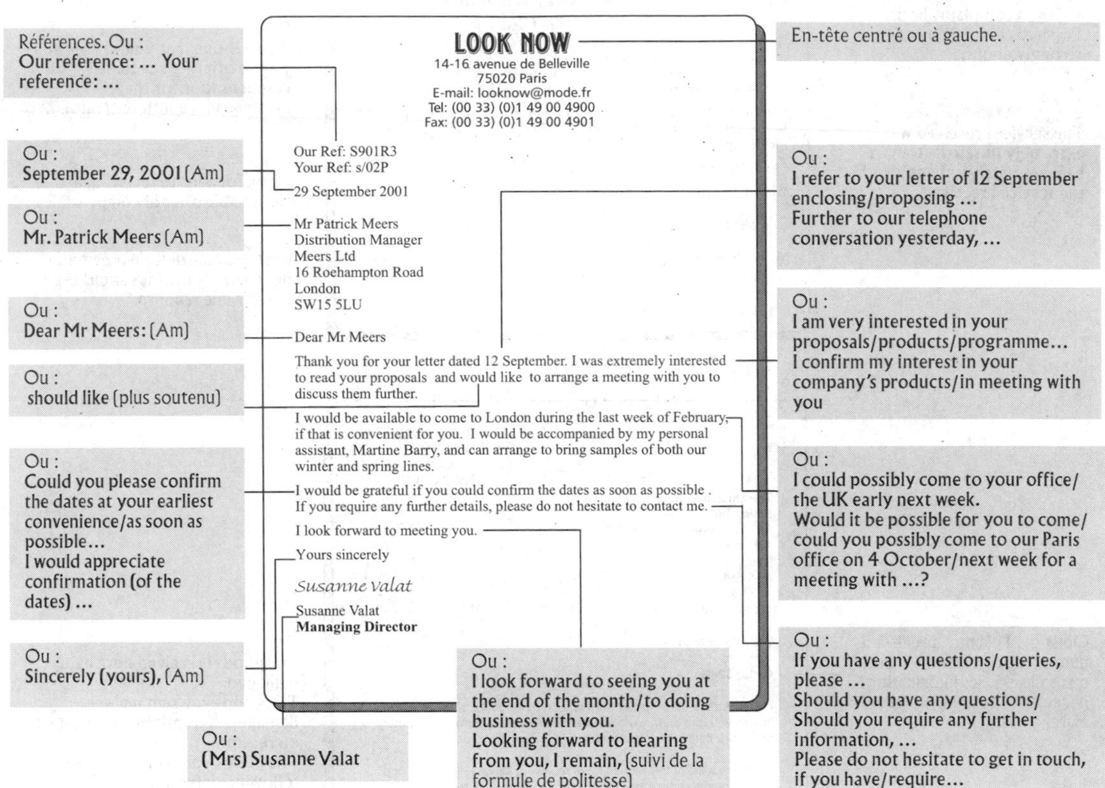

Références. Ou : Our reference: ... Your reference: ...

Ou : September 29, 2001 (Am)

Ou : Mr. Patrick Meers (Am)

Ou : Dear Mr Meers: (Am)

Ou : should like (plus soutenu)

Ou : Could you please confirm the dates at your earliest convenience/as soon as possible... I would appreciate confirmation (of the dates) ...

Ou : Sincerely (yours), (Am)

Ou : (Mrs) Susanne Valat

LOOK NOW
14-16 avenue de Belleville
75020 Paris
E-mail: looknow@mode.fr
Tel: (00 33) (0)1 49 00 4900
Fax: (00 33) (0)1 49 00 4901

Our Ref: S901R3
Your Ref: s/02P

29 September 2001

Mr Patrick Meers
Distribution Manager
Meers Ltd
16 Roehampton Road
London
SW15 5LU

Dear Mr Meers

Thank you for your letter dated 12 September. I was extremely interested to read your proposals and would like to arrange a meeting with you to discuss them further.

I would be available to come to London during the last week of February, if that is convenient for you. I would be accompanied by my personal assistant, Martine Barry, and can arrange to bring samples of both our winter and spring lines.

I would be grateful if you could confirm the dates as soon as possible. If you require any further details, please do not hesitate to contact me.

I look forward to meeting you.

Yours sincerely

Susanne Valat

Susanne Valat
Managing Director

Ou : I look forward to seeing you at the end of the month/to doing business with you. Looking forward to hearing from you, I remain, (suivi de la formule de politesse)

En-tête centré ou à gauche.

Ou : I refer to your letter of 12 September enclosing/proposing ... Further to our telephone conversation yesterday, ...

Ou : I am very interested in your proposals/products/programme... I confirm my interest in your company's products/in meeting with you

Ou : I could possibly come to your office/the UK early next week. Would it be possible for you to come/could you possibly come to our Paris office on 4 October/next week for a meeting with ...?

Ou : If you have any questions/queries, please ... Should you have any questions/ Should you require any further information, ... Please do not hesitate to get in touch, if you have/require...

Suite à un rendez-vous

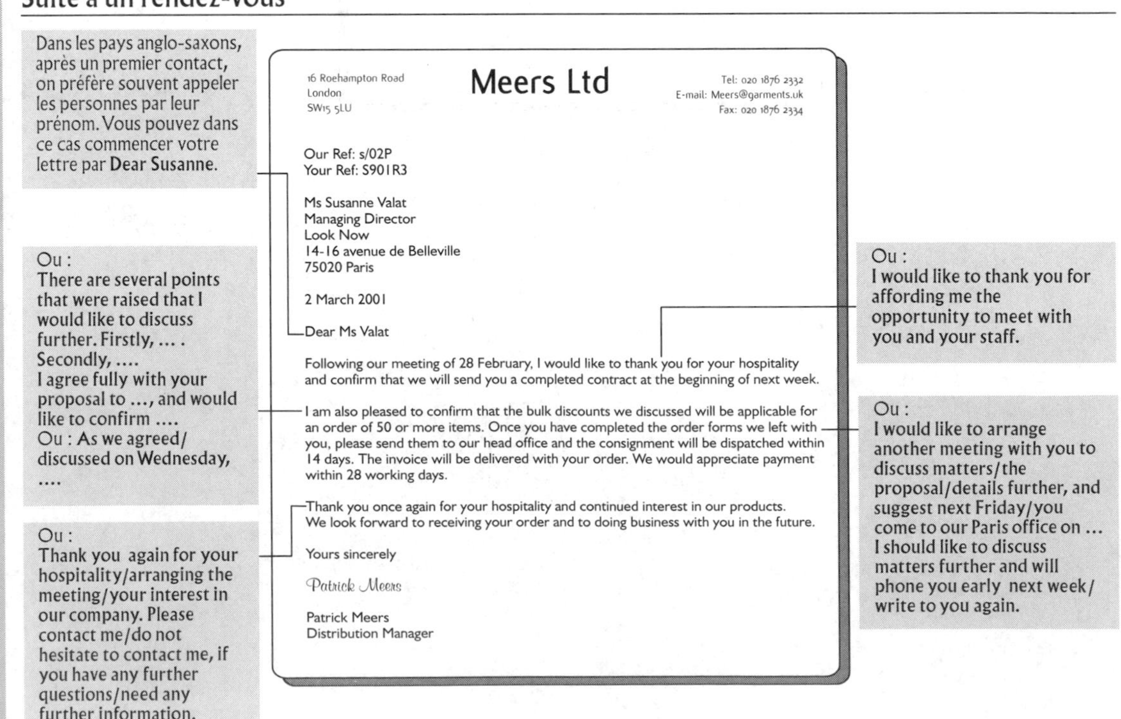

Dans les pays anglo-saxons, après un premier contact, on préfère souvent appeler les personnes par leur prénom. Vous pouvez dans ce cas commencer votre lettre par **Dear Susanne.**

Ou : There are several points that were raised that I would like to discuss further. Firstly, ... Secondly, ... I agree fully with your proposal to ..., and would like to confirm .... Ou : As we agreed/discussed on Wednesday, ...

Ou : Thank you again for your hospitality/arranging the meeting/your interest in our company. Please contact me/do not hesitate to contact me, if you have any further questions/need any further information.

16 Roehampton Road
London
SW15 5LU

Meers Ltd

Tel: 020 1876 2332
E-mail: Meers@garments.uk
Fax: 020 1876 2334

Our Ref: s/02P
Your Ref: S901R3

Ms Susanne Valat
Managing Director
Look Now
14-16 avenue de Belleville
75020 Paris

2 March 2001

Dear Ms Valat

Following our meeting of 28 February, I would like to thank you for your hospitality and confirm that we will send you a completed contract at the beginning of next week.

I am also pleased to confirm that the bulk discounts we discussed will be applicable for an order of 50 or more items. Once you have completed the order forms we left with you, please send them to our head office and the consignment will be dispatched within 14 days. The invoice will be delivered with your order. We would appreciate payment within 28 working days.

Thank you once again for your hospitality and continued interest in our products. We look forward to receiving your order and to doing business with you in the future.

Yours sincerely

Patrick Meers

Patrick Meers
Distribution Manager

Ou : I would like to thank you for affording me the opportunity to meet with you and your staff.

Ou : I would like to arrange another meeting with you to discuss matters/the proposal/details further, and suggest next Friday/you come to our Paris office on ... I should like to discuss matters further and will phone you early next week/write to you again.

Réponse à une demande de renseignements

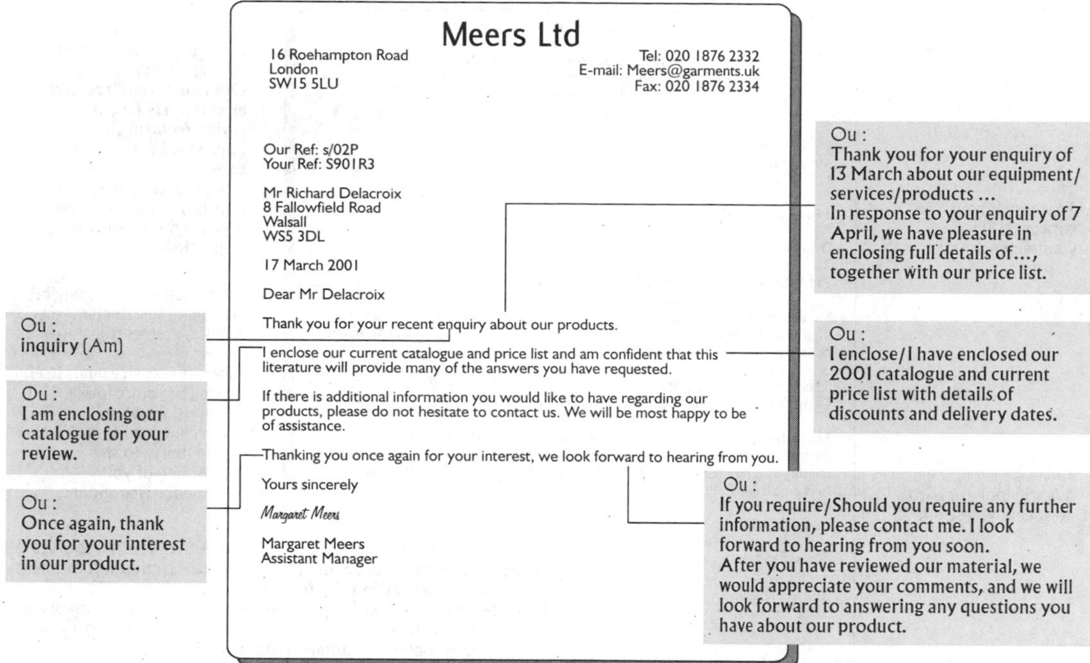

Meers Ltd

16 Roehampton Road
London
SW15 5LU

Tel: 020 1876 2332
E-mail: Meers@garments.uk
Fax: 020 1876 2334

Our Ref: s/02P
Your Ref: S901R3

Mr Richard Delacroix
8 Fallowfield Road
Walsall
WS5 3DL

17 March 2001

Dear Mr Delacroix

Thank you for your recent enquiry about our products.

I enclose our current catalogue and price list and am confident that this literature will provide many of the answers you have requested.

If there is additional information you would like to have regarding our products, please do not hesitate to contact us. We will be most happy to be of assistance.

Thanking you once again for your interest, we look forward to hearing from you.

Yours sincerely

Margaret Meers

Margaret Meers
Assistant Manager

Ou :
inquiry (Am)

Ou :
I am enclosing our catalogue for your review.

Ou :
Once again, thank you for your interest in our product.

Ou :
Thank you for your enquiry of 13 March about our equipment/services/products ...
In response to your enquiry of 7 April, we have pleasure in enclosing full details of..., together with our price list.

Ou :
I enclose/I have enclosed our 2001 catalogue and current price list with details of discounts and delivery dates.

Ou :
If you require/Should you require any further information, please contact me. I look forward to hearing from you soon.
After you have reviewed our material, we would appreciate your comments, and we will look forward to answering any questions you have about our product.

Réponse à une réclamation

La lettre d'excuse reprend la structure de la lettre de réclamation.

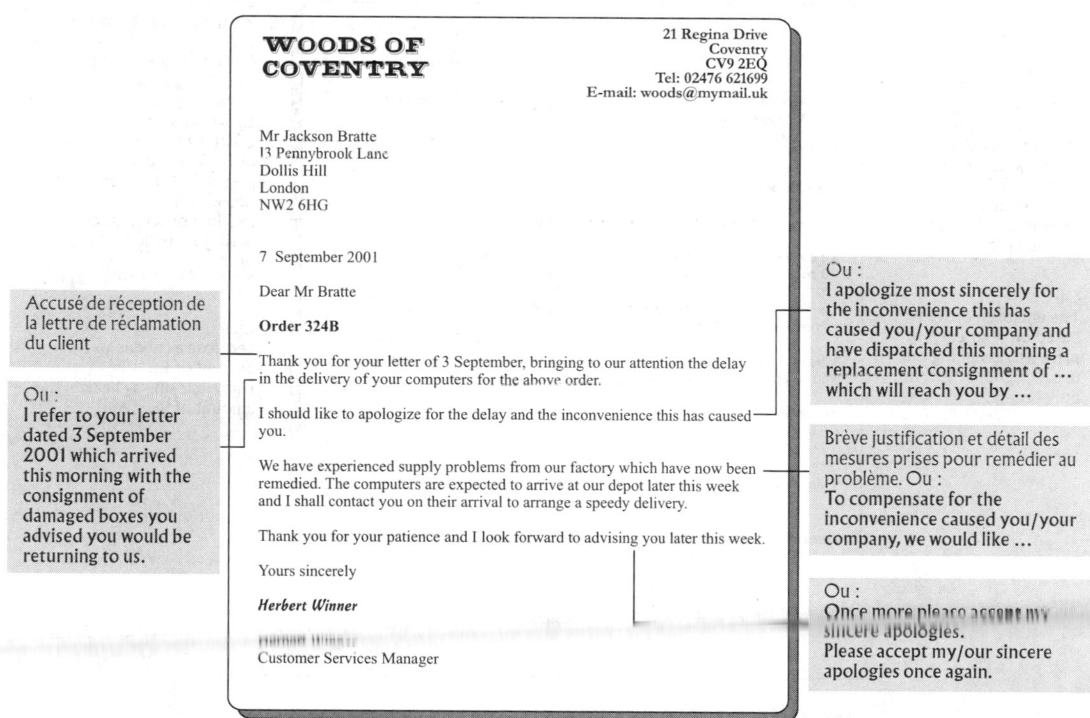

WOODS OF COVENTRY

21 Regina Drive
Coventry
CV9 2EQ
Tel: 02476 621699
E-mail: woods@mymail.uk

Mr Jackson Bratte
13 Pennybrook Lane
Dollis Hill
London
NW2 6HG

7 September 2001

Dear Mr Bratte

Order 324B

Thank you for your letter of 3 September, bringing to our attention the delay in the delivery of your computers for the above order.

I should like to apologize for the delay and the inconvenience this has caused you.

We have experienced supply problems from our factory which have now been remedied. The computers are expected to arrive at our depot later this week and I shall contact you on their arrival to arrange a speedy delivery.

Thank you for your patience and I look forward to advising you later this week.

Yours sincerely

Herbert Winner

[illegible]
Customer Services Manager

Accusé de réception de la lettre de réclamation du client

Ou :
I refer to your letter dated 3 September 2001 which arrived this morning with the consignment of damaged boxes you advised you would be returning to us.

Ou :
I apologize most sincerely for the inconvenience this has caused you/your company and have dispatched this morning a replacement consignment of ... which will reach you by ...

Brève justification et détail des mesures prises pour remédier au problème. Ou :
To compensate for the inconvenience caused you/your company, we would like ...

Ou :
Once more please accept my sincere apologies.
Please accept my/our sincere apologies once again.

Publipostage

BRACON SA
24 rue du Chatillon
13101 Aix-en-Provence Cedex 789
Tel: 04 56 76 76 77 E-mail: bracon@fiesta.fr
Nico Software Inc

98 Howard Street
Manchester
M28 2SG

13 December 2001

Dear Sir or Madam

Publishing Opportunities in Europe

We are an established publisher of European trade and business journals with high visibility throughout Europe. We are currently offering special advertising rates and benefits to new customers.

This is an excellent opportunity for your company to increase its share of the IT market in the dynamic European marketplace.

Please find enclosed two copies of our journals, with our compliments. If you wish to pursue our offer or require any further information, please contact our enquiry line on Freefone 0800 39853. I look forward to hearing from you and to our possible future partnership.

Yours faithfully

Muriel Delahais

Muriel Delahais
Sales Director

Ou :
To whom it may concern: (Br)
Gentlemen: (Am)

Ou :
We will look forward to seeing you soon.

Présentation de la société et objet de la lettre. Autres tournures utiles :
Our firm recently received an extremely favourable review from/in ... which we hope may be of some interest to you.
It is our great pleasure to inform you that our new product line is ready for your inspection.

Introduction des arguments destinés à susciter l'intérêt du lecteur. Autres tournures utiles :
Since our service lends itself so well to your type of business, we would appreciate having an opportunity to speak with you or one of your representatives about ...

Invitation à prendre contact avec la société. Autres tournures utiles :
Please contact me at (telephone), so that we can arrange a convenient time to meet. I will be looking forward to your call.
Please feel free to either drop in or make an appointment with one of our staff at any time.
Thank you for being a customer of our firm.
We invite you to call for an appointment to visit our display room/factory/shop.

Commande

48 rue Beaubourg
75003 Paris
Tel: 00 33 1 40 28 91 00

Brooke's Books
188 Belvidere Road
Glasgow
G64 2JP

23 June 2001

Dear Sir or Madam

Please send me the following items from your summer catalogue:

10 copies of "Learn English the Easy Way", Intermediate, Scot Press. Ref: 4356K
10 copies of "Improve your Ps and Qs", Scot Press. Ref 5367Q

I enclose a cheque made payable to you for £267.50, which includes the cost of postage and packaging.

I look forward to receiving confirmation of my order, and would be obliged if you would advise me in advance of the planned delivery date.

Yours faithfully

Pierre Sabire

Pierre Sabire

Ou :
Gentlemen: (Am).
To whom it may concern:
Cette dernière formule s'utilise en anglais britannique dans la correspondance administrative lorsqu'on ne connaît pas le nom du destinataire.

Ou :
The enclosed order is based on your current price list, assuming our usual discount of ... on bulk orders.

Ou :
We would like to place an order for the following items, in the sizes and quantities specified below.
I refer to your letter of 5 June enclosing your catalogue for 2001. I would like to place an order for/to order ...
Please find enclosed our order no. 471 for ...
I wish to order... as advertised in the July issue of ...

Ou :
I enclose a cheque to the amount of £... (Br)
I am enclosing a check in the amount of $... (Am)

▪ Réponse

Dear Mr Sabire
Dear Customer

Thank you for your order no ... It is receiving our immediate attention and will be dispatched to you by ... Please allow 28 days for delivery.

This is to acknowledge receipt of your order no ... dated ..., and to advise you that the goods will be dispatched within 7 working days.

We acknowledge receipt of your order of 12 July, which will be dispatched within 14 days.

We cannot accept responsibility for goods damaged in transit.

I hope we may continue to receive your valued custom.

Ou :

We regret that we will be unable to fulfill your order for ...

We regret that the goods you ordered are temporarily out of stock/we no longer stock the goods you ordered.

Facture

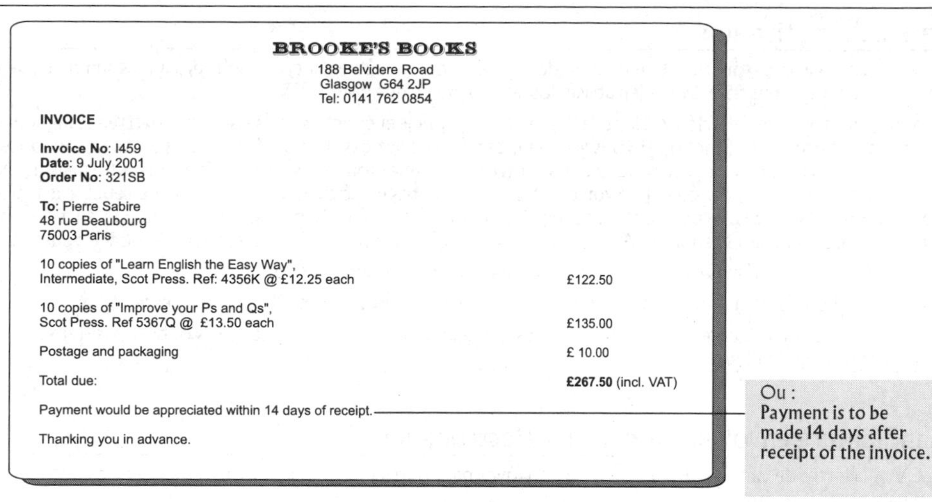

BROOKE'S BOOKS
188 Belvidere Road
Glasgow G64 2JP
Tel: 0141 762 0854

INVOICE

Invoice No: I459
Date: 9 July 2001
Order No: 321SB

To: Pierre Sabire
48 rue Beaubourg
75003 Paris

10 copies of "Learn English the Easy Way", Intermediate, Scot Press. Ref: 4356K @ £12.25 each	£122.50
10 copies of "Improve your Ps and Qs", Scot Press. Ref 5367Q @ £13.50 each	£135.00
Postage and packaging	£ 10.00
Total due:	**£267.50** (incl. VAT)

Payment would be appreciated within 14 days of receipt.

Thanking you in advance.

Ou : Payment is to be made 14 days after receipt of the invoice.

Lettre de rappel

Our records indicate that payment on your account is overdue to the amount of £ ... If the amount has already been paid, please disregard this notice. If you have not yet posted your payment, please use the enclosed envelope to send payment in full.

Thank you in advance for your anticipated co-operation in this matter.

Ou : in the amount of ... (Am)

Ou : mailed (Am)

Deuxième rappel

On 12 July 2001 we notified you of your overdue account for order no. ...

To date we still have not received payment for the above order.

Please give this matter your most urgent attention. Payment must be made within the next ten days.

Envoi du règlement

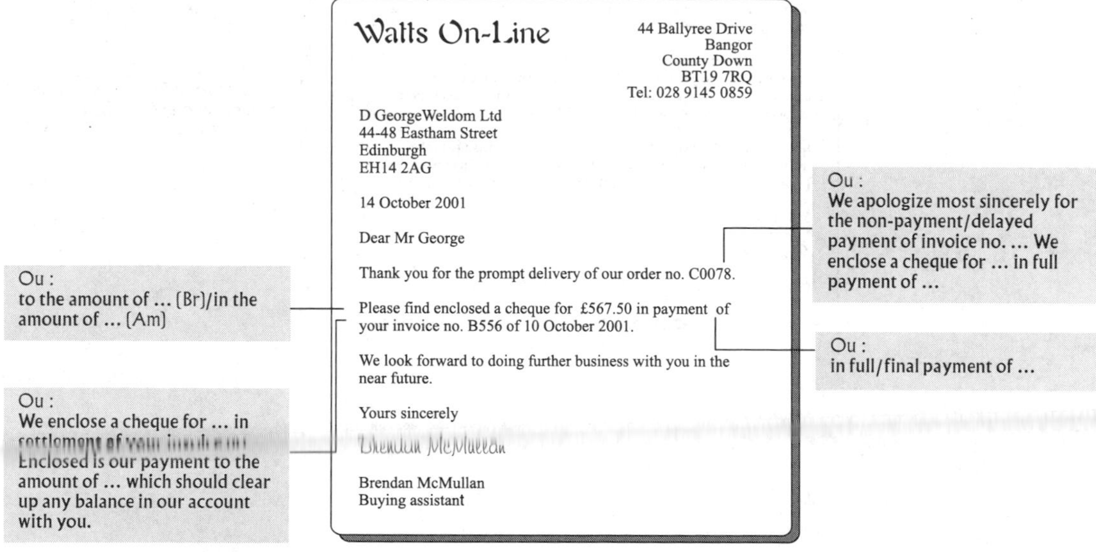

Watts On-Line

44 Ballyree Drive
Bangor
County Down
BT19 7RQ
Tel: 028 9145 0859

D GeorgeWeldom Ltd
44-48 Eastham Street
Edinburgh
EH14 2AG

14 October 2001

Dear Mr George

Thank you for the prompt delivery of our order no. C0078.

Please find enclosed a cheque for £567.50 in payment of your invoice no. B556 of 10 October 2001.

We look forward to doing further business with you in the near future.

Yours sincerely

Brendan McMullan
Buying assistant

Ou : to the amount of ... (Br)/in the amount of ... (Am)

Ou : We enclose a cheque for ... in settlement of your invoice no. ... Enclosed is our payment to the amount of ... which should clear up any balance in our account with you.

Ou : We apologize most sincerely for the non-payment/delayed payment of invoice no. ... We enclose a cheque for ... in full payment of ...

Ou : in full/final payment of ...

Recherche d'emploi

Lettre de motivation

Dans les pays anglo-saxons, la lettre de candidature doit toujours être dactylographiée, sauf si l'annonce spécifie qu'il faut envoyer une lettre manuscrite. Le papier utilisé doit être le même que pour le CV.

Comme pour toute lettre d'affaires, le style doit être clair, concis et courtois. Adressez votre lettre à la personne responsable, en précisant son nom et sa fonction si vous les connaissez. N'oubliez pas de rappeler les références de l'annonce et le poste pour lequel vous êtes candidat. Si vous ne joignez pas votre CV, donnez toutes les informations utiles (formation, expérience professionnelle, compétences, diplômes). Si votre lettre est accompagnée d'un CV, il est inutile de répéter les informations qui s'y trouvent déjà. Dans ce cas, vous devez susciter l'intérêt du lecteur, en faisant ressortir vos compétences et en démontrant que vous possédez les qualités requises. Vous pouvez reprendre certains mots clés utilisés dans l'annonce pour retenir son attention.

L'expérience et les diplômes que vous mentionnez doivent correspondre au poste proposé.

Vous devez montrer dans votre lettre que vous connaissez l'entreprise et qu'elle vous intéresse.

Expliquez en quoi votre expérience et vos qualités correspondent au profil demandé. N'oubliez pas d'ajouter que vous êtes disponible pour un entretien.

Candidature envoyée par courrier électronique

Le CV et la lettre de candidature peuvent être envoyés par courrier électronique. Il est préférable d'envoyer également une version papier par la poste.

▪ Demande de stage

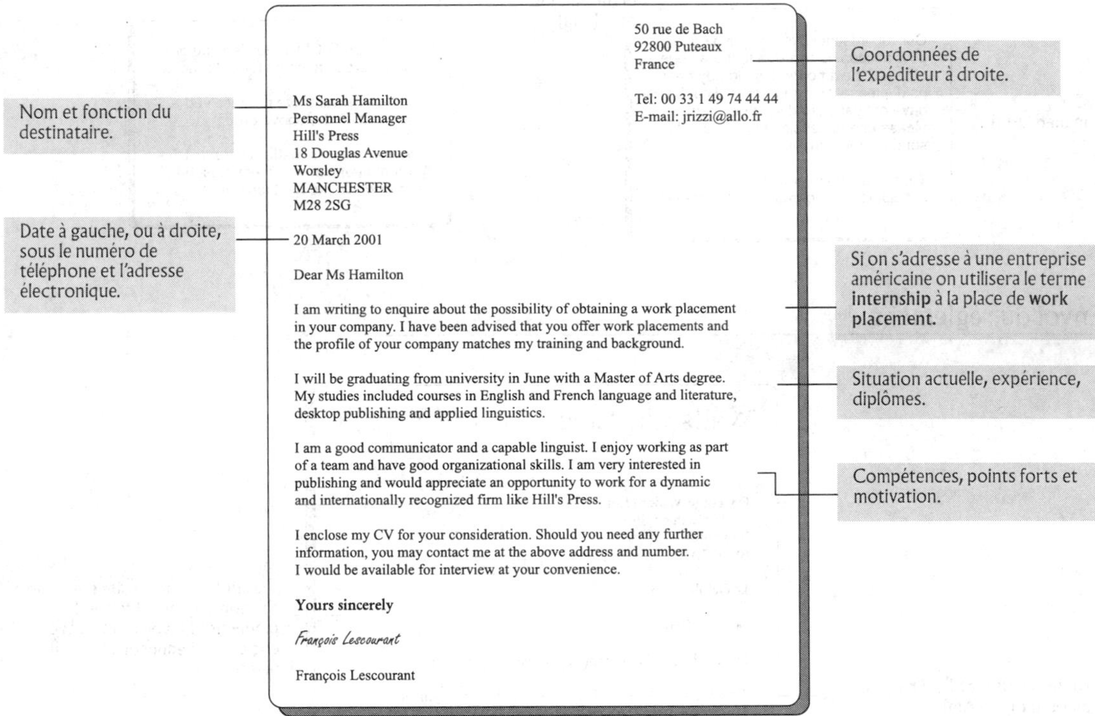

50 rue de Bach
92800 Puteaux
France

Tel: 00 33 1 49 74 44 44
E-mail: jrizzi@allo.fr

Ms Sarah Hamilton
Personnel Manager
Hill's Press
18 Douglas Avenue
Worsley
MANCHESTER
M28 2SG

20 March 2001

Dear Ms Hamilton

I am writing to enquire about the possibility of obtaining a work placement in your company. I have been advised that you offer work placements and the profile of your company matches my training and background.

I will be graduating from university in June with a Master of Arts degree. My studies included courses in English and French language and literature, desktop publishing and applied linguistics.

I am a good communicator and a capable linguist. I enjoy working as part of a team and have good organizational skills. I am very interested in publishing and would appreciate an opportunity to work for a dynamic and internationally recognized firm like Hill's Press.

I enclose my CV for your consideration. Should you need any further information, you may contact me at the above address and number.
I would be available for interview at your convenience.

Yours sincerely

François Lescourant

François Lescourant

Coordonnées de l'expéditeur à droite.
Nom et fonction du destinataire.
Date à gauche, ou à droite, sous le numéro de téléphone et l'adresse électronique.
Si on s'adresse à une entreprise américaine on utilisera le terme **internship** à la place de **work placement**.
Situation actuelle, expérience, diplômes.
Compétences, points forts et motivation.

▪ Candidature spontanée

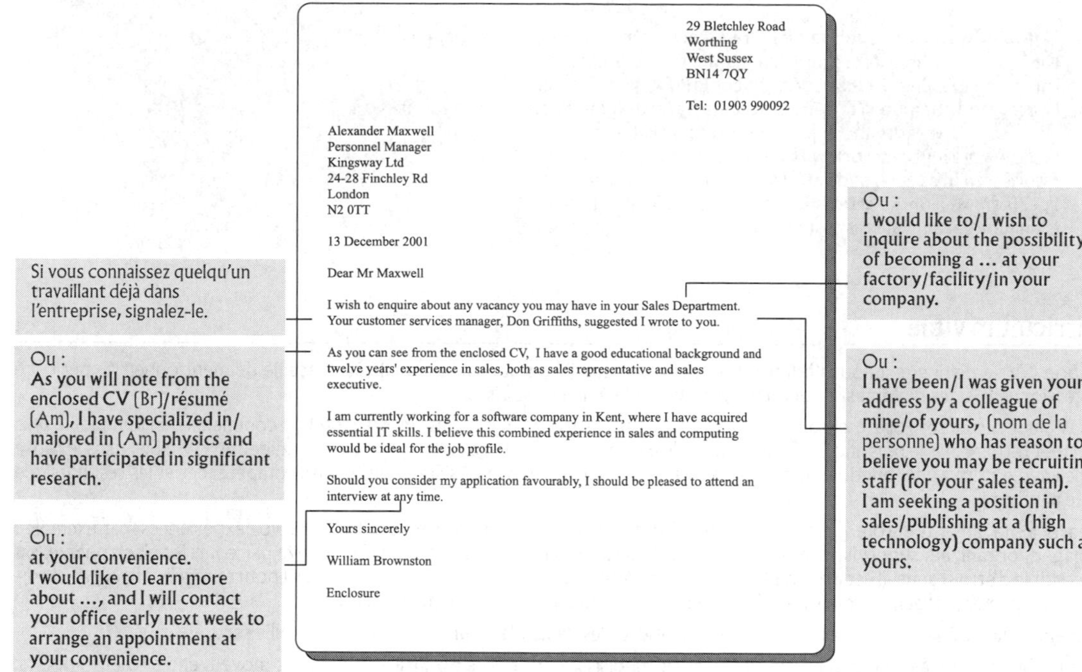

29 Bletchley Road
Worthing
West Sussex
BN14 7QY

Tel: 01903 990092

Alexander Maxwell
Personnel Manager
Kingsway Ltd
24-28 Finchley Rd
London
N2 0TT

13 December 2001

Dear Mr Maxwell

I wish to enquire about any vacancy you may have in your Sales Department. Your customer services manager, Don Griffiths, suggested I wrote to you.

As you can see from the enclosed CV, I have a good educational background and twelve years' experience in sales, both as sales representative and sales executive.

I am currently working for a software company in Kent, where I have acquired essential IT skills. I believe this combined experience in sales and computing would be ideal for the job profile.

Should you consider my application favourably, I should be pleased to attend an interview at any time.

Yours sincerely

William Brownston

Enclosure

Si vous connaissez quelqu'un travaillant déjà dans l'entreprise, signalez-le.

Ou :
As you will note from the enclosed CV (Br)/résumé (Am), I have specialized in/ majored in (Am) physics and have participated in significant research.

Ou :
at your convenience.
I would like to learn more about ..., and I will contact your office early next week to arrange an appointment at your convenience.

Ou :
I would like to/I wish to inquire about the possibility of becoming a ... at your factory/facility/in your company.

Ou :
I have been/I was given your address by a colleague of mine/of yours, (nom de la personne) who has reason to believe you may be recruiting staff (for your sales team).
I am seeking a position in sales/publishing at a (high technology) company such as yours.

Réponse à une annonce

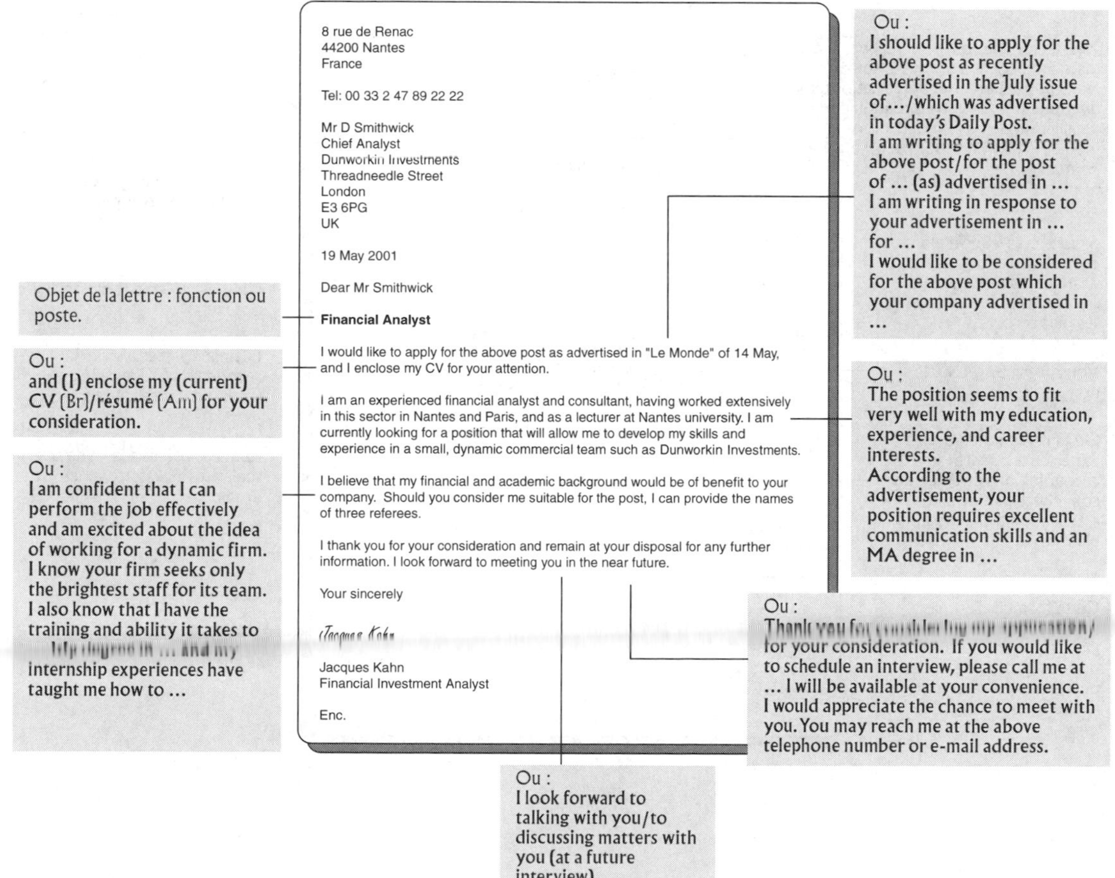

8 rue de Renac
44200 Nantes
France

Tel: 00 33 2 47 89 22 22

Mr D Smithwick
Chief Analyst
Dunworkin Investments
Threadneedle Street
London
E3 6PG
UK

19 May 2001

Dear Mr Smithwick

Financial Analyst

I would like to apply for the above post as advertised in "Le Monde" of 14 May, and I enclose my CV for your attention.

I am an experienced financial analyst and consultant, having worked extensively in this sector in Nantes and Paris, and as a lecturer at Nantes university. I am currently looking for a position that will allow me to develop my skills and experience in a small, dynamic commercial team such as Dunworkin Investments.

I believe that my financial and academic background would be of benefit to your company. Should you consider me suitable for the post, I can provide the names of three referees.

I thank you for your consideration and remain at your disposal for any further information. I look forward to meeting you in the near future.

Your sincerely

Jacques Kahn

Jacques Kahn
Financial Investment Analyst

Enc.

Objet de la lettre : fonction ou poste.

Ou :
and (I) enclose my (current) CV (Br)/résumé (Am) for your consideration.

Ou :
I am confident that I can perform the job effectively and am excited about the idea of working for a dynamic firm. I know your firm seeks only the brightest staff for its team. I also know that I have the training and ability it takes to [illegible] degree in ... and my internship experiences have taught me how to ...

Ou :
I should like to apply for the above post as recently advertised in the July issue of.../which was advertised in today's Daily Post.
I am writing to apply for the above post/for the post of ... (as) advertised in ...
I am writing in response to your advertisement in ... for ...
I would like to be considered for the above post which your company advertised in ...

Ou :
The position seems to fit very well with my education, experience, and career interests.
According to the advertisement, your position requires excellent communication skills and an MA degree in ...

Ou :
Thank you for [illegible]/ for your consideration. If you would like to schedule an interview, please call me at ... I will be available at your convenience.
I would appreciate the chance to meet with you. You may reach me at the above telephone number or e-mail address.

Ou :
I look forward to talking with you/to discussing matters with you (at a future interview).

Tournures utiles :

I know how to/I can operate a cash register/a computer/power equipment
I am computer literate/a good communicator/a good organizer
I am a capable linguist/can speak fluent English and German
I have good computer/IT/language/editing/communication/organizational skills
I can learn new tasks and enjoy/can accept a challenge
I enjoy working/can work with a variety of people
I work well in a team, and can also work under pressure
I perform well under stress/am good with difficult customers
I can handle multiple tasks simultaneously

Curriculum vitae

Un bon CV se distingue aujourd'hui par sa concision (deux pages au maximum). Il est conseillé de mentionner l'expérience professionnelle et les diplômes en fonction du poste et de l'entreprise visés.

Le CV peut respecter l'ordre chronologique ou adopter l'ordre chronologique inversé, où l'on commence par l'emploi le plus récent et termine par le plus ancien. Ce format est le plus courant. Il est également possible de rédiger un CV ciblé, dans le cadre d'une candidature à une fonction ou à un secteur professionnel précis, en insistant plus sur les compétences et les résultats que sur le parcours.

Les articles (**a**, **an** et **the**) sont généralement omis. Vous pouvez utiliser des verbes pour décrire vos expériences, par exemple : **managed, organized, supervised, designed, co-ordinated, developed**, etc. Dans un CV envoyé par courrier électronique, ou susceptible d'être scanné, il est préférable d'utiliser des substantifs et des mots clés que le logiciel pourra reconnaître, par exemple : **management, organization, supervision, design, co-ordination, development of**, etc.

Ne mentionnez pas les références sur le CV. Si l'employeur les demande, imprimez-les sur une feuille séparée.

Si vous envoyez votre CV par courrier électronique, choisissez une police ordinaire et un corps moyen, entre 10 et 14 points. N'insérez pas de tableaux ni de graphiques et évitez d'utiliser des caractères italiques ou soulignés.

▪ Diplômé anglais ayant une première expérience

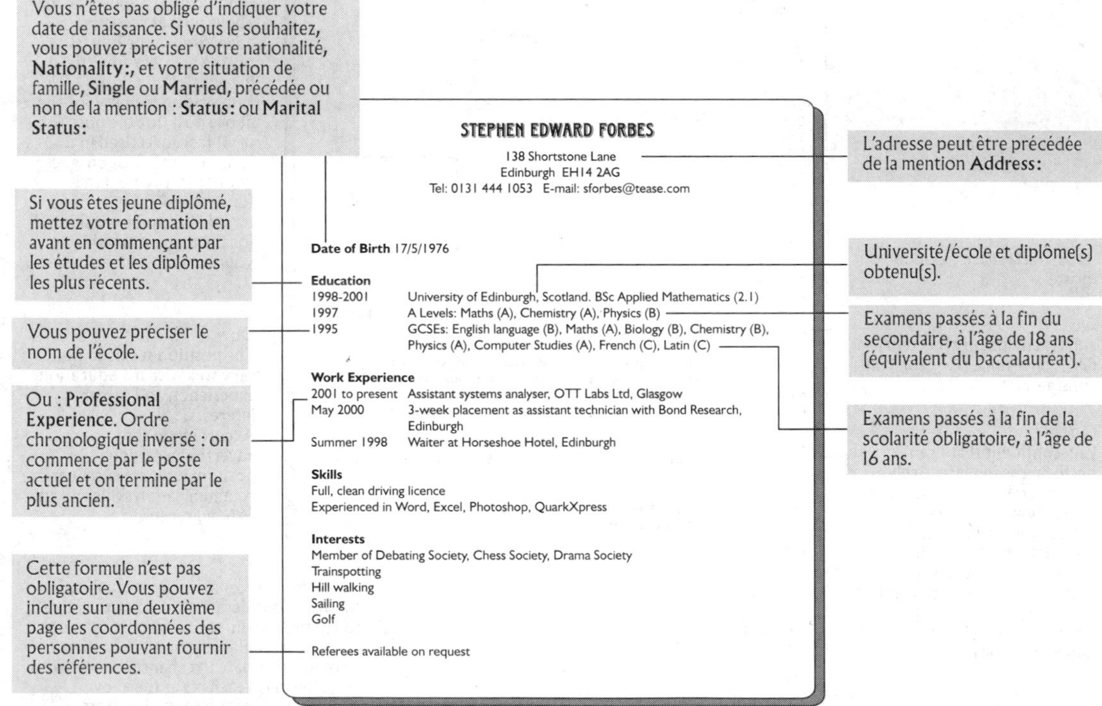

Vous n'êtes pas obligé d'indiquer votre date de naissance. Si vous le souhaitez, vous pouvez préciser votre nationalité, **Nationality:**, et votre situation de famille, **Single** ou **Married**, précédée ou non de la mention : **Status:** ou **Marital Status:**

STEPHEN EDWARD FORBES
138 Shortstone Lane
Edinburgh EH14 2AG
Tel: 0131 444 1053 E-mail: sforbes@tease.com

L'adresse peut être précédée de la mention **Address:**

Date of Birth 17/5/1976

Si vous êtes jeune diplômé, mettez votre formation en avant en commençant par les études et les diplômes les plus récents.

Education

1998-2001	University of Edinburgh, Scotland. BSc Applied Mathematics (2.1)
1997	A Levels: Maths (A), Chemistry (A), Physics (B)
1995	GCSEs: English language (B), Maths (A), Biology (B), Chemistry (B), Physics (A), Computer Studies (A), French (C), Latin (C)

Université/école et diplôme(s) obtenu(s).

Vous pouvez préciser le nom de l'école.

Examens passés à la fin du secondaire, à l'âge de 18 ans (équivalent du baccalauréat).

Examens passés à la fin de la scolarité obligatoire, à l'âge de 16 ans.

Work Experience

2001 to present	Assistant systems analyser, OTT Labs Ltd, Glasgow
May 2000	3-week placement as assistant technician with Bond Research, Edinburgh
Summer 1998	Waiter at Horseshoe Hotel, Edinburgh

Ou : **Professional Experience**. Ordre chronologique inversé : on commence par le poste actuel et on termine par le plus ancien.

Skills
Full, clean driving licence
Experienced in Word, Excel, Photoshop, QuarkXpress

Interests
Member of Debating Society, Chess Society, Drama Society
Trainspotting
Hill walking
Sailing
Golf

Referees available on request

Cette formule n'est pas obligatoire. Vous pouvez inclure sur une deuxième page les coordonnées des personnes pouvant fournir des références.

- Cadre anglais

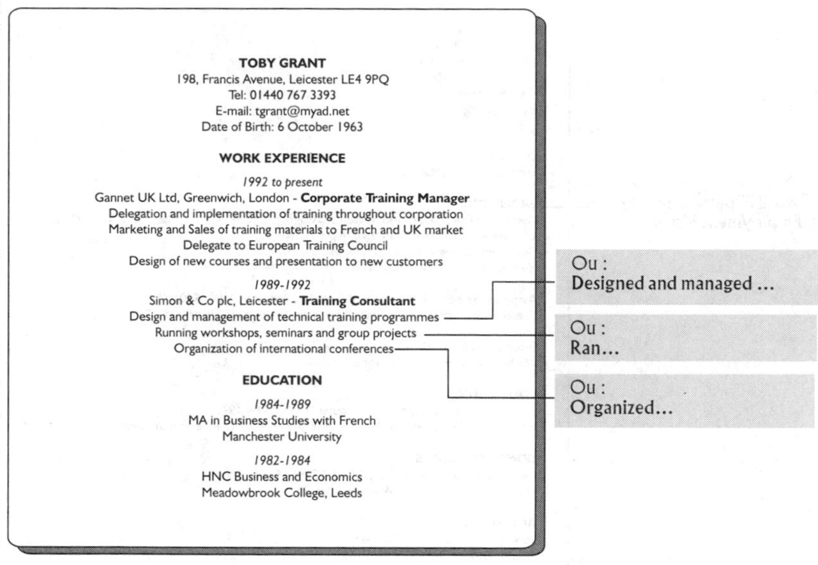

TOBY GRANT
198, Francis Avenue, Leicester LE4 9PQ
Tel: 01440 767 3393
E-mail: tgrant@myad.net
Date of Birth: 6 October 1963

WORK EXPERIENCE

1992 to present
Gannet UK Ltd, Greenwich, London - **Corporate Training Manager**
Delegation and implementation of training throughout corporation
Marketing and Sales of training materials to French and UK market
Delegate to European Training Council
Design of new courses and presentation to new customers

1989-1992
Simon & Co plc, Leicester - **Training Consultant**
Design and management of technical training programmes
Running workshops, seminars and group projects
Organization of international conferences

EDUCATION

1984-1989
MA in Business Studies with French
Manchester University

1982-1984
HNC Business and Economics
Meadowbrook College, Leeds

Ou :
Designed and managed ...

Ou :
Ran...

Ou :
Organized...

- Diplômé américain ayant une première expérience

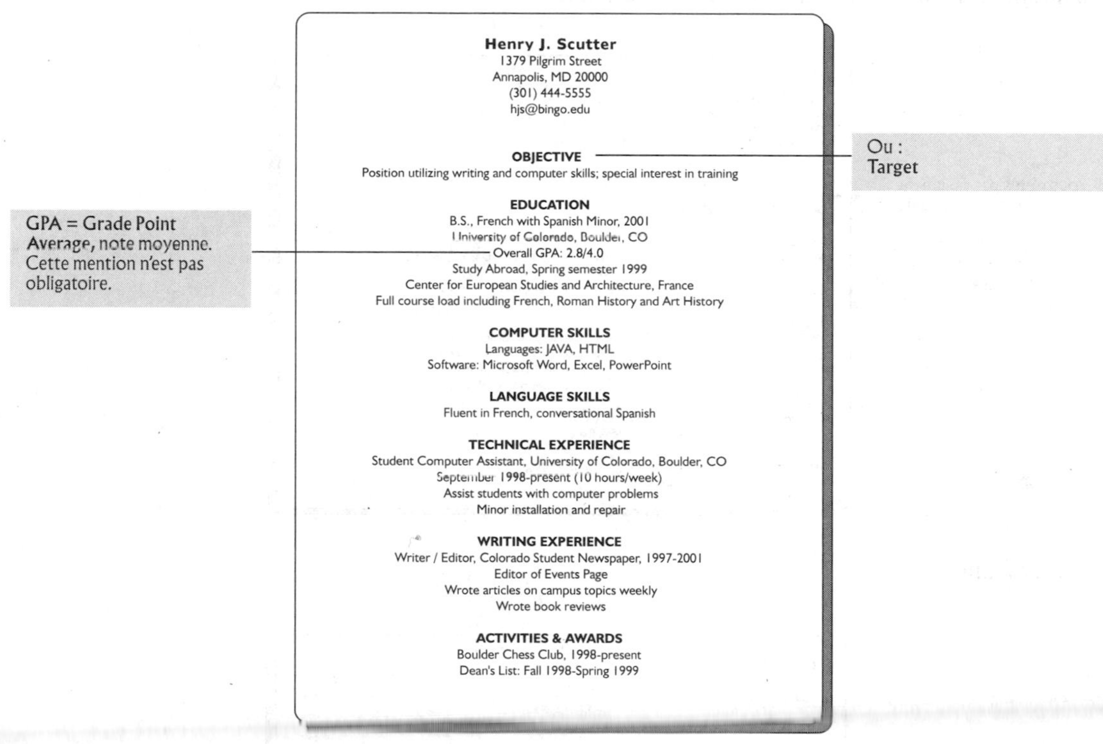

Henry J. Scutter
1379 Pilgrim Street
Annapolis, MD 20000
(301) 444-5555
hjs@bingo.edu

OBJECTIVE
Position utilizing writing and computer skills; special interest in training

EDUCATION
B.S., French with Spanish Minor, 2001
University of Colorado, Boulder, CO
Overall GPA: 2.8/4.0
Study Abroad, Spring semester 1999
Center for European Studies and Architecture, France
Full course load including French, Roman History and Art History

COMPUTER SKILLS
Languages: JAVA, HTML
Software: Microsoft Word, Excel, PowerPoint

LANGUAGE SKILLS
Fluent in French, conversational Spanish

TECHNICAL EXPERIENCE
Student Computer Assistant, University of Colorado, Boulder, CO
September 1998-present (10 hours/week)
Assist students with computer problems
Minor installation and repair

WRITING EXPERIENCE
Writer / Editor, Colorado Student Newspaper, 1997-2001
Editor of Events Page
Wrote articles on campus topics weekly
Wrote book reviews

ACTIVITIES & AWARDS
Boulder Chess Club, 1998-present
Dean's List: Fall 1998-Spring 1999

Ou :
Target

GPA = Grade Point Average, note moyenne. Cette mention n'est pas obligatoire.

▪ Cadre américain

Ou :
Work Experience
Employment history

JESSICA O'GARA
725 Boulder Henry Dr.,
Blacksburg, VA 24060
(540) 961-6666
jogara@vt.edu

OBJECTIVE
Product Designer/Manager

EXPERIENCE
Computer Consultant and Systems Designer, Systems Go Inc, Blacksburg, VA, 1994-present
Troubleshoot hardware and software problems
Design and test new operating systems
Head up large team of consultants

Assistant Systems Consultant, Benson Inc, Redmond, WA, 1990-1994
Created Web pages and customized computer systems for clients in the Redmond area

Intern, JCN Corp., Redmond, WA, June-August 1990
Worked as software design engineer intern.

EDUCATION
Bachelor of Science Degree in Computer Science, May 1990
Virginia Polytechnic Institute & State University (Virginia Tech), Blacksburg, VA

Il n'est pas nécessaire de développer cette section lorsque l'accent est mis sur l'expérience professionnelle.

COMPUTER SKILLS
Languagues and Software : B, CC, Java, HTML, Excel, Word
Operating Systems : Unix, Windows, Mac OS

ACTIVITIES
Society of Manufacturing Engineers
Aircraft Owners and Pilots Association

▪ Diplômé français ayant une première expérience

Vous n'êtes pas obligé de préciser votre nationalité ou votre âge. Ces informations, tout comme la situation de famille, sont souvent omises.

Isabelle Murat
40, impasse de la Colline
75003 Paris
Tel: (00 33) (0)1 40 30 40 40
E-mail: imurat@ubet.fr

Nationality French
Date of Birth 13/2/1980

Professional Experience

April/May 2000	Three-month placement at Cabinet Desmoulin, Paris Customer Services
Summer 1999	Organiser in school summer camp, Port-de-Bouc

Education

1998-2000	Ecole Technique Supérieure, Bordeaux Three-year diploma course in Civil Engineering
1997-1998	Baccalauréat S (equivalent A Levels) in: Maths, Physics, Chemistry, Biology, French, English, Geography, History

Languages	French, English (fluent) German, Greek (basic)
Interests	Horse-riding, mountaineering Opera singing

▪ Cadre français

Laurent Marie
25, rue des Arquebusiers
76000 Rouen
Tel: 02 24 24 45 73
E-mail: mariel@battisto.com.fr

Human Resources Consultant

Work Experience

1991 - present	Human Resources Consultant, Cabinet Battisto-Langlade, Rouen Advising companies on accounting, recruitment strategies
1987 - 1990	Personnel Manager, Conseil général, Le Havre Recruiting, planning of training programmes, staff follow-up
1985 - 1986	Assistant to Personnel Manager, Société Pierre et Fils, Le Havre

Education

1983	Master of Business Administration, Boston University
1981 - 1982	DEA 'Langage et Médias' - Paris X
1980	Master's Degree in History - Paris IV
1976	Baccalauréat (equivalent A Levels), specialising in Maths, Académie de Paris.

Other Experience
Year spent in Africa (1984/5) as part of a mission with the voluntary medical aid organisation, "Médecins sans frontières"
Member of a voluntary association promoting adult literacy

Languages Fluent English and Spanish

Computer Skills Mac OS, Word, Excel

Abréviations et acronymes utilisés dans la correspondance générale

a/c	account (compte)
ack.	acknowledge
add.	addendum (addenda)
AGM	annual general meeting (assemblée générale annuelle)
am, a.m.	ante meridiem, morning (du matin)
AOB	any other business (questions diverses)
approx.	approximately (approximativement)
APR	annual percentage rate (taux effectif global)
asap, a.s.a.p.	as soon as possible (dès que possible)
av.	average (moyenne)
bal.	balance (solde)
b/d	banker's draft (chèque bancaire)
bc., bcc.	blind (carbon) copy (copie cachée d'une note de service, d'une lettre)
b/e	bill of exchange (lettre de change)
bk	bank; book (banque; livre)
bkcy, bkpt	bankruptcy, bankrupt (faillite, en faillite)
B/L, bl	bill of lading (connaissement)
b/s	bill of sale (acte de vente, contrat de vente)
BST	British Summer Time (heure d'été en Grande-Bretagne)
c.	circa (environ)
CB	cash book (livre de caisse)
cc	carbon copy (copie à)
CEO	chief executive officer (PDG)
CET	Central European Time (heure de l'Europe centrale)
CFO	chief financial officer (chef comptable)
chq	cheque (chèque)
c.i.f., CIF	cost, insurance, freight (coût, assurance et fret)
C/O	care of; carried over; cash order (aux bons soins de; reporté; ordre au comptant)
Co	company; county (entreprise; comté)
COD	cash on delivery (paiement à la livraison)
Conf	confirm; conference (confirmez; conférence)
contd, cont'd	continued (suite)
CV	curriculum vitae
DD	direct debit (prélèvement automatique)
del.	delivery; delivered (livraison; livré)
Dir	director (directeur)
Dr	Doctor (docteur, médecin)
E&OE	errors and omissions excepted (sauf erreur ou omission)
eg	for example (par exemple)
EGM	extraordinary general meeting (assemblée générale extraordinaire)
enc(s)	enclosure(s) (pièce(s) jointe(s))
ETA	estimated time of arrival (heure d'arrivée prévue)
FAO	for the attention of (à l'attention de)
ff	following (suite à)
HM	His/Her Majesty (eg: HMC = Her Majesty's Customs) (Sa Majesté le Roi/la Reine)
ie, i.e.	in other words (c'est-à-dire)
Inc., Incorp	incorporated (SA)
incl.	included, including (joint(e), y compris)
infm., info	information
inst	of this month (courant, de ce mois)
L/C	letter of credit (lettre de crédit)
Ltd	limited company (SARL)
MD	managing director (PDG)
mgr.	manager (directeur, dirigeant, responsable)
mtg.	meeting (réunion)
NB	nota bene
OD	overdraft (découvert, solde débiteur)
OHP	overhead projector (rétroprojecteur)
ono	or nearest offer (prix à débattre)
p.a.	per annum (par an)
p&p	postage and packing (frais d'emballage et d'expédition)
PAYE	pay as you earn (retenue de l'impôt sur le revenu à la base ou à la source)
P/L	profit and loss (pertes et profits)
PLC	public limited company (SA)
pm, p.m.	post meridiem (de l'après-midi/du soir)
p.o.	postal order (mandat postal)
pp	post procurationem, on behalf of (au nom de)
pps	additonal postscript (post postscriptum)
Pres.	president
Prof.	professor
ps	postscript (postscriptum)
PTO	please turn over (tournez la page svp)
rc'd	received (reçu)
re	with reference to (objet, à propos de, en référence à)
Ref	reference (référence)
req, reqd	required (requis)
retd	retired (retraité)
sae	stamped addressed envelope (enveloppe timbrée)
sase	self-addressed stamped envelope (enveloppe timbrée à son propre nom)
SO	standing order (virement automatique)
tbc	to be confirmed (à confirmer)
ult.	ultimo, last (dernier)
viz	namely (à savoir, c'est-à-dire)
VP	vice-president
yf	Yours faithfully (cordialement)
ys	Yours sincerely (cordialement)

COMMUNICATION EN ANGLAIS

La télécopie

Quelques conseils pour la rédaction de documents transmis par télécopieur ou fax :

- Ne mentionnez que les informations essentielles.
- Vous pouvez adopter un style télégraphique et utiliser des abréviations et des acronymes pour remplacer des mots, voire des expressions entières. Seules les abréviations reconnues doivent être employées (voir p. 55)
- Veillez au ton général du message : les messages courts et factuels peuvent sembler froids. Il est donc conseillé de terminer par une formule de politesse amicale, telle que "Best Wishes".

Dans une entreprise

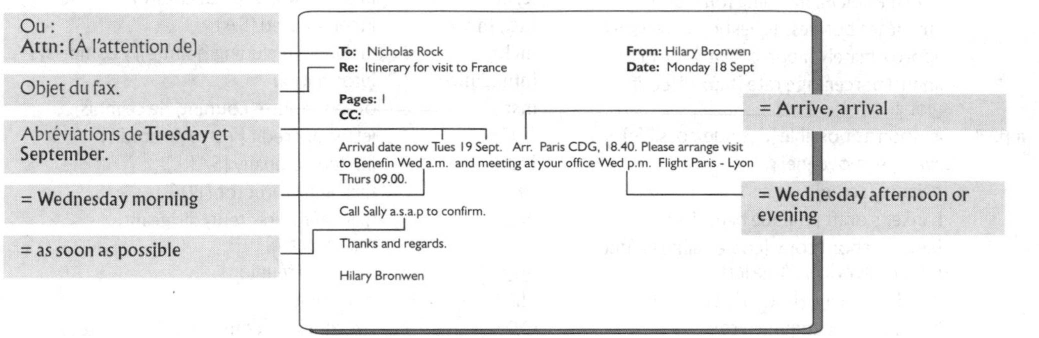

To: Nicholas Rock **From:** Hilary Bronwen
Re: Itinerary for visit to France **Date:** Monday 18 Sept
Pages: 1
CC:

Arrival date now Tues 19 Sept. Arr. Paris CDG, 18.40. Please arrange visit to Benefin Wed a.m. and meeting at your office Wed p.m. Flight Paris - Lyon Thurs 09.00.

Call Sally a.s.a.p to confirm.

Thanks and regards.

Hilary Bronwen

Pour confirmer une réservation

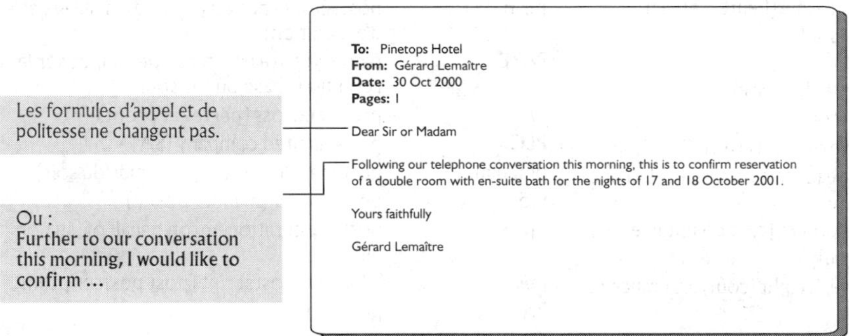

To: Pinetops Hotel
From: Gérard Lemaître
Date: 30 Oct 2000
Pages: 1

Dear Sir or Madam

Following our telephone conversation this morning, this is to confirm reservation of a double room with en-suite bath for the nights of 17 and 18 October 2001.

Yours faithfully

Gérard Lemaître

Les formules d'appel et de politesse ne changent pas.
Ou :
Further to our conversation this morning, I would like to confirm ...

Le courrier électronique

Le courrier électronique étant un moyen de communication rapide, le style des messages est souvent familier et télégraphique et l'emploi des abréviations et des acronymes est très courant. Selon la netiquette, ou code de conduite sur le réseau, il est déconseillé d'écrire un message tout en majuscules car cela pourrait être interprété comme un signe de mauvaise humeur.

Les formules d'appel traditionnelles (**Dear ...**) sont généralement omises. Si vous connaissez bien votre correspondant, vous pouvez commencer par une formule familière telle que **Hello** ou **Hi**, suivie du prénom de la personne.

Message interne

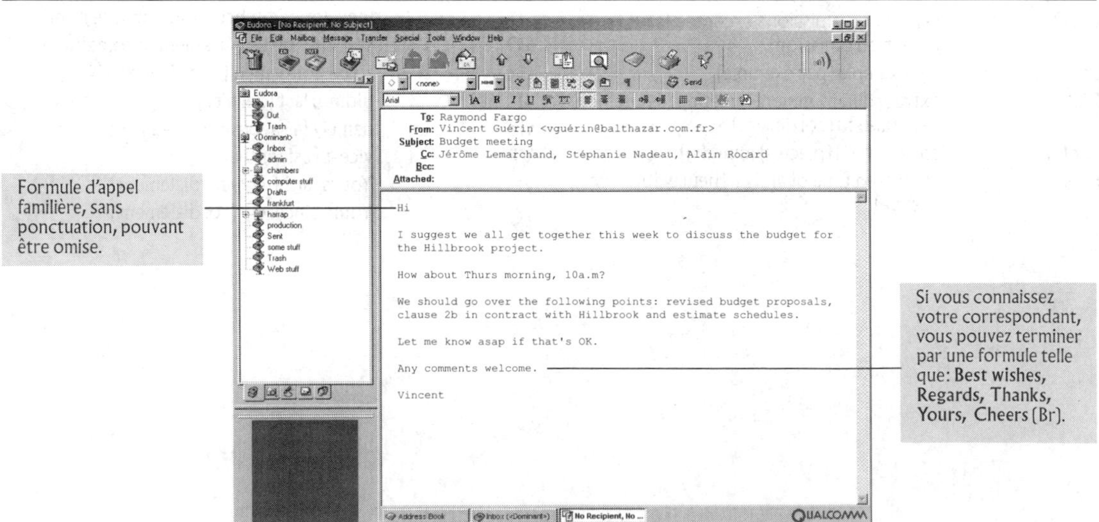

To: Raymond Fargo
From: Vincent Guérin <vguérin@balthazar.com.fr>
Subject: Budget meeting
Cc: Jérôme Lemarchand, Stéphanie Nadeau, Alain Rocard
Bcc:
Attached:

Hi

I suggest we all get together this week to discuss the budget for the Hillbrook project.

How about Thurs morning, 10a.m?

We should go over the following points: revised budget proposals, clause 2b in contract with Hillbrook and estimate schedules.

Let me know asap if that's OK.

Any comments welcome.

Vincent

Eudora - [No Recipient, No Subject]
Formule d'appel familière, sans ponctuation, pouvant être omise.
Si vous connaissez votre correspondant, vous pouvez terminer par une formule telle que: Best wishes, Regards, Thanks, Yours, Cheers (Br).
QUALCOMM

Message d'une entreprise à une autre

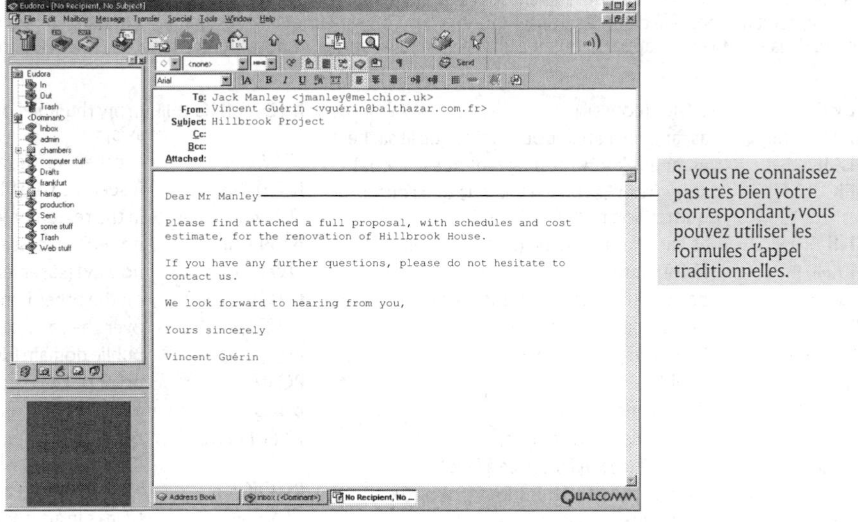

To: Jack Manley <jmanley@melchior.uk>
From: Vincent Guérin <vguérin@balthazar.com.fr>
Subject: Hillbrook Project
Cc:
Bcc:
Attached:
Dear Mr Manley
Please find attached a full proposal, with schedules and cost estimate, for the renovation of Hillbrook House.
If you have any further questions, please do not hesitate to contact us.
We look forward to hearing from you,
Yours sincerely
Vincent Guérin

Si vous ne connaissez pas très bien votre correspondant, vous pouvez utiliser les formules d'appel traditionnelles.

Réservation

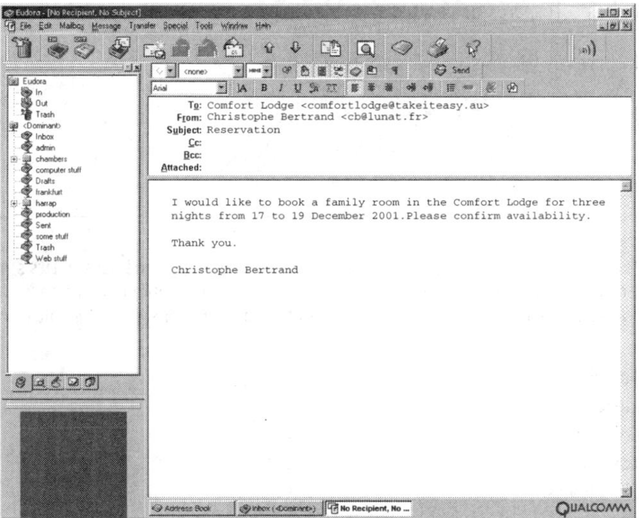

To: Comfort Lodge <comfortlodge@takeiteasy.au>
From: Christophe Bertrand <cb@lunat.fr>
Subject: Reservation
Cc:
Bcc:
Attached:
I would like to book a family room in the Comfort Lodge for three nights from 17 to 19 December 2001.Please confirm availability.
Thank you.
Christophe Bertrand

Message au fournisseur d'accès

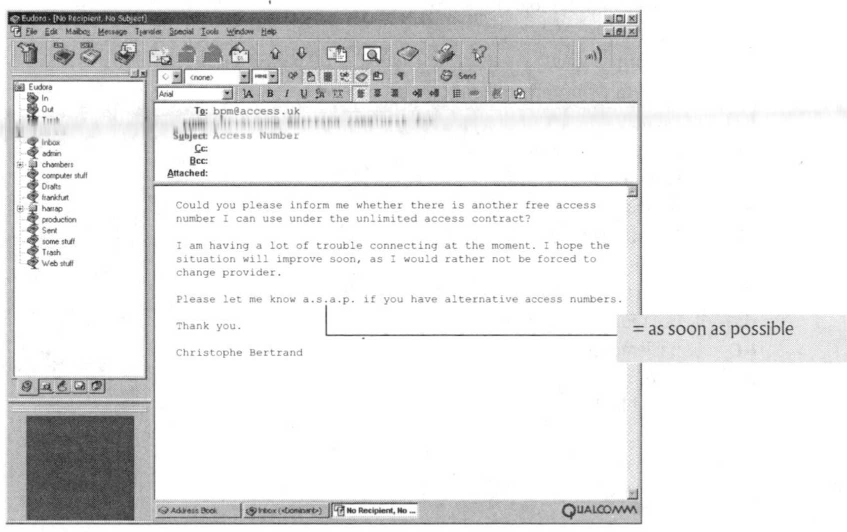

To: bpm@access.uk
Subject: Access Number
Cc:
Bcc:
Attached:
Could you please inform me whether there is another free access number I can use under the unlimited access contract?
I am having a lot of trouble connecting at the moment. I hope the situation will improve soon, as I would rather not be forced to change provider.
Please let me know a.s.a.p. if you have alternative access numbers.
Thank you.
Christophe Bertrand

= as soon as possible

Abréviations utilisées dans le courier électronique et les forums

Les abréviations et acronymes qui suivent sont couramment employés dans le courrier électronique et les forums de discussion. Il est cependant conseillé de ne les utiliser que lorsque l'on est sûr que le destinataire connaît leur signification. Les abréviations suivies de la mention *Fam* appartiennent à un registre plus familier et doivent être réservées à une correspondance plus relâchée.

Adv	advice (conseil)
AFAICT *Fam*	as far as I can tell (pour autant que je sache)
AFAIK *Fam*	as far as I know (pour autant que je sache)
AFK	away from keyboard (indique que l'on va quitter son poste)
AIUI *Fam*	as far as I understand (si j'ai bien compris)
B4 *Fam*	before (avant)
BAK	back at keyboard (de retour devant l'écran)
BBL *Fam*	be back later (je reviens)
BTW *Fam*	by the way (à propos)
cld	could
Doc	document
EOF	end of file (fin de fichier)
F2F *Fam*	face to face (en face, face à face)
FAQ	frequently asked questions (foire aux questions)
FOC	free of charge (gratuit, gratuitement)
Foll	following, to follow (suivant, à suivre)
FYI	for your information (pour ton information)
HTH *Fam*	hope this helps (j'espère que cela te sera utile)
IIRC *Fam*	if I recall correctly (si mes souvenirs sont bons)
IMO, IMHO *Fam*	in my (humble) opinion (à mon (humble) avis)
IOW *Fam*	in other words (autrement dit)
ISTM *Fam*	it seems to me (il me semble que)
ITRO *Fam*	in the region of (environ)
NRN *Fam*	no reply necessasry (réponse facultative)
NW! *Fam*	no way! (sûrement pas!)
OTOH *Fam*	on the other hand (d'un autre côté)
OTT *Fam*	over the top (excessif)
PD	public domain (domaine public)
POV	point of view (point de vue)
prhps	perhaps (peut-être)
RTFM *très Fam*	read the f***ing manual (regarde dans le manuel, nom de Dieu!)
RUOK *Fam*	are you OK? (ça va?)
TIA *Fam*	thanks in advance (merci d'avance)
TNX *Fam*	thanks (merci)
TVM *Fam*	thanks very much (merci beaucoup)
VR	virtual reality (réalité virtuelle)
WRT *Fam*	with regard to (en ce qui concerne)
urgt	urgent

Émoticons

Les habitués du réseau ont souvent recours aux émoticons pour nuancer leurs propos. Ces petits symboles obtenus à l'aide des caractères du clavier forment un visage que l'on découvre en penchant la tête à gauche. Comme les abréviations, les émoticons doivent être réservés à la correspondance amicale. Quelques exemples d'émoticons, parmi les plus courants :

:-)	joie ; ironie
:-))	grande joie
:-D	éclats de rire
:-(	tristesse ; désaccord
:-((	grande tristesse
:'-(	pleurs
:-ıı	colère
:-C	grande colère
:-O	surprise ; choc
;-)	clin d'œil
:-ı	froncement de sourcils
(:-)	chauve
:-)›	barbu
:-)X	porteur de nœud papillon
3:-)	vache
8-)	porteur de lunettes
ı-)	sommeil
:-i	fumeur
:-?	fumeur de pipe
:-\	doute
Cı:-)	porteur de chapeau melon
d:-)	porteur de casquette
ı-O	bâillements
:-*	bise
*‹ :-)	père Noël

Les petites annonces

Il peut être difficile de lire une annonce dans une langue étrangère lorsqu'on ne connaît pas les abréviations employées. Vous trouverez dans les exemples et les listes qui suivent les formes abrégées les plus couramment utilisées dans les petites annonces.

Emploi

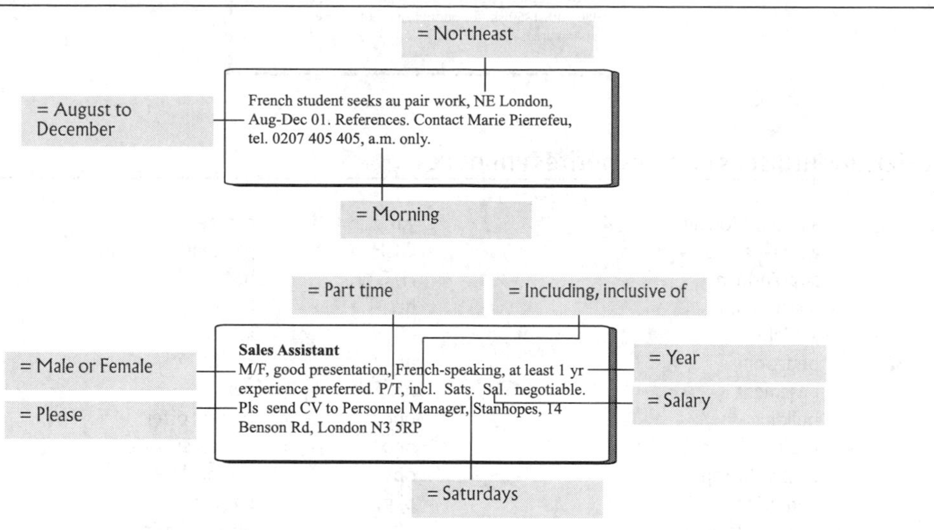

= Northeast
= August to December
French student seeks au pair work, NE London, Aug-Dec 01. References. Contact Marie Pierrefeu, tel. 0207 405 405, a.m. only.
= Morning
= Part time
= Including, inclusive of
= Male or Female
= Please
Sales Assistant
M/F, good presentation, French-speaking, at least 1 yr experience preferred. P/T, incl. Sats. Sal. negotiable. Pls send CV to Personnel Manager, Stanhopes, 14 Benson Rd, London N3 5RP
= Year
= Salary
= Saturdays

Vente

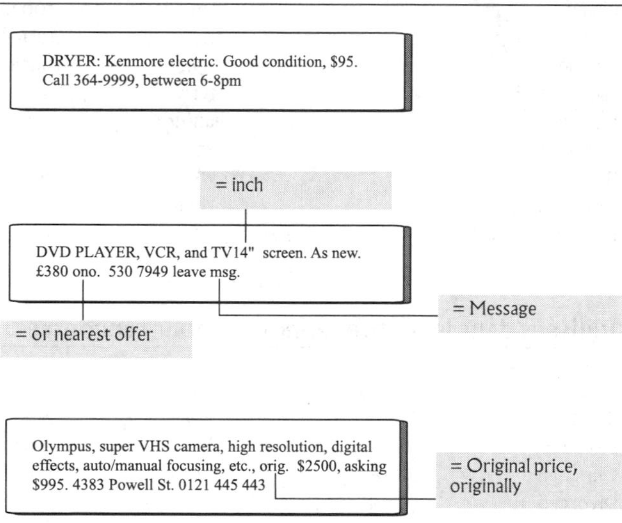

DRYER: Kenmore electric. Good condition, $95. Call 364-9999, between 6-8pm
= inch
DVD PLAYER, VCR, and TV14" screen. As new. £380 ono. 530 7949 leave msg.
= Message
= or nearest offer
Olympus, super VHS camera, high resolution, digital effects, auto/manual focusing, etc., orig. $2500, asking $995. 4383 Powell St. 0121 445 443
= Original price, originally

Immobilier

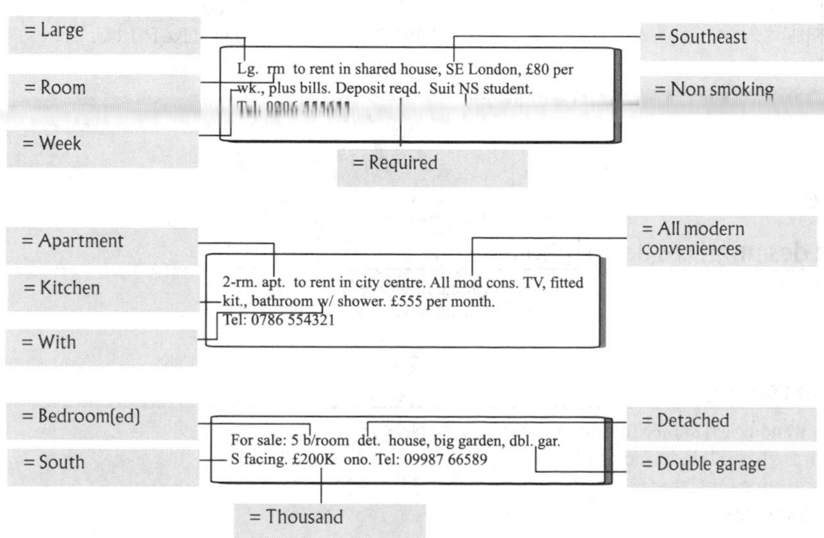

= Large
= Room
= Week
Lg. rm to rent in shared house, SE London, £80 per wk., plus bills. Deposit reqd. Suit NS student.
= Southeast
= Non smoking
= Required
= Apartment
= Kitchen
= With
2-rm. apt. to rent in city centre. All mod cons. TV, fitted kit., bathroom w/ shower. £555 per month. Tel: 0786 554321
= All modern conveniences
= Bedroom(ed)
= South
For sale: 5 b/room det. house, big garden, dbl. gar. S facing. £200K ono. Tel: 09987 66589
= Detached
= Double garage
= Thousand

Rencontres

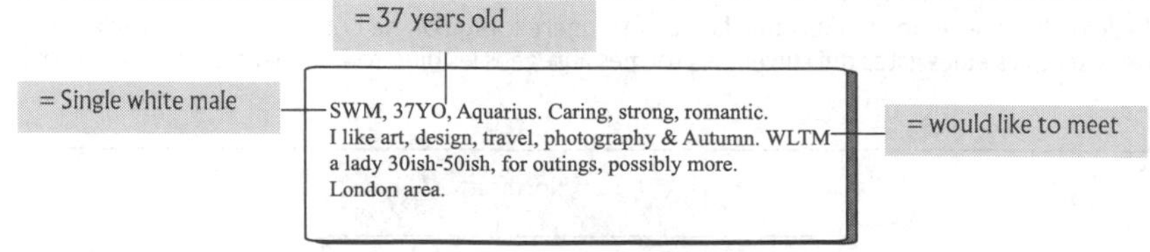

= 37 years old
= Single white male
SWM, 37YO, Aquarius. Caring, strong, romantic.
I like art, design, travel, photography & Autumn. WLTM
a lady 30ish-50ish, for outings, possibly more.
London area.
= would like to meet

Abréviations utilisées dans les petites annonces

AC	air conditioning	gar.	garage
adj.	adjoining	GCH	gas central heating
appt.	appointment	H/CW	hot/cold water
apt.	apartment	hr.	hour
avail.	available	kit.	kitchen
bedrm., BR	bedroom	m.	month
bsmt.	basement	nr.	near
bldg.	building	obo	or best offer
bus.	business	ono	or nearest offer
c/h	central heating	opt.	optional
cond.	condition	pkg.	parking
del.	deliver; delivery	PR	public relations
det.	detached	ref.	reference
din.	dining	rm.	room
dr.	door	sal.	salary
dbl.	double	sgl.	single
ea.	each	terr.	terrace
elec.	electric	unfurn.	unfurnished
exch.	exchange	vac.	vacancy
fl.	floor	wk.	week
ft.	foot, feet	wpm	words per minute
furn.	furniture, furnished	yr	year

Abréviations ulilisées dans les petites annonces pour rencontres

A	Asian	NBM	Never Been Married
B	Black	ND	Non Drinker
Bi	Bisexual	NS	Non Smoker
C	Christian	P	Professional
D	Divorced	S	Single
F	Female	SD	Social Drinker
G	Gay	SI	Similar Interests
GSOH	Good Sense of Humour	SOH	Sense of Humour
H	Hispanic	W	White
ISO	In Search Of	W/	With
LTR	Long Term Relationship	Wi	Widowed
M	Male	WLTM	Would Like To Meet
NA	Native American	YO	Years Old

Le téléphone

Prononciation des numéros de téléphone

20995 — Two oh double nine five (Br)
Two zero double nine five (Am)

Pour obtenir un renseignement

- Can I have directory enquiries (Br) *or* directory assistance (Am) please?
- I'm trying to get through to a London number.
- What is the (country) code for Canada?
- How do I get an outside line?

Pour demander un interlocuteur

Hello,
- could I speak to ...?
- can I speak to ...?
- I'd like to speak to ...
- (could I have) extension 593 please?

Pour répondre à un appel

- Robert McQueen speaking, can I help you?
- Hello, this is ...
- Yes, speaking (pour confirmer que l'on est bien la personne demandée)
- Hold on/hold please, I'll (just) get him/her.
- I'm sorry, he's/she's not here. Can I take a message?
- I'm afraid he's away on business/out of the office/off sick/on holiday/on vacation (Am)

Pour laisser un message

Sur un répondeur :

- I'm returning your call.
- I'll be in London next week, perhaps we can ...
- I'd like to talk to you about ...
- Could you call me back, so we can discuss ...?

À une autre personne :

- Could you ask him/her to call me on ...?
- Could you tell him/her I won't be able to ...?
- I'll call back later.
- I need to speak to him/her urgently.
- Please ask him/her to confirm. Thank you.

Pour demander une confirmation

- Could you spell that please?
- Could you speak a bit more slowly please?
- I'm sorry I didn't catch that. Could you repeat that please?
- Let me check, 11 a.m. Wednesday 10th. Yes, that's fine.

Pour conclure un appel

- Thank you, I look forward to seeing you on Wednesday. Goodbye.
- Thank you for your help.

Message de répondeur téléphonique

- We are unable to take your call at the moment/I am not here at the moment. Please leave a message after the tone.

Allusions anglaises

L'une des innovations de ce dictionnaire est la présence de notes explicatives portant sur les allusions. On entend par allusion toute expression dont les connotations et le référent sont évidents pour tous les gens d'une même culture. Les expressions allusives proviennent de la culture classique ou populaire, de la littérature ou encore de la publicité. Les notes explicatives doivent permettre à l'utilisateur de comprendre des expressions a priori impénétrables utilisées dans l'autre langue. Dans chaque cas, la note explicative éclaire le lecteur sur l'origine de l'expression et la façon dont on l'emploie. Ont été sélectionnées les expressions les plus courantes et les plus intéressantes. Les allusions qui figurent dans le corps du dictionnaire ont été regroupées ci-après pour en faciliter la consultation.

ALONE
I want to be alone
Il s'agit d'une phrase prononcée par Greta Garbo dans le film *Grand Hotel* ("Grand Hôtel") (1932), qui évoque immanquablement la célèbre actrice.

On prononce cette phrase avec l'accent scandinave, en référence à Greta Garbo et souvent par dérision, lorsque quelqu'un annonce qu'il désire qu'on le laisse seul de façon quelque peu théâtrale.

AMUSE
We are not amused
Cette expression fait allusion à une réflexion qu'aurait faite la reine Victoria pour marquer sa désapprobation, après avoir entendu une histoire osée de la bouche d'un de ses courtisans.

De nos jours, il est courant de l'employer en réponse à quelqu'un qui a fait une remarque qu'on ne trouve pas drôle ou qu'on juge malvenue.

ANGRY
Angry Young Men
Il s'agit du nom qui fut donné à un groupe de jeunes auteurs britanniques dans les années 50 parmi lesquels figuraient John Osborne, John Arden, Alan Sillitoe et Kingsley Amis. "Les Jeunes Gens en colère" explorèrent le thème de l'aliénation sociale et s'insurgèrent contre les valeurs et le conformisme de la société anglaise de l'époque.

Aujourd'hui on utilise cette expression à propos de toute jeune personne exprimant des opinions radicales.

BEACH
We shall fight them on the beaches
Ces mots ("nous les combattrons sur les plages") furent prononcés par Churchill dans un de ses discours les plus fameux pendant la Deuxième Guerre mondiale, dans lequel il encourageait les Britanniques à se préparer à lutter en cas de débarquement nazi.

Aujourd'hui encore on utilise cette formule métaphoriquement pour exprimer sa volonté farouche de continuer le combat et de ne jamais s'avouer vaincu.

BECAUSE
Because it's there
Cette phrase ("parce qu'il est là") est censée être la réponse donnée par l'alpiniste britannique George Mallory lorsqu'on lui demanda pourquoi il désirait être le premier à faire l'ascension de l'Everest.

Aujourd'hui on utilise cette formule de façon allusive pour expliquer pourquoi on décide de s'atteler à une tâche particulièrement ardue.

BELL
The bells, the bells
Dans *The Hunchback of Notre-Dame*, la traduction anglaise de *Notre-Dame de Paris* de Victor Hugo, Quasimodo s'exclame "the bells, the bells!" lorsqu'il entend sonner les cloches de la cathédrale.

Pour plaisanter, il arrive que l'on prononce ces paroles en prenant une grosse voix lorsque l'on entend sonner des cloches, pour évoquer le personnage de Quasimodo.

BIG
Big brother is watching you
Cette formule ("Big Brother vous surveille") est tirée du roman de George Orwell *1984*, dans lequel Big Brother personnifie l'état tout-puissant et omniprésent.

Le terme "Big Brother" est entré dans la langue pour décrire tout état totalitaire, et l'expression **Big Brother is watching you** s'utilise souvent sur le mode humoristique à propos d'un gouvernement ou de tout autre forme d'autorité perçus comme impersonnels et envahissants.

BOLDLY
To boldly go
Il s'agit certainement du "split infinitive" le plus célèbre de la langue anglaise, présent dans la formule **to boldly go where no man has gone before** ("s'aventurer là où nul n'est jamais allé") qui figure au commencement de chaque épisode de la série américaine de science-fiction *Star Trek*, qui débuta dans les années 60.

On utilise fréquemment cette expression de façon humoristique en allusion à la série télévisée lorsque quelqu'un se lance dans une aventure dont l'issue est incertaine.

BRAVE
Brave new world
Il s'agit du titre d'un roman de science-fiction de l'écrivain anglais Aldous Huxley (publié en 1932) et d'une allusion à un vers de Shakespeare dans *La Tempête*. Il est intéressant de noter que le titre français du roman est *Le Meilleur des mondes*, une allusion au *Candide* de Voltaire.

L'expression **brave new world** s'utilise à propos de tout changement de société provoqué par les progrès de la science. On parlera par exemple de **the brave new world of genetic manipulation** ("l'ère de la manipulation génétique").

BREACH
Once more into the breach, dear friends
Cette phrase ("encore une fois sur la brèche, les amis") est extraite d'un passage de *Henry V* de Shakespeare, lorsque le roi s'adresse à ses soldats pour les encourager avant la bataille d'Azincourt.

Aujourd'hui on utilise cette phrase sur le mode humoristique lorsque l'on entreprend une tâche difficile, et souvent avant un deuxième essai.

BREAKFAST
To believe six impossible things before breakfast
Il s'agit d'une formule tirée d'un passage de l'œuvre de Lewis Carrol *Through the Looking-Glass* ("De l'autre côté du miroir") (1872), dans lequel la reine confie à Alice que lorsqu'elle avait son âge il lui arrivait de "croire jusqu'à six choses impossibles avant le petit déjeuner.

On utilise aujourd'hui cette phrase lorsque quelqu'un doit assimiler de nombreuses connaissances ou bien s'adapter à une situation radicalement nouvelle. Parfois on ne garde que la seconde partie de la phrase (**before breakfast**) lorsque quelqu'un a fait quelque chose très rapidement. Ainsi on pourra dire **They are only short novels, I used to read two of them before breakfast** ("ces romans sont très courts, il m'arrivait d'en lire deux avant le petit déjeuner").

BUTLER
The butler did it
Il s'agit de la formule consacrée des romans policiers et des pièces de théâtre du début du XXème siècle dont l'action se déroule traditionnellement dans un manoir de campagne. Le majordome y est en effet le principal suspect et bien souvent l'assassin. On utilise cette formule – que l'on peut traduire par "c'est le majordome qui a fait le coup" – pour faire allusion à ce style de récit ou bien de façon humoristique lorsqu'on essaie de deviner qui est le responsable d'une mauvaise action.

What the butler saw
A l'origine cette formule ("ce que vit le majordome") figurait sur les visionneuses à pièces installées dans les stations balnéaires anglaises et invitait le spectateur à jouer au voyeur en lui promettant des scènes osées. L'auteur dramatique Joe Orton fit de cette phrase le titre d'une de ses pièces dans les années 60.

Cette expression évoque le refoulement sexuel associé à l'époque victorienne, mais s'utilise également pour décrire une situation dans laquelle quelqu'un assiste à une scène intime à l'insu des participants ou bien a accès à des informations censées être confidentielles.

CANDID
Smile, you're on Candid Camera
Il s'agit du slogan d'une émission de télévision britannique des années 70 dont l'équivalent français est "La Caméra invisible", dans laquelle des gens étaient filmés à leur insu dans des situations cocasses. **Smile, you're on Candid Camera** ("Souriez, c'est pour la caméra invisible") était la formule utilisée par les animateurs de l'émission pour annoncer aux participants qu'ils venaient d'être filmés.

On utilise aujourd'hui cette expression de façon humoristique lorsque l'on photographie ou lorsque l'on filme quelqu'un.

CATCH-22
Cette formule provient du roman éponyme de Joseph Heller, publié en 1961, dans lequel **catch-22** est le nom donné à une situation sans issue. Pendant la deuxième guerre mondiale, un pilote de l'armée américaine essaie de trouver un prétexte pour ne pas partir en mission. Mais le règlement stipule que seul un pilote reconnu comme malade mental peut être dispensé de mission; tout pilote qui cherche à être exempté montre qu'il a conscience du danger encouru en mission, et fait par là même preuve de sa santé mentale, et doit donc continuer à voler. Autrement dit, seuls peuvent être dispensés ceux qui ne cherchent pas à l'être.

On utilise cette expression pour parler de toute situation en forme de cercle vicieux. On dira par exemple **it's a catch-22 situation, I can't get a job without experience, but I can't get experience without a job** ("c'est une situation sans issue: je ne peux pas trouver de travail sans expérience préalable, mais je ne pas acquérir d'expérience sans travail").

CEASE

It has ceased to be

Il s'agit d'une formule extraite de l'un des sketchs les plus célèbres de la troupe de comiques britannique Monty Python, dans lequel le client d'un magasin d'animaux venait se plaindre qu'on lui avait vendu un perroquet mort. Le client décrivait l'état du perroquet au vendeur en utilisant de nombreuses périphrases, dont l'une était **it has ceased to be** ("il n'est plus"). Aujourd'hui on utilise cette expression de façon humoristique pour parler de quelque chose qui n'existe plus ou qui n'a plus cours.

CHRISTMAS

It will (all) be over by Christmas

Il s'agit de la célèbre formule qui avait cours au tout début de la Première Guerre mondiale en Grande-Bretagne lorsque nombreux étaient ceux qui croyaient que la victoire contre les Allemands serait acquise avant Noël 1914.

Aujourd'hui on utilise cette phrase de manière allusive lorsqu'on estime que quelqu'un fait preuve d'un excès d'optimisme en s'imaginant que telle ou telle chose sera terminée dans les temps. On pourra dire par exemple **This project is a nightmare – Don't worry, it will all be over by Christmas** (ce projet est un vrai cauchemar – ne t'en fais pas, on aura fini d'ici Noël).

COME

Come on down!

Il s'agit de la formule consacrée du jeu télévisé *The Price is Right* (dont l'équivalent français est *Le Juste prix*) qui débuta en 1957 aux États-Unis, et dans les années 80 en Grande-Bretagne. L'animateur de l'émission prononçait ces paroles ("Descendez!") pour inviter les membres du public sélectionnés pour participer au jeu à venir le rejoindre sur la scène.

Aujourd'hui on utilise cette formule plaisamment pour dire à quelqu'un d'approcher ou bien pour indiquer à quelqu'un qui doit prononcer un discours ou se produire sur scène qu'il est temps de prendre place.

Come up and see me sometime...

Cette formule fut utilisée pour la première fois par Mae West dans le film de 1933 *She Done Him Wrong* (dont le titre français est "Lady Lou"); la citation exacte était en fait **Why don't you come up sometime, see me?** ("Pourquoi est-ce que tu ne monterais pas un de ces jours, pour me voir?"). Il s'agit de l'archétype de l'invitation au badinage. Encore aujourd'hui on utilise cette formule en imitant l'air canaille de Mae West.

CONTENDER

I could have been a contender

Il s'agit d'une formule extraite du film d'Elia Kazan de 1954 *On the Waterfront* ("Sur les quais"). C'est Terry Malloy, le personnage interprété par Marlon Brando, qui déclare en s'adressant à son frère, interprété par Rod Steiger, **I could have been a contender**" ("j'aurais pu devenir quelqu'un"). On utilise cette phrase pour exprimer une certaine mélancolie et les regrets que l'on éprouve en pensant aux occasions que l'on n'a pas su saisir.

COUNTRY

Your country needs you

Cette phrase ("la patrie vous réclame") figurait sur les affiches qui appelaient les Britanniques à s'engager dans l'armée, au début de la Première Guerre mondiale. On y voyait Lord Kitchener, ministre de la Guerre, l'index pointé vers la personne regardant l'affiche. L'idée fut reprise par les Américains avec l'Oncle Sam à la place de Lord Kitchener et le slogan **I want you** ("J'ai besoin de vous").

Aujourd'hui on utilise l'expression dans tout appel à la nation, comme dans l'exemple suivant: **Thinking about becoming a nurse? Call this number now, your country needs you** ("La carrière d'infirmière vous intéresse? Composez ce numéro dès maintenant, le pays a besoin de vous.").

CRÈME

The crème de la crème

Cette expression hyperbolique et faussement française fut popularisée par l'ouvrage de la romancière écossaise Muriel Spark *The Prime of Miss Jean Brodie* ("Le Bel Âge de Miss Brodie") (1961). Dans ce roman, Miss Brodie est institutrice à Édimbourg et elle utilise cette expression à propos de ses élèves préférées.

Aujourd'hui on utilise cette formule pour parler de ce qui se fait de mieux dans un domaine donné. On dira par exemple **the company only recruits the crème de la crème of recent graduates** ("cette entreprise ne recrute que le gratin des diplômés").

CUNNING

I have a cunning plan

La série télévisée comique *Blackadder* a été diffusée pendant de nombreuses années en Grande-Bretagne. Baldrick, qui en était l'un des personnages principaux et qui était particulièrement stupide, inventait toujours des stratagèmes qu'il présentait à son maître précédés de la formule **I have a cunning plan** ("J'ai un plan des plus ingénieux").

Aujourd'hui on utilise cette phrase sur le mode humoristique en référence à la série télévisée ou bien lorsque quelqu'un est sur le point d'expliquer un projet qu'il a conçu.

CUP

The cup that cheers

"Le breuvage qui réconforte"; il s'agit du slogan d'une vieille publicité pour une marque de thé. Aujourd'hui, on utilise cette expression pour parler du thé en général; on pourra dire par exemple **this café makes the best cup that cheers for miles around** ("ce café sert le meilleur thé à des lieux à la ronde").

CURIOUS

Curiouser and curiouser

Cette expression trouve son origine dans *Alice in Wonderland* ("Alice au pays des merveilles") de Lewis Carroll (1865), lorsqu'Alice prend conscience de l'étrangeté du pays où elle a échoué.

On utilise cette expression ("de plus en plus étrange") pour exprimer sa surprise ou sa perplexité, parfois de façon ironique comme dans l'exemple suivant: **hmmm, curiouser and curiouser, first she goes away for the weekend unexpectedly, then she gets a new hairstyle, then she keeps mentioning her "friend" Lawrence** ("tiens, c'est de plus en plus étrange, d'abord elle part en week-end sans prévenir, ensuite elle change de coiffure, et en plus elle n'arrête pas de parler de son "ami" Lawrence"). C'est sans doute parce que cette formule est grammaticalement incorrecte qu'elle a marqué les esprits (la forme correcte serait en effet **more and more curious**).

DARK

Dark Satanic mills

Cette formule ("Les sombres et diaboliques usines") est tirée du cantique *Jerusalem*, inspiré d'un poème de William Blake de 1804 (le poème est connu sous le titre *Jerusalem* mais son titre diffère en réalité de celui du cantique). Ces mots évoquent la transformation du paysage du nord d'Angleterre survenue avec la révolution industrielle. Aujourd'hui on les cite volontiers pour parler de cette période de l'histoire d'Angleterre ou bien pour évoquer tout paysage industriel hideux et oppressant.

DENMARK

Something is rotten in the state of Denmark

Cette célèbre formule ("Il y a quelque chose de pourri au royaume du Danemark") provient de *Hamlet* (Acte I, scène 4) de William Shakespeare où elle est prononcée par Marcellus, qui s'inquiète des intrigues qui se nouent au sein du royaume.

Aujourd'hui cette phrase est souvent utilisée, notamment dans la presse, pour parler d'une situation où règne la corruption, dans le monde politique ou bien dans une organisation par exemple. Le terme **the state of Denmark** est alors remplacé par le terme approprié comme dans l'exemple suivant: **the recent revelations have shown that there is something rotten at the heart of the British civil service** ("les dernières révélations prouvent qu'il y a quelque chose de pourri au cœur de l'administration britannique").

DIFFERENT

And now for something completely different

Cette expression ("Et maintenant passons à tout autre chose") était souvent utilisée pour assurer la transition entre les sketches dans l'émission de télévision *Monty Python's Flying Circus*, de la célèbre troupe de comiques britanniques. Ces paroles étaient prononcées avec un accent aristocratique sur un ton qui évoquait celui des anciens présentateurs de la BBC.

Aujourd'hui on utilise cette expression sur le mode humoristique lorsque l'on change de sujet de conversation.

DISGUSTED

Disgusted of Tunbridge Wells

Tunbridge Wells est une ville très bourgeoise située dans le Kent, au sud de Londres. En anglais britannique cette phrase (que l'on pourrait traduire par "signé: un habitant dégoûté de Tunbridge Wells") fait référence à un certain type d'Anglais aisé et généralement réactionnaire qui envoie volontiers des lettres rageuses aux journaux pour se plaindre de tel ou tel aspect de la société dans laquelle nous vivons.

DREAM

I have a dream

Cette célèbre formule est extraite d'un discours que prononça Martin Luther King à Washington au cours d'un rassemblement du mouvement pour les droits civiques en 1963. Dans son discours il parlait de l'Amérique dont il rêvait, où tous les citoyens seraient égaux et vivraient ensemble dans l'harmonie.

Aujourd'hui on utilise cette phrase pour parler de tout projet, toute idée nouvelle qui nous tient particulièrement à cœur. On pourra dire par exemple **I have a dream that one day everyone will have access to a computer** ("je rêve qu'un jour chacun puisse avoir accès à un ordinateur").

EARLY

Here's one I made earlier

L'émission éducative britannique *Blue Peter*, diffusée sur le petit écran depuis de nombreuses années, comprend souvent des séquences de travaux manuels et de cuisine. Les animateurs présentent toujours le produit fini à la caméra en prononçant les mots **here's one I made earlier** ("en voici un que j'ai confectionné au préalable").

On utilise cette phrase de façon humoristique lorsqu'on montre à quelqu'un une chose que l'on a réalisée.

EASTERN

Full of Eastern promise

Il s'agit du slogan utilisé dans la publicité pour la barre chocolatée Fry's Turkish Delight des années 50 aux années 70, slogan que l'on pourrait traduire librement par "toute la saveur de l'Orient".

Aujourd'hui on utilise cette formule de façon allusive à propos de toute chose considérée comme exotique ou provenant d'Asie; on pourra dire par exemple **the new restaurant offers a menu full of Eastern promise with the emphasis on Chinese-influenced food** ("ce nouveau restaurant propose un menu plein des saveurs de l'Orient avec une forte influence chinoise").

ELEMENTARY

Elementary my dear Watson

Cette expression ("élémentaire, mon cher Watson") a pour origine les romans de Conan Doyle où apparaissent le détective Sherlock Holmes et son associé le Docteur Watson. Ce sont les mots que prononcent invariablement Holmes avant d'expliquer à Watson comment il est parvenu à résoudre une énigme. On utilise cette formule de façon humoristique lorsque l'on explique quelque chose à quelqu'un.

EVENING

Evenin' all!

Cette expression ("bonsoir à tous!") était la formule que prononçait l'acteur Jack Warner au début de chaque épisode de la série policière britannique *Dixon of Dock Green* qui fut diffusée à la télévision de 1955 à 1976. Aujourd'hui, on utilise cette phrase en référence aux policiers de la vieille école ou bien simplement en guise de salut.

EVERYDAY

An everyday story of ... folk

À l'origine, le sous-titre du feuilleton radiophonique britannique *The Archers*, diffusé depuis 1951, était la formule **an everyday story of farming folk** ("la chronique d'une famille d'agriculteurs").

Aujourd'hui on utilise cette formule en anglais britannique de façon allusive et souvent sur le mode ironique en parlant du sujet d'un livre ou d'un film. On dira par exemple **NYPD Blue is more than just an everyday story of New York police folk** ("New York Police Blues est plus que la simple chronique de policiers new-yorkais").

EYE

Eyes on the prize

Il s'agit d'une phrase extraite d'une chanson du mouvement pour les droits civils, aux États-Unis: "I know one thing we did right/ Was the day we started to fight/Keep your eyes on the prize/Hold on, hold on" ("je sais que l'on a eu raison d'entamer la lutte, ne perdez jamais votre objectif de vue, tenez bon, tenez bon"). Cette phrase symbolise la lutte menée par le mouvement pour les droits civils en Amérique et figure dans de nombreux titres de livres et de films. On l'utilise également dans toute situation où des gens luttent pour l'obtention de droits civils, quel que soit le pays.

En anglais américain, on utilise aussi cette expression de façon allusive lorsque quelqu'un doit se concentrer sur l'objectif à atteindre; on dira par exemple **this year the Pistons need to keep their eyes firmly on the prize of the championship** ("cette année les Pistons doivent faire tout leur possible pour gagner le championnat").

FAMOUS

Famous for fifteen minutes

Le peintre américain Andy Warhol déclara en 1968 qu' "à l'avenir tout le monde [aurait] droit à son quart d'heure de célébrité".

La formule est maintenant entrée dans la langue pour parler du caractère éphémère de la célébrité, et est souvent utilisée dans la structure **to have one's fifteen minutes of fame** ("connaître son quart d'heure de célébrité"), comme dans l'exemple suivant **I had my fifteen minutes of fame in 1999 when I appeared as an interviewee on Belgian television** ("j'ai connu mon quart d'heure de célébrité en 1999 lorsque j'ai été interviewé par une chaîne de télévision belge").

FEE

Fee fie fo fum

Cette formule vient du conte de fées anglais *Jack and the Beanstalk* ("Jack et le haricot magique") dans lequel un ogre à la poursuite du jeune Jack déclare **Fee fie fo fum, I smell the blood of an Englishman, be he alive or be he dead, I'll crush his bones to make my bread** ("Fee fie fo fum, je sens le sang d'un Anglais, qu'il soit mort ou vif, je lui broierai les os pour en faire de la farine pour mon pain").

Ces mots n'ont aucune signification particulière mais on les utilise de façon allusive lorsqu'on s'amuse à imiter un ogre, ou bien à propos d'une personne agressive ou coléreuse. On pourra dire par exemple **he can't go around fee-fie-fo-fumming and shouting at everyone. Sometimes he would do better just to stop and listen** ("il ne devrait pas s'énerver comme ça et crier sur tout le monde. Il ferait mieux de se calmer et d'écouter les autres").

FINE

Their finest hour

Churchill utilisa cette formule dans une déclaration adressée à ses compatriotes en 1940, destinée à encourager ces derniers à résister de toutes leurs forces contre l'ennemi, en leur promettant que la postérité se souviendrait de cette époque comme de "leur heure la plus glorieuse".

Aujourd'hui on utilise cette expression de manière allusive à propos de la période la plus mémorable de la vie ou de la carrière de quelqu'un. On dira par exemple **she always felt that her time as a doctor in Africa was her finest hour** ("elle a toujours considéré que la période durant laquelle elle était médecin en Afrique fut le meilleur moment de son existence").

This is another fine mess you've gotten us into

Il s'agit d'une formule utilisée par Oliver Hardy, le plus gros des membres du célèbre duo comique américain Laurel et Hardy. Chaque fois que les deux compères se retrouvent en difficulté et quelles que soient les circonstances, Hardy s'en prend à Laurel en ces termes: **this is another fine mess you've gotten us into** ("tu nous as encore mis dans de beaux draps!"). On utilise aujourd'hui cette phrase sur le mode humoristique dans toute situation similaire.

FOLK

That's all folks!

Les dessins animés de Bugs Bunny se terminaient généralement avec ces mots qui s'inscrivaient sur l'écran. On utilise aujourd'hui cette phrase ("c'est fini, les amis!") en allusion au dessin animé, pour indiquer à un auditoire que l'on a terminé.

FORCE

May the force be with you

Il s'agit d'une formule qui provient du film de science-fiction *Star Wars* ("La Guerre des étoiles"), réalisé par George Lucas en 1977. Les personnages qui luttaient pour le triomphe du bien dans l'univers se quittaient généralement sur ces mots ("que la force soit avec toi").

On utilise parfois cette phrase de façon humoristique, à l'écrit ou à l'oral, pour souhaiter bonne chance à quelqu'un. On dira par exemple: **have a good business trip, and may the force be with you, you'll need it** ("j'espère que ton voyage d'affaires se passera bien, et que la force soit avec toi, tu en auras besoin").

FRANKLY

Frankly my dear, I don't give a damn

Cette phrase ("franchement ma chère, je m'en fiche complètement") provient du film *Gone With the Wind* ("Autant en emporte le vent") (1939), où elle est prononcée par Rhett Butler, le personnage incarné par Clark Gable, et est adressée à sa femme Scarlett O'Hara, jouée par Vivien Leigh. Le film est une adaptation du roman éponyme de Margaret Mitchell (1936), où apparaît cette phrase mais sans le mot "frankly".

Aujourd'hui on utilise cette formule pour exprimer son indifférence ou bien en n'en gardant que la première partie (**frankly, my dear**), pour exprimer une opinion sans ambages.

FRIEND

How to win friends and influence people

Il s'agit du titre d'un ouvrage de l'auteur américain Dale Carnegie publié en 1937, que l'on pourrait traduire par "comment se faire des amis et influencer autrui".

On utilise cette formule de manière allusive lorsque quelqu'un vient de dire une grossièreté ou vient de se comporter comme un rustre; on dira alors **he won't win friends and influence people that way** ("ce n'est pas comme ça qu'il se fera des amis et qu'il influencera autrui"); ou encore lorsque quelqu'un est mené par l'ambition: **he's got his eyes set on the top job and is desperately trying to win friends and influence people to help him get there** ("il est décidé à devenir patron et il fait tout ce qu'il peut pour se faire des amis et influencer autrui afin d'atteindre son objectif").

FULL

To do a Full Monty

Cette phrase est une allusion au film britannique *The Full Monty*, qui fut un très gros succès en 1997, et qui est l'histoire d'un groupe de chômeurs de Sheffield qui décident de devenir strip-teaseurs.

L'expression **the full Monty** existait déjà avant le film dans le sens "absolument tout", mais le film a donné naissance à cette nouvelle formule (**to do a Full Monty**) qui signifie "faire un strip-tease intégral". On pourra dire par exemple: **every Saturday night drunken youths spill out of pubs and do a full Monty in the middle of the High Street** ("le samedi soir des jeunes sortent du pub complètement saouls et se mettent à poil au milieu de la rue principale").

GENTLE

Do not go gentle into that good night

Il s'agit du premier vers du poème éponyme de Dylan Thomas, publié en 1952, dans lequel le poète invite le lecteur à profiter de la vie et à ne pas accepter son destin de mortel sans se révolter **rage, rage against the dying of the light** ("insurge-toi, n'accepte pas la mort du jour").

On utilise cette phrase ("n'entre pas sans violence dans cette bonne nuit") de façon allusive à propos de la vieillesse et de la mort. On dira par exemple **the artist refused to go gentle into that good night, and was more prolific in his last years than at any other time of his life** ("le peintre refusa de s'avouer vaincu par la vieillesse et fut plus productif que jamais pendant les dernières années de sa vie").

GO

Do not pass go, (do not collect £200/ $200)

Au Monopoly les joueurs tirent parfois une carte qui les envoie sur la case "prison". Sur cette carte sont inscrits les mots **do not pass go, do not collect £200** (ou bien **do not collect $200** s'il s'agit de la version américaine).

Cette phrase, dont la version française est "ne passez pas par la case départ, ne recevez pas 20 000 francs", est utilisée de façon allusive et sur le mode humoristique dans différents contextes: on dira par exemple **you do that again and you're going straight to jail, Bill. Do not pass go, do not collect $200** ("refais ça, Bill, et je t'assure que tu iras droit en prison).

On peut également utiliser cette expression lorsque quelqu'un essaie de mener un projet à bien mais rencontre des obstacles: **the country is trying hard to get back on its feet but because of the civil war it has not even been allowed to pass go, let alone collect £200** ("le pays fait de son mieux pour se rétablir mais la guerre civile n'arrange rien, bien au contraire").

Go ahead, make my day

C'est la formule prononcée par l'inspecteur Harry Callahan (incarné par Clint Eastwood) dans le film *Sudden Impact* (1983) lorsqu'il se trouve confronté à un gangster. Il s'agit d'une façon d'encourager le bandit à se servir de son arme afin de pouvoir l'abattre en état de légitime défense: "allez, vas-y, fais-moi plaisir". On utilise cette formule par allusion au film et en réaction à une personne qui vient de proférer des menaces. Ainsi, le président Reagan s'en servit en s'adressant à des travailleurs qui menaçaient de se mettre en grève.

GOOD
You've never had it so good
Ce slogan a été utilisé pour la première fois aux États-Unis en 1952 par les Démocrates. Il signifie "vous êtes aujourd'hui plus prospères que jamais". En Grande-Bretagne, ce slogan est associé au Premier ministre conservateur Harold Macmillan qui l'utilisa dans un discours en 1957. Aujourd'hui, on utilise cette formule sur le mode ironique lorsqu'une situation n'encourage pas du tout à l'optimisme.

GOTCHA!
Il s'agit du titre qui fit la une du journal *The Sun* lorsque le navire argentin General Belgrano fut coulé par les Britanniques durant la guerre des Malouines. Ce mot, qui est la transcription phonétique des termes **got you!** (je t'ai eu!), est aujourd'hui utilisé de façon allusive: il est devenu le symbole de la frénésie nationaliste qui s'empara de la Grande-Bretagne à cette période, ainsi que du chauvinisme de la presse populaire britannique.

GREEN
This green and pleasant land
Il s'agit d'un vers extrait du cantique 'Jerusalem', d'après un poème de William Blake de 1804 (le poème est connu sous le même nom bien que le titre en soit différent). On chante très souvent ce cantique dans les écoles et au cours des manifestations sportives, à tel point qu'il est presque devenu un second hymne national.
On utilise la formule **this green and pleasant land** ("ce pays vert et plaisant") par allusion au cantique et à propos de l'Angleterre; elle véhicule une vision idéalisée et quelque peu désuète du pays.

HAPPILY
And they all lived happily ever after
Il s'agit de la formule qui clôt tous les contes de fées en anglais ("et tous vécurent heureux pour toujours"), dont l'équivalent français est "ils vécurent heureux et eurent beaucoup d'enfants".
Aujourd'hui on utilise cette phrase de façon allusive et parfois sur le mode sarcastique, comme dans l'exemple suivant: **Neil and Maggie were supposed to live happily ever after but actually divorced after six months** ("Neil et Maggie étaient censés vivre heureux et avoir beaucoup d'enfants mais finalement ils ont divorcé au bout de six mois").

HOME
Don't try this at home
Il s'agit d'un conseil donné aux spectateurs dans les émissions de télévision dans lesquelles figurent des tours dangereux et des cascades. Aujourd'hui, cette formule ("n'essayez pas de faire cela chez vous") est toujours utilisée par les présentateurs de télévision avec une pointe d'ironie et d'une manière plus générale par toute personne qui est sur le point de tenter quelque chose de dangereux.

HOUSTON
Houston, we have a problem
Ce sont les mots que prononça le commandant de la mission Apollo 13 (en 1970) à l'intention du centre de contrôle à Houston au Texas, lorsqu'il s'aperçut que la capsule spatiale connaissait de graves problèmes techniques.
Aujourd'hui, on utilise cette formule ("Houston, nous avons un problème") pour indiquer à quelqu'un que quelque chose ne va pas. Il faut noter que le mot "Houston" est toujours prononcé à l'américaine, même par les Britanniques.

HUMBUG
Bah humbug
Dans *A Christmas Carol* ("Un Conte de Noël") de Charles Dickens, le personnage principal, Ebenezer Scrooge, est avare et misanthrope et rejette toute occasion de se réjouir en prononçant les mots **bah humbug!** ("sornettes que tout cela!").
On utilise généralement cette expression sur le mode humoristique pour gronder quelqu'un qui fait preuve d'avarice ou qui joue les rabat-joie.

HURT
If it's not (*or* **it ain't**) **hurting, it's not** (*or* **it ain't**) **working**
Cette phrase ("si ça ne fait pas mal, c'est que ça ne marche pas") fut popularisée au début des années 90 par le Premier ministre britannique John Major, qui voulait dire par là que si l'on veut obtenir des résultats en matière d'économie, il faut être prêt à faire des sacrifices.
On utilise aujourd'hui cette formule dans des contextes autres que politiques pour justifier des mesures d'austérité, ou bien pour encourager un patient lors d'un traitement douloureux (un régime de remise en forme éprouvant, par exemple).

JAW
Jaw-jaw is better than war-war
Churchill déclara lors d'un discours prononcé à la Maison Blanche en 1954 **"Talking jaw is better than going to war"** ("Mieux vaut discuter que de faire la guerre"). Cependant, c'est la formule **Jaw-jaw is better than war-war** qui est passée à la postérité.
On utilise cette expression aujourd'hui pour dire qu'il est toujours préférable de parlementer avec ses ennemis afin de résoudre un différend de façon pacifique.

LAND
A land fit for heroes
Cette expression ("un pays digne de ses héros") trouve son origine dans un discours que le Premier ministre britannique Lloyd George prononça en 1918. Il y expliquait la façon dont il envisageait l'avenir de son pays au sortir de la Première Guerre mondiale, et déclarait qu'il incombait au gouvernement de faire de la Grande-Bretagne **a fit country for heroes to live in** ("un pays qui ferait honneur à ses héros").
On utilise aujourd'hui cette formule dans sa version modifiée et souvent sur le mode ironique en parlant de la façon dont un pays traite ses soldats. On dira par exemple **if the returning veterans hoped for a land fit for heroes, they were to be sadly disappointed** ("si, une fois de retour au pays, les anciens combattants s'étaient imaginé trouver un pays digne de héros, ils allaient être amèrement déçus").

LEAD
Lead on, MacDuff
Cette phase ("après toi, MacDuff") est une déformation d'un vers de *Macbeth* de Shakespeare, dans un passage où Macbeth défie à l'épée son ennemi MacDuff en prononçant les mots **lay on, MacDuff** ("frappe, MacDuff").
On utilise la version modifiée de cette phrase de façon humoristique lorsque l'on demande à quelqu'un d'ouvrir la marche.

LEAP
One small step for a man, one giant leap forward for mankind
Il s'agit des mots que prononça Neil Armstrong lorsqu'il devint le premier homme à marcher sur la Lune le 20 juillet 1969 : "un petit pas pour l'homme, un pas de géant pour l'humanité".
On utilise aujourd'hui cette formule en référence aux mots d'Armstrong pour mettre en contraste le caractère apparemment anodin d'un phénomène et l'ampleur de son effet, comme **it's a small step for nanotechnology but a giant leap forward for computers** ("c'est un petit pas pour la nanotechnologie mais un pas de géant pour les ordinateurs").

LIE
Lie back and think of England
Peu de gens savent que la phrase à l'origine de cette formule ("allonge-toi et pense à l'Angleterre") fut prononcée par Lady Hillingdon en 1912, mais elle n'en évoque pas moins dans l'esprit de tous l'époque victorienne et son idéologie. En fait la phrase exacte était **I lie down on my bed, close my eyes, open my legs, and think of England** ("je m'allonge sur mon lit, je ferme les yeux, j'écarte les jambes, et je pense à l'Angleterre").
Aujourd'hui on utilise cette phrase dans son contexte d'origine à propos d'une femme qui accepte à contrecœur d'avoir des rapports sexuels, et de manière générale pour parler d'une attitude caractérisée par un certain stoïcisme, comme dans l'example **I know life's tough for you at the moment working out there in the Antarctic but you'll just have to lie back and think of England** ("je sais que la vie n'est pas facile pour toi qui travailles là-bas dans l'Antarctique, mais il faut que tu prennes ton mal en patience").

LIVE
To live fast, die young and leave a beautiful corpse
À l'origine, cette phrase provient du titre d'un film de 1949 mis en scène par Nicholas Ray intitulé *Knock on Any Door* ("Les Ruelles du malheur"), dont le personnage principal, un marginal joué par John Derek, voulait "vivre vite, mourir jeune et laisser un beau cadavre". Aujourd'hui cette formule est davantage associée aux personnages de rebelles qu'incarnaient James Dean et d'autres jeunes acteurs des années 50 et 60, et à la vie trépidante qu'ils menaient dans la réalité.
Cette formule est généralement utilisée dans sa version tronquée (**live fast and die young**) pour faire référence à un style de vie débridé. On dira par exemple **I don't like these modern pop stars and their live fast, die young attitude** ("je n'aime pas les vedettes de la musique pop d'aujourd'hui qui ne pensent qu'à s'amuser sans jamais penser aux conséquences").

LOOK
Here's looking at you kid
Ce sont les mots que prononce Rick Blaine, le personnage incarné par Humphrey Bogart dans le film *Casablanca* (1942), lorsqu'il dit adieu à la femme qu'il aime, jouée par Ingrid Bergman.
Aujourd'hui on utilise souvent cette phrase en référence au film lorsque l'on porte un toast à quelqu'un.

MAGICAL
A magical mystery tour
Il s'agit du titre d'un album des Beatles de 1967, que l'on pourrait traduire par "voyage mystère". Aujourd'hui on utilise cette expression à propos d'un long trajet dont la destination est incertaine; on dira par exemple **the guide led us on a magical mystery tour around the Kent countryside in search of the country pub that he remembered from his youth** ("le guide nous a fait parcourir la campagne du Kent dans tous les sens à la recherche d'un pub qu'il connaissait dans sa jeunesse").

MAN
A man's gotta do what a man's gotta do
Il s'agit d'une phrase que l'on associe généralement aux vieux westerns dans lesquels les héros expriment leur détermination à agir en hommes, en dépit du danger.
Cette formule ("un homme, un vrai, ne recule pas devant l'obstacle") s'utilise aujourd'hui de façon allusive et sur le mode ironique lorsque quelqu'un doit exécuter une tâche simple (l'équivalent français est "quand il faut y aller, il faut y aller").

MASKED
Who was that masked man?
Il s'agit d'une formule extraite de la série télévisée américaine des années 50 *Zorro*, dans laquelle le héros éponyme porte un masque.

On utilise aujourd'hui cette formule ("qui est cet homme masqué?") sur le mode humoristique lorsque l'on demande à connaître l'identité de quelqu'un que l'on ne connaît pas ou que l'on n'a fait qu'apercevoir.

MEANWHILE
Meanwhile, back at the ranch
Il s'agit d'une phrase qui évoque les séries télévisées américaines réalisées dans les années 60 et 70 dont l'action se déroulait au Far-West, telles que *The High Chaparral* ("Chaparral" en français). La continuité du récit était assurée par un récitant qui prononçait ces mots ("pendant ce temps, au ranch") pour introduire une séquence qui avait lieu au ranch où la famille des héros habitait. Aujourd'hui, on utilise souvent cette phrase sur le mode humoristique à la place de **meanwhile** ("pendant ce temps").

MENTION
Don't mention the war
Cette phrase vient de la série comique britannique des années 70 *Fawlty Towers*, dans laquelle John Cleese joue le rôle de Basil Fawlty, le patron d'un hôtel situé quelque part sur la côte sud de l'Angleterre. Dans un épisode intitulé *The Germans*, des clients allemands séjournent dans l'hôtel; Basil Fawlty a reçu un coup sur la tête et n'arrête pas de répéter à ses employés **whatever you do, don't mention the war** ("surtout, ne parlez pas de la guerre") mais lui-même ne cesse de faire référence à la Seconde Guerre mondiale en parlant aux clients allemands.

Le sketch est tellement connu qu'aujourd'hui cette phrase est souvent utilisée par les Britanniques de façon humoristique lorsqu'ils parlent des Allemands.

MONEY
Show me the money
Cette phrase ("fais-moi voir l'argent") vient du film américain *Jerry Maguire* (1996), dans lequel Tom Cruise joue le rôle d'un manager sportif. L'un de ses clients, incarné par Cuba Gooding, prononce ces mots à maintes reprises lors de négociations.

On utilise cette phrase de façon allusive en anglais américain dans des contextes similaires, comme dans l'exemple suivant: **forget about the free CDs and baseball caps, just show me the money** ("les casquettes de base-ball et les CDs gratuits ne m'intéressent pas, parlons argent"), ou bien lorsqu'on réclame une somme due: **I won the bet, so show me the money** ("j'ai gagné le pari, alors donne-moi mon argent").

NOT!
Le film américain *Wayne's World* (1992), avec Mike Myers dans le rôle principal, est à l'origine de plusieurs expressions d'usage courant. La plus célèbre d'entre elles est sans doute le mot **not** utilisé de façon exclamative et sur le mode ironique pour exprimer exactement le contraire de ce que l'on vient de dire.

NUNNERY
Get thee to a nunnery
Ce sont les mots que prononce Hamlet dans l'œuvre éponyme de Shakespeare, lorsqu'il rejette Ophélia.

Aujourd'hui cette phrase ("retire-toi dans un couvent") est utilisée de manière allusive et non sans un certain sexisme lorsqu'un homme demande à une femme de partir, ou encore pour conseiller à quelqu'un de pratiquer l'abstinence sexuelle.

OVER
They think it's all over (...it is now)
Ces mots, précédés de la phrase **some people are on the pitch...** ("il y a quelques personnes sur le terrain"), furent prononcés par Kenneth Wolstenholme, commentateur sportif de la BBC, au moment où Geoff Hurst marqua un dernier but pour l'Angleterre dans les dernières secondes de la finale de la Coupe du monde de football de 1966, qui vit l'Angleterre l'emporter face à la République fédérale d'Allemagne.

Aujourd'hui on utilise cette expression ("ils croient que c'est terminé,... maintenant, c'est terminé") en anglais britannique lorsque quelqu'un s'imagine à tort qu'une chose est terminée, ou bien au moment même où cette chose s'achève.

OVERPAID
Overpaid, oversexed and over here
Cette phrase (que l'on attribue à l'artiste de music-hall anglais Tommy Trinder) était utilisée pendant la Seconde Guerre mondiale par certains Britanniques jaloux du succès que remportaient auprès des femmes les soldats américains basés en Grande-Bretagne. Cette formule, que l'on pourrait traduire par "surpayés, surexcités et sur place" est encore utilisée aujourd'hui à propos de certains étrangers qui séjournent en Grande-Bretagne, mais souvent avec des modifications. Ainsi on pourra dire à propos d'un boy's-band américain: **overhyped, overeager and over here** ("surfaits, trop enthousiastes et chez nous").

PART
Reaches the parts that other beers can't reach
Il s'agit du slogan d'une série de publicités pour la bière Heineken pendant les années 70 dans lesquelles la bière était censée conférer des pouvoirs spéciaux à ceux qui la consommaient. Aujourd'hui on utilise encore cette formule ("atteint les parties que les autres bières ne peuvent atteindre"), en remplaçant le mot **beers** par un autre pour décrire les qualités de quelque chose de façon humoristique. On dira par exemple **she makes tea that reaches the parts that other tea cannot reach** ("elle fait du thé vraiment excellent"), ou **this tour reaches the parts of Scotland that others don't** ("ce circuit touristique explore les coins d'Écosse que les autres ignorent").

PLAY
Play it again Sam
Cette formule célèbre ("joue-le encore, Sam"), que l'on attribue au film *Casablanca*, n'est en fait pas prononcée dans le film. Le personnage incarné par Ingrid Bergman dit au pianiste du Rick's Bar **play it once Sam, for old times' sake** ("joue-le une fois, Sam, en souvenir du bon vieux temps").

Aujourd'hui on utilise cette formule en allusion au film lorsque l'on demande à quelqu'un de refaire quelque chose, et particulièrement lorsqu'il s'agit de rejouer un air de musique.

PORLOCK
The person from Porlock
Cette formule ("la personne de Porlock") est une allusion au poète anglais Samuel Taylor Coleridge. Ce dernier était dans sa maison du Somerset en train de composer son poème *Kubla Khan*, inspiré par un rêve qui lui était venu sous l'effet de l'opium, lorsqu'un visiteur (la personne de Porlock) vint l'interrompre pour une affaire sans importance. Coleridge fut dans l'incapacité de terminer son poème comme il l'espérait.

Aujourd'hui, on utilise cette formule de façon allusive pour parler d'un importun qui vient interrompre quelqu'un et lui fait perdre son inspiration. Ainsi on pourra dire **I knew that I would be alone all day and that no person from Porlock was likely to interrupt me** ("je savais que je serais seul toute la journée et que personne ne viendrait me déranger").

POUND
Pound of flesh
Cette formule ("une livre de chair") vient du *Marchand de Venise*, de Shakespeare, pièce dans laquelle Shylock vient réclamer son dû à Antonio (une livre de la chair de ce dernier) comme dédommagement pour n'avoir pas tenu ses engagements. Aujourd'hui on utilise cette expression pour parler des conditions exactes d'un contrat ou d'une façon plus générale en référence à une somme d'argent qu'un débiteur est dans l'incapacité de payer. On pourra dire par exemple **We're barely able to make ends meet as it is, the last thing we need is the taxman asking for his pound of flesh** ("on a déjà du mal à joindre les deux bouts, on n'a vraiment pas besoin que le percepteur vienne nous réclamer de l'argent").

PRESUME
Dr Livingstone, I presume
Ce sont les mots que Sir Henry Stanley aurait adressés au Docteur Livingstone lorsqu'il le retrouva dans la jungle africaine où il s'était perdu en 1871. Stanley avait été envoyé à la recherche de l'explorateur par un journal américain. Cette phrase ("Docteur Livingstone, je présume") est utilisée sur le mode humoristique lorsqu'on fait la connaissance de quelqu'un dont on a entendu parler auparavant, le plus souvent en remplaçant **Doctor Livingstone** par le nom de la personne en question.

PROTEST
The lady protests too much, methinks
Cette phrase ("la dame fait trop de serments, me semble-t-il") vient de *Hamlet* de Shakespeare, et est prononcée par Gertrude lorsqu'elle assiste à la représentation de la *Souricière*, la pièce écrite par son fils Hamlet, et dans laquelle le personnage de la reine, calqué sur la reine Gertrude elle-même, jure de ne jamais se remarier après la mort de son mari.

On utilise cette expression en plaçant **methinks** en début de phrase et en ajoutant la forme archaïque **doth** avant le verbe, lorsqu'on estime que quelqu'un proteste trop de son innocence pour être honnête. On se sert souvent de l'expression à propos de l'attitude de personnes de sexe féminin, mais pas exclusivement; ainsi on pourra dire **the minister has spoken loudly on the issue, but methinks he doth protest too much** ("le ministre a beaucoup parlé du problème, et son insistance même me semble suspecte").

PUBLISH
Publish and be damned
Il s'agit de la réponse que fit Lord Wellington à une femme qui menaçait de révéler qu'elle avait eu une aventure avec lui.

On utilise couramment cette formule lorsque, comme Wellington, on défie quelqu'un de publier une information ("publiez si vous voulez et allez au diable!"), ou pour afficher son indifférence quant aux conséquences que pourrait avoir une révélation: **we're going to publish and be damned** ("on publiera, advienne que pourra").

QUIET
All quiet on the Western front
Il s'agit du titre anglais du roman *À l'Ouest rien de nouveau* de l'écrivain allemand Erich Maria Remarque ainsi que du film de Lewis Milestone.

Aujourd'hui on utilise cette phrase de façon allusive et sur le mode humoristique (et en la modifiant si nécessaire) à propos d'une période d'accalmie dans une situation de crise, ou bien pour dire qu'il ne se passe grand-chose comme dans l'exemple suivant: **How's things up there in Helsinki? – Oh, you know, all quiet on the Northern front** ("comment ça va, là-haut, à Helsinki? – rien à signaler").

READ
Read my lips
Il s'agit d'un extrait de la formule utilisée par George Bush lors de sa campagne électorale de 1988, avant son élection à la présidence des États-Unis. La formule complète était: **read my lips, no new taxes** ("regardez bien mes lèvres: pas d'augmentation des impôts"). Aujourd'hui on utilise cette expression pour insister sur le fait que ce que l'on dit est vrai.

REBEL
Rebel without a cause
Il s'agit du titre original de *La Fureur de vivre*, un film de Nicholas Ray de 1955 dans lequel James Dean joue le rôle d'un fils de bonne fa-

mille. L'interprétation de James Dean et son personnage de jeune rebelle ténébreux a fait de l'acteur l'incarnation d'une jeunesse inquiète et en rupture avec son milieu.

Aujourd'hui, on utilise cette formule à propos du type de personnage interprété par James Dean dans ce film.

ROOM

No room at the inn

Cette phrase provient de la nativité lorsque Joseph et Marie se virent refuser l'accès à l'auberge de Bethléem et trouvèrent refuge dans une étable. On utilise cette formule ("il n'y a aucune chambre de libre dans l'auberge") de façon allusive lorsqu'un hôtel est complet ou lorsqu'un hôpital ne peut accueillir de nouveaux patients, par exemple.

RUMOUR

Rumours of my death have been greatly exaggerated

Cette phrase ("les rumeurs concernant ma mort sont très exagérées") aurait été prononcée par Mark Twain après qu'un journal avait annoncé son décès par erreur.

Aujourd'hui on utilise cette phrase lorsque l'on veut démentir une rumeur ou une idée reçue. On pourra dire par exemple **rumours of the death of vinyl records have been greatly exaggerated** ("les rumeurs concernant la fin des disques vinyle sont très exagérées").

SCARLET

The Scarlet Pimpernel

Le Mouron rouge est le titre français du roman de la Baronne Orczy *The Scarlet Pimpernel* (1905), ainsi que le surnom de Sir Percy Blakeney, qui en est le personnage principal. L'histoire se déroule pendant la Révolution française et Blakeney, qui est passé maître dans l'art du déguisement, aide des membres de l'aristocratie française à s'enfuir en Angleterre. Il parvient toujours à échapper à ses poursuivants, comme en témoigne le passage suivant: **They seek him here, they seek him there, Those Frenchies seek him everywhere, Is he in Heaven or is he in Hell?, That damned elusive pimpernel** ("les Français le cherchent partout mais jamais ne l'attrapent, est-il au ciel ou en enfer, ce sacré mouron rouge?").

Aujourd'hui on utilise cette citation (ou simplement le terme **Scarlet Pimpernel**) sur le ton de la plaisanterie à propos de quelqu'un d'introuvable ou avec qui il est particulièrement difficile d'entrer en contact.

SHE

She who must be obeyed

Il s'agit d'une expression tirée de *She* ("Elle"), un roman d'aventures publié en 1887 par l'auteur anglais Henry Rider Haggard. Cette expression ("celle à qui l'on doit obéir") y désignait la reine Ayesha, qui régnait sur le royaume de Kôr.

Aujourd'hui, on utilise cette phrase sur le mode humoristique à propos de toute femme qui inspire le respect et une certaine crainte, qu'elle soit supérieure hiérarchique, mère ou épouse. On pourra dire par exemple **I've got to go into work early tomorrow. She who must be obeyed has called a meeting for 8.30** ("il faut que je sois au travail plus tôt que d'habitude demain, j'ai une réunion avec la patronne à 8h30"). Cette allusion a été popularisée par l'auteur anglais John Mortimer et sa série de romans *Rumpole of the Bailey*, dans lesquels le héros éponyme utilise cette expression à propos de sa femme.

SHIP

I see no ships

Il s'agit d'une phrase qu'aurait prononcée l'amiral Nelson lors de la bataille de Copenhague en 1801. Nelson était borgne et lorsque ses officiers l'informèrent que des navires de guerre danois approchaient, il aurait levé sa lunette vers son mauvais œil et aurait déclaré **I see no ships** ("je ne vois aucun navire"), donnant ainsi l'occasion à la flotte anglaise d'engager le combat, et de le gagner.

Aujourd'hui, on utilise cette expression en allusion à Nelson lorsque quelqu'un fait exprès de ne pas remarquer quelque chose.

SIT

Are you sitting comfortably? (Then I'll begin)

Cette expression ("Êtes-vous assis confortablement? Je peux donc commencer") est la formule d'introduction classique que l'on prononce avant de raconter une histoire à des enfants. Le narrateur de l'émission de radio britannique *Listen with Mother* l'employait systématiquement avant chaque récit.

Aujourd'hui, cette expression témoigne d'une attitude quelque peu condescendante de la part de celui qui l'emploie. On l'utilise lorsqu'on veut capter l'attention de personnes inattentives ou bien sur le mode humoristique avant un discours.

SLIP

Do you mind if I slip into something more comfortable?

Cette formule ("Est-ce que ça vous dérange si j'enfile quelque chose de plus confortable?") a pour origine *Hell's Angels* ("Les Anges de l'Enfer"), un film américain de 1930 avec Jean Harlow. La phrase exacte que prononce l'actrice est **would you be shocked if I changed into something more comfortable?** ("est-ce que ça vous choquerait si j'enfilais quelque chose de plus confortable?") Cette formule évoque les vedettes féminines du cinéma américain des années 30 et 40 et notamment les scènes dans lesquelles celles-ci font des numéros de charme en revêtant des tenues sexy.

Aujourd'hui on utilise cette phrase en allusion à l'air séducteur de Jean Harlow, le plus souvent sur le mode humoristique.

SLOUGH

Slough of Despond

Il s'agit d'une allusion à l'œuvre allégorique de l'écrivain puritain anglais John Bunyan, *The Pilgrim's Progress* ("Le Voyage du pèlerin"). L'histoire raconte les tribulations du héros, qui entreprend un pèlerinage en quête du paradis céleste. En chemin, il rencontre toutes sortes d'obstacles, parmi lesquels figure un marécage profond et redoutable, le Slough of Despond, symbolisant l'abîme du désespoir mais que le héros arrive néanmoins à traverser.

L'expression est couramment utilisée pour évoquer de façon facétieuse un état d'abattement et de découragement, généralement passager. Par exemple, **it took him several weeks to emerge from this slough of despond** ("il lui a fallu plusieurs semaines pour sortir de son abattement").

SPECTRE

Spectre at the feast

Cette formule est tirée de l'acte III du *Macbeth* de Shakespeare. Au cours d'un banquet, Macbeth est pris de délire lorsqu'apparaît le fantôme de Banquo, l'ancien camarade qu'il vient de faire assassiner, et dévoile ainsi sa culpabilité; la fête est gâchée et les invités s'enfuient.

On emploie l'expression lorsque la présence indésirable de quelqu'un à une réunion fait l'effet d'une douche froide. Par exemple, **his first wife turned up at the wedding like the spectre at the feast** ("en venant au mariage, sa première épouse a véritablement joué les trouble-fête").

START

I've started so I'll finish

Le jeu télévisé britannique *Mastermind* fut diffusé de 1972 à 1997. Les concurrents de ce jeu portant sur la culture générale devaient répondre au plus grand nombre de questions possible en l'espace de deux minutes. Si l'animateur était en train de poser une question lorsque retentissait la sonnerie qui annonçait la fin du temps imparti, il prononçait rituellement ces mots ("j'ai commencé, je vais donc finir") avant de finir de lire la question au concurrent.

Aujourd'hui, on utilise cette phrase par allusion au jeu télévisé lorsqu'on est interrompu.

STARTER

Starter for 10

University Challenge est un jeu télévisé britannique qui fait s'opposer deux équipes composées d'étudiants de deux universités britanniques. L'animateur pose des questions valant 10 points aux deux équipes. L'équipe qui appuie la première sur le bouton et donne la bonne réponse a le droit de répondre à trois autres questions, valant cinq points chacune. La première question donnant droit aux trois suivantes s'appelle **starter for 10** ("première question pour 10 points").

On utilise cette formule sur le mode humoristique par allusion au jeu lorsqu'on pose une question difficile à quelqu'un, comme dans l'exemple suivant: **OK, cleverclogs, here's your starter for ten: why do...** ("puisque tu es si malin que ça, essaie de répondre à cette question: pourquoi est-ce que...").

STEPFORD

The Stepford wives

Il s'agit du titre original d'un film américain de 1974 tiré du roman éponyme de Ira Levin (en français "Les Femmes de Stepford"). Stepford est une petite ville américaine où toutes les femmes semblent trouver l'épanouissement complet dans leur rôle de ménagères et de femmes au foyer; il s'avère par la suite que les hommes se sont débarrassés de leurs épouses et les ont remplacées par des androïdes.

On utilise l'expression **Stepford wife** à propos d'une femme qui semble obsédée par les tâches ménagères ou bien qui a le regard vide.

TAKE

Take me to your leader

Il s'agit de la formule prononcée par les extraterrestres fraîchement débarqués sur terre dans les vieux films de science-fiction et adressée au premier terrien rencontré. On emploie cette phrase ("menez-moi jusqu'à votre chef") de façon humoristique lorsque, dans une situation donnée, on désire parler au responsable.

THREE

Three pipe problem

Dans certaines histoires de *Sherlock Holmes*, de Conan Doyle, le célèbre détective emploie l'expression **a three pipe problem** ("un problème à trois pipes") à propos de certaines énigmes particulièrement difficiles à résoudre, qui nécessitent une période de réflexion correspondant au temps qu'il faut pour fumer trois pipes afin d'élaborer une stratégie. On emploie cette expression par allusion à Sherlock Holmes à propos de tout problème ardu qui demande beaucoup de réflexion.

TIME

I may be some time

Ce sont les mots ("je risque d'en avoir pour un certain temps") qu'aurait prononcés le capitaine Oates lorsqu'il sortit de la tente qu'il occupait avec le capitaine Scott au cours de leur expédition de 1912 au pôle sud. Oates souffrait de gelures multiples et afin de ne pas ralentir la progression de ses camarades, il décida de se sacrifier en disparaissant dans la tourmente. Cet épisode est censé symboliser les qualités d'héroïsme et d'abnégation associées au caractère britannique.

Aujourd'hui, on emploie cette formule par allusion à Oates sur le mode humoristique lorsque l'on sort d'une pièce ou bien lorsqu'on va aux toilettes.

TIN

Does exactly what it says on the tin

Il s'agit du slogan d'une publicité britannique pour la marque de peinture et de vernis Ronseal. Le message de la publicité est direct et simple et vise à donner une impression de fiabilité: "fait exactement ce qui est écrit sur la boîte".

Aujourd'hui on emploie cette expression en anglais britannique lorsqu'une chose correspond exactement à ce que l'on en attendait. On dira par exemple **the Comprehensive Guide to Pop Trivia website is really cool – it does exactly what it says on the tin, it's got everything** ("le site web du Guide complet de la musique pop est vraiment chouette – le titre ne ment pas: il est vraiment complet.").

TONIGHT

Not tonight, Josephine

On raconte en Grande-Bretagne que Napoléon Bonaparte aurait prononcé ces mots en réponse à sa femme Joséphine, qui l'invitait à la rejoindre au lit.

Aujourd'hui on emploie cette expression ("pas ce soir, Joséphine") pour plaisanter et en prenant l'accent français dans des circonstances similaires ou bien lorsqu'on décline une invitation, comme dans l'exemple suivant: **Do you want to go out for a drink? – not tonight, Josephine** ("est-ce que tu veux aller prendre un verre ce soir? – pas ce soir Joséphine").

TWIRL

Give us a twirl

Le jeu télévisé britannique *The Generation Game*, diffusé depuis les années 70, fut présenté pendant de nombreuses années par Bruce Forsyth. Il prononçait ces mots ("retourne-toi!") au début de chaque émission lorsqu'apparaissait sa jeune et séduisante assistante Anthea Redfern vêtue d'une nouvelle robe. Il lui demandait de faire un tour sur elle-même pour que le public puisse l'admirer.

On emploie cette expression par allusion au *Generation Game* en guise de compliment à une femme élégamment vêtue.

USUAL

Round up the usual suspects

Il s'agit de l'ordre que le policier interprété par Claude Raines donne à ses hommes dans le film *Casablanca*.

On emploie fréquemment cette formule ("allez me chercher les suspects habituels") par allusion au film lorsqu'on demande à quelqu'un de rassembler des gens, ou bien, dans sa version tronquée, pour parler d'un groupe de personnes déterminé, comme dans l'exemple suivant: **all the usual suspects were there at the party** ("il y avait la bande habituelle à la soirée").

WALTER MITTY

Il s'agit d'une allusion au personnage principal du roman de l'écrivain américain James Thurber, *The Secret Life of Walter Mitty*, (1947). Ce personnage, homme tout à fait ordinaire mais doté d'une imagination très vive, essaie continuellement d'échapper à sa vie monotone en s'imaginant être le héros de toutes sortes d'aventures, au point de vivre davantage dans un monde imaginaire que dans la réalité.

On évoque son nom pour désigner toute personne au caractère rêveur qui essaie de compenser la monotonie de la vie quotidienne à travers son imagination.

WAY

We have ways of making you talk

Il s'agit de la formule prononcée par les membres de la Gestapo dans les films de guerre anglais des années 50 et 60 lorsqu'ils interrogent des prisonniers de guerre britanniques.

Aujourd'hui, on emploie cette expression ("nous avons les moyens de vous faire parler") pour plaisanter en prenant l'accent allemand lorsqu'on veut obtenir une information de quelqu'un.

WEEKEND

Anything for the weekend, sir?

Cette formule ("vous désirez quelque chose pour le week-end, Monsieur?") était jadis utilisée en Grande-Bretagne par les coiffeurs pour hommes pour proposer des préservatifs à leurs clients.

Cette expression ou sa version tronquée **something for the weekend** ("quelque chose pour le week-end") s'emploie aujourd'hui lorsqu'il est question de s'adonner à une activité particulière pendant le week-end ou bien pour évoquer une certaine lubricité qui serait typique du caractère britannique.

WELL

Didn't he/she do well?

Le jeu télévisé britannique *The Generation Game* fut présenté pendant de nombreuses années par un nommé Bruce Forsyth. Cette expression ("il/elle s'est bien débrouillé(e), vous ne trouvez pas?") était l'une des petites phrases qu'il employait immanquablement au cours de l'émission. Il utilisait cette formule en s'adressant au public lorsqu'un concurrent venait de terminer une épreuve.

Aujourd'hui, on emploie cette expression pour féliciter quelqu'un sur un ton légèrement condescendant.

WEST

Go West young man

On attribut cette phrase ("va vers l'Ouest, jeune homme") à John Soule, journaliste américain de l'Indiana qui l'aurait employée pour la première fois en 1851. Il s'agit d'une allusion à la colonisation de l'ouest américain mais on emploie cette formule dans d'autres contextes, lorsque quelqu'un part en voyage vers l'Ouest, quel que soit le pays où il se trouve, ou bien en l'adaptant en remplaçant "ouest" par un autre terme. On utilise aussi cette expression pour encourager quelqu'un à faire preuve d'ambition et à se déplacer de façon à trouver du travail.

WHITE

The white man's burden

Cette expression provient du titre d'un poème de l'écrivain anglais Rudyard Kipling publié en 1899, dans lequel il fait l'éloge du colonialisme, justifié selon lui par la supériorité culturelle de l'empire britannique. Le "fardeau" auquel le titre fait référence est la mission civilisatrice de l'homme blanc colonisateur. Le titre du poème devint le slogan des impérialistes de l'époque.

L'expression est aujourd'hui souvent utilisée de façon ironique pour désigner l'attitude raciste et condescendante des impérialistes.

WOODSHED

Something nasty in the woodshed

Il s'agit d'une allusion à un roman comique anglais, *Cold Comfort Farm* (1932), de Stella Gibbons. Parmi les personnages excentriques qui figurent dans le roman se trouve une vieille dame, Aunt Ada Doom, qui répète sans cesse la phrase "I saw something nasty in the woodshed"("J'ai vu quelque chose d'horrible dans le bûcher"), en se remémorant une expérience traumatisante qui a eu lieu dans son enfance. La nature de cette expérience reste inexpliquée.

L'expression est couramment utilisée, souvent de façon humoristique, pour désigner une chose ou un événement mal élucidé mais dont on soupçonne la nature louche ou néfaste.

WORTHY

We are not worthy!

Cette formule ("nous ne méritons pas cet honneur") vient du film comique américain de 1992 *Wayne's World* . Tout comme dans le film, on emploie cette expression sur le mode humoristique en se prosternant pour exprimer son admiration pour quelqu'un, le plus souvent une vedette de la musique pop ou du sport.

WRETCHED

Wretched refuse

Ces mots (que l'on pourrait traduire par "le rebut") sont extraits du poème *New Colossus* (1883) de la poétesse américaine Emma Lazarus. Ce poème est inscrit sur le piédestal de la Statue de la Liberté, à l'entrée du port de New York. Y figurent également les vers **Give me your tired your poor, Your huddled masses yearning to breathe free** ("donne-moi tes exténués, tes pauvres, qui en rangs pressés aspirent à vivre libres").

On emploie cette formule en anglais américain à propos des immigrants des siècles passés mais également à propos de ceux d'aujourd'hui.

Divisions administratives (anglais)

Comtés anglais

Comté	Centre administratif	Abréviation
Avon[1]	Bristol	
Bedfordshire	Bedford	Beds
Berkshire	Reading	Berks
Buckinghamshire	Aylesbury	Bucks
Cambridgeshire	Cambridge	Cambs
Cheshire	Chester	Ches
Cleveland[1]	Middlesbrough	
Cornwall	Truro	Corn
Cumbria[1]	Carlisle	
Derbyshire	Matlock	Derby
Devon	Exeter	
Dorset	Dorchester	
Durham	Durham	Dur
Essex	Chelmsford	
Gloucestershire	Gloucester	Glos
Greater London[1]	-	
Greater Manchester[1]	-	
Hampshire	Winchester	Hants
Hereford and Worcester[1]	Worcester	
Hertfordshire	Hertford	Herts
Humberside[1]	Hull	
Isle of Wight	Newport	IOW
Kent	Maidstone	
Lancashire	Preston	Lancs
Leicestershire	Leicester	Leics
Lincolnshire	Lincoln	Lincs
Merseyside[1]	Liverpool	
Norfolk	Norwich	
Northamptonshire	Northampton	Northants
Northumberland	Newcastle upon Tyne	Northumb
Nottinghamshire	Nottingham	Notts
Oxfordshire	Oxford	Oxon
Shropshire	Shrewsbury	
Somerset	Taunton	Som
Staffordshire	Stafford	Staffs
Suffolk	Ipswich	
Surrey	Kingston upon Thames	
Sussex, East	Lewes	
Sussex, West	Chichester	
Tyne and Wear[1]	Newcastle	
Warwickshire	Warwick	War
West Midlands[1]	Birmingham	W Midlands
Wiltshire	Trowbridge	Wilts
Yorkshire, North	Northallerton	N Yorks
Yorkshire, South	Barnsley	S Yorks
Yorkshire, West	Wakefield	W Yorks

[1] Les comtés créés en 1974 ont été formés de la façon suivante:

Avon: une partie du Somerset et du Gloucestershire
Cleveland: une partie du comté de Durham et du Yorkshire
Cumbria: Cumberland, Westmoreland, et une partie du Lancashire et du Yorkshire
Greater London: Londres et la plus grande partie du Middlesex
Greater Manchester: une partie du Lancashire, du Cheshire et du Yorkshire
Hereford and Worcester: Hereford et la plus grande partie du Worcestershire
Humberside: une partie du Yorkshire et du Lincolnshire
Merseyside: une partie du Lancashire et du Cheshire
Tyne and Wear: une partie du Northumberland et du comté de Durham
West Midlands: une partie du Staffordshire, du Warwickshire et du Worcestershire

Écosse

Division administrative[1]	Centre administratif
Aberdeen City	Aberdeen
Aberdeenshire	Aberdeen
Angus	Forfar
Argyll and Bute	Lochgilphead
Clackmannanshire	Alloa
Dumfries and Galloway	Dumfries
Dundee City	Dundee
East Ayrshire	Kilmarnock
East Dunbartonshire	Kirkintillock
East Lothian	Haddington
East Renfrewshire	Giffnock
Edinburgh, City of	Edinburgh
Falkirk	Falkirk
Fife	Glenrothes
Glasgow City	Glasgow
Highland	Inverness
Inverclyde	Greenock
Midlothian	Dalkeith
Moray	Elgin
North Ayrshire	Irvine
North Lanarkshire	Motherwell
Orkney Islands	Kirkwall
Perth and Kinross	Perth
Renfrewshire	Paisley
Scottish Borders	Newton St Boswells
Shetland Islands	Lerwick
South Ayrshire	Ayr
South Lanarkshire	Hamilton
Stirling	Stirling
West Dunbartonshire	Dumbarton
Western Isles (Eilean Siar, Comhairle nan)	Stornoway
West Lothian	Livingston

[1] Les comtés d'Écosse ont été remplacés par 9 "regional councils" et 53 "district councils" en 1975, qui furent eux-mêmes remplacés par 29 "unitary authorities" ou "council areas" (divisions administratives) en avril 1996, les 3 "islands councils" (pour l'ouest de l'Écosse) restant inchangés.

Comtés irlandais

Comté	Centre administratif
Carlow	Carlow
Cavan	Cavan
Clare	Ennis
Cork	Cork
Donegal	Lifford
Dublin	Dublin
Galway	Galway
Kerry	Tralee
Kildare	Naas
Kilkenny	Kilkenny
Laoighis (Leix)	Portlaoise
Leitrim	Carrick
Limerick	Limerick
Longford	Longford
Louth	Dundalk
Mayo	Castlebar
Meath	Trim
Monaghan	Monaghan
Offaly	Tullamore
Roscommon	Roscommon
Sligo	Sligo
Tipperary	Clonmel
Waterford	Waterford
Westmeath	Mullingar
Wexford	Wexford
Wicklow	Wicklow

Pays de Galles

Division administrative	Centre administratif
Anglesey, Isle of	Llangefni
Blaenau Gwent	Ebbw Vale
Bridgend	Bridgend
Caerphilly	Hengoed
Cardiff	Cardiff
Carmarthenshire	Carmarthen
Ceredigion	Aberaeron
Conwy	Conwy
Denbighshire	Ruthin
Flintshire	Mold
Gwynedd	Caernarfon
Merthyr Tydfil	Merthyr Tydfil
Monmouthshire	Cwmbran
Neath Port Talbot	Port Talbot
Newport	Newport
Pembrokeshire	Haverfordwest
Powys	Llandrindod
Wells	
Rhondda, Cynon, Taff	Clydach Vale
Swansea	Swansea
Torfaen	Pontypool
Vale of Glamorgan	Barry
Wrexham	Wrexham

Irlande du Nord

Division administrative	Centre administratif
Antrim	Antrim
Ards	Newtownards
Armagh	Armagh
Ballymena	Ballymena
Ballymoney	Balleymoney
Banbridge	Banbridge
Belfast	
Carrickfergus	Carrickfergus
Castlereagh	Belfast
Coleraine	Coleraine
Cookstown	Cookstown
Craigavon	Craigavon
Derry	
Down	Downpatrick
Dungannon	Dungannon
Fermanagh	Enniskillen
Larne	Larne
Limavady	Limavady
Lisburn	Lisburn
Magherafelt	Magherafelt
Moyle	Ballycastle
Newry and Mourne	Newry
Newtownabbey	Newtownabbey
North Down	Bangor
Omagh	Omagh
Strabane	Strabane

États des États-Unis d'Amérique

Deux abréviations figurent après le nom de chaque État: la première est l'abréviation courante, la seconde est celle utilisée dans le code postal (ZIP code).

Alabama (Ala; AL)
Date d'entrée dans l'union 1819 (22e)
Surnom Heart of Dixie, Yellowhammer State
Capitale Montgomery

Alaska (Alaska; AK)
Date d'entrée dans l'union 1959 (49e)
Surnom The Last Frontier
Capitale Juneau

Arizona (Ariz; AZ)
Date d'entrée dans l'union 1912 (48e)
Surnom Grand Canyon State
Capitale Phoenix

Arkansas (Ark; AR)
Date d'entrée dans l'union 1836 (25e)
Surnom Natural State
Capitale Little Rock

California (Calif; CA)
Date d'entrée dans l'union 1850 (31e)
Surnom Golden State
Capitale Sacramento

Colorado (Colo; CO)
Date d'entrée dans l'union 1876 (38e)
Surnom Centennial State
Capitale Denver

Connecticut (Conn; CT)
Date d'entrée dans l'union 1788 (5e)
Surnom Nutmeg State, Constitution State
Capitale Hartford

Delaware (Del; DE)
Date d'entrée dans l'union 1787 (1er)
Surnom Diamond State, First State
Capitale Dover

District of Columbia (DC; DC)
Capitale Washington

Florida (Fla; FL)
Date d'entrée dans l'union 1845 (27e)
Surnom Sunshine State
Capitale Tallahassee

Georgia (Ga; GA)
Date d'entrée dans l'union 1788 (4e)
Surnom Peach State
Capitale Atlanta

Hawaii (Hawaii; HI)
Date d'entrée dans l'union 1959 (50e)
Surnom Aloha State
Capitale Honolulu

Idaho (Idaho; ID)
Date d'entrée dans l'union 1890 (43e)
Surnom Gem State
Capitale Boise

Illinois (Ill; IL)
Date d'entrée dans l'union 1818 (21e)
Surnom Prairie State
Capitale Springfield

Indiana (Ind; IN)
Date d'entrée dans l'union 1816 (19e)
Surnom Hoosier State
Capitale Indianapolis

Iowa (Iowa; IA)
Date d'entrée dans l'union 1846 (29e)
Surnom Hawkeye State
Capitale Des Moines

Kansas (Kans; KS)
Date d'entrée dans l'union 1861 (34e)
Surnom Sunflower State
Capitale Topeka

Kentucky (Ky; KY)
Date d'entrée dans l'union 1792 (15e)
Surnom Bluegrass State
Capitale Frankfort

Louisiana (La; LA)
Date d'entrée dans l'union 1812 (18e)
Surnom Pelican State
Capitale Baton Rouge

Maine (Maine; ME)
Date d'entrée dans l'union 1820 (23e)
Surnom Pine Tree State
Capitale Augusta

Maryland (Md; MD)
Date d'entrée dans l'union 1788 (7e)
Surnom Old Line State
Capitale Annapolis

Massachusetts (Mass; MA)
Date d'entrée dans l'union 1788 (6e)
Surnom Bay State
Capitale Boston

Michigan (Mich; MI)
Date d'entrée dans l'union 1837 (26e)
Surnom Wolverine State, Great Lake State
Capitale Lansing

Minnesota (Minn; MN)
Date d'entrée dans l'union 1858 (32e)
Surnom North Star State
Capitale St Paul

Mississippi (Miss; MS)
Date d'entrée dans l'union 1817 (20e)
Surnom Magnolia State
Capitale Jackson

Missouri (Mo; MO)
Date d'entrée dans l'union 1821 (24e)
Surnom Show-Me State
Capitale Jefferson City

Montana (Mont; MT)
Date d'entrée dans l'union 1889 (41e)
Surnom Treasure State
Capitale Helena

Nebraska (Nebr; NE)
Date d'entrée dans l'union 1867 (37e)
Surnom Cornhusker State
Capitale Lincoln

Nevada (Nev; NV)
Date d'entrée dans l'union 1864 (36e)
Surnom Silver State, Sagebrush State
Capitale Carson City

New Hampshire (NH; NH)
Date d'entrée dans l'union 1788 (9e)
Surnom Granite State
Capitale Concord

New Jersey (NJ; NJ)
Date d'entrée dans l'union 1787 (3e)
Surnom Garden State
Capitale Trenton

New Mexico (N Mex; NM)
Date d'entrée dans l'union 1912 (47e)
Surnom Land of Enchantment
Capitale Santa Fe

New York (NY; NY)
Date d'entrée dans l'union 1788 (11e)
Surnom Empire State
Capitale Albany

North Carolina (NC: NC)
Date d'entrée dans l'union 1789 (12e)
Surnom Tar Heel State
Capitale Raleigh

North Dakota (N Dak; ND)
Date d'entrée dans l'union 1889 (39e)
Surnom Peace Garden State
Capitale Bismarck

Ohio (Ohio; OH)
Date d'entrée dans l'union 1803 (17e)
Surnom Buckeye State
Capitale Columbus

Oklahoma (Okla; OK)
Date d'entrée dans l'union 1907 (46e)
Surnom Sooner State
Capitale Oklahoma City

Oregon (Oreg; OR)
Date d'entrée dans l'union 1859 (33e)
Surnom Beaver State
Capitale Salem

Pennsylvania (Pa; PA)
Date d'entrée dans l'union 1787 (2e)
Surnom Keystone State
Capitale Harrisburg

Rhode Island (RI; RI)
Date d'entrée dans l'union 1790 (13e)
Surnom Plantation State
Capitale Providence

South Carolina (SC; SC)
Date d'entrée dans l'union 1788 (8e)
Surnom Palmetto State
Capitale Columbia

South Dakota (S Dak; SD)
Date d'entrée dans l'union 1889 (40e)
Surnom Coyote State
Captiale Pierre

Tennessee (Tenn; TN)
Date d'entrée dans l'union 1796 (16e)
Surnom Volunteer State
Capitale Nashville

Texas (Tex; TX)
Date d'entrée dans l'union 1845 (28e)
Surnom Lone Star State
Capitale Austin

Utah (Utah; UT)
Date d'entrée dans l'union 1896 (45e)
Surnom Beehive State
Capitale Salt Lake City

Vermont (Vt; VT)
Date d'entrée dans l'union 1791 (14e)
Surnom Green Mountain State
Capitale Montpelier

Virginia (Va; VA)
Date d'entrée dans l'union 1788 (10e)
Surnom Old Dominion State
Capitale Richmond

Washington (Wash; WA)
Date d'entrée dans l'union 1889 (42e)
Surnom Evergreen State
Capitale Olympia

West Virginia (W Va; WV)
Date d'entrée dans l'union 1863 (35e)
Surnom Mountain State
Capitale Charleston

Wisconsin (Wis; WI)
Date d'entrée dans l'union 1848 (30e)
Surnom Badger State
Capitale Madison

Wyoming (Wyo; WY)
Date d'entrée dans l'union 1890 (44e)
Surnom Equality State
Capitale Cheyenne

États et territoires australiens

Nom	Capitale
Australian Capital Territory	Canberra
New South Wales	Sydney
Northern Territory	Darwin
Queensland	Brisbane
South Australia	Adelaide
Tasmania	Hobart
Victoria	Melbourne
Western Australia	Perth

Provinces canadiennes

Nom	Capitale
Alberta	Edmonton
British Columbia	Victoria
Manitoba	Winnipeg
New Brunswick	Fredericton
Newfoundland	St John's
Northwest Territories and Nunavut	Yellowknife
Nova Scotia	Halifax
Ontario	Toronto
Prince Edward Island	Charlottetown
Quebec	Quebec City
Saskatchewan	Regina
Yukon Territory	Whitehorse

MILITARY RANKS/GRADES MILITAIRES

Military Ranks

The classification and naming of military ranks varies considerably between different countries and languages. The following tables are designed to facilitate the translation of this terminologically complicated subject, and to allow comparisons to be made between the terms used in different English- and French-speaking countries. It should be stressed that precise word-for-word translation is not strictly possible, and that in all cases terms placed on the same line are the closest equivalents. Details of duties and roles will differ to a greater or lesser degree.

The dark blue line marks the division between commissioned and non-commissioned ranks. The alternating blue and white lines have been used simply to aid consultation.

Grades Militaires

L'appellation des différents grades des armées varie considérablement en fonction des pays. Les tableaux suivants ont été conçus pour faciliter la tâche du traducteur s'aventurant sur le terrain miné des hiérarchies militaires. Ils lui permettront d'établir des correspondances entre les grades des armées des pays anglophones et francophones. Il faut noter qu'il est rare que les grades coïncident exactement d'un pays à l'autre, et à ce titre les termes figurant sur une même ligne constituent des équivalents plutôt que des traductions exactes.

La ligne bleu foncé sépare les grades d'officiers de ceux de sous-officiers. L'alternance de bleu et de blanc est destinée à faciliter la consultation des tableaux.

Air Force/Armée de l'air

RAF Armée de l'air britannique	USAF Armée de l'air américaine	RCAF Armée de l'air canadienne - anglais	RCAF - French Armée de l'air canadienne - français	Belgian Airforce Armée de l'air belge	French Airforce Armée de l'air française
Marshal of the Royal Air Force	General of the Air Force	Marshal of the RCAF	Maréchal de l'ARC		Chef d'état-major de l'Armée de l'Air
Air Chief Marshal	General	General	Général		Général d'armée aérienne
Air Marshal	Lieutenant General	Lieutenant General	Lieutenant-général	Lieutenant-général	Général de corps aérien
Air Vice Marshal	Major General	Major General	Major-général	Général-major	Général de division aérienne
Air Commodore	Brigadier General	Brigadier General	Brigadier-général	Général de brigade	Général de brigade aérienne
Group Captain	Colonel	Colonel	Colonel	Colonel	Colonel
Wing Commander	Lieutenant Colonel	Lieutenant Colonel	Lieutenant-colonel	Lieutenant-colonel	Lieutenant-colonel
Squadron Leader	Major	Major	Major	Major	Commandant
				Capitaine-commandant	
Flight Lieutenant	Captain	Captain	Capitaine	Capitaine	Capitaine
Flying Officer	First Lieutenant	Lieutenant	Lieutenant	Lieutenant	Lieutenant
Pilot Officer	Second Lieutenant	Second Lieutenant	Sous-lieutenant	Sous-lieutenant	Sous-lieutenant
Officer Cadet	Air Force Cadet	Officer Cadet	Élève-officier		Aspirant
Warrant Officer	Chief Master Sergeant of Air Force	Chief Warrant Officer	Adjudant-chef	Major	Major
	Chief Master Sergeant	Master Warrant Officer	Adjudant-maître	Adjudant-chef	Adjudant-chef
	Senior Master Sergeant	Warrant Officer	Adjudant	Adjudant	Adjudant
Flight Sergeant	Master Sergeant			Premier sergent- major	
	Technical Sergeant			Sergent-chef	Sergent-chef
	Staff Sergeant				
Sergeant	Sergeant	Sergeant	Sergent	Sergent	Sergent
Corporal	Senior Airman	Master Corporal	Caporal-chef	Caporal-chef	Caporal-chef
Senior Aircraftman	Airman First Class	Corporal	Caporal	Caporal	Caporal
Leading Aircraftman	Airman	Private	Soldat	1er Soldat	Aviateur de 1ère classe
Aircraftman	Airman Basic				Aviateur

MILITARY RANKS/GRADES MILITAIRES

Navy/Marine

Royal Navy (RN) Marine de guerre britannique	US Navy (USN) Marine de guerre américaine	Royal Canadian Navy (RCN) Marine de guerre canadienne - français	Canadian Navy (RCN) - French Marine de guerre canadienne - français	Belgian Navy Marine de guerre blege	French Navy Marine nationale
Admiral of the Fleet	Fleet Admiral	Admiral of the Fleet	Amiral de la Flotte		Amiral de France
Admiral	Admiral	Admiral	Amiral		Amiral
Vice-Admiral	Vice-Admiral	Vice-Admiral	Vice-amiral	Vice-amiral	Vice-amiral d'escadre
Rear-Admiral	Rear-Admiral (upper half)	Rear-Admiral	Contre-amiral	Amiral de division	Vice-amiral
Commodore	Rear-Admiral (lower half)	Commodore	Commodore	Amiral de flottille	Contre-amiral
Captain	Captain	Captain	Capitaine de vaisseau	Capitaine de vaisseau	Capitaine de vaisseau
Commander	Commander	Commander	Capitaine de frégate	Capitaine de frégate	Capitaine de frégate
Lieutenant Commander	Lieutenant Commander	Lieutenant Commander	Capitaine de corvette	Capitaine de corvette	Capitaine de corvette
Lieutenant	Lieutenant	Lieutenant	Lieutenant de vaisseau	Lieutenant de vaisseau	Lieutenant de vaisseau
Sub-Lieutenant	Lieutenant Junior Grade	Sub-Lieutenant	Enseigne de vaisseau de 1ère classe	Enseigne de vaisseau de 1ère classe	Enseigne de vaisseau de 1ère classe
Sub-Lieutenant	Ensign	Acting Sub-Lieutenant	Enseigne de vaisseau de 2e classe	Enseigne de vaisseau de 2e classe	Enseigne de vaisseau de 2e classe
Midshipman	Midshipman	Naval Cadet	Aspirant		Aspirant
Warrant Officer	Warrant Officer	Warrant Officer	Adjudant	Maître principal chef	Major
Fleet Chief Petty Officer	Master Chief Petty Officer	Chief Petty Officer, 1st Class	Premier maître de 1ère classe	Maître principal	Maître principal
Chief Petty Officer	Chief Petty Officer	Chief Petty Officer, 2nd Class	Premier maître de 2e classe	Premier maître	Premier maître
	Petty Officer 1st Class	Petty Officer 1st Class	Maître de 1ère classe	Maître	Maître
Petty Officer	Petty Officer 2nd Class	Petty Officer 2nd Class	Maître de 2e classe	Second maître	Second maître
Leading Rate or Rating	Petty Officer 3rd Class	Master Seaman	Matelot-chef	Quartier-maître	Quartier-maître de 1ère classe
		Leading Seaman	Matelot de 2e classe		Quartier-maître de 2e classe
Able or Ordinary Rate or Rating	Seaman	Able Seaman	Matelot de 1ère classe	Matelot de 1ère classe	Matelot breveté
Junior Rate or Rating	Seaman Apprentice	Ordinary Seaman	Matelot 2e classe	Matelot	Matelot
			Matelot 3ème classe		

MILITARY RANKS/GRADES MILITAIRES

Army/Armée de la terre

British Army Armée de terre britannique	US Army Armée de terre américaine	Canadian Army - English Armée de terre canadienne - anglais	Canadian Army - French Armée de terre canadienne - français	French Army Armée de terre française	Belgian Army Armée de terre belge	Swiss Army Armée de terre suisse
Field-Marshal	General of the Army			Maréchal de France		
General	General	General	Général	Général d'armée		Général
Lieutenant-General	Lieutenant-General	Lieutenant-General	Lieutenant-général	Général de corps d'armée	Lieutenant-général	Commandant de corps
Major-General	Major-General	Major-General	Major-général	Général de division	Général-major	Divisionnaire
Brigadier	Brigadier-General	Brigadier-General	Brigadier-général	Général de brigade	Général de brigade	Brigadier
Colonel	Colonel	Colonel	Colonel	Colonel	Colonel	Colonel
Lieutenant-Colonel	Lieutenant-Colonel	Lieutenant-Colonel	Lieutenant-colonel	Lieutenant-colonel	Lieutenant-colonel	Lieutenant-colonel
Major	Major	Major	Major	Chef de bataillon, Commandant	Major	Major
					Capitaine-commandant	
Captain	Captain	Captain	Capitaine	Capitaine	Capitaine	Capitaine
Lieutenant	First Lieutenant	Lieutenant	Lieutenant	Lieutenant	Premier lieutenant	Premier lieutenant
Second Lieutenant	Second Lieutenant	Second Lieutenant	Sous-lieutenant	Sous-lieutenant	Lieutenant	Lieutenant
Officer cadet	Officer cadet	Officer cadet	Élève-officier	Aspirant		
Warrant Officer 1st Class	Chief Warrant Officer 4-5	Chief Warrant Officer	Adjudant-chef	Major	Adjudant-major	Adjudant d'état-major
	Chief Warrant Officer 2-3	Master Warrant Officer	Adjudant maître	Adjudant-chef	Adjudant-chef	
Warrant Officer 2nd Class	Warrant Officer 1	Warrant officer	Adjudant	Adjudant	Adjudant	Adjudant
Sergeant Major	Sergeant Major	Sergeant Major	Sergent-major	Sergent-major	Premier sergent-major	Sergent-major
Staff Sergeant	Master Sergeant			Sergent-chef	Premier sergent	
	Sergeant 1st Class			Sergent (de carrière)		
	Staff Sergeant					
Sergeant	Sergeant	Sergeant	Sergent	Sergent	Sergent	Sergent
Corporal	Corporal	Master corporal	Caporal-chef	Caporal-chef	Caporal-chef	Caporal
Lance Corporal	Private 1st Class	Corporal	Caporal	Caporal, brigadier	Caporal	Appointé
				Soldat 1ère classe	Soldat 1ère classe	
Private	Private	Private	Soldat	Soldat	Soldat	Soldat

English-French Abbreviations
Abréviations anglais-français

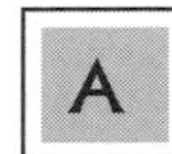

A *Elec* (*written abbr* **ampere**) A

a. *Agr* (*written abbr* **acre**) = 4047m², ≃ demi-hectare *m*

AA [ˌeɪ'eɪ] **1** *adj Mil* (*abbr* **anti-aircraft**) DCA *f*; **AA fire/guns** tir *m*/canons *mpl* de DCA

2 *n* (**a**) (*abbr* **Automobile Association**) = automobile club britannique et compagnie d'assurances, qui garantit le dépannage de ses adhérents et propose des services touristiques et juridiques, ≃ ACF *m*, ≃ TCF *m*

(**b**) (*abbr* **Alcoholics Anonymous**) AA *mpl*; **an AA meeting** une réunion des alcooliques anonymes

(**c**) (*abbr* **Advertising Association**) = organisme britannique dont le rôle est de veiller à la qualité des publicités et de défendre les intérêts des annonceurs et des agences de publicité

(**d**) *Am Univ* (*abbr* **Associate in Arts**) *(person)* = titulaire d'un diplôme universitaire américain de lettres; *(qualification)* diplôme *m* universitaire américain de lettres

AAA *n* (**a**) [ˌθriː'eɪz] *Formerly Sport* (*abbr* **Amateur Athletics Association**) = ancien nom de la fédération britannique d'athlétisme (remplacé en octobre 1991 par la "British Athletics Federation") (**b**) [ˌeɪeɪ'eɪ] (*abbr* **American Automobile Association**) = automobile club américain, ≃ ACF *m*, ≃ TCF *m*

A & E [ˌeɪənd'iː] *n Med* (*abbr* **accident and emergency**) service *m* des urgences, urgences *fpl*

AARP [ˌeɪeɪɑː'piː] *n* (*abbr* **American Association of Retired Persons**) = association américaine de retraités *(constituant un groupe de pression)*

AAU [ˌeɪeɪ'juː] *n Am Sport* (*abbr* **Amateur Athletic Union**) = organisme chargé de superviser les manifestations sportives, en particulier dans les universités

AAUP [ˌeɪeɪjuː'piː] *n* (*abbr* **American Association of University Professors**) = syndicat américain des professeurs d'université

AB¹ [ˌeɪ'biː] *n* (**a**) *Am Univ* (*abbr* **Artium Baccalaureus**) *(person)* = titulaire d'une [illegible] de lettres; *(qualification)* licence *f* de lettres (**b**) *Br Naut* (*abbr* **able-bodied seaman**) matelot *m* de deuxième classe

AB² (*written abbr* **Alberta**) Alberta *f*

ABA [ˌeɪbiː'eɪ] *n* (**a**) (*abbr* **Amateur Boxing Association**) Association *f* de boxe amateur (**b**) *Law* (*abbr* **American Bar Association**) = association d'avocats américains qui sert de centre d'information et de formation continue à ses membres

abbr, abbrev (**a**) (*written abbr* **abbreviation**) abréviation *f* (**b**) (*written abbr* **abbreviated**) abrégé

ABC [ˌeɪbiː'siː] *n* (**a**) *Banking* (*abbr* **activity-based costing**) coûts *mpl* par activité (**b**) (*abbr* **American Broadcasting Company**) = chaîne de télévision américaine (**c**) (*abbr* **Australian Broadcasting Corporation**) = chaîne de télévision australienne

ABD [ˌeɪbiː'diː] *n Am Univ* (*abbr* **all but dissertation**) = personne qui n'a plus qu'à rédiger sa thèse pour obtenir son doctorat

ABM [ˌeɪbiː'em] *n Mil* (*abbr* **anti-ballistic missile**) ABM *m*

A-bomb *n Mil* (*abbr* **atom bomb**) bombe *f* A

ABS [ˌeɪbiː'es] *n Aut* (*abbr* **Anti-lock Braking System**) ABS *m*

ABTA ['æbtə] *n* (*abbr* **Association of British Travel Agents**) = association des agences de voyage britanniques

AC [ˌeɪ'siː] *n* (**a**) *Br Sport* (*abbr* **athletics club**) club *m* d'athlétisme (**b**) *Elec* (*abbr* **alternating current**) courant *m* alternatif (**c**) *Tech* (*abbr* **air conditioning**) climatisation *f*

.ac [ˌeɪ'siː, æk] *Comput* (*abbr* **academic**) = abréviation désignant les universités et les sites éducatifs dans les adresses électroniques britanniques

a/c *Br Banking & Fin* (*written abbr* **account**) c

ACAS ['eɪkæs] *n Ind* (*abbr* **Advisory, Conciliation and Arbitration Service**) = organisme britannique de conciliation et d'arbitrage des conflits du travail, ≃ conseil *m* de prud'hommes

AC/DC [ˌeɪsiː'diːsiː] *n Elec* (*abbr* **alternating current/direct current**) CA/CC *m*

ACE [ˌeɪsiː'iː] *n Am Mil* (*abbr* **Army Corps of Engineers**) **the ACE** le Génie

ACGB [ˌeɪsiːˌdʒiː'biː] *n* (*abbr* **Arts Council of Great Britain**) = organisme public britannique de promotion des arts

ACH [ˌeɪsiː'eɪtʃ] *n Banking* (*abbr* **automated clearing house**) chambre *f* de compensation automatisée

ACL [ˌeɪsiː'el] *n Anat* (*abbr* **anterior cruciate ligament**) ligament *m* croisé antérieur

ACLU [ˌeɪsiːˌel'juː] *n Pol* (*abbr* **American Civil Liberties Union**) = ligue américaine des droits du citoyen

ACORN ['eɪkɔːn] *n Mktg* (*abbr* **A Classification Of Residential Neighbourhoods**) = classement des différents types de quartiers résidentiels existant en Grande-Bretagne en 39 catégories, utilisé par les entreprises pour mieux cibler leurs clients potentiels lors de campagnes commerciales

ACP [ˌeɪsiː'piː] *n* (**a**) *Geog* (*abbr* **African, Caribbean and Pacific**) **the ACP countries** les pays africains, des Caraïbes et du Pacifique (**b**) (*abbr* **American College of Physicians**) = académie [illegible] États-Unis

ACPO ['ækpəʊ] *n* (*abbr* **Association of Chief Police Officers**) = syndicat d'officiers supérieurs de la police britannique

ACS [ˌeɪsiː'es] *n* (*abbr* **American Cancer Society**) = association américaine de lutte contre le cancer

ACT [ˌeɪsiː'tiː] *n Sch* (*abbr* **American College Test**) = examen de fin d'études secondaires aux États-Unis

ACTT [ˌeɪsiːˌtiː'tiː] *n Formerly* (*abbr* **Association of Cinematographic, Television and Allied Technicians**) = ancien syndicat britannique des techniciens du cinéma et de l'audiovisuel, aujourd'hui remplacé par "BECTU"

AD [ˌeɪ'diː] **1** *adv* (*abbr* **Anno Domini**) apr. J.-C.; **in 3 AD** en l'an 3 (après Jésus-Christ *ou* de notre ère)

2 *n* (**a**) *Mil* (*abbr* **active duty**) service *m* actif (**b**) *Cin & Theat* (*abbr* **art director**) directeur(trice) *m,f* artistique

ADC [ˌeɪdiː'siː] *n* (**a**) *Mil* (*abbr* **aide-de-camp**) aide *m* de camp (**b**) *Am* (*abbr* **Aid to Dependent Children**) = aide pour enfants assistés (**c**) *Tech* (*abbr* **analogue-digital converter**) CAN *m*

ADHD [ˌeɪdiːˌeɪtʃ'diː] *n Med* (*abbr* **attention deficit hyperactivity disorder**) syndrome *m* hyperkinétique de l'enfant, syndrome *m* de l'enfant hyperactif

adj. *Mil* (*written abbr* **adjutant**) adjt

adjt. *Mil* (*written abbr* **adjutant**) adjt

admin ['ædmɪn] *n Fam* (*abbr* **administration**) *(work)* travail *m* administratif ❑; *(department)* administration ❑ *f*; **admin tasks** tâches *fpl* administratives; **are you (in) sales or admin?** vous êtes au service des ventes ou à l'administration?

ADP [ˌeɪdiː'piː] *n Comput* (*abbr* **automatic data processing**) traitement *m* automatique des données

ADR [ˌeɪdiː'ɑː(r)] *n Fin* (*abbr* **American Depositary Receipt**) certificat *m* américain de dépôt

ADSL [ˌeɪdiːˌes'el] *n Comput* (*abbr* **asymmetric digital subscriber line**) LNPA *f*

ADT [ˌeɪdiː'tiː] *n* (*abbr* **Atlantic Daylight Time**) = heure d'été des Provinces Maritimes du Canada et d'une partie des Caraïbes

advt (*written abbr* **advertisement**) *(for product, service)* publicité *f*; *(for job, event, accommodation)* (petite) annonce *f*

AEA [ˌeɪiː'eɪ] *n* (**a**) *Br* (*abbr* **Atomic Energy Authority**) ≃ CEA *f* (**b**) *Am* (*abbr* **Actors' Equity Association**) = syndicat de comédiens aux États-Unis

AEC [ˌeɪiː'siː] *n Am* (*abbr* **Atomic Energy Commission**) ≃ CEA *f*

AEEU [ˌeɪiːˌiː'juː] *n* (*abbr* **Amalgamated Engineering and Electrical Union**) = syndicat britannique de l'industrie mécanique

AF [ˌeɪ'ef] *n Am* (*abbr* **Air Force**) armée *f* de l'air

AFB [ˌeɪef'biː] *n Am* (**a**) (*abbr* **air force base**) base *f* aérienne (**b**) (*abbr* **American Foundation for the Blind**) = institution américaine pour les aveugles

AFC [ˌeɪef'siː] *n* (**a**) *Aviat & Tech* (*abbr* **automatic flight control**) commande *f* automatique de vol (**b**) *Rad* (*abbr* **automatic frequency control**) correcteur *m* automatique de fréquence (**c**) (*abbr* **American Football Conference**) = division de la fédération nationale de football américain (NFL), comprenant quinze équipes

AFDC [ˌeɪefˌdiː'siː] *n Admin* (*abbr* **Aid to Families with Dependent Children**) = type d'allocations familiales destinées tout particulièrement aux familles monoparentales

AFL [ˌeɪef'el] *n Sport* (*abbr* **American Football League**) = ligue professionnelle de football américain

AFL-CIO [ˌeɪef'elˌsiːaɪ'əʊ] *n Admin & Ind* (*abbr* **American Federation of Labor and Congress of Industrial Organizations**) = la plus grande confédération syndicale américaine

AFM [ˌeɪef'em] *n TV* (*abbr* **assistant floor manager**) régisseur *m* de plateau adjoint

AFT [ˌeɪef'tiː] *n* (*abbr* **American Federation of Teachers**) = syndicat américain d'enseignants

AG *Am* (*written abbr* **Attorney General**) ≃ ministre *m* de la Justice

AGC [ˌeɪdʒiː'siː] *n Rad & Elec* (*abbr* **Automatic Gain Control**) antifading *m*

AGM [ˌeɪdʒiː'em] *n Br Admin* (*abbr* **annual general meeting**) AGA *f*

AGR [ˌeɪdʒiː'ɑː(r)] *n Tech* (*abbr* **advanced gas-cooled reactor**) AGR *m*

AHA [ˌeɪeɪtʃ'eɪ] *Chem* (*abbr* **alpha-hydroxy acid**) **1** *n* AHA *m*

2 *comp* (*moisturizer, product*) aux acides de fruits

AI [ˌeɪ'aɪ] *n* (**a**) (*abbr* **Amnesty International**) Amnesty International (**b**) *Comput* (*abbr* **artificial intelligence**) IA *f* (**c**) *Biol* (*abbr* **artificial insemination**) insémination *f* artificielle

AIB [ˌeɪaɪ'biː] *n* (*abbr* **Accident Investigation Bureau**) = commission d'enquête sur les accidents en Grande-Bretagne

AID [ˌeɪaɪ'diː] *n* (**a**) *Biol* (*abbr* **artificial insemination by donor**) IAD *f* (**b**) *Am Admin & Econ* (*abbr* **Agency for International Development**) = agence américaine pour le développement international

AIDA [aɪ'iːdə] *n Mktg* (*abbr* **attention-interest-desire-action**) AIDA *m*

AIDS, Aids [eɪdz] *Med* (*abbr* **acquired immune deficiency syndrome**) **1** *n* sida *m*, SIDA *m*, Sida *m*

2 *comp* (*clinic*) pour sidéens

▸▸ ***Aids patient*** sidéen(enne) *m,f*; ***Aids research*** recherche *f* sur le sida; ***Aids specialist*** sidologue *mf*; ***Aids sufferer*** sidéen (-enne) *m,f*, malade *mf* atteint(e) du sida; ***the Aids virus*** le virus du sida

AIH [ˌeɪaɪ'eɪtʃ] *n Biol* (*abbr* **artificial insemination by husband**) IAC *f*

AIM [ˌeɪaɪ'em] *n Br St Exch* (*abbr* **Alternative Investment Market**) = marché hors-cote rattaché à la Bourse de Londres

AIO [ˌeɪaɪ'əʊ] *n Mktg* (*abbr* **activities, interests and opinions**) AIO

▸▸ ***AIO research*** étude *f* AIO

AK (*written abbr* **Alaska**) Alaska *m*

aka [ˌeɪkeɪ'eɪ] *adv* (*abbr* **also known as**) alias

AL (*written abbr* **Alabama**) Alabama *m*

Alas. (*written abbr* **Alaska**) Alaska *m*

A level *n* (*abbr* **Advanced level**) (*in England, Wales and Northern Ireland*) **A levels, A level exams** ≃ baccalauréat *m*; **he teaches A level physics** ≃ il est professeur de physique en terminale; **he has an A level in Maths** il a un diplôme de maths niveau bac; **to take one's A levels** ≃ passer son bac

ALF [ˌeɪel'ef] *n* (*abbr* **Animal Liberation Front**) = mouvement britannique militant pour la défense des droits des animaux

ALGOL, Algol ['ælgɒl] *n Comput* (*abbr* **algorithmic oriented language**) ALGOL *m*

alkie, alky ['ælkɪ] (*pl* **alkies**) *n Fam* (**a**) (*abbr* **alcoholic**) alcolo *mf*, poivrot(e) *m,f* (**b**) *Am* (*abbr* **alcohol**) gnôle *f*

▸▸ *Am* ***alkie cooking*** = fabrication clandestine d'alcool

.alt [ɔːlt] *n Comput* (*abbr* **alternative**) (*in newsgroups*) = abréviation désignant des forums de discussion qui peuvent porter sur toutes sortes de sujets

Alta. (*written abbr* **Alberta**) Alberta *f*

ALU [ˌeɪel'juː] *n Comput* (*abbr* **arithmetic and logic unit**) unité *f* arithmétique et logique

AM [ˌeɪ'em] *n* (**a**) *Am Univ* (*abbr* **Master of Arts**) (*person*) = titulaire d'une maîtrise de lettres; (*qualification*) maîtrise *f* de lettres (**b**) *Tel* (*abbr* **amplitude modulation**) AM (**c**) *Pol* (*abbr* **(Welsh) Assembly Member**) = membre de l'assemblée galloise

a.m. [ˌeɪ'em] *adv* (*abbr* **ante meridiem**) du matin; **at 2 a.m.** à 2 heures du matin

AMA [ˌeɪem'eɪ] *n* (**a**) *Med* (*abbr* **American Medical Association**) = ordre américain des médecins (**b**) *Mktg* (*abbr* **American Marketing Association**) = institut américain de marketing

Amex ['æmeks] *n* (**a**) *St Exch* (*abbr* **American Stock Exchange**) = deuxième place boursière des États-Unis (**b**) *Fin* (*abbr* **American Express**®) American Express®

amp [æmp] *n* (**a**) *Elec* (*abbr* **ampere**) ampère *m*; **13-amp plug** fiche *f* de 13 ampères (**b**) *Fam* (*abbr* **amplifier**) ampli *m*

amt (*written abbr* **amount**) (*quantity*) quantité *f*; (*sum*) montant *m*

ANA [ˌeɪen'eɪ] *n* (**a**) *Press* (*abbr* **American Newspaper Association**) = syndicat américain de la presse écrite (**b**) *Med* (*abbr* **American Nurses Association**) = syndicat américain d'infirmiers

ANC [ˌeɪen'siː] *n Pol* (*abbr* **African National Congress**) ANC *m*

anon. (*written abbr* **anonymous**) anon.

ANSI [ˌeɪenˌes'aɪ] *n Admin & Ind* (*abbr* **American National Standards Institute**) association *f* américaine de normalisation, = AFNOR *f*

ANTA [ˌeɪenˌtiː'eɪ] *n* (*abbr* **American National Theater and Academy**) = organisation américaine dont le rôle est de promouvoir l'art théâtral

Anzac ['ænzæk] *n Mil* (*abbr* **Australia-New Zea-land Army Corps**) = soldat néo-zélandais ou australien

▸▸ ***Anzac Day*** = date anniversaire du débarquement des alliés australiens et néo-zélandais à Gallipoli en Turquie, le 25 avril 1915

ANZUS ['ænzəs] *n Mil* (*abbr* **Australia, New Zealand, United States**) = alliance entre l'Australie, la Nouvelle-Zélande et les États-Unis

aob, AOB [ˌeɪəʊ'biː] *n Admin* (*abbr* **any other business**) ≃ divers

aocb, AOCB [ˌeɪəʊˌsiː'biː] *n Admin* (*abbr* **any other competent business**) ≃ affaires diverses

AONB [ˌeɪəʊˌen'biː] *n Br* (*abbr* **area of outstanding natural beauty**) = zone naturelle protégée

AP [ˌeɪ'piː] *n* (**a**) (*abbr* **American Plan**) pension *f* complète (**b**) *Press* (*abbr* **Associated Press**) AP *f*

APB [ˌeɪpiː'biː] *n Am* (*abbr* **all points bulletin**) = message radio diffusé par la police concernant une personne recherchée

APEX ['eɪpeks] *n Br* (*abbr* **advance purchase excursion**) = tarif préférentiel sujet à des restrictions de délai d'achat

API [ˌeɪpiː'aɪ] *n Press* (*abbr* **American Press Institute**) = association de journalistes américains

APO [ˌeɪpiː'əʊ] *n Mil* (*abbr* **Army Post Office**) = service postal de l'armée

appro ['æprəʊ] *n Br Fam Com* (*abbr* **approval**) **on appro** à *ou* sous condition❑, à l'essai❑

approx. (*written abbr* **approximately**) approx., env

APR [ˌeɪpiː'ɑː(r)] *n Fin* (**a**) (*abbr* **annual** *or* **annualized percentage rate**) TEG *m* (**b**) (*abbr* **annual purchase rate**) taux *m* annuel

Apr. (*written abbr* **April**) avr

APS [ˌeɪpiː'es] (*abbr* **advanced photo system**) **1** *n* APS *m inv*

2 *adj* (*camera*) APS (*inv*)

APT [ˌeɪpiː'tiː] *n* (**a**) *Br Rail* (*abbr* **advanced passenger train**) = train à grande vitesse, ≃ TGV *m* (**b**) *Fin* (*abbr* **arbitrage pricing theory**) théorie *f* de l'évaluation arbitrage

apt. (*written abbr* **apartment**) appt

AQ [ˌeɪ'kjuː] *n* (*abbr* **achievement quotient**) = quotient d'aptitude obtenu en divisant l'âge d'aptitude par l'âge réel du sujet

AR (*written abbr* **Arkansas**) Arkansas *m*

ARA [ˌeɪɑː'reɪ] *n* (*abbr* **Associate of the Royal Academy**) = membre associé de la "Royal Academy"

ARAM [ˌeɪɑːˌreɪ'em] *n Mus* (*abbr* **Associate of the Royal Academy of Music**) = membre associé de la "Royal Academy of Music"

ARC [ˌeɪɑː'siː] *n* (**a**) *Med* (*abbr* **aids-related complex**) ARC *m* (**b**) (*abbr* **American Red Cross**) **the ARC** la Croix-Rouge américaine

ARCM [ˌeɪɑːˌsiː'em] *n Mus* (*abbr* **Associate of the Royal College of Music**) = membre associé du "Royal College of Music"

ARIBA [ə'riːbə] *n* (*abbr* **Associate of the Royal Institute of British Architects**) = membre associé du "Royal Institute of British Architects"

Ariz (*written abbr* **Arizona**) Arizona *m*

ARP [ˌeɪɑː'piː] *n Br Hist* (*abbr* **air-raid precautions**) (*measures*) = mesures de défense civile lors des bombardements aériens pendant la Deuxième Guerre mondiale; **the ARP** (*organization*) = organisation chargée de mettre en œuvre les mesures de défense civile lors des bombardements aériens pendant la Deuxième Guerre mondiale

▸▸ ***ARP warden*** = agent chargé de faire appliquer les mesures de défense civile lors des bombardements aériens pendant la Deuxième Guerre mondiale

ARR [ˌeɪɑː'rɑː(r)] *n Acct* (*abbr* **accounting rate of return**) taux *m* de rendement comptable

arr. (*written abbr* **arrives**) (*on timetable*) arrive

artic [ɑː'tɪk] *n Br Fam* (*abbr* **articulated lorry**) semi-remorque *m*

ARV [ˌeɪɑː'viː] *n* (**a**) *Bible* (*abbr* **American Revised Version**) = traduction américaine de la Bible (**b**) *Med* (*abbr* **aids-related virus**) ARV *m*

AS[1] [ˌeɪ'es] *n Am Univ* (*abbr* **Associate in Science**) (*person*) = titulaire d'un diplôme universitaire américain de sciences; (*qualification*) = diplôme universitaire américain de sciences

AS[2] (*written abbr* **American Samoa**) Samoa *fpl* américaines

ASA [ˌeɪes'eɪ] *n* (**a**) *Br* (*abbr* **Advertising Standards Authority**) ≃ BVP *m* (**b**) (*abbr* **American Standards Association**) association *f* américaine de normalisation, ≃ AFNOR *f* (**c**) *Phot* (*abbr* **American Standards Association**) ASA *f*; **ASA/DIN exposure index** graduations *fpl* ASA/DIN; **an ASA 100 film, a 100 ASA film** une pellicule 100 ASA (**d**) *Br* (*abbr* **Amateur Swimming Association**) fédération *f* de natation

asap [ˌeɪeseɪ'piː] *adv* (*abbr* **as soon as possible**) aussitôt *ou* dès que possible; **we need to reply asap** il faut qu'on réponde dès que possible

ASC [ˌeɪes'siː] *n* (*abbr* **American Society of Cinematographers**) = société américaine des chefs-opérateurs

ASCII ['æskɪ] *Comput* (*abbr* **American Standard Code for Information Interchange**) *n* ASCII *m*; **in ASCII** en ASCII

▸▸ ***ASCII art*** art *m* ASCII; ***ASCII code*** code *m* ASCII; ***ASCII file*** fichier *m* ASCII; ***ASCII text*** texte *m* ASCII; ***ASCII value*** valeur *f* ASCII

ASCU [ˌeɪesˌsiː'juː] *n Am Univ* (*abbr* **Association of State Colleges and Universities**) = association des établissements universitaires d'État aux États-Unis

ASE [ˌeɪes'iː] *n* (*abbr* **American Stock Exchange**) = deuxième place boursière des États-Unis

ASEAN [ˌeɪesˌiːeɪ'en] *n* (*abbr* **Association of South East Asian Nations**) ANASE *f*

ASH [æʃ] *n* (*abbr* **Action on Smoking and Health**) = ligue antitabac britannique

ASL [ˌeɪes'el] *n* (*abbr* **American Sign Language**) = langage des signes utilisé aux États-Unis

ASLEF ['æzlef] *n Rail* (*abbr* **Associated Society of Locomotive Engineers and Firemen**) = syndicat des cheminots en Grande-Bretagne

ASM [ˌeɪes'em] *n* (**a**) *Mil* (*abbr* **air-to-surface missile**) ASM *m* (**b**) *Theat* (*abbr* **assistant stage manager**) régisseur *m* général

ASPCA [ˌeɪesˌpiːsiːˈeɪ] *n* (*abbr* **American Society for the Prevention of Cruelty to Animals**) = société protectrice des animaux aux États-Unis, ≃ SPA *f*

ASR [ˌeɪesˈɑː(r)] *n Am* (*abbr* **air-sea rescue**) sauvetage *m* air-mer

ass (*written abbr* **assistant**) assistant(e) *m,f*

assoc (**a**) (*written abbr* **association**) association *f* (**b**) (*written abbr* **associated**) associé

asst (*written abbr* **assistant**) assistant(e) *m,f*

AST [ˌeɪesˈtiː] *n* (*abbr* **Atlantic Standard Time**) = heure d'hiver des Provinces Maritimes du Canada et d'une partie des Caraïbes

ASTMS [ˈæstiːmz, ˌeɪesˌtiːemˈes] *n* (*abbr* **Association of Scientific, Technical and Managerial Staffs**) = ancien syndicat britannique des personnels scientifiques, techniques et administratifs

ASV [ˌeɪesˈviː] *n* (*abbr* **American Standard Version**) = traduction américaine de la Bible

ATB [ˌeɪtiːˈbiː] *n* (*abbr* **all-terrain bike**) VTT *m*

ATC [ˌeɪtiːˈsiː] *n* (**a**) (*abbr* **air traffic control**) contrôle *m* du trafic aérien (**b**) (*abbr* **Air Training Corps**) = unité de formation de l'armée de l'air britannique

ATM [ˌeɪtiːˈem] *n* (**a**) *Banking* (*abbr* **automated teller machine**) DAB *m*, *Can* guichet *m* (bancaire) automatique, *Suisse* bancomat *m* (**b**) *Comput* (*abbr* **asynchronous transfer mode**) ATM *m*, commutation *f* temporelle asynchrone

atm. (*written abbr* **atmosphere**) atm

ATOL [ˌæˈtɒl] *n* (*abbr* **air travel organizer's licence**) licence *m* d'organisateur de voyages par avion

ATP [ˌeɪtiːˈpiː] *n Sport* (*abbr* **Association of Tennis Professionals**) ATP *f*

attn (*written abbr* **for the attention of**) attn, à l'attention de

Atty. Gen. (*written abbr* **Attorney General**) (*in US*) ≃ ministre *m* de la Justice

ATV [ˌeɪtiːˈviː] *n* (*abbr* **all-terrain vehicle**) véhicule *m* tout terrain

ATW [ˌeɪtiːˈdʌbəljuː] *adv* (*abbr* **around the world**) autour du monde

AUEW [ˌeɪjuːˌiːˈdʌbəljuː] *n Formerly Ind* (*abbr* **Amalgamated Union of Engineering Workers**) = ancien syndicat britannique de l'industrie mécanique, aujourd'hui remplacée par l'AEEU

Aug. (*written abbr* **August**) août *m*

AUP [ˌeɪjuːˈpiː] *n Comput* (*abbr* **Acceptable Use Policy**) = code de conduite défini par un fournisseur d'accès à l'Internet

AUR [ˌeɪjuːˈɑː(r)] *n Acct & Fin* (*abbr* **asset utilization ratio**) taux *m* d'utilisation des actifs

AUT [ˌeɪjuːˈtiː] *n Univ* (*abbr* **Association of University Teachers**) = syndicat britannique d'enseignants d'université

AV [ˌeɪˈviː] **1** *n Br Bible* (*abbr* **Authorized Version**) = la version anglaise de la Bible de 1611, autorisée par le roi Jacques Ier d'Angleterre
2 *adj* (*abbr* **audiovisual**) audio-visuel

Av. (*written abbr* **avenue**) av

AVC [ˌeɪviːˈsiː] *n Fin* (*abbr* **additional voluntary contribution**) supplément *m* de cotisation retraite (*payé volontairement*)

AVCO [ˈævˌkəʊ] *n Fin* (*abbr* **average cost**) coût *m* moyen

avdp. (*written abbr* **avoirdupois**) avoirdupoids *m*

Ave. (*written abbr* **avenue**) av

AVP [ˌeɪviːˈpiː] *n* (*abbr* **assistant vice-president**) = vice-président adjoint

AWACS [ˈeɪwæks] *n Aviat & Mil* (*abbr* **airborne warning and control system**) AWACS *m*

AWB [ˌeɪdʌbəljuːˈbiː] *n Com* (*abbr* **air waybill**) LTA *f*

AWOL [ˈeɪwɒl] (*abbr* **absent without leave**) *adj Mil* **to be/to go AWOL** être absent/s'absenter sans permission; *Fig Hum* **to go AWOL** (*person*) disparaître de la circulation; (*object*) disparaître; **my keys have gone AWOL** mes clés ont disparu, impossible de retrouver mes clés

AYH [ˌeɪwaɪˈeɪtʃ] *n* (*abbr* **American Youth Hostels**) = association américaine des auberges de jeunesse

AZ (*written abbr* **Arizona**) Arizona *m*

AZT [ˌeɪzedˈtiː] *n Med* (*abbr* **azidothymidine**) AZT *f*

B

b (**a**) (*written abbr* **billion**) milliard *m* (**b**) (*written abbr* **born**) né

BA [ˌbiːˈeɪ] *n* (**a**) *Univ* (*abbr* **Bachelor of Arts**) (*person*) = titulaire d'une licence de lettres; (*qualification*) licence *f* de lettres; **to have a BA in history** ≃ avoir une licence en histoire; **John Smith, BA** ≃ John Smith, licencié ès lettres/droit/*etc* (**b**) (*abbr* **British Academy**) = organisme public d'aide à la recherche dans le domaine des lettres (**c**) (*abbr* **British Airways**) British Airways

BAA [ˌbiːeɪˈeɪ] *n Com & Aviat* (*abbr* **British Airports Authority**) = organisme autonome responsable des aéroports en Grande-Bretagne

BACS [bæks] *n Banking* (*abbr* **Bankers' Automated Clearing Services**) système *m* électronique de compensation de chèques; **to pay by BACS** payer par virement électronique

BAE [ˌbiːeɪˈiː] *n Am* (*abbr* **Bachelor of Arts in Education**) (*person*) = titulaire d'une licence de sciences de l'éducation; (*qualification*) licence *f* de sciences de l'éducation

BAFTA [ˈbæftə] *n Cin & TV* (*abbr* **British Academy of Film and Television Awards**) **BAFTA (award)** = prix récompensant les meilleurs films et émissions de télévision en Grande-Bretagne

BALPA [ˈbælpə] *n Aviat* (*abbr* **British Airline Pilots' Association**) = syndicat britannique des pilotes de ligne

b and b, B & B [ˌbiːənˈbiː] *n* (*abbr* **bed and breakfast**) chambre *f* et petit déjeuner, chambre *f* d'hôte

BAOR [ˌbiːeɪəʊˈɑː(r)] *n Mil* (*abbr* **British Army of the Rhine**) = forces britanniques en Allemagne

Bart. (*written abbr* **baronet**) baronnet *m*

BASIC [ˈbeɪsɪk] *n Comput* (*abbr* **beginner's all-purpose symbolic instruction code**) basic *m*

BASW [ˌbiːeɪˌesˈdʌbəljuː] *n* (*abbr* **British Association of Social Workers**) = syndicat britannique des travailleurs sociaux

BATF [ˌbiːeɪˌtiːˈef] *n Am* (*abbr* **Bureau of Alcohol, Tobacco and Firearms**) = organisme gouvernemental américain dont le rôle est de veiller à ce que les lois concernant les boissons alcoolisées, le tabac et les armes à feu soient respectées

BB [ˌbiːˈbiː] *n* (**a**) (*abbr* **Boys' Brigade**) = organisation protestante de scoutisme pour garçons (**b**) (*abbr* **double black**) = sur un crayon à papier, indique une mine grasse (**c**) *Am* (*abbr* **bail bond**) cautionnement *m*
►► *Am* ***BB gun*** fusil *m* à air comprimé

BBB [ˌbiːbiːˈbiː] *n Am* (*abbr* **Better Business Bureau**) = organisme dont la vocation est de faire respecter la déontologie professionnelle dans le secteur tertiaire

BBC [ˌbiːbiːˈsiː] *n* (*abbr* **British Broadcasting Corporation**) **the BBC** la BBC (*office national britannique de radiodiffusion*); **BBC1** = chaîne généraliste de la BBC; **BBC2** = chaîne à vocation culturelle de la BBC
►► ***BBC English*** = l'anglais tel qu'il était parlé sur la BBC et qui servait de référence pour la "bonne" prononciation; ***BBC World Service*** = émissions radiophoniques de la BBC diffusées dans le monde entier

bbl. (*written abbr* **barrel**) baril *m*

BBQ [ˌbiːbiːˈkjuː] *n* (*abbr* **barbecue**) barbecue *m*

BBS [ˌbiːbiːˈes] *n Comput* (*abbr* **bulletin board system**) serveur *m* télématique, *Can* babillard *m*

BC¹ [ˌbiːˈsiː] (*abbr* **before Christ**) av. J–C.; **in the year 25 BC** en l'an 25 avant Jésus-Christ

BC² (*written abbr* **British Columbia**) Colombie-Britannique *f*

Bcc [ˌbiːsiːˈsiː] *n Comput* (*abbr* **blind carbon copy**) copie *f* cachée

BCCI [ˌbiːsiːˌsiːˈaɪ] *n Banking* (*abbr* **Bank of Credit and Commerce International**) BCCI *f*

BCD [ˌbiːsiːˈdiː] *n Comput* (*abbr* **binary-coded decimal**) DCB *m*

BCE [ˌbiːsiːˈiː] *n* (*abbr* **Board of Customs and Excise**) = douane britannique

BCG [ˌbiːsiːˈdʒiː] *n Med* (*abbr* **bacille Calmette-Guérin**) BCG *m*
►► ***BCG vaccination*** vaccin *m* BCG

BD [ˌbiːˈdiː] *n* (**a**) (*abbr* **Bachelor of Divinity**) (*person*) = titulaire d'une licence de théologie; (*qualification*) licence *f* de théologie (**b**) *Am Fin* (*abbr* **bank draft**) traite *f* bancaire

BDS [ˌbiːdiːˈes] *n* (*abbr* **Bachelor of Dental Science**) (*person*) = titulaire d'une licence de chirurgie dentaire; (*qualification*) licence *f* de chirurgie dentaire

BE [ˌbiːˈiː] *n* (*abbr* **Bank of England**) Banque *f* d'Angleterre

b/e *Fin* (*written abbr* **bill of exchange**) lettre *f* de change

BECTU [ˈbektuː] *n Cin, TV & Theat* (*abbr* **Broadcasting, Entertainment, Cinematograph and Theatre Union**) = syndicat britannique des techniciens du cinéma, du théâtre et de l'audiovisuel

BEd [ˌbiːˈed] *n Br* (*abbr* **Bachelor of Education**) (*person*) = titulaire d'une licence de sciences de l'éducation; (*qualification*) licence *f* de sciences de l'éducation

Beds (*written abbr* **Bedfordshire**) le Bedfordshire, = comté dans le sud de l'Angleterre

BEng [ˌbiːˈeŋ] *n Br Univ* (*abbr* **Bachelor of Engineering**) (*person*) = titulaire d'une licence d'ingénierie; (*qualification*) licence *f* d'ingénierie

bens *Admin* (*written abbr* **benefits**) allocations *fpl*

Berks. (*written abbr* **Berkshire**) le Berkshire, = comté dans le sud de l'Angleterre

BeV *Phys & Elec* (*written abbr* **billion electron volts**) GeV

bf¹ [ˌbiːˈef] *n Br Fam* (*abbr* **bloody fool**) crétin(e) *m,f*

bf² *Typ* (*written abbr* **boldface**) caractères *mpl* gras

b/f *Acct* (*written abbr* **brought forward**) reporté

BFA [ˌbiːefˈeɪ] *n Am* (*abbr* **Bachelor of Fine Arts**) (*person*) = titulaire d'un diplôme universitaire d'art, de musique ou de théâtre; (*qualification*) = diplôme universitaire d'art, de musique ou de théâtre

BFI [ˌbiːefˈaɪ] *n* (*abbr* **British Film Institute**) = organisme britannique de promotion du cinéma (aide à la réalisation notamment)

BFPO [ˌbiːefpiːˈəʊ] *n Mil* (*abbr* **British Forces Post Office**) = mention figurant dans l'adresse des militaires britanniques

bhp [ˌbiːeɪtʃˈpiː] *n Aut* (*abbr* **brake horsepower**) puissance *f* au frein

BIA [ˌbiːaɪˈeɪ] *n Am* (*abbr* **Bureau of Indian Affairs**) Bureau *m* des affaires indiennes

BIFU [ˈbɪfuː] *n* (*abbr* **The Banking, Insurance and Finance Union**) = syndicat britannique des employés du secteur financier

BIM [ˌbiːaɪˈem] *n Com* (*abbr* **British Institute of Management**) = organisme britannique dont la fonction est de renseigner et de conseiller les entreprises en matière de gestion, ainsi que de promouvoir l'enseignement de cette discipline

BinHex [bɪnˈheks] *n Comput* (*abbr* **Binary Hexadecimal**) BinHex

BIOS [ˈbaɪɒs] *n Comput* (*abbr* **basic input/output system**) BIOS *m*

BIS [ˌbiːaɪ'es] *n* (*abbr* **Bank for International Settlements**) BRI *f*
bk (**a**) (*written abbr* **bank**) banque *f* (**b**) (*written abbr* **book**) livre *m*
BL [ˌbiː'el] *n* (**a**) (*abbr* **Bachelor of Law(s)**) *(person)* = titulaire d'une licence de droit; *(qualification)* licence *f* de droit (**b**) (*abbr* **Bachelor of Letters**) *(person)* = titulaire d'une licence de lettres; *(qualification)* licence *f* de lettres (**c**) *Am* (*abbr* **Bachelor of Literature**) *(person)* = titulaire d'une licence de littérature; *(qualification)* licence *f* de littérature
bl *Com* (*written abbr* **bill of lading**) connaissement *m*
bldg (*written abbr* **building**) bât.
BLit [ˌbiː'lɪt] *n* (*abbr* **Bachelor of Literature**) *(person)* = titulaire d'une licence de littérature; *(qualification)* licence *f* de littérature
BLitt [ˌbiː'lɪt] *n Br Univ* (*abbr* **Bachelor of Letters**) *(person)* = titulaire d'une licence de littérature; *(qualification)* licence *f* de littérature
BLM [ˌbiːel'em] *n Am Admin* (*abbr* **Bureau of Land Management**) = services de l'aménagement du territoire aux États-Unis
BLS [ˌbiːel'es] *n Am* (*abbr* **Bureau of Labor Statistics**) = institut de statistiques du travail aux États-Unis
BLT [ˌbiːel'tiː] *n* (*abbr* **bacon, lettuce and tomato**) = sandwich avec du bacon, de la laitue et de la tomate
Blvd (*written abbr* **boulevard**) bd, boul
BM [ˌbiː'em] *n* (**a**) (*abbr* **Bachelor of Medicine**) *(person)* = titulaire d'une licence de médecine; *(qualification)* licence *f* de médecine (**b**) (*abbr* **British Museum**) **the BM** le British Museum
BMA [ˌbiːem'eɪ] *n Med* (*abbr* **British Medical Association**) = ordre britannique des médecins
BMJ [ˌbiːem'dʒeɪ] *n* (*abbr* **British Medical Journal**) = organe de la "British Medical Association"
BMus *n* (*written abbr* **Bachelor of Music**) *(person)* = titulaire d'une licence de musique; *(qualification)* licence *f* de musique
BMX [ˌbiːem'eks] *n* (*abbr* **bicycle motorcross**) *(bicycle)* VTT *m*; *(sport, activity)* cyclo-cross *m inv*
bn (*written abbr* **billion**) milliard *m*
BNP [ˌbiːen'piː] *n Pol* (*abbr* **British National Party**) = parti d'extrême-droite britannique
BO [ˌbiː'əʊ] *n Fam* (*abbr* **body odour**) odeur *f* corporelle ❑; **he's got BO** il sent mauvais
B of E [ˌbiːəv'iː] *n* (*abbr* **Bank of England**) Banque *f* d'Angleterre
BoT [ˌbiːəʊ'tiː] *n* (*abbr* **Board of Trade**) *(in UK)* ministère *m* du Commerce; *(in US)* chambre *f* de commerce
BP [ˌbiː'piː] *n Med* (*abbr* **blood pressure**) pression *f* artérielle
Bp *Rel* (*written abbr* **bishop**) Mgr
bpd [ˌbiːpiː'diː] *Petr* (*abbr* **barrels per day**) barils *mpl* par jour
BPhil [ˌbiː'fɪl] *n* (*abbr* **Bachelor of Philosophy**) *(person)* = titulaire d'un diplôme intermédiaire entre le MA et le PhD; *(qualification)* = diplôme intermédiaire entre le MA et le PhD
bpi [ˌbiːpiː'aɪ] *Comput* (*abbr* **bits per inch**) bits *mpl* par pouce
bpm [ˌbiːpiː'em] *Mus* (*abbr* **beats per minute**) temps *mpl* par minute
bps [ˌbiːpiː'es] *Comput* (*abbr* **bits per second**) bits *mpl* par seconde
BR [ˌbiː'ɑː(r)] *n Formerly* (*abbr* **British Rail**) = société des chemins de fer britanniques
Br (**a**) (*written abbr* **British**) britannique (**b**) *Rel* (*written abbr* **brother**) *(preceding name of monk)* F
Brig. *Mil* (*written abbr* **brigadier**) général *m* de brigade; **Brig. Smith** le général de brigade Smith
Bros., bros. (*written abbr* **brothers**) Frères
BS [ˌbiː'es] *n* (**a**) *Br* (*abbr* **British Standard/Standards**) = indique que le chiffre qui suit renvoie au numéro de la norme fixée par l'Institut britannique de normalisation (**b**) *Am Univ* (*abbr* **Bachelor of Science**) *(person)* = titulaire d'une licence de sciences; *(qualification)* licence *f* de sciences (**c**) *Am very Fam* (*abbr* **bullshit**) conneries *fpl*
bs *Com* (*written abbr* **bill of sale**) acte *m ou* contrat *m* de vente
BSA [ˌbiːes'eɪ] *n* (*abbr* **Boy Scouts of America**) = association américaine de scouts
BSC [ˌbiːes'siː] *n* (*abbr* **British Steel Corporation**) = entreprise sidérurgique, aujourd'hui privatisée
BSc [ˌbiːes'siː] *n Br* (*abbr* **Bachelor of Science**) *(person)* = titulaire d'une licence de sciences; *(qualification)* licence *f* de sciences
BSE [ˌbiːes'iː] *n Vet* (*abbr* **bovine spongiform encephalopathy**) EBS *f*
BSI [ˌbiːes'aɪ] *n* (*abbr* **British Standards Institution**) = association britannique de normalisation, ≃ AFNOR *f*
BSkyB [ˌbiːskaɪ'biː] *n TV* (*abbr* **British Sky Broadcasting**) = société de diffusion de chaînes de télévision par satellite
BSM [ˌbiːes'em] *n Aut* (*abbr* **British School of Motoring**) = école de conduite britannique
BST [ˌbiːes'tiː] *n* (*abbr* **British Summer Time**) = heure d'été britannique
BT [ˌbiː'tiː] *n* (*abbr* **British Telecom**) = société britannique de télécommunications
Bt. (*written abbr* **baronet**) baronnet *m*
bt/fwd *Acct* (*written abbr* **brought forward**) reporté
BTU [ˌbiːtiː'juː] *n Phys* (*abbr* **British thermal unit**) BTU
BTW *Comput* (*written abbr* **by the way**) *(in e-mail messages)* à propos
Bucks (*written abbr* **Buckinghamshire**) le Buckinghamshire, = comté dans le sud de l'Angleterre
BUPA ['buːpə] *n* (*abbr* **British United Provident Association**) = association d'assurance-maladie privée
BVM (*written abbr* **Blessed Virgin Mary**) **the BVM** la Sainte Vierge
b/w (*written abbr* **black and white**) NB
BYO [ˌbiːwaɪ'əʊ] *n* (*abbr* **bring your own**) = restaurant non autorisé à vendre des boissons alcoolisées mais où l'on a la possibilité d'apporter sa propre bouteille
BYOB [ˌbiːwaɪˌəʊ'biː] *n* (*abbr* **bring your own bottle**) = "apportez une bouteille", inscription que l'on trouve sur un carton d'invitation à une soirée ou qui indique qu'un restaurant n'est pas autorisé à vendre d'alcool et que l'on peut donc en apporter pour accompagner son repas
BYOD [ˌbiːwaɪˌəʊ'diː] *n Am* (*abbr* **bring your own drink**) = **BYOB**

C (**a**) (*written abbr* **Celsius, Centigrade**) C (**b**) (*written abbr* **century**) s; **C16** XVIème s
c (**a**) (*written abbr* **cent(s)**) ct (**b**) (*written abbr* **circa**) vers
C1 [ˌsiː'wʌn] *n Sport* (*abbr* **Canadian canoe 1**) C1 *m*
C2 [ˌsiː'tuː] *n Sport* (*abbr* **Canadian canoe 2**) C2 *m*
CA[1] [ˌsiː'eɪ] *n* (**a**) (*abbr* **Consumers' Association**) = association britannique des consommateurs (**b**) *Br* (*abbr* **chartered accountant**) expert-comptable *m*
CA[2] (**a**) (*written abbr* **Central America**) Amérique *f* centrale (**b**) (*written abbr* **California**) Californie *f*
c/a (**a**) *Banking* (*written abbr* **capital account**) compte *m* de capitaux (**b**) *Com* (*written abbr* **credit account**) compte *m* créditeur (**c**) *Banking* (*written abbr* **current** *or* **cheque** *or Am* **checking account**) C/C *m*, CCB *m*
ca. (*written abbr* **circa**) vers
CAA [ˌsiːeɪ'eɪ] *n Aviat* (**a**) *Br* (*abbr* **Civil Aviation Authority**) = organisme britannique de réglementation de l'aviation civile (**b**) *Am Formerly* (*abbr* **Civil Aeronautics Authority**) = organisme américain de contrôle des compagnies aériennes
CAB [ˌsiːeɪ'biː] *n* (**a**) *Br* (*abbr* **Citizens' Advice Bureau**) = en Grande-Bretagne, bureau où les citoyens peuvent obtenir des conseils d'ordre juridique, social etc (**b**) *Am Formerly Aviat* (*abbr* **Civil Aeronautics Board**) = organisme américain de réglementation de l'aviation civile
CACI [ˌsiːeɪˌsiː'aɪ] *n Mktg* (*abbr* **California Analysis Centers Inc**) = institut international de sondages
CAD[1] [ˌsiːeɪ'diː] *n Com* (*abbr* **cash against documents**) comptant *m* contre documents
CAD[2] [kæd] *n Comput* (*abbr* **computer-assisted design**) CAO *f*
CADCAM ['kædkæm] *n Comput* (*abbr* **computer-assisted design and manufacture**) CFAO *f*
CAE [ˌsiːeɪ'iː] *n Comput* (*abbr* **computer-aided engineering**) IAO *f*
CAF [ˌsiːeɪ'ef] *n Com* (*abbr* **cost and freight**) C et F
CAI [ˌsiːeɪ'aɪ] *n* (**a**) *Comput* (*abbr* **computer-aided instruction**) EAO *m* (**b**) *Ind* (*abbr* **Confederation of Australian Industry**) = confédération du patronat australien
CAL [ˌsiːeɪ'el, kæl] *n Comput* (*abbr* **computer-assisted learning**) EAO *m*
cal. (*written abbr* **calorie**) cal
CAM [ˌsiːeɪ'em, kæm] *n Comput* (*abbr* **computer-aided manufacture**) FAO *f*
Cambs. (*written abbr* **Cambridgeshire**) Cambridgeshire *m*
CAMRA ['kæmrə] *n Br* (*abbr* **Campaign for Real Ale**) = association britannique d'amateurs de bières traditionnelles
Can. (*written abbr* **Canada**) Canada *m*
C&F, C and F [ˌsiːənd'ef] *n Com* (*abbr* **cost and freight**) C et F
C&G, C and G [ˌsiːən'dʒiː] *n Sch* (*abbr* **City and Guilds**) = diplôme britannique d'enseignement technique
C&I, C and I [ˌsiːənd'aɪ] *n Com* (*abbr* **cost and insurance**) C & A
C & W [ˌsiːən'dʌbəljuː] *n* (*abbr* **country and western (music)**) country and western *f*
Cantab. *Univ* (*written abbr* **Cantabrigiensis**) = de l'université de Cambridge
CAP [ˌsiːeɪ'piː, kæp] *n EU* (*abbr* **Common Agricultural Policy**) PAC *f*
CAPM [ˌsiːeɪˌpiː'em, ˌkæp'em] *n* (*abbr* **capital asset pricing model**) MÉDAF *m*
caps [kæps] *npl* (**a**) *Typ & Comput* (*abbr* **capital letters**) majuscules *fpl*; **put in small caps** à imprimer en petites capitales (**b**) (*abbr* **capsules**) capsules *fpl*, gélules *fpl*
►► ***caps lock*** verrouillage *m* des majuscules; ***caps lock key*** touche *f* de verrouillage des majuscules
Capt. (*written abbr* **captain**) cap
Cards (*written abbr* **Cardiganshire**) Cardiganshire *m*
CARE [keə(r)] *n* (*abbr* **Cooperative for American Relief Everywhere**) = organisation humanitaire américaine
►► ***CARE package*** envoi *m* humanitaire; *Fig* = colis plein de friandises envoyé par un proche
CASE [keɪs] *n Comput* (*abbr* **computer-aided software engineering**) ingénierie *f* des systèmes assistée par ordinateur
CASM ['kæzəm] *n Br Comput* (*abbr* **computer-aided sales and marketing**) vente *f* et marketing *m* assistés par ordinateur
CAT[1] [kæt] *n Med* (*abbr* **computerized axial tomography**) TDM *f*
►► ***CAT scan*** scanographie *f*; ***CAT scanner*** scanographe *m*
CAT[2] [ˌsiːeɪ'tiː] *n Comput* (*abbr* **computer-aided teaching**) EAO *m*
CATV [ˌsiːeɪˌtiː'viː] *n Am* (*abbr* **community antenna television**) télévision *f* par câble

CB [ˌsiː'biː] *n* (**a**) (*abbr* **Citizens' Band**) CB *f* (**b**) (*abbr* **Companion of (the Order of) the Bath**) = distinction honorifique britannique

CBAT [ˌsiːbiːˌeɪ'tiː] *n Am Formerly* (*abbr* **college board achievement test**) = examen d'entrée à l'université aux États-Unis

CBC [ˌsiːbiː'siː] *n* (**a**) (*abbr* **Canadian Broadcasting Corporation**) = office national canadien de radiodiffusion (**b**) *Med* (*abbr* **complete blood count**) hémogramme *m*

CBD [ˌsiːbiː'diː] *n Am* (*abbr* **cash before delivery**) règlement *m* avant livraison

CBE [ˌsiːbiː'iː] *n* (*abbr* **Companion of (the Order of) the British Empire**) = distinction honorifique britannique

CBI [ˌsiːbiː'aɪ] *n* (*abbr* **Confederation of British Industry**) = association du patronat britannique, ≃ CNPF *m*

CBR [ˌsiːbiː'ɑː(r)] *comp Chem* (*abbr* **chemical, bacteriological and radiation**) chimique, bactériologique et radioactif

CBS [ˌsiːbiː'es] *n* (*abbr* **Columbia Broadcasting System**) = chaîne de télévision américaine

CBT [ˌsiːbiː'tiː] *n Am Fin* (*abbr* **Chicago Board of Trade**) Chambre *f* de commerce de Chicago

CC (*written abbr* **county council**) ≃ conseil *m* général

cc [ˌsiː'siː] **1** *n* (*abbr* **cubic centimetre**) cm^3
2 *vt* (*abbr* **carbon copy**) pcc; **to cc sb sth, to cc sth to sb** envoyer une copie de qch à qn

CCA [ˌsiːsiː'eɪ] *n* (**a**) *Acct* (*abbr* **current cost accounting**) comptabilité *f* en coûts actuels (**b**) *Am Hist* (*abbr* **Circuit Court of Appeals**) = cour d'appel du système judiciaire des États-Unis avant 1948

CCI [ˌsiːsiː'aɪ] *n* (*abbr* **Chamber of Commerce and Industry**) CCI *f*

CCTV [ˌsiːsiːˌtiː'viː] *n* (*abbr* **closed-circuit television**) télévision *f* en circuit fermé

CCU [ˌsiːsiː'juː] *n Med* (*abbr* **coronary care unit**) unité *f* de soins coronariens

CD[1] [ˌsiː'diː] *n* (**a**) (*abbr* **compact disc**) CD *m*; **on CD** sur CD (**b**) (*abbr* **Civil Defence**) protection *f* civile (**c**) (*abbr* **certificate of deposit**) certificat *m* de dépôt
▸▸ ***CD burner*** graveur *m* de CD; ***CD player*** lecteur *m* de CD; ***CD rack*** casier *m* de rangement pour CD; ***CD writer*** graveur *m* de CD

CD[2] (*written abbr* **Corps Diplomatique**) CD

CDC [ˌsiːdiː'siː] *n Am Med* (*abbr* **Center for Disease Control**) = aux États-Unis, institut fédéral de recherche sur les causes et la prévention des maladies

cd/fwd *Acct* (*written abbr* **carried forward**) reporté

CDI [ˌsiːdiː'aɪ] *n Comput* (*abbr* **compact disc interactive**) CDI *m*

Cdr *Mil* (*written abbr* **commander**) Cdt

CD-R [ˌsiːdiː'ɑː(r)] *n* (**a**) (*abbr* **compact disc recorder)** graveur *m* de disque compact (**b**) (*abbr* **compact disc recordable)** CD-R *m*

Cdre (*written abbr* **Commodore**) (**a**) *Mil* commodore *m (officier de rang inférieur au contre-amiral et supérieur au capitaine de vaisseau)* (**b**) *Naut (of merchant ships)* chef *m* de convoi *(of shipping line)* doyen *m* (des capitaines); *(of yacht club)* président *m*

CD-ROM [ˌsiːdiː'rɒm] *n Comput* (*abbr* **compact disc read-only memory**) CD-ROM *m*, CD-Rom *m*, *Offic* DOC *m*, *Offic* cédérom *m*
▸▸ *Comput* ***CD-ROM burner*** graveur *m* de CD-ROM; *Comput* ***CD-ROM drive*** lecteur *m* de CD-ROM, *Offic* lecteur *m* de disque optique; *Comput* ***CD-ROM newspaper*** journal *m* sur CD-ROM; *Comput* ***CD-ROM reader*** lecteur de CD-ROM

CD-RW [ˌsiːdiːɑː'dʌbəljuː] *n Comput* (*abbr* **compact disc rewritable)** CD *m* réinscriptible

CDT [ˌsiːdiː'tiː] *n* (**a**) *Am* (*abbr* **Central Daylight Time**) = heure d'été du centre des États-Unis (**b**) *Br Sch* (*abbr* **craft, design and technology**) = matière enseignée dans le secondaire qui comprend travaux manuels et technologie

CDV [ˌsiːdiː'viː] *n Comput* (*abbr* **compact disc video**) CDV *m*, CD vidéo *m*

CDW [ˌsiːdiː'dʌbəljuː] *n Ins* (*abbr* **collision damage waiver**) = suppression de franchise pour les dommages causés aux véhicules

CE [ˌsiː'iː] *n* (*abbr* **Church of England**) Église *f* anglicane

CEEB [ˌsiːiːˌiː'biː] *n Am Univ* (*abbr* **College Entry Examination Board**) = commission d'admission dans l'enseignement supérieur aux États-Unis

CEO [ˌsiːiː'əʊ] *n Com & Ind* (*abbr* **chief executive officer**) P-DG *m*

cert. (*written abbr* **certificate**) certificat *m*; **a cert. 18 film** un film interdit aux moins de 18 ans

CertEd [sɜːt'ed] *n Br Univ* (*abbr* **Certificate in Education**) = diplôme universitaire britannique en sciences de l'éducation

CET [ˌsiːiː'tiː] *n* (**a**) (*abbr* **Central European Time**) heure *f* de l'Europe centrale (**b**) *EU* (*abbr* **common external tariff**) tarif *m* extérieur commun

CF [ˌsiː'ef] *n Am Com* (*abbr* **cost and freight**) C et F

c/f *Acct* (*written abbr* **carried forward**) reporté

cf. (*written abbr* **confer**) cf

CFC [ˌsiːefˈsiː] *n Chem* (*abbr* **chlorofluorocarbon**) CFC *m*

cfi [ˌsiːef'aɪ] *n Com* (*abbr* **cost, freight and insurance**) caf, CAF

CFL [ˌsiːef'el] *n* (*abbr* **Canadian Football League**) – ligue professionnelle canadienne de football américain

CFO [ˌsiːef'əʊ] *n Am* (*abbr* **Chief Financial Officer**) chef *m* comptable, chef *m* de la comptabilité

CFR [ˌsiːef'ɑː(r)] *n Am* (*abbr* **Code of Federal Regulations**) ≃ Journal *m* officiel

CFS [ˌsiːef'es] *n Med* (*abbr* **chronic fatigue syndrome**) encéphalomyélite *f* myalgique, syndrome *m* de fatigue chronique

CFSP [ˌsiːefes'piː] *n EU* (*abbr* **Common Foreign and Security Policy**) PESC *f*

CFTC [ˌsiːefˌtiː'siː] *n Fin* (*abbr* **Commodity Futures Trading Commission**) = organisme fédéral chargé de réglementer les marchés des options et des contrats à terme de marchandises aux États-Unis

CG [ˌsiː'dʒiː] *n* (*abbr* **coastguard**) garde-côte *m*

cg (*written abbr* **centigram**) cg

CGA [ˌsiːdʒiː'eɪ] *n Phot* (*abbr* **colour graphics adapter**) adaptateur *m* graphique couleur, CGA *m*

CGI [ˌsiːdʒiː'aɪ] *n Comput* (**a**) (*abbr* **common gateway interface**) interface *f* commune de passerelle, CGI *f* (**b**) (*abbr* **computer-generated images**) images *fpl* de synthèse

CGT [ˌsiːdʒiː'tiː] *n Fin* (*abbr* **capital gains tax**) impôt *m* sur les plus-values

CH [ˌsiː'eɪtʃ] *n* (**a**) (*abbr* **Companion of Honour**) = décoration britannique remise aux citoyens qui ont rendu des services à l'État, ≃ chevalier *m* de la Légion d'honneur (**b**) *Banking & Fin* (*abbr* **clearing house**) chambre *f* de compensation

ch (*written abbr* **central heating**) ch. cent

ch. (*written abbr* **chapter**) chap

CHAPS [tʃæps] *n Br Banking* (*abbr* **clearing house automated payment system**) ≃ SIT *m*

ChB [ˌsiːeɪtʃ'biː] *n Univ* (*abbr* **Bachelor of Surgery**) *(person)* = titulaire d'un diplôme sanctionnant trois années d'études de médecine; *(qualification)* = diplôme sanctionnant trois années d'études de médecine

ChE (*written abbr* **chemical engineer**) ingénieur *m* chimiste

chemo ['kiːməʊ] *n Fam Med* (*abbr* **chemotherapy**) chimio *f*

Ches. (*written abbr* **Cheshire**) Cheshire *m*

CHIPS [tʃɪps] *n Am Banking* (*abbr* **Clearing House Interbank Payment System**) ≃ SIT *m*

CI[1] (*written abbr* **Channel Islands**) îles *fpl* Anglo-Normandes

CI[2] [ˌsiː'aɪ] *n* (**a**) *Am* (*abbr* **counter-intelligence**) contre-espionnage *m* (**b**) *Math* (*abbr* **confidence interval**) IC *m*

CIA [ˌsiːaɪ'eɪ] *n Am* (*abbr* **Central Intelligence Agency**) CIA *f*

CIC *Mil* (*written abbr* **commander-in-chief**) commandant *m* en chef, généralissime *m*

CICB [ˌsiːaɪˌsiː'biː] *n Br* (*abbr* **Criminal Injuries Compensation Board**) = organisme gouvernemental dont le rôle est de dédommager les victimes d'actes criminels

CID [ˌsiːaɪ'diː] *n* (*abbr* **Criminal Investigation Department**) = police judiciaire britannique, ≃ PJ *f*

cif, CIF [ˌsiːaɪ'ef] *n Com* (*abbr* **cost, insurance and freight**) CAF, caf

CIM [ˌsiːaɪ'em] *n* (**a**) *Comput* (*abbr* **computer-integrated manufacturing**) CFAO *f* (**b**) (*abbr* **Chartered Institute of Marketing**) = institut britannique de marketing

C-in-C *Mil* (*written abbr* **Commander-in-Chief**) commandant *m* en chef, généralissime *m*

CIS [ˌsiːaɪ'es] *n* (*abbr* **Commonwealth of Independent States**) CEI *f*

CISC [ˌsiːaɪˌes'siː] *n* (*abbr* **complex instruction set computer**) CISC *m*

CITES [ˌsaɪ'tiːz] *n* (*abbr* **Convention on International Trade in Endangered Species**) CITES *f*

CJD [ˌsiːdʒeɪ'diː] *n Med* (*abbr* **Creutzfeld-Jakob disease**) MCJ *f*; **new variant CJD** nouveau variant *m* de MCJ

Cl *Chem* (*written abbr* **chlorine**) Cl

cl (*written abbr* **centilitre**) cl

CLEP [ˌsiːelˌiː'piː] *n Am* (*abbr* **College Level Examination Program**) = examen d'entrée à l'université aux États-Unis

CLI [ˌsiːel'aɪ] *n Fin* (*abbr* **cost-of-living index**) indice *m* du coût de la vie

Cllr (*written abbr* **Councillor**) conseiller(ère) *m,f*

CLU [ˌsiːel'juː] *n Am* (*abbr* **Civil Liberties Union**) = ligue américaine des droits du citoyen

cm (*written abbr* **centimetre**) cm

Cmdr *Mil* (*written abbr* **Commander**) Cdt

CMI [ˌsiːem'aɪ] *n Med & Vet* (*abbr* **cell-mediated immunity**) immunité *f* cellulaire

CMO [ˌsiːem'əʊ] *n Am Fin* (*abbr* **collateralized mortgage obligation**) obligation *f* garantie par une hypothèque

CMOS ['siːmɒs] *n Comput* (*abbr* **complementary metal oxide silicon**) CMOS

CMV [ˌsiːem'viː] *n Med* (*abbr* **cytomegalovirus**) CMV *m*

CMYK [ˌsiːemˌwaɪ'keɪ] *n Comput* (*abbr* **cyan, magenta, yellow, black**) CMJN

CNAA [ˌsiːenˌeɪ'eɪ] *n Br* (*abbr* **Council for National Academic Awards**) = organisme non universitaire délivrant des diplômes en Grande-Bretagne

CND [ˌsiːen'diː] *n Br* (*abbr* **Campaign for Nuclear Disarmament**) = en Grande-Bretagne, mouvement pour le désarmement nucléaire

CNN [ˌsiːen'en] *n TV* (*abbr* **Cable News Network**) réseau *m* d'informations américain diffusé par câble et satellite

CNS [ˌsiːen'es] *n Biol* (*abbr* **central nervous system**) système *m* nerveux central

CO[1] [ˌsiː'əʊ] *n Mil* (**a**) (*abbr* **commanding officer**) commandant *m* (**b**) (*abbr* **conscientious objector**) objecteur *m* de conscience

CO[2] (*written abbr* **Colorado**) Colorado *m*

Co.[1] [kəʊ] *n* (*abbr* **company**) Cie; *Fig* **Jane and co** Jane et compagnie

Co.[2] (*written abbr* **county**) comté *m*

c/o [ˌsiː'əʊ] (*abbr* **care of**) chez

COBOL ['kəʊbɒl] *n Comput* (*abbr* **Common Business-Oriented Language**) cobol *m*

COD [ˌsiːəʊ'diː] *adv Com* (*abbr Br* **cash on delivery**, *Am* **collect on delivery**) **to send sth COD** envoyer qch contre remboursement; **all goods are sent COD** toutes les marchandises doivent être payées à la livraison

C of C [ˌsiːəv'siː] *n* (*abbr* **Chamber of Commerce**) chambre *f* de commerce

C of E [ˌsiːəv'iː] (*abbr* **Church of England**) **1** *n* Église *f* anglicane
2 *adj* anglican; **he's C of E** il appartient à l'Église anglicane

C of I [ˌsiːəv'aɪ] *n* (*abbr* **Church of Ireland**) Église *f* d'Irlande (*branche de l'Église anglicane*)

C of S [ˌsiːəv'es] *n* (**a**) (*abbr* **Church of Scotland**) Église *f* d'Écosse (**b**) *Am* (*abbr* **Chief of Staff**) secrétaire *m* général de la Maison Blanche

COGS [ˌsiːəʊˌdʒiː'es] *n Acct* (*abbr* **cost of goods sold**) coût *m* des produits vendus

COHSE ['kəʊzɪ] *n Br Admin* (*abbr* **Confederation of Health Service Employees**) = ancien syndicat des employés des services de santé en Grande-Bretagne

COI [ˌsiːəʊ'aɪ] *n Admin* (*abbr* **Central Office of Information**) = service public d'information en Grande-Bretagne

COL [ˌsiːəʊ'el] *n* (*abbr* **cost of living**) coût *m* de la vie

Col. *Mil* (*written abbr* **colonel**) Col

col (*written abbr* **column**) col

COLA ['kəʊlə] *n Am Fin* (*abbr* **cost-of-living adjustment**) augmentation *f* de salaire indexée sur le coût de la vie

Colo (*written abbr* **Colorado**) Colorado *m*

Comecon ['kɒmɪkɒn] *n* (*abbr* **Council for Mutual Economic Assistance**) le Comecon

Comintern ['kɒmɪntɜːn] *n Pol* (*abbr* **Communist International**) Komintern *m*

.comp *Comput* (*written abbr* **computers**) (*in newsgroups*) = abréviation désignant les forums de discussion qui ont pour thème l'informatique

comsat ['kɒmsæt] *n* (*abbr* **communications satellite**) satellite *m* de communication

Con. (**a**) (*written abbr* **constable**) agent *m* (*de police*) (**b**) *Pol* (*written abbr* **conservative**) conservateur

conchy ['kɒnʃɪ] (*pl* **conchies**) *n Br Fam Pej* (*abbr* **conscientious objector**) objecteur *m* de conscience ❑

Conn (*written abbr* **Connecticut**) Connecticut *m*

Cons *Pol* (*written abbr* **Conservative**) conservateur(trice) *m,f*

cont. (**a**) (*written abbr* **contents**) contenu *m*; (*in book*) table *f* des matières (**b**) (*written abbr* **continued**) suite

cont'd, contd (*written abbr* **continued**) suite *f*; **cont'd on p14** suite à la page 14; **to be cont'd** à suivre

co-op ['kəʊˌɒp] (*abbr* **co-operative society**) **1** *n* coopérative *f*, coop *f*
2 Co-op *n Br* **the Co-op** la Coop

CORE [kɔː(r)] *n Am* (*abbr* **Congress On Racial Equality**) = ligue américaine contre le racisme

Corn (*written abbr* **Cornwall**) Cornouailles *f*

Corp. (**a**) *Com* (*written abbr* **corporation**) Cie (**b**) *Mil* (*written abbr* **corporal**) caporal *m*

COS [ˌsiːəʊ'es] *n Com* (*abbr* **cash on shipment**) = paiement à l'expédition

cos[1] [kɒs] *n Math* (*abbr* **cosine**) cos

cos[2] [kɒz] *conj Fam* (*abbr* **because**) parce que ❑

CP [ˌsiː'piː] *n* (*abbr* **Communist Party**) PC *m*

c/p *Com* (*written abbr* **carriage paid**) pp

cp. (*written abbr* **compare**) cf

CPA [ˌsiːpiː'eɪ] *n Am* (*abbr* **certified public accountant**) ≃ expert-comptable *m*

cpa [ˌsiːpiː'eɪ] *n* (*abbr* **critical path analysis**) analyse *f* du chemin critique

CPI [ˌsiːpiː'aɪ] *n Com & Econ* (*abbr* **Consumer Price Index**) IPC *m*

cpi [ˌsiːpiː'aɪ] *Comput* (*abbr* **characters per inch**) cpp

Cpl *Mil* (*written abbr* **corporal**) caporal *m*

cpm (*written abbr* **copies per minute**) cpm

CP/M [ˌsiːpiː'em] *n* (*abbr* **control program for microcomputers**) CP/M *m*

CPR [ˌsiːpiː'ɑː(r)] *n Med* (*abbr* **cardiopulmonary resuscitation**) réanimation *f* cardiorespiratoire

CPS [ˌsiːpiː'es] *n Law* (*abbr* **Crown Prosecution Service**) ≃ ministère *m* public

cps [ˌsiːpiː'es] *Comput* (*abbr* **characters per second**) cps

CPSA [ˌsiːpiːˌes'eɪ] *n Admin* (*abbr* **Civil and Public Services Association**) = syndicat de la fonction publique

CPU [ˌsiːpiː'juː] *n Comput* (*abbr* **central processing unit**) unité *f* centrale (de traitement)

CPVE [ˌsiːpiːˌviː'iː] *n Br Sch* (*abbr* **Certificate of pre-vocational education**) = examen d'accès à une formation professionnelle pour les élèves désirant poursuivre leurs études après le GCSE mais ne souhaitant pas passer les "A levels"

CR [ˌsiː'ɑː(r)] *n Typ & Comput* (*abbr* **carriage return**) retour *m* chariot

cr. (**a**) (*written abbr* **credit**) crédit *m* (**b**) (*written abbr* **creditor**) créancier(ère) *m,f*

CRC [ˌsiːɑː'siː] *n* (**a**) *Typ* (*abbr* **camera-ready copy**) copie *f* prête pour la reproduction (**b**) *Am* (*abbr* **Civil Rights Commission**) = organisme gouvernemental qui veille au respect des droits civiques

CRE [ˌsiːɑː'riː] *n* (*abbr* **Commission for Racial Equality**) = commission contre la discrimination raciale

Cres. *Br* (*written abbr* **Crescent**) rue *f*

CRN [ˌsiːɑː'ren] *n Com* (*abbr* **customs registered number**) numéro *m* d'enregistrement douanier

CRO [ˌsiːɑː'rəʊ] *n Br Com* (*abbr* **Companies Registration Office**) = institut britannique où sont enregistrées toutes les informations concernant les entreprises du pays

CRT [ˌsiːɑː'tiː] *n* (*abbr* **cathode-ray tube**) (**a**) (*in TV set*) tube *m* cathodique (**b**) *Am* (*work station*) poste *m* de travail

CSA [ˌsiːes'eɪ] *n* (**a**) *Hist* (*abbr* **Confederate States of America**) États *mpl* confédérés d'Amérique (**b**) *Br Admin* (*abbr* **Child Support Agency**) = en Grande-Bretagne, organisme gouvernemental qui décide du montant des pensions alimentaires et les prélève au besoin

CSC [ˌsiːes'siː] *n Admin* (*abbr* **Civil Service Commission**) = commission de recrutement des fonctionnaires

CSCE [ˌsiːessiː'iː] *n EU* (*abbr* **Council for Security and Cooperation in Europe**) CSCE *f*

CSD [ˌsiːes'diː] *n Banking & St Exch* (*abbr* **Central Securities Depository**) depositaire *m* national de titres

CSE [ˌsiːes'iː] *n Formerly Sch* (*abbr* **Certificate of Secondary Education**) = ancien brevet de l'enseignement secondaire en Grande-Bretagne, aujourd'hui remplacé par le GCSE

CSEU [ˌsiːesˌiː'juː] *n Br* (*abbr* **Confederation of Shipbuilding and Engineering Unions**) = confédération britannique des syndicats de la construction navale et de la mécanique

CSM [ˌsiːes'em] *n Mil* (*abbr* **Company Sergeant-Major**) adjudant *m*

CST [ˌsiːes'tiː] *n Am* (*abbr* **Central Standard Time**) heure *f* d'hiver du centre des États-Unis

CSU [ˌsiːes'juː] *n Br* (*abbr* **Civil Service Union**) = syndicat britannique de la fonction publique

CSV [ˌsiːes'viː] *npl Comput* (*abbr* **comma-separated values**) valeurs *fpl* séparées par des virgules

CSYS [ˌsiːesˌwaɪ'es] *n Scot Sch* (*abbr* **Certificate of Sixth Year Studies**) = certificat sanctionnant une année d'étude supplémentaire facultative avant l'entrée à l'université, en Écosse

CT[1] [ˌsiː'tiː] *n Med* (*abbr* **computerized tomography**) TDM *f*; **a CT (scan)** une scanographie

CT[2] (*written abbr* **Connecticut**) Connecticut *m*

ct (*written abbr* **carat**) ct

CTC [ˌsiːtiː'siː] *n* (*abbr* **city technology college**) = collège technique britannique, généralement établi dans des quartiers défavorisés

cu. (*written abbr* **cubic**) **cu. cm** cm^3; **cu. metre** m^3

cu.in. (*written abbr* **cubic inch(es)**) pouce *m* cube

CV [ˌsiː'viː] **1** *n* (*abbr* **curriculum vitae**) CV *m*
2 *adj* (*abbr* **cardio-vascular**) cardio-vasculaire; **a CV workout** une séance de cardio-training

CV joint [ˌsiː'viː-] *n Aut* (*abbr* **constant velocity joint**) joint *m* de cardan

CVP [ˌsiːviː'piː] *n Fin* (*abbr* **cost-volume-profit**) étude *f* de coût-efficacité

CVR [ˌsiːviː'ɑː(r)] *n Fin* (*abbr* **contingent value right**) CVG *m*

CVS [ˌsiːviː'es] *n Med* (*abbr* **chorionic villus sampling**) prélèvement *m* des villosités choriales

CW [ˌsiː'dʌbəljuː] *Rad & Tech* (*abbr* **continuous waves**) **1** *npl* ondes *fpl* entretenues
2 *n* (*Morse code*) morse *m*

cwo, CWO *Com* (*written abbr* **cash with order**) payable à la commande

cwt (*written abbr* **hundredweight**) *Br* = 50,8 kg, (poids *m* de) 112 livres *fpl*; *Am* = 45,36 kg, (poids *m* de) 100 livres *fpl*

CYO [ˌsiːwaɪ'əʊ] *n Am* (*abbr* **Catholic Youth Organization**) = association de jeunes catholiques aux États-Unis

CZ [*Br* ˌsiː'zed, *Am* ˌsiː'ziː] *n Am Geog* (*abbr* **Canal Zone**) zone *f* du canal de Panama

D *Am* (*written abbr* **democrat, democratic**) démocrate

d (**a**) (*written abbr* **penny**) = symbole du penny anglais jusqu'en 1971 (**b**) (*written abbr* **died**) **d 1913** mort en 1913

DA [ˌdiː'eɪ] *n* (**a**) *Am Law* (*abbr* **District Attorney**) ≃ Procureur *m* de la République; **the DA's office** le parquet (**b**) (*abbr* **duck's arse**) = coiffure masculine populaire dans les années cinquante (cheveux courts plaqués vers l'arrière)

D/A *Com* (*written abbr* **documents against acceptance**) documents *mpl* contre acceptation

DAC [ˌdiːeɪ'siː] *n* (*abbr* **Development Assistance Committee**) CAD *m*

D and C, D & C [ˌdiːən'siː] *n Med* (*abbr* **dilation and curettage**) (dilation *f* et) curetage *m*

DAR [ˌdiːeɪ'ɑː(r)] *n* (*abbr* **Daughters of the American Revolution**) = organisme à tendance nationaliste et conservatrice regroupant des femmes descendant des patriotes de la guerre d'Indépendance aux États-Unis

DAT [ˌdiːeɪ'tiː, dæt] *n* (*abbr* **digital audio tape**) DAT *m*
►► ***DAT cartridge*** cartouche *f* DAT; ***DAT drive*** lecteur *m* DAT, lecteur *m* de bande audionumérique

dB *Phys* (*written abbr* **decibel**) dB

DBA [ˌdiːbiː'eɪ] *n* (*abbr* **Doctor of Business Administration**) docteur *m* en gestion

dbase *n Comput* (*written abbr* **database**) BD *f*

DBE [ˌdiːbiː'iː] *n Br* (*abbr* **Dame Commander of the Order of the British Empire**) = distinction honorifique britannique pour les femmes

DBMS [ˌdiːbiːˌem'es] *n Comput* (*abbr* **database management system**) SGBD *m*

DBS [ˌdiːbiː'es] *n* (*abbr* **direct broadcasting by satellite**) télédiffusion *f* directe par satellite

DC [ˌdiː'siː] *n* (**a**) *Elec* (*abbr* **direct current**) CC (**b**) *Am Fam* (*abbr* **District of Columbia**) DC (**c**) (*abbr* **Detective Constable**) ≃ inspecteur(trice) *m,f* de police

DCC [ˌdiːsiːˈsiː] *(abbr* **digital compact cassette**) DCC *f*

DCF [ˌdiːsiːˈef] *n Fin (abbr* **discounted cash flow**) cash-flow *m* actualisé, flux *mpl* de trésorerie actualisés

DD [ˌdiːˈdiː] *n* (**a**) *Univ (abbr* **Doctor of Divinity**) *(person)* = titulaire d'un doctorat en théologie; *(qualification)* doctorat *m* en théologie (**b**) *Comput (abbr* **double density**) double densité *f* (**c**) *Am Mil (abbr* **dishonorable discharge**) = exclusion de l'armée pour manquement à l'honneur

D/D *Fin (written abbr* **direct debit**) prélèvement *m* automatique

dd. *(written abbr* **delivered**) livré

DDE [ˌdiːdiːˈiː] *n Comput (abbr* **dynamic data exchange**) DDE *m*

DDS [ˌdiːdiːˈes] *n Univ (abbr* **Doctor of Dental Science**) *(person)* = titulaire d'un doctorat en dentisterie; *(qualification)* doctorat *m* en dentisterie

DDT [ˌdiːdiːˈtiː] *n Chem (abbr* **dichlorodiphenyltrichloroethane**) DDT *m*

DE *(written abbr* **Delaware**) Delaware *m*

DEA [ˌdiːiːˈeɪ] *n Am (abbr* **Drug Enforcement Administration**) = agence américaine de lutte contre la drogue

Dec. *(written abbr* **December**) déc

DEd [ˌdiːˈed] *n Univ (abbr* **Doctor of Education**) *(person)* = titulaire d'un doctorat en sciences de l'éducation; *(qualification)* doctorat *m* en sciences de l'education

Del *(written abbr* **Delete**) *(on keyboard)* Suppr

Del. *(written abbr* **Delaware**) Delaware *m*

deli [ˈdelɪ] *n Fam (abbr* **delicatessen**) (**a**) *(fine foods shop)* épicerie *f* fine; *(food shop)* ≃ traiteur *m* (**b**) *Am (restaurant)* ≃ restaurant *m* traiteur

►► ***deli counter*** *(in supermarket)* rayon *m* traiteur

Dem. *Am (written abbr* **Democrat(ic)**) démocrate

demo [ˈdeməʊ] *(pl* **demos**) *n Fam (abbr* **demonstration**) (**a**) *(protest)* manif *f*

(**b**) *(of band, singer)* disque *m*/cassette *f*/ vidéo *f* de démonstration ❑

(**c**) *(of device, system)* démonstration *f*; **we received a demo of the new software system** quelqu'un est venu nous faire une démonstration du nouveau logiciel

►► *Comput* ***demo disk*** disquette *f* de démonstration *ou* d'évaluation; ***demo tape*** bande *f* démo; *Comput* ***demo version*** version *f* de démonstration *ou* d'évaluation

dep *(written abbr* **departure/departs**) dép

dept. *(written abbr* **department**) service *m*

DEQ [ˌdiːiːˈkjuː] *adj Com (abbr* **delivered ex quay**) DEQ

DES [ˌdiːiːˈes] *n Formerly Admin (abbr* **Department of Education and Science**) = ancien ministère britannique de l'Éducation et de la Recherche scientifique

des res [ˌdezˈrez] *n Br Fam (abbr* **desirable residence**) *(flat)* bel appartement ❑ *m*; *(house)* belle maison ❑ *f*

Det. *(written abbr* **detective**) **Det. Jenkins** l'inspecteur Jenkins

DETR [ˌdiːiːˌtiːˈɑː(r)] *n Br (abbr* **Department of the Environment, Transport and the Regions**) = ministère britannique de l'Environnement, des Transports et des Régions

DF [ˌdiːˈef] *n (abbr* **Direction Finder**) radiogoniomètre *m*

DFC [ˌdiːefˈsiː] *n Mil (abbr* **Distinguished Flying Cross**) = distinction honorifique des armées de l'air américaine et britannique

DFE [ˌdiːefˈiː] *n Admin (abbr* **Department for Education**) ministère *m* de l'Éducation

DFM [ˌdiːefˈem] *n Mil (abbr* **Distinguished Flying Medal**) = médaille des armées de l'air américaine et britannique

DG [ˌdiːˈdʒiː] **1** *n (abbr* **director-general**) directeur(trice) *m,f* général(e)

2 *adv (written abbr* **Deo Gratias**) Dieu merci

DH [ˌdiːˈeɪtʃ] *n Br Admin (abbr* **Department of Health**) ministère *m* de la Santé

DHSS [ˌdiːeɪtʃˌesˈes] *n* (**a**) *Br Formerly Admin (abbr* **Department of Health and Social Security**) = ancien nom du ministère britannique de la Santé et de la Sécurité sociale (**b**) *Am Admin (abbr* **Department of Health and Social Services**) ≃ ministère *m* de la Santé

dial. *(written abbr* **dialect**) dial.

DIN [dɪn] *n (abbr* **Deutsche Industrie Norm**) (indice *m*) DIN *f*

dinky *(abbr* **double income no kids yet**) *Fam Hum* **1** *n* = membre d'un couple à deux revenus sans enfants

2 *comp (lifestyle etc)* de couple à deux revenus sans enfants

Dip. *(written abbr* **diploma**) diplôme *m*

DipEd [ˌdɪpˈed] *n Br Univ (abbr* **Diploma in Education**) ≃ CAPES *m*

dir (**a**) *Admin (written abbr* **director**) directeur(trice) *m,f* (**b**) *Comput (written abbr* **directory**) répertoire *m*

disc. *(written abbr* **discount**) esc.

Dist. Atty *Am (written abbr* **district attorney**) ≃ procureur *m* de la République

DIY [ˌdiːaɪˈwaɪ] *Br (abbr* **do-it-yourself**) **1** *n* bricolage *m*

2 *comp* de bricolage

►► ***DIY expert*** spécialiste *m* du bricolage; ***DIY shop*** magasin *m* de bricolage; ***DIY superstore*** grande surface *f* de bricolage

DJ [ˌdiːˈdʒeɪ] **1** *n* (**a**) *(abbr* **disc jockey**) DJ *m* (**b**) *Fam (abbr* **dinner jacket**) smoking ❑ *m*

2 *vi (work as DJ)* travailler comme DJ; **he DJ's every Friday night at the Volcano** il travaille comme DJ au Volcano tous les vendredis soir

DJIA [ˌdiːdʒeɪˌaɪˈeɪ] *n Am St Exch (abbr* **Dow Jones Industrial Average**) DJIA *m*

dl *(written abbr* **decilitre**) dl

DLit [ˌdiːˈlɪt] *n Univ (abbr* **Doctor of Literature**) *(person)* = titulaire d'un doctorat ès lettres; *(qualification)* doctorat *m* ès lettres

DLitt [ˌdiːˈlɪt] *n Univ (abbr* **Doctor of Letters**) *(person)* = titulaire d'un doctorat ès lettres; *(qualification)* doctorat *m* ès lettres

DLO [ˌdiːelˈəʊ] *n (abbr* **dead-letter office**) = bureau où est entreposé le courrier dont les destinataires sont introuvables

DM[1] *(written abbr* **Deutsche Mark**) DM

DM[2] [ˌdiːˈem] *n (abbr* **direct mail**) publipostage *m*

dm *(written abbr* **decimetre**) dm

DMA [ˌdiːemˈeɪ] *n Comput (abbr* **direct memory access**) accès *m* direct à la mémoire

DMs [ˌdiːˈemz] *npl Br Fam (abbr* **Doc Martens**®) Docs *fpl*, Doc Martens® *fpl*

DMus [ˌdiːˈmjuːz] *n Univ (abbr* **Doctor of Music**) *(person)* = titulaire d'un doctorat en musique; *(qualification)* doctorat *m* en musique

DMV [ˌdiːemˈviː] *n Am Admin (abbr* **Department of Motor Vehicles**) = service des immatriculations et des permis de conduire aux États-Unis

DMZ [ˌdiːemˈzed] *n (abbr* **demilitarized zone**) zone *f* démilitarisée

DNA [ˌdiːenˈeɪ] *n Biol (abbr* **deoxyribonucleic acid**) ADN *m*

►► ***DNA fingerprinting*** analyse *f* de l'empreinte génétique; ***DNA profiling*** séquençage *m* de l'ADN

DNR [ˌdiːenˈɑː(r)] *n Med (abbr* **do not resuscitate**) ne pas réanimer *(mention figurant sur le dossier de patients ne souhaitant pas être réanimés)*

DNS [ˌdiːenˈes] *n Comput (abbr* **Domain Name System**) système *m* de nom de domaine, DNS *m*

do. *(written abbr* **ditto**) do

DOA [ˌdiːəʊˈeɪ] *Med (abbr* **dead on arrival**) **1** *n* personne *f* morte *ou* décédée avant l'arrivée à l'hôpital

2 *adj* mort *ou* décédé avant l'arrivée à l'hôpital

d.o.b., DOB *(written abbr* **date of birth**) date *f* de naissance

DOD [ˌdiːəʊˈdiː] *n Am Admin (abbr* **Department of Defense**) = ministère américain de la Défense

DOE [ˌdiːəʊˈiː] *n Am Admin (abbr* **Department of Energy**) = ministère américain de l'Énergie

DoE [ˌdiːəʊˈiː] *n Br Formerly Admin (abbr* **Department of the Environment**) = ministère britannique de l'Environnement

DOI [ˌdiːəʊˈaɪ] *n Am Admin (abbr* **Department of the Interior**) = ministère américain de l'Intérieur

DOJ [ˌdiːəʊˈdʒeɪ] *n Am Admin (abbr* **Department of Justice**) = ministère américain de la Justice

dol *(written abbr* **dollar**) dol(l)

dorm [dɔːm] *n Fam (abbr* **dormitory**) (**a**) *(room)* dortoir ❑ *m* (**b**) *Am Univ* résidence *f* universitaire ❑

►► *Am Univ* ***dorm mother*** surveillante ❑ *f*

Dors *(written abbr* **Dorset**) Dorset *m*

DOS [dɒs] *n Comput (abbr* **disk operating system**) DOS *m*

►► ***DOS command*** commande *f* du DOS; ***DOS prompt*** indicatif *m* (du) DOS, invite *f* du DOS; ***DOS switch*** clé *f ou* paramètre *m* du DOS

DOT [ˌdiːəʊˈtiː] *n Am Admin (abbr* **Department of Transportation**) = ministère des Transports

doz. *(written abbr* **dozen**) douz

DP [ˌdiːˈpiː] *n* (**a**) *Comput (abbr* **data processing**) TD *m* (**b**) *(abbr* **disabled person**) handicapé(e) *m,f*

DPH [ˌdiːpiːˈeɪtʃ] *n (abbr* **Diploma in Public Health**) diplôme *m* de santé publique

DPh [ˌdiːpiːˈeɪtʃ] *n (abbr* **Doctor of Philosophy**) *(person)* = titulaire d'un doctorat de 3ème cycle; *(qualification)* = doctorat de 3ème cycle

DPhil [ˌdiːˈfɪl] *n (abbr* **Doctor of Philosophy**) *(person)* = titulaire d'un doctorat de 3ème cycle; *(qualification)* = doctorat de 3ème cycle

dpi [ˌdiːpiːˈaɪ] *Comput (abbr* **dots per inch**) dpi, ppp

DPP [ˌdiːpiːˈpiː] *n Br Law (abbr* **Director of Public Prosecutions**) ≃ procureur *m* général

DPT [ˌdiːpiːˈtiː] *n Med (abbr* **diphtheria, pertussis, tetanus**) DCT *m*

dpt *(written abbr* **department**) service *m*

DPW [ˌdiːpiːˈdʌbəljuː] *n Br Admin (abbr* **Department of Public Works**) ≃ ministère *m* de l'Équipement

Dr (**a**) *(written abbr* **Doctor**) **Dr Jones** *(on envelope)* Dr Jones; **Dear Dr Jones** *(in letter)* Monsieur, Madame; *(less formal)* Cher Monsieur, Chère Madame; *(if acquainted)* Cher Docteur (**b**) *(written abbr* **drive**) allée *f*

dr (**a**) *(written abbr* **debtor**) débiteur(trice) *m,f* (**b**) *(written abbr* **dram**) drachme *m* (**c**) *(written abbr* **drachma**) drachme *f*

DRAM [ˈdiːræm] *n Comput (abbr* **dynamic random access memory**) DRAM *f*

DSC [ˌdiːesˈsiː] *n Br Mil (abbr* **Distinguished Service Cross**) = décoration de l'armée britannique

DSc [ˌdiːesˈsiː] *n Univ (abbr* **Doctor of Science**) *(person)* = titulaire d'un doctorat en sciences; *(qualification)* doctorat *m* en sciences

DSL [ˌdiːesˈel] *n Comput (abbr* **Digital Subscriber Line**) ligne *f* d'abonné numérique, DSL *m*

DSM [ˌdiːesˈem] *n Br Mil (abbr* **Distinguished Service Medal**) = décoration de l'armée britannique

DSO [ˌdiːesˈəʊ] *n Br Mil (abbr* **Distinguished Service Order**) = décoration de l'armée britannique

DSS [ˌdiːesˈes] *n Br Admin (abbr* **Department of Social Security**) = ministère britannique de la Sécurité sociale

DST [ˌdiːesˈtiː] *n Am (abbr* **daylight saving time**) heure *f* d'été

DT [ˌdiːˈtiː] *n Comput (abbr* **data transmission**) transmission *f* de données

DTI [ˌdiːtiːˈaɪ] *n Br Admin (abbr* **Department of Trade and Industry**) = ministère britannique du Commerce et de l'Industrie

DTP [ˌdiːtiːˈpiː] *n Comput* (*abbr* **desktop publishing**) PAO *f*
▸▸ ***DTP operator*** opérateur(trice) *m,f* de PAO; ***DTP software*** logiciel *m* de PAO

DTp [ˌdiːtiːˈpiː] *n Br Admin* (*abbr* **Department of Transports**) ≃ ministère *m* des Transports

DT's [ˌdiːˈtiːz] *npl Fam* (*abbr* **delirium tremens**) delirium tremens❑ *m*; **to have the DT's** avoir une crise de delirium tremens

DTT [ˌdiːtiːˈtiː] *n* (*abbr* **digital terrestrial television**) télévision *f* numérique terrestre

DU [ˌdiːˈjuː] *n Chem* (*abbr* **depleted uranium**) uranium *m* appauvri

DUI [ˌdiːjuːˈaɪ] *n* (*abbr* **driving under the influence**) conduite *f* en état d'ivresse

dunno [dəˈnəʊ] *exclam Fam* (*abbr* **I don't know**) j'sais pas!

Dur (*written abbr* **Durham**) comté *m* de Durham

DV [ˌdiːˈviː] *adv* (*abbr* **Deo volente**) si Dieu le veut

DVD [ˌdiːviːˈdiː] *n Comput* (*abbr* **Digital Versatile Disk, Digital Video Disk**) DVD *m*, disque *m* vidéo numérique

DVD-ROM [ˌdiːviːˌdiːˈrɒm] *n* (*abbr* **Digital Versatile Disk read-only memory**) DVD-ROM *m*, DVD-Rom *m*

DVLA [ˌdiːviːˌelˈeɪ] *n Br* (*abbr* **Driver and Vehicle Licensing Agency**) = service des immatriculations et des permis de conduire en Grande-Bretagne

DVLC [ˌdiːviːˌelˈsiː] *n Br Formerly* (*abbr* **Driver and Vehicle Licensing Centre**) = service des immatriculations et des permis de conduire en Grande-Bretagne

DVM [ˌdiːviːˈem] *n Am Univ* (*abbr* **Doctor of Veterinary Medicine**) = titulaire d'un diplôme en médecine vétérinaire

DVT [ˌdiːviːˈtiː] *n Med* (*abbr* **deep-vein thrombosis**) TVP *f*

DWB [ˌdiːdʌbəljuːˈbiː] *n Am* (*abbr* **Driving While Black**) **he was stopped for DWB** un policier l'a fait se ranger sur le bord de la route pour contrôler ses papiers pour la seule raison qu'il est noir

DWEM [dwem] *n* (*abbr* **dead white European male**) = écrivain, musicien etc européen blanc mort depuis longtemps

DWI [ˌdiːdʌbəljuːˈaɪ] *n Am* (*abbr* **driving while intoxicated**) conduite *f* en état d'ébriété

E¹ [iː] *n Fam Drugs slang* (*abbr* **ecstasy**) (*drug, pill*) ecsta *f*

E² (**a**) (*written abbr* **East**) E (**b**) (*written abbr* **English**) anglais

EA [ˌiːˈeɪ] *n Am Sch* (*abbr* **educational age**) âge *m* pédagogique

ea. (*written abbr* **each**) **£3.00 ea.** 3 livres pièce

E and OE, E&OE [ˌiːəndˈəʊiː] *n Com* (*abbr* **errors and omissions excepted**) SEO

EAS [ˌiːeɪˈes] *n Br Com* (*abbr* **Enterprise Allowance Scheme**) fonds *m* d'aide à la création d'entreprise

EBIT [ˌiːbiːˌaɪˈtiː] *npl Fin* (*abbr* **earnings before interest and tax**) bénéfices *mpl* avant impôts et charges

EBRD [ˌiːbiːˌɑːˈdiː] *n Pol* (*abbr* **European Bank for Reconstruction and Development**) BERD *f*

EBU [ˌiːbiːˈjuː] *n* (*abbr* **European Broadcasting Union**) Union *f* européenne de radiodiffusion, UER *f*

EBV [ˌiːbiːˈviː] *n Med* (*abbr* **Epstein-Barr Virus**) EBV *m*

EC [ˌiːˈsiː] *n Pol* (*abbr* **European Community**) CE *f*

ECB [ˌiːsiːˈbiː] *n Com* (*abbr* **European Central Bank**) BCE *f*

ECG [ˌiːsiːˈdʒiː] *n Med* (**a**) (*abbr* **electrocardiogram**) ECG *m* (**b**) (*abbr* **electrocardiograph**) ECG *m*

ECGD [ˌiːsiːˌdʒiːˈdiː] *n Com* (*abbr* **Export Credits Guarantee Department**) = organisme d'assurance pour le commerce extérieur, ≃ COFACE *f*

ECH (*written abbr* **electric central heating**) chauffage *m* central électrique

ECM [ˌiːsiːˈem] *n Am* (*abbr* **European Common Market**) = Marché commun européen

ECN [ˌiːsiːˈen] *n St Exch* (*abbr* **electronic communications network**) = marché électronique privé

ECOFIN [ˈiːkəʊˌfɪn] *n Fin* (*abbr* **Economic and Financial Council of Ministers**) Conseil *m* Ecofin

ECP [ˌiːsiːˈpiː] *n Fin* (*abbr* **euro-commercial paper**) billet *m* de trésorerie (*émis sur le marché des eurodevises*)

ECSC [ˌiːsiːˌesˈsiː] *n Pol* (*abbr* **European Coal & Steel Community**) CECA *f*

ECSDA [ˌiːsiːˌesdiːˈeɪ] *n Fin* (*abbr* **European Central Securities Depositories Association**) association *f* européenne des dépositaires centraux de titres

ECT [ˌiːsiːˈtiː] *n Med* (*abbr* **electroconvulsive therapy**) traitement *m* par électrochocs

ECU [ˈeɪkjuː] *n* (*abbr* **European Currency Unit**) ECU *m*, écu *m*

ED [ˌiːˈdiː] *n Admin* (*abbr* **Employment Department**) ≃ ministère *m* du Travail

ed.¹ [ed] *n* (**a**) (*abbr* **editor**) éd., édit (**b**) (*abbr* **education**) éducation *f*

ed.² (**a**) (*written abbr* **edited**) sous la dir. de, coll (**b**) (*written abbr* **edition**) éd., édit (**c**) (*written abbr* **education**) éduc

EdD [ˌedˈdiː] *n Am* (*abbr* **Doctor of Education**) (*person*) docteur *m* en sciences de l'éducation; (*qualification*) doctorat *m* en sciences de l'éducation

EDF [ˌiːdiːˈef] *n Pol* (*abbr* **European Development Fund**) FED *m*

EDGAR [ˈedgə(r)] *n Fin* (*abbr* **electronic data gathering, analysis and retrieval**) = banque de données créée par la commission américaine des opérations de Bourse (le SEC), qui contient toutes sortes d'informations sur de nombreux fonds communs de placement et entreprises publiques

EDI [ˌiːdiːˈaɪ] *n* (**a**) *Comput* (*abbr* **Electronic Data Interchange**) EDI *m* (**b**) *Fin* (*abbr* **European Data Interchange**) EED *m*

EdM [edˈem] *n Am* (*abbr* **Master of Education**) (*person*) = titulaire d'une maîtrise en sciences de l'éducation; (*qualification*) maîtrise *f* en sciences de l'éducation

EDP [ˌiːdiːˈpiː] *n Comput* (*abbr* **electronic data processing**) traitement *m* électronique de l'information

EDT [ˌiːdiːˈtiː] *n Am* (*abbr* **Eastern Daylight Time**) heure *f* d'été de l'Est

.edu [ˈedjuː] *Comput* (*abbr* **education**) = abréviation désignant les universités et les sites éducatifs dans les adresses électroniques

EE [ˌiːˈiː] *n* (*abbr* **electrical engineer**) ingénieur *m* électricien

EEB [ˌiːiːˈbiː] *n* (*abbr* **European Environmental Bureau**) BEE *m*

EEA [ˌiːiːˈeɪ] *n Pol* (*abbr* **European Economic Area**) EEE *m*

EEC [ˌiːiːˈsiː] *n Formerly Pol* (*abbr* **European Economic Community**) CEE *f*

EEG [ˌiːiːˈdʒiː] *n Med* (**a**) (*abbr* **electroencephalogram**) EEG *m* (**b**) (*abbr* **electroencephalograph**) EEG *m*

EENT [ˌiːiːˌenˈtiː] *n Med* (*abbr* **eye, ear, nose and throat**) ophtalmologie *f* et ORL *f*

EEOC [ˌiːiːˌəʊˈsiː] *n Am Admin* (*abbr* **Equal Employment Opportunities Commission**) = commission pour l'égalité des chances d'emploi aux États-Unis

EEPROM [ˈiːprɒm] *n Comput* (*abbr* **electrically erasable programmable ROM**) EEPROM *f*

EET [ˌiːiːˈtiː] *n* (*abbr* **Eastern European Time**) heure *f* de l'Europe orientale

EFL [ˌiːefˈel] *n* (*abbr* **English as a foreign language**) = anglais langue étrangère

EFT [eft] *n Comput* (*abbr* **electronic funds transfer**) transfert *m* de fonds électronique

EFTA [ˈeftə] *n* (*abbr* **European Free Trade Association**) AELE *f*, AEL-E *f*

EFTPOS [ˈeftpɒs] *n Comput* (*abbr* **electronic funds transfer at point of sale**) transfert *m* de fonds électronique sur point de vente

EFTS [efts] *n Comput* (*abbr* **electronic funds transfer system**) = système électronique de transfert de fonds

eg [ˌiːˈdʒiː] *adv* (*abbr* **exempli gratia**) par exemple

EGA [ˌiːdʒiːˈeɪ] *n Comput* (*abbr* **enhanced graphics adapter**) EGA *m*

EGM [ˌiːdʒiːˈem] *n Com* (*abbr* **extraordinary general meeting**) AGE *f*

EHO [ˌiːeɪtʃˈəʊ] *n* (*abbr* **environmental health officer**) inspecteur(trice) *m,f* de la santé publique

EIA [ˌiːaɪˈeɪ] *n* (*abbr* **environmental impact assessment**) étude *f* d'impact sur l'environnement

EIB [ˌiːaɪˈbiː] *n* (*abbr* **European Investment Bank**) BEI *f*

EID [ˌiːaɪˈdiː] *npl Biol & Med* (*abbr* **emerging infectious diseases**) maladies *fpl* infectieuses émergentes

EIS [ˌiːaɪˈes] *n* (*abbr* **Educational Institute of Scotland**) = syndicat écossais d'enseignants

EKG [ˌiːkeɪˈdʒiː] *n Am Med* (*abbr* **electrocardiogram**) ECG *m*

el [el] *n Am Fam* (*abbr* **elevated railroad**) métro *m* aérien❑

ELT [ˌiːelˈtiː] *n* (*abbr* **English language teaching**) = enseignement de l'anglais

EMA [ˌiːemˈeɪ] *n Fin* (*abbr* **European Monetary Agreement**) AME *m*

emcee [ˌemˈsiː] *Fam* (*abbr* **master of ceremonies**) **1** *n* maître *m* de cérémonies❑; *Rad & TV* animateur(trice)❑ *m,f*
2 *vt* animer❑

emf, EMF [ˌiːemˈef] *n* (**a**) *Elec* (*abbr* **electromotive force**) force *f* électromotrice (**b**) (*abbr* **European Monetary Fund**) FME *m*

EMI [ˌiːemˈaɪ] *n* (*abbr* **European Monetary Institute**) IME *m*

EMS [ˌiːemˈes] *n Formerly Fin* (*abbr* **European Monetary System**) SME *m*

EMT [ˌiːemˈtiː] *n Med* (*abbr* **emergency medical technician**) = technicien médical des services d'urgence

EMU [ˌiːemˈjuː] *n Pol & Fin* (*abbr* **economic and monetary union**) UME *f*

EN [ˌiːˈen] *n Br* (*abbr* **enrolled nurse**) = infirmière diplômée

enc. (**a**) (*written abbr* **enclosure**) PJ (**b**) (*written abbr* **enclosed**) ci-joint

encl. (**a**) (*written abbr* **enclosure**) PJ (**b**) (*written abbr* **enclosed**) ci-joint

ENE (*written abbr* **east-north-east**) E-NE

ENG [ˌiːenˈdʒiː] *n* (*abbr* **electronic news gathering**) journalisme *m* électronique de télévision

ENO [ˌiːenˈəʊ] *n* (*abbr* **English National Opera**) opéra *m* national d'Angleterre

Ens (*written abbr* **Ensign**) (**a**) *Br Mil* (*officier m*) porte-étendard *m* (**b**) *Am Naut* enseigne *m* de vaisseau de deuxième classe

ENT [ˌiːenˈtiː] *Med* (*abbr* **ear, nose & throat**)
1 *n* ORL *f*
2 *adj* ORL

EOC [ˌiːəʊˈsiː] *n Admin* (*abbr* **Equal Opportunities Commission**) = commission pour l'égalité des chances en matière d'emploi en Grande-Bretagne

EONIA [iːˈəʊnɪə] *n St Exch* (*abbr* **Euro Overnight Index Average**) EONIA *m*, TEMPÉ *m*

EP [ˌiːˈpiː] *n* (**a**) (*abbr* **extended play**) super 45 tours *m*, EP *m* (**b**) *Am* (*abbr* **European Plan**) chambre *f* sans pension

EPA [ˌiːpiːˈeɪ] *n* (*abbr* **Environmental Protection Agency**) = agence américaine pour la protection de l'environnement

EPNS [ˌiːpiːenˈes] *n* (*abbr* **electroplated nickel silver**) rudz *m*

EPO [ˌiːpiːˈəʊ] *n Physiol* (*abbr* **erythropoietin**) EPO *f*

EPOS [ˈiːpɒs] *n Comput* (*abbr* **electronic**

point of sale) = point de vente électronique

EPROM ['iːprɒm] *n Comput* (*abbr* **erasable programmable read-only memory**) mémoire *f* morte effaçable

EPS [ˌiːpiː'es] *n* (**a**) *Fin* (*abbr* **earnings per share**) BPA *m* (**b**) *Comput* (*abbr* **encapsulated PostScript**) EPS *m*

ER[1] [ˌiː'ɑː(r)] *n Am Med* (*abbr* **emergency room**) urgences *fpl*

ER[2] (*written abbr* **Elizabeth Regina**) = emblème de la reine Élisabeth

ERA ['ɪərə] *n Am* (*abbr* **Equal Rights Amendment**) = projet de loi américain rejeté en 1982 qui posait comme principe l'égalité des individus quels que soient leur sexe, leur religion ou leur race

ERDF [ˌiːɑːˌdiː'ef] *n Fin* (*abbr* **European Regional Development Fund**) FEDER *m*

ERIC ['erɪk] *n Am* (*abbr* **Educational Resources Information Center**) = centre d'information américain sur l'éducation

ERISA [ə'riːsə] *n Am* (*abbr* **Employee Retirement Income Security Act**) = loi américaine sur les pensions de retraite

ERM [ˌiːɑː'rem] *n Formerly Fin* (*abbr* **exchange rate mechanism**) mécanisme *m* de change (du SME)

Ernie ['ɜːnɪ] *n Br Fam* (*abbr* **Electronic Random Number Indicator Equipment**) = en Grande-Bretagne, ordinateur qui sert au tirage des numéros gagnants des bons à lots

ERW [ˌiːɑː'dʌbəljuː] *n Mil* (*abbr* **enhanced radiation weapon**) arme *f* à rayonnement renforcé

ESA [ˌiːes'eɪ] *n* (**a**) (*abbr* **European Space Agency**) ESA *f*, ASE *f* (**b**) *Ecol* (*abbr* **Environmentally Sensitive Area**) = zone de protection de la nature désignée par l'Union européenne où les agriculteurs doivent utiliser des méthodes traditionnelles

ESE (*written abbr* **east-south-east**) E-SE

ESL [ˌiːes'el] *n* (*abbr* **English as a Second Language**) = l'anglais comme deuxième langue

ESN [ˌiːes'en] *adj Old-fashioned* (*abbr* **educationally subnormal**) en retard sur le plan scolaire

ESOL [ˌiːesˌəʊ'el] *n Am* (*abbr* **English for Speakers of Other Languages**) = anglais langue étrangère

ESOP [ˌiːesˌəʊ'piː] *n* (*abbr* **employee** *Br* **share** *or Am* **stock ownership plan**) plan *m* d'actionnariat des salariés

ESP [ˌiːes'piː] *n* (**a**) (*abbr* **extrasensory perception**) perception *f* extrasensorielle (**b**) (*abbr* **English for special purposes**) = anglais spécialisé

esp. (*written abbr* **especially**) particulièrement

Esq. (*written abbr* **Esquire**) **Gregor Clark, Esq.** M.Gregor Clark

ESRC [ˌiːesˌɑː'siː] *n Br* (*abbr* **Economic and Social Research Council**) = organisme chargé de distribuer des subventions pour la recherche en sciences sociales

EST [ˌiːes'tiː] *n* (*abbr* **Eastern Standard Time**) heure *f* normale de l'Est

est [est] *n Psy* (*abbr* **Erhard Seminars Training**) = méthode de formation [illegible]gique créée par Werner Erhard

est. (**a**) (*written abbr* **established**) **est. 1890** fondé en 1890 (**b**) (*written abbr* **estimated**) **est. cost** coût évalué à

estd., est'd. (*written abbr* **established**) **estd. 1890** fondé en 1890

ET [ˌiː'tiː] *n* (**a**) *Br* (*abbr* **Employment Training**) = programme gouvernemental en faveur des chômeurs de longue durée (**b**) (*abbr* **extraterrestrial**) extraterrestre *mf*

ETA [ˌiːtiː'eɪ] *n Aviat* (*abbr* **estimated time of arrival**) HPA *f*; **our ETA is 2300 hours** l'heure d'arrivée prévue est 23 heures

et al. [ˌet'æl] *adv* (*abbr* **et alia**) et autres

etc. (*written abbr* **et cetera**) etc

ETD [ˌiːtiː'diː] *n Aviat* (*abbr* **estimated time of departure**) HPD *f*

ETU [ˌiːtiː'juː] *n Br* (*abbr* **Electrical Trades Union**) = syndicat britannique d'électriciens

ETV [ˌiːtiː'viː] *n Am* (*abbr* **Educational Television**) = chaîne de télévision éducative et culturelle

EU [ˌiː'juː] *n* (*abbr* **European Union**) UE *f*; **EU policy** politique *f* communautaire; **the EU member states** les États *mpl* membres de l'UE; **imports to the EU** les importations *fpl* vers l'UE

Euratom [jʊər'ætəm] *n* (*abbr* **European Atomic Energy Community**) CEEA *f*

EURIBOR ['jʊərɪbɔː(r)] *n Fin* (*abbr* **Euro Interbank Offered Rate**) EURIBOR *m*, TIBEUR *m*

Euro-MP *n EU* (*abbr* **European Member of Parliament**) député *m ou* parlementaire *m* européen

EVA [ˌiːviː'eɪ] *n* (**a**) *Astron* (*abbr* **extravehicular activity**) = activité qui a lieu en dehors d'un engin spatial (**b**) (*abbr* **economic value added**) VAE *f*

EVC [ˌiːviː'siː] *n Mktg* (*abbr* **economic value to the customer**) valeur *f* économique apportée au consommateur

excl. (*written abbr* **excluding**) non compris; **excl. taxes** HT

exec [ɪg'zek] *n* (*abbr* **executive**) cadre *m*

expat [ˌeks'pæt] *Fam* (*abbr* **expatriate**) **1** *n* expatrié(e) ❑ *m,f*

2 *adj (Briton, American etc)* expatrié ❑; *(bar, community)* d'expatriés ❑

ext. (*written abbr* **extension**) poste *m*; **ext. 4174** poste 4174

extn. (*written abbr* **extension**) poste *m*; **extn. 421** poste 421

F (**a**) (*written abbr* **Fahrenheit**) F (**b**) (*written abbr* **franc**) F (**c**) *Chem* (*written abbr* **fluorine**) F (**d**) *Phys* (*written abbr* **farad**) F (**e**) *Phys* (*written abbr* **force**) F (**f**) *Phys* (*written abbr* **frequency**) F (**g**) (*written abbr* **false**) F

f (**a**) (*written abbr* **fathom**) brasse *f (mesure)* (**b**) (*written abbr* **female**) f (**c**) (*written abbr* **feminine**) f, fém (**d**) *Math* (*written abbr* **function of**) f de (**e**) *Mus* (*written abbr* **forte**) f

f.a., FA[1] [e'feɪ] *n* (*abbr* **fanny adams**) *Br Fam* **sweet f.a.** que dalle

FA[2] [e'feɪ] *n* (*abbr* **Football Association**) **the FA** = la Fédération britannique de football

►► ***the FA cup*** = championnat de football

FAA [ˌefeɪ'eɪ] *n Am* (*abbr* **Federal Aviation Administration**) = direction fédérale de l'aviation civile américaine

faa [ˌefeɪ'eɪ] *adj Com* (*abbr* **free of all average**) franc de toute avarie

FAO [ˌefeɪ'əʊ] *n* (*abbr* **Food and Agriculture Organization**) FAO *f*

fao (*written abbr* **for the attention of**) à l'attention de

FAQ [ˌefeɪ'kjuː] **1** *adv Br Com* (*abbr* **free alongside quay**) FLQ

2 *n Comput* (*abbr* **frequently asked questions**) FAQ

►► *Comput* ***FAQ file*** fichier *m* FAQ

faq [ˌefeɪ'kjuː] *n Com* (*abbr* **fair average quality**) qualité *f* loyale et marchande

FAS [ˌefeɪ'es] *adv Br Com* (*abbr* **free alongside ship**) FLB, FLQ

FBI [ˌefbiː'aɪ] *n Am* (*abbr* **Federal Bureau of Investigation**) **the FBI** le FBI

►► ***FBI agent*** agent *m* du FBI

FC [ˌef'siː] *n* (*abbr* **Football Club**) FC *m*

FCC [ˌefsiː'siː] *n Am* (*abbr* **Federal Communications Commission**) = conseil fédéral de l'audiovisuel aux États-Unis, ≃ CSA *m*

FCL-FCL *Com* (*written abbr* **full container load-full container load**) FCL-FCL

FCL-LCL *Com* (*written abbr* **full container load-less than container load**) FCL-LCL

FCO [ˌefsiː'əʊ] *n Br* (*abbr* **Foreign and Commonwealth Office**) **the FCO** le Foreign Office, le ministère britannique des Affaires étrangères

FD[1] [ˌef'diː] *n Am* (*abbr* **Fire Department**) brigade *f* des pompiers

FD[2] (**a**) *Br* (*written abbr* **Fidei Defensor**) = Défenseur de la foi (**b**) *Comput* (*written abbr* **floppy disk**) disquette *f*

FDA [ˌefdiː'eɪ] *n* (*abbr* **Food and Drug Administration**) = organisme officiel chargé de contrôler la qualité des aliments et de délivrer les autorisations de mise sur le marché pour les produits pharmaceutiques

FDD *Comput* (*written abbr* **floppy disk drive**) unité *f* de disquette

FDIC [ˌefdiːˌaɪ'siː] *n Am* (*abbr* **Federal Deposit Insurance Corporation**) = organisme garantissant la sécurité des dépôts dans les banques qui en sont membres

FDR [ˌefdiː'ɑː(r)] *pr n* (*abbr* **Franklin D Roosevelt**) Franklin Delano Roosevelt

Feb. (*written abbr* **February**) févr

Fed[1] [fed] *n Am* (**a**) *Fin* (*abbr* **Federal Reserve Board**) banque *f* centrale (des États-Unis) (**b**) *Fin* (*abbr* **Federal Reserve (System)**) (système *m* de) Réserve *f* fédérale (**c**) *Fin* (*abbr* **Federal Reserve Bank**) banque *f* membre de la Réserve fédérale (**d**) *Fam* (*abbr* **Federal Agent**) agent *m* du FBI ❑

Fed[2] *Am* (**a**) (*written abbr* **federal**) fédéral (**b**) (*written abbr* **federation**) fédération *f*

►► ***Fed funds*** fonds *mpl* fédéraux

fem [fem] *adj* (*abbr* **feminine**) fém.

FEMA ['fiːmə] *n* (*abbr* **Federal Emergency Management Agency**) = agence gouvernementale américaine pour la prévention des catastrophes et l'aide aux sinistrés

ff (*written abbr* **and the following**) et suiv., sqq.

FFA [ˌefef'eɪ] *n* (*abbr* **Future Farmers of America**) = organisation nationale d'étudiants en agriculture

FGA [ˌefdʒiː'eɪ] *adj Ins* (*abbr* **free of general average**) FCA

FH *Br* (*written abbr* **fire hydrant**) borne *f* à incendie

FHA [ˌefeɪtʃ'eɪ] *n Am* (*abbr* **Federal Housing Administration**) = organisme de gestion des logements sociaux aux États-Unis

FICA [ˌefaɪˌsiː'eɪ] *n Am* (*abbr* **Federal Insurance Contributions Act**) = loi américaine régissant les cotisations sociales

FIFA ['fiːfə] *n* (*abbr* **Fédération Internationale de Football Association**) FIFA *f*

FIFO ['fiːfəʊ] *n Comput & Ind* (*abbr* **first in, first out**) PEPS

Fimbra ['fɪmbrə] *n Br Formerly* (*abbr* **Financial Intermediaries, Managers and Brokers Regulatory Association**) = organisme britannique contrôlant les activités des courtiers d'assurances

FIS [ˌefaɪ'es] *n Br* (*abbr* **Family Income Supplement**) ≃ complément *m* familial

FL, Fla (*written abbr* **Florida**) Floride *f*

fl. oz. (*written abbr* **fluid ounce**) once *f* liquide

FM [ˌe'fem] *n* (**a**) (*abbr* **frequency modulation**) FM *f*; **FM radio** (radio *f*) FM *f*; **broadcast on FM only** diffusion en FM seulement (**b**) *Br Mil* (*abbr* **field marshal**) maréchal *m*

FMB [ˌefem'biː] *n Am* (*abbr* **Federal Maritime Board**) = conseil supérieur de la Marine marchande aux États-Unis

FMCG [ˌefemˌsiː'dʒiː] *npl Mktg* (*abbr* **fast-moving consumer goods**) biens *mpl* de consommation à forte rotation

FMCS [ˌefemˌsiː'es] *n Am* (*abbr* **Federal Mediation and Conciliation Services**) = organisme américain de conciliation des conflits du travail

FO [ˌe'fəʊ] *n* (**a**) *Mil* (*abbr* **field officer**) officier *m* supérieur (**b**) *Br Mil* (*abbr* **flying officer**) lieutenant *m* de l'armée de l'air (**c**) *Br* (*abbr* **Foreign Office**) **the FO** le Foreign Office, le ministère britannique des Affaires étrangères

fob, FOB [ˌefəʊ'biː] *adv Com & Naut* (*abbr* **free on board**) FOB

FOE [ˌefəʊ'iː] *n* (**a**) (*abbr* **Friends of the Earth**) AT *mpl* (**b**) *Am* (*abbr* **Fraternal Order of Eagles**) = organisation caritative américaine

FOI [ˌefəʊ'aɪ] *n* (*abbr* **freedom of information**) liberté *f* d'information

foll (*written abbr* **following**) suiv

FOOTSIE, Footsie ['fʊtsɪ] *n St Exch* (*abbr* **Financial Times-Stock Exchange 100 Index**) = principal indice boursier du 'Financial Times' basé sur la valeur de 100 actions cotées à la Bourse de Londres

FOR [ˌefəʊ'ɑː(r)] *adv Com* (*abbr* **free on rail**) franco wagon

forex ['fɔːreks] *n Fin* (*abbr* **foreign exchange**) devises *fpl* étrangères
▸▸ ***forex trading*** transactions *fpl* en devises étrangères

FOT [ˌefəʊ'tiː] *adj* (*abbr* **free on truck**) franco camion

FP [ˌef'piː] *n* (**a**) (*abbr* **former pupil**) ancien(enne) élève *mf* (**b**) *Am* (*abbr* **fire-plug**) bouche *f* d'incendie

FPA [ˌefpiː'eɪ] **1** *adj Ins* (*abbr* **free of particular average**) FAP
2 *n Br* (*abbr* **Family Planning Association**) = association pour le planning familial

FPO [ˌefpiː'əʊ] *n Am Naut* (*abbr* **Fleet Post Office**) = mention figurant dans l'adresse des membres de la marine américaine

FPU [ˌefpiː'juː] *n Comput* (*abbr* **floating-point unit**) FPU *f*, coprocesseur *m* arithmétique

FQDN [ˌefkjuːˌdiː'en] *n Comput* (*abbr* **Fully Qualified Domain Name**) nom *m* de domaine complet

Fr (**a**) *Rel* (*written abbr* **Father**) P (**b**) (*written abbr* **France**) France *f* (**c**) *Fin* (*written abbr* **franc**) franc *m* (**d**) (*written abbr* **friar**) F

FRA [ˌefɑː'reɪ] *n Fin* (*abbr* **Future Rate Agreement, Forward Rate Agreement**) ATF *m*

frat [fræt] *n Am Fam* (*abbr* **fraternity**) = confrérie d'étudiants
▸▸ ***frat rat*** = membre d'une confrérie d'étudiants

FRB [ˌefɑː'biː] *n Am Fin* (*abbr* **Federal Reserve Board**) = conseil d'administration des banques centrales américaines

FRCD [ˌefɑːˌsiː'diː] *n Banking* (*abbr* **floating-rate certificate of deposit**) = certificat de dépôt à taux flottant

FRCM [ˌefɑːˌsiː'em] *n Br* (*abbr* **Fellow of the Royal College of Music**) = membre du "Royal College of Music"

FRCP [ˌefɑːˌsiː'piː] *n Br* (*abbr* **Fellow of the Royal College of Physicians**) = membre du "Royal College of Physicians"

FRCS [ˌefɑːˌsiː'es] *n Br* (*abbr* **Fellow of the Royal College of Surgeons**) = membre du "Royal College of Surgeons"

FRCVS [ˌefɑːˌsiːviː'es] *n Br* (*abbr* **Fellow of the Royal College of Veterinary Surgeons**) = membre du "Royal College of Veterinary Surgeons"

FRG [ˌefɑː'dʒiː] *n* (*abbr* **Federal Republic of Germany**) RFA *f*

Fri. (*written abbr* **Friday**) ven

FRN [ˌefɑː'ren] *n Banking* (*abbr* **floating-rate note**) effet *m* à taux flottant

FRS [ˌefɑː'res] *n* (**a**) (*abbr* **Fellow of the Royal Society**) ≃ membre *m* de l'Académie des sciences (**b**) *Am* (*abbr* **Federal Reserve System**) (système *m* de) Réserve *f* fédérale

FSA [ˌefes'eɪ] *n* (**a**) *Fin* (*abbr* **Financial Services Authority**) = organisme gouvernemental britannique chargé de contrôler les activités du secteur financier (**b**) (*abbr* **Food Standards Agency**) = organisme britannique de contrôle de la sécurité alimentaire

FSH [ˌefes'eɪtʃ] *n Biol* (*abbr* **follicle-stimulating hormone**) hormone *f* folliculo-stimulante, FSH *f*

FT [ˌef'tiː] *n Press* (*abbr* **Financial Times**) Financial Times *m*
▸▸ *St Exch* ***FT Index*** (**a**) (*abbr* **Financial Times-(Industrial) Ordinary Share Index**) = indice boursier du 'Financial Times' basé sur la valeur de 30 actions cotées à la Bourse de Londres (**b**) (*abbr* **Financial Times-Stock Exchange 100 Index**) = principal indice boursier du 'Financial Times' basé sur la valeur de 100 actions cotées à la Bourse de Londres

ft (**a**) (*written abbr* **foot**) pied *m* (**b**) (*written abbr* **fort**) fort *m*

FTC [ˌeftiː'siː] *n Am* (*abbr* **Federal Trade Commission**) = commission fédérale chargée de veiller au respect de la concurrence sur le marché

FTP [ˌeftiː'piː] *Comput* **1** *n* (*abbr* **File Transfer Protocol**) protocole *m* de transfert de fichiers
2 *vt* télécharger par FTP
▸▸ ***FTP server*** serveur *m* FTP; ***FTP site*** site *m* FTP

FT-SE index ['fʊtsɪ-] *n St Exch* (*abbr* **Financial Times-Stock Exchange 100 Index**) = principal indice boursier du 'Financial Times' basé sur la valeur de 100 actions cotées à la Bourse de Londres

fwd. (*written abbr* **forward**) vers l'avant

fwy *Am* (*written abbr* **freeway**) autoroute *f*

FX [ˌef'eks] *n Fin* (*abbr* **foreign exchange**) devises *fpl* étrangères
▸▸ ***FX broker, FX dealer*** cambiste *mf*, courtier(ère) *m,f* en devises; ***FX market*** marché *m* des changes; ***FX option*** option *f* sur devises; ***FX transfer*** transfert *m* de devises

FY *Fin* (*written abbr* **fiscal year**) année *f* fiscale *ou* d'exercice

FYI (*written abbr* **for your information**) à titre indicatif

G¹ [dʒiː] *n* (**a**) *Phys* conductance *f* (**b**) *Am Fam* (*abbr* **grand**) (*thousand dollars*) mille dollars *mpl*; **he earns 50G a year** il gagne cinquante mille dollars par an

G² (**a**) (*written abbr* **good**) B (**b**) *Austr Cin* (*written abbr* **general (audience)**) = tous publics

g (**a**) (*written abbr* **gramme**) g (**b**) (*written abbr* **gravity**) g

GA¹ [ˌdʒiː'eɪ] *n Ins* (*abbr* **general average**) avarie *f* commune

GA² (*written abbr* **Georgia**) Géorgie *f*

GAA [ˌdʒiːeɪ'eɪ] *n* (*abbr* **Gaelic Athletic Association**) = association qui œuvre pour le développement des sports irlandais traditionnels, notamment le football gaélique

GAAP [ˌdʒiːeɪˌeɪ'piː] *npl Acct* (*abbr* **generally-accepted accounting principles**) PCGR *mpl*

gal. (*written abbr* **gallon**) gallon *m*

gall. (*written abbr* **gallon**) gallon *m*

GAO [ˌdʒiːeɪ'əʊ] *n Am* (*abbr* **General Accounting Office**) = Cour des comptes américaine

GATT [gæt] *n Fin* (*abbr* **General Agreement on Tariffs and Trade**) GATT *m*

GB¹ [ˌdʒiː'biː] *n* (*abbr* **Great Britain**) G-B *f*; **GB plate** plaque *f* GB; *Aut* **GB sticker** autocollant *m* GB

GB² *Comput* (*written abbr* **gigabyte**) Go

GBH [ˌdʒiːbiː'eɪtʃ] *n Law* (*abbr* **grievous bodily harm**) coups *mpl* et blessures *fpl*; *Br Fam* **to give sb GBH of the earholes** raser qn

GC [ˌdʒiː'siː] *n Br* (*abbr* **George Cross**) = distinction honorifique britannique

GCE [ˌdʒiːsiː'iː] *n Formerly Sch* (*abbr* **General Certificate of Education**) = certificat britannique de fin d'études secondaires en deux étapes (O level et A level) dont la première est aujourd'hui remplacée par le "GCSE"

GCH *Br* (*written abbr* **gas central heating**) chauffage *m* central au gaz

GCHQ [ˌdʒiːsiːˌeɪtʃ'kjuː] *n Br* (*abbr* **Government Communications Headquarters**) = centre d'interception des télécommunications étrangères en Grande-Bretagne

GCSE [ˌdʒiːsiːˌes'iː] *n Sch* (*abbr* **General Certificate of Secondary Education**) = premier examen de fin de scolarité en Grande-Bretagne

GD [ˌdʒiː'diː] *adj Am very Fam* (*abbr* **goddamn(ed)**) foutu, sacré; **he's a GD fool** c'est un sacré con

Gdns. (*written abbr* **Gardens**) = abréviation écrite du terme "Gardens", qui est le nom donné à certaines rues en Grande-Bretagne

GDP [ˌdʒiːdiː'piː] *n Econ* (*abbr* **gross domestic product**) PIB *m*

GDR [ˌdʒiːdiː'ɑː(r)] *n* (*abbr* **German Democratic Republic**) RDA *f*

Gds (*written abbr* **Gardens**) = abréviation écrite du terme "Gardens", qui est le nom donné à certaines rues en Grande-Bretagne

GEC [ˌdʒiːiː'siː] *n Br* (*abbr* **General Electric Company**) = société britannique fabriquant des produits électriques, électroniques et de télécommunications

GED [ˌdʒiːiː'diː] *n Am Sch* (*abbr* **general equivalency diploma**) = aux États-Unis, diplôme d'études secondaires pour adultes souvent obtenu par correspondance

GEMM [ˌdʒiːiːˌem'em] *n Fin* (*abbr* **gilt-edged market maker**) teneur *m* de marché de premier ordre

Gems [dʒemz] *n Ecol* (*abbr* **Global Environment Monitoring System**) système *m* mondial de surveillance continue de l'environnement

Gen (*written abbr* **general**) G

gen. (*written abbr* **general, generally**) gén

GHQ [ˌdʒiːeɪtʃ'kjuː] *n* (*abbr* **general headquarters**) GQG *m*

GHz (*written abbr* **gigahertz**) GHz

GI [ˌdʒiː'aɪ] *n Fam* (*abbr* **Government Issue**) (*soldier*) soldat *m* américain ❑, GI *m*
▸▸ ***GI bill*** = loi adoptée aux États-Unis en 1944, accordant certains avantages aux combattants de la Seconde Guerre mondiale (notamment la possibilité de poursuivre leurs études); ***GI bride*** épouse *f* (étrangère) d'un GI; ***GI Joe*** = surnom collectif des soldats américains, notamment pendant la Seconde Guerre mondiale

GIF [gɪf] *n Comput* (*abbr* **Graphics Interchange Format**) GIF *m*

GIFT [gɪft] *n* (*abbr* **gamete intrafallopian transfer**) FIVETE *f*

GIGO ['gaɪgəʊ, ˌdʒiːaɪˌdʒiː'əʊ] *n Comput* (*abbr* **garbage in, garbage out**) GIGO

GLC [ˌdʒiːel'siː] *n Formerly* (*abbr* **Greater London Council**) = ancien organe administratif du grand Londres

Glos (*written abbr* **Gloucestershire**) Gloucestershire *m*

GM [ˌdʒiː'em] *adj* (**a**) (*abbr* **genetically modified**) génétiquement modifié (**b**) (*abbr* **grant maintained**) subventionné (*par l'État*); **a GM school** une école privée subventionnée (*acceptant en échange un droit de regard de l'État sur la gestion de ses affaires*) (**c**) (*abbr* **General Motors**) General Motors *f*
▸▸ ***GM food*** aliments *mpl* génétiquement modifiés

gm (*written abbr* **gram**) g

GMAT [ˌdʒiːemˌeɪ'tiː] *n Am Univ* (*abbr* **Graduate Management Admissions Test**) = test d'admission dans le 2ème cycle de l'enseignement supérieur aux États-Unis

GMB [ˌdʒiːem'biː] *n Br* (*abbr* **General, Municipal, Boilermakers and Allied Trades Union**) = important syndicat britannique

GMC [ˌdʒiːem'siː] *n* (**a**) (*abbr* **general management committee**) comité *m* de direction (**b**) *Br* (*abbr* **General Medical Council**) ≃ conseil *m* de l'ordre des médecins (**c**) (*abbr* **General Motors Corporation**) General Motors *f*

GMO [ˌdʒiːemˈəʊ] *n* (*abbr* **genetically-modified organism**) OGM *m*

GMT [ˌdʒiːemˈtiː] *n* (*abbr* **Greenwich Mean Time**) GMT *m*

GMWU [ˌdʒiːemˌdʌbəljuːˈjuː] *n Br* (*abbr* **General and Municipal Workers' Union**) = syndicat britannique des employés des collectivités locales

GNP [ˌdʒiːenˈpiː] *n Econ* (*abbr* **gross national product**) PNB *m*

GNVQ [ˌdʒiːenˌviːˈkjuː] *n Br Sch* (*abbr* **General National Vocational Qualification**) = formation professionnelle sur deux ans que l'on peut suivre à partir de seize ans

GOC [ˌdʒiːəʊˈsiː] *n Mil* (*abbr* **General Officer Commanding/Commanding-in-Chief**) = général commandant en chef

GOM [ˌdʒiːəʊˈem] *n* (*abbr* **Grand Old Man**) **the GOM of English theatre/American novels** le doyen des hommes de théâtre anglais/des romanciers américains

GOP [ˌdʒiːəʊˈpiː] *n Am* (*abbr* **Grand Old Party**) = le parti républicain aux États-Unis

Gov (**a**) (*written abbr* **government**) gouvernement *m* (**b**) (*written abbr* **governor**) gouverneur *m*

govt (*written abbr* **government**) gouv.

GP [ˌdʒiːˈpiː] *n* (*abbr* **general practitioner**) (médecin *m*) généraliste *mf*, *Can* omnipracticien(enne) *m,f*

GPA [ˌdʒiːpiːˈeɪ] *n Am Sch* (*abbr* **grade point average**) moyenne *f*

GPMU [ˌdʒiːpiːˌemˈjuː] *n Br* (*abbr* **Graphical, Paper and Media Union**) = syndicat britannique des ouvriers du livre

GPO [ˌdʒiːpiːˈəʊ] *n* (**a**) *Br Formerly* (*abbr* **General Post Office**) **the GPO** = titre officiel de la Poste britannique avant 1969 (**b**) *Am* (*abbr* **Government Printing Office**) **the GPO** = maison d'édition publiant les ouvrages ou documents émanant du gouvernement, ≃ Imprimerie *f* nationale

GPS [ˌdʒiːpiːˈes] *n* (*abbr* **global positioning system**) GPS *m* (*système de navigation par satellite*)

gr (**a**) (*written abbr* **gramme(s)**) g (**b**) (*written abbr* **gross**) brut

GRACE [greɪs] *n Tel* (*abbr* **group routing and charging equipment**) automatique *m*

grad [græd] *n Am Fam* (*abbr* **graduate**) diplômé(e) ❑ *m,f*

▸▸ ***grad school*** = école où l'on poursuit ses études après la licence

GRE [ˌdʒiːɑːˈriː] *n Am* (*abbr* **Graduate Record Exam**) = test de niveau avant l'entrée dans une "graduate school"

GRSM [ˌdʒiːɑːˌresˈem] *n Br* (*abbr* **Graduate of the Royal Schools of Music**) = diplômé du conservatoire de musique britannique

GS¹ (*written abbr* **General Staff**) EM *m*

GS² [ˌdʒiːˈes] *n* (*abbr* **general secretary**) secrétaire *mf* général(e)

GSM [ˌdʒiːesˈem] *n Tel* (*abbr* **global system for mobile communication**) GSM *m*

gsm [ˌdʒiːesˈem] *n Typ* (*abbr* **grams per square metre**) grammage *m* (du papier)

GST [ˌdʒiːesˈtiː] *n Can Fin* (*abbr* **goods and services tax**) TPS *f*

GSW [ˌdʒiːesˈdʌbəljuː] *n Med* (*abbr* **gunshot wound**) blessure *f* par balle

gt (*written abbr* **great**) grand

GU (*written abbr* **Guam**) Guam

GUI [ˈguːiː] *n Comput* (*abbr* **graphical user interface**) interface *f* utilisateur graphique

gynae [ˈgaɪnɪ] *adj Br Fam* (*abbr* **gynaecological**) (*department, ward*) de gynécologie ❑; **a gynae nurse** une infirmière du service de gynécologie ❑

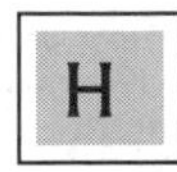

h [eɪtʃ] *n Fam Drugs slang* (*abbr* **heroin**) héro *f*, blanche *f*

h & c (*written abbr* **hot and cold**) eau *f* courante chaude et froide

hankie, hanky [ˈhæŋkɪ] (*pl* **hankies**) *n Fam* (*abbr* **handkerchief**) mouchoir ❑ *m*

Hants (*written abbr* **Hampshire**) Hampshire

Hazchem *Br* (*written abbr* **hazardous chemicals**) (*sign*) produits dangereux

HB [ˌeɪtʃˈbiː] *n Br* (*abbr* **hard-black**) (*on pencils*) HB

H-bomb *n* (*abbr* **hydrogen bomb**) bombe *f* H

HCF [ˌeɪtʃsiːˈef] *n Math* (*abbr* **highest common factor**) PGCD *m*

HD [ˌeɪtʃˈdiː] *Comput* (**a**) (*abbr* **hard disk**) DD (**b**) (*abbr* **high density**) HD

HDD [ˌeɪtʃdiːˈdiː] *n Comput* (*written abbr* **hard disk drive**) unité *f* de disque dur

HDTV [ˌeɪtʃdiːˌtiːˈviː] *n* (*abbr* **high definition television**) TVHD *f*

HE¹ (**a**) (*written abbr* **high explosive**) explosif *m* puissant (**b**) (*written abbr* **His/Her Excellency**) S Exc, SE

HE² [ˌeɪtʃˈiː] *n Br* (*abbr* **higher education**) enseignement *m* supérieur

Herts (*written abbr* **Hertfordshire**) Hertfordshire *m*

HEW [ˌeɪtʃiːˈdʌbəljuː] *n Am Formerly* (*abbr* **Department of Health, Education and Welfare**) = ancien ministère américain de l'Éducation et de la Santé publique

Hex [heks] *adj Comput* (*abbr* **hexadecimal**) hexadécimal

HF [ˌeɪtʃˈef] *n Rad* (*abbr* **high frequency**) HF *f*

HGH [ˌeɪtʃdʒiːˈeɪtʃ] *n Biol* (*abbr* **human growth hormone**) hormone *f* de croissance

HGV [ˌeɪtʃdʒiːˈviː] *n Br* (*abbr* **heavy goods vehicle**) PL *m*

▸▸ ***HGV licence*** permis *m* PL

HI (*written abbr* **Hawaii**) Hawaii *f*, Hawaï *f*

hi-fi [ˈhaɪˌfaɪ] (*abbr* **high fidelity**) **1** *n* (**a**) (*UNCOUNT*) hi-fi *f inv* (**b**) (*stereo system*) chaîne *f* (hi-fi); (*radio*) radio *f* (hi-fi)

2 *comp* (*equipment, recording*) hi-fi (*inv*)

▸▸ ***hi-fi system*** chaîne *f* (hi-fi)

HIP [ˌeɪtʃaɪˈpiː] *n Am* (*abbr* **health insurance plan**) assurance *f* médicale

hi-res [ˈhaɪrez] *adj Fam Comput* (*abbr* **high-resolution**) (à) haute résolution ❑

HIV [ˌeɪtʃaɪˈviː] *n Med* (*abbr* **human immunodeficiency virus**) VIH *m*, HIV *m*; **to be HIV negative** être séronégatif; **to be HIV positive** être séropositif

▸▸ ***HIV case*** cas *m* de séropositivité; ***HIV patients*** patients *mpl* séropositifs

hl (*written abbr* **hectolitre**) hl

HM [ˌeɪtʃˈem] *n* (*abbr* **His/Her Majesty**) SM

HMG [ˌeɪtʃemˈdʒiː] *n Br Admin* (*abbr* **His/Her Majesty's Government**) = expression utilisée sur des documents officiels en Grande-Bretagne

HMI [ˌeɪtʃemˈaɪ] *n Br Sch* (*abbr* **His/Her Majesty's Inspector**) = inspecteur de l'éducation nationale en Grande-Bretagne

HMMV [ˈhʌmviː] *n Am* (*abbr* **high-mobility multipurpose vehicle**) = sorte de grosse jeep utilisée pour le transport de troupes

HMO [ˌeɪtʃemˈəʊ] *n Am* (*abbr* **Health Maintenance Organization**) = aux États-Unis, clinique de médecine préventive où l'on peut aller lorsqu'on a certains contrats d'assurance

HMP [ˌeɪtʃemˈpiː] *n Br* (*abbr* **His/Her Majesty's Prison**) = abréviation qui précède les noms de prison en Grande-Bretagne

HMS [ˌeɪtʃemˈes] *n Br Naut* (*abbr* **His/Her Majesty's Ship**) = dénomination officielle précédant le nom de tous les bâtiments de guerre de la marine britannique

HMSO [ˌeɪtʃemˌesˈəʊ] *n Br Typ* (*abbr* **His/Her Majesty's Stationery Office**) = maison d'édition publiant les ouvrages ou documents approuvés par le Parlement, les ministères et autres organismes officiels, ≃ l'Imprimerie *f* nationale

HNC [ˌeɪtʃenˈsiː] *n Br* (*abbr* **Higher National Certificate**) = brevet de technicien en Grande-Bretagne, ≃ BTS *m*

HND [ˌeɪtʃenˈdiː] *n Br* (*abbr* **Higher National Diploma**) = brevet de technicien supérieur en Grande-Bretagne, ≃ DUT *m*

HO [ˌeɪtʃˈəʊ] *n Br* (**a**) (*abbr* **Home Office**) ≃ ministère *m* de l'Intérieur (**b**) *Med* (*abbr* **House Officer**) ≃ interne *mf*

Hon. *Br* (*written abbr* **honourable**) honorable

hon. *Br* (*written abbr* **honorary**) honoraire

Hons. *Br Univ* (*written abbr* **honours degree**) = diplôme universitaire obtenu avec mention

Hon. Sec. (*written abbr* **honorary secretary**) secrétaire *mf* honoraire

HOV [ˌeɪtʃəʊˈviː] *n Am* (*abbr* **High Occupancy Vehicle**) = voiture transportant au moins deux passagers

▸▸ ***HOV lane*** = voie d'autoroute réservée aux automobiles occupées par au moins deux passagers

hp¹, HP¹ [ˌeɪtʃˈpiː] *n Br* (*abbr* **hire purchase**) **to buy sth on hp** acheter qch à crédit

hp², HP² (*written abbr* **horsepower**) CV

HQ [ˌeɪtʃˈkjuː] *n Mil* (*abbr* **headquarters**) QG *m*

HR [ˌeɪtʃˈɑː(r)] *n* (*abbr* **human resources**) RH *fpl*

hr (**a**) (*written abbr* **hour**) h (**b**) *Am Sport* (*written abbr* **home run**) coup *m* de circuit (*coup de batte qui permet au batteur de marquer un point en faisant un tour complet en une seule fois*)

HRH (*written abbr* **His/Her Royal Highness**) SAR

HRM [ˌeɪtʃɑːˈrem] *n* (*abbr* **human resource management**) GRH *f*

hrs (*written abbr* **hours**) h

HRT [ˌeɪtʃɑːˈtiː] *n Med* (*abbr* **hormone replacement therapy**) traitement *m* hormonal substitutif

HS *Am* (*written abbr* **high school**) lycée *m*

HSC [ˌeɪtʃesˈsiː] *n Austr* (*abbr* **Higher School Certificate**) ≃ baccalauréat *m*

HSE [ˌeɪtʃesˈiː] *n* (*abbr* **Health and Safety Executive**) inspection *f* du travail

HST [ˌeɪtʃesˈtiː] *n* (**a**) (*abbr* **high speed train**) ≃ TGV *m* (**b**) (*abbr* **Hawaiian Standard Time**) heure *f* d'Hawaii

HT (**a**) (*written abbr* **high tension**) HT (**b**) *Sport* (*written abbr* **half-time**) mi-temps *f*

ht (*written abbr* **height**) hauteur *f*

HTML [ˌeɪtʃtiːˌemˈel] *n Comput* (*abbr* **Hypertext Markup Language**) HTML *m*

▸▸ ***HTML editor*** éditeur *m* HTML

HTTP [ˌeɪtʃtiːtiːˈpiː] *n Comput* (*abbr* **Hypertext Transfer Protocol**) protocole *m* HTTP

▸▸ ***HTTP server*** serveur *m* Web

HUAC [ˈhjuːæk] *n Am Hist* (*abbr* **House Un-American Activities Committee**) = organisme maccarthyste de répression anticommuniste fondé en 1938 et dissous en 1975

HUD [hʌd] *n Am Formerly* (*abbr* **Department of Housing and Urban Development**) = ancien ministère américain de l'Urbanisme et du Logement

hypo [ˈhaɪpəʊ] *Fam* **1** *n Drugs slang* (*abbr* **hypodermic**) shooteuse *f*, pompe *f*

2 *adj Physiol* (*abbr* **hypoglycaemic**) hypoglycémiant ❑; **to be hypo** (*permanently*) faire de l'hypoglycémie ❑; (*temporarily*) avoir une crise d'hypoglycémie ❑

Hz *Elec & Phys* (*written abbr* **hertz**) Hz

I. (*written abbr* **island**) île *f*

IA (*written abbr* **Iowa**) Iowa *m*

IAAF [ˌaɪdʌbəleɪˈef] *n* (*abbr* **International Amateur Athletics Federation**) FIAA *f*

IAEA [ˌaɪeɪˌiːˈaɪ] *n* (*abbr* **International Atomic Energy Agency**) AIEA *f*

IAP [ˌaɪeɪˈpiː] *n Comput* (*abbr* **Internet Access Provider**) fournisseur *m* d'accès à l'Internet

IASC [ˌaɪeɪˌesˈsiː] *n Fin* (*abbr* **International Accounting Standards Committee**) comité *m* international des normes comptables

IATA [aɪˈɑːtə, iːˈɑːtə] *n* (*abbr* **International Air Transport Association**) IATA *f*

IBA [ˌaɪbiːˈeɪ] *n Br Formerly* (*abbr* **Independent Broadcasting Authority**) = organisme d'agrément et de coordination des stations de radio et chaînes de télévision du secteur privé en Grande-Bretagne
IBC [ˌaɪbiːˈsiː] *n Press* (*abbr* **inside back cover**) troisième *f* de couverture
IBEW [ˈaɪbjuː] *n* (*abbr* **International Brotherhood of Electrical Workers**) = syndicat international d'électriciens
ibid (*written abbr* **ibidem**) ibid
IBOR [ˈaɪbɔː(r)] *n Fin* (*abbr* **interbank offered rate**) taux *m* interbancaire offert
IBRD [ˌaɪbiːˌɑːˈdiː] *n* (*abbr* **International Bank for Reconstruction and Development**) BIRD *f*
IBS [ˌaɪbiːˈes] *n Med* (*abbr* **irritable bowel syndrome**) syndrôme *m* du côlon irritable
IC [ˌaɪˈsiː] *n Comput* (*abbr* **integrated circuit**) circuit *m* intégré
►► ***IC card*** carte *f* à circuits intégrés
i/c [ˌaɪˈsiː] (*abbr* **in charge of**) responsable de
ICA [ˌaɪsiːˈeɪ] *n Br* (*abbr* **Institute of Contemporary Arts**) = centre d'art moderne à Londres
ICAO [ˌaɪsiːˌeɪˈəʊ] *n* (*abbr* **International Civil Aviation Organization**) OACI *f*
ICBM [ˌaɪsiːˌbiːˈem] *n* (*abbr* **intercontinental ballistic missile**) ICBM *m*
ICC [ˌaɪsiːˈsiː] *n* (**a**) (*abbr* **International Chamber of Commerce**) CCI *f* (**b**) *Am* (*abbr* **Interstate Commerce Commission**) = commission fédérale américaine réglementant le commerce entre les États
ICJ [ˌaɪsiːˈdʒeɪ] *n Law* (*abbr* **International Court of Justice**) CIJ *f*
ICR [ˌaɪsiːˈɑː(r)] *n Am* (*abbr* **Institute for Cancer Research**) = institut américain de recherche sur le cancer
ICT [ˌaɪsiːˈtiː] *n* (*abbr* **information and communication technology**) informatique *f*
ICU [ˌaɪsiːˈjuː] *n Med* (*abbr* **intensive care unit**) unité *f* de soins intensifs
ID[1] [ˌaɪˈdiː] (*pl* **ID's**, *pt & pp* **ID'd**, *cont* **ID'ing**) **1** *n (UNCOUNT)* (*abbr* **identification**) (**a**) *(documents)* papiers *mpl*; **do you have any ID?** vous avez une pièce d'identité? (**b**) *Comput* numéro *m* d'identification
2 *vt* (*abbr* **identify**) **to ID sb** identifier qn; **to be** *or* **to get ID'd** subir un contrôle d'identité
►► ***ID card*** carte *f* d'identité
ID[2] (*written abbr* **Idaho**) Idaho
IDB [ˌaɪdiːˈbiː] *n Fin* (*abbr* **inter-dealer broker**) courtier *m* intermédiaire
IDD [ˌaɪdiːˈdiː] *n Tel* (*abbr* **international direct dialling**) indicatif *m* du pays
IDE [ˌaɪdiːˈiː] *n Comput* (*abbr* **integrated drive electronics**) IDE *m*
ie [ˈaɪˌiː] *adv* (*abbr* **id est**) c'est-à-dire, à savoir
IEEE [ˌaɪiːˌiːˈiː] *n Comput* (*abbr* **Institute of Electronic and Electrical Engineers**) IEEE *m*
IFA [ˌaɪefˈeɪ] *n Fin* (*abbr* **independent financial adviser**) conseiller(ère) *m,f* financier(ère) indépendant(e)
IFC [ˌaɪefˈsiː] *n* (**a**) *Typ* (*abbr* **inside front cover**) deuxième *f* de couverture (**b**) *Fin* (*abbr* **International Finance Corporation**) SFI *f*
IKBS [ˌaɪkeɪˌbiːˈes] *n Comput* (*abbr* **intelligent knowledge-based system**) système *m* expert
IL (*written abbr* **Illinois**) Illinois *m*
ILA [ˌaɪelˈeɪ] *n* (*abbr* **International Longshoremen's Association**) = syndicat international de dockers
ILEA [ˌaɪelˌiːˈeɪ, ˈɪlɪə] *n Br Formerly Sch* (*abbr* **Inner London Education Authority**) **the ILEA** = organisme qui, jusqu'en 1990, était chargé de gérer les services londoniens de l'enseignement
ill. (*written abbr* **illustration**) ill
ILO [ˌaɪeˈləʊ] *n Ind* (*abbr* **International Labour Organization**) OIT *f*
ILWU [ˈɪljuː] *n* (*abbr* **International Longshoremen's and Warehousemen's Union**) = syndicat international de dockers et de magasiniers
IMF [ˌaɪemˈef] *n Fin* (*abbr* **International Monetary Fund**) FMI *m*
IMR [ˌaɪemˈɑː(r)] *n* (*abbr* **infant mortality rate**) taux *m* de mortalité infantile
IMRO [ˈɪmrəʊ] *n Br Formerly* (*abbr* **Investment Management Regulatory Organization**) = organisme britannique contrôlant les activités de banques d'affaires et de gestionnaires de fonds de retraite
in. (*written abbr* **inch(es)**) inch *m*, pouce *m*
Inc. *Am* (*written abbr* **incorporated**) ≃ SARL
inc. (*written abbr* **inclusive**) **12–15 April inc** du 12 au 15 avril inclus
incl. (**a**) (*written abbr* **inclusive**) inclus; **from 14 to 23 November incl.** du 14 au 23 novembre inclus; **incl. of gas and electricity** gaz et électricité compris (**b**) (*written abbr* **including**) avec; **incl. VAT** TVA comprise; **350 francs incl. VAT** 350 FF TTC
Ind (**a**) (*written abbr* **Independent**) indépendant (**b**) (*written abbr* **Indiana**) Indiana *m*
Indy [ˈɪndɪ] *n Fam* (*abbr* **Indianapolis**) Indianapolis ❑
►► ***Indy car*** = type de voiture de course, aux États-Unis; ***the Indy 500*** = course automobile qui se déroule à Indianapolis, aux États-Unis
INF [ˌaɪenˈef] *npl Mil* (*abbr* **intermediate range nuclear forces**) FNI *fpl*
INLA [ˌaɪenˌelˈeɪ] *n* (*abbr* **Irish National Liberation Army**) Armée *f* de libération nationale irlandaise, INLA *f*
INS [ˌaɪenˈes] *n Am* (*abbr* **Immigration and Naturalization Service**) = services américains de contrôle de l'immigration
ins (**a**) (*written abbr* **insurance**) asse. (**b**) (*written abbr* **inches**) pouces
INSET [ˈɪnset] *n Br Sch* (*abbr* **in-service training**) formation *f* permanente *ou* continue pour les enseignants
inst. *Old-fashioned Com* (*written abbr* **instant**) courant; **of the 9th inst.** du 9 courant *ou* de ce mois
INTUC [ˈɪntʌk] *n* (*abbr* **Indian National Trade Union Congress**) = confédération de syndicats indiens
I/O *Comput* (*written abbr* **input/output**) E/S *f*
IOC [ˌaɪəʊˈsiː] *n Sport* (*abbr* **International Olympic Committee**) CIO *m*
IOM (*written abbr* **Isle of Man**) île *f* de Man
IOU [ˌaɪəʊˈjuː] *n* (*abbr* **I owe you**) reconnaissance *f* de dette
IOW (*written abbr* **Isle of Wight**) île *f* de Wight
IP [ˌaɪˈpiː] *n Comput* (*abbr* **Internet Protocol**)
►► ***IP address*** adresse *f* IP; ***IP number*** numéro *m* IP
IPCC [ˌaɪpiːˌsiːˈsiː] *n* (*abbr* **Intergovernmental Panel on Climate Change**) GIEC *m*
IPO [ˌaɪpiːˈəʊ] *n Am St Exch* (*abbr* **initial public offering**) introduction *f* en Bourse
IQ [ˌaɪˈkjuː] *n* (*abbr* **intelligence quotient**) QI *m*
IRA [ˌaɪɑːˈreɪ] *n* (**a**) (*abbr* **Irish Republican Army**) IRA *f* (**b**) *Am Fin* (*abbr* **individual retirement account**) plan *m* d'épargne retraite personnel
IRBM [ˌaɪɑːˌbiːˈem] *n* (*abbr* **intermediate range ballistic missile**) IRBM *m*
IRC [ˌaɪɑːˈsiː] *n Comput* (*abbr* **Internet Relay Chat**) IRC *m*, service *m* de bavardage Internet, dialogue *m* en direct
►► ***IRC channel*** canal *m* IRC, canal *m* de dialogue en direct
IRFU [ˌaɪɑːrˌefˈjuː] *n* (*abbr* **Irish Rugby Football Union**) = fédération irlandaise de rugby
IRN [ˌaɪɑːˈren] *n* (*abbr* **Independent Radio News**) = agence de presse radiophonique
IRO [ˌaɪɑːˈrəʊ] *n* (*abbr* **International Refugee Organization**) = organisation humanitaire pour les réfugiés
IRR [ˌaɪɑːˈrɑː(r)] *n Fin* (*abbr* **internal rate of return**) taux *m* de rentabilité interne
IRS [ˌaɪɑːˈres] *n Am Fin* (*abbr* **Internal Revenue Service**) **the IRS** ≃ le fisc
IS [ˌaɪˈes] *n* (*abbr* **information system**) système *m* informatique
ISA [ˈaɪsə] *n Br Fin* (*abbr* **individual savings account**) ≃ PEA *m*
ISBN [ˌaɪesˌbiːˈen] *n* (*abbr* **International Standard Book Number**) ISBN *m*
ISDN [ˌaɪesˌdiːˈen] (*abbr* **integrated services digital network**) **1** *n* RNIS *m*
2 *vt Fam* **to ISDN sth** envoyer qch par RNIS ❑
►► ***ISDN card*** carte *f* RNIS; ***ISDN line*** ligne *f* RNIS; ***ISDN modem*** modem *m* RNIS *ou* Numéris
ISO [ˌaɪesˈəʊ] *n* (*abbr* **International Standards Organization**) ISO *f*
ISOC [ˌaɪesˌəʊˈsiː] *n Comput* (*abbr* **Internet Society**) = organisation non gouvernementale chargée de veiller à l'évolution de l'Internet
ISP [ˌaɪesˈpiː] *n Comput* (*abbr* **Internet Service Provider**) fournisseur *m* d'accès à l'Internet
ISTC [ˌaɪesˌtiːˈsiː] *n* (*abbr* **Iron and Steel Trades Confederation**) = syndicat britannique des ouvriers de la sidérurgie
IT [ˌaɪˈtiː] *n* (*abbr* **information technology**) technologie *f* de l'information; **she's our IT expert** c'est notre spécialiste en informatique; **IT has revolutionized the way we do business** l'informatique a complètement transformé le monde du commerce
ITA [ˌaɪtiːˈeɪ] *n* (*abbr* **Initial Teaching Alphabet**) **the ITA** = alphabet en partie phonétique parfois utilisé pour l'enseignement de la lecture
ITC [ˌaɪtiːˈsiː] *n Br* (*abbr* **Independent Television Commission**) = commission de surveillance des télévisions britanniques privées
ITN [ˌaɪtiːˈen] *n Br* (*abbr* **Independent Television News**) = service d'actualités télévisées pour les chaînes relevant de l'"ITC"
ITV [ˌaɪtiːˈviː] *n Br* (*abbr* **Independent Television**) = sigle désignant les programmes diffusés par les chaînes relevant de l'"ITC"
IUCD [ˌaɪjuːˌsiːˈdiː] *n* (*abbr* **intrauterine contraceptive device**) stérilet *m*
IUD [ˌaɪjuːˈdiː] *n* (*abbr* **intrauterine device**) stérilet *m*
IV [ˌaɪˈviː] *Med* (*abbr* **intravenous**) **1** *n* perfusion *f* intraveineuse
2 *adj* intraveineux
3 *adv* par voie intraveineuse
►► ***IV drip*** perfusion *f* intraveineuse; ***IV push*** pompe *f* de perfusion sous pression
IVF [ˌaɪviːˈef] *n* (*abbr* **in vitro fertilization**) FIV *f*
IWW [ˌaɪdʌbəljuːˈdʌbəljuː] *n* (*abbr* **Industrial Workers of the World**) IWW *m*, = syndicat révolutionnaire américain actif au début du XXème siècle
IYHF [ˌaɪwaɪˌeɪtʃˈef] *n* (*abbr* **International Youth Hostel Federation**) FIAJ *f*

JA [ˌdʒeɪˈeɪ] *n* (*abbr* **judge advocate**) assesseur *m (d'un tribunal militaire)*
J/A, j/a *Banking* (*written abbr* **joint account**) compte *m* joint
JAG [ˌdʒeɪeɪˈdʒiː] *n* (*abbr* **judge advocate general**) assesseur *m* général
Jan. (*written abbr* **January**) janv
JANET [ˈdʒænɪt] *n Comput* (*abbr* **Joint Academic Network**) = réseau Internet composé d'universités et d'organismes de recherche britanniques
JAP [dʒæp] *n Am Fam Pej* (*abbr* **Jewish American princess**) = jeune Juive américaine issue d'une famille aisée
Jas. (*written abbr* **James**) James
jato [ˈdʒeɪtəʊ] *n Aviat* (*abbr* **jet-assisted take-off**) décollage *m* (avec fusées) JATO
►► ***jato unit*** fusées *fpl* JATO
JC [ˌdʒeɪˈsiː] *n Fam* (*abbr* **Jesus Christ**) J.-C.

JCR [ˌdʒeɪsiː'ɑː(r)] *n Br Univ* (*abbr* **junior common room**) ≃ foyer *m* des étudiants

JCS [ˌdʒeɪsiː'es] *npl Am* (*abbr* **Joint Chiefs of Staff**) = organe consultatif du ministère américain de la Défense, composé des chefs d'état-major des trois armées

JD [ˌdʒeɪ'diː] *n Am* (**a**) (*abbr* **Justice Department**) ≃ le ministère de la Justice (**b**) (*abbr* **Doctor of Jurisprudence**) ≃ docteur *m* en droit

JFK [ˌdʒeɪef'keɪ] *n* (*abbr* **John Fitzgerald Kennedy**) (**a**) *(person)* John Kennedy (**b**) *(airport)* aéroport *m* JFK *(de New York)*

JIT [ˌdʒeɪaɪ'tiː] *adj* (*abbr* **just-in-time**) juste à temps, JAT
 ►► ***JIT distribution*** distribution *f* JAT; ***JIT production*** production *f* JAT; ***JIT purchasing*** achat *m* JAT

Jnr (*written abbr* **Junior**) **Michael Roberts Jnr** Michael Roberts fils

Joburg, Jo'burg ['dʒəʊbɜːg] *n* (*abbr* **Johannesburg**) Johannesburg *m*

JP [ˌdʒeɪ'piː] *n Br Law* (*abbr* **Justice of the Peace**) ≃ juge *m* d'instance

JPEG ['dʒeɪpeg] *n Comput* (*abbr* **Joint Photographic Experts Group**) (format *m*) JPEG *m*

Jr. (*written abbr* **Junior**) junior, fils

Jul. (*written abbr* **July**) juill

Jun. (**a**) (*written abbr* **June**) juin (**b**) (*written abbr* **Junior**) junior, fils

Junr (*written abbr* **Junior**) **Douglas Ross Junr** Douglas Ross fils

K¹, k [keɪ] *n* (**a**) *Comput* (*abbr* **kilobyte**) K, Ko; **how many K are left?** combien de Ko reste-t-il?; **720K diskette** disquette *f* de 720 Ko
 (**b**) (*abbr* **thousand**) K
 (**c**) *Fam* (*abbr* **thousand pounds**) **he earns 30K** il gagne 30 000 livres ❑
 (**d**) *Fam* (*abbr* **kilometre(s)**) kilomètre(s) ❑ *m(pl)*; **a 10K race** une course de 10 kilomètres
 ►► *Am Mil* ***K ration*** ration *f* (alimentaire)

K² (*written abbr* **Knight**) chevalier *m*

KB [ˌkeɪ'biː] *n Comput* (*abbr* **kilobyte**) Ko *m*

Kb [ˌkeɪ'biː] *n Comput* (*abbr* **kilobit**) Kb *m*

KBE [ˌkeɪbiː'iː] *n Br* (*abbr* **Knight (Commander of the Order) of the British Empire**) Chevalier *m* de l'Ordre de l'Empire britannique

Kbps [ˌkeɪbiːˌpiː'es] *n Comput* (*abbr* **kilobits per second**) Kb/s

KC [ˌkeɪ'siː] *n Br Law* (*abbr* **King's Counsel**) = avocat de la Couronne

kcal (*written abbr* **kilocalorie**) Kcal

KCB [ˌkeɪsiː'biː] *n Br* (*abbr* **Knight Commander (of the Order) of the Bath**) Chevalier *m* Commandeur de l'Ordre du Bain

kd [ˌkeɪ'diː] *adj* (*abbr* **knocked down**) = livré en kit à monter soi-même

KG [ˌkeɪ'dʒiː] *n Br* (*abbr* **Knight of the (Order of the) Garter**) Chevalier *m* de l'Ordre de la Jarretière

kg (*written abbr* **kilogram(me)**) kg

KGB [ˌkeɪdʒiː'biː] *n Formerly* (*abbr* **Komitet Gosudarstvennoi Bezopasnosti**) KGB *m*
 ►► ***KGB agent*** agent *m* du KGB; ***KGB officer*** officier *m* du KGB

kHz (*written abbr* **kilohertz**) kHz

KIA [ˌkeɪaɪ'eɪ] *adj Am Mil* (*abbr* **killed in action**) tué au combat

kilo ['kiːləʊ] (*pl* **kilos**) *n* (*abbr* **kilogram(me)**) kilo *m*

KIPS [kɪps] *n Comput* (*abbr* **kilo instructions per second**) = millier d'instructions par seconde

KISS [kɪs] *adj Am Fam* (*abbr* **keep it simple, stupid**) = sobre et simple

KKK [ˌkeɪkeɪ'keɪ] *n Am* (*abbr* **Ku Klux Klan**) Ku Klux Klan *m*

km (*written abbr* **kilometre**) km

km/h (*written abbr* **kilometres per hour**) km/h

KO [ˌkeɪ'əʊ] (*pl* **KO's**, *pt & pp* **KO'd**, *cont* **KO'ing**) *Fam* (*abbr* **knockout**) **1** *n* K-O *m*
 2 *vt* mettre K-O; *(in boxing)* battre par K-O

KP [ˌkeɪ'piː] *n Am Fam Mil slang* (*abbr* **kitchen police**) **looks like we're on KP tonight** on dirait qu'on est de corvée de cuisine ce soir

kph (*written abbr* **kilometres per hour**) km/h

KS¹ [ˌkeɪ'es] *n Med* (*abbr* **Kaposi's sarcoma**) sarcome *m* de Kaposi

KS² (*written abbr* **Kansas**) Kansas *m*

KT (*written abbr* **Knight**) chevalier *m*

kV (*written abbr* **kilovolt**) kV

kW (*written abbr* **kilowatt**) kW

kWh (*written abbr* **kilowatt-hour**) kWh

KY (*written abbr* **Kentucky**) Kentucky *m*

L (**a**) (*written abbr* **lake**) lac *m* (**b**) (*written abbr* **large**) L (**c**) (*written abbr* **left**) g (**d**) (*written abbr* **learner**) = lettre apposée sur une voiture et signalant un apprenti conducteur (en Grande-Bretagne)

l (*written abbr* **litre**) l

LA¹ [ˌel'eɪ] *n* (*abbr* **Los Angeles**) Los Angeles *m*

LA² (*written abbr* **Louisiana**) Louisiane *f*

Lab (*written abbr* **Labour, Labour Party**) parti *m* travailliste

lab [læb] **1** *n* (**a**) (*abbr* **laboratory**) labo *m* (**b**) *Fam* (*abbr* **labrador**) labrador ❑ *m*
 2 *comp (book)* de laboratoire
 ►► ***lab assistant*** laborantin(e) *m,f*, assistant(e) *m,f* de laboratoire; ***lab coat*** blouse *f*

LAMDA ['læmdə] *n* (*abbr* **London Academy of Music and Dramatic Art**) = conservatoire de musique et d'art dramatique, à Londres

LAN [læn] *n Comput* (*abbr* **local area network**) réseau *m* local

Lancs (*written abbr* **Lancashire**) Lancashire *m*

lang *Sch & Univ* (*written abbr* **language**) langue *f*

lat (*written abbr* **latitude**) lat.

LAUTRO ['laʊtrəʊ] *n Br* (*abbr* **Life Assurance and Unit Trust Regulatory Organization**) = organisme britannique contrôlant les activités de compagnies d'assurance-vie et de SICAV

LAV [ˌeleɪ'viː] *n Med* (*abbr* **lymphadenopathy associated virus**) LAV *m*

LAX (*written abbr* **Los Angeles Airport**) = sigle désignant l'aéroport international de Los Angeles

LB (*written abbr* **Labrador**) Labrador *m*

lb (*written abbr* **pound**) **3 lb** *or* **lbs** 3 livres

LBJ [ˌelbiː'dʒeɪ] *n* (*abbr* **Lyndon Baines Johnson**) Lyndon Johnson

LBO [ˌelbiː'əʊ] *n Fin* (*abbr* **leveraged buy-out**) rachat *m* d'entreprise financé par l'endettement

lbw [ˌelbiː'dʌbljuː] *n Br Sport* (*abbr* **leg before wicket**) = au cricket, faute d'un joueur qui intercepte avec sa jambe une balle qui allait frapper le guichet

LC [ˌel'siː] *n Am* (*abbr* **Library of Congress**) bibliothèque *f* du Congrès *(équivalent américain de la Bibliothèque nationale)*

lc *Typ* (*written abbr* **lower case**) bdc

L/C *Com* (*written abbr* **letter of credit**) lettre *f* de crédit

LCD [ˌelsiː'diː] *n Comput* (*abbr* **liquid crystal display**) affichage *m* à cristaux liquides, LCD *m*
 ►► ***LCD screen*** écran *m* LCD

LCL *Com* (*written abbr* **less than container load**) conteneur *m* chargé en partie

LCM [ˌelsiː'em] *n Math* (*abbr* **lowest common multiple**) PPCM *m*

LD [ˌel'diː] *n Pharm* (*abbr* **lethal dose**) dose *f* létale *ou* mortelle

Ld (*written abbr* **lord**) Lord

LDR [ˌeldiː'ɑː(r)] *n Electron* (*abbr* **light dependent resistor**) LDR *m*

L-driver *n Br* (*abbr* **learner-driver**) = personne qui apprend à conduire

LDS [ˌeldiː'es] *n* (*abbr* **Licentiate in Dental Surgery**) *(person)* = titulaire d'un diplôme en chirurgie dentaire; *(qualification)* diplôme *m* en chirurgie dentaire

LEA [ˌeliː'eɪ] *n Br Admin & Sch* (*abbr* **local education authority**) = organisme chargé de l'enseignement au niveau régional

LED [ˌeliː'diː] *n Comput* (*abbr* **light-emitting diode**) DEL *f*, LED *f*
 ►► ***LED display*** affichage *m* (par) LED

Leics (*written abbr* **Leicestershire**) Leicestershire *m*

LEM [lem] *n Astron* (*abbr* **lunar excursion module**) module *m* lunaire

LEP [ˌeliː'piː] *n* (**a**) *Am* (*abbr* **Limited English Proficiency**) = niveau d'expression moyen en anglais (**b**) (*abbr* **Large Electon-Positron Collider**) LEP *m*

LETS [lets] *n Com* (*abbr* **Local Exchange Trading System**) = système d'échange de services dans une communauté donnée, basé sur une monnaie nominale

lh [ˌel'eɪtʃ] *Mus* (*abbr* **left hand**) main *f* gauche

LI (*written abbr* **Long Island**) Long Island

Lib [lɪb] *n* (*abbr* **Liberal**) libéral(e) *m,f*
 ►► ***Lib Dem*** **1** *n* = membre du parti libéral démocrate **2** *adj* libéral démocrate

lib [lɪb] *n Fam* (*abbr* **liberation**) libération ❑ *f*

Lib-Lab *adj Br Fam* (*abbr* **Liberal-Labour**) *(agreement, talks)* entre libéraux et travaillistes; **a Lib-Lab pact** un accord entre libéraux et travaillistes

LIBOR ['laɪbɔː(r)] *n Br Fin* (*abbr* **London Inter-Bank Offer Rate**) ≃ TIOP *m*

Lieut *Mil* (*written abbr* **lieutenant**) Lieut.

Lieut-Col *Mil* (*written abbr* **Lieutenant-Colonel**) Lieut.-Col.

LIFFE [laɪf, 'lɪfɪ] *n Fin* (*abbr* **London International Financial Futures Exchange**) = marché à terme britannique d'instruments financiers, ≃ MATIF *m*

LIFO ['laɪfəʊ] *n Com & Fin* (*abbr* **last in, first out**) DEPS

Lincs (*written abbr* **Lincolnshire**) Lincolnshire *m*

LISA [ˌelaɪˌes'eɪ] *n Br Fin* (*abbr* **long-term individual savings account**) plan *m* de retraite en actions

lit [lɪt] *n Fam* (*abbr* **literature**) **she teaches English lit** elle enseigne la littérature anglaise ❑
 ►► ***lit crit*** critique *f* littéraire ❑

litho ['lɪθəʊ, 'laɪðəʊ] **1** *adj* (*abbr* **lithographic**) lithographique
 2 *n* (**a**) (*abbr* **lithograph**) lithographie *f* (**b**) (*abbr* **lithography**) lithographie *f*

LLB [ˌelel'biː] *n* (*abbr* **Bachelor of Laws**) *(person)* = titulaire d'une licence de droit; *(qualification)* licence *f* de droit

LLD [ˌelel'diː] *n* (*abbr* **Doctor of Laws**) *(person)* docteur *m* en droit; *(qualification)* doctorat *m* en droit

LLM [ˌelel'em] *n* (*abbr* **Master of Laws**) *(person)* = titulaire d'une maîtrise de droit; *(qualification)* maîtrise *f* de droit

LMBO [ˌelemˌbiː'əʊ] *n Fin* (*abbr* **leveraged management buy-out**) = rachat d'entreprise par les salariés

LMS [ˌelem'es] *n Admin* (*abbr* **local management of schools**) = système où l'administration des écoles publiques est confiée à l'échelon local

LMT [ˌelem'tiː] *n* (*abbr* **Local Mean Time**) = heure locale

LNG [ˌelen'dʒiː] *n* (*abbr* **liquefied natural gas**) GNL *m*

loc. cit. (*written abbr* **loco citato**) loc. cit.

log [lɒg] *n Math* (*abbr* **logarithm**) log *m*

long. (*written abbr* **longitude**) long.

LOOM [luːm] *n Am* (*abbr* **Loyal Order of the Moose**) = association caritative américaine

lox [lɒks] *n* (*abbr* **liquid oxygen**) oxygène *m* liquide

LP [ˌelˈpiː] *n* (*abbr* **long-player**) **an LP** un 33 tours

LPG [ˌelpiːˈdʒiː] *n* (*abbr* **liquefied petroleum gas**) GPL *m*, *Belg* LPG *m*

LPN [ˌelpiːˈen] *n* (*abbr* **licensed practical nurse**) = aide infirmière diplômée

LQ [ˌelˈkjuː] *Comput* (*abbr* **letter quality**) qualité *f* courrier
▸▸ ***LQ printer*** imprimante *f* de qualité courrier

LRAM [ˌelɑːˌreɪˈem] *n* (*abbr* **Licentiate of the Royal Academy of Music**) = membre de la "Royal Academy of Music"

LSAT [ˌelesˌeɪˈtiː] *n* (*abbr* **Law School Admissions Test**) = aux États-Unis, test d'admission aux études de droit

LSD[1] [ˌelesˈdiː] *n* (*abbr* **lysergic acid diethylamide**) LSD *m*

LSD[2], **lsd** *n Formerly* (*abbr* **librae, solidi, denarii**) = symboles représentant les "pounds", les "shillings" et les "pence" de l'ancienne monnaie britannique avant l'adoption du système décimal en 1971

LSE [ˌelesˈiː] *n* (**a**) *Univ* (*abbr* **London School of Economics**) = grande école de sciences économiques et politiques à Londres (**b**) *St Exch* (*abbr* **London Stock Exchange**) = la Bourse de Londres

LSI [ˌelesˈaɪ] *n Comput* (*abbr* **large scale integration**) intégration *f* à grande échelle

LSO [ˌelesˈəʊ] *n* (*abbr* **London Symphony Orchestra**) = orchestre symphonique de Londres

LT[1] [ˌelˈtiː] *n* (*abbr* **London Transport**) = régie des transports londoniens

LT[2] (*written abbr* **low tension**) BT

Lt. *Mil* (*written abbr* **lieutenant**) Lieut.

LTA [ˌeltiːˈeɪ] *n* (*abbr* **Lawn Tennis Association**) = la Fédération britannique de tennis

Ltd, ltd (*written abbr* **limited**) ≃ SARL, *Can* limité; **Smith and Sons Ltd** ≃ Smith & Fils, SARL

LULAC [ˈluːlæk] *n* (*abbr* **League of United Latin-American Citizens**) = ligue américaine pour la défense des droits de la population d'origine latino-américaine

LV (*written abbr* **luncheon voucher**) Ticket-Restaurant® *m inv*

LW *Rad* (*written abbr* **long wave**) GO

LWOP [ˈelwɒp] *n Am* (**a**) (*abbr* **leave without pay**) congé *m* sans solde (**b**) (*abbr* **life without parole**) = réclusion criminelle à perpétuité sans possibilité de remise en liberté conditionnelle

LWT [ˌeldʌbəljuːˈtiː] *n* (*abbr* **London Weekend Television**) = chaîne de télévision relevant de l'ITC

M (*written abbr* **medium**) M

m (**a**) (*written abbr* **metre**) m (**b**) (*written abbr* **million**) M (**c**) (*written abbr* **mile**) mile *m*

MA[1] [ˌemˈeɪ] *n* (**a**) *Univ* (*abbr* **Master of Arts**) (*in England, Wales and US* → *person*) = titulaire d'une maîtrise de lettres; (→ *qualification*) maîtrise *f* de lettres; (*in Scotland* → *person*) = titulaire du premier examen universitaire, équivalent de la licence; (→ *qualification*) = premier examen universitaire, équivalent de la licence; **to have an MA in Russian** avoir une maîtrise/licence de russe; **Susan Long, MA** Susan Long, Maîtrise de lettres/licenciée ès lettres (**b**) (*abbr* **military academy**) école *f* militaire

MA[2] (*written abbr* **Massachusetts**) Massachusetts *m*

mac [mæk] *n Br Fam* (*abbr* **mackintosh**) imper *m*

MACRS [ˌemeɪˌsiːɑːˈres] *n Am Acct* (*abbr* **modified accelerated cost recovery system**) = méthode d'amortissement accéléré

MAD [mæd] *n* (**a**) *Am Nucl* (*abbr* **mutual assured destruction**) = équilibre de la terreur (**b**) *Acct* (*abbr* **mean absolute deviation**) écart *m* moyen absolu

MADD [mæd] *n Am* (*abbr* **Mothers Against Drunk Driving**) = association américaine de lutte contre l'alcool au volant, fondée par la mère d'une enfant tuée par un conducteur en état d'ébriété

MAFF [mæf] *n Br* (*abbr* **Ministry of Agriculture, Fisheries and Food**) ≃ ministère *m* de l'Agriculture

mag [mæg] *adj* (*abbr* **magnetic**)
▸▸ ***mag tape*** bande *f* magnétique; ***mag tape cassette*** cassette *f* à bande magnétique; ***mag tape reader*** lecteur *m* de bandes magnétiques

maglev [ˈmæglev] *n Transp* (*abbr* **magnetic levitation**) lévitation *f* magnétique
▸▸ ***maglev train*** train *m* à lévitation magnétique

MAG welding [mæg-] *n Tech* (*abbr* **metallic active-gas**) soudage *m* MAG

MAI [ˌemeɪˈaɪ] *n Fin* (*abbr* **multilateral agreement on investment**) AMI *m*

Maj. *Mil* (*written abbr* **Major**) ≃ Cdt; *Can & Belg* Maj.

Maj. Gen. *Mil* (*written abbr* **Major General**) ≃ général *m* de division; *Belg* ≃ général-major *m*, *Suisse* ≃ divisionnaire *m*, *Can* ≃ major-général *m*

Man (*written abbr* **Manitoba**) Manitoba *m*

Manc [mæŋk] *n Br Fam* (*abbr* **Mancunian**) (*inhabitant*) habitant(e) *m,f* de Manchester; (*native*) originaire *mf* de Manchester

M&A [ˌemənˈeɪ] *n Fin* (*abbr* **mergers and acquisitions**) fusions et acquisitions *fpl*

Manit (*written abbr* **Manitoba**) Manitoba *m*

MAP [mæp] *n Am* (*abbr* **Modified American Plan**) = dans un hôtel américain, séjour en demi-pension

Mar. (*written abbr* **March**) mars *m*

MARV [mɑːv] *n Mil* (*abbr* **manoeuvrable re-entry vehicle**) MARV *m*

MASH [mæʃ] *n Am* (*abbr* **mobile army surgical hospital**) = hôpital militaire de campagne

Mass. (*written abbr* **Massachusetts**) Massachusetts *m*

matric [məˈtrɪk] *n Br Fam Univ* (*abbr* **matriculation**) inscription ❑ *f*
▸▸ ***matric card*** carte *f* d'étudiant ❑

MATV [ˌemeɪˌtiːˈviː] *n Br* (*abbr* **Master Antenna Television**) télévision *f* à antenne maîtresse

MAV [ˌemeɪˈviː] *n* (*abbr* **micro air vehicle**) microdrone *m* (*avion espion téléguidé en modèle réduit*)

max [mæks] (*abbr* **maximum**) **1** *n* max *m*; *Am Fam* **to the max** (*totally*) un max; **did you have a good time? – to the max!** tu t'es bien amusé? – vachement bien!, un max!
2 *adv Fam* (*at the most*) maxi; **it'll take three days max** ça prendra trois jours maxi
3 *vt Am Fam* **to max an exam** = obtenir le maximum de points à un examen

MB (**a**) *Comput* (*written abbr* **megabyte**) Mo (**b**) (*written abbr* **Manitoba**) Manitoba *m*

Mb *n Comput* (*written abbr* **megabit**) Mb

MBA [ˌembiːˈeɪ] *n Univ* (*abbr* **Master of Business Administration**) (*person*) = titulaire d'une maîtrise de gestion; (*qualification*) maîtrise *f* de gestion, MBA *m*

MBBS [ˌembiːˌbiːˈes] *n Univ* (*abbr* **Bachelor of Medicine and Surgery**) (*person*) = titulaire d'une licence de médecine et de chirurgie; (*qualification*) licence *f* de médecine et de chirurgie

MBE [ˌembiːˈiː] *n* (*abbr* **Member of the Order of the British Empire**) (*award*) ordre *m* de l'Empire britannique; (*person*) = membre de l'ordre de l'Empire britannique

MBI [ˌembiːˈaɪ] *n Fin* (*abbr* **management buy-in**) apport *m* de gestion

MBO [ˌembiːˈəʊ] *n Br Fin* (**a**) (*abbr* **management buy-out**) rachat *m* d'une société par la direction (**b**) (*abbr* **management by objectives**) gestion *f* ou direction *f* par objectifs

Mbps *Comput* (*written abbr* **megabits per second**) mbps

MBS [ˌembiːˈes] *n Fin* (*abbr* **mortgage-backed security**) titre *m* garanti par des créances hypothécaires

MC [ˌemˈsiː] *n* (**a**) (*abbr* **master of ceremonies**) (*at reception*) maître *m* de cérémonie; (*on TV show*) présentateur *m* (**b**) *Br Mil* (*abbr* **Military Cross**) = distinction militaire britannique (**c**) *Am* (*abbr* **Member of Congress**) membre *m* du Congrès (**d**) *Am Mil* (*abbr* **Marine Corps**) Marines *mpl*

MCAT [ˌemsiːˌeɪˈtiː] *n Am* (*abbr* **Medical College Admissions Test**) = test d'admission aux études de médecine aux États-Unis

MCC [ˌemsiːˈsiː] *n* (*abbr* **Marylebone Cricket Club**) = célèbre club de cricket de Londres

MCG [ˌemsiːˈdʒiː] *n* (*abbr* **Melbourne Cricket Ground**) = principal terrain de cricket de Melbourne

MCP [ˌemsiːˈpiː] *n Fam* (*abbr* **male chauvinist pig**) phallo *m*, macho *m*

MD[1] [ˌemˈdiː] *n* (**a**) (*abbr* **Doctor of Medicine**) docteur *m* en médecine (**b**) (*abbr* **managing director**) P-DG *m*

MD[2] (*written abbr* **Maryland**) Maryland *m*

MDF [ˌemdiːˈef] *n* (*abbr* **medium-density fibreboard**) MDF *m*, panneaux *mpl* de fibres de moyenne densité

MDMA [ˌemdiːˌemˈeɪ] *n* (*abbr* **methylenedioxymethamphetamine**) MDMA *f*

MDS [ˌemdiːˈes] *n* (*abbr* **Master of Dental Surgery**) (*person*) = titulaire d'une maîtrise de médecine dentaire; (*qualification*) maîtrise *f* de médecine dentaire

MDT [ˌemdiːˈtiː] *n Am* (*abbr* **Mountain Daylight Time**) heure *f* d'été des montagnes Rocheuses

ME [ˌemˈiː] *n* (**a**) (*UNCOUNT*) *Med* (*abbr* **myalgic encephalomyelitis**) encéphalomyélite *f* myalgique (**b**) *Am* (*abbr* **medical examiner**) médecin *m* légiste

Me (*written abbr* **Maine**) Maine *m*

MEd [ˌemˈed] *n Univ* (*abbr* **Master of Education**) (*person*) = titulaire d'une maîtrise en sciences de l'éducation; (*qualification*) maîtrise *f* en sciences de l'éducation

MEng [ˌemˈeŋ] *n Univ* (*abbr* **Master of Engineering**) (*person*) = titulaire d'une maîtrise d'ingénierie; (*qualification*) maîtrise *f* d'ingénierie

MEP [ˌemiːˈpiː] *n EU* (*abbr* **Member of the European Parliament**) député *m* à l'Assemblée européenne, membre *m* du Parlement européen

Merc [mɜːk] *n Fam* (*abbr* **Mercedes**) Mercedes ❑ *f*

Messrs, Messrs. [ˈmesəz] *npl* (*abbr* **Messieurs**) MM *mpl*

Met [met] *n Fam* (**a**) *Am* (*abbr* **Metropolitan Opera**) **the Met** le Metropolitan Opera ❑ (*opéra de New York*) (**b**) *Am* (*abbr* **Metropolitan Museum of Art**) = un des principaux musées américains, à New York (**c**) *Br* (*abbr* **Metropolitan Police**) police *f* londonienne ❑
▸▸ *Br Met* ***Met Office*** = services météorologiques britanniques

meths [meθs] *n Br Fam* (*abbr* **methylated spirits**) alcool *m* à brûler ❑
▸▸ ***meths drinker*** = alcoolique qui boit de l'alcool à brûler

Mex [meks] *Am Fam* (*abbr* **Mexican**) **1** *n* = terme injurieux désignant un Mexicain
2 *adj* mexicain

MFA [ˌemefˈeɪ] *n Univ* (*abbr* **Master of Fine Arts**) (*person*) = titulaire d'une maîtrise en beaux-arts; (*qualification*) maîtrise *f* en beaux-arts

mfd *Com* (*written abbr* **manufactured**) fabriqué

mfr (*written abbr* **manufacturer**) fabricant *m*

mg (*written abbr* **milligram**) mg

Mgr (**a**) *Rel* (*written abbr* **Monseigneur, Monsignor**) Mgr (**b**) (*written abbr* **manager**) directeur(trice) *m,f*

MHC [ˌemeɪtʃˈsiː] *n Med* (*abbr* **major histocompatibility complex**) CMH *m*

MHR [ˌemeɪtʃ'ɑː(r)] *n Am Pol* (*abbr* **Member of the House of Representatives**) membre *m* de la Chambre des représentants

MHz *Elec* (*written abbr* **megahertz**) MHz

MI[1] (**a**) (*written abbr* **Michigan**) Michigan *m* (**b**) *Comput* (*written abbr* **machine intelligence**) IA *f*

MI[2] [ˌem'aɪ] *n Med* (*abbr* **myocardial infarction**) infarctus *m* du myocarde

MI5 [ˌemaɪ'faɪv] *n Br* (*abbr* **Military Intelligence 5**) = service de contre-espionnage britannique

MI6 [ˌemaɪ'sɪks] *n Br* (*abbr* **Military Intelligence 6**) = service de renseignements britannique

MIA [ˌemaɪ'eɪ] *Mil* (*abbr* **missing in action**) **1** *n* soldat *m* porté disparu
2 *adj* porté disparu au combat

Mich. (*written abbr* **Michigan**) Michigan *m*

MICR [ˌemaɪˌsiː'ɑː(r)] *n Comput* (*abbr* **magnetic ink character recognition**) RMC *f*

Middx (*written abbr* **Middlesex**) Middlesex *m*

MIDI ['mɪdɪ] *n Comput* (*abbr* **musical instrument digital interface**) MIDI *m*

MIG welding [mɪg-] *n Tech* (*abbr* **metallic-electrode inert gas**) soudage *m* MIG

mike [maɪk] *n Fam* (*abbr* **microphone**) micro *m*

MIME [maɪm] *n Comput* (*abbr* **Multipurpose Internet Mail Extensions**) (protocole *m*) MIME *m*

Min. (*written abbr* **ministry**) ministère *m*

min. (**a**) (*written abbr* **minute**) min (**b**) (*written abbr* **minimum**) min

Minn (*written abbr* **Minnesota**) Minnesota *m*

mips [mɪps] *n Comput* (*abbr* **million instructions per second**) MIPS *m*

MIRAS ['maɪræs] *n Br Formerly Fin* (*abbr* **Mortgage Interest Relief at Source**) = système par lequel les intérêts dus à une société de crédit immobilier sont déductibles des impôts

MIRV [mɜːv] *n Mil* (*abbr* **multiple independently targeted re-entry vehicle**) MIRV *m*

MIS [ˌemaɪ'es] *n* (**a**) *Comput* (*abbr* **management information system**) système *m* intégré de gestion (**b**) *Mktg* (*abbr* **marketing information system**) système *m* d'information marketing

misc (*written abbr* **miscellaneous**) divers

Miss (*written abbr* **Mississippi**) Mississippi *m*

MIT [ˌemaɪ'tiː] *n Am* (*abbr* **Massachusetts Institute of Technology**) l'Institut *m* de Technologie du Massachusetts

mk, MK (*written abbr* **mark**) version *f*

mkt (*written abbr* **market**) marché *m*

ml (*written abbr* **millilitre**) ml

MLA [ˌeme'leɪ] *n* (*abbr* **Member of the Legislative Assembly**) membre *m* de l'Assemblée législative *(en Irlande du Nord, en Australie, en Inde et au Canada)*

MLC [ˌemel'siː] *n* (*abbr* **Member of the Legislative Council**) membre *m* du Conseil législatif *(en Australie, en Inde)*

MLitt [ˌem'lɪt] *n Univ* (*abbr* **Master of Literature, Master of Letters**) *(person)* = titulaire d'une maîtrise de lettres; *(qualification)* maîtrise *f* de lettres

MLM [ˌeme'lem] *n Mktg* (*abbr* **multi-level marketing**) VRC *f*

MLR [ˌemel'ɑː(r)] *n Br Formerly Fin* (*abbr* **minimum lending rate**) taux *m* de base

mm (*written abbr* **millimetre**) mm

MMC [ˌemem'siː] *n Com* (*abbr* **Monopolies and Mergers Commission**) = commission britannique veillant au respect de la législation antitrust

MMF [ˌemem'ef] *n St Exch* (*abbr* **money market fund**) ≃ SICAV *f* monétaire

MMR [ˌemem'ɑː(r)] *n Med* (*abbr* **measles, mumps and rubella**) vaccin *m* contre la rougeole, les oreillons et la rubéole

MMX [ˌemem'eks] *n Comput* (*abbr* **multimedia extensions**) MMX *m*

MN[1] [ˌem'en] *n Br* (*abbr* **Merchant Navy**) marine *f* marchande

MN[2] (*written abbr* **Minnesota**) Minnesota *m*

MNA [ˌemen'eɪ] *n Can* (*abbr* **Member of the National Assembly**) *(in Quebec)* MAN *m*

MO[1] [ˌem'əʊ] *n* (**a**) (*abbr* **medical officer**) *Ind* médecin *m* du travail; *Mil* médecin *m* militaire (**b**) (*abbr* **modus operandi**) *(of criminal)* façon *f* d'agir (**c**) (*abbr* **money order**) mandat-poste *m*

MO[2] (*written abbr* **Missouri**) Missouri *m*

MOD [ˌeməʊ'diː] *n Br* (*abbr* **Ministry of Defence**) ministère *m* de la Défense

mod cons [-kɒnz] *npl Br Fam* (*abbr* **modern conveniences**) **all mod cons** tout confort ❑, tt. conf

Mods [mɒdz] *npl Br Univ* (*abbr* **(Honour) Moderations**) *(at Oxford University)* = premier examen pour le grade de "Bachelor of Arts"

MOH [ˌeməʊ'eɪtʃ] *n Br* (*abbr* **Medical Officer of Health**) directeur(trice) *m,f* de la santé publique

MOMA ['məʊmə] *n Am* (*abbr* **Museum of Modern Art**) = musée d'art moderne à New York

MOMI ['məʊmɪ] *n* (*abbr* **Museum of the Moving Image**) = musée de l'image à Londres

MON [ˌeməʊ'en] *n Aut* (*abbr* **motor octane numbers**) IOM *m*

Mon. (*written abbr* **Monday**) Lu

mono ['mɒnəʊ] (*pl* **monos**) **1** *n* (**a**) (*abbr* **monophony**) monophonie *f*; **in mono** en mono (**b**) *Am Fam* (*abbr* **mononucleosis**) mononucléose *f* (infectieuse) ❑
2 *adj* (*abbr* **monophonic**) mono *(inv)*, monophonique; **mono record player** électrophone *m* mono

Mont (*written abbr* **Montana**) Montana *m*

MOR [ˌeməʊ'ɑː(r)] *adj* (*abbr* **middle-of-the-road**) *(music)* grand public *(inv)*; *Pej* passe-partout *(inv)*

MORI ['mɒrɪ] *n Br* (*abbr* **Market & Opinion Research Institute**) = institut britannique de sondage

MOS [ˌeməʊ'es] *n Electron* (*abbr* **metal oxide semiconductor**) MOS *m*

MOT [ˌeməʊ'tiː] (*pt & pp* **MOT'd** [ˌeməʊ'tiːd], *cont* **MOT'ing** [ˌeməʊ'tiːɪŋ]) *Br* (*abbr* **Ministry of Transport**) **1** *n* (**a**) *Formerly (ministry)* ministère *m* des Transports
(**b**) *(certificate)* = contrôle technique annuel obligatoire pour les véhicules de plus de trois ans; **that old car of yours will never pass its MOT** ta vieille voiture n'obtiendra jamais son certificat de contrôle technique
2 *vt* **to have one's car MOT'd** soumettre sa voiture au contrôle technique
►► ***MOT certificate*** = contrôle technique annuel obligatoire pour les véhicules de plus de trois ans

MP [ˌem'piː] *n* (**a**) (*abbr* **Military Police**) PM *f* (**b**) *Br & Can* (*abbr* **Member of Parliament**) ≃ député *m*; **the MP for Finchley** le député de Finchley (**c**) *Can* (*abbr* **Mounted Policeman**) policier *m*

MP3 [ˌempiː'θriː] *n Comput* (*abbr* **MPEG1 Audio Layer**) (format *m*) MPEG *m*

MPC [ˌempiː'siː] *n Fin* (*abbr* **monetary policy committee**) = comité formé de quatre membres de la Banque d'Angleterre et de quatre économistes nommés par le gouvernement, dont l'un des rôles est de fixer les taux d'intérêt

MPEG ['emˌpeg] *n Comput* (*abbr* **Moving Pictures Expert Group)** (format *m*) MPEG *m*

mpg [ˌempiː'dʒiː] *n* (*abbr* **miles per gallon**) consommation *f* d'essence; **my old car did 20 mpg** mon ancienne voiture faisait *ou* consommait 3,5 litres au cent

mph [ˌempiː'eɪtʃ] *n* (*abbr* **miles per hour**) miles *mpl* à l'heure; **100 mph** ≃ 160 km/h

MPhil [ˌem'fɪl] *n Univ* (*abbr* **Master of Philosophy**) *(person)* = titulaire d'une maîtrise de lettres; *(qualification)* maîtrise *f* de lettres

mps [ˌempiː'es] *n* (*abbr* **master production schedule)** plan *m* de production principal

MPV [ˌempiː'viː] *n Aut* (*abbr* **multi-purpose vehicle**) monospace *m*

Mr ['mɪstə(r)] *n* (*abbr* **mister**) M., Monsieur; **Mr Brown** M. Brown; **Mr President** Monsieur le Président; *Fam* **no more Mr Nice Guy!** j'en ai assez d'être la bonne pâte!; *Fam Fig* **he's a regular Mr Fixit** on peut toujours compter sur lui pour trouver une solution
►► *Fam* ***Mr Big*** le chef, le patron ❑; *Fam* ***Mr Right*** l'homme idéal ❑, le prince charmant; **she's waiting for Mr Right** elle attend le prince charmant *ou* l'homme de ses rêves

MRC [ˌemɑː'siː] *n Br* (*abbr* **Medical Research Council**) = institut de recherche médicale situé à Londres

MRCP [ˌemɑːˌsiː'piː] *n Br* (*abbr* **Member of the Royal College of Physicians**) = membre du "Royal College of Physicians"

MRCS [ˌemɑːˌsiː'es] *n Br* (*abbr* **Member of the Royal College of Surgeons**) = membre du "Royal College of Surgeons"

MRCVS [ˌemɑːsiːˌviː'es] *n Br* (*abbr* **Member of the Royal College of Veterinary Surgeons**) = membre du "Royal College of Veterinary Surgeons"

MRI [ˌemɑː'raɪ] *n* (*abbr* **magnetic resonance imaging**) IRM *f*

MRM [ˌemɑː'rem] *n* (*abbr* **mechanically-recovered meat**) viande *f* séparée mécaniquement

mrp [ˌemɑː'piː] *n Mktg* (*abbr* **manufacturer's recommended price**) prix *m* conseillé par le fabricant

MRS [ˌemɑː'res] *n Mktg* (*abbr* **Market Research Society**) = société d'étude de marché britannique

Mrs ['mɪsɪz] *n* (*abbr* **mistress**) Mme, Madame; **Mrs Brown** Mme Brown
►► ***Mrs Beeton*** = célèbre auteur anglais de livres de cuisine au dix-neuvième siècle; *Br Fam* ***Mrs Mop*** *(cleaner)* femme *f* de ménage ❑; **I'm not your Mrs Mop, you know!** hé, je ne suis pas ta bonne!

MS[1] [ˌem'es] *n* (**a**) *Med* (*abbr* **multiple sclerosis**) SEP *f* (**b**) *Am Univ* (*abbr* **Master of Science**) *(person)* = titulaire d'une maîtrise de sciences; *(qualification)* maîtrise *f* de sciences

MS[2] (**a**) (*written abbr* **Mississippi**) Mississippi *m* (**b**) (*written abbr* **manuscript**) ms

Ms [mɪz, məz] *n* = titre que les femmes peuvent utiliser au lieu de "Mrs" ou "Miss" pour éviter la distinction entre les femmes mariées et les célibataires

ms. (*pl* **mss**) (*written abbr* **manuscript**) ms

MSA [ˌemes'eɪ] *n Univ* (*abbr* **Master of Science in Agriculture**) *(person)* = titulaire d'une maîtrise en sciences agricoles; *(qualification)* maîtrise *f* en sciences agricoles

MSB [ˌemes'biː] *n Comput* (*abbr* **most significant bit/byte**) = bit de poids fort

MSC [ˌemes'siː] *n Formerly* (*abbr* **Manpower Services Commission**) = agence britannique pour l'emploi, aujourd'hui remplacée par la "Training Agency", ≃ ANPE *f*

MSc [ˌemes'siː] *n Br Univ* (*abbr* **Master of Science**) *(person)* = titulaire d'une maîtrise de sciences; *(qualification)* maîtrise *f* de sciences

MS-DOS [ˌemes'dɒs] *n Comput* (*abbr* **Microsoft Disk Operating System**) MS-DOS *m*

MSF [ˌemes'ef] *n Br* (*abbr* **Manufacturing, Science, Finance**) = confédération syndicale britannique

MSG [ˌemes'dʒiː] *n* (*abbr* **monosodium glutamate**) glutamate *m* de sodium

Msgr *Rel* (*written abbr* **Monsignor**) Mgr

MSP [ˌemes'piː] *n* (*abbr* **Member of the Scottish Parliament**) député *m* du parlement écossais

mss (*written abbr* **manuscripts**) manuscrits *mpl*

MST [ˌemes'tiː] *n* (*abbr* **Mountain Standard Time**) heure *f* d'hiver des montagnes Rocheuses

MSW [ˌemes'dʌbəljuː] *n Univ* (*abbr* **Master**

of Social Work) *(person)* = titulaire d'une maîtrise en travail social; *(qualification)* maîtrise *f* en travail social

MT[1] [ˌem'tiː] *n Comput* (*abbr* **machine translation**) TA *f*

MT[2] (*written abbr* **Montana**) Montana *m*

Mt (*written abbr* **mount**) Mt

MTBF [ˌemtiːˌbiː'ef] *n Comput* (*abbr* **mean time between failures**) moyenne *f* de temps entre deux pannes

MTFA [ˌemtiːˌef'eɪ] *n Fin & EU* (*abbr* **medium-term financial assistance**) aide *f* financière à moyen terme

MTN [ˌemtiː'en] *n Fin* (*abbr* **medium-term note**) bon *m* à moyen terme (négociable)

MUD [ˌemjuː'diː] *n Comput* (*abbr* **multi-user dungeon**) environnement *m* MUD

MusB ['mʌzbiː], **MusBac** ['mʌzbæk] *n Univ* (*abbr* **Bachelor of Music**) *(person)* = titulaire d'une licence de musique; *(qualification)* licence *f* de musique

MusD ['mʌzdiː], **MusDoc** ['mʌzdɒk] *n Univ* (*abbr* **Doctor of Music**) *(person)* = titulaire d'un doctorat en musique; *(qualification)* doctorat *m* en musique

muso ['mjuːzəʊ] *n Br Fam* (*abbr* **musician**) musico *m*

MV [ˌem'viː] *n* (**a**) *Elec* (*abbr* **megavolt(s)**) MV (**b**) *Naut* (*abbr* **motor vessel**) bateau *m* à moteur

MVP [ˌemviː'piː] *n Am Sport* (*abbr* **most valuable player**) = titre décerné au meilleur joueur d'une équipe

MW [ˌem'dʌbəljuː] *n* (**a**) *Elec* (*abbr* **megawatt(s)**) MW (**b**) *Rad* (*abbr* **Medium Wave**) PO *fpl*

MX [ˌem'eks] *n* (*abbr* **missile-experimental**) = missile américain MX

MYOB [ˌemwaɪˌəʊ'biː] *exclam* (*abbr* **mind your own business**) occupez-vous de vos affaires!

N (*written abbr* **North**) N

'n' [ən] *conj Fam* (*abbr* **and**) et ❑; **fish 'n' chips** poisson-frites ❑ *m*

NA [ˌen'eɪ] *n Am* (*abbr* **Narcotics Anonymous**) = association américaine d'aide aux toxicomanes

n/a, N/A (*written abbr* **not applicable**) s.o.

NAACP [ˌeneɪˌeɪsiː'piː] *n Am* (*abbr* **National Association for the Advancement of Colored People**) = ligue américaine pour la défense des droits de la population noire

Naafi ['næfɪ] *n Br Mil* (*abbr* **Navy, Army, and Air Force Institutes**) *(organization)* = organisme approvisionnant les forces armées britanniques en biens de consommation; *(canteen)* cantine *f* militaire; *(shop)* magasin *m* réservé aux militaires

NACU [ˌeneɪsiː'juː] *n Am* (*abbr* **National Association of Colleges and Universities**) = association des établissements d'enseignement supérieur américains

NAFTA ['næftə] *n* (*abbr* **North American Free Trade Agreement**) ALENA *m*

NALGO ['nælgəʊ] *n Br Formerly* (*abbr* **National and Local Government Officers' Association**) = ancien syndicat de la fonction publique en Grande-Bretagne

NAM [ˌeneɪ'em] *n Am* (*abbr* **National Association of Manufacturers**) = organisation patronale américaine

NAPA [ˌeneɪˌpiː'eɪ] *n Am* (*abbr* **National Association of Performing Artists**) = syndicat américain des gens du spectacle

NAS [ˌeneɪ'es] *n Am* (*abbr* **National Academy of Sciences**) = académie américaine des sciences

NASA ['næsə] *n Am* (*abbr* **National Aeronautics and Space Administration**) NASA *f*

Nasdaq ['næzdæk] *n St Exch* (*abbr* **National Association of Securities Dealers Automated Quotation**) le Nasdaq *(Bourse américaine des valeurs technologiques)*

NAS/UWT [ˌeneɪ'esˌjuːdʌbəljuː'tiː] *n Br* (*abbr* **National Association of Schoolmasters/Union of Women Teachers**) = syndicat d'enseignants et de chefs d'établissement en Grande-Bretagne

NATO ['neɪtəʊ] *n* (*abbr* **North Atlantic Treaty Organization**) l'OTAN *f*

NAV [ˌeneɪ'viː] *n Fin* (*abbr* **net asset value**) valeur *f* d'actif net

NB (**a**) (*written abbr* **nota bene**) NB (**b**) (*written abbr* **New Brunswick**) Nouveau-Brunswick *m*

NBA [ˌenbiː'eɪ] *n* (**a**) *Am* (*abbr* **National Basketball Association**) = fédération américaine de basket-ball (**b**) *Am* (*abbr* **National Boxing Association**) = fédération américaine de boxe (**c**) *Formerly Com* (*abbr* **net book agreement**) = accord entre maisons d'édition et libraires stipulant que ces derniers n'ont le droit de vendre aucun ouvrage à un prix inférieur à celui fixé par l'éditeur

NBC [ˌenbiː'siː] **1** *n TV* (*abbr* **National Broadcasting Company**) = chaîne de télévision américaine

2 *adj* (*abbr* **nuclear, biological and chemical**) NBC

►► ***NBC suit*** survêtement *m* de protection NBC; ***NBC weapons*** armes *fpl* NBC

nbg [ˌenbiː'dʒiː] *adj Br Fam* (*abbr* **no bloody good**) nul

NBS [ˌenbiː'es] *n Am* (*abbr* **National Bureau of Standards**) = service américain des poids et mesures

NBV [ˌenbiː'viː] *n Fin* (*abbr* **net book value**) valeur *f* comptable nette

NC (**a**) (*written abbr* **no charge**) gratuit (**b**) (*written abbr* **North Carolina**) Caroline *f* du Nord

NCAA [ˌensiːˌeɪ'eɪ] *n Am* (*abbr* **National Collegiate Athletic Association**) = association interuniversitaire traitant des questions sportives, aux États-Unis

NCB [ˌensiː'biː] *n Br Formerly* (*abbr* **National Coal Board**) = ancien nom des charbonnages britanniques

NCC [ˌensiː'siː] *n* (**a**) *Br Ecol* (*abbr* **Nature Conservancy Council**) = organisme britannique de protection de la nature (**b**) (*abbr* **National Curriculum Council**) = conseil responsable de l'établissement des programmes scolaires en Angleterre et au pays de Galles

NCCL [ˌensiːˌsiː'el] *n* (*abbr* **National Council for Civil Liberties**) = en Grande-Bretagne, ligue de défense des droits du citoyen luttant contre toute forme de discrimination

NCO [ˌensiː'əʊ] *n Mil* (*abbr* **non-commissioned officer**) sous-officier *m*

NCT [ˌensiː'tiː] *n* (*abbr* **National Childbirth Trust**) = organisation de conseil aux femmes enceintes

NCU [ˌensiː'juː] *n* (*abbr* **National Communications Union**) = syndicat des salariés qui travaillent dans les télécommunications

NCVQ [ˌensiːˌviː'kjuː] *n* (*abbr* **National Council for Vocational Qualifications**) = organisme britannique responsable de la formation professionnelle

ND (*written abbr* **North Dakota**) Dakota *m* du Nord

NDP [ˌendiː'piː] *n Fin* (*abbr* **net domestic product**) produit *m* intérieur net

NDPB [ˌendiːˌpiː'biː] *n Br Pol* (*abbr* **non-departmental public body**) = organisme semi-public

NE (**a**) (*written abbr* **Nebraska**) Nebraska *m* (**b**) (*written abbr* **New England**) Nouvelle-Angleterre *f* (**c**) (*written abbr* **north-east**) NE

NEC [ˌeniː'siː] *n Br* (*abbr* **National Exhibition Centre**) = parc d'expositions près de Birmingham en Angleterre

NEDC [ˌeniːˌdiː'siː] *n Br Formerly* (*abbr* **National Economic Development Council**) = agence nationale britannique de développement économique supprimée en 1992

neg (*written abbr* **negotiable**) négociable, à débattre

NESTA ['nestə] *n* (*abbr* **National Endowment for Science, Technology and the Arts**) = organisme indépendant d'aide financière aux artistes, inventeurs et scientifiques, à partir de fonds provenant de la Loterie nationale

NF[1] [ˌen'ef] *n* (*abbr* **National Front**) = parti britannique d'extrême droite, ≃ Front *m* national

NF[2] (*written abbr* **Newfoundland**) Terre-Neuve *f*

NFL [ˌenef'el] *n* (*abbr* **National Football League**) = fédération nationale de football américain

NFP [ˌenef'piː] *n* (*abbr* **natural family planning**) = contraception par des moyens naturels

NFT [ˌenef'tiː] *n* (*abbr* **National Film Theatre**) = cinéma d'art et d'essai londonien qui fait partie du "British Film Institute"

NFU [ˌenef'juː] *n* (*abbr* **National Farmers' Union**) = syndicat britannique d'exploitants agricoles

NG [ˌen'dʒiː] *n* (*abbr* **National Guard**) Garde *f* nationale *(milice nationale américaine composée de volontaires)*

NGA [ˌendʒiː'eɪ] *n* (*abbr* **National Graphical Association**) = syndicat britannique d'imprimeurs

NGO [ˌendʒiː'əʊ] *n* (*abbr* **non-governmental organization**) ONG *f*

NH (*written abbr* **New Hampshire**) New Hampshire *m*

NHI [ˌeneɪtʃ'aɪ] *n Br* (*abbr* **National Health Insurance**) = système britannique de sécurité sociale

NHL [ˌeneɪtʃ'el] *n* (*abbr* **National Hockey League**) = fédération nationale américaine de hockey sur glace

NHS [ˌeneɪtʃ'es] *n Br* (*abbr* **National Health Service**) ≃ Sécurité *f* sociale

►► ***NHS number*** numéro *m* de Sécurité sociale

NI[1] [ˌen'aɪ] *n Br* (*abbr* **national insurance**) = système britannique de sécurité sociale

NI[2] (*written abbr* **Northern Ireland**) Irlande *f* du Nord

NIC [ˌenaɪ'siː] *n* (**a**) (*abbr* **newly-industrialized country**) pays *m* en voie d'industrialisation, NPI *m* (**b**) (*abbr* **national insurance contributions**) cotisations *fpl* à la Sécurité sociale

NICAM ['naɪkæm] *n* (*abbr* **near-instantaneous companded audio multiplex**) Nicam *m*

NIF [ˌenaɪ'ef] *n Fin* (*abbr* **note issue facility**) autorisation *f* d'émettre les billets de banque

NIH [ˌenaɪ'eɪtʃ] *n Am* (*abbr* **National Institutes of Health**) = ensemble de centres de recherche médicale aux États-Unis

Nimby ['nɪmbɪ] *n Fam* (*abbr* **not in my backyard**) = personne qui, tout en se montrant d'accord sur le principe, est peu encline à voir un projet (de construction le plus souvent) se réaliser à proximité de chez elle

NJ (*written abbr* **New Jersey**) New Jersey *m*

NLF [ˌenel'ef] *n* (*abbr* **National Liberation Front**) FLN *m*

NLM [ˌenel'em] *n Comput* (*abbr* **netware loadable module**) module *m* logiciel téléchargeable

NLP [ˌenel'piː] *n* (*abbr* **natural language processing**) TALAN *m*

NLQ [ˌenel'kjuː] *n Comput* (*abbr* **near letter quality**) = qualité quasi-courrier

NLRB [ˌenelˌɑː'biː] *n Am* (*abbr* **National Labor Relations Board**) = organisme américain de conciliation et d'arbitrage des conflits du travail

NM (*written abbr* **New Mexico**) Nouveau-Mexique *m*

NMD [ˌenem'diː] *n* (*abbr* **National Missile Defence**) projet *m* NMD *(programme de défense antimissiles américain)*

NME [ˌenem'iː] *n Press* (*abbr* **New Musical Express**) = hebdomadaire anglais de musique rock

NMR [ˌene'mɑː(r)] *n Med* (*abbr* **nuclear magnetic resonance**) RMN *f*

NNE (*written abbr* **north-north-east**) N-NE

NNP [ˌenen'piː] *n* (*abbr* **net national product**) produit *m* national net

NNW (*written abbr* **north-north-west**) N-NW

No., no. (*written abbr* **number**) No, no

NOC [ˌenəʊ'siː] *n* (*abbr* **National Olympic Committee**) Comité *m* olympique national

non obst. (*written abbr* **non obstante**) nonobstant

Norf (*written abbr* **Norfolk**) Norfolk *m*

Northants (*written abbr* **Northamptonshire**) Northamptonshire *m*

Northd (*written abbr* **Northumberland**) Northumberland *m*

Northumb (*written abbr* **Northumberland**) Northumberland *m*

Nos., nos. (*written abbr* **numbers**) no

Notts (*written abbr* **Nottinghamshire**) Nottinghamshire *m*

Nov. (*written abbr* **November**) nov

NOW [naʊ] *n Am* (*abbr* **National Organization for Women**) = organisation féministe américaine

NP[1] (*written abbr* **notary public**) notaire *m*

NP[2] [ˌen'piː] *n* (*abbr* **New Providence**) île *f* de la Nouvelle-Providence

NPD [ˌenpiː'diː] *n Mktg* (*abbr* **new product development**) développement *m* de nouveaux produits

NPV [ˌenpiː'viː] *n Acct* (*abbr* **net present value**) VAN *f*, valeur *f* actuelle nette
▸▸ ***NPV rate*** taux *m* d'actualisation

nr (*written abbr* **near**) près de

NRA [ˌenɑː'reɪ] *n* (**a**) *Am* (*abbr* **National Rifle Association**) = association américaine défendant le droit au port d'armes (**b**) *Br* (*abbr* **National Rivers Authority**) = organisme britannique chargé de veiller à la propreté des cours d'eau en Angleterre et au pays de Galles

NRC [ˌenɑː'siː] *n* (*abbr* **Nuclear Regulatory Commission**) = agence américaine chargée de veiller au respect des normes de sécurité dans le convoyage et l'utilisation de matériaux radioactifs

NREM [ˌenɑːˌriː'em] *n* (*abbr* **non-rapid eye movement**) **NREM sleep** sommeil *m* lent

NRS [ˌenɑː'res] *n* (*abbr* **national readership survey**) étude *f* nationale sur le lectorat

NRT [ˌenɑː'tiː] *n* (*abbr* **nicotine replacement therapy**) thérapie *f* de désaccoutumance à la nicotine *(patch, gomme nicotinique etc)*

NRV [ˌenɑː'viː] *n Fin* (*abbr* **net realizable value**) valeur *f* réalisable nette

NS (**a**) (*written abbr* **Nova Scotia**) Nouvelle-Écosse *f* (**b**) *Ir* (*written abbr* **national school**) école *f* primaire

NSAID [ˌenesˌeɪaɪ'diː] *n Med* (*abbr* **non-steroidal anti-inflammatory drug**) anti-inflammatoire *m* non stéroïde

NSC [ˌenes'siː] *n Am* (*abbr* **National Security Council**) = organisme chargé de superviser la politique militaire de défense du gouvernement des États-Unis

NSF[1] [ˌenes'ef] *n* (*abbr* **National Science Foundation**) = organisme indépendant américain d'aide à la recherche scientifique

NSF[2] (*written abbr* **not sufficient funds**) fonds *mpl* insuffisants

NSPCC [ˌenesˌpiːsiː'siː] *n Br* (*abbr* **National Society for the Prevention of Cruelty to Children**) = association britannique de protection de l'enfance

NSU [ˌenes'juː] *n Med* (*abbr* **nonspecific urethritis**) urétrite *f* non spécifique

NSW (*written abbr* **New South Wales**) Nouvelle-Galles *f* du Sud

NT [ˌen'tiː] *n* (**a**) (*abbr* **New Testament**) NT *m* (**b**) *Ir* (*abbr* **national teacher**) instituteur (trice) *m,f* (**c**) (*abbr* **National Trust**) = organisme non gouvernemental britannique assurant la conservation de certains paysages et monuments historiques (**d**) (*abbr* **(Royal) National Theatre**) = grand théâtre londonien subventionné par l'État

NTS [ˌentiː'es] *n* (*abbr* **National Trust for Scotland**) = organisme non gouvernemental assurant la conservation du patrimoine naturel et historique écossais

NTSB [ˌentiːˌes'biː] *n* (*abbr* **National Transportation Safety Board**) = agence du gouvernement américain chargée des questions de sécurité dans le domaine des transports

NUAAW [ˌenjuːˌeɪeɪ'dʌbəljuː] *n Br* (*abbr* **National Union of Agricultural and Allied Workers**) = syndicat britannique des employés du secteur agricole

NUCPS [ˌenjuːˌsiːpiː'es] *n Br* (*abbr* **National Union of Civil and Public Servants**) = syndicat britannique des employés de la fonction publique

NUJ [ˌenjuː'dʒeɪ] *n Br* (*abbr* **National Union of Journalists**) = syndicat britannique des journalistes

NUM [ˌenjuː'em] *n* (*abbr* **National Union of Mineworkers**) = syndicat britannique des mineurs

num lock ['nʌm-] *n Comput* (*abbr* **number lock**) verr num; **the num lock is on** le pavé numérique est verrouillé
▸▸ ***num lock key*** touche *f* de verrouillage du pavé numérique

NUPE ['njuːpɪ] *n Formerly* (*abbr* **National Union of Public Employees**) = ancien syndicat britannique des employés de la fonction publique

NUR [ˌenjuː'ɑː(r)] *n Formerly* (*abbr* **National Union of Railwaymen**) = ancien syndicat britannique des employés des chemins de fer

NURMTW [ˌenjuːɑːˌremtiː'dʌbəljuː] *n* (*abbr* **National Union of Rail, Maritime and Transport Workers**) = syndicat britannique des cheminots, gens de mer et routiers

NUS [ˌenjuː'es] *n Br* (*abbr* **National Union of Students**) ≃ UNEF *f*

NUT [ˌenjuː'tiː] *n* (*abbr* **National Union of Teachers**) = syndicat britannique d'enseignants

NV (*written abbr* **Nevada**) Nevada *m*

NVQ [ˌenviː'kjuː] *n* (*abbr* **National Vocational Qualification**) = diplôme britannique professionnel national

NW (*written abbr* **north-west**) N-O

NWT (*written abbr* **Northwest Territories**) Territoires *mpl* du Nord-Ouest

NY (*written abbr* **New York**) *(city)* New York *m; (state)* État *m* de New York

NYC (*written abbr* **New York City**) New York *m*

NYMEX [ˌenwaɪˌemiː'eks] *n St Exch* (*abbr* **New York Mercantile Exchange**) = marché à terme des produits pétroliers de New York

nympho ['nɪmfəʊ] *n Fam* (*abbr* **nymphomaniac**) nympho *f*

NYSE [ˌenwaɪˌes'iː] *n St Exch* (*abbr* **New York Stock Exchange**) = la bourse de New York

NZ (*written abbr* **New Zealand**) Nouvelle-Zélande *f*

O (*written abbr* **Ohio**) Ohio *m*

O & M [ˌəʊənd'em] *n* (*abbr* **organization and methods**) O et M *f*

OAP [ˌəʊeɪ'piː] *n Br* (*abbr* **old age pensioner**) retraité(e) *m,f*; **students and OAPs half price** *(sign)* ≃ étudiants et carte vermeille demi-tarif

OAS [ˌəʊeɪ'es] *n* (**a**) (*abbr* **Organization of American States**) OÉA *f* (**b**) (*abbr* **Organisation armée secrète**) OAS *f*

OAU [ˌəʊeɪ'juː] *n* (*abbr* **Organization of African Unity**) OUA *f*

OB [ˌəʊ'biː] *n TV* (*abbr* **outside broadcast**) émission *f* réalisée en dehors des studios

OBE [ˌəʊbiː'iː] *n* (*abbr* **Officer of the Order of the British Empire**) = distinction honorifique britannique

o.b.o. (*written abbr* **or best offer**) à déb.

OC [ˌəʊ'siː] *n Mil* (*abbr* **Officer Commanding**) chef *m* de corps

OCAS [ˌəʊsiːˌeɪ'es] *n* (*abbr* **Organization of Central American States**) ODEAC *f*

OCR [ˌəʊsiː'ɑː(r)] *n Comput* (**a**) (*abbr* **optical character reader**) lecteur *m* (à reconnaissance) optique de caractères (**b**) (*abbr* **optical character recognition**) OCR *f*
▸▸ ***OCR software*** logiciel *m* d'OCR

Oct. (*written abbr* **October**) oct.

OD [ˌəʊ'diː] (*pt & pp* **OD'd**, *cont* **OD'ing**) **1** *n* (**a**) *Fam* (*abbr* **overdose**) overdose ❑ *f* (**b**) (*abbr* **overdraft**) découvert *m*
2 *adj* (*abbr* **overdrawn**) à découvert
3 *vi Fam* faire une overdose (**on** de); **I've OD'd on pizzas/soap operas lately** j'ai tellement mangé de pizzas/regardé de feuilletons télé ces derniers temps que j'en suis dégoûté

ODA [ˌəʊdiː'eɪ] *n Br Formerly* (*abbr* **Overseas Development Administration**) = ancien nom du secrétariat d'État à la Coopération

OECD [ˌəʊiːˌsiː'diː] *n* (*abbr* **Organization for Economic Cooperation and Development**) OCDE *f*

OEEC [ˌəʊiːˌiː'siː] *n Formerly* (*abbr* **Organization for European Economic Cooperation**) OECE *f*

OEM [ˌəʊiː'em] *n* (*abbr* **original equipment manufacturer**) constructeur *m* de systèmes originaux, OEM *m*

Offer ['ɒfə(r)] *n Br Formerly* (*abbr* **Office of Electricity Regulation**) = organisme britannique chargé de contrôler les activités des compagnies régionales de distribution d'électricité

offie ['ɒfɪ] *n Br Fam* (*abbr* **off-licence**) = magasin autorisé à vendre des boissons alcoolisées à emporter

Ofgas ['ɒfˌgæs] *n Formerly* (*abbr* **Office of Gas Supply**) = organisme britannique chargé de contrôler les activités des compagnies régionales de distribution de gaz

Ofgem ['ɒfˌdʒem] *n* (*abbr* **Office of the Gas and Electricity Markets**) = nouvel organisme britannique qui a remplacé les anciens "Ofgas" et "Offer"

Oflot ['ɒfˌlɒt] *n* (*abbr* **Office of the National Lottery**) = organisme britannique chargé de contrôler la loterie nationale

Ofsted ['ɒfˌsted] *n* (*abbr* **Office for Standards in Education**) = organisme britannique chargé de contrôler le système d'éducation nationale

OFT [ˌəʊef'tiː] *n* (*abbr* **Office of Fair Trading**) = organisme britannique de défense des consommateurs et de régulation des pratiques commerciales

Oftel ['ɒfˌtel] *n Br* (*abbr* **Office of Telecommunications**) = organisme britannique chargé de contrôler les activités des sociétés de télécommunications

Ofwat ['ɒfˌwɒt] *n* (*abbr* **Office of Water Supply**) = organisme britannique chargé de contrôler les activités des compagnies régionales de distribution des eaux

OH (*written abbr* **Ohio**) Ohio *m*

ohc [ˌəʊeɪtʃ'siː] *n* (*abbr* **overhead camshaft**)
▸▸ ***ohc engine*** moteur *m* ACT

OHMS (*written abbr* **On His/Her Majesty's Service**) = tampon apposé sur le courrier administratif britannique

OHP [ˌəʊeɪtʃ'piː] *n* (*abbr* **overhead projector**) rétroprojecteur *m*

OI [ˌəʊ'aɪ] *n* (*abbr* **opportunistic infection**) infection *f* opportuniste

OID [ˌəʊaɪ'diː] *n Fin* (*abbr* **original issue discount bond**) obligation *f* à prime d'émission

oiro (*written abbr* **offers in the region of**) **oiro £100** 100 livres à débattre

OJ ['əʊˌdʒeɪ] *n Fam* (*abbr* **orange juice**) jus *m* d'orange ❑

OJT [ˌəʊdʒeɪ'tiː] *n Am* (*abbr* **on-the-job training**) formation *f* en entreprise

OK (*written abbr* **Oklahoma**) Oklahoma *m*

Okla (*written abbr* **Oklahoma**) Oklahoma *m*

OLE [ˌəʊel'iː] *n Comput* (*abbr* **object linking and embedding**) OLE *m*

OM [ˌəʊ'em] *n* (*abbr* **Order of Merit**) ordre *m* du Mérite

OMB [ˌəʊem'biː] *n* (*abbr* **Office of Management and Budget**) = organisme fédéral américain chargé de préparer le budget

Omov, OMOV ['əʊmɒv] *n* (*abbr* **one member one vote**) = système de scrutin "un homme, une voix"

ON (*written abbr* **Ontario**) Ontario *m*

ONC [ˌəʊen'siː] *n* (*abbr* **Ordinary National Certificate**) = brevet de technicien en Grande-Bretagne

OND [ˌəʊen'diː] *n* (*abbr* **Ordinary National Diploma**) = brevet de technicien en Grande-Bretagne

o.n.o. [ˌəʊen'əʊ] *adv Br* (*abbr* **or near/nearest offer**) **£100 o.n.o.** 100 livres à débattre

Ont. (*written abbr* **Ontario**) Ontario *m*

OP [ˌəʊ'piː] *adj Typ* (*abbr* **out of print**) épuisé

op [ɒp] *n Fam Med & Mil* (*abbr* **operation**) opération ❑ *f*; **she has to have an op on her knee** il faut qu'elle se fasse opérer le genou ❑

op. (*written abbr* **opus**) op.

op. cit. [ˌɒp'sɪt] (*abbr* **opere citato**) op. cit.

OPEC ['əʊpek] *n* (*abbr* **Organization of Petroleum Exporting Countries**) OPEP *f*; **the OPEC countries** les pays *mpl* membres de l'OPEP

OPEIC [ˌəʊpiːˌiːaɪ'siː] *n Fin* (*abbr* **open-ended investment company**) SICAV *f*, société *f* d'investissement à capital variable

opp (*written abbr* **opposite**) en face

OR¹ [ˌəʊ'ɑː(r)] *n Am Fam* (*abbr* **operating room**) salle *f* d'op

OR² (*written abbr* **Oregon**) Oregon

Ore (*written abbr* **Oregon**) Oregon *m*

Oreg (*written abbr* **Oregon**) Oregon *m*

ORT [ˌəʊɑː'tiː] *n Med* (*abbr* **oral rehydration therapy**) = réhydratation par ingestion d'une solution d'eau, de glucose et de sel

OS¹ [ˌəʊ'es] *n* **(a)** (*abbr* **ordinary seaman**) matelot *m* breveté **(b)** *Comput* (*abbr* **operating system**) système *m* d'exploitation **(c)** (*abbr* **Ordnance Survey**) ≃ IGN *m* **(d)** *Austr* (*abbr* **overseas**) à l'étranger

OS² (*written abbr* **outsize**) grande taille *f*

O/S (*written abbr* **out of stock**) épuisé

OSCE [ˌəʊesˌsiː'iː] *n* (*abbr* **Organization for Security and Cooperation in Europe**) OSCE *f*

OSD [ˌəʊes'diː] *n* (*abbr* **optical scanning device**) lecteur *m* optique

OSHA [ˌəʊesˌeɪtʃ'eɪ] *n* (*abbr* **Occupational Safety and Health Administration**) = aux États-Unis, direction de la sécurité et de l'hygiène au travail

OT [ˌəʊ'tiː] *n* **(a)** (*abbr* **Old Testament**) AT *m* **(b)** (*abbr* **occupational therapy**) ergothérapie *f*

OTC [ˌəʊtiː'siː] **1** *n Br Sch* (*abbr* **Officer Training Corps**) corps *m* de formation des officiers

2 *adj St Exch* (*abbr* **over the counter**) hors cote

OTE [ˌəʊtiː'iː] *npl Mktg* (*abbr* **on-target earnings**) salaire *m* de base plus commissions

OTH [ˌəʊtiː'eɪtʃ] *n Mktg* (*abbr* **opportunity to hear**) ODE *f*

OTS [ˌəʊtiː'es] *n Mktg* (*abbr* **opportunity to see**) ODV *f*

OTT [ˌəʊtiː'tiː] *adj Br Fam* (*abbr* **over-the-top**) **that's a bit OTT!** c'est un peu exagéré!; **there was no need to be quite so OTT about it** ce n'était pas la peine d'en faire toute une histoire; **the house is nice, but the decor's a bit OTT** la maison est bien, mais la décoration est un peu lourdingue; **it's a bit OTT to call him a fascist** c'est un peu exagéré de le traiter de fasciste; **he went completely OTT when he heard what she'd said** il a pété les plombs quand il a appris ce qu'elle avait dit

OU [ˌəʊ'juː] *n Br Univ* (*abbr* **Open University**) = organisme d'enseignement universitaire par correspondance doublé d'émissions de télévision et de radio

Oxfam ['ɒksfæm] *n* (*abbr* **Oxford Committee for Famine Relief**) = association caritative britannique

▸▸ ***Oxfam shop*** = magasin où l'œuvre de bienfaisance Oxfam vend des articles d'occasion et d'artisanat au profit du tiers-monde

Oxon (*written abbr* **Oxfordshire**) Oxfordshire *m*

Oxon. (*written abbr* **Oxoniensis**) = de l'université d'Oxford

oz. (*written abbr* **ounce**) once *f*

P **(a)** (*written abbr* **president**) président *m* **(b)** (*written abbr* **prince**) Pce

p [piː] *n* **(a)** (*abbr* **penny**) penny *m* **(b)** (*abbr* **pence**) pence *mpl*

p. (*written abbr* **page**) p.

PA¹ [ˌpiː'eɪ] *n* **(a)** *Br* (*abbr* **personal assistant**) (*of executive*) assistant(e) *m,f*; (*with secretarial duties*) secrétaire *mf* de direction

(b) (*abbr* **public address system**) système *m* de sonorisation, sono *f*; **departure times will be announced over the PA** les horaires de départ seront annoncés par haut-parleur

(c) *Am* (*abbr* **physician's assistant**) médecin-assistant *m*

(d) (*abbr* **Press Association**) = la principale agence de presse britannique

(e) (*abbr* **production assistant**) assistant(e) *m,f* de production

PA² (*written abbr* **Pennsylvania**) Pennsylvanie *f*

p.a. (*written abbr* **per annum**) par an

PABX [ˌpiːeɪbiː'eks] *n Tel* (*abbr* **private automatic branch exchange**) = autocommutateur privé

PAC [ˌpiːeɪ'siː] *n Am* (*abbr* **political action committee**) = comité qui réunit des fonds pour soutenir une cause politique

Paki ['pækɪ] *n Br Fam* (*abbr* **Pakistani**) = terme raciste désignant un Pakistanais

▸▸ ***Paki shop*** = épicerie de quartier tenue par un Pakistanais

PAL [pæl] *n TV* (*abbr* **phase alternation line**) PAL *f*

p & h (*written abbr* **postage and handling**) frais *mpl* de port et d'emballage

P & L [ˌpiːən'el] *n* **(a)** (*abbr* **profit and loss**) pertes *fpl* et profits *mpl*

(b) (*abbr* **profit and loss account, profit and loss statement**) compte *m* de résultat; **we can see from the P & L that developing the product is not a viable option** le compte de résultat montre clairement qu'il ne serait pas rentable de développer ce produit

(c) (*abbr* **profit and loss form**) compte *m* d'exploitation

▸▸ ***P & L account*** compte *m* de résultat; ***P & L form*** compte *m* d'exploitation; ***P & L statement*** compte *m* de résultat

p & p [ˌpiːən'piː] *n Br* (*abbr* **postage and packing**) frais *mpl* de port et d'emballage

para ['pærə] *n* **(a)** (*abbr* **paragraph**) par. **(b)** *Fam Mil* (*abbr* **paratrooper**) para *m*

PAX [ˌpiːeɪ'eks] *n Tel* (*abbr* **private automatic exchange**) central *m* automatique privé

PAYE [ˌpiːeɪˌwaɪ'iː] *n Br Fin* (*abbr* **pay-as-you-earn**) prélèvement *m* de l'impôt à la source

PB [ˌpiː'biː] *n Sport* (*abbr* **personal best**) record *m* personnel; **he ran a PB in the 200 m** il a battu son propre record *ou* son record personnel sur 200 m

PBS [ˌpiːbiː'es] *n Am* (*abbr* **Public Broadcasting Service**) = société américaine de production télévisuelle

PBX [ˌpiːbiː'eks] *n Br Tel* (*abbr* **private branch exchange**) = autocommutateur privé

pc¹, PC¹ [ˌpiː'siː] *n* **(a)** *Comput* (*abbr* **personal computer**) PC *m*, micro *m*; **available for the PC** disponible en version PC **(b)** (*abbr* **postcard**) carte *f* postale

▸▸ *Comput* ***PC disk*** disquette *f* pour PC

PC² **1** *n* **(a)** (*abbr* **police constable**) agent *m* de police **(b)** (*abbr* **privy councillor**) = membre du Conseil privé

2 *adj* (*abbr* **politically correct**) politiquement correct

pc² (*written abbr* **per cent**) pc

p/c (*written abbr* **petty cash**) petite caisse *f*

PCAS ['piːkæs] *n Br Formerly* (*abbr* **Polytechnics Central Admissions System**) = organisme britannique autrefois responsable des entrées dans les "polytechnics"

PCB [ˌpiːsiː'biː] *n* **(a)** *Electron* (*abbr* **printed circuit board**) carte *f* de *ou* à circuits imprimés **(b)** *Chem* (*abbr* **polychlorinated biphenyl**) PCB *m*

PCI [ˌpiːsiː'aɪ] *n Comput* (*abbr* **peripheral component interface**) PCI *m*

pcm (*written abbr* **per calendar month**) par mois

PCMCIA [ˌpiːsiː'emˌsiːaɪ'eɪ] *n Comput* (*abbr* **PC memory card international association**) PCMCIA *m*

PCN [ˌpiːsiː'en] *n Tel* (*abbr* **personal communications network**) réseau *m* de téléphonie mobile

PCP [ˌpiːsiː'piː] *n Chem* (*abbr* **phencyclidine**) PCP *f*

PCR [ˌpiːsiː'ɑː(r)] *n* (*abbr* **polymerase chain reaction**) réaction *f* en chaîne par polymérase, amplification *f* génique

PCV [ˌpiːsiː'viː] *n Br* (*abbr* **passenger carrying vehicle**) véhicule *m* de transport en commun

PD [ˌpiː'diː] *n Am* (*abbr* **police department**) service *m* de police

pd (*written abbr* **paid**) payé

PDA [ˌpiːdiː'eɪ] *n Comput* (*abbr* **personal digital assistant**) agenda *m* électronique de poche, assistant *m* numérique de poche

PDF [ˌpiːdiː'ef] *n Comput* (*abbr* **portable document format**) (format *m*) PDF *m*

pdq [ˌpiːdiː'kjuː] *adv Fam* (*abbr* **pretty damn quick**) illico presto

PDSA [ˌpiːdiːˌes'eɪ] *n Br* (*abbr* **People's Dispensary for Sick Animals**) = association de soins aux animaux malades

PDT [ˌpiːdiː'tiː] *n Am* (*abbr* **Pacific Daylight Time**) heure *f* d'été du Pacifique

PE [ˌpiː'iː] *n* (*abbr* **physical education**) EPS *f*

pecs [peks] *npl Fam* (*abbr* **pectoral muscles**) pectoraux ❑ *mpl*; **he's got a great set of pecs** il a des super pectoraux

ped Xing *Am* (*written abbr* **pedestrian crossing**) passage *m* clouté *ou* piétons

PEI (*written abbr* **Prince Edward Island**) l'île *f* du Prince-Édouard

Penn, Penna (*written abbr* **Pennsylvania**) Pennsylvanie *f*

PEP [pep] *n Br Formerly Fin* (*abbr* **personal equity plan**) ≃ PEA *m*

p/e ratio [ˌpiː'iː-] *n St Exch* (*abbr* **price-earnings ratio**) ratio *m ou* rapport *m* cours-bénéfices, PER *m*

Perl [pɜːl] *n Comput* (*abbr* **practical extraction and report language**) langage *m* Perl

perp [pɜːp] *n Am Fam Crime slang* (*abbr* **perpetrator**) auteur ❑ *m*

PEST [pest] *n Mktg* (*abbr* **political, economic, sociological, technological**) = facteurs politiques, économiques, sociaux et technologiques

PET [pet] *n Med* (*abbr* **positron emission tomography**) tomographie *f* par émission de positrons

PETA ['petə] *n Am* (*abbr* **People for the Ethical Treatment of Animals**) = association américaine de défense des droits des animaux, opposée notamment à la vivisection

Pfc, PFC [ˌpiːefˈsiː] *n Am Mil* (*abbr* **private first class**) soldat *m* de première classe

PFI [ˌpiːefˈaɪ] *n* (*abbr* **private finance initiative**) partenariat *m* public-privé

PFLP [ˌpiːefˌelˈpiː] *n* (*abbr* **Popular Front for the Liberation of Palestine**) FPLP *m*

PG [ˌpiːˈdʒiː] **1** *adj Cin* (*abbr* **parental guidance**) = désigne un film dont certaines scènes peuvent choquer, ≃ tous publics *(l'accord des parents étant souhaitable)*

2 *n Br* (*abbr* **paying guest**) pensionnaire *mf*

PGA [ˌpiːdʒiːˈeɪ] *n* (*abbr* **Professional Golfers Association**) PGA *f (association des golfeurs professionnels)*

PGCE [ˌpiːdʒiːˌsiːˈiː] *n Br Sch* (*abbr* **postgraduate certificate in education**) = diplôme d'enseignement

PGP [ˌpiːdʒiːˈpiː] *n Comput* (*abbr* **Pretty Good Privacy**) (logiciel *m* de chiffrement) PGP *m*

PH [ˌpiːˈeɪtʃ] *n Am Mil* (*abbr* **Purple Heart**) = médaille décernée aux blessés de guerre

PHA [ˌpiːeɪtʃˈeɪ] *n Am* (*abbr* **Public Housing Administration**) = services du logement social aux États-Unis

PhD [ˌpiːeɪtʃˈdiː] *n* (*abbr* **Doctor of Philosophy**) *(person)* = titulaire d'un doctorat de 3ème cycle; *(qualification)* = doctorat de 3ème cycle; **to have a PhD in Maths** avoir un doctorat en maths

▸▸ ***PhD student*** étudiant(e) *m,f* inscrit(e) en doctorat; ***PhD thesis*** thèse *f* de doctorat

Phys Ed [ˈfɪzˌed] *n Am* (*abbr* **physical education**) éducation *f* physique

physio [ˈfɪzɪəʊ] (*pl sense* (**b**) **physios**) *n Fam* (**a**) (*abbr* **physiotherapy**) kiné *f* (**b**) (*abbr* **physiotherapist**) kiné *mf*

PI [ˌpiːˈaɪ] *n Am* (*abbr* **private investigator**) détective *m* privé

PIA [ˌpiːaɪˈeɪ] *n Br Fin* (*abbr* **personal investment authority**) = organisme chargé de surveiller les activités des conseillers financiers indépendants et de protéger les petits investisseurs

PIBOR [ˈpaɪbɔː(r)] *n* (*abbr* **Paris Interbank Offered Rate**) TIOP *m*, PIBOR *m*

PID [ˌpiːaɪˈdiː] *n Med* (*abbr* **pelvic inflammatory disease**) syndrome *m* inflammatoire pelvien

PIMS [pɪmz] *n Mktg* (*abbr* **profit impact of marketing strategy**) IRSM *m*

PIN [pɪn] *n* (*abbr* **personal identification number**) code *m* confidentiel *(d'une carte bancaire)*

▸▸ ***PIN number*** code *m* confidentiel *(d'une carte bancaire)*

PIP [pɪp] *n Comput* (*abbr* **peripheral interchange program**) logiciel *m* de commutation de périphérique

PJs [ˈpiːdʒeɪz] *npl Fam* (*abbr* **pyjamas**) pyjama *m*

pkg (*written abbr* **package**) paquet *m*, colis *m*

pkt (*written abbr* **packet**) paquet *m*

pkwy *Am* (*written abbr* **parkway**) grand boulevard *m* bordé d'arbres

Pl. (*written abbr* **place**) rue *f*

pl (*written abbr* **plural**) pl

PLC, plc [ˌpiːelˈsiː] *n* (**a**) *Br Com* (*abbr* **public limited company**) ≃ SA *f*; **Scandia PLC** ≃ Scandia SA (**b**) *Mktg* (*abbr* **product lifecycle**) cycle *m* de vie du produit

PLO [ˌpiːelˈəʊ] *n* (*abbr* **Palestine Liberation Organization**) OLP *f*

PLP [ˌpiːelˈpiː] *n Br* (*abbr* **Parliamentary Labour Party**) députés *mpl* du Parti travailliste

PLR [ˌpiːelˈɑː(r)] *n* (*abbr* **Public Lending Right**) = droit d'auteur versé pour les ouvrages prêtés par les bibliothèques

PM [ˌpiːˈem] *n* (**a**) (*abbr* **Prime Minister**) Premier ministre *m* (**b**) (*abbr* **post mortem**) autopsie *f*

p.m. [ˌpiːˈem] *adv* (*abbr* **post meridiem**) de l'après-midi; **3 p.m.** 3 heures de l'après-midi, 15 heures; **at 11 p.m.** à 11 heures du soir, à 23 heures

PMG [ˌpiːemˈdʒiː] *n Br* (**a**) *Fin* (*abbr* **Paymaster General**) Trésorier-payeur-général *m* britannique (**b**) (*abbr* **Postmaster General**) ≃ ministre *m* des Postes et Télécommunications, *Can* Ministre *m* des Postes

PMS [ˌpiːemˈes] *n Am* (*abbr* **premenstrual syndrome**) syndrome *m* prémenstruel

PMT [ˌpiːemˈtiː] *n Br* (*abbr* **premenstrual tension**) syndrome *m* prémenstruel

P/N *Com* (*written abbr* **promissory note**) billet *m* à ordre, effet *m* à ordre

PO[1] [ˌpiːˈəʊ] *n* (*abbr* **Post Office**) poste *f*

▸▸ ***PO Box*** BP *f*, boîte *f* postale

PO[2] (**a**) (*written abbr* **postal order**) mandat *m* postal (**b**) *Naut* (*written abbr* **petty officer**) second maître *m*

POA [ˌpiːəʊˈeɪ] *n Br* (*abbr* **Prison Officers' Association**) = syndicat des agents pénitentiaires en Grande-Bretagne

POB [ˌpiːəʊˈbiː] *n* (*abbr* **post office box**) boîte *f* postale, BP *f*

POD [ˌpiːəʊˈdiː] *adv Am Com* (*abbr* **pay on delivery**) **to send sth POD** envoyer qch contre remboursement; **all goods are sent POD** toutes les marchandises doivent être payées à la livraison

POE [ˌpiːəʊˈiː] *n* (**a**) (*abbr* **port of embarkation**) port *m* d'embarquement (**b**) (*abbr* **port of entry**) port *m* de débarquement

POP [ˌpiːəʊˈpiː] *n* (**a**) *Comput* (*abbr* **post office protocol**) protocole *m* POP (**b**) *Comput* (*abbr* **point of presence**) point *m* de présence, point *m* d'accès (**c**) *Mktg* (*abbr* **point of purchase**) lieu *m* d'achat, lieu *m* de vente

pop. (*written abbr* **population**) population *f*

POS [ˌpiːəʊˈes] *n Com* (*abbr* **point of sale**) PDV *m*

POTUS *Am* (*written abbr* **President of the United States**) = président des États-Unis d'Amérique

POV [ˌpiːəʊˈviː] *n TV & Cin* (*abbr* **point of view**) angle *m* du regard

POW [ˌpiːəʊˈdʌbəljuː] *n* (*abbr* **prisoner of war**) PG *m*

pp [ˌpiːˈpiː] (*abbr* **per procurationem**) **1** *adv* **pp Jane Smith** pp Jane Smith

2 *vt* **shall I pp it?** est-ce que je signe à votre/sa place?

pp. (*written abbr* **pages**) pp.; **see pp. 44 to 47** voir pp. 44 à 47

PPB [ˌpiːpiːˈbiː] *n Acct* (*abbr* **planning-programming-budgeting system**) système *m* de planification-programmation-budgétisation, rationalisation *f* des choix budgétaires

PPD [ˌpiːpiːˈdiː] *adj Com* (*abbr* **prepaid**) port payé par le destinataire

PPE [ˌpiːpiːˈiː] *n Br* (*abbr* **philosophy, politics and economics**) = philosophie, science politique et science économique (cours à l'université d'Oxford)

ppm (**a**) (*written abbr* **parts per million**) ppm (**b**) (*written abbr* **pages per minute**) ppm

PPP [ˌpiːpiːˈpiː] *n Comput* (*abbr* **point-to-point protocol**) protocole *m* PPP, protocole *m* point à point

PPS [ˌpiːpiːˈes] *n* (**a**) *Br* (*abbr* **parliamentary private secretary**) = en Grande-Bretagne, député qui assure la liaison entre un ministre et la Chambre des communes (**b**) (*abbr* **post postscriptum**) PPS

ppsi (*written abbr* **pounds per square inch**) = livres au pouce carré (mesure de pression)

ppv [ˌpiːpiːˈviː] *TV* (*abbr* **pay-per-view**) **1** *n* système *m* de télévision à la carte

2 *adj* à la carte

PQ [ˌpiːˈkjuː] *n Can* (**a**) (*abbr* **Province of Quebec**) province *f* de Québec (**b**) (*abbr* **Parti québécois**) PQ *m*

PR[1] [ˌpiːˈɑː(r)] *n* (**a**) (*abbr* **public relations**) relations *fpl* publiques, RP *fpl*; **we need better PR** il nous faut améliorer nos relations publiques; **a skilful PR man** un homme qui excelle dans les relations publiques; **who does their PR?** qui est-ce qui s'occupe de leurs relations publiques? (**b**) *Pol* (*abbr* **proportional representation**) RP *f*

▸▸ ***PR agency*** agence *f* conseil en communication; ***PR company*** société *f* conseil en communication; ***PR consultancy*** agence *f* conseil en communication; ***PR consultant*** conseil *m* en communication

PR[2] (**a**) (*written abbr* **Puerto Rico**) Porto Rico (**b**) *Am Pej* (*written abbr* **Puerto Rican**) Portoricain(e) *m,f*

Pr. (*written abbr* **prince**) Pce

PRAM [præm] *n Comput* (*abbr* **programmable random access memory**) RAM *f* programmable

prelim [ˈpriːlɪm] **1** *n* (*abbr* **preliminary exam**) *Univ* examen *m* préliminaire; *Scot Sch* examen *m* blanc

2 prelims *npl Typ* (*abbr* **preliminary pages**) pages *fpl* liminaires *(précédant le corps de l'ouvrage)*

Pres. (*written abbr* **president**) président *m*

PRM [ˌpiːɑːˈrem] *n* (*abbr* **personnel resource management**) GRH *f*

PRO [ˌpiːɑːˈrəʊ] *n* (**a**) (*abbr* **public relations officer**) responsable *mf* des relations publiques (**b**) *Br* (*abbr* **Public Record Office**) ≃ Archives *fpl* nationales

pro [prəʊ] (*pl* **pros**) **1** *n Fam* (**a**) (*abbr* **professional**) pro *mf*; **to turn pro** passer pro; **she was a real pro** *(actress, singer etc)* c'était une vraie pro

(**b**) (*abbr* **professional**) *(at sports club)* pro *mf*

(**c**) (*abbr* **prostitute**) professionnelle *f*

2 *adj Fam* (*abbr* **professional**) pro

▸▸ *Am* ***pro ball*** *(baseball)* base-ball *m* professionnel; *Golf* ***pro shop*** pro shop *m*, *Can* boutique *f* du pro

Prof. (*written abbr* **professor**) Pr

prof [prɒf] *n Fam* (*abbr* **professor**) prof *mf*

PROM [prɒm] *n Comput* (*abbr* **programmable read-only memory**) PROM *f inv*

prop. (*written abbr* **proprietor**) propriétaire *mf*

Pros. Atty *Am Law* (*written abbr* **prosecuting attorney**) ≃ procureur *m*

prox *Old-fashioned* (*written abbr* **proximo**) du mois prochain

PRP [ˌpiːɑːˈpiː] *n* (*abbr* **performance-related pay**) salaire *m* au mérite

PS [ˌpiːˈes] *n* (*abbr* **postscript**) PS *m*

PSAT [ˌpiːesˌeɪˈtiː] *n Am Sch* (*abbr* **Preliminary Scholastic Aptitude Test**) = examen blanc préparant au "SAT"

PSB [ˌpiːesˈbiː] *n Rad & TV* (*abbr* **public-service broadcasting**) émissions *fpl* de service public

PSBR [ˌpiːesˌbiːˈɑː(r)] *n Br Fin* (*abbr* **public sector borrowing requirement**) = besoins d'emprunt du secteur public non couverts par les rentrées fiscales

psi [ˌpiːesˈaɪ] *n Phys* (*abbr* **pounds per square inch**) = livres au pouce carré (mesure de pression)

PST [ˌpiːesˈtiː] *n Am* (*abbr* **Pacific Standard Time**) heure *f* du Pacifique

PSTN [ˌpiːesˌtiːˈen] *n Tel* (*abbr* **Public Switched Telephone Network**) RTC *m*

PSV [ˌpiːesˈviː] *n Br Formerly* (*abbr* **public service vehicle**) véhicule *m* de transport en commun

PT[1] [ˌpiːˈtiː] *n* (**a**) (*abbr* **physical training**) EPS *f* (**b**) *Am* (*abbr* **physical therapy**) kinésithérapie *f*

▸▸ ***PT instructor*** professeur *mf* d'éducation physique

PT[2] *n* (*abbr* **patrol torpedo**)

▸▸ ***PT boat*** = vedette rapide utilisée par les forces américaines pendant la Seconde Guerre mondiale

pt (**a**) (*written abbr* **pint**) pinte *f* (**b**) (*written abbr* **point**) point *m*

Pt. (*written abbr* **point**) *(on map)* Pte

PTA [ˌpiːtiːˈeɪ] *n Sch* (*abbr* **parent-teacher association**) = association de parents d'élèves et de professeurs

Pte. *Br Mil* (*written abbr* **private**) soldat *m* de deuxième classe

PTO[1] [ˌpiːtiːˈəʊ] *n Am Sch* (*abbr* **parent-teacher organization**) = association de parents d'élèves et de professeurs
PTO[2] *Br* (*written abbr* **please turn over**) TSVP
PTV [ˌpiːtiːˈviː] *n* (**a**) (*abbr* **pay television**) = télévision à péage (**b**) (*abbr* **public television**) = programmes télévisés éducatifs
Pty (*written abbr* **proprietary company**) SARL *f*
pub. (*written abbr* **published**) publié
pud [pʊd] *n Br Fam* (*abbr* **pudding**) dessert ❑ *m*
P/V *Fin* (*written abbr* **profit-volume ratio**) rapport *m* profit sur ventes, ratio *m* de volume de bénéfices
PVC [ˌpiːviːˈsiː] *n* (*abbr* **polyvinyl chloride**) PVC *m*
PVS [ˌpiːviːˈes] *n Med* (*abbr* **persistent vegetative state**) état *m* végétatif chronique
Pvt. (*written abbr* **private**) soldat *m* de deuxième classe
PW [ˌpiːˈdʌbəljuː] *n Br* (*abbr* **policewoman**) femme *f* policier
pw (*written abbr* **per week**) p.sem
PWA [ˌpiːdʌbəljuːˈeɪ] *n* (*abbr* **person with AIDS**) sidéen(enne) *m,f*
PWR [ˌpiːdʌbəljuːˈɑː(r)] *n Nucl & Phys* (*abbr* **pressurized-water reactor**) REP *m*
PX [ˌpiːˈeks] *n Am Mil* (*abbr* **post exchange**) = économat pour les militaires et leurs familles
PYO (*written abbr* **pick your own**) (*sign*) cueillette à la ferme

Q (*written abbr* **Queen**) (*in chess*) D
q (*written abbr* **quart**) ≃ litre *m*
QA (*written abbr* **quality assurance**) garantie *f* de qualité
QC [ˌkjuːˈsiː] *n* (**a**) *Br Law* (*abbr* **Queen's Counsel**) ≃ bâtonnier *m* de l'ordre (**b**) (*abbr* **quality control**) contrôle *m* de (la) qualité
QE2 [ˌkjuːiːˈtuː] *n Br Naut* (*abbr* **Queen Elizabeth II**) = grand paquebot de luxe
QED [ˌkjuːiːˈdiː] *adv* (*abbr* **quod erat demonstrandum**) CQFD
QIP [ˌkjuːaɪˈpiː] *n* (*abbr* **quality improvement programme**) programme *m* d'amélioration de la qualité
QM [ˌkjuːˈem] *n Mil* (*abbr* **Quartermaster**) (**a**) (*in army*) commissaire *m*; *Hist* intendant *m* (**b**) (*in navy*) officier *m* de manœuvre
QMG [ˌkjuːemˈdʒiː] *n Mil* (*abbr* **Quartermaster General**) ≃ Directeur *m* de l'Intendance (militaire)
QSO [ˌkjuːesˈəʊ] *n Astron* (*abbr* **quasi-stellar object**) objet *m* quasistellaire, QSO *m*
qt (*written abbr* **quart**) ≃ litre *m*
qty (*written abbr* **quantity**) qté
quad [kwɒd] *n* (**a**) (*abbr* **quadruplet**) quadruplé(e) *m,f* (**b**) (*abbr* **quadrangle**) cour *f* (**c**) *Typ* cadrat *m* (**d**) *Elec* quarte *f*
quango [ˈkwæŋgəʊ] (*pl* **quangos**) *n Br* (*abbr* **quasiautonomous non-governmental organization**) = organisme semi-public
quin [kwɪn] *n Br* (*abbr* **quintuplet**) quintuplé(e) *m,f*
quint [kwɪnt] *n Am* (*abbr* **quintuplet**) quintuplé(e) *m,f*
qv (*written abbr* **quod vide**) = expression renvoyant le lecteur à une autre entrée dans une encyclopédie

R[1] [ɑː(r)] *adj Am* (*abbr* **restricted**) = indique qu'un film est interdit aux moins de 17 ans
R[2] (**a**) (*written abbr* **right**) dr (**b**) (*written abbr* **river**) rivière *f* (**c**) (*written abbr* **Réaumur**) R (**d**) *Am* (*written abbr* **Republican**) républicain (**e**) *Br* (*written abbr* **Rex**) = suit le nom d'un roi (**f**) *Br* (*written abbr* **Regina**) = suit le nom d'une reine (**g**) *Geom* (*written abbr* **radius**) R (**h**) (*written abbr* **road**) rue *f* (**i**) (*written abbr* **rand**) R
RA [ɑːˈreɪ] *n* (**a**) (*abbr* **rear admiral**) contre-amiral *m* (**b**) (*abbr* **Royal Academician**) = membre de la "Royal Academy" (**c**) (*abbr* **Royal Academy**) Académie *f* royale britannique (*académie des beaux-arts*)
RAAF [ræf] *n Austr* (*abbr* **Royal Australian Air Force**) = armée de l'air australienne
RAC [ˌɑːreɪˈsiː] *n Br* (*abbr* **Royal Automobile Club**) **the RAC** = automobile club britannique et compagnie d'assurances qui garantit le dépannage de ses adhérents et propose des services touristiques et juridiques, ≃ ACF *m*, ≃ TCF *m*
RADA [ˈrɑːdə] *n Br* (*abbr* **Royal Academy of Dramatic Art**) = conservatoire britannique d'art dramatique
RAF [ˌɑːreɪˈef] *n Br* (*abbr* **Royal Air Force**) = armée de l'air britannique
RAM[1] [ræm] *n Comput* (*abbr* **random access memory**) RAM *f*, mémoire *f* vive
►► ***RAM chip*** puce *f* de mémoire vive; ***RAM disk*** mémoire *f* à disque
RAM[2] [ˌɑːreɪˈem] *n* (*abbr* **Royal Academy of Music**) = conservatoire national de musique de Londres
RAMC [ˌɑːreɪˌemˈsiː] *n Br* (*abbr* **Royal Army Medical Corps**) = service de santé des armées britanniques
RAN [ˌɑːreɪˈen] *n Austr* (*abbr* **Royal Australian Navy**) = marine de guerre australienne
R & B [ˌɑːrənˈbiː] *n* (*abbr* **rhythm and blues**) rhythm and blues *m*
R & D [ˌɑːrənˈdiː] *n* (*abbr* **research and development**) recherche *f* et développement *m*, R-D *f*
►► ***R & D department*** bureau *m* d'études; ***R & D director*** directeur(trice) *m,f* de recherche et développement; ***R & D expenditure*** dépenses *fpl* pour la recherche et le développement
R and R, R&R [ˌɑːrənˈdɑː(r)] *n Am Mil* (*abbr* **rest and recreation**) permission *f*; *Fam Fig* **she went on holiday for some R and R** elle est allée en vacances pour se reposer un peu ❑
Rasta [ˈræstə] (*abbr* **Rastafarian**) **1** *n* rasta *mf*
2 *adj* rasta (*inv*)
RBI [ˌɑːbiːˈaɪ] *n Am Sport* (*abbr* **runs batted in**) = points marqués par le batteur
RC [ˌɑːˈsiː] *n* (**a**) (*abbr* **Roman Catholic**) catholique *mf* (**b**) (*abbr* **Red Cross**) Croix-Rouge *f*
RCA [ˌɑːsiːˈeɪ] *n* (*abbr* **Royal College of Art**) = école de beaux-arts, à Londres
RCAF [ˌɑːsiːˌeɪˈef] *n Can* (*abbr* **Royal Canadian Air Force**) = armée de l'air canadienne
RCCh (*written abbr* **Roman Catholic Church**) Église *f* catholique
RCMP [ˌɑːsiːˌemˈpiː] *n Can* (*abbr* **Royal Canadian Mounted Police**) Gendarmerie *f* royale du Canada
RCN [ˌɑːsiːˈen] *n Can* (*abbr* **Royal Canadian Navy**) = marine de guerre canadienne
Rd (*written abbr* **road**) rue *f*
RDA [ˌɑːdiːˈeɪ] *n* (*abbr* **recommended daily allowance**) recommandation *f* quotidienne officielle (*en vitamines, sels minéraux etc*)
RDBMS [ˌɑːdiːˌbiːemˈes] *n Comput* (*abbr* **relational database management system**) SGBDR *m*
RE[1] [ˌɑːˈriː] *n* (*abbr* **religious education**) éducation *f* religieuse
RE[2] (*written abbr* **Royal Engineers**) génie *m* militaire britannique
rec. (*written abbr* **received**) reçu
recd, rec'd (*written abbr* **received**) reçu
ref[1], **ref.** (*written abbr* **reference**) réf.; **your ref** v/réf.; **our ref** n/réf.
ref[2] [ref] *n Br Fam Sport* (*abbr* **referee**) arbitre ❑ *m*
reg[1] (*written abbr* **registered**) **reg trademark** marque *f* déposée
reg[2] [redʒ] *Br Fam* (*abbr* **registration**) immatriculation ❑ *f*; **what reg is your car?** ta voiture est de quelle année? ❑
regd (*written abbr* **registered**) **regd trademark** marque *f* déposée
regt (*written abbr* **regiment**) régiment *m*
REM [ˌɑːriːˈem] *n* (*abbr* **rapid eye movement**) mouvements *mpl* oculaires rapides
►► ***REM sleep*** sommeil *m* paradoxal
rem [rem] *n Nucl* (*abbr* **roentgen equivalent man**) rem *m*
REMIC [ˌɑːriːˌemaɪˈsiː] *n Am Fin* (*abbr* **real estate mortgage investment conduit**) obligation *f* garantie par hypothèque
rents [rents] *npl Am Fam* (*abbr* **parents**) vieux *mpl*, renps *mpl*
Rep *Am* (**a**) (*written abbr* **Representative**) ≃ député *m* (**b**) (*written abbr* **Republican**) républicain(e) *m,f*
rep [rep] *n* (**a**) *Fam* (*abbr* **representative**) représentant(e) ❑ *m,f*, VRP ❑ *m*
(**b**) *Br Fam* (*abbr* **repertory**) (*theatre*) théâtre *m* de répertoire ❑; **to be** *or* **to work in rep** faire partie d'une troupe de répertoire, faire du théâtre de répertoire
(**c**) *Fam* (*abbr* **reputation**) réputation ❑ *f*
(**d**) *Fam* (*abbr* **repetition**) (*in physical training*) mouvement ❑ *m*; **twenty reps on each piece of equipment** vingt mouvements sur chaque machine
repo [ˈriːpəʊ] **1** *n* (**a**) *Am Fam St Exch* (*abbr* **repossession**) réméré ❑ *m*
(**b**) (*abbr* **repurchase**) rachat *m*; *St Exch & Banking* réméré *m*
2 *vt Fam* (*abbr* **repossess**) saisir ❑
►► *St Exch & Banking* ***repo agreement*** opération *f* de réméré *ou* de prise en pension, opération *f* repo; *Am Fam* ***repo man*** ≃ huissier *m* (*chargé par une société de saisir des meubles etc non payés*); *St Exch & Banking* ***repo operation*** opération *f* de réméré *ou* de prise en pension, opération *f* repo; ***repo rate*** taux *m* de réméré *ou* de prise en pension
repro [ˈriːprəʊ] (*pl* **repros**) *n Fam Typ* (*abbr* **reproduction**) (épreuve *f*) repro *f*
►► ***repro head*** tête *f* de lecture ❑
Repub. *Am* (*written abbr* **Republican**) républicain
retd (*written abbr* **retired**) à la retraite
rev [rev] *n Fam Aut* (*abbr* **revolution**) tour ❑ *m*; **3,000 revs per minute** 3000 tours par minute
►► ***rev counter*** compte-tours ❑ *m inv*
Rev. (*written abbr* **Reverend**) révérend *m*
Revd (*written abbr* **reverend**) révérend *m*
REX [ˌɑːriːˈeks] *n* (*abbr* **real-time executive routine**) = superviseur en temps réel
RF [ˌɑːˈref] *n* (*abbr* **radio frequency**) fréquence *f* radio
RFC (*written abbr* **Rugby Football Club**) = club de rugby
RFU [ˌɑːrefˈjuː] *n Br Sport* (*abbr* **Rugby Football Union**) = fédération anglaise de rugby
RGB [ˌɑːdʒiːˈbiː] *n Comput* (*abbr* **red, green and blue**) RVB *m*
RGN [ˌɑːdʒiːˈen] *n Br Formerly* (*abbr* **registered general nurse**) infirmier(ère) *m,f* diplômé(e) d'État (*remplacé en 1992 par "RN"*)
Rgt (*written abbr* **regiment**) rég
Rh (*written abbr* **rhesus**) Rh
►► ***Rh factor*** (facteur *m*) rhésus *m*
RI[1] [ˌɑːˈraɪ] *n* (*abbr* **religious instruction**) instruction *f* religieuse
RI[2] (*written abbr* **Rhode Island**) Rhode Island *m*
RIBA [ˌɑːraɪˌbiːˈeɪ] *n Br* (*abbr* **Royal Institute of British Architects**) = institut d'architectes, à Londres
RIE [ˌɑːraɪˈiː] *n Fin* (*abbr* **recognized investment exchange**) marché *m* d'investissement agréé
RIP [ˌɑːraɪˈpiː] *n* (**a**) (*abbr* **rest in peace**) RIP (**b**) *Comput & Typ* (*abbr* **Raster Image Processor**) processeur *m* d'image tramée, RIP *m*

RISC [rɪsk] *n Comput (abbr* **reduced instruction set chip** *or* **computer**) RISC *m*

RMT [ˌɑːrem'tiː] *n Br (abbr* **National Union of Rail, Maritime and Transport Workers**) = syndicat britannique des cheminots et des gens de mer

RN [ˌɑː'ren] *n Br* (**a**) *(abbr* **Royal Navy**) marine *f* nationale britannique (**b**) *(abbr* **registered nurse**) *(nurse)* infirmier(ère) *m,f* diplômé(e) (d'État) (**c**) *(qualification)* diplôme *m* (d'État) d'infirmier

RNA [ˌɑːren'eɪ] *n Biol (abbr* **ribonucleic acid**) ARN *m*

RNIB [ˌɑːrenˌaɪ'biː] *n (abbr* **Royal National Institute for the Blind**) = institution britannique pour les aveugles

RNLI [ˌɑːrenˌel'aɪ] *n (abbr* **Royal National Lifeboat Institution**) = société britannique de sauvetage en mer

RNZAF [ˌɑːrenˌzedeɪ'ef] *n (abbr* **Royal New Zealand Air Force**) = armée de l'air néo-zélandaise

RNZN [ˌɑːrenˌzed'en] *n (abbr* **Royal New Zealand Navy**) = marine de guerre néo-zélandaise

ROCE [ˌɑːrəʊˌsiː'iː] *n Fin (abbr* **return on capital employed**) retour *m* sur capital immobilisé

ROI [ˌɑːrəʊ'aɪ] *n Fin (abbr* **return on investment**) retour *m* sur investissement(s)

roid [rɔɪd] *n Am Fam (abbr* **steroid**) **roids** stéroïdes ❑ *mpl*

▸▸ ***roid rage*** = état d'agressivité extrême causé par l'absorption de stéroïdes

Roller [ˌrəʊlə(r)] *n Br Fam (abbr* **Rolls-Royce**®) Rolls Royce® ❑ *f*

ROM [rɒm] *n Comput (abbr* **read-only memory**) mémoire *f* morte, (mémoire *f*) ROM *f*

RON ['rəʊn] *n Petr (abbr* **Research Octane Number**) IOR *m*

ROS [ˌɑːrəʊ'es] *n Fin (abbr* **return on sales**) retour *m* sur ventes

RoSPA ['rɒspə] *n Br (abbr* **Royal Society for the Prevention of Accidents**) = association britannique pour la prévention des accidents

ROTC [ˌɑːrəʊˌtiː'siː, 'rɒtsɪ] *n Mil (abbr* **Reserve Officer Training Corps**) = préparation militaire proposée par l'armée de terre américaine aux étudiants désireux de se faire payer leurs études, en échange de quoi ces derniers s'engagent à passer quatre ans dans l'armée

RP [ˌɑː'piː] *n Ling (abbr* **received pronunciation**) = prononciation de l'anglais britannique considérée comme la norme

RPB [ˌɑːpiː'biː] *n (abbr* **recognized professional body**) = organisme professionnel agréé

RPI [ˌɑːpiː'aɪ] *n Br Fin (abbr* **Retail Price Index**) indice *m* des prix de détail

RPM [ˌɑːpiː'em] *n (abbr* **retail price maintenance**) prix *m* imposé

rpm [ˌɑːpiː'em] *n Tech (abbr* **revolutions per minute**) tr/min

RPO [ˌɑːpiː'əʊ] *n (abbr* **Royal Philharmonic Orchestra**) = orchestre philharmonique basé à Londres

RPV [ˌɑːpiː'viː] *n Mil (abbr* **remotely piloted vehicle**) véhicule *m* télécommandé *ou* téléguidé

RR [ˌɑː'rɑː(r)] (**a**) *Am (written abbr* **railroad**) chemin *m* de fer (**b**) *Am (written abbr* **rural route**) = route de campagne desservie par le facteur (**c**) *(written abbr* **Right Reverend**) **RR James Brown** le très révérend James Brown

RRP [ˌɑːrɑː'piː] *n Br (abbr* **recommended retail price**) prix *m* recommandé, prix *m* conseillé

RS [ˌɑː'res] *n Br (abbr* **Royal Society**) Académie *f* des sciences britannique

RSA [ˌɑːres'eɪ] *n* (**a**) *Br (abbr* **Royal Society of Arts**) Société *f* royale des arts (**b**) *(abbr* **Republic of South Africa**) Afrique *f* du Sud (**c**) *(abbr* **Royal Scottish Academy**) Académie *f* écossaise des beaux-arts

RSC [ˌɑːres'siː] *n Br (abbr* **Royal Shakespeare Company**) = célèbre troupe de théâtre basée à Stratford-on-Avon et à Londres

RSFSR [ˌɑːresˌefes'ɑː(r)] *n (abbr* **Russian Soviet Federal Socialist Republic**) RSFSR *f*; **in the RSFSR** en RSFSR

RSI [ˌɑːres'aɪ] *n (UNCOUNT) Med (abbr* **repetitive strain** *or* **stress injury**) lésions *fpl* attribuables au travail répétitif

RSJ [ˌɑːres'dʒeɪ] *n Constr (abbr* **rolled steel joist**) solive *f* en I

RSM [ˌɑːres'em] *n* (**a**) *Mil (abbr* **regimental sergeant major**) ≃ adjudant-chef *m* (**b**) *Br (abbr* **Royal School of Music**) École *f* royale de musique (**c**) *Br (abbr* **Royal Society of Medicine**) Fondation *f* de médecine britannique

RSNO [ˌɑːresˌen'əʊ] *n (abbr* **Royal Scottish National Orchestra**) = orchestre national d'Écosse

RSPB [ˌɑːresˌpiː'biː] *n (abbr* **Royal Society for the Protection of Birds**) = ligue britannique pour la protection des oiseaux

RSPCA [ˌɑːresˌpiːsiː'eɪ] *n (abbr* **Royal Society for the Prevention of Cruelty to Animals**) = société britannique protectrice des animaux, ≃ SPA *f*

RSPCC [ˌɑːresˌpiːsiː'siː] *n Br (abbr* **Royal Society for the Prevention of Cruelty to Children**) ≃ Fondation *f* pour l'enfance

RSV [ˌɑːres'viː] *n Bible (abbr* **Revised Standard Version**) = traduction américaine de la Bible établie en 1952

RSVP [ˌɑːresˌviː'piː] *(abbr* **répondez s'il vous plaît**) RSVP

RT [ˌɑː'tiː] *n Biol (abbr* **reverse transcriptase**) transcriptase *f* inverse

RTA [ˌɑːtiː'eɪ] *n (abbr* **road traffic accident**) accident *m* de la route

RTE [ˌɑːtiː'iː] *n (abbr* **Radio Telefis Éireann**) = office de radio et de télévision irlandais

RTGS [ˌɑːtiːˌdʒiː'es] *n Fin (abbr* **Real-Time Gross Settlement**) RTGS *m*

▸▸ ***RTGS system*** système *m* RTGS

Rt Hon *Br (written abbr* **Right Honourable**) = titre utilisé pour s'adresser à certains hauts fonctionnaires ou à quelqu'un ayant un titre de noblesse

RTM [ˌɑːtiː'em] *n (abbr* **registered trademark**) marque *f* déposée

Rt Rev *(written abbr* **Right Reverend**) **the Rt Rev James Brown** le très révérend James Brown

RTW [ˌɑːtiː'dʌbəljuː] *n (abbr* **round the world**) tour *m* du monde

RU [ˌɑː'juː] *n (abbr* **Rugby Union**) *(sport)* rugby *m* (à quinze); *(authority)* fédération *f* de rugby

RUC [ˌɑːjuː'siː] *n (abbr* **Royal Ulster Constabulary**) = corps de police d'Irlande du Nord

RUF [ˌɑːjuː'ef] *n Fin (abbr* **revolving underwriting facility**) facilité *f* renouvelable de prise ferme

RV [ˌɑː'viː] *n* (**a**) *Bible (abbr* **Revised Version**) = traduction anglaise de la Bible faite en 1885 (**b**) *Am (abbr* **recreational vehicle**) camping-car *m*

S (**a**) *(written abbr* **south**) S (**b**) *(written abbr* **small**) *(on clothes label)* S

SA¹ [ˌes'eɪ] *n (abbr* **Salvation Army**) Armée *f* du salut

SA² (**a**) *(written abbr* **South Africa**) Afrique *f* du Sud (**b**) *(written abbr* **South America**) Amérique *f* du Sud

SAD [ˌeseɪ'diː] *n (abbr* **seasonal affective disorder**) dépression *f* saisonnière

s.a.e., sae, SAE [ˌeseɪ'iː] *n (abbr* **stamped addressed envelope**) enveloppe *f* timbrée *(portant l'adresse à laquelle elle doit être renvoyée)*; **please return the form with an s.a.e.** veuillez renvoyer le formulaire ainsi qu'une enveloppe timbrée à votre adresse

SAG [sæg] *n Am (abbr* **Screen Actors' Guild**) = syndicat américain des acteurs

SALT [sɔːlt, sɒlt] *n (abbr* **Strategic Arms Limitation Talks** *or* **Treaty**) SALT *m*

▸▸ ***SALT talks*** négociations *fpl* SALT

SAM [sæm] *n (abbr* **surface-to-air missile**) missile *m* sol-air

S&L [ˌesə'nel] *n Am (abbr* **savings and loan association**) ≃ société *f* de crédit immobilier

S&M [ˌesən'dem] *n Fam* (**a**) *(abbr* **sadomasochism**) sadomasochisme ❑ *m* (**b**) *(abbr* **sales & marketing**) ventes *fpl* et marketing ❑

sarge [sɑːdʒ] *n Fam (abbr* **sergeant**) sergent ❑ *m*

sarnie ['sɑːnɪ] *n Br Fam (abbr* **sandwich**) sandwich ❑ *m*, casse-dalle *m*

SAS [ˌeseɪ'es] *n Br Mil (abbr* **Special Air Service**) = commando d'intervention spéciale de l'armée britannique

SASE [ˌeseɪˌes'iː] *n Am (abbr* **self-addressed stamped envelope**) enveloppe *f* timbrée *(portant l'adresse à laquelle elle doit être renvoyée)*

Sask *(written abbr* **Saskatchewan**) Saskatchewan *m*

SAT [sæt, ˌeseɪ'tiː] *n* (**a**) *Am (abbr* **Scholastic Aptitude Test**) = examen d'entrée à l'université aux États-Unis (**b**) *Br (abbr* **Standard Assessment Task**) = dans le cadre du "National Curriculum", contrôle des connaissances auquel doivent se soumettre les élèves de 7, 11 et 14 ans

Sat. *(written abbr* **Saturday**) sam

sax [sæks] *n Fam (abbr* **saxophone**) saxo *m*

SAYE [ˌeseɪˌwaɪ'iː] *n Br Fin (abbr* **save-as-you-earn**) = plan d'épargne à contributions mensuelles produisant des intérêts exonérés d'impôts

SBA [ˌesbiː'eɪ] *n Am (abbr* **Small Business Administration**) = organisme fédéral américain d'aide aux petites entreprises

SBS [ˌesbiː'es] *n (abbr* **sick building syndrome**) = syndrome comprenant des maux de tête etc qu'on retrouve chez des personnes résidant ou travaillant dans des bâtiments équipés de la climatisation, *Can* ≃ syndrome *m* des bâtiments malsains

SBU [ˌesbiː'juː] *n (abbr* **strategic business unit**) DAS *m*, UAS *f*

SC¹ [ˌes'siː] *n Law (abbr* **Supreme Court**) Cour *f* suprême *(des États-Unis)*

SC² *(written abbr* **South Carolina**) Caroline *f* du Sud

S/C *(written abbr* **self-contained**) *(flat)* indépendant

SCART [skɑːt] *n Elec (abbr* **Syndicat des Constructeurs d'Appareils Radiorécepteurs et Téléviseurs**)

▸▸ ***SCART cable*** câble *m* péritel®; ***SCART plug*** prise *f* péritel®

SCE [ˌessiː'iː] *n Sch (abbr* **Scottish Certificate of Education**) = examen de fin d'études secondaires en Écosse

SCF [ˌessiː'ef] *n (abbr* **Save the Children Fund**) = organisme international d'assistance à l'enfance

SCG [ˌessiː'dʒiː] *n (abbr* **Sydney Cricket Ground**) = célèbre terrain de cricket de Sydney où se jouent des matches internationaux

schizo ['skɪtsəʊ] *Fam (abbr* **schizophrenic**) *(pl* **schizos**) **1** *adj* schizo; *Fig (mad)* cinglé
2 *n* schizo *mf*; *Fig (mad person)* cinglé(e) *m,f*

.sci *Comput (written abbr* **science**) *(in Internet newsgroups)* = abréviation désignant les forums de discussion scientifiques

SCID [skɪd] *n Med (abbr* **severe combined immunodeficiency**) syndrome *m* de déficience immune combinée sévère, déficit *m* immunitaire combiné sévère

sci-fi ['saɪfaɪ] *Fam (abbr* **science fiction**) **1** *n* SF *f*
2 *adj* de SF

SCR [ˌessiː'ɑː(r)] *n Br (abbr* **senior common room**) = salle des étudiants de troisième cycle

SCSI ['skʌzɪ] *n Comput (abbr* **small compu-**

ter systems interface) SCSI *f*
►► ***SCSI card*** carte *f* SCSI

SD (*written abbr* **South Dakota**) Dakota *m* du Sud

SDI [ˌesdiːˈaɪ] *n Mil* (*abbr* **strategic defence initiative**) initiative *f* de défense stratégique

SDLP [ˌesdiːˌelˈpiː] *n* (*abbr* **Social Democratic and Labour Party**) = parti politique d'Irlande du Nord

SDP [ˌesdiːˈpiː] *n* (*abbr* **Social Democratic Party**) Parti *m* social démocrate

SDRAM [ˌesdiːˈræm] *n Comput* (*abbr* **synchronous dynamic random access memory**) SDRAM *f*

SDRs [ˌesdiːˈɑːz] *npl Econ* (*abbr* **special drawing rights**) DTS *mpl*

SE (*written abbr* **south-east**) S-E

SEA [ˌesiːˈeɪ] *n EU* (*abbr* **Single European Act**) AUE *m*

SEAQ [ˌesiːˌeɪˈkjuː] *n* (*abbr* **Stock Exchange Automated Quotations System**) système *m* de cotation automatisé

SEATO [ˈsiːtəʊ] *n Formerly* (*abbr* **Southeast Asia Treaty Organization**) OTASE *f*

SEC [ˌesiːˈsiː] *n* (*abbr* **Securities and Exchange Commission**) = commission américaine des opérations de Bourse, ≃ COB *f*

sec [sek] *n Fam* (*abbr* **second**) seconde❑ *f*, instant❑ *m*; **in a sec!** une seconde!; **I'll only be a sec** j'en ai pour une seconde

SECAM [ˈsiːkæm] *n TV* (*abbr* **séquentiel couleur à mémoire**) Secam *m*

secy (*written abbr* **secretary**) secr

semi [ˈsemɪ] *n Fam* (**a**) *Br* (*abbr* **semi-detached house**) maison *f* jumelée❑ (**b**) (*abbr* **semifinal**) demi-finale❑ *f* (**c**) *Am, Austr & NZ* (*abbr* **semitrailer**) semi *m*

SEN [ˌesiːˈen] *n* (*abbr* **State Enrolled Nurse**) aide-soignant(e) *m,f* diplômé(e)

Sen. (*written abbr* **Senator**) sénateur *m*

sen. (*written abbr* **senior**) (*in rank*) (de grade) supérieur; **John Brown sen.** John Brown père

Sept. (*written abbr* **September**) sept

SERPS [sɜːps] *n Br* (*abbr* **State Earnings-Related Pension Scheme**) = régime de retraite minimal en Grande-Bretagne

sesh [seʃ] *n Br Fam* (*abbr* **session**) **to have a drinking sesh** se pinter; **we had a bit of a sesh last night** on s'en est donné hier soir

SET[1] [ˌesiːˈtiː] *n Tel* (*abbr* **satellite experimental terminal**) SET *m*

SET[2]® *n Comput* (*written abbr* **secure electronic transaction**) SET *f*

SF [ˌesˈef] (*abbr* **science fiction**) **1** *n* SF *f*
2 *adj* de SF

SFA [ˌesefˈeɪ] *n* (*abbr* **Scottish Football Association**) Fédération *f* écossaise de football

SFO [ˌesefˈəʊ] *n* (*abbr* **Serious Fraud Office**) = service britannique de la répression des fraudes

sfx [ˌesefˈeks] *n Cin* (*abbr* **special effects**) effets *mpl* spéciaux

SG [ˌesˈdʒiː] *n* (*abbr* **Surgeon General**) (**a**) *Mil* médecin-général *m* (**b**) *Am Admin* chef *m* des services de santé

SGML [ˌesdʒiːˌemˈel] *n Comput* (*abbr* **Standard Generated Mark-up Language**) SGML *m*

Sgt (*written abbr* **sergeant**) Sgt

Shaef [ʃeɪf] *n* (*abbr* **Supreme Headquarters, Allied Expeditionary Force, World War II**) SHAEF *m*, Commandement *m* suprême des forces expéditionnaires alliées

SHAPE [ʃeɪp] *n* (*abbr* **Supreme Headquarters Allied Powers Europe**) SHAPE *m*

s/he (*written abbr* **she/he**) il ou elle

SHO [ˌeseɪtʃˈəʊ] *n Br Med* (*abbr* **Senior House Officer**) ≃ interne *mf* (*de rang supérieur au "house officer"*)

SI [ˌesˈaɪ] *n* (**a**) (*abbr* **Système International**) SI *m* (**b**) (*in golf*) (*abbr* **stroke index**) stroke index *m*, coefficient *m* de difficulté
►► ***SI unit*** unité *f* SI

SIB [ˌesaɪˈbiː] *n* (*abbr* **Securities and Investments Board**) = commission britannique des opérations de Bourse, ≃ COB *f*

SIDS [sɪdz] *n Med* (*abbr* **sudden infant death syndrome**) mort *f* subite du nourrisson

SIG [ˌesaɪˈdʒiː] *n Am* (*abbr* **special interest group**) groupe *m* d'intérêt

SIM [sɪm] *n* (*abbr* **subscriber identity module**)
►► ***SIM card*** (*in mobile phone*) carte *f* SIM

SIMM [sɪm] *n Comput* (*abbr* **single in-line memory module**) SIMM *m*

simp [sɪmp] *n Am Fam Pej* (*abbr* **simpleton**) andouille *f*, crétin(e) *m,f*

sis [sɪs] *n Fam* (*abbr* **sister**) frangine *f*, sœurette *f*

SK *Can* (*written abbr* **Saskatchewan**) Saskatchewan *m*

skin [skɪn] *n Fam* (*abbr* **skinhead**) skinhead❑ *mf*, skin *mf*

SLAPP [slæp] *n Am* (*abbr* **strategic lawsuit against public participation**) = procès intenté par une société à des activistes, visant à intimider ces derniers et stopper leur action

SLIP [slɪp] *n Comput* (*abbr* **serial line Internet protocol**) protocole *m* SLIP

slo-mo [ˈsləʊməʊ] *adj Fam* (*abbr* **slow-motion**) au ralenti❑

SLR [ˌeselˈɑː(r)] *n Phot* (*abbr* **single-lens reflex**) reflex *m* à un objectif

SM [ˌesˈem] *n Mil* (*abbr* **sergeant major**) sergent-chef *m*

s/m [ˌesˈem] *n* (*abbr* **sadomasochism**) sadomasochisme *m*

SME [ˌesemˈiː] *n* (*abbr* **small and medium-sized enterprise**) PME *f*

SMS [ˌesemˈes] *n Tel* (*abbr* **short message service**) service *m* SMS

SMSA [ˌesemˌesˈeɪ] *n Am* (*abbr* **Standard Metropolitan Statistical Area**) = zone urbaine utilisée comme base d'études statistiques

SMTP [ˌesemˌtiːˈpiː] *n Comput* (*abbr* **Simple Mail Transfer Protocol**) protocole *m* SMTP

SNO [ˌesenˈəʊ] *n* (**a**) *Formerly* (*abbr* **Scottish National Orchestra**) = ancien nom de l'orchestre national d'Écosse (**b**) (*abbr* **Scottish National Opera**) = compagnie nationale écossaise d'opéra

SNP [ˌesenˈpiː] *n* (*abbr* **Scottish National Party**) = parti indépendantiste écossais fondé en 1934

Snr (*written abbr* **Senior**) **Ralph Todd Snr** Ralph Todd père

SO (*written abbr* **standing order**) prélèvement *m* (bancaire) automatique

So. (**a**) (*written abbr* **South**) S (**b**) (*written abbr* **Southern**) S

SOAS [ˈsəʊæs] *n* (*abbr* **School of Oriental and African Studies**) = école des études orientales et africaines de Londres

sob, SOB [ˌesəʊˈbiː] *n Am very Fam* (*abbr* **son of a bitch**) salaud *m*, fils *m* de pute

Soc [sɒk] *n* (*abbr* **Society**) ≃ club *m* (*abréviation utilisée dans la langue parlée notamment par les étudiants pour désigner les différents clubs universitaires*)

.soc *Comput* (*written abbr* **social**) (*in newsgroups*) = abréviation désignant les forums de discussion qui ont pour thème les faits de société

SOFFEX [ˈsɒfeks] *n St Exch* (*abbr* **Swiss Options and Financial Futures Exchange**) SOFFEX *f* (*Bourse suisse pour le négoce des options et des contrats à terme*)

SOGAT [ˈsəʊgæt] *n Br* (*abbr* **Society of Graphical and Allied Trades**) = syndicat britannique des métiers du graphisme

Som. (*written abbr* **Somerset**) Somerset *m*

SOP [ˌesəʊˈpiː] *n* (*abbr* **standard operating procedure**) = marche à suivre normale

soph [sɒf] *n Am Fam* (*abbr* **sophomore**) étudiant(e) *m,f* de deuxième année❑

SOR (*written abbr* **sale or return**) **to buy sth on an SOR basis** acheter qch à condition

SOS [ˌesəʊˈes] *n* (*abbr* **save our souls**) SOS *m*; **to send out an SOS** lancer un SOS; **we received an SOS call** *or* **message** nous avons reçu un SOS; *Fig* **relief organizations are sending out an SOS for food and clothing** les organisations d'aide demandent d'urgence de la nourriture et des vêtements

SP [ˌesˈpiː] *n* (*abbr* **starting price**) *Horseracing* cote *f* au départ; *Br Fam Fig* **to give sb the SP (on)** mettre qn au parfum (à propos de *ou* concernant)

spag bol [ˌspægˈbɒl] *n Br Fam* (*abbr* **spaghetti bolognese**) spaghettis *mpl* (à la) bolognaise❑

SPCA [ˌespiːˌsiːˈeɪ] *n Am* (*abbr* **Society for the Prevention of Cruelty to Animals**) = société américaine protectrice des animaux, ≃ SPA *f*

SPCC [ˌespiːˌsiːˈsiː] *n Am* (*abbr* **Society for the Prevention of Cruelty to Children**) = société américaine pour la protection de l'enfance

spec [spek] *n* (*abbr* **specification**) spécifications *fpl*

specs [speks] *npl Fam* (*abbr* **spectacles**) carreaux *mpl*, hublots *mpl*

SPF [ˌespiːˈef] *n* (*abbr* **sun protection factor**) indice *m* de protection solaire

SPUC [spʌk] *n* (*abbr* **Society for the Protection of the Unborn Child**) = ligue américaine contre l'avortement

Sq. (*written abbr* **Square**) (*in addresses*) ≃ Place

sq. ft. (*written abbr* **square foot/feet**) pied(s) carré(s)

SQL [ˌeskjuːˈel] *n Comput* (*abbr* **structured query language**) SQL *m*
►► ***SQL engine*** processeur *m* SQL

Sqn. Ldr. *Br Mil* (*written abbr* **Squadron Leader**) ≃ commandant *m*, *Belg & Can* ≃ major *m*

Sr (**a**) (*written abbr* **senior**) **Ralph Todd Sr** Ralph Todd père (**b**) (*written abbr* **sister**) sœur *f*

SRAM [ˈesræm] *n Comput* (*abbr* **static random access memory**) mémoire *f* vive statique

SRC [ˌesɑːˈsiː] *n* (**a**) *Br* (*abbr* **students' representative council**) = comité étudiant (**b**) (*abbr* **Science Research Council**) = conseil de la recherche scientifique

SRN [ˌesɑːˈren] *n Br* (*abbr* **State Registered Nurse**) infirmier(ère) *m,f* diplômé(e) (*remplacé en 1992 par "Registered Nurse"*)

SRO[1] [ˌesɑːˈrəʊ] *Br St Exch* (*abbr* **self-regulatory organization**) organisme *m* autoréglementé *ou* autonome

SRO[2] *Am* (*written abbr* **single room occupancy**) = tarif pour une seule personne (*d'une chambre d'hôtel*)

SRU [ˌesɑːˈjuː] *n* (*abbr* **Scottish Rugby Union**) = association écossaise de rugby à quinze

SRV [ˌesɑːˈviː] *n* (*abbr* **space rescue vehicle**) véhicule *m* spatial de sauvetage

SS [ˌesˈes] *n* (**a**) *Naut* (*abbr* **steamship**) = initiales précédant le nom des navires de la marine marchande; **the SS Norfolk** le Norfolk (**b**) (*abbr* **Schutzstaffel**) **the SS** les SS; **an SS officer** un officier SS

SSA [ˌesesˈeɪ] *n Am* (*abbr* **Social Security Administration**) ≃ Sécurité *f* sociale

SSAE [ˌesesˌeɪˈiː] *n Am* (*abbr* **stamped self-addressed envelope**) enveloppe *f* timbrée (*portant l'adresse à laquelle elle doit être renvoyée*); **please return the form with an SSAE** veuillez renvoyer le formulaire ainsi qu'une enveloppe timbrée à votre adresse

SSE (*written abbr* **south-south-east**) S-SE

SSL [ˌesesˈel] *n Comput* (*abbr* **secure sockets layer**) protocole *m* SSL

SSN [ˌesesˈen] *n Am* (*abbr* **social security number**) numéro *m* de Sécurité sociale

SSP [ˌesesˈpiː] *n* (*abbr* **statutory sick pay**) = indemnité de maladie versée par l'employeur

SSRI [ˌesesˌɑːˈraɪ] *n Pharm* (*abbr* **Selective Serotonin Re-uptake Inhibitor**) ISRS *m*, inhibiteur *m* sélectif de recapture de la sérotonine

SSSI [ˌesesˌesˈaɪ, ˌtrɪpəlesˈaɪ] *n Br* (*abbr* **Site of Special Scientific Interest**) = en Grande-Bretagne, site déclaré d'intérêt scientifique

SST [ˌeses'tiː] *n* (*abbr* **supersonic transport**) transport *m* supersonique

SSW (*written abbr* **south-south-west**) S-SO, S-SW

ST (*written abbr* **Standard Time**) heure *f* légale

St (**a**) (*written abbr* **saint**) St, Ste (**b**) (*written abbr* **street**) rue *f*

st (*written abbr* **stone**) (*unit of weight*) ≃ 6 kg

stache [stæʃ] *n Am Fam* (*abbr* **mustache**) bacchantes *fpl*, moustagache *f*

Staffs (*written abbr* **Staffordshire**) Staffordshire *m*

START [stɑːt] *n* (*abbr* **Strategic Arms Reduction Talks**) négociations *fpl* START

STD [ˌestiː'diː] *n* (**a**) *Br Tel* (*abbr* **subscriber trunk dialling**) automatique *m* (interurbain) (**b**) (*abbr* **sexually transmitted disease**) MST *f*

►► ***STD code*** indicatif *m* de zone

stew [stjuː] *n Am Fam* (*abbr* **stewardess**) hôtesse *f* de l'air ❑

St. Ex. (*written abbr* **stock exchange**) Bourse *f*

stg (*written abbr* **sterling**) sterling *inv*

STOL [stɒl] *n* (*abbr* **short takeoff and landing**) (*system*) décollage *m* et atterrissage *m* courts; (*aircraft*) ADAC *m*

STUC [ˌestiːjuː'siː] *n* (*abbr* **Scottish Trades Union Congress**) = section écossaise de la confédération des syndicats britanniques

STV [ˌestiː'viː] *n* (**a**) *Pol* (*abbr* **single transferable vote**) scrutin *m* uninominal préférentiel avec report de voix (**b**) *Am* (*abbr* **subscription television**) chaînes *fpl* à péage

Sun. (*written abbr* **Sunday**) dim.

Supt. (*written abbr* **superintendent**) ≃ commissaire *m* (de police)

SVGA [ˌesviːˌdʒiː'eɪ] *n Comput* (*abbr* **super video graphics array**) SVGA *m*

►► ***SVGA monitor*** moniteur *m* SVGA

SVQ [ˌesviː'kjuː] *n* (*abbr* **Scottish Vocational Qualification**) = diplôme de formation professionnelle sur le lieu de travail délivré en Écosse

SW (**a**) (*written abbr* **short wave**) OC (**b**) (*written abbr* **south-west**) S-O

SWALK [swɔːk] *n Fam* (*abbr* **sealed with a loving kiss**) ≃ doux baisers (*écrit sur une enveloppe contenant une lettre d'amour*)

SWAPO ['swɑːpəʊ] *n* (*abbr* **South West Africa People's Organization**) SWAPO *f*

SWOT [swɒt] *n Mktg* (*abbr* **strengths, weaknesses, opportunities, threats**) forces, faiblesses, opportunités et menaces *fpl*

►► ***SWOT analysis*** analyse *f* des forces, faiblesses, opportunités et menaces

sync, synch [sɪŋk] *n Fam* (*abbr* **synchronization**) synchronisation ❑ *f*; **to be in/out of sync** être/ne pas être synchro; **the engine is a bit out of sync** le moteur ne tourne pas très rond ❑

►► ***sync pulse*** *TV* impulsion *f* de synchronisation; *Cin* signal *m* de synchronisation

SYSOP ['sɪsɒp] *n Comput* (*abbr* **Systems Operator**) sysop *m*, opérateur *m* système

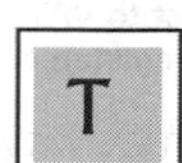

TA [ˌtiː'eɪ] *n* (**a**) *Br Mil* (*abbr* **Territorial Army**) armée *f* territoriale (**b**) *Am & Can Univ* (*abbr* **teaching assistant**) = étudiant de deuxième cycle qui assure quelques heures de cours en échange d'une bourse d'études

TAB [tæb] *n Med* (*abbr* **typhoid-paratyphoid A and B**) (vaccin *m*) TAB *m*; **he's had a TAB injection** on lui a fait le TAB

tache [tæʃ] *n Fam* (*abbr* **moustache**) bacchantes *fpl*

TARGET ['tɑːgɪt] *n Fin* (*abbr* **Trans-European Automated Real-Time Gross Settlement Transfer System**) TARGET *m*

TASS [tæs] *n Formerly* (*abbr* **Telegraphic Agency of the Soviet Union**) TASS *f*

TAT [ˌtiːeɪ'tiː] *n Mktg* (*abbr* **thematic apperception test**) TAT *m*

TB [ˌtiː'biː] *n* (*abbr* **tuberculosis**) tuberculose *f*

tbs., tbsp. (*written abbr* **tablespoon(ful)**) cs

TCP® [ˌtiːsiː'piː] *n Br* (*abbr* **trichlorophonoxyacetic acid**) = désinfectant utilisé pour nettoyer des petites plaies ou pour se gargariser

TCP/IP [ˌtiːsiː'piːˌaɪ'piː] *n Comput* (*abbr* **transmission control protocol/Internet protocol**) TCP-IP

TD [ˌtiː'diː] *n* (**a**) (*abbr* **Treasury Department**) ministère *m* des Finances (**b**) *Ir Pol* (*abbr* **Teachta Dála**) ≃ député(e) *m,f* (**c**) *Sport* (*abbr* **touchdown**) essai *m*

TEC [tek] *n* (*abbr* **Training and Enterprise Council**) = centre d'emploi et de formation

tech [tek] *n Br Fam Sch* (*abbr* **technical college**) ≃ IUT ❑ *m*

TEFL ['tefəl] *n* (*abbr* **Teaching (of) English as a Foreign Language**) enseignement *m* de l'anglais langue étrangère

tel. (*written abbr* **telephone**) tél

telco ['telkəʊ] *n* (*abbr* **telecommunications company**) société *f* de télécommunications

telecom ['telɪkɒm] *n* (*UNCOUNT*) (*abbr* **telecommunications**) télécoms *fpl*

temp [temp] **1** *n* (*abbr* **temporary employee**) intérimaire *mf*

2 *adj* **to do temp work** faire de l'intérim

3 *vi* faire de l'intérim

temp. (*written abbr* **temperature**) temp

Ter. *Br* (*written abbr* **terrace**) = rangée de maisons attenantes et identiques

Terr. (*written abbr* **terrace**) = rangée de maisons attenantes et identiques

TESL ['tesəl] *n* (*abbr* **Teaching (of) English as a Second Language**) enseignement *m* de l'anglais langue seconde

TESOL ['tiːsɒl] *n* (*abbr* **Teaching English to Speakers of Other Languages**) enseignement *m* de l'anglais aux étrangers *ou* comme langue étrangère

TESSA ['tesə] *n* (*abbr* **tax-exempt special savings account**) = en Grande-Bretagne, plan d'épargne exonéré d'impôt

Tex (*written abbr* **Texas**) Texas *m*

TFT [ˌtiːef'tiː] *n Electron* (*abbr* **thin film transistor**) transistor *m* en couche mince

TGIF [ˌtiːdʒiːˌaɪ'ef] *exclam Fam* (*abbr* **thank God it's Friday!**) encore une semaine de tirée!

TGWU [ˌtiːdʒiːˌdʌbəljuː'juː] *n Ind* (*abbr* **Transport and General Workers' Union**) = le plus grand syndicat interprofessionnel britannique

thou [θaʊ] (*pl* **inv** *or* **thous**) *n* (**a**) *Fam* (*abbr* **thousand**) mille ❑ *m inv* (**b**) (*abbr* **thousandth of an inch**) millième *m* de pouce

Thur (*written abbr* **Thursday**) jeu

Thurs (*written abbr* **Thursday**) jeu

TIF [ˌtiːaɪ'ef] *n Rail* (*abbr* **transport international ferroviaire**) TIF *m*

TIFF [tɪf] *n Comput* (*abbr* **Tagged Image File Format**) format *m* TIFF

TIG welding [tɪg-] *n Tech* (*abbr* **tungsten-electrode inert gas**) soudure *f* à l'arc au tungstène

TIR [ˌtiːaɪ'ɑː(r)] *n Transp* (*abbr* **transports internationaux routiers**) TIR *m*

TKO [ˌtiːkeɪ'əʊ] *n Boxing* (*abbr* **technical knockout**) K-O *m* technique

TLC [ˌtiːel'siː] *n Fam* (*abbr* **tender loving care**) affection ❑ *f*; **she just needs a bit of TLC** elle a juste besoin d'un peu d'affection

TLS [ˌtiːel'es] *n Press* (*abbr* **Times Literary Supplement**) = supplément littéraire du 'Times'

TM[1] [ˌtiː'em] *n* (*abbr* **transcendental meditation**) MT *f*

TM[2] (*written abbr* **trademark**) MD

TN (*written abbr* **Tennessee**) Tennessee *m*

TNT [ˌtiːen'tiː] *n Chem* (*abbr* **trinitrotoluene**) TNT *m*

TOPS [tɒps] *n Br* (*abbr* **Training Opportunities Scheme**) = programme du recyclage professionnel en Grande-Bretagne

tote [təʊt] *n Br Horseracing* (*abbr* **totalizator**) pari *m* mutuel

tpi *Comput* (*written abbr* **tracks per inch**) pistes *fpl* par pouce

TQC [ˌtiːkjuː'siː] *n* (*abbr* **total quality control**) QG *f*

TQM [ˌtiːkjuː'em] *n* (*abbr* **total quality management**) gestion *f* de la QG

TRAM [træm] *n Comput* (*abbr* **transputer module**) module *m* de transputer

trans. (*written abbr* **translated, translation**) trad.

treas. (*written abbr* **treasurer**) trés

trig [trɪg] *n Fam* (*abbr* **trigonometry**) trigo *f*

t-RNA [ˌtiːɑːˌren'eɪ] *n* (*abbr* **transfer RNA**) ARN *m* de transfert

TRO [ˌtiːɑː'rəʊ] *n Law* (*abbr* **temporary restraining order**) injonction *f* du tribunal

Trot [trɒt] *n Fam Pej Pol* (*abbr* **Trotskyist**) trotskiste ❑ *mf*

tsp. (*written abbr* **teaspoon(ful)**) cc

TSS [ˌtiːes'es] *n Med* (*abbr* **toxic shock syndrome**) SCT *m*

TT [ˌtiː'tiː] **1** *adj* (*abbr* **teetotal**) qui ne boit jamais d'alcool

2 *n Sport* (*abbr* **Tourist Trophy**) **the TT races** = courses de moto sur l'île de Man

TTL [ˌtiːtiː'el] *adj Phot* (*abbr* **through the lens**)

►► ***TTL flash*** flash *m* TTL; ***TTL measurement*** mesure *f* TTL *ou* à travers l'objectif

TTP [ˌtiːtiː'piː] *n Comput* (*abbr* **trusted third party**) (*for Internet transactions*) TPC *f*

TU [ˌtiː'juː] *n Ind* (*abbr* **trade union**) syndicat *m*

TUC [ˌtiːjuː'siː] *n Br Ind* (*abbr* **Trades Union Congress**) = confédération des syndicats britanniques; **the TUC annual conference** le congrès annuel des syndicats

Tue., Tues. (*written abbr* **Tuesday**) mar

tux [tʌks] *n Fam* (*abbr* **tuxedo**) smoking *m*

TV[1] [ˌtiː'viː] (*abbr* **television**) **1** *n* TV *f*

2 *comp* (*programme, set*) de télé; (*star*) de la télé

►► ***TV advertisement*** publicité *f* télévisée; ***TV advertising*** publicité *f* télévisée; ***TV campaign*** campagne *f* télévisuelle; ***TV commercial*** spot *m*; ***TV dinner*** plateau-repas *m*, repas *m* tout prêt *ou* prêt à consommer (*que l'on mange devant la télé*); ***TV movie*** téléfilm *m*; *Mktg* ***TV viewing panel*** panel *m* de téléspectateurs

TV[2] *n Fam* (*abbr* **transvestite**) travelo *m*

TVM [ˌtiːviː'em] *n* (*abbr* **television movie**) téléfilm *m*

TVP [ˌtiːviː'piː] *n Culin* (*abbr* **textured vegetable protein**) protéine *f* végétale texturée

TX (*written abbr* **Texas**) Texas *m*

U[1] [juː] *n Cin* (*abbr* **universal**) = désigne un film tous publics en Grande-Bretagne

U[2] (*written abbr* **unionist**) unioniste

UAE [ˌjuːeɪ'iː] *n* (*abbr* **United Arab Emirates**) EAU *mpl*

UAR [ˌjuːeɪ'ɑː(r)] *n* (*abbr* **United Arab Republic**) RAU *f*

UAW [ˌjuːeɪ'dʌbəljuː] *n Am* (*abbr* **United Automobile Workers**) = syndicat américain de l'industrie automobile

UB40 [ˌjuːbiː'fɔːtɪ] *n Br Formerly* (*abbr* **unemployment benefit form 40** (*card*) = carte de pointage pour bénéficier de l'allocation de chômage; *Fam (person)* chômeur(euse) *m,f*

UBR [ˌjuːbiːˈɑː(r)] *n Fin (abbr* **uniform business rate**) = taxe assise sur la valeur des locaux commerciaux, ≃ taxe *f* professionnelle

UCAS [ˈjuːkæs] *n Br (abbr* **University and College Admissions Service**) = organisme centralisant les demandes d'inscription dans les universités britanniques

UCATT [ˈjuːkæt] *n Br (abbr* **Union of Construction, Allied Trades and Technicians**) = syndicat britannique des employés du bâtiment

UCCA [ˈʌkə] *n Br Formerly (abbr* **Universities Central Council on Admissions**) = organisme centralisant les demandes d'inscription dans les universités britanniques

UCITS [ˌjuːsiːaɪˌtiːˈes] *n Fin (abbr* **undertakings for collective investment in transferables**) OPCVM *m*

UCL [ˌjuːsiːˈel] *n Br (abbr* **University College, London**) = l'une des facultés de l'Université de Londres

UCLA [ˈʌklə] *n Am (abbr* **University of California at Los Angeles**) UCLA *f*, = partie de l'université de Californie située à Los Angeles, célèbre pour la qualité de ses équipes de sport

UCW [ˌjuːsiːˈdʌbəljuː] *n Br (abbr* **Union of Communication Workers**) = syndicat britannique des communications

UDA [ˌjuːdiːˈeɪ] *n (abbr* **Ulster Defence Association**) = organisation paramilitaire protestante d'Irlande du Nord, déclarée hors la loi en 1992

UDC [ˌjuːdiːˈsiː] *n Br Admin (abbr* **Urban District Council**) = conseil d'une communauté urbaine

UDI [ˌjuːdiːˈaɪ] *n (abbr* **Unilateral Declaration of Independence**) = déclaration unilatérale d'indépendance

UDM [ˌjuːdiːˈem] *n Br (abbr* **Union of Democratic Mineworkers**) = syndicat britannique de mineurs

UDR [ˌjuːdiːˈɑː(r)] *n Br Formerly (abbr* **Ulster Defence Regiment**) = ancien régiment de réservistes d'Irlande du Nord qui fait aujourd'hui partie du "Royal Irish Regiment"

UEFA [juːˈeɪfə] *n (abbr* **Union of European Football Associations**) UEFA *f*

UFC [ˌjuːefˈsiː] *n Br (abbr* **Universities Funding Council**) = organisme répartissant les crédits entre les universités en Grande-Bretagne

UFO [ˌjuːefˈəʊ, ˈjuːfəʊ] *n (abbr* **unidentified flying object**) OVNI *m*, ovni *m*

UGC [ˌjuːdʒiːˈsiː] *n Br (abbr* **University Grants Committee**) = organisme répartissant les crédits entre les universités en Grande-Bretagne

UHF [ˌjuːeɪtʃˈef] *n (abbr* **ultrahigh frequency**) UHF *f*

UHT [ˌjuːeɪtʃˈtiː] *adj (abbr* **ultra heat treated**) UHT

UK [ˌjuːˈkeɪ] *(abbr* **United Kingdom**) **1** *n* Royaume-Uni *m*; **in the UK** au Royaume-Uni

2 *comp* du Royaume-Uni

UKAEA [ˌjuːkeɪˌeɪiːˈeɪ] *n Br (abbr* **United Kingdom Atomic Energy Authority**) = commissariat britannique à l'énergie atomique

uke [juːk] *n Fam (abbr* **ukulele**) guitare *f* hawaïenne ❑, ukulélé ❑ *m*

ult *Old-fashioned (written abbr* **ultimo**) du mois dernier

UMIST [ˈjuːmɪst] *n Br (abbr* **University of Manchester Institute of Science and Technology**) = institut de science et de technologie de l'université de Manchester, en Grande-Bretagne

UMW [ˌjuːemˈdʌbəljuː] *n Am (abbr* **United Mineworkers of America**) = syndicat américain de mineurs

UN [ˌjuːˈen] *(abbr* **United Nations**) **1** *n* **the UN** l'ONU *f*, l'Onu *f*

2 *comp* de l'ONU

►► ***UN peacekeeping forces*** les casques *mpl* bleus; ***UN resolution*** résolution *f* de l'ONU; ***the UN security council*** le Conseil de sécurité de l'ONU

UNCSTD [ˌjuːensiːˌestiːˈdiː] *n (abbr* **United Nations Conference on Science and Technology for Development**) CSTD *f*

UNCTAD [ˈʌŋktæd] *n (abbr* **United Nations Conference on Trade and Development**) CNUCED *f*

undies [ˈʌndɪz] *npl Fam (abbr* **underwear**) sous-vêtements *mpl* féminins

UNEF [ˈjuːnef] *n (abbr* **United Nations Emergency Force**) FUNU *f*

UNESCO [juːˈneskəʊ] *n (abbr* **United Nations Educational, Scientific and Cultural Organization**) Unesco *f*

UNHCR [ˌjuːenˌeɪtʃsiːˈɑː(r)] *n (abbr* **United Nations High Commission for Refugees**) HCR *m*

uni [ˈjuːnɪ] *n Fam* (**a**) *Br (abbr* **university**) fac *f*, *Suisse* Uni *f*; **he's doing law at uni** il fait une fac de droit (**b**) *Am (abbr* **uniform**) uniforme ❑ *m*

UNICEF [ˈjuːnɪsef] *(abbr* **United Nations International Children's Emergency Fund**) *n* Unicef *m*

UNIDO [juːˈniːdəʊ] *n (abbr* **United Nations Industrial Development Organization**) ONUDI *f*

Univ. *(written abbr* **university**) Univ.

UNIX® [ˈjuːnɪks] *n Comput (abbr* **Uniplexed Information and Computing System**) UNIX *m*

UNO [ˈjuːnəʊ, ˌjuːenˈəʊ] *n (abbr* **United Nations Organization**) ONU *f*

Unprofor [ˈʌnprəʊfɔː(r)] *n (abbr* **United Nations Protection Force**) FORPRONU *f*

UP [ˌjuːˈpiː] *n (abbr* **unit price**) PU *m*

UPS [ˌjuːpiːˈes] *n Comput (abbr* **uninterruptible power supply**) onduleur *m*

URL [ˌjuːɑːˈrel] *n Comput (abbr* **uniform resource locator**) (adresse *f*) URL *m*

US [ˌjuːˈes] *(abbr* **United States**) **1** *n* **the US** les USA *mpl*, les États-Unis *mpl*; **in the US** aux USA, aux États-Unis

2 *comp* des États-Unis, américain

USA [ˌjuːesˈeɪ] *n* (**a**) *(abbr* **United States of America**) **the USA** les USA *mpl*, les États-Unis *mpl*; **in the USA** aux USA, aux États-Unis (**b**) *(abbr* **United States Army**) = armée des États-Unis

USAF [ˌjuːesˌeɪˈef] *n (abbr* **United States Air Force**) = armée de l'air des États-Unis

USAID [ˌjuːesˌeɪaɪˈdiː] *n (abbr* **United States Agency for International Development**) = agence américaine d'aide au développement

USB [ˌjuːesˈbiː] *n Comput (abbr* **universal serial bus**) norme *f* USB, port *m* série universel

USCG [ˌjuːesˌsiːˈdʒiː] *n (abbr* **United States Coast Guard**) = service de surveillance côtière américain

USDA [ˌjuːesˌdiːˈeɪ] *n (abbr* **United States Department of Agriculture**) = ministère américain de l'Agriculture

USDAW [ˈʌzdɔː] *n (abbr* **Union of Shop, Distributive and Allied Workers**) = syndicat britannique des personnels de la distribution

USDI [ˌjuːesˌdiːˈaɪ] *n (abbr* **United States Department of the Interior**) = ministère américain de l'Intérieur

USES [ˌjuːesˌiːˈes] *n (abbr* **United States Employment Service**) = services américains de l'emploi

USIA [ˌjuːesˌaɪˈeɪ] *n (abbr* **United States Information Agency**) = agence américaine de renseignements

USM [ˌjuːesˈem] *n* (**a**) *Am (abbr* **United States Mail**) ≃ la Poste *(aux États-Unis)* (**b**) *Am (abbr* **United States Mint**) ≃ la Monnaie *(aux États-Unis)* (**c**) *St Exch (abbr* **unlisted securities market**) marché *m* hors cote, second marché *m*

USMC [ˌjuːesˌemˈsiː] *n (abbr* **United States Marine Corps**) = corps des marines américains

USN [ˌjuːesˈen] *n (abbr* **United States Navy**) = marine de guerre des États-Unis

USO [ˌjuːesˈəʊ] *n (abbr* **United Service Organization**) = organisme organisant des activités culturelles pour les forces armées américaines

USP [ˌjuːesˈpiː] *n Mktg (abbr* **unique selling point** *or* **proposition**) proposition *f* unique de vente

USPHS [ˌjuːesˌpiːeɪtʃˈes] *n (abbr* **United States Public Health Service**) = direction américaine des Affaires sanitaires et sociales

USS [ˌjuːesˈes] *n (abbr* **United States Ship**) = initiales précédant le nom des navires américains; **the USS Washington** le Washington

USSR [ˌjuːesˌesˈɑː(r)] *n Formerly (abbr* **Union of Soviet Socialist Republics**) **the USSR** l'URSS *f*; **in the USSR** en URSS

usu. *(written abbr* **usually**) d'habitude

USW [ˌjuːesˈdʌbəljuː] *n Rad* (**a**) *(abbr* **ultrashort wave**) OUC *f* (**b**) *(abbr* **ultrasonic wave**) onde *f* ultrasonore

UT *(written abbr* **Utah**) Utah *m*

UV [ˌjuːˈviː] *n (abbr* **ultra-violet**) UV *m*

UV-A, UVA [ˌjuːviːˈeɪ] *n (abbr* **ultra-violet-A**) UVA *m*

UV-B, UVB [ˌjuːviːˈbiː] *n (abbr* **ultra-violet-B**) UVB *m*

UVF [ˌjuːviːˈef] *n (abbr* **Ulster Volunteer Force**) = organisation paramilitaire déclarée hors la loi, favorable au maintien de l'Irlande du Nord au sein du Royaume-Uni

UWIST [ˈjuːwɪst] *n Br (abbr* **University of Wales Institute of Science and Technology**) = institut de science et de technologie de l'université du pays de Galles

V *(written abbr* **volt**) V

v (**a**) *(written abbr* **velocity**) v (**b**) *(written abbr* **verb**) v (**c**) *(written abbr* **verse**) v (**d**) *(written abbr* **versus**) contre (**e**) *(written abbr* **vide**) v

VA¹ [ˌviːˈeɪ] *n Am (abbr* **Veterans Administration**) Bureau *m* des anciens combattants

VA² *(written abbr* **Virginia**) Virginie *f*

vac [væk] *n Br Fam (abbr* **vacation**) vacances ❑ *fpl*; **the Easter vac** les vacances de Pâques

VAD [ˌviːeɪˈdiː] *n (abbr* **Voluntary Aid Detachment**) = infirmières britanniques volontaires pendant la Première Guerre mondiale

vag [veɪg] *n Am Fam (abbr* **vagrant**) clodo *mf*

VAN [væn] *n Comput (abbr* **value-added network**) réseau *m* à valeur ajoutée

V and A [ˌviːənˈeɪ] *n Br (abbr* **Victoria and Albert Museum**) = grand musée londonien des arts décoratifs

VAT [væt, ˌviːeɪˈtiː] *n Br Fin (abbr* **value added tax**) TVA *f*; **exclusive of** *or* **excluding VAT** hors TVA; **subject to VAT** soumis à la TVA; **to be VAT registered** être assujetti à la TVA

►► ***VAT credit*** crédit *m* de TVA; ***VAT man*** = inspecteur *m* de la TVA; ***VAT rate*** taux *m* de TVA; ***VAT registration number*** code *m* assujetti TVA; ***VAT return*** déclaration *f* de TVA; ***VAT statement*** état *m* TVA

VC [ˌviːˈsiː] *n* (**a**) *Br Mil (abbr* **Victoria Cross**) Victoria Cross *f* (**b**) *Br Univ (abbr* **vice-chancellor**) ≃ président *m* d'université (**c**) *(abbr* **vice-chairman**) VP *m* (**d**) *Am Hist (abbr* **Vietcong**) Viêt-cong *mf*

vCJD [ˌviːsiːˌdʒeɪˈdiː] *n Med (abbr* **new-variant Creutzfeldt-Jakob disease**) vMCJ *m*

VCR [ˌvi:si:'ɑ:(r)] *n* (*abbr* **video cassette recorder**) magnétoscope *m*

VCT [ˌvi:si:'ti:] *n Fin* (*abbr* **venture capital trust**) FCPR *m*

VD [ˌvi:'di:] *n* (*UNCOUNT*) (*abbr* **venereal disease**) MST *f*

►► ***VD clinic*** centre *m* de traitement des maladies vénériennes

VDT [ˌvi:di:'ti:] *n Comput* (*abbr* **visual display terminal**) moniteur *m*

VDU [ˌvi:di:'ju:] *n Comput* (*abbr* **visual display unit**) moniteur *m*

►► *Comput* ***VDU operator*** personne *f* travaillant sur écran

VED [ˌvi:i:'di:] *n* (*abbr* **vehicle excise duty**) taxe *f*, impôt *m* direct

VE day [ˌvi:'i:-] *n* (*abbr* **Victory in Europe Day**) = jour de l'armistice du 8 mai 1945

veggie ['vedʒɪ] *Fam* (*abbr* **vegetarian**) **1** *n* végétarien(enne) ❑ *m,f*

2 *adj* végétarien ❑

vet[1] [vet] *n* (*abbr* **veterinary surgeon, veterinary**) vétérinaire *mf*

vet[2] *Am Fam* (*abbr* **veteran**) **1** *n* ancien combattant ❑ *m*, vétéran ❑ *m*

2 *adj* (*association, rally*) d'anciens combattants ❑

VFD [ˌvi:ef'di:] *n Am* (*abbr* **voluntary fire department**) = pompiers bénévoles aux États-Unis

VG (*written abbr* **very good**) TB

VGA [ˌvi:dʒi:'eɪ] *n Comput* (*abbr* **Video Graphics Array**) VGA *m*

►► ***VGA monitor*** moniteur *m* VGA

vgc (*written abbr* **very good condition**) tbe

VHF [ˌvi:eɪtʃ'ef] *n* (*abbr* **very high frequency**) VHF *f*

VHS [ˌvi:eɪt'es] *n* (*abbr* **video home system**) VHS *m*

VI (*written abbr* **Virgin Islands**) îles *fpl* Vierges

vibes [vaɪbz] *npl Fam* (**a**) *Mus* (*abbr* **vibraphone**) vibraphone ❑ *m* (**b**) (*abbr* **vibrations**) atmosphère ❑ *f*, ambiance ❑ *f*; **they give off really good/bad vibes** avec eux le courant passe vraiment bien/ne passe vraiment pas; **I get really bad vibes from her** je la sens vraiment mal; **I don't like the vibes in this place** je n'aime pas l'ambiance ici

VIN [ˌvi:aɪ'en] *n* (*abbr* **vehicle identification number**) numéro *m* d'immatriculation

VIP [ˌvi:aɪ'pi:] (*abbr* **very important person**) **1** *n* VIP *mf*, personnalité *f*, personnage *m* de marque

2 *comp* (*guests, visitors*) de marque, éminent, très important; **to give sb the VIP treatment** traiter qn comme un personnage de marque; **we got VIP treatment** on nous a réservé un accueil princier, on nous a traités comme des rois

►► ***VIP lounge*** (*in airport*) = salon d'accueil réservé aux personnages de marque

VISTA ['vɪstə] *n Am* (*abbr* **Volunteers in Service to America**) = programme américain d'aide aux personnes les plus défavorisées

viz [vɪz] *adv* (*abbr* **videlicet**) c.-à-d.

VJ [ˌvi:'dʒeɪ] *n* (*abbr* **Video Jockey**) présentateur(trice) *m,f* de (vidéo)clips

VJ Day *n* (*abbr* **Victory in Japan Day**) = jour de la victoire des alliés sur le Japon, le 15 août 1945

VLF [ˌvi:el'ef] *n* (*abbr* **very low frequency**) VLF *f*

VLSI [ˌvi:elˌes'aɪ] *n Comput* (*abbr* **very large-scale integration**) VLSI *f*

VOA [ˌvi:əʊ'eɪ] *n Am Rad* (*abbr* **Voice of America**) = station de radio américaine émettant dans le monde entier

VOD [ˌvi:əʊ'di:] *n* (*abbr* **video on demand**) vidéo *f* à la demande

vol. (*written abbr* **volume**) vol

VP [ˌvi:'pi:] *n* (*abbr* **vice-president**) VP *m*

VPL [ˌvi:pi:'el] *n Fam* (*abbr* **visible panty line**) = contours du slip visibles sous les vêtements

VR [ˌvi:'ɑ:(r)] *Br* (*abbr* **Victoria Regina**) la Reine Victoria

VRAM ['vi:ræm] *n Comput* (*abbr* **video random access memory**) VRAM *f*

VRML [ˌvi:ɑ:ˌrem'el] *n Comput* (*abbr* **virtual reality modelling language**) VRML *m*

vs (*written abbr* **versus**) contre

VSO [ˌvi:es'əʊ] *n Br* (*abbr* **Voluntary Service Overseas**) = coopération technique à l'étranger (non rémunérée)

VSOP [ˌvi:esˌəʊ'pi:] *n* (*abbr* **very special old pale**) VSOP

VT, Vt (*written abbr* **Vermont**) Vermont *m*

VTOL ['vi:tɒl] *n Aviat* (*abbr* **vertical takeoff and landing**) (*system*) décollage *m* et atterrissage *m* vertical; (*plane*) ADAV *m*

VTR [ˌvi:ti:'ɑ:(r)] *n* (*abbr* **video tape recorder**) magnétoscope *m*

vv (**a**) (*written abbr* **verses**) v. (**b**) (*written abbr* **versus**) contre

W (**a**) (*written abbr* **west**) O (**b**) (*written abbr* **watt**) w

W3 [ˌdʌbəlju:'θri:] *n Comput* (*abbr* **World Wide Web**) W3 *m*, le Web *m*

WA (**a**) (*written abbr* **Washington (State)**) État *m* de Washington (**b**) (*written abbr* **Western Australia**) Australie-Occidentale *f*

WAAC [wæk] *n Br Hist* (*abbr* **Women's Army Auxiliary Corps**) = pendant la Seconde Guerre mondiale, section féminine auxiliaire de l'armée de terre britannique

WAAF [wæf] *n Br Hist* (*abbr* **Women's Auxiliary Air Force**) = pendant la Seconde Guerre mondiale, section féminine auxiliaire de l'armée de l'air britannique

WALL [wɔ:l] *n Comput* (*abbr* **Web-assisted language learning**) enseignement *m* des langues assisté par la Toile

WAN [wæn] *n Comput* (*abbr* **wide area network**) réseau *m* longue distance

WAP [wæp] *n Comput & Tel* (*abbr* **wireless application protocol**) WAP *m*

►► ***WAP phone*** téléphone *f* WAP

Warks (*written abbr* **Warwickshire**) Warwickshire *m*

Wash (*written abbr* **Washington**) Washington *f*

Wasp, WASP [wɒsp] *n Am* (*abbr* **White Anglo-Saxon Protestant**) = Blanc d'origine anglo-saxonne et protestante, appartenant aux classes aisées et influentes

WATS [wɒts] *n Tel* (*abbr* **Wide Area Telephone Service**) = service téléphonique qui propose un forfait pour les appels longue distance

WBA [ˌdʌbəlju:bi:'eɪ] *n* (*abbr* **World Boxing Association**) WBA *f*

WBC [ˌdʌbəlju:bi:'si:] *n* (*abbr* **World Boxing Council**) WBC *m*

WBO [ˌdʌbəlju:bi:'əʊ] *n* (*abbr* **World Boxing Organization**) WBO *f*

WC [ˌdʌbəlju:'si:] *n* (*abbr* **water closet**) W-C *mpl*

WCC [ˌdʌbəlju:si:'si:] *n* (*abbr* **World Council of Churches**) COE *m*

w/e (*written abbr* **week ending**) semaine se terminant

Wed. (*written abbr* **Wednesday**) mer

WEU [ˌdʌbəlju:i:'ju:] *n Pol* (*abbr* **Western European Union**) UEO *f*

WFP [ˌdʌbəlju:ef'pi:] *n* (*abbr* **World Food Programme**) PAM *m*

WFTU [ˌdʌbəlju:efˌti:'ju:] *n* (*abbr* **World Federation of Trade Unions**) FSM *f*

WHO [ˌdʌbəlju:eɪtʃ'əʊ] *n* (*abbr* **World Health Organization**) OMS *f*

WI[1] [ˌdʌbəlju:'aɪ] **1** *n* (*abbr* **Women's Institute**) = association britannique de femmes particulièrement active en milieu rural, à qui l'on prête une image démodée

2 *npl* (*abbr* **West Indies**) Antilles *fpl*

WI[2] (*written abbr* **Wisconsin**) Wisconsin *m*

Wilts (*written abbr* **Wiltshire**) Wiltshire *m*

WIMP [wɪmp] *n Comput* (*abbr* **window, icon, mouse, pointer**) interface *f* WIMP

WIP [ˌdʌbəlju:aɪ'pi:] *n Acct* (*abbr* **work in progress**) travail *m* en cours, encours *m* de production de biens

Wis (*written abbr* **Wisconsin**) Wisconsin *m*

wk (*written abbr* **week**) sem

Wm. (*written abbr* **William**) William

WNW (*written abbr* **west-north-west**) O-NO

WO [ˌdʌbəlju:'əʊ] *n Br Mil* (*abbr* **warrant officer**) adjt

Worcs (*written abbr* **Worcestershire**) Worcestershire *m*

WORM [wɜ:m] *Comput* (*abbr* **write once read many times**) WORM

WP[1] [ˌdʌbəlju:'pi:] *n* (**a**) (*abbr* **word processing**) TTX *m*, traitement *m* de texte (**b**) (*abbr* **word processor**) machine *f* à traitement de texte

WP[2] (*written abbr* **weather permitting**) si le temps le permet

WPC [ˌdʌbəlju:pi:'si:] *n Br* (*abbr* **woman police constable**) = femme agent de police; **WPC Roberts** l'agent Roberts

wpm (*written abbr* **words per minute**) mots/min

WRAC [ræk] *n Br* (*abbr* **Women's Royal Army Corps**) = section féminine de l'armée de terre britannique

WRAF [ræf] *n Br* (*abbr* **Women's Royal Air Force**) = section féminine de l'armée de l'air britannique

WRNS [renz] *n Br* (*abbr* **Women's Royal Naval Service**) = section féminine de la marine de guerre britannique

WRU [ˌdʌbəlju:ɑ:'ju:] *n Sport* (*abbr* **Welsh Rugby Union**) = association galloise de rugby à quinze

WRVS [ˌdʌbəlju:ɑ:ˌvi:'es] *n Br* (*abbr* **Women's Royal Voluntary Service**) = association de femmes au service des déshérités

WSW (*written abbr* **west-south-west**) O-SO

wt. (*written abbr* **weight**) poids

WTO [ˌdʌbəlju:ti:'əʊ] *n* (*abbr* **World Trade Organization**) OMC *f*

WV, WVa (*written abbr* **West Virginia**) Virginie-Occidentale *f*

WW (*written abbr* **World War**) guerre *f* mondiale

WWF [ˌdʌbəlju:dʌbəlju:'ef] *n* (*abbr* **World-wide Fund for Nature**) WWF *m*

WWJD [ˌdʌbəlju:dʌbəlju:ˌdʒeɪ'di:] *Am* (*abbr* **what would Jesus do?**) = slogan souvent arboré sur un bracelet, exhortant celui qui le porte à faire le bien dans ses actions quotidiennes

WWW [ˌdʌbəlju:dʌbəlju:'dʌbəlju:] *n Comput* (*abbr* **world wide web**) WWW, W3

WY (*written abbr* **Wyoming**) Wyoming *m*

Wyo (*written abbr* **Wyoming**) Wyoming *m*

WYSIWYG ['wɪzɪwɪg] *n & adj Comput* (*abbr* **what you see is what you get**) tel écran-tel écrit *m*, tel-tel *m*, Wysiwyg *m*

►► ***WYSIWYG display*** affichage *m* tel écran-tel écrit *ou* tel-tel *ou* Wysiwyg

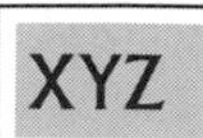

X (**a**) (*written abbr* **kiss**) = formule affectueuse placée après la signature à la fin d'une lettre (**b**) (*written abbr* **Christ**) Christ *m*

XL [ˌeks'el] *n* (*abbr* **extra-large**) XL *m*

Xmas (*written abbr* **Christmas**) Noël *m*

XML [ˌeksem'el] *n Comput* (*abbr* **Extensible Markup Language**) XML *m*

Y (**a**) (*written abbr* **yen**) y (**b**) (*written abbr* **yuan**) yuan

Y2K [ˌwaɪtuːˈkeɪ] (*abbr* **year 2000**) **1** *n* l'an *m* 2000

2 *adj Comput* **Y2K compatible, Y2K compliant** conforme à l'an 2000

yd (*written abbr* **yard**) yd

YHA [ˌwaɪeɪtʃˈeɪ] *n Br* (*abbr* **Youth Hostels Association**) = fédération unie des auberges de jeunesse

YMCA [ˌwaɪemˌsiːˈeɪ] *n* (*abbr* **Young Men's Christian Association**) = association chrétienne de jeunes gens (surtout connue pour ses centres d'hébergement)

YOI [ˌwaɪəʊˈaɪ] *n Br* (*abbr* **Young Offenders' Institution**) = centre de détention pour mineurs

YOP [jɒp] *n Br* (*abbr* **Youth Opportunities Programme**) *(programme)* ≃ TUC *mpl*; *(worker)* ≃ tuciste *mf*

Yorks. (*written abbr* **Yorkshire**) Yorkshire *m*

yr (*written abbr* **year**) année *f*

YT (*written abbr* **Yukon Territory**) territoire *m* du Yukon

YTS [ˌwaɪtiːˈes] *n Br* (*abbr* **Youth Training Scheme**) *(programme)* = programme gouvernemental britannique d'insertion des jeunes dans la vie professionnelle; *(person)* = personne participant au programme "YTS"

yuppie [ˈjʌpɪ] (*abbr* **young upwardly mobile professional**) **1** *n* yuppie *mf*, ≃ jeune cadre *m* dynamique

2 *adj (club)* pour jeunes cadres dynamiques; *(lifestyle, neighbourhood)* de yuppies

►► ***yuppie flu*** encéphalomyélite *f* myalgique

YWCA [ˌwaɪdʌbəljuːˌsiːˈeɪ] *n* (*abbr* **Young Women's Christian Association**) = association chrétienne de jeunes filles (surtout connue pour ses centres d'hébergement)

ZBB [*Br* ˌzedbiːˈbiː, *Am* ˌziːbiːˈbiː] *n Fin* (*abbr* **zero-base budgeting**) BBZ *m*

Abbreviations Used in this Dictionary

Abréviations utilisées dans ce dictionnaire

gloss [introduces an explanation]	=	glose [introduit une explication]
cultural equivalent [introduces a translation which has a roughly equivalent status in the target language]	≃	équivalent culturel [introduit une traduction aux connotations comparables]
abbreviation	*abbr, abrév*	abréviation
accounting	*Acct*	comptabilité
adjective	*adj*	adjectif
administration	*Admin*	administration
adverb	*adv*	adverbe
agriculture	*Agr*	agriculture
American English	*Am*	anglais américain
anatomy	*Anat*	anatomie
antiquity	*Antiq*	antiquité
archaic	*Arch*	archaïque
archaeology	*Archeol, Archéol*	archéologie
architecture	*Archit*	architecture
slang	*Arg*	argot
article	*art*	article
insurance	*Assur*	assurances
astrology	*Astrol*	astrologie
astronomy	*Astron*	astronomie
Australian English	*Austr*	anglais d'Australie
cars	*Aut*	automobile
auxiliary	*aux*	auxiliaire
aviation	*Aviat*	aviation
Belgian French	*Belg*	belgicisme
biology	*Biol*	biologie
botany	*Bot*	botanique
British English	*Br*	anglais britannique
Canadian French	*Can*	canadianisme
carpentry	*Carp*	menuiserie
catholicism	*Cathol*	catholicisme
ceramics	*Cer, Cér*	céramique
chemistry	*Chem, Chim*	chimie
cinema	*Cin*	cinéma
commerce	*Com*	commerce
compound-forming noun	*comp*	nom à fonction adjectivale
comparative	*compar*	comparatif
accounting	*Compta*	comptabilité
computing	*Comput*	informatique
conjunction	*conj*	conjonction
building industry	*Constr*	bâtiment

continuous form	*cont*	forme progressive
cooking	*Culin*	cuisine
definite	*def, déf*	défini
ecology	*Ecol, Écol*	écologie
economics	*Econ, Écon*	économie
electricity	*Elec, Élec*	électricité
electronics	*Electron, Électron*	électronique
English	*Eng*	anglais d'Angleterre
entomology	*Entom*	entomologie
especially	*esp*	surtout
European Union	*EU*	Union européenne
euphemism	*Euph*	euphémisme
exclamation	*exclam*	exclamation
feminine	*f*	féminin
familiar	*Fam*	familier
figurative use	*Fig*	sens figuré
finance	*Fin*	finance
feminine plural noun	*fpl*	nom féminin pluriel
football	*Ftbl*	football
geography	*Geog, Géog*	géographie
geology	*Geol, Géol*	géologie
geometry	*Geom, Géom*	géométrie
grammar	*Gram*	grammaire
gymnastics	*Gym*	gymnastique
heraldry	*Her, Hér*	héraldique
history	*Hist*	histoire
horticulture	*Hort*	horticulture
humorous	*Hum*	humoristique
hunting	*Hunt*	chasse
fish	*Ich*	poissons
industry	*Ind*	industrie
insurance	*Ins*	assurances
indefinite	*indef, indéf*	indéfini
invariable	*inv*	invariable
Irish English	*Ir*	anglais d'Irlande
journalism	*Journ*	journalisme
law	*Jur*	droit
linguistics	*Ling*	linguistique
masculine	*m*	masculin
mathematics	*Math*	mathématique
medicine	*Med, Méd*	médecine
carpentry	*Menuis*	menuiserie
meteorology	*Met*	météorologie
metallurgy	*Metal, Métal*	métallurgie
meteorology	*Météo*	météorologie
military	*Mil*	militaire
mineralogy	*Miner, Minér*	minéralogie